P9-EGJ-549

ENCYCLOPEDIA OF ASSOCIATIONS®

AN ASSOCIATIONS UNLIMITED REFERENCE

ISSN 0071-0202

ENCYCLOPEDIA OF ASSOCIATIONS®

AN ASSOCIATIONS UNLIMITED REFERENCE

A Guide to More Than 25,000 National and International Organizations, Including: Trade, Business, and Commercial; Environmental and Agricultural; Legal, Governmental, Public Administration, and Military; Engineering, Technological, and Natural and Social Sciences; Educational; Cultural; Social Welfare; Health and Medical; Public Affairs; Fraternal, Nationality, and Ethnic; Religious; Veterans', Hereditary, and Patriotic; Hobby and Avocational; Athletic and Sports; Labor Unions, Associations, and Federations; Chambers of Commerce and Trade and Tourism; Greek Letter and Related Organizations; Fan Clubs.

46th EDITION

VOLUME 1

NATIONAL ORGANIZATIONS OF THE U.S.

PART 1 (SECTIONS 1-6)
ENTRIES 1-11220

Kristy A. Swartout, Project Editor

Detroit • New York • San Francisco • New Haven, Conn • Waterville, Maine • London

GALE
CENGAGE Learning

Encyclopedia of Associations, 46th Edition

Product Management: David Forman

Project Editor: Kristy Swartout

Editorial: Tara Atterberry, Verne Thompson

Composition and Electronic Capture: Gary Oudersluys

Manufacturing: Rita Wimberley

For product information and technology assistance, contact us at
Gale Customer Support, 1-800-877-4253.
For permission to use material from this text or product,
submit all requests online at **www.cengage.com/permissions.**
Further permissions questions can be emailed to
permissionrequest@cengage.com

While every effort has been made to ensure the reliability of the information presented in this publication, Gale, a part of Cengage Learning, does not guarantee the accuracy of the data contained herein. Gale accepts no payment for listing; and inclusion in the publication of any organization, agency, institution, publication, service, or individual does not imply endorsement of the editors or publisher. Errors brought to the attention of the publisher and verified to the satisfaction of the publisher will be corrected in future editions.

EDITORIAL DATA PRIVACY POLICY: Does this product contain information about you as an individual? If so, for more information about our editorial data privacy policies, please see our Privacy Statement at www.gale.cengage.com.

Gale
27500 Drake Rd.
Farmington Hills, MI, 48331-3535

ISBN-13: 978-1-4144-2006-6 (vol. 1, 3-part set)
ISBN-10: 1-4144-2006-4 (vol. 1, 3-part set)
ISBN-13: 978-1-4144-2007-3 (vol. 1, part 1)
ISBN-10: 1-4144-2007-2 (vol. 1, part 1)
ISBN-13: 978-1-4144-2008-0 (vol. 1, part 2)
ISBN-10: 1-4144-2008-0 (vol. 1, part 2)
ISBN-13: 978-1-4144-2009-7 (vol. 1, part 3)
ISBN-10: 1-4144-2009-9 (vol. 1, part 3)
ISBN-13: 978-1-4144-2010-3 (vol. 2)
ISBN-10: 1-4144-2010-2 (vol. 2)

ISSN 0071-0202

Printed in the United States of America
1 2 3 4 5 6 7 12 11 10 09 08

Contents

The Value of Associations to American Society

In a nation that always has encouraged individualism, Americans always have felt the need to belong. Driven by the knowledge that they can achieve more through group efforts than they can individually, Americans have made associations one of the most powerful forces in the United States today.

The enormous impact associations have on the life of each American every day cannot be overestimated. Reflecting the fact that nine out of ten Americans belong to at least one association, the activities undertaken by associations in the U.S. impart numerous social and economic benefits, including:

- Educating their members and the public;
- Setting professional standards of conduct;
- Setting and enforcing product safety and quality standards;
- Stimulating and organizing volunteerism;
- Informing the public on key issues;
- Developing and disseminating information;
- Establishing forums for the exchange of information and ideas;
- Ensuring representation for private interests;
- Exercising and supporting political choice;
- Employing millions of Americans.

Research conducted on behalf of the American Society of Association Executives reveals:

- Nine out of ten Americans belong to an association; one out of four belongs to four or more associations.
- 95% of associations offer education courses on technical and scientific matters, business practices, etc. to their members and the public.
- Associations spend only about 10% of their revenues on political activities, with primary expenditures being professional development, printing and publishing and developing codes of ethics and professional and safety standards that govern a host of professions and disciplines in this country.
- Associations promote volunteerism, logging nearly 200 million volunteer hours in community service per year.

Most associations exist to serve their members, be they companies in an industry, professionals, or individuals who share an interest. Associations serve their members in many ways but, above all, they do for the membership that which individual members cannot do for themselves as effectively.

Despite the myriad ways associations advance America, they remain largely misunderstood and invisible. The work of associations is often done quietly and behind the scenes; public perceptions, therefore, vary widely about what associations are and the contributions they make. The examples that follow provide some general insight into the range and diversity of association contributions.

Educating Workers and the Public

Associations play a leading role in the education of the American workforce, making education perhaps their most important activity. By creating effective forums for the exchange of information and ideas within all industries and professions, associations often are in the forefront of significant technological discoveries and advancements that enrich the lives of all Americans.

Advancing Safety, Health, and Quality

Associations voluntarily set various standards that play a key role in protecting consumer safety and health and in helping ensure products meet measurable requirements for performance, quality, and even compatibility and interchangeability.

Aiding Professional Competence and Exemplary Conduct

Associations strengthen virtually every profession by establishing and enforcing professional standards and codes of ethics, augmenting the public's trust that professionals with identical titles deliver competent and similar services. While the seed of professional expertise is sown in undergraduate and graduate training and state licensing procedures, associations advance and nurture the professions by encouraging the peer review process, by offering courses that meet legal requirements, and by assuring standards that often form the basis for disciplinary action.

Unearthing New Data

Many institutions, including the federal government, depend heavily on associations for the statistical information they research, gather, and analyze. These research-related activities enable businesses and professions to function more efficiently and help identify important new directions for social improvements.

Reaching Out to Others

Mobilizing volunteers in areas of expertise tied closely to the trade, profession, or cause they represent, associations have united their members' talents to meet many pressing social or economic needs. In recent years, for example, associations have united their members' talents to promote literacy, find missing children, improve the condition of health care facilities, provide eye care to the poor, offer fire safety education, aid victims of natural disasters, administer medical care to the homeless, help the elderly file their tax returns, and help reduce a state budgetary deficit.

Since the infancy of the United States of America, the American reliance on associations to perform work for the benefit of all has increased rather than decreased and with it the scope, sophistication, and significance of association activities. All of us are the beneficiaries.

American Society of Association Executives

1575 I St., NW

Washington, DC 20005-1168

(888) 950-2723

The *Encyclopedia of Associations (EA),* Volume 1, is the only comprehensive source of detailed information concerning more than 25,000 nonprofit American membership organizations of national scope. For over fifty years and through 45 earlier editions, *EA's* listing of associations and professional societies is unsurpassed as a 'switchboard' connecting persons needing information to highly qualified sources.

Frequently, a phone call, fax, or email to one of the thousands of organizations formed around a specific interest or objective produces more information faster than research in books, periodicals, and other printed materials.

Organizations often operate with small, volunteer staffs. *Many such groups have requested that all written inquiries be accompanied by stamped, self-addressed envelopes.* Replies can then be expedited and costs to the organization kept to a minimum.

Preparation of This Edition

The editorial objective for each edition of *EA* is complete verification or updating of existing entries and the identification and description of new or previously unlisted organizations. This intensive effort includes direct contact by correspondence and telephone with non-responding groups.

Scope of the Encyclopedia

The organizations described in *EA* fall into the following seven general categories:

National, nonprofit membership associations, which represent the largest number of organizations listed;

International associations, which are generally North American in scope and membership or binational, representing a direct link between the United States and another country or region; also includes American or North American sections, chapters, or divisions of associations headquartered outside of the United States;

Local and regional associations, only if their subjects or objectives are national in interest;

Nonmembership organizations, if they disseminate information to the public as well as to the researcher;

For-profit associations, if their names suggest that they are nonprofit organizations;

Defunct associations, which appear only in the index with the appropriate 'defunct' annotation;

Untraceable associations, which are listed without address with the annotation 'address unknown since [edition year]' in place of contact information. (After requests for updated information have remained unanswered for two editions, these associations are listed in the index only, with the annotation 'address unknown.')

Available in Electronic Formats

Licensing. National Organizations of the U.S. is available for licensing. The complete database is provided in a fielded format and is deliverable on such media as disk or CD-ROM. For more information, contact Gale's Business Development Group at 1-800-877-GALE, or visit us on our web site at www.gale.com/bizdev.

Online. The complete *Encyclopedia of Associations (EA)* series (including associations listed in the international and regional, state and local editions) is available online as File 114 through The Dialog Corporation's DIALOG service and as File ENASSC through LexisNexis. For more information, contact The Dialog Corporation, 11000 Regency Parkway, Ste. 10, Cary, NC 27511, phone: (919) 462-8600; toll-free: 800-3-DIALOG; or LexisNexis, PO Box 933, Dayton, OH 45401-0933, phone: (937) 865-6800, toll-free: 800-227-4908.

Associations Unlimited. *Associations Unlimited* is a modular approach to the *Encyclopedia of Associations* database, allowing customers to select the pieces of the series that they want to purchase.

The four modules include each of the *EA* series (national, international, and regional) as well as one module featuring U.S. government data on more than 450,000 nonprofit organizations.

Associations Unlimited is available on a subscription basis through InfoTrac, Gale's online information resource that features an easy-to-use end-user interface, powerful search capabilities, and ease of access through the World-Wide Web. For more information, call 800-877-GALE.

The complete *EA* database is also available through InfoTrac as part of *Gale's Ready Reference Shelf.*

Acknowledgments

The editors are grateful to the large number of organization officials in the United States and abroad who generously responded to our requests for updated information, provided additional data by telephone, fax, email or website and helped in the shaping of this edition with their comments and suggestions throughout the year. Special thanks go to Jeannine M. James for her research contributions. Appreciation is also extended to the American Society of Association Executives for its ongoing support.

Comments and Suggestions Welcome

Matters pertaining to specific listings in *EA,* as well as suggestions for new listings, should be directed to Kristy Swartout, Editor, *Encyclopedia of Associations.*

Please write or call:
Encyclopedia of Associations
Gale
27500 Drake Rd.
Farmington Hills, MI 48331-3535

Phone: (248) 699-4253
Toll-free: 800-347-GALE
Fax: (248) 699-8075
Email: Kristy.Swartout@Cengage.com

Descriptive Listings

Entries in *EA* are arranged into 18 subject sections, as outlined on the Contents page. Within each section, organizations are arranged in alphabetical order, with numeric listings appearing first, according to the assigned principal subject keyword that appears as a subhead above the organization names. An alphabetical list of keywords used throughout *EA* follows the 'Abbreviations and Symbols' list. Within each keyword, entries are listed alphabetically by organization name.

Access to entries is facilitated by the alphabetical *Name and Keyword Index* found in Part 3 of this edition. An explanation of this index follows the discussion of the sample entry.

Sample Entry

The number preceding each portion of the sample entry designates an item of information that might be included in an entry. Each numbered item in the sample entry is explained in the paragraph of the same number following the diagram.

▮1▮ Storytelling

▮2▮ 3348 ■ **▮3▮** Association of Eclectic Storytellers **▮4▮** (AES)
▮5▮ 123 Amanda Ave.
PO Box 1992
Eldridge, NY 13201
▮6▮ Ph: (315)555-9500
▮7▮ Free: (800)555-2000
Fax: (315)555-9505
Telex: 123456
▮8▮ E-mail: harmersway@aes.org
▮9▮ Website: http://www.aes.org
▮10▮ Contact: Grant Smith, Pres.

▮11▮ Founded: 1950. **▮12▮ Members:** 150,000. **▮13▮ Membership Dues:** individual, $50 (annual). **▮14▮ Staff:** 15. **▮15▮ Budget:** $1,000,000. **▮16▮ Regional Groups:** 10. **Local Groups:** 20. **▮17▮ Languages:** English, Dutch. **▮18▮ Multinational. ▮19▮ Description:** Professional society of storytellers, focusing on storytellers that enjoy eclectic themes and others with an interest in this field. Promotes the study and tradition of storytelling. Conducts special programs for various types of audiences. Sponsors special seminars and courses on traditional forms of storytelling. **▮20▮ Libraries: Type:** lending. **Holdings:** 15,000; archival material, artwork, books, periodicals. **Subjects:** folktales, traditional stories, fairytales. **▮21▮ Awards:** Yaeko Abe Excellence Endowment. **Frequency:** annual. **Type:** monetary. • Michelle Eads's Founder Prize. **Frequency:** quarterly. **Type:** recognition. **▮22▮ Computer Services:** database on literature • publishing capabilities. **▮23▮ Telecommunication Services:** electronic bulletin board, (201)836-7569 • teleconference • teletype. **▮24▮ Committees:** Career Counseling; Cultural Studies; History of Stories. **Divisions:** Education; Literature. **▮25▮ Affiliated With:** Storytelling Institute. **▮26▮ Also Known As:** Story Time Society. **▮27▮ Formerly:** (1975) Storytelling Society of America. **▮28▮ Publications:** *AES News*, monthly. Newsletter. Contains happenings in the storytelling world, book reviews, and listing of seminars and courses offered. **▮29▮ Price:** $25. **▮30▮ ISSN:** 1234-5678. **▮31▮ Circulation:** 5000. **▮32▮ Advertising:** accepted. **▮33▮ Alternate Formats:** online. **▮34▮ Also Cited As:** *American Society of Eclectic Storytellers*. **▮35▮ Conventions/Meetings:** annual (with exhibits) - 2008 Sept. 14-16, Ypsilanti, MI; 2009 Nov. 1-9, Boulder, CO.

Description of Numbered Elements

▮1▮ Keyword. In each of the sections, keywords are given as subheadings and listed alphabetically. Organizations are listed in alphabetical order under their principal keyword subheading. Since the listings are arranged by keyword, the user will find organizations having similar interests grouped together within each keyword subheading.

▮2▮ Entry Number. Entries are numbered sequentially and the entry number (rather than the page number) is used in the Name and Keyword Index to refer to the organization. To facilitate location of the entries in the text, the first entry number on each left-hand page and the last entry number on each right-hand page are provided at the top outer corners of the pages.

▮3▮ Organization Name. The formal name is given; 'The' and 'Inc.' are omitted in most listings, unless they are an integral part of the acronym used by the association.

▮4▮ Acronym. Indicates the short form or abbreviation of the organization's name, usually composed of the initial letter or syllable of each word in it.

▮5▮ Address. The address is generally that of the permanent national headquarters, or of the chief official for groups that have no permanent office.

▮6▮ Telephone Numbers. These are listed when furnished by the organization.

7 Toll-free, Fax, and Telex. These are listed when furnished by the organization.

8 E-mail. This is listed when furnished by the organization.

9 Website. The primary web address for the organization or contact person listed.

10 Chief Official and Title. The name of a full-time executive, an elected officer, or other contact person designated by the association is provided.

11 Founding Date. Indicates the year in which the organization was formed. If the group has changed its name, the founding date is for the earliest name by which it was known. If, however, the group was formed by a merger or supersedes another group, the founding date refers to the year in which this action took place.

12 Members. The figure represents individuals, firms, institutions, other associations, or a combination of these categories. Since membership constantly fluctuates, the figure listed should be considered an approximation. If an organization describes itself as nonmembership, such notation is made in the entry preceding the descriptive text.

13 Membership Dues. Fees required of members as reported by the organization. Dues often vary according to membership category.

14 Staff. Many associations operate with a small paid or volunteer staff. The fact that an organization has no paid staff does not mean it has a limited program. Many groups carry on extensive activities through volunteer workers and committees.

15 Budget. The approximate annual budget for all activities is listed as reported by the organization.

16 Regional, State, and Local Groups. Indicates the number of regional, state, and local associations, chapters, clubs, councils, and posts affiliated with the national organization.

17 Languages. The official and/or working languages of the organization are listed, if other than English.

18 Geographic Scope. The boldface word **Multinational** indicates a multinational scope of the organization; otherwise, the geographic scope is assumed to be National.

19 Description. The description briefly outlines the membership, purpose, and activities of the association. Where no description is given, the title of the group usually is self-explanatory; in some cases, no summary of activities could be obtained.

20 Libraries. Provides information for organizations that maintain a library. Includes type of collection, holdings, and subject matter of collection, if available.

21 Awards. Provides information for organizations that offer awards. Includes name, frequency, type, and recipient of award.

22 Computer Services. Lists computer-based services offered by the organization, including online services and databases, bibliographic or other search services, automated mailing list services, and electronic publishing capabilities.

23 Telecommunication Services. Notes special communications services sponsored by the organization. Services included are hotlines, electronic mail/bulletin boards, and telephone referrals.

24 Subgroups. Lists those subgroups, including committees, sections, divisions, councils, departments, etc., that give an indication of the activities of the group, as distinguished from such administrative committees such as membership, finance, and convention. This information often supplements the description (see paragraph 19) by providing details about the organization's programs and fields of interest. Geographic divisions are omitted.

25 Affiliated With. Lists organizations sponsored by or directly related to the listed group. Organizations listed under this rubric can be found in *EA* or in *International Organizations.*

26 Also Known As. If the group is also known by another name, legally doing business under another name, or otherwise operates under a name different than its official title, that name is provided here.

27 Supersessions, Mergers, and Former Names. If the group superseded another organization or was formed by a merger, the original organizations are listed. Former names and the date of change to a new name, if available, are also listed.

28 Publications. The official publications are listed in alphabetical order with frequencies. When available, a brief description of the publication is provided. Additional publications, such as newspaper columns, are listed following the words 'Also publishes.' When provided, languages in which the publications are available are noted. If the group has indicated that no publications are issued, this is noted in the entry's main body.

29 Price. The figures are as provided by the organization.

30 ISSN. The International Standard Serial Number is a unique code for the purpose of identifying a specific serial publication. It is listed when provided by the organization; not all publications have been assigned an ISSN.

31 Circulation. This figure is as reported by the organization.

32 Advertising. Indicates whether or not the association accepts advertising in the publication.

33 Alternate Formats. Notes online, CD-ROM, diskette, and microform (includes microfiche and microfilm) availability.

34 Also Cited As. Lists any alternate or former names of the publication.

▮35▮ Conventions/Meetings. The frequency of national or international sessions and the dates and locations (city, state, and country) of the association's conventions, meetings, or conferences are given, if available at the time of publication. Also noted is the inclusion of commercial exhibits. If the group has indicated that no conventions or meetings are held, this is noted in the entry's main body.

Name and Keyword Index

A comprehensive alphabetical Name and Keyword index is provided in Part 3 of this edition of the Encyclopedia. Note that *each reference refers to the entry number, rather than the page on which the entry is listed.* Alphabetization rules ignore articles, prepositions, and conjunctions. A collection of references in this index would appear this way:

▮1▮ Amer. Soc. of Earth Sciences **[6359]**, 123 Salina St., Syracuse, NY 13201 (315)222-950
▮2▮ Earth Sciences, Amer. Soc. of **[6359]**
▮3▮ Earth Sciences Soc., USA **[★6359]**
▮4▮ **Geology**
Amer. Soc. of Earth Sciences **[6359]**
▮5▮ *Highways* Asphalt Recycling and Reclaiming Assn **[3728]**
▮6▮ Natl. Soc. of Constitutional Training —Address unknown since 1988
▮7▮ Soc. for the Advancement of Space Travel—Defunct
▮8▮ Turkish Air Assn. **[IO]**

Description of Numbered Index References

▮1▮ Each association's primary reference includes the mailing address and telephone number of the group.

▮2▮ Associations are alphabetized by important words in the name. These references aid in locating organizations whose correct name is unknown to the user.

▮3▮ Any reference with a ★ preceding the entry number indicates that the organization is not listed separately, but is mentioned within the description of another entry. These references would include the organization's former or alternate name as well as names of important committees, projects, or programs.

▮4▮ Associations appear alphabetically by primary and added keywords (see keyword list in this volume). These references allow the user to access all organizations within a particular field of interest.

▮5▮ Keywords that are italicized are added keywords and do not appear as subject headings within a section.

▮6▮ Organizations that are untraceable are noted as 'address unknown.'

▮7▮ Defunct associations are listed as such.

▮8▮ This index includes references to associations listed in the *Encyclopedia of Associations: International Organizations.*

Geographic Index

Entries in *EA*'s Geographic Index are listed according to the state in which the organization's headquarters are located. They are then sub-arranged by city and listed alphabetically according to the names of the organizations within each city.

A sample entry is shown below.

▮1▮ Amer. Soc. of Earth Sciences ▮2▮ [3348]
▮3▮ 123 Salina St.
PO Box 1992
Allen Park, NY 13201
▮4▮ Ph: (315)555-9500
▮5▮ Patsy, Mrs. Rachel, Pres.

Description of Numbered Elements

▮1▮ Organization Name. The formal name is given; 'The' and 'Inc.' are omitted in most listings, unless they are an integral part of the acronym used by the association.

▮2▮ Entry Number. Refers to the sequential entry number (rather than the page number) assigned to the organization's main entry in Volume 1, where other details concerning membership, objectives and activities, and publications can be found.

▮3▮ Address. The address is generally that of the permanent national headquarters, or of the chief official for groups that have no permanent offices. The city appears in **boldface.**

▮4▮ Telephone Number. A telephone number is listed when furnished by the organization.

▮5▮ Chief Official and Title. Lists the name of a full-time executive, an elected officer, or other contact person designated by the association.

Executive Index

Entries in *EA*'s Executive Index are listed alphabetically according to the surname of the chief executive of the organization. When an individual is listed as the chief executive of more than one organization, entries are arranged by organization name.

A sample entry is shown below.

▮1▮ Patsy, Mrs. Rachel, Pres.
▮2▮ Amer. Soc. of Earth Sciences ▮3▮ [3348]
▮4▮ 123 Salina St.
PO Box 1992
Allen Park, NY 13201
▮5▮ Ph: (315)555-9500

Description of Numbered Elements

▮1▮ Chief Official and Title. Lists the name of a full-time executive, an elected officer, or other contact person designated by the association.

▮2▮ Organization Name. The formal name is given; 'The' and 'Inc.' are omitted in most listings, unless they are an integral part of the acronym used by the association.

▮3▮ Entry Number. Refers to the sequential entry number (rather than the page number) assigned to the organization's main entry in Volume 1, where other details concerning membership, objectives and activities, and publications can be found.

▮4▮ Address. The address is generally that of the permanent national headquarters, or of the chief official for groups that have no permanent offices.

▮5▮ Telephone Number. A telephone number is listed when furnished by the organization.

Geographic Abbreviations

United States and U.S. Territories

AK	Alaska
AL	Alabama
AR	Arkansas
AZ	Arizona
CA	California
CO	Colorado
CT	Connecticut
DC	District of Columbia
DE	Delaware
FL	Florida
GA	Georgia
GU	Guam
HI	Hawaii
IA	Iowa
ID	Idaho
IL	Illinois
IN	Indiana
KS	Kansas
KY	Kentucky
LA	Louisiana
MA	Massachusetts
MD	Maryland
ME	Maine
MI	Michigan
MN	Minnesota
MO	Missouri
MS	Mississippi
MT	Montana
NC	North Carolina
ND	North Dakota
NE	Nebraska
NH	New Hampshire
NJ	New Jersey
NM	New Mexico
NV	Nevada
NY	New York
OH	Ohio
OK	Oklahoma
OR	Oregon
PA	Pennsylvania
PR	Puerto Rico
RI	Rhode Island
SC	South Carolina
SD	South Dakota
TN	Tennessee
TX	Texas
UT	Utah
VA	Virginia
VI	Virgin Islands
VT	Vermont
WA	Washington
WI	Wisconsin
WV	West Virginia
WY	Wyoming

Table of Abbreviations Used in Addresses and the Index

Acad	Academy
AFB	Air Force Base
Amer	American
APO	Army Post Office
Apt	Apartment
Assn	Association
Ave	Avenue
Bd	Board
Bldg	Building
Blvd	Boulevard
Br	Branch
Bur	Bureau
c/o	Care of
Co	Company
Coll	College
Comm	Committee
Commn	Commission
Conf	Conference
Confed	Confederation
Cong	Congress
Corp	Corporation
Coun	Council
Ct	Court
Dept	Department
Div	Division
Dr	Drive
E	East
Expy	Expressway
Fed	Federation
Fl	Floor
Found	Foundation
FPO	Fleet Post Office
Ft	Fort
Fwy	Freeway
Govt	Government
GPO	General Post Office
Hwy	Highway
Inc	Incorporated
Inst	Institute
Intl	International
Ln	Lane
Ltd	Limited
Mfrs	Manufacturers
Mgt	Management
Mt	Mount
N	North
Natl	National
NE	Northeast
No	Number
NW	Northwest
Pkwy	Parkway
Pl	Place
PO	Post Office
Prof	Professor
Rd	Road
RD	Rural Delivery
RFD	Rural Free Delivery
Rm	Room
RR	Rural Route
Rte	Route
S	South
SE	Southeast
Sect	Section
Soc	Society

Sq	Square
St	Saint, Street
Sta	Station
Ste	Sainte, Suite
Subcomm	Subcommittee
Subcommn	Subcommission
SW	Southwest
Terr	Terrace, Territory
Tpke	Turnpike
T.V.	Television
UN	United Nations
Univ	University
U.S.	United States
U.S.A.	United States of America
W	West

Currency Abbreviations and Definitions

Arranged by Currency Abbreviation

Abbr.	Currency Unit	Country
$	U.S. dollar	American Samoa, British Virgin Islands, Guam, Marshall Islands, Federated States of Micronesia, U.S.
$A	Australian dollar	Australia, Kiribati, Nauru, Norfolk Island, Tuvalu
$B	Belizean dollar	Belize
$b	boliviano	Bolivia
$F	Fijian dollar	Fiji
œ	pound sterling	England, Northern Ireland, Scotland, Wales
œC	Cyprus pound	Cyprus
œE	Egyptian pound	Egypt
œG	Gibraltar pound	Gibraltar
œS	Sudanese pound	Sudan
Syr	Syrian pound	Syria
A	Argentinian austral	Argentina
Af	afghani	Afghanistan
AF	Aruban florin	Aruba
AS	Austrian Schilling	Austria
B	balboa	Panama
B$	Bahamian dollar	Bahamas
BD	Bahraini dinar	Bahrain
BD$	Barbados dollar	Barbados
BFr	Belgian franc	Belgium
Bht	baht	Thailand
Bm$	Bermuda dollar	Bermuda
Br$	Brunei dollar	Brunei Darussalam
Bs	bolivar	Venezuela
C	colon	Costa Rica, El Salvador
Cd	cedi	Ghana
C$	Canadian dollar	Canada
C$	new cordoba	Nicaragua
CFP	Colonial Francs Pacifique	New Caledonia
ChP	Chilean peso	Chile
CI$	Cayman Island dollar	Cayman Islands
CoP	Colombian peso	Colombia
Cr$	cruzado	Brazil
CRs	Ceylon rupee	Sri Lanka
CuP	Cuban peso	Cuba
D	dalasi	Gambia
DA	dinar	Algeria
Db	dobra	Sao Tome and Principe
DFr	Djibouti franc	Djibouti
Dg	dong	Vietnam
Dh	dirham	Morocco
Din	dinar	Bosnia-Hercegovina, Croatia, Macedonia, Slovenia, Yugoslavia
DKr	Danish krone	Denmark, Faroe Islands, Greenland
DM	Deutsche Mark	Germany
DP	Dominican peso	Dominican Republic
Dr	drachma	Greece
Ec	escudo	Cape Verde
EC$	East Caribbean dollar	Antigua-Barbuda, Dominica, Grenada, Montserrat, St.Christopher-Nevis, St. Lucia, St. Vincent and the Grenadines
ECU	European currency unit	European Economic Community
E$	Ethiopian birr	Ethiopia
Eg	emalangeni	Swaziland
Esc	escudo	Portugal
EUR	Euro	Austria, Belgium, Finland, France, Germany, Greece, Ireland, Italy, Luxembourg, Netherlands, Portugal, Spain
f	florin	Netherlands
FM	Finnish mark	Finland
Fr	franc	Andorra, France, French Guiana, Guadeloupe, Martinique, Monaco, Reunion Island, St. Pierre and Miquelon
FrB	Burundi franc	Burundi
Fr CFA	Communaute Financiere Africaine franc	Benin, Burkina Faso, Cameroon, Central African Republic, Chad, Comoros, Congo, Cote d'Ivoire, Equatorial Guinea, Gabon, Mali, Niger, Senegal, Togo
Ft	forint	Hungary
G	gourde	Haiti
GBP	Guinea-Bissau peso	Guinea-Bissau
G$	Guyana dollar	Guyana
GFr	Guinea franc	Guinea
Gs	guarani	Paraguay
HK$	Hong Kong dollar	Hong Kong
ID	Iraqi dinar	Iraq
IKr	Icelandic krona	Iceland
IRœ	Irish pound	Republic of Ireland
IS	Israel shekel	Israel
It	inti	Peru
J$	Jamaican dollar	Jamaica
JD	Jordanian dinar	Jordan
K	kina	Papua New Guinea
K	new kip	Laos
Kcs	koruna	Czech Republic, Slovakia
KD	Kuwaiti dinar	Kuwait
KSh	Kenyan shilling	Kenya
Ky	kyat	Myanmar (Burma)
Kz	kwanza	Angola
L	leu	Romania
L$	Liberian dollar	Liberia
LD	Libyan dinar	Libya
Le	leone	Sierra Leone
LFr	Luxembourg franc	Luxembourg
Lk	lek	Albania
Lp	lempira	Honduras
L£	Lebanese pound	Lebanon
Lr	lira	Italy, San Marino
Lv	leva	Bulgaria
M$	Malaysian dollar	Malaysia
MFr	Malagasy franc	Madagascar
MKw	Malawi kwacha	Malawi
Ml	maloti	Lesotho
ML	Maltese lira	Malta

MP	Mexican peso	Mexico
MRs	Mauritius rupee	Mauritius
MRu	Maldivian rufiya	Maldives
Mt	metical	Mozambique
N	naira	Nigeria
NAf	Antillean florin	Netherlands Antilles
Ng	ngultrum	Bhutan
NKr	Norwegian krone	Norway
NP	nuevo peso	Uruguay
NRs	Nepalese rupee	Nepal
NTs	New Taiwanese dollar	Taiwan
NZ$	New Zealand dollar	Cook Islands, New Zealand, Niue
Og	ouguiya	Mauritania
P	pula	Botswana
PP	Philippine peso	Philippines
PRs	Pakistan rupee	Pakistan
Ptas	peseta	Spain
Ptcs	pataca	Macao
Q	quetzal	Guatemala
QRl	riyal	Qatar
R	rand	South Africa, Namibia
Rb	ruble	Armenia, Azerbaijan, Belarus, Estonia, Georgia, Kazakhstan, Kirgizstan, Latvia, Lithuania, Moldova, Russia, Tajikstan, Turkmenistan, Ukraine, Uzbekistan
RFr	Rwandan franc	Rwanda
riel	riel	Cambodia
Rl	Iranian rial	Iran
Rlo	rial Omani	Oman
Rp	rupiah	Indonesia
Rs	rupee	India
S	sucre	Ecuador
S$	Singapore dollar	Singapore
Sf	Suriname florin	Suriname
SFr	Swiss franc	Switzerland, Liechtenstein
SI$	Solomon Island dollar	Soloman Islands
SKr	Swedish krona	Sweden
SRl	Saudi riyal	Saudi Arabia
SRs	Seychelles rupee	Seychelles
SSh	Somali shilling	Somalia
T$	pa'anga	Tonga
TD	Tunisian dinar	Tunisia
Tg	tugrik	Mongolia
Tk	taka	Bangladesh
TL	Turkish lira	Turkey
TSh	Tanzanian shilling	Tanzania
TT$	Trinidad and Tobagoan dollar	Trinidad and Tobago
USh	Ugandan shilling	Uganda
V	vatu	Vanuatu
W	won	Democratic People's Republic of Korea, Republic of Korea
Y	yen	Japan
YRl	Yemen rial	Yemen
Yu	yuan	People's Republic of China
Z	Zaire	Zaire
Z$	Zimbabwe dollar	Zimbabwe
ZKw	Zambian kwacha	Zambia
Zl	zloty	Poland

Keyword List

Following is a list of keywords used in EA. The section(s) in which each keyword appears are listed after each keyword. Within each keyword, entries are arranged alphabetically by organization name.

Accounting

1 ■ Professional Accounting Society of America (PASA)
PO Box 251451
Los Angeles, CA 90025
E-mail: info@thepasa.org
URL: http://www.thepasa.org
Contact: Boomer Butler, Contact
Founded: 2005. **Description:** Represents entry-level and mid-level associates working at accounting firms across America. Addresses the issues that affect entry-level and mid-level accounting professionals. Serves as a voice for everyone in the public accounting industry. **Awards:** CPA Exam Achievement Award. **Frequency:** annual. **Type:** recognition. **Recipient:** for CPA candidates who score exceptionally well on one or more particular exam sections. **Publications:** Journal. Alternate Formats: online ● Annual Report, annual. Alternate Formats: online.

Accounting

2 ■ Accountants Global Network (AGN)
2851 S Parker Rd., Ste.850
Aurora, CO 80014
Ph: (303)743-7880
Fax: (303)743-7660
E-mail: rhood@agn.org
URL: http://www.agn.org
Contact: Rita Hood, Exec. Dir.
Founded: 1978. **Multinational. Description:** Represents and promotes the fields of separate and independent accounting and consulting firms serving business organizations.

3 ■ Accreditation Council for Accountancy and Taxation (ACAT)
1010 N Fairfax St.
Alexandria, VA 22314-1574
Free: (888)289-7763
Fax: (703)549-2512
E-mail: info@acatcredentials.org
URL: http://www.acatcredentials.org
Contact: Peg D. Kirkpatrick, Dir.
Founded: 1973. **Staff:** 3. **Description:** Strives to raise professional standards and improve the practices of accountancy and taxation. Identifies persons with demonstrated knowledge of the principles and practices of accountancy and taxation. Ensures the continued professional growth of accredited individuals by setting stringent continuing education requirements. Fosters increased recognition for the profession in the public, private, and educational sectors. **Awards:** High Scorer Award. **Frequency:** semiannual. **Type:** recognition. **Recipient:** for the highest score on accountancy exam. **Study Groups:** Exam Technical Advisory Panel. **Affiliated With:** National Society of Accountants. **Formerly:** (1990) Accreditation Council for Accountancy. **Publications:** *Accreditation Council for Accountancy and Taxation—Directory*, annual. Alternate Formats: online ● *Action Letter*, semiannual. Newsletters. Alternate Formats: online. **Conventions/Meetings:** board meeting - 3/year.

4 ■ Affiliated Conference of Practicing Accountants International (ACPA)
Address Unknown since 2008
URL: http://acpa.careerbank.com
Founded: 1978. **Members:** 78. **Staff:** 2. **Regional Groups:** 3. **Local Groups:** 2. **Multinational. Description:** Certified public and chartered accounting firms. Encourages the interchange of professional and legislative information among members with the aim of: enhancing service and technical and professional competency; maintaining effective management administration and practice development; increasing public awareness of members' capabilities. Facilitates availability and use of specialists and industry expertise among members in areas such as manufacturing, real estate, legal and medical services, finance, wholesaling, retailing, and municipal government. Makes client referrals; compiles revenue, operating expense, and cost ratio comparisons among firms. **Committees:** Quality Control; Regional Management. **Subgroups:** Asian Activity Centre; Computer; Construction; Employee Benefits; International Tax Network; Law Firms; Litigation and Forensic Services; Manufacturing; Multimedia; Real Estate; Tax. **Also Known As:** ACPA International. **Publications:** *ACPA Worldwide Brochure* ● *Perspective*. Newsletter. Includes committee, networks, and membership updates and international news. ● Directory, annual. **Price:** included in membership dues. **Circulation:** 5,000 ● Also makes available press kit. **Conventions/Meetings:** semiannual regional meeting ● annual Worldwide Conference - international conference, seminar and roundtable discussion format (exhibits).

5 ■ AGN International - North America (AGN-NA)
2851 S Parker Rd., Ste.850
Aurora, CO 80014
Ph: (303)743-7880
Free: (800)782-2272
Fax: (303)743-7660
E-mail: rhood@agn.org
URL: http://www.agn-na.org
Contact: Rita Hood, Exec. Dir.
Founded: 1978. **Members:** 52. **Staff:** 3,803. **Budget:** $900,000. **Description:** Certified public accounting firms. Provides networking resources, technical and marketing assistance, and staff training programs to members. Compiles statistics. Maintains networking share groups. **Libraries: Type:** reference. **Holdings:** audiovisuals, books. **Subjects:** accounting, auditing, marketing, tax, management. **Awards:** Chairman's Award. **Frequency:** annual. **Type:** recognition. **Recipient:** for volunteer who has devoted significant time to the organization. **Computer Services:** database ● mailing lists. **Absorbed:** (2002) TAG International. **Formerly:** (1998) Continental Association of CPA Firms. **Publications:** *AGW International World-wide Link*, quarterly. Newsletter ● *Client Newsletter*, quarterly ● *Tax Brochures* ● Brochures ● Also publishes materials for clients in the construction industry, health care profession, manufacturers, and law firms. **Conventions/Meetings:** congress ● semiannual convention (exhibits).

6 ■ Alliance of Practicing Certified Public Accountants (APCPA)
12149 Fremont St.
Yucaipa, CA 92399
Ph: (909)705-7505
Fax: (909)790-7646
E-mail: bmvalek@earthlink.net
Contact: Mr. Bernard Valek CPA, Pres.
Founded: 1988. **Members:** 5,000. **Membership Dues:** regular, $95 (annual). **Staff:** 10. **Description:** Represents and promotes practicing certified public accountants.

7 ■ American Accounting Association (AAA)
5717 Bessie Dr.
Sarasota, FL 34233-2330
Ph: (941)921-7747
Fax: (941)923-4093
E-mail: office@aaahq.org
URL: http://aaahq.org
Contact: Tracey Sutherland, Exec. Dir.
Founded: 1916. **Members:** 10,000. **Membership Dues:** individual, $145 (annual) ● student, $25 (annual). **Staff:** 16. **Description:** Professors and practitioners of accounting. Promotes worldwide excellence in accounting education, research and practice. **Awards: Frequency:** periodic. **Type:** fellowship. **Recipient:** to PhD candidates in accounting. **Telecommunication Services:** electronic mail, tracey@aaahq.org ● electronic mail, joe@aaahq.org. **Formerly:** (1935) American Association of University Instructors in Accounting. **Publications:** *Accounting Education News*, periodic. Newsletter ● *Accounting Horizons*, quarterly. Journal. **Price:** free for members; $60.00 /year for nonmembers ● *Accounting Review*, quarterly. Journal. Contains scholarly articles on all aspects of accounting; includes annual index. **Price:** free for members; $90.00 /year for nonmembers ● *Issues in Accounting Education*, quarterly. Journal. **Price:** free for members; $30.00 /year for nonmembers ● Also publishes special studies. **Conventions/Meetings:** annual meeting (exhibits) - always August. 2008 Aug. 3-6, Orange, CA; 2009 Aug. 2-5, New York, NY.

8 ■ American Association of Attorney-Certified Public Accountants (AAA-CPA)
3921 Old Lee Hwy., Ste.71A
Fairfax, VA 22030
Ph: (703)352-8064
Free: (888)288-9272
Fax: (703)352-8073
E-mail: info@attorney-cpa.com
URL: http://www.attorney-cpa.com
Contact: Kenneth D. Goodman Esq., Pres.
Founded: 1964. **Members:** 1,350. **Membership Dues:** educator, government employee, $65 (annual)

● regular, international, $210 (annual) ● associate, student, $35 (annual) ● life, $2,500. **Staff:** 3. **Budget:** $430,000. **State Groups:** 19. **Description:** Represents persons who are licensed both as attorneys and as certified public accountants (CPAs). Promotes high professional and ethical standards; seeks to safeguard and defend the professional and legal rights of attorney-CPAs. Conducts research on dual licensing and dual practice; maintains speakers' bureau, placement service. Has compiled a list of attorney-CPAs in the United States; conducts biennial economic and practice survey. Maintains liaison with bar associations and accounting groups and offers referral service of potential clients. State groups conduct extensive self-education programs. **Computer Services:** Mailing lists. **Committees:** Continuing Education; Cooperation With Bar and Accounting Groups; Ethics and Opinions; Relations With Government Groups. **Publications:** *American Association of Attorney-Certified Public Accountants—Membership List*, periodic. Membership Directory. Contains a computer printout or pressure-sensitive mailing labels. **Price:** $135.00 ● *The Attorney-CPA*, quarterly. Newsletter. Contains updates on dual license regulations. **Price:** $30.00/year. ISSN: 0571-8279. **Circulation:** 1,800. **Advertising:** accepted. Alternate Formats: online ● *Attorney-CPA Directory*, annual. Membership Directory. **Price:** $160.00. **Circulation:** 1,500. **Advertising:** accepted. **Conventions/Meetings:** annual meeting (exhibits) - 2008 June 22-29, Amelia Island, FL.

9 ■ American Institute of Certified Public Accountants (AICPA)

1211 Ave. of the Americas
New York, NY 10036-8775
Ph: (212)596-6001
Free: (888)777-7077
Fax: (212)596-6030
E-mail: bmelancon@aicpa.org
URL: http://www.aicpa.org
Contact: Barry C. Melancon, Pres./CEO

Founded: 1887. **Members:** 330,000. **Membership Dues:** public accounting, law and consulting, $185-$380 (annual) ● business, industry, $185-$345 (annual) ● education, government, associate, $180 (annual) ● retired, inactive, $95 (annual) ● student, $35 (annual) ● non-CPA section associate, $95 (annual). **Staff:** 575. **Description:** Professional society of accountants certified by the states and territories. Responsibilities include establishing auditing and reporting standards; influencing the development of financial accounting standards underlying the presentation of U.S. corporate financial statements; preparing and grading the national Uniform CPA Examination for the state licensing bodies. Conducts research and continuing education programs and oversight of practice. Maintains over 100 committees including Accounting Standards, Accounting and Review Services, AICPA Effective Legislation Political Action, Auditing Standards, Taxation, Consulting Services, Professional Ethics, Quality Review, Women and Family Issues, and Information Technology. **Additional Websites:** http://www.cpa2biz.com. **Divisions:** Academic and Career Development Team; Accounting Standards Team; Assurance Services Webtrust; Audit and Attest Standards Team; Center for Excellence in Financial Management; Communications/Public Relations Team; Congressional and Political Affairs Team; Consulting Services Membership; Examinations Team; Information Technology Membership Section and Credential; International Services; PCPS: The AICPA Alliance for CPA Firms; Peer Review; Personal Financial Planning Team; Professional Ethics; Professional Standards and Services-Washington; SEC Practice; State Societies and Regulatory Affairs Team; Taxation Topics; Technical Hotline Team. **Publications:** *The CPA Letter*, bimonthly, published online monthly. Newsletter. ISSN: 0094-792X. Alternate Formats: online.

10 ■ American Society of Tax Professionals (ASTP)

PO Box 1213
Lynnwood, WA 98046-1213
Ph: (425)774-1996
Free: (877)674-1996
Fax: (425)672-0461
E-mail: carol.kraemer1@verizon.net
Contact: Carol L. Kraemer CCCE, Exec. Dir.

Founded: 1987. **Members:** 150. **Membership Dues:** active, $65 (annual). **Staff:** 1. **State Groups:** 3. **Description:** Tax preparers, accountants, attorneys, bookkeepers, accounting services, and public accounting firms seeking to uphold high service standards in professional tax preparation. Works to enhance the image of tax professionals and make tax practice more profitable; keep members abreast of tax law and service and delivery changes; promote networking among members for mutual assistance. Offers continuing education and training courses and public relations and marketing planning and preparation services. Supports Certified Tax Preparer Program. **Boards:** Directors. **Committees:** Nominating. **Supersedes:** National Association of Income Tax Practitioners. **Publications:** *Tax Professional's Update*, bimonthly. Newsletter. Contains tax preparation changes, practice management and building tips, and calendar of events. **Price:** included in membership dues. **Circulation:** 210. **Advertising:** accepted. **Conventions/Meetings:** annual Educational Tax Conference (exhibits) - always in fall.

11 ■ American Society of Women Accountants (ASWA)

8405 Greensboro Dr., Ste.800
McLean, VA 22102-5120
Ph: (703)506-3265
Free: (800)326-2163
Fax: (703)506-3266
E-mail: aswa@aswa.org
URL: http://www.aswa.org
Contact: Karen J. Gunther, Pres.

Founded: 1938. **Members:** 5,000. **Membership Dues:** regular/dual, affiliate, $100 (annual) ● student/associate, $33 (annual). **Staff:** 18. **Budget:** $600,000. **Regional Groups:** 6. **Local Groups:** 96. **Description:** Professional society of women accountants, educators, and others in the field of accounting dedicated to the achievement of personal, professional, and economic potential. Assists women accountants in their careers and promotes development in the profession. Conducts educational and research programs. **Libraries: Type:** reference. **Awards:** ASWA Scholarship Award. **Frequency:** annual. **Type:** scholarship. **Recipient:** for undergraduate students majoring in accounting. **Publications:** *The Edge*, bimonthly. Magazine. Includes calendar of events and listing of new officers and directors. **Advertising:** accepted. **Conventions/Meetings:** annual conference (exhibits) - always fall.

12 ■ American Woman's Society of Certified Public Accountants (AWSCPA)

136 S Keowee St.
Dayton, OH 45402
Ph: (937)222-1872
Free: (800)297-2721
Fax: (937)222-5794
E-mail: info@awscpa.org
URL: http://www.awscpa.org
Contact: Mary B. Riley CPA, Pres.

Founded: 1933. **Members:** 1,500. **Membership Dues:** individual, professional friend (with $25 application fee plus affiliate fee), $125 (annual) ● student friend (with $10 application fee plus affiliate fee), $30 (annual). **Staff:** 10. **Local Groups:** 35. **Description:** Citizens who hold Certified Public Accountant certificates as well as those who have passed the CPA examination but do not have certificates. Works to improve the status of professional women and to make the business community aware of the professional capabilities of the woman CPA. Conducts semiannual statistical survey of members; offers specialized education and research programs. **Awards:** Authorship Award. **Frequency:** annual. **Type:** recognition. **Recipient:** for a major contribution to accounting literature ● Educator of the Year Award. **Frequency:** annual. **Type:** recognition. **Recipient:** for exceptional, effective teaching of accounting at a two or four-year college ● National Scholarships. **Frequency:** annual. **Type:** scholarship. **Recipient:** to individuals aspiring to become CPAs ● Public Service Award. **Frequency:** annual. **Type:** recognition. **Recipient:** for outstanding service outside the accounting profession ● Woman CPA of the Year Award. **Frequency:** annual. **Type:** recognition. **Recipient:** for exemplary service to the AWSCPA and the accounting profession. **Telecommunication Services:** electronic mail, mbrileycpa@mindspring.com. **Publications:** *AWSCPA Newsletter*, quarterly ● *Issues Paper* ● *Membership Roster*. Membership Directory. **Circulation:** 1,500. **Conventions/Meetings:** annual conference (exhibits).

13 ■ Association for Accounting Administration (AAA)

136 S Keowee St.
Dayton, OH 45402
Ph: (937)222-0030
Fax: (937)222-5794
E-mail: aaainfo@cpaadmin.org
URL: http://www.cpaadmin.org
Contact: Kimberly A. Fantaci, Exec. Dir.

Founded: 1984. **Members:** 600. **Membership Dues:** administrator, consultant SIG, Vendor SIG, $275 (annual) ● subsequent (additional member from different office), $225 (annual) ● subsequent (additional member from the same office), $175 (annual) ● ATA SIG, $100 (annual). **Staff:** 10. **Budget:** $250,000. **Local Groups:** 14. **Description:** Promotes the profession of accounting administration and office management in accounting firms and corporate accounting departments. Sponsors activities, including consulting and placement services, seminars, salary and trends surveys, and speakers' bureau. Provides a forum for representation and exchange. Offers group purchasing opportunities. **Libraries: Type:** not open to the public; lending. **Holdings:** 250. **Subjects:** personnel, firm administration, management. **Awards:** Achievement, Commitment and Excellence Award. **Frequency:** annual. **Type:** recognition. **Recipient:** for leadership and the individual's strategic impact on the firm's profit and growth ● Distinguished Service Award. **Frequency:** annual. **Type:** recognition. **Recipient:** for individuals who have made outstanding contributions to the association and the profession. **Committees:** Education; Newsletter; Public Relations; Special Projects. **Formerly:** (1993) Association of Accounting Administrators. **Publications:** *AAA Report*, bimonthly. Newsletters. **Circulation:** 600. **Advertising:** accepted ● Membership Directory, annual. **Conventions/Meetings:** annual symposium (exhibits).

14 ■ Association of Chartered Accountants in the United States (ACAUS)

341 Lafayette St., Ste.4246
New York, NY 10012-2417
Ph: (212)334-2078
Fax: (212)431-5786
E-mail: admin@acaus.org
URL: http://www.acaus.org
Contact: Guy Langford, Pres.

Founded: 1980. **Members:** 6,000. **Membership Dues:** regular, $95 (annual) ● retiree, $25 (annual). **Staff:** 3. **Budget:** $75,000. **State Groups:** 40. **Local Groups:** 14. **Description:** Chartered accountants from England, Wales, Scotland, Ireland, Canada, Australia, New Zealand, and South Africa in commerce and public practice. Represents the interests of chartered accountants; promotes career development and international mobility of professionals. Offers educational and research programs. Maintains speakers' bureau and placement service. **Libraries: Type:** reference. **Holdings:** clippings. **Subjects:** international mobility and licensing of professionals. **Awards:** Chartered Accountants/Beta Alpha Psi Scholarship. **Frequency:** annual. **Type:** scholarship ● Chartered Accountants International Education Award. **Frequency:** annual. **Type:** monetary. **Computer Services:** database ● mailing lists. **Telecommunication Services:** electronic mail, info@networknyc.com. **Publications:** *Chartered Accountants US Newsletter*, quarterly. **Price:** free. **Circulation:** 1,500. **Advertising:** accepted ● *Member's Directory and Handbook*, annual. Membership Directory. **Circu-**

lation: 1,500. **Advertising:** accepted. **Conventions/Meetings:** annual dinner - usually October in New York.

15 ■ Association of Insolvency and Restructuring Advisors (AIRA)
221 Stewart Ave., Ste.207
Medford, OR 97501
Ph: (541)858-1665
Fax: (541)858-9187
E-mail: aira@airacira.org
URL: http://www.airacira.org
Contact: Grant W. Newton CIRA, Pres.-Elect
Founded: 1981. **Members:** 1,500. **Membership Dues:** government/education, $75 (annual) ● regular, $225 (annual). **Staff:** 4. **Budget:** $235,000. **Description:** Certified and licensed public accountants, attorneys, examiners, trustees, and receivers. Seeks to define and develop the accountant's role provided by the Bankruptcy Reform Act of 1978 and to improve accounting skills used in insolvency cases. Promotes the primary role of creditors in insolvency situations and the enforcement of ethical standards of practice. Seeks to develop judicial reporting standards for insolvency and provide technical, analytical, and accounting skills necessary in insolvent situations. Works to educate others in the field of the role of the accountant in order to foster better working relationships. Provides information about legislative issues that affect members and testifies before legislative bodies. Offers technical referral service. Administers the Certified Insolvency and Restructuring Advisor (CIRA) program. **Awards:** Kroll Zolfo Cooper/Randy Waits Awards. **Frequency:** annual. **Type:** recognition. **Recipient:** for the top three test scores on the CIRA exam. **Formerly:** (1985) National Association of Accountants in Insolvencies; (1999) Association of Insolvency Accountants. **Publications:** *Association of Insolvency and Restructuring Advisors Membership Directory*, annual. **Price:** included in membership dues. **Circulation:** 1,500 ● *Association of Insolvency and Restructuring Advisors Newsletter*, bimonthly. Includes information on conferences. **Price:** included in membership dues. Alternate Formats: online ● *Certified Insolvency and Reorganization and Restructuring Advisors Directory*, annual. **Conventions/Meetings:** annual Bankruptcy and Restructuring - conference, includes technical tax update and basic bankruptcy seminars (exhibits).

16 ■ Association of Latino Professionals in Finance and Accounting (ALPFA)
801 S Grand Ave., Ste.400
Los Angeles, CA 90017
Ph: (213)243-0004
Fax: (213)243-0006
E-mail: acepero@bdo.com
URL: http://www.alpfa.org
Contact: Alfredo Cepero CPA, Pres.
Founded: 1982. **Members:** 2,000. **Membership Dues:** associate, general, $120 (annual) ● life, $1,200 ● student, $20 (annual). **Staff:** 1. **Languages:** English, Spanish. **Description:** Hispanic certified public accountants from the private and public sectors, accounting firms, universities, and banks. Maintains and promotes professional and moral standards of Hispanics in the accounting field. Assists members in practice development and develops business opportunities for members. Sponsors continuing professional education seminars; provides employment services. **Awards: Frequency:** annual. **Type:** scholarship. **Recipient:** for an accounting student. **Telecommunication Services:** electronic mail, ceo@national.alpfa.org. **Committees:** Fundraising; Scholarship. **Formerly:** (1982) American Associations of Spanish Speaking CPA's; (2002) American Association of Hispanic CPAs. **Publications:** *La Cuenta*, quarterly. Newsletter. **Price:** included in membership dues. **Circulation:** 2,500. **Advertising:** accepted. Alternate Formats: online ● Membership Directory, annual. **Conventions/Meetings:** annual convention (exhibits).

17 ■ Association of Practicing Certified Public Accountants (AP-CPA)
Address Unknown since 2008
Founded: 1968. **Members:** 320. **Membership Dues:** individual CPA, $65 (annual). **Staff:** 1. **Description:** Provides seminars and courses that are approved by local CPAs. **Computer Services:** database, CPA directory ● mailing lists ● online services, bulletin board. **Publications:** *CPA Practitioner*, 9/year. Newsletter. **Conventions/Meetings:** monthly board meeting and meeting - 9/year.

18 ■ BKR International (BKR)
19 Fulton St., Ste.306
New York, NY 10038
Ph: (212)964-2115
Free: (800)BKR-INTL
Fax: (212)964-2133
E-mail: bkr@bkr.com
URL: http://www.bkr.com
Contact: Maureen M. Schwartz, Exec. Dir.
Founded: 1972. **Members:** 143. **Staff:** 6. **Budget:** $800,000. **Multinational. Description:** Accounting firms in the U.S. and abroad. Seeks to create an international group of competent professional firms, which will provide full services in major markets of the world and enable member firms to send and receive referrals. Helps reduce operating costs of member firms by: developing consolidated purchasing arrangements for services and supplies at the lowest possible cost; developing recruiting programs, marketing materials, and advertising to reduce the collective recruiting effort of group members; expanding the group to reduce the burden on individual member firms and increase their potential scope of services. Compiles statistics to provide member firms with data helpful to sound management decisions. Organizes clinical and administrative peer reviews to insure quality and provide management with professional counsel. Develops forms, procedures, and manuals to provide guidance and accommodate the needs of partners. Conducts 12 continuing education programs per year in all areas of expertise. **Computer Services:** database, directory of specialists ● database, mergers and acquisitions. **Committees:** Accounting and Auditing; Business Development; Construction; Human Resource; International Business; Manufacturing; MAS; Medical/Dental; Peer Review; Practice Management; Professional Development; Prototype; Resolution Trust Corporation; Taxation. **Formerly:** (1989) National CPA Group. **Publications:** *Roster*, semiannual. Membership Directory ● *Worldwide Bulletin*, bimonthly. Newsletter. Alternate Formats: online ● Brochures ● Also publishes marketing programs and updates. **Conventions/Meetings:** semiannual conference ● annual meeting.

19 ■ Clearinghouse for Volunteer Accounting Services (CVAS)
920 Hampshire Rd., Ste.A-29
Westlake Village, CA 91361
Ph: (805)495-6755
Fax: (805)374-2257
E-mail: info@cvas-ca.org
URL: http://www.cvas-usa.org
Contact: Paul H. Glass, Pres./Exec. Dir.
Founded: 1985. **Staff:** 3. **Description:** Works to match nonprofit organizations with pro bono accounting services required. **Programs:** Board Member Placement; Reduced Fee Audit; Technical Assistance; Technical Question and Answer. **Publications:** Newsletter, quarterly. Alternate Formats: online.

20 ■ Community Banking Advisory Network (CBAN)
10831 Old Mill Rd., Ste.400
Omaha, NE 68154
Ph: (402)778-7922
Free: (888)475-4476
Fax: (402)778-7931
E-mail: info@bankingcpas.com
URL: http://www.bankingcpas.com
Contact: Nancy Drennen, Exec. Dir.
Founded: 1995. **Members:** 19. **Membership Dues:** firm, $1,695 (annual). **Staff:** 3. **National Groups:** 19. **For-Profit. Description:** Certified Public Accounting (CPA) firms providing financial and consulting services to community banks. Seeks to advance CPA services to the community banking industry. Sponsors continuing education and training courses; conducts industry and member surveys; facilitates formation of joint ventures; makes available marketing assistance; facilitates resource sharing among members. **Publications:** *Community Banking Advisor*, quarterly. Newsletter. Addresses financial news and issues for Community banks. Alternate Formats: online. **Conventions/Meetings:** annual Community Banking Track at Super Conference, networking and Education events (exhibits).

21 ■ Construction Industry CPAs/Consultants Association (CICPAC)
15011 E Twilight View Dr.
Fountain Hills, AZ 85268
Ph: (480)836-0300
Free: (800)864-0491
Fax: (480)836-0400
E-mail: jcorcoran@cicpac.com
URL: http://www.cicpac.com
Contact: John J. Corcoran CPA, Exec. Dir.
Description: Certified Public Accounting (CPA) firms providing financial and consulting services to construction companies. Seeks to advance CPA services to the construction industries. Sponsors continuing education and training courses; conducts industry and member surveys; facilitates formation of joint ventures; makes available marketing assistance; facilitates resource sharing among members. **Publications:** *CICPAC Membership Directory*, periodic. **Conventions/Meetings:** annual conference - 2008 July 30-Aug. 1, Chicago, IL.

22 ■ Controllers Council (CC)
c/o Institute of Management of Accountants
10 Paragon Ave.
Montvale, NJ 07645-1718
Ph: (201)573-9000
Free: (800)638-4427
E-mail: roberta.booker@conference-board.org
URL: http://www.imanet.org/communities_controllers.asp
Contact: Roberta Booker, Council Rep.
Founded: 1985. **Members:** 2,000. **Membership Dues:** regular, $4,000 (annual). **Staff:** 2. **Budget:** $150,000. **Description:** Chief financial officers, corporate, divisional, group, and plant controllers; others with financial or accounting backgrounds who have responsibilities equivalent with those of controllers. Provides a means by which controllers may exchange information on and keep abreast of professional and career-related subjects. Member interest group of the Institute of Management Accountants (IMA). **Affiliated With:** Institute of Management Accountants. **Publications:** *Controllers Update*, monthly. Newsletter. Gives a management perspective on such topics as cost control, performance measurement, productivity improvement, and tax laws and regulations. **Price:** $75.00 /year for members; $215.00 /year for nonmembers. ISSN: 8756-5676. **Circulation:** 2,000. Alternate Formats: online. **Conventions/Meetings:** annual Roundtable Seminars - meeting and conference.

23 ■ Council of Petroleum Accountants Societies (COPAS)
3900 E Mexico Ave., Ste.602
Denver, CO 80210
Ph: (303)300-1131
Free: (877)992-6727
Fax: (303)300-3733
E-mail: natlofc@copas.org
URL: http://www.copas.org
Contact: Susan H. Jones, Exec. Dir.
Founded: 1961. **Members:** 2,800. **Membership Dues:** limited, $80 (annual). **Staff:** 3. **Local Groups:** 24. **Description:** Accountants, managers, and controllers employed in the petroleum industry. Formulates and disseminates accounting practices and pronouncements. Conducts research and educational programs. Operates speaker's bureau. **Telecommunication Services:** electronic mail, execdir@copas.org. **Committees:** Audit; Editorial; Education; Financial Reporting; Joint Interest; Revenue; Small Oil and Gas Companies; Tax. **Publications:** *Accounts*, quarterly. Magazine. Features updates of organizational activities. **Price:** available to members only. **Circulation:** 2,800. **Advertising:** accepted ●

Brochure. **Conventions/Meetings:** semiannual meeting - always April and October.

24 ■ CPA Associates International (CPAAI)
Meadows Off. Complex
301 Rte. 17 N
Rutherford, NJ 07070
Ph: (201)804-8686
Fax: (201)804-9222
E-mail: homeoffice@cpaai.com
URL: http://www.cpaai.com
Contact: Howard K. Lewis, Chm.
Founded: 1957. **Members:** 148. **Staff:** 4. **Regional Groups:** 4. **Languages:** English, French, Spanish. **Description:** Independent firms of Certified Public Accountants (CPAs) offering professional accounting, auditing, tax, and management advisory services. Fosters exchange of ideas and information among members; works to improve the profitability and practice of the accounting profession. **Committees:** Accounting and Assurance; Auto Dealers; Business Valuation; Construction and Real Estate; Employee Benefits; Family Business; Financial Institutions; Information Technology; Investment Planning; Litigation Services; Manufacturing; Marketing; Medical Professionals; Not for Profit and Government Services; Peer Review; Practice Management; SEC Practice; Tax. **Formerly:** (1992) CPA Associates. **Publications:** *Business Insights*, quarterly. Newsletter ● *Client Newsletter Tax Outlook*, quarterly. Discusses proposed changes in federal tax laws and their effect on both corporations and individuals. ● *Client Newsletters* ● *Construction Client Newsletter*, quarterly. Focuses on CPA services for members' clients. ● *CPA Associates Directory*, annual. Lists member firms in the United States and abroad. **Circulation:** 3,000 ● *CPAAI Update*, semimonthly. Newsletter. Updates member firms on association and member developments. ● *Medical Professionals Client Newsletter*, quarterly. Provides information on CPA services available to members' clients. ● *Year-End Tax Planning Guide*, annual. Covers legislative and financial developments and practical tax information for the purpose of year-end tax planning. **Price:** free, for members and members' clients. **Circulation:** 24,000. **Conventions/Meetings:** annual meeting, with seminars ● roundtable, by telephone ● periodic seminar.

25 ■ CPA Auto Dealer Consultants Association (CADCA)
PO Box 542055
Omaha, NE 68154
Ph: (402)964-3805
Free: (888)475-4476
Fax: (402)964-3736
E-mail: info@autodealercpas.net
URL: http://www.autodealercpas.net
Contact: Nancy Drennen, Exec. Dir.
Founded: 1996. **Members:** 31. **Membership Dues:** firm, $1,800 (annual). **Staff:** 3. **For-Profit. Description:** Certified Public Accounting (CPA) firms providing financial and consulting services to automobile dealers. Seeks to advance CPA services to automobile dealers. Sponsors continuing education and training courses; conducts industry and member surveys; facilitates formation of joint ventures; makes available marketing assistance; facilitates resource sharing among members. **Telecommunication Services:** electronic mail, nancyd@autodealercpas.net. **Publications:** *Auto Focus*, quarterly. Newsletter. Contains information on auto dealerships. **Price:** $2,000.00/year. **Conventions/Meetings:** semiannual Education and Networking Conference (exhibits).

26 ■ CPA Manufacturing Services Association (MSA)
One Valmont Plz., 4th Fl.
Omaha, NE 68154-5214
Ph: (402)964-3805
Free: (888)475-4476
Fax: (402)964-3736
E-mail: info@manufacturingcpas.com
URL: http://www.manufacturingcpas.com
Contact: Nancy Drennen, Exec. Dir.
Membership Dues: $1,595 (annual). **Description:** Certified Public Accounting (CPA) firms providing financial and consulting services to the manufacturing industries. Seeks to advance CPA services to manufacturers. Sponsors continuing education and training courses; conducts industry and member surveys; facilitates formation of joint ventures; makes available marketing assistance; facilitates resource sharing among members. **Publications:** *Client*, periodic. Newsletter ● Membership Directory, periodic.

27 ■ CPAmerica International
11801 Res. Dr.
Alachua, FL 32615
Ph: (386)418-4001
Free: (800)992-2324
Fax: (386)418-4002
E-mail: info@cpamerica.org
URL: http://www.afai.com
Contact: Douglas H. Thompson Jr., Pres./CEO
Founded: 1978. **Members:** 25. **Multinational. Description:** Provides programs and services to CPA firms, including courses, professional training, networking, peer and practice reviews, surveys, and marketing products. **Publications:** Newsletter ● Brochures. **Conventions/Meetings:** annual conference.

28 ■ DFK International/USA (DFK/USA)
c/o Jay Hauck, Exec. Dir.
1255 23rd St. NW, Ste.200
Washington, DC 20037-1174
Ph: (202)452-1588
Fax: (202)833-3636
E-mail: exec@dfkusa.com
URL: http://www.dfkusa.com
Contact: Jay Hauck, Exec. Dir.
Founded: 1979. **Members:** 27. **Staff:** 3. **Description:** Provides member firms with a forum to share practice-management information and technical expertise, leadership development training, opportunities for business referral, and the resources to serve clients on a national and international level.

29 ■ Financial Accounting Standards Board (FASB)
401 Merritt 7
PO Box 5116
Norwalk, CT 06856-5116
Ph: (203)847-0700
Fax: (203)849-9714
E-mail: clklimek@f-a-f.org
URL: http://www.fasb.org
Contact: Ms. Christine Klimek, Communications Mgr.
Founded: 1973. **Description:** Establishes standards of financial accounting and reporting for private-sector entities, including businesses and not-for-profit organizations. **Libraries: Type:** not open to the public. **Holdings:** archival material, articles, books, business records, clippings, periodicals. **Committees:** Investors Technical Advisory; Private Company Financial Reporting; Small Business Advisory. **Councils:** Financial Accounting Standards Advisory; User Advisory. **Task Forces:** Emerging Issues.

30 ■ Forensic Accountants Society of North America (FASNA)
4248 Park Glen Rd.
Minneapolis, MN 55416
Ph: (952)928-4668
Fax: (952)929-1318
E-mail: info@fasna.org
URL: http://www.fasna.org
Contact: Roger Nearmyer CPA, Pres.
Founded: 1996. **Members:** 8. **Membership Dues:** $300 (monthly). **Budget:** $50,000. **Regional Groups:** 10. **Description:** Serves as a resource center for member firms. Provides training and support in all aspects of forensic accounting (investigative accounting and auditing). **Publications:** *FASNA Forum*, bimonthly. Newsletter. Alternate Formats: online.

31 ■ Foundation for Accounting Education (FAE)
3 Park Ave., 18th Fl.
New York, NY 10016-5991
Ph: (212)719-8300
Free: (800)633-6320
Fax: (212)719-3364
E-mail: aschmelkin@nysscpa.org
URL: http://www.nysscpa.org
Contact: Alan Schmelkin, Managing Dir. for Operations
Founded: 1972. **Staff:** 17. **Budget:** $5,000,000. **Description:** Conducts educational and technical programs, seminars, workshops, and conferences for CPAs in private practice and industry. **Divisions:** CPE Operations; Firm Sales; Marketing and Educational Services; Self-Study. **Publications:** *Catalog of Education Programs*, annual. **Circulation:** 33,000 ● *Update*, monthly. Report.

32 ■ Hospitality Financial and Technology Professionals (HFTP)
11709 Boulder Ln., Ste.110
Austin, TX 78726-1832
Ph: (512)249-5333
Free: (800)646-4387
Fax: (512)249-1533
E-mail: frank.wolfe@hftp.org
URL: http://www.hftp.org
Contact: Frank Wolf CAE, Exec. VP/CEO
Founded: 1953. **Members:** 3,800. **Membership Dues:** individual, $295 (annual). **Staff:** 14. **Budget:** $2,300,000. **Local Groups:** 53. **Description:** Accountants, financial officers and MIS managers in 50 countries working in hotels, resorts, casinos, restaurants, and clubs. Develops uniform system of accounts. Conducts education, training, and certification programs; offers placement service; maintains hall of fame. **Awards: Frequency:** annual. **Type:** scholarship. **Formerly:** National Association of Hotel Accountants; (1975) National Association of Hotel and Motel Accountants; (1998) International Association of Hospitality Accountants. **Publications:** *The Bottomline*, bimonthly. Journal. Contains articles on hospitality technology, management, accounting and other issues pertinent to the IAHA and allied industries. **Price:** included in membership dues; $50.00 for nonmembers. ISSN: 0279-1889. **Circulation:** 3,800. **Advertising:** accepted. Alternate Formats: online ● *Membership and Resource Guide*, annual. Contains membership information. **Conventions/Meetings:** Club and Hotel Controllers - conference (exhibits) ● annual convention, with tradeshow (exhibits).

33 ■ Institute of Internal Auditors (IIA)
247 Maitland Ave.
Altamonte Springs, FL 32701-4201
Ph: (407)937-1100
Fax: (407)937-1101
E-mail: iia@theiia.org
URL: http://www.theiia.org
Contact: Dave A. Richards, Pres.
Founded: 1941. **Members:** 90,000. **Membership Dues:** individual, $115 (annual) ● educational, $65 (annual) ● student/retired, $30 (annual) ● sustaining, $50 (annual) ● special (Gaming Audit Group and CSA Center Sections), $40 (annual) ● life, $2,100 ● special (CAE Services Program Section), $100 (annual). **Staff:** 100. **Budget:** $13,000,000. **Local Groups:** 210. **Description:** Members in internal auditing, governance, internal control, IT audit, education, and security. Provides comprehensive professional, educational and development opportunities; standards and other professional practice guidance; and certification programs. **Libraries: Type:** reference. **Holdings:** 2,000. **Awards:** Bradford Cadmus Memorial Award. **Frequency:** annual. **Type:** recognition. **Recipient:** for service and accomplishments to profession ● **Frequency:** annual. **Type:** grant. **Recipient:** for doctoral research ● Thurston Award. **Frequency:** annual. **Type:** recognition. **Recipient:** for best article in journal ● Victor Z. Brink Award. **Frequency:** annual. **Type:** recognition. **Recipient:** for outstanding service to internal auditing profession. **Computer Services:** Information services, internal auditing resources ● online services,

discussion groups. **Boards:** Internal Auditing Standards; Regents. **Committees:** Academic Relations; Advanced Technology; Business and Industry Relations; Conferences; Educational Product; Government Relations; International Relations; Professional Issues; Quality Assurance; Research Foundation; Seminars. **Divisions:** Certifications and Standards; Educational Services; Membership Services; Practices and Communications; Quality Auditing; Technology. **Publications:** *AuditWire*, bimonthly. Newsletter. Alternate Formats: online ● *Connections*, quarterly ● *IIA Educator*, semiannual. Newsletter. Alternate Formats: online ● *Internal Auditor*, bimonthly. Magazine. Covers current issues and includes book reviews. **Advertising:** accepted. Alternate Formats: online ● *Professional Development and Educational Products*, semiannual. Catalog. Contains descriptions of all seminar courses/textbooks, research reports, and videos. ● Reports, periodic ● Also publishes textbooks and produces audio/video programs. **Conventions/Meetings:** annual international conference - usually June ● periodic seminar.

34 ■ Institute of Management Accountants (IMA)
10 Paragon Dr.
Montvale, NJ 07645
Ph: (201)573-9000
Free: (800)638-4427
Fax: (201)474-1600
E-mail: ima@imanet.org
URL: http://www.imanet.org
Contact: Paul A. Sharman ACMA, Pres./CEO
Founded: 1919. **Members:** 70,000. **Membership Dues:** professional, $185 (annual) ● student, $37 (annual) ● academic, $93 (annual). **Staff:** 80. **Budget:** $17,000,000. **Regional Groups:** 24. **Local Groups:** 280. **Description:** Management accountants in industry, public accounting, government, and academia; other persons interested in internal and management uses of accounting. Conducts research on accounting methods and procedures and the management purposes served. Established Institute of Certified Management Accountants (see separate entry) to implement and administer examinations for the Certified Management Accountant (CMA) program and the Certified in Financial Management (CFM) program. Annually presents chapter medals for competition, manuscripts and for the highest scores on the CMA Examination. Offers continuing education programs comprising courses, conferences, and a self-study program in management accounting areas. Offers ethics counseling services for members by telephone. Sponsors the Foundation for Applied Research. **Libraries: Type:** reference. **Holdings:** 20,000; archival material, books, periodicals. **Subjects:** accounting, financial management. **Awards:** James Bulloch Awards. **Frequency:** annual. **Type:** recognition. **Recipient:** for professors ● **Frequency:** annual. **Type:** scholarship. **Recipient:** for students and IMA chapters. **Committees:** Academic Relations; Education; Ethics; Finance; Financial Reporting; Information; Management Accounting Practices; Member Interest Groups; Professional Issues; Regional Operations; Research; Technology. **Formerly:** (1957) National Association of Cost Accountants; (1991) National Association of Accountants. **Publications:** *Management Accounting Quarterly*. Journal. Includes articles on merging practical experience and theoretical knowledge. **Price:** included in membership dues; $60.00 for nonmembers. ISSN: 1528-5359. **Circulation:** 65,000. Alternate Formats: online ● *Strategic Finance*, monthly. Magazine. Includes articles on corporate financial management and accounting. **Price:** included in membership dues; $140.00/year for corporate libraries; $93.00/year for nonprofit U.S. libraries; $140.00 /year for libraries outside U.S. ISSN: 1524-833X. **Circulation:** 65,000. **Advertising:** accepted. Alternate Formats: microform; online ● *Strategic TechNotes*, semimonthly. Newsletter. **Price:** free. Alternate Formats: CD-ROM; diskette ● Books. **Conventions/Meetings:** annual conference, with show (exhibits) - 2008 June 14-18, Tampa, FL.

35 ■ Interamerican Accounting Association (IAA)
275 Fountainebleau Blvd., Ste.245
Miami, FL 33172
Ph: (305)225-1991
Fax: (305)225-2011
E-mail: oficina@contadoresaic.org
URL: http://www.contadoresaic.org
Contact: Victor Manuel Abreu Paez, Exec. Dir.
Founded: 1949. **Members:** 33. **Staff:** 4. **Budget:** $500,000. **Regional Groups:** 3. **Languages:** English, Portuguese, Spanish. **Multinational. Description:** National associations representing 1,100,000 accountants in the Americas. Objectives are to maintain high technical and ethical standards for the accounting profession; further accounting as a scientific discipline by fostering contacts between members and institutions of higher learning; provide members with information on current accounting practices and concepts; encourage members to establish ties with accounting groups worldwide; assure that professional services rendered by members contribute to the social and economic development of their community. Operates speakers' bureau. **Libraries: Type:** reference. **Holdings:** archival material. **Subjects:** Interamerican accounting. **Awards:** Meritorious Accountant of the Americas. **Frequency:** biennial. **Type:** recognition ● **Frequency:** biennial. **Type:** recognition. **Recipient:** for ethical and technical merit. **Telecommunication Services:** electronic mail, servicios@contadoresaic.org. **Committees:** Accounting Research; Auditing Standards and Practices; Economic and Fiscal Integration; Education; Ethics and Professional Practice; Financial and Management; Internal Auditing; Public Sector; Small and Medium Organizations Management; Systems and Technology Information; University Accreditation. **Affiliated With:** International Federation of Accountants. **Foreign language name:** Asociacion Interamericana de Contabilidad. **Formerly:** (1974) Interamerican Accounting Conference. **Publications:** *IAA Directory* (in English and Spanish), biennial. **Circulation:** 2,500 ● *Interamerican Accounting Magazine* (in English, Portuguese, and Spanish), quarterly ● *Interamerican Bulletin* (in English, Portuguese, and Spanish), monthly ● Also publishes studies conducted by technical committees. **Conventions/Meetings:** biennial Conferencia Interamericana de Contabilidad - conference ● semiannual regional meeting and seminar.

36 ■ International Federation of Accountants (IFAC)
545 5th Ave., 14th Fl.
New York, NY 10017
Ph: (212)286-9344 (212)471-8702
Fax: (212)286-9570
E-mail: julissaguevara@ifac.org
URL: http://www.ifac.org
Contact: Julissa Guevara, Member Relations Assoc.
Founded: 1977. **Members:** 163. **Staff:** 10. **Budget:** $1,200,000. **Languages:** English, French, Spanish. **Multinational. Description:** Accounting bodies recognized by law or general consensus representing over 1,000,000 individuals in 78 countries. Seeks to achieve international technical, ethical, and educational guidelines and standards for the accountancy profession. Fosters cooperation among members and encourages development of regional groups with similar goals. **Libraries: Type:** reference. **Holdings:** 200. **Subjects:** international accountancy. **Awards:** Sempier Award. **Frequency:** quinquennial. **Type:** recognition. **Boards:** International Accounting Education Standards; International Auditing and Assurance Standards; International Public Sector Accounting Standards. **Committees:** Compliance Advisory Panel; Developing Nations; International Ethics Standards Board for Accountants; Professional Accountants in Business; Small and Medium Practices. **Publications:** *International Federation of Accountants—Annual Report*. Reviews the federation's activities in the past year. Provides a description of IFAC and financial statements. **Circulation:** 3,000 ● Newsletter, quarterly. Covers worldwide meetings and activities of interest to accountants. Includes calendar of events. **Circulation:** 3,000. **Conventions/Meetings:** quinquennial congress (exhibits).

37 ■ International Group of Accounting Firms (IGAF)
3235 Satellite Blvd., Bldg. 400, Ste.300
Duluth, GA 30096
Ph: (678)417-7730
Fax: (678)999-3959
E-mail: kmead@igaf.org
URL: http://www.igaf.org
Contact: Kevin Mead, Pres./Exec. Dir.
Founded: 1977. **Members:** 125. **Staff:** 5. **Regional Groups:** 330. **National Groups:** 59. **Multinational. Description:** Works to ensure that the standard for accounting, auditing, and management services are maintained. **Computer Services:** Online services, message board. **Publications:** Annual Report, annual.

38 ■ Law Firm Services Association (LFSA)
10831 Old Mill Rd., Ste.400
Omaha, NE 68154
Ph: (402)778-7922
Free: (888)475-4476
Fax: (402)778-7931
E-mail: info@lawfirmcpas.com
Contact: Nancy Drennen, Exec.Dir.
Membership Dues: general, $1,595. **Description:** Certified public accountant (CPA) firms providing financial and consulting services to law firms. Seeks to enhance members' ability to serve the legal community. Facilitates resource sharing and the establishment of joint ventures among members; provides marketing services to members; conducts industry surveys; sponsors continuing professional development and training courses. **Computer Services:** Mailing lists. **Publications:** Membership Directory ● Brochure.

39 ■ Leading Edge Alliance (LEA)
621 Cedar St.
St. Charles, IL 60174
Ph: (630)513-9814
Fax: (630)524-9014
URL: http://www.leadingedgealliance.com
Contact: Karen Kehl-Rose, Pres.
Multinational. Description: Represents independently owned accounting and consulting firms. Provides business development, professional training and education, and peer-to-peer networking opportunities. Offers business advisory expertise and experience and conducts accounting, tax and consulting services. **Publications:** *Edge Magazine*. **Price:** included in membership dues. Alternate Formats: online.

40 ■ Medical Dental Hospital Business Associates (MDHBA)
350 Poplar Ave.
Elmhurst, IL 60126
Ph: (630)941-8100
Fax: (630)359-4274
E-mail: info@mdhba.org
URL: http://www.mdhba.org
Contact: Mr. Michael J. Bandy, Exec. Dir.
Founded: 1939. **Members:** 75. **Membership Dues:** associate, $150 (annual). **Staff:** 2. **Description:** Accounts receivable management companies. Provides educational programs and services for members and the healthcare industry; sets quality standards; promotes business integrity. Offers services and benefits for medical and hospital accounts receivable collection management agencies. Provides three levels of certification. **Awards:** Elmer Award. **Frequency:** annual. **Type:** recognition. **Recipient:** to member esteemed by the past President Council as having made the most significant contribution to organizational activities ● Lifetime Achievement Award. **Frequency:** annual. **Type:** recognition. **Recipient:** for a member who has made innumerable and valuable contributions to the healthcare industry as a leader, teacher and consultant ● Pinnacle Award. **Frequency:** annual. **Type:** recognition. **Recipient:** for member agencies who have received recognition from clients ● President's Award. **Frequency:** annual. **Type:** recognition. **Recipient:** for an individual who did the most to advance the organization's interests during his or her tenure as president ● Robert T. Hellrung Award. **Frequency:** annual. **Type:** recognition. **Recipient:** to individuals who have made major contributions to the association during his or her term of office. **Programs:** Certified Profes-

sional Business Executive. **Publications:** *News and Views*, biweekly. Newsletter. Provides association updates, industry news and feature articles relative to the industry. **Circulation:** 75. Alternate Formats: online. **Conventions/Meetings:** biennial convention, for medical and hospital business personnel (exhibits).

41 ■ Moore Stephens North America (MSNA)
One Penn Plz.
250 W 34th St., 36th Fl.
New York, NY 10119
Ph: (212)896-3946
Fax: (212)849-6901
E-mail: theteam@msnainc.org
URL: http://www.msnainc.com
Contact: Steven E. Sacks CPA, Exec. Dir.

Founded: 1966. **Members:** 51. **Membership Dues:** $7,500 (annual). **Staff:** 4. **Budget:** $1,300,000. **National Groups:** 3. **Languages:** English, Spanish. **For-Profit. Multinational. Description:** North American public accounting and consulting firms. Aids certified public accounting firms in increasing, expanding, and diversifying their practices. Capitalizes on diversity of resources resident throughout the network to build a stronger revenue base for all members. Sponsors training programs in areas such as industry niche development, service niche development tax, staff, and computer auditing; conducts tax and management seminars. Compiles statistics. Offers networking forums, marketing assistance, and technology consulting to member firms. **Libraries: Type:** reference. **Holdings:** 750; periodicals. **Subjects:** accounting and consulting. **Computer Services:** Online services, networking requests, referrals worldwide. **Telecommunication Services:** electronic mail, ssacks@msnainc.org. **Committees:** Audit and Accounting; Automation and Technology; Business Valuation; Human Resources; Internal Auditing Services; International Tax; Litigation Support/Receivership Services; M&A; Management Services; Marketing; Practice Development; Tax. **Publications:** *MSNA Membership Directory*, annual. **Circulation:** 3,500. Alternate Formats: online ● *MSNA Networker*, monthly. Newsletter. Reports membership activities. **Circulation:** 3,500. Alternate Formats: online ● Brochures.

42 ■ National Asian American Society of Accountants (NAASA)
c/o Marc Bernardo, CPA, Treas.
PO Box 8689
New York, NY 10116
E-mail: dylan.jeng@naasa.org
URL: http://www.naasa.org
Contact: Dylan Jeng CPA, Sec.

Membership Dues: regular, $75 (annual) ● student, $25 (annual). **Description:** Enhances the influence and presence of Asian Americans in the accounting profession. Cultivates growth of accounting knowledge. Advances business development opportunities. **Telecommunication Services:** electronic mail, jenny.wei@naasa.org ● electronic mail, marc.bernardo@naasa.org. **Committees:** Professional Development; Public Relations; Student Affairs.

43 ■ National Associated CPA Firms (NACPAF)
136 S Keowee St.
Dayton, OH 45402
Ph: (937)222-1024
Fax: (937)222-5794
E-mail: email@nacpaf.com
URL: http://www.nacpaf.com
Contact: Kim Fantaci, Exec. Dir.

Founded: 1979. **Members:** 50. **Staff:** 5. **Regional Groups:** 3. **Description:** Professional accounting firms. Strives to increase public awareness of the accounting industry; seeks to expand member firms' ability to serve clients on an international basis; disseminates information to members in order to improve technical and professional competence; maintains management, administration and practice developments of member firms. **Conventions/Meetings:** annual meeting.

44 ■ National Association of Black Accountants (NABA)
7249-A Hanover Pkwy.
Greenbelt, MD 20770
Ph: (301)474-6222
Free: (888)571-2939
Fax: (301)474-3114
E-mail: customerservice@nabainc.org
URL: http://www.nabainc.org
Contact: Charlisa Watson, Interim Exec. Dir.

Founded: 1969. **Members:** 5,500. **Membership Dues:** regular student, $20 (annual) ● regular professional, $120 (annual) ● academia, senior, $65 (annual). **Staff:** 8. **Budget:** $2,500,000. **Local Groups:** 130. **Description:** Minority students and professionals currently working, or interested in the fields of accounting, finance, technology, consulting or general business. Seeks, promotes, develops, and represents the interests of current and future minority business professionals. **Awards: Frequency:** annual. **Type:** scholarship. **Recipient:** for ethnic minorities; GPA, leadership, volunteer activities, essay, financial aid. **Publications:** *Achieve*, 3/year. Newsletter. Contains pertinent information for aspiring business students. **Circulation:** 5,000 ● *NewsPlus*, quarterly. Newsletter. Provides a communication mechanism of key topics of interest within the accounting, finance and business professions. **Price:** free for members; $20.00 /year for nonmembers. **Circulation:** 9,000. **Advertising:** accepted ● *Spectrum*, annual. Journal. Addresses current and potential accounting and general business issues. **Price:** free for members; $20.00 /year for nonmembers. **Circulation:** 5,000. **Advertising:** accepted. **Conventions/Meetings:** annual convention (exhibits).

45 ■ National Association of Certified Valuation Analysts (NACVA)
1111 Brickyard Rd., Ste.200
Salt Lake City, UT 84106-5401
Ph: (801)486-0600
Free: (800)677-2009
Fax: (801)486-7500
E-mail: nacva1@nacva.com
Contact: Parnell Black, CEO

Founded: 1991. **Members:** 6,000. **Membership Dues:** practitioner, $430 (annual) ● professional and academician, $215 (annual) ● government employee, associate and student, $125 (annual). **Staff:** 35. **Regional Groups:** 4. **State Groups:** 48. **For-Profit. Multinational. Description:** Consultants who provide valuation and litigation services, enterprise value building, and fraud deterrence services, including liquidation or reorganization, mergers or acquisitions, mediation and arbitration, sale of business, succession planning, bankruptcy and foreclosure, estate and gift taxes, initial public offerings, franchise valuation, buy/sell agreements, and more. Offers accreditation of Certified Valuation Analyst (CVA), Accredited Valuation Analyst (AVA), Certified Forensic Financial Analyst (CFFA), and Certified Fraud Deterrence Analyst (CFD); conducts educational training programs and exams; develops valuation software; provides consulting and information research services; offers business valuation marketing tools. Maintains Speakers' Bureau and Mentor Support Groups. **Libraries: Type:** reference; open to the public. **Holdings:** 270; archival material, audiovisuals, books, business records, clippings, periodicals. **Subjects:** business valuation, business. **Awards:** Circle of Light. **Frequency:** annual. **Type:** recognition. **Recipient:** for attained instructor of the year prior ● Instructor of the Year. **Frequency:** annual. **Type:** recognition ● Outstanding Members. **Frequency:** bimonthly. **Type:** recognition. **Recipient:** to members who have provided a tremendous amount of support to the organization. **Computer Services:** database, of valuations. **Boards:** Ethics Oversight; Executive Advisory; Fraud Deferrence; Litigation Forensics; Valuation Credentialing. **Committees:** Annual Conference Planning; Course Review; Exam and Grading; Government Relations; Ideas and Technology; Practice Development; Quality Enhancement; Standards; State Chapters. **Publications:** *NACVA U.S. Guide to Valuation Professionals*. Directory. Contains database of members and credentialed members by city and state. **Price:** free. **Circulation:** 150,000. **Advertising:** accepted. Alternate Formats: online; CD-ROM ● *The Value Examiner*, bimonthly. Magazine. **Price:** $185.00 single copy. ISSN: 1094-3137. **Circulation:** 10,000. **Advertising:** accepted. Alternate Formats: online ● *The Value of Membership*, annual. Report ● Brochures. **Advertising:** accepted ● Manuals. Features business valuation training. ● Also offers Business Valuation Manager Pro Software and Professional Reports Writer software. **Conventions/Meetings:** annual Consultants - conference and trade show, with over 50 speakers on popular topics in business valuation, litigation support, fraud deterrence and detection, and a variety of other consulting disciplines (exhibits) ● Consultants' Training Institutes (CTI) - seminar, educational program (exhibits) - 3/year, summer, fall and winter ● monthly Executive Advisory Board - board meeting.

46 ■ National Association of Forensic Accountants (NAFA)
2455 E Sunrise Blvd., Ste.1201
Fort Lauderdale, FL 33304-3115
Ph: (954)535-5556
Free: (800)523-3680
Fax: (954)537-4942
E-mail: mail@nafanet.com
URL: http://www.nafanet.com

Description: Professional investigative accounting firms providing claims support to the insurance industry and claims litigation clients. **Publications:** *Accounting and Claims*. Newsletter. Alternate Formats: online.

47 ■ National Conference of CPA Practitioners (NCCPAP)
22 Jericho Tpke.
Mineola, NY 11501
Ph: (516)333-8282
Free: (888)488-5400
Fax: (516)333-4099
E-mail: office@nccpap.org
URL: http://www.nccpap.org
Contact: Dennis Scott CPA, Pres.

Founded: 1979. **Members:** 1,200. **Membership Dues:** sole practitioner, $220 (annual) ● CPA Firm, $250 (annual) ● retired, $400 (annual). **Staff:** 3. **Regional Groups:** 7. **State Groups:** 4. **Local Groups:** 2. **Description:** Represents the interests of CPA regional and local accounting firms. Works to enhance the professionalism of local firms. Works with the IRS and local and national government. **Libraries: Type:** reference. **Holdings:** books, periodicals, photographs. **Subjects:** accounting. **Awards:** Gold Award. **Frequency:** annual. **Type:** recognition. **Recipient:** for service to NCCPAP and community involvement. **Committees:** Issues; Tax. **Publications:** *NCCPAP News and Views*, bimonthly. Newsletter. **Price:** free for members. **Advertising:** accepted. **Conventions/Meetings:** annual conference - always October ● quarterly regional meeting ● seminar.

48 ■ National Society of Accountants (NSA)
1010 N Fairfax St.
Alexandria, VA 22314
Ph: (703)549-6400
Free: (800)966-6679
Fax: (703)549-2984
E-mail: members@nsacct.org
URL: http://www.nsacct.org
Contact: John G. Ams, Exec. VP

Founded: 1945. **Members:** 13,500. **Membership Dues:** active and associate, international associate, $179 (annual) ● educator associate, $54 (annual) ● student associate, $30 (annual). **Staff:** 21. **Budget:** $3,750,000. **Description:** Professional organization and its affiliates represent 30,000 members who provide auditing, accounting, tax preparation, financial and estate planning, and management services to approximately 19 million individuals and business clients. Most members are sole practitioners or partners in small to mid-size accounting firms. **Libraries: Type:** reference. **Holdings:** periodicals, photographs. **Awards: Frequency:** annual. **Type:** scholarship. **Recipient:** for 33 accounting students. **Committees:** Professional Development; Right to

Practice. **Councils:** Accreditation Council for Accountancy and Taxation; Scholarship Foundation. **Doing business as:** (2000) National Society of Public Accountants. **Publications:** *Income and Fees of Accountants in Public Practice*, triennial. Report. Surveys report analyzing statistics of the economics of the public accounting profession. **Price:** $65.00/ copy for members; $120.00/copy for nonmembers ● *NPA Magazine*, 6/year. Covers taxes, accounting, accounting standards, and related issues; includes book reviews, legislative news, and classified ads. **Price:** $20.00/year. ISSN: 0027-9978. **Circulation:** 15,000. **Advertising:** accepted. Alternate Formats: online ● Yearbook, annual. **Conventions/Meetings:** annual convention (exhibits) - always August.

49 ■ National Society of Accountants for Cooperatives (NSAC)
136 S Keowee St.
Dayton, OH 45402
Ph: (937)222-6707
Fax: (937)222-5794
E-mail: info@nsacoop.org
URL: http://www.nsacoop.org
Contact: Ronald P. Hennen, Pres.
Founded: 1935. **Members:** 1,650. **Membership Dues:** regular, $150 (annual) ● retired, $50 (annual). **Staff:** 7. **Budget:** $325,000. **Regional Groups:** 11. **Description:** Employees of cooperatives, certified public accountants, auditors, chief financial officers, attorneys, and bankers. Unites persons performing accounting, auditing, financial, and legal services for cooperative and non-profit associations. Holds technical sessions annually. Compiles statistics. **Libraries: Type:** reference. **Holdings:** 55. **Subjects:** cooperative accounting, financial reporting by cooperatives. **Awards:** Silver Bowl Award. **Type:** recognition ● Silver Pen Award. **Type:** recognition. **Committees:** Accounting and Auditing; Audit and Finance; Chapter Development; Convention Planning and Resource; Membership Development; Small Cooperative; Tax; TCA. **Publications:** *The Cooperative Accountant*, quarterly. Journal. **Price:** $90.00 for nonmembers in U.S.; $120.00 for nonmembers outside U.S.; included in membership dues. **Circulation:** 1,750. **Advertising:** accepted ● *Financial Reporting by Cooperatives*, annual. **Price:** $150.00 for members (3-year subscription); $225.00 for nonmembers (3-year subscription) ● *Membership Directory and Resource Guide*, annual. Includes resource guide. ● *News and Views*, quarterly. Newsletter ● *Welcome to Cooperatives.* Provides a description of cooperatives and what they do. **Conventions/Meetings:** annual convention, includes technical program - always first week of August ● seminar, for cooperative use.

50 ■ Not-For-Profit Services Association (NSA)
One Valmont Plz., 4th Fl.
Omaha, NE 68154
Ph: (402)964-3805
Free: (888)475-4476
Fax: (402)964-3736
E-mail: info@nonprofitcpas.com
URL: http://www.nonprofitcpas.com
Contact: Nancy Drennen, Exec. Dir.
Founded: 1994. **Members:** 16. **Membership Dues:** firm, $1,200 (annual). **Staff:** 3. **Description:** CPA firms. Provides financial and consulting services to non-profit organizations; provides e-mail network, consulting, and management services. Maintains speakers' bureau. **Publications:** *NSA Members' Bulletin*, quarterly. **Conventions/Meetings:** semiannual conference ● roundtable and meeting, covering technical, management, and marketing issues.

51 ■ Polaris International North American Network (PINAN)
3700 Crestwood Pkwy., Ste.350
Duluth, GA 30096
Ph: (770)279-4560
Fax: (770)279-4566
E-mail: rbeilfuss@pkfnan.org
URL: http://www.pkfnan.org
Contact: Rudolf Beilfuss, Pres.
Founded: 1969. **Members:** 75. **Staff:** 18. **Description:** Independent certified public accounting firms practicing on a regional or local basis. Objectives are to: strengthen accounting practices; increase competency and quality of service; provide a practice management program; maintain technical competence in accounting principles and auditing standards; make available a reservoir of specialists who are immediately accessible to members; provide for the sharing of skills, knowledge and experience. Offers technical, marketing, and public relations support; promotes continuing professional education; facilitates networking. Conducts 4 staff development, 2 tax training, and 3 manager/partner training courses per year; operates committees and task forces. **Committees:** Accounting and Auditing; Commercial Lenders; Consulting Services; Continuing Professional Education; Firm Management; Healthcare Services; Legal Services; Long Range Planning; Membership; Practice Development; Tax. **Formerly:** (1998) Associated Regional Accounting Firms. **Publications:** *Management Services Update.* Report ● *Marketing Services Update*, bimonthly. Report ● *Pictorial Directory*, annual ● *Resource Directory*, annual ● *Resource Guide*, annual. Manual ● *Technical Services Update*, bimonthly. Report ● Brochures ● Handbooks ● Manuals ● Membership Directory, annual ● Newsletters ● Report, quarterly. **Conventions/Meetings:** annual Firm Management - conference, with seminar and members' meeting.

52 ■ Society of Depreciation Professionals (SDP)
8100-M4 Wyoming Blvd. NE, No. 228
Albuquerque, NM 87113
Ph: (505)867-9513
Fax: (505)867-0917
E-mail: sdp@his.com
Contact: Rod Daniel, Exec. Sec.
Founded: 1986. **Members:** 200. **Membership Dues:** associate, senior, student, $40 (annual). **Staff:** 1. **Budget:** $50,000. **Description:** Accountants and other individuals with an interest in the depreciation of assets. Promotes "professionalism and ethics within the art of depreciation." Serves as a forum for the discussion of issues affecting depreciation; sponsors continuing professional development courses for members. **Awards: Frequency:** periodic. **Type:** recognition. **Telecommunication Services:** electronic bulletin board. **Publications:** *Journal of the Society of Depreciation Professionals*, annual. **Price:** included in membership dues; $15.00/issue for nonmembers; $10.00 each, for nonmembers (for 10 or more copies) ● Newsletter, triennial. **Price:** included in membership dues ● Membership Directory. **Conventions/Meetings:** periodic conference.

53 ■ Society of Insurance Financial Management (SIFM)
PO Box 9001
Mount Vernon, NY 10552
Ph: (914)966-3180
Fax: (914)966-3264
E-mail: sifm@cinn.com
URL: http://www.sifm.org
Contact: Christopher T. McNulty, Pres.
Founded: 1960. **Members:** 600. **Membership Dues:** individual, $125 (annual). **Staff:** 1. **Budget:** $100,000. **Description:** Insurance company officers and employees in financial management departments. **Committees:** Accounting; Reinsurance; Statutory; Tax and Legislative. **Formed by Merger of:** Association of Casualty Accountants and Statisticians and Insurance Accountants Association. **Formerly:** Society of Insurance Accountants. **Conventions/Meetings:** annual conference.

Acquisitions

54 ■ Alliance of Merger and Acquisition Advisors (AMAA)
150 N Michigan Ave., Ste.2700
Chicago, IL 60601
Ph: (312)856-9590
Free: (877)844-2535
Fax: (312)729-9800
E-mail: info@amaaonline.org
URL: http://www.amaaonline.com
Contact: Mr. Michael Nall, Founder
Founded: 1999. **Members:** 400. **Membership Dues:** individual, $495 (annual). **Staff:** 5. **Regional Groups:** 4. **For-Profit. Description:** Serves the educational and resource needs of mergers and acquisitions professionals. Helps members improve their level of knowledge to better market and deliver their advisory services. Maintains the highest recognized standards of professional excellence for corporate advisory and transaction services. **Computer Services:** database, advisor directory ● information services, mergers and acquisitions resources ● online services, bulletin. **Conventions/Meetings:** semiannual conference (exhibits) - every winter.

Actors

55 ■ Television Audience Screen Extras Guild (TASEG)
Guild Penthouse
LaFong Tower
8311 54th Ave. S
Seattle, WA 98118-4702
Ph: (206)725-0873
Contact: Paul Martin, Founder/CEO
Founded: 2002. **Members:** 2,800. **Membership Dues:** life, $350. **Staff:** 6. **Budget:** $600,000. **State Groups:** 4. **Local Groups:** 1. **Description:** Represents studio audiences in network/cable network television industry assuring living wages for services rendered. Seeks legislation in the United States Congress requiring television networks and cable networks and production companies to begin to pay their television studio audience extra actors a fair living wage. Works with chambers of commerce/visitors bureaus in the three major television markets, to increase the longevity of the visits to Los Angeles, New York City, and Chicago, by travellers who work as extra-actor-talents in the television industry. **Awards:** Gene Buck/TASEG Memorial Award. **Frequency:** annual. **Type:** recognition. **Recipient:** to television/cable network and/or television production company that best epitomizes aims of the Guild.

Adhesives

56 ■ Adhesive and Sealant Council (ASC)
7979 Old Georgetown Rd., Ste.500
Bethesda, MD 20814
Ph: (301)986-9700
Fax: (301)986-9795
E-mail: info@ascouncil.org
URL: http://www.ascouncil.org
Contact: Joseph Stevenson, Dir. of Member Services
Founded: 1958. **Members:** 130. **Staff:** 10. **Budget:** $1,600,000. **Description:** Firms manufacturing and selling adhesives and sealants in either solid or liquid form; raw materials and equipment suppliers; consulting firms. Provides training, information, and interaction for members. Offers educational programs that communicate the advantages of adhesives and sealants over other types of fasteners. Represents the industry in regulatory and government affairs. **Libraries: Type:** open to the public. **Holdings:** archival material, articles, papers, reports. **Subjects:** technical and business/marketing related. **Awards:** ASC Award. **Frequency:** annual. **Type:** recognition. **Recipient:** for an individual contributing to industry technology and civic programs. **Telecommunication Services:** electronic mail, joe.stevenson@ascouncil.org. **Committees:** Convention; Government Relations; Leadership Conference; Membership; Statistical; Technical. **Formerly:** Rubber and Plastic Adhesive and Sealant Manufacturers Council. **Publications:** *Catalyst*, 3/year. Newsletter. **Circulation:** 2,500. **Advertising:** accepted. Alternate Formats: online ● *Global Market Survey Report*, biennial. Reports on markets and trends for adhesives and sealants. **Price:** $575.00 for members; $1,175.00 for nonmembers. Alternate Formats: CD-ROM ● Membership

Directory, annual. **Conventions/Meetings:** semiannual convention (exhibits) - every spring and fall.

57 ■ Pressure Sensitive Tape Council (PSTC)
PO Box 609
Northbrook, IL 60062
Ph: (847)562-2630
Fax: (847)562-2631
E-mail: info@pstc.org
URL: http://www.pstc.org
Contact: Glen R. Anderson, Exec. VP
Founded: 1953. **Members:** 26. **Staff:** 3. **Budget:** $700,000. **Description:** Manufacturers of cellophane, cloth, paper, plastic, and rubber pressure sensitive tape products. Maintains research on test methods and standards of nomenclature, and on characteristics of products under all conditions of humidity and temperature. Offers educational events and publications. **Awards:** Carl A. Dahlquist Award. **Frequency:** annual. **Type:** recognition. **Recipient:** for research in adhesive tape technology. **Telecommunication Services:** electronic mail, ganderson@pstc.org. **Committees:** Marketing; Regulatory; Statistical; Technical. **Publications:** *Proceedings of the Annual Technical Seminars*, annual. **Price:** $30.00 in U.S.; $35.00 in Canada and Mexico; $40.00 outside North America ● *PSTC 2003-2004 Tape Products Directory*, annual. Describes pressure sensitive tape products manufactured by members and lists principal uses of the products. **Price:** $60.00 in U.S.; $65.00 in Canada and Mexico; $75.00 outside North America ● *Test Methods Manual (14th Edition)*, annual. Contains information for testing the performance of pressure sensitive tape. **Price:** $80.00 in U.S.; $85.00 in Canada and Mexico; $95.00 outside North America. **Conventions/Meetings:** annual seminar, presentation of latest technological advances in the industry (exhibits).

58 ■ Sealant Waterproofing and Restoration Institute (SWR Institute)
14 W 3rd St., Ste.200
Kansas City, MO 64105
Ph: (816)472-7974
Fax: (816)472-7765
E-mail: info@swrionline.org
URL: http://www.swrionline.org
Contact: Ms. Debra Nemec, VP
Founded: 1976. **Members:** 180. **Membership Dues:** senior, $250 (annual) ● associate, $600 (annual) ● contractor, $600-$1,200 (annual) ● manufacturer, $1,200-$1,500 (annual). **Staff:** 5. **Budget:** $100,000. **Multinational. Description:** Sealant contractors; suppliers of sealants and related products; other interested persons. Works to: promote exchange of ideas for the development of the highest standards and operating efficiency within the industry; develop industry-wide standards and specifications; improve conditions affecting the sealant and waterproofing industry. **Telecommunication Services:** electronic mail, debn@robstan.com. **Committees:** Clear Water Repellent Handbook; Editorial Advisory; Strategic Planning; Validation. **Formerly:** (1989) Sealant and Waterproofers Institute. **Publications:** *A Practical Guide to Waterproofing Exterior Walls*, 5/year. Manual. **Price:** $44.95 for members; $59.95 for nonmembers ● *The Applicator*, quarterly. Journal. **Price:** $36.00 /year for nonmembers; included in membership dues. **Advertising:** accepted ● *Applying Liquid Sealants: An Applicator Training Program*, annual. Manual. Comprehensive training program for the application of liquid sealants, comes with video. **Price:** $159.00 ● *Below Grade Waterproofing Manual*. **Price:** $50.00 for nonmembers; $40.00 for members ● *Clearwater Repellent Manual*, annual. Includes glossary, production comparison, spec, monograph, and performance test criteria. **Price:** $65.95 for nonmembers ● *Sealants: The Professionals' Guide*. Annual Reports. Features a comprehensive overview of sealants. **Price:** $50.00 for nonmembers; $40.00 for members ● *Technical Bulletin Series*. Bulletins. **Price:** $29.95 for members; $35.95 for nonmembers. **Conventions/Meetings:** semiannual meeting, business and networking (exhibits) - usually winter and fall.

Administrative Services

59 ■ Association of Celebrity Personal Assistants (ACPA)
914 Westwood Blvd.
PMB 507
Los Angeles, CA 90024-2905
Ph: (310)281-7755
E-mail: contact@celebrityassistants.org
URL: http://www.celebrityassistants.org
Contact: Kimberly Logan, Pres.
Founded: 1992. **Members:** 100. **Membership Dues:** full, $150 (annual) ● non-resident, $75 (annual). **Description:** Individuals acting as personal assistants to celebrities. Promotes professional development of members. Serves as a forum for networking, job referral, and information exchange among members. Conducts educational programs; compiles statistics. **Libraries: Type:** not open to the public. **Subjects:** stalking, privacy, professional development, networking. **Computer Services:** Mailing lists, of members ● online services, job bank ● online services, referral support. **Publications:** *Best of the Best: A Resource Guide for the Celebrity Personal Assistant*, annual. Book. Contains information of interest to celebrity personal assistants. **Price:** free for members; $25.00 /year for nonmembers. **Circulation:** 100. **Advertising:** accepted ● *The Right Hand*, bimonthly. Newsletter. Contains information of interest to celebrity personal assistants. **Price:** free for members; $50.00 /year for nonmembers. **Circulation:** 300. **Advertising:** accepted. **Conventions/Meetings:** monthly board meeting ● monthly meeting - always in Los Angeles, CA.

60 ■ Association of Certified Professional Secretaries (ACPS)
Address Unknown since 2007
Founded: 1985. **Members:** 150. **Membership Dues:** individual or association, $50 (annual). **Regional Groups:** 1. **State Groups:** 2. **Description:** Certified professional secretaries and their professional societies. Represents members' interests and supports members' ongoing professional development. Maintains support groups; facilitates communication among members; provides continuing professional education programs. **Awards:** Jacqueline Kaiser Scholarship. **Frequency:** annual. **Type:** scholarship. **Computer Services:** database ● mailing lists. **Publications:** *ACPS Connection*, 6/year. Newsletter. **Price:** free. ISSN: 1079-4913. **Advertising:** not accepted. **Conventions/Meetings:** quarterly board meeting ● annual meeting.

61 ■ Association for Financial Technology (AFT)
c/o Kurt Guenther, Pres.
230 Sci. Dr., Ste.800
Norcross, GA 30092-2904
Free: (800)879-1996
Fax: (770)409-1735
E-mail: aft@aftweb.com
URL: http://www.aftweb.com
Contact: Kurt Guenther, Pres.
Founded: 1972. **Members:** 75. **Membership Dues:** corporate, $1,000 (annual). **Staff:** 2. **Description:** Computer centers providing data processing services to banks, savings and loan associations, credit unions, and other financial institutions. Acts as clearinghouse for the exchange of information and ideas in all areas of computer technology, operations, and production. Also acts as a liaison with other industry-related organizations. Represents members' interests before governmental regulatory agencies. Compiles statistics. **Awards:** James E. Stoner Memorial Scholarship. **Type:** scholarship. **Formerly:** (1975) Multi-Bank Data Processing Organization; (1998) National Association of Bank Servicers. **Publications:** *AFTech Letter*, quarterly. Newsletter. **Price:** available to members and select others. **Circulation:** 350. **Advertising:** accepted. Alternate Formats: online. **Conventions/Meetings:** annual meeting - every fall ● semiannual meeting - every spring.

62 ■ Black Data Processing Associates (BDPA)
6301 Ivy Ln., Ste.700
Greenbelt, MD 20770
Ph: (301)220-2180 (301)220-2181
Free: (800)727-BDPA
Fax: (301)220-2185
E-mail: president@bdpa.org
URL: http://www.bdpa.org
Contact: Gina L. Billings, Pres.
Founded: 1975. **Members:** 5,000. **Membership Dues:** professional, $75 (annual) ● student, $15 (annual). **Staff:** 5. **Budget:** $1,487,000. **State Groups:** 53. **Local Groups:** 53. **Description:** Represents persons employed in the information processing industry, including electronic data processing, electronic word processing, and data communications; others interested in information processing. Seeks to accumulate and share information processing knowledge and business expertise in order to increase the career and business potential of minorities in the information processing field. Conducts professional seminars, workshops, tutoring services, and community introductions to data processing. Makes annual donation to the United Negro College Fund. **Awards:** Dr. Jesse L. Bemley Scholarship Award. **Frequency:** annual. **Type:** scholarship. **Recipient:** for high school computer competition winners ● **Type:** scholarship. **Recipient:** to qualified high school graduates. **Computer Services:** database, resume ● online services, subscriber services. **Committees:** Communications; Corporate Relations; Education; Speakers' Bureau. **Formerly:** (1996) BDPA Information Technology Thought Leaders. **Publications:** *National Journal*, quarterly. **Circulation:** 16,000. **Advertising:** accepted ● Chapters publish their own newsletters. **Conventions/Meetings:** Career Fair, Tech Expo - conference ● annual Looking at Tomorrow Today - conference and seminar (exhibits).

63 ■ Executive Women International (EWI)
515 S 700 E, Ste.2A
Salt Lake City, UT 84102
Ph: (801)355-2800
Free: (877)4EWI-NOW
Fax: (801)355-2852
E-mail: ewi@executivewomen.org
URL: http://www.executivewomen.org
Contact: Suzette Smith, Exec. Dir.
Founded: 1938. **Members:** 5,000. **Membership Dues:** member-at-large, $140 (annual). **Staff:** 5. **Budget:** $600,000. **Regional Groups:** 5. **National Groups:** 85. **Multinational. Description:** Individuals holding key positions in business professions. Conducts networking educational and charitable programs. **Awards:** Adult Students in Scholastic Transition. **Frequency:** annual. **Type:** scholarship. **Recipient:** for twelve need-based non-traditional students ● Executive Women International Scholarship Program. **Frequency:** annual. **Type:** scholarship. **Recipient:** for six high school juniors in participating areas. **Computer Services:** database ● mailing lists ● online services. **Programs:** Academy Online; Adult Students in Scholastic Transition; Certified Professionals; Scholarship. **Formerly:** (1977) Executives' Secretaries. **Publications:** *Executive Women International Directory*, annual. Contains addresses and key persons from each member firm. **Price:** $8.25 available to members only. **Circulation:** 5,000. **Advertising:** accepted ● *Pulse*, annual. Magazine. Contains professional development and educational articles, as well as an EWI year in review. **Price:** $8.00/copy. **Circulation:** 4,500. **Advertising:** accepted. Alternate Formats: online ● *Pulse*, bimonthly. Newsletter. Contains professional development and educational articles. **Advertising:** accepted. Alternate Formats: online. **Conventions/Meetings:** annual Leadership Conference - meeting and convention (exhibits) - always in fall. 2008 Sept. 18-20, Palm Springs, CA.

64 ■ Health Care Executive Assistants (HCEA)
1 N Franklin
Chicago, IL 60606
Ph: (312)422-3702

Fax: (312)422-4575
E-mail: hcea@aha.org
URL: http://www.hceaonline.org
Contact: Ms. Alyse Kittner, Marketing Coor.
Members: 600. **Membership Dues:** regular, $125 (annual) ● retired, $45 (annual) ● Tennessee regional/national, Mississippi regional/national, $150 (annual). **Staff:** 5. **Description:** Executive assistants, administrative assistants and other professionals reporting to health care management or employed in other health care organizations. Promotes professional development, leadership and excellence for its members. **Awards:** Conference Awards. **Frequency:** annual. **Type:** recognition. **Recipient:** for active members ● Conference Scholarship Award. **Frequency:** annual. **Type:** scholarship. **Recipient:** for members. **Telecommunication Services:** electronic bulletin board, for members only. **Councils:** Advisory. **Programs:** Scholarship Award. **Working Groups:** Diversity; E-Communications; Nominations; Planning. **Publications:** *Notations*, quarterly. Newsletter. **Price:** included in membership dues. **Advertising:** accepted. Alternate Formats: online. **Conventions/ Meetings:** annual conference, for novice and experienced health care executive assistants and administrators.

65 ■ Information Systems Audit and Control Association and Foundation (ISACA)
3701 Algonquin Rd., Ste.1010
Rolling Meadows, IL 60008
Ph: (847)253-1545
Fax: (847)253-1443
E-mail: membership@isaca.org
URL: http://www.isaca.org
Contact: Everett C. Johnson Jr., Intl. Pres.
Founded: 1969. **Members:** 50,000. **Membership Dues:** individual, $120 (annual) ● student, $25 (annual). **Staff:** 50. **Local Groups:** 140. **Multinational. Description:** Acts as a harmonizing source for IT control practices and standards all over the world. Serves its members and other constituencies by providing education, research (through its affiliated Foundation), a professional certification, conferences and publications. **Committees:** Academic Relations; Audit; Certification; Education; Marketing; Membership; Research; Standards; Test Maintenance; Ways and Means. **Also Known As:** Electronic Data Processing Auditors Association. **Formerly:** (1977) EDP Auditors Association. **Publications:** *CobiT*. Book. Contains comprehensive set of control objectives/ management and audit guidelines for information systems. **Price:** $225.00 for nonmembers; $115.00 for members ● *Global Communique*, bimonthly. Newsletter. **Price:** free, for members only ● *Information Systems Control Journal*, bimonthly. **Price:** $75.00 in U.S.; $90.00 outside U.S. ISSN: 1076-4100. **Circulation:** 31,000. **Advertising:** accepted. Also Cited As: *EDP Auditors Journal*. **Conventions/ Meetings:** annual Conference on Computer Audit, Control, and Security (exhibits) - usually in May in North America, Europe, Asia Pacific and Latin America ● annual international conference (exhibits) - usually July.

66 ■ International Association of Administrative Professionals (IAAP)
10502 NW Ambassador Dr.
PO Box 20404
Kansas City, MO 64195-0404
Ph: (816)891-6600
Fax: (816)891-9118
E-mail: rstroud@iaap-hq.org
URL: http://www.iaap-hq.org
Contact: Rick Stroud, Communications Mgr.
Founded: 1942. **Members:** 40,000. **Membership Dues:** professional in U.S. and Canada, $58 (annual) ● student in U.S. and Canada, $24 (annual) ● associate in U.S. and Canada, $155 (annual) ● professional outside U.S. and Canada, $78 (annual) ● student outside U.S. and Canada, $44 (annual) ● associate outside U.S. and Canada, $175 (annual). **Staff:** 26. **Budget:** $3,500,000. **Regional Groups:** 6. **State Groups:** 37. **Local Groups:** 700. **Multinational. Description:** Professional organization of administrative professionals. Sponsors Administrative Professionals Day/Week. Establishes Research and Educational Foundation to develop research and educational projects for secretaries, management, and educators. Sponsors continuing education programs. **Awards:** Certified Administrative Professional Certification. **Type:** recognition ● Certified Professional Secretary Certification. **Type:** recognition. **Recipient:** for successful completion of examinations in behavioral science in business, business law, economics and management, accounting, office administration and communication, and office technology. **Computer Services:** Mailing lists, rental-postal. **Telecommunication Services:** electronic mail, service@iaap-hq.org. **Absorbed:** (1950) Secretaries International; (1986) National Association of Collegiate Secretaries. **Formerly:** (1981) National Secretaries Association (International); (1998) Professional Secretaries International. **Publications:** *Bits & Bytes*, periodic. Newsletter. ISSN: 0037-0622. **Circulation:** 36,000. Alternate Formats: online ● *OfficePro*, 9/year. Magazine. **Price:** $22.00 in U.S. ISSN: 0037-0622. **Circulation:** 36,000. **Advertising:** accepted. Alternate Formats: online. **Conventions/Meetings:** annual Professional Education Conference - workshop and seminar - during spring ● annual International Convention and Education Forum (exhibits) - during summer. 2008 July 27-30, New Orleans, LA; 2009 July 26-29, Minneapolis, MN; 2010 July 18-21, Boston, MA.

67 ■ International Association for Human Resource Information Management (IHRIM)
PO Box 1086
Burlington, MA 01803-6086
Free: (800)804-3983
Fax: (781)998-8011
E-mail: moreinfo@ihrim.org
URL: http://www.ihrim.org
Contact: Lynne Mealy, Pres./CEO
Founded: 1978. **Members:** 3,500. **Membership Dues:** student, $50 (annual) ● faculty, $80 (annual) ● full, $295 (annual) ● full, $500 (biennial). **State Groups:** 20. **National Groups:** 9. **Description:** Human resource, payroll, and data processing professionals; others concerned with the development, maintenance, and operation of automated human resource systems. Provides a forum for exchanging experiences, acquiring information, and discussing common needs and problems relating to human resource systems. Works to enhance capabilities for effective and efficient human resource management. Conducts activities on the local, national, and international level. Offers programs and job posting services. Operates resource center, member referral network, and vendor fairs. **Awards:** Chairman's Award. **Frequency:** annual. **Type:** recognition. **Recipient:** to an individual who has made an outstanding contribution to human resource information management ● Excellence Award. **Frequency:** annual. **Type:** recognition. **Recipient:** for exemplary volunteer service and/or overseeing a project that has a positive impact to IHRIM ● Partners Award. **Frequency:** annual. **Type:** recognition. **Recipient:** to an organization that has made a significant contribution to the practice of human resource information management ● The Summit Award. **Frequency:** annual. **Type:** recognition. **Recipient:** for contribution to organization's goals and objectives in its strategic plan. **Computer Services:** Electronic publishing, journal (IHRIM e-Journal) and newsletter (IHRIM Wire) ● mailing lists, of members. **Special Interest Groups:** Global; Privacy and Security; Small to Mid Sized. **Formerly:** (1998) Association of Human Resource Systems Professionals. **Publications:** *Conference Program*. **Advertising:** accepted ● *HR: Funny Side Up*. Book. **Price:** $39.00 for nonmembers; $29.00 for members ● *IHRIM Journal*, bimonthly. Magazine ● *IHRIM Link*, bimonthly. Magazine. Covers association business reports, reports on chapter activities, program announcements, training programs, and legislative issues. **Price:** $60.00/year. **Circulation:** 5,000. **Advertising:** accepted ● *Out of Site: An Inside Look at Outsourcing*. Book. **Price:** $49.00 for nonmembers; $29.00 for members ● *Remote Control: A Practitioner's Guide to Managing Virtual Teams*. Book. **Price:** $29.00 for members; $39.00 for nonmembers. **Conventions/Meetings:** annual HRM Strategies Conference and Technology Exposition (exhibits) - 2009 Apr. 19-22, San Diego, CA ● seminar and workshop.

68 ■ International Virtual Assistants Association (IVAA)
561 Keystone Ave., Ste.309
Reno, NV 89503
Free: (888)259-2487
Fax: (888)259-2487
E-mail: president@ivaa.org
URL: http://www.ivaa.org
Contact: Candy Beauchamp, Pres.
Members: 650. **Membership Dues:** regular, $75 (annual). **Multinational. Description:** Represents the interests of virtual assistants. Works for the professional education and development of the virtual assistant. Educates the public on the role and function of the profession. Builds alliances, coalitions and affiliations to foster networking opportunities. Offers Certified Virtual Assistant (CVA) exam, Ethics Check exam, and Certified Real Estate Support Specialist (CRESS) exam.

69 ■ Legal Secretaries International
2302 Fannin St., Ste.500
Houston, TX 77002-9136
Ph: (713)659-7617 (206)903-8891
Fax: (713)659-7641
E-mail: vicepresident@legalsecretaries.org
URL: http://www.legalsecretaries.org
Contact: Jan Sullivan CBJA, VP
Founded: 1995. **Members:** 890. **Membership Dues:** individual, $35 (annual) ● retiree, $17 (annual). **Staff:** 9. **State Groups:** 4. **Local Groups:** 16. **Description:** Consists of individuals who are presently or formerly employed in or interested in the legal secretarial profession. Responds to the educational and networking needs of legal secretaries, as an affordable means of increasing knowledge, skills, and networking opportunities. **Publications:** *Basic Training Manual for Legal Secretaries*. **Price:** $35.00 in U.S., plus shipping and handling; $20.00 in Canada, plus shipping and handling ● Journal, quarterly. **Price:** $5.00. **Advertising:** accepted. **Conventions/ Meetings:** semiannual meeting.

70 ■ MEMA Information Services Council (MISC)
10 Lab. Dr.
PO Box 13966
Research Triangle Park, NC 27709-3966
Ph: (919)406-8830
Fax: (919)549-8733
E-mail: info@miscouncil.org
URL: http://www.miscouncil.org
Contact: Chris Gardner, VP
Founded: 1972. **Members:** 72. **Membership Dues:** manufacturer, $650 (annual) ● affiliate, $750 (annual) ● affiliate (includes sponsorship), $2,750 (annual). **Staff:** 3. **Description:** Serves as a forum for industry interaction, education and idea exchange regarding matters of common interest to MIS managers and related executives in the automotive manufacturing industry. **Awards:** Aftermarket Web Challenge. **Frequency:** annual. **Type:** recognition. **Recipient:** for web application excellence. **Committees:** X.12; XML. **Affiliated With:** Motor and Equipment Manufacturers Association. **Formerly:** (1992) Automotive Manufacturers EDP Council. **Publications:** *Membership Roster*, annual. Membership Directory. **Conventions/ Meetings:** annual conference - in fall.

71 ■ NALS, the Association for Legal Professionals
8159 E 41st St.
Tulsa, OK 74120
Ph: (918)582-5188
Fax: (918)582-5907
E-mail: info@nals.org
URL: http://www.nals.org
Contact: Saundra Bates, Membership Services Mgr.
Founded: 1929. **Members:** 6,000. **Membership Dues:** individual, $135 (annual) ● educator, judge, attorney, $45 (annual) ● student, $19 (annual) ● life,

$750. **State Groups:** 40. **Local Groups:** 575. **Description:** Legal secretaries and others employed in work of a legal nature in law offices, banks, and courts. Sponsors legal secretarial training courses and awards those passing a two-day examination the rating of Certified Professional Legal Secretary. **Telecommunication Services:** electronic mail, bates@nals.org. **Committees:** Award of Excellence; Continuing Education; Legal Training Course; Manual; PLS Certification. **Sections:** Specialty Education. **Formerly:** (1940) California Federation of Legal Secretaries; (1950) Legal Secretaries, Inc.; (1999) National Association of Legal Secretaries International. **Publications:** *Career Legal Secretary*. Book ● *Law*, quarterly. **Price:** $40.00/year in Canada. **Advertising:** accepted ● *Manual for Lawyer's Assistant*. Book. **Conventions/Meetings:** annual National Forum and Education Conference - meeting (exhibits) - always October.

72 ■ National Association of Executive Secretaries and Administrative Assistants (NAESAA)
900 S Washington St., Ste.G-13
Falls Church, VA 22046
Ph: (703)237-8616
Fax: (703)533-1153
E-mail: headquarters@naesaa.com
URL: http://www.naesaa.com
Contact: Ruth Ludeman, Exec. Dir.
Founded: 1975. **Members:** 10,000. **Membership Dues:** individual, $39 (annual) ● individual online, $36 (annual) ● platinum, $69 (annual) ● platinum online, $66 (annual). **Staff:** 4. **Budget:** $100,000. **For-Profit. Description:** Professional secretaries united to bring added stature to their profession and to create for members the benefits that are normally limited to members of specialized professional and fraternal groups. Sponsors biennial secretarial salary survey. **Awards: Frequency:** annual. **Type:** scholarship. **Recipient:** for members. **Formerly:** (1997) National Association of Executive Secretaries. **Publications:** *The Executary*, 11/year. Newsletter. Provides articles of interest to executive secretaries, administrative assistants, and secretaries. **Price:** free for members; $26.00 /year for nonmembers in U.S.; $36.00 /year for nonmembers in Canada; $41.00 /year for nonmembers outside U.S. and Canada. **Circulation:** 7,000. **Advertising:** accepted ● *Improving Communication in the Workplace* ● *Moving Up: A Career Path Guide for the Executive Secretary* ● *Stress Management in the Workplace—Coping Skills for the Executive Secretary*. **Conventions/Meetings:** annual conference (exhibits).

73 ■ National Secretarial Association (NSA)
PO Box 35215
Chicago, IL 60707-0215
Ph: (708)453-0080
Fax: (708)453-0083
E-mail: nsa@rentamark.com
Founded: 1974. **Members:** 35,000. **Membership Dues:** individual, $25 (annual) ● business, $100 (annual) ● corporate sponsor, $250 (annual). **Staff:** 10. **Description:** Secretaries and other administrative support personnel. Seeks to increase members' public visibility and professional influence. Provides trademark licensing and product and service enforcement services to support members' activities. Serves as a major platform for employers to locate administrative assistants on the net. **Libraries: Type:** reference. **Holdings:** 10,000. **Subjects:** secretarial studies. **Awards:** Secretary of the Year. **Frequency:** annual. **Type:** recognition. **Computer Services:** Mailing lists. **Also Known As:** (2000) Administrative Assistant Association. **Publications:** *National Secretarial Journal*, annual. Contains articles submitted by authors via email. **Circulation:** 40,872. **Advertising:** accepted. Alternate Formats: online. **Conventions/Meetings:** annual convention.

74 ■ Office Business Center Association International (OBCAI)
15000 Commerce Pkwy., Ste.C
Mount Laurel, NJ 08054
Ph: (856)439-1076
Free: (800)237-4741
Fax: (856)439-0525
E-mail: info@officebusinesscenters.com
URL: http://www.obcai.org
Contact: Mr. Sam Albrecht, Exec. Dir.
Founded: 1985. **Members:** 950. **Membership Dues:** company, $460-$1,000 (annual) ● associate, $525 (annual). **Staff:** 4. **Budget:** $500,000. **Description:** Owners and operators of office business centers; associate members are vendors who provide products and services to the industry. (Office business centers offer professionals flexible leasing and operating arrangements for fully equipped office facilities and support services.) Promotes the advancement of the office business center industry as an alternative to conventional office space or home office. Sponsors seminars and workshops to develop effective operating, management, and marketing techniques. Conducts national, regional, and local network program. **Computer Services:** database, international office business centers. **Formerly:** (1993) Executive Suite Network; (2002) Executive Suite Association. **Conventions/Meetings:** annual international conference and convention, four days of educational programming (exhibits).

75 ■ Society of Corporate Secretaries and Governance Professionals
521 5th Ave.
New York, NY 10175
Ph: (212)681-2000 (212)681-2012
Fax: (212)681-2005
E-mail: dsmith@governanceprofessionals.org
URL: http://www.governanceprofessionals.org
Contact: David W. Smith, Pres.
Founded: 1946. **Members:** 4,000. **Membership Dues:** general, $575 (annual). **Staff:** 13. **Regional Groups:** 25. **Description:** Corporate secretaries, assistant secretaries, officers and executives of corporations, and others interested in corporate practices and procedures. Conducts surveys and research. Sponsors educational programs for members. Maintains a central information and reference service. **Committees:** Audit; Compensation; Corporate Practices; Educational Programs; Executive Steering; National Conference; Public Company Affairs; Securities Law. **Formerly:** (2005) American Society of Corporate Secretaries. **Publications:** *Compensation of the Corporate Secretary*, annual ● *The Corporate Secretary*, 10/year ● *The Corporate Secretary and Governance Professional*, periodic. Newsletter. Features up-to-date news and information on a variety of topics of interest to members. **Price:** free for members. Alternate Formats: online ● Annual Report, annual. Alternate Formats: online. **Conventions/Meetings:** annual conference - always June or July. 2008 June 25-29, Boca Raton, FL; 2009 June 24-28, San Diego, CA; 2010 July 7-11, Chicago, IL.

76 ■ Special Interest Group for Business Data Processing and Management (SIGBDP)
Address Unknown since 2008
Founded: 1960. **Members:** 4,265. **Description:** A special interest group of the Association for Computing Machinery (see separate entry). Primary interest is in the use of computers in the business environment. Places emphasis on pragmatic business information systems that utilize advanced technology where beneficial. Areas of interest include: long-range planning for information systems; information systems cost/benefit analysis techniques; database/data communication systems approaches and selection; distributed processing; applied telecommunications; large-scale systems design, development, testing, and implementation; developing management and user-oriented information systems; developing unstructured decision support systems; managing and controlling application development; chargeback and budgeting tec hniques; data security and privacy; personnel development and career-pathing for the information systems staff; improving productivity in application development; office automation and business information systems. Designs projects to survey and critique research in specific subject areas. Organizes technical sessions and seminars at the National Computer Conferences and the ACM annual conferences. **Publications:** *Database*, quarterly ● Proceedings. **Conventions/Meetings:** annual meeting.

Advertising

77 ■ Advertising Club of New York (ACNY)
235 Park Ave. S, 6th Fl.
New York, NY 10003-1405
Ph: (212)533-8080
Fax: (212)533-1929
E-mail: gina@theadvertisingclub.org
URL: http://www.theadvertisingclub.org
Contact: Gina Grillo, Exec. Dir.
Founded: 1906. **Members:** 1,800. **Membership Dues:** platinum, $5,000 (annual) ● gold, $3,000 (annual) ● silver, $1,500 (annual) ● individual, $175 (annual) ● corporate associate, $125 (annual) ● academic, $100 (annual) ● young professional, $75 (annual). **Staff:** 10. **Description:** Professionals in advertising, publishing, marketing, and business. Sponsors educational and public service activities, promotional and public relations projects, and talks by celebrities and advertising persons. Conducts annual advertising and marketing course, which offers classes in copywriting, special graphics, verbal communication, advertising production, sale promotion, marketing and management. Sponsors competitions and charitable programs. **Awards:** ANDY Award. **Frequency:** annual. **Type:** recognition. **Recipient:** for creative excellence in all phases of advertising. **Committees:** Brain Game; International ANDY Awards; Mediaction; Programs. **Affiliated With:** American Advertising Federation. **Formerly:** (1915) Advertising Men's League of New York. **Publications:** *ACNY Membership Roster*, annual. Membership Directory ● *The Advertising Club Insider*, quarterly. Newsletter. Alternate Formats: online ● *ANDY Souvenir Journal*, annual ● *Auction Catalogue and Program*, annual. **Conventions/Meetings:** monthly luncheon, includes panel discussion.

78 ■ Advertising Council (AC)
261 Madison Ave., 11th Fl.
New York, NY 10016-2303
Ph: (212)922-1500
Free: (800)933-7727
Fax: (212)922-1676
E-mail: info@adcouncil.org
URL: http://www.adcouncil.org
Contact: Peggy Conlon, Pres./CEO
Founded: 1942. **Staff:** 42. **Budget:** $12,000,000. **Description:** Founded and supported by American business, media, and advertising sectors to conduct public service advertising campaigns. Encourages advertising media to contribute time and space and advertising agencies to supply creative talent and facilities to further timely national causes. Specific campaigns include: Drug Abuse Prevention; AIDS Prevention; Teen-Alcoholism; Child Abuse; Crime Prevention; Forest Fire Prevention. **Awards:** Public Service Award. **Frequency:** annual. **Type:** recognition ● Silver Bell Award. **Frequency:** annual. **Type:** recognition. **Committees:** Campaigns Review; Industries Advisory; Media; Public Issues Advisory. **Publications:** *PSA Bulletin*, bimonthly. Newsletter. **Circulation:** 15,000. Alternate Formats: online ● *Report to the American People*, annual. **Conventions/Meetings:** annual dinner - always November, New York City ● annual luncheon ● quadrennial meeting - always in Washington, DC.

79 ■ Advertising and Marketing International Network (AMIN)
c/o B. Vaughn Sink, Exec. Dir.
12323 Nantucket
Wichita, KS 67235
Ph: (316)531-2342
E-mail: vaughn.sink@shscom.com
URL: http://www.aminworldwide.com
Contact: B. Vaughn Sink, Exec. Dir.
Founded: 1932. **Members:** 34. **Membership Dues:** $4,000 (annual). **Multinational. Description:** Comprised of cooperative worldwide network of non-

competing independent advertising agencies organized to provide facilities and branch office services for affiliated agencies. **Formerly:** Continental Advertising Agency Network. **Publications:** *AMIN Directory*, annual. **Conventions/Meetings:** annual seminar, media, creative, financial, public relations, and management ● annual Senior Management - meeting.

80 ■ Advertising Specialty Association for Printers (ASAP)
14015 Long Shadow
Houston, TX 77015
Ph: (713)330-1452
Fax: (713)330-1418
E-mail: asap@aol.com
URL: http://www.adspecialtyshops.com
Contact: G. Duckworth, Pres.
Founded: 1988. **Members:** 1,500. **Membership Dues:** regular, $100 (annual). **Description:** Supports and represents qualified distributors of advertising specialty products (promotional products). **Computer Services:** Online services, printshop. **Publications:** *ASAP Directory of Sources* ● *Promotional Products Catalog*. Alternate Formats: online ● Newsletter, monthly ● Newsletter, weekly. Alternate Formats: online.

81 ■ Advertising Women of New York (AWNY)
25 W 45th St., Ste.403
New York, NY 10036
Ph: (212)221-7969
Fax: (212)221-8296
E-mail: awny@awny.org
URL: http://www.awny.org
Contact: Liz Schroeder, Exec. Dir.
Founded: 1912. **Members:** 1,240. **Membership Dues:** resident, $125 (annual) ● supporting, $150 (annual) ● young executive, $65 (annual) ● associate/non-resident, $50 (annual). **Staff:** 3. **Local Groups:** 1. **Description:** Women in advertising and related industries that provides a forum for professional growth, serves as catalyst for enhancement and advancement of women; promotes philanthropic endeavors. Conducts events of interest and benefit to members and non-members involved in the industry. Membership concentrated in the metropolitan New York area. **Committees:** Advertising Career Conference; Agency; Big Events; Cannes Advertising Film Festival; Good, Bad and Ugly Awards; Hospitality; Marketing/Public Relations; Media; Membership Development; Young Executives. **Publications:** *Advertising Women of New York—Annual Roster*. Membership Directory. **Price:** free, for members only. **Circulation:** 1,100. **Conventions/Meetings:** semiannual assembly ● periodic luncheon and breakfast ● periodic seminar.

82 ■ AEM Marketing Council (MC)
6737 W Washington St., Ste.2400
Milwaukee, WI 53214-5647
Ph: (414)272-0943 (414)298-4123
Free: (866)AEM-0442
Fax: (414)272-1170
URL: http://www.aem.org
Contact: Kris Flitcroft, Chair
Founded: 1939. **Members:** 250. **Description:** Advertising and marketing executives of equipment manufacturers and their advertising agencies directly interested in the marketing, advertising and sales promotion of construction equipment. **Awards:** Measures of Success. **Frequency:** annual. **Type:** recognition. **Recipient:** for outstanding marketing communications in the off-road equipment manufacturing industry. **Formerly:** (1979) Construction Equipment Advertisers; (1991) Construction Equipment Advertisers and Public Relations Council; (2002) CIMA Marketing Communications Council; (2002) AEM Marketing Communications Council.

83 ■ American Advertising Federation (AAF)
1101 Vermont Ave. NW, Ste.500
Washington, DC 20005-6306
Ph: (202)898-0089
Fax: (202)898-0159
E-mail: aaf@aaf.org
URL: http://www.aaf.org
Contact: Wally S. Snyder, Pres./CEO
Founded: 1967. **Members:** 45,000. **Staff:** 28. **Budget:** $4,122,561. **Local Groups:** 210. **Description:** Works to advance the business of advertising as a vital and essential part of the American economy and culture through government and public relations; professional development and recognition; community service, social responsibility and high standards; and benefits and services to members. Operates Advertising Hall of Fame, Hall of Achievement, and National Student Advertising Competition. Maintains Speaker's Bureau. **Awards:** ADDY Awards. **Frequency:** annual. **Type:** trophy. **Recipient:** for advertising excellence ● Advertising Hall of Achievement. **Frequency:** annual. **Type:** recognition. **Recipient:** for less than 40 age group ● National Student Advertising Competition. **Frequency:** annual. **Type:** recognition ● Silver Medal Award. **Type:** medal. **Recipient:** to outstanding advertising executives and students. **Committees:** Academic; Advertising Hall of Achievement; Government Affairs; Legal Affairs. **Formed by Merger of:** (1968) Advertising Federation of America; (1968) Associated Advertising Clubs of the World. **Publications:** *American Advertising Federation—Government Report*, monthly. Newsletter. Covers government and legislative issues affecting advertising. **Circulation:** 6,000 ● *American Advertising Magazine*, quarterly. Journal. Contains advertising industry information; includes calendar of events, listings of new members, news of awards, and legislative updates. **Circulation:** 48,000. **Advertising:** accepted ● *Communicator*, monthly. Newsletter. For college chapter members. **Circulation:** 5,000 ● *Newsline*, monthly. Newsletter. **Price:** free to AD Club officers. **Circulation:** 600. **Conventions/Meetings:** annual conference - always fall ● annual Government Affairs - conference - always March, Washington, DC ● annual National Advertising - conference (exhibits) - always June.

84 ■ American Association of Advertising Agencies (AAAA)
405 Lexington Ave., 18th Fl.
New York, NY 10174-1801
Ph: (212)682-2500
Fax: (212)682-8391
E-mail: tfinneran@aaaa.org
URL: http://www.aaaa.org
Contact: O. Burtch Drake, Pres./CEO
Founded: 1917. **Members:** 484. **Staff:** 65. **Budget:** $14,000,000. **Regional Groups:** 4. **Local Groups:** 27. **Description:** Fosters development of the advertising industry; assists member agencies to operate more efficiently and profitably. Sponsors member information and international services. Maintains 47 committees. Conducts government relations. **Libraries: Type:** not open to the public. **Subjects:** advertising, marketing. **Awards:** O'Toole Award. **Frequency:** annual. **Type:** trophy. **Recipient:** for creative excellence in advertising. **Publications:** *AAAA Publications Catalog*, periodic. Lists publications. ● *The Reporter*, bimonthly. Newsletter. Alternate Formats: online ● *Roster of Members*, annual. Directory. **Conventions/Meetings:** annual conference, for Company Executive Officers ● annual conference and trade show, for media (exhibits).

85 ■ American Council of Highway Advertisers (ACHA)
Address Unknown since 2007
Founded: 1936. **Members:** 70. **Staff:** 3. **Budget:** $300,000. **Description:** Commercial enterprises on private property along public highways. **Committees:** Executive; Highway Advertisers Political Action; Legislative. **Formerly:** (1949) American Highway Sign Association; (1985) Roadside Business Association. **Publications:** *Washington Morning Line*, monthly. Newsletter. Includes updates on legislative and regulatory development. **Price:** free to members. **Circulation:** 300. **Advertising:** not accepted. **Conventions/Meetings:** annual general assembly - always fall.

86 ■ American Society of Dermatological Retailers (ASDR)
c/o Dr. Jeffrey Lauber, MD, Medical Dir.
320 Superior Ave., No. 395
Newport Beach, CA 92663-2511
Ph: (949)646-9098 (949)646-9099
Free: (800)469-3739
Fax: (949)646-7298
E-mail: info@epex.com
URL: http://www.epex.com
Contact: Dr. Jeffrey Lauber MD, Medical Dir.
Founded: 1989. **Members:** 10. **Staff:** 2. **Budget:** $50,000. **Regional Groups:** 1. **State Groups:** 1. **Local Groups:** 1. **Languages:** English, Spanish. **For-Profit**. **Description:** Board certified dermatologists. Promotes ethical and professional marketing standards for skin care products. Conducts educational and research programs; sponsors competitions. Compiles statistics; maintains speakers' bureau, hall of fame, and museum. **Libraries: Type:** reference. **Holdings:** 2,000; archival material, artwork, audiovisuals, books, clippings, periodicals. **Subjects:** skin care product development. **Awards:** Best Product Award. **Frequency:** annual. **Type:** recognition ● **Type:** scholarship. **Recipient:** for outstanding achievement. **Computer Services:** database ● mailing lists. **Publications:** *Epex Quarterly*. Contains information on advancing skin products ethically. **Price:** free. **Advertising:** accepted ● *Health and Beauty*, periodic ● *Skin Saver*, annual. Newsletter. **Price:** free. **Advertising:** accepted. **Conventions/Meetings:** annual conference and board meeting, presentations, posters, sessions (exhibits) - always first week of December.

87 ■ ARF - Advertising Research Foundation (ARF)
432 Park Ave. S
New York, NY 10016
Ph: (212)751-5656
Fax: (212)319-5265
E-mail: info@thearf.org
URL: http://www.thearf.org
Contact: Robert L. Barocci, Pres./CEO
Founded: 1936. **Members:** 355. **Staff:** 20. **Description:** Advertisers, advertising agencies, research organizations, associations, and the media are regular members of the foundation; colleges and universities are associate members. Objectives are to: further scientific practices and promote greater effectiveness of advertising and marketing by means of objective and impartial research; develop new research methods and techniques; analyze and evaluate existing methods and techniques, and define proper applications; establish research standards, criteria, and reporting methods. Compiles statistics and conducts research programs. **Libraries: Type:** reference. **Holdings:** 2,500; clippings, periodicals, reports. **Subjects:** advertising, marketing. **Awards:** David Ogilvy Award. **Frequency:** annual. **Type:** recognition. **Recipient:** for excellence in the application of research in the creation of marketing campaigns ● Michael J. Naples Award. **Frequency:** annual. **Type:** recognition. **Recipient:** for leadership in the marketing, advertising, and media research industry. **Absorbed:** (1977) Center for Marketing Communication. **Also Known As:** Advertising Research Foundation. **Publications:** *ARF Transcript Proceedings*, periodic. Includes transcripts of papers delivered at ARF conferences and Key Issues Workshops. **Price:** $50.00/copy for members; $75.00/copy for nonmembers ● *Journal of Advertising Research*, bimonthly. Reports on advertising and market research. **Price:** $110.00/year in U.S.; $140.00/year outside U.S. ISSN: 0021-8499. **Circulation:** 4,700. **Advertising:** accepted. Alternate Formats: microform. Also Cited As: *JAR* ● Reports. **Conventions/Meetings:** periodic regional meeting.

88 ■ Association of Free Community Papers (AFCP)
PO Box 1989
Idaho Springs, CO 80452
Free: (877)203-2327
Fax: (781)459-7770

E-mail: afcp@afcp.org
URL: http://www.afcp.org
Contact: Craig S. McMullin, Exec. Dir.

Founded: 1950. **Members:** 385. **Membership Dues:** regular, $100 (annual) ● associate, $200 (annual). **Staff:** 2. **Budget:** $4,000,000. **State Groups:** 14. **Multinational. Description:** Represents publishers of nearly 3,000 free circulation papers and shopping/advertising guides. Offers national classified advertising placement service and national marketing for industry recognition. Conducts charitable programs. Sponsors competitions and compiles industry statistics. **Awards:** Distinguished Service Award. **Frequency:** annual. **Type:** recognition. **Recipient:** for members ● Publisher of the Year. **Frequency:** annual. **Type:** recognition. **Recipient:** for excellence in free paper publishing. **Formerly:** (1987) National Advertising Network, Inc. **Publications:** *Free Paper Ink*, monthly. Magazine. **Price:** included in membership dues. **Circulation:** 2,500. **Advertising:** accepted. Alternate Formats: online. **Conventions/Meetings:** annual conference and trade show (exhibits).

89 ■ Association of Hispanic Advertising Agencies (AHAA)

8201 Greensboro Dr., 3rd Fl.
McLean, VA 22102
Ph: (703)610-9014 (212)500-9400
Fax: (703)610-9005
E-mail: info@ahaa.org
URL: http://www.ahaa.org
Contact: Horacio Gavilan CMP, Exec. Dir.

Founded: 1996. **Members:** 170. **Membership Dues:** associate, $2,000-$10,000 (annual) ● individual, $500 (annual) ● student, $25 (annual) ● faculty, $100 (annual) ● general (based on annual billings), $1,500-$7,500 (annual). **Staff:** 14. **Budget:** $500,000. **Languages:** English, Spanish. **Description:** Advertising and marketing firms targeting Hispanic consumers. Seeks to "grow, strengthen and protect the Hispanic marketing and advertising industry." Promotes professional advancement of advertising and marketing personnel working with Hispanic markets. Conducts educational programs to raise awareness of Hispanic markets in the United States in the advertising industry. **Awards:** Advertising Age Hispanic Creative Advertising Awards. **Frequency:** annual. **Type:** recognition. **Publications:** *The AHAA Red Book*, annual. Directory. Serves as a standard directory of Hispanic advertising agencies. **Advertising:** accepted ● *Conexion AHAA*, monthly. Newsletter. Alternate Formats: online. **Conventions/Meetings:** semiannual conference - always spring and fall.

90 ■ Association of Independent Commercial Producers (AICP)

3 W 18th St., 5th Fl.
New York, NY 10011
Ph: (212)929-3000
Fax: (212)929-3359
E-mail: info@aicp.com
URL: http://www.aicp.com
Contact: Matthew Miller, Pres./CEO

Founded: 1972. **Members:** 500. **Staff:** 12. **Regional Groups:** 8. **Description:** Represents the interests of companies that specialize in producing television commercials for advertisers and agencies, and the businesses that furnish supplies and services to this industry. Serves as a collective voice for the industry before government and business councils, and in union negotiations; disseminates information; works to develop industry standards and tools; provides professional development; and markets American production. **Libraries: Type:** reference; not open to the public. **Holdings:** video recordings. **Awards:** The AICP Show: The Art and Technique of the American Television Commercial. **Frequency:** annual. **Type:** recognition. **Recipient:** for the best commercial filmmaking in 24 crafts categories ● The Jay B. Eisenstat Award. **Frequency:** periodic. **Type:** recognition. **Recipient:** for distinguished service in the television commercial production industry ● Jay Eisenstat Memorial Scholarship. **Type:** scholarship ● **Type:** recognition. **Computer Services:** Information services, production bulletins emailed to members ● online services, member services via website. **Telecommunication Services:** electronic mail, mattm@aicp.com. **Committees:** Finance; International Relations; Labor. **Programs:** The AICP Show: The Art and Technique of the American Television Commercial. **Publications:** *AICP Membership Directory*, annual. **Price:** $55.00 for nonmembers; free for members. **Advertising:** accepted ● *AICP National Newsletter*. **Conventions/Meetings:** annual show and lecture (exhibits) - premieres every June, followed by international tour.

91 ■ Association of National Advertisers (ANA)

708 Third Ave.
New York, NY 10017-4270
Ph: (212)697-5950 (202)296-1883
Fax: (212)661-8057
E-mail: rliodice@ana.net
URL: http://www.ana.net
Contact: Robert D. Liodice, Pres./CEO

Founded: 1910. **Members:** 343. **Staff:** 32. **Description:** Serves the needs of members by providing marketing and advertising industry leadership in traditional and e-marketing, legislative leadership, information resources, professional development and industry-wide networking. Maintains offices in New York City and Washington, DC. **Awards:** Robert V. Goldstein Award. **Frequency:** annual. **Type:** recognition. **Recipient:** for distinguished service as an Advertising Council Campaign Director. **Committees:** Advertising and Market Research; Advertising Financial Management; Advertising Management; Business-to-Business Marketing; Corporate Communications; Global Marketing; Government Relations; Multicultural Marketing; New Technologies; Print Advertising; Production Management; Promotion Marketing; Radio Advertising; Sponsorship and Event Marketing; Telephone Directory Advertising; Television Advertising. **Publications:** *The Advertiser*, bimonthly. Magazine. **Price:** $30.00 /year for nonmembers; free for members. **Advertising:** accepted. **Conventions/Meetings:** annual Advertising Financial Management Conference ● annual Agency Relationship Forum - conference ● annual conference and trade show ● annual Family Friendly Programming Forum - conference ● annual Multicultural Marketing Conference ● annual Sponsorship and Event Marketing Conference ● annual Television Advertising Forum - conference.

92 ■ Automotive Communications Council (ACC)

7101 Wisconsin Ave., Ste.1300
Bethesda, MD 20814
Ph: (240)333-1089
Fax: (301)654-3299
E-mail: acc@aftermarket.org
URL: http://www.acc-online.org
Contact: Tom Marx, Pres.

Founded: 1941. **Members:** 60. **Membership Dues:** $295 (annual). **Description:** Marketing, advertising, and/or sales promotion executives of manufacturing concerns, a substantial portion of whose products are sold through independent automotive wholesalers. Provides forum for exchange of views and opinions on needs of automotive trade and encourages study and research to increase advertising effectiveness. **Awards:** ACC Promotional Achievement Awards. **Frequency:** annual. **Type:** recognition. **Recipient:** to automotive wholesalers. **Telecommunication Services:** electronic mail, tmarx@themarxgrp.com. **Committees:** History; Internet; Marketing Awards; Meeting Agenda; Meeting Sites; Public Relations. **Formerly:** Automotive Advertisers Council. **Conventions/Meetings:** semiannual conference - every spring and fall.

93 ■ BPA Worldwide (BPA)

Two Corporate Dr., 9th Fl.
Shelton, CT 06484
Ph: (203)447-2800
Fax: (203)447-2900
E-mail: info@bpaww.com
URL: http://www.bpaww.com
Contact: Glenn J. Hansen, Pres./CEO

Founded: 1931. **Members:** 4,300. **Staff:** 37. **Budget:** $12,000,000. **Description:** Provides global audited data to the marketing, media, and information industries. **Awards:** Circulation Publicity Award. **Frequency:** annual. **Type:** recognition. **Telecommunication Services:** electronic mail, ghansen@bpai.com. **Committees:** Auditing Policies; Circulation Managers; Healthcare Services; Media Managers; Yellow Pages Advisory. **Divisions:** Business Publications; Electronic Media; Special Interest Consumer Magazines. **Formerly:** Controlled Circulations Audit; Business Publications Audit of Circulation; (2004) BPA International. **Publications:** *Comparability Update*, bimonthly ● *Directory to BPA Membership and Marketing Compatibility Programs*, annual ● *Forum*, quarterly. Newsletter. For membership. **Circulation:** 4,300. Alternate Formats: online ● Annual Report, annual. Alternate Formats: online. **Conventions/Meetings:** quarterly conference, continued education seminars for media buyers, advertising sales people, circulation managers and interactive media professionals.

94 ■ Business Marketing Association (BMA)

401 N Michigan Ave., Ste.1200
Chicago, IL 60611
Ph: (312)822-0005
Free: (800)664-4262
Fax: (312)822-0054
E-mail: bma@marketing.org
URL: http://www.marketing.org
Contact: John Favalo, Chm.

Founded: 1922. **Members:** 4,000. **Membership Dues:** international, $185 (annual) ● professional/individual, $90 (annual). **Staff:** 4. **Budget:** $1,000,000. **Local Groups:** 22. **Multinational. Description:** Business-to-business marketing and communications professionals working in business, industry and the professions. Develops and delivers benefits, services, information, skill enhancement, and networking opportunities to help members grow, develop, and succeed throughout business-to-business careers. **Libraries: Type:** not open to the public; reference. **Holdings:** 200; archival material, articles, monographs, papers, periodicals, reports. **Awards:** G.D. Crain Award. **Frequency:** annual. **Type:** recognition. **Recipient:** to a member who has exhibited exceptional dedication and support to the organization ● W.A. Marsteller Award. **Frequency:** annual. **Type:** recognition. **Recipient:** to a senior-level marketing executive who supports business-to-business marketing and communications. **Computer Services:** Electronic publishing. **Formerly:** (1959) National Industrial Advertisers Association; (1974) Association of Industrial Advertisers; (1993) Business/Professional Advertising Association. **Publications:** *The Business to Business Marketer*, 10/year. Magazine. Provides information for business-to-business marketing strategies and tactics. **Price:** included in membership dues; $50.00 /year for nonmembers. ISSN: 1073-4538. **Circulation:** 5,000. **Advertising:** accepted. Alternate Formats: online ● *Tuesday Marketing Notes*, weekly. Newsletter. **Conventions/Meetings:** annual conference - always June ● annual Pro-Comm Awards Competition.

95 ■ Cabletelevision Advertising Bureau (CAB)

830 Third Ave., 2nd Fl.
New York, NY 10022
Ph: (212)508-1200
Fax: (212)832-3268
E-mail: cynthiap@cabletvadbureau.com
URL: http://www.onetvworld.org
Contact: Cynthia Perkins-Roberts, Contact

Founded: 1981. **Staff:** 30. **Description:** Ad-supported cable networks. Provides marketing and advertising support to members and promotes the use of cable by advertisers and ad agencies locally, regionally, and nationally. **Libraries: Type:** open to the public. **Holdings:** books, periodicals. **Subjects:** cable industry, cable advertising. **Awards:** Cable Advertising Awards. **Frequency:** annual. **Type:**

recognition. **Recipient:** for cable sales executives. **Publications:** *Cable Network Profiles*, annual. Book. Provides summaries of national ad-supported cable networks. **Advertising:** accepted ● *TV Facts*, annual. Book. **Advertising:** accepted. **Conventions/ Meetings:** annual Cable Advertising - conference (exhibits) - always April in New York City ● annual Local Cable Sales Management - conference.

96 ■ Children's Advertising Review Unit (CARU)
70 W 36th St.
New York, NY 10018
Free: (866)334-6272
E-mail: caru@caru.bbb.org
URL: http://www.caru.org
Contact: Elizabeth Lascoutx, Dir.
Founded: 1972. **Staff:** 6. **Local Groups:** 1. **Description:** Participants include advertisers and advertising agencies. Monitors and evaluates child-directed advertising in all media; reviews advertising prior to its release upon request. Seeks voluntary change when advertising is found to be inaccurate, misleading, or otherwise inconsistent with the association's Self-Regulatory Guidelines for Children's Advertising. Acts as arbitrator in cases where the truthfulness of advertising claims comes under question by a competitor and entertains consumer complaints. Maintains Advisory Board to gather and disseminate information on the ways in which children perceive and understand advertising, and to revisit guidelines to ensure they remain current. Provides a Safe Harbor program under COPPA for the association's supporters. **Computer Services:** database, advertising challenges arbitrated by CARU. **Publications:** *A Parent's Guide: Advertising and Your Child*. Brochure ● *Self-Regulatory Guidelines for Children's Advertising*. Brochure. **Conventions/Meetings:** annual conference ● lecture and workshop, for lawyers, media representatives, educators, and other interested parties ● annual meeting, for advisory board.

97 ■ Digital Distribution of Advertising for Publications (DDAP)
1421 Prince St., Ste.230
Alexandria, VA 22314
Ph: (425)707-2713 (703)837-1066
Fax: (703)837-1072
E-mail: ddapinfo@idealliance.org
URL: http://www.ddap.org
Contact: David Steinhardt, Exec. Dir.
Founded: 1992. **Membership Dues:** member of IDEAlliance, $195 (annual) ● non-member of IDEAlliance, $295 (annual). **Description:** Focuses on digital delivery of advertising, advocating the use of accredited file formats in digital workflows and supporting the members' transition to digital ads by providing educational seminars, software tools and onsite consultation to build solid business practices.

98 ■ eBusiness Association (eBA)
PO Box 804
Adams Basin, NY 14410-0804
Ph: (585)234-1322
E-mail: rpenders@ebusinessassociation.org
URL: http://www.ebusinessassociation.org
Contact: Eric Hunt, Pres.
Founded: 1995. **Members:** 300. **Membership Dues:** student, $25 (annual) ● individual/professional, $95 (annual) ● corporate/executive - bronze, $275 (annual) ● corporate/executive - silver, $575 (annual) ● corporate/executive - gold, $950 (annual). **Staff:** 2. **Budget:** $25,000. **Regional Groups:** 1. **Description:** Corporations advertising on the Internet; professionals engaged in developing Internet marketing and advertising strategies and campaigns. Seeks to advance the practice of online advertising, marketing and business; promotes professional development of members. Represents members' interests before government agencies, industry associations, and the public. Conducts research and educational programs; sponsors advocacy campaigns; maintains speakers' bureau. **Awards:** eBusiness Association Scholarship. **Frequency:** annual. **Type:** scholarship. **Recipient:** to outstanding undergraduate student attending local academic institution or high school senior with plans to attend an institution ● eBusiness Executive of the Year Award. **Frequency:** annual. **Type:** recognition. **Recipient:** to local ebusiness practitioners for their professional success and role in advancement of "e" in their workplace or community. **Computer Services:** Online services, publication. **Telecommunication Services:** electronic mail, ldwyer@ebusinessassociation.org. **Formerly:** (2001) Internet Marketing and Advertising Association. **Publications:** *IMAA News Group*, quarterly. Newsletter. **Price:** free for members. **Advertising:** accepted. Alternate Formats: online. **Conventions/Meetings:** monthly board meeting and regional meeting.

99 ■ Eight Sheet Outdoor Advertising Association (ESOAA)
PO Box 2680
Bremerton, WA 98310-0344
Ph: (360)377-9867
Free: (800)874-3387
Fax: (360)377-9870
E-mail: davidjacobs@esoaa.com
URL: http://www.esoaa.com
Contact: David D. Jacobs, Exec. Dir.
Founded: 1953. **Members:** 140. **Membership Dues:** plant (varies with the number of panels), $150-$750 (annual) ● supplier/associate, $250 (annual). **Staff:** 2. **Budget:** $180,000. **Regional Groups:** 5. **Description:** Promotes the use of 8-sheet poster panels in outdoor advertising. (8-sheet signs are smaller than the usual 24-sheet ones, and are most commonly composed of 1 or 3 sheets covering an area of 6 x 12 feet.). **Awards: Frequency:** annual. **Type:** recognition. **Formerly:** (1980) Junior Panel Outdoor Advertising Association. **Publications:** *Display*, monthly. Newsletter. Includes updates and supplements to the Rates and Allotments book. **Price:** free, for members only. **Circulation:** 350. **Advertising:** accepted ● *Eight Sheet Outdoor Advertising Association-Sources: A Guide to Suppliers of Outdoor Materials and Services*, annual. Directory. Lists suppliers to the 8-sheet outdoor billboard industry; arranged by specialty. Includes definitions of basic industry terms. **Price:** free. **Circulation:** 800. **Advertising:** accepted ● *Rates and Allotments: 8 Sheet Poster Panels in the Top Population Ranked Markets*, annual. Directory. Covers rates and allotments for 8 sheet outdoor billboards; includes brief guide to 8-sheet outdoor advertising. **Price:** free for members, advertisers, and agencies; $35.00/issue for nonmembers. **Circulation:** 2,000. **Advertising:** accepted. **Conventions/ Meetings:** annual conference (exhibits).

100 ■ Healthcare Marketing and Communications Council (HMC)
1525 Valley Center Pkwy., Ste.150
Bethlehem, PA 18017
Ph: (610)868-8299
Fax: (610)868-8387
E-mail: info@hmc-council.org
URL: http://www.hmc-council.org
Contact: Mary L. Lacquaniti CAE, Exec. Dir.
Founded: 1934. **Members:** 1,400. **Membership Dues:** regular, $175 (annual) ● regular, $315 (biennial). **Staff:** 6. **Budget:** $2,500,000. **Description:** Sponsors targeted management development seminars for healthcare marketing and communication personnel. Offers education, information, and networking opportunities. **Awards:** Kathryn M. Amin Scholarship. **Frequency:** annual. **Type:** scholarship ● Terence E. Downer Scholarship. **Frequency:** annual. **Type:** scholarship. **Recipient:** to students pursuing a career in healthcare marketing or communications ● Win Gerson Scholarship. **Frequency:** annual. **Type:** scholarship. **Telecommunication Services:** electronic mail, mary@hmc-council.org. **Formerly:** Pharmaceutical Advertising Council; (1979) Pharmaceutical Advertising Club. **Publications:** *HMC News*, 9/year. Newsletter. **Price:** included in membership dues. **Advertising:** accepted ● Membership Directory, annual. **Price:** available to members only. **Conventions/Meetings:** seminar and luncheon - 8/year, January-May and September-November ● annual seminar, for healthcare marketing and communication personnel; conducted at Dartmouth College.

101 ■ Inflatable Advertising Dealers Association (IADA)
136 S Keowee St.
Dayton, OH 45402
Ph: (937)222-1024
Fax: (937)222-5794
E-mail: info@inflatableads.com
URL: http://www.inflatableads.com
Contact: Kimberly Fantaci, Exec. Dir.
Founded: 1992. **Members:** 110. **Membership Dues:** dealer, $225 (annual). **Staff:** 2. **Description:** Endeavors to be the voice of the inflatable industry. Provides and promotes a better understanding of the functions of inflatable advertising and its values. **Awards:** IADA Hall of Fame. **Frequency:** annual. **Type:** recognition.

102 ■ Interactive Advertising Bureau (IAB)
116 E 27th St., 7th Fl.
New York, NY 10016
Ph: (212)380-4700 (212)380-4717
URL: http://www.iab.net
Contact: Randall Rothenberg, Pres.
Founded: 1996. **Membership Dues:** general, $7,000 (annual) ● associate, $5,000 (annual). **Multinational. Description:** Companies actively engaged in the sale of advertising delivered on the Internet. Evaluates and recommends standards and practices, fields research and educates the advertising industry about the use of online and digital advertising. Publishes reports, updates members on key activities in online advertising, sponsors meetings and seminars. **Committees:** Hispanic; Interactive Advertising Games; Sponsorship. **Councils:** Agency Relations; Research. **Task Forces:** Ad Sizes; Measurement; Rich Media Guidelines. **Publications:** *IAB Informer*, monthly. Newsletter. Features the industry news and research and includes latest IAB conferences, products and services. Alternate Formats: online. **Conventions/ Meetings:** annual meeting ● seminar.

103 ■ Intermarket Agency Network (IAN)
5307 S 92nd St.
Hales Corners, WI 53130
Ph: (414)425-8800
Fax: (414)425-0021
E-mail: bille@nonbox.com
URL: http://www.intermarketnetwork.com
Contact: Bill Eisner, Exec. Dir.
Founded: 1967. **Members:** 19. **Staff:** 1. **Description:** An active network of high-powered marketing/ communications agencies in the United States, Canada, Central and South America, and Europe. **Formerly:** (1999) Intermarket Association of Advertising Agencies. **Conventions/Meetings:** semiannual conference - spring and fall.

104 ■ International Advertising Association (IAA)
521 5th Ave., Ste.1807
New York, NY 10175
Ph: (212)557-1133
Fax: (212)983-0455
E-mail: iaa@iaaglobal.org
URL: http://www.iaaglobal.org
Contact: Nubia Martinez, Exec. Asst.
Founded: 1938. **Members:** 5,000. **Membership Dues:** global corporate, $10,000 (annual) ● regional corporate, $7,000 (annual) ● national corporate, $4,000 (annual) ● organization, $405 (annual) ● individual, $200 (annual) ● academic, $85 (annual). **Staff:** 10. **Regional Groups:** 62. **State Groups:** 105. **Description:** Global network of advertisers, advertising agencies, the media and related services, spanning 99 countries. Demonstrates to governments and consumers the benefits of advertising as the foundation of diverse, independent media. Protects and advances freedom of commercial speech and consumer choice, encourages greater practice and acceptance of advertising self-regulation, provides a forum to debate emerging professional marketing communications issues and their consequences in the fast-changing world environment, and takes the lead in state-of-the-art professional development through education and training for the marketing communications industry of tomorrow. Conducts research on such topics as restrictions and taxes on advertis-

ing, advertising trade practices and related information, and advertising expenditures around the world. Sponsors IAA Education Program. Has compiled recommendations for international advertising standards and practices. **Libraries: Type:** reference. **Holdings:** audiovisuals, books, clippings, monographs, periodicals. **Subjects:** advertising/marketing communications, regulatory issues affecting the industry. **Awards: Frequency:** biennial. **Type:** recognition. **Recipient:** for distinguished service in the field of international advertising and marketing ● Samir Fares Award. **Frequency:** biennial. **Type:** recognition. **Recipient:** to an individual in recognition of career achievement in the IAA and of outstanding service in furthering the objectives of the association. **Computer Services:** Online services, comprehensive association information and industry links. **Telecommunication Services:** electronic mail, nubia@iaa-global.org. **Formerly:** (1954) Export Advertising Association. **Publications:** *The Case for Advertising Self-Regulation.* Booklet ● *IAA Annual Report*, annual ● *IAA Membership Directory*, annual. Covers the advertising industry, with emphasis on the value of advertising, freedom of commercial speech, and consumer choice. **Price:** free for members; $15.00/copy for nonmembers; $80.00 /year for nonmembers. **Circulation:** 4,000 ● *IAA Weekly*. Newsletter. Alternate Formats: online ● *Monographs on Severely Restricted or Forbidden Advertising Practices.* Pamphlets ● Pamphlets. **Conventions/Meetings:** biennial World Advertising - congress (exhibits) ● annual World Education - conference.

105 ■ International Communications Agency Network (ICOM)
PO Box 490
Rollinsville, CO 80474-0490
Ph: (303)258-9511
Fax: (303)484-4087
E-mail: info@icomagencies.com
URL: http://www.icomagencies.com
Contact: Mr. Gary Burandt, Exec. Dir.

Founded: 1950. **Members:** 84. **Membership Dues:** regular, $2,650 (annual) ● in Latin America, $1,500 (annual). **Staff:** 2. **Budget:** $350,000. **Regional Groups:** 4. **National Groups:** 30. **Languages:** English, Spanish. **Multinational. Description:** Network of non-competing advertising agencies. Provides an interchange of management information, international facilities, and branch office service for partner agencies. Provides discounts on syndicated services and access to 1000 computer databases. **Libraries: Type:** not open to the public. **Holdings:** business records. **Awards:** Creative Award. **Frequency:** annual. **Type:** recognition. **Telecommunication Services:** electronic mail, burandt@icomagencies.com. **Formerly:** (1998) International Federation of Advertising Agencies. **Publications:** *Agency Client Lists*, monthly. Directories. **Price:** available to members only. Alternate Formats: online ● *Best Practices* ● *Facts About Membership*, semiannual ● *The Globe*, monthly. Newsletter. **Advertising:** accepted. Alternate Formats: online ● *Member Surveys* ● *Membership Roster*, annual. Membership Directory. Includes monthly updates. **Conventions/Meetings:** annual International Management Conference, for members only ● annual North American Regional Management Meeting - regional meeting.

106 ■ International Vintage Poster Dealers Association (IVPDA)
PO Box 501
New York, NY 10113-0501
E-mail: info@ivpda.com
URL: http://www.ivpda.com

Founded: 1996. **Members:** 60. **Multinational. Description:** Educates the public, collectors and buyers about vintage posters. Promotes the appreciation of vintage posters around the world. Provides strict guidelines to ensure the authenticity of the posters offered for sale. **Computer Services:** Online services, vintage poster resources. **Publications:** Brochure. Alternate Formats: online.

107 ■ Los Angeles Advertising Agencies Association (LAAAA)
4223 Glencoe Ave., Ste.C-100
Marina del Rey, CA 90292
Ph: (310)823-7320
Fax: (310)823-7325
E-mail: submissions@laaaa.com
URL: http://www.laaaa.com
Contact: Susan Franceschini, Exec.Dir.

Founded: 1946. **Members:** 175. **Staff:** 6. **Description:** Assists heads of advertising agencies in the Western U.S. to operate their agencies more effectively and profitably. Offers assistance to agency management and staff. Provides a forum for discussion and exchange of information. Promotes members' interests. **Awards:** Lifetime Achievement Award/Leader of the Year. **Frequency:** annual. **Type:** recognition. **Recipient:** for individuals who have made significant impact on the Los Angeles advertising community. **Computer Services:** Mailing lists. **Formerly:** (1956) Southern California Advertising Agencies Association; (2002) Western States Advertising Agencies Association. **Publications:** Newsletter, quarterly. Alternate Formats: online. **Conventions/Meetings:** annual conference.

108 ■ Mailing and Fulfillment Service Association (MFSA)
1421 Prince St., Ste.410
Alexandria, VA 22314-2806
Ph: (703)836-9200
Free: (800)333-6272
Fax: (703)548-8204
E-mail: mfsa-mail@mfsanet.org
URL: http://www.mfsanet.org
Contact: David A. Weaver, Pres./CEO

Founded: 1920. **Members:** 700. **Membership Dues:** business (based on sales volume), $1,335-$5,600 (annual) ● sole practitioner, $535 (annual) ● foreign (based on sales volume), $395-$850 (annual) ● associate/supplier (based on number of location), $1,535-$3,200 (annual). **Staff:** 11. **Budget:** $2,000,000. **Local Groups:** 8. **Description:** Commercial direct mail producers, letter shops, mailing list houses, fulfillment operations, and advertising agencies. Conducts special interest group meetings. Offers specialized education; conducts research programs. **Awards:** L.V. Luke Kaiser Educational Award. **Frequency:** annual. **Type:** recognition. **Recipient:** for individuals who have contributed to the advancement of education pertaining to mail and fulfillment service ● Leo G. Bill Bernheimer Award. **Frequency:** annual. **Type:** recognition. **Recipient:** for exceptional dedication and service to MFSA ● Miles Kimball Medallion. **Frequency:** annual. **Type:** medal. **Recipient:** for individuals who have made the greatest contribution to the advancement of direct mail industry ● Robert M. Huse Chapter Achievement Award. **Frequency:** annual. **Type:** recognition. **Recipient:** for chapter members with outstanding contributions to MFSA. **Telecommunication Services:** electronic mail, daweaver@mfsanet.org. **Committees:** Chapter Leaders; Education Content; Fulfillment; Government Affairs; Membership Development; Postal and Government; Publications and Member Services; Risk; Technology. **Formerly:** (2001) Mail Advertising Service Association International. **Publications:** *MFSA Wage Salary, and Fringe Benefit Survey*, semiannual. Features report on wages, salaries, and fringe benefits for the mailing service industry data arranged by region and sales volume. **Price:** $300.00 for members; $400.00 for nonmembers ● *Performance Profiles: The Financial Ratios for the Mailing Service Industry*, annual. Report. Provides operating and financial ratios from data submitted by member firms; allows firms to evaluate their performance and determine their position. **Price:** $300.00 for members; $500.00 for nonmembers ● *Postscripts*, monthly. Newsletter. Keeps members up-to-date on industry news, contains articles from members, equipment exchange, and upcoming meetings. **Price:** available to members only. **Circulation:** 2,000. **Advertising:** accepted. Alternate Formats: online ● *Who's Who: MASA's Buyers' Guide to Blue Ribbon Mailing Services*, annual. Membership Directory. Lists members by geographic region and the services rendered; includes suppliers to the mailing industry. Contains a resident list exchange directory. **Price:** free. **Advertising:** accepted. **Conventions/Meetings:** Customer Service and Project Management Conference ● annual Fulfillment Conference ● annual Mailer Strategies - conference ● annual Mailer's Expo - conference ● annual Mid-Winter Executive Conference - held in January ● annual Production Management Seminar - conference.

109 ■ Marketing and Advertising Global Network (MAGNET)
1017 Perry Hwy., Ste.5
Pittsburgh, PA 15237
Ph: (412)366-6850 (412)779-5393
Fax: (412)366-6840
E-mail: mxdirector@verizon.net
URL: http://www.magnetglobal.org
Contact: Cheri D. Gmiter, Exec. Dir./Controller

Founded: 1946. **Members:** 40. **Membership Dues:** regular, $6,500 (annual). **Staff:** 1. **Budget:** $250,000. **Regional Groups:** 2. **Languages:** Danish, English, Finnish, French, German, Spanish. **Multinational. Description:** Cooperative network of non-competing advertising, marketing, merchandising, and public relations agencies. Aims to bring about, through mutual cooperation, greater accomplishment and efficiency in the management of member advertising agencies. Other goals are: to raise standards of the advertising agency business through the exchange of information relative to agency management and all phases of advertising; to exchange information on all common problems, such as management, sales development, market studies, agency functions, and operations. Aims to inform the general public of current global marketing trends. **Libraries: Type:** not open to the public. **Holdings:** archival material, biographical archives, business records, maps, periodicals, video recordings. **Awards:** Indie Awards Competition. **Frequency:** annual. **Type:** recognition. **Recipient:** body of work for each agency's previous year. **Computer Services:** database, clients; their products and services. **Formerly:** (1958) Midwestern Advertising Agency Network; (1999) Mutual Advertising Agency Network. **Publications:** *MAGNET Matters*, 3/year. Newsletter. Contains recap of activities of all member agencies. **Price:** $1.00. **Circulation:** 125 ● *This Week at MAGNET*, weekly. Newsletter. Contains members' activities and pertinent market news about advertising and marketing. **Price:** $1.00. Alternate Formats: online. **Conventions/Meetings:** annual General Membership Meetings ● workshop.

110 ■ Mobile Marketing Association (MMA)
75 Manhattan Dr., Ste.204
Boulder, CO 80303
Ph: (303)415-2550
Fax: (303)499-0952
E-mail: mma@mmaglobal.com
URL: http://mmaglobal.com
Contact: Laura Marriott, Exec. Dir.

Members: 400. **Membership Dues:** general, $5,000 (annual) ● startup, $2,500 (annual) ● individual, $1,000 (annual). **Multinational. Description:** Represents agencies, advertisers, hand held device manufacturers, wireless operators and service providers, retailers, software and services providers, and any company focused on the potential of marketing via the mobile channel. Strives to stimulate the growth of mobile marketing and its associated technologies. Establishes standards and practices for sustainable growth. **Awards:** Best Use of Mobile Marketing Award. **Frequency:** annual. **Type:** recognition. **Recipient:** to the company that used mobile marketing in an innovative manner ● Innovation Award. **Frequency:** annual. **Type:** recognition. **Recipient:** to a company that has demonstrated and applied new products or technology which significantly contribute to the growth of the industry ● Outstanding Individual Achievement in Mobile Marketing. **Frequency:** annual. **Type:** recognition. **Recipient:** to an individual who exhibits impressive leadership and selfless dedication to growing the mobile marketing industry. **Telecommunication Services:** electronic mail, laura.marriott@mmaglobal.com. **Publications:** *International Journal of Mobile Marketing*, semiannual. Provides a medium for academics, students and industry professionals from around the world. **Price:** $75.00 /year for members; $45.00 per copy for members; $100.00 /year for nonmembers;

$70.00 per copy for nonmembers. Also Cited As: *IJMM* ● *MMA Messenger*, monthly. Newsletter. Contains information about mobile marketing and the mobile space. Alternate Formats: online.

111 ■ National Advertising Division Council of Better Business Bureaus (NAD)
70 W 36th St., 13th Fl.
New York, NY 10018
Ph: (212)705-0120
E-mail: sharris@nad.bbb.org
URL: http://www.nadreview.org
Contact: Sheryl Harris, Marketing Dir.
Founded: 1971. **Description:** A division of the Council of Better Business Bureaus. Functions as the self-regulatory mechanism of the U.S. advertising industry in conjunction with the National Advertising Review Board. Seeks to maintain high standards of truth and accuracy in advertising. Investigates advertising that is thought to contain falsehoods about or misrepresentations of a product; acts as arbitrator in cases where an advertisement's veracity has been challenged by a competitor and the public interest is involved. Monitors television, radio, and print advertising and initiates challenges of advertisements judged to contain false or misleading information or images. Does not participate in challenges to advertising that are based on matters of taste, political or issue positions, or possibly unlawful business practices. **Libraries: Type:** reference. **Subjects:** NAD Case Reports. **Telecommunication Services:** electronic mail, rpersaud@narc.bbb.org. **Affiliated With:** BBB Wise Giving Alliance; National Advertising Review Board. **Publications:** *Do's and Don'ts in Advertising Copy*, periodic ● *NAD Case Report*, monthly. Includes synopses of advertising challenges adjudicated in the preceding month. ● Proceedings. **Conventions/Meetings:** biennial workshop, on trends in claim substantiation.

112 ■ National Advertising Review Board (NARB)
70 W 36th St., 13th Fl.
New York, NY 10018
Ph: (212)705-0114
E-mail: bhopewell@narc.bbb.org
URL: http://www.narbreview.org
Contact: Howard Bell, Chm.
Founded: 1971. **Description:** Individuals from industry and the public. Sponsored by the National Advertising Review Council for the purpose of sustaining high standards of truth and accuracy in national advertising. Aims to maintain a self-regulatory mechanism that responds constructively to public complaints about national advertising and which significantly improves advertising performance and credibility. **Libraries: Type:** reference. **Holdings:** 84; reports. **Subjects:** advertising disputes. **Publications:** *NARB Panel Reports*. **Conventions/Meetings:** annual meeting - usually in New York City.

113 ■ National Association of Publishers' Representatives (NAPR)
54 Cove Rd.
Huntington, NY 11743
Ph: (631)223-2200
E-mail: napr@naprassoc.com
URL: http://www.naprassoc.com
Contact: Armand Villiger, Exec. Dir.
Founded: 1950. **Members:** 265. **Membership Dues:** individual, $200 (annual). **Staff:** 2. **Budget:** $30,000. **Regional Groups:** 3. **Description:** Independent publishers' representatives selling advertising space for more than one publisher of consumer, industrial, direct response, and trade publications. **Computer Services:** database ● mailing lists. **Formerly:** (1981) Association of Publishers' Representatives. **Publications:** *NAPR Newsletter*, monthly. **Price:** included in membership dues. **Advertising:** accepted. Alternate Formats: online ● Membership Directory, annual. **Advertising:** accepted. **Conventions/Meetings:** monthly meeting, with lunch ● quarterly meeting.

114 ■ Outdoor Advertising Association of America (OAAA)
1850 M St. NW, Ste.1040
Washington, DC 20036
Ph: (202)833-5566
Fax: (202)833-1522
E-mail: kklein@oaaa.org
URL: http://www.oaaa.org
Contact: Ken Klein, Exec. VP for Government Relations
Founded: 1891. **Members:** 1,100. **Staff:** 14. **Regional Groups:** 5. **State Groups:** 46. **Description:** Firms owning, erecting, and maintaining standardized poster panels and painted display advertising facilities. Aims to provide leadership, services, and standards to promote, protect and advance the outdoor advertising industry. **Awards:** OBIE Award. **Frequency:** annual. **Type:** recognition. **Recipient:** to agencies for excellence in outdoor advertising ● Outdoor Media Plan Awards. **Frequency:** annual. **Type:** recognition. **Recipient:** for efficient and effective outdoor media plans that maximize the synergies between media and creative strategies within an available budget. **Committees:** Legislative; Marketing; Membership and Communications; Standards and Procedures, and Executive. **Councils:** Alternative; Street Furniture; Suppliers; Transit. **Absorbed:** (2002) Shelter Advertising Association. **Conventions/Meetings:** biennial convention (exhibits).

115 ■ Point-of-Purchase Advertising International (POPAI)
1600 Duke St., Ste.400
Alexandria, VA 22314
Ph: (703)373-8800 (703)373-8808
Fax: (703)373-8801
E-mail: info@popai.com
URL: http://www.popai.com
Contact: Richard K. Blatt, Pres./CEO
Founded: 1938. **Members:** 1,000. **Staff:** 20. **Description:** Producers and suppliers of point-of-purchase advertising signs and displays and national and regional advertisers and retailers interested in use and effectiveness of signs, displays, and other point-of-purchase media. Conducts student education programs; maintains speakers' bureau. **Libraries: Type:** reference. **Holdings:** articles, books. **Subjects:** marketing. **Awards:** Merchandising Award. **Frequency:** annual. **Type:** recognition. **Computer Services:** Mailing lists. **Telecommunication Services:** electronic mail, dblatt@popai.com. **Committees:** Educational Relations; Exhibit; Research; Retail; Scholarship; Trade Practices; Wire Fabricator. **Task Forces:** Canadian. **Formerly:** (2000) Point-of-Purchase Advertising Institute. **Publications:** *Better Marketing at the Point-of-Purchase*. Book ● *Exhibit Directory*, periodic ● *Harvard Business School Case History: L'Eggs Products Incorporated*. Book ● *Industry Magazine*, periodic ● *Merchandising Yearbook Awards*, annual. Lists award-winning displays and signs. **Price:** $75.00/copy. **Circulation:** 3,000 ● *Point of Purchase* **Advertising:** A Marketing In-Store Arsenal. Book ● *POPAI News*, bimonthly. Magazine. Covers research in retailing, marketing, and merchandising. **Price:** $35.00/year. **Circulation:** 24,000. **Advertising:** accepted. **Conventions/Meetings:** annual European Awards and Tradeshow - trade show.

116 ■ Promotional Products Association International (PPAI)
3125 Skyway Cir. N
Irving, TX 75038-3526
Ph: (972)252-0404
Free: (888)IAM-PPAI
Fax: (972)258-3007
E-mail: steves@ppa.org
URL: http://www.ppa.org
Contact: Steve Slagle CAE, Pres./CEO
Founded: 1903. **Members:** 7,000. **Membership Dues:** supplier, distributor, $60 (annual) ● international, $266 (annual) ● associate, $700 (annual) ● franchisor, $1,087-$2,952 (annual) ● franchisee, $100 (annual) ● marketing, $672 (annual) ● supplier representative, $240 (annual), **Staff:** 65. **Budget:** $15,000,000. **Regional Groups:** 28. **Multinational. Description:** Suppliers and distributors of promotional products including incentives, imprinted ad specialties, premiums, and executive gifts. Promotes industry contacts in 60 countries. Holds executive development and sales training seminars. Conducts research and compiles statistics. Administers industry advertising and public relations program. Maintains speakers' bureau. Conducts trade shows, regional training, publishes educational resources. **Libraries: Type:** reference. **Holdings:** 200. **Subjects:** management, professional development, technology, sales management. **Awards:** Distributor Web Award. **Frequency:** annual. **Type:** recognition. **Recipient:** for distributor members who have developed creative and effective business internet websites for the promotional products industry ● Golden Pyramid Competition. **Frequency:** annual. **Type:** recognition. **Recipient:** for outstanding use of promotional products in business promotions, individual contribution to industry ● Industry Hall of Fame. **Frequency:** annual. **Type:** recognition. **Recipient:** to industry individuals for outstanding contributions to the promotional products industry ● Supplier Web Award. **Frequency:** annual. **Type:** recognition. **Recipient:** for supplier members who have developed creative and effective business internet websites for the promotional products industry ● Suppliers Golden Achievement. **Frequency:** annual. **Type:** recognition. **Recipient:** for PPAI suppliers. **Computer Services:** database ● mailing lists ● online services. **Committees:** Advertising and Public Relations; Awards; Conventions; Distributors; Education; Government and Legal Affairs; International Strategic Planning; Marketing Information and Research; Membership Services; Suppliers; Technology. **Formed by Merger of:** Specialty Advertising National Association; Specialty Advertising Guild International. **Formerly:** (1970) Specialty Advertising Association; (1993) Specialty Advertising Association International. **Publications:** *Distributor Update*, monthly. Newsletter. Alternate Formats: online ● *PPB Newslink*. Newsletter. Alternate Formats: online ● *Promotional Products Association International—Membership Directory and Reference Guide*, annual. **Price:** available to members only. **Circulation:** 6,000. **Advertising:** accepted ● *Promotional Products Business*, monthly. Magazine. Provides industry and association news, government and legislative information, and general business articles; includes index. **Price:** $48.00 /year for members; $62.00 /year for nonmembers. ISSN: 0195-0495. **Circulation:** 12,500. **Advertising:** accepted ● *Supplier Update*, biweekly. Newsletter. Alternate Formats: online ● Also produces educational and promotional publications and audiovisual resources. **Conventions/Meetings:** semiannual trade show (exhibits) - always January.

117 ■ Radio Advertising Bureau (RAB)
1320 Greenway Dr., Ste.500
Irving, TX 75038-2587
Ph: (212)681-7214
Free: (800)232-3131
Fax: (212)681-7217
E-mail: jhaley@rab.com
URL: http://www.rab.com
Contact: Jeffrey M. Haley, Pres./CEO
Founded: 1951. **Members:** 7,000. **Staff:** 50. **Budget:** $5,500,000. **Description:** Includes radio stations, radio networks, station sales representatives, and allied industry services, such as producers, research firms, schools, and consultants. Calls on advertisers and agencies to promote the sale of radio time as an advertising medium. Sponsors program to increase professionalism of radio salespeople, awarding Certified Radio Marketing Consultant designation to those who pass examination. Sponsors regional marketing conferences. Conducts extensive research program into all phases of radio sales. Issues reports on use of radio by national, regional, and local advertisers. Speaks before conventions and groups to explain benefits of radio advertising. Sponsors Radio Creative Fund. Compiles statistics. **Libraries: Type:** reference. **Holdings:** 500; archival material, books, clippings, periodicals. **Subjects:** advertising, retailing, demographics, marketing. **Awards:** Radio-Mercury Award. **Frequency:** annual. **Type:** recognition. **Recipient:** for radio advertising. **Computer Services:** database, co-op advertising ● database, marketing information. **Telecommunication Services:** electronic mail, member_response@rab.com. **Committees:** Sales Advisory; Small Market Advisory. **Formerly:** Broadcast Advertising Bureau. **Publications:**

Guide to Competitive Media, biennial. Book. Explains differences in major media as advertising agents. Alternate Formats: online ● *RAB Instant Background: Profiles of 100 Businesses*, annual. Provides marketing and demographic information on different product categories. Includes statistics and annual index. **Circulation:** 15,000. Alternate Formats: CD-ROM; online ● *RAB Media Fact Book*, annual. Overviews the commercial radio industry in the United States. Contains statistics, graphs, and tables covering radio audience types. Alternate Formats: CD-ROM; online ● *Radio Co-op Sources*, annual. Directory. Lists co-op advertising plans, arranged by advertiser category; separate listing of manufacturers with 100 percent co-op plans. Includes index. ● *Radio Sales Today*, semiweekly. **Price:** included in membership dues. **Circulation:** 3,825. **Advertising:** accepted ● *Retail Marketing Kit*, monthly. **Conventions/Meetings:** annual Managing Sales Conference - symposium (exhibits).

118 ■ Retail Advertising and Marketing Association (RAMA)

325 7th St. NW, Ste.1100
Washington, DC 20004-2818
Ph: (202)661-3052
Fax: (202)737-2849
E-mail: perweilerp@rama-nrf.com
URL: http://www.rama-nrf.org
Contact: Peter Perweiler, Mgr., Marketing Communications

Founded: 1952. **Members:** 1,500. **Membership Dues:** individual, $125 (annual) ● corporate, $875 (annual). **Staff:** 5. **Budget:** $1,000,000. **Description:** Persons in retail sales promotion, advertising, and marketing, and persons serving retailers in promotional capacities. Elects one professional to the Retail Advertising Hall of Fame. Conducts research programs. **Awards:** RACie Awards. **Frequency:** annual. **Type:** trophy. **Recipient:** for advertising. **Telecommunication Services:** electronic mail, gilmorek@rama-nrf.com ● electronic mail, perweilerp@nrf.com. **Affiliated With:** National Retail Federation. **Formerly:** (1991) Retail Advertising Conference; (2003) Retail Advertising and Marketing Association, International. **Publications:** *RAMA Bulletin*. Newsletter. **Advertising:** accepted. Alternate Formats: online ● *RAMA Report*, annual ● *Retail Sales Outlook*, quarterly. Newsletter. Alternate Formats: online ● *Stores*, monthly. Magazine. **Price:** free for members and retailers; $120.00 for nonmembers and nonretailer. **Advertising:** accepted. Alternate Formats: online. **Conventions/Meetings:** annual competition, for best print and broadcast ads (exhibits) ● annual conference (exhibits).

119 ■ Southern Classified Advertising Managers Association (SCAMA)

c/o Hugh J. Rushing, Exec. Off.
PO Box 531335
Mountain Brook, AL 35253-1335
Ph: (205)823-3448
Fax: (205)823-3449
E-mail: hrushing@usit.net
URL: http://www.scama.com
Contact: Hugh J. Rushing, Exec. Off.

Founded: 1947. **Members:** 250. **Membership Dues:** advertising (depends on circulation), $95-$195 (annual) ● associate, $220 (annual). **Staff:** 1. **Budget:** $180,000. **Description:** Represents and promotes Southern classified advertising managers. **Publications:** *The SCAMA Bulletin*, monthly. **Advertising:** accepted ● *SCAMA Scoop*, 11/year. Newspaper. Reaches key decision makers in newspapers throughout the 17-state SCAMA region. **Advertising:** accepted. **Conventions/Meetings:** Sales and Education Conference ● Telephone Sales Conference.

120 ■ Syndicated Network Television Association (SNTA)

630 Fifth Ave., Ste.2320
New York, NY 10111
Ph: (212)259-3740
Fax: (212)259-3770
E-mail: mburg@snta.com
URL: http://www.snta.com
Contact: Mitch Burg, Pres.

Description: Represents television program syndicators, whose programs air nationwide on network and independent stations. Communicates to advertisers, their agencies and media planners and buyers the benefits of syndication. Makes information on syndication readily available to the advertising community. **Publications:** *Syndication Insider*. Newsletter. **Price:** free.

121 ■ Television Bureau of Advertising (TVB)

3 E 54th St., 10th Fl.
New York, NY 10022-3108
Ph: (212)486-1111
Fax: (212)935-5631
E-mail: info@tvb.org
URL: http://www.tvb.org
Contact: Christopher J. Rohrs, Pres.

Founded: 1954. **Members:** 550. **Staff:** 20. **Description:** Television stations, station sales representatives, and program producers/syndicates. Strives to increase advertiser dollars to U.S. spot television. Represents television stations to the advertising community. **Libraries:** **Type:** not open to the public. **Holdings:** 200. **Subjects:** broadcasting. **Awards:** TVB Automotive Commercial Competition. **Frequency:** annual. **Type:** recognition. **Telecommunication Services:** electronic mail, crohrs@tvb.org. **Committees:** E-Business; National Sales Advisory; NSAC Research; Sales Advisory. **Conventions/Meetings:** annual conference (exhibits).

122 ■ Trade Promotion Management Associates (TPMA)

1055 Parsippany Blvd., Ste.405
Parsippany, NJ 07054
Ph: (646)442-3703
Fax: (973)263-1974
E-mail: headquarters@tpmaww.com
URL: http://www.tradepromo.org
Contact: Mr. Mike Kantor, Managing Dir.

Founded: 1989. **Members:** 150. **Membership Dues:** manufacturer, retailer, $1,800 (annual) ● service provider, $4,200 (annual). **Staff:** 6. **Budget:** $500,000. **Description:** Represents manufacturers, retailers, media outlets, advertising agencies and providers of enabling technology. Serves as the industry's resource for information and education on all types of trade allowance programs, including the latest industry regulations. Gathers the latest research and trends from industry experts, and distributes information from industry-leading organizations. Serves as the industry's premier resource allowing trading partners to get the maximum value out of their channel marketing programs. **Awards:** Hall of Fame Award. **Frequency:** annual. **Type:** recognition. **Recipient:** for significant contribution to coop/MPF industry. **Formerly:** (2005) National Association for Promotional and Advertising Allowances. **Publications:** *Trade Promotion Outlook*, weekly. Newsletter. Contains current views and events of the association. **Price:** free for members. **Circulation:** 3,000. **Advertising:** accepted. Alternate Formats: online ● *Trading Partner Practices*, bimonthly. Journal. **Price:** included in membership dues. Alternate Formats: online. **Conventions/Meetings:** semiannual conference, discussion of advanced strategies and ready solutions for greatest performance measurement challenges; highlights case studies (exhibits) - in September.

123 ■ Traffic Audit Bureau for Media Measurement (TAB)

212 Madison Ave., Ste.1504
New York, NY 10016
Ph: (212)972-8075
Fax: (212)972-8928
E-mail: inquiry@tabonline.com
URL: http://www.tabonline.com
Contact: Joseph C. Philport, Pres./CEO

Founded: 1933. **Members:** 560. **Membership Dues:** advertiser, $418-$1,276 (annual) ● associate, $418 (annual) ● advertising agency, media buying services (minimum), $1,000 (annual) ● plant operator (minimum), $2,000 (annual). **Staff:** 10. **Description:** Advertisers, advertising agencies, operators of outdoor advertising plants, bus shelter advertising companies, and backlighted display and painted bulletin companies. Sets standard practices for the evaluation of circulation and visibility of outdoor advertising; issues statements on the circulation values of outdoor advertising plants. Encourages standardization of terminology and practices in the industry. Seeks to educate those involved in out-of-home media on ways of developing circulation data for advertising sites. Compiles statistics. **Telecommunication Services:** electronic mail, joephilport@tabonline.com. **Committees:** Audit Development; Audit Policies and Procedures; Conference; Data Standards and Policy; IT Steering; Marketing; VAI/Research. **Formed by Merger of:** Out-of-Home Measurement Bureau; Traffic Audit Bureau. **Publications:** *Building Accountability for Out of Home Media*. Brochure. Alternate Formats: online ● *Calculating Daily Effective Circulation (DEC)*. Brochure. Alternate Formats: online ● *Planning for Out-of-Home Media*. Book. **Price:** $49.00 each (1-5 copies); $44.00 each (6-9 copies); $40.00 each (10 or more copies) ● *Standard Procedures for the Evaluation of Outdoor Advertising* ● *TABBriefs*. Newsletter. Alternate Formats: online ● *Tabulations*, quarterly. Newsletter ● *What You Should Know About the New TAB Audit*. Brochure. Alternate Formats: online. **Conventions/Meetings:** annual Conference and Marketing Expo, for buyers, sellers and suppliers to OOH industry (exhibits).

124 ■ Transworld Advertising Agency Network (TAAN)

7920 Summer Lake Ct.
Fort Myers, FL 33907
Ph: (239)433-0669
Fax: (239)433-1366
E-mail: info@taan.org
URL: http://www.taan.org
Contact: Gary Lessner, Pres.

Founded: 1936. **Members:** 47. **Staff:** 2. **Budget:** $120,000. **Description:** Independently owned advertising agencies that cooperate for exchange of management education and information, reciprocal service, and personal local contact. Allows members to seek aid of other members in campaign planning, creative services, merchandising, public relations, publicity, media, research, and test facilities. Conducts annual expertise audit. **Telecommunication Services:** electronic mail, gary@taan.org. **Formerly:** (1975) Transamerican Advertising Agency Network. **Publications:** *TAAN Newsletter*, quarterly ● *Transcript*, semiannual. **Conventions/Meetings:** semiannual conference and workshop - February/August.

125 ■ Utility Communicators International (UCI)

c/o Elliot Boardman, Exec. Dir.
1818 Country Creek Ct.
Magnolia, TX 77354
Ph: (936)271-5005
Fax: (936)271-5060
E-mail: eboardman@att.net
URL: http://www.uci-online.com
Contact: Elliot Boardman, Exec. Dir.

Founded: 1921. **Members:** 300. **Membership Dues:** individual, $275 (annual) ● corporate (includes 3 members; add $150 for each additional member), $700 (annual). **Staff:** 1. **Regional Groups:** 6. **Description:** Advertising and public relations directors of electric, gas, water, telephone, and other utility companies and allied industries. Sponsors utility advertising/communications contest. **Awards:** Better Communications. **Frequency:** annual. **Type:** recognition. **Recipient:** for energy companies. **Formerly:** (1977) Public Utilities Advertising Association; (1989) Public Utilities Communicators Association. **Publications:** *UCI—Membership Directory*, annual. **Price:** included in membership dues. **Circulation:** 400 ● *UCI—Newsletter*, bimonthly. Reports on membership activities; includes information on advertising and public relations. **Price:** included in membership dues. **Circulation:** 400 ● Proceedings. **Conventions/Meetings:** annual conference ● annual meeting ● annual workshop (exhibits).

Advertising Auditors

126 ■ Audit Bureau of Circulations (ABC)
900 N Meacham Rd.
Schaumburg, IL 60173-4968
Ph: (847)605-0909
Fax: (847)605-0483
E-mail: service@accessabc.com
URL: http://www.accessabc.com
Contact: Michael J. Lavery, Pres./Managing Dir.
Founded: 1914. **Staff:** 250. **Regional Groups:** 30. **Description:** Represents advertisers, advertising agencies, and publishers of daily and weekly newspapers, farm publications, consumer magazines, and business publications in the United States and Canada. Issues standardized statements on the circulation of publisher members; verifies the figures shown in these statements by auditors' examination of publishers' records; disseminates circulation data. Provides academic associate support; conducts forums and seminars. **Libraries: Type:** reference. **Computer Services:** database, Circulation Data Bank. **Committees:** Business Publications Buyer Advisory; Business Publications Industry; Canadian Newspaper Buyers' Advisory; Data Bank Users Group; Farm Publication Buyers Advisory; Farm Publishers Advisory; Interactive Media; Interactive Technical; Magazine Buyers Advisory; Magazine Directors Advisory; NAA/ABC Liaison; Newspaper Buyers Advisory; Young Media Professionals. **Subcommittees:** NAA Circulation. **Task Forces:** Canadian Coupon; U.S. Coupon. **Publications:** *ABC—Membership Roster*, annual. Membership Directory. Arranged alphabetically and geographically. **Price:** free. **Circulation:** 6,000 ● *Audit Bureau of Circulations—Supplemental Data Reports*, periodic. Includes data on the cost of a single issue of a publication or one day's gross distribution. **Price:** included in membership dues; $2.75 for nonmembers ● *Audit Report*, annual. Presents a verified report of publisher members' circulation claims. **Price:** $2.15 ● *Bylaws and Rules*, annual ● *Canadian Circulation of U.S. Magazines*, annual. **Price:** $35.00 for members ● *Canadian Daily/Weekly Newspaper Circulation Factbook*, annual. Report. Analyzes the circulation of daily and weekly newspapers by counties, major markets, and five-year trends. **Price:** $50.00/issue for members. ISSN: 0098-2520. **Circulation:** 450 ● *County Penetration Reports*, semiannual. Helps advertisers identify the newspapers that will most effectively reach their customers. **Price:** included in membership dues ● *Daily Newspaper Circulation Rate Book*, annual. Contains a listing of daily U.S. and Canadian newspapers. Includes weekly, monthly, and single copy circulation rates. **Price:** $10.00 /year for members ● *FAS-FAX Reports*, semiannual. Four-volume compilation of reports of the most current summary circulation information for U.S. and Canadian periodicals. ● *Magazine Market Coverage Reports*, annual. Reports for media buyers and planners covering circulation data for ABC-audited U.S. magazines, farm, and business publications. **Price:** $75.00/copy for members ● *Magazine Trend Report*, annual. Presents a five-year trend report of circulation, advertising page rates, and subscription and newsstand information. **Price:** $115.00/copy for members ● *News Bulletin*, 3/year. Newsletter. Announces changes to the ABC rules, bylaws, and reports. **Circulation:** 13,000 ● *Newspaper Blue Books*. **Price:** $395.00 daily (in U.S.); $95.00 weekly (in U.S.); C$45.00 daily (in Canada); C$68.00 weekly (in Canada) ● *Periodical Blue Books*. **Price:** $320.00 periodical; $210.00 magazines; $115.00 business publications; $23.00 farm publications ● *Periodical Statement Library*, semiannual. Catalog. Includes publisher's circulation statements. Available in 7 volumes. **Price:** available to members only ● *Publishers' Statements*, semiannual. Provides six-month circulation averages as submitted by publishers. ● Annual Report, annual. Includes financial statements. **Price:** free for members, libraries, and colleges. **Circulation:** 6,000 ● Bulletins ● Videos. **Conventions/Meetings:** annual conference, focuses on a different industry topic each year.

127 ■ Certified Audit of Circulations (CAC)
155 Willowbrook Blvd., 4th Fl.
Wayne, NJ 07470
Ph: (973)785-3000
Free: (800)346-1357
Fax: (973)785-8341
E-mail: mstoecklin@certifiedaudit.com
URL: http://www.certifiedaudit.com
Contact: Mark Stoecklin, CEO
Founded: 1956. **Membership Dues:** advertiser/agency, $25 (annual). **Description:** Provides objective, accurate and reliable reporting of circulation data and market information to members. **Conventions/Meetings:** semiannual meeting and board meeting.

128 ■ Publishers Information Bureau (PIB)
810 7th Ave., 24th Fl.
New York, NY 10019
Ph: (212)872-3722
Fax: (212)753-2768
E-mail: pib@magazine.org
URL: http://www.magazine.org
Contact: Wayne Eadie, Pres.
Founded: 1945. **Members:** 250. **Staff:** 2. **Description:** Measures the amount and type of advertising in magazines and reports this information monthly through printed and electronic formats; service prepared by TNSMI/Competitive Media Reporting (contracting agent). **Computer Services:** database, consumer magazine information. **Committees:** Technical Advisory. **Publications:** *Publishers Information Bureau—Reports*, monthly. Alternate Formats: online. Also Cited As: *PIB Reports*.

Aerospace

129 ■ Aeronautical Repair Station Association (ARSA)
121 N Henry St.
Alexandria, VA 22314-2903
Ph: (703)739-9543
Fax: (703)739-9488
E-mail: arsa@arsa.org
URL: http://www.arsa.org
Contact: Sarah MacLeod, Exec. Dir.
Founded: 1984. **Members:** 700. **Membership Dues:** regular (based on number of employees), $250-$1,500 (annual) ● associate, $500 (annual) ● corporate, $7,500 (annual) ● individual, $100 (annual). **Staff:** 2. **Description:** Represents FAA-certified repair stations, suppliers and distributors. Assists members on regulatory and legislative issues before the FAA and other governmental agencies. **Libraries: Type:** reference. **Holdings:** articles. **Telecommunication Services:** electronic mail, sarahsays@arsa.org. **Absorbed:** (1985) Airline Services Association. **Publications:** *The Hotline*, monthly. Newsletter. **Advertising:** accepted. Alternate Formats: online ● *Legal Briefs Compendium*. Handbook. Alternate Formats: online ● *Model Domestic Repair Station Manual*. Alternate Formats: online. **Conventions/Meetings:** annual symposium.

130 ■ Aerospace Industries Association of America (AIA)
1000 Wilson Blvd., Ste.1700
Arlington, VA 22209-3928
Ph: (703)358-1000
Fax: (703)358-1012
E-mail: michelle.princi@aia-aerospace.org
URL: http://www.aia-aerospace.org
Contact: John W. Douglass, Pres./CEO
Founded: 1919. **Members:** 96. **Membership Dues:** associate (based on company's sales), $3,000-$5,000 (annual). **Staff:** 51. **Budget:** $8,000,000. **Description:** Represents manufacturers of commercial, military and business aircraft, helicopters, aircraft engines, missiles, spacecraft, and related components and equipment. Maintains Aerospace Research Center. Compiles statistics. **Libraries: Type:** not open to the public. **Holdings:** books, periodicals, reports. **Committees:** Compensation Practices; Cost Principles; Defense Trade; Economic Advisory; Electronic Enterprise Integration; Environmental, Safety and Health; Export Controls; Industrial Security; Intellectual Property. **Councils:** Communications; International; Procurement and Finance. **Departments:** Supply Chain Management; Technical Operations. **Divisions:** Civil Aviation; Space Systems. **Affiliated With:** Council of Defense and Space Industry Associations. **Formerly:** (1945) Aeronautical Chamber of Commerce of America; (1959) Aircraft Industries Association of America. **Publications:** *Aerospace Facts and Figures*, annual. Book. Provides statistical and analytical information on aircraft production, missile programs, space programs and air transportation. **Price:** $60.00 for nonmembers; $45.00 for members. ISSN: 0898-4425. **Circulation:** 3,000 ● *Aerospace Industries Association of America—Annual Report* ● *AIA Update*, bimonthly. Newsletter. Alternate Formats: online ● *Executive Report*, quarterly. Contains news and information about AIA members. Alternate Formats: online ● *The Future of Aerospace Standardization Report*. Provides recommendations to strengthen the U.S. aerospace standards infrastructure. ● *Integrated Space Operations Summit Panel Report*. Alternate Formats: online ● *Security and Policy Review Handbook*. Alternate Formats: online.

131 ■ Air, Inc. - Aviation Information Resources
1777 Phoenix Pkwy., Bldg. 100, Ste.105
Atlanta, GA 30349
Ph: (404)592-6500
Free: (800)JET-JOBS
Fax: (404)592-6515
E-mail: airinfo@airapps.com
URL: http://www.jet-jobs.com
Contact: Kit Darby, Pres.
Founded: 1989. **Members:** 10,000. **Membership Dues:** web, $139 (annual) ● full, $159 (annual). **Staff:** 40. **For-Profit. Description:** Provides career planning service for pilots. Includes services such as reference publications for job hunting. **Formerly:** (2001) Air - Aviation Information Resources. **Publications:** *Airline Fleet/Simulator Directory*, annual. Contains current fleets by model at the largest 130 U.S. airlines, and 530 U.S. full-motion simulators. **Price:** $29.95. **Circulation:** 10,000. **Advertising:** accepted. Alternate Formats: online ● *Airline Info and Address Directory*, annual. Contains addresses, contacts, fleets, bases, minimum qualifications, pay and benefits for the major, national, jet, non-jet and startup airlines. **Price:** $33.95. **Circulation:** 10,000. **Advertising:** accepted ● *Airline Pilot Application Handbook*. **Price:** $34.95. **Advertising:** accepted ● *Airline Pilot Career Developmental System*. **Price:** included in membership dues ● *Airline Pilot Career Guide*. **Price:** $32.95. **Advertising:** accepted ● *Airline Pilot Careers*, monthly. Magazine. Contains career, financial, and legal information of interest to prospective commercial pilots. **Price:** $29.95/year. **Circulation:** 20,000. **Advertising:** accepted. Alternate Formats: online ● *Airline Pilot Job Monthly*. Newsletter. **Price:** $99.00. Alternate Formats: online ● *Airline Pilot Salary Survey*, annual. Journal. **Price:** $35.00. **Advertising:** accepted ● *Airline Simulator Training Manual*. **Price:** $54.95. **Advertising:** accepted ● *Airline Test Kit*. **Price:** $39.00. **Advertising:** accepted. **Conventions/Meetings:** quarterly Airline Pilot Career Seminar and Job Fair, pilots learn about the industry; hiring and meeting with airline recruiters.

132 ■ Air Traffic Control Association (ATCA)
1101 King St., Ste.300
Alexandria, VA 22314
Ph: (703)299-2430
Fax: (703)299-2437
E-mail: info@atca.org
URL: http://www.atca.org
Contact: Peter F. Dumont, Pres.
Founded: 1956. **Members:** 2,500. **Membership Dues:** corporate, $1,000 (annual) ● individual, $130 (annual). **Staff:** 9. **Budget:** $2,000,000. **Multinational. Description:** Air traffic controllers; private, commercial, and military pilots; private and business aircraft owners and operators; aircraft and electronics engineers; airlines, aircraft manufacturers, and electronic and human engineering firms. Promotes the establishment and maintenance of a safe and efficient air traffic control system. Conducts special

surveys and studies on air traffic control problems. Participates in aviation community conferences. **Libraries: Type:** not open to the public. **Awards:** ATCA Air Traffic Control Specialist of the Year Award. **Frequency:** annual. **Type:** recognition. **Recipient:** to an individual military or civilian air traffic control specialist acting in a non-supervisory capacity ● ATCA Airway Transportation Systems Specialist of the Year. **Frequency:** annual. **Type:** recognition. **Recipient:** to an individual military or civilian airway facilities technician acting in a non-supervisory capacity ● ATCA Industrial Award. **Frequency:** annual. **Type:** recognition. **Recipient:** to an industry or group of industries for outstanding achievement or contribution that has added to the quality, safety, or efficiency of the air traffic control system ● ATCA Small and Disadvantaged Business Award. **Frequency:** annual. **Type:** recognition. **Recipient:** to a small business owned and controlled by socially and economically disadvantaged individuals ● The Charles E. Varnell Memorial Award for Small Business. **Frequency:** annual. **Type:** recognition. **Recipient:** to a company classified as a small business, for outstanding achievement or contribution that has added to the quality, safety, or efficiency of the air traffic control system ● Earl F. Ward Memorial Award. **Frequency:** annual. **Type:** medal. **Recipient:** to a group for outstanding achievement during the previous year that has added to the quality, safety, or efficiency of the air traffic control system ● General E.R. Quesada Memorial Award. **Frequency:** annual. **Type:** medal. **Recipient:** for outstanding achievement and contribution during the previous year as a manager in the air traffic control system ● George W. Kriske Memorial Award. **Frequency:** annual. **Type:** medal. **Recipient:** for an outstanding career that has added to the quality, safety, or efficiency of the air traffic control system ● The Lingiam Odems Memorial Award. **Frequency:** annual. **Type:** medal. **Recipient:** for air traffic control specialists of the military ● William A. Parenteau Memorial Award. **Frequency:** annual. **Type:** medal. **Recipient:** to an individual for outstanding achievement during the previous year that has added to the quality, safety, or efficiency of the air traffic control system. **Telecommunication Services:** electronic mail, pete.dumont@atca.org. **Committees:** Air Traffic Control; ATC Engineering and Development; Aviation Education; Awards; Nominating; Professional Ethics and Standards; Publications; Publicity and Public Relations. **Publications:** *Air Traffic Control Bulletin*, monthly. **Price:** available to members only. ISSN: 0400-1915 ● *Fall Conference Proceedings*, annual. ISSN: 0192-8740 ● *Journal of Air Traffic Control*, quarterly. ISSN: 1064-3818. **Advertising:** accepted. **Conventions/Meetings:** annual International Technical Conference (exhibits) ● annual meeting (exhibits).

133 ■ Air Transport Association of America (ATA)

1301 Pennsylvania Ave. NW, Ste.1100
Washington, DC 20004-7017
Ph: (202)626-4000 (202)626-4172
Fax: (202)626-4181
E-mail: ata@airlines.org
URL: http://www.airlines.org
Contact: James C. May, Pres./CEO

Founded: 1936. **Members:** 28. **Membership Dues:** tiered level, $5,000-$25,000 (annual) ● industry backbone level (maximum), $75,000 (annual). **Staff:** 120. **Description:** Airlines engaged in transporting persons, goods, and mail by aircraft between fixed terminals on regular schedules. **Libraries: Type:** reference. **Holdings:** 12,000. **Subjects:** transportation texts, civil aviation history. **Committees:** Senior Advisory. **Councils:** Energy; Engineering and Maintenance; Environment; Government Affairs; Law; Safety; Security. **Publications:** *Air Transport*, annual. Report. **Price:** $20.00 ● *Airline Handbook*. Alternate Formats: online ● Reports ● Also publishes fact sheets, press releases, studies, speeches, testimonies, and specifications.

134 ■ Aircraft Electronics Association (AEA)

4217 S Hocker
Independence, MO 64055-0963
Ph: (816)373-6565
Fax: (816)478-3100
E-mail: info@aea.net
URL: http://www.aea.net
Contact: Paula Derks, Pres.

Founded: 1958. **Members:** 1,250. **Membership Dues:** regular in U.S. and Canada, $260-$770 (annual) ● associate in U.S. and Canada, $770-$2,600 (annual) ● corporate/commercial operator in U.S. and Canada, $670-$2,300 (annual) ● academic, $275 (annual) ● regular outside U.S. and Canada, $345-$825 (annual). **Staff:** 6. **Budget:** $1,000,000. **Description:** Companies engaged in the sales, engineering, installation, and service of electronic aviation equipment and systems. Seeks to: advance the science of aircraft electronics; promote uniform and stable regulations and uniform standards of performance; establish and maintain a code of ethics; gather and disseminate technical data; advance the education of members and the public in the science of aircraft electronics. Offers supplement type certificates, test equipment licensing, temporary FCC licensing for new installations, spare parts availability and pricing, audiovisual technician training, equipment and spare parts loan, profitable installation, and service facility operation. Provides employment information, equipment exchange information and service assistance on member installations anywhere in the world. **Awards:** Associate Member of the Year Award. **Frequency:** annual. **Type:** recognition. **Recipient:** for associate members ● Avionics Training Excellence. **Frequency:** annual. **Type:** recognition. **Recipient:** to members with total commitment to training ● Member of the Year Award. **Frequency:** annual. **Type:** recognition. **Recipient:** for regular members. **Publications:** *Avionics News*, monthly. Magazine. **Price:** $132.00/year. **Circulation:** 6,500. **Advertising:** accepted. Alternate Formats: online. **Conventions/Meetings:** annual trade show (exhibits) - 2009 Apr. 1-4, Dallas, TX; 2010 Apr. 7-10, Orlando, FL; 2011 Mar. 30-Apr. 2, Reno, NV.

135 ■ Aircraft Owners and Pilots Association (AOPA)

421 Aviation Way
Frederick, MD 21701
Ph: (301)695-2000
Free: (800)USA-AOPA
Fax: (301)695-2375
E-mail: aopahq@aopa.org
URL: http://www.aopa.org
Contact: Phil Boyer, Pres.

Founded: 1939. **Members:** 404,000. **Membership Dues:** individual, $39 (annual) ● life, $2,500. **Staff:** 210. **Budget:** $43,700,000. **Description:** Represents general aviation pilots and owners, 60 percent of U.S. are members, as are three-quarters of the nation's general aviation aircraft owners. Works to make flying safer, less expensive, and more fun. **Libraries: Type:** reference. **Awards:** Joseph B. Hartranft, Jr. "Doc" Award. **Frequency:** annual. **Type:** monetary. **Recipient:** for significant contributions to the advancement of general aviation ● Laurence P. Sharples Perpetual Award. **Frequency:** annual. **Type:** monetary. **Recipient:** for individuals whose life's work is beyond the field of general aviation ● Max Karant Awards for Excellence in Aviation Journalism. **Frequency:** annual. **Type:** monetary. **Recipient:** for TV, radio, and print. **Publications:** *AOPA Flight Training Magazine*, monthly. **Price:** $18.00 /year for members. **Circulation:** 90,000. **Advertising:** accepted ● *AOPA Pilot*, monthly. Magazine. **Price:** available to members only. ISSN: 0001-2084. **Circulation:** 360,253. **Advertising:** accepted. Alternate Formats: online ● *AOPA's Airport Directory*. Alternate Formats: online ● *AOPA's Aviation U.S.A.*, semiannual. Serves as guide to approximately 5,400 public-use and 1,900 private-use airports, seaplane bases, and heliports in the United States. **Price:** first copy free for members; $24.95 for nonmembers; $12.50 for additional copies. **Advertising:** accepted ● Newsletters. Alternate Formats: online ● Annual Report, annual. **Conventions/Meetings:** annual convention, with product demonstrations and static aircraft display (exhibits) ● annual meeting and seminar (exhibits) - first Saturday of June ● annual trade show (exhibits) - 2008 Nov. 6-8, San Jose, CA; 2009 Nov. 5-7, Tampa, FL.

136 ■ Airline Industrial Relations Conference (AIRCON)

1300 19th St. NW, Ste.750
Washington, DC 20036-1609
Ph: (202)861-7550
Fax: (202)861-7557
E-mail: staff@aircon.org
URL: http://www.aircon.org
Contact: Donald W. Maliniak, Pres.

Founded: 1971. **Members:** 22. **Staff:** 4. **Description:** U.S. scheduled air carriers. Exchanges industrial relations information. **Also Known As:** AIR Conference. **Publications:** *Airline Employee Wage Rates and Benefit Surveys* ● *Digest of Airline Arbitration Awards* ● *Directory of Airline Industrial Relations Officials*, periodic ● *Weekly Review of Collective Bargaining* ● Newsletter, bimonthly. **Conventions/Meetings:** quarterly conference.

137 ■ Airports Council International - North America (ACI-NA)

1775 K St. NW, Ste.500
Washington, DC 20006
Ph: (202)293-8500
Free: (888)424-7767
Fax: (202)331-1362
E-mail: memberservices@aci-na.aero
URL: http://www.aci-na.org
Contact: Greg Principato, Pres.

Founded: 1991. **Members:** 163. **Membership Dues:** platinum, $16,500 (annual) ● diamond, $11,100 (annual) ● gold, $6,100 (annual) ● silver, $3,000 (annual) ● airport related business, $4,100 (annual) ● small business, $1,750 (annual) ● government, nonprofit, $720 (annual) ● sole proprietor, $665 (annual). **Staff:** 28. **Description:** Represents local, regional, and state governing organizations that own and operate commercial airports in the U.S., Canada, and Bermuda. Represents a variety of industries that provide products and services to the air transportation industry. **Committees:** Business Information Technologies; Commissioners; Economic Affairs; Environmental Affairs; Facilitation Group; Governmental Affairs; Legal Affairs; Marketing and Communications; Operations and Technical Affairs; Public Security and Safety; Small Airports. **Councils:** Canada Airports. **Affiliated With:** Airports Council International - Switzerland. **Publications:** *ACI-NA Hotlights*, weekly. Bulletin. Alternate Formats: online ● *Airport Highlights*, monthly. Newsletter. **Price:** $495.00 for nonmembers; $250.00 for members; $125.00 for libraries and students. **Circulation:** 2,300. **Advertising:** accepted. Alternate Formats: online ● *Centerlines*. Magazine. **Price:** included in membership dues. Alternate Formats: online ● *Worldwide Airport Traffic Report*, annual ● Handbooks ● Surveys. **Conventions/Meetings:** annual conference - 2008 Sept. 21-24, Boston, MA ● annual Excellence in Communications Contest - competition.

138 ■ American Association of Airport Executives (AAAE)

601 Madison St., Ste.400
Alexandria, VA 22314
Ph: (703)824-0500
Fax: (703)820-1395
E-mail: member.services@airportnet.org
URL: http://www.aaae.org
Contact: Charles M. Barclay AAE, Pres.

Founded: 1928. **Members:** 4,500. **Membership Dues:** executive, affiliate, $225 (annual) ● participating, $275 (annual) ● associate, $325 (annual) ● corporate, $715 (annual) ● military, $150 (annual) ● academic, $40 (annual). **Staff:** 50. **Budget:** $10,000,000. **Description:** Represents airport management personnel at public use airports nationwide. Offers specialized educational seminars; conducts examination for and awards professional designation of AAE (Accredited Airport Executive). **Libraries: Type:** reference; open to the public. **Holdings:** 4,600. **Subjects:** airport related material. **Telecommunication Services:** electronic mail, charles.barclay@aaae.org. **Committees:** Academic Relations; Airline Economics and Air Service; Airport Training; Audit; Diversity; Environmental Services; General Aviation; Information Technology. **Publications:** *Airport Maga-*

zine, bimonthly. **Price:** $45.00/year. **Advertising:** accepted. Alternate Formats: online ● *Airport Report*, semimonthly. Newsletter. **Advertising:** accepted. Alternate Formats: online ● *Airport Report Express*, semiweekly. Newsletter. Alternate Formats: online. **Conventions/Meetings:** semiannual conference ● annual conference (exhibits) - always May or September ● annual International Airport Facilities Conference and Exposition.

139 ■ American Helicopter Society (AHS)

217 N Washington St.
Alexandria, VA 22314-2538
Ph: (703)684-6777
Fax: (703)739-9279
E-mail: staff@vtol.org
URL: http://www.vtol.org
Contact: Morris E. Rhett Flater, Exec. Dir.

Founded: 1943. **Members:** 6,000. **Membership Dues:** regular in U.S. and Canada, $65 (annual) ● international, $80 (annual) ● student in U.S. and Canada, $25 (annual) ● student outside U.S. and Canada, $45 (annual) ● regular in U.S. and Canada (age 30 and under), $40 (annual) ● international (age 30 and under), $60 (annual) ● retired over 60, active military in U.S. and Canada, $35 (annual) ● retired over 60, active military (international), $55 (annual) ● educational, $250 (annual) ● corporate: class a (with annual revenues greater than $100 million), $8,250 (annual) ● corporate: class b (with annual revenues of $50-100 million), $5,250 (annual) ● corporate: class c (with annual revenues of $10-50 million), $2,250 (annual) ● corporate: class d (with annual revenues of less than $10 million), $950 (annual) ● corporate: consulting firm, government agency, association, $350 (annual). **Staff:** 6. **Budget:** $1,000,000. **Regional Groups:** 7. **Local Groups:** 21. **Multinational. Description:** Represents aircraft designers, engineers, government personnel, operators, and industry executives in over 40 countries interested in V/STOL aircraft. (V/STOL stands for Vertical/Short Takeoff and Landing.) Conducts research and educational and technical meetings concerning professional training and updated information. **Libraries: Type:** reference. **Holdings:** 10,700; archival material, books, papers, video recordings. **Subjects:** vertical flight, aeronautics. **Awards:** AHS Fellows. **Frequency:** annual. **Type:** fellowship. **Recipient:** for society members whose work towards the interest of the industry constitutes an outstanding achievement ● Captain William J. Kossler, USCG Award. **Frequency:** annual. **Type:** recognition. **Recipient:** for the greatest achievement in practical application or operation of rotary wing aircraft ● Dr. Alexander Klemin Award. **Frequency:** annual. **Type:** recognition. **Recipient:** for notable achievement in the advancement of rotary wing aeronautics ● Frederick L. Feinberg Award. **Frequency:** annual. **Type:** recognition. **Recipient:** for the helicopter pilot who had the most outstanding achievement during the preceding year ● Grover E. Bell Award. **Frequency:** annual. **Type:** recognition. **Recipient:** for research and experimentation in helicopter development in the U.S. ● Gruppo Agusta International Helicopter Fellowship Award. **Frequency:** annual. **Type:** fellowship. **Recipient:** for the most significant contribution to international vertical flight cooperation by an individual or group ● Harry T. Jensen Award. **Frequency:** annual. **Type:** recognition. **Recipient:** for an outstanding contribution to the improvement of helicopter reliability, maintainability, and/or safety through improved design during the preceding year ● Honorary Fellows. **Frequency:** annual. **Type:** fellowship. **Recipient:** for society members whose work towards the interest of the AHS constitutes an outstanding achievement ● Howard Hughes Award. **Frequency:** annual. **Type:** recognition. **Recipient:** for outstanding improvement in fundamental helicopter technology brought to fruition during the previous year ● Igor I. Sikorsky International Trophy. **Frequency:** annual. **Type:** trophy. **Recipient:** for the company that designed and built a world record-breaking helicopter ● Paul E. Haueter Award. **Frequency:** annual. **Type:** recognition. **Recipient:** for significant contribution to the development of VTOL aircraft other than helicopters ● Vertical Flight Foundation Scholarship. **Frequency:** annual. **Type:** scholarship. **Recipient:** for students. **Computer Services:** Bibliographic search ● database, membership ● mailing lists. **Telecommunication Services:** electronic mail, rflater@vtol.org. **Committees:** Acoustics; Aerodynamics; Aircraft Design; Avionics and Systems; Crash Safety; Crew Stations and Human Factors Engineering; Dynamics; Education; Flight Simulation; Handling Qualities; Health And Usage Monitoring Systems; History; Integrated Manufacturing Process and Control Technology; Operations; Product Support; Propulsion; Scholarship; STOVL Technology; Structures and Materials; Test and Evaluation. **Publications:** *American Helicopter Society—Proceedings*, annual. Contains technical papers presented at the annual AHS forum, covering helicopter research and operation. **Price:** $205.00 /year for members; $255.00 /year for nonmembers; $20.00 single paper for members; $25.00 single paper for nonmembers. **Circulation:** 550. Alternate Formats: CD-ROM ● *Journal of the American Helicopter Society*, quarterly. Contains papers selected by peer review for managers and engineers in the vertical flight industry; includes detailed page of instructions. **Price:** $115.00 /year for nonmembers in U.S.; $20.00 /year for members; $135.00 /year for nonmembers outside U.S.; $30.00/issue for nonmembers in U.S. ISSN: 0002-8711. **Circulation:** 7,500 ● *Specialists' Meeting Proceedings*. **Price:** $105.00 for members (full proceedings); $145.00 for nonmembers (full proceedings); $20.00 for members (single paper); $25.00 for nonmembers (single paper). Alternate Formats: CD-ROM ● *Vertiflite*, quarterly. Magazine. Includes technical articles, calendar of meetings, and book reviews; for engineers and managers in the vertical flight industry worldwide. **Price:** $115.00 /year for members in U.S.; $135.00 /year for members outside U.S.; $30.00/back issue in U.S. ISSN: 0042-4455. **Circulation:** 8,000. **Advertising:** accepted. Alternate Formats: online ● Papers. **Conventions/Meetings:** annual Forum and Technology Display - convention, three-day vertical flight technical conference (exhibits) - always spring.

140 ■ Aviation Development Council (ADC)

141-07 20th Ave., Ste.404
Whitestone, NY 11357
Ph: (718)746-0212
Fax: (718)746-1006
E-mail: root@aviationdevelopmentcouncil.org
URL: http://www.aviationdevelopmentcouncil.org
Contact: Bill Huisman, Dir.

Founded: 1963. **Members:** 96. **Staff:** 2. **Description:** U.S. and foreign scheduled air carriers serving the New York-New Jersey metropolitan area; Port Authority of New York and New Jersey; Allied Pilots Association; and Air Line Pilots Association, International. Aims to explore, evaluate, and recommend to the proper authorities measures in various fields that will afford possible relief to people affected by noise of aircraft. Initiates public information on significant developments in the metropolitan area. Compiles runway analysis data on New York City area airports. Administers industry funded outreach programs designed to encourage local purchasing; administers "crime and security watch" programs for JFK, LGA & EWR. **Computer Services:** Record retrieval services, CATER (collection and analysis of terminal records). **Affiliated With:** Air Line Pilots Association, International; Allied Pilots Association. **Formerly:** National Air Transport Coordinating Committee.

141 ■ Aviation Distributors and Manufacturers Association (ADMA)

100 N 20th St., 4th Fl.
Philadelphia, PA 19103-1443
Ph: (215)564-3484
Fax: (215)963-9784
E-mail: adma@fernley.com
URL: http://www.adma.org
Contact: Michael J. Mitkus, Exec. Dir.

Founded: 1943. **Members:** 75. **Staff:** 3. **Description:** Wholesalers and manufacturers of general aviation aircraft parts, supplies, and equipment. Strives to further the development of the aviation marketplace through the services and products produced and distributed by members. **Awards:** Aviation Education Award. **Frequency:** annual. **Type:** recognition. **Recipient:** for excellence in aviation education ● Janice Marie Dyer Award. **Frequency:** annual. **Type:** recognition. **Recipient:** for excellence in aviation education. **Additional Websites:** http://www.fernley.com. **Telecommunication Services:** electronic mail, mmitkus@fernley.com. **Publications:** *Aviation Education News Bulletin*, bimonthly ● *The Flight Plan*, bimonthly. Newsletter. Alternate Formats: online ● Directory, annual. **Price:** included in membership dues; $150.00 for nonmembers ● Newsletters ● Membership Directory. **Conventions/Meetings:** semiannual meeting.

142 ■ Aviation Industry CBT Committee (AICC)

PO Box 472
Sugar City, ID 83448-0472
Ph: (208)496-1136
Fax: (208)496-5136
E-mail: admin@aicc.org
URL: http://www.aicc.org
Contact: Dr. Scott Bergstrom, Admin.

Founded: 1988. **Members:** 120. **Membership Dues:** voting, $2,500 (annual) ● airline voting, $1,500 (annual) ● observer, $1,000 (annual). **Staff:** 2. **Multinational. Description:** International Computer-Based Training (CBT) hardware and software vendors, airlines, and airplane manufacturers. Creates guidelines for interoperability of airline CBT hardware and software systems and intercompatibility of Computer Managed Instruction (CMI) systems with CBT systems. Operates an independent testing laboratory to verify compliance with established guidelines. **Computer Services:** Mailing lists ● online services, forum. **Programs:** AICC Compliance Logo. **Subcommittees:** Communication; Computer Managed Instruction; Digital Electronic Library Systems; Independent Test Lab; Management and Processes; Training Infrastructure; Training Technology. **Also Known As:** Aviation Industry Computer-Based Training Committee. **Publications:** *AICC Guidelines and Recommendations*. Pamphlets. Includes series of pamphlets explaining usage of association's standards manuals. **Conventions/Meetings:** meeting - 3/year.

143 ■ Aviation Maintenance Foundation International (AMFI)

Address Unknown since 2007

Founded: 1971. **Members:** 4,600. **Membership Dues:** active, $250 (annual) ● IA, $350 (annual) ● student, $130 (annual) ● school, $1,250 (annual) ● FBO, $1,750 (annual) ● corporate, $10,000 (annual). **Staff:** 6. **Budget:** $650,000. **Description:** Trade association consisting of licensed aircraft mechanics, students, and schools as well as companies involved in the aviation maintenance industry. To promote and improve the industry through education and research. Conducts surveys and market studies. Appoints professional aviation maintenance delegates to foreign countries. Sponsors competitions. Conducts seminars; maintains speakers' bureau and placement service; compiles statistics. Operates charitable program; compiles statistics. **Awards: Type:** recognition. **Recipient:** for service to the industry ● **Type:** scholarship. **Recipient:** through the Aviation Maintenance Education Fund. **Publications:** *AMFI Industry News*, bimonthly. Newsletter. Industry and membership newsletter covering aviation maintenance; includes research and survey reports. **Price:** free, for members only. **Circulation:** 6,000 ● *Industry Report*, annual. **Price:** $150.00/copy ● *Job Opportunities Listing*, monthly. Directory. Contains job listings for aircraft mechanics. **Price:** free, for members only ● *Samolyot*, quarterly. Magazine. Russian aviation/aerospace magazine. **Price:** $95.00/year ● Also publishes aviation maintenance educational materials. **Conventions/Meetings:** biennial Aviation Maintenance Symposium, for aviation maintenance executives - always October.

144 ■ Avionics Maintenance Conference (AMC)

c/o Aeronautical Radio, Inc.
2551 Riva Rd.
Annapolis, MD 21401

Ph: (410)266-2008
Free: (800)633-6882
Fax: (410)266-2047
E-mail: samuel.buckwalter@arinc.com
URL: http://www.arinc.com/amc
Contact: Samuel Buckwalter, Contact
Founded: 1949. **Staff:** 3. **Description:** Avionics maintenance professionals from commercial airlines, airframe manufacturers, avionics suppliers, and government organizations. Seeks to improve safety and reliability and reduce the costs of operating and supporting avionics equipment. Contributes to reduce the growth of avionics maintenance costs per flight hour despite growth in avionics capital costs. Conducts projects such as: the establishment of a standard language source document for writing automatic test programs; definition of an economic alternative to costly dedicated automatic test systems provided by manufacturers; development of an industry standard for automated preparation of test software; specification of documentation standards for software-based avionics; coordination of technical training needs for maintenance; and development of voluntary standards for the avionics industry. **Committees:** TG-111 Future Concepts of Maintenance; TG-115 Electronic Library System; TG-103 Test Equipment Guidance. **Publications:** *Conference Program*, annual ● *Conference Report*, annual. Alternate Formats: online ● *Plane Talk*, monthly. Newsletter. **Circulation:** 800. Alternate Formats: online ● Booklet. **Conventions/Meetings:** annual conference (exhibits).

145 ■ Cargo Airline Association (CAA)
1220 19th St. NW, Ste.400
Washington, DC 20036
Ph: (202)293-1030
Fax: (202)293-4377
E-mail: info@cargoair.org
URL: http://www.cargoair.org
Contact: Stephen A. Alterman, Pres.
Founded: 1948. **Members:** 27. **Description:** Represents the interests of all-cargo air carriers. **Telecommunication Services:** electronic mail, salterman@cargoair.org. **Formerly:** (1979) Air Freight Forwarders Association of America; (1998) Air Freight Association of America.

146 ■ Caterpillar Club (CC)
c/o Milkweed Cafe
901 Wilson St.
Pinckneyville, IL 62274-1552
Fax: (253)399-4677
E-mail: cindy@milkweedcafe.com
URL: http://www.milkweedcafe.com/ClubCathome.htm
Contact: Cindy Hepp, Contact
Founded: 1922. **Members:** 28,000. **Description:** Represents airmen and individuals who have successfully used a parachute to save their lives. Bestows caterpillar pin to members; sponsored by Switlik Parachute Company.

147 ■ Council of Defense and Space Industry Associations (CODSIA)
1000 Wilson Blvd., Ste.1800
Arlington, VA 22209
Ph: (703)243-2020
Fax: (703)243-8539
E-mail: info@codsia.org
URL: http://www.codsia.org
Contact: Timothy M. Nunnally-Olsen, Admin. Off.
Founded: 1964. **Members:** 8. **Description:** Comprised of Aerospace Industries Association, Contract Services Association, Electronic Industries Alliance, National Defense Industrial Association, Manufacturer's Alliance/MAPI, American Electronics Association, Professional Services Council, and American Shipbuilding Association. Provides a central channel of communications in order to simplify, expedite, and improve industry-wide consideration of the many policies, regulations, problems, and questions of broad application involved in procurement actions by the Department of Defense, National Aeronautics and Space Administration, the Office of Federal Procurement Policy, the General Services Administration, and other procurement agencies of the federal government. **Committees:** Operating; Policy. **Affiliated With:** AeA - Advancing the Business of Technology; Aerospace Industries Association of America; Contract Services Association of America; Electronic Industries Alliance; Manufacturers Alliance/MAPI; Professional Services Council; Shipbuilders Council of America.

148 ■ Flight Safety Foundation (FSF)
601 Madison St., Ste.300
Alexandria, VA 22314-1756
Ph: (703)739-6700
Fax: (703)739-6708
E-mail: wahdan@flightsafety.org
URL: http://www.flightsafety.org
Contact: William R. Voss, Pres./CEO
Founded: 1947. **Members:** 900. **Membership Dues:** corporate, $3,000-$4,999 (annual) ● subscriber, $5,000-$9,999 (annual) ● contributor (maximum), $14,999 (annual) ● patron (maximum), $24,999 (annual) ● benefactor (minimum), $25,000 (annual). **Staff:** 14. **Budget:** $2,500,000. **Description:** Aerospace manufacturers, domestic and foreign airlines, insurance companies, fuel and oil companies, schools, and miscellaneous organizations having an interest in the promotion of safety in flight. Sponsors safety audits. Compiles statistics. **Libraries: Type:** reference; open to the public. **Holdings:** 1,000; archival material, articles, audiovisuals, books, periodicals, reports. **Subjects:** aviation safety. **Awards:** Admiral Luis de Florez Flight Safety Award. **Frequency:** annual. **Type:** recognition. **Recipient:** to journalists with significant contributions to aviation safety awareness ● Aviation Week and Space Technology Distinguished Service Award. **Frequency:** annual. **Type:** recognition. **Recipient:** to the people and organizations responsible for major advances in aviation safety ● Business Aviation Meritorious Service Award. **Frequency:** annual. **Type:** recognition. **Recipient:** for outstanding service and contributions to corporate aviation safety ● FSF Cecil A. Brownlow Publication Award. **Frequency:** annual. **Type:** recognition. **Recipient:** to journalists with significant contributions to aviation safety awareness ● Heroism Award. **Frequency:** annual. **Type:** recognition. **Recipient:** for heroism outside normal levels of duty and ability ● Honeywell Bendix Trophy for Aviation Safety. **Frequency:** annual. **Type:** trophy. **Recipient:** to individuals or institutions with outstanding contributions to aerospace safety ● Joe Chase Award. **Frequency:** annual. **Type:** recognition. **Recipient:** for outstanding contributions to the aviation maintenance profession ● Laura Taber Barbour Air Safety Award. **Frequency:** annual. **Type:** recognition. **Recipient:** for significant or group effort contributing to improving aviation safety. **Computer Services:** Online services, general organization, membership, and publications information. **Committees:** Corporate Advisory; European Advisory; Icarus; International Advisory. **Publications:** *Airport Operations*, bimonthly. Newsletter. **Price:** $280.00 for nonmembers; included in membership dues. Alternate Formats: online ● *Annual Index*, annual ● *Aviation Mechanics Bulletin*, bimonthly. Magazine. Features specific aspects of maintenance. **Price:** $280.00 for nonmembers; included in membership dues ● *Cabin Crew Safety*, bimonthly. Newsletter. Reports on the safety of the aircraft's crew members. **Price:** $280.00 for nonmembers; included in membership dues ● *Flight Safety Digest*, monthly. Magazine. Tackles subject that is of special importance to the aviation community. **Price:** $520.00 for nonmembers; included in membership dues. Also Cited As: *FSD* ● *Helicopter Safety*, bimonthly. Newsletter. Discusses the unique concerns of rotary-wing aircraft pilots and operations personnel. **Price:** $280.00 for nonmembers; included in membership dues ● *Human Factors and Aviation Medicine*, bimonthly. Newsletter. Contains information important to the training and performance of all aviation professionals. **Price:** $280.00 for nonmembers; included in membership dues ● Report ● Also publishes studies. **Conventions/Meetings:** annual Corporate Aviation Safety Seminar - conference (exhibits) - always spring ● annual International Air Safety Seminar - always fall.

149 ■ General Aviation Manufacturers Association (GAMA)
1400 K St. NW, Ste.801
Washington, DC 20005
Ph: (202)393-1500
Fax: (202)842-4063
E-mail: webmaster@gama.aero
URL: http://www.gama.aero
Contact: Peter J. Bunce, Pres./CEO
Founded: 1970. **Members:** 50. **Staff:** 12. **Description:** Manufacturers of aviation airframes, engines, avionics, and components. Seeks to create a better climate for the growth of general aviation. **Awards:** Dr. Harold S. Wood Award for Excellence. **Frequency:** annual. **Type:** recognition. **Recipient:** to a college student attending a National Intercollegiate Flying Association member college or university program ● Harold Wood Scholarship. **Frequency:** annual. **Type:** scholarship. **Recipient:** for students involved with aviation extra curricular activities, service, contributions to NIFA, and service to school. **Computer Services:** Mailing lists. **Committees:** Communications; Flight Operations Policy; International Affairs; Product Liability and Legal Issues; Safety Affairs; Security Issues; Technical Policy. **Subcommittees:** Accident Investigation; Avionics and Electronic Systems; Government Research Coordinating; Propeller Damage Tolerance. **Working Groups:** Cockpit Standardization. **Publications:** *G.A. Shipment Report*, quarterly. Alternate Formats: online ● *General Aviation Is.* ● *General Aviation Statistical Databook*, annual. Alternate Formats: online ● *Learn to Fly* ● Also distributes printed material on the aviation industry and airport development.

150 ■ Helicopter Association International (HAI)
1635 Prince St.
Alexandria, VA 22314-2818
Ph: (703)683-4646
Free: (800)435-4976
Fax: (703)683-4745
E-mail: questions@rotor.com
URL: http://www.rotor.com
Contact: Matthew S. Zuccaro, Pres.
Founded: 1948. **Members:** 2,750. **Membership Dues:** regular (operator), $300-$2,600 (annual) ● associate A (based on annual revenue), $5,450-$11,850 (annual) ● associate B (based on annual revenue), $275-$2,000 (annual) ● sustaining, pilot, mechanic/technician, $80 (annual) ● student, $35 (annual). **Staff:** 32. **Budget:** $5,000,000. **Multinational. Description:** Owners, operators, helicopter enthusiasts, and affiliated companies in the civil helicopter industry. Receives and disseminates information concerning the use, operation, hiring, contracting, and leasing of helicopters. Maintains a collection of current helicopter service bulletins and technical data; organizes safety seminars, continuing education courses, and helicopter operator management courses; and maintains a maintenance malfunction information database. **Libraries: Type:** reference. **Holdings:** archival material. **Awards:** Aviation Maintenance Technician Safety Award. **Frequency:** annual. **Type:** recognition. **Recipient:** for helicopter maintenance technicians ● Operator Safety Award. **Frequency:** annual. **Type:** recognition. **Recipient:** for regular members, firms and operators of helicopters ● Pilot Safety Award. **Frequency:** annual. **Type:** recognition. **Recipient:** for helicopter pilots ● Salute to Excellence. **Frequency:** annual. **Type:** recognition. **Recipient:** for individuals or organizations with outstanding achievements in the civil helicopter industry. **Computer Services:** database. **Telecommunication Services:** electronic mail, matt.zuccaro@rotor.com. **Committees:** Acoustics/Environmental; Aerial Applications; Air Medical; Economics; Flight Operations; Fly Neighborly; Government Contracting; Government Services; Helicopter Tour Operators; Heliport; Human Resources; Insurance; Legislative; Manufacturers'; Offshore; Regulations; Restricted Category Aircraft; Safety; Technical; Utilities, Patrol and Construction. **Formerly:** (1951) California Helicopter Association; (1981) Helicopter Association of America. **Publications:** *Helicopter Annual*, annual. Membership Directory. Guides civil

helicopter industry. Includes helicopter and avionics specifications, industry statistics, and directories of HAI members. **Price:** free for members; $50.00/issue for nonmembers. ISSN: 0639-5728. **Circulation:** 18,000. **Advertising:** accepted ● *Heliport Directory*, biennial. Lists public and private use heliports in the United States, Puerto Rico, and the Virgin Islands. **Price:** $15.00 for members; $20.00 for nonmembers. Alternate Formats: CD-ROM ● *Heliport/Vertiport Development Guide*, periodic. Directory. Services operators, community planners, and heliport developers. Includes list of heliport consultants. **Price:** $100.00/issue for members; $125.00/issue for nonmembers ● *Maintenance Update*, quarterly. Newsletter. Reports on service difficulty reports, air worthiness directives, and technical bulletins of interest to helicopter operators. **Price:** $25.00 /year for members; $50.00 /year for nonmembers. **Circulation:** 1,400 ● *Operations Update*, monthly. Newsletter. Reports government and industry activities affecting helicopter operators. **Price:** $25.00 /year for members; $50.00 /year for nonmembers. **Circulation:** 1,800 ● *Preliminary Accident Reports and Technical Notes*, quarterly. Newsletter. Covers accident summaries. **Price:** $25.00 for regular members and associates; $50.00 for nonmembers. **Circulation:** 1,800 ● *Rotor: By the Industry - For the Industry*, quarterly. Magazine. Covers developments in the helicopter industry worldwide, emphasizing safety, regulatory, and technical matters. **Price:** $15.00 in U.S.; $25.00 outside U.S. ISSN: 0897-831X. **Circulation:** 17,000. **Advertising:** accepted ● *Rotorgram*, weekly. Newsletter. Alternate Formats: online. **Conventions/Meetings:** annual Heli-Expo - meeting, world's largest event devoted exclusively to the civil helicopter industry (exhibits).

151 ■ Helicopter Foundation International (HFI)

1635 Prince St.
Alexandria, VA 22314-2818
Ph: (703)683-4646
E-mail: webmanager@rotor.com
URL: http://www.hfi.rotor.com
Contact: G.E. Newton Jr., Chm.

Founded: 1983. **Description:** Works to preserve helicopter history. Collects and preserves historical data on the helicopter industry. Maintains comprehensive collection of scale model helicopters and files. **Libraries: Type:** by appointment only. **Holdings:** photographs. **Subjects:** scale models of helicopters. **Awards:** HFI Heritage Hall of Fame. **Frequency:** annual. **Type:** recognition. **Recipient:** for lifetime achievement in helicopter industry. **Committees:** Founders. **Affiliated With:** Helicopter Association International. **Formerly:** (1984) International Helicopter Foundation.

152 ■ Helicopter Safety Advisory Conference (HSAC)

c/o Joseph Gross, Treas.
BHP Billiton Petroleum, Inc.
1360 Post Oak Blvd., Ste.150
Houston, TX 77056-3020
Ph: (713)499-5452
Fax: (713)985-8224
E-mail: joe.gross@bhpbilliton.com
URL: http://www.hsac.org
Contact: Casey Lowery, Chm.

Founded: 1978. **Members:** 120. **Membership Dues:** regular, associate, $1,000 (annual). **Description:** Helicopter operators who transport workers to and from offshore oil drilling sites and supply the rigs; manufacturers and others involved in the process. Promotes safety and seeks to improve operations through establishment of standards of practice. Aims to develop a common radio frequency. Standardizes traffic flow procedures. Establishes in-flight rules developed in cooperation with the Federal Aviation Administration. Seeks to coordinate efforts with the military regarding offshore military maneuvers. Conducts educational programs; compiles operational and safety statistics. **Awards: Type:** recognition. **Committees:** FAA/HSAC Federal Aviation Administration Interface; Government Liaison; Heliport and Airways; Industry Liaison; Military Liaison; Standardization and Safety; Technical Advisory Liaison. **Working Groups:** Federal Aviation Administration Interface; Gulf of Mexico; Heliport Design; Industry Liaison; Military Liaison; Organization; Passenger Briefing Film; Standardization; Traffic Control/Base Operating Agreements. **Publications:** *Area Agreements Booklet* ● *Offshore Design Guide/Heliports*, semiannual ● *Sensitive Area Handbook*. Alerts pilots on environmental issues. **Conventions/Meetings:** conference - 3/year.

153 ■ International Association of Air Travel Couriers (IAATC)

PO Box 1832
Ames, IA 50010
Ph: (515)292-2458
E-mail: info_request@iaatc.com
URL: http://www.courier.org
Contact: Kathy Craig, Pres.

Founded: 1989. **Members:** 9,876. **Membership Dues:** individual in U.S., $45 (annual) ● individual outside U.S., $50 (annual). **Staff:** 7. **For-Profit. Description:** Serves as a clearinghouse for the air courier industry from the consumer stand point. Tracks every known courier route in the world and publishes their flight schedules. Updates listings twice-daily; accessible by fax or computer. Publishes newsletters and publications on bargain travel. **Libraries: Type:** reference. **Holdings:** 1,500; articles, books, maps. **Subjects:** travel. **Computer Services:** Online services. **Publications:** *The Shoestring Traveler*, bimonthly. Reports. Features trip reports. **Price:** $48.00/year. ISSN: 1082-5304. **Circulation:** 24,000. **Advertising:** accepted ● *Travel Guide*, monthly. Magazine. Includes discount flight information, guide to internet travel, and schedules of air couriers. **Price:** $48.00/year. ISSN: 1082-3859. **Circulation:** 25,000. **Advertising:** accepted. Alternate Formats: online.

154 ■ International Coordinating Council of Aerospace Industries Associations (ICCAIA)

1000 Wilson Blvd., Ste.1700
Arlington, VA 22209-3901
Ph: (703)358-1000
Fax: (703)358-1011
E-mail: info@iccaia.org
URL: http://www.aia-aerospace.org/iccaiatest/commi.htm
Contact: Mr. Remy Nathan, Sec.

Founded: 1972. **Members:** 5. **Description:** Aerospace Industries Association of America, Aerospace Industries Association of Canada, Association Europeenne des Constructeurs de Material Aerospatial, and Society of Japanese Aerospace Companies, Aerospace Industries Association of Brazil. Works as the official observer organization for the manufacturing of the industry to the International Civil Aviation Organization. Works for the development and advancement of the industry. **Publications:** none. **Committees:** Aircraft Noise and Engine Emissions; Airworthiness; Communication, Navigation, and Surveillance/Air Traffic Management. **Conventions/Meetings:** annual meeting.

155 ■ International Council of Aircraft Owner and Pilot Associations (IAOPA)

421 Aviation Way
Frederick, MD 21701
Ph: (301)695-2220
Fax: (301)695-2375
E-mail: iaopa@aopa.org
URL: http://www.iaopa.org
Contact: Phil Boyer, Pres.

Founded: 1962. **Members:** 56. **National Groups:** 51. **Multinational. Description:** Pilots represented by member groups who fly general aviation airplanes for business and recreational purposes. Facilitates the movement of general aviation aircraft for peaceful purposes; develops airports, air routes, communications, navigation facilities, and services designed and operated to fill the needs of general aviation. Works to eliminate barriers that impede the utilization of general aviation aircraft for international flights. **Publications:** *IAOPA Bulletin*, quarterly. Newsletter. **Price:** free. Alternate Formats: online. **Conventions/Meetings:** assembly ● biennial conference and general assembly.

156 ■ International Society of Transport Aircraft Trading (ISTAT)

401 N Michigan Ave.
Chicago, IL 60611
Ph: (312)321-5169
Fax: (312)673-6579
E-mail: istat@istat.org
URL: http://www.istat.org
Contact: Michael Platt, Pres.

Founded: 1983. **Members:** 1,500. **Membership Dues:** individual, $400 (annual) ● corporate (includes 6 members; add $200 for each additional member), $1,750 (annual). **Staff:** 5. **Budget:** $2,000,000. **Multinational. Description:** Professionals engaged in the purchase, sale, financing, manufacturing, appraising, and leasing of commercial aircraft. Seeks to facilitate communication among those involved in aviation and supporting industries related to the exchange of transport category aircraft. **Awards:** The ISTAT Award. **Frequency:** annual. **Type:** recognition. **Recipient:** for entrepreneurial excellence in aviation and air finance. **Publications:** *JeTrader*, quarterly. Newsletter. Reports on issues of importance to the members, membership, industry, conferences, exhibitions and worldwide activity in the marketplace. **Circulation:** 1,200. **Advertising:** accepted. Alternate Formats: online ● Membership Directory, annual. Lists members alphabetically and by category. **Conventions/Meetings:** annual conference, focus on aviation-related topics on an international scope (exhibits).

157 ■ International Society of Women Airline Pilots (ISWAP)

2250 E Tropicana Ave., Ste.19-395
Las Vegas, NV 89119-6573
Ph: (772)228-6719
E-mail: updownarch@aol.com
URL: http://www.iswap.org
Contact: Kelly Woods, Sec.

Founded: 1978. **Members:** 420. **Membership Dues:** full, $55 (annual). **Staff:** 9. **Multinational. Description:** Women airline pilots employed as flight crewmembers or holding seniority numbers with a major air carrier that operates at least 1 aircraft with a gross weight of 90,000 pounds or more. Fosters international cooperation and exchange among women in the profession. Operates information bank for women interested in entering the field. Maintains speakers' bureau and biographical archives. Recognizes members attaining the rank of captain. **Libraries: Type:** not open to the public. **Holdings:** books, video recordings. **Formerly:** (1984) International Social Affiliation of Women Airline Pilots. **Publications:** *International Society of Women Airline Pilots Membership Roster*, annual. Membership Directory. **Price:** available to members only. ISSN: 1536-3066. **Circulation:** 450. Alternate Formats: online ● *International Society of Women Airline Pilots Newsletter*, quarterly. **Price:** available to members only. **Circulation:** 450. Alternate Formats: online. **Conventions/Meetings:** annual meeting - always second week of May.

158 ■ National Aeronautic Association (NAA)

1737 King St., Ste.220
Alexandria, VA 22314
Ph: (703)527-0226
Free: (800)644-9777
Fax: (703)527-0229
E-mail: naa@naa.aero
URL: http://www.naa.aero
Contact: Jonathan Gaffney, Pres.

Founded: 1905. **Members:** 3,000. **Membership Dues:** individual, $39-$250 (annual) ● life, $1,000. **Staff:** 7. **Budget:** $1,000,000. **Local Groups:** 1. **Description:** Persons interested in the progress and development of American general and military aviation. Supervises sporting aviation competitions and official world records in aeronautics and astronautics, model flying, gliding, soaring, parachuting, hang gliding, ballooning, and helicopters. **Awards:** Elder Statesman of Aviation Award. **Frequency:** annual. **Type:** recognition. **Recipient:** for lifetime contribution

● Frank G. Brewer Trophy. **Frequency:** annual. **Type:** trophy. **Recipient:** for significant contribution ● Katharine Wright Award. **Frequency:** annual. **Type:** recognition. **Recipient:** for a woman who has contributed to the success of others, or made a personal contribution to the advancement of the art, sport and science of aviation and space flight ● MacKay Trophies. **Frequency:** annual. **Type:** trophy. **Recipient:** for the most meritorious flight of the year ● Robert J. Collier Trophy. **Frequency:** annual. **Type:** trophy. **Recipient:** for greatest achievement of the previous year ● Wright Brothers Memorial Trophy. **Frequency:** annual. **Type:** trophy. **Recipient:** for lifetime civilian service. **Divisions:** Academy of Model Aeronautics; Balloon Federation of America; Helicopter Club of America; International Aerobatics Club; Soaring Society of America; United States Hang Gliding Association; United States Parachute Association; United States Ultralight Association (see separate entries). **Absorbed:** (1922) Aero Club of America. **Formerly:** (2004) National Aeronautic Association of the U.S.A. **Publications:** *NAA Aero Magazine*, bimonthly. **Price:** included in membership dues. **Advertising:** accepted ● *National Aeronautics Newsletter*, bimonthly. Presents general news on aerospace developments, general and sport aviation, and world records and competition. **Price:** included in membership dues. **Circulation:** 6,300. **Advertising:** accepted ● *World and United States Aviation and Space Records*, annual. Book. Contains compilation of all U.S. and world records. **Price:** included in membership dues; $24.95 for nonmembers. **Conventions/Meetings:** luncheon, with guest speaker - 10/year.

159 ■ National Air Carrier Association (NACA)

1000 Wilson Blvd., Ste.1700
Arlington, VA 22209
Ph: (703)358-8060
E-mail: rpriddy@naca.cc
URL: http://www.naca.cc
Contact: Ronald N. Priddy, Pres.

Founded: 1962. **Members:** 14. **Membership Dues:** full (with earnings greater than $150 million), $2,400 (monthly) ● full (with earnings less than $150 million), $1,800 (monthly). **Staff:** 4. **Budget:** $500,000. **Description:** Represents U.S. certificated airlines specializing in low-cost scheduled and air charter operations. Assists members in the promotion of air transportation and serves as a liaison between members and U.S. government bodies that regulate air transportation. **Councils:** Maintenance; Operations; Safety and Security.

160 ■ National Air Transportation Association (NATA)

4226 King St.
Alexandria, VA 22302
Ph: (703)845-9000
Free: (800)808-6282
Fax: (703)845-8176
E-mail: enews@nata.aero
URL: http://www.nata.aero
Contact: James K. Coyne, Pres.

Founded: 1940. **Members:** 1,945. **Membership Dues:** associate, $750 (annual) ● affiliate, $250 (annual) ● Airline Services Council (based on number of employees), $2,500-$5,000 (annual) ● regular (maximum; based on number of employees), $8,400 (annual). **Staff:** 19. **Description:** Represents the interests of aviation businesses nationwide. Provides vital aviation services to the airlines, the military, and business/corporate/individual aircraft owners and operators; services includes fueling, maintenance, and flight instruction. **Libraries: Type:** reference. **Holdings:** archival material. **Subjects:** aviation. **Awards: Type:** recognition. **Committees:** Air Charter; Aircraft Maintenance and System; Airports; Business Management; Flight Training; Safety and Security; Update. **Councils:** Airline Services. **Formed by Merger of:** National Aviation Trades Association; National Air Transportation Conferences. **Publications:** *Fact Finder*, periodic ● *General Aviation Operations*, quarterly ● *Industry Barometer*, annual ● *NATAnews*, monthly. Newsletter. Alternate Formats: online ● *Wage and Salary Handbook*, annual ● Annual Report, annual ● Membership Directory, annual. **Conventions/Meetings:** annual convention ● annual FBO Leadership - conference (exhibits).

161 ■ National Association of Flight Instructors (NAFI)

EAA Aviation Ctr.
PO Box 3086
Oshkosh, WI 54903-3086
Ph: (920)426-6801
Fax: (920)426-6865
E-mail: nafi@eaa.org
URL: http://www.nafinet.org
Contact: Rusty Sachs, Exec. Dir.

Founded: 1967. **Members:** 5,100. **Membership Dues:** regular, $39 (annual). **Staff:** 2. **Description:** Flight instructors certified by the Federal Aviation Administration. Works to raise the professional standards of the flight instructor through education and organization. Serves as a central point for dissemination of knowledge, methodology, and new information relative to flight instruction. Supports improved legislation concerning pilot training, certification, and aviation regulations. Works with all segments of the industry for improvement of flight education, efficiency, and safety. Compiles statistics. **Awards:** Flight Instructor Hall of Fame. **Frequency:** annual. **Type:** recognition. **Recipient:** for flight instructors. **Publications:** *Flying*. Magazine ● *NAFI Mentor*, monthly. Magazine. **Price:** included in membership dues. **Advertising:** accepted. Alternate Formats: online.

162 ■ National Business Aviation Association (NBAA)

1200 18th St. NW, Ste.400
Washington, DC 20036-2527
Ph: (202)783-9000 (202)783-9450
Fax: (202)331-8364
E-mail: info@nbaa.org
URL: http://www.nbaa.org
Contact: Edward M. Bolen, Pres./CEO

Founded: 1947. **Members:** 3,200. **Membership Dues:** corporate (single or multi-engine), $175-$400 (annual) ● corporate (turboprop and helicopter), $275-$1,000 (annual) ● corporate (jet), $375-$2,000 (annual) ● associate, $350-$1,500 (annual) ● affiliate, $400-$2,000 (annual). **Staff:** 31. **Description:** Companies owning and operating aircraft for business use, suppliers, and maintenance and air fleet service companies. Compiles statistics; provides literature for researchers and students. **Libraries: Type:** reference. **Holdings:** articles, books, reports, video recordings. **Subjects:** business aircraft operations. **Awards:** American Spirit Award. **Type:** recognition. **Recipient:** for an individual who has exemplified courage and service to others ● Flying Safety Award. **Frequency:** annual. **Type:** recognition. **Recipient:** for business aircraft operations ● Gold Wing Award. **Frequency:** annual. **Type:** recognition. **Recipient:** for excellent, accurate, and insightful reports ● Platinum Wing Award. **Frequency:** annual. **Type:** recognition. **Recipient:** for lifetime achievement and excellence in journalism. **Committees:** Air Space/Air Traffic Control; Airports/Heliports; Corporate Aviation Management; Flight Attendants; International Operators; Operations; Tax; Technical. **Affiliated With:** International Business Aviation Council. **Formerly:** (1949) Corp. Aircraft Owners Association; (1998) National Business Aircraft Association. **Publications:** *Business Aviation Fact Book*, annual. **Price:** free ● *Maintenance and Operations Bulletin*, semiannual. **Price:** free ● *Management Guide*. Manual ● *National Business Aircraft Association—Membership Directory*, periodic. **Price:** available to members only ● *NBAA Update*, weekly. Newsletter. Alternate Formats: online ● Reports. **Conventions/Meetings:** annual meeting ● seminar - 6-12/year ● workshop.

163 ■ Ninety-Nines, International Organization of Women Pilots

4300 Amelia Earhart Rd.
Oklahoma City, OK 73159
Ph: (405)685-7969
Free: (800)994-1929
Fax: (405)685-7985
E-mail: 99s@ninety-nines.org
URL: http://www.ninety-nines.org
Contact: Pat Prentiss, Pres.

Founded: 1929. **Members:** 6,100. **Membership Dues:** regular in U.S., $75 (annual) ● regular in Canada, $67 (annual) ● overseas, $54 (annual) ● academic pilot, future woman pilot, $30 (annual) ● student, $20 (annual). **Staff:** 3. **Budget:** $400,000. **Regional Groups:** 21. **State Groups:** 197. **Local Groups:** 197. **Multinational. Description:** Represents women pilots. Fosters a better understanding of aviation. Encourages cross-country flying; provides consulting service and gives indoctrination flights; flies missions for charitable assistance programs; endorses air races. Develops programs and courses for schools and youth organizations and teaches ground school subjects. Participates in flying competitions. Maintains resource center and women's aviation museum. Conducts lecture on personal aviation experience, and charitable event. Compiles statistics. **Libraries: Type:** reference. **Holdings:** 700; archival material. **Subjects:** women's achievements in aviation. **Awards:** Amelia Earhart Memorial Scholarship for Women Pilots. **Frequency:** annual. **Type:** scholarship. **Recipient:** for members taking advanced flight training or courses in specialized branches of aviation ● Future Woman Pilot Awards. **Frequency:** annual. **Type:** recognition. **Recipient:** for woman pilot members ● Maule Tailwheel Training Award. **Frequency:** annual. **Type:** recognition. **Recipient:** for members in tailwheel training ● Research Scholar Grants. **Frequency:** periodic. **Type:** grant. **Recipient:** to specialized, professional scholar members. **Computer Services:** Information services, women interested in aviation careers ● mailing lists, membership. **Committees:** Aerospace Archives Librarian; Airmarking; Audio Visual Education; Flying Activities; Historian; NIFA Award; Public Relations; Safety Education; Scrapbook. **Also Known As:** International Organization of Women Pilots. **Formerly:** (1998) Ninety-Nines International Women Pilots. **Publications:** *History of the Ninety-Nines*. Book ● *International Women Pilots*, bimonthly. Magazine. **Price:** included in membership dues; $20.00 /year for nonmembers. **Circulation:** 7,000. **Advertising:** accepted ● *Ninety-Nines, International Women Pilots—Membership Directory*, annual. **Price:** free. **Circulation:** 7,000 ● Brochures. **Conventions/Meetings:** annual conference - 2008 Aug. 7-10, Anchorage, AK ● annual meeting and convention (exhibits) - always in July ● seminar, on safety education.

164 ■ Organization of Black Airline Pilots (OBAP)

8630 Fenton St., Ste.126
Silver Spring, MD 20910
Ph: (703)753-2047
Free: (800)JET-OBAP
E-mail: nationaloffice@obap.org
URL: http://www.obap.org
Contact: Karl Minter, Pres.

Founded: 1976. **Members:** 900. **Membership Dues:** associate, probationary pilot, $100 (annual) ● corporate, institutional, $1,000 (annual) ● student, $25 (annual) ● captain (major national airline/corporate), $500 (annual) ● first officer (major/national airline/corporation), captain (regional airline), $250 (annual) ● second officer, first officer (regional airline), $150 (annual). **Regional Groups:** 5. **Description:** Cockpit crew members of commercial air carriers, corporate pilots, and other interested individuals. Seeks to enhance minority participation in the aerospace industry. Maintains liaison with airline presidents and minority and pilot associations. Conducts lobbying efforts, including congressional examinations into airline recruitment practices. Provides scholarships; cosponsors Summer Flight Academy for Youth. Offers job placement service and charitable program; operates speakers' bureau; compiles statistics on airline hiring practices. **Awards:** Scholarship/Professional Pilot Development Program. **Frequency:** annual. **Type:** scholarship. **Recipient:** for experience, interest, need and potential. **Computer Services:** database, job placement bank ● mailing lists. **Committees:** Aviation Medicine. **Publi-**

cations: *PIREP*, monthly. Newsletter. **Price:** included in membership dues. **Advertising:** accepted. Alternate Formats: online. **Conventions/Meetings:** semiannual conference (exhibits) - always April and August.

165 ■ Professional Aviation Maintenance Association (PAMA)
400 Commonwealth Dr.
Warrendale, PA 15096
Ph: (724)772-4092
Free: (866)865-7262
Fax: (724)772-4064
E-mail: hq@pama.org
URL: http://www.pama.org
Contact: Mr. Brian Finnegan, Pres.
Founded: 1972. **Members:** 4,300. **Membership Dues:** regular, associate, $49 (annual) ● company, $650 (annual) ● student, $10 (annual). **Staff:** 4. **Regional Groups:** 35. **Description:** Airframe and powerplant (A&P) technicians and aviation industry-related companies. Strives to increase the professionalism of the individual aviation technician through greater technical knowledge and better understanding of safety requirements. Establishes communication among technicians throughout the country. Fosters and improves methods, skills, learning, and achievement in the aviation maintenance field. **Awards:** Aviation Technician of the Year Award. **Frequency:** annual. **Type:** recognition. **Recipient:** for technicians ● Joe Chase Award. **Type:** recognition. **Recipient:** to an individual who has shown outstanding personal achievement in improving the knowledge, safety, and dignity of the Aircraft Technician ● PAMA/ATP Award. **Type:** recognition. **Recipient:** to a regular PAMA member who is employed as an aircraft technician ● Student Scholarship. **Frequency:** annual. **Type:** scholarship. **Recipient:** for Airframe, Powerplant, and Avionics students. **Publications:** *Membership Directory and Information Guide*, annual. **Price:** included in membership dues. **Advertising:** accepted ● *Your Career in Aviation Maintenance*. Booklet ● Also publishes technical reports and press releases. **Conventions/Meetings:** annual Aviation Maintenance - symposium and trade show (exhibits).

166 ■ Regional Airline Association (RAA)
2025 M St. NW, Ste.800
Washington, DC 20036-3309
Ph: (202)367-1170
Fax: (202)367-2170
E-mail: raa@raa.org
URL: http://www.raa.org
Contact: Roger Cohen, Pres.
Founded: 1975. **Members:** 402. **Membership Dues:** associate, $650 (annual). **Staff:** 5. **Description:** Regional air carriers engaged in the transportation of passengers, cargo, or mail on a scheduled basis; persons, companies, and organizations engaged in pursuits related to commercial aviation; colleges and universities, state and local governments, and state aviation associations. Responds to community, consumer, and public needs for air transportation and aviation facilities and to help establish a healthy business, regulatory, and legislative climate that enables members to profit through service to the nation and the flying public. Supports programs for improving safety and reliability of air transportation and air commerce; provides a forum for exchange of ideas and information. **Formerly:** (1975) Commuter Airline Association of America; (1981) Commuter Airline Association. **Publications:** *Annual Report of the Regional Airline Association*, annual. Contains statistical report and directory. **Price:** $75.00/copy. **Circulation:** 2,700. **Advertising:** accepted. Alternate Formats: CD-ROM ● *Regional Horizons*, bimonthly. Newsletter. Alternate Formats: online. **Conventions/Meetings:** annual convention and meeting, for training and education (exhibits).

167 ■ Seaplane Pilots Association (SPA)
3859 Laird Blvd.
Lakeland, FL 33811
Ph: (863)701-7979
Free: (888)SPA-8923
Fax: (863)701-7588
E-mail: spa@seaplanes.org
URL: http://www.seaplanes.org
Contact: Dr. James McManus, Exec. Dir.
Founded: 1972. **Members:** 7,200. **Membership Dues:** individual, $45 (annual) ● overseas, $55 (annual). **Staff:** 3. **Budget:** $500,000. **Description:** Seaplane pilots and other individuals interested in water flying. Aims to promote water flying among both aviation and non-aviation groups and to protect the rights of seaplane operators with regard to national, state, and local access to lakes, rivers, and waterways worldwide. Disseminates information to seaplane pilots and non-pilot members; locates training facilities for members and water flying enthusiasts; organizes annual national and regional safety seminars and fly-in activities. Lobbies on behalf of water flying operators. Compiles statistics; conducts educational programs. **Libraries: Type:** reference. **Holdings:** audiovisuals, books, business records, periodicals. **Subjects:** water flying. **Awards:** Pilot of the Year Award. **Frequency:** annual. **Type:** recognition. **Computer Services:** database, members. **Committees:** Awards. **Formerly:** (1980) U.S. Seaplane Pilots Association. **Publications:** *Water Flying*, bimonthly. Magazine. Covers seaplane regulatory, operational, safety, and industry news; includes regional report. **Price:** included in membership dues; $17.50 /year for nonmembers. ISSN: 0733-1754. **Circulation:** 8,500. **Advertising:** accepted ● *Water Flying Annual*, annual. Magazine. Covers aircraft reports, tips, and techniques to improve flying. Includes travel features and directories of dealers of equipment and floats. **Price:** free for members; $10.00/issue for nonmembers. ISSN: 0733-1754. **Circulation:** 7,000. **Advertising:** accepted ● *Water Landing Directory*, biennial. Includes state listings of regulations and landing areas for seaplanes, with descriptions of facilities and services available at landing areas. **Price:** $19.00 for members; $38.00 for nonmembers. ISSN: 0894-5667. **Circulation:** 2,500. **Advertising:** accepted.

168 ■ United States Pilots Association (USPA)
483 S Kirkwood Rd., No. 10
St. Louis, MO 63122
Ph: (314)849-8772
Fax: (309)215-6323
E-mail: jan@hoynacki.com
URL: http://www.uspilots.org
Contact: Jan Hoynacki, Exec. Dir.
Founded: 1981. **Members:** 5,000. **Membership Dues:** individual/associate, $35 (annual). **Staff:** 1. **State Groups:** 10. **Local Groups:** 50. **Description:** Aircraft pilots and individuals interested in aviation. Works to: promote aviation safety and pilot education; improve and strengthen the aviation industry at both the state and local levels; facilitate communication among members; coordinate activities of state and local aviation associations. **Committees:** Air Tours; Airport Development; Awards; Disaster Relief; Education; Legislation; Meetings; Public Relations; Rules and Regulation; Safety. **Publications:** *America's Flyways*, monthly. Magazine. **Price:** included in membership dues. **Circulation:** 6,600. **Advertising:** accepted ● *USPA Directory*, annual. **Price:** available to members only. **Conventions/Meetings:** quarterly board meeting.

Africa

169 ■ Corporate Council on Africa (CCA)
1100 17th St. NW, Ste.1100
Washington, DC 20036
Ph: (202)835-1115
Fax: (202)835-1117
E-mail: cca@africacncl.org
URL: http://www.africacncl.org
Contact: Stephen Hayes, Pres.
Founded: 1993. **Membership Dues:** small business ($6 million gross revenue per year or less), $3,000 (annual) ● medium business ($6-$500 million gross revenue per year), $5,000 (annual) ● large business (above $500 million gross revenue per year), $10,000 (annual). **Multinational. Description:** Strengthens and facilitates the commercial relationship between the United States and the African continent. Raises the profile of Africa in the US business community. Works closely with governments, multilateral groups and businesses to improve the African continent's trade and investment climate. Provides members with business networks, trade and investment opportunities, and the promotion of commercial operations in Africa. **Publications:** *The Africa Journal*, quarterly. Provides a synopsis of important trade policy and political developments in Africa. **Price:** included in membership dues. **Circulation:** 3,500. Alternate Formats: online ● Brochure. Alternate Formats: online.

African-American

170 ■ National Black Business Council (NBBC)
600 Corporate Pointe, Ste.1010
Culver City, CA 90230
Ph: (310)568-5000
Free: (888)264-6222
E-mail: nbbc.admin@nbbc.org
URL: http://www.nbbc.org
Contact: Rosalind Pennington, Pres./CEO
Description: Aims to create and advance black businesses; advocates for expansion of black business procurement.

Agents

171 ■ Association of Authors' Representatives (AAR)
676A 9th Ave., No. 312
New York, NY 10036
Ph: (212)252-3695 (212)840-5777
E-mail: info@aar-online.org
URL: http://www.aar-online.org
Contact: Joanne Brownstein, Admin. Sec.
Founded: 1991. **Members:** 360. **Membership Dues:** full, $150 (annual). **Description:** Literary and dramatic agents who market books, plays, and other literary and dramatic material. **Formed by Merger of:** Society of Authors' Representatives; Independent Literary Agents Association. **Publications:** *Canon of Ethics*. Alternate Formats: online ● Brochure. **Price:** $7.00 plus postage ● Brochure ● Membership Directory ● Also publishes brochure.

172 ■ Association of Talent Agents (ATA)
9255 Sunset Blvd., Ste.930
Los Angeles, CA 90069
Ph: (310)274-0628
Fax: (310)274-5063
E-mail: shellie@agentassociation.com
URL: http://www.agentassociation.com
Contact: Karen Stuart, Exec. Dir.
Founded: 1937. **Members:** 120. **Membership Dues:** new (initial), $1,000. **Staff:** 2. **Description:** Talent agencies that have clients in the Screen Actors Guild, American Federation of Television and Radio Artists, Directors Guild of America, Writers Guild of America, East, and Writers Guild of America, West (see separate entries). Negotiates terms of franchise agreements with these guilds and maintains liaison with their representatives. Assists members with contract problems, interpretations, rulings, residual matters, and arbitrations. Employs legal counsel to prepare opinions upon request and to file briefs in arbitrations and labor commission hearings. Maintains liaison with labor commission representatives in San Francisco and Los Angeles, CA, and intervenes on behalf of individual members having special problems. Conducts seminars and symposia. **Libraries: Type:** reference. **Holdings:** books, monographs, periodicals. **Subjects:** law, arbitration, minority rights, legislative history. **Awards:** Distinguished Agent. **Frequency:** periodic. **Type:** recognition. **Computer Services:** database, SAG residual information; available to members only. **Formerly:** Artists Managers Guild. **Publications:** Bulletin. **Conventions/Meetings:** annual meeting.

173 ■ Coalition of Exclusive Agent Associations (CEAA)
c/o Donald P. Cassell, Pres.
791 Aquahart Rd., Ste.101
Glen Burnie, MD 21061
Ph: (410)768-5040
Fax: (410)768-5041
E-mail: d.cassell@verizon.net
Contact: Donald P. Cassell, Pres.
Description: Represents and promotes professional exclusive agents. **Publications:** *The Agents' Voice*, quarterly. Newsletter. **Advertising:** accepted ● *The Mirror*, bimonthly. Newsletter ● *The NAAFA News*, biweekly. Newsletter. Contains supplements of The Agents' Voice. Alternate Formats: online ● *The NIICA News*. Newsletter. **Advertising:** accepted ● *The Voice*, quarterly. Newsletter. **Advertising:** accepted.

174 ■ National Conference of Personal Managers (NCOPM)
PO Box 50008
Henderson, NV 89016-0008
Ph: (702)837-1170 (610)366-1700
Fax: (702)255-2256
E-mail: askncopm@ncopm.com
URL: http://www.ncopm.com
Contact: Mr. Clinton Ford Billups Jr., Natl. Pres.
Founded: 1967. **Members:** 275. **Membership Dues:** individual, $180 (annual). **Staff:** 11. **Local Groups:** 2. **Description:** Represents personal managers for artists in the entertainment industry. **Telecommunication Services:** electronic mail, ncopmse@earthlink.net. **Formed by Merger of:** Conference of Personal Managers, West; Conference of Personal Managers, East. **Publications:** *NCOPM Newsletter*, quarterly. **Conventions/Meetings:** periodic Division Meetings.

175 ■ North American Performing Arts Managers and Agents (NAPAMA)
459 Columbus Ave., No. 133
New York, NY 10024
Free: (888)745-8759
E-mail: info@napama.org
URL: http://www.napama.org
Contact: Laura Colby, Pres.
Founded: 1976. **Members:** 115. **Membership Dues:** organizational, $300-$450 (annual) ● business associate, $300 (annual) ● individual/self-managed artist/member artist or staff/emeritus, $150 (annual) ● student, $50 (annual). **Description:** Managers of performing artists; public relations specialists; publishers; related businesses. Works to strengthen the community of artists' managers; encourages excellence in the profession. Acts as a source of influence in the industry and as a forum for the exchange of information. Provides experts in arts management to other professional organizations for speaking engagements and workshops. Participates in panels for professionals. **Libraries: Type:** reference. **Holdings:** archival material. **Awards:** NAPAMA Award for Excellence in Presenting the Performing Arts. **Frequency:** annual. **Type:** monetary. **Recipient:** for distinguished colleague presenter. **Formerly:** (2003) National Association Performing Arts Managers and Agent. **Publications:** *NAPAMA News*, quarterly. Newsletter. **Price:** $25.00 for nonmembers; included in membership dues. **Advertising:** accepted. **Conventions/Meetings:** annual conference - always December, in New York City ● symposium - 2-3/year.

176 ■ Sporting Goods Agents Association (SGAA)
PO Box 998
Morton Grove, IL 60053
Ph: (847)296-3670
Fax: (847)827-0196
E-mail: sgaa998@aol.com
URL: http://www.sgaaonline.org
Contact: Don Leonard, Pres.
Founded: 1934. **Members:** 1,000. **Membership Dues:** principal, $200 (annual) ● associate, additional partner, $50 (annual). **Staff:** 2. **Budget:** $400,000. **National Groups:** 180. **Multinational. Description:** Represents manufacturers' agents whose goal is to provide free legal counsel for members and additional product lines from manufacturers, and to improve the image of the independent agent. Offers placement service. **Awards:** Appreciation Award. **Frequency:** annual. **Type:** recognition. **Recipient:** to outstanding manufacturers ● Lifetime Sales Career Award. **Frequency:** annual. **Type:** recognition. **Recipient:** to members. **Formerly:** (1977) Sporting Goods Representatives Association. **Publications:** *Q & A for agent and manufacturer*. Brochure. **Price:** $15.00 for agents ● *SGAA Membership Roster*. Directory. Lists member agents, territories covered, and product lines by categories. **Price:** $200.00. Alternate Formats: diskette ● Newsletter, monthly ● Yearbook, annual. **Conventions/Meetings:** annual meeting (exhibits) ● seminar, for training.

Agricultural Equipment

177 ■ Association of Equipment Manufacturers (AEM)
6737 W Washington St., Ste.2400
Milwaukee, WI 53214
Ph: (414)272-0943
Free: (866)AEM-0442
Fax: (414)272-1170
E-mail: aem@aem.org
URL: http://www.aem.org
Contact: Dennis E. Eagan, Chm.
Founded: 1894. **Members:** 700. **Staff:** 49. **Budget:** $9,000,000. **Multinational. Description:** Provides business development services on a global basis for companies that manufacture equipment, products and services used worldwide in the agricultural, construction, industrial, mining, forestry, and utility fields. **Councils:** Ag Equipment; Attachment Manufacturers; Compact Loader/Compact Excavator; Earthmoving and Mining Equipment; Farm Equipment; Farmstead Equipment Association; Forestry Equipment; Industrial/Agricultural Mower Manufacturers. **Formed by Merger of:** (2002) Construction Industry Manufacturers Association; (2002) Equipment Manufacturers Institute. **Publications:** *AEM Advisor*, periodic. Newsletter. **Price:** free for members ● Booklets. **Conventions/Meetings:** annual conference ● triennial trade show (exhibits) ● annual World of Asphalt - convention and trade show (exhibits).

178 ■ Equipment Manufacturers Council (EMC)
c/o American Feed Industry Association
1501 Wilson Blvd., Ste.1100
Arlington, VA 22209
Ph: (703)524-0810
Fax: (703)524-1921
E-mail: afia@afia.org
URL: http://www.afia.org/Committees_and_Councils.html
Contact: Keith Kepperson, Contact
Founded: 1987. **Members:** 175. **Description:** A council of the American Feed Industry Association. Serves as a trade association for feed and grain equipment manufacturers. **Telecommunication Services:** electronic mail, kepperson@afia.org. **Publications:** *Educator*, semiannual. Newsletter ● *Feed Gram*, biweekly. Newsletter. **Price:** free with membership. **Circulation:** 2,200. **Conventions/Meetings:** annual conference ● biennial show.

179 ■ Farm Equipment Manufacturers Association (FEMA)
1000 Executive Pkwy., Ste.100
St. Louis, MO 63141-6369
Ph: (314)878-2304
Fax: (314)878-1742
E-mail: info@farmequip.org
URL: http://www.farmequip.org
Contact: Richard W. Heiniger, Pres.
Founded: 1950. **Members:** 700. **Membership Dues:** regular, in North America, $235-$920 (annual) ● foreign in North America, $600 (annual) ● supplier associate, marketing associate, $350 (annual). **Staff:** 6. **Budget:** $500,000. **For-Profit. Description:** Manufacturers of "shortlines" (specialized farm equipment). **Awards:** Harold Halter Scholarship. **Frequency:** annual. **Type:** monetary. **Recipient:** for high school students. **Councils:** Auger Product; Hay Handling Product; Post Hole Digger Product; Rotary Cutter Manufacturers; Tillage and Ground Engaging Equipment Product; Wagon Product. **Formerly:** (1956) Allied Farm Equipment Manufacturers Association. **Publications:** *Faxliner*, weekly. Newsletter. **Circulation:** 1,000 ● *Informa Economics Daily Policy Report*. Alternate Formats: online ● *Membership/Product Directory*, monthly. Membership Directory. Alternate Formats: online ● *Shortliner*, semimonthly. Newsletter. Covers the shortline industry. Includes crop reports, legislative updates, job listings, agricultural show listings, and statistics. **Price:** free, for members only. **Circulation:** 1,000. Alternate Formats: online ● Bulletins ● Surveys. Alternate Formats: online. **Conventions/Meetings:** annual convention - always fall ● Spring Management Clinic - meeting - always spring.

180 ■ Farm Equipment Wholesalers Association (FEWA)
PO Box 1347
Iowa City, IA 52244
Ph: (319)354-5156
Fax: (319)354-5157
E-mail: info@fewa.org
URL: http://www.fewa.org
Contact: Patricia A. Collins, Exec. VP
Founded: 1945. **Members:** 200. **Membership Dues:** associate, $295 (annual) ● wholesaler (based on total annual sales), $350-$1,375 (annual) ● offshore, $825 (annual). **Staff:** 2. **Budget:** $225,000. **Multinational. Description:** Independent wholesaler-distributors of shortline and specialty farm equipment, light industrial tractors, lawn and garden tractors, turf care equipment, estate and park maintenance equipment, power vehicles for outdoor recreation and sports, and related supply items. **Publications:** *Tips*, monthly. Newsletter. **Price:** available to members only. Alternate Formats: online ● Membership Directory, annual. **Price:** $50.00 plus shipping and handling. **Conventions/Meetings:** annual convention, with industry showcase and tabletop booth show (exhibits).

181 ■ International Silo Association (ISA)
E106 Church Rd.
Luxemburg, WI 54217
Ph: (920)655-3301
E-mail: info@silo.org
URL: http://www.silo.org
Contact: Joe Shefchik, Pres.
Founded: 1907. **Members:** 50. **Staff:** 3. **Budget:** $30,000. **Regional Groups:** 2. **Description:** Manufacturers of silos, crop processing containers, and related storage structures for agricultural products. Extends the use of ensilage through education and research. Compiles statistics. **Awards:** Honorary Member Award. **Type:** recognition. **Recipient:** for contributions to the association ● Zur Craine Award. **Type:** recognition. **Recipient:** for contributions to the industry. **Committees:** Education and Promotions; Marketing; Monolithic Construction; Research; Safety; Silo Operator's Manual; Standards; Waste Management. **Formerly:** (1956) National Association of Silo Manufacturers; (1979) National Silo Association. **Publications:** *Silo Operator's Manual* ● Membership Directory, annual ● Newsletter, bimonthly ● Papers. **Conventions/Meetings:** annual convention - always January.

182 ■ Irrigation Association (IA)
6540 Arlington Blvd.
Falls Church, VA 22042-6638
Ph: (703)536-7080
Fax: (703)536-7019
E-mail: deborah@irrigation.org
URL: http://www.irrigation.org
Contact: Deborah M. Hamlin CAE, Exec. Dir.
Founded: 1949. **Members:** 1,700. **Membership Dues:** individual, $150 (annual) ● technical, $100 (annual) ● life - technical, $500 ● retired, $60 (annual) ● life - retired, $300 ● student, $30 (annual). **Staff:** 12. **Budget:** $2,500,000. **State Groups:** 38. **Local Groups:** 5. **Languages:** English, Spanish. **Multinational. Description:** Manufacturers, distribu-

tors, dealers, designers, engineers, technicians, students, educators, sports facility managers, park and university grounds managers, golf course/resort designers and managers, government administrators, and contractors. Offers government relations, education courses, and certification programs. **Awards:** Crawford Reid Memorial Award. **Frequency:** periodic. **Type:** recognition. **Recipient:** for significant achievements in the promotion of proper irrigation techniques and procedures ● Industry Achievement Award. **Frequency:** annual. **Type:** recognition. **Recipient:** to individuals within the industry ● Irrigation Person of the Year. **Frequency:** annual. **Type:** recognition. **Recipient:** for major contributions by an individual outside the industry ● National Water and Energy Conservation Award. **Frequency:** periodic. **Type:** recognition. **Recipient:** for significant achievement in the conservation of water and energy ● Partner of the Year. **Frequency:** periodic. **Type:** recognition. **Recipient:** to a person or group with exceptional contributions or distinctive accomplishments in areas allied with, or an integral part of the irrigation industry. **Computer Services:** Online services. **Committees:** Awards and Honors; Certification; Communications; Education; Legislative; Research; Standards; State Relations; Technical Conference Program; Water Management. **Divisions:** Agriculture; Golf; Turf/Landscape; Water Features. **Subgroups:** Aeration and Fountain; Affiliates. **Absorbed:** (1979) International Drip Irrigation Association. **Formerly:** (1977) Sprinkler Irrigation Association. **Publications:** *E-Times*, monthly. Newsletter. **Price:** free for members. Alternate Formats: online ● *Irrigation Association—Membership Directory and Buyers' Guide*, annual. Contains list of members and their products and certified irrigation designers. **Price:** free for members; $25.00 for nonmembers. **Circulation:** 2,000. **Advertising:** accepted ● *Irrigation Association—Technical Conference Proceedings*, annual. **Conventions/Meetings:** annual International Irrigation Show - meeting (exhibits) - 2008 Nov. 2-4, Anaheim, CA.

183 ■ National Clay Pot Manufacturers (NCPM)
PO Box 485
Jackson, MO 63755
Ph: (573)243-3138
Fax: (573)243-3130
E-mail: vlkasten@ceramousa.com
Contact: Stone Manes, Pres.

Founded: 1956. **Members:** 12. **Description:** Manufacturers of red clay flower pots. **Conventions/Meetings:** conference - every 9 to 10 months.

184 ■ National Greenhouse Manufacturers Association (NGMA)
4305 N Sixth St., Ste.A
Harrisburg, PA 17110
Ph: (717)238-4530
Free: (800)792-NGMA
Fax: (717)238-9985
E-mail: ngma@ngma.com
URL: http://www.ngma.com
Contact: Steve Woods Hortica, Assoc. Chm.

Founded: 1958. **Members:** 85. **Membership Dues:** structural/component manufacturer and service, $900 (annual) ● university, $25 (annual) ● affiliate, $50 (annual). **Staff:** 2. **Description:** Manufacturers and distributors of greenhouses and supplies to greenhouse manufacturers. Provides continued education through meetings. **Libraries: Type:** open to the public. **Holdings:** 1. **Subjects:** all aspects of greenhouse standards available to public. **Committees:** Advertising; Agenda; Codes and Ethics; Environmental/Electrical; Glazing; Government Relations; Scholarship. **Divisions:** Associates; Components; Structural Engineering. **Subcommittees:** By-Laws; Greenhouse Fire Prevention. **Publications:** *Insights*, quarterly. Newsletter. **Price:** included in membership dues ● Also publishes structural, cooling and ventilating, heating, glazing, retrofit, and insect screening standards. **Conventions/Meetings:** semiannual conference.

185 ■ North American Equipment Dealers Association (NAEDA)
1195 Smizer Mill Rd.
Fenton, MO 63026-3480
Ph: (636)349-5000
Fax: (636)349-5443
E-mail: kindingerp@naeda.com
URL: http://www.naeda.com
Contact: Paul E. Kindinger, Pres./CEO

Founded: 1900. **Members:** 5,000. **Membership Dues:** associate, $500 (annual). **Staff:** 18. **Regional Groups:** 18. **For-Profit. Description:** Retailers of farm equipment, implements, light industrial equipment, outdoor power equipment, and related supplies. Conducts programs on management training, and governmental and trade relations. **Formerly:** (1962) National Retail Farm Equipment Association; (1988) National Farm and Power Equipment Dealers Association. **Publications:** *Buyer's Guide*, annual. Magazine. Features the names, including trade and product names of more than 2000 of the equipment industry's manufacturers and suppliers. **Price:** $35.00 plus shipping and handling. Alternate Formats: online ● *Guides 2000 - OPE*, annual. Guide for evaluating used outdoor power equipment. Includes rental information. ISSN: 0735-6676 ● *Guides 2000—Tractors, Combines and Accessories*, quarterly. Book. Guide for evaluating used tractors, combines, and accessories. ISSN: 0162-6809. Alternate Formats: CD-ROM ● *NAEDA Equipment Dealer*, monthly. Magazine. Provides management and marketing information for farm, lawn and garden, and industrial equipment dealers. **Price:** $15.00 /year for members; $20.00/year for associate members; $40.00 direct. ISSN: 0014-7834. **Circulation:** 12,500. **Advertising:** accepted. **Conventions/Meetings:** annual convention.

Agriculture

186 ■ Compost Tea Industry Association (CTIA)
PO Box 71894
Eugene, OR 97401
Ph: (541)345-2855
E-mail: info@compostea.org
URL: http://www.compostea.org
Contact: Michael Alms, Co-Founder

Membership Dues: business premium, $250 (annual) ● business standard, $100 (annual) ● academic, nonprofit, $75 (annual) ● individual sustaining, $50 (annual) ● student, press, general public, $25 (annual). **Description:** Provides a unified voice for the compost tea industry. Provides marketing opportunities for the products and services of members. Creates a forum for information exchange in the industry. Conducts research, education, and outreach programs.

187 ■ Independent Professional Seedsmen Association (IPSA)
2320 S 48th St., Ste.102
Lincoln, NE 68506-5810
Ph: (402)483-2571
Fax: (402)489-2394
E-mail: ipsagreg@aol.com
URL: http://www.ipsaweb.com
Contact: Tom Burrus, Pres.

Founded: 1989. **Members:** 249. **Membership Dues:** regular (seed company; based on annual sales), $500-$1,250 (annual) ● associate (non-seed company), $500 (annual) ● association, $400 (annual). **Description:** Enhances the competitiveness of professional seedsmen. Promotes the interests and capabilities of family-owned companies. **Libraries: Type:** reference. **Holdings:** photographs. **Subjects:** specimen. **Awards:** IPSA Student Recognition Award. **Frequency:** annual. **Type:** scholarship. **Recipient:** for students who are pursuing degrees in or related fields of agriculture. **Committees:** Business Development; Research. **Publications:** Newsletter. Alternate Formats: online. **Conventions/Meetings:** annual meeting, with workshops - every January.

Aircraft

188 ■ National Aircraft Appraisers Association (NAAA)
7 W Square Lake Rd.
Bloomfield Hills, MI 48302
Ph: (248)758-2333
Fax: (248)769-6084
E-mail: naaa@plane-values.com
URL: http://www.plane-values.com
Founded: 1980. **Members:** 250. **Membership Dues:** regular, $750 (annual). **Description:** Dedicated to the standardization of the aircraft appraisal process.

189 ■ National Aircraft Resale Association (NARA)
320 King St., Ste.250
Alexandria, VA 22314
Ph: (703)671-8273
Fax: (703)671-5848
E-mail: slsheets@nara-dealers.com
URL: http://www.nara-dealers.com
Contact: Susan Sheets, Pres.
Members: 30. **Description:** Dealers and brokers of pre-owned aircraft. Committed to maintaining ethical standards; provides technically advanced information and marketing tools to members.

Alcoholic Beverages

190 ■ African American Wine Tasting Society (AAWTS)
PO Box 681
Powder Springs, GA 30127
Ph: (770)943-3649
Free: (888)239-5705
Fax: (770)437-1756
E-mail: info@aawts.org
URL: http://aawts.org
Contact: Pamela Roebuck, Contact
Membership Dues: crus classe', $75 (annual) ● grands cru classe', $200 (annual). **Local Groups:** 9. **Description:** Supports the achievement and professional development of African-Americans in the wine industry. Promotes the appreciation, education and responsible enjoyment of wine. **Computer Services:** Online services, feedback form. **Telecommunication Services:** electronic mail, aawts@aawts.org. **Publications:** Newsletter, quarterly.

191 ■ America Homebrewers Association (AHA)
736 Pearl St.
Boulder, CO 80302
Ph: (303)447-0816
Free: (888)822-6273
Fax: (303)447-2825
E-mail: info@brewersassociation.org
URL: http://www.beertown.org/homebrewing/index.html
Contact: Charlie Papazian, Pres.
Founded: 1978. **Members:** 15,000. **Membership Dues:** individual, $38 (annual) ● family, $43 (annual). **Staff:** 2. **Description:** Strives to serve amateur and commercial brewers. Encourages the responsible consumption of beer as an alcohol-containing beverage. **Libraries: Type:** open to the public. **Holdings:** archival material, articles, books, clippings, periodicals. **Subjects:** beer, brewing. **Awards:** National Homebrew. **Frequency:** annual. **Type:** recognition. **Recipient:** for outstanding homebrewed beer, mead and cider being produced by amateur brewers worldwide. **Divisions:** Brewers Publications and Series Books; Brewing Matters; Institute for Brewing Studies. **Publications:** *Zymurgy*, bimonthly. Magazine. **Price:** included in membership dues. **Conventions/Meetings:** Great American Beer Festival.

192 ■ American Bartenders' Association (ABA)
Address Unknown since 2008
Founded: 1983. **For-Profit. Description:** Works to improve the image of bartenders and their profes-

sion. Encourages higher quality among mixologists and the maintenance of professional standards within the wine and spirits industry. Fosters improved relations between government, the public, and the alcohol industry. Serves as public information source; provides for exchange of information on merchandising, marketing, and buying of alcohol as well as discussion of problems. Operates bookstore. **Libraries: Type:** reference. **Holdings:** artwork, books, clippings, periodicals. **Publications:** *ABA Bookstore*, periodic. Catalog. Alternate Formats: online ● *Mixin'*, quarterly. Newsletter. For and about people in the beverage business. Includes book reviews, statistics, research reports, new products, and drink recipes. Alternate Formats: online ● *The Quickie Wine Course.*

193 ■ American Beverage Licensees (ABL)
5101 River Rd., Ste.108
Bethesda, MD 20816-1560
Ph: (301)656-1494
Fax: (301)656-7539
E-mail: wiles@ablusa.org
URL: http://www.ablusa.org
Contact: Harry G. Wiles, Exec. Dir.
Founded: 2002. **Members:** 20,000. **Membership Dues:** diamond, $25,000 (annual) ● platinum, $15,000 (annual) ● gold, $10,000 (annual) ● silver, $5,000 (annual) ● bronze, $2,500 (annual) ● national associate affiliate, $1,000 (annual). **Staff:** 5. **Budget:** $800,000. **State Groups:** 50. **Description:** Federation of associations of alcohol beverage retailers. **Awards:** Retailer of the Year Award. **Frequency:** annual. **Type:** recognition. **Recipient:** for each state affiliate. **Absorbed:** (2003) National Licensed Beverage Association. **Formerly:** National Retail Liquor Package Stores Association; (1992) National Liquor Stores Association; (2003) National Association of Beverage Retailers. **Publications:** *News and Views*, quarterly ● Directory, annual. **Conventions/Meetings:** annual convention (exhibits).

194 ■ American Sommelier Association (ASA)
580 Broadway, Ste.716
New York, NY 10012
Ph: (212)226-6805
Fax: (212)226-6407
E-mail: office@americansommelier.org
URL: http://www.americansommelier.org
Contact: Andrew F. Bell, Pres./CEO
Membership Dues: individual, $136 (annual). **Description:** Represents the interests of individuals and corporations dedicated to enhancing the appreciation of wine. Raises the level of wine knowledge through education and training. Provides a forum for dialogues about wine. Promotes the enjoyment of wine. **Publications:** Newsletter. Alternate Formats: online.

195 ■ Association of African American Vintners (AAAV)
PO Box 2168
Sonoma, CA 95476
Ph: (707)933-0556
Fax: (707)933-0557
E-mail: info@aaavintners.org
URL: http://www.aaavintners.org
Contact: Vance Sharp III, Pres.
Membership Dues: general, $500 (annual) ● associate, $250 (annual) ● friend - consumer, $100 (annual). **Description:** Increases the quality of wine communications to the general public, with special emphasis on African-Americans.

196 ■ Association of Winery Suppliers (AWS)
575 W Coll. Ave., Ste.103
Santa Rosa, CA 95401
Ph: (707)573-3901
Fax: (707)573-3933
Contact: Michael D. Larsen, Exec. Dir.
Founded: 1983. **Members:** 34. **Description:** United States suppliers of services, materials, or equipment used in the winery industry that have at least 20 active accounts with wineries. **Publications:** *Bankruptcy Report*, periodic. **Conventions/Meetings:** annual meeting - always fall, Marin County, CA.

197 ■ Beer Institute (BI)
122 C St. NW, Ste.350
Washington, DC 20001
Ph: (202)737-2337
Free: (800)379-BREW
Fax: (202)737-7004
E-mail: info@beerinstitute.org
URL: http://www.beerinstitute.org
Contact: Jeff Becker, Pres.
Founded: 1986. **Members:** 100. **Staff:** 11. **Budget:** $2,000,000. **Description:** Brewers, importers, and suppliers to the industry. Committed to the development of public policy and to the values of civic duty and personal responsibility. **Publications:** *Beer Institute Bulletin*, quarterly. Alternate Formats: online ● *Brewers Almanac*, annual. Provides information on the U.S. brewing industry including total production, shipment, and sales. Includes statistics and charts. ● *Membership*. Brochure. Alternate Formats: online ● Pamphlets. Contains information on alcohol awareness and drunk driving. ● Newsletters. Alternate Formats: online. **Conventions/Meetings:** annual meeting, for members only.

198 ■ Brewers Association (BA)
PO Box 1679
Boulder, CO 80306
Ph: (303)447-0816
Free: (888)822-6273
Fax: (303)447-2825
E-mail: info@brewersassociation.org
URL: http://www.brewersadvocate.org
Contact: Charlie Papazian, Pres./Founder
Founded: 1942. **Members:** 250. **Staff:** 3. **Description:** Represents micro and regional brewers of beer. Aims to promote and protect American Craft Beer and American Craft Brewers and the community of brewing enthusiasts. **Additional Websites:** http://www.beertown.org. **Formed by Merger of:** (2005) Association of Brewers and Brewers' Association of America. **Formerly:** (1941) Small Brewers Association; (1948) Small Brewers Committee. **Publications:** *BAA Bulletin*, 8/year. Newsletter. Provides information on legislative, economic, and legal issues. **Price:** included in membership dues. **Circulation:** 350. Alternate Formats: CD-ROM. **Conventions/Meetings:** annual conference (exhibits) - always October/November.

199 ■ Distilled Spirits Council of the United States (DISCUS)
1250 Eye St. NW, Ste.400
Washington, DC 20005
Ph: (202)628-3544
Fax: (202)682-8888
E-mail: fcoleman@discus.org
URL: http://www.discus.org
Contact: Dr. Peter H. Cressy, Pres./CEO
Founded: 1973. **Members:** 24. **Staff:** 56. **Description:** Serves as national trade association of producers and marketers of distilled spirits sold in the U.S. Provides statistical and legal data for industry and the public and serves as public information source; conducts educational programs. **Convention/Meeting:** none. **Libraries: Type:** reference. **Holdings:** 3,500; periodicals. **Subjects:** alcohol abuse, alcoholism, liquor industry, prohibition. **Committees:** Affairs; Code Review; Distilled Spirits Political Action; Fire Protection; Government Relations; International Affairs; Laws and Regulations; Military Sales; Public Affairs; Research and Statistics; Technical; Transportation. **Special Interest Groups:** Industry. **Absorbed:** Tax Council-Alcoholic Beverage Industries. **Formed by Merger of:** Distilled Spirits Institute; Licensed Beverage Industries; Bourbon Institute. **Publications:** *Summary of State Laws and Regulations Relating to Distilled Spirits*, biennial. Handbook. **Price:** $17.00/copy ● Brochures.

200 ■ El Dorado Winery Association (EDWA)
PO Box 1614
Placerville, CA 95667
Ph: (916)966-5008
Free: (800)306-3956
E-mail: info@eldoradowines.org
URL: http://www.eldoradowines.org
Contact: Jolaine Collins, Contact
Founded: 1980. **Members:** 17. **Membership Dues:** regular, $300 (annual). **Staff:** 300. **Budget:** $150,000. **Description:** Works to educate consumers regarding the consumption, recognition, and development of El Dorado County grapes and wine.

201 ■ Flair Bartenders' Association (FBA)
104 E Fairview Ave., No. 283
Meridian, ID 83642-1733
Ph: (208)888-3146
E-mail: info@barflair.org
URL: http://www.barflair.org
Contact: Jim Allison, Pres./CEO
Founded: 1998. **Members:** 15,000. **Staff:** 1. **For-Profit. Multinational. Description:** Aims to help teach the art of flair and to develop the sport of freestyle or extreme bartending. Supports all styles of performance bartending in a safe and fun manner. **Computer Services:** Online services, forum.

202 ■ Home Wine and Beer Trade Association (HWBTA)
c/o Dee Roberson, Exec. Dir.
PO Box 1373
Valrico, FL 33595
Ph: (813)685-4261
Fax: (813)681-5625
E-mail: dee@hwbta.org
URL: http://www.hwbta.org
Contact: Dee Roberson, Exec. Dir.
Founded: 1979. **Members:** 510. **Membership Dues:** retailer, $100 (annual) ● wholesaler/manufacturer, $250-$500 (annual) ● alumni/publisher/author, $25 (annual). **Staff:** 1. **Multinational. Description:** Manufacturers, wholesalers, retailers, authors, and editors having a commercial interest in the home beermaking and winemaking trade. Promotes the development and growth of home brewing, home winemaking, and associated trades. Sponsors wine competition. **Awards:** HWBTA Service Award. **Frequency:** annual. **Type:** recognition. **Recipient:** for an individual who has contributed outstanding service to the industry. **Computer Services:** Online services, locator service. **Committees:** Wine Competition. **Publications:** *Advocate*, bimonthly. Newsletter. **Price:** free for members. **Advertising:** accepted. **Conventions/Meetings:** annual conference and seminar (exhibits).

203 ■ International Center for Alcohol Policies (ICAP)
1519 New Hampshire Ave. NW
Washington, DC 20036
Ph: (202)986-1159
Fax: (202)986-2080
E-mail: webmaster@icap.org
URL: http://www.icap.org
Contact: Marcus Grant, Pres.
Founded: 1995. **Staff:** 8. **Multinational. Description:** Works towards "the conviction that beverage alcohol deserves to be treated with respect, both by producers and consumers." Develops partnerships with government and non-government organizations, the beverage alcohol industry, and the scientific and public health communities. **Publications:** *ICAP Reports*. Alternate Formats: online ● Books ● Articles. Alternate Formats: online ● Journals. Alternate Formats: online.

204 ■ Minnesota Beer Wholesalers Association (MBWA)
701 4th Ave. S, Ste.1710
Minneapolis, MN 55415
Ph: (612)604-4400 (612)604-2588
Fax: (612)604-2598
E-mail: email@mnbwa.com
URL: http://www.mnbwa.com
Contact: Michael D. Madigan, Pres.
Founded: 1945. **Members:** 42. **Staff:** 4. **Description:** Representatives of state beer wholesale associations. Promotes the welfare of beer association executives and beer wholesalers. Provides speakers; sponsors legislative conferences; compiles statistics. Bestows annual awards. **Telecommunication Ser-**

vices: electronic mail, madigan@mnbwa.com. **Formerly:** Beer Distributors Secretaries of America; State Beer Wholesalers Secretaries; (1946) National Association of State Beer Association Secretaries; (1977) State Beer Association of Executives of America; (2000) Wholesale Beer Association Executives of America. **Publications:** *Exectic Exhortations*, bimonthly ● *MBWA Directory*, annual ● *WBAE Directory*, annual. **Conventions/Meetings:** annual conference.

205 ■ National Association of Bar and Tavern Owners (NABTO)
PO Box 11578
Fort Lauderdale, FL 33339
Ph: (954)776-7017
Fax: (954)772-9341
Contact: David Jett, Pres.
Founded: 1993. **Members:** 25,000. **Membership Dues:** regular, associate, $100 (annual). **Staff:** 20. **Budget:** $2,000,000. **State Groups:** 13. **Local Groups:** 12. **Description:** Individual bar and tavern owners. Works to unite the local associations from the U.S. into one national association. Provides small bar owners with advantages of large franchises such as cost and management consulting and legal services. Lobbies at the local, state, and national level; offers health and insurance. Sponsors competitions; maintains speakers' bureau. **Computer Services:** database. **Publications:** *Top Gun Newsletter*, weekly. **Advertising:** accepted ● Newsletter. **Circulation:** 20,000. **Conventions/Meetings:** annual Convention and National Sports Tournament - conference, with billiard championship (exhibits) - usually October or November.

206 ■ National Association of Beverage Importers (NABI)
932 Hungerford Dr., Unit 12A
Rockville, MD 20850
Ph: (240)453-9998
Fax: (240)453-9358
E-mail: beverageimporters@nabi-inc.org
URL: http://www.nabi-inc.org
Contact: William T. Earle, Pres.
Founded: 1934. **Members:** 70. **Membership Dues:** associate, $2,000 (annual). **Staff:** 2. **Budget:** $500,000. **Description:** Represents importers of alcoholic beverages. Compiles and reports statistics from Bureau of Census and Internal Revenue sources. **Committees:** Beer; Champagne and Sparkling Wines; Cognac, Armagnac and Calvados; Customs; Freight; French Wine; German Wine; Italian Wine; Legal and Judicial Affairs; Rioja Wine. **Formerly:** (1978) National Association of Alcoholic Beverage Importers. **Publications:** *National Association of Beverage Importers—Statistical Report*, annual. Covers industry arranged by products. Compares arrivals and tax payments for each beverage. **Price:** free for members; $100.00 for nonmembers ● *Statistics and Member Letter*, periodic. Bulletin. **Advertising:** accepted. **Conventions/Meetings:** annual symposium - always fourth Thursday in March, Washington, DC.

207 ■ National Beer Wholesalers Association (NBWA)
1101 King St., Ste.600
Alexandria, VA 22314-2944
Ph: (703)683-4300
Free: (800)300-6417
Fax: (703)683-8965
E-mail: info@nbwa.org
URL: http://www.nbwa.org
Contact: Craig A. Purser CAE, Pres.
Founded: 1938. **Members:** 1,835. **Membership Dues:** distributor (per $1 million annual beer sales), $295 (annual) ● brewer/importer (based on sales barrel), $250-$10,000 (annual) ● vendor (silver), $250 (annual) ● vendor (gold), $500 (annual) ● vendor (platinum), $1,000 (annual). **Staff:** 25. **Budget:** $6,000,000. **Description:** Independent wholesalers of malt beverages and affiliates of the malt beverage industry. Conducts specialized education programs. **Libraries: Type:** reference. **Subjects:** malt beverages. **Computer Services:** Mailing lists, of members. **Committees:** Political Action. **Formerly:** (1983) National Beer Wholesalers' Association of America. **Publications:** *Distributor Productivity Report*, biennial. **Price:** $350.00 for participants ● *NBWA Beer Perspectives*, biweekly. Newsletter. **Price:** included in membership dues ● *NBWA Buyer's Guide*, annual. **Price:** $25.00 ● *NBWA Compensation and Benefits Study*, biennial. **Price:** $100.00 for participants. Alternate Formats: online; CD-ROM; diskette ● *NBWA Legislative and Regulatory Issues Alert*, periodic ● *NBWA Who's Who*, annual ● Annual Report, annual. **Price:** free ● Handbook, annual. **Conventions/Meetings:** annual conference - always fall.

208 ■ North American Brewers' Association (NABA)
601 W 19th St.
Idaho Falls, ID 83402
Ph: (208)705-2667
E-mail: info@northamericanbrewers.org
URL: http://www.northamericanbrewers.org
Contact: Leon Wolfram, Contact
Founded: 1996. **Multinational. Description:** Aims to promote and secure beer's role in culture and society. Works to advance brewing quality and consumer education. Sanctions beer festivals and brewing competitions. Facilitates collaboration and camaraderie among members. **Awards:** North American Beer Awards. **Frequency:** annual. **Type:** medal. **Recipient:** for commercially produced beers from active breweries.

209 ■ Sommelier Society of America (SSA)
PO Box 20080
West Village Sta.
New York, NY 10014
Ph: (212)679-4190
Fax: (212)255-8959
E-mail: info@sommeliersocietyofamerica.org
URL: http://www.sommeliersocietyofamerica.org
Contact: Mr. Robert R. Moody III, Chm.
Founded: 1954. **Members:** 300. **Membership Dues:** non-resident, $125 (annual) ● company, $600. **Staff:** 5. **Regional Groups:** 1. **State Groups:** 3. **Local Groups:** 1. **Description:** Sommeliers (wine captains and wine stewards); members of the restaurant, hospitality and catering industry; distributors; wine importers and producers; retail wine merchants; wine connoisseurs. Educates and shares information about wines and spirits. Conducts Wine Captains Seminar twice yearly. Holds events and tasting of fine wines and liquors. **Additional Websites:** http://www.winestudy.org. **Telecommunication Services:** electronic mail, info@winestudy.org. **Committees:** Entertainment; International; School; Special Events; Tasting. **Conventions/Meetings:** annual meeting and dinner.

210 ■ Tasters Guild International (TG)
c/o Joe Borrello, Pres./CEO
1515 Michigan NE
Grand Rapids, MI 49503
Ph: (616)454-7815
Fax: (616)459-9969
E-mail: joeb@tastersguild.com
URL: http://www.tastersguild.com
Contact: Joe Borrello, Pres./CEO
Founded: 1987. **Membership Dues:** personal/family, $45 (annual) ● corporate affiliation/single unit, $225 (annual) ● winery, restaurant, $125 (annual). **Regional Groups:** 65. **Description:** Endeavors to educate consumers and spread the word of responsible wine and food consumption. **Publications:** *Tasters Guild*, 3/year. Journal. Contains articles and also sponsors yearly travel excursions for members to all corners of the wine world.

211 ■ Wine and Spirits Shippers Association (WSSA)
11800 Sunrise Valley Dr., Ste.332
Reston, VA 20191
Ph: (703)860-2300
Free: (800)368-3167
Fax: (703)860-2422
E-mail: info@wssa.com
URL: http://www.wssa.com
Contact: Louis Healey, Pres.
Founded: 1976. **Members:** 420. **Membership Dues:** general, $100 (annual). **Staff:** 12. **Budget:** $1,000,000. **Description:** Importers, exporters, and distributors of beverages and allied products. Provides members with services, either directly or through agents, that allow for the efficient and economical transportation of products between foreign sources to destinations within the U.S., and from sources within the U.S; offers members reduced ocean freight rates. Qualifies and operates as a shippers association as defined in the Shipping Act of 1984. **Libraries: Type:** not open to the public. **Subjects:** beverages' transportation.

212 ■ Wine and Spirits Wholesalers of America (WSWA)
805 15th St. NW, Ste.430
Washington, DC 20005
Ph: (202)371-9792
Fax: (202)789-2405
E-mail: craig.wolf@wswa.org
URL: http://www.wswa.org
Contact: Craig Wolf, Pres./CEO
Founded: 1943. **Members:** 530. **Membership Dues:** diamond, $10,000 (annual) ● platinum, $6,000 (annual) ● gold, $3,000 (annual) ● silver, $1,000 (annual). **Staff:** 11. **Budget:** $2,100,000. **State Groups:** 43. **Description:** Represents wholesale distributors of domestic and imported wine and distilled spirits. **Councils:** Leadership Development. **Affiliated With:** Wine and Spirits Shippers Association. **Publications:** *Upfront*, monthly. Newsletter. Covers industry, business, and association activities. **Price:** available to members only. **Circulation:** 1,300 ● *WSWA Member Roster and Industry Directory*, annual. Lists alcohol beverage industry members, suppliers, associations, and trade media. Includes index of individuals and firms. **Price:** $100.00/copy. **Conventions/Meetings:** annual convention (exhibits).

213 ■ World Association of the Alcohol Beverage Industries (WAABI)
PO Box 191
Mason, OH 45040-0191
Ph: (513)675-3443
E-mail: barry.becton@diageo.com
URL: http://www.waabi.org
Contact: Barry Becton, Pres.
Founded: 1944. **Members:** 4,000. **Membership Dues:** national, $20 (annual). **Staff:** 1. **Budget:** $100,000. **Regional Groups:** 4. **State Groups:** 15. **Local Groups:** 26. **For-Profit. Description:** Volunteer men and women working together for personal growth and for the benefit of the legal alcohol beverage industry. Local groups contribute time and money in support of civic and charitable projects. **Formerly:** (1991) National Women's Association of Allied Beverage Industries. **Publications:** *Industry World*, bimonthly. Newsletter. Covers the alcohol beverage industry; includes association activities. **Price:** free for members. **Circulation:** 3,000. Alternate Formats: online. **Conventions/Meetings:** annual convention.

Amusement Parks

214 ■ National Association of Amusement Ride Safety Officials (NAARSO)
PO Box 638
Brandon, FL 33509-0638
Ph: (813)661-2779
Free: (800)669-9053
Fax: (813)685-5117
E-mail: joe@naarso.com
URL: http://www.naarso.com
Contact: Joseph D. Gallagher, Pres.
Membership Dues: individual, $50 (annual). **Description:** Represents amusement ride inspectors representing jurisdictional agencies, insurance companies, private consultants, safety professionals, and federal government agencies. Promotes amusement ride safety. **Publications:** Newsletter, quarterly.

Price: included in membership dues ● Membership Directory. **Price:** included in membership dues. Alternate Formats: online. **Conventions/Meetings:** seminar.

Animal Science

215 ■ American Registry of Professional Animal Scientists (ARPAS)
1111 N Dunlap Ave.
Savoy, IL 61874
Ph: (217)356-5390
Fax: (217)398-4119
E-mail: arpas@assochq.org
URL: http://www.arpas.org
Contact: Darrell D. Johnson, Pres.
Membership Dues: regular, $85 (annual). **Description:** Consultants; companies providing products and services; producers, commodity organizations, and related food industries; university, extension, and government staff; and professional societies and related organizations. Strives to be the standard for certified professionals in animal sciences industries. **Affiliated With:** American Dairy Science Association; American Meat Science Association; American Society of Animal Science; Poultry Science Association. **Publications:** Newsletter, 3/year. Alternate Formats: online.

Antiques

216 ■ Antiques and Collectibles Associations (ACA)
PO Box 4389
Davidson, NC 28036
Ph: (704)895-9088
Free: (800)287-7127
Fax: (704)895-0230
E-mail: angie@acna.us
URL: http://www.antiqueandcollectible.com
Contact: Jim Tucker, Exec. Dir./Co-Founder
Founded: 1991. **Members:** 4,000. **Membership Dues:** dealer, promoter, mall owner, $50 (annual) ● corporate, $300 (annual). **Staff:** 7. **Description:** Largest trade association in the antiques and collectibles industry. Provides benefit programs, information, educational opportunities and representation. Strives to create a public awareness and promotes professionalism. **Libraries: Type:** reference; not open to the public. **Publications:** *World of Antiques & Collectibles*, bimonthly. Newsletter. **Circulation:** 3,500. **Advertising:** accepted ● Brochure. **Conventions/Meetings:** annual convention and trade show (exhibits) ● bimonthly seminar.

217 ■ Antiques Council
PO Box 1508
Warren, MA 01083
Ph: (413)436-7064
Fax: (413)436-7066
E-mail: info@antiquescouncil.com
URL: http://www.antiquescouncil.com
Contact: Marty Shapiro, VP
Founded: 1990. **Members:** 80. **Multinational. Description:** Improves the confidence of the public in antiques and their dealers through education, service, and example. Provides management services to charities that hold antiques shows as fund raisers. Offers the general public education about antiques. **Publications:** Newsletter.

218 ■ Association of Restorers and Council of Craftsmen and Artists (AOR)
8 Medford Pl.
New Hartford, NY 13413
Ph: (315)733-1952
Free: (800)260-1829
Fax: (315)724-7231
E-mail: aorcca@adelphia.net
URL: http://www.assoc-restorers.com
Contact: Andrea Daley, Pres./Co-Founder
Founded: 1997. **Membership Dues:** regular, in U.S., $95 (annual) ● regular, outside U.S., $105 (annual) ● extended benefit, in U.S., $125 (annual) ● extended benefit, outside U.S., $135 (annual). **Description:** Restorers of antiques and antique dealers, appraisers, insurance adjusters, and collectors. Seeks to advance the practice of antique restoration. Encourages exchange of information and sharing of techniques among members; serves as a clearinghouse on antique restoration. Makes available discounts on antique restoration products and services to members. **Computer Services:** database, antique restoration. **Formerly:** (2003) Association of Restorers. **Publications:** Newsletter, quarterly. **Conventions/Meetings:** periodic convention.

219 ■ World Antique Dealers Association (WADA)
Address Unknown since 2007
Founded: 1995. **Membership Dues:** $50 (annual). **Regional Groups:** 8. **Description:** Antique dealers, educators, authors, auctioneers, show managers, and museum professionals dedicated to the promotion and preservation of the antiques profession and fair and honest representation of antiques. Seeks to build a more professional and reliable approach to the purchase and sale of antiques. Establishes standards to clearly price merchandise, refund purchase money if merchandise is found to be other than represented. Receives and transmits pertinent information, actively engages in curbing unethical practices, and promotes the dignity of the antiques profession. Conducts seminars and study groups. **Libraries: Type:** reference. **Holdings:** books. **Subjects:** antiques. **Committees:** Ethics; Publicity. **Formerly:** (1994) Branched from: Associated Antique Dealers of America. **Publications:** *WADA News*, monthly. Newsletter. Covers membership activities; includes list of new members. **Price:** free to members. **Advertising:** accepted ● Membership Directory, annual. **Conventions/Meetings:** annual conference.

Apparel

220 ■ Accessories Council
390 Fifth Ave., Ste.710
New York, NY 10018
Ph: (212)947-1135
Fax: (212)947-9258
URL: http://www.accessoriescouncil.org
Contact: Karen Giberson, Pres.
Founded: 1995. **Membership Dues:** associate, $1,000 (annual) ● company (with over $5 million annual revenues), $2,000 (annual) ● company (with less than $2 million annual revenues), $500 (annual). **Description:** Designers, manufacturers, retailers, wholesalers, industry suppliers, press writers and editors, PR professionals. Strives to provide accessory-related information to its members.

221 ■ American Apparel and Footwear Association (AAFA)
1601 N Kent St., Ste.1200
Arlington, VA 22209
Ph: (703)524-1864 (703)797-9037
Free: (800)520-2262
Fax: (703)522-6741
E-mail: mrust@apparelandfootwear.org
URL: http://www.apparelandfootwear.org
Contact: Kevin M. Burke, Pres./CEO
Founded: 1962. **Members:** 670. **Membership Dues:** company (less than $10 million in sales), $2,500 (annual) ● company (over $5 billion in sales), $110,000 (annual) ● supplier (maximum; over $3 billion in sales), $30,150 (annual) ● footwear division (maximum; over $116 million domestic sales), $31,850 (annual) ● international affiliate, $5,000-$15,000 (annual). **Staff:** 19. **Description:** Manufacturers of infants', children's, boys', girls', juniors', men's, and women's wearing apparel; associate members are suppliers of fabrics, equipment, accessories, and services to the apparel industry. Operates the Apparel Foundation; offers placement service through newsletter. Compiles statistics. **Awards: Type:** recognition. **Committees:** Apparel Quality; Apparel Research; Associate Member; Communications; Domestic Production and Contracting; Education; 807 Operations; Financial Management; Government Contracts; Human Resources; Legal; Management Systems; Marketing; Membership; Quick Response Leadership; Textile Relations; Trade Policy. **Councils:** Intimate Apparel. **Divisions:** American Apparel Education Foundation; Headwear; Swimwear Industry Manufacturers Association; Technical Advisory; Western. **Absorbed:** Textile Merchants and Associated Industries of Chicago; Textile Merchants and Associated Industries of St. Louis; (1965) Pacific Coast Garment Manufacturers Association; (1971) Corset and Brassiere Association of America; (1971) Lingerie Industry Council; (1974) New England Rainwear Manufacturers Association; (1993) National Outerwear and Sportswear Association. **Formed by Merger of:** (2001) Fashion Association; (2001) Footwear Industries of America; (2001) American Apparel and Footwear Manufacturers Association; Southern Garment Manufacturers Association; National Association of Skirt, Pajama and Sportswear Manufacturers. **Formerly:** (2001) American Apparel Manufacturers Association. **Publications:** *AAFA Directory of Members and Associate Members*, annual. Membership Directory. **Price:** $100.00/copy. **Advertising:** accepted ● *AAFA News*, monthly. Newsletter ● *Apparel Import Digest*, annual ● *Apparel Plant Wages Survey*, annual ● *Apparel Research Notes*, periodic ● *Apparel Sales/Marketing Compensation Survey*, annual ● *Apparel Trends*, quarterly ● *Committee Manual*, annual ● *Focus: Economic Profile*, annual ● *Personnel Policy Survey*, biennial ● *Technical Advisory Committee Bulletin*, periodic ● *Technical Advisory Committee Research Paper*, annual. **Conventions/Meetings:** annual Bobbin Show/Convention - trade show (exhibits) - always fall in Atlanta, GA ● annual meeting - always spring in Colorado Springs, CO ● periodic seminar.

222 ■ American Apparel Producers' Network (AAPN)
PO Box 720693
Atlanta, GA 30358
Ph: (404)843-3171
Fax: (413)702-3226
E-mail: source@aapnetwork.net
URL: http://www.aapnetwork.net
Contact: Sue C. Strickland, Exec. Dir.
Founded: 1980. **Members:** 210. **Membership Dues:** corporate, $1,600 (annual). **Staff:** 2. **Budget:** $100,000. **Multinational. Description:** Represents apparel contractors, manufacturers, and suppliers of goods and services to the industry. Provides sourcing programs. **Awards:** Don Strickland Memorial Scholarship. **Frequency:** annual. **Type:** scholarship. **Recipient:** for a student in apparel manufacturing at Southern Tech. **Computer Services:** Online services, sourcing, color catalogs, fax broadcasting. **Committees:** Education; Social; Sourcing; Technical Support. **Formerly:** (1985) Southern Apparel Contractors Association; (1986) American Apparel Producers Association; (1998) American Apparel Contractors Association. **Publications:** *Guide to Sourcing American Made Apparel*, annual. Directory. Features listings indexed by type of apparel produced and by services provided. **Price:** $25.00. **Circulation:** 2,000. **Advertising:** accepted ● Journal. **Price:** $15.00 for non-members ● Membership Directory. **Conventions/Meetings:** semiannual conference and seminar - spring and fall.

223 ■ American Cloak and Suit Manufacturers Association (ACSMA)
Address Unknown since 2007
Founded: 1919. **Members:** 100. **Staff:** 3. **Description:** Contractors producing women's coats and suits for wholesalers and other manufacturers. Represents contractors and manufacturers in contractual relations with International Ladies' Garment Workers' Union (see separate entry).

224 ■ Apparel Graphics Institute
58 Boston Dr., Ste.1000
Ocean Pines, MD 21811
Ph: (410)641-7300

E-mail: markvenit@cs.com
Contact: Mark L. Venit, Dir.

Founded: 1992. **Members:** 526. **Membership Dues:** standard, $1,850 (annual). **Staff:** 3. **Description:** Serves apparel decorators by providing information unavailable elsewhere. Focuses on management and financial consulting, industry-specific data and research, and educational programs, trade shows, and conventions. **Libraries: Type:** not open to the public. **Holdings:** books, business records, monographs, periodicals. **Subjects:** apparel, screen printing, embroidery.

225 ■ Apparel Manufacturers Association (AMA)

1601 N Kent St., Ste.1200
Arlington, VA 22209
Ph: (703)797-9037 (703)524-1864
Free: (800)520-2262
Fax: (703)522-6741
E-mail: mrust@apparelandfootwear.org
Contact: Mr. Kevin Burke, Pres./CEO

Founded: 1935. **Members:** 430. **Staff:** 15. **Budget:** $5,000,000. **Description:** Represents manufacturers of ladies' garments. Aims to negotiate arbitration of labor problems within the apparel industry. **Formed by Merger of:** National Dress Manufacturers Association; Popular Priced Dress Manufacturers Group.

226 ■ Asian American Importers Association

1407 Broadway, Ste.2106
New York, NY 10018-3617
Ph: (212)239-8120
Fax: (212)239-0776
E-mail: icilimited@aol.com
Contact: Roger Menda, Contact

Founded: 1994. **Members:** 75. **Membership Dues:** individual, $300 (annual). **Staff:** 2. **Description:** Apparel and textile importers, and manufacturers and traders. **Formerly:** (2000) Indo American Garment Association. **Conventions/Meetings:** monthly board meeting.

227 ■ Associated Corset and Brassiere Manufacturers (ACBM)

Address Unknown since 2008

Founded: 1933. **Members:** 25. **Staff:** 2. **Description:** Trade ass'n representing manufacturers of girdles, brassieres, and foundation garments. **Conventions/Meetings:** annual meeting - always New York City.

228 ■ Association of Knitwear Designers (AKD)

c/o Diane Zangl, Pres.
W3090 County Rd. Y
Lomira, WI 53048
Ph: (920)583-4298
Fax: (920)583-3515
E-mail: stitchwi@dotnet.com
URL: http://www.knitwear-designers.org
Contact: Diane Zangl, Pres.

Founded: 1988. **Members:** 55. **Membership Dues:** professional (publishing, teacher, production knitter, retailer and yarn manufacturer/importer), associate in U.S., $35 (annual) ● associate, professional outside U.S., $40 (annual). **Staff:** 8. **Multinational. Description:** Promotes the art and business of knitting. Provides networking, professional accreditation, and help to freelance knitwear designers worldwide. **Libraries: Type:** reference. **Holdings:** 100; books, video recordings. **Subjects:** textiles, design, knitwear, color theory. **Formerly:** (2006) Professional Knitwear Designers Guild. **Publications:** *Design Lines*, bimonthly. Newsletter. Covers member accomplishments, business opportunities, new products and industry news. **Price:** free for members ● *Teachers Directory*, annual. Lists teaching professionals who have been accredited by AKD, their credentials, classes, and fees charged. **Price:** free. **Conventions/Meetings:** seminar.

229 ■ Clothing Manufacturers Association of the U.S.A. (CMA)

Address Unknown since 2008

Founded: 1933. **Members:** 100. **Membership Dues:** associate; U.S.A.-based member, $150 (annual) ● outside U.S.A., $200 (annual). **Staff:** 2. **Description:** Manufacturers of men's and boys' tailored clothing; suppliers of products or services used by clothing manufacturers. Provides assistance to members on labor and government relations. Sponsors seminars and conferences on subjects of interest to men's clothing manufacturers and suppliers of products and services they use. Compiles production, economic, and financial statistics. **Libraries: Type:** not open to the public; reference. **Holdings:** 85. **Subjects:** statistics, production, sales labor relations, compilation of presentations at annual seminars. **Publications:** *Members News Bulletin*, periodic. **Price:** available to members only. **Circulation:** 200 ● *Statistical Report on Profit, Sales, Production and Marketing Trends for the Men's and Boys' Tailored Clothing Industry*, annual. Statistics of annual U.S. production, imports, and exports of men's and boys' tailored clothing. Includes industry profits on sales and net worth. **Price:** $30.00/copy ● Reports. Contains reports on special economic, financial, production and merchandising statistics. **Conventions/Meetings:** periodic Manufacturing & Management Seminar - usually May or September.

230 ■ Council of Fashion Designers of America (CFDA)

1412 Broadway, Ste.2006
New York, NY 10018
Ph: (212)302-1821
Fax: (212)768-0515
E-mail: info@cfda.com
URL: http://www.cfda.com
Contact: Diane von Furstenberg, Pres.

Founded: 1962. **Members:** 280. **Membership Dues:** designer, $500 (annual). **Staff:** 4. **Description:** Persons of "recognized ability, standing, and integrity, who are actively engaged in creative fashion design in the United States, in the fields of wearing apparel, fabrics, accessories, jewelry, or related products." (Membership is individual and does not extend to the firm or associates.) Seeks "to further the position of fashion design as a recognized branch of American art and culture, to advance its artistic and professional standards, to establish and maintain a code of ethics and practices of mutual benefit in professional, public, and trade relations, and to promote and improve public understanding and appreciation of the fashion arts through leadership in quality and taste". **Awards:** Council of Fashion Designers of America Award. **Frequency:** annual. **Type:** recognition. **Recipient:** for excellence in the field. **Committees:** Scholarship. **Conventions/Meetings:** annual dinner, includes presentation.

231 ■ Custom Tailors and Designers Association of America (CTDA)

PO Box 41331
Cleveland, OH 44141
Ph: (440)526-8860
Free: (888)248-CTDA
Fax: (440)526-9593
E-mail: info@ctda.com
URL: http://www.ctda.com
Contact: Davide Cotugno, Publicity Chm.

Founded: 1880. **Members:** 350. **Membership Dues:** merchant, $325 (annual) ● associate, $575 (annual). **Staff:** 1. **Budget:** $200,000. **Regional Groups:** 12. **Local Groups:** 18. **Description:** Designers and makers of men's custom tailored outerwear and clothing. **Libraries: Type:** reference. **Subjects:** fashion. **Formerly:** Merchant Tailors and Designers Association of America. **Publications:** *Custom Tailor: The Only Business Journal of Custom Tailoring*, 3/year. Covers association activities. Includes index of advertisers, annual National Research Pattern, and membership roster. **Price:** included in membership dues. **Circulation:** 700. **Advertising:** accepted ● Newsletter, quarterly. **Conventions/Meetings:** annual convention ● annual meeting (exhibits) - always in February.

232 ■ Educational Foundation for the Fashion Industries (EFFI)

7th Ave. at 27th St.
Bldg. C, Rm. 204
New York, NY 10001
Ph: (212)217-7999
Fax: (212)594-9206
E-mail: effivive@fitsuny.edu

Founded: 1944. **Staff:** 8. **Description:** Labor and management representatives of the fashion industries. Serves as an advisory body to the Fashion Institute of Technology on the initiation and evaluation of curriculum offerings relative to current industrial needs and trends and on the placement of graduates according to their aptitudes and interests. Provides funds for scholarships and development. **Formerly:** Educational Foundation for the Apparel Industry.

233 ■ Fashion Exports New York

c/o New York Fashion International
275 7th Ave., 9th Fl.
New York, NY 10001
Ph: (212)366-6160
Fax: (212)366-6162
E-mail: info@nyfi.org
URL: http://www.fashionexportsny.org

Founded: 1991. **Multinational. Description:** Fashion manufacturers. Works to assist New York manufacturers to export overseas and promote New York fashion internationally. Conducts foreign market research; organizes exhibitions.

234 ■ Fashion Group International (FGI)

8 W 40th St., 7th Fl.
New York, NY 10018
Ph: (212)302-5511
Fax: (212)302-5533
E-mail: pmaffei@fgi.org
URL: http://www.fgi.org
Contact: Margaret Hayes, Pres.

Founded: 1930. **Members:** 5,000. **Membership Dues:** student, $35 (annual) ● executive, $60-$70 (annual) ● associate, $45 (annual). **Staff:** 14. **Description:** Fashion, apparel, accessories, beauty and home industries. Works to advance professionalism in fashion and its related lifestyle industries with a particular emphasis on the role and development of women. Provides a public forum for examination of important contemporary issues in fashion and the business of fashion. Works to present timely information regarding national and global trends and to attain greater recognition of women's achievements in business and to promote career opportunities in fashion. **Awards:** Rising Star Awards. **Frequency:** annual. **Type:** recognition. **Recipient:** to individuals who are upcoming stylemakers of the future.

235 ■ Fashion Outreach

Address Unknown since 2007

Description: Fashion industry professionals. Works to educate and provide role models for youths that are interested in a career in fashion. Provides mentoring, conducts symposiums. **Awards:** Scholarship. **Type:** recognition.

236 ■ Fur Information Council of America (FICA)

8424 A Santa Monica Blvd., No. 860
West Hollywood, CA 90069
Ph: (323)782-1700
Fax: (323)651-1417
E-mail: info@fur.org
URL: http://www.fur.org
Contact: Alison Landau, Contact

Founded: 1958. **Members:** 300. **Membership Dues:** retailer, wholesaler (with total yearly sales of over $1 million), $1,000 (annual) ● retailer, wholesaler (with total yearly sales of less than $1 million), $500 (annual). **Staff:** 6. **Description:** Fur retailers, manufacturers, and others involved in the fur industry. Aims to promote the fur industry and foster high standards, quality, and craftsmanship. Conducts public relations and advertising work. Committed to the wise use and humane care of animals; develops programs to ensure high standards for animal welfare in the fur industry; works with wildlife biologists to promote sound wildlife management. **Formerly:** American Fur Industry. **Publications:** *American Fur Industry Fashion-Newsletter*, annual. Promotes fur and conservation of fur-bearing animals. Includes fashion and conservation reports. **Price:** free. **Circulation:** 3,000 ● *Furs Naturally*. Booklet. **Conventions/Meetings:** semiannual board meeting ● show, fur fashions for retailers and the press.

237 ■ Greater Blouse, Skirt and Undergarment Association (GBSUA)
1359 Broadway, Ste.1814
New York, NY 10018
Ph: (212)563-5052
Fax: (212)563-5373
E-mail: info@greaterblouse.org
Contact: Teddy Lai, Exec. Dir.
Founded: 1933. **Members:** 300. **Membership Dues:** regular, $85 (monthly). **Staff:** 5. **Budget:** $600,000. **Local Groups:** 300. **Languages:** Chinese, English, Spanish. **Description:** Represents contractors in the ladies' blouses, sportswear, underwear, and negligee industry. Conducts charitable programs. **Awards:** Lifetime Achievement Award. **Type:** recognition ● Man of the Year. **Frequency:** annual. **Type;** recognition. **Affiliated With:** National Association of Blouse Manufacturers; New York Skirt and Sportswear Association. **Formerly:** (1969) Greater Blouse and Skirt Contractors Association. **Publications:** *Greater Voice*, monthly. Newsletter. **Price:** free. **Circulation:** 800. **Advertising:** accepted ● Annual Report, annual. **Conventions/Meetings:** monthly workshop.

238 ■ Headwear Information Bureau (HIB)
302 W 12th St., PHC
New York, NY 10014
Ph: (212)627-8333
E-mail: milicase@aol.com
URL: http://www.hatsworldwide.com
Contact: V. Casey Bush, Exec. Dir./Founder
Founded: 1989. **Members:** 80. **Membership Dues:** student, supplier, new milliner, $25 (monthly). **Staff:** 2. **Description:** Headwear and Millinery manufacturers, importers, and suppliers for men and women's hats. Promotes the wearing of hats by women and men of all ages. Disseminates fashion information; conducts promotional and educational campaigns; handles press relations and designer store appearances. Operates speakers' bureau and charitable program; compiles statistics. **Awards:** Millinery Designer of the Year. **Frequency:** annual. **Type:** recognition. **Recipient:** for designers. **Formerly:** (1989) Millinery Institute of America; (1997) Millinery Information Bureau. **Publications:** *Milligram*, bimonthly. Newsletter. **Price:** available to members only.

239 ■ The Hosiery Association (THA)
7421 Carmel Executive Park, Ste.200
Charlotte, NC 28226
Ph: (704)365-0913
Fax: (704)362-2056
E-mail: info@hosieryassociation.com
URL: http://www.hosieryassociation.com
Contact: Sally Kay, Pres./CEO
Founded: 1905. **Members:** 425. **Membership Dues:** hosiery, supplier, international (minimum), $600 (annual) ● hosiery, supplier, international (maximum), $12,000 (annual). **Staff:** 9. **Budget:** $1,200,000. **Regional Groups:** 7. **State Groups:** 7. **Description:** Hosiery manufacturers and suppliers. Develops standards for hosiery measurement. Sponsors annual "Celebrate Hosiery" to educate consumers on hosiery varieties. Conducts field visitations for assistance in technical areas. Compiles statistics; conducts research programs. Operates Group Purchasing Program. **Libraries: Type:** reference. **Subjects:** hosiery. **Computer Services:** database, member access. **Telecommunication Services:** electronic mail, sally.kay@hosieryassociation.com. **Committees:** Human Resources; Public Relations and Marketing. **Formerly:** (1999) National Association of Hosiery Manufacturers. **Publications:** *Hosiery News*, monthly. Magazine. Covers legislative and regulatory issues; technology and equipment; new hosiery products at retail; hosiery production, shipments, and foreign trade. **Price:** included in membership dues. ISSN: 0742-8065. **Circulation:** 2,400. **Advertising:** accepted. Alternate Formats: online ● *Industry Directory of Manufacturers, Marketers, Distributors, Suppliers*, periodic. **Price:** $100.00 for nonmembers; $50.00 for members. **Advertising:** accepted ● *THA Directory of Hosiery Manufacturers and Mill Suppliers*, periodic ● *THA Directory of Hosiery Mill Suppliers*, periodic ● Also publishes information on legislation and trade practice rules; disseminates career booklets to high school students. **Conventions/Meetings:** International Hosiery Exposition - trade show (exhibits) - always April/May in Charlotte, NC.

240 ■ Infant and Juvenile Manufacturers Association (IJMA)
Address Unknown since 2008
Founded: 1912. **Members:** 15. **Description:** Manufacturers of children's apparel.

241 ■ International Association of Clothing Designers and Executives (IACDE)
835 NW 36th Terr.
Oklahoma City, OK 73118
Ph: (405)602-8037
Fax: (405)602-8038
E-mail: newyorkiacde@cox.net
URL: http://www.iacde.com
Contact: David M. Schmida, Exec. Dir.
Founded: 1911. **Members:** 300. **Membership Dues:** industrial chapter, $700 (annual) ● manufacturing executive, retail tailoring director/executive, designer and education chapter, $400 (annual). **Staff:** 2. **Budget:** $300,000. **Local Groups:** 10. **Description:** Men's and women's apparel designers. Forecasts clothing styles for manufacturers and retailers. Compiles statistics. Conducts research programs; sponsors placement service. **Libraries: Type:** reference. **Holdings:** archival material. **Subjects:** fashion. **Awards:** IDA Awards for Design Excellence. **Frequency:** annual. **Type:** recognition. **Recipient:** for the designer with a winning presentation ● Industrial Chapter Scholarship. **Frequency:** annual. **Type:** scholarship. **Recipient:** for a student with a winning essay. **Committees:** Industry Fashion Coordinating; Textile Study. **Formerly:** (1919) National Association of Clothing Designers; (1998) International Association of Clothing Designers. **Publications:** *Design News*. Newsletter. Alternate Formats: online ● *International Association of Clothing Designers—Convention Yearbook*, annual ● *Style Forecast*, semiannual ● Newsletter, quarterly. **Conventions/Meetings:** semiannual conference - always in April/May and September/October.

242 ■ International Formalwear Association (IFA)
401 N Michigan Ave.
Chicago, IL 60611-4267
Ph: (312)321-5139
Fax: (312)321-5150
E-mail: ifa@formalwear.org
URL: http://www.formalwear.org
Contact: Karen A. Hurley, Exec. Dir.
Founded: 1972. **Members:** 350. **Membership Dues:** specialist (based on number of retail stores), $195-$795 (annual) ● supplier (based on annual gross sales), $295-$895 (annual). **Staff:** 195. **Budget:** $500,000. **Description:** Specialists working to promote the formalwear industry. Conducts educational programs through seminars and exhibitions. **Awards:** Black Tie Award. **Frequency:** annual. **Type:** recognition. **Recipient:** for service to the formalwear industry. **Formerly:** (1987) American Formalwear Association. **Publications:** *Formalwords*, bimonthly. Newsletter. Provides information on marketing, merchandising, advertising, management, sales, and related business topics. **Price:** available to members only. **Circulation:** 700. **Advertising:** accepted. Alternate Formats: online ● *IFA Membership Directory*, annual. **Advertising:** accepted. **Conventions/Meetings:** annual trade show (exhibits).

243 ■ International Wooden Bow Tie Club (IWBTC)
24B Rosemary Ln.
Middlefield, CT 06455
Ph: (860)349-9328
Free: (800)974-3557
Fax: (860)349-1455
URL: http://www.woodbowties.com
Contact: Peter Burch MD, Pres.
Membership Dues: regular, $49. **Multinational. Description:** Represents wooden bow tie enthusiasts. Promotes the manufacture of wooden bow ties. Facilitates cooperation and communication among members. **Publications:** Newsletter. Alternate Formats: online.

244 ■ Ladies Apparel Contractors Association (LACA)
Address Unknown since 2008
Founded: 1964. **Members:** 100. **Staff:** 3. **Description:** Apparel contractors. Conducts labor negotiations, legislative activities, and other services for members. **Formerly:** (1977) Popular Price Dress Contractors Association. **Supersedes:** United Popular Dress Manufacturers Association. **Conventions/Meetings:** seminar.

245 ■ National Association of Blouse Manufacturers (NABM)
Address Unknown since 2008
Founded: 1933. **Members:** 150. **Staff:** 5. **Description:** Manufacturers of women's blouses.

246 ■ National Association of Fashion and Accessory Designers (NAFAD)
Address Unknown since 2007
Founded: 1949. **Members:** 240. **Regional Groups:** 2. **State Groups:** 2. **Local Groups:** 12. **Description:** Persons engaged in the field of fashion design or other allied fields. Fosters the development of the black fashion designer; encourages integration of members in all phases of the fashion industry through the extension of educational and economic opportunities. Disseminates information; holds workshops and fashion seminars; maintains Black Historical Museum of Fashion Dolls. **Libraries: Type:** reference. **Awards: Type:** scholarship. **Committees:** Doll Project; Fashion Show Scholarship; Standards; Time and Place. **Affiliated With:** National Association for the Advancement of Colored People. **Publications:** *Membership Roster*, annual ● Newsletter, semiannual. **Conventions/Meetings:** annual conference (exhibits) - always July 3.

247 ■ National Association of Men's Sportswear Buyers (NAMSB)
c/o Theresa Ochs, Exec. Dir.
NAMSB Found.
PO Box 227
Millwood, NY 10546
Ph: (212)685-4550
Fax: (212)685-4688
E-mail: tochs@namsb.org
URL: http://www.namsb.org
Contact: Theresa Ochs, Exec. Dir.
Founded: 1954. **Members:** 1,500. **Membership Dues:** men's wear retailer, $10 (annual). **Staff:** 4. **Description:** Sponsors trade shows for buyers of clothes for men's wear stores. Conducts media interviews to discuss men's wear and educational programs. **Libraries: Type:** reference. **Holdings:** video recordings. **Subjects:** men's fashion. **Publications:** *NAMSB News*, monthly. Newsletter. Contains information on men's fashion. **Price:** available to members only. **Circulation:** 1,500 ● Videos. **Conventions/Meetings:** semiannual Vibestyle - trade show (exhibits) - usually January, March, June, or October in New York City.

248 ■ National Association of Uniform Manufacturers and Distributors (NAUMD)
16 E 41st St., Ste.700
New York, NY 10017
Ph: (212)869-0670
Fax: (212)575-2847

E-mail: rjlerman@naumd.com
URL: http://www.naumd.com
Contact: Mr. Richard J. Lerman, Pres.
Founded: 1933. **Members:** 350. **Membership Dues:** manufacturer/associate, $995-$3,500 (annual) ● dealer/distributor, $395-$1,500 (annual). **Staff:** 4. **Description:** Represents the uniform and career apparel industry. Provides programs and services to individuals involved in the career apparel industry and offers specialized programs for mill suppliers, manufacturers, dealers, and distributors. **Awards:** Best Dressed Police Department. **Frequency:** annual. **Type:** recognition ● Image of the Year Award. **Frequency:** annual. **Type:** recognition. **Formerly:** (1997) Uniform Manufacturers Exchange. **Publications:** *FYI NAUMD*, quarterly. Newsletter. Alternate Formats: online ● *NAUMD Membership Directory and Resource Guide*, annual. **Price:** free for members; $100.00 for nonmembers. **Conventions/Meetings:** annual convention (exhibits).

249 ■ National Costumers Association (NCA)
121 N Bosart Ave.
Indianapolis, IN 46201
Ph: (317)351-1940
Free: (800)NCA-1321
Fax: (317)351-1941
E-mail: office@costumers.org
URL: http://www.costumers.org
Contact: Jennifer Skarstedt, Sec.-Treas.
Founded: 1923. **Members:** 375. **Membership Dues:** rental/retail shop, retail only shop, costume professional, manufacturer/wholesaler, basic, $195 (annual) ● affiliate, $80 (annual) ● web link, $25 (annual) ● deluxe (including buyer's group), $390 (annual). **Staff:** 2. **Budget:** $400,000. **Description:** Designers, producers, and renters of costumes for all occasions. Works to establish and maintain professional and ethical standards of business in the costume industry. Encourage and promote a greater and more diversified use of costumes in all fields of human activity. Offers Play Plot, Book services; conducts educational programs during conventions; buyer's group discounts, website listing, book service, and debt recovery source. **Libraries: Type:** reference. **Subjects:** costume design. **Awards:** Memorial Award. **Type:** recognition. **Recipient:** for outstanding costuming in a variety of categories ● Scholarships. **Type:** scholarship. **Computer Services:** Online services, source list, guide book, plot service. **Additional Websites:** http://hdacshow.org. **Committees:** Awards; Costume Show; Dance Apparel; Halloween; Historian; Memorial Fund; Trade Show. **Publications:** *National Costumers Association—Membership Roster*, annual. Membership Directory. Contains listing of manufacturers, wholesalers and distributors, as well as retail members. **Price:** free, for members only. **Circulation:** 600. **Advertising:** accepted. Alternate Formats: CD-ROM; online ● *National Costumers Magazine*, 8/year. Covers association activities; tips, tricks and trends for costuming industry. **Price:** free, for members only. **Circulation:** 600. **Advertising:** accepted. Also Cited As: *The Costumer* ● *Operations Guide Book*, periodic. Covers operations, organization, management, and wardrobe. Includes buyer's guide. **Price:** free, for members only. **Circulation:** 200. Alternate Formats: online. **Conventions/Meetings:** annual convention and trade show (exhibits) - every summer ● annual Halloween Dance Apparel and Costume Show - trade show (exhibits) - every March.

250 ■ National Fashion Accessories Association (NFAA)
350 5th Ave., Ste.2030
New York, NY 10118
Ph: (212)947-3424
Fax: (212)629-0361
E-mail: gemini@geminishippers.com
URL: http://www.accessoryweb.com
Contact: Sara Mayes, Pres.
Founded: 1916. **Members:** 100. **Staff:** 8. **Description:** Manufacturers and importers of handbags and accessories. Services include credit group, product safety and environmental regulation advice, discounted rates on ocean carrier service contracts, and weekly quota and customs information. **Special Interest Groups:** Legal and Governmental Affairs. **Also Known As:** Fashion Accessories Shippers Association. **Formerly:** (1986) National Handbag Association. **Publications:** *How to Sell Accessories*. Booklet. **Price:** $1.00.

251 ■ National Knitwear and Sportswear Association (NKSA)
Address Unknown since 2007
URL: http://www.asktmag.com
Founded: 1918. **Members:** 200. **Staff:** 10. **Description:** Represents the knit- and sportswear industry in support of domestic knitwear production before government agencies and in relation to other industries and the public; manages publicity and promotional campaigns for industry products. Conducts technical studies and standardization programs; also holds design and technical seminars. Sponsors and manages periodic Yarn Fair, International, CAD ExpoPlus, Knitting Arts Expo and Trimmings, Accessories, and Fabrics Expo (TAFE) expositions. **Computer Services:** database. **Additional Websites:** http://www.cadexpo.com. **Formerly:** (1981) National Knitted Outerwear Association. **Publications:** *American Sportwear & Knitting Times*, monthly. Magazine. **Price:** $40.00/yr. ISSN: 0023-2300. **Circulation:** 8,000. **Advertising:** accepted. Alternate Formats: diskette ● *Buyers' Guide Directory*, annual. **Price:** $25.00 plus 2.50 shipping/handling ● Handbooks. **Conventions/Meetings:** annual Yarn Fair/Cad Expo - show (exhibits) - always August.

252 ■ Neckwear Association of America (NAA)
Address Unknown since 2007
Founded: 1947. **Members:** 100. **Description:** Men's neckwear manufacturers, tie fabric producers, suppliers, and related industries. Conducts various consumer and trade promotional activities. **Awards: Type:** recognition. **Committees:** Public Relations. **Formerly:** (1979) Men's Tie Foundation. **Publications:** *Neckwear Industry Directory*, biennial ● *Tie Lines*, periodic. Newsletter ● Papers.

253 ■ New York Coat and Suit Association (NYCSA)
Address Unknown since 2008
Founded: 1961. **Members:** 175. **Staff:** 10. **Description:** Manufacturers of women's and misses' coats and suits. **Formed by Merger of:** Industrial Council of Cloak, Suit and Skirt Manufacturers; Merchants Ladies Garment Association.

254 ■ New York Skirt and Sportswear Association (NYSSA)
Address Unknown since 2008
Founded: 1933. **Members:** 32. **Staff:** 2. **Budget:** $270,000. **Description:** Manufacturers of women's skirts, slacks, coordinates, and other sportswear. **Formerly:** (1977) National Skirt and Sportswear Association. **Publications:** Bulletin, periodic. **Conventions/Meetings:** annual conference - always October.

255 ■ Professional Apparel Association (PAA)
994 Old Eagle School Rd., Ste.1019
Wayne, PA 19087-1866
Ph: (610)971-4850
Free: (800)722-7712
Fax: (610)971-4859
E-mail: info@proapparel.com
Contact: Sharon Tannahill, Exec. Dir.
Founded: 1984. **Members:** 35. **Membership Dues:** associate, $1,000 (annual) ● retail associate, $100 (annual) ● manufacturer, $5,000 (annual). **Staff:** 3. **Budget:** $200,000. **Description:** Seeks to enhance the growth of the professional apparel industry by educating uniform retailers. **Publications:** *PAA Uniformer*, quarterly. Newsletter. Contains educational articles for retailers. Advertising is accepted from members only. **Price:** free for members. **Circulation:** 500. **Advertising:** accepted. **Conventions/Meetings:** biennial trade show, for manufacturers of health care and hospitality uniforms, shoes, accessories (exhibits).

256 ■ Professional Association of Custom Clothiers (PACC)
56 S 33rd Ave., No. 220
St. Cloud, MN 56301
Ph: (320)240-2007
Free: (877)755-0303
Fax: (320)240-2011
E-mail: admin@paccprofessionals.org
URL: http://www.paccprofessionals.org
Contact: Tina Colombo, Pres.
Founded: 1991. **Members:** 700. **Membership Dues:** intern, $88 (annual) ● formal, $135 (annual) ● resource, $300 (annual) ● retired, $55 (annual) ● educational, $210 (annual) ● student, $25 (annual). **Staff:** 1. **Budget:** $126,000. **Regional Groups:** 7. **Local Groups:** 19. **Description:** Represents dressmakers, tailors, and alteration and home decoration specialists; interested others. Encourages the interchange of ideas among individuals involved in the custom clothing industry. Promotes professions in the industry; represents members' interests. Conducts educational and training programs. **Publications:** *PACC News*, quarterly. Newsletter. **Price:** $35.00/year. **Circulation:** 800. **Advertising:** accepted. Alternate Formats: online. **Conventions/Meetings:** annual conference ● seminar.

257 ■ Sunglass Association of America (SAA)
390 N Bridge St.
LaBelle, FL 33935
Ph: (863)612-0085
Fax: (863)612-0250
E-mail: info@sunglassassociation.com
URL: http://www.sunglassassociation.com
Contact: Tibor Gross, Pres.
Founded: 1970. **Members:** 80. **Membership Dues:** regular (maximum; domestic), $14,000 (annual) ● associate (international), $2,000-$5,000 (annual) ● affiliate, $2,000 (annual). **Staff:** 3. **Description:** Leads, represents, and promotes the sunglass or reader industry by giving market information, statistics, training and industry trends. Provides member guidance regarding regulatory and standards compliance. Advocates responsible regulations and industry standards. **Publications:** Brochures ● Membership Directory, semiannual. **Conventions/Meetings:** annual conference - always fall in various locations.

258 ■ Underfashion Club (UC)
326 Field Rd.
Clinton Corners, NY 12514
Ph: (845)758-6405
Fax: (845)758-2546
E-mail: underfashionclub@frontiernet.net
URL: http://www.underfashionclub.org
Contact: Barry Ross, Pres.
Founded: 1958. **Members:** 500. **Membership Dues:** individual, $75 (annual). **Description:** Executives engaged in the design, production, promotion, management, and distribution of the foundation, lingerie, sleepwear, and loungewear industries at the manufacturer, supplier, buyer, merchandise manager, and store principal levels. Engages in charitable activities. Sponsors scholarship programs for high school and college students in intimate apparel studies. **Libraries: Type:** reference; open to the public; by appointment only. **Holdings:** archival material, articles, audiovisuals, books, clippings, periodicals. **Subjects:** intimate apparel industry. **Awards:** Femmy. **Frequency:** annual. **Type:** recognition. **Recipient:** for leaders of the intimate apparel industry. **Committees:** Program; Scholarship. **Formerly:** Corset and Brassiere Women's Club. **Publications:** *News Briefs*, quarterly. Newsletter. **Circulation:** 800. Alternate Formats: online. **Conventions/Meetings:** competition ● seminar.

259 ■ Western-English Trade Association (WETA)
451 E 58th Ave., No. 4323
Denver, CO 80216-8468
Ph: (303)295-2001
Fax: (303)295-6108

E-mail: weta@netway.net
URL: http://www.wetaonline.com
Contact: Glenda Chipps, Exec. Dir.
Founded: 1963. **Members:** 130. **Membership Dues:** corporate manufacturer, $450-$1,290 (annual) ● corporate retailer, $240-$840 (annual) ● associate, $450 (annual) ● individual, $180 (annual). **Staff:** 1. **Budget:** $150,000. **Description:** Manufacturers and suppliers of Western and English tack equipment and apparel. Provides forum for communication within the industry. Monitors legislation; gathers marketing data and manufacturing statistics for the industry. Operates speakers' bureau. **Awards:** Tradition of the American West. **Frequency:** annual. **Type:** recognition. **Telecommunication Services:** electronic mail, info@wetaonline.com. **Committees:** Awards; Computerization; Industry Information Center; Marketing; Member Services. **Formerly:** (1976) Western Apparel and Equipment Manufacturers Association; (2003) Western and English Manufacturers Association. **Publications:** *WETA Watch*, quarterly. Newsletter. Alternate Formats: online. **Conventions/Meetings:** annual All Industry Conference and Showcase - seminar, new product introduction; held in conjunction with the Western and English Retailers Association (exhibits).

260 ■ World Shoe Association (WSA)
15821 Ventura Blvd., Ste.415
Encino, CA 91436
Ph: (818)379-9400
Free: (888)62-SHOES
Fax: (818)379-9410
E-mail: accounting@wsashow.com
URL: http://www.wsashow.com
Contact: Mitch Fisherman, Pres.
Multinational. Description: Footwear executives. Aims to promote a higher standard of ethics and encourage a spirit of cooperation in the industry. Sponsors trade shows, job opportunity listings. **Conventions/Meetings:** semiannual trade show (exhibits).

261 ■ Worldwide Responsible Apparel Production (WRAP)
2200 Wilson Blvd., Ste.601
Arlington, VA 22201
Ph: (703)243-0970
Free: (877)524-9727
Fax: (703)243-8247
E-mail: info@wrapapparel.org
URL: http://www.wrapapparel.org
Contact: Steven A. Jesseph, Vice Chm./Pres./CEO
Multinational. Description: Promotes humane, ethical and lawful conditions and practices in manufacturing facilities all over the world. Grants certification to individual factories for compliance with its principles and procedures concerning issues of fair pay, workers' dignity, safe and secure conditions and environmental impact. Conducts various training programs to educate workers, factory managers, and government inspectors about issues related to global supply chains and their workers. **Publications:** Handbooks (in Chinese, English, Russian, and Spanish). Alternate Formats: online.

262 ■ Young Menswear Association (YMA)
36 W 20th St., 3rd Fl.
New York, NY 10011
Ph: (212)594-6422
Fax: (212)594-9349
E-mail: the-yma@att.net
URL: http://the-yma.com
Contact: Harry Harrison, Contact
Founded: 1937. **Members:** 650. **Staff:** 1. **Description:** Individuals associated with any aspect of the men's apparel industry. Seeks to further the interests of young people involved in the menswear industry. Raises funds to endow textile/apparel college programs. Sponsors orientation seminars; holds fashion shows at dinners and luncheons. Raises funds to endow textile and apparel college programs at selected schools. Maintains hall of fame. **Awards:** AMY Award. **Frequency:** annual. **Type:** recognition. **Recipient:** for leadership in the apparel and textile industry ● **Frequency:** annual. **Type:** recognition. **Recipient:** for apparel-related industry executives with industry citizenship record of contributions ● YMA Scholarship. **Type:** scholarship. **Recipient:** for textile and apparel students. **Telecommunication Services:** electronic mail, hharrison@ymafashionscholarshipfund.org. **Committees:** Scholarship; Scholarship Dinner Awards; Special Events; Sports Outing. **Formerly:** (1972) Young Men's Association of the Men's Apparel Industry; (1980) Young Menswear Association of Men's Apparel Industry.

Appliances

263 ■ Appliance Parts Distributors Association (APDA)
4700 W Lake Ave.
Glenview, IL 60025
Ph: (847)375-4713 (847)375-4814
Free: (800)621-0298
Fax: (866)879-7505
E-mail: apda@apda.com
URL: http://www.apda.com
Contact: Fred Lambert, Pres.
Founded: 1937. **Members:** 79. **Membership Dues:** business organization (plus $50/branch), $1,000 (annual). **Staff:** 2. **Description:** Wholesale distributors of appliance parts, supplies, and accessories. Promotes the sale of appliance parts through independent parts distributors. **Committees:** Business Control Systems; Cost of Doing Business; Manufacturers Relations; Service Training; Standardization. **Formerly:** Appliance Parts Jobbers Association. **Publications:** *Membership Roster*, periodic. Directory. **Conventions/Meetings:** semiannual conference.

264 ■ Association of Home Appliance Manufacturers (AHAM)
1111 19th St. NW, Ste.402
Washington, DC 20036
Ph: (202)872-5955
Fax: (202)872-9354
E-mail: info@aham.org
URL: http://www.aham.org
Contact: Jill A. Notini, Dir., Communications and Marketing
Founded: 1967. **Members:** 160. **Staff:** 14. **Description:** Companies manufacturing major and portable appliances; supplier members provide products and services to the appliance industry. Major areas of activity include: market research and reporting of industry statistics; development of standard methods for measuring appliance performance and certification of certain characteristics of room air conditioners, refrigerators, freezers, humidifiers, dehumidifiers, and room air cleaners; public relations and press relations. Represents the appliance industry before government at the federal, state, and local levels. **Libraries: Type:** reference. **Holdings:** archival material, audiovisuals, books, clippings, periodicals. **Subjects:** appliance industry. **Awards:** Hail Award. **Frequency:** annual. **Type:** recognition. **Recipient:** for members only. **Telecommunication Services:** electronic mail, jnotini@aham.org. **Boards:** Major Appliance Division; Portable Appliance Division. **Committees:** Appliance Recycling Information Center Advisory; Legal Operations Advisory. **Departments:** Government Relations; Marketing and International Trade. **Task Forces:** Air Cleaner Certification Promotion; Annual Meeting Advisory. **Absorbed:** (2004) Vacuum Cleaner Manufacturers Association. **Formed by Merger of:** American Home Laundry Manufacturers Association; Consumer Products Division of the National Electrical Manufacturers Association. **Publications:** *AHAM Factory Shipment Release*, monthly. Contains press release and statistics on major appliance factory shipments. **Price:** $300.00/year (via fax only). ISSN: 1072-3501. **Circulation:** 1,000 ● *AHAM Major Home Appliance Industry Factbook*. **Price:** $75.00/copy. ISSN: 1072-3579 ● *AHAM Membership Directory*, annual. **Price:** free for members; $150.00 for nonmembers. **Circulation:** 1,400 ● *Directory of Certified Dehumidifiers*, semiannual. Lists certified brands and models of dehumidifiers. Includes dehumidification selection guide for consumers. **Price:** $5.00/copy. **Circulation:** 6,000 ● *Directory of Certified Humidifiers*, semiannual. Contains a listing of AHAM-certified brands and models of humidifiers. Includes humidification selection guide for consumers. **Price:** $5.00/copy. **Circulation:** 4,500 ● *Directory of Certified Refrigerators and Freezers*, semiannual. Describes AHAM Certification Program for refrigerators and freezers; provides energy, mechanical, and storage capacity data in tabular arrangement. **Price:** $7.50/issue. **Circulation:** 6,000 ● *Directory of Certified Room Air Conditioners*, semiannual. Describes AHAM Certification Program for room air conditioners and gives data in tabular form for cooling capacity and energy requirements. **Price:** $7.50/issue. **Circulation:** 7,200 ● *MACAP Statistical Report*, annual. Contains a detailed tabular statistical report about complaints received by the MACAP concerning appliances. **Price:** free. **Circulation:** 700 ● *Trends and Forecasts*. Report. Contains trends and forecasts of domestic and export shipments of major appliances. **Conventions/Meetings:** annual meeting - always in spring.

265 ■ Gas Appliance Manufacturers Association (GAMA)
2107 Wilson Blvd., Ste.600
Arlington, VA 22201-3042
Ph: (703)525-7060
Fax: (703)525-6790
E-mail: membership@gamanet.org
URL: http://www.gamanet.org
Contact: Jack Klimp, Pres./CEO
Founded: 1935. **Members:** 240. **Membership Dues:** general associate, $1,000 (annual) ● utility associate, $1,000-$3,000 (annual). **Staff:** 20. **Description:** Composed of manufacturers of gas, oil, and electric space heating and water heating equipment for residential, commercial, and industrial applications, and associated components and accessories. Scope includes gas and oil central furnaces and boilers; gas, oil, and electric water heaters; gas space heaters; gas-fired commercial cooking equipment; gas-fired industrial heating equipment; and equipment used in the production, transmission, and distribution of natural gas. **Telecommunication Services:** electronic mail, info@gamanet.org ● electronic mail, information@gamanet.org. **Divisions:** Burner; Controls; Corrugated Stainless Steel Tubing; Direct-Fired; Direct Heating; Food Service Equipment; Fuel Cell Group; Furnace; Gas Air Conditioning; Gas Appliance Connector; Gas Detector; Gas Equipment and Services; Gas Venting Products; Hydronics Institute; Industrial Forced Air; Infrared; Instantaneous Water Heater Group; Motor and Blower; Power Generation; Relief Valve Group; Vent-Free; Water Heaters. **Absorbed:** (1967) Institute of Appliance Manufacturers. **Formerly:** (1946) Association of Gas Appliance and Equipment Manufacturers. **Publications:** *Patent Digest*, monthly. Report. Contains information on patents of interest to appliance and equipment manufacturers. **Price:** $105.00/copy ● *Statistical Highlights*, monthly. **Conventions/Meetings:** annual conference and meeting - 2009 May 16-19, Santa Ana Pueblo, NM.

266 ■ National Appliance Parts Suppliers Association (NAPSA)
c/o Sherry Harrell, Pres.
4015 W Marshall Ave.
Longview, TX 75604-4916
Ph: (903)759-3983
Free: (888)309-9676
E-mail: info@napsaweb.org
URL: http://www.napsaweb.org
Contact: Sherry Harrell, Pres.
Founded: 1966. **Members:** 250. **Membership Dues:** wholesaler/distributor, $500 (annual) ● subscriber, $450 (annual) ● manufacturers' representative, $125 (annual). **Staff:** 5. **Regional Groups:** 5. **Description:** Wholesale distributors of replacement parts for major home appliance. Promotes and supports good relations among groups in the supply and distribution of appliance service parts. Sponsors Young Executives Society of NAPSA to prepare younger generations for leadership in the appliance parts wholesale and distribution industry, and to handle problems

characteristic of family businesses. **Telecommunication Services:** electronic mail, sherry@appliancepartsco.com. **Publications:** *National Appliance Parts Suppliers Association—Membership Directory*, annual ● *National Appliance Parts Suppliers Association—Results*, quarterly. Newsletter. Alternate Formats: online. **Conventions/Meetings:** annual convention (exhibits) - always in October.

267 ■ National Appliance Service Association (NASA)
PO Box 2514
Kokomo, IN 46904
Ph: (765)453-1820
Fax: (765)453-1895
E-mail: nasahq@sbcglobal.net
URL: http://www.nasa1.org
Contact: Carrie Giannakos, Exec. Dir.

Founded: 1949. **Members:** 150. **Staff:** 1. **Description:** Owners of factory-authorized portable appliance repair centers servicing small electrical appliances and commercial food equipment. Promotes the interests and welfare of the commercial-domestic appliance service industry. **Committees:** Member Services. **Publications:** *NASA News*, monthly. Newsletter. Includes articles of interest to the independent service dealer and appliance manufacturer. **Price:** included in membership dues ● Membership Directory, annual. **Circulation:** 600. **Advertising:** accepted. **Conventions/Meetings:** annual convention, with tradeshow (exhibits).

268 ■ Vacuum Dealers Trade Association (VDTA)
2724 2nd Ave.
Des Moines, IA 50313-4933
Ph: (515)282-9101
Free: (800)367-5651
Fax: (515)282-4483
E-mail: mail@vdta.com
URL: http://www.vdta.com
Contact: Tim Devick, Membership Dir.

Founded: 1981. **Members:** 2,200. **Membership Dues:** independent retail dealer, $100 (annual) ● independent manufacturer representative/independent educator, $75 (annual) ● associate, $500 (annual). **Staff:** 11. **Budget:** $1,000,000. **Description:** Vacuum cleaner and sewing machine dealers, manufacturers, and distributors. Seeks to increase the independent vacuum cleaner and sewing machine dealer's share of the market and provide a forum for continuing education. Develops certification program for service operations; has developed code of ethics. Compiles statistics. **Libraries: Type:** reference. **Holdings:** 2,000. **Subjects:** sales, motivational, business. **Telecommunication Services:** electronic mail, tim2@vdta.com. **Publications:** *Central Vac Professional*. Magazine. Provides advertising opportunities for manufacturers, suppliers, and distributors wanting to reach the retail floor care and home sewing market. Alternate Formats: online ● *Floor Care Professional*. Magazine. Features current industry news, business tips and new product development. Alternate Formats: online ● *Phone Directory and Product Guide*, annual. **Advertising:** accepted ● *Sewing and Embroidery Professional*. Magazine. Features home sewing, embroidery, quilting, notions and accessories dealer. ● *VDTA News*, monthly. Magazine. Features association and industry news. **Price:** free. **Circulation:** 20,000. **Advertising:** accepted. **Conventions/Meetings:** annual convention and show ● annual Floor Care and Sewing Professional Regional Summer Show - show and seminar (exhibits) - July or August ● annual meeting (exhibits).

Appraisers

269 ■ Accredited Review Appraisers Council (ARAC)
303 W Cypress St.
San Antonio, TX 78212
Free: (800)486-3676
Fax: (210)225-8450
E-mail: djd@lincoln-grad.org
URL: http://arac.lincoln-grad.org
Contact: Deborah J. Deane, Contact

Founded: 1987. **Members:** 400. **Membership Dues:** association, candidate, $50 (annual). **Staff:** 18. **Description:** Individuals interested or involved in real estate who seek to advance the profession of appraisal review. Establishes standards for review and accuracy in appraisal of real estate properties. Assists in curriculum development. Researches federal and state regulations affecting the industry. Provides a forum for the exchange of information and ideas. Grants the designation of Accredited in Appraisal Review to an individual who has successfully completed the required education and appraisal report, and has maintained a code of ethics. Conducts educational programs. **Awards:** Accredited in Appraisal Review. **Type:** recognition. **Recipient:** for an individual who has successfully completed the required education and appraisal report. **Computer Services:** database. **Committees:** Code of Ethics; Education; Standards. **Publications:** *Accredited Review Appraiser*, quarterly. Newsletter. Covers federal legislation and other issues. **Price:** free for members. **Circulation:** 1,000. Alternate Formats: online ● *The Registry*, annual. Membership Directory. Alternate Formats: online. **Conventions/Meetings:** annual conference (exhibits).

270 ■ American Academy of State Certified Appraisers (AASCA)
1438-F W Main St.
Ephrata, PA 17522-1345
Ph: (717)721-3500
Free: (800)640-7601
Fax: (717)721-3515
E-mail: info@intercorpinc.net
Contact: John J. Matternas, Exec. Dir.

Founded: 1991. **Members:** 4,500. **Membership Dues:** regular, $125 (annual). **Staff:** 2. **Description:** Works to advance the interests of state certified real estate appraisers. **Publications:** Newsletter, quarterly. **Advertising:** accepted.

271 ■ American Society of Agricultural Appraisers (ASAA)
PO Box 186
Twin Falls, ID 83303-0186
Ph: (208)733-2323
Free: (800)488-7570
Fax: (208)733-2326
E-mail: ag@amagappraisers.com
URL: http://www.amagappraisers.com
Contact: Jay Proost, Exec. Dir.

Founded: 1980. **Members:** 784. **Membership Dues:** individual, $395 (annual). **Staff:** 5. **Budget:** $300,000. **For-Profit. Description:** Appraisers of livestock, farm equipment, and other agricultural properties, supplies, and products. Promotes adherence to high standards of ethics and practice in the field of agricultural appraising. Sponsors educational programs. **Publications:** *The Appraiser*. Handbook. Serves as a guide for a successful career in the appraisal business. **Price:** included in membership dues. **Conventions/Meetings:** periodic seminar.

272 ■ American Society of Appraisers (ASA)
555 Herndon Pkwy., Ste.125
Herndon, VA 20170
Ph: (703)478-2228
Free: (800)ASA-VALU
Fax: (703)742-8471
E-mail: asainfo@appraisers.org
URL: http://www.appraisers.org
Contact: Laurie M. Saunders, Exec. VP

Founded: 1952. **Members:** 6,000. **Membership Dues:** student affiliate, $60 ● affiliate, $200 ● affiliate in Canada, $175 ● individual, $390 ● individual in Canada, $320. **Staff:** 30. **Budget:** $4,000,000. **Local Groups:** 83. **Description:** Professional appraisal educator, testing, and accrediting society. Sponsors mandatory recertification program for all members. Offers a consumer information service to the public. **Libraries: Type:** reference. **Subjects:** appraisal. **Telecommunication Services:** electronic mail, laurie@appraisers.org. **Programs:** Principles of Valuation Courses. **Sections:** Appraisal Review and Management; Business Valuation; Gems and Jewelry; Machinery/Technical Specialties; Personal Property; Real Property. **Absorbed:** Association of Governmental Appraisers. **Formed by Merger of:** American Society of Technical Appraisers; Technical Valuation Society. **Publications:** *ASA Professional Magazine*, quarterly. **Price:** free for members ● *Business Valuation Review*, quarterly. Journal. **Price:** $50.00 /year for nonmembers; $45.00 for members in U.S.; $60.00 for members outside U.S. ISSN: 0882-2875 ● *Directory of Professional Appraisal Services*, annual ● *The MTS Journal*, quarterly. **Price:** $40.00 for nonmembers; $25.00 for members. ISSN: 0897-960X ● *Personal Property Journal*, quarterly. **Price:** $35.00 for nonmembers; $25.00 for members ● *Real Property Journal*, 3/year. **Price:** $30.00/year ● Audiotapes ● Monographs ● Many additional appraisal-related publications; call (703)478-2228 for a publications catalog or an educational catalog. **Conventions/Meetings:** annual International Appraisal Conference (exhibits) - 2008 Aug. 3-6, Minneapolis, MN.

273 ■ American Society of Farm Equipment Appraisers (ASFEA)
PO Box 186
Twin Falls, ID 83303-0186
Ph: (208)733-2323
Free: (800)488-7570
Fax: (208)733-2326
E-mail: farm@amagappraisers.com
URL: http://www.amagappraisers.com/farmeqip.htm

Founded: 1984. **Members:** 600. **Staff:** 5. **Budget:** $300,000. **Description:** Professional appraisers of farm equipment. Seeks to establish and maintain standards of ethics, practice, and training in the field of farm equipment appraising. Recruits individuals with expertise in judging the value of farm equipment; bestows certification to qualified individuals; provides training and performance criteria to aspiring farm equipment appraisers.

274 ■ American Society of Farm Managers and Rural Appraisers (ASFMRA)
950 S Cherry St., Ste.508
Denver, CO 80246-2664
Ph: (303)758-3513
Fax: (303)758-0190
E-mail: info@asfmra.org
URL: http://www.asfmra.org
Contact: Ray L. Brownfield, Pres.

Founded: 1929. **Members:** 2,500. **Membership Dues:** accredited, $520 (annual) ● professional, $415 (annual) ● candidate/associate, $350 (annual) ● affiliate, $240 (annual) ● academic, $180 (annual) ● student, $25 (annual) ● inactive, $80 (annual) ● retired, $145 (annual). **Staff:** 12. **Budget:** $1,400,000. **State Groups:** 37. **Description:** Professional farm managers, appraisers, lenders, consultants, educators and researchers in farm and ranch management and/or rural appraisal. Bestows registered ARA (Accredited Rural Appraiser), Accredited Agricultural Consultant (ACC), AFM (Accredited Farm Manager) and RPRA (Real Property Review Appraiser) designations. Operates management and appraisal schools, Internet course offerings. Maintains placement service. **Libraries: Type:** reference. **Holdings:** archival material. **Awards:** D. Howard Doane Award. **Frequency:** annual. **Type:** recognition. **Recipient:** to a person who has contributed to agriculture and the agricultural profession ● Distinguished Service in Agriculture. **Frequency:** annual. **Type:** recognition. **Recipient:** for distinguished service to agriculture other than directly in the farm management and rural appraisal professions ● Meritorious Service in Communications. **Frequency:** annual. **Type:** recognition. **Recipient:** for individuals, company, or association in communications who promoted goodwill between producers and consumers of agricultural products. **Computer Services:** database, records and publication, qualified appraisers and farm managers. **Committees:** Accrediting; Appraisal Education; Appraisal Review; Awards; Continuing Education; Crop Talk; Editorial; Ethics; Government Relations; Management Education; Membership Recruitment/Retention;

Membership Services; Public Relations. **Affiliated With:** American Society of Agricultural Consultants; American Society of Appraisers; Appraisal Institute; Appraisal Institute of Canada; International Association of Assessing Officers; International Right of Way Association; National Alliance of Independent Crop Consultants; National Association of Independent Fee Appraisers; National Association of Master Appraisers. **Formerly:** (1936) American Society of Farm Managers. **Publications:** *American Society of Farm Managers and Rural Appraisers-General Membership Directory*, annual. **Price:** included in membership dues. Alternate Formats: online ● *Appraisal of Rural Property, 2nd Edition*. Manual. **Price:** $54.00 for members; $59.00 for nonmembers ● *Appraising Easements, 3rd Edition*. Manual. **Price:** $30.00 for members; $35.00 for nonmembers ● *The Dictionary of Real Estate Appraisal, 4th Edition*. Manual. **Price:** $70.00 for members; $80.00 for nonmembers ● *Farm Management Manual* ● *FMRA News*, bimonthly. Newsletter. **Price:** $24.00 ● *Journal of the American Society of Farm Managers and Rural Appraisers*, annual. **Price:** included in membership dues; $24.00 /year for nonmembers ● *Minerals Appraisal Symposium Proceedings*. Manual. **Price:** $95.00 each ● *Real Estate Valuation in Litigation, 2nd Edition*. Manual. **Price:** $44.00 for members; $48.00 for nonmembers. **Conventions/Meetings:** annual meeting (exhibits) ● seminar.

275 ■ Appraisal Institute (AI)
HQ Off.
550 W Van Buren St., Ste.1000
Chicago, IL 60607
Ph: (312)335-4100
Fax: (312)335-4400
E-mail: info@appraisalinstitute.org
URL: http://www.appraisalinstitute.org
Contact: Fred Grubbe, CEO

Founded: 1991. **Members:** 21,000. **Membership Dues:** associate, $310 (annual) ● affiliate, $190 (annual) ● student affiliate, $50 (annual). **Staff:** 100. **Regional Groups:** 10. **State Groups:** 102. **Description:** General appraisers who hold the MAI designation, and residential members who hold the SRA designation. Enforces Code of Professional Ethics and Standards of Professional Appraisal Practice. Confers one general designation, the MAI, and one residential designation, the SRA. Provides training in valuation of residential and income properties, market analysis, and standards of professional appraisal practice. Sponsors courses in preparation for state certification and licensing; offers continuing education programs for designated members. **Libraries: Type:** reference. **Holdings:** 1,800; books, monographs, periodicals. **Subjects:** real estate appraisal. **Awards:** Appraisal Institute Education Trust Scholarship. **Type:** scholarship. **Recipient:** for individuals concentrating in real estate appraisal, land economics, real estate or allied fields ● Minority and Women Scholarships. **Type:** scholarship. **Recipient:** for minority and women college students pursuing academic degrees in real estate appraisal or related fields. **Computer Services:** database ● online services. **Telecommunication Services:** electronic mail, information@appraisalinstitute.org. **Committees:** Political Action. **Formed by Merger of:** (1991) American Institute of Real Estate Appraisers; Society of Real Estate Appraisers. **Publications:** *Appraisal Institute Directory of Designated Members*, annual. Membership Directory. **Price:** free. **Circulation:** 30,000. **Advertising:** accepted. Alternate Formats: CD-ROM; online ● *The Appraisal Journal*, quarterly. **Price:** free for members; $48.00 for nonmembers. Alternate Formats: online. Also Cited As: *TAJ* ● *The Appraisal of Real Estate, 12th Edition*, quarterly. Book. **Price:** $60.00 for members; $70.00 for nonmembers ● *Appraiser News in Brief*, 8/year. Newsletter. **Price:** free for members; $30.00/year for students; $35.00 /year for nonmembers ● *Appraising Residential Property, 3rd Edition*, 8/year. Newsletter. **Price:** $44.00 for members; $48.00 for nonmembers ● *The Dictionary of Real Estate Appraisal, 4th Edition*. Book. **Price:** $70.00 for members; $80.00 for nonmembers. Alternate Formats: CD-ROM ● *Education Catalog*, annual. **Price:** free for members; $30.00/year for students; $35.00 /year for nonmembers ● *MarketSource*, quarterly. Catalog. **Price:** $100.00 /year for members and affiliates; $150.00 /year for nonmembers ● *Products and Services Catalog*, annual. Magazine. **Price:** free ● *Real Estate Valuation in Litigation, 2nd Edition*, annual. Catalog. **Price:** $44.00 for members; $48.00 for nonmembers ● *Valuation Insights and Perspectives*, quarterly. Magazine. **Price:** free for members; $30.00/year for students; $35.00 /year for nonmembers. **Conventions/Meetings:** semiannual conference and seminar (exhibits) - June and December.

276 ■ Appraisers Association of America (AAA)
386 Park Ave. S, 20th Fl., Ste.2000
New York, NY 10016
Ph: (212)889-5404
Fax: (212)889-5503
E-mail: aaa@appraisersassoc.org
URL: http://www.appraisersassoc.org
Contact: Aleya Lehmann, Exec. Dir.

Founded: 1949. **Members:** 800. **Membership Dues:** basic, certified, $525 (annual) ● student affiliate, $75 (annual) ● friend, $100 (annual). **Staff:** 4. **Budget:** $500,000. **Regional Groups:** 9. **Description:** Professional society of appraisers of personal property such as: Americana; antiques; armor; art objects; bibelot; books; bronzes; china and porcelain; clocks and watches; coins; crystal and glass; curios; diamonds and jewelry; enamels; etchings; fine art; firearms; furniture; furs; graphic art; guns; household furnishings; ivories; leather goods; lighting fixtures; linens and lace; miniatures; music; musical instruments; oriental art; paintings; pewter; pianos; primitive art; prints; rugs; sculpture; Sheffield plate; silver and silverware; stamps; steins and tankards; taxes; and woodcarvings. **Libraries: Type:** reference. **Holdings:** books, periodicals. **Subjects:** personal property, auction records. **Telecommunication Services:** electronic mail, appraisers@appraisersassoc.org. **Publications:** *The Appraiser*, quarterly. Newsletter. **Price:** $90.00/year. ISSN: 1080-1510. **Circulation:** 2,000 ● *Appraisers Association of America—Membership Directory*, biennial. **Conventions/Meetings:** monthly lecture.

277 ■ Association of Machinery and Equipment Appraisers (AMEA)
315 S Patrick St.
Alexandria, VA 22314
Ph: (703)836-7900
Free: (800)537-8629
Fax: (703)836-9303
E-mail: amea@amea.org
URL: http://www.amea.org
Contact: John S. Greene CEA, Pres.

Founded: 1983. **Members:** 285. **Membership Dues:** regular, $395 (annual) ● associate, $600 (annual). **Staff:** 2. **Budget:** $120,000. **Description:** Accredited and certified appraisers of metalworking, woodworking, chemical, and food processing machinery and equipment. Allows persons and industries such as finance and insurance companies and machinery owners needing appraisals to deal directly with accredited appraisers. Accredits professional appraisers meeting the association's standards of ethics and proficiency in evaluation procedures. **Telecommunication Services:** electronic mail, jgreene@fl-sales.com. **Publications:** *AMEA Appraiser*, quarterly. Newsletter. **Price:** free. **Circulation:** 5,000. Alternate Formats: online ● *Standards and Procedures of Professional Appraisal Ethics and Practice*, annual. **Price:** free ● Membership Directory, annual. **Price:** free. **Circulation:** 10,000.

278 ■ Collector Car Appraisers Association (CCAA)
Address Unknown since 2008

Founded: 1980. **Members:** 25. **Staff:** 2. **Description:** Licensed and bonded individuals with at least ten years' experience in dealing with antique, classic, and special interest collector cars. Certifies members to act as expert witnesses in lawsuits and arbitration; recommends car appraisers who determine the value of the car and the cost and value of rebuilding. Plans to provide referral services to persons interested in restoring cars. **Libraries: Type:** reference. **Holdings:** 3,740; archival material, books, photographs.

279 ■ Equipment Appraisers Association of North America (EAANA)
1270 State Rte. 30
Clinton, PA 15026
Free: (800)790-1053
Fax: (724)899-2001
E-mail: mail@eaana.org
URL: http://www.eaana.org
Contact: Valerie Rakowski, Admin. Sec.

Founded: 1990. **Members:** 120. **Membership Dues:** associate, $100 (annual) ● Certified Senior Appraiser, candidate, $250 (annual). **Multinational. Description:** Provides a professional appraisal society representing all aspects of the machinery and equipment industries. Seeks to establish and maintain standards of ethics, practice and training in the field of equipment appraising. Complies with the Uniform Standards of Professional Appraisal Practice (USPAP). **Publications:** Newsletter. Alternate Formats: online.

280 ■ Foundation of Real Estate Appraisers (FREA)
4907 Morena Blvd., No. 1415
San Diego, CA 92117
Free: (800)882-4410
Fax: (858)273-8026
E-mail: info@frea.com
URL: http://www.frea.com

Founded: 1991. **Members:** 10,000. **Membership Dues:** appraiser, $850-$895 (annual) ● home inspector, $2,995-$3,295 (annual). **Description:** Represents real estate appraisers and home inspectors. **Computer Services:** database, National Data Collective. **Publications:** *The Communicator*, quarterly. Magazine. **Price:** free. **Circulation:** 125,000. **Advertising:** accepted.

281 ■ Independent Automotive Damage Appraisers Association (IADA)
PO Box 12291
Columbus, GA 31917-2291
Free: (800)369-4232
Fax: (888)IADA-NOW
E-mail: admin@iada.org
URL: http://www.iada.org
Contact: John Williams, Exec. VP

Founded: 1947. **Members:** 108. **Staff:** 2. **Budget:** $2,000,000. **Regional Groups:** 5. **State Groups:** 46. **Description:** Professional automobile damage appraisal firms that evaluate damaged automobiles for insurance companies, self-insured fleets, and rental car companies. Seeks to establish professional standards and to facilitate the exchange of information on automobile appraisals techniques and repairs technology. **Programs:** 20-Point Appraisal. **Publications:** *IADA Service Directory*, annual. Lists automotive service locations nationwide. **Price:** free. **Circulation:** 9,000. **Advertising:** accepted. Alternate Formats: online. **Conventions/Meetings:** annual seminar (exhibits) ● annual Vehicle Repair Conference.

282 ■ Institute of Business Appraisers (IBA)
PO Box 17410
Plantation, FL 33318
Ph: (954)584-1144
Fax: (954)584-1184
E-mail: ibahq@go-iba.org
URL: http://www.go-iba.org
Contact: Michelle G. Miles Esq., Exec. Dir.

Founded: 1978. **Members:** 3,000. **Membership Dues:** individual, $395 (annual). **Staff:** 9. **Budget:** $500,000. **Regional Groups:** 7. **Local Groups:** 3. **Description:** Individuals involved or with interested in the practice of business valuation and appraisal. Seeks to educate the public in matters relating to business valuation and appraisal; to support legislation establishing minimum standards of competence for persons offering these services; to promulgate a code of ethics for all members to observe. Conducts advancement programs that include the awards of the professional designation's Certified Business Appraiser (CBA) and Business Valuator Accredited in Litigation to qualifying members. Maintains referral program and Speaker's Bureau; compiles statistics. Offers educational programs. **Libraries: Type:** reference. **Holdings:** 17,000; archival material, articles, books, clippings, monographs, periodicals. **Subjects:** business appraisal. **Computer Services:** Bibliographic search, business valuation ● database, market ● mailing lists. **Caucuses:** Atlanta BV; St. Louis BV. **Divisions:** CPA. **Publications:** *Basic Business Appraisal*. Features a self-study course. ● *Business Appraisal Practice*, semiannual. Journal. **Price:** $60.00 for members; $90.00 for nonmembers ● *IBA Applicants Handbook*. **Price:** $20.00 for members; $35.00 for nonmembers ● *Institute of Business Appraisers—Newsletter*, quarterly. Covers association and industry news. Alternate Formats: online ● Monographs ● Audiotapes ● Distributes workbooks. **Conventions/Meetings:** annual conference (exhibits) ● seminar.

283 ■ International Society of Appraisers (ISA)
1131 SW 7th St., Ste.105
Renton, WA 98055
Ph: (206)241-0359
Free: (888)472-4732
Fax: (206)241-0436
E-mail: isa@isa-appraisers.org
URL: http://www.isa-appraisers.org
Contact: Jorge N. Sever, Exec. Dir.
Founded: 1979. **Members:** 1,400. **Membership Dues:** individual, $400 (annual). **Staff:** 8. **Budget:** $980,000. **State Groups:** 17. **Description:** Represents personal property appraisers. Seeks to provide the public with a network of appraisal specialists who have been pre-screened by ISA. Conducts educational opportunities for members, the consumer public, and other affinity groups. Offers Certified Appraiser of Personal Property Program, education, testing, and certification program. Compiles statistics; maintains speakers' bureau. Offers free appraisal referral service in the U.S. and Canada. **Awards:** Media Award. **Frequency:** annual. **Type:** recognition. **Recipient:** for an article promoting professionals in appraising. **Computer Services:** database, appraiser referral service ● database, member ● mailing lists, of members. **Telecommunication Services:** electronic mail, isaed@isa-appraisers.org. **Committees:** Antiques and Residential Contents; Appraisal Studies; Awards; Conference; Designation and Review; Electronic Information Service; Ethics; Fine Art; Gems and Jewelry; Machinery and Equipment; Nominating; Public Relations; Scholarship; Specialty Studies. **Publications:** *ISA Professional Appraisers Information Exchange*. Newsletter. **Price:** $1.00. **Circulation:** 2,500. **Advertising:** accepted. Alternate Formats: online ● Membership Directory, annual. Contains a list of members with specialty, city-state, zip code, and company indexes. **Price:** $15.00. **Circulation:** 1,600. **Advertising:** accepted. **Conventions/Meetings:** annual International Conference on Personal Property Appraising - meeting, materials and service pertaining to appraising (exhibits).

284 ■ National Association of Independent Fee Appraisers (NAIFA)
401 N Michigan Ave., Ste.2200
Chicago, IL 60611
Ph: (312)321-6830
Fax: (312)673-6652
E-mail: info@naifa.com
URL: http://www.naifa.com
Contact: Oliver Yandle CAE, Exec. VP
Founded: 1961. **Members:** 4,000. **Membership Dues:** affiliate, $195 (annual) ● associate, $245 (annual) ● candidate, $325 (annual) ● regular, ADP, $475 (annual). **Staff:** 18. **Budget:** $2,000,000. **Regional Groups:** 9. **State Groups:** 50. **Local Groups:** 200. **Description:** Appraisers for real estate groups, savings and loan associations, title insurance groups, governmental agencies, and related industries. Raises the standards of the appraisal profession. Sponsors career training and professional development programs. Conducts general and applied research in real estate and related fields. **Libraries: Type:** reference. **Subjects:** real estate appraisal. **Telecommunication Services:** electronic mail, oliver_yandle@naifa.com. **Commissions:** National Education. **Publications:** *Appraiser-Gram*, quarterly. Newsletter. Covers association activities as well as developments in the real estate appraisal industry. Includes association course schedule. **Price:** free for members. **Circulation:** 5,000 ● *National Convention Proceedings*, annual ● *Technical Manual*, periodic ● Membership Directory, annual. Includes recertification status of members and chapter affiliation. **Price:** free for members. **Circulation:** 5,000 ● Also publishes workbooks.

285 ■ National Association of Real Estate Appraisers (NAREA)
1224 N Nokomis NE
Alexandria, MN 56308
Ph: (320)763-7626
Fax: (320)763-9290
E-mail: narea@iami.org
URL: http://www.iami.org
Contact: Robert G. Johnson, Exec. Dir.
Founded: 1966. **Members:** 10,000. **Membership Dues:** CREA designation, CVC designation, RPM designation, $195 (annual) ● CCRA designation, $245 (annual) ● CREA and CCRA dual designation, $295 (annual) ● CLAT designation, affiliate, $95 (annual). **Budget:** $3,000,000. **Description:** Real estate appraisers. Aims to make available the services of the most highly qualified real estate appraisers. Offers certification to members. **Libraries: Type:** not open to the public. **Holdings:** 752; books. **Subjects:** real estate. **Awards:** Appraiser of the Year. **Frequency:** annual. **Type:** recognition. **Recipient:** for real estate appraisers. **Computer Services:** database ● mailing lists ● online services. **Publications:** *The Appraisal Times*, bimonthly. Newsletter. **Price:** $29.50. **Advertising:** accepted. Alternate Formats: online ● *NAREA Real Estate Appraisal Newsletter*, bimonthly ● *National Association of Real Estate Appraisers—Directory of Designated Members*, annual ● Books. **Conventions/Meetings:** annual conference (exhibits) - always October in Las Vegas, NV.

286 ■ National Society of Appraiser Specialists (NSAS)
303 W Cypress St.
PO Box 12528
San Antonio, TX 78212-0528
Ph: (210)271-0781 (210)225-2897
Free: (800)486-3676
Fax: (210)225-8450
URL: http://pcb.lincoln-grad.org
Contact: Rachel Phelps, Exec. Dir.
Founded: 1988. **Members:** 1,200. **Membership Dues:** associate, $55 (annual). **Staff:** 4. **Description:** Works to provide information, education and board certification in three appraisal specialties: manufactured housing valuation, business valuation and expert witness. **Libraries: Type:** not open to the public. **Holdings:** 800. **Subjects:** real estate, appraisals, environmental. **Computer Services:** database. **Publications:** *The Agenda*, quarterly. Newsletter. **Circulation:** 2,500. **Conventions/Meetings:** annual National Education Conference (exhibits).

287 ■ Professional Women's Appraisal Association (PWAA)
1224 N Nokomis NE
Alexandria, MN 56308-5072
Ph: (320)763-7626
Fax: (320)763-9290
Contact: Deborah S. Johnson, Exec. Dir.
Founded: 1986. **Members:** 1,424. **Membership Dues:** individual, $195 (annual). **Staff:** 6. **Budget:** $192,000. **Regional Groups:** 8. **Description:** Women appraisers in government agencies and national banks; independent professional appraisers. Provides a support system for women real estate appraisers. Offers continuing education classes in appraisal trends, technical methods, and legislation regarding the appraisal industry. Conducts research; maintains library. **Computer Services:** Mailing lists, membership. **Affiliated With:** National Association of Real Estate Appraisers. **Publications:** *The Woman Appraiser*, monthly. Newsletter. **Conventions/Meetings:** annual conference (exhibits).

Architecture

288 ■ American Institute of Architecture Students (AIAS)
1735 New York Ave. NW
Washington, DC 20006
Ph: (202)626-7472
Fax: (202)626-7414
E-mail: mailbox@aias.org
URL: http://www.aias.org
Contact: Michael V. Geary CAE, Exec. Dir.
Membership Dues: student, $45 (annual) ● individual affiliate in U.S., $60 (annual) ● high school affiliate in U.S., $20 (annual) ● individual affiliate outside U.S., $90 (annual) ● high school affiliate outside U.S., $40 (annual). **Description:** Promotes excellence in architecture education, training and practice. **Publications:** *Crit*, semiannual. Magazine. Presents information devoted to the work and critical thoughts of architecture students. **Price:** $25.00 /year for libraries in U.S. and Canada; $100.00 /year for libraries outside U.S. and Canada. **Circulation:** 6,200. **Advertising:** accepted. **Conventions/Meetings:** annual convention.

289 ■ American Society of Architectural Illustrators (ASAI)
3301 N Garden Ln.
Avondale, AZ 85392
Ph: (623)433-8782
Fax: (623)444-7420
E-mail: hq@asai.org
URL: http://www.asai.org
Contact: Ms. Tamara Prezioso, Exec. Dir.
Founded: 1986. **Members:** 500. **Membership Dues:** individual in North America, $170 (annual) ● individual overseas, $205 (annual) ● student, $35 (annual) ● firm, $300 (annual). **Multinational. Description:** Aims to foster communication among architectural illustrators. Raises the standards of architectural illustration and acquaints the public with the importance of such drawing as integral to the practice of architecture. **Awards:** Best Formal Drawing Award. **Type:** recognition ● Best Sketch Drawing Award. **Type:** recognition ● Hugh Ferriss Memorial Prize. **Type:** recognition ● Juror's Awards. **Type:** recognition. **Publications:** *Architecture in Perspective*, annual. Book. Features selected entries from the Architecture In Perspective Exhibition. **Price:** $30.00. **Conventions/Meetings:** annual Architecture In Perspective - competition, held at the annual convention (exhibits) ● annual convention, with banquet, seminars, discussion groups, sketch tours.

290 ■ Association of Licensed Architects (ALA)
PO Box 687
Barrington, IL 60011-0687
Ph: (847)382-0630
Fax: (847)382-8380
E-mail: ala@licensedarchitect.org
URL: http://www.licensedarchitect.org
Contact: Steven Pate FALA, Pres.
Founded: 1999. **Membership Dues:** professional, $80 (annual) ● senior (over 65 years old), $50 (annual) ● affiliate, $100 (annual) ● associate, $50 (annual) ● student, $15 (annual) ● Europe, $30 (annual) ● Far East, $35 (annual). **Multinational. Description:** Seeks to advance the architectural profession through education. Supports and improves the profession's role in the built environment. Aims to adress the critical issues confronting the architectural profession. **Computer Services:** Information services, job postings. **Telecommunication Services:** electronic mail, spate@ruckpate.com. **Publications:** *Licensed Architect*, quarterly. Magazine. **Circulation:** 6,500.

291 ■ Association for Women in Architecture (AWA)
22815 Frampton Ave.
Torrance, CA 90501-5034
Ph: (310)534-8466

Fax: (310)257-6885
E-mail: president@awa-la.org
URL: http://www.awa-la.org
Contact: Kate Svoboda-Spanbock, Pres.
Founded: 1922. **Members:** 180. **Membership Dues:** professional, associate, $60 (annual) ● member at large, intern, student, retired, $30 (annual). **Description:** Promotes the position of women in architecture and related fields. Provides support to its members, especially those starting out in their professions and running their own firms, by developing educational programs, lectures and tours, and by providing opportunities for mentoring and mutual support. **Awards:** AWA Scholarship Awards. **Frequency:** annual. **Type:** scholarship. **Recipient:** for students studying architecture; must be residents of California. **Committees:** Book Salon; Career Counseling - Mentoring; Exhibits - Special Projects; Newsletter; Programs - Architectural Tours - Publicity - Public Relations; Ways and Means. **Programs:** Scholarship. **Publications:** Membership Directory, annual. **Price:** included in membership dues ● Newsletter, quarterly. **Price:** included in membership dues. **Conventions/Meetings:** monthly Educational Programs - meeting, with speakers ● annual party - every first Saturday in December.

292 ■ Council of Latin-American Students of Architecture (CLEAUSA)
7500 Glenoaks Blvd.
Burbank, CA 91510
Ph: (818)513-5372
Fax: (818)352-2253
E-mail: cleausa@vaxb.woodbury.edu
URL: http://www.geocities.com/~cleausa
Contact: Guillermo Honles, Pres.
Founded: 1994. **Members:** 50. **Staff:** 20. **Languages:** English, Spanish. **Multinational. Description:** Represents architectural students of Latin American heritage. Promotes Latin American culture.

293 ■ Graham Foundation
4 W Burton Pl.
Chicago, IL 60610-1416
Ph: (312)787-4071
E-mail: info@grahamfoundation.org
URL: http://www.grahamfoundation.org
Contact: Roberta Feldman, Pres.
Founded: 1956. **Staff:** 6. **Description:** Works to support efforts relating to architecture. Hosts lectures and exhibitions. **Awards:** Carter H. Manny Award. **Frequency:** annual. **Type:** grant. **Recipient:** for academic dissertations by promising scholars who are presently candidates for a doctoral degree ● Graham Foundation Grant. **Frequency:** periodic. **Type:** grant. **Recipient:** for institutions and individuals who support activities that focus on architecture and the built environment.

Archives

294 ■ Academy of Certified Archivists (ACA)
90 State St., Ste.1009
Albany, NY 12207
Ph: (518)463-8644
Fax: (518)463-8656
E-mail: aca@caphill.com
URL: http://www.certifiedarchivists.org
Contact: Judith G. Cetina PhD, Pres.
Founded: 1989. **Membership Dues:** $50 (annual). **Description:** Supports and promotes standards of professional archival practice; defines the knowledge and abilities necessary to be an archivist and achieve certification; promotes the employment of Certified Archivists. **Publications:** *ACA News*. Newsletter. **Price:** free ● *Handbook for Archival Certification*. Alternate Formats: online ● Membership Directory. Alternate Formats: online.

Art

295 ■ American Art Deco Dealers Association (AADDA)
PO Box 2454
Cordova, TN 38088-2454
E-mail: aadda@bellsouth.net
URL: http://www.aadda.org
Membership Dues: regular, $100 (annual) ● associate, $50 (annual). **Description:** Establishes confidence between the members and the public in buying, trading and selling of art deco and art nouveau collectibles. Promotes the interest of the art deco and art nouveau collectible trade. **Committees:** Charitable Activities; Events; Fundraising; Professional Standards and Ethics.

296 ■ Antique Tribal Art Dealers Association (ATADA)
215 Sierra SE
Albuquerque, NM 87108
Ph: (415)863-3173
Fax: (415)431-1939
E-mail: acek33@aol.com
URL: http://www.atada.org
Contact: Alice Kaufman, Exec. Dir.
Founded: 1988. **Description:** Represents individuals interested in antiques and art objects. Ensures that objects have been properly acquired and fall within the restrictions of laws concerning cultural sensitivity.

297 ■ Art and Antique Dealers League of America (AADLA)
1040 Madison Ave.
New York, NY 10021
Ph: (212)879-7558
Fax: (212)772-7197
E-mail: secretary@artantiquedealersleague.com
URL: http://www.artantiquedealersleague.com
Contact: Robert Israel, Pres.
Founded: 1926. **Members:** 94. **Staff:** 1. **Description:** Represents retailers and wholesalers of antiques and art objects. **Convention/Meeting:** none. **Formerly:** Antique and Decorative Arts League. **Publications:** Membership Directory, triennial. **Price:** free for members.

298 ■ Art Dealers Association of America (ADAA)
575 Madison Ave.
New York, NY 10022
Ph: (212)940-8590
Fax: (212)940-6484
E-mail: adaa@artdealers.org
URL: http://www.artdealers.org
Contact: Roland J. Augustine, Pres.
Founded: 1962. **Members:** 162. **Staff:** 5. **Description:** Art dealers united to promote the highest standards of connoisseurship, scholarship, and ethical practice within the profession and to increase public awareness of the role and responsibilities of reputable art dealers. Works with museums and scholars on activities and problems of mutual concern; cooperates with domestic and international government agencies on art matters and offers assistance and expertise to these agencies; advises on legislation and other governmental activity regarding the fine arts; seeks to identify and remove fake works of art from the marketplace. Appraises, for tax purposes only, works of art donated to nonprofit institutions. **Formerly:** (1962) National Association of Fine Art Dealers. **Publications:** *Art Dealers Association of America Directory*, annual. Membership Directory. Contains list of members and activities. **Price:** free.

299 ■ International Guild of Glass Artists (IGGA)
c/o Katherine Bell, Membership Dir.
4735 Waverly Ln.
Jacksonville, FL 32210
Fax: (904)388-4213
E-mail; jpreston43@cfl.rr.com
URL: http://www.igga.org
Contact: John Emery, Chm.
Founded: 1993. **Membership Dues:** regular, in U.S., $25-$150 (annual) ● regular, in Canada and Mexico, $30-$175 (annual) ● international, $40-$195 (annual). **Multinational. Description:** Represents the interests of artists, artisans, and craftspeople who work with glass as a crafts and art medium. Promotes public appreciation and understanding of glass art. Represents members on questions affecting their financial, commercial, and industrial interests. **Computer Services:** database, members by location. **Publications:** *Common Ground: Glass*, quarterly. Newsletter. Contains technical information and the latest IGGA news.

300 ■ National Antique and Art Dealers Association of America (NAADAA)
220 E 57th St.
New York, NY 10022
Ph: (212)826-9707
Fax: (212)832-9493
E-mail: inquiries@naadaa.org
URL: http://www.naadaa.org
Contact: Leon J. Dalva, Pres.
Founded: 1954. **Members:** 40. **Description:** Art and antique dealers who handle antiques and works of art of the highest quality. Safeguards the interests of those who buy, sell, and collect antiques and works of art. Sponsors periodic exhibitions; maintains speakers' bureau. **Libraries: Type:** not open to the public. **Subjects:** antiques, arts. **Publications:** Membership Directory, annual.

301 ■ National Association of Artists and Crafters (NAAC)
c/o Founding Comm.
8630-M Guilford Rd.
PMB No. 300
Columbia, MD 21046
Ph: (410)744-2296
E-mail: info@nationalaac.org
URL: http://www.nationalaac.org
Contact: M. Blacker, Exec. Dir.
Membership Dues: artisan, $65 (annual) ● artisan, $115 (biennial) ● associate, $85 (annual) ● associate, $150 (biennial). **Description:** Seeks to protect the work, creativity, livelihood and marketing rights of artists and crafters. Advocates for the passage of a National Arts and Crafts Act. Promotes the establishment of a standardized set of ethics and standards for use by all promoters and event organizers. Promotes the right of artists to protect copyrighted products or goods from fraudulent sources such as retailers and "arts and crafts vendors". **Computer Services:** Information services, evaluating promoters ● information services, legal issues and national legislation. **Publications:** *The Artisan World*, quarterly. Newsletter.

302 ■ Private Art Dealers Association (PADA)
PO Box 872, Lenox Hill Sta.
New York, NY 10021
Ph: (212)572-0772
Fax: (212)572-8398
E-mail: pada99@msn.com
URL: http://www.pada.net
Contact: Robert Dance, Pres.
Founded: 1990. **Languages:** English, French, Spanish. **Description:** Qualified art dealers. Offers fine art appraisal service that provides tax valuations for estate purposes and donations to charitable institutions at competitive rates; supports scholarship; encourages colleagues, museum professionals and collectors to use services and member network of art world specialists. **Awards:** PADA Award. **Frequency:** annual. **Type:** monetary. **Publications:** Membership Directory. Alternate Formats: online. **Conventions/Meetings:** lecture and symposium ● annual meeting and dinner.

303 ■ Watermark Association of Artisans (WAA)
150 US Hwy. 158 E
Camden, NC 27921
Ph: (252)338-0853
Free: (800)982-8337
Fax: (252)338-1444
URL: http://www.albemarle-nc.com/camden/watermark
Contact: Dianne Sprouse, Exec. Dir.
Founded: 1978. **Members:** 945. **Membership Dues:** worker-owner, $100 (annual). **Staff:** 6. **Budget:** $1,000,000. **For-Profit. Description:** Craft produc-

ers. Serves as a marketing cooperative for members. Provides technical assistance to craft organizations worldwide; offers training programs at the state and national levels. Offers internship program in marketing and technical assistance. Operates speakers' bureau. **Conventions/Meetings:** annual meeting.

304 ■ Western Association for Art Conservation (WAAC)
c/o Alexis Miller, Sec.
Balboa Art Conservation Center
PO Box 3755
San Diego, CA 92163-1755
Ph: (619)236-9702
Fax: (619)236-0141
E-mail: lxs2002@hotmail.com
URL: http://palimpsest.stanford.edu/waac
Contact: Alexis Miller, Sec.
Founded: 1975. **Members:** 525. **Membership Dues:** individual in U.S. and Canada, $30 (annual) ● individual outside U.S. and Canada, $35 (annual) ● institution in U.S. and Canada, $35 (annual) ● institution outside U.S. and Canada, $40 (annual). **Budget:** $44,000. **Regional Groups:** 1. **Multinational. Description:** Art conservators and restorers; museum scientists; individuals providing art-related services. Provides a forum for professional exchange between members; though founded to serve Eastern states, membership and information are extended internationally. **Formerly:** (1977) Western Association of Art Conservators. **Publications:** *A Guide to Handling Anthropological Museum Collections* (in English and Spanish). Book. **Price:** $8.95 post paid ● *Loss Compensation Postprints*, 3/year. Newsletter. Includes listings of employment training opportunities, feature articles, and regional news. **Price:** $12.50 post paid; $10.00/back issues. ISSN: 1052-0066. **Circulation:** 525 ● *WAAC Newsletter* (in English and Spanish), 3/year. Includes listings of employment training opportunities, feature articles, and regional news. **Price:** $8.95 included in membership dues; $10.00/back issues. ISSN: 1052-0066. **Circulation:** 525. **Conventions/Meetings:** annual conference, with presentation of papers.

Artists

305 ■ Artists Rights Society (ARS)
536 Broadway, 5th Fl.
New York, NY 10012
Ph: (212)420-9160
Fax: (212)420-9286
E-mail: info@arsny.com
URL: http://www.arsny.com
Contact: Dr. Theodore H. Feder, Pres.
Founded: 1987. **Multinational. Description:** Represents visual artists and their intellectual property interests worldwide; lobbies state and federal legislatures for stronger, more effective artists' rights laws. **Telecommunication Services:** electronic mail, tfeder@arsny.com.

306 ■ Guild of Fine Craftsmen and Artisans
c/o Leland R.S. Torrence
17 Vernon Ct.
Woodbridge, CT 06525
Ph: (203)397-8505
Fax: (203)389-7516
E-mail: info@lelandtorrenceenterprises.com
URL: http://www.lelandtorrenceenterprises.com/guild.html
Contact: Leland R.S. Torrence, Contact
Founded: 1995. **Description:** Works for the preservation of standards in the restoration trades. **Conventions/Meetings:** workshop.

Arts

307 ■ Association of Science Fiction and Fantasy Artists (ASFA)
PO Box 15131
Arlington, TX 76015-7311
E-mail: alyconart@yahoo.com
URL: http://www.asfa-art.org
Contact: Jannie Shea, Sec.
Founded: 1982. **Members:** 600. **Membership Dues:** regular, in U.S., $40 (annual) ● regular, in Canada, $45 (annual) ● regular, outside U.S. and Canada, $50 (annual) ● life, $800 ● corporate, $130 (annual) ● associate, $25 (annual). **Regional Groups:** 5. **Description:** Amateur and professional artists, art directors, art show managers, publishers, collectors or anyone interested in the science fiction and fantasy art genre. Serves as educational association dedicated to the artistic, literary and charitable purposes concerning the visual arts of science fiction, fantasy, mythology and related topics. Provides networking, information and technical services. Promotes public awareness of the art. **Libraries: Type:** not open to the public. **Holdings:** 200; periodicals. **Awards:** Chesley Awards. **Frequency:** annual. **Type:** recognition. **Recipient:** for individual works and achievements during the previous year. **Computer Services:** Online services, web gallery for members. **Publications:** *ASFA Quarterly*. Magazine. Contains informative articles, how-to advise, artists' profiles, interviews with art directors, and upcoming events. **Circulation:** 600. **Advertising:** accepted. **Conventions/Meetings:** annual meeting.

308 ■ Complex Weavers (CW)
1615 4th Ave. N
Seattle, WA 98109
E-mail: alcorn@nwlink.com
URL: http://www.complex-weavers.org
Contact: Frances Alcorn, Membership Chair
Membership Dues: regular, in U.S., $25 (annual) ● regular, in U.S., $50 (biennial) ● regular, in Canada and Mexico, $30 (annual) ● regular, in Canada and Mexico, $60 (biennial) ● regular, outside North America, $35 (annual) ● regular, outside North America, $70 (biennial). **Description:** Promotes complex weaving through education, information, and technology; encourages research, documentation and innovative ideas as well as information exchange. **Libraries: Type:** reference; lending. **Holdings:** books, periodicals. **Subjects:** textile samples. **Awards: Type:** recognition. **Recipient:** for excellence in complex weaving. **Publications:** Journal, 3/year. Contains information shared by members. **Advertising:** accepted ● Membership Directory, biennial. Includes contact information, equipment and areas of interest. **Conventions/Meetings:** regional meeting ● biennial seminar and conference.

309 ■ International Fine Print Dealers Association (IFPDA)
250 W 26th St., Ste.405
New York, NY 10001
Ph: (212)674-6095
Fax: (212)674-6783
E-mail: info@ifpda.org
URL: http://www.ifpda.org
Contact: Michele Senecal, Exec. Dir.
Founded: 1987. **Members:** 160. **Membership Dues:** general, $750 (annual). **Multinational. Description:** Ensures high ethical standards and quality among fine print dealers. Promotes greater appreciation of fine prints among art collectors and the general public. **Awards:** International Fine Print Dealers Association Book Award. **Frequency:** annual. **Type:** recognition. **Recipient:** for outstanding publication in the field of fine prints. **Publications:** Membership Directory, annual. **Price:** $10.00. **Advertising:** accepted. Alternate Formats: online.

310 ■ Mid Atlantic Fiber Association (MAFA)
PO Box 5053
Delanco, NJ 08075
E-mail: communications@mafafiber.org
URL: http://www.mafafiber.org
Contact: Cheryl Migliarini, Pres.
Members: 64. **State Groups:** 8. **Description:** Supports the fiber arts; dedicated to educating and promoting participation in fiber crafts; advances public interest in hand-weaving and related activities. **Awards:** Allen Fannin Memorial Scholarship. **Type:** scholarship. **Recipient:** to deserving students ● Grants. **Type:** grant. **Recipient:** for the member of the guilds. **Committees:** By-Law; Nominations. **Publications:** *Threadlines*, quarterly. Newsletter ● Brochure. **Conventions/Meetings:** biennial conference ● periodic conference, mini-conferences ● semiannual meeting.

Arts and Crafts

311 ■ International Society of Glass Beadmakers (ISGB)
1120 Chester Ave., No. 470
Cleveland, OH 44114
Free: (888)742-0242
Fax: (216)696-2582
E-mail: president@isgb.org
URL: http://www.isgb.org
Contact: Ms. Gwynne Rukenbrod, Exec. Dir.
Founded: 1993. **Membership Dues:** student, $30 (annual) ● business, $100 (annual) ● corporate, $250 (annual) ● life, $2,000 ● individual, $55 (annual) ● family (2 adults at the same address and children under the age of 18), $75 (annual). **Multinational. Description:** Promotes the growth and recognition of the art of glass beadmaking. Facilitates communication and mentoring among members. Educates the public about the process of beadmaking and the artistic value of glass beads. **Publications:** *The Glass Bead*, quarterly. Newsletter. **Price:** included in membership dues. **Advertising:** accepted ● Membership Directory, annual. **Price:** included in membership dues.

Asbestos

312 ■ Asbestos Cement Product Producers Association
PMB 114
1235 Jefferson Davis Hwy.
Arlington, VA 22202
Ph: (514)861-1153
Fax: (514)861-1152
E-mail: aia@chrysotile.com
Contact: Mr. Clement Godbout, Pres.
Founded: 1972. **Members:** 11. **Staff:** 1. **Budget:** $26,500. **Multinational. Description:** Promotes and defends the use of asbestos cement building materials. **Libraries: Type:** reference; open to the public. **Holdings:** books, monographs, periodicals. **Subjects:** a/c pipes and sheets.

Associations

313 ■ Alliance for Nonprofit Management
1899 L St. NW, 6th Fl.
Washington, DC 20036
Ph: (202)955-8406
Fax: (202)721-0086
E-mail: info@allianceonline.org
URL: http://www.allianceonline.org
Contact: Tangie Newborn, Chair
Founded: 1997. **Members:** 477. **Membership Dues:** individual, $200 (annual) ● full-time student, $50 (annual) ● organization (with operating budget less than $500,000), $250 (annual) ● organization (with operating budget from $500,000-$999,999), $500 (annual) ● organization (with operating budget from $1,000,000-$4,999,999), $750 (annual) ● organization (with operating budget from $5,000,000 up), $1,000 (annual). **Staff:** 5. **Budget:** $900,000. **Description:** Member organizations and individuals devoted to building the capacity of non-profit organizations in order to increase their effectiveness. **Awards:** Terry McAdam Book Award. **Frequency:** annual. **Type:** recognition. **Recipient:** for the book with the greatest contribution to nonprofit management. **Computer Services:** Online services, publication. **Formed by Merger of:** (1999) Non-profit Management Association and Support Centers of America. **Publications:** *Gold Book*, monthly. Highlights the success stories in non-profit capacity build-

ing. **Price:** $20.00. Alternate Formats: online ● *NMA Members Directory*, annual. Membership Directory ● *Pulse!*, bimonthly. Newsletter. Features latest events, research, technology and tools in the non-profit sector. **Price:** free. **Circulation:** 2,600. Alternate Formats: online. **Conventions/Meetings:** annual conference - 2008 July 9, Dearborn, MI.

314 ■ AMCinstitute (AMCi)

100 N 20th St., 4th Fl.
Philadelphia, PA 19103-1443
Ph: (215)564-3484
Fax: (215)963-2175
E-mail: info@amcinstitute.org
URL: http://www.iaamc.org
Contact: Suzanne C. Pine, Exec. VP

Founded: 1963. **Members:** 170. **Membership Dues:** provisional status, $655 (annual) ● active (based on annual income), $790-$16,500 (annual) ● independent company (without national distribution or multiple locations; with sales under $3,000,000), $600 (annual) ● independent company (without national distribution or multiple locations; with sales over $3,000,000), $1,200 (annual) ● convention bureau, $1,800 (annual) ● hotel chain, $2,500 (annual). **Staff:** 4. **Budget:** $3,470,000. **Description:** Management companies serving a number of associations on a professional basis (but not executives serving more than one association in an employee relationship). Membership employs nearly 3,000 association management professionals and serves over 1,200 associations with annual budgets exceeding 960 million dollars and serving nearly 1.7 million members. **Libraries: Type:** reference. **Holdings:** audiovisuals, books. **Awards:** G.W. Bostrum Award for Service Quality & Excellence. **Frequency:** annual. **Type:** recognition. **Telecommunication Services:** electronic bulletin board ● electronic mail, spine@amcinstitute.org. **Committees:** Associate Member Relations; Communications; Meetings; Public Relations and Marketing/External Communications. **Formerly:** (1977) Multiple Association Management Institute; (1996) Institute of Association Management Companies; (2006) International Association of Association Management Companies. **Conventions/Meetings:** semiannual conference and meeting - winter and summer.

315 ■ American Society of Association Executives (ASAE)

1575 I St. NW
Washington, DC 20005
Ph: (202)371-0940 (202)626-2723
Free: (888)950-2723
Fax: (202)371-8315
E-mail: pr@asaenet.org
URL: http://www.asaecenter.org
Contact: John H. Graham IV, Pres./CEO

Founded: 1920. **Members:** 23,700. **Membership Dues:** association professional staff, $265 (annual) ● association chief executive, $295 (annual) ● industry partner, consultant, $395 (annual) ● full-time student, $30 (annual) ● young professional, $100 (annual). **Staff:** 110. **Budget:** $20,000,000. **Description:** Professional society of paid executives of international, national, state, and local trade, professional, and philanthropic associations. Seeks to educate association executives on effective management, including: the proper objectives, functions, and activities of associations; the basic principles of association management; the legal aspects of association activity; policies relating to association management; efficient methods, procedures, and techniques of association management; the responsibilities and professional standards of association executives. Maintains information resource center. Conducts resume, guidance, and consultation services; compiles statistics in the form of reports, surveys, and studies; carries out research and education. Maintains ASAE Services Corporation to provide special services and ASAE Foundation to do future-oriented research and make grant awards. Offers executive search services and insurance programs. Provides CEO center for chief staff executives. Conducts Certified Association Executive (CAE) program. **Libraries: Type:** open to the public. **Holdings:** 1,400. **Subjects:** associations, nonprofit management. **Awards:** Academy of Leaders Awards. **Type:** recognition. **Recipient:** to an individual industry partner who has made especially outstanding contributions to the advancement of the association profession ● ASAE Fellows. **Type:** scholarship. **Recipient:** for leading thinkers and doers in the association ● Associations Advance America Awards. **Frequency:** annual. **Type:** recognition. **Recipient:** for outstanding associations and suppliers ● Associations Make a Better World Awards. **Frequency:** annual. **Type:** recognition. **Recipient:** for outstanding examples of activities carried out by associations ● Banff Centre Scholarship Award. **Type:** scholarship. **Recipient:** for executive level participants ● Key Award. **Type:** recognition. **Recipient:** for outstanding accomplishment and contributions to the association ● Sentinel Award. **Frequency:** periodic. **Type:** recognition. **Recipient:** for members of Congress. **Computer Services:** database. **Telecommunication Services:** information service, fax-on-demand, (800)622-2723. **Programs:** Certified Association Executive. **Sections:** Association Management Companies; Chapter Relations; Communication; Education; Executive Management; Finance and Administration; Government Relations; International; Legal; Marketing; Meetings and Expositions; Membership Development; Technology. **Formerly:** (1956) American Trade Association Executives. **Publications:** *Association Management*, monthly. Magazine. Includes in-depth articles and how-to tips on all areas of association management, and an index in spring issue; also includes book reviews. **Price:** included in membership dues; $30.00 /year for nonmembers. **Circulation:** 25,000. **Advertising:** accepted. Alternate Formats: microform; CD-ROM; online ● *Journal of Association Leadership*. Provides a source of insight and research for associations and their leaders. **Price:** $30.00 for members; $45.00 for nonmembers ● *Leadership: The Magazine for Volunteer Association Leaders*, annual. Includes theory and practical methods on the role of volunteer officers and directors in associations. **Price:** $5.00/issue. **Circulation:** 45,000. **Advertising:** accepted ● *Who's Who in Association Management*, annual. Membership Directory. Lists of ASAE members. Also includes names and descriptions of vendors supplying services to the association community. **Price:** first copy free for members; $60.00/ additional copy; $150.00/copy for nonmembers. **Circulation:** 25,000. **Advertising:** accepted ● Also publishes market research reports, compensation studies, meeting trends, operating ratio report, and section newsletters. **Conventions/Meetings:** annual conference and meeting (exhibits) ● annual conference (exhibits) ● annual Strategic Leadership Forum - conference.

316 ■ Center for Excellence in Association Leadership (CEAL)

236 W Portal Ave., No. 782
San Francisco, CA 94127
Ph: (650)355-4094
Fax: (650)359-3611
E-mail: info@cealweb.com
URL: http://www.cealweb.com
Contact: Patricia A. Hudson CAE, Pres.

Multinational. Description: Dedicated to developing new and innovative programs, products, and services that will strengthen the effectiveness of the volunteer and staff leadership team. **Computer Services:** Mailing lists. **Subgroups:** Knowledge Exchange Group. **Publications:** *Beyond Membership Marketing*. Book. **Price:** $19.95 ● Articles.

317 ■ DMA Nonprofit Federation (DMANF)

1615 L St. NW, Ste.1100
Washington, DC 20036
Ph: (202)628-4380 (202)861-2498
Fax: (202)628-4383
E-mail: nonprofitfederation@the-dma.org
URL: http://www.the-dma.org/nonprofitfederation
Contact: Ms. Xenia Boone Esq., Exec. Dir.

Founded: 1982. **Members:** 400. **Membership Dues:** organization, $600 (annual). **Staff:** 3. **Budget:** $750,000. **Description:** Trade and lobbying group for non-profit organizations that use direct and online marketing to raise funds and communicate with members. Sponsors professional development conferences and seminars, lobbies on state and federal legislation, regulation, and standards related to direct marketing and related issues. Provides information about and participants in litigation affecting nonprofits. Promotes the overall welfare of non-profits. Represents health care charities, social service agencies, religious groups, colleges and universities and fraternal organizations. **Awards:** Nonprofit Advancement Award. **Frequency:** annual. **Type:** recognition ● Nonprofit Organization of the Year. **Frequency:** annual. **Type:** recognition ● Nonprofit Public Service Award. **Type:** recognition. **Recipient:** for an outstanding public service to the nonprofit community. **Formerly:** Nonprofit Mailers Federation; (2001) National Federation of Nonprofits. **Publications:** *Journal of The DMA Nonprofit Federation*, quarterly. **Price:** free for members and corporate partners; $35.00 /year for nonmembers. **Circulation:** 600. **Advertising:** accepted. Alternate Formats: CD-ROM; online ● *News Update*, biweekly. Newsletter. Alternate Formats: online ● Papers ● Reports. **Conventions/Meetings:** annual New York Nonprofit Conference ● annual Washington Nonprofit Conference - February/March, Washington, DC.

318 ■ Foundation for Educational Futures (FEF)

PO Box 6381
New York, NY 10150-6381
Free: (800)285-1310
E-mail: tgv1233@netzero.net
Contact: Thomas G. Voss, Pres.

Founded: 1983. **Staff:** 3. **Languages:** Chinese, English, French. **Multinational. Description:** Assists educational institutions, nonprofit agencies, and cultural associations worldwide in institutional governance, policy programs, asset development, fund development, and financial management. Provides academic and corporate advisers (usually retired) to evaluate avenues for improvement of the client organization. **Conventions/Meetings:** annual board meeting.

319 ■ National Association for Membership Development

Address Unknown since 2007

Description: The only professional society solely dedicated to the support and effectiveness of membership development professionals in the United States and abroad. **Formerly:** (1992) National Association of Membership Directors of Chambers of Commerce.

320 ■ National Council of Nonprofit Associations (NCNA)

1101 Vermont Ave. NW, Ste.1002
Washington, DC 20005-1525
Ph: (202)962-0322
Fax: (202)962-0321
E-mail: ncna@ncna.org
URL: http://www.ncna.org
Contact: Audrey R. Alvarado PhD, Exec. Dir.

Founded: 1989. **Members:** 56. **Membership Dues:** individual, $200 (annual) ● organization, $400 (annual). **Staff:** 4. **Budget:** $750,000. **Regional Groups:** 2. **State Groups:** 45. **Description:** Strives to advance the role and capacity of the nonprofit sector in civil society and supports the state and regional associations of nonprofit organizations. **Libraries: Type:** not open to the public. **Holdings:** 200; books, business records, periodicals. **Subjects:** general nonprofit management. **Programs:** Peer Consulting. **Projects:** State Assistance. **Publications:** *NCNA Notes from the Road*, bimonthly. Newsletter ● *Nonprofit Policy News*, monthly. Newsletter. Features articles about federal and state legislation affecting non-profits. **Price:** free for members. Alternate Formats: online ● *SPARC Change*, quarterly. Newsletter. **Price:** free for members. Alternate Formats: online ● *State By State*. Manual ● *What You Need to Know*, biweekly. Newsletter. **Price:** free for members. Alternate Formats: online ● Also publishes public policy updates. **Conventions/Meetings:** annual conference (exhibits) ● annual Regional Membership Meeting - always spring.

321 ■ Society of National Association Publications (SNAP)
8405 Greensboro Dr., No. 800
McLean, VA 22102
Ph: (703)506-3285
Fax: (703)506-3266
E-mail: snapinfo@snaponline.org
URL: http://www.snaponline.org
Contact: Robert Fromberg, Pres.

Founded: 1963. **Members:** 750. **Membership Dues:** publication (based on advertising revenues), $295-$995 (annual) ● associate (based on annual gross revenues), $295-$695 (annual). **Staff:** 3. **Budget:** $400,000. **State Groups:** 2. **Local Groups:** 2. **Description:** Publications owned, operated, or controlled by voluntary associations and societies, including organizations with licensing and certification functions; associate, institutional, and student members. Develops high standards of editorial and advertising content and publishing practices; represents, promotes, and advances the common interests of publications of voluntary associations and societies. Compiles statistics; sponsors seminars and resource network. **Awards:** EXCEL Awards. **Frequency:** annual. **Type:** recognition. **Recipient:** for excellence in association publishing. **Computer Services:** Mailing lists. **Committees:** Award; Editorial; Marketing; Production; Publication Management. **Publications:** *Association Publishing*, bimonthly. Magazine. **Price:** included in membership dues. **Circulation:** 1,000. **Advertising:** accepted ● *SNAP In Touch*, biweekly. Newsletter. Provides timely articles and industry news to members. Alternate Formats: online ● *Who's Who in SNAP*, annual. Membership Directory. Includes buyers' guide of products offered to association/society publications; includes list of SNAP publication members. **Price:** free for members; $300.00 for nonmembers. **Circulation:** 750. **Advertising:** accepted ● Reports. **Conventions/Meetings:** semiannual Publications Management Conference (exhibits).

322 ■ Society for Nonprofit Organizations (SNPO)
5820 Canton Center Rd., Ste.165
Canton, MI 48187-2683
Ph: (734)451-3582
Fax: (734)451-5935
E-mail: info@snpo.org
URL: http://www.snpo.org
Contact: Katie Burnham-Laverty, Co-Founder/Pres./CEO

Founded: 1983. **Members:** 4,000. **Membership Dues:** individual, $59 (annual) ● organization, $115 (annual) ● electronic (paperless), $39 (annual) ● affiliate, $15 (annual). **Staff:** 7. **Multinational. Description:** Brings together those who serve in the nonprofit world in order to build a strong network of professionals throughout the country; provides a forum for the exchange of information, knowledge, and ideas on strengthening and increasing productivity within nonprofit organizations and among their leaders. Mission is accomplished through the publication of Nonprofit World magazine, educational programs offered by the Learning Institute, and other communications with its members. **Libraries: Type:** reference. **Holdings:** 21; archival material, articles, audio recordings, books, periodicals, video recordings. **Subjects:** nonprofit management, board governance, fundraising, strategic planning, resource development, social entrepreneurship. **Computer Services:** Online services, archive of over 700 management articles. **Divisions:** Learning Institute. **Publications:** *Funding Alert*, monthly. Newsletter. Provides current information on available grants and profiles a new foundation. **Price:** free for members. **Advertising:** accepted. Alternate Formats: online ● *Nonprofit World*, bimonthly. Journal. Includes tips on board governance, creative fundraising ideas, legal advice, legislative updates, profiles of nonprofit organizations, book reviews. **Price:** free for members; $79.00 /year for nonmembers. **Advertising:** accepted. Alternate Formats: CD-ROM. **Conventions/Meetings:** seminar and workshop.

Attorneys

323 ■ American College of Construction Lawyers (ACCL)
1030 15th St. NW, Ste.870
Washington, DC 20005
E-mail: contact@accl.org
URL: http://www.accl.org
Contact: Robert J. Smith, Sec.

Founded: 1987. **Members:** 115. **Membership Dues:** individual, $475 (annual). **Staff:** 3. **Budget:** $75,000. **Description:** Senior lawyers involved in construction law; membership is limited to lawyers who have demonstrated skill, experience, and high standards of professional and ethical conduct in the practice or in the teaching of construction law. Focuses on excellence in the special practice of construction law. Offers advanced professional educational programs; contributes to solving construction industry legal problems; provides a forum for development and exchange of ideas. **Conventions/Meetings:** board meeting - 3/year ● annual convention - always February.

324 ■ State Capital Global Law Firm Group
1747 Pennsylvania Ave. NW, Ste.1200
Washington, DC 20006
Ph: (202)659-6601
Fax: (202)659-6641
E-mail: inquiry@statecapitallaw.org
URL: http://www.statecapitallaw.org
Contact: J. Phil Carlton, CEO

Founded: 1989. **Members:** 120. **Multinational. Description:** Represents Independent law firms. Works to serve the diverse needs of business in a global economy. **Computer Services:** database, member firms. **Formerly:** (2003) State Capital Law Firm Group. **Publications:** *Lobbying, PACs and Campaign Finance: 50 State Handbook* ● *The Newest New Federalism: The 50 States vs. Business.* Report. Contains information about business regulations. ● *State Capital Global Law Firm Group 2006 Member Firm Directory*, annual. Contains contact information and a short profile of member firms. **Conventions/Meetings:** annual International Meeting ● annual United States Meeting - 2008 Oct. 2-4, San Francisco, CA.

325 ■ USFN-America's Mortgage Banking Attorneys (USFN)
c/o Ms. Alberta E. Hultman, CAE, Exec. Dir./CEO
14471 Chambers Rd., Ste.260
Tustin, CA 92780
Ph: (714)838-7167
Free: (800)635-6128
Fax: (714)573-2650
E-mail: info@usfn.org
URL: http://www.usfn.org
Contact: Ms. Alberta E. Hultman CAE, Exec. Dir./CEO

Founded: 1988. **Members:** 145. **Staff:** 6. **Budget:** $1,500,000. **Description:** Works as a national resource network of law firms, trustee companies, and affiliated business support firms serving the mortgage industry. Provides education, training and information resources to the mortgage servicing industry, as well as onsite education for clients. **Libraries: Type:** reference. **Holdings:** articles. **Subjects:** information about the mortgage industry. **Awards:** USFN Awards of Excellence. **Frequency:** annual. **Type:** recognition. **Recipient:** for excellent service. **Computer Services:** Information services, servicing topics. **Formerly:** US Foreclosure Network. **Publications:** *National Mortgage Servicer's Reference Directory*, annual. Alternate Formats: CD-ROM ● *USFN e-Update*, monthly. Newsletter. Alternate Formats: online ● *USFN Report*, quarterly. Newsletter. Contains news publications about the industry. Alternate Formats: online. **Conventions/Meetings:** Default Servicing Seminars - 3/year ● annual Legal Issues Seminar ● annual Meeting/Education Retreat - conference.

Auctions

326 ■ National Auctioneers Association (NAA)
8880 Ballentine
Overland Park, KS 66214
Ph: (913)541-8084
Fax: (913)894-5281
E-mail: bob@auctioneers.org
URL: http://www.auctioneers.org
Contact: Robert A. Shively CAE, Exec. Dir.

Founded: 1949. **Members:** 6,319. **Membership Dues:** individual, $250 (annual) ● virtual, associate, $175 (annual) ● affiliate, $450 (annual) ● retired, $125 (annual) ● life, $5,000. **Staff:** 16. **Budget:** $3,000,000. **State Groups:** 45. **Multinational. Description:** Professional auctioneers. Provides continuing education classes for auctioneers, promotes use of the auction method of marketing in both the private and public sectors. Encourages the highest ethical standards for the profession. **Awards: Type:** recognition. **Recipient:** for the most professional manner of advertising. **Computer Services:** Mailing lists, of members. **Absorbed:** (2003) Auction Marketing Institute. **Publications:** *The Auctioneer*, monthly. Magazine. Reports on current trends in the auction profession and auctioneering methods; includes directory, affiliate reports, and information on new members. **Price:** free for members. ISSN: 1070-0137. **Circulation:** 5,927. **Advertising:** accepted ● Brochures. **Conventions/Meetings:** annual convention (exhibits) ● annual meeting and workshop (exhibits) ● seminar, for continuing education.

327 ■ National Auto Auction Association (NAAA)
5320 Spectrum Dr., Ste.D
Frederick, MD 21703
Ph: (301)696-0400 (508)626-7000
Fax: (301)631-1359
E-mail: naaa@naaa.com
URL: http://www.naaa.com
Contact: Greg Kobel, Pres.

Founded: 1948. **Members:** 309. **Membership Dues:** regular, $800 (annual). **Staff:** 6. **Budget:** $890,000. **Regional Groups:** 4. **Description:** Owners/operators of wholesale automobile and truck auctions; associate members are car and truck manufacturers, insurers of checks and titles, car and truck rental companies, publishers of auto price guide books, and others connected with the industry. Maintains hall of fame. **Awards:** Hall of Fame. **Frequency:** annual. **Type:** recognition. **Committees:** Dealer Affairs; Independent Auction Advisory; Institutional Seller Affairs; National Site Selection; Quad-Zone. **Publications:** *National Auto Auction Association—Membership Directory*, annual. **Price:** $15.00. **Circulation:** 12,000 ● *On the Block*, quarterly. Newsletter. Alternate Formats: online. **Conventions/Meetings:** annual Convention and Equipment and Services Exposition (exhibits) - always September or October.

Audiovisual

328 ■ Association for Information Media and Equipment (AIME)
PO Box 9844
Cedar Rapids, IA 52409-9844
Ph: (319)654-0608
Fax: (319)654-0609
E-mail: bettyge@mchsi.com
URL: http://www.aime.org
Contact: Betty Gorsegner Ehlinger, Exec. Dir.

Founded: 1986. **Members:** 125. **Membership Dues:** institutional, $150 (annual) ● corporate, $250 (annual). **Staff:** 1. **Description:** Producers and distributors of nontheatrical film/video and video related technologies; organizations that use film and video related technologies; manufacturer/vendors of related equipment and services; interested others. Promotes the use of motion media in the instructional and informational fields; works to educate schools and libraries regarding copyright laws as applied to film and video; offers networking opportunities among members and the sharing of information; lobbies for increased funds for school media materials; compiles statistics; sponsors market research. **Publications:** *AIME News*, quarterly. Newsletter. **Price:** $35.00/ year ● *Copyright Information Packet.* Article. **Price:** $19.95 ● *Copyright Law: What Every School, College and Public Library Should Know and Copyright: New Issues.* Video. Includes 2 programs on one cassette. **Price:** $59.95 for members.

329 ■ Communications Media Management Association (CMMA)
20423 State Rd. 7, Ste.F6-491
Boca Raton, FL 33498
Ph: (561)988-2681
E-mail: cmma@cmma.org
URL: http://www.cmma.net
Contact: Jody B. Rosen APR, Exec. Dir.
Founded: 1946. **Members:** 160. **Membership Dues:** active, $350 (annual) ● associate, $275 (annual) ● retired, $55 (annual). **Staff:** 1. **Budget:** $75,000. **Regional Groups:** 6. **Description:** Professional association of managers of communications media departments of business, education, or government. Aims to provide networking and educational opportunities for communications media managers that build peer professional relationships, facilitate leadership development, deepen managerial skills, expand technical knowledge, and develop skills in business strategy. **Libraries: Type:** not open to the public; reference. **Holdings:** biographical archives, business records, papers, photographs, reports, video recordings. **Subjects:** member and association history. **Awards: Type:** recognition. **Formerly:** (1946) Industrial Audio-Visual Association; (1980) Audiovisual Management Association. **Publications:** *Visions*, quarterly. Newsletter. Provides reports on meetings and regional activities. Includes technical reports. **Price:** available to members only. Alternate Formats: online ● Membership Directory. **Conventions/Meetings:** annual conference, open to all communication media managers (exhibits) - always fall ● annual Professional Development Conference, for members, their guests, and those pursuing membership (exhibits) - always spring.

330 ■ Independent Professional Representatives Organization (IPRO)
34157 W 9 Mile Rd.
Farmington Hills, MI 48335
Ph: (248)474-0522
Free: (800)420-4268
E-mail: ray@avreps.org
URL: http://www.avreps.org
Contact: Raymond Wright, Exec. Dir.
Founded: 1988. **Members:** 80. **Staff:** 3. **Description:** Representatives of manufacturers and dealers in the audiovisual industry. Seeks to improve the professional image of members and strengthen relationships among manufacturers, retailers, and representatives. Promotes education of and communication among members. **Publications:** *IPRO Words*, quarterly. Newsletter ● Directory ● Newsletter, weekly. **Price:** free for members. Alternate Formats: online. **Conventions/Meetings:** annual conference and seminar.

331 ■ InfoComm International
11242 Waples Mill Rd., Ste.200
Fairfax, VA 22030-6079
Ph: (703)273-7200
Free: (800)659-7469
Fax: (703)278-8082
E-mail: customerservice@infocomm.org
URL: http://www.infocomm.org
Contact: Randal A. Lemke PhD, Exec. Dir.
Founded: 1939. **Members:** 2,500. **Membership Dues:** silver (commercial AV company), gold (organization and commercial AV branch), $400 ● gold (commercial AV company), platinum (organization), $800 ● platinum (commercial AV company), $1,200 ● silver (organization), $200 ● silver (commercial AV branch), $100 ● platinum (commercial AV branch), $600 ● commercial AV affiliate, $75 ● associate, $150 ● student, $25. **Staff:** 40. **Multinational. Description:** Represents for-profit individuals and organizations that derive revenue from the commercialization or utilization of communications technology. Ensures the credibility and desirability of its members' products and services by representing the communications industry to the public, business, education, and governments. **Awards:** ICIA Achievement Awards. **Frequency:** annual. **Type:** recognition. **Recipient:** for excellence in all phases of the communications industry. **Telecommunication Services:** electronic mail, membership@infocomm.org. **Absorbed:** (1982) Association of Media Producers. **Formerly:** (1947) National Association of Visual Education Dealers; (1983) National Audio-Visual Association; (2006) International Communications Industries Association. **Publications:** *Directory of Multimedia Equipment, Software, and Services* ● *ICIA Membership Directory*, annual. Includes dealers, independent design consultants, software developers, manufacturers, producers, representatives and associates. **Price:** free for members; $100.00 for nonmembers ● *InfoCommunity News*, quarterly. Newsletter. Contains news of the audiovisual, communication, and presentation electronics industry. **Price:** included in membership dues. ISSN: 1070-4426. **Circulation:** 3,500. **Advertising:** accepted. Alternate Formats: online ● Newsletters. Alternate Formats: online ● Surveys. **Conventions/Meetings:** annual convention and seminar (exhibits) - always June.

332 ■ International Society of Communication Specialists (ISCS)
201 Blue Sky Dr.
Marietta, GA 30068-3511
Ph: (770)973-0662
Fax: (770)973-1410
E-mail: ecs91@aol.com
Contact: Edward Sanner, Exec. Dir.
Founded: 1983. **Members:** 54. **Membership Dues:** regular, company, $300 (annual). **Staff:** 2. **Description:** Provides communications to America's trade and professional associations, primarily through audio-videotape, CD and CD-Rom; promotes these media as means of communication within organizations or companies. **Conventions/Meetings:** annual meeting - always in January.

333 ■ Video Software Dealers Association (VSDA)
16530 Ventura Blvd., Ste.400
Encino, CA 91436-4551
Ph: (818)385-1500
Free: (800)955-8732
Fax: (818)385-0567
E-mail: vsdaoffice@vsda.org
URL: http://www.vsda.org
Contact: Crossan R. Andersen, Pres.
Founded: 1981. **Members:** 3,000. **Staff:** 24. **Budget:** $8,000,000. **Regional Groups:** 48. **Description:** Retailers and distributors of videocassettes and videodiscs; associate members are major studios or independent companies that produce video programming and manufacturers of video games, accessories, and other goods and services for the video software industry. Represents and acts as spokesperson for the video software merchandising industry. Conducts statistical survey of video retailing; offers legal counsel representing members' interests in Washington, DC. Offers seminars on management and inventory control. **Libraries: Type:** reference. **Awards:** DVD Certification Program. **Type:** recognition. **Recipient:** for impressive growth and sale of DVDs ● DVD Technical Awards. **Frequency:** annual. **Type:** recognition. **Recipient:** for an outstanding DVD product ● Home Entertainment Awards. **Frequency:** annual. **Type:** recognition. **Recipient:** for outstanding videos ● VSDA Retailer of the Year. **Frequency:** annual. **Type:** recognition. **Recipient:** for the best retailer. **Committees:** Convention; Education; Election Review; Government Affairs; Home Entertainment Awards Nominating; Loss Prevention; Marketing; Membership and Chapter Development; New Technology; Retail Advisory; Scholarship. **Publications:** *Inside VSDA*. Magazine ● *VSDA Video Voice*, monthly. Newsletter. Covers convention, events, contests, and industry promotions. **Price:** included in membership dues. **Circulation:** 6,000. **Advertising:** accepted ● Annual Report, annual. **Price:** $19.95 for members; $54.95 for nonmembers ● Membership Directory. Alternate Formats: online. **Conventions/Meetings:** annual convention and trade show (exhibits) - every January ● East Coast Video Show.

Audiovisual Communications

334 ■ Visual Resources Association (VRA)
c/o Liz Edgar Hernandez, Membership Services Coor.
4201 Wilson Blvd., No. 110-331
Box 331
Arlington, VA 22203-1859
Ph: (202)422-4876
E-mail: macie.hall@jhu.edu
URL: http://www.vraweb.org
Contact: Ms. Virginia Hall, Pres.
Founded: 1983. **Members:** 800. **Membership Dues:** full, $35-$110 (annual) ● student, retiree, $25 (annual) ● contributor, $150-$299 (annual) ● patron, $300 (annual) ● institutional outside North America, $125 (annual). **Regional Groups:** 11. **Multinational. Description:** Slide and photograph curators; electronic media professionals; film and video librarians; photo archivists; slide, microfilm, and digital image producers; rights and reproduction officials; photographers; art historians; and others concerned with visual materials. Works to study visual materials, their history, production, conservation, classification, and accessibility. **Awards:** Distinguished Service Award. **Frequency:** annual. **Type:** recognition. **Recipient:** for individuals who have made significant contributions to the field of visual resources ● Nancy DeLaurier Award. **Frequency:** annual. **Type:** recognition. **Recipient:** for distinguished achievement in visual resources. **Computer Services:** Mailing lists. **Committees:** Data Standards; Digital Initiatives Advisory; Intellectual Property Rights. **Affiliated With:** College Art Association. **Publications:** *Image Stuff*, quarterly. Newsletter. **Price:** included in membership dues. Alternate Formats: online ● *VRA Bulletin*, quarterly. Journal. **Price:** included in membership dues. **Circulation:** 800. **Advertising:** accepted ● Membership Directory. **Conventions/Meetings:** annual conference ● annual meeting, informational sessions of professional interest (exhibits).

Automatic Identification

335 ■ AIM
125 Warrendale-Bayne Rd., Ste.100
Warrendale, PA 15086
Ph: (724)934-4470 (412)965-6229
Fax: (724)934-4495
E-mail: info@aimglobal.org
URL: http://www.aimglobal.org
Contact: Daniel P. Mullen, Pres.
Founded: 1972. **Members:** 999. **Staff:** 6. **Description:** Serves as a trade association for the automatic identification data captures technology industry. **Libraries: Type:** reference. **Holdings:** archival material, audiovisuals, books, clippings, periodicals. **Subjects:** automatic data collection technologies. **Awards:** Don Percival Award. **Frequency:** annual. **Type:** recognition. **Recipient:** for outstanding technical contributions in the application of automatic data collection technology ● Richard R. Dilling Award. **Frequency:** annual. **Type:** scholarship. **Recipient:** for furthering the growth of the automatic data collection industry through important applications and new technology. **Additional Websites:** http://www.aim-na.org. **Committees:** Education; Marketing; Membership. **Formerly:** (1983) Automatic Identification Manufacturers Association; (1993) Automatic Identification Manufacturers; (2001) AIM U.S.A. **Publications:** *Yearbook and Buyers' Guide*, annual ● Newsletter ● Also publishes a glossary, materials describing products and their capabilities, manuals, and bibliographies; produces filmstrips and other materials; distributes books on bar code, RFID, RF Data Communications, systems integration, and

magnetic stripe technologies. **Conventions/Meetings:** annual Frontline Solutions Europe - trade show ● annual Frontline Solutions USA - trade show, features education and demonstrations of AIDC products (exhibits) ● annual Meeting and Knowledge Networking Forum.

336 ■ Association for Automatic Identification and Mobility North America (AIM NA)
c/o Mary Lou Bosco
125 Warrendale-Bayne Rd.
Warrendale, PA 15086
Ph: (724)934-5688
Fax: (724)934-5688
E-mail: marylou@aim-na.org
URL: http://www.aim-na.org
Contact: Mr. A. Tee Migliori, Pres.
Membership Dues: domestic/associate, $945 (annual) ● international, $2,500 (annual). **Description:** Promotes and advances the interests of the automatic identification industry. Accelerates the growth and use of ADIC technologies and services. Compiles and issues basic trade information.

337 ■ GS1 US
Princeton Pike Corporate Ctr.
1009 Lenox Dr., Ste.202
Lawrenceville, NJ 08648
Ph: (609)620-0200 (937)435-3870
Fax: (609)620-1200
E-mail: info@gs1us.org
URL: http://www.uc-council.org
Contact: Mr. Miguel A. Lopera, CEO
Founded: 1972. **Members:** 250,000. **Staff:** 150. **Languages:** English, German, Spanish. **Description:** Develops and implements standard-based, global supply chain solutions. Operates two wholly owned subsidiaries, UCCnet and RosettaNet, and co-manages the global EAN.UCC System with EAN International. Manages the United Nations Standard Products and Services Code (UNSPSC) for the United Nations Development Programme (UNDP). Evaluates the effects of brand and size demand, competitor actions, pricing policy, and shelf location of merchandise. Administers Universal Product Code and Symbol (UPC), Uniform Communications Standard (UCS), Warehouse Information Network Standard (WINS), and Voluntary Inter-Industry Communications Standard (VICSEDI). **Formerly:** (1976) Uniform Grocery Product Code Council; (1985) Uniform Product Code Council; (2005) Uniform Code Council. **Publications:** *Application Identifier Manual* ● *DATA Communication Guidelines*. Manual ● *EDI Architecture Guide* ● *Marking Guidelines for General Merchandise/Apparel*. Manual ● *Seminar Schedule and Support Materials*, periodic. Lists meetings, seminars, educational videos, and publications. ● *Shipping Container Code and Symbol Specification Manual* ● *Symbol Location Guidelines*. Manual ● *Symbol Specification Manual* ● *UCC/EAN Code 128 Shipping Container Manual* ● *UCS Architecture Guide* ● *UCS/DSD Implementation and User Guide*. Manual ● *UCS/WINS Directory*, semiannual. Membership Directory. **Price:** free ● *UCS/WINS Standards Manual* ● *VICS EDI Directory*, semiannual. Membership Directory. **Price:** free ● *VICS EDI Standards Manual* ● *VICS 856 Guidelines Manual* ● Annual Report, annual. Alternate Formats: online. **Conventions/Meetings:** annual UConnect Conference, for users - usually May.

338 ■ Integrated Business Communications Alliance (IBCA)
81 Cottage St.
Doylestown, PA 18901
Ph: (215)489-1722
E-mail: kelleyt@quadii.com
URL: http://www.ibcaweb.org
Founded: 1986. **Members:** 175. **Membership Dues:** company, $500 (annual) ● trade association, $1,350 (annual). **Staff:** 5. **Budget:** $180,000. **Description:** Represents a number of commodity groups including the heating, air conditioning, plumbing, gas, fasteners, and refrigeration industries. Promotes use of bar coding by distributors. Seeks to assist companies that wish to use a standardized bar code system for "electronic data capture and exchange". **Libraries: Type:** reference. **Holdings:** books, video recordings. **Subjects:** technology-related topics. **Formerly:** (1998) Industry Bar Code Alliance. **Publications:** *The Bar Code Implementation Guide: Using Bar Codes in Distribution*. Book. **Price:** $69.95 ● *Compliance Labeling.How to Do It*. Book ● *Getting Started With Bar Codes: A Systematic Guide*. Book. **Price:** $89.95 ● *IBCA Bar Code Application Guidelines*.

339 ■ Optical Product Code Council (OPCC)
1700 Diagonal Rd., Ste.500
Alexandria, VA 22314
Ph: (703)548-4560
Fax: (703)548-4580
E-mail: vca@visionsite.org
URL: http://www.opccouncil.org
Contact: Kendall Blake, Contact
Founded: 1984. **Members:** 100. **Staff:** 1. **Description:** Trade association composed of the Optical Laboratories Association. Works to assist the optical industry in serving the interest of consumers by overseeing the administration of an optical product bar code. Establishes standards and guidelines for the assigning of optical product bar codes in order to facilitate the ordering and processing of eyeware. **Publications:** none. **Convention/Meeting:** none.

Automation

340 ■ Ebix Users Association (EUA)
Address Unknown since 2008
URL: http://www.eua.org
Membership Dues: general (based on number of users), $400-$750 (annual). **Description:** Represents independent agencies using ebix.com, Inc.'s products. Promotes profitability and professionalism through the use of automation. Represents members' technology concerns for future product development. Maintains and enhances member communications. Implements comprehensive automation education programs on regional and national levels. **Publications:** Newsletter. Alternate Formats: online.

Automotive Education

341 ■ Council of Advanced Automotive Trainers (CAAT)
632 Gamble Dr.
Lisle, IL 60532
Ph: (630)963-4051
Free: (800)922-2894
E-mail: tommettner@cs.com
URL: http://www.caat.org
Contact: Tom Mettner, Pres.
Founded: 1995. **Membership Dues:** individual, $100 (annual) ● training agency-per trainer (3 or more applicants), $50 (annual). **Description:** Provides support for professional automotive educators and trainers.

Automotive Industries

342 ■ American Salvage Pool Association (ASPA)
PMB 709
2100 Roswell Rd., Ste.200 C
Marietta, GA 30062
Ph: (678)560-6678 (678)645-2118
Fax: (678)560-9112
E-mail: natalie@aspa.com
URL: http://www.aspa.com
Contact: Natalie Nardone CMP, Exec. Dir.
Founded: 1975. **Members:** 172. **Membership Dues:** regular, $900-$5,600 (annual) ● associate, $300 (annual). **Staff:** 1. **Budget:** $350,000. **Regional Groups:** 4. **Description:** Salvage and storage pool owners and related industries. (The salvage pool industry provides a market for insurance companies, banks, and other businesses to "pool" together salvaged, theft recovered, and water damaged vehicles in order to sell them at more competitive prices, usually through auctions.) Encourages ethical business practices and facilitates exchange of information among members. Assists members in developing educational resources for salvage pool operations. Monitors legislative activities. **Committees:** Commu/Marketing; Convention; Education; Federal Legislative; Finance; Info Resources, Commerce; Info Resources, Services; Insurance Advisory; Legislative Monitoring; Membership/Bylaws; Past Presidents'; Regional Group. **Publications:** *ASPA Flash*, periodic. Bulletin. Contains member specific information. **Circulation:** 200. **Advertising:** accepted. Alternate Formats: diskette ● *ASPA Membership Directory*, annual. **Circulation:** 3,500. **Advertising:** accepted ● *ASPA Report*, quarterly. Newsletter. Includes committee reports, annual report, and membership activities information. Alternate Formats: online. **Conventions/Meetings:** annual convention (exhibits) - usually April.

343 ■ Association of International Automobile Manufacturers (AIAM)
2111 Wilson Blvd., Ste.1150
Arlington, VA 22201
Ph: (703)525-7788
Fax: (703)525-8817
E-mail: techaffrs@aiam.org
URL: http://www.aiam.org
Contact: Michael J. Stanton, Pres./CEO
Founded: 1964. **Members:** 17. **Staff:** 11. **Budget:** $2,900,000. **Description:** Companies that manufacture automobiles or automotive equipment and that import into, or export to, the U.S. Purposes are: to act as a clearinghouse for information, especially with regard to proposed state and federal regulations in the automobile industry as they bear upon imported automobiles; and to report proposed regulations by state or federal governments pertaining to equipment standards, licensing, and other matters affecting members. **Committees:** Consumer Relations; Emissions; Government Relations; Safety. **Formerly:** (1966) Imported Car Group; (1990) Automobile Importers of America. **Publications:** Handbooks. Alternate Formats: online.

344 ■ Automobile Film Club of America
10 Cross St.
Staten Island, NY 10304
Ph: (718)447-2255
Fax: (718)447-2289
E-mail: autofilm3@aol.com
URL: http://www.autofilmclub.com
Contact: Ralph Lucci, Contact
Founded: 1992. **Multinational**. **Description:** Works to supply vehicles and equipment for the film industry throughout the world. Helps to ensure that the production runs smoothly by providing modern facilities and vast inventory. Maintains a database of vehicles.

345 ■ Automotive Hall of Fame (AHF)
21400 Oakwood Blvd.
Dearborn, MI 48124-4078
Ph: (313)240-4000
Fax: (313)240-8641
E-mail: felicia@thedrivingspirit.org
URL: http://www.automotivehalloffame.org
Contact: Jeffrey K. Leestma, Pres.
Founded: 1939. **Members:** 700. **Staff:** 5. **Local Groups:** 20. **Description:** Individuals who have been or are now engaged in the automotive industry or related industries. Dedicated in 1976, the Automotive Hall of Fame contains exhibits and histories of the people of the industry. Perpetuates the memory of pioneers in the automotive industry among present and future generations. Cooperates with business schools and colleges that have automotive-related courses. Elects automotive pioneers to Automotive Hall of Fame annually. **Libraries: Type:** reference. **Holdings:** books. **Subjects:** automotive pioneers. **Awards:** College Scholarship. **Frequency:** annual. **Type:** scholarship. **Recipient:** for automotive students ● Distinguished Service Citation. **Frequency:** annual. **Type:** recognition. **Recipient:** for superior

performance (engaged in or retired from auto industry) ● Inductees. **Frequency:** annual. **Type:** recognition. **Recipient:** for deceased or retired automotive industry individuals who have made a dramatic impact ● Industry Leader of the Year. **Frequency:** annual. **Type:** recognition. **Recipient:** for outstanding industry leadership ● Young Leadership and Excellence Award. **Frequency:** annual. **Type:** recognition. **Recipient:** to young automotive men or women 35 and under who have demonstrated significant potential. **Formerly:** (1957) Automobile Old Timers; (1971) Automotive Old Timers; (1982) Automotive Organization Team.

346 ■ Automotive Industry Action Group (AIAG)

26200 Lahser Rd., Ste.200
Southfield, MI 48033-7100
Ph: (248)358-3003 (248)358-3570
Fax: (248)358-3253
E-mail: order_inquiry@aiag.org
URL: http://www.aiag.org
Contact: Brian L. Vautaw, Chm.

Founded: 1982. **Members:** 1,500. **Staff:** 60. **Budget:** $12,000,000. **Description:** Corporations seeking to improve productivity in the automotive industry. Fosters cooperation among on-highway and off-highway vehicle manufacturers and suppliers. Disseminates information about current industry developments to members. Develops and implements formal standards for manufacturers and suppliers. Sponsors educational and training seminars. **Awards:** Outstanding Achievement Award. **Frequency:** annual. **Type:** recognition. **Recipient:** for volunteers who benefit AIAG and the automotive industry. **Subgroups:** Collaborative Engineering; Electronic Commerce; Materials Management; Occupational Health and Safety; Quality; Truck and Heavy Equipment. **Publications:** *ActionLINE*, monthly. Magazine. **Price:** free for members. **Circulation:** 30,000. **Advertising:** accepted ● *Member Source Book*, annual. Membership Directory ● *Standards/Conventions*, periodic. Journal ● Catalog. **Conventions/Meetings:** annual Auto-Tech - conference, includes 120 educational sessions (exhibits).

347 ■ Automotive Market Research Council (AMRC)

PO Box 13966
Research Triangle Park, NC 27709-3966
Ph: (919)549-4800
Fax: (919)549-4824
E-mail: info@amrc.org
URL: http://www.amrc.org
Contact: Nancy Wang, Pres.

Founded: 1966. **Members:** 100. **Membership Dues:** company, $500 (annual) ● additional individual, $75 (annual). **Description:** Represents manufacturers of automotive service equipment, automotive parts, components, subassemblies, accessories as original or replacement equipment, and employees whose principal responsibility is market research analysis and business planning. Promotes more complete, prompt, and accurate gathering and dissemination of marketing data; seeks to increase the reliability of forecasts of demand in the industry; works to improve the professional abilities of market analysis. Works with government agencies to improve collection of statistics. **Committees:** Aftermarket; Associations; Automotive Materials; Commercial Vehicle; Heavy Duty Aftermarket; Information Services; International Research; Light Vehicle Original Equipment; Market Research and Planning; Off-Highway. **Publications:** *Automotive Data Bibliography*, biennial ● *Automotive Market Research Council—Newsletter*, periodic ● *International Bibliography*, periodic ● *Semiannual Vehicle Forecasts*. **Conventions/Meetings:** semiannual conference and seminar.

348 ■ Automotive Presidents Council (APC)

c/o Motor and Equipment Manufacturers Association
PO Box 13966
Research Triangle Park, NC 27709-3966
Ph: (919)549-4800
Fax: (919)549-4824
E-mail: info@mema.org
URL: http://www.mema.org
Contact: Robert E. McKenna, Pres./CEO

Founded: 1982. **Members:** 60. **Description:** Presidents and chief executive officers of leading manufacturing companies producing automotive parts, equipment, accessories, tools, paint, and refinishing supplies. Provides a forum in which chief executives can discuss areas of mutual interest or top management problems, share ideas, and exchange solutions. **Affiliated With:** Motor and Equipment Manufacturers Association.

349 ■ Automotive Trade Association Executives (ATAE)

8400 Westpark Dr.
McLean, VA 22102
Ph: (703)821-7072
Fax: (703)556-8581
URL: http://www.atae.info
Contact: Ray W. Shennan, Founder

Members: 107. **Description:** Executives of state and local automotive dealer associations. **Formerly:** (1984) Automotive Trade Association Managers. **Conventions/Meetings:** semiannual conference ● regional meeting ● annual seminar.

350 ■ Automotive Trade Policy Council (ATPC)

1350 I St. NW, Ste.1060
Washington, DC 20005
Ph: (202)789-0030
Fax: (202)789-0054
E-mail: scollins@autotradecouncil.org
URL: http://www.autotradecouncil.org
Contact: Stephen J. Collins, Pres.

Description: Represents the common international economic, trade and investment interests of member companies. Serves as the primary advocate for the member companies' common positions with the principal agencies for international trade and economic policy of the U.S. Government. Prepares consensus policy positions and supporting materials. Provides a forum for member companies to discuss and coordinate best approaches to common international challenges.

351 ■ Automotive Training Managers Council (ATMC)

101 Blue Seal Dr. SE, Ste.101
Leesburg, VA 20175
Ph: (703)669-6670
Fax: (703)669-6126
E-mail: info@atmc.org
URL: http://www.atmc.org
Contact: Al Ebron, Pres.

Founded: 1984. **Members:** 130. **Membership Dues:** individual, $325 (annual). **Staff:** 1. **Budget:** $120,000. **Description:** Directors of training for automotive and truck parts manufacturers and aftermarket suppliers. Seeks to enhance the role of automotive aftermarket training managers through the exchange of ideas and opinions among training experts. Encourages and works to establish high standards in the development of training programs for increased training effectiveness. Offers educational programs; conducts research. **Awards:** Training Achievement Award. **Frequency:** annual. **Type:** recognition. **Recipient:** for warehouse distributors, wholesalers, retailers, service dealers, and installers who develop effective training programs. **Committees:** Achievement Awards; Conference and Meeting; Heavy Duty; Membership/PR; Technology; Training Awards. **Publications:** *Technician Retention Guide*. **Conventions/Meetings:** semiannual conference - always spring and fall.

352 ■ Automotive Undercar Trade Organization (AUTO)

7101 Wisconsin Ave., Ste.1300
Bethesda, MD 20814
Ph: (301)654-6664
Fax: (301)654-3299
E-mail: kimberlee.berry@aftermarket.org
URL: http://www.undercar.org
Contact: Malcolm Sissmore, Pres.

Membership Dues: service facility, $90 (annual) ● service affiliate, $10 (annual) ● warehouse distributor/associate/manufacturer's representative, $175 (annual) ● manufacturer, $500 (annual). **Description:** Provides guidelines for self-regulation and certification. Provides opportunities for networking with industry leaders and learning about additional business opportunities. **Publications:** Newsletter, monthly. Contains industry information, association updates and business opportunities. **Price:** included in membership dues. Alternate Formats: online. **Conventions/Meetings:** biennial conference.

353 ■ Automotive Women's Alliance (AWA)

PO Box 4305
Troy, MI 48099-4305
Ph: (248)643-6590
Fax: (248)643-9685
URL: http://www.automotivewomensalliance.com
Contact: Susan West, Pres.

Founded: 2001. **Members:** 300. **Membership Dues:** regular, $85 (annual) ● gold, $150 (annual) ● student, $25 (annual). **Multinational. Description:** Represents and supports women in automotive and affiliated industries. **Awards:** AWAF Education Scholarship. **Frequency:** quarterly. **Type:** scholarship. **Recipient:** for young women who are choosing a career in the automotive industry ● Global Scholarship. **Frequency:** annual. **Type:** scholarship. **Recipient:** to women in all aspects of the automotive and affiliated industries. **Committees:** AWAF Education Scholarship; Event; Marketing; Mentoring; Professional Development; Sponsorship. **Councils:** Executive Advisory. **Publications:** *Member Roster*. Directory ● *Up To Speed*, quarterly. Newsletter. **Advertising:** accepted ● Brochure. **Conventions/Meetings:** seminar.

354 ■ Car Care Council (CCC)

7101 Wisconsin Ave., Ste.1300
Bethesda, MD 20814
Ph: (240)333-1088
E-mail: marcella.tilli@aftermarket.org
URL: http://www.carcare.org
Contact: Rich White, Exec. Dir.

Founded: 1969. **Staff:** 2. **Languages:** English, Spanish. **Description:** Works as the source of information for the "Be Car Care Aware" consumer education campaign promoting the benefits of regular vehicle care, maintenance and repair to consumers. **Libraries: Type:** reference. **Holdings:** articles. **Awards:** Women's Automotive Communications Awards. **Frequency:** annual. **Type:** recognition. **Subgroups:** Women's Board. **Publications:** *Car Care Chronicles*, quarterly. Newsletter. **Price:** free. Alternate Formats: online.

355 ■ Commercial Vehicle Safety Alliance (CVSA)

c/o Mr. Stephen F. Campbell, Exec. Dir.
1101 17th St. NW, Ste.803
Washington, DC 20036
Ph: (202)775-1623
Fax: (202)775-1624
E-mail: cvsahq@cvsa.org
URL: http://www.cvsa.org
Contact: Mr. Stephen F. Campbell, Exec. Dir.

Founded: 1982. **Members:** 70. **Staff:** 9. **Budget:** $3,000,000. **Multinational. Description:** Local, state, provincial, territorial and federal motor carrier safety officials and industry representatives from the United States, Canada, and Mexico. Promotes commercial motor vehicle safety and security by providing leadership to enforcement, industry and policy makers. **Telecommunication Services:** electronic mail, stephenc@cvsa.org. **Publications:** *Guardian*, quarterly. Magazine. Alternate Formats: online. **Conventions/Meetings:** annual conference (exhibits) - always in the spring ● annual workshop (exhibits) - always in the fall.

356 ■ Heavy-Duty Business Forum (HDBF)
10 Lab. Dr.
PO Box 13966
Research Triangle Park, NC 27709-3966
Ph: (919)406-8808
Fax: (919)549-4824
E-mail: info@hdma.org
URL: http://www.hdma.org/membership/benefits.php
Contact: Tim Kraus, Exec. Dir.
Founded: 1977. **Members:** 50. **Membership Dues:** individual, $450 (annual). **Staff:** 2. **Budget:** $50,000. **Description:** A division of the Heavy Duty Manufacturers Association. Executives engaged in the manufacturing and marketing of products for the heavy-duty vehicle industry (membership is limited to 50 and by invitation only). Serves as a forum for idea and information exchange among members. **Publications:** none. **Affiliated With:** Motor and Equipment Manufacturers Association. **Conventions/Meetings:** semiannual conference - always May and November.

357 ■ Heavy Duty Distribution Association (HDDA)
4600 East-West Hwy., Ste.300
Bethesda, MD 20814
Ph: (301)654-6664
Fax: (301)654-3299
E-mail: hdda@aftermarket.org
URL: http://www.hdda.org
Contact: Lee Kadrich, VP
Founded: 1988. **Members:** 160. **Staff:** 40. **Description:** Serves aftermarket distributors manufacturers of parts and services for commercial vehicles in North America, especially the heavy duty aftermarket. **Publications:** Newsletter, biweekly. **Conventions/Meetings:** annual convention.

358 ■ International Association of Quality Technicians in the Automotive Industry
c/o Rachel Vandongen
9705 Sterling
Allen Park, MI 48101
Contact: Rachel VanDongen, Sec.
Founded: 1999. **Staff:** 4. **Multinational. Description:** Represents the interests of individuals employed in quality assurance and control areas of automotive manufacturing industries throughout the world.

359 ■ International Automotive Remarketers Alliance (IARA)
PO Box 431
Mount Arlington, NJ 07856
Ph: (973)398-2774
Fax: (973)398-2731
E-mail: info@iaraonline.org
URL: http://www.iaraonline.org
Contact: Steve Houston, Pres.
Founded: 2001. **Description:** Aims for the continuous improvement of the vehicle remarketing industry. Provides a forum in which members are able to maximize remarketed vehicle portfolio values. Facilitates standardization of processes within the industry. **Awards:** Circle Of Excellence Award. **Frequency:** annual. **Type:** recognition. **Recipient:** to an individual who has clearly demonstrated outstanding contributions to the betterment of society and to the remarketing industry ● IARA Remarketing Industry Recognition Award. **Frequency:** annual. **Type:** recognition. **Recipient:** for outstanding contributions to the remarketing industry. **Publications:** *Automotive Remarketer*. Newsletter.

360 ■ International Manufacturers Representatives Association (IMRA)
PO Box 702678
Tulsa, OK 74170
Fax: (918)743-5443
E-mail: onewhitedog@msn.com
Contact: Mert Dale, Sec.-Treas.
Founded: 1958. **Members:** 18. **For-Profit. Description:** Manufacturers' representatives who are specialists in representing manufacturers of automotive refinishing supplies and related products for auto body repair. Assists manufacturers in locating reputable representatives. Supplies information on the advantages of using manufacturers' representative as opposed to a company direct salesman. **Conventions/Meetings:** annual International Autobody Congress & Exposition - conference (exhibits) - December.

361 ■ National Association of Dealer Counsel (NADC)
7250 Parkway Dr., Ste.510
Hanover, MD 21076-1343
Ph: (410)712-4037
Fax: (410)712-4038
E-mail: contact@dealercounsel.com
URL: http://www.dealercounsel.com
Contact: Jack Tracey CAE, Interim Exec. Dir.
Founded: 2004. **Members:** 400. **Membership Dues:** full, trade association executive, dealer, $585 (annual) ● fellow, $200 (annual) ● associate, $1,500 (annual). **Staff:** 2. **Budget:** $300,000. **Description:** Provides a forum for members to share information, common experience, advice, help and answers to questions on manufacturer franchise issues, lemon laws, vehicle finance and regulatory complexities, insurance laws, tax laws, multiple regulatory requirements, buy and sell agreements, rights of first refusal, employment laws and the many other issues facing dealers and their counsel today. **Computer Services:** database, member directory ● mailing lists, member-only listserv ● online services, member forum. **Publications:** *Headlights*, monthly. Newsletter. Alternate Formats: online ● *Spot Delivery*, monthly. Newsletter. Provides updates on legal issues that affect automobile dealership operations.

362 ■ National Association of Fleet Administrators (NAFA)
125 Village Blvd., Ste.200
Princeton Forrestal Village
Princeton, NJ 08540
Ph: (609)720-0882 (609)986-1055
Fax: (609)452-8004
E-mail: info@nafa.org
URL: http://www.nafa.org
Contact: Phillip E. Russo CAE, Exec. Dir.
Founded: 1957. **Members:** 4,000. **Membership Dues:** full, $440 (annual) ● associate, $350 (annual) ● full affiliate, $440 (annual) ● regional affiliate, $350 (annual) ● international full, $685 (annual) ● international associate, $595 (annual) ● international web subscriber, $180 (annual) ● student, $45 (annual). **Staff:** 14. **Budget:** $3,000,000. **Regional Groups:** 33. **Description:** Persons responsible for the administration of a motor vehicle fleet of 25 or more units for a firm not commercially engaged in the sale, rental, or lease of motor vehicles. Compiles statistics. Maintains placement service and speakers' bureau; conducts research programs. Operates Fleet Information Resource Center. Sponsors professional Certified Automotive Fleet Manager certification. **Libraries: Type:** not open to the public. **Subjects:** fleet management. **Awards:** Distinguished Service Award. **Frequency:** annual. **Type:** recognition. **Recipient:** for exemplary professional and personal contributions to the industry, society, and/or community ● Larry Goill Quality Fleet Management Idea Award. **Frequency:** annual. **Type:** recognition. **Recipient:** to individuals whose creative ideas have improved fleet management. **Committees:** Editorial; Education; Law Enforcement; Light Trucks; Public Service Fleets; Safety. **Programs:** Advanced Fleet Management; Basic Principles of Fleet Management; Masters' Forums; Outsourcing Fleet Management. **Publications:** *Fleet Executive*, 8/year. Magazine. Contains in-depth stories designed to educate, inform and facilitate fleet managers to excel in their jobs. **Price:** included in membership dues. **Advertising:** accepted. Alternate Formats: online ● *Fleet Manager's Manual*. For fleet managers. ● *FleetFocus*, biweekly. Newsletter. Includes legislative news, quarterly safety results, calendar of events, and list of job openings. **Price:** included in membership dues. **Circulation:** 4,000. Alternate Formats: online ● *NAFA Annual Reference Book*. Provides data on tires, vehicle service recommendations, results of association surveys, vehicle specifications, EPA gas mileage figures, etc. **Price:** free for members and affiliates; $35.00 /year for nonmembers. **Circulation:** 5,000. **Advertising:** accepted ● *NAFA Roster*, annual. Membership Directory. Lists all members and affiliates arranged alphabetically by company name, chapter affiliation, and industry type. **Price:** available to members only. **Circulation:** 4,000. **Advertising:** accepted ● *NAFA's Fleet Executive*, monthly. Journal. Provides articles on fleet management, reports on important automotive developments, and news of interest to members and affiliates. Includes index. **Price:** free for members, affiliates, and advertisers; $48.00 /year for nonmembers. **Circulation:** 4,000. **Advertising:** accepted. **Conventions/Meetings:** annual Fleet Management Institute - meeting (exhibits).

363 ■ National Auto Body Council (NABC)
PO Box 3007
Mechanicsville, VA 23116
Free: (888)667-7433
Fax: (866)498-7433
E-mail: info@autobodycouncil.org
URL: http://www.autobodycouncil.org
Contact: Russell Thrall III, Pres.
Founded: 1994. **Members:** 400. **Membership Dues:** corporate, $5,000 (annual) ● individual, $100 (annual) ● prestige, $250 (annual) ● premier, $500 (annual) ● pinnacle, $1,000 (annual). **Staff:** 1. **Budget:** $125,000. **Description:** Members from the collision repair industry. Seeks to promote pride in professionalism and increase consumer confidence. **Awards:** Pride Awards. **Frequency:** annual. **Type:** recognition. **Recipient:** for outstanding charitable acts by industry members. **Telecommunication Services:** electronic mail, russ@thrall3.com. **Publications:** *The Good News*, quarterly. Newsletter. Highlights the best of the collision industry. **Price:** free for members. **Circulation:** 500. Alternate Formats: online.

364 ■ Overseas Automotive Council (OAC)
PO Box 13966
10 Lab. Dr.
Research Triangle Park, NC 27709-3966
Ph: (919)406-8810
Fax: (919)549-4824
E-mail: oac@mema.org
URL: http://www.oac-intl.org
Contact: Rafaat N. Kureshi, Pres.
Founded: 1923. **Members:** 700. **Membership Dues:** domestic, $200-$400 (annual) ● international, $175 (annual). **Budget:** $200,000. **Description:** Multifaceted resource for individuals involved in the international marketing and sales of automotive products manufactured in the United States. Provides a forum, which enhances the prestige of the American automotive industry, promoting friendly trade relationships with understanding of the various cultures involved. **Libraries: Type:** reference. **Holdings:** archival material. **Formerly:** (1992) Overseas Automotive Club. **Publications:** *Global Report*, monthly. Newsletter. Alternate Formats: online ● *Overseas Automotive Council—Membership Roster*, annual. Membership Directory. Lists members engaged in the overseas automotive trade of the U.S. Includes advertising index, cross-index of products sold by members, and calendar. **Circulation:** 1,000. **Conventions/Meetings:** luncheon and conference - 4-5/year.

365 ■ Society of Automotive Analysts (SAA)
3300 Washtenaw Ave., Ste.220
Ann Arbor, MI 48104-4200
Ph: (734)677-3518
Fax: (734)677-2407
E-mail: cybersaa@cybersaa.org
URL: http://www.cybersaa.org
Contact: Robert E. Barba, Exec. Dir.
Founded: 1987. **Members:** 600. **Membership Dues:** individual, $125 (annual). **Staff:** 2. **Budget:** $250,000. **Description:** Aims to be the leading organization providing access to candid opinions and analyses of the global automotive industry. Comprises of automotive firm analysts and executives, stock market analysts and other interested individuals. Promotes professional interaction in the automobile industry. Maintains automobile industry contacts. Holds joint seminars with universities, manufacturers' associa-

tions and other industry groups. **Awards:** SAA Scholarship. **Frequency:** annual. **Type:** scholarship. **Computer Services:** Mailing lists, of members. **Committees:** Education; Scholarship. **Publications:** *AutoBeat ASIA*, weekly, every Monday morning. Newsletter. **Price:** free for members ● *AutoBeat Daily*. Newsletter. **Price:** free for members ● Membership Directory. Alternate Formats: online. **Conventions/Meetings:** annual Automotive Outlook - international conference (exhibits) ● annual Strategic Planning Summit - conference, brings together leading automotive research, forecasting and consulting firms to address a variety of pertinent issues.

366 ■ Truck Manufacturers Association (TMA)
1225 New York Ave. NW, Ste.300
Washington, DC 20005-6156
Ph: (202)638-7825
Fax: (202)737-3742
E-mail: contacttma@truckmfgs.org
URL: http://www.truckmfgs.org
Contact: Robert M. Clarke, Pres.
Founded: 1995. **Members:** 8. **Staff:** 2. **Budget:** $450,000. **Multinational. Description:** Represents the major North American manufacturers of medium and heavy duty trucks to the governmental entities that regulate the industry.

367 ■ Women's Automotive Association International (WAAI)
PO Box 2535
Birmingham, MI 48012
Ph: (248)646-5250
Fax: (248)646-6721
E-mail: lhswaai@aol.com
URL: http://www.waai.com
Contact: Lorraine H. Schultz, Founder/CEO
Founded: 1995. **Membership Dues:** regular, $90 (annual) ● associate, $50 (annual) ● sustaining, $130 (annual) ● student, $25 (annual). **Multinational. Description:** Recognizes the achievements of women in the automotive industry. Provides educational e-news to automotive career-focused individuals. Builds relationships through networking and other interactive forums. Encourages growth through mentoring, educational endeavors, and scholarships. **Awards:** Professional Achievement Award. **Frequency:** annual. **Type:** recognition. **Recipient:** to a professional woman in the automotive industry in recognition of her commitment, professionalism, and success in the automotive industry ● Spirit of Leadership Award. **Frequency:** annual. **Type:** recognition. **Recipient:** to professional women in the automotive industry in recognition of their significant accomplishments in their profession, community, and family.

Automotive Manufacturers

368 ■ Alliance of Automobile Manufacturers
1401 Eye St. NW, Ste.900
Washington, DC 20005
Ph: (202)326-5500
Fax: (202)326-5598
E-mail: info@autoalliance.org
URL: http://www.autoalliance.org
Contact: Dave McCurdy, Pres./CEO
Founded: 1999. **Members:** 9. **Multinational. Description:** New car and light truck manufacturers. Works to improve the environment and motor vehicles safety. Strives to seek harmonization of global standards; promotes market-based, cost-effective solutions in preference to mandates on public policy issues; provides industry information and data with global perspective; provides industry forum for issues; and provides essential industry interface with other organizations and coalitions.

369 ■ Ambulance Manufacturers Division (AMD)
c/o National Truck Equipment Association
37400 Hills Tech Dr.
Farmington Hills, MI 48331-3414
Ph: (248)489-7090
Free: (800)441-NTEA
Fax: (248)489-8590
E-mail: info@ntea.com
URL: http://www.ntea.com
Contact: Jim Carney, Exec. Dir.
Founded: 1975. **Members:** 45. **Membership Dues:** full/associate, $250 (annual) ● distributor (based on annual volume sales), $650-$1,700 (annual) ● manufacturer (based on annual volume sales), $950-$2,700 (annual). **Description:** A division of the National Truck Equipment Association. Manufacturers of ambulance, rescue, and emergency vehicles, and related emergency apparatus and equipment. Works to expand and improve the market segment; acquires, preserves, and disseminates information on the role of emergency vehicles; improves relationships with other industry segments; promotes product innovations and assists in the development of industry safety standards and programs. **Libraries: Type:** reference. **Subjects:** performance standards for ambulances. **Additional Websites:** http://www.worktrucks.com. **Affiliated With:** National Truck Equipment Association. **Publications:** *AMD Standards 001-015*. Provides performance standards for ambulances. **Price:** free. Alternate Formats: online ● Membership Directory. **Conventions/Meetings:** semiannual meeting.

370 ■ Association of Automotive Aftermarket Distributors/Parts Plus (AAAD)
3085 Fountainside Dr., No. 210
Germantown, TN 38138
Ph: (901)682-9090
Free: (800)727-8112
Fax: (901)682-9098
E-mail: info@networkhq.org
URL: http://www.partsplus.com
Contact: Michael Lambert, Pres.
Founded: 1977. **Members:** 34. **Staff:** 22. **Budget:** $5,000,000. **Description:** Represents the independent automotive warehouse distributors. Purchases and markets automotive replacement parts through wholesale/retail auto parts stores. Conducts marketing activities. **Formerly:** (2002) Association of Automotive Aftermarket Distributors. **Publications:** *Car Care Center Newsletter* ● *Parts Plus Magazine*, bimonthly. **Circulation:** 5,500. **Conventions/Meetings:** Business/Marketing - conference.

371 ■ Auto International Association (AIA)
7101 Wisconsin Ave., Ste.1300
Bethesda, MD 20814
Ph: (301)654-6664
Fax: (301)654-3299
E-mail: aaia@aftermarket.org
URL: http://aiaglobal.org
Contact: Lee Kadrich, Staff Liaison
Founded: 1983. **Members:** 400. **Staff:** 20. **Description:** Manufacturers/importers, distributors/retailers, subcontractors, and manufacturers' representatives supporting the import automotive aftermarket products industry. Works to promote and protect the interests of the import auto and accessories industry. Offers Import Parts Specialist certification program for sales personnel. Produces annual AIA World Auto Parts Conference. Compiles statistics. **Awards: Frequency:** annual. **Type:** recognition. **Recipient:** for excellence in developing high quality products and innovative marketing programs for import cars or trucks. **Committees:** Educational Services; VMPG Vehicle Manufacturers Parts Group. **Publications:** *AIA Facts*, biweekly. Newsletter. Alternate Formats: online ● *AIA Update*, monthly. Newsletter. Provides information on automotive parts and accessories. Includes membership profiles and new product information. **Price:** included in membership dues. **Circulation:** 500. **Advertising:** accepted ● Membership Directory, annual. **Conventions/Meetings:** annual show and trade show, largest North American auto show (exhibits) ● World Auto Parts - conference.

372 ■ Autobody Craftsman Association (ACA)
c/o Alpine Auto Body
PO Box 820230
Vancouver, WA 98662
Ph: (206)575-8893
Free: (800)526-3792
E-mail: info@acanw.com
URL: http://www.acanw.com
Contact: William Parkins, Pres.
Founded: 1977. **Members:** 150. **Membership Dues:** independent repair shop, $36-$79 (monthly) ● associate, out of state, $24-$49 (monthly) ● educational, $19 (monthly). **Staff:** 1. **Budget:** $225,000. **Description:** Autobody designers and engineers. Maintains statistics. Sponsors educational, research, and charitable programs. Offers placement services. **Libraries: Type:** reference. **Affiliated With:** Society of Collision Repair Specialists. **Publications:** *Autobody Craftsman Association Directory*, biennial. **Price:** $49.95/copy. **Circulation:** 500. **Advertising:** accepted ● *Collision World News*, monthly. Newsletter. **Price:** $24.00/year. **Circulation:** 3,000. **Advertising:** accepted. **Conventions/Meetings:** annual meeting.

373 ■ Automatic Transmission Rebuilders Association (ATRA)
2400 Latigo Ave.
Oxnard, CA 93030
Ph: (805)604-2000
Free: (866)GO4-ATRA
Fax: (805)604-2027
E-mail: membership@atra.com
URL: http://www.atra.com
Contact: Charles Ed Doyle Jr., Sec.-Treas.
Founded: 1954. **Members:** 2,700. **Membership Dues:** rebuilder, supplier, $85 (monthly) ● technical subscriber, $70 (monthly). **Staff:** 27. **Description:** Transmission rebuilders and suppliers. Provides a basis for cross-country guarantees among members; and formulates basic advertising format incorporating the association emblem and logo. Conducts automatic transmission service and repair clinics. **Telecommunication Services:** electronic mail, a1e@classicnet.net. **Departments:** Audio Visual; Technical. **Publications:** *ATRA Scene*, annual. Magazine ● *The Good Guys*, 10/year. Newsletter ● *Membership Roster*, 1-2/year. Directory ● Bulletins ● Manuals ● Also publishes service information letters. **Conventions/Meetings:** annual trade show (exhibits).

374 ■ Automotive Aftermarket Industry Association (AAIA)
7101 Wisconsin Ave., Ste.1300
Bethesda, MD 20814-3415
Ph: (301)654-6664
Fax: (301)654-3299
E-mail: aaia@aftermarket.org
URL: http://www.aftermarket.org
Contact: Kathleen Schmatz, Pres./CEO
Founded: 1999. **Members:** 8,243. **Membership Dues:** supplier, $650-$7,500 (annual) ● buyer, $400-$7,500 (annual) ● associate, $375-$1,400 (annual) ● trade press, $250 (annual) ● educational institution, $275 (annual) ● program group, $1,000 (annual) ● agency/manufacturers' representative, $275-$750 (annual). **Staff:** 38. **Budget:** $7,000,000. **Multinational. Description:** Automotive parts and accessories retailers, distributors, manufacturers, and manufacturers' representatives. Conducts research and compiles statistics. Conducts seminars and provides specialized education program. **Libraries: Type:** reference. **Subjects:** aftermarket management resources. **Awards:** Industry Leadership Award. **Frequency:** annual. **Type:** recognition. **Computer Services:** Mailing lists, of members. **Telecommunication Services:** electronic mail, kathleen.schmatz@aftermarket.org. **Committees:** Category Management; Education Rep; Electronic Information Management; Government Affairs; Market Research; Marketing Communications; Member Development; Member Services; Show; Strategic Planning; Technology Standards and Solutions. **Divisions:** Communications; Data Services; International Trade; Manufacturer's Representative; Technical Services. **Publications:** *Aftermarket Insider*, bimonthly. Magazine. **Price:** included in membership dues. **Circulation:** 8,000 ● *APAA Who's Who*, annual. Directory. Lists companies and the products in the exhibits at the annual APAA Show. **Price:** free to those attending the APAA Show. **Circulation:** 15,000. **Advertis-**

ing: accepted ● *Facts*, weekly or biweekly. Newsletters. Features up-to-the-minute industry and association news. **Price:** included in membership dues. Alternate Formats: online ● *Foreign Buyers Directory*, annual. **Conventions/Meetings:** annual Automotive Aftermarket Products Expo (AAPEX) - convention and trade show, international exhibition of automotive parts, accessories, tools and service equipment (exhibits) - always October.

375 ■ Automotive Engine Rebuilders Association (AERA)
330 Lexington Dr.
Buffalo Grove, IL 60089-6933
Ph: (847)541-6550
Free: (888)326-2372
Fax: (888)329-2372
E-mail: john@aera.org
URL: http://www.aera.org
Contact: John Goodman, Pres./CEO
Founded: 1922. **Members:** 4,100. **Membership Dues:** associate, $295-$570 (annual) ● active, $295-$550 (annual) ● engine builder/installer, $285-$540 (annual) ● engine builder/installer (international), $320-$575 (annual) ● active (international), $325-$590 (annual) ● associate (international), $340-$600 (annual) ● government, $350 (annual) ● government (international), $380 (annual) ● school, $200 (annual) ● school (international), $245 (annual). **Staff:** 12. **Budget:** $1,500,000. **Multinational. Description:** Wholesalers of automotive replacement parts and equipment with machine shop operations; associate members are suppliers of parts, equipment, tools, and services to the rebuilder members. Acts as clearinghouse for automotive jobber machine shop information. **Awards:** Charles W. Yount Distinguished Service Award. **Type:** recognition. **Telecommunication Services:** additional toll-free number, technical, (888)324-2372. **Formerly:** National Cylinder Grinders Association. **Publications:** *Automotive Engine Rebuilders Association—Technical Bulletin*, monthly. Describes technical changes in specification of light- and heavy-duty engines. **Price:** included in membership dues; $75.00 for nonmembers in U.S.; $85.00 for nonmembers outside U.S. **Circulation:** 4,100 ● *Connecting Rod Manual*, semiannual. **Price:** included in membership dues; $69.00/copy for nonmembers. **Circulation:** 4,100 ● *Crankshaft Manual*, semiannual. Identifies automotive engine crankshafts by casting/forging number. **Price:** included in membership dues; $59.00/copy for nonmembers. **Circulation:** 4,100 ● *Cylinder Head and Block Identification Guide*, annual. Manual. Identifies automotive engine cylinder heads and blocks by casting number. **Price:** included in membership dues; $59.00/copy for nonmembers. **Circulation:** 4,100 ● *Shop Talk*, monthly. Newsletter. Contains association and industry information. **Price:** included in membership dues. **Circulation:** 4,100. Alternate Formats: online ● Booklets. **Conventions/Meetings:** annual show and seminar, on operating machine equipment, parts and supplies (exhibits) - always odd-numbered years.

376 ■ Automotive Lift Institute (ALI)
PO Box 85
Cortland, NY 13045
Ph: (607)756-7775
Fax: (607)756-0888
E-mail: info@autolift.org
URL: http://www.autolift.org
Contact: Bob O'Gorman, Pres.
Founded: 1945. **Members:** 18. **Staff:** 4. **Budget:** $500,000. **Description:** Manufacturers and marketers of automotive lifts in the U.S. and Canada whose products have been listed and certified by an OSHA. Promotes safety standards in automotive lifts industry. **Committees:** Automotive Liaison; Engineering; Public Relations; Safety; Standards. **Sections:** Heavy Duty Mobile Lifts; In-Ground Hydraulic Automotive Lifts; Surface-Mounted Automotive Lifts. **Publications:** *ANSI/ALI ALCTV-1998 Safety Standard for the Construction, Testing and Validation of Automotive Lifts* ● *ANSI/ALI ALIS-2001 Safety Standard for Installation and Service of Automotive Lifts* ● *ANSI/ALI ALOIM-2000 Safety Standard for Operation, Inspection and Maintenance of Automotive Lifts* ● *Guide to Lifting Points for Frame Engaging Lifts*, annual ● *Lifting It Right Video & Manual*. Includes instructor's quiz. ● *Membership List of Manufacturers of ALI/ETL Certified Lifts*, periodic. Membership Directory ● *Safety Tips*. Wall chart. ● *Uniform Warning Labels*. Features pictographic safety decals. **Conventions/Meetings:** semiannual meeting, for members only.

377 ■ Automotive Occupant Restraints Council (AORC)
1081 Dove Run Rd., Ste.403
Lexington, KY 40502
Ph: (859)269-4240
Fax: (859)269-4241
E-mail: info@aorc.org
URL: http://www.aorc.org
Contact: Wendell C. Lane Jr., Chm.
Founded: 1965. **Members:** 54. **Membership Dues:** system manufacturer, $50,000 (annual) ● component manufacturer, $6,000 (annual) ● material manufacturer, $4,000 (annual) ● sponsoring, $3,000 (annual). **Staff:** 2. **Budget:** $250,000. **Description:** Manufacturers of motor vehicle occupant restraint systems and of primary and secondary component materials and supplies. Undertakes research; cooperates with other organizations in promulgating performance standards; and promotes the installation and use of safety belts and air bags. Conducts public education program on air bags and seat belts. **Awards:** Path Finder Award. **Frequency:** annual. **Type:** recognition. **Recipient:** for vision and leadership in auto and occupant safety. **Committees:** Air Bag Inflator; Air Bag Inflator Recycling/Disposal; Occupant Ejection Protection; Safety, Health and Environmental; Seat Belt Technical; Sensing and Active Safety; Systems Performance and Numerical Analysis; UN Air Bag Transportation and Classification. **Formerly:** (1969) American Seat Belt Council; (1978) American Safety Belt Council; (1989) American Seat Belt Council. **Supersedes:** Automobile Safety Belt Institute. **Conventions/Meetings:** annual meeting - always March.

378 ■ Automotive Refrigeration Products Institute (ARPI)
Address Unknown since 2007
URL: http://www.imaca.org
Founded: 1983. **Members:** 10. **Description:** Companies involved in the manufacture, sale, and distribution of automotive refrigeration products. Promotes the establishment of industry standards. **Publications:** none. **Committees:** Environmental Activities; Technical Standards. **Conventions/Meetings:** semiannual meeting.

379 ■ Automotive Warehouse Distributors Association (AWDA)
7101 Wisconsin Ave., Ste.1300
Bethesda, MD 20814
Ph: (301)654-6664
Fax: (301)654-3299
E-mail: info@awda.org
URL: http://www.awda.org
Contact: Tim Sturdevant, Chm.
Founded: 1947. **Members:** 335. **Budget:** $2,000,000. **Description:** Warehouse distributors of automotive parts and supplies; manufacturers of automotive parts and suppliers; publishers. Compiles statistics. **Awards:** Automotive Leader of the Year. **Frequency:** annual. **Type:** recognition. **Recipient:** to an aftermarket professional who has contributed to the industry in a unique and significant manner ● AWDA Memorial Scholarship Award. **Frequency:** annual. **Type:** scholarship. **Recipient:** to someone who has shown extraordinary devotion to duty in supporting the association and its many needs ● Martin Fromm Lifetime Achievement Award. **Frequency:** annual. **Type:** recognition. **Recipient:** to industry leaders who exemplify Fromm's unique dedication to AWDA ● Pursuit of Excellence Awards. **Frequency:** annual. **Type:** recognition. **Recipient:** to individuals or companies for their outstanding support of AWDA programs. **Committees:** Financial Statistics and Market Research; Government Affairs; Logistics and Technology; Marketing Communications; Store Operations and Sales; Young Executives Society. **Councils:** Manufacturers Advisory. **Publications:** *AWDA Facts*, biweekly. Newsletter. Features market research, industry news, legislative and regulatory actions, and association activities and services. **Price:** included in membership dues. Alternate Formats: online ● *AWDA News*, bimonthly. Newsletter. Contains industry news and events, association updates, legal bulletins, and university news. **Price:** included in membership dues. **Circulation:** 1,700 ● *Leadership Directory*, annual. **Price:** $10.00 for members; $200.00 for nonmembers ● *Life in the Fast Lane: Careers in the Automotive Aftermarket*. Video. Contains introduction to the wide variety of industry career opportunities in the automotive aftermarket. **Price:** $6.00 each for schools; $9.00 each for individuals ● *Washington Alert/Legal Bulletin*, monthly. **Conventions/Meetings:** annual conference ● workshop.

380 ■ Battery Council International (BCI)
401 N Michigan Ave., 24th Fl.
Chicago, IL 60611-4267
Ph: (312)644-6610
Fax: (312)527-6640
E-mail: info@batterycouncil.org
URL: http://www.batterycouncil.org
Contact: Maurice A. Desmarais CAE, Exec. VP
Founded: 1924. **Members:** 175. **Staff:** 3. **Budget:** $1,300,000. **Multinational. Description:** Manufacturers, suppliers of materials, and national distributors of lead-acid storage batteries. Recommends industry standards; compiles statistics. **Committees:** Data Book; Deep Cycle and Electrical Vehicle Battery; Environmental; Industrial Battery and Charger; Industrial Health; Industry Relations; Materials; Membership; Product Information; Product Safety; Technical. **Formerly:** (1940) National Battery Manufacturers Association; (1970) Association of American Battery Manufacturers. **Publications:** *Battery Council International—News*, periodic. Newsletter. Contains association and industry news; includes graphs, statistical information, committee reports, convention news, and news about members. **Price:** free. **Circulation:** 725. Also Cited As: *BCI News* ● *The Battery Man*. Magazine. **Advertising:** accepted ● *Battery Replacement Data Book*, annual. Features tables giving information on group sizing numbers for replacement batteries in various makes of automobiles, trucks, buses, and tractors. **Price:** $1.20 each, for members (10,000 copies/shipment); $1.60 each, for nonmembers (10,000 copies/shipment). **Circulation:** 65,000. Alternate Formats: CD-ROM ● *Battery Service Manual*, periodic. Serves as a technical manual for consumers and technical engineers on automotive batteries. **Price:** $2.75 each, for members (1,000 copies per shipment); $3.50 each, for nonmembers (1,000 copies per shipment). **Circulation:** 100,000. Alternate Formats: CD-ROM ● *Battery Technical Manual*, periodic. Includes standards and recommendations for testing lead-acid batteries and components. **Price:** $99.00 1-10 copies (for members); $89.00 11-24 copies (for members); $125.00 1-10 copies (for nonmembers); $115.00 11-24 copies (for nonmembers). Alternate Formats: CD-ROM ● *Failure Modes of Batteries Removed From Service*. Report. **Price:** $6.00 for nonmembers, plus shipping and handling ● Proceedings. Alternate Formats: CD-ROM. **Conventions/Meetings:** annual meeting, equipment for manufacture of lead-acid batteries (exhibits).

381 ■ Brake Manufacturers Council (BMC)
PO Box 13966
Research Triangle Park, NC 27709-3966
Ph: (919)549-4800
Fax: (919)549-8496
E-mail: bmc@mema.org
URL: http://www.brakecouncil.org
Contact: Richard Johnston, Chm.
Founded: 1973. **Members:** 28. **Membership Dues:** company, $2,500 (annual). **Staff:** 2. **Description:** Manufacturers of brake system parts who supply both the original equipment automotive market and the automotive replacement parts market. **Formerly:** Brake System Parts Manufacturers Council. **Conventions/Meetings:** annual meeting.

382 ■ Commercial Vehicle Solutions Network (CVSN)
5121 Bowden Rd., Ste.303
Jacksonville, FL 32216-5950
Ph: (904)737-2900
Fax: (904)636-9881
E-mail: info@cvsn.org
URL: http://www.cfshq.com
Contact: Angelo Volpe, Exec. VP

Founded: 1967. **Members:** 217. **Membership Dues:** regular, $1,000 (annual). **Staff:** 5. **Description:** Represents heavy-duty truck parts and service aftermarket. **Libraries: Type:** lending. **Holdings:** audio recordings, books, video recordings. **Subjects:** general business. **Telecommunication Services:** electronic mail, avolpe@cvsn.org. **Committees:** Planning; Reciprocal Warranty; Research. **Formed by Merger of:** (2006) Council of Fleet Specialists and National Wheel and Rim Association. **Publications:** *Buyers Guide and Services Directory*, annual ● *Heavy-Duty*, bimonthly. Newsletter. Contains the latest industry news and educational articles including full coverage of meetings and conferences. **Conventions/Meetings:** annual Business Forum - meeting.

383 ■ Equipment and Tool Institute (ETI)
134 W Univ. Dr., Ste.206
Rochester, MI 48307
Ph: (248)656-5080
Fax: (603)971-2375
E-mail: info@etools.org
URL: http://www.etools.org
Contact: John D. Wiedemann, Pres.

Founded: 1947. **Members:** 70. **Membership Dues:** company in North America (with annual sales of under $10 million to over $50 million), $5,000-$10,000 (annual). **Staff:** 4. **Budget:** $1,500,000. **Description:** Manufacturers of automotive service equipment and tools. **Libraries: Type:** reference; not open to the public. **Holdings:** archival material. **Subjects:** vehicle specifications. **Awards:** Founders Award. **Type:** recognition. **Recipient:** for contributions to the institute. **Committees:** .42-Volt; Inspection and Maintenance; On-Board Diagnostic & Protocol Interface Review. **Subgroups:** Collision Repair; Shop Management and Information Software; Undercar; Underhood. **Publications:** *ETI News and Views*, quarterly. **Circulation:** 1,200. Alternate Formats: online ● *Who's Who in Service Tools and Equipment*, annual. Directory. Lists manufacturers of automotive service equipment and tools. **Conventions/Meetings:** annual conference.

384 ■ Filter Manufacturers Council (FMC)
PO Box 13966
Research Triangle Park, NC 27709-3966
Ph: (919)549-4800 (919)406-8817
Free: (800)993-4583
Fax: (919)406-1306
E-mail: rbumpass@mema.org
URL: http://www.filtercouncil.org
Contact: Robin Bumpass, Contact

Founded: 1971. **Members:** 26. **Staff:** 2. **Multinational. Description:** Worldwide manufacturers of filters for automotive and industrial companies. Keeps members informed of governmental actions relating to the filter industry. Provides regulatory assistance to commercial generators of used vehicular oil filters, and a forum for discussions of issues affecting the industry. **Computer Services:** database, covering state regulations regarding used oil filters and recycling methods. **Committees:** Catalog; Environmental; Marketing; Technical. **Affiliated With:** Motor and Equipment Manufacturers Association. **Formerly:** (1988) Automotive Filter Manufacturers Council. **Publications:** *FMC Environmental News*. Newsletter. Alternate Formats: online ● *Technical Service Bulletin* (in English, French, and Spanish), periodic. Contains information on the applications and uses of filters. **Price:** free. **Conventions/Meetings:** semiannual conference - always March or April and October.

385 ■ Friction Materials Standards Institute (FMSI)
23 Woodland Rd., Ste.B-3
Madison, CT 06443
Ph: (203)245-8425
Fax: (203)245-8537
E-mail: fmsiinc@aol.com
URL: http://www.fmsi.org
Contact: Patrick T. Healey, Exec. Dir.

Founded: 1948. **Members:** 96. **Staff:** 2. **Budget:** $140,000. **Multinational. Description:** U.S. manufacturers of brake linings and/or clutch facings; foreign manufacturers and U.S. manufacturers of brake shoes or materials or tools for friction materials assembly. Has established an industry-wide numbering and cataloging system for brake linings so that replacement linings can be correctly and quickly installed. "Efforts are aimed towards meaningful and effective federal brake lining regulation." Involved with the environmental and occupational health considerations of the industry. **Committees:** Brake Performance Study; Data Book and Technical; Health and Environmental Affairs. **Formerly:** (1948) Brake Lining Manufacturers Association; (1949) Clutch Facing and Brake Lining Standards Institute. **Publications:** *Automotive Data Book*, annual. Catalog. **Price:** $305.00 includes postage and handling ● *Brake Block Identification Catalog*, periodic ● Bulletin, monthly ● Catalogs. **Conventions/Meetings:** annual meeting.

386 ■ Heavy Duty Representatives Association (HDRA)
4015 Marks Rd., Ste.2B
Medina, OH 44256-8316
Ph: (330)725-7160
Free: (800)763-5717
Fax: (330)722-5638
E-mail: trucksvc@aol.com
URL: http://hdra.org
Contact: Cara R. Giebner, Contact

Founded: 1973. **Members:** 70. **Membership Dues:** agency, $375 (annual). **Staff:** 1. **Multinational. Description:** Persons or agencies selling parts and accessories to the heavy-duty vehicle market including manufacturers and aftermarket distributors. Promotes the use of the HDRA Code of Ethics in all business activities within the heavy-duty industry. Programs are directed toward advising members on current problems and solutions needed. **Publications:** *Profile Directory*, annual ● *Representative Locator Services*. Directory ● Directory. **Conventions/Meetings:** semiannual National Truck Show - meeting.

387 ■ Industrial Truck Association (ITA)
1750 K St. NW, Ste.460
Washington, DC 20006
Ph: (202)296-9880
Fax: (202)296-9884
URL: http://www.indtrk.org
Contact: Jim Malvaso, Pres.

Founded: 1924. **Members:** 145. **Membership Dues:** associate, $6,000 (annual) ● regular, $2,450-$8,000 (annual). **Staff:** 5. **Budget:** $1,200,000. **Description:** Manufacturers of powered industrial lift trucks, electric storage batteries, tires, engines, attachments, and hydraulic systems for powered industrial lift trucks. **Committees:** Canada; Engineering; Lawyers; Statistics; Suppliers. **Formerly:** (1951) Electric Industrial Truck Association. **Publications:** Membership Directory, annual. **Price:** free. **Conventions/Meetings:** annual meeting.

388 ■ International Truck Parts Association (ITPA)
7127 Braeburn Pl.
Bethesda, MD 20817
Ph: (202)544-3090
Fax: (301)229-7331
E-mail: venlo@itpa.com
URL: http://www.itpa.com
Contact: Venlo Wolfsohn, Exec. Dir.

Founded: 1974. **Members:** 120. **Membership Dues:** company, $450 (annual). **Staff:** 1. **Budget:** $30,000. **Description:** Represents Companies specializing in the purchase and sale of used and rebuilt heavy-duty truck components. **Awards:** Lifetime Achievement Award. **Type:** recognition. **Recipient:** for contributions to the association and the industry. **Conventions/Meetings:** annual meeting.

389 ■ Japan Automobile Manufacturers Association, Washington Office (JAMA)
1050 17th St. NW, Ste.410
Washington, DC 20036
Ph: (202)296-8537
Fax: (202)872-1212
E-mail: cpowers@porternovelli.com
URL: http://www.jama.org
Contact: Charley Powers, Contact

Founded: 1967. **Members:** 13. **Languages:** English, Japanese. **Description:** Trade association representing Japanese automobile manufacturers. Promotes the development of the automobile industry. Conducts research programs involving vehicle production, trade policy, overseas investment, and parts procurement; exchanges information with other sectors of the industry. **Libraries: Type:** reference. **Holdings:** papers. **Subjects:** industry related information. **Publications:** *Japan Auto Trends*, quarterly. Newsletter. Provides in-depth coverage of the industry. Alternate Formats: online ● *The Motor Industry of Japan*, annual. Report ● *Motor Vehicle Statistics*, annual ● *Press Releases*, monthly. Newspaper ● Brochures, periodic. Alternate Formats: online. **Conventions/Meetings:** periodic meeting.

390 ■ Light Truck Accessory Alliance (LTAA)
c/o Specialty Equipment Market Association
PO Box 4910
Diamond Bar, CA 91765
Ph: (909)396-0289
Fax: (909)860-0184
E-mail: ltaa@sema.org
URL: http://www.sema.org/ltaa
Contact: Ron DiVincenzo, Chm.

Founded: 1989. **Members:** 650. **Description:** Manufacturers and retailers of truck caps and light truck accessories; corporations with a business interest in the truck cap and light truck accessory industry. (Truck caps are used to enclose the cargo beds of pickup trucks). Seeks to educate the public about the importance of truck caps and other light truck accessories. Develops industry standards for product quality and service. Sponsors educational programs and national advertising campaign. Conducts research; compiles statistics. **Awards:** Ron Webster Memorial Award. **Frequency:** annual. **Type:** recognition. **Recipient:** for industry engineering excellence. **Computer Services:** database, dealers and manufacturers of light truck accessories. **Formerly:** (1991) Truck Cap Industry Association; (2001) Truck Cap and Accessory Association; (2005) Truck Cap and Accessory Alliance - a SEMA Council. **Publications:** *LTAA News*, bimonthly. Newsletter. **Price:** included in membership dues ● *Market Research Study of Pickup Truck Owners*. Report ● *SEMA Member Directory*, annual. Membership Directory. Contains member listings and services in the automotive specialty industry. **Price:** $99.95 each. **Circulation:** 7,000. **Advertising:** accepted. **Conventions/Meetings:** annual Light Truck Accessory Expo - trade show and seminar, produced by SEMA and TCAA (exhibits) - always January/February ● periodic seminar.

391 ■ Limousine Industry Manufacturers Organization (LIMO)
3603 Fredericksburg Rd.
San Antonio, TX 78201
Ph: (210)732-5466
Free: (800)34-FLEET
Fax: (210)732-5488
E-mail: lcwsales@lcwlimo.com
URL: http://www.lcwlimo.com
Contact: Ken Boyar, CEO

Founded: 1989. **Members:** 14. **Membership Dues:** regular, $3,000 (annual). **Staff:** 4. **Budget:** $60,000. **Description:** Seeks to aid and ensure industry compliance with Federal Motor Vehicle Safety Standards. Informs members on current events and issues that may affect the industry. **Conventions/Meetings:** annual convention and meeting, product expo (exhibits).

392 ■ Motor and Equipment Manufacturers Association (MEMA)
10 Lab. Dr.
PO Box 13966
Research Triangle Park, NC 27709-3966
Ph: (919)549-4800
Fax: (919)549-4824
E-mail: info@mema.org
URL: http://www.mema.org
Contact: Robert E. McKenna, Pres./CEO

Founded: 1904. **Members:** 700. **Staff:** 90. **Budget:** $14,000,000. **National Groups:** 22. **Languages:** English, French, Italian, Japanese, Spanish. **Description:** Manufacturers of automotive and heavy-duty original equipment and aftermarket components, maintenance equipment, chemicals, accessories, refinishing supplies, tools, and service equipment united for research into all aspects of the automotive and heavy-duty markets. Provides manufacturer-oriented services and programs including marketing consultation for the automotive industry; federal and state legal, safety, and legislative representation and consultation; personnel services; manpower development workshops; international information. Cosponsors Automotive Aftermarket Industry Week, largest automotive aftermarket tradeshow in western hemisphere. Co-sponsors Pan-American Automotive Components/Accessories Expo in Mexico City. Maintains credit reporting service covering wholesalers, retailers, chain stores, and warehouse distributors; offers electronic order-entry, price-update, and electronic document exchange services through MEMA/Transnet and MEMA/Ansinet systems. Maintains international liaison. Maintains U.S. Automotive Parts Industry Japan Office in Yokohama, the United States Automotive Parts Industry European Office, Brussels, U.S. Pan American Automotive Industry Office in Mexico City and office in Sao Paulo, Brazil. Also have offices in Washington, DC and Detroit, Michigan. Compiles statistics on automotive and heavy duty OE market. **Awards:** Triangle Award. **Frequency:** periodic. **Type:** recognition. **Recipient:** for industry service. **Committees:** Anti-Counterfeiting; Automotive Emissions; Credit; Engineering; Government Relations; Industry Relations; International Trade; Legal and Legislative; Marketing; MIS; Research; Safety; Traffic and Transportation. **Councils:** Automotive Chemical Manufacturers; Automotive Chief Financial Executives; Automotive Exhaust Systems Manufacturers; Automotive Freight Transportation; Automotive Human Resource; Automotive MIS; Automotive Presidents; Automotive Public Relations; Brake Manufacturers; Filter Manufacturers; Heavy Duty Brake Manufacturers; Overseas Automotive. **Divisions:** ABS Education Alliance; Auto International Association; Automotive Cooling Systems Institute; Heavy-Duty Business Forum; Heavy Duty Manufacturers Association; Original Equipment Suppliers Association; Transportation Safety Equipment Institute; Tune-Up Manufacturers Institute. **Subgroups:** Financial Services; Management Information Systems; MEMA/Transnet. **Publications:** *Asia-Pacific Automotive Insight*, monthly ● *Automotive Distributor Trends and Financial Analysis*, periodic ● *Automotive Industry Status Report*, annual ● *Automotive Jobbers in the U.S.A.*, biennial ● *Car Maintenance in the U.S.A.*. Directory ● *Credit and Sales Reference Directory*, 3/year ● *Distributors Financial Analysis* ● *Europe Automotive Insight*, monthly ● *Executive Compensation and Benefits Practices*, annual ● *Foreign Vehicle Maintenance in the U.S.A.* ● *Heavy Duty Truck Maintenance in the U.S.A.*, biennial ● *International Buyer's Guide of U.S. Automotive and Heavy Duty Products*, biennial ● *Latin America Automotive Insights*, monthly ● *Legislative Insight*, biweekly ● *Market Analysis*, bimonthly. Newsletter. Alternate Formats: online ● *Motor Vehicle Market Report*. **Price:** $200.00 for nonmembers ● *Personnel Insight*, monthly. Newsletter. **Advertising:** accepted ● *Sales Force Compensation and Benefits Practice*, annual. Report ● *Topline News*, weekly. Newsletter. Alternate Formats: online ● *Washington Insider*, weekly. Newsletter. Alternate Formats: online. **Conventions/Meetings:** biennial Heavy Duty Dialogue Conference - seminar, on domestic and overseas marketing, federal trade regulations, credit, and collections (exhibits).

393 ■ National Association of Trailer Manufacturers (NATM)
1320 SW Topeka Blvd.
Topeka, KS 66612-1817
Ph: (785)272-4433
Fax: (785)272-4455
E-mail: natm@natm.com
URL: http://www.natm.com
Contact: Pam O'Toole, Exec. Dir.

Founded: 1987. **Members:** 670. **Membership Dues:** associate (supplier to the industry), $600 (annual) ● regular (trailer manufacturer), $700 (annual) ● branch, $100 (annual). **Staff:** 7. **Budget:** $700,000. **Description:** Manufacturers producing bumper pull and gooseneck trailers weighing less than 26,000 pounds; producers of trailer parts and providers of services to the industry. Promotes the growth of the mid-size trailer industry. Represents members' interests before government agencies, industry organizations, and the public. Facilitates exchange of information among members. Gathers and disseminates information on federal regulations affecting the trailer manufacturing industry. Makes available workers compensation and product liability insurance programs. Compiles statistics. **Awards:** Associate Member of the Year. **Frequency:** annual. **Type:** recognition. **Recipient:** for an associate member who has made outstanding contributions to NATM ● Bill Bernhardt Award. **Frequency:** annual. **Type:** recognition. **Recipient:** for an individual who has made significant contributions to NATM and the trailer manufacturing industry. **Computer Services:** database ● mailing lists. **Committees:** Early Warning Reporting; Past Presidents. **Programs:** Guidelines Compliance. **Formerly:** (1993) National Association of Livestock Trailer Manufacturers. **Publications:** *Directory and Buyer's Guide*, annual. **Advertising:** accepted ● *Guidelines for Recommended Minimum Manufacturing Practices for Light and Medium Duty Trailers*. Manual. **Price:** included in membership dues. Alternate Formats: CD-ROM ● *Tracks*, bimonthly. Newsletter. **Price:** included in membership dues; $100.00 for nonmembers. **Circulation:** 1,000. **Advertising:** accepted. Alternate Formats: online. **Conventions/Meetings:** quarterly board meeting (exhibits) ● annual convention (exhibits) - every February.

394 ■ National Automotive Parts Association (NAPA)
2999 Circle 75 Pkwy.
Atlanta, GA 30339
Free: (877)805-6272
E-mail: customersupport@napaonline.com
URL: http://www.napaonline.com
Contact: Steve Handschuh, Contact

Founded: 1925. **Members:** 4. **Staff:** 70. **Description:** Distributors of automobile parts, accessories, and supplies. **Committees:** Data Processing; Marketing; Merchandising; Operations; Sales Promotion; Training. **Publications:** *Autocare News*, monthly. Newsletter. Covers topics of interest to NAPA auto parts storeowners and operators. ● *NAPA News*, 3/year. Newspaper. Reports on subjects to help any professional mechanic or serious do-it-yourself. Offered to the public through NAPA AUTO PARTS stores. **Price:** free. **Circulation:** 300,000 ● *National Automotive Parts Association—Outlook*, 10/year. Magazine. Contains advertising and marketing techniques used to aid NAPA auto parts storeowners; also serves as a forum for the exchange of ideas. **Price:** included in membership dues. **Circulation:** 17,500. **Advertising:** accepted ● *Update*, monthly. Informs owners and managers of NAPA auto parts stores of services available from NAPA. **Conventions/Meetings:** semiannual meeting (exhibits) ● biennial National Business Conference.

395 ■ National Truck Equipment Association (NTEA)
37400 Hills Tech Dr.
Farmington Hills, MI 48331-3414
Ph: (248)489-7090
Free: (800)441-NTEA
Fax: (248)489-8590
E-mail: info@ntea.com
URL: http://www.ntea.com
Contact: James Carney, Exec. Dir.

Founded: 1964. **Members:** 1,600. **Membership Dues:** manufacturer, $950-$2,700 (annual) ● distributor, $650-$1,700 (annual) ● distributor branch, $325 (annual). **Staff:** 24. **Budget:** $3,500,000. **Description:** Serves as a trade group for commercial truck, truck body, truck equipment, trailer and accessory manufacturers and distributors. Advises members of current federal regulations affecting the manufacturing and installation of truck bodies and equipment; works to enhance the professionalism of management and improve profitability in the truck equipment business. **Libraries: Type:** not open to the public. **Holdings:** periodicals. **Subjects:** commercial truck industry, fleet and utility, association industries. **Computer Services:** Information services, industry statistics ● information services, technical resources ● mailing lists, labels, disk. **Telecommunication Services:** electronic mail, jim@ntea.com. **Divisions:** Ambulance Manufacturers; American Institute of Service Body Manufacturers; Articulating Crane Council of North America; Body and Hoist Manufacturers; Manufacturers Council of Small School Buses; Mid-Size Bus Manufacturers Association; Snow Control Equipment Manufacturers; Towing Equipment Manufacturers Association; Van Body Manufacturers. **Affiliated With:** Ambulance Manufacturers Division. **Publications:** *Dump Body and Conversion Hoist Charts*, periodic. **Price:** 1st copy free for members; $10.00 additional copy for members; $20.00 for nonmembers ● *Excise Tax Bulletin*, periodic. Concise report on timely excise tax activities affecting the truck equipment industry. **Price:** $2.00/issue, for members; $4.00/issue, for nonmembers. **Circulation:** 1,600 ● *Federal Excise Reference Tax Manual*. Compilation of all FET bulletins, quarterlies, and enquiries published since 1983. Update service available. **Price:** $149.00 for members; $298.00 for nonmembers ● *Membership Roster and Product Directory*, annual. Lists distributors, manufacturers and suppliers of commercial trucks, truck bodies, truck equipment, trailers and accessories. **Price:** $10.00 /year for members, quantity discount available; $50.00 /year for nonmembers. **Circulation:** 15,000. **Advertising:** accepted ● *NTEA News*, monthly. Newsletter. Provides information on current legislative, regulatory, and judicial issues. Includes information on financial management, taxes, and member news. **Price:** $3.00/issue, for members; $6.00/issue, for nonmembers. **Circulation:** 1,600 ● *Publications & Resources Catalog* ● *Technical Report*, periodic. Covers engineering and design and product compatibility for truck chassis manufacturers. **Price:** $4.00/issue, for members; $8.00/issue, for nonmembers. **Circulation:** 1,600 ● *Truck Equipment Handbook* ● *Vehicle Certification Guide* ● *Washington Update*, monthly. Covers legislative developments in Congress and reports on current and pending state and federal regulations affecting the truck equipment industry. **Price:** $4.00/issue, for members; $8.00/issue, for nonmembers. **Circulation:** 1,600. **Conventions/Meetings:** The Work Truck Show and Annual NTEA Convention - convention and trade show, commercial trucks, bodies, trailers and equipment (exhibits).

396 ■ PGI
Address Unknown since 2008
URL: http://pgi.com

Founded: 1990. **For-Profit**. **Description:** Engages in business involved with kit cars and their components. (A kit car is a replica of a custom made car, but it is built on an inexpensive chassis). **Absorbed:** (1988) Speciality Automotive Manufacturers Association. **Formerly:** (2000) Epic Enterprises.

397 ■ Specialty Equipment Market Association (SEMA)
PO Box 4910
Diamond Bar, CA 91765-0910
Ph: (909)396-0289
Fax: (909)860-0184

E-mail: member@sema.org
URL: http://www.sema.org
Contact: Christopher Kersting CAE, Pres./CEO
Founded: 1963. **Members:** 5,000. **Staff:** 72. **Budget:** $17,000,000. **Description:** Manufacturers, retailers, sales representatives, distributors, motorsports sanctioning groups, and other firms related to the automotive high performance and custom vehicle industry. Represents the industry to governmental agencies and consumer groups. Coordinates and conducts research; assists in writing of regulations and codes; collects and disseminates information; compiles statistics. **Libraries: Type:** reference. **Holdings:** reports. **Awards:** Manufacturers' Representative of the Year. **Frequency:** annual. **Type:** recognition ● Person of the Year Award. **Frequency:** annual. **Type:** recognition ● SEMA Hall of Fame Award. **Frequency:** annual. **Type:** recognition. **Recipient:** for industry achievers ● Warehouse Distributor of the Year. **Type:** recognition. **Committees:** Automotive Restoration Market Organization; Educational Services; International Trade; Manufacturers Representatives; Market Study; Motorsports Parts Manufacturers; Professional Restylers Organization; Public Relations; SEMA Scholarship Fund; SEMA Show; SEMAPAC; Street Rod Marketing Alliance; Technical; Youth Awareness. **Councils:** Sport Compact; Truck Cap & Accessory Alliance. **Formerly:** (1966) Speed Equipment Manufacturers Association; (1979) Specialty Equipment Manufacturers Association. **Publications:** *Fast Facts*, monthly. Bulletin. **Price:** included in membership dues. **Circulation:** 5,000. **Advertising:** accepted ● *SEMA Membership Directory*, annual ● *SEMA News*, monthly. Journal. **Circulation:** 30,000. **Advertising:** accepted. **Conventions/Meetings:** annual trade show, exhibits include automotive performance parts and accessories (exhibits).

398 ■ Specialty Vehicle Institute of America (SVIA)
2 Jenner St., Ste.150
Irvine, CA 92618-3812
Ph: (949)727-3727
Free: (800)887-2887
Fax: (949)727-4216
E-mail: tyager@svia.org
URL: http://www.svia.org
Contact: Mr. Thomas Yager, VP
Founded: 1983. **Members:** 10. **Staff:** 40. **Budget:** $6,000,000. **Description:** Trade association representing U.S. distributors of all-terrain vehicles (ATVs). Fosters and promotes safe and responsible use of ATVs through public information and education, operator training, government relations and technical programs.

399 ■ Spring Research Institute (SRI)
3034 N Fleming Cir.
Shelbyville, IN 46176
Ph: (317)398-3822
E-mail: johndthomson@comcast.net
Contact: John D. Thomson, Pres.
Founded: 1933. **Members:** 12. **Staff:** 3. **Description:** Manufacturers of aftermarket leaf springs, which are used in trucks and passenger vehicles. Works to keep members informed of developments in manufacturing and marketing of leaf springs. **Publications:** Manuals. **Conventions/Meetings:** semiannual meeting.

400 ■ Truck Mixer Manufacturers Bureau (TMMB)
900 Spring St.
Silver Spring, MD 20910
Ph: (301)587-1400
Fax: (301)587-1605
E-mail: bgarbini@tmmb.org
URL: http://www.tmmb.org
Contact: Robert Garbini, Exec. Sec.
Founded: 1944. **Members:** 10. **Staff:** 5. **Description:** Provides technical support to manufacturers of truck mixer drums. Sets nationally-recognized standards for the manufacture of truck mixer drum equipment. **Affiliated With:** National Ready Mixed Concrete Association. **Publications:** *TMMB 100-01 Truck Mixer, Agitator and Front Discharge Concrete Carrier Standards*. **Price:** free. **Conventions/Meetings:** annual meeting - always November.

401 ■ Truck Trailer Manufacturers Association (TTMA)
1020 Princess St.
Alexandria, VA 22314-2247
Ph: (703)549-3010
Fax: (703)549-3014
E-mail: ttma@erols.com
URL: http://www.ttmanet.org
Contact: Richard P. Bowling, Pres.
Founded: 1941. **Members:** 225. **Staff:** 6. **Multinational. Description:** Manufacturers of commercial trailers; manufacturers of supplies for the truck trailer industry. **Committees:** Convention; Product Liability; Site Selection; Tank Conference Engineering. **Divisions:** Tank Conference. **Publications:** *Truck Trailer Manufacturers Association—Directory*, annual. **Price:** free for members; $135.00 for nonmembers ● Bulletin, monthly. Contains summaries of current legislation, research, statistics, and other information affecting trailer and tank manufacturers. **Price:** free for members; $375.00 /year for nonmembers. **Conventions/Meetings:** annual convention.

402 ■ Tune-Up Manufacturers Council (TMC)
10 Lab. Dr.
PO Box 13966
Research Triangle Park, NC 27709-3966
Ph: (919)549-4800
Fax: (919)549-4824
E-mail: info@tune-up.org
URL: http://www.tune-up.org
Contact: Arthur W. Daigneault, Sec.-Treas.
Founded: 1973. **Members:** 9. **Membership Dues:** regular, $1,000 (annual). **Staff:** 2. **Description:** Manufacturers, producers or marketers of aftermarket tune-up components and emission test equipment. **Telecommunication Services:** electronic mail, adaigneault@generalcable.com. **Formerly:** (1981) Tune-up Manufacturers Institute. **Conventions/Meetings:** annual meeting.

Automotive Services

403 ■ American Automobile Association (AAA)
c/o AAA Mid-Atlantic
One River Pl.
Wilmington, DE 19801
Ph: (302)299-4700
Free: (800)763-9900
URL: http://www.aaa.com
Contact: Robert Darbelnet, Pres./CEO
Founded: 1902. **Members:** 40,000,000. **Membership Dues:** basic, $71 (annual) ● plus, $106 (annual) ● plus RV, $136 (annual). **Description:** Federation of automobile clubs (1,000 offices) providing domestic and foreign travel services, emergency road services, and insurance. Sponsors public services for traffic safety, better highways, more efficient and safer cars, energy conservation, and improvement of motoring and travel conditions. **Libraries: Type:** reference. **Holdings:** 14,000. **Subjects:** travel, transportation safety, business, automotive. **Additional Websites:** http://www.aaamidatlantic.com. **Committees:** Business Strategies; Public and Government Relations; Service Quality and Performance Standards. **Publications:** *Digest of Motor Laws*, annual. Booklet ● *Maps and Tour Books*, annual ● *Sportsmanlike Driving*, periodic.

404 ■ American International Automobile Dealers Association (AIADA)
211 N Union St., Ste.300
Alexandria, VA 22314
Ph: (703)519-7800
Free: (800)GOAIADA
Fax: (703)519-7810
E-mail: goaiada@aiada.org
URL: http://www.aiada.org
Contact: John H. Hawkins, Chm.
Founded: 1970. **Members:** 10,000. **Membership Dues:** regular, $250-$975 (annual). **Staff:** 13. **Budget:** $3,000,000. **Description:** Trade association for America's international nameplate automobile dealerships and their employees who sell and service automobiles manufactured in the U.S. and abroad. Works to preserve a free market for international automobiles in the U.S. and is dedicated to increasing public awareness of the benefits the industry provides. **Awards:** David H. Gezon Lifetime Achievement Award. **Frequency:** annual. **Type:** recognition. **Telecommunication Services:** electronic mail, membership@aiada.org. **Formerly:** (1972) Volkswagen American Dealers Association; (1980) American Imported Automobile Dealers Association. **Publications:** *AIADA News*, monthly. Newsletter ● *AIADA's Showroom*, 9/year. Magazine. **Circulation:** 12,000. **Advertising:** accepted ● Newsletters. Alternate Formats: online. **Conventions/Meetings:** annual American-International Automotive Congress - convention and meeting - always May ● annual meeting and luncheon.

405 ■ Automotive Body Parts Association (ABPA)
PO Box 820689
Houston, TX 77282-0689
Ph: (281)531-0809
Free: (800)323-5832
Fax: (281)531-9411
E-mail: srodman1@sbcglobal.net
URL: http://www.autobpa.com
Contact: Stanley A. Rodman, Exec. Dir.
Founded: 1980. **Members:** 210. **Membership Dues:** company (with 1-250 employees), $125-$300 (quarterly) ● company (with 251 to more than 1000 employees), $500-$1,000 (quarterly). **Staff:** 3. **Budget:** $450,000. **Multinational. Description:** Represents the industry interests of distributors, suppliers and manufacturers of independently produced collision replacement parts such as bumpers, fenders, hoods, doors, lights, radiators, etc., and is also involved with the recycling of both steel bumpers and urethane and rubber bumper fascias. **Awards:** Associate Member Award of Merit. **Type:** recognition ● Award of Merit. **Type:** recognition ● Hall of Fame Award. **Type:** recognition. **Computer Services:** Mailing lists, of members. **Committees:** Budget; Bylaws; Electronic Processing; Executives; Industry Liaison; Long Range Planning; Member Services; Membership; Recyclers Division. **Councils:** Legislative/Regulation. **Formerly:** (1984) Aftermarket Body Parts Distributors Association; (1987) Aftermarket Body Parts Association. **Publications:** *Body Language*, 10-11/year. Newsletter. Provides information on aftermarket auto parts, new association policies, and industry and members' news. ISSN: 1526-8918. **Circulation:** 480. **Advertising:** accepted ● *Collision Parts Journal*, semiannual. Provides information for industry and insurance companies on collision parts, their availability, and suppliers. Includes reports on new products. **Circulation:** 2,300. **Advertising:** accepted ● *International Collision Parts Industry Suppliers Guide and Membership Roster*. Directory. **Advertising:** accepted ● Also publishes membership roster and International Industry supplies guide. **Conventions/Meetings:** semiannual conference (exhibits) ● annual trade show (exhibits) - always spring.

406 ■ Automotive Fleet and Leasing Association (AFLA)
c/o Paul Hanscom, Exec. Dir.
1000 Westgate Dr.
St. Paul, MN 55114
Ph: (651)203-7247
Fax: (651)290-2266
E-mail: info@aflaonline.com
Contact: Paul Hanscom, Exec. Dir.
Founded: 1969. **Members:** 320. **Membership Dues:** regular, $200 (annual) ● alumnus/alumna, $100 (annual). **Staff:** 2. **Budget:** $500,000. **Description:** New car dealers, fleet administrators, leasing companies, drive-away companies, auto manufacturers, and

consultants. Provides a forum for the exchange of information between related segments of the fleet and leasing industry. Seeks to build working relationships with professionals in all phases of the industry, develop new ideas that will help the industry continue to grow, and help the industry find ways to operate more efficiently and profitably. **Libraries: Type:** not open to the public. **Holdings:** articles. **Awards:** Professional Fleet Manager of the Year, McGarvey Award. **Frequency:** annual. **Type:** monetary. **Recipient:** for lifetime dedication ● Top Fleet Dealer Award. **Frequency:** annual. **Type:** monetary. **Computer Services:** Mailing lists, of members. **Publications:** *Annual Meeting and Conference Journal*, annual. Magazine. Includes membership roster, conference agenda, speaker biographies, information on conference site, and feature articles. **Circulation:** 3,000. **Advertising:** accepted ● *The Forum*, quarterly. Newsletter. Includes information for automotive fleet dealers and leasing agencies. Covers important events, new legislation, and government programs. **Price:** included in membership dues. **Conventions/Meetings:** semiannual conference - always spring and fall.

407 ■ Automotive Maintenance and Repair Association (AMRA)

7910 Woodmont Ave., Ste.760
Bethesda, MD 20814
Ph: (301)634-4955 (301)634-4954
Fax: (202)318-0378
E-mail: amra@motorist.org
URL: http://www.4amra.com
Contact: Mr. Larry Hecker, Pres.
Founded: 1994. **Members:** 170. **Membership Dues:** manufacturer, supplier, $500-$15,000 (annual) ● trade press, $100 (annual) ● consultant, law firm, $250 (annual). **Staff:** 5. **Budget:** $500,000. **Multinational. Description:** Multi-bay automotive repair shops and their suppliers, automotive manufacturers, manufacturers' representatives, trade associations, and the automotive trade press. Promotes ethical and effective practice of automotive repair and maintenance; works to improve relations between auto owners and automotive service providers. Facilitates communication and cooperation between members and government bodies responsible for regulating automotive inspection procedures. Creates and enforces inspection and communication standards of ethics and practice; conducts research and educational programs; accredits repair shops that adhere to these standards. **Publications:** *Directions*, quarterly. Newsletter. **Price:** free for members ● *e-Directions*, semimonthly. Newsletter. **Price:** free for members ● *How to Find Your Way Under the Hood and Around the Car*, biennial, 7 editions issued biennially. Brochure ● *Uniform Inspection and Communications Standards for Automotive Systems*, biennial, 7 editions issued biennially. Handbook.

408 ■ Automotive Oil Change Association (AOCA)

12810 Hillcrest, Ste.221
Dallas, TX 75230
Ph: (972)458-9468
Free: (800)331-0329
Fax: (972)458-9539
E-mail: info@aoca.org
URL: http://www.aoca.org
Contact: Stephen Christie, Exec. Dir.
Founded: 1987. **Members:** 1,200. **Membership Dues:** regular in U.S., $350 (annual) ● regular outside U.S., $275 (annual) ● associate, $1,000 (annual). **Staff:** 6. **Budget:** $1,000,000. **Description:** Owners and operators of oil change shops. Works to solve problems and advance interests of members. Offers group insurance and credit card program. Compiles statistics; disseminates information, employee training programs. **Libraries: Type:** reference. **Awards:** Member of the Year. **Frequency:** annual. **Type:** recognition. **Recipient:** for outstanding contribution to the association's growth & enhanced programs and/or the oil change industry. **Computer Services:** Mailing lists. **Formerly:** (1993) National Association of Independent Lubes. **Publications:** *Oil Changing Times*, bimonthly. Newsletter. **Price:** $40.00/year. **Circulation:** 1,500. **Advertising:** accepted. **Conventions/Meetings:** annual Fast Lube Expo - convention and trade show, educational forum for business management & technical information (exhibits).

409 ■ Automotive Parts Remanufacturers Association (APRA)

4215 Lafayette Center Dr., Ste.3
Chantilly, VA 20151-1243
Ph: (703)968-2772
Fax: (703)968-2878
E-mail: mail@apra.org
URL: http://www.apra.org
Contact: William C. Gager, Pres.
Founded: 1941. **Members:** 1,800. **Membership Dues:** rebuilder, $205-$1,835 (annual) ● manufacturer/core supplier, $715-$3,865 (annual) ● manufacturer representative, $270-$465 (annual) ● European company (rebuilder), $600-$1,000 (annual) ● European company (supplier), $600 (annual) ● international company, $715-$3,865 (annual). **Staff:** 9. **Budget:** $2,000,000. **Multinational. Description:** Remanufacturers of automotive and truck parts (on exchange basis) and suppliers of component parts. Provides technical material; sponsors technical seminars, meetings and conventions under the name "International BIG R Show". **Libraries: Type:** reference. **Holdings:** papers. **Awards: Type:** recognition. **Recipient:** for distinguished service. **Additional Websites:** http://www.bigrshow.com. **Divisions:** Air Conditioning; Brake Systems; Clutch; CV and Rack; Electrical; European; Fuel Systems; Heavy Duty Brake; Heavy Duty Transmission, Driveline and Axle; Management; Volume Transmission; Water Pump. **Formerly:** (2004) Automotive Parts Rebuilders Association. **Publications:** *Automotive Parts Remanufacturers Association—Membership Directory*, annual. **Price:** included in membership dues; $900.00 /year for nonmembers. **Circulation:** 2,000. **Advertising:** accepted ● *Global Connection*, monthly. Newspaper. **Circulation:** 20,000. **Advertising:** accepted ● *International Big R Show Showguide*, annual. Catalogs. **Circulation:** 3,000. **Advertising:** accepted. **Conventions/Meetings:** annual International BIG R Show - convention (exhibits) - always fall.

410 ■ Automotive Service Association (ASA)

PO Box 929
Bedford, TX 76095-0929
Ph: (817)283-6205 (706)724-0900
Free: (800)272-7467
Fax: (817)685-0225
E-mail: asainfo@asashop.org
URL: http://www.asashop.org
Contact: Ron Pyle, Pres.
Founded: 1951. **Members:** 12,000. **Membership Dues:** associate, $495 (annual) ● educational, $50 (annual). **Staff:** 32. **Budget:** $7,000,000. **State Groups:** 14. **Local Groups:** 200. **National Groups:** 15. **Description:** Automotive service businesses including body, paint, and trim shops, engine rebuilders, radiator shops, brake and wheel alignment services, transmission shops, tune-up services, and air conditioning services; associate members are manufacturers and wholesalers of automotive parts, and the trade press. Represents independent business owners and managers before private agencies and national and state legislative bodies. Promotes confidence between consumer and the automotive service industry, safety inspection of motor vehicles, and better highways. **Libraries: Type:** reference. **Divisions:** Collision; Mechanical. **Formed by Merger of:** (1986) Automotive Service Councils; Independent Automotive Service Association. **Publications:** *AutoInc*, monthly. Journal. Covers technical and management information of interest to members; contains shop profiles, legislative news, and industry events. **Price:** included in membership dues; $25.00 /year for nonmembers. ISSN: 0199-6908. **Circulation:** 14,000. **Advertising:** accepted. Alternate Formats: online ● *Collision Repair Report*, monthly. Newsletter. Specialty publication for members of the ASA Collision Division. ● *Mechanical Dispatch*, monthly. Specialty publication for members of the ASA Mechanical Division. ● Pamphlets. Contains consumer awareness information. **Conventions/Meetings:** annual Congress of Automotive Repair and Service CARS, management and technical seminars ● annual International Autobody Congress and Exposition (NACE) - seminar and trade show.

411 ■ Car Wash Owners and Suppliers Association (COSA)

1822 South St.
Racine, WI 53404
Ph: (262)639-4393
Contact: Ed Holbus, Pres.
Founded: 1983. **Description:** Fosters a better public image and improve the operation of the car wash industry. **Formerly:** (1984) Car Wash Manufacturers and Suppliers Association. **Conventions/Meetings:** annual meeting.

412 ■ Dealers Alliance (DA)

Continental Plz.
401 Hackensack Ave.
Hackensack, NJ 07601
Ph: (201)342-4542
Fax: (201)342-3997
E-mail: fda@dealersalliance.org
URL: http://www.dealersalliance.org
Contact: A. Michell Van Vorst, Exec. Dir.
Founded: 1983. **Members:** 1,700. **Budget:** $170,000. **Description:** Franchised new car dealers throughout the U.S. concerned with issues such as pricing, overdealering, product identification, financing, and recognition of the dealer as the manufacturer's greatest asset. Opposes new car subsidies to fleets; provides advice to dealers concerning warranty audits, market representation plans, unfair distribution, policy board problems, sales promotion problems, and other problem areas. **Telecommunication Services:** electronic mail, michell@dealersalliance.org. **Formed by Merger of:** Chevrolet Dealers Alliance; Ford Dealers Alliance. **Publications:** *FDA Newsletter*, monthly. **Price:** available only to Ford and Lincoln-Mercury dealers. **Circulation:** 6,000 ● Brochures ● Also publishes dealer help folders. **Conventions/Meetings:** annual conference.

413 ■ Ford Motor Minority Dealers Association (FMMDA)

16000 W 9 Mile Rd., Ste.603
Southfield, MI 48075
Ph: (248)557-2500
Free: (800)247-0293
Fax: (248)557-2882
E-mail: fmmdafacts@aol.com
URL: http://www.fmmda.org
Contact: Dr. A.V. Fleming, Exec. Dir./CEO
Founded: 1980. **Members:** 550. **Membership Dues:** small business supporter, $1,000 (annual) ● patron, $5,000 (annual) ● bronze sponsor, $7,500 (annual) ● silver sponsor, $10,000 (annual) ● gold sponsor, $20,000 (annual) ● platinum sponsor, $30,000 (annual) ● millennium sponsor, $50,000 (annual). **Staff:** 4. **Description:** Minority-owned car dealerships. Promotes professional standards of minority dealerships. Strives to increase the number of minority dealerships. **Awards: Type:** scholarship. **Recipient:** for minority students. **Formerly:** (2001) Ford, Lincoln, Mercury Minority Dealers Association. **Publications:** *FMMDA Facts*, bimonthly. Newsletter. **Advertising:** accepted. Alternate Formats: online ● Directory, annual. **Conventions/Meetings:** bimonthly board meeting ● annual competition, golf tournament - usually June ● annual convention.

414 ■ Gasoline and Automotive Service Dealers Association (GASDA)

78 Harvard Ave., Ste.260
Stamford, CT 06902
Ph: (203)327-4773
Fax: (203)323-6935
E-mail: info@gasda.org
URL: http://www.gasda.org
Contact: Michael Fox, Exec. Dir.
Founded: 1931. **Members:** 1,500. **Membership Dues:** $35 (monthly). **Staff:** 8. **Description:** Owners/operators or dealers of service stations or automotive repair facilities; interested individuals. Aims to

educate, inform, and help increase professionalism of members and of the industry. Offers periodic technical training clinics, and other educational programs including advanced automotive technical training, prepaid group legal services plan and group health insurance, and liaison with government agencies. Informs members of political and legislative action or changes affecting their industry. **Formerly:** Gasoline Merchants. **Publications:** *Gasoline and Automotive Service Dealers Association—Bulletin*, monthly. **Price:** available to members only. **Circulation:** 1,000 ● *Gasoline and Automotive Service Dealers Association—Trade Directory and Buyers Guide*, annual. Contains randomly arranged advertisements of companies who offer services in the field. Indexed by subject and alphabetically by company name. **Price:** free. **Circulation:** 6,500. **Advertising:** accepted ● *Tel-U-Gram*, monthly. Includes brief news items in single-page format. **Price:** available to members only. **Circulation:** 1,000. **Conventions/Meetings:** annual meeting.

415 ■ Inter-Industry Conference on Auto Collision Repair
5125 Trillium Blvd.
Hoffman Estates, IL 60192-3600
Free: (800)422-7872
Fax: (847)590-1215
E-mail: tom.mcgee@i-car.com
URL: http://www.i-car.com
Contact: Thomas McGee Jr., Pres./CEO
Founded: 1979. **Members:** 85. **Membership Dues:** individual, educational partner, $500 (annual) ● corporate, $2,500 (annual) ● sustaining, $5,000 (annual). **Staff:** 65. **Budget:** $12,000,000. **Regional Groups:** 10. **State Groups:** 50. **Local Groups:** 275. **National Groups:** 3. **Languages:** English, French, Spanish. **Description:** Automobile manufacturers, collision repair shops, insurance companies, tool, equipment, and supply manufacturers, vocational institutions, and related industrial organizations such as auto dismantlers and recyclers, appraisers, and technical publishers. Works to improve the quality, safety, and efficiency of collision repair, especially on newly manufactured fuel-efficient automobiles, through education in the collision repair and insurance industries. Serves as a forum providing for communication among insurance claims representatives, body shop owners and managers, and interested individuals. Conducts classes to improve skills of repair technicians, insurance claims personnel, and other interested individuals. Offers courses on unibody repair, refinishing, plastic repair, electronics, steering and suspension and advanced vehicle systems; also conducts collision repair research. Offers welding qualification test through its Welding Qualification Program. **Awards:** Achievement Award. **Frequency:** annual. **Type:** recognition. **Recipient:** for local activity versus goal ● Founder's Award. **Frequency:** annual. **Type:** recognition. **Recipient:** for an individual in each region who exemplifies the I-CAR Volunteer spirit ● Regional Instructor of the Year Award. **Frequency:** annual. **Type:** recognition. **Recipient:** to one instructor in each region who most exemplifies the I-CAR presence in the classroom. **Telecommunication Services:** additional toll-free number, (800)590-1215. **Committees:** Course Development; Field Advisory; Finance; Instructor Advisory; Technical Advisory. **Programs:** Advanced Vehicle Systems; Collision Repair; Electronics; Enhanced Delivery; MIG Welding Certification; Plastics Repair; Refinishing; Steering and Suspension; Welding Qualification. **Also Known As:** I-CAR. **Publications:** *Communications*. Bulletins. Alternate Formats: online ● *How-To-Handbook*. Alternate Formats: online ● *I-CAR E-newsletter*, biweekly. **Price:** free. Alternate Formats: online ● Bulletins. **Conventions/Meetings:** annual conference, regional ● annual meeting.

416 ■ International Carwash Association (ICA)
401 N Michigan Ave., Ste.2200
Chicago, IL 60611-4267
Ph: (312)321-5199
Free: (888)ICA-8422
Fax: (312)245-1085
E-mail: ica@smithbucklin.com
URL: http://www.carcarecentral.com
Contact: Frank Lash, Pres.
Founded: 1982. **Members:** 3,000. **Membership Dues:** conveyor, distributor, $195 (annual) ● self service, $135 (annual) ● in-bay automatic, $135 (annual) ● manufacturer/supplier, $645 (annual). **Staff:** 20. **Budget:** $3,500,000. **Multinational. Description:** Membership consists of car wash and detail operators, manufacturers, and supplier's distributors. Promotes the car wash industry by providing educational opportunities to members and gathering information on the industry and its customer. **Libraries: Type:** reference. **Holdings:** books, periodicals. **Subjects:** car wash industry. **Formed by Merger of:** International Carwash Association; National Carwash Council. **Publications:** *ICA Directory and Buyer's Guide*, annual ● *ICA News*, monthly. Newsletter ● ICA study of consumer Car Washing Attitudes and Habits. **Conventions/Meetings:** seminar ● annual trade show, with educational and business speakers (exhibits) - 2009 Apr. 2-4, Las Vegas, NV; 2010 Apr. 22-24, Las Vegas, NV.

417 ■ International Midas Dealers Association (IMDA)
14 W 3rd St., Ste.200
Kansas City, MO 64152
Ph: (972)489-0602 (816)472-8870
Free: (877)543-6203
Fax: (816)472-7765
E-mail: tdsnook@sbcglobal.net
URL: http://www.imdaonline.org
Contact: Terry Snook, Exec. Dir.
Founded: 1971. **Members:** 425. **Membership Dues:** association, $100 (quarterly). **Staff:** 5. **Budget:** $350,000. **Multinational. Description:** Midas auto service shop franchisees. **Formerly:** (1998) National Midas Dealers Association. **Publications:** *Franchise Focus*, bimonthly. Newsletter. **Advertising:** accepted. **Conventions/Meetings:** annual convention (exhibits).

418 ■ National Association of Emergency Vehicle Technicians (NAEVT)
151 Lexington Rd.
Shirley, NY 11967
Free: (800)466-2388
E-mail: adminassist@naevt.org
URL: http://www.naevt.org
Contact: Cheryl Benson, Admin. Asst.
Founded: 1991. **Members:** 2,200. **Membership Dues:** municipal, individual, $50 (annual) ● corporate, $400 (annual). **Description:** Promotes and supports the profession of Emergency Vehicle Technicians (EVT). Facilitates training, education, and legislation, and provides a national and international voice for the technician. Helps elevate the standards of emergency vehicle maintenance and the EVT Profession through the Commission's EVT certification/testing programs. Addresses issues of the mechanics and technicians. **Awards:** Technician of the Year. **Frequency:** annual. **Type:** recognition. **Recipient:** to recognize the accomplishments of emergency vehicle technicians. **Telecommunication Services:** electronic mail, president@naevt.org. **Publications:** *The Technician*. Newsletter. **Price:** included in membership dues.

419 ■ National Association of Fleet Resale Dealers (NAFRD)
396 Clarkston Dr.
Smyrna, TN 37167
Ph: (615)355-5225
Fax: (615)825-7794
E-mail: kimg@nafrd.com
URL: http://www.nafrd.com
Contact: Kim Glasscock, Exec. Dir.
Founded: 1984. **Members:** 110. **Membership Dues:** associate, affiliate, $750 (annual) ● regular, $1,200 (annual) ● industry partner, $100 (annual). **Budget:** $200,000. **Description:** Used car wholesalers dealing exclusively with large fleets. Encourages members to employ effective marketing methods and to conduct businesses soundly and ethically. Seeks a favorable public image of wholesale used cars and the used car industry. Serves as a forum for exchange of ideas and information; monitors legislation. **Computer Services:** Mailing lists, of members. **Committees:** Education; Legislation; Public Relations. **Publications:** *Annual Business Survey*, annual. Includes comprehensive view of used fleet marketing. ● *Inside Tracks*, quarterly. Newsletter. **Price:** free for members. **Advertising:** accepted. Alternate Formats: online ● *NAFRD Resource Guide*, annual. Membership Directory. **Advertising:** accepted. **Conventions/Meetings:** semiannual conference ● annual conference ● meeting - always mid-year.

420 ■ National Automobile Dealers Association (NADA)
8400 Westpark Dr.
McLean, VA 22102
Ph: (703)821-7000 (703)821-7113
Free: (800)252-6232
E-mail: nadainfo@nada.org
URL: http://www.nada.org
Contact: Phillip D. Brady, Pres.
Founded: 1917. **Members:** 19,500. **Membership Dues:** automobile/light truck dealer (based on annual sales volume), $90-$550 (annual) ● heavy/medium duty truck dealer (based on annual sales volume), $180-$420 (annual) ● regular, in Canada and Mexico, $315 (annual) ● dealer outside U.S., $455 (annual). **Staff:** 400. **Budget:** $10,000,000. **State Groups:** 57. **Local Groups:** 55. **Description:** Franchised new car and truck dealers. Provides representation for franchised new car and truck dealers in the areas of government, industry, and public affairs. Offers management services and retirement and insurance programs to member dealers. Maintains National Automobile Dealers Charitable Foundation. **Awards: Type:** recognition. **Recipient:** for achievement and service to the industry. **Committees:** Communications/Public Relations; Dealers Election Action; Dealership Operations; Government Relations; Industry Relations. **Publications:** *American Truck Dealers Division Newsletter*, monthly ● *AutoExec*, monthly. Magazine. Alternate Formats: online ● *DEAC Report*, quarterly. Newsletter ● *Dealers Business Guide*, annual. Directory ● *NADA Facts Weekly*. Newsletter ● *Official Used Car Guide Book*, monthly ● *Society of Automotive Sales Professional Report*, quarterly. Newsletter ● Also publishes management guides and career books. **Conventions/Meetings:** annual convention, for medium and heavy duty truck dealers (exhibits) ● annual convention, for new car dealers (exhibits) ● annual convention, launch and promote new products and services (exhibits) - 2009 Jan. 24-27, New Orleans, LA; 2010 Feb. 13-16, Orlando, FL ● annual Washington Conference - convention.

421 ■ National Automotive Finance Association (NAFAssociation)
7250 Parkway Dr., Ste.510
Hanover, MD 21076-1343
Ph: (410)712-4036
Free: (800)463-8955
Fax: (410)712-4038
E-mail: information@nafassociation.com
URL: http://www.nafassociation.com
Contact: Jack Tracey, Exec. Dir.
Founded: 1996. **Members:** 120. **Membership Dues:** business (sliding scale up to $5000), $1,250 (annual). **Staff:** 2. **Budget:** $350,000. **Description:** Serves the non-prime automotive lending industry. Creates and publishes standards of financial reporting; conducts research measuring growth and changes in credit terms and practices in the industry; develops code of industry responsibility. **Committees:** Legal; Research. **Publications:** *Nonprime Times*, quarterly. Newsletter. **Conventions/Meetings:** annual Non-Prime Auto Lending Conference, for lenders and dealers (exhibits).

422 ■ National Automotive Radiator Service Association (NARSA)
15000 Commerce Pkwy., Ste.C
Mount Laurel, NJ 08054
Ph: (856)439-1575 (856)642-4409
Free: (800)551-3232
Fax: (856)439-9596

E-mail: info@narsa.org
URL: http://www.narsa.org
Contact: Mike Dwyer, Exec. Dir.
Founded: 1954. **Members:** 1,600. **Membership Dues:** regular, $250-$350 (annual) ● associate (based on gross sales), $575-$2,300 (annual) ● retired, $35 (annual). **Staff:** 10. **Budget:** $1,300,000. **Regional Groups:** 6. **Description:** Represents operators of automotive radiator and air conditioning repair shops and cooling system service businesses as well as manufacturers and suppliers for the trade. Maintains hall of fame. **Awards: Type:** recognition. **Computer Services:** Mailing lists ● online services, registration for meetings, trade show, and conferences; member and subscription applications. **Committees:** Educational and Technical; Legislative and Government; Marketing and Merchandising; Publications and Communications. **Publications:** *Automotive Cooling Journal*, monthly. Contains news, views, profiles, and technology of the automotive heat repair and manufacturing industry. Includes advertisers index. **Price:** $30.00/year. **Circulation:** 10,000. **Advertising:** accepted ● *NARSA Service Reports*, bimonthly. Newsletter. Features technical information for use by NARSA members. **Circulation:** 1,800 ● Membership Directory, annual. **Conventions/Meetings:** annual convention, features displays of latest products and services for the cooling system service aftermarket (exhibits).

423 ■ National Independent Automobile Dealers Association (NIADA)
2521 Brown Blvd.
Arlington, TX 76006
Ph: (817)640-3838 (434)983-2073
Free: (800)682-3837
Fax: (817)649-5866
E-mail: mike@niada.com
URL: http://www.niada.com
Contact: Michael R. Linn, Exec. VP/CEO
Founded: 1946. **Members:** 19,000. **Staff:** 14. **Budget:** $3,100,000. **State Groups:** 35. **For-Profit. Description:** Individuals, companies, or corporations licensed by their states as dealers to buy and sell used motor vehicles; associate members are businesses related to or associated with the buying or selling of motor vehicles. Gathers and disseminates information relative to the used car industry; represents used car dealers before regulatory and legislative bodies; provides educational and other programs to help used car dealers understand their responsibilities; works for the betterment of the automobile industry. Works closely with local and state independent automobile dealers' associations and others concerning dealers and the public. Maintains code of fair dealing for members. Conducts seminars, meetings, and professional training programs. Maintains speakers' bureau, services for children, and charitable programs. Sponsors competitions; compiles statistics. **Awards:** Crystal Eagle Award. **Frequency:** biennial. **Type:** trophy. **Recipient:** to top qualifying membership recruiters who recruit a minimum of 100 new members over a two-year period ● Eagle Award. **Frequency:** annual. **Type:** recognition. **Recipient:** to top qualifying membership recruiters who recruit a minimum of 20 new members in one year ● National Quality Dealer Award. **Frequency:** annual. **Type:** medal. **Recipient:** for outstanding service to the industry and his/her community ● Ring of Honor. **Frequency:** annual. **Type:** recognition. **Recipient:** to an allied industry executive for outstanding performance and leadership to automobile industry ● Scholarship Award. **Frequency:** annual. **Type:** scholarship. **Recipient:** to high school seniors that are children or grandchildren of a NIADA member in good standing ● State Executive of the Year. **Frequency:** annual. **Type:** recognition. **Recipient:** to an executive for outstanding services to his/her association. **Formerly:** (1955) National Used Car Dealers Association. **Publications:** *Dealer Connection*, quarterly. Newsletter. Contains licensed independent used car dealers nationwide pertinent up-to-date information about the used car industry. **Advertising:** accepted ● *Used Car Dealer*, monthly. Magazine. Provides information of interest to used car dealers. Includes advertisers index, calendar of events, auto auction directory, and member profiles. **Price:** included in membership dues; $6.00/issue for nonmembers; $120.00 /year for nonmembers. **Circulation:** 16,000. **Advertising:** accepted. Alternate Formats: online ● *Used Car Industry Report*, annual. Contains snapshot of what trends are currently shaping and driving the used motor vehicle industry. **Price:** included in membership dues; $250.00 each additional copy. **Advertising:** accepted. **Conventions/Meetings:** annual convention and trade show, over 150 exhibits (exhibits) - always June. 2008 June 24-28, Grapevine, TX.

424 ■ National Institute for Automotive Service Excellence (ASE)
101 Blue Seal Dr. SE, Ste.101
Leesburg, VA 20175
Ph: (703)669-6600
Free: (888)ASE-TEST
Fax: (703)669-6127
E-mail: webmaster@asecert.org
URL: http://www.asecert.org
Contact: Tim Zilke, Pres.
Founded: 1972. **Members:** 400,000. **Staff:** 50. **Description:** Governed by a 40-member board of directors selected from all sectors of the automotive service industry and from education, government, and consumer groups. Encourages and promotes the highest standards of automotive service in the public interest. Conducts continuing research to determine the best methods for training automotive technicians; encourages the development of effective training programs. Tests and certifies the competence of automobile, medium/heavy truck, collision repair, school bus and engine machinist technicians as well as parts specialists. **Libraries: Type:** reference. **Holdings:** articles. **Awards:** Top Scoring Technician Awards. **Frequency:** annual. **Type:** monetary. **Committees:** Collision Repair/Refinish; Consumer Relations; Industry Relations; Medium/Heavy Truck; Nominations; Operations. **Affiliated With:** National Automotive Technicians Education Foundation. **Also Known As:** Auto Service Excellence. **Publications:** *ASE Blue Seal Tech News*, quarterly. Newsletter. Contains news of ASE technicians and their employers. **Price:** free. **Circulation:** 500,000. Alternate Formats: online ● *ASE Catalogs of Tests*, annual. Booklet. Includes bibliographic listing of training materials for upgrading technicians' skills in automotive repair; sample test questions; and task lists. **Price:** free individual copies ● *ASE Certification Test Registration Booklet*, semiannual. Includes registration for technicians who wish to become ASE certified. Provides registration information and sample questions. **Price:** free. **Circulation:** 1,800,000. **Conventions/Meetings:** semiannual board meeting - always May and November.

425 ■ National Windshield Repair Association (NWRA)
PO Box 569
Garrisonville, VA 22463
Ph: (540)720-7484
Fax: (540)720-3470
E-mail: nwra@nwraassociation.org
Contact: Paul Syfko, Pres.
Founded: 1994. **Membership Dues:** regular, $150 (annual) ● multilevel ($25 per additional locations), associate, $2,500 (annual) ● supplier, $500 (annual). **Description:** Represents professionals working in the windshield repair industry. **Publications:** *Auto Glass Repair and Replacement*. Magazine. Also Cited As: *AGRR* ● *NWRA News*. Newsletter.

426 ■ New York State Association of Service Stations and Repair Shops (NYSASSRS)
6 Walker Way
Albany, NY 12205
Ph: (518)452-4367
E-mail: state@nysassrs.com
URL: http://www.nysassrs.com
Contact: Ralph Bombardiere, Exec. Dir.
Founded: 1967. **Members:** 6,000. **Staff:** 3. **State Groups:** 7. **Description:** Service station dealers united for: passage of national, state, and local legislation supportive of the service station dealer; promotion of fraternity and unity among dealers in New York State and throughout the country; achievement of the highest standards of service and safety for the motoring public. Conducts trade exhibits and seminars in automotive mechanics. **Libraries: Type:** open to the public. **Holdings:** articles. **Awards:** Certificate of Achievement. **Frequency:** annual. **Type:** recognition. **Recipient:** for service to the association. **Formerly:** (1990) New York State Association of Service Stations; (2002) New York State Association of Service Stations. **Publications:** *The Review News*, quarterly. Newsletter. **Advertising:** accepted ● Newsletter. Alternate Formats: online. **Conventions/Meetings:** annual conference ● periodic trade show.

427 ■ Service Specialists Association (SSA)
4015 Marks Rd., Ste.2B
Medina, OH 44256-8316
Ph: (330)725-7160
Free: (800)763-5717
Fax: (330)722-5638
E-mail: trucksvc@aol.com
URL: http://www.truckservice.org
Contact: Cara Giebner, Ed.
Founded: 1981. **Members:** 200. **Staff:** 1. **Description:** Persons, firms, or corporations who have operated a full line truck repair shop for at least one year with a sufficient inventory to service the market area. Affiliate members are suppliers to the suspension industry. Provides a forum for the dissemination and understanding of technical information and to advance the interests of the wholesaler and installer segments of the aftermarket industry. Provides a voice in Washington, DC, through membership in the National Association of Wholesaler-Distributors (see separate entry) and informs members of pending legislation pertaining to the industry. Sponsors profit management seminars and technical clinics. **Formerly:** Suspension Specialists Association; (1989) Spring Service Association, Suspension Specialists. **Publications:** *The Leaf*, quarterly. Newsletter. Provides information of use to owners and operators of full line truck service shops. Includes technical notices and calendar of events. **Price:** free. **Circulation:** 500. **Conventions/Meetings:** annual convention (exhibits) - usually October.

428 ■ Society of Collision Repair Specialists (SCRS)
PO Box 909
Prosser, WA 99350
Ph: (708)598-3384 (949)272-3838
Free: (877)841-0660
Fax: (877)851-0660
E-mail: info@scrs.com
URL: http://www.scrs.com
Contact: Dan Risley, Exec. Dir.
Founded: 1982. **Members:** 7,800. **Membership Dues:** regular, $300 (annual) ● platinum, $1,000 (annual) ● affiliate, $350 (annual) ● company, $1,250 (annual) ● corporate, $5,000 (annual). **Staff:** 3. **Budget:** $300,000. **Local Groups:** 3. **Description:** Businesses; associations; individual owners and managers of auto collision repair shops, suppliers, insurance and educational associates. Distributes management and technical information; maintains industry standards; works to promote professionalism within the industry. **Libraries: Type:** reference. **Holdings:** articles, periodicals. **Awards:** Industry Achievement Award. **Frequency:** annual. **Type:** recognition. **Recipient:** for people who have done a specific deed or created a specific product, which has helped the industry ● Lifetime Achievement Award. **Frequency:** annual. **Type:** recognition. **Recipient:** for people who have given generously to the aid of their respective homeland. **Committees:** Aftermarket Parts Review; Communication Standards; Insurance Programs; Labor Time Review; Publications; Training Programs. **Conventions/Meetings:** annual meeting and seminar ● seminar and workshop, for managers and owners, industry issues, concerns and electronic technology.

429 ■ Towing and Recovery Association of America (TRAA)
2121 Eisenhower Ave., Ste.200
Alexandria, VA 22314

Ph: (703)684-7713
Free: (800)728-0136
Fax: (703)684-6720
E-mail: towserver@aol.com
URL: http://www.towserver.net
Contact: Harriet Cooley, Exec. Dir.
Founded: 1979. **Members:** 1,600. **Membership Dues:** regular, $210 (annual) ● manufacturer, $500 (annual) ● allied, $400 (annual) ● certified tower, $40 (annual) ● organization's driver, $50 (annual) ● women of the organization, $30 (annual) ● regular, $245 (annual). **Staff:** 4. **Budget:** $635,000. **State Groups:** 40. **Description:** Tow truck owners or operators; associate members are wrecker and accessory manufacturers and vendors. Aims to upgrade and promote the industry. Promotes uniform legislation; offers specialized education and National Driver Certification Program. **Libraries: Type:** reference. **Holdings:** archival material, clippings. **Awards: Type:** recognition. **Computer Services:** Mailing lists, of members. **Committees:** Awards; Legislative and Political Action; Trade Show and Convention; Truck and Equipment Specifications. **Publications:** *National Towing News*, monthly. Newspaper. Presents current information on legislative and regulatory issues affecting the industry. Includes industry updates, tax tips and association news. **Price:** included in membership dues. **Circulation:** 1,800. **Advertising:** accepted ● *TRAA Membership Directory*, annual. **Conventions/Meetings:** annual meeting and trade show (exhibits).

430 ■ Truck-Frame and Axle Repair Association (TARA)
c/o Wayne G. Reich, Admin./Consultant
3741 Enterprise Dr. SW
Rochester, MN 55902
Free: (800)232-8272
Fax: (507)529-0380
E-mail: w.g.reich@att.net
URL: http://www.taraassociation.com
Contact: Wayne G. Reich, Admin./Consultant
Founded: 1966. **Members:** 107. **Staff:** 1. **Budget:** $50,000. **Description:** Owners and operators of heavy-duty truck repair facilities and their mechanics; allied and associate members are manufacturers of heavy-duty trucks and repair equipment, engineers, trade press and insurance firms. Seeks to help members share skills and technical knowledge and keep abreast of new developments and technology to better serve customers in areas of minimum downtime, cost and maximum efficiency. Conducts studies and surveys regarding safety, fuel conservation and heavy-duty truck maintenance and repairs. Has formed TARA's Young Executives to help make young people at members' repair facilities more proficient in normal business functions and to ensure the future of the Association. **Committees:** Insurance Liaison; Manufacturing Liaison. **Publications:** *TARA News*, monthly. Newsletter. **Price:** free. **Circulation:** 1,500. Alternate Formats: online ● *Tek Info*, semiannual. Features technical information on vehicle changes. **Price:** available to members only ● *Truck-Frame and Axle Repair Association—Membership Directory*, annual. **Price:** free. **Circulation:** 10,000. **Conventions/Meetings:** semiannual conference.

431 ■ Used Truck Association (UTA)
909 Eagles Landing Pkwy., Ste.140-216
Stockbridge, GA 30281
Free: (877)438-7882
E-mail: contact@uta.org
URL: http://www.uta.org
Contact: Steve Nadolson, Pres. Emeritus
Founded: 1988. **Members:** 100. **Membership Dues:** professional, $100 (annual) ● corporate, $350 (annual). **Description:** Truck dealerships with substantial used truck sales; truck manufacturers. Promotes professionalism among members; works to elevate the image of the used truck sales business. Monitors federal regulatory developments affecting used truck sales; conducts lobbying activities. **Awards:** Marvin F. Gordon Lifetime Achievement Award. **Frequency:** annual. **Type:** recognition. **Recipient:** for individuals who have made significant contributions to the used truck industry. **Formerly:** (2003) Used Truck Sales Network. **Publications:** *Industry Watch*, monthly. Newsletter. Contains information on the association. **Price:** included in membership dues. Alternate Formats: online. **Conventions/Meetings:** annual meeting (exhibits) - always first Sunday after Memorial Day ● semiannual Sales and Employee Training Seminar.

Aviation

432 ■ Airline Pilots Security Alliance (APSA)
2526 Vineyard Ln.
Crofton, MD 21114
Ph: (615)479-4140
E-mail: apsa@secure-skies.org
URL: http://www.secure-skies.org
Contact: Capt. David Mackett, Pres.
Description: Works to shape public opinion and policy by educating pilots and the general public to improve airport and airline security. Advocates firearms for pilots.

433 ■ Aviation Crime Prevention Institute (ACPI)
PMB 306
226 N Nova Rd.
Ormond Beach, FL 32174
Ph: (386)341-7270
Free: (800)969-5473
Fax: (386)615-3378
E-mail: acpiusa@aol.com
URL: http://www.acpi.org
Contact: Robert J. Collins, Pres.
Founded: 1986. **Membership Dues:** attorney, $300 (annual). **Staff:** 1. **Budget:** $90,000. **Multinational. Description:** Helps law enforcement agencies locate and recover stolen aircraft and avionics equipment. Compiles and distributes detailed information on stolen aircraft and equipment; maintains contact with persons specializing in recovering aircraft from foreign countries. Educates the public on the importance of airport security; conducts airport security evaluations. **Computer Services:** database, covers stolen aircraft and equipment. **Supersedes:** International Aviation Theft Bureau. **Conventions/Meetings:** semiannual meeting.

434 ■ Aviation Safety Alliance (ASA)
601 Madison St., Ste.300
Alexandria, VA 22314
Ph: (703)739-6700
Fax: (703)739-6000
E-mail: scoughlin@aviationsafetyalliance.org
Contact: Susan Coughlin, Pres./CEO
Founded: 1998. **Description:** Aims to enhance public understanding of high safety standards and strong safety record of the commercial and general aviation industry. **Divisions:** Aviation Safety Alliance Education Fund. **Conventions/Meetings:** seminar.

435 ■ Black Pilots of America (BPA)
PO Box 7463
Pine Bluff, AR 71611
Ph: (504)214-7346
E-mail: president@bpapilots.org
URL: http://www.bpapilots.org
Contact: Col. Palmer Sullins Jr., Pres.
Founded: 1997. **Members:** 1,010. **Membership Dues:** regular, associate, $70 (annual) ● student, family, $20 (annual). **Regional Groups:** 15. **Description:** Trains African Americans to participate and advance in various areas within the field of aviation. Encourages youth to enter the field of aviation. Promotes opportunities in field of aviation by lecturing in schools. Encourages recognition of the contributions of blacks in aviation. Members are from all walks of life and backgrounds. Membership is open to anyone who understands and abides by the Aims and Purposes outlined in the BPA Constitution and Bylaws. **Awards:** Top Gun. **Frequency:** annual. **Type:** trophy. **Recipient:** to a pilot demonstrating the highest degree of proficiency during the Memorial Day Weekend Fly-In. **Committees:** Bylaws; Fundraising; Information Management; Skyhook Activities; Skyhook Rules; Summer Flight Academy Coordinating; Sunshine. **Councils:** Internationational Black Aerospace. **Publications:** *BPA ATIS*, quarterly. Newsletter. Alternate Formats: online ● *NOTAM*, monthly. Bulletin. Provides vital information to current members. Alternate Formats: online. **Conventions/Meetings:** annual Summer Flight Academy - workshop, flight training for youth 15 to 19 years of age - 2008 July 12-26, Houston, TX - **Avg. Attendance:** 24.

436 ■ International Aviation Ground Support Association (IAGSA)
201 Park Washington Ct.
Falls Church, VA 22046-4527
Ph: (703)533-0251
Fax: (703)241-5603
E-mail: info@iagsa.org
URL: http://www.iagsa.org
Contact: Clay Tyeryar, Exec. Dir.
Founded: 2003. **Membership Dues:** annual sales under $2 million, $500 ● annual sales $2 million or more, $1,000. **Multinational. Description:** Unites ground support equipment manufacturers and suppliers. Influences associations that represent the industry's customers. Provides the industry voice to global governing authorities.

437 ■ International Aviation Womens Association (IAWA)
PO Box 1088
Edgewater, MD 21037
Ph: (410)571-1990
E-mail: info@iawa.org
URL: http://www.iawa.org
Contact: Julie H. Ellis, Pres.
Founded: 1988. **Members:** 200. **Membership Dues:** full, $150 (annual) ● government employee, $125 (annual). **Budget:** $30,000. **Multinational. Description:** Represents and supports women of achievement in all facets of aviation and aerospace including airline, airport, insurance, finance, legal, manufacturing, operations and government. Members must be executives, managers or professionals with at least five years experience in the aviation industry, or equivalent experience.

438 ■ Latin American Aeronautical Association (ALA)
5100 S Collins
Arlington Airport
Arlington, TX 76018
Ph: (817)284-0431
Fax: (817)284-0433
E-mail: ala@ala.aero
URL: http://www.ala.aero
Founded: 1989. **Membership Dues:** general, $35 (annual). **Languages:** English, Portuguese, Spanish. **Multinational. Description:** Seeks to provide the Latin American aviation community an organizational link to the global aviation industry. Strives to close the communication and information gap between the aviation industry and the Latin American community. **Computer Services:** database, aviation directory ● online services, aviation dictionary ● online services, aviation encyclopedia. **Publications:** Magazine (in English, Portuguese, and Spanish). Contains articles, reviews and current events. **Price:** included in membership dues. **Advertising:** accepted. Alternate Formats: online.

439 ■ National Gay Pilot's Association (NGPA)
PO Box 7271
Dallas, TX 75209-0271
Ph: (214)336-0873
Fax: (214)350-0447
E-mail: info@ngpa.org
URL: http://www.ngpa.org
Members: 630. **Membership Dues:** individual, $55 (annual) ● family, $75 (annual) ● individual outside U.S., $65 (annual) ● family outside U.S., $85 (annual) ● college student, $20 (annual). **Description:** Provides a social and professional network for gay and lesbian aviators. Encourages gays and lesbians to begin piloting careers. Fosters equal treatment of

gay and lesbian aviators. Promotes aviation safety. **Libraries: Type:** lending. **Holdings:** 100; video recordings. **Subjects:** aviation. **Awards:** NGPA Education Fund. **Frequency:** annual. **Type:** scholarship. **Recipient:** for individuals pursuing a career as a professional pilot. **Publications:** *NGPA News*, quarterly. Magazine. Contains programs, news and upcoming activities and events. **Price:** included in membership dues ● Newsletter, monthly. Alternate Formats: online. **Conventions/Meetings:** annual Cape Cod Classic - meeting.

440 ■ World Airline Entertainment Association (WAEA)
8201 Greensboro Dr., Ste.300
McLean, VA 22102
Ph: (703)610-9021
Free: (866)890-7356
Fax: (703)610-9005
E-mail: info@waea.org
URL: http://www.waea.org
Contact: Sue Pinfold, Sec.
Founded: 1979. **Members:** 400. **Membership Dues:** airline, $350 (annual) ● vendor, $500 (annual). **Staff:** 7. **Budget:** $2,000,000. **Description:** Promotes airline entertainment. Conducts educational programs. **Libraries: Type:** not open to the public; reference. **Holdings:** articles, reports. **Awards:** Avion Award. **Frequency:** annual. **Type:** trophy. **Recipient:** for best flight entertainment in print, audio, and video. **Computer Services:** database, members only. **Publications:** *Avion Magazine*, quarterly. **Price:** free for members. **Advertising:** accepted ● *WAEA Conference Handbook*, annual. **Price:** free for members. **Advertising:** accepted ● Membership Directory, annual. Includes member's contact names, titles, addresses, phone, fax, e-mail and web addresses. **Price:** free for members. **Advertising:** accepted. **Conventions/Meetings:** annual conference, for the IFE professional (exhibits) - 2008 Sept. 8-11, Long Beach, CA; 2009 Oct. 19-22, Kuala Lumpur, Malaysia.

Awards

441 ■ Awards and Recognition Association (ARA)
4700 W Lake Ave.
Glenview, IL 60025
Ph: (847)375-4800 (901)385-0400
Free: (800)344-2148
Fax: (877)734-9380
E-mail: info@ara.org
URL: http://www.ara.org
Contact: Ed Hunt, Pres.
Founded: 1980. **Members:** 4,500. **Membership Dues:** full retailer, $195 (annual) ● branch retail/franchisee, $115 (annual) ● full supplier, $490 (annual) ● supplier branch/franchisee/representative, $85 (annual) ● affiliate, associate, $595 (annual). **Staff:** 15. **Regional Groups:** 7. **State Groups:** 55. **Description:** Awards and recognition industry retailers and suppliers. Advances the business growth of recognition specialists. **Awards:** ARA Hall of Fame. **Frequency:** annual. **Type:** recognition. **Recipient:** to honor the creative foresight and organizing ability of those who have shaped the awards and engraving industry ● Best Trade Show Product and Best Booth Display. **Type:** recognition ● Certified Recognition Specialist (CSR). **Type:** recognition ● Founders Award. **Frequency:** annual. **Type:** recognition. **Recipient:** for contributions to the association ● Retailer of the Year Award. **Frequency:** annual. **Type:** recognition. **Recipient:** for most creative and quality-oriented retailer companies ● Sportsmanship Award. **Frequency:** annual. **Type:** recognition. **Recipient:** to a Division I college football player who exemplifies sportsmanship both on and off the field ● Supplier Member of the Year. **Frequency:** annual. **Type:** recognition. **Recipient:** for contributions to the association ● Volunteer Member of the Year. **Frequency:** annual. **Type:** recognition. **Recipient:** for contributions to the association. **Committees:** Education; Trade Shows. **Formed by Merger of:** American Award Manufacturers Association; Trophy Dealers of America. **Formerly:** (1993) Trophy Dealers and Manufacturers Association. **Publications:** *ARA Membership Directory and Buyers Guide*, annual. Lists dealers, manufacturers, and products sold by ARA manufacturers found under 450 categories. **Price:** available to members only. **Circulation:** 4,500. **Advertising:** accepted ● *Recognition Review*, monthly. Magazine. Covers association news, chapter news, business and technical features. Includes lists of new members. **Price:** included in membership dues. **Circulation:** 9,000. **Advertising:** accepted. **Conventions/Meetings:** quarterly trade show (exhibits).

Bail

442 ■ American Bail Coalition
1725 Desales St. NW, Ste.800
Washington, DC 20036
Ph: (202)659-6547
Free: (800)375-8390
Fax: (202)296-8702
E-mail: dnabic@aol.com
URL: http://www.americanbailcoalition.com
Contact: William B. Carmichael, Pres.
Founded: 1992. **Members:** 5. **Description:** Bail insurance companies. Defends and expands the role of the commercial surety bail with the American justice system. **Formerly:** (2004) National Association of Bail Insurance Companies.

Baking

443 ■ Allied Trades of the Baking Industry (ATBI)
c/o Cereal Food Processors, Inc.
2001 Shawnee Mission Pkwy.
Mission Woods, KS 66205
Ph: (913)890-6300
E-mail: t.miller@cerealfood.com
URL: http://www.atbi.org
Contact: Gary Cain, Pres.
Founded: 1920. **Members:** 1,000. **Membership Dues:** regular, $50 (annual). **Staff:** 2. **Regional Groups:** 8. **Description:** Salespeople from the allied trades servicing the baking industry. Promotes the industry through cooperative service to national, state, and local bakery associations; encourages mutual understanding and goodwill between the baking industry and the allied trades. Carries out promotional and service activities. **Publications:** *The Allied Tradesman*, semiannual. Newsletter. **Price:** free. **Advertising:** accepted ● Handbook. Contains information on baking schools and scholarships. **Conventions/Meetings:** semiannual meeting.

444 ■ American Bakers Association (ABA)
1300 I St. NW, Ste.700 W
Washington, DC 20005
Ph: (202)789-0300
Fax: (202)898-1164
E-mail: info@americanbakers.org
URL: http://www.americanbakers.org
Contact: Robb MacKie, Pres./CEO
Founded: 1897. **Members:** 300. **Membership Dues:** allied (dues based on gross sales), $1,300-$2,500 (annual) ● baker (minimum; dues based on gross sales), $1,000 (annual) ● allied, $1,690-$3,250 (annual). **Staff:** 14. **Budget:** $3,000,000. **Description:** Manufacturers and wholesale distributors of bread, rolls, and pastry products; suppliers of goods and services to bakers. Conducts seminars and expositions. **Publications:** *ABA Bulletin*, biweekly. Newsletter. **Conventions/Meetings:** annual convention.

445 ■ American Institute of Baking (AIB)
1213 Bakers Way
PO Box 3999
Manhattan, KS 66505-3999
Ph: (785)537-4750
Free: (800)633-5137
Fax: (785)537-1493
E-mail: info@aibonline.org
URL: http://www.aibonline.org
Contact: James Munyon, Pres./CEO
Founded: 1919. **Members:** 890. **Membership Dues:** regular, $500 (annual). **Staff:** 150. **Budget:** $16,440,000. **Languages:** English, French, Spanish. **Description:** Baking research and educational center. Conducts basic and applied research, educational and hands-on training, and in-plant sanitation and worker safety audits. Maintains museum. Provides bibliographic and reference service. Serves as registrar for ISO-9000 quality certification. **Libraries: Type:** reference. **Holdings:** 11,350; archival material, books, periodicals, reports. **Subjects:** baking, food science, food legislation, ISO 9000, food safety. **Awards:** AIB Scholarship. **Frequency:** annual. **Type:** scholarship. **Recipient:** for students accepted for course in Baking Science & Technology or Maintenance Engineering (most are limited to U.S. citizens). **Computer Services:** database, about food and baking technology. **Committees:** Educational Advisory; Scientific Advisory. **Departments:** AIBRS (ISO-9000 Registration Service); Communications; Food Safety & Hygiene; Information Services; Nutrition Labeling Program; Occupational Safety; Research; School of Baking. **Also Known As:** AIB International. **Publications:** *AIB—Maintenance Bulletin*, bimonthly. Covers maintenance engineering and related topics. **Price:** $18.50/year in U.S.; $33.00/year outside U.S.; $7.50/copy outside U.S.; $5.00/copy in U.S. **Circulation:** 880 ● *American Institute of Baking—Technical Bulletin*, monthly. Covers developments in baking research and sanitation. **Price:** $475.00 complete set of back issues; $50.00 updated CD; $5.00/copy in U.S.; $7.50/copy outside U.S. **Circulation:** 1,700. Alternate Formats: CD-ROM; online ● *Bakers Way*, quarterly. Newsletter. **Price:** included in membership dues ● Bibliographies. Covers bagels, hearth breads, tortillas, pizza, biscuits, cookies, food safety, enzymes, and ISO 9000. ● Also publishes training materials and books and manuals on food safety and production standards, and food labeling law.

446 ■ American Pie Council (APC)
PO Box 368
Lake Forest, IL 60045
Ph: (847)371-0170
Fax: (847)371-0199
E-mail: apc@piecouncil.org
URL: http://www.piecouncil.org
Contact: Linda Hoskins, Exec. Dir.
Membership Dues: regular, $35 (annual) ● senior/student, $25 (annual) ● professional, $75 (annual) ● business, $100-$2,500 (annual). **Description:** Works for the preservation of the American pie heritage; promotes awareness, enjoyment and consumption of pies. Sponsors National Pie Day. **Telecommunication Services:** electronic bulletin board, consumers bulletin board with a recipe and tips section. **Committees:** Pie Marketing. **Publications:** *Pie Times*, quarterly. Newsletter. Features pie news, recipes and secrets from top pie bakers. **Price:** included in membership dues. Alternate Formats: online. **Conventions/Meetings:** annual The Great American Pie Festival ● annual National Pie Championships - competition, for amateurs, professionals and commercial pie bakers compete for best pie categories.

447 ■ American Society of Baking
533 1st St. E
Sonoma, CA 95476
Ph: (707)935-0103
Free: (866)920-9885
Fax: (707)935-0174
E-mail: tmatthias@asbe.org
URL: http://www.asbe.org
Contact: Thomas D. Kuk, Pres.
Founded: 1924. **Members:** 2,900. **Membership Dues:** individual, $145 (annual) ● international, $160 (annual). **Staff:** 3. **Description:** Professional organization of persons engaged in bakery production; chemists, production supervisors, engineers, technicians, and others from allied fields. Maintains information service and library references to baking and related subjects. **Libraries: Type:** not open to the public. **Subjects:** baking industry. **Telecommunica-**

tion Services: electronic mail, asbe@asbe.org. **Committees:** Engineers Information Service; Research and Study; Safety; Sanitation. **Formerly:** (1999) American Society of Bakery Engineers. **Publications:** *Letter*, quarterly ● Bulletin, periodic ● Proceedings, annual. **Conventions/Meetings:** annual meeting - always Chicago, IL.

448 ■ Baking Industry Sanitation Standards Committee (BISSC)

PO Box 3999
Manhattan, KS 66505-3999
Ph: (785)537-4750
Free: (866)342-4772
Fax: (785)565-6060
E-mail: bissc@bissc.org
URL: http://www.bissc.org
Contact: Mr. Jon Anderson, Exec. Dir./Sec.

Founded: 1949. **Members:** 120. **Membership Dues:** company, $350 (annual). **Staff:** 3. **Budget:** $200,000. **National Groups:** 5. **Description:** Industry association representing 120 bakery equipment manufacturers. Seeks to establish standards of sanitation in bakery food processing equipment. Receives advisory assistance from national and international public health and food sanitation groups. Develops and publishes sanitation standards for the baking industry. Offers an equipment certification program for bakery equipment conforming to BISSC standards (annual). **Telecommunication Services:** electronic mail, janderson@aibonline.org. **Publications:** *ANSI/BISSC/Z50.2-2003 Sanitation Standard*, quadrennial. Manual. Alternate Formats: online. Also Cited As: *BISSC Sanitation Standards for Bakery Equipment* ● *Design Handbook for Easily Cleanable Equipment*. Alternate Formats: online ● *Directory of BISSC Registered Companies*, annual. Lists registered firms and individual certification authorizations. Alternate Formats: online. **Conventions/Meetings:** annual meeting, membership meeting in the morning and board of directors meeting in the afternoon - always in Chicago, IL.

449 ■ BEMA, The Baking Industry Suppliers Association (BEMA)

7101 Coll. Blvd., Ste.1505
Overland Park, KS 66210
Ph: (913)338-1300
Fax: (913)338-1327
E-mail: info@bema.org
URL: http://www.bema.org
Contact: Kerwin Brown, Pres./CEO

Founded: 1918. **Members:** 202. **Membership Dues:** regular, $1,250 (annual). **Staff:** 2. **Budget:** $1,000,000. **Multinational. Description:** Baking and food industries. **Awards:** BEMA Scholarship. **Frequency:** annual. **Type:** scholarship. **Recipient:** for outstanding individuals in the baking industry ● Lifetime Achievement Award. **Frequency:** annual. **Type:** recognition. **Telecommunication Services:** electronic mail, office@bema.org. **Affiliated With:** Baking Industry Sanitation Standards Committee. **Also Known As:** (1993) Bakery Equipment Manufacturers Association. **Formerly:** (2003) BEMA. **Publications:** *Bakery Equipment, Product & Service Guide*, quadrennial. Membership Directory. Includes subject index. **Price:** free. **Circulation:** 300 ● *BEMA Newsletter*, quarterly. **Circulation:** 300. **Conventions/Meetings:** annual conference and workshop - usually June. 2008 June 26-July 1, Newport, RI ● quadrennial International Baking Industry Exposition - trade show ● quadrennial meeting.

450 ■ Biscuit and Cracker Manufacturers Association (B&CMA)

6325 Woodside Ct., Ste.125
Columbia, MD 21046
Ph: (443)545-1645
Fax: (410)290-8585
E-mail: kkinter@thebcma.org
URL: http://www.thebcma.org
Contact: Kathy Kinter, Contact

Founded: 1901. **Members:** 300. **Staff:** 5. **Budget:** $800,000. **Description:** Bakers of crackers and cookies; suppliers to the industry. Sponsors the Cookie and Cracker Manufacturing Correspondence Course. **Awards:** Vander Heide Award. **Frequency:** annual. **Type:** recognition. **Recipient:** for the graduate with highest GPA. **Absorbed:** (1965) Biscuit Bakers Institute. **Publications:** Directory, annual. **Conventions/Meetings:** annual conference (exhibits) - 2008 Sept. 14-17, Chantilly, VA ● annual convention.

451 ■ Bread Bakers Guild of America

3203 Maryland Ave.
North Versailles, PA 15137
Ph: (412)823-2080
Fax: (412)823-2495
E-mail: info@bbga.org
URL: http://www.bbga.org
Contact: Gina Renee Piccolino, Exec. Dir.

Founded: 1993. **Members:** 1,300. **Membership Dues:** individual, $75 (annual) ● educational, instructor, $60 (annual) ● student, $45 (annual) ● business, $120-$900 (annual). **Staff:** 2. **Budget:** $280,000. **Multinational. Description:** Bakeries, baking and cooking instructors and students, industry suppliers, and other individuals with an interest in bread. Seeks to "provide education in the field of artisan baking and the production of high quality bread products." Serves as a clearinghouse on bread baking; conducts educational and training programs. **Awards:** Awards for Excellence. **Frequency:** periodic. **Type:** recognition. **Computer Services:** database ● mailing lists. **Telecommunication Services:** electronic mail, membership@bbga.org. **Publications:** *Bread Lines*, quarterly. Newsletter. Alternate Formats: online ● Books. **Conventions/Meetings:** periodic seminar.

452 ■ Independent Bakers Association (IBA)

PO Box 3731
Washington, DC 20007
Ph: (202)333-8190 (267)238-3887
Fax: (202)337-3809
E-mail: independentbaker@yahoo.com
URL: http://www.mindspring.com/~independentbaker
Contact: Nicholas A. Pyle, Pres.

Founded: 1967. **Members:** 415. **Membership Dues:** baker representative, $425 (annual) ● baker senator, allied president, $1,100 (annual) ● baker governor, $1,815 (annual) ● baker president, $2,200 (annual) ● allied representative, $275 (annual) ● allied senator, $550 (annual) ● allied governor, $825 (annual). **Staff:** 4. **Budget:** $350,000. **Description:** Trade association representing small-medium wholesale bakers and allied trade members. Represents independent wholesale bakers on federal legislative and regulatory issues. Offers annual Smith-Schaus-Smith internships. **Libraries: Type:** reference; open to the public. **Holdings:** photographs. **Committees:** National Affairs; Peanut Users; Political Education. **Councils:** Young Presidents. **Publications:** *Bagel Bits*, bimonthly. Newsletter. Contains news about the bagel industry. **Price:** free ● *The Independent*, annual. Newsletter. Provides legislative updates and industry news of concern to independent bakers. Includes annual conference report. **Price:** free for industry only. **Circulation:** 3,000 ● *Legislative and Regulatory Update*, monthly. Newsletter ● *News Release*, biweekly. Newsletter. **Conventions/Meetings:** annual convention ● annual convention, west coast membership meeting - every fall ● annual convention, membership meeting - every winter ● meeting - 3/year.

453 ■ Quality Bakers of America Cooperative (QBA)

1055 Parsippany Blvd., Ste.201
Parsippany, NJ 07054
Ph: (973)263-6970
Fax: (973)263-0937
E-mail: info@qba.com
URL: http://www.qba.com
Contact: Norm Trapp, Contact

Founded: 1922. **Members:** 83. **Staff:** 21. **Description:** Independent national and international wholesale bakeries; composed of three major consulting divisions: marketing, manufacturing and technical research. Offers expertise in business strategy and management, product development, marketing and consumer research, process development, training and procurement. **Telecommunication Services:** electronic mail, ntrapp@qba.com. **Conventions/Meetings:** annual meeting.

454 ■ Retailer's Bakery Association (RBA)

8201 Greensboro Dr., Ste.300
McLean, VA 22102
Ph: (703)610-9035 (703)610-0272
Free: (800)638-0924
Fax: (703)610-9005
E-mail: info@rbanet.com
URL: http://www.rbanet.com
Contact: Susan Nicholas CAE, Exec. VP

Founded: 1918. **Members:** 3,500. **Membership Dues:** allied - corporate, $250 (annual) ● allied - gold, $750 (annual) ● school, $150 (annual) ● student, $50 (annual) ● retail, $250-$750 (annual). **Staff:** 4. **Budget:** $2,000,000. **Regional Groups:** 15. **Languages:** English, Spanish. **Description:** Independent and in-store bakeries, food service, specialty bakeries (2500), suppliers of ingredients, tools and equipment (780); other (220). Provides information, management, production, merchandising, and small business services. **Libraries: Type:** reference. **Holdings:** books. **Subjects:** retail baking. **Computer Services:** Mailing lists, of members. **Formerly:** Associated Bakers of America - Retail and Wholesale; (1925) Retail Bakers Association of America; (1938) Associated Bakers of America; (1978) Associated Retail Bakers of America; (1981) Retail Merchant Bakers of America; (1995) Retail Bakers of America. **Publications:** *RBA Bakers Rack*, 10/year. Newsletter. Includes legal news and production and management topics; association news and practical information on baking. Contains calendar of events. **Price:** $65.00 /year for members. **Circulation:** 3,500. **Advertising:** accepted. Also Cited As: *RBA Insight*. **Conventions/Meetings:** annual American Bakery Expo - convention (exhibits).

455 ■ Wholesale Variety Bakers Association (WVBA)

c/o Steve Baldinger, Pres.
215 Eva St.
St. Paul, MN 55107
Ph: (651)224-5761
Fax: (651)224-9047
Contact: Steve Baldinger, Pres.

Founded: 1964. **Members:** 20. **Description:** Bakeries. Facilitates exchange of information among members and between members and other bakeries. **Conventions/Meetings:** semiannual meeting.

Banking

456 ■ American Association of Bank Directors (AABD)

4701 Sangamore Rd., Ste.P-15
Bethesda, MD 20816
Ph: (301)263-9841
Fax: (301)229-2443
E-mail: info@aabd.org
URL: http://www.aabd.org
Contact: David H. Baris Esq., Exec. Dir.

Founded: 1989. **Members:** 2,000. **Membership Dues:** institution, $695 (annual) ● associate, $750 (annual) ● individual, $295 (annual). **Staff:** 3. **Description:** Bank and saving institution directors. Provides information, education and advocacy before federal and state banking regulators as well as the United States Congress; conducts educational programs; compiles statistics. **Libraries: Type:** by appointment only. **Holdings:** books. **Subjects:** banking. **Computer Services:** database. **Publications:** *A Bank Director's Guide to Internal Investigations*. Book. **Price:** free for premium member; $10.00 for basic member; $12.50 for nonmembers ● *Bank Director News*, periodic. Newsletter. Contains articles written about current topics affecting bank directors. **Price:** included in membership dues ● *Report of Task Force on Asset Freezes of Bank Directors and Officers*. **Price:** free for premium member; $15.00 for basic member; $25.00 for nonmembers. **Conventions/Meetings:** annual convention.

457 ■ American Bankers Association (ABA)
1120 Connecticut Ave. NW
Washington, DC 20036
Ph: (202)663-5000 (202)663-5129
Free: (800)BANKERS
Fax: (202)663-7543
E-mail: custserv@aba.com
URL: http://www.aba.com
Contact: Ed Yingling, Pres./CEO

Founded: 1875. **Members:** 8,000. **Staff:** 410. **Budget:** $62,000,000. **Description:** Members are principally commercial banks and trust companies; combined assets of members represent approximately 90&percent; of the U.S. banking industry; approximately 94&percent; of members are community banks with less than $500 million in assets. Seeks to enhance the role of commercial bankers as preeminent providers of financial services through communications, research, legal action, lobbying of federal legislative and regulatory bodies, and education and training programs. Serves as spokesperson for the banking industry; facilitates exchange of information among members. Maintains the American Institute of Banking, an industry-sponsored adult education program. Conducts educational and training programs for bank employees and officers through a wide range of banking schools and national conferences. Maintains liaison with federal bank regulators; lobbies Congress on issues affecting commercial banks; testifies before congressional committees; represents members in U.S. postal rate proceedings. Serves as secretariat of the International Monetary Conference and the Financial Institutions Committee for the American National Standards Institute. Files briefs and lawsuits in major court cases affecting the industry. Conducts teleconferences with state banking associations on such issues as regulatory compliance; works to build consensus and coordinate activities of leading bank and financial service trade groups. Provides services to members including: public advocacy; news media contact; insurance program providing directors and officers with liability coverage, financial institution bond, and trust errors and omissions coverage; research service operated through ABA Center for Banking Information; fingerprint set processing in conjunction with the Federal Bureau of Investigation; discounts on operational and income-producing projects through the Corporation for American Banking. Conducts conferences, forums, and workshops covering subjects such as small business, consumer credit, agricultural and community banking, trust management, bank operations, and automation. Sponsors ABA Educational Foundation and the Personal Economics Program, which educates schoolchildren and the community on banking, economics, and personal finance. **Libraries: Type:** reference. **Holdings:** 75,000. **Subjects:** banking, money, economics, finance, law. **Awards: Type:** fellowship. **Recipient:** to academicians ● **Type:** fellowship. **Recipient:** to financial journalists. **Telecommunication Services:** hotline, (800)551-2572. **Subgroups:** Corporation for American Banking; Institute of Certified Bankers; Minbane Capital Corp. **Affiliated With:** ABA Marketing Network. **Publications:** *ABA Bank Compliance*, bimonthly. Magazine. **Price:** $160.00 for members; $250.00 for nonmembers. Alternate Formats: online ● *ABA Banking Journal*, monthly. Provides immediate access to banking's inner circles and the behind-the-scenes activities, which are shaping the banking industry. **Price:** $18.00/copy in U.S. and Canada; $75.00/copy outside U.S. and Canada; $295.00/year outside U.S. and Canada. ISSN: 0194-5947. **Circulation:** 32,000. **Advertising:** accepted. Alternate Formats: online ● *AIB Alert*, bimonthly. **Price:** included in membership dues ● *Bank Operations Bulletin*, monthly. **Price:** $75.00 for members; $110.00 for nonmembers ● *Bank Security & Fraud Prevention*, monthly ● *Bankers News*, biweekly. Newspaper. Covers national trends and developments in the banking industry, and legislative, regulatory, and judicial news related to banking. **Price:** $48.00 for members; $96.00 for nonmembers. **Circulation:** 20,000 ● *Commercial Lending Review*, quarterly. Published by Institutional Investor (endorsed by ABA). **Price:** $84.00 for members; $140.00 for nonmembers ● *Consumer Credit Delinquency Bulletin*, quarterly ● *Employee Benefits Quarterly*. Newsletter. **Price:** $80.00 for members; $120.00 for nonmembers ● *Journal of Agricultural Lending*, quarterly. **Price:** $60.00 for members; $90.00 for nonmembers ● *Network News*, 3/year. Newsletter. **Price:** included in membership dues ● *Retail Delivery Strategies*, quarterly. **Price:** $139.00 for members; $219.00 for nonmembers ● *Securities Processing Digest*, quarterly. **Price:** $90.00 for members; $135.00 for nonmembers ● *Trends*, bimonthly. **Price:** $105.00 for members; $166.00 for nonmembers ● *Trust and Financial Advisor*, quarterly. **Price:** $125.00 for members; $190.00 for nonmembers ● *Trust Letter*, monthly. **Price:** $100.00 for members; $150.00 for nonmembers. **Conventions/Meetings:** annual meeting.

458 ■ American Council of State Savings Supervisors (ACSSS)
c/o Andrea M. Falzarano, CAE, Exec. Dir.
PO Box 1904
Leesburg, VA 20177
Ph: (703)669-5440
Fax: (703)669-5441
E-mail: amfalz@acsss.org
URL: http://www.acsss.org
Contact: Andrea M. Falzarano CAE, Exec. Dir.

Founded: 1939. **Members:** 100. **Staff:** 1. **Budget:** $100,000. **Description:** Active members are state savings association supervisors; associate members are savings associations; affiliate members are suppliers to the financial services industry. Purposes are to: increase the usefulness and effectiveness of state departments having direct supervision over state chartered savings associations; obtain more uniform methods among departments of savings associations; secure proper consideration of questions regarding the supervision and examination of savings associations; encourage modernization of state laws and regulatory procedures relating to savings associations; broaden public understanding of the function of and need for strong and viable state chartered savings systems; preserve and protect the dual savings system; ensure that state chartered savings associations receive equal benefits from the federal government; protect and improve the health of the industry as a whole. **Formerly:** (1987) National Association of State Savings and Loan Supervisors. **Publications:** *State Advisor*, monthly. Newsletter. Alternate Formats: online. **Conventions/Meetings:** annual seminar - always spring.

459 ■ American League of Financial Institutions (ALFI)
Address Unknown since 2007

Founded: 1948. **Members:** 49. **Staff:** 5. **Description:** Federal and state chartered minority savings and loan associations in 25 states and the District of Columbia. Undertakes programs to increase the income of and savings flow into the associations including a direct solicitation effort; provides counseling and technical assistance for member associations; offers consultant services to assist individual associations and groups wishing to organize new associations or acquire existing associations with development potential; collects, organizes, and distributes materials that will aid member associations. Conducts research to improve investment capability, resolve common management problems, and evaluate statistical data on an industry-wide basis to develop and institute training programs for management personnel. Conducts research programs. **Committees:** Banking; Housing. **Affiliated With:** America's Community Bankers. **Formerly:** (1983) American Savings and Loan Leagues. **Publications:** *ALFI Focus Magazine*, periodic ● *Directory of Members and Associate Members*, periodic. Membership Directory. **Conventions/Meetings:** annual meeting (exhibits).

460 ■ The American Safe Deposit Association (TASDA)
PO Box 519
Franklin, IN 46131
Ph: (317)738-4432 (573)874-8430
Fax: (317)738-5267
E-mail: tasda1@aol.com
URL: http://www.tasda.com
Contact: Joyce A. McLin, Exec. Dir.

Founded: 1924. **Members:** 1,850. **Membership Dues:** associate, $110 (annual) ● individual, $60 (annual) ● corporate (add $50 for each branch), $1,000 (annual). **Staff:** 2. **Budget:** $130,000. **State Groups:** 64. **Description:** Federation of state and local associations of banks, trust companies, and other firms engaged in the safe deposit business. **Additional Websites:** http://www.americansafedeposit.org. **Telecommunication Services:** electronic mail, john_merrill@boonebank.com. **Formerly:** (1947) National Safe Deposit Advisory Council. **Publications:** *Access*, quarterly. Magazine ● *Educational Bulletin*, 10/year. Newsletter. **Conventions/Meetings:** annual conference - May/June ● seminar, covers senior management and safe deposit basics.

461 ■ America's Community Bankers (ACB)
900 19th St. NW, Ste.400
Washington, DC 20006
Ph: (202)857-3100
Fax: (202)296-8716
E-mail: info@acbankers.org
URL: http://www.acbankers.org
Contact: Mark E. Macomber, Chm.

Founded: 1992. **Members:** 2,100. **Staff:** 120. **Description:** Savings and loan associations, savings banks, cooperative banks, and state and local savings and loan association leagues in all U.S. states and territories; associate members are institutions and firms providing products or services to the savings business. Serves the savings institution business and the public interest by furthering thrift and home ownership. Encourages private investment in the purchase of homes; works for the development of safe, efficient operating methods for member institutions; promotes the improvement of statutes and regulations affecting the savings and community banking business and the public interest. Conducts studies of operating procedures; provides specialized services in the field of funds acquisition, mortgage lending, public relations, accounting procedures, advertising, business development, marketing, economic forecasting, statistical data and trends, and policy formation. Sponsors management and legislative workshops and clinics; analyzes federal rules, regulations, and laws pertaining to taxation and housing legislation, or otherwise affecting savings institution groups. **Absorbed:** (1993) National Council of Savings Institutions. **Formed by Merger of:** United States League of Savings Institutions; National Council of Community Bankers. **Formerly:** (1998) Savings and Community Bankers of America. **Publications:** *Corporate Finance Letter*. Covers structuring loans to facilitate the sale of real estate owned and making allowances for credit losses. **Price:** $195.00 /year for members; $395.00 /year for nonmembers. **Circulation:** 170 ● *Data Bank*, monthly. Newsletter. Tracks complex changes in interest rates, the housing market, and the U.S. economy. **Price:** $85.00 /year for members; $170.00 /year for nonmembers. **Circulation:** 4,700 ● *Directors and Trustees Digest*, monthly. Provides updates on the latest in board management relations, significant legislation and regulations, and legal fiduciary responsibilities. **Price:** $24.00 /year for members; $50.00 /year for nonmembers. **Circulation:** 11,525 ● *Federal Guide Highlights*, monthly. Summary of federal regulations, laws, and rules affecting savings and community banking institutions. **Price:** $455.00 /year for members; $650.00 /year for nonmembers; $815.00 /year for nonmembers (for supplements). **Circulation:** 3,200. Alternate Formats: online ● *Reg/Ops*, monthly. Newsletter ● *Supervisory Service*. Covers regulatory activities of agencies such as the FDIC and OTS. Contains annotations, interpretations, and comments ruling on agency matters. **Price:** $290.00 /year for members; $425.00 /year for nonmembers; $300.00 /year for members (for supplements); $525.00 /year for nonmembers (for supplements) ● *Trustees and Directors Handbook*. Covers fiduciary responsibilities, meeting the "business judgment" rule, and changes in indemnification and liability insurance standards. **Price:** $95.00 /year for members; $225.00 /year for nonmembers. **Circulation:** 365 ● *Washington Perspective*, weekly. Covers congressional and regulatory actions. **Price:** $155.00 /year for members; $350.00 /year for nonmembers. **Circulation:** 3,200. Alternate Formats: online. **Conventions/Meetings:** periodic conference ● annual meeting.

462 ■ Arab Bankers Association of North America (ABANA)

c/o Brenda Murad, Exec. Dir.
PO Box 2249
Grand Central Sta.
New York, NY 10163
Ph: (212)599-3030
Fax: (212)599-3131
E-mail: bmurad@arabbankers.org
URL: http://www.arabbankers.org
Contact: Laura Osman, Pres.
Founded: 1983. **Members:** 2,400. **Membership Dues:** individual, $150-$200 (annual) ● institutional, $2,000 (annual) ● student, $50 (annual). **Staff:** 2. **Multinational. Description:** Promotes financial and banking relations between the Arab world and North America. Fosters improved relations, information-sharing and understanding between the Arab and American public and private financial sectors. Promotes the exchange of banking, financial and monetary information in both international and regional dimensions, with particular emphasis on the Arab world and North America. **Awards:** Lifetime Achievement Award. **Frequency:** annual. **Type:** recognition. **Recipient:** for an individual in recognition of his or her distinguished achievements and pioneering contributions to banking and finance. **Computer Services:** database, membership directory ● information services, reports and analyses; Arab banks; resource links ● online services, institutional member links. **Committees:** Communications; Nominations; Programs; Strategy. **Publications:** *ABANA Review*, quarterly. Journal. Features activities of ABANA, guest articles, interviews and institutional spotlights. **Circulation:** 2,200. **Advertising:** accepted. Alternate Formats: online. **Conventions/Meetings:** annual dinner, includes awarding ceremonies.

463 ■ Association of Certified Anti-Money Laundering Specialists (ACAMS)

Brickell Bayview Center
80 SW 8th St., Ste.2350
Miami, FL 33130
Ph: (305)373-0020
Free: (866)459-2267
Fax: (305)373-7788
E-mail: info@acams.org
URL: http://www.acams.org
Contact: Gregory Calpakis, Exec. Dir.
Founded: 2001. **Members:** 2,800. **Membership Dues:** private, $225 (annual) ● public, $150 (annual) ● academic, $125 (annual) ● student, $50 (annual). **Languages:** English, Spanish. **Multinational. Description:** Promotes the development and implementation of sound anti-money laundering policies and procedures. Advances the knowledge, skills, and experience of professionals dedicated to detecting and preventing money laundering through education, certification, and training. **Publications:** *ACAMS Connection*, biweekly. Bulletin. Provides timely information on a variety of anti-money laundering subjects. **Price:** free for members. Alternate Formats: online ● *ACAMS Today*, bimonthly. Newsletter. Contains articles about member benefits, education programs, special events, and legislative and regulatory developments. **Price:** free for members.

464 ■ Association for Management Information in Financial Services (AMIfs)

3895 Fairfax Ct.
Atlanta, GA 30339
Ph: (770)444-3557
Fax: (770)444-9084
E-mail: ami@amifs.org
URL: http://www.amifs.org
Contact: Kevin W. Link CPA, Exec. Dir.
Founded: 1980. **Members:** 600. **Membership Dues:** individual, $350 (annual) ● corporate, $1,200 (annual). **Staff:** 1. **Budget:** $500,000. **Description:** Employees of commercial banks, trust companies, savings and loan banks, mutual savings banks, credit unions, federal reserve, or bank holding companies interested in management accounting and cost analysis. Also open to employees of companies that directly serve the financial services industry. Works to develop and improve financial analysis principles and practices in the banking industry; provide a research and education program for members; stimulate fellowship among members. Recognizes educational achievement and professional competence. Conducts Bank Cost and Management Accounting Certificate Program. **Libraries: Type:** not open to the public. **Holdings:** 15; periodicals. **Subjects:** finance for banking professionals. **Formerly:** National Association for Bank Cost Analysis; (1998) National Association for Bank, Cost, and Management Accounting. **Publications:** *Journal of Performance Management*, 3/year. Features articles on various areas of management accounting and outstanding presentations from association conferences and workshops. **Price:** included in membership dues; $200.00 /year for nonmembers in U.S.; $210.00 /year for nonmembers outside U.S. ISSN: 1070-941X. **Circulation:** 650. Alternate Formats: CD-ROM; online. Also Cited As: *AMIfs Journal* ● Bulletin, quarterly. Provides information on conferences and workshops. Includes calendar of events. **Price:** included in membership dues. **Circulation:** 600. **Advertising:** accepted. **Conventions/Meetings:** annual conference (exhibits) ● bimonthly workshop, subjects include customer, organizational and product profitability measurement, and performance analysis.

465 ■ Association of Military Banks of America (AMBA)

PO Box 3335
Warrenton, VA 20188
Ph: (540)347-3305
Fax: (540)347-5995
E-mail: christiane.jacobs@ambahq.org
URL: http://www.ambahq.org
Contact: Christiane Jacobs, Admin. Asst.
Founded: 1959. **Members:** 130. **Membership Dues:** total parent bank asset, $175-$325 (annual) ● associate corporate (non-voting), $200 (annual) ● associate individual (non-voting), $50 (annual) ● associate corporate/industrial (non-voting), $400 (annual). **Budget:** $135,000. **Description:** Banks operating on military bases and/or specializing in providing banking services to military personnel; military banking facilities designated by the U.S. Treasury Department; commercial and industrial corporations involved in the financial industry; interested individuals. Promotes the use of military banks by those living on or employed at military bases. Seeks to establish meaningful interaction and facilitate exchange of information among members; coordinates interbank transactions. Assists the military establishment and military personnel with their banking activities; develops and coordinates bank programs, special studies, and analyses. Provides member banks with reference materials, government regulations, and legislation; opposes measures judged contrary to members' interests. Sponsors marketing campaigns for banking services tailored to military needs. **Publications:** *Association of Military Banks of America Newsletter*, bimonthly. Reports on workshop proceedings and U.S. Department of Defense activities. Alternate Formats: online ● *Banking Institutions Serving Military and Government Personnel*, annual. **Conventions/Meetings:** periodic seminar ● annual workshop.

466 ■ ATM Industry Association (ATMIA)

PO Box 452
Brookings, SD 57006-0452
E-mail: mike@atmia.com
URL: http://www.atmia.com
Contact: Michael Lee, CEO
Founded: 1997. **Members:** 1,050. **Budget:** $2,000,000. **Regional Groups:** 8. **Multinational. Description:** Consists of financial institutions, independent ATM deployers, network processors, manufacturers, consultancies, research houses. Works for the advancement and proliferation of automated teller machines. Very involved in ATM security. Holds international annual ATM conferences. **Additional Websites:** http://www.atmiaconferences.com.

467 ■ Bank Administration Institute (BAI)

1 N Franklin St., Ste.1000
Chicago, IL 60606-3421
Ph: (312)683-2464
Free: (888)284-4078
Fax: (312)683-2373
E-mail: info@bai.org
URL: http://www.bai.org
Contact: Deborah L. Bianucci, Pres./CEO
Founded: 1924. **Membership Dues:** regular, $1,000 (annual). **Staff:** 120. **Description:** Works to improve the competitive position of banking companies through strategic research and educational offerings. **Libraries: Type:** reference. **Holdings:** articles, reports. **Telecommunication Services:** additional toll-free number, order, registration, and customer service number, (800)375-5543. **Commissions:** Audit, Compliance, Security and Fiduciary Services; Finance, Treasury and Capital Markets; Human Resources; Lending; Operations and Technology; Payments; Retail Banking. **Formerly:** (1959) National Association for Bank Auditors and Controllers; (1967) NABAC, The Association for Bank Audit, Control and Operation. **Publications:** *Bank Fraud*, monthly. Newsletter. Details fraud cases and provides information on preventive measures. **Price:** $174.00/year. ISSN: 1065-8165 ● *Banking Strategies*, bimonthly. Magazine. Provides strategic insight on emerging issues for bankers. **Price:** $59.00/year in U.S.; $89.00/year outside U.S. ● *Compliance Alert*, biweekly. Analyzes federal laws and rules, including impact statements and discussion of long-term implications. **Price:** $385.00/year.

468 ■ Bank Information Center (BIC)

1100 H St. NW, Ste.650
Washington, DC 20005
Ph: (202)737-7752
Fax: (202)737-1155
E-mail: info@bicusa.org
URL: http://www.bicusa.org
Contact: Bruce Jenkins, Acting Exec. Dir.
Founded: 1987. **Staff:** 9. **Budget:** $1,000,000. **Languages:** English, French, Spanish. **Description:** Serves as clearinghouse for information on multilateral development bank funded projects. Monitors projects and provides information and documents to overseas nongovernmental organizations that are assessing the environmental, social, and economic impact of these projects in specific countries. Promotes reform in information, social, and environmental policies at the multilateral development banks. **Libraries: Type:** not open to the public. **Holdings:** articles, books. **Subjects:** international development issues, multilateral development bank information. **Computer Services:** database, development, environmental policy, and multilateral development banks. **Conventions/Meetings:** conference.

469 ■ Bankers' Association for Finance and Trade (BAFT)

1120 Connecticut Ave. NW, 5th Fl.
Washington, DC 20036
Ph: (202)663-7575 (202)663-5013
Fax: (202)663-5538
E-mail: baft@aba.com
URL: http://www.baft.org
Contact: Rebecca Morter, Exec. Dir.
Founded: 1921. **Members:** 170. **Membership Dues:** service firm (based on number of employees), $1,000-$5,000 (annual). **Staff:** 8. **Budget:** $1,000,000. **Description:** Internationally active U.S. banks and non-bank financial services companies, service organizations and non-U.S. banks that have a keen interest in U.S. regulatory and market developments. Works to promote and improve techniques for international banking, trade, finance and investment between the U.S. and its trading partners. Conducts educational seminars and lectures. **Libraries: Type:** not open to the public. **Holdings:** articles, books, periodicals. **Subjects:** international banking, trade and regulatory issues. **Computer Services:**

database. **Committees:** Program Oversight; Project Finance; Regulatory & Legislation; Small Business Export Finance; Trade Finance. **Formerly:** (2001) Bankers' Association for Foreign Trade. **Publications:** *BAFT For Your Information*, quarterly. Newsletter ● *BAFT Lead Line* ● *Focus: Trade Finance*, quarterly. Newsletter. Covers legislative and regulatory developments. **Circulation:** 6,000. **Conventions/Meetings:** conference ● annual meeting and convention (exhibits).

470 ■ Consumer Bankers Association (CBA)
1000 Wilson Blvd., Ste.2500
Arlington, VA 22209-3912
Ph: (703)276-1750 (703)276-3884
Fax: (703)528-1290
E-mail: membership@cbanet.org
URL: http://www.cbanet.org
Contact: Cece S. Sutton, Chair
Founded: 1919. **Membership Dues:** student lending associate, small business associate, $2,100 (annual) ● automotive finance associate, $3,700 (annual) ● collections and home equity associate, $2,700 (annual) ● small business, student lending, compliance/CRA/fair lending associate, $2,100 (annual) ● education non-profit associate, $1,600 (annual). **Staff:** 20. **Budget:** $5,000,000. **Description:** Federally insured deposit-taking institutions. Sponsors Graduate School of Retail Bank Management at the University of Virginia. **Computer Services:** database ● mailing lists. **Committees:** Automobile Finance; Community Reinvestment; Consumer Investments; Education Funding; Home Equity; Small Business Banking. **Councils:** Alternative Retail Delivery; Education; Government Relations; Membership/Communications. **Formerly:** (1946) Morris Plan Bankers Association. **Publications:** *CBA Report*, monthly. Newsletter. Covers regulatory, legislative, judicial, and industry news. Includes index, books reviews, and membership profiles. **Price:** free for members and selected journalists. **Circulation:** 6,500.

471 ■ Electronic Funds Transfer Association (EFTA)
11350 Random Hills Rd., Ste.800
Fairfax, VA 22030
Ph: (703)934-6052 (610)918-1161
Fax: (703)934-6058
E-mail: melanierenner@efta.org
URL: http://www.efta.org
Contact: Kurt Helwig, Pres./CEO
Founded: 1977. **Members:** 900. **Membership Dues:** company, $20,000 (annual) ● individual, $5,000 (annual) ● government, $1,250 (annual). **Staff:** 6. **Description:** Financial institutions, credit card companies, ATM owners, networks and processors, hardware and software manufacturers and e-commerce companies dedicated to the advancement of electronic payment systems and commerce. **Libraries: Type:** reference. **Holdings:** 1,500; articles, books, periodicals, reports. **Subjects:** EFT. **Awards:** Robert A. Mooney Distinguished Service Award. **Frequency:** annual. **Type:** recognition. **Recipient:** for outstanding service to advance EFT over a career. **Telecommunication Services:** electronic mail, kurthelwig@efta.org. **Subgroups:** Consumer Issues; eCommerce Enablers; eCommerce Payments; Electronic Benefits Transfer; Legal and Regulatory Issues. **Also Known As:** The EFT Association. **Formed by Merger of:** Electronic Money Council; Electronic Funds Transfer Association. **Publications:** *EFTA News*, quarterly. Newsletter. **Price:** included in membership dues.

472 ■ Electronic Transactions Association (ETA)
1101 16th St. NW, Ste.402
Washington, DC 20036
Ph: (202)828-2635
Free: (800)695-5509
Fax: (202)828-2639
E-mail: thomas.goldsmith@electran.org
URL: http://www.electran.org
Contact: Ms. Carla Balakgie, Exec. Dir.
Founded: 1990. **Members:** 400. **Membership Dues:** financial institution, $1,000-$2,500 (annual) ● service provider, $650-$3,000 (annual). **Staff:** 17. **Budget:** $1,000,000. **National Groups:** 7. **Multinational. Description:** Represents companies who help facilitate electronic payment transactions and settlement on behalf of merchants and others. Provides leadership through education, advocacy and the exchange of information. **Libraries: Type:** open to the public. **Awards: Frequency:** annual. **Type:** recognition. **Recipient:** for outstanding member service or performance. **Computer Services:** database. **Committees:** Awards and Recognition; Best Practices; Editorial Advisory; Education; Emerging Markets; Exhibitor Advisory; Expo Network Steering; Government Relations. **Formerly:** (1998) Bankcard Services Association. **Publications:** *Transaction Trends*, monthly. Magazine. Covers trends and issues related to electronic payments. **Price:** $150.00/year. **Circulation:** 1,000. **Advertising:** accepted. Alternate Formats: online. **Conventions/Meetings:** annual meeting (exhibits).

473 ■ Environmental Bankers Association (EBA)
510 King St., Ste.410
Alexandria, VA 22314
Ph: (703)549-0977
Fax: (703)548-5945
E-mail: eba@envirobank.org
URL: http://www.envirobank.org
Contact: D. Jeffery Telego, Exec. Co-Dir.
Founded: 1994. **Members:** 64. **Membership Dues:** financial institution, $700-$1,400 (annual) ● sustaining, associate, $300 (annual) ● affiliate, $1,450 (annual) ● international development bank, $750 (annual). **Staff:** 2. **Budget:** $150,000. **Description:** Banks and financial services organizations, law firms, consultants, and insurers interested in environmental risk management and liability issues. Aims to help members preserve net income and assets from environmental liability issues resulting from lending and trust activities. Updates members on environmental risk management programs, auditing procedures, legislation and government regulation, environmental banking case law, and environmental insurance/risk management procedures. **Libraries: Type:** reference; not open to the public. **Holdings:** 50; books, clippings, periodicals. **Subjects:** environmental lender liability insurance, EPA and FDIC regulations, environment risk management. **Publications:** *BanKNotes*, quarterly. Newsletter. **Price:** $50.00/year. **Advertising:** accepted ● *Your Financial Institution and The Environment*. **Conventions/Meetings:** semiannual meeting (exhibits) - always January and June ● seminar.

474 ■ Farm Credit Council (FCC)
50 F St. NW, Ste.900
Washington, DC 20001-1530
Ph: (202)626-8710 (202)879-0843
Free: (800)525-2345
Fax: (202)626-8718
E-mail: boscia@fccouncil.com
URL: http://www.fccouncil.com
Contact: Kenneth E. Auer, Pres./CEO
Founded: 1983. **Members:** 6. **Staff:** 10. **Budget:** $2,650,000. **Description:** Represents the Farm Credit System, a nationwide system of cooperative financial institutions that lends to agriculture and rural America. Makes loans to agricultural producers, rural homebuyers, farmer cooperatives, and rural utilities. Finances the export of U.S. agricultural commodities. **Telecommunication Services:** electronic mail, auer@fccouncil.com. **Publications:** *CAP Brochure*, annual. **Price:** $1.75 for members. Alternate Formats: online ● *The Insider*, biweekly. Newsletter. **Price:** free, for members only. **Conventions/Meetings:** annual conference (exhibits).

475 ■ Financial Markets Association - U.S.A. (FMA USA)
c/o Peter Wadkins, Pres.
PO Box 156
Parlin, NJ 08859
Ph: (212)645-5111 (732)316-0384
E-mail: info@fma-usa.org
URL: http://www.fma-usa.org
Contact: Peter Wadkins, Pres.
Founded: 1957. **Members:** 300. **Membership Dues:** international, corporate associate, $100 (annual). **Description:** Individuals engaged by banks in foreign exchange trading and deposit dealing; brokers in these markets. Encourages public and professional education in foreign exchange and furthers awareness of the effect of foreign exchange on economics and finance. Fosters better relations among members and strives to improve professional responsibility and the market environment. Works with other organizations and government officials and agencies. Conducts annual seminar for junior traders, semiannual seminar for senior traders, educational meetings, and presentations. **Formerly:** Forex Club of North America; (1988) Forex Association of North America; (2001) Forex U.S.A. **Publications:** *Forex Newsletter*, quarterly. **Conventions/Meetings:** annual International Congress - meeting ● periodic National Congress - meeting.

476 ■ Financial and Security Products Association (FSPA)
5300 Sequoia NW, Ste.205
Albuquerque, NM 87120
Ph: (505)839-7958
Free: (800)843-6082
Fax: (505)839-0017
E-mail: info@fspa1.com
URL: http://www.fspa1.com
Contact: John M. Vrabec, Exec. Dir.
Founded: 1973. **Members:** 296. **Membership Dues:** manufacturer, dealer, $395 (annual). **Staff:** 2. **Budget:** $250,000. **Description:** Represents independent companies who manufacture, sell, install and service products provided primarily to financial institutions. **Formerly:** (1977) National Independent Bank Equipment Suppliers Association; (2004) National Independent Bank Equipment and Systems Association. **Publications:** *Business Owners*, bimonthly. Alternate Formats: online ● *Membership Directory & Buyers Guide*, annual ● Newsletter, monthly. **Advertising:** accepted. **Conventions/Meetings:** annual meeting, with trade show and educational sessions (exhibits).

477 ■ Financial Services Round Table
1001 Pennsylvania Ave. NW, Ste.500 S
Washington, DC 20004
Ph: (202)289-4322
Fax: (202)628-2507
E-mail: info@fsround.org
URL: http://www.fsround.org
Contact: Steve Bartlett, Pres./CEO
Members: 295. **Staff:** 15. **Description:** Companies registered with the Federal Reserve Board under the Bank Holding Company Act of 1956. **Telecommunication Services:** electronic mail, steve@fsround.org. **Committees:** Emerging Issues; Government Relations; Lawyers; Legislative Policy. **Formed by Merger of:** Association of Bank Holding Companies; Association of Reserve City Bankers. **Formerly:** (1976) Association of Registered Bank Holding Companies; (1999) Banker's Round Table. **Publications:** *Bank Holding Company Facts*, annual ● *Financial Services Fact*. Book. ISSN: 1537-6257. **Conventions/Meetings:** annual meeting - always fall.

478 ■ Financial Women International (FWI)
1027 W Roselawn Ave.
Roseville, MN 55113
Ph: (651)487-7632
Free: (866)236-2007
Fax: (651)489-1322
E-mail: info@fwi.org
URL: http://www.fwi.org
Contact: Nancy Kinder, Pres.
Founded: 1921. **Members:** 2,000. **Membership Dues:** active, allied, virtual, $199 (annual) ● retired, interim, student, $79 (annual). **Staff:** 1. **State Groups:** 41. **Local Groups:** 230. **Description:** Individuals working in or with the financial services industry. Maintains FWI Educational Foundation. **Computer Services:** database ● mailing lists. **Telecommunication Services:** additional toll-free num-

ber, (866)807-6081. **Formerly:** (1991) National Association of Bank Women. **Publications:** *FWI News*, bimonthly. Newsletter. Alternate Formats: online ● Brochures. **Conventions/Meetings:** annual conference - always September.

479 ■ Hellenic American Bankers Association (HABA)
PO Box 7244
New York, NY 10150
Ph: (212)421-1057
E-mail: administrator@haba.org
URL: http://www.haba.org
Contact: James Hansel, Pres.

Founded: 1982. **Members:** 200. **Membership Dues:** individual, $150 (annual). **Staff:** 1. **Budget:** $50,000. **Languages:** English, Greek. **Description:** Greek-American banking and finance professionals. Works to promote the professional growth of members. Conducts educational, social, and charitable programs. Maintains speakers' bureau. **Awards:** Executive of the Year. **Frequency:** annual. **Type:** recognition. **Recipient:** for overall contributions to business and community. **Committees:** Activities; Media and Public Relations; New Membership. **Formerly:** (1998) ISSHII Association. **Publications:** *HABA Bank Notes*, quarterly. Newsletter. **Circulation:** 500 ● *Who's Who Among Greek Americans in Banking and Finance*, triennial. Directory. **Circulation:** 500. **Conventions/Meetings:** monthly meeting - September through June, every 6 weeks.

480 ■ Independent Community Bankers of America (ICBA)
1615 L St. NW, Ste.900
Washington, DC 20036
Ph: (202)659-8111
Free: (800)422-8439
Fax: (202)861-5503
E-mail: info@icba.org
URL: http://www.icba.org
Contact: Camden R. Fine, Pres./CEO

Founded: 1930. **Members:** 5,000. **Membership Dues:** corporate bronze, $1,150 (annual) ● corporate silver, $2,250 (annual) ● corporate gold, $3,750 (annual). **Staff:** 130. **Budget:** $12,000,000. **Description:** Provides legislative and regulatory information and representation for community financial institutions and opposes "concentration of banking and commercial powers". Provides credit and debit cards, travelers checks, insurance, bank investment, mutual funds, credit and debit card programs, mortgages, check purchase protection, and group purchasing programs. **Libraries:** **Type:** reference; lending; not open to the public. **Holdings:** 1,500; books, clippings, periodicals. **Subjects:** banking structure issues, small bank operations. **Awards:** National Community Bank Service Awards. **Type:** recognition. **Computer Services:** Online services. **Committees:** Agriculture-Rural America; Bank Education; Bank Services; Executive; Federal Legislation; Independent Community Bankers Political Action; Lending; Marketing; Payments and Technology; Policy Development; Regulation Review; Tax. **Subgroups:** ICBA Bancard; ICBA Credit Life Reinsurance Co.; ICBA Financial Services Corporation; ICBA Mortgage Corporation; ICBA Securities Corporation. **Formerly:** (1999) Independent Bankers Association of America. **Publications:** *Community Bank Director Quarterly*. Newsletter. **Price:** included in membership dues. **Circulation:** 14,000 ● *Community Bank Purchasing Guide* ● *Compliance Bulletin*, periodic ● *Compliance Deskbook* ● *ICBA Community Reinvestment Act Deskbook*. Journal ● *Independent Banker*, monthly. Magazine. Features articles for community bankers on banking operations, industry trends, and association activities. Includes calendar of events. **Price:** $60.00 /year for nonmembers; $18.00 /year for members. ISSN: 0019-3674. **Advertising:** accepted. Alternate Formats: microform; online ● *Washington Weekly Report*. Newsletter. Concerned with current federal banking legislation and regulation. **Price:** included in membership dues; $20.00 /year for nonmembers. ISSN: 0274-5127 ● Annual Report, annual. Summarizes association activities and developments in banking during the past year; includes lists of ICBA staff and board of directors. ● Pamphlets ● Videos, annual. Summarizes association activities and developments in banking during the past year; includes lists of IBAA staff and board of directors. **Conventions/Meetings:** annual National Convention and Techworld - convention and seminar (exhibits).

481 ■ Institute of International Bankers (IIB)
299 Park Ave., 17th Fl.
New York, NY 10171
Ph: (212)421-1611
Fax: (212)421-1119
E-mail: iib@iib.org
URL: http://www.iib.org
Contact: Lawrence R. Uhlick, CEO

Founded: 1966. **Members:** 500. **Staff:** 5. **Budget:** $2,000,000. **Multinational. Description:** Individuals representing non-U.S. banks with offices in the United States. Seeks to foster and develop knowledge of international banking and credit. Provides medium for exchange of ideas and discussion of common problems. **Committees:** Legislative and Regulatory; Liaison. **Subcommittees:** Human Resources; Tax. **Formerly:** (1987) Institute of Foreign Bankers. **Publications:** *Global Survey of Regulatory and Market Developments in Banking, Securities and Insurance*, annual ● *Institute News*, bimonthly. Newsletter ● *Institute of International Bankers—Membership Directory*, annual. **Price:** included in membership dues. **Circulation:** 1,000 ● *International Banking Focus*, bimonthly. Newsletter. **Conventions/Meetings:** annual Breakfast Dialogue - meeting ● annual conference and dinner - always December.

482 ■ Institute of International Finance (IIF)
1333 H St. NW, Ste.800E
Washington, DC 20005-4770
Ph: (202)857-3600
Fax: (202)775-1430
E-mail: info@iif.com
URL: http://www.iif.com
Contact: Josef Ackermann, Chm.

Founded: 1983. **Members:** 320. **Staff:** 60. **Budget:** $15,000,000. **Description:** Financial institutions. Seeks to improve upon the process of sovereign lending, trade and project financing, and the long-term efficiency of international credit markets. Functions are to gather accurate economic information on individual countries; to discuss economic plans, assumptions, and financing needs with borrower countries; to serve as a focal point for dialogue between the international banking community and multilateral institutions, central banks, and bank supervisory authorities; to support members' risk management, asset allocation, and business development in emerging markets. **Libraries:** **Type:** reference. **Holdings:** 1,000; books, periodicals. **Subjects:** economic and financial statistics of emerging markets. **Publications:** *Economic Review*, monthly ● Annual Report, annual. **Price:** free ● Brochure. **Conventions/Meetings:** quarterly board meeting.

483 ■ International Financial Services Association (IFSA)
9 Sylvan Way, Ste.130
Parsippany, NJ 07054-3817
Ph: (973)656-1900
Fax: (973)656-1915
E-mail: info@intlbanking.org
URL: http://www.ifsaonline.org
Contact: Dan Taylor, Pres./CEO

Founded: 1924. **Members:** 600. **Membership Dues:** full, $5,225 (annual) ● associate, $2,975 (annual) ● supplier, $7,250 (annual) ● individual, $500 (annual). **Staff:** 5. **Budget:** $2,000,000. **Regional Groups:** 8. **Description:** Banks involved in international banking operations. Provides a forum to solve operational problems currently facing the global financial service community. Conducts research; sponsors educational programs. **Computer Services:** Online services. **Committees:** Bank-to-Bank Reimbursements; Collections; Letters of Credit; Loan and Discount; Payments/Investigations; Product Management; Regulatory/Compliance; Rules; SWIFT; Technology; Treasury Operations. **Formed by Merger of:** (1988) Council on International Banking; Western Council on International Banking; Mid-America Council on International Banking. **Formerly:** (1998) U.S. Council on International Banking. **Publications:** *Documentary Credit World*. Journal. Also Cited As: *DCW* ● *Network*, quarterly. Newsletter. **Price:** available to members only. **Conventions/Meetings:** annual conference (exhibits) ● seminar.

484 ■ Loan Syndications and Trading Association (LSTA)
366 Madison Ave., 15th Fl.
New York, NY 10017
Ph: (212)880-3000
Fax: (212)880-3040
E-mail: ataylor@lsta.org
URL: http://www.lsta.org
Contact: Allison Taylor, Exec. Dir.

Founded: 1995. **Members:** 265. **Membership Dues:** full dealer/full other, $25,000 (annual) ● full institution, $13,000 (annual) ● other associate, $12,500 (annual) ● associate institution/other affiliate, $8,000 (annual) ● affiliate legal firm, $10,000 (annual). **Staff:** 13. **Multinational. Description:** Advances the interests of the marketplace as a whole and promotes the orderly development of a fair, efficient, liquid, transparent and professional trading market for loans. Fosters the development of policies and market practices designed to promote just and equitable marketplace principles. Seeks to enhance public understanding of the corporate loan market. **Publications:** *The Handbook of Loan Syndications and Trading*. **Price:** $129.00 ● Bulletin, monthly. Outlines important LSTA initiatives and topical items of particular interest to the loan market. **Price:** included in membership dues.

485 ■ Mortgage Bankers Association (MBA)
1919 Pennsylvania Ave. NW
Washington, DC 20006-3404
Ph: (202)557-2700
Free: (800)793-6222
E-mail: membership@mortgagebankers.org
URL: http://www.mortgagebankers.org
Contact: John M. Robbins, Chm.

Founded: 1914. **Members:** 2,700. **Membership Dues:** international affiliate, $1,000 (annual) ● regular, $350 (annual) ● associate, $2,500-$10,000 (annual). **Staff:** 140. **Description:** Principal lending and investor interests in the mortgage finance field, including mortgage banking firms, commercial banks, life insurance companies, title companies, and savings and loan associations. Seeks to improve methods of originating, servicing, and marketing loans of residential and income-producing properties through industry education and cooperation with federal agencies and the Congress. Holds clinics on all aspects of the mortgage finance business. Sponsors School of Mortgage Banking, and correspondence courses and web-based training on mortgage subjects for member personnel. Collects statistics and conducts research on the industry. **Libraries:** **Type:** reference. **Holdings:** 6,500; periodicals. **Subjects:** commercial and residential finance. **Awards:** FW Thompson Award. **Frequency:** annual. **Type:** recognition. **Recipient:** for excellence in communication and marketing programs. **Committees:** Affordable Housing; Commercial Mortgage and Asset Management; Commercial Real Estate Finance; Communications and Marketing; CRED Statistics, Research, and Management; CREF Communications; Diversity; Education; Fair Lending; Financial Management; Legal Issues; Legislative; Loan Administration; Multi-Family Housing; Quality Assurance; Regulatory Compliances; Residential Loan Production; Secondary and Capital Markets; State and Local MBA Liaison; Technology; Wholesale Lending. **Formerly:** (2003) Mortgage Bankers Association of America. **Publications:** *Income and Cost for Origination and Servicing of 1 to 4 Unit Residential Loans*, annual. Provides breakdowns of revenues and costs associated with origination and servicing of one- to four-unit residential loans. **Price:** $100.00 for members; $200.00 for nonmembers ● *MBA Directory of Members*, annual. Membership Directory. Includes statistics. **Price:** $60.00 for members. **Circulation:** 5,000 ● *Mortgage Banking: The Magazine of Real Estate Finance*, monthly.

Includes book reviews and mortgage banking statistics; contains annual index to the previous year and advertisers' index. **Price:** $40.00/year. ISSN: 0027-1241. **Circulation:** 11,000. **Advertising:** accepted. Alternate Formats: microform ● *National Delinquency Survey*, quarterly. Newsletter. Reports on delinquency rates by state, region, and nationally for various types of residential loans; includes foreclosures data. ● Brochures. **Conventions/Meetings:** annual convention (exhibits).

486 ■ NACHA: The Electronic Payments Association

13450 Sunrise Valley Dr., Ste.100
Herndon, VA 20171
Ph: (703)561-1100
Free: (800)487-9180
Fax: (703)787-0996
E-mail: info@nacha.org
URL: http://www.nacha.org
Contact: Elliott McEntee, Pres./CEO

Founded: 1974. **Members:** 600. **Membership Dues:** affiliate, $600-$1,200 (annual) ● corporate (based on gross revenue), $2,000-$5,500 (annual) ● direct, $4,500 (annual). **Staff:** 50. **Budget:** $5,000,000. **Regional Groups:** 34. **Description:** Automated Clearing House (ACH) association. Provides an interregional exchange for electronic debits and credits among ACHs and to establish and administer nationwide standards and operating rules for ACHs. Conducts national seminars and conferences on ACH operations and products; sponsors annual Payments and Electronic Commerce Institute; sponsors Accredited ACH Professional (AAP) program. Sponsors national marketing campaign; compiles statistics. **Awards:** NACHA Payment Systems Excellence Award. **Frequency:** annual. **Type:** recognition. **Recipient:** for outstanding contributions to improve payment systems. **Computer Services:** Online services. **Committees:** Education and Training; Marketing; Rules and Operations. **Councils:** Affiliates; Bill Payment; Cross Border; Electronic Benefits Transfer; Electronic Check; Financial; Internet. **Absorbed:** (2004) National Council for Uniform Interest Compensation. **Formerly:** (1999) National Automated Clearing House Association. **Publications:** *ACH Risk Management Handbook* ● *ACH Rules*, annual. Contains operating rules and guidelines for national electronic payments network. Includes index. ● *Electronic Payments Journal*, bimonthly. Newsletter ● *Electronic Payments Review and Buyer's Guide*, annual. Directory. **Circulation:** 15,000. **Advertising:** accepted. Alternate Formats: online ● *Payments Systems Report*, monthly. Newsletter. Covers developments and policy issues involving ACHs. Includes information on successful programs and calendar of events. **Price:** $95.00 for members; $150.00 for nonmembers. **Circulation:** 3,300. **Advertising:** accepted ● *UCC 4A and the Automated Clearing House System* ● Audiotapes ● Brochures. **Conventions/Meetings:** annual PAYMENTS - conference (exhibits).

487 ■ National Association of Affordable Housing Lenders (NAAHL)

1300 Connecticut Ave. NW
Washington, DC 20036
Ph: (202)293-9850
Fax: (202)293-9852
E-mail: info@naahl.org
URL: http://www.naahl.org
Contact: Judy Kennedy, Pres./CEO

Founded: 1988. **Members:** 1,000. **Membership Dues:** associate, $500 (annual) ● nonprofit (based on fund balance), $500-$1,000 (annual) ● general (based on asset/origination), $1,000-$5,000 (annual). **Staff:** 3. **Budget:** $500,000. **Description:** Supports organizations that invest private capital in low-income communities, including banks and loan consortia and non-profit providers. Sponsors Forums on Banking and Housing Finance. Represents members' interests before Congress and government agencies. **Libraries: Type:** not open to the public. **Publications:** *Affordable Housing and Community Development Best Practices Guide*. **Price:** $15.00 ● *Building Sustainable Communities: Best Practices in Community Development Lending*. Paper. **Price:** $15.00 plus shipping and handling ● *Directions in Affordable Housing Finance*, quarterly. Newsletter. **Price:** $139.00 /year for nonmembers; free for members ● *Loan Consortia Source Book*. **Price:** $35.00 ● *Washington Update*, monthly. Newsletter. **Conventions/Meetings:** conference, national and regional forums on affordable housing lending - 3/year.

488 ■ National Association of Equity Source Banks (NAESB)

10451 Mill Run Cir., Ste.400
Owings Mills, MD 21117
Ph: (410)363-3698
E-mail: nahbb@msn.com
Contact: Rudolph Lewis, Pres.

Founded: 2000. **Description:** Private investors and venture capital firms. Promotes investments in microeconomic enterprises from urban and rural areas with certified business models and franchises (these models must be third party verified from a business development institution authorized by the Association).

489 ■ National Association of Mortgage Brokers (NAMB)

7900 Westpark Dr., Ste.T309
McLean, VA 22102
Ph: (703)342-5900 (703)342-5850
Fax: (703)342-5905
E-mail: georgehanzimanolis@namb.org
URL: http://www.namb.org
Contact: George Hanzimanolis CMC, Pres.

Founded: 1973. **Members:** 24,000. **Membership Dues:** professional, $120 (annual) ● associate, $45 (annual) ● affiliate, $95 (annual). **Staff:** 13. **Budget:** $4,900,000. **State Groups:** 39. **Local Groups:** 50. **Description:** Mortgage brokers seeking to increase professionalism and to foster business relationships among members. Offers three levels of professional certification. Focuses on education and government affairs. **Awards:** Broker of the Year. **Frequency:** annual. **Type:** recognition. **Recipient:** to a member who typifies the NAMB professional broker. **Committees:** Education; Legislative; Political Action. **Divisions:** Certified Mortgage Consultant. **Formed by Merger of:** American Institute of Mortgage Brokers; Society of Mortgage Consultants. **Publications:** *National Mortgage Broker*, monthly. Magazine. **Circulation:** 10,000. **Advertising:** accepted. **Conventions/Meetings:** annual convention (exhibits).

490 ■ National Association of Mortgage Planners (NAMP)

Address Unknown since 2008
URL: http://www.namp.org

Membership Dues: individual/corporate/company, $295 (annual) ● associate (individual), $195 (annual) ● affiliate (individual/corporate/company), $495 (annual). **Description:** Promotes and nurtures the highest level of professionalism in the practice of fiduciary-based mortgage planning. Provides the expertise, guidance and skills necessary to obtain the best mortgage to meet the needs of clients. **Telecommunication Services:** electronic mail, memberinfo@namp.org ● electronic mail, consumerinfo@namp.org.

491 ■ National Association of Professional Mortgage Women (NAPMW)

PO Box 2016
Edmonds, WA 98020-9516
Ph: (425)775-6589
Free: (800)827-3034
Fax: (425)771-9588
E-mail: info@napmw.org
URL: http://www.napmw.org
Contact: Sue Barnett, Pres.

Founded: 1964. **Members:** 3,200. **Membership Dues:** basic, $98 ● bronze, $107 ● silver, $152 ● gold, $242. **Staff:** 3. **Budget:** $400,000. **Regional Groups:** 5. **Local Groups:** 60. **Languages:** English, Spanish. **Description:** Supports professional and personal development for individuals in the mortgage lending industry. Aims to maintain high standards of professional conduct and to encourage the educational advancement of women in the industry. Believes in equal recognition and professional opportunities for women. Offers professional designations through the Institute of Mortgage Lending. **Committees:** Convention; Credentials; Education; Extension; History Book; Internal Audit; Leadership Materials; Technology. **Publications:** *Notes and Deeds*, quarterly. Newsletter. Keeps members up-to-date on key industry developments, issues and activities of the Association and its members. **Price:** included in membership dues; $49.00 for nonmembers. **Circulation:** 3,500. **Advertising:** accepted. **Conventions/Meetings:** annual convention (exhibits) - always May ● semiannual regional meeting and workshop.

492 ■ National Bankers Association (NBA)

1513 P St. NW
Washington, DC 20005
Ph: (202)588-5432
Fax: (202)588-5443
E-mail: nahart@nationalbankers.org
URL: http://www.nationalbankers.org
Contact: Norma Alexander Hart, Pres.

Founded: 1927. **Members:** 64. **Membership Dues:** affiliate, $2,000 (annual) ● associate, $250 (annual). **Budget:** $360,000. **Regional Groups:** 5. **Description:** Minority banking institutions owned by minority individuals and institutions. Serves as an advocate for the minority banking industry. Organizes banking services, government relations, marketing, scholarship, and technical assistance programs. Offers placement services; compiles statistics. **Awards: Type:** recognition. **Computer Services:** database. **Formerly:** (1951) National Negro Bankers Association. **Publications:** *NBA Today*, semiannual. Magazine. **Price:** included in membership dues; $5.00 /year for nonmembers. **Circulation:** 5,000. **Advertising:** accepted. **Conventions/Meetings:** annual convention (exhibits) ● periodic regional meeting.

493 ■ National Finance Adjusters (NFA)

PO Box 3855
Baltimore, MD 21217
Ph: (410)728-2400
Fax: (410)523-8336
E-mail: homeoffice@nfa.org
URL: http://www.nfa.org
Contact: Jack Barnes, Contact

Founded: 1947. **Members:** 203. **Membership Dues:** general, $400 (annual). **Description:** Members of the vehicle lending/leasing industry and professional collateral recovery specialists. Offers education and expertise to lending institutions in the field of skip tracing, vehicle title service, transporting, locksmithing, and remarketing collateral. Publishes numerous articles regarding repossession. Each member is covered by a $1,000,000 Client Security Bond. **Conventions/Meetings:** Repossession - seminar.

494 ■ National Home Equity Mortgage Association (NHEMA)

1301 Pennsylvania Ave. NW, Ste.500
Washington, DC 20004
Ph: (202)347-1210
Free: (800)342-1121
Fax: (202)347-1171
E-mail: jzeltzer-dc@nhema.org
Contact: Jeffrey L. Zeltzer, Pres./Exec. Dir.

Founded: 1974. **Members:** 180. **Membership Dues:** associate, $1,000-$5,000 (annual) ● correspondent, $495 (annual) ● active, $1,500-$30,000 (annual). **Staff:** 4. **Budget:** $500,000. **Description:** Serves home equity mortgage; members are drawn from national, regional and local financial institutions. **Committees:** Capital Markets; Communications; E-Commerce; Education; Government and Public Affairs; International Affairs; Legislative; Speakers' Bureau. **Publications:** *Buyer/Seller Profile*, semiannual. Describes products and services offered by members. **Price:** included in membership dues. **Circulation:** 400 ● *Equity*, bimonthly. Magazine. **Price:** included in membership dues. **Advertising:** accepted ● *Equity Update*, biweekly. Newsletter. Alternate Formats: online ● *Federal Regulation of Second Mortgage Lending*, annual. Explains federal laws and regulations governing second mortgage lending. **Price:** included in membership dues. **Circulation:** 400 ● *NSMA Equity*, quarterly. Provides information on lending equity. Includes membership profiles and calendar of events. **Price:** free. **Circulation:** 1,000. **Advertising:** accepted ● *NSMA Legislative Report*, 3/year. Provides information on state legislation affecting the industry and legal maximum interest rates for second mortgages arranged by state. **Price:** free for members. **Circulation:** 500 ● *Receivables and Delinquency Report*, monthly. **Price:** free for members. **Circulation:** 500 ● *Washington Update*, monthly ● Annual Report, annual. Alternate Formats: online ● Reports. Alternate Formats: online. **Conventions/Meetings:** annual conference.

495 ■ National Marine Bankers Association (NMBA)
200 E Randolph Dr., Ste.5100
Chicago, IL 60601
Ph: (312)946-6260 (312)946-6200
Fax: (312)946-0388
E-mail: bmcardle@nmma.org
URL: http://www.marinebankers.org
Contact: Bernice McArdle, Mgr.

Founded: 1980. **Members:** 80. **Membership Dues:** company (plus $100 initiation fee), $445 (annual). **Staff:** 1. **Description:** Banks, savings institutions, and financial service firms that extend credit to consumers, retailers, and manufacturers of recreational boating equipment. Provides a forum in which lenders can exchange information on developing recreational boating loan programs. Promotes the extension of credit to recreational boating manufacturers, retailers, and consumers. Educates financial institutions on correct methods of underwriting and securing consumer loans and wholesale financing through Marine Lender Workshops. Compiles national statistics on marine financing. **Awards:** William B. Otto III Marine Lending Industry Service Award. **Frequency:** annual. **Type:** recognition. **Recipient:** for individuals within the marine industry who have given their time and energy to the NMBA. **Affiliated With:** National Marine Manufacturers Association. **Publications:** *Business of Pleasure Boats*, quarterly. Newsletter. Contains information for recreational marine lenders. **Price:** free. **Circulation:** 500. Alternate Formats: online ● *Lender's Boating Handbook*. Available for loan-out only. No longer published. ● *Summary of Annual Marine Lending Survey*, annual. Annual Reports. **Price:** included in membership dues; $295.00 for nonmembers. **Conventions/Meetings:** annual conference, 3-day program featuring education programs and latest services for the industry (exhibits) - usually held in August or September ● annual Marine Lending Workshop, comprehensive 2-day program for marine finance professionals engaged in direct and indirect retail lending - usually held in December.

496 ■ Retired Western Union Employees Association (RWUEA)
PO Box 413
Montgomery, NY 12549
E-mail: rwueasecy@jmsn.com
URL: http://www.rwuea.com
Contact: John Skelton, Pres.

Members: 3,000. **Membership Dues:** regular, $7 (annual). **Description:** Represents past and present Western Union employees; historically, represented the interests of pensioners in Western Union's bankruptcy proceedings. **Publications:** Membership Directory, every two or three years ● Newsletter, quarterly. **Price:** included in membership dues. **Conventions/Meetings:** quarterly meeting.

497 ■ Retirement Industry Trust Association (RITA)
c/o Scott McCartan, Treas.
Millennium Trust Company LLC
820 Jorie Blvd.
Oak Brook, IL 60523
Ph: (630)368-5600
E-mail: smccartan@mtrustcompany.com
URL: http://www.r-i-t-a.org
Contact: Scott McCartan, Treas.

Members: 20. **Membership Dues:** regular, $350 (annual). **Description:** Retirement trusts. Represents members' interests. Conducts educational programs; compiles statistics. **Telecommunication Services:** electronic mail, kclick@matrixbancorp.com. **Conventions/Meetings:** semiannual conference - always spring and fall.

498 ■ Risk Management Association
1801 Market St., Ste.300
Philadelphia, PA 19103-1628
Ph: (215)446-4000
Free: (800)677-7621
Fax: (215)446-4101
E-mail: member@rmahq.org
URL: http://www.rmahq.org/RMA
Contact: Maurice H. Hartigan II, Pres./CEO

Founded: 1914. **Members:** 18,000. **Membership Dues:** associate, $50 (annual) ● professional, $195 (annual) ● student, $15 (annual). **Staff:** 80. **Budget:** $17,000,000. **Regional Groups:** 9. **Local Groups:** 120. **National Groups:** 7. **Description:** Commercial and savings banks, and savings and loan, and other financial services companies. Conducts research and professional development activities in areas of loan administration, asset management, and commercial lending and credit to increase professionalism. **Libraries: Type:** reference. **Holdings:** archival material, books, monographs, periodicals. **Subjects:** commercial lending and credit. **Awards:** Award for Journalistic Excellence. **Frequency:** annual. **Type:** monetary. **Recipient:** to the most outstanding articles published in the RMA Journal during the preceding calendar year ● National Paper Writing Competition Award. **Frequency:** annual. **Type:** monetary. **Recipient:** for RMA associates writing an outstanding paper on commercial lending. **Computer Services:** Online services, publication. **Committees:** Accounting Policy; Agricultural Lending; Award for Journalistic Excellence; Consumer Risk Management; Credit Information and Exchange; Credit Portfolio Management; Loan Management Seminar Board of Regents; Private Lending; Real Estate Lending; Securities Lending; Small Business Banking; Statement Studies; Young Professionals. **Councils:** Community Bank; Credit Risk Managers; Global Relations; Leadership Development; Portfolio Management; Professional Development; Regulatory Relations and Communications. **Divisions:** Agency Relations; Credit Management; Global Relations; Information Products; Lending/Finance; Marketing; Professional Development; Relationship Consulting. **Formerly:** (1997) Robert Morris Associates-Association of Bank Loan and Credit Officers; (2000) Robert Morris Associates/Association of Lending and Credit Risk. **Publications:** *Member Roster*, annual. Directory ● *RMA Annual Statement Studies*, annual. Contains composite balance sheets, income and trend data, and ratios for nearly 500 industries. **Price:** $134.00/copy for nonmembers. **Circulation:** 50,000. Alternate Formats: CD-ROM; online ● *The RMA Journal*, 10/year. Covers commercial lending and credit issues. Includes book reviews, technology update, and legislative and regulatory news. **Price:** $60.00 for members; $95.00 for nonmembers; $85.00 for members (foreign); $140.00 for nonmembers (foreign). ISSN: 1082-6271. **Circulation:** 23,000. Alternate Formats: microform; online ● Books ● Monographs. **Conventions/Meetings:** annual International Securities Lending - conference ● annual Lending and Credit Risk Management - conference (exhibits) - always fall ● annual Loan Management Seminar - workshop ● roundtable, on lending.

499 ■ Urban Financial Services Coalition
1212 New York Ave. NW, Ste.950
Washington, DC 20005
Ph: (202)289-8335
Fax: (202)842-0567
E-mail: ufsc@ufscnet.org
URL: http://www.ufscnet.org
Contact: Andrew T. Carr, Pres.

Founded: 1974. **Members:** 2,000. **Membership Dues:** national, $125 (annual). **Budget:** $500,000. **National Groups:** 47. **Description:** Minority professionals in the financial services industry. Supports minority bankers, insurance, and investment professionals. Communicates information and sponsors programs to further careers for minority bankers. Utilizes member resources to solve problems of minority entrepreneurs and others who need financial advice. Sponsors programs to support future minority bankers. **Awards:** UFSC Scholarship Fund. **Frequency:** annual. **Type:** scholarship. **Recipient:** for minority banking students. **Formerly:** (2002) National Association of Urban Bankers. **Publications:** *Conference Brochure* ● *Conference Journal*, annual. **Advertising:** accepted. Alternate Formats: CD-ROM; online ● *Urban Banker*, quarterly. Newsletter. **Advertising:** accepted. **Conventions/Meetings:** annual conference (exhibits) - always June.

500 ■ Western Independent Bankers (WIB)
600 Montgomery St., Ste.1200
San Francisco, CA 94111
Ph: (415)352-2323
Fax: (415)352-2314
E-mail: info@wib.org
URL: http://www.wib.org
Contact: Nancy E. Sheppard, Pres./CEO

Founded: 1937. **Members:** 400. **Membership Dues:** bank (based on bank assets), $575-$4,500 (annual) ● associate (based on number of employees), $1,100-$1,875 (annual). **Description:** Represents and promotes community-oriented banks and savings and loans in Western U.S. states and territories. **Divisions:** Western Independent Bankers Service Corporation. **Publications:** *Interactive Director's CD ROM*. Helps explain the risks and precautions facing bankers and directors. Alternate Formats: CD-ROM ● *VIP NewsWire*, monthly. Newsletter. Highlights new features of endorsed products and services. Alternate Formats: online ● *Western Banking Magazine*, bimonthly. Features articles on the industry and WIB education and services. **Advertising:** accepted. Alternate Formats: online ● *What Really Is Expected of Me? The Bank Directors Guidebook*. Handbook. Published in conjunction with Laurel Management Systems, Inc. **Price:** $20.00 for members, plus shipping and handling of $3; $30.00 for nonmembers, plus shipping and handling of $3. **Conventions/Meetings:** annual Conference for Bank Presidents, Senior Officers and Directors, with sessions (exhibits) - always March ● annual Marketing Conference - conference and lecture, with sessions (exhibits) ● annual Technology Summit - conference, with speakers and sessions.

Batteries

501 ■ Portable Rechargeable Battery Association (PRBA)
1776 K St., 4th Fl.
Washington, DC 20006
Ph: (202)719-4978
E-mail: gkerchner@prba.org
URL: http://www.prba.org
Contact: Charlie Monahan, Chm.

Multinational. Description: Promotes the portable rechargeable battery industry on legislative, regulatory, and standards issues at state, federal, and international levels; facilitates collection for recycling of SSLA batteries; addresses issues on other rechargeable battery recycling; aims to develop criteria for international environmental labeling of rechargeable battery products both nationally and internationally; disseminates information on regulatory and legislative developments to members; seeks ways to improve efficiency and cost-effectiveness for the industry. **Publications:** *PRBA Battery Reclamation*. Manual. Contains information to assist members to comply with laws regulating rechargeable batteries, both nationally and internationally. **Price:** $495.00/manual, plus shipping and handling; $195.00 for annual (calendar year) updates.

Beekeeping

502 ■ American Beekeeping Federation (ABF)
PO Box 1337
Jesup, GA 31598-1038

Ph: (912)427-4233
Fax: (912)427-8447
E-mail: info@abfnet.org
URL: http://www.abfnet.org
Contact: Daniel Weaver, Pres.

Founded: 1943. **Members:** 1,200. **Membership Dues:** hobbyist, $35 (annual) ● sideliner, $100 (annual) ● commercial, $250 (annual) ● President's Club, $500 (annual) ● President's Club Silver, $1,000 (annual) ● President's Club Gold, $1,500 (annual). **Staff:** 4. **Budget:** $150,000. **Description:** Commercial and avocational beekeepers, suppliers, bottlers, packers, and others affiliated with the honey industry. Promotes the industry and serves as an representative before legislative bodies; makes recommendations and helps secure appropriations for research programs. Operates the Honey Defense Fund, which works to insure the purity of honey marketed in the U.S. Sponsors American Honey Queen Program. **Awards:** 4-H Essay Contest. **Frequency:** annual. **Type:** monetary. **Recipient:** to active 4-H Club members. **Committees:** Audit; Convention; Honey Queen; Honey Show; Legislative; Research and Technical; Resolutions. **Programs:** American Honey Queen. **Formerly:** National Federation of Beekeepers Associations. **Publications:** *Honey Recipe Leaflet*, annual ● *Membership Directory-Classified*, annual. Membership Directories ● Newsletter, bimonthly. Provides up-to-date information on happenings in the beekeeping industry. **Advertising:** accepted. Alternate Formats: online ● Membership Directory, biennial ● Also issues informational releases. **Conventions/Meetings:** annual convention (exhibits) ● annual meeting (exhibits) - always January.

Beverages

503 ■ American Beverage Association (ABA)

1101 16th St. NW
Washington, DC 20036-4803
Ph: (202)463-6732 (202)463-6770
Fax: (202)659-5349
E-mail: info@ameribev.org
URL: http://www.ameribev.org
Contact: Ms. Susan K. Neely, Pres./CEO

Founded: 1919. **Members:** 1,865. **Membership Dues:** international affiliate, $300 (annual). **Staff:** 36. **Budget:** $7,000,000. **State Groups:** 47. **Description:** Active members are bottlers and distributors of soft drinks and franchise companies; associate members are suppliers of materials and services. Conducts government affairs activities on the national and state levels, discussion of industry problems, and general improvement of operating procedures. Conducts research on beverage laws. **Libraries: Type:** reference. **Holdings:** 500; articles, books, papers. **Subjects:** beverage industry. **Awards: Frequency:** annual. **Type:** scholarship. **Recipient:** for college students to attend National Recycling Coalition Congress. **Committees:** Environmental Affairs; Federal Affairs; Membership; Scientific and Regulatory Affairs; State and Local Affairs. **Absorbed:** National Bottlers Association; National Bottlers Protective Association. **Formerly:** (1967) American Bottlers of Carbonated Beverages; (2004) National Soft Drink Association. **Publications:** *Membership Directory and Buyer's Guide*, annual. **Price:** included in membership dues; $350.00 for nonmembers. **Advertising:** accepted.

504 ■ American Beverage Institute (ABI)

1090 Vermont Ave. NW, Ste.800
Washington, DC 20005
Ph: (202)463-7110
Free: (800)843-8877
URL: http://www.abionline.org
Contact: Richard Berman, Gen. Counsel

Founded: 1991. **Members:** 200. **Description:** Provides public information regarding the consumption of adult beverages. Offers research and educational programs. **Publications:** *ABI News*. Newsletter. **Price:** included in membership dues. Alternate Formats: online. **Conventions/Meetings:** periodic conference.

505 ■ Beverage Network (BN)

c/o John Craven, Ed.
1 Miffin Pl., 3rd Fl.
Cambridge, MA 02138
Ph: (617)715-9670 (617)715-9675
Fax: (617)812-7740
E-mail: jcraven@bevnet.com
URL: http://www.bevnet.com
Contact: John Craven, Ed.

Founded: 1986. **Members:** 200. **Description:** Beverage distributors dealing primarily in "new wave specialty non-alcoholic" products and some specialty food items. Serves as a forum for the exchange of information among members. Assists members in identifying new products. **Publications:** Bulletin, periodic. **Conventions/Meetings:** periodic meeting.

506 ■ Dr Pepper Bottlers Association (DPBA)

PO Box 906
Rowlett, TX 75030
Ph: (972)475-7397
Contact: Bob Birdsong, Sec.

Founded: 1965. **Members:** 453. **Staff:** 1. **Description:** Dr Pepper soft drink franchise bottlers. Promotes better business relations. **Conventions/Meetings:** annual meeting.

507 ■ International Beverage Dispensing Equipment Association (IBDEA)

3837 Naylors Ln.
Baltimore, MD 21208
Ph: (410)602-0616
Free: (877)40-IBDEA
Fax: (410)486-6799
E-mail: ibdea@cornerstoneassoc.com
URL: http://www.ibdea.org
Contact: Marvin Howard, Exec. Dir.

Founded: 1971. **Members:** 250. **Membership Dues:** regular, $325 (annual). **Staff:** 2. **Budget:** $250,000. **Multinational. Description:** Represents companies in the business of selling, renting, leasing, and servicing beverage dispensing equipment to the U.S. food and beverage industry. Combines forces to create better buying power with suppliers. **Formerly:** National Beverage Dispensing Equipment Association; (1983) National Soda Dispensing Equipment Association. **Publications:** *IBDEA News Bulletin*, monthly. Newsletter ● *IBDEA Report*, quarterly. Newsletter. **Advertising:** accepted ● Membership Directory, annual. **Price:** available to members only. **Advertising:** accepted. **Conventions/Meetings:** annual convention, with workshops, tradeshow, hospitality, networking (exhibits).

508 ■ International Beverage Packaging Association (IBPA)

c/o Brian Bishop, Pres.
Anheuser-Busch, Inc.
Fort Collins, CO 80524
E-mail: info@ibpa.org
URL: http://www.ibpa.org
Contact: Brian Bishop, Pres.

Founded: 1947. **Members:** 750. **Membership Dues:** individual, $40 (annual). **Staff:** 7. **Budget:** $20,000. **Regional Groups:** 7. **Local Groups:** 7. **Description:** Beverage industry personnel interested in the concerns of the beverage packaging industry, including soft drink, beer, bottled water, juice manufacturers and packagers, allied suppliers. **Awards:** NBPA Chapter Awards. **Frequency:** annual. **Type:** recognition ● Richard F. Heaney Memorial Scholarship Fund. **Frequency:** annual. **Type:** scholarship. **Recipient:** to college students who showed an interest in a beverage-packaging career. **Committees:** Scholarship. **Formerly:** (1986) Brewers and Beverage Packaging Association; (2000) National Beverage Packaging Association. **Publications:** *IBPA's Voice*. Newsletter. **Advertising:** accepted. **Conventions/Meetings:** Beverage Technology - seminar and trade show.

509 ■ International Bottled Water Association (IBWA)

1700 Diagonal Rd., Ste.650
Alexandria, VA 22314
Ph: (703)683-5213
Free: (800)WATER11
Fax: (703)683-4074
E-mail: ibwainfo@bottledwater.org
URL: http://www.bottledwater.org
Contact: Joseph K. Doss, Pres.

Founded: 1958. **Members:** 700. **Staff:** 14. **Budget:** $4,000,000. **Multinational. Description:** Bottled water plants; distributors; manufacturers of bottled water supplies; international bottlers, distributors and suppliers. Conducts seminars and technical research. **Awards:** Aqua Awards. **Frequency:** annual. **Type:** recognition. **Recipient:** for outstanding advertising/public relations. **Programs:** Educational; Governmental Relations; Public Relations; Technical Training. **Formed by Merger of:** American Bottled Water Association; Council of Natural Waters. **Publications:** *Bottled Water Reporter*, bimonthly. Magazine. Includes statistics, feature articles, and lists new products and technologies. **Price:** $50.00 for nonmembers in U.S. and Canada; $100.00 for nonmembers outside U.S. and Canada; included in membership dues. **Advertising:** accepted ● *IBWA Audit Handbook*. Assists members in preparing for the annual plant inspection. **Price:** $25.00 for members; $1,500.00 for nonmembers ● *IBWA Membership Roster*, annual. Membership Directory. Lists all IBWA members in four sections. **Price:** $25.00 for members; $1,500.00 for nonmembers. **Advertising:** accepted. **Conventions/Meetings:** annual convention and trade show (exhibits).

510 ■ Juice Products Association (JPA)

1156 15th St. NW, Ste.900
Washington, DC 20005
Ph: (202)785-3232
Fax: (202)223-9741
E-mail: jpa@kellencompany.com
URL: http://www.juiceproducts.org
Contact: Richard E. Cristol, Pres.

Founded: 1957. **Members:** 123. **Membership Dues:** regular, $4,250 (annual) ● associate, $3,750 (annual). **Staff:** 1. **Description:** Promotes research, technology, and communication within the juice processing industry. Seeks uniform standards of quality, advertising, and labeling practices; monitors rules and regulations of the Food and Drug Administration; disseminates information on regulatory actions, pending legislation, marketing data, commodity information, and antitrust developments. **Libraries: Type:** not open to the public. **Subjects:** fruits, juice products. **Awards:** D. Glynn Davies/Juice Products Association Scholarship. **Frequency:** annual. **Type:** scholarship. **Recipient:** to a junior student who has demonstrated a keen interest in the fruit juice industry. **Committees:** Governmental Affairs; Technical Affairs. **Absorbed:** Processed Apples Institute. **Formed by Merger of:** (2003) National Juice Products Association and Processed Apples Institute. **Formerly:** National Orange Juice Association; National Association of Citrus Juice Processors. **Publications:** *Membership Roster*, annual. Membership Directory ● Bulletin, periodic. **Advertising:** accepted ● Also publishes anti-trust compliance guides and model record retention programs. **Conventions/Meetings:** annual conference.

511 ■ National Coffee Association of U.S.A. (NCA)

15 Maiden Ln., Ste.1405
New York, NY 10038-4003
Ph: (212)766-4007
Fax: (212)766-5815
E-mail: info@ncausa.org
URL: http://www.ncausa.org
Contact: Robert F. Nelson, Pres./CEO

Founded: 1911. **Members:** 185. **Membership Dues:** roaster (based on annual volume), $250-$75,000 (annual) ● green coffee broker/importer, $1,250-$36,800 (annual) ● retailer (based on number of locations), $250-$2,000 (annual) ● foreign/grower, $250-$750 (annual) ● allied, $1,600 (annual) ● wholesaler/

distributor, $300-$5,000 (annual). **Staff:** 5. **Budget:** $1,200,000. **Description:** Green coffee importers, jobbers, brokers, and agents; instant coffee and liquid extract processors; roasters and allied coffee industries; exporters; retailers. Promotes sound business relations and mutual understanding among members of the trade, and to increase coffee consumption. Collects and publishes consumer, market and technical information on the coffee industry. **Libraries: Type:** reference. **Holdings:** 600. **Subjects:** coffee, caffeine. **Additional Websites:** http://www.coffee-science.org. **Committees:** Armed Services; Government Affairs; Information & Education; Market Research; Producer; Public Relations; Technical. **Formerly:** (1939) Associated Coffee Industries of America. **Publications:** *Coffee Reporter*, monthly. Newsletter. Contains general business information for the coffee industry including import data, technical developments and government regulations. **Price:** free for members; $65.00 /year for nonmembers in U.S.; $75.00 /year for nonmembers outside U.S. **Circulation:** 500 ● *CoffeeTrax*, quarterly. Bulletin. Contains U.S. import-export information. **Price:** $100.00 /year for members; $115.00 /year for nonmembers ● *National Coffee Drinking Trends*, annual. Report. Provides statistics on the US coffee consumption patterns. **Price:** $185.00 for members; $350.00 for nonmembers ● *US Coffee Industry Review 2005*. Report. **Price:** $1,500.00 for members; $2,000.00 for nonmembers. **Conventions/Meetings:** annual conference ● annual convention.

512 ■ Royal Crown Bottlers Association (RCBA)

Address Unknown since 2008

Founded: 1964. **Members:** 30. **Staff:** 1. **Description:** Bottlers of Royal Crown Cola. Purposes are to: represent Royal Crown franchised bottlers; promote business cooperation among members and between bottlers and the parent company. **Committees:** Executive; Marketing. **Affiliated With:** American Beverage Association. **Publications:** *Roster and By-Laws*, annual. **Conventions/Meetings:** annual meeting.

513 ■ Specialty Coffee Association of America (SCAA)

330 Golden Shore, Ste.50
Long Beach, CA 90802
Ph: (562)624-4100
Fax: (562)624-4101
E-mail: coffee@scaa.org
URL: http://www.scaa.org
Contact: Mary Petitt, Pres.

Founded: 1982. **Members:** 2,500. **Membership Dues:** coffee-oriented retailer, coffee cart/kiosk/drive thru, grower/exporter/ producer, $195 (annual) ● roaster wholesaler, roaster retailer, importer/green broker, allied/ distributor, restaurant, office coffee service, $405 (annual) ● culinary professional, $215 (annual) ● restaurant (over $10,000,001), $775 (annual) ● associate, $285 (annual). **Staff:** 12. **Budget:** $3,000,000. **Description:** Coffee roasters, green coffee brokers, retailers, distributors, and others involved in the gourmet coffee industry. Provides business, professional, promotional, and educational assistance in the areas of cultivation, processing, preparation, and marketing of specialty coffee; increase consumer awareness, understanding, and consumption of specialty coffee. Provides a forum for discussion of the purpose and unified character of the industry and represents members in national and regional coffee concerns. Distributes posters, surveys, articles, and other promotional information; develops coffee education curricula for culinary school programs. Maintains reference materials. Sponsors tastings of specialty coffees. **Libraries: Type:** reference. **Holdings:** 1; books. **Subjects:** coffee. **Awards:** Achievement Awards. **Frequency:** annual. **Type:** recognition. **Recipient:** to members who have made outstanding contributions to the organization ● The Golden Cup. **Frequency:** annual. **Type:** recognition. **Recipient:** to coffee retailers who demonstrate the best overall business practices ● Mose Drachman Sales and Service Award. **Frequency:** annual. **Type:** recognition. **Recipient:** for excellence in specialty coffee sales and service. **Publications:** *In Good Taste*, bimonthly. Newsletter ● Brochures ● Membership Directory, annual. **Conventions/Meetings:** annual conference (exhibits) ● periodic seminar.

514 ■ Tea Association of the U.S.A. (TA)

420 Lexington Ave., Ste.825
New York, NY 10170
Ph: (212)986-9415
Fax: (212)697-8658
E-mail: info@teausa.com
URL: http://teausa.org
Contact: Joseph P. Simrany, Pres.

Founded: 1899. **Members:** 115. **Membership Dues:** packer (based on packs per annum), $1,050-$28,350 (annual) ● importer/trader (based on annual sales), $1,050-$7,350 (annual) ● associate (based on annual revenue), $785-$3,930 (annual). **Staff:** 3. **Description:** Packers, importers, brokers, agents, and other firms dedicated to the interests and growth of the U.S. tea industry. **Libraries: Type:** reference; open to the public. **Holdings:** 200; books, periodicals. **Subjects:** tea. **Additional Websites:** http://www.teausa.com. **Telecommunication Services:** electronic mail, simrany@teausa.com. **Committees:** Arbitration; Brewing, Tasting and Standards; Consumer Packaging; Convention; Directors Nominating; Events; Executive; Finance; Foreign Affairs; Legislative; Membership; Officers Nominating; Raw Material Packaging; Tea Information; Tea World; Technical Standards; Transportation and Systems. **Subgroups:** Specialty Tea Registry. **Affiliated With:** Tea Council of the United States of America. **Publications:** *Tea Bits*, quarterly. Newsletter. **Price:** available to members only. **Conventions/Meetings:** annual conference ● annual convention.

515 ■ Tea Board of India

Address Unknown since 2007

Founded: 1960. **Members:** 700. **Staff:** 4. **Budget:** $300,000. **Description:** Indian tea producers and exporters. Promotes Indian tea and develops new markets for tea in the U.S. and Canada. Sets quality control standards for tea packers. Serves as a liaison between buyers and suppliers and among tea packers. Provides feedback to the Indian tea industry about market conditions in the U.S. and Canada.

516 ■ Tea Council of the United States of America (TC)

420 Lexington Ave., Ste.825
New York, NY 10170
Ph: (212)986-9415
Fax: (212)697-8658
E-mail: info@teausa.com
URL: http://www.teausa.org
Contact: Joseph P. Simrany, Pres.

Founded: 1950. **Members:** 100. **Membership Dues:** packer (based on packs per annum), $164,000 (annual) ● importer/trader (based on annual sales), $142-$6,745 (annual) ● associate (based on annual revenue), $405-$2,430 (annual). **Staff:** 4. **Description:** Represents companies and countries trading tea in the U.S. Works to increase tea consumption. **Libraries: Type:** reference. **Holdings:** 200; books, periodicals. **Subjects:** tea. **Affiliated With:** Tea Association of the U.S.A. **Publications:** *Tea World*, annual. Magazine. **Price:** included in membership dues ● *TeaBits*, quarterly. Newsletter. **Price:** included in membership dues. **Conventions/Meetings:** annual World Tea Forum - meeting.

Bicycle

517 ■ International Federation of Bike Messenger Associations (IFBMA)

PO Box 191443
San Francisco, CA 94119-1443
E-mail: ifbma@messengers.org
URL: http://www.messengers.org/ifbma
Contact: Joel Metz, Contact

Founded: 1998. **Membership Dues:** regular, $5. **Multinational. Description:** Ensures the successful realization of an annual Cycle Messenger World Championships. Fosters a spirit of cooperation and community amongst bicycle messengers worldwide. Promotes the use of pedal power for commercial purposes. **Awards:** Markus Cook Award. **Frequency:** annual. **Type:** recognition. **Recipient:** for people who inspire and empower the wider messenger community. **Telecommunication Services:** electronic mail, magpie@messengers.org. **Publications:** *CMC Organizer's Guidebook*. Alternate Formats: online.

Billiards

518 ■ American Cuemakers Association (ACA)

c/o Russ Espiritu, Chm.
6162 Hwy. 18
Brandon, MS 39042
Ph: (601)825-7077
Fax: (601)825-7077
E-mail: aca@cuemakers.org
URL: http://www.cuemakers.org
Contact: Russ Espiritu, Chm.

Founded: 1992. **Membership Dues:** voting, $300 (annual) ● probationary, $200 (annual) ● merchandising, $100 (annual) ● associate, $50 (annual). **Description:** Promotes American-made cue as a unique collectible art form. Advances the art of cuemaking. Establishes and maintains high standards for American-made cue and cue products. **Awards:** Appreciation Award. **Frequency:** periodic. **Type:** recognition. **Recipient:** for outstanding contribution and dedication to custom cue industry. **Committees:** Ethics; Hall of Fame; Long Range Planning; Trade Show.

519 ■ International Cuemakers Association (ICA)

c/o Chris Hightower, Intl. Dir.
444 Flint Hill Rd.
Aragon, GA 30104
Ph: (770)684-7004
E-mail: ica@internationalcuemakers.com
URL: http://www.internationalcuemakers.com
Contact: Chris Hightower, Intl. Dir.

Membership Dues: cuemaker, cue-manufacturer, cue-repairman, apprentice, supplier/merchant, $100 (annual) ● associate, $75 (annual). **Multinational. Description:** Promotes and elevates custom cue making as a true form of collectible art and a precision sports instrument. Helps provide a forum for cuemakers. Encourages and assists all members to excel in their craft.

Biotechnology

520 ■ Biotechnology Industry Organization (BIO)

1201 Maryland Ave. SW, Ste.900
Washington, DC 20024
Ph: (202)962-9200
Fax: (202)962-9201
E-mail: info@bio.org
URL: http://www.bio.org
Contact: James C. Greenwood, Pres./CEO

Founded: 1993. **Members:** 1,100. **Membership Dues:** corporate (based on revenues and number of employees), $860-$41,500 (annual) ● associate (based on number of employees), $3,500-$21,000 (annual) ● affiliate, center, $2,000 (annual) ● industrial/environmental (maximum), $125,000 (annual). **Staff:** 73. **Budget:** $25,000,000. **State Groups:** 24. **Description:** Represents biotechnology companies, academic institutions, state biotechnology centers and related organizations in all 50 U.S. states and 33 other nations. Members are involved in the research and development of healthcare, agricultural, industrial and environmental biotechnology products. **Libraries: Type:** reference. **Holdings:** books, clippings, periodicals. **Subjects:** biotechnology. **Awards:** Governor of the Year. **Frequency:** annual. **Type:** recognition ● High School Essay Contest. **Type:** recognition ● Legislator of the Year. **Frequency:** annual. **Type:** recognition ● Student Science Project Contest. **Type:** recognition. **Committees:** Agricultural and Environmental; Communications; Education; Financial

Management; Government Relations; Manufacturing/Product Commercialization; Marketing/Business Development; Patent and Regulatory Affairs; Research and Development. **Formed by Merger of:** (1993) Association of Biotechnology Companies; Industrial Biotechnology Association. **Publications:** *BIO News*, bimonthly. Newsletter. Focuses on federal regulatory and legislative developments affecting the biotechnology industry; also covers association news. **Price:** included in membership dues. **Circulation:** 5,000. Alternate Formats: online ● *Milestones*, annual. Annual Report. Alternate Formats: online ● Bulletin, periodic. **Price:** free for members ● Prepares monthly columns for biotechnology journals. **Conventions/Meetings:** annual BIO Europe - conference - usually November ● annual BIO Venture Forum - conference - usually September/October ● annual CEO and Investor Conference - usually February ● annual conference, with over 600 speakers, 120 workshops and 250 exhibitors (exhibits) - always May/June ● annual Human Resources Conference - usually October ● annual international conference.

521 ■ Organization of Regulatory and Clinical Associates (ORCA)
PO Box 3490
Redmond, WA 98073
Ph: (206)464-0825
E-mail: info@orcanw.org
URL: http://www.orcanw.org
Contact: Drew Queen, Pres.
Founded: 1993. **Members:** 138. **Membership Dues:** regular, $90 (annual). **Staff:** 6. **Budget:** $25,000. **Description:** Represents individuals providing services to the biological, biotechnological, pharmaceutical, and medical equipment industries in areas including regulatory affairs, quality assurance, and clinical research. Facilitates communication and mutual support among members. Conducts educational programs. **Conventions/Meetings:** monthly meeting.

Blacksmiths

522 ■ American Farrier's Association (AFA)
4059 Iron Works Pkwy., Ste.1
Lexington, KY 40511
Ph: (859)233-7411
Fax: (859)231-7862
E-mail: farriers@americanfarriers.org
URL: http://www.americanfarriers.org
Contact: Dave Ferguson CJF, Pres.
Founded: 1971. **Members:** 3,300. **Membership Dues:** regular, $150 (annual) ● student, $35 (annual). **Staff:** 4. **Budget:** $600,000. **State Groups:** 50. **Description:** Practicing farriers (blacksmiths who shoe horses). Promotes interest in the art and science of the farrier; informs the public, particularly horseowners, of the quality and standard of service to which they are entitled; assists those who want to enter the trade; assists the farrier in furthering his skills; cooperates with related associations to further the interests of the equine industry. Sponsors the American Farrier's Team for participation in international competitions in Canada and the United Kingdom. Conducts research. **Libraries: Type:** reference. **Holdings:** video recordings. **Awards:** Administration Award. **Frequency:** annual. **Type:** recognition. **Recipient:** for outstanding ability to organize and implement farrier functions ● Edward Martin Humanitarian. **Frequency:** annual. **Type:** recognition. **Recipient:** for an active effort to promote goodwill in the farrier profession ● Journalism. **Frequency:** annual. **Type:** recognition. **Recipient:** for meritorious service in collecting, editing and presenting information of interest to farriers ● Outstanding Educator. **Frequency:** annual. **Type:** recognition. **Recipient:** for outstanding service and dedication to the field of farrier education ● Sharon Walker Association Newsletter Award. **Frequency:** annual. **Type:** recognition. **Recipient:** for the best newsletter from an AFA chapter or recognized group ● Walt Taylor Award. **Frequency:** annual. **Type:** recognition. **Recipient:** for unlimited service, distinguished contributions and unselfish devotion to the farrier industry. **Computer Services:** Mailing lists, of members. **Telecommunication Services:** electronic mail, daveferguson@americanfarriers.org. **Committees:** Certification Education and Activities; Contest Rules; Cultural Exchange. **Divisions:** Educators. **Publications:** *AFA Membership Directory*, annual. **Price:** included in membership dues ● *AFA Newsletter*, bimonthly. **Price:** included in membership dues. **Circulation:** 2,600 ● *Industry Directory*, annual ● *Presidents Newsletter*, monthly ● *Professional Farrier*, bimonthly. Journal. **Conventions/Meetings:** annual convention (exhibits) - 2009 Feb. 25-28, Chattanooga, TN; 2010 Feb. 23-27, Portland, OR.

523 ■ Artist-Blacksmith's Association of North America (ABANA)
c/o LeeAnn Mitchell, Central Office Admin.
PO Box 816
Farmington, GA 30638-0816
Ph: (706)310-1030
Fax: (706)769-7147
E-mail: abana@abana.org
URL: http://www.abana.org
Contact: LeeAnn Mitchell, Central Office Admin.
Founded: 1973. **Members:** 5,000. **Membership Dues:** regular, $55 (annual) ● senior citizen (age 65 plus), $50 (annual) ● foreign, $65 (annual) ● student, library, $45 (annual) ● contributory, $100. **Staff:** 3. **Budget:** $288,209. **Regional Groups:** 65. **Multinational. Description:** Represents amateur and professional blacksmiths, artists and farriers interested in promoting the art of blacksmithing. **Awards:** Bealer Award. **Frequency:** annual. **Type:** recognition. **Recipient:** for outstanding service to the field of blacksmithing ● Joe Humble Award. **Frequency:** annual. **Type:** recognition. **Recipient:** to an affiliate newsletter editor. **Computer Services:** database ● mailing lists. **Telecommunication Services:** information service. **Publications:** *The Anvil's Ring*, quarterly. Journal. For blacksmiths containing trade articles, tips, and techniques; includes association news and calendar of events. **Price:** free for members. ISSN: 0889-177X. **Circulation:** 4,600. **Advertising:** accepted ● *Hammer's Blow*, quarterly. Journal. Hands-on, how-to newsletter for members, with tips, techniques and projects. ● Also makes available videotapes for rental to members. **Conventions/Meetings:** biennial conference (exhibits).

524 ■ National Blacksmiths and Weldors Association (NBWA)
c/o James E. Holman, Information Off.
PO Box 123
Arnold, NE 69120
Ph: (308)848-2913
E-mail: dhart@ndsupernet.com
URL: http://www.horseshoes.com/assoc/national-blacksmiths/nbwa
Contact: James E. Holman, Information Off.
Founded: 1875. **Members:** 566. **Membership Dues:** regular, $40 (annual). **Staff:** 1. **Budget:** $500. **State Groups:** 6. **Local Groups:** 30. **Description:** Blacksmiths, weldors, manufacturing machine shops, and general repair shops. Works to disseminate general and technical information through newsletters, seminars, state and national conventions, and district meetings. Maintains hall of fame and speakers' bureau. Conducts charitable programs. **Libraries: Type:** reference. **Holdings:** periodicals. **Subjects:** blacksmithing history. **Awards:** Blacksmith of the Year Award. **Frequency:** annual. **Type:** recognition. **Recipient:** for blacksmiths. **Publications:** *Modern Blacksmith*, bimonthly. Newsletter. Includes obituaries. **Price:** included in membership dues; $20.00 /year for nonmembers. **Circulation:** 350. **Advertising:** accepted ● *National Blacksmiths and Weldors Association—Directory of Members*, periodic. Membership Directory. **Conventions/Meetings:** annual conference, only for suppliers of equipment (exhibits).

Blind

525 ■ National Association of Blind Merchants (NABM)
1223 Lake Plaza Dr., Ste.D
Colorado Springs, CO 80906
Ph: (719)527-0488
Free: (866)543-6808
E-mail: kevanworley@blindmerchants.org
URL: http://www.blindmerchants.org
Contact: Kevan Worley, Pres.
Description: Seeks to improve business opportunities and quality of life for the blind. Provides a means of collective action for blind business people. Promotes the vocational, economic, business, cultural and social advancement of the blind. Strives to maximize opportunities under the Randolph-Sheppard Act. **Computer Services:** Information services, 50 Points of Profit ● information services, Randolph-Sheppard Act ● mailing lists. **Programs:** BLAST. **Affiliated With:** National Federation of the Blind. **Publications:** *Presidential Reports*, annual. Alternate Formats: online.

Boating

526 ■ Metal Boat Society (MBS)
PO Box 61856
Vancouver, WA 98666
Ph: (360)695-4100
Fax: (360)993-1600
E-mail: info@metalboatsociety.org
URL: http://www.metalboatsociety.org
Contact: Steve Hayward, Pres.
Members: 500. **Membership Dues:** regular in U.S., $35 (annual) ● regular in Canada, $40 (annual) ● regular outside U.S. and Canada, $55 (annual) ● commercial, $195 (annual). **Multinational. Description:** Works for the promotion, design and building of metal boats. Serves as a forum for metal boat builders, owners and buyers. **Computer Services:** Online services, forum. **Publications:** *Metal Boat Quarterly*. Magazine. **Price:** included in membership dues. Alternate Formats: online. Also Cited As: *MBQ*.

527 ■ Sail America
850 Aquidneck Ave., Unit B-4
Middletown, RI 02842-7244
Ph: (401)841-0900
Free: (800)817-SAIL
Fax: (401)847-2044
E-mail: info@sailamerica.com
URL: http://www.sailamerica.com
Founded: 1991. **Description:** Promotes the growth of the sailing industry. **Conventions/Meetings:** trade show.

528 ■ States Organization for Boating Access (SOBA)
200 E Randolph Dr., Ste.5100
Chicago, IL 60601
Ph: (312)946-6283
Fax: (312)946-0388
E-mail: info@sobaus.org
URL: http://www.sobaus.org
Contact: Ed Poolos, Pres.
Founded: 1986. **Members:** 100. **Membership Dues:** voting, $600 (annual) ● associate, $500 (annual) ● advisory, $300 (annual) ● individual, $125 (annual) ● affiliated professional, $50 (annual). **Description:** Individuals interested in recreational boating facilities. Provides information regarding the construction, maintenance, financing, and administration of recreational boating facilities to state program administrators charged with their management. **Awards:** Meritorious Service Award. **Frequency:** annual. **Type:** recognition. **Recipient:** to a state agency ● Outgoing President Award. **Type:** recognition ● Outstanding Project Awards. **Frequency:** annual. **Type:** recognition. **Recipient:** to an agency, group, or corporation for quality, unique, useful, economical or innovative projects ● Outstanding Service Award. **Frequency:** annual. **Type:** recognition. **Recipient:** to an individual who has made either a one-time or continuing contribution to improved access for boaters and anglers to the nation's public waters ● Professional Service Award. **Frequency:** annual. **Type:** recognition. **Recipient:** to individual or group of volunteers ● Special Recognition Award. **Frequency:** annual. **Type:** recognition. **Recipient:** to individual, group,

organization or political subdivision ● State Boating Access Program Excellence Award. **Frequency:** annual. **Type:** recognition. **Recipient:** to a state agency ● State CVA Program Excellence Award. **Frequency:** annual. **Type:** recognition. **Recipient:** to a state agency ● William H. Ivers Award. **Frequency:** annual. **Type:** recognition. **Recipient:** to an individual who has contributed at least 15 years to the design, construction, management or administration of boat access facilities. **Committees:** Clean Vessel/Boating Infrastructure; Conference/Awards; Design/Development/Operations; Outreach/Education/Technology. **Publications:** *CVA Lifecycle Pump out Study Report*. **Price:** $32.00 hardcopy; $3.50 CD. Alternate Formats: CD-ROM ● *Design Handbook and Operations and Maintenance Guidelines*. **Price:** $46.50 for members; $74.50 for nonmembers ● *Video Guide to Building a Better Boat Ramp*. Includes footage taken during the actual construction and pushing of boat ramps. **Price:** $12.50 for members; $29.99 for nonmembers ● Newsletter, quarterly ● Proceedings. **Price:** $10.00. **Conventions/Meetings:** annual conference - usually in September or October. 2008 Oct. 13-17, Norfolk, VA.

Books

529 ■ Association of Booksellers for Children (ABC)

c/o Kristen McLean, Exec. Dir.
6538 Collin Ave., No. 168
Miami Beach, FL 33141
Ph: (617)390-7759 (715)256-9186
Fax: (617)344-0540
E-mail: kristen@abfc.com
URL: http://www.abfc.com
Contact: Kristen McLean, Exec. Dir.

Founded: 1986. **Members:** 400. **Membership Dues:** bookstore, associate, $85 (annual) ● publisher, sponsor (base), $200 (annual) ● author, illustrator, self-publisher, publisher rep/literary agent, $50 (annual). **Staff:** 1. **Budget:** $200,000. **Description:** Works to encourage quality standards and service in the children's book industry. Promotes public awareness of the importance of children's literature; provides a forum for communication among members; offers support to booksellers; conducts educational programs; and offers children's services. **Awards:** ABC Choices Award. **Frequency:** annual. **Type:** recognition. **Recipient:** to members' favorite titles ● E.B. White Read Aloud Award. **Frequency:** annual. **Type:** recognition. **Recipient:** for a book that reflects the universal read aloud standards. **Computer Services:** Mailing lists. **Publications:** *ABC Choices for Children*, annual. Catalog. Features a full-color promotional catalog for use by member stores. Alternate Formats: online ● Newsletter, quarterly. Alternate Formats: online ● Membership Directory, annual. **Conventions/Meetings:** annual convention.

530 ■ Independent Online Booksellers Association (IOBA)

c/o Sandra L. Morris, Membership Sec.
Nan's Book Shop
350 N Main St.
Glen Ellyn, IL 60137-5065
E-mail: info@ioba.org
URL: http://www.ioba.org
Contact: David Friedman, Pres.

Membership Dues: business, $60 (annual) ● associate, $35 (annual) ● apprentice, $30 (annual) ● supporting, $20 (annual). **Description:** Promotes internet bookselling. Promotes the interests of internet booksellers. Maintains high ethical and professional standards for booksellers. Promotes trust between consumers and booksellers by providing a safe online environment for the purchase and sale of books. Raises awareness of online bookselling. **Computer Services:** database, members' directory ● information services, book conditioning definitions ● information services, book terminology ● mailing lists. **Committees:** Education; Ethics; Internet Operations; Public Relations. **Publications:** *The Standard*, quarterly. Magazine. ISSN: 1542-0493. Alternate Formats: online.

Bowling

531 ■ International Bowling Pro Shop and Instructors Association (IBPSIA)

615 Six Flags Dr.
Arlington, TX 76011-6305
Ph: (817)649-0079
Free: (800)659-9444
Fax: (817)633-2940
E-mail: bill@ibpsia.com
URL: http://www.ibpsia.com
Contact: Bill Supper, Exec. Dir.

Founded: 1990. **Members:** 700. **Membership Dues:** regular in North America, $250 (annual) ● regular, affiliate outside North America, $275 (annual) ● regular branch, $150 (annual) ● associate in North America, $450 (annual) ● associate outside North America, $475 (annual). **Description:** Represents bowling pro shop and instructional professionals. Compiles statistics. Conducts educational programs. **Formerly:** (1998) National Bowling Pro Shop and Instructors Association. **Publications:** *Directory and Buyers Guide*, annual. Membership Directory. **Price:** free for members ● *The Industry Standard*, bimonthly. Newspaper. **Price:** free for members. **Circulation:** 8,000. **Advertising:** accepted. Also Cited As: *Pro Shop Today*. **Conventions/Meetings:** annual conference ● annual convention (exhibits) - always July.

Bridal Services

532 ■ American Society of Wedding Professionals (ASWP)

268 Griggs Ave.
Teaneck, NJ 07666
Ph: (973)472-1800
Free: (800)526-0497
Fax: (973)574-7626
E-mail: lawrence@carroll.com
URL: http://www.sellthebride.com
Contact: Brian D. Lawrence, Exec. Off.

Founded: 1992. **Members:** 100. **Membership Dues:** student, $129 (annual) ● new business, $129 (annual) ● junior wedding professional, $129 (annual) ● senior wedding professional, $129 (annual) ● wedding supplier, $129 (annual). **Staff:** 2. **Local Groups:** 2. **Description:** Professionals in the wedding industry. Promotes the wedding professional and educates brides on the experience of working with a consultant. Provides trends, etiquette, marketing, consulting information, directory listing, referrals, networking, and co-op advertising. Offers local forums for information exchange among members. Compiles statistics and conducts educational programs and seminars. **Libraries: Type:** reference. **Holdings:** audio recordings, books, clippings, periodicals. **Subjects:** general business, marketing, wedding planning, wedding etiquette, international weddings, wedding industry, bridal statistics. **Subcommittees:** Bride Education; Meeting Planning; Membership News; Public Relations. **Publications:** *The Wedding Expert's Guide to Sales and Marketing*. Book. Leading marketing manual in the wedding industry. **Price:** $80.00 ● *WedPro News*, monthly. Newsletter. **Price:** included in membership dues. **Advertising:** accepted. **Conventions/Meetings:** annual conference ● quarterly seminar.

533 ■ Association of Bridal Consultants (ABC)

56 Danbury Rd., Ste.11
New Milford, CT 06776
Ph: (860)355-0464
Fax: (860)354-1404
E-mail: office@bridalassn.com
URL: http://www.bridalassn.com
Contact: David M. Wood III, Pres.

Founded: 1981. **Members:** 3,800. **Membership Dues:** novice, $165 (annual) ● consultant, $245 (annual) ● vendor, $175 (annual) ● corporate, $550 (annual). **Staff:** 13. **Budget:** $1,000,000. **State Groups:** 24. **National Groups:** 3. **For-Profit. Multinational. Description:** Represents independent bridal and wedding consultants; persons employed by companies in wedding-related businesses and novices looking to get into the business. Strives to improve professionalism and recognition of bridal and wedding consultants. Offers professional development program, start-up manual and seminars. Provides advertising, publicity, referrals, and information services. Operates speakers' bureau; compiles statistics. **Libraries: Type:** reference. **Holdings:** 75; audiovisuals, books. **Subjects:** weddings, business management, consulting. **Awards:** "Miss Dorothy" Heart. **Frequency:** annual. **Type:** recognition. **Recipient:** for passion to the industry ● "Miss Dorothy" Scholarship. **Frequency:** annual. **Type:** scholarship. **Recipient:** for outstanding novice member. **Supersedes:** American Association of Professional Bridal Consultants. **Publications:** *ABCDialogue*, bimonthly. Newsletter. Includes articles about wedding fashions, floral arrangements, photography, jewelry, etiquette, advertising, and public relations. **Price:** $24.00. ISSN: 1053-9107. **Circulation:** 3,800. **Advertising:** accepted ● *The Bridal Show: Planner's Handbook*. Consists of a guide to developing and marketing a successful bridal show. ISSN: 1079-2708 ● *Ethnic and Specialty by Wedding Guide*, periodic. Handbook. Contains background and etiquette for various ethnic and specialty weddings. Alternate Formats: diskette; online ● *Retail Resource Directory*, semiannual. Details on more than 1,000 manufacturers/suppliers of wedding-related goods and services. ISSN: 1079-2708 ● *Weddings As A Business*. Manual. A guide for new consultants, from concept to first consultation. ISSN: 9627-4872. **Conventions/Meetings:** annual Business of Brides - seminar and workshop (exhibits) - always begins in second Sunday of November; location varies.

534 ■ Bridal Association of America (BAOA)

531 H St.
Bakersfield, CA 93304
Ph: (661)633-1949
Fax: (661)633-9199
E-mail: kyle@bridalassociationofamerica.com
URL: http://www.bridalassociationofamerica.com
Contact: Mr. Kyle Brown, Exec. Dir.

Founded: 1999. **Membership Dues:** local, $10 (monthly) ● national, $66 (monthly). **Description:** Provides free and accessible information on wedding planning and on how to adjust on living life as a couple. Provides a forum for wedding professionals to express their own approaches and styles when it comes to their own wedding products and services. **Computer Services:** Information services, wedding planning timeline; weddings facts and stories ● online services, find a wedding professional. **Publications:** *The Wedding Book*. Contains tips and suggestions on planning a wedding. **Price:** free for members.

535 ■ National Black Bridal Association (NBBA)

c/o Dion Magee, Pres.
3401 Ramey Dr.
Arlington, TX 76014
Ph: (817)784-8515
Free: (866)302-2897
E-mail: info@nationalbba.com
URL: http://www.nationalbba.com
Contact: Dion Magee, Pres.

Description: Professional experts in the wedding industry dedicated to African-American weddings. Aims to provide the highest level of excellence in all areas of wedding planning. Assists in achieving cultural and elegant wedding experiences. Provides wedding budgets, consultation and referral programs. **Telecommunication Services:** electronic mail, dion@nationalbba.com. **Publications:** *Black Bride & Groom*, annual. Magazine. **Price:** $4.95/issue, plus shipping and handling. Alternate Formats: online.

536 ■ National Bridal Service (NBS)

1004 W Thompson St., Ste.205
Richmond, VA 23230
Ph: (804)342-0055

Fax: (804)342-6062
E-mail: info@nationalbridal.com
URL: http://nationalbridal.com
Contact: Doris Nixon, Pres.
Founded: 1951. **Members:** 800. **Staff:** 16. **Budget:** $5,000,000. **For-Profit. Description:** Represents bridal, jewelry, and gift stores. Makes available management support services including employee training, advertising, merchandising, financial and market research. **Awards:** Registered Bridal Consultant. **Type:** recognition. **Recipient:** for members; must complete home study course. **Publications:** *The Groom's Corner*, annual. Newsletter ● *Momentum*, bimonthly. Newsletter ● *One Perfect Day*, periodic ● *The Why's and Wherefore's of Wedding Traditions*, annual. **Conventions/Meetings:** semiannual meeting and seminar.

537 ■ Weddings Beautiful Worldwide
1004 N Thompson St., Ste.205
Richmond, VA 23230
Ph: (804)342-6061
Fax: (804)342-6062
E-mail: info@weddingsbeautiful.com
URL: http://weddingsbeautiful.com
Contact: Ms. Nancy Tucker, Pres.
Founded: 1954. **Members:** 600. **Languages:** English, Japanese. **Multinational. Description:** Provides Certified Wedding Specialist training for independent wedding consultants, planners, and coordinators. Association membership provides support, information, newsletter and national advertising benefits. **Computer Services:** Online services, home study course. **Telecommunication Services:** electronic mail, nancy@weddingsbeautiful.com. **Formerly:** (2004) Association of Wedding Planners Worldwide. **Publications:** *The Grooms Corner*. Booklet. **Price:** included in membership dues ● *One Perfect Day*. Booklet. **Price:** included in membership dues ● *The Why's and Wherefore's of Wedding Traditions*. Brochure. **Price:** included in membership dues ● Newsletter, bimonthly. **Conventions/Meetings:** semiannual seminar.

Bridge

538 ■ International Association for Bridge Maintenance and Safety (IABMAS)
c/o Prof. Dan M. Frangopol, Pres.
ATLSS Ctr.
Lehigh Univ.
117 ATLSS Dr., Imbt Labs
Bethlehem, PA 18015-4729
Ph: (610)758-6103
Fax: (610)758-4115
E-mail: iabmas@civil.colorado.edu
URL: http://iabmas.org
Contact: Prof. Dan M. Frangopol, Pres.
Founded: 1999. **Multinational. Description:** Encompasses all aspects of bridge maintenance, safety and management. Seeks to address all issues concerning bridge repair and rehabilitation, bridge management systems, bridge owners' needs, financial planning, investment and other economic implications. Promotes international cooperation and advancement in the fields of bridge maintenance, safety and management for the purpose of enhancing the welfare of the society. **Telecommunication Services:** electronic mail, dan.frangopol@lehigh.edu. **Conventions/Meetings:** biennial international conference (exhibits) - 2008 July 13-17, Seoul, Republic of Korea.

539 ■ National Steel Bridge Alliance (NSBA)
1 E Wacker Dr., Ste.700
Chicago, IL 60601-1802
Ph: (312)670-7010 (312)670-7012
Fax: (312)670-5403
E-mail: abnee@nsbaweb.org
URL: http://www.steelbridges.org
Contact: Conn Abnee, Exec. Dir.
Membership Dues: active fabricator, $550 (annual) ● class I affiliate, $500 (annual) ● class II affiliate, $250 (annual) ● class III affiliate, $150 (annual). **Description:** Represents the interests of individuals interested in the development, promotion and construction of cost effective steel bridges. Aims to serve customers and members with state-of-the-art design and construction of steel bridges. Strives to make steel the desired material for bridges. **Awards:** Prize Bridge Awards. **Frequency:** annual. **Type:** recognition. **Recipient:** for significant and innovative steel bridges constructed within the US. **Publications:** *Steel Bridge News*, quarterly. Newsletter. Alternate Formats: online.

Broadcasters

540 ■ Collegiate Broadcasters, Inc. (CBI)
UPS - Hershey Square Ctr.
1152 Mae St.
Hummelstown, PA 17036
Free: (877)ASK-CBI1
E-mail: chair@collegebroadcasters.org
URL: http://www.askcbi.org
Contact: Mr. Ron Bland, Chm.
Membership Dues: regular, $100 (annual) ● regular, $265 (triennial). **Description:** Represents students involved in radio, television, webcasting and other media ventures. **Computer Services:** Mailing lists, email lists ● online services, public list, FS list. **Publications:** *CBInsights*, quarterly. Newsletter. **Price:** included in membership dues. **Circulation:** 1,400. **Advertising:** accepted. Alternate Formats: online.

541 ■ National Association of Shortwave Broadcasters (NASB)
10400 NW 240th St.
Okeechobee, FL 34972
Ph: (863)763-0281
Fax: (863)763-1034
E-mail: nasbmem@rocketmail.com
URL: http://www.shortwave.org
Contact: Jeff White, Pres.
Founded: 1990. **Description:** Serves the interests of FCC licensed international broadcasters. Advocates for advancement of the industry. Disseminates information among shortwave broadcasters. **Publications:** Newsletter, bimonthly. **Conventions/Meetings:** annual meeting, for broadcasters to relay information to one another.

Broadcasting

542 ■ Academy of Television Arts and Sciences (ATAS)
5220 Lankershim Blvd.
North Hollywood, CA 91601-3109
Ph: (818)754-2800 (818)754-2810
Fax: (818)761-2827
E-mail: membership@emmys.org
URL: http://www.emmys.org
Contact: Dick Askin, Chm./CEO
Founded: 1948. **Members:** 10,997. **Membership Dues:** active (plus $10 one-time processing fee), $160 (annual) ● associate, academic faculty (plus $10 one-time processing fee), $85 (annual) ● academic student, $25 (annual). **Staff:** 51. **Description:** Professionals in the television and film industry. Aims to advance the arts and sciences of television through services to the industry in education, preservation of television programs, and information and community relations; to foster creative leadership in the television industry. Sponsors Television Academy Hall of Fame. Maintains library on television credits and historical material, the Television Academy Archives, and archives at UCLA of over 35,000 television programs. Offers internships to students. Holds luncheon and speakers series and meetings on problems of the various crafts. **Awards:** Daytime Emmy Awards. **Frequency:** annual. **Type:** recognition ● Los Angeles Area Emmy Award. **Frequency:** annual. **Type:** recognition. **Recipient:** for local programming in the LA area ● Primetime Emmy Awards. **Frequency:** annual. **Type:** recognition ● Student Video Award. **Frequency:** annual. **Type:** recognition. **Committees:** Activities; Awards; Student Activities. **Formerly:** (1977) Hollywood Chapter of National Academy of Television Arts and Sciences. **Publications:** *Debut*, semiannual. Newsletter. Contains information on educational programs and services of the academy including information on internships and video/film competitions and awards. **Price:** included in membership dues ● *Emmy Directory*, annual. Contains list of primetime, daytime, and Los Angeles-area Emmy nominees and winners, in loose-leaf format. **Price:** $10.00 ● *Emmy Magazine*, bimonthly. Includes interviews, book reviews, and articles covering new technology and old shows. **Price:** $28.00/year in U.S.; $42.00/year in Canada; $65.00/year outside U.S. and Canada (airmail). **Circulation:** 14,000. **Advertising:** accepted. Alternate Formats: microform. **Conventions/Meetings:** seminar ● symposium.

543 ■ Advanced Television Systems Committee (ATSC)
1750 K St. NW, Ste.1200
Washington, DC 20006
Ph: (202)872-9160
Fax: (202)872-9161
E-mail: mricher@atsc.org
URL: http://www.atsc.org
Contact: Mark Richer, Pres.
Founded: 1983. **Members:** 55. **Membership Dues:** organizational (maximum; based on annual gross revenues), $15,300 (annual). **Staff:** 3. **Description:** Sponsored by the Joint Committee on Intersociety Coordination. Members of the television and motion picture industry united to develop voluntary international standards in the area of advanced digital television systems. **Committees:** Distribution; Planning; Production. **Subgroups:** Technology and Standards.

544 ■ American Sportscasters Association (ASA)
225 Broadway, Ste.2030
New York, NY 10007
Ph: (212)227-8080
Fax: (212)571-0556
E-mail: lschwa8918@aol.com
URL: http://www.americansportscastersonline.com
Contact: Louis O. Schwartz, Pres./Founder/Ed.
Founded: 1979. **Members:** 500. **Membership Dues:** basic, $50 (annual) ● associate, $100 (annual) ● student, $35 (annual). **Staff:** 3. **Budget:** $200,000. **Description:** Radio and television sportscasters. Sponsors seminars, clinics, and symposia for aspiring announcers and sportscasters. Compiles statistics. Operates Speaker's Bureau, placement service, hall of fame, and biographical archives. Maintains American Sportscaster Hall of Fame Trust. Is currently implementing Hall of Fame Museum, Community Programs. **Libraries: Type:** reference. **Holdings:** 200; photographs. **Subjects:** sports, broadcasting. **Awards:** Graham McNamee Award. **Frequency:** annual. **Type:** recognition. **Recipient:** to a former sportscaster ● Hall of Fame Award. **Frequency:** annual. **Type:** recognition. **Recipient:** to sportscasters who gave voice to sports history's greatest moments ● Humanitarian Award. **Frequency:** annual. **Type:** recognition ● International Sportscaster of the Year. **Frequency:** annual. **Type:** recognition ● Mel Allen Service Award. **Frequency:** annual. **Type:** recognition ● Sports Legend of the Year. **Frequency:** annual. **Type:** recognition ● Sports Personality of the Year. **Frequency:** annual. **Type:** recognition ● Sportscaster of the Year/Play by Play/Studio Host/Color Analyst/Reporter. **Frequency:** annual. **Type:** recognition. **Telecommunication Services:** electronic mail, info@americansportscastersonline.com. **Publications:** *Insiders Sportsletter*, quarterly. Newsletter. Includes annual *Hall of Fame Journal*. **Price:** included in membership dues, available to members only. **Circulation:** 2,000. **Advertising:** accepted. **Conventions/Meetings:** annual Hall of Fame Dinner.

545 ■ American Women in Radio and Television (AWRT)
8405 Greensboro Dr., Ste.800
McLean, VA 22102
Ph: (703)506-3290

Fax: (703)506-3266
E-mail: info@awrt.org
URL: http://www.awrt.org
Contact: Maria Efantis Brennan CAE, Pres.
Founded: 1951. **Membership Dues:** professional, $110 (annual) ● entry level, $85 (annual) ● retired, $50 (annual) ● student, $30 (annual). **Staff:** 3. **Regional Groups:** 5. **Local Groups:** 40. **Description:** Professionals in administrative, creative, or executive positions in broadcasting and related industries (radio, television, cable, entertainment, information, networks, etc.) as well as advertising, government, and charitable agencies, corporations, and service organizations, whose work is substantially devoted to radio and television. Maintains AWRT Educational Foundation, chartered 1960. **Awards:** Gracie Allen Awards. **Frequency:** annual. **Type:** recognition. **Recipient:** for positive and realistic portrayals of the roles, issues, and concerns of women ● Silver Satellite. **Type:** recognition. **Recipient:** for outstanding accomplishment in the field of broadcasting. **Telecommunication Services:** electronic mail, mbrennan@awrt.org. **Projects:** AWRT: Empowering America; Professional Seminars; Stop Sexual Harassment; Symposium on Careers. **Publications:** *Making Waves*, quarterly. Magazine. **Price:** included in membership dues. **Advertising:** accepted ● *News and Views*, monthly. **Price:** included in membership dues ● Membership Directory, annual. **Advertising:** accepted ● Manuals. **Conventions/Meetings:** periodic competition.

546 ■ Associated Press Broadcasters (APB)
c/o AP Broadcast News Center
1825 K St. NW, Ste.800
Washington, DC 20006-1232
Ph: (202)736-1108
Free: (800)821-4747
Fax: (202)736-1107
E-mail: wxwilliams@ap.org
URL: http://www.apbroadcast.com
Contact: James R. Williams III, VP/Dir. of Broadcast Services
Founded: 1941. **Members:** 6,000. **State Groups:** 50. **Description:** Broadcast stations in the United States that are members of the Associated Press. Advances journalism through radio and television. Cooperates with the AP in order to make available accurate and impartial news. Serves as a liaison between radio and television stations that are members of the AP and representatives of those stations. **Awards:** APB National Awards. **Frequency:** annual. **Type:** recognition. **Recipient:** to stations for news coverage and enterprise. **Committees:** Awards; Freedom of Information; News Access; Radio; Technology; Television. **Formerly:** (1970) Associated Press Radio-Television Association; (1974) Associated Press Broadcasters Association. **Conventions/Meetings:** semiannual board meeting.

547 ■ Association of America's Public Television Stations (AAPTS)
666 Eleventh St. NW, Ste.1100
Washington, DC 20001
Ph: (202)654-4200 (202)654-4209
Fax: (202)654-4236
E-mail: jeffrey@apts.org
URL: http://www.apts.org
Contact: Jeffrey Davis, Communications VP
Founded: 1980. **Members:** 156. **Staff:** 19. **Budget:** $2,900,000. **Description:** Public television licensees whose goal is to organize efforts of public television stations in areas of planning and research, and in representation before the government. Maintains current information on the public television system including such areas as licensee characteristics, financing, and industry trends; makes projections on system growth and income. Monitors social, economic, and demographic trends that have an impact on public television services. Prepares and disseminates general information about public television to policymaking agencies, the press, and the public. **Awards:** Grassroots Award. **Frequency:** annual. **Type:** recognition. **Recipient:** to a person at a public television station ● 21st Century. **Frequency:** annual. **Type:** recognition. **Recipient:** to a person at a public television station. **Formerly:** (1980) Association for Public Broadcasting; (1990) National Association of Public Television Stations; (1990) Association for Public Broadcasting. **Publications:** *Communique*, quarterly. Newsletter. Alternate Formats: online ● *Research Studies*, annual. Booklet. Alternate Formats: online ● *Transitions*, quarterly. Newsletter. Alternate Formats: online ● *Update*, quarterly. Newsletter. Alternate Formats: online. **Conventions/Meetings:** annual Capitol Hill Day - conference - always spring in Washington, DC.

548 ■ Association of Independents in Radio (AIR)
PO Box 220400
Boston, MA 02122
Free: (877)937-2477
E-mail: inquiry@airmedia.org
URL: http://www.airmedia.org
Contact: Sue Schardt, Exec. Dir.
Founded: 1988. **Members:** 535. **Description:** Represents and promotes producers and other professionals working in public radio. **Computer Services:** Information services, email discussion list ● online services, conferences, mentoring, regional training. **Telecommunication Services:** electronic mail, dbrandon@airmedia.org. **Publications:** *AIR Producers Directory*. **Advertising:** accepted. Alternate Formats: online ● *AIRSPACE*, quarterly. Journal. **Price:** free for members. **Advertising:** accepted. Alternate Formats: online ● *Awards Directory*. **Advertising:** accepted. Alternate Formats: online ● *Fellowships and Grants Directory*. **Advertising:** accepted. Alternate Formats: online ● *Local Station Directory*. **Advertising:** accepted. Alternate Formats: online. **Conventions/Meetings:** meeting ● workshop.

549 ■ Association for Maximum Service Television (MSTV)
4100 Wisconsin Ave. NW
PO Box 9897
Washington, DC 20016
Ph: (202)966-1956
Fax: (202)966-9617
E-mail: sbaurenfeind@mstv.org
URL: http://www.mstv.org
Contact: David L. Donovan, Pres.
Founded: 1956. **Members:** 450. **Staff:** 6. **Description:** Aims to assure the maintenance and development of an effective nationwide system of free, over-the-air television, based on local broadcast stations that provide community-oriented service of maximum technical quality. Promotes protection against interference and degradation of the public's broadcast service and opportunities for local stations to use advanced television. **Telecommunication Services:** electronic mail, ddonovan@mstv.org. **Committees:** Engineering. **Formerly:** (1990) Association of Maximum Service Telecasters. **Publications:** *Membership Brochure* ● *Membership Newsletter*, periodic.

550 ■ Black Broadcasters Alliance (BBA)
Address Unknown since 2008
URL: http://www.thebba.org/about.html
Founded: 1997. **Membership Dues:** corporate, $1,000 (annual) ● gold sponsor, $20,000 ● silver sponsor, $10,000 ● bronze sponsor, $5,000. **Description:** African American broadcasters. Working to better educate and assist those who seek career opportunities in the industry with a great emphasis on increasing African American representation in ownership, management, engineering and sales. Exercise the right to inform, lobby and influence not only the public but also local and national governmental bodies as to equal participation in the industry. **Publications:** *Communique*, semiannual. Newsletter. Features information on the latest technology and news about BBA and the broadcast industry. **Conventions/Meetings:** annual Golf Classic and Awards Dinner - always August ● annual Media Conference - always September.

551 ■ Black College Radio Organization (BCR)
PO Box 3191
Atlanta, GA 30302
Ph: (404)523-6136
Fax: (404)523-5467
E-mail: bcrmail@aol.com
URL: http://www.blackcollegeradio.com
Description: Provides forum for black colleges and universities to acquire information for the construction and maintenance of college radio and television stations. **Awards:** Broadcaster of the Year. **Frequency:** annual. **Type:** recognition ● Station of the Year. **Frequency:** annual. **Type:** recognition. **Publications:** Newsletter, monthly. **Conventions/Meetings:** annual convention.

552 ■ Broadcast Cable Credit Association (BCCA)
550 W Frontage Rd., Ste.3600
Northfield, IL 60093
Ph: (847)881-8757
Fax: (847)784-8059
E-mail: info@bccacredit.com
URL: http://www.bccacredit.com
Contact: Mary M. Collins, Pres./CEO
Founded: 1972. **Members:** 410. **Staff:** 7. **Budget:** $1,000,000. **Languages:** English, Spanish. **For-Profit. Description:** A subsidiary of the Broadcast Cable Financial Management Association (see separate entry). Television and radio stations; cable television networks; national sales representatives. Provides industry specific credit reports on individual agencies, advertisers, or buying services (local or national). **Libraries: Type:** not open to the public. **Awards:** Lifetime Achievement. **Frequency:** annual. **Type:** recognition. **Recipient:** for a member who has made significant contribution to the association. **Telecommunication Services:** electronic mail, mcollins@bcfm.com. **Affiliated With:** Broadcast Cable Financial Management Association. **Formerly:** (1985) BCA-Credit Information; (1990) Broadcast Credit Association. **Publications:** *BCCA Credit Handbook*, annual. Manual. Credit and collection manual. **Price:** $29.95 for members; $79.95 for nonmembers ● *Credit and Collection Survey* ● *The Financial Manager for the Media Professional/Credit Topics*, bimonthly. Newsletter. **Price:** $49.00/year. **Advertising:** accepted ● *Update*, monthly. Newsletter. **Conventions/Meetings:** annual conference and seminar, held in conjunction with BCFM (exhibits) ● monthly Distance Learning - seminar, educational telephone conference forums.

553 ■ Broadcast Cable Financial Management Association (BCFM)
550 W Frontage Rd., Ste.3600
Northfield, IL 60093
Ph: (847)716-7000
Fax: (847)716-7004
E-mail: info@bcfm.com
URL: http://www.bcfm.com
Contact: Mary M. Collins, Pres./CEO
Founded: 1961. **Members:** 1,000. **Staff:** 5. **Budget:** $1,000,000. **Description:** Chief financial officers, controllers, chief accountants, credit managers, auditors, business and personnel managers, corporation officers, owners, and other executives who perform or supervise the function of financial management of radio, television, and cable television operations. Dedicated in serving top management at television, radio and cable companies and in furthering the interests of the industry. Develops and maintains progressive concepts of controllership, treasurership, and related financial management functions in the broadcasting-telecasting industry. Operates the Broadcast Cable Credit Association (see separate entry), which provides credit information on advertising agencies, advertisers or buying services. **Awards:** Avatar. **Frequency:** annual. **Type:** monetary. **Recipient:** for an industry leader. **Computer Services:** database, membership disk available at a fee. **Telecommunication Services:** electronic mail, mcollins@bcfm.com. **Committees:** Accounting Standards; Cable; Human Resources; Industry Education; Information Technology; Member Services; Membership Marketing; Music License; New Media; Programming; Radio; Tax. **Affiliated With:** Broadcast Cable Credit Association. **Formerly:** (1977) Institute of Broadcasting Financial Management; (1990) Broadcast Financial Management Association. **Publica-**

tions: *Broadcast Cable Credit Association Credit Manual.* **Price:** $29.95 for members; $75.00 for nonmembers ● *Broadcast Cable Financial Management Association—Membership Directory*, annual. **Price:** available to members only. Alternate Formats: online ● *The Financial Manager*, bimonthly. Journal. Covers accounting, FCC, personnel matters, tax, and information systems. **Price:** included in membership dues; $49.00 /year for nonmembers. **Circulation:** 2,000 ● *Operational Guidelines*, periodic. Includes information on credit and collections, broadcast accounting, internal controls, risk and insurance, trade and barter, and records retention. **Price:** $5.00/issue for members; $100.00 for nonmembers - accounting; $35.00 for nonmembers - all other guides; free for new members ● *Understanding Broadcast and Cable Finance*. Handbook. Contains information for nonfinancial radio, TV, or cable manager. **Price:** $15.00 for members; $49.95 for nonmembers ● *Update*, monthly. Newsletter. **Conventions/Meetings:** annual conference (exhibits).

554 ■ Broadcast Designer's Association (BDA)

9000 W Sunset Blvd., Ste.900
Los Angeles, CA 90069
Ph: (310)788-7600 (310)789-1509
Fax: (310)788-7616
E-mail: brett@ashyagency.com
URL: http://www.bda.tv
Contact: Brett Ashy, Chm.

Founded: 1978. **Members:** 1,800. **Membership Dues:** associate, freelance, $199 (annual) ● executive, $495 (annual) ● academic, $99 (annual) ● student, $50 (annual). **Staff:** 12. **Budget:** $5,400,000. **Multinational. Description:** Designers, artists, art directors, illustrators, photographers, animators, and other motion graphic professionals in the electronic media industry; educators and students; commercial and industrial companies that manufacture products related to design. Seeks to promote understanding between designers, clients, and management; to stimulate innovative ideas and techniques; to encourage and provide a resource for young talents; and to provide a forum for discussion on industry issues and concerns. Maintains placement service; conducts surveys and compiles statistics. **Libraries: Type:** reference. **Awards:** BDA International Design Award. **Frequency:** annual. **Type:** recognition. **Recipient:** for excellence in various categories of media design ● **Frequency:** annual. **Type:** scholarship. **Formerly:** (1998) Broadcast Designers Association International; (2000) BDA International. **Publications:** *BDA Directory/DNA*, annual. **Price:** included in membership dues ● *BDA News*, weekly. Newsletter ● *DNA*, annual. Magazine ● Also publishes a series of design books. **Conventions/Meetings:** annual meeting ● annual PROMAX/BDA Conference - seminar (exhibits).

555 ■ Broadcasters' Foundation of America

7 Lincoln Ave.
Greenwich, CT 06830
Ph: (203)862-8577
Fax: (203)629-5739
E-mail: ghastings@broadcastersfoundation.org
URL: http://broadcastersfoundation.org
Contact: Gordon H. Hastings, Pres./CEO

Founded: 1947. **Members:** 1,400. **Membership Dues:** general, $150 (annual). **Staff:** 1. **Regional Groups:** 5. **State Groups:** 2. **Description:** Provides financial assistance to broadcasters who are in acute need. **Libraries: Type:** reference. **Holdings:** 25,340; archival material, audio recordings, books, clippings, periodicals, photographs. **Subjects:** radio and television broadcasting history. **Awards:** Golden Mike Award. **Frequency:** annual. **Type:** recognition. **Recipient:** for excellence in broadcasting. **Formerly:** (1947) Twenty Year Club; (1957) Radio Pioneers Club; (1976) Broadcast Pioneers; (2006) Broadcasters' Foundation. **Publications:** *On the Air*, quarterly. Newsletter. **Circulation:** 2,500. **Conventions/Meetings:** annual Pioneer Breakfast - general assembly, in conjunction with National Association of Broadcasters - usually April in Las Vegas, NV.

556 ■ Coalition Opposing Signal Theft (COST)

1724 Massachusetts Ave. NW
Washington, DC 20036
Ph: (202)775-3684
Fax: (202)775-3696
E-mail: ocst@ncta.com
Contact: Neilda Sid, Asst. Dir.

Founded: 1986. **Description:** Participants are representatives from the cable television, sports, and film programming industries, including manufacturers, producers, and distributors of programs. Provides support to the National Cable T.V. Association's Office of Cable Signal Theft. Sends representatives to national and regional trade shows to offer information and advice regarding cable signal theft. **Affiliated With:** National Cable and Telecommunications Association. **Publications:** *Secure Signals*, as needed. Newsletter. **Price:** available to members only.

557 ■ Country Radio Broadcasters (CRB)

819 18th Ave. S
Nashville, TN 37203
Ph: (615)327-4487
Fax: (615)329-4492
E-mail: info@crb.org
URL: http://www.crb.org
Contact: Ed Salamon, Exec. Dir.

Founded: 1970. **Staff:** 4. **Budget:** $1,000,000. **Description:** Seeks to advance and promote the study of the science of broadcasting through the mutual exchange of ideas by conducting seminars and workshops, as well as providing scholarships to broadcasting students. **Awards:** Artist Humanitarian Award. **Frequency:** annual. **Type:** recognition. **Recipient:** for humanitarian achievements of a country music artist ● Career Achievement Award. **Frequency:** annual. **Type:** recognition. **Recipient:** for an individual, artist or act that has made a significant contribution to the development and promotion of country music and country radio ● Country Music DJ Hall of Fame. **Frequency:** annual. **Type:** recognition. **Recipient:** for individuals who have made significant contributions to the country radio/music industry ● Country Radio Hall of Fame. **Frequency:** annual. **Type:** recognition. **Recipient:** for an individual who has contributed to the preservation and enhancement of country music as an art form and started at least 25 years ago ● President's Award. **Frequency:** annual. **Type:** recognition. **Recipient:** for an individual who has made a significant contribution to the marketing, production, growth and development of the Country Radio Seminar ● Radio Humanitarian Award. **Frequency:** annual. **Type:** recognition. **Recipient:** for full time country radio stations for their efforts to improve the quality of life for communities they serve. **Formerly:** Organization of Country Radio Broadcasters. **Publications:** *CRB Program Book and Directory*, annual. **Advertising:** accepted ● Newsletter, quarterly. **Conventions/Meetings:** annual meeting and seminar ● seminar, for professional development.

558 ■ CTAM - Cable and Telecommunications Association for Marketing

201 N Union St., Ste.440
Alexandria, VA 22314
Ph: (703)549-4200 (703)837-6567
Fax: (703)837-6571
E-mail: info@ctam.com
URL: http://www.ctamnetforum.com/eweb/DynamicPage.aspx?site=ctamPublic&WebCode=GL00_Hom e
Contact: Char Beales, Pres./CEO

Founded: 1975. **Members:** 5,600. **Membership Dues:** national, $295 (annual) ● chapter, $25-$35 (annual). **Staff:** 34. **Budget:** $5,000,000. **Local Groups:** 19. **Description:** Network of cable and telecommunications professionals dedicated to the pursuit of marketing excellence. Provides its members with competitive marketing resources including education, research, networking and leadership opportunities. **Libraries: Type:** not open to the public. **Holdings:** 300. **Subjects:** cable and telecommunications marketing. **Awards:** Chairman's Award. **Frequency:** periodic. **Type:** recognition. **Recipient:** for extraordinary contribution to CTAM or to the industry ● CTAM Hall of Fame. **Frequency:** annual. **Type:** recognition. **Recipient:** for the most notable, most influential and most memorable marketing campaigns from cable's past and its present ● Grand TAM Award. **Frequency:** annual. **Type:** recognition. **Recipient:** to an individual who has contributed to the future of the industry through leadership, marketing and education ● Mark Award. **Frequency:** annual. **Type:** recognition. **Recipient:** for effective marketing ● One of a Kind Award. **Frequency:** periodic. **Type:** recognition. **Recipient;** to an industry executive chosen by former CTAM board members ● Rainmaker Award. **Frequency:** annual. **Type:** recognition. **Recipient:** for members who have played an essential role in supporting CTAM's priority of helping the cable business to grow ● TAMI Awards. **Frequency:** annual. **Type:** recognition. **Recipient:** for members who have contributed significantly to the overall success and growth of the organization. **Committees:** Basic Customer Growth; Customer Service; New Cable; New Revenue Sources; Pay Per View; Premium TV; Research. **Formerly:** Cable Television Administration and Marketing Society; (1998) Cable and Telecommunications: A Marketing Society; (2002) CTAM, The Marketing Society for the Cable and Telecommunications Industry. **Publications:** *CTAM Pulse*, 10/year. Magazine. Includes the results of research studies. **Price:** included in membership dues ● *CTAM Quarterly Journal.* **Price:** included in membership dues. **Advertising:** accepted. **Conventions/Meetings:** annual conference.

559 ■ Hollywood Radio and Television Society (HRTS)

13701 Riverside Dr., Ste.205
Sherman Oaks, CA 91423
Ph: (818)789-1182
Fax: (818)789-1210
E-mail: info@hrts.org
URL: http://www.hrts.org
Contact: Dave Ferrara, Exec. Dir.

Founded: 1947. **Members:** 1,000. **Membership Dues:** regular (includes $100 initiation fee), $285 (annual) ● corporate, $13,500 (annual). **Staff:** 4. **Description:** Persons involved in radio, television, broadcasting, and advertising, including program and commercial producers and radio and television networks and studios seeking to promote the broadcasting industry. Sponsors monthly luncheon featuring top industry and government speakers. Sponsors seminars on the business and creative aspects of broadcasting and competitions. Maintains film and audio library of outstanding radio and television commercials. **Awards:** International Broadcasting Award. **Frequency:** annual. **Type:** recognition. **Recipient:** for the best radio and television commercials. **Affiliated With:** American Advertising Federation; International Radio and Television Society Foundation. **Publications:** *Hollywood Radio and Television Society—Roster*, annual. Directory ● *International Broadcasting Awards Book*, annual ● *Society Views*, quarterly. Newsletter. Alternate Formats: online ● *SPIKE*, quarterly. Journal.

560 ■ International Academy of Television Arts and Sciences

888 7th St., 5th Fl.
New York, NY 10019
Ph: (212)489-6969
Fax: (212)489-6557
E-mail: camille.bidermann-roizen@iemmys.tv
URL: http://www.iemmys.tv
Contact: Ms. Camille Bidermann-Roizen, Sr. VP/Exec. Dir.

Founded: 1968. **Members:** 430. **Membership Dues:** regular, $1,000 (annual). **Staff:** 6. **Multinational. Description:** Officers of organizations active in the international television community. Seeks to further the arts and sciences of international television by bestowing an Emmy Award for excellence in television programming in the categories of Drama Series, TV Movie, Comedy, Non-Scripted Entertainment, Documentary, Arts Programming, and Children and Young People. Provides forum for discussion of issues affecting the television industry internationally.

Awards: George Movshon Fellowship. **Frequency:** annual. **Type:** fellowship. **Recipient:** for young professionals from foreign countries to come to the U.S. to learn about the U.S. television industry ● Joan Wilson Memorial Scholarship. **Type:** scholarship. **Recipient:** for a student or professional engaged in writing, producing, or directing drama for television. **Formerly:** (2004) International Council - National Academy of Television Arts and Sciences. **Publications:** *International Emmy Almanac*, annual. Magazine. Covers the television industry globally, focusing on the International Emmy Awards. Includes statistics, calendar of events, and advertisers' index. **Price:** $7. 50/copy. **Advertising:** accepted. **Conventions/Meetings:** annual International Emmy Awards Gala - meet - always November, New York City, NY.

561 ■ International Association of Broadcast Monitors (IABM)
c/o Clara McNamara, Exec. Dir./Librarian
PO Box 422
Meriden, NH 03770
Ph: (603)469-3054
Free: (800)236-1741
Fax: (603)469-3135
E-mail: info@iabm.com
URL: http://www.iabm.com
Contact: Clara McNamara, Exec. Dir./Librarian
Founded: 1981. **Members:** 130. **Membership Dues:** monitoring company/associate, $550 (annual) ● affiliate, $50 (annual) ● supporting, $650 (annual). **Staff:** 1. **Multinational. Description:** Companies that monitor radio and/or television transmissions, newspaper clippings, and advertising checking; interested others. Provides a forum for the exchange of information in the broadcast monitoring industry; facilitates cooperative action among members. **Publications:** Membership Directory, annual. Contains list of members. **Conventions/Meetings:** annual conference and convention, with seminar - always October ● annual meeting - regional meetings every April or May held in Eastern US, Western US and Europe.

562 ■ International Nanocasting Association (INA)
1010 N Central Ave.
Glendale, CA 91202
Ph: (320)210-1857
E-mail: info@nanocasting.org
URL: http://www.nanocasting.org
Contact: Valerie Geller, Contact
Multinational. Description: Accelerates the growth of commercial Internet radio and nanocasting. Supports the commercialization and expansion of Internet radio and podcasting. Promotes exchange of insight, knowledge and strategy about how to develop a viable market for Internet radio and podcasting. Identifies and promotes best practices in the industry.

563 ■ International Radio and Television Society Foundation (IRTS)
420 Lexington Ave., Ste.1601
New York, NY 10170
Ph: (212)867-6650
Fax: (212)867-6653
E-mail: membership@irts.org
URL: http://www.irts.org
Contact: Joyce M. Tudryn, Pres.
Founded: 1952. **Members:** 1,900. **Membership Dues:** sponsor, $100-$149 (annual) ● friend, $50-$74 (annual) ● associate, $75-$99 (annual) ● patron, $150-$499 (annual) ● benefactor, $500-$999 (annual) ● pacesetter (minimum), $1,000 (annual). **Staff:** 8. **Description:** Individuals interested in management, sales, or executive production in the radio, television, and cable industries and their allied fields. Seeks to educate members through seminars. Conducts summer internships for college students majoring in communications. **Awards:** Barry Sherman Fellowship. **Frequency:** annual. **Type:** fellowship. **Recipient:** for outstanding students ● Coltrin Case Study Award. **Frequency:** annual. **Type:** recognition. **Recipient:** to the winning team of the Case Study Competition ● IRTS Foundation Award. **Frequency:** annual. **Type:** recognition. **Recipient:** to an outstanding media figure or personality ● IRTS Gold Medal. **Frequency:** annual. **Type:** medal. **Recipient:** for outstanding contribution to or achievement in broadcasting, broadcast advertising, or cable ● IRTS Stanton Fellow Award. **Frequency:** annual. **Type:** recognition. **Recipient:** for outstanding contribution to electronic media education ● Stephen K. Nenno Inspirational Fellow Award. **Frequency:** annual. **Type:** recognition. **Recipient:** for an inspirational student leader ● Stephen M. Coltrin Professor of the Year. **Frequency:** annual. **Type:** recognition. **Recipient:** for outstanding contribution to communications education. **Affiliated With:** National Broadcasting Society - Alpha Epsilon Rho. **Formed by Merger of:** Radio Executives Club; American Television Society. **Formerly:** (1962) Radio and Television Executive Society; (1994) International Radio and Television Society. **Publications:** *International Radio and Television Society Foundation—Roster Yearbook*, annual. Contains listing of current membership and annual events. **Price:** included in membership dues. **Circulation:** 3,000. **Advertising:** accepted. **Conventions/Meetings:** luncheon and dinner, holds approximately 45 events each season ● annual seminar.

564 ■ Junior Hollywood Radio and Television Society (JHRTS)
PO Box 16173
Beverly Hills, CA 90209
Fax: (818)789-1210
E-mail: membership@jhrts.com
URL: http://www.jhrts.com
Contact: Malene Sam, Co-Pres.
Founded: 2000. **Membership Dues:** regular, $40 (annual). **Description:** Represents assistants, coordinators, and associates from all areas of the entertainment industry. Promotes professional development of its members through facilitation of lectures and sessions. Fosters fellowship among its members. **Telecommunication Services:** electronic mail, malene.sam@cbs.com. **Affiliated With:** Hollywood Radio and Television Society.

565 ■ Manufacturers Radio Frequency Advisory Committee (MRFAC)
899-A Harrison Dr. SE
Leesburg, VA 20175
Ph: (703)669-0320
Free: (800)262-9206
Fax: (703)669-0322
E-mail: info@mrfac.com
URL: http://www.mrfac.com
Contact: Marv McKinley, Pres.
Founded: 1970. **Description:** An authorized Federal Communications Commission frequency coordinator for communications and operating systems below 800 megahertz, providing radio frequency coordination to the nation's manufacturers and private interests. **Telecommunication Services:** electronic mail, jpakla@mrfac.com. **Committees:** Computer; Frequency Coordination; Publicity; Regulatory. **Formerly:** (1954) National Association of Manufacturers. **Publications:** *MRFAC Newsletter*, monthly. **Conventions/Meetings:** meeting - 3/year.

566 ■ Media Rating Council (MRC)
370 Lexington Ave., Ste.902
New York, NY 10017
Ph: (212)972-0300
Fax: (212)972-2786
E-mail: staff@mediaratingcouncil.org
URL: http://www.mediaratingcouncil.org
Contact: George W. Ivie, Exec. Dir.
Founded: 1964. **Members:** 97. **Staff:** 3. **Description:** Broadcast and cable trade associations, media owners, advertising agencies, cable networks, and national networks including National Association of Broadcasters, Television Bureau of Advertising, Radio Advertising Bureau, Cable Advertising Bureau (see separate entries). Establishes minimum standards for electronic media ratings surveys. Commissions audits by CPA firms of the collection and processing of data gathered by audience measurement services, including A.C. Nielsen, Arbitron, Statistical Research Inc., and Mediafax. **Convention/Meeting:** none. **Affiliated With:** National Association of Broadcasters; Radio Advertising Bureau; Television Bureau of Advertising. **Formerly:** (1982) Broadcast Rating Council; (1998) Electronic Media Rating Council.

567 ■ National Academy of Television Arts and Sciences (NATAS)
5220 Lankershim Blvd.
North Hollywood, CA 91601-3109
Ph: (818)754-2810 (818)754-2800
Fax: (818)761-2827
E-mail: pprice@emmyonline.tv
URL: http://www.emmyonline.org
Contact: Peter O. Price, Pres./CEO
Founded: 1947. **Members:** 14,000. **Staff:** 10. **Local Groups:** 17. **Description:** Persons engaged in television performing, art directing, cinematography, directing, taping, tape editing, choreography, engineering, film editing, music, production, and writing. Advances the arts and sciences of television and fosters creative leadership in the television industry for artistic, cultural, educational, and technological progress; recognizes outstanding achievements in the television industry by conferring annual awards for excellence (Emmy Awards). Utilizes a television film and tape library at UCLA, California. Sponsors workshops and seminars; maintains library. **Computer Services:** database, Emmy Awards Directory. **Additional Websites:** http://www.emmys.org. **Committees:** Awards; International; Issues; Legal. **Publications:** *Local Newsletter*, bimonthly ● *NATAS News*, quarterly. **Price:** $25.00/year. ISSN: 1062-9637. **Circulation:** 12,000 ● *National Emmy Awards Directory*, periodic ● *Television Quarterly*. Trade publication. Includes articles and book reviews. **Price:** $25.00/year; $6.00/issue. ISSN: 0040-2796. **Circulation:** 12,000. **Advertising:** accepted. Alternate Formats: microform. **Conventions/Meetings:** meeting - always June and November, New York City.

568 ■ National Association of Black Owned Broadcasters (NABOB)
1155 Connecticut Ave. NW, Ste.600
Washington, DC 20036
Ph: (202)463-8970
Fax: (202)429-0657
E-mail: nabob@nabob.org
URL: http://www.nabob.org
Contact: James L. Winston, Exec. Dir./Gen. Counsel
Founded: 1976. **Members:** 150. **Membership Dues:** standard (maximum), $5,000 (annual) ● associate, $450-$2,000 (annual) ● individual, $150 (annual) ● student, $50 (biennial). **Staff:** 3. **Regional Groups:** 5. **Description:** Black broadcast station owners; black formatted stations not owned or controlled by blacks; organizations having an interest in the black consumer market or black broadcast industry; individuals interested in becoming owners; and communications schools, departments, and professional groups and associations. Represents the interests of existing and potential black radio and television stations. Works with the Office of Federal Procurement Policy to determine which government contracting major advertisers and advertising agencies are complying with government initiatives to increase the amount of advertising dollars received by minority-owned firms. Conducts lobbying activities; provides legal representation for the protection of minority ownership policies. Sponsors annual Communications Awards Dinner each March. Conducts workshops; compiles statistics. **Awards: Frequency:** annual. **Type:** recognition. **Recipient:** to the most prestigious names in entertainment, communications and public service. **Computer Services:** Mailing lists, black-owned broadcast facilities. **Divisions:** Information. **Also Known As:** National Black Owned Broadcasters Association. **Publications:** *Black-Owned Station Directory*, quarterly ● *NABOB News*, monthly. Newsletter. **Conventions/Meetings:** meeting - always March and September.

569 ■ National Association of Broadcasters (NAB)
1771 N St. NW
Washington, DC 20036
Ph: (202)429-5300
Fax: (202)429-4199

E-mail: nab@nab.org
URL: http://www.nab.org
Contact: David K. Rehr, CEO/Pres.
Founded: 1922. **Members:** 7,500. **Membership Dues:** non-commercial radio station, $360 (annual) ● commercial radio station, $45-$750 (monthly) ● associate, $500-$3,000 (annual) ● international station, $500 (annual) ● public television, $83 (monthly). **Staff:** 165. **Description:** Representatives of radio and television stations and networks; associate members include producers of equipment and programs. Seeks to ensure the viability, strength, and success of free, over-the-air broadcasters; serves as an information resource to the industry. Monitors and reports on events regarding radio and television broadcasting. Maintains Broadcasting Hall of Fame. Offers minority placement service and employment clearinghouse. **Libraries: Type:** reference. **Holdings:** 10,000; archival material, books, clippings, monographs, periodicals. **Subjects:** broadcasting. **Awards:** Belva B. Brissett Award. **Frequency:** annual. **Type:** recognition ● Best of the Best Award. **Frequency:** annual. **Type:** recognition ● Crystal Awards. **Frequency:** annual. **Type:** recognition ● Distinguished Service Award. **Frequency:** annual. **Type:** recognition ● Engineering Achievement in Radio Award. **Frequency:** annual. **Type:** recognition ● Engineering Achievement in Television Award. **Frequency:** annual. **Type:** recognition ● **Frequency:** annual. **Type:** grant. **Recipient:** for research in broadcasting ● Grover Cobb Memorial Award. **Frequency:** annual. **Type:** recognition ● Mal Beville Award. **Frequency:** annual. **Type:** recognition ● Marconi Radio Award. **Frequency:** annual. **Type:** recognition ● National Radio Award. **Frequency:** annual. **Type:** recognition ● Service to Children Television Awards. **Frequency:** annual. **Type:** recognition ● Spirit of Broadcasting Award. **Type:** recognition. **Committees:** Children's Television; Future of Radio Broadcasting; Future of TV Broadcasting; On-Air Initiatives. **Absorbed:** (1951) Television Broadcasters Association; (1985) Daytime Broadcasters Association; (1986) National Radio Broadcasters Association. **Formerly:** (1958) National Association of Radio and Television Broadcasters. **Publications:** *Broadcast Engineering Conference Proceedings*, annual ● *Member Services Catalog*, annual. Serves as a resource guide of available products and services. ● *RadioWeek*, weekly. Provides information to members. **Advertising:** accepted ● *TV Today*, weekly. Provides information to members. **Advertising:** accepted ● Monographs. **Conventions/Meetings:** annual convention (exhibits) - always held in Las Vegas, NV during April ● annual Future's Summit - meeting ● annual trade show (exhibits).

570 ■ National Association of Farm Broadcasting (NAFB)

PO Box 500
Platte City, MO 64079
Ph: (816)431-4032
Fax: (816)431-4087
E-mail: info@nafb.com
URL: http://www.nafb.com
Contact: Bill O'Neill, Exec. Dir.
Founded: 1944. **Members:** 701. **Membership Dues:** student, $25 (annual) ● Allied Industry Council, $200 (annual) ● Management Council, $100 (annual). **Staff:** 5. **Budget:** $1,000,000. **Regional Groups:** 3. **Description:** Radio and television farm directors actively engaged in broadcasting or telecasting farm news and information; associate members are persons with agricultural interests who are affiliated with advertising agencies, government agencies, farm organizations, and commercial firms. Works to improve quantity and quality of farm programming and serve as a clearinghouse for new ideas in farm broadcasting. Provides placement information. **Telecommunication Services:** electronic mail, bill@nafb.com. **Committees:** Awards; Broadcast/Promotion; Convention Courtesy; Ethics; Farm City Week; Farm Safety; Marketing and Promotion Advisory; New Members; NFBS; Past Presidents; Photography; Professional Improvement; Publicity; Radio; Resolutions; Strategic Planning; Television; Trade Talk; Washington Watch. **Formerly:** (1956) National Association of Radio Farm Directors; (1964) National Association of Television-Radio Farm Directors; (2005) National Association of Farm Broadcasters. **Publications:** *Chats*, monthly. Newsletter. **Circulation:** 1,000 ● *National Association of Farm Broadcasters—Directory*, annual. **Conventions/Meetings:** annual Trade Talk - convention (exhibits) - always November.

571 ■ National Association of Television Program Executives (NATPE)

5757 Wilshire Blvd., Penthouse 10
Los Angeles, CA 90036-3681
Ph: (310)453-4440 (310)857-1621
Fax: (310)453-5258
E-mail: info@natpe.org
URL: http://www.natpe.org
Contact: Rick Feldman, Pres./CEO
Founded: 1963. **Members:** 4,100. **Membership Dues:** corporate, $700 (annual) ● professional, $195 (annual) ● educational, $95 (annual). **Staff:** 20. **Multinational. Description:** Program directors of television stations, networks, and multiple station groups; persons engaged in television programming (including cable, DBS and multimedia) or production; representatives of related businesses, such as station representatives, advertising agencies, film and package show producers and distributors and research organizations. Seeks to contribute to the improvement of television programming by providing a forum for discussion of ideas and exchange of information concerning programming, production and related fields. Maintains NATPE Educational Foundation. Sponsors faculty development program, seminars and international exchange program. Sponsors six faculty internships. **Awards:** Brandon Tartikoff Legacy Awards. **Frequency:** annual. **Type:** recognition. **Recipient:** for television professionals who exhibit extraordinary contributions in the process of creating television programming ● Faculty Development Grant. **Frequency:** annual. **Type:** grant. **Recipient:** to college and university educators in order that they may gain first hand experience in a professional media environment. **Publications:** *Guide to North American Media*, semiannual. **Circulation:** 5,000 ● *NATPE Show Guide*, annual. **Circulation:** 10,000. **Conventions/Meetings:** annual conference (exhibits) - always January ● meeting.

572 ■ National Broadcast Association for Community Affairs (NBACA)

Address Unknown since 2007
Founded: 1974. **Members:** 285. **Membership Dues:** radio, $95 (annual) ● television, $195 (annual) ● partners, $235 (annual). **Staff:** 2. **Budget:** $200,000. **Regional Groups:** 6. **Description:** Professionals from radio and television industries seeking to promote public affairs programming and improve community relations. Offers educational programs. **Awards:** Community Service Award. **Frequency:** annual. **Type:** recognition. **Recipient:** for outstanding performance in addressing community concerns. **Publications:** *NBACA News*, quarterly. Newsletter. Provides information on industry issues, profiles of successful public affairs projects, and how-to articles. **Circulation:** 285. **Conventions/Meetings:** annual convention.

573 ■ National Cable and Telecommunications Association (NCTA)

25 Massachusetts Ave. NW, Ste.100
Washington, DC 20001
Ph: (202)222-2300 (202)222-2500
Fax: (202)222-2514
E-mail: webmaster@ncta.com
URL: http://www.ncta.com
Contact: Kyle E. McSlarrow, Pres./CEO
Founded: 1952. **Membership Dues:** affiliate, $1,000 (annual) ● associate (maximum; based on total gross revenue from direct and indirect U.S. sales), $28,000 (annual) ● cable programmer (maximum; based on gross sales), $82,112 (annual) ● cable system (maximum; based on quarterly revenues), $31,770 (annual). **Staff:** 100. **Description:** Franchised cable operators, programmers, and cable networks; associate members are cable hardware suppliers and distributors; affiliate members are brokerage and law firms and financial institutions; state and regional cable television associations cooperate, but are not affiliated, with the organization. Serves as national medium for exchange of experiences and opinions through research, study, discussion, and publications. Represents the cable industry before Congress, the Federal Communications Commission and various courts on issues of primary importance. Conducts research program in conjunction with National Academy of Cable Programming. Sponsors, in conjunction with Motion Picture Association of America, the Coalition Opposing Signal Theft, an organization designed to deter cable signal theft and to develop anti-piracy materials. Provides promotional aids and information on legal, legislative and regulatory matters. Compiles statistics. **Awards: Type:** recognition. **Recipient:** for outstanding contributions by individuals to the growth and development of the industry. **Committees:** Engineering; Independent Operators; Music Licensing; National Satellite; Network ACE; Regulatory Policy; State/Local Government; Telecommunications. **Affiliated With:** Motion Picture Association of America. **Formerly:** (1969) National Community Television Association; (2001) National Cable Television Association. **Publications:** *Cable Developments*, annual. Serves as a reference guide. ● *Cable Industry Overview*, semiannual. Report. **Conventions/Meetings:** annual National Cable Show - convention, exposition and tradeshow (exhibits).

574 ■ National Cable Television Institute (NCTI)

9697 E Mineral Ave.
Centennial, CO 80112
Ph: (303)797-9393
Free: (866)575-7206
Fax: (303)797-9394
E-mail: info@jonesncti.com
URL: http://www.ncti.com
Contact: Thomas W. Brooksher, Pres./CEO
Founded: 1968. **Staff:** 30. **Description:** Provides comprehensive broadband training for the cable television industry. Offers career training resources and courses in areas ranging from customer service procedures to optical fiber system design, installation, and maintenance. **Additional Websites:** http://www.jonesncti.com. **Publications:** *Spanish/English CATV Dictionary* (in English and Spanish). Book. Contains illustrated dictionary of CATV and Broadband terminology describing numerous cable television terms. **Price:** $29.95 plus shipping and handling. **Conventions/Meetings:** workshop, CATV/broadband overview and cable TV design workshops.

575 ■ National Federation of Community Broadcasters (NFCB)

1970 Broadway, Ste.1000
Oakland, CA 94612
Ph: (510)451-8200
Fax: (510)451-8208
E-mail: comments@nfcb.org
URL: http://www.nfcb.org
Contact: Carol Pierson, Pres./CEO
Founded: 1975. **Members:** 200. **Membership Dues:** individual, $125 (annual) ● organization (based on budget), $225-$950 (annual) ● participant (maximum; based on 1.1&percent; of a station's yearly income), $3,650 (annual). **Staff:** 5. **Budget:** $300,000. **National Groups:** 200. **Description:** Independent, community-licensed radio and radio production organizations. Fosters the development of public policy at the legislative, regulatory and administrative levels; aids the growth of community-oriented radio stations and advances the public interest in mass communications; seeks an equitable distribution of federal funds appropriated for noncommercial broadcasting and develops support for community-oriented broadcast projects; facilitates the exchange of program materials, information and technical expertise; assists in the organization and expansion of new and innovative broadcast stations throughout the U.S. Provides services and consultation. **Awards:** Community Radio Program Award. **Frequency:** annual. **Type:** recognition. **Recipient:** for outstanding

programs produced by and/or aired on community licensed radio stations in areas of public affairs, news and entertainment ● Volunteer of the Year. **Frequency:** annual. **Type:** recognition. **Recipient:** for a station volunteer who provided extraordinary service over a significant period of time to the station and the community. **Telecommunication Services:** electronic mail, carol@nfcb.org. **Projects:** Low Power FM; National Youth in Radio Training; Rural Programming Initiative. **Publications:** *Audiocraft: Tools and Techniques of Audio Production*, monthly. Book. Includes calendar of events, listing of job openings, and legislative and regulatory updates. **Price:** $33.00 for nonmembers; $25.00 for members ● *Community Radio News*, monthly. Newsletter. Includes calendar of events, listing of job openings, and legislative and regulatory updates. **Price:** $75.00/year ● *The NFCB Public Radio Legal Handbook: A Guide to FCC Rules and Regulations.* **Price:** $75.00 hard copy for members; $129.00 hard copy for nonmembers; $45.00 online subscription for members; $70.00 online subscription for nonmembers. Alternate Formats: online ● *NFCB's Guide to Underwriting for Public Radio.* Handbook. **Price:** $20.00 for members; $35.00 for nonmembers ● *Starting an LPFM Station.* Book. **Price:** $50.00 plus shipping and handling. **Conventions/Meetings:** annual Community Radio Conference - competition, for community radio stations/ program producers (exhibits) ● workshop.

576 ■ National Translator Association (NTA)
5611 Kendall Ct., Ste.2
Arvada, CO 80002
Ph: (303)465-5742 (303)378-8209
Fax: (303)940-8442
E-mail: stcl@comcast.net
URL: http://www.tvfmtranslators.com
Contact: Byron W. St. Clair, Pres.
Founded: 1967. **Members:** 200. **Membership Dues:** general, $200 (annual) ● sustaining organization (minimum), $500 (annual). **Staff:** 3. **Description:** Operators of translator television and FM stations; manufacturers and suppliers of equipment, as well as licensure applicants. Promotes and preserves the transmission of television and FM signals to all parts of the U.S., with emphasis upon service to unserved and underserved communities. Sponsors seminars conducted by professional leaders of industry and government on topics such as engineering and technical requirements, issues of channel allocation, ownership policies, legal concerns, operating procedures and programming options. **Formerly:** (1984) National Translator LPTV Association. **Publications:** *NTA Translator*, quarterly. Newsletter. **Conventions/Meetings:** annual convention.

577 ■ PROMAX
9000 W Sunset Blvd., Ste.900
Los Angeles, CA 90069
Ph: (310)788-7600 (310)789-1505
Fax: (310)788-7616
E-mail: michael.d.benson@abc.com
URL: http://www.promax.tv
Contact: Mike Benson, Chm.
Founded: 1956. **Members:** 2,000. **Membership Dues:** executive, $495 (annual) ● associate, $199 (annual) ● academic, $99 (annual) ● student, $50 (annual). **Staff:** 12. **Budget:** $4,400,000. **Multinational. Description:** Advertising, public relations, and promotion managers of cable, radio, and television stations, systems and networks; syndicators. Seeks to: advance the role and increase the effectiveness of promotion and marketing within the industry, related industries, and educational communities. Conducts workshops and weekly fax service for members. Operates employment service. Maintains speakers' bureau, hall of fame, and resource center with print, audio, and visual materials. **Awards:** Muse Award. **Frequency:** annual. **Type:** recognition. **Recipient:** for excellence in promotion and marketing. **Computer Services:** Online services, message board. **Formerly:** (1985) Broadcasters' Promotion Association; (1993) Broadcast Promotion and Marketing Executives; (2003) PROMAX International. **Publications:** *Image DNA*, 3/year. Magazine. Includes news profiles, editorials, features, and technologies that affect the electronic media; membership information; interchange of ideas. **Price:** included in membership dues. **Circulation:** 2,000. **Advertising:** accepted ● *PROMAX—Membership Roster and Service Directory*, annual. Includes product/service listings arranged geographically and services, membership, and company indexes. **Price:** free for members. **Circulation:** 2,000. **Advertising:** accepted ● Book. Covers broadcast advertising and promotions. **Conventions/Meetings:** annual conference.

578 ■ Public Broadcasting Management Association
PO Box 50008
Columbia, SC 29250
Ph: (803)799-5517
Fax: (803)771-4831
E-mail: chuck@pbma.org
URL: http://www.pbma.org
Contact: Chuck McConnell, Exec. Dir.
Founded: 1981. **Members:** 300. **Budget:** $230,000. **Description:** Represents finance, human resources, information systems, and administrative managers in public broadcasting. **Formerly:** (1997) Public Telecommunications Financial Management Association. **Publications:** *BottomLine*, weekly. Newsletter. Alternate Formats: online. **Conventions/Meetings:** annual conference, tabletops by vendors serving the field (exhibits).

579 ■ Public Radio News Directors Incorporated (PRNDI)
c/o Jonathan Ahl, Treas.
1501 W Bradley Ave.
Peoria, IL 61625
Ph: (309)677-2773
Fax: (309)677-3462
E-mail: ahl@bradley.edu
URL: http://www.prndi.org
Contact: Jonathan Ahl, Treas.
Founded: 1985. **Members:** 100. **Membership Dues:** independent producer/educator/network personnel/ other news personnel, $90 (annual) ● sponsor, $190 (annual) ● 5 or more news staff, $200 (annual) ● 3 to 4 news staff, $150 (annual) ● 1 or 2 news staff, $120 (annual). **Budget:** $50,000. **Description:** Conducts educational programs; holds competitions. **Libraries: Type:** open to the public. **Holdings:** archival material. **Awards:** PRNDI Award of Journalistic Excellence. **Frequency:** annual. **Type:** recognition. **Publications:** Newsletter, quarterly. **Conventions/ Meetings:** annual conference - July.

580 ■ Radio-Television Correspondents Association (RTCA)
c/o Senate Radio-TV Gallery
U.S. Capitol, Rm. S-325
Washington, DC 20510
Ph: (202)224-6421
Fax: (202)224-4882
E-mail: mike_mastrian@saa.senate.gov
URL: http://www.senate.gov/galleries/radiotv
Contact: Michael J. Mastrian, Dir.
Founded: 1939. **Members:** 3,000. **Description:** Comprises of correspondents, reporters, and news analysts assigned to cover Congress for radio and television broadcasting stations and networks. **Awards:** Joan Shorenstein Barone Award. **Frequency:** annual. **Type:** monetary. **Recipient:** for excellence in Washington-based national affairs/ public policy reporting. **Formerly:** Radio Correspondents Association.

581 ■ Radio-Television News Directors Association (RTNDA)
1600 K St. NW, Ste.700
Washington, DC 20006-2806
Ph: (202)659-6510 (202)467-5214
Free: (800)80-RTNDA
Fax: (202)223-4007
E-mail: rtnda@rtnda.org
URL: http://rtnda.org
Contact: Barbara Cochran, Pres.
Founded: 1946. **Members:** 3,600. **Membership Dues:** radio news director/manager, educator, $130 (annual) ● radio news staff, $110 (annual) ● TV news director/manager, associate, $190 (annual) ● TV news staff, $140 (annual) ● online and emerging media news professional, $135 (annual) ● new professional, $85 (annual) ● student, $65 (annual) ● government, $175 (annual) ● retired, $60 (annual) ● associate, $525 (annual). **Staff:** 15. **Budget:** $3,250,000. **Description:** Comprises of heads of news departments for broadcast and cable stations and networks; associate members are journalists engaged in the preparation and presentation of broadcast news and teachers of electronic journalism; other members represent industry services, public relations departments of business firms, public relations firms, and networks. Works to improve standards of electronic journalism; defends rights of journalists to access news; promotes journalism training to meet specific needs of the industry. Operates placement service and speakers' bureau. **Awards:** Edward R. Murrow Award. **Frequency:** annual. **Type:** recognition. **Recipient:** for news reporting and outstanding contribution to electronic journalism ● Paul White Award. **Frequency:** annual. **Type:** recognition. **Recipient:** for an individual's lifetime contribution to electronic journalism ● RTANDA/UNITY Award. **Frequency:** annual. **Type:** recognition. **Recipient:** to news organizations that show an ongoing commitment to covering the diversity of the communities they serve ● RTNDA Rob Downey Citation. **Frequency:** annual. **Type:** recognition. **Recipient:** for exceptional service to the RTNDA board of directors. **Committees:** Career Information; Freedom of Scholarship. **Formerly:** (1952) National Association of Radio News Directors. **Publications:** *Careers in Radio and Television.* Booklet. Describes careers. ● *Job Bulletin*, biweekly. **Price:** included in membership dues ● *Radio-Television News Directors Association—Membership Directory and Resource Guide*, semiannual. **Price:** available to members only ● *RTNDA Communicator*, monthly. Magazine. Covers radio and television journalism as well as industry activities. **Price:** included in membership dues. ISSN: 0033-7153. **Circulation:** 4,400. **Advertising:** accepted ● Brochures. **Conventions/Meetings:** annual international conference (exhibits) ● seminar ● workshop.

582 ■ Society of Broadcast Engineers (SBE)
9102 N Meridian St., Ste.150
Indianapolis, IN 46260
Ph: (317)846-9000
Fax: (317)846-9120
E-mail: jporay@sbe.org
URL: http://www.sbe.org
Contact: John L. Poray CAE, Exec. Dir.
Founded: 1964. **Members:** 5,700. **Membership Dues:** individual, reinstatement, associate, $63 (annual) ● student, $20 (annual) ● youth, $10 (annual) ● sustaining, $575 (annual). **Staff:** 6. **Budget:** $681,000. **Local Groups:** 107. **Multinational. Description:** Broadcast engineers, students, and broadcast professionals in closely allied fields. Promotes professional abilities of members and provides information exchange. Provides support to local chapters. Maintains certification program; represents members' interests before the Federal Communications Commission and other governmental and industrial groups. Offers educational workshops and seminars. Provides volunteer frequency coordination service for the nation's broadcasters. **Libraries: Type:** not open to the public. **Holdings:** 13; video recordings. **Subjects:** technical/regulatory issues. **Awards:** Broadcast Engineer of the Year. **Frequency:** annual. **Type:** recognition. **Recipient:** for broadcasting achievement ● Educator of the Year. **Frequency:** annual. **Type:** recognition ● Ennes Scholarship. **Frequency:** annual. **Type:** scholarship. **Recipient:** for interest in broadcast engineering career ● Fellow. **Frequency:** annual. **Type:** fellowship ● Technology Award. **Frequency:** annual. **Type:** recognition. **Recipient:** for outstanding product development using latest technology. **Computer Services:** Online services, job listings, resume service. **Telecommunication Services:** electronic mail, mclappe@sbe.org. **Committees:** Awards; Certification; Chapter Liaison; Conference; EAS; Education; Electronic Communications; FCC Liaison;

Finance; Frequency Coordination; Futures; Industry Relations; International; Membership; Nominations; Publications; Sustaining Membership. **Publications:** *Chief Radio Operator Handbook*. Manual. **Price:** $35.00 for members; $65.00 for nonmembers ● *SBE Guide to Writing Station Operation Manuals*. **Price:** $52.00 ● *SBE Handbook for Radio Operators*. **Price:** $42.00 ● *SBE Introduction to DTV-RF*. Manual ● *SBE Membership Directory*, annual. Lists members alphabetically and geographically. **Price:** 1st copy free for members; $35.00/additional copy for members. **Circulation:** 5,600. **Advertising:** accepted ● *SBE Signal*, bimonthly. Newsletter. Contains information on SBE programs, issues, and individuals. **Price:** included in membership dues, available to members only. **Circulation:** 5,600. **Advertising:** accepted ● *SBE Television Operators Handbook* ● *Short Circuits*, monthly. Newsletter. Contains information for members and non-members. Alternate Formats: online. **Conventions/Meetings:** annual conference, broadcast equipment trade show (exhibits).

583 ■ Television Operators Caucus (TOC)
c/o Mary Jo Manning, Coor.
1776 K St. NW
Washington, DC 20006
Ph: (202)719-7090
Fax: (202)719-7049
E-mail: mmanning@wrf.com
Contact: Mary Jo Manning, Coor.
Founded: 1984. **Description:** Participants are executive officers in charge of operating full-service television station groups in the U.S. Provides forum for the definition and discussion of public policy regulatory and other issues faced by members. Conducts activities on behalf of members.

584 ■ Traffic Directors Guild of America (TDGA)
26000 Avenida Aeropuerto No. 114
San Juan Capistrano, CA 92675
Ph: (949)429-7063
Fax: (509)471-5765
E-mail: tdga@earthlink.net
URL: http://www.tdga.org
Contact: Larry Keene, CEO
Membership Dues: primary, $37 (annual) ● primary, $67 (biennial). **Description:** Fosters pride in the profession of Traffic Director. Promotes the contributions provided to the Radio and Television Broadcasting Industry. Seeks to enhance careers through information, cooperative services and education. **Telecommunication Services:** electronic mail, larrykeene@earthlink.net. **Publications:** Reports.

585 ■ Women in Cable Telecommunications (WICT)
PO Box 791305
Baltimore, MD 21279-1305
Ph: (703)234-9810 (703)234-9801
Fax: (703)817-1595
E-mail: bfmosley@wict.org
URL: http://www.wict.org
Contact: Benita Fitzgerald Mosley, Pres./CEO
Founded: 1979. **Members:** 5,000. **Membership Dues:** entry level, $75 (annual) ● regular, $175 (annual) ● executive, $275 (annual) ● full-time student, $35 (annual). **Staff:** 16. **Budget:** $1,800,000. **Regional Groups:** 22. **Description:** Empowers and educates women to achieve their professional goals by providing opportunities for leadership, networking and advocacy. **Awards:** Accolades. **Frequency:** annual. **Type:** recognition. **Recipient:** for individuals who significantly influence customers, subscribers, employees and viewers in the industry through their passion, presence and power ● Millennium Award. **Frequency:** semiannual. **Type:** recognition. **Programs:** ESPN Coaching; Executive Mentoring; Mentoring. **Formerly:** (1994) Women in Cable. **Publications:** *The Catalyst*. Newsletter. Alternate Formats: online ● *Insights*, quarterly. Newsletter. **Circulation:** 3,500 ● *WICT Wire*. Newsletter. Alternate Formats: online ● Membership Directory, annual. **Circulation:** 4,000. **Advertising:** accepted. **Conventions/Meetings:** annual Women's Leadership Summit - conference.

Building Industries

586 ■ Affordable Housing Tax Credit Coalition (AHTCC)
1900 K St. NW, Ste.1200
Washington, DC 20006
Ph: (202)419-2025
Fax: (202)828-3738
E-mail: info@taxcreditcoalition.org
URL: http://www.taxcreditcoalition.org
Contact: Victoria E. Spielman, Exec. Dir.
Founded: 1988. **Members:** 115. **Membership Dues:** public agency, nonprofit developer, service provider, $500 (annual) ● professional, $3,500 (annual) ● developer, $3,000 (annual) ● investor, $6,000 (annual) ● broker, lender, $75,000 (annual) ● syndicator, $15,000 (annual). **Staff:** 3. **Budget:** $250,000. **Description:** Developers, syndicators, and other building industries and nonprofit organizations concerned with the low-income housing tax credit, which was established on a temporary basis in 1988. Promotes permanent extension of the low-income housing tax credit, which was achieved in 1993. Seeks to insure passage of legislation favorable to members in all matters relating to the low-income housing tax credit. Represents members' interests before government agencies and industry organizations; conducts educational programs for tax credit professionals; sponsors competitions. **Libraries:** **Type:** by appointment only. **Holdings:** audio recordings, video recordings. **Subjects:** low-income housing tax credit. **Awards:** Charles L. Edson Tax Credit Excellence Awards. **Frequency:** annual. **Type:** monetary. **Recipient:** for the most outstanding Low Income Housing Tax Credit (LIHTC) projects. **Publications:** *Preserver*, monthly. Newsletter. **Price:** available to members only ● Brochure. **Conventions/Meetings:** quarterly board meeting.

587 ■ Air Barrier Association of America (ABAA)
1600 Boston-Providence Hwy.
Walpole, MA 02081
Free: (866)956-5888
Fax: (866)956-5819
E-mail: abaa@airbarrier.org
URL: http://www.airbarrier.org
Contact: Paul J. Fox CDT, Chm.
Founded: 2001. **Description:** Promotes the use and benefits of air barrier systems. Seeks to raise the standard of proficiency in the industry through the ABAA On-Site Quality Assurance Program. Furthers continuing education in the industry. Offers training and education programs for all stakeholders in the air barrier industry.

588 ■ American Architectural Manufacturers Association (AAMA)
1827 Walden Off. Sq., Ste.550
Schaumburg, IL 60173-4287
Ph: (847)303-5664
Fax: (847)303-5774
E-mail: rwalker@aamanet.org
URL: http://www.aamanet.org
Contact: Rich Walker, Pres./CEO
Founded: 1936. **Members:** 280. **Membership Dues:** corporate (base), $25,000 (annual) ● professional individual, $100 (annual) ● professional firm, $250 (annual) ● professional educator, student, $50 (annual). **Staff:** 17. **Budget:** $3,000,000. **Regional Groups:** 2. **Description:** Provides performance standards, product certification and educational programs for the fenestration industry, including product testing and market research. **Libraries:** **Type:** reference. **Holdings:** books, business records, periodicals. **Committees:** Certification Policy; Code Policy; Consumer Education; Market Development; Marketing Research; Technical Policy. **Divisions:** Architectural/Heavy Commercial Window and Door; Curtainwall and Storefront; Mobile/Manufactured Housing Components; Residential/Commercial Window and Door; Residential Sheet Products. **Absorbed:** (1971) Aluminum Siding Association. **Formed by Merger of:** Aluminum Window Manufacturers Association; Sliding Glass Door and Window Institute. **Formerly:** (1984) Architectural Aluminum Manufacturers Association. **Publications:** *American Architectural Manufacturers Association-AAMANET.work*, 3/year. Newsletter. Provides technical information. **Price:** free ● *American Architectural Manufacturers Association—Certified Products Directory*, annual. Provides information in tabular form for products, which bear the AAMA label. **Price:** $10.00/year. Alternate Formats: online ● *Industry Statistical Review and Forecast*. Contains market data. ● *North American Industry Market Studies*, biennial. Includes in-depth market research by product and material, regional studies, and a channel distribution study. **Price:** $3,300.00 for the first CD-ROM. Alternate Formats: CD-ROM ● Also publishes voluntary industry product specifications, test methods, technical information reports, etc. **Conventions/Meetings:** board meeting ● annual meeting ● semiannual meeting (exhibits) - usually summer and fall ● quarterly regional meeting.

589 ■ American Composites Manufacturers Association (ACMA)
1010 N Glebe Rd., Ste.450
Arlington, VA 22201
Ph: (703)525-0511
Fax: (703)525-0743
E-mail: info@acmanet.org
URL: http://www.acmanet.org
Contact: Monty Felix, Pres.-Elect
Founded: 1979. **Members:** 800. **Membership Dues:** manufacturer (annual sales volume of under $1 million to $25 million), $500-$3,400 (annual) ● manufacturer (annual sales volume from $25 to $150 million), $4,800-$10,900 (annual) ● manufacturer (annual sales volume from $150 to over $300 million), $16,000 (annual) ● supplier (annual sales volume of under $1 million to $10 million), $1,500-$3,800 (annual) ● supplier (annual sales volume from $10 million to $75 million), $7,400-$13,500 (annual) ● supplier (maximum; annual sales volume from $75 million to over $300 million), $26,200 (annual) ● general, $200 (annual) ● national association, press, $530 (annual) ● regional association, $160 (annual) ● student, $80 (annual) ● manufacturer's representative, $320 (annual) ● consultant, $500 (annual) ● distributor (annual sales volume of under $1 million to $25 million), $1,500-$3,400 (annual) ● distributor (annual sales volume from $25 to $150 million), $4,800-$10,900 (annual) ● distributor (maximum; annual sales volume from $150 to over $300 million), $17,500 (annual). **Staff:** 14. **Budget:** $3,000,000. **Description:** Companies engaged in the hand lay up or spray up of fiberglass in open molds or engaged in filament winding or resin transfer molding. Products requiring this process include boats, swimming pools, and bathroom fixtures. Conducts educational and research programs; compiles statistics. Sponsors product specialty seminars. **Awards:** Gary B. Multanen/CM Magazine. **Frequency:** annual. **Type:** scholarship. **Recipient:** for a student ● President's Award. **Frequency:** annual. **Type:** recognition. **Telecommunication Services:** electronic mail, acmainfo@acmanet.org. **Committees:** Government Affairs; RMC: Process Safety Management. **Councils:** Fiberglass Grating Manufacturers; Pultrusion Industry; Resin Management. **Divisions:** Bath; Corrosion; Custom Molders. **Absorbed:** (2001) Suppliers of Advanced Composite Materials Association. **Formerly:** (1991) Fiberglass Fabrication Association; (2003) Composites Fabricators Association. **Publications:** *Composites Manufacturing*, monthly. Magazine. **Circulation:** 10,000. **Advertising:** accepted. Also Cited As: *CM* ● *Government Matters*, monthly. Newsletter ● *Membership Directory/Buyer's Guide*, annual. **Conventions/Meetings:** annual convention and seminar (exhibits).

590 ■ American Fiberboard Association (AFA)
853 N Quentin Rd., Ste.317
Palatine, IL 60067
Ph: (847)934-8394
Fax: (847)934-8394

E-mail: afa@fiberboard.org
URL: http://www.fiberboard.org
Contact: Louis Wagner, Exec. Dir.
Founded: 1991. **Members:** 5. **Staff:** 1. **Budget:** $150,000. **Multinational. Description:** Fiberboard manufacturing companies. Provides research and fiberboard certification to members. **Libraries: Type:** not open to the public. **Publications:** Brochure. **Conventions/Meetings:** semiannual meeting - spring/fall.

591 ■ American Shipbuilding Association (ASA)

600 Pennsylvania Ave. SE, Ste.305
Washington, DC 20003-4345
Ph: (202)544-8170
Fax: (202)544-8252
E-mail: asa@usships.org
URL: http://usships.org
Contact: Cynthia L. Brown, Pres.
Founded: 1994. **Members:** 6. **Staff:** 2. **Description:** Six private sector shipyards. Aims to preserve the U.S. naval shipbuilding industrial base. Promotes the importance of American shipbuilding to the public and the government. **Awards:** Bateman Award. **Frequency:** annual. **Type:** recognition. **Recipient:** for outstanding individuals dedicated to supporting the shipbuilding industry. **Computer Services:** database ● mailing lists ● online services, Sea Power Forum. **Publications:** *American Shipbuilder*, monthly. Newsletter. **Circulation:** 1,000. **Conventions/Meetings:** quarterly board meeting.

592 ■ American Society of Home Inspectors (ASHI)

932 Lee St., Ste.101
Des Plaines, IL 60016-6546
Ph: (847)759-2820
Free: (800)743-2744
Fax: (847)759-1620
E-mail: robp@ashi.org
URL: http://www.ashi.org
Contact: Robert J. Paterkiewicz CAE, Exec. Dir.
Founded: 1976. **Members:** 6,000. **Membership Dues:** candidate, $295 (annual) ● individual, $395 (annual) ● affiliate, $645 (annual). **Staff:** 15. **Budget:** $4,000,000. **Regional Groups:** 80. **Languages:** English, French, Spanish. **Description:** Professional home inspectors whose goals are to: establish home inspector qualifications; set standards of practice for home inspections; adhere to a code of ethics; keep the concept of "objective third party" intact; inform members of the most advanced methods and techniques, and educate consumers on the value of home inspections. Conducts seminars through local chapters. **Telecommunication Services:** electronic mail, hq@ashi.org. **Publications:** *The Reporter*, monthly. Magazine. Includes general industry information. **Price:** $45.00/year. **Circulation:** 6,000. **Advertising:** accepted ● Also publishes standards of practice, pamphlets, and technical proceedings of seminars, conferences and consumer brochures. **Conventions/Meetings:** annual InspectionWorld - conference (exhibits).

593 ■ Architectural Woodwork Institute (AWI)

46179 Westlake Dr., Ste.120
Potomac Falls, VA 20165
Ph: (571)323-3636
Fax: (571)323-3630
E-mail: pduvic@awinet.org
URL: http://www.awinet.org
Contact: Philip Duvic, Exec. VP
Founded: 1953. **Members:** 850. **Membership Dues:** manufacturer (based on total gross sales), $600-$2,400 (annual) ● supplier, $700-$1,100 (annual) ● small company, $50 (monthly) ● major player, $200 (monthly) ● affiliate ($75 for the first time), $25 (annual) ● full-time student, $20 (annual). **Staff:** 6. **Budget:** $1,200,000. **Regional Groups:** 29. **Description:** Manufacturers of architectural woodwork products (casework, fixtures, and paneling) and associated suppliers of equipment and materials. Works to: raise industry standards; research new and improved materials and methods; publish technical data helpful in the design and use of architectural woodwork. Conducts seminars and training course. **Awards:** Award of Excellence. **Type:** recognition. **Absorbed:** Millwork Cost Bureau. **Publications:** *AWI Quality Standards Guide*, periodic. **Price:** $10.00 for members; $100.00 for nonmembers. Alternate Formats: CD-ROM ● *Design Solutions*, quarterly. Journal. Includes detailed drawings for architects, interior designers, real estate developers, and building owners. **Price:** $25.00/year. ISSN: 0277-3538. **Circulation:** 30,000. **Advertising:** accepted ● *Newsbriefs*, monthly. Newsletter ● *Source Book*, annual. Membership Directory. **Conventions/Meetings:** annual convention and meeting (exhibits).

594 ■ Asphalt Emulsion Manufacturers Association (AEMA)

3 Church Cir.
PMB 250
Annapolis, MD 21401
Ph: (410)267-0023
Fax: (410)267-7546
E-mail: krissoff@aema.org
URL: http://www.aema.org
Contact: Michael Krissoff, Exec. Dir.
Founded: 1973. **Members:** 150. **Membership Dues:** international, North American manufacturer, $2,500 (annual) ● supplier, $3,000 (annual) ● contractor, individual, $500 (annual) ● North American manufacturer plant (maximum), $10,000 (annual). **Staff:** 2. **Budget:** $250,000. **Description:** Seeks to foster: advancement and improvement of the asphalt emulsion industry; expanded and more efficient use of emulsion as a result of an improved state of the art; provision of information to users through guide specifications and answers to specific questions. **Awards:** Hall of Fame Award. **Frequency:** annual. **Type:** recognition. **Recipient:** for an individual who has made a substantial contribution to the development of the emulsion industry ● Recognition of Achievement Award. **Frequency:** annual. **Type:** recognition. **Recipient:** for an individual who has made a significant contribution to emulsion technology. **Committees:** Environmental and Regulatory Issues; International Technical; Maintenance Technology; Paving Technology. **Publications:** *Basic Asphalt Emulsion Manual*. Gives a basic understanding of asphalt emulsions. **Price:** $15.00/book for members; $18.00/book for nonmembers; $35.00/CD-ROM for members; $50.00/CD-ROM for nonmembers. Alternate Formats: CD-ROM ● Brochures. **Price:** $45.00/package for members; $65.00/package for nonmembers. Alternate Formats: CD-ROM ● Membership Directory, annual ● Newsletter, quarterly ● Proceedings. **Price:** $30.00. **Conventions/Meetings:** annual board meeting - every fall ● annual meeting and seminar - every spring ● annual symposium - 2008 Sept. 24-26, Arlington, VA.

595 ■ Asphalt Institute (AI)

2696 Res. Park Dr.
Lexington, KY 40511-8480
Ph: (859)288-4960
Fax: (859)288-4999
E-mail: info@asphaltinstitute.org
URL: http://www.asphaltinstitute.org
Contact: Mr. Peter T. Grass, Pres.
Founded: 1919. **Members:** 75. **Staff:** 26. **Budget:** $3,000,000. **Multinational. Description:** Composed of petroleum asphalt/bitumen producers, manufacturers and affiliated businesses. Promotes the use, benefits, and quality performance of petroleum asphalt through environmental marketing, research, engineering, and technical development, and through the resolution of issues affecting the industry. **Libraries: Type:** open to the public. **Subjects:** asphalt. **Formerly:** (1929) Asphalt Association. **Publications:** *Asphalt*, 3/year. Magazine. Includes schedule of workshops and seminars for asphalt users, producers, and others concerned with the asphalt industry. **Price:** free (restricted circulation). **Circulation:** 18,000. **Advertising:** accepted. Alternate Formats: online ● Directory, annual ● Brochure. Alternate Formats: online ● Also publishes specifications, engineering manuals, booklets, catalog, and audiovisuals on asphalt construction. **Conventions/Meetings:** annual board meeting.

596 ■ Asphalt Pavement Alliance (APA)

c/o Asphalt Institute
PO Box 14052
Lexington, KY 40512
Ph: (859)288-4960
Free: (877)APA-0077
Fax: (859)288-4999
E-mail: publications@asphaltalliance.com
URL: http://www.asphaltalliance.com
Contact: Brian Clark, Contact
Description: Furthers the use and quality of Hot Mix Asphalt pavements. Facilitates the exchange of information on all aspects of the asphalt industry. Promotes the use of asphalt in the construction and maintenance of roads through research, technology transfer, engineering, education and innovation. **Awards:** Perpetual Pavement Awards. **Frequency:** annual. **Type:** recognition. **Recipient:** to owners of asphalt pavements who are at least 35 years old and have never had a structural failure. **Telecommunication Services:** electronic mail, bclark@asphaltinstitute.org.

597 ■ Asphalt Roofing Manufacturers Association (ARMA)

1156 15th St. NW, Ste.900
Washington, DC 20005
Ph: (202)207-0917
Fax: (202)223-9741
E-mail: info@asphaltroofing.org
URL: http://asphaltroofing.org
Contact: Russell K. Snyder, Exec. VP
Founded: 1915. **Members:** 52. **Staff:** 5. **Budget:** $1,100,000. **Description:** Manufacturers of asphalt shingles, rollgoods, built-up roofing systems (BUR) and modified bitumen roofing systems. Compiles statistics. **Awards:** Presidential Leadership Award. **Frequency:** annual. **Type:** recognition. **Committees:** Built-Up Roofing; Codes; Communications; Executive; Industry; Modified Bitumen; Research/Residential. **Formerly:** (1970) Asphalt Roofing Industry Bureau. **Publications:** *ARMA eNewsletter*, quarterly. Alternate Formats: online ● *ARMA Government Issues Newsletter*, quarterly ● *Asphalt Roofing Manufacturers Association—Newsletter*, semiannual. **Price:** free, for members only ● *Publication and Audio-Visual Directory*, biennial. Contains descriptions and prices of literature and audiovisual materials used by roofing manufacturers. **Price:** free ● *Residential Asphalt Roofing Manual* ● *Residential, Built-up Roofing, and Modified Bitumen* ● Membership Directory, annual. **Conventions/Meetings:** semiannual board meeting - always November.

598 ■ Associated Air Balance Council (AABC)

1518 K St. NW
Washington, DC 20005
Ph: (202)737-0202
Fax: (202)638-4833
E-mail: info@aabc.com
URL: http://www.aabchq.com
Contact: Kenneth M. Sufka, Exec. Dir.
Founded: 1965. **Members:** 146. **Membership Dues:** regular, $500 (monthly). **Staff:** 5. **Description:** Certified test and balance engineers. Works to upgrade air testing and balancing within the building industry through exchange of technical information and professional standards. Offers recommendations to the manufacturing segment concerning air-handling equipment and to the professional sector regarding design of air handling systems. Holds Apprenticeship Training Program for Balancing Technicians; conducts testing and balancing seminars for engineers. **Telecommunication Services:** electronic mail, aabchq@aol.com. **Committees:** Technical. **Publications:** *International Certified Agency Directory*, annual. Lists certified AABC test and balance agencies, arranged geographically. Includes alphabetical index of member companies. **Price:** free. **Circulation:** 30,000. Also Cited As: *AABC Directory* ● *TAB Journal*, quarterly. **Price:** $24.00/year. **Advertising:** accepted. Alternate Formats: online ● *Technician Training Videos*. **Price:** $495.00 for nonmembers; $195.00 for members ● Manuals.

599 ■ Associated Construction Distributors International (ACD)
PO Box 14552
Des Moines, IA 50306-3552
Ph: (515)964-1335
Fax: (515)964-7668
E-mail: acdi@acdi.net
URL: http://www.acdi.net
Contact: Tom Goetz, Exec. VP

Founded: 1974. **Members:** 36. **Staff:** 3. **Budget:** $300,000. **Description:** Independent construction material and equipment distributors specializing in concrete and masonry supplies and equipment. Promotes improved communication and greater professionalism among members. Maintains library; conducts annual financial statistical survey of member firms; sponsors occasional technical seminars. **Telecommunication Services:** electronic mail, tgoetz@acdi.net. **Publications:** *Associated Construction Distributors International—Directory*, annual ● Bulletin, periodic. **Conventions/Meetings:** semiannual congress - always spring and fall.

600 ■ Association of Millwork Distributors (AMD)
10047 Robert Trent Jones Pkwy.
New Port Richey, FL 34655-4649
Ph: (727)372-3665
Fax: (727)372-2879
E-mail: rleone@amdweb.com
URL: http://www.amdweb.com
Contact: Rosalie Leone, Exec. Dir.

Founded: 1964. **Members:** 1,100. **Membership Dues:** distributor (based on sales), $1,000-$2,500 (annual) ● associate manufacturer, $1,000 (annual) ● associate manufacturer's representative, $500 (annual). **Staff:** 7. **Budget:** $1,800,000. **Description:** Wholesale distributors of windows, door, millwork, and related products. Conducts research and statistical studies. Offers millwork home study course and audiovisual program dealing with product knowledge; furnishes group insurance. Compiles statistics. **Libraries: Type:** reference. **Awards:** Ron Taylor Award. **Type:** recognition. **Recipient:** for an individual who represents the highest values, integrity, and character. **Computer Services:** database ● online services, discussion board. **Committees:** Annual Convention Program; Education; Exhibit Hall; Industry Standards and Certification; Long Range and Strategic Planning; Ron Taylor Award. **Formed by Merger of:** (1964) Northern Sash and Door Jobbers Association; (1964) Southern Sash and Door Jobbers Association. **Formerly:** (2005) National Sash and Door Jobbers Association. **Publications:** *AMD News*, monthly. Newsletter. Alternate Formats: online ● *Labor Law Highlights*, periodic ● *Membership Directory and Products' Guide*, annual ● Bulletin, periodic ● Also publishes sales reports and financial operations summary. **Conventions/Meetings:** annual convention, for members of the millwork industry (exhibits) ● semiannual executive committee meeting.

601 ■ Association of Modified Asphalt Producers (AMAP)
PO Box 270006
St. Louis, MO 63127
Ph: (314)843-2627
E-mail: amap@sbcglobal.net
URL: http://www.modifiedasphalt.org
Contact: Bob Berkley, Exec. Dir.

Membership Dues: producer, supplier, $2,000 (annual) ● associate, $850 (annual) ● friend, $85 (annual). **Description:** Represents individuals committed to informing owners, contractors, and specifying agencies about the performance and economic benefits of modified asphalt binders for bituminous pavements. Serves as a voice on issues pertaining to modified asphalt. Encourages User-Producer agencies toward the use of higher performing binders. Evaluates and communicates advancements in modified asphalt technology. Promotes standardization of asphalt binder testing procedures. **Libraries: Type:** reference. **Holdings:** papers.

602 ■ Association of the Wall and Ceiling Industries - International (AWCI)
513 W Broad St., Ste.210
Falls Church, VA 22046
Ph: (703)538-1600 (703)538-1602
Fax: (703)534-8307
E-mail: info@awci.org
URL: http://www.awci.org
Contact: Michael Heering, Pres.

Founded: 1918. **Members:** 2,000. **Membership Dues:** supplier or distributor, contractor in U.S., manufacturer, $585 (annual) ● contractor in Canada and international, general, $295 (annual) ● life (maximum), $12,000. **Staff:** 14. **Budget:** $4,000,000. **Regional Groups:** 15. **Multinational. Description:** Acoustical tile, drywall, demountable partitions, lathing and plastering, fireproofing, light-gauge steel framing, stucco and exterior insulation finish systems contractors, suppliers and manufacturers. **Libraries: Type:** reference. **Holdings:** 7,500; articles, books, periodicals, video recordings. **Subjects:** walls and ceiling information. **Awards:** Excellence in Construction Safety Award. **Frequency:** annual. **Type:** recognition ● Pinnacle Award. **Frequency:** annual. **Type:** recognition. **Committees:** Apprenticeship; Convention; Education; Labor Liaison; Safety; Suppliers; Technical. **Affiliated With:** Foundation of the Wall and Ceiling Industry. **Publications:** *Buyer's Guide for the Wall and Ceiling Industry*, annual. Directory. Provides information for consumers. **Price:** $30.00/year. **Circulation:** 2,000. **Advertising:** accepted ● *Construction Dimensions Magazine*, monthly. Journal. **Price:** $30.00/year. **Circulation:** 24,000. **Advertising:** accepted ● *Information Resources*. Catalog ● *Technical Information* ● *Who's Who in the Wall and Ceiling Industry*, annual. **Price:** $45.00. **Circulation:** 2,000. **Advertising:** accepted ● Newsletter, monthly. **Circulation:** 2,000. **Conventions/Meetings:** annual convention and trade show (exhibits) - usually March or April.

603 ■ Automated Builders Consortium
1445 Donlon St., Ste.16
Ventura, CA 93003
Ph: (805)642-9735
Free: (800)344-BLDR
Fax: (805)642-8820
E-mail: info@automatedbuilder.com
URL: http://www.automatedbuilder.com
Contact: Donald O. Carlson, Founder

Founded: 1993. **Members:** 350. **Membership Dues:** regular, $250 (annual) ● auxiliary, $250 (annual) ● associate, $250 (annual). **Staff:** 1. **Budget:** $110,000. **Description:** Advocates for inner city factories that build housing and other modular structures for use in the inner city and elsewhere. **Publications:** *Module*, quarterly. Newsletter. **Circulation:** 750. **Conventions/Meetings:** annual meeting (exhibits).

604 ■ Brick Industry Association (BIA)
1850 Centennial Park Dr., Ste.301
Reston, VA 20191
Ph: (703)620-0010 (703)674-1537
Fax: (703)620-3928
E-mail: brickinfo@bia.org
URL: http://www.bia.org
Contact: Richard A. Jennison, Pres./CEO

Founded: 1934. **Members:** 250. **Staff:** 13. **Budget:** $3,000,000. **Regional Groups:** 8. **Description:** Manufacturers and distributors of clay brick. Promotes clay brick with the goal of increasing its market share. **Libraries: Type:** reference. **Holdings:** 2,000; articles, books, periodicals. **Subjects:** engineering and ceramics pertinent to masonry construction. **Awards:** Brick in Architecture Awards. **Frequency:** biennial. **Type:** recognition. **Recipient:** for the best architectural project ● Brick Paving Design Awards. **Frequency:** biennial. **Type:** recognition. **Recipient:** for creative uses of clay paver. **Additional Websites:** http://www.gobrick.com. **Telecommunication Services:** electronic mail, jennison@bia.org. **Committees:** Engineering and Research; Government Relations; Manpower Development; Marketing Promotion. **Absorbed:** (1969) Structural Clay Products Research Foundation; (1999) National Association of Brick Distributors. **Formed by Merger of:** American Face Brick Association; Brick Manufacturers Association; National Paving Brick Association; Structural Clay Tile Association. **Formerly:** (1972) Structural Clay Products Institute; (1999) Brick Institute of America. **Publications:** *Annual Sales and Marketing Report*, annual ● *BIA News*, monthly. Magazine. **Price:** $30.00/year. **Circulation:** 2,000. **Advertising:** accepted ● *Brick in Architecture*, quarterly. Magazine ● *Brick News Online*, semimonthly. Newsletter. **Advertising:** accepted. Alternate Formats: online ● *Builder Notes*, bimonthly ● *Directory of Manufacturers*, annual ● *Technical Notes on Brick Construction*, bimonthly. Bulletins. **Price:** $75.00. Alternate Formats: online. **Conventions/Meetings:** annual The Brick Show - conference (exhibits).

605 ■ Bridge Grid Flooring Manufacturers Association (BGFMA)
300 E Cherry St.
North Baltimore, OH 45872
Ph: (419)257-3561
Free: (877)257-5499
Fax: (419)257-2200
E-mail: mkaczinski@dsbrown.com
URL: http://www.bgfma.org
Contact: Mark Kaczinski, Exec. Dir.

Founded: 1985. **Members:** 5. **Staff:** 1. **Description:** Manufacturers of bridge grid decks; associate members are suppliers of steel used in the construction of bridge grid decks. Seeks to increase the use of steel bridge grid decks by promoting their use among consultants, state bridge engineers, bridge owners, and other specifying agencies. Conducts research, in conjunction with universities, on engineering characteristics of steel grid decks. Maintains speakers' bureau. **Libraries: Type:** open to the public. **Committees:** Technical. **Publications:** *Gridline*, quarterly. Newsletter. Contains case studies and product information. **Circulation:** 2,800 ● Catalog ● Also publishes informational material. **Conventions/Meetings:** semiannual board meeting.

606 ■ Building Futures Council (BFC)
2300 Wilson Blvd., Ste.400
Arlington, VA 22201
Ph: (703)837-5365 (703)837-5414
Fax: (703)837-5406
E-mail: bfc@agc.org
URL: http://www.thebfc.com
Contact: Damian P. Hill, Asst. Exec. Dir.

Membership Dues: sustaining, corporate, $1,250 (annual) ● small business, public sector, non-profit, $500 (annual) ● associate, retiree, $300 (annual). **Description:** Represents building and construction industry decision makers concerned with the challenges and rewards of the built environment. Seeks to identify critical issues encountered in the building and construction process. Advocates for the establishment of standard productivity measures to improve efficiency in the construction industry. **Telecommunication Services:** electronic mail, hilld@agc.org. **Affiliated With:** Associated General Contractors of America. **Publications:** Papers. Alternate Formats: online ● Reports. Alternate Formats: online.

607 ■ Building Material Dealers Association (BMDA)
12540 SW Main St., Ste.200
Tigard, OR 97223-6198
Ph: (503)624-0561
Free: (800)666-2632
Fax: (503)620-1016
E-mail: bmda@bmda.com
URL: http://www.bmda.com

Founded: 1915. **Membership Dues:** full, $32 (monthly) ● associate, $10 (monthly) ● notice, $14 (monthly). **Description:** Working to continue being a computerized membership company providing "notices of right to a lien".

608 ■ Building Materials Reuse Association (BMRA)
545 Ridge Ave.
State College, PA 16803
Free: (800)990-2672
URL: http://www.ubma.org
Contact: Brad Guy, Pres.

Membership Dues: government, business, $95 (annual). **Description:** Represents those involved in acquisition and/or redistribution of used building materials. **Formerly:** (2005) Used Building Materials Association. **Conventions/Meetings:** conference.

609 ■ Building Trades Employers' Association (BTEA)
1430 Broadway, 8th Fl.
New York, NY 10018
Ph: (212)704-9745
Fax: (212)704-4367
E-mail: jnastasi@bteany.com
URL: http://www.robex.com
Contact: Louis J. Coletti, Pres./CEO

Description: Promotes building trade employers. **Additional Websites:** http://www.bteany.com. **Publications:** Newsletter. **Circulation:** 3,500. Alternate Formats: online ● Report. Alternate Formats: online.

610 ■ Cellulose Insulation Manufacturers Association (CIMA)
136 S Keowee St.
Dayton, OH 45402
Ph: (937)222-2462
Free: (888)881-2462
Fax: (937)222-5794
E-mail: info@cellulose.org
URL: http://www.cellulose.org
Contact: Mr. Daniel Lea, Exec. Dir.

Founded: 1982. **Members:** 38. **Staff:** 3. **Budget:** $400,000. **Description:** Manufacturers of cellulose insulation. Promotes quality control; represents the interests of the industry. Supports research into the characteristics and performance of cellulose insulation. **Libraries: Type:** not open to the public. **Holdings:** archival material, articles. **Subjects:** energy, recycling, insulation performance. **Awards:** Floyd England Award. **Frequency:** annual. **Type:** recognition. **Computer Services:** Mailing lists, cellulose insulation producers. **Telecommunication Services:** electronic mail, dlea@advmgtconcepts.com. **Committees:** Technical. **Formerly:** (1992) Cellulose Industry Standards Enforcement Program. **Conventions/Meetings:** annual Membership Meeting - general assembly.

611 ■ Ceramic Tile Distributors Association (CTDA)
800 Roosevelt Rd., Bldg. C, Ste.312
Glen Ellyn, IL 60137
Free: (800)938-CTDA
Fax: (630)790-3095
E-mail: info@ctdahome.org
URL: http://www.ctdahome.org
Contact: Douglas Miles, Pres.

Founded: 1978. **Members:** 500. **Membership Dues:** regular, allied company, associate with less than $10 million annual sales, $600 (annual) ● associate with more than $10 million annual sales, $1,100 (annual) ● independent agent (3 or less employees), $200 (annual). **Staff:** 3. **Description:** Wholesale distributors and manufacturers of ceramic tile and related products. Promotes the increase of sales volumes in the ceramic tile industry through educational programs and networking. Promotes independent ceramic tile distributors and represents their interests. Provides technical information; compiles statistics. Sponsors competitions. Maintains insurance program for members and speakers' bureau. **Programs:** Color/Shade Variation. **Formerly:** (1985) Ceramic Tile Distributors of America. **Publications:** *Tile Management Quarterly*. Newsletter. Includes member and industry news. **Price:** included in membership dues. **Circulation:** 700 ● Membership Directory, annual. **Price:** $250.00 for nonmembers; included in membership dues.

612 ■ Concrete Reinforcing Steel Institute (CRSI)
933 N Plum Grove Rd.
Schaumburg, IL 60173-4758
Ph: (847)517-1200
Free: (800)328-6306
Fax: (847)517-1206
E-mail: sendean@crsi.org
URL: http://www.crsi.org
Contact: Robert J. Risser Jr., Pres.

Founded: 1924. **Members:** 180. **Membership Dues:** professional, $125 (annual). **Staff:** 19. **Description:** Producers, fabricators, and distributors of reinforcing steel bars used in reinforced concrete construction. Conducts research; provides technical information on reinforced concrete design and construction practices. **Telecommunication Services:** electronic mail, brisser@crsi.org. **Committees:** Bar Producers; Codes; Concrete Formwork; Engineering Practice; Epoxy Coatings; Marketing; Reinforcing Bar Supports. **Absorbed:** (1985) Fusion Bonded Coaters Association. **Publications:** *Design*. Handbook ● *Manual of Standard Practice* ● *Shop Talk*, quarterly. Newsletter ● Also publishes technical aids and promotional materials. **Conventions/Meetings:** annual convention.

613 ■ Construction Employers Association (CEA)
1646 N California Blvd., Ste.500
Walnut Creek, CA 94596-4148
Ph: (925)930-8184
Fax: (925)930-9014
E-mail: mwwalton@cea-ca.org
URL: http://www.cea-ca.org
Contact: William Stronck, Pres.

Founded: 1911. **Members:** 350. **Budget:** $500,000. **Local Groups:** 282. **Description:** Works with trade unions and local, state and federal agencies to promote job safety. Conducts apprenticeship programs. **Conventions/Meetings:** bimonthly board meeting.

614 ■ Construction Owners Association of America (COAA)
2859 Paces Ferry Rd.
Overlook III, Ste.420
Atlanta, GA 30339
Ph: (770)433-0820
Free: (800)994-2622
Fax: (404)577-3551
E-mail: coaa@coaa.org
URL: http://www.coaa.org
Contact: Kim J. Fisher, Managing Exec.

Founded: 1994. **Members:** 350. **Membership Dues:** regular, $350 (annual) ● associate, corporate, $1,000 (annual). **Staff:** 3. **State Groups:** 5. **Description:** Represents public and private owners and developers of construction projects all across America. Aims to make a significant and lasting impact on the construction industry by educating its membership and by providing a collective voice for owners and developers of construction projects. **Awards:** Construction Owners Project Leadership Award. **Frequency:** annual. **Type:** recognition. **Recipient:** to owners who demonstrate exceptional leadership and project management skills. **Committees:** Automation; Awards; Chapter; Communications/Editorial; Documents; Education. **Publications:** *The Owner's Perspective*, semiannual. Magazine. **Price:** included in membership dues. **Circulation:** 13,000. **Advertising:** accepted ● Membership Directory, annual. **Price:** free for members. **Conventions/Meetings:** semiannual Construction Owners Leadership Conference - conference and seminar (exhibits) - every spring and fall. 2008 Nov. 19-12, Tampa, FL.

615 ■ Cool Roof Rating Council (CRRC)
1738 Excelsior Ave.
Oakland, CA 94602
Ph: (510)485-7175
Free: (866)465-2523
Fax: (510)482-4421
E-mail: info@coolroofs.org
URL: http://www.coolroofs.org
Contact: Ted Pope, Admin. Dir.

Founded: 1998. **Membership Dues:** class A - regular (manufacturer, distributor, supplier), $700 (annual) ● class A - trade association, $1,200 (annual) ● class B - regular, $300 (annual) ● class B - sustaining, $2,500 (annual). **Description:** Works to develop methods for evaluating and labeling the solar reflectance and thermal emittance of roofing products. Implements and communicates radiative energy performance rating systems for roof surfaces. Supports research into energy related radiative properties of roofing surfaces. Provides education and objective support to parties interested in understanding and comparing various roofing options. **Publications:** *Rated Products Directory*. Alternate Formats: online ● *Roofing Reflections*. Newsletter. Alternate Formats: online.

616 ■ Cooling Technology Institute (CTI)
2611 FM 1960 W, Ste.A-101
Houston, TX 77068-3730
Ph: (281)583-4087
Fax: (281)537-1721
E-mail: vmanser@cti.org
URL: http://www.cti.org
Contact: Virginia A. Manser, Admin.

Founded: 1950. **Members:** 400. **Membership Dues:** corporate, $495 (annual) ● individual, affiliate, $140 (annual). **Staff:** 3. **Budget:** $800,000. **Description:** Seeks to improve the technology, design and performance of water conservation apparatus. Develops standard specifications for cooling towers; provides inspection services. Conducts research through technical subcommittees. Sponsors projects; maintains speakers' bureau. **Libraries: Type:** open to the public. **Holdings:** reports. **Subjects:** cooling towers. **Committees:** Acceptance Test Procedure; Commercial Tower Certification Program; End User Benefits; Engineering Standards; Information Services; International Expansion; Performance; Technology; Water Conservation; Water Treating; Wood Maintenance. **Formerly:** (2001) Cooling Tower Institute. **Publications:** *Cooling Tower Institute—Bibliography of Technical Papers*, periodic. Lists available technical papers presented at meetings sponsored by the institute, arranged within the four categories of engineering standards. **Price:** free. **Circulation:** 6,800. **Advertising:** accepted ● *CTI Book of Performance Curves*. **Price:** $240.00 for members; $300.00 for nonmembers ● *CTI News*, quarterly. Newsletter. Covers institute activities and items of general interest concerning cooling towers. **Price:** free ● *Journal of the Cooling Tower Institute*, semiannual. Provides technical information professionals responsible for the construction specifications, testing, maintenance, and operation of cooling towers. **Price:** free to individuals in U.S.; $30.00 /year for libraries and individuals outside U.S. **Advertising:** accepted ● Papers ● Reports ● Also publishes standard specifications. **Conventions/Meetings:** semiannual conference and workshop - always February and July ● seminar.

617 ■ Design-Build Institute of America (DBIA)
1100 H St. NW, Ste.500
Washington, DC 20005-5476
Ph: (202)682-0110
Free: (866)692-0110
Fax: (202)682-5877
E-mail: dbia@dbia.org
URL: http://www.dbia.org
Contact: Walker Lee Evey, Pres.

Founded: 1993. **Members:** 875. **Membership Dues:** student, $45 (annual) ● academic/non-profit, government/agency, private facility owner, $99 (annual) ● practitioner, $199-$299 (annual) ● at-risk firm, consolidator (based on corporate revenues/billings), $750-$10,000 (annual) ● A/E or E/A, specialty contractor (based on corporate revenues/billings), $750-$5,000 (annual) ● professional firm, insurance, attorney, $2,500 (annual) ● public agency, academic institution, $500 (annual). **Staff:** 18. **Budget:** $4,000,000. **Regional Groups:** 10. **Description:** Companies and individuals concerned with integrated architecture, engineering, and construction services; related companies and service providers including financial institutions, real estate agencies, and building operators. Promotes DesignBuild project delivery, through which professional design and construction of buildings is arranged for under a single source responsibility contract. Develops standards of ethics and practice for the industry. **Libraries: Type:** not open to the public. **Holdings:** 200; articles, periodicals, reports. **Subjects:** design-build. **Awards:** Brunelleschi Lifetime Achievement Award. **Frequency:** annual. **Type:** recognition. **Recipient:** for individuals who have made significant contributions to the design and construction industry ● Distinguished Design-Build Leadership Award. **Frequency:** annual. **Type:** recognition. **Recipient:** for individuals who have demonstrated leadership in the advancement of best design-build practices ● National Design-Build Project Awards. **Frequency:** annual. **Type:** recognition. **Publications:** *Dateline*, monthly. Journal. **Advertising:** accepted ● *Design-Build*, quarterly. Magazine. **Advertising:** accepted. Alternate Formats: online ● *Design-Build Documents*, periodic. Report ● *Design-Build Manual of Practice*. Alternate Formats: CD-ROM ● *FYI Literature Review*, bimonthly. Directory ● Membership Directory, annual. **Conventions/Meetings:** annual Integrated Products and Services Expo - conference (exhibits) ● monthly meeting.

618 ■ EIFS Industry Members Association (EIMA)

3000 Corporate Center Dr., Ste.270
Morrow, GA 30260
Ph: (770)968-7945
Free: (800)294-3462
Fax: (770)968-5818
E-mail: eifsinfo@eima.com
URL: http://www.eima.com
Contact: Steve Klamke, Exec. Dir.

Founded: 1981. **Members:** 325. **Staff:** 2. **Budget:** $2,000,000. **Description:** Represents the exterior insulation and finish systems industry. Aims to improve the exterior insulation industry and to widen the use of its products through collective action. Conducts educational and research programs. **Awards:** Excellence in EIFS Construction. **Frequency:** annual. **Type:** recognition. **Recipient:** for new construction and renovation construction in current year. **Committees:** Education; Technical. **Formerly:** (1981) Exterior Insulation Manufacturers Association. **Publications:** Also publishes series of industry guideline specifications and standards and other technical documents. **Conventions/Meetings:** annual convention.

619 ■ Energy and Environmental Building Association (EEBA)

6520 Edenvale Blvd., Ste.112
Eden Prairie, MN 55346
Ph: (952)881-1098
Fax: (952)881-2048
E-mail: inquiry@eeba.org
URL: http://www.eeba.org
Contact: Kathleen Guidera, Exec. Dir.

Founded: 1982. **Members:** 2,700. **Membership Dues:** individual (1st year), $195 ● individual, $175 (annual) ● small business (1st year), $275 ● small business, $250 (annual) ● corporate (1st year), $495 ● corporate, $475 (annual). **Staff:** 3. **Budget:** $500,000. **Description:** Professional association of builders, architects, consultants, designers, researchers, educators, government agencies, suppliers, and manufactures. Promotes the awareness, education, and development of energy-efficient and environmentally responsible buildings and communities. **Boards:** Directors. **Formerly:** (2001) Energy Efficient Building Association. **Publications:** *The EEBA Builders Guide- Cold Climate; Mixed Climate; Hot/Humid Climate; and Hot/Dry Climate*. Booklets. **Price:** $45.00 ● *EEBA New Water Management Guide*. Handbook. **Price:** $18.00 ● *EEBA News*, quarterly. Newsletter. **Advertising:** accepted. Alternate Formats: online ● Brochures. **Conventions/Meetings:** annual Excellence in Building Conference - meeting (exhibits) - 2008 Oct. 21-23, Phoenix, AZ ● workshop and seminar.

620 ■ Environmental Information Association (EIA)

6935 Wisconsin Ave., Ste.306
Chevy Chase, MD 20815-6112
Ph: (301)961-4999
Free: (888)343-4342
Fax: (301)961-3094
E-mail: info@eia-usa.org
URL: http://www.eia-usa.org
Contact: Brent Kynoch, Managing Dir.

Founded: 1983. **Members:** 1,000. **Membership Dues:** individual, $105 (annual) ● pioneer student, $35 (annual) ● organization, $400 (annual) ● executive, $1,000 (annual). **Staff:** 5. **Regional Groups:** 12. **Description:** Individuals and corporations concerned about environmental management and control. Collects and disseminates information concerning environmental risks in buildings to interested professionals, building owners, and the public. Serves as a clearinghouse of information on effective environmental management. Promotes high standards of professionalism among members. Maintains Asbestos Abatement Worker and Training Program and offers operations and maintenance programs for management. Provides consulting and referral service to members on health issues. Maintains speakers' bureau; compiles statistics. **Libraries: Type:** reference. **Awards:** Snider Lifetime Achievement Award. **Frequency:** annual. **Type:** recognition. **Recipient:** for long term involvement in the environmental profession and industry. **Computer Services:** Mailing lists ● online services, discussion board. **Committees:** Education; Environmental Audits; Ethics; Insurance and Bonding; Lead Worker Training; National Asbestos Examinations and Registrations System; Operations-and-Maintenance; Permanent Conference; Public Relations/Marketing; Radon Regulatory Affairs; Safety and Health; Sampling and Analytical; Site Selection; Suppliers and Equipment; Survey, Design, and Administration; Technical Services. **Formerly:** NAC - Environmental Information Association; (1992) National Asbestos Council. **Publications:** *Environmental Choices and a Technical Journal*, quarterly. Magazine. **Advertising:** accepted ● *Technical Supplement*, periodic. Covers laboratory/ field analysis and monitoring techniques, and environmental control methodologies. ● Membership Directory, annual. **Advertising:** accepted. **Conventions/ Meetings:** annual Environmental Management - conference (exhibits) - always spring ● periodic seminar, for professional development.

621 ■ Expanded Shale Clay and Slate Institute (ESCSI)

2225 Murray Holladay Rd., Ste.102
Salt Lake City, UT 84117
Ph: (801)272-7070
Fax: (801)272-3377
E-mail: info@escsi.org
URL: http://www.escsi.org

Founded: 1952. **Members:** 10. **Staff:** 3. **State Groups:** 14. **Local Groups:** 1. **National Groups:** 3. **Description:** Manufacturers of rotary kiln produced shale, clay, and slate lightweight aggregate. Promotes the extensive use of rotary kiln produced lightweight aggregate in the concrete masonry, ready-mix, and precast markets. Disseminates educational materials to the building industry based on research and development. Works with other technical organizations to maintain product quality, life-safety, and professional integrity throughout the construction industry and related building code bodies. **Libraries: Type:** reference. **Holdings:** clippings, periodicals. **Subjects:** lightweight aggregate. **Awards:** Frank G. Erskine Award. **Frequency:** annual. **Type:** recognition. **Recipient:** for outstanding achievement in lightweight aggregate industry ● Manufacturer's Safety Awards. **Type:** recognition. **Recipient:** for no lost time accidents. **Committees:** Asphalt; Educational; Geotechnical; Marketing; Masonry; Process Technology; Special Uses; Structural. **Formerly:** (1955) Expanded Shale Institute. **Publications:** *Expanded Shale Clay and Slate Institute—Information Sheets*, periodic. Covers a specific aspect of the industry. **Price:** free ● *Special Bulletin*, periodic ● Membership Directory, annual ● Newsletter, quarterly. **Conventions/Meetings:** semiannual conference.

622 ■ Finishing Contractors Association (FCA)

8150 Leesburg Pike, Ste.1210
Vienna, VA 22182
Ph: (703)448-9001
Fax: (703)448-9002
E-mail: fca@finishingcontractors.org
URL: http://www.finishingcontractors.org
Contact: Vincent R. Sandusky, CEO

Founded: 1997. **Members:** 1,400. **Membership Dues:** individual, $250 (annual). **Staff:** 4. **Budget:** $1,000,000. **Local Groups:** 23. **National Groups:** 28. **Description:** Union finishing contractors in the following market sectors: drywall finishing, glass/glazing flooring, painting/decorating, signs/display and other related industries. Engages in governmental affairs and labor-management relations activities designed to provide a competitive advantage for its members over the non-union contractor. **Computer Services:** Online services, membership lists by state. **Committees:** Drywall Finishing; Flooring; Glass/ Glazing; Government Relations; Labor; Marketing; Membership; Painting/Decorating; Signs/Display; Workforce. **Affiliated With:** American Society of Association Executives; Associated Specialty Contractors; International Foundation of Employee Benefit Plans. **Publications:** *Finishing News*, quarterly. Newsletter. Updates members on programs, products and services. **Price:** included in membership dues. **Circulation:** 11,000. Alternate Formats: online. **Conventions/Meetings:** board meeting - 3/year.

623 ■ Floor Installation Association of North America (FIANA)

PO Box 5505
Granbury, TX 76049
Ph: (817)326-2615
Free: (888)883-4262
Fax: (817)326-4097
E-mail: info@fiana.org
URL: http://www.fiana.org
Contact: Jim Lee, Pres.

Multinational. Description: Represents the interests of manufacturers or distributors of floor installation products and flooring accessories. Works with other flooring industry associations in developing training programs for floor covering installers. Develops materials for distribution to members that would forward the objective of a higher degree of professionalism in the manufacturing and distribution of floor installation products. **Computer Services:** Online services, discussion forum. **Telecommunication Services:** electronic mail, jglee@alltel.net. **Committees:** Public Relations; Training Development. **Publications:** Newsletter. Alternate Formats: online.

624 ■ Foundation of the Wall and Ceiling Industry (FWCI)

c/o Association of the Wall and Ceiling Industry
513 W Broad St., Ste.210
Falls Church, VA 22046
Ph: (703)538-1600 (703)538-1615
Fax: (703)534-8307
E-mail: awci-cares@awci.org
URL: http://www.awci.org/thefoundation.shtml
Contact: Alfons-Jean Knauf, Pres.

Founded: 1978. **Staff:** 1. **Budget:** $50,000. **Description:** National and local contractors, manufacturers of construction products, architects, specifiers, and distributors/suppliers of wall and ceiling products. Seeks to support and expand the wall and ceiling industry's educational and research activities. Operates information clearinghouse. **Libraries: Type:** reference; lending; open to the public. **Holdings:** 10,000; archival material, audiovisuals, books, clippings, periodicals. **Subjects:** industry specifications, model codes, government regulations. **Awards:** Foundation Scholarship. **Frequency:** annual. **Type:** grant. **Affiliated With:** Association of the Wall and Ceiling Industries - International. **Publications:** *Single Source Document on Fire-rated Portland Cement-based Plaster Assemblies* ● *Standard Practice for the Testing and Inspections of Field Applied Sprayed Fire-Resistive Materials: An Annotated Guide* ● *Tolerances, Variations, and Pre-Existing Site Conditions*. Includes annual updates. ● AWCI Employee Safety Handbook; AWCI Employee Safety Handbook, Spanish edition; AWCI Tool Box Talks. **Conventions/Meetings:** annual meeting (exhibits).

625 ■ General Building Contractors Association (GBCA)
36 S 18th St.
PO Box 15959
Philadelphia, PA 19103-0959
Ph: (215)568-7015
Fax: (215)568-3115
E-mail: palmer3rd@gbca.net
URL: http://www.gbca.net
Contact: Walter P. Palmer III, Pres./CEO

Founded: 1724. **Members:** 350. **Membership Dues:** affiliate, $910 (annual) ● associate, $1,010 (annual). **Staff:** 14. **Description:** Building contractors. Seeks to serve members' needs as they relate to the construction industry. Represents members before labor and industrial organizations; makes available programs and services to members; facilitates networking among general building contractors. **Publications:** *Construction Today*, quarterly. Magazine. Serves as a regional construction magazine. **Advertising:** accepted. Alternate Formats: CD-ROM; online.

626 ■ Glazing Industry Code Committee (GICC)
2945 SW Wanamaker Dr., Ste.A
Topeka, KS 66614-5321
Ph: (785)271-0208
Fax: (785)271-0166
E-mail: gicc@glazingcodes.org
URL: http://www.glazingcodes.org
Contact: Stan Smith, Admin.

Founded: 1983. **Members:** 19. **Membership Dues:** company, $5,200 (annual). **Budget:** $95,000. **Description:** Trade association for the glazing industry. Represents members' interests before the model building codes. **Publications:** Newsletter. Alternate Formats: online ● Papers. Alternate Formats: online. **Conventions/Meetings:** biennial board meeting.

627 ■ Home Builders Institute (HBI)
1201 15th St. NW, 6th Fl.
Washington, DC 20005
Ph: (202)371-0600
Free: (800)795-7955
Fax: (202)266-8999
E-mail: postmaster@hbi.org
URL: http://hbi.org
Contact: Bill Paul, Chm.

Founded: 1983. **Description:** Strives to help builders enhance their professionalism through continuing education and certificate programs. Conducts training seminars.

628 ■ Insulated Steel Door Institute (ISDI)
Address Unknown since 2008

Founded: 1975. **Members:** 6. **Staff:** 4. **Description:** Manufacturers of insulated steel door systems for residential applications, united for development of performance specifications and standards. **Committees:** Technical. **Publications:** *Industry Standards Promulgated by the ISDI-Promo Material.* **Conventions/Meetings:** annual meeting; **Avg. Attendance:** 8.

629 ■ International Association for the Retractable Awning Industry
c/o Lily Harrison
16677 Racho Rd.
Taylor, MI 48180
Ph: (734)383-4082
Contact: Ms. Lily Harrison, Exec.Dir.

Founded: 1948. **Staff:** 10. **Multinational. Description:** Represents the interests of retractable awning manufacturers throughout the world.

630 ■ International Cast Polymer Association (ICPA)
1010 N Glebe Rd., Ste.450
Arlington, VA 22201
Ph: (703)525-0320
Free: (800)414-4272
Fax: (703)525-0743
E-mail: icpa@icpa-hq.org
URL: http://www.icpa-hq.org
Contact: Timothy Hill, Pres.

Founded: 1974. **Members:** 330. **Staff:** 5. **Budget:** $900,000. **Regional Groups:** 7. **Description:** Firms and corporations that make cast polymer products (such as cast marble vanity tops and solid surface countertops); firms and corporations that supply raw materials and production equipment to manufacturers of cast polymer products. Promotes the merits of cast polymer products to their markets; works to expand these markets for the benefit of manufacturers, suppliers, and sellers of these products; firms that fabricate/install cast polymer products. Develops and promotes industry-wide standards of product quality and acceptability for the protection of purchasers of cast polymer products. Represents the cast polymer industry before government, code bodies, and regulatory agencies of all types. Defends the industry against unwarranted regulations and seeks to guarantee its source and supply of raw materials; helps members improve their skills as businessmen; educates the public on how the industry sells its products. Works to develop reliable industry-wide market data to guide members in planning operations; strives to advance the interests of the industry and of members within the boundaries set by law. Participates in standards, product testing, technical exchange, marketing and business educational activities, production data, and informal exchanges. Conducts research programs; compiles statistics. **Libraries: Type:** reference. **Holdings:** audiovisuals, books, periodicals, video recordings. **Subjects:** manufacture, safety, OSHA. **Awards:** Pinnacle Award. **Frequency:** annual. **Type:** recognition. **Recipient:** for manufacturer members only ● **Type:** recognition. **Computer Services:** Mailing lists, of members. **Committees:** Education; Government Affairs; Marketing; Research and Development; Technical. **Councils:** Solid Surface; Suppliers. **Formerly:** (1974) National Association of Cultured Marble Manufacturers; (1993) Cultured Marble Institute. **Publications:** *Cast Polymer Connection*, bimonthly. Magazine. Features articles related to technical/industry topics, regulatory, business, and marketing. **Price:** included in membership dues; $35.00 /year for nonmembers in U.S., Canada, and Mexico. **Circulation:** 3,000. **Advertising:** accepted ● *Installation Manual.* **Price:** $40.00 for members; $80.00 for nonmembers ● *The Resource—ICPA's Membership/Product Directory*, annual. Contains a listing of ICPA manufacturer and supplier members. **Price:** included in membership dues; $500.00 for nonmembers ● Brochures. Contains technical, safety, and regulation information. ● Bulletins. Contains technical, safety, and regulation information. **Conventions/Meetings:** annual Polycon - trade show and convention (exhibits) ● periodic workshop and seminar.

631 ■ International Door Association (IDA)
PO Box 246
West Milton, OH 45383-0246
Ph: (937)698-8042
Free: (800)355-4432
Fax: (937)698-6153
E-mail: info@longmgt.com
URL: http://www.doors.org
Contact: Christopher S. Long, Managing Dir.

Founded: 1996. **Members:** 2,000. **Membership Dues:** installing/servicing dealer, $350 (annual) ● subscribing dealer, subscribing associate, $100 (annual) ● primary industry manufacturer/vendor, $550 (annual). **Description:** Individuals and companies who manufacture, sell, or install overhead garage doors and openers. Aims to promote the industry and increase training and educational opportunities. Sets a code of business practices; compiles statistics. Conducts seminars. **Awards:** International Door Association Scholarship. **Frequency:** annual. **Type:** scholarship. **Recipient:** for employees and immediate family members ● **Type:** recognition. **Committees:** Affiliates Relations and Conference; Communications; Heritage and Nominating; International Garage Door Exposition; Membership; Strategic Planning. **Formerly:** (1986) Door and Operator Dealers of America; (1998) Door and Operator Dealers Association. **Publications:** *Door and Operator Industry Magazine*, bimonthly. Includes articles published online. **Advertising:** accepted. Alternate Formats: online ● *Employee Safety and Health Manual.* Contains safety and health topics. **Price:** $25.00 for members; $50.00 for nonmembers ● *IDA Dealership Marketing Manual.* Contains information and important suggestions in all-out marketing effort. **Price:** $150.00 for members; $300.00 for nonmembers ● *IDA Sample Employment Manual.* Designed to assist door dealers in drafting an employment manual. **Price:** $25.00 for members ● Membership Directory. Lists all IDA members. **Price:** $40.00 for members. Alternate Formats: CD-ROM.

632 ■ International Slurry Surfacing Association (ISSA)
3 Church Cir.
PMB 250
Annapolis, MD 21401
Ph: (410)267-0023 (785)825-5303
Fax: (410)267-7546
E-mail: krissoff@slurry.org
URL: http://www.slurry.org
Contact: Michael R. Krissoff, Exec. Dir.

Founded: 1962. **Members:** 225. **Membership Dues:** active, $2,500 (annual) ● government agency, $100 (annual) ● international, $1,500 (annual) ● associate, $500 (annual) ● affiliate, $100 (annual). **Staff:** 3. **Budget:** $400,000. **Multinational. Description:** Dedicated to the interests, education, and success of slurry surfacing professionals and corporations around the world. Promotes ethics and quality. Provides members with information, technical assistance, and ongoing opportunities for networking and professional development. **Libraries: Type:** reference. **Holdings:** audiovisuals. **Subjects:** pavement maintenance and rehabilitation. **Awards:** President's Award. **Frequency:** annual. **Type:** recognition. **Recipient:** for innovation and contracting excellence. **Committees:** Industry Relations; Promotion; Safety; Specification; Technical Development. **Formerly:** (1990) International Slurry Seal Association. **Publications:** *ISSA Report*, quarterly. Newsletter. **Price:** included in membership dues. **Advertising:** accepted. Alternate Formats: online ● *Technical Bulletin*, periodic ● Membership Directory, annual. **Conventions/Meetings:** annual convention - always February ● annual Slurry Systems - workshop (exhibits) ● annual World Congress - meeting, heavy paving machinery (exhibits).

633 ■ International Window Film Association (IWFA)
PO Box 3871
Martinsville, VA 24115-3871
Ph: (276)666-4932
Fax: (276)666-4933
E-mail: admin@iwfa.com
URL: http://iwfa.com/industry.htm
Contact: Darrell L. Smith, Exec. Dir.

Founded: 1990. **Members:** 1,500. **Membership Dues:** manufacturer, $10,000 (annual) ● distributor in U.S. and Canada, $2,500 (annual) ● dealer in U.S., $175 (annual) ● international distributor (sells film outside U.S. and Canada), $375 (annual) ● dealer - international, $135 (annual) ● supplier (raw materials), $2,000 (annual) ● supplier (equipment/accessories), sub-distributor, $500 (annual) ● chapter (international), $2,000 (annual). **Staff:** 3. **Budget:** $1,000,000. **Multinational. Description:** Manufacturers, distributors, suppliers, and installers of solar control, safety and security film for windows in automobiles, houses, and commercial buildings. Acts as a forum for communication and works to increase professionalism in the window film industry. Maintains educational programs and speakers' bureau. **Libraries: Type:** reference; lending; not open to the public. **Holdings:** 100; audiovisuals. **Subjects:** business. **Committees:** Business Practices; Education; International; Legislative; Member Services; Outreach. **Affiliated With:** Institute for Business and Home Safety; National Glass Association; Protective Glazing Council. **Publications:** *Flat Glass Training Manual*, annual. Includes educational guide. **Price:** $29.95 each. **Circulation:** 25,000 ● Newsletter, quarterly.

Circulation: 9,000. **Conventions/Meetings:** annual meeting, held in conjunction with SEMA Show (exhibits) - always October or November in Las Vegas, NV.

634 ■ Italian Trade Commission (ITC)
33 E 67th St.
New York, NY 10021-5949
Ph: (212)980-1500
Fax: (212)758-1050
E-mail: newyork@newyork.ice.it
URL: http://www.investinitaly.com
Contact: Aniello Musella, Exec. Dir./Trade Commissioner
Founded: 1980. **Staff:** 4. **Languages:** English, Italian. **Description:** Promotes the Italian tile industry. Informs retailers, distributors, architects, builders, and other consumers of the availability of Italian ceramic tile in the U.S. Disseminates educational materials. Compiles statistics; conducts research programs. **Computer Services:** database, list of distributors, importers, and manufacturers. **Additional Websites:** http://www.italtrade.com. **Formerly:** (1997) Italian Tile Center. **Publications:** *Buyer's Guide to Italian Ceramic Tile*, annual. Booklet. Features a guide to Italian manufacturers and their products. **Price:** free ● *Guide to Ceramic Tile*. Booklet ● *Tile News*, semiannual. Newsletter. **Price:** free. **Conventions/Meetings:** annual seminar, subjects include the design, selection, and installation of Italian tile.

635 ■ Maple Flooring Manufacturers Association (MFMA)
60 Revere Dr., Ste.500
Northbrook, IL 60062
Ph: (847)480-9138
Free: (888)480-9138
Fax: (847)480-9282
E-mail: mfma@maplefloor.org
URL: http://www.maplefloor.org
Contact: Madhuri Carson, Contact
Founded: 1897. **Members:** 200. **Membership Dues:** sport floor contractor, distributor, $500 (annual) ● allied manufacturer, $1,500 (annual). **Staff:** 4. **Budget:** $500,000. **Multinational. Description:** Manufacturers and installers of Northern Maple hardwood flooring. Establishes uniform grades and standards for hard maple. **Computer Services:** Mailing lists ● online services. **Committees:** Advisory; Architectural; Marketing; Technical. **Absorbed:** (1994) Wood and Synthetic Flooring Institute. **Publications:** *Game Markings Manual*. Alternate Formats: online ● *Source Book*, annual. **Conventions/Meetings:** annual convention, for allied product manufacturers (exhibits).

636 ■ Materials and Methods Standards Association (MMSA)
4000 Pinemont
Houston, TX 77292
URL: http://www.mmsa.ws
Contact: Leigh Hightower, Pres.
Founded: 1962. **Members:** 43. **Description:** Corporations, firms, and individuals engaged in the manufacture and sale of products in the ceramic tile and dimensional stone industries. Establishes standards of quality and performance of materials and methods for installation and use. Participates in the writing of industry standards with the Tile Council of America, American National Standards Institute, and Marble Institute of America. **Committees:** ANSI Sealants; Special Tile Setting Mortars; Waterproofing and Crack Isolation Membrane. **Formerly:** (1977) Mortar Manufacturers Standards Association. **Publications:** Bulletins. Alternate Formats: online. **Conventions/Meetings:** annual conference, held in conjunction with coverings - always March.

637 ■ Metal Building Manufacturers Association (MBMA)
1300 Sumner Ave.
Cleveland, OH 44115-2851
Ph: (216)241-7333
Fax: (216)241-0105
E-mail: mbma@mbma.com
URL: http://www.mbma.com
Contact: Mr. Charles M. Stockinger, Gen. Mgr.
Founded: 1956. **Members:** 55. **Staff:** 6. **Description:** Manufacturers of metal building and roofing systems. Conducts research programs and compiles statistics. Associate members - suppliers. **Awards:** Graduate Fellowship Awards. **Type:** monetary. **Recipient:** for students pursuing Master's degree ● Manufacturer Safety Awards. **Frequency:** annual. **Type:** recognition. **Computer Services:** database. **Committees:** Certification; Construction; Insurance; Manufacturing; Marketing Communications; Statistics; Technical. **Publications:** *AISC-MB Certified Excellence Brochure*. **Price:** $3.00 ● *Bay Industries High Profile Case Study*. Brochure. **Price:** $1.00 ● *BHP Coated Steel Corp. High Profile Case Study*. Brochure. **Price:** $1.00 ● *Cold Hard Facts*. Brochure. **Price:** $4.00 ● *Commercial Solutions*. Brochure. **Price:** $4.00 ● *Industrial Solutions*. Brochure. **Price:** $4.00 ● *Institutional Solutions*. Brochure. **Price:** $4.00 ● *Landstar/Inway High Profile Case Study*. Brochure. **Price:** $1.00 ● *Standing Seam Metal Roofing Solutions*. Brochure. **Price:** $4.00.

638 ■ Metal Construction Association (MCA)
4700 W Lake Ave.
Glenview, IL 60025-1485
Ph: (847)375-4718 (610)966-2430
Fax: (877)665-2234
E-mail: mca@metalconstruction.org
URL: http://www.metalconstruction.org
Contact: T.A. Bus, Pres.
Founded: 1983. **Members:** 100. **Membership Dues:** manufacturer, coil coater, metal producer, $13,000 (annual) ● distributor, accessory, $8,000 (annual) ● fabricator, onsite rollformer, pre-engineered metal building, affiliate, $3,000 (annual) ● associate, $1,000 (annual). **Staff:** 5. **Description:** Promotes the metal construction industry in order to expand the use of all metals used in construction, including structure erection, estimating, and bookkeeping. Compiles statistics. **Libraries: Type:** not open to the public; reference. **Holdings:** articles, papers, periodicals, reports. **Awards:** Larry Swaney Award. **Frequency:** annual. **Type:** recognition ● President's Awards. **Frequency:** annual. **Type:** scholarship ● Student Design Competition. **Frequency:** annual. **Type:** scholarship. **Councils:** Commercial Roofing; MCM Fabricators; Metal-Forming Equipment; Residential Roofing; Wall Panel. **Publications:** *A Primer on Diaphragm Design Manual*. **Price:** $50.00 for members; $100.00 for nonmembers ● *Metal Construction Association—Membership Directory*, annual. Contains company index and personnel index. **Price:** free for members and select others ● *Metal Construction Association—Newsletter*, 3/year. Includes technical articles, meeting reviews, committee reports, minutes, and calendar of events. **Price:** free for members and select others. Alternate Formats: online. **Conventions/Meetings:** semiannual conference ● annual conference and meeting - always January ● annual Metalcon International - trade show (exhibits).

639 ■ Metal Framing Manufacturers Association (MFMA)
401 N Michigan Ave.
Chicago, IL 60611-4267
Ph: (312)644-6610
Fax: (312)321-4098
E-mail: mfma@sba.com
URL: http://www.metalframingmfg.org
Contact: Mr. Jack M. Springer, Exec. Dir.
Founded: 1981. **Members:** 8. **Membership Dues:** firm, $2,000 (annual). **Staff:** 2. **Budget:** $2,000. **Description:** Manufacturers of ferrous and nonferrous metal framing systems. Promotes the use of metal framing (continuous slot metal channel) systems; develops industry standards; collects industry statistics. **Convention/Meeting:** none. **Libraries: Type:** reference. **Subjects:** metal framing, standard MFMA-No. 4. **Committees:** Statistics; Technical. **Publications:** *Uses for Metal Framing - Metal Framing Standard*.

640 ■ National Academy of Building Inspection Engineers (NABIE)
PO Box 522158
Salt Lake City, UT 84152
Free: (800)294-7729
Fax: (801)583-1531
E-mail: director@nabie.org
URL: http://www.nabie.org
Contact: Don Liszkay, Pres.
Founded: 1989. **Members:** 135. **Membership Dues:** professional, intern, correspondent, international, student, $175 (annual) ● executive, $225 (annual) ● diplomate, fellow, $275 (annual). **Staff:** 1. **Description:** State-registered professional engineers. Strives to lead and advance the integrity, value and understanding of the practice of professional engineering as it applies to the inspection, investigation, and evaluation of buildings and homes. Affinity group of the National Society of Professional Engineers. **Affiliated With:** National Society of Professional Engineers. **Publications:** *NABIE Examiner*, quarterly. Newsletter. **Price:** included in membership dues.

641 ■ National Asphalt Pavement Association (NAPA)
5100 Forbes Blvd.
Lanham, MD 20706
Ph: (301)731-4748
Free: (888)468-6499
Fax: (301)731-4621
E-mail: mcervarich@hotmix.org
URL: http://www.hotmix.org
Contact: Mike Acott, Pres.
Founded: 1955. **Members:** 750. **Staff:** 25. **Budget:** $4,000,000. **State Groups:** 38. **Languages:** English, Spanish. **Description:** Manufacturers and producers of scientifically proportioned Hot Mix Asphalt for use in all paving, including highways, airfields, and environmental usages. Membership includes hot mix producers, paving contractors, equipment manufacturers, engineering consultants, and others. Supports research and publishes information on: producing, stockpiling, and feeding of the aggregate to the manufacturing facility; drying; methods of screening, storing, and proportioning in the manufacturing facility; production of the hot mix asphalt; transporting mix to paver; lay down procedure and rolling; general workmanship; and related construction practices and materials. Commits to product quality, environmental control, safety and health, and energy conservation. Conducts training programs on a variety of technical and managerial topics for industry personnel. Maintains speakers' bureau and Hot Mix Asphalt Hall of Fame. **Libraries: Type:** not open to the public. **Holdings:** 2,000; articles, books, periodicals. **Subjects:** asphalt pavement technology. **Awards:** Community Involvement Awards. **Frequency:** annual. **Type:** recognition. **Recipient:** for excellence in community relations programs ● Hot Mix Asphalt Hall of Fame. **Frequency:** annual. **Type:** recognition. **Recipient:** for individual contributions ● Quality in Construction Awards. **Type:** recognition. **Recipient:** for superior construction of hot mix asphalt pavements ● Sheldon G. Hayes Award. **Frequency:** annual. **Type:** recognition. **Recipient:** for outstanding workmanship in asphalt paving. **Additional Websites:** http://www.OwnYourRoad.com, http://www.asphaltjobs.com, http://www.beyondRoads.com. **Telecommunication Services:** electronic mail, macott@hotmix.org. **Committees:** Asphalt Pavement Alliance; Asphalt Research and Technology; Awards; Dues, Finance and Audit; Environmental, Safety and Plant Operations; Hot Mix Asphalt Hall of Fame Selection; Marketing; Nominating; Superpave Implementation. **Formerly:** (1965) National Bituminous Concrete Association. **Publications:** *HMAT*, bimonthly. Magazine. Provides information on technical development and application in the hot mix asphalt paving industry. Also contains association and industry news. **Price:** free. **Circulation:** 30,000. **Advertising:** accepted ● *NAPA Membership Directory*, annual. **Price:** available to members only ● *National Asphalt Pavement Association—Publications Catalog*, annual. Lists films and publications produced by NAPA. Includes subject, alphabetical, and film/videotape indexes. **Price:** free ● *Practical Paving*, semiweekly. Newsletter. **Price:**

available to members only. **Circulation:** 3,500 ● Booklets. **Conventions/Meetings:** annual meeting - 2009 Jan. 25-28, San Diego, CA ● annual World of Asphalt Show and Conference - trade show, technical, management, and marketing (exhibits) - 2009 Mar. 9-12, Orlando, FL; 2010 Feb. 15-18, Cincinnati, OH.

642 ■ National Association of Independent Resurfacers (NAIR)

5806 W 127th St.
Alsip, IL 60803
Ph: (708)371-8237
Fax: (708)371-8283
E-mail: nairbowlanecare@msn.com
URL: http://www.nairbowl.org
Contact: Nancy Surprenant, Exec. Sec.

Founded: 1973. **Members:** 100. **Description:** Individuals and firms in the business of resanding and refinishing bowling lanes. Purposes are: to cooperate with proprietors; to improve safety standards, finishes, and equipment, thus reducing fire hazards; to convince the insurance industry that insuring resurfacers is a good investment; to enhance the status of the resurfacing industry and give resurfacers a representative voice in the bowling industry; to keep abreast of federal, state, and local legislation affecting resurfacers; to exchange ideas for resurfacers' mutual benefit. Conducts resurfacers training school and sales training seminar. **Awards:** Tom Nonnenmacher Industry Service Award. **Frequency:** annual. **Type:** recognition. **Recipient:** for significant service and dedication to NAIR and the bowling industry. **Committees:** Industry Relations; Safety and Training; Technical. **Publications:** *NAIR Membership Directory*, periodic. Includes listing of services offered. **Price:** available to members only. **Advertising:** accepted ● *NAIR News*, quarterly. Newsletter. **Price:** available to members only. Alternate Formats: online.

643 ■ National Association of the Remodeling Industry (NARI)

780 Lee St., Ste.200
Des Plaines, IL 60016
Ph: (847)298-9200
Free: (800)611-NARI
Fax: (847)298-9225
E-mail: info@nari.org
URL: http://www.nari.org
Contact: Gwen Biasi, Dir. of Marketing and Communications

Founded: 1982. **Members:** 7,000. **Staff:** 12. **Regional Groups:** 7. **State Groups:** 54. **Local Groups:** 80. **Description:** Represents remodeling contractors, manufacturers of remodeling/building products, lending institutions, and wholesalers and distributors. Promotes the common business interests of those engaged in the home improvement and remodeling industries. Encourages ethical conduct, good business practices, and professionalism in the remodeling industry. Conducts seminars, workshops, and promotional programs and has developed an extensive certification program. Local NARI chapters monitor legislations and regulations affecting the industry. **Awards:** Contractor of the Year Award. **Frequency:** annual. **Type:** recognition. **Recipient:** for outstanding remodeling projects across the country. **Telecommunication Services:** electronic mail, gbiasi@nari.org. **Committees:** Awards; Education; Ethics; Government Affairs; Strategic Planning and Research. **Councils:** Contractors; Distributors; Manufacturers. **Formed by Merger of:** (1982) National Remodelers Association; (1982) National Home Improvement Council. **Publications:** *Remodeler's Journal*, bimonthly. **Price:** available to members only. **Conventions/Meetings:** annual Evening of Excellence - banquet.

644 ■ National Association of Store Fixture Manufacturers (NASFM)

4651 Sheridan St., Ste.470
Hollywood, FL 33021
Ph: (954)893-7300
Fax: (954)893-7500
E-mail: nasfm@nasfm.org
URL: http://www.nasfm.org
Contact: Klein Merriman, Exec. Dir.

Founded: 1956. **Members:** 600. **Membership Dues:** company based outside North America, $750 (annual) ● company with a North American presence (based on total plant square footage and number of employees), $1,200-$2,300 (annual) ● associate, $1,475 (annual) ● designer (based on number of employees), $250-$1,000 (annual) ● company, $450 (annual) ● retail, $250 (annual) ● student, $25 (annual). **Staff:** 10. **Budget:** $1,000,000. **Description:** Represents the interests of store fixtures manufacturers and suppliers. Provides networking opportunities for members. Conducts educational programs, benchmarking surveys and other resources for manufacturers. **Awards:** Retail Design Award. **Frequency:** annual. **Type:** recognition. **Recipient:** for store designers. **Committees:** Associate Member; Convention; Costing and Estimating Seminar; Manufacturing Seminar; Membership Development; Project Management Seminar; Retail Design Awards; Retail Marketing. **Publications:** *Industry Performance Report*, annual. Alternate Formats: online ● *NASFM Store Fixture Buyer's Guide & Membership Directory*, annual. Includes members with product descriptions, manufacturing capabilities and geographic areas served. **Price:** free for members; $175.00 for nonmembers. **Circulation:** 12,000. **Advertising:** accepted. Alternate Formats: online ● Magazine, bimonthly. Contains issues and events specific to store fixture manufacturing. **Price:** $48.00 in North America; $75.00 outside North America; $25.00 back issue. **Circulation:** 8,000. **Advertising:** accepted. **Conventions/Meetings:** annual GlobalShop - show - 2009 Mar., Las Vegas, NV ● meeting - 3/year.

645 ■ National Association of Waterproofing and Structural Repair Contractors (NAWSRC)

c/o Claudia J. Clemons, Exec. Dir.
8015 Corporate Dr., Ste.A
Baltimore, MD 21236
Ph: (410)931-3332
Free: (800)245-6292
Fax: (410)931-2060
E-mail: info@nawsrc.org
URL: http://www.nawsrc.org
Contact: Claudia J. Clemons, Exec. Dir.

Founded: 1981. **Members:** 180. **Membership Dues:** ordinary, $795 (annual). **Staff:** 2. **Description:** Waterproofing contractors. Represents members' interests before industry organizations, government agencies, and the public. Conducts educational programs. **Computer Services:** database ● electronic publishing. **Telecommunication Services:** electronic mail, nawsrc@managementalliance.com. **Programs:** Above Grade Waterproofing Certification; Structural Repair Certification; Waterproofing Certification. **Publications:** *NAWSRC Foundation News*, quarterly. Newsletter. **Price:** included in membership dues. **Circulation:** 180. **Advertising:** accepted. Alternate Formats: online. **Conventions/Meetings:** annual convention, for suppliers (exhibits) ● annual meeting (exhibits).

646 ■ National Council of Acoustical Consultants (NCAC)

7150 Winton Dr., Ste.300
Indianapolis, IN 46268
Ph: (317)328-0642
Fax: (317)328-4629
E-mail: info@ncac.com
URL: http://www.ncac.com
Contact: Jackie Williams, Exec. Dir.

Founded: 1962. **Members:** 130. **Description:** Firms of acoustical consultants. Focuses on the management and related concerns of professional acoustical consulting firms and safeguards the interests of the individuals they serve. Sponsors educational programs; maintains Speaker's Bureau. **Telecommunication Services:** electronic mail, jwilliams@ncac.com. **Committees:** Acoustical Instrumentation Accreditation; Canons of Ethics Review; Communications Policy; Government Agency Liaison; Insurance; Manufacturers Liaison; Professional Advertising; Professional Practice; Professional Society Liaison. **Affiliated With:** Acoustical Society of America; Institute of Noise Control Engineering. **Publications:** Membership Directory, biennial ● Newsletter, quarterly. Provides news of developments affecting acoustical consulting businesses. **Advertising:** accepted. Alternate Formats: online.

647 ■ National Council of the Housing Industry (NCHI)

1201 15th St. NW
Washington, DC 20005
Ph: (202)266-8200 (202)266-8243
Free: (800)368-5242
Fax: (202)266-8521
E-mail: bmcmurray@nahb.com
URL: http://www.nahb.org
Contact: Barbara McMurray, Staff VP

Founded: 1964. **Members:** 235,000. **Membership Dues:** corporate, $7,000 (annual). **Staff:** 4. **Budget:** $600,000. **Description:** Manufacturers of goods and services for the American housing industry. Provides support for the effort of the industry to fill the housing needs of American families. **Libraries: Type:** reference. **Holdings:** 12,000. **Committees:** Building Materials Issues; Education; Government Affairs; Marketing. **Task Forces:** The New American Home. **Affiliated With:** National Association of Home Builders. **Formerly:** (1975) National Housing Center Council. **Publications:** *Nations Building News*, periodic. Newspaper. **Conventions/Meetings:** conference ● annual meeting (exhibits) ● seminar.

648 ■ National Fenestration Rating Council (NFRC)

6305 Ivy Ln., Ste.140
Greenbelt, MD 20770
Ph: (301)589-1776
Fax: (301)589-3884
E-mail: info@nfrc.org
URL: http://www.nfrc.org
Contact: James C. Benney, Exec. Dir.

Founded: 1990. **Members:** 200. **Membership Dues:** regular, manufacturer/supplier (with below $1 million annual sales), $400 (annual) ● manufacturer/supplier (with $1 million to $10 million annual sales), $750-$1,500 (annual) ● manufacturer/supplier (with $11 million to $50 million annual sales), $3,000-$5,500 (annual) ● manufacturer/supplier (with $51 million to $300 million annual sales), $8,500-$12,500 (annual) ● manufacturer/supplier (with above $300 million annual sales), $17,500 (annual). **Staff:** 8. **Budget:** $1,000,000. **Description:** Individuals, organizations, and corporations interested in production, regulation, promotion, and development of technology related to fenestration products. Develops national voluntary energy performance rating system for fenestration products; coordinates certification and labeling activities to ensure uniform rating application. Promotes consumer awareness of fenestration ratings in an effort to encourage informed purchase of windows, doors, and skylights. Conducts efficiency testing. Maintains speakers' bureau; conducts educational and research programs. **Libraries: Type:** reference. **Affiliated With:** Alliance to Save Energy; American Architectural Manufacturers Association; American Society of Heating, Refrigerating and Air-Conditioning Engineers; International Window Film Association; Window and Door Manufacturers Association. **Publications:** *An Introduction to NFRC*. Brochure ● *NFRC 100-1: Procedure for Determining Fenestration Product Thermal Properties*. **Price:** $40.00 for members; $75.00 for nonmembers ● *NFRC 200-93: Procedure for Determining Fenestration Solar Heat Gain at Normal Incidence* ● *NFRC Update*, quarterly. Newsletter. **Price:** free. **Circulation:** 3,000 ● Annual Report, annual ● Also produces software and ratings procedures. **Conventions/Meetings:** semiannual meeting.

649 ■ National Housing Endowment

1201 15th St. NW
Washington, DC 20005
Ph: (202)266-8483
Free: (800)368-5242
Fax: (202)266-8177

E-mail: nhe@nahb.com
URL: http://www.nationalhousingendowment.com
Contact: Bruce S. Silver, Pres./CEO
Founded: 1987. **Staff:** 2. **Budget:** $475,000. **Description:** Works to 'build a foundation' to help make the American dream of homeownership a reality for present and future generations. Provides a permanent source of funds to address long-term industry concerns at the national level. Helps the industry to develop more effective approaches to home building. Enhances the ways to educate and train future generations of leaders in residential construction and increase the body of knowledge on housing issues. Supports innovative and effective programs that further Education, Training, and Research. **Awards:** Builders Achievement Award for Community Service. **Frequency:** annual. **Type:** recognition ● Home Builders Care Project of the Year Award. **Frequency:** annual. **Type:** recognition ● Various Scholarships Awards. **Frequency:** annual. **Type:** scholarship. **Recipient:** for students pursuing careers in residential construction and building related industries. **Programs:** Challenge/Build/Grow Grant Initiative. **Affiliated With:** National Association of Home Builders. **Publications:** *Blueprint*. Newsletter ● Brochure. Alternate Formats: online.

650 ■ National One Coat Stucco Association (NOCSA)

1615 W Abram St., Ste.L
Arlington, TX 76013
Ph: (817)461-3351
Free: (888)461-3352
Fax: (817)461-3351
URL: http://www.nocsa.org
Contact: Wayne James CAE, Exec. Dir.
Description: Promotes the manufacturing and installation of quality one coat stucco. Seeks to uphold the standards that are set for the stucco industry. Facilitates an online continuing education course for architects and design professionals. **Publications:** Membership Directory, annual ● Newsletter.

651 ■ National Pavement Contractors Association (NPCA)

PO Box 57
Mineral Wells, TX 76068-0057
Ph: (940)327-8041
E-mail: info@pavementpro.com
URL: http://www.pavementpro.org
Membership Dues: single service contractor, $185 (annual) ● limited multiple service contractor, $195 (annual) ● limited residential-only maintenance contractor, $225 (annual) ● multiple residential only service/multiple commercial-only service contractor, $235 (annual) ● multiple residential only service/multiple commercial-only service contractor (with paving), $250 (annual) ● contractor offering multiple services for both commercial and residential clients, $250 (annual) ● contractor providing any number of full-range services for both commercial and residential clients, $275 (annual). **Description:** Provides pavement customers with reliable information and sample specifications. Promotes excellence of service, quality of performance and profitable growth for professional pavement contractors. Facilitates nationwide advertising, networking, training and professional improvement of members and their employees. **Computer Services:** Online services, message board. **Additional Websites:** http://pavementpro.com. **Publications:** *55 News*. Newsletter. **Price:** included in membership dues. Alternate Formats: online.

652 ■ National Slag Association (NSA)

25 Stevens Ave., Bldg. A
West Lawn, PA 19609
Ph: (610)670-0701
Fax: (610)670-0702
E-mail: info@nationalslagassoc.org
URL: http://www.nationalslagassoc.org
Contact: Terry R. Wagaman, Pres.
Founded: 1918. **Members:** 78. **Staff:** 2. **Description:** Comprises of organizations actively engaged in iron and steel slag processing, refining, and/or the marketing of these slags; organizations that are actively involved in activities directly connected with the iron and steel slag industry such as users, manufacturer's of equipment, suppliers, and service firms. Seeks to communicate and exchange pertinent slag industry information to the membership. Supports and promotes iron and steel slag interests at all levels, provides initiative and leadership, fosters humanistic and user-friendly levels of communications, and nurtures a positive relationship with all governmental and environmental agencies and the steel slag industry. **Libraries: Type:** reference. **Holdings:** archival material, audiovisuals, books, clippings, periodicals. **Subjects:** slag blast furnace, steel. **Awards:** Plant Safety Awards. **Frequency:** annual. **Type:** recognition. **Committees:** Cement Manufacturing Technology; Marketing; Plant Operators; Safety; Technical. **Publications:** *Slag Runner*, quarterly. Newsletter. Informs the membership of iron and steel slag industry news and activities. **Price:** available to members only. Alternate Formats: online. **Conventions/Meetings:** semiannual meeting, with guest speakers and members speaking on industry-related topics - every spring and fall.

653 ■ National Sunroom Association (NSA)

1300 Sumner Ave.
Cleveland, OH 44115-2851
Ph: (216)241-7333
Fax: (216)241-0105
E-mail: info@nationalsunroom.org
URL: http://www.nationalsunroom.org
Contact: Dean A. Schwartz, Pres.
Founded: 1997. **Membership Dues:** manufacturer (based on sales volume), $2,000-$6,000 (annual) ● affiliate, $3,000 (annual) ● affiliate organization, $500 (annual) ● dealer/sponsor, $75 (annual). **Description:** Manufacturers and constructors of sunrooms, patio rooms, and solariums. Seeks to advance members' commercial and regulatory interests. Represents members before government agencies, industrial organizations, media, and the public. Serves as a clearinghouse on sunrooms and related technologies. **Awards:** Design Award. **Frequency:** annual. **Type:** recognition. **Recipient:** for top sunroom designs. **Computer Services:** database, list of NSA dealer members across the United States. **Committees:** Code; Program; Standards; Technical; Website and Design Awards. **Publications:** *NSA Membership*. Brochure ● *NSA Sunroom News*, quarterly. Newsletter. Alternate Formats: online.

654 ■ National Town Builders' Association (NTBA)

3220 N St. NW, No. 238
Washington, DC 20007
Ph: (202)333-1902
Fax: (202)333-0223
E-mail: info@ntba.net
URL: http://www.ntba.net
Contact: David Mayfield, Pres.
Membership Dues: company, $2,500 (annual). **Description:** Promotes growth and development of traditional neighborhoods and town centers. Strives to enhance the skills and meet the business needs of members through peer networking and collaborative education. Facilitates communication and collaboration among members and town builders.

655 ■ National Wood Flooring Association (NWFA)

111 Chesterfield Indus. Blvd.
Chesterfield, MO 63005
Ph: (636)519-9663
Free: (800)422-4556
Fax: (636)519-9664
E-mail: info@nwfa.org
URL: http://www.woodfloors.org
Contact: Ken Schumacher CR, Chm.
Founded: 1985. **Members:** 3,300. **Membership Dues:** firm, $395 (annual) ● branch, $50 (annual). **Staff:** 15. **Budget:** $3,200,000. **Multinational. Description:** Individuals, firms, and corporations engaged in the manufacture, distribution, installation, or sale of wood flooring and allied products. Purposes are to: unite all segments of the wood flooring industry; coordinate marketing and advertising programs of members; educate professionals and consumers about the benefits of wood flooring; increase the market share of the wood flooring industry. Works to develop product standards and a code of professional ethics within the industry. Sponsors training seminars for management and sales personnel; conducts promotional programs on the care and maintenance of wood floors. Disseminates information on new products and services; maintains speakers' bureau; compiles statistics. Maintains hall of fame on wood floor products and installation. Offers a certification program for sanders, finishers, inspectors, sales personnel and installers. **Libraries: Type:** not open to the public. **Holdings:** 1,500; articles. **Subjects:** wood and the environment. **Awards:** Wood Floor of the Year. **Frequency:** annual. **Type:** recognition. **Recipient:** voted by wood flooring professionals. **Additional Websites:** http://www.nwfa.org. **Committees:** Installation Guidelines; Membership; Promotion and Public Relations; Regional Seminars; Technical and Education. **Publications:** *Hardwood Floors Magazine*, bimonthly. **Circulation:** 24,000. **Advertising:** accepted ● *NWFA Installation Guidelines* ● *NWFA The Log*, monthly. Newsletter ● *NWFA Wood Flooring Manual*. **Conventions/Meetings:** annual convention (exhibits).

656 ■ NOFMA: The Wood Flooring Manufacturers Association

22 N Front St., Ste.660
Memphis, TN 38103
Ph: (901)526-5016
Fax: (901)526-7022
E-mail: info@nofma.org
URL: http://www.nofma.org
Contact: Timm Locke, Exec. VP
Founded: 1909. **Members:** 27. **Membership Dues:** associate, $1,500 (annual). **Staff:** 7. **Description:** Manufacturers of wood flooring. Promotes standardization; conducts grade labeling and inspection service; maintains research program in grading, handling, and installation; compiles statistics. **Formerly:** Oak Flooring Manufacturers of United States; Southern Oak Flooring Industries; (2002) National Oak Flooring Manufacturers Association. **Publications:** *Official Flooring Grading Rules* ● Brochures. **Conventions/Meetings:** Certified Wood Flooring Inspector Schools - meeting - 3/year; usually April, July and November in Memphis, TN ● semiannual Hardwood Flooring Installation School - workshop - usually March and September in Memphis, TN.

657 ■ North American Association of Floor Covering Distributors (NAFCD)

401 N Michigan Ave., Ste.2200
Chicago, IL 60611
Ph: (312)321-6836
Fax: (312)673-6962
E-mail: info@nafcd.org
URL: http://www.nafcd.org
Contact: Maurice A. Desmarais CAE, Exec. VP
Founded: 1971. **Members:** 285. **Membership Dues:** distributor, $995 (annual) ● manufacturer, manufacturer's agent, allied, $1,095 (annual). **Staff:** 3. **Budget:** $500,000. **Description:** Floor covering distributors and firms selling to them. Aims to promote, protect, and advance the best interests of wholesale floor covering distribution; to foster sound business principles in all phases of floor covering wholesaling; to increase the use of wholesale floor covering products by the retailer; to improve understanding between manufacturers and wholesalers of floor covering products, and increase distribution of floor covering and related products through wholesale distribution channels; to improve the conditions under which the industry must operate; to collect and disseminate pertinent industry data; to assist its members through education, research, and training. **Libraries: Type:** not open to the public. **Awards:** Young Executive of the Year. **Frequency:** annual. **Type:** scholarship. **Committees:** Floor Covering Adhesive Manufacturers. **Formerly:** (2007) National Association of Floor Covering Distributors. **Publications:** *National Association of Floor Covering Distributors—Industry Chart Book*, annual. Serves as an industry chart book. **Price:** $50.00 for members; $150.00 for nonmembers ● *National Association of Floor Cover-*

ing Distributors—Membership, annual. Membership Directory ● *News and Views*, bimonthly. Newsletter ● Book, semiannual. Features a compensation study. **Conventions/Meetings:** biennial conference ● annual convention, quality education tailored to floor covering industry ● monthly meeting, educational teleconference ● semiannual regional meeting.

658 ■ North American Building Material Distribution Association (NBMDA)

401 N Michigan Ave.
Chicago, IL 60611
Ph: (312)321-6845
Free: (888)747-7862
Fax: (312)644-0310
E-mail: info@nbmda.org
URL: http://www.nbmda.org
Contact: Kevin Gammonley, Exec. VP

Founded: 1952. **Members:** 400. **Membership Dues:** allied, $495 (annual) ● associate (based on annual gross sales), $995-$3,595 (annual) ● distributor (based on annual gross sales), $795-$4,595 (annual). **Staff:** 5. **Budget:** $1,200,000. **Description:** Building material distributors and manufacturers operating in more than 1500 locations. Represents the industry when appropriate. Distributes member and industry information; provides networking opportunities to distributors and manufacturers in the building material industry. Maintains education foundation; provides charitable programs. **Telecommunication Services:** electronic mail, exec@nbmda.org. **Committees:** Canadian Affairs; Distribution; Education; Government Relations; Marketing and Communications; Technology. **Formerly:** (1995) National Building Material Distributors Association. **Publications:** *Channels*, bimonthly. Newsletter. Includes industry news, calendar of events, business tips, and statistics. **Price:** included in membership dues. **Circulation:** 1,500. **Advertising:** accepted. Alternate Formats: online ● *NBMDA Membership and Product Directory*, annual. **Price:** $795.00 for nonmembers ● *NBMDA Survey Series*, 2-3/year. Includes comprehensive surveys exclusive to the building products industry. ● *The Sales Trainer: A Bi-Monthly Digest of Marketing Techniques for Aggressive Salespeople*, bimonthly. Monograph. **Price:** included in membership dues. **Circulation:** 1,700. Alternate Formats: online ● Annual Report, annual. Contains association news, industry statistics, and committee reports. **Price:** included in membership dues. **Circulation:** 1,500. **Conventions/Meetings:** annual convention and conference, for management (exhibits) ● Executive Management Conference.

659 ■ North American Insulation Manufacturers Association (NAIMA)

44 Canal Center Plz., Ste.310
Alexandria, VA 22314
Ph: (703)684-0084
Fax: (703)684-0427
E-mail: insulation@naima.org
URL: http://www.naima.org
Contact: Kenneth Mentzer, Pres./CEO/Treas.

Founded: 1933. **Members:** 14. **Staff:** 10. **Budget:** $4,000,000. **Description:** Manufacturers of fiberglass, rock wool, and slag wool insulation products. Promotes energy efficiency and environmental preservation through the use of fiberglass, rock wool, and slag wool insulation products. Encourages safe production and use of insulation materials. **Committees:** Product; Service. **Programs:** Health and Safety Partnership; Insulation Energy Appraisal; National Insulation Training; Train the Trainer. **Formerly:** Mineral Insulation Manufacturers Association. **Publications:** Publishes standard reports and material on the uses of insulation in houses and buildings.

660 ■ North American Laminate Flooring Association (NALFA)

1747 Pennsylvania Ave. NW, Ste.1000
Washington, DC 20006
Ph: (202)785-9500
Fax: (202)835-0243
E-mail: information@nalfa.com
URL: http://www.nalfa.com
Contact: Bill Dearing, Pres.

Founded: 1997. **Multinational. Description:** Represents manufacturers of laminate flooring products. Seeks to create voluntary product performance standards for laminate flooring in North America. Aspires to bring about product satisfaction to laminate flooring customers. Provides careful assessment of laminate flooring quality. **Awards:** Lammy Awards. **Frequency:** annual. **Type:** recognition. **Recipient:** for individuals and companies who made a significant contribution to the laminate flooring industry.

661 ■ Polyisocyanurate Insulation Manufacturers Association (PIMA)

7315 Wisconsin Ave., Ste.400E
Bethesda, MD 20814
Ph: (301)654-0000
Fax: (301)951-8401
E-mail: pima@pima.org
URL: http://www.polyiso.org
Contact: Jared O. Blum, Pres.

Founded: 1987. **Members:** 30. **Staff:** 2. **Budget:** $1,000,000. **Description:** Companies and individuals involved in the manufacture of polyisocyanurate roofing and wall insulations; associate members are suppliers to the industry. Promotes the industry and represents its legislative and regulatory interests at the state and federal levels; develops product application standards. Addresses issues such as toxicity, building codes, fire performance, energy conservation, environmental effects of insulation, and the import industry. Conducts research; sponsors educational programs; compiles statistics. **Committees:** Industry Promotion; Technical. **Publications:** *PIMA Online*, 5/year. Newsletter. Alternate Formats: online. **Conventions/Meetings:** annual meeting.

662 ■ Porcelain Enamel Institute (PEI)

PO Box 920220
Norcross, GA 30010
Ph: (770)281-8980
Fax: (770)281-8981
E-mail: penamel@aol.com
URL: http://www.porcelainenamel.com
Contact: Cullen Hackler, Exec. VP/Sec.

Founded: 1930. **Members:** 80. **Membership Dues:** steel company (based on the previous year sales), $2,625-$6,850 (annual) ● enameller (based on the previous year sales), $2,100-$5,250 (annual) ● supplier (chemical to end user), $1,575 (annual) ● supplier (raw materials other than frit or base metals), $3,700 (annual) ● supplier (equipment; based on dollar sales from the previous year), $1,575-$3,700 (annual) ● supplier (frit manufacturing), $6,000-$36,000 (annual) ● company (not currently listed in other categories), $1,050 (annual). **Staff:** 2. **Budget:** $450,000. **Description:** Trade association of the porcelain enamel industry. Manufacturers of major appliances, sanitary ware, architectural porcelain enamel, signs, and other porcelain enamel products; suppliers to the industry such as producers of steel, aluminum, and porcelain enamel frit; chemical companies. Conducts market development and promotion programs, develops test methods for evaluation of porcelain enamel properties, and maintains weather resistance testing sites jointly with the National Bureau of Standards. Serves as information clearinghouse. **Libraries: Type:** reference. **Holdings:** 100; books. **Subjects:** porcelain enameling and coatings. **Awards:** Long-Oliver Distinguished Service Award. **Frequency:** annual. **Type:** recognition. **Computer Services:** database, of papers and presenters ● mailing lists ● online services. **Committees:** Marketing; Meetings; Membership; Technical. **Affiliated With:** American Ceramic Society; Ceramic Manufacturers Association; Enamelist Society. **Publications:** *Technical Forum*, annual. Proceedings. **Price:** $15.00. **Circulation:** 1,250. Also Cited As: *Ceramic Engineering and Science Proceedings* ● Newsletter, bimonthly ● Also publishes data on test methods, standards, and construction of porcelain enamel. **Conventions/Meetings:** annual meeting, technical forum (exhibits) ● annual Technical Forum - conference, with porcelain enameling technology and materials.

663 ■ Post-Tensioning Institute (PTI)

8601 N Black Canyon Hwy., Ste.103
Phoenix, AZ 85021
Ph: (602)870-7540
Fax: (602)870-7541
E-mail: info@post-tensioning.org
URL: http://post-tensioning.org
Contact: Theodore L. Neff, Exec. Dir.

Founded: 1976. **Members:** 800. **Membership Dues:** associate A, post tensioning, $2,500 (annual) ● associate B (based on sales), $1,600-$2,600 (annual) ● affiliate/consulting company/installing company, $770 (annual) ● foreign post-tensioning, $900 (annual) ● foreign associate A, $600 (annual) ● foreign associate B, $300 (annual) ● professional, in North America, $95 (annual) ● professional, partial year, in North America, $60 ● professional, outside North America, $125 (annual) ● professional, partial year, outside North America, $75 ● association, $1,200 (annual) ● student, $40 (annual). **Staff:** 5. **Budget:** $1,200,000. **Description:** Post-tensioning material fabricators, manufacturers of prestressing steel and P/T accessories and supplies, concrete construction organizations, professional engineers, architects, and contractors. Seeks to advance the use of post-tensioning materials through research, technical development, and marketing efforts. Compiles information of benefit to users of post-tensioning materials. Cooperates in the adoption and maintenance of standard specifications for the design, fabrication, and installation of post-tensioning materials. Conducts research programs. **Libraries: Type:** not open to the public. **Telecommunication Services:** electronic mail, tedneff@post-tensioning.org. **Boards:** Technical Advisory. **Committees:** Cable-Stayed Bridges; Grouting Specifications; Post-Tensioning Systems Certification; Prestressed Rock and Soil Anchor; Slab-on-Ground; Strategic Planning; Training and Certification of Unbonded Post-Tensioning Field Personnel; Unbonded Tendons. **Publications:** *Design, Construction and Maintenance of Cast-in-place Post-Tensioned Concrete Parking Structures.* Manual. **Price:** $60.00 ● *Guide Specification for Grouting of Post-Tension Structures.* **Price:** $28.00 for nonmembers; $17.00 for members ● *PTI Membership Directory*, annual. **Price:** included in membership dues; $80.00 for nonmembers. **Circulation:** 1,200. **Advertising:** accepted ● *PTI Newsletter*, quarterly ● *Technical Notes*, periodic. **Price:** $2.00 for members; $3.00 for nonmembers; included in professional membership subscription. **Circulation:** 1,200. **Conventions/Meetings:** semiannual board meeting ● seminar ● workshop, for certification.

664 ■ Residential Energy Services Network (RESNET)

PO Box 4561
Oceanside, CA 92052-4561
Ph: (760)806-3448
E-mail: info@natresnet.org
URL: http://www.resnet.us
Contact: Steve Baden, Exec. Dir.

Founded: 1995. **Membership Dues:** associate, $100 (annual) ● certified rater, $200 (annual). **Description:** Aims to uphold the national standards for home energy ratings. Provides services concerning policy issues that affect consumer demand and housing industry support for residential energy efficiency. Serves as the portal by which consumers, the home energy rating industry, residential energy and, and the housing and mortgage industry can secure up-to-date information on residential energy performance and energy efficient financing options and packages. **Awards:** RESNET Industry Innovation Award. **Frequency:** annual. **Type:** recognition. **Recipient:** to an organization that has developed and implemented the most innovative program or policy ● RESNET Market Transformation Award. **Frequency:** annual. **Type:** recognition. **Recipient:** to an organization/rater that has made the most significant contribution to penetrating their housing market with rating services while maintaining the quality of the services ● RES-

NET Program Leadership Award. **Frequency:** annual. **Type:** recognition. **Recipient:** for outstanding contribution a residential energy efficiency, building performance, or financing initiative has made to the rating industry. **Telecommunication Services:** electronic mail, sbaden@resnet.us. **Publications:** *RESNET Notes*, monthly. Newsletter. **Price:** included in membership dues ● Annual Report. Alternate Formats: online. **Conventions/Meetings:** annual Building Performance Conference.

665 ■ Resilient Floor Covering Institute (RFCI)
401 E Jefferson St., Ste.102
Rockville, MD 20850
Ph: (301)340-8580
Fax: (301)340-7283
E-mail: info@rfci.com
URL: http://www.rfci.com
Contact: Douglas W. Wiegand, Managing Dir.
Founded: 1929. **Members:** 25. **Staff:** 2. **Budget:** $700,000. **Description:** Supports the manufacturers of vinyl composition tile, solid vinyl tile, or sheet vinyl and rubber tile and people who use its products. Provides technical information and data regarding the resilient flooring industry. **Committees:** Promotional; Technical Affairs. **Formerly:** (1957) Asphalt Tile Institute; (1973) Asphalt and Vinyl Asbestos Tile Institute; (1976) Resilient Tile Institute. **Publications:** *Recommended Work Practices for the Removal of Resilient Floor Coverings.* Booklet. Contains information on the recommended removal procedures of resilient floor coverings. **Price:** free. Alternate Formats: online. **Conventions/Meetings:** semiannual conference - always May and October.

666 ■ Roofing Industry Committee on Weather Issues (RICOWI)
c/o Patty Wood-Shields, Exec. Dir.
4721 Covenant Way
Powder Springs, GA 30127
Ph: (770)726-7194
Fax: (678)567-1759
E-mail: paws01@ricowi.com
URL: http://www.ricowi.com
Contact: Patty Wood-Shields, Exec. Dir.
Founded: 1990. **Membership Dues:** sponsor, $1,200 (annual) ● affiliate, $300 (annual). **Description:** Encourages and coordinates research on roof issues including wind, hail, energy efficiency, and durability effects. Seeks to accelerate the establishment of new or improved industry consensus standard practices for weather design and testing. Aims to improve the understanding of roof weather concepts and issues within the building community.

667 ■ Rubber Pavements Association (RPA)
1801 S Jentilly Ln., Ste.A-2
Tempe, AZ 85281-5738
Ph: (480)517-9944
Free: (888)517-9944
Fax: (480)517-9959
E-mail: dougc@rubberpavements.org
URL: http://www.rubberpavements.org
Contact: Douglas D. Carlson, Exec. Dir.
Founded: 1985. **Members:** 34. **Membership Dues:** producer/user, $2,000 (annual) ● associate, $550 (annual) ● individual, $35 (annual) ● affiliate, $75 (annual) ● non-blender, $1,000 (annual). **Staff:** 4. **Budget:** $580,000. **Multinational. Description:** Suppliers and processors of Asphalt-Rubber paving products. Promotes the efficient use of ground scrap tire rubber in asphalt products. Conducts national and international seminars; presents technical papers and films. Maintains bibliography; operates speakers' bureau. **Libraries: Type:** open to the public. **Holdings:** 1,000; reports, video recordings. **Subjects:** Asphalt-rubber. **Awards:** Outstanding Achievement Award. **Frequency:** annual. **Type:** recognition ● Outstanding Program Award. **Frequency:** annual. **Type:** recognition. **Telecommunication Services:** electronic mail, gdickerson@rubberpavements.org. **Boards:** Technical Advisory. **Affiliated With:** American Highway Users Alliance; Tire Industry Association. **Formerly:** Asphalt Rubber Producers Group. **Publications:** *The RPA News*, quarterly. Newsletter. Contains educational materials about Asphalt-Rubber. **Price:** free for members. **Circulation:** 6,500. Alternate Formats: online.

668 ■ Safety Glazing Certification Council (SGCC)
PO Box 730
Sackets Harbor, NY 13685-0730
Ph: (315)646-2234
Fax: (315)646-2297
E-mail: staff@amscert.com
URL: http://www.sgcc.org
Contact: John G. Kent, Contact
Founded: 1971. **Members:** 155. **Staff:** 3. **Description:** Manufacturers of safety glazing products, building code administrators, and others responsible for the safety of the public. Maintains certification and testing program for safety glazing material used in buildings. Certification activities include: accrediting laboratories to conduct safety glazing testing; initial and periodic testing by an accredited laboratory, and complaint testing in the event of a substantiated complaint; formal appeals procedure. **Committees:** Certification. **Publications:** *SGCC Certified Products Directory*, semiannual. **Conventions/Meetings:** semiannual conference.

669 ■ Scaffold Industry Association (SIA)
PO Box 20574
Phoenix, AZ 85036-0574
Ph: (602)257-1144
Free: (866)687-7115
Fax: (602)257-1166
E-mail: info@scaffold.org
URL: http://www.scaffold.org
Contact: John R. Miller, Pres.
Founded: 1972. **Members:** 1,000. **Membership Dues:** regular, voting (domestic/international; based on annual gross volume), $850-$950 (annual) ● regular, voting, branch (domestic/international; based on number of member branches), $100-$300 (annual) ● allied (domestic/international), $850 (annual) ● affiliate (domestic/international), $550 (annual). **Staff:** 8. **Budget:** $1,500,000. **Description:** Firms or individuals that manufacture, sell, or contract for the erection and/or rental of scaffolding, aerial platforms, and shoring or for any device used in the support of workers, material, or equipment. Includes activities such as meetings, educational seminars, research, and accident prevention insurance programs for members. Provides safety training aids such as videos, slides, warning signs and a scaffolder training program. **Telecommunication Services:** electronic mail, jrm@millstonecorp.com. **Committees:** Audit; Budget; Bylaws and Resolutions; Convention; Nominating; Oversight; Strategic Planning. **Councils:** Adjustable Scaffold; Fall Protection Equipment; Industrial Scaffold; International; Mast Climbing; Permanent Installation; Platform; Supported Scaffolds; Suspended Scaffolds. **Formerly:** (1975) Scaffold Contractors Association. **Publications:** *Scaffold Industry*, monthly. Magazine. Contains articles, news and information tailored specifically for the access industry. **Price:** included in membership dues; $10.00/issue for nonmembers; $85.00 /year for nonmembers. **Advertising:** accepted ● *Scaffold Industry Association—Membership Directory and Handbook*, annual. Includes both company and individual listings; also provides OSHA scaffold standards, and grading rules for scaffold planks. **Price:** free for members; $125.00 for nonmembers. **Circulation:** 3,000. **Advertising:** accepted ● *Scaffold Industry Association—Newsletter*, monthly. Covers industry developments in safety, accident prevention, litigation, insurance, and business practices; also provides calendar of events. **Circulation:** 2,000. **Advertising:** accepted. **Conventions/Meetings:** annual conference and seminar (exhibits) - July. 2008 July 16-27, Denver, CO.

670 ■ Scaffolding, Shoring and Forming Institute (SSFI)
1300 Sumner Ave.
Cleveland, OH 44115
Ph: (216)241-7333
Fax: (216)241-0105
E-mail: ssfi@ssfi.org
URL: http://www.ssfi.org
Contact: Chris Johnson, Managing Dir.
Founded: 1960. **Members:** 17. **Staff:** 3. **Description:** Manufacturers of scaffolding, shoring, and forming. Establishes recommended criteria and inspection guidelines for the proper and safe use of scaffolding, shoring, and forming in concrete construction. **Formerly:** Steel Scaffolding and Shoring Institute; (1980) Scaffolding, Shoring and Forming Institute. **Conventions/Meetings:** annual conference.

671 ■ Steel Deck Institute (SDI)
PO Box 25
Fox River Grove, IL 60021
Ph: (847)458-4647
Fax: (847)458-4648
E-mail: steve@sdi.org
URL: http://www.sdi.org
Contact: Steven A. Roehrig, Managing Dir.
Founded: 1936. **Members:** 26. **Staff:** 2. **Budget:** $300,000. **Description:** Represents manufacturers of steel decks; associate members are manufacturers of allied products. Formulates and publishes design specifications; conducts and sponsors research and test programs; compiles statistics. **Publications:** *Composite Steel Deck Design Handbook.* **Price:** $50.00 ● *Manual of Construction with Steel Deck.* **Price:** $21.00 ● *Roof Deck Construction Handbook.* **Price:** $22.00 ● *Steel Deck Diaphragm Design Manual.* Contains information and design examples for the design of steel deck diaphragms. **Price:** $95.00 ● *Steel Deck Institute Design Manual for Composite Decks, Form Decks, and Roof Decks*, biennial. Contains information on standard steel decks, acoustical and long span decks, pour stop, and cantilevers. **Price:** $35.00. **Conventions/Meetings:** annual conference ● seminar.

672 ■ Steel Door Institute (SDI)
c/o Wherry Associates
30200 Detroit Rd.
Cleveland, OH 44145-1967
Ph: (440)899-0010
Fax: (440)892-1404
E-mail: leh@wherryassoc.com
URL: http://www.steeldoor.org
Contact: J.J. Wherry, Managing Dir.
Founded: 1954. **Members:** 11. **Staff:** 4. **Description:** Represents manufacturers of standard, all-metal doors and frames used in commercial applications. Aims to promote the use of steel doors and frames in the construction industry. **Publications:** *SDI Fact File.* Contains information on commercial application of steel doors and frames. **Price:** $50.00. Alternate Formats: CD-ROM; online. **Conventions/Meetings:** meeting - 3/year.

673 ■ Steel Joist Institute (SJI)
3127 Mr. Joe White Ave.
Myrtle Beach, SC 29577-6760
Ph: (843)626-1995
Fax: (843)626-5565
E-mail: sji@steeljoist.org
URL: http://www.steeljoist.org
Contact: Sam Mahdavi, Pres.
Founded: 1928. **Members:** 15. **Staff:** 2. **Description:** Manufacturers engaged in the production of open web, longspan, and deep longspan steel joists; K-, LH-, and DLH-series; and joist girders. Formulates standards for design, manufacture, and use; assists in the development of building code regulations. Conducts seminars. **Committees:** Engineering Practice; Executive; Publicity; Research. **Publications:** *Safe Erection of Steel Joists* (in English and Spanish). Video. **Price:** $125.00 ● *75-Year Manual 1928-2003.* **Price:** $85.00. Alternate Formats: online ● *Standard Specifications, Load Tables, and Weight Tables for Steel Joists and Joist Girders.* Catalog. Includes technical digests. **Price:** $25.00. Alternate Formats: online.

674 ■ Steel Window Institute (SWI)
1300 Sumner Ave.
Cleveland, OH 44115-2851
Ph: (216)241-7333

Fax: (216)241-0105
E-mail: swi@steelwindows.com
URL: http://www.steelwindows.com
Contact: Susan Young, Exec. Sec.
Founded: 1920. **Members:** 9. **Staff:** 3. **Description:** Manufacturers of solid section steel windows. Provides the public with general and technical information concerning the industry's products. **Publications:** *An Architect's Guide to Steel Windows* ● *The First 12 Reasons to Buy Steel Windows* ● Brochures. Provides information on energy. **Conventions/Meetings:** annual meeting.

675 ■ Structural Insulated Panel Association (SIPA)
PO Box 1699
Gig Harbor, WA 98335
Ph: (253)858-7472
Fax: (253)858-0272
E-mail: help@sips.org
URL: http://www.sips.org
Contact: Bill Wachtler, Exec. Dir.
Founded: 1990. **Members:** 215. **Membership Dues:** manufacturer (maximum, based on annual production level), $30,000 (annual) ● supplier (group 1), $10,000 (annual) ● supplier (group 2), $5,000 (annual) ● dealer, distributor, $1,000 (annual) ● associate, $300 (annual) ● builder/design professional, $125 (annual). **Staff:** 3. **Budget:** $250,000. **Description:** Trade association for the Structural Insulated Panel (SIP) industry. Promotes increased use and acceptance of SIPs by building designers, contractors, regulators, and homeowners. Serves as a clearinghouse for information on SIPs; develops industry standards for manufacturing and ethical practice; facilitates communication and cooperation among members. Conducts educational programs; sponsors competitions. **Publications:** *Building With Structural Insulated Panels (SIPs)*. Book. **Price:** $34.95 for nonmembers; $27.96 for members ● *OnSite@SIPA*, quarterly. Newsletter. **Circulation:** 5,500. Alternate Formats: online. **Conventions/Meetings:** periodic board meeting (exhibits) ● periodic conference (exhibits).

676 ■ Stucco Manufacturers Association (SMA)
2402 Vista Nobleza
Newport Beach, CA 92660
Ph: (949)640-9902
Fax: (949)640-9911
E-mail: info@stuccomfgassoc.com
URL: http://www.stuccomfgassoc.com
Contact: Norma S. Fox, Exec. Dir.
Founded: 1957. **Members:** 45. **Membership Dues:** regular, $2,000 (annual) ● associate, $1,000 (annual). **Description:** Manufacturers of stucco products in North America and their related suppliers. Promotes the products manufactured by the members, while holding high standards. Maintains the highest levels of product quality, business ethics and professionalism among the membership and the building industry. **Awards:** Stucco Design Award. **Frequency:** semiannual. **Type:** recognition. **Publications:** Bulletins. Alternate Formats: online. **Conventions/Meetings:** luncheon - 6-8/year.

677 ■ Submersible Wastewater Pump Association (SWPA)
1866 Sheridan Rd., Ste.201
Highland Park, IL 60035-2545
Ph: (847)681-1868
Fax: (847)681-1869
E-mail: swpaexdir@sbcglobal.net
URL: http://www.swpa.org
Contact: Charles Stolberg, Exec. Dir.
Founded: 1976. **Members:** 50. **Membership Dues:** pump manufacturer (based on industry sales), $2,670-$6,450 (annual) ● component manufacturer, $1,135 (annual) ● associate (non-manufacturer), $295 (annual) ● component manufacturer subsidiary, $515 (annual) ● pump manufacturer subsidiary, $1,050 (annual). **Staff:** 5. **Description:** Represents manufacturers of submersible wastewater pumps and pumping systems for municipal and industrial applications; manufacturers of component parts and accessory items for those pumps and systems, and companies who provide services to users of those products, including consulting engineers, distributors, rep organizations, service shops, systems packagers and publishers. **Libraries: Type:** not open to the public. **Holdings:** 150; articles, books, software. **Subjects:** submersible wastewater pumps, lift stations, accessory items, component parts, grinder pumps. **Committees:** Grinder Pumps in Pressure Sewers; Marketing; Technical. **Publications:** *Start-Up and Field Checkout Procedures Manual for Submersible Lift Stations*. Contains different levels of procedures based on available equipment to be used in conjunction with the pump manufacturer's instruction manual. **Price:** $6.00 ● *Submersible Sewage Pumping Systems Handbook*. Provides technical information and assistance for those responsible for designing, installing, and operating lift stations using submersible pumps. **Price:** $27.95 ● *Submersible Wastewater Pump Association—Annual Membership Roster and Product Reference Guide*. Membership Directory. Lists manufacturers of submersible pumps for municipal and industrial wastewater applications, and their suppliers. Includes product reference guide. ● *The Very Versatile Submersible*. Video ● Brochures. **Conventions/Meetings:** annual meeting, with plant tour and membership meeting - always March/April/May ● annual meeting, business meeting with speakers on current industry issues, legislative and industry outlook - usually in September or October, in conjunction with WEFTEC. 2008 Oct. 18-22, Chicago, IL.

678 ■ Sump and Sewage Pump Manufacturers Association (SSPMA)
PO Box 647
Northbrook, IL 60065-0647
Ph: (847)559-9233
Fax: (847)559-9235
E-mail: hdqtrs@sspma.org
URL: http://www.sspma.org
Contact: Pamela W. Franzen, Managing Dir.
Founded: 1956. **Members:** 32. **Staff:** 2. **Multinational. Description:** Manufacturers of residential sump pumps (cellar drainers) and sewage pumps. Seeks to: develop and promulgate quality standards; implement a certification and labeling program for all products conforming to these standards; investigate market size and activity; promote improved provisions in building codes on the use of sump and sewage pumps. **Committees:** Codes; Promotion and Technical. **Formerly:** (1981) Sump Pump Manufacturers Association. **Publications:** *Domestic Sump, Effluent, and Sewage Pump Standards*. Brochures ● *Effluent Pumps for Onsite Wastewater Treatment: Selecting the Right Pump for the Job*. Video. Alternate Formats: CD-ROM ● *Guidelines for Sizing Sewage Pumps* ● *Installation Guides for Sump Pumps* ● *Installation/Maintenance for Sewage Pumps* ● *Selection, Sizing, and Maintenance Guidelines for Sump, Sewage, and Effluent Pumps* ● *Trouble Shooting Chart for Sump Pumps*. **Conventions/Meetings:** semiannual board meeting and dinner.

679 ■ Tesla Engine Builders Association (TEBA)
5464 N Port Washington Rd., No. 293
Milwaukee, WI 53217-4925
E-mail: teba@execpc.com
URL: http://www.teslaengine.org
Founded: 1993. **Membership Dues:** contributing in U.S., $10 (annual) ● associate in U.S., $20 (annual) ● full in U.S., $35 (annual) ● supporting in U.S., $45 (annual) ● sustaining in U.S., $65 (annual) ● corporate, $600 (annual) ● contributing in Canada and Mexico, $12 (annual) ● associate in Canada and Mexico, $25 (annual) ● full in Canada and Mexico, $40 (annual) ● supporting in Canada and Mexico, $50 (annual) ● sustaining in Canada and Mexico, $70 (annual) ● contributing elsewhere, $15 (annual) ● associate elsewhere, $30 (annual) ● full elsewhere, $55 (annual) ● supporting elsewhere, $65 (annual) ● sustaining elsewhere, $90 (annual). **Description:** Provides accurate information and assistance to those interested in building reproductions of Tesla's engine that would perform properly. **Publications:** *TEBA News*, quarterly. Newsletter. **Price:** $8.95/issue ● Manual. **Price:** included in membership dues.

680 ■ Tile Council of North America (TCNA)
100 Clemson Res. Blvd.
Anderson, SC 29625
Ph: (864)646-8453
Fax: (864)646-2821
E-mail: info@tileusa.com
URL: http://www.tileusa.com
Contact: Eric Astrachan, Exec. Dir.
Founded: 1945. **Members:** 84. **Membership Dues:** regular, $1,200 (annual) ● associate, associate installation material (based on corporate sales), $1,000-$7,500 (annual) ● associate art, studio (based on sales of $1 million or less), $250-$750 (annual) ● affiliated product manufacturer, $1,000-$2,000 (annual). **Staff:** 7. **Budget:** $1,000,000. **For-Profit. Description:** Manufacturers of domestic ceramic tile for floors, walls, and related products. Promotes increase in the marketability of ceramic tile. Conducts testing program on tile and tile installation materials. Supervises international licensing program with 16 licensees. Compiles statistics. **Formerly:** (2003) Tile Council of America. **Publications:** *Directory of Manufacturers of Ceramic Tile and Related Products*, annual ● *Handbook for Ceramic Tile Installation*, annual. Provides detailed drawings and installation specification guidelines for 101 installation methods. **Price:** $9.00 each (1-9 copies); $7.00 each (10-99 copies); $5.00 each (100 plus copies). Alternate Formats: CD-ROM ● *TileFlash*, monthly. Newsletter. Alternate Formats: online. **Conventions/Meetings:** semiannual meeting - always May and October.

681 ■ Tile Roofing Institute (TRI)
230 E Ohio St., Ste.400
Chicago, IL 60611-3265
Ph: (312)670-4177
Free: (888)321-9236
Fax: (312)644-8557
E-mail: info@tileroofing.org
URL: http://www.tileroofing.org
Contact: Richard K. Olson, Technical Dir.
Founded: 1975. **Members:** 35. **Staff:** 3. **Budget:** $350,000. **Regional Groups:** 1. **Description:** Manufacturers and suppliers of clay and concrete roofing tiles; cement companies; mineral pigment producers; and others furnishing equipment and materials for manufacturing roof tiles. Promotes the use of "fire-safe" roof construction, especially clay and concrete tile roofs; educates the architectural, design, and construction industries regarding the advantages of tile roofs; presents to the home-owning public the advantages and economies of tile roofs. Conducts international programs for architects, builders, building inspectors, and roofing contractors; provides sound/slide presentations, speakers, mailers, and specifications relating to tile roof construction. **Committees:** Advertising and Promotion; Codes and Standards; Technical. **Formerly:** (2001) National Tile Roofing Manufacturers Association; (2004) Roof Tile Institute. **Publications:** *Manual of Concrete Roof Tile Installation*. **Conventions/Meetings:** semiannual conference.

682 ■ Timber Frame Business Council (TFBC)
217 Main St.
Hamilton, MT 59840
Ph: (406)375-0713
Free: (888)560-9251
Fax: (406)375-6401
E-mail: info@timberframe.org
URL: http://www.timberframe.org
Contact: Robert Best, Pres.
Founded: 1995. **Membership Dues:** sustaining company, $1,500 (annual) ● regular company, $1,000 (annual) ● small company, $500 (annual) ● sustaining supplier, $900 (annual) ● regular supplier, $600 (annual) ● professional associate, $200 (annual). **Description:** Builders and designers of timber frame homes, panel manufacturers, and other related businesses. Strives to enhance the quality, integrity, and marketability of the timber frame industry. **Publications:** *TFBC News and Notes*, monthly. Newsletter.

Alternate Formats: online. **Conventions/Meetings:** semiannual conference - 2008 Nov. 5-9, Rockport, ME; 2009 Mar. 25-29, Sunriver, OR.

683 ■ Truss Plate Institute (TPI)
218 N Lee St., Ste.312
Alexandria, VA 22314
Ph: (703)683-1010
Fax: (866)501-4012
E-mail: charlie@tpinst.org
URL: http://www.tpinst.org
Contact: Charlie Goehring, Dir. of Inspection Services

Founded: 1960. **Members:** 400. **Membership Dues:** associate, $300 (annual). **Staff:** 3. **Languages:** English, Spanish. **Description:** Firms manufacturing metal connector plates for wood trusses; firms producing trusses; suppliers of materials for trusses. Develops consensus design criteria in accordance with ANSI's accredited procedures for the development and coordination of American National Standards. Disseminates information to the public, including design specifications, truss bracing recommendations, and a quality control manual; conducts statistical survey and research programs. **Libraries: Type:** reference. **Awards:** Stanley Suddarth Scholarship. **Frequency:** annual. **Type:** scholarship. **Recipient:** for demonstrated interest in wood engineering. **Computer Services:** database. **Committees:** Allowable Stress Design; Load Resistance Factor Design; Technical Advisory; Truss Load Test. **Absorbed:** (1980) Component Manufacturers Council of the Truss Plate Institute. **Publications:** *ANSI/TPI National Design Standard for Metal Plate Connected Wood Truss Construction* ● *DSB-89 Recommended Design Specification for Temporary Bracing of Metal Plate Connected Wood Trusses* ● *HIB-91 Handling, Installing, and Bracing* ● *TPI News*, quarterly ● Membership Directory, annual ● Reports. Alternate Formats: online ● Also makes available truss, safety, and specialty tags.

684 ■ US Green Building Council
1800 Massachusetts Ave. NW, Ste.300
Washington, DC 20036
Ph: (202)742-3792
Free: (800)795-1747
Fax: (202)828-5110
E-mail: info@usgbc.org
URL: http://www.usgbc.org
Contact: S. Richard Fedrizzi, Pres./CEO

Founded: 1993. **Members:** 400. **Membership Dues:** product manufacturer, service contractor, distributor, building control, $500-$12,500 (annual) ● corporate, retail, $1,000-$5,000 (annual) ● utility/energy service company, $750-$3,500 (annual) ● nonprofit, environmental organization, $300-$750 (annual) ● professional society, trade association, $500-$5,000 (annual) ● professional firm, $300-$3,500 (annual) ● contractor, builder, $300-$5,000 (annual) ● educational institution, $300-$2,000 (annual) ● federal government, government owned-contractor operated labs, $750-$1,000 (annual). **Staff:** 6. **Description:** Product manufacturers. Committed to the adoption of green building practices, technologies, policies, and standards. **Committees:** LEED; Organizational; Technical Advisor. **Publications:** *Sustainable Building Technical Manual*. Alternate Formats: online ● *USGBC Update*, monthly. Newsletter. Contains articles on council activities and initiatives. Alternate Formats: online.

685 ■ Vinyl Siding Institute (VSI)
1201 15th St. NW, Ste.220
Washington, DC 20005
Ph: (202)587-5100
Free: (888)FOR-VSI-1
Fax: (202)587-5127
E-mail: vsi@vinylsiding.org
URL: http://www.vinylsiding.org
Contact: Jery Y. Huntley, Pres.

Founded: 1976. **Members:** 50. **Membership Dues:** polymeric producer, $12,900 (annual) ● manufacturer ($300-$399 million siding and accessories sales), $198,600 (annual) ● manufacturer ($200-$299 million siding and accessories sales), $159,000 (annual) ● manufacturer ($100-$199 million siding and accessories sales), $104,500 (annual) ● manufacturer ($50-$99 million siding and accessories sales), $75,740 (annual) ● manufacturer (less than $50 million siding and accessories sales), $30,880 (annual) ● resin manufacturer, $29,700 (annual) ● consultant/testing lab, $1,188 (annual) ● supplier (up to $20 million sales), $3,564-$11,880 (annual) ● supplier (more than $20 million sales), $17,820 (annual) ● manufacturer ($400-$499 million siding and accessories sales), $275,000 (annual) ● manufacturer ($500 million or greater siding and accessories sales), $357,600 (annual). **Staff:** 4. **Description:** A division of The Society of the Plastics Industry (see separate entry). Vinyl siding manufacturers and suppliers. Compiles statistics. **Awards:** Awards of Distinction. **Frequency:** annual. **Type:** recognition. **Recipient:** for outstanding remodeling and new construction contractors for vinyl siding installations ● Member of the Year. **Frequency:** annual. **Type:** recognition. **Recipient:** for contributions to the Vinyl Siding Industry. **Committees:** Certification; Code and Regulatory; Technical. **Affiliated With:** Society of the Plastics Industry. **Formerly:** Thermoplastic Exterior Building Division of the Society of the Plastics Industry. **Publications:** Also provides application teaching kit for carpentry teachers. **Conventions/Meetings:** semiannual conference, held in conjunction with the Vinyl Window and Door Institute.

686 ■ Window and Door Manufacturers Association (WDMA)
1400 E Touhy Ave., Ste.470
Des Plaines, IL 60018
Ph: (847)299-5200
Free: (800)223-2301
Fax: (847)299-1286
E-mail: wdma@wdma.com
URL: http://www.wdma.com
Contact: Dave Beeken, Pres.

Founded: 1927. **Members:** 140. **Staff:** 9. **Description:** Manufacturers of doors, windows, frames, and related products. Fosters, promotes, and protects members' interests; encourages product use. Establishes quality and performance standards; conducts research in all areas of door and window manufacture. Issues seals of approval for wood preservative treatment, hardwood doors, and window unit manufacture. **Committees:** Building Codes and Regulations - Door Division; Building Codes and Regulations - Window Division; Environmental Stewardship; Exterior Fenestration Standards; Hallmark Certification; Interior Door Standards; Promotion and Education; Statistics and Research; Strategic Vision; Technical Review; Treatments, Coatings and Composites. **Absorbed:** (1975) Ponderosa Pine Woodwork Association. **Formerly:** (1927) National Door Manufacturers Association; (1949) National Woodwork Manufacturers Association; (1999) National Wood Window and Door Association. **Publications:** *Membership and Product Directory*, annual. Provides membership information. **Price:** free ● *Millwork Sources of Supply*, annual. Directory ● *WDMA Newsletter*, monthly ● Also publishes literature on industry standards, test methods, fire doors, and proper care and finishing of windows, sashes, doors, and frames. **Conventions/Meetings:** semiannual meeting - always August and February.

687 ■ Wire Reinforcement Institute (WRI)
942 Main St., Ste.300
Hartford, CT 06103
Free: (800)552-4974
Fax: (860)808-3009
E-mail: wwrinfo@wirereinforcementinstitute.org
URL: http://www.wirereinforcementinstitute.org
Contact: Richard Wagner, Chm.

Founded: 1930. **Members:** 27. **Membership Dues:** regular, in U.S. (based on annual shipment of WWR), $7,160-$9,550 (annual) ● regular, outside U.S. (based on annual shipment of WWR), $1,700-$6,654 (annual) ● associate (based on business volume per annum), $1,504-$6,329 (annual) ● professional, $55 (annual). **Staff:** 1. **Multinational. Description:** Manufacturers of steel welded wire reinforcement (WWR), sometimes referred to as fabric, mesh or WWF and wire products for concrete construction. Works to disseminate technical information and extend the use of welded wire reinforcement through scientific and market research, consumer education, engineering, product development, and general construction technology. Provides technical service to users and specifiers of welded wire reinforcement such as architects, consulting engineers, contractors, and governmental department engineers. Conducts research programs on properties and performance of welded wire reinforcement. **Libraries: Type:** reference. **Subjects:** welded wire fabric. **Committees:** Engineering Practices; Executive; Marketing; Product Development. **Subcommittees:** Building and Paving; Codes and Standards; Pipe and Box Culvert; Structural. **Publications:** *Design of Slab-On-Ground Foundations*. Contains design, construction, and inspection aid for consulting engineers. **Price:** free ● *Manual of Standard Practice-Structural Welded Wire Reinforcement*. Includes product information and material specifications and properties. **Price:** free ● *Performance Study of Large Slabs On Grade*. Report. Includes documentation to validate interim design procedure of the included Design Procedure for Industrial Slabs Reinforced with Welded Wire Fabric. **Price:** free ● *Pipe Fabric Guide*. Contains current WRI publications on concrete pipe and precast boxes; includes information on welded wire fabric and ASTM specifications on wire. **Price:** $35.00 ● *Potential Gains Through Welded Wire Fabric Reinforcement*. Reprint. Contains comparison of time and cost savings of welded wire fabric over rebar. **Price:** $2.00. **Conventions/Meetings:** semiannual board meeting - every spring and fall.

688 ■ Wood Moulding and Millwork Producers Association (WMMPA)
507 1st St.
Woodland, CA 95695
Ph: (530)661-9591
Free: (800)550-7889
Fax: (530)661-9586
E-mail: info@wmmpa.com
URL: http://wmmpa.com
Contact: Kellie A. Schroeder, Exec. VP/Sec.

Founded: 1963. **Members:** 120. **Staff:** 3. **Budget:** $590,000. **Multinational. Description:** Represents manufacturers of wood mouldings and millwork. Provides promotion, standardization, and marketing information services. **Libraries: Type:** open to the public. **Subjects:** industry standards. **Awards:** Warren C. Jimerson Award. **Frequency:** annual. **Type:** recognition. **Recipient:** for an individual who has made an outstanding contribution to the industry. **Computer Services:** database, member locator. **Committees:** General Management; International Affairs; Marketing; Standards. **Affiliated With:** Softwood Export Council. **Formerly:** (1968) Western Wood Moulding Producers; (1978) Wood Moulding and Millwork Producers. **Publications:** *Case 'n Base News*, monthly. Newsletter. Provides information on housing starts, building permits, median prices, unsold homes, and other economic news. **Price:** free. **Advertising:** accepted. Alternate Formats: CD-ROM ● *Safety Newsletter*, monthly. **Circulation:** 120 ● *Tree to Trim* (in English, French, German, Japanese, and Spanish). Books. Covers how to use wood mouldings. **Price:** $15.00 ● *Wood Moulding and Millwork Producers Association—Products and Services Membership Directory*, annual. **Price:** $12.00/copy ● Brochures. **Conventions/Meetings:** semiannual conference - always February and August.

689 ■ Wood Truss Council of America (WTCA)
6300 Enterprise Ln.
Madison, WI 53719
Ph: (608)274-4849
Fax: (608)274-3329
E-mail: wtca@sbcindustry.com
URL: http://www.sbcindustry.com
Contact: Kirk Grundahl PE, Exec. Dir.

Founded: 1983. **Members:** 750. **Membership Dues:** regular (based on sales volume), $414-$14,040 (annual) ● associate, $648 (annual) ● professional, $125 (annual) ● builder/framer (based on sales volume),

$125-$14,040 (annual). **Staff:** 26. **Regional Groups:** 30. **Multinational. Description:** Manufacturers and suppliers of structural wood components. Promotes the interests of members, manufacturers, and suppliers of related products. Encourages the use of structural wood components; supports research and development; provides educational services. **Libraries: Type:** reference. **Holdings:** books, clippings, periodicals. **Subjects:** wood industry. **Computer Services:** Online services, truss knowledge. **Telecommunication Services:** electronic mail, kgrundahl@qualtim.com. **Committees:** BCMC; Engineering and Technology; Legislative; Management and Business Insurance; Marketing; Membership; Nominating; Quality Control. **Publications:** *Metal Plate Connected Wood Trusses*. Handbook. Contains guide to the design and use of metal-plate connected wood trusses in construction. **Price:** $50.00/copy for members; $100.00/copy for nonmembers ● *Structural Building Components*, monthly. Magazine. Covers legislative, technological, managerial, and other developments in the structural component industry. Includes calendar of events. **Circulation:** 8,000. **Advertising:** accepted. Alternate Formats: online ● Membership Directory, annual ● Annual Report, annual. **Conventions/Meetings:** annual Building Component and Manufacturers Conference, with educational seminars (exhibits).

Business

690 ■ Accounting and Finance Benchmarking Consortium
c/o The Benchmarking Network
4606 FM 1960 W, Ste.250
Houston, TX 77069-9949
Ph: (281)440-5044
Fax: (281)440-6677
E-mail: info@afbc.org
URL: http://www.afbc.org
Founded: 1998. **Members:** 4,900. **Staff:** 14. **Budget:** $2,000,000. **Description:** Accounting and finance managers of corporations with an interest in benchmarking. Promotes the use of benchmarking, wherein businesses compare their processes with those of their competitors, as a means of improving corporate efficiency and profitability. Facilitates exchange of information among members; conducts target operations, procurement, development, and maintenance studies; identifies model business practices. **Conventions/Meetings:** annual meeting.

691 ■ American and African Business Women's Alliance (AABWA)
1100 17th St. NW, Ste.1100
Washington, DC 20036
Ph: (202)263-3520
Fax: (202)835-1117
E-mail: aabwa@earthlink.net
URL: http://www.aabwa.com
Contact: Sandra E. Saunders, Vice Chair/Founder
Founded: 2001. **Membership Dues:** African individual, $100 (annual) ● American individual, $250 (annual) ● government, student (American), $100 (annual) ● government, student (African), $50 (annual). **Multinational. Description:** Represents business and professional women from America and Africa engaged in trade and investment. Fosters business opportunities and access to markets through networks, linkages, mentoring and leadership development for women. Seeks to increase international and intra-Africa trade and investment by encouraging business partnerships within the African continent and with the United States. **Computer Services:** database, business directory ● database, listings of export, import, investment and joint venture opportunities.

692 ■ American Association of Business Valuation Specialists (AABVS)
PO Box 13089
Tallahassee, FL 32317
Ph: (850)878-3134
Fax: (850)878-1291
Contact: Robert S. Rhinehart, Pres./CEO
Founded: 1995. **Members:** 100. **Membership Dues:** regular, student, $40 (annual) ● associate, $60 (annual). **Staff:** 2. **Budget:** $50,000. **Description:** People interested in the field of business valuation who agree to achieve the BVS designation. Regulates the certification of professionals.

693 ■ American Business Women's Association (ABWA)
9100 Ward Pkwy.
PO Box 8728
Kansas City, MO 64114-0728
Ph: (816)361-6621
Free: (800)228-0007
Fax: (816)361-4991
E-mail: abwa@abwa.org
URL: http://www.abwa.org
Contact: Robin Necci, Natl. Pres.
Founded: 1949. **Members:** 50,000. **Membership Dues:** basic, $75 (annual) ● express network, $100 (annual) ● full-time student, $35 (annual) ● express network student, company connection, $50 (annual). **Staff:** 30. **Local Groups:** 1,000. **Description:** Women in business, including women owning or operating their own businesses, women in professions, and women employed in any level of government, education, or retailing, manufacturing, and service companies. Provides opportunities for businesswomen to help themselves and others grow personally and professionally through leadership, education, networking support, and national recognition. Offers leadership training, business skills training and business education; special membership options for retired businesswomen and the Company Connection for business owners, a resume service, credit card and programs, various travel and insurance benefits. Sponsors American Business Women's Day and National Convention and regional conferences held annually. **Awards:** Local Woman of the Year. **Frequency:** annual. **Type:** recognition ● **Type:** scholarship. **Recipient:** for women students ● Stephen Bufton Memorial Educational Fund. **Frequency:** annual. **Type:** scholarship ● Top Ten Business Women of ABWA. **Frequency:** annual. **Type:** recognition. **Recipient:** for outstanding career achievements, community involvement, professional development and educational accomplishments. **Computer Services:** database. **Publications:** *The Company Connection*, bimonthly. Newsletter. **Price:** free for Company Connection members. **Advertising:** accepted ● *The Leadership Edge*, quarterly. Newsletter. **Price:** free to chapter officers. **Circulation:** 7,200. **Advertising:** accepted ● *Prime Time Connection*, quarterly. Newsletter. **Price:** free for retired members. **Circulation:** 13,000. **Advertising:** accepted ● *Women in Business*, bimonthly. Magazine. Features informative articles covering a range of topics that are of interest to businesswomen and entrepreneurs. **Price:** $20.00 for nonmembers in U.S.; $24.00 for nonmembers outside U.S.; included in membership dues. ISSN: 0043-7441. **Circulation:** 55,000. **Advertising:** accepted ● Also publishes training materials. **Conventions/Meetings:** annual convention and meeting (exhibits) ● regional meeting and conference (exhibits) - 9/year.

694 ■ American Businesspersons Association (ABA)
Hillsboro Executive Ctr. N
350 Fairway Dr., Ste.200
Deerfield Beach, FL 33441-1834
Ph: (954)571-1877
Free: (800)221-2168
Fax: (954)571-8582
E-mail: membership@assnservices.com
URL: http://www.aba-assn.com
Contact: Jack Furnari, Exec. Dir.
Founded: 1972. **Members:** 1,200. **Membership Dues:** individual, $35 (annual) ● individual, $85 (triennial). **Staff:** 15. **Description:** Owners of businesses and individuals in executive, managerial, and sales capacities. Provides substantial discounts, affordable insurance, products and other special services to members. **Computer Services:** database. **Publications:** *Forum*, quarterly. Newsletter. **Price:** included in membership dues. **Circulation:** 1,200.

695 ■ American Entrepreneurs for Economic Growth (AEEG)
1655 N Fort Myer Dr., Ste.850
Arlington, VA 22209
Ph: (703)524-3743
Fax: (703)524-3940
E-mail: achappell@aeeg.org
URL: http://www.aeeg.com
Contact: Allyson Chappell, Contact
Founded: 1992. **Members:** 12,000. **Description:** Seeks to organize entrepreneurs to be advocates for capital formation, investment incentives and other public policy issues that affect entrepreneurial companies. Strives to create a legislative and regulatory environment that promotes entrepreneurship in America. **Affiliated With:** National Venture Capital Association. **Publications:** Newsletter, quarterly. Contains legislative and regulatory information and entrepreneurial experiences. Alternate Formats: online.

696 ■ Asian Business League of San Francisco (ABL-SF)
564 Market St., Ste.404
San Francisco, CA 94104
Ph: (415)350-9023
E-mail: info@ablsf.org
URL: http://www.ablsf.org
Contact: John Lee, Chm.
Founded: 1980. **Members:** 150. **Membership Dues:** individual, $75 (annual) ● non-profit, $100 (annual) ● business owner, $150 (annual) ● corporate, $1,500 (annual). **Staff:** 2. **Regional Groups:** 3. **Description:** Seeks to promote and further the success of Asian Americans in business. Provides its members with seminars and opportunities to meet with other business leaders in the community, to participate in the advocacy to issues important to Asian Americans and to learn and share pertinent information about the current economic and business climate on both local and international level. **Telecommunication Services:** electronic mail, ablsf@aol.com. **Publications:** *ABL-SF Directory*, annual ● *Asian Business*, quarterly. Newsletter ● *The Asian Business Link*, quarterly. Newsletter. **Conventions/Meetings:** periodic conference ● periodic seminar.

697 ■ Asian Women in Business (AWIB)
358 5th Ave., Ste.504
New York, NY 10001
Ph: (212)868-1368
Fax: (212)868-1373
E-mail: info@awib.org
URL: http://www.awib.org
Contact: Rana Quraishi, Contact
Founded: 1995. **Membership Dues:** individual, $125 (annual) ● student, $50 (annual) ● sustaining, $250 (annual) ● small business, $500 (annual) ● corporate, $1,000 (annual) ● sponsor, $5,000 (annual). **Description:** Asian-American women in business. Seeks to enable Asian-American women to achieve their entrepreneurial potential. Serves as a clearinghouse on issues affecting small business owners; provides technical assistance and other support to members; sponsors business and entrepreneurial education courses. **Libraries: Type:** reference. **Subjects:** women, business, Asian American. **Awards:** Entrepreneurial Leadership Award. **Frequency:** annual. **Type:** recognition. **Recipient:** for Asian-American businesswomen. **Computer Services:** Mailing lists, of members. **Publications:** Newsletter, quarterly. Features business-related articles for women. **Price:** included in membership dues. **Advertising:** accepted. Alternate Formats: CD-ROM.

698 ■ Association Chief Executives Council (ACEC)
Address Unknown since 2007
Founded: 1988. **Members:** 100. **Membership Dues:** individual, $200 (annual). **Budget:** $6,000. **Description:** CEOs who manage trade associations, professional societies, and other non-profit organizations. Plans, pursues, and achieves association and

personal goals through mutual support, collaboration and sharing of ideas, experience, services and programs. Organizes CEO forums which offer support group help in strict confidentiality. **Publications:** Newsletter, periodic. **Circulation:** 50. **Conventions/Meetings:** monthly CEO Forum - conference; **Avg. Attendance:** 15.

699 ■ Association for Corporate Growth (ACG)

616 N North Ct., Ste.210
Palatine, IL 60067-8156
Ph: (847)934-5425
Free: (877)358-2220
Fax: (847)934-6089
E-mail: acghq@tcag.com
URL: http://www.acg.org
Contact: Daniel A. Varroney, Pres./CEO

Founded: 1954. **Members:** 9,000. **Membership Dues:** individual, $250 (annual). **Staff:** 10. **Budget:** $2,000,000. **Regional Groups:** 42. **Multinational. Description:** Representatives of firms that manufacture a wide range of consumer and industrial products; supply services closely related to the planning and growth activities of such companies. Provides a forum for the exchange of ideas related to external and internal growth including acquisitions and divestitures, joint ventures, and new or expanded products and services. Assists members in improving their management skills and techniques in the field of corporate growth. **Awards:** Emerging Company Award. **Frequency:** annual. **Type:** recognition. **Recipient:** for companies demonstrating outstanding performance ● Outstanding Corporate Growth. **Frequency:** annual. **Type:** recognition. **Recipient:** for companies demonstrating outstanding performance. **Formerly:** Association for Corporate Growth and Diversification. **Publications:** *ACG Network*, monthly. Newsletter. **Circulation:** 6,000. **Advertising:** accepted. Alternate Formats: online ● *Association for Corporate Growth—Membership Directory*, annual. **Price:** available to members only ● *Mergers and Acquisitions, the Dealmaker's Journal*, monthly. **Conventions/Meetings:** annual Intergrowth - international conference - every spring.

700 ■ Association for Enterprise Integration (AFEI)

2111 Wilson Blvd., Ste.400
Arlington, VA 22201
Ph: (703)247-9474 (703)247-2597
Fax: (703)522-3192
E-mail: info@afei.org
URL: http://www.afei.org
Contact: David Chesebrough, Pres.

Founded: 1984. **Staff:** 3. **Description:** Strives to advance enterprise integration and electronic business practices for industries and governments. **Affiliated With:** National Defense Industrial Association.

701 ■ Association for International Business (AIB)

725 G St.
Salida, CO 81201
Ph: (719)539-0500
Free: (800)359-5166
Fax: (719)539-6925
E-mail: director@aibcenter.com
URL: http://www.creditman.co.uk/internat/aiblink.html
Contact: Ray Gabriel, Managing Dir.

Founded: 1997. **Members:** 15,000. **Membership Dues:** basic professional, $18 (annual) ● life, $1,200. **Staff:** 5. **Budget:** $100,000. **Regional Groups:** 3. **Multinational. Description:** Global business community whose members are in all areas of International business. Provides a network for the international business community where members can provide and share information, resources, and help with problem solving. Hosts in 70 countries to assist visitors. Conducts a mentorship program. **Libraries: Type:** reference. **Holdings:** articles, clippings, periodicals. **Subjects:** all areas of International business. **Publications:** *International Business Discussion Group*, daily.

702 ■ Association of Master of Business Administration Executives (AMBA)

Address Unknown since 2008

Founded: 1970. **Description:** Private corporation organized by Master of Business Administration executives to serve their professional, career, and financial needs. Compiles statistics. **Libraries: Type:** reference. **Also Known As:** Association of MBA Executives. **Publications:** *AMBA Network News*, quarterly. Newsletter ● *MBA Employment Guide*, semiannual.

703 ■ Auto Suppliers Benchmarking Association (ASBA)

4606 FM 1960 W, Ste.250
Houston, TX 77069-9949
Ph: (281)440-5044
Fax: (281)440-6677
URL: http://www.asbabenchmarking.com
Contact: Mark T. Czarnecki, Pres.

Founded: 1996. **Members:** 2,000. **Staff:** 14. **Budget:** $2,000,000. **Description:** Automotive supplier firms with an interest in benchmarking. Promotes the use of benchmarking, wherein businesses compare their processes with those of their competitors, as a means of improving corporate efficiency and profitability. Facilitates exchange of information among members; conducts target operations, procurement, development, and maintenance studies; identifies model business practices. **Formerly:** (2000) Auto Suppliers Benchmarking Consortium. **Conventions/Meetings:** annual meeting and roundtable.

704 ■ Beyster Institute

UC Washington Ctr.
1608 Rhode Island Ave. NW
Washington, DC 20036
Ph: (202)833-4617 (858)822-6000
Fax: (202)293-0634
E-mail: info@beysterinstitute.ucsd.edu
URL: http://www.beysterinstitute.org
Contact: Ray Smilor, Exec. Dir.

Founded: 1986. **Membership Dues:** visionary contributor, $5,000 ● trailblazer contributor, $2,500-$4,999 ● catalyst contributor, $1,000-$2,499 ● forward thinker contributor, $500-$999 ● team player contributor, $100-$499. **Staff:** 14. **Description:** Helps entrepreneurs and executives use employee ownership and equity compensation as a fair and effective means of motivating the workforce and improving performance. Provides information, workshops and consulting services. **Also Known As:** (2003) Foundation for Enterprise Development. **Publications:** *Leading Companies*, monthly. Magazine. Covers topics domestically and internationally. **Price:** free. Alternate Formats: online ● Annual Report, annual. Alternate Formats: online ● Newsletter, periodic. **Price:** included in membership dues.

705 ■ British-American Business Council (BABC)

52 Vanderbilt Ave., 20th Fl.
New York, NY 10017
Ph: (212)661-5660
Fax: (212)661-1886
E-mail: info@babinc.org
URL: http://www.babc.org
Contact: Daniel S. Glaser, Chm.

Founded: 1987. **Members:** 3,000. **Membership Dues:** sponsor, $1,500 (annual) ● corporate, $450 (annual). **Multinational. Description:** British and American businesses. Strives to provide a forum in which members can exchange information and ideas. Hosts various programs and activities. **Publications:** *UK & USA*, biennial. Magazine. Alternate Formats: online ● Newsletter, quarterly.

706 ■ Business Modeling and Integration Domain Task Force (BMIDTF)

Bldg. A, Ste.300
140 Kendrick St.
Needham, MA 02494
Ph: (781)444-0404
Fax: (781)444-0320
E-mail: info@omg.org
URL: http://www.bpmi.org
Contact: Dr. Richard Soley, Chm./Exec. Dir.

Founded: 2000. **Membership Dues:** government, $12,000 (annual) ● trial, $2,000 (annual) ● analyst, $1,500 (annual) ● university, $500 (annual). **Description:** Aims to empower all companies, across all industries, to develop and operate business processes that span multiple applications and business partners, behind the firewall and over the Internet. **Libraries: Type:** reference. **Holdings:** articles, papers. **Subjects:** business process management. **Computer Services:** Mailing lists ● online services. **Formed by Merger of:** (2005) Business Process Management Initiative and Object Management Group.

707 ■ Business for Social Responsibility (BSR)

111 Sutter St., 12th Fl.
San Francisco, CA 94104
Ph: (415)984-3200
Fax: (415)984-3201
E-mail: web@bsr.org
URL: http://www.bsr.org
Contact: Mats Lederhausen, Chm.

Founded: 1992. **Members:** 1,400. **Membership Dues:** corporate (based on annual gross revenue), $1,000-$30,000 (annual) ● associate (based on annual operating budget), $400-$1,600 (annual). **Multinational. Description:** Large, small, and medium-sized businesses. Promotes responsible business behavior and serves as a resource to companies striving to make ethical business decisions. **Publications:** *BSR Weekly*. Newsletter. Alternate Formats: online. **Conventions/Meetings:** annual conference.

708 ■ Canadian-American Business Council (CABC)

1900 K St. NW
Washington, DC 20006
Ph: (202)496-7430
Fax: (202)496-7756
E-mail: sgreenwood@mckennalong.com
URL: http://www.canambusco.org
Contact: Scotty Greenwood, Exec. Dir.

Founded: 1987. **Members:** 125. **Membership Dues:** individual, $250 (annual) ● SME, $2,500 (annual) ● corporate, $5,000 (annual) ● corporate sponsor, $10,000 (annual) ● sustaining partner (minimum), $25,000 (annual). **Staff:** 4. **Languages:** English, French. **Description:** Individuals, corporations, institutions, and organizations with an interest in trade between the United States and Canada. Promotes free trade. Gathers and disseminates information; maintains speakers' bureau. **Awards:** Canadian-American Business Achievement Award. **Frequency:** annual. **Type:** recognition. **Telecommunication Services:** electronic mail, jmorris@mckennalong.com. **Publications:** *CABCommunique* (in English and French), bimonthly. Newsletter. **Advertising:** accepted. Alternate Formats: online. **Conventions/Meetings:** monthly luncheon ● periodic Pharmaceuticals Conference.

709 ■ Center for Family Business

Address Unknown since 2007

Founded: 1962. **Members:** 5,000. **Staff:** 5. **Budget:** $1,000,000. **Description:** Presidents, owner/managers, founders, and inheritors of family-owned businesses and independent, private, or closely held companies. Develops educational programs for its members in the areas of business management, management succession, and business continuity. Provides consulting services. Conducts promotion, research, and public relations activities on behalf of its membership. **Formerly:** (1962) University Services Institute. **Publications:** *Beyond Survival*. Book. A discussion of business ownership and management. **Price:** $25.00 including S & H. Alternate Formats: CD-ROM ● *Inside the Family Business*. Book ● *Outside Directors in the Family Owned Business*. Book ● *Someday This Will All Be.Whose? The Lighter Side of Family Business*. Book. A book of cartoons accumulated by Leon Danco and friends. **Price:** $30.00

including S & H. **Conventions/Meetings:** annual seminar - always Cleveland, OH.

710 ■ Center for International Private Enterprise (CIPE)
1155 15th St. NW, Ste.700
Washington, DC 20005
Ph: (202)721-9200
Fax: (202)721-9250
E-mail: cipe@cipe.org
URL: http://www.cipe.org
Contact: John D. Sullivan PhD, Exec. Dir.
Founded: 1983. **Staff:** 30. **Budget:** $7,000,000. **Description:** Encourages the growth of voluntary business organizations and private enterprise systems abroad, such as chambers of commerce, trade associations, employers' organizations, and business-oriented research groups, particularly in developing countries. Helps business communities abroad strengthen their organizational capabilities; creates exchanges among business leaders and institutions to strengthen the international private enterprise system; encourages development of active business participation in the political process. Activities include: developing leadership training for association executives and their voluntary leadership to strengthen business institutions; developing communications programs and educational materials for youth, employees, women's groups, academic institutions, government officials, political leaders, and other audiences to encourage entrepreneurship. **Computer Services:** Mailing lists, of members. **Affiliated With:** U.S. Chamber of Commerce. **Publications:** *Economic Reform Today*, quarterly. Magazine. **Circulation:** 26,000. **Conventions/Meetings:** Strengthening Women's Business Organizations - meeting (exhibits).

711 ■ Chief Executive Officers Club
4 W 22nd St., 10th Fl.
New York, NY 10010
Ph: (212)925-7911
Fax: (212)925-7463
E-mail: mail@ceoclubs.org
URL: http://ceoclubs.org
Contact: Joseph R. Mancuso, Pres.
Founded: 1978. **Members:** 3,000. **Membership Dues:** entrepreneurial, $495 (annual) ● life, $6,500. **Staff:** 8. **Description:** Serves as a management resource for entrepreneurial managers and their professional advisers. Selects and makes available publications on developing business plans, organizing an entrepreneurial team, attracting venture capital, and obtaining patents, trademarks, and copyrights. Develops, collects, and disseminates information on business trends, new laws and regulations, and tax guidance. Conducts intensive-study courses and seminars. Has identified stages of the entrepreneurial process and, through essays and audiocassettes, addresses problems pertinent to each stage. **Libraries: Type:** reference. **Subjects:** small business, venture capital. **Computer Services:** Online services, ordering information. **Telecommunication Services:** electronic mail, jmancuso@ceoclubs.org. **Councils:** Presidential Advisory. **Programs:** CEO Clubs Exclusive Health; CEO Clubs PPO Plans. **Formerly:** (1999) Center for Entrepreneurial Management. **Publications:** *Entrepreneurial Manager: The Entrepreneur's Source of Useful Information*, monthly. Newsletter. Includes calendar of events. **Price:** free for members; $71.00 /year for nonmembers. ISSN: 0272-0396. Alternate Formats: online ● Brochure. Alternate Formats: online ● Articles. Alternate Formats: online.

712 ■ Chief Executives Organization (CEO)
7920 Norfolk Ave., Ste.400
Bethesda, MD 20814-2507
Ph: (301)656-9220
Fax: (301)656-9221
E-mail: info@ceo.org
URL: http://www.ceo.org
Contact: Brian Biondy, Exec. Dir.
Founded: 1958. **Members:** 1,900. **Membership Dues:** individual, $1,150 (annual). **Staff:** 18. **Description:** Invited members of the Young Presidents' Organization who have reached the age of 49, the mandatory "retirement" age for YPO. (Young Presidents' Organization comprises presidents of corporations with gross annual revenue of at least one million dollars and a minimum of 50 employees, of nonindustrial corporations with revenue of two million dollars and 25 employees, or of banking corporations with average deposits of 15 million dollars and 25 employees. Each member must have been elected president of a corporation before reaching the age of 40.) Sponsors educational programs. **Telecommunication Services:** electronic mail, membership@ceo.org. **Affiliated With:** Young Presidents' Organization. **Formerly:** (1982) Chief Executives Forum. **Publications:** *Compass*, quarterly ● Membership Directory, annual. **Price:** included in membership dues. **Conventions/Meetings:** monthly conference.

713 ■ Committee of 200 (C200)
980 N Michigan Ave., Ste.1575
Chicago, IL 60611-7540
Ph: (312)255-0296
Fax: (312)255-0789
E-mail: info@c200.org
URL: http://www.c200.org
Contact: Susan Gilpin, Pres.
Founded: 1982. **Members:** 470. **Membership Dues:** regular, $1,200 (annual) ● international, $900 (annual). **Staff:** 3. **Budget:** $1,670,000. **Regional Groups:** 5. **Description:** Represents women executives who are recognized as leaders in their industries (though originally intended to have a membership of 200 top-ranking businesswomen, the committee is no longer limited to 200). Encourages successful entrepreneurship by women and the active participation of women business owners and senior corporate executives in business, economic, social, and educational concerns. Seeks to strengthen the influence of women business leaders. Provides forum for exchange of ideas and enhancement of business opportunities for women. **Libraries: Type:** not open to the public. **Awards:** C200 Scholar Awards. **Frequency:** semiannual. **Type:** scholarship. **Recipient:** to outstanding first-year women MBA students ● Luminary Awards. **Frequency:** annual. **Type:** recognition. **Recipient:** to outstanding women business leaders and innovators. **Programs:** Case Study; Growing Entrepreneurs Mentoring. **Publications:** *Update*, semiannual. Newsletter. Alternate Formats: online ● Articles. Alternate Formats: online. **Conventions/Meetings:** annual conference, with business meeting - always fall.

714 ■ Council for Ethical Leadership (CEE)
92 Jefferson Ave., Ste.108
Columbus, OH 43215
Ph: (614)221-8661
Fax: (614)221-8707
E-mail: councilforethicsineconomics@businessethics.org
URL: http://www.businessethics.org
Contact: Michael Distelhorst, Pres.
Founded: 1982. **Members:** 150. **Staff:** 3. **Budget:** $340,000. **Description:** Leaders in business, education, and the professions. Seeks to "strengthen the ethical fabric of business and economic life". Facilitates the development of international networks of businesspeople interested in economic ethics; sponsors educational programs and develops and distributes educational materials; advises and supports communities wishing to implement character educational programs; makes available consulting services. **Formerly:** (2007) Council for Ethics in Economics. **Publications:** *Ethical Leadership*, 3/year. Newsletter. Alternate Formats: online.

715 ■ Council of Growing Companies (CGC)
Address Unknown since 2007
Members: 1,200. **Staff:** 6. **Local Groups:** 20. **Description:** Entrepreneurs and chief executive officers, founders and owners of high-growth companies. Members strive for continual success by sharing their ideas, experience and solutions. Operates mentoring and internship programs.

716 ■ Customer Satisfaction Measurement Association (CSMA)
c/o The Benchmarking Network
4606 FM 1960 W, Ste.250
Houston, TX 77069-9949
Ph: (281)440-5044
Free: (800)856-8546
Fax: (281)440-6677
E-mail: csmainfo@csmassociation.org
URL: http://www.csmassociation.org
Contact: Mark Czarnecki, Pres.
Founded: 1998. **Members:** 4,500. **Staff:** 14. **Budget:** $2,000,000. **Description:** Employees responsible for consumer satisfaction measurement with an interest in benchmarking. Promotes the use of benchmarking, wherein businesses compare their processes with those of their competitors, as a means of improving corporate efficiency and profitability. Facilitates exchange of information among members; conducts target operations, procurement, development, and maintenance studies; identifies model business practices. **Conventions/Meetings:** annual meeting and roundtable.

717 ■ Dealer Management Association (DMA)
239 Drakeside Rd.
Hampton, NH 03842
Ph: (603)926-8000
Free: (800)370-3362
Fax: (603)926-4505
E-mail: contact@dmagroup.com
URL: http://www.dmagroup.com
Founded: 1979. **Staff:** 15. **For-Profit. Description:** Provides CEO's, presidents, and owners of privately owned and operated companies with strategic planning and Net Profit Improvement consulting programs, sales and general skills training, accounting services, market research, family business successorship, new sales, development, website design, website marketing, manufacturing and wholesale distribution consulting. **Libraries: Type:** not open to the public. **Holdings:** 3,700; articles, books, periodicals. **Subjects:** business, finance, government. **Also Known As:** DMA Group. **Publications:** *Family Business Matters Newsletter*, monthly. **Conventions/Meetings:** quarterly workshop, management training.

718 ■ Entrepreneurs' Organization (EO)
500 Montgomery St., Ste.500
Alexandria, VA 22314
Ph: (703)519-6700
Fax: (703)519-1864
E-mail: info@eonetwork.org
URL: http://www.eonetwork.org
Contact: Mr. Tim Young, Dir. of Marketing
Founded: 1987. **Members:** 6,600. **Membership Dues:** individual, $1,200 (annual). **Staff:** 50. **Budget:** $8,000,000. **Regional Groups:** 4. **Local Groups:** 65. **National Groups:** 38. **Multinational. Description:** Entrepreneurs under the age of 50 who have either founded, co-founded, are a controlling shareholder of, or own a firm with annual gross revenues exceeding $1000000 (membership is by invitation only). Engages leading entrepreneurs to learn and grow. Serves as a focal point for networking and development of members through small group learning sessions, regular local chapter social and learning events, and global conference-based education programs. **Libraries: Type:** reference. **Holdings:** archival material. **Formerly:** (2005) Young Entrepreneurs' Organization. **Publications:** *Octane*, quarterly. Newsletter. Alternate Formats: online ● *Overdrive*, monthly. Newsletter. Alternate Formats: online. **Conventions/Meetings:** periodic Universities and Leadership Conference - meeting (exhibits).

719 ■ The Entrepreneurship Institute (TEI)
3592 Corporate Dr., Ste.101
Columbus, OH 43231
Ph: (614)895-1153
Free: (800)736-3592
E-mail: tei@tei.net
URL: http://www.tei.net
Contact: Dr. Jan W. Zupnick, Pres.
Founded: 1976. **Members:** 550. **Membership Dues:** presidential, $99 (annual) ● stewardship for advisory

board contributor, $3,300 (annual). **Staff:** 18. **Budget:** $1,500,000. **State Groups:** 20. **Description:** Provides encouragement and assistance to entrepreneurs who operate companies with revenue in excess of $1 million. Unites financial, legal, and community resources to help foster the success of companies. Promotes sharing of information and interaction between members. Operates President's forums and projects which are designed to improve communication between businesses, develop one-to-one business relationships between small and mid-size businesses and local resources, provide networking, and stimulate the growth of existing companies. **Libraries: Type:** reference. **Holdings:** audiovisuals, books, software. **Subjects:** growth strategies, accounting, finance, investments 401K. **Computer Services:** Information services, membership directory. **Doing business as:** Presidents Forum. **Publications:** *The President's Forum*, monthly. Newsletter. Contains articles written by expert resources on subjects affecting growing companies. **Price:** free for members; $99.00 for nonmembers. **Conventions/Meetings:** periodic meeting and lecture, for local groups of company presidents.

720 ■ Ethics and Compliance Officer Association (ECOA)

411 Waverley Oaks Rd., Ste.324
Waltham, MA 02452-8420
Ph: (781)647-9333
Fax: (781)647-9399
E-mail: support@theecoa.org
URL: http://www.theecoa.org
Contact: Keith T. Darcy, Exec. Dir.

Founded: 1991. **Members:** 250. **Membership Dues:** basic, $950 (annual) ● sponsoring partner, $3,500 (annual) ● associate, $200 (annual). **Staff:** 4. **Description:** Managers of ethics, compliance, and business conduct programs. Offers educational business ethics and compliance programs; conducts national research; and provides free job-listing service. **Libraries: Type:** by appointment only. **Subjects:** codes, gifts and gratuities, job descriptions, ethnics and compliance. **Formerly:** (2006) Ethics Officer Association. **Publications:** *ECOA News*. Newsletter. **Circulation:** 2,000. Alternate Formats: online ● Membership Directory ● Brochure. **Conventions/Meetings:** annual conference and convention, networking ● Sponsoring Partner Forum - seminar, think tanks, networking.

721 ■ Financial Services and Banking Benchmarking Association (FSBBA)

4606 FM 1960 W, Ste.250
Houston, TX 77069-9949
Ph: (281)440-5044
Fax: (281)440-6677
URL: http://www.fsbba.org
Contact: Mark T. Czarnecki MBA, Contact

Founded: 1998. **Members:** 5,000. **Staff:** 14. **Budget:** $2,000,000. **Description:** Employees of banking and financial services corporations with an interest in benchmarking. Promotes the use of benchmarking, wherein businesses compare their processes with those of their competitors, as a means of improving corporate efficiency and profitability. Facilitates exchange of information among members; conducts target operations, procurement, development, and maintenance studies; identifies model business practices. **Conventions/Meetings:** annual meeting.

722 ■ Home-Based Working Moms (HBWM)

c/o Lesley Spencer Pyle, Founder/Pres.
PO Box 1628
Spring, TX 77383-1628
Ph: (281)350-4495
E-mail: hbwm@hbwm.com
URL: http://www.hbwm.com
Contact: Lesley Spencer Pyle, Founder/Pres.

Founded: 1995. **Members:** 700. **Membership Dues:** individual, $69 (annual) ● renewal, $64 (annual). **Staff:** 1. **Description:** Individuals who work at home or would like to. Promotes working at home as an option for people in applicable positions; seeks to enhance the careers of members currently working at home. Serves as a forum for exchange of information among members. Makes available member matching service. Advocates for creation of more work-at-home opportunities by American businesses. **Computer Services:** database ● mailing lists. **Additional Websites:** http://www.edirectoryofhomebasedcareers.com, http://www.hiremymom.com. **Formerly:** (1996) Work at Home Moms. **Publications:** *Basics of Starting a Home Business*. Pamphlet ● *How to Promote Your Home Business*. Pamphlet ● *Our Place*, 10/year. Newsletter. **Advertising:** accepted ● *Over 200 Home Business Opportunities*. Pamphlet ● *Tips for Selecting a Home Business*. Pamphlet ● *Twenty Ways to Cut Your Living Expenses*. Pamphlet ● *Work-At-Home Kit*. Book. Includes a workbook.

723 ■ Human Resources Benchmarking Association (HRBA)

c/o The Benchmarking Network
4606 FM 1960 W, Ste.250
Houston, TX 77069-9949
Ph: (281)440-5044
Free: (800)856-8546
Fax: (281)440-6677
URL: http://www.hrba.org
Contact: Mark Czarnecki, Pres.

Founded: 1998. **Members:** 4,000. **Staff:** 14. **Budget:** $2,000,000. **Description:** Human resources professionals of corporations with an interest in benchmarking. Promotes the use of benchmarking, wherein businesses compare their processes with those of their competitors, as a means of improving corporate efficiency and profitability. Facilitates exchange of information among members; conducts target operations, procurement, development, and maintenance studies; identifies model business practices. **Conventions/Meetings:** annual meeting and roundtable.

724 ■ Hungarian-U.S. Business Council

c/o Chamber of Commerce of the U.S.
1615 H St. NW
Washington, DC 20062-2000
Ph: (202)463-5460
Fax: (202)463-3114
E-mail: europe@uschamber.com
URL: http://www.uschamber.org
Contact: Thomas J. Donohue, Pres./CEO

Founded: 1975. **Members:** 50. **Membership Dues:** annual revenue over $50 million, $5,000 (annual) ● annual revenue under $50 million, $3,000 (annual). **Multinational. Description:** Executive firms having significant actual or potential trade involvement with Hungary, including coverage of policy issues related to Russia, Ukraine, Belarus, Turkey, Iran, the Caucasus and Central Asia. Provides a forum for discussing trade and investment issues and formulation of policy issues to promote and expand economic relations between the U.S. and Hungary. **Libraries: Type:** not open to the public. **Holdings:** articles, books, periodicals. **Subjects:** international trade, investment. **Publications:** *Bridging the Atlantic*. Book. Describes how eight small American businesses succeeded in Europe. **Price:** $19.95 plus shipping and handling ($4/book) ● *Europe and Eurasia Business Committee Dispatch*, weekly. Newsletter. Provides current Information on regulations, legislation and specific industries for Central/Eastern Europe, New Independent States, Turkey and Iran. **Price:** included in membership dues; $350.00 /year for nonmembers. **Conventions/Meetings:** periodic conference and convention.

725 ■ Information Systems Management Benchmarking Consortium (ISMBC)

4606 FM 1960 W, Ste.250
Houston, TX 77069-9949
Ph: (281)440-5044
Fax: (281)440-6677
E-mail: info@ismbc.org
URL: http://www.ismbc.org
Contact: Mark Czanecki, Pres.

Founded: 1998. **Members:** 8,000. **Staff:** 14. **Budget:** $2,000,000. **Description:** Information systems managers with an interest in benchmarking. Promotes the use of benchmarking, wherein businesses compare their processes with those of their competitors, as a means of improving corporate efficiency and profitability. Facilitates exchange of information among members; conducts target operations, procurement, development, and maintenance studies; identifies model business practices. **Publications:** *ebusiness Newsletter*, weekly. Features announcements of benchmarking studies. **Price:** free. **Circulation:** 40,000. Alternate Formats: online. **Conventions/Meetings:** periodic meeting.

726 ■ Institute of Certified Business Counselors (ICBC)

18615 Willamette Dr.
West Linn, OR 97068
Free: (877)ICB-CORG
Fax: (503)292-8237
E-mail: inquiry@i-cbc.org
URL: http://www.i-cbc.org
Contact: Jeff Adam, Pres.

Founded: 1975. **Members:** 180. **Membership Dues:** individual, $100 (annual). **Staff:** 2. **Budget:** $50,000. **Description:** Bankers, consultants, accountants, attorneys, appraisers, merger and acquisition specialists, estate planners, financial consultants, and business brokers active in the continuation, evaluation, financing, or marketing of privately held businesses. Offers training and advice on how to buy or sell a business, including information on what to look for in a prospective deal. Maintains speakers' bureau. **Telecommunication Services:** electronic mail, jeffadam@comcast.net. **Publications:** *CBC Roster*, annual. Directory. Contains list of company members. **Price:** free for members. **Circulation:** 200 ● *The Certified Business Counselor*, bimonthly. Newsletter. **Price:** free for members. **Circulation:** 200. Alternate Formats: online. **Conventions/Meetings:** annual conference ● semiannual conference.

727 ■ Institute for International Entrepreneurship

Address Unknown since 2007

Founded: 1987. **Languages:** Russian, Spanish. **Multinational. Description:** Supports international exchange with former Soviet Countries. Trains individuals from around the world in business and nonprofit development, marketing, and technology. Offers a speakers bureau, educational, charitable, and research programs. **Libraries: Type:** reference; not open to the public. **Holdings:** articles, books. **Subjects:** business, management, international relations. **Awards: Type:** scholarship. **Computer Services:** Electronic publishing. **Publications:** *Doing Business with International Partners*. **Conventions/Meetings:** periodic convention and conference.

728 ■ The International Alliance for Women (TIAW)

8405 Greensboro Dr., Ste.800
McLean, VA 22102-5120
Ph: (703)506-3284
Free: (866)533-8429
Fax: (905)305-1548
E-mail: info@tiaw.org
URL: http://www.tiaw.org
Contact: Stephanie MacKendrick, Pres.

Founded: 1980. **Members:** 50,000. **Membership Dues:** individual, $150 (annual) ● supporting, $300 (annual) ● sustaining, $500 (annual). **Multinational. Description:** Local networks comprising 50,000 professional and executive women in 12 countries; individual businesswomen without a network affiliation are alliance associates. Promotes recognition of the achievements of women in business. Encourages placement of women in senior executive positions. Maintains high standards of professional competence among members. Facilitates communication on an international scale among professional women's networks and their members. Represents members' interests before policymaking business and government. Sponsors programs that support equal opportunity and enhance members' business and professional skills. Operates appointments and directors service. Maintains speakers' bureau. **Libraries: Type:** reference. **Holdings:** archival material. **Subjects:** women in business. **Awards:** Mandy Goetz 21st Century Award. **Frequency:** annual. **Type:** recognition. **Recipient:** to a member who has made an outstanding contribution to the association ● World of Difference Award. **Frequency:** annual. **Type:** recognition. **Recipient:** to a woman who has made a difference in the advancement of women. **Committees:** Directors Resource Bank; Membership; Program; Structure; Visibility. **Councils:** Network of Representatives. **Programs:** Daughters; Microenterprise Development. **Formerly:** (1986) National Alliance of Professional and Executive Women's Networks; (2003) The International Alliance, An Association of Executive and Professional Women. **Publications:** *eBulletins*. **Price:** included in membership dues. Alternate Formats: online ● *eConnections*, bimonthly. Newsletter. Includes calendar of events and research updates. **Price:** included in membership dues; $35.00 /year for nonmembers. **Circulation:** 5,000. **Advertising:** accepted. Alternate Formats: online ● Membership Directory, annual. **Conventions/Meetings:** board meeting - 3/year ● annual conference (exhibits) ● regional meeting ● seminar and symposium ● Washington Briefing - meeting.

729 ■ International Association for Documentation Technologies (IADT)

Address Unknown since 2007

Members: 500. **Description:** Promotes the strength of the forms and systems industry. **Formerly:** (2003) International Business Forms Industries. **Publications:** *PaperTronix*, bimonthly. Magazine. Features in-depth articles covering critical issues and trends within the industry. **Conventions/Meetings:** annual conference.

730 ■ International Association of Merger and Acquisition Professionals (IMAP)

525 SW 5th St.
Des Moines, IA 50309
Ph: (515)282-8192
Fax: (515)282-9117
E-mail: info@imap.com
URL: http://www.imap.com
Contact: Mary Mycka, Exec. Dir.

Founded: 1971. **Members:** 60. **Staff:** 1. **Description:** Firms with experience in the merger/acquisition field that meet the association's criteria of professional background and financial ability (primarily specialists in selling, buying, and merging medium-sized businesses with sales in the range of 1 to 100 million dollars); allied members include individuals and firms that provide auxiliary services for the completion of merger/acquisition transactions. Purposes are: promotion of the science of merger/acquisition consultancy; encouragement of educational and training material in the field; enhancement of the image and professional standing of industry specialists; expeditious but confidential distribution of business information on available merger or acquisition prospects. **Formerly:** International Association Merger and Acquisition Consultants. **Publications:** *M & A Insider*, quarterly. Newsletter. **Price:** available to members only. **Circulation:** 28,000 ● Reports. Alternate Formats: online. **Conventions/Meetings:** semiannual conference.

731 ■ International Call Center Benchmarking Consortium (ICCBC)

c/o The Benchmarking Network
4606 FM 1960 W, Ste.250
Houston, TX 77069-9949
Ph: (281)440-5044
Free: (800)856-8546
Fax: (281)440-6677
E-mail: info@iccbc.org
URL: http://www.iccbc.org
Contact: Mark Czarnecki, Pres.

Founded: 1997. **Members:** 4,000. **Staff:** 14. **Budget:** $2,000,000. **Description:** Corporations that manage call centers. Promotes the use of benchmarking, wherein businesses compare their processes with those of their competitors, as a means of improving corporate efficiency and profitability. Facilitates exchange of information among members; conducts target operations, procurement, development, and maintenance studies; identifies model business practices. **Formerly:** (2000) Call Center Benchmarking Network. **Conventions/Meetings:** annual meeting and roundtable.

732 ■ International Downtown Association (IDA)

1250 H St. NW, 10th Fl.
Washington, DC 20005
Ph: (202)393-6801
Fax: (202)393-6869
E-mail: question@ida-downtown.org
URL: http://www.ida-downtown.org
Contact: David M. Feehan, Pres.

Founded: 1954. **Members:** 690. **Membership Dues:** organization, agency (based on the size of operating budget), corporate (based on gross revenue), $225-$2,550 (annual) ● individual, academic, $300 (annual) ● student virtual, $50 (annual) ● international virtual, $100 (annual). **Staff:** 4. **Budget:** $500,000. **Multinational. Description:** Represents vital and livable urban centers. Works to build partnerships that anchor the well-being of towns, cities and regions throughout the world. **Libraries: Type:** reference. **Subjects:** towns, cities, regions. **Awards:** IDA Downtown Achievement Awards. **Frequency:** annual. **Type:** recognition. **Recipient:** for exemplary downtown and town center projects. **Telecommunication Services:** electronic mail, dfeehan@ida-downtown.org. **Formerly:** (1985) International Downtown Executives Association. **Publications:** *Downtown News Briefs*, quarterly. Newsletter. Includes case studies of city districts, new member listings, job openings, and IDA conference wrap-up. **Price:** free for members; $50.00 /year for nonmembers. ISSN: 0891-1029. **Circulation:** 600 ● *International Downtown Association—Membership Directory and Buyers' Guide*, annual. Lists member organizations, corporations, agencies, and individuals involved in the improvement of downtowns and their adjacent neighborhoods. **Price:** available to members only ● Books ● Brochures ● Handbooks ● Reports ● Annual Reports, annual. Alternate Formats: online ● Brochure. Alternate Formats: online ● Also publishes position statements. **Conventions/Meetings:** annual conference, with speakers (exhibits) ● annual workshop - always in spring.

733 ■ International Executive Service Corps (IESC)

1900 M St. NW, Ste.500
Washington, DC 20036
Ph: (202)589-2600
Free: (800)243-4372
Fax: (202)326-0289
E-mail: iesc@iesc.org
URL: http://www.iesc.org
Contact: Spencer T. King, Pres./CEO

Founded: 1964. **Staff:** 45. **Description:** Provides technical and managerial assistance to enterprises, organizations and government bodies in emerging democracies and developing countries. Focuses on the knowledge, skill and experience of its 12,000 industry experts. Maintains a network of experts that includes high-level professionals drawn from nearly every area of private enterprise, government and non-governmental organizations; Geekcorps division includes experts in communications and information technology and is committed to closing the digital divide. **Libraries: Type:** reference. **Holdings:** books, periodicals. **Subjects:** information technology. **Awards:** Frank Pace Award. **Frequency:** annual. **Type:** recognition. **Recipient:** for outstanding project of the year. **Programs:** Accra Technology Skills Transfer; Africa Fast Track Trade; BizAIDs; Global Trade and Technology Network; Jordan-US Business Partnership; Technology Initiative for the Private Sector. **Projects:** Morocco Fast Track Trade. **Publications:** Annual Report, annual. Alternate Formats: online ● Newsletters. Alternate Formats: online ● Brochure. Alternate Formats: online.

734 ■ International Function Point Users Group (IFPUG)

191 Clarksville Rd.
Princeton Junction, NJ 08550
Ph: (609)799-4900
Fax: (609)799-7032
E-mail: ifpug@ifpug.org
URL: http://www.ifpug.org
Contact: Tom Cagley, Pres.

Founded: 1984. **Members:** 1,200. **Membership Dues:** individual, $185 (annual) ● corporate ($425 for each additional in metropolitan area), $625 (annual) ● worldwide corporate, $1,875 (annual) ● affiliate, $675-$1,850 (annual) ● student ($60, with electronic counting practices manual), $50 (annual). **Multinational. Description:** Works to increase the "effectiveness of its members' information technology environments through the applications of function point analysis and other software measurement techniques". **Telecommunication Services:** electronic mail, coribabor@cmasolutions.com. **Committees:** Applied Programs; Counting Standards; Education and Conference; Marketing and Communications. **Subgroups:** Academic Affairs; International Software Benchmarking Standards; International Standards Organization. **Publications:** *A World of Information*, quarterly. Newsletter. Alternate Formats: online ● *Function Point Counting Standard*. Manual. **Price:** $75.00 for members; $150.00 for nonmembers. Alternate Formats: diskette. **Conventions/Meetings:** annual conference - 2008 Sept. 14-19, Washington, DC.

735 ■ International Management Development Association (IMDA)

PO Box 216
Hummelstown, PA 17036
Ph: (717)566-3054
Fax: (717)566-1191
E-mail: execdirector@imda.cc
URL: http://www.imda.cc
Contact: Dr. Fahri Karakaya, Network Mgr.

Founded: 1987. **Membership Dues:** institutional, $250 (annual) ● individual, $60 (annual) ● student, $40 (annual). **Multinational. Description:** Provides interdisciplinary and global platform for the exchange of ideas in the pursuit of professional growth and opportunities for academics, practitioners and public policy makers. Focuses on management development through the transfer of information and knowledge, learning, cooperation and exchange of personnel. Promotes and organizes the exchange of professors, administrators and managers between developed and developing countries. **Telecommunication Services:** electronic mail, imda-l@umassd.edu ● electronic mail, f1karakaya@umassd.edu. **Publications:** *IMDA NEWS*. Newsletter. **Price:** included in membership dues ● *Journal of Transnational Management Development*, quarterly. Examines management research, teaching and development issues. **Price:** included in membership dues ● Membership Directory. **Price:** included in membership dues. **Conventions/Meetings:** annual congress, jointly organized and hosted by Sarajevo Graduate School of Business.

736 ■ International Ombudsman Association (IOA)

203 Towne Centre Dr.
Hillsborough, NJ 08844-4693
Ph: (908)359-0246
Fax: (908)842-0376
E-mail: info@ombudsassociation.org
URL: http://www.ombudsassociation.org
Contact: Janis Schonauer, Pres.

Founded: 1982. **Members:** 600. **Membership Dues:** regular, $195 (annual) ● affiliate, $145 (annual) ● retiree, $45 (annual) ● associate, $160 (annual). **Staff:** 1. **Multinational. Description:** Individuals actively engaged in the practice of organizational ombudsmanry, as designated neutrals. Works to enhance the quality and value of the ombudsman function by: establishing and communicating appropriate standards of excellence for the profession; developing and disseminating ethical guidelines for organizational ombudspeople; training new and experienced ombuds practitioners in complaint handling skills and principles of effective practice; communicating the latest developments of the profession; and fostering appropriate forums to share common interests and strengthen skills. **Committees:** Communication; Conference Planning; Curriculum Development;

Research; Standards; Strategic Alliances; Strategic Planning. **Formed by Merger of:** (2005) The Ombudsman Association; (2005) University and College Ombuds Association. **Formerly:** (1984) Corporate Ombudsman Association. **Publications:** *Neutrality*. Booklet. Discusses the aspects and value of neutrality by the ombuds. **Price:** included in membership dues; $13.00 for nonmembers ● *The Ombuds Confidentiality Privilege*. Booklet. Written for practicing ombuds and/or organizations considering an ombuds function. Deals with the aspect of ombuds confidentiality. **Price:** $8.50 for members; $13.00 for nonmembers ● *Ombudsman Handbook*, periodic. Includes information for newly appointed organizational Ombuds or people considering an Ombuds function in their organization. **Price:** $35.00 for members; $125.00 for nonmembers ● *Ombudsman News*, quarterly. Newsletter. Includes legal issues, profiles of practicing organizational ombuds, training information, etc. **Price:** included in membership dues. **Advertising:** accepted ● *Options Functions and Skills*. Booklet. Discusses the role of the ombuds in organizations. **Price:** $8.50 for members; $13.00 for nonmembers ● *Reprisal, Retaliation and Redress*. Booklet. Written for practicing ombuds dealing with potential retaliation problems within the work area. **Price:** $5.00 for members; $10.00 for nonmembers ● *Why an Organizational Ombudsman*. Booklet. Discusses the reasons organizations might consider having an ombuds function. **Price:** $8.50 for members; $13.00 for nonmembers. **Conventions/Meetings:** annual conference - usually April or May.

737 ■ Internet Alliance (IA)

c/o Emily T. Hackett, Exec. Dir.
1111 19th St. NW, Ste.1100
Washington, DC 20035-5782
Ph: (202)861-2476
E-mail: info@internetalliance.org
URL: http://www.internetalliance.org
Contact: Emily T. Hackett, Exec. Dir.

Founded: 1981. **Members:** 70. **Staff:** 5. **Budget:** $1,000,000. **Description:** Companies offering Internet services. Seeks to "build the confidence and trust necessary for the Internet to become the global mass market medium of the 21st century". Represents members' commercial and regulatory interests; conducts promotional activities; facilitates communication and cooperation among members. **Computer Services:** database, FOCUS. **Telecommunication Services:** electronic mail, emilyh@internetalliance.org. **Councils:** Law Enforcement and Security. **Subgroups:** Internet State Coalition; Public Policy. **Affiliated With:** Direct Marketing Association. **Absorbed:** Internet Local Advertising and Commerce Association; (1994) National Association for Interactive Services. **Formerly:** (1992) Videotex Industry Association. **Publications:** *CyberBrief*, daily. **Price:** included in membership dues. **Circulation:** 400. Alternate Formats: online.

738 ■ Invest to Compete Alliance (ITCA)

1010 Pennsylvania Ave. SE
Washington, DC 20003
Ph: (202)546-4995
Fax: (202)544-7926
E-mail: jcampbell@campbell-crane.com
Contact: Garland Miller, Exec. Dir.

Founded: 1985. **Members:** 25,000. **Membership Dues:** $60,000 (annual). **Staff:** 6. **Budget:** $400,000. **Languages:** English, Spanish. **Description:** Individuals and corporations in the manufacturing and service industries. Works to address the impact of tax legislation, especially the loss of investment tax credit, upon the business community. Offers educational forums to update members on legislative issues affecting their industries. Sponsors meetings with tax and trade policymakers. **Publications:** none. **Conventions/Meetings:** annual congress, with congressional leadership seminar.

739 ■ Kauffman Center for Entrepreneurial Leadership

4801 Rockhill Rd.
Kansas City, MO 64110-2046
Ph: (816)932-1000
E-mail: info@kauffman.org

Founded: 1992. **Description:** Works to accelerate entrepreneurship in America. **Programs:** Adult Entrepreneurship; Children and Youth Entrepreneurship; College Entrepreneurship; Social Entrepreneurship.

740 ■ Latin Business Association (LBA)

120 S San Pedro St., Ste.530
Los Angeles, CA 90012
Ph: (213)628-8510
Fax: (213)628-8519
E-mail: membership@lbausa.com
URL: http://www.lbausa.com
Contact: Ruben Guerra, Chm./CEO

Founded: 1976. **Members:** 1,200. **Membership Dues:** full, $250 (annual) ● corporate, $2,500 (annual) ● associate, $300 (annual) ● amigo, $75 (annual) ● distinguished full, $1,000 (annual) ● international, $195 (annual) ● life, $10,000. **Staff:** 10. **Description:** Latino business owners and corporations. Assists Latino business owners to develop their businesses. **Libraries: Type:** reference. **Holdings:** 250; books. **Subjects:** business, management, leadership. **Awards:** Scholarship of Latino Business Owners. **Type:** scholarship. **Publications:** *Latin Business Association Business Directory*, periodic ● *Latin Business Association Business Journal*, monthly ● *Latin Business Association Business Newsletter*, monthly. **Advertising:** accepted. **Conventions/Meetings:** monthly meeting (exhibits) - every 3rd Thursday ● monthly seminar.

741 ■ Mountains and Plains Booksellers Association (MPBA)

19 Old Town Sq., Ste.238
Fort Collins, CO 80524
Ph: (970)484-5856
Free: (800)752-0249
Fax: (970)407-1479
E-mail: info@mountainsplains.org
URL: http://www.mountainsplains.org
Contact: Lisa D. Knudsen, Exec. Dir.

Members: 528. **Membership Dues:** associate/active, $65 (annual). **Staff:** 2. **Description:** Supports independent bookstores; promotes literacy and defends freedom of speech and of the press. **Awards:** MPBA Literacy Grants. **Frequency:** annual. **Type:** grant. **Recipient:** to support non-profit literacy programs ● Regional Book Awards. **Type:** recognition. **Programs:** Book Sense. **Publications:** *MPBA Handbook*, annual, published in January. Provides detailed information on member stores, member publishers, and sales reps in the region. ● *Regional Catalogue* ● Newsletter, 5-6/year. Highlights regional news and activities. **Conventions/Meetings:** seminar - every spring ● annual trade show - in fall.

742 ■ National Association for Female Executives (NAFE)

60 E 42nd St., Ste.2700
New York, NY 10165
Ph: (212)351-6451
Free: (800)927-6233
Fax: (212)351-6486
E-mail: nafe@nafe.com
URL: http://www.nafe.com
Contact: Paula Damiano, Newsletter Ed.

Founded: 1972. **Members:** 60,000. **Membership Dues:** individual in U.S., $39 (annual) ● individual outside U.S., $49 (annual). **Staff:** 8. **Local Groups:** 200. **For-Profit. Description:** Represents and supports professional women and women business owners; provides resources and services through education, networking, and public advocacy to empower members to achieve career success and financial security. **Awards:** Women of Achievement Awards. **Frequency:** annual. **Type:** recognition. **Telecommunication Services:** electronic mail, paula.damiano@nafe.com. **Publications:** *NAFE E-Newsletter*, biweekly. Alternate Formats: online ● *NAFE Magazine*, quarterly. Includes book reviews and calendar of events. **Price:** included in membership dues. ISSN: 0199-2880. **Circulation:** 150,000. **Advertising:** accepted. Alternate Formats: online. **Conventions/Meetings:** periodic Breakfast Clubs - meeting.

743 ■ National Association of Professional Asian American Women (NAPAW)

304 Oak Knoll Terr.
Rockville, MD 20850
Ph: (301)785-8585
E-mail: info@napaw.org
URL: http://www.napaw.org
Contact: Vivian C. Kim MA, Natl. Chair

Founded: 1987. **Description:** Represents the professional interests of Asian-American women. Promotes continued personal and professional development; works to enhance career opportunities. Encourages greater visibility of Asian-American women in public decision-making. Conducts educational programs. **Publications:** *NAPAW Newsletter*, periodic. **Conventions/Meetings:** monthly meeting - always first Thursday.

744 ■ National Association of Women Business Owners (NAWBO)

8405 Greensboro Dr., Ste.800
McLean, VA 22102
Ph: (703)506-3268
Free: (800)556-2926
Fax: (703)506-3266
E-mail: national@nawbo.org
URL: http://www.nawbo.org
Contact: Erin M. Fuller CAE, Exec. Dir.

Founded: 1975. **Members:** 8,000. **Membership Dues:** supporting, sustaining, established business owner, $100 (annual) ● emerging business, student, retired, $50 (annual) ● at-large, $120 (annual). **Staff:** 10. **Budget:** $2,000,000. **Regional Groups:** 5. **Local Groups:** 80. **Description:** Represents and promotes women-owned businesses to shape economic and public policy. **Awards:** NAWBO(R)/Guardian Diversity Best Practices Award. **Frequency:** annual. **Type:** recognition. **Recipient:** to a chapter that embraces diversity among its members ● Woman Business Owner of the Year. **Frequency:** annual. **Type:** recognition. **Recipient:** for participation and business success. **Computer Services:** database ● online services, member directory. **Telecommunication Services:** electronic mail, efuller@nawbo.org. **Committees:** Political Action. **Councils:** Corporate and Economic Development; Member Services; Public Policy. **Affiliated With:** Center for Women's Business Research. **Formerly:** (1976) Association of Women Business Owners. **Publications:** *Leader Bulletin*, monthly. Newsletter. Informs NAWBO's volunteer leaders on principles of chapter management. **Price:** included in membership dues. Alternate Formats: online ● *NAWBOTime*, bimonthly. Newsletter. Includes calendar of events. **Price:** included in membership dues. **Circulation:** 8,000. Alternate Formats: online ● Books. **Conventions/Meetings:** annual Public Policy Days - meeting (exhibits) - always in February ● annual Women's Business Conference (exhibits) - always in June.

745 ■ National Association of Women MBAs (NAWMBA)

c/o Rice University
PO Box 2932
Houston, TX 77252
E-mail: director@mbawomen.org
URL: http://www.mbawomen.org
Contact: Tonya Olpin, Exec. Dir.

Founded: 1979. **Members:** 400. **Membership Dues:** chapter school, $150 (annual) ● student - unaffiliated with chapter, $30 (annual) ● alumnus, professional, $40 (annual). **Staff:** 4. **Description:** Provides networking opportunities for its members. Increases communication among graduate business schools regarding their initiatives to educate and support women in business. **Formerly:** (2005) Graduate Women in Business.

746 ■ National Business Incubation Association (NBIA)

20 E Circle Dr., No. 37198
Athens, OH 45701-3571
Ph: (740)593-4331
Fax: (740)593-1996

E-mail: info@nbia.org
URL: http://www.NBIA.org
Contact: Dinah Adkins, Pres./CEO

Founded: 1985. **Members:** 975. **Membership Dues:** incubation professional, $375 (annual) ● associate, $250 (annual) ● consultant, vendor, $525 (annual) ● corporate, $1,050 (annual). **Staff:** 17. **Budget:** $950,000. **Regional Groups:** 1. **State Groups:** 14. **Description:** Incubator developers and managers; corporate joint venture partners, venture capital investors; economic development professionals. (Incubators are business assistance programs providing business consulting services and financing assistance to start-up and fledgling companies.) Helps newly formed businesses to succeed. Educates businesses and investors on incubator benefits; offers specialized training in incubator formation and management. Conducts research and referral services; compiles statistics; maintains speakers' bureau; publishes information relevant to business incubation and growing companies. **Libraries: Type:** not open to the public. **Subjects:** business incubation, entrepreneurship. **Awards:** Incubator Innovation Award. **Frequency:** annual. **Type:** recognition. **Recipient:** for incubator program innovation that benefits clients ● Incubator of the Year. **Frequency:** annual. **Type:** recognition. **Recipient:** for excellence in business incubation programs ● Outstanding Incubator Client. **Frequency:** annual. **Type:** recognition. **Recipient:** to outstanding client firms of NBIA member incubation programs ● Outstanding Incubator Graduate. **Frequency:** annual. **Type:** recognition. **Recipient:** to outstanding firms. **Computer Services:** database, research ● mailing lists. **Programs:** Forums; Partner. **Publications:** *NBIA Insights*, monthly. Newsletter. Serves the nonmembers of NBIA in the entrepreneurship support industry. **Circulation:** 10,000. **Advertising:** accepted. Alternate Formats: online ● *NBIA Memberabilia*, biweekly. Newsletter. **Price:** included in membership dues. **Advertising:** accepted. Alternate Formats: online ● *NBIA Review*, bimonthly. Newsletter. Contains news, features, reviews, how to articles and other material related to helping entrepreneurial businesses grow. **Price:** included in membership dues; $89.99 /year for nonmembers. **Circulation:** 1,000. **Advertising:** accepted. Alternate Formats: online ● *NBIA Updates*, bimonthly. Newsletter. **Price:** included in membership dues. **Circulation:** 1,620. **Advertising:** accepted. Alternate Formats: online ● Books. Contains business incubation monographs. Alternate Formats: online ● Handbooks. **Conventions/Meetings:** annual International Conference on Business Incubation, with award ceremony (exhibits).

747 ■ National Executive Service Corps (NESC)

29 W 38th St., 8th Fl.
New York, NY 10018
Ph: (212)269-1234
Fax: (212)269-0959
E-mail: questions@nesc.org
URL: http://www.nesc.org
Contact: Marvin B. Berenblum, CEO/Chm.

Founded: 1977. **Staff:** 11. **Budget:** $1,200,000. **National Groups:** 39. **Description:** Provides management and business advisory services to non-profit educational, health care, social services, cultural, and religious organizations. Supplies services through experienced and senior-leveled business people who act as volunteer management consultants. **Telecommunication Services:** electronic mail, mterry@nesc.org. **Affiliated With:** National Executive Service Corps. **Publications:** *NESCene*. Newsletter. Alternate Formats: online ● Annual Report, annual. Alternate Formats: online. **Conventions/Meetings:** annual conference.

748 ■ National Family Business Council (NFBC)

1640 W Kennedy Rd.
Lake Forest, IL 60045
Ph: (847)295-1040
Fax: (847)295-1898
E-mail: jmnfbc@msn.com
Contact: John E. Messervey, Pres.

Founded: 1976. **Description:** Serves as a consulting group and resource center on family-owned businesses. Offers consultation, speakers' bureau, and other communications with other family businesses; sponsors regional seminars on problems unique to family businesses. Conducts surveys. **Libraries: Type:** reference. **Holdings:** articles, books, periodicals. **Supersedes:** Sons of Bosses International. **Publications:** *Family Business Letter*, periodic. Newsletter ● *Resource Guide to Family Business*, periodic. **Conventions/Meetings:** annual conference.

749 ■ National Federation of Municipal Analysts (NFMA)

PO Box 14893
Pittsburgh, PA 15234-0893
Ph: (412)341-4898
Fax: (412)341-4894
E-mail: lgood@nfma.org
URL: http://www.nfma.org
Contact: Lisa Good, Exec. Dir.

Founded: 1983. **Members:** 1,000. **Membership Dues:** individual, $80 (annual). **Staff:** 2. **Regional Groups:** 8. **Description:** Municipal analysts' societies and affiliated individual members. Promotes professionalism in municipal credit analysis and furthers the skills of its members through educational programs, industry communication and other means. **Awards: Frequency:** annual. **Type:** recognition. **Computer Services:** database, membership directory. **Publications:** *Municipal Analysts Bulletin*, 3/year. **Circulation:** 1,000. Alternate Formats: online. **Conventions/Meetings:** annual conference (exhibits).

750 ■ National Hispanic Corporate Council (NHCC)

1530 Wilson Blvd., Ste.110
Arlington, VA 22209
Ph: (703)807-5137
Fax: (703)842-7924
E-mail: csoto@nhcc-hq.org
URL: http://www.nhcc-hq.org
Contact: Carlos Soto, Pres./CEO

Founded: 1985. **Members:** 90. **Membership Dues:** corporate, $5,000 (annual). **Staff:** 2. **Description:** Corporate think tank serving Fortune 1000 companies and their representatives as a principal resource for information, expertise and counsel about Hispanic issues affecting corporate objectives, and to advocate for increased employment, leadership and business opportunities for Hispanics in corporate America. **Libraries: Type:** reference. **Subjects:** Hispanic market, language, household trends, corporate America, consumer trends. **Computer Services:** database, open to members only ● mailing lists, open to members only ● online services, open to members only. **Publications:** *NHCC News*, quarterly. Newsletter. **Price:** free for members. **Advertising:** accepted. **Conventions/Meetings:** conference and general assembly, with case studies - 3/year.

751 ■ National Indian Business Association (NIBA)

1730 Rhode Island Ave. NW, Ste.501
Washington, DC 20036
Ph: (202)223-3766
Fax: (202)955-5605
E-mail: niba@nibanetwork.org
URL: http://www.nibanetwork.org
Contact: Mr. Pete Homer, Pres./CEO

Founded: 1992. **Membership Dues:** individual, $150 (annual) ● tribal, $1,000 (annual) ● corporate, $5,000 (annual) ● VIP, $10,000 (annual). **Description:** Promotes American-Indian and Alaskan Native business development through education, communication and advocacy. Assists in the advancement of Native business development by providing information, programs and services to address the unique needs of American-Indian and Alaskan Native business owners, entrepreneurs and governments. Works to expand economic and business opportunities for American-Indian and Alaskan Natives. **Computer Services:** database, business ● information services, tax incentive resources ● mailing lists. **Programs:** Business Development Pilot. **Publications:** Newsletter. Alternate Formats: online.

752 ■ National Nurses in Business Association (NNBA)

PO Box 561081
Rockledge, FL 32956-1081
Ph: (321)633-4610
Free: (877)353-8888
E-mail: bemis@nnba.net
URL: http://www.nnba.net
Contact: Patricia A. Bemis, Pres.

Founded: 1985. **Members:** 600. **Membership Dues:** full, $99 (annual) ● corporate, $500 (annual). **Budget:** $75,000. **For-Profit. Description:** Promotes, supports, educates, and provides a comprehensive network for nurse entrepreneurs. **Libraries: Type:** reference. **Awards:** Living Legend Award. **Frequency:** annual. **Type:** recognition ● Nurses in Business Hall of Fame. **Frequency:** annual. **Type:** recognition. **Recipient:** to nurses who have made significant contributions to other nurses in business. **Computer Services:** Electronic publishing, e-zine. **Publications:** *Business Training for Registered Nurses* ● *Directory of Nurses in Business*, annual. Contains membership directory with description of business owned by members. **Price:** $129.00. **Advertising:** accepted. Alternate Formats: CD-ROM ● *Emergency Nursing Bible*. **Price:** $54.95 for nonmembers; $49.45 for members ● *NNBA Update*, monthly. Newsletter. Alternate Formats: online ● *Nurse Entrepreneurs: Tales of Nurses in Business*. Book. **Price:** $22.45 for members; $24.95 for nonmembers. **Conventions/Meetings:** Making Money in Healthcare: Self-Employment Opportunities for Nurses - seminar - April, June, September, November ● annual Nurse Entrepreneur Convention and Reunion (exhibits) - in October.

753 ■ National Retail Hobby Stores Association (NRHSA)

214 N Hale St.
Wheaton, IL 60187
Ph: (630)510-4596
Fax: (630)510-4501
E-mail: info@nrhsa.org
URL: http://www.nrhsa.org
Contact: Janet Svazas, Exec. Dir.

Membership Dues: retail, $120 (annual). **Multinational. Description:** Addresses the interests and needs of hobby retailers. Acts as a link between manufacturers, distributors and retailers. Researches and develops marketing and advertising strategies for retailers. Facilitates networking among its members. **Additional Websites:** http://www.coolhobbyshops.com. **Committees:** Advertising and Marketing; Education. **Councils:** HVI Advisory. **Programs:** Buy, Sell and Trade; Claim Assistance; Health; Insurance; Paper and Ink. **Publications:** *The Link*, bimonthly. Newsletter. **Conventions/Meetings:** annual trade show.

754 ■ National Society of Hispanic MBAs (NSHMBA)

1303 Walnut Hill Ln., Ste.100
Irving, TX 75038
Ph: (214)596-9338
Free: (877)467-4622
Fax: (214)596-9325
E-mail: lhassler@nshmba.org
URL: http://www.nshmba.org
Contact: Lourdes M. Hassler, CEO

Founded: 1988. **Members:** 4,400. **Membership Dues:** student, $20 (annual) ● professional, $65 (annual) ● life, $1,000 ● executive, $250 (annual). **Staff:** 10. **Budget:** $1,700,000. **Regional Groups:** 26. **State Groups:** 26. **Languages:** English, Spanish. **Description:** Hispanic MBA professional business network dedicated to economic and philanthropic advancement. **Awards:** Brillante Award. **Frequency:** annual. **Type:** recognition. **Recipient:** to outstanding leaders whose work and contributions reflect the society's mission ● **Type:** scholarship. **Recipient:** to MBA students. **Computer Services:** database. **Pub-**

lications: *The Bottom Line*, monthly. Newsletter. **Price:** included in membership dues. **Advertising:** accepted. **Conventions/Meetings:** annual Career Fair - conference (exhibits) ● annual conference (exhibits) - 2008 Oct. 9-11, Atlanta, GA; 2009 Oct. 8-10, Minneapolis, MN ● monthly meeting.

755 ■ North American Association of Inventory Services (NAAIS)
PO Box 120145
St. Paul, MN 55112
Free: (888)529-DATA
Fax: (651)631-9149
E-mail: lneumann@risinventory.com
URL: http://www.naais.com
Contact: Lee J. Neumann, Assoc. Dir.

Founded: 1982. **Members:** 45. **Membership Dues:** regular, $325 (annual). **Multinational. Description:** Represents Independent inventory services; individuals interested in the inventory industry; individuals outside the industry who have performed notable service. Promotes activities aimed at enabling the inventory service to operate efficiently and maintain high standards of conduct. Provides a clearinghouse and medium for the benefit of owners of businesses and shops involving the utilization and maintenance of product inventories. Considers and deals with problems of operation and management, such as those associated with customer accounts and employment. Disseminates business information on the inventory service industry. Maintains speakers' bureau; compiles statistics. **Awards:** Joe Gohs Scholarship Award. **Frequency:** annual. **Type:** scholarship. **Recipient:** to employees and their dependents involved in post high school studies. **Publications:** *NAAIS Newsletter*. Alternate Formats: online. **Conventions/Meetings:** semiannual meeting (exhibits) - in May and November.

756 ■ Organization of Pakistani Entrepreneurs of North America (OPEN)
4 Maxwell Cir.
Hudson, MA 01749
Ph: (781)266-2141
Fax: (781)266-2141
E-mail: info@open-us.org
URL: http://www.open-us.org

Founded: 1998. **Membership Dues:** general (New England chapter), $25 (annual) ● general (New York chapter), $150 (annual) ● charter (Silicon Valley chapter), $500 (annual) ● general (Silicon Valley chapter), $50 (annual) ● student (Silicon Valley chapter), $30 (annual). **Description:** Provides networking opportunities for Pakistani entrepreneurs and professionals in high-tech industries in the Nascent Community of Massachusetts. **Telecommunication Services:** electronic mail, rsvp@open-us.org.

757 ■ Outsourcing Institute (OI)
Jericho Atrium
500 N Broadway, Ste.141
Jericho, NY 11753
Ph: (516)681-0066 (631)261-6810
Fax: (516)215-6810
E-mail: info@outsourcing.com
URL: http://www.outsourcing.com
Contact: Frank J. Casale, Founder/Chm./CEO

Founded: 1993. **Members:** 500. **Staff:** 20. **For-Profit. Description:** Represents corporations making use of outside resources and services. Serves as a clearinghouse on the strategic use of outside resources. Conducts research, executive events, publications and educational programs. **Publications:** Also publishes Custom research and industry white papers.

758 ■ Pakistani American Business Executives Association (PABE)
23105 Kashiwa Ct.
Torrance, CA 90505
Ph: (310)534-1505
Fax: (310)534-1424
E-mail: plodhie@ledtronics.com
URL: http://www.pabe.org
Contact: Mr. Pervaiz Lodhie, Chm.

Multinational. Description: Represents business leaders from Pakistan and the United States. Seeks to foster and facilitate trade and investment between Pakistan and the United States. Mentors new businesses to the international market place.

759 ■ POWERLUNCH!
c/o The Employment Support Center
1556 Wisconsin Ave. NW
Washington, DC 20007
Ph: (202)628-2919
Fax: (202)628-2919
E-mail: jobclubs@hotmail.com
URL: http://www.angelfire.com/biz/jobclubs
Contact: Ms. Ellie Wegener, Founder/Exec. Dir.

Founded: 1984. **Members:** 100. **Membership Dues:** unemployed/part-time, $50 (annual) ● employed/full-time, $100 (annual). **Staff:** 2. **Description:** Seeks to enhance networking capabilities by matching an individual seeking a specific type of information with an expert in that field. Capitalizes on the concept "it's not what you know, but who you know". Activities are currently limited to the Washington, DC, area; plans to expand nationally. Teaches facilitators how to start self-help groups for job seekers. **Libraries: Type:** open to the public. **Holdings:** 200. **Subjects:** employment, job-search skills, entrepreneurship, life goals. **Subcommittees:** Capitol Hill Career Support. **Affiliated With:** Center for Nonprofit Advancement; National Neighborhood Coalition. **Publications:** *ESC Newsline*. Newsletter ● *The Self-Help Bridge to Employment*, quarterly. Handbook. Describes history of the ESC and how to start job clubs. **Price:** $25.00 includes postage ● Also publishes calendar of events. **Conventions/Meetings:** weekly Job Club - meeting, unemployed exchange job info, jobs and support, and self-help strategies.

760 ■ Procurement and Supply Chain Benchmarking Association (PASBA)
c/o The Benchmarking Network
4606 FM 1960 W, Ste.250
Houston, TX 77069-9949
Ph: (281)440-5044
Free: (800)856-8546
Fax: (281)440-6677
URL: http://www.pasba.com
Contact: Mark T. Czarnecki MBA, Contact

Founded: 1998. **Members:** 4,000. **Staff:** 14. **Budget:** $2,000,000. **Description:** Procurement and supply chain managers of corporations with an interest in benchmarking. Promotes the use of benchmarking, wherein businesses compare their processes with those of their competitors, as a means of improving corporate efficiency and profitability. Facilitates exchange of information among members; conducts target operations, procurement, development, and maintenance studies; identifies model business practices. **Publications:** *eBenchmarketing*, weekly. Newsletter. Includes articles about new trends in benchmarking, information about open studies and links to other benchmarking sites. **Price:** free. Alternate Formats: online. **Conventions/Meetings:** annual meeting and roundtable.

761 ■ Professional Scripophily Trade Association (PSTA)
c/o Bob Kerstein, Pres.
PO Box 223795
Chantilly, VA 20153
Ph: (703)579-4209
Free: (888)786-2576
Fax: (703)995-4422
E-mail: bob@psta.com
URL: http://www.psta.com
Contact: Bob Kerstein, Pres.

Founded: 2004. **Description:** Promotes the study and collection of scripophily for collectors, researchers, and for the interpretation and preservation of financial history. Helps support educational projects, programs, and seminars to help collectors and the general public gain a better understanding of scripophily, finance and business history.

762 ■ Representative of German Industry and Trade (RGIT)
1627 I St. NW, Ste.550
Washington, DC 20006
Ph: (202)659-4777
Fax: (202)659-4779
E-mail: info@rgit-usa.com
URL: http://www.rgit-usa.com
Contact: Bernhard Welschke, Pres.

Founded: 1988. **Members:** 37. **Staff:** 350. **Languages:** English, German. **Description:** Organizations representing 95&percent; of private industry in Germany. Provides data concerning economic developments and the economic environment in Germany. **Formerly:** (2000) Federation of German Industries. **Publications:** *Report to Patrons*, periodic. **Conventions/Meetings:** periodic seminar ● periodic workshop.

763 ■ Singapore American Business Association (SABA)
333 Twin Dolphin Dr., Ste.145
Redwood City, CA 94065
Ph: (415)252-1150
Fax: (415)252-1160
E-mail: sabausa@aol.com
URL: http://www.saba-usa.org
Contact: Ms. Isabelle Lee, Exec. Dir.

Founded: 1992. **Membership Dues:** individual, $50 (annual) ● student, $20 (annual) ● corporate, $1,200 (annual). **Multinational. Description:** Serves as a catalyst for business opportunities, inquiries, investments and introductions between Northern America, Singapore and Asia. Provides leadership for local and regional organizations to create and expand Pacific Rim market opportunities. Facilitates cooperation among Asian and North American professionals doing business on either side of the Pacific. **Publications:** *The Monitor*. Newsletter. **Price:** included in membership dues. **Advertising:** accepted ● Membership Directory. **Price:** included in membership dues. Alternate Formats: online.

764 ■ Social Venture Network (SVN)
PO Box 29221
San Francisco, CA 94129-0221
Ph: (415)561-6501
Fax: (415)561-6435
E-mail: svn@svn.org
URL: http://www.svn.org
Contact: Deb Nelson, Exec. Dir.

Founded: 1987. **Members:** 400. **Membership Dues:** basic, $1,000 (annual) ● partner, $2,000 (annual) ● supporting, $2,500 (annual) ● sponsoring, $5,000 (annual) ● affiliate, $500 (annual) ● mission, $10,000 (annual) ● leadership, $25,000 (annual) ● mission - life, $100,000. **Description:** Aims to build a just and sustainable world through business. Promotes new models and leadership for socially and environmentally sustainable business through initiatives, information services and forums. **Computer Services:** database, SVNet ● online services, library. **Publications:** *Network News*, quarterly. Newsletter. Features new member information and initiatives. ● *The Networker*, biweekly. Newsletter. Provides information about timely projects, events and issues. Alternate Formats: online ● Membership Directory. Alternate Formats: online.

765 ■ U.S. Council of Better Business Bureaus (CBBB)
4200 Wilson Blvd., Ste.800
Arlington, VA 22203-1838
Ph: (703)276-0100
Fax: (703)525-8277
URL: http://www.bbb.org
Contact: Steven J. Cole, Pres./CEO

Founded: 1912. **Members:** 300,000. **Staff:** 120. **Budget:** $17,300,000. **Local Groups:** 123. **Multinational. Description:** Promotes ethical relationships between businesses and the public through self-regulation, consumer and business education, and service excellence. **Computer Services:** Online services, BBB. **Divisions:** Better Business Bureau Wise Giving Alliance; Children's Advertising Review Unit; National Advertising. **Programs:** Dispute

Resolution Services & Mediation Training; Nationwide System of BBBs. **Publications:** *BBB Wise Giving Guide*, quarterly ● *We Build Trust*. Brochure. Alternate Formats: online ● Reports. **Conventions/Meetings:** annual assembly.

766 ■ United States Council for International Business (USCIB)
1212 Ave. of the Americas
New York, NY 10036
Ph: (212)354-4480
Fax: (212)575-0327
E-mail: membership@uscib.org
URL: http://www.uscib.org
Contact: William G. Parrett, Chm.
Founded: 1945. **Members:** 300. **Membership Dues:** company, $10,000 (annual) ● association, law firm, $5,000 (annual). **Staff:** 45. **Budget:** $6,131,500. **Description:** Serves as the U.S. National Committee of the International Chamber of Commerce. Enables multinational enterprises to operate effectively by representing their interests to intergovernmental and governmental bodies and by keeping enterprises advised of international developments having a major impact on their operations. Serves as: U.S. representative to the International Organization of Employers; national affiliate to the U.S.A. Business and Industry Advisory Committee to the BIAC. Operates ATA Carnet export service, which enables goods to be shipped overseas duty-free for demonstration and exhibition. Sponsors seminars and luncheon briefings. **Awards:** International Leadership Award. **Frequency:** annual. **Type:** recognition. **Recipient:** for individuals who make outstanding contributions to international trade and investment. **Committees:** Arbitration; Banking; Biotechnology; Competition; Corporate Responsibility; Customs and Trade Facilitation; Economies in Transition; Finance and Oversight. **Formerly:** (1949) United States Associates of the International Chamber of Commerce; (1962) USA-BIAC; (1982) United States Council of the International Chamber of Commerce. **Publications:** *Business and Environment*, periodic. Newsletter. Alternate Formats: online ● *Corporate Handbook Series* ● *USCIB Newsletter*, monthly. Reports on council programs and committees. Contains information on International Chamber of Commerce, and International Organization of Employers. **Price:** free for members; $25.00 /year for nonmembers. **Conventions/Meetings:** annual dinner - always in New York City.

767 ■ Workflow and Reengineering International Association (WARIA)
2436 N Fed. Hwy., No. 374
Lighthouse Point, FL 33064
Ph: (954)782-3376
Free: (800)74-WARIA
Fax: (954)782-6365
E-mail: waria04@waria.com
URL: http://www.waria.com
Contact: Layna Fischer, Pres./CEO
Founded: 1992. **Members:** 3,000. **Membership Dues:** individual, $200 (annual) ● student, $60 (annual). **Description:** Identifies and clarifies issues that are common to users of workflow, electronic commerce, knowledge management and those who are in the process of re-engineering their organizations. **Awards:** Global Excellence in Workflow Award. **Frequency:** annual. **Type:** recognition. **Recipient:** for innovation and excellence in workflow implementations. **Computer Services:** database ● mailing lists.

768 ■ World Presidents' Organization (WPO)
110 S Union St., Ste.200
Alexandria, VA 22314-3351
Ph: (703)684-4900
Fax: (703)684-4955
E-mail: info@wpo.org
URL: http://www.wpo.org
Contact: Robert Strade, COO
Founded: 1970. **Members:** 4,800. **Staff:** 26. **Multinational. Description:** Corporate executives, all of whom are former members of the Young Presidents' Organization (see separate entry). Functions as a graduate school for former members of YPO. Strives to provide high quality program content and to keep members well-informed on major topics through contact with the world's leading authorities. Conducts seminars. **Formerly:** (1992) World Business Council. **Publications:** *World Presidents Organization—Express*, monthly. Newsletter. Provides information concerning WPO programs and activities. **Price:** free for members. **Circulation:** 3,500. **Conventions/Meetings:** meeting - 8/year.

769 ■ Young Presidents' Organization (YPO)
600 E Las Colinas Blvd., Ste.1000
Irving, TX 75039
Ph: (972)587-1500
Free: (800)773-7976
E-mail: askypo@ypo.org
URL: http://www.ypo.org
Contact: Les Ward, CFO/COO
Founded: 1950. **Members:** 11,000. **Local Groups:** 162. **Multinational. Description:** Presidents or chief executive officers of corporations with minimum of 50 employees; each member must have been elected president before his/her 40th birthday and must retire by June 30th the year after his/her 50th birthday. Assists members in becoming better presidents through education and idea exchange. Conducts courses for members and spouses, in business, arts and sciences, world affairs, and family and community life, during a given year at various locations, including graduate business schools. **Publications:** *Worldwide*. **Conventions/Meetings:** seminar.

770 ■ Young Women Social Entrepreneurs (YWSE)
1684 Washington St., No. 5
San Francisco, CA 94109
Ph: (415)378-4417
E-mail: contactus@ywse.org
URL: http://www.ywse.org
Contact: Sara Ellis, Contact
Membership Dues: general, $75 (annual). **Description:** Serves women, primarily ages 25-40, with socially conscious agenda who are founders and leaders within businesses, non-profits, and government organizations. Aims to promote young women entrepreneurs by providing training and development, access to resources, and networking opportunities. **Computer Services:** Mailing lists.

Business and Commerce

771 ■ Consuming Industries Trade Action Coalition (CITAC)
2000 L St. NW, Ste.835
Washington, DC 20036
Ph: (202)316-3046
E-mail: info@citac.info
URL: http://www.citac.info
Contact: Steve Alexander, Exec. Dir.
Description: Represents manufacturers and organizations committed to promoting a trade arena where U.S. consuming industries and their workers have access to global markets for imports that enhance the international competitiveness of American firms. Seeks to increase the involvement and influence of consuming industries in the trade debate. Provides education and awareness programs for consuming industries and their employees. **Telecommunication Services:** electronic mail, steve.alexander@citac.info.

772 ■ International Association for Contract and Commercial Management (IACCM)
90 Grove St.
Ridgefield, CT 06877
Ph: (203)431-8741
Fax: (203)431-9305
E-mail: info@iaccm.com
URL: http://www.iaccm.com
Contact: Tim Cummins, Pres./CEO
Founded: 1999. **Members:** 5,000. **Membership Dues:** individual, $150 (annual) ● corporate, $2,500 (annual). **Regional Groups:** 4. **Multinational. Description:** Brings together a global community of senior contracts, sourcing, and commercial management executives and managers. Aims to help members develop innovation, best practices, and operational excellence within their organizations, and ultimately, through sharing goals and methods. Provides services and knowledge required to enable organizational and professional excellence in contracting and commercial management. Raises the international status, profile and professionalism of commercial contracting and negotiators handling both buy and sell transactions. Promotes the role of contracts and negotiation professionals in industry and commerce. **Libraries: Type:** reference. **Awards: Frequency:** periodic. **Type:** fellowship. **Recipient:** for a fellow with outstanding experience and performance in his/her career ● Negotiations Challenge. **Type:** recognition. **Recipient:** for a company that won in the negotiations challenge. **Councils:** Advisory. **Special Interest Groups:** Contract Management Community of Interest; Women In Commitment Management. **Publications:** *Annual Salary Survey*, annual. Report ● *IACCM Benchmarking Survey*, annual. Report ● *IACCM Top 10 Negotiated Terms Report*, annual ● *Updates*, monthly. Newsletter. Alternate Formats: online.

773 ■ Korean American Society of Entrepreneurs (KASE)
2882 Sand Hill Rd., Ste.100
Menlo Park, CA 94025
E-mail: mail@kase.org
URL: http://www.kase.org
Contact: Keibock Lee, Co-Founder/Chm.
Membership Dues: regular, $40 (annual). **Description:** Brings together entrepreneurs, engineers, corporate executives, venture capitalists, and other professionals with roots or interests in Korea. Fosters and supports network of Korean Americans interested in starting or playing key roles in companies in the United States. Facilitates the professional development, networking, and mentoring of its members. Provides information on all areas related to its members' interests.

774 ■ National Council of Asian American Business Associations (NCAABA)
PO Box 2157
Walnut, CA 91789
Ph: (831)425-4502 (909)861-9670
E-mail: jamieb@national-caaba.org
URL: http://www.national-caaba.org
Contact: Jamie Borromeo, Exec. Dir.
Description: Serve as the voice of Asian Pacific American business owners in the United States. Works to effect positive change in the areas of economic development, public contracting and private procurement, and public and fiscal policies that impact Asian Pacific American businesses and communities at large. Seeks to create opportunities in the social, political, and economic sectors for the Asian Pacific American business community. **Telecommunication Services:** electronic mail, nicolea@national-caaba.org. **Publications:** Newsletter, monthly.

775 ■ United States-Indonesia Society (USINDO)
1625 Massachusetts Ave. NW, Ste.550
Washington, DC 20036-2260
Ph: (202)232-1400
Fax: (202)232-7300
E-mail: usindo@usindo.org
URL: http://www.usindo.org
Contact: Alphonse F. La Porta, Pres.
Founded: 1994. **Membership Dues:** full time student, $25 (annual) ● friend/professional, $120-$239 (annual) ● friend, $240-$10,000 (annual) ● society, $50,000 (annual) ● corporate subscriber, $5,000-$9,999 (annual) ● organization supporter, $1,500-$4,999 (annual). **Multinational. Description:** Expands understanding of Indonesia and of the importance of the United States-Indonesia relationship. Works with leaders in government and non-governmental organizations, educators, the media, business, and the general public. Provides information and promotes education about United States-

Indonesia relationship. **Publications:** *USINDO News*, biennial. Newsletter. **Price:** included in membership dues. Alternate Formats: online.

776 ■ US-Ireland Alliance
2800 Clarendon Blvd., No. 502 W
Arlington, VA 22201
Ph: (703)841-5843
E-mail: vargo@us-irelandalliance.org
URL: http://www.us-irelandalliance.org
Contact: Trina Vargo, Pres.
Founded: 1998. **Multinational. Description:** Represents groups and individuals with a strong interest in Irish affairs. Works to consolidate existing relations between the United States and Ireland (North and South) and build that relationship for the future. Educates the American public about the United States and Ireland relationship. **Awards:** George J. Mitchell Scholarship. **Frequency:** annual. **Type:** scholarship. **Recipient:** for individuals who have outstanding record of leadership and academic excellence. **Publications:** Newsletter, annual. Alternate Formats: online.

Business Products

777 ■ Original Equipment Suppliers Association (OESA)
1301 W Long Lake Rd., Ste.225
Troy, MI 48098
Ph: (248)952-6401
Fax: (248)952-6404
E-mail: info@oesa.org
URL: http://www.oesa.org
Contact: Neil De Koker, Pres./CEO
Founded: 1998. **Members:** 400. **Membership Dues:** regular (based on total annual automotive sales), $750-$17,500 (annual) ● affiliate, $3,000 (annual) ● divisional, $1,000 (annual). **Staff:** 11. **Description:** Represents and supports original equipment suppliers. **Councils:** Automotive Human Resources; Automotive Presidents; Automotive Public Relations; E-Business; Environmental; Legal Issues; Sales and Marketing; Peer Groups; Small and Medium Suppliers. **Publications:** *Automotive Industry Review*, annual ● *Automotive Supplier News*, monthly. Newsletter ● Bulletin. **Conventions/Meetings:** annual conference and meeting ● seminar and workshop.

Business Studies

778 ■ Global Business and Technology Association (GBATA)
PO Box 2686
Huntington Station, NY 11746
Ph: (516)876-3408 (516)876-3292
Fax: (631)462-9578
E-mail: gbatadelener@oldwestbury.edu
URL: http://www.gbata.com
Contact: Dr. Nejdet Delener, Pres./Founder
Founded: 1998. **Members:** 2,000. **Multinational. Description:** Represents the interests of individuals committed to the advancement of knowledge related to the theory and practice of international business and technology. Promotes research pertaining to business and technology issues facing the Global marketplace. Improves the communication and exchange of information concerning business and technology issues among interested college and university faculty members. **Publications:** *Journal of Global Business and Technology*. Presents articles on variety of topics in international business and technology. **Price:** $85.00 per year (corporate, institution, library), plus shipping and handling; $45.00 /year for individuals, plus shipping and handling. Also Cited As: *JGBAT*. **Conventions/Meetings:** annual conference.

Cable Television

779 ■ American Cable Association (ACA)
One Parkway Ctr., Ste.212
Pittsburgh, PA 15220
Ph: (412)922-8300
Fax: (412)922-2110
E-mail: aca@americancable.org
URL: http://www.americancable.org
Contact: Matthew M. Polka, Pres./CEO
Founded: 1993. **Members:** 930. **Membership Dues:** cable operator (with 0-200 subscribers), $25 (quarterly) ● cable operator (with 201-400 subscribers), $50 (quarterly) ● associate, $800 (annual). **Description:** Represents the interests of independent cable television businesses and smaller cable systems across the United States. Elevates the concerns of its members before the Congress, the Federal Communications Commission and other agencies of the federal government. Helps its members to stay competitive through a legislative and regulatory framework designed to boost their economic potential. **Publications:** *ACAction*, monthly. Newsletter. Contains news and information about the association and its activities. **Price:** included in membership dues. Alternate Formats: online ● *Independent Cable News*, monthly. Magazine.

780 ■ Cable Television Laboratories (CableLabs)
c/o Michael M. Schwartz, Sr. VP for Communications
858 Coal Creek Cir.
Louisville, CO 80027-9750
Ph: (303)661-9100
Fax: (303)661-9199
E-mail: m.schwartz@cablelabs.com
URL: http://www.cablelabs.com
Contact: Michael M. Schwartz, Sr. VP for Communications
Founded: 1988. **Staff:** 80. **Description:** Cable television companies (as defined by the Cable Act) located in North, Central, or South America, and cable operators. Designed to keep the cable television industry on the leading edge of technology and services. **Publications:** *SPECS News and Technology*. Newsletter. Alternate Formats: online.

781 ■ National Cable Television Cooperative (NCTC)
11200 Corporate Ave.
Lenexa, KS 66219-1392
Ph: (913)599-5900
Fax: (913)599-5903
URL: http://www.cabletvcoop.org
Contact: Michael Pandzik, Pres./CEO
Founded: 1984. **Members:** 1,000. **Description:** Represents independent cable television companies. Purchases programming, hardware and services in order to remain competitive.

Career Counseling

782 ■ Association of Career Professionals International
204 E St. NE
Washington, DC 20002
Ph: (202)547-6377
Fax: (202)547-6348
E-mail: info@acpinternational.org
URL: http://www.iacmp.org
Contact: Annette Summers, Exec. Dir.
Founded: 1989. **Members:** 2,000. **Membership Dues:** professional, $165 (annual) ● student, $80 (annual) ● international corporate supplier, $625 (annual). **Multinational. Description:** Promotes the global development of the career management profession. **Formerly:** (2003) International Association of Career Management Professionals. **Publications:** *Career Voice International*, quarterly. Newsletter. Alternate Formats: online. **Conventions/Meetings:** annual conference.

Carriages

783 ■ Carriage Operators of North America (CONA)
PO Box 554
Norfolk, CT 06058
Ph: (860)542-5222
Free: (866)602-2662
E-mail: membership@cona.org
URL: http://www.cona.org
Contact: Steve Podhajecki, Contact
Membership Dues: general, $100 (annual). **Multinational. Description:** Promotes the welfare of carriage animals. Fosters quality carriage and customer service. Provides open communication on the operation and management of the carriage trade. **Publications:** Newsletter. **Conventions/Meetings:** annual convention.

Celtic

784 ■ North American Celtic Buyers Association (NACBA)
27 Addison Ave.
Rutherford, NJ 07070
Ph: (201)842-9922
Fax: (201)804-9143
E-mail: info@celticbuyers.com
URL: http://www.celticbuyers.com
Contact: Neville Gardner, Pres.
Membership Dues: general/associate, $150 (annual). **Multinational. Description:** Represents professional Celtic retailers in North America. Facilitates communication among businesses involved in Celtic retailing in the USA and Canada. Develops and implements programs of value to its members. **Telecommunication Services:** electronic mail, neville@ptd.net. **Publications:** Newsletter, 3 to 4 issues per year. **Price:** included in membership dues.

Ceramics

785 ■ Association of American Ceramic Component Manufacturers (AACCM)
735 Ceramic Pl., Ste.100
Westerville, OH 43081-8720
Ph: (614)794-5821
Fax: (614)794-5882
E-mail: aaccm@acers.org
URL: http://www.aaccm.org
Founded: 1992. **Description:** Aims to expand the market for manufactured ceramic components by enhancing processes. Increases the public and industry education and awareness of ceramic applications. Addresses concerns relative to market requirement, raw material supply and fabrication technology. Promotes the industry to domestic and international markets. **Computer Services:** Information services, ceramics resources.

786 ■ Ceramic Manufacturers Association (CerMA)
c/o Myra Warne, Exec. Dir.
47 N Fourth St.
Zanesville, OH 43701
Ph: (740)588-0828
Fax: (740)588-0273
E-mail: myrawarne@yahoo.com
URL: http://www.cerma.org
Contact: Myra Warne, Exec. Dir.
Founded: 1925. **Members:** 300. **Membership Dues:** individual, $95 (annual) ● corporate, $300 (annual) ● corporate associate, $25 (annual). **Staff:** 5. **Languages:** English, German, Spanish. **Description:** Businesses involved in the manufacture and supply of ceramic products and services. Addresses problems in the production, supply, supervision, and marketing of ceramic products. Promotes the welfare of ceramic, glass, and cement manufacturers; stimulates public interest in the profession; provides a forum for the exchange of information among manufacturers. Sponsors plant tours educational programs. **Computer Services:** Mailing lists, member roster. **Formerly:** (1986) Ohio Ceramics Association; (1990) American Association of Ceramic Industries. **Publications:** Magazine. **Price:** included in membership dues. **Conventions/Meetings:** semiannual conference and seminar (exhibits) - every spring and fall. 2009 May 21-23, Pittsburgh, PA.

787 ■ International Ceramic Association (ICA)
c/o Helen Daum, Treas.
17098 Pheasant Meadow Ln. SW
Prior Lake, MN 55372
Ph: (952)447-6421
E-mail: ceramicteacher@msn.com
URL: http://www.ceramic-ica.com
Contact: Helen Daum, Treas.
Founded: 1958. **Members:** 3,000. **Membership Dues:** raw material, $200 (annual) ● manufacturer, $100 (annual) ● distributor, $50 (annual) ● retailer, teacher, China painter, doll, finished ceramicist, $25 (annual) ● affiliate, $65 (annual) ● individual, hobbyist, $15 (annual). **Staff:** 1. **Local Groups:** 90. **National Groups:** 6. **Description:** Manufacturers, distributors, dealers, teachers, and finished ceramists in 7 countries. Conducts promotional activities; seeks to improve relations between the industry and raw material suppliers, transportation companies, and governments. Recommends standards for sales policy and buying, pricing, and inventory; promotes standardization of entries and judging at shows. Encourages improved teaching methods; conducts pilot programs for the handicapped; organizes teachers' meetings, business seminars, and competitions. Maintains International Ceramic Association Educational Foundation. Operates hall of fame. **Awards: Frequency:** annual. **Type:** recognition. **Divisions:** Affiliate Association; Distributors; Manufacturers; Retailers; Teachers. **Formerly:** (1982) National Ceramic Association. **Publications:** *Blue Book*, annual ● *Judging Manual* ● *Teachers' Manual* ● *Trade Journal*, quarterly. **Conventions/Meetings:** annual meeting (exhibits).

788 ■ Refractory Ceramic Fibers Coalition (RCFC)
c/o Dana Bishop
2300 N St. NW
Washington, DC 20037
Ph: (202)663-9188
Fax: (202)354-5230
E-mail: rcfc@buffnet.net
URL: http://www.rcfc.net
Contact: Dana Bishop, Contact
Members: 3. **Description:** Develops and promotes proper work practices and standards for the Refractory Ceramic Fibers (RCFs) industry. Conducts health research and disseminates information on the proper handling and use of RCFs. **Computer Services:** Information services, handling practices for health products and applications; quantitative risk assessment for RCF. **Programs:** Product Stewardship. **Publications:** *ACGIH Update*. Report. Provides update on the decision of the American Conference of Governmental Industrial Hygiene (ACGIH) on RCF harmful particles. Alternate Formats: online ● *Customer Self-Monitoring Program Overview for Airborne Fiber*. Report. Alternate Formats: online ● *Summary of Health Studies of Workers Manufacturing Refractory Ceramic Fibers*. Report. Alternate Formats: online ● *Work Practice Guide for Refractory Ceramic Fiber Products*. Booklet. Alternate Formats: online ● *Workplace Guidelines*. Handbook. Contains proper guidelines on RCF after service removal, batching, blanket cutting and finishing operations. Alternate Formats: online.

Chambers of Commerce

789 ■ National Association of Chamber Ambassadors (NACA)
PO Box 1198
Seminole, TX 79360
Free: (800)411-6222
E-mail: printplus@totacc.com
URL: http://www.chamberambassadors.com
Contact: Frank Sherman, Pres.
Founded: 1986. **Membership Dues:** ambassador, $25 (annual) ● life, $200. **Description:** Assists chambers of commerce in establishing ambassador groups. Strengthens existing ambassador groups by providing education, materials and information. Provides a forum for the exchange of ideas between ambassadors. Offers various enrichment opportunities for all chamber ambassador groups, public relations and welcoming committees. **Publications:** *The Ambassador*, quarterly. Newsletter. Features ideas and activities of other member groups. **Price:** included in membership dues.

Chefs

790 ■ American Culinary Federation (ACF)
180 Center Place Way
St. Augustine, FL 32095
Ph: (904)824-4468
Free: (800)624-9458
Fax: (904)825-4758
E-mail: hcramb@acfchefs.net
URL: http://www.acfchefs.org
Contact: Heidi Cramb, Exec. Dir. of Operations
Founded: 1929. **Members:** 20,500. **Staff:** 29. **Local Groups:** 240. **Description:** Aims to promote the culinary profession and provide on-going educational training and networking for members. Provides opportunities for competition, professional recognition, and access to educational forums with other culinary experts at local, regional, national, and international events. Operates the National Apprenticeship Program for Cooks and pastry cooks. Offers programs that address certification of the individual chef's skills, accreditation of culinary programs, apprenticeship of cooks and pastry cooks, professional development, and the fight against childhood hunger. **Libraries: Type:** reference. **Holdings:** books. **Subjects:** hospitality industry. **Awards:** Chef of the Year Award. **Frequency:** annual. **Type:** recognition. **Recipient:** for an individual who was selected by members and committee ● Hospitality Industry Scholarships. **Frequency:** annual. **Type:** scholarship. **Recipient:** for individuals working in the hospitality industry. **Publications:** *Art and Science of Food Preparation* ● *Culinary Olympic Cookbook* ● *National Culinary Review*, monthly. Magazine. **Price:** $50.00/year. **Advertising:** accepted ● Also publishes accompanying student and teacher guides. **Conventions/Meetings:** annual regional meeting and competition, educational seminars, techniques, trends, and culinary competitions (exhibits).

791 ■ American Personal and Private Chef Association (APPCA)
4572 Delaware St.
San Diego, CA 92116
Free: (800)644-8389
Fax: (619)294-2436
E-mail: info@personalchef.com
URL: http://www.personalchef.com
Contact: Candy Wallace, Exec. Dir.
Membership Dues: general, $150 (annual). **Local Groups:** 9. **Description:** Promotes the advancement of personal and private chefs. Facilitates communication, networking with colleagues, continuing education, online mentoring, support and exchange of ideas among members. **Libraries: Type:** reference. **Holdings:** 2; articles, audio recordings, books, photographs, software, video recordings. **Subjects:** personal and private chefs. **Awards:** Chef of the Year. **Frequency:** annual. **Type:** recognition. **Recipient:** for significant contribution to the industry ● Scholarship Award. **Frequency:** 3/year. **Type:** scholarship. **Computer Services:** Information services, chef resources ● online services, discussion forum. **Formerly:** (2007) American Personal Chef Association. **Publications:** *Ala Minute*, bimonthly. Newsletter. Contains upcoming events and training, articles, and recipes. **Price:** free for members. Alternate Formats: online ● *Personal Chef Specialty Skills DVD Library*, quadrennial. Videos. **Price:** $149.00 free, for members only. Alternate Formats: CD-ROM.

792 ■ Chefs de Cuisine Association of America (CCAA)
Address Unknown since 2008
Founded: 1916. **Members:** 410. **Membership Dues:** allied, $100 (annual) ● regular, $75 (annual). **Staff:** 1. **Description:** Professional executive chefs; chefs who own restaurants; pastry chefs for hotels, clubs, and restaurants. Maintains 350 volume library and placement service for members. **Libraries: Type:** reference. **Holdings:** 350. **Awards: Type:** recognition. **Recipient:** for individuals who promote the profession. **Formerly:** (1964) Executive Chefs de Cuisine Association of America. **Publications:** *Chef's Edge*, bimonthly. Newsletter. Alternate Formats: online ● Yearbook. **Conventions/Meetings:** competition ● annual dinner - always October.

793 ■ United States Personal Chef Association (USPCA)
610 Quantum Rd. NE
Rio Rancho, NM 87124
Ph: (505)994-6372
Free: (800)995-2138
E-mail: customerservice@uspca.com
URL: http://www.uspca.com
Founded: 1991. **Members:** 5,000. **Membership Dues:** premier, $299 (annual) ● associate, $299 (annual) ● student, $79 (annual). **Staff:** 16. **Budget:** $2,100,000. **State Groups:** 44. **Multinational. Description:** Promotes the personal chef; committed in advancing the profession of personal chef as a legitimate career choice in the culinary arts field; ensures the credibility of the personal chef with the industry-wide implementation of Educational Standards of Knowledge. **Publications:** *Personal Chef Magazine*, bimonthly. Contains information of true value to the working professional and is the only printed trade publication for the Personal Chef industry. **Price:** included in membership dues. **Advertising:** accepted. Alternate Formats: online.

794 ■ Women Chefs and Restaurateurs (WCR)
455 S Fourth St., Ste.650
Louisville, KY 40202
Ph: (502)581-0300
Free: (877)927-7787
Fax: (502)589-3602
E-mail: elynn@hqtrs.com
URL: http://www.womenchefs.org
Contact: Emily B. Lynn, Exec. Dir.
Founded: 1993. **Members:** 2,300. **Membership Dues:** executive, $195 (annual) ● chef/restaurant/culinary professional, $95 (annual) ● beginning restaurant professional, $55 (annual) ● friend, $140 (annual) ● small business, $280 (annual) ● corporate, $1,650 (annual) ● student, $45 (annual). **Staff:** 3. **Description:** Seeks to educate and advance women in the restaurant industry. **Awards: Frequency:** annual. **Type:** scholarship ● Women Who Inspire Awards. **Frequency:** annual. **Type:** recognition. **Recipient:** for women involved in foodservice industry. **Computer Services:** database ● mailing lists, for sale to members only ● online services. **Formerly:** (1998) International Association of Women Chefs and Restaurateurs. **Publications:** *Entrez*, quarterly. Newsletter. **Advertising:** accepted. Alternate Formats: online. **Conventions/Meetings:** annual conference ● semiannual regional meeting.

Chemicals

795 ■ Acrylonitrile Group (AN)
1250 Connecticut Ave. NW, Ste.700
Washington, DC 20036
Ph: (202)419-1500
Fax: (202)659-8037
E-mail: angroup@regnet.com
URL: http://www.angroup.org
Contact: Robert J. Fensterheim, Exec. Dir.
Founded: 1981. **Members:** 8. **Staff:** 2. **Budget:** $500,000. **Description:** Producers and users of acrylonitrile concerned with the health, safety, environmental, and other regulatory matters regarding the manufacture, distribution, storage, and use of acrylonitrile. Supports research on acrylonitrile, used in the production of synthetic acrylic and mod-acrylic fibers, plastic resin, nitrile rubber automotive components, and nylon 66. **Committees:** Communications;

Environment; Epidemiology; Health and Science; Process/Transportation Safety; Toxicology. **Conventions/Meetings:** annual board meeting.

796 ■ Alkylphenols and Ethoxylates Research Council (APERC)
1250 Connecticut Ave., Ste.700
Washington, DC 20036
Ph: (202)419-1506
Free: (866)APERC-NA
Fax: (202)659-8037
E-mail: info@aperc.org
URL: http://www.aperc.org
Contact: Robert J. Fensterheim, Exec. Dir.
Founded: 1998. **Members:** 5. **Description:** Promotes the safe use of APs and AP derivatives through research, product stewardship and outreach efforts. Advocates science-based public policy. Communicates findings of research, regulatory issues to industry, academia, government and media. Sponsors research to advance scientific understanding of health and environmental safety of alkylphenol products.

797 ■ Alliance for Responsible Atmospheric Policy
2111 Wilson Blvd., Ste.850
Arlington, VA 22201
Ph: (703)243-0344
Fax: (703)243-2874
E-mail: info@arap.org
URL: http://www.arap.org
Contact: David Stirpe, Exec. Dir.
Founded: 1980. **Members:** 250. **Description:** Users and producers of Chlorofluorocarbon (CFC) chemicals and their alternatives; businesses and companies that use or produce chlorofluorocarbons and their alternatives. Ensures scientifically sound and economically and socially effective government policies pertaining to ozone protection. (Chlorofluorocarbons are a family of compounds containing carbon, chlorine, fluorine, and sometimes hydrogen that are used primarily as refrigerants, specialty solvents, and agents for foamed plastics). **Computer Services:** Mailing lists, for periodic announcement and updates. **Committees:** Communications and Science; Government Relations; International; Legal; Science Advisor. **Formerly:** (1993) Alliance for Responsible CFC Policy. **Conventions/Meetings:** conference (exhibits).

798 ■ American Chemistry Council (ACC)
1300 Wilson Blvd.
Arlington, VA 22209
Ph: (703)741-5000
Fax: (703)741-6050
URL: http://www.americanchemistry.com
Contact: Jack N. Gerard, Pres./CEO
Founded: 1872. **Members:** 195. **Staff:** 300. **Budget:** $110,000,000. **Description:** Represents the leading companies engaged in the business of chemistry. Members apply the science of chemistry to make innovative products and services that make people's lives "better, healthier and safer." Improves environmental, health and safety performance through "Responsible Care"(R), common sense advocacy designed to address major public policy issues, and health and environmental research and product testing. **Computer Services:** Mailing lists, of members. **Councils:** American Plastics; Chlorine Chemistry; Expandable Polystyrene Resin Suppliers; Polyolefins Fire Performance. **Subgroups:** Air; Alliance for the Polyurethanes Industry; Automotive Work; Building and Construction Work; CHEMSTAR; CHEMSTREC; Distribution; Energy; Good Chemistry; Health; Market Access; Plant Operations; Polycarbonate; Product Stewardship; Public Health; Responsible Care TM; Rigid Plastic Packaging Institute; Science Policy; Spray Polyurethane Foam Alliance; Strategic Science (LRI); Tax; Underground Injection Control; Waste; Water. **Formerly:** (2000) Chemical Manufacturers Association; (2003) American Chemical Council. **Publications:** *Chemistry Business, The Journal of the American Chemistry Council*, 10/year. Magazine. **Price:** free for members ● *Membership Directory and Resource Guide*, annual. **Price:** available to members only. **Conventions/Meetings:** annual Leadership Conference - meeting - every fall.

799 ■ American Fire Safety Council (AFSC)
1909 K St. NW, Ste.400
Washington, DC 20006
Ph: (202)419-3269
Fax: (202)955-6215
E-mail: info@fire-safety.net
URL: http://www.fire-safety.net
Contact: Mike Heimowitz, Program Mgr.
Founded: 1973. **Members:** 35. **Staff:** 2. **Description:** Companies that manufacture and/or distribute chemicals and are active in fire safety through chemical technology, and companies or organizations interested in fire retardants. Encourages greater fire safety through chemical technology. Serves as a forum for dissemination of information on new developments, new applications, and current testing procedures. Conducts formal panel presentations and technical symposia. Bestows annual Russell C. Kidder Memorial Scholarship for college level work in fire retardancy. **Committees:** Codes and Standards Committee for Construction and Electrical and Electronic Products; Liaison; Technical; Upholstered Furniture. **Formerly:** (2003) Fire Retardant Chemicals Association. **Publications:** Proceedings, semiannual. Contains proceedings from semi-annual conferences. **Conventions/Meetings:** semiannual conference.

800 ■ Basic Acrylic Monomer Manufacturers (BAMM)
17260 Vannes Ct.
Hamilton, VA 20158
Ph: (540)751-2093
Fax: (540)751-2094
E-mail: ehunt@adelphia.net
URL: http://www.bamm.net
Contact: Elizabeth K. Hunt, Exec. Dir.
Founded: 1986. **Members:** 5. **Staff:** 2. **Budget:** $500,000. **Description:** U.S. manufacturers of basic acrylic monomers (chemicals used in the production of paints, varnishes, and plastics). Sponsors and publishes studies relating to safe procedures for producing basic acrylic monomers; disseminates health, safety, and environmental information to members. **Formerly:** (1999) Basic Acrylic Monomer Manufacturers Association.

801 ■ Center for Chemical Process Safety (CCPS)
3 Park Ave., 19th Fl.
New York, NY 10016-5991
Ph: (212)591-7237
Fax: (212)591-8883
E-mail: ccps@aiche.org
URL: http://www.aiche.org/ccps
Contact: Scott Berger, Dir.
Founded: 1985. **Members:** 87. **Budget:** $2,000,000. **Description:** Chemical and hydrocarbon manufacturers; engineering firms. Purpose is to study process safety issues in the chemical and hydrocarbon industries and publish and disseminate the results. Is concerned with safety in the manufacture, handling, and storage of toxic and reactive materials and those scientific and engineering practices that can prevent episodic events involving the release of potentially hazardous materials. Conducts research on hazard evaluation procedures, bulk storage and handling of toxic or reactive materials, plant operating procedures, safety training, and dispersion modeling. Seeks to enhance the personal, professional, and technical development of engineers in process plant safety. **Computer Services:** Online services, Process Safety Incident Database. **Boards:** Advisory; Managing. **Committees:** Planning; Technical Steering. **Affiliated With:** American Institute of Chemical Engineers. **Formerly:** Center for Chemical Plant Safety. **Publications:** *Guidelines for Chemical Process Safety Series*. Book. Covers all aspects of process safety. ● Annual Report, annual ● Catalog ● Proceedings. **Conventions/Meetings:** annual meeting - 2008 Nov. 16-21, Philadelphia, PA ● annual Risk, Reliability, and Security - conference, for equipment vendors, consultants (exhibits) ● seminar ● symposium.

802 ■ Chemical Coaters Association International (CCAI)
PO Box 54316
Cincinnati, OH 45254
Ph: (513)624-6767
Free: (800)926-2848
Fax: (513)624-0601
E-mail: aygoyer@one.net
URL: http://www.ccaiweb.com
Contact: Anne Goyer, Exec. Dir.
Founded: 1970. **Members:** 1,000. **Membership Dues:** individual, $85 (annual) ● custom coater, $150-$300 (annual) ● standard corporate, $1,195 (annual) ● gold corporate, $1,695 (annual) ● platinum corporate, $1,995 (annual). **Staff:** 3. **Budget:** $110,000. **Local Groups:** 11. **Description:** Industrial users of organic finishing systems; suppliers of chemicals, equipment, and paints. Works toward the improvement of decorative, functional, and performance standards of chemical coatings. Encourages members to continue improvements in application technology. Provides coating industry with representation to public authorities and government agencies. Sponsors research and educational programs to control environmental pollution. Maintains placement service. Provides speaker's bureau. **Libraries: Type:** reference. **Subjects:** coating industry. **Awards: Type:** recognition. **Formerly:** (1991) Chemical Coater Association. **Publications:** *Chemical Coaters Association—Newsletter*, quarterly. Includes publications list and calendar of events. **Price:** free for members. **Circulation:** 1,200 ● *Finishing Touch*, quarterly. Newsletter. Contains news of chapter events, finishing industry news and member highlights. **Price:** free for members. **Circulation:** 1,000. **Advertising:** accepted ● Membership Directory, annual. **Price:** available to members only. **Conventions/Meetings:** annual meeting.

803 ■ Chemical Producers and Distributors Association (CPDA)
1430 Duke St.
Alexandria, VA 22314
Ph: (703)548-7700
Fax: (703)548-3149
E-mail: warren@cpda.com
URL: http://www.cpda.com
Contact: Dr. Warren Stickle, Pres.
Members: 86. **Description:** Represents the interests of small to medium-sized pesticide companies in federal legislative and regulatory affairs. Aims to "reduce the costly regulations, which provide no significant increase in the protection of the environment or human health and safety.". **Publications:** Annual Report, annual.

804 ■ Chlorinated Paraffins Industry Association (CPIA)
1250 Connecticut Ave. NW, Ste.700
Washington, DC 20036
Ph: (202)419-1500
Fax: (202)659-8037
E-mail: info@regnet.com
URL: http://www.regnet.com/cpia
Contact: Robert J. Fensterheim, Exec. Dir.
Founded: 1984. **Members:** 2. **Description:** Manufacturers, distributors, and users of chlorinated paraffins. (Chlorinated paraffins are used in the manufacture of products such as lubricants, plastics, and flame retardants.) Serves as a clearinghouse for health, safety, and environmental data relating to production, distribution, use, and disposal of chlorinated paraffins. Represents the industry in regulatory and legislative matters. **Publications:** *Status Report: Chlorinated Paraffins*, periodic ● Also publishes handbook on the management of used metalworking oils containing chlorinated paraffins.

805 ■ Chlorine Institute (CI)
1300 Wilson Blvd.
Arlington, VA 22209
Ph: (703)741-5760

Fax: (703)741-6068
E-mail: aonna@cl2.com
URL: http://www.chlorineinstitute.org
Contact: Autumn Onna, Proj. Coor.
Founded: 1924. **Members:** 220. **Membership Dues:** North American producer, packager/bleach producer, associate, $3,900 (annual) ● overseas producer, $7,640 (annual). **Staff:** 12. **Budget:** $2,500,000. **Description:** Manufacturers of chlorine and caustic soda; other members are packagers of chlorine and manufacturers of equipment for chlorine production and handling. Promotes safe production and handling of chlorine, caustic soda, caustic potash sodium hypochlorite and hydrogen chloride. Caustic soda and caustic potash are co-products of chlorine. Compiles statistics on chlorine capacity and production. **Libraries: Type:** not open to the public. **Awards:** Safety Awards. **Frequency:** annual. **Type:** recognition. **Recipient:** for producers and packagers. **Committees:** Anhydrous Hydrogen Chloride; CHLORine Emergency Plan; Communications; Environment and Health; Hydrochloric Acid; Mercury Issues Management Steering; Packaging; Plant Operations and Safety; Properties, Analysis and Specifications; Sodium Hypochlorite; Storage and Transport; Transportation. **Publications:** *CI Insider*. Newsletter ● Manuals ● Pamphlets ● Also publishes publication lists, drawings, and related material; produces audiovisual aids. **Conventions/Meetings:** semiannual meeting and conference (exhibits) ● annual meeting.

806 ■ Consumer Specialty Products Association (CSPA)
900 17th St. NW, Ste.300
Washington, DC 20006
Ph: (202)872-8110 (202)833-7302
Fax: (202)872-8114
E-mail: ccathcart@cspa.org
URL: http://www.cspa.org
Contact: Christopher Cathcart, Pres./COO
Founded: 1914. **Members:** 250. **Staff:** 38. **Description:** Represents manufacturers, marketers, formulators, and suppliers of household, industrial, and personal care chemical specialty products such as pesticides, cleaning products, disinfectants, sanitizers, and polishes. Maintains liaison with federal and state agencies and public representatives; provides information and sponsors seminars on governmental activities and scientific developments. Develops consumer education information. **Awards:** Charles Aldrdice Award. **Type:** recognition ● Murray Glauberman. **Type:** scholarship. **Computer Services:** Electronic publishing, Air Insider ● electronic publishing, Scientific Insider. **Committees:** Government Affairs Advisory; Scientific Affairs. **Councils:** Small Business. **Divisions:** Aerosol Products; Air Care; Antimicrobials; Cleaning Products; Industrial and Automotive; Pest Management Products; Polishes and Floor Maintenance. **Formerly:** (1948) National Association Insecticide and Disinfectant Manufacturers; (2003) Chemical Specialties Manufacturers Association. **Publications:** *Executive Newswatch*, monthly. Newsletter. Alternate Formats: online ● *Formulators' Forum*, semiannual. Newsletter. Features pertinent topics of member interest. ● *Results for Industry: Annual Report*, annual ● Also publishes test methods and standards and compilations of laws and regulations. **Conventions/Meetings:** annual board meeting ● competition ● semiannual conference and trade show.

807 ■ CropLife America (CLA)
1156 15th St. NW
Washington, DC 20005
Ph: (202)296-1585
Fax: (202)463-0474
E-mail: webmaster@croplifeamerica.org
URL: http://www.croplifeamerica.org
Contact: Jay J. Vroom, Pres./CEO
Founded: 1933. **Members:** 78. **Staff:** 40. **Budget:** $10,000,000. **Description:** Fosters the interests of the general public and member companies by promoting innovative and environmentally sound manufacture, distribution and use of crop protection and production technologies for safe, high quality, affordable, abundant food, fiber and other crops. **Committees:** Biotechnology; Communications; International Affairs; Law; Registration; State Affairs; Washington Representatives. **Councils:** Legislative Affairs Oversight; Public Affairs Oversight; Scientific and Regulatory Oversight. **Departments:** Communications; Legal; Legislative; Public Affairs; Regulatory; Science. **Formerly:** (1933) Agricultural Insecticides and Fungicide Manufacturers Association; (1949) Agricultural Insecticide and Fungicide Association; (1994) National Agricultural Chemicals Association; (2002) American Crop Protection Association. **Publications:** *This Week and Next*, weekly ● Bulletin, periodic ● Manuals ● Annual Report, annual. Alternate Formats: online. **Conventions/Meetings:** annual meeting - always in September.

808 ■ Ethylene Oxide Sterilization Association (EOSA)
PO Box 33361
Washington, DC 20033
Ph: (630)928-1758
Free: (800)235-5030
Fax: (202)557-3836
E-mail: info@eosa.org
URL: http://www.eosa.org
Contact: Kathleen Hoffman, Pres.
Founded: 1995. **Members:** 46. **Staff:** 4. **Budget:** $250,000. **Description:** Represents contract sterilizers; suppliers, manufacturers, and remanufacturers of abatement equipment and systems, laboratory services, analytical/monitoring equipment and systems, electronics/process controls, sterilant, packaging, employee safety equipment, medical devices, medical disposables and sterilizers. Works to educate industry, regulators, and the public on the uses and benefits of Ethylene Oxide. **Committees:** Regulatory; Safety; Scientific. **Conventions/Meetings:** semiannual general assembly, general membership.

809 ■ Halogenated Solvents Industry Alliance (HSIA)
1300 Wilson Blvd.
Arlington, VA 22209
Ph: (703)741-5780
Free: (888)594-4742
Fax: (703)741-6077
E-mail: info@hsia.org
URL: http://www.hsia.org
Contact: Stephen P. Risotto, Exec. Dir.
Founded: 1980. **Members:** 200. **Membership Dues:** solvent user, product formulator, trade association, $100 ● solvent distributor/recycler, industry consultant, $200 ● equipment manufacturer, $500. **Description:** Represents producers, users and distributors of halogenated solvents, and equipment manufacturers. Develops constructive programs on problems involving halogenated solvents. Seeks fair legislation and regulations for the industry. Provides industry comments and information to government agencies; represents the industry at regulatory and legislative hearings. Serves as sponsoring body for working groups concentrating on issues of concern to specific segments of the solvent industry. **Computer Services:** Information services, chlorinated solvents resources. **Telecommunication Services:** electronic mail, contact@hsia.org. **Committees:** Health and Science; International (Europe and Japan); Regulatory Affairs; Stewardship and Outreach. **Publications:** *Halogenated Solvents Industry Alliance—Newsletter*, bimonthly. Includes list of documents available from HSIA. **Price:** available to members only ● *Solvents Update*, monthly. Newsletter. Covers government regulations in progress and HSIA activities. **Price:** available to members only. Alternate Formats: online.

810 ■ Industrial Chemical Research Association (ICRA)
Address Unknown since 2007
Founded: 1985. **Members:** 4,037. **Staff:** 3. **Budget:** $6,500,000. **Description:** Manufacturers, marketers, researchers, formulators, salesmen, and suppliers of industrial chemical products. Goal is to promote research, safe practices, improved selling efficiency, and fellowship among members. Maintains speakers' bureau; provides educational and research programs. **Libraries: Type:** reference. **Awards: Type:** recognition. **Divisions:** Aerosol; Automotive Chemicals; Detergent and Cleaning Compounds; Disinfectants and Sanitizers; Insecticides and Pesticides; Political Action; Waxes, Polishes, and Floor Finishes. **Publications:** *Industrial Chemical Research Association—Newsletter*, periodic. **Price:** free, for members only. **Circulation:** 30,000. **Conventions/Meetings:** competition ● annual conference.

811 ■ Institute for Polyacrylate Absorbents (IPA)
c/o Synthetic Organic Chemical Manufacturers Association
1850 M St. NW, Ste.700
Washington, DC 20036-5810
Ph: (202)721-4100 (301)651-5051
Fax: (202)296-8120
E-mail: info@socma.com
URL: http://www.socma.org
Contact: John F. Murray CAE, Exec. Dir.
Founded: 1985. **Members:** 13. **Staff:** 2. **Budget:** $500,000. **Multinational. Description:** Addresses the "scientific, regulatory, and related issues which may impact upon health, safety, and environmental aspects of the manufacture, use and disposal of fluid-absorbing polyacrylates". **Additional Websites:** http://www.socma.com, http://www.superabsorbents.com. **Divisions:** Personal Absorbent Products Council. **Affiliated With:** Synthetic Organic Chemical Manufacturers Association.

812 ■ Materials Technology Institute (MTI)
1215 Fern Ridge Pkwy., Ste.206
St. Louis, MO 63141-4408
Ph: (314)576-7712
Fax: (314)576-6078
E-mail: mtiadmin@mti-global.org
URL: http://www.mti-global.org
Contact: Dr. Debby Ehret, Operations Dir.
Founded: 1977. **Members:** 52. **Staff:** 8. **Multinational. Description:** Chemical processors and their suppliers. Conducts studies on the deterioration of materials and equipment used in the industry and institutes projects aimed at solving these problems. **Additional Websites:** http://www.mtiproducts.org. **Formerly:** (2004) Materials Technology Institute of the Chemical Process Industries. **Publications:** *MTI Communications*, 3/year. Newsletter. Includes information on projects and publications; lists new members. ● Annual Report, annual ● Manuals ● Reports. **Conventions/Meetings:** meeting - 3/year in February, June and October.

813 ■ Methacrylate Producers Association (MPA)
17260 Vannes Ct.
Hamilton, VA 20158
Ph: (540)751-2093
Fax: (540)751-2094
URL: http://www.mpausa.org
Contact: Elizabeth K. Hunt, Exec. Dir.
Founded: 1987. **Members:** 4. **Staff:** 1. **Budget:** $400,000. **Description:** Manufacturers and importers of methacrylate monomers. Gathers and disseminates health, safety, and environmental information. Evaluates and publishes assessments of industry health, safety, and environmental risks. **Publications:** *Methacrylic Acid Safe Handling Manual*.

814 ■ Methyl Chloride Industry Association (MCIA)
555 11th St. NW, Ste.1000
Washington, DC 20004-1327
Ph: (202)637-2200
Fax: (202)637-2201
E-mail: william.rawson@lw.com
URL: http://www.lw.com
Contact: William K. Rawson, Contact
Founded: 1981. **Description:** Aims to serve the industry needs with respect to government regulation of methyl chloride (chloromethane). Works to participate effectively and responsibly in rule-making proceedings before the Environmental Protection Agency relating to a proposed test rule for methyl

chloride under the Toxic Substances Control Act. Prepares comments on regulations; represents the industry at hearings. **Convention/Meeting:** none. **Publications:** none.

815 ■ National Association of Chemical Distributors (NACD)
1560 Wilson Blvd., Ste.1250
Arlington, VA 22209
Ph: (703)527-6223
Fax: (703)527-7747
E-mail: nacdpublicaffairs@nacd.com
URL: http://www.nacd.com
Contact: Peter Y. Hess, Chm.

Founded: 1971. **Members:** 265. **Membership Dues:** regular (based on total company sales, including all subsidiaries and branches), $1,675-$29,650 (annual) ● professional (for each member company employee), $400 (annual) ● regular affiliate, non-chemical handler affiliate, $950 (annual) ● chemical handler affiliate, $1,500 (annual) ● chemical supplier affiliate, $1,950 (annual). **Staff:** 7. **Budget:** $1,400,000. **Regional Groups:** 5. **Description:** Represents chemical distributor companies that purchase and take title of chemical products from manufacturers. Promotes professionalism in the chemical distribution industry. **Awards:** Awards of Commendation. **Type:** recognition. **Recipient:** for service to the industry. **Committees:** Annual Meeting; Canadian Liaison; Chemical Distribution Advancement; Communications and Publications; Distributors' Code; Education and Training; Government Affairs and Political Education; Insurance; International Affairs; Member Performance Profile; Sales and Professional Development; Supplier Relations. **Publications:** *Action Alerts*, periodic. Bulletin ● *Chemical Distributor*, 10/year. Magazine. **Price:** $49.00/year ● *Government Affairs Update*, periodic ● Membership Directory, annual. **Price:** available to members only. **Conventions/Meetings:** annual conference - always spring in Washington, DC ● annual seminar and trade show - always in fall.

816 ■ National Lime Association (NLA)
200 N Glebe Rd., Ste.800
Arlington, VA 22203
Ph: (703)243-5463
Fax: (703)243-5489
E-mail: natlime@lime.org
URL: http://www.lime.org
Contact: Arline M. Seeger, Exec. Dir./Gen. Counsel

Founded: 1902. **Members:** 20. **Staff:** 5. **Budget:** $811,000. **Description:** Manufacturers of lime products (quicklime and hydrated lime) used in steel manufacture, soil stabilization, building construction, air pollution control, and water treatment. Conducts research; operates educational programs. **Libraries: Type:** open to the public. **Holdings:** articles, books, periodicals. **Subjects:** lime products. **Computer Services:** database. **Publications:** *Hoover's Water Supply and Treatment*. Manual. **Price:** $39.95/copy ● *Lime Facts*. Handbook. **Price:** $10.00/copy ● *Lime Handling, Application and Storage*. Manual. **Price:** $19.95/copy ● *Lime Lites*, quarterly. Newsletter. Contains articles and technical information. Alternate Formats: online ● *Lime Stabilization Construction Manual*. **Conventions/Meetings:** annual convention, for members only - usually in May ● annual convention.

817 ■ Phosphate Chemicals Export Association (PhosCHEM)
c/o Chris Reynolds
PO Box 3320
Northbrook, IL 60062
Ph: (847)849-4305
Fax: (847)849-4693
E-mail: info@phoschem.com
URL: http://www.phoschem.com
Contact: Chris Reynolds, Contact

Founded: 1975. **Members:** 4. **Description:** Represents producing and exporting companies of phosphate chemicals. Assists in the exporting and selling of phosphate chemicals. **Telecommunication Services:** electronic mail, cpreynolds@potashcorp.com.

818 ■ Pine Chemicals Association (PCA)
3350 Riverwood Pkwy. SE, Ste.1900
Atlanta, GA 30339
Ph: (770)984-5340
Fax: (770)984-5341
E-mail: wjones@pinechemicals.org
URL: http://www.pinechemicals.org
Contact: Walter L. Jones, Pres./COO

Founded: 1947. **Members:** 40. **Staff:** 2. **Budget:** $500,000. **Description:** Represents manufacturers of chemical products (other than pulp, paper, and paper products) produced by, or from, wood pulp industry products. Sponsors educational and management meetings. Collects statistical data. **Awards:** Recovery Awards. **Frequency:** annual. **Type:** recognition. **Recipient:** for members. **Committees:** Environmental, Health, Safety; Information; Membership. **Formerly:** (1958) Tall Oil Association; (1999) Pulp Chemicals Association. **Publications:** *Naval Stores: Production, Chemistry and Utilization*. Book. **Price:** $160.00 for members; $180.00 for nonmembers ● *Standard Test Methods for Tall Oil Products*. **Price:** $15.00 for members; $25.00 for nonmembers ● *Sulfate Turpentine Recovery*. **Price:** $5.00 for members; $15.00 for nonmembers ● *Tall Oil*. **Price:** $35.00 for members; $50.00 for nonmembers. Alternate Formats: CD-ROM ● *Tall Oil and Its Uses-II*. **Price:** $30.00 for members; $40.00 for nonmembers. **Conventions/Meetings:** annual international conference.

819 ■ Sales Association of the Chemical Industry (SACI)
Address Unknown since 2008

Founded: 1921. **Members:** 350. **Budget:** $50,000. **Description:** Sales agents, distributors, and individuals engaged in sales or sales promotion for American chemical manufacturers, exporting companies for American manufacturers, personnel of publications and advertising agencies in chemical and allied industries, and purchasing agents of American chemical manufacturers. Works to increase selling efficiency, foster high sales ethics, and promote fellowship among members. Sponsors golf outings; conducts sales clinics and research programs; provides speakers on selling; helps unemployed members find jobs. **Formerly:** (1973) Salesmen's Association of the American Chemical Industry. **Publications:** *SACI Slants*, quarterly. Newsletter. Covers association activities. Includes calendar of events and career opportunities. **Price:** free to members, press, and prospective members. **Circulation:** 400. **Advertising:** accepted. Alternate Formats: CD-ROM ● *Sales Association of the Chemical Industry Roster and By-Laws*, periodic. Membership Directory.

820 ■ SB Latex Council (SBLC)
1250 Connecticut Ave. NW, Ste.700
Washington, DC 20036
Ph: (202)419-1500
Fax: (202)659-8037
E-mail: info@regnet.com
URL: http://www.regnet.com/sblc
Contact: Robert J. Fensterheim, Exec. Dir.

Founded: 1988. **Members:** 4. **Staff:** 2. **Description:** Manufacturers of styrene butadiene latex. Promotes the safe use of styrene butadiene latex. Liaises with government agencies; sponsors health and safety studies. **Formerly:** Styrene Butadiene Latex Manufacturers Council (SBLMC).

821 ■ Silicones Environmental, Health and Safety Council (SEHSC)
2325 Dulles Corner Blvd., Ste.500
Herndon, VA 20171
Ph: (703)788-6570
Fax: (703)788-6545
E-mail: sehsc@sehsc.com
URL: http://www.sehsc.com
Contact: Reo Menning, Exec. Dir.

Founded: 1976. **Members:** 6. **Staff:** 3. **Budget:** $4,000,000. **Description:** Organosilicones manufacturers. Coordinates programs dealing with health, environmental, and safety issues of interest to the industry. Disseminates scientifically sound information regarding silicones. **Formerly:** (1993) Silicones Health Council.

822 ■ Soap and Detergent Association (SDA)
1500 K St. NW, Ste.300
Washington, DC 20005
Ph: (202)347-2900
Fax: (202)347-4110
E-mail: info@cleaning101.com
URL: http://www.cleaning101.com
Contact: Brian Sansoni, VP

Founded: 1926. **Members:** 100. **Staff:** 19. **Description:** Represents manufacturers of household, industrial and institutional cleaning products, their ingredients and finished packaging, and oleochemical producers. Advances the public understanding of the safety and benefits of cleaning products and protecting the ability of its members to formulate products that best meet consumer needs. Serves its members and the public by developing and sharing information about industry products with the technical community, policy makers, childcare and health professionals, educators, media and consumers. **Libraries: Type:** reference. **Holdings:** 1,500. **Subjects:** cleaning products. **Committees:** Consumer Education; International; Public Relations; Research, Technology and Regulation. **Formed by Merger of:** Glycerine Producers Association; Fatty Acid Producers' Council. **Formerly:** (1984) Glycerine and Fatty Acid Producers Association; (1996) Glycerine and Oleochemicals Association. **Publications:** *Cleanliness Facts*, bimonthly. Annual Reports. **Circulation:** 100. **Conventions/Meetings:** annual convention and meeting - always in January.

823 ■ Styrene Information and Research Center (SIRC)
1300 Wilson Blvd., Ste.1200
Arlington, VA 22209
Ph: (703)741-5010
Fax: (703)741-6010
E-mail: sirc@styrene.org
URL: http://www.styrene.org
Contact: Jack Snyder, Exec. Dir.

Founded: 1987. **Members:** 80. **Staff:** 4. **Budget:** $2,000,000. **Description:** Styrene manufacturers and users. (Styrene is a colorless liquid used with other materials to form synthetic rubbers.) Provides public information on health-related issues involving styrene; responds to phone queries. Works to ensure the health and safety of those who are exposed to styrene. Conducts research and disseminates medical, scientific, and technical information to managers, employees, plant communities, federal, state, and local officials, the public, and the media. **Telecommunication Services:** electronic mail, jack_snyder@styrene.org. **Committees:** Steering and Operating. **Task Forces:** Membership and Funding; Public Affairs; Science and Technology. **Publications:** *SIRC Bulletin*, periodic. Includes information on regulatory decisions requiring action or compliance. ● *SIRC Executive Update*, as needed ● *SIRC Review*, periodic. Covers research and technical studies. ● Brochures. **Conventions/Meetings:** annual meeting.

824 ■ The Sulphur Institute (TSI)
1140 Connecticut Ave. NW, Ste.612
Washington, DC 20036
Ph: (202)331-9660
Fax: (202)293-2940
E-mail: sulphur@sulphurinstitute.org
URL: http://www.sulphurinstitute.org
Contact: Robert J. Morris, Pres.

Founded: 1960. **Members:** 32. **Staff:** 7. **Budget:** $1,500,000. **Languages:** Chinese, English, French. **Multinational. Description:** International organization supported by the sulphur industry to promote and expand the use of sulphur in all forms worldwide. **Libraries: Type:** reference. **Telecommunication Services:** electronic mail, tsiadmin@sulphurinstitute.org. **Publications:** *Sulphur Outlook: The State of the Sulphur Industry Today with Forecasts to 2015*, biennial, odd-numbered years. Report. Features sulphur market research report. **Price:** $3,500.00/copy. **Conventions/Meetings:** annual World Sulphur - symposium.

825 ■ Swimming Pool Water Treatment Professionals (SPWTP)
21939 Camille Dr.
Nuevo, CA 92567
Ph: (949)364-1990 (909)928-1050
Fax: (949)858-9607
E-mail: assocofc@aol.com
URL: http://www.spwtp.org
Contact: Chip Bury, Pres.
Founded: 1992. **Description:** Promotes swimming pool companies specializing in the application of pure gas chlorine to residential swimming pools; strives to increase public awareness while reducing misconceptions concerning residential gas chlorinators; conducts educational programs promoting professionalism and safety with respect to the use of gas chlorine; performs research on gas chlorine and pH dynamics. **Formerly:** (2001) National Association of Gas Chlorinators. **Publications:** *Chlorine Applicator's Study Guide*. Aims to create the foundation for a self-regulating industry. ● *Minimum Recommended Safety Guidelines*. Aims to create the foundation for a self-regulating industry. **Conventions/Meetings:** annual conference ● annual seminar, held during the Western Pool and Spa Show ● periodic seminar, offers basic safety training, medical management of chlorine exposure, a safe handling review, regulatory issues updates, and more.

826 ■ Synthetic Amorphous Silica and Silicates Industry Association (SASSI)
Address Unknown since 2007
Founded: 1981. **Members:** 9. **Description:** Manufacturers and firms involved with synthetic amorphous silica and silicates, which are synthetically produced chemical compounds used as flow and anticaking agents because of their ability to absorb water. Other uses include: in silicone rubber, as a reinforcing aid; in paints, as flattening agents and thickeners; in dentifrices, as a polishing agent; in foods, as flavor carriers; in beer, as a stabilizer. Objective is to further industrial, governmental, and public understanding of synthetic amorphous silica and sililicate health and safety data. **Publications:** none.

827 ■ Synthetic Organic Chemical Manufacturers Association (SOCMA)
1850 M St. NW, Ste.700
Washington, DC 20036-5810
Ph: (202)721-4100 (202)721-4120
Fax: (202)296-8120
E-mail: info@socma.com
URL: http://www.socma.com
Contact: Joseph Acker, Pres.
Founded: 1921. **Members:** 300. **Staff:** 45. **Budget:** $25,000,000. **Description:** Represents manufacturers of synthetic organic chemicals, which are products manufactured from coal, natural gas, crude petroleum, and certain natural substances such as vegetable oils, fats, proteins, carbohydrates, rosin, grains, and their derivatives. **Committees:** Air; Commercial Services; Communications; Emergency Planning and Community Right-to-Know Act; Employee and Process Safety; Environmental; Government Affairs; Hazardous Waste; Informex; International Trade; Occupational Safety and Health; Public Policy; Responsible Care; Small Business; Toxic Substances Control; Water. **Subgroups:** Association Management Center; Marketing and Member Services; Meetings and Expositions; Public Affairs. **Affiliated With:** Acrylonitrile Group; Commercial Development and Marketing Association; ETAD North America - Ecological and Toxicological Association of Dyes and Organic Pigments Manufacturers; Tributyl Phosphate Task Force. **Publications:** *Chemical Bond Express*, weekly. Newsletter. Alternate Formats: online ● *Commercial Guide*, annual. Magazine. Contains over 150 company listings. **Price:** $60.00/copy. **Circulation:** 15,000. **Advertising:** accepted ● *SOCMA Newsletter*, bimonthly. Provides information on legislative and regulatory developments affecting the industry, chemical exposure risks, and business opportunities. **Price:** free for members ● *Synthetic Organic Chemical Manufacturers Association—Annual Report to Membership*. Covers previous years' activities and accomplishments, legislative and regulatory affairs, member programs, and information services. **Price:** free ● *Synthetic Organic Chemical Manufacturers Association—Membership Directory*, annual. Provides description of member companies and names and addresses of key personnel with each company. **Price:** free for members ● Also publishes Responsible Care Manuals and newsletters, regulatory compliance guides. **Conventions/Meetings:** Custom Chemical Services Trade Show (exhibits) ● annual dinner, attended by 550 chemical industry executives - always December, in New York City ● annual meeting (exhibits) - always in May.

828 ■ Tributyl Phosphate Task Force (TBPTF)
c/o SOCMA VISIONS
1850 M St. NW, Ste.700
Washington, DC 20036-5810
Ph: (202)721-4154
Fax: (202)296-8120
E-mail: helmest@socma.com
URL: http://www.socma.org
Contact: C. Tucker Helmes PhD, Sr. Dir.
Founded: 1987. **Members:** 3. **Staff:** 1. **Description:** Manufacturers, processors, and importers of tributyl phosphate. Coordinates testing programs; monitors regulatory developments concerning health and environmental issues related to tributyl phosphate. **Affiliated With:** Synthetic Organic Chemical Manufacturers Association.

Child Care

829 ■ National Association of Nannies (NAN)
PMB 2004
25 Rte. 31 S, Ste.C
Pennington, NJ 08534
Free: (800)344-6266
Fax: (636)475-7207
E-mail: info@nannyassociation.com
Contact: Kristen Kanoski, Pres.
Founded: 1992. **Membership Dues:** working nanny, $50 (annual) ● student nanny, $25 (annual) ● educator, employer, $75 (annual) ● business owner, $125 (annual). **Description:** Promotes public awareness of the nanny as a profession and a legitimate career choice. Increases public awareness of quality issues on in-home child care. Encourages professional pay and professional respect for nannies. **Publications:** *NAN Newsletter*, bimonthly. Contains updates on the nanny industry. Alternate Formats: online.

Chiropractic

830 ■ Academy of Forensic and Industrial Chiropractic Consultants (AFICC)
c/o Thomas Bakman, DC, Pres.
18800 Delaware St., No. 150
Huntington Beach, CA 92648
Ph: (714)841-5333
Fax: (714)841-5303
E-mail: tbakmen@socal.rr.com
URL: http://aficc.tripod.com
Contact: Thomas Bakman DC, Pres.
Founded: 1988. **Membership Dues:** fellow, $450 (annual) ● associate, $150 (annual) ● student faculty, $25 (annual). **Description:** Expands knowledge of forensic medical legal practice, involving applied expertise and evaluation in workers' compensation, personal injury, malpractice, rehabilitation, and industrial consulting. **Telecommunication Services:** electronic mail, dryamada@aol.com. **Publications:** Articles. Alternate Formats: online. **Conventions/Meetings:** seminar.

Churches

831 ■ National Association of Church Design Builders (NACDB)
1000 Ballpark Way
Arlington, TX 76011
Ph: (817)200-2622
Free: (866)416-2232
Fax: (817)275-4519
E-mail: sskelton@nacdb.com
URL: http://www.nacdb.com
Contact: Greg Barron, Pres.
Description: Strives for excellence in church design building with focus on the needs of local churches. Provides information to church authorities, which will be helpful in determining the facilities that are suitable for the style and function of the church that they serve. Conducts seminars on church architecture and construction trends. **Awards:** NACDB Full Membership Awards. **Frequency:** annual. **Type:** recognition. **Recipient:** for ethical behavior and high standard of quality in all products and services rendered by members. **Publications:** Newsletter. Contains news and articles about church design building. Alternate Formats: online.

Cleaning Industry

832 ■ Carpet Cleaners Institute of the Northwest (CCINW)
PMB 40
2421 S Union Ave., Ste.L-1
Tacoma, WA 98405
Ph: (253)759-5762 (253)472-9686
Free: (877)692-2469
Fax: (253)761-9134
E-mail: info@ccinw.org
URL: http://www.ccinw.org
Contact: Matt O'Haleck, Pres.
Membership Dues: professional, $350 (annual). **Staff:** 4. **Multinational. Description:** Represents and promotes the carpet cleaning industry. **Affiliated With:** Restoration Industry Association. **Conventions/Meetings:** annual convention and trade show ● meeting.

Clubs

833 ■ Club Managers Association of America (CMAA)
1733 King St.
Alexandria, VA 22314
Ph: (703)739-9500
Fax: (703)739-0124
E-mail: cmaa@cmaa.org
URL: http://www.cmaa.org
Contact: James B. Singerling CCM, CEO
Founded: 1927. **Members:** 6,000. **Membership Dues:** student, $50 (annual) ● retired, $60 (annual) ● faculty, $100 (annual). **Staff:** 37. **Budget:** $7,500,000. **State Groups:** 50. **Description:** Professional managers and assistant managers of private golf, yacht, athletic, city, country, luncheon, university, and military clubs. Encourages education and advancement of members and promotes efficient and successful club operations. Provides reprints of articles on club management. Supports courses in club management. Compiles statistics; maintains management referral service. **Awards: Type:** scholarship. **Committees:** Premier Club Services; Student Development. **Publications:** *Club Management Magazine*, bimonthly. Includes association and industry news, new product reviews, and calendar of events. **Price:** $21.95/year. **Advertising:** accepted ● *Club Managers Association of America—Yearbook*, annual. **Price:** available to members only ● *Contemporary Club Management*. Book. Contains information on club management. ● *Job Descriptions in the Club Industry*. Monograph ● *Outlook*, monthly. Newsletter. Includes columns on association affairs and allied association news. **Price:** free for members; $15.00 /year for nonmembers. Alternate Formats: online ● *Private Club Administration* ● *Uniforms System of Accounts for Clubs*. Monograph. **Conventions/Meetings:** annual World Conference on Club Management.

834 ■ International Military Community Executives Association (IMCEA)
1530 Dunwoody Village Pkwy., Ste.203
Atlanta, GA 30338
Ph: (770)396-2101

Fax: (770)396-2198
E-mail: imcea@imcea.com
URL: http://www.imcea.com
Contact: Sari Jill Schneider, Exec. Dir.
Founded: 1972. **Members:** 800. **Membership Dues:** position, $225 (annual) ● associate, $495 (annual) ● retired/inactive, affiliate, $50 (annual). **Staff:** 3. **Multinational. Description:** Army, Navy, Air Force, Marine, and Coast Guard personnel who manage military clubs, golf courses, bowling centers, and other recreation facilities. Fosters communication among morale, welfare, and recreation personnel. Facilitates cooperation on regional, national, and international levels. Encourages recruitment activities. Promotes retention of club executives by improving working climates and conditions. Conducts seminars on management training. **Awards:** Associate Council Achievement Award. **Frequency:** annual. **Type:** recognition ● Hall of Fame. **Frequency:** annual. **Type:** recognition ● Memorial Scholarship Award. **Frequency:** annual. **Type:** scholarship ● MWR Leadership Award. **Frequency:** annual. **Type:** recognition. **Recipient:** for senior officials ● Roy C. Olson Award. **Frequency:** annual. **Type:** recognition. **Recipient:** for outstanding contributions to military MWR. **Telecommunication Services:** electronic mail, sarischneider@imcea.com. **Committees:** Annual Conference; Awards; Certification; Chapter Relations; Education; Long-Range Planning; Public Relations; Publications. **Publications:** *MWR Today*, monthly. Magazine. **Price:** $30.00/year; $2.50 single copy. **Circulation:** 9,000 ● Membership Directory, annual. **Advertising:** accepted. **Conventions/Meetings:** annual conference (exhibits) - always in May ● workshop, one-day throughout the United States; sponsored in conjunction with local chapters - in fall.

835 ■ National Club Association (NCA)
1201 15th St., Ste.450
Washington, DC 20005
Ph: (202)822-9822
Free: (800)625-6221
Fax: (202)822-9808
E-mail: natlclub@natlclub.org
URL: http://www.natlclub.org
Contact: Susanne Wegrzyn, Pres./CEO
Founded: 1961. **Members:** 1,000. **Membership Dues:** regular (social, athletic, recreational club), $695-$2,995 (annual) ● associate outside U.S., $700 (annual) ● regular, outside U.S., $695 (annual) ● group (minimum), $2,600 (annual) ● group (maximum), $33,975 (annual) ● associate (domestic), $650 (annual). **Staff:** 10. **Budget:** $1,100,000. **Description:** Represents the business and legal interests of private clubs. Analyzes proposed laws and regulations affecting clubs; compiles statistics and economic data; drafts model legislation; and acts as a general center of information about club matters. **Telecommunication Services:** electronic mail, wegrzyn@nationalclub.org. **Councils:** Associate; Presidents; Regional. **Publications:** *Club Director*, bimonthly. Magazine. **Advertising:** accepted ● *Clubhouse Trends*, bimonthly. Newsletter. Highlights and analyzes current trends affecting the private club industry. **Circulation:** 10,000 ● *Private Club*, annual. Directory. Serves as a reference guide for club decision-makers. **Circulation:** 10,000 ● Monographs ● Reports.

Coaching

836 ■ International Coach Federation (ICF)
2365 Harrodsburg Rd., Ste.A325
Lexington, KY 40504
Ph: (859)219-3580
Free: (888)423-3131
Fax: (859)226-4411
E-mail: icfoffice@coachfederation.org
URL: http://www.coachfederation.org
Contact: Pamela Richarde, Pres.
Members: 10,500. **Membership Dues:** single, $195 (annual) ● group (based on the number of employees), $156-$175 (annual). **Multinational. Description:** Builds, supports and preserves the integrity of the coaching profession. Provides programs to maintain and upgrade the standards of the profession. Researches and develops programs in the legal, regulatory and credentialing areas that will serve coaches and their clients. **Telecommunication Services:** electronic mail, president@coachfederation.org ● electronic mail, customerservice@coachfederation.org ● electronic mail, membership@coachfederation.org ● additional toll-free number, (888)329-2423. **Publications:** *Coaching World*. Newsletter. Contains information and strategies to assist coaches. **Price:** included in membership dues. Alternate Formats: online. **Conventions/Meetings:** annual international conference.

Coal

837 ■ American Coal Foundation (ACF)
101 Constitution Ave. NW, Ste.525 E
Washington, DC 20001-2133
Ph: (202)463-9875
Free: (800)325-8677
Fax: (202)463-9876
E-mail: info@teachcoal.org
URL: http://www.teachcoal.org
Contact: Alma Hale Paty, Acting Exec. Dir.
Founded: 1981. **Staff:** 1. **Description:** Promotes public education focusing on the importance of coal as America's most abundant fuel source. Disseminates classroom materials, including booklets, videos, coal samples, and science activity kits. Sponsors and participates in educator conventions and teacher workshops. **Publications:** *Coal Poster* ● *Coal Sample Kit*. Includes four samples. ● *Electricity Poster* ● *Let's Learn More About Coal*. Booklet ● *Mining Reclamation Poster* ● *Power From Coal* ● *What Everyone Should Know About Coal*. Booklet ● *What Everyone Should Know About Electricity from Coal*. Booklet ● *What Everyone Should Know About Land Reclamation*. Booklet. **Conventions/Meetings:** annual meeting ● workshop, with hands-on classroom activities and lectures on different aspects of the coal industry.

838 ■ American Coke and Coal Chemicals Institute (ACCCI)
1140 Connecticut Ave. NW, Ste.705
Washington, DC 20036
Ph: (202)452-7198
Fax: (202)463-6573
E-mail: information@accci.org
URL: http://www.accci.org
Contact: Bruce Steiner, Pres.
Founded: 1944. **Members:** 210. **Membership Dues:** associate, academic, $75 (annual) ● builder, supplier, transportation, $1,129 (annual) ● metallurgical coal producer, $1,896 (annual). **Staff:** 4. **Budget:** $600,000. **Description:** Producers of oven coke and coal chemicals; producers of metallurgical coal; tar distillers; producers of chemicals and suppliers to the industry. **Awards:** Max Edward Safety Award. **Frequency:** annual. **Type:** recognition. **Committees:** Coal Chemicals; Coke; Government Relations; Industry Supplier; International; Manufacturing, Environment, Safety and Health. **Publications:** *Actionline*, annual. Newsletter. Alternate Formats: online ● *Foundry Facts*, semiannual. Bulletin. Provides technical information on the coke and coal chemicals industry. **Price:** free. **Circulation:** 850. **Conventions/Meetings:** annual meeting - always fall, in White Sulphur Springs, WV ● annual meeting - always in spring.

839 ■ Association of Bituminous Contractors (ABC)
815 Connecticut Ave. NW, Ste.620
Washington, DC 20006
Ph: (202)785-4440
Fax: (202)331-8049
Contact: William H. Howe, Sec.-Gen./Counsel
Founded: 1968. **Members:** 250. **Description:** Independent and general contractors who build coal mines and coal mine facilities. Aims to facilitate collective bargaining with the International Union United Mine Workers of America (see separate entry) and to institute health and safety programs relating to the coal mine construction industry. **Committees:** Health and Safety.

840 ■ Bituminous Coal Operators' Association (BCOA)
1500 K St. NW
Washington, DC 20005-1209
Ph: (202)783-3195
Fax: (202)783-4862
Contact: Charles Perkins, Sec.-Treas.
Founded: 1950. **Members:** 19. **Staff:** 4. **Budget:** $3,000,000. **Description:** Firms engaged in mining bituminous coal. Promotes improved industrial relations among member coal operators and their employees represented by the International Union United Mine Workers of America. Concerned with the negotiation of wages, hours, and conditions of employment. Promotes mine safety and the improvement of mining methods. **Affiliated With:** United Mine Workers of America. **Conventions/Meetings:** meeting - usually second Tuesday in May, Washington, DC.

841 ■ Coal Exporters Association of the United States (CEA)
c/o National Mining Association
101 Constitution Ave. NW, Ste.500 E
Washington, DC 20001-2133
Ph: (202)463-2600
Fax: (202)463-2666
E-mail: craulston@nma.org
URL: http://www.nma.org
Founded: 1945. **Members:** 20. **Staff:** 1. **Description:** Exporters of coal and coke. Promotes and encourages the reliable export of quality coals from the United States. **Affiliated With:** National Mining Association. **Formerly:** Coal Exporters of the United States. **Publications:** *International Coal Review*, monthly. Bulletin. Features information on monthly exports of U.S. coal. **Price:** $100.00/copy. **Conventions/Meetings:** biennial conference and symposium - every spring, in Europe.

842 ■ Coal Technology Association (CTA)
601 Suffield Dr.
Gaithersburg, MD 20878
Ph: (301)294-6080
Fax: (301)294-7480
E-mail: barbarasak@aol.com
URL: http://www.coaltechnologies.com
Contact: Barbara A. Sakkestad, VP
Founded: 1975. **Members:** 20. **Membership Dues:** class A, $15,000 (annual) ● class B, $7,500 (annual) ● class C, $5,000 (annual) ● class D, $2,000 (annual). **Staff:** 1. **Budget:** $250,000. **Description:** Consists of firms engaged in providing supportive materials and services for the transportation, production, or industrial use of coal. Fosters the development and growth of the coal industry through development of coal technologies. **Committees:** Communications; Technical. **Formerly:** (1984) Slurry Transport Association; (1987) Slurry Technology Association. **Publications:** *Inside Pipeline*, monthly. Newsletter. Includes conference reports. **Price:** free for members ● *Proceedings of International Technical Conferences on Coal Utilization and Fuel Systems*, annual. Provides complete text of all presentations, with illustrations, graphs, and equations. **Price:** $395.00 for nonmembers; free for conference attendees. ISSN: 0739-5825. **Conventions/Meetings:** annual International Technical Conference on Coal Utilization and Fuel Systems, provides reports on innovative evolving technologies, new fuels and equipment for newer generation (exhibits) - always spring.

843 ■ Coal Trading Association (CTA)
2001 Jefferson Davis Hwy., Ste.1004
Arlington, VA 22202-3617
Ph: (703)418-0392
Fax: (703)416-0014

E-mail: info@coaltrade.org
URL: http://www.coaltrade.org
Contact: Robert E. McLean CAE, Exec. Dir.
Founded: 1999. **Membership Dues:** corporate (voting), $2,000 (annual) ● nonprofit, government, academic institution (non-voting), $150 (annual) ● corporate (nonvoting), $750 (annual). **Description:** Promotes efficient and effective coal trading practices, policies, and procedures to service members and the public; encourages and facilitates information exchange among members, professionals and technical groups; and provides education and training.

844 ■ National Coal Transportation Association (NCTA)

4 W Meadow Lark Ln., Ste.100
Littleton, CO 80127-5718
Ph: (303)979-2798
Fax: (303)973-1848
E-mail: tom@nationalcoaltransportation.org
URL: http://www.nationalcoaltransportation.org
Contact: Thomas C. Canter, Exec. Dir.
Founded: 1974. **Members:** 80. **Membership Dues:** regular, individual, associate, $1,250 (annual). **Staff:** 3. **Description:** Represents electric utilities and coal producing companies. Promotes the export of coal from the United States; facilitates the transportation of coal throughout the U.S. Encourages the exchange of information and ideas about coal transport. Conducts seminars on maintenance and repair of coal transport railroad cars. Monitors state and federal legislation affecting the industry. Sponsors research projects. Maintains speakers' bureau; participates in charitable activities. **Libraries: Type:** reference. **Awards: Type:** fellowship ● **Type:** scholarship ● WCTA Transportation Award. **Frequency:** annual. **Type:** recognition. **Recipient:** to an outstanding student. **Computer Services:** Mailing lists. **Committees:** Education; Environmental; Operations and Maintenance; Regulatory. **Formerly:** (2004) Western Coal Transportation Association. **Publications:** *General Membership Meeting and Conference Transcript*, quarterly. Newsletter ● *Proceedings of Annual and Interim Conferences*, quarterly ● *Spring Meeting and Conference Transcript*, annual ● Brochures. **Conventions/Meetings:** annual conference - always spring. 2009 Apr. 12-15, Nashville, TN ● annual meeting and conference - 2008 Sept. 8-10, Denver, CO ● annual Operations and Maintenance - conference - always June. 2008 June 15-19, Bay Harbor, MI.

845 ■ National Council of Coal Lessors (NCCL)

902 Oakbridge Dr.
Hurricane, WV 25526
Contact: Nick Carter, Pres.
Founded: 1951. **Description:** Represents interests of Coal Lessors.

846 ■ National Mining Association

101 Constitution Ave. NW, Ste.500 E
Washington, DC 20001-2133
Ph: (202)463-2600
Fax: (202)463-2666
E-mail: craulston@nma.org
URL: http://www.nma.org
Contact: Kraig R. Naasz, Pres./CEO
Founded: 1917. **Members:** 400. **Staff:** 80. **Budget:** $7,000,000. **Description:** Producers and sellers of coal and hardrock minerals, equipment manufacturers, distributors, equipment suppliers, other energy suppliers, consultants, utility companies, and coal transporters. Serves as liaison between the industry and federal government agencies. Keeps members informed of legislative and regulatory actions. Works with industry, consumers, and government agencies on mining industry issues. Seeks improved conditions for export of steam and metallurgical coal. Collects, analyzes, and distributes industry statistics; makes special studies of competitive fuels, coal and metal markets, production and consumption forecasts, and industry planning. **Awards:** Excellence in Mining Education Sentinels of Safety Awards and Reclamation Awards. **Frequency:** annual. **Type:** recognition. **Divisions:** Government Affairs; Law; Policy and Statistical Analysis; Public and Constituent Relations; Trade, Environment, and Transportation. **Absorbed:** (1953) Bituminous Coal Institute; (1960) American Coal Sales Association; (1987) Mining and Reclamation Council. **Formerly:** National Coal Association. **Publications:** *Coal Data*, annual. Report. Contains data in chart and tabular form on coal production, consumption, stocks, and distribution over the past five years. **Price:** included in membership dues; $75.00/copy for nonmembers - domestic; $85.00/copy for nonmembers - foreign ● *Coal - Energy for the Next Decade and Beyond* ● *Coal Industry Employment/Production*, annual. Reports. Provides statistics on coal industry manhours, injury counts, and production, arranged by volume of mine production, state, and region. **Price:** included in membership dues; $35.00 /year for nonmembers in U.S.; $45.00 /year for nonmembers outside U.S. ● *Coal Transportation Statistics*, annual. Provides data on equipment, tonnage handled, and revenue received by coal-carrying railroads. **Price:** included in membership dues; $40.00 /year for nonmembers in U.S.; $45.00 /year for nonmembers outside U.S. ● *Electric Utility Coal Stockpiles*, annual. Provides annual days supply figures for coal-fired utility plants with an annual coal consumption of more than 100,000 tons. **Price:** included in membership dues; $50.00 /year for nonmembers ● *International Coal*, annual. Report. Contains compilations of world coal reserves and production, energy consumption, and crude steel production. **Price:** included in membership dues; $150.00/copy for nonmembers in U.S.; $165.00/copy for nonmembers outside U.S. ● *International Coal Review*, monthly. Newsletter. Reports statistics in tabular format on world coal reserves and production, energy consumption, and crude steel production. **Price:** included in membership dues; $100.00 /year for nonmembers in U.S.; $150.00 /year for nonmembers outside U.S. ● *Mining Voice: The National Magazine of Coal, Hardrock Minerals, Environmental and Energy Issues*, bimonthly. Covers surface and underground coal and hardrock mineral mining, the association, government regulations, environmental issues, and other news. **Price:** included in membership dues; $36.00 /year for nonmembers in U.S.; $72.00 /year for nonmembers outside U.S. **Circulation:** 6,000. **Advertising:** accepted ● *Mining Week*, weekly. Newsletter. Reports on legislation, research and development, mining activity, and industry trends. **Price:** included in membership dues; $100.00 /year for nonmembers in U.S.; $150.00 /year for nonmembers outside U.S. ● *Power Plant Deliveries*, monthly. Report. Provides coverage on the cost and quality of oil and gas deliveries to electric power plants. **Price:** included in membership dues; $500.00 /year for nonmembers in U.S.; $550.00 /year for nonmembers outside U.S. ● *Steam Electric Market Analysis*, monthly. Contains information on coal consumption, stockpiles, and power generation fuels, arranged by fuel type. **Price:** included in membership dues; $300.00 /year for nonmembers in U.S.; $350.00 /year for nonmembers outside U.S. ● *Weekly Statistical Summary*. Newsletter. Reports on coal production and consumption, electrical output, and steel production. Includes information on coal and petroleum prices. **Price:** included in membership dues; $100.00 /year for nonmembers in U.S.; $150.00 /year for nonmembers outside U.S. ● Also publishes forecasts, synthetic fuels studies, and educational materials. **Conventions/Meetings:** annual meeting, mining equipment, suppliers, machinery - always June.

847 ■ Pennsylvania Coal Association (PCA)

212 N 3rd St., Ste.102
Harrisburg, PA 17101-1588
Ph: (717)233-7909
Free: (800)COAL-NOW
Fax: (717)231-7610
E-mail: pacoal1@aol.com
Contact: George Ellis, Pres.
Founded: 1988. **Members:** 150. **Staff:** 4. **Description:** Mining and coal companies, equipment manufacturers, and engineers. Lobbies on behalf of the coal mining industry; informs members of state and federal rules and regulations. **Awards:** Reclamation Awards. **Type:** recognition. **Affiliated With:** National Mining Association. **Formed by Merger of:** Keystone Bituminous Coal Association; Pennsylvania Coal Mining Association. **Publications:** *Coal Data*, annual ● *Coal Quarterly* ● *Pennsylvania Coal Monthly* ● Directory, annual. **Conventions/Meetings:** meeting - always August.

848 ■ Rocky Mountain Coal Mining Institute (RMCMI)

8057 S Yukon Way
Littleton, CO 80128-5510
Ph: (303)948-3300
Fax: (303)948-1132
E-mail: mail@rmcmi.org
URL: http://www.rmcmi.org
Contact: Karen L. Inzano, Exec. Dir.
Founded: 1912. **Members:** 540. **Membership Dues:** individual, $100 (annual) ● senior, $40 (annual). **Staff:** 1. **Budget:** $500,000. **Description:** Coal industry persons, including producers, users, equipment manufacturers, suppliers, coal transporters, lawyers, bankers, and others. Promotes the use of western coal through education. **Libraries: Type:** reference. **Holdings:** audiovisuals. **Subjects:** coal mining. **Awards:** RMCMI Scholarship. **Frequency:** annual. **Type:** scholarship. **Recipient:** for college sophomore or junior students pursuing careers in mining and residents of AZ, CO, MT, NM, ND, TX, UT or WY. **Publications:** *RMCMI Reporter*, quarterly. Newsletters. **Circulation:** 850. **Advertising:** accepted. Alternate Formats: online. **Conventions/Meetings:** annual convention - last Sunday through Tuesday in June ● annual State Meetings.

Coatings

849 ■ Aluminum Anodizers Council (AAC)

1000 N Rand Rd., No. 214
Wauconda, IL 60084
Ph: (847)526-2010
Fax: (847)526-3993
E-mail: mail@anodizing.org
URL: http://www.anodizing.org
Contact: Ms. Pat Alterio, Admin. Asst.
Founded: 1987. **Members:** 83. **Membership Dues:** professional, $75 (annual) ● associate, $550 (annual) ● firm, $750-$2,000 (annual) ● supplier, $1,875-$2,100 (annual). **Staff:** 3. **Budget:** $250,000. **Description:** Companies involved in anodizing aluminum coil, extrusions and parts. (Anodization is a process that uses electrolysis, or electrically-induced chemical decomposition, to coat metal with a protective layer.) Sets color consistency standards. Promotes the anodizing industry. Conducts surveys. **Computer Services:** Online services, web forum. **Committees:** Environmental and Regulatory Compliance; Hardcoat Anodizing; Marketing; Program Planning; Technical and Standards. **Formerly:** (1992) Architectural Anodizers Council. **Publications:** *Anodizing Newsline*, bimonthly. Newsletter. Contains news on industry events, member activities, marketing tips and technical information. **Price:** free, for members only ● *Regulatory Roundup*, periodic. Newsletter. **Price:** free, for members only. Alternate Formats: online. **Conventions/Meetings:** annual Anodizing Conference (exhibits) - September/October ● periodic Anodizing Essentials - workshop - typically twice a year on a regional rotation.

850 ■ American Galvanizers Association (AGA)

6881 S Holy Cir., Ste.108
Centennial, CO 80112
Ph: (720)554-0900
Free: (800)468-7732
Fax: (720)554-0909
E-mail: aga@galvanizeit.org
URL: http://www.galvanizeit.org
Contact: Phil G. Rahrig, Marketing Dir.
Founded: 1935. **Members:** 150. **Membership Dues:** regular, domestic associate, $2,520 (annual) ● foreign, $1,575 (annual) ● sustaining, $13,125-$1,680 (annual). **Staff:** 10. **Budget:** $900,000. **Multinational. Description:** After-fabrication hot dip

galvanizers applying a zinc coating to iron and steel; material and equipment suppliers and service companies. Activities include educational seminars; technical service and development, industry forecasting and analysis; and marketing. **Libraries: Type:** not open to the public. **Holdings:** 500; articles. **Subjects:** corrosion protection. **Awards:** Galvanizing Excellence Awards. **Frequency:** annual. **Type:** recognition. **Telecommunication Services:** electronic mail, prahrig@galvanizeit.org. **Committees:** Market Development; Sustaining Members; Technical Services. **Formerly:** (1989) American Hot Dip Galvanizers Association. **Publications:** *American Galvanizers Association—Directory*, annual. Membership Directory. Includes suppliers. **Price:** free for members and restricted others. **Circulation:** 1,000. **Advertising:** accepted ● Also publishes technical literature. **Conventions/Meetings:** annual conference - always spring.

851 ■ Association of Industrial Metallizers, Coaters and Laminators (AIMCAL)

201 Springs St.
Fort Mill, SC 29715
Ph: (803)802-7820
Fax: (803)802-7821
E-mail: aimcal@aimcal.org
URL: http://www.aimcal.org
Contact: Craig S. Sheppard, Exec. Dir.

Founded: 1970. **Members:** 230. **Membership Dues:** converter, supplier, associate, $1,870 (annual) ● trade press, $935 (annual) ● premium, $2,495 (annual). **Staff:** 4. **Budget:** $1,000,000. **Description:** Metallizers, coaters, and laminators; producers of metallized film and/or paper on continuous rolls; manufacturers of metallizing, coating, and laminating equipment; suppliers of plastic films, papers, and adhesives. The end uses of the product are films and papers, solar control films, reflective insulation, decorative films and papers, and packaging. Monitors related legislative activities; reports on current industry developments. Conducts technical seminars. **Computer Services:** Mailing lists. **Formerly:** (1973) Vacuum Metallizers Association. **Publications:** *AIMCAL News*, quarterly. Newsletter. **Price:** free to industry. **Circulation:** 1,000 ● *AIMCAL Sourcebook*, annual. Directory ● *Metallizing Technical Reference*, annual ● *Technical Proceedings* ● Also publishes technical proceedings.

852 ■ National Association of Pipe Coating Applicators (NAPCA)

c/o Merritt B. Chastain, Jr., Managing Dir.
8570 Bus. Park Dr.
Shreveport, LA 71105
Ph: (318)227-2769
Fax: (318)222-0482
URL: http://www.napca.com
Contact: Merritt B. Chastain Jr., Managing Dir.

Founded: 1965. **Members:** 135. **Staff:** 3. **Budget:** $290,000. **Multinational. Description:** Business firms engaged in the application of exterior or interior pipe coatings to steel pipe at established facilities using permanently located equipment; associate members are companies engaged in the manufacture or sale of materials, supplies, equipment, or services used by applicators of protective pipe coatings and line pipe manufacturers. Promotes application of pipe coatings in permanent yards, encourages high standards of workmanship, and develops standardized specifications for materials. Encourages research to improve materials. **Libraries: Type:** reference. **Subjects:** coating application, association history. **Awards:** Hall of Fame Award. **Frequency:** annual. **Type:** recognition. **Recipient:** for outstanding contribution to the plant pipe coating industry. **Computer Services:** Mailing lists, of members. **Committees:** Advertising; Business Ethics; Environmental; Materials Specifications. **Conventions/Meetings:** annual convention.

853 ■ National Coil Coating Association (NCCA)

1300 Sumner Ave.
Cleveland, OH 44115-2851
Ph: (216)241-7333
Fax: (216)241-0105
E-mail: ncca@coilcoating.org
URL: http://www.coilcoating.org
Contact: John Addington, Contact

Founded: 1962. **Members:** 129. **Membership Dues:** professional, $1,250 (annual) ● non-coater, coater (based on annual sales revenue), $2,750-$8,500 (annual). **Staff:** 6. **Budget:** $1,000,000. **Description:** Manufacturers of continuously coated metal coil other than metal-plated coil; associate members are producers of metal coil sheet and suppliers of equipment, material, or services used in continuous coating of metal coil. Seeks to raise quality standards of decorative and functional coated metal coil and to stimulate improvements in the mechanical, technical, and manufacturing phases of the industry. Maintains speakers' bureau and hall of fame; compiles statistics. **Libraries: Type:** reference. **Subjects:** coating, paint. **Awards:** Hall of Fame. **Frequency:** annual. **Type:** recognition. **Recipient:** for outstanding contributions to the organization and the coil coating industry ● Pollution Prevention Award. **Frequency:** annual. **Type:** recognition. **Recipient:** for coater and non-coater members. **Telecommunication Services:** electronic mail, jaddington@taol.com. **Committees:** Government Relations; Marketing; Program Planning; Technical. **Publications:** *Coil Lines*, quarterly. Newsletter. Includes meeting news. **Price:** included in membership dues ● *National Coil Coaters Association—Proceedings*, semiannual. Meeting and technical marketing papers of the association. **Price:** $25.00 for nonmembers; $10.50 for members ● Membership Directory, annual. **Price:** available to members only ● Brochure. **Conventions/Meetings:** annual meeting (exhibits) - always fall.

854 ■ Powder Coating Institute (PCI)

2121 Eisenhower Ave., Ste.401
Alexandria, VA 22314
Ph: (703)684-1770
Free: (800)988-COAT
Fax: (703)684-1771
E-mail: pci-info@powdercoating.org
URL: http://www.powdercoating.org
Contact: Gregory J. Bocchi, Exec. Dir.

Founded: 1981. **Members:** 320. **Membership Dues:** affiliate in North America, $95 (annual) ● affiliate outside North America, $150 (annual) ● company (category 1-3), $1,800-$7,200 (annual) ● company (category 4), $2,400-$4,800 (annual) ● company (category 5), $500-$1,000 (annual) ● company (category 6), $1,000 (annual). **Staff:** 4. **Description:** Individuals and businesses that manufacture, sell, or develop powder coating materials and equipment. Promotes the application and use of powder coating technology among industrial finishers; disseminates information to both consumers and the industry on the value and performance of powder coating; supports educational programs in the industrial coating/finishing field; updates members, governmental departments, and regulatory agencies on the activities and developments concerning the manufacture, application, and proper handling of powder coatings. Presents technical papers at conferences of related organizations and prepares articles for the media on the powder coating industry. **Libraries: Type:** reference. **Holdings:** articles, audiovisuals. **Telecommunication Services:** electronic mail, gbocchi@powdercoating.org. **Committees:** Application and Recovery Equipment; Custom Powder Coaters; Health and Safety/Test Procedures; Industry Communications; Raw Materials Suppliers; Technical; Trade Show. **Publications:** *PCI Information*, annual. Brochure. Lists institute members and their products and services; includes description of the institute and its purposes. **Price:** free ● *Powder Coating Institute—Directory*, annual. Membership Directory. **Price:** available to members only ● *Powder Coating Institute—Newsletter*, bimonthly. Includes meetings schedule. **Price:** available to members only. **Circulation:** 450 ● *Powder Coating Institute—Tech Briefs*, periodic. Provides technical information on powder coating materials, equipment, applications, health and safety, and terms and definitions. **Price:** free ● *Powder Coating - The Complete Finisher's Handbook* ● *Powder Coatings*. Brochure. **Conventions/Meetings:** annual meeting - always May ● annual Powder Coating Technical Conference and Trade Show - trade show and conference - always fall.

855 ■ Roof Coatings Manufacturers Association (RCMA)

1156 - 15th St. NW, Ste.900
Washington, DC 20005
Ph: (202)207-0919
Fax: (202)223-9741
E-mail: questions@roofcoatings.org
URL: http://www.roofcoatings.org
Contact: Chris Salazar, Pres.

Founded: 1983. **Members:** 60. **Membership Dues:** associate, $3,000 (annual) ● affiliate (1st year), $2,400 ● affiliate (2nd year), $3,600 (annual) ● contributory, $1,200 (annual). **Staff:** 3. **Budget:** $300,000. **Description:** Corporations involved in the manufacture and distribution of cold-process protective roof coatings. Represents manufacturers and suppliers; conducts market research on the size, volume, and number of roof coating companies in the U.S; provides financial management surveys, business studies, industry statistics, and technical information. Sponsors educational and training seminars. **Libraries: Type:** reference. **Awards:** Martin Davis Award. **Frequency:** annual. **Type:** recognition. **Recipient:** for an industry leader recognized by peers. **Computer Services:** database ● mailing lists. **Committees:** Annual Conference Planning; Communications; Government Affairs; Technical. **Councils:** Associates; Past Presidents; White Coatings. **Publications:** *RCMA Government Issues*, quarterly. Newsletter ● *RCMA Report*, bimonthly. Newsletter. Includes research materials and information on committee activities. **Price:** included in membership dues. Also Cited As: *Roof Coatings Manufacturers Association Bulletin* ● *Roof Coatings Manufacturers Association Membership Directory*, annual ● *Surface Preparation Document* ● *VDC/VDS Guide*. **Conventions/Meetings:** annual convention (exhibits) - always January.

856 ■ Society of Vacuum Coaters (SVC)

71 Pinon Hill Pl. NE
Albuquerque, NM 87122
Ph: (505)856-7188
Fax: (505)856-6716
E-mail: svcinfo@svc.org
URL: http://www.svc.org
Contact: Vivienne Harwood Mattox, Exec. Dir.

Founded: 1957. **Members:** 1,020. **Membership Dues:** individual, $95 (annual) ● individual in North America, $135 (annual) ● individual outside North America, $150 (annual) ● student, $40-$70 (annual) ● corporate sponsor, $500 (annual). **Staff:** 2. **Budget:** $900,000. **Description:** Vacuum coating industry organizations and others concerned with capabilities of vacuum coating and thin film technology. Provides a common medium of inter-communications for the many and widely separated persons and groups interested in the vacuum coating process. Directs attention toward problems and factors concerned with the outstanding use of vacuum metallizing plastic, metal, and glass substrates. Sponsors educational programs and equipment exhibits. **Libraries: Type:** open to the public. **Awards:** Mentor Award. **Frequency:** annual. **Type:** recognition. **Recipient:** for outstanding contributions to the development of vacuum coating technology ● Nathaniel Sugerman Memorial Award. **Frequency:** annual. **Type:** monetary. **Recipient:** for outstanding technical achievement. **Committees:** Contamination Control; Custom Processors; Decorative and Functional Coating; Education and Training; Large Area Rigid Coatings; Optical Coating; Plasma Processes; Process Control and Monitoring; Suppliers; Thin Film and Media Technology; Vacuum Technology and Industrial Thin Films; Vacuum Web Coating; Web Coaters. **Publications:** *Products and Services Directory*, annual. **Price:** free. **Advertising:** accepted. Alternate Formats: online ● *SVC Conference Proceedings*, annual. **Price:** included in membership dues; $115.00 for nonmembers. **Advertising:** accepted. Alternate Formats: online ● *SVC News Bulletin*, 3/year, every spring, summer, and fall. **Circulation:** 8,000. **Adver-**

tising: accepted. Alternate Formats: online ● Membership Directory, annual. **Advertising:** accepted ● CD-ROM of conference proceedings. **Conventions/Meetings:** annual Technical Conference, technical meeting with educational program (exhibits).

857 ■ Thermoset Resin Formulators Association (TRFA)
c/o Jerilyn J. Church, CAE, Exec. Dir.
800 Roosevelt Rd., Bldg. C, Ste.312
Glen Ellyn, IL 60137
Ph: (630)942-6596
Fax: (630)790-3095
E-mail: info@trfa.org
URL: http://www.trfa.org
Contact: Jerilyn J. Church CAE, Exec. Dir.
Membership Dues: formulator, supplier (based on sales volume), $500-$5,000 (annual) ● distributor (based on sales volume), $500-$1,000 (annual). **Description:** Serves the needs and interests of all thermoset resin formulators and suppliers. Provides a forum for sharing and interaction among members. Offers its members access to formulator and supplier market trend information. **Publications:** Newsletter, quarterly. **Price:** included in membership dues. **Conventions/Meetings:** annual meeting (exhibits).

Collectibles

858 ■ CIMTA
4244 Spring Creek Ln.
Bellingham, WA 98226
Ph: (360)733-5721
Free: (866)326-9386
Fax: (360)733-5169
E-mail: 2006@cimta.org
URL: http://www.cimta.org
Contact: Sue Weber, Pres.
Founded: 1980. **Members:** 267. **Membership Dues:** regular, $135 (annual) ● supporting, $60 (annual). **Description:** Individuals who create and sell handcrafted miniature objects to miniatures shops; interested others. Aims to provide a forum to allow handcrafting miniaturists to meet with shop owners. **Telecommunication Services:** electronic mail, sweber553011@aol.com. **Committees:** Nominating. **Also Known As:** Cottage Industry Miniaturists Trade Association, Inc. **Publications:** *CIMTA Ink*, semiannual. Newsletter. **Price:** included in membership dues ● Book. **Price:** included in membership dues. **Conventions/Meetings:** semiannual trade show (exhibits).

859 ■ Gift Association of America (GAA)
115 Rolling Hills Rd.
Johnstown, PA 15905-5225
Ph: (814)288-1460
Fax: (814)288-1483
E-mail: info@giftassn.com
Contact: Michael L. Russo, Chm./Pres.
Founded: 1952. **Members:** 850. **Membership Dues:** retail, $65 (annual) ● wholesale, industry affiliate, foreign affiliate, $115 (annual). **Staff:** 2. **Budget:** $55,000. **Description:** Retailers, wholesalers, and industry affiliate of gifts, china, glass, and decorative accessories. Sponsors seminars at gift shows and European market tours. **Formerly:** (1982) Gift and Decorative Accessories Association of America. **Publications:** *GAA News*, quarterly. Newsletter. Contains president's letter, association program news, and new members listing. **Price:** included in membership dues. **Circulation:** 1,000. **Advertising:** accepted ● *How to Shop A Gift Show* ● Membership Directory, annual. **Price:** available to members only ● Booklets. **Price:** included in membership dues. **Conventions/Meetings:** semiannual board meeting - always August and February in New York City.

860 ■ Gift and Collectibles Guild (GCG)
PO Box A3294
Chicago, IL 60690
Ph: (312)236-3930 (312)379-2935
Fax: (312)346-7004
E-mail: info@giftandcollectiblesguild.org
Contact: Karen Feil, Managing Dir.
Founded: 1977. **Members:** 100. **Membership Dues:** voting (manufacturer), non-voting associate (publisher, rep, artist), $295 (annual). **Staff:** 1. **Description:** Firms engaged in the manufacture or importation of limited edition prints, collector plates, figurines, dolls, miniatures, ornaments, diecast cars, and bells and the artists and suppliers to the industry. Promotes collecting as a hobby. Sponsors charitable and educational programs; compiles statistics. **Libraries: Type:** not open to the public. **Awards:** Retailer of the Year. **Frequency:** annual. **Type:** recognition. **Formerly:** Collectibles and Giftmakers Guild; (1989) Collector Platemakers Guild; (2001) Collectibles and Platemakers Guild. **Publications:** *Giftware News*. Magazine ● *Guild Member News*, bimonthly. Newsletter. Covers current events in the limited edition and collectibles industry. **Price:** free, for members only. **Advertising:** accepted. **Conventions/Meetings:** annual Collectibles Show - trade show, wholesale market for collectibles retailers followed by a consumer show (exhibits).

861 ■ International Inflatable Products and Games Association (IIP&GA)
10 E Athens Ave., Ste.208
Ardmore, PA 19003
Ph: (610)645-6940
Fax: (610)645-6943
E-mail: tapmag@kanec.com
URL: http://www.iipga.com
Contact: Scott C. Borowsky, Pres./Exec. Ed.
Founded: 1994. **Members:** 650. **Membership Dues:** primary, $300 (annual) ● affiliate, $150 (annual) ● associate, $100 (annual). **Staff:** 10. **Description:** Manufacturers, wholesalers-distributors, resort gift shops, and others associated with the souvenir and novelty industry. Conducts trade promotion activities for the industry. Plans to collect trade statistics and information on such topics as new merchandising methods; domestic and foreign distribution, including imports and exports; freight rates; production; stocks of goods on hand; and shipments. Sponsors competitions. Maintains speakers' bureau. **Awards:** Innovator Award. **Frequency:** annual. **Type:** recognition. **Recipient:** for selected members. **Formerly:** (2001) Souvenir and Novelty Trade Association; (2005) Souvenir and Gift Novelty Trade Association. **Publications:** *Inflatable News*, annual. Magazine. **Price:** free for members. **Advertising:** accepted ● *Souvenirs, Gifts, and Novelties Magazine*, 8/year. Includes news, trends, and survey results for the souvenir industry, supplier guide, megaback survey issue, t-shirt and collectible preview. **Price:** $40.00/year in U.S.; $45.00/year outside U.S. **Circulation:** 43,085. **Advertising:** accepted ● *Tourist Attractions and Parks*, 7/year. Magazine. Covers management of theme and amusement parks, carnivals, arcades, zoos, museums, arenas, stadiums, and concessions. **Price:** $49.00/year in U.S.; $55.00/year outside U.S. **Circulation:** 33,083. **Advertising:** accepted. **Conventions/Meetings:** annual Leisure Entertainment Expo - seminar, with theme, resort, gifts (exhibits).

862 ■ National Association of Limited Edition Dealers (NALED)
332 Hurst Mill N
Bremen, GA 30110
Ph: (770)537-1970
Free: (800)446-2533
E-mail: naledoffice@aol.com
URL: http://www.naled.org
Contact: Helen Yanek, Pres.
Founded: 1976. **Members:** 400. **Membership Dues:** retailer, $150 (annual) ● associate (based on levels), $225-$750 (annual) ● sales representative, $50 (annual). **Staff:** 2. **Budget:** $250,000. **Description:** Retailers, manufacturers, artists, and sales representatives of limited edition and collectible items such as figurines, plates, and prints. Seeks to enhance the hobby of limited edition collecting. Conducts dealer educational seminars and workshops on how to effectively serve the limited edition and collecting customer. **Awards:** Achievement Awards. **Frequency:** annual. **Type:** recognition. **Recipient:** for quality of product or service ● Eugene Freedman Humanitarian Award. **Frequency:** annual. **Type:** recognition. **Recipient:** to an individual or company with exceptional service to the industry. **Committees:** Budget and Finance; Catalog; Membership; Personnel; Program; Publications/Advertising; Source Pool Nomination; Technology. **Publications:** *The NALED Complete SourceBook for Gift & Collectibles Retailers*, annual. Serves as guide to collectible and gift vendors and their policies. Contains retailing techniques for increasing collectibles sales. **Price:** $29.95. **Advertising:** accepted ● *NALED Directory of Members*, annual. Membership Directory ● *News and Views*, quarterly. Newsletter. Includes industry news and opinion. **Conventions/Meetings:** annual International Collectible Exposition - convention and trade show (exhibits) - last week of June, Rosemont, IL.

Collectors

863 ■ Antiques and Collectibles Dealer Association (ACDA)
c/o Antiques and Collectibles Association
PO Box 4389
Davidson, NC 28036
Ph: (704)895-9088
Free: (800)287-7127
Fax: (704)895-0230
E-mail: info@antiqueandcollectible.com
URL: http://www.antiqueandcollectible.com/acda.shtml
Contact: Angie Becker, Pres./CEO
Founded: 1991. **Membership Dues:** general, $45 (annual). **Description:** Provides member dealers with benefit programs to enhance their businesses. Creates public awareness of the antiques and collectibles industry. Promotes professionalism in the antiques and collectibles industry. Offers dealers and the public with educational opportunities to improve their knowledge of the things they collect, buy and sell. **Publications:** Newsletter, quarterly.

864 ■ Antiques and Collectibles National Association (ACNA)
PO Box 4389
Davidson, NC 28036
Ph: (704)895-9088
Free: (800)287-7127
Fax: (704)895-0230
E-mail: angie@acna.us
URL: http://www.acna.us
Founded: 1991. **Description:** Protects the antiques and collectibles business by developing insurance and other benefit programs. Fosters professionalism and profitability within the industry. Seeks to enhance credibility with the buying public. **Conventions/Meetings:** biennial symposium, with informative speakers and interactive panel discussions.

865 ■ Professional Autograph Dealers Association (PADA)
PO Box 1729W
Murray Hill Sta.
New York, NY 10016
Free: (888)338-4338
Fax: (866)639-1240
E-mail: padamail@padaweb.org
URL: http://www.padaweb.org
Contact: Steven L. Hoskin, Pres.
Founded: 1996. **Members:** 49. **Multinational. Description:** Represents autograph dealers working to encourage interest in and appreciation of the field of autograph collecting. Promotes high standards of business ethics, professionalism and service in the trade. **Publications:** Membership Directory. **Conventions/Meetings:** annual Autograph Show.

Color

866 ■ Color Association of the United States (CAUS)
315 W 39th St., Studio 507
New York, NY 10018
Ph: (212)947-7774

Fax: (212)594-6987
E-mail: caus@colorassociation.com
URL: http://www.colorassociation.com
Contact: Margaret Walch, Dir.

Founded: 1915. **Members:** 1,000. **Membership Dues:** general, $1,050 (annual). **Description:** Issues color forecasts to members representing dyestuffs, paints, automobiles, airplanes, home furnishings, textiles, men's, women's, and children's wear, hosiery, plastics, cosmetics, manufacturers, retailers, publications, advertising agencies, and other fields. Offers consultations. **Libraries: Type:** reference. **Holdings:** archival material. **Subjects:** colored swatches dating back to 1915, U.S. Armed Forces color standards, color standards. **Committees:** Children's Color; Interiors; Men's Colors; Women's Colors. **Formerly:** The Textile Color Card Association of America. **Publications:** *CAUS/Forecast Colors/ Children's/Women's/Men's/Interior Colors*, monthly. A fabric-swatched forecast card published in three categories: men's, women's and children's interior. Interior color forecasts are silk screens. **Price:** included in membership dues. **Circulation:** 1,000 ● *CAUS Newsletter*, monthly. Covers such topics as apparel and interior design, fashion, and marketing. Includes book reviews. **Price:** included in membership dues. **Circulation:** 2,000 ● *The Color Compendium*. Book ● *Color Forecasts* ● *Living Colors*. Book. Contains definition guide to historical and contemporary colors. ● *Standard Color Reference of America*, 10/year. Provides over two hundred silk-swatched examples in mat and shiny surface of shades of colors. **Price:** $400.00 for members; $550.00 for nonmembers ● Also publishes textile color standards. **Conventions/Meetings:** seminar ● bimonthly trade show, presentation of various topics related to color and current forecasts (exhibits).

867 ■ Color Marketing Group (CMG)

5845 Richmond Hwy., No. 410
Alexandria, VA 22303
Ph: (703)329-8500
Fax: (703)329-0155
E-mail: cmg@colormarketing.org
URL: http://www.colormarketing.org
Contact: Jaime E. Stephens, Exec. Dir.

Founded: 1962. **Members:** 1,100. **Membership Dues:** regular, $715 (annual) ● academic, $410 (annual) ● non-participating, $1,600 (annual). **Staff:** 6. **Budget:** $1,900,000. **Regional Groups:** 5. **National Groups:** 4. **Multinational. Description:** International group of professionals who forecast colors for consumer and contract markets. Examines color as it applies to the profitable marketing of products and services. Provides a forum for the exchange of ideas for all phases of color marketing, including styling, design, trends, merchandising, sales, education, and research. **Computer Services:** Information services, color forecasting resources. **Committees:** Consumer and Contract Color Directions; Consumer and Contract Colors Current; Consumer Inter-Industry; Contract Color Design; Design; Trend Catalyst. **Publications:** *CMG Directory*, annual. Membership Directory. **Advertising:** accepted ● *CMG News Update*, monthly. Newsletter. **Price:** included in membership dues. Alternate Formats: online ● *Color Cards*, semiannual. Reports ● *Color Chips*, semiannual. Newsletter. **Price:** included in membership dues ● *Roving Tradeshow Color Trend Reports*, monthly. **Conventions/Meetings:** semiannual international conference - every spring and fall. 2008 Nov. 7-11, Phoenix, AZ.

868 ■ Color Pigments Manufacturers Association (CPMA)

PO Box 20839
Alexandria, VA 22320-1839
Ph: (703)684-4044
Fax: (703)684-1795
E-mail: cpma@cpma.com
URL: http://www.pigments.org
Contact: J. Lawrence Robinson, Pres.

Founded: 1925. **Members:** 50. **Staff:** 5. **Budget:** $1,000,000. **Description:** Manufacturers of inorganic and organic color pigments. Disseminates technical, regulatory, and legislative information on laboratory testing, toxicity, and subjects of general interest to manufacturers of pigments. **Committees:** Cadmium Pigments; Carbazole Violet Pigments; Complex Inorganic Colors Pigments; Diarylide Pigments; Education; Education and Communication; Hazard Communications; International Commercial Relations; Iron Oxide Pigments; Lead Chromate; Monoarylide Yellow Pigments; Monoazo and Related Pigments; Nominating; Phthalocyanine Pigments; Scientific; Transportation/Traffic. **Formerly:** (1993) Dry Color Manufacturers Association. **Publications:** *Catalog of Official Statements, Studies, and Publications of the Color Pigments Manufacturers Association*, annual. **Price:** free ● *Color Pigments Manufacturers Association—Annual Report*. **Price:** free ● *CPMA Executive Update*, monthly. Newsletter. **Price:** free, for members only ● *CPMA Membership Handbook and Directory*, annual. **Price:** free, for members only ● Bulletins. Includes topics on international trade, the environmental, and legislation. **Conventions/Meetings:** annual International Color Pigments Conference - meeting (exhibits).

869 ■ International Association of Color Manufacturers (IACM)

1620 I St. NW, Ste.925
Washington, DC 20006
Ph: (202)293-5800
Fax: (202)463-8998
E-mail: bbursiek@therobertsgroup.net
URL: http://www.iacmcolor.org
Contact: Glenn Roberts, Exec. Dir.

Founded: 1972. **Members:** 4. **Description:** Serves as certified food color manufacturers. Aims to acquire and maintain Food and Drug Administration approval of color additives for foods. **Convention/Meeting:** none. **Publications:** none. **Committees:** Certified Color; Exempt Color. **Formerly:** (1993) Certified Color Manufacturers Association.

870 ■ International Color Consortium (ICC)

1899 Preston White Dr.
Reston, VA 20191
Ph: (703)264-7200
Fax: (703)620-0994
E-mail: ksmythe@npes.org
URL: http://www.color.org
Contact: Kip Smythe, Sec.

Founded: 1993. **Members:** 70. **Membership Dues:** corporate, $2,500 (annual). **Budget:** $250,000. **Multinational. Description:** Represents and promotes standardization and evolution of an open, vendor-neutral, cross-platform color management system architecture and components. **Publications:** Annual Report, annual ● Articles.

Commodities

871 ■ National Sweet Sorghum Producers and Processors Association (NSSPPA)

c/o Morris Bitzer, Exec. Sec.
2049 Rebel Rd.
Lexington, KY 40503
Ph: (859)806-3358
Fax: (859)257-7874
E-mail: mbitzer@uky.edu
URL: http://www.ca.uky.edu/nssppa
Contact: Morris Bitzer, Exec. Sec.

Membership Dues: regular/associate/supporter, $20 (annual). **Description:** Provides a mechanism for communication among sweet sorghum producers and processors. Provides a mechanism for the sweet and sorghum industry to express its needs and interests to researchers, extension workers, government officials and regulators, suppliers of equipment materials, servicers, buyers and consumers. Acts as an advisory body for all activities related to sweet sorghum. **Publications:** *Sorghum Treasures*. Book. Contains recipes using sweet sorghum. **Price:** $4.00/ issue for members; $6.00/issue for nonmembers.

Communications

872 ■ American Association of Paging Carriers (AAPC)

441 N Crestwood Dr.
Wilmington, NC 28405
Free: (866)301-2272
Fax: (910)792-9733
E-mail: info@pagingcarriers.org
URL: http://www.pagingcarriers.org
Contact: Bruce Deer, Pres.

Membership Dues: carrier, $500-$7,000 (annual) ● carrier - more than 100000 units, $9,000 (annual) ● carrier - national footprint, $25,000 (annual) ● individual, $250 (annual) ● vendor - gold level, $5,000 (annual) ● vendor - silver level, $2,500 (annual) ● vendor - bronze level, $1,000 (annual). **Description:** Provides an effective forum for the discussion and progression of issues relating to the paging industry. Monitors and addresses regulatory and legal matters as a unified organization. Provides research on the development of the industry and its current prospective markets. **Computer Services:** Online services, message board ● online services, newsroom. **Committees:** Paging Technical. **Publications:** Newsletter. Alternate Formats: online.

873 ■ American Society of Professional Communicators (ASPC)

4885 McKnight Rd., Ste.325
Pittsburgh, PA 15237
Ph: (412)625-4094
E-mail: info@asprocomm.com
URL: http://www.asprocomm.com
Contact: Shawn Bannon, Pres.

Founded: 2000. **Membership Dues:** individual, $125 (annual). **Description:** Works to create a platform for education, innovation and the recognition of excellence among professional communicators. Provides resources and encourages communicators to share best practices and professional experiences with one another. **Awards:** ASPC Annual Report Award. **Frequency:** annual. **Type:** recognition. **Recipient:** for outstanding annual report work ● ASPC Masters Communication Award. **Frequency:** annual. **Type:** recognition. **Recipient:** for excellence and innovation in professional communications. **Publications:** *ASPC Quarterly*. Newsletter. Contains articles about the field of communications by and for professional communicators.

874 ■ Association for Women in Communications (AWC)

3337 Duke St.
Alexandria, VA 22314
Ph: (703)370-7436
Fax: (703)370-7437
E-mail: info@womcom.org
URL: http://www.womcom.org
Contact: Ms. Pamela Valenzuela CAE, Exec. Dir.

Founded: 1909. **Members:** 4,000. **Membership Dues:** professional, $99 (annual) ● collegiate, graduate student, new graduate, retired, $29 (annual) ● executive communicator, $159 (annual) ● entrepreneur, $84 (annual). **Staff:** 5. **Budget:** $350,000. **Regional Groups:** 100. **Description:** Professional association of journalism and communications. **Awards:** Clarion Awards. **Frequency:** annual. **Type:** recognition. **Recipient:** for excellence in communication fields ● International Matrix Award. **Frequency:** annual. **Type:** recognition. **Recipient:** for achieving the highest level of professional excellence in communication ● Rising Star Award. **Frequency:** annual. **Type:** recognition. **Recipient:** for outstanding contributions to school and community ● Ruth Weyand Award. **Frequency:** annual. **Type:** recognition. **Recipient:** for a labor attorney who worked tirelessly for women's rights in the workplace. **Absorbed:** (2003) Women in Advertising and Marketing. **Formerly:** (1972) Theta Sigma Phi; (1996) Women in Communications. **Publications:** *AWC Communique*, bimonthly. Newsletters. Covers the national and chapter organizations' news, and individual members' news. **Circulation:** 4,000. **Advertising:** accepted. Alternate Formats: online ● *The Intercom*, monthly. Newsletter. Alternate Formats: online ● *The Matrix*, quarterly. Magazine. Alternate Formats: online. **Conventions/Meetings:** annual National Professional Conference (exhibits) - 2008 Oct. 10-14, Atlanta, GA - **Avg. Attendance:** 200; 2009 Oct. 12-16, Seattle, WA - **Avg. Attendance:** 200.

875 ■ Copywriter's Council of America (CCA)
CCA Bldg.
PO Box 102
Middle Island, NY 11953-0102
Ph: (631)924-8555 (631)924-3888
Fax: (631)924-3890
E-mail: cca4dmcopy@att.net
URL: http://lgroup.addr.com/freelance.htm
Contact: Roger Dextor, Exec. VP/Creative Dir.
Founded: 1964. **Members:** 550. **Membership Dues:** associate, $95 (annual) ● professional, $125 (annual) ● corporate, $200 (annual). **Staff:** 6. **Description:** Advertising copywriters, marketing and public relations consultants, copyeditors, proofreaders, and other individuals involved in print, radio, broadcast, video, and telecommunications. Provides freelance work; acts as agent for members; negotiates on members' behalf. Serves as a forum for professional and social contact between freelance communications professionals. Offers courses on copywriting, direct marketing, mail order, publishing screenplays, and how to get published. Conducts charitable programs. Maintains speakers' bureau, hall of fame, and word processing consultation service. **Awards: Type:** recognition. **Computer Services:** Electronic publishing ● mailing lists. **Formerly:** (1978) Direct Response Creative Association. **Publications:** *Business Communication Resource Guide*. Lists books, special reports, audiocassettes, and other resources from the association. ● *The Digest*, quarterly. Newsletter. Includes fee schedules, information on marketing and self-promotion, and articles on contract negotiation, retainers, and rates. **Price:** included in membership dues. **Circulation:** 1,300 ● Audiotapes ● Books ● Reports. **Conventions/Meetings:** competition ● annual seminar and workshop (exhibits).

876 ■ Council of Communication Management (CCM)
65 Enterprise
Aliso Viejo, CA 92656
Ph: (973)453-8854 (309)766-3434
Free: (866)463-6226
Fax: (949)715-6931
E-mail: membership@ccmconnection.com
URL: http://www.ccmconnection.com
Contact: Bill Furtkevic, Pres.
Founded: 1955. **Members:** 250. **Membership Dues:** regular, $300 (annual). **Staff:** 1. **Budget:** $80,000. **Description:** Managers, consultants, and educators who work at the policy level in organizational communication. Serves as a network through which members can help one another advance the practice of communications in business. **Libraries: Type:** reference. **Computer Services:** Mailing lists, of members ● online services, forum. **Formerly:** (1985) Industrial Communication Council. **Publications:** *CCM Communicator*, bimonthly. Newsletter. **Circulation:** 250. **Advertising:** accepted. Alternate Formats: online ● Books ● Membership Directory, annual. Alternate Formats: online ● Reports. **Conventions/Meetings:** annual conference and seminar.

877 ■ Enterprise Communications Association (ECA)
1901 Pennsylvania Ave. NW, 5th Fl.
Washington, DC 20006
Ph: (202)467-4868
Fax: (202)872-1331
E-mail: info@encomm.org
URL: http://www.encomm.org
Contact: Mary I. Bradshaw, Exec. Dir.
Membership Dues: supplier, sales channel company, reseller, distributor, $1,000-$10,000 (annual) ● individual, $500 (annual) ● professional services firm, $1,000 (annual). **Description:** Promotes growth of healthy markets and effective sales path for converged voice, video and data communications solutions. **Telecommunication Services:** electronic mail, mary@encomm.org. **Committees:** Channel Issues Forum; Education; End-User Outreach; Events; Finance; Industry Futures and Research; Media Relations; Membership Development; Operations; Public Policy. **Programs:** Channel CEO Forums; Sales Training for Convergence Solutions; Technical Training for Technical Personnel. **Publications:** *ECA Alert*, monthly. Newsletter. Alternate Formats: online.

878 ■ Enterprise Computer Telephony Forum (ECTF)
c/o ComTIA
1815 S Meyers Rd., Ste.300
Oakbrook Terrace, IL 60181-5228
Ph: (510)608-5915
Fax: (510)608-5917
E-mail: ectf@comptia.org
URL: http://www.comptia.org/sections/ectf
Founded: 1995. **Description:** Suppliers, developers, systems integrators, and users of computer telephony technologies. Seeks to "bring interoperability to computer telephony". Serves as a forum for the discussion and evaluation of emerging computer telephony technologies; develops and tests interoperability techniques; incorporates and augments computer telephony standards; publicizes interoperability agreements. **Committees:** Technical.

879 ■ International Association of Business Communicators (IABC)
1 Hallidie Plz., Ste.600
San Francisco, CA 94102-2818
Ph: (415)544-4700
Free: (800)776-4222
Fax: (415)544-4747
E-mail: service_centre@iabc.com
URL: http://www.iabc.com
Contact: Julie Freeman, Pres.
Founded: 1970. **Members:** 13,000. **Membership Dues:** regular, $40 (annual) ● student, retiree, $43 (annual) ● life, $1,000. **Staff:** 27. **Budget:** $3,679,554. **Regional Groups:** 12. **Local Groups:** 98. **Multinational. Description:** Represents Communication managers, public relations directors, writers, editors, audiovisual specialists, and others in the public relations and organizational communication field that use a variety of media to communicate with internal audiences (employees, management, association members, and leaders) and external audiences (media, customers, dealers, investors, and government). Conducts research in the communication field and encourages establishment of college-level programs in organizational communication. Offers accreditation program; conducts surveys on employee communication effectiveness and media trends. **Libraries: Type:** reference. **Subjects:** organizational communication. **Awards:** Chairman's Award. **Frequency:** annual. **Type:** recognition. **Recipient:** for an IABC volunteer ● Chapter Management Award. **Frequency:** annual. **Type:** recognition. **Recipient:** for the most outstanding IABC chapter ● Excellence in Communication Leadership. **Frequency:** annual. **Type:** recognition. **Recipient:** for a nonmember of IABC ● Fellow Designation. **Frequency:** annual. **Type:** recognition. **Recipient:** for outstanding leaders ● Gold Quill. **Frequency:** annual. **Type:** recognition. **Recipient:** for communicators ● Lifetime Foundation Friend Award. **Frequency:** annual. **Type:** recognition. **Recipient:** for individuals who supported the Foundation. **Telecommunication Services:** electronic mail, jfreeman@iabc.com. **Formed by Merger of:** American Association of Industrial Editors; International Council of Industrial Editors; Corporate Communicators Canada. **Publications:** *Communication World*, bimonthly. Magazine. For those in the public relations and organizational communication fields. **Price:** $199.00 for nonmembers. **Circulation:** 20,000. **Advertising:** accepted. **Conventions/Meetings:** annual international conference (exhibits).

880 ■ Joint Users of Siemens Technologies United States (JUST-US)
401 N Michigan Ave.
Chicago, IL 60611
Ph: (312)321-6804 (214)645-7410
Fax: (312)245-1081
E-mail: just-us@just-us.org
URL: http://www.just-us.org
Contact: Mary Beth Roman, Exec. Dir.
Founded: 1985. **Members:** 600. **Membership Dues:** general, $300 (annual). **Staff:** 10. **Description:** Strives to serve Siemens Information and Communication Networks users and aims to help members achieve success. **Publications:** *Information Exchange Newsletter*. Includes updates, special offers from Siemens, and user success stories. ● Membership Directory. Alternate Formats: online. **Conventions/Meetings:** annual conference and workshop.

881 ■ MultiService Forum (MSF)
48377 Fremont Blvd., Ste.117
Fremont, CA 94538
Ph: (510)492-4050 (510)492-4052
Fax: (510)492-4001
E-mail: info@msforum.org
URL: http://www.msforum.org
Contact: Julianne Fitzpatrick, Exec. Dir./Marketing Program Mgr.
Founded: 1998. **Membership Dues:** principal, $18,750 (annual) ● small company, not-for-profit principal, $7,500 (annual) ● individual, educational, $500 (annual). **Staff:** 2. **Multinational. Description:** Works for the deployment of open communications systems that realize economic benefits, which result from flexible support of network services using multiple infrastructure technologies. Focuses on the development of architecture and industry agreements that enable interoperability and innovation in a rapidly evolving environment. Maintains speakers' bureau. **Formerly:** (2005) Multiservice Switching Forum. **Publications:** Newsletter. Alternate Formats: online. **Conventions/Meetings:** annual Technical Committee Meeting.

882 ■ National Association of Minority Media Executives (NAMME)
7950 Jones Br. Dr.
McLean, VA 22107
Ph: (703)854-7178 (703)854-7179
Free: (888)968-7658
Fax: (703)854-7181
E-mail: info@namme.org
URL: http://www.namme.org
Contact: Neil Foote, Chm.
Founded: 1990. **Members:** 400. **Membership Dues:** individual, $150-$400 (annual) ● corporate, $1,750-$3,750 (annual) ● life, $5,000 ● educational institution, $500 (annual). **Staff:** 4. **Budget:** $250,000. **Description:** Senior minority managers and executives. Strives to increase the number of minorities in senior management positions and to promote diversity in the communications industry. Conducts research and educational programs. Provides executive development for members, and management training and mentoring for new members. Creates forums and alliances to bring media companies and organizations together to discuss multi-cultural issues and generate strategies and solutions. **Awards:** Catalyst Awards. **Frequency:** annual. **Type:** recognition. **Recipient:** for excellence in print, broadcast and new media ● Lawrence Young Breakthrough Award. **Frequency:** annual. **Type:** recognition ● Lifetime Achievement in Diversity. **Frequency:** annual. **Type:** recognition. **Recipient:** to individuals effective in hiring, promoting, and developing minorities ● Robert C. Maynard Legend Award. **Frequency:** annual. **Type:** recognition. **Computer Services:** Mailing lists, of members. **Publications:** *NAMME Newsletter*, monthly. **Price:** free for members. **Circulation:** 500. **Advertising:** accepted. Alternate Formats: online. **Conventions/Meetings:** banquet ● board meeting - 2008 July 23, Chicago, IL ● annual conference, with executive development sessions and discussion of media issues (exhibits) - 2008 July 22, Chicago, IL.

883 ■ New York Women in Communications, Inc. Foundation (NYWICIF)
355 Lexington Ave., 15th Fl.
New York, NY 10017-6603
Ph: (212)297-2133 (212)297-2124
Fax: (212)370-9047
E-mail: mungaro@kellencompany.com
URL: http://www.nywici.org/foundation
Contact: Maria Ungaro, Exec. Dir.
Founded: 1968. **Staff:** 3. **Budget:** $200,000. **Description:** Serves a vanguard for transformational

leadership, influencing the work culture through: identifying, developing and sustaining leaders; offering a new approach for leadership parity for women and men; and integrating Communications as critical to organizational success. **Libraries: Type:** reference. **Holdings:** archival material, periodicals. **Awards:** The Vanguard Award. **Frequency:** biennial. **Type:** scholarship. **Computer Services:** Mailing lists. **Also Known As:** (1998) The Vanguard Foundation. **Formerly:** (2006) Women in Communications Foundation. **Publications:** *The Vanguard Digest*, quarterly. Newsletter ● Brochure. **Conventions/Meetings:** biennial conference and board meeting.

884 ■ Professional Insurance Communicators of America (PICA)
PO Box 68700
Indianapolis, IN 46268-0700
Ph: (317)875-5250
Fax: (317)879-8408
E-mail: jwright@namic.org
URL: http://www.pro-ins-coa.org
Contact: Janet E.H. Wright APR, Publications Mgr.
Founded: 1954. **Members:** 45. **Membership Dues:** full, single, $275 (annual) ● full, corporate, $325 (annual) ● single, associate, $300 (annual) ● corporate, associate, $375 (annual) ● affiliate, $300 (annual) ● professional, $150 (annual). **Staff:** 1. **Budget:** $12,000. **Description:** Insurance industry communicators. Dedicated to the continuing education and professional development of its members and the positive promotion of the insurance industry to its audiences. Provides educational tools to insurance editors to increase professionalism. Fosters communication among members. **Libraries: Type:** lending. **Awards:** Editorial Awards of Excellence. **Frequency:** annual. **Type:** recognition. **Recipient:** for best photo, best news story, and best four-color magazine. **Publications:** *Communique*, periodic. Newsletter. **Conventions/Meetings:** annual workshop.

885 ■ Satellite Industry Association (SIA)
1730 M St. NW, Ste.600
Washington, DC 20036
Ph: (202)349-3650 (202)349-3651
Fax: (202)349-3622
E-mail: info@sia.org
URL: http://www.sia.org
Contact: Patricia Cooper, Pres.
Founded: 1995. **Membership Dues:** executive (minimum; based on annual revenue from commercial space related activities), $16,000 (annual) ● executive (maximum; based on annual revenue from commercial space related activities), $40,000 (annual) ● associate (based on annual revenue from commercial space related activities), $5,000-$16,000 (annual). **Description:** Represents the U.S. commercial satellite industry; promotes the use of satellite technology in global communications. **Working Groups:** International Trade and Industry Statistics; Launch Policies; Satellite Licensing; Spectrum Allocation and Regulation. **Publications:** Annual Report, annual. Alternate Formats: online ● Reports. Alternate Formats: online.

886 ■ Society for Technical Communication (STC)
901 N Stuart St., Ste.904
Arlington, VA 22203-1822
Ph: (703)522-4114
Fax: (703)522-2075
E-mail: stc@stc.org
URL: http://www.stc.org
Contact: Susan Burton, Exec. Dir.
Founded: 1953. **Members:** 23,000. **Membership Dues:** classic, $80-$150 (annual) ● student, $50-$55 (annual) ● limited, $70-$130 (annual). **Staff:** 15. **Budget:** $4,000,000. **Local Groups:** 155. **Multinational. Description:** Writers, editors, educators, scientists, engineers, artists, publishers, and others professionally engaged in or interested in the field of technical communication; companies, corporations, organizations, and agencies interested in the aims of the society. Seeks to advance the theory and practice of technical communication in all media. Sponsors high school writing contests. **Awards: Frequency:** annual. **Type:** recognition. **Recipient:** to members for outstanding art, audiovisuals, and publications ● **Type:** scholarship. **Computer Services:** Mailing lists, of members. **Formed by Merger of:** (1953) Technical Publishing Society; Society of Technical Writers and Editors. **Formerly:** (1971) Society of Technical Writers and Publishers. **Publications:** *Intercom*, 10/year. Magazine. **Circulation:** 23,000. **Advertising:** accepted. Alternate Formats: CD-ROM; online ● *Technical Communication*, quarterly. Journal. Includes articles about the practical application of technical communication. **Price:** included in membership dues. **Advertising:** accepted ● Proceedings, annual. Alternate Formats: CD-ROM. **Conventions/Meetings:** annual conference, focuses on the arts and sciences of technical communication; includes more than 250 educational presentations; offers opportunities for networking (exhibits) - 2009 May 3-6, Atlanta, GA.

Community Development

887 ■ Business Alliance for Local Living Economies (BALLE)
165 11th St.
San Francisco, CA 94103
Ph: (415)255-1108
E-mail: info@livingeconomies.org
URL: http://www.livingeconomies.org
Contact: Don Shaffer, Natl. Coor.
Founded: 2001. **Members:** 12,000. **Membership Dues:** network, $500 (annual). **Multinational. Description:** Represents individuals dedicated to building local living economies. Seeks to build long-term economic empowerment and prosperity through local business ownership, economic justice, cultural diversity, and environmental stewardship. Advocates public policies that strengthen independent local businesses and farms, promote economic equity, and protect the environment. Supports the growth and development of community-based business. **Telecommunication Services:** electronic mail, don@livingeconomies.org. **Publications:** *Living Economy Newsletter*, monthly. Alternate Formats: online.

Computer Aided Design

888 ■ International Association of Webmasters and Designers (IAWMD)
11924 Forest Hill Blvd.
Executive Ste.22-276
Wellington, FL 33414
Ph: (561)248-5507
Fax: (561)828-0495
URL: http://www.iawmd.com
Contact: Darin I. Carter III, Chm.
Founded: 1997. **Members:** 310,000. **Membership Dues:** professional, student, new, $79 (annual) ● corporate, $550 (annual). **Multinational. Description:** Promotes trust and confidence on the Internet through voluntary self-regulation and administration, as well as webmaster and web surfer interaction. **Awards:** Diamond Web Awards. **Frequency:** annual. **Type:** recognition. **Recipient:** for websites that achieved levels of excellence ● Golden Web Awards. **Frequency:** annual. **Type:** recognition. **Recipient:** for websites that achieved levels of excellence. **Publications:** *Member News Briefs*. Newsletter. Contains news and information about the association.

Computer Science

889 ■ RapidIO Trade Association
12343 Hymeadow Dr., Ste.2R
Austin, TX 78750
Ph: (512)401-2900
Fax: (512)401-2902
E-mail: tom.cox@rapidio.org
URL: http://www.rapidio.org
Contact: Tom Cox, Exec. Dir.
Founded: 1997. **Members:** 41. **Membership Dues:** steering committee, $25,000 (annual) ● sponsoring, $15,000 (annual) ● regular, $9,500 (annual) ● auditing participant, $2,500 (annual). **Description:** Promotes development and adoption of new interconnect technology called RapidIO architecture for increased bandwidth, lower costs, faster time-to-market. **Publications:** *RapidIO Connections*, periodic. Newsletter. Contains product updates and status reports on the progress of the various RapidIO Trade Association working groups. **Price:** free. Alternate Formats: online.

Computer Software

890 ■ Open Applications Group
PO Box 4897
Marietta, GA 30061
Ph: (678)715-7588
Fax: (770)234-6036
E-mail: dconnelly@openapplications.org
URL: http://www.openapplications.org
Contact: David Connelly, Pres./CEO
Founded: 1994. **Membership Dues:** individual, $250 (annual) ● educational institution, $5,000 (annual). **Staff:** 3. **Multinational. Description:** Software vendors. Focuses on best practices and process-based XML content for eBusiness and Application Integration; strives for a unified standard for eBusiness and application software interoperability.

891 ■ Open Data Acquisition Association (ODAA)
Address Unknown since 2008
Founded: 1998. **Membership Dues:** for voting members with annual net sales of $4.999 million and below, $500 (annual) ● for voting members with annual net sales of $5 to $9.999 million, $2,500 (annual) ● for voting members with annual net sales of $10 to $24.999 million, $5,000 (annual) ● for voting members with annual net sales of $25 million or higher, $12,500 (annual). **Multinational. Description:** Provides users of data acquisition systems with a universal, open standard that allows interoperability between PC-based data acquisition hardware and software solutions from multiple vendors. **Libraries: Type:** reference. **Subjects:** software, interface, communication, hardware. **Committees:** Technical Specifications.

892 ■ Open DeviceNet Vendor Association (ODVA)
c/o Technology and Training Center
4220 Varsity Dr., Ste.A
Ann Arbor, MI 48108-5006
Ph: (734)975-8840
Fax: (734)922-0027
E-mail: odva@odva.org
URL: http://www.odva.org
Contact: Katherine Voss, Exec. Dir.
Multinational. Description: Supports the use, research and development of network technologies based on the Common Industrial Protocol (CIP). Includes DeviceNet, EtherNet/IP CIP Safety and CIP Sync. Assists manufacturers and users of CIP-based networks through tools, training and marketing activities. Offers conformance testing to ensure that products built to the specifications operate in multi-vendor systems. **Boards:** Technical Review. **Publications:** *DeviceNet Product Catalog*. Contains description, pricing, and features of DeviceNet products. Alternate Formats: online.

Computer Users

893 ■ U.S. Internet Industry Association (USIIA)
1800 Diagonal Rd., Ste.600
Alexandria, VA 22314
Ph: (703)647-7440 (703)924-0006
Fax: (703)647-6009

E-mail: info.3@usiia.org
URL: http://www.usiia.org
Contact: David P. McClure, Pres./CEO
Founded: 1994. **Members:** 300. **Membership Dues:** academic, non-profit, $500 (annual) ● corporate (with $1 million - $50 million annual revenues), $150-$3,000 (annual) ● corporate (with $50 million - $1 billion annual revenues), $7,500-$25,000 (annual) ● corporate (with $1 billion or above annual revenues), $30,000 (annual). **Staff:** 2. **Budget:** $300,000. **Description:** Works to foster and promote the growth of online communication and electronic commerce worldwide through legislative advocacy and professional services. Works with individuals and companies involved in the creation, management, and growth of computer-based, remote-access communication systems, including internet and online services. **Special Interest Groups:** Education; ISP; Legal and Legislative Issues; Media and Publishing; Online Services. **Publications:** *AOP Code of Professional Standards.* Booklet ● *USIIA Bulletin*, 40/year. **Price:** $150.00/year. **Conventions/Meetings:** annual conference and board meeting.

Computers

894 ■ ACM SIGGRAPH
PO Box 11414
New York, NY 10286-1414
Ph: (212)626-0500 (212)626-0510
Free: (800)342-6626
Fax: (212)944-1318
E-mail: acmhelp@acm.org
URL: http://www.siggraph.org
Contact: Alyn Rockwood, VP
Members: 7,000. **Membership Dues:** regular, $35 (annual) ● full-time student, $25 (annual) ● Eurographics, $28 (annual). **Multinational. Description:** Diverse group of researchers, artists, developers, filmmakers, scientists, and other professionals who share an interest in computer graphics and interactive techniques. Values integrity, passion, excellence, volunteerism and cross-disciplinary interaction. Sponsors annual SIGGRAPH conference, focused symposia, chapters in cities throughout the world, awards, grants, educational resources, online resources, a public policy program, traveling art show, and the SIGGRAPH Video Review. **Libraries: Type:** reference. **Subjects:** digital library. **Awards:** Computer Graphics Achievement Award. **Frequency:** annual. **Type:** recognition. **Recipient:** for outstanding achievement in computer graphics and interactive techniques ● Outstanding Service Award. **Frequency:** biennial. **Type:** recognition. **Recipient:** for extraordinary service to SIGGRAPH by a volunteer ● Significant New Researcher Award. **Frequency:** annual. **Type:** recognition. **Recipient:** for a researcher who made a recent significant contribution to the field of computer graphics ● Steven A. Coons Award. **Frequency:** biennial. **Type:** recognition. **Recipient:** for lifetime contribution to computer graphics and interactive techniques. **Affiliated With:** Association for Computing Machinery. **Formerly:** (2003) National Computer Graphics Association. **Publications:** *Computer Graphics*, quarterly. Newsletter. Alternate Formats: online ● *SIGGRAPH Video Review*. Lists video and DVD publication. Alternate Formats: online ● Annual Report, annual. Alternate Formats: online. **Conventions/Meetings:** annual conference (exhibits) - 2008 Aug. 11-15, Los Angeles, CA ● seminar ● symposium ● workshop.

895 ■ American Association of Computer Rental Professionals (AACRP)
Adams Hill Rd., Box 34
South Newfane, VT 05351
Free: (877)846-6404
E-mail: info@american-computer-rentals.org
URL: http://www.american-computer-rentals.org
Contact: Marilyn Whitehead, Exec. Dir.
Founded: 1997. **Description:** Provides meeting planners, conference organizers, trade show consultants and temporary staffing agencies with techniques and resources for planning PC and laptop rental needs and other related equipment for all purposes. Represents computer rental retailers and wholesalers from across the United States. Develops standards to help end users plan, track and measure results of service. **Computer Services:** database, certified vendors.

896 ■ American Association of Webmasters (AAWM)
7017 Litchfield Rd., No. 331
Glendale, AZ 85307
Ph: (623)202-5613
E-mail: info@aawebmasters.com
URL: http://www.aawebmasters.com
Contact: Donna Snyder, CEO/Founder
Founded: 2002. **Membership Dues:** regular, $49 (annual) ● deluxe, $79 (annual) ● life, $19. **Description:** Represents individuals committed to providing quality websites that are of a positive and informative nature to the Internet community. Advances the profession of website creation and management. Facilitates communication and cooperation among members. **Awards:** Bronze Award. **Frequency:** annual. **Type:** recognition. **Recipient:** for website with good layout and design and is user friendly for its visitors ● Gold Award. **Frequency:** annual. **Type:** recognition. **Recipient:** for website with original design, graphics and material ● Silver Award. **Frequency:** annual. **Type:** recognition. **Recipient:** for website with interesting content and is user friendly ● Site of the Year Award. **Frequency:** annual. **Type:** recognition. **Recipient:** for outstanding website design. **Publications:** Newsletter, monthly. Alternate Formats: online ● Brochure. Alternate Formats: online.

897 ■ Association of Service and Computer Dealers International (ASCDI)
131 NW 1st Ave.
Delray Beach, FL 33444
Ph: (561)266-9016
Fax: (561)266-9017
E-mail: jmarion@ascdi.com
URL: http://www.ascdi.com
Contact: Joseph Marion, Pres.
Founded: 1981. **Members:** 160. **Membership Dues:** regular, $900 (annual). **Staff:** 3. **Description:** Dealers, brokers, and lessors of computer hardware, who emphasize mid-range systems such as the IBM AS/400, S/38, and S/36. Enforces the code of ethics established by the Computer Dealers and Lessors Association. **Committees:** Ethics; Industry Relations. **Formerly:** American Society of Computer Dealers. **Publications:** Membership Directory, periodic. **Conventions/Meetings:** semiannual conference - always spring and fall.

898 ■ Computing Technology Industry Association (CompTIA)
1815 S Meyers Rd., Ste.300
Oakbrook Terrace, IL 60181-5228
Ph: (630)678-8300
Fax: (630)678-8384
E-mail: information@comptia.org
URL: http://www.comptia.org
Contact: John Venator, Pres./CEO
Founded: 1982. **Members:** 22,000. **Staff:** 150. **Budget:** $53,000,000. **For-Profit. Description:** Trade association of more than 19,000 companies and professional IT members in the rapidly converging computing and communications market. Has members in more than 89 countries and provides a unified voice for the industry in the areas of e-commerce standards, vendor-neutral certification, service metrics, public policy and workforce development. Serves as information clearinghouse and resource for the industry; sponsors educational programs. **Computer Services:** database, research companies providing information to the computer industry. **Sections:** Certification; Document Management; E-commerce; IT Services; Public Policy; Workforce Development. **Task Forces:** Electronic Commerce. **Absorbed:** (1990) Computer Industry Council. **Formerly:** Association of Better Computer Dealers; ABCD: The Microcomputer Industry Association. **Publications:** *Computing Channels*, monthly. Magazine. Covers emerging technologies and industry trends. **Circulation:** 19,000. Alternate Formats: online ● Membership Directory, annual. **Conventions/Meetings:** annual Breakaway - conference (exhibits).

899 ■ Distributed Computing Industry Association (DCIA)
2838 Cox Neck Rd., Ste.200
Chester, MD 21619
Ph: (410)476-7965
E-mail: info@dcia.info
URL: http://www.dcia.info
Contact: Marty Lafferty, CEO
Description: Engages in the development and adoption of business and technical standards and practices to advance the commercial development of online consumer-based distribution systems. Represents all sectors of the distributed computing industry, including content providers, software developers/distributors and service-and-support companies. **Publications:** *DCINFO*, weekly. Newsletter. Alternate Formats: online.

900 ■ Geospatial Information and Technology Association (GITA)
14456 E Evans Ave.
Aurora, CO 80014
Ph: (303)337-0513
Fax: (303)337-1001
E-mail: info@gita.org
URL: http://www.gita.org
Contact: Robert M. Samborski, Exec. Dir.
Founded: 1982. **Members:** 2,200. **Membership Dues:** individual, $125 (annual) ● student, $25 (annual) ● individual (with Geo Tech Report), $429 (annual). **Staff:** 11. **Budget:** $2,000,000. **Regional Groups:** 17. **Languages:** English, Spanish. **Description:** Represents utilities, government, oil and gas companies, and the telecommunications industry; vendors, service companies, and consultants. Focuses on excellence in geospatial information technologies. Promotes education and the exchange of information in the industry. Maintains speakers' bureau. **Libraries: Type:** open to the public. **Holdings:** reports. **Subjects:** GIS, AM/FM, SCADA. **Awards:** Ed Forrest Education Program. **Frequency:** annual. **Type:** scholarship. **Recipient:** for studies in the field of GIS. **Computer Services:** Mailing lists ● online services, membership list. **Telecommunication Services:** electronic mail, bsamborski@gita.org. **Committees:** Chapter Relations; Conference; Education; Membership. **Formerly:** (1998) AM/FM International. **Publications:** *Annual Conference Proceedings*, annual ● *Geospatial Technology Report*. **Price:** $259.00 for members; $399.00 for nonmembers ● *GIS for Oil and Gas Conference*. Proceedings ● *GITA—Membership Directory*, annual. Lists individual and corporate members with descriptions of each company or project. **Price:** free for members ● *Networks*, bimonthly. Newsletter. Includes user profiles, survey results, industry news, association news, and product information. **Price:** free for members. **Circulation:** 2,200. **Advertising:** accepted. Alternate Formats: online ● Also publishes conference and symposium proceedings. **Conventions/Meetings:** annual conference, educational sessions for the AM/FM/GIS industry (exhibits).

901 ■ HTML Writers Guild (HWG)
119 E Union St., Ste.F
Pasadena, CA 91103
E-mail: help@iwanet.org
URL: http://www.hwg.org
Contact: Richard Brinegar, Exec. Dir.
Founded: 1998. **Members:** 123,000. **Membership Dues:** full, $49 (annual). **National Groups:** 150. **Multinational. Description:** Web authors, including beginners, hobbyists, students, and professionals. Supports network dedicated to providing resources, support, and representation to Internet web creators. Offers online classes. **Computer Services:** Mailing lists. **Publications:** *HWG-News*, monthly. Newsletter. Contains information important to members such as new services and new mailing lists. Alternate Formats: online.

902 ■ Independent Computer Consultants Association (ICCA)
11131 S Towne Sq., Ste.F
St. Louis, MO 63123
Ph: (314)892-1675
Free: (800)774-4222
Fax: (314)487-1345
E-mail: info@icca.org
URL: http://www.icca.org
Contact: Joyce Burkard, Exec. Dir.
Founded: 1976. **Members:** 1,200. **Membership Dues:** consultant, associate, $200 (annual) ● individual (chapter), $50-$100 (annual). **Staff:** 3. **Budget:** $350,000. **Local Groups:** 20. **Description:** Provides a national network of independent computer consultants. Supports the success of independent computer consultants in providing professional services to clients. Members objectively support the best computer or software solutions in all areas of the computer industry, from hardware design to systems integration to employee training. Membership is open to individuals, partnerships, and corporations providing consulting assistance in computer related areas. **Telecommunication Services:** electronic mail, execdirector@icca.org. **Committees:** Communications; Education; External Relations; Government Relations. **Publications:** *The Independent*, bimonthly. Newsletter. **Price:** included in membership dues. **Advertising:** accepted ● *Tax and Handbook for Consultants and Clients*. **Conventions/Meetings:** annual conference (exhibits).

903 ■ Information Storage Industry Consortium (INSIC)
3655 Ruffin Rd., Ste.335
San Diego, CA 92123-1833
Ph: (858)279-7230
Fax: (858)279-8591
E-mail: insic@insic.org
URL: http://www.insic.org
Contact: Dr. Paul D. Frank, Exec. Dir.
Founded: 1991. **Membership Dues:** associate, $500 (annual) ● limited, $5,000 (annual) ● government organization, $22,000 (annual) ● corporate (less than or equal to $1 billion annual gross revenues), $11,000 (annual) ● non-storage company (greater than $1 billion annual gross corporate revenues), $22,000 (annual) ● storage company (greater than $1 billion annual gross corporate revenues), $55,000 (annual). **Staff:** 7. **Description:** Brings together companies and universities involved in computer data storage research, united to accomplish mutual goals. Creates and manages joint precompetitive research programs among its members. Performs studies to develop long-term roadmaps for various data storage technologies. **Programs:** Advanced Magnetic Tape Storage Technology Research; Data Storage Devices and Systems Research; Extremely High Density Recording Research; Heat Assisted Magnetic Recording Research. **Formerly:** National Storage Industry Consortium. **Publications:** *NSIC News*, 3/year. Newsletter. **Conventions/Meetings:** annual meeting ● periodic meeting ● quarterly meeting.

904 ■ Information Technology Industry Council (ITI)
1250 Eye St. NW, Ste.200
Washington, DC 20005
Ph: (202)737-8888
Fax: (202)638-4922
E-mail: rdawson@itic.org
URL: http://www.itic.org
Contact: Rhett Dawson, Pres./CEO
Founded: 1916. **Members:** 28. **Staff:** 30. **Budget:** $3,000,000. **Description:** Represents manufacturers of information technology products. Serves as secretariat and technology for ANSI-accredited standards committee x3 information technology group. Conducts public policy programs; compiles industry statistics. **Awards:** Public Policy Award. **Frequency:** annual. **Type:** recognition. **Telecommunication Services:** electronic mail, kkriner@itic.org. **Committees:** Electronic Commerce; Federal IT; Intellectual Property; Regulatory Policy; Tax; Telecommunications; Trade Policy; Workforce. **Formerly:** (1961) Office Equipment Manufacturers Institute; (1972) Business Equipment Manufacturers Association; (1994) Computer and Business Equipment Manufacturers Association. **Publications:** *Issue Brief*, periodic. **Price:** available on request ● *Washington Letter*, biweekly. Newsletter ● Annual Report, annual. **Price:** free ● Directory, annual. **Price:** available to members only. **Conventions/Meetings:** semiannual meeting.

905 ■ International Association for Computer Systems Security (IACSS)
6 Swathmore Ln.
Dix Hills, NY 11746
Ph: (631)499-1616
Fax: (631)462-9178
E-mail: iacssjalex@aol.com
URL: http://iacss.com
Contact: Robert J. Wilk CSSP, Pres./Founder
Founded: 1981. **Members:** 800. **Staff:** 14. **Budget:** $400,000. **Regional Groups:** 3. **Description:** Organizations and individuals in 32 countries interested in the security of their computerized information systems. Offers a testing program to certify individuals as Computer Systems Security Professionals; upholds a code of professional ethics. Supports continuing education through workshops; furthers awareness of security issues both within the industry and the government. Conducts in-house management security awareness programs and monthly seminars and workshops; distributes information on state-of-the-art methods of protecting computer and communication resources. Maintains speakers' bureau, sponsors lectures, and compiles statistics. Presents Distinguished Service Award. **Divisions:** Computer Systems Security Consulting and Design; Computer Systems Security Education and Training. **Task Forces:** Biometric Access Control Systems; Communicating Systems; Computer-Related Crime Legislation; Computer Virus Control; Contingency Planning for Back-Up and Disaster Recovery; Data and Software Security; Data Privacy Legislation; EDP Audit and Control; Hardware Security; Office Automation Security; Organizing and Administering the EDP Security Program; PC Security and Control; Personal Computer Controls; Physical Access Controls; Risk Management; Transitional Data Flow. **Publications:** *Computer Systems Security Newsletter*, quarterly ● *Proceedings Regional 1 IACSS Conference*, periodic ● *Proceedings Regional 2 IACSS Conference*, periodic ● *Security and Control of Your PC/Micro Network*. Book ● Brochures ● Papers. **Conventions/Meetings:** Network Security, Audit and Control - workshop and regional meeting - 8/year.

906 ■ Internet Society
1775 Wiehle Ave., Ste.102
Reston, VA 20190-5109
Ph: (703)326-9880
Fax: (703)326-9881
E-mail: info@isoc.org
URL: http://www.isoc.org
Contact: Lynn St. Amour, Pres.
Founded: 1992. **Members:** 14,000. **Membership Dues:** non-profit - professional, $1,250 (annual) ● for-profit organization - professional, $2,500 (annual) ● non-profit - principal, $2,500 (annual) ● for-profit organization - principal, $5,000 (annual) ● non-profit - executive, $5,000 (annual) ● for-profit organization - executive, $10,000 (annual) ● start-up organization, $1,000 (annual) ● for-profit sustaining gold, $50,000 (annual) ● non-profit sustaining gold, $25,000 (annual) ● patron, $500 (annual) ● benefactor, $250 (annual) ● supporter, $125 (annual) ● contributor, $75 (annual). **Staff:** 7. **Budget:** $5,000,000. **Regional Groups:** 81. **Languages:** English, French. **Description:** Technologists, developers, educators, researchers, government representatives, and business people. Seeks to ensure global cooperation and coordination for the Internet and related internetworking technologies and applications. Supports the development and dissemination of standards for the Internet. Promotes the growth of Internet architecture and Internet-related education and research. Encourages assistance to technologically developing countries in implementing local Internet infrastructures. **Awards:** Jonathan B. Postel Memorial Service Award. **Frequency:** annual. **Type:** monetary. **Recipient:** for an individual who has made outstanding contributions in service to the data communications community. **Boards:** Internet Architecture. **Task Forces:** Internet Engineering; Internet Research. **Publications:** *ISOC Forum*, monthly. Newsletter. Contains information on Internet and industry developments. **Price:** included in membership dues. Alternate Formats: online ● *ISP Column*. Article. Alternate Formats: online. **Conventions/Meetings:** annual conference, premier international event for Internet and internet-working professionals (exhibits) ● annual Symposium on Network and Distributed System Security - conference - usually February/March.

907 ■ North American Computer Service Association (NACSA)
Address Unknown since 2007
Founded: 1982. **Members:** 1,000. **Membership Dues:** individual, companies, associates, $50 (annual). **Staff:** 10. **Budget:** $250,000. **Languages:** English, Spanish. **For-Profit. Description:** Computer service and repair companies; suppliers to the industry; computer repair schools; professional consultants. Promotes orderly growth for the computer service industry and assists members with tasks such as contract negotiation, training, legislative liaison, and parts and supplies purchasing. Maintains placement service members and acquisition. **Libraries: Type:** open to the public. **Holdings:** 5,000. **Subjects:** business management, computer, software. **Awards:** Annual Good Business Award. **Frequency:** annual. **Type:** recognition. **Recipient:** excellence. **Committees:** Education; Legislative; National Accreditation Council (NAC). **Absorbed:** (1982) International Association Service Companies. **Publications:** *Readout Computer Service and Repair (Magazine)*, monthly. Newsletter. **Price:** included in membership; $15.00/year nonmembers. **Circulation:** 5,000. **Advertising:** accepted ● *Technical Bulletins*, periodic ● Also publishes market letters, consulting studies and sponsored research. **Conventions/Meetings:** annual conference, members and associates (exhibits) - always 1st weekend in November ● quarterly regional meeting.

908 ■ Portable Computer and Communications Association (PCCA)
PO Box 680
Hood River, OR 97031
Ph: (541)490-5140
Fax: (419)831-4779
E-mail: pcca@pcca.org
URL: http://www.pcca.org
Contact: Gloria Kowalski, Dir.
Founded: 1993. **Membership Dues:** associate, $2,500 (annual) ● executive, $5,000 (annual) ● affiliate, $750 (annual) ● individual, $100 (annual). **Description:** Messaging, paging, and wireless networks; software developers and vendors. Promotes development of software and hardware standards for interoperable mobile computing and communications. Represents members' interests. Conducts research and educational programs. **Committees:** Mobile Connectivity; Standards. **Publications:** *PCCA Newsletter*, bimonthly. Alternate Formats: online. **Conventions/Meetings:** quarterly board meeting.

909 ■ Professional Association for SQL Server (PASS)
203 N LaSalle, Ste.2100
Chicago, IL 60601
Ph: (604)899-6009
Fax: (604)899-1269
E-mail: info@sqlpass.org
URL: http://www.sqlpass.org
Contact: Kevin Kline, Pres.
Membership Dues: premium, $150 (annual). **Staff:** 14. **Description:** Committed to providing a forum for education, facilitate networking, and influence the direction of SQL Server and related products and services. **Publications:** *SQL Server Standard*, bimonthly. Journal. **Price:** $24.99 in U.S.; $39.99 in Canada; $46.99 outside U.S. and Canada. **Advertising:** accepted. Alternate Formats: online.

910 ■ RSPA
4115 Taggart Creek Rd.
Charlotte, NC 28208-5479
Ph: (704)357-3124
Fax: (704)357-3127
E-mail: info@gorspa.org
URL: http://www.rspassn.org
Contact: Joe Finizio, Exec. Dir.
Founded: 1948. **Members:** 480. **Membership Dues:** company (based on revenue level), $300-$4,000 (annual) ● associate, $300 (annual). **Staff:** 30. **Budget:** $20,000,000. **Description:** Independent dealers who sell and service cash registers and computerized point-of-sale systems. Seeks to have manufacturers distribute their products through dealer organizations, rather than through individually established sales organizations. Furnishes sales and service aids to members; conducts management, sales, and service seminars; maintains speakers' bureau. Operates Parts Center, which offers cash register equipment and POS parts to members and non-members. **Awards: Type:** recognition ● RSPA Scholarship Fund. **Frequency:** annual. **Type:** scholarship. **Recipient:** for children and grandchildren of members and their employees. **Telecommunication Services:** electronic mail, jfinizio@gorspa.org. **Formerly:** (2002) Retail Solutions Providers Association; (2004) IRCDA/SDA. **Publications:** *RSPA Connect*, 10/year. Journal. Provides industry and association news, and new product information. **Advertising:** accepted. Alternate Formats: online ● *RSPA Membership Directory*, annual. **Conventions/Meetings:** annual convention (exhibits).

911 ■ United States Internet Service Provider Association (US ISPA)
c/o Kate Dean
700 12th St. NW, Ste.700E
Washington, DC 20005
Ph: (202)904-2351
E-mail: kdean@usispa.org
URL: http://www.usispa.org
Contact: Kate Dean, Contact
Founded: 1991. **Members:** 150. **Membership Dues:** partial, $15,000 (annual) ● full, $25,000 (annual). **Staff:** 6. **Description:** Consists of Public Data Internetwork service providers united to promote and encourage development of the public data communications internetworking services industry. Provides a neutral forum for the exchange of ideas and information. Serves as a clearinghouse of resources. Develops positions on legislative and policy issues of interest to members. Assists member networks in the establishment of, and adherence to, operational, technical, and administrative policies and standards necessary to ensure fair, open, and competitive operations and communication. **Councils:** Security. **Working Groups:** Policy. **Formerly:** (2004) Commercial Internet Exchange Association. **Conventions/Meetings:** periodic meeting.

912 ■ VITA
PO Box 19658
Fountain Hills, AZ 85269
Ph: (480)837-7486
E-mail: info@vita.com
URL: http://www.vita.com
Contact: Ray Alderman, Exec. Dir.
Founded: 1984. **Members:** 130. **Membership Dues:** regular, $2,500 (annual) ● sponsor, $25,000 (annual). **Staff:** 3. **Description:** Represents vendors and users that are having common market interest in real-time, modular embedded computing systems. Has accredited as an American National Standards Institute (ANSI) developer and a submitter of Industry Trade Agreements to the IEC. Provides its members with the ability to develop and to promote open technology standards.

Concrete

913 ■ American Concrete Pavement Association (ACPA)
500 New Jersey Ave. NW, 7th Fl.
Washington, DC 20001
Ph: (202)638-2272
Fax: (202)638-2688
E-mail: acpa@pavement.com
URL: http://www.pavement.com
Contact: Gerald Voigt PE, Pres.
Founded: 1964. **Members:** 750. **Staff:** 20. **Regional Groups:** 20. **Description:** Contractors, cement companies, equipment manufacturers, material service suppliers, ready mixed concrete producers, consultants, trucking companies/material haulers and others allied with the concrete pavement industry. Advocates the use of concrete pavement for highways, airports, streets, and roads. **Awards:** Excellence in Concrete Pavements Awards. **Frequency:** annual. **Type:** recognition. **Recipient:** for contractors, engineers and owners ● Hartmann-Hirschman Award. **Frequency:** annual. **Type:** recognition. **Recipient:** for outstanding leadership and dedication to advancing the use of concrete pavements. **Publications:** *Concrete Pavement Progress*, bimonthly. Newsletter. **Conventions/Meetings:** annual convention.

914 ■ American Concrete Pumping Association (ACPA)
606 Enterprise Dr.
Lewis Center, OH 43035-9432
Ph: (614)431-5618
Fax: (614)431-6944
E-mail: christi@concretepumpers.com
URL: http://www.concretepumpers.com
Contact: Christi Collins, Exec. Dir.
Founded: 1974. **Members:** 450. **Membership Dues:** trailer pump (0-6 units; plus $20/additional pump), $300 (annual) ● boom pump (1 pump; plus $35/additional boom pump), $335 (annual) ● line pump (add $20/line), $335 (annual) ● distributor of concrete pumps/equipment, $665 (annual) ● boom manufacturer, $4,000 (annual) ● small line pump manufacturer, $2,000 (annual) ● systems and parts manufacturer, $1,600 (annual) ● affiliated professional, $500 (annual) ● individual, $125 (annual). **Staff:** 4. **Budget:** $500,000. **Description:** Concrete pumping companies; manufacturers, distributors, and suppliers of concrete pumps and related services; architects, ready-mix suppliers, engineers, testing labs, and allied persons. Seeks to: increase the use of concrete pumping; improve the conditions under which it is utilized; promote goodwill within the industry and with the public. Promotes safety precautions. **Libraries: Type:** open to the public. **Awards:** Richard E. Henry Award. **Frequency:** annual. **Type:** recognition. **Recipient:** for an industry person promoting concrete pumping industry ● Safe ACPA Certified Operator of the Year. **Frequency:** annual. **Type:** recognition. **Recipient:** for service and promotion of concrete pumping. **Computer Services:** database, member certification ● mailing lists, of members ● online services, certification. **Committees:** Chapters; Finance; Manufacturing; Marketing; Members; Methods; Safety; Standards. **Supersedes:** Concrete Pumpers Association of Southern California. **Publications:** *ACPA Safety Videos*. **Price:** $20.00 for members. **Advertising:** accepted ● *Concrete Pumping*, quarterly. Magazine. Promotes concrete pumping. **Price:** included in membership dues. **Circulation:** 10,000. **Advertising:** accepted ● *Safety Books* ● *The Update*, bimonthly. Newsletter. **Price:** included in membership dues ● Booklets. **Conventions/Meetings:** annual World of Concrete - seminar and board meeting (exhibits) - usually January.

915 ■ American Portland Cement Association (APCA)
1330 Connecticut Ave. NW, Ste.1250
Washington, DC 20036
Ph: (202)408-9494
Fax: (202)408-0877
E-mail: info@apca.com
Contact: Richard C. Creighton, Pres.
Founded: 1985. **Members:** 44. **Staff:** 13. **Budget:** $2,400,000. **Description:** Manufacturers of Portland cement. Conducts governmental affairs activities. Compiles statistics. **Committees:** Political Action. **Formerly:** American Cement Trade Alliance; (1993) American Cement Alliance; (2005) American Portland Cement Alliance. **Conventions/Meetings:** annual Political Partners for Concrete Results - conference, cement and concrete industry government affairs conference - always in Washington, DC.

916 ■ American Shotcrete Association (ASA)
38800 Country Club Dr.
Farmington Hills, MI 48331
Ph: (248)848-3780
Fax: (248)848-3740
E-mail: info@shotcrete.org
URL: http://www.shotcrete.org
Contact: Thomas H. Adams, Exec. Dir.
Founded: 1998. **Members:** 200. **Membership Dues:** organization, $750 (annual) ● individual, $250 (annual) ● employee of public authority and agency, $50 (annual). **Staff:** 2. **Budget:** $300,000. **Description:** Represents professionals and companies within the shotcrete industry. Promotes the use of shotcrete by educating, encouraging, and supporting all persons and organizations benefiting from the use of this concrete placement method. Focuses on providing current and accurate information to all in the industry who wish to improve the quality and expand the use of shotcrete. **Libraries: Type:** open to the public. **Publications:** *Shotcrete Magazine*, quarterly. Features case studies, technical articles, news of the shotcrete industry, and new product information. **Circulation:** 5,000. **Advertising:** accepted ● Manual (in English, French, and Spanish). **Price:** $3.00 for members; $5.00 for nonmembers. **Conventions/Meetings:** semiannual board meeting and executive committee meeting - always spring and fall ● annual meeting, held in conjunction with the World of Concrete.

917 ■ Architectural Precast Association (APA)
6710 Winkler Rd., Ste.8
Fort Myers, FL 33919
Ph: (239)454-6989
Fax: (239)454-6787
E-mail: info@archprecast.org
URL: http://www.archprecast.org
Contact: Fred L. McGee, Exec. Dir.
Founded: 1966. **Members:** 260. **Membership Dues:** producer (based on annual gross sales), $4,600-$7,100 (annual) ● associate, $1,500 (annual) ● professional, $750 (annual). **Description:** Manufacturers and suppliers of precast concrete elements for building construction. Promotes the dissemination of educational materials related to the manufacture and use of precast concrete; encourages interest in precast concrete throughout the construction industry; advocates the adoption of the standards and specifications of the association. **Awards:** APA Award for Design and Manufacturing Excellence. **Frequency:** annual. **Type:** recognition. **Recipient:** for members ● Tom Cory Memorial Scholarship. **Frequency:** annual. **Type:** scholarship. **Recipient:** for members/students. **Committees:** Awards; Certification; Education; Promotion; Technical. **Publications:** *Architectural Impressions*, annual. Magazine ● *Architectural Precaster*, bimonthly. Newsletter. **Price:** available to members only ● *Material of Choice*. Video ● Membership Directory, annual. **Conventions/Meetings:** annual convention - usually in March ● annual Fall Production - workshop - usually September or October.

918 ■ Autoclaved Aerated Concrete Products Association (AACPA)
3701 County Rd. 544 E
Haines City, FL 33844
Ph: (863)422-6360
Fax: (863)419-2068
E-mail: info@aacpa.org
URL: http://www.aacpa.org
Contact: Jeannie Taylor, Membership Chair
Founded: 1999. **Members:** 30. **Membership Dues:** producer/associate, $25,000 (annual) ● major supplier, $2,500 (annual) ● supplier, $1,000 (annual) ● non-supplier, $500 (annual). **Staff:** 3. **Description:** Promotes the autoclaved aerated concrete products industry.

919 ■ Cast Stone Institute (CSI)
PO Box 68
Lebanon, PA 17042
Ph: (717)272-3744
Fax: (717)272-5147
E-mail: staff@caststone.org
URL: http://www.caststone.org
Contact: Jan Boyer, Exec. Dir.
Founded: 1917. **Members:** 41. **Membership Dues:** associate, $500 (annual) ● producer, $5,000 (annual). **Staff:** 11. **Budget:** $70,000. **Description:** Architects, engineers, cast stone manufacturers, and concrete technologists. Works to improve the quality and promote the use of cast stone, a refined architectural precast building stone. Conducts educational and research programs. **Awards:** Design and Manufacturing Excellence. **Frequency:** annual. **Type:** recognition. **Recipient:** for excellence in design and manufacturing of cast stone elements. **Committees:** AIA Project; Design Competition; Educational Standards/Website; Ethics; Plant Certification; Promotion; Strategic Planning; Technical. **Publications:** *Cast in Stone*, quarterly. Newsletter. **Conventions/Meetings:** semiannual conference and board meeting.

920 ■ Cement Employers Association (CEA)
122 E Broad St., 2nd Fl.
Bethlehem, PA 18018
Ph: (610)868-8060
Fax: (610)861-2884
E-mail: emcgehee@cementemployers.com
Contact: Elton McGehee, Exec. Dir.
Founded: 1936. **Members:** 32. **Staff:** 2. **Budget:** $250,000. **Description:** Cement companies. Aims to improve labor and employee relations. **Libraries: Type:** reference. **Conventions/Meetings:** annual conference.

921 ■ Concrete Anchor Manufacturers Association (CAMA)
136 S Main St., No. 2E
St. Charles, MO 63301
Ph: (314)889-7116
Fax: (314)725-6592
E-mail: info@concreteanchors.org
URL: http://www.concreteanchors.org
Contact: James A. Burchers, Exec. Dir.
Founded: 1994. **Members:** 21. **Membership Dues:** manufacturer, $3,150 (annual) ● associate-technical/professional, $315 (annual) ● associate-institution/regular, $30 (annual). **Staff:** 2. **Budget:** $50,000. **Description:** Provides a unified voice for the concrete anchoring industry; strives to advance the uses of anchoring systems; develops uniform codes and standards; and provides a forum for industry concerns.

922 ■ Concrete Corrosion Inhibitors Association (CCIA)
11836 Goya Dr.
Potomac, MD 20854
Ph: (301)340-7368
E-mail: info@corrosioninhibitors.org
URL: http://www.corrosioninhibitors.org
Contact: Arnie Rosenberg, Exec. Dir.
Founded: 1999. **Members:** 6. **Staff:** 3. **Multinational. Description:** Promotes the use and understanding of corrosion-inhibiting admixtures in concrete. **Publications:** Newsletter. Alternate Formats: online.

923 ■ Concrete Sawing and Drilling Association (CSDA)
11001 Danka Way N, Ste.1
St. Petersburg, FL 33716
Ph: (727)577-5004
Fax: (727)577-5012
E-mail: info@csda.org
URL: http://www.csda.org
Contact: Patrick O'Brien, Exec. Dir.
Founded: 1972. **Members:** 500. **Membership Dues:** contractor (based on gross sales), $505-$2,650 (annual) ● manufacturer, $1,050-$5,300 (annual) ● distributor, $780-$2,375 (annual) ● overseas contractor, $345 (annual) ● affiliate, $605 (annual). **Staff:** 4. **Budget:** $900,000. **Multinational. Description:** Contractors, manufacturers, and affiliated members from the concrete construction and renovation industry. Promotes the use of professional sawing and drilling contractors and their methods. Believes that concrete cutting with diamond tools offers the industry many benefits, including reduced downtime, precision cutting, maintenance of structural integrity, reduced noise, dust and debris, limited-access cutting, and the ability to cut heavily reinforced concrete. **Libraries: Type:** reference. **Holdings:** articles, books, periodicals, reports, video recordings. **Computer Services:** database, concrete cutting firms and specifiers ● mailing lists. **Telecommunication Services:** electronic mail, pat@csda.org. **Committees:** Convention; Election; International; Long Range Planning; Manufacturer; Marketing; Safety; Standards and Specifications; Training. **Publications:** *Concrete Openings*, quarterly. Magazine. Features job stories to demonstrate the capabilities of diamond tools in cutting concrete. **Price:** included in membership dues. ISSN: 1093-6483. **Circulation:** 15,000. **Advertising:** accepted. Alternate Formats: online ● *Resource Guide & Membership Directory*, annual. **Circulation:** 10,000. **Conventions/Meetings:** quarterly board meeting ● annual convention, with technology fair (exhibits).

924 ■ Concrete Tile Manufacturers Association (CTMA)
PO Box 6225
Buena Park, CA 90622
Ph: (714)535-0791
Free: (800)970-2862
Fax: (714)535-0244
E-mail: themfg@gmail.com
URL: http://www.concretetile.org
Description: Represents individuals and businesses involved in the manufacture and supply of concrete tile products and services. Promotes the use of concrete tile products through research, educational activities and marketing. **Publications:** *Concrete Tile Tales*. Newsletter ● *CTMA Technical Bulletin*.

925 ■ Insulating Concrete Form Association (ICFA)
1730 Dewes St., Ste.No. 2
Glenview, IL 60025
Ph: (847)657-9730
Free: (888)864-4232
Fax: (847)657-9728
E-mail: icfa@forms.org
URL: http://www.forms.org
Contact: Kent Stumpe, Chm.
Founded: 1995. **Membership Dues:** associate, $3,000 (annual) ● contributing associate, $5,000 (annual) ● ready-mix, $500 (annual) ● distributor, $250 (annual) ● contractor, $200 (annual) ● professional, $350 (annual). **Description:** Promotes the use of insulating concrete form system. Supports the development of industry standards for insulating concrete forms. **Awards:** Excellence Award. **Frequency:** annual. **Type:** recognition. **Recipient:** for significant contribution to the ICF industry. **Computer Services:** database, leads ● database, member list ● information services, insulating concrete forms resources. **Publications:** *ICFA Dialog*, quarterly. Newsletters. **Price:** included in membership dues. **Advertising:** accepted ● *ICFA Informer*, monthly. Newsletter. Contains industry news and activities. Alternate Formats: online.

926 ■ Interlocking Concrete Pavement Institute (ICPI)
1444 I St. NW, Ste.700
Washington, DC 20005-2210
Ph: (202)712-9036
Fax: (202)408-0285
E-mail: icpi@icpi.org
URL: http://www.icpi.org
Contact: Charles A. McGrath CAE, Exec. Dir.
Founded: 1993. **Members:** 800. **Membership Dues:** contractor, local associate, local dealer (non-voting), $250 (annual) ● design professional, informational (non-voting), $500 (annual) ● dealer, $1,000 (annual) ● international contractor (non-voting), $1,500 (annual) ● associate in North America (voting, based on annual sales), $2,000-$10,000 (annual) ● producer in U.S., Canada and Mexico (voting, based on number of machines), $2,000-$25,000 (annual). **Staff:** 6. **Budget:** $1,400,000. **Multinational. Description:** Producers, contractors and suppliers to the interlocking concrete pavement industry. Develops product and installation specifications for concrete pavers, contractor certification programs, and curriculum for training installers and university students. Provides technical support to design professionals. **Libraries: Type:** reference. **Holdings:** 1,100; articles, books. **Subjects:** interlocking concrete pavements. **Committees:** Construction; Dues/By-Laws/Membership; Executive; Expo/Convention; Marketing; Technical. **Publications:** *Activities Update*, biennial. Newsletter. Contains membership news. **Advertising:** accepted ● *Interlocking Concrete Pavement Magazine*, quarterly. Contains industry news, technical articles, and summaries of technical papers. **Price:** free. **Circulation:** 21,000. **Advertising:** accepted. Alternate Formats: online ● Manuals. Covers designs for street, port, industrial, and airport pavements. ● Membership Directory, annual ● Also publishes brochures and technical manuals series on design, installation, and maintenance of interlocking concrete pavements. **Conventions/Meetings:** annual meeting - usually February ● meeting - usually late summer or early fall ● triennial Sustainable Paving for Our Future - conference.

927 ■ International Concrete Repair Institute (ICRI)
3166 S River Rd., Ste.132
Des Plaines, IL 60018
Ph: (847)827-0830
Fax: (847)827-0832
E-mail: kelly.page@icri.org
URL: http://www.icri.org
Contact: Marty Sobelman, Pres.
Founded: 1988. **Members:** 1,400. **Membership Dues:** supporting, $2,915 (annual) ● distributor, consultant, $325 (annual) ● architect and manufacturer's representative, $180 (annual) ● individual, government agency, union, facility owner, $150 (annual) ● government employee and educator, $80 (annual) ● student, union apprentice, $35 (annual) ● contractor/manufacturer (based on annual gross income), $325-$1,750 (annual). **Staff:** 7. **Budget:** $580,000. **Local Groups:** 21. **Description:** Contractors, manufacturers, suppliers, engineers, architects, consultants, distributors, and manufacturing representatives. Develops guidelines for the concrete repair industry. Conducts educational programs. Maintains speakers' bureau. Operates technical activity committees. **Libraries: Type:** reference. **Holdings:** audio recordings, periodicals, video recordings. **Subjects:** concrete repair. **Awards:** Awards for Outstanding Concrete Repair Projects. **Frequency:** annual. **Type:** recognition. **Recipient:** for uniqueness, use of state-of-the art methods and technology, use of materials, functionality, value engineering, and aesthetics. **Boards:** Directors. **Committees:** Administrative; Awards; Coatings and Water Proofing; Corrosion; Education; Fellows; Technical. **Formerly:** (1993) International Association of Concrete Repair Specialists. **Publications:** *Concrete Repair Bulletin*, bimonthly. Magazine. Includes association and chapter news, new product information, case histories, technical features, and industry news. **Price:** free. ISSN: 1055-2936. **Circulation:** 14,000. **Advertising:** accepted. Alternate Formats: online ● *Who's Who in Concrete Repair*, annual. Membership Directory. **Circulation:** 2,000. **Advertising:** accepted ● Also issues technical guidelines. **Conventions/Meetings:** semiannual convention (exhibits) - always spring and fall. 2008 Oct. 29-31, St. Louis, MO ● annual meeting.

928 ■ International Grooving and Grinding Association (IGGA)
12573 Rte. 9W
West Coxsackie, NY 12192
Ph: (518)731-7450
Fax: (518)731-7490

E-mail: jroberts@pavement.com
URL: http://www.igga.net
Contact: John Roberts, Exec. Dir.
Founded: 1972. **Members:** 44. **Budget:** $100,000. **Multinational. Description:** Businesses licensed to engage in the pavement grooving and grinding contracting business; manufacturers and suppliers of parts for the industry. Serves highway, airport, and commercial authorities by supplying information, data, and advice on the safety-grooving process and the long-range economy of grinding new pavement to meet required surface tolerances. Makes presentations at technical functions. **Committees:** Educational; Promotional. **Publications:** *Groovers and Grinders*, quarterly. Newsletter. Reports on pavement, grinding, and texturing. **Price:** free for members of the industry. **Circulation:** 3,500 ● *Minutes of Meetings*, quarterly ● Bulletins ● Reports ● Also publishes related literature, specifications, and articles. **Conventions/Meetings:** annual conference (exhibits).

929 ■ National Concrete Masonry Association (NCMA)

13750 Sunrise Valley Dr.
Herndon, VA 20171-4662
Ph: (703)713-1900 (703)713-1908
Fax: (703)713-1910
E-mail: ncma@ncma.org
URL: http://www.ncma.org
Contact: Mark B. Hogan PE, Pres.
Founded: 1918. **Members:** 500. **Membership Dues:** producer (based on the last fiscal year's production), $1,091-$27,254 (annual) ● associate, $2,905-$22,745 (annual) ● international (add $579/additional mailings), $1,577 (annual) ● CM affiliate in U.S. and Canada, $698 (annual) ● CM affiliate outside U.S. and Canada, $803 (annual). **Staff:** 29. **Budget:** $5,000,000. **Languages:** English, Spanish. **Description:** Manufacturers of concrete masonry units (concrete blocks), segmental retaining wall units and paving block; associate members are machinery, cement, and aggregate manufacturers. Conducts testing and research on masonry units and masonry assemblies. Compiles statistics. **Libraries: Type:** reference. **Holdings:** 4,000; articles, books, periodicals, reports. **Subjects:** concrete masonry, masonry engineering, energy conservation. **Awards:** Design Awards of Excellence. **Frequency:** annual. **Type:** monetary ● Honorary Membership. **Frequency:** annual. **Type:** monetary ● **Frequency:** annual. **Type:** scholarship. **Computer Services:** database ● information services, engineered masonry. **Departments:** Publications. **Programs:** Industry Leadership; Information Resources; Peer Interaction; Technical Support. **Formerly:** (1995) Concrete Paver Institute. **Publications:** *CM News*, monthly. Magazine. Focuses on the manufacturing and marketing of concrete masonry products, and the managing of production plants. Includes book reviews. **Price:** free. **Circulation:** 4,500. **Advertising:** accepted. Alternate Formats: CD-ROM; online; magnetic tape ● *Concrete Masonry Designs*. Distributed to architects, engineers and specifiers. **Circulation:** 100,000 ● *NCMA TEK*, monthly. Manual. Features technical publication for architects, engineers, and builders using concrete masonry. **Price:** $100.00 hard copy; $35.00 CD. Alternate Formats: CD-ROM ● Membership Directory. **Price:** $12.00 for members. Alternate Formats: online ● Reports ● Articles. Alternate Formats: online. **Conventions/Meetings:** annual Manufactured Concrete Products Exposition - convention (exhibits).

930 ■ National Precast Concrete Association (NPCA)

10333 N Meridian St., Ste.272
Indianapolis, IN 46290-1081
Ph: (317)571-9500
Free: (800)366-7731
Fax: (317)571-0041
E-mail: bibitz@precast.org
URL: http://www.precast.org
Contact: Ty Gable CAE, Pres.
Founded: 1965. **Members:** 900. **Membership Dues:** professional, $275 (annual) ● associate, $1,500 (annual) ● producer (based on sales), $1,200-$2,700 (annual) ● branch/multiple location, $1,200 (annual). **Staff:** 26. **Budget:** $5,000,000. **Description:** Producers of precast concrete products in all categories (small stock, agricultural, architectural, utility, and sewage disposal systems); suppliers to the industry; those interested in the technical and educational aspects of precast concrete. Promotes the use of quality precast concrete; advocates improvement of techniques for the purpose of developing high standards of quality. Encourages cooperation between concrete products producers and architects, engineers, real estate developers, contractors, and government officials. Operates plant certification program promoting quality control and safety. Fosters the exchange of information. **Awards: Type:** recognition ● **Type:** scholarship. **Telecommunication Services:** electronic mail, npca@precast.org ● electronic mail, technical@precast.org. **Committees:** Building Products; Grease Interceptor; Manholes; Marketing; Pipe; Septic Tank; Stormwater Products; Technical. **Affiliated With:** American Concrete Pipe Association; Interlocking Concrete Pavement Institute; National Concrete Masonry Association. **Publications:** *Directory of Members and Precast Products*, annual. Provides geographical listing of members with a brief description of the company and its products. **Price:** $300.00/copy for nonmembers. **Circulation:** 1,000. **Advertising:** accepted ● *MC: The Voice of the Manufactured Concrete Products Industry*, bimonthly. Magazine. Provides legislative and regulatory updates, and industry news. Also includes an insert supplement update. **Price:** free. **Circulation:** 8,000. **Advertising:** accepted ● *Precast Solutions*, quarterly. Magazine. Contains information about the uses and benefits of precast concrete. **Circulation:** 14,000. **Advertising:** accepted. Alternate Formats: online. **Conventions/Meetings:** annual Manufactured Concrete Products Exposition - convention and trade show (exhibits) - always winter ● annual convention and workshop - always fall. 2008 Sept. 18-22, Ottawa, ON, Canada; 2009 Oct. 1-4, Hilton Head Island, SC; 2010 Oct. 21-25, Vancouver, BC, Canada.

931 ■ National Ready Mixed Concrete Association (NRMCA)

900 Spring St.
Silver Spring, MD 20910
Ph: (301)587-1400
Free: (888)846-7622
Fax: (301)585-4219
E-mail: info@nrmca.org
URL: http://www.nrmca.org
Contact: Robert A. Garbini PE, Pres.
Founded: 1930. **Members:** 12. **Membership Dues:** producer (minimum; with less than 20,001 cubic yards production), $350 (annual) ● associate (based on gross sales), $1,000-$5,000 (annual) ● contractor, $1,000 (annual). **Staff:** 2. **Description:** Concrete plant manufacturers. Develops engineering standards with a view toward simplification and standardization of sizes, capacities, and other criteria associated with the manufacture of concrete plants. Performs services leading to higher quality concrete plant equipment. **Libraries: Type:** reference. **Holdings:** reports. **Awards:** Driver of the Year Award. **Frequency:** annual. **Type:** recognition. **Recipient:** for ready mixed concrete truck drivers ● Environmental Excellence Award. **Frequency:** annual. **Type:** recognition. **Recipient:** for producers with outstanding contributions to protecting the environment and maintaining sound management practice in their operations ● Excellence in Training Award. **Frequency:** annual. **Type:** recognition. **Recipient:** for ready mixed concrete producer members ● Joseph E. Carpenter Award. **Frequency:** annual. **Type:** recognition. **Recipient:** for individuals with outstanding lifetime contributions to the ready mixed concrete industry in the field of operations, safety or environmental ● Richard D. Gaynor Award. **Frequency:** annual. **Type:** recognition. **Recipient:** for individuals with lifetime contributions to the ready mixed industry in the technical field. **Telecommunication Services:** electronic mail, rgarbini@nrmca.org. **Departments:** Communications; Education; Engineering; Environmental; Government Affairs; Marketing/Promotion. **Divisions:** Control System Manufacturers; Plant Mixer Manufacturers. **Formerly:** (2000) Concrete Plant Manufacturers Bureau. **Publications:** *Concrete InFocus*, quarterly. Magazine. **Advertising:** accepted. Alternate Formats: online ● *Concrete Plant Standards*. **Price:** free to qualified personnel ● *Construction Manual: Concrete and Formwork*. **Price:** $17.75 ● *Truck Driver's Manual*. **Price:** $10.00 for members; $40.00 for nonmembers ● Videos ● Surveys, annual ● Concrete Plant Standards-Metric Version, Concrete Plant Mixer Standards, Bin or Silo Capacity Rating and Method of Computation, and Recommended Guide Specifications for Batching Equipment and Control Systems in Concrete Batch Plants. **Conventions/Meetings:** annual board meeting ● annual meeting - always April, Scottsdale, AZ.

932 ■ Ornamental Concrete Producers Association (OCPA)

502 Kay Ave. SE
Bemidji, MN 56601
Ph: (218)751-1982
Fax: (218)751-2186
E-mail: delpreus@paulbunyan.net
URL: http://www.ornamentalconcrete.org
Contact: Del R. Preuss, Exec. Dir.
Founded: 1991. **Members:** 500. **Membership Dues:** producer/apprentice/allied, $50 (annual). **Staff:** 1. **Budget:** $400,000. **Description:** Producers of ornamental concrete products. Seeks to advance the ornamental concrete and related industries. Conducts educational programs; sponsors competitions; holds mold auctions. **Libraries: Type:** not open to the public. **Holdings:** video recordings. **Subjects:** ornamental concrete. **Computer Services:** database. **Publications:** *Ornamental Observer*, bimonthly. Newsletter. **Circulation:** 600. **Advertising:** accepted. **Conventions/Meetings:** annual convention and board meeting (exhibits) - September or October.

933 ■ Portland Cement Association (PCA)

5420 Old Orchard Rd.
Skokie, IL 60077-1053
Ph: (847)966-6200 (847)972-9170
Fax: (847)966-8389
E-mail: info@cement.org
URL: http://www.cement.org
Contact: John P. Gleason Jr., Pres.
Founded: 1916. **Members:** 43. **Staff:** 110. **Budget:** $25,000,000. **Description:** Companies in the U.S. and Canada. Seeks to improve and extend the uses of Portland cement and concrete through market promotion, research and development, educational programs, and representation with governmental entities. Conducts research on concrete technology and durability; concrete pavement design; load-bearing capacities, field performance, and fire resistance of concrete; transportation, building, and structural uses of concrete. Operates Construction Technology Laboratories, which conducts research and technical services in construction materials, products, and applications. Sponsors a public affairs program in Washington, DC. **Libraries: Type:** reference. **Holdings:** 100,000; archival material, books, monographs, periodicals, reports. **Subjects:** concrete technology, cement chemistry, construction. **Councils:** Administrative; Government Affairs; Market Promotion; Research and Technical. **Publications:** *Executive Report*, weekly. Newsletter. Alternate Formats: online ● Reports. Includes technical, promotional publications. ● Manuals ● Videos. **Conventions/Meetings:** semiannual meeting - every spring and fall.

934 ■ Precast/Prestressed Concrete Institute (PCI)

209 W Jackson Blvd., No. 500
Chicago, IL 60606-6938
Ph: (312)786-0300 (312)360-3204
Fax: (312)786-0353
E-mail: info@pci.org
URL: http://www.pci.org
Contact: James G. Toscas, Pres.
Founded: 1954. **Members:** 2,000. **Membership Dues:** producer in U.S., $6,300 (annual) ● producer outside U.S., $850 (annual) ● associate, $1,650 (annual) ● professional in U.S., $110 (annual) ● professional outside U.S., $140 (annual) ● professional

intern in U.S., $50 (annual) ● professional intern outside U.S., $75 (annual). **Staff:** 25. **Regional Groups:** 15. **Description:** Manufacturers, suppliers, educators, engineers, technicians, and others interested in the design and construction of prestressed concrete. Compiles statistics. Maintains 17 committees, including marketing, technical and research committees. **Telecommunication Services:** electronic mail, memberservices@pci.org. **Publications:** *ASCENT*, quarterly. Magazine. Illustrates the latest in precast and prestressed concrete products and systems. **Advertising:** accepted. Alternate Formats: online ● *Journal of the Precast/Prestressed Concrete Institute*, bimonthly. Reports the latest technological advances in precast and prestressed concrete design, manufacture, and application. **Price:** $44.00/ year. **Advertising:** accepted. Alternate Formats: online. Also Cited As: *Journal of PCI* ● *The Professional*, quarterly. Newsletter. Alternate Formats: online ● Membership Directory, periodic. **Price:** free for members; $150.00 for nonmembers ● Handbooks ● Manuals ● Newsletter, periodic ● Reports ● Reprints. **Conventions/Meetings:** annual meeting (exhibits).

935 ■ Slag Cement Association (SCA)
12926 Dairy Ashford Rd., Ste.160
Sugar Land, TX 77478
Ph: (281)242-1258
Fax: (281)242-1293
E-mail: info@slagcement.org
URL: http://www.slagcement.org
Contact: Jan R. Prusinski PE, Exec. Dir.
Description: Represents producers and shippers of slag cement in the Unites States. Promotes the increased use of slag cement. Educates specifiers and other end-users on slag cement's varied attributes, benefits and uses. Fosters greater understanding about slag cement through research and development.

Conservation

936 ■ American River Touring Association (ARTA)
24000 Casa Loma Rd.
Groveland, CA 95321
Ph: (209)962-7873
Free: (800)323-2782
Fax: (209)962-4819
E-mail: arta@arta.org
URL: http://www.arta.org
Founded: 1963. **Description:** Aims to introduce the public to wilderness and to involve them in river rafting trips that are safe, meaningful and beneficial to both the individual and the environment. Conducts safe river trips which promote a sense of involvement and fulfillment, and foster an appreciation for the wilderness.

Construction

937 ■ American Construction Inspectors Association (ACIA)
12995 6th St., Ste.69
Yucaipa, CA 92399-2549
Ph: (909)795-3039
Free: (888)867-ACIA
Fax: (909)795-4039
E-mail: office@acia.com
URL: http://www.acia.com
Contact: Woneta Carnes, Exec. Dir.
Founded: 1956. **Members:** 1,200. **Membership Dues:** general, $210 (annual) ● professional, $280 (annual) ● affiliate, $350 (annual) ● associate, $140 (annual) ● student, $25 (annual) ● professional gold (one-time fee), $2,100. **Staff:** 3. **Budget:** $250,000. **Regional Groups:** 7. **Local Groups:** 16. **National Groups:** 2. **Description:** Represents construction inspectors. Aims to advance and improve the profession of detailed construction inspection. **Boards:** Registered Construction Inspectors. **Publications:** *The Inspector*, bimonthly. Magazine. Contains technical information for the construction industry. **Price:** free for members. **Circulation:** 1,000. **Advertising:** accepted. Alternate Formats: online. **Conventions/ Meetings:** annual conference and symposium (exhibits) - first weekend of November.

938 ■ American Fence Association (AFA)
800 Roosevelt Rd., Bldg. C-312
Glen Ellyn, IL 60137
Ph: (630)942-6598
Free: (800)822-4342
Fax: (630)790-3095
E-mail: kbailey731@aol.com
URL: http://www.americanfenceassociation.com
Contact: Lynn Hayworth, Pres.-Elect
Founded: 1962. **Members:** 2,400. **Membership Dues:** associate, $365 (annual) ● chapter, $500 (annual). **Staff:** 6. **Budget:** $1,960,000. **State Groups:** 25. **Description:** Fence contractors, manufacturers, and wholesalers; associate members are general contractors, architects, and insurance companies. Promotes the fence industry in 17 countries. Sponsors field training school and certification program. **Awards:** Ambassador. **Frequency:** annual. **Type:** recognition. **Recipient:** for individuals with devoted service to the association ● Chapter of the Year. **Frequency:** annual. **Type:** recognition. **Recipient:** to a chapter ● Distinguished Service. **Frequency:** annual. **Type:** recognition. **Recipient:** for individuals with great contribution to the fence industry ● Fence Project of the Year. **Frequency:** annual. **Type:** recognition. **Recipient:** for fence project that raises the standard for originality ● Hall of Fame. **Frequency:** annual. **Type:** recognition. **Recipient:** to individuals who have given their time and effort for the association ● Outstanding Committee Achievement. **Frequency:** annual. **Type:** recognition. **Recipient:** to committees and task force chair ● Past Presidents. **Frequency:** annual. **Type:** recognition. **Recipient:** for individuals with essential support and dedication. **Computer Services:** database, on industry. **Committees:** Awards; Business Partners; Certification; FENCETECH; Field Training School; Gate Operators; Insurance and Safety; Underground Utilities. **Divisions:** Deck and Railing; Manufacturers Association; Vinyl Fence. **Formerly:** International Fence Industry Association. **Publications:** *Davison Fence Blue Book*, annual. Directory. Contains profiles for fence contractors, manufacturers and suppliers in the fence industry. **Price:** $125.00 ● *Fence Sense*, monthly. Newsletter. **Circulation:** 1,700. Alternate Formats: online ● *FencePost*, bimonthly. Magazine. Contains information on the association and its entire fence industry. ISSN: 1082-2062. **Circulation:** 12,000. **Advertising:** accepted ● *Who's Who In AFA*, biennial. Membership Directory. Contains annual listing of members. **Advertising:** accepted. **Conventions/Meetings:** annual FENCETECH - convention and trade show (exhibits) - usually January or February.

939 ■ Associated Owners and Developers (AOD)
PO Box 4163
McLean, VA 22103-4163
Ph: (703)734-2397
Free: (888)999-2536
Fax: (703)734-2908
E-mail: aod@cbrmag.com
URL: http://www.constructionchannel.net/aod
Contact: Harvey L. Kornbluh, Chm./CEO
Membership Dues: individual, group government/ university (up to 3 individuals), $250 (annual) ● organization, $500 (annual) ● affiliate, $1,000 (annual) ● individual government or university, $125 (annual). **Description:** Works to support the needs of owners and developers involved in the construction process. **Committees:** Annual Seminar; Contract Documents Development; Overview; Strategic Planning. **Subcommittees:** Owner/Construction Manager; Owner/Design-Builder; Owner/Design Professional; Owner/General Contractor. **Publications:** *The AOD Monitor*, quarterly. Newsletter. Alternate Formats: online.

940 ■ Construction Industry Round Table (CIRT)
1101 17th St. NW, Ste.608
Washington, DC 20036-4734
Ph: (202)466-6777
Fax: (202)466-6767
E-mail: cirt@cirt.org
URL: http://www.cirt.org
Contact: Mark A. Casso Esq., Pres.
Founded: 1998. **Members:** 100. **Description:** Represents the interests of CEOs from architectural, engineering and construction firms doing business in the United States. Enhances and develops strong management approaches through networking and peer interaction. Seeks to improve the industry's image and relationships with public and private clients. **Conventions/Meetings:** semiannual conference - every spring and fall.

941 ■ Construction Innovation Forum (CIF)
6494 Latcha Rd.
Walbridge, OH 43465
Ph: (419)725-3108
Fax: (419)725-3079
E-mail: info@cif.org
URL: http://www.cif.org
Contact: Mr. Timothy A. Alter, Chm.
Founded: 1987. **Members:** 25. **Staff:** 1. **Budget:** $50,000. **Multinational. Description:** Seeks to recognize and encourage innovation that improves quality and reduces cost of construction. **Awards:** Construction Scholarship Program. **Type:** scholarship. **Recipient:** to graduate student ● NOVA Award. **Frequency:** 5/year. **Type:** recognition. **Recipient:** for innovations that have had positive, important effects on construction to improve quality and reduce cost. **Computer Services:** database, nominations, with 560 innovations. **Conventions/Meetings:** annual banquet ● annual Reload Classic Golf Outing Sponsorship - meeting.

942 ■ Crane Certification Association of America (CCAA)
PO Box 87907
Vancouver, WA 98687-7907
Ph: (360)834-3805
Free: (800)447-3402
Fax: (360)834-3507
E-mail: admin@ccaaweb.net
URL: http://www.ccaaweb.net
Contact: Jody Terrell, Office Asst.
Membership Dues: regular, voting, associate, $495 (annual) ● additional, $99 (annual). **Description:** Provides construction workers certification. **Publications:** Newsletter, semiannual. Features items of interest, including OSHA regulations and highlights of previous meetings. **Advertising:** accepted.

943 ■ Equipment Managers Council of America (EMCA)
PO Box 794
South Amboy, NJ 08879-0794
Ph: (908)309-3905
Fax: (732)721-0754
E-mail: fubarology@aol.com
URL: http://www.emca.org
Contact: Bob Lynch, Pres.
Members: 400. **Membership Dues:** individual, $35 (annual) ● corporate, $100 (annual). **Description:** Improves the equipment intensive industries, including construction, mining, utilities, demolition, recycling, solid waste, municipalities, and transportation. **Publications:** Newsletter, monthly. **Conventions/ Meetings:** monthly meeting and seminar.

944 ■ Firestop Contractors International Association (FCIA)
4415 W Harrison St., No. 322a
Hillside, IL 60162
Ph: (708)202-1108
Fax: (708)449-0837
E-mail: info@fcia.org
URL: http://www.fcia.org
Contact: Bill McHugh, Exec. Dir.
Founded: 1998. **Members:** 130. **Membership Dues:** manufacturer, $3,000 (annual) ● voting, $1,150 (annual) ● associate, contractor, distributor, international associate, $300 (annual) ● branch, $300 (annual). **Staff:** 2. **Description:** Building construction contractors. Provides and maintains information for installa-

tion of firestop materials and systems. Promote life safety. **Committees:** Accreditation; Codes; Education; Marketing; Program; Technical. **Publications:** *FCIA E-News*, 10/year. Newsletter. Alternate Formats: online ● *FCIA Manual of Practice*. **Price:** $305.00 for members, plus shipping and handling; $905.00 for nonmembers, plus shipping and handling. Alternate Formats: online ● *FM 4991 Brochure*. Alternate Formats: online ● Articles. Alternate Formats: online. **Conventions/Meetings:** annual conference and trade show, with committee meetings.

945 ■ Foundation for Pavement Preservation (FP2)
8613 Cross Park Dr.
Austin, TX 78754
Free: (866)862-4587
E-mail: fppexdir@aol.com
URL: http://www.fp2.org
Contact: Gerry Eller, Exec. Dir.
Founded: 1992. **Staff:** 1. **Budget:** $500,000. **Nonmembership. Description:** Represents individual involved in Pavement Preservation. Promotes pavement preservation internationally. **Publications:** *Pavement Preservation Journal*. **Advertising:** accepted. Alternate Formats: online ● Annual Report. Alternate Formats: online.

946 ■ Quartzite Rock Association (QRA)
PO Box 661
Sioux Falls, SD 57101
Ph: (605)339-1520
E-mail: info@quartzite.com
URL: http://www.quartzite.com
Description: Works to promote quality quartzite aggregates for construction, landscape, and decorative architectural applications. **Publications:** *Quartzite Quotes*, quarterly. Newsletter. Alternate Formats: online.

947 ■ Residential Construction Employers Council (RCEC)
3041 Woodcreek Dr., Ste.101
Downers Grove, IL 60515
Ph: (630)512-0552
Fax: (630)512-0554
E-mail: rcec@rcec-res-build.com
URL: http://www.aboutrcec.org
Contact: Ms. Lou Couper, Exec. VP
Founded: 1966. **Members:** 170. **Staff:** 5. **Description:** Works to represent the residential housing industry. Conducts educational seminars and safety programs. Negotiates carpenter collective bargaining agreements. **Committees:** Annual Dinner; ByLaws; Code; Combined Craft; Construction Management Certification; Golf Outing; Legislative; MidResCom. **Councils:** Residential Production. **Programs:** Industry Scholarships; Internship; Risk Management; Safety; Tuition Reimbursement; University Scholarships. **Publications:** *Residential Report*, bimonthly. Newsletter. **Circulation:** 1,900 ● *Roster and Labor Guide*, annual. **Circulation:** 500 ● *Safety Newsletter*, bimonthly. **Conventions/Meetings:** monthly board meeting ● periodic seminar.

948 ■ Residential Construction Workers' Association (ASTRACOR)
3660D Wheeler Ave.
Alexandria, VA 22304
Ph: (703)212-8294
E-mail: info@astracor.org
URL: http://www.astracor.org
Contact: Clayton Sinyai PhD, Dir.
Description: Represents the interests of residential construction workers. Aims to improve the lives of all workers employed in residential construction. Provides job and social service referrals. Informs workers of their rights and benefits and provides training in different construction trades.

949 ■ SPRI
77 Rumford Ave., Ste.3B
Waltham, MA 02453
Ph: (781)647-7026
Fax: (781)647-7222
E-mail: info@spri.org
URL: http://www.spri.org
Contact: Linda King, Managing Dir.
Founded: 1982. **Members:** 55. **Multinational. Description:** Represents and promotes sheet membrane and component suppliers to the commercial roofing industry. **Publications:** *SPRI Flexible Membrane Roofing: A Professional's Guide to Specifications*. Alternate Formats: CD-ROM ● *SPRI Safety Guide*.

950 ■ Western Council of Construction Consumers (WCCC)
31320 Via Colinas, Ste.120
Westlake Village, CA 91362
Ph: (818)735-4733
Fax: (818)735-4738
E-mail: andy@wccc.org
URL: http://www.wccc.org
Contact: Andrew C. Wiktorowicz PE, Exec. Dir.
Founded: 1972. **Membership Dues:** contractor, vendor, subcontractor (based on annual revenues), $725-$4,500 (annual) ● professional services (based on annual revenues), $725-$2,100 (annual) ● private sector (based on annual revenues), $2,200-$8,750 (annual) ● public sector (based on annual revenues), $1,900 (annual). **Description:** Promotes professional development, improved company operations and maintenance, safety, quality and cost-effective construction to consumers. **Publications:** *WCCConnection*, quarterly. Newsletter. Alternate Formats: online. **Conventions/Meetings:** annual conference.

Consulting

951 ■ Airport Consultants Council (ACC)
908 King St., Ste.100
Alexandria, VA 22314
Ph: (703)683-5900
Fax: (703)683-2564
E-mail: paulah@acconline.org
URL: http://www.acconline.org
Contact: Ms. Paula P. Hochstetler, Pres.
Founded: 1978. **Members:** 230. **Membership Dues:** associate, $1,650 (annual) ● executive, participating, $2,150 (annual). **Staff:** 4. **Budget:** $500,000. **Multinational. Description:** Represents firms that provide airport architecture, design, engineering, security, marketing, and environmental services, air service development, and airport products and materials. Reviews industry issues and represents members before Congress and federal agencies. Conducts educational programs, and research programs. **Libraries: Type:** reference. **Subjects:** airports and aviation issues. **Awards:** Aviation Award of Excellence. **Frequency:** annual. **Type:** recognition. **Computer Services:** Mailing lists, of members. **Committees:** Events; Government Affairs; Operations; Services; Special Projects; Technical. **Publications:** *ACC Membership Directory*, annual. Contains a listing of member firms and their services. **Price:** free ● *ACCess Outlook*, weekly. Report. Lists airport RFPs and business opportunities. Alternate Formats: online ● *AirportConsulting*, quarterly. Newsletter. **Price:** included in membership dues. **Circulation:** 600. **Advertising:** accepted. Alternate Formats: online. **Conventions/Meetings:** annual Airport Planning, Design and Construction - symposium, focuses on planning and development, landside/terminal facilities development, airside/airfield facility ● annual conference and seminar, with professional programs highlighting major airport consulting issues relating to the business interests of its members (exhibits) - always 2nd week of November; Sunday-Wednesday.

952 ■ Alliance of Professional Consultants (APC)
PO Box 441350
Aurora, CO 80044
Ph: (303)607-7566
Fax: (303)699-2852
E-mail: ray@corlyx.com
URL: http://www.apconsultants.org
Contact: Pat Hanafee, Pres.
Membership Dues: professional, affiliate, associate, $130 (annual) ● corporate, $495 (annual). **Description:** Represents the interests of professional consultants and consulting companies. Seeks to elevate the level of educational, professional and ethical standards of business consulting. Facilitates the referral of high quality consultants to the regional business community. **Publications:** Newsletter, quarterly.

953 ■ American Association of Insurance Management Consultants (AAIMCO)
c/o Mr. Thomas M. Braniff, Pres.
8980 Lakes at 610 Dr., Ste.100
Houston, TX 77054
Ph: (713)664-6424
Fax: (713)524-3350
E-mail: thomas@aaimco.com
URL: http://www.aaimco.com
Contact: Mr. Thomas M. Braniff, Pres.
Founded: 1978. **Members:** 35. **Membership Dues:** $250 (annual). **Description:** Consists of individuals who devote a substantial portion of their services to insurance consulting, risk management activities, legal representation relating to insurance issues; as well as education and professional development training, employment consulting, and other technical and management advice to the insurance industry. Advises and assists the insurance industry and seeks to achieve professional recognition for insurance management consultants. Mediates the exchange of ideas; sets standards of service and performance; maintains a code of ethics; offers a referral service and a series of educational conferences and seminars. Operates speakers' bureau; offers placement services; compiles statistics. **Publications:** Newsletter, quarterly. Alternate Formats: online. **Conventions/Meetings:** annual conference.

954 ■ American Consultants League (ACL)
c/o ETR
245 NE 4th Ave., Ste.102
Delray Beach, FL 33483
Free: (866)344-7200
E-mail: support@earlytorise.com
URL: http://www.americanconsultantsleague.com
Contact: Robert W. Bly, Contact
Founded: 1983. **Members:** 1,000. **Membership Dues:** individual, $139 (annual). **Staff:** 3. **Budget:** $100,000. **For-Profit. Multinational. Description:** Full-time and part-time consultants in varied fields of expertise. Provides assistance to consultants in establishing and managing the business component of their consultancies; offers marketing and legal advice. Maintains the Consultants Institute, which offers a home study program and bestows Certified Professional Consultants designation upon completion of program. Conducts research programs; compiles statistics. **Convention/Meeting:** none. **Awards:** Chartered Consultant. **Type:** recognition. **Divisions:** Consultants' Library. **Publications:** *Consulting Intelligence*, bimonthly. Newsletter. **Price:** included in membership dues; no longer accept outside subscriptions. ISSN: 0887-0314. **Circulation:** 1,200. **Advertising:** accepted ● *Consulting Tips*, monthly. Newsletter. Alternate Formats: online.

955 ■ American Society of Theatre Consultants (ASTC)
c/o Edgar L. Lustig, Sec./CFO
12226 Mentz Hill Rd.
St. Louis, MO 63128
Ph: (314)843-9218
Fax: (314)843-4955
E-mail: elustig@swbell.net
URL: http://www.theatreconsultants.org
Contact: Edgar L. Lustig, Sec./CFO
Founded: 1983. **Members:** 49. **Staff:** 1. **Multinational. Description:** Professional theatre consultants. Seeks to improve the planning and construction of theatres and public assembly facilities. Fosters and works to further the interests of owners, users, and audience members in the design, use, and enjoyment of theatres. Serves as a forum for the exchange

of ideas and technical information; promotes high standards in the field. Informs theatre owners, planners, and users of members' services. Collects and disseminates information on designing and furnishing theatres. Conducts study and research activities in conjunction with related organizations and interested individuals. Maintains speakers' bureau. **Publications:** *The ASTC Letter*, annual. Newsletter. **Price:** free. **Conventions/Meetings:** annual conference.

956 ■ Association of Certified Turnaround Professionals (ACTP)
150 S Wacker Dr., Ste.900
Chicago, IL 60606
Ph: (312)578-6900
Fax: (312)578-8336
E-mail: info@actp.org
URL: http://www.actp.org
Contact: Ms. Nicole Gibby, Relations Mgr.

Founded: 1993. **Members:** 410. **Membership Dues:** individual, $195 (annual). **Staff:** 2. **Description:** Works as an independent certifying body, created by the Turnaround Management Association, for Certified Turnaround Professionals, the consultants, turnaround practitioners, accountants, executives, and lenders that assists struggling companies. Provides examination information, conducts exams for certification. **Commissions:** Blue Ribbon.

957 ■ Association of Image Consultants International (AICI)
100 E Grand Ave., Ste.330
Des Moines, IA 50309
Ph: (515)282-5500
Fax: (515)243-2049
E-mail: info@aici.org
URL: http://www.aici.org
Contact: Karen Brunger CIP, Pres.

Founded: 1990. **Members:** 500. **Membership Dues:** student, sustaining, $165 (annual) ● associate/affiliate, $275 (annual). **Staff:** 1. **Local Groups:** 12. **Description:** Personal color, style, wardrobe, and image planning consultants. Promotes quality service for clients; aids in establishing working relations between retail stores and consultants; assists community colleges in offering accredited image consulting programs; maintains standards of professionalism for members in the image consulting industry. Provides continuing education and training; maintains speakers' bureau. **Awards:** Image Makers Merit for Industry Excellence Award. **Frequency:** annual. **Type:** recognition. **Formed by Merger of:** Association of Image Consultants; Association of Fashion and Image Consultants. **Publications:** *Association of Image Consultants International Newsletter*, quarterly. Contains shopping and consulting updates and chapter news; includes convention information. **Price:** $15.00/year. **Conventions/Meetings:** annual conference (exhibits).

958 ■ Association of Philanthropic Counsel (APC)
1901 N Roselle Rd., Ste.920
Schaumburg, IL 60195
Ph: (704)940-7386
Free: (800)957-5666
Fax: (847)885-8393
E-mail: info@apcinc.org
URL: http://www.apcinc.org
Contact: Cindy Savage, Admin. Dir.

Founded: 1996. **Members:** 40. **Membership Dues:** associate, $500 (annual) ● regular, $1,000 (annual). **Staff:** 15. **Budget:** $65,000. **Description:** Professional consultants providing assistance and services to nonprofit, public sector organizations. Promotes high standards of ethics and practice among philanthropic counselors. Facilitates professional advancement of members. Conducts educational programs; maintains speakers' bureau. **Computer Services:** database ● mailing lists. **Conventions/Meetings:** semiannual board meeting ● semiannual Education Conference.

959 ■ Association of Professional Communication Consultants (APCC)
c/o Dr. Kenneth W. Davis, Pres.
8910 Purdue Rd., Ste.480
Indianapolis, IN 46268
Ph: (317)616-1810
Free: (866)616-3397
Fax: (317)616-1811
E-mail: ken@komei.com
URL: http://www.consultingsuccess.org
Contact: Dr. Kenneth W. Davis, Pres.

Founded: 1982. **Members:** 150. **Membership Dues:** student, $15 (annual) ● regular/international, $50 (annual). **Multinational. Description:** Consultants, trainers, writers and editors who work in corporate, private, government, and academic settings. Promotes the profession of communication. Provides networking opportunities and information on business operation and consulting problems. Conducts educational programs. **Awards:** Excellence in Communication Training. **Frequency:** annual. **Type:** recognition. **Recipient:** to a member for outstanding training program ● Excellence in Professional Communication. **Frequency:** annual. **Type:** recognition. **Recipient:** to a member for outstanding communication project ● Honor Roll of Excellence in Communication. **Frequency:** annual. **Type:** recognition. **Recipient:** for outstanding commitment to excellent communication. **Telecommunication Services:** electronic bulletin board, listserv for members only. **Formerly:** Association of Professional Writing Consultants. **Publications:** *Consulting Success*, quarterly. Newsletter. **Price:** $50.00/year. **Circulation:** 200. **Advertising:** accepted ● Membership Directory. **Price:** $50.00 for nonmembers; free for members. **Conventions/Meetings:** annual Consulting Institute - workshop, morning session is about consulting issues, afternoon session hands-on practical issues.

960 ■ Association of Professional Consultants (APC)
PO Box 51193
Irvine, CA 92619-1193
Ph: (949)675-9222
Free: (800)745-5050
Fax: (800)977-3272
E-mail: apc@consultapc.org
URL: http://www.consultapc.org
Contact: Mo Aiken, Pres.

Founded: 1983. **Members:** 250. **Membership Dues:** general, $325 (annual) ● out of area, $275 (annual). **Description:** Professional consultants. Aids and guides members in the improvement of their professional abilities. **Formerly:** (2004) American Association of Professional Consultants. **Publications:** *The Consultant's Journal*, annual ● *The Consultant's Voice*, monthly. Newsletter. **Price:** available to members only. **Circulation:** 500. **Advertising:** accepted ● Membership Directory, annual. **Conventions/Meetings:** periodic regional meeting.

961 ■ Association of Professional Material Handling Consultants (APMHC)
8720 Red Oak Blvd., Ste.201
Charlotte, NC 28217
Ph: (704)676-1190
Fax: (704)676-1199
E-mail: jnofsinger@mhia.org
URL: http://www.mhia.org/PS/PS_APMHC_WhatIsAPMHC.cfm
Contact: John B. Nofsinger, CEO

Founded: 1959. **Members:** 32. **Description:** Professional and independent material handling consultants; individuals who perform similar functions within multi-plant corporations. Promotes the art and science of material handling; aims to elevate the profession of the material handling consultant and establishes codes of ethics, conduct, and qualifications. Develops, maintains, and enforces rigorous membership requirements and high standards of ethical professional practice which will make membership in the association a recognized mark of experience, stability, competence, reliability, and character. Encourages the publication of technical papers and books and the interchange of thought, ideas, and methods between members and cooperates with government agencies, educational institutions, public bodies, and engineering societies to increase the usefulness of the profession. **Publications:** *Membership Roster*, semiannual. Membership Directory. **Conventions/Meetings:** semiannual meeting.

962 ■ Consultants Consortium
c/o Mr. Henry D. Lewis, CFRE, Pres.
1730 M St. NW, Ste.801
Washington, DC 20036
Ph: (202)463-8929
Fax: (301)986-8647
E-mail: devconassc@aol.com
URL: http://www.consultants-consortium.com
Contact: Mr. Henry D. Lewis CFRE, Pres.

Founded: 1992. **Members:** 100. **Membership Dues:** individual, $50 (annual). **Budget:** $5,000. **Description:** Represents the interests of independent consultants residing in and serving the Washington, DC Metropolitan area. Provides opportunities for members to broaden their professional education, capabilities and professionalism. **Libraries: Type:** not open to the public. **Holdings:** archival material, business records. **Awards:** The Stewart Macdonald Award. **Frequency:** periodic. **Type:** recognition. **Recipient:** for activities that benefit the practice/field of consulting and/or benefit the organization. **Computer Services:** database, list of members with contact information and areas of expertise. **Telecommunication Services:** information service, listserv of members only. **Publications:** Newsletter, monthly. **Price:** included in membership dues ● Membership Directory, annual ● Bulletin. **Conventions/Meetings:** annual meeting.

963 ■ Foodservice Consultants Society International (FCSI)
455 S 4th St., Ste.650
Louisville, KY 40202
Ph: (502)583-3783
Fax: (502)589-3602
E-mail: fcsi@fcsi.org
URL: http://www.fcsi.org
Contact: Cindy Wyant, Exec. Dir.

Founded: 1945. **Members:** 1,000. **Membership Dues:** professional, $385 (annual) ● senior associate, $325 (annual) ● associate, $50 (annual) ● corporate (based on annual sales volume), $1,000-$1,900 (annual) ● corporate division, $485 (annual) ● individual allied, $450 (annual) ● student, $25 (annual). **Staff:** 6. **Regional Groups:** 8. **Description:** Works to promote client usage of services provided by members. Promotes ethical industry practices; disseminates information; develops accreditation programs; conducts educational and research programs; maintains speakers' bureau. **Awards:** Green. **Frequency:** annual. **Type:** recognition. **Recipient:** for positive environmental impact ● Service. **Frequency:** annual. **Type:** recognition ● Trendsetter. **Frequency:** annual. **Type:** recognition. **Computer Services:** Mailing lists, of members. **Publications:** *The Consultant*, quarterly. Magazine. **Price:** $40.00/year in North America; $55.00/year outside North America. **Circulation:** 2,000. **Advertising:** accepted. **Conventions/Meetings:** annual conference - always September or October.

964 ■ Image Industry Council International/Institute for Image Management
PO Box 190007
San Francisco, CA 94119
Ph: (415)863-2573
Fax: (415)840-0655
E-mail: marily@image360.com
URL: http://www.image360.com
Contact: Marily Mondejar, Founder/Exec. Dir.

Founded: 1988. **Members:** 376. **Membership Dues:** corporate, $2,000 ● active, $150 ● associate, $200 ● subscriber, $110. **Staff:** 3. **Budget:** $250,000. **Description:** Maintains speakers' bureau. Conducts educational and research programs. **Libraries: Type:** not open to the public; reference. **Holdings:** artwork, audiovisuals, books, clippings, periodicals. **Subjects:** image management, color analysis, wardrobe strategies, grooming, etiquette. **Awards:** Award of Excellence. **Frequency:** annual. **Type:** recognition. **Recipi-**

ent: for significant contribution to the image industry ● Image Consultant of the Year. **Frequency:** annual. **Type:** recognition. **Recipient:** for significant contribution to the image industry. **Computer Services:** database ● mailing lists. **Conventions/Meetings:** annual meeting (exhibits) - always September.

965 ■ International Association of Protocol Consultants (IAPC)
PO Box 6150
McLean, VA 22106-6150
Ph: (703)555-1212
Fax: (703)555-1212
E-mail: iapc@protocolconsultants.org
URL: http://www.protocolconsultants.org
Contact: Alinda Lewris, Founder
Founded: 2002. **Multinational. Description:** Advances the practice of protocol, etiquette and civility worldwide. Increases educational opportunities in learning more about corporate/international protocol, diplomatic/government protocol, business etiquette and civility. Raises public awareness of the critical need for international cooperation in civility, ethics and integrity. **Awards:** IAPC Outstanding Achievement Award. **Frequency:** annual. **Type:** recognition. **Boards:** Advisory; Education Review. **Publications:** *Protocol Today*. Newsletter. Features trends in the protocol and etiquette industry. Alternate Formats: online.

966 ■ International Guild of Professional Consultants (IGPC)
5703 Red Bug Lake Rd., Ste.403
Winter Springs, FL 32708
Ph: (407)687-7853
Free: (888)244-9541
Fax: (407)678-8173
E-mail: info@igpc.org
URL: http://igpc.org
Membership Dues: individual, $295 (annual). **Multinational. Description:** Encourages excellence in the consulting profession. Furthers professionalism among consultants through programs and support services that enhance the quality of services and the profitability of consulting practices. Addresses the needs of members through professional certification, development seminars and workshops, distribution of printed materials and individual coaching. **Telecommunication Services:** electronic mail, igpc@igpc.org. **Publications:** *Powerlines*, bimonthly. Newsletter. Contains ideas, pointers, techniques and news from the consulting industry. **Price:** included in membership dues. **Advertising:** accepted ● Report, bimonthly. Features topical and relevant issues. ● Magazines, weekly. **Price:** included in membership dues. Alternate Formats: online.

967 ■ International Society of Hospitality Consultants (ISHC)
c/o Lori E. Raleigh, Exec. Dir.
411 6th St. S, No. 204
Naples, FL 34102
Ph: (239)436-3915 (703)684-6681
Fax: (239)436-3916
E-mail: lraleighishc@aol.com
URL: http://www.ishc.com
Contact: Lori E. Raleigh, Exec. Dir.
Founded: 1989. **Members:** 173. **Membership Dues:** professional association, $1,000 (annual). **Staff:** 2. **National Groups:** 16. **Multinational. Description:** Consultants qualified by experience, training, and knowledge to express ideas concerning hospitality industry related issues. Provides expertise to hotels, restaurants, clubs, and travel related businesses. **Awards:** Pioneer Award-Europe. **Frequency:** annual. **Type:** recognition ● Pioneer Award-US. **Frequency:** annual. **Type:** recognition. **Computer Services:** database, membership directory ● online services, library. **Publications:** *CapEx 2000 Report* (in English and Spanish), quadrennial. **Price:** $295.00. **Conventions/Meetings:** annual conference.

968 ■ National Association of Computer Consultant Businesses (NACCB)
1420 King St., Ste.610
Alexandria, VA 22314
Ph: (703)838-2050
Fax: (703)838-3610
E-mail: staff@naccb.org
URL: http://www.naccb.org
Contact: Mark Roberts, CEO
Founded: 1987. **Members:** 500. **Membership Dues:** company (based on annual revenues), $1,000-$10,000 (annual). **Staff:** 8. **Budget:** $2,000,000. **Regional Groups:** 17. **Description:** Businesses that provide the services of highly technical professionals, such as computer programmers, systems analysts, engineers, to clients in need of temporary technical support. Promotes legal and economic environment favorable to the technical services industry, including protection of a firm's freedom to choose either employees or independent contractors when supplying services to clients. Encourages professional standards in the industry; serves as a support mechanism for members. Provides industry-specific educational information and insurance discounts. **Telecommunication Services:** electronic mail, roberts@naccb.org. **Committees:** Benefits; Government Affairs; Membership; Public Relations. **Publications:** *Business Owner's Manual*. **Price:** available to members only ● *Directory of Members Firms*, periodic. Membership Directory. **Price:** available to members only ● *NACCB Monitor*, quarterly. Magazine ● *NACCB Newsletter*, quarterly. Includes business tips and information on legislative developments. **Price:** available to members only. **Circulation:** 500. **Advertising:** accepted. **Conventions/Meetings:** annual conference (exhibits) - always fall.

969 ■ Professional and Technical Consultants Association (PATCA)
PO Box 2261
Santa Clara, CA 95055
Ph: (408)971-5902
Free: (800)74-PATCA
Fax: (866)746-1053
E-mail: info@patca.org
URL: http://www.patca.org
Contact: Tonia Forbus, Exec. Dir.
Founded: 1975. **Members:** 300. **Membership Dues:** affiliate, $125 (annual) ● associate, full, company, $395 (annual) ● non-consultant employee, $60 (annual). **Staff:** 2. **Description:** Represents Independent consultants active in the support of business, industry, and government. Serves as a referral service to aid independent consultants in marketing their services as well as to assist those seeking their services. **Libraries: Type:** open to the public. **Holdings:** 2. **Subjects:** consulting. **Computer Services:** database, consultant search. **Committees:** Benefits; Directory; Ethics and Client Satisfaction; Internet; Marketing and Public Relations; Mentor; Program. **Programs:** Referral. **Publications:** *PATCA Directory of Consultants*, annual. Membership Directory. Includes brief biographical statements. **Price:** $15.00/copy. **Circulation:** 5,000. Alternate Formats: online ● *PATCA Newsletter*, monthly. Includes calendar of events, legislative report, membership profiles and topics of interest to consultants. **Advertising:** accepted ● *PATCA Survey of Rates and Business Practices*, biennial. Contains statistics presented in tabular form on consulting rates and business practices. **Price:** included in membership dues; $25.00 for nonmembers ● Journal, quarterly. Contains timely information of interest to PATCA members. **Price:** included in membership dues. **Conventions/Meetings:** monthly meeting and dinner, for the exchange of information and networking - every 2nd Thursday.

Consumers

970 ■ Consumer Trends Forum International (CTFI)
7076 Drinkard Way
Mechanicsville, VA 23111
Ph: (804)559-6519
Fax: (804)559-4087
E-mail: info@consumerexpert.org
URL: http://www.consumerexpert.org
Contact: Marge Ryerson, Pres.
Founded: 1998. **Members:** 250. **Membership Dues:** professional, $150 (annual) ● supporting, $120 (annual) ● corporate, $600 (annual) ● student (online), $25 (annual). **Staff:** 1. **Multinational. Description:** Provides global trend information and networking resources to assist members to identify and integrate trends into the design and marketing of consumer goods and services; educates businesses to interpret impact of trends on consumer needs and expectations. Hosts an annual Consumer Trends Forum with speakers addressing consumer trends. **Formerly:** (2003) Consumer Science Business Professionals. **Publications:** *Trendline*, biweekly. Report. Contains email report. **Conventions/Meetings:** annual Consumer Trends Forum - conference.

Containers

971 ■ Aluminum Foil Container Manufacturers Association (AFCMA)
10 Vecilla Ln.
Hot Springs Village, AR 71909
Ph: (501)922-7425
Fax: (501)922-0383
E-mail: info@afcma.org
URL: http://www.afcma.org
Contact: Edward T. Doyle, Exec. Sec.-Treas.
Founded: 1955. **Members:** 12. **Staff:** 2. **Description:** Manufacturers of aluminum foil containers for food products. **Telecommunication Services:** electronic mail, eddoyle@suddenlink.net. **Conventions/Meetings:** semiannual conference.

972 ■ Associated Cooperage Industries of America (ACIA)
2100 Gardiner Ln., Ste.100-E
Louisville, KY 40205-2947
Ph: (502)459-6113
Fax: (502)459-6114
E-mail: aciainc@acia.net
URL: http://www.acia.net
Contact: Mrs. Polly Wagner, Sec.-Treas.
Founded: 1934. **Members:** 54. **Membership Dues:** regular, $400 (annual). **Staff:** 1. **Description:** Serves as contact point for members; disseminates information about the wooden barrel, with emphasis on white oak; promotes the common interest of those in the industry. **Committees:** Export; Forestry; Statistics; Technical. **Divisions:** Barrel and Keg; Stave and Heading. **Publications:** *Associated Cooperage Industries of America—Newsletter*, quarterly. **Price:** available to members only ● Membership Directory, periodic. **Conventions/Meetings:** annual convention, with forum - always fall.

973 ■ Association of Independent Corrugated Converters (AICC)
PO Box 25708
Alexandria, VA 22313
Ph: (703)836-2422
Free: (877)836-2422
Fax: (703)836-2795
E-mail: info@aiccbox.org
URL: http://www.aiccbox.org
Contact: A. Steven Young, Pres.
Founded: 1974. **Members:** 1,056. **Membership Dues:** overseas regular, $450 (annual) ● company in U.S. (based on annual sales), $950-$3,500 (annual) ● associate company in U.S. (based on number of employees), $950-$3,500 (annual). **Staff:** 9. **Budget:** $2,000,000. **Regional Groups:** 13. **State Groups:** 10. **National Groups:** 3. **Languages:** English, Spanish. **Multinational. Description:** Independent boxmakers united to provide a forum for discussion of mutual problems and initiate programs to assist sheet plants and independent corrugators. Seeks to provide a voice for independents. Offers educational, purchasing, and self-insurance programs. Conducts sales seminars and compiles statistical surveys. Sponsors package competitions. **Awards:** Hall of Fame Award. **Frequency:** annual. **Type:** recognition. **Recipient:** for those who have made significant contributions to the independent sector of the corrugated packaging industry ● Packaging Design Competition Awards. **Frequency:** biennial. **Type:** recognition. **Recipient:** for independent corrugators

and sheet plant manufacturers ● Safe Shop Award. **Frequency:** biennial. **Type:** recognition. **Recipient:** for outstanding performance in box plant safety ● Student Design Competition Award. **Frequency:** annual. **Type:** monetary. **Recipient:** for an outstanding student's work design in corrugated packaging. **Computer Services:** Information services, industry-related. **Telecommunication Services:** electronic mail, syoung@aiccbox.org. **Publications:** *Anti-Trust Compliance Manual.* Provides policy guidelines for adhering to the nation's antitrust laws, covering price fixing and price discrimination. **Price:** $7.00 for members; $20.00 for nonmembers ● *Boxscore* ● *The Business Owner* ● *Profile of the Independent Corrugated Converter*, biennial. Report. Provides statistical and visual portrayal of the independent sector of the corrugated container industry. **Price:** $75.00 for members; $150.00 for nonmembers ● *Quarterly Business Conditions* ● *Salary, Hourly Wage and Benefit Survey*, biennial. **Price:** $145.00 for members; $195.00 for nonmembers ● *Sales Compensation Survey*, biennial. **Price:** $125.00 for members; $175.00 for nonmembers ● Membership Directory, annual. Includes listings of AICC's independent boxplant members and industry suppliers. **Price:** $175.00 for members; $250.00 for nonmembers. Alternate Formats: online. **Conventions/Meetings:** semiannual meeting.

974 ■ Can Manufacturers Institute (CMI)

1730 Rhode Island Ave. NW, Ste.1000
Washington, DC 20036
Ph: (202)232-4677
Fax: (202)232-5756
E-mail: sreilly@cancentral.com
URL: http://www.cancentral.com
Contact: Sean M. Reily, VP, Public Relations and Research

Founded: 1938. **Members:** 25. **Membership Dues:** manufacturer and supplier (minimum), $5,000 (annual). **Staff:** 7. **Budget:** $2,000,000. **Description:** Represents can makers and can industry suppliers. Aims to foster the prosperity of the industry and bring value to its members in a cost effective way. **Computer Services:** Information services, industry-related. **Committees:** Can Standards; Environmental Quality; Food Can; Government Relations; Health and Safety; Market Data; Public Policy; Public Relations; Regulatory Affairs. **Absorbed:** (1973) Carbonated Beverage Container Manufacturers Association. **Publications:** *Can Shipments Report*, quarterly. **Price:** $265.00 ● *Cans: A Visual History* ● *Directory of Can Manufacturers and Industry Suppliers*, biennial ● *Executive Focus*, quarterly. Newsletter ● *Federal/State Review*, monthly ● Booklets. **Conventions/Meetings:** annual meeting.

975 ■ Closure Manufacturers Association (CMA)

PO Box 1358
Kilmarnock, VA 22482
Ph: (804)435-9580
Fax: (804)435-2203
E-mail: cmadc@rivnet.net
URL: http://www.cmadc.org
Contact: Darla Jean Williamson, Pres.

Founded: 1984. **Members:** 40. **Staff:** 1. **Budget:** $250,000. **Description:** Metal and plastic closure manufacturers for all types of containers and suppliers to the closure industry as well as plastic container manufacturers. Conducts public relations, marketing, technical, and government and congressional liaison activities for member companies and has established industry standards for metal and plastic closures. **Committees:** Child-Resistant Closures; Closure Promotion; Closure Technical. **Affiliated With:** Glass Packaging Institute. **Formerly:** Closure Committee of the Glass Packaging Institute. **Publications:** *Closure Report*, 3/year. Newsletter. Features articles covering lids, bottlecaps, and other closures. Alternate Formats: online ● Bulletins. Alternate Formats: CD-ROM. **Conventions/Meetings:** annual conference - always spring.

976 ■ Composite Can and Tube Institute (CCTI)

50 S Pickett St., Ste.110
Alexandria, VA 22304-7206
Ph: (703)823-7234
Fax: (703)823-7237
E-mail: ccti@cctiwdc.org
URL: http://www.cctiwdc.org
Contact: Kristine Garland, Exec. VP

Founded: 1933. **Members:** 100. **Membership Dues:** associate, $1,800 (annual) ● packaging educator, $60 (annual) ● packaging student, $35 (annual) ● Independent Manufacturers' Council, $500 (annual) ● international industry, $1,000-$2,100 (annual) ● industry (maximum), $41,270 (annual). **Staff:** 4. **Multinational. Description:** Manufacturers of composite cans, tubes, cores, ribbon blocks, cones, bobbins, mailing packages, spools, and related items. Compiles statistics. **Committees:** Composite Can; Government and Environmental Relations; Human Resources; Safety; Technical; Vendors Technical. **Councils:** Independent Manufacturers. **Formerly:** (1970) National Fibre Can and Tube Association. **Publications:** *Cantube Bulletin*, bimonthly. Newsletter. **Advertising:** accepted. Alternate Formats: online ● *Industry Directory*, annual. Lists manufacturers of paperboard products worldwide, and CCTI supplier members. ● *Industry Marketing Report*, triennial. **Price:** $300.00 for members; $600.00 for nonmembers ● *Technical Notebook* ● Also publishes technical documents, recommended industry standards, standard testing procedures, and guidelines. **Conventions/Meetings:** annual meeting (exhibits).

977 ■ Container Market Committee (CMC)

c/o American Iron and Steel Institute
1140 Connecticut Ave. NW, Ste.705
Washington, DC 20036
Ph: (202)452-7100
Fax: (202)463-6573
E-mail: rfatzinger@steel.org
URL: http://www.steel.org
Contact: Robert Fatzinger, Contact

Founded: 1908. **Members:** 7. **Staff:** 2. **Description:** A committee of the American Iron and Steel Institute (see separate entry). Promotes the market for industry products, which include food and beverage cans, general purpose containers, lids for glass containers and shipping containers. Coordinates investigations, activities, and promotional programs with other interested groups. Conducts product application research. Maintains speakers' bureau; compiles statistics; sponsors educational programs. **Convention/Meeting:** none. **Libraries: Type:** reference. **Holdings:** periodicals. **Affiliated With:** American Iron and Steel Institute; Steel Recycling Institute. **Formerly:** (1987) Committee of Tin Mill Product Producers. **Publications:** *SPC in the Steel Industry.* Booklet. Contains information on steel processing. **Price:** $6.00 ● *Statistical Report*, annual. **Price:** $250.00 CD-ROM/email; $300.00 paper. Alternate Formats: CD-ROM; online ● Reports ● Membership Directory, annual ● Also produces a marketing information kit.

978 ■ Containerization and Intermodal Institute (CII)

960 Holmdel Rd., Bldg. 2, Ste.201
Holmdel, NJ 07733
Ph: (732)817-9131
Free: (800)231-8244
Fax: (732)817-9133
E-mail: info@containerization.org
URL: http://containerization.org
Contact: Barbara Yeninas, Exec. Dir.

Founded: 1960. **Description:** Shippers of freight, lessors, and manufacturers of containers, accessories, and equipment; transportation and material handling specialists; marine insurance representatives; port authorities; transportation companies, common carriers, and other corporate and individual members concerned with containerization, including modern cargo containers and van-type containers. Disseminates information on intermodal transportation; Maintains speakers' bureau. **Awards:** Connie Awards. **Frequency:** annual. **Type:** recognition. **Recipient:** for individuals who have demonstrated leadership in furthering containerization and intermodalism. **Formerly:** (1968) Bulk Packaging and Containerization Institute; (1979) Containerization Institute. **Conventions/Meetings:** conference (exhibits) - 3-4/year.

979 ■ Fiberglass Tank and Pipe Institute (FPTPI)

11150 S Wilcrest Dr., Ste.101
Houston, TX 77099-4343
Ph: (281)568-4100
Fax: (281)568-9998
E-mail: info@fiberglasstankandpipe.com
URL: http://www.fiberglasstankandpipe.com
Contact: Sullivan D. Curran PE, Exec. Dir.

Founded: 1987. **Members:** 8. **Staff:** 2. **Budget:** $500,000. **Description:** Manufacturers of fiberglass reinforced thermosetting plastic tanks and piping. Promotes and protects the interests and image of members. Disseminates information; maintains speakers' bureau. **Libraries: Type:** not open to the public. **Holdings:** 500; books. **Subjects:** standards, regulations, codes, underground and aboveground storage tanks piping, fittings. **Publications:** *FRP Pipe Installation Checklist*, annual. Manual ● *FRP Tank Remanufacturing Practice*, annual. Manual. Contains procedure and guidelines. ● Papers. Alternate Formats: online. **Conventions/Meetings:** semiannual board meeting - always spring and fall.

980 ■ Film and Bag Federation (FBF)

c/o Society of the Plastics Industry, Inc.
1667 K St. NW, Ste.1000
Washington, DC 20006
Ph: (202)974-5218
Fax: (202)296-7675
E-mail: ddempsey@socplas.org
URL: http://www.plasticbag.com
Contact: Mr. Kevin Ott, Exec. Dir.

Founded: 1985. **Members:** 60. **Membership Dues:** $2,000 (annual). **Description:** Represents plastic bag manufacturing companies and suppliers involved in retail packaging. Seeks to facilitate communication among plastic bag manufacturers and keep members informed of recent technological developments in the industry. **Formerly:** (1999) Plastic Bag Association. **Publications:** Newsletter, quarterly. **Conventions/Meetings:** semiannual conference, of plastic film and bag processors, resin suppliers and machiners, equipment and services providers - in fall.

981 ■ Flexible Intermediate Bulk Container Association (FIBCA)

PO Box 24792
Minneapolis, MN 55424
Free: (866)600-8880
Fax: (661)339-0023
E-mail: info@fibca.com
URL: http://www.fibca.com
Contact: Lewis Anderson, Exec. VP

Founded: 1984. **Members:** 54. **Membership Dues:** corporate, $1,500 (annual). **Staff:** 1. **Multinational. Description:** Flexible intermediate bulk container manufacturers and other companies with an interest in the industry. Works to develop minimum standards of testing and performance for FIBCs. Acts as forum for the advancement of the FIBC industry through meetings, publications, seminars, and other programs. Serves as voice and advocate of industry needs before local, state, and national governments. **Libraries: Type:** not open to the public. **Publications:** Newsletter, semiannual. **Price:** free for members. **Conventions/Meetings:** semiannual conference - always May and October/November.

982 ■ Glass Packaging Institute (GPI)

700 N Fairfax St., Ste.510
Alexandria, VA 22314
Ph: (703)684-6359
Fax: (703)684-6048
E-mail: info@gpi.org
URL: http://www.gpi.org
Contact: Joseph J. Cattaneo, Pres.

Founded: 1945. **Members:** 43. **Membership Dues:** associate (minimum or 0.0003 of sales), $5,000 (annual) ● associate (if a company chooses not to disclose its sales level), $7,500 (annual). **Staff:** 5. **Budget:** $1,800,000. **Regional Groups:** 1. **Descrip-**

tion: Glass container manufacturers and suppliers. Promotes the manufacture, use, and recycling of glass containers and closures. Develops and evaluates testing procedures and equipment; conducts experimental activities in glass packaging; develops designs and specifications for glass containers and finishes; conducts advertising and promotional campaigns for the generic products; develops and maintains constructive relationships with various public and government agencies at the local, regional, state, and national levels. **Telecommunication Services:** electronic mail, jcattaneo@gpi.org. **Committees:** Academic; Closures; Marketing; Recycling; Technical. **Formerly:** (1976) Glass Container Manufacturers Institute. **Publications:** *Teacher's Guide to Class Container Recycling.* **Conventions/Meetings:** annual conference.

983 ■ Industrial Metal Containers and Wire Decking, a Product Section of the Material Handling Industry (IMC&WD)
8720 Red Oak Blvd., Ste.201
Charlotte, NC 28217
Ph: (704)676-1190
Fax: (704)676-1199
E-mail: jnofsinger@mhia.org
Contact: John B. Nofsinger, CEO
Founded: 1972. **Members:** 10. **Staff:** 2. **Description:** Individual proprietorships, partnerships, corporations, and other enterprises that are members of the Material Handling Institute and are involved in the manufacture and sale of steel and wire industrial containers and their components. Aims to promote the best and widest possible market, consistent with the user's best interests. Develops and promotes standard nomenclature and a code of ethics within the industry. Serves as liaison among members, related trade associations, product sections, and private and governmental groups establishing standards and safety codes affecting the industry; coordinates efforts of such organizations. Compiles and disseminates industry statistics. **Telecommunication Services:** electronic mail, ahowie@mhia.org ● electronic mail, ctringali@mhia.org. **Formerly:** (1999) Industrial Medal Containers, Section of the Material Handling Institute. **Publications:** *Membership Roster*, periodic. Membership Directory ● *Specifications for Design and Utilization of Industrial Metal Containers* ● Also prepares and distributes educational and publicity materials. **Conventions/Meetings:** semiannual meeting.

984 ■ Institute of International Container Lessors (IICL)
555 Pleasantville Rd., Ste.140 S
Briarcliff Manor, NY 10510
Ph: (914)747-9100
Fax: (914)747-4600
E-mail: info@iicl.org
URL: http://www.iicl.org
Contact: Henry F. White Jr., Pres.
Founded: 1971. **Members:** 3. **Staff:** 5. **Multinational. Description:** Companies throughout the world engaged in leasing marine cargo containers and chassis to ship operators and others. Stresses the contribution to world trade made by the container and chassis leasing industry; suggests actions to be taken by intergovernmental agencies that will benefit the industry and take into account safety, environment, and efficiency. Coordinates standard activities with the International Organization for Standardization and the American National Standards Institute. Publishes series of technical manuals. Sponsors container testing, inspector certification, and other instructional and communications programs. **Awards:** Chassis Inspector's Award. **Frequency:** annual. **Type:** recognition. **Recipient:** for an individual with the highest score on the chassis inspector's certification examination ● Container Inspector's Award. **Frequency:** annual. **Type:** recognition. **Recipient:** for an individual with the highest score on the container inspector's certification examination. **Committees:** Legal and Tax; Technology. **Publications:** *Guide for Container Equipment Inspection*, periodic. Manual ● *The IICL Newsletter*, 2-3/year. Alternate Formats: online ● *Inspection Directory*, annual. Alternate Formats: online ● *Technical Bulletin*, periodic. Alternate Formats: online ● Manuals ● Also publishes other inspection guides, repair manuals, recommendations, testing reports.

985 ■ International Corrugated Case Association (ICCA)
25 NW Point Blvd., Ste.510
Elk Grove Village, IL 60007
Ph: (847)364-9600
Fax: (847)364-9639
E-mail: hmarshall@iccanet.org
URL: http://www.iccanet.org
Contact: Heather Marshall, Pres.
Founded: 1961. **Members:** 37. **Staff:** 2. **Multinational. Description:** Promotes the welfare of the worldwide corrugated industry. Supports and supplements the programs and activities of member associations. Addresses the needs of the worldwide corrugated container industry. Collects and disseminates information about corrugated products, issues, services and resources throughout the world. **Working Groups:** Good Manufacturing Practices/Food Contact; Lightweighting; Plastic Penetration; Retail Requirements; RFID/Tracking-Tracing. **Affiliated With:** Association of Independent Corrugated Converters; Fibre Box Association. **Formerly:** Association Internationale des Fabricants de Caisses en Carton Ondule. **Conventions/Meetings:** biennial conference.

986 ■ National Association of Container Distributors (NACD)
1601 Bond St., Ste.101
Naperville, IL 60563
Ph: (630)544-5052
Fax: (630)544-5055
E-mail: info@nacd.net
URL: http://www.nacd.net
Contact: Dennis Sipe, Chm.
Founded: 1924. **Members:** 36. **Staff:** 3. **Description:** Represents packaging distributors who supply bottles, lubes, pumps, sprayers, and related components. Services include warehousing and labeling. **Awards:** Package Awards. **Frequency:** annual. **Type:** recognition ● **Type:** scholarship. **Recipient:** for packaging school. **Telecommunication Services:** electronic mail, dennysipe@all-pak.com. **Publications:** *Container News*, periodic. Newsletter. **Price:** included in membership dues. Alternate Formats: online ● Membership Directory, annual. **Conventions/Meetings:** annual competition and convention ● annual meeting.

987 ■ National Paperbox Association (NPA)
113 S West St., 3rd Fl.
Alexandria, VA 22314
Ph: (703)684-2212
Fax: (703)683-6920
E-mail: npahq@paperbox.org
URL: http://www.paperbox.org
Contact: Scott Miller, Exec. VP
Founded: 1918. **Members:** 250. **Membership Dues:** active (based on net sales), $1,000-$6,500 (annual) ● associate, $2,000 (annual). **Staff:** 3. **Budget:** $650,000. **Regional Groups:** 4. **Description:** Independent package converters, including manufacturers of rigid (set-up) and folding paper boxes; suppliers to the industry. Aims to further the development, use, and sale of members' products; to deal with common industry problems; to foster greater operating economies and efficiencies. Represents the industry before legislative and regulatory bodies. Conducts technical workshops and seminars on sales, marketing, costing, computers, and management methods. Compiles statistics. **Awards: Type:** recognition. **Committees:** Folding Carton; Rigid Box. **Formerly:** (1969) National Paper Box Manufacturers Association; (1979) National Paper Box Association; (1992) National Paper Box and Packaging Association. **Publications:** *Key Business Ratio*. Manual. **Price:** $53.50 for members; $78.50 for nonmembers ● *The Packet*, quarterly. Newsletter. Includes management information, government updates, membership news, and tips on production cost saving and methods. **Price:** free, for members only. **Circulation:** 450. **Advertising:** accepted ● Membership Directory, annual. **Price:** $150.00. **Circulation:** 500 ● Booklets. **Conventions/Meetings:** annual meeting (exhibits) - always April or May ● annual seminar (exhibits).

988 ■ National Wood Tank Institute (NWTI)
PO Box 2755
Philadelphia, PA 19120
Ph: (215)329-9022
Fax: (215)329-1177
E-mail: jackhillman@woodtank.com
URL: http://www.woodtank.com
Contact: Jack Hillman, Sec.
Founded: 1942. **Members:** 9. **Description:** Corporations, individuals, partnerships, or associations within the U.S. and Canada engaged, in whole or in part, in the manufacture of any type of wood tank, wood vat, or wood pipe for any purpose. Seeks to advance the interests of members and to increase the use of their products. Prepares and disseminates information regarding the proper selection, installation, use, and maintenance of wood tanks and wood pipe; exchanges knowledge for the benefit of the industry. Works to improve manufacturing methods and practices, establish acceptable standards, and engage in product research. **Libraries: Type:** open to the public. **Publications:** *Specifications for Wood Tanks and Pipe Technical Bulletin No. S-82*. **Price:** free ● *Wood Tanks and Pipe for Corrosive Applications*. Bulletin. **Conventions/Meetings:** annual meeting.

989 ■ National Wooden Pallet and Container Association (NWPCA)
1421 Prince St., Ste.340
Alexandria, VA 22314-2805
Ph: (703)519-6104
Fax: (703)519-4720
E-mail: bscholnick@palletcentral.com
URL: http://www.nwpca.com
Contact: Bruce N. Scholnick, Pres./CEO
Founded: 1947. **Members:** 525. **Membership Dues:** domestic industry (based on annual sales volume), $500-$5,000 (annual) ● international industry (based on annual sales volume), $800-$1,500 (annual) ● associate (based on annual sales volume), $1,325-$2,350 (annual) ● end user, $800 (annual). **Staff:** 10. **Budget:** $1,500,000. **Description:** Manufacturers, recyclers, and distributors of pallets, containers, reels, and other unit load bases used in warehousing, distribution, and logistics. Compiles industry information; develops national product standards; conducts market research. **Additional Websites:** http://www.palletcentral.com. **Committees:** Education; Membership; Research; Standards; Trade Promotion. **Councils:** Container; Recyclers. **Formed by Merger of:** National Wooden Box Association; National Wooden Pallet Manufacturers Association. **Publications:** *Pallet Central*, monthly. Newsletter. **Advertising:** accepted ● Directory, annual ● Handbooks ● Pamphlets. **Conventions/Meetings:** annual Leadership Conference and Expo - meeting (exhibits) - always February.

990 ■ Pacific Coast Paper Box Manufacturers' Association (PCPBMA)
c/o Paperboard Packaging Council
201 N Union St., Ste.220
Alexandria, VA 22314
Ph: (703)836-3300
Fax: (703)836-3290
E-mail: jbrown@ppcnet.org
URL: http://www.ppcnet.org
Contact: James Brown CAE, Exec. Dir.
Founded: 1911. **Members:** 48. **Staff:** 1. **Budget:** $48,500. **Local Groups:** 2. **Description:** Represents folding carton and rigid carton manufacturers. Furthers the success and development of paperboard packaging in the territory west of the Rocky Mountains. Offers statistical, and labor data summary programs for members. Conducts technical and production seminars and employee training in plant and equipment operations. Sponsors student design-school competition. **Awards:** Safety Award. **Frequency:** annual. **Type:** recognition. **Recipient:** for safety record ● Student Design-School Competition.

Frequency: annual. **Type:** recognition. **Recipient:** for the best boxes and cartons produced by class. **Committees:** Carton Competition; Insurance; Safety. **Divisions:** Folding Box; Rigid Box; Suppliers. **Publications:** *Labor Data Manual*, quarterly ● *Safety Super*, monthly. **Conventions/Meetings:** annual convention - always June ● annual meeting.

991 ■ Paper Shipping Sack Manufacturers' Association (PSSMA)
520 E Oxford St.
Coopersburg, PA 18036
Ph: (610)282-6845
Fax: (610)282-6921
E-mail: admin@pssma.org
URL: http://www.pssma.com
Contact: Richard E. Storat, Pres.

Founded: 1933. **Members:** 50. **Staff:** 2. **Budget:** $400,000. **Description:** Manufacturers of multi-wall (3-4-5-6 walls) paper shipping sacks designed for packaging and shipping products in domestic and export commerce. **Awards:** Plant Safety Award. **Frequency:** annual. **Type:** recognition. **Recipient:** for plant in size category with best safety record. **Computer Services:** database, management information system. **Committees:** Associate; Information; Marketing; Production; Technical. **Formerly:** Rope Paper Sack Manufacturers Association. **Publications:** *Color Guide*. Features a natural and bleached Kraft color guide for multi-wall bags. **Price:** $276.00/set of 12 ● *Hazardous Material Packaging Guide*. Includes guidelines to DOT regulations for multi-wall bags. **Price:** $110.00/set of 10 ● *PSSMA Reference Guide - For the Paper Shipping Sack Industry*. Introduces the complexity and diverse nature of the paper shipping sack industry. **Price:** $11.00 for nonmembers ● *Recovery Directory*. **Price:** $100.00/set of 10. **Conventions/Meetings:** annual meeting ● semiannual Production Managers' Seminars.

992 ■ Plastic Shipping Container Institute (PSCI)
1700 Pennsylvania Ave. NW, Ste.400
Washington, DC 20006
Ph: (202)349-4190
Fax: (202)349-4199
E-mail: info@pscionline.org
URL: http://www.pscionline.org
Contact: David H. Baker, Gen. Counsel

Founded: 1976. **Members:** 42. **Staff:** 1. **Budget:** $150,000. **Description:** Manufacturers of plastic shipping containers and component parts; producers of virgin high-density polyethylene; companies engaged in performance evaluation. Promotes the use of plastic pails through educational and public relations campaigns and assists various regulatory bodies in the development of regulations affecting the industry. Seeks to improve service to the consumer and to keep abreast of new technical developments, rules, and regulations affecting the industry. Conducts research and testing projects. **Telecommunication Services:** electronic mail, membership@psconline.org ● electronic mail, dhbakerlaw@aol.com. **Committees:** Educational/Promotional; Regulatory; Technical. **Conventions/Meetings:** semiannual meeting and seminar - usually February and September.

993 ■ Recycled Paperboard Technical Association (RPTA)
920 Davis Rd., Ste.306
Elgin, IL 60123
Ph: (847)622-2544
Fax: (847)622-2546
E-mail: rpta@rpta.org
URL: http://www.rpta.org
Contact: Mr. Dave Ruby, Exec. Dir.

Founded: 1953. **Members:** 27. **Staff:** 4. **Budget:** $600,000. **Description:** All members manufacture recycled paperboard from recovered fiber. Conducts research on technical developments in recycled boxboard. **Formerly:** (1991) Boxboard Research and Development Association. **Conventions/Meetings:** annual meeting - always second week of May in Chicago, IL.

994 ■ Reusable Industrial Packaging Association (RIPA)
8401 Corporate Dr., Ste.450
Landover, MD 20785
Ph: (301)577-3786
Fax: (301)577-6476
E-mail: prankin@igc.org
URL: http://www.reusablepackaging.org
Contact: Paul W. Rankin, Pres.

Founded: 1942. **Members:** 160. **Membership Dues:** reconditioner, manufacturer, dealer, broker in U.S., voting international, $2,150-$35,700 (annual) ● reconditioner, manufacturer, dealer, broker in Canada, $1,100-$17,800 (annual) ● manufacturer, $5,500-$1,500 (annual) ● packager, $425 (annual) ● supplier, associate, $2,150 (annual) ● non-voting international, $975 (annual). **Staff:** 4. **Description:** Reconditioners, dealers, and suppliers of the steel drum reconditioning industry. Represents the industrial packaging business in North America. Serves as a focal point for the industry's collective action on legislative issues, regulatory, standards, and legal matters at the international, national and state levels. **Committees:** Steel Drum; Technical. **Formerly:** (1986) National Barrel and Drum Association; (1998) Association of Container Reconditioners. **Publications:** *Digest of Hazardous Materials Regulations* ● *Membership and Industrial Supply Directory*, annual. Membership Directory ● *Ordering New Steel Drums for Hazardous Materials Transportation*. Booklet. **Price:** $2.95 for members; $3.75 for nonmembers ● *Responsible Container Management* ● *Responsible Packaging Management Booklet*. **Price:** $3.25 for nonmembers (1-100 copies); $3.00 for members (100 or more copies); $4.00/copy for nonmembers ● *Reusable Packaging*, monthly. Newsletter ● *Technical Forum*, annual. **Conventions/Meetings:** triennial international conference ● annual meeting - always November.

995 ■ Steel Shipping Container Institute (SSCI)
1101 14th St. NW, Ste.S-1001
Washington, DC 20005
Ph: (202)408-1900
Fax: (202)408-1972
E-mail: ssci_office@steelcontainers.com
URL: http://www.steelcontainers.com
Contact: Leonard H. Berenfield, Chm.

Founded: 1944. **Members:** 57. **Membership Dues:** regular (based on sales), $6,415-$50,000 (annual) ● associate, $5,304 (annual) ● international, $1,500 (annual). **Staff:** 3. **Description:** Manufacturers of steel drums, barrels, pails, accessories, fittings, equipment, and materials used by the industry. Underwrites U.S. Bureau of Census monthly report on steel pail and drum production. Sponsors development programs on container design, safety features, testing, quality control, and product protection systems. **Telecommunication Services:** electronic mail, lberenfield@berenfield.com. **Committees:** Federal Regulations; Industrial Relations; Market Development; Technical Projects; Traffic Advisory. **Publications:** *Color Selector for New Steel Drums and Pails* ● *Drum Buyer's Guide* ● *Pail Buyer's Guide* ● *SSCI Guide for Export Shippers of Hazardous Materials* ● *Steel Shipping Container Institute—Reporter*, periodic. **Price:** free ● Annual Report, annual. **Price:** available to members only ● Directory, periodic. **Price:** available to members only ● Newsletter, periodic. **Conventions/Meetings:** annual meeting.

996 ■ Steel Tank Institute and Steel Plate Fabricators Association (STI/SPFA)
570 Oakwood Rd.
Lake Zurich, IL 60047
Ph: (847)438-8265
Fax: (847)438-8766
E-mail: info@steeltank.com
URL: http://www.steeltank.com
Contact: Wayne B. Geyer PE, Exec. VP

Founded: 1916. **Members:** 200. **Staff:** 15. **Budget:** $2,000,000. **Multinational. Description:** Trade association for manufacturers of steel underground and above ground storage tanks. Develops fabrication standards for secondary containment, corrosion control and thermal insulation. Conducts research and development, quality control, and marketing programs. Sponsors educational programs. **Libraries: Type:** reference. **Holdings:** artwork, audiovisuals, books, clippings, periodicals. **Awards:** Quality Awards. **Frequency:** annual. **Type:** recognition ● Safety Award of Achievement. **Frequency:** annual. **Type:** recognition. **Recipient:** for the highest achievements in safe performance ● Safety Award of Excellence. **Frequency:** annual. **Type:** recognition. **Recipient:** for outstanding safety performance ● Steel Pipe Fabricated Project of the Year. **Frequency:** annual. **Type:** recognition ● Steel Pipeline Project of the Year. **Frequency:** annual. **Type:** recognition ● Steel Plate Fabricated Product of the Year. **Frequency:** annual. **Type:** recognition ● Steel Tank of the Year. **Frequency:** annual. **Type:** recognition. **Committees:** Member Services; Safety and Health; Technical. **Programs:** Pipe Certification. **Sections:** Field Erected Tank; Pressure Vessel & Special Fabricated Products; Shop Fabricated Atmospheric Tanks; Steel Pipe. **Publications:** *Membership Roster*, annual. Membership Directory ● *Tank Talk*, bimonthly. Newsletter. Alternate Formats: online. **Conventions/Meetings:** semiannual conference (exhibits) - always February and August.

997 ■ Steel Tube Institute of North America (STINA)
2000 Ponce de Leon, Ste.600
Coral Gables, FL 33134
Ph: (305)421-6326
Fax: (305)443-1603
E-mail: stina@steeltubeinstitute.org
URL: http://www.steeltubeinstitute.org
Contact: William Wolfe, Exec. Dir.

Founded: 1930. **Members:** 75. **Membership Dues:** active (minimum), $3,005 (annual) ● associate, $3,850 (annual). **Staff:** 3. **Budget:** $1,500,000. **Description:** Manufacturers of tube and pipe formed from flat rolled carbon or stainless steel. Disseminates information to tubing users; recommends new tube uses; encourages research and development; fosters efficient production and expands proven uses for both carbon and stainless steel tubing. Maintains technical information center. **Libraries: Type:** open to the public. **Holdings:** 100. **Subjects:** tube and pipe production, product applications, producer and capabilities, design aid. **Computer Services:** Mailing lists, of members. **Committees:** AS Welded Mechanical; Drawn Over Mandrel; Hollow Structural Sections; Manufacturing/Technical; Mechanical Tube; Stainless; Standard Pipe; Standards, Codes, and Public Relations; Supplier Relations. **Formerly:** Formed Steel Tube Institute; (1988) Welded Steel Tube Institute. **Publications:** Also publishes tables and technical papers. **Conventions/Meetings:** semiannual convention and conference.

998 ■ Tank Conference of the Truck Trailer Manufacturers Association (TCTTMA)
1020 Princess St.
Alexandria, VA 22314
Ph: (703)549-3010
Fax: (703)549-3014
E-mail: ttma@erols.com
URL: http://www.ttmanet.org
Contact: Richard P. Bowling, Pres.

Founded: 1937. **Description:** Manufacturers of transportation tanks for the hauling by truck of liquid and dry bulk commodities. **Formerly:** (1941) National Truck Tank Association; (1962) National Truck Tank and Trailer Tank Institute. **Publications:** Bulletin, weekly ● Directory, annual. **Conventions/Meetings:** annual meeting.

999 ■ Textile Bag and Packaging Association (TBPA)
c/o Maxine Shapiro, Sec.
3181-306 Charlevoix SE
Grand Rapids, MI 49546
Ph: (616)942-9654
Free: (800)543-3400

E-mail: sccasharpir@aol.com
URL: http://www.textilepackaging.org
Contact: Maxine Shapiro, Sec.

Founded: 1933. **Members:** 175. **Membership Dues:** regular, $400 (annual). **Staff:** 2. **Budget:** $70,000. **Description:** Represents manufacturers, distributors, and recyclers of new, reclaimed, and processed paper, burlap, polypropylene, and cotton bags; distributors of other packaging products. **Formerly:** (1968) National Burlap Bag Dealers Association; (1984) Textile Bag Processors Association. **Publications:** *Grab Bag*, biennial. Newsletter. **Advertising:** accepted ● *Textile Bag and Packaging Association Roster Book*, biennial. **Price:** free, for members only. **Advertising:** accepted ● *Who's Who in Textile Bag and Packaging*, biennial. Directory. **Price:** available to members only. **Advertising:** accepted. **Conventions/Meetings:** semiannual convention and meeting (exhibits).

Contractors

1000 ■ ADSC: The International Association of Foundation Drilling

Pacific Ctr. I
14180 Dallas Pkwy., Ste.510
Dallas, TX 75254
Ph: (214)343-2091
Fax: (214)343-2384
E-mail: adsc@adsc-iafd.com
URL: http://www.adsc-iafd.com
Contact: S. Scot Litke, Exec. Dir.

Founded: 1971. **Members:** 600. **Membership Dues:** category I contractor, $4,640 (annual) ● category II contractor, $2,460 (annual) ● category III contractor, $1,500 (annual) ● category IV contractor, $600 (annual). **Staff:** 6. **Budget:** $725,000. **Description:** Contracting firms, suppliers, design engineers, and educators engaged in the design and construction of drilled shafts and foundations under water and on land. Promotes the education of the engineering community on the advantages of using the drilled shaft foundation concept and on the economies and permanency therein. Conducts 5 to 7 seminars each year. Provides film service; maintains speakers' bureau. Compiles statistics; conducts research programs; develops standards and specifications. **Libraries: Type:** reference. **Holdings:** 150. **Awards:** Design Award. **Frequency:** annual. **Type:** recognition ● Outstanding Contractor Award. **Frequency:** annual. **Type:** recognition ● Outstanding Service Award. **Frequency:** annual. **Type:** recognition ● Safety Awards. **Frequency:** annual. **Type:** recognition. **Recipient:** for universities. **Telecommunication Services:** electronic mail, slitke@adsc-iafd.com. **Committees:** Associate Member; Awards; Earth Retention Subcontracting; Education; Health and Safety; History; Industry Advancement; Membership; Oversight; Residential; Site Selection; Standards and Specifications; Strategic Planning; Supervisory Personnel Training Institute; Technical Affiliates. **Formerly:** (2000) Association of Drilled Shaft Contractors; (2005) International Association of Foundation Drilling. **Publications:** *ADSC Directory*, annual. Membership Directory. Lists all members with cross-references. **Price:** free for members; $75.00/issue for nonmembers. **Circulation:** 1,250. **Advertising:** accepted ● *Association of Drilled Shaft Contractors—Technical Library Catalog*, periodic. Contains technical reference materials for soil and structural engineers, architects, specification writers and engineering students. **Price:** free ● *Drilled Shaft Inspectors Manual* ● *Drilled Shafts: Construction Procedures and Design Methods, the FHWA Manual* ● *Foundation Drilling*, 8/year. Journal. Devoted to the international affairs of the foundation drilling industry. Includes research reports and calendar of events. **Price:** included in membership dues; $60.00 /year for nonmembers. ISSN: 0274-5184. **Circulation:** 2,000. **Advertising:** accepted ● *Foundations in Problem Soils: A Guide to Lightly Loaded Foundation Construction for Challenging Soil and Site Conditions* ● Reports. **Conventions/Meetings:** annual meeting.

1001 ■ American Society of Concrete Contractors (ASCC)

2025 S Brentwood Blvd., Ste.105
St. Louis, MO 63144
Ph: (314)962-0210
Free: (866)788-2722
Fax: (314)968-4367
E-mail: questions@ascconline.org
URL: http://www.ascconline.org
Contact: Michael J. Schneider, Chm.

Founded: 1964. **Members:** 700. **Membership Dues:** contractor, $795-$995 (annual) ● associate, $850 (annual) ● sustaining, $2,000 (annual) ● individual, $250 (annual). **Staff:** 4. **Budget:** $850,000. **Description:** General contractors and subcontractors working with concrete; allied businesses, such as ready-mix producers, equipment manufacturers, and other suppliers and distributors. Seeks to: stimulate professional responsibility and reliability; encourage the research and development of concrete; facilitate technical and practical education; enhance the public image of concrete and improve its competitive position among basic building materials; broaden markets for concrete construction. **Awards:** Safety Award. **Frequency:** annual. **Type:** recognition. **Committees:** Annual Conference; Bylaws; CEO Forum; Education and Training; Education, Research and Development Foundation; Insurance; Liaison; Nominating; Strategic Planning. **Councils:** Decorative Concrete; Manufacturers Advisory; Safety and Risk Management. **Formerly:** (1998) American Society for Concrete Construction. **Supersedes:** National Concrete Contractors Association. **Publications:** *ASCC Insurance Bulletins*. Contains brief discussions of insurance issues affecting the concrete contractor. **Price:** $20.00 for nonmembers; $10.00 for members ● *ASCC Membership Directory*, annual. Contains lists of all members of ASCC and DCC. **Price:** included in membership dues ● *ASCC Safety Manual*. Contains the elements of an effective safety program for the concrete contractor. **Price:** $395.00 for nonmembers; $75.00 for members ● *ASCC Troubleshooting Newsletter*. Newsletters. Contains the answers to tough questions from the ASCC Concrete Hotline. **Price:** $35.00 for members; $70.00 for nonmembers ● *Basic Safety Rules for Construction* (in English and Spanish). Book. Contains brief discussions of insurance issues affecting the concrete contractor. **Price:** $4.00 for nonmembers; $2.50 for members ● *Concrete Construction and Concrete Concepts*. Magazine. **Price:** free for members ● *Construction Spanish Pocket Dictionary* (in English and Spanish). Book. Includes hundreds of words and phrases translated from English to Spanish, and Spanish to English. **Price:** $8.00 for nonmembers; $6.00 for members ● *Employee Safety Orientation* (in English and Spanish). Video. Serves as a tool to welcome new employees and introduce them to the basics of safety on a concrete construction job site. **Price:** $59.95 for nonmembers; $39.95 for members. **Conventions/Meetings:** annual ASCC CEO Forum - meeting, for presidents, owners, CEOs of concrete contracting companies - always July ● annual conference - always September. 2008 Sept. 11-13, San Antonio, TX ● annual meeting, for all members - always January or February.

1002 ■ American Sports Builders Association (ASBA)

8480 Baltimore Natl. Pike, No. 307
Ellicott City, MD 21043
Ph: (410)730-9595
Free: (866)501-2722
Fax: (410)730-8833
E-mail: info@sportsbuilders.org
URL: http://sportsbuilders.org
Contact: Carol T. Hogan CAE, Exec. VP

Founded: 1965. **Members:** 300. **Membership Dues:** provisional/ancillary, $435 (annual) ● professional, $490 (annual) ● builder, $815 (annual) ● associate/affiliate, $1,090 (annual). **Staff:** 3. **Budget:** $400,000. **Description:** Contractors who install running tracks, synthetic turf fields, tennis courts and indoor sports surfaces; manufacturers who supply basic materials for construction; accessory suppliers, designers, architects, and consultants of facilities. Provides guidelines for tennis court construction, running track construction, fencing, synthetic turf field construction and lighting. Offers certification and awards programs. **Awards:** Outstanding Indoor Tennis Facility Award. **Frequency:** annual. **Type:** recognition ● Outstanding Outdoor Tennis Facility Award. **Frequency:** annual. **Type:** recognition ● Outstanding Residential Tennis Court/Facility Award. **Frequency:** annual. **Type:** recognition ● Outstanding Track/Facility Award. **Frequency:** annual. **Type:** recognition. **Computer Services:** Information services, construction guidelines/buyer's guides. **Telecommunication Services:** electronic mail, carol@assochq.com. **Divisions:** Associate/Affiliate; Indoor Facilities; Professionals; Tennis; Track. **Publications:** *American Sports Builders Association—Newsline*, quarterly. Newsletter. Includes association news, technical articles, information on new products, membership profile, book reviews, and calendar of events. Alternate Formats: online. Also Cited As: *ASBA Newsletter* ● *Buyers Guide for Tennis Court Construction*, periodic. Booklet. **Price:** free ● *Buyer's Guide for Track Construction*, periodic. Booklet. **Price:** free ● *Running Tracks: A Construction and Maintenance Manual*, semiannual. Covers running tracks, including diagrams and construction information. **Price:** $39.95 plus postage and handling. **Advertising:** accepted ● *Tennis and Track Construction Guidelines*, periodic. Manual. Covers all aspects of tennis court design, construction, surfaces, equipment, amenities and accessories. **Price:** $39.95 ● *Tennis Courts: A Construction and Maintenance Manual*, biennial. Covers all aspects of tennis court design, construction, surfaces, equipment, amenities and accessories. **Price:** $39.95 plus postage and handling. **Advertising:** accepted ● Membership Directory, annual. Includes advertisers' index and list of builders, suppliers, architects, and designers of tennis courts and running tracks by company name. **Price:** free. **Advertising:** accepted. **Conventions/Meetings:** annual convention (exhibits).

1003 ■ American Subcontractors Association (ASA)

1004 Duke St.
Alexandria, VA 22314-3588
Ph: (703)684-3450
Free: (888)374-3133
Fax: (703)836-3482
E-mail: asaoffice@asa-hq.com
URL: http://www.asaonline.com
Contact: David H. Bradbury, Pres.

Founded: 1966. **Members:** 5,500. **Membership Dues:** individual, $270 (annual). **Staff:** 11. **Budget:** $1,500,000. **Local Groups:** 51. **Description:** Construction subcontractors of trades and specialties such as foundations, concrete, masonry, steel, mechanical, drywall, electrical, painting, plastering, roofing, and acoustical. Formed to deal with issues common to subcontractors. Works with other segments of the construction industry in promoting ethical practices, beneficial legislation, and education of construction subcontractors and suppliers. Manages the Foundation of the American Subcontractors Association (FASA). **Telecommunication Services:** electronic mail, dbradbury@asa-hq.com. **Publications:** *Action ASA*, monthly. Newsletter. Contains news for ASA volunteer leaders. Also available via email. Alternate Formats: online ● *ASA Today*, weekly. Newsletter. Reports on business, legal, and legislative issues of concern to the subcontracting industry. **Circulation:** 7,000 ● *The Contractor's Compass*, quarterly. Magazine. Serves as an educational journal for the construction industry. **Circulation:** 7,000. **Conventions/Meetings:** annual Business Forum & Convention (exhibits).

1004 ■ Associated Builders and Contractors (ABC)

4250 N Fairfax Dr., 9th Fl.
Arlington, VA 22203-1607
Ph: (703)812-2000
Fax: (703)812-8200
E-mail: gotquestions@abc.org
URL: http://www.abc.org
Contact: Kirk Pickerel, Pres./CEO

Founded: 1950. **Members:** 19,000. **Staff:** 75. **Budget:** $12,500,000. **Local Groups:** 81. **Description:**

Construction contractors, subcontractors, suppliers, and associates. Aims to foster and perpetuate the principles of rewarding construction workers and management on the basis of merit. Sponsors management education programs and craft training; also sponsors apprenticeship and skill training programs. Disseminates technological and labor relations information. **Libraries: Type:** reference. **Holdings:** archival material. **Awards:** Beam Club Man on the Year. **Frequency:** annual. **Type:** recognition. **Recipient:** for top membership recruitment ● Contractor of the Year. **Frequency:** annual. **Type:** recognition ● Excellence in Construction. **Frequency:** annual. **Type:** recognition. **Recipient:** for outstanding safety or project difficulty. **Computer Services:** Online services, construction referral service. **Telecommunication Services:** electronic mail, pickerel@abc.org. **Committees:** Business Development; Bylaws and Policy; Contract Documents; Craft Training; Diversity; Insurance; Legal Rights & Strategy; Legislative; Management Education; Pension; Political Action; Safety, Environment and Health; Skilled Trades Exploring. **Councils:** Metal Building Contractors. **Departments:** Communications; Finance; Government Affairs; Insurance; Member Services. **Task Forces:** Mold. **Affiliated With:** National Center for Construction Education and Research. **Publications:** *ABC Today*, semimonthly. Magazine. Includes news for merit shop contractors. **Price:** included in membership dues; $60.00 /year for nonmembers. **Advertising:** accepted ● *National Membership Directory and Users' Guide*, annual ● Manuals ● Videos. **Conventions/Meetings:** annual convention, with entertainment and speakers (exhibits).

1005 ■ Associated General Contractors of America (AGC)
2300 Wilson Blvd., Ste.400
Arlington, VA 22201
Ph: (703)548-3118 (703)837-5343
Free: (800)242-1767
Fax: (703)548-3119
E-mail: info@agc.org
URL: http://www.agc.org
Contact: Stephen E. Sandherr, CEO
Founded: 1918. **Members:** 34,416. **Staff:** 81. **Budget:** $18,000,000. **Local Groups:** 100. **Description:** General construction contractors; subcontractors; industry suppliers; service firms. Provides market services through its divisions. Conducts special conferences and seminars designed specifically for construction firms. Compiles statistics on job accidents reported by member firms. Maintains 65 committees, including joint cooperative committees with other associations and liaison committees with federal agencies. **Awards:** AGC Education and Research Fund Scholarships. **Type:** scholarship ● Build/America Awards. **Frequency:** annual. **Type:** recognition. **Recipient:** for innovative and outstanding achievements by general contractors ● Willis Safety Awards. **Frequency:** annual. **Type:** recognition. **Recipient:** for safety. **Divisions:** Building; Collective Bargaining; Construction Economics; Contract Documents; Education; Equal Opportunity; Heavy; Highway; Industrial; Information; International Construction; Legal; Legislative; Manpower and Training; Municipal Utilities; Open Shop; Safety; Tax and Fiscal. **Publications:** *AGC Membership Directory and Buyers' Guide*, annual. **Price:** $35.00 /year for members; $250.00 /year for nonmembers. **Advertising:** accepted ● *Associated General Contractors of America—News and Views*, biweekly. Newsletter. **Price:** free for members; $100.00 /year for nonmembers. **Circulation:** 22,000 ● *Constructor*, monthly. Magazine. Contains information for general contractors engaged in construction. **Price:** $15.00 /year for members; $250.00 /year for nonmembers. ISSN: 0162-6191. **Circulation:** 44,000. **Advertising:** accepted ● Manuals ● Videos ● Also publishes guides, model contract documents, studies, and checklists. **Conventions/Meetings:** annual Construction Exposition - convention (exhibits) - usually March ● annual meeting - always mid-year.

1006 ■ Associated Specialty Contractors (ASC)
3 Bethesda Metro Ctr., Ste.1100
Bethesda, MD 20814
Ph: (703)548-3118
E-mail: dgw@necanet.org
URL: http://www.assoc-spec-con.org
Contact: Daniel G. Walter, Pres.
Founded: 1950. **Members:** 9. **Membership Dues:** regular, $2,700 (annual). **Budget:** $50,000. **Description:** Works to promote efficient management and productivity. Coordinates the work of specialized branches of the industry in management information, research, public information, government relations and construction relations. Serves as a liaison among specialty trade associations in the areas of public relations, government relations, and with other organizations. Seeks to avoid unnecessary duplication of effort and expense or conflicting programs among affiliates. Identifies areas of interest and problems shared by members, and develops positions and approaches on such problems. **Libraries: Type:** reference. **Holdings:** archival material. **Committees:** Government Affairs; Industry Relations. **Formerly:** (1973) Council of Mechanical Specialty Contracting Industries. **Publications:** *Contract Documents*. Book.

1007 ■ Association of Diving Contractors International (ADCI)
5206 FM 1960 W, Ste.202
Houston, TX 77069-4406
Ph: (281)893-8388
Fax: (281)893-5118
E-mail: pnewsum@adc-int.org
URL: http://www.adc-int.org
Contact: Phil Newsum, Exec. Dir.
Founded: 1968. **Members:** 500. **Membership Dues:** individual, $25 (annual) ● general (1), $500 (annual) ● general (2), $750 (annual) ● general (3), $1,400 (annual) ● general (4), $3,750 (annual) ● general (5), $4,800 (annual) ● general (6), $5,750 (annual) ● supporting, $750 (annual) ● associate (based on annual revenues), $500-$1,000 (annual). **Staff:** 4. **Budget:** $300,000. **Regional Groups:** 4. **National Groups:** 39. **Multinational. Description:** Represents commercial diving and underwater contractors, manufacturers, and suppliers of diving equipment and related products. Promotes communication, education, and safety throughout the international commercial diving and underwater industry worldwide. Compiles statistics, prepares and develops safety related video films. **Computer Services:** database. **Committees:** Civil Engineering Diving; DOT Operator Qualifications; Safety; Technical. **Formerly:** (2000) Association of Diving Contractors. **Publications:** *ADC Consensus Standards for Commercial Diving Operations*. Manual. **Price:** $43.00 ● *Underwater Magazine*, quarterly. Covers marine technology and underwater vehicles. **Price:** $50.00/year outside U.S. **Advertising:** accepted. Alternate Formats: online ● Videos. **Conventions/Meetings:** annual Underwater Intervention - convention and trade show, with international diving symposium (exhibits).

1008 ■ Ceilings and Interior Systems Construction Association (CISCA)
1500 Lincoln Hwy., Ste.202
St. Charles, IL 60174
Ph: (630)584-1919
Fax: (630)584-2003
E-mail: info@cisca.org
URL: http://www.cisca.org
Contact: Bonny Luck, Exec. Dir.
Founded: 1949. **Members:** 600. **Membership Dues:** contractor, $640 (annual) ● distributor, $730 (annual) ● manufacturer, $880 (annual) ● associate/manufacturer's representative, $440 (annual) ● overseas manufacturer, $545 (annual) ● other overseas manufacturer, $365 (annual) ● branch (contractor, distributor, manufacturer, manufacturer's representative, associate), $135 (annual) ● dual, $150-$450 (annual). **Staff:** 6. **Multinational. Description:** International trade association for the advancement of the interior commercial construction industry. Provides quality education, resources and a forum for communication among its members. **Awards:** Construction Excellence Award. **Frequency:** annual. **Type:** recognition ● DeGelleke Award. **Frequency:** annual. **Type:** recognition. **Committees:** Acoustical; Distributor Planning; Education and Training; GRG and Safety; Industry Relations; Labor Relations; Security Ceilings; Wall Panel. **Programs:** Acoustics Academy; Ceilings and Wall Systems Training; CISCA Supervisory Leadership and Management Skills Seminar; Executive Development; Professional Selling Skills; Sales Training. **Formerly:** (1969) National Acoustical Contractors Association; (1985) Ceilings and Interior Systems Contractors Association. **Publications:** *Acoustical Ceilings Use and Practice* ● *Ceiling Systems*. Handbook ● *Interior Construction*, bimonthly. Magazine. For sellers, installers, and buyers of interior finishing systems. Includes editorials, product news, supplier news, and calendar of events. **Price:** $35.00/year. ISSN: 0888-0387. **Circulation:** 15,000. **Advertising:** accepted ● Manuals. **Conventions/Meetings:** annual meeting (exhibits).

1009 ■ Ceramic Tile Institute of America (CTIOA)
12061 Jefferson Blvd.
Culver City, CA 90230-6219
Ph: (310)574-7800
Fax: (310)821-4655
E-mail: ctioa@earthlink.net
URL: http://www.ctioa.org
Contact: Thomas Brady CTC, Dir.
Membership Dues: regular, $50 (monthly) ● contributor, associate, $100 (monthly) ● donor, $250 (monthly) ● patron, $500 (monthly) ● benefactor, $750 (monthly) ● Bronze Circle, $1,000 (monthly) ● Silver Circle, $1,500 (monthly) ● Gold Circle, $2,000 (monthly) ● Platinum Circle, $2,500 (monthly). **Description:** Tile contractors, setters, finishers, manufacturers, and distributors; individuals interested in the tile industry or working in a related field. Promotes the use of tile and disseminates information on the development and improvement of tile and its installation; seeks to upgrade the tile industry through research and development. Encourages and assists in providing well-trained industry employees; offers counseling. **Publications:** Brochures. **Conventions/Meetings:** annual meeting and seminar (exhibits) - always February, in Los Angeles, CA.

1010 ■ Certified Contractor's Network (CCN)
134 Sibley Ave.
Ardmore, PA 19003
Free: (866)868-7895
Fax: (610)642-5842
E-mail: admin@contractors.net
URL: http://www.contractors.net
Contact: Gail McNeill, VP/Gen. Mgr.
Founded: 1996. **Description:** Works to make independent contractors more successful and profitable, while assisting them to provide better and more professional services and products for their customers and to provide an alternative to industry consolidation, but have the benefits of a national organization along with national name awareness. **Publications:** *Successful Construction Investment*. Brochure. **Price:** $50.00/copy ● *ToolBox*, monthly. Newsletter.

1011 ■ Concrete Foundations Association (CFA)
PO Box 204
113 W 1st St.
Mount Vernon, IA 52314
Ph: (319)895-6940
Free: (866)232-9255
Fax: (320)213-5556
E-mail: info@cfawalls.org
URL: http://www.cfawalls.org
Contact: J. Edward Sauter, Exec. Dir.
Founded: 1975. **Members:** 330. **Membership Dues:** professional (engineer/architect), $175 (annual) ● contractor (based on gross annual revenue), $400-$600 (annual) ● local supplier, $250 (annual) ● national supplier, $1,000 (annual). **Staff:** 4. **Budget:** $280,000. **Description:** Contractors, suppliers, and manufacturers engaged in poured concrete wall construction. Promotes poured concrete wall construction and works to improve the quality of the product; serves as a forum for the exchange of ideas, techniques, and methods. Prepares and distributes technical information on products and methods

related to special needs; informs members of new trends, specifications, codes, rules, and regulations regarding the industry. Reviews EPA, OSHA, and other governmental agency practices and regulations as they affect the industry and represents the industry before governmental agencies. **Awards:** Contractor of the Year Award. **Frequency:** annual. **Type:** recognition. **Recipient:** for contribution to industry ● Robert D. Sawyer Award. **Frequency:** annual. **Type:** recognition. **Recipient:** for contribution to industry. **Telecommunication Services:** electronic mail, esauter@cfawalls.org. **Formerly:** (1991) Poured Concrete Contractors Association. **Publications:** *Concrete Facts Newsletter*, bimonthly. **Circulation:** 750. **Advertising:** accepted. **Conventions/Meetings:** annual meeting (exhibits) - 2009 July 29-Aug. 1, Amelia Island, FL ● seminar.

1012 ■ Construction Financial Management Association (CFMA)

29 Emmons Dr., Ste.F-50
Princeton, NJ 08540
Ph: (609)452-8000
Fax: (609)452-0474
E-mail: info@cfma.org
URL: http://www.cfma.org
Contact: William M. Schwab, Pres./CEO

Founded: 1981. **Members:** 7,000. **Membership Dues:** general, $300 (annual) ● associate, $400 (annual). **Staff:** 20. **Budget:** $3,000,000. **Local Groups:** 87. **Description:** Contractors, subcontractors, architects, real estate developers, and engineers; associate members are equipment and material suppliers, accountants, lawyers, bankers, and others involved with the financial management of the construction industry. Provides a forum for the exchange of ideas; coordinates educational programs dedicated to improving the professional standards of financial management in the construction industry. Offers expanded national programs, technical assistance, and industry representation. Conducts research programs; maintains speakers' bureau and placement service; compiles statistics. **Libraries: Type:** open to the public. **Holdings:** 9. **Subjects:** industry analysis. **Awards:** Danny Parrish Leadership Award. **Frequency:** annual. **Type:** recognition ● Debra Hahn Memorial Award. **Frequency:** annual. **Type:** recognition ● Joe Quigley Memorial Award. **Frequency:** annual. **Type:** recognition ● **Type:** scholarship. **Committees:** Accounting and Reporting; Budget and Finance; Chapter Formation; Chapter Support; Conference Planning; Construction Industry Liaison; Education; Membership; Tax and Legislative Affairs; Technology. **Publications:** *CFMA Building Profits*, bimonthly. Magazine. Features tax and accounting alerts, risk management updates, employment and career opportunities, and technical articles. **Price:** included in membership dues. **Circulation:** 7,000. **Advertising:** accepted ● *CFMA's Construction Industry Annual Financial Survey*, annual ● *CFMA's Information Technology Survey for the Construction Industry*, biennial. **Advertising:** accepted ● *The Source*, annual. Membership Directory. **Conventions/Meetings:** annual conference (exhibits) - May.

1013 ■ Deep Foundations Institute (DFI)

326 Lafayette Ave.
Hawthorne, NJ 07506
Ph: (973)423-4030
Fax: (973)423-4031
E-mail: dfihq@dfi.org
URL: http://www.dfi.org
Contact: Theresa Rappaport, Exec. Dir.

Founded: 1976. **Members:** 1,490. **Membership Dues:** individual, $95 (annual) ● corporate class I, $650 (annual) ● corporate class II, $950 (annual) ● corporate class III, $1,300 (annual) ● affiliate, noncommercial organization, $300 (annual) ● employee of corporate member, $75 (annual) ● student, government employee, $50 (annual). **Staff:** 4. **Budget:** $250,000. **Multinational. Description:** Individuals concerned with pilings, caissons, and other deep support for structures or deep excavations; consulting firms, foundation contractors, project owners, educators, and service, materials, and equipment suppliers. Aims to advance knowledge in the design, installation, and permanent stability of deep foundations for all types of structures. Seeks to: promote cooperation and improve communication between members; encourage and participate in the application of technological research to deep foundation design, construction, and project completion. Interests include: planning for and installation of H-section, timber, pipe, concrete, and sheet piles; consideration of problems encountered in environmental regulations and building codes; encouraging developments in pile materials and equipment for installation; stimulating improvements in communication and education in the area of deep foundations. Encourages and gives direction to practical research; conducts seminars. **Libraries: Type:** open to the public. **Holdings:** 50; video recordings. **Subjects:** technical manuals, meeting proceedings, journals. **Awards:** Distinguished Service Award. **Frequency:** annual. **Type:** recognition. **Recipient:** for career achievement ● Outstanding Project Award. **Frequency:** annual. **Type:** recognition. **Recipient:** for ingenuity in design/constructing of deep foundation projects. **Telecommunication Services:** electronic mail, trappaport@dfi.org. **Committees:** Augered Cast in Place Pile; Drilled Shaft; Driven Pile; Micropiles; Seismic and Lateral Loads; Slurry Wall; Soil Mixing; Testing and Evaluation. **Publications:** *Augured Cast-In-Place Pile Manual*. Contains model-specific information. **Price:** $12.00 for members; $22.00 for nonmembers ● *Deep Foundations*, quarterly. Magazine ● *Drilled Shaft Inspector's Manual* ● *Drilled Shaft Inspectors Video* ● *Glossary of Foundations Terms*. Manual. **Conventions/Meetings:** annual Conference on Deep Foundations (exhibits) - always October ● periodic international conference.

1014 ■ Directional Crossing Contractors Association (DCCA)

Address Unknown since 2007

Founded: 1991. **Members:** 95. **Membership Dues:** regular, $1,500 (annual) ● associate, $1,000 (annual) ● technical affiliate, $150 (annual). **Staff:** 2. **Description:** Promotes the interests of the directional crossing industry & educates the public regarding directional crossing issues & technology. **Task Forces:** Drilling Contractors Assn (DCCA Europe); Membership/Marketing; Networking; Operator Training; Risk Management/Contact; Safety; Scholarship/Grant. **Conventions/Meetings:** annual symposium, with discussion on relevent issues in Directional Crossing.

1015 ■ Engineering Contractors Association (ECA)

8310 Florence Ave.
Downey, CA 90240
Ph: (562)861-0929
Free: (800)293-2240
Fax: (562)923-6179
E-mail: info.eca@verizon.net
URL: http://www.ecaonline.net
Contact: Cynthia Miramontes, Pres.

Founded: 1976. **Members:** 250. **Membership Dues:** associate contractor, $575 (quarterly) ● contractor (3-5 unions), $600-$5,500 (quarterly) ● affiliate, $500 (quarterly) ● alumnus, $50 (quarterly) ● contractor (1-2 unions), $600-$3,300 (quarterly). **Staff:** 3. **Budget:** $250,000. **Description:** Engineering construction contractors and suppliers. Represents members in labor and legislation matters and negotiates disputes within the industry. **Libraries: Type:** reference. **Holdings:** archival material. **Committees:** Labor; Legislative; Public Agencies; Safety. **Affiliated With:** American Public Works Association. **Formed by Merger of:** (1976) Underground Engineering Contractors' Association; Engineering and Grading Contractors Association. **Publications:** *ECA Directory and Buyer's Guide*, annual ● *ECA Magazine*, monthly. **Advertising:** accepted. **Conventions/Meetings:** annual meeting - always August, El Monte, CA ● annual trade show.

1016 ■ Floor Covering Installation Contractors Association (FCICA)

7439 Millwood Dr.
West Bloomfield, MI 48322
Ph: (248)661-5015
Free: (877)TO-FCICA
Fax: (248)661-5018
E-mail: info@fcica.com
URL: http://www.fcica.com
Contact: Kimberly Oderkirk, Exec. VP

Founded: 1982. **Members:** 202. **Membership Dues:** installation contractor (based on number of installers), $350-$950 (annual) ● associate (silver), $700 (annual) ● associate (gold), $1,250 (annual) ● associate (platinum), $2,500 (annual) ● consultant/inspector (based on number of employees), $350-$700 (annual). **Staff:** 1. **Budget:** $250,000. **Description:** Installation contractors, carpet manufacturers, and suppliers to the installation trade. Aims to establish acceptable levels of performance for the carpet installation industry; to promote standards of business ethics; to encourage quality installations. Acts as liaison with retailers, manufacturers, and suppliers; represents the industry before government agencies regarding proposed or enacted regulation and legislation. Fosters the sale and use of the industry's products and services. Serves as clearinghouse for resolving problems of mutual interest inside and outside the industry. Assists local installation workrooms/ contractors' groups. Sponsors training programs. **Awards: Type:** recognition. **Committees:** Associates; Convention Planning; FIT; Industry Relations; Marketing; Membership Services. **Publications:** *Bottom Line*, quarterly. Newsletter. **Price:** free for members. **Circulation:** 600. **Advertising:** accepted ● *Bottom Line E-News*, biweekly. Newsletter. **Price:** free for members. **Circulation:** 800. **Advertising:** accepted ● Membership Directory, annual. **Conventions/Meetings:** annual Catch the Wave of Opportunity - board meeting and convention (exhibits) ● annual Mid-Year Meeting - board meeting and executive committee meeting.

1017 ■ Gunite/Shotcrete Contractors Association (G/SCA)

Address Unknown since 2007

Founded: 1951. **Members:** 35. **Membership Dues:** structural contractor, $900 (annual) ● nonstructural contractor, $650 (annual) ● supplier, $500 (annual) ● professional, $150 (annual). **Staff:** 1. **Description:** Contractors specializing in Gunite and Shotcrete construction; equipment manufacturers and material suppliers for the industry. (Gunite and Shotcrete are trademarks used for mixtures of cement, sand, and water applied by pneumatic pressure through a specially adapted hose.) Primary aim is to disseminate information on standards for the Gunite and Shotcrete industry. Conducts research on developments within the industry and supplies technical data and specifications to the design sector. Makes available speakers upon request. Maintains database containing current information on the methods, techniques, and applications of Gunite and Shotcrete in all phases of construction and makes recommendations on proper equipment and material usage. **Affiliated With:** American Concrete Institute; American Society for Testing and Materials. **Formerly:** (1988) Gunite Contractors Association; (1994) Gunite/Shotcrete Association. **Publications:** *Gunite and Air-Placed Concrete for Subterranean Basement Walls* ● *Gunite and Shotcrete*, periodic ● *Membership List*, quarterly ● Brochures ● Bulletin, periodic. **Conventions/Meetings:** annual World of Concrete - meeting (exhibits).

1018 ■ Independent Electrical Contractors (IEC)

4401 Ford Ave., Ste.1100
Alexandria, VA 22302-1432
Ph: (703)549-7351 (703)549-7352
Free: (800)456-4324
Fax: (703)549-7448
E-mail: info@ieci.org
URL: http://www.ieci.org
Contact: Larry Mullins, Exec. VP/CEO

Founded: 1957. **Members:** 3,200. **Staff:** 15. **Budget:** $1,600,000. **State Groups:** 74. **Description:** Independent electrical contractors, small and large, primarily open shop. Promotes the interests of members; works to eliminate "unwise and unfair business practices" and to protect its members against "unfair or unjust taxes and legislative enactments."

Sponsors electrical apprenticeship programs; conducts educational programs on cost control and personnel motivation. Represents independent electrical contractors to the National Electrical Code panel. Conducts surveys on volume of sales and purchases and on type of products used. Has formulated National Pattern Standards for Apprentice Training for Electricians. **Libraries: Type:** reference. **Holdings:** archival material. **Awards: Frequency:** annual. **Type:** recognition. **Telecommunication Services:** electronic mail, lmullins@ieci.org. **Committees:** Apprenticeship; Awards; Code Review; Convention; Drug Abuse and Safety; Insurance; Legislative; Public Relations; Training. **Formerly:** (1980) Associated Independent Electrical Contractors of America. **Publications:** *IEC Connection*, biweekly. Newsletter. **Price:** included in membership dues. **Circulation:** 10,000. **Advertising:** accepted ● *IEC Insights*, bimonthly. Magazine. **Price:** included in membership dues. **Circulation:** 1,000. **Advertising:** accepted. Alternate Formats: CD-ROM; online ● Membership Directory, annual. **Advertising:** accepted ● Also publishes pre- and post-convention specials and training booklets. **Conventions/Meetings:** annual convention and trade show (exhibits) ● annual workshop, on legislation.

1019 ■ Independent Professional Painting Contractors Association of America (IPPA)

Address Unknown since 2008

Founded: 1982. **Members:** 40. **Membership Dues:** $125 (annual). **Staff:** 1. **Budget:** $3,000. **Languages:** English, German. **Description:** Professional contractors, open shop painting contractors, paperhangers, decorators, sign painters, drywall contractors, or tradesmen in related fields. Goals are: to represent and promote open shop contractors; to improve skills and provide information to members; to provide major medical and group liability insurance while working for better safety standards and quality control. Encourages the institution of youth apprenticeship and exchange programs between the U.S. and European countries. Maintains educational programs; provides job and manpower referrals; makes available troubleshooting consultation to members. Conducts program requiring paint companies to label their products so that professional painters can better determine the nature of the health hazards (if any) the ingredients in the paint may pose; investigates the legitimacy of member firms. Provides training program; conducts 10 workshop/seminars per year. Maintains small library and manpower and job referral services. Conducts hands on seminar on faux finishings, graining, glacing, marbleizing and others. **Libraries: Type:** not open to the public. **Holdings:** 15; video recordings. **Subjects:** painting, paperhanging, spraying, fan, finish, technique, method of applications, restorations of wood, faux finishings, graining, rag rolling. **Computer Services:** Mailing lists. **Committees:** Charity; Insurance; Membership; Winterwork. **Publications:** *Flyers & Insurance, Business Matter*, monthly. **Price:** free to members. **Circulation:** 100 ● *The Independent Brushstroke*. **Price:** included in membership dues. **Conventions/Meetings:** monthly seminar and workshop (exhibits) - always second Thursday of the month, Huntington, NY (except July and August).

1020 ■ Instrument Contracting and Engineering Association (ICEA)

c/o Nick Theisen Exec. Dir.
4312 Rochard Ln.
Fort Mill, SC 29707-5851
Ph: (704)905-0319
Fax: (803)547-7697
E-mail: ntheisen@carolina.rr.com
URL: http://www.instrumentcontractors.com
Contact: Nick Theisen, Exec. Dir.

Founded: 1984. **Members:** 40. **Staff:** 2. **Description:** Contractors who install pneumatic and electronic control mechanisms for robotic and automated systems in industrial facilities such as nuclear power plants, fossil fuel power stations, refineries, and steel mills. Seeks to improve and promote the instrumentation industry. Coordinates interaction with other groups in the construction industry. Engages in labor negotiations. **Conventions/Meetings:** annual meeting ● seminar.

1021 ■ Instrument Technicians Labor-Management Cooperation Fund

Address Unknown since 2007

Founded: 1987. **Members:** 50. **Staff:** 2. **Description:** Contractor companies contributing to a joint labor-management fund for promoting the instrumentation industry. Encourages better labor relations and engages in technical activities. **Committees:** Labor Relations; Promotion; Technical. **Conventions/Meetings:** annual meeting.

1022 ■ Insulation Contractors Association of America (ICAA)

1321 Duke St., Ste.303
Alexandria, VA 22314
Ph: (703)739-0356
Fax: (703)739-0412
E-mail: icaa2007@insulate.org
URL: http://www.insulate.org
Contact: Mel Tabor, Pres.

Founded: 1977. **Members:** 200. **Membership Dues:** general, provisional, associate contractor (single location), $625-$1,250 (annual) ● associate industry, $625-$1,875 (annual) ● other associate, $775 (annual) ● corresponding associate, $325 (annual). **Staff:** 5. **Budget:** $300,000. **State Groups:** 13. **Description:** Residential and commercial insulation contractors; manufacturing and supplier associates. Seeks to develop industry standards; promotes energy conservation in old and new buildings through proper specifications and applications of insulation; represents interests of the industry at all government levels; promotes exchange of information among insulation contractors. Sponsors seminars, field surveys, and research. **Libraries: Type:** not open to the public. **Holdings:** 30. **Committees:** Commercial; Marketing; Technical. **Publications:** *ICAA News*, monthly. Newsletter. Includes listing of new products, news, members and calendar of events. **Price:** available to members only. **Circulation:** 1,000. **Advertising:** accepted ● *Insulation Contractors Association of America—Bulletin*, periodic. Includes technical, marketing, member, and directors' bulletins providing information on aspects of each function. **Circulation:** 2,000 ● *Insulation Contractors Report*, bimonthly. Newsletter ● *Insulation Industry Buyer's Guide*, annual. Directory. Lists contractor members and manufacturers, and supplier associate members by firm name. Includes indexes of geographical and personal names. **Price:** $10.00/issue. **Circulation:** 2,000. **Advertising:** accepted ● Brochures. **Conventions/Meetings:** annual convention and trade show (exhibits).

1023 ■ International Association of Geosynthetic Installers (IAGI)

PO Box 18012
St. Paul, MN 55118
Ph: (651)554-1895
Fax: (651)450-6167
E-mail: iagi@iagi.org
URL: http://www.iagi.org
Contact: Laurie Honnigford, Managing Dir.

Founded: 1995. **Members:** 110. **Membership Dues:** installer, associate, $300 (annual). **Staff:** 2. **Budget:** $30,000. **Languages:** English, French. **Multinational. Description:** Works to advance geosynthetic installation and construction technologies. **Awards:** Approved Installation Contractor Award. **Frequency:** annual. **Type:** recognition. **Recipient:** for professional installers of geomembrane products ● Certified Welding Technicians. **Type:** recognition. **Programs:** HDPE Certification - Certified Welding Technician. **Publications:** *White Paper on Improving Geomembrane Installations*. Alternate Formats: online ● Membership Directory, biennial. **Circulation:** 16,000 ● Newsletter, quarterly. Addresses issues, news, and events affecting the geosynthetics installation community. **Price:** included in membership dues. Alternate Formats: online. **Conventions/Meetings:** annual conference.

1024 ■ International Builders Exchange Executives (IBEE)

4047 Naco Perrin, Ste.201A
San Antonio, TX 78232
Ph: (210)653-3900
Free: (877)MYBXNET
Fax: (210)653-3912
E-mail: info@bxnetwork.org
URL: http://www.bxnetwork.org
Contact: Brenda L. Romano, Exec. VP

Founded: 1948. **Members:** 103. **Membership Dues:** regular, $500 (annual) ● corporate, $1,250 (annual). **Staff:** 3. **Local Groups:** 103. **Multinational. Description:** Provides services, advocacy and training for executive managers of builders' exchange and other construction-related associations. **Libraries: Type:** by appointment only. **Holdings:** archival material, articles, artwork, audiovisuals, clippings, software. **Awards:** Dan Patrick Award, Management Award. **Frequency:** annual. **Type:** recognition. **Recipient:** to members. **Computer Services:** Information services, access to construction news and information at the local level. **Committees:** Award; Education; Public Relations. **Also Known As:** (2003) The Builders Exchange Network. **Publications:** *Construction Executive Report*, bimonthly. Newsletters. **Advertising:** accepted. Alternate Formats: online. Also Cited As: *CER* ● *Membership Roster*, annual. Membership Directory. **Circulation:** 1,000. **Conventions/Meetings:** annual banquet and board meeting.

1025 ■ International Certified Floorcovering Installers Association (CFI)

2400 E Truman Rd.
Kansas City, MO 64127
Ph: (816)231-4646
Fax: (816)231-4343
E-mail: cfiguy@earthlink.net
URL: http://www.cfi-installers.org
Contact: Jim Walker, CEO/Exec. Dir.

Founded: 1993. **Members:** 14,000. **Multinational. Description:** Identifies and certifies, according to skill and knowledge, professional flooring installers. Offers commercial or residential customers an opportunity to engage the services of an installation specialist who "guarantees the work with the assurance of a worthwhile and lasting purchase.". **Computer Services:** Online services, message board. **Committees:** Certification; Chapter; Complaint; Installation Standards; Internet Communications; Marketing. **Publications:** *The CFI Professional*, quarterly. Newsletter. Contains chapter and member news, educational items, training and certification dates and industry news. **Price:** free for members; $35.00 for nonmembers.

1026 ■ International Institute for Lath and Plaster (IILP)

PO Box 1663
Lafayette, CA 94549
Ph: (925)283-5160 (760)837-9094
Fax: (925)283-5161
E-mail: frank@fenunes.com
URL: http://www.iilp.org
Contact: Walter F. Pruter, Pres.

Founded: 1976. **Staff:** 2. **Description:** Industry-wide federation of lathing and plastering contractors, labor organizations, and manufacturers of lathing and plastering supplies. Promotes use of lath and plaster. **Libraries: Type:** reference. **Telecommunication Services:** electronic mail, wf.pruter@gte.net. **Formed by Merger of:** (1994) Associated Institutes for Lath and Plaster; International Council for Lathing and Plastering.

1027 ■ International Masonry Institute (IMI)

The James Brice House
42 East St.
Annapolis, MD 21401
Ph: (410)280-1305 (301)229-1001
Free: (800)803-0295
Fax: (301)261-2855

E-mail: masonryquestions@imiweb.org
URL: http://www.imiweb.org
Contact: Joan Baggett Calambokidis, Pres.
Founded: 1970. **Regional Groups:** 5. **State Groups:** 7. **Local Groups:** 1. **Nonmembership. Description:** Joint labor/management trust fund of the International Union of Bricklayers and Allied Craftworkers and union masonry contractors. Aims for the advancement of quality masonry construction through national and regional training, promotion, advertising and labor management relations programs in the U.S. and Canada. Provides support and materials for local/regional masonry promotion groups in the U.S. and Canada, and cooperates with national groups and organizations promoting the industry. Sponsors craft training and research programs. Offers educational programs. Maintains museum. **Libraries: Type:** reference. **Holdings:** books, clippings, periodicals, reports. **Subjects:** masonry construction, design, installation. **Awards:** Golden Trowel Award. **Frequency:** periodic. **Type:** recognition. **Recipient:** for union built masonry projects. **Computer Services:** database, bibliographic ● online services, computer software for architectural schools. **Telecommunication Services:** hotline, masonry, (800)464-0988 ● hotline, training, (800)562-7464. **Programs:** Apprenticeship and Training; Labor/Management Relations; Market Promotion; Research and Development; Tile Promotion. **Affiliated With:** International Union of Bricklayers and Allied Craftworkers. **Absorbed:** Masonry Research Foundation; (1986) Masonry Industry Committee. **Publications:** *IMI Today*, bimonthly. Newsletter. **Circulation:** 10,000. Alternate Formats: online ● Pamphlets ● Also publishes pictorial and technical publications. **Conventions/Meetings:** annual Mason Industry Educational Conference, with seminars and general session.

1028 ■ International Playground Contractors Association (NPCAI)

PO Box 2364
Salt Lake City, UT 84110-2364
Free: (888)908-9519
Fax: (801)355-2788
E-mail: npca@playground-contractors.org
URL: http://www.playground-contractors.org
Contact: Sylvia Salazar, Exec. Dir.
Founded: 1997. **Membership Dues:** manufacturer, $750 (annual) ● qualified contractor, $100 (annual) ● general, $250 (annual). **Multinational. Description:** Aims to advance the playground building industry. Promotes playground installation as a legitimate contracting profession within the playground industry. Seeks to uphold the standards of playground installation by helping professionals expand and strengthen their professional skills. Supports playground safety programs, guidelines and standards that foster playground safety. **Publications:** *NPCAI Professional Directory*, annual. **Advertising:** accepted ● *The Playbook*, quarterly. Magazine. **Advertising:** accepted ● *The Playground Connection*, monthly. Newsletter. Alternate Formats: online ● *Playground Construction School*, 3/year. Brochure. Alternate Formats: online.

1029 ■ International Union of Bricklayers and Allied Craftsworkers

620 F St. NW
Washington, DC 20004
Ph: (202)783-3788
Free: (888)880-8222
E-mail: askbac@bacweb.org
URL: http://www.bacweb.org
Contact: John J. Flynn, Pres.
Founded: 1987. **Members:** 5,000. **Staff:** 3. **Multinational. Description:** Contractors engaged in masonry work, including pointing, cleaning, and caulking masonry walls and the installation of all types of masonry products. Promotes the masonry contracting industry for employers of craftworkers. Represents members in legislation and before the public; works with other construction associations; conducts labor negotiations. Operates speakers' bureau and charitable program; compiles statistics. **Libraries: Type:** reference. **Holdings:** biographical archives. **Awards:** Canadian Bates Scholarship. **Frequency:** annual. **Type:** scholarship. **Recipient:** for high school students ● Craft Award. **Frequency:** annual. **Type:** trophy. **Recipient:** for local unions and workers ● U.S. Bates Scholarship. **Frequency:** annual. **Type:** scholarship. **Recipient:** for high school students. **Additional Websites:** http://www.imiweb.org. **Committees:** Labor Relations; Promotion; Technical Subjects. **Funds:** International Health; International Pension. **Programs:** Harry C. Bates Scholarship. **Projects:** Millenium Morning. **Affiliated With:** International Masonry Institute. **Formerly:** (2004) International Council of Employers of Bricklayers and Allied Craftsworkers. **Publications:** *BAC Journal*, bimonthly. Magazine ● *ICE Voice*, quarterly. Newsletter. **Conventions/Meetings:** competition ● seminar.

1030 ■ Joint Industry Board of the Electrical Industry (JIBEI)

158-11 Harry Van Arsdale Jr. Ave.
Flushing, NY 11365
Ph: (718)591-2000
Fax: (718)969-2293
URL: http://www.jibei.org
Contact: Dr. Gerald Finkel, Chm.
Founded: 1943. **Description:** Electrical contractors. Represents members in labor-management relations. Conducts educational programs. Administers benefit funds. **Convention/Meeting:** none. **Publications:** none. **Libraries: Type:** reference. **Holdings:** archival material, artwork, audiovisuals, books, business records, clippings. **Subjects:** labor. **Awards: Frequency:** annual. **Type:** scholarship. **Recipient:** for children of members. **Committees:** Political Action.

1031 ■ Log Home Builders Association of North America (LHBANA)

14241 NE Woodinville-Duvall Rd., Ste.345
Woodinville, WA 98072-8564
Ph: (360)794-4469
E-mail: info@loghomebuilders.org
URL: http://www.loghomebuilders.org
Contact: Skip Ellsworth, Pres.
Founded: 1965. **Members:** 45,000. **Membership Dues:** life, $795. **Staff:** 3. **Local Groups:** 1. **Description:** Log home builders (professional and nonprofessional); interested individuals. Sponsors a three-month apprenticeship program to train and certify journeymen log home builders; a telephone hotline for answering questions about log homes. **Libraries: Type:** open to the public. **Holdings:** 4,500; articles. **Subjects:** log home construction, log home history, tools, and construction in general. **Awards:** Log Home Builder's Award. **Frequency:** monthly. **Type:** scholarship. **Telecommunication Services:** electronic mail, skip@loghomebuilders.org. **Formerly:** (1976) Log House Association of North America; (2003) Log House Builder's Association of North America. **Publications:** Brochure. Contains apprenticeship information. ● Journal, annual ● Newsletter, periodic ● Plans to publish directory. **Conventions/Meetings:** annual conference (exhibits).

1032 ■ Mason Contractors Association of America (MCAA)

33 S Roselle Rd.
Schaumburg, IL 60193
Ph: (847)301-0001 (410)795-3300
Free: (800)536-2225
Fax: (847)301-1110
URL: http://www.masoncontractors.org
Contact: Jeff Buczkiewicz, Exec. Dir.
Founded: 1950. **Members:** 1,500. **Membership Dues:** contractor, $560-$3,000 ● national associate, $2,000 ● chapter associate, $300. **Staff:** 10. **Budget:** $2,000,000. **Regional Groups:** 9. **State Groups:** 34. **Local Groups:** 78. **Description:** Masonry construction firms. Conducts specialized education and research programs. Compiles statistics. **Awards:** International Excellence in Masonry. **Frequency:** annual. **Type:** recognition. **Recipient:** for contractors/architects. **Committees:** Apprenticeship; Contract Research; Education; Legislative; Masonry Marketing; Membership; Safety; Technical. **Publications:** *Masonry*, monthly. Magazine. **Price:** $20.00/year. **Circulation:** 16,000. **Advertising:** accepted. **Conventions/Meetings:** annual Masonry Showcase - competition, premier tradeshow for mason contractors (exhibits) ● annual trade show (exhibits).

1033 ■ Mechanical Contractors Association of America (MCAA)

1385 Piccard Dr.
Rockville, MD 20850-4329
Ph: (301)869-5800
Free: (800)556-3653
Fax: (301)990-9690
E-mail: membership@mcaa.org
URL: http://www.mcaa.org
Contact: John R. Gentille, Exec. VP/CEO
Founded: 1889. **Members:** 2,200. **Staff:** 29. **Budget:** $7,000,000. **Local Groups:** 80. **Description:** Contractors who furnish, install, and service piping systems and related equipment for heating, cooling, refrigeration, ventilating, and air conditioning systems. Works to standardize materials and methods used in the industry. Conducts business overhead, labor wage, and statistical surveys. Maintains dialogue with key officials in building trade unions. Promotes apprenticeship training programs. Conducts seminars on contracts, labor estimating, job cost control, project management, marketing, collective bargaining, contractor insurance, and other management topics. Promotes methods to conserve energy in new and existing buildings. Sponsors Industrial Relations Council for the Plumbing and Pipe Fitting Industry. **Committees:** Industry Improvement Funds; International Pipe Trades Joint Trading; Labor Estimating Manual; Management Methods; Manufacturer/Supplier Liaison; Project Managers Education; Safety and Health; Technology. **Councils:** Industrial Relations; National Safety; Piping Industry Collective Bargaining. **Departments:** Mechanical Contracting Foundation; Mechanical Service Contractors of America; National Certified Pipe Welding Bureau; Plumbing Contractors of America. **Affiliated With:** National Environmental Balancing Bureau. **Formerly:** Heating and Piping and Air Conditioning Contractors National Association; Heating and Piping Contractors National Association; National Association of Master Steam and Hot Water Fitters. **Publications:** *MCAA National Update*, weekly. Newsletter. Alternate Formats: online ● *MSCA News*, bimonthly. Newsletter ● *NCPW Bulletin*, semiannual ● *Reporter*, monthly. Newsletter. Alternate Formats: online ● Also publishes management and training aids. **Conventions/Meetings:** annual convention (exhibits).

1034 ■ National Association of Elevator Contractors (NAEC)

1298 Wellbrook Cir., Ste.A
Conyers, GA 30012
Ph: (770)760-9660
Free: (800)900-6232
Fax: (770)760-9714
E-mail: info@naec.org
URL: http://www.naec.org
Contact: Teresa Shirley, Exec. Dir.
Founded: 1951. **Members:** 680. **Membership Dues:** contractor in U.S., associate contractor in U.S., supplier in U.S., professional in U.S., $495 (annual) ● contractor outside U.S., associate contractor outside U.S., supplier outside U.S., professional outside U.S., $595 (annual) ● dual (contractor/supplier) in U.S., $990 (annual) ● dual (contractor/supplier) outside U.S., $1,190 (annual). **Staff:** 5. **Description:** Contractors who install and service elevators and lift equipment; suppliers of complete elevators and components. **Telecommunication Services:** electronic mail, teresa@naec.org ● additional toll-free number, (888)847-7530. **Committees:** Accessibility; Convention Host; Executive Office Building Maintenance; Future Directions; NEII Performance Standards. **Task Forces:** CET Business Review; CET Program Review; Convention Review. **Conventions/Meetings:** annual conference - always spring ● annual convention (exhibits) - always fall.

1035 ■ National Association of Home Builders (NAHB)

1201 15th St. NW
Washington, DC 20005
Ph: (202)266-8200
Free: (800)368-5242

Fax: (202)266-8400
E-mail: info@nahb.com
URL: http://www.nahb.org
Contact: Jerry M. Howard, Exec. VP/CEO
Founded: 1942. **Members:** 208,000. **Membership Dues:** international associate/builder, $500. **Staff:** 460. **Local Groups:** 824. **Description:** Single and multifamily home builders, commercial builders, and others associated with the building industry. Lobbies on behalf of the housing industry and conducts public affairs activities to increase public understanding of housing and the economy. Collects and disseminates data on current developments in home building and home builders' plans through its Economics Department and nationwide Metropolitan Housing Forecast. Maintains NAHB Research Center, which functions as the research arm of the home building industry. Sponsors seminars and workshops on construction, mortgage credit, labor relations, cost reduction, land use, remodeling, and business management. Compiles statistics; offers charitable program, spokesman training, and placement service; maintains speakers' bureau, and Hall of Fame. Subsidiaries include the National Council of the Housing Industry. Maintains over 50 committees in many areas of construction; operates National Commercial Builders Council, National Council of the Multifamily Housing Industry, National Remodelers Council, and National Sales and Marketing Council. **Libraries: Type:** reference. **Holdings:** 35,000; archival material, audiovisuals, books, clippings, periodicals. **Subjects:** housing, building/construction, mortgage finance, business management, housing policy, regulatory issues, smart growth. **Awards: Type:** recognition. **Computer Services:** Electronic publishing, e-newsletter ● electronic publishing, Lexis Intranet Publisher ● online services, catalog database. **Telecommunication Services:** electronic mail, jhoward@nahb.com. **Formerly:** (2003) National Association of Home Builders of the U.S. **Publications:** *Builder Magazine*, monthly ● *Forecast of Housing Activity*, monthly ● *Housing and Construction Summaries*. Alternate Formats: online ● *Housing Economics*, monthly ● *Housing Market Statistics*, monthly ● *Land Development Magazine*, quarterly. **Price:** $40.00 ● *Nation's Building News*, semimonthly. Newsletter. Provides the latest information concerning the housing industry, including finance, legislation, new technologies, and membership news. ISSN: 8750-6580. **Circulation:** 161,417. **Advertising:** accepted. Alternate Formats: online ● Bibliographies ● Booklets ● Manuals ● Also publishes bibliographies, booklets, and manuals. **Conventions/Meetings:** annual International Builders' Show - convention and show (exhibits) ● annual meeting (exhibits).

1036 ■ National Association of Minority Contractors (NAMC)

1300 Pennsylvania Ave. NW, Ste.700
Washington, DC 20004
Ph: (202)347-8259
Free: (866)688-6262
Fax: (202)789-7349
E-mail: national@namcline.org
URL: http://www.namcline.org
Contact: Al Barber, Pres.
Founded: 1969. **Members:** 5,000. **Membership Dues:** regular, $400 (annual) ● associate, $500 (annual) ● major corporate partner, $5,000 (annual). **Staff:** 4. **State Groups:** 25. **National Groups:** 2. **Description:** Minority construction contractors and major corporations wishing to do business with minority contractors. Identifies procurement opportunities; provides specialized training; acts as national advocate for minority construction contractors. Holds workshops and seminars; compiles statistics. **Awards:** Founders Award. **Frequency:** annual. **Type:** recognition ● Local Minority Contractor of the Year. **Frequency:** annual. **Type:** recognition ● Major Corporate Partner of the Year. **Frequency:** annual. **Type:** recognition ● Minority Builders Hall of Famé. **Frequency:** periodic. **Type:** recognition. **Computer Services:** Mailing lists, minority contractors by trade and location. **Absorbed:** (1983) Associated Minority Contractors of America. **Publications:** *Building Concerns*, quarterly. Newsletter. **Advertising:** accepted ● *Legislative Bulletin*, periodic ● *Procurement Bulletin*, periodic. **Conventions/Meetings:** annual conference - always June ● annual Fall Chapters and Affiliates Conference - meeting - September/October, Washington, DC.

1037 ■ National Association of Miscellaneous, Ornamental and Architectural Products Contractors (NAMOA)

10382 Main St., Ste.200
PO Box 280
Fairfax, VA 22038
Ph: (703)591-1870
Fax: (703)591-1895
Contact: Fred H. Codding, Pres.
Founded: 1969. **Members:** 185. **Staff:** 6. **Budget:** $175,000. **Regional Groups:** 8. **National Groups:** 2. **Description:** Companies engaged primarily in the erection and fabrication of miscellaneous, ornamental, and architectural products, particularly metals; associate members are suppliers of services and materials. Seeks to inform members on technological methods or advances that increase operational efficiency, safety standards, and welfare. Serves as spokesman for members in dealing with the federal and local governments, the architectural and engineering professions, and the public. Advises members on congressional legislation, wage settlements throughout the U.S., and other matters that affect the industry. Conducts studies on apprenticeship and manpower programs, equal employment in the construction industry, and labor relations. **Committees:** Apprenticeship; Joint Industry Advisory Jurisdictional Disputes; Labor Liaison; Public Affairs; Safety. **Publications:** Membership Directory, periodic ● Newsletter, monthly. **Conventions/Meetings:** annual meeting.

1038 ■ National Association of Ordnance and Explosive Waste Contractors (NAOC)

c/o Suzy McKinney, Sec.
Zapata Engg.
6302 Fairview Rd., Ste.600
Charlotte, NC 28210
Ph: (704)378-4910
Fax: (704)358-8342
E-mail: scmckinney@zapeng.com
URL: http://www.naoc.org
Contact: Suzy McKinney, Sec.
Founded: 1995. **Members:** 33. **Membership Dues:** large business (more than 500 employees), $3,850 (annual) ● small business (less than 500 employees), $2,750 (annual) ● small business (with less than $5M in annual revenue), $1,375 (annual). **Description:** Companies that perform OEW (Ordnance and Explosive Waste) studies or remediation. Promotes the interests of its members and the public in all aspects of OEW remediation projects. Serves as an industry voice to work with government representatives and clients to develop and coordinate improved standards for industry workers. **Formerly:** (2003) National Association of OEW Contractors. **Conventions/Meetings:** annual Equine Affaire - trade show (exhibits) - usually in Columbus, OH.

1039 ■ National Association of Reinforcing Steel Contractors (NARSC)

PO Box 280
Fairfax, VA 22038
Ph: (703)591-1870
Fax: (703)591-1895
E-mail: info@narsc.com
URL: http://www.narsc.com
Contact: Mr. Fred H. Codding, Pres.
Founded: 1969. **Members:** 410. **Staff:** 8. **Budget:** $200,000. **Regional Groups:** 9. **State Groups:** 2. **Description:** Companies engaged primarily in the placing of reinforcing steel and post-tensioning systems; associate members are suppliers of services and materials. Serves as a unified voice for reinforcing steel contractors. Disseminates information on topics such as trade practices, construction techniques, efficient operation, safety standards, and welfare. Advises members on congressional legislation, wage settlements throughout the country, and other matters. Conducts studies on apprenticeship and training, equal employment, and labor relations. **Awards: Frequency:** annual. **Type:** recognition. **Committees:** Apprenticeship; Joint Industry Advisory Groups; Jurisdictional Disputes; Labor Liaison; Public Affairs; Reinforcing Steel Promotion; Safety. **Publications:** Membership Directory, periodic ● Newsletter, monthly. **Conventions/Meetings:** annual meeting.

1040 ■ National Association of State Contractors Licensing Agencies (NASCLA)

PO Box 14941
Scottsdale, AZ 85267
Ph: (602)485-3941
Fax: (602)923-7218
E-mail: info@nascla.org
URL: http://www.nascla.org
Contact: Greg Crow, Acting Pres.
Founded: 1962. **Membership Dues:** business, $750 (annual) ● state, $475 (annual) ● associate, $125 (annual) ● affiliate, $50 (annual). **Description:** Assists its members in striving for the better regulation of the construction industry to protect the health, welfare and safety of the general public. Assists licensing agencies to develop licensing laws and rules. Provides education programs for the construction industry. **Publications:** Newsletter, quarterly. Alternate Formats: online.

1041 ■ National Association of Women in Construction (NAWIC)

327 S Adams St.
Fort Worth, TX 76104
Ph: (817)877-5551
Free: (800)552-3506
Fax: (817)877-0324
E-mail: nawic@nawic.org
URL: http://www.nawic.org
Contact: Dede Hughes, Exec. VP
Founded: 1955. **Members:** 6,000. **Membership Dues:** active chapter, $205 (annual) ● corporate chapter, $280 (annual) ● student chapter, $45 (annual) ● at-large, $180 (annual) ● student-at-large, $35 (annual) ● international, $140 (annual). **Staff:** 9. **Budget:** $700,000. **Regional Groups:** 14. **Local Groups:** 189. **Multinational. Description:** Seeks to enhance the success of women in the construction industry. **Awards:** NAWIC Founders Scholarship. **Frequency:** annual. **Type:** scholarship. **Recipient:** for students of engineering construction or architecture. **Telecommunication Services:** electronic mail, dedeh@nawic.org. **Committees:** Construction Industry; Legislative Awareness; Membership; Parliamentarian; Professional Education; Strategic Plan; Tradeswomen. **Councils:** Owners. **Publications:** *NAWIC IMAGE*, bimonthly. Magazine. **Price:** $15.00 /year for members in U.S.; $35.00 /year for nonmembers in U.S.; $45.00/year outside U.S. **Circulation:** 6,500. **Advertising:** accepted. **Conventions/Meetings:** annual convention, with educational seminars - 2008 Sept. 3-6, New Orleans, LA.

1042 ■ National Council of Erectors, Fabricators and Riggers (NCEFR)

10382 Main St., Ste.200
PO Box 3687
Fairfax, VA 22038
Ph: (703)591-1870
Fax: (703)591-1895
Contact: Fred H. Codding, Pres.
Founded: 1969. **Nonmembership. Description:** Ironworker employer associations. **Affiliated With:** National Association of Miscellaneous, Ornamental and Architectural Products Contractors; National Association of Reinforcing Steel Contractors; Specialized Carriers and Rigging Association. **Conventions/Meetings:** periodic meeting.

1043 ■ National Demolition Association

16 N Franklin St., Ste.203
Doylestown, PA 18901-3536
Ph: (215)348-4949 (513)241-1116
Free: (800)541-2412
Fax: (215)348-8422

E-mail: info@demolitionassociation.com
URL: http://www.demolitionassociation.com
Contact: Drew Lammers, Pres.
Founded: 1972. **Members:** 850. **Membership Dues:** regular (based on gross sales), $575-$875 (annual) ● associate and international, $575 (annual) ● student, $20 (annual). **Staff:** 3. **Budget:** $1,000,000. **Regional Groups:** 2. **Local Groups:** 3. **Description:** Demolition contractors and equipment manufacturers. Seeks to foster goodwill and to encourage the exchange of ideas among the public and members. **Libraries: Type:** not open to the public. **Holdings:** 500; articles, books, papers, periodicals. **Subjects:** demolition. **Awards:** Lifetime Achievement Award. **Frequency:** annual. **Type:** recognition. **Recipient:** for service to National Demolition Association, the demolition industry and the community. **Telecommunication Services:** electronic mail, drachel@rachelcontracting.com. **Formerly:** (2004) National Association of Demolition Contractors. **Publications:** *Demolition*, bimonthly. Magazine. Provides information on government standards, safety hazards, and new products for the demolition industry. Contains news of association activities. **Price:** included in membership dues; $40.00 /year for nonmembers. **Circulation:** 5,000. **Advertising:** accepted ● *Demolition Safety Manual*, annual ● *National Demolition Association—Membership List*, periodic. Membership Directory. **Price:** available to members only ● Also publishes 10 common misconceptions about the demolition industry. **Conventions/Meetings:** annual convention (exhibits).

1044 ■ National Drilling Association (NDA)

3511 Center Rd., Ste.8
Brunswick, OH 44212
Ph: (330)220-6436 (724)746-9100
Free: (877)632-4748
Fax: (216)803-9900
E-mail: info@nda4u.com
URL: http://www.nda4u.com
Contact: Larry Gibel, Pres.
Founded: 1992. **Members:** 250. **Membership Dues:** affiliate, $270 (annual) ● government, $160 (annual) ● retired, $80 (annual) ● contractor (with gross annual sales of up to $2.5 million), $325 (annual) ● manufacturer (with gross annual sales of up to $1 million), $590 (annual) ● manufacturer (with gross annual sales of $1M to $2M), $890 (annual) ● manufacturer (with gross annual sales of $2M to $5M), $1,470 (annual) ● manufacturer (with gross annual sales of $5M to $10M), $1,765 (annual) ● manufacturer (with gross annual sales of over $10M), $2,000 (annual) ● contractor (with gross annual sales of over $2.5M), $640 (annual). **Staff:** 5. **Budget:** $150,000. **Regional Groups:** 3. **Multinational. Description:** Corporations, partnerships, and individuals engaged in the manufacture, sale, and use of rotary or percussion drilling rigs and equipment; branch offices of member companies. Promotes the interests of the industry and fosters commerce and trade in the contract drilling business. Serves as liaison among members and legislative bodies. **Libraries: Type:** reference. **Holdings:** articles, books, papers, periodicals, reports. **Committees:** Diamond Core Drill Manufacturers Association. **Formed by Merger of:** (1995) National Drilling Contractors Association; International Drilling Federation. **Publications:** *Drill Bits*, biennial. Magazine. **Circulation:** 10,000. **Advertising:** accepted. **Conventions/Meetings:** annual board meeting and convention (exhibits).

1045 ■ National Electrical Contractors Association (NECA)

3 Bethesda Metro Ctr., Ste.1100
Bethesda, MD 20814
Ph: (301)657-3110
Fax: (301)215-4500
E-mail: webmaster@necanet.org
URL: http://www.necanet.org
Contact: John M. Grau, CEO
Founded: 1901. **Members:** 4,200. **Membership Dues:** company, $150 (annual). **Staff:** 80. **Budget:** $14,500,000. **Local Groups:** 119. **Description:** Contractors erecting, installing, repairing, servicing, and maintaining electric wiring, equipment, and appliances. Provides management services and labor relations programs for electrical contractors; conducts seminars for contractor sales and training. Conducts research and educational programs; compiles statistics. Sponsors honorary society, the Academy of Electrical Contracting. **Awards:** Coggeshall. **Frequency:** annual. **Type:** recognition ● Comstock. **Frequency:** annual. **Type:** recognition ● Industry Partner. **Frequency:** annual. **Type:** recognition ● McGraw. **Frequency:** annual. **Type:** recognition. **Committees:** Codes and Standards; Electrical Construction Political Action; Government Affairs; Labor Relations; Management Development; Manpower Development; Marketing; Research. **Formerly:** (1930) Electrogists International. **Publications:** *A Comparison of Operational Cost of Union vs. Non-Union Contractors*. Booklet. **Price:** $20.00 for nonmembers; $10.00 for members ● *Electrical Contractor Magazine*, monthly. **Circulation:** 90,000. **Advertising:** accepted ● *Electrical Design Library* ● *Electrical Maintenance Pays Dividends*. Booklet. **Price:** $10.00 for nonmembers; $4.00 for members ● *Electro Fact File*, bimonthly ● *NECA Manual of Labor Units*. **Price:** $99.00 for nonmembers; $30.00 for members ● *NECA News*, weekly ● *NECA Standard of Installation* ● *This is NECA*. Booklet. **Price:** $10.00 for nonmembers; $4.00 for members. **Conventions/Meetings:** annual meeting, with show (exhibits) - always October.

1046 ■ National Electrical Contractors Council (NECC)

c/o Associated Builders and Contractors
4250 N Fairfax Dr., 9th Fl.
Arlington, VA 22203
Ph: (703)812-2000 (703)812-2006
Fax: (703)812-8201
E-mail: gotquestions@abc.org
URL: http://www.abc.org/wmspage.cfm?parm1=970
Contact: M. Kirk Pickerel, Pres./CEO
Founded: 1983. **Members:** 3,500. **Regional Groups:** 82. **Description:** Serves as a council of the Associated Builders and Contractors (see separate entry). Aims to provide assistance to merit shop contractors (individuals awarded construction jobs based on the lowest bidding and best qualifications, regardless of union or non-union affiliation). Conducts educational programs. **Telecommunication Services:** electronic mail, electrical@abc.org. **Programs:** Craft Training; Management Training; Peer Group Participation; Trade Show Participation. **Affiliated With:** Associated Builders and Contractors. **Formerly:** (1990) Electrical Trade Council. **Publications:** *Construction Executive*, monthly. Magazine. **Advertising:** accepted. **Conventions/Meetings:** annual Electrical Contractors Conference - meeting (exhibits).

1047 ■ National Frame Builders Association (NFBA)

4840 Bob Billings Pkwy.
Lawrence, KS 66049-3862
Ph: (785)843-2444
Free: (800)557-6957
Fax: (785)843-7555
E-mail: nfba@nfba.org
URL: http://www.nfba.org
Contact: John Fullerton, VP
Founded: 1971. **Members:** 700. **Staff:** 12. **Budget:** $500,000. **Regional Groups:** 8. **State Groups:** 8. **Description:** Construction contractors specializing in post frame structures for agricultural, residential, industrial and commercial uses. Seeks to enhance the image of the industry and improve management and construction techniques. Conducts educational programs on safety and other vital matters. **Awards:** Bernon G. Perkins. **Frequency:** annual. **Type:** recognition. **Recipient:** for contribution to the post-frame industry ● Building of the Year. **Frequency:** annual. **Type:** recognition. **Recipient:** to any building erected by a member that utilizes post-frame construction to a minimum of 50&percent; of the building structure. **Telecommunication Services:** electronic mail, john.fullerton@nfba.org ● electronic mail, tom.knight@nfba.org. **Committees:** Chapter Presidents; Convention; Executive/Finance; Membership; Safety; Technical and Research. **Councils:** Supplier. **Publications:** *Frame Building News*, 5/year. Magazine. **Price:** free. **Circulation:** 32,000. **Advertising:** accepted ● *Supplier News*, quarterly. Newsletter ● Newsletter, quarterly. **Conventions/Meetings:** annual Frame Building Expo - convention, products/services involved with or applying to post-frame construction (exhibits) - always winter.

1048 ■ National Insulation Association (NIA)

99 Canal Center Plz., Ste.222
Alexandria, VA 22314
Ph: (703)683-6422
Fax: (703)549-4838
E-mail: mjones@insulation.org
URL: http://www.insulation.org
Contact: Michele Jones, Exec. VP
Founded: 1953. **Members:** 700. **Membership Dues:** associate, $3,000 (annual) ● active (maximum; varies by revenue level), $7,885 (annual) ● holding company, $685 (annual) ● international affiliate, $1,110 (annual) ● consultant/manufacturer's representative, $1,250 (annual). **Staff:** 9. **Budget:** $2,000,000. **Regional Groups:** 6. **Description:** Insulation contractors, distributors, and manufacturers. **Telecommunication Services:** electronic mail, cschattgen@spi-co.com. **Committees:** Associates; Distribution; Growing the Insulation Industry; Health and Safety; Labor; Merit Contractor; Metal Building Laminators; Refractory Contractor; Technical; Technical Information; Web Site. **Formerly:** (1970) Insulation Distributor Contractors National Association; (1989) National Insulation Contractors Association; (1997) National Insulation and Abatement Contractors Association. **Publications:** *Estimator's Handbook* ● *Insulation Outlook*, monthly. Magazine. **Price:** free in U.S. and Canada. **Advertising:** accepted ● *Manufacturers Technical Literature*. **Advertising:** accepted ● *National Industries and Commercial Standards Manual*. Manuals. Provides self-study programs on commercial and industrial insulation applications. ● *NIA News*, monthly. Newsletter ● *Safety Handbook*. **Conventions/Meetings:** annual convention.

1049 ■ National Mechanical Contractors Council (NMCC)

c/o Associated Builders and Contractors
4250 N Fairfax Dr., 9th Fl.
Arlington, VA 22203-1607
Ph: (703)812-2000
Fax: (703)812-8235
E-mail: mechanical@abc.org
URL: http://www.abc.org
Contact: Crissi McGlynn, Dir., National Councils
Founded: 1983. **Regional Groups:** 80. **Description:** A council of Associated Builders and Contractors. Seeks to meet the needs of workers in sheet metal, plumbing, heating, ventilation, and air conditioning. **Telecommunication Services:** electronic mail, mcglynn@abc.org. **Programs:** Craft Training; Management Training; Peer Group Participation; Trade Show Participation. **Affiliated With:** Associated Builders and Contractors. **Formerly:** (1992) National Mechanical Trade Council. **Publications:** *Construction Executive*. Magazine. **Advertising:** accepted. **Conventions/Meetings:** annual Mechanical Contractors Conference (exhibits).

1050 ■ National Restaurant Association Multi-Unit Architects, Engineers and Construction Officers (MAECO)

c/o National Restaurant Association
1200 17th St. NW
Washington, DC 20036
Ph: (202)973-3678 (202)331-5900
Free: (800)424-5156
Fax: (202)331-2429
E-mail: jcolindres@dineout.org
URL: http://www.restaurant.org/studygroups/maeco/index.cfm
Contact: Dawn Sweeney, Pres./CEO
Members: 700. **Description:** Professional architects, engineers, and construction officers from member companies of the National Restaurant Association (see separate entry) who are involved in the construc-

tion and equipping of food service and hospitality facilities. Provides a forum for the sharing of common goals, concerns, ideas, and problems. **Computer Services:** Mailing lists, of members. **Conventions/ Meetings:** semiannual meeting - always spring and fall.

1051 ■ National Roofing Contractors Association (NRCA)
10255 W Higgins Rd., Ste.600
Rosemont, IL 60018-5607
Ph: (847)299-9070
Free: (800)323-9545
Fax: (847)299-1183
E-mail: nrca@nrca.net
URL: http://www.nrca.net
Contact: Bill Good, Exec. VP
Founded: 1886. **Members:** 5,000. **Membership Dues:** contractor (based on sales volume), $725-$8,750 ● manufacturer (based on sales volume), $3,000-$8,000 ● distributor (based on sales volume), $1,250-$6,000 ● raw material provider, $2,000 ● service provider, $1,000 ● firm (architect/engineer/ consultant), $995. **Staff:** 65. **Budget:** $14,000,000. **Description:** Roofing, roof deck, and waterproofing contractors and industry-related associate members. Assists members to successfully satisfy their customers through technical support, testing and research, education, marketing, government relations, and consultation. **Committees:** Contractor Management; Education Operating; Government Relations; Health; Insurance; International Relations; Labor; Quality Management; Safety; Steep Roofing; Substance Abuse; Technical and Research. **Programs:** Technical. **Publications:** *NRCA Roofing and Waterproofing Manual* ● *Professional Roofing*, monthly. Magazine. **Circulation:** 22,000. **Advertising:** accepted ● *Roofing Materials Guide* ● Directory, annual. **Advertising:** accepted. **Conventions/Meetings:** annual convention (exhibits) - always February or March ● annual trade show.

1052 ■ National Terrazzo and Mosaic Association (NTMA)
201 N Maple Ave., Ste.208
Purcellville, VA 20132
Ph: (540)751-0930
Free: (800)323-9736
Fax: (540)751-0935
E-mail: info@ntma.com
URL: http://www.ntma.com
Contact: Wayne T. Grazzini, Pres.
Founded: 1924. **Members:** 150. **Staff:** 5. **Budget:** $500,000. **Description:** Contractors who install terrazzo and mosaic work; firms that produce or manufacture materials. Provides information to building owners, architects, builders, and terrazzo contractors. Conducts research on installation methods. **Awards:** Honor Awards. **Frequency:** annual. **Type:** recognition. **Publications:** *Design Book* ● *Terrazzo and Mosaic Catalog* ● Directory, annual ● Also publishes technical data and standard specifications for terrazzo. **Conventions/Meetings:** annual convention and conference (exhibits).

1053 ■ National Tile Contractors Association (NTCA)
PO Box 13629
Jackson, MS 39236
Ph: (601)939-2071
Fax: (601)932-6117
E-mail: bart@tile-assn.com
URL: http://www.tile-assn.com
Contact: Bart Bettiga, Exec. Dir.
Founded: 1947. **Members:** 800. **Membership Dues:** domestic, $425 (annual) ● foreign, $525 (annual). **Staff:** 4. **Description:** Members are installer-contractors; distributors, manufacturers, and importers are affiliate members. Promotes the ceramic tile industry; provides educational programs. **Committees:** Technical. **Formerly:** (1988) Association of Tile, Terrazzo, Marble Contractors and Affiliates. **Publications:** *Buyer's Guide*, annual. Includes directory. ● *NTCA Reference Manual*. **Price:** included in membership dues ● *TileLetter*, monthly. Magazine. **Advertising:** accepted. **Conventions/Meetings:** annual meeting (exhibits) ● workshop and seminar, for members and interested individuals - 75-100/year.

1054 ■ National Utility Contractors Association (NUCA)
4301 N Fairfax Dr., Ste.360
Arlington, VA 22203-1627
Ph: (703)358-9300
Free: (800)662-6822
Fax: (703)358-9307
E-mail: bill@nuca.com
URL: http://www.nuca.com
Contact: Bill Hillman, CEO
Founded: 1964. **Members:** 2,000. **Membership Dues:** contractor, $1,000 (annual) ● associate, $600 (annual) ● institution, $400 (annual). **Staff:** 18. **Budget:** $3,500,000. **Local Groups:** 44. **Description:** Utility contractors engaged in construction of utility lines (pipes for storm and sanitary sewers and drainage, water lines, cables, ducts, conduits, and other utility work) and related projects such as sanitation, sewage disposal, and irrigation; suppliers to the industry. Represents interest of contractors in legislative and public hearings on the local, state, and national levels, with regard to promulgation of state and local codes and federal programs relating to needs of communities for proper utilities, water pollution programs, urban renewal, area redevelopment, and public works that may affect utility contractors. Fosters safety education. Conducts surveys. **Awards:** Ditchdigger of the Year Award. **Frequency:** annual. **Type:** recognition. **Recipient:** to a contractor member who has made a significant contribution to NUCA and the underground utility construction industry ● We Dig America Award. **Frequency:** annual. **Type:** recognition. **Recipient:** to a nonmember who has made a significant contribution to NUCA and the underground utility construction industry ● William H. Feather Safety Award. **Type:** recognition. **Recipient:** for safety excellence. **Committees:** Awards; Budget and Finance; Education; Government Relations; Insurance and Documents; Member and Chapter Relations; Nominating; Political Action; Safety; Scholarship; Trenchless Technology. **Councils:** Chapter Executive Director's. **Publications:** *National Utility Contractors Association Membership Directory*, annual. Appears in June issue of Utility Contractor Magazine. **Price:** included in membership dues. **Circulation:** 26,000. **Advertising:** accepted. Alternate Formats: online ● *The NUCA Report*, weekly. Newsletter. Alternate Formats: online ● *NUCA Safety News*, bimonthly. Newsletter. Covers safety issues affecting the underground utility construction industry. **Price:** free, for members only. Alternate Formats: online ● *Utility Contractor*, monthly. Magazine. Includes buyer's guide in September issue. **Price:** included in membership dues. ISSN: 0192-0359. **Circulation:** 26,000. **Advertising:** accepted. **Conventions/Meetings:** board meeting - 3/year ● annual Utility Construction EXPO - convention (exhibits) - usually in February or March.

1055 ■ National Utility Locating Contractors Association (NULCA)
2563 Capital Medical Blvd.
Tallahassee, FL 32308
Ph: (850)531-8352
Fax: (850)531-8344
E-mail: info@nulca.org
URL: http://www.nulca.org
Contact: Robert E. Shively, Pres.
Founded: 1994. **Membership Dues:** company, $250-$6,000 (annual) ● associate, $250 (annual) ● individual, One-Call center, excavation contractor, $100 (annual) ● vendor sponsor, $2,000 (annual) ● general vendor, $500 (annual). **Multinational. Description:** Aims to define, establish and maintain high standards and practices in the underground utility contract locating industry. Ensures the safety of the general public, excavators and locating employees. Promotes and supports research for the underground facility locators locating industry. Encourages practical application of scientific and technical knowledge related to the underground facility locating industry for the benefit of public health, safety and comfort. **Telecommunication Services:** electronic mail, president@nulca.org. **Publications:** *NULCA News*, bimonthly. Newsletter. **Price:** included in membership dues. Alternate Formats: online.

1056 ■ NEA - The Association of Union Constructors (NEA)
1501 Lee Hwy., Ste.202
Arlington, VA 22209-1109
Ph: (703)524-3336
Fax: (703)524-3364
E-mail: tmustard@tauc.org
URL: http://www.nea-online.org
Contact: Stephen R. Lindauer, CEO
Founded: 1969. **Members:** 125. **Membership Dues:** regular (level I), $3,000 (annual) ● regular (level II), $5,000 (annual) ● regular (level III), $9,000 (annual) ● regular (level IV), $12,000 (annual) ● associate, $2,500 (annual). **Staff:** 8. **Description:** Active members are union construction companies. Associate members are engaged in the manufacture of products and equipment or providing services generally used in the construction industry. Objectives include developing industry standards, communicating governmental regulations to members, promoting safe work practices, and expanding opportunities for job training and increasing job skills. Represents the industry engaged in the construction industry before all divisions of government. Conducts activities with labor organizations to prevent strikes and promote cooperation with labor groups in areas of mutual interest. Conducts research. **Awards:** NEA Craftsman Award. **Frequency:** annual. **Type:** recognition. **Recipient:** for ingenuity and innovation in construction ● NEA Safety Award. **Type:** recognition. **Committees:** Apprenticeship; Labor; Maintenance; Marketing; Safety and Health. **Formerly:** (2001) National Erectors Association. **Publications:** *The Construction User*, quarterly. Magazine. **Advertising:** accepted. Alternate Formats: online ● *NEA Notes Newsletter*, monthly ● Membership Directory, annual. **Conventions/Meetings:** annual meeting, with speakers and programs (exhibits).

1057 ■ Painting and Decorating Contractors of America (PDCA)
1801 Park 270 Dr., Ste.220
St. Louis, MO 63146
Ph: (314)514-7322
Free: (800)332-PDCA
Fax: (314)514-9417
E-mail: ihoren@pdca.org
URL: http://www.pdca.org
Contact: Dr. Ian R. Horen CAE, CEO
Founded: 1884. **Members:** 3,100. **Membership Dues:** national affiliate, $330 (annual) ● international, $145 (annual) ● national associate (based on sales), $1,250-$2,500 (annual). **Staff:** 6. **Budget:** $1,900,000. **State Groups:** 33. **Local Groups:** 250. **Description:** Painting and wall covering contractors. Operates educational and charitable programs. Compiles statistics. **Libraries: Type:** reference. **Awards:** A.E. Robert Friedman/PDCA Scholarship. **Frequency:** annual. **Type:** scholarship. **Recipient:** for an individual nominated by a PDCA contractor member ● Picture It Painted Professionally (PIPP) Award. **Frequency:** annual. **Type:** trophy. **Recipient:** to outstanding projects of professional painting and decorating contractors ● Safety Awards. **Frequency:** annual. **Type:** trophy. **Recipient:** for companies who have made a commitment to safety in the workplace. **Computer Services:** database, of contractor members. **Committees:** Apprentice Training; Commercial Painting; Cost and Estimating; Education; Government Relations; Industrial Painting; Insurance and Safety; Manpower Training; National Trade; Residential Painting; Specifications; Technical Services; Wallcovering. **Publications:** *Hazardous Waste Handbook* ● *Painting and Wallcovering Contractor*, bimonthly. Magazine. **Advertising:** accepted ● *PDCA Directory*, annual. Membership Directory ● *PDCA Technical Standards*. **Conventions/Meetings:** annual PACE - convention and trade show, supplier and manufacturers of products to paint and wallcovering industry (exhibits) - always March.

1058 ■ Pile Driving Contractors Association (PDCA)
PO Box 66208
Orange Park, FL 32065
Ph: (904)215-4771
Free: (888)311-7322
Fax: (904)264-9531
E-mail: info@piledrivers.org
URL: http://www.piledrivers.org
Contact: Stevan A. Hall, Exec. Dir.
Founded: 1995. **Members:** 390. **Membership Dues:** contractor, $350-$725 (annual) ● associate, $725 (annual) ● technical affiliate, $95 (annual) ● student, $25 (annual). **Staff:** 1. **Budget:** $300,000. **Description:** Works to promote and increase the use of driven piles for deep foundations and earth retention systems. **Committees:** Communications; Education; Environment; Market Development; Technical. **Publications:** *Design and Construction of Driven Pile Foundations Workshop Manual*. **Price:** $74.95 for members; $84.95 for nonmembers; $59.95 each (more than 10 orders) ● *The Federal Highway Administration Design and Construction of Driven Pile Foundations Workshop Manual*. **Price:** $84.95 ● *PDCA Member Directory*, annual. Membership Directory ● *PileDrivers.org*, quarterly. Magazine. **Advertising:** accepted. **Conventions/Meetings:** annual roundtable (exhibits) - always in winter.

1059 ■ Plumbing-Heating-Cooling Contractors Association (PHCC)
PO Box 6808
Falls Church, VA 22046
Ph: (703)237-8100
Free: (800)533-7694
Fax: (703)237-7442
E-mail: naphcc@naphcc.org
URL: http://www.phccweb.org
Contact: Dwight "Ike" L. Casey, Exec. VP
Founded: 1883. **Members:** 5,000. **Membership Dues:** active, $387 (annual) ● associate, $1,126 (annual). **Staff:** 22. **Budget:** $3,000,000. **Regional Groups:** 237. **State Groups:** 51. **Local Groups:** 212. **Description:** Federation of state and local associations of plumbing, heating, and cooling contractors. Seeks to advance sanitation, encourage sanitary laws, and generally improve the plumbing, heating, ventilating, and air conditioning industries. Conducts apprenticeship training programs, workshops, seminars, political action committee, educational and research programs. **Telecommunication Services:** electronic mail, casey@naphcc.org. **Committees:** Apprenticeship; Industrial Relations; Insurance; Legislative; Membership; Political Action; Safety; Scholarship; Technical. **Departments:** Communications/Marketing Administration; Convention/Meetings; Educational Foundation; Finance; Government Relations; Technical and Training Services. **Formerly:** (1953) National Association of Master Plumbers; (1962) National Association of Plumbing Contractors; (2000) National Association of Plumbing-Heating-Cooling Contractors. **Publications:** *Connection*, semimonthly. Newsletter. **Price:** included in membership dues. **Circulation:** 6,000 ● *Leadership Directory*, annual ● Videos. Contains technical, safety, estimating, and business information. **Conventions/Meetings:** annual convention and trade show (exhibits).

1060 ■ Power and Communication Contractors Association (PCCA)
103 Oronoco St., Ste.200
Alexandria, VA 22314
Ph: (703)212-7734
Free: (800)542-7222
Fax: (703)548-3733
E-mail: info@pccaweb.org
URL: http://www.pccaweb.org
Contact: Greg Johnson, Gen. Dir.
Founded: 1945. **Members:** 500. **Membership Dues:** associate/contractor, $1,000 (annual). **Staff:** 4. **Budget:** $500,000. **Description:** Contractors engaged in electrical power and communication line construction. Offers group insurance. **Committees:** Associate Advisory; Government Affairs; Insurance; Safety. **Councils:** Cable Television Contractors; Power Contractors; Telephone Contractors. **Publications:** *Buyer's Catalog*, annual. **Advertising:** accepted ● *Communication Construction Directory*. **Advertising:** accepted ● *Convention Program*, annual. **Advertising:** accepted ● *PCCA Directory and Buyer's Guide*, annual. **Price:** free for members; $25.00 additional copy for members; $90.00 for nonmembers ● *Power and Communication Contractor*, monthly. Magazine. **Advertising:** accepted ● Membership Directory, annual. **Price:** free for members. **Advertising:** accepted. **Conventions/Meetings:** annual convention ● annual meeting.

1061 ■ Professional Construction Estimators Association of America (PCEA)
PO Box 680336
Charlotte, NC 28216
Ph: (704)489-1494
Free: (877)521-7232
Fax: (704)489-1495
E-mail: pcea@pcea.org
URL: http://www.pcea.org
Contact: Kim Lybrand, Exec. Mgr.
Founded: 1956. **Members:** 1,000. **Membership Dues:** individual, $295 (annual). **Staff:** 1. **Regional Groups:** 5. **Local Groups:** 13. **Description:** Professional construction estimators. Objectives are to further recognition of construction estimating as a professional field of endeavor; to collect and disseminate information; to research and solve problems related to the construction industry; to establish educational programs for youth and promote construction estimating as a career; to maintain ethical standards. **Awards:** Rudy Barnes Award. **Frequency:** annual. **Type:** recognition. **Recipient:** for excellence in the field ● Ted G. Wilson Scholarship. **Frequency:** annual. **Type:** scholarship. **Recipient:** for deserving students; one recipient in each state that has an established chapter (NC, SC, VA, GA and FL). **Publications:** *Estimator*, quarterly. Newsletter. **Circulation:** 1,000. **Advertising:** accepted. Alternate Formats: online ● *National PCEA Directory*, annual. **Advertising:** accepted. **Conventions/Meetings:** annual convention and meeting ● seminar.

1062 ■ Professional Women in Construction (PWC)
315 E 56th St.
New York, NY 10022-3730
Ph: (212)486-7745
Fax: (212)486-0228
E-mail: pwcusa1@aol.com
URL: http://www.pwcusa.org
Contact: Lenore Janis, Pres./Co-Founder
Founded: 1980. **Members:** 500. **Membership Dues:** individual, $225 (annual) ● corporate B (with 10 or less employees), $450 (annual) ● corporate A (with 11 or more employees), $750 (annual) ● business (sole proprietor/consultant with 3 or less employees), $275 (annual) ● student (matriculating), $65 (annual). **Staff:** 4. **Regional Groups:** 2. **Description:** Management-level women and men in construction and allied industries; owners, suppliers, architects, engineers, field personnel, office personnel, and bonding/surety personnel. Provides a forum for exchange of ideas and promotion of political and legislative action, education, and job opportunities for women in construction and related fields; forms liaisons with other trade and professional groups; develops research programs. Strives to reform abuses and to assure justice and equity within the construction industry. Sponsors mini-workshops. Maintains Action Line, which provides members with current information on pertinent legislation and on the association's activities and job referrals. **Awards:** Project of the Year. **Frequency:** annual. **Type:** recognition. **Recipient:** for major construction projects utilizing woman-owned businesses ● Salute to Women of Achievement. **Frequency:** annual. **Type:** recognition. **Recipient:** for the outstanding woman in construction industry. **Task Forces:** Architects/Engineers; Management Field Personnel; Management Office Personnel; Owners; Suppliers; Surety/Insurance. **Publications:** *Calendar of Events*, monthly ● *e-PWC*, quarterly. Newsletter. **Circulation:** 5,000. **Advertising:** accepted. Alternate Formats: online. **Conventions/Meetings:** monthly Developers' Forums - meeting, with networking (exhibits) ● annual Holiday Dinner Dance ● annual trade show, with MBD workshop and opportunity fair (exhibits).

1063 ■ Roof Consultants Institute (RCI)
1500 Sunday Dr., Ste.204
Raleigh, NC 27607
Ph: (919)859-0742
Free: (800)828-1902
Fax: (919)859-1328
E-mail: jbirdsong@rci-online.org
URL: http://www.rci-online.org
Contact: James R. Birdsong, Exec. Dir./CEO
Founded: 1983. **Members:** 1,700. **Membership Dues:** professional, $373 (annual) ● professional/industry affiliate, associate, $236 (annual) ● industry, $421 (annual) ● quality assurance observer, $133 (annual) ● facility manager, $103 (annual) ● student, $61 (annual). **Staff:** 10. **Budget:** $1,600,000. **Regional Groups:** 8. **State Groups:** 4. **Description:** Individuals organized to promote the field of roof consultation. (Roof consultants are individuals that provide advice to architects, engineers, and building owners on the latest and most appropriate technology in the roofing industry.) Maintains certification program; conducts research in roofing technology. **Awards:** H.W. Busching Memorial Scholarship. **Type:** scholarship. **Additional Websites:** http://www.rci-mercury.com. **Committees:** Annual Convention; Building Envelope; Bylaws; Chapter Development; Education; Ethics; Jury of Fellows; Publications. **Publications:** *Interface*, 11/year. Journal. Contains technical articles and papers, and timely coverage of industry news and events. **Price:** $90.00/year in U.S.; $110.00/year outside U.S. **Circulation:** 2,500. **Advertising:** accepted ● *International Directory of Roofing Professionals*. **Circulation:** 3,500. **Advertising:** accepted ● Membership Directory. **Conventions/Meetings:** annual conference (exhibits) ● annual convention and trade show (exhibits) ● monthly meeting.

1064 ■ Roofing Industry Educational Institute (RIEI)
10255 W Higgins Rd., Ste.600
Rosemont, IL 60018-5607
Ph: (847)299-9070
Fax: (847)299-1183
E-mail: nrca@nrca.net
URL: http://www.nrca.net/rp/related/riei
Contact: Bill Good CAE, Exec. VP
Founded: 1979. **Staff:** 6. **Budget:** $1,000,000. **Description:** Participants are contractors, architects, specifiers, owners, consultants, and others involved in the roofing industry. Conducts seminars and educational programs covering all aspects of roofing, highlighting design, installation, and maintenance including topics such as thermal insulation, vapors and condensation, and fire and codes. Provides referral service and presents diplomas. **Libraries:** **Type:** reference. **Awards:** The Charlie Raymond Award. **Frequency:** annual. **Type:** recognition. **Recipient:** to a member who has recruited the most number of new members during a calendar year ● The Gold Circle Award. **Frequency:** annual. **Type:** recognition. **Recipient:** for members from around the world with outstanding contributions to the roofing industry. **Committees:** Curriculum; Publication Review. **Publications:** *Catalog of Education Materials* ● *Roofing Industry Educational Institute—Information Letter*, quarterly. Newsletter. Contains articles on roofing technology and extracts from new industry papers. Includes seminar and conference schedules. **Price:** free. **Circulation:** 28,000 ● Manuals ● Videos ● Produces slide presentations. **Conventions/Meetings:** seminar.

1065 ■ Sheet Metal Industry Promotion Plan (SMIPP)
Address Unknown since 2007
Founded: 1961. **Members:** 80. **Staff:** 2. **Description:** Heating, air conditioning, ventilating, roofing, and sheet metal contractors in Cuyahoga, Ashtabula, Geauga, and Lake counties of Ohio. Promotes quality sheet metal installations and pride in workmanship. Disseminates information on fabrication and

erection of sheet metal construction. Has drawn up standards for mechanical sheet metal work; standards are to be adhered to by union members and participating contractors in fabrication and erection on residential, commercial, and industrial work involving sheet metal. Sponsors training classes for journeymen on sheet metal layout, heliarc welding, mechanical drawing, electric welding, balancing, and blueprint reading. **Publications:** none. **Conventions/Meetings:** annual convention - usually October ● bimonthly meeting.

1066 ■ Tile Contractors Association of America (TCAA)
4 E 113th Terr.
Kansas City, MO 64114
Free: (800)655-8453
Fax: (816)767-0194
E-mail: info@tcaainc.org
URL: http://www.tcaainc.org
Contact: Patty Nolte, Exec. Dir.
Founded: 1903. **Members:** 130. **Membership Dues:** active contractor and supplier, $800 (annual) ● retired supplier, $75 (annual) ● retired contractor, $25 (annual). **Staff:** 3. **Description:** Ceramic tile contractors in the United States. Encourages the use of ceramic tile by the building industry and better and more economical methods for installation of ceramic tile. **Awards:** Cesery Award. **Frequency:** annual. **Type:** recognition. **Telecommunication Services:** electronic mail, patty@ccainc.org. **Committees:** Labor; Legal; Membership; Nominating; Scholarship; Technical. **Formerly:** (1936) Tile and Mantel Contractors Association of America. **Publications:** *9300 Contractor*, bimonthly. Newsletter. Alternate Formats: online. **Conventions/Meetings:** annual conference (exhibits).

1067 ■ Tilt-Up Concrete Association (TCA)
PO Box 204
Mount Vernon, IA 52314
Ph: (319)895-6911
Fax: (320)213-5555
E-mail: info@tilt-up.org
URL: http://www.tilt-up.org
Contact: J. Edward Sauter, Exec. Dir.
Founded: 1986. **Members:** 450. **Membership Dues:** national associate, $1,100 (annual) ● local associate, $600 (annual) ● contractor, $750 (annual) ● educator, student, $75 (annual) ● professional firm, developer, owner, consultant, $500 (annual) ● sustaining, $2,000 (annual). **Staff:** 4. **Budget:** $300,000. **Multinational. Description:** Engineers, suppliers, contractors, and others involved in tilt-up construction. Advocates the use of tilt-up construction through promotion and training. (Tilt-up construction is a process of casting wall panels at the building site and then standing or tilting them up. The process saves on transportation and production cost because the panels are produced quickly, don't have to be moved, and can be made to large specifications.) Conducts seminars and educational programs; offers technical assistance. **Awards:** Achievement Awards. **Frequency:** annual. **Type:** recognition. **Recipient:** for advancement of industry, unique application, aesthetics and quality. **Computer Services:** database ● mailing lists. **Telecommunication Services:** electronic mail, bsaltzman@tilt-up.org. **Committees:** Awards; Education; Meetings; Promotion; Technical. **Councils:** Global Associate's. **Subcommittees:** Construction/Safety; Engineering. **Task Forces:** Seismic Performance. **Publications:** *The Architecture of Tilt-Up*. Manual. Features engineering and construction fundamentals. **Price:** $103.00 plus shipping and handling ● *TCA eNews*. Newsletter. Alternate Formats: online ● *Tilt UP News*, quarterly. Magazine. **Price:** $15.00. **Circulation:** 4,000. **Advertising:** accepted. **Conventions/Meetings:** annual convention ● annual meeting ● biennial Tilt-Up Symposium - conference (exhibits).

1068 ■ Women Construction Owners and Executives, U.S.A. (WCOE, USA)
4401A Connecticut Ave. NW
Washington, DC 20008
Free: (800)788-3548
Fax: (425)294-8898
E-mail: info@wcoeusa.org
URL: http://www.wcoeusa.org
Contact: Deborah Wilder, Pres.
Founded: 1984. **Members:** 100. **Membership Dues:** individual, $200 (annual) ● corporate, associate, $250 (annual) ● gold, $500 (annual). **Staff:** 1. **Budget:** $100,000. **Regional Groups:** 7. **Description:** Promotes the interests of women construction owners and executives. Provides legislation, business, educational, and networking opportunities. **Awards:** President's Phoenix Award. **Frequency:** annual. **Type:** recognition. **Recipient:** for service to the association. **Committees:** By-Laws; Legislative; Long Range Planning and Financial Development; Public Relations; Turning Point. **Publications:** *The Turning Point*, monthly. Newsletter. Up To Date Legislative, Business, Trade (Industry) Info. & Assoc. News. **Price:** $50.00/year. **Circulation:** 1,000. **Advertising:** accepted. Alternate Formats: online. **Conventions/Meetings:** annual meeting and conference (exhibits).

Cooperatives

1069 ■ Co-op America
1612 K St. NW, Ste.600
Washington, DC 20006
Ph: (202)872-5307
Free: (800)584-7336
Fax: (202)331-8166
E-mail: info@coopamerica.org
URL: http://www.coopamerica.org
Contact: Alisa Gravitz, Exec. Dir.
Founded: 1982. **Members:** 67,500. **Membership Dues:** individual, family - sliding scale, $20 (annual) ● business - sliding scale, $75 (annual). **Staff:** 35. **Budget:** $3,500,000. **Description:** Seeks to create a socially just and environmentally sustainable economy. Educates people on how to spend and invest their money in a manner that supports the ultimate goal of social and environmental responsibility. Encourages irresponsible corporations to become more responsible corporate citizens. Provides services to members, including socially-responsible financial planning tools, long distance phone service, and a travel service. **Convention/Meeting:** none. **Computer Services:** Mailing lists, will trade/rent list to like-minded organizations. **Telecommunication Services:** TDD, (202)873-5362. **Programs:** Boycotts; Fair Trade; Green Business; Green Energy; Living Green; Responsible Shopper; Sweatshops; Woodwise. **Publications:** *Co-op America Quarterly*. Magazine. Provides coverage and solutions to social and environmental issues. **Price:** included in membership dues. **Circulation:** 50,000. **Advertising:** accepted. Alternate Formats: online ● *Financial Planning Handbook*. Contains tips and resources about responsible saving and investing. **Price:** included in membership dues; $11.95 for nonmembers ● *National Green Pages*, annual. Directory. Lists 2,000 socially and environmentally responsible businesses nationwide. **Price:** included in membership dues; $7.95 for nonmembers. ISSN: 1064-8729. **Circulation:** 80,000. **Advertising:** accepted ● *Real Money*, bimonthly. Newsletter. **Price:** included in membership dues. **Circulation:** 2,000.

1070 ■ Cooperative Association of Tractor Dealers (CATD)
Crescent Ctr.
6075 Poplar Ave., Ste.125
Memphis, TN 38119
Ph: (901)333-8600
Fax: (901)333-8640
E-mail: loans@catdloans.com
URL: http://www.catdloans.com
Contact: Shellie G. McCain, Pres.
Founded: 1981. **Members:** 57. **Staff:** 4. **Description:** Caterpillar tractor dealers. Special purpose finance cooperative which provides low-interest loans to members, primarily for inventory financing. **Telecommunication Services:** electronic mail, sgm@catdloans.com. **Publications:** Annual Report, annual. **Conventions/Meetings:** annual meeting.

1071 ■ Cooperative Business International (CBI)
5898 Cleveland Ave.
Columbus, OH 43231-6884
Ph: (614)839-2700
Fax: (614)839-2709
E-mail: info@cbi-global.com
URL: http://www.cbi-global.com
Contact: Robert W. Clark, Pres./CEO
Founded: 1984. **Description:** Promotes and facilitates business opportunities among business cooperatives worldwide. Seeks to link cooperatives into mutually beneficial business relationships. Provides assistance with finance, management, sourcing of needed goods, transportation, market information, investment, consulting, marketing, brokering, and technology transfers. Offers technical assistance to cooperatives in developing countries in areas such as: financing of business development; conversion of surplus food commodities into cash capital; application to donor commodities; finance marketing; quality control; export preparation; cost analysis; financial management and distribution. **Telecommunication Services:** electronic mail, cbi@cbi-global.com. **Affiliated With:** National Cooperative Business Association. **Conventions/Meetings:** annual conference and seminar (exhibits) ● periodic International Cooperative Business Seminar.

1072 ■ Cooperative Grocers' Information Network (CGIN)
PO Box 399
Arcata, CA 95518
Ph: (707)445-4849
Fax: (707)445-1808
E-mail: info@cgin.coop
URL: http://www.cgin.coop
Contact: Gail Graham, Pres.
Founded: 1997. **Membership Dues:** primary (retail food cooperative), $175 (annual) ● associate (organization), $325 (annual) ● associate (individual), $125 (annual). **Description:** Supports the growth and development of retail food cooperatives. Seeks to boost the economic potential of retail food cooperatives. Improves business conditions of retail food cooperatives by providing educational services and conducting research activities. Strives to strengthen retail food cooperatives by facilitating the sharing and development of resources among its members. **Telecommunication Services:** electronic mail, admin@cgin.coop. **Publications:** Annual Report. Alternate Formats: online.

1073 ■ National Cooperative Business Association (NCBA)
1401 New York Ave. NW, Ste.1100
Washington, DC 20005
Ph: (202)638-6222
Fax: (202)638-1374
E-mail: ncba@ncba.coop
URL: http://www.ncba.org
Contact: Paul Hazen, Pres./CEO
Founded: 1916. **Members:** 450. **Membership Dues:** individual, $52 (annual) ● twin pines, $105 (annual) ● life, $525. **Staff:** 35. **Description:** Local, state, regional, and national cooperative business organizations including farm supply, agricultural marketing, insurance, banking, housing, health care, consumer goods and services, student, worker, fishery, and other cooperatives. Represents, strengthens, and expands cooperative businesses. Programs include: supporting the development of cooperative businesses in the U.S; developing and providing technical assistance to cooperatives in developing nations; representing American cooperatives in Washington, DC and abroad; promoting and developing commercial relations among the world's cooperatives. Operates Cooperative Action for Congressional Trust. Supports the Cooperative Hall of Fame, and the Cooperative Development Foundation. Maintains hall of fame. **Committees:** Political Action. **Departments:** Domestic Operations; International Business Development. **Divisions:** Communications; Government Relations; Member Services. **Publications:** *Cooperative Business Journal*, 10/year. **Price:** $15.00/year in U.S.; $25.00/year outside U.S. ISSN: 0893-3391. **Cir-**

culation: 5,000. **Advertising:** accepted ● Annual Report, annual. Alternate Formats: online. **Conventions/Meetings:** annual conference (exhibits) - always in Washington, DC.

1074 ■ National Cooperative Grocers Association (NCGA)

389 E Coll. St.
Iowa City, IA 52240
Ph: (319)466-9029
URL: http://www.ncga.coop
Contact: Robynn Shrader, CEO

Founded: 1999. **Members:** 109. **Description:** Supports the development of cooperative businesses in the United States. Serves as a business services cooperative for natural food coops located throughout the United States. Unifies natural food coops to optimize operational and marketing resources, strengthen purchasing power, and offer more value to natural food coop owners and shoppers.

Cordage

1075 ■ Cordage Institute (CI)

994 Old Eagle School Rd., Ste.1019
Wayne, PA 19087
Ph: (610)971-4854
Fax: (610)971-4859
E-mail: info@ropecord.com
URL: http://www.ropecord.com
Contact: Robert H. Ecker, Exec. Dir.

Founded: 1920. **Members:** 85. **Membership Dues:** regular (based on annual sales), $500-$3,000 (annual) ● associate, affiliate, $2,750 (annual) ● reseller, specialty supplier, $600 (annual) ● technical, $500 (annual) ● academic, $50 (annual). **Staff:** 3. **Budget:** $300,000. **Description:** Represents manufacturers of natural and synthetic fiber cordage, in constructions, industry suppliers, consultants, and machinery manufacturers. Offers standard technical information and educational programs. Operates Speaker's Bureau. Compiles statistics. **Libraries: Type:** reference. **Holdings:** 15. **Subjects:** cordage, rope, twines. **Awards:** Merit. **Frequency:** annual. **Type:** recognition. **Recipient:** for service to the industry. **Computer Services:** database, specifications ● mailing lists, cordage, rope and twine manufacturers. **Telecommunication Services:** electronic mail, ecker@mmco1.com. **Committees:** Government Affairs; Product Liability; Technical. **Absorbed:** (1990) American Cordage and Netting Manufacturers. **Publications:** *Cordage Directory*, quarterly. Contains listings of cordage manufacturers and their capabilities. **Price:** free ● *Fiber Rope Technical Manual*. Contains information on basic properties, safe use, inspections guideline, working loads, cordage and rope engineering, and structural components. ● *Ropecord News*, bimonthly. Newsletter. Features cordage industry news, technical information, and statistics. **Price:** $45.00/year in U.S., Canada, and Mexico; $95.00/year elsewhere. **Circulation:** 900. **Advertising:** accepted ● *Standard Test Methods for Fiber Rope*, annual. Features standards for testing all fiber strength members, including instructions for making terminations and determining physical properties. **Price:** $30.00/issue. **Conventions/Meetings:** annual conference and symposium ● annual meeting.

Correctional

1076 ■ Corrections Technology Association (CTA)

c/o Paul Lewin, Pres.
Colorado Dept. of Corrections
2862 S Circle Dr., Ste.407
Colorado Springs, CO 80906
Ph: (719)226-4811
E-mail: paul.lewin@doc.state.co.us
URL: http://www.correctionstech.org
Contact: Paul Lewin, Pres.

Description: Develops standards for common business functions in corrections. Serves as a forum for technology executives in the field of corrections. Provides a vehicle to identify current, new, and emerging technologies as a means to advise and promote sharing of information throughout the corrections community. **Computer Services:** Online services, forum. **Committees:** Ad Hoc; Annual; Operating. **Special Interest Groups:** Technology. **Conventions/Meetings:** annual conference.

Cosmetology

1077 ■ Aesthetics International Association (AIA)

2611 N Beltline Rd., Ste.140
Sunnyvale, TX 75182
Ph: (972)203-8530
Free: (877)968-7539
Fax: (972)226-2339
E-mail: aiathekey@aol.com
URL: http://www.beautyworks.com/aia
Contact: Patricia Strunk, Sec./Assoc. Publisher

Founded: 1972. **Members:** 1,000. **Membership Dues:** student, $30 (semiannual) ● professional, $125 (annual). **Staff:** 2. **Regional Groups:** 1. **Local Groups:** 1. **Languages:** English, Spanish. **For-Profit. Description:** Aestheticians (persons licensed to manage or own a skin care salon) and students of certified schools; associate members are manufacturers and distributors representing the cosmetic industry. Seeks to improve the education and upgrade the standards of aestheticians, cosmetologists, and related persons in the industry. Promotes public awareness of research results and information relating to the professions of aesthetics and cosmetology. Educates the public and the aesthetic and cosmetology professions through seminars and lectures. Conducts charitable and research programs. **Libraries: Type:** open to the public. **Holdings:** audio recordings, books, video recordings. **Subjects:** aesthetics, aromatherapy, massage. **Additional Websites:** http://www.dermascope.com. **Committees:** AIACEU Exam; AIACEU Schools and Salons; Dermascope; Legal Service Referral; Legislation; Make-Up; Manufacturing Liaison; National Education; Research. **Formerly:** (1998) Aestheticians International Association. **Publications:** *AIA Newsletter*, quarterly. **Circulation:** 1,500 ● *Dermascope*, bimonthly. Magazine. Provides information and techniques on skin care, make-up, and body therapy; also reports information on cancer. **Price:** $35.00/year; $60.00/2 years. **Circulation:** 15,000. **Advertising:** accepted. **Conventions/Meetings:** congress.

1078 ■ Association of Cosmetologists and Hairdressers (ACH)

Address Unknown since 2007

Founded: 1985. **Members:** 4,311. **Staff:** 6. **Budget:** $3,000,000. **Description:** Cosmetologists and beauticians; beauty product manufacturers, wholesalers, buyers, and retailers. Seeks to keep members informed of current trends in the beauty culture industry. Conducts demonstrations. Compiles statistics. Sponsors educational programs. **Libraries: Type:** reference. **Awards: Type:** recognition. **Formerly:** (1986) Association of Cosmetologists. **Publications:** *Bulletin Update*, quarterly ● Newsletter, quarterly. **Conventions/Meetings:** annual meeting - always December or January ● seminar and workshop ● trade show.

1079 ■ Hair International/Associated Master Barbers and Beauticians of America (HI/AMBBA)

Address Unknown since 2007

Founded: 1924. **Members:** 1,000. **Staff:** 2. **Description:** Barber styling and cosmetology school and business owners and employees; manufacturers. Operates speakers' bureau; conducts hairstyling show, classes, and seminars. **Divisions:** National Educational Council. **Formerly:** (1984) Associated Master Barbers and Beauticians of America. **Publications:** *Hair International News*, bimonthly. Magazine. **Price:** $25.00/year in U.S.; $30.00/year in Canada. ISSN: 0887-803X. **Circulation:** 800. **Advertising:** accepted ● *Standardized Textbook of Barbering and Styling*. **Conventions/Meetings:** triennial meeting (exhibits).

1080 ■ Intercoiffure America

c/o Joy Warner, Membership Chair
154 Rte. 206
Chester, NJ 07930
Ph: (908)879-6211
Free: (800)442-3007
Fax: (908)879-3286
E-mail: ebersohlady@aol.com
URL: http://www.intercoiffure.us
Contact: Joy Warner, Membership Chair

Founded: 1915. **Members:** 260. **Membership Dues:** regular, $695 (annual). **Description:** Owners of beauty salons in the United States and Canada who meet the ethical standards set down by Intercoiffure. Seeks to "make the women of America the best in hair fashion". **Formerly:** (1966) Internationale des Coiffures de Dames. **Conventions/Meetings:** semiannual conference - always in New York City ● semiannual show, presents hair fashions for the press in New York City.

1081 ■ International Chain Salon Association (ICSA)

207 E Ohio St., No. 361
Chicago, IL 60611
Free: (866)444-ICSA
Fax: (815)609-5139
E-mail: mmelaniphy@icsa.cc
URL: http://www.icsa.cc
Contact: Margie Melaniphy, Contact

Members: 60. **Budget:** $60,000. **Description:** Beauty salon chains. Collects and processes data on industry standards; proactively works to affect the outcome of pending legislation and regulations governing the cosmetology industry; provides continuing education programs on management issues to members; works for free exchange of corporate information, solutions to common problems, advertising ideas, and incentive programs amongst members; takes part in and supports other industry associations. **Committees:** Legislative Action. **Formerly:** (1985) National Beauty Salon Chain Association. **Publications:** *Link Up*, quarterly. Newsletter. Alternate Formats: online ● Membership Directory, annual. Alternate Formats: online ● Bulletin, periodic ● Reports. **Conventions/Meetings:** conference - every 9 months.

1082 ■ Nail Manufacturers Council (NMC)

c/o Professional Beauty Association
15825 N 71st St.
Scottsdale, AZ 85254
Ph: (312)245-1575
Free: (800)468-2274
Fax: (312)245-1080
E-mail: dschoon@cox.net
URL: http://www.probeauty.org/about/committees/nmc
Contact: Doug Schoon, Co-Chm.

Founded: 1989. **Members:** 41. **Staff:** 2. **Description:** Division of American Beauty Association. Nail product manufacturers and marketers. Promotes unity within the nail product industry. Works to: elevate safety standards; maintain high ethical standards in advertising; increase public awareness of nail care. Lobbies the government concerning issues that affect the industry. Acts as a forum for the exchange of information. Maintains safety guidelines. **Committees:** Communications; Safety and Standards. **Affiliated With:** Professional Beauty Association.

1083 ■ National Association of Barber Boards of America (NABBA)

c/o Charles Kirkpatrick, Exec. Off.
2708 Pine St.
Arkadelphia, AR 71923
Ph: (501)682-2806
Fax: (501)682-5073

E-mail: nabba@iocc.com
URL: http://www.nationalbarberboards.com
Contact: Charles Kirkpatrick, Exec. Off.

Founded: 1935. **Members:** 50. **Membership Dues:** state, $200 (annual) ● delegate, $150 (annual). **Staff:** 2. **Regional Groups:** 200. **State Groups:** 50. **Description:** Represents state boards of barber examiners. Promotes the exchange of information among state barber boards and state agencies that examine, license, and regulate the barber industry. Improves standards and procedures for examining barbers and regulates the barber industry. Furthers continuing education and development of curricula for educating barbers. Devises procedures for ensuring that consumers are informed and protected. Maintains library. **Awards:** Conference Attendance. **Frequency:** annual. **Type:** recognition. **Recipient:** for more than 20 years of attendance. **Formerly:** (1986) National Association of Boards of Barbers Examiners of America; (2005) National Association of Barber Boards. **Conventions/Meetings:** annual conference - always 3rd Monday of September.

1084 ■ National Beauty Culturists' League (NBCL)
25 Logan Cir. NW
Washington, DC 20005-3725
Ph: (202)332-2695
Fax: (202)332-0940
E-mail: nbcl@bellsouth.net
URL: http://www.nbcl.org
Contact: Dr. Katie B. Catalon, Pres.

Founded: 1919. **Members:** 10,000. **Membership Dues:** sustaining, $200 (annual) ● individual, $100 (annual) ● beauty school student, $50 (annual) ● corporate, $500 (annual). **State Groups:** 39. **Local Groups:** 250. **Description:** Beauticians, cosmetologists, and beauty products manufacturers. Encourages standardized, scientific, and approved methods of hair, scalp, and skin treatments. Offers scholarships and plans to establish a research center. Sponsors: National Institute of Cosmetology, a training course in operating and designing and business techniques; National Beauty Week. Maintains hall of fame; conducts research programs; compiles statistics. **Committees:** Charity; Education; Scholarship. **Formerly:** (1920) National Hair System Culture League. **Conventions/Meetings:** annual trade show.

1085 ■ National Cosmetology Association (NCA)
401 N Michigan Ave., 22nd Fl.
Chicago, IL 60611
Ph: (312)527-6765
Fax: (312)464-6118
E-mail: nca1@ncacares.org
URL: http://www.ncacares.org
Contact: Marlene Bridge, Pres.

Founded: 1921. **Members:** 30,000. **Membership Dues:** student, $75 (annual) ● professional, $115 (annual). **Staff:** 10. **Budget:** $1,500,000. **State Groups:** 50. **Local Groups:** 600. **Description:** Owners of cosmetology salons; cosmetologists. Sponsors: National Cosmetology Month; National Beauty Show. Provides special sections for estheticians, school owners, salon owners, and nail technicians. Maintains hall of fame. Conducts educational and charitable programs. **Libraries: Type:** reference. **Holdings:** archival material. **Subjects:** hair, esthetics, nails, cosmetology. **Absorbed:** (1985) CIDESCO United States of America; (1985) Skin Care Association of America. **Formerly:** (1986) National Hairdressers and Cosmetologists Association. **Publications:** *American Salon Magazine*, annual. **Price:** included in membership dues ● Newsletter, monthly. Alternate Formats: online.

1086 ■ Professional Beauty Association (PBA)
15825 N 71st St., Ste.100
Scottsdale, AZ 85254
Ph: (480)281-0424
Free: (800)468-2274
Fax: (480)905-0708
E-mail: info@probeauty.org
URL: http://www.probeauty.org
Contact: Steve Sleeper, Exec. Dir.

Founded: 1985. **Members:** 250. **Membership Dues:** business (with annual gross of $500,000 to $10 million), $175-$1,000 (annual) ● business (with annual gross of $10 million to 100 million or more), $1,500-$7,500 (annual) ● associate, $1,500 (annual). **Staff:** 7. **Budget:** $350,000. **Description:** Manufacturers and manufacturers' representatives of beauty and barber products, cosmetics, equipment, and supplies used in or resold by beauty salons or barbershops. Promotes the beauty industry; works to ensure product safety; disseminates information. Holds educational seminars; organizes charity events. **Awards:** Outstanding Achievement Award. **Type:** recognition. **Councils:** Distributor Leadership; Governing; Manufacturer Leadership; Salon and Spa Leadership. **Affiliated With:** Nail Manufacturers Council. **Formed by Merger of:** United Beauty Association; National Beauty and Barber Manufacturers Association. **Formerly:** (2005) American Beauty Association. **Publications:** *PBA Progress*, 3/year, every fall, summer and spring. Newsletter. **Conventions/Meetings:** Cosmoprof North America - show.

1087 ■ Society of Permanent Cosmetic Professionals (SPCP)
69 N Broadway
Des Plaines, IL 60016
Ph: (847)635-1330
Fax: (847)635-1326
E-mail: elizfhowell@hotmail.com
URL: http://www.spcp.org
Contact: Elizabeth Finch Howell CPCP, Pres.

Founded: 1990. **Membership Dues:** regular, $195 (annual). **Multinational**. **Description:** Permanent cosmetic professionals. Dedicated to promoting safety, excellence and professional standards for the industry; provides education and industry guidelines. **Telecommunication Services:** electronic mail, dixie@classicbeautyconcepts.com. **Publications:** *Eyebrow Design Video*. **Price:** $45.00 for members ● *SPCP 10-Year Journal*. Contains compilation of valuable newsletter articles. **Price:** $99.00/set; $79.00/set (for trainers only, minimum of 5 order) ● Newsletter, quarterly. Contains membership information, trainer programs, publicity activities, legislative updates, education, and insider information. **Price:** included in membership dues. **Conventions/Meetings:** annual convention.

1088 ■ World International Nail and Beauty Association (WINBA)
1221 N Lake View Ave.
Anaheim, CA 92807
Ph: (714)779-9892
Free: (800)541-9838
Fax: (714)779-9971
E-mail: dkellenberger@inmnails.com
Contact: David Kellenberger, VP

Founded: 1981. **Members:** 13,000. **Budget:** $250,000. **State Groups:** 16. **Description:** Professionals in the nail and skin care industries. Objectives are to: represent the manicure and skin care industry; promote the effective use and application of manicuring and skin care products and equipment; provide a means for mutual communication and joint study; represent the industry before state boards, the Food and Drug Administration, and other regulatory agencies. Conducts seminars; secures discounts on supplies; offers special conducts public relations program; sponsors research and educational programs; compiles statistics. Maintains speakers' bureau and placement service. **Libraries: Type:** reference. **Holdings:** biographical archives. **Awards: Type:** recognition. **Recipient:** for best in nail art, makeup application, and hair styling. **Computer Services:** database ● mailing lists ● online services. **Committees:** Educational Programs; Professional Training; World Congress of Nail Artist Political Action; World International Judging. **Publications:** *Encyclopedia of Nails*, periodic ● *Nail and Beauty Emporium Buyer's Catalog and Guide*, quarterly. **Price:** free. **Circulation:** 50,000. **Advertising:** accepted ● *National Aesthetician and Nail Artist*, quarterly ● *WINBA Catalog of Trade Shows*, periodic. **Circulation:** 50,000. **Advertising:** accepted. Alternate Formats: online ● *World International Nail and Beauty Association—Buyer's Guide*, periodic ● *World International Nail and Beauty Association—Magazine*, periodic ● *World International Nail and Beauty Association—Membership Directory*, periodic ● *World International Nail and Beauty Association—Newsletter*, periodic ● Brochures. **Conventions/Meetings:** semiannual World Champion Beauty Trade Show (exhibits).

Cotton

1089 ■ American Cotton Shippers Association (ACSA)
88 Union Ave., Ste.1204
Memphis, TN 38103
Ph: (901)525-2272
Fax: (901)527-8303
E-mail: bmay@acsa-cotton.org
URL: http://www.acsa-cotton.org
Contact: William E. May, Sr. VP, Foreign and Domestic Operations

Founded: 1924. **Members:** 425. **Membership Dues:** active/associate, $300 (annual). **Staff:** 10. **Description:** Four affiliated regional cotton shippers' associations comprised of firms of merchants and exporters of raw cotton in bales. **Committees:** Data Systems and Information Development; Domestic Mills and Overland Transportation; Foreign Affairs and Ocean Transportation; Futures Contracts; National Affairs; Primary Buyers/Mill Service Agents; Quality/Quotations and Technical Standards; Rules, By-Laws, and Fair Practices. **Conventions/Meetings:** annual convention - always May.

1090 ■ Cotton Council International (CCI)
1521 New Hampshire Ave. NW
Washington, DC 20036
Ph: (202)745-7805
Fax: (202)483-4040
E-mail: cottonusa@cotton.org
URL: http://www.cottonusa.org
Contact: David L. Burns, Chm.

Founded: 1956. **Staff:** 25. **Budget:** $15,000,000. **Description:** Representatives of all segments of the U.S. cotton industry. Works as an international cotton sales promotion organization cooperating with cotton interests in foreign countries. **Computer Services:** Mailing lists. **Publications:** *Buyers' Guide to U.S. Cotton*, annual. Handbook. Alternate Formats: online ● Also publishes maps. **Conventions/Meetings:** annual meeting.

1091 ■ Cotton Foundation
c/o Bill Norman
PO Box 820284
Memphis, TN 38112
Ph: (901)274-9030
Fax: (901)725-0510
URL: http://www.cotton.org/foundation/index.cfm
Contact: Clyde Sharp, Pres.

Founded: 1955. **Members:** 72. **Staff:** 2. **Budget:** $1,000,000. **Description:** Corporations interested in supporting research and educational programs to promote markets for cotton. Offers grants to public and private institutions, and occasionally to industrial firms, for fundamental and applied research pertaining to cotton production and processing. **Libraries: Type:** open to the public. **Holdings:** 6. **Subjects:** cotton insects, weeds, physiology, harvest. **Awards:** Harry S. Baker Distinguished Service Award for Cotton. **Frequency:** annual. **Type:** recognition. **Recipient:** for an individual who has provided extraordinary service, leadership, and dedication to the U.S. cotton industry ● Oscar Johnston Lifetime Achievement Award. **Frequency:** annual. **Type:** recognition. **Recipient:** to an individual (deceased) who served the cotton industry through the NCC. **Formerly:** (1970) Foundation for Cotton Research and Education. **Publications:** *Journal of Cotton Science*, quarterly.

Alternate Formats: online; CD-ROM ● Annual Report, annual ● Brochures. **Conventions/Meetings:** annual conference.

1092 ■ Cotton Incorporated (CI)
6399 Weston Pkwy.
Cary, NC 27513
Ph: (919)678-2220
Fax: (919)678-2230
E-mail: kbrannigan@cottoninc.com
URL: http://www.cottoninc.com
Contact: Berrye J. Worsham III, Pres./CEO
Founded: 1971. **Description:** Represents 45,000 cotton producers for research and promotion. **Formerly:** Cotton Producers' Institute.

1093 ■ Cotton Warehouse Association of America (CWAA)
1156 15th St. NW, Ste.315
Washington, DC 20005
Ph: (202)331-2121
Fax: (202)331-2112
E-mail: cwaa@cottonwarehouse.org
URL: http://www.cottonwarehouse.org
Contact: Tommy Malin, Chm.
Founded: 1969. **Members:** 250. **Membership Dues:** associate, $250 (annual). **Description:** Promotes the interests of cotton manufacturers and conducts research. **Committees:** Cotton Warehouse Government Relations; Industry Liaison and Technology; Insurance and Internal Affairs; Legislative and Government Policy; Operations. **Supersedes:** NA Cotton Compress and Cotton Warehouse Association. **Publications:** *Cotton Comments*, monthly ● Membership Directory, annual. **Conventions/Meetings:** annual meeting - always June.

1094 ■ National Cotton Batting Institute (NCBI)
4322 Bloombury St.
Southaven, MS 38672
Ph: (662)449-0000
Fax: (662)449-0046
E-mail: info@natbat.com
URL: http://www.natbat.com
Contact: Fred W. Middleton, Exec. Sec.-Treas.
Founded: 1954. **Members:** 28. **Staff:** 1. **Budget:** $24,750. **Description:** Cotton felt manufacturers and their fiber suppliers. Aims to expand use of cotton cushioned products such as bedding, furniture through advertising, promotion, and product improvement. Participates with other cotton organizations in research on flame retardant, cotton batting and combustion toxicity. **Libraries: Type:** not open to the public. **Conventions/Meetings:** annual board meeting ● annual meeting.

1095 ■ National Cotton Council of America (NCC)
PO Box 820285
Memphis, TN 38182-0285
Ph: (901)274-9030
Fax: (901)725-0510
E-mail: info@cotton.org
URL: http://www.cotton.org
Contact: Dr. Mark D. Lange, Pres./CEO
Founded: 1938. **Members:** 21,794. **Description:** Delegates from 19 cotton producing states, named by their respective producer, ginner, warehousemen, merchant, cooperative, textile manufacturer, and cottonseed crusher organizations in each state. Seeks to increase consumption of U.S. cotton and cottonseed products. Conducts public relations, economic, and technical activities. Represents cotton interests in Washington, DC. Maintains Committee for the Advancement of Cotton as political action arm. **Libraries: Type:** reference. **Holdings:** books, business records, clippings, monographs, periodicals. **Subjects:** agriculture, USDA reports, textiles. **Divisions:** Communication Services; Economic Services; Field Services; Finance; Foreign Operations; Information Services; Production; Technical Services; Washington Operation. **Publications:** *Cotton Economic Review*, monthly. Newsletter. Reports economic developments in the cotton industry. Alternate Formats: online ● *Cotton Physiology Today*, monthly. Newsletter. Concerns cotton plant physiology. Alternate Formats: online ● *Cotton's Week*, weekly. Newsletter. Provides information to council members. **Price:** free for members; $250.00 /year for nonmembers ● Reports. Covers council's program. **Conventions/Meetings:** annual Belwide Cotton Production Conference (exhibits) - always January ● annual conference.

1096 ■ National Cotton Ginners' Association (NCGA)
PO Box 820285
Memphis, TN 38182-0285
Ph: (901)274-9030
Fax: (901)725-0510
URL: http://www.cotton.org/ncga
Contact: Harrison Ashley, Exec. VP
Founded: 1936. **Members:** 1,500. **Staff:** 1. **Regional Groups:** 2. **State Groups:** 6. **Description:** Cotton ginners. Sponsors short courses on cotton ginning. **Awards:** Ginner of the Year Award. **Frequency:** annual. **Type:** recognition. **Recipient:** for an outstanding member. **Committees:** Ginning Technology; Safety. **Publications:** *Conference Proceedings*, annual. Presents research on public and private ginning. **Price:** free for members. **Circulation:** 2,000 ● *Hazard Communication: A Program Guide for Cotton Gins*. Booklet. **Conventions/Meetings:** annual conference.

1097 ■ Southern Cotton Association (SCA)
88 Union Ave., Ste.1204
Memphis, TN 38103
Ph: (901)525-2272 (901)380-4511
Fax: (901)527-8303
E-mail: mfarrish@weilbros.com
URL: http://www.southerncottonassociation.com
Contact: Michael Farrish, Pres.
Founded: 1916. **Members:** 100. **Staff:** 2. **Description:** Cotton merchants and allied cotton interest groups. Keeps members informed of matters relating to cotton, and represents their views to state and federal government bodies (principally departments of agriculture) regarding legislation and rulings affecting cotton. Maintains ten committees. **Affiliated With:** American Cotton Shippers Association. **Publications:** *SCA Membership Directory*, annual ● Also issues circulars to members. **Conventions/Meetings:** biennial convention and meeting, with committees' meetings.

1098 ■ Southern Cotton Ginners Association (SCGA)
874 Cotton Gin Pl.
Memphis, TN 38106
Ph: (901)947-3104
Fax: (901)947-3103
E-mail: mary.stice@southerncottonginners.org
URL: http://www.southerncottonginners.org
Contact: Mary Stice, Admin. Asst.
Founded: 1967. **Members:** 325. **Membership Dues:** associate, $100 (annual). **Staff:** 4. **Budget:** $300,000. **Regional Groups:** 4. **Description:** Cotton ginners; associate members are firms serving the industry, such as oil mills, warehouses, banks, and chemical companies. Offers educational and informational services to cotton gin management, keeping them informed of federal and state regulations. Conducts seminars on safety, insurance, proper record keeping practices, and OSHA air pollution control requirements; also engages in research concerning the disposal of cotton gin waste. Offers placement service; compiles statistics. **Publications:** *Blue Book of Cotton Ginners*, annual ● *Southern Cotton Ginners Association—Confidential Newsletter*, monthly. Alternate Formats: online. **Conventions/Meetings:** annual conference (exhibits) - always in Memphis, TN.

Counseling

1099 ■ Chi Sigma Iota (CSI)
PO Box 35448
Greensboro, NC 27425-5448
Ph: (336)841-8180
Fax: (336)841-8180
E-mail: info@csi-net.org
URL: http://www.csi-net.org
Contact: Thomas J. Sweeney PhD, Exec. Dir.
Founded: 1985. **Members:** 48,000. **Membership Dues:** initial, $35 (annual) ● renewal, $25. **Staff:** 2. **Budget:** $330,000. **National Groups:** 275. **Multinational. Description:** Counselors-in-training, counselor educators, and professional counselors. Strives to recognize outstanding achievement and service within the counseling profession. **Awards:** Chapter and Individual Member Awards. **Frequency:** annual. **Type:** recognition. **Recipient:** for chapters and members with outstanding achievement and service ● **Frequency:** annual. **Type:** fellowship. **Recipient:** for active members ● Fellowships and Internships. **Frequency:** annual. **Type:** monetary. **Recipient:** for emerging leaders ● Research Grants. **Frequency:** annual. **Type:** monetary. **Recipient:** for members. **Computer Services:** Online services, chapter and member support and resources. **Publications:** *Exemplar*, 3/year. Newsletter. **Circulation:** 8,500. Alternate Formats: online. **Conventions/Meetings:** annual conference.

Crafts

1100 ■ Craft Organization Development Association (CODA)
c/o Linda Van Trump, Managing Dir.
PO Box 51
Onia, AR 72663
Ph: (870)746-4396
E-mail: info@codacraft.org
URL: http://www.codacraft.org
Contact: Tim Glotzbach, Chm.
Founded: 1986. **Members:** 150,000. **Membership Dues:** individual, $50-$75 (annual) ● non-profit, $100 (annual) ● for profit/business, $150 (annual) ● sponsor, $500 (annual). **State Groups:** 36. **Multinational. Description:** Promotes the appreciation and understanding of crafts. Provides opportunities for professional development and education. Supports issues important to the crafts industry. **Computer Services:** Mailing lists. **Committees:** Survey. **Publications:** *The Coda Survey: The Impact of Crafts on the National Economy*. Report. **Price:** $15.00 for members; $25.00 for nonmembers ● Newsletter, quarterly. Alternate Formats: online.

Credit

1101 ■ Printing Industry Credit Executives (PICE)
1100 Main St.
Buffalo, NY 14209
Free: (800)226-0722
Fax: (716)878-0479
E-mail: agcisupport@abc-amega.com
URL: http://www.pice.com
Contact: Andrea Deljanovan, Pres.
Founded: 1977. **Members:** 130. **Membership Dues:** individual, $900 (annual). **Staff:** 10. **Regional Groups:** 1. **Description:** Printers. Provides a forum for the exchange of information; provides educational programs on credit management. **Telecommunication Services:** electronic bulletin board, credit information. **Publications:** *PICE Update*, semiannual. Newsletter. **Conventions/Meetings:** semiannual conference and lecture - always March and September ● workshop.

Credit Unions

1102 ■ American Association of Credit Union Leagues (AACUL)
c/o Credit Union National Association
PO Box 4312
Madison, WI 53701-0431
Ph: (608)231-4000
Free: (800)356-9655

Fax: (608)231-4858
E-mail: searl@cuna.coop
URL: http://www.cuna.org/league/index.html
Contact: Scott Earl, VP

Members: 51. **Budget:** $210,000. **Description:** Represents credit union leagues who are members of the Credit Union National Association.

1103 ■ American Credit Union Mortgage Association (ACUMA)

PO Box 400955
Las Vegas, NV 89140
Ph: (702)933-2007
Free: (877)442-2862
Fax: (702)949-3590
E-mail: bdorsa@acuma.org
URL: http://www.acuma.org
Contact: Robert Dorsa, Pres.

Founded: 1996. **Members:** 200. **Membership Dues:** regular, $395 (annual) ● associate, $850 (annual). **Staff:** 3. **Description:** Credit unions providing real estate lending services. Promotes adherence to high standards of ethics and practice in the issuing of mortgage loans. Represents members' interests before regulatory agencies and industrial associations; conducts research and educational programs; maintains speakers' bureau; compiles statistics. **Libraries: Type:** reference. **Holdings:** audio recordings, periodicals, video recordings. **Subjects:** real estate lending services. **Computer Services:** Mailing lists, of members. **Formed by Merger of:** (1999) American Credit Union Mortgage Association and American CU Housing Alliance. **Publications:** *ACUMA Pipeline*, quarterly. Newsletter. **Conventions/Meetings:** periodic board meeting ● semiannual conference.

1104 ■ Association of Credit Union Internal Auditors (ACUIA)

PO Box 1926
Columbus, OH 43216-1926
Free: (866)254-8128
Fax: (614)221-2335
E-mail: acuia@acuia.org
URL: http://www.acuia.org
Contact: Brad L. Feldman MPA, Exec. Dir.

Founded: 1989. **Members:** 600. **Membership Dues:** regular (internal auditor), $200-$400 (annual) ● supervisory/audit, $100 (annual) ● associate, $400 (annual). **Regional Groups:** 3. **Description:** Professional credit union internal auditors. Dedicated to the practice of internal auditing in credit unions. **Awards:** Best Article Award. **Frequency:** annual. **Type:** recognition. **Recipient:** for the best published article from the quarterly magazine ● Best Practice Award. **Frequency:** annual. **Type:** recognition. **Recipient:** for a newly developed auditing routine/procedure/audit program that contributes to an effective audit ● Chairman's Excellence in Service Award. **Frequency:** annual. **Type:** recognition. **Recipient:** to volunteer who gave an outstanding service for the year ● Terry McEachern Internal Auditor of the Year Award. **Frequency:** annual. **Type:** recognition. **Recipient:** to an internal auditor who has made a significant contribution to the internal audit profession and to the credit union industry. **Publications:** *The Audit Report*, quarterly. Magazine. **Price:** free for members. **Advertising:** accepted. Alternate Formats: online ● *Internal Audit Guide*. Book. Includes a set of administrative procedures and internal audit programs. **Price:** $125.00 for members (electronic copy); $350.00 for nonmembers (electronic copy); $135.00 for members (CD); $360.00 for nonmembers (CD). Alternate Formats: CD-ROM. **Conventions/Meetings:** annual Roundup - conference, with seminar (exhibits) - 2008 June 24-27, Seattle, WA - **Avg. Attendance:** 225; 2009 June 16-19, Boston, MA.

1105 ■ Council of General Motors Credit Unions (CGMCU)

c/o Terry Frazer, Dir.
1814 Crawford's Ferry Rd.
Hartwell, GA 30643
E-mail: dterryfrazer@aol.com
URL: http://www.ccacu.com
Contact: Harold Foster, Pres.

Founded: 1965. **Members:** 80. **Description:** Credit unions serving General Motors Company employees. Aims to establish a liaison between members and General Motors. Promotes discussion of mutual problems; conducts educational sessions. **Conventions/Meetings:** annual conference.

1106 ■ Credit Union Executives Society (CUES)

PO Box 14167
Madison, WI 53708-0167
Ph: (608)271-2664
Free: (800)252-2664
Fax: (608)271-2303
E-mail: cues@cues.org
URL: http://www.cues.org
Contact: Tim Greisch, Membership Services Supervisor

Founded: 1962. **Members:** 3,500. **Membership Dues:** individual, $625 (annual) ● retired, $110 (annual). **Staff:** 45. **Budget:** $8,000,000. **Description:** Advances the professional development of credit union CEOs, senior management and directors. Serves as an international membership association dedicated to the professional development of credit union CEOs, senior management and directors. **Awards:** CUES Executive of the Year. **Frequency:** annual. **Type:** recognition ● CUES Financial Suppliers Forum Supplier of the Year. **Frequency:** annual. **Type:** recognition ● CUES Future Leader Award. **Frequency:** annual. **Type:** recognition ● CUES Golden Mirror Award. **Frequency:** annual. **Type:** recognition. **Recipient:** for outstanding marketing achievements ● CUES Hall of Fame. **Frequency:** annual. **Type:** recognition ● CUES Marketer of the Year. **Frequency:** annual. **Type:** recognition ● CUES Technology Executive of the Year. **Frequency:** annual. **Type:** recognition ● DEF Director of the Year. **Frequency:** annual. **Type:** recognition ● Outstanding Council. **Type:** recognition. **Divisions:** Directors Educational Forum; Financial Suppliers Forum. **Formerly:** (1970) CUES Managers Society. **Publications:** *Compensation Manual*, annual. Survey. Contains salary survey data of members. **Price:** $129.00 for members; $179.00 for nonmembers ● *Credit Union Executives Society—Membership Directory*, annual ● *Credit Union Management Magazine*, monthly. **Advertising:** accepted. Alternate Formats: online ● *CUES FYI*, weekly. Newsletter. Alternate Formats: online ● Newsletter ● Manuals. **Conventions/Meetings:** annual convention (exhibits).

1107 ■ Credit Union National Association (CUNA)

PO Box 431
Madison, WI 53701-0431
Ph: (608)231-4000
Free: (800)356-9655
Fax: (608)231-4263
E-mail: dorothy@cuna.org
URL: http://www.cuna.org
Contact: Daniel A. Mica, Pres./CEO

Founded: 1934. **Members:** 9,000. **Staff:** 185. **State Groups:** 52. **Description:** Serves as trade association serving more than 90&percent; of credit unions in the U.S. through their respective state leagues with a total membership of more than 77 million persons. (A credit union is a member-owned, nonprofit institution formed to encourage saving and to offer low interest loans to members, usually people working for the same employer, belonging to the same association, or living in the same community.) Promotes credit union membership, use of services, and organization of new credit unions. Seeks to perfect credit union laws; aids in the development of new credit union services, including new payment systems techniques; assists in the training of credit union officials and employees; compiles statistics, annually, by state. Offers charitable program. **Libraries: Type:** reference. **Holdings:** archival material, books, business records, monographs, periodicals. **Awards:** Dora Maxwell Social Responsibility Recognition Award. **Frequency:** annual. **Type:** recognition. **Recipient:** for credit unions that help other people or strengthen the structure of a community ● Louise Herring Award for Philosophy in Action. **Frequency:** annual. **Type:** recognition. **Recipient:** for credit unions that demonstrate extraordinary practical application of the philosophy of their actual operations. **Councils:** Credit Union Legislative Action. **Affiliated With:** Defense Credit Union Council; National Federation of Community Development Credit Unions; World Council of Credit Unions. **Formerly:** (1971) CUNA International. **Publications:** *Credit Union Directors Newsletter*, monthly. Provides ideas and advice on policy matters and considerations for the credit union's board of directors. **Price:** $88.00/year. ISSN: 1058-1561. **Circulation:** 8,166. Alternate Formats: online ● *Credit Union Executive Newsletter*, biweekly. Includes monthly four-page supplement called the *Economic Report*. **Price:** $210.00/year. ISSN: 1068-2120. **Circulation:** 2,438. Alternate Formats: online ● *Credit Union Magazine*, monthly. Journal. For credit union officials, management, staff, and committee members. Includes statistics and employment listings. **Price:** $53.00/year. ISSN: 0011-1066. **Circulation:** 47,000. **Advertising:** accepted. Alternate Formats: microform; online ● *Credit Union Newswatch*, weekly. Newsletter. Contains news and information on legislative, regulatory affairs, industry development and association activities. **Price:** $125.00/year. ISSN: 0889-5597. **Circulation:** 16,000. Alternate Formats: online ● *Everybody's Money*, quarterly. Magazine. Serves as a promotional piece for credit unions and an educational tool for their members. **Price:** $99.00/year (minimum order of 100 subscriptions). ISSN: 0423-8710. **Circulation:** 426,053. **Conventions/Meetings:** annual Governmental Affairs Conference - meeting (exhibits) ● annual National Credit Union Symposium - convention, educational conference for a professional and volunteer (exhibits).

1108 ■ Defense Credit Union Council (DCUC)

601 Pennsylvania Ave. NW
South Bldg., Ste.600
Washington, DC 20004-2601
Ph: (202)638-3950
Fax: (202)638-3410
E-mail: dcuc1@cuna.com
URL: http://www.dcuc.org
Contact: Roland A. Arteaga, Pres./CEO

Founded: 1963. **Members:** 300. **Staff:** 6. **Budget:** $300,000. **Description:** Credit unions serving Department of Defense military and civilian personnel. Aims to assist credit unions serving DOD personnel with problems peculiar to military installations and personnel, and to maintain close liaison with DOD. **Awards:** Distinguished Service Award. **Frequency:** annual. **Type:** recognition. **Recipient:** for individuals outside the council for service to defense credit unions. **Telecommunication Services:** electronic mail, bthompson@cuna.com. **Publications:** *Alert*, monthly, except August. Newsletter. Includes regulations and policies, member news, obituaries, and membership directory updates. **Price:** $15.00 /year for members; $25.00 /year for nonmembers. **Circulation:** 850. **Advertising:** accepted. Alternate Formats: online ● *Directory of Defense Credit Unions*, annual. Membership Directory. Includes name of chief executive officer and assets to nearest hundred dollars. **Price:** $45.00/issue for members; $95.00/issue for nonmembers ● *Statistical Report of Defense Credit Unions*, annual. Includes assets, loans, deposits, services offered, and employees. **Price:** free for members; $50.00/issue for nonmembers. **Circulation:** 800 ● Also publishes studies on Defense Credit Unions. **Conventions/Meetings:** annual conference (exhibits).

1109 ■ Education Credit Union Council (ECUC)

c/o Lorraine Zerfas, Exec. Dir.
PO Box 7558
Spanish Fort, AL 36577
Ph: (251)626-3399
Fax: (251)626-3565
E-mail: ecuclbw@aol.com
URL: http://www.ecuc.org
Contact: Lorraine Zerfas, Exec. Dir.

Founded: 1972. **Members:** 345. **Membership Dues:** credit union, $350 (annual). **Description:** Credit unions serving educational communities. Provides an opportunity for credit unions to exchange ideas and information. Educates credit union CEOs and their "official families". Encourages the organization of local and regional independent education credit union groups for the purpose of exchanging ideas. Compiles statistics. **Awards: Type:** scholarship. **Publications:** *Chalktalk*, bimonthly. Newsletter. Alternate Formats: online ● *Directory of Education Credit Unions*, biennial. Alternate Formats: online. **Conventions/Meetings:** annual conference (exhibits).

1110 ■ Information Technologies Credit Union Association (ITCUA)
PO Box 160
Del Mar, CA 92014-0160
Ph: (858)792-3883
Fax: (858)792-3884
E-mail: itcua@itcua.org
URL: http://www.itcua.org
Contact: Kathy Clark, Exec. Dir.
Founded: 1959. **Members:** 290. **Membership Dues:** regular (based on asset), $350-$700 (annual). **Staff:** 3. **Budget:** $230,000. **Description:** Represents telecommunication and technology credit unions. Conducts educational training programs. **Telecommunication Services:** electronic mail, kathy@itcua.org. **Formerly:** International Telephone Credit Union Association. **Publications:** *Connection*, quarterly. Newsletter. **Circulation:** 300 ● *ITCUA Directory*, annual. **Conventions/Meetings:** annual Strategic Summit - conference.

1111 ■ LICU
1 Credit Union Plz.
24 McKinley Ave.
Endicott, NY 13760
Ph: (607)754-7900
Free: (800)434-1776
Fax: (607)754-9772
E-mail: redmondson@atlanticcu.org
URL: http://www.licuplus.org
Contact: Larry Nonemaker, Contact
Founded: 1975. **Members:** 29. **Staff:** 1. **Budget:** $100,000. **Description:** Member credit unions in the U.S. and Canada. Provides a network for information sharing. Compiles statistics. **Divisions:** Benefit Trust; Insurance Trust; Pension Trust. **Formerly:** (1995) League of IBM Employees Credit Unions. **Publications:** *LICU Directory*, annual ● *LICU News and Views Newsletter*, quarterly. **Conventions/Meetings:** semiannual meeting (exhibits) - spring and fall.

1112 ■ National Association of Credit Union Chairmen (NACUC)
PO Box 160
Del Mar, CA 92014-0160
Ph: (858)792-3883
Free: (888)987-4247
Fax: (858)792-3884
E-mail: celeste@nacuc.org
URL: http://www.nacuc.org
Contact: Celeste Shelton, Exec. Dir.
Founded: 1976. **Members:** 200. **Membership Dues:** corporate, $300 (annual). **Staff:** 3. **Budget:** $200,000. **Description:** Credit union chairmen. Provides a forum to exchange information on common problems and solutions and to discuss programs to improve the role of the credit union chairman. **Formerly:** National Association of Credit Union Presidents. **Publications:** *Exchange*, quarterly. Newsletter. **Circulation:** 300. Alternate Formats: online ● *NACUC Membership Directory*, annual. **Conventions/Meetings:** annual Chairmen's Roundtable Forum - conference.

1113 ■ National Association of Credit Union Services Organizations (NACUSO)
PMB 3419 Via Lido, No. 135
Newport Beach, CA 92663
Ph: (949)645-5296
Free: (888)462-2870
Fax: (949)645-5297
E-mail: info@nacuso.org
URL: http://www.nacuso.org
Contact: Thomas C. Davis, Pres./CEO
Founded: 1985. **Members:** 400. **Membership Dues:** associate, $250 (annual) ● primary, $750 (annual) ● contributory, $1,250 (annual). **Staff:** 3. **Budget:** $350,000. **Description:** Credit union service organizations and their employees. Promotes professional advancement of credit union service organization staff; seeks to insure adherence to high standards of ethics and practice among members. Conducts research and educational programs; formulates and enforces standards of conduct and practice; maintains speakers' bureau; compiles statistics. **Libraries: Type:** reference. **Holdings:** periodicals. **Subjects:** credit union service. **Awards:** CUSO of the Year. **Frequency:** annual. **Type:** recognition. **Computer Services:** database ● mailing lists ● online services. **Publications:** *National CUSO Directory*, annual ● Brochure. **Conventions/Meetings:** annual conference ● semiannual convention.

1114 ■ National Association of Credit Union Supervisory and Auditing Committees (NACUSAC)
PO Box 160
Del Mar, CA 92014
Free: (800)287-5949
Fax: (858)792-3884
E-mail: nacusac@nacusac.org
URL: http://www.nacusac.org
Contact: Kathy Clark, Exec. Dir.
Founded: 1985. **Members:** 220. **Membership Dues:** regular, $400 (annual) ● associate, $500 (annual). **Staff:** 3. **Budget:** $230,000. **Description:** Credit union supervisory and auditing committees. Designed to provide leadership, support and education to enhance the capability of credit union supervisory and auditing committee members. **Awards:** Golden Service Award. **Frequency:** annual. **Type:** recognition. **Recipient:** for an outstanding individual. **Publications:** *NACUSAC News*, quarterly. Newsletter. **Price:** free for members. **Circulation:** 600. **Conventions/Meetings:** annual conference, offers networking and educational opportunities for supervisory and auditing committees (exhibits) - 2008 June 18-21, Denver, CO.

1115 ■ National Association of Federal Credit Unions (NAFCU)
3138 10th St. N
Arlington, VA 22201-2149
Ph: (703)522-4770
Free: (800)336-4644
Fax: (703)524-1082
E-mail: fbecker@nafcu.org
URL: http://www.nafcu.org
Contact: Fred R. Becker Jr., Pres./CEO
Founded: 1967. **Members:** 863. **Membership Dues:** regular (with asset of less than $1 million), $100 (annual). **Staff:** 65. **Budget:** $10,000,000. **Description:** Serves as federally chartered credit unions united for financial reform legislation and regulations impacting members. Provides information on the latest industry developments and proposed and final regulations issued by the National Credit Union Administration, the Federal Reserve, and other regulatory agencies. Represents members' interests before federal regulatory bodies and Congress. Maintains speakers' bureau and research information service; offers placement service; compiles statistics and holds educational conferences. **Computer Services:** database, all federally insured credit unions. **Additional Websites:** http://www.nafcunet.org. **Committees:** Awards; Education; Legislative; PAC; Regulatory. **Publications:** *The Federal Credit Union*, bimonthly. Magazine. Reports on trends, issues, opportunities, and the law within the industry. Includes advertisers' index and buyers' guide. **Price:** included in membership dues; $100.00 /year for nonmembers. **Advertising:** accepted. Alternate Formats: online ● *Final Regulations*, periodic. Lists and analyzes regulations in their final form. ● *NAFCU's Annual Membership Handbook*, annual. Lists members cross-referenced by region, asset size, field of membership, and chief executive officer. **Price:** available to members only ● *National Association of Federal Credit Unions Update*, weekly. Newsletter. Reports on federal legislation and regulations affecting credit unions. Provides membership news and activities. **Price:** included in membership dues; $350.00 /year for nonmembers. Alternate Formats: online ● *Regulatory Alerts*, periodic. Analyzes the impact of proposed regulation on credit unions; includes actual language of the draft of the featured regulation. ● *Regulatory Compliance*, monthly. Newsletter. Alternate Formats: online. **Conventions/Meetings:** annual conference (exhibits) ● annual Congressional Caucus ● Regulatory Compliance - seminar, on regional and special interests.

1116 ■ National Council of Postal Credit Unions (NCPCU)
PO Box 160
Del Mar, CA 92014-0160
Ph: (858)792-3883
Fax: (858)792-3884
E-mail: ncpcu@ncpcu.org
URL: http://www.ncpcu.org
Contact: Will Yarborough, Chm.
Founded: 1984. **Membership Dues:** credit union (based on assets), $100-$1,000 (annual). **Description:** Postal credit unions. Offers programs that target the special interests of postal credit unions. **Publications:** *Postal Courier*, quarterly. Newsletter. **Price:** free for members. **Circulation:** 300. **Conventions/Meetings:** annual conference.

1117 ■ National Credit Union Management Association (NCUMA)
4989 Rebel Trail
Atlanta, GA 30327
Ph: (404)255-6828 (678)777-7463
Fax: (404)851-1752
E-mail: kanchors@ncuma.com
URL: http://www.ncuma.com
Contact: Kathy Anchors, Contact
Founded: 1949. **Members:** 7,000. **Description:** Credit unions whose assets exceed one million dollars. Helps credit union managers, officers, and board members deal with the problems involved in managing large credit unions. Provides information on new methods and ideas designed to increase efficiency and aid marketing; acts as a forum for the exchange of information. Offers specialized seminars. Conducts statistical surveys of credit union finances. Sponsors competitions. **Awards: Frequency:** annual. **Type:** recognition ● Tune Awards. **Frequency:** annual. **Type:** recognition. **Recipient:** for management excellence. **Conventions/Meetings:** annual conference (exhibits) - always fall ● annual seminar - every summer.

1118 ■ National Federation of Community Development Credit Unions (NFCDCU)
116 John St., 33rd Fl.
New York, NY 10038
Ph: (212)809-1850
Free: (800)437-8711
Fax: (212)809-3274
E-mail: info@cdcu.coop
URL: http://www.natfed.org
Contact: Clifford N. Rosenthal, Exec. Dir.
Founded: 1974. **Members:** 170. **Membership Dues:** associate (individual), $50 (annual) ● associate (organizing committee), $95 (annual) ● associate (league, association), $600 (annual) ● associate (non-profit organization), $220 (annual) ● associate (with under $10,000,000 in assets), $220 (annual) ● associate (with over $10,000,000 in assets), $600 (annual) ● policy (based on annual credit union's assets), $100-$4,125 (annual) ● community development partner (based on credit union's assets), $1,000-$5,000 (annual). **Staff:** 17. **Budget:** $1,100,000. **Description:** Consists of credit unions serving low-income communities. Represents the concerns of community development credit unions. Provides capital resources, advocacy, training and technical assistance to community development credit unions throughout the country. **Telecommunication Services:** electronic mail, crosenthal@cdcu.coop. **Programs:** Capitalization. **Special Interest Groups:** Faith-Based Credit Union Network;

Latino Credit Union Network; Youth Credit Union Network. **Publications:** *Faithful Stewardship (1995).* Manual. **Price:** $19.00 ● *Organizing Credit Unions: A Manual (1995).* **Price:** $98.00. **Conventions/Meetings:** annual conference (exhibits) - always May.

1119 ■ World Council of Credit Unions (WOCCU)
PO Box 2982
Madison, WI 53705
Ph: (608)395-2000
Fax: (608)395-2001
E-mail: mail@woccu.org
URL: http://www.woccu.org
Contact: Pete Crear, CEO
Founded: 1970. **Members:** 26. **Staff:** 50. **Languages:** English, French, Spanish. **Description:** Serves as a worldwide representative organization of credit unions that is "the world's leading advocate, platform for innovation, and development agency for credit unions". Includes members such as regional and national credit union associations, cooperative associations and business service organizations. (Organizations and individuals can also support the Council through its Supporter category). **Libraries: Type:** reference. **Holdings:** 3,000; books, periodicals. **Subjects:** credit unions in developing and developed countries. **Awards:** Distinguished Service Award. **Frequency:** annual. **Type:** recognition. **Recipient:** for contributions to credit union development ● WYCUP Scholarship. **Frequency:** annual. **Type:** scholarship. **Recipient:** for individuals 35 or under who have made a significant contribution within their own credit union or organization. **Computer Services:** Mailing lists. **Supersedes:** World Division CUNA International. **Publications:** *Credit Union World* (in English and Spanish), quarterly. Magazine. Serves as a source for international credit union information. Alternate Formats: online ● *International Credit Union Statistics* (in English, French, and Spanish), annual. Features a compilation of country-by-country, regional, and international credit union statistics of member nations. **Conventions/Meetings:** annual conference, with speakers and educational breakout sessions ● triennial International Credit Union Forum - meeting ● annual International Credit Union Leadership Institute - meeting.

Cryonics

1120 ■ Cryonics Institute (CI)
24355 Sorrentino Ct.
Clinton Township, MI 48035
Ph: (586)791-5961
Fax: (586)792-7062
E-mail: cryonics@cryonics.org
URL: http://www.cryonics.org
Contact: Ben Best, Pres.
Founded: 1976. **Members:** 603. **Membership Dues:** option two, $120 (annual) ● life, $1,250. **Staff:** 3. **Multinational. Description:** Offers cryopreservation services for humans, pets and tissue/DNA. Researches and educates about Cryonics. **Computer Services:** Information services, resources on the topic of cryonics. **Publications:** *The Immortalist*, bimonthly, usually January, March, May, July, September, and November. Magazine. **Price:** free for members (one per household). **Advertising:** accepted. Alternate Formats: online.

Crystallography

1121 ■ United States Faceters Guild (USFG)
c/o Jeff Ford, Treas.
2410 N 2nd St.
Kalamazoo, MI 49009
E-mail: artandsandy@netscape.com
URL: http://www.usfacetersguild.org
Contact: Art Kavan, Pres.
Founded: 1990. **Membership Dues:** general, $18 (annual). **Description:** Strives to promote the art and skill of faceting. Sponsors and assists in managing faceting competitions and educating competitors. Develops and promotes uniform rules for faceting competitions within the USA and other countries. Seeks to expand the knowledge of natural and manmade crystals. Serves as a national repository and clearing house for faceting designs, published materials, and educational information for faceters. **Computer Services:** database, faceting diagrams ● database, USFG certified cutters ● information services, faceting facts. **Telecommunication Services:** electronic mail, jeffinkazoo@sbcglobal.net. **Publications:** Newsletter, quarterly. Includes information about upcoming faceting competitions. **Price:** included in membership dues; $2.50 in U.S. and Canada; $3.00 in all other countries.

Culinary Arts

1122 ■ Black Culinarian Alliance (BCA)
55 W 116th St., Ste.234
New York, NY 10026
Ph: (646)548-2949 (646)548-1886
Free: (800)308-8188
Fax: (212)283-7157
E-mail: info@thebca.net
URL: http://www.blackculinarians.com
Contact: Alex Askew, Pres.
Founded: 1998. **Membership Dues:** student, $45 (annual) ● general, $60 (annual) ● chef/manager, $100 (annual) ● executive management, $200 (annual) ● life, $500. **Description:** Seeks to create exposure and provide educational and professional opportunities for culinary and hospitality professionals of color. Provides educational and employment resources, job coaching, mentoring, assistance with placement and networking support to Black culinarians. Exposes inner-city high school students to the culinary arts through a series of workshops. **Awards:** Heritage Award. **Frequency:** annual. **Type:** recognition. **Recipient:** for individuals who have left a mark for others to follow ● James Lewis Award. **Frequency:** annual. **Type:** recognition. **Recipient:** for individuals whose persistence and fortitude outweigh the obstacles that culinary professionals of color face ● Jefferson Evans Award. **Frequency:** annual. **Type:** recognition. **Recipient:** for individuals who have exhibited culinary excellence in the hospitality industry ● Lifetime Ambassador Award. **Frequency:** annual. **Type:** recognition. **Recipient:** for individuals who have contributed guidance, support and vision to the development and benefit of the alliance. **Also Known As:** The BCA. **Publications:** Newsletter.

1123 ■ Les Dames d'Escoffier International (LDEI)
PO Box 4961
Louisville, KY 40204
Ph: (502)456-1851
Fax: (502)456-1821
E-mail: ldei@aecmanagement.com
URL: http://www.ldei.org
Contact: Mr. Greg Jewell, Exec. Dir.
Founded: 1987. **Members:** 1,250. **Staff:** 1. **Regional Groups:** 27. **Multinational. Description:** Chefs and restaurateurs, cookbook authors, food journalists and historians, wine professionals, food publicists, culinary educators, hospitality executives. Consists of women who have achieved success in their professions and also contributes significantly to their communities. Offers mentoring to students and supports food related charitable organizations. Maintains speakers' bureau. **Awards:** Grande Dame Award. **Frequency:** biennial. **Type:** recognition. **Recipient:** for extraordinary and unusual contributions to the fields of food, wine, other fine beverage, nutrition, the arts of the table, or other related fields ● **Type:** grant. **Recipient:** to culinary students ● MFK Fisher Award. **Frequency:** biennial. **Type:** recognition. **Recipient:** for works published in books, magazines, newspapers or the internet in the last 12 months ● **Type:** scholarship. **Recipient:** to culinary students. **Publications:** Brochures. Alternate Formats: online.

1124 ■ Research Chefs Association (RCA)
1100 Johnson Ferry Rd., Ste.300
Atlanta, GA 30342
Ph: (404)252-3663
Fax: (404)252-0774
E-mail: rca@kellencompany.com
URL: http://www.culinology.org
Contact: John D. Folse CEC, Pres.
Founded: 1996. **Members:** 2,000. **Membership Dues:** chef/affiliate, $125 (annual) ● associate, $375 (annual) ● student, $25 (annual). **Description:** Represents Research chefs. Promotes professional and educational development of culinary and technical information for the food industry; establishes standards and procedures for certification. **Awards:** Awards of Excellence. **Frequency:** annual. **Type:** recognition. **Recipient:** to individuals or companies who have demonstrated excellence ● Gary Holleman Award for Excellence in Technology/Communications. **Frequency:** annual. **Type:** recognition. **Recipient:** for advances in the food industry in the field of technology, communications or both. **Committees:** Annual Conference. **Publications:** *Culinology*, quarterly. Magazine. Features special editorial sections to describe food industry practices as they relate to the discipline of Culinology. **Price:** included in membership dues ● *Culinology Currents*, quarterly. Newsletter. Contains information of interest to members. **Price:** included in membership dues. Alternate Formats: online ● *Food Product Design*. Journal. **Price:** included in membership dues. **Conventions/Meetings:** annual conference ● annual convention and trade show ● regional meeting ● workshop, with panel discussions and general sessions focused on issues in the field of culinary research and development.

Dairy Products

1125 ■ 3-A Sanitary Standards Committees, Inc. (3-A SSCI)
6888 Elm St., Ste.2D
McLean, VA 22101
Ph: (703)790-0295
Fax: (703)761-6284
E-mail: trugh@3-a.org
URL: http://www.3-a.org
Contact: Timothy R. Rugh CAE, Exec. Dir.
Founded: 2002. **Members:** 5. **Staff:** 2. **Budget:** $400,000. **Description:** Participants include manufacturers and users of dairy and food equipment; state and local sanitarians, U.S. Public Health Service and the USDA. Provides the dairy and food industries with voluntary sanitary standards on a national level. Establishes and updates dairy and food equipment and machinery standards. **Libraries: Type:** not open to the public. **Holdings:** monographs. **Subjects:** standards for sanitary design, construction of food and dairy equipment to meet domestic and international regulations. **Awards:** 3-A Bronze Plaque. **Frequency:** periodic. **Type:** recognition. **Recipient:** for outstanding service to the 3-A sanitary standards program. **Committees:** Sanitary Procedures; Sanitary Standards Subcommittee of the Dairy Industry; Task; Technical and Standards. **Affiliated With:** International Association for Food Protection. **Publications:** *Mark of Compliance; 3-A story* (in English and Spanish). Report. Features agenda and meeting minutes. **Price:** free. **Circulation:** 1,700. Alternate Formats: online ● *3-A Index of Standards*. Alternate Formats: online ● *3-A Progress Report*, 2-3/year ● *3-A Sanitary Standards*, periodic ● *3-A Story* ● *3-A Symbol Holders List*. **Conventions/Meetings:** annual meeting, to review tentative standards - usually third full week of May in Milwaukee, WI.

1126 ■ All Star Dairy Association (ASDA)
PO Box 911050
Lexington, KY 40591-1050
Ph: (859)255-3644
Free: (800)930-3644
Fax: (859)255-3647
URL: http://www.allstardairy.com
Contact: Jeff Sterne, Exec. Dir.
Founded: 1958. **Members:** 275. **Staff:** 8. **Budget:** $1,000,000. **For-Profit. Description:** Dairy and ice cream companies. Develops a national trademark and creates advertising and merchandising for

members who use the trademark. Encourages economical and efficient operation through improved packaging, group purchasing, quality control, sales, trade, and other services. Offers group purchasing of supplies for members. **Awards:** John O. Utterback College Scholarship. **Frequency:** annual. **Type:** scholarship. **Recipient:** to member employees and/or their dependents. **Publications:** Directory. **Conventions/Meetings:** annual conference (exhibits) ● annual convention, covers subjects such as lowering health insurance costs and hiring practices.

1127 ■ Allied Purchasing Company (APC)
PO Box 1249
Mason City, IA 50402
Free: (800)247-5956
Fax: (800)635-3775
E-mail: carol@alliedpurchasing.com
URL: http://www.alliedpurchasing.com
Contact: Carol Peterson, CEO
Founded: 1937. **Members:** 800. **Description:** Represents dairies, ice cream plants and soft drink bottlers. Collaborates to obtain group purchasing rates on equipment, ingredients, services, and supplies. **Formerly:** (1983) United Dairy. **Publications:** *Membership List*, annual. Membership Directory. **Conventions/Meetings:** annual meeting.

1128 ■ American Butter Institute (ABI)
2101 Wilson Blvd., Ste.400
Arlington, VA 22201
Ph: (703)243-5630
Fax: (703)841-9328
E-mail: aminer@nmpf.org
URL: http://www.butterinstitute.org
Contact: Anuja Miner, Dir. of Membership Services
Founded: 1908. **Members:** 31. **Staff:** 4. **Description:** Represents butter manufacturers, processors, packagers, and distributors based on volume. Aims to promote and protect the interests and welfare of the butter industry. **Libraries: Type:** not open to the public. **Committees:** Marketing. **Conventions/Meetings:** annual conference and board meeting.

1129 ■ American Cheese Society (ACS)
304 W Liberty St., Ste.201
Louisville, KY 40202
Ph: (502)583-3783
Fax: (502)589-3602
E-mail: acs@hqtrs.com
URL: http://www.cheesesociety.org
Contact: Marci Wilson, Exec. Dir.
Founded: 1983. **Members:** 1,200. **Membership Dues:** associate, $90 (annual) ● individual, $160 (annual) ● small business, $450 (annual) ● corporate/society sponsor, $790 (annual) ● multi-unit business, $1,975 (annual). **Staff:** 3. **Description:** Represents producers, manufacturers, retailers, distributors, and others interested in the specialty and farmstead cheese industry. Aims to promote cheese appreciation and to provide useful information on cheese making in a farm, house, or a manufacturing plant environment. Includes activities such as annual conferences, cheese tasting, and workshops on cheese making. Conducts discussions on the technical and economical aspects of cheese making. Sponsors competitions; maintains Speaker's Bureau. **Computer Services:** Mailing lists. **Telecommunication Services:** electronic mail, mwilson@hqtrs.com. **Publications:** *A Guide to American Specialty and Farmstead Cheeses*, quarterly. Newsletter. **Advertising:** accepted ● Newsletter, periodic. **Conventions/Meetings:** annual conference, educational.

1130 ■ American Dairy Products Institute (ADPI)
116 N York St.
Elmhurst, IL 60126
Ph: (630)530-8700
Fax: (630)530-8707
E-mail: info@adpi.org
URL: http://www.adpi.org
Contact: James J. Page, CEO
Founded: 1925. **Members:** 225. **Staff:** 6. **Description:** Manufacturers of condensed, evaporated, dry milk, whey products and cheese; affiliate members are manufacturers and dealers of equipment or suppliers of services for the industry; utilization members are end-users of processed dairy products. Promotes market expansion and standards research. Conducts technical and educational services; assists in the development of sanitary standards and the establishment of grades for condensed, evaporated, dry milks, whey products, and cheese. **Libraries: Type:** reference. **Subjects:** chemistry, biology, economics, dairy science. **Awards:** Award of Merit. **Frequency:** annual. **Type:** recognition. **Recipient:** for meritorious service to industry. **Telecommunication Services:** electronic mail, jjpage@adpi.org. **Committees:** Affiliate Member; Dairy Products Marketing; Evaporated Milks; Lactose; Technical; 3-A Sanitary Standards. **Absorbed:** Evaporated Milk Association. **Formed by Merger of:** (1986) American Dry Milk; Whey Products Institute. **Publications:** *Census of Utilization Publications*, annual. **Advertising:** accepted ● *Standards for Grades of Dry Milks, Including Methods of Analysis (Bulletin 916)*. Covers dry milk standards and methods of analysis. **Price:** $15.00 for members; $25.00 for nonmembers, domestic; $35.00 for nonmembers, international ● *Statistical Reports*, monthly ● *Utilization Reports*, annual ● *Whey & Whey Products: Definitions, Compositions, Standard Methods of Analysis (Bulletin W-16)*. Covers whey and whey products including methods of analysis. **Price:** $15.00 for members; $25.00 for nonmembers, domestic; $35.00 for nonmembers, international ● Pamphlets. Contains information on technical product usage subjects. **Conventions/Meetings:** annual conference, joint conference with the American Butter Institute (exhibits) - usually April and May, in Chicago, IL.

1131 ■ Cheese Importers Association of America (CIAA)
204 E St. NE
Washington, DC 20002
Ph: (202)547-0899
Fax: (202)547-6348
E-mail: info@theciaa.org
URL: http://www.theciaa.org
Contact: Thomas Gellert, Sec.
Founded: 1943. **Members:** 160. **Staff:** 2. **Description:** Represents importers, brokers, steamship lines, warehousemen, and firms interested in the importation of cheese. **Publications:** Newsletter, periodic.

1132 ■ Dairy Management, Inc. (DMI)
10255 W Higgins Rd., Ste.900
Rosemont, IL 60018-5616
Ph: (847)803-2000
Free: (800)853-2479
Fax: (847)803-2077
URL: http://www.dairyinfo.com
Contact: Joe Bavido, Contact
Founded: 1915. **Members:** 24. **Staff:** 20. **Local Groups:** 27. **Description:** Operates under the auspices of the United Dairy Industry Association. Milk producers, milk dealers, and manufacturers of butter, cheese, ice cream, dairy equipment, and supplies. Conducts programs of nutrition research and nutrition education in the use of milk and its products. **Formerly:** (2000) National Dairy Council. **Publications:** *Current Awareness*, bimonthly ● *Dairy Council Digest*, bimonthly. Newsletter. Provides current nutrition research to health professionals; includes annual index. ISSN: 0011-5568. **Circulation:** 75,000 ● *Nutrition News*, quarterly ● Catalogs. Lists nutrition education materials and curricula.

1133 ■ Food Processing Suppliers Association (FPSA)
1451 Dolley Madison Blvd., Ste.200
McLean, VA 22101-3850
Ph: (703)761-2600
Fax: (703)761-4334
E-mail: info@fpsa.org
URL: http://www.fpsa.org
Contact: Stephen C. Schlegel, Pres./CEO
Founded: 1911. **Members:** 600. **Membership Dues:** company (below $8 million annual revenues), $1,000 (annual) ● company (over $8 million annual revenues), $1,500 (annual). **Staff:** 13. **Languages:** English, Spanish. **Description:** Manufacturers and distributors of dairy and food processing and packaging equipment, machinery, ingredients, and supplies. Provides marketing and technical services to member firms. Compiles market statistics. **Awards:** IAFIS/ASAE Food Engineering Award. **Frequency:** biennial. **Type:** recognition. **Recipient:** for outstanding original contributions in research, development, design or management of food processing equipment or processes ● M.E. Franks Scholarship. **Frequency:** annual. **Type:** scholarship. **Recipient:** to undergraduate and graduate students of U.S. or Canadian citizenship majoring in food science. **Computer Services:** database, IMIS. **Committees:** Employee Relations; Marketing; Pension; Public Relations; Students Judging; Technical; 3-A Sanitary Standards. **Absorbed:** (1976) National Association of Food and Dairy Equipment Manufacturers. **Formed by Merger of:** (2005) International Association of Food Industry Suppliers; (2005) International Association of Food Industry Suppliers and Food Processing Machinery Association. **Formerly:** Dairy and Ice Cream Machinery and Supplies Association; (1963) Dairy Industries Supply Association; (1998) Dairy and Food Industries Supply Association. **Publications:** *Global Food MegaTrends*, quarterly. Bulletins. Contains highlights of important exporting news. **Circulation:** 500 ● *IAFIS—Directory of Membership Products and Services*, biennial. Membership Directory. **Price:** free. Alternate Formats: online ● *IAFIS—Reporter*, monthly. Newsletter. Includes list of new members. **Circulation:** 1,400. **Conventions/Meetings:** annual conference, with educational and networking opportunities ● annual Process Expo - trade show (exhibits) - 2008 Nov. 9-13, Chicago, IL.

1134 ■ International Dairy Foods Association (IDFA)
1250 H St. NW, Ste.900
Washington, DC 20005
Ph: (202)737-4332
Fax: (202)331-7820
E-mail: membership@idfa.org
URL: http://www.idfa.org
Contact: Cindy Cavallo, Membership Sr. Mgr.
Founded: 1990. **Members:** 525. **Staff:** 55. **Budget:** $10,000,000. **Multinational. Description:** Umbrella organization providing services such as government relations, regulatory affairs monitoring, marketing, public relations, seminars, and general management to 3 constituent organizations: Milk Industry Foundation, National Cheese Institute, and International Ice Cream Association. Represents processors, manufacturers, and distributors of dairy products. Addresses industry concerns such as international trade, product labeling, quality assurance, sanitation, and many other issues. Holds workshops, seminars, and other training and educational programs. **Affiliated With:** Milk Industry Foundation; National Cheese Institute. **Publications:** *Dairy Facts*, annual. Handbook. Includes statistics and trends of milk production and consumption. **Price:** $45.00 ● Membership Directory. **Price:** $495.00 ● Also publishes a variety of reference and training manuals. **Conventions/Meetings:** annual convention, with dairy business and policy discussion ● biennial Worldwide Food Exposition - convention (exhibits) - 2009 Oct. 28-31, Chicago, IL.

1135 ■ Milk Industry Foundation (MIF)
c/o International Dairy Foods Association
1250 H St. NW, Ste.900
Washington, DC 20005-3952
Ph: (202)737-4332
Fax: (202)331-7820
E-mail: membership@idfa.org
URL: http://www.idfa.org
Contact: Mr. Brian Haugh, Chm.
Founded: 1908. **Members:** 110. **Staff:** 55. **Multinational. Description:** Represents processors of fluid milk and milk products. Advocates before government and regulatory bodies on behalf of members. **Libraries: Type:** reference. **Committees:** MIF and LLCA Legislative and Economic Policy; MIF Regulating. **Affiliated With:** International Dairy Foods Association; National Cheese Institute. **Formerly:** (1920) International Milk Dealers Association. **Publi-**

cations: *MIF Labeling Manual*. Alternate Formats: online ● *Milk Facts*, annual. Booklet.

1136 ■ National Cheese Institute (NCI)
c/o International Dairy Foods Association
1250 H St. NW, Ste.900
Washington, DC 20005-3952
Ph: (202)737-4332
Fax: (202)331-7820
E-mail: membership@idfa.org
URL: http://www.idfa.org
Contact: Mr. Kevin Ponticelli, Chm.
Founded: 1927. **Members:** 70. **Staff:** 55. **Description:** Represents manufacturers, processors, marketers, assemblers, and distributors of cheese and cheese products; advocates before government and regulatory bodies on behalf of members. **Committees:** Legislative/Regulatory Policy and Economic Policy; Marketing; Regulatory. **Affiliated With:** International Dairy Foods Association; Milk Industry Foundation. **Publications:** *Cheese Facts*, annual. Booklet ● *NCI Labeling Manual*. Alternate Formats: online.

1137 ■ National Ice Cream Retailers Association (NICRA)
1028 W Devon Ave.
Elk Grove Village, IL 60007
Ph: (847)301-7500
Fax: (847)301-8402
E-mail: info@nicyra.org
URL: http://www.nicyra.org
Contact: Lynda Utterback, Exec. Dir.
Founded: 1933. **Members:** 550. **Membership Dues:** active, $175 (annual) ● supplier, $200 (annual). **Staff:** 2. **Budget:** $110,000. **Description:** Represents frozen dessert retailers that operate ice cream and frozen yogurt dipping stores or parlors. Provides free and frank exchange of information among members so that all may improve their operations, increase profits and prosper. **Awards:** Bryce Thomson Scholarship Fund. **Frequency:** annual. **Type:** recognition. **Recipient:** for full-time or part-time employees of active members ● Person of the Year. **Frequency:** annual. **Type:** recognition. **Recipient:** for an outstanding member ● Promotion of the Year. **Frequency:** annual. **Type:** recognition. **Formerly:** National Association of Retail Ice Cream Manufacturers; (1989) National Ice Cream Retailers Association; (2003) National Ice Cream and Yogurt Retailers Association. **Publications:** *NICRA Bulletin*, monthly. **Circulation:** 550. **Advertising:** accepted ● *NICRA Yearbook*, annual. **Conventions/Meetings:** annual convention (exhibits) - 2008 Nov. 12-15, St. Petersburg, FL.

1138 ■ National Yogurt Association (NYA)
2000 Corporate Ridge, Ste.1000
McLean, VA 22102
Ph: (703)821-0770
Fax: (703)821-1350
E-mail: lsarasin@affi.com
URL: http://www.aboutyogurt.com
Contact: Leslie G. Sarasin CAE, Pres.
Founded: 1986. **Members:** 8. **Staff:** 3. **Budget:** $1,000,000. **Description:** Manufacturers and marketers of live and active culture yogurt products; suppliers to the industry. Sponsors health and medical research for yogurt with live and active cultures and serves as an information source to the trade and the general public.

1139 ■ Quality Chekd Dairies
1733 Park St.
Naperville, IL 60563
Ph: (630)717-1110
Fax: (630)717-1126
E-mail: qchekd@qchekd.com
Contact: Peter W. Horvath, Managing Dir.
Founded: 1945. **Members:** 40. **Staff:** 12. **Description:** Represents dairy foods processors. Has members that combine the Quality Chekd trademark with their dairy's name and logotype. Provides marketing and advertising program, and plant operation and production counsel. Arranges for group purchasing of supplies and ingredients. **Awards:** **Type:** recognition. **Recipient:** for superior performance by members in marketing and production. **Committees:** Marketing; Production; Purchasing. **Formerly:** (1950) Quality Chekd Ice Cream Association. **Publications:** *Scope*, bimonthly.

1140 ■ United Dairy Industry Association (UDIA)
Address Unknown since 2008
Founded: 1970. **Members:** 60. **Regional Groups:** 9. **Description:** Aims to promote the sale and consumption of U.S.-produced milk and milk products. Sponsors the advertising and sales promotion campaigns of the American Dairy Association and the nutrition research and education programs of the National Dairy Council. Maintains reference library. **Publications:** none. **Libraries:** **Type:** reference. **Conventions/Meetings:** annual conference.

1141 ■ Wisconsin Cheese Makers' Association (WCMA)
8030 Excelsior Dr., Ste.305
Madison, WI 53717-1950
Ph: (608)828-4550
Fax: (608)828-4551
E-mail: office@wischeesemakersassn.org
URL: http://www.wischeesemakersassn.org
Contact: John T. Umhoefer, Exec. Dir.
Founded: 1891. **Members:** 300. **Staff:** 3. **Description:** Active licensed cheese plants; active licensed cheese making employees; suppliers of goods and services to the industry. Seeks to educate members for better work in the art of making cheese, the care and management of factories, and the sale of the product. Works to curb competency in the business and enforce laws that will protect the manufacturer against deceitful imitations. **Awards:** **Frequency:** annual. **Type:** recognition. **Publications:** *Convention Book*, annual ● Newsletter, monthly. **Conventions/Meetings:** biennial International Cheese Technology Exposition - convention (exhibits) - always April, even years ● biennial Wisconsin Cheese Industry Conference - convention.

Dance

1142 ■ United Dance Merchants of America (UDMA)
376 Main Rd.
Granville, MA 01034
Ph: (413)357-8500
Free: (800)304-8362
Fax: (413)357-8889
E-mail: office@udma.org
URL: http://www.udma.org
Contact: Rick Ferreira, Pres.
Founded: 1959. **Members:** 80. **Membership Dues:** full, $500 (annual) ● associate, $300 (annual). **Staff:** 1. **Description:** Manufacturers and distributors of such items as dance costumes and shoes; publishers and distributors of dance-related publications. Provides a forum for communication among firms; conducts special education programs. Holds symposia. Participates in planning activities for National Dance Week. **Computer Services:** Mailing lists. **Publications:** *Update*, quarterly. Newsletter ● Membership Directory. Alternate Formats: online. **Conventions/Meetings:** semiannual meeting - always January and July ● annual show (exhibits).

Data Processing

1143 ■ Software Contractors' Guild
3 Country Club Dr., No. 303
Manchester, NH 03102
E-mail: admin@scguild.com
URL: http://www.scguild.com
Contact: David Keeney, Admin.
Membership Dues: regular, $20 (annual). **Multinational. Description:** Provides a way for clients and agents to locate the best qualified contractor for them. Promotes software contracting and disseminates information relative to software contracting. **Telecommunication Services:** electronic mail, keeney@scguild.com.

Debt Collection

1144 ■ ACA International (ACA)
PO Box 390106
Minneapolis, MN 55439
Ph: (952)926-6547
Fax: (952)926-1624
E-mail: aca@acainternational.org
URL: http://www.acainternational.org
Contact: Gary D. Rippentrop CAE, CEO
Founded: 1939. **Members:** 5,400. **Membership Dues:** attorney, $360 (annual) ● affiliate, $600 (annual) ● collection and related company, $165 (annual) ● creditor international (based on number of employees), $165-$5,000 (annual). **Staff:** 70. **State Groups:** 44. **Description:** Collection services handling overdue accounts for retail, professional, and commercial credit grantors. Maintains specialized programs in the areas of healthcare, checks, and government which provide services for members who work with credit grantors in these areas. Conducts research. Offers specialized education; compiles statistics. **Libraries:** **Type:** reference. **Holdings:** 400. **Awards:** ACA Academy Scholar and Fellow Degrees. **Frequency:** annual. **Type:** recognition. **Recipient:** for participants in the ACA International-sponsored meetings and seminars and other educational programs ● Charles F. Lindemann Certified Instructor of the Year. **Frequency:** annual. **Type:** recognition. **Recipient:** for outstanding educator ● Enterprises Award of Merit. **Frequency:** annual. **Type:** recognition. **Recipient:** to a member who has made the most outstanding contribution to ACA International Enterprises ● Fred Kirschner Instructor Achievement Award. **Frequency:** annual. **Type:** recognition. **Recipient:** to certified instructors who have reached milestones in their volunteer teaching careers with ACA ● Honorary Membership. **Frequency:** annual. **Type:** recognition. **Recipient:** to members who are no longer active in the credit and collection industry and have made noteworthy achievements and furtherance of the association and the industry ● International Foundation Fellow Award. **Frequency:** annual. **Type:** recognition. **Recipient:** for an individual member or unit ● James K. Erickson Continuous Service. **Frequency:** annual. **Type:** recognition. **Recipient:** to a member who has made contributions to the associations for at least 10 consecutive years ● Member of the Year. **Frequency:** annual. **Type:** recognition. **Recipient:** for members who have made the most significant contributions to the credit and collection industry during the past 12 months ● Red Coat (Membership) Award. **Frequency:** annual. **Type:** recognition. **Recipient:** for members who promoted the advantages of belonging to the organization and recruited five or more new members during the fiscal year ● Unit Certificate of Excellence. **Frequency:** annual. **Type:** recognition. **Recipient:** for units ● Unit Leader of the Year. **Frequency:** annual. **Type:** recognition. **Recipient:** to an individual who has made the most contribution to his/her unit during the past year. **Computer Services:** database, IMIS. **Committees:** Creditors; Education; Ethics; Legislative; Members' Attorney Program; Membership; Online; Public Relations; Vendor Advisory. **Formerly:** (2003) American Collectors Association. **Publications:** *ACA Roster and Buyers Guide*. Membership Directory. **Circulation:** 3,600. **Advertising:** accepted. Alternate Formats: online ● *Collector*, monthly. Magazine. Covers the consumer credit and debt collection industry. Includes regulation, agency management, and collection techniques information. **Price:** free for members; $70.00 /year for nonmembers. **Circulation:** 7,000. **Advertising:** accepted ● *Consumer Trends*, monthly. Newsletter. **Price:** free for members ● *Cred-Alert*, monthly. Bulletin. Provides information for credit grantors and collectors. **Price:** $48.00 /year for nonmembers. **Circulation:** 29,000 ● *Management Trends*, bimonthly. Newsletter. Contains information on management and employment issues

that pertain to any industry. **Conventions/Meetings:** annual convention and board meeting (exhibits).

1145 ■ American Recovery Association (ARA)
5525 N MacArthur Blvd., Ste.135
Irving, TX 75038
Ph: (972)755-4755
Fax: (972)870-5755
E-mail: homeoffice@americanrecoveryassn.org
URL: http://www.repo.org
Contact: Tom Crosby, Pres.
Founded: 1965. **Members:** 500. **Membership Dues:** individual, $600-$1,300 (annual). **Staff:** 6. **Description:** Independent repossession agencies that recover collateral on defaulted installment contracts for lending institutions including banks, credit unions, finance companies, leasing companies, and savings and loan associations. Offers services throughout the U.S., Mexico, part of Canada, Germany, Puerto Rico and the Virgin Islands. Conducts educational seminars on laws and procedures affecting the repossession industry. Maintains speakers' bureau. **Telecommunication Services:** electronic mail, repo2@comcast.net. **Committees:** Association History and Records; Bond Trustee; Budget and Dues; By-Laws/Legislation; Computer Technology/Development; Grievance; Insurance/Member Benefits. **Formerly:** (1972) American Repossessors Association. **Supersedes:** Repossessions Division of American Collectors Association. **Publications:** *American Recovery Association—Membership Directory*, annual. **Price:** free. **Circulation:** 120,000 ● *American Recovery Association—News and Views*, monthly. Newsletter. Contains information for professional finance adjusters and repossession specialists. **Price:** free. **Circulation:** 45,000. **Conventions/Meetings:** annual meeting (exhibits) - always July.

1146 ■ Debt Buyers' Association (DBA)
8201 Greensboro Dr., Ste.300
McLean, VA 22102
Ph: (703)610-0224
Fax: (703)610-9005
E-mail: info@dbainternational.org
URL: http://www.dbainternational.org
Contact: Roger Knauf, Exec. Dir.
Founded: 1996. **Members:** 423. **Membership Dues:** standard, $595 (annual). **Staff:** 2. **Multinational. Description:** Represents buyers committed to building a reliable and credible market for delinquent receivables. **Computer Services:** database, Super Search: buyers and sellers. **Publications:** Newsletter. **Conventions/Meetings:** annual convention and conference, with tie-in meetings.

1147 ■ International Association of Commercial Collectors (IACC)
4040 W 70th St.
Minneapolis, MN 55435
Ph: (952)925-0760
Fax: (952)926-1624
E-mail: iacc@commercialcollector.com
URL: http://www.commercialcollector.com
Contact: Ted M. Smith CAE, Exec. Dir.
Founded: 1970. **Members:** 350. **Membership Dues:** agency, $350 (annual) ● associate, $250 (annual). **Staff:** 3. **Budget:** $150,000. **Multinational. Description:** Debt collection professionals who are specialists in the recovery of commercial accounts receivable. **Telecommunication Services:** electronic mail, smitht@commercialcollector.com. **Committees:** Agency Certification; Associate Membership; Convention/Meetings; Education; Grievance; Legislation; Nominating; PR/Advertising. **Formerly:** American Commercial Collectors Association. **Publications:** *Blue Book of Commercial Collectors*, annual. Membership Directory. **Price:** available to members only. **Circulation:** 350. **Advertising:** accepted. Alternate Formats: online ● *Commercial Collection Guidelines for Credit Grantors*. Booklet ● *Scope*, monthly. Newsletter. **Price:** available to members only. **Circulation:** 350. **Conventions/Meetings:** annual conference (exhibits) ● Strategic Management Conference.

Defense

1148 ■ Aircraft Carrier Industrial Base Coalition (ACIBC)
700 13th St. NW, Ste.1000
Washington, DC 20005
Ph: (202)585-2018
Fax: (202)383-0079
E-mail: info@acibc.org
URL: http://www.acibc.org
Contact: Gerald A. Nicholson, Co-Chm.
Founded: 2004. **Description:** Represents businesses that supply components and services for U.S. Navy aircraft carriers. Seeks to preserve the strength of the U.S. Navy's aircraft carrier force structure. Promotes the value of the aircraft carrier industrial base as a vital part of the nation's overall defense structure by educating policymakers and other stakeholders. Serves as an advocate for congressional funding of carrier programs.

1149 ■ Submarine Industrial Base Council (SIBC)
1399 New York Ave. NW, Ste.550
Washington, DC 20005
Ph: (202)207-3633
Fax: (202)575-3400
E-mail: sibc@submarinesuppliers.org
URL: http://www.submarinesuppliers.org
Contact: James Jelinek, Co-Chm.
Founded: 1992. **Members:** 4,000. **Description:** Aims to educate policymakers and the public about the nation's ability to design, build and maintain submarines. Promotes the importance of the submarine industrial base as a vital part of the nation's overall defense structure. Encourages its members to engage in dialogue with decision and policy makers.

Dentistry

1150 ■ Hellenic American Dental Society (HADS)
PO Box 4803
Oak Brook, IL 60523-4803
Ph: (847)698-1180
E-mail: info@hads.com
URL: http://www.hads.com
Contact: Dr. George A. Mandelaris, Pres.
Founded: 1963. **Membership Dues:** individual, $75 (annual). **Description:** Dentists, dental hygienists, and dental technicians of Greek descent, promoting Hellenic heritage. **Awards: Frequency:** annual. **Type:** scholarship. **Committees:** Scholarship. **Publications:** Newsletter, periodic. **Price:** included in membership dues.

Design

1151 ■ American Association of Human Design Practitioners (HDP)
PO Box 1716
Taos, NM 87571
E-mail: support@humandesignsystem.net
URL: http://www.humandesignsystem.net
Contact: Zeno Dickson, Pres.
Membership Dues: student, $40 (annual) ● practitioner, $60 (annual) ● practitioner, $150 (triennial) ● practitioner - life, $800. **Description:** Promotes study, research, professional practice and dissemination of human design system. Bridges human design practitioners and brings the human design system into a wider audience. Promotes the exchange of ideas among human design practitioners and students.

1152 ■ Foundation for Design Integrity (FDI)
1950 N Main St.
PO Box 139
Salinas, CA 93906
Ph: (650)326-1867
Fax: (831)449-7040
E-mail: designintegrity@msn.com
Founded: 1994. **Members:** 116. **Budget:** $40,000. **Multinational. Description:** Promotes ethical practice in the interior and architectural products industries.

1153 ■ National Association of Visual Merchandisers (NAVM)
15304 Rainbow 1, Ste.201
Austin, TX 78734
Membership Dues: individual, $50 (annual) ● retailer/employer, $100 (annual) ● supplier, $150 (annual). **Description:** Promotes respect for the field of visual merchandising. Recognizes visual merchandisers as key players in the retail world. **Computer Services:** database, directory of members ● online services, discussion forum. **Publications:** Newsletter, quarterly. Alternate Formats: online.

1154 ■ Society of Boat and Yacht Designers (SBYD)
117 E Louisa St., No. 268
Seattle, WA 98102-3203
Ph: (801)225-6060
E-mail: info@sbyd.org
URL: http://www.sbyd.org
Contact: Don Robertson, Pres.
Membership Dues: regular, $45 (annual) ● student, $30 (annual). **Description:** Provides a forum for the exchange of ideas and information relative to small craft marine industry. **Telecommunication Services:** electronic mail, drobert@efortress.com. **Publications:** *Ballast*, quarterly. Newsletter. Contains news and information on past and future meetings. Alternate Formats: online ● *Sextant*, annual. Journal. Alternate Formats: online ● Proceedings, periodic. Alternate Formats: online. **Conventions/Meetings:** weekly meeting, with speakers, features tours of design and construction facilities - every Saturday.

Detergent

1155 ■ Handcrafted Soap Makers Guild (HSMG)
3416 Primm Ln.
Birmingham, AL 35216
Ph: (205)823-5517
Free: (866)900-7627
Fax: (205)823-2760
E-mail: info@soapguild.org
URL: http://www.soapguild.org
Contact: Marie Gale, Pres.
Founded: 1998. **Membership Dues:** basic - soapmaker, vendor, $80 (annual) ● benefactor - friend, $150 (annual) ● benefactor - supporter, $250 (annual) ● benefactor - patron, $500 (annual). **Multinational. Description:** Promotes the handcrafted soap industry. Acts as a center of communication among soap makers. Circulates information that will be beneficial to soap makers. Provides an online forum to facilitate exchange of information between soap makers and to create a venue where beginners can seek advice and assistance from experienced soap makers. **Awards:** Longevity Award. **Frequency:** annual. **Type:** recognition. **Recipient:** for members who have maintained their memberships for a prolonged period of time ● President's Volunteer of the Year. **Frequency:** annual. **Type:** recognition. **Recipient:** to a member who has rendered outstanding voluntary service to the association ● Soapers Showcase Awards. **Frequency:** annual. **Type:** recognition. **Recipient:** for the best soaps displayed at the annual conference. **Telecommunication Services:** electronic mail, marieg@soapguild.org. **Publications:** *The Handcrafted Soap Maker*, quarterly. Journal. Contains articles of interest to soapmakers, advertisements from vendors and information about the association and its activities. **Price:** included in membership dues. **Advertising:** accepted ● Brochures. **Price:** included in membership dues. Alternate Formats: online. **Conventions/Meetings:** annual conference, with demonstrations and workshops (exhibits).

Disabled

1156 ■ Accessibility Equipment Manufacturers Association (AEMA)
PO Box 380
Metamora, IL 61548-0380
Free: (800)514-1100
Fax: (309)923-7964
E-mail: info@aema.com
URL: http://www.aema.com
Contact: Stephen Whittenberg, Pres.

Founded: 1990. **Membership Dues:** manufacturer (based on sales volume of accessibility equipment), $400-$6,000 (annual) ● associate, $200 (annual). **Description:** Promotes awareness of accessibility equipment, including the design, installation and servicing of vertical, inclined and horizontal conveying systems that are used to provide access and/or egress for physically challenged people in public and residential areas. (Accessibility products are platform lifts, wheelchair lifts, access elevators, residence elevators, stairway chairlifts, and similar products). **Computer Services:** Information services. **Publications:** *Accessibility News*. Newsletter. Features up-to-date information on industry news and events. **Price:** included in membership dues. Alternate Formats: online.

Disposable Products

1157 ■ Foodservice and Packaging Institute (FPI)
150 S Washington St., Ste.204
Falls Church, VA 22046
Ph: (703)538-2800
Fax: (703)538-2187
E-mail: fpi@fpi.org
URL: http://www.fpi.org
Contact: John R. Burke, Pres.

Founded: 1933. **Members:** 25. **Membership Dues:** converter (minimum), $4,500 ● supplier (minimum), $7,000 ● converter (maximum), $35,000 ● supplier (maximum), $40,000. **Staff:** 3. **Budget:** $625,000. **Languages:** English, French, Spanish. **Description:** Manufacturers of raw material and machinery; suppliers and distributors of: single-use cups, plates, and related items for service of food and/or beverages; nestable containers for food packaging and containers for oven usage, placemats and doilies, egg cartons, and trays for prepackaging meat and produce. Promotes sanitation and the environmentally responsible use of food and beverage packaging. Compiles market data. **Awards:** QSR/FPI Foodservice Packaging Awards. **Frequency:** annual. **Type:** recognition. **Recipient:** for distinctive packaging used in foodservice applications ● Samuel J. Crumbine Consumer Protective Award. **Frequency:** annual. **Type:** recognition. **Recipient:** for an outstanding local health department. **Computer Services:** Mailing lists, of members. **Committees:** Market Development; Marketing and Communications; Public Affairs; Safety Management; Technical. **Divisions:** Egg Packaging; Food Packaging; Linen and Lace; Supplier. **Absorbed:** (1971) Food Tray and Board Association; (1973) Egg Packaging Association. **Formed by Merger of:** Paper Cup and Container Institute; Paper Plate Association; Linen and Lace Paper Institute. **Formerly:** (1967) Plate, Cup, Container, and Doily Institute; (1971) Plate, Cup, and Container Institute; (1987) Single Service Institute. **Publications:** *Council Communications*, semiannual. Newsletter ● *Executive Briefs*, biweekly. Newsletter ● *In the Loop*, semiannual. Newsletter. Alternate Formats: online ● *Packaging Innovation Insights*, semiannual. Newsletter. **Price:** free ● *Single Service News*, semiannual. Newsletter. Covers industry news and association and member activities. Includes information on publications and events of interest. **Price:** free for members and related trade associations. **Circulation:** 300. Alternate Formats: online ● Annual Report, annual. Alternate Formats: online ● Brochures. **Conventions/Meetings:** annual meeting - 2008 Oct. 15-16, New Orleans, LA.

1158 ■ Manufacturers Representatives of America (MRA)
PO Box 150229
Arlington, TX 76015
Ph: (682)518-6008
Fax: (682)518-6476
E-mail: assnhqtrs@aol.com
URL: http://www.mra-reps.com
Contact: Pamela L. Bess, Exec. Dir.

Founded: 1978. **Members:** 450. **Membership Dues:** representative, $505-$770 (annual) ● manufacturer, $650 (annual) ● associate, $515 (annual). **Staff:** 2. **Budget:** $180,000. **Description:** Independent manufacturers' representatives handling paper and plastic disposable products, and sanitary supplies. Aims to improve agent sales skills, market coverage, and customer service and to establish more effective agent/principal communications. **Publications:** *Manufacturers Representatives of America-Newsline*, quarterly. Newsletter. Covers membership activities. **Price:** included in membership dues. **Conventions/Meetings:** annual seminar - always spring.

Do It Yourself Aids

1159 ■ Home Improvement Research Institute (HIRI)
3922 Coconut Palm Dr., 3rd Fl.
Tampa, FL 33619
Ph: (813)627-6750 (813)627-6976
Fax: (813)627-7063
E-mail: aangel@hiri.org
URL: http://www.hiri.org
Contact: Angie Angel, Admin. Coor.

Founded: 1981. **Members:** 58. **Membership Dues:** full, $10,000 (annual) ● associate, $9,000 (annual). **Staff:** 3. **Description:** Companies serving the home improvement market. (The home improvement industry is defined as manufacturers, wholesalers, retailers, and others catering to the personal, economic, and material needs of consumers who undertake home improvement projects on their own.) Gathers data and initiates research on the industry on behalf of its members. **Formerly:** (1989) Do-It-Yourself Research Institute. **Publications:** *E-Business Tracking Study*, semiannual. Survey. **Price:** $495.00 ● *Home Improvement Reference Guide*, annual. Book. Contains demographic and housing trends in the U.S. market. **Price:** $395.00/copy. ISSN: 8750-2569. Alternate Formats: CD-ROM ● *Product Category*. Reports. Provides information on product category market size. **Price:** $1,595.00 each ● *Product Purchase Tracking Study*, biennial. **Price:** $3,295.00 for nonmembers; $595.00/product category. Alternate Formats: online ● *Remodeler Study*, biennial. **Price:** $2,995.00/copy; $495.00/product category. **Conventions/Meetings:** annual conference, for members - held in the fall ● annual Data Dialogue - conference.

Dog

1160 ■ Association of Pet Dog Trainers (APDT)
150 Executive Center Dr.
Box 35
Greenville, SC 29615
Free: (800)PET-DOGS
Fax: (864)331-0767
E-mail: information@apdt.com
URL: http://www.apdt.com
Contact: Jackie Powell, Operations Mgr.

Founded: 1993. **Members:** 5,000. **Membership Dues:** full, associate, $100 (annual). **Description:** Individual trainers. Seeks to advance the profession of pet dog trainer; promotes awareness of the profession and dog-friendly training to veterinarians as well as the public. **Awards:** APDT Outstanding Trainer of the Year. **Frequency:** annual. **Type:** recognition. **Recipient:** for a member who exemplifies the APDT spirit through their commitment to the organization ● Dogwise John Fisher Scholarship. **Frequency:** annual. **Type:** scholarship. **Recipient:** for an article about modern positive reinforcement ● Outstanding Member of the Year. **Frequency:** annual. **Type:** recognition. **Recipient:** for a member who exemplifies the APDT spirit through training of dogs. **Computer Services:** database ● mailing lists. **Telecommunication Services:** electronic mail, execdir@apdt.com. **Committees:** Awards; Conference. **Publications:** *Chronicle of the Dog*, bimonthly. Newsletter. Contains information to keep members abreast of contemporary pet dog training techniques, and articles of interest. **Price:** $50.00 for members. **Advertising:** accepted ● *Members News Bulletin Online*. Alternate Formats: online. **Conventions/Meetings:** annual conference and trade show.

1161 ■ International Association of Canine Professionals (IACP)
PO Box 560156
Montverde, FL 34756-0156
Ph: (407)469-2008
Free: (877)THE-IACP
E-mail: iacpadmin@mindspring.com
URL: http://www.dogpro.org
Contact: Martin Deeley, Exec. Dir.

Membership Dues: affiliate, $35 (annual) ● associate, $50 (annual) ● professional, $75 (annual). **Multinational**. **Description:** Provides support and representation for all professional occupations involved with any aspect of canine management, health, training and husbandry. Seeks to maintain the highest standards of professional and business practice among canine professionals. Encourages responsible dog ownership. Provides and assists members with opportunities for further education, development of skills, and hands on experience. **Awards:** Conference Scholarship. **Frequency:** annual. **Type:** scholarship. **Recipient:** for young adults interested in careers in the dog professions. **Telecommunication Services:** electronic mail, iacp@mindspring.com. **Publications:** *SafeHands Journal*, quarterly. Provides education and articles of interest and value to canine professionals. **Price:** included in membership dues. Alternate Formats: online ● Articles. Alternate Formats: online.

Dollhouses

1162 ■ Cottage Industry Miniaturists Trade Association (CIMTA)
4244 Spring Creek Ln.
Bellingham, WA 98226
Ph: (716)355-3651 (716)627-4644
Free: (866)326-9386
Fax: (360)733-5169
E-mail: 2006@cimta.org
URL: http://www.cimta.org/cimta.htm
Contact: Nicole Minnick, Acting Pres.

Members: 294. **Membership Dues:** handcrafter, $135 (annual) ● supporting, $100 (annual). **Description:** Presents programs that deal with the unique problems facing the handcrafter of miniatures within the miniatures industry. **Telecommunication Services:** electronic mail, nicole444@verizon.net. **Publications:** *CIMTA Ink*, biennial. Newsletter.

Door

1163 ■ American Association of Automatic Door Manufacturers (AAADM)
1300 Sumner Ave.
Cleveland, OH 44115-2851
Ph: (216)241-7333
Fax: (216)241-0105
E-mail: aaadm@aaadm.com
URL: http://www.aaadm.com
Contact: Don Morbe, Pres.

Founded: 1994. **Members:** 14. **Staff:** 3. **Description:** Manufacturers of automatically operated pedestrian doors. (Automatic folding, sliding and swinging doors used in grocery stores and other businesses.) Works to promote the industry and provide a forum for members to communicate. Offers certification program for inspectors. **Committees:** Certification. **Publications:** *Automatic Door*. Newsletter. Includes managerial column, feature articles and latest information about the industry. **Conventions/Meetings:** semiannual meeting.

1164 ■ Institutional Locksmiths' Association (ILA)
PO Box 24772
Philadelphia, PA 19111
E-mail: brotherkeyman@aol.com
URL: http://www.ilanational.org
Contact: Kurt Kloeckner CJIL, Pres.
Founded: 1983. **Members:** 900. **Membership Dues:** regular, student, corporate individual, $50 (annual) ● associate, $100 (annual) ● corporate (based on annual gross sales), $300-$1,000 (annual). **Budget:** $24,000. **Regional Groups:** 15. **State Groups:** 13. **Description:** Promotes the goals of its member. Sponsors educational programs. **Libraries: Type:** not open to the public. **Holdings:** audiovisuals. **Subjects:** locksmithing, security. **Awards: Frequency:** annual. **Type:** scholarship. **Committees:** By-Law and Policy; Publications. **Programs:** Certification. **Publications:** *Key Issues*, quarterly. Newsletter. **Circulation:** 1,250. **Advertising:** accepted. **Conventions/Meetings:** annual conference.

Drums

1165 ■ Percussion Marketing Council (PMC)
PO Box 33252
Cleveland, OH 44133
Ph: (440)582-7006
Fax: (440)230-1346
E-mail: kbdustman@aol.com
URL: http://www.playdrums.com
Contact: Karl Dustman, Co-Exec. Dir.
Founded: 1995. **Multinational. Description:** Represents drum and percussion manufacturers, suppliers, and dealers. Promotes drumming as a positive experience for all individuals regardless of age, gender, musical background, economic means, education, or geographic location. Seeks to expand both the percussion market and demand for percussion instruments through the increased visibility of all forms of percussion. Provides professional marketing and advertising campaigns, programs, and activities that bring increased public awareness to drumming. **Publications:** Newsletter. Alternate Formats: online.

E-Commerce

1166 ■ eMarketing Association (eMA)
105 Franklin St., No. 16-129
Westerly, RI 02891
Ph: (401)315-2194
Fax: (408)884-2461
E-mail: admin@emarketingassociation.com
URL: http://www.emarketingassociation.com
Contact: Robert Fleming CeM, Pres.
Founded: 1997. **Membership Dues:** platinum corporate, $2,995 (annual) ● corporate, $995 (annual) ● professional, $175 (annual) ● associate, $125 (annual) ● student, $75 (annual). **Multinational. Description:** Represents the interests of e-marketing professionals. Strives to enrich the marketing community and its members through recognition, research, advocacy, education and services. Advocates ethical practices in Search Engine Optimization (SEO), eMail marketing and website promotion. **Committees:** Educational; Legislative.

1167 ■ WECAI Network
7100 Pembroke Rd.
Miramar, FL 33023
Ph: (954)625-6606
Free: (877)947-3667
Fax: (954)964-3135
E-mail: info@wecai.org
URL: http://www.wecai.org
Contact: Heidi Richards, Founder/CEO
Founded: 2002. **Membership Dues:** basic, $77 (annual) ● charter, $97 (annual) ● charter elite, $197 (annual) ● life (global), $397. **Multinational. Description:** Promotes the development of e-commerce among women. Encourages the growth of existing business and industry while offering guidance to new firms or individuals seeking assistance through its educational resources. Provides opportunities for women's personal and professional development through networking and programs on topics related to doing business on the web. **Awards:** Golden Mouse Award. **Frequency:** annual. **Type:** recognition. **Recipient:** to distinguished businesswomen who have made a difference in their respective communities. **Telecommunication Services:** electronic mail, heidi@wecai.org. **Publications:** *eMonday News*, weekly. Newsletter. **Price:** included in membership dues ● *WECommerce News*, monthly. Magazine. **Price:** included in membership dues. Alternate Formats: online.

Economic Development

1168 ■ GALA: Globalization and Localization Association (GALA)
23 Main St.
Andover, MA 01810
Ph: (206)329-2596
Fax: (815)346-2361
E-mail: info@gala-global.org
URL: http://www.gala-global.org
Contact: Ms. Laura Brandon, Development Mgr.
Founded: 2002. **Membership Dues:** institution, $500 (annual). **Multinational. Description:** Promotes local communication as an indispensable component of a global strategy. Consists of companies that are experts in language services and technologies field. Deploys sophisticated and proven tools and processes to help global enterprises understand in-country issues, language and needs. Represents the interests of the translation, internationalization, localization and globalization industry and provides a forum to discuss issues, create innovative solutions and present a joint voice within the industry. **Committees:** Events; Promotion; Standards; Technology. **Publications:** *GALAxy*, quarterly. Newsletter.

1169 ■ New America Alliance (NAA)
6688 N Central Expy., Ste.625
Dallas, TX 75206
Ph: (214)466-6410
Free: (866)414-7508
Fax: (214)466-6415
E-mail: rmontoya@naaonline.org
URL: http://www.naaonline.org
Contact: Regina Montoya, CEO
Membership Dues: Latino MBA, $2,500 (annual) ● associate, $7,500 (annual) ● general, $10,000 (annual) ● corporate, $25,000 (annual). **Description:** Focuses on increasing access to capital markets and financing for Latino businesses. Promotes the participation and influence of American Latinos on corporate and pension fund boards. Expands the participation and influence of American Latinos in federal and state financial institutions. Invests in the higher education of American Latinos in the fields of business and finance.

Economics

1170 ■ America Business Conference (ABC)
1828 L St. NW, Ste.908
Washington, DC 20036
Ph: (202)822-9300
Fax: (202)467-4070
E-mail: member@americanbusinessconference.org
URL: http://www.americanbusinessconference.org
Contact: Mardie Pergler, Contact
Founded: 1981. **Description:** Men and women who are either the chief executive, chairman, or president of a company with annual revenues of $25 million or more and growing. Conducts activities and meetings in Washington pertaining to economic growth. Provides reports on topics of economic growth interest. **Publications:** Reports.

1171 ■ Bionomics Institute
2173 E Francisco Blvd., Ste.C
San Rafael, CA 94901
Ph: (415)454-1800
Fax: (415)454-7460
Contact: Michael Rothschild, Pres.
Description: Seeks to educate corporate leaders, policy makers, and the general public about bionomics. **Publications:** *Bionomics: Economy as Ecosystem*, periodic. Book. **Price:** $17.95. **Conventions/Meetings:** annual conference ● seminar.

1172 ■ Group of Thirty
1726 M St., Ste.200
Washington, DC 20036
Ph: (202)331-2472
Fax: (202)785-9423
E-mail: info@group30.org
URL: http://www.group30.org
Contact: Dr. Jacob A. Frenkel, Chm.
Founded: 1978. **Members:** 38. **Description:** Aims at promoting deep understanding of international economic and financial issues. Explores the international repercussions of decisions taken in the public and private sectors, and examines the choices available to market practitioners and policy makers. **Computer Services:** Information services, news ● mailing lists, of members. **Publications:** *External Transparency in Trade Policy*. Paper. Focuses on trade policy-making at the national level and the implications for the future of the WTO. **Price:** $10.00 ● *Global Clearing and Settlement: A Plan of Action*. Report. Contains twenty recommendations that constitute a plan of action for global clearing and settlement. ● *Is it Possible to Preserve the European Social Model*. Paper. Addresses the current slow growth rate of the EU. **Price:** $10.00 ● *Occasional Papers Series*. Features a study on economic and financial issues for policy makers. ● *Sharing the Gains from Trade: Reviving the Doha Round*. Report. Focuses on three issues discussed at the Doha Round negotiations. **Price:** $20.00.

1173 ■ International Society for Ecological Economics (ISEE)
c/o Marsha Kopan
PO Box 44194
West Allis, WI 53214
Ph: (414)453-0030
Fax: (877)230-5110
E-mail: secretariat@ecoeco.org
URL: http://www.ecoeco.org
Contact: Joan Martinez-Alier, Pres.
Founded: 1989. **Members:** 2,200. **Staff:** 2. **Regional Groups:** 9. **Multinational. Description:** Encourages the integration of the study of ecology and economy through education, events, research, and outreach to address these issues and more. **Publications:** *Ecological Economics*. Journal. **Price:** included in membership dues ● Newsletter, semiannual. **Price:** included in membership dues. Alternate Formats: online. **Conventions/Meetings:** meeting.

Education

1174 ■ Association of Specialized and Professional Accreditors (ASPA)
c/o Cynthia A. Davenport, Exec. Dir.
1020 W Byron St., Ste.8G
Chicago, IL 60613-2987
Ph: (773)525-2160 (330)672-2220
Fax: (773)525-2162
E-mail: aspa@aspa-usa.org
URL: http://www.aspa-usa.org
Contact: Cynthia A. Davenport, Exec. Dir.
Founded: 1993. **Members:** 45. **Membership Dues:** institution (depends on organization size), $6,000 (annual). **Staff:** 9. **Budget:** $250,000. **Description:** Specialized and Professional Accreditors. Works to promote quality and integrity in non-governmental specialized and professional accreditation of post-secondary programs and institutions, provide a forum for discussion and analysis, address accreditation issues in educational, governmental and public policy

contexts and communicate with the public about accreditation. **Affiliated With:** Accreditation Commission for Acupuncture and Oriental Medicine; Accreditation Council for Pharmacy Education; Accreditation Review Commission on Education for the Physician Assistant; Accrediting Bureau of Health Education Schools; American Association of Family and Consumer Sciences; American Association for Marriage and Family Therapy; American Council for Construction Education; American Dental Association; American Library Association; American Occupational Therapy Association; American Optometric Association; American Physical Therapy Association; American Psychological Association; American Society of Landscape Architects; American Speech Language Hearing Association; American Veterinary Medical Association; Association of Advanced Rabbinical and Talmudic Schools; Bureau of Professional Education of the American Osteopathic Association; Commission on Accreditation of Allied Health Education Programs; Council on Accreditation of Nurse Anesthesia Educational Programs; Council on Education for Public Health; Council for Interior Design Accreditation; Council on Podiatric Medical Education; Council on Rehabilitation Education; Council on Social Work Education; Joint Review Committee on Education in Radiologic Technology; Liaison Committee on Medical Education; National Accrediting Agency for Clinical Laboratory Sciences; National Architectural Accrediting Board; National Association of Industrial Technology; National Association of Schools of Art and Design; National Association of Schools of Dance; National Association of Schools of Music; National Association of Schools of Theatre; National Council for Accreditation of Teacher Education; National League for Nursing; National Recreation and Park Association; Society of American Foresters. **Publications:** *ASPA News*, semiannual, every January and July. Newsletter. Posted to website one month after hard copy is mailed. **Conventions/Meetings:** annual conference - always fall ● annual conference - always spring. 2009 Mar. 29-31, WASHINGTON, DC.

Educators

1175 ■ Conference on English Leadership (CEL)
c/o National Council of Teachers of English
1111 W Kenyon Rd.
Urbana, IL 61801-1096
Ph: (217)328-3870
Free: (877)369-6283
Fax: (217)328-9645
E-mail: public_info@ncte.org
URL: http://www.ncte.org/groups/cel
Contact: Henry Kiernan, Chm.
Founded: 1970. **Membership Dues:** regular, $65 (annual). **Description:** English department leaders and other English educators. Commits to a common interest in English program development and teacher training; dedicated to meeting the professional needs of English department chairs, English/Language Arts curriculum supervisors, and others having supervisory roles in the areas of English/Language Arts education from elementary through secondary levels. **Awards:** Award for Exemplary Leadership. **Frequency:** annual. **Type:** recognition. **Recipient:** to an NCTE member who is an outstanding English language arts educator and leader ● English Leadership Quarterly Best Article. **Frequency:** annual. **Type:** recognition. **Recipient:** for articles published in the CEL journal English Leadership Quarterly in the previous school year. **Publications:** *English Leadership Quarterly*. Journal. **Price:** included in membership dues. ISSN: 0738-1409. **Circulation:** 2,000. **Advertising:** accepted. Alternate Formats: online. **Conventions/Meetings:** annual Significant Seeing: Seeing Significance - convention.

Elections

1176 ■ National Association of State Election Directors (NASED)
12543 Westella, Ste.100
Houston, TX 77077-3929
Ph: (281)752-6200
E-mail: services@nased.org
URL: http://www.nased.org
Contact: Brad Bryant, Pres.
Founded: 1989. **Description:** Works to assure free and fair elections with accurate results. **Conventions/Meetings:** annual meeting - every summer. 2008 June 26-28, Jackson Hole, WY.

Electrical

1177 ■ Action Committee for Rural Electrification (ACRE)
c/o Pennsylvania Rural Electric Association
PO Box 1266
Harrisburg, PA 17108
Ph: (717)233-5704
E-mail: russ_biggica@prea.com
URL: http://www.prea.com/Political/Acre.htm
Contact: Russ Biggica, Dir.
Founded: 1967. **Members:** 25,000. **Staff:** 3. **Description:** Represents rural electric cooperative directors, managers, consumers and employees. Advocates support for rural electrification. **Affiliated With:** National Rural Electric Cooperative Association. **Conventions/Meetings:** annual meeting.

1178 ■ Consumer Electronics Association TechHome Division
1919 S Eads St.
Arlington, VA 22202
Ph: (703)907-7600 (703)907-7650
Free: (866)858-1555
Fax: (703)907-7675
E-mail: cea@ce.org
URL: http://www.ce.org/Membership/Divisions/103.asp
Contact: Gary Shapiro, Pres./CEO
Founded: 2002. **Description:** Represents the entire channel for home control and networking products. Board is composed of manufacturers, integrators and distributors. Mission is to increase sales and support of consumer electronics products by professional integrators. **Awards:** Mark of Excellence Awards. **Frequency:** annual. **Type:** recognition. **Recipient:** for the best in home control and networking products, services and installations. **Committees:** Education; Events; Market Research; Marketing; Member Support; Nominations. **Working Groups:** Awards; Industry Training; Rating System. **Formerly:** (2003) Home Automation Association. **Publications:** *CEA Government Alert*, biweekly ● *TechHome Guide to Home Networks*. Alternate Formats: online ● Papers. Alternate Formats: online.

1179 ■ ELECTRI International - The Foundation for Electrical Contraction
3 Bethesda Metro Ctr., Ste.1100
Bethesda, MD 20814-6302
Ph: (301)215-4538
Fax: (301)215-4536
E-mail: rja@necanet.org
URL: http://www.electri.org
Contact: Russell J. Alessi, Pres.
Founded: 1901. **Description:** Represents electrical contractors. Aims to improve the contractor's ability to work efficiently and effectively. **Formerly:** (2005) Electrical Contracting Foundation.

1180 ■ Electrical Apparatus Service Association (EASA)
1331 Baur Blvd.
St. Louis, MO 63132
Ph: (314)993-2220
Fax: (314)993-1269
E-mail: easainfo@easa.com
URL: http://www.easa.com
Contact: Linda J. Raynes CAE, Pres./CEO
Founded: 1933. **Members:** 2,600. **Membership Dues:** entrance fee (new), $125 ● company (with 1-5 employees), $432 (annual) ● company (with 6-10 employees), $453 (annual) ● company (with 11-25 employees), $547 (annual) ● company (with 26-50 employees), $828 (annual) ● company (with 51 or more employees), $1,182 (annual). **Staff:** 16. **Budget:** $2,900,000. **Regional Groups:** 10. **Local Groups:** 34. **Multinational. Description:** Electrical apparatus service and sales firms. Establishes standards for rebuilding electric motors, generators, and transformers. Maintains extensive data files on rewinding and repair of electrical equipment. Sponsors and presents seminar programs geared to the needs of those in the electrical repair industry. **Awards:** EASA Exceptional Achievement and Service Award. **Frequency:** annual. **Type:** recognition. **Recipient:** to a member with outstanding contribution to the industry. **Computer Services:** database ● mailing lists ● online services. **Telecommunication Services:** electronic mail, lraynes@easa.com. **Formerly:** (1960) National Industrial Service Association. **Publications:** *CURRENTS*, monthly. Magazine. Contains technical articles and member information. ● *Motor Rewinding Data*. Alternate Formats: microform ● *Technical Manual* ● Yearbook, annual. **Conventions/Meetings:** annual convention (exhibits).

1181 ■ Electrical Equipment Representatives Association (EERA)
638 W 39th St.
Kansas City, MO 64111
Ph: (816)561-5323
Fax: (816)561-1249
E-mail: info2005@eera.org
URL: http://www.eera.org
Contact: William J. Chowanec, Pres.
Founded: 1948. **Members:** 102. **Membership Dues:** individual, $1,100 (annual). **Staff:** 3. **Budget:** $140,000. **Description:** Represents sales agents for manufacturers of electrical equipment used by utilities, industrial firms, and the government. **Awards:** EERA Scholarships. **Frequency:** annual. **Type:** scholarship. **Recipient:** for sons, daughters, grandsons, granddaughters of members and employees. **Committees:** Directory; Finance; Industry Relations; Membership; Scholarship; Trade Relations. **Publications:** *Electrical Equipment Representatives Association-Directory*, annual. Contains lists of territory, represented manufacturers, and photographs of proprietors. Includes calendar of events and individuals index. **Price:** free for members and electrical manufacturers. **Circulation:** 1,000. **Conventions/Meetings:** annual conference.

1182 ■ Electrical Generating Systems Association (EGSA)
1650 S Dixie Hwy., Ste.500
Boca Raton, FL 33432-7462
Ph: (561)750-5575
Fax: (561)395-8557
E-mail: e-mail@egsa.org
URL: http://www.egsa.org
Contact: Jalane L. Kellough, Exec. Dir.
Founded: 1965. **Members:** 600. **Membership Dues:** manufacturer, energy management company, $825 (annual) ● manufacturer's rep, distributor/dealer, full associate, $285 (annual) ● regular associate, $200 (annual) ● retiree, $90 (annual). **Staff:** 8. **Budget:** $1,000,000. **Description:** Manufacturers, distributor/dealers, and manufacturers' representatives of devices used to generate electrical power through the use of an internal combustion engine or a gas turbine coupled to a generator. Conducts training programs and publishes material on On-Site Power Generation. **Libraries: Type:** reference. **Subjects:** standards. **Awards:** The David I. Coren Memorial Scholarship. **Frequency:** annual. **Type:** scholarship. **Recipient:** for students pursuing a career in power generation industry. **Computer Services:** database, suppliers of products and services ● mailing lists. **Telecommunication Services:** electronic mail, j.kellough@egsa.org. **Committees:** Codes and Standards Surveillance; Communications and Conventions; Distributor/Dealer; Education; Government Relations; International Trade; Marketing Trends; Membership. **Formerly:** Engine Generator Set Manufacturers Association; (1983) Electrical Generating Systems Marketing Association. **Publications:** *Electrical Generating Systems Association—Buyer's Guide and Member Services Directory*, annual. Lists leading companies for emergency, standby, and

supplementary electrical needs. **Price:** $6.00 plus shipping and handling. **Advertising:** accepted ● *On-Site Power Generation: A Reference Book.* Covers on-site power equipment use. **Price:** $110.00 for members; $185.00 for nonmembers ● *Powerline*, bimonthly. Magazine. Lists publications, industry personnel promotions, new members, and company awards. **Price:** $5.00/issue. **Circulation:** 1,500. **Advertising:** accepted ● Videos. Features convention presentations. **Conventions/Meetings:** semiannual convention ● annual convention, with speakers.

1183 ■ Electrical Manufacturing and Coil Winding Association (EMCWA)
PO Box 278
Imperial Beach, CA 91933
Ph: (619)435-3629
Free: (800)984-3629
Fax: (619)435-3639
E-mail: info@emcwa.org
URL: http://www.emcw.org
Contact: Chuck Thurman, Exec. Dir.
Founded: 1974. **Members:** 500. **Membership Dues:** company (in U.S., Canada and Mexico), $300 (annual) ● professional, associate (in U.S., Canada and Mexico), $50 (annual) ● professional, associate (in U.S., Canada and Mexico), $75 (annual) ● student, $10 (annual) ● company in other country, $350 (annual). **Staff:** 2. **Description:** Electric motor, coil, and transformer manufacturers, suppliers, firms and individuals with an interest in the field. Promotes the welfare of the motor and coil manufacturing industry; and sponsors career enrichment courses, workshops, and technical conference programs. Maintains hall of fame. **Formerly:** (1993) International Coil Winding Association. **Publications:** *Electrical Manufacturing and Coil Winding Association—Membership Directory*, annual ● *Electrical Manufacturing and Coil Winding Proceedings*, annual. Presents a collection of presentations on emerging technologies related to manufacturing electric products. **Price:** $50.00. **Circulation:** 1,800. Alternate Formats: CD-ROM ● *EMCW News*, quarterly. Newsletter. **Advertising:** accepted. Alternate Formats: online. **Conventions/Meetings:** annual conference and trade show, with materials and equipment used in manufacturing electrical products (exhibits).

1184 ■ Electricity Consumers Resource Council (ELCON)
1333 H St. NW
West Tower, 8th Fl.
Washington, DC 20005
Ph: (202)682-1390
Fax: (202)289-6370
E-mail: elcon@elcon.org
URL: http://www.elcon.org
Contact: John A. Anderson, Pres./CEO
Founded: 1976. **Members:** 38. **Staff:** 5. **Description:** Represents large industrial consumers of electricity. Promotes the development of coordinated and rational federal and state policies that will assure an adequate, reliable and efficient supply of electricity for all users at competitive prices. Has member companies come from virtually every segment of the manufacturing community. **Libraries: Type:** reference. **Telecommunication Services:** electronic mail, janderson@elcon.org ● electronic mail, jhughes@elcon.org. **Committees:** Federal Relations; Legal; Technical. **Publications:** *ELCON Report*, quarterly. Alternate Formats: online ● Brochures ● Membership Directory ● Reports. Alternate Formats: online. **Conventions/Meetings:** annual workshop, addresses current electricity issues.

1185 ■ Energy Telecommunications and Electrical Association (ENTELEC)
5005 Royal Ln., Ste.190
Irving, TX 75063
Free: (888)503-8700
Fax: (972)915-6040
E-mail: blaine@entelec.org
URL: http://www.entelec.org
Contact: Blaine Siske, Exec. Mgr.
Founded: 1928. **Members:** 170. **Membership Dues:** corporate, associate, $495 (annual) ● individual, $250 (annual). **Staff:** 4. **Budget:** $250,000. **Description:** Telecommunications superintendents, engineers, and technicians for petroleum and gas pipelines, refineries, and allied firms interested in the construction, maintenance, and operation of automation systems, communication systems, and electrical power installations. **Committees:** Education/Training; Long Range Planning; Nominating; Technical Advisory. **Formerly:** (1979) Petroleum Industry Electrical Association. **Publications:** *ENTELEC News*, bimonthly. Magazine. **Price:** $25.00/year. **Circulation:** 9,000. **Advertising:** accepted. **Conventions/Meetings:** annual conference, telecommunications products and services (exhibits).

1186 ■ International Association of Electrical Inspectors (IAEI)
PO Box 830848
Richardson, TX 75083-0848
Ph: (972)235-1455
Free: (800)786-4234
Fax: (972)235-6858
E-mail: iaei@iaei.org
URL: http://www.iaei.org
Contact: James W. Carpenter, CEO/Exec. Dir.
Founded: 1928. **Members:** 25,000. **Membership Dues:** inspector, associate, $90 (annual). **Staff:** 14. **Budget:** $3,600,000. **Regional Groups:** 6. **Local Groups:** 115. **Multinational. Description:** State, federal, county, city, industrial, utility, and insurance electrical inspectors; associate members are electricians, contractors, manufacturers, engineers, architects, and wiremen. Promotes the safe use of electrical wiring and equipment in compliance with the National Electrical Code and other electrical codes. Conducts educational programs. **Awards:** Presidential Medal of Honor. **Frequency:** annual. **Type:** recognition. **Computer Services:** Mailing lists, of members. **Telecommunication Services:** electronic mail, jcarpenter@iaei.org. **Publications:** *Analysis of the National Electrical Code 1999.* Book ● *Analysis of the National Electrical Code 1996.* Book ● *Analysis of the National Electrical Code 1993.* Book ● *Ferms Fast Finder Index.* Book ● *IAEI Membership Directory*, annual. **Price:** $10.95. **Circulation:** 1,000. **Advertising:** accepted ● *IAEI News*, bimonthly. Magazine. **Price:** $65.00/year; $45.00 for educational institution. **Circulation:** 25,500. **Advertising:** accepted ● *Neon Installation Manual* ● *One- and Two-Family Dwelling Electrical Systems.* Book ● *Soares Book on Grounding* ● *2002 NEC Study Guides: Electrical One- and Two-Family Dwellings, Electrical General, and Electrical Plan Review.*

1187 ■ International Electrical Testing Association (NETA)
2700 W Centre Ave., Ste.A
Portage, MI 49024
Ph: (269)488-6382
Free: (888)300-NETA
Fax: (269)488-6383
E-mail: neta@netaworld.org
URL: http://www.netaworld.org
Contact: Jayne M. Tanz, Exec. Dir.
Founded: 1972. **Members:** 1,500. **Membership Dues:** individual, company, $75 (annual) ● affiliate, $135 (annual) ● international associate, $250 (annual). **Staff:** 4. **Budget:** $1,000,000. **Description:** Independent firms involved in testing, analysis, and maintenance of electrical power systems; firms supplying construction, maintenance, engineering, or similar services to the power systems industry; interested individuals. Seeks to represent, promote, and advance the interests of the electrical testing industry through safety and technical advancements, sound competition, establishment of standards, and dissemination of related data. Offers training programs and technical certification. Provides technical support in procedures and specifications. **Libraries: Type:** not open to the public. **Awards:** Outstanding Achievement in the Industry. **Frequency:** annual. **Type:** recognition. **Recipient:** for service to the electrical testing industry. **Committees:** Codes and Standards; Government; Safety; Technical. **Formerly:** (1984) National Electrical Testing Association. **Publications:** *NETA Acceptance Testing Specifications*, quadrennial. Manual. Contains specifications for electrical acceptance testing. **Price:** $95.00 bound version; $135.00 CD-Rom or download version. Alternate Formats: diskette; CD-ROM ● *NETA Maintenance Testing Specifications.* Manual. Contains specifications for electrical maintenance testing. **Price:** $125.00 bound; $175.00 CD-Rom; $165.00 download version. Alternate Formats: diskette; CD-ROM ● *NETA World*, quarterly. Journal. Includes safety and technical tips and calendar of events. **Price:** included in membership dues; $40.00 for nonmembers. **Circulation:** 6,000. **Advertising:** accepted ● *Technical Conference Papers.* Covers annual technical conference. **Price:** $25.00 plus shipping and handling. **Conventions/Meetings:** annual conference and seminar (exhibits) - always March.

1188 ■ International League of Electrical Associations (ILEA)
12165 W Center Rd., Ste.59
Omaha, NE 68144
Ph: (402)330-7227
Fax: (402)330-7283
E-mail: info@electricalcouncil.com
URL: http://www.ileaweb.org
Contact: R.E. Morris, Exec. Mgr.
Founded: 1936. **Members:** 35. **Membership Dues:** with annual budget of $500,000 or more, $400 (annual) ● with annual budget of $100,000 to $500,000, $300 (annual) ● with annual budget of $100,000 or less, $250 (annual). **Budget:** $50,000. **Multinational. Description:** Serves as a federation of local organizations representing electrical utilities, contractors, distributors, dealers, manufacturers, and representatives. Aims to facilitate interchange throughout the U.S. and Canada. Conducts local and regional cooperative programs. **Awards:** Golden Globes. **Frequency:** annual. **Type:** recognition. **Formerly:** (1978) International Association of Electrical Leagues. **Publications:** *Keeping Current*, monthly. Newsletter. Contains information on member leagues and ILEA events and updates. Alternate Formats: online ● Membership Directory, annual. Contains the contact information of members. **Conventions/Meetings:** annual conference - every summer.

1189 ■ International Sign Association
707 N St. Asaph St.
Alexandria, VA 22314
Ph: (703)836-4012 (703)836-4014
Fax: (703)836-8353
E-mail: lori.anderson@signs.org
URL: http://www.signs.org
Contact: Lori Anderson, Pres./CEO
Founded: 1944. **Members:** 2,200. **Membership Dues:** company (based on number of employees), $95-$1,650 ● national division, $1,650 ● international division, $250 ● supplier (based on last four quarters' gross sales), $2,000-$10,000 ● distributor division, $950 ● related organization, $575 ● affiliated association division, associate division, $100 ● manufacturer's representative, $300 ● business identity division, $75. **Staff:** 14. **Budget:** $4,000,000. **Regional Groups:** 9. **Multinational. Description:** Manufacturers, users, and suppliers of on-premise signs and sign products produced by more than 400,000 employees in all 50 states and 69 countries. Exists to support, promote and improve the $30 billion-a-year sign industry, which sustains the nation's nearly $3 trillion-a-year retail industry. **Libraries: Type:** reference. **Holdings:** books. **Awards:** Kirk L. Brimley Distinguished Service Award. **Frequency:** annual. **Type:** recognition. **Recipient:** to a member who has demonstrated outstanding dedication and service to the association ● Sign Design Award. **Frequency:** annual. **Type:** recognition. **Recipient:** for outstanding designs. **Computer Services:** Mailing lists, of members. **Committees:** Education; Government Relations; Marketing; Technical; Trade Show. **Divisions:** Architectural Signage and Graphics; Corporate Identity; Custom Sign Companies; Digital Signage and Graphics; National Sign Companies; Sign Product Manufacturers; Sign Supply Distributors. **Absorbed:** (1978) Institute of Signage Research. **Formerly:** (1995) National Electric Sign Association. **Publications:** *ISA-Membership Direc-*

tory, annual. **Price:** included in membership dues; $250.00/copy for nonmembers. **Circulation:** 2,300. **Advertising:** accepted. Alternate Formats: online ● Also publishes safety and training manuals, legislative bulletins, and publications dealing with permits, sign codes, and zoning issues. **Conventions/Meetings:** annual trade show (exhibits).

1190 ■ National Association of Electrical Distributors (NAED)

1100 Corporate Square Dr., Ste.100
St. Louis, MO 63132
Ph: (314)991-9000
Free: (888)791-2512
Fax: (314)991-3060
E-mail: info@naed.org
URL: http://www.naed.org
Contact: Thomas Naber, Pres./Publisher

Founded: 1908. **Members:** 4,000. **Staff:** 28. **Budget:** $6,000,000. **Regional Groups:** 4. **Description:** Serves as wholesale distributors of electrical supplies and apparatus. Aims to serve and protect the electrical distribution channel; maintains several committees. **Telecommunication Services:** electronic mail, tnaber@naed.org. **Committees:** Performance Analysis. **Councils:** Associates Advisory; Channel Advantage Partnership; Eastern Region; Government Affairs; Industry Education; Manufacturer's Sales and Marketing; South Central Region. **Formerly:** (1928) Electrical Supply Jobbers Association; (1949) National Electric Wholesalers Association. **Publications:** *The Electrical Distributor*, monthly. Magazine. Presents through articles, features, and mail surveys, information on industry issues, management and operating methods, marketing opportunities. **Price:** free for members; $12.00 /year for nonmembers. ISSN: 0422-8707. **Circulation:** 28,000. **Advertising:** accepted ● *NAED Newsline*, weekly. Newsletter ● *Performance Analysis Report*. **Price:** free to survey participants; $300.00 for non-participants ● Directories, periodic. **Price:** $275.00 for nonmembers. Alternate Formats: online ● Annual Report, annual. Alternate Formats: online. **Conventions/Meetings:** annual National Electrical Leadership Summit - meeting - 2009 May 16-20, Fort Lauderdale, FL; 2010 May 15-19, Chicago, IL; 2011 May 15-19, Las Vegas, NV.

1191 ■ National Electrical Manufacturers Association (NEMA)

1300 N 17th St., Ste.1752
Rosslyn, VA 22209
Ph: (703)841-3200
Fax: (703)841-5900
E-mail: communications@nema.org
URL: http://www.nema.org
Contact: Evan R. Gaddis, Pres./CEO

Founded: 1926. **Members:** 430. **Membership Dues:** basic, $2,500 (annual) ● small company, $500-$2,500 (annual) ● associate, $1,000 (annual). **Staff:** 90. **Budget:** $17,000,000. **Multinational. Description:** Aims to maintain and improve quality and reliability of products; insure safety standards in manufacture and use of products; organize and act upon members' interests in productivity, competition from overseas suppliers, energy conservation and efficiency, marketing opportunities, economic matters, and product liability. Develops product standards covering such matters as nomenclature, ratings, performance, testing, and dimensions; actively participates in regional and international standards process for electrical products; participates in developing National Electrical Code and National Electrical Safety Codes, and advocates their acceptance by state and local authorities; conducts regulatory and legislative analyses on issues of concern to electrical manufacturers; compiles and issues market data of all kinds, and statistical data on such factors as sales, new orders, unfilled orders, cancellations, production, and inventories. Sponsors geographical projects, advisory services, and statistical and management services. **Awards:** Bernard H. Falk Award. **Frequency:** annual. **Type:** recognition. **Recipient:** for outstanding achievement in technology, management, marketing, international trade, education, public affairs, or any other field important to the electro industry ● Kite and Key Award. **Frequency:** annual. **Type:** recognition. **Recipient:** for individuals who have advanced the interests of the electrical industry through active and sustained involvement in the affairs of the organization. **Committees:** Codes and Standards; Environmental Affairs; Government Affairs; International Trade; Product Liability. **Councils:** Economics and Statistics; Marketing; Public Relations. **Departments:** Engineering; Public Affairs; Statistical and Management Services. **Divisions:** Automation; Building Equipment; Diagnostic Imaging and Therapy Systems; Electronic Equipment; Industrial Equipment; Insulating Materials; Lighting Equipment; Power Equipment; Wire and Cable. **Programs:** Semiannual Sales Survey/Industry Information. **Formed by Merger of:** Associated Manufacturers of Electrical and Supplies; Electric Power Club. **Publications:** *Directory of Member Companies*, periodic ● *Electroindustry*. Magazine. **Advertising:** accepted. Alternate Formats: online ● *Executive Update*, monthly ● *National Electrical Manufacturers Association—Publications and Materials Catalog*, semiannual. Includes price and ordering information and alpha-numerical index. **Price:** free ● *Tech Alert*, bimonthly ● Brochures, monthly. Alternate Formats: online ● Also publishes manuals, guidebooks, and other material on wiring, installing equipment, lighting, and standards. **Conventions/Meetings:** annual meeting and conference - always November.

1192 ■ National Electrical Manufacturers Representatives Association (NEMRA)

660 White Plains Rd., Ste.600
Tarrytown, NY 10591-5172
Ph: (914)524-8650
Free: (800)446-3672
Fax: (914)524-8655
E-mail: nemra@nemra.org
URL: http://www.nemra.org
Contact: Henry P. Bergson, Pres.

Founded: 1969. **Members:** 1,100. **Membership Dues:** company (add $80 per additional person; maximum of 50 persons), $650-$4,570 (annual) ● manufacturer, $2,000 (annual). **Staff:** 10. **Budget:** $1,700,000. **Regional Groups:** 41. **Description:** North American trade association dedicated to promoting continuing education, professionalism, and the use of independent manufacturers representatives in the electrical industry. Offers professional development programs in business management and sales training, and offers a proprietary computer system for independent electrical representatives. Sponsors educational programs; compiles statistics; and holds an annual networking conference for its representative members and their manufacturers. **Awards:** NEMRA Educational Scholarship Fund Awards. **Frequency:** annual. **Type:** scholarship. **Recipient:** for children of employees and principals of member representative agencies. **Committees:** Industry Relations; Manufacturers' Group; Professional Development Program. **Publications:** *The Insider*, quarterly. Newsletter ● *NEMRA Locator*, annual. Membership Directory ● *REPconnections*, quarterly ● *Viewpoint*, annual. Covers issues in the electric industry. ● Also publishes industry guidelines. **Conventions/Meetings:** annual conference - 2009 Mar. 17-21, San Diego, CA; 2010 Feb. 16-20, New York, NY.

1193 ■ National Regap Network

PO Box 454
Cary, IL 60013-0454
Ph: (847)217-1836 (847)622-5440
Free: (800)379-2341
E-mail: matras@regap.org
URL: http://www.regap.org
Contact: John Matras, Dir.

Founded: 1997. **Members:** 200. **Description:** Commits in finding responsible homes for retired racing greyhounds. Educates the public about the excellent, loving and devoted pets they make. **Publications:** *REGAP Review*, quarterly. Newsletter. **Conventions/Meetings:** annual Adopter Reunion Picnic.

1194 ■ National Rural Electric Cooperative Association (NRECA)

4301 Wilson Blvd.
Arlington, VA 22203
Ph: (703)907-5500
Fax: (703)907-5511
E-mail: nreca@nreca.coop
URL: http://www.nreca.org
Contact: Patrick Lavigne, Media and Public Relations Dir.

Founded: 1942. **Members:** 1,000. **Membership Dues:** silver (associate), $1,250 (annual) ● gold (associate), $6,500 (annual) ● platinum (associate), $12,000 (annual). **Staff:** 650. **Budget:** $87,000,000. **Regional Groups:** 10. **Description:** Rural electric cooperative systems, public power districts, and public utility districts in 46 states. Conducts activities such as: legislative representation; energy and regulatory; management institutes; professional conferences; training and consulting services; insurance and safety programs; international program; wage and salary surveys. **Telecommunication Services:** electronic mail, patrick.lavigne@nreca.coop. **Committees:** Community and Economic Development; Consumer Action; Insurance and Employee Welfare; Lawyers; Legislative; Management Issues; Marketing and Energy Services; Power and Generation; Power and Water Resources; Public and Member Relations; Resolutions; Telecommunications. **Publications:** *Electric Co-Op Today*, weekly. Newspaper. Covers legislative, regulatory, and political issues affecting rural electrification. **Price:** $75.00/year. ISSN: 0747-4784. **Circulation:** 15,000 ● *Facts About America's Consumer-Owned Rural Electric Systems* ● *Management Quarterly*. Journal. **Price:** $25.00/year. ISSN: 0025-1860 ● *Rural Electrification Magazine*, monthly. Covers the electric cooperative industry for directors and employees of member systems. **Price:** $60.00 in U.S.; $80.00 outside U.S. **Circulation:** 36,800. **Advertising:** accepted ● Annual Report, annual. Alternate Formats: online. **Conventions/Meetings:** annual meeting (exhibits).

1195 ■ North American Electric Reliability Council (NERC)

116-390 Village Blvd.
Princeton, NJ 08540-5721
Ph: (609)452-8060
Fax: (609)452-9550
E-mail: info@nerc.com
URL: http://www.nerc.com
Contact: Richard P. Sergel, Pres./CEO

Founded: 1968. **Members:** 10. **Staff:** 45. **Budget:** $12,000,000. **Regional Groups:** 10. **Description:** Represents regional reliability councils composed of electric utility systems, independent power producers, power marketers, and brokers who are concerned about the reliability of the bulk electric supply in North America. Operates virtually all of the generation and transmission facilities in the 48 continental United States, the 9 bordering provinces of Canada, and a portion of the Mexican power system which is interconnected with that of California. Reviews regional and interregional reliability periodically and acts as a means for exchange of information on planning and operating matters relating to reliability of transmission systems and adequacy of bulk electricity supply in North America. Maintains numerous technical subcommittees. **Computer Services:** database, Electric Supply & Demand (ES&D) ● database, Generating Availability Data System (GADS) ● database, provides aggregate utility forecasts of electricity supply/demand, fuel use, and other energy topics during the next ten years ● database, Spare Transformer ● database, System Disturbances. **Committees:** Compliance Enforcement and Certification; Critical Infrastructure Protection; Market; Operating; Planning; Standards Authorization. **Formerly:** (1981) National Electric Reliability Council. **Publications:** *NERC News*, monthly. Newsletter. Alternate Formats: online ● *Reliability Assessment*, annual. Report. Reviews the overall reliability of the North American bulk power systems. Includes statistics. ● *Summer Assessment*, annual. Features assessment of electric power supply and demand for the upcoming summer.

● *Winter Assessment*, annual. Features assessment of electric power supply and demand for the upcoming winter. ● Annual Report, annual. Alternate Formats: online. **Conventions/Meetings:** quarterly board meeting.

1196 ■ Professional Electrical Apparatus Recyclers League (PEARL)
4255 S Buckley Rd., No. 118
Aurora, CO 80013
Free: (877)AT-PEARL
Fax: (888)996-3296
E-mail: pearl@pearl1.org
URL: http://www.pearl1.org
Contact: Bill Schofield, Pres.
Founded: 1997. **Members:** 55. **Membership Dues:** voting, $2,000 (annual) ● affiliate, $1,500 (annual). **Staff:** 1. **Budget:** $150,000. **Description:** Recyclers of electrical apparatus, vendors, and associates. Aims to create a marketable distinction in quality, safety, and integrity. **Publications:** *PEARL News*, quarterly. Newsletter. Alternate Formats: online ● *PEARL Reconditioning Standards*. Alternate Formats: online. **Conventions/Meetings:** annual conference.

1197 ■ Relay and Switch Industry Association (RSIA)
2500 Wilson Blvd.
Arlington, VA 22201
Ph: (703)907-8021
E-mail: rwillis@ecaus.org
URL: http://www.ec-central.org/RSIA
Contact: Robert Willis, Exec. Dir.
Founded: 1947. **Members:** 34. **Membership Dues:** regular, $2,000 (annual) ● associate technical, $1,000 (annual). **National Groups:** 35. **Description:** Manufacturers of relays. Works to standardize technical ratings, nomenclature, and testing methods; disseminates information to relay users and manufacturers. **Libraries: Type:** reference. **Holdings:** books. **Awards:** College of Relay Engineers. **Frequency:** annual. **Type:** recognition. **Recipient:** for best technical paper. **Committees:** Education; Marketing; Military Specification Coordinating; Non-Military Relay Specifications; Relay Handbook; Reliability. **Affiliated With:** Electronic Industries Alliance. **Formerly:** (2004) National Association of Relay Manufacturers. **Publications:** *Engineers' Relay Handbook*, periodic. **Price:** $60.00 for members; $90.00 for nonmembers. **Circulation:** 100,000 ● *International Relay Conference Proceedings*, annual. **Price:** $60.00/issue for members; $70.00/issue for nonmembers. **Conventions/Meetings:** annual International Relay Conference - meeting, technical paper conference (exhibits) - always 3rd week of April ● periodic symposium.

1198 ■ SMMA - The Motor and Motion Association (SMMA)
PO Box P182
South Dartmouth, MA 02748
Ph: (508)979-5935 (508)979-5933
Fax: (508)979-5845
E-mail: info@smma.org
URL: http://www.smma.org
Contact: Elizabeth B. Chambers, Exec. Dir.
Founded: 1975. **Members:** 150. **Membership Dues:** regular, $995 (annual) ● affiliate, $495 (annual). **Staff:** 2. **Budget:** $211,000. **Multinational. Description:** Original equipment manufacturers, users, suppliers, and others involved in the manufacture of fractional and subfractional horsepower motors and controls. Serves as a forum for exchange of information among members; gathers and disseminates industry information. Compiles technical reference materials; represents members before government bodies. **Committees:** Benchmarking; Government and Regulatory Affairs; Marketing Communications; Motor and Motion College; Technology. **Formerly:** (1993) Small Motor Manufacturer Association; (1998) SMMA - The Association for Electric Motors, Their Control and Application; (2003) Small Motors and Motion Association. **Conventions/Meetings:** annual Fall Technical Conference, focuses on technical topics (exhibits) ● annual Spring Management Conference, emphasizes management issues for motor and motion industry (exhibits).

1199 ■ Wiring Harness Manufacturer's Association (WHMA)
7500 Flying Cloud Dr., Ste.900
Eden Prairie, MN 55344
Ph: (952)253-6225
Fax: (952)835-4774
E-mail: whma@whma.org
URL: http://www.whma.org
Contact: Lyle C. Fahning, Chm.
Founded: 1993. **Members:** 170. **Membership Dues:** regular (based on annual sales volume), $350-$650 (annual) ● supplier, $1,600 (annual). **Staff:** 5. **Budget:** $100,000. **Description:** International wiring harness and cord set manufacturers. Strives to provide a cooperative forum for which member companies can network to resolve their specific goals and help address industry problems. Provides a cooperative exchange program for excess inventory among members. Lobbies for government action in the best interest of the industry. Offers educational courses. Sets universal technical and product specification standards. Compiles statistics on human resource issues and business benchmarking trends. **Awards: Type:** recognition. **Computer Services:** database ● mailing lists. **Telecommunication Services:** electronic mail, lfahning@tseinc.net. **Publications:** *Wire Taps*, quarterly. Membership Directory. **Price:** included in membership dues; $10.00 for nonmembers ● *Wiring Harness News*, bimonthly. Newsletter. Features story about the industry and announcements of events. Includes managerial columns. **Price:** included in membership dues ● Newsletter, semiannual. **Price:** included in membership dues. **Conventions/Meetings:** annual conference (exhibits) ● annual convention and seminar (exhibits) - always spring ● annual meeting - always spring.

1200 ■ Women's International Network of Utility Professionals (WiNUP)
PO Box 817
Fergus Falls, MN 56538-0817
Ph: (218)731-1651 (320)284-2299
Fax: (320)284-2299
E-mail: drexler@runestone.net
URL: http://www.winup.org
Contact: Theresa Drexler, Exec. Dir.
Founded: 1923. **Members:** 250. **Membership Dues:** international, $66 (annual) ● members-at-large, $4 (annual) ● chapter (based on state chapters), $4-$15 (annual). **Staff:** 1. **Budget:** $40,000. **Local Groups:** 15. **Description:** Women and men holding positions connected with the electrical industry or allied fields in roles such as communicator, educator, information specialist, and researcher. Seeks to provide opportunities for professional growth and development; increase knowledge and understanding among members of issues affecting the electric and allied fields; and educate the public. Acts as a forum, promotes research, conducts workshops, and reviews new audiovisual and printed materials. **Awards:** Julia Kiene Fellowship in Electrical Energy. **Frequency:** annual. **Type:** scholarship. **Recipient:** to students engaging in graduate work toward an advanced degree in any phase of electrical energy ● Louisan Mamer Scholarship. **Type:** scholarship. **Recipient:** for advanced education in the energy field ● Lyle Mamer Fellowship. **Frequency:** annual. **Type:** scholarship. **Recipient:** to students engaging in graduate work toward an advanced degree in any phase of electrical energy ● Member Scholarship. **Frequency:** annual. **Type:** scholarship. **Recipient:** to a member who desires to further his/her education. **Formerly:** (2001) Electrical Women's Roundtable. **Publications:** *Connection*, quarterly. Newsletter. Addresses the efficient use of electrical energy from an administrative standpoint. **Price:** included in membership dues. Alternate Formats: online ● *Energy Update*. Bulletin. Alternate Formats: online ● Membership Directory, annual. **Circulation:** 500 ● Brochures. **Conventions/Meetings:** annual conference.

1201 ■ World Sign Associates (WSA)
Address Unknown since 2008
Founded: 1947. **Members:** 170. **Membership Dues:** company, $70 (monthly). **Staff:** 3. **Budget:** $450,000. **Regional Groups:** 8. **Description:** Custom electrical sign manufacturers. Works to promote and protect the electrical sign industry. Conducts seminars on sales techniques, manufacturing, and labor relations; sponsors educational programs on sign construction, maintenance, new products, and technology. **Publications:** Brochure ● Manuals ● Newsletter, quarterly. **Conventions/Meetings:** annual conference.

Electronic Publishing

1202 ■ Electronic Literature Organization (ELO)
Maryland Inst. for Tech. in the Humanities
B0131 McKeldin Lib.
Univ. of Maryland
College Park, MD 20742
Ph: (301)314-6545
E-mail: hdevinney@gmail.com
URL: http://www.eliterature.org
Contact: Helen DeVinney, Managing Dir.
Founded: 1999. **Membership Dues:** basic, $25 (annual) ● student, $15 (annual) ● contributing, $50 (annual). **Languages:** English, Spanish. **Description:** Strives to facilitate and promote the writing, publishing, and reading of literature in electronic media. **Projects:** Preservation, Archiving and Dissemination. **Publications:** *Acid-Free Bits: Recommendations for Long-Lasting Electronic Literature*. Pamphlet. **Price:** free. Alternate Formats: online ● *Born-Again Bits: A Framework for Migrating Electronic Literature*. Report. **Price:** free. Alternate Formats: online ● *Electronic Literature Directory*. Alternate Formats: online ● *State of the Arts*. Book. **Price:** free. Alternate Formats: online; CD-ROM.

Electronics

1203 ■ AeA - Advancing the Business of Technology (AeA)
601 Pennsylvania Ave. NW, North Bldg., Ste.600
Washington, DC 20004
Ph: (202)682-9110
Free: (800)284-4232
Fax: (202)682-9111
E-mail: csc@aeanet.org
URL: http://www.aeanet.org
Contact: William T. Archey, Pres./CEO
Founded: 1943. **Members:** 3,500. **Staff:** 110. **Regional Groups:** 18. **State Groups:** 20. **Multinational. Description:** High-tech trade association representing the technology spectrum from software, semiconductors and computer, to Internet technology, advanced electronics and telecommunications systems and services; works as voice of the U.S. technology community. **Libraries: Type:** reference. **Holdings:** books, periodicals. **Awards:** AEA Medal of Achievement. **Frequency:** annual. **Type:** medal ● Legislator of the Year. **Frequency:** annual. **Type:** recognition. **Computer Services:** Mailing lists, of members. **Committees:** Customs; Environment and Occupational Health; Europe; Export Controls; Government Business; Human Resources; Industry in Japan; Industry Statistics; International Competitiveness; Membership and Council Affairs; National Competitiveness; Public Affairs; State; Tax; Technology, Manufacturing, and Infrastructure; Total Quality Commitment; Trade and Investment; World-Class Work Force. **Formerly:** West Coast Electronics Manufacturers Association; Western Electronics Manufacturers Association. **Publications:** *Cybercities: A City-by-City Overview of the High-Technology Industry*. Reprint. Includes data on high-tech employment, wages, establishments, and payroll since 1993 for nation's top sixty technology metropolitan areas. ● *CyberEducation* ● *Cybernation 2.0*. Evaluates 60 global technology markets and assesses the competitiveness of the U.S. high-tech industry. **Price:** $95.00 for members; $190.00 for nonmembers ● *Cyberstates*, annual. Provides national and state tech trends on employment, exports, and venture capital investments. ● Surveys.

1204 ■ Asian American MultiTechnology Association (AAMA)
PO Box 7522
Menlo Park, CA 94026-7522
Ph: (650)738-1480
Fax: (650)738-1486
E-mail: aama@aamasv.com
URL: http://www.aamasv.com
Contact: Ms. Leilynne Fong, Exec. Dir.
Founded: 1979. **Members:** 1,100. **Membership Dues:** student, $25 (annual) ● individual, $100 (annual) ● life, $1,000 ● corporate (gold), $1,000 (annual) ● corporate (platinum), $5,000 (annual) ● corporate (diamond), $10,000 (annual). **Description:** Promotes the success of the Asia America region's technology enterprises. Through its diverse programs ranging from monthly Speakers Series to the Asia-Silicon Valley Technology Investment Conference, the association provides a forum in which members can network, exchange ideas and share resources to promote and build one another's companies and careers, ultimately benefiting the larger Pacific Rim technological community. **Awards:** Entrepreneurial and Community Leadership. **Frequency:** annual. **Type:** recognition. **Programs:** AAMA China Expansion; Annual Connect Conference; Charter Member; Monthly Speaker Series; Strategic Alliances; VC/Entrepreneur. **Conventions/Meetings:** annual banquet ● annual Pacific Rim Conference.

1205 ■ Association for High Technology Distribution (AHTD)
N19 W24400 Riverwood Dr.
Waukesha, WI 53188
Ph: (262)696-3490
Fax: (262)523-9091
E-mail: ahtd@ahtd.org
URL: http://www.ahtd.org
Contact: George Otte Jr., Pres.
Founded: 1985. **Members:** 280. **Staff:** 4. **Description:** High technology distributors and manufacturing affiliates. Promotes an open forum for discussion among members of the industrial automation high technology distribution industry. **Formerly:** (1997) Association of High Tech Distributors; (2004) Association for High Tech Distribution. **Publications:** *AHTD Quarterly Profitability Report*. Alternate Formats: online ● *Association of High Tech Distributors Network Newsletter*, quarterly ● *The Five Pillars of Financial Success in Distribution*. Report. Alternate Formats: online ● *Innovations*, monthly. Newsletter. Alternate Formats: online ● *Profile for a Successful ASP/Manufacturer Partnership Selling Technology Based Products*. Brochure. **Price:** free. Alternate Formats: online ● Membership Directory, periodic ● Directories. Alternate Formats: online. **Conventions/Meetings:** semiannual meeting - always spring and fall.

1206 ■ Association of Loudspeaker Manufacturers and Acoustics International (ALMA International)
PO Box 180093
Boston, MA 02118
Ph: (617)314-6977
Fax: (617)848-9935
E-mail: management@almainternational.org
URL: http://www.almainternational.org
Contact: Stu Lumsden, Pres.
Founded: 1964. **Members:** 125. **Membership Dues:** full, $500 (annual) ● subsidiary, educational, $225 (annual) ● individual, $100 (annual) ● student, $35 (annual). **Staff:** 3. **Description:** A global organization consisting of companies of all sizes, individual consultants and students. Aims to provide the loudspeaker industry a forum for the exchange of technical information to continually improve the design and manufacture of loudspeakers and related products. **Awards:** **Type:** recognition. **Formerly:** (2002) American Loudspeaker Manufacturers Association. **Publications:** *ALMANews*, semiannual, winter and spring. Newsletter. **Advertising:** accepted. **Conventions/Meetings:** semiannual general assembly and seminar (exhibits) ● symposium and seminar.

1207 ■ Blue-ray Disc Association (BDA)
c/o Makoto Morise, Sec.
10 Universal City Plz., T-100
Universal City, CA 91608
Ph: (818)301-1891
Fax: (818)301-1893
E-mail: morisem@us.panasonic.com
URL: http://www.blu-raydisc.com
Contact: Makoto Morise, Sec.
Founded: 2002. **Members:** 70. **Membership Dues:** contributor, $20,000 (annual) ● general, $3,000 (annual). **Multinational. Description:** Promotes the interest in creating, upholding and adopting the Blue-ray Disc formats in optical storage devices. Encourages research, development and manufacturing of any Blue-ray Disc products in the market. Ensures BD products are implemented by licensees according to the intent of the specifications. **Computer Services:** Information services, technical and product information ● online services, product category. **Committees:** Compliance; Joint Technical; Promotion. **Working Groups:** BD ROM Physical Specifications; File System and Command Set; Systems Compatibility; Test Specification; Verification Service. **Publications:** *Deep Blu*. Newsletter. Contains news and commentary about Blu-ray Disc. Alternate Formats: online.

1208 ■ Chinese American Semiconductor Professional Association (CASPA)
3555 Ryder St.
Santa Clara, CA 95051
Ph: (408)245-5638
Fax: (408)245-5638
E-mail: caspa@ix.netcom.com
URL: http://www.caspa.com
Contact: Lie-Szu Juang, Pres.
Founded: 1991. **Membership Dues:** life, $100 ● general, $20 (annual) ● overseas, $30 (annual). **Multinational. Description:** Provides networking and business expansion. Facilitates collaboration and communication among professionals and companies in the semiconductor industry. **Computer Services:** Mailing lists. **Publications:** Newsletter, quarterly. Alternate Formats: online ● Newsletter, biweekly. Alternate Formats: online ● Proceedings, annual.

1209 ■ Consumer Electronics Association (CEA)
1919 S Eads St.
Arlington, VA 22202
Ph: (703)907-7600 (703)907-7650
Free: (866)858-1555
Fax: (703)907-7675
E-mail: cea@ce.org
URL: http://www.ce.org
Contact: Gary Shapiro, Pres./CEO
Members: 2,200. **Membership Dues:** regular - minimum (based on annual product sales), $750 (annual) ● regular - maximum (based on annual product sales), $30,000 (annual) ● retailer - minimum (based on annual product sales), $350 (annual) ● retailer - maximum (based on annual product sales), $20,000 (annual) ● dealer, in U.S. and Canada, $399-$499 (annual) ● mobile electronic division associate, $150-$3,500 (annual) ● international affiliate, $500 (annual) ● associate - minimum (based on annual product sales), $1,000 (annual) ● associate - maximum (based on annual product sales), $35,000 (annual). **Description:** Manufacturers of consumer technology and electronics products. Strives to aid members in growth through connections, education, exposure, and by providing information. Hosts workshops and educational programs. **Awards:** Demmy Awards. **Frequency:** annual. **Type:** recognition. **Recipient:** for excellence in demonstration material ● Mark of Excellence Awards. **Frequency:** annual. **Type:** recognition. **Recipient:** to manufacturers, distributors, and installing dealers. **Divisions:** Communications; Market Research; PARA; Public Policy; Technical Education and Services. **Absorbed:** (2004) Professional Audiovideo Retailers Association. **Publications:** *Consumer Electronics Vision*, bimonthly. Magazine. **Advertising:** accepted. Alternate Formats: online.

1210 ■ Electronic Components Certification Board (ECCB)
c/o Mr. Joe V. Chapman, Sec.-Treas.
PO Box 9041
Midland, TX 79708
Ph: (432)697-9970
Fax: (915)694-5705
E-mail: info@eccb.org
URL: http://www.eccb.org
Contact: Mr. Joe V. Chapman, Sec.-Treas.
Founded: 1982. **Members:** 18. **Staff:** 3. **Description:** Users and suppliers of electronic components; interested individuals. Monitors the activities of national and international standards-setting bodies, including the International Electrotechnical Commission, the Electronic Industries Association, and Underwriters Laboratories. **Publications:** Publishes standards and guides. **Conventions/Meetings:** semiannual meeting.

1211 ■ Electronic Distribution Show and Conference (EDS)
222 S Riverside Plz., Ste.2160
Chicago, IL 60606
Ph: (312)648-1140
Fax: (312)648-4282
E-mail: eds@edsc.org
URL: http://www.edsc.org
Contact: Gretchen Oie-Weghorst, Contact
Founded: 1937. **Members:** 500. **Staff:** 3. **Description:** Suppliers who sell to electronic distributors. Exhibitors at EDS are primarily manufacturers of electronic components (wire, cable, capacitors, resistors, batteries, etc; test equipment; accessories; publications; etc.) plus suppliers of goods and services used by distributors (software, insurance, bar code equipment, etc.).

1212 ■ Electronic Industries Alliance (EIA)
2500 Wilson Blvd.
Arlington, VA 22201
Ph: (703)907-7500 (703)907-7590
E-mail: mflanigan@eia.org
URL: http://www.eia.org
Contact: Matthew Flanigan, Interim Pres./CEO
Founded: 1924. **Members:** 1,500. **Staff:** 16. **Budget:** $26,000,000. **Description:** Seeks for the competitiveness of the American producer, represents all companies involved in the design and manufacture of electronic components, parts, systems and equipment for communications, industrial, government and consumer uses. **Councils:** Environmental Issues; Government Procurement Relations; Legislative Affairs. **Affiliated With:** Telecommunications Industry Association. **Absorbed:** (1965) Magnetic Reading Industry Association; (1974) Association of Electronic Manufacturers; (1979) Institute of High Fidelity. **Formerly:** (1950) Radio Manufacturers Association; (1953) Radio Television Manufacturers Association; (1957) Radio Electronics Television Manufacturers Association; (2001) Electronic Industries Association. **Publications:** *EIA Publications Index/EIA Trade Directory*, annual. Includes list of prices, descriptions, and ordering information. **Price:** free. **Conventions/Meetings:** annual conference - always fall ● annual convention - always spring ● annual roundtable.

1213 ■ Electronics Representatives Association (ERA)
300 W Adams St., Ste.617
Chicago, IL 60606
Ph: (312)527-3050
Free: (800)776-7377
Fax: (312)527-3783
E-mail: info@era.org
URL: http://www.era.org
Contact: Raymond J. Hall, Vice Chm.
Founded: 1935. **Members:** 1,000. **Membership Dues:** manufacturer, $595 (annual). **Staff:** 10. **Budget:** $1,400,000. **Local Groups:** 24. **Description:** Professional field sales organizations selling components and materials; computer, instrumentation, and data communications products; audiovisual, security, land/mobile communications and commercial sound components, and consumer products to the electronics industry. Sponsors insurance programs and

educational conference for members. **Libraries: Type:** not open to the public. **Holdings:** archival material. **Awards: Type:** recognition. **Formerly:** (1942) Representatives of Radio Parts Manufacturers; (1959) Representatives of Electronic Products Manufacturers. **Publications:** *Lines Available*, weekly. Bulletin. Lists of electronics manufacturers seeking representation for their lines. **Price:** included in membership dues; $449.00 for nonmembers. **Circulation:** 1,500. Alternate Formats: online ● *Locator of Professional Field Sales Organizations*, annual. Directory. Lists of electronics manufacturing sales firms representing the United States, the Caribbean, Canada, Europe, and the Far East. **Price:** $75.00. **Circulation:** 5,000 ● *Representor*, quarterly. Magazine. Covers association and industry news. **Price:** $24.00 for members; $48.00 for nonmembers. **Circulation:** 5,000. **Advertising:** accepted. Alternate Formats: online. **Conventions/Meetings:** annual Management and Marketing Conference (exhibits).

1214 ■ ETA International - Electronics Technicians Association, International (ETA)

5 Depot St.
Greencastle, IN 46135
Ph: (765)653-8262 (765)653-4301
Free: (800)288-3824
Fax: (765)653-4287
E-mail: eta@eta-i.org
URL: http://www.eta-i.org
Contact: Richard L. Glass, Pres.

Founded: 1978. **Members:** 5,000. **Membership Dues:** individual, $25 (annual) ● regular, outside U.S., $55 (annual) ● institution (includes 4 individuals), $250 (annual). **Staff:** 17. **Budget:** $650,000. **Regional Groups:** 1. **State Groups:** 1. **Local Groups:** 25. **National Groups:** 2. **Multinational. Description:** Skilled electronics technicians. Provides placement service; offers certification examinations for electronics technicians and satellite, fiber optics, and data cabling installers. Compiles wage and manpower statistics. Administers FCC Commercial License examinations and certification of computer network systems technicians and web and internet specialists. **Libraries: Type:** reference. **Holdings:** 300; audiovisuals, monographs, video recordings. **Subjects:** technical, business training, employment, customer relations. **Awards:** Educator of the Year Award. **Frequency:** annual. **Type:** recognition. **Recipient:** for an outstanding educator who has made significant contributions to the technical industry over the previous year ● President's Award. **Frequency:** annual. **Type:** recognition ● Technician of the Year Award. **Frequency:** annual. **Type:** recognition. **Computer Services:** database, electronic certification exam ● electronic publishing, high-tech news online ● online services, electronics technician examination quiz ● online services, membership and product ordering from the ETA website. **Telecommunication Services:** electronic bulletin board, TechTalk forums offer interactive communications for visitors. **Committees:** Audio Video Distribution; Avionics. **Divisions:** Antenna Experts Group; Certified Technicians; Communications Technicians; Electronic Educators; Satellite Dealers Association, Inc.; Shop Owners. **Absorbed:** (1996) Satellite Dealers Association Inc. **Publications:** *High Tech News*, monthly. Journal. Contains industry news, association news, listing of all newly certified technicians (20 categories). **Price:** $25.00/year. ISSN: 1092-9592. **Circulation:** 4,000. **Advertising:** accepted ● *Management Update*, monthly. Included in High Tech News. **Conventions/Meetings:** annual Service Retail Convention - seminar, on service of general electronics and retail servicers, as well as specific aspects of the master antenna and satellite television business (exhibits) ● annual workshop, for technician training and business management.

1215 ■ Fabless Semiconductor Association (FSA)

3 Lincoln Center
5430 LBJ Freeway, Ste.280
Dallas, TX 75240
Ph: (972)866-7579
Free: (888)322-5195
Fax: (972)239-2292
E-mail: jshelton@fsa.org
URL: http://www.fsa.org
Contact: Jodi Shelton, Exec. Dir.

Founded: 1994. **Membership Dues:** start-up supplier, semiconductor company (with $0 - 5 million annual revenues), $2,500 (annual) ● semiconductor company (with $5 - 50 million annual revenues), $5,000-$10,000 (annual) ● semiconductor company (with $50 - 100 million annual revenues), $15,000 (annual) ● semiconductor company (with $100 - 500 million annual revenues), $20,000 (annual) ● semiconductor company (with more than $500 million annual revenues), $25,000 (annual) ● supplier (3 years or greater), industry partner, $5,500 (annual) ● organization, association, government, educational partner, $3,500 (annual) ● individual partner, $1,000 (annual). **Multinational. Description:** Provides a forum for global collaboration between fabless companies and their partners. Identifies, debates, and discusses business issues. Provides members with research and resources. Works to enable fabless companies to gain greater market share and success. **Awards:** Best Financially Managed Company. **Frequency:** annual. **Type:** recognition. **Recipient:** to company that excelled most in terms of financial indices ● Dr. Morris Chang Exemplary Leadership Award. **Frequency:** annual. **Type:** recognition. **Recipient:** for outstanding achievement and unique contribution to the fabless sector ● Fabless Start-Up to Watch. **Frequency:** annual. **Type:** recognition. **Recipient:** to company that demonstrates the greatest likelihood of achieving the next phase of growth ● Industry's Most Respected Private Fabless Company. **Frequency:** annual. **Type:** recognition. **Recipient:** to private company most respected by members in terms of product, vision and strategy ● Industry's Most Respected Public Fabless Company. **Frequency:** annual. **Type:** recognition. **Recipient:** to public company most respected by members in terms of product, vision and strategy. **Computer Services:** Information services, semiconductor industry resources ● mailing lists. **Subcommittees:** Business Management Systems; Education; Intellectual Property; Mixed-Signal, RF Foundry; Modeling; SiP; Standard Foundry Process Qualification; Supply-Chain Performance.

1216 ■ HomePlug Powerline Alliance

2400 Camino Ramon, Ste.375
San Ramon, CA 94583
Ph: (925)275-6630
Fax: (925)886-3614
E-mail: help@homeplug.org
URL: http://www.homeplug.org
Contact: Matt Theall, Pres.

Founded: 2000. **Membership Dues:** participant, $15,000 (annual) ● adopter, $5,000 (annual). **Description:** Seeks to enable and promote rapid availability adoption and implementation of cost effective, interoperable and standards-based home powerline networks and products. Educates the business and consumer communities on the value of powerline networking products. Fosters competition in the development of new powerline networking products. **Publications:** *HomePlug Newsletter* (in Chinese, English, and Japanese). Contains news and other information on HomePlug AV products. **Price:** included in membership dues. Alternate Formats: online.

1217 ■ Industry Coalition on Technology Transfer (ICOTT)

Address Unknown since 2007

Founded: 1983. **Members:** 4. **Membership Dues:** trade association, $5,500 (annual). **Budget:** $25,000. **Description:** Members are American Association of Exporters and Importers, Electronic Industries Alliance, Semiconductor Equipment and Materials International, and Semiconductor Industry Association. Monitors and addresses U.S. regulations on technology transfer. **Affiliated With:** American Association of Exporters and Importers; Electronic Industries Alliance; SEMI International; Semiconductor Industry Association. **Conventions/Meetings:** monthly meeting.

1218 ■ International Association of Electronics Recyclers (IAER)

PO Box 16222
Albany, NY 12212-6222
Free: (888)989-4237
Fax: (877)989-4237
E-mail: info@iaer.org
URL: http://www.iaer.org
Contact: Peter R. Muscanelli, Chm./Founder/Pres.

Membership Dues: large company, $995 (annual) ● small and start-up company, $695 (annual) ● nonprofit organization, $495 (annual). **Multinational. Description:** Represents the interests of electronics recyclers and related organizations. **Publications:** *IAER Electronics Recycling Newsletter*, monthly. **Advertising:** accepted. Alternate Formats: online.

1219 ■ International Auto Sound Challenge Association (IASCA)

2129 S Ridgewood Ave.
South Daytona, FL 32119
Ph: (386)322-1551
Fax: (386)761-1740
E-mail: paul@iasca.com
URL: http://www.iasca.com
Contact: Paul Papadeas, Pres.

Founded: 1987. **Members:** 3,000. **Membership Dues:** individual, $25 (annual). **Staff:** 11. **Description:** Manufacturers, retailers, and representatives/distributors of auto stereos; other interested individuals. Promotes the automotive stereo industry; holds sound quality and security contests; conducts consumer education. **Awards: Type:** recognition. **Formerly:** (1989) National Autosound Challenge Association. **Publications:** Newsletter, monthly ● Also publishes marketing reports. **Conventions/Meetings:** semiannual Consumer Electronics - show and workshop ● annual International Electronics Expo - meeting.

1220 ■ International Society of Certified Electronics Technicians (ISCET)

3608 Pershing Ave.
Fort Worth, TX 76107-4527
Ph: (817)921-9101
Free: (800)946-0201
Fax: (817)921-3741
E-mail: info@iscet.org
URL: http://www.iscet.org
Contact: Mack Blakely, Exec. Dir.

Founded: 1970. **Members:** 2,000. **Membership Dues:** individual, $35 (annual) ● individual, $60 (biennial) ● life, $425. **Staff:** 8. **Budget:** $300,000. **Languages:** English, Spanish. **Description:** Technicians in 50 countries who have been certified by the society. Seeks to provide a fraternal bond among certified electronics technicians, raise their public image, and improve the effectiveness of industry education programs for technicians. Offers training programs in new electronics information. Maintains library of service literature for consumer electronic equipment, including manuals and schematics for out-of-date equipment. Offers all FCC licenses. Sponsors testing program for certification of electronics technicians in the fields of audio, communications, computer, consumer, industrial, medical electronics, radar, radio-television, and video. **Awards: Type:** recognition. **Computer Services:** Mailing lists. **Publications:** *ISCET Update*, quarterly. Newsletter. Includes job listings. **Price:** included in membership dues. **Circulation:** 2,000. **Advertising:** accepted ● *ProService Magazine*. **Conventions/Meetings:** annual National Professional Service Convention - convention and trade show, electronics technical seminars, management seminars, and sponsored events (exhibits) ● periodic trade show.

1221 ■ IPC - Association Connecting Electronics Industries

3000 Lakeside Dr., 309 S
Bannockburn, IL 60015
Ph: (847)615-7100
Fax: (847)615-7105

E-mail: dmcguirk@ipc.org
URL: http://www.ipc.org
Contact: Dennis P. McGuirk, Pres./CEO
Founded: 1957. **Members:** 2,850. **Membership Dues:** primary site, $1,000 (annual) ● additional facility, $800 (annual) ● independent PCB fabricator, independent EMSI provider, $600 (annual) ● government agency, academic technical liaison, $250 (annual). **Staff:** 100. **Budget:** $11,500,000. **Description:** Company members are producers and users of printed circuit boards and electronics assemblies. Supports over 100 committees writing industry standards, guidelines, and specifications. Compiles statistics; conducts research programs. Provides training and education programs to enhance workforce development and industry competitiveness. **Libraries: Type:** reference. **Holdings:** archival material, artwork, clippings, periodicals. **Subjects:** printed circuit boards and assemblies. **Councils:** Assembly Market Research; California Circuits Association; Designers; SMEMA; Technology Market Research. **Formerly:** (1978) Institute of Printed Circuits; (1999) Institute for Interconnecting and Packaging Electronic Circuits. **Publications:** *IPC Review*, monthly. Newsletter. **Circulation:** 6,000 ● Also publishes standards, guidelines, and specifications. **Conventions/Meetings:** annual Electronics Assembly Process Exhibition and Conference - convention and trade show (exhibits) ● annual IPC Printed Circuits Expo - conference and trade show (exhibits).

1222 ■ JEDEC
2500 Wilson Blvd., Ste.220
Arlington, VA 22201-3834
Ph: (703)907-7515
Fax: (703)907-7583
E-mail: johnk@jedec.org
URL: http://www.jedec.org
Contact: John J. Kelly, Pres.
Founded: 1958. **Members:** 250. **Membership Dues:** company (1 committee participation), $4,000 (annual) ● company (2 committees), $6,000 (annual) ● company (3 committees), $8,000 (annual) ● company (4 or more committees), $10,000 (annual). **Staff:** 10. **Budget:** $2,500,000. **Description:** Manufacturers and users of semiconductors and solid state products concerned with technical matters. Develops standards, test methods, and specifications for solid state components. Administers type designation system, assigning and identifying part numbers to solid state components. Maintains liaison with U.S. government agencies and foreign trade associations, like JEITA and IEC. Founding sector of Electronic Industries Alliance. Maintains 50 engineering committees. **Affiliated With:** Electronic Industries Alliance. **Formerly:** (2003) Joint Electron Device Engineering Council. **Publications:** *EIA/JEDEC Standards and Engineering Publications*, annual. Catalog. **Price:** free. **Conventions/Meetings:** quarterly board meeting ● annual meeting - always spring.

1223 ■ National Electronic Distributors Association (NEDA)
1111 Alderman Dr., Ste.400
Alpharetta, GA 30005
Ph: (678)393-9990
Fax: (678)393-9998
E-mail: admin@nedassoc.org
URL: http://www.nedassoc.org
Contact: Robin B. Gray Jr., Exec. VP
Founded: 1937. **Members:** 250. **Membership Dues:** distributor (minimum), associate, $750 (annual) ● distributor (maximum), $50,000 (annual) ● international distributor, $1,500 (annual) ● manufacturer, $1,000-$5,000 (annual). **Staff:** 8. **Budget:** $1,300,000. **Local Groups:** 2. **Description:** Represents authorized distributors and manufacturers of electronic components. Conducts research. Compiles statistical reports and surveys. **Awards:** Channel Marketing Awards. **Frequency:** annual. **Type:** recognition. **Recipient:** for distributors and manufacturers. **Divisions:** Maintenance, Repair and Operations; Test, Measurement, and Control. **Affiliated With:** National Association of Wholesaler-Distributors. **Formerly:** (1937) National Radio Parts Distributors. **Publications:** *Distribution Business Index Report*, monthly. **Price:** $595.00 /year for nonmembers ● *Distributor Productivity Report*, annual. **Price:** $295.00 for non-participating members; $395.00 for nonmembers ● *NEDA News*, monthly. Newsletter. **Price:** available to members only. **Advertising:** accepted. Alternate Formats: online ● Membership Directory, annual. **Price:** $395.00 for nonmembers; $30.00 for members. **Advertising:** accepted. **Conventions/Meetings:** annual conference, executive - always fall ● annual Electronic Distribution Show - trade show (exhibits) - May, Las Vegas.

1224 ■ National Electronics Service Dealers Association (NESDA)
3608 Pershing Ave.
Fort Worth, TX 76107-4527
Ph: (817)921-9061
Fax: (817)921-3741
E-mail: info@nesda.com
URL: http://www.nesda.com
Contact: Mack Blakely, Exec. Dir.
Founded: 1963. **Members:** 1,900. **Membership Dues:** full, $240 (annual). **Staff:** 6. **Budget:** $400,000. **Regional Groups:** 15. **State Groups:** 22. **Local Groups:** 3. **Description:** Local and state electronic service associations and companies representing 4200 individuals. Provides educational assistance in electronic training to public schools; supplies technical service information on business management training to electronic service dealers. Offers certification, apprenticeship, and training programs through International Society of Certified Electronics Technicians. Compiles statistics on electronics service business; conducts technical service and business management seminars. **Awards:** Associate Leadership Excellence Award. **Frequency:** annual. **Type:** recognition. **Recipient:** for an associate organization ● Best Local Publication. **Frequency:** annual. **Type:** recognition. **Recipient:** for outstanding publication ● Everett Pershing Memorial Membership Award. **Frequency:** annual. **Type:** recognition. **Recipient:** for an outstanding member of NESDA ● Leo Shumavon Award. **Frequency:** annual. **Type:** recognition. **Recipient:** for NESDA members ● M.L. Fineburgh, Sr., Award of Excellence. **Frequency:** annual. **Type:** recognition. **Recipient:** for an individual who performs exceptional service to NESDA ● National Friend of Service. **Frequency:** annual. **Type:** recognition. **Recipient:** for a national company or individual ● Outstanding Associate President Award. **Frequency:** annual. **Type:** recognition. **Recipient:** for an associate organization president ● Outstanding Committee Chairperson Award. **Frequency:** annual. **Type:** recognition. **Recipient:** for an outstanding committee chairperson ● Person of the Year. **Frequency:** annual. **Type:** recognition. **Recipient:** for an outstanding individual ● Richard Mildenberger Outstanding NESDA Officer. **Frequency:** annual. **Type:** recognition. **Recipient:** for outstanding NESDA officers. **Computer Services:** Mailing lists. **Committees:** Apprenticeship; Business Management; CATV; Consumer Affairs; Extended Warranties; Government Relations; Industry Relations; Serviceability; Surveys and Facts; Warranty Standards. **Absorbed:** (1986) National Association of Television and Electronic Servicers of America. **Formerly:** (1973) National Electronic Associations; (1984) National Electronic Service Dealers Association. **Publications:** *Industry Alert*, periodic. Newsletter. Contains information important to electronics servicers. **Price:** included in membership dues. **Circulation:** 1,000 ● *Legislative Alert*, periodic. **Price:** included in membership dues. **Circulation:** 1,000 ● *NESDA—Update*, bimonthly. Newsletter. Provides information on legislation, regulations, legal, and industry news. **Price:** included in membership dues. **Circulation:** 1,000 ● *Pro-service Directory and Yearbook*, annual. Lists parts distributors, service contract vendors/administrators, software/systems vendors, and manufacturers. **Price:** $25.00. **Circulation:** 5,000. **Advertising:** accepted ● *Proservice Magazine*, bimonthly. **Price:** included in membership dues. Alternate Formats: online. **Conventions/Meetings:** annual National Professional Service Convention - convention and trade show, suppliers to the service industry (exhibits) ● annual Western Regional Convention.

1225 ■ National Systems Contractors Association (NSCA)
625 1st St. SE, Ste.420
Cedar Rapids, IA 52401
Ph: (319)366-6722
Free: (800)446-6722
Fax: (319)366-4164
E-mail: nsca@nsca.org
URL: http://www.nsca.org
Contact: Christy Block, Dir. of Marketing and Communication
Founded: 1980. **Members:** 3,000. **Membership Dues:** corporate, $400 (annual). **Staff:** 18. **Budget:** $2,500,000. **Description:** Contractors for electronics systems and for sound and communications equipment. Aims to provide a means for evaluation and analysis on matters of concern to sound and electronics systems contractors and to obtain group benefits. Encourages communication and exchange of ideas among members; offers educational programs and in-house training. **Libraries: Type:** reference. **Holdings:** articles. **Subjects:** business, sales, marketing, management. **Computer Services:** Mailing lists. **Formerly:** (1994) National Sound and Communications Association. **Publications:** *Building Connections*, bimonthly. Newsletter ● *Business Owner*, bimonthly. Newsletter. **Conventions/Meetings:** annual Systems Integration Expo - convention (exhibits).

1226 ■ North America Chinese Semiconductor Association (NACSA)
PO Box 61086
Sunnyvale, CA 94088-1086
Ph: (408)428-5112
E-mail: nacsaman@yahoo.com
URL: http://www.nacsa.com
Contact: Greg Ye, Dir.
Founded: 1996. **Members:** 1,000. **Membership Dues:** general, $25 (annual). **Multinational. Description:** Represents the interests of professionals dedicated to the advancement of Chinese professionals in high-tech industries. Strengthens networking among professionals. Fosters entrepreneurship among ethnic Chinese. Promotes the exchange in the global semiconductor and information technology industries. **Special Interest Groups:** Entrepreneurship. **Publications:** Annual Report. **Price:** included in membership dues.

1227 ■ North American Retail Dealers Association (NARDA)
4700 W Lake Ave.
Glenview, IL 60025
Ph: (847)375-4713
Free: (800)621-0298
Fax: (866)879-7505
E-mail: nardasvc@narda.com
URL: http://www.narda.com
Contact: Thomas Drake, Pres./CEO
Founded: 1943. **Members:** 2,000. **Membership Dues:** regular, $295 (annual) ● affiliate, $4,500 (annual) ● associate, $8,000 (annual) ● allied, $2,000 (annual). **Staff:** 8. **Description:** Firms engaged in the retailing of electronic and electrical devices and components. Promotes and represents members' interests. Makes available services to members including: legal and technical consulting; employee screening; bank card processing; long-distance phone discounts; financial statements analysis; in-store promotion kits; customer check authorization. Advocates for members' interests before federal regulatory bodies; disseminates information on new regulations affecting members. Conducts educational programs. **Libraries: Type:** not open to the public. **Holdings:** books. **Subjects:** retail, general management. **Awards:** NARDA Scholarship Foundation Awards. **Frequency:** annual. **Type:** scholarship. **Recipient:** to members pursuing higher education in business ● Pinnacle of Promotion. **Frequency:** annual. **Type:** recognition. **Recipient:** for best retail promotion. **Programs:** CEA CEKnowHow; CEA Small Business; CFC Refrigerant Recovery Certification; Foundation Scholarships; Institute of Retail and Service Center Management; University; Vision. **Publications:** *Compensation and Benefits Report* ● *Cost of Doing Business Report* ● *Cost of Doing Business*

Survey ● *Custom Employee Manual* ● *NARDA Independent Retailer*, monthly. Newsletter. **Price:** included in membership dues. **Circulation:** 1,700 ● *Who's Who*, annual. Directory ● Audiotape ● Newsletter, biweekly. **Price:** included in membership dues. **Conventions/Meetings:** semiannual Institute of Retail and Service Management - conference and trade show.

1228 ■ SEMI International (SEMI)
3081 Zanker Rd.
San Jose, CA 95134
Ph: (408)943-6900
Fax: (408)428-9600
E-mail: semihq@semi.org
URL: http://wps2a.semi.org/wps/portal
Contact: Stanley T. Myers, Pres./CEO
Founded: 1970. **Members:** 1,400. **Membership Dues:** corporate, $2,000-$60,000 (annual) ● associate, $1,000-$14,000 (annual) ● allied, $500 (annual) ● affiliate, $750-$7,500 (annual) ● start-up company, $500 (annual) ● individual, $150 (annual) ● student, $45 (annual) ● retired, $75 (annual). **Staff:** 125. **Multinational. Description:** Firms, corporations, and individuals engaged in supplying fabrication equipment, materials, or services to the semiconductor industry. Develops voluntary technical standards for the semiconductor industry. Conducts SEMI Technical Education Programs (STEP) and annual Information Services Seminar (ISS) forecast. Operates industry program; offers market statistics. **Awards:** Akira Inoue Award. **Type:** recognition. **Recipient:** for individuals in industry and academia ● Bob Graham Award. **Type:** recognition. **Recipient:** for outstanding individuals in marketing ● SEMMY Awards. **Frequency:** annual. **Type:** recognition. **Recipient:** for outstanding contributions by equipment and materials suppliers to the semiconductor industry. **Computer Services:** Online services, DIALOG and RLIN searches for members on a cost recovery basis. **Committees:** Education; Government Relations; Information Services; Programs; SEMMY Award; Shows; Standards. **Formerly:** (1989) Semiconductor Equipment and Materials Institute; (2002) Semiconductor Equipment and Materials International. **Publications:** *Book of SEMI Standards*, annual. Compendium developed by committees of industry volunteers providing complete listings of approved semiconductor manufacturing equipment. **Price:** $150.00 for complete eleven-volume set ● *Information Strategy Symposium: The Business Outlook for the Semiconductor Equipment and Materials Industry*, annual. Contains economic forecasts. **Price:** $450.00 for members (with discount). Also Cited As: *ISS Forecast* ● *SEMI Japan News*, monthly. Newsletter. Covers the institute's activities in Japan. Written in Japanese. **Price:** free for members ● *SEMICON Technical Proceedings*, 7/year. Book. Contains information from the Institute's technical symposia held in Europe, Japan, Korea, and the United States. **Price:** $55.00/book (with discount for members) ● Membership Directory, annual. Lists of companies and individuals providing equipment, materials, and services to the semiconductor industry. **Price:** $100.00 for members (with discount) ● Also publishes Silicon Valley genealogy chart; produces posters, films, and videos. **Conventions/Meetings:** meeting and symposium - 7/year.

1229 ■ Semiconductor Industry Association (SIA)
181 Metro Dr., Ste.450
San Jose, CA 95110-1344
Ph: (408)436-6600
Fax: (408)436-6646
E-mail: mailbox@sia-online.org
URL: http://www.sia-online.org/home.cfm
Contact: George M. Scalise, Pres.
Founded: 1977. **Members:** 40. **Staff:** 12. **Budget:** $4,400,000. **Description:** Companies that produce semiconductor products such as discrete components, integrated circuits, and microprocessors. Compiles industry trade statistics. Affiliate: Semiconductor Research Corporation and SEMATECH. **Libraries: Type:** reference. **Awards: Type:** recognition. **Committees:** Communications; Environmental; Facilities and Building Standards; Law; Occupational Health; Technology; Trade and Public Policy; Trade Statistics. **Publications:** *Annual Databook*, annual ● *Circuit*, quarterly. Newsletter. **Price:** free. **Circulation:** 3,000 ● *Semiconductor Industry Association—Status Report and Industry Directory*. Provides review of association-sponsored programs; includes graphs and charts of key industry statistics and analyses by industry experts. **Price;** $85.00 ● *World Semiconductor Trade Statistics*, semiannual. Reports. Provides data on orders and shipments of U.S., European, and Japanese semiconductor manufacturers in all world markets. **Price:** $2,200.00/year ● Proceedings ● Reports ● Also publishes essays. **Conventions/Meetings:** quarterly executive committee meeting ● annual meeting and dinner, with forecast.

1230 ■ Variable Electronic Components Institute (VECI)
PO Box 1070
Vista, CA 92085-1070
Ph: (760)631-0178
Fax: (760)631-7827
E-mail: veci2@cox.net
URL: http://www.veci-vrci.com
Contact: Stanley Kukawka, Exec. Dir.
Founded: 1960. **Members:** 30. **Multinational. Description:** Compiles market statistics and develops industry standards for potentiometers and encoders. **Formerly:** (1964) Precision Potentiometer Manufacturers Association; (1998) Variable Resistive Components Institute. **Conventions/Meetings:** semiannual meeting.

1231 ■ Wire and Cable Industry Suppliers Association (WCISA)
1867 W Market St.
Akron, OH 44313
Ph: (330)864-2122
Fax: (330)864-5298
E-mail: info@wcisa.org
Contact: Michael J. McNulty, Exec. Dir.
Founded: 1996. **Members:** 90. **Membership Dues:** company, $300 (annual). **Multinational. Description:** Represents the interests of suppliers of wire and cable machinery and equipment, materials, process accessories and controls in North America. Promotes members' products and services by providing the members with promotion, representation, networking, social opportunities and services at domestic and international wire and cable trade shows and conferences. **Publications:** Membership Directory. Alternate Formats: online.

Elevators

1232 ■ Elevator Escalator Safety Foundation (EESF)
362 Pinehill Dr.
Mobile, AL 36606-1715
Ph: (251)479-2199
Free: (888)RIDE-SAFE
Fax: (251)479-7099
E-mail: info@eesf.org
URL: http://www.eesf.org
Contact: Barbara Allen, Exec. Dir.
Description: Promotes public awareness on the safe and proper use of elevators, escalators and moving walks through informational programs; seeks to educate young children, adults and seniors in order to reduce accidents and incidents. Sponsors the National Elevator Escalator Safety Awareness Week. **Programs:** A Safe Ride; Safe-T Rider. **Publications:** *Insider*, periodic. Newsletter. Alternate Formats: online ● Brochures. Alternate Formats: online.

Employee Benefits

1233 ■ American Society of Pension Professionals and Actuaries (ASPPA)
4245 N Fairfax Dr., Ste.750
Arlington, VA 22203
Ph: (703)516-9300
Fax: (703)516-9308
E-mail: asppa@asppa.org
URL: http://www.aspa.org
Contact: Brian H. Graff Esq., Exec. Dir./CEO
Founded: 1966. **Members:** 6,000. **Membership Dues:** affiliate, $346 (annual) ● designated, reinstatement, $440 (annual) ● retired, government employee, $50 (annual). **Staff:** 27. **Local Groups:** 14. **Description:** Aims to educate pension actuaries, consultants, administrators, and other benefits professionals. Seeks to preserve and enhance the private pension system as part of the development of a cohesive and coherent national retirement income policy. **Awards:** Educator's Award. **Frequency:** annual. **Type:** recognition. **Recipient:** to an outstanding educator from the ASPPA membership who has made a significant contribution to retirement plan education ● Harry T. Eidson Founder's Award. **Frequency:** annual. **Type:** recognition. **Recipient:** for individuals who have made the greatest contribution to ASPPA and/or private pension system ● Martin Rosenberg Academic Achievement Award. **Frequency:** semiannual. **Type:** monetary. **Recipient:** for top performing candidates on credential education and exams ● Presidential Scholarship. **Frequency:** annual. **Type:** scholarship. **Recipient:** to deserving junior year student. **Computer Services:** Mailing lists, of members. **Committees:** Conference and Programs; Continuing Education; Education and Examination; Government Affairs; Membership. **Programs:** Finance and Budget; Interpersonal Relations; Long Range Planning; Nominating; NRIP; Technology. **Formerly:** (2005) American Society of Pension Actuaries. **Publications:** *ASSPA Journal*, bimonthly. Newsletter. Provides semi-annual listing of proposed and final regulations. **Circulation:** 6,000 ● *The Candidate Connection*, 3/year. Alternate Formats: online ● Yearbook, annual. Contains names, addresses, phone numbers, and companies of members. **Price:** available to members only. **Circulation:** 5,000. **Conventions/Meetings:** annual conference (exhibits) ● annual meeting, provides a unique, interactive environment for retirement sales and investment professionals (exhibits) - 2009 Mar. 22-24, San Diego, CA; 2010 Mar. 14-16, Orlando, FL.

1234 ■ Council on Employee Benefits (CEB)
4910 Moorland Ln.
Bethesda, MD 20814
Ph: (301)664-5940
Fax: (301)664-5944
E-mail: scanfield@ceb.org
URL: http://www.ceb.org
Contact: Shane Canfield, Exec. Dir.
Founded: 1946. **Members:** 225. **Membership Dues:** company, $1,500 (annual). **Staff:** 3. **Description:** Employers seeking informal exchange of experiences and information on the design, financing, and administration of employee benefit programs, both domestic and international. Provides a medium for the exchange of ideas, information, and statistics; sponsors or conducts research projects on benefits; makes known its views on legislative matters affecting employee benefits. Conducts research. **Committees:** Finance; Information Exchange; Planning; Professional Placement. **Formerly:** (1950) Federation of Employee Benefit Association; (1961) Council on Employee Benefit Plans. **Publications:** Newsletter ● Membership Directory. Alternate Formats: online. **Conventions/Meetings:** annual Benefits and the Bottom Line - conference, for members only - held in spring ● annual meeting.

1235 ■ Employee Benefit Research Institute (EBRI)
2121 K St. NW, Ste.600
Washington, DC 20037-1896
Ph: (202)659-0670
Fax: (202)775-6312
E-mail: info@ebri.org
URL: http://www.ebri.org
Contact: Dallas L. Salisbury, Pres./CEO
Founded: 1978. **Members:** 142. **Membership Dues:** sustaining, $28,500 (annual) ● full, $15,000 (annual) ● associate, $7,500 (annual) ● contributing, $4,000 (annual) ● subscriber, $1,500 (annual). **Staff:** 14.

Budget: $3,000,000. **Description:** Corporations, consulting firms, banks, insurance companies, unions, and others with an interest in the future of employee benefit programs. Purpose is to contribute to the development of effective and responsible public policy in the field of employee benefits through research, publications, educational programs, seminars, and direct communication. Sponsors a broad range of studies on retirement income, health, disability, and other benefit programs; disseminates study results. Maintains research library with information on employee benefit programs. **Libraries: Type:** not open to the public. **Holdings:** 4,000; audiovisuals, books, clippings, monographs, periodicals. **Subjects:** employee benefits, retirement income, economic security, health insurance. **Awards:** The EBRI Lillywhite Award. **Frequency:** annual. **Type:** recognition. **Recipient:** for distinguished career in the investment management and employee benefits fields. **Committees:** Program. **Affiliated With:** American Savings Education Council. **Publications:** *EBRI Databook on Employee Benefits*, periodic. Handbook. **Price:** $99.00. Alternate Formats: online ● *EBRI Issue Brief*, monthly. Monograph. Provides evaluations of evolving employee benefit issues and trends and analyses of employee benefit program policies and proposals. **Price:** $25.00/issue. ISSN: 0887-137X. Alternate Formats: online ● *EBRI Notes*, monthly. Newsletter. Provides released employee benefit statistical findings. **Price:** $25.00/issue. ISSN: 1085-4452 ● *EBRI Pension Investment Report*, periodic. Provides data on assets in the private and public pension systems and the performance of pension investment. Covers historical data. **Price:** included in membership dues; $500.00/issue for nonmembers. ISSN: 0889-4396 ● *EBRI Policy Forums*, semiannual. Proceedings ● *Washington Bulletin*, biweekly. Includes information on congressional activities as they relate to employee benefits. **Price:** included in membership dues ● Also publishes consumer education series and policy studies.

1236 ■ Employers Association
3020 W Arrowood Rd.
Charlotte, NC 28273
Ph: (704)522-8011
Fax: (704)522-8105
E-mail: info@employersassoc.com
URL: http://www.employersassoc.com
Contact: Kenny L. Colbert SPHR, Pres.

Founded: 1958. **Members:** 850. **Membership Dues:** company, $475-$3,100 (annual). **Staff:** 20. **Budget:** $3,900,000. **Regional Groups:** 1. **Description:** Works to promote human resources services. Provides information on wage and salary, workers compensation, and worker safety; conducts human resources and computer training programs; offers consulting and industrial relations services. **Convention/Meeting:** none. **Libraries: Type:** reference; not open to the public. **Holdings:** articles, audiovisuals, books, clippings, periodicals. **Subjects:** human resources. **Awards:** Babcock Award. **Frequency:** annual. **Type:** recognition. **Recipient:** for human resources professionals. **Publications:** *Management Report*, monthly. Newsletter.

1237 ■ Employers Council on Flexible Compensation (ECFC)
927 15th St. NW, Ste.1000
Washington, DC 20005
Ph: (202)659-4300
Fax: (202)371-1467
E-mail: info@ecfc.org
URL: http://www.ecfc.org
Contact: Lewis Freeman, Pres.

Founded: 1981. **Members:** 800. **Membership Dues:** corporate, non-profit, public sector, $995 (annual) ● service provider (based on number of employees), $1,925-$5,900 (annual). **Staff:** 4. **Budget:** $1,500,000. **Description:** Represents employers and service providers who have implemented or are interested in flexible compensation plans allowing employees to choose from a variety of benefits packages. Promotes flexible compensation plans including cafeteria plans, health reimbursement arrangements, cash-or-deferred plans, and other defined contribution plans. Monitors legislation and represents members' interests before Congress. Lobbies to preserve and simplify the flexible compensation provisions of the Internal Revenue Code. **Committees:** Washington Representatives. **Projects:** Cafeteria Plan Regulation; Cash or Deferred Compensation Regulations; Tax Legislation. **Publications:** *ECFC Flex Reporter*, quarterly. Newsletter. **Conventions/Meetings:** annual conference (exhibits) - always March, Washington, DC ● annual Flex Plan Symposium - always August.

1238 ■ ERISA Industry Committee (ERIC)
1400 L St. NW, Ste.350
Washington, DC 20005
Ph: (202)789-1400
Fax: (202)789-1120
E-mail: eric@eric.org
URL: http://www.eric.org
Contact: Mark J. Ugoretz, Pres.

Founded: 1976. **Members:** 127. **Membership Dues:** regular, $15,000 (annual). **Staff:** 7. **Description:** Large corporations that sponsor employee pension, health, and other benefit programs. Represents the concerns of major employers regarding policy, legislative, judicial, and regulatory matters involving the administration of private retirement, health, and other employee benefit plans. Issues briefings to members' congressional representatives. Operates speakers' bureau. (ERISA is an acronym for the Employee Retirement Income Security Act of 1974.). **Telecommunication Services:** electronic mail, tgodbout@eric.org. **Committees:** Emerging Pension Issues; Fiduciary Responsibility; Health and Welfare Benefits; Legal; Retirement Security. **Task Forces:** Social Security. **Publications:** *ERIC Executive Report*, bimonthly. Newsletter. **Price:** included in membership dues. **Conventions/Meetings:** quarterly conference and workshop.

1239 ■ Global Equity Organization (GEO)
1442 E Lincoln Ave., No. 487
Orange, CA 92865
Ph: (714)630-2908
Fax: (253)423-8390
E-mail: mholly@globalequity.org
URL: http://www.globalequity.org
Contact: Pam Stetson, Exec. Dir.

Founded: 1999. **Membership Dues:** academic, governmental/regulatory agency, $100 (annual) ● provider, $295-$7,500 (annual). **Multinational. Description:** Provides a forum for an open exchange between members of the latest information involving the use of equity-based employee compensation in the global community. Promotes high standards of competence, professionalism, and performance in the administration of share plans. Obtains and disseminates information on the subject of share plans. Encourages the exchange of ideas and mutual assistance. Facilitates the association of professionals handling all aspects of global share plans. **Awards:** Best Communications. **Frequency:** annual. **Type:** recognition. **Recipient:** to employees for the most effective and appropriate means of communication materials used to help achieve the plan's objectives ● Best in Financial Education. **Frequency:** annual. **Type:** recognition. **Recipient:** for companies that extends responsibility to employees beyond the implementation of a share plan ● Best Plan Effectiveness. **Frequency:** annual. **Type:** recognition. **Recipient:** for companies that have spent time and energy developing a stock plan that works towards those various corporate objectives ● Best Use of Technology. **Frequency:** annual. **Type:** recognition. **Recipient:** to companies with innovative, appropriate, easy to use electronic communications ● GEO Award for Financial Education. **Frequency:** annual. **Type:** recognition. **Recipient:** to a company who has implemented a Financial Education program that recognizes the importance of the provision of independent and objective advice to employees ● Most Innovative and Creative Design. **Frequency:** annual. **Type:** recognition. **Recipient:** for inventive and creative stock plans. **Telecommunication Services:** electronic mail, pstetson@globalequity.org. **Publications:** Newsletter. **Price:** included in membership dues.

1240 ■ International Foundation of Employee Benefit Plans (IFEBP)
PO Box 69
Brookfield, WI 53008-0069
Ph: (262)786-6700 (262)786-6710
Free: (888)334-3327
Fax: (262)786-8670
E-mail: membership@ifebp.org
URL: http://www.ifebp.org
Contact: Joseph J. Burke, Pres./Chm.

Founded: 1954. **Members:** 35,000. **Membership Dues:** organization in U.S., $625 (annual) ● individual in U.S., $295 (annual) ● organization in Canada, $825 (annual) ● individual in Canada, $390 (annual). **Staff:** 140. **Budget:** $20,000,000. **Description:** Provides sources for employee benefits and compensation information and education, including seminars and conferences, books, and an information center, CEBS, and Certificate Series. Conducts more than 100 educational programs. Provides Internet job and resume posting service. **Libraries: Type:** reference. **Holdings:** 12,000; books, periodicals. **Subjects:** employee benefits, human resources, compensation. **Computer Services:** database, Employee Benefits InfoSource. **Boards:** Canadian; Corporate; Public Employee. **Committees:** Accountants; Actuaries/Consultants; Administrators; Attorneys; Benefit Communications; Canadian CEBS; Canadian Education; Canadian Government/Industry Relations; Canadian Investment; Canadian Public Service; CEBS; Continuing Education; Corporate Educational Services; Educational Program; Executive; Executive Financial Review; Government Liaison; Health Care Management and Coalition; Investment Management; Research; Trustees. **Councils:** Past Presidents. **Affiliated With:** International Society of Certified Employee Benefit Specialists. **Formerly:** (1973) National Foundation of Health, Welfare and Pension Plans. **Supersedes:** National Foundation of Health, Welfare and Pension Plans, Trustees and Administrators. **Publications:** *Benefits & Compensation Digest*, monthly. Newsletter. Provides information on employee benefits. **Price:** $100.00 included in publication package. ISSN: 1550-4190. **Circulation:** 35,000. **Advertising:** accepted. Alternate Formats: online ● *Employee Benefits Legal-Legislative Reporter*, monthly. Bulletin. Summarizes legal and legislative developments affecting employee benefits. **Price:** included in membership dues. ISSN: 0458-9599. **Circulation:** 35,000. **Conventions/Meetings:** annual Employee Benefits Conference - meeting (exhibits) - 2008 Oct. 19-22, Miami, FL - **Avg. Attendance:** 6000; 2009 Nov. 8-11, Orlando, FL.

1241 ■ International Society of Certified Employee Benefit Specialists (ISCEBS)
PO Box 209
Brookfield, WI 53008-0209
Ph: (262)786-8771
Fax: (262)786-8650
E-mail: iscebs@iscebs.org
URL: http://www.iscebs.org
Contact: Daniel W. Graham, Exec. Dir.

Founded: 1981. **Members:** 3,900. **Membership Dues:** regular, $175 (annual) ● unemployed, retired, student, $165 (annual). **Staff:** 3. **Local Groups:** 50. **Description:** Graduates of the Certified Employee Benefit Specialist Program, co-sponsored by the International Foundation of Employee Benefit Plans and the Wharton School of the University of Pennsylvania. Promotes continuing education and professional development of employee benefit practitioners through courses and seminars. **Telecommunication Services:** electronic mail, dang@iscebs.org. **Committees:** Local Chapter; Membership; Professional Development; Strategic Planning; Symposium Planning. **Affiliated With:** International Foundation of Employee Benefit Plans. **Publications:** *Benefits Quarterly*. Journal. Features articles on problems and issues regarding employee benefits. Includes index of authors and articles, arranged in broad subject categories. **Price:** included in membership dues;

$100.00 /year for nonmembers. ISSN: 8756-1263. **Circulation:** 17,000. **Advertising:** accepted. Alternate Formats: CD-ROM; online ● *International Society of Certified Employee Benefit Specialists—Membership Directory*, annual. Lists members by name, geographical region, and industry. **Price:** included in membership dues. **Circulation:** 3,900 ● *International Society of Certified Employee Benefit Specialists—Newsbriefs*, bimonthly. Newsletter. Contains news of the society and its local chapters, articles on trends and innovations in the field, summaries of articles in current periodicals. **Price:** included in membership dues. ISSN: 0731-4531 ● Surveys. Alternate Formats: online. **Conventions/Meetings:** annual symposium.

1242 ■ National Coordinating Committee for Multiemployer Plans (NCCMP)
815 16th St. NW
Washington, DC 20006
Ph: (202)737-5315
Fax: (202)737-1308
E-mail: nccmp@nccmp.org
URL: http://www.nccmp.org
Contact: Randy G. DeFrehn, Exec. Dir.
Founded: 1975. **Members:** 230. **Membership Dues:** regular (based on plan size), $3,000-$7,500 (annual) ● contributing, sustaining, $25,000 (annual). **Staff:** 3. **Description:** International trade unions and jointly administered employee benefit trust funds. Promotes the interests of organizations that provide retirement security, health, and other welfare benefits to individuals working in industries that, due to their structure, would not otherwise provide sufficient pension and welfare benefits. Lobbies before Congress and federal regulatory agencies and participates in judicial proceedings affecting multiemployer plans and participants. **Conventions/Meetings:** annual conference - fall.

1243 ■ National Employee Benefits Institute (NEBI)
Address Unknown since 2007
Founded: 1977. **Members:** 100. **Staff:** 6. **Description:** Fortune 1000 corporations with an interest in employee benefits legislation and regulation. Works to improve government regulation of employee benefits. Supports and introduces what the institute considers realistic legislation. Invites government spokespersons, legislators, and regulators to speak at special meetings. Conducts educational programs. **Awards:** Congressional Representative of the Year. **Frequency:** annual. **Type:** recognition. **Recipient:** for a member of Congress or the Senate involved in employee benefits legislation. **Conventions/Meetings:** semiannual meeting.

1244 ■ National Institute of Pension Administrators (NIPA)
401 N Michigan Ave., Ste.2200
Chicago, IL 60611
Free: (800)999-6472
Fax: (312)245-1085
E-mail: nipa@nipa.org
URL: http://www.nipa.org
Contact: Laura J. Rudzinski, Exec. Dir.
Founded: 1983. **Members:** 800. **Membership Dues:** regular, associate, $325 (annual) ● firm A (with 25 employees or fewer), $750 (annual) ● firm B (with 26 employees or more), $1,500 (annual) ● student, $162 (annual). **Staff:** 7. **Budget:** $1,000,000. **Local Groups:** 14. **Description:** Individuals with at least a year of experience in pension administration, full-time pension administration employees, and interested individuals. Sponsors educational program for the accreditation of pension administrators and a series of regional programs relative to pension/profit-sharing programs and administration. **Publications:** *PLAN Horizons*, quarterly. Newsletter. **Price:** included in membership dues. **Advertising:** accepted. Alternate Formats: online ● Membership Directory. **Conventions/Meetings:** annual Business Management Conference - meeting - always January ● annual conference (exhibits) - always May.

1245 ■ Society of Professional Benefit Administrators (SPBA)
Two Wisconsin Cir., Ste.670
Chevy Chase, MD 20815
Ph: (301)718-7722
Fax: (301)718-9440
E-mail: spba@erols.com
URL: http://users.erols.com/spba
Contact: Frederick D. Hunt Jr., Pres.
Founded: 1975. **Members:** 430. **Membership Dues:** regular, $3,500 (annual). **Staff:** 6. **Budget:** $1,750,000. **Description:** Third Party Administration (TPA), contract employee benefit plan administration firms. Member firms provide out-of-house professional benefit administration and claims services for client employee benefit plans. Estimated 2/3 of USA employees benefit plans use TPA's. Deals with employee benefits and such issues as: the Employee Retirement Income Security Act; tax; health coverage; self-funding of benefit plans. Promotes public understanding and acceptance of contract administration and employee benefits. Assists government legislative and regulatory bodies in better understanding and coordinating different laws and their impact. **Publications:** *Directory of TPA Firms*, annual. Book. Lists independent Third Party Administration firms, including services offered, clients served, and geographical and size descriptions. **Price:** $395.00. **Circulation:** 5,000 ● *SPBA Update*, periodic. Newsletter. Features informal memo to members covering legislative, regulatory, and legal proceedings pertaining to employee benefits and plan administration. **Price:** free for members. **Circulation:** 3,300 ● *State TPA Licensing Statutes*, annual. Contains a survey of state TPA licensing laws, with contact information and analysis of each. **Price:** $500.00. **Circulation:** 4,000. **Conventions/Meetings:** semiannual conference, for members only - always spring in Washington, DC, and fall in various locations.

1246 ■ WEB - Worldwide Employee Benefits Network
1700 Pennsylvania Ave. NW, Ste.400
Washington, DC 20006-4707
Free: (888)795-6862
Fax: (202)318-8778
E-mail: info@webnetwork.org
URL: http://www.webnetwork.org
Contact: Diane Morgenthaler, Pres.
Founded: 1982. **Members:** 2,000. **Membership Dues:** associate, $65 (annual) ● individual, $150 (annual) ● government, $95 (annual) ● corporate, $680 (annual). **Staff:** 1. **Budget:** $350,000. **Regional Groups:** 3. **State Groups:** 1. **Local Groups:** 24. **Description:** Supports and furthers the development of employee benefits professionals from diverse disciplines through topical educational meetings, publications and networking opportunities. **Computer Services:** Mailing lists, of members. **Formerly:** (1992) WEB; (1997) Working in Employee Benefits; (1998) Web Network of Employee Benefits; (2001) Web Network of Professional Benefits. **Publications:** *Benefits Insider*, monthly. Newsletter. Alternate Formats: online ● *JobBank*, 11/year. Newsletter. **Advertising:** accepted ● *Network*, 10/year. Newsletter. Contains industry updates, technical articles, and association news. **Circulation:** 2,500 ● Membership Directory, annual. Alternate Formats: online ● Brochure. Alternate Formats: online. **Conventions/Meetings:** biennial board meeting ● semiannual President's Meeting - April and September.

1247 ■ Workplace Benefits Association
9221 Ravenna Rd., Ste.No. D8
Twinsburg, OH 44087
Ph: (330)425-8399
Free: (888)282-1765
Fax: (330)425-8489
E-mail: wpodgurski@aol.com
URL: http://www.benefitsmarketing.org
Contact: Walt Podgurski CLU, Chm./CEO
Membership Dues: regular, $29 (annual). **Description:** Recognizes and acknowledges best practice in workplace benefits. Helps to improve the process and result for the service providers, consultants, employers and employees. Assists employers and employees in financial planning and security. **Publications:** Brochure. Includes members' company logo and contact information. **Price:** included in membership dues. **Conventions/Meetings:** annual conference, with networking opportunities, sales and marketing (exhibits).

Employee Ownership

1248 ■ ESOP Association
1726 M St. NW, Ste.501
Washington, DC 20036
Ph: (202)293-2971
Free: (866)366-3832
Fax: (202)293-7568
E-mail: esop@esopassociation.org
URL: http://www.esopassociation.org
Contact: J. Michael Keeling CAE, Pres.
Founded: 1978. **Members:** 2,400. **Membership Dues:** corporate (based on the number of participants), $575-$3,780 (annual) ● affiliate, $525 (annual) ● professional, $630 (annual) ● educational, $140 (annual). **Staff:** 10. **Budget:** $3,000,000. **State Groups:** 19. **Description:** Companies with employee stock ownership plans; associate members are lawyers, accountants, appraisers, actuaries, brokers, management and benefit consultants, and bankers specializing in working with ESOP. Acts as national information clearinghouse for the press and public interested in the concept of employee ownership; provides forum for the exchange of ideas, experience, and advice among members; lobbies for favorable legislation and regulation on national and state levels; produces and distributes communications material to educate employees on stock ownership. Holds seminars and roundtables. Compiles statistics; maintains speakers' bureau. **Libraries: Type:** reference. **Awards:** AACE Awards. **Type:** recognition. **Committees:** Finance; Legal and Regulatory; Ownership Culture; Valuation. **Formed by Merger of:** (1982) ESOP Council of America; National Association of ESOP Companies. **Publications:** *The ESOP Association Membership Directory*, annual. Lists companies with employee stock ownership and individuals who provide services to ESOP companies; listed alphabetically, by name and expertise. **Price:** $250.00 ● *ESOP Report and Profile*, 11/year. Newsletter. Reports latest developments in employee stock ownership plans as affected by Congressional action and regulations by the Department of Labor and IRS. **Price:** free for members. **Circulation:** 2,200 ● *How the ESOP Really Works*, periodic. Introduction to legal and business mechanics of ESOP. **Price:** $10.00 for members; $40.00 for nonmembers. **Circulation:** 1,800 ● Brochures ● Handbook ● Reports. **Conventions/Meetings:** competition ● annual conference - always May in Washington, DC ● annual seminar, about repurchase obligation.

1249 ■ ICA Group
1 Harvard St., Ste.200
Brookline, MA 02445
Ph: (617)232-8765
Fax: (617)232-9545
E-mail: ica@ica-group.org
URL: http://www.ica-group.org
Contact: Newell Lessell, Pres.
Founded: 1978. **Members:** 800. **Staff:** 7. **Budget:** $850,000. **Languages:** English, Spanish. **Description:** Seeks to create and strengthen worker-owned and controlled businesses (worker cooperatives) in low income and blue-collar communities. Provides full business development assistance. Services include: initial feasibility review for a plant closing response, conversion, or start-up; financing advice and brokering; management assistance; advice on democratic decision-making structures; implementation of work force education programs. Works both directly with employee groups and through sponsoring organizations. Conducts work force education and board training to ICA client cooperatives. Develops labor/management cooperation programs. Believes that employee-owned companies show increased profits due partly to workers' attitudes, as

they are working for themselves, not an outside owner; and that community economic development is enhanced, because as the work force owns the company, profits remain within the community, discouraging poverty and capital flight. **Computer Services:** Online services, business planning and financial monitoring. **Departments:** Business/Education; Legal. **Formerly:** (1991) Industrial Cooperative Association. **Publications:** *The Design of Governance Systems for Small Workers' Cooperatives.* Paper. **Price:** $5.00 ● *ICA Model Bylaws for a Worker Cooperative (version III).* Paper. **Price:** $95.00 book (plus $5.25 postage); $50.00 diskette. Alternate Formats: diskette ● *ICA News & Events*, semiannual. Newsletter. Alternate Formats: online ● *Illustrated Guide to the Internal Capital Accounts System.* Paper. **Price:** $6.00 ● *The Massachusetts Law for Worker Cooperatives: MGL Chapter 157A.* Paper. **Price:** $5.00 ● *Organizing Worker Cooperatives.* Paper. **Price:** $5.00 ● *Putting Democracy to Work: A Practical Guide for Starting Worker-Owned Businesses.* Book. **Price:** $19.95 plus $3.98 postage ● *What is a Workers' Cooperative?.* Paper. **Price:** $1.00 ● *Worker Cooperatives and Basic Orientation.* Paper. **Price:** $5.00/copy ● *Workers' Cooperatives: The Question of Legal Structure.* Paper. **Price:** $3.00 ● Annual Report, annual. Alternate Formats: online ● Also publishes papers covering employee stock ownership plans, various case studies and surveys and the Mondragon Cooperatives. **Conventions/Meetings:** annual Introduction to Worker Ownership - workshop.

1250 ■ National Center for Employee Ownership (NCEO)
1736 Franklin St., 8th Fl.
Oakland, CA 94612
Ph: (510)208-1300
Fax: (510)272-9510
E-mail: nceo@nceo.org
URL: http://www.nceo.org
Contact: Corey Rosen, Exec. Dir./Co-Founder
Founded: 1981. **Members:** 3,500. **Membership Dues:** regular, in U.S., $80 (annual) ● consultant, in U.S., $265 (annual) ● regular, outside U.S., $90 (annual) ● consultant, outside U.S., $275 (annual) ● full-time student/teacher in U.S., $35 (annual) ● full-time student/teacher outside U.S., $45 (annual). **Staff:** 12. **Budget:** $1,200,000. **Regional Groups:** 1. **Description:** Researchers, companies, unions, associations, consultants, and other individuals. Promotes an increased awareness and understanding of employee ownership of companies. Sponsors research projects. Maintains referral service; operates clipping service. Compiles lists of employee-owned companies in the United States. **Computer Services:** database, for consultants. **Publications:** *Employee Ownership Report*, bimonthly. Newsletter. Provides news and articles on legal, financial, and regulatory developments, case studies, and reviews of resources and research. Indexed annually. **Price:** free for members. **Circulation:** 1,800. Alternate Formats: online ● *Journal of Employee Ownership Law and Finance*, quarterly. **Price:** $75.00 /year for members; $100.00 /year for nonmembers. ISSN: 1046-7491. **Circulation:** 335 ● *Membership, Publications, and Services.* Catalog. Alternate Formats: online ● Monographs ● Video ● Books ● Bulletin. Contains news about upcoming events, new features and NCEO projects. **Price:** free. Alternate Formats: online ● Audiotapes. Alternate Formats: CD-ROM. **Conventions/Meetings:** annual conference - always spring ● seminar ● semiannual workshop - always fall and spring.

Employers

1251 ■ American Society of Employers (ASE)
23815 Northwestern Hwy.
Southfield, MI 48075-7713
Ph: (248)353-4500
Fax: (248)353-1224
E-mail: mschroeder@aseonline.org
URL: http://www.aseonline.org
Contact: Mary Schroeder, Pres.
Founded: 1902. **Description:** Offers members compensation and benefit surveys, HR research, workforce development, employee opinion surveys, customized and public training, management and assessment center testing, job posting services, HR assessments, labor relation services, and peer networking. **Libraries: Type:** reference; lending; not open to the public. **Holdings:** articles, books, periodicals. **Subjects:** human resources. **Publications:** *Everythingpeople*, monthly. Magazine ● *Everythingpeople This Week!.* Newsletter. Alternate Formats: online ● Newsletter, monthly. **Circulation:** 1,300.

Employment

1252 ■ American Council on International Personnel (ACIP)
1212 New York Ave. NW, Ste.800
Washington, DC 20005
Ph: (202)371-6789
Fax: (202)371-5524
E-mail: info@acip.com
URL: http://www.acip.com
Contact: Lynn Shotwell, Exec. Dir.
Founded: 1971. **Members:** 250. **Membership Dues:** regular, $500 (annual). **Staff:** 5. **Description:** Corporations and institutions organized to serve the business community in matters involving immigration-related issues. Disseminates information on current immigration laws and practices. Sponsors conferences and symposia to inform personnel managers and the corporate counsel of international companies and industries of immigration-related policies. **Telecommunication Services:** electronic mail, lynn_shotwell@acip.com. **Publications:** *ACIP Newsletter*, bimonthly. **Price:** available to members only ● *Immigration Handbook: Employment of Foreign Nationals.* **Conventions/Meetings:** annual meeting.

1253 ■ American Payroll Association (APA)
660 N Main Ave., Ste.100
San Antonio, TX 78205-1217
Ph: (210)226-4600
Free: (800)398-8681
Fax: (210)226-4027
E-mail: apa@americanpayroll.com
URL: http://www.americanpayroll.org
Contact: Dan Maddux, Exec. Dir.
Founded: 1982. **Members:** 17,500. **Membership Dues:** individual, $165 (annual). **Staff:** 60. **Budget:** $13,500,000. **Regional Groups:** 8. **Local Groups:** 105. **Description:** Payroll employees. Works to increase members' skills and professionalism through education and mutual support. Represents the interest of members before legislative bodies. Conducts training courses. Operates speakers' bureau; conducts educational programs. Administers the certified payroll professional program of recognition. **Awards:** Donald W. Sharper Education Grant. **Frequency:** annual. **Type:** scholarship. **Recipient:** for dedication to payroll industry and continuing education. **Telecommunication Services:** electronic mail, chapterrelations@americanpayroll.org ● phone referral service, (210)224-6406. **Committees:** American Payroll Institute, Inc.; Automated Clearing House; Learning System Advisory; Professional Certification. **Task Forces:** Government Affairs; Large Employer. **Publications:** *APA Basic Guide to Payroll*, annual. Book. **Price:** $142.95 ● *APA Directory*, annual. **Price:** included in membership dues. **Circulation:** 17,500. **Advertising:** accepted ● *APA Guide to Payroll Practice and Management.* Manual. **Price:** $129.95 ● *Guide to Global Payroll Management.* Book. **Price:** $134.95 for members; $149.95 for colleagues; $164.95 for nonmembers ● *Payroll Currently*, biweekly. Newsletter. Tracks payroll compliance changes. **Price:** $279.00. **Circulation:** 2,200 ● *The Payroll Source*, annual. Includes a comprehensive payroll compliance reference and study guide. **Price:** $194.95 for members; $219.95 for colleagues; $239.95 for nonmembers. **Circulation:** 5,000. Alternate Formats: CD-ROM ● *Your Paycheck Factbook.* **Price:** $9.95. **Conventions/Meetings:** seminar and workshop ● annual congress, with 90 Workshops and 100-vendor Exhibit Hall (exhibits) - 2009 May 19-23, Long Beach, CA; 2010 May 25-29, Potomac, MD; 2012 May 6-10, Kissimmee, FL.

1254 ■ American Staffing Association (ASA)
277 S Washington St., Ste.200
Alexandria, VA 22314-3675
Ph: (703)253-2020
Fax: (703)253-2053
E-mail: asa@americanstaffing.net
URL: http://www.americanstaffing.net
Contact: Pat Rohe, Chair
Founded: 1966. **Members:** 1,600. **Membership Dues:** active company (with aggregate gross sales of $500,000 to over $1,200,000,000), $520-$68,770 (annual) ● associate, $450 (annual) ● regular outside U.S. (with office in only one country), $500 (annual) ● regular, outside U.S. (with offices in two or more countries), $1,000 (annual). **Staff:** 30. **Budget:** $6,000,000. **State Groups:** 69. **Description:** Promotes and represents the staffing industry through legal and legislative advocacy, public relations, education, and the establishment of high standards of ethical conduct. **Awards:** Communications Awards. **Frequency:** annual. **Type:** recognition. **Recipient:** for advertising, public relations, and publications ● Leadership Hall of Fame. **Frequency:** annual. **Type:** recognition. **Recipient:** for leadership in the association and industry. **Computer Services:** Mailing lists, of members. **Committees:** Chapter Relations; Convention; Foundation; Health Care Services; International; Labor Services; Leadership Award; Legal/Legislative; Member Education; Member Services; Membership; Nominating; Past Chairmen; Political Action; Public Relations. **Formerly:** Institute of Temporary Services; (1995) National Association of Temporary Services; (2000) National Association of Temporary and Staffing Services. **Publications:** *ASA Managers Guide to Employment Law.* Book ● *Co-Employment Guide.* Handbook. **Price:** $40.00 for members; $60.00 for nonmembers ● *Membership and Resource Directory* ● *Staffing Law.* Book. **Price:** $35.00 /year for members; $295.00 /year for nonmembers; $55.00/year for business and education industry ● *Staffing Success*, bimonthly. Magazine. Monitors current trends in the industry, each issue focusing on a specific topic; also covers association activities; contains book reviews. **Price:** $360.00 /year for nonmembers; $90.00 /year for members; $120.00/year for business and education industry. **Circulation:** 2,500. **Advertising:** accepted. Alternate Formats: online ● *Staffing Week*, weekly, every Monday. Newsletter. Alternate Formats: online ● Brochures ● Reports. Alternate Formats: online ● Audiotapes. **Price:** $49.00 for members; $149.00 for nonmembers; $4.00 6-audiocassette storage album; $6.00 12-audiocassette storage album. Alternate Formats: CD-ROM. **Conventions/Meetings:** annual Staffing World - meeting (exhibits).

1255 ■ Association of Career Management Consulting Firms International (AOCFI)
204 E St. NE
Washington, DC 20002
Ph: (202)547-6344
Fax: (202)547-6348
E-mail: acf@acfinternational.org
URL: http://www.aocfi.org
Contact: Annette Summers, Exec. Dir.
Founded: 1982. **Members:** 125. **Membership Dues:** regular, $220 (annual). **Staff:** 3. **Budget:** $300,000. **Regional Groups:** 1. **Description:** Represents firms providing displaced employees, who are sponsored by their organization, with counsel and assistance in job searching and the techniques and practices of choosing a career. Develops, improves and encourages the art and science of outplacement consulting and the professional standards of competence, objectivity, and integrity in the service of clients. Cooperates with other industrial, technical, educational, professional, and governmental bodies in areas of mutual interest and concern. **Libraries: Type:** open to the public. **Subjects:** outplacement services. **Computer Services:** Mailing lists, of members. **Telecommunication Services:** electronic mail, als@acfinternational.org. **Formerly:** Association of Outplacement Consulting Firms; (1998) As-

sociation of Outplacement Consulting Firms International. **Publications:** *World Wire*, quarterly. Newsletter. **Price:** free. **Advertising:** accepted ● Membership Directory, annual. **Conventions/Meetings:** annual conference (exhibits).

1256 ■ Association of Executive Search Consultants (AESC)
12 E 41st St., 17th Fl.
New York, NY 10017
Ph: (212)398-9556
Free: (877)THE-AESC
Fax: (212)398-9560
E-mail: aesc@aesc.org
URL: http://www.aesc.org
Contact: Peter M. Felix, Pres.

Founded: 1959. **Members:** 160. **Staff:** 15. **Languages:** English, French, German. **Multinational. Description:** Represents executive search consulting firms worldwide, establishes professional and ethical standards for its members, and serves to broaden public understanding of the executive search process. Specialized form of management consulting, conducted through an exclusive engagement with a client organization. **Awards:** Eleanor Raynolds Award. **Frequency:** annual. **Type:** recognition. **Recipient:** for commitment to volunteerism ● Gardner Heidrick Award. **Frequency:** annual. **Type:** recognition. **Recipient:** for contribution to executive search. **Computer Services:** database, senior executive profiles ● online services, searchable list of members. **Additional Websites:** http://www.bluesteps.com. **Telecommunication Services:** electronic mail, pmf@aesc.org. **Committees:** Communications/Marketing; Ethics and Professional Practices; Government Affairs; Membership. **Councils:** The Americas Membership; Asia Pacific Marketing and PR; Asia Pacific Membership. **Formerly:** (1982) Association of Executive Recruiting Consultants. **Publications:** *eSearch Connection*, monthly. Newsletter. Alternate Formats: online. **Conventions/Meetings:** annual AESC European Conference (exhibits) ● annual AESC North American Conference (exhibits).

1257 ■ Association of Manpower Franchise Owners (AMFO)
c/o Jane A. Svinicki, CAE, Exec. Dir.
6737 W Washington St., Ste.1420
Milwaukee, WI 53214
Ph: (414)276-2651 (414)276-8488
Fax: (414)276-7704
E-mail: info@amfo.org
URL: http://www.amfo.org
Contact: Jane A. Svinicki CAE, Exec. Dir.

Founded: 1971. **Description:** Serves as a forum for exchange of ideas and information among members; acts as liaison between members and the parent company. Studies and critiques procedures and policies of Manpower International; solicits suggestions from members regarding smooth operation of a temporary employee service. Provides formalized procedure for resolution of grievances among members and between members and the parent company. **Conventions/Meetings:** semiannual board meeting.

1258 ■ A.W.A.R.E. - American Workforce Alliance for Responsible Economics
Address Unknown since 2007

Membership Dues: unemployed, $10 (annual) ● underemployed, $15 (annual) ● student, $20 (annual) ● regular, $35 (annual) ● family, $60 (annual) ● small business sponsorship, $125 (annual) ● cornerstone contributor, $250 (annual) ● foundation benefactor, $500 (annual) ● life standing, $1,000. **Description:** Seeks to "unify the American workforce-American citizens and permanent residents-across all industries and occupations to safeguard the American middle class standard of living and economic security.". **Computer Services:** Online services, American Joblog. **Telecommunication Services:** electronic mail, membership@rescueamericanjobs.org. **Publications:** *Status Report*, quarterly. **Conventions/Meetings:** Activist Seminars.

1259 ■ Disability Management Employer Coalition (DMEC)
5173 Waring Rd., Ste.134
San Diego, CA 92120-2705
Free: (800)789-3632
Fax: (619)303-6855
E-mail: admin.dir@dmec.org
URL: http://www.dmec.org
Contact: Kathleen Cuban, Admin. Dir.

Founded: 1992. **Members:** 1,225. **Membership Dues:** employer in U.S. (2 individuals), $350 (annual) ● corporate employer (based on the number of persons), $525-$3,550 (annual) ● supporting in U.S. (based on the number of persons), $475-$2,300 (annual) ● sole proprietor, $285 (annual) ● employer outside U.S., $100 (annual) ● supporting outside U.S., $125 (annual). **Staff:** 5. **Budget:** $700,000. **Regional Groups:** 17. **State Groups:** 17. **Local Groups:** 17. **National Groups:** 17. **Description:** Health, disability, and workers' compensation professionals. Provides educational opportunities and "fosters the development of model programs with the goal of reducing the impact of the cost of disability to employers while assisting disabled employees in returning to work". **Libraries: Type:** not open to the public. **Subjects:** return to work, baby boomers, annual salary survey. **Publications:** *Boom or Bust - Baby Boomers*. **Price:** $65.95 for nonmembers; $53.00 for members ● *Modified Duty Return to Work Workbook*. **Price:** $95.00 each. Alternate Formats: CD-ROM ● *RTW Statutory Guide*. **Price:** $32.95 for nonmembers; $26.00 for members ● *Year 2001 Salary Survey*. **Price:** $40.00 each. **Conventions/Meetings:** annual Integration Magic: Incorporating the Human Element - conference, with disability-related products (exhibits).

1260 ■ Employee Involvement Association (EIA)
PO Box 2307
Dayton, OH 45401-2307
Ph: (937)586-3724
Fax: (937)586-3699
E-mail: eia@meinet.com
URL: http://www.eianet.org
Contact: Ms. Fran Rickenbach CAE, Exec. Dir.

Founded: 1952. **Members:** 300. **Membership Dues:** organizational, $250 (annual) ● individual, $70 (annual) ● associate, $290 (annual) ● student, $35 (annual). **Budget:** $200,000. **Regional Groups:** 9. **Multinational. Description:** Represents finance, commerce, industry, and government professionals. Dedicated to the worth, contributions, and benefits of employee suggestion systems and other employee involvement processes. Supports communication between employees and employer for the purpose of exchanging ideas. **Awards:** Communicator of the Year. **Frequency:** annual. **Type:** recognition. **Recipient:** for an individual who has best communicated the EI program within the company ● Executive Leadership Award. **Frequency:** annual. **Type:** recognition. **Recipient:** for the CEO or top manager who has provided significant support to the EI program within the company ● Idea/Evaluator of the Year Award. **Frequency:** annual. **Type:** recognition ● Statistical Awards. **Frequency:** annual. **Type:** recognition. **Recipient:** to EIA member organizations. **Formerly:** (1967) National Association of Suggestion Systems. **Publications:** *Ideas and Inspirations*, monthly. Newsletter. Presents information concerning employee suggestion systems at member organizations. Includes calendar of events. **Price:** free for members. **Circulation:** 300. **Advertising:** accepted. Alternate Formats: online ● *Statistical Report*, annual. Booklet. Contains benchmarking report of statistical data from member organizations. **Price:** free to organizational and associate members; $50.00 extra copy for members; $150.00 for nonmembers. **Circulation:** 300. **Conventions/Meetings:** annual Training, Networking, and Awards Conference, with break out sessions, and presentation of the Association's annual statistical awards, Association awards, and Idea and Evaluator of the Year awards (exhibits).

1261 ■ Employee Relocation Council/Worldwide ERC
1717 Pennsylvania Ave. NW, Ste.800
Washington, DC 20006
Ph: (202)857-0857 (202)857-0905
Fax: (202)659-8631
E-mail: webmaster@erc.org
URL: http://www.erc.org
Contact: H. Cris Collie CAE, Exec. VP

Founded: 1964. **Members:** 12,000. **Membership Dues:** corporate, government, professional ERC, $165 (annual) ● real estate appraiser, $299 (annual) ● relocation service company, $595 (annual) ● real estate broker, $565 (annual). **Staff:** 50. **Budget:** $12,000,000. **Regional Groups:** 40. **Description:** Representatives of major corporations that transfer personnel and representatives from the relocation service industry. Seeks to study, evaluate, and communicate information on practices and procedures in relocation of employees, so that the transfer may be accomplished with maximum efficiency and minimum disruption to the employee, his or her family, and the employer. Compiles statistics on corporate relocation trends and practices, monitors and promotes legislation in concert with government relations activities. **Libraries: Type:** reference. **Holdings:** audio recordings. **Awards: Type:** recognition. **Telecommunication Services:** electronic mail, ccollie@erc.org. **Departments:** Globility; Human Resources and Finance/Accounting; International Initiatives; Mobility; Professional Development; Research; Tax and Legal; Web Strategy and Services. **Formerly:** (1973) Employee Relocation Real Estate Advisory Council. **Publications:** *Broker's Market Analysis and Strategy Report*. Manual. **Price:** $50.00 for members; $125.00 for nonmembers ● *ERC Global Workforce Service Directory*, annual. **Advertising:** accepted. Alternate Formats: CD-ROM; online ● *Globility*. Newsletter. Alternate Formats: online ● *MOBILITY*, monthly. Magazine. **Price:** $48.00/year. ISSN: 0195-8194. **Advertising:** accepted ● *Worldwide ERC Advantage*. Newsletter. Alternate Formats: online ● Reports. Alternate Formats: online. **Conventions/Meetings:** annual meeting and conference (exhibits) - always May ● annual symposium (exhibits) ● annual workshop, covers the topic of employee relocation and international assignment management - always October.

1262 ■ FACE Intel - Former and Current Employees of Intel
7349 Cross Dr.
Citrus Heights, CA 95610
E-mail: kenh7@faceintel.com
URL: http://www.faceintel.com
Contact: Ken Hamidi, Contact

Founded: 1996. **Description:** Works to influence positive human resource policies and practices and create true long-term employment opportunities at Intel; to abolish its predatory Ranking and Rating system and replace it with a true performance review system, which will only be based on merits of employees performance; to stop age, disability, gender, race, and ethnicity discriminations.

1263 ■ Independent Educational Services (IES)
Address Unknown since 2007

Founded: 1968. **Members:** 550. **Membership Dues:** company, $1,000 (annual). **Staff:** 25. **Budget:** $2,000,000. **Regional Groups:** 1. **Description:** Nonprofit consulting, head search, and teacher recruitment organization. Furnishes to independent (private) schools dossiers of qualified candidates for teaching and administrative positions. Offers to teachers and prospective teachers information concerning current requirements and qualifications for positions in the field of education and vacancies for which they qualify. Conducts searches for heads of schools. Offers specialized placement workshops, consulting, and in-service programs to independent schools. **Supersedes:** Cooperative Bureau for Teachers. **Publications:** *IES Profile*, periodic. Bulletin. **Advertising:** accepted. **Conventions/Meetings:** semiannual conference.

1264 ■ Industrial Foundation of America (IFA)
402 E San Antonio Ave.
Boerne, TX 78006
Ph: (830)249-7899
Free: (800)592-1433
Fax: (800)628-2397
E-mail: ifasmith@gvtc.com
URL: http://www.ifa-america.com
Contact: Bill Smith, Exec. Dir.
Founded: 1960. **Members:** 750. **Membership Dues:** regular, $125 (annual). **Staff:** 5. **Languages:** English, Spanish. **Description:** Provides education and screening of prospective employees for a safe and healthy workplace. **Libraries: Type:** reference; not open to the public. **Holdings:** archival material, articles, books, business records, periodicals. **Subjects:** health and safety.

1265 ■ International Association of Corporate and Professional Recruitment (IACPR)
327 N Palm Dr., Ste.201
Beverly Hills, CA 90210
Ph: (310)550-0304 (310)550-8050
Fax: (206)202-4838
E-mail: office@iacpr.org
URL: http://www.iacpr.org
Contact: Nancie S. Whitehouse, Chair
Founded: 1978. **Members:** 300. **Membership Dues:** individual, $400 (annual). **Staff:** 4. **Budget:** $400,000. **Regional Groups:** 4. **Multinational. Description:** Human resources executives and executive search professionals who are leaders in executive recruitment and retention. Serves as a communications network for sharing information and solving problems within the corporate recruiting industry. **Awards:** Professional Recruiters Ovation Award. **Frequency:** annual. **Type:** recognition. **Committees:** Professional Practices. **Formerly:** (1991) National Association of Corporate and Professional Recruiters; (1997) International Association of Corporate and Professional Resources. **Publications:** *Impact*, semiannual. Newsletter ● *Quick Takes*, bimonthly. Newsletter. **Conventions/Meetings:** annual international conference - 2008 Oct. 5-7, New York, NY.

1266 ■ International Association of Employment Web Sites (IAEWS)
2052 Shippan Ave.
Stamford, CT 06902
Ph: (203)964-1888
Fax: (203)964-1877
E-mail: director@employmentwebsites.org
URL: http://www.employmentwebsites.org
Contact: Peter Weddle, Exec. Dir.
Membership Dues: organization (based on organization's revenue), $450-$10,000 (annual). **Multinational. Description:** Serves as a reliable source of information about the services, practices and status of the global online employment industry. Supports a range of initiatives to bring its members' contributions to the attention of the public, the media, and the government. Provides a forum for its members to discuss, ratify and promulgate standards of operation that will benefit job seekers, employers and recruiters who access their web sites. **Publications:** Report, quarterly.

1267 ■ International Public Management Association for Human Resources (IPMA-HR)
1617 Duke St.
Alexandria, VA 22314
Ph: (703)549-7100
Fax: (703)684-0948
E-mail: ipma@ipma-hr.org
URL: http://www.ipma-hr.org
Contact: Neil Reichenberg, Exec. Dir.
Founded: 1973. **Members:** 7,500. **Membership Dues:** individual/consultant, $145 (annual) ● international agency, $500 (annual) ● agency/associate, $330-$2,195 (annual) ● online individual, $100 (annual) ● emeritus, $70 (annual) ● student, $35 (annual). **Staff:** 20. **Budget:** $3,000,000. **Regional Groups:** 4. **Local Groups:** 53. **Multinational. Description:** Seeks to improve human resource practices in government through provision of testing services, advisory service, conferences, professional development programs, research, and publications. Sponsors seminars, conferences, and workshops on various phases of public personnel administration. Compiles statistics. **Libraries: Type:** reference. **Holdings:** 10,000. **Awards:** Agency Award for Excellence. **Frequency:** annual. **Type:** recognition. **Recipient:** for an agency member of IPMA ● Honorary Life Membership. **Frequency:** annual. **Type:** recognition. **Recipient:** for distinguished service in upholding the purposes of IPMA ● Warner W. Stockberger Achievement Award. **Frequency:** annual. **Type:** recognition. **Recipient:** for individual and outstanding contributions to the field of public personnel. **Committees:** Awards; Chapter Development and Relations; Conference Program; Fellowship; Human Rights; International; Nominating; Publications; Resolutions; Technology. **Programs:** International Training Conference; Regional and Section Conferences. **Formed by Merger of:** Public Personnel Association; Society for Personnel Administration. **Formerly:** (2004) International Personnel Management Association. **Publications:** *Agency Issues*, biweekly. Newsletter. Summarizes recent regulations and legislation affecting public sector personnel management. **Price:** free, for agency members only. **Circulation:** 2,500 ● *International Personnel Management Association*, annual. Membership Directory. **Price:** included in membership dues; $150.00 for nonmembers. **Circulation:** 6,000. **Advertising:** accepted ● *IPMA News*, monthly. Newsletter. Covers public sector human resource topics, legislation, professional development opportunities and membership activities. **Price:** included in membership dues. **Circulation:** 6,000. **Advertising:** accepted ● *Public Personnel Management*, quarterly. Journal. Features articles on labor relations, assessment issues, comparative personnel policies, and governmental reform. **Price:** included in membership dues; $75.00 in U.S. and Canada; $50.00 online. ISSN: 0091-0260. **Circulation:** 7,000. **Advertising:** accepted. Alternate Formats: microform; online. **Conventions/Meetings:** annual International Training - conference (exhibits).

1268 ■ National Association for Alternative Staffing (NAAS)
3535 S Woodland Cir.
Quinton, VA 23141
Ph: (804)932-9159
Free: (888)436-NAAS
Fax: (804)932-9461
E-mail: roleary@naas-net.org
URL: http://www.naas-net.org
Contact: Kenneth Wood, Pres.
Founded: 1991. **Membership Dues:** general, $500 (annual). **Description:** Increases awareness of human resources outsourcing and professional employer organizations. Equips members with the tools needed for changing regulatory environment.

1269 ■ National Association for the Employment of Americans (NAEA)
Address Unknown since 2007
Membership Dues: $15 (annual) ● unemployed, $5 (annual). **Description:** "NAEA is a unified voice to speak for the merits of the American workforce and to denounce those forces that would reduce the United States to economic depression and foreign domination.". **Publications:** Reports.

1270 ■ National Association of Executive Recruiters (NAER)
c/o Hall and Associates
1 E Wacker Dr., Ste.2600
Chicago, IL 60601
Ph: (847)885-1453
E-mail: naerinfo@naer.org
URL: http://www.naer.org
Contact: Jim Schneider, Chm.
Founded: 1984. **Members:** 50. **Membership Dues:** regular, $750 (annual). **Staff:** 1. **Description:** Executive recruitment and search specialist firms providing counsel and assistance in identifying and hiring candidates for middle- and senior-level management positions. Promotes and enhances the public image, awareness, and understanding of the executive search profession. Serves as a forum for exchange of ideas among members; conducts educational programs and owners' roundtable. Maintains code of ethics and professional practice guidelines. **Publications:** Membership Directory, annual. Includes listing by name, firm, and field of specialty. **Conventions/Meetings:** annual meeting and seminar, roundtable conference discussion.

1271 ■ National Association of Part-Time and Temporary Employees (NAPTE)
5800 Barton, Ste.201
PO Box 3805
Shawnee, KS 66203
Ph: (913)962-7740
E-mail: napte-champion@worldnet.att.net
URL: http://www.members.tripod.com/~napte
Contact: Preston L. Conner, Pres.
Founded: 1994. **Membership Dues:** individual, $20 (annual). **Description:** Promotes the economic and social interests of persons working on a part-time, contingent, or temporary basis through research, advocacy, and member services. Offers short-term portable health insurance. **Libraries: Type:** reference. **Holdings:** books, clippings, periodicals. **Subjects:** economic and labor trends, career development, public policy. **Publications:** *NAPTE Tempo*, bimonthly. Newsletter. **Price:** included in membership dues. **Advertising:** accepted ● Also publishes career development materials.

1272 ■ National Association of Personnel Services (NAPS)
The Village at Banner Elk, Ste.108
PO Box 2128
Banner Elk, NC 28604
Ph: (828)898-4929
Fax: (828)898-8098
E-mail: conrad.taylor@recruitinglife.com
URL: http://www.recruitinglife.com
Contact: Conrad Taylor, Pres.
Founded: 1961. **Members:** 1,780. **Membership Dues:** company, $2,400 (annual) ● firm ($9.95/additional office), $39 (monthly) ● individual, $120 (annual) ● allied (vendor), $49 (monthly). **Staff:** 7. **Budget:** $1,800,000. **Description:** Private employment and temporary service firms. Compiles statistics on professional agency growth and development; conducts certification program and educational programs. Association is distinct from former name of National Association of Personnel Consultants. **Computer Services:** Mailing lists, of members. **Committees:** Certification; Education; Ethics; Governmental Affairs; Retained Search; Temporary Help. **Absorbed:** American Institute of Employment Counseling. **Formed by Merger of:** Employment Agencies (Protective) Association; National Association of Employment Agencies; National Employment Board. **Formerly:** (1978) National Employment Association; (1992) National Association of Personnel Consultants. **Publications:** *Inside NAPS*, 8/year. Newsletter. **Price:** $60.00/year. **Circulation:** 4,000. **Advertising:** accepted ● Membership Directory, annual. **Price:** free for members. Alternate Formats: online. **Conventions/Meetings:** annual conference (exhibits) - always September/October.

1273 ■ National Association of Professional Employer Organizations (NAPEO)
901 N Pitt St., Ste.150
Alexandria, VA 22314
Ph: (703)836-0466
Fax: (703)836-0976
E-mail: info@napeo.org
URL: http://www.napeo.org
Contact: Milan P. Yager, Exec. VP
Founded: 1984. **Members:** 500. **Membership Dues:** associate, $750 (annual) ● regular (for every 1 million in annual payroll), $130 (annual). **Staff:** 13. **Budget:** $4,000,000. **Regional Groups:** 4. **State Groups:** 12. **Description:** Professional employer organizations. Seeks to enhance professionalism in the professional employer industry. Sponsors educational and public information programs. Maintains speakers' bureau; compiles statistics. **Libraries: Type:** reference. **Awards: Type:** recognition. **Computer Services:** database, membership list. **Com-**

mittees: Accounting Practices; Convention and Educational Services; Government Affairs; Public Relations. **Formerly:** (1994) National Staff Leasing Association. **Publications:** *PEO Insider*, 10/year. Magazine. **Price:** included in membership dues; $150.00 /year for nonmembers. **Advertising:** accepted ● Directory, annual. **Conventions/Meetings:** annual Legal & Legislative Conference - May. 2009 May 17-19, Arlington, VA ● annual Professional Employee Conference and Marketplace - convention and trade show (exhibits) - always fall; September/October. 2008 Sept. 15-17, Phoenix, AZ.

1274 ■ National Association of Public Sector Equal Opportunity Officers (NAPSEO)

c/o Sharon Ofuani
City of Tallahassee Equal Opportunity Dept.
300 S Adams St.
Tallahassee, FL 32301
Ph: (850)891-8290
Fax: (850)891-8733
E-mail: ofuanis@talgov.com
URL: http://www.talgov.com
Contact: Sharon Ofuani, Contact

Founded: 1983. **Members:** 125. **Membership Dues:** active, $75 (annual) ● associate, $75 (annual) ● affiliate, $100 (annual). **Description:** Equal employment opportunity officers and coordinators, human resources managers, employee relations directors, attorneys, lawmakers, consultants, community relations specialists, and other associated professionals in the public sector. Promotes the professionalism of equal opportunity workers and an understanding of diversity as means for improving the quality of life for all citizens. Serves as a resource for the public and private sectors through education and training. Provides recruitment assistance for professional, technical, and executive/managerial positions. Acts as a clearinghouse for members on effective problem solving and decision making. **Publications:** Book. Covers opportunities featuring results of independent research and papers on equal opportunity and affirmative action. ● Newsletter. Covers issues affecting public sector employees at all levels. **Conventions/Meetings:** annual conference and workshop.

1275 ■ National Association of Teachers' Agencies (NATA)

Address Unknown since 2008

Founded: 1914. **Members:** 20. **Membership Dues:** regular/provisional, $250 (annual). **Budget:** $20,000. **Description:** Private employment agencies engaged primarily in the placement of teaching and administration personnel. Works to standardize records and promote a strong ethical sense in the placement field. Maintains speakers' bureau. **Libraries: Type:** reference. **Holdings:** archival material. **Committees:** Conference; Ethics. **Absorbed:** Association of Teachers Agencies of the South. **Publications:** *NATA Notes*, quarterly. Newsletter. **Advertising:** accepted. **Conventions/Meetings:** annual conference - always October or November.

1276 ■ National Hire American Citizens Society

Address Unknown since 2008

Membership Dues: individual, $30 (annual) ● student, $15 (annual). **Description:** Dedicated to the "protection and promotion of the American citizen professional. Aims to advance the American public's welfare and promote the professional, social, and economic interests of the American citizen professional; to promote the hiring of American citizens, to stimulate the dialogue with American business and political leaders for a return to the concepts of American workers first and foremost, and to promote our American heritage of American workers and an American wage".

1277 ■ North American Alliance for Fair Employment (NAFFE)

30 Harrison Ave., 4th Fl.
Boston, MA 02111
Ph: (617)482-6300
Fax: (617)842-7300
E-mail: info@fairjobs.org
URL: http://www.fairjobs.org

Description: Exists as "an alliance of organizations across a broad range of constituencies affected by problems associated with nonstandard work, such as part-time, temporary and contract employment". Stands for equal treatment (pay, benefits and protections under law) regardless of employment status. Serves its members as part of the broader fight to ensure that working people have the right and opportunity to provide for themselves, their families and their communities. **Committees:** Health and Safety; Immigration; Message/Media/Public Education; Organizing; Policy; Prison Labor; Research/Analysis; Temp Work. **Publications:** *Know Your Rights*. Brochure. Alternate Formats: online ● *News & Comment*. Newsletter. Alternate Formats: online ● *Web Directory*. Alternate Formats: online ● Reports. Alternate Formats: online ● Papers. Alternate Formats: online.

1278 ■ The Organization for the Rights of American Workers (TORAW)

PO Box 2354
Meriden, CT 06450-1454
E-mail: feedback@toraw.org
URL: http://www.toraw.org

Membership Dues: individual, $25 (annual) ● student, $10 (annual). **Description:** Acts as a worker advocacy group "demanding that U.S. jobs be preserved first and foremost for American citizens." Strives to "guarantee that U.S. citizens and permanent green card status immigrants are gainfully employed before non-immigrant foreign workers are imported to fill positions.". **Publications:** *TORAW Reports*. Newsletter. Alternate Formats: online ● Reports.

1279 ■ Profit Sharing/401(k) Council of America (PSCA)

20 N Wacker Dr., Ste.3700
Chicago, IL 60606
Ph: (312)419-1863
Fax: (312)419-1864
E-mail: psca@psca.org
URL: http://www.psca.org
Contact: David L. Wray, Pres.

Founded: 1947. **Members:** 1,200. **Membership Dues:** associate (based on number of eligible plan participants), $295-$3,900 (annual) ● affiliate, $295 (annual). **Staff:** 7. **Description:** Sponsors sharing of information and working together to preserve a favorable regulatory environment for profit sharing and 401(K) plans. Collects best practices information and shares it with members through faxes, publications, conferences and a technical assistance hotline. Supports plan sponsors and participants in Washington through Congressional lobbying. **Awards:** PSCA Signature Award. **Frequency:** annual. **Type:** recognition. **Recipient:** to PSCA staff. **Committees:** Communication and Education; Legal and Legislative; National Conference Planning; Provider Advisory; Research. **Affiliated With:** Profit Sharing/401(k) Education Foundation. **Formerly:** Council of Profit Sharing Industries; (1996) Profit Sharing Council of America. **Publications:** *Buying Guide*, annual. Membership Directory ● *Defined Contribution Insights*, monthly. Magazine. Includes articles about best practices in profit sharing and 401 (K) plan design, administration, investment, compliance, communication and education. **Price:** included in membership dues. **Circulation:** 2,500. **Advertising:** accepted. Alternate Formats: online ● *Profit Sharing Handbook*. **Price:** $40.00 for nonmembers; $25.00 for members ● *PSCA Executive Report*, monthly. Newsletter. Focuses on legislative, regulatory, and judicial developments affecting profit sharing and 401 plans. **Price:** included in membership dues. **Circulation:** 1,200 ● *Take Control: How to Save Now for Retirement*. Pamphlet. Alternate Formats: online ● Survey, annual. **Price:** included in membership dues; $195.00 for nonmembers ● Annual Report, annual. Alternate Formats: online ● Papers. Alternate Formats: online. **Conventions/Meetings:** annual conference (exhibits) - always September ● annual Midwest Regional Conference - meeting - always March ● annual Washington Forum - meeting - always March.

1280 ■ Profit Sharing/401(k) Education Foundation

20 N Wacker Dr., Ste.3700
Chicago, IL 60606
Ph: (312)419-1863
Fax: (312)419-1864
E-mail: psca@psca.org
URL: http://www.psca.org
Contact: David L. Wray, Pres.

Founded: 1951. **Description:** Seeks to gather and disseminate information regarding the experiences of companies with profit sharing, 401 (K) employee stock ownership, and participative programs. Serves as resource in the design and operation of these programs; studies the potential of profit sharing programs in solving human and economic problems such as motivation, inflation, productivity, industrial relations, quality-of-life, and retirement income. Compiles statistics. **Awards:** Signature Awards. **Frequency:** annual. **Type:** recognition. **Recipient:** for excellence in profit sharing or 401(k) plan communication. **Affiliated With:** Profit Sharing/401(k) Council of America. **Formerly:** Profit Sharing Research Foundation. **Publications:** *Defined Contributions Insights*, bimonthly. Magazine ● *Executive Report*, monthly. Newsletter ● *Profit Sharing: Philosophy, Practice, Benefits to Society*. Book. Discusses the versatility of profit sharing. **Price:** $7.25. **Conventions/Meetings:** annual conference (exhibits).

1281 ■ Recruiters Online Network (RON)

c/o Minnie Ahlstrand
135 Bishops Curve
Berlin, CT 06037-3703
Free: (800)364-8425
Fax: (888)752-8425
E-mail: info@recruitersonline.com
URL: http://www.recruitersonline.com
Contact: Anthony Rossi, Exec. Dir.

Members: 7,000. **Membership Dues:** regular, $995 (annual). **Description:** Recruiters, employment agencies, and employment professionals. Committed to the progress of using the Internet and other technologies for employee search and placement.

1282 ■ Save U.S. Jobs (SUJ)

Address Unknown since 2008

Membership Dues: individual, $25 (annual). **Description:** "Save U.S. Jobs.biz was organized in Silicon Valley as a direct result of the growing and alarming trend of U.S. companies shipping well-paying American jobs to foreign shores." Mission is to plan direct action events, such as mass phone and email campaigns, company-specific nonviolent marches, sit-ins and boycotts. **Computer Services:** Electronic publishing, monthly newsletter ● online services, forum.

1283 ■ WorldatWork

14040 N Northsight Blvd.
Scottsdale, AZ 85260
Ph: (480)951-9191 (480)922-2020
Free: (877)951-9191
Fax: (480)483-8352
E-mail: customerrelations@worldatwork.org
URL: http://www.worldatwork.org
Contact: Anne C. Ruddy CPCU, Pres.

Founded: 1955. **Members:** 25,000. **Membership Dues:** practitioner/consultant in U.S., $320 (annual) ● practitioner/consultant in Canada, $410 (annual) ● practitioner/consultant outside U.S. and Canada, $370 (annual) ● academic/university professor in U.S., $115 (annual) ● academic/university professor in Canada, $130 (annual) ● academic/university professor outside U.S. and Canada, $150 (annual) ● student in U.S., $55 (annual) ● student in Canada, $65 (annual) ● student outside U.S. and Canada, $90 (annual). **Staff:** 115. **Local Groups:** 80. **Multinational. Description:** Dedicated to knowledge leadership in compensation, benefits and total rewards, focusing on disciplines associated with attracting, retaining and motivating employees. Offers CCP, CBP, and GRP certification and education programs, conducts surveys, research and provides networking opportunities. **Libraries: Type:** reference. **Holdings:** periodicals. **Awards:** Keystone Award. **Frequency:**

annual. **Type:** recognition. **Recipient:** to an individual with significant contributions to the field. **Computer Services:** Mailing lists, of members ● online services, information resources. **Formerly:** (1955) Ohio Wage and Salary Association; (1963) Midwest Compensation Association; (2000) American Compensation Association. **Publications:** *The Conference Insider*. Newsletter. Alternate Formats: online ● *Salary Budget Survey*. **Price:** $125.00 ● *Workspan*, monthly. Magazine. Includes special features and news about practices in the profession. **Price:** included in membership dues; $95.00 /year for nonmembers. **Circulation:** 25,000. **Advertising:** accepted ● *Workspan Weekly*. Newsletter. **Price:** included in membership dues; $49.95 for nonmembers ● *WorldatWork Journal*, quarterly. Features peer-reviewed, strategic and scholarly articles. **Price:** included in membership dues; $125.00 /year for nonmembers. ISSN: 1068-0918. **Circulation:** 25,000 ● Annual Report, annual. Alternate Formats: online ● Audiotapes. Alternate Formats: online ● Numerous additional publications, surveys and reports available. See Web site for details. **Conventions/Meetings:** annual conference (exhibits) - always summer. 2009 May 31-June 3, Seattle, WA.

Energy

1284 ■ Alliance of Energy Suppliers
c/o Edison Electric Institute
701 Pennsylvania Ave. NW
Washington, DC 20004-2696
Ph: (202)508-5000 (202)508-5571
E-mail: rmcmahon@eei.org
URL: http://www.eei.org
Contact: Richard McMahon, Exec. Dir.
Membership Dues: associate (based on company's annual revenues), $4,000-$6,000 (annual). **Description:** Promotes and supports the commercial interests of power producers and marketers. **Committees:** Energy Supply Executive Advisory; Policy Committee on Energy Supply. **Task Forces:** Energy Supply Policy; Rail; Renewable Energy. **Affiliated With:** Edison Electric Institute. **Publications:** *Alliance Express*. Newsletter. **Price:** free.

1285 ■ Business Council for Sustainable Energy (BCSE)
1620 Eye St. NW, Ste.501
Washington, DC 20006
Ph: (202)785-0507
Fax: (202)785-0514
E-mail: bcse@bcse.org
URL: http://www.bcse.org
Contact: Lisa Jacobson, Exec. Dir.
Founded: 1992. **Membership Dues:** associate/supporter - minimum, $2,500 (annual) ● associate/supporter - maximum, $15,000 (annual) ● board - minimum, $5,000 (annual) ● board - maximum, $25,000 (annual). **Staff:** 1. **Description:** Natural gas, energy efficiency, electric utility, and renewable energy executives. Strives to realize the nation's economic, environmental, and national security goals; implement cost-effective programs and policies that recognize environmental attributes of various energy sources; provide technological response to environmental issues; and reduce reliance on imported fossil fuels. **Publications:** *Climate Change and Business*, 10/year. Report. Contains information on climate change.

1286 ■ Consortium for Energy Efficiency (CEE)
98 N Washington St., Ste.101
Boston, MA 02114-1918
Ph: (617)589-3949
Fax: (617)589-3948
E-mail: mhoffman@cee1.org
URL: http://www.cee1.org
Contact: Marc Hoffman, Exec. Dir.
Founded: 1991. **Membership Dues:** utility (without mandated program), $2,575-$6,180 (annual) ● state agency, $3,090 (annual) ● national government agency, $6,180 (annual) ● research and development lab, $773 (annual) ● energy-efficiency organization, $773 (annual) ● individual, $155 (annual) ● administrator (based on the number of customers), $2,575-$18,540 (annual). **Description:** Promotes the manufacture and purchase of energy-efficient products and services. Advocates lasting structural and behavioral changes in the marketplace, resulting in the increased adoption of energy-efficient technologies. **Libraries: Type:** reference; open to the public. **Holdings:** articles, papers. **Subjects:** energy, gas, efficiency. **Publications:** Newsletter, quarterly. Contains information about the industry and the current activities of the organization. ● Annual Report, annual. Alternate Formats: online. **Conventions/Meetings:** board meeting.

1287 ■ National Alliance of Clean Energy Business Incubators
c/o Lawrence M. Murphy, PhD
1617 Cole Blvd.
Golden, CO 80401-3393
Ph: (303)275-3050
E-mail: lawrence_murphy@nrel.gov
URL: http://www.cleanenergyalliance.com
Contact: Lawrence M. Murphy PhD, Contact
Founded: 2000. **Description:** Provides business and financial services tailored to the needs of the clean energy community. Strengthens its network and welcomes new energy companies, venture firms, angel investors, nonprofits, government organizations, and others committed to supporting the clean energy industry. Provides services that gives members a competitive advantage over other clean energy start-ups.

1288 ■ National Energy Marketers Association (NEM)
3333 K St. NW, Ste.110
Washington, DC 20007
Ph: (202)333-3288
Fax: (202)333-3266
E-mail: info@energymarketers.com
URL: http://www.energymarketers.com
Contact: Craig Goodman, Pres.
Multinational. Description: Represents the wholesale and retail marketers of energy, telecom and financial related products and services throughout the US, Canada and the UK. Helps resolve issues that delay competition. Advocates for neutral standards of conduct that protect all market participants. Promotes policies that encourage investments in new technology.

Engineering

1289 ■ American Society of Validation Engineers (ASVE)
Address Unknown since 2008
URL: http://www.asve.org
Founded: 2002. **Membership Dues:** individual, $99 ● student, $79. **Multinational. Description:** Advocates for excellence in the education and practice of Verification and Validation Engineering. Enhances the technical competency of members. Encourages the free flow of ideas and knowledge exchange.

Engines

1290 ■ Association of Diesel Specialists (ADS)
PO Box 13966
Research Triangle Park, NC 27709-3966
Ph: (919)406-8804
Fax: (919)406-1306
E-mail: info@diesel.org
URL: http://www.diesel.org
Contact: David A. Fehling, Exec. Dir.
Founded: 1956. **Members:** 850. **Membership Dues:** service, diesel engine service in U.S. and Canada, $595 (annual) ● service, diesel engine service outside U.S. and Canada, $275 (annual) ● technical training, $350 (annual) ● allied equipment manufacturer, service provider (initial fee), $395 ● associate, $295 (annual) ● manufacturer, replacement parts manufacturer, distributor, $1,295 (annual) ● diesel engine manufacturer, vehicle manufacturer, allied equipment manufacturer, service provider, $795 (annual). **Staff:** 2. **Budget:** $800,000. **Languages:** English, Spanish. **Multinational. Description:** Corporations and technically oriented professionals engaged in the sale and service of fuel injection, governor, supercharger, and turbocharger systems, and interested in improving the technology and servicing of these systems. Provides members with technical information and business management support. Sponsors a Parts Finder Program that compiles a monthly listing of obsolescent or surplus parts for sale by ADS members in the United States and Canada. Offers an ADS Nationwide Warranty Program which allows members to cooperate with each other and provide warranty service for transient customers. Conducts semiannual "TechCert" exams in cooperation with the National Institute for Automotive Service Excellence to certify diesel technicians. **Committees:** Business Management; Canadian General; Certification; Communications; Convention Planning; Exhibits; Latin American General; Liaison; Manufacturers; Membership; Technical Education. **Programs:** ADS TechCert Diesel Technician. **Publications:** *ADS International Directory of Members, Products and Services*, annual. Membership Directory. **Price:** $20.00 each; $750.00 set of 50 ● *Nozzle Chatter*, bimonthly. Newsletter. Contains news of association and diesel industry. **Price:** free for members. **Circulation:** 3,000. **Advertising:** accepted. Alternate Formats: online ● Bulletins. Alternate Formats: online ● Also publishes specifications for repairs, tips for more efficient service methods, and other technical materials. **Conventions/Meetings:** annual convention and trade show (exhibits) - always early August.

1291 ■ Engine Manufacturers Association (EMA)
2 N LaSalle St., Ste.2200
Chicago, IL 60602
Ph: (312)827-8700
Fax: (312)827-8737
E-mail: ema@enginemanufacturers.org
URL: http://www.enginemanufacturers.org
Contact: Jed R. Mandel, Pres.
Founded: 1968. **Members:** 29. **Staff:** 5. **Budget:** $8,500,000. **Description:** Producers of internal combustion engines for all applications except those used exclusively for automobiles and aircraft. Conducts research and development programs on noise, smoke, and other emissions from internal combustion engines. **Telecommunication Services:** electronic mail, jmandel@emamail.org. **Committees:** Alternate Fuels; Diesel Fuel Quality; Diesel Health Effects Issues Group; Emissions Group; Engine Coolants; Engine Lubricants; Environmental Activities; Fluids Group; Grounds Care and Utility; Heavy Duty On-Highway; Locomotive Engine; Marine Engine; Mobile Off-Highway; Public Policy Group; Public Relations; State Legislative; Stationary; Statistics; Washington Legislative. **Subcommittees:** APBF-DEC Policy Steering; Diesel Health Steering; Locomotive Test Procedure; Nonroad Emissions Testing. **Task Forces:** Calibration Standards; Engine Test Facilities. **Supersedes:** Internal Combustion Engine Institute. **Publications:** *EMA Information Directory*. Alternate Formats: online ● *Engine Fluids Data Book*, biennial. Manual. Contains information on lube oil physical and chemical properties. **Price:** $100.00 first edition, plus shipping and handling ● *SCR-Urea Infrastructure Implementation Study Final Report*. Alternate Formats: online. **Conventions/Meetings:** annual board meeting.

1292 ■ Outdoor Power Equipment Aftermarket Association (OPEAA)
1726 M St. NW, Ste.1101
Washington, DC 20036
Ph: (202)775-8605
Fax: (202)833-1577
E-mail: opeaa@opeaa.org
URL: http://www.opeaa.org
Contact: John Fogle, Pres.
Founded: 1986. **Members:** 75. **Membership Dues:** corporate, $450-$4,700 (annual) ● international/affili-

ate, $600 (annual). **Staff:** 3. **Budget:** $250,000. **Multinational. Description:** Manufacturers and distributors of aftermarket parts. Promotes adherence to high product quality standards by members. Encourages the use of aftermarket replacement parts in outdoor power equipment such as lawnmowers and chainsaws; works to ensure unrestrained trade in the industry. **Awards:** Bill Nelson Scholarship Endowment. **Frequency:** annual. **Type:** scholarship. **Recipient:** to outstanding high school graduate. **Councils:** Senior Advisory. **Publications:** *Cutting Edge*, quarterly. Newsletter. Contains news about the association and its members. **Price:** free. **Advertising:** accepted. Alternate Formats: online ● Membership Directory, annual. **Conventions/Meetings:** annual convention ● annual meeting.

1293 ■ Outdoor Power Equipment and Engine Service Association (OPEESA)

c/o Nancy Cueroni, Exec. Dir.
37 Pratt St.
Essex, CT 06426-1159
Ph: (860)767-1770
Fax: (860)767-7932
E-mail: executivedirector@opeesa.com
URL: http://www.opeesa.com
Contact: Nancy Cueroni, Exec. Dir.

Founded: 2001. **Members:** 152. **Staff:** 2. **Description:** Works to lead the outdoor power equipment industry in customer service through the promotion and sale of original equipment parts utilizing a professional service dealer distribution network. **Absorbed:** (2003) Outdoor Power Equipment Distributors Association. **Publications:** *Dealer Success Series*. Video. **Price:** $79.95 ● *Ope-In-The-Know*. Newsletter. Alternate Formats: online ● Brochures ● Catalog ● Manual ● Membership Directory, annual. **Conventions/Meetings:** annual convention.

1294 ■ Outdoor Power Equipment Institute (OPEI)

341 S Patrick St.
Old Town
Alexandria, VA 22314
Ph: (703)549-7600
Fax: (703)549-7604
E-mail: pgoodell@opei.org
URL: http://www.opei.org
Contact: Mr. William G. Harley, Pres./CEO

Founded: 1952. **Members:** 81. **Membership Dues:** associate, $5,000 (annual). **Staff:** 8. **Budget:** $4,500,000. **Description:** Manufacturers of lawn mowers, garden tractors, snow throwers, utility vehicles, chainsaws, motor tillers, shredder/grinders, edger/trimmers, leaf vacuums, log splitters, stump cutters, chippers and sprayers, and major components. Compiles statistics and forecasting information; sponsors industry trade shows; produces comprehensive consumer education materials on safety and other industry issues; hosts' annual member meeting; represents members' interests on important legislative and regulatory issues. **Committees:** Communications; Human Resources; Marketing; Product Liability and Government Relations; Statistical; Technical Advisory; Traffic. **Formerly:** (1960) Lawn Mower Institute. **Publications:** *Association Insider*, monthly. Newsletter. Covers association activities on behalf of members. **Price:** free for members ● *Export-Import Report*, quarterly ● *Traffic Report*, monthly ● Membership Directory, annual. **Conventions/Meetings:** annual International Lawn, Garden, and Power Equipment Expo - trade show, more than 500 exhibitors (exhibits) ● annual meeting.

1295 ■ Production Engine Remanufacturers Association (PERA)

28203 Woodhaven Rd.
Edwards, MO 65326
Ph: (417)998-5057
Fax: (417)998-5056
E-mail: nancieboland@pera.org
URL: http://www.pera.org
Contact: Nancie Boland, Contact

Founded: 1946. **Members:** 150. **Membership Dues:** remanufacturer, $1,000-$1,500 (annual) ● remanufacturer subsidiary, $550 (annual) ● trade press, $400 (annual) ● sales agency, manufacturer's representative, manufacturer subsidiary, $200 (annual) ● manufacturer, $800-$1,250 (annual) ● core supplier, $1,050-$1,500 (annual). **Staff:** 2. **Budget:** $300,000. **Description:** Production line combustion engine remanufacturers; manufacturers and representatives supplying material and parts to remanufacturers. Assists members in operating more productive and profitable businesses by: conducting seminars and meetings; publishing legislative, management, and technical bulletins. **Libraries: Type:** reference. **Awards:** Associate Member of the Year Award. **Frequency:** annual. **Type:** recognition. **Recipient:** for meritorious service to the engine remanufacturing industry ● Engine Remanufacturer of the Year Award. **Frequency:** annual. **Type:** recognition. **Recipient:** for meritorious service to the automotive industry. **Computer Services:** database, core identification for engine components. **Additional Websites:** http://www.enginedatasource.com. **Committees:** Government Affairs; Industry Methods; Industry Statistics; Legislative; Technical. **Divisions:** Ladies Auxiliary. **Formerly:** (1969) Western Engine Rebuilders Association; (1973) Production Engine Rebuilders Association. **Publications:** *Engine Application and Identification Catalog*, annual. Lists engines by make and model year; includes cubic inches, liters, bores, and numbers for block casting, crank forging, head casting and crank kits. **Price:** $20.00 for nonmembers ● *EngiNews*, monthly. Newsletter. **Price:** included in membership dues. **Circulation:** 480. Alternate Formats: online ● *Production Engine Remanufacturers Association—Membership Directory and Handbook*, annual. Lists remanufacturers alphabetically and by state, manufacturers, representatives, core suppliers, trade presses, and major association events. **Price:** included in membership dues; $500.00 for nonmembers ● Membership Directory, annual. **Conventions/Meetings:** annual convention, business and social program focused on the need of the owners and managers of large engine remanufacturing companies and their suppliers - every fall ● annual Technical/Marketing Conference - in spring.

Entertainment

1296 ■ American Amusement Machine Association (AAMA)

450 E Higgins Rd., Ste.201
Elk Grove Village, IL 60007
Ph: (847)290-9088
Fax: (847)290-9121
E-mail: information@coin-op.org
URL: http://www.coin-op.org
Contact: Michael R. Rudowicz, Pres.

Founded: 1981. **Members:** 225. **Membership Dues:** manufacturer, distributor, $1,800 (annual) ● associate, $745 (annual). **Staff:** 4. **Budget:** $2,000,000. **Multinational. Description:** Manufacturers and distributors of coin machines; parts suppliers and others interested in promoting and protecting the amusement machine industry. Seeks solutions to the problem of copyright infringement by foreign manufacturers, and legislative and regulatory problems facing the industry and manufacturers. Works to improve the image of the coin-operated amusement industry. Presents views to governmental decision-makers. Operates American Amusement Machine Charitable Foundation. **Committees:** ASI Show; Budget; Distributor; Education; Enforcement; Foreign Business Development; Government Relations; Industry Promotion; Nominating; Personnel; Standardization; Video Content. **Affiliated With:** Amusement and Music Operators Association. **Formed by Merger of:** International Association of Amusement Parks & Attractions. **Publications:** *Loose Change*, monthly. Newsletter. **Price:** available to members only. **Circulation:** 550. Alternate Formats: online ● Manual, periodic ● Membership Directory, annual. **Price:** included in membership dues. **Advertising:** accepted. **Conventions/Meetings:** annual Amusement Showcase International - trade show (exhibits) - always spring ● EXIME - trade show ● annual meeting (exhibits).

1297 ■ American Dinner Theatre Institute (ADTI)

1275 E Waterloo Rd.
Akron, OH 44306
Ph: (330)724-9855
Free: (800)362-4100
Fax: (330)724-2232
E-mail: carouseldt@carouseldinnertheatre.com
URL: http://www.carouseldinnertheatre.com
Contact: David W. Slaght, Pres.

Founded: 1972. **Members:** 16. **Staff:** 1. **Description:** Owner/operators of dinner theatres. Seeks to: advance the construction, maintenance, management, and operation of professional year-round dinner theatres; promote good theatrical productions and wholesome food services; encourage the free exchange of information and experience among members and other persons. **Libraries: Type:** reference. **Holdings:** archival material. **Subjects:** theater. **Publications:** *American Dinner Theatre Institute—Newsletter*, monthly. Includes schedule of productions in member dinner theatres. **Price:** free for members ● Membership Directory, annual. **Price:** available to members only. **Conventions/Meetings:** semiannual meeting.

1298 ■ Amusement Industry Manufacturers and Suppliers International (AIMS)

Banco Bus. Park
1061 Main St., Bin No. 28
North Huntingdon, PA 15642
Ph: (724)864-3862
Fax: (724)864-8035
E-mail: info@aimsintl.org
URL: http://www.aimsintl.org
Contact: John P. Hinde, Exec. Dir.

Founded: 1926. **Members:** 480. **Membership Dues:** active, full, $360 (annual) ● associate, $100 (annual). **Staff:** 5. **Budget:** $250,000. **Languages:** English, Spanish. **Description:** Represents manufacturers and suppliers of amusement riding devices and equipment used by amusement parks, carnivals, and traveling amusement companies. Exchanges information on safety, maintenance, state laws, transportation, and credit. Works to develop safety programs and codes at the federal and state levels; carries out public relations activities; and cooperates with the ASTM to develop voluntary standards for amusement rides and devices. **Awards:** Safety Awards. **Frequency:** annual. **Type:** recognition. **Recipient:** for safety in the amusement industry. **Computer Services:** database, membership list ● online services, trade show, sales leads. **Committees:** Public Relations; Safety. **Affiliated With:** Showmen's League of America; World Waterpark Association. **Formerly:** (1934) Manufacturers Division, National Association of Amusement Parks; (1996) American Recreational Equipment Association. **Publications:** *AIMSAFE*, quarterly. Contains safety-related information. **Price:** $2.00. **Circulation:** 1,500. **Advertising:** accepted. **Conventions/Meetings:** annual Safety Seminar, features classes on safety, equipment and management (exhibits) - always January.

1299 ■ Amusement and Music Operators Association (AMOA)

33 W Higgins Rd., Ste.830
South Barrington, IL 60010
Ph: (847)428-7699
Free: (800)937-2662
Fax: (847)428-7719
E-mail: amoa@amoa.com
URL: http://www.amoa.com
Contact: Jack Kelleher, Exec. VP

Founded: 1948. **Members:** 1,775. **Membership Dues:** operator (based on number of full-time employees), $250-$1,580 (annual) ● associate A (distributor), associate B (supplier), associate C, $400 (annual) ● associate B (manufacturer), $500 (annual) ● classified, $250 (annual). **Staff:** 3. **Budget:** $2,500,000. **Description:** Firms engaged in the coin-operated music, vending, and amusement business. Sponsors juke box and amusement game award programs; compiles industry statistics. Conducts research; offers specialized education programs. **Awards:** Rick Holley Memorial Music Scholarship.

Frequency: annual. **Type:** scholarship. **Recipient:** for students of University of Florida ● Wayne E. Hesch Memorial Scholarship. **Frequency:** annual. **Type:** scholarship. **Recipient:** to individuals endorsed by an AMOA member company. **Telecommunication Services:** electronic mail, jackamoa@aol.com. **Boards:** Industry Directors. **Committees:** Education Foundation; Expo Education/Seminars; Expo Hesch Promotion; Expo Planning; Government Relations; Industry Promotion; Industry Standardization/Technology; Jukebox Promotion; National Dart Association; Notre Dame Program; PAC Fundraising; Tradeshow Enhancement. **Councils:** Past Presidents'. **Subcommittees:** Information Privacy and Security; Jukebox Licensing; Video Content. **Task Forces:** Expo International Attendee; New Director. **Formerly:** (1976) Music Operators of America. **Publications:** *Amusement and Music Operators Association—Roster of Members*, annual. Membership Directory. **Price:** $50.00 additional copy (1st copy is free). **Advertising:** accepted. Alternate Formats: online ● *The Edge*, bimonthly. Newsletter. Alternate Formats: online ● *Policy Guidebook*. Alternate Formats: online. **Conventions/Meetings:** annual International Exposition of Games and Music - convention (exhibits) ● annual regional meeting and seminar ● annual trade show (exhibits).

1300 ■ Coalition of Asian Pacifics in Entertainment (CAPE)
PO Box 251855
Los Angeles, CA 90025
Ph: (310)278-2313
E-mail: info@capeusa.org
URL: http://www.capeusa.org
Contact: Wenda Fong, Chair

Founded: 1991. **Membership Dues:** regular, $75 (annual) ● student, $25 (annual) ● corporate, $300 (annual). **Description:** Supports Asian Pacifics in the arts and entertainment. Increases the social, educational and professional opportunities for Asian Pacifics in the entertainment industry. Serves as a forum for Asian Pacifics in feature film, television, video, publishing, music and other entertainment fields to share common interests and concerns through such programs as screenings, panels, workshops, and hosted conversations with notable executives and artists. **Programs:** CAPE Pitch Lab.

1301 ■ Game Manufacturer Association (GAMA)
280 N High St., Ste.230
Columbus, OH 43215
Ph: (614)255-4500
Fax: (614)255-4499
E-mail: ed@gama.org
URL: http://www.gama.org
Contact: Anthony J. Gallela, Exec. Dir.

Founded: 1977. **Members:** 300. **Membership Dues:** club/convention, communicating, $50 (annual) ● retailer, $125 (annual) ● associate, $100 (annual) ● full, $400 (annual) ● wholesale/distributor, $300 (annual) ● vendor, $200 (annual). **Staff:** 5. **Budget:** $1,000,000. **Multinational. Description:** Manufacturers and distributors of games. Provides a forum for those involved in the purchase, sale, and manufacture of games. Maintains hall of fame and Speaker's Bureau; sponsors educational, research, and charitable programs. **Awards:** Merit of Service. **Frequency:** annual. **Type:** recognition. **Recipient:** for an individual or group with significant recent contribution to the game industry or to GAMA ● Origin Award. **Frequency:** annual. **Type:** recognition. **Recipient:** for excellence in hobby games publishing. **Committees:** Industry Watch; Mentorship. **Divisions:** Retail; Wholesale. **Publications:** *GAMA in Motion*, monthly. Newsletter. Contains news and announcements regarding GAMA business. Alternate Formats: online ● *GAMA Membership Directory*, annual. Contains information and industry data. **Price:** $10.00. **Circulation:** 5,000. **Advertising:** accepted ● *GAMA News*, bimonthly. Newsletter ● *Gama Source Book* ● *Inside Our Industry*. **Circulation:** 5,000 ● *The Manufacturer's Handbook*. **Price:** $20.00 for nonmembers ● *The Retailers Handbook*. Covers all aspects of running a hobby game store. **Price:** $50.00 for nonmembers ● Annual Report, annual. Alternate Formats: online. **Conventions/Meetings:** seminar ● annual trade show, new products, company showcase (exhibits) - always March.

1302 ■ Global Mobile Entertainers Association (GMEA)
121 N Baldwin St.
Johnson City, NY 13790
Ph: (607)729-1485
Free: (877)352-7762
E-mail: art@globalmobile.org
URL: http://www.globalmobile.org
Contact: Art Bradlee, Exec. Dir.

Membership Dues: regular, $122 (annual). **Multinational. Description:** Represents individuals interested in the art of entertaining. Educates the media and the masses about Mobile Entertainment as a musical entertainment of choice. Facilitates communication and cooperation among members. **Publications:** Newsletter, periodic. Alternate Formats: online.

1303 ■ International Association of Amusement Parks and Attractions (IAAPA)
1448 Duke St.
Alexandria, VA 22314
Ph: (703)836-4800
Fax: (703)836-9678
E-mail: cbray@iaapa.org
URL: http://www.iaapa.org
Contact: Charlie Bray, Pres./CEO

Founded: 1918. **Members:** 5,000. **Membership Dues:** amusement facility in U.S. (based on annual gross revenue), $410-$3,275 (annual) ● amusement facility outside U.S. (based on annual gross revenue), $290-$2,300 (annual) ● amusement facility in Western Europe, EUR 255-EUR 2,035 (annual) ● manufacturer, supplier, consultant, individual, $355 (annual). **Staff:** 35. **Budget:** $12,000,000. **Multinational. Description:** Operators of amusement parks, theme parks, tourist attractions, water parks, zoos, aquariums, museums, miniature golf courses, and family entertainment centers; manufacturers and suppliers of amusement equipment and services. Conducts research programs; compiles statistics; hosts annual convention and trade show; publishes periodicals. **Libraries: Type:** reference. **Subjects:** amusement industry. **Awards:** Brass Ring Award. **Frequency:** annual. **Type:** recognition. **Recipient:** for amusement facilities worldwide ● **Frequency:** periodic. **Type:** recognition. **Computer Services:** database, industry article ● mailing lists, of members. **Committees:** Audit; Education; Family Entertainment Centers; Government Relations; Investment; Nominating; Planning. **Councils:** World. **Formed by Merger of:** (1920) National Association of Amusement Parks; National Outdoor Showmen's Association. **Formerly:** (1934) National Association of Amusement Parks, Pools, and Beaches; (1962) International Association of Amusement Parks. **Publications:** *Carousel of Capitols*, quarterly. Newsletter. Alternate Formats: online ● *Funworld*, 11/year. Magazine. Features aspects of the amusement business including safety, thrill rides, financial issues, and profiles of member and nonmember facilities. **Price:** one subscription is free for members; $45.00 /year for nonmembers; $5.00/ issue. **Circulation:** 8,500. **Advertising:** accepted. Alternate Formats: online ● *International Directory and Buyer's Guide*, annual. Features a membership guide with profiles of parks and suppliers. **Price:** $135.00. Alternate Formats: CD-ROM ● *Regulatory Tracking Report*, monthly. Alternate Formats: online ● Manual ● Proceedings ● Annual Report, annual. Alternate Formats: online. **Conventions/Meetings:** annual Attractions Expo - convention and trade show (exhibits).

1304 ■ International Association of Haunted Attractions (IAHA)
1508 Rolling Hills Dr.
Niles, MI 49120
Fax: (574)280-5802
E-mail: woodsofterror@yahoo.com
URL: http://www.hauntedhouseassociation.org
Contact: Eddie McLaurin, Pres.

Membership Dues: individual, $100 (annual) ● business, $200 (annual) ● associate, $75 (annual) ● family, $50 (annual). **Multinational. Description:** Represents professional haunters, actors, set designers, haunted house suppliers, and other related vendors. Assists and advances the haunted house industry through communication, education, and information. Provides a forum for members to communicate with fellow haunters in order to exchange ideas, information, experiences, and concerns. **Publications:** *IAHA E-Zine Newsletter*. **Price:** included in membership dues.

1305 ■ International Association for the Leisure and Entertainment Industry (IALEI)
10 Briarcrest Sq.
Hershey, PA 17033
Ph: (717)533-0534
Free: (888)464-6498
Fax: (717)533-0535
E-mail: tracy@ialei.com
URL: http://www.ialei.org
Contact: Tracy Sarris, Exec. Dir.

Founded: 1993. **Members:** 600. **Membership Dues:** entertainment facility, $300 (annual) ● associate, $375 (annual) ● entertainment developer, $400 (annual) ● additional location, $50 (annual). **Staff:** 5. **Budget:** $500,000. **Description:** Works to promote the family entertainment and recreation center industry. Conducts educational programs; holds competitions; compiles statistics; **Awards:** Golden Token Awards. **Frequency:** annual. **Type:** recognition. **Computer Services:** database ● mailing lists. **Formerly:** (2000) International Association of Family Entertainment Centers. **Publications:** *Fun Extra*, monthly. Newsletter. **Circulation:** 1,000. **Advertising:** accepted. **Conventions/Meetings:** annual Fun Expo - trade show (exhibits).

1306 ■ International Entertainment Buyers Association (IEBA)
PO Box 128376
Nashville, TN 37212
Ph: (615)251-9000
Free: (888)999-4322
Fax: (615)251-9001
E-mail: info@ieba.org
URL: http://www.ieba.org
Contact: Patti Burgart, Exec. Dir.

Founded: 1970. **Members:** 530. **Membership Dues:** active/associate, $125 (annual) ● supporting, $150 (annual). **Staff:** 1. **Multinational. Description:** Talent buyers and sellers, artists, managers, agents, venue operators and managers, and entertainment organizations; others with an interest in the entertainment industry, including advertisers, promoters, lighting, sound, and film technicians, and staging, production, and music businesses. Promotes professional advancement of members; seeks to ensure provision of high quality entertainment purchasing services to customers. Serves as a clearinghouse on talent agencies and upcoming performances; facilitates exchange among members; represents members' commercial and professional interests. **Awards:** All Access Award. **Frequency:** annual. **Type:** recognition ● Harry Peebles Foundation Award. **Frequency:** annual. **Type:** recognition. **Computer Services:** Mailing lists. **Publications:** *IEBA News*, monthly. Newsletter. Contains the latest information on industry happenings and legislative trends. **Circulation:** 530. **Advertising:** accepted. Alternate Formats: online. **Conventions/Meetings:** annual conference.

1307 ■ International Federation of Festival Organizations
4230 Stansbury Ave., Ste.105
Sherman Oaks, CA 91423
Ph: (818)789-7596
Fax: (818)784-9141

E-mail: morenfidof@aol.com
URL: http://www.morenofidof.org
Contact: Prof. Armando Moreno, Pres.
Founded: 1966. **Membership Dues:** regular, $200 (annual) ● corporate, $1,000 (annual). **Budget:** $50,000. **Languages:** English, French, German, Italian, Spanish. **Multinational. Description:** Individuals and organizations in 72 countries in television, radio, tourism, recording, and related industries that work with festivals or cultural events. Works to: coordinate festivals and events; establish a calendar and coordinate dates; render professional advice and assistance. Sponsors charitable and educational programs. Maintains liaison with United Nations Educational, Scientific and Cultural Organization. **Libraries: Type:** not open to the public. **Holdings:** 463; periodicals. **Subjects:** festivals and cultural events worldwide. **Awards:** Distant Accords. **Frequency:** annual. **Type:** recognition. **Recipient:** for following statues, cooperation, promotion of intercultural relations, promotion of artists and talents ● Festival of the Year. **Type:** recognition. **Recipient:** for talented young artists ● FIDOF Golden Ring of Friendship. **Frequency:** annual. **Type:** recognition. **Recipient:** for the media/press supporting "peace and friendship through music and arts" ● Man of the Year. **Type:** recognition. **Recipient:** for talented young artists ● Medals for Peace. **Frequency:** quarterly. **Type:** recognition ● Person of the Year. **Frequency:** annual. **Type:** recognition ● Ring of Friendship. **Frequency:** annual. **Type:** recognition. **Computer Services:** database ● mailing lists. **Boards:** Directors. **Affiliated With:** International Music Council; United Nations Educational, Scientific and Cultural Organization. **Also Known As:** Federation Internationale des Organizations de Festivals. **Publications:** *FIDOF Monthly Bulletin* (in English, French, German, Italian, and Spanish). Contains news of festivals and cultural events; includes calendar of events. **Price:** included in membership dues. **Circulation:** 700. **Advertising:** accepted ● Also publishes letters and calendar of festivals. **Conventions/Meetings:** annual congress and meeting, promotional materials about festivals and cultural events (exhibits) - always January in Cannes, France ● annual general assembly - always January, Cannes, France.

1308 ■ International Festivals and Events Association (IFEA)

2603 Eastover Terr.
Boise, ID 83706
Ph: (208)433-0950
Fax: (208)433-9812
E-mail: schmader@ifea.com
URL: http://www.ifea.com
Contact: Steve Schmader CFEE, Pres./CEO
Founded: 1956. **Members:** 2,700. **Staff:** 15. **Budget:** $1,400,000. **Multinational. Description:** Festival and event professionals, including large and small events, festivals, fairs, sporting events, sponsors, parks and recreation departments, municipalities, convention and visitors' bureaus, chambers of commerce, consultants, theme parks, volunteers, suppliers, services providers and others. Works to advance festivals and events throughout the world, providing benefits to members through information publications, seminars, annual convention and trade show, state/regional and international affiliate partners and programs, a professional certification program and ongoing networking channels. **Libraries: Type:** reference. **Holdings:** 35; books, video recordings. **Subjects:** sponsorship, event operations, parades, event ideas. **Awards:** Haas & Wilkerson Pinnacle Awards. **Frequency:** annual. **Type:** recognition ● Miller Brewing Company Hall of Fame. **Frequency:** annual. **Type:** recognition ● Zambelli Fireworks Internationale Volunteer of the Year Award. **Frequency:** annual. **Type:** recognition. **Computer Services:** Mailing lists, available for purchase by members and nonmembers. **Formerly:** International Festivals Association. **Publications:** *Affiliate Connection*. Newsletter. Alternate Formats: online ● *Convention Marketing Brochure*. Alternate Formats: online ● *Convention Program*, annual. Book. Schedule and guide for annual convention. **Price:** included with convention registration. **Circulation:** 800. **Advertising:** accepted ● *ie: The Business of International Events*, quarterly. Magazine. Includes industry updates, trends and issues. **Price:** included in membership dues; $50.00 for nonmembers; $25.00 additional subscription for members. **Circulation:** 3,000. **Advertising:** accepted ● *Roster*, annual. Membership Directory. **Price:** free for members. Alternate Formats: online. **Conventions/Meetings:** annual International Festivals & Events Convention and Expo Experience, for top executive directors of festivals and events worldwide and suppliers to this industry (exhibits).

1309 ■ International Laser Display Association (ILDA)

7062 Edgeworth Dr.
Orlando, FL 32819
Ph: (407)797-7654
Fax: (503)344-3770
E-mail: mail@laserist.org
URL: http://www.laserist.org
Contact: Mr. Patrick Murphy, Exec. Dir.
Founded: 1986. **Members:** 125. **Membership Dues:** non-profit, individual, $125 (annual) ● student, $50 (annual) ● corporate/associate (with billings over $1,000,000), $1,000 (annual) ● corporate/associate (with billings $500,000 to $1,000,000), $500 (annual) ● corporate/associate (with billings USD $500,000 and below), $250 (annual). **Staff:** 1. **Multinational. Description:** Advances the use of laser displays in art, entertainment, and education. **Awards:** ILDA Awards for artistic achievement. **Frequency:** annual. **Type:** trophy. **Recipient:** for outstanding laser displays ● ILDA Awards for technical achievement. **Frequency:** annual. **Type:** trophy. **Recipient:** for technical advancements in the field of laser displays ● ILDA Career Achievement Award. **Frequency:** annual. **Type:** trophy. **Recipient:** to an individual who has made significant contributions to laser shows and displays. **Committees:** Awards; Ethics; Membership Status; Safety; Technical. **Publications:** *The Laserist*, quarterly. Magazine. **Price:** included in membership dues. **Circulation:** 1,500. **Advertising:** accepted. Alternate Formats: online. **Conventions/Meetings:** annual conference.

1310 ■ International Recreational Go-Kart Association (IRGA)

1113 Belle Pl.
Fort Worth, TX 76107
Ph: (817)738-3344
Fax: (817)738-6622
E-mail: info@irga.us
URL: http://www.irga.us
Contact: Steven W. Hix, Exec. Dir.
Founded: 1991. **Members:** 400. **Membership Dues:** associate (state/government), $50 (annual) ● operator/supplier, $250 (annual) ● manufacturer, $500 (annual). **Staff:** 3. **For-Profit. Description:** Business people interested in the continued growth and success of concession go-karting and family entertainment centers. Seeks to open lines of communication and provide an effective forum for the go-karting industry. Offers educational programs and statistical information. Maintains speakers bureau. **Libraries: Type:** reference; open to the public. **Holdings:** audiovisuals, books, clippings, periodicals, video recordings. **Subjects:** concession go-karting information, family entertainment center industry materials. **Awards: Type:** recognition. **Computer Services:** Mailing lists, of members. **Committees:** Standards and Guidelines. **Publications:** *Right Track*, annual. Newsletter. **Price:** included in membership dues. **Circulation:** 2,500. **Advertising:** accepted ● Brochure ● Bulletin. **Conventions/Meetings:** annual board meeting, general membership - usually in November.

1311 ■ International Special Events Society (ISES)

401 N Michigan Ave.
Chicago, IL 60611-4267
Ph: (312)321-6853
Free: (800)688-4737
Fax: (312)673-6953
E-mail: info@ises.com
URL: http://www.ises.com
Contact: Connie Riley, Pres.
Founded: 1987. **Members:** 3,200. **Membership Dues:** individual, corporate, $449 (annual) ● non-profit, $349 (annual). **Staff:** 349. **Budget:** $1,000,000. **Regional Groups:** 6. **Local Groups:** 30. **For-Profit. Description:** Special events planners, caterers, designers, event marketers, technical experts, transportation and destination professionals. Seeks to educate, advance, and promote special events. **Awards:** Esprit. **Frequency:** annual. **Type:** recognition. **Telecommunication Services:** electronic mail, connie@tskorman.com. **Publications:** *Event World*, monthly. Magazine. **Circulation:** 25,000. **Advertising:** accepted ● *ISES Membership Directory*, annual. **Conventions/Meetings:** annual Professional Development Conference - usually August. 2008 Aug. 21-23, St. Petersburg, FL.

1312 ■ International Ticketing Association (INTIX)

330 W 38th St., No. 605
New York, NY 10018
Ph: (212)629-4036
Fax: (212)629-8532
E-mail: info@intix.org
URL: http://www.intix.org
Contact: Jeffrey Larris, Pres.
Founded: 1979. **Members:** 1,400. **Membership Dues:** organization (first member), $225 (annual) ● organization, vendor (second member), $150 (annual) ● supporting organization, $275 (annual) ● Chairman's Circle (organization, vendor, individual), $500 (annual) ● vendor (first member), contributing, $250 (annual) ● supporting vendor, $350 (annual) ● regular, $200 (annual) ● retired, $50 (annual) ● student, $25 (annual). **Staff:** 5. **Budget:** $1,000,000. **Multinational. Description:** Ticket managers and directors, treasurers, financial and marketing and systems directors, and others involved in the marketing, selling, and manufacture of tickets in the performing arts and sports fields. Promotes growth and development in the ticket management industry. Works to: advance and upgrade management techniques and systems; maintain high standards of professionalism in box office management; monitor and analyze technological advances in ticket selling and accounting. Acts as an information exchange and resource center for addressing control and service issues. Provides advisory, consulting, and reference services, and job opportunity information and referral services. Compiles statistics. **Awards:** Outstanding Box Office of the Year Award. **Frequency:** annual. **Type:** recognition ● Outstanding Ticketing Professional of the Year. **Frequency:** annual. **Type:** recognition ● Patricia G. Spira Lifetime Achievement Award. **Frequency:** annual. **Type:** recognition ● Spirit Award. **Frequency:** annual. **Type:** recognition. **Computer Services:** Mailing lists. **Committees:** Awards; Conference; Ethics, Standards and Certification; Exhibitor Relations; Nominating; Peer Consulting; Sponsorship. **Task Forces:** Gift. **Formerly:** (1997) Box Office Management International. **Publications:** *INTIX e-Bulletin*, monthly. Newsletter. Includes news from the association, promotions, replacements, and clips from industry news sources. **Price:** included in membership dues ● *INTIX Membership Directory*, annual ● Also publishes Dictionary of Ticketing Terms. **Conventions/Meetings:** annual conference and trade show (exhibits) - always January in North America ● conference, with tabletop tradeshow - summer.

1313 ■ National Association of Casino Party Operators (NACPO)

PO Box 2165
Poulsbo, WA 98370
Free: (800)355-8259
E-mail: info@nacpo.com
URL: http://www.nactpo.com
Founded: 1992. **Members:** 50. **Membership Dues:** regular, $300 (annual). **Staff:** 3. **Description:** Casino party operators, party planners, party rental shop owners, theme party and special events operators, and others involved in casino party rental business.

Strives to strengthen the casino and theme party industry and advance the industry into more geographical markets. Promotes members' interests. **Formerly:** (2004) National Association of Casino and Theme Party Operators. **Publications:** *Casino and Theme Party Operators Association Newsletter*, quarterly. Includes articles on industry developments, guest writer column, and helpful business services. **Price:** included in membership dues ● *Suppliers and Manufacturers Directory*, periodic ● Membership Directory, periodic. **Conventions/Meetings:** annual conference and trade show (exhibits) - every July.

1314 ■ National Association of Mobile Entertainers (NAME)
PO Box 144
Willow Grove, PA 19090
Ph: (215)658-1193
Free: (800)434-8274
E-mail: name@djkj.com
URL: http://www.djkj.com
Contact: Bruce Keslar, Natl. Dir.
Membership Dues: company, $125 (annual) ● corporate, $200 (annual) ● associate, $75 (annual). **Description:** Promotes the professions of mobile DJs, nightclub DJs, and KJs; assists party planners and brides. Provides liability and equipment coverage for mobile entertainers. **Publications:** *National Entertainer*, bimonthly. Magazine.

1315 ■ National Association of Theatre Owners (NATO)
PO Box 77318
Washington, DC 20013-7318
Ph: (202)962-0054
Fax: (202)962-0370
E-mail: nato@natodc.com
URL: http://www.natoonline.org
Contact: Kathy Conroy, Exec. Dir.
Founded: 1948. **Membership Dues:** theatre owner, per screen, $40 (annual). **Staff:** 12. **Regional Groups:** 4. **State Groups:** 33. **Languages:** English, Spanish. **Multinational. Description:** Owners, operators and executives of motion picture theaters. Provides services to assist theater owners in successfully operating their theaters including monitoring legislative and technological advancements; compiles statistics. **Awards:** NATO Stars of the Year. **Frequency:** annual. **Type:** recognition. **Recipient:** for box office stars. **Formed by Merger of:** (1993) Allied States Association of Motion Picture Exhibitors; Theatre Owners of America. **Publications:** *Encyclopedia of Exhibition*, annual. Directory. Contains statistics on the economics of theatre and concession apparatus. Lists film distributors and producers and film releases. **Price:** $100.00/copy, plus shipping and handling. **Circulation:** 5,000. **Advertising:** accepted ● *In Focus*, monthly. Magazine. Reports on box office performance of current films, industry profiles, and business and legal developments affecting motion picture theater owners. **Price:** $70.00 in U.S.; $85.00 outside U.S. ISSN: 0279-120X. **Circulation:** 5,000. **Advertising:** accepted. Alternate Formats: online. **Conventions/Meetings:** annual board meeting (exhibits) - October/November ● annual Show East - trade show and convention - always October/November, Orlando, FL ● annual Show West - trade show and convention - always March and April, Las Vegas, NV.

1316 ■ National Association of Ticket Brokers (NATB)
214 N Hale St.
Wheaton, IL 60187
Ph: (630)510-4594
Fax: (630)510-4501
E-mail: darren@gscgrouppr.com
URL: http://www.natb.org
Contact: Jason Berger, Pres.
Founded: 1994. **Members:** 175. **Membership Dues:** company (1 to 3 employees), $975 (annual) ● company (4 to 6 employees), $1,300 (annual) ● company (7 or more employees), $1,625 (annual). **Staff:** 2. **Budget:** $150,000. **Regional Groups:** 6. **Description:** Ticket brokers. Represents the interests of the Ticket Brokering industry by promoting consumer protection, and educating the public. **Conventions/Meetings:** meeting.

1317 ■ National Ballroom and Entertainment Association (NBEA)
c/o John Matter, Exec. Dir.
2799 Locust Rd.
Decorah, IA 52101-7600
Ph: (563)382-3871
E-mail: nbea@oneota.net
URL: http://www.nbea.com
Contact: John Matter, Exec. Dir.
Founded: 1947. **Members:** 450. **Membership Dues:** active, $150 (annual) ● entertainment, $90 (annual) ● friend, $25 (annual). **Description:** Represents owners and operators of ballrooms; entertainment members are band leaders and others in positions related to live music dancing. **Formerly:** (1971) National Ballroom Operators Association; (1976) Entertainment Operators of America. **Publications:** *National Ballroom and Entertainment Association—Newsletter*, quarterly. Intended for establishments using live music for dancing. Includes association activities. **Price:** free for members. **Circulation:** 400. **Advertising:** accepted. **Conventions/Meetings:** annual conference and seminar.

1318 ■ National Caricaturist Network (NCN)
c/o Tracey Iverson, Mgr.
922 W Dayton St.
Ferndale, MI 48220
E-mail: prez@caricature.org
URL: http://www.caricature.org
Contact: Roger Hurtado, Pres.
Founded: 1988. **Members:** 350. **Membership Dues:** professional, $55 (annual) ● associate, $40 (annual) ● student, $45 (annual) ● gold, $80 (annual). **Description:** Works to promote public interest in the art of caricature. Conducts educational and charitable programs; holds competitions; maintains speakers' bureau. **Awards:** Golden Nosey. **Frequency:** annual. **Type:** recognition. **Recipient:** for the best caricaturist of the year. **Computer Services:** Mailing lists. **Publications:** *Exaggerated Features*, quarterly. Newsletter. **Price:** included in membership dues. **Circulation:** 400. **Advertising:** accepted. **Conventions/Meetings:** board meeting and convention ● annual convention - usually March.

1319 ■ National Caves Association (NCA)
PO Box 280
Park City, KY 42160
Ph: (270)749-2228
Fax: (270)749-2428
E-mail: info@cavern.com
URL: http://www.cavern.com
Contact: Susan Berdeaux, Contact
Founded: 1965. **Members:** 91. **Membership Dues:** show cave, $650 (annual). **Staff:** 1. **Regional Groups:** 10. **Description:** Publicly and privately owned show caves and caverns-caves developed for public visitation. All are natural caves or caverns beneath the surface of the earth. Presents these underground wonders to the visitor with good taste, courtesy and hospitality during tours at regularly scheduled times. Promotes the preservation and conservation of these natural resources. **Awards:** NCA/NSS Award. **Frequency:** annual. **Type:** monetary. **Recipient:** for best research paper. **Committees:** Insurance; International Liaison; Legislative; NSS/NCA Liaison; Promotion Strategies; Show Cave Liaison. **Affiliated With:** American Cave Conservation Association. **Publications:** *Caves and Caverns*. Video. Describes caves and how they are formed. For use in schools and libraries. **Price:** $25.00 free 10-day loan to school or library. Alternate Formats: magnetic tape ● *Caves and Caverns Directory*, annual. Brochure. Lists NCA member show caves. Includes location map, address, and phone number, and color photos of cave interiors. **Price:** free ● *NCA Cave Talk*, bimonthly. Newsletter. **Price:** available to members only. **Conventions/Meetings:** annual convention, invitation only (exhibits) - always fall.

1320 ■ National Club Industry Association of America (NCIAA)
67 Wall St., 22nd Fl.
New York, NY 10005
Ph: (917)779-0496
Free: (866)558-4255
E-mail: info@nciaa.org
URL: http://www.nciaa.com
Contact: Kris Sweeton, Pres./CEO
Founded: 1989. **Members:** 40,000. **Membership Dues:** club industry license, $25 (annual) ● label/booking/agent/promoter directory listing, $100 (annual) ● apprentice, $125 (annual) ● professional, $175 (annual) ● partner (based on annual rate), $300-$500 (annual) ● basic/club/venue/booking agent/promoter/broker, $350 (annual) ● vendor directory listing, $1,000 (annual). **Multinational. Description:** Represents the interests of DJs, clubs, promoters, record companies, producers, suppliers, manufacturers and service providers. Promotes the club and electronic music industry. Serves as the national governing body of the club industry. **Publications:** Newsletter, monthly.

1321 ■ National Park Hospitality Association (NPHA)
129 Park St. NE, Ste.B
Vienna, VA 22180
Ph: (703)242-1999
Fax: (703)242-1992
E-mail: info@nphassn.org
URL: http://www.nphassn.org
Contact: Todd C. Hull, Contact
Founded: 1919. **Members:** 150. **Membership Dues:** associate, $500 (annual). **Staff:** 4. **Description:** Represents private concessionaires operating in the U.S. national parks. Acts as liaison between members and the National Park Service and Congress. **Libraries: Type:** not open to the public. **Holdings:** 250. **Subjects:** national parks. **Formerly:** Conference of National Park Concessionaires. **Publications:** *Directory of NPS Concessionaires*. Alternate Formats: online ● *NPHA News*, periodic. Newsletter ● Membership Directory, biennial ● Brochure. Alternate Formats: online. **Conventions/Meetings:** semiannual conference - always March in Washington, DC, and October in various locations.

1322 ■ North American Association of Ventriloquists (NAAV)
c/o Maher Ventriloquists Studios
PO Box 420
Littleton, CO 80160-0420
Ph: (303)346-6819
Fax: (720)344-2907
E-mail: maherstudios@earthlink.net
Contact: Clinton Detweiler, Dir.
Founded: 1940. **Members:** 1,700. **Staff:** 2. **Description:** Amateur, semiprofessional, and professional ventriloquists and puppeteers. Disseminates information on ventriloquists and ventriloquist activities, including regional convention information and reports; assists members in answering questions and solving problems related to ventriloquism; reviews current industry products and assists members in locating supplies and instruction. **Convention/Meeting:** none. **Publications:** *Newsy Vents*, quarterly. Newsletter.

1323 ■ Organization of Black Screenwriters (OBS)
Address Unknown since 2008
URL: http://www.obswriter.com
Founded: 1988. **Membership Dues:** professional, $90 (annual) ● general, $65 (annual) ● affiliate, $45 (annual) ● student, $35 (annual) ● international, $115 (annual). **Multinational. Description:** Seeks to address the lack of black writers represented within the entertainment industry. Assists in the creation of works for film and television. Encourages freedom of expression through quality writing and filmmaking. **Computer Services:** Online services, forum ● online services, poll. **Committees:** Agent Outreach; Celebration of Excellence Awards; "Dinner With." Series; Fundraising; Guest Speakers; OBS Reality Shows/OBS Productions; Producer Outreach; Public Rela-

tions/Media Development. **Conventions/Meetings:** monthly meeting - every 1st Saturday.

1324 ■ Outdoor Amusement Business Association (OABA)
1035 S Semoran Blvd., Ste.1045A
Winter Park, FL 32792
Ph: (407)681-9444
Free: (800)517-OABA
Fax: (407)681-9445
E-mail: oaba@aol.com
URL: http://www.oaba.org
Contact: Robert W. Johnson, Pres.
Founded: 1965. **Members:** 5,000. **Membership Dues:** carnival, $500-$1,500 (annual) ● manufacturer/supplier, $200 (annual) ● independent ride owner, attraction/acts owner, amusement rental, carnival executive, $125 (annual) ● concession owner, $100 (annual) ● fair/festival, associate, $50 (annual). **Staff:** 4. **Budget:** $650,000. **Description:** Represents executives and employees of carnivals and fairs; ride owners; independent food and games concessionaires; manufacturers and suppliers of equipment. Promotes and lobbies on behalf of the interests of the outdoor amusement industry; provides a center for dissemination of information. **Committees:** Concessionaires; Continuing Education; Ethical Standards; Legislative; Public Relations; Safety. **Publications:** *Midway Marquee*, annual. Directory. **Price:** $15.00. **Circulation:** 7,000. **Advertising:** accepted ● *OABA News*, monthly. Newsletter. **Price:** $2.00. **Circulation:** 5,000. **Advertising:** accepted. **Conventions/Meetings:** annual Amusement Industry Expo - convention, for carnival industry (exhibits) ● seminar and trade show.

1325 ■ Talent Managers Association (TMA)
4804 Laurel Canyon Blvd., No. 611
Valley Village, CA 91607
Ph: (310)205-8495
Fax: (818)765-2903
E-mail: support@talentmanagers.org
URL: http://www.talentmanagers.org
Contact: Steven Nash, Pres.
Membership Dues: general, $450 (annual). **Description:** Promotes the highest standards of professional ethics and behavior in the practice of talent management. Seeks to enhance the entertainment industry through the presence and involvement of talent managers. **Awards:** Seymour Heller Award. **Frequency:** annual. **Type:** recognition. **Recipient:** for outstanding contribution to the talent management profession. **Computer Services:** Information services, talent manager resources ● online services, message board. **Publications:** *Academy Players*. Directory. **Price:** free for members; $90.00 4 months subscription.

1326 ■ Themed Entertainment Association (TEA)
175 E Olive Ave., Ste.100
Burbank, CA 91502
Ph: (818)843-8497
Fax: (818)843-8477
E-mail: info@teaconnect.org
URL: http://www.themeit.com
Contact: Gene Jeffers, Exec. Dir.
Founded: 1992. **Members:** 800. **Membership Dues:** company (based on number of employees), $325-$2,100 (annual) ● individual associate, $175 (annual) ● branch listing, $200 (annual) ● student, $50 (annual). **Staff:** 3. **Multinational. Description:** Promotes the location-based entertainment industry, including theme parks, entertainment centers, casino/resorts, museums, themed restaurants, and themed retail. **Awards:** THEA Awards. **Frequency:** annual. **Type:** recognition. **Recipient:** for outstanding quality projects. **Publications:** *Project Development Chart*. **Price:** $10.00 additional copies, plus shipping and handling ● *TEA Project Development Guidelines, 2nd Edition*. Handbook. Provides important aspects of project development process, including Project Development Process Chart. **Price:** $75.00 for members and their employees, plus shipping and handling; $275.00 for nonmembers, plus shipping and handling. Also Cited As: *PDG Book* ● *TEA Sourcebook*. Directory. Details member companies and their products and services. **Price:** included in membership dues; $25.00 additional member copies, and for nonmembers, plus shipping and handling. Alternate Formats: CD-ROM. **Conventions/Meetings:** annual Awards Gala - banquet ● international conference and board meeting.

1327 ■ Western Fairs Association (WFA)
1776 Tribute Rd., Ste.210
Sacramento, CA 95815-4495
Ph: (916)927-3100 (916)404-3187
Fax: (916)927-6397
E-mail: wfa@fairsnet.org
URL: http://www.fairsnet.org
Contact: Stephen J. Chambers, Exec. Dir.
Founded: 1945. **Members:** 2,000. **Membership Dues:** service, $225-$525 (annual) ● associate fair, $190-$790 (annual) ● festival, special event, $175 (annual) ● agricultural resource, $75 (annual) ● affiliate, $125 (annual). **Staff:** 5. **Budget:** $650,000. **Description:** State and county fairs, carnival operators, food concessionaires, entertainment agents, and commercial exhibitors. Seeks to improve conditions in the fair industry by maintaining good relations with governmental agencies. Maintains hall of fame. Compiles statistics. **Libraries: Type:** reference. **Subjects:** fair management, fair financing, horse racing, breeding, other agricultural and fair subjects. **Awards:** Merrit Award. **Frequency:** annual. **Type:** recognition. **Committees:** Achievement Awards; Administrative Relations; Agriculture and Education; Area Chairs; County Fairs; Marketing; Professional Development; Showcase. **Publications:** *Fair Dealer*, quarterly. Magazine. Reports on industry activities; provides informational and educational materials for members. Includes information on new members. **Price:** included in membership dues; $35.00 /year for nonmembers. **Circulation:** 2,200. **Advertising:** accepted ● *Western Fairs Association—Date List and Membership Directory*, annual. Lists member fairs located throughout western United States and Canada including attendance figures of previous year and size of fair. **Price:** included in membership dues; $225.00/copy for nonmembers. **Circulation:** 2,200. **Advertising:** accepted. Alternate Formats: online ● *WFA Newsletter*, quarterly. Describes current legislative action, association events and member activities. **Conventions/Meetings:** annual competition and meeting (exhibits).

1328 ■ World Robotic Boxing Association (WRBA)
Address Unknown since 2007
Founded: 1986. **Members:** 148. **Staff:** 5. **For-Profit. Description:** Organization for enthusiasts of robotic boxing.

1329 ■ World Waterpark Association (WWA)
8826 Santa Fe Dr., Ste.310
Overland Park, KS 66212
Ph: (913)599-0300
Fax: (913)599-0520
E-mail: memberservices@waterparks.com
URL: http://www.waterparks.org
Contact: Rick Root, Pres./CEO
Founded: 1980. **Members:** 1,350. **Membership Dues:** park (with an annual attendance of below 250000), $325 (annual) ● supplier (with an annual attendance of 250000 or more), $525 (annual). **Staff:** 6. **Budget:** $1,000,000. **Languages:** English, Spanish. **Description:** Water leisure amusement facilities; suppliers of products and services. Provides a forum for the discussion of information related to the water amusement park industry. Furthers safety and profitability in the water leisure industry through educational conferences and publications. Maintains placement service; compiles statistics. **Awards:** WWA Executive Board Award. **Frequency:** annual. **Type:** recognition ● WWA Media Award. **Frequency:** annual. **Type:** recognition. **Computer Services:** Mailing lists ● online services. **Telecommunication Services:** electronic mail, rroot@watersparks.org. **Committees:** Safety and Standards. **Formerly:** (1985) American Waterpark Association. **Publications:** *Buyers' Guide*, annual. Lists suppliers to the waterpark industry. **Advertising:** accepted. Alternate Formats: online ● *Considerations for Operating Safety*. Handbook ● *Splash* (in English and Spanish), 9/year. Magazine. Published for developers. **Advertising:** accepted ● *Waterpark Development & Expansion Guide*, annual. **Price:** included in membership dues; $250.00 for nonmembers ● Magazine, 10/year. Provides special insight into the specifics of the waterpark industry. **Price:** included in membership dues. **Conventions/Meetings:** annual meeting and symposium (exhibits) - always fall ● seminar, covers the topics of risk management, developing a facility, marketing, expansion, certified pool operator's course, international development, and family entertainment centers.

Environmental Quality

1330 ■ National Association of Mold Professionals (NAMP)
3250 Old Farm Ln., Ste.1
Walled Lake, MI 48390
Ph: (248)669-5673
E-mail: info@moldpro.org
URL: http://www.moldpro.org
Membership Dues: personal, $295 (annual) ● corporate, $495 (annual). **Description:** Seeks to promote and develop the mold inspection and remediation industry. Provides education and authoritative credentials for mold professionals. Conducts promotional activities designed to educate the public and to instill the value of performing certified mold inspections as a perfunctory part of real estate transactions. **Computer Services:** database, mold inspectors and remediators. **Publications:** Newsletter. Features relevant issues and subjects important to mold inspectors and remediators.

1331 ■ National Organization of Remediators and Mold Inspectors (NORMI)
22174 Prats Rd.
Abita Springs, LA 70420
Free: (877)251-2296
Fax: (866)211-4324
URL: http://www.normi.org
Contact: D. Douglas Hoffman, CEO
Description: Represents certified IAQ/mold inspectors and certified mold remediators. Improves the indoor living environment through educating the public and training professionals. Identifies problems and offers solutions to improve indoor air and drinking water quality. **Libraries: Type:** reference. **Holdings:** articles. **Subjects:** mold.

Estate Management

1332 ■ Society of Trust and Estate Practitioners USA (STEP USA)
7 Times Sq.
New York, NY 10036-7311
Ph: (914)636-2531
E-mail: marian.kramer@step.org
URL: http://www.step.org
Contact: Marian Kramer, Admin.
Founded: 1991. **Membership Dues:** full, associate, $325 (annual) ● student, $150 (annual) ● retired, non-earner, $75 (annual). **Description:** Aims to bring together all practitioners in the field of trusts and estates. Raises the public profile of trust and estate work as a profession in its own right. Advances knowledge and learning in trusts, estates and allied subjects. Encourages and promotes the study of trusts and estate practice. Provides education, training, representation and networking for its members. **Publications:** *STEP Journal USA Supplement*, semiannual.

Ethics

1333 ■ Council of Ethical Organizations
214 S Payne St.
Alexandria, VA 22314
Ph: (703)683-7916

Fax: (703)299-8836
E-mail: membership@corporateethics.com
URL: http://www.corporateethics.com
Contact: Mark J. Pastin PhD, Pres./Chm.
Founded: 1980. **Membership Dues:** organizational, $2,600 (annual) ● organizational, $4;200 (biennial) ● individual, $500 (annual) ● individual, $800 (biennial). **Description:** Promotes ethical and legal conduct of business, government and the professions. **Special Interest Groups:** Health Ethics Trust. **Publications:** *Best Practices in Healthcare Compliance Programs*. Book ● *Compliance Case Study Library: A Training & Educational Resource*. Book. **Price:** $150.00 for members; $195.00 for nonmembers ● *Ethical Organizations Fact Sheet* ● *Hard Problems of Management: Gaining the Ethics Edge*. Book. **Price:** $35.00 plus shipping and handling ● *Hotline Handbook: A Guide for Implementing & Operating Hotlines* ● *Hotline & Investigations Handbook: A Guide for Implementing & Operating Hotlines & Conducting Compliance Investigations*. **Price:** $100.00 for members; $100.00 for nonmembers ● *Pastin Report on Best Compliance Practices*. **Price:** included in membership dues. Alternate Formats: online ● *Strategy Book for Healthcare Compliance Officers*. **Price:** $275.00 plus shipping and handling.

Exhibitors

1334 ■ American Veterinary Exhibitors Association (AVEA)

Address Unknown since 2007
Founded: 1936. **Members:** 100. **Membership Dues:** $250 (annual). **Description:** Manufacturers and dealers of products for the veterinary profession. To give firms exhibiting at veterinary conventions a voice in planning the time, place, program, and facilities of such meetings; to cooperate and consult with veterinary associations in matters of mutual interest. **Publications:** *American Veterinary Exhibitors Association—Schedule of Conventions: Membership Roster*, annual. List of member companies and schedule of major veterinary meetings with exhibits. **Price:** free to members. **Advertising:** not accepted ● *AVEA Newsletter*, quarterly. Covers veterinary convention exhibitions and the veterinary industry in general. Includes meeting minutes and annual financial statement. **Price:** free, for members only. **Conventions/Meetings:** Convention Booth Exhibit Competitions (exhibits) ● semiannual meeting, in conjunction with American Veterinary Medical Association and North American Veterinary Conference.

1335 ■ Center for Exhibition Industry Research (CEIR)

8111 LBJ Fwy., Ste.750
Dallas, TX 75251
Ph: (972)687-9242
Fax: (972)692-6020
E-mail: info@ceir.org
URL: http://www.ceir.org
Contact: Douglas L. Ducate, Pres./CEO
Founded: 1978. **Members:** 900. **Membership Dues:** general, $695 (annual) ● exhibitor, academic, $195 (annual). **Staff:** 4. **Budget:** $1,000,000. **Description:** Promotes the growth, awareness and value of exhibitions and other face-to-face marketing events by producing and delivering research-based knowledge tools. Consists of exhibition organizers, service providers, exhibitors, CVBs and facilities. **Libraries: Type:** reference. **Holdings:** 150; articles, books, clippings, periodicals, reports. **Subjects:** industry marketing, professional development, history, growth, trends. **Computer Services:** database, provides custom reports. **Committees:** Research/Product. **Formerly:** (1995) Trade Show Bureau. **Publications:** *CEIR Direct*, bimonthly. Newsletter ● *Face-to-Face Marketing*. Reports ● *Guru Reports* ● *The Power of Exhibitions*. Reports ● Catalog. Features CEIR publications and reports. **Conventions/Meetings:** annual meeting - always May, Washington, DC.

1336 ■ Educational Exhibitors Association (EEA)

c/o VMS, Inc.
805 Airway Dr.
Allegan, MI 49010-8516
Ph: (269)673-2200
Fax: (269)673-9509
Contact: Lydia E. Walsh, Exec. Dir.
Founded: 1922. **Members:** 100. **Membership Dues:** regular, $125 (annual). **Staff:** 1. **Budget:** $20,000. **Description:** Companies selling to schools. Promotes and supports school conferences and trade shows. **Awards:** SHIP Citation. **Frequency:** 3/year. **Type:** recognition ● SHIP Citation for Excellence in Education. **Frequency:** annual. **Type:** recognition. **Recipient:** available through three educational associations; also for scholarships to teachers in vocational education. **Publications:** *Show List*, semiannual. **Price:** free, for members only. **Circulation:** 120. Alternate Formats: online.

1337 ■ Exhibit Designers and Producers Association (EDPA)

1100 Johnson Ferry Rd., Ste.300
Atlanta, GA 30342
Ph: (404)303-7310
Fax: (404)252-0774
E-mail: pdicks@edpa.com
URL: http://www.edpa.com
Contact: Peter A. Dicks, Exec. Dir.
Founded: 1954. **Members:** 370. **Membership Dues:** regular (based on annual gross industry sales), $595-$2,045 (annual) ● supplier associate, $995 (annual) ● associate, $295 (annual) ● student, $35 (annual) ● international chapter, $495 (annual) ● supplier associate branch, $395 (annual). **Multinational. Description:** Firms designing and building exhibits for trade shows and museums. Conducts educational and research programs. **Awards:** Ambassador Award. **Frequency:** annual. **Type:** recognition. **Recipient:** for a member who has made outstanding contributions to the organization and to the industry ● E-Cubed Awards. **Frequency:** annual. **Type:** recognition. **Recipient:** for innovative approaches to exhibit design ● Hazel Hays Award. **Frequency:** annual. **Type:** recognition. **Recipient:** for distinguished contribution to the exhibit industry. **Programs:** Cost-Savings Benefits. **Publications:** *EDP Action News*, bimonthly. Newsletter. Serves as official news magazine of EDPA. **Advertising:** accepted ● *EDPA.COMmunications*, monthly. Newsletter. **Advertising:** accepted. Alternate Formats: online ● *EDPA Today*, quarterly. Newsletter. **Advertising:** accepted. Alternate Formats: online ● Membership Directory. **Advertising:** accepted. **Conventions/Meetings:** annual convention, educational meeting for exhibit industry (exhibits).

1338 ■ Exhibitor Appointed Contractor Association (EACA)

2214 NW 5th St.
Bend, OR 97701
Ph: (541)317-8768
Fax: (541)317-8749
E-mail: jimwurm@eaca.com
URL: http://www.eaca.com
Contact: Jim Wurm, Exec. Dir.
Founded: 1998. **Membership Dues:** corporate (regular/associate), $75 (quarterly) ● sole proprietor (regular), $250 (annual) ● area corporate (regular), $500 (annual) ● regional corporate (regular), $1,500 (annual) ● national corporate (regular), $3,500 (annual) ● corporate sponsor (regular), $7,500 (annual) ● sole proprietor (associate), $250 (annual) ● area corporate (associate), $500 (annual) ● regional corporate (associate), $1,500 (annual) ● national corporate (associate), $3,500 (annual) ● corporate sponsor (associate), $7,500 (annual). **Description:** Promotes service excellence on the showfloor by improving working conditions of those contractors and other floor professionals that provide exhibit services. **Publications:** *Showfloor Buzz*, weekly. Newsletter. Contains late breaking news that affects the industry, companies and jobs. **Price:** included in membership dues. Alternate Formats: online ● Report. **Conventions/Meetings:** annual conference, with Town Hall meeting, showfloor olympics.

1339 ■ Exposition Operations Society (EOS)

c/o Stephen A. Schuldenfrei, Pres.
PO Box 949
Framingham, MA 01701-0949
Ph: (508)544-1527
Free: (877)272-EXPO
Fax: (508)435-0280
E-mail: info@expoops.com
URL: http://www.expoops.com
Contact: Stephen A. Schuldenfrei, Pres.
Founded: 2000. **Members:** 50. **Membership Dues:** individual, $250 (annual) ● corporate, $1,000 (annual) ● associate, $450 (annual). **Staff:** 1. **Budget:** $125,000. **Multinational. Description:** Operations/logistics professionals who share tactical ideas, experiences, and challenges. Provides information and solutions for the benefit of the members and their organizations. **Computer Services:** Mailing lists, of members. **Formerly:** (2000) Society of Independent Show Organizers. **Publications:** *Mid Month Memo*, monthly. Newsletter. Alternate Formats: online. **Conventions/Meetings:** annual Executive Conference ● annual meeting, forum.

1340 ■ Healthcare Convention and Exhibitors Association (HCEA)

1100 Johnson Ferry Rd., Ste.300
Atlanta, GA 30342
Ph: (404)252-3663
Fax: (404)252-0774
E-mail: hcea@kellencompany.com
URL: http://www.hcea.org
Contact: Eric Allen, Exec. VP
Founded: 1930. **Members:** 700. **Membership Dues:** regular, in U.S., $595 (annual) ● regular/associate outside U.S., supporting in U.S., $695 (annual) ● associate in U.S. (single contact), $299 (annual) ● associate in U.S. (multiple contacts), $595 (annual) ● supporting outside U.S., $795 (annual). **Staff:** 7. **Multinational. Description:** Works to increase effectiveness and efficiency of healthcare conventions and exhibitions as an educational and marketing medium; promotes the value of exhibits. Provides forum for exchange of mutually beneficial information and ideas. **Awards:** Distinguished Service Award. **Type:** recognition. **Recipient:** for individuals who have made significant contributions to the association or to the industry. **Computer Services:** Mailing lists. **Committees:** Association/Industry Partnering; Education and Industry Networking; Information Resource; International; Marketing and Public Relations; Membership. **Formerly:** (1973) Medical Exhibitors Association; (1990) Health Care Exhibitors Association. **Publications:** *AIP Alert*. Newsletter. **Price:** single issue free ● *Association Alert*, semiannual. Newsletter. Contains news for healthcare convention and exhibition organizers. **Price:** free. **Circulation:** 2,500 ● *Conventional Wisdom*. Pamphlet. **Price:** included in membership dues; $1.00 for nonmembers ● *Exhibitors Advisory Councils Booklet*. **Price:** single copy free ● *Guidelines for U.S. Health Care Conventions*. **Price:** single copy free. Alternate Formats: online ● *HCEA Directory of Healthcare Meetings and Conventions*, semiannual. Includes chronological, geographical, and keyword indexes. **Price:** included in membership dues; $245.00 for nonmembers; $69.00 extra copy for members. **Advertising:** accepted ● *Inbox Informer*, monthly. Newsletter. Alternate Formats: online ● *Insight*, semiannual. Magazine. **Price:** included in membership dues; $29.00 /year for nonmembers ● Also publishes brochures and special reports. **Conventions/Meetings:** annual meeting, 4-day summit (exhibits) ● annual trade show and meeting, only healthcare-specific exhibit marketing educational meeting in US (exhibits).

1341 ■ International Association of Butterfly Exhibitions (IABE)

PO Box 240757
St. Paul, MN 55124
Ph: (952)212-4757
Fax: (952)953-9133
E-mail: info@butterflyexhibitions.org
URL: http://www.butterflyexhibitions.org
Contact: Martin Feather, Pres.
Founded: 2001. **Membership Dues:** regular, $125 (annual) ● flagship, $500 (annual) ● individual, $40 (annual) ● regular, EUR 100 (annual) ● flagship, EUR 415 (annual) ● individual, EUR 35 (annual). **Multinational. Description:** Advances the international but-

terfly exhibition industry through representation, communication, education, and marketing. Accepts sponsorships from butterfly livestock breeders/suppliers or other corporations (including future exhibitors) that are interested in promoting butterfly exhibitions. Maintains an online directory of member facilities. **Publications:** *The International Flutterings*, quarterly. Newsletter. **Price:** included in membership dues.

1342 ■ International Association for Modular Exhibitry (IAME)
Address Unknown since 2007
Founded: 1987. **Members:** 47. **Description:** Companies united to promote the use of modular exhibitry. Works to create an orderly industry and foster a competitive and beneficial arena for modular exhibit manufacturers. Plans to: establish an industry code of ethics; facilitate the interchange of information through exhibitions and forums; encourage networking of modular distributors; promote the research and development of new materials, methods, and applications for modular exhibitry. Sponsors designers' competitions. Operates speakers' bureau; compiles statistics. **Publications:** Newsletter, quarterly. **Conventions/Meetings:** quarterly meeting.

1343 ■ International Defense Equipment Exhibitors Association (IDEEA)
6233 Nelway Dr.
McLean, VA 22101
Ph: (703)760-0762
Fax: (703)760-0764
E-mail: qwhiteree@ideea.com
URL: http://www.ideea.com
Contact: Quentin Whiteree, Pres.
Founded: 1986. **Staff:** 3. **For-Profit. Description:** Promotes international cooperation between the United States and the 19 allied countries that have reciprocal defense procurement agreements with the U.S. **Also Known As:** IDEEA Inc. **Publications:** *ComDef Handbook*, annual. Directory. Lists exhibitions. **Advertising:** accepted ● *Common Defense Forum*, monthly. Newsletter. Focuses on a different country each month. **Circulation:** 21,000. **Advertising:** accepted ● Also publishes transcripts of technical sessions and symposia. **Conventions/Meetings:** annual ComDet - meeting (exhibits) - March and August ● annual conference.

1344 ■ International Sport Show Producers Association (ISSPA)
c/o Dianne Seymour, Exec. Sec.
PO Box 480084
Denver, CO 80248-0084
Ph: (303)892-6800
Free: (800)457-2434
Fax: (303)892-6322
E-mail: dseymour@iei-expos.com
URL: http://www.sportshow.org
Contact: Dianne Seymour, Exec. Sec.
Founded: 1970. **Members:** 17. **Description:** Member association of the Northern Ontario Tourist Outfitters Association and American Sportfishing Association. Producers of public events involving the exhibition of sporting goods, including fishing tackle, boating and marine equipment, recreational vehicles, hunting, and travel destinations, boats. **Publications:** *Sports and Vacation Show Directory and Calendar*, annual. **Price:** free. **Conventions/Meetings:** annual meeting, members only - usually June/July.

1345 ■ International Trade Exhibitions in France (ITEF)
1611 N Kent St., Ste.903
Arlington, VA 22209
Ph: (703)522-5000
Free: (888)522-5001
Fax: (703)522-5005
E-mail: usa@promosalons.com
URL: http://www.promosalons.fr/accueil.php
Contact: Mr. Philippe Bazin, Pres.
Founded: 1970. **Members:** 80. **Staff:** 5. **Languages:** English, French. **Description:** Organizers for trade shows held in France at which more than 25&percent; of the exhibitors or attendees come from other countries. Promotes France as a venue for international trade shows. **Publications:** *The Calendar* (in English, French, and Spanish), annual. Directory. **Circulation:** 5,000.

1346 ■ National Association of Consumer Shows (NACS)
147 SE 102nd Ave.
Portland, OR 97216
Ph: (503)253-0832
Free: (800)728-6227
Fax: (503)253-9172
E-mail: info@publicshows.com
URL: http://www.publicshows.com
Contact: Jim Fricke, Pres.
Founded: 1987. **Members:** 250. **Membership Dues:** regular, associate, $245 (annual). **Staff:** 3. **Description:** Show producers and suppliers. Conducts educational programs. **Computer Services:** database, show sales ● mailing lists, of members. **Publications:** *NACS Show Producer*, bimonthly. Newsletter. **Circulation:** 250. **Advertising:** accepted ● Directory, annual. **Price:** included in membership dues. **Advertising:** accepted. **Conventions/Meetings:** bimonthly board meeting ● annual convention and trade show.

1347 ■ National Catholic Educational Exhibitors (NCEE)
2621 Dryden Rd., Ste.300
Dayton, OH 45439
Ph: (937)293-1415
Free: (800)523-4625
Fax: (937)293-1310
Contact: Bret Thomas, Exec. Dir.
Founded: 1950. **Members:** 383. **Membership Dues:** corporate, $150 (annual). **Description:** Companies selling to Catholic schools and exhibiting at national, regional, and diocesan educational meetings. **Awards:** J.P. Walsh Scholarship. **Frequency:** annual. **Type:** scholarship. **Recipient:** for a member's child ● **Type:** recognition. **Recipient:** for 25 years of service. **Affiliated With:** National Catholic Educational Association. **Publications:** *National Catholic Educational Exhibitors—Membership Directory*, annual. Includes a classified directory of products. **Price:** free. **Circulation:** 500 ● *NCEE News*, quarterly. Newsletter. Provides list of school and diocesan exhibits and meetings and features on new members. **Price:** free for members only. **Circulation:** 500. **Conventions/Meetings:** annual meeting - always Easter week.

1348 ■ Society of Independent Show Organizers (SISO)
7000 W Southwest Hwy.
Chicago Ridge, IL 60415
Ph: (708)361-0900
Free: (877)YES-SISO
Fax: (708)361-6166
E-mail: siso@tradeshownet.com
URL: http://www.siso.org
Contact: Mary Beth Rebedeau, Exec. Dir.
Founded: 1990. **Members:** 200. **Membership Dues:** company, $295-$1,825 (annual). **Description:** Independent consumer and trade show organizers. Dedicated to the advancement of the consumer and trade show industry; provides members with business experience, show management experience, unbiased answers, current news, and industry leadership. **Computer Services:** Electronic publishing, NewsNow! Bulletin. **Programs:** Neil Grossman Trade Show Industry Internship. **Publications:** *Update*, weekly. Newsletter ● Newsletter, monthly ● Membership Directory, semiannual. **Conventions/Meetings:** annual CEO Forum - meeting, focuses on special needs of company presidents, CEOs, and CFOs - held in late summer ● annual conference, open to senior management of for-profit trade shows and event production companies - held in spring.

1349 ■ Trade Show Exhibitors Association (TSEA)
2301 S Lake Shore Dr., Ste.1005
Chicago, IL 60616
Ph: (312)842-8732
Fax: (312)842-8744
E-mail: tsea@tsea.org
URL: http://www.tsea.org
Contact: Stephen Schuldenfrei, Pres.
Founded: 1966. **Members:** 2,000. **Membership Dues:** active company ($125 each additional member), $800 ● active individual, $295 ● allied individual, $500 ● allied company ($200 each additional member), $1,350 ● academic institution, $150 ● student, $35. **Staff:** 11. **Budget:** $2,000,000. **Regional Groups:** 6. **Description:** Exhibitors working to improve the effectiveness of trade shows as a marketing tool. Purposes are to promote the progress and development of trade show exhibiting; to collect and disseminate trade show information; conduct studies, surveys, and stated projects designed to improve trade shows; to foster good relations and communications with organizations representing others in the industry; to undertake other activities necessary to promote the welfare of member companies. Sponsors Exhibit Industry Education Foundation and professional exhibiting seminars; the forum series of educational programs on key issues affecting the industry. Maintains placement services; compiles statistics. **Libraries: Type:** reference. **Holdings:** periodicals. **Awards:** Chairman's Award. **Frequency:** annual. **Type:** recognition. **Recipient:** for an individual member who has made contributions to the association ● Distinguished Service Award. **Frequency:** annual. **Type:** recognition. **Recipient:** for an individual member who has made a significant contribution to the exposition industry ● President's Award. **Frequency:** annual. **Type:** recognition. **Recipient:** for an individual who embodies the spirit of excellence in dealing with TSEA and the industry. **Computer Services:** Mailing lists. **Formerly:** (1983) National Trade Show Exhibitors Association; (1997) International Exhibitors Association. **Publications:** *How to Develop a Successful Exhibit Marketing Plan*, periodic. Serves as a desk reference covering exhibit marketing. **Price:** free, for members only. **Circulation:** 2,000 ● *Trade Show Ideas Magazine*, monthly. Includes research reports, statistical analysis, and information on new products. **Price:** free for members. **Circulation:** 2,500. **Advertising:** accepted ● Membership Directory, annual. **Price:** free for members; $55.00 for nonmembers. **Circulation:** 2,000 ● Reports. Alternate Formats: online ● Articles. Alternate Formats: online ● Also publishes periodic special management reports, budget guide, salary survey, international exhibitors handbook and guide, and position statements. **Conventions/Meetings:** conference ● annual meeting (exhibits) - always July or August.

1350 ■ World Council for Venue Management (WCVM)
Address Unknown since 2008
URL: http://www.venue.org
Founded: 1997. **Multinational. Description:** Represents public assembly venue industry professionals and facilities. Seeks to enhance communication and professional development to facilitate knowledge and understanding of the public assembly venue industry.

Explosives

1351 ■ Institute of Makers of Explosives (IME)
1120 19th St. NW, Ste.310
Washington, DC 20036-3605
Ph: (202)429-9280
Fax: (202)293-2420
E-mail: info@ime.org
URL: http://www.ime.org
Contact: J. Christopher Ronay, Pres.
Founded: 1913. **Members:** 40. **Staff:** 8. **Description:** Provides technically accurate information and recommendations concerning explosive materials and their uses. Serves as a source of reliable information. Conducts national blasting cap safety education program. **Committees:** Environmental Affairs; Legal Affairs; Safety and Health; Technical;

Transportation and Distribution. **Publications:** *Safety Library Series.* **Conventions/Meetings:** quarterly meeting.

1352 ■ National Fireworks Association (NFA)
8224 NW Bradford Ct.
Kansas City, MO 64151
Ph: (816)505-3589
E-mail: info@nationalfireworks.org
URL: http://www.nationalfireworks.org
Contact: Bob Blake, VP
Founded: 1992. **Members:** 400. **Membership Dues:** full, $375 (annual) ● associate, $150 (annual) ● friend, $30 (annual). **Staff:** 2. **Budget:** $50,000. **Description:** Seeks to preserve the use of fireworks in the U.S. Monitors legislation and lobbies on behalf of members; conducts educational and charitable programs; and holds competitions. **Telecommunication Services:** electronic mail, nlblogin@nationalfireworks.org. **Publications:** *NFA News*, monthly. Newsletter. **Price:** free for members. **Circulation:** 500. **Advertising:** accepted. **Conventions/Meetings:** annual board meeting and trade show (exhibits) ● annual regional meeting.

Farriers

1353 ■ Brotherhood of Working Farriers Association (BWFA)
c/o Ralph Casey, Pres./Exec. Dir.
14013 E Hwy. 136
Lafayette, GA 30728
Ph: (706)397-8047
Fax: (706)397-8047
E-mail: farrierhdq@aol.com
URL: http://www.bwfa.net
Contact: Ralph Casey, Pres./Exec. Dir.
Founded: 1989. **Members:** 8,000. **Membership Dues:** farrier, certified farrier, $85 (annual) ● horse owner, $35 (annual) ● life, $450 ● veterinarian, company, $250 (annual) ● foreign, $150 (annual). **Staff:** 3. **Description:** Offers clinics and education on hoofcare, trimming and shoeing for the public and horse owners through the National Farrier Referral Program and Farrier Certification and Continuing Education Programs for farriers. Provides its members with discounts on AFLAC Insurance Plans (accidental, cancer, health and life), the Injured Farriers Fund and pension plan/retirement for all members. Sponsors the television show, Horseshoe' Time aired on the Dish Network and Cable. Maintains Farriers Hall of Fame and museum at the Georgia headquarters. Co-sponsors the West Quest Cowboy Cancer Crusade events. Supports the National Equine & Hoof Research Foundation, Inc. **Publications:** *National Business News Bulletin* ● Articles. Alternate Formats: online.

1354 ■ Guild of Professional Farriers
2020 Pennsylvania Ave. NW, No. 800
Washington, DC 20006
Ph: (301)898-6990
Fax: (301)898-0564
E-mail: horseu@earthlink.net
URL: http://www.guildfarriers.org
Contact: Henry Heymering, Pres.
Founded: 1996. **Membership Dues:** regular, $100 (annual). **Description:** Promotes and represents the professional farrier. **Publications:** *New Guild Chronicle.* Magazine. **Price:** included in membership dues. Alternate Formats: online.

1355 ■ Sisterhood of Shoers
804 Vann St.
Vidalia, GA 30474
E-mail: horseshoer@yahoo.com
URL: http://www.horseshoes.com/assoc/national/sisterhood/contact.htm
Contact: Meg Oliver, Pres.
Membership Dues: regular, $40 (annual). **Description:** Promotes women in the art and trade of horseshoeing.

1356 ■ World Farriers Association (WFA)
PO Box 1102
Albuquerque, NM 87103
Ph: (505)345-7550
E-mail: wfassoc@msn.com
URL: http://www.horseshoes.com/assoc/intrnatl/wfa/homepage.htm
Founded: 1984. **Membership Dues:** organizational (origination fee), $200 ● organizational (plus $1/member), $100 (annual) ● individual, associate (origination fee), $50 ● individual/associate, $25 (annual) ● commercial (origination fee), $200 ● commercial, $100 (annual). **Multinational. Description:** Works for the well being of all hoofed animals, including asses, donkeys, mules and horses, as well as other species and hybrids of single-hoofed creatures by promoting the ethics and skills of the farrier industry.

Feed

1357 ■ American Feed Industry Association (AFIA)
1501 Wilson Blvd., Ste.1100
Arlington, VA 22209
Ph: (703)524-0810
Fax: (703)524-1921
E-mail: afia@afia.org
URL: http://www.afia.org
Contact: Joel Newman, Pres./CEO
Founded: 1909. **Members:** 690. **Membership Dues:** international, $1,800 (annual) ● association, $1,200 (annual). **Staff:** 17. **Budget:** $2,000,000. **State Groups:** 32. **Description:** Manufacturers of formula feed and pet food; suppliers to feed manufacturers; other trade related associations. Maintains Equipment Manufacturing Council. **Awards:** Distinguished Service Award. **Frequency:** annual. **Type:** recognition ● Environmental Awards. **Frequency:** annual. **Type:** recognition. **Recipient:** for operating facilities, management and employees who have made improvements in the reduction of waste ● Feed Mill of the Year. **Frequency:** annual. **Type:** recognition. **Recipient:** for national publicity in trade media ● Food Safety Innovation Awards. **Frequency:** annual. **Type:** recognition. **Recipient:** for firms and organizations responsible for pioneering new feed safety methods ● Member of the Year. **Frequency:** annual. **Type:** recognition ● Truck Fleet of the Year. **Frequency:** annual. **Type:** recognition. **Recipient:** for national publicity in trade media. **Computer Services:** database, buyer's guide. **Telecommunication Services:** electronic mail, jnewman@afia.org. **Committees:** Aquaculture; Environmental; Equipment Manufacturers Council Executive; Feed Control; Information Technology; International; Laboratory; Liquid Feed; Manufacturing; Marketing and Professional Development; Membership; Nutrition Council Executive; Pet Food Council Executive; Purchasing; Safety and Health. **Councils:** AFIA-Alfalfa Processors Council Members; Credit and Finance; Ingredient Suppliers Executive; Quality; Women in Ag. **Affiliated With:** Animal Agriculture Alliance. **Absorbed:** National Feed Ingredients Association; National Mineral Feed Association; (2002) American Alfalfa Processors Association. **Formerly:** (1975) Midwest Feed Manufacturers Association; (1985) American Feed Manufacturers Association; (2002) American Feed Industry Association. **Publications:** *Feed Control Comment*, monthly. **Price:** available to members only ● *Feed Manufacturing Technology* ● *Feedgram*, biweekly. Newsletter. Provides news in the feed industry and updates on state, federal, regulatory and legislative affairs affecting the feed industry. **Price:** available to members only ● *Publications Catalog* ● *SafetyGram*, monthly. Newsletter ● Membership Directory, annual. **Price:** $25.00 for members; $100.00 for nonmembers. **Advertising:** accepted. **Conventions/Meetings:** annual convention ● biennial Expo - show, largest exhibition of feed manufacturing and related industries (exhibits).

1358 ■ National Alfalfa and Forage Alliance (NAFA)
4630 Churchill St., No. 1
St. Paul, MN 55126
Ph: (651)484-3888
Fax: (651)638-0756
E-mail: nafa@comcast.net
URL: http://www.alfalfa.org
Contact: Beth Nelson, Pres./Exec. Dir.
Founded: 1953. **Members:** 600. **Membership Dues:** diamond, $20,000 (annual) ● platinum, $10,000 (annual) ● gold, $5,000 (annual) ● silver, $1,500 (annual) ● associate, $500 (annual). **Budget:** $100,000. **Description:** Alfalfa seed growers. Promotes the use of alfalfa. Facilitates the exchange of ideas and information among researchers. **Awards:** Alfalfa Awards Program. **Frequency:** annual. **Type:** recognition. **Recipient:** for the expenses to National Alfalfa symposium. **Formerly:** (2003) Alfalfa Council; (2006) National Alfalfa Alliance. **Publications:** *Alfalfa Talk*, quarterly. Newsletter. **Circulation:** 2,000 ● Also publishes leaflets. **Conventions/Meetings:** semiannual Alfalfa Intensive Training Seminar ● annual symposium (exhibits).

1359 ■ National Grain and Feed Association (NGFA)
1250 Eye St. NW, Ste.1003
Washington, DC 20005-3922
Ph: (202)289-0873
Fax: (202)289-5388
E-mail: ngfa@ngfa.org
URL: http://www.ngfa.org
Contact: Kendell W. Keith, Pres.
Founded: 1896. **Members:** 1,000. **Staff:** 15. **Regional Groups:** 2. **State Groups:** 33. **Description:** One thousand grain, feed and processing firms. Country terminal and export elevators; feed mills; cash grain and feed merchandisers; commodity futures brokers and commission merchants; processors; millers; and allied industries. Represents and provides services for grain and grain-related commercial businesses. Focuses on achieving beneficial agricultural growth that will provide a healthy environment for production, merchandising, handling, warehousing, feed and processing businesses. Seeks to ensure a wholesome, high quality and adequate food and feed supply for domestic and world consumers by protecting, promoting and enhancing the integrity and interests of U.S. grain handling, warehousing, merchandising, feed and processing businesses. **Committees:** Arbitration Appeals; Executive; Food and Feed Safety; Grain Grades and Weights; International Trade/Agricultural Policy; Marketing; Rail Arbitration Rules; Rail Shipper/Receiver; Research; Risk Management; Safety, Health and Environmental Quality; Strategic Issues; Trade Rules; Waterborne Commerce. **Councils:** Country Elevator; Feed Industry. **Formerly:** (1896) Grain and Feed Dealers National Association. **Publications:** *Annual Directory/Yearbook*, annual. Includes names, addresses, phone numbers, fax numbers, key contacts, locations, and types of business of all NGFA member companies. **Price:** free for members; $150.00 for nonmembers. **Circulation:** 5,000. **Advertising:** accepted ● *Committee Action* ● *Feed Quality Assurance Program*, quarterly ● *Grain Book*, triennial ● *Industry Info-Line*, periodic ● *NGFA Newsletter*, biweekly ● *Trade Rules*, annual. Booklet. **Conventions/Meetings:** annual convention - always March ● annual Country Elevator Council/Feed Industry Council - conference and trade show - always early December.

1360 ■ National Hay Association (NHA)
102 Treasure Island Causeway
St. Petersburg, FL 33706
Ph: (727)367-9702
Free: (800)707-0014
Fax: (727)367-9608
E-mail: haynha@aol.com
URL: http://nationalhay.org
Contact: Donald F. Kieffer, Exec. Dir.
Founded: 1895. **Members:** 650. **Membership Dues:** regular, $260 (annual). **Staff:** 1. **Budget:** $200,000. **Description:** Hay shippers, dealers, brokers, producers, and others interested in the hay industry. **Awards:** Haymaker of the Year. **Frequency:** annual. **Type:** recognition. **Recipient:** for the member who has made contribution to USA hay and forge industry.

Committees: Arbitration; Export; Grades; Hay Grades; Legislative; Statistical; Trade Questions; Transportation. **Publications:** *Hay There!*, monthly. Magazine. Provides information on markets, production, storage, and packaging. **Price:** free for members. **Advertising:** accepted ● *National Hay Association—News Release*, periodic. Reports dates of upcoming meetings, previous meeting minutes, and updates on specific issues. **Price:** free ● *National Hay Association—Yearbook and Membership Directory*, annual. **Price:** included in membership dues. **Advertising:** accepted ● Bulletins ● Membership Directory. **Conventions/Meetings:** annual conference and convention (exhibits).

1361 ■ Wild Bird Feeding Industry (WBFI)
1305 N Tahoe Trail
Sioux Falls, SD 57110-6410
Free: (888)839-1237
Fax: (605)275-6697
E-mail: info@wbfi.org
URL: http://www.wbfi.org
Contact: Susan M. Hays CMP, Exec. Dir.
Founded: 1984. **Members:** 150. **Staff:** 3. **Description:** Represents manufacturers, processors, packers, distributors, and retailers of birdseed, bird feeders, and related products. Promotes responsible feeding to enhance the consumer's experience. Publishes 6 Steps to turn your Backyard into a Sanctuary for Birds, a consumer education publication. **Publications:** *Chronicles*, quarterly. Newsletter. Alternate Formats: online. **Conventions/Meetings:** annual meeting.

Fencing

1362 ■ Chain Link Fence Manufacturers Institute (CLFMI)
10015 Old Columbia Rd., Ste.B-215
Columbia, MD 21046
Ph: (301)596-2583
Fax: (301)596-2594
E-mail: clfmihq@aol.com
URL: http://codewriters.com/asites/main-pub.cfm?usr=clfma
Contact: Mark Levin CAE, Exec. VP
Founded: 1960. **Members:** 52. **Staff:** 2. **Description:** Firms engaged in the manufacture of chain link fencing. Provides a forum in which members can meet to be educated and exchange ideas on operations and management; promotes use of chain link fence. Collects statistics; works with consumers and governments to develop standards and specifications with the goal of upgrading the quality of the product. **Awards:** Design Award. **Frequency:** annual. **Type:** recognition. **Recipient:** for licensed architects and unique usage of chain link fence. **Committees:** AFA Liaison; Bar Coding; Design Award; General Technical; Industry Promotion; Legislative Action; Membership; Product Promotion; Statistics. **Publications:** *Fact Guide to Chain Link Fences*. Booklets ● *Field Inspection Guide*. Booklets. Alternate Formats: online ● *Link Letter*, monthly ● *Product Manual: Step-by-Step Installation Guide*. Booklets. Alternate Formats: online ● *Today's Chain Link*. Pamphlets. Alternate Formats: online ● Reports. Alternate Formats: online. **Conventions/Meetings:** semiannual conference.

Fertilizer

1363 ■ Agricultural Retailers Association (ARA)
1156 15th St. NW, Ste.302
Washington, DC 20005
Ph: (202)457-0825
Free: (800)535-6272
Fax: (202)457-0864
E-mail: ara@aradc.org
URL: http://www.aradc.org
Contact: Jack Eberspacher, Pres./CEO
Founded: 1954. **Members:** 1,000. **Membership Dues:** associate, $600 (annual) ● retailer/distributor (maximum; based on total number of sales), $25,000 (annual) ● manufacturer (maximum; based on total number of sales), $30,000 (annual). **Staff:** 6. **Budget:** $1,500,000. **Description:** Retailers, manufacturers, and suppliers of fertilizers and agrochemicals; equipment manufacturers; retail affiliations; and state association affiliates. **Formed by Merger of:** (1992) National Fertilizer Solutions Association; (1992) National AgriChemical Retailers Association. **Formerly:** National Nitrogen Solutions Association. **Publications:** *Retailer Facts*. Newsletter. **Price:** included in membership dues. **Conventions/Meetings:** annual convention (exhibits).

1364 ■ Fertilizer Industry Round Table (FIRT)
c/o Ms. Peggy Long
1701 S Highland Ave.
Baltimore, MD 21224
Ph: (410)276-4466
Fax: (410)276-0241
E-mail: peggyl@ajsackett.com
URL: http://www.firt.org
Contact: Ms. Peggy Long, Contact
Founded: 1951. **Description:** Participants include production, technical, and research personnel in the fertilizer industry. Acts as a forum for discussion of technical and production problems. **Publications:** Proceedings, annual. **Price:** $35.00/copy. **Conventions/Meetings:** annual meeting - always in October or November.

1365 ■ The Fertilizer Institute (TFI)
Union Center Plz.
820 1st St. NE, Ste.430
Washington, DC 20002
Ph: (202)962-0490
Fax: (202)962-0577
E-mail: informationtfi@tfi.org
URL: http://www.tfi.org
Contact: Ford West, Pres.
Founded: 1970. **Members:** 300. **Staff:** 22. **Regional Groups:** 48. **Description:** Producers, manufacturers, retailers, trading firms, and equipment manufacturers. Represents members in various legislative, educational, and technical areas. Provides information and public relations programs. **Formed by Merger of:** Agricultural Nitrogen Institute; National Plant Food Institute. **Publications:** *Directory of Fertilizer References*, annual ● *Fertilizer Facts and Figures*, annual ● *Fertilizer Institute—Action Letter*, monthly. Newsletter. Includes information of interest to TFI members. ● *Fertilizer Record*, periodic. Newsletter. Includes information of interest to TFI members. ● Also produces and distributes motion pictures and visual aids. **Conventions/Meetings:** annual Fertilizer Marketing Business - meeting - always February ● annual Fertilizer Outlook and Technology Conference ● annual World Fertilizer Conference.

Fibers

1366 ■ Fiber Economics Bureau (FEB)
1530 Wilson Blvd., Ste.690
Arlington, VA 22209
Ph: (703)875-0432
Fax: (703)875-0907
E-mail: diane@afma.org
URL: http://www.fibereconomics.com
Contact: Diane Bayatafshar, Business Mgr.
Founded: 1935. **Multinational. Description:** Provides statistics on the U.S. manufactured fiber industry and its products, including acrylic, nylon, polyester, olefin, rayon, glass fiber, and others. **Additional Websites:** http://www.fibersource.com. **Telecommunication Services:** electronic mail, feb@afma.org. **Affiliated With:** American Fiber Manufacturers Association. **Publications:** *Fiber Organon*, monthly. Journal. Contains the latest information on industry trends, tables and charts. **Price:** $350.00/year in U.S.; $400.00/year outside U.S. ● *Manufactured Fiber Fact Book*. **Price:** $5.00 for members; $10.00 for nonmembers, plus shipping and handling ● *Manufactured Fiber Review*, monthly. Report. Contains latest industry trends, tables, and charts. **Price:** $350.00/year ● *Manufactured Fibers - A Technical Video*. **Price:** $30.00 for members; $35.00 for nonmembers, plus shipping and handling ● *World Directory of Manufactured Fiber Producers*, annual. **Price:** $145.00/copy.

Film

1367 ■ Association of Cinema and Video Laboratories (ACVL)
c/o Chip Wilkinson, Pres.
630 Ninth Ave.
New York, NY 10036
Ph: (212)586-4822
Fax: (212)582-3744
E-mail: cfw2447@rcn.com
URL: http://www.acvl.org
Contact: Chip Wilkinson, Pres.
Founded: 1953. **Members:** 58. **Membership Dues:** laboratory/associate in North America, $600 (annual) ● laboratory/associate outside North America, $250 (annual). **Description:** Motion picture film or video transfer laboratories; non-laboratory firms with allied interests. Provides a forum for the exchange of ideas in connection with the technical, administrative, and managerial problems of the motion picture and video laboratory industry. Concerns include: government relations; public and industry relations; product specifications; improvement of technical practices and procedures; other areas of interest to film and video laboratories. **Formerly:** Association of Cinema Laboratories. **Publications:** *ACVL Handbook*. Acquaints users of motion picture laboratory services with terminology, pre-print preparation. **Price:** $19.95 in U.S. **Conventions/Meetings:** annual conference (exhibits) - every spring.

1368 ■ Association of Film Commissioners International (AFCI)
314 N Main
Helena, MT 59601
Ph: (406)495-8040
Fax: (406)495-8039
E-mail: info@afci.org
URL: http://www.afci.org
Contact: Bill Lindstrom, CEO
Founded: 1975. **Members:** 310. **Membership Dues:** regular, $750 (annual). **Staff:** 2. **Budget:** $900,000. **Multinational. Description:** Government representatives responsible, in their respective cities, states, regions, and countries, for the attraction and development of, and services to, the motion picture and television industries; private sector businesses with activities directly or indirectly affected by film commissions. Facilitates exchange of information among members; takes policy positions on issues when appropriate. Offers members greater visibility in the industry than would be possible on an individual basis and promotes industry growth. Conducts educational programs. Compiles statistics; maintains speakers' bureau. **Awards:** Crystal Vision Award. **Frequency:** annual. **Type:** recognition. **Recipient:** for contribution to the organization ● Dutch Horton Award. **Frequency:** annual. **Type:** recognition. **Computer Services:** database, production personnel and film commissioners. **Telecommunication Services:** electronic mail, bill@afci.org. **Boards:** Advisory; Directors. **Formerly:** (1988) Association of Film Commissioners. **Publications:** *AFCI Locations*, annual. Journal. Contains location production and information on state film commissions. **Price:** free. **Circulation:** 15,000. **Advertising:** accepted ● *AFCI Members List*, monthly. Newsletter ● *AFCI Newsletter*, quarterly. Magazine ● *Locations*, annual. Magazine. **Advertising:** accepted. **Conventions/Meetings:** annual Cineposium and Film Commission Fundamentals - trade show (exhibits).

1369 ■ Construction and Agricultural Film Manufacturers Association (CAFMA)
Address Unknown since 2007
URL: http://www.cafma.org
Founded: 1989. **Members:** 3. **Membership Dues:** ordinary, $20,000 (annual). **Staff:** 1. **Budget:** $100,000. **Description:** Manufacturers of polyethyl-

ene plastic sheeting products used in construction, industrial, and agricultural applications. Promotes the plastic film industry. Represents members' interests. **Conventions/Meetings:** annual conference and board meeting.

1370 ■ International Recording Media Association (IRMA)
182 Nassau St., Ste.204
Princeton, NJ 08542
Ph: (609)279-1700
Fax: (609)279-1999
E-mail: info@recordingmedia.org
URL: http://www.recordingmedia.org
Contact: Charles Van Horn, Pres.
Founded: 1970. **Members:** 450. **Membership Dues:** company (with annual audio/video/data revenue of up to $2.5 million), $1,000 (annual) ● company (with annual audio/video/data revenue of $2.5-7.5 million), $2,100 (annual) ● company (with annual audio/video/ data revenue of $7.5-15 million), $4,000 (annual) ● company (with annual audio/video/data revenue of $15-25 million), $5,600 (annual) ● company (with annual audio/video/data revenue of $25-50 million), $7,700 (annual) ● company (with annual audio/video/ data revenue of $50-100 million), $8,500 (annual) ● company (with annual audio/video/data revenue of over $100 million), $9,500 (annual). **Staff:** 9. **Budget:** $1,300,000. **Multinational. Description:** Serves as the advocate for the growth and development of all recording media and as a forum for the exchange of information regarding global trends and innovations. Provides members an opportunity to join forces and be a strong industry voice allowing them to grow and expand their business. Encompasses all facets of the recording media. **Awards:** Gold Video Award. **Type:** recognition. **Recipient:** for sales by volume and dollar amount ● Platinum Video Award. **Type:** recognition. **Recipient:** for sales by volume and dollar amount. **Computer Services:** Online services, source directory. **Telecommunication Services:** electronic mail, cvanhorn@recordingmedia.org. **Committees:** Blank Audio and Videotape Statistical; Canadian Statistical; Data Media Statistical; Forum Program Planning; Strategic Planning. **Programs:** Anti-Piracy Compliance. **Formerly:** ITA - International Association of Magnetic and Optical Media Manufacturers and Related Industries; (1980) International Tape Association; (1990) International Tape/Disc Association. **Publications:** *IRMA International Source Directory*, annual. Describes products and services of IRMA member companies. Includes product, services, and company indexes. **Price:** free. **Circulation:** 10,000. **Advertising:** accepted ● *Mediaware*, 9/year. Magazine. **Circulation:** 10,000. **Advertising:** accepted. **Conventions/Meetings:** annual meeting and seminar.

1371 ■ Motion Picture Sound Editors (MPSE)
10061 Riverside Dr.
PMB Box 751
Toluca Lake, CA 91602-2560
Ph: (818)506-7731
Fax: (818)506-7732
E-mail: mail@mpse.org
URL: http://www.MPSE.org
Contact: Ms. Bobbi Banks, Pres.
Founded: 1953. **Members:** 400. **Membership Dues:** affiliate (US), $135 (annual) ● active, Foley (US), $150 (annual) ● student, $35 (annual) ● international, $100 (annual). **Staff:** 1. **Description:** Motion picture sound editors. **Awards:** Ethel Crutcher Scholarship. **Frequency:** annual. **Type:** scholarship. **Recipient:** for student. **Telecommunication Services:** electronic mail, office@mpse.org. **Publications:** *Golden Reel Awards Guide*, annual. **Conventions/Meetings:** monthly board meeting.

1372 ■ Women in Animation (WIA)
PO Box 17706
Encino, CA 91416
Ph: (818)759-9596
E-mail: info@womeninanimation.org
URL: http://www.womeninanimation.org
Contact: Janet Nagel, Pres.
Founded: 1994. **Members:** 400. **Membership Dues:** professional, $50 (annual) ● student, $25 (annual). **Staff:** 1. **Regional Groups:** 5. **Multinational. Description:** Promotes women in animation; provides networking opportunities; offers free or low-cost classes and seminars. **Libraries: Type:** reference. **Holdings:** archival material, audio recordings. **Subjects:** interviews with animation pioneers. **Awards:** Phyllis Craig Scholarship Fund. **Frequency:** annual. **Type:** scholarship. **Recipient:** to U.S. citizen/student. **Publications:** *Work In Progress*, quarterly. Newsletter. Contains news and articles. **Price:** included in membership dues. **Circulation:** 1,000. **Advertising:** accepted. Alternate Formats: online. **Conventions/ Meetings:** annual meeting ● quarterly regional meeting.

1373 ■ Women in Film and Video (WIFV)
3628 12th St. NE
Washington, DC 20017
Ph: (202)429-9438
Fax: (202)429-9440
E-mail: membership@wifv.org
URL: http://www.wifv.org
Contact: Melissa Houghton, Exec. Dir.
Founded: 1979. **Members:** 1,200. **Membership Dues:** student, $40 (annual) ● professional, $100 (annual) ● executive, $175 (annual) ● corporate, $300 (annual). **Staff:** 2. **Description:** Individuals, businesses, and organizations promoting women in the film and video industries. Seeks to advance the professional development and achievement of women in film, video, and related media. Promotes equality of opportunity within the film and video industries. Provides professional support to members; sponsors professional mentoring programs; serves as a clearinghouse on women in film, video, and related video. Conducts technical and professional educational programs in areas including screenwriting, directing, business and legal issues, editing, and lighting. Maintains network linking professional women in the film and video industries. **Awards:** Women of Vision Awards. **Frequency:** annual. **Type:** recognition. **Committees:** Communications; Development; Image Makers; Programming; WIFTI; Women of Vision Awards Gala. **Publications:** Membership Directory, annual. **Circulation:** 1,500. **Advertising:** accepted ● Newsletter, monthly. Alternate Formats: online. **Conventions/Meetings:** annual Awards Gala - meeting - always in Washington, DC ● monthly board meeting - always in Washington, DC ● annual Job Fair - trade show - always in Washington, DC ● annual Professional Development Seminar - always in Washington, DC ● monthly Wednesday One - workshop - always in Washington, DC.

Film Industry

1374 ■ Academy of Motion Picture Arts and Sciences (AMPAS)
8949 Wilshire Blvd.
Beverly Hills, CA 90211-1907
Ph: (310)247-3000
E-mail: ampas@oscars.org
URL: http://www.oscars.org
Contact: Bruce Davis, Exec. Dir.
Founded: 1927. **Members:** 6,316. **Staff:** 100. **Description:** Represents motion picture producers, directors, writers, cinematographer, editors, actors, and craftsmen. **Libraries: Type:** reference. **Holdings:** archival material, books, films, photographs. **Subjects:** film history. **Awards:** Nicholl Fellowships in Screenwriting. **Frequency:** annual. **Type:** fellowship. **Recipient:** for screenwriting students ● **Type:** recognition. **Recipient:** for student films ● Student Academy Awards. **Frequency:** annual. **Type:** recognition. **Recipient:** for outstanding achievements in motion picture production. **Telecommunication Services:** information service, motion picture reference, (213)247-3020. **Publications:** *Academy Players Directory*, 3/year ● *Annual Index of Motion Picture Credits*, annual ● Union List of Motion Picture Scripts.

1375 ■ Alliance of Motion Picture and Television Producers (AMPTP)
15503 Ventura Blvd.
Encino, CA 91436
Ph: (818)995-3600
URL: http://www.amptp.org
Contact: J. Nicholas Counter, Pres.
Founded: 1982. **Members:** 350. **Staff:** 14. **Description:** Major motion picture and television producing companies. **Supersedes:** Association of Motion Picture and Television Producers.

1376 ■ American Cinema Editors (ACE)
100 Universal City Plz.
2282 Verna Fields Bldg., Rm. 190
Universal City, CA 91608
Ph: (818)777-2900
Fax: (818)733-5023
E-mail: amercinema@earthlink.net
URL: http://www.ace-filmeditors.org
Contact: Alan Heim ACE, Pres.
Founded: 1950. **Members:** 385. **Staff:** 1. **Description:** Invitational society of professional motion picture and television film editors. Sponsors production and distribution of motion picture films on film editing entitled Basic Principles of Film Editing, and Interpretation and Values. Conducts Visiting Editor program at schools; maintains speakers' bureau. **Awards:** ACE Eddie Award. **Frequency:** annual. **Type:** recognition. **Recipient:** for best film editing and career achievement ● Golden Eddie Filmmaker of the Year. **Frequency:** annual. **Type:** recognition. **Telecommunication Services:** electronic mail, lea@perceptionpr.com ● electronic mail, gena@perceptionpr.com. **Publications:** *Cinemaeditor*, quarterly. Magazine. Contains emphasis on editors and editing. **Price:** $15.00/year, domestic; $36.00/year, international. **Advertising:** accepted. Alternate Formats: online. **Conventions/Meetings:** annual meeting - always spring, Los Angeles, CA.

1377 ■ American Society of Cinematographers (ASC)
PO Box 2230
Hollywood, CA 90078
Ph: (323)969-4333
Free: (800)448-0145
Fax: (323)882-6391
E-mail: office@theasc.com
URL: http://www.theasc.com
Contact: Richard Crudo, Pres.
Founded: 1919. **Members:** 415. **Membership Dues:** invitational, $400 (annual). **Staff:** 12. **Description:** Professional directors of photography in motion picture and television photography and others affiliated with cinematography. **Libraries: Type:** reference. **Holdings:** archival material. **Awards:** ASC Board of Governors Award. **Frequency:** annual. **Type:** recognition. **Recipient:** to an individual who has made significant and enduring contributions to advancing the art of filmmaking ● ASC Presidents Award. **Frequency:** annual. **Type:** recognition. **Recipient:** to an individual who made exceptional contributions to advancing the art and craft of filmmaking ● International Achievement Award. **Frequency:** annual. **Type:** recognition. **Recipient:** to an individual who compiled their main body of work outside the United States ● Lifetime Achievement Award. **Frequency:** annual. **Type:** recognition. **Recipient:** to a cinematographer whose body of work has made an important and enduring impression on the art of filmmaking ● Mini-Series Award. **Frequency:** annual. **Type:** recognition ● Movie of the Week. **Frequency:** annual. **Type:** recognition ● Pilot Award. **Frequency:** annual. **Type:** recognition ● Regular Series Award. **Frequency:** annual. **Type:** recognition. **Publications:** *American Cinematographer*, monthly. Magazine. **Price:** $5.00. **Circulation:** 26,582. **Advertising:** accepted ● *American Cinematographer Manual*. **Advertising:** accepted ● *American Cinematographer Video Manual* ● *ASC Cinema Workshop*. Book ● *Reflections: Twenty-One Cinematographers at Work*. Book. **Conventions/Meetings:** annual ASC Awards for Outstanding Achievement in Cinematography - show (exhibits) - usually February.

1378 ■ Association of Commercial Stock Image Licensors (ACSIL)
400 W 55th St., Ste.14G
New York, NY 10019
Ph: (212)956-3893

Fax: (212)956-3893
E-mail: jill.hawkins@acsil.org
URL: http://www.acsil.org
Contact: Jill Hawkins, Exec. Dir.
Founded: 2003. **Membership Dues:** associate, $1,500 (annual) ● full, $2,500 (annual). **Description:** Promotes and advances the professional interests of the stock footage industry. Represents the stock image industry's position to governmental bodies, other trade associations and NGOs on policy and trade issues. Raises the profile of stock footage as a creative source for all markets through education, dissemination of information, promotion, research and networking.

1379 ■ Black Stuntmen's Association (BSA)
Address Unknown since 2007
Founded: 1966. **Members:** 34. **Staff:** 4. **Description:** Men and women (ages 18 to 50) who are members of the Screen Actors Guild and the American Federation of Television and Radio Artists (see separate entries). Serves as an agency for stuntpeople in motion pictures and television. Conducts stunt performances at various local schools. Plans to operate school for black stuntpeople. Offers placement service. **Libraries: Type:** reference. **Holdings:** films. **Subjects:** television and motion picture. **Affiliated With:** American Federation of Television and Radio Artists; Screen Actors Guild.

1380 ■ Digital Cinema Society
PO Box 1973
Studio City, CA 91614
Ph: (818)762-2214
E-mail: mathers@digitalcinemasociety.org
URL: http://www.digitalcinemasociety.org
Contact: James Mathers, Pres./Co-Founder
Founded: 2004. **Members:** 2,000. **Membership Dues:** regular, $30 (annual). **Multinational. Description:** Works to educate and inform the entertainment industry about digital motion picture production, delivery and exhibition. Addresses the information needs of producers, directors, cinematographers, post-production specialists, and exhibitors. Seeks to examine all media, solutions, services, and technologies in the field of digital cinema. **Publications:** Newsletter, monthly. **Price:** included in membership dues. Alternate Formats: online.

1381 ■ Independent Feature Project (IFP)
c/o Michelle Byrd, Exec. Dir.
104 W 29th St., 12th Fl.
New York, NY 10001-5310
Ph: (212)465-8200
Fax: (212)465-8525
E-mail: mbyrd@ifp.org
URL: http://www.ifp.org
Contact: Michelle Byrd, Exec. Dir.
Founded: 1979. **Members:** 3,000. **Membership Dues:** dual region, $150 (annual) ● film fanatic, $70 (annual) ● student, $65 (annual) ● filmmaker, $100 (annual) ● international, $125 (annual) ● corporate, $2,000 (annual). **Staff:** 10. **Budget:** $2,500,000. **Regional Groups:** 5. **Description:** Independent film producers and directors. Promotes the production and distribution of independent feature films. Maintains information service on development, financing, and distribution. Conducts seminars and screenings. **Libraries: Type:** not open to the public. **Holdings:** 1,500; periodicals. **Subjects:** independent film. **Awards:** Gordon Parks Award. **Frequency:** annual. **Type:** recognition. **Recipient:** for excellence in screenwriting and directing ● Gotham Award. **Frequency:** annual. **Type:** monetary. **Recipient:** for excellence in film production and direction. **Computer Services:** database, files of films, personnel, distributors, and market research. **Telecommunication Services:** electronic mail, mtabbot@ifp.org ● electronic mail, advertise@ifp.org. **Programs:** Mentorship. **Publications:** *Development Guide*, annual. Journal. **Price:** $25.00/copy ● *Filmmaker Magazine*, quarterly. Covers independent film. **Price:** included in membership dues; $7.50/copy, for nonmembers. ISSN: 1063-8954. **Circulation:** 20,000. **Advertising:** accepted ● *IFP Calendar*, monthly. Newsletter. Lists IFP events, film festivals, organization news, and member news. **Circulation:** 3,000. **Advertising:** accepted ● *Independent Feature Film Market Catalogue*. **Price:** $25.00/copy. **Circulation:** 10,000 ● *Industry Directory*. **Price:** $25.00/copy. **Circulation:** 10,000. **Conventions/Meetings:** annual American Independents at Berlin - show, held in conjunction with the Berlin Film Festival (exhibits) - always February ● annual Independent Feature Film Market - conference, with workshops (exhibits) - always September.

1382 ■ Independent Film and Television Alliance (IFTA)
10850 Wilshire Blvd., 9th Fl.
Los Angeles, CA 90024-4321
Ph: (310)446-1000
Fax: (310)446-1600
E-mail: info@ifta-online.org
URL: http://www.ifta-online.org
Contact: Michael Ryan, Chm.
Founded: 1980. **Members:** 150. **Membership Dues:** company, $6,000 (annual). **Staff:** 30. **Budget:** $8,000,000. **Multinational. Description:** Trade association for the worldwide independent film and television industry. Contributes to negotiations with foreign producer associations; develops standardized theatrical, TV and video contracts for international distribution. Established and maintains the IFTA International Arbitration Tribunal, a system through which prominent entertainment attorneys throughout the world assist members and consenting clients in reaching equitable and binding agreements. Facilitates the formulation of policies, standardized private practices and language contracts, and the exchange of information and experience among members. Produces the American Film Market (AFM), the largest international motion picture trade event in the world. **Libraries: Type:** reference. **Holdings:** archival material. **Awards:** AFMA Honors. **Frequency:** annual. **Type:** recognition. **Recipient:** for achievements in independent motion pictures. **Computer Services:** database, members only: international box office reports, buyers guide, territorial fact book. **Committees:** Export Alliance; Legal; Market Advisory; New Technology Opportunities; Producers; Television. **Formerly:** (2004) American Film Marketing Association. **Publications:** *IFTA Bulletin*, weekly. Contains email updates on association and industry matters. **Price:** free. **Circulation:** 1,014. Alternate Formats: online. **Conventions/Meetings:** annual American Film Market - trade show, attracts national film distribution executives from 70 countries (exhibits) - 2008 Nov. 5-12, Santa Monica, CA - **Avg. Attendance:** 8000.

1383 ■ International Animated Film Society, ASIFA - Hollywood
2114 Burbank Blvd.
Burbank, CA 91506
Ph: (818)842-8330 (818)842-4691
Fax: (818)842-5645
E-mail: info@asifa-hollywood.org
URL: http://www.asifa-hollywood.org
Contact: Antran Manoogian, Pres.
Founded: 1972. **Members:** 1,700. **Membership Dues:** student, $30 (annual) ● general, $75 (annual) ● outside U.S., $100 (annual) ● patron, $150 (annual) ● corporate, $6,000 (annual). **Staff:** 1. **Regional Groups:** 50. **Languages:** English, French, Russian. **Description:** Represents professional animation artists, fans, and students of animation. Works to promote and advance the art of animation. **Awards:** Annie Award. **Frequency:** annual. **Type:** recognition. **Recipient:** for outstanding achievement and creative excellence in the art of animation ● Babbitt Fund Scholarship. **Frequency:** annual. **Type:** scholarship. **Recipient:** for a college student pursuing a career in animation ● Bosustow Fund. **Frequency:** annual. **Type:** scholarship. **Recipient:** for a graduating high school senior pursuing a career in animation ● June Foray Award. **Frequency:** annual. **Type:** recognition ● Winsor McCay Award. **Frequency:** annual. **Type:** recognition. **Formerly:** International Animated Film Society - Hollywood. **Publications:** *Annie Awards Annual Program Book*, annual. **Price:** $12.00. **Circulation:** 2,000. **Advertising:** accepted ● *ASIFA-Hollywood News*, 3/year. Newsletter. **Conventions/Meetings:** periodic AniFest! - conference, convention and collectors show for the animation fan (exhibits) ● periodic Animation Opportunities Expo - convention and meeting, job fair for those trying to enter field of animation (exhibits).

1384 ■ International Association of Audio Visual Communicators (IAAVC)
57 W Palo Verde Ave.
PO Box 250
Ocotillo, CA 92259-0250
Ph: (760)358-7000
Fax: (760)358-7569
E-mail: sheemonw@cindys.com
URL: http://www.cindys.com
Contact: Phillip N. Shuey, Exec. Dir.
Founded: 1957. **Members:** 6,950. **Membership Dues:** individual, $50 (annual). **Staff:** 4. **Regional Groups:** 32. **Multinational. Description:** Media producers, managers, and creative and technical people in industry, government, education, and technical, promotional, and enrichment fields. **Libraries: Type:** reference. **Subjects:** competition categories and award winners. **Awards:** International Competition Cinema in Industry (CINDY). **Frequency:** semiannual. **Type:** recognition. **Recipient:** for films, videotapes, slide films, audio, and online and offline interactive multimedia productions ● Visual Communicators Department of the Year Awards. **Frequency:** annual. **Type:** recognition. **Committees:** Political Action. **Formerly:** (1969) Industry Film Producers Association; (1975) Information Film Producers of America; (1985) IFPA Film and Video Communicators; (1992) Association of Visual Communicators. **Conventions/Meetings:** competition and workshop, with video screenings (exhibits) - usually March and September ● periodic meeting ● seminar (exhibits).

1385 ■ International Documentary Association (IDA)
1201 W 5th St., Ste.M320
Los Angeles, CA 90017
Ph: (213)534-3600
Fax: (213)534-3610
E-mail: sandra@documentary.org
URL: http://www.documentary.org
Contact: Sandra J. Ruch, Exec. Dir.
Founded: 1982. **Members:** 2,800. **Membership Dues:** individual, $85 (annual) ● student, $45 (annual) ● international, $65 (annual) ● partner, $150 (annual) ● university, friend, $500 (annual) ● corporate, $1,000 (annual). **Staff:** 10. **Budget:** $750,000. **Multinational. Description:** Individuals and organizations involved in nonfiction film and video. Objectives are: to promote nonfiction film and video; to encourage the progress of the documentary arts and sciences; to support the efforts of nonfiction film and videomakers throughout the world. Provides a forum for documentaries and allied members of the film and video industries to meet and discuss areas of mutual interest related to all aspects of nonfiction film and video arts, sciences, production, financing, and distribution. Holds screenings of all Oscar-nominated documentaries. **Awards:** Career Achievement Award. **Frequency:** annual. **Type:** recognition ● IDA Awards. **Frequency:** annual. **Type:** recognition ● Preservation and Scholarship. **Frequency:** annual. **Type:** scholarship. **Telecommunication Services:** electronic mail, tracie@documentary.org. **Committees:** Membership; Outreach; Publications; Screenings; Website. **Also Known As:** International Documentary Foundation. **Publications:** *International Documentary*, 10/year. Magazine. Contains information solely dedicated to the documentary form. **Price:** included in membership dues. ISSN: 1077-9361. **Circulation:** 3,000. **Advertising:** accepted. Alternate Formats: online ● *Membership Directory and Survival Guide*, biennial. **Conventions/Meetings:** triennial conference.

1386 ■ International Motion Picture and Lecturers Association (IMPALA)
Address Unknown since 2008
Founded: 1972. **Members:** 70. **Membership Dues:** regular, $125 (annual) ● associate, $80 (annual).

Description: Travelogue film producers and lecturers. Aims to tour the U.S. narrating travelogues and to foster fellowship among members. Conducts annual film festival of internationally produced travelogue films. **Awards:** Nancy Award. **Frequency:** annual. **Type:** recognition. **Recipient:** for the best travel photo of the year. **Formerly:** Travelogues by IMPALA (International Motion Picture and Lecturers Association). **Supersedes:** Film Lecturers Association. **Publications:** *Impala Communique - President's Newsletter*, quarterly. **Price:** free to members ● *Membership Roster*, annual ● *Travelogue Magazine*, semiannual. Includes travel filmmakers' experiences, recent productions, technical information. **Price:** $5.00/ issue; $7.00/year. **Circulation:** 2,000. **Advertising:** accepted. **Conventions/Meetings:** annual Travel Adventure Cinema Society - convention (exhibits) - always December.

1387 ■ Large Format Cinema Association (LFCA)

c/o Jeannie Moore, Exec. Dir.
28241 Crown Valley Pkwy.
PMB 401
Laguna Niguel, CA 92677
Ph: (949)831-1142
Fax: (949)831-4948
E-mail: jmoore@lfca.org
Contact: Jeannie Moore, Exec. Dir.

Founded: 1995. **Membership Dues:** student, $50 (annual) ● individual, $100 (annual) ● institution, $150 (annual) ● corporate, $250 (annual) ● sustaining, $1,250 (annual) ● patron, $5,000 (annual). **Description:** Fosters the growth of the large screen entertainment industry. Promotes interaction among large format film professionals, film students and the general public through educational programs and activities. **Computer Services:** Mailing lists. **Publications:** *Original Cinema*. Newsletter ● Newsletter. Alternate Formats: online.

1388 ■ Media Communications Association International (MCA-I)

c/o Susan M. Rees, Exec. Dir.
2810 Crossroads Dr., Ste.3800
Madison, WI 53718
Ph: (608)443-2464
Fax: (608)443-2474
E-mail: info@mca-i.org
URL: http://www.mca-i.org
Contact: Susan M. Rees, Exec. Dir.

Founded: 1973. **Members:** 3,000. **Membership Dues:** individual, $160 (annual) ● organization (includes 3 people, $155 each additional member), $455 (annual) ● student, $43 (annual) ● commercial silver, $2,500 (annual) ● commercial bronze, $1,250 (annual) ● commercial gold, $5,500 (annual) ● commercial platinum, $7,500 (annual) ● life, $1,000-$2,000 ● retired, $45 (annual). **Staff:** 2. **Budget:** $400,000. **Local Groups:** 91. **Multinational. Description:** Individuals engaged in multimedia communications needs analysis, scriptwriting, producing, directing, consulting, and operations management in the video, multimedia, and film fields. Seeks to advance the benefits and image of media communications professionals. **Libraries: Type:** reference. **Holdings:** video recordings. **Subjects:** Golden Reel: achievements in media excellence. **Awards:** Golden Reel. **Frequency:** annual. **Type:** recognition ● **Frequency:** annual. **Type:** recognition ● Silver Reel. **Frequency:** annual. **Type:** recognition ● Technical Achievement. **Frequency:** annual. **Type:** recognition. **Recipient:** for service to the association and advancement of the industry in a technological or management support area. **Telecommunication Services:** electronic mail, execdirect@mca-i.org. **Formed by Merger of:** (1973) Industrial Television Society; National Industrial Television Association. **Formerly:** International Industrial Television Association; (2000) International Television Association. **Publications:** *MCA-I News*, quarterly. Newsletter. **Price:** available to members only. **Circulation:** 6,000. **Advertising:** accepted ● *Media Communications International Association*, annual. Membership Directory. **Price:** available to members only. **Circulation:** 6,000. **Advertising:** accepted. **Conventions/Meetings:** annual international conference (exhibits) ● periodic seminar and workshop.

1389 ■ Motion Picture Association of America (MPAA)

15503 Ventura Blvd.
Encino, CA 91436
Ph: (818)995-6600
Fax: (818)382-1795
URL: http://www.mpaa.org
Contact: Dan Glickman, Chm./CEO

Founded: 1922. **Members:** 8. **Staff:** 120. **Description:** Represents principal producers and distributors of motion pictures in the U.S. Serves as an advocate of the American motion picture, home video, and television industries; activities also include preserving and protecting the rights of copyright owners; fighting censorship and restrictive attacks on First Amendment rights of motion picture, television, and home video producers; and directing anti-piracy programs to protect U.S. films, television programming, and home video throughout the U.S. **Affiliated With:** Alliance of Motion Picture and Television Producers. **Formerly:** (1945) Motion Picture Producers and Distributors of America.

1390 ■ National Association of Latino Independent Producers (NALIP)

PO Box 1247
Santa Monica, CA 90406
Ph: (310)395-8880
Fax: (310)395-8811
E-mail: info@nalip.org
URL: http://www.nalip.org
Contact: Kathryn Galan, Exec. Dir.

Founded: 1999. **Membership Dues:** student, $20 (annual) ● individual, $50 (annual) ● professional/ executive, $150 (annual) ● joint (with IDA), $110 (annual) ● organization, $200 (annual). **Staff:** 3. **State Groups:** 8. **Description:** Represents the professional needs of Latino/Latina independent producers. Promotes the advancement, development and funding of Latino/Latina film and media arts. Supports both grassroots and community-based producers/ media makers along with publicly funded and industry-based producers. **Publications:** *Latinos in the Industry*, biweekly. Newsletter. Contains information about NALIP programs and services. **Price:** free. **Circulation:** 4,000. **Advertising:** accepted. Alternate Formats: online. **Conventions/Meetings:** annual conference.

1391 ■ National Association of Video Distributors (NAVD)

1092 N Forest Oak
Henderson, KY 42420
Ph: (270)826-9423
Fax: (270)826-9424
Contact: Bill Burton, Exec. Dir.

Founded: 1981. **Members:** 35. **Membership Dues:** regular corporate, associate corporate, $3,000 (annual). **Staff:** 3. **Budget:** $300,000. **Description:** Wholesale distributors of home video software including discs and cassettes. Promotes the home video products industry. Conducts industry-wide programs in areas such as public, government, and industry relations. **Committees:** Credit; Operations. **Publications:** *National Association of Video Distributors—Membership Directory*, annual. **Price:** free, for members only. **Circulation:** 50. **Conventions/Meetings:** annual conference.

1392 ■ Producers Guild of America (PGA)

8530 Wilshire Blvd., Ste.450
Beverly Hills, CA 90211-3115
Ph: (310)358-9020
Fax: (310)358-9520
E-mail: info@producersguild.org
URL: http://www.producersguild.org
Contact: Vance Van Petten, Exec. Dir.

Founded: 1950. **Members:** 2,700. **Membership Dues:** Producer Council, $935 (annual) ● AP Council/ New Media Council, $460 (annual) ● coordinator, $110 (annual). **Staff:** 7. **Description:** Represents, protects and promotes the interests of members of the producing team in film, television and new media. **Awards:** Golden Laurel Awards. **Frequency:** annual. **Type:** recognition. **Recipient:** for best-produced motion picture (theatrically released) and TV show (episodic and long form) ● Oscar Micheaux Award. **Frequency:** annual. **Type:** recognition. **Recipient:** for an individual whose achievements in film and television have been accomplished despite difficult odds. **Boards:** Directors. **Committees:** Events; Golden Laurel Awards. **Formerly:** (1950) Screen Producers Guild. **Publications:** *PGA Networker*, quarterly. Newsletter. **Price:** included in membership dues ● *Produced By*, quarterly. Magazine. **Price:** included in membership dues. **Circulation:** 3,500. **Advertising:** accepted. **Conventions/Meetings:** monthly board meeting ● annual meeting (exhibits).

1393 ■ Stuntmen's Association of Motion Pictures (SAMP)

10660 Riverside Dr., 2nd Fl., Ste.E
Toluca Lake, CA 91602
Ph: (818)766-4334
Fax: (818)766-5943
E-mail: info@stuntmen.com
URL: http://www.stuntmen.com
Contact: Steve Kelso, Pres.

Founded: 1961. **Members:** 123. **Staff:** 1. **Description:** Men who do stunt work in motion pictures and television and who belong to the Screen Actors Guild and/or the American Federation of Television and Radio Artists Associations activities are primarily fraternal and charitable. Also seeks to improve working conditions for stuntmen and encourages members to uphold high professional standards. **Computer Services:** Information services, members' sizes, abilities and equipment. **Telecommunication Services:** electronic mail, board@stuntmen.com. **Committees:** Safety; Work. **Publications:** *Stuntmen's Directory*, biennial ● Newsletter, monthly. Alternate Formats: online. **Conventions/Meetings:** bimonthly meeting.

1394 ■ Stuntwomen's Association of Motion Pictures (SWAMP)

12457 Ventura Blvd., No. 208
Studio City, CA 91604-2411
Ph: (818)762-0907
Fax: (818)762-9534
E-mail: stuntwomen@stuntwomen.com
URL: http://www.stuntwomen.com

Founded: 1967. **Members:** 37. **Description:** Represents stunt actresses and stunt coordinators who belong to the Screen Actors Guild and/or to the American Federation of Television and Radio Artists (see separate entries) and who have worked as professional stuntwomen for a minimum of five years. **Councils:** Safety in Motion Pictures and TV. **Publications:** Report, monthly. Lists all current shows and movies in production that needs stunt people or coordinators. **Conventions/Meetings:** monthly meeting - every 3rd Thursday.

1395 ■ Wedding and Event Videographers Association International (WEVA)

8499 S Tamiami Trail
PMB 208
Sarasota, FL 34238
Ph: (941)923-5334
Fax: (941)921-3836
E-mail: info@weva.com
URL: http://www.weva.com
Contact: Roy Chapman, Founder/Chm.

Founded: 1995. **Membership Dues:** regular, $170. **Multinational. Description:** Professional wedding and event videographers. Serves as a trade organization representing members' commercial interests. Provides educational programs and resources to wedding and event videographers. **Awards:** Creative Excellence Award. **Frequency:** annual. **Type:** recognition. **Recipient:** for outstanding achievement in professional wedding and event videography. **Publications:** *The Business of Wedding and Special Event Videography*. Book. **Price:** $45.00 for members; $49.00 for nonmembers ● *Wedding and Event Videography Resource Guide*. Magazine.

1396 ■ Women in Film (WIF)
8857 W Olympic Blvd., Ste.201
Beverly Hills, CA 90211
Ph: (310)657-5144
Fax: (310)657-5154
E-mail: info@wif.org
URL: http://www.wif.org
Contact: Jane Fleming, Pres.

Founded: 1973. **Members:** 2,400. **Membership Dues:** individual, $125 (annual) ● associate, $75 (annual) ● FWIF, $250 (annual). **Staff:** 10. **Budget:** $100,000. **Description:** Supports women in the film and television industry and serves as a network for information on qualified women in the entertainment field. Sponsors screenings and discussions of pertinent issues. Provides speakers' bureau. Maintains Women in Film Foundation, which offers financial assistance to women for education, research, and/or completion of film projects. **Awards:** Crystal Awards. **Frequency:** annual. **Type:** recognition. **Recipient:** to men and women for their contributions toward improving the image and increasing participation of women in the industry ● Film Finishing Fund. **Frequency:** annual. **Type:** grant. **Recipient:** for films in the post-production process. **Publications:** *WIF Directory*, annual. **Price:** included in membership dues; $10.00 for nonmembers. **Circulation:** 3,000. **Advertising:** accepted ● *WIF Reel News*, bimonthly. Newsletter. **Conventions/Meetings:** annual Crystals Awards Luncheon (exhibits) - always June ● annual Oscar Viewing Party - always evening of Academy Awards presentation ● annual Women In Film Festival ● workshop, lectures and discussions on directing, producing, contract negotiation, writing, production development, acting, and technical crafts.

Finance

1397 ■ Advertising Media Credit Executives Association (AMCEA)
8840 Columbia 100 Pkwy.
Columbia, MD 21045-2158
Ph: (410)992-7609
Fax: (410)740-5574
E-mail: amcea@amcea.org
URL: http://www.amcea.org
Contact: Michael Murphy, Pres.

Founded: 1953. **Members:** 300. **Membership Dues:** individual, $200 (annual) ● print media (based on number of circulation), $245-$395 (annual) ● broadcast (TV, radio, cable), $270 (annual) ● associate, $395 (annual). **Staff:** 1. **Budget:** $75,000. **Description:** Credit executives for advertising media such as newspapers, magazines, radio, and television. Provides information for exchange of ideas on credit management methods and procedures; encourages study in advanced educational courses in fundamentals, such as business law, finance, banking, accounting, and economics. **Awards:** Credit Executive of the Year Award. **Frequency:** annual. **Type:** recognition. **Publications:** *News and Views*, quarterly. Newsletter. **Advertising:** accepted. Alternate Formats: online. **Conventions/Meetings:** annual conference (exhibits) - always third week of October.

1398 ■ American Escrow Association (AEA)
211 N Union St., Ste.100
Alexandria, VA 22314
Ph: (703)519-1240
E-mail: hq@a-e-a.org
URL: http://www.a-e-a.org
Contact: Lois L. Mayabb, State Dir.

Membership Dues: associate/affiliate, $100 (annual). **Description:** Furthers the education and professionalism of the escrow industry. Enhances the education of escrow/settlement professionals. Increases the public knowledge and understanding of escrow and closing services. Coordinates legislative efforts throughout the United States. **Programs:** Education Partners. **Publications:** *Federal Update*. Newsletter. Alternate Formats: online.

1399 ■ American Finance Association (AFA)
c/o Blackwell Publishing
Membership Services
350 Main St.
Malden, MA 02148
Ph: (781)388-8532
Free: (800)835-6770
Fax: (781)388-8232
E-mail: pyle@haas.berkeley.edu
URL: http://www.afajof.org
Contact: Kenneth French, Pres.

Founded: 1940. **Members:** 7,500. **Membership Dues:** regular, in U.S., $40 (annual) ● online only, $35 (annual) ● student, $10 (annual). **Staff:** 2. **Budget:** $350,000. **Description:** College and university professors of economics and finance, bankers, treasurers, analysts, financiers, and others interested in financial problems; libraries and other institutions. Seeks to improve public understanding of financial problems and to provide for exchange of analytical ideas. Areas of special interest include: corporate finance, investments, banking, and international and public finance. **Publications:** *Journal of Finance*, bimonthly. Contains book reviews and research reports. **Price:** included in membership dues. ISSN: 0022-1082. **Circulation:** 7,500. **Advertising:** accepted. **Conventions/Meetings:** annual meeting, held in conjunction with Allied Social Sciences Association (exhibits) - always first weekend in January.

1400 ■ Asian Financial Society (AFS)
PO Box 568
Bowling Green Sta.
New York, NY 10274-0568
Ph: (212)479-8405
E-mail: afswww@yahoo.com
URL: http://www.geocities.com/afswww

Founded: 1984. **Membership Dues:** individual, $50 (annual). **Description:** Fosters business relationships and opportunities for growth for professionals in the Asian financial community. **Computer Services:** Mailing lists ● online services, message board. **Publications:** *AFS Exchange*, quarterly. Newsletter. **Conventions/Meetings:** bimonthly seminar and/dinner.

1401 ■ Asset Managers Forum (AMF)
360 Madison Ave.
New York, NY 10017-7111
Ph: (646)637-9200
Fax: (646)637-9118
E-mail: jsack@sifma.org
URL: http://www.theassetmanager.com
Contact: Jason Jesner, Chm.

Members: 54. **Membership Dues:** associate, $11,500 (annual) ● assets management firm (with more than 250 billion assets), $13,500 (annual) ● assets management firm (with 100-249 billion assets), $12,000 (annual) ● assets management firm (with 40-99 billion assets), $10,000 (annual) ● assets management firm (with 10-39 billion assets), $8,500 (annual) ● assets management firm (with less than 10 billion assets), $6,000 (annual). **Multinational. Description:** Serves as a unified voice for buyside operations professionals in addressing major securities operations, accounting, legal and regulatory compliance, and market practices initiatives. Offers its members a range of services and activities designed to assist them in the strategic development and day-to-day management of their operations. **Computer Services:** Information services, regulatory and legislative releases. **Committees:** Accounting Policy; Compliance; Corporate Actions; Operations Benchmarking; Pricing; Steering; Swaps. **Subgroups:** Senior Executives. **Publications:** Newsletter, monthly. Alternate Formats: online ● Monographs. Includes lists of regulatory reforms, proposed rules, concept releases, and legislation. Alternate Formats: online.

1402 ■ Association of Chinese Finance Professionals (ACFP)
240 Hazelwood Ave.
San Francisco, CA 94127
E-mail: acfp_us@yahoo.com
URL: http://www.acfp.net
Contact: Dr. William Ren, Pres.

Membership Dues: regular, $25 (annual). **Description:** Promotes cooperation between U.S. and China in the fields of commercial and investment banking, asset management, insurance, corporate finance, financial planning and financial software. Provides a forum for finance professionals to exchange ideas and discuss experiences. **Publications:** *Chinese American Finance* (in Chinese and English). Newsletter. Alternate Formats: online ● *Monthly Gazette*. Newspaper. Alternate Formats: online.

1403 ■ Association for Financial Professionals (AFP)
4520 E West Hwy., Ste.750
Bethesda, MD 20814
Ph: (301)907-2862
Fax: (301)907-2864
E-mail: afp@afponline.org
URL: http://www.afponline.org
Contact: James A. Kaitz, Pres./CEO

Founded: 1979. **Members:** 14,000. **Membership Dues:** full, $295 (annual). **Staff:** 70. **Budget:** $15,000,000. **Regional Groups:** 62. **Description:** Seeks to establish a national forum for the exchange of concepts and techniques related to improving the management of treasury and the careers of professionals through research, education, publications, and recognition of the treasury management profession through a certification program. Conducts educational programs. Operates career center. **Libraries: Type:** lending; reference; not open to the public. **Holdings:** archival material, books, periodicals. **Subjects:** treasury management, corporate finance, banking. **Awards:** Scholar's Award. **Frequency:** annual. **Type:** scholarship. **Recipient:** for undergraduate and graduate students ● TMA Pinnacle Award. **Frequency:** annual. **Type:** grant. **Recipient:** for a corporate practitioner. **Computer Services:** database, members, seminar attendees, interested individuals. **Boards:** Editorial Advisory. **Committees:** Audit; Certification; Government Relations; Nominating. **Programs:** Certified Cash Manager. **Task Forces:** Affiliate Officers' Meeting; Annual Conference Program Planning; ANSI ASC X12 Standards; Cash Management Conferences Program; CCM Body of Knowledge; Credentials; Federal Electronic Tax Payments; Financial EDI Conference Planning; Item Writers; Negotiating Wire Transfers; Retail Industry; Service Codes; Treasure's Teleconference; VCC5. **Formerly:** Cash Management Practitioners Association; (1991) National Corporate Cash Management Association; (2000) Treasury Management Association. **Publications:** *AFP Exchange*, bimonthly. Magazine. **Price:** free for members; $90.00 for nonmembers ● *Corporate Financial Risk Management*. Book. **Price:** $66.00 for members; $96.00 for nonmembers ● *The Corporate Guide to Payments System Risk*. Book. **Price:** $40.50 for members; $60.50 for nonmembers ● *M&A From Planning to Integration: Executing Acquisitions and Increasing Shareholder Value*. Book. **Price:** $45.00 for members; $65.00 for nonmembers. **Conventions/Meetings:** annual conference, comprehensive treasury management forum; offers more than 130 concurrent educational sessions (exhibits).

1404 ■ Association of Trade and Forfaiting in the Americas (AFTA)
c/o Gregory J. Bernardi, Pres./Treas.
1180 Ave. of the Americas, Ste.2020
New York, NY 10022
Ph: (212)377-2012
Fax: (212)377-2018
E-mail: greg.bernardi@forfaiting.com
URL: http://afia-forfaiting.org
Contact: Gregory J. Bernardi, Pres./Treas.

Multinational. Description: Fosters and promotes international trade finance. Serves as a medium of exchange of information between organizations with an interest in forfaiting and international trade finance. Offers advice and counsel to interested parties involved in trade finance.

1405 ■ Business Products Credit Association (BPCA)
607 Westridge Dr.
O'Fallon, MO 63366
Ph: (636)272-3005
Fax: (636)272-2973
E-mail: service@bpca.org
URL: http://www.bpca.org
Founded: 1875. **Members:** 235. **Staff:** 6. **National Groups:** 7. **Description:** Member-owned credit association serving businesses. Assists members in protecting their accounts receivable. Provides credit reporting services, collection service letters, and business alert reports. Conducts educational programs; compiles statistics. **Awards:** Credit Executive of the Year. **Frequency:** annual. **Type:** recognition. **Computer Services:** database, Internet Service Provider and Web Page Design and Management ● online services, Specialized Trade Association Interchange Reporting System. **Subgroups:** Jan/San Industry Credit; National Deduction and Resolution; Office Furniture Industry Credit; Office Products Industry Credit; Promotional Products/Ad Specialty; School Supply Industry Credit. **Publications:** *Ledger*, semiannual. Newsletter. **Advertising:** accepted ● Brochure ● Bulletin, periodic. **Conventions/Meetings:** annual Credit and Financial Conference, educational programs.

1406 ■ Chinese Finance Association (TCFA)
c/o Guang Guo, Membership Off.
Moody's KMV
100 Broadway, 12th Fl.
New York, NY 10005
E-mail: guoguang88@hotmail.com
URL: http://www.aimhi.com/VC/tcfa
Contact: Li Wei, Chm.
Membership Dues: general, $40 (annual). **Multinational. Description:** Promotes Chinese finance, business, economy, financial institutions and financial markets. **Boards:** Advisory. **Publications:** *Working Papers*. Alternate Formats: online ● Newsletter. **Conventions/Meetings:** annual conference ● annual meeting.

1407 ■ Clearpoint Financial Solutions
8000 Franklin Farms Dr.
Richmond, VA 23229
Free: (877)877-1995
Fax: (804)236-3816
E-mail: customerservice@clearpointfs.org
URL: http://www.clearpointcreditcounselingsolutions.org
Founded: 1979. **Staff:** 150. **Description:** Provides consumer credit counseling services to all consumers in need. Strives to increase financial literacy.

1408 ■ Community Financial Services Association (CFSA)
515 King St., Ste.300
Alexandria, VA 22314
Ph: (703)684-1029
Fax: (703)684-1219
E-mail: cfsa@multistate.com
URL: http://www.cfsa.net
Contact: John A. McIntyre, Exec. Dir.
Founded: 1999. **Members:** 150. **Membership Dues:** sustaining, $214,500 (annual) ● platinum, $71,500 (annual) ● advisory/industry partner, $21,450 (annual) ● general/vendor, $7,150 (annual) ● associate, $2,860 (annual). **Staff:** 17. **Description:** Works to promote laws and regulations that balance the interests of the payday advance industry with consumers. Supports and encourages responsible industry practices. **Publications:** *First Friday*. Newsletter. Alternate Formats: online. **Conventions/Meetings:** annual Fall Legislative Conference - usually in Washington, DC ● annual meeting and conference, open to the public - usually February.

1409 ■ Consumer Data Industry Association (CDIA)
1090 Vermont Ave. NW, Ste.200
Washington, DC 20005-4905
Ph: (202)371-0910
Free: (866)696-7227
Fax: (202)371-0134
E-mail: cdia@cdiaonline.org
URL: http://www.cdiaonline.org
Contact: Betty Byrnes, Contact
Founded: 1906. **Members:** 1,100. **Membership Dues:** associate, $600 (annual) ● base, $75 (annual). **Staff:** 27. **Description:** Serves as international association of credit reporting and collection service offices. Maintains hall of fame and biographical archives; conducts specialized educational programs. Offers computerized services and compiles statistics. **Awards:** **Type:** recognition. **Recipient:** for international achievement ● **Type:** recognition. **Recipient:** for credit. **Computer Services:** Online services, e-OSCAR (Online Solution for Complete and Accurate Reporting) ● online services, e-store. **Committees:** CSD; Legislative; Standard. **Divisions:** Collection Service; Credit Reporting; Specialized Reporting. **Formerly:** (2002) Associated Credit Bureaus. **Publications:** *Communicator*, monthly. Newsletter. Includes calendar of events. **Price:** included in membership dues. **Circulation:** 2,800. **Advertising:** accepted ● *International CSD Forwarding Roster*, annual ● *International Reporting Roster*, annual ● *Update*, periodic. Bulletin. **Conventions/Meetings:** periodic executive committee meeting.

1410 ■ Credit Card Users of America (CCUA)
Address Unknown since 2007
Founded: 1986. **Members:** 1,100. **Description:** Credit card holders and companies. Works for the enforcement of existing laws regarding credit card use and companies. Supports the rights of credit card users. **Publications:** *What Every Credit Card User Needs to Know*. Book.

1411 ■ Credit Professionals International (CPI)
525 B N Laclede Sta. Rd.
St. Louis, MO 63119
Ph: (314)961-0031
Fax: (314)961-0040
E-mail: creditpro@creditprofessionals.org
URL: http://www.creditprofessionals.org
Contact: Esther Brinkley, VP
Founded: 1937. **Members:** 700. **Membership Dues:** local association, $80 (annual) ● direct, $120 (annual) ● member-at-large, $100 (annual). **Budget:** $100,000. **Regional Groups:** 7. **Local Groups:** 80. **Description:** Represents individuals employed in credit or collection departments of business firms or professional offices. Conducts educational program in credit work. Sponsors Career Club composed of members who have been involved in credit work for at least 25 years. **Libraries:** **Type:** reference. **Holdings:** audio recordings. **Awards:** Credit Professional of the Year Award. **Frequency:** annual. **Type:** recognition. **Formerly:** (1965) Credit Women's Breakfast Clubs of North America; (1987) Credit Women - International; (1990) CWI: Credit Professionals. **Publications:** *The Credit Connection*, quarterly. Newsletter. **Price:** $15.00 for members; $20.00 for nonmembers ● *The Credit Professional*, annual. Magazine. **Price:** $10.00 for members; $15.00 for nonmembers ● *Educational Manual*, annual. **Price:** $3.00 for members; $5.00 for nonmembers. **Conventions/Meetings:** annual conference.

1412 ■ Credit Research Foundation (CRF)
8840 Columbia 100 Pkwy.
Columbia, MD 21045
Ph: (410)740-5499
Fax: (410)740-4620
E-mail: crf_info@crfonline.org
URL: http://www.crfonline.org
Contact: Alex Behm, Chm.
Founded: 1949. **Members:** 500. **Membership Dues:** associate, $110 (annual) ● international, $350 (annual) ● corporate, $795 (annual) ● premier, $1,295 (annual) ● premier plus, $2,000 (annual) ● vendor, $2,500 (annual). **Staff:** 7. **Budget:** $1,000,000. **Description:** Represents credit, financial, and working capital executives of manufacturing and banking concerns. Aims to create a better understanding of the impact of credit on the economy. Plans, supervises, and administers research and educational programs. Conducts surveys on economic conditions, trends, policies, practices, theory, systems, and methodology. Sponsors formal educational programs in credit and financial management. Maintains library on credit, collections, and management. **Committees:** Education; Research. **Publications:** *Compensation of Credit Executives*, biennial. Report. Presents annual compensation, number of customer accounts handled, and number of credit people supervised. Includes compensation data. **Price:** $49.95 ● *Credit and Financial Management Review*, quarterly. Journal ● *Credit Professional's Handbook*. **Price:** $100.00 ● *CRF News*, quarterly. Newsletter ● *National Summary of Domestic Trade Receivables*, quarterly. Newsletter. Provides benchmarks on the basis of which credit executives may develop forecasts and compare the general condition of their trade receivables. **Price:** free for members; $175.00 /year for nonmembers ● Papers. **Conventions/Meetings:** annual conference - always May.

1413 ■ Dominicans on Wall Street (DOWS)
160 E 48th St., Apt. 2L
New York, NY 10017
E-mail: info@dows.ws
URL: http://www.dows.ws
Contact: Robert Abreu, Sec.
Founded: 1997. **Membership Dues:** professional, $50 (annual) ● student, $25 (annual). **Multinational. Description:** Advances the professional development of its members. Keeps track of the developments in the Dominican Republic's capital markets and securities exchange. Assures the educational achievement of Dominican youth. Serves as a link between the Dominican Republic and Dominican professionals working with U.S. and international financial markets. **Publications:** Newsletter. Alternate Formats: online.

1414 ■ Eastern Finance Association (EFA)
c/o David R. Lange, Exec. Dir.
Auburn Montgomery
School of Bus.
PO Box 244023
Montgomery, AL 36124-4023
E-mail: membershipservices@blackwellpublishers.co.uk
URL: http://www.easternfinance.org
Contact: David R. Lange, Exec. Dir.
Founded: 1965. **Members:** 750. **Membership Dues:** individual, $32 (annual) ● library, $125 (annual). **Description:** College and university professors and financial officers; libraries. Provides a meeting place for persons interested in any aspect of finance, including financial management, investments, and banking. Sponsors research competitions. **Awards:** Distinguished Scholar. **Frequency:** annual. **Type:** recognition ● Outstanding Paper Awards. **Frequency:** annual. **Type:** recognition. **Formerly:** (1972) Appalachian Finance Association. **Publications:** *Financial Review*, quarterly. Journal. Publishes research and reviews in all areas of finance. ISSN: 0732-8516. **Circulation:** 1,800. **Conventions/Meetings:** annual conference and workshop (exhibits) ● annual meeting.

1415 ■ Emerging Markets Private Equity Association (EMPEA)
1055 Thomas Jefferson St. NW, Ste.240
Washington, DC 20007
Ph: (202)449-1155
Fax: (202)449-1165
E-mail: empea@empea.net
URL: http://www.empea.net
Contact: Dr. Roger S. Leeds, Chm.
Founded: 2004. **Membership Dues:** charter, $10,000 (annual) ● full, $1,000-$3,000 (annual) ● limited partner, $1,500 (annual) ● associate, $3,000 (annual). **Staff:** 3. **Multinational. Description:** Works to serve private equity and venture capital firms and institutional investors in the emerging markets of Asia, Eastern Europe, Africa, Latin America and the Middle East. Strengthens the performance of private equity investing in emerging markets by helping private equity firms and other stakeholders address industry challenges that are "pan-emerging-market" in nature.

Telecommunication Services: electronic mail, info@empea.net. **Committees:** Governance; Program. **Publications:** Newsletter, quarterly ● Brochure.

1416 ■ Financial Executives International (FEI)
200 Campus Dr.
Florham Park, NJ 07932-0674
Ph: (973)765-1000 (973)765-1001
Fax: (973)765-1018
E-mail: mcangemi@fei.org
URL: http://www.fei.org
Contact: Michael P. Cangemi, Pres./CEO
Founded: 1931. **Members:** 15,200. **Membership Dues:** active, $475 (annual) ● academic, $150 (annual). **Staff:** 50. **Budget:** $8,000,000. **Local Groups:** 86. **Multinational. Description:** Professional organization of corporate financial executives performing duties of chief financial officer, controller, treasurer, or vice-president-finance. Sponsors research activities through its affiliated Financial Executives Research Foundation. Maintains offices in Toronto, Canada, and Washington, DC. **Committees:** Benefits Finance; Corporate Finance; Corporate Reporting; Finance and IT; Globalization; Government Business; Private Companies; Taxation. **Formerly:** (1962) Controllers Institute of America; (2001) Financial Executives Institute. **Publications:** *FEI Express*, biweekly. Newsletter. **Price:** $39.00/year. **Circulation:** 15,000. **Advertising:** accepted. Alternate Formats: online ● *Financial Executive*, 10/year. Magazine. Examines the latest developments in business, government, and economics. **Price:** $59.00/year in U.S.; $79.00/year outside U.S. **Circulation:** 19,000. **Advertising:** accepted. Alternate Formats: online ● Also publishes special studies. **Conventions/Meetings:** annual Current Financial Reporting Issues - conference - always November. 2008 Nov. 13-14, New York, NY ● annual Financial Executives Summit - conference.

1417 ■ Financial Executives Research Foundation (FERF)
200 Campus Dr.
Florham Park, NJ 07932-0674
Ph: (973)765-1000 (973)765-1064
Fax: (973)765-1018
E-mail: cgraziano@fei.org
URL: http://www.fei.org
Contact: Cheryl de Mesa Graziano, VP for Research and Operations
Founded: 1944. **Staff:** 5. **Budget:** $1,000,000. **Description:** Sponsors and publishes research in business management, with emphasis on corporate financial management issues. Maintains inquiry services. **Libraries: Type:** reference. **Affiliated With:** Financial Executives International. **Formerly:** (1959) Controllership Foundation; (1962) Controllers Institute Research Foundation. **Publications:** *Global Update*, quarterly. Newsletter. Alternate Formats: online ● Monographs ● Reports. Alternate Formats: online ● Also publishes Issues Alerts for FEI members.

1418 ■ Financial Managers Society (FMS)
100 W Monroe, Ste.810
Chicago, IL 60603
Ph: (312)578-1300 (312)630-3425
Free: (800)275-4367
Fax: (312)578-1308
E-mail: info@fmsinc.org
URL: http://www.fmsinc.org
Contact: Dick Yingst, Pres./CEO
Founded: 1949. **Members:** 1,600. **Membership Dues:** regular, $425 (annual) ● affiliate, $495 (annual). **Staff:** 7. **Budget:** $1,700,000. **Local Groups:** 10. **Description:** Works for the needs of finance and accounting professionals from banks, thrifts and credit unions. Offers career-enhancing education, specialized publications, national leadership opportunities, and worldwide connections with other industry professionals. **Councils:** Accounting; Finance; Internal Audit; Strategic Issues. **Formerly:** (1969) Society of Savings and Loan Controllers; (1975) National Society of Controllers and Financial Officers of Savings Institutions; (1982) Financial Managers Society for Savings Institutions. **Publications:** *Financial Managers Society—Membership and Peer Consulting Directory*, annual. Membership Directory. Lists executives and managers of financial institutions who volunteer their advice to other members in specific areas of expertise. Alternate Formats: online ● *Financial Managers Update*, biweekly. Newsletter. Includes regulatory checklist, accounting checklist, and calendar of events. **Price:** free for members. ISSN: 8755-5751. **Circulation:** 1,600 ● *Internal Audit Manual Update*. **Price:** $325.00 for nonmembers; $275.00 for members. Alternate Formats: CD-ROM ● *Record Retention Manual*. **Price:** $185.00 for nonmembers; $150.00 for members. Alternate Formats: CD-ROM ● Also publishes technical publications on asset/liability management, investment management, accounting and regulatory topics. **Conventions/Meetings:** annual National Financial Managers Conference and Business Show (exhibits) ● workshop, covering topics such as interest rate risk, profitability measurement, and investment portfolio management.

1419 ■ Financial Markets Association (FMA)
c/o Carlene Crnkovich, Sec.
U.S. Bancorp Center
800 Nicollet Mall
Minneapolis, MN 55402
Ph: (212)645-5111 (612)340-9121
E-mail: info@fma-usa.org
URL: http://www.fma-usa.org
Contact: Peter C. Wadkins, Pres.
Founded: 1990. **Members:** 325. **Membership Dues:** international, corporate associate, $100 (annual). **Staff:** 1. **Budget:** $160,000. **Description:** Accountants, brokers, retail and investment bankers. Dedicated to meeting the needs of the financial industry for capital markets, fiduciary services, data processing, banking, asset/liability management, broker/dealer activities and investment advisory services. Offers educational seminars. **Computer Services:** Mailing lists. **Publications:** *Market Solutions*, quarterly. Newsletter ● Brochures. **Conventions/Meetings:** annual Compliance Conference ● annual Legal Conference ● annual Operations Conference ● annual Supercourse Conference.

1420 ■ Financial Planning Association (FPA)
4100 E Mississippi Ave., Ste.400
Denver, CO 80246-3053
Ph: (303)759-4910
Free: (800)322-4237
Fax: (303)759-0749
E-mail: marv.tuttle@fpanet.org
URL: http://www.fpanet.org
Contact: Marvin W. Tuttle Jr., Exec. Dir./CEO
Founded: 2000. **Members:** 30,000. **Membership Dues:** individual, financial planner, $295 (annual) ● corporate, $7,500 (annual) ● broker/dealer, corporate media company, $3,995 (annual) ● student, $145 (annual). **Staff:** 80. **Budget:** $15,000,000. **Local Groups:** 100. **Description:** Works to support the financial planning process in order to help people achieve their goals and dreams. Believes that everyone needs objective advice to make smart financial decisions and that when seeking the advice of a financial planner, the planner should be a CFP professional. **Awards:** Chapter Recognition Awards. **Frequency:** annual. **Type:** recognition. **Recipient:** for local chapters, varies according to recognition level. **Departments:** Broker-Dealer Relations; Career Development; Chapter Relations; Corporate Relations; Education; Government Relations; Journal of Financial Planning; Meetings; Membership and Marketing; Public Relations; Research and Community Development; Technology. **Formerly:** (1965) International Association for Financial Planning; (1971) Institute of Certified Financial Planners. **Publications:** *FPA This Week*, weekly. Newsletter. Contains updates on FPA happenings and current industry events. Alternate Formats: online ● *Journal of Financial Planning*, monthly. Magazine. **Price:** included in membership dues. **Circulation:** 52,000. **Advertising:** accepted. **Conventions/Meetings:** annual Broker/Dealer Conference (exhibits) - always January/February ● annual Retreat - conference ● annual Success Forum - convention (exhibits) - usually September/October.

1421 ■ Financial Women's Association of New York (FWA)
215 Park Ave. S, Ste.1713
New York, NY 10003
Ph: (212)533-2141
Fax: (212)982-3008
E-mail: fwaoffice@fwa.org
URL: http://www.fwa.org
Contact: Nancy Sellar, Exec. Dir.
Founded: 1956. **Members:** 1,100. **Membership Dues:** full, $295 (annual) ● associate, $140 (annual) ● retired, $150 (annual). **Description:** Persons of professional status in the field of finance in the New York metropolitan area. Works to promote and maintain high professional standards in the financial and business communities; provide an opportunity for members to enhance one another's professional contacts; achieve recognition of the contribution of women to the financial and business communities; encourage other women to seek professional positions within the financial and business communities. Activities include educational trips to foreign countries; college internship program including foreign student exchange; high school mentorship program; Washington and international briefings; placement service for members. Maintains speakers' bureau. **Awards:** Career Achievement Award. **Frequency:** annual. **Type:** recognition ● Woman of the Year Award. **Frequency:** annual. **Type:** recognition. **Recipient:** to a distinguished woman from the public and private sector for her achievements, leadership and professionalism. **Telecommunication Services:** electronic mail, nsellar@fwa.org. **Committees:** College Connections; Community Affairs; Distinguished Speakers; Education; Entrepreneur; Government; High School; International Affairs; Leaders and Legends; Lifestyle Program; Lifestyles; Professional Development. **Formerly:** (1968) Young Women's Investment Association of New York; (1971) Young Women's Financial Association of New York. **Publications:** *Financial Women's Association of New York—Directory*, annual. Includes listings by firm and occupation. Includes photographs. **Price:** free for members. **Circulation:** 1,100 ● Newsletter, 11/year. Includes listing of new members. **Price:** free for members; $90.00 /year for nonmembers. **Circulation:** 1,300. **Conventions/Meetings:** semiannual meeting.

1422 ■ Forius Business Credit Resources
PO Box 59149
Minneapolis, MN 55459-0149
Ph: (612)341-9600
Free: (800)279-6226
Fax: (612)341-9648
E-mail: info@forius.com
URL: http://www.forius.com
Contact: Don Mosher CAE, Pres.
Founded: 1896. **Members:** 1,300. **Staff:** 30. **Regional Groups:** 6. **Local Groups:** 18. **National Groups:** 13. **Description:** Represents credit executives and owners of distribution and manufacturing companies. Promotes mutually beneficial ideas on credit techniques and methods. Provides a forum for the exchange of credit information. **Computer Services:** Online services, commercial credit information. **Also Known As:** National Association of Credit Management North Central. **Formerly:** National Radiator Manufacturing Credit Association; (1986) National Radiator Core Manufacturing Credit Association; (2006) NACM North Central. **Conventions/Meetings:** semiannual conference.

1423 ■ Global Association of Risk Professionals (GARP)
111 Town Square Pl., Ste.1215
Jersey City, NJ 07310
Ph: (201)719-7210
Fax: (201)222-5022
E-mail: rich.apostolik@garp.com
URL: http://www.garp.com
Contact: Greg Winsper, Contact
Members: 67,000. **Membership Dues:** individual, fellow, $100 (annual) ● student, $50 (annual). **Multi-**

national. Description: Represents banks, investment management firms, government agencies, regulatory agencies, academic institutions, and corporations from more than 167 countries on six continents around the globe. Aims to encourage and enhance communications between risk professionals, practitioners, and regulators worldwide. Works on expanding views and increasing recognition of the global risk management community. **Libraries: Type:** reference. **Holdings:** articles, books, papers. **Subjects:** financial risk management. **Awards:** Risk Manager of the Year. **Frequency:** annual. **Type:** recognition. **Recipient:** to the most outstanding risk manager. **Publications:** *GARP Risk Review*, bimonthly. Magazine. Features articles about trends, strategies and best practices affecting financial risk management. **Price:** included in membership dues.

1424 ■ International Association of Financial Engineers (IAFE)
560 Lexington Ave., 9th Fl.
New York, NY 10022
Ph: (212)317-7479
Fax: (212)527-2927
E-mail: main@iafe.org
URL: http://www.iafe.org
Contact: David Jaffe, Exec. Dir.
Founded: 1992. **Membership Dues:** student, $25 (annual) ● academic, $100 (annual) ● practitioner, $200 (annual). **Multinational. Description:** Seeks to develop and advance financial engineering as a formal discipline and profession. Provides a forum for the exchange of ideas on topics of relevance and interest to the financial engineering community. Facilitates interaction and communication between the practitioners of quantitative finance and the academic financial community. Raises awareness of the value of the field to industry. **Publications:** *The Journal of Derivatives*, quarterly. Includes research articles on the field of financial engineering. **Price:** included in membership dues ● Newsletter, quarterly. Contains reviews on recent activities by the organization. **Price:** included in membership dues. Alternate Formats: online.

1425 ■ International Association of Registered Financial Consultants (IARFC)
PO Box 42506
2507 N Verity Pkwy.
Middletown, OH 45042-0506
Ph: (513)424-6395
Free: (800)532-9060
Fax: (513)424-5752
E-mail: director@iarfc.org
URL: http://www.iarfc.org
Contact: Judith Fisette-Losz, Exec. Dir.
Founded: 1984. **Members:** 2,500. **Membership Dues:** RFC and general, RFA, $100 (annual). **Staff:** 3. **Multinational. Description:** Financial professionals gathered to foster public confidence in the financial planning profession. Helps financial consultants exchange planning techniques. Offers educational programs and professional certifications. **Awards:** Loren Dunton Memorial Award. **Frequency:** annual. **Type:** recognition. **Recipient:** for significant contribution to financial services profession ● President's Award. **Frequency:** annual. **Type:** recognition. **Recipient:** to members for their contributions to the organization. **Computer Services:** database, web search of advisors. **Telecommunication Services:** electronic mail, stephanie@iarfc.org. **Publications:** *The Register*, bimonthly. Newsletter. **Circulation:** 1,600. **Advertising:** accepted. **Conventions/Meetings:** annual conference (exhibits).

1426 ■ International Consortium on Governmental Financial Management (ICGFM)
444 N Capitol St., Ste.234
Washington, DC 20001
Ph: (202)624-8461
Fax: (202)624-5473
E-mail: icgfm@yahoo.com
URL: http://www.icgfm.org
Contact: Ms. Nina Powell, Exec. Dir.
Membership Dues: individual, $100 (annual) ● organization, $250 (annual) ● sustaining, $1,000 (annual). **Multinational. Description:** Represents elected officials, permanent civil servants, accountants, financial managers, and others with an interest in government spending and investments. Promotes responsible management and expenditure of public funds. Conducts research and educational programs. **Publications:** *ICGFM Newsletter* (in English and Spanish). **Price:** included in membership dues ● *Public Fund Digest*, semiannual. Journal. Contains research and practices in Government Financial Management. **Price:** $10.00. Alternate Formats: online.

1427 ■ International Energy Credit Association (IECA)
8325 Lantern View Ln.
St. John, IN 46373
Ph: (219)365-7313
Fax: (219)365-0327
E-mail: rprco@aol.com
URL: http://www.ieca.net
Contact: Robert Raichle CCE, Exec. VP
Founded: 1923. **Members:** 700. **Membership Dues:** individual, $300 (annual). **Staff:** 2. **Budget:** $500,000. **Description:** Credit executives of petroleum and energy related companies and vendors to the field. Conducts educational seminars. **Awards:** Outstanding New Member. **Type:** recognition. **Computer Services:** database. **Committees:** Canadian; Commercial; Crude Oil and Refined Products; Education; European; Gas Liquids and Electricity. **Formerly:** (1992) American Petroleum Credit Association; (1998) International Petroleum Credit Association. **Publications:** *IECA Journal*, 3/year. Newsletter. **Price:** included in membership dues. **Conventions/Meetings:** annual conference (exhibits) - every spring. 2009 Mar., Dana Point, CA ● annual conference - every fall. 2008 Oct., Scottsdale, AZ; 2009 Oct., Orlando, FL.

1428 ■ International Newspaper Financial Executives (INFE)
21525 Ridgetop Cir., Ste.200
Sterling, VA 20166
Ph: (703)421-4060
Fax: (703)421-4068
E-mail: infehq@infe.org
URL: http://www.infe.org
Contact: Greg Robinson, Pres.
Founded: 1947. **Members:** 1,000. **Membership Dues:** active individual (based on average daily newspaper circulation), $290-$745 (annual) ● associate, $745 (annual) ● academic, $80 (annual) ● retired, $35 (annual). **Staff:** 5. **Budget:** $750,000. **Description:** Controllers, chief accountants, auditors, business managers, treasurers, secretaries and related newspaper executives, educators, and public accountants. Conducts research projects on accounting methods and procedures for newspapers. Offers placement service; maintains Speaker's Bureau. Produces conferences and seminars. **Libraries: Type:** not open to the public. **Computer Services:** Online services, members' forum; poll. **Committees:** Benchmarking; Communications; Conference Entertainment; Conference Marketing; Conference Program; Group/Corporate Executives. **Formerly:** (1984) Institute of Newspaper Controllers and Finance Officers. **Publications:** *INFe-letter*, weekly. Newsletter. **Advertising:** accepted. Alternate Formats: online ● *INFE Membership Roster*, annual. Membership Directory ● *Newspaper Financial Executive Journal*, quarterly. **Price:** included in membership dues; $150.00 /year for nonmembers. ISSN: 0028-9558. **Advertising:** accepted ● Manuals. Covers newspaper accounting. ● Reports. Covers newspaper accounting. **Conventions/Meetings:** annual conference (exhibits).

1429 ■ International Society of Financiers (ISF)
Address Unknown since 2008
Founded: 1979. **Members:** 250. **Staff:** 2. **Budget:** $70,000. **For-Profit. Multinational. Description:** Membership in more than 50 countries includes; real estate, minerals, commodities, and import-export brokers; corporate, industrial, and private lenders; and other financial professionals. Provides information and referrals on major domestic and international financial projects and transactions, and fosters integrity and professionalism among members. **Libraries: Type:** reference. **Publications:** *International Financier: Information and Referrals on International Projects Requiring the Expertise of Members Throughout the Free World*, monthly. Newsletter. **Price:** included in membership dues; available to members only. **Circulation:** 250.

1430 ■ I.T. Financial Management Association (ITFMA)
PO Box 30188
Santa Barbara, CA 93130
Ph: (805)687-7390
Fax: (805)687-7382
E-mail: info@itfma.com
URL: http://www.itfma.com
Contact: Terence Quinlan, Exec. Off.
Founded: 1988. **Members:** 1,000. **Membership Dues:** individual, $100 (annual) ● corporate (15 or less members), $500 (annual) ● corporate (16-30 members), $1,000 (annual) ● corporate (31-45 members), $1,500 (annual). **Staff:** 2. **Budget:** $200,000. **For-Profit. Description:** Individuals and corporations interested in the financial management of information technology (IT) organizations. Works for the education and improvement of members and the industry. Offers certification in IT financial management. Conducts peer studies, in-house seminars, and chargeback system reviews. Operates educational programs. **Libraries: Type:** reference. **Holdings:** articles. **Awards:** Decade of Contribution Award. **Frequency:** annual. **Type:** recognition. **Recipient:** for the most dedicated and prolific speakers who have participated for a minimum of ten years at ITFMA conferences ● Education Certification. **Frequency:** annual. **Type:** recognition. **Recipient:** for accounting, controllership, chargeback and ABCM, asset management, performance management and benchmarking, government financial management, and telecom financial management. **Formerly:** (1997) Financial Management for Data Processing; (2002) I.S. Financial Management Association. **Publications:** *Journal of IT Financial Management*, triennial. Includes association news. **Price:** free for members. **Circulation:** 1,100 ● Also publishes articles on chargeback and IT cost accounting, readings in chargeback for information technology, readings in IT financial management, IT financial planning, controlling, evaluating, pricing, and decision-making. **Conventions/Meetings:** semiannual conference.

1431 ■ Latin American Venture Capital Association (LAVCA)
28 E Jackson Blvd., Ste.1700
Chicago, IL 60604
Ph: (503)239-7449
Fax: (312)922-0955
E-mail: rdenies@lavca.org
URL: http://www.lavca.org
Contact: Ramona W. DeNies, Research Dir.
Founded: 2002. **Membership Dues:** fund management company (based on capital under management), $750-$10,000 (annual) ● corporate investor, $5,000 (annual) ● institutional investor, service provider, $2,000 (annual) ● official institution, academic institution, $500 (annual). **Staff:** 1. **Languages:** English, Portuguese, Spanish. **Description:** Promotes the growth of the private equity and venture capital industry in Latin America and the Caribbean. Advocates on behalf of the industry by disseminating information to the media, promoting the region to investors and supporting efforts to improve the regulatory framework. Conducts research on industry trends, performance and policy environment. Develops model documents, industry guides and standards. **Publications:** *LAVCA Reporter*, monthly. Newsletter. Keeps readers abreast of important industry announcements, upcoming events and new resources. **Price:** free. **Circulation:** 1,300. Alternate Formats: online.

1432 ■ Media Credit Association (MCA)
Address Unknown since 2007
Founded: 1903. **Members:** 800. **Staff:** 3. **Description:** Offers a credit guideline service to members of

the Magazine Publishers of America. Conducts annual survey on magazine credit industry practices. **Awards:** Quoin Award. **Frequency:** annual. **Type:** recognition. **Computer Services:** database, payment histories of advertising agencies and direct accounts. **Affiliated With:** Magazine Publishers of America. **Formerly:** (1972) Periodical Publishers Association. **Publications:** *Credit Management Newsletter*, monthly. Provides a review of pertinent monthly statistics. **Advertising:** not accepted. **Conventions/Meetings:** conference - 3/year, always March, June, November; New York City; **Avg. Attendance:** 75.

1433 ■ Medical Banking Project
320 Main St., Ste.230
Franklin, TN 37064
Ph: (615)794-2009
Fax: (615)794-1481
E-mail: info@mbproject.org
URL: http://www.mbproject.org
Contact: John Casillas, Founder/Chm.
Founded: 2001. **Membership Dues:** individual, $350 (annual) ● affiliate, $5,000 (annual) ● nonprofit organization that delivers healthcare, $500-$2,500 (annual) ● for profit/nonprofit organization that does not deliver healthcare organization (based on annual revenue), $500-$10,000 (annual). **Description:** Represents and supports the medical banking industry. **Publications:** *The Medical Banking Report*, bimonthly. Newsletter. Contains policy updates and industry-leading news. **Price:** $495.00/year. Alternate Formats: online ● *2001/2 HIPAA Readiness Survey for Financial Institutions*. Report. **Price:** included in membership dues; $50.00 for nonmembers. **Conventions/Meetings:** roundtable.

1434 ■ Motion Picture and Television Credit Association (MPTCA)
4102 W Magnolia Blvd., Ste.A
Burbank, CA 91505
Ph: (818)729-0220
Fax: (818)729-0225
E-mail: mptca1@msn.com
Contact: Seta Kasparian, Exec. Dir.
Founded: 1966. **Members:** 103. **Membership Dues:** company, $1,200 (annual). **Staff:** 3. **Description:** Motion picture and television credit executives. **Formerly:** (1969) Motion Picture and Television Credit Managers Association. **Conventions/Meetings:** monthly luncheon ● periodic seminar.

1435 ■ National Association of Corporate Treasurers (NACT)
12100 Sunset Hills Rd., Ste.130
Reston, VA 20190
Ph: (703)437-4377
Fax: (703)435-4390
E-mail: nact@nact.org
URL: http://www.nact.org
Contact: Mark Peterson, Chm.
Founded: 1982. **Members:** 800. **Membership Dues:** individual, $500 (annual). **Staff:** 3. **Budget:** $400,000. **Regional Groups:** 9. **Description:** Serves as a forum for high-level finance executives who perform all or a substantial part of the duties of corporate treasurership. Seeks to produce and facilitate the exchange of information relevant to the management of corporate treasury operations. Sponsors general sessions on such topics as Cash Management Issues for the 90's, Corporate Finance, Data Processing/Electronic Services, International Liquidity Management. Offers job clearinghouse services. **Committees:** Annual Meeting; Benefits Finance; Corporate Finance; Day of Technical Discussion; International Finance; Investors Relations; Job Clearinghouse; Media Relations; Membership; New Products; Newsletter; Revolving Credit Facilities; Risk Management; Small Company Treasury Issues; Telediscussions; Treasury Operations. **Publications:** *Annual Meeting Program*. **Circulation:** 1,500. **Advertising:** accepted ● *News and Notes*, bimonthly. Newsletter. **Circulation:** 1,500. **Advertising:** accepted ● Membership Directory, annual. **Circulation:** 1,500. **Advertising:** accepted. **Conventions/Meetings:** semiannual meeting - always January or February and October ● annual meeting.

1436 ■ National Association of Credit Management (NACM)
8840 Columbia 100 Pkwy.
Columbia, MD 21045
Ph: (410)740-5560
Free: (800)955-8815
Fax: (410)740-5574
E-mail: robins@nacm.org
URL: http://www.nacm.org
Contact: Robin D. Schauseil CAE, Pres./COO
Founded: 1896. **Members:** 35,000. **Staff:** 35. **Local Groups:** 60. **Description:** Credit and financial executives representing manufacturers, wholesalers, financial institutions, insurance companies, utilities, and other businesses interested in business credit. Promotes sound credit practices and legislation. Conducts Graduate School of Credit and Financial Management at Dartmouth College, Hanover, NH. **Libraries: Type:** lending; reference; not open to the public. **Holdings:** archival material, audiovisuals, books, monographs, papers. **Awards:** Certified Credit Executive. **Type:** recognition ● Graduate School Achievement. **Type:** recognition. **Computer Services:** Mailing lists. **Departments:** FGIB-NACM International Subsidiary; Legislative; Loss Prevention. **Formerly:** (2001) National Institute of Credit. **Publications:** *Business Credit*, 10/year. Magazine. ISSN: 0897-0181. **Circulation:** 36,800. **Advertising:** accepted. Alternate Formats: online ● *Credit Executives Handbook* ● *Digest of Commercial Laws* ● *Manual of Credit and Commercial Laws*, annual. **Price:** $70.00. **Conventions/Meetings:** annual Credit Congress and Exposition - convention (exhibits) - always May or June ● workshop.

1437 ■ National Association of Financial and Estate Planning (NAFEP)
525 E 4500 S, No. F-100
Salt Lake City, UT 84107
Ph: (801)266-9900
Fax: (801)266-1019
E-mail: ashley@nafep.com
URL: http://www.nafep.com
Contact: Mike Janko, Pres.
Founded: 1993. **Members:** 200. **Membership Dues:** associate, $100 (annual) ● affiliate, $50 (annual). **Staff:** 8. **Description:** Represents financial and estate planners. **Libraries: Type:** reference. **Holdings:** books. **Subjects:** estate planning. **Boards:** Advisory. **Publications:** *Premier I Living Trust*. Brochure ● *Premier II Life Estate Trust*. Brochure ● *Premier III Children's/Gifting Trust*. Brochure ● *Premier V Life Insurance Trust*. Brochure ● *Premier VI Private Annuity/Trust*. Brochure.

1438 ■ National Association of Payment Professionals (NAOPP)
c/o Steve Schwimmer, Pres.
PO Box 324
Syosset, NY 11791-0324
Ph: (516)746-6363
E-mail: schwimmer@naopp.com
URL: http://www.naopp.com
Contact: Steve Schwimmer, Pres.
Founded: 2003. **Membership Dues:** MLS, $99 ● MLSO/ISO, $500 ● vendor, $1,000. **Multinational. Description:** Provides education, benefits, liaison/representation and certification to individuals selling in the payment processing industry. Assists independent sales professionals in improving their businesses. Provides resources vital to the success of payment process professionals.

1439 ■ National Association of Settlement Purchasers (NASP)
c/o Peachtree Settlement Funding
3301 Quantum Blvd., 2nd Fl.
Boynton Beach, FL 33426
Free: (800)821-7773
Fax: (800)600-7161
E-mail: information@settlementfunding.com
URL: http://www.lumpsum.com
Contact: Ms. Deborah Benaim, VP
Founded: 1997. **Members:** 200. **Membership Dues:** associate, $195 (annual). **Staff:** 2. **Budget:** $2,400,000. **Description:** Finance companies that purchase structured settlements from individuals for a lump sum (structured settlements are received by individuals as redress for personal injury or other liability). Seeks to insure ethical practice in the trading of structured settlements; promotes advancement of the structured settlement purchasing industry. Serves as a clearinghouse on the purchase of structured settlements; lobbies for reform of regulations governing the trade in structured settlements. **Additional Websites:** http://www.settlementfunding.com. **Formerly:** (1999) National Settlement Purchasers Association.

1440 ■ National Chemical Credit Association (NCCA)
c/o Michael Meyers, Servicing Sec.
1100 Main St.
Buffalo, NY 14209-2356
Ph: (716)878-2807
Fax: (716)887-0479
E-mail: michael.meyers@abc-amega.com
URL: http://www.ncca1.org
Contact: Michael Meyers, Servicing Sec.
Founded: 1938. **Members:** 175. **Staff:** 4. **Description:** Represents chemical companies. Aims to facilitate the exchange of commercial credit information among leaders of the chemical industry, as well as provide continual professional education to its members. Sponsors monthly educational programs at divisional meetings. **Libraries: Type:** reference. **Holdings:** reports. **Subjects:** credit, finance. **Computer Services:** database, credit. **Divisions:** Agricultural; Animal Health; Chemical; International; Plastic. **Publications:** *Roster*, annual. Membership Directory ● Newsletter, quarterly. **Price:** included in membership dues. **Conventions/Meetings:** annual conference ● quarterly meeting (exhibits).

1441 ■ National Rural Utilities Cooperative Finance Corporation (NRUCFC)
2201 Cooperative Way
Herndon, VA 20171
Ph: (703)709-6700
Free: (800)424-2954
Fax: (703)709-6785
E-mail: membercenter@nrucfc.org
URL: http://www.nrucfc.org
Contact: Sheldon C. Petersen, CEO
Founded: 1969. **Staff:** 150. **Description:** Rural electric cooperative distribution systems, power supply systems, regional and statewide associations, one national association, and associate members. Based on the concepts of member-ownership and self-help, the purpose of the cooperative is to arrange financing for the programs and projects of its rural electric system members. Provides rural electric system members with a continuing source of private capital to supplement loan funds made available by the Rural Utilities Service. **Departments:** Administration; Legal; Loan. **Publications:** *CFC Report*, quarterly. Newsletter. Covers CFC activities, rural utility financing, and rural electric systems. **Price:** free. **Circulation:** 16,000 ● *National Rural Utilities Cooperative Finance Corporation—News in Brief*, weekly. Newsletter. Contains information for select leaders of rural electric systems cooperatives. **Price:** available to members only. **Circulation:** 1,200. **Conventions/Meetings:** annual meeting.

1442 ■ Native American Finance Officers Association (NAFOA)
PO Box 50637
Phoenix, AZ 85076-0637
Ph: (928)567-1007
Fax: (928)567-3994
E-mail: edwin@nafoa.org
URL: http://www.nafoa.org
Contact: Edwin Kane, Pres.
Founded: 1982. **Members:** 150. **Membership Dues:** student (Indian), $10 (annual) ● individual (Indian), $50 (annual) ● tribe (Indian), $250 (annual) ● associate individual (non-Indian), $500 (annual) ● associate corporate (non-Indian), $2,000 (annual). **Description:** Improves the quality of financial and business management of Native American governments and businesses. Promotes tribal sovereignty through

sound financial management. Develops scholarship training and internship program for Native American students and tribal employees. **Publications:** Newsletter, quarterly.

1443 ■ Network Branded Prepaid Card Association (NBPCA)
PO Box 180
Sherborn, MA 01770
Ph: (508)655-6107
Fax: (508)655-3026
E-mail: nbpca@nbpca.com
URL: http://www.nbpca.com
Contact: Marilyn Bochicchio, Pres./Exec. Dir.
Founded: 2005. **Members:** 38. **Membership Dues:** corporate, $25,000 (annual). **Description:** Contributes to the continued growth and success of the network branded prepaid card industry. Represents the collective interests of the network branded prepaid card industry. Fosters a positive climate conducive to the continued growth and acceptance of network branded prepaid cards.

1444 ■ Print Alliance Credit Exchange (PACE)
c/o ABC - Amega, Inc.
1100 Main St.
Buffalo, NY 14209
Ph: (716)887-9515
Fax: (716)887-9599
E-mail: jeff.markley@abc-amega.com
URL: http://www.gopace.com
Contact: Jeff Markley, VP, Credit Information
Founded: 1965. **Members:** 100. **Description:** Manufacturers or designers of business forms or graphic media, selling to dealers, distributors, office supply, copy stores, or end users. Promotes the collection, computation, and exchange of factual ledger experience information by members. Compiles statistics. **Divisions:** Western Forms Manufacturers Credit Interchange. **Formerly:** (1997) Forms Manufacturers Credit Interchange; (2004) Print Associates Credit Exchange. **Conventions/Meetings:** semiannual conference.

1445 ■ Private Equity CFO Association (PECFOA)
c/o Citizens Bank
101 Park Ave., 11th Fl.
New York, NY 10178
Ph: (212)401-3894
Fax: (212)401-3275
E-mail: liz.lambert@citizensbank.com
URL: http://www.privateequitycfo.org
Contact: Liz Lambert, Exec. Dir.
Founded: 2001. **Members:** 560. **Description:** Provides networking opportunities for members to share best practices. Responds to and addresses industry and professional issues of current interest. Develops programs that will provide education to association members. Improves and strengthens the flow of information among members.

1446 ■ Professional Women Controllers (PWC)
PO Box 950085
Oklahoma City, OK 73195-0085
Free: (800)232-9792
E-mail: info@pwcinc.org
URL: http://www.pwcinc.org
Contact: Lynette Jamison, Pres.
Founded: 1978. **Members:** 600. **Membership Dues:** associate, $78 (annual) ● active, $156 (annual) ● corporate, $400 (annual) ● student, $39 (annual). **Budget:** $60,000. **Description:** Women controllers. Promotes the advancement of women within the financial industry. Represents members' interests; facilitates networking among women controllers; and makes available educational programs. **Awards:** Honorary Membership Award. **Frequency:** annual. **Type:** recognition. **Recipient:** for commitment in furthering PWC's goals ● Manager of the Year. **Frequency:** annual. **Type:** recognition ● National Commendation Award. **Frequency:** annual. **Type:** recognition. **Recipient:** to an individual/group ● President's Award. **Frequency:** annual. **Type:** recognition. **Recipient:** to an individual who supported the president above and beyond the norm ● Regional Director's Award. **Frequency:** annual. **Type:** recognition. **Recipient:** to an individual who supported the regional director above and beyond the norm. **Telecommunication Services:** electronic mail, president@pwcinc.org. **Publications:** *WATCH*, 3/year. Newsletter. **Price:** included in membership dues. **Advertising:** accepted. **Conventions/Meetings:** annual conference (exhibits).

1447 ■ Society of Certified Credit Executives (SCCE)
PO Box 390106
Minneapolis, MN 55439
Ph: (952)926-6547
Fax: (952)926-1624
E-mail: scce@collector.com
URL: http://www.acainternational.org
Contact: Sandy Wesner, Mgr.
Founded: 1961. **Members:** 4,000. **Description:** A division of the International Credit Association (see separate entry). Credit executives who have been certified through SCCE's professional certification programs. Seeks to improve industry operations while expanding the knowledge of its members. Maintains placement service. **Awards:** Outstanding Fellow Award. **Frequency:** annual. **Type:** recognition. **Committees:** Certification Application Review; District Liaison; Employment Referral Service. **Publications:** *Who's Who of Credit Management*, annual. Newsletter. **Conventions/Meetings:** annual meeting and convention - always May or June.

1448 ■ Society of Cost Estimating and Analysis (SCEA)
527 Maple Ave. E, Ste.301
Vienna, VA 22180
Ph: (703)938-5090
Fax: (703)938-5091
E-mail: scea@sceaonline.net
URL: http://www.sceaonline.net
Contact: Robyn Kane, Sec.
Founded: 1990. **Members:** 2,000. **Membership Dues:** general, $55 (annual). **Staff:** 3. **Budget:** $400,000. **Local Groups:** 12. **Description:** Works to improve cost estimating and analysis in government and industry and to enhance the professional competence and achievements of its members. Administers a professional certification program leading to the designation of Certified Cost Estimator/Analyst; offers extensive literature in the field through its Professional Development Program. Goals of the Society include enhancing the profession of cost estimating and analysis, fostering the professional growth of its members, enhancing the understanding and application of cost estimating, analysis and related disciplines throughout government and industry and providing forums and media through which current issues of interest to the profession can be addressed and advances in the state-of-the-art can be shared. **Formed by Merger of:** (1990) Institute of Cost Analysis; National Estimating Society. **Publications:** *Journal of Cost Analysis & Management*, annual. Presents scholarly papers on cost estimating and analysis and related disciplines. **Price:** $40.00/year; $50.00 foreign subscription. ISSN: 0882-3871. **Circulation:** 3,000 ● *National Estimator*, semiannual. **Price:** $30.00 /year for nonmembers; free, for members only. **Circulation:** 3,000. **Advertising:** accepted. Alternate Formats: online. **Conventions/Meetings:** annual National Training Workshop (exhibits).

1449 ■ Society of Medical Banking Excellence (SOMBEX)
c/o The Medical Banking Project
320 Main St., Ste.230
Franklin, TN 37064
Ph: (615)794-2009
Fax: (615)794-1481
E-mail: members@mbproject.org
URL: http://www.mbproject.org/sombex-info.php
Contact: Evelyn Marquez, Contact
Founded: 2001. **Description:** Seeks to advance the creation of digital infrastructures to be used to test and implement EDI processing techniques and analytics in medical payment channels. **Working Groups:** Charity; CyberWar; Healthcare Credit Practices; HIPAA Compliance; Workflow Automation. **Publications:** Directory. Alternate Formats: online.

1450 ■ Society of Quantitative Analysts (SQA)
PO Box 539
Webster, NY 14580-0539
Free: (800)918-7930
E-mail: sqa@sqa-us.org
URL: http://www.sqa-us.org
Contact: David Carleton CAE, Mgr.
Founded: 1989. **Members:** 300. **Membership Dues:** regular, $150 (annual) ● academic, $75 (annual) ● student, $25 (annual). **Description:** Works for the application of new and innovative techniques in finance, with particular emphasis on the use of quantitative techniques in investment and risk management. Sponsors a half-day program in the fall and a Fuzzy Day seminar in the spring on an exploratory topic. **Conventions/Meetings:** monthly meeting.

1451 ■ Western Payments Alliance (WPA)
685 Market St., Ste.540
San Francisco, CA 94105
Ph: (415)433-1230
Fax: (415)433-1370
E-mail: info@wespay.org
URL: http://www.wespay.org
Contact: Peter Yeatrakas AAP, Pres./CEO
Founded: 1876. **Members:** 1,100. **Membership Dues:** associate, $625 (annual) ● regular, institution, $400 (annual). **Staff:** 10. **Description:** Represents financial institutions and others involved in payments systems in the U.S. **Awards:** A.R. Zipf Award for Payments Systems Innovation. **Type:** recognition ● George E. Lowther Award for Outstanding Service to the Payments Industry. **Type:** recognition ● Russell L. Fenwick Award for Payments System Leadership. **Type:** recognition. **Departments:** Accounting; ACH Rules; Check Services; Education Services. **Publications:** *Notes*, quarterly. Newsletter. Alternate Formats: online. **Conventions/Meetings:** annual conference ● annual Payments Symposium - 2008 Sept. 7-9, Las Vegas, NV ● monthly Tele-seminars.

1452 ■ Women in Housing and Finance (WHF)
717 Princess St.
Alexandria, VA 22314
Ph: (703)683-4742
Fax: (703)683-0018
E-mail: whf@whfdc.org
URL: http://www.whfdc.org
Contact: Ali Solis, Pres.
Founded: 1979. **Members:** 600. **Membership Dues:** private sector organization, $125 (annual) ● government/public service organization, $100 (annual) ● associate, $65 (annual). **Local Groups:** 1. **Description:** Professionals employed in the fields of housing or finance. Provides women finance professionals with the opportunity for continued professional development through interaction with others with similar interests. Promotes educational development of women in housing and finance; provides members with services and benefits to help them attain higher levels of expertise. Sponsors social events for members; holds receptions for congressional and regulatory leaders; conducts monthly luncheon and programs featuring speakers from federal agencies, Congress, and the private sector. Sponsors career development workshops. Activities are concentrated in the Washington, DC, area. **Committees:** Professional Development. **Task Forces:** Housing; Insurance; International; Legislative; Regulatory; Securities; Technology. **Publications:** *Women in Housing and Finance—Membership Directory*, annual. **Price:** free, for members only ● Newsletter, 10/year. **Conventions/Meetings:** annual meeting - always June in Washington, DC.

Financial Planning

1453 ■ American Association of Daily Money Managers (AADMM)
174 Crestview Dr.
Bellefonte, PA 16823
Free: (877)326-5991
Fax: (814)355-2452
E-mail: info@aadmm.com
URL: http://www.aadmm.com
Contact: Marcia Turner, Pres.
Membership Dues: active, affiliate, $175 (annual) ● agency/business, $325 (annual). **Description:** Works to advance the daily money management industry. **Publications:** Newsletter ● Directory. **Conventions/Meetings:** meeting ● seminar.

1454 ■ American Money Management Group (AMMG)
5755 N Point Pkwy., Ste.57
Alpharetta, GA 30022-1145
Ph: (678)297-9500
Free: (877)974-9800
Fax: (678)297-9514
E-mail: info@ammg.us
URL: http://www.ammg.us
Contact: Richard A. Alford, Pres.
Founded: 1980. **Members:** 3,000. **State Groups:** 3. **Description:** Provides money management and financial planning services. **Formerly:** (1980) American Buyers Federation; (2004) American Money Management Association.

1455 ■ Association of African American Financial Advisors (AAAA)
3 Bethesda Metro Ctr., Ste.700
Bethesda, MD 20814
Ph: (301)961-1507
E-mail: info@aaafa.org
URL: http://www.aaafa.org
Contact: Lanta Evans-Motte, Pres.
Founded: 2001. **Membership Dues:** general, $100 (annual). **Description:** Seeks to develop and foster professional relationships among African American professionals working in the financial advisory industry. Provides assistance and nurturing for those families that seek to improve their opportunities for participating and prospering financially in an economically progressive society. Strives to create support networks for minority financial professionals. Provides a forum for further education, training and visibility of its members. **Awards:** Association of African American Financial Advisors Scholarship and Internship Awards. **Frequency:** annual. **Type:** scholarship. **Recipient:** to outstanding minority students pursuing undergraduate degrees in business, while demonstrating strong leadership abilities, integrity, and a commitment to their communities.

1456 ■ Association for Financial Counseling and Planning Education (AFCPE)
1500 W 3rd Ave., Ste.223
Columbus, OH 43212
Ph: (614)485-9650 (225)578-1726
Fax: (614)485-9621
E-mail: sburns@afcpe.org
URL: http://www.afcpe.org/pages/index.cfm
Contact: Sharon A. Burns PhD, Exec. Dir.
Founded: 1983. **Members:** 850. **Membership Dues:** regular, $100 (annual). **Staff:** 5. **Budget:** $400,000. **Description:** Researchers, academics, financial counselors, and financial planners. Aims to improve service to their clients through education. **Awards:** Distinguished Fellow. **Frequency:** annual. **Type:** recognition. **Recipient:** to a colleague ● Financial Counselor of the Year. **Frequency:** annual. **Type:** recognition. **Recipient:** to a member who has contributed outstanding work in financial counseling ● Mary Ellen Edmondson Educator of the Year. **Frequency:** annual. **Type:** recognition. **Recipient:** to a member with dedicated service to teaching and/or outreach ● Outstanding Consumer Information. **Frequency:** annual. **Type:** recognition. **Recipient:** to the author and/or publisher of widely distributed educational materials ● Outstanding Educational Program. **Frequency:** annual. **Type:** recognition. **Recipient:** to a program that has demonstrated an impact in the field of financial counseling and planning ● Outstanding Financial Counseling and/or Planning Center. **Frequency:** annual. **Type:** recognition. **Recipient:** to a center that has demonstrated its effectiveness in its local community. **Programs:** Accredited Credit Counselor; Accredited Financial Counselor; Certified Housing Counselor. **Publications:** *Financial Counseling and Planning*, semiannual. Journal. Contains researches concerning financial management and counseling techniques and tools. **Price:** included in membership dues ● *The Standard*, quarterly. Newsletter. Contains news regarding financial education and financial counseling. **Circulation:** 850. Alternate Formats: online. **Conventions/Meetings:** annual conference, with 4 general sessions, 20 breakout sessions (exhibits).

1457 ■ Association of Independent Trust Companies (AITCO)
8 S Michigan Ave., Ste.1000
Chicago, IL 60603
Ph: (312)223-1611
Fax: (312)580-0165
E-mail: aitco@gss.net
URL: http://www.aitco.net
Contact: Troy Kennedy, Pres.
Members: 150. **Membership Dues:** regular, resource, special, community bank, $950 (annual) ● vendor, $1,000 (annual) ● associate, $550 (annual). **Staff:** 4. **Description:** Independent financial counselors, asset managers and trustees who are governed by the same state and federal requirements applicable to the trust departments of large banks. **Computer Services:** Online services, internet community of members. **Publications:** *The Advisor*, quarterly. Newsletter. **Price:** included in membership dues. **Advertising:** accepted. **Conventions/Meetings:** annual conference (exhibits).

1458 ■ Association of PVO Financial Managers (APVOFM)
19 S Compo Rd.
Westport, CT 06880
Ph: (203)226-3650
Fax: (203)226-3652
E-mail: info@apvofm.org
URL: http://www.apvofm.org
Contact: Alison N. Smith, Exec. Dir.
Membership Dues: organizational, $500 (annual). **Multinational**. **Description:** Represents organizations and individuals with an interest in the financial management of nonprofit organizations. Addresses the needs and concerns of international development/ relief groups. Strengthens the financial management of the international development non-profit community through sharing knowledge, improving professional skills, and working as an advocate. Acts as a resource for information exchange. **Publications:** *Tie Lines*. Newsletter. **Price:** included in membership dues.

1459 ■ Certified Financial Planner Board of Standards (CFP Board)
1670 Broadway, Ste.600
Denver, CO 80202-4809
Ph: (303)830-7500
Free: (888)CFP-MARK
Fax: (303)860-7388
E-mail: mail@cfpboard.org
URL: http://www.cfp.net
Contact: Ms. Jina Martingano, Mgr., External Relations
Founded: 1985. **Staff:** 36. **Budget:** $4,500,000. **Nonmembership**. **Description:** Certifies individuals who meet its initial and ongoing certification standards to use the CFP(R) certification marks. Works to benefit the public by fostering professional standards in personal financial planning. **Telecommunication Services:** electronic mail, humanresources@cfpboard.org ● additional toll-free number, certificant line, (800)487-1497. **Boards:** Directors. **Commissions:** Disciplinary and Ethics. **Councils:** Examinations. **Formerly:** (1994) International Board of Standards and Practices for Certified Financial Planners. **Publications:** *CFP Board Report*, monthly. Newsletter. **Circulation:** 58,000 ● *It's Your Turn*, monthly. Newsletter. Provides information about financial matters and the benefits of financial planning. **Circulation:** 19,000 ● *Mark of Quality*. Brochure. Describes the certification requirements of the CFP mark, and offers guidance on choosing a financial planner. ● *10 Questions to Ask When Choosing a Financial Planner*. Brochure. Provides guidelines and checklist for interviewing financial planners. Alternate Formats: online ● *What You Should Know About Financial Planning*, periodic. Brochure. Explains financial planning, its benefits, and what consumers should expect from the financial planning process. Alternate Formats: online ● *Why You Should Choose a Certified Financial Planner Practitioner*, periodic. Brochure. Promotes the value of choosing a certified financial planner practitioner and highlights a CFP practitioner's competency. ● Annual Report, annual. **Circulation:** 35,000. Alternate Formats: online.

1460 ■ Fifty Plus Financial Network
c/o American Money Management Group
5755 N Point Pkwy., Ste.57
Alpharetta, GA 30022-1145
Ph: (678)297-9500
Free: (877)974-9800
Fax: (678)297-9514
E-mail: info@ammg.us
URL: http://www.ammg.us
Contact: Richard A. Alford, Pres.
Description: Provides money management and financial planning services for persons age 50 plus.

1461 ■ Financial Services Technology Network (FSTN)
8 S Michigan Ave., Ste.1000
Chicago, IL 60603
Ph: (312)782-4951
Fax: (312)580-0165
Contact: John Doyle, Pres.
Description: Financial services firms. Promotes development and introduction of new technologies in the field of financial services. Conducts SAS 70 audits and reviews SEI Trust computer software systems of members; conducts educational programs; facilitates exchange of information among members.

1462 ■ Fixed Income Analysts Society (FIASI)
244 Fifth Ave., Ste.L230
New York, NY 10001
Ph: (212)726-8100
E-mail: fiasi@fiasi.org
URL: http://www.fiasi.org
Contact: Lauren Nausser, Exec. Dir.
Founded: 1975. **Members:** 300. **Membership Dues:** full, $160 (annual) ● academic, $80 (annual) ● associate, $50 (annual) ● student, $25 (annual). **Staff:** 1. **Description:** Corporate research analysts and portfolio managers involved in high yield, asset, mortgage backed, and municipal research. **Awards:** Hall of Fame Award. **Frequency:** annual. **Type:** recognition. **Recipient:** to outstanding practitioners for their lifetime achievements in the advancement of the analysis of fixed income securities. **Computer Services:** Mailing lists. **Publications:** *Bonds-Eye*, periodic. Newsletter ● *Membership Brochure*. Alternate Formats: online. **Conventions/Meetings:** monthly conference.

1463 ■ Forum for Investor Advice
PO Box 3216
Mercerville, NJ 08619
Fax: (609)890-8037
E-mail: investoradvice@optonline.net
URL: http://www.investoradvice.org
Contact: Barbara Levin, Exec. Dir.
Founded: 1994. **Members:** 70. **Description:** Financial services organizations including mutual fund companies, securities firms, and banks and insurance companies. Promotes increased public awareness of the availability and effectiveness of financial and investment services provided by members. Gathers and disseminates information; conducts public relations and promotional activities; sponsors continu-

ing professional development courses for financial services providers. **Publications:** *Do You Really Need a Financial Advisor?*. Brochure ● *Getting Help Made All the Difference*. Brochure ● *Managing Investment Risk*. Booklet ● *Media Directory*, periodic.

1464 ■ IAB Partners
462 E 800 N
Orem, UT 84097
Ph: (801)805-1361
Fax: (801)224-4457
E-mail: support@iabweb.com
URL: http://www.iabnew.com/about.html
Contact: Greg Stuart, Pres./CEO

Founded: 1982. **Description:** Promotes the interests and financial security of families, through benefits packages for both consumers and small business owners. **Programs:** Money Back Reward; New Dimension. **Formerly:** (1982) Family Security Coalition; (1987) International Association of Businesses. **Publications:** *IABusiness Review*, quarterly. Newsletter. **Conventions/Meetings:** annual meeting.

1465 ■ National Association of Christian Financial Consultants (NACFC)
1055 Maitland Center Commons Blvd.
Maitland, FL 32751
Ph: (407)644-9793
Free: (877)966-2232
E-mail: info@nacfc.org
URL: http://www.nacfc.org
Contact: Wesley Pennington, Exec. Dir.

Founded: 1997. **Membership Dues:** regular, $150 (annual). **Description:** Represents investment professionals committed to investment and financial planning disciplines centered upon biblical principles. Provides educational resources, fellowship support, and biblical standards for professional investment counselors. Seeks to integrate Bible-based principles within financial counseling practices. **Telecommunication Services:** electronic mail, wes@nacfc.org. **Publications:** Newsletter, quarterly. Includes articles delivering practical training on implementing biblical wisdom. **Price:** included in membership dues ● Brochure. Alternate Formats: online. **Conventions/Meetings:** annual conference, with speakers (exhibits).

1466 ■ National Association of Estate Planners and Councils (NAEPC)
1120 Chester Ave., Ste.470
Cleveland, OH 44114
Free: (866)226-2224
Fax: (216)696-2582
E-mail: admin@naepc.org
URL: http://www.naepc.org
Contact: Gary L. Flotron MBA, Pres.

Founded: 1962. **Members:** 20,000. **Membership Dues:** council (with 100 or fewer individual), $100 (annual) ● council (with more than 100 individual), $200 (annual) ● individual, $80 (annual). **Staff:** 2. **Local Groups:** 200. **Description:** Life underwriters, trust officers, attorneys, and Certified Public Accountants. Forms new estate planning councils; promotes cooperation among the disciplines of estate planning; publicizes the need for estate planning. Sponsors the Accredited Estate Planner and Estate Planning Law Specialist designations. **Formerly:** (2002) National Association of Estate Planning Councils. **Publications:** *Business Week Magazine*, weekly. **Price:** $39.97 for members (51 issues) ● *NAEPC News*, quarterly. Newsletter. Alternate Formats: online ● *Trusts & Estates Magazine*. **Price:** $199.00/year. **Conventions/Meetings:** annual conference (exhibits) - always fall.

1467 ■ National Association of Independent Public Finance Advisors (NAIPFA)
PO Box 304
Montgomery, IL 60538-0304
Ph: (630)896-1292
Free: (800)624-7321
Fax: (209)633-6265
E-mail: rhoban@naipfa.com
URL: http://www.naipfa.com
Contact: Roseanne M. Hoban, Exec. Dir.

Founded: 1990. **Membership Dues:** business, $3,000 (annual) ● individual, $100 (annual) ● associate, $750 (annual). **Description:** Firms that specialize in providing financial advice on bond sales and financial planning to public agencies. Promotes common interests of members. Seeks to build credibility and recognition of financial advisory firms through a public relations plan. Maintains high ethical and professional standards. Maintains a Board of Review to ensure members' compliance to standards; provides educational materials to independent financial advisors. Responds to legislative needs of member firms and the public agencies they serve. **Publications:** *NAIPFA News*. Newsletter. Alternate Formats: online ● Directory, annual. **Conventions/Meetings:** annual conference - 2008 Oct. 15-17, Seattle, WA ● semiannual seminar.

1468 ■ National Association of Personal Financial Advisors (NAPFA)
3250 N Arlington Heights Rd., Ste.109
Arlington Heights, IL 60004
Ph: (847)483-5400
Free: (800)366-2732
Fax: (847)483-5415
E-mail: info@napfa.org
URL: http://www.napfa.org
Contact: Ellen Turf, CEO

Founded: 1983. **Members:** 1,130. **Membership Dues:** registered financial advisor, provisional, $475 (annual) ● financial services affiliate, $350 (annual) ● academic affiliate, $150 (annual) ● student affiliate, $100 (annual) ● full-time college/university student, $35 (annual). **Staff:** 10. **Budget:** $1,900,000. **Regional Groups:** 4. **Local Groups:** 26. **Description:** Full-time, fee-only financial planners. Serves as a network for fee-only planners to discuss issues relating to practice management, client services, and investments selection. Works to encourage and advance the practice of fee-only financial planning by developing the skills of members and increasing the awareness of fee-only financial planning of consumers. **Awards:** Distinguished Service Award. **Frequency:** annual. **Type:** recognition. **Recipient:** for a NAPFA member or staff ● Special Membership Award. **Frequency:** annual. **Type:** recognition. **Recipient:** for a NAPFA member or staff. **Computer Services:** Mailing lists, of members. **Committees:** Education; Ethics; Government Affairs; Membership; Policy Review; Public Awareness. **Publications:** *NAPFA Advisor*, monthly. Magazine. **Price:** included in membership dues; $85.00 for nonmembers. **Advertising:** accepted ● *NAPFA Membership Directory*, annual ● *NAPFA NewsLink*, bimonthly. Newsletter ● Brochures. **Conventions/Meetings:** annual Advanced Planners Conference ● Basic Training - meeting ● meeting - 5/year ● quarterly regional meeting (exhibits) - in Midwest, Northeast/Mid-Atlantic, South and West.

1469 ■ National Association of Stock Plan Professionals (NASPP)
PO Box 21639
Concord, CA 94521-0639
Ph: (925)685-9271
Fax: (925)930-9284
E-mail: naspp@naspp.com
URL: http://www.naspp.com
Contact: Barbara Baksa, Exec. Dir.

Founded: 1992. **Members:** 6,000. **Membership Dues:** individual, $495 (annual) ● corporate, $495 (annual) ● corporate (for up to 3 members), $595 (annual). **Staff:** 6. **Regional Groups:** 4. **State Groups:** 32. **Local Groups:** 30. **For-Profit. Description:** Compensation and human resources professionals, stock plan administrators, securities and tax attorneys, accountants, corporate secretaries, transfer agents, stockbrokers, and software vendors. Dedicated to providing opportunities for professional and educational advancement to members; provides networking, education and information resources. **Publications:** *The Stock Plan Advisor*, quarterly. Newsletter. Provides an advisory service for stock plan professionals. **Price:** included in membership dues. ISSN: 1539-0659. **Advertising:** accepted. Alternate Formats: online. **Conventions/Meetings:** annual conference and workshop.

1470 ■ National Center for Home Equity Conversion (NCHEC)
360 N Robert St., No. 403
St. Paul, MN 55101
URL: http://www.reverse.org
Contact: Ken Scholen, Founder

Founded: 1981. **Description:** Acts as a clearinghouse for information on reverse mortgages for the elderly. Offers educational publications. **Publications:** *Reverse Mortgages for Beginners*. Book.

1471 ■ Registered Financial Planners Institute (RFPI)
2001 Cooper Foster Park Rd.
Amherst, OH 44001
Ph: (440)282-7176
Fax: (440)282-8027
E-mail: info@rfpi.com
URL: http://rfpi.com
Contact: Ade J. Schreiber, Pres.

Founded: 1983. **Members:** 300. **Membership Dues:** collective, $150 (annual) ● affiliate, $75 (annual). **Staff:** 2. **Regional Groups:** 2. **State Groups:** 5. **Local Groups:** 3. **For-Profit. Description:** Registered financial planners, including insurance and real estate agents, attorneys, accountants, certified public accounts, bankers, securities, and stockbrokers. Promotes professionalism in financial planning for individuals and businesses, and ensures that work conforms to high standards of competence, impartiality, and confidentiality. Offers study programs in the form of classroom seminars and correspondence course programs. Sponsors research program and referral service; maintains speakers' bureau. Bestows designation of Registered Financial Planner (RFP) upon qualified members. **Publications:** *Financial Planning Strategies*, monthly. Newsletter. **Price:** included in membership dues. **Advertising:** accepted. Alternate Formats: online ● *20-20*, quarterly. Newsletter. **Price:** included in membership dues. Alternate Formats: online ● *Your Personal Financial Planning*, monthly. Newsletter. **Price:** available to members only. **Advertising:** accepted ● Newsletter, quarterly. **Conventions/Meetings:** annual convention.

1472 ■ Viatical and Life Settlement Association of America (VLSAA)
Address Unknown since 2008

Founded: 1995. **Members:** 40. **Membership Dues:** voting, $6,000 (annual) ● provisional, associate, $3,000 (annual). **Staff:** 2. **Budget:** $300,000. **Description:** Seeks to inform the public and state and federal legislators and officials about viatical settlements. A viatical settlement addresses the critical financial priorities of the terminally ill by providing the opportunity to convert their existing life insurance into cash, enabling them to receive a significant portion of their life insurance benefit at a time when they most need or want additional financial resources. The association also advocates the needs and interests of viators and VAA members before Congress and state legislatures and regulatory agencies. **Computer Services:** Information services ● mailing lists. **Formerly:** (2000) Viatical Association of America. **Publications:** *Viatical Fax*, periodic. Newsletter. **Price:** included in membership dues. **Conventions/Meetings:** semiannual convention.

Finishing

1473 ■ Mass Finishing Job Shops Association (MFJSA)
808 13th St.
East Moline, IL 61244-1628
Ph: (309)755-1101

Fax: (309)755-1121
URL: http://www.mfjsa.com
Contact: Jerry Stenger, Chm.
Founded: 1981. **Members:** 43. **Membership Dues:** associate, $350 (annual). **Staff:** 1. **Description:** Represents tumbling, vibratory, and other mass finishing and blasting job shops. Mass finishing includes deburring, cleaning, and surface finishing of metal and other materials. Promotes ethical practices of mass finishing job shops; encourages pride in workmanship. Provides forum for exchange of information, ideas, and developments in the field. Conducts specialized education program and research; compiles statistics. **Conventions/Meetings:** semiannual conference.

1474 ■ National Association for Surface Finishing (NASF)
1155 15th St. NW, Ste.500
Washington, DC 20005
Ph: (202)457-8404
Fax: (202)530-0659
E-mail: jflatley@nasf.org
URL: http://www.nasf.org
Contact: John Flatley, Exec. Dir.
Founded: 1951. **Members:** 160. **Membership Dues:** supplier (based on annual sales revenue), $1,100-$10,100 (annual) ● institutional, $375 (annual) ● domestic, $125 (annual) ● foreign, $100 (annual) ● student, retired, $62 (annual). **Staff:** 1. **Budget:** $390,000. **Regional Groups:** 1. **Description:** Companies manufacturing metal finishing equipment, materials, and processes, including basic metals, chemicals, and compounds; suppliers of services for metal finishing of all types; distributors. Sponsors metal finishing clinics for industrial groups; promotes the use of established standards to acquaint buyers of plated and finished products with the means of specifying a high-quality finish. **Libraries:** **Type:** not open to the public. **Awards:** August P. Munning Award. **Frequency:** annual. **Type:** recognition. **Boards:** Surface Finishing Market Research. **Committees:** Chemical/Pretreatment/Technical; Distributors; Equipment; Marketing; Membership Promotion; Metals and Commodities. **Programs:** Government Relations. **Subgroups:** International Promotion. **Formed by Merger of:** (2006) Metal Finishing Suppliers' Association, National Association of Metal Finishers and American Electroplaters and Surface Finishers Society. **Formerly:** (1927) International Fellowship Society. **Publications:** *Safety Tips Booklet* ● *Supplier News*, quarterly. Newsletter ● Membership Directory, annual. **Conventions/Meetings:** annual conference (exhibits) ● annual Washington Forum - meeting (exhibits).

Fire Protection

1475 ■ International Kitchen Exhaust Cleaning Association (IKECA)
12339 Carroll Ave.
Rockville, MD 20852
Ph: (301)230-0099
Fax: (301)231-4871
E-mail: info@ikeca.org
URL: http://www.ikeca.org
Contact: Glenn Fellman, Exec. Dir.
Founded: 1988. **Members:** 170. **Staff:** 4. **Budget:** $150,000. **Description:** Promotes restaurant fire safety. Provides professional cleaning services. **Publications:** *The Journal*, quarterly. Newsletter. **Circulation:** 250. **Advertising:** accepted. **Conventions/Meetings:** annual meeting (exhibits).

1476 ■ National Fireproofing Contractors Association (NFCA)
PO Box 1571
Westford, MA 01886
Free: (866)250-4111
Fax: (978)250-9788
E-mail: nfca@nfca-online.org
URL: http://www.nfca-online.org
Contact: Hubert T. Dudley, Exec. Dir.
Membership Dues: associate, $500 (annual) ● contractor, $1,000 (annual) ● supplier, $2,000 (annual). **Description:** Represents contractors who install passive fireproofing products to protect building structural materials from fire. Develops standards and quality control procedures for the application of fireproofing products. Provides educational programs for the fire protection industry. Provides design assistance to the contractor, specification writers and design community.

Firearms

1477 ■ American Custom Gunmakers Guild (ACGG)
22 Vista View Ln.
Cody, WY 82414-9606
Ph: (307)587-4297
Fax: (307)587-4297
E-mail: acgg@acgg.org
URL: http://www.acgg.org
Contact: Jan Billeb, Exec. Dir.
Founded: 1983. **Members:** 350. **Membership Dues:** associate (individual), $85 (annual) ● associate (corporate), $140 (annual) ● associate (gunsmithing student), $45 (annual) ● associate (Canadian/foreign), $115 (annual) ● regular (stockmaker, metalsmith, engraver and metalfinisher), $150 (annual). **Description:** Seeks to preserve and promote the art of fine custom gun making. **Awards:** Gunsmithing Student Grant-in-Aid. **Frequency:** annual. **Type:** scholarship. **Recipient:** to a gunsmithing student attending annual convention. **Publications:** *Directory of Custom Gun making Services*, biennial. Includes listing of specialties. **Price:** $5.00. **Circulation:** 1,000 ● *Directory of Regular Members*, biennial ● *Gunmaker*, quarterly. Journal. **Advertising:** accepted ● *Realizing Your Dream: A Client's Guide to Building a Custom Gun*. Booklet. **Price:** $20.00. **Conventions/Meetings:** annual Firearms Engravers and Gunmakers Exhibition - show (exhibits) ● meeting ● annual seminar.

1478 ■ National Association of Federally Licensed Firearms Dealers (NAFLFD)
2400 E Las Olas Blvd., No. 397
Fort Lauderdale, FL 33301
Ph: (954)467-9994
Fax: (954)463-2501
E-mail: webmaster@amfire.com
URL: http://www.amfire.com
Contact: Andrew Molchan, Pres.
Founded: 1972. **Members:** 12,000. **Membership Dues:** individual, $35 (annual). **Staff:** 12. **Description:** Persons licensed by the federal government to sell firearms. Provides firearm retailers with low-cost liability insurance, current information on new products for the industry, and retail business guidance. Distributes pro-firearms, legislative, and production and sales information concerning the industry. Compiles statistics on firearm production, importation, and exportation. **Awards:** Product Award of Merit. **Frequency:** annual. **Type:** recognition. **Recipient:** for manufacturers of firearms, cutlery, archery, and optics. **Computer Services:** database, on firearms. **Publications:** *AFI Shot Show Magazine*, annual. **Circulation:** 110,000. **Advertising:** accepted ● *American Firearms Industry*, monthly. Magazine. Covers the firearms, archery, cutlery, and outdoor sports equipment industries; emphasizes products and retailing. **Price:** $35.00/year. ISSN: 0164-8136. **Circulation:** 60,000. **Advertising:** accepted ● *American Firearms Industry Buying Directory*, annual. Lists manufacturers and suppliers of hunting equipment; also lists notable people in history who developed firearms, archery, and cutlery weapons. **Price:** $10.00/copy for members; $20.00/copy for nonmembers. **Circulation:** 60,000. **Advertising:** accepted. Also Cited As: *AFI's Buying Directory* ● *Firearms Disposition and Requisition Log Book*. **Conventions/Meetings:** annual Firearms Trade Expo - convention (exhibits).

1479 ■ National Association of Firearms Retailers (NAFR)
11 Mile Hill Rd.
Newtown, CT 06470
Ph: (203)426-1320
Fax: (203)426-1087
E-mail: nafr@nssf.org
URL: http://www.nafr.org
Membership Dues: shooting range developer/not-for-profit shooting range, $75 (annual) ● for profit range/firearm retailer, $75-$250 (annual). **Description:** Addresses the interests and needs of firearm retailers. Helps restore the professional firearms retailer's image as a responsible businessman and community citizen. Increases profitability through more effective management. Provides opportunities to members to participate in professionally designed and administered programs. **Libraries:** **Type:** lending. **Holdings:** books, video recordings. **Affiliated With:** National Shooting Sports Foundation. **Publications:** Newsletter. Alternate Formats: online.

1480 ■ National Firearms Act Trade and Collectors Association (NFATCA)
PO Box 855
Winchester, KY 40392
Ph: (703)263-7676
E-mail: teresa@jtdistributing.com
URL: http://www.nfatca.org
Contact: John Brown, Pres.
Founded: 2005. **Membership Dues:** life, $25,000 ● plankholder, silver, $1,000 (annual) ● dealer, $500 (annual) ● collector, $250 (annual). **Description:** Represents the National Firearms Act (NFA) trade and collectors community. Unites the NFA community, manufacturers, dealers and collectors alike. Focuses on solving the problems of the NFA community. Facilitates communication and cooperation among members. **Publications:** *NFA Handbook*.

1481 ■ National Reloading Manufacturers Association (NRMA)
1 Centerpointe Dr., Ste.550
Lake Oswego, OR 97035
URL: http://www.reload-nrma.com/orderform.html
Contact: Greg Chevalier, Exec. Sec.
Members: 22. **Description:** Promotes interest in handloading of ammunition by all potential users. Manufactures and improves reloading tools, equipment, and supplies. Conducts consumer and trade promotion programs and publicity. **Publications:** *Reloading Catalog of Catalogs*. Contains reloading information and all leading reloading manufacturers. **Price:** $10.00 plus shipping and handling ● *Reloading Video*. Covers the basics of reloading, with detailed operations in rifle, pistol and shotshell reloading. **Price:** $9.95 plus shipping and handling ● *Set Yourself Up To Reload*. Booklet. Includes list of equipment, accessories and components to start reloading. **Price:** $5.00 plus shipping and handling ● Also publishes promotional and educational literature. **Conventions/Meetings:** annual conference.

1482 ■ Sporting Arms and Ammunitions Manufacturers Institute (SAAMI)
c/o Flintlock Ridge Office Center
11 Mile Hill Rd.
Newtown, CT 06470-2359
Ph: (203)426-4358 (203)426-1320
Fax: (203)426-1087
E-mail: info@nssf.org
URL: http://www.saami.org
Contact: Rick Patterson, Managing Dir.
Founded: 1926. **Members:** 17. **Staff:** 3. **Description:** Producers of firearms, ammunition, and propellants. Promotes and facilitates voluntary compliance with industry performance standards for sporting ammunitions. **Telecommunication Services:** electronic mail, rpatterson@nssf.org. **Committees:** Environment; Legal and Legislative; Regulatory Affairs; Technical.

Fishing Industries

1483 ■ At-sea Processors Association (APA)
c/o Stephanie Madsen, Exec. Dir.
PO Box 32817
Juneau, AK 99803
Ph: (206)285-5139

E-mail: msavey@atsea.org
URL: http://www.atsea.org
Contact: Stephanie Madsen, Exec. Dir.
Membership Dues: associate (based on annual level of economic interaction), $500-$2,000 (annual). **Staff:** 5. **Description:** US flag catcher/processor vessels that participate in the healthy and abundant groundfish fisheries of the Bering Sea. Committed to working with fishery managers, scientists, environmentalists and members of the fishing industry to ensure the continued health and sustainability of marine resources.

1484 ■ International Institute of Fisheries Economics and Trade (IIFET)
Dept. of Agricultural and Rsrc. Economics
Oregon State Univ.
Corvallis, OR 97331-3601
Ph: (541)737-1439 (541)737-1416
Fax: (541)737-2563
E-mail: iifet@oregonstate.edu
URL: http://oregonstate.edu/Dept/IIFET
Contact: Ann L. Shriver, Exec. Dir.
Founded: 1982. **Members:** 500. **Membership Dues:** individual, $75 (annual) ● institutional/corporate, $500 (annual) ● student, $25 (annual) ● library, $200 (annual). **Staff:** 2. **Multinational. Description:** Individuals from the fisheries industry, government, and universities. Objectives are to: promote discussion on factors affecting seafood trade and fisheries management; facilitate cooperative research projects and data exchange. **Awards:** Best Student Paper Award. **Frequency:** biennial. **Type:** recognition. **Recipient:** for the best paper by a graduate student presented at IIFET biennial conference ● Distinguished Service Award. **Frequency:** biennial. **Type:** recognition. **Recipient:** for major contribution to Fisheries Economics. **Computer Services:** Mailing lists, of members. **Committees:** Global Groundfish Markets Research Group; Salmon Network; Socioeconomics Network. **Formerly:** (1982) Institute for the Cooperative Study of International Sea-food Markets. **Publications:** *Conference Proceedings*, biennial. Contains papers presented at IIFET conferences. ● *IIFET Newsletter*, semiannual. Provides information on association activities, new publications, conferences and workshops, and the fishing industry. **Price:** free for members; free introductory copy for nonmembers ● Membership Directory, annual. **Price:** available to members only. **Conventions/Meetings:** biennial conference, on fisheries and seafood economics (exhibits) - always summer.

1485 ■ North American Association of Fisheries Economists (NAAFE)
c/o IIFET
Dept. of Agriculture and Rsrc. Economics
Oregon State Univ.
Corvallis, OR 97331-3601
Ph: (541)737-1416
Fax: (541)737-2563
E-mail: ann.l.shriver@oregonstate.edu
URL: http://oregonstate.edu/Dept/IIFET/NAAFE/Home.html
Contact: Dr. Lee G. Anderson, Pres.
Founded: 2001. **Members:** 100. **Membership Dues:** regular, $60 (biennial) ● student, $30 (biennial). **Staff:** 2. **Multinational. Description:** Industry, government, and academic fisheries economists. Promotes fisheries management, aquaculture, other marine resources, seafood industry, domestic or international trade in seafood, or similar issues. **Conventions/Meetings:** biennial Economics Forum - conference and workshop, with general sessions to strengthen communication across the fisheries economist profession - held in odd-numbered years.

1486 ■ Norwegian Seafood Export Council (NSEC)
Address Unknown since 2008
URL: http://www.seafood.no/worldwide
Founded: 1991. **Languages:** English, Norwegian. **Multinational. Description:** Engages in the export of seafood. Represents members' interests; gathers and disseminates information regarding Norwegian fisheries and seafood trade; compiles statistics.

Flag

1487 ■ Flag Manufacturers Association of America (FMAA)
15000 Commerce Pkwy., Ste.C
Mount Laurel, NJ 08054
Ph: (856)439-0500
Fax: (856)439-0525
E-mail: fmaa@ahint.com
URL: http://www.fmaa-usa.com
Contact: Sandy Van Lieu, Chair
Founded: 2003. **Membership Dues:** manufacturer, $10,000 (annual) ● related industry, $3,500-$10,000 (annual) ● sponsor, $1,000-$2,500 (annual). **Description:** Represents United States flag manufacturers and suppliers. Educates and promotes the quality, variety and proper use of flags manufactured in the United States. Facilitates the exchange of information within the industry. Assists members in maintaining compliance to existing standards/laws on matters relating to the development and enhancement of the United States manufactured flag industry. **Publications:** Newspaper, quarterly. **Price:** included in membership dues.

1488 ■ National Independent Flag Dealers Association (NIFDA)
214 N Hale St.
Wheaton, IL 60187
Ph: (630)510-4528
Free: (877)544-FLAG
Fax: (630)510-4501
E-mail: info@nifda.org
URL: http://www.flaginfo.com
Contact: Ms. Terry Stevenson, Exec. Dir.
Founded: 1987. **Members:** 130. **Membership Dues:** dealer, associate, manufacturer (with tradeshow), $425 (annual). **Staff:** 2. **Budget:** $75,000. **Description:** Flag retailers and suppliers. Promotes flag merchants whose products are made in the U.S.A. and high standards of ethics and service. Provides referral services and networking opportunities. **Awards:** Golden Grommet. **Frequency:** periodic. **Type:** recognition. **Computer Services:** Electronic publishing ● mailing lists ● online services. **Publications:** *NIFDA News*, bimonthly. Newsletter. **Advertising:** accepted ● Membership Directory. **Conventions/Meetings:** annual conference (exhibits).

Florists

1489 ■ American Floral Industry Association (AFIA)
PO Box 420244
Dallas, TX 75342-0244
Ph: (214)742-2747
Fax: (214)742-2648
E-mail: afia@afia.net
URL: http://www.afia.net
Contact: Ronald D. Poling CAE, Pres.
Founded: 1994. **Members:** 211. **Membership Dues:** regular, $500 (annual) ● affiliate, $250 (annual). **Staff:** 2. **Description:** Strives to act as the national organization for importers, domestic manufacturers, wholesalers, retailers, overseas suppliers, manufacturers sales representatives, etc., of artificial, botanical, Christmas and floral products and accessories. **Awards:** AFIA Scholarship Awards. **Frequency:** annual. **Type:** scholarship. **Recipient:** for member company, employee or dependent. **Formerly:** (2002) American Flower Importers Association. **Publications:** *AFIA Trends*, quarterly. Newsletter. Contains membership information. Alternate Formats: online. **Conventions/Meetings:** semiannual Holiday and Home Expo - trade show (exhibits) - in January and June.

1490 ■ American Institute of Floral Designers (AIFD)
720 Light St.
Baltimore, MD 21230
Ph: (410)752-3318
Fax: (410)752-8295
E-mail: aifd@assnhqtrs.com
URL: http://www.aifd.org
Contact: Thomas C. Shaner CAE, Exec. Dir.
Founded: 1965. **Members:** 1,500. **Membership Dues:** individual, $250 (annual). **Budget:** $1,000,000. **Regional Groups:** 6. **Description:** Active floral designers, associates, retired floral designers, and other individuals. Works to promote the profession and art of floral design. Maintains student chapter. **Awards:** AIFD Award of Design Influence. **Frequency:** periodic. **Type:** recognition. **Recipient:** to a floral designer whose creative work over the years has significantly and positively influenced the direction of American floral design ● AIFD Award of Merit - Industry. **Frequency:** annual. **Type:** recognition. **Recipient:** to members of the floral industry who are serving a crucial role in advancing the industry ● Award of Distinguished Service to AIFD. **Frequency:** annual. **Type:** recognition. **Recipient:** to a member who has demonstrated outstanding service to the institute ● Special Award of Recognition. **Frequency:** periodic. **Type:** recognition. **Recipient:** for meritorious and dedicated service to the institute. **Publications:** *Focal Points*, quarterly. Newsletter. **Conventions/Meetings:** annual Phenomenon - symposium.

1491 ■ Association of Specialty Cut Flower Growers (ASCFG)
PO Box 268
Oberlin, OH 44074
Ph: (440)774-2887
Fax: (440)774-2435
E-mail: ascfg@oberlin.net
Contact: Judy Laushman, Exec. Dir.
Founded: 1988. **Members:** 600. **Membership Dues:** company in U.S. and Canada, international company, $175 (annual) ● additional company, $75 (annual) ● educator, $110 (annual) ● student, cooperative extension, $45 (annual) ● life, $2,000. **Staff:** 1. **Regional Groups:** 8. **Description:** Works to promote the specialty cut flower industry. **Telecommunication Services:** electronic bulletin board. **Publications:** *The Cut Flower Quarterly*. Newsletter. **Circulation:** 1,000. **Advertising:** accepted. **Conventions/Meetings:** annual conference ● regional meeting - 3/year.

1492 ■ International Freeze-Dry Floral Association (IFDFA)
c/o Connie Johnson, Pres.
320 Scandia Ave.
Des Moines, IA 50315
Ph: (515)953-2211
Free: (888)554-9706
E-mail: gardensoftheheart@yahoo.com
URL: http://www.ifdfa.org
Contact: Connie Johnson, Pres.
Founded: 1990. **Members:** 144. **Membership Dues:** regular, $335 (annual). **Regional Groups:** 4. **Description:** Growers, freeze-dry processors, retail florists, home-based crafters, students, educators, suppliers, researchers, and interested individuals. Promotes the interest and improvement in freeze-dried product industry. Encourages the interaction between the different service industries. Compiles and disseminates information on the production of freeze-drieds. Conducts research on the production and marketing of freeze-dried florals and botanicals. **Publications:** *Freeze-Dry Quarterly*. Newsletter. Provides information on industry trends and advances in technology and procedures. **Advertising:** accepted ● Directory. Lists all members and brief profile of their product lines and services. **Advertising:** accepted. **Conventions/Meetings:** annual conference (exhibits) ● annual Trade Fair - meeting.

1493 ■ Society of American Florists (SAF)
1601 Duke St.
Alexandria, VA 22314-3406
Ph: (703)836-8700
Free: (800)336-4743
Fax: (703)836-8705
E-mail: info@safnow.org
Contact: Peter J. Moran, Exec. VP/CEO
Founded: 1884. **Members:** 15,000. **Staff:** 30. **Budget:** $2,000,000. **Description:** Growers, wholesalers, retailers, and allied tradesmen in the floral industry.

Lobbies Congress on behalf of the industry; sponsors educational programs; promotes the floral industry; prepares materials for consumers and for high school and college students; provides business resources. Sponsors Floricultural Hall of Fame, American Academy of Floriculture, and Professional Floral Commentators International. Compiles statistics; sponsors competitions. **Awards: Type:** recognition. **Telecommunication Services:** electronic mail, memberinfo@safnow.org. **Councils:** Retailer; Wholesaler. **Formerly:** (1981) Society of American Florists and Ornamental Horticulturists; (1985) SAF - The Center for Commercial Floriculture. **Publications:** *Dateline: Washington*, 21/year. Newsletter ● *Floral Management*, monthly. Magazine. Informs members of developments in the floral industry; features articles on marketing, government trends, and business practices. **Price:** included in membership dues; $24.00 /year for nonmembers. **Circulation:** 22,967. **Advertising:** accepted. **Conventions/Meetings:** annual Congressional Action Days - meeting - usually March ● annual meeting and conference - always September ● annual Pest Management Conference - meeting and conference.

1494 ■ Teleflora
PO Box 60910
Los Angeles, CA 90060-0910
Free: (800)835-3356
E-mail: service@teleflora.com
URL: http://www.teleflora.com
Contact: Gregg Coccari, Pres.
Founded: 1934. **For-Profit. Description:** Provides service for retail florists who exchange orders by telegraph and telephone for delivery anywhere in the world. **Formerly:** Telegraph Delivery Service.

1495 ■ Wholesale Florist and Florist Supplier Association (WF&FSA)
147 Old Solomons Island Rd., Ste.302
Annapolis, MD 21401
Ph: (410)573-0400
Free: (888)289-3372
Fax: (410)573-5001
E-mail: info@wffsa.org
URL: http://www.wffsa.org
Contact: Jim Wanko, Exec. VP
Founded: 1926. **Members:** 1,300. **Membership Dues:** wholesale, supplier, associate, $495-$1,495 (annual) ● sales representative, $250 (annual). **Staff:** 12. **Budget:** $2,500,000. **Regional Groups:** 6. **Description:** Proprietorships, partnerships or corporations conducting wholesale businesses in fresh flowers, greens, or plants, or engaged in the manufacture and/or wholesaling of florist supplies; others actively engaged in the floral industry are associate members. Preserves and strengthens the wholesale florists' position in the floral industry. Provides a unified voice to promote the wholesalers' contributions to the industry. **Awards:** Leland T. Kintzele Award. **Frequency:** annual. **Type:** recognition. **Recipient:** for outstanding and distinguished service to the industry. **Telecommunication Services:** electronic mail, jwanko@wffsa.org. **Committees:** Communications and Public Relations; Education; Product Audio Tapes; Special Projects; Supply/Demand Advisory; Transportation; Young Executive Group. **Formerly:** (1961) Wholesale Commission Florists of America; (2006) Wholesale Florists and Florist Suppliers of America. **Publications:** *Link Magazine*, 10/year. Covers management and sales techniques, business topics, transportation news, legislative updates, and other developments in the floral industry. **Price:** $20.00 /year for members; $30.00 for nonmembers. **Advertising:** accepted. **Conventions/Meetings:** regional meeting ● seminar ● annual trade show - always in Atlanta, GA.

Food

1496 ■ American Frozen Food Institute (AFFI)
2000 Corporate Ridge, Ste.1000
McLean, VA 22102
Ph: (703)821-0770
Fax: (703)821-1350
E-mail: info@affi.com
URL: http://www.affi.com
Contact: Leslie G. Sarasin, Pres./CEO
Founded: 1942. **Members:** 550. **Membership Dues:** marketing associate, $250 (annual) ● international processor, $2,200 (annual). **Staff:** 18. **Description:** Frozen food processors and allied industry companies who work for the advancement of the frozen food industry. Seeks to improve consumer understanding and acceptance of frozen foods and to increase sales of frozen products through promotional and communications programs. Sponsors retail trade study, consumer and industry education on care and handling of frozen foods. Promotes a cooperative relationship between frozen food processors, suppliers and marketing associates. Represents the frozen food industry before federal, state and local governments. Conducts research to improve the quality of frozen food products. **Committees:** Attorneys; Distribution and Logistics; Environment Issues; International Trade; Microbiology; Political Action; Seafood; Statistics; Western Technical. **Divisions:** Category Promotion; Distribution; Regulatory and Technical Affairs. **Absorbed:** (1969) California Freezers Association; (1982) Frozen Onion Ring Packers Council; (1986) Frozen Foods Action Communications Team. **Formerly:** National Association of Frozen Food Packers. **Publications:** *AFFI Capital Connection*, weekly. Newsletter ● *Frozen Food Pack Statistics* ● *Membership Directory and Buyer's Guide*, annual ● Reports. **Conventions/Meetings:** annual Western Frozen Food Convention - meeting and convention - always February.

1497 ■ American Institute of Food Distribution
1 Broadway, 2nd Fl.
Elmwood Park, NJ 07407
Ph: (201)791-5570
Fax: (201)791-5222
E-mail: info@foodinstitute.com
URL: http://www.foodinstitute.com
Contact: Mark S. Allen, Pres./CEO
Founded: 1928. **Members:** 2,200. **Membership Dues:** regular, $725 (annual). **Staff:** 14. **Multinational. Description:** Canners, packers, freezers, manufacturers, brokers, wholesalers, retailer-cooperatives, chains, independent retailers, growers, trade associations, banks, advertising and government agencies, supply houses, and others working for or with the food trades. Serves as central information service for the food trades. Issues statistical and analytical digests on food distribution and related topics. **Convention/Meeting:** none. **Libraries: Type:** reference. **Subjects:** food industry. **Computer Services:** Electronic publishing, annual studies and weekly and monthly reports ● electronic publishing, monthly Producer Price Index FAX report. **Telecommunication Services:** electronic mail, questions@foodinstitute.com. **Publications:** *Complying with OSHA* ● *FI Daily Email Update*. Newsletters. **Circulation:** 7,500. **Advertising:** accepted. Alternate Formats: online ● *Food Business Mergers and Acquisitions*, annual ● *Food Industry Review*, annual ● *Food Institute Report*, weekly ● *Food Markets in Review*, annual ● *HAACP and U.S. Food Safety Guide* ● *International Profiles* ● *OSHA Manual* ● *Recall Manual*, periodic ● *Regulatory Directory*, periodic ● *U.S. Food Labeling Guide*, periodic.

1498 ■ American Spice Trade Association (ASTA)
2025 M St. NW, Ste.800
Washington, DC 20036
Ph: (202)367-1127
Fax: (202)367-2127
E-mail: info@astaspice.org
URL: http://www.astaspice.org
Contact: Susan Brown, Pres.
Founded: 1907. **Members:** 250. **Membership Dues:** active (maximum), $65,000 (annual) ● broker/agent (first income producer), $4,000 (annual) ● associate, $1,800 (annual). **Staff:** 4. **Budget:** $900,000. **Regional Groups:** 3. **Description:** Works to foment the export of American spices. Promotes the interests of the American spice industry. **Sections:** Technical; Trading and Manufactured Products. **Publications:** *American Spice Trade Association—Membership Roster*, annual. Membership Directory ● *ASTA Analytical Methods*. Article ● *Spice Letter/Broadcast Fax*, monthly. Article. **Price:** available to members only ● Books, periodic ● Brochures ● Catalog ● Manuals ● Reprints ● Also publishes audiovisual materials. **Conventions/Meetings:** annual convention.

1499 ■ American Sugar Alliance (ASA)
2111 Wilson Blvd., Ste.600
Arlington, VA 22201
Ph: (703)351-5055
Fax: (703)351-6698
E-mail: info@sugaralliance.org
URL: http://www.sugaralliance.org
Contact: Vickie Myers, Exec. Dir.
Founded: 1983. **Members:** 300. **Staff:** 5. **Description:** Domestic producers, processors, and refiners of sugar beets, and sugarcane; labor organizations; allied organizations that supply goods and services to the domestic sweetener producing industry. Works to increase public awareness of the international economic and political factors influencing sweetener production; seeks increased support from consumers and the government for a U.S. sugar policy that is favorable to domestic sugar and sweetener producers; strives to maintain among domestic producers the ability to meet the sweetener needs of the U.S. **Formerly:** (1988) U.S. Sweetener Producers Group. **Publications:** *Washington Report*, monthly. Newsletter. **Price:** included in membership dues. **Circulation:** 500. **Conventions/Meetings:** annual International Sweetener Symposium - 2009 Aug. 1-5, Park City, UT; 2010 July 31-Aug. 4, Vail, CO ● seminar.

1500 ■ American Wholesale Marketers Association (AWMA)
2750 Prosperity Ave., Ste.530
Fairfax, VA 22031
Ph: (703)208-3358
Free: (800)482-2962
Fax: (703)573-5738
E-mail: info@awmanet.org
URL: http://www.awmanet.org
Contact: Scott Ramminger, Pres./CEO
Founded: 1991. **Members:** 1,500. **Membership Dues:** wholesale distributor (based on the number of employees), $515-$3,600 ● manufacturer, importer (based on the annual sales volume), $285-$2,835 (annual) ● broker, sales representative (based on the number of employees), $170-$565 (annual) ● retailer, foreign distributor, other allied, $515 (annual). **Staff:** 8. **Budget:** $3,000,000. **Description:** Represents the interests of distributors of convenience products. Its members include wholesalers, retailers, manufacturers, brokers and allied organizations from across the U.S. and abroad. Programs include strong legislative representation in Washington and a broad spectrum of targeted education, business and information services. Sponsors the country's largest show for candy and convenience related products in conjunction with its semi-annual convention. **Awards:** Hall of Fame, Deans. **Frequency:** annual. **Type:** recognition. **Telecommunication Services:** electronic mail, scottr@awmanet.org. **Formed by Merger of:** National Candy Wholesalers Association; National Association of Tobacco Distributors. **Publications:** *Buying Guide and Membership Directory*, annual. **Price:** $200.00 ● *Distribution Channels*, monthly. Magazine. **Price:** $36.00 /year for nonmembers; $66.00 /year for nonmembers (international). **Circulation:** 11,500. **Advertising:** accepted. Alternate Formats: online ● Newsletters. Alternate Formats: online ● Reports. **Conventions/Meetings:** annual Real Deal Expo - convention (exhibits) ● annual Summit and Business Exchange - meeting and conference, features business sessions and scheduled meetings between distributors and suppliers - every September.

1501 ■ Animal Agriculture Alliance
PO Box 9522
Arlington, VA 22219
Ph: (703)562-5160

E-mail: info@animalagalliance.org
URL: http://www.animalagalliance.org
Contact: Ms. Kay Johnson, Exec. VP
Founded: 1987. **Staff:** 3. **Budget:** $250,000. **Description:** Provides educational information about U.S. animal agriculture's contribution to the American consumer's quality of life. Serves as umbrella organization for feed, livestock, and poultry groups to deliver consistent messages to consumers. Provides information on animal agriculture as it relates to animal well-being, food safety, and environmental safety. Works to dispel misconceptions that animals raised for food and other products are mistreated and that a diet containing meat, milk, and eggs is unhealthy. Encourages and sponsors scientific research and educational programs. **Libraries: Type:** open to the public. **Holdings:** articles. **Subjects:** animal agriculture, animal rights, animal care and handling guides, food safety, nutrition. **Computer Services:** database ● mailing lists ● online services. **Boards:** Trustees. **Formerly:** (2002) Animal Industry Foundation. **Publications:** *Alliance Newsletter*, monthly. Contains information on current issues and events related to animal agriculture, animal welfare, food safety, and nutrition as well as animal rights. **Price:** free to contributors. **Circulation:** 3,200 ● *Animal Agriculture: Myths and Facts*. Video ● *Show Animal Care and Handling Guide*. Book.

1502 ■ Association for Dressings and Sauces (ADS)
1100 Johnson Ferry Rd., Ste.300
Atlanta, GA 30342
Ph: (404)252-3663
Fax: (404)252-0774
E-mail: ads@kellencompany.com
URL: http://www.dressings-sauces.org
Contact: Richard E. Cristol, Pres.
Founded: 1933. **Members:** 175. **Membership Dues:** manufacturing (maximum), $34,109 (annual) ● supplier (maximum), $10,201 (annual). **Staff:** 8. **Description:** Manufacturers of mayonnaise, salad dressing, and condiment sauces; associate members are industry suppliers. Administers technical, quality assurance, and regulatory programs. Conducts consumer awareness programs. **Formerly:** Mayonnaise and Salad Dressing Manufacturers Association; (1974) Mayonnaise and Salad Dressing Institute. **Publications:** *Horseradish on the Side* ● *Horseradish - The Secret Ingredient*. Booklet ● *Mayonnaise - The Misunderstood Dressing*. Brochure ● *Salad Dressing Isn't Just for Salads Anymore*. Brochure ● *Wisconsin Cheese and Horseradish*. **Conventions/Meetings:** annual meeting - 2008 Oct. 5-7, Naples, FL ● annual Technical Conference (exhibits).

1503 ■ Association of Food Industries (AFI)
3301 Rte. 66, Ste.205, Bldg. C
Neptune, NJ 07753
Ph: (732)922-3008
Fax: (732)922-3590
E-mail: info@afius.org
URL: http://afi.mytradeassociation.org
Contact: Barbara Harloe, Chair
Founded: 1906. **Members:** 370. **Membership Dues:** import/export agent, $1,040-$1,940 (annual) ● importer/exporter, $1,040-$2,685 (annual) ● associate/overseas, $495 (annual). **Staff:** 5. **Budget:** $500,000. **Description:** Food processors, importers, and import agents nationally; food brokers in the New York metropolitan market and overseas food exporters. Maintains arbitration tribunal, government relations, and information services. **Divisions:** National Honey Packers and Dealers Association (see separate entry); North American Olive Oil Association; Nut and Agricultural Products; Processed Foods. **Affiliated With:** North American Olive Oil Association. **Absorbed:** Olive Oil Association of America. **Formed by Merger of:** Bean Association; Dried Fruit Association of New York; Food Brokers Association. **Formerly:** (1982) Association of Food Distributors. **Publications:** *Import Statistics*, monthly ● *Standard Import Contract*. Bulletins ● Newsletter, bimonthly. **Conventions/Meetings:** annual convention.

1504 ■ California Olive Association (COA)
980 9th St., Ste.230
Sacramento, CA 95814
Ph: (916)444-9260
Fax: (916)444-2746
E-mail: billg@clfp.com
Contact: Bill Grigg, Sec.-Treas.
Founded: 1920. **Members:** 2. **Staff:** 1. **Description:** Canners of black ripe olives. Conducts olive industry programs. **Committees:** International Trade & Government Affairs; Technical Advisory.

1505 ■ Calorie Control Council (CCC)
5775 Peachtree-Dunwoody Rd., Ste.500-G
Atlanta, GA 30342
Ph: (404)252-3663
Fax: (404)252-0774
E-mail: ccc@kellencompany.com
URL: http://www.caloriecontrol.org
Contact: Robin Steagall, Contact
Founded: 1966. **Members:** 60. **Description:** Represents manufacturers of low-calorie and reduced-fat foods and beverages. Works to maintain and enhance communication among the industry, government and regulatory bodies, scientific and medical professionals, and consumers. Responds to inquiries for information and references. Conducts research; evaluates data. Maintains speakers' bureau. **Committees:** Fat Task Force; Government Affairs; Legal; Light Foods and Beverages; Polyol; Public Relations; Technical/Scientific. **Publications:** *Calorie Control Council—Commentary*, semiannual. Newsletter. Summarizes scientific, regulatory, and other developments related to sweeteners, fat substitutes, dietetic foods and beverages, etc. **Price:** free. ISSN: 1049-1791. **Circulation:** 15,000. Alternate Formats: online ● *Fat Replacers: Food Ingredients for Healthy Eating* ● *Winning By Losing - A Guide to Effective Weight Control* ● Brochures. Subjects include acesulfame K, aspartame, saccharin, isomalt, xylitol, HSH, sorbitol, lactitol and sucralose, maltitol, olestra. **Conventions/Meetings:** annual Building Consumer Confidence - meeting (exhibits).

1506 ■ Chocolate Manufacturers Association of the U.S.A. (CMA)
8320 Old Courthouse Rd., Ste.300
Vienna, VA 22182
Ph: (703)790-5750 (703)790-5011
Fax: (703)790-5752
E-mail: info@candyusa.org
URL: http://www.candyusa.org
Contact: Lynn Bragg, Pres.
Founded: 1923. **Members:** 11. **Staff:** 7. **Budget:** $2,000,000. **Description:** Represents manufacturers of cocoa and chocolate products, including solid chocolate products with added fruit, nuts, cereals, or other foods. Finances American Cocoa Research Institute (see separate entry). Compiles statistics. **Additional Websites:** http://www.chocolateusa.org. **Telecommunication Services:** electronic mail, lynn.bragg@chocolateusa.org. **Committees:** International Cocoa; Legislative and Regulatory; Public Relations; Scientific. **Affiliated With:** World Cocoa Foundation. **Formerly:** (1958) Association of Cocoa and Chocolate Manufacturers of the U.S. **Publications:** *The Sweet Journal*, periodic. **Conventions/Meetings:** annual conference.

1507 ■ Cocoa Merchants' Association of America (CMAA)
World Financial Ctr.
One N End Ave., 13th Fl.
New York, NY 10282-1101
Ph: (212)201-8819
Fax: (212)785-5475
E-mail: cmaa@cocoamerchants.com
URL: http://www.cocoamerchants.com
Contact: Lori Trimarchi, Exec. Dir.
Founded: 1924. **Members:** 111. **Membership Dues:** regular class A, $6,500 (annual) ● regular class B, $4,500 (annual) ● associate trade, $3,000 (annual) ● associate, $1,000 (annual). **Budget:** $400,000. **Description:** Dealers and importers of raw cocoa beans and cocoa products. Provides arbitration in contract disputes. Maintains speakers' bureau and a voluntary warehouse inspection program; conducts traffic and orientation seminars; compiles statistics. **Libraries: Type:** reference. **Holdings:** monographs, periodicals. **Subjects:** cocoa bean production. **Committees:** Arbitration; Physical Operations. **Programs:** Warehouse Inspection. **Conventions/Meetings:** periodic convention (exhibits) ● triennial meeting.

1508 ■ Corn Refiners Association (CRA)
1701 Pennsylvania Ave., Ste.950
Washington, DC 20006
Ph: (202)331-1634
Fax: (202)331-2054
URL: http://www.corn.org
Contact: Audrae Erickson, Pres.
Founded: 1913. **Members:** 9. **Staff:** 7. **Budget:** $1,000,000. **Description:** Corn refining firms that manufacture corn starches, sugars, syrups, oils, feed and alcohol by wet process. **Libraries: Type:** not open to the public. **Awards:** Outstanding Paper Awards in Cereal, Carbohydrate Chemistry. **Frequency:** annual. **Type:** monetary. **Formerly:** (1923) American Manufacturers Association of Products From Corn; (1932) Associated Corn Products Manufacturers; (1966) Corn Industries Research Foundation. **Publications:** *Corn Annual*, annual. Report. Features articles on the state of the industry. Includes statistical report on corn shipments, supply and consumption in the U.S. and abroad. **Price:** free. **Circulation:** 8,000. Alternate Formats: online ● Pamphlets. Contains information on corn refining and products. **Conventions/Meetings:** biennial conference, corn utilization and technology (exhibits).

1509 ■ Flavor and Extract Manufacturers Association of the United States (FEMA)
1620 I St. NW, Ste.925
Washington, DC 20006
Ph: (202)293-5800
Fax: (202)463-8998
E-mail: ccook@therobertsgroup.net
URL: http://www.femaflavor.org
Contact: Cathy Cook, Communications Dir.
Founded: 1909. **Members:** 130. **Staff:** 12. **Description:** Firms engaged in the manufacture and sale of flavoring extracts, flavors, flavoring ingredients, and syrups; food processors and other flavor users; manufacturers, wholesalers, and jobbers who supply the industry. **Committees:** Alcohol Tax; Communications; Flavor Ingredients; Flavor Labeling; Government Relations; Information Technology; International Regulatory Affairs; Safety Evaluation; Technical; Vanilla. **Formerly:** Flavoring Extract Manufacturers Association of the U.S. **Publications:** Proceedings, annual. **Conventions/Meetings:** annual meeting.

1510 ■ Food Ingredient Distributors Association (FIDA)
4646 W Jefferson, Ste.200
Fort Wayne, IN 46804
Ph: (260)432-3033
Fax: (260)436-4057
E-mail: ld@proparkwest.com
URL: http://www.fidassoc.com
Contact: Kathy Kennedy, Pres.
Description: Seeks to increase the value of food ingredient distribution services. Promotes professionalism, growth, value of services, training and the development of standards and practices for the food ingredient distribution industry. **Conventions/Meetings:** annual meeting, open to all members - usually held in April or May.

1511 ■ Food Institute (FI)
1 Broadway
Elmwood Park, NJ 07407
Ph: (201)791-5570
Fax: (201)791-5222
E-mail: questions@foodinstitute.com
URL: http://www.foodinstitute.com
Contact: Mark S. Allen, Pres./CEO
Founded: 1928. **Members:** 2,200. **Membership Dues:** general in U.S., $725 (annual) ● general in Canada, $800 (annual) ● general outside U.S. and Canada, $859 (annual). **Multinational. Description:** Growers, food processors, importers, exporters,

brokers, wholesalers, supermarket chains, independent retailers, food industry suppliers, food service distributors, advertising and banking executives, and government officials. Strives to provide food industry-related information to its members. **Publications:** *The Food Institute Report*, weekly. **Price:** included in membership dues; $395.00 /year for nonmembers ● *Get It Out, Get It Right, Get It Over! Avoiding Food Product Recalls*. Report. Contains information on avoiding food product recalls. **Price:** $95.00/copy ● *2000 Edition of Food Business Mergers and Acquisitions*, annual. Report. Contains information on food industry mergers during 2000. **Price:** $295.00 for members.

1512 ■ Food Shippers Association of North America (FSANA)
13240 Northup Way, No. 14
Bellevue, WA 98005
Ph: (425)649-0555
Fax: (425)643-5222
E-mail: bobweiss@fsana.org
URL: http://www.fsana.org
Contact: Robert Weiss, Independent Admin.
Founded: 1996. **Description:** Works to enable export and import companies to maintain their competitiveness in the global marketplace. **Telecommunication Services:** electronic mail, aprilthanos@fsana.org.

1513 ■ Fresh Produce Association of the Americas (FPAA)
PO Box 848
Nogales, AZ 85628-0848
Ph: (520)287-2707
Fax: (520)287-2948
E-mail: info@freshfrommexico.com
URL: http://www.freshfrommexico.com
Contact: Lee Frankel, Pres.
Founded: 1943. **Members:** 120. **Membership Dues:** general, $1,500 (annual). **Staff:** 6. **Languages:** English, Japanese, Spanish. **Description:** Importers, brokers, and suppliers of fruits and vegetables. Ensures market access of high quality produce throughout the world. Facilitates international trade by working with government officials, retailers, purchasers, growers, and consumer groups. Provides information on the safety of imported produce. **Divisions:** Custom House Broker; Grape; Mango; San Diego; Tomato. **Publications:** *FPAA Member Update*, weekly. Newsletter. **Price:** free, for members only. **Circulation:** 130 ● Directory. **Conventions/Meetings:** annual convention (exhibits).

1514 ■ Fresh Produce and Floral Council
16700 Valley View Ave., Ste.130
La Mirada, CA 90638
Ph: (714)739-0177
Fax: (714)739-0226
E-mail: fpfc@aol.com
URL: http://www.fpfc.org/home.htm
Contact: Linda Stine, Pres.
Founded: 1965. **Members:** 630. **Membership Dues:** corporate, $495 (annual) ● student, $50 (annual). **Staff:** 3. **Budget:** $800,000. **Description:** Individuals involved with growing, shipping, wholesaling, brokerage, distributing, or retailing of produce and/or floral items. Strives to stimulate the promotion and sale of fresh fruit, vegetables and floral products, improve the communication between all segments of the industries, and to be more economically efficient. **Publications:** *Fresh Digest*, bimonthly. Newsletter. **Advertising:** accepted. Alternate Formats: online.

1515 ■ Frozen Potato Products Institute (FPPI)
2000 Corporate Ridge, Ste.1000
McLean, VA 22102
Ph: (703)821-0770
Fax: (703)821-1350
E-mail: mgill@affi.com
Contact: Susan M. Siemietkowski, Exec. Dir.
Founded: 1958. **Members:** 7. **Description:** Processors of frozen potato products. **Affiliated With:** American Frozen Food Institute. **Conventions/Meetings:** annual meeting.

1516 ■ The Glutamate Association - U.S. (TGA)
PO Box 14266
Washington, DC 20044-4266
Ph: (202)783-6135
URL: http://www.msgfacts.com
Founded: 1977. **Members:** 12. **Description:** Represents manufacturers, distributors, and processed food users of glutamic acid and its salts, including monosodium glutamate (MSG). Gathers and disseminates information on glutamates; sponsors research on glutamates and food safety; supports public information programs concerning glutamates; provides technical and scientific assistance to industry and government; represents the industry in governmental affairs. **Publications:** *Monosodium Glutamate: A Look at the Facts*. Brochure. Contains information on MSG and its effect as food ingredient. Alternate Formats: online. **Conventions/Meetings:** annual meeting - always spring.

1517 ■ Greek Food and Wine Institute (GFWI)
34-80 48th St.
Long Island City, NY 11101
Ph: (718)729-5277
E-mail: info@gfwi.org
URL: http://www.gfwi.org
Founded: 1992. **Members:** 18. **Staff:** 6. **Languages:** English, Greek. **Description:** Food, wine and spirits producers, importers, and distributors from Greece and the U.S. Educates food and wine trade and consumers about the quality, variety, uses, and healthfulness of Greek foods, wines, and spirits. Conducts educational programs. **Publications:** *Gastronomia*, semiannual. Newsletter. Includes recipes, articles on institute activities, educational articles on Greek food, wine, and spirits, membership news and upcoming events. **Price:** free. **Circulation:** 7,500. **Advertising:** accepted ● *Greek Wine Manual: Guide Sommeliers & Wine Professionals*. **Conventions/Meetings:** annual board meeting, members, prospective members and press - always fall.

1518 ■ Grocery Manufacturers Association/Food Products Association (GMA/FPA)
1305 I St. NW, Ste.300
Washington, DC 20037
Ph: (202)337-9400 (202)639-5918
Fax: (202)337-4508
E-mail: info@gmabrands.com
URL: http://www.gmabrands.com
Contact: Cal Dooley, Pres./CEO
Founded: 1908. **Members:** 129. **Membership Dues:** associate (partner), $25,000 (annual) ● associate (affiliate), $10,000 (annual). **Staff:** 50. **Budget:** $12,000,000. **Description:** Global manufacturers of food and nonfood products sold in the United States. **Additional Websites:** http://www.fpa-food.org. **Committees:** Consumer Affairs; Coupon Advisory; Distribution; International Affairs; Legal; Political Action; Tax; Technical; Washington Representatives. **Absorbed:** (2003) Association of Sales and Marketing Companies. **Formed by Merger of:** (2007) Grocery Manufacturers of America and Food Products Association. **Publications:** *GMA Executive Update*, weekly. Newsletter. Alternate Formats: online ● *State Legislative Report*, weekly ● *Washington Report*, monthly. Newsletter. **Conventions/Meetings:** annual Executive Conference, for top industry executives and retail partners.

1519 ■ Guard Society (GS)
c/o Food Processing Machinery Association
1451 Dolley Madison Blvd., Ste.200
McLean, VA 22101
Ph: (703)761-2600
Fax: (703)761-4334
E-mail: info@fpsa.org
URL: http://www.processfood.com/programs/guard-society.cfm
Contact: Dr. George Melnykovich, Pres.
Founded: 1986. **Members:** 400. **Membership Dues:** individual, $25 (annual) ● life, $300. **Description:** Individuals in and suppliers to the food processing industry. Provides recognition to individuals with many years of service. Supports the industry through promotional work, assistance at exhibits at national and local meetings, and hospitality to visitors to industry-related events. Maintains speakers' bureau. **Awards:** Outstanding Young Professional Service Award. **Frequency:** annual. **Type:** recognition. **Recipient:** to a person less than 40 years of age for outstanding service and potential leadership. **Formed by Merger of:** Old Guard Society; Young Guard Society. **Publications:** *The Guard Society News and Views*. Newsletter. Alternate Formats: online ● *Guard Society Update*, quarterly ● Membership Directory, annual. **Conventions/Meetings:** annual meeting, held in conjunction with the Food Processing Machinery and Supplies Association.

1520 ■ Home Baking Association (HBA)
2931 SW Gainsboro Rd.
Topeka, KS 66614-4413
Ph: (785)478-3283
Fax: (785)478-3024
E-mail: hbapatton@aol.com
URL: http://www.homebaking.org
Contact: Keith Dierberg, Pres.
Founded: 1943. **Members:** 39. **Staff:** 2. **Budget:** $160,000. **Description:** Millers, blenders, home baking ingredient companies and suppliers allied with the sale of home baking supplies nationally. Promotes use of these products through educational campaign to encourage baking in the home. Conducts intensive marketing management seminars. **Libraries: Type:** reference. **Subjects:** teaching materials. **Awards:** Most Outstanding Family and Consumer Sciences Teacher Award. **Frequency:** annual. **Type:** recognition. **Formerly:** Self-Rising Flour Institute; (1990) Self-Rising Flour and Corn Meal Program. **Conventions/Meetings:** annual convention.

1521 ■ International Council of Grocery Manufacturers Associations (ICGMA)
1350 I St. NW, Ste.300
Washington, DC 20005
Ph: (202)337-9400
Fax: (202)337-4508
E-mail: info@icgma.com
URL: http://www.icgma.com
Contact: Monica Gonzalez, Sec.
Founded: 1982. **Members:** 20. **Multinational. Description:** Grocery manufacturers' associations of Australia, Austria, Belgium, Brazil, Canada, Denmark, France, Germany, Italy, Japan, Mexico, New Zealand, South Africa, Switzerland, the United Kingdom, the United States, and Venezuela. Promotes high standards in the manufacture and distribution of grocery products. Coordinates activities of grocery manufacturers worldwide. **Formerly:** (1993) International Assembly of Grocery Manufacturers Associations. **Conventions/Meetings:** annual meeting.

1522 ■ International Dairy-Deli-Bakery Association (IDDBA)
PO Box 5528
Madison, WI 53705-0528
Ph: (608)310-5000
Fax: (608)238-6330
E-mail: iddba@iddba.org
URL: http://www.iddba.org
Contact: Carol Christison, Exec. Dir.
Founded: 1964. **Members:** 1,200. **Membership Dues:** corporate (regular), $450 (annual) ● corporate (retail), $200 (annual) ● corporate (DSD distributor), $250 (annual). **Staff:** 22. **Multinational. Description:** Companies and organizations engaged in the production, processing, packaging, marketing, promotion, and/or selling of cheese and cheese products, bakery, or delicatessen and delicatessen-related items. Aims to further the relationship between manufacturing, production, marketing and distribution channels utilized in the delivery of deli, dairy, and bakery foods to the marketplace. Develops and disseminates information concerning deli, dairy, and bakery foods. **Awards:** Undergraduate/Graduate Scholarships. **Frequency:** annual. **Type:** scholarship. **Recipient:** to high school seniors and current or returning college or vocational/technical school students. **Committees:** Bakery Steering; Dairy Steer-

ing; Deli Steering; Market Research; Products and Services; Program. **Departments:** Education. **Programs:** Food Safety Certification Reimbursement. **Formerly:** (1978) Wisconsin Cheese Seminar; (1978) National Cheese Seminar; (1979) International Cheese and Deli Seminar; (1985) International Cheese and Deli Association; (1991) International Dairy-Deli-Bakery Association. **Publications:** *Dairy-Deli-Bake Digest*, monthly. Newsletter. Contains industry news. **Price:** included in membership dues. **Circulation:** 14,500 ● *Dairy-Deli-Bake Wrap-up*, quarterly. Newsletter. Includes conference report. **Price:** included in membership dues; available to others in related industries. **Circulation:** 14,500 ● *IDDBA and You*, monthly. Newsletter. Alternate Formats: online ● *IDDBA Legis-Letter*. Newsletter. **Price:** included in membership dues. Alternate Formats: online ● *Trainer's Tool Kit*. Newsletter ● *What's In Store*, annual. Report. Trends report on dairy, deli, bakery, and cheese centers. **Price:** $399.00 for nonmembers; included in membership dues ● *Who's Who in Dairy-Deli-Bakery*, periodic. Membership Directory. Features alphabetical, geographical and business classifications for member companies. **Price:** free free, for members only. **Circulation:** 1,200 ● Reports. Includes information on consumer purchasing behavior and attitudes. ● Books ● Videos ● Also distributes audiovisual training materials CD ROMs, and tapes on merchandising. **Conventions/Meetings:** annual conference and seminar (exhibits) - always June.

1523 ■ International Food Additives Council (IFAC)
5775 Peachtree-Dunwoody Rd., Ste.500G
Atlanta, GA 30342
Ph: (404)252-3663
Fax: (404)252-0774
E-mail: ifac@kellencompany.com
Contact: Lyn O. Nabors, Pres.
Founded: 1980. **Members:** 9. **Staff:** 3. **Description:** Consists of manufacturers of food additives and businesses using food additives. Aims to: gather and disseminate information on food additives; represent members' interests; provide technical and scientific assistance. Sponsors research; compiles statistics. **Libraries: Type:** reference. **Holdings:** archival material, audiovisuals, books, periodicals. **Publications:** *Food Additives*. Brochure. **Conventions/Meetings:** annual meeting - usually December.

1524 ■ International Food and Agribusiness Management Association (IAMA)
333 Blocker Bldg.
2124 TAMU
College Station, TX 77843-2124
Ph: (979)845-2118
Fax: (979)862-1487
E-mail: iama@tamu.edu
URL: http://www.ifama.org
Contact: Dr. Jerome Siebert, Exec. VP
Founded: 1990. **Members:** 700. **Membership Dues:** student (full time), $60 (annual) ● professional, $125 (annual) ● institutional, $500 (annual) ● corporate (based on annual revenues), $500-$5,000 (annual) ● president's club, $10,000 (annual). **Staff:** 3. **Multinational. Description:** Stimulates strategic thinking across the food and fiber systems. Serves as a forum for people involved in the food and agribusiness management. **Computer Services:** database, membership directory ● online services, discussion forum. **Caucuses:** Executive Education. **Task Forces:** Contribution of Technology to Supply Chains; Economic and Social Development; Education and Knowledge Transfer; Effective Food Chain Management; Focus Area; Food Safety and Food Security. **Publications:** *Chain Letter*, quarterly. Newsletter. Contains current events associated with the global food chain. ● Annual Report. **Conventions/Meetings:** annual conference, with forum, symposium and case.

1525 ■ International Food Information Council (IFIC)
1100 Connecticut Ave. NW, Ste.430
Washington, DC 20036
Ph: (202)296-6540
Fax: (202)296-6547
E-mail: foodinfo@ific.org
URL: http://ific.org
Contact: Jeff Strei, Dir.
Founded: 1985. **Members:** 31. **Staff:** 22. **Budget:** $2,000,000. **Languages:** English, Spanish. **Description:** Serves as an information and educational resource on nutrition and food safety. Provides science-based information to journalists, health professionals, educators, government officials and other opinion leaders who communicate with the public. **Telecommunication Services:** electronic mail, strei@ific.org. **Committees:** Caffeine; Children's Nutrition; Dietary Fats; Food Biotechnology; MSG. **Publications:** *Food Insight*, bimonthly. Newsletter. Contains current topics in food safety and nutrition. **Price:** free. Alternate Formats: online ● *Guidelines*, bimonthly. Book. Includes tips to scientists, public relations professionals and journalists. Alternate Formats: online ● Brochures, 2-4/year. Provides information on nutrition, food safety, and food ingredients.

1526 ■ International Foodservice Manufacturers Association (IFMA)
2 Prudential Plz.
180 N Stetson Ave., Ste.4400
Chicago, IL 60601
Ph: (312)540-4400
Fax: (312)540-4401
E-mail: ifma@ifmaworld.com
URL: http://www.ifmaworld.com
Contact: Michael J. Licata, Pres./CEO
Founded: 1952. **Members:** 680. **Membership Dues:** regular (based on per million sales over), $25,645 (annual) ● associate (minimum), $2,400 (annual) ● international, $900 (annual). **Staff:** 18. **Multinational. Description:** National and international manufacturers and processors of food, food equipment, and related products for the away-from-home food market. Associate and allied members provide support services to the industry through marketing, publishing, distribution, consulting, promotion, research, advertising, public relations, and brokering. Activities are aimed at marketing, merchandising, sales training, and market research. Compiles statistics. **Awards:** Gold Plate Award. **Frequency:** annual. **Type:** recognition. **Recipient:** to the nation's top operator talent ● Silver Plate Award. **Frequency:** annual. **Type:** recognition. **Recipient:** to the nation's top operator talent. **Committees:** Awards; COEX Conference Planning; Education; International; Market Data; Publishers Activity; Sales and Marketing Conference Planning; Small Business Advisory; Solid Waste Solutions. **Task Forces:** Nonfood; Operator Advisory. **Formerly:** (1959) Institutional Food Manufacturers of America; (1964) Institutional Food Manufacturers Association; (1970) Institutional Food-Service Manufacturers Association. **Publications:** *IFMA World*, 9/year. Newsletter. Includes membership activity information. **Price:** available to members only. **Circulation:** 3,000. Alternate Formats: online ● Membership Directory, annual. **Price:** free for members. Alternate Formats: online ● Books ● Handbooks ● Reports ● Also publishes forecast data, chain restaurant market data; casual dining data; multiple concept data; Canadian and Mexican information, international markets report; compensation survey and top 100 specialty chain data. **Conventions/Meetings:** annual Chain Operators Exchange - conference, for foodservice operators and suppliers ● annual Foodservice Sales and Marketing - conference - always May in Chicago, IL ● annual Forecast and Outlook - seminar - always September ● annual Presidents Conference - meeting - always November ● periodic seminar.

1527 ■ International Frozen Food Association (IFFA)
2000 Corporate Ridge, Ste.1000
McLean, VA 22102
Ph: (703)821-0770
Fax: (703)821-1350
E-mail: info@affi.com
Contact: Leslie G. Sarasin, Deputy Dir. Gen.
Founded: 1973. **Multinational. Description:** Companies and associations engaged in some aspect of the production, distribution, or marketing of frozen food, and firms supplying goods and services in support of those activities. Objectives are to: encourage sound development of the frozen food industry and the production of high quality frozen food in sanitary plants; encourage practical trade in frozen foods through development of appropriate standards of identity, quality, sanitation, labeling, and other trade factors; provide a clearinghouse of industry information, news, and technical reports to implement the above. **Projects:** Physical Distribution; Product Standards; Scientific Research; Trade Relations. **Affiliated With:** American Frozen Food Institute. **Conventions/Meetings:** seminar ● symposium.

1528 ■ International Glutamate Technical Committee (IGTC)
1100 Johnson Ferry Rd.
Atlanta, GA 30342
Ph: (404)252-3663
Fax: (404)252-0774
Contact: Andrew Ebert PhD, Chm.
Founded: 1969. **Members:** 50. **Staff:** 4. **Regional Groups:** 7. **Languages:** Chinese, English, French, Japanese, Korean. **Multinational. Description:** Associations engaged in the manufacture, sale, and commercial use of glutamates; researchers. Gathers and disseminates scientific research data on the use and safety of monosodium glutamate; designs and implements research protocols and provides financial assistance for such research; promotes acceptance of MSG as a food ingredient and "glutamate" as its generic term. Represents members' collective interest. Conducts research programs. **Publications:** none. **Libraries: Type:** reference. **Holdings:** books, monographs, periodicals. **Subjects:** basic medicine, biochemistry, food science. **Awards: Type:** grant ● **Type:** monetary. **Conventions/Meetings:** annual meeting.

1529 ■ International Hydrolyzed Protein Council (IHPC)
555 13th St. NW
Washington, DC 20004-1109
Ph: (202)637-5926
Fax: (202)637-5910
Contact: Martin J. Hahn, Contact
Founded: 1976. **Members:** 20. **Description:** Individuals, firms, and corporations who use or produce hydrolyzed proteins. (Hydrolyzed proteins are extracted from crops such as soybeans, and then broken down into amino acids to be used in the production of flavor enhancer products such as soy sauce or bullion cubes.) Conducts scientific research on the composition, manufacture, and use of hydrolyzed proteins. Works to disseminate research results to the industry, customers, regulatory authorities, and the public. **Conventions/Meetings:** annual board meeting.

1530 ■ International Jelly and Preserve Association (IJPA)
5775 Peachtree-Dunwoody Rd., Ste.500-G
Atlanta, GA 30342
Ph: (404)252-3663
Fax: (404)252-0774
E-mail: webmaster@jelly.org
URL: http://www.jelly.org/homepage.html
Contact: Pamela A Chumley, Exec. Dir.
Founded: 1945. **Members:** 75. **Staff:** 5. **Budget:** $170,000,000. **Description:** Manufacturers of fruit spreads, such as fruit butters, jams, jellies, marmalades, pie fillings, and preserves; producers of bakers' supplies; brokers; suppliers of packaging materials. Works to maintain standards for the preserve industry. Cooperates with federal, state, and municipal authorities to promote uniformity of laws and regulations regarding the industry. Promotes a wider use of fruit spread products; disseminates information to members. Compiles statistics. **Formerly:** National Preservers Association. **Publications:** Manuals. Covers quality assurance techniques, safety procedures, waste management, and raw materials purchase guidelines. ● Membership Directory, annual. **Conventions/Meetings:** annual meeting.

1531 ■ International Maple Syrup Institute (IMSI)
c/o Larry Myott, Exec. Sec.
5014 Rte. 7
Ferrisburg, VT 05456
Ph: (802)877-2250
Fax: (802)877-6659
E-mail: larry.myott@uvm.edu
URL: http://www.internationalmaplesyrupinstitute.com
Contact: Larry Myott, Exec. Sec.
Founded: 1975. **Members:** 25,000. **Staff:** 1. **Regional Groups:** 30. **State Groups:** 13. **Languages:** English, French. **Multinational. Description:** Maple syrup producers, packers, equipment suppliers, government representatives, and extension officers. Promotes the development of the pure maple syrup industry through promotional activities and the improvement of production techniques. Conducts seminars and research programs. Supports or resists legislation which favors or is unfavorable towards the maple syrup industry or its members. **Publications:** *The Pure Maple Syrup Logo (Use and Care Manual).* **Conventions/Meetings:** annual general assembly and convention (exhibits) - always September or October.

1532 ■ International Technical Caramel Association (ITCA)
c/o McKenna Long & Aldridge LLP
1900 K St. NW, Ste.100
Washington, DC 20006
Ph: (202)496-7111
Fax: (202)496-7281
E-mail: fhigginbotham@mckennalong.com
Contact: Francine Higginbotham, Administrator
Founded: 1976. **Members:** 6. **Description:** Companies that produce and use caramel coloring in their products. (Caramel coloring is used in drugs, cosmetics, and foods and beverages such as soft drinks, baked goods, ice cream, and beer.) Promotes public health and safety in the use of caramel coloring. Organizes scientific research projects to study the effects and work to improve the ingredient; disseminates results. Publications: none. **Conventions/Meetings:** annual meeting.

1533 ■ International Wheat Gluten Association (IWGA)
9300 Metcalf Ave., Ste.300
Overland Park, KS 66212
Ph: (913)381-8180
Fax: (913)381-8836
E-mail: pbunn@fbolaw.com
URL: http://www.iwga.net
Contact: G. Peter Bunn III, Gen. Counsel
Founded: 1979. **Members:** 12. **Membership Dues:** regular, $2,000 (annual). **Staff:** 2. **Description:** Producers of wheat gluten and wheat starch. Promotes and expands the utilization of wheat gluten and wheat starch through sponsored technical projects, advertising, and public relations efforts. Conducts research on new uses of wheat gluten. Compiles statistics on worldwide wheat gluten production, import and export, and end-use. **Libraries: Type:** reference. **Subjects:** standard test methods, production application. **Committees:** Promotion and Technical; Regulatory Affairs; Statistical. **Publications:** *Bake Test Methods Manual* ● Membership Directory, annual. **Price:** free. **Conventions/Meetings:** annual conference and meeting.

1534 ■ Italian Wine and Food Institute (IWFI)
PO Box 789
New York, NY 10150-0789
Ph: (212)867-4111
Fax: (212)867-4114
E-mail: iwfi@aol.com
URL: http://www.italianwineandfoodinstitute.com
Contact: Dr. Lucio Caputo, Pres.
Founded: 1984. **Members:** 71. **Membership Dues:** ordinary/associate, $3,000 (annual). **Staff:** 6. **Budget:** $1,000,000. **Description:** Producers, importers, distributors, and marketers of Italian wines and foods. Promotes a positive image of Italian wines and foods among U.S. consumers. Serves as a liaison between the Italian wine and food industry and government, business, and consumers. Supports legislation to stimulate free trade between Italy and the U.S. Holds wine-tastings, prepares market reports, organizes trip to Vinitaly, International Wine Exhibition in Verona, Italy. **Libraries: Type:** not open to the public. **Subjects:** wine, food. **Awards:** Special Achievement - Man/Woman of the Year. **Frequency:** annual. **Type:** recognition. **Recipient:** for individuals who have made outstanding contributions to the industry. **Committees:** Food Advisory; Wine Advisory. **Also Known As:** (1994) CAPUTO. **Publications:** *Discovering Italian Wines*, bimonthly. Bulletins. Covers market and production. **Price:** $300.00 ● *Gala Italia*, bimonthly. Newsletter. Contains information about the American wine market. ● *Market Research on the Wines in the U.S.*. **Price:** $250.00 ● *Notiziario*, bimonthly. Newsletter. Contains information about the American wine market. ● *Notizie in Breve*, bimonthly. Book. **Conventions/Meetings:** semiannual assembly - April and December.

1535 ■ Les Amis d'Escoffier Society of New York
787 Ridgewood Rd.
Millburn, NJ 07041
Ph: (212)414-5820 (973)564-7575
Fax: (973)379-3117
E-mail: kurt@escoffier-society.com
URL: http://www.escoffier-society.com
Contact: Kurt Keller, Exec. Dir./Treas.
Founded: 1936. **Members:** 1,650. **Membership Dues:** regular, $125 (annual). **Regional Groups:** 27. **State Groups:** 2. **Local Groups:** 18. **National Groups:** 29. **Languages:** English, French. **Multinational. Description:** An educational organization of professionals in the food and wine industries. Maintains museum, speakers' bureau, hall of fame, and placement service. Sponsors charitable programs. **Libraries: Type:** reference. **Subjects:** news. **Awards:** Escofferr Chair and Scholarships. **Frequency:** annual. **Type:** recognition ● **Type:** scholarship. **Publications:** Newsletter (in English and French), monthly. **Price:** free. **Conventions/Meetings:** competition ● semiannual meeting.

1536 ■ Mexican American Grocers Association (MAGA)
405 N San Fernando Rd.
Los Angeles, CA 90031
Ph: (323)227-1565
Fax: (323)227-6935
E-mail: maga727@sbcglobal.net
URL: http://www.maga.org
Contact: Steven Soto, Pres./CEO
Founded: 1977. **Description:** Mexican American retail grocers. Committed to information sharing between the grocer industry and the U.S. Mexican/Latino community.

1537 ■ National Alliance for Food Safety and Security (NAFSS)
c/o James H. Denton, Sec.
1260 W Maple Ave., Rm. 0-114
Univ. of Arkansas
Fayetteville, AR 72701
Ph: (501)575-3699
Fax: (501)575-3026
E-mail: jdenton@uark.edu
URL: http://www.nafssfoodsafety.org
Contact: James H. Denton, Sec.
Founded: 1998. **Description:** Improves the safety and security of food supply to ensure the public's health and to enhance national and international food system. Meets the emerging food safety needs of the industry in the areas of food production, processing, transportation, retail and food service. Initiates food safety projects. Addresses global issues on food safety. Conducts research to enhance the safety of food products in the food service, retail environment and market distribution. **Computer Services:** database, alliance member directory. **Publications:** Newsletters ● Annual Report.

1538 ■ National Association of Chewing Gum Manufacturers (NACGM)
15000 Commerce Pkwy., Ste.C
Mount Laurel, NJ 08054
Ph: (856)439-0500
Fax: (856)439-0525
E-mail: nacgm@ahint.com
URL: http://www.nacgm.org
Contact: Robert B. Waller Jr., Exec. Dir.
Founded: 1918. **Members:** 25. **Staff:** 3. **Description:** Manufacturers of chewing gum. **Committees:** Technical. **Publications:** *The Story of Chewing Gum.* Pamphlet. **Conventions/Meetings:** semiannual meeting.

1539 ■ National Association of Flavors and Food-Ingredient Systems (NAFFS)
3301 Rte. 66, Bldg. C, Ste.205
Neptune, NJ 07753
Ph: (732)922-3218
Fax: (732)922-3590
E-mail: info@naffs.org
URL: http://naffs.mytradeassociation.org
Contact: Paula Boudjouk, Pres.
Founded: 1917. **Members:** 105. **Membership Dues:** full, $500 (annual) ● associate, $400 (annual). **Staff:** 5. **Budget:** $50,000. **Description:** Represents manufacturers, processors and suppliers of fruits, flavors, syrups, stabilizers, emulsifiers, colors, sweeteners, cocoa and related food ingredients. **Formerly:** (1975) National Fruit and Syrup Manufacturers Association; (2003) National Association of Fruits, Flavors and Syrups. **Publications:** *Newswire*, semimonthly. Newsletter. **Price:** included in membership dues. Alternate Formats: online ● *Report of Convention Proceedings*, annual. **Advertising:** accepted ● Yearbook, ANN. **Advertising:** accepted. Alternate Formats: online ● Brochure. Alternate Formats: online. **Conventions/Meetings:** annual convention - always September/October ● meeting - 3/year.

1540 ■ National Association of Flour Distributors (NAFD)
c/o Jean La Corte, Pres.
PO Box 610
Montville, NJ 07045
Ph: (973)402-1801 (410)796-0203
Fax: (973)316-6668
E-mail: jean@thecompassgroupinc.com
URL: http://www.thenafd.com
Contact: Jean La Corte, Pres.
Founded: 1919. **Members:** 225. **Membership Dues:** individual, $200 (annual). **Budget:** $160,000. **Regional Groups:** 6. **Local Groups:** 3. **Description:** Jobbers, distributors, brokers, mill representatives and bakery allied manufacturers, engaged in the distribution of bakery flours. **Awards:** Wilson P. Tanner Award. **Frequency:** annual. **Type:** scholarship. **Recipient:** for outstanding service to the organization. **Affiliated With:** National Association of Wholesaler-Distributors. **Publications:** *The Flour Distributor*, semiannual. Newsletter ● Membership Directory, annual. **Conventions/Meetings:** annual convention - always May.

1541 ■ National Association for the Specialty Food Trade (NASFT)
120 Wall St., 27th Fl.
New York, NY 10005
Ph: (212)482-6440
Fax: (212)482-6459
E-mail: customerservice@specialtyfood.com
URL: http://www.specialtyfood.com
Contact: Ann Daw, Pres.
Founded: 1952. **Members:** 2,800. **Membership Dues:** general, $200-$600 (annual). **Staff:** 42. **Description:** Represents manufacturers, distributors, processors, importers, retailers, and brokers of specialty and gourmet foods. **Awards:** sofi awards. **Frequency:** annual. **Type:** recognition. **Recipient:** to outstanding specialty foods. **Publications:** *Show Directory*, periodic. **Price:** $30.00 for purchase after the show ● *Specialty Food Magazine*, 10/year. Provides excellent advertising vehicle for specialty food marketers to reach over 30,100 members of the buying trade. **Price:** $134.00 international; $45.00

domestic. **Advertising:** accepted. **Conventions/Meetings:** competition - 3/year. 2008 June 29-July 1, New York, NY.

1542 ■ National Barbecue Association (NBBQA)
1306-A W Anderson Ln.
Austin, TX 78757
Ph: (512)454-8626
Free: (888)909-2121
Fax: (512)454-3036
E-mail: nbbqa@assnmgmt.com
URL: http://www.nbbqa.org
Contact: Don McCullough CAE, Exec. VP
Founded: 1991. **Members:** 600. **Membership Dues:** individual in U.S., affiliate, $50 (annual) ● business in U.S., affiliated association, $150 (annual) ● individual in Canada, $60 (annual) ● business in Canada, $160 (annual) ● individual outside U.S. and Canada, $85 (annual) ● business outside U.S. and Canada, $185 (annual). **Staff:** 2. **Budget:** $225,000. **Description:** Industry professionals and barbecue enthusiasts including restaurants, caterers, specialty equipment retailers, grill manufacturers and distributors, smoker manufacturers and distributors, food product suppliers and distributors, sauces and spice distributors, backyard hobbyists. **Awards:** Award of Excellence and People's Choice. **Frequency:** annual. **Type:** recognition. **Recipient:** for barbecue sauces/rubs/marinades. **Publications:** *National Barbecue News*, monthly. Newsletter. **Price:** available to members only. **Circulation:** 1,500. **Advertising:** accepted ● *NBBQA Annual Membership Directory*, annual ● *NBBQA Barbecue Buyers' Guide*, annual. Directory. **Price:** $25.00. **Advertising:** accepted ● Brochure. Alternate Formats: online. **Conventions/Meetings:** annual conference and trade show, with outdoor cooking demonstrations (exhibits).

1543 ■ National Center for Food Safety and Technology (NCFST)
6502 S Archer Rd.
Summit, IL 60501-1957
Ph: (708)563-1576 (708)563-8267
Fax: (708)563-1873
E-mail: nnoka@iit.edu
URL: http://www.ncfst.iit.edu
Contact: Dr. Martin Cole, Dir.
Founded: 1988. **Description:** Consortium of leading food companies, FDA, Illinois Institute of Technology and university-based scientists. Works to ensure the safety of food processing and packaging technologies. **Committees:** Technical Advisory. **Special Interest Groups:** Allergens and Food Contaminants; Food Defense; Food Packaging; Food Processing; Microbiology. **Publications:** *Food Safety Watch*, 3/year. Newsletter. Reports activities of the center and technical briefs related to research. **Circulation:** 1,000. Alternate Formats: online. **Conventions/Meetings:** annual symposium.

1544 ■ National Confectioners Association of the U.S. (NCA)
8320 Old Courthouse Rd., Ste.300
Vienna, VA 22182
Ph: (703)790-5750
Free: (800)433-1200
Fax: (703)790-5752
E-mail: info@candyusa.org
URL: http://www.candyusa.org
Contact: Susan S. Smith, Sr. VP for Public Affairs
Founded: 1884. **Members:** 700. **Staff:** 27. **Budget:** $5,000,000. **Description:** Represents manufacturers of confectionery products; suppliers to the industry. Conducts research and technical and governmental services; provides information to the public; conducts annual confectionery technology course at the University of Wisconsin, Madison; gathers statistics on the industry. **Additional Websites:** http://www.ecandy.com. **Committees:** All Candy Expo; Political Action; Public Relations; Research; Technical; Trade Relations. **Affiliated With:** Chocolate Manufacturers Association of the U.S.A.; World Cocoa Foundation. **Publications:** *A Year of Confectionery*, annual. Magazine. **Conventions/Meetings:** annual All Candy Expo - convention, for manufacturers of confectionery to showcase products for buyers; not open to public (exhibits).

1545 ■ National Country Ham Association (NCHA)
PO Box 948
Conover, NC 28613
Ph: (828)466-2760
Free: (800)820-4426
Fax: (828)466-2770
E-mail: eatham@countryham.org
URL: http://www.countryham.org
Founded: 1992. **Members:** 50. **State Groups:** 6. **Description:** Represents country ham producers in the United States. Members include processors, suppliers, and academic advisors. **Computer Services:** Mailing lists. **Affiliated With:** American Association of Meat Processors. **Publications:** *Country Ham Cookbook*. Includes recipes of all country cured meats. ● *Taste the Tradition*. Brochure. Contains innovative recipes from chefs across the country. **Circulation:** 8,000 ● Survey. Features attitudes and opinions on marketing. **Conventions/Meetings:** annual meeting, with workshops.

1546 ■ National Frozen Pizza Institute (NFPI)
2000 Corporate Ridge, Ste.1000
McLean, VA 22102
Ph: (703)821-0770
Fax: (703)821-1350
URL: http://www.affi.com/nfpi/nfpihomepage.htm
Contact: Robert L. Garfield, Exec. Dir./Sec.
Founded: 1975. **Members:** 40. **Membership Dues:** packer (based on annual gross sales for the most recent fiscal year), $440-$7,150 (annual) ● associate, $650 (annual). **Description:** Aims to advance the interests of the frozen pizza industry. Monitors federal regulatory agency activities affecting frozen pizza processors and serves as an information resource for the trade and general public about the nutrition, value and convenience of frozen pizza and pizza products. **Committees:** Food Service; Retail; Technical and Regulatory. **Affiliated With:** American Frozen Food Institute. **Publications:** Membership Directory, biennial. **Conventions/Meetings:** annual meeting - always fall in Washington, DC or Chicago, IL.

1547 ■ National Frozen and Refrigerated Foods Association (NFRA)
PO Box 6069
Harrisburg, PA 17112
Ph: (717)657-8601
Fax: (717)657-9862
E-mail: info@nfraweb.org
URL: http://www.nfraweb.org
Contact: Nevin B. Montgomery, Pres./CEO
Founded: 1945. **Members:** 450. **Membership Dues:** foodservice operator, retailer/wholesaler, international, $485 (annual) ● logistics provider, $760-$1,230 (annual) ● supplier, $1,020 (annual) ● manufacturer, $1,490-$11,670 (annual) ● distributor, $900-$3,935 (annual) ● sales agent/broker, $670 (annual) ● local frozen food association, $100 (annual). **Staff:** 8. **Multinational. Description:** Comprised of over 400 member companies representing all segments of the frozen and refrigerated dairy foods industry. Promotes the sales and consumption of frozen and refrigerated foods through education, training, research, sales planning and menu development, and provides a forum for industry dialogue. Sponsors National Frozen Food Month, in March; June Dairy Month; June and July Ice Cream and Novelties Promotion; Frozen and Refrigerated Foods Festival, in October; and Bring Us To Your Table! Freezer Favorites. **Awards:** Golden Penguin Award. **Frequency:** annual. **Type:** recognition. **Recipient:** for outstanding promotion of March National Frozen Food Month. **Telecommunication Services:** electronic mail, nevin@nfraweb.org. **Committees:** Buying Group; Foodservice Marketing; Government Relations; Ice Cream/Novelties; National Distributors; National Frozen Food Month; School Foodservice. **Councils:** Foodservice; Manufacturer Advisory; Retail. **Absorbed:** Foodservice Organization of Distributors. **Formerly:** (1945) National Wholesale Frozen Food Distributors Association; (1955) National Frozen Food Distributors Association; (2002) National Frozen Food Association. **Publications:** *A Golden Opportunity*. Brochure. Alternate Formats: online ● *Editorial Kit*, annual ● *Frozen Food Book of Knowledge* ● *National Frozen Food Association Directory*, annual. Lists executives, products, and capabilities of NFFA member companies. **Price:** $195.00 for nonmembers. **Circulation:** 3,500. **Advertising:** accepted ● *Program and Directory*. Handbook. **Advertising:** accepted ● *2003 Planning Guide* ● *Year End Report*, annual. Annual Report. **Price:** $10.00 for members; $50.00 for nonmembers. Alternate Formats: online ● Newsletters. Alternate Formats: online ● Membership Directory, annual. **Price:** $25.00 for members; $195.00 for nonmembers. **Advertising:** accepted ● Books ● March National Frozen Food Month Idea Book Editorial Kit, Research Study on Activity Based Cost Management, Retail Consumer Study. **Conventions/Meetings:** annual meeting - always October ● annual Retail Executive Conference - workshop, with speakers - always April.

1548 ■ National Honey Board (NHB)
11409 Bus. Park Cir., Ste.210
Firestone, CO 80504
Ph: (303)776-2337
Fax: (303)776-1177
E-mail: americanhoney@hughes.net
URL: http://www.honey.com
Contact: Buddy Ashurst, Chm.
Founded: 1986. **Staff:** 9. **Budget:** $3,500,000. **Description:** Focuses on honey research, marketing, and promotion.

1549 ■ National Honey Packers and Dealers Association (NHPDA)
3301 Rte. 66, Ste.205, Bldg. C
Neptune, NJ 07753
Ph: (732)922-3008
Fax: (732)922-3590
E-mail: info@nhpda.org
URL: http://www.mytradeassociation.org/nhpda
Contact: Bob Bauer, Exec. VP
Founded: 1950. **Members:** 40. **Membership Dues:** packer, importer, international, associate, $600 (annual). **Staff:** 5. **Description:** Represents cooperative and independent processors, packers, and dealers of honey at either the wholesale or retail level. Offers members information on testing facilities for honey analysis. Consults with Department of Agriculture on research programs in the field of honey marketing. **Publications:** Newsletter, distributed on a regular basis. Features subjects of interest and importance to the members. ● Annual Report, annual. **Conventions/Meetings:** annual meeting - usually January.

1550 ■ National Pasta Association (NPA)
1156 15th St. NW, Ste.900
Washington, DC 20005
Ph: (202)637-5888
Fax: (202)223-9741
E-mail: info@ilovepasta.org
URL: http://www.ilovepasta.org
Contact: Jula J. Kinnaird, Pres.
Founded: 1904. **Members:** 80. **Staff:** 4. **Budget:** $1,000,000. **Description:** Manufacturers of pasta in the U.S. and suppliers to the industry. Seeks to improve manufacturer and supplier efficiency. Conducts agricultural and technical research programs. Sponsors U.S. pasta product public relations program and pasta/durum wheat technical course. **Committees:** Government Relations; Industry Affairs; Internal Affairs; Pasta Product Promotion; Technical Affairs. **Formerly:** (1981) National Macaroni Manufacturers Association. **Publications:** *National Pasta Association—FYI*, biweekly. Newsletter. Provides information on new products, commodities, mergers, and trends within the industry. **Price:** available to members only ● *Pasta Industry Directory*, annual. Lists, by category, pasta manufacturers and industry suppliers, including contact names. **Price:** $50.00/issue. **Advertising:** accepted ● *Pasta Journal*, bimonthly. Provides information on the pasta industry; includes new products. **Price:** $18.00 for members in U.S.; $35.00

for nonmembers in U.S.; $28.50 for members outside U.S.; $45.00 for nonmembers outside U.S. ISSN: 8750-9393. **Circulation:** 850. **Advertising:** accepted ● Also publishes consumer brochures. **Conventions/ Meetings:** annual meeting.

1551 ■ National Poultry and Food Distributors Association (NPFDA)
958 McEver Rd. Extension, Unit B-8
Gainesville, GA 30504
Ph: (770)535-9901
Free: (877)845-1545
Fax: (770)535-7385
E-mail: info@npfda.org
URL: http://www.npfda.org
Contact: Kristin McWhorter, Exec. Dir./Sec.
Founded: 1967. **Members:** 250. **Membership Dues:** branch location, $100 (annual) ● independent/ processor distributor, broker/trader/market specialist, supply/transportation company, $450 (annual). **Staff:** 2. **Budget:** $200,000. **Description:** Distributors, processors, and food brokers; supply and transportation companies. Provides benefits, services, and network opportunities to industry companies giving them the competitive advantage, lowering their costs, and increasing their profits. Provides market information. **Libraries: Type:** reference. **Holdings:** audiovisuals, books, clippings, periodicals. **Awards:** Industry Lifetime Achievement Award. **Frequency:** annual. **Type:** recognition. **Recipient:** for an individual active in the poultry industry with significant contributions ● Member of the Year Award. **Frequency:** annual. **Type:** recognition. **Recipient:** for services to industry, the Association, and the consuming public ● NPFDA Scholarship Foundation. **Frequency:** annual. **Type:** scholarship. **Recipient:** for a junior or senior enrolled in poultry or related degree. **Computer Services:** Online services, members' only section, directory. **Telecommunication Services:** electronic bulletin board. **Committees:** Financial; Handbook; Legislative; Man of the Year; Meetings; Membership; Nominating; Scholarship. **Formerly:** (1993) National Independent Poultry and Food Distributors Association. **Publications:** *NPFDA Membership Directory*, annual. **Price:** included in membership dues; $50.00 for nonmembers. **Circulation:** 300. **Advertising:** accepted ● *NPFDA News*, monthly. Newsletter. **Price:** included in membership dues. **Circulation:** 250. **Advertising:** accepted ● Directory, annual. **Price:** included in membership dues; $50.00 for nonmembers. **Circulation:** 300. **Advertising:** accepted. **Conventions/Meetings:** annual convention - always January ● annual meeting, for membership - fall ● annual Poultry Suppliers Showcase - trade show (exhibits) ● annual seminar, with networking and sports.

1552 ■ National Seasoning Manufacturers Association (NSMA)
c/o Dr. Richard H. Alsmeyer, Exec. Dir.
2527 Mill Race Rd.
Frederick, MD 21701
Ph: (301)694-0419 (301)299-8009
Fax: (301)299-7523
E-mail: alsmeyerfood@isp.com
Contact: Dr. Richard H. Alsmeyer, Exec. Dir.
Founded: 1972. **Members:** 21. **Membership Dues:** voting, corporate, $750 (annual). **Staff:** 1. **Budget:** $20,000. **Multinational. Description:** Food seasoning manufacturers; producers of meat curing compounds, flavors, supplies, services, and equipment used for the seasoning and preserving of food products. Seeks to promote and continue scientific study and research in the food seasoning industry, and to improve relations between the industry, related associations, and U.S. food regulatory agencies. **Libraries: Type:** reference; not open to the public. **Holdings:** archival material. **Committees:** Government Liaison; Trade Relations. **Formerly:** (1981) National Association of Meat Seasoning Manufacturers; (1984) National Association of Meat and Food Seasoning Manufacturers. **Publications:** Newsletter, quarterly. **Price:** free, for members only. **Conventions/Meetings:** annual conference (exhibits) - usually July ● annual meeting, held in conjunction with Institute of Food Technologists.

1553 ■ National Sugar Ingredient Marketing Association
Address Unknown since 2007
Founded: 1903. **Members:** 52. **Membership Dues:** $400 (annual). **Staff:** 1. **Description:** Persons and businesses selling sugar to food processors, grocery retailers, and wholesalers. Purposes are: to promote the interests of all those engaged in the sugar industry including sellers, buyers, and brokers; to define, establish, and maintain rules and regulations for the sound, ethical, and progressive conduct of the sugar brokerage business; to eliminate unfair and unlawful business practices in the sugar industry. Holds meetings and discussions; encourages the exchange of ideas and opinions among members. Compiles and disseminates statistical and other information relating to the industry and sugar brokerage business. **Publications:** *N.S.B.A. Newsletter*, bimonthly. **Conventions/Meetings:** annual meeting.

1554 ■ Network of Ingredient Marketing Specialists (NIMS)
c/o Mr. Kenneth W. Reynolds, Exec. Dir.
630 Village Trace NE, Bldg. 15, Ste.A
Marietta, GA 30067
Ph: (770)989-0049
Fax: (770)956-7498
E-mail: kreynolds@nimsgroup.com
URL: http://www.nimsgroup.com
Contact: Mr. Kenneth W. Reynolds, Exec. Dir.
Founded: 1981. **Members:** 17. **Staff:** 1. **Description:** Food ingredient manufacturers' representatives. Serves as a referral service for food producers and distributors seeking food ingredient sales representation in various regions of the U.S. and Canada. **Formerly:** (1993) National Ingredient Marketing Specialists; (1998) Northamerican Ingredient Marketing Specialists. **Conventions/Meetings:** annual Sales and Marketing Meeting.

1555 ■ North American Natural Casing Association (NANCA)
c/o Leon Van Leeuwen Corp.
494 8th Ave., Ste.805
New York, NY 10001
Ph: (212)695-4980
Fax: (212)695-7153
E-mail: nanca18hq@yahoo.com
URL: http://www.nanca.org
Contact: Howard deWied, Sec./Exec. VP
Founded: 1990. **Members:** 35. **Staff:** 1. **Budget:** $128,000. **Multinational. Description:** Seeks to respond to issue and service needs unique to the North American segment of the natural casing industry. **Committees:** Government Affairs; Industry Image/Public Relations. **Publications:** *NANCA News*, quarterly. Newsletter. **Circulation:** 100. Alternate Formats: online. **Conventions/Meetings:** annual meeting and convention.

1556 ■ Peanut and Tree Nut Processors Association (PTNPA)
PO Box 59811
Potomac, MD 20859-9811
Ph: (301)365-2521
Fax: (301)365-7705
E-mail: rbarker@ptnpa.org
URL: http://www.ptnpa.org
Contact: Russell E. Barker, Pres./CEO
Founded: 1969. **Members:** 160. **Membership Dues:** active (based on the quantity of nuts packaged/ processed for the most recent fiscal year), $1,400-$5,000 (annual) ● associate; $1,150 (annual). **Staff:** 3. **Description:** Represents manufacturers of peanut butter, peanut butter sandwiches, packaged nuts, salted nuts, and other peanut and tree nut products, as well as suppliers of goods and services to the industry. **Committees:** Technical. **Absorbed:** Peanut Butter Sandwich and Cookie Manufacturers Association. **Formed by Merger of:** Peanut Butter Manufacturers Association; Peanut and Nut Salters Association. **Formerly:** Peanut Butter and Nut Processors Association; (1979) Peanut Butter Manufacturers and Nut Salters Association. **Publications:** Membership Directory, annual ● Newsletter, periodic. **Conventions/Meetings:** annual convention and trade show (exhibits) - always January.

1557 ■ Pickle Packers International (PPI)
1620 I St. NW, Ste.925
Washington, DC 20006
Ph: (202)331-2456
Fax: (202)463-8998
E-mail: bbursiek@therobertsgroup.net
URL: http://ilovepickles.org
Contact: Richard Hentschel, Exec. VP
Founded: 1893. **Members:** 188. **Membership Dues:** manufacturer, associate, broker, $1,500 (annual). **Staff:** 3. **Description:** Represents the interests of pickle and sauerkraut manufacturers, salters, salt stockbrokers and suppliers. **Awards:** Hall of Fame Award. **Type:** recognition. **Recipient:** for an individual who has contributed the most to the pickle industry. **Formerly:** (1963) National Pickle Packers Association. **Publications:** Directory, annual. **Price:** available to members only. **Conventions/Meetings:** annual conference and meeting ● biennial Fall Business Conference - meeting - always held in even-numbered years ● biennial Pickle Fair - meeting (exhibits) - always held in odd-numbered years.

1558 ■ PMCA: An International Association of Confectioners
2980 Linden St., Ste.E3
Bethlehem, PA 18017
Ph: (610)625-4655
Fax: (610)625-4657
E-mail: info@pmca.com
URL: http://www.pmca.com
Contact: Yvette Thomas, Admin. Dir.
Founded: 1907. **Members:** 435. **Membership Dues:** associate/active in U.S., $250 (annual) ● associate/ active outside U.S., $275 (annual). **Staff:** 2. **Multinational. Description:** Manufacturers and suppliers of confectionery and chocolate products. Conducts research and educational programs. **Libraries: Type:** reference. **Holdings:** 1,000; books. **Subjects:** research and production, confectionery technology. **Awards:** Graduate Confectionary Fellowship at Penn State. **Frequency:** biennial. **Type:** scholarship. **Recipient:** for food science, chemistry, chemical engineering, or biology students. **Committees:** Education and Training; Finance; Membership; PMCA Research; Production Conference. **Formerly:** (1992) Association of Manufacturers of Confectionary and Chocolate; (1999) Pennsylvania Manufacturing Confectioner's Association. **Publications:** *Annual Production Conference Proceedings*, annual. **Price:** $40.00. Alternate Formats: CD-ROM ● *PMCA News Update*, quarterly. Newsletter. **Circulation:** 890. **Conventions/Meetings:** annual Production Conference - seminar and conference, confectionery production (exhibits).

1559 ■ Popcorn Institute (PI)
401 N Michigan Ave., Ste.2200
Chicago, IL 60611-4267
Ph: (312)644-6610 (312)673-4883
Fax: (312)527-6783
E-mail: gbertalmio@smithbucklin.com
Contact: Ms. Deirdre Flynn, Exec. Dir.
Founded: 1943. **Members:** 25. **Staff:** 2. **Budget:** $18,000. **Description:** Represents companies engaged in popcorn processing and trade management activities as well as government relations. Provides a platform for discussion on the popcorn industry. Maintains hall of fame for retired members who have made contributions to the industry. **Absorbed:** (1960) Popcorn Processors Association.

1560 ■ Refrigerated Foods Association (RFA)
2971 Flowers Rd. S, Ste.266
Atlanta, GA 30341
Ph: (770)452-0660
Fax: (770)455-3879
E-mail: info@refrigeratedfoods.org
URL: http://www.refrigeratedfoods.org
Contact: Judy Stokes Gervais, Founding Exec. Dir.
Founded: 1980. **Members:** 200. **Membership Dues:** associate, $700 (annual) ● manufacturer (based on annual sales volume), $700-$4,150 (annual) ● affili-

ate, $2,000 (annual) ● professional/academic, $50 (annual). **Staff:** 2. **Budget:** $400,000. **Description:** Represents firms or individuals involved in the manufacture of refrigerated foods; others interested in the industry. Seeks to advance the use and distribution of refrigerated foods; discusses problems common to the industry. **Libraries: Type:** reference. **Holdings:** books, reports. **Subjects:** refrigerated foods. **Telecommunication Services:** electronic mail, terry@refrigeratedfoods.org. **Committees:** Conference; Environmental; Foundation; International; Marketing; New Ideas; Publicity; Retention; Technical. **Councils:** Young Managers. **Formerly:** (1992) Salad Manufacturers Association. **Publications:** *Chill In! Membership Bulletin*. Includes membership news and updates on association's activities. **Price:** free. **Advertising:** accepted ● *Chilled News Review and Technical Newsletter*, 5/year. Covers technical and marketing aspects of the industry; includes news of projects, conventions, and expositions. **Price:** free. **Advertising:** accepted ● *Quarterly Technical Newsletter* ● Membership Directory, biennial. Lists contact names, addresses, e-mails, web sites and product information on the entire membership. **Price:** available to members only. Alternate Formats: online. **Conventions/Meetings:** annual conference, includes exhibition in even-numbered years (exhibits) - usually late February/early March.

1561 ■ Retail Confectioners International (RCI)
1807 Glenview Rd.
Glenview, IL 60025
Ph: (847)724-6120
Free: (800)545-5381
Fax: (847)724-2719
E-mail: van@retailconfectioners.org
URL: http://www.retailconfectioners.org
Contact: Van Billington, Exec. Dir.
Founded: 1917. **Members:** 600. **Membership Dues:** manufacturing retailer (based on annual candy sales volume), $150-$785 (annual) ● supplier (based on number of employees), $565-$1,130 (annual) ● manufacturing retailer-retired, $85 (annual). **Staff:** 2. **Budget:** $500,000. **Description:** Manufacturing retail confectioners who make and sell their own candies through directly owned retail candy shops; associates are suppliers to the industry. Provides education, promotion, and legislative and information service. Monitors legislative activities that affect the industry at state and national levels. Holds comprehensive two-week course and one-week specialized course on retail candy making biennially. **Awards: Type:** recognition. **Formerly:** Associated Retail Confectioners of the U.S.; (1970) Associated Retail Confectioners of North America. **Publications:** *Kettle Talk*, bimonthly. Newsletter. Includes confection recipes. **Price:** free for members. **Circulation:** 600. **Advertising:** accepted ● *Retail Confectioners International Bulletins*, periodic ● Membership Directory, annual. **Advertising:** accepted. **Conventions/Meetings:** annual convention (exhibits) - always June.

1562 ■ Snack Food Association (SFA)
1600 Wilson Blvd., Ste.650
Arlington, VA 22209
Ph: (703)836-4500
Free: (800)628-1334
Fax: (703)836-8262
E-mail: sfa@sfa.org
URL: http://www.sfa.org
Contact: James A. McCarthy, Pres./CEO
Founded: 1937. **Members:** 800. **Staff:** 13. **Budget:** $3,000,000. **Description:** Manufacturers of potato chips, pretzels, corn chips, tortilla chips, popcorn, cheese snacks, pork rinds, cookies, crackers, nuts, meat snacks, fruit snacks, and grain-based snacks; associate members are suppliers and distributors of fats and oils, packaging supplies, machinery, seasonings, and potato and corn growers. **Telecommunication Services:** electronic mail, jmccarthy@sfa.org. **Committees:** Legislative; Marketing; Production; Sales and Merchandising; Snack Pac; Technical. **Formerly:** National Potato Chip Institute; (1975) Potato Chip Institute, International; (1986) Potato Chip/Snack Food Association. **Publications:** *Snack Food and Wholesale Bakery*, monthly. Magazine. Features information on the latest industry news, marketing updates, technical advances and international developments in the snack food industry. ● *The Snack Report*, weekly. Newsletter. Contains up-to-date information on association activities while also highlighting snack food industry news and events. **Price:** included in membership dues. Alternate Formats: online ● *State of the Industry Report*, annual. Examines domestic sales of snack food by category. ● *Who's Who in the International Snack Food Industry*, annual. Directory. Provides information on all SFA member companies including key contacts, brands, products produced, number of employees and distribution methods. **Conventions/Meetings:** annual SNAXPO - trade show, for the snack food industry (exhibits).

1563 ■ Soy Protein Council (SPC)
1255 23rd St. NW
Washington, DC 20037-1174
Ph: (202)467-6610
Fax: (202)466-4949
E-mail: spinfo@spcouncil.org
URL: http://www.spcouncil.org
Contact: David A. Saunders, Exec. VP
Founded: 1971. **Members:** 3. **Staff:** 2. **Description:** Persons, firms, and corporations regularly engaged within the U.S. in the actual processing and sale of soy proteins or food products containing soy proteins. Seeks to: promote the acceptance of soy protein products; provide the public and industry with information concerning use and benefits of soy protein products; assist legislative and regulatory bodies in developing laws and policies relating to soy protein products; collect pertinent statistical and other industry information. **Publications:** *Soy Protein Products: Characteristics, Nutritional Aspects, and Utilization*. Book. Provides an overview of the key benefits of soy protein products. **Price:** one copy free. **Conventions/Meetings:** periodic board meeting ● seminar, for foreign industry and government officials.

1564 ■ Sugar Association (SA)
1300 L St. NW, Ste.1001
Washington, DC 20005
Ph: (202)785-1122
Fax: (202)785-5019
E-mail: sugar@sugar.org
URL: http://www.sugar.org
Contact: Andrew C. Briscoe, Pres./CEO
Founded: 1943. **Members:** 23. **Staff:** 10. **Budget:** $2,000,000. **Description:** Represents processors, refiners, and growers of beet sugar and cane sugar. Disseminates scientifically based information on the nutritional and health aspects of sucrose. Promotes research. Sponsors educational programs on sugar and its role in a balanced diet. **Libraries: Type:** reference. **Holdings:** 3,500. **Subjects:** sugar. **Publications:** *Fit for Life*. Brochure. **Price:** free ● *On Your Mark*, quarterly. Newsletter. Covers nutrition and fitness emphasizing recent developments concerning sugar and health. **Price:** free. **Circulation:** 8,000 ● *Refining and Processing Sugar*. Brochure. **Price:** free ● *Sugar Consumption. The Truth*. Brochure. Provides accurate data based on USDA information of sugar consumption in the United States. **Price:** free ● *Sugar Note and News*, quarterly. Report. Features reports on current topics of interest to sugar users and producer. **Circulation:** 4,000 ● Booklets ● Brochures ● Videos. **Conventions/Meetings:** annual meeting.

1565 ■ Tortilla Industry Association (TIA)
8201 Greensboro Dr., Ste.300
McLean, VA 22102
Ph: (703)610-9036 (703)610-0258
Fax: (703)610-9005
E-mail: info@tortilla-info.com
URL: http://www.tortilla-info.com
Contact: Roberto Quinones, Exec. Dir.
Founded: 1990. **Members:** 180. **Membership Dues:** affiliate, $2,000 (annual) ● associate, $500 (annual) ● regular (based on annual sales), $500-$2,000 (annual). **Staff:** 2. **Budget:** $500,000. **Languages:** English, Spanish. **Multinational. Description:** Companies engaged in manufacturing tortillas; suppliers, food brokers, and Mexican restaurant owners are affiliate or associate members. Promotes the increased consumption of tortillas and provides management assistance to members. **Awards:** Research Award. **Frequency:** annual. **Type:** monetary. **Recipient:** for best papers related to tortilla products. **Publications:** *Tortilla Industry News*, quarterly. Newsletter. **Price:** free. **Circulation:** 3,000. **Conventions/Meetings:** annual convention and trade show (exhibits) ● biennial Tortilla Industry Seminar, technical, marketing and management subject presentation.

1566 ■ UniPro Foodservice
2500 Cumberland Pkwy., Ste.600
Atlanta, GA 30339
Ph: (770)952-0871
Fax: (770)952-0872
E-mail: info@uniprofoodservice.com
URL: http://www.uniprofoodservice.com
Contact: Jim Kite, Chm.
Founded: 1988. **Members:** 300. **Description:** Wholesale food distributing companies selling or distributing food products and related merchandise to public or private foodservice operations. Members control their own national label on more than 15,000 canned and frozen food items and related supplies, maintenance items, and paper products. Secures reputable manufacturers and processors of foods to use under the CIFC label. Provides members with consolidated purchasing power to secure competitive pricing arrangements, national advertising, national sales network and other sales assistance, promotions, and marketing information. Conducts sales training seminars and offers field sales assistance to member salesmen. **Formed by Merger of:** National Institutional Food Distributors Association; North American Foodservice Companies. **Formerly:** (1998) ComSource Independent Foodservice Companies. **Conventions/Meetings:** UniPro - meeting - 1-2/year; usually fall or spring. 2008 Oct. 19-22, Washington, DC.

1567 ■ United States Beet Sugar Association (USBSA)
1156 15th St. NW, Ste.1019
Washington, DC 20005
Ph: (202)296-4820
Fax: (202)331-2065
E-mail: usbsa@beetsugar.org
URL: http://www.beetsugar.org
Contact: James Johnson, Pres.
Founded: 1911. **Members:** 10. **Staff:** 4. **Description:** Represents beet sugar processing companies. **Libraries: Type:** reference. **Holdings:** 5,000. **Committees:** Political Action. **Formerly:** (1914) United States Beet Sugar Industry; (1926) United States Sugar Manufacturers Association. **Publications:** Directory, annual. **Price:** free. **Conventions/Meetings:** annual meeting.

1568 ■ U.S. Canola Association (USCA)
600 Pennsylvania Ave. SE, Ste.320
Washington, DC 20003
Ph: (202)969-8113
Fax: (202)969-7036
E-mail: jgordley@gordley.com
URL: http://www.uscanola.com
Contact: John Gordley, Exec. Dir.
Founded: 1989. **Members:** 50. **Membership Dues:** allied industry board, $10,000 (annual) ● allied industry, $5,000 (annual) ● associate, $500 (annual) ● grower, $25 (annual) ● introductory industry, $2,500 (annual). **Staff:** 6. **Description:** Producers, companies, and associations promoting the U.S. canola and rapeseed industries. (Canola is the edible form of rapeseed that is used most commonly in the production of cooking oil and animal foods.) Works for legislation that encourages agricultural production of canola and rapeseed; monitors Canadian rapeseed tariffs. Promotes industry standards. **Committees:** Budget and Finance; Crop Production; Government Relations; Market Development; Membership; Public Relations; Research and Technology. **Conventions/Meetings:** annual meeting - every spring.

1569 ■ Vermont Maple Industry Council (VMIC)
c/o Timothy Perkins
Proctor Maple Res. Center
PO Box 233
Underhill, VT 05489
Ph: (802)899-9926
E-mail: timothy.perkins@uvm.edu
Contact: Timothy Perkins, Contact
Founded: 1956. **Members:** 33. **Description:** Maple syrup and sugar producers, processors, manufacturers, blenders, packers, and retailers. Assists in the development of maple marketing and research policy in Vermont. **Conventions/Meetings:** quarterly meeting.

1570 ■ Vinegar Institute (VI)
1100 Johnson Ferry Rd., Ste.300
Atlanta, GA 30342
Ph: (404)252-3663
Fax: (404)252-0774
E-mail: vi@kellencompany.com
URL: http://www.versatilevinegar.org
Contact: Pamela A. Chumley, Pres.
Founded: 1964. **Members:** 45. **Membership Dues:** active (minimum), $1,640 (annual) ● international, $1,147 (annual) ● associate, $1,093-$2,733 (annual). **Staff:** 3. **Budget:** $110,000,000. **Description:** Represents manufacturers and bottlers of vinegar and suppliers to the industry. Seeks to improve the quality of vinegar and increase its acceptance to the consumer. **Libraries: Type:** reference. **Holdings:** books, periodicals. **Subjects:** vinegar. **Committees:** Scientific. **Publications:** Membership Directory, annual. **Price:** included in membership dues. **Conventions/Meetings:** annual convention and meeting (exhibits).

Food Equipment

1571 ■ Commercial Food Equipment Service Association (CFESA)
2216 W Meadowview Rd., Ste.100
Greensboro, NC 27407
Ph: (336)346-4700
Free: (877)414-4127
Fax: (336)346-4745
E-mail: info@cfesa.com
URL: http://www.cfesa.com
Contact: Carla Strickland, Exec. Dir.
Founded: 1963. **Members:** 400. **Membership Dues:** affiliate, associate, supporting, $650 (annual). **Staff:** 4. **Regional Groups:** 6. **Description:** Represents firms that repair food preparation equipment used by restaurants, hotels, and institutions. Provides training and education for members and their employees. **Libraries: Type:** reference. **Holdings:** audiovisuals. **Subjects:** technical training. **Telecommunication Services:** electronic mail, cstrickland@cfesa.com. **Committees:** Board Development; Business Technology; Conference Planning; Education/Training; Industry Recruitment; Installation; Marketing; Service Standards. **Formerly:** (1981) Commercial Food Equipment Service Agencies of America. **Publications:** *Commercial Food Equipment Service Association—Directory*, annual ● *On Target*, bimonthly. Newsletter. **Advertising:** accepted. Alternate Formats: online ● Membership Directory, annual. Contains lists of all members alphabetically and geographically. Alternate Formats: online. **Conventions/Meetings:** semiannual conference, educational forums - always spring and fall.

1572 ■ FISA
1207 Sunset Dr.
Greensboro, NC 27408
Ph: (336)274-6311
Fax: (336)691-1839
E-mail: stella@fisanet.org
URL: http://www.fisanet.org
Contact: Stella Jones, Exec. Dir.
Founded: 1968. **Members:** 110. **Membership Dues:** regular (distributor, manufacturer), $735 (annual) ● associate, $425 (annual). **Staff:** 5. **Budget:** $35,000. **Description:** Represents distributors and manufacturers of equipment and supplies for the sanitary processing industries. Provides a medium for strengthening the distribution channel. **Awards:** Manufacturer of the Year. **Frequency:** annual. **Type:** recognition. **Affiliated With:** National Association of Wholesaler-Distributors. **Formerly:** Food Industries Suppliers Association. **Publications:** *Distributors News*, quarterly. Newsletter. Includes industry happenings and business management information. **Price:** included in membership dues. Alternate Formats: online ● Papers. **Price:** included in membership dues ● Reports. **Price:** included in membership dues. **Conventions/Meetings:** annual conference - every fall ● seminar and symposium.

1573 ■ Food Equipment Manufacturers Association (FEMA)
Address Unknown since 2008
Members: 32. **Membership Dues:** $650 (annual). **Staff:** 2. **Description:** Commercial kitchen equipment fabricators. Works to promote improved labor and industrial relationships in the food industry. Conducts research to improve product quality and to improve design and construction of equipment. **Conventions/Meetings:** semiannual meeting - always February and September.

1574 ■ Foodservice Equipment Distributors Association (FEDA)
2250 Point Blvd., Ste.200
Elgin, IL 60123-7887
Ph: (224)293-6500
Fax: (224)293-6505
E-mail: feda@feda.com
URL: http://www.feda.com
Contact: Raymond W. Herrick CAE, Exec. VP
Founded: 1933. **Members:** 325. **Membership Dues:** special first-year, $195 ● regular (based on the class), $480-$1,680 (annual) ● branch service, $230 (annual). **Staff:** 4. **Regional Groups:** 12. **Description:** Distributors of foodservice equipment, such as ovens, ranges, dishwashing machines, china, utensils, and cutlery for hotels, restaurants, and institutions. Conducts specialized education programs. **Awards: Type:** recognition. **Telecommunication Services:** electronic bulletin board, FEDA/AutoQuotes Liaison. **Formerly:** (1972) Food Service Equipment Industry. **Publications:** *Education Foundation News*. Newsletter. Alternate Formats: online ● *FEDA News and Views*, bimonthly. Magazine. **Price:** $15.00 /year for members; $60.00 /year for nonmembers. ISSN: 0746-9675. **Circulation:** 1,600. **Advertising:** accepted. Alternate Formats: online ● Membership Directory, periodic. **Price:** $100.00 for nonmembers ● Brochure. Alternate Formats: online. **Conventions/Meetings:** annual convention - 2009 Mar. 25-29, Las Vegas, NV; 2010 Mar. 17-21, Indian Wells, CA; 2011 Mar. 30-Apr. 3, Phoenix, AZ.

1575 ■ Manufacturers' Agents for the Foodservice Industry (MAFSI)
2814 Spring Rd., Ste.211
Atlanta, GA 30339
Ph: (770)433-9844
Fax: (770)433-2450
E-mail: info@mafsi.org
URL: http://www.mafsi.org
Contact: Alison Cody, Exec. Dir.
Founded: 1949. **Members:** 600. **Membership Dues:** agent, $385-$1,525 (annual) ● associate, $580 (annual). **Staff:** 3. **Budget:** $750,000. **Regional Groups:** 26. **Description:** Independent manufacturers' representative firms selling equipment, furnishings, and supplies to dealers and users. Sponsors annual mini manufacturer sales meetings. Conducts specialized education programs. **Awards:** All-Industry Awards. **Frequency:** annual. **Type:** recognition ● Bill H. Loveless Chapter of the Year Award. **Frequency:** annual. **Type:** recognition. **Recipient:** to an outstanding chapter ● Jack Pressberg Memorial Scholarship Fund. **Type:** scholarship ● Lifetime Membership Award. **Frequency:** annual. **Type:** recognition. **Recipient:** to an individual who has contributed to the food service industry through significant national involvement and is retired from the industry ● Market Mover Award. **Frequency:** annual. **Type:** recognition. **Recipient:** to individuals and/or organizations who through action, achievement and philosophy, demonstrated leadership qualities that are significant to the advancement of the representative function and foodservice industry ● Pacesetter Award. **Frequency:** annual. **Type:** recognition. **Recipient:** to individuals who have worked for MAFSI agent member companies only, for demonstrating the highest degree of devotion and distinguished service in conjunction with MAFSI projects and activities ● Special Recognition Award. **Frequency:** annual. **Type:** recognition. **Recipient:** to MAFSI agent members who have made significant contributions to a local region. **Boards:** OutFront Editorial Advisory. **Committees:** Education; Growth and Development; Industry Trends and Research; Public Relations; Strategic Alliance; Technology. **Formerly:** (1975) Manufacturers Agents for Food Service Industry; (1993) Marketing Agents for Food Service Industry. **Publications:** *Outfront*, quarterly. Magazine. Contains information on running a better rep agency. **Price:** included in membership dues. **Circulation:** 2,000. **Advertising:** accepted. Alternate Formats: online ● *Principles of Decision*. Manual. **Price:** $35.00. Alternate Formats: online; CD-ROM ● Membership Directory ● Annual Report, annual. Alternate Formats: online. **Conventions/Meetings:** annual conference (exhibits) - 2008 Sept. 17-20, Tucson, AZ; 2009 Sept. 23-25, Toronto, ON, Canada; 2010 Sept. 22-24, San Antonio, TX; 2011 Sept. 21-23, Hilton Head, SC.

1576 ■ North American Association of Food Equipment Manufacturers (NAFEM)
161 N Clark St., Ste.2020
Chicago, IL 60601
Ph: (312)821-0201
Fax: (312)821-0202
E-mail: info@nafem.org
URL: http://www.nafem.org
Contact: Deirdre T. Flynn, Exec. VP
Founded: 1948. **Members:** 700. **Membership Dues:** associate, $2,500 (annual). **Staff:** 30. **Description:** Represents manufacturers of commercial food service equipment and supplies for restaurant, hotel, and institutional use. Conducts certification program. **Awards:** Doctorate of Foodservice. **Frequency:** annual. **Type:** recognition. **Recipient:** to individuals who have contributed to the industry. **Committees:** Allied End-User; FCSI Liaison; Government Relations; Industry Education and Certification; Information Technology; International; MAFSI Liaison; Market Research; Sales and Marketing; Service Managers. **Formerly:** (1994) National Association of Food Equipment Manufacturers. **Publications:** *NAFEM for Operators*, quarterly. Newsletter. **Price:** available to operators. Alternate Formats: online ● *NAFEM in Print*, quarterly. Magazine. **Price:** free for members. **Advertising:** accepted. Alternate Formats: online. **Conventions/Meetings:** biennial trade show and seminar, food equipment manufacturers (exhibits).

Food Service

1577 ■ Association of Correctional Food Service Affiliates (ACFSA)
406 Surrey Woods Dr.
St. Charles, IL 60174
Ph: (630)513-4736
Fax: (630)513-4653
E-mail: info@acfsa.org
URL: http://www.acfsa.org
Contact: William St. John, Exec. Dir.
Founded: 1969. **Members:** 1,400. **Membership Dues:** food service professional, $69 (annual) ● professional partner, $384 (annual) ● institutional, $134 (annual) ● associate professional partner, $109 (annual) ● retired, $34 (annual) ● chapter professional partner, $159 (annual). **Staff:** 4. **Budget:** $500,000. **Regional Groups:** 4. **State Groups:** 15. **Multinational. Description:** Food service professionals from federal, state and county correctional institutions and vendors that serve them. Works to advance skills and professionalism through education, information and networking. **Awards:** Chapter of

the Year. **Frequency:** annual. **Type:** recognition. **Recipient:** for innovative chapter activities, meetings, attendance at conference and other association activities ● Food Service Employee of the Year. **Frequency:** annual. **Type:** monetary. **Recipient:** for excellence in foodservice supervision and training production, peer recognition ● Food Service Operator of the Year. **Frequency:** annual. **Type:** monetary. **Recipient:** for excellence in foodservice supervision and training production, peer recognition. **Telecommunication Services:** electronic mail, bstjohn@acfsa.org. **Committees:** Certified Food Service Professional; Membership; Resource; Vendor Relations. **Affiliated With:** American Jail Association; Association of Correctional Food Service Affiliates. **Formerly:** (2006) American Correctional Food Service Association. **Publications:** *Food Service Manual.* **Price:** $53.00 for members; $74.00 for nonmembers ● *Insider Magazine*, quarterly. Covers food service programs in correctional and detention facilities. **Price:** included in membership dues. **Circulation:** 1,700. **Advertising:** accepted ● Membership Directory, annual. Geographic listing of members and separate list professional partner members; contains category listings of professional partners by business type. **Price:** included in membership dues. **Advertising:** accepted. **Conventions/Meetings:** annual International Conference (exhibits) - usually in August. 2008 Aug. 24-28, North Charleston, SC ● annual Spring Training Conference (exhibits) - usually in April.

1578 ■ Association of Correctional Food Service Affiliates
4248 Park Glen Rd.
Minneapolis, MN 55416
Ph: (952)928-4658
Fax: (952)929-1318
E-mail: info@acfsa.org
URL: http://www.acfsa.org
Description: Foodservice personnel working in the correctional environment. Sponsors publications and conferences that help its members improve management skills; promotes professionalism and informs members of industry developments. **Conventions/Meetings:** annual conference.

1579 ■ Association of Pizza Delivery Drivers (APDD)
Address Unknown since 2008
URL: http://www.pizzadeliverydrivers.org
Description: Aims to advance the profession and improve the lives of pizza delivery drivers. Seeks to address the major issues that are common to delivery drivers. **Computer Services:** Information services, crimes against drivers ● online services, business chat ● online services, discussion board ● online services, driver's chat. **Telecommunication Services:** electronic mail, apdd@cox.net.

1580 ■ Council of Independent Restaurants of America (CIRA)
c/o Don Luria, Pres.
3500 E Sunrise Dr.
Tucson, AZ 85718
Ph: (520)577-8181
Fax: (520)577-9015
E-mail: info@dineoriginals.com
URL: http://www.dineoriginals.com
Contact: Don Luria, Pres.
Founded: 1998. **Members:** 750. **Membership Dues:** individual, $150 (annual). **Staff:** 2. **Budget:** $250,000. **Regional Groups:** 16. **Description:** Fine-dining restaurateurs. Represents the interest of independent operators; establishes a marketing program meeting the challenges of the national dinner-house restaurant chains. **Telecommunication Services:** electronic mail, president@dineoriginals.com. **Conventions/Meetings:** annual Chapter Leadership Conference.

1581 ■ Foodservice Sales and Marketing Association (FSMA)
9192 Red Br. Rd., Ste.200
Columbia, MD 21045
Ph: (410)715-6672
Free: (888)488-0688
Fax: (410)997-9387
E-mail: info@fsmaonline.com
URL: http://www.fsmaonline.com
Contact: Rick Abraham, Pres./CEO
Founded: 2003. **Description:** Works to promote sales and marketing agencies as the preferred method for manufacturers to come to market. Serves as the national voice of the foodservice sales agency community. Enhances relationships among manufacturers, agencies, customers and other key stakeholders in the foodservice industry. **Telecommunication Services:** electronic mail, rabraham@fsmaonline.com.

1582 ■ International Association of Culinary Professionals (IACP)
304 W Liberty St., Ste.201
Louisville, KY 40202
Ph: (502)581-9786
Free: (800)928-4227
Fax: (502)589-3602
E-mail: iacp@hqtrs.com
URL: http://www.iacp.com
Contact: Rosemary Barron, Pres.
Founded: 1978. **Members:** 4,000. **Membership Dues:** professional, $220 (annual) ● cooking school, $360 (annual) ● small business, $420 (annual) ● corporate, $995 (annual). **Staff:** 9. **Budget:** $1,100,000. **Multinational. Description:** Represents cooking school owners, food writers, chefs, caterers, culinary specialists, directors, teachers, cookbook authors, food stylists, food photographers, student/apprentices, and individuals in related industries in 20 countries. Promotes the interests of cooking schools, teachers, and culinary professionals. Encourages the exchange of information and education. Promotes professional standards and accreditation procedures. Maintains a Foundation to award culinary scholarships and grants. **Awards:** Bert Greene Memorial Award. **Frequency:** annual. **Type:** recognition. **Recipient:** for excellence in food journalism ● Cooking School (Avocational). **Type:** recognition ● Cooking School (Vocational). **Frequency:** annual. **Type:** recognition ● Cooking Teacher of the Year. **Frequency:** annual. **Type:** recognition ● Corporate-Consumer Educational and Communications Materials. **Frequency:** annual. **Type:** recognition ● Entrepreneur/Business Person. **Type:** recognition ● Humanitarian. **Frequency:** annual. **Type:** recognition ● IACP Awards of Excellence. **Frequency:** annual. **Type:** recognition. **Recipient:** for members who are experts and leaders in their field ● IACP Cookbook Awards. **Frequency:** annual. **Type:** recognition. **Recipient:** for outstanding food and beverage publications ● Lifetime Achievement. **Frequency:** annual. **Type:** recognition. **Computer Services:** database, job bank ● mailing lists ● online services, bulletin board. **Committees:** Awards and Recognition; Certification; Chefs and Restaurateurs; Cooking Schools and Teachers; Corporate; Culinary Experience; Ethics; Food History; International; Kids in the Kitchen; Test Kitchen Professionals. **Sections:** Entrepreneurs; Food Photographers and Stylists; Food Writing and Publishing; Marketing Communicators. **Formerly:** Association of Cooking Schools; International Association of Cooking Schools; International Association of Cooking Professionals. **Publications:** *Frontburner*, monthly. Newsletter. **Price:** included in membership dues ● *International Association of Culinary Professionals Food Forum Quarterly*. Newsletter. Contains membership and association activities news. Lists new members. **Price:** included in membership dues. **Circulation:** 4,000. **Advertising:** accepted. **Conventions/Meetings:** annual international conference (exhibits).

1583 ■ International Flight Service Association (IFSA)
1100 Johnson Ferry Rd., Ste.300
Atlanta, GA 30342
Ph: (404)252-3663
Fax: (404)252-0774
E-mail: ifsa@kellencompany.com
URL: http://www.ifsanet.com
Contact: Pam Chumley, Exec. Admin.
Founded: 1972. **Members:** 450. **Membership Dues:** airline, railway, $250 (annual) ● caterer, supplier, $600 (annual). **Staff:** 7. **Description:** Works to serve the needs and interests of the airline and railway personnel, in-flight and railway caterers and suppliers responsible for providing passenger foodservice on regularly scheduled travel routes. **Libraries: Type:** open to the public. **Holdings:** 1. **Subjects:** catering the in-flight food service industry. **Awards:** President's Award. **Frequency:** annual. **Type:** recognition. **Recipient:** for individuals or a group with outstanding achievements in the areas of humanitarian service, dedication to the industry and its associations, and to the improvement of the environment. **Committees:** Allied Advisory; Asia Pacific; Communications; Conference Planning; Education; Government Affairs Education; Latin America; Membership Development. **Programs:** Membership Referral. **Formerly:** (1995) International Inflight Food Service Association; (1998) Inflight Food Service Association; (2006) International Inflight Food Service Association. **Publications:** *IFCA/IFSA Review*, quarterly. Magazine. **Price:** $50.00/year. **Circulation:** 4,500. **Advertising:** accepted ● *Onboard IFSA*, monthly. Newsletter. Provides the latest information about all IFSA happenings. Alternate Formats: online ● Brochure. Alternate Formats: online. **Conventions/Meetings:** annual meeting and conference (exhibits) ● annual trade show (exhibits).

1584 ■ International Food Service Executives Association (IFSEA)
2609 Surfwood Dr.
Las Vegas, NV 89128
Ph: (702)430-9217
Fax: (702)430-9223
E-mail: hq@ifsea.com
URL: http://www.ifsea.com
Contact: Greg Hobby, Exec. VP
Founded: 1901. **Members:** 1,600. **Membership Dues:** active, active duty, allied, apprentice, retired, $49 (annual) ● student, $20 (annual) ● corporate operator (regional), $300 (annual) ● corporate operator (national)/corporate supplier (regional), $500 (annual) ● corporate supplier (national), $1,000 (annual) ● active international, $35 (annual) ● retired/allied international, $25 (annual) ● apprentice international, $15 (annual) ● student international, $10 (annual). **Staff:** 2. **Budget:** $500,000. **State Groups:** 30. **Description:** Owners, managers, stewards, caterers, proprietors, purchasing agents, dietitians, and other management-level personnel of hotels, clubs, restaurants, cafeterias, schools, hospitals, institutions, and airlines. Associate members are providers of goods and services to the food service industry. Seeks to raise standards in the food service industry by educating members. Underwrites scholarships; provides assistance to universities and other educational institutions establishing programs for professional food service training. Maintains Certified Food Executive Program, through which individuals in the food service industry who have demonstrated outstanding leadership capabilities receive certification training. **Libraries: Type:** reference. **Awards:** Armed Forces John L. Hennessy Award. **Frequency:** annual. **Type:** trophy. **Recipient:** for members ● Worthy Goal Scholarship. **Frequency:** annual. **Type:** scholarship. **Recipient:** for full time students. **Boards:** Job. **Committees:** Certified Food Executive; Certified Food Manager; Military Foodservice Evaluation. **Funds:** Worthy Goal Annual Scholarship. **Programs:** Ask A Specialist - Free consulting; Awards; Certification; Conference; E-Learning; Food Safety; Member Development; Military Excellence Awards; Recommended Restaurants Nationwide; Scholarship. **Formerly:** Executive Stewards and Caterers Association; (1957) International Stewards and Caterers Association; (1975) Food Service Executives Association. **Publications:** *Hotline Magazine*, quarterly. Contains calendar of events. Alternate Formats: online ● *Inside Scoop*, bimonthly ● Brochure. Alternate Formats: online. **Conventions/Meetings:** semiannual conference - 2009 Apr. 2-5, Atlanta, GA; 2010 Mar. 11-14, Reno, NV.

1585 ■ International Foodservice Distributors Association (IFDA)
201 Park Washington Ct.
Falls Church, VA 22046-4521
Ph: (703)532-9400

Fax: (703)538-4673
E-mail: sbarrett@ifdaonline.org
URL: http://www.ifdaonline.org
Contact: Mark S. Allen, Pres./CEO
Founded: 2003. **Members:** 135. **Membership Dues:** foodservice distributor (based on sales), $975-$165,000 (annual) ● allied (based on sales), $5,000-$15,000 (annual) ● associate (based on sales), $2,500-$7,500 (annual). **Multinational. Description:** Advocates the interests of the foodservice distribution community in government and industry affairs. **Publications:** *Daily Update*. Newsletter. Features food industry news and developments. Alternate Formats: online ● *Hazard Analysis and Critical Control Points (HACCP) Guidelines for Food Distributors*. Manual. Features particular issues faced by food distributors. **Price:** $195.00 for members; $345.00 for nonmembers ● *Kellers' Official OSHA Safety Training Handbook*. Contains safety advice on 22 of OSHA's hottest topics. **Price:** $5.50 for members; $7.25 for nonmembers ● *OSHA for Transportation: Key Compliance Topics*. Manual. Contains guidance on key OSHA regulations. **Price:** $145.00 for members; $165.00 for nonmembers ● *Truck Driver Handbook*. Contains practical information for drivers. **Price:** $3.00 for members; $3.40 for nonmembers.

1586 ■ Multicultural Foodservice and Hospitality Alliance (MFHA)

PO Box 25661
Providence, RI 02905
Ph: (401)461-6342
Fax: (401)461-9004
E-mail: info@mfha.net
URL: http://www.mfha.net
Contact: Gerry Fernandez, Pres.
Founded: 1998. **Members:** 600. **Membership Dues:** individual, $250 (annual) ● educational institution, government agency, non-profit organization, $100 (annual). **Staff:** 6. **Budget:** $1,000,000. **Languages:** English, Portuguese, Spanish. **Description:** Food service industry. Provides education, facilitation and information. **Publications:** *Fusion*, quarterly. Newsletter. Contains information about the association and its members. Alternate Formats: online ● *MFHA Straight Talk*. Newsletter. Alternate Formats: online. **Conventions/Meetings:** annual conference - 2008 Aug. 10-12, Chicago, IL.

1587 ■ National Association of Church Food Service (NACFS)

PO Box 550413
Atlanta, GA 30355
Ph: (404)261-1794 (404)240-8217
Fax: (404)240-8276
E-mail: carolyn@prumc.org
URL: http://www.nacfs.org
Contact: Carolyn B. Clayton CFSR, CEO
Founded: 1989. **Members:** 225. **Membership Dues:** regular ($100 for new member), $85 (annual) ● retired, $25 (annual) ● second membership from same church, $45 (annual). **State Groups:** 10. **Local Groups:** 15. **Description:** Individuals involved in production of food at a church. Offers certification to become a certified church food service director. Conducts educational and charitable programs. **Computer Services:** database. **Publications:** Membership Directory ● Newsletter, monthly. **Conventions/Meetings:** annual conference ● annual seminar.

1588 ■ National Association of College and University Food Services (NACUFS)

2525 Jolly Rd., Ste.280
Okemos, MI 48864-3680
Ph: (517)332-2494
Fax: (517)332-8144
E-mail: rfmeyer@unr.edu
URL: http://www.nacufs.org
Contact: Joseph H. Spina PhD, Exec. Dir.
Founded: 1958. **Members:** 1,075. **Membership Dues:** institutional (based on annual food service revenues), $190-$600 (annual) ● industry, $525 (annual) ● associate, $150 (annual) ● retired, $50 (annual) ● student, $25 (annual). **Staff:** 8. **Budget:** $1,600,000. **Regional Groups:** 9. **Description:** Food services in operation at colleges or universities; residence halls; student centers. Advances and promotes the highest standards of food preparation and service on college and university campuses. Provides information and assistance to members through discussions, researches and publications. **Awards:** Clark E. DeHaven Scholarship Trust. **Frequency:** annual. **Type:** recognition. **Recipient:** for outstanding leadership ● Theodore W. Minah Distinguished Service Award. **Frequency:** annual. **Type:** recognition. **Recipient:** for the most outstanding food service operator. **Computer Services:** database, members. **Telecommunication Services:** electronic mail, jhspina@msu.edu. **Committees:** Education; Finance; Food and Nutrition Awareness; Food Service Internship; Industry Advisory; Marketing; Membership; Strategic Planning. **Publications:** *Campus Dining Today*, quarterly. Magazine. **Price:** included in membership dues. **Circulation:** 3,100. **Advertising:** accepted ● *Job Opportunities Bulletin*. Features website postings. **Price:** included in membership dues. **Circulation:** 2,600. Alternate Formats: online ● *NACUFS Directory*, annual. Membership Directory. **Advertising:** accepted ● *NACUFS News*, weekly. Newsletter. Alternate Formats: online. **Conventions/Meetings:** annual conference (exhibits).

1589 ■ National Association of Concessionaires (NAC)

35 E Wacker Dr., Ste.1816
Chicago, IL 60601
Ph: (312)236-3858
Fax: (312)236-7809
E-mail: info@naconline.org
URL: http://www.naconline.org
Contact: Charles A. Winans, Exec. Dir.
Founded: 1944. **Members:** 900. **Membership Dues:** full, $545 (annual) ● associate, $75 (annual). **Staff:** 4. **Budget:** $700,000. **Regional Groups:** 10. **Description:** Represents popcorn processors, manufacturers, and merchandisers; operators of food and beverage concessions in theaters, amusement parks, sports arenas, and other recreational facilities; equipment manufacturers and suppliers. Works to professionalize the concession industry. Provides information services and audiovisual training programs for concession managers and employees. Maintains certification program for concession industry. **Awards: Frequency:** annual. **Type:** scholarship. **Recipient:** for NAC members or their children pursuing a college degree. **Committees:** Public Affairs. **Divisions:** Diversified Concessionaire; Equipment Manufacturers; Popcorn Processor, Manufacturer-Wholesaler, and Merchandiser; Suppliers; Theatre Concessionaire. **Programs:** Association Cruise; Concession Manager Certification; Executive Concession Manager Certification; Insurance. **Formerly:** National Association of Popcorn Manufacturers; International Popcorn Association; Popcorn and Concessions Association. **Publications:** *Concession Profession*, semiannual. Magazine. Contains membership directory in winter issue. **Price:** free for members. **Circulation:** 6,000. **Advertising:** accepted. Alternate Formats: online ● *Concessionworks*, semiannual. Newsletter. **Price:** available to members only. **Circulation:** 2,000. Alternate Formats: online. **Conventions/Meetings:** annual convention and trade show, for members of the concessions industry (exhibits) - usually June.

1590 ■ National Food Service Management Institute (NFSMI)

PO Drawer 188
Univ. of Mississippi
6 Jeanette Philips Dr.
University, MS 38677-0188
Ph: (662)915-7658
Free: (800)321-3054
Fax: (800)321-3061
E-mail: nfsmi@olemiss.edu
URL: http://www.nfsmi.org
Contact: Dr. Charlotte Oakley, Exec. Dir.
Founded: 1989. **Staff:** 31. **Budget:** $4,000,000. **Description:** Seeks to be the leader in providing education, research, and resources to promote excellence in child nutrition programs. Provides information, conducts applied research, and offers training and education opportunities using appropriate technology. **Libraries: Type:** by appointment only. **Holdings:** 3,000; archival material, audiovisuals, books, clippings, photographs, reports. **Subjects:** school food service, child nutrition program, computer-based instructional program, food safety, nutrition education, food service management, recipe, health promotion, applied research, customer service, procurement, financial management. **Computer Services:** Electronic publishing ● information services. **Publications:** *Insight*, quarterly. Newsletter. Communicates research and projects in reader-friendly terms. Alternate Formats: online ● *Mealtime Memo for Child Care* (in English and Spanish), bimonthly. Contains fact sheet for the Child and Adult Care Food Program. Alternate Formats: online ● *Resource Guide*. Catalog. Details publications, research reports, and videos of the NFSMI. **Price:** free for members ● *Update*, semiannual. Newsletter. Communicates projects, research reports, workshops and other activities. **Price:** free for members. Alternate Formats: online. **Conventions/Meetings:** convention, participates in state and national food service conventions.

1591 ■ National Independent Concessionaires Association (NICA)

6671 13th Ave. N, Ste.1B
St. Petersburg, FL 33710
Ph: (727)346-9302
Fax: (727)346-9312
E-mail: cgnica@nicainc.org
URL: http://www.nicainc.org
Contact: David J. Schlabach CFE, Exec. Dir.
Members: 1,200. **Membership Dues:** regular voting, business, carnival, associate, fair/festival with over 75,000 attendance, $125 (annual) ● regular voting spousal, employee, fair/festival with under 75,000 attendance, $75 (annual). **Description:** Represents independent concessionaires within the food, retail sales, games and entertainment industry. Provides business services to members. Organizes food shows and business expos. **Awards:** NICA Scholarship. **Frequency:** annual. **Type:** scholarship. **Recipient:** for NICA members, their children and grandchildren. **Telecommunication Services:** electronic mail, dsnica@nicainc.org. **Publications:** *NICA News*, monthly. Newsletter. Includes information on current industry issues and concerns. **Price:** included in membership dues ● Membership Directory, annual. Provides a detailed information on each NICA member. **Price:** included in membership dues.

1592 ■ National Society for Healthcare Foodservice Management (HFM)

355 Lexington Ave., 15th Fl.
New York, NY 10017
Ph: (212)297-2166
Fax: (212)370-9047
E-mail: info@hfm.org
URL: http://www.hfm.org
Contact: Mary Angela Miller, Pres.
Founded: 1988. **Members:** 3,475. **Membership Dues:** operator, healthcare executive, sponsored associate, affiliate, $175 (annual) ● second operator, second healthcare executive, educator, second affiliate, $125 (annual) ● sponsored operator, $150 (annual) ● second sponsored operator, $100 (annual) ● student, $25 (annual) ● inactive operator, $50 (annual) ● inactive operator (life), $250 ● associate, $700 (annual). **Description:** Independent non-contract healthcare foodservice department directors and suppliers. Seeks to promote the independent non-contract operation of foodservice in healthcare and provide members with the tools for success. **Conventions/Meetings:** annual conference - 2008 Sept. 15-19, Hot Springs, VA.

1593 ■ Roundtable for Women in Foodservice (RWF)

Address Unknown since 2007
Description: Individuals, suppliers and service professionals in the food service industry trade. Dedicated to the development and improvement of women's careers in all segments of the industry; provides education, mentoring, and networking with emphasis on women's careers in corporate and

entrepreneurial operator, supplier, and service areas of the industry; creates forum between male and female restaurant operators, foodservice directors, and culinarians. **Awards:** Pacesetter Awards. **Type:** recognition ● Scholarship Awards. **Type:** scholarship. **Publications:** Newsletter.

1594 ■ Society for Foodservice Management (SFM)
304 W Liberty St., Ste.201
Louisville, KY 40202
Ph: (502)583-3783
Fax: (502)589-3602
E-mail: sfm@hqtrs.com
URL: http://www.sfm-online.org
Contact: Mary Gratzer, Exec. Dir.
Founded: 1979. **Members:** 2,000. **Membership Dues:** active, $350 (annual) ● associate, $550 (annual) ● emeritus, $75 (annual) ● student, $25 (annual). **Staff:** 8. **Description:** Operates or maintains food service and vending facilities in businesses and industrial plants, or supply food products, equipment, or other essential industry services. Serves the needs and interests of onsite employee food service executives and management. Provides an opportunity for the exchange of experiences and opinions through study, discussion, and publications; develops greater efficiency and more economical methods of providing high-quality food and service at a reasonable cost; assists members in solving specific operating and management problems; keeps pace with the rapidly changing conditions of the employee food service segment of the industry. Develops and encourages the practice of high standards and professional conduct among management and executive personnel; provides job placement and management personnel recruiting service; sends representative to the U.S. Air Force Hennessey Award Team, which selects the Air Force base having the most superior food service. **Telecommunication Services:** electronic mail, mgratzer@hqtrs.com. **Publications:** *FactsFax*, bimonthly. Newsletter ● *Journal of Foodservice Systems*, quarterly. Covers food service systems analysis, design, implementation, and management. Includes index, research reports, and case histories. **Price:** included in membership dues; $40.00 /year for nonmembers. ISSN: 0196-4283. **Circulation:** 150. **Advertising:** accepted ● *SFM Membership and Networking Directory*, annual. Membership Directory. **Conventions/Meetings:** annual conference and regional meeting (exhibits).

1595 ■ Women's Foodservice Forum (WFF)
Southpoint Off. Ctr.
1650 W 82nd St., Ste.650
Bloomington, MN 55431
Ph: (952)358-2100 (952)358-2101
Free: (866)368-8008
Fax: (952)358-2119
E-mail: info@womensfoodserviceforum.com
URL: http://www.womensfoodserviceforum.com
Contact: Mary Bentley, Pres./CEO
Founded: 1989. **Members:** 2,200. **Membership Dues:** professional, $250 (annual) ● educator, $150 (annual). **Staff:** 3. **Description:** Strives to promote leadership development and career advancement of executive women for the benefit of the foodservice industry. **Publications:** *Open Doors*. Newsletter. Alternate Formats: online.

Footwear

1596 ■ Boot and Shoe Travelers Association of New York (BSTA/NY)
50 W 34th St., Ste.8A6
New York, NY 10001
Ph: (212)564-1069
Fax: (212)564-0513
E-mail: bootshoeny@aol.com
URL: http://www.bootshoeny.com
Contact: Amy Carickhoff, Exec. Dir.
Founded: 1939. **Members:** 400. **Membership Dues:** individual, $60 (annual). **Staff:** 1. **Description:** Sales representatives in the footwear and allied industries united to provide benefits, services, and assistance to members. **Conventions/Meetings:** semiannual Metropolitan New York Shoe Market - trade show, footwear presentations to the trade (exhibits).

1597 ■ Footwear Distributors and Retailers of America (FDRA)
1319 F St., Ste.700
Washington, DC 20004
Ph: (202)737-5660
Fax: (202)638-2615
E-mail: ptmangione@fdra.org
URL: http://www.fdra.org
Contact: Peter Mangione, Pres.
Founded: 1944. **Members:** 63. **Staff:** 5. **Description:** Volume shoe store chains. Conducts traffic, foreign sourcing, customs, leadership and employment relations' seminars. **Computer Services:** database, member organizations. **Telecommunication Services:** electronic mail, lproctor@fdra.org. **Committees:** Customs; Government Affairs; Taxation; Traffic; Transportation. **Councils:** Distribution; Footwear Traffic. **Formerly:** Popular Price Shoe Retailer Association; Footwear Retailers of America; (1965) National Association of Shoe Chain Stores; (1969) Volume Footwear Retailers Association; (1985) Volume Footwear Retailers of America. **Publications:** *Labor Digest*, bimonthly ● *Traffic Bulletin*, periodic ● Bulletin, monthly. Alternate Formats: online. **Conventions/Meetings:** annual conference (exhibits).

1598 ■ National Shoe Retailers Association (NSRA)
7150 Columbia Gateway Dr., Ste.G
Columbia, MD 21046-1151
Ph: (410)381-8282
Fax: (410)381-1167
E-mail: info@nsra.org
URL: http://www.nsra.org
Contact: Phil Wright, Chm.
Founded: 1912. **Members:** 2,500. **Membership Dues:** voting (based on annual sales volume), $190-$1,100 (annual) ● international, $220 (annual) ● affiliate, $300 (annual). **Staff:** 17. **Budget:** $1,000,000. **Regional Groups:** 5. **Description:** Proprietors of independent shoe stores, and stores with major shoe departments. Provides business services and professional development programs including bankcard processing, shipping, freight discounts, free website listing, employee training; conducts research; monitors legislation. **Libraries: Type:** reference. **Holdings:** 500; archival material, business records, clippings, periodicals. **Subjects:** footwear, business start up, employee relations, marketing. **Awards:** Retail Excellence Awards. **Frequency:** annual. **Type:** recognition. **Telecommunication Services:** electronic mail, scott@nsra.org. **Publications:** *Business Performance Report*, biennial. Contains survey on costs of doing business. **Price:** $75.00 for members; $150.00 for nonmembers. **Circulation:** 4,000. **Advertising:** accepted ● *Shoe Retailing Today*, bimonthly. Magazine. **Price:** $35.00. **Circulation:** 7,000. **Advertising:** accepted. **Conventions/Meetings:** semiannual conference, business techniques and trends (exhibits) - always August and February ● biennial Leadership Conference - meeting, held day before World Shoe Association Show.

1599 ■ Pedorthic Footwear Association (PFA)
2025 M St. NW, Ste.800
Washington, DC 20036
Ph: (202)367-1145
Free: (800)673-8447
Fax: (202)367-2145
E-mail: info@pedorthics.org
URL: http://www.pedorthics.org
Contact: Brian Lagana, Exec. Dir.
Founded: 1958. **Members:** 2,100. **Membership Dues:** regular (company), $300 (annual) ● associate, $85 (annual) ● regular (individual), $210 (annual) ● affiliate, medical, $100 (annual) ● student, $135 (annual) ● vendor, manufacturer, $750 (annual). **Staff:** 12. **Budget:** $1,250,000. **Languages:** English, Spanish. **For-Profit. Multinational. Description:** Professionals involved in the field of pedorthics. (Pedorthics is the design, manufacture, fit and modification of shoes and foot orthoses to alleviate foot problems caused by disease, overuse, or injury). **Libraries: Type:** reference. **Holdings:** 100; archival material, books, business records, clippings, periodicals. **Subjects:** orthopedic footwear and conservative care of the foot. **Awards:** Aristotle Mirones. **Frequency:** annual. **Type:** scholarship. **Recipient:** for individuals below 18 years old ● Seymour Lefton, Vendor of the Year. **Frequency:** annual. **Type:** recognition. **Computer Services:** Mailing lists. **Telecommunication Services:** electronic mail, brian@pedorthics.org. **Committees:** Education; Government Affairs; Marketing/Communications; Membership. **Formerly:** Prescription Footwear Association. **Publications:** *Current Pedorthics*, bimonthly. Magazine. **Price:** $35.00 for nonmembers; included in membership dues. **Circulation:** 4,800. **Advertising:** accepted ● *When the Shoe Fits*. Video. **Price:** $150.00 for members; $250.00 for nonmembers. **Conventions/Meetings:** annual symposium (exhibits) - always October or November.

1600 ■ Shoe Service Institute of America (SSIA)
18 School St.
North Brookfield, MA 01535
Ph: (508)867-7732
E-mail: webmaster@ssia.info
URL: http://www.ssia.info
Contact: John McLoughlin, Pres.
Founded: 1904. **Members:** 120. **Membership Dues:** repairer/retailer, $25 (annual) ● wholesaler, $50 (annual) ● supplier, $100 (annual). **Staff:** 4. **Budget:** $250,000. **Description:** Finders (wholesalers) of shoe repair supplies and equipment. Supplier members are manufacturers, tanners, and distributors. **Libraries: Type:** open to the public. **Awards:** Silver Cup. **Frequency:** annual. **Type:** recognition. **Recipient:** for excellence in shoe repair retailing. **Computer Services:** database, member manufacturers ● database, member retailers ● information services, consumer resources ● online services, chat room ● online services, forum. **Formerly:** (1949) National Leather and Shoe Finders Association. **Publications:** *Bookkeeping System* ● *Finders Directory* ● *Intercom* ● *Legal Advisory* ● *Shoe Service Institute of America—Membership Directory*, annual. **Price:** available to members only ● *SSIA Educational Series* ● *Suppliers Directory*. **Conventions/Meetings:** annual meeting (exhibits).

1601 ■ Two/Ten Footwear Foundation
1466 Main St.
Waltham, MA 02451
Ph: (781)736-1500
Free: (800)FIND-210
Fax: (781)736-1555
E-mail: pmeill@twoten.org
URL: http://www.twoten.org
Contact: Peggy Kim Meill, Pres.
Founded: 1939. **Members:** 14,000. **Membership Dues:** life, $390 ● general, $50 (annual). **Staff:** 25. **Description:** Workers in the shoe, leather and allied industries. (Foundation derives its name from its previous location, 210 Lincoln St., which was known as the leather and shoe center in Boston, MA.) Aims to provide assistance to people in the footwear, leather and allied trades who may be in financial need; promote the general welfare of those engaged in the shoe industry. Operates gerontology services programs for shoe people 55 years and over. Maintains job placement, health planning and retirement services. **Awards:** T. Kenyon Holly Memorial Award. **Frequency:** annual. **Type:** recognition. **Recipient:** for philanthropic service to the general community by a member of the footwear industry ● Two/Ten Scholarship. **Type:** scholarship. **Recipient:** to the children of workers in the footwear or allied industries. **Telecommunication Services:** electronic mail, mhehir@twoten.org. **Committees:** Endowment; Investment; Job Placement; Leadership Enrichment; Pension; Public Relations; Relief Fund; Scholarship; Social Service; Young Leadership. **Formerly:** (1974) Two/Ten Associates; (1984) Two/Ten National Foundation; (1990) Two/Ten Foundation. **Publications:** *New Findings Quarterly*. Newsletter. Covers retire-

ment and concerns of the aging. **Price:** included in membership dues ● *Two/Ten Today*, quarterly. Newsletter. Contains information on membership activities. **Price:** free for members. **Circulation:** 12,000 ● Also publishes booklets, brochures, magazines and pamphlets. **Conventions/Meetings:** annual dinner ● annual meeting - always November or December, Boston, MA.

1602 ■ United Shoe Retailers Association (USRA)
c/o Linda Hauss, Exec. Dir.
PO Box 4931
West Hills, CA 91308
Ph: (818)703-6062
Fax: (818)703-6063
E-mail: linda@usraonline.org
URL: http://usraonline.org
Contact: Linda Hauss, Exec. Dir.
Founded: 1977. **Members:** 500. **Membership Dues:** shoe retailer, $95 (annual). **Staff:** 9. **Description:** Represents and promotes the independent shoe retailer. **Programs:** Networking. **Formerly:** (2005) Western Shoe Retailers Association. **Publications:** *Networking Directory* ● *Shoe Times*, quarterly. Newsletter. **Conventions/Meetings:** annual seminar, with workshops, networking and golf tournament (exhibits) - always May.

Forest Industries

1603 ■ American Hardwood Export Council (AHEC)
1111 19th St. NW, Ste.800
Washington, DC 20036
Ph: (202)463-2720 (202)463-2774
Fax: (202)463-2787
E-mail: michael_snow@afandpa.org
URL: http://www.ahec.org
Contact: Michael Snow, Exec. Dir.
Founded: 1989. **Members:** 124. **Membership Dues:** exporting company (maximum), $7,500 (annual) ● exporting association (maximum), $9,000 (annual) ● associate/supporting, $1,100 (annual) ● sponsor, $1,250 (annual). **Staff:** 4. **Description:** Represents exporting companies and hardwood trade associations that serve the hardwood lumber industry. Promotes the export of U.S. hardwood lumber worldwide. **Computer Services:** Mailing lists, of members. **Formed by Merger of:** (1988) Hardwood Export Trade Council; (1988) National Lumber Exporters Association. **Publications:** *U.S. Hardwood Exporter*. Brochure. **Conventions/Meetings:** annual meeting, in conjunction with National Hardwood Lumber Association - always fall ● semiannual meeting.

1604 ■ American Loggers Council (ALC)
PO Box 966
Hemphill, TX 75948
Ph: (409)625-0206
Fax: (409)625-0207
E-mail: americanlogger@aol.com
URL: http://www.americanloggers.org
Contact: Charles Johns, Pres.
Founded: 1994. **Membership Dues:** individual logger (based on number of employees), $100-$400 (annual) ● associate - consumer, supplier (Platinum), $5,000 (annual) ● associate - consumer, supplier (Gold), $2,000 (annual) ● associate - consumer, supplier (Silver), $1,000 (annual) ● associate - consumer, supplier (Bronze), associate - organization, $500 (annual) ● associate - individual, $250 (annual). **Description:** Seeks to enhance the logging profession. Provides a unified voice on logging issues. Cooperates with public, industrial and private timberland owners to further sustainable forestry practices.

1605 ■ California Forestry Association (CFA)
1215 K St., Ste.1830
Sacramento, CA 95814-3947
Ph: (916)444-6592
Fax: (916)444-0170
E-mail: cfa@foresthealth.org
URL: http://www.foresthealth.org
Contact: David A. Bischel, Pres.
Founded: 1952. **Members:** 230. **Membership Dues:** supporting, $368 (annual) ● affiliate, $100 (annual). **Staff:** 7. **Budget:** $1,600,000. **Description:** Companies and individuals committed to environmentally sound policies, sustainable use of renewable resources, and responsible forestry. Provides advocacy services before California state and Federal legislatures. Maintains electronic information services. Distributes information to regulatory agencies, public and private organizations, and individuals. **Awards: Type:** scholarship. **Telecommunication Services:** electronic mail, davidb@cwo.com. **Committees:** Environmental Affairs; Forest Practice; Legal Affairs; Legislative Affairs; Public Resources; Wildlife. **Formed by Merger of:** (1988) California Forest Protective Association; Western Timber Association. **Formerly:** (1991) Timber Association of California. **Publications:** *California Forests*, quarterly. Magazine. **Circulation:** 5,000. **Advertising:** accepted. **Conventions/Meetings:** annual conference - always winter.

1606 ■ Forest Industries Telecommunications (FIT)
1565 Oak St.
Eugene, OR 97401
Ph: (541)485-8441
Fax: (541)485-7556
E-mail: license@landmobile.com
URL: http://www.landmobile.com
Contact: Kenton E. Sturdevant, Exec. VP
Founded: 1947. **Members:** 2,200. **Staff:** 6. **Budget:** $500,000. **Regional Groups:** 3. **Description:** Represents the forest products industry in communication matters before the Federal Communications Commission (FCC). Provides radio license assistance to members, distribution of FCC rules and regulations and advice to the forest products. **Libraries: Type:** not open to the public. **Holdings:** 500; books, periodicals. **Subjects:** telecommunication, radio communications. **Computer Services:** database, FCC license. **Committees:** Legislative; Personnel; Policy. **Formerly:** Forest Industries Radio Communications. **Publications:** *Two-Way Transmissions*, quarterly. Newsletter. Includes radio communications subjects for Forest Products Radio Service licensees and FIT members, and legislative and regulatory updates of the FCC. **Circulation:** 2,300 ● Also publishes operators' manual, various technical papers and publications relating to FCC matters. **Conventions/Meetings:** annual meeting, business and membership meeting - always October or November.

1607 ■ Forest Resources Association (FRA)
600 Jefferson Plz., Ste.350
Rockville, MD 20852-1157
Ph: (301)838-9385
Fax: (301)838-9481
E-mail: fra@forestresources.org
URL: http://www.forestresources.org
Contact: Mr. Neil Ward, Dir. of Communications
Founded: 1934. **Members:** 1,700. **Staff:** 17. **Budget:** $1,800,000. **Regional Groups:** 6. **Description:** Provides a forum to members of the forest resources community-foresters, loggers, landowners, and product manufacturers-where they can meet to solve problems and leverage opportunities within the wood fiber supply chain. Promotes sharing of information, facilitates networking, coordinates activism, serves as a change agent, structures problem-solving workshops, and provides education for members. **Awards:** Outstanding Forestry Activist. **Frequency:** annual. **Type:** recognition. **Recipient:** for outstanding activism in support of the forest-based industries ● Outstanding Logger Award. **Frequency:** annual. **Type:** recognition. **Recipient:** for outstanding performance in timber harvesting as a business ● Outstanding Technical Writing. **Frequency:** annual. **Type:** recognition. **Recipient:** to the author of the finest member-written article the association has published in the previous calendar year. **Telecommunication Services:** electronic mail, nward@forestresources.org. **Formerly:** (2000) American Pulpwood Association. **Publications:** *Forest Operations Review*, quarterly. Magazine. Includes articles and technical briefs of interest to industrial foresters and logging contractors. **Price:** free for members; $160.00 for nonmembers in U.S.; $290.00 for nonmembers outside U.S. **Circulation:** 4,500. **Advertising:** accepted. Alternate Formats: online ● *FRA Bulletin*, periodic. Newsletter. Provides updates and analysis on industry and policy developments. **Price:** free for members; $160.00 for nonmembers in U.S.; $290.00 for nonmembers outside U.S. ISSN: 1529-0522. **Circulation:** 2,100. **Advertising:** accepted. Alternate Formats: online ● Also issues statistical reports and topical publications. **Conventions/Meetings:** annual meeting, policy meetings and educational sessions (exhibits).

1608 ■ Intermountain Forest Association (IFA)
3731 N Ramsey Rd., Ste.110
Coeur d'Alene, ID 83815
Ph: (208)667-4641
Fax: (208)664-0557
E-mail: info@intforest.org
URL: http://www.ifia.com
Contact: James S. Riley, Pres.
Founded: 1986. **Members:** 40. **Staff:** 6. **Description:** Companies within the timber industry. Seeks to provide a unified voice for the industry; promotes a sustained and perpetual timber yield. Monitors federal legislation on industry-related issues. Compiles statistics. **Formed by Merger of:** Inland Forest Resource Council; Idaho Forest Industry Council; Intermountain Forestry Services. **Formerly:** (2002) Intermountain Forest Industry Association. **Conventions/Meetings:** annual meeting - always December in Coeur d'Alene, ID.

1609 ■ International Wood Products Association (IWPA)
4214 King St. W
Alexandria, VA 22302
Ph: (703)820-6696
Fax: (703)820-8550
E-mail: info@iwpawood.org
URL: http://www.iwpawood.org
Contact: Brent J. McClendon CAE, Exec. VP
Founded: 1956. **Members:** 196. **Membership Dues:** new (initial), $1,890 ● new (based on annual sales volume), $1,890-$8,295 (annual) ● associate (initial for domestic/overseas), $600 ● associate (domestic), $1,365 (annual) ● associate (overseas), $1,130 (annual). **Staff:** 4. **Budget:** $500,000. **Description:** Importers, processors, manufacturers, and distributors of imported wood products; steamship companies; customs brokers, etc. Membership figure represents participants from 30 countries. Promotes acceptance and use of imported wood products; develops product standards; compiles statistics; supports good forestry management. **Awards:** Hall of Fame and Distinguished Service. **Type:** recognition. **Recipient:** for excellence in the imported wood products industry. **Committees:** C.U.R.E.; Engineered Panel Products; Government Affairs; Lumber/Lumber Products; Plywood; Veneer. **Formerly:** (1956) Imported Hardwood Plywood Association of America; (1969) Imported Hardwood Plywood Association; (1982) Imported Hardwood Products Association; (1994) International Hardwood Products Association. **Publications:** *Import Statistics*, quarterly ● *Imported Wood: The Guide to Applications, Sources and Trends*, annual. Magazine. **Price:** $15.00 per additional copy; free (initial copy) ● *Legislative Activities*, quarterly. **Conventions/Meetings:** annual World of Wood - convention (exhibits).

1610 ■ New England Kiln Drying Association (NEKDA)
c/o Scott Ferland, Pres.
36 Frost St.
Brattleboro, VT 05301
E-mail: kilndry@kilndry.com
URL: http://www.esf.edu/nekda
Contact: Scott Ferland, Pres.
Founded: 1951. **Members:** 500. **Membership Dues:** supporting, $60 (annual) ● individual, $20 (annual).

Description: Individuals and firms involved or interested in the drying of wood in kilns. Disseminates information on the drying of wood to the wood-using industry and other interested persons. Conducts workshops and technical meeting. **Additional Websites:** http://www.kilndry.com/macgregormill.html. **Publications:** *Drying Eastern White Pine* ● *NEKDA Membership Directory*, annual ● Newsletter, periodic. **Conventions/Meetings:** semiannual meeting.

1611 ■ North American Wholesale Lumber Association (NAWLA)
3601 Algonquin Rd., Ste.400
Rolling Meadows, IL 60008
Ph: (847)870-7470
Free: (800)527-8258
Fax: (847)870-0201
E-mail: info@lumber.org
URL: http://www.lumber.org
Contact: Nicholas R. Kent, Pres./CEO
Founded: 1893. **Members:** 657. **Membership Dues:** wholesaler, $995-$2,220 (annual) ● manufacturer, $675-$1,345 (annual) ● service affiliate, $840 (annual) ● branch, $320 (annual). **Staff:** 8. **Budget:** $2,000,000. **Description:** Wholesale distributors of lumber, wood products, and complementary products. Aids members with procedure for settling trade disputes. Provides weeklong course for wholesale lumber traders. Compiles statistics. Provides networking opportunities at regional, and annual meetings, trade show, and NAWLA Traders Market. **Telecommunication Services:** electronic mail, nrkent@nawla.org. **Committees:** Awards; Business Services; Communications; Education; Information Services; Magellan Club; Membership; Traders Market; Western Red Cedar Lumber Advisory. **Departments:** Group Insurance. **Formerly:** National Wholesale Lumber Dealers Association; National-American Wholesale Lumber Association. **Publications:** *NAWLA Distribution Directory*, annual. **Price:** $95.00 ● *North American Wholesale Lumber Association—Membership Bulletin*, monthly ● Manual ● Surveys. **Conventions/Meetings:** annual conference.

1612 ■ Northeastern Loggers Association (NELA)
PO Box 69
Old Forge, NY 13420
Ph: (315)369-3078
Free: (800)318-7561
Fax: (315)369-3736
E-mail: jphaneuf@nothernlogger.com
URL: http://www.northernlogger.com
Contact: Joseph E. Phaneuf, Exec. Dir.
Founded: 1952. **Members:** 2,200. **Membership Dues:** individual (class I-VI), $32-$375 (annual) ● associate (class A1-A3), $75-$200 (annual) ● individual, $21 (annual). **Staff:** 6. **Budget:** $1,000,000. **Description:** Timberland owners, independent loggers, professional foresters, and primary wood products industries. Works to improve the industry in the Northeast and educate the public about the policies, practices, and products of the industry. Maintains Forest Industries Exhibit Hall. Cooperates in research by public and private agencies. Operates museum; conducts educational program. **Libraries: Type:** not open to the public. **Holdings:** video recordings. **Subjects:** safety, forestry, wood supply. **Awards: Frequency:** annual. **Type:** recognition. **Recipient:** for outstanding service and management within the forest products industry. **Telecommunication Services:** additional toll-free number, (800)318-7562. **Committees:** Awards; Safety. **Absorbed:** (1956) Northeastern Wood Utilization Council. **Publications:** *Northern Logger and Timber Processor*, monthly. Journal. Covers the logging and saw milling industries in the Northeast and the Great Lakes states. Includes book reviews and recent literature. **Price:** $12.00/year; $18.00/24 issues; $25.00/36 issues. ISSN: 0029-3156. **Circulation:** 13,600. **Advertising:** accepted. **Conventions/Meetings:** annual Northeastern Forest Product Equipment Expo - trade show (exhibits).

1613 ■ Northwest Forestry Association (NFA)
1500 SW 1st Ave., Ste.700
Portland, OR 97201
Ph: (503)222-9505
Fax: (503)222-3255
E-mail: nfa@woodcom.seagull.com
URL: http://www.batnet.com/woodcom/nfa/index.html
Founded: 1987. **Members:** 80. **Staff:** 7. **Budget:** $736,000. **Description:** Manufacturers of forest products in Oregon and Washington organized to promote forestry throughout the region in order to assure a permanent industry and a stable economy. Works to: keep informed on current changes affecting the forest products industry; cooperate with agencies on resource management issues and assist these agencies in the implementation of resource management. Seeks to inform the public on matters concerning the Northwest forest products industry. **Committees:** Legal; Technical; Wildlife. **Formed by Merger of:** Industrial Forestry Association; Northwest Pine Association. **Publications:** *Forestry Forum*, semimonthly. Newsletter. **Conventions/Meetings:** annual meeting - always April or May.

1614 ■ Northwestern Lumber Association (NLA)
1405 Lilac Dr. N, No. 130
Minneapolis, MN 55422
Ph: (763)544-6822
Free: (800)331-0193
Fax: (763)595-4060
E-mail: nlassn@nlassn.org
URL: http://www.nlassn.org
Contact: Paula Siewert, Pres.
Founded: 1890. **Members:** 1,500. **Staff:** 10. **Description:** Building materials dealers in Iowa, Minnesota, North Dakota, and South Dakota; associate members are distributors, manufacturers, and allied industries. **Telecommunication Services:** electronic mail, psiewertnla@megapathdsl.net. **Affiliated With:** National Lumber and Building Material Dealers Association. **Formerly:** Northwestern Lumbermen's Association. **Publications:** *Building Material Retailer*, monthly. Magazine. For lumber dealers, manufacturers, and suppliers selling volume trade to contractor market. **Price:** included in membership dues; $18.00 /year for nonmembers. **Circulation:** 30,000. **Advertising:** accepted ● *Building Products Connection*, bimonthly. Magazine ● *Dealer Reference Manual and Buyers' Guide*. Alternate Formats: CD-ROM ● *Northwestern Lumbermen's Association—Dealer Reference Manual*, annual. Membership Directory. Contains trade name and advertisers' index, buyer's guide of manufacturers, and suppliers and product listings. **Price:** free for members; $75.00 /year for nonmembers ● *Northwestern Scene*, monthly. Newsletter. **Conventions/Meetings:** annual Northwestern Building Products Expo - convention.

1615 ■ Pacific Logging Congress (PLC)
PO Box 1281
Maple Valley, WA 98038
Ph: (425)413-2808
Fax: (425)413-1359
E-mail: pacificlogging@aol.com
URL: http://www.pacificloggingcongress.org
Contact: Rikki Wellman, Exec. Dir.
Founded: 1909. **Members:** 400. **Membership Dues:** company in U.S. (based on number of employees), $50-$500 (annual) ● company in Canada (based on number of employees), $85-$830 (annual). **Staff:** 1. **Budget:** $100,000. **Regional Groups:** 8. **Multinational. Description:** Logging firms, manufacturers of wood products and logging equipment, and distributors in Canada, New Zealand, and the United States. **Publications:** none. **Conventions/Meetings:** annual convention (exhibits) ● quadrennial In the Woods Demo Show - convention (exhibits).

1616 ■ Pacific Lumber Exporters Association (PLEA)
1260 NW Waterhouse Ave., Ste.150
Beaverton, OR 97006
Ph: (503)439-6000
Fax: (503)439-6330
E-mail: info@lumber-exporters.org
URL: http://lumber-exporters.org
Contact: Paul Owen, Pres.
Founded: 1923. **Members:** 50. **Membership Dues:** exporting, $150 (annual). **Local Groups:** 1. **Languages:** Chinese, English, Japanese, Korean. **Multinational. Description:** Exporters of wood products from the states of Washington, Oregon, and Idaho. Works cooperatively with sawmills, lumber inspection bureaus, and steamship conferences. **Conventions/Meetings:** dinner and meeting - 3/year.

1617 ■ Pacific Lumber Inspection Bureau (PLIB)
33442 First Way S, Ste.300
Federal Way, WA 98003
Ph: (253)835-3344
Fax: (253)835-3371
E-mail: info@plib.org
Contact: Ted Smith, Pres.
Founded: 1903. **Members:** 50. **Staff:** 7. **Budget:** $1,000,000. **Description:** Lumber grading association of manufacturers in Oregon, Washington and British Columbia. Approved by American Lumber Standards Committee (see separate entry) and Canadian Lumber Standards Accreditation Board for grading and grade stamping of softwood lumber. Issues certificates on domestic and export lumber shipments. **Publications:** *Export "R" List Grading and Dressing Rules*. Booklet. Contains grading and dressing rules for export lumber. **Price:** $4.50. **Conventions/Meetings:** semiannual board meeting - always June and December ● annual meeting.

1618 ■ Redwood Inspection Service (RIS)
c/o California Redwood Association
405 Enfrente Dr., Ste.200
Novato, CA 94949
Ph: (415)382-0662
Free: (888)225-7339
Fax: (415)382-8531
E-mail: info@calredwood.org
URL: http://www.calredwood.org
Contact: Charles J. Jourdain, VP
Founded: 1961. **Members:** 14. **Staff:** 5. **Description:** A division of California Redwood Association. Lumber manufacturers authorized by the Department of Commerce to develop and supervise redwood lumber grading. Provides schools to train individuals in lumber grading. **Committees:** Redwood Quality Standards. **Publications:** *Standard Specifications for Grades of California Redwood Lumber*. Book. Serves as the official grade-rule book for redwood lumber industry. **Price:** $5.00.

1619 ■ Softwood Export Council (SEC)
520 SW 6th Ave., Ste.810
Portland, OR 97204-1514
Ph: (503)248-0406
Fax: (503)248-0399
E-mail: info@softwood.org
URL: http://www.softwood.org
Contact: Craig L. Larsen, Pres.
Founded: 1998. **Members:** 16. **Membership Dues:** individual, $125 (annual) ● small company (with under $1 million in sales), $250 (annual) ● large company (with over $1 million in sales), $375 (annual). **Staff:** 2. **Multinational. Description:** Coordinates overseas market development activities for the U.S. softwood industry with the Foreign Agricultural Service; aids American Exports of softwood products by providing information and assistance to agents, importers, designers, and users of these products in other countries. **Publications:** *Softwood Export Council Newsletter*, quarterly. Alternate Formats: online. **Conventions/Meetings:** annual board meeting - every December.

1620 ■ Southeastern Lumber Manufacturers Association (SLMA)
PO Box 1788
Forest Park, GA 30298
Ph: (404)361-1445
Fax: (404)361-5963
E-mail: info@slma.org
URL: http://www.slma.org
Contact: Stephen H. Rountree, Pres.
Founded: 1962. **Members:** 225. **Membership Dues:** treater, $1,500 (annual) ● associate, $500 (annual). **Staff:** 7. **Budget:** $1,800,000. **Description:** Independent southeastern lumber manufacturers. Represents

and coordinates efforts of membership to alleviate local, regional, and national problems that affect independent southeastern lumber manufacturing industry. Conducts marketing and promotional activities. **Committees:** Forestry and Environmental Affairs; Governmental Affairs; Hardwood Marketing; Pine Marketing; Production and Management Issues. **Publications:** *Management Update Weekly*. Newsletter ● Membership Directory, annual ● Reports. **Conventions/Meetings:** annual meeting and conference (exhibits) - usually August.

1621 ■ Southern Cypress Manufacturers Association (SCMA)
400 Penn Center Blvd., Ste.530
Pittsburgh, PA 15235
Free: (877)607-SCMA
Fax: (412)829-0844
URL: http://www.cypressinfo.org
Contact: Gene Wengert, Pres.
Founded: 1905. **Members:** 19. **Staff:** 1. **Budget:** $20,000. **Description:** Producers of Cypress lumber and manufacturers of other Cypress products. **Publications:** *Cypress: The Distinction You Deserve*. Brochure. Contains consumer information. ● *SCMA Buyer's Guide and Directory*, periodic. **Price:** free. Alternate Formats: online. **Conventions/Meetings:** annual conference.

1622 ■ Southern Forest Products Association (SFPA)
2900 Indiana Ave.
Kenner, LA 70065
Ph: (504)443-4464
Fax: (504)443-6612
E-mail: mail@sfpa.org
URL: http://www.sfpa.org
Contact: Digges Morgan, Pres.
Founded: 1915. **Members:** 240. **Membership Dues:** associate, $500 (annual) ● active (maximum), $350,000 (annual). **Staff:** 20. **Budget:** $4,027,265. **Description:** Southern pine lumber manufacturers. Conducts market development and product promotional programs. **Additional Websites:** http://www.southernpine.com. **Telecommunication Services:** electronic mail, dmorgan@sfpa.org. **Committees:** Exposition Advisory; Government Affairs; Marketing. **Affiliated With:** American Forest and Paper Association; APA: The Engineered Wood Association; Southeastern Lumber Manufacturers Association. **Publications:** *Mill Activity Summary*, weekly ● *SFPA Newsletter*, weekly. Covers forest products, timber resources, market development activities, transportation, lumber manufacturing, and business and association news. **Price:** free for members; $50.00 /year for nonmembers. **Circulation:** 1,000 ● *Southern Pine Production Update*, monthly. **Conventions/Meetings:** annual board meeting, includes membership meeting ● biennial Forest Products Machinery and Equipment Exposition - trade show and meeting ● annual meeting, with membership meetings (exhibits) - always spring.

1623 ■ Southern Pine Inspection Bureau (SPIB)
c/o Bob Browder, Dir.
PO Box 10915
Pensacola, FL 32524-0915
Ph: (850)434-2611
Fax: (850)433-5594
URL: http://www.spib.org
Contact: Bob Browder, Dir.
Founded: 1940. **Description:** Develops grading standards for southern pine lumber and provides an inspection service and system of grade-marking. Sponsored by Southern Pine Lumber Manufacturers. **Conventions/Meetings:** semiannual meeting.

1624 ■ Southern Pressure Treaters' Association (SPTA)
PO Box 3219
Pineville, LA 71361-3219
Ph: (318)619-8589
Fax: (318)767-1388
E-mail: sptala@bellsouth.net
URL: http://www.spta.org
Contact: April James, Exec. Dir.
Founded: 1954. **Members:** 50. **Staff:** 1. **Budget:** $75,000. **Description:** Manufacturers who apply preservative pressure treatment (there are four basic preservatives: creosote, waterborne salts, pentachlorophenol, and fire retardants) to such products as utility and building poles, pilings, railroad ties, fence posts, lumber, laminated timbers, and floor blocks. Sponsors college seminars and compiles statistics. **Awards:** Safety and Service. **Frequency:** annual. **Type:** recognition. **Recipient:** for OSHA standards. **Committees:** Arrangements; Environmental; Forestry; Insurance; Marketing and Education; Plant Operations; Safety; Standards; Traffic. **Publications:** *Product-Mix Information*, quarterly ● *Safety-Disabling Injury Reporting*, annual ● *Wage and Working Conditions Survey*, annual ● Newsletter, periodic. **Conventions/Meetings:** semiannual conference - always January and June.

1625 ■ Timber Framers Guild (TFG)
PO Box 60
Becket, MA 01223
Ph: (413)623-9926 (603)835-2077
Free: (888)453-0879
Fax: (888)453-0879
E-mail: info@tfguild.org
URL: http://www.tfguild.org
Contact: Will Beemer, Exec. Dir.
Founded: 1984. **Members:** 1,700. **Membership Dues:** individual in U.S. and Canada, $85 (annual) ● family in U.S. and Canada, $25 (annual) ● student in U.S. and Canada, individual outside U.S. and Canada, $50 (annual). **Staff:** 4. **Budget:** $300,000. **Multinational. Description:** Teaches members and the general public about the craft of timber frame construction through publications, conferences, and workshops. **Computer Services:** database ● mailing lists. **Publications:** *Timber Framing*, quarterly. Journal. **Price:** $25.00/year. **Circulation:** 2,000. **Advertising:** accepted. **Conventions/Meetings:** annual conference - 2009 Mar. 25-29, Sunriver, OR.

1626 ■ Timber Products Manufacturers (TPM)
951 E 3rd Ave.
Spokane, WA 99202-2215
Ph: (509)535-4646
Free: (877)535-4646
Fax: (509)534-6106
E-mail: tpm@tpmrs.com
URL: http://www.tpmrs.com
Contact: Charles M. Fox, Pres.
Founded: 1916. **Members:** 220. **Staff:** 8. **Description:** Works as full-service employer association offering human resource and safety and risk management consulting, employee benefits and training. **Awards:** Old Timers Award. **Frequency:** biennial. **Type:** recognition. **Recipient:** for employees serving in timber industry for over 40 years ● President's Award. **Frequency:** annual. **Type:** recognition. **Recipient:** for outstanding service to the association and the industry. **Telecommunication Services:** electronic mail, cfox@tpmrs.com. **Committees:** Safety and Health; Training. **Formerly:** (1969) Timber Products Manufacturers Association. **Publications:** *Frontline*, monthly. Newsletter. Publication for front line supervisors. **Circulation:** 400 ● *Management Bulletin*, monthly ● Also publishes periodic information pieces. **Conventions/Meetings:** quarterly board meeting.

1627 ■ Washington Forest Protection Association (WFPA)
724 Columbia St. NW, Ste.250
Olympia, WA 98501
Ph: (360)352-1500
Fax: (360)352-4621
E-mail: info@wfpa.org
URL: http://www.wfpa.org
Contact: Peter Heide, Dir. of Forest Management
Founded: 1908. **Members:** 52. **Staff:** 17. **Languages:** English, German. **Description:** Owners of timberland in Washington. Advocates public policies favorable to the forest products industry. **Committees:** Communication; Environmental Affairs; Environmental Education; Forest Management; Forest Taxation; Government Relations; Legal. **Publications:** *FYI*, quarterly. Newsletter. Contains research summary. ● Annual Report, annual. **Conventions/Meetings:** annual meeting.

1628 ■ West Coast Lumber Inspection Bureau (WCLIB)
PO Box 23145
Tigard, OR 97281
Ph: (503)639-0651
Fax: (503)684-8928
E-mail: info@wclib.org
URL: http://www.wclib.org
Contact: Bradley E. Shelley, Exec. VP
Founded: 1941. **Members:** 150. **Staff:** 16. **Description:** Manufacturers of lumber and related products predominantly in the Douglas Fir region of western Washington, western Oregon, and northern California. Offers membership nationwide. Supervises manufacturing practices, grade stamping, inspecting, and reinspecting of lumber and treated wood. Principal species graded include Douglas Fir, Hem-Fir, Hemlock, Sitka Spruce, Spruce-Pine-Fir South, West Coast Hemlock, Western Red Cedar, and White Fir. **Telecommunication Services:** electronic mail, bshelley@wclib.org. **Publications:** Publishes grading rules. **Conventions/Meetings:** annual meeting - always April in Portland, OR.

1629 ■ Western Building Material Association (WBMA)
PO Box 1699
Olympia, WA 98507
Ph: (360)943-3054
Fax: (360)943-1219
E-mail: casey@wbma.org
URL: http://www.wbma.org
Contact: Casey Voorhees, Exec. Dir.
Founded: 1903. **Members:** 550. **Membership Dues:** associate, $295 (annual) ● regular, $95 (annual) ● manpower, $225-$795 (annual) ● regular (initiation), $225. **Staff:** 5. **Regional Groups:** 6. **Description:** Retail lumber and building material dealers in states of Alaska, Hawaii, Idaho, Montana, Oregon, and Washington. Seeks to further and protect the interests of retail lumber dealers. Services include: classes, workshops, and seminars; group insurance and pension; printing of business forms; government and legislative action; information clearinghouse; training courses for personnel. Maintains a learning resource center. Conducts educational programs. **Libraries: Type:** reference; lending; not open to the public. **Holdings:** 500; audiovisuals, books, periodicals. **Subjects:** business, industry related. **Awards:** Distinguished Dealer of the Year. **Frequency:** annual. **Type:** recognition. **Recipient:** for service to community, state, federal, industry. **Committees:** Education; Insurance Trust; Legislative; Long Range; Pension Trust; Safety; Scholarship; Young Westerners. **Affiliated With:** National Lumber and Building Material Dealers Association. **Formerly:** (1967) Western Retail Lumbermen's Association. **Publications:** *Western Building Material Association—Management Guide*, monthly. Bulletin ● *Western Building Material Association—Newsletter*, monthly ● *Western News*, monthly. Bulletin. Contains information on legislative and government affairs and management and personnel development. **Price:** available to members only. **Circulation:** 700. Alternate Formats: online. **Conventions/Meetings:** annual Building Products Showcase - convention (exhibits) - always November ● annual conference - always spring ● annual Young Westerners Club Conference.

1630 ■ Western Hardwood Association (WHA)
PO Box 1095
Camas, WA 98607
Ph: (360)835-1600
Fax: (360)835-1900
E-mail: wha@westernhardwood.org
URL: http://www.westernhardwood.org
Contact: David A. Sweitzer, Sec./Mgr.
Founded: 1955. **Members:** 105. **Membership Dues:** regular, $550 (annual) ● affiliate, $350 (annual) ●

small woodland owner, $50 (annual) ● gold, $1,000 (annual). **Staff:** 1. **Description:** Timberland owners, sawmill operators, manufacturers, wholesalers, and lumber brokers; manufacturers of furniture, pallets, kitchen cabinets, veneer, and cut stock. Works to conserve, utilize, and promote Pacific coast hardwoods. Sponsors education programs in hardwood grading. Compiles statistics on production of lumber and other products by members. **Committees:** Economic Research; Grading Rules; Legislative; Promotion; Raw Material Supply. **Formerly:** (1983) Northwest Hardwood Association. **Publications:** *The Hardwood Stand*, monthly. **Circulation:** 325. **Advertising:** accepted ● *Western Hardwood Association—Membership Roster*, annual. Membership Directory. **Price:** free ● Brochures. **Conventions/Meetings:** annual conference (exhibits) - always spring ● annual Grading School - meeting.

1631 ■ Western Wood Products Association (WWPA)
522 SW 5th Ave., Ste.500
Portland, OR 97204-2122
Ph: (503)224-3930
Fax: (503)224-3934
E-mail: info@wwpa.org
URL: http://www.wwpa.org
Contact: Michael R. O'Halloran, Pres./CEO
Founded: 1964. **Members:** 120. **Staff:** 32. **Budget:** $4,000,000. **Description:** Represents lumber manufacturers in 12 Western states and Alaska. Delivers lumber grade inspection and quality control, technical support, product/market support and statistical services to Western sawmills. **Committees:** Economic Services; Export; Product Support; Quality Standards. **Formed by Merger of:** (1964) West Coast Lumbermen's Association; (1964) Western Pine Association. **Conventions/Meetings:** annual meeting - always spring.

Forest Products

1632 ■ Alliance for Environmental Technology (AET)
1250 24th St. NW, Ste.300
Washington, DC 20037
Free: (800)999-PULP
E-mail: info@aet.org
URL: http://www.aet.org
Contact: Douglas C. Pryke, Exec. Dir.
Multinational. Description: Chemical manufacturers and forest product companies. Seeks to improve the environmental performance of the pulp and paper industry. Supports the use of chlorine dioxide bleaching. **Publications:** *AET Newsplash*, bimonthly. Newsletter ● *ECF: The Sustainable Technology*. Brochure. Alternate Formats: online.

1633 ■ American Institute of Timber Construction (AITC)
7012 S Revere Pkwy., Ste.140
Centennial, CO 80112
Ph: (303)792-9559
Fax: (303)792-0669
E-mail: info@aitc-glulam.org
URL: http://www.aitc-glulam.org
Contact: R. Michael Caldwell, Exec. VP
Founded: 1952. **Members:** 500. **Membership Dues:** supplier, $505 (annual) ● associate, $155 (annual) ● professional, $55 (annual) ● student, $30 (annual). **Staff:** 7. **Budget:** $800,000. **Description:** Manufacturers of structural glued laminated timber; affiliate members are subcontractors who design, shop, fabricate, and assemble structural timber framing; associate members are firms or organizations connected with engineered timber construction; professional members are engineers, architects, building code officials, and professors; supplier members are companies furnishing industry supplies. Develops timber construction standards and specifications and timber design and construction publications. Conducts quality control and inspection program. Conducts research to develop technical construction data and information on structural glued laminated timber. Advises architects, engineers, building code officials, and others on qualities of engineered timber construction. **Libraries: Type:** reference. **Subjects:** structural glued laminated timber. **Telecommunication Services:** electronic mail, rmc@aitc-glulam.org. **Boards:** Technical Review. **Committees:** Marketing Advisory; Technical Advisory. **Departments:** Inspection Bureau. **Publications:** *Lam Lines*, quarterly. Newsletter. **Price:** free. **Circulation:** 500 ● *Timber Construction Manual* ● Also publishes construction standards, technical notes, and other publications; produces slides and design and visual aids. **Conventions/Meetings:** annual general assembly (exhibits) - always in April.

1634 ■ American Lumber Standard Committee (ALSC)
PO Box 210
Germantown, MD 20875-0210
Ph: (301)972-1700
Fax: (301)540-8004
E-mail: alsc@alsc.org
URL: http://www.alsc.org
Contact: Thomas D. Searles, Pres.
Founded: 1922. **Members:** 28. **Staff:** 12. **Budget:** $1,600,000. **Multinational. Description:** Members appointed by the Department of Commerce to represent producers, consumers, and specifiers of softwood lumber. Establishes and maintains standards for size, grade, and other matters; elects an independent board of review to approve softwood lumber grading rules and accredit agencies that audit treating plants and accredit agencies that audit pallet, box and crate manufacturers for international trade. **Telecommunication Services:** electronic mail, rreck@alsc.org. **Committees:** National Grading Rule. **Programs:** Treated Wood; Untreated Wood; Wood Packaging Material. **Formerly:** (1941) Central Committee on Lumber Standards. **Publications:** *Accredited Agencies for Supervisory and Lot Inspection of Pressure-Treated Wood Products*. **Price:** free ● *ALSC Agencies Typical Grade Stamps*. **Conventions/Meetings:** annual meeting - always in November.

1635 ■ American Walnut Manufacturers Association (AWMA)
PO Box 5046
Zionsville, IN 46077
Ph: (317)873-8780
Fax: (317)873-8780
E-mail: fryelarryr@aol.com
URL: http://www.walnutassociation.org
Contact: Larry R. Frye, Exec. Dir.
Founded: 1912. **Members:** 8. **Membership Dues:** manufacturer, $1,800 (annual). **Staff:** 1. **Budget:** $18,000. **Description:** Manufacturers of hardwood veneer and lumber, especially American black walnut. Seeks to improve the sale of products made from hardwoods through advertising, promotion, sales education, and product improvement; also promotes good forest management. **Libraries: Type:** reference. **Holdings:** 240. **Subjects:** wood technology, furniture design and construction, forestry production. **Awards: Type:** recognition. **Committees:** Forestry; Promotion; Walnut Lumber. **Formerly:** (1985) Fine Hardwoods American Walnut Association; (1998) Fine Hardwood Veneer Association/American Walnut Manufacturers Association. **Publications:** *American Black Walnut*. Brochure ● Membership Directory, periodic ● Pamphlets. **Conventions/Meetings:** annual meeting, held in conjunction with the National Hardwood Lumber Association.

1636 ■ American Wood-Preservers' Association (AWPA)
PO Box 361784
Birmingham, AL 35236-1784
Ph: (205)733-4077
Fax: (205)733-4075
E-mail: email@awpa.com
URL: http://www.awpa.com
Contact: Colin McCown, Exec. VP
Founded: 1904. **Members:** 1,200. **Membership Dues:** regular (includes $10 application fee), $85-$160 (annual). **Staff:** 2. **Budget:** $250,000. **Description:** Aims to promulgate voluntary wood preservation standards. **Awards:** Award of Merit. **Frequency:** annual. **Type:** recognition. **Recipient:** for distinguished service in furthering the purposes of the association. **Publications:** *AWPA Book of Standards*, annual. Handbook. Covers preservatives and treatments. **Price:** $90.00 for members; $250.00 for nonmembers. ISSN: 1534-195X. **Circulation:** 1,000. Alternate Formats: CD-ROM. Also Cited As: *American Wood Preservers' Association Standards* ● *AWPA Proceedings*, annual. **Price:** $125.00/copy. ISSN: 0066-1198. **Circulation:** 800. **Advertising:** accepted. **Conventions/Meetings:** annual international conference, general meeting in which papers are presented and committees report on the development of standards - always in April/May. 2009 Apr. 19-21, San Antonio, TX ● annual meeting, technical committees meet to develop standards for wood protection - every September.

1637 ■ APA: The Engineered Wood Association
7011 S 19th
Tacoma, WA 98466
Ph: (253)565-6600
Fax: (253)565-7265
E-mail: help@apawood.org
URL: http://www.apawood.org
Contact: Dennis Hardman, Pres.
Founded: 1936. **Members:** 120. **Staff:** 145. **Budget:** $14,000,000. **Description:** Manufacturers of structural panel products, oriented strand board and composites. Conducts trade promotion through advertising, publicity, merchandising, and field promotion. Maintains quality supervision in accordance with U.S. product standards, APA performance standards, and APA trademarking. Conducts research to improve products, applications, and manufacturing techniques. Sponsors Engineered Wood Research Foundation (see separate entry); compiles statistics. **Libraries: Type:** reference. **Subjects:** structural panel products. **Awards:** APA Safety Awards. **Frequency:** annual. **Type:** recognition. **Recipient:** for mill safety. **Committees:** Environmental Affairs; International Markets; Marketing; Quality Services; Technical Services. **Affiliated With:** Engineered Wood Technology Association. **Formerly:** (1964) Douglas Fir Plywood Association; (1994) American Plywood Association. **Publications:** *The Engineered Wood Connection*, periodic. Newsletter. Features a broad range of engineering design topics. Alternate Formats: online ● *Engineered Wood Journal*. **Advertising:** accepted ● *Management Report*, monthly ● *Plywood Statistics*, periodic ● Also publishes application guides and product data inventories. **Conventions/Meetings:** annual meeting (exhibits).

1638 ■ Appalachian Hardwood Manufacturers, Inc. (AHMI)
PO Box 427
High Point, NC 27261
Ph: (336)885-8315
Fax: (336)886-8865
E-mail: info@appalachianwood.org
URL: http://www.appalachianwood.org
Contact: Tom Inman, Pres.
Founded: 1928. **Members:** 201. **Membership Dues:** producer within the Appalachian region (based on monthly production), $150-$200 (monthly) ● distributor (based on annual sales), $500-$2,000 (annual) ● land owner and supplier, $500 (annual) ● consulting forester, $100 (annual) ● consumer, $250 (annual). **Staff:** 3. **Description:** Promotes Appalachian hardwoods. **Awards: Type:** recognition. **Telecommunication Services:** electronic mail, tom@appalachianwood.org. **Divisions:** Distributor; Forestry. **Formerly:** (1932) Appalachian Hardwood Club. **Publications:** *Appalachian Hardwood*, annual. Yearbook ● *Hardwood Forests of the Eastern U.S. - A Quite Success Story*. Video ● *Lessons in Appalachian Forestry* ● *The Standard*, monthly. Newsletter. Contains information about the association and its members and the forest product industry. ● *Your Wood Fact Book* ● Membership Directory, annual ● Brochure. **Conventions/Meetings:** annual convention - always in February ● annual Inter-Industry Meeting - always in

October ● annual Summer Family Conference - always in July.

1639 ■ California Redwood Association (CRA)
405 Enfrente Dr., Ste.200
Novato, CA 94949
Ph: (415)382-0662
Free: (888)225-7339
Fax: (415)382-8531
E-mail: info@calredwood.org
URL: http://www.calredwood.org
Contact: Christopher F. Grover, Pres.
Founded: 1916. **Members:** 5. **Staff:** 6. **Description:** Represents manufacturers of redwood lumber products. Serves as a source of technical information for all who study, sell, or buy redwood products. **Committees:** Promotion. **Publications:** *All Decked Out Redwood Decks*. Book. **Price:** $30.00 single copy ● *Fancy Fences and Gates*. Book. **Price:** $21.00 single copy ● *Landscape Architecture*. Booklet. Features specifying guides for redwood garden applications. **Price:** $1.50 single copy ● *Redwood Design Gallery*. Booklet. Features decks, fences, arbors, trellises and gates made from redwood. Includes photos. **Price:** $2.50 single copy ● *Redwood: Frequently Asked Questions*. Booklet. **Price:** $3.60 single copy ● Also publishes data files. **Conventions/Meetings:** annual meeting - always second Tuesday of September in Eureka, CA.

1640 ■ Cedar Shake and Shingle Bureau (CSSB)
PO Box 1178
Sumas, WA 98295-1178
Ph: (604)820-7700
Fax: (604)820-0266
E-mail: info@cedarbureau.com
URL: http://www.cedarbureau.org
Contact: Lynne Christensen MBA, Dir. of Operations
Founded: 1915. **Members:** 400. **Membership Dues:** manufacturer, $200 (monthly) ● distributor/broker/wholesaler, $1,100 (annual) ● retailer and approved installer, $750 (annual) ● associate, $300 (annual) ● subsidiary (same company), $150 (annual) ● subsidiary (different company), $160 (annual). **Staff:** 8. **Multinational. Description:** Represents shake and shingle manufacturers, distributors, brokers, retailers, wholesalers, installers, and care/maintenance contractors in North America. Promotes the common interests of members involved in wood roofing and sidewall business. Experienced in administering quality assurance, lobbying for building code acceptance of members' products, quality marketing services, and support and protection of the viability of the industry. Bureau's Certi-labels are widely recognized in the industry as a symbol of quality. **Formed by Merger of:** Red Cedar Shingle Bureau; Handsplit Red Cedar Shake Association. **Formerly:** (1988) Red Cedar Shingle and Handsplit Shake Bureau. **Publications:** *Certi-label Confidence*. Brochure ● *Certi-Talk*, quarterly. Newsletter. Provides membership with bureau and industry updates. ● *Membership Directory and Buyer's Guide*, semiannual. Lists manufacturers, products, and services rendered. **Price:** free for members ● *New Roof Construction Manual* ● Also publishes a variety of product brochures. **Conventions/Meetings:** annual meeting - usually late summer or early fall.

1641 ■ Coalition for Fair Lumber Imports (CFLI)
975 F St. NW
Washington, DC 20004
Ph: (202)862-3686
Fax: (202)862-1093
E-mail: zoltan@4fairlumber.com
URL: http://www.fairlumbercoalition.org
Contact: Steve Swanson, Chm.
Founded: 1985. **Staff:** 2. **Budget:** $1,500,000. **Regional Groups:** 6. **State Groups:** 15. **Description:** U.S.-based producers of softwood lumber products. Seeks to "restore fair market competition to the softwood lumber market, and to promote long-term resolution to the problem of subsidized Canadian softwood lumber into the United States." Conducts educational programs to raise public awareness of softwood lumber market issues; conducts lobbying activities to secure trade regulations ensuring fair competition between members and their counterparts overseas. **Publications:** Newsletter, bimonthly.

1642 ■ Composite Lumber Manufacturers Association (CLMA)
1156 15th St. NW, Ste.900
Washington, DC 20005
Ph: (202)207-0906
Fax: (202)223-9741
E-mail: info@compositelumber.org
URL: http://www.compositelumber.org
Contact: Penny Alston, Admin. Mgr.
Founded: 2005. **Membership Dues:** regular, $30,000 (annual) ● associate (based on annual sales), $2,500-$5,000 (annual) ● contributory, $5,000 (annual) ● affiliate, $10,000 (annual). **Description:** Represents manufacturers and suppliers of composite lumber to the residential and commercial building construction markets. Promotes the values and use of composite lumber products. Enhances sustained market growth through code and standards organization representation. Promotes composite lumber materials to raise awareness for the industry and members. Serves as a technical and market information resource for the industry. **Telecommunication Services:** electronic mail, palston@kellencompany.com.

1643 ■ Composite Panel Association (CPA)
18922 Premiere Ct.
Gaithersburg, MD 20879-1574
Ph: (301)670-0604
Fax: (301)840-1252
E-mail: tjulia@cpamail.org
URL: http://www.pbmdf.com
Contact: Tom Julia, Pres.
Founded: 1960. **Members:** 36. **Staff:** 12. **Budget:** $1,648,400. **Multinational. Description:** Works as a North American trade association for the particleboard, medium density fiberboard (MDF) industries, hardboard, and for other compatible products. Dedicated in increasing the acceptance and use of industry products and providing for the general welfare of the industry. **Libraries: Type:** reference; not open to the public. **Holdings:** articles, books, periodicals. **Subjects:** wood products, standards, particle board. **Awards:** Robert E. Dougherty Award. **Frequency:** annual. **Type:** scholarship. **Committees:** Member Services; Production Management; Promotion; Technical. **Affiliated With:** Composite Wood Council. **Absorbed:** (2003) American Hardboard Association; (2004) Laminating Materials Association. **Formerly:** (1997) National Particleboard Association. **Publications:** *Buyer's and Specifiers Guide to Particle Board and MDF* (in English, French, and Spanish), annual. Brochure. **Price:** free ● *CPA/CWC Promotional Video*. **Price:** available to members only ● *Second Wave*, semiannual. Magazine. Alternate Formats: online ● Newsletter, weekly. **Price:** free, for members only. Alternate Formats: online. **Conventions/Meetings:** semiannual meeting - every spring and fall.

1644 ■ Cork Institute of America
c/o Dodge Regupol, Inc.
715 Fountain Ave.
Lancaster, PA 17601
Ph: (717)295-3400
Fax: (717)295-3414
E-mail: info@corkinstitute.com
URL: http://www.corkinstitute.com
Contact: Arthur Dodge Sr., Contact
Founded: 1933. **Members:** 15. **Membership Dues:** regular, $100 (annual). **Budget:** $20,000. **Languages:** English, Portuguese. **Description:** Promotes knowledge about the bark of the cork oak, commonly used as bottle stoppers, bulletin boards, gaskets, flooring, and many specialties. Disseminates technical literature to interested individuals. **Publications:** *Cork*. Book. Features the history of cork and its uses. **Price:** $28.00. **Conventions/Meetings:** biennial meeting - always New York.

1645 ■ Cork Quality Council
1160 Terrace Dr.
Forestville, CA 95436
Ph: (707)824-5831
E-mail: info@corkqc.com
URL: http://www.corkqc.com
Contact: Peter Weber, Dir.
Members: 7. **Description:** Devotes itself to education and quality control procedures concerning natural cork and the wine industry. **Computer Services:** database ● information services, cork quality control procedures ● information services, winery procedures ● online services. **Also Known As:** Natural Cork Quality Council.

1646 ■ Engineered Wood Technology Association (EWTA)
c/o APA - The Engineered Wood Association
7011 S 19th St.
Tacoma, WA 98466
Ph: (253)565-6600 (253)620-7237
Fax: (253)565-7265
E-mail: terry.kerwood@apawood.org
URL: http://www.apawood.org
Contact: Terry Kerwood, Managing Dir.
Founded: 1944. **Members:** 178. **Membership Dues:** associate, $1,200 (annual). **Staff:** 2. **Description:** Represents manufacturers of construction and industrial panels and related products; associate members. Sponsors research programs on improvement in panel production processes and techniques. **Awards:** Supplier of the Year Award. **Frequency:** annual. **Type:** recognition. **Recipient:** to members. **Affiliated With:** APA: The Engineered Wood Association. **Formerly:** Plywood Research Foundation; (2006) Engineered Wood Research Foundation. **Conventions/Meetings:** annual meeting.

1647 ■ Hardwood Distributor's Association (HDA)
c/o Heidler Hardwood Lumber, Co.
2559 S Damen Ave.
Chicago, IL 60608
Ph: (773)847-7444
Fax: (773)847-7833
URL: http://www.hardwooddistributors.net
Contact: Chuck Bice, Pres.
Founded: 1933. **Members:** 70. **Description:** Promotes the interests of Hardwood distributors. **Formerly:** (1985) National Wholesale Lumber Distributing Yard Association. **Conventions/Meetings:** annual conference, held in conjunction with National Hardwood Lumber Association - always October.

1648 ■ Hardwood Manufacturers Association (HMA)
400 Penn Center Blvd., Ste.530
Pittsburgh, PA 15235
Ph: (412)829-0770
Free: (800)373-9663
Fax: (412)829-0844
E-mail: info@hardwood.org
URL: http://www.hardwoodinfo.com
Contact: Susan Regan, Exec. VP
Founded: 1935. **Members:** 116. **Staff:** 10. **Description:** Represents manufacturers of hardwood lumber and hardwood products. Conducts promotion program; compiles statistics. **Awards:** Robert B. Hendricks/Hardwood Manufacturers Association Scholarship. **Frequency:** annual. **Type:** scholarship. **Recipient:** for a student enrolled in the college of agricultural and life sciences at the University of Wisconsin-Madison and the University of Wisconsin Foundation. **Formerly:** (1984) Southern Hardwood Producers; (1984) NF Association; (1984) Southern Hardwood Lumber Manufacturers Association. **Supersedes:** Hardwood Manufacturers Institute. **Publications:** *Hardwood Expressions* ● *HMA Link*, monthly. **Conventions/Meetings:** annual convention (exhibits) - always March ● annual Production Meeting and Exposition.

1649 ■ Hardwood Plywood and Veneer Association (HPVA)
1825 Michael Faraday Dr.
PO Box 2789
Reston, VA 20195-0789
Ph: (703)435-2900
Fax: (703)435-2537
E-mail: hpva@hpva.org
URL: http://www.hpva.org
Contact: Bill Altman, Pres.
Founded: 1921. **Members:** 195. **Membership Dues:** associate, $1,380 (annual) ● Engineered Hardwood Flooring Council (maximum; based on annual sales), $12,000 (annual) ● plywood manufacturer (maximum), $12,880 (annual) ● supplier, $3,120 (annual) ● veneer manufacturer, $1,200-$7,500 (annual) ● wholesale distributor, $1,080 (annual). **Staff:** 11. **Budget:** $1,400,000. **Description:** Manufacturers and finishers of hardwood plywood; and engineered wood flooring, manufacturers and sales agents of veneer; suppliers of glue, machinery, and other products related to the industry; stocking distributors. Conducts laboratory testing of plywood, adhesives, finishes, flamespread, formaldehyde emissions, structural, and smoke density. Performs glue bond, flamespread, formaldehyde emissions, and structural listing services. Provides public relations, advertising, marketing, and technical services to members. Represents the industry in legislative matters and keeps members informed on tariff and trade actions. **Libraries: Type:** reference. **Holdings:** 300. **Subjects:** hardwood plywood and veneer manufacturing and uses. **Telecommunication Services:** electronic mail, baltman@hpva.org. **Committees:** Marketing; Technical. **Divisions:** Cut-to-Size; Finish; Laminated Hardwood Flooring; Natural Resources; Stock Panel; Stocking Distributors; Supplier; Veneer. **Absorbed:** (1957) Southern Plywood Manufacturers Association; (1999) Fine Hardwood Veneer Association. **Formerly:** (1964) Hardwood Plywood Institute; (1992) Hardwood Plywood Manufacturers Association. **Publications:** *Executive Brief*, quarterly. Newsletter ● *Hardwood Plywood*. Handbook. **Price:** $15.00 for members; $20.00 for nonmembers ● *Hardwood Plywood and Veneer News*, monthly. Newsletter. **Advertising:** accepted ● *Where to Buy Hardwood Plywood and Veneer*, annual. Lists manufacturers of wood, sales agents, suppliers to these industries and wholesale stocking distributors. **Price:** $15.00 plus shipping and handling ● Also publishes executive briefs, standards, and design guides. **Conventions/Meetings:** semiannual conference - always spring and fall.

1650 ■ Lignin Institute
5775 Peachtree-Dunwoody Rd., Bldg. G, Ste.500
Atlanta, GA 30342
Ph: (404)252-3663 (678)303-3036
Fax: (404)252-0774
E-mail: li@kellencompany.com
URL: http://www.lignin.org
Contact: Peter Dicks, Pres.
Founded: 1990. **Members:** 24. **Staff:** 3. **Budget:** $90,000. **Multinational. Description:** Serves as trade association for manufacturers and distributors of lignin products. (Lignin is an amorphous polymeric substance that together with cellulose forms the woody cell walls of plants.) Works to improve public awareness and recognition of lignin as a safe and useful product. Collects and provides information on the characteristics, qualities, production, sales, and uses of lignin products. Facilitates communication and cooperation within the industry and with government agencies. Informs members of legislative and regulatory initiatives affecting the industry. Conducts research. **Libraries: Type:** reference. **Holdings:** 225. **Telecommunication Services:** electronic mail, pdicks@kellencompany.com. **Subcommittees:** Dust Control. **Publications:** *Dialogue*, periodic. Newsletter. Alternate Formats: online. **Conventions/Meetings:** semiannual meeting.

1651 ■ Mulch and Soil Council (MSC)
10210 Leatherleaf Ct.
Manassas, VA 20111-4245
Ph: (703)257-0111
Fax: (703)257-0213
E-mail: info@mulchandsoilcouncil.org
URL: http://www.mulchandsoilcouncil.org
Contact: Robert C. LaGasse CAE, Exec. Dir.
Founded: 1972. **Members:** 84. **Membership Dues:** regular (maximum; based on annual sales), $15,000 (annual) ● affiliate, $1,500 (annual) ● associate, $1,000 (annual) ● foreign, $500 (annual) ● non-profit, $295 (annual). **Staff:** 2. **Budget:** $150,000. **Description:** Individuals and firms actively engaged in the production of bark and soil products; persons or firms providing services to the industry; persons or firms supplying products to the industry. Purposes are to: provide an exchange of business ideas and information; better serve the public through quality environmentally protective products. Acts as clearinghouse for information and the means for members to work together for mutual benefit. Serves as industry spokesman at national and state levels. **Awards:** Safety Award. **Frequency:** annual. **Type:** recognition. **Recipient:** for outstanding performance. **Telecommunication Services:** electronic mail, execdir@mulchandsoilcouncil.org. **Formerly:** (1987) National Bark Producers Association; (2002) National Bark and Soil Producers Association. **Publications:** *Bark and Soil Producers Product Index* ● *Bark is Best*. Video ● *NBSPA Membership Directory*, annual ● *News, Notes and Quotes*, monthly. Newsletter ● *Producers Report*, quarterly. Newsletter. Covers association and industry news. Includes statistical report of bark product shipments. **Price:** available to members only. **Circulation:** 300 ● *Special Regional Releases*, periodic. **Conventions/Meetings:** annual meeting, with educational programs.

1652 ■ National Hardwood Lumber Association (NHLA)
6830 Raleigh LaGrange Rd.
Memphis, TN 38134
Ph: (901)377-1818
Fax: (901)382-6419
E-mail: info@nhla.com
URL: http://www.nhla.com
Contact: Mark Barford, Exec. Dir.
Founded: 1898. **Members:** 1,800. **Membership Dues:** active (maximum; based on annual sales and number of branch location), $8,565 (annual) ● associate in Canada, sustaining, inspector, $645 (annual) ● individual, $70 (annual) ● institution, $175 (annual) ● foreign (associate, sustaining), $775 (annual). **Staff:** 40. **Budget:** $4,000,000. **Multinational. Description:** United States, Canadian and International hardwood lumber and veneer manufacturers, distributors, and consumers. Inspects hardwood lumber. Maintains inspection training school. Conducts management and marketing seminars for the hardwood industry. Promotes research in hardwood timber management and utilization. Promotes public awareness of the industry. **Libraries: Type:** reference. **Holdings:** 1,000. **Awards:** Forest Stewardship Award. **Frequency:** annual. **Type:** recognition. **Telecommunication Services:** electronic mail, m.barford@nhla.com. **Committees:** Education; Forest Resources; Government and Public Affairs; Hardwood Research; Inspection; Rules. **Absorbed:** Hardwood Research Council. **Publications:** *An Illustrated Guide to Hardwood Lumber Grades*. **Price:** $5.00 for members; $7.00 for nonmembers ● *Forest Resource Factbook* ● *Hardwood Matters*, monthly. Magazine. **Price:** free for members. **Circulation:** 2,500. **Advertising:** accepted ● *National Hardwood Lumber Association—Buyer's Guide*, annual. Newsletter. **Price:** $500.00 for nonmembers; $60.00 for members. **Circulation:** 2,000. Alternate Formats: CD-ROM ● *Rules for the Measurement and Inspection of Hardwood and Cypress Lumber* (in English, French, German, and Spanish). Books. **Price:** $7.00 for nonmembers; $5.00 for members ● Videos. **Conventions/Meetings:** annual convention (exhibits) - always September.

1653 ■ National Lumber and Building Material Dealers Association (NLBMDA)
900 2nd St. NE, Ste.305
Washington, DC 20002
Ph: (202)547-2230
Free: (800)634-8645
Fax: (202)547-7640
E-mail: shawn@dealer.org
URL: http://www.dealer.org
Contact: Shawn Conrad, Pres.
Founded: 1916. **Members:** 8,000. **Membership Dues:** manufacturer, service council, $5,000 (annual). **Staff:** 8. **Budget:** $1,500,000. **Regional Groups:** 20. **Description:** Represents more than 8,000 lumber and building material companies with over 400,000 employees, 20 state and regional associations and the industry's leading manufacturers and service providers. **Awards:** Excellence in Human Resources. **Frequency:** annual. **Type:** recognition ● Grassroots Award. **Frequency:** annual. **Type:** recognition ● Member of Congress Award. **Frequency:** annual. **Type:** recognition ● Safety Award. **Frequency:** annual. **Type:** recognition. **Boards:** Lumber and Building Materials Institute; Lumber Dealers Political Action. **Committees:** BMAE; Executive; Government Affairs; Industry Summit Oversight; Nominating. **Councils:** Manufacturers and Services. **Formerly:** National Retail Lumber Dealers Association. **Publications:** *Cost of Doing Business*, annual. Report. **Price:** $225.00 for members; $375.00 for nonmembers ● *Forklift and You*. Manual ● *NLBMDA Advocate*, monthly. Newsletter. Alternate Formats: online ● *Nuts & Bolts*. Manual ● *ProSales*, monthly. Magazine. Contains product information, sales techniques, industry trends and dealer profiles. **Price:** free for members. **Advertising:** accepted ● *Risk Management Best Practices*. Manual ● *Your National Perspective*, quarterly. Newsletters. **Advertising:** accepted. **Conventions/Meetings:** annual Industry Summit - convention, with speakers and table top exhibits (exhibits) - usually fall ● annual Legislative Conference (exhibits) - usually spring.

1654 ■ Northeastern Lumber Manufacturers Association (NELMA)
272 Tuttle Rd.
Cumberland, ME 04021
Ph: (207)829-6901
Fax: (207)829-4293
E-mail: info@nelma.org
URL: http://www.nelma.org
Contact: Jeff Easterling, Pres.
Founded: 1933. **Members:** 400. **Staff:** 10. **Description:** Manufacturers of hardwood and softwood lumber and timber products in the New England states, New York, and Pennsylvania. Promotes the interests of the northeastern lumber manufacturing industry. Encourages uniformity, efficiency, and economy in the manufacture, gradation, distribution, and use of lumber and timber products. Encourages the use of lumber and timber products and the conservation and renewal of forest resources by improved forest utilization and practices. Conducts economic research on forest and other industry problems, and technical and other investigations of the properties and uses of wood. Collects and disseminates statistics and other economic information. Presents the views of the industry to other organizations, the government, and the public. Sponsors annual two-week training school for softwood lumber graders. **Committees:** Dimension Species; Grading; Loss Control; Marketing; Pine Species. **Publications:** *Ask NELMA*, monthly. Newsletter. **Advertising:** accepted. Alternate Formats: online ● *Dimensional Lumber*. Brochure ● *Eastern White Pine*. Brochure ● *Northeastern Lumber Manufacturers Association—Buyer's Guide and Membership Directory*, annual. Contains listing of lumber manufacturing and associate members and their products. **Price:** free ● *Standard Grading Rules for Northeastern Lumber*. Booklet. **Conventions/Meetings:** semiannual convention - always March and September.

1655 ■ Northeastern Retail Lumber Association (NRLA)
585 N Greenbush Rd.
Rensselaer, NY 12144
Ph: (518)286-1010
Free: (800)292-6752
Fax: (518)286-1755

E-mail: rferris@nrla.org
URL: http://www.nrla.org
Contact: Rita Ferris CAE, Pres.
Founded: 1894. **Members:** 1,300. **Membership Dues:** retail (maximum; based on sales volume), $6,000 (annual) ● associate, $100-$1,650 (annual). **Staff:** 25. **Regional Groups:** 13. **State Groups:** 7. **Description:** Retail lumber and building material dealers in the Northeast. Conducts educational, legislative, and government affairs programs. Sponsors seminars and workshops in sales training, products, and legislation. **Formerly:** (1989) Northeastern Retail Lumberman's Association. **Publications:** *Lumber Co-Operator*, biennial. Magazine. Provides marketing and industry information. Includes new product information. **Price:** $25.00 /year for members; $35.00 /year for nonmembers. ISSN: 0024-7294. **Circulation:** 3,400. **Advertising:** accepted ● *The Source*, annual. Directory. **Price:** $80.00. ISSN: 0024-7294. **Circulation:** 2,000. **Advertising:** accepted. **Conventions/Meetings:** annual convention (exhibits).

1656 ■ Wood Component Manufacturers Association (WCMA)
741 Butlers Gate, Ste.100
Marietta, GA 30068
Ph: (770)565-6660
Fax: (770)565-6663
E-mail: wcma@woodcomponents.org
URL: http://www.woodcomponents.org
Contact: Steve Lawser CAE, Exec. Dir.
Founded: 1929. **Members:** 150. **Membership Dues:** general (based on annual product shipment), $1,000-$3,000 (annual). **Staff:** 3. **Description:** Manufacturers of wood parts for the furniture, kitchen cabinet, and building industries, including interior trim moldings, stair treads and risers, thresholds, and paneling; industrial users. Establishes grading rules and standards. Offers seminars in cost accounting, marketing, and production techniques. Conducts plant tours among members. **Committees:** Grading Rules. **Formerly:** National Dimension Manufacturers Association; (1984) Hardwood Dimension Manufacturers Association. **Publications:** *Moisture and Wood*. Video. **Price:** $15.00 single copy ● *Rules and Specifications for Dimension and Woodwork*. Book. **Price:** $5.00 single copy ● Newsletter, periodic ● Also publishes grading rules. **Conventions/Meetings:** annual convention and meeting, includes educational displays (exhibits).

1657 ■ Wood Products Manufacturers Association (WPMA)
PO Box 761
Westminster, MA 01473-0761
Ph: (978)874-5445
Fax: (978)874-9946
E-mail: woodprod@wpma.org
URL: http://www.wpma.org
Contact: Philip A. Bibeau, Exec. Dir.
Founded: 1929. **Members:** 417. **Membership Dues:** manufacturing (based on number of employees), $495-$1,125 (annual) ● associate, $650 (annual). **Staff:** 5. **Description:** Manufacturers of component parts, turned and shaped wood products, moulding, millwork, manufacturer's representatives, wholesalers, suppliers of lumber, machinery, and service providers in the industry. **Libraries: Type:** reference. **Holdings:** audiovisuals. **Awards:** PEES. **Frequency:** annual. **Type:** grant. **Formerly:** Wood-Turners Service Bureau; (1978) Wood Turners and Shapers Association. **Publications:** *Wood Products Manufacturers Association—Benefit Survey*, annual. Report. **Price:** free ● *Wood Products Manufacturers Association—Newsletter*, monthly ● Membership Directory, annual. **Price:** free, for members only. **Advertising:** accepted. **Conventions/Meetings:** semiannual conference (exhibits) - always April and September ● annual trade show (exhibits).

Forestry

1658 ■ World Forest Institute (WFI)
c/o World Forestry Center
4033 SW Canyon Rd.
Portland, OR 97221
Ph: (503)488-2130 (503)228-1367
Fax: (503)228-4608
E-mail: sarawu@worldforestry.org
URL: http://wfi.worldforestrycenter.org
Contact: Sara Wu, Dir.
Founded: 1989. **Membership Dues:** regular, $500 (annual). **Description:** Wood processing mills, industry associations, parks and timberlands, forestry schools, government agencies. Works as the information services division of the World Forestry Center; expands access to information on international markets, new products, evolving technologies, wood species and characteristics and new industry trends; provides research services. **Publications:** *The Changing World of Forest Management*. Reports. **Price:** $75.00 hard copy ● *Managing Risk in the Evolving World of Timberland Investments*. Reports. **Price:** $95.00 hard copy; $75.00 digital copy ● Books. **Price:** $70.00 hard copy; $50.00 digital copy ● Catalog, annual ● Article. **Conventions/Meetings:** conference, forestry ● tour, for study.

Fragrances

1659 ■ American Society of Perfumers (ASP)
PO Box 1551
West Caldwell, NJ 07007
Ph: (201)991-0040
Fax: (201)991-0073
E-mail: arebeck@aromatec.com
URL: http://www.perfumers.org
Contact: Alice Rebeck, Chair
Founded: 1947. **Members:** 300. **Description:** Perfumers; apprentice perfumers. Seeks to further the art and science of perfumery. Conducts educational programs. **Conventions/Meetings:** annual symposium.

1660 ■ Chemical Sources Association (CSA)
c/o Diane Davis
3301 Rte. 66, Ste.205, Bldg. C
Neptune, NJ 07753
Ph: (732)922-3008
Fax: (732)922-3590
E-mail: diane@afius.org
URL: http://www.chemicalsources.org
Contact: Diane Davis, Contact
Founded: 1969. **Members:** 85. **Membership Dues:** corporate, $325 (annual). **Description:** Representatives of flavor and fragrance manufacturers. Purpose is to find suppliers and manufacturers for rare or hard-to-obtain chemicals and essential oils used in the flavor and fragrance industry. Compiles statistics. **Awards: Type:** recognition. **Publications:** *Natural Source Listing Food Ingredients*, periodic. **Conventions/Meetings:** annual meeting - always May ● monthly meeting - always first Thursday, September-May.

1661 ■ Fragrance Foundation
145 E 32nd St.
New York, NY 10016-6002
Ph: (212)725-2755
Fax: (212)779-9058
E-mail: info@fragrance.org
URL: http://www.fragrance.org
Contact: Mary Ellen Lapsansky, Exec. Dir.
Founded: 1949. **Members:** 170. **Staff:** 8. **Multinational. Description:** Fragrance manufacturers, suppliers to the trade, publications, package designers, analysts, and advertising agencies. Seeks to educate consumers on the pleasures, use and care of fragrance and allied products. Initiates public relations programs. **Libraries: Type:** by appointment only. **Holdings:** 1,000. **Awards:** Circle of Champions. **Frequency:** annual. **Type:** recognition. **Recipient:** for excellence in business ● FiFi Awards. **Frequency:** annual. **Type:** recognition. **Recipient:** for creativity in the fragrance industry. **Telecommunication Services:** electronic mail, mlapsansky@fragrance.org. **Publications:** *Aromatic Pleasures and the Bath*. Booklet. Explores the pleasures and art of the bath - past, present and future. **Price:** $5.00 for members; $7.00 for nonmembers ● *The Facts and Fun of Fragrance*. Booklet. Addresses today's teens' heightened interest in scents. **Price:** $5.00 for members; $7.00 for nonmembers ● *Fragrance and Olfactory Dictionary*. Booklet. Contains definitions of ingredients, techniques, language of fragrance and olfactory references. **Price:** $5.00 for members; $7.00 for nonmembers ● *The History, The Mystery, The Enjoyment of Fragrance*. Booklet. Contains capsule history of the fragrance world. **Price:** $5.00 for members; $7.00 for nonmembers ● *The Male Fragrance Adventure*. Booklet. Traces history of usage, describes ingredients and provides a fragrance guide for men. **Price:** $5.00 for members; $7.00 for nonmembers ● *Reference Guide*, annual. Contains up-to-date listing of fragrances available in America at the time of publication. **Price:** $85.00 for members; $100.00 for nonmembers ● *Scents of Time*. Video. Contains review of the "Scents of Time" Exhibition featuring the 17th Century through the 1960s, in VHS format. **Price:** $65.00 ● Also publishes other booklets. **Conventions/Meetings:** annual FiFi Awards - show, honoring the fragrance industry's creative achievements.

1662 ■ Fragrance Materials Association of the U.S. (FMA)
1620 I St. NW, Ste.925
Washington, DC 20006
Ph: (202)293-5800
Fax: (202)463-8998
E-mail: ccook@therobertsgroup.net
URL: http://www.fmafragrance.org
Contact: Glenn Roberts, Exec. Dir.
Founded: 1979. **Members:** 110. **Description:** Represents manufacturers of fragrance and fragrance ingredients. **Committees:** Education and Program; Export-Import; Government Relation; Instrumental Analysis and Specifications; Scientific Affairs; Trademarks; Transportation. **Supersedes:** Essential Oil Association of the U.S.A. **Conventions/Meetings:** annual meeting.

1663 ■ Research Institute for Fragrance Materials (RIFM)
50 Tice Blvd.
Woodcliff Lake, NJ 07677
Ph: (201)689-8089
Fax: (201)689-8090
E-mail: rifm@rifm.org
URL: http://www.rifm.org
Contact: Dr. Ladd W. Smith, Pres.
Founded: 1966. **Members:** 70. **Membership Dues:** manufacturer (minimum), $4,000 (annual) ● purchaser (minimum), $100,000 (annual) ● supporting (minimum), $13,400 (annual) ● associate, $2,425 (annual). **Staff:** 18. **Multinational. Description:** Conducts research into the safety of materials which comprise the ingredients for fragrances. **Computer Services:** database, on the safe use of fragrance materials. **Affiliated With:** International Fragrance Association. **Publications:** Report. Alternate Formats: online ● Brochure. Alternate Formats: online.

1664 ■ Sense of Smell Institute (SOSI)
145 E 32nd St., 8th Fl.
New York, NY 10016-6002
Ph: (212)725-2755
Fax: (212)779-9072
E-mail: info@senseofsmell.org
URL: http://www.senseofsmell.org
Contact: Annette Green, Chair
Founded: 1982. **Staff:** 2. **Multinational. Description:** Provides financial support to doctors and clinical researchers who study aromas and their effect on human behavior. Conducts educational programs relating to olfaction. **Libraries: Type:** reference. **Subjects:** psychology of fragrance, aroma-chology, aromatherapy. **Awards:** Corporate Vision Award. **Frequency:** annual. **Type:** recognition. **Recipient:** for a corporation that has successfully applied aromachology research to product development ● Richard B. Salomon Award. **Frequency:** annual. **Type:** recognition. **Recipient:** for increasing public awareness of the role the sense of smell plays in daily lives ● Sense of Smell Award. **Frequency:** annual. **Type:** recognition. **Recipient:** for research achievement in

area of olfaction. **Committees:** Industry Advisory; Scientific Advisory. **Formerly:** (1993) Fragrance Research Fund; (2001) Olfactory Research Fund. **Publications:** *Aging Well With Your Sense of Smell.* Book. **Price:** $10.00. **Conventions/Meetings:** periodic seminar.

Franchising

1665 ■ American Association of Franchisees and Dealers (AAFD)
3500 5th Ave., Ste.103
PO Box 81887
San Diego, CA 92138-1887
Ph: (619)209-3775
Free: (800)733-9858
Fax: (619)209-3777
E-mail: benefits@aafd.org
URL: http://www.aafd.org
Contact: Robert L. Purvin Jr., Chm./CEO
Founded: 1992. **Members:** 5,000. **Membership Dues:** franchisee, $290 ● associate, $119 ● supporting, franchisor, $500 ● life, $5,000. **Staff:** 6. **Budget:** $500,000. **Regional Groups:** 60. **Description:** Franchise business owners. Represents the interests of franchise business owners. Seeks to bring fairness to franchising. Maintains legal and financial referral services, speakers' bureau, and suppliers network; conducts research and educational programs; compiles statistics. **Libraries: Type:** not open to the public. **Awards:** Fair Franchising Seal. **Frequency:** periodic. **Type:** recognition. **Computer Services:** Online services, email communities; member guide; co-op and commerce marketplace. **Committees:** AAFD Purchasing; Fair Franchising Standards. **Councils:** Legislative; Trade Association. **Sections:** Trademark Chapters. **Publications:** *Franchisee Voice*, quarterly. Newsletter. **Price:** included in membership dues. **Circulation:** 5,000. **Advertising:** accepted. Alternate Formats: online. **Conventions/Meetings:** annual Total Quality Franchising - meeting and symposium (exhibits).

1666 ■ American Franchisee Association (AFA)
53 W Jackson Blvd., Ste.1157
Chicago, IL 60604
Ph: (312)431-0545
Fax: (312)431-1469
E-mail: info@franchisee.org
URL: http://www.franchisee.org
Contact: Susan P. Kezios, Pres.
Founded: 1993. **Members:** 16,000. **Membership Dues:** individual, $100 (annual) ● independent franchisee, $25 (annual). **Staff:** 3. **Description:** Works to promote and enhance the economic interests of small business franchisees; promote the growth and development of members' enterprises; assist in the formation of independent franchisee associations; offer support, assistance, and legal referral services to members. **Publications:** *E-news*, monthly. Newsletter. Alternate Formats: online ● *Forming an Independent Franchisee Association - A Turn-Key Approach.* **Price:** $49.95 plus shipping and handling ● *How to Form an Association?*. Video. Features three speakers, each from a different franchise brand, who shared the experiences of forming their independent franchisee associations. **Price:** $30.00 plus shipping and handling.

1667 ■ Culligan Dealers Association of North America (CDANA)
c/o JSJ Productions, Inc.
14101 Hwy. 290 W, Bldg. 1600B
Austin, TX 78737
Ph: (512)894-4106
Fax: (512)858-0486
E-mail: susangibson@austin.rr.com
URL: http://www.cdana.org
Contact: Susan Gibson, Exec. Dir.
Membership Dues: regular, $235 (annual). **Multinational. Description:** Represents independent franchisees and distributors of quality water products and services. Protects and enhances members' economic interests. Provides a forum to exchange information, ideas and talents. Promotes programs to leverage the collective purchasing and bargaining power held by members. **Publications:** *Connection*, quarterly. Magazine. Features informational and educational articles of interest to all phases of the independent Culligan dealer operation. **Price:** included in membership dues. **Advertising:** accepted. Alternate Formats: online ● Membership Directory, annual. **Price:** included in membership dues.

1668 ■ International Franchise Association (IFA)
1501 K St. NW, Ste.350
Washington, DC 20005
Ph: (202)628-8000 (202)662-0780
Fax: (202)628-0812
E-mail: ifa@franchise.org
URL: http://www.franchise.org
Contact: Cecelia Bond, Exec. Asst.
Founded: 1960. **Members:** 30,000. **Membership Dues:** franchisor (minimum), $1,100 (annual) ● international (franchisor), $1,500 (annual) ● individual (franchisee), $100-$200 (annual) ● organizational (franchisee), $100-$500 (annual) ● supplier, $2,500 (annual). **Staff:** 30. **Budget:** $5,000,000. **Description:** Firms in 100 countries utilizing the franchise method of distribution for goods and services in all industries. **Libraries: Type:** reference. **Holdings:** 500; books, clippings, periodicals. **Awards: Type:** recognition. **Telecommunication Services:** electronic mail, cbond@franchise.org. **Committees:** Ethical Standards; Finance, Audit, and Budget; Franchisee Relations; Franchising Political Action; International Affairs; Legal/Legislative; Marketing and Public Affairs; Minorities and Women in Franchise. **Councils:** Franchise Suppliers; Past Chairmen. **Publications:** *Franchise Opportunities Guide*, semiannual. Directory. **Price:** $21.00. **Advertising:** accepted ● *Franchising World Magazine*, bimonthly. **Conventions/Meetings:** annual Legal Symposium ● periodic workshop ● annual convention - 2009 Feb. 14-17, San Diego, CA; 2010 Feb. 6-9, San Antonio, TX; 2011 Feb. 12-15, Las Vegas, NV.

1669 ■ National Franchisee Association (NFA)
1201 Roberts Blvd., Ste.100
Kennesaw, GA 30144
Ph: (678)797-5160
Fax: (678)797-5170
E-mail: amy@namgllc.com
URL: http://www.nfabk.org
Contact: Joseph Anghelone, Chm.
Founded: 1988. **Members:** 1,200. **Membership Dues:** $25 (annual). **Staff:** 10. **Budget:** $5,000,000. **Regional Groups:** 19. **Multinational. Description:** Federation of associations representing owners of Burger King restaurant franchises. Promotes members' interests. **Committees:** Diversity Affairs; Franchise Relations; Marketing Advisory; Operations, Technology and Profitability. **Formerly:** (2003) National Franchise Association. **Publications:** *Flame*, quarterly. Magazine. Contains relevant articles for Burger King owners. **Circulation:** 1,500. **Advertising:** accepted. Alternate Formats: CD-ROM; online. **Conventions/Meetings:** annual trade show and convention (exhibits).

1670 ■ North American Association of Subway Franchisees (NAASF)
95 Merrick Way, Ste.710
Coral Gables, FL 33134
Ph: (305)448-8553
Free: (866)590-9865
Fax: (305)448-8753
E-mail: info@naasf.org
URL: http://www.naasf.org
Contact: Jim Hansen, CEO
Membership Dues: Bronze Club, DA associate, patron, $100 (annual) ● Silver Club, $250 (annual) ● Gold Club, $500 (annual) ● Platinum Club, associate, $1,000 (annual) ● Diamond Club, $2,500 (annual). **Multinational. Description:** Represents Subway franchisees in North America. Seeks and develops ideas, processes, plans and procedures that will provide Subway Franchisees the tools to operate professional, competitive and profitable businesses. **Publications:** *NAASF Newswire*, monthly. Magazine. Alternate Formats: online. **Conventions/Meetings:** annual convention (exhibits).

1671 ■ Women in Franchising (WIF)
53 W Jackson Blvd., Ste.1157
Chicago, IL 60604
Ph: (312)431-1467
Fax: (312)431-1469
E-mail: spkezios@womeninfranchising.com
URL: http://www.womeninfranchising.com
Contact: Susan P. Kezios, Pres.
Founded: 1987. **For-Profit. Description:** Assists women interested in all aspects of franchise business development including those buying a franchised business and those expanding their businesses via franchising. Provides franchise technical assistance in both of these areas. Surveys the industry on the status of women. **Publications:** *Buying a Franchise: How to Make the Right Choice.* Audiotape. **Price:** $49.95/copy, plus shipping and handling ($6) ● *Growing Your Business: The Franchise Option.* Audiotape. **Price:** $49.95 plus shipping and handling ($6).

Freelance

1672 ■ Working Today
45 Main St., Ste.710
Brooklyn, NY 11201
Ph: (718)222-1099 (718)532-1515
Free: (800)856-9981
Fax: (718)222-4440
E-mail: membership@freelancersunion.org
URL: http://www.freelancersunion.org
Contact: Sara Horowitz, Founder/Exec. Dir.
Founded: 1995. **Description:** Independent workforce, freelancers, consultants, independent contractors, temps, part-timers, the self-employed, and contingent employees. Works to promote the interests of independent workers by providing services and practical tools to independent workers, access to health insurance and free consumer-oriented legal, tax and retirement planning advice. Provides education and advocates for policy changes that are suited to today's independent workforce. **Publications:** Newsletter, 3/year.

Fruits and Vegetables

1673 ■ Apple Processors Association (APA)
1100 17th St. NW, 10th Fl.
Washington, DC 20036
Ph: (202)785-6710
Fax: (202)331-4212
E-mail: pweller@agriwashington.org
URL: http://www.appleprocessors.org
Contact: Paul S. Weller Jr., Pres.
Founded: 1987. **Members:** 28. **Staff:** 4. **Budget:** $175,000. **Description:** Represents processors of apple juice and sauce; suppliers of apple juice containers. Produces apple juice and sauce from whole apples rather than from apple concentrate. Serves as a forum for discussion of improved processing techniques. Conducts lobbying activities and research and educational programs. **Publications:** *Apagram*, quarterly. Newsletter. **Circulation:** 500. **Advertising:** accepted. **Conventions/Meetings:** annual Raw Products Committee - meeting ● annual seminar - always November in Washington, DC.

1674 ■ Association of Fruit and Vegetable Inspection and Standardization Agencies (AFVISA)
c/o Thomas Smith, Pres.
1100 Bank St., Rm. 804
Richmond, VA 23219
Ph: (804)786-3548
Fax: (804)371-7785

E-mail: tsmith@vdacs.state.va.us
URL: http://www.afvisa.org
Contact: Thomas Smith, Pres.
Founded: 1986. **Description:** Aims to promote and attain uniformity and understanding among states, member agencies, the federal government, and related agencies on inspection and standardization of fresh products. Provides a forum where member agencies' personnel can formulate and promote policies for maintaining and implementing effective standardization services.

1675 ■ North American Bramble Growers Research Foundation (NABG-RF)
c/o Debby Wechsler, Exec. Sec.
1138 Rock Rest Rd.
Pittsboro, NC 27312
Ph: (919)542-3687
Fax: (919)542-4037
E-mail: nabga@mindspring.com
URL: http://www.raspberryblackberry.com/local.cfm?doc=webdocs/AboutNABG-RF.htm
Contact: Debby Wechsler, Exec. Sec.
Founded: 1998. **Members:** 200. **Membership Dues:** grower, $85 (annual) ● bramble researcher, extension, student, $40 (annual). **Staff:** 1. **Budget:** $12,000. **Description:** Professional association dedicated to the advancement of the raspberry and blackberry industry. Provides comprehensive information on bramble production and the advancement of the industry. **Publications:** *The Bramble*, quarterly. Newsletter. Contains bramble and marketing information. **Price:** included in membership dues. **Advertising:** accepted. Alternate Formats: online ● *Proceedings of NABGA Annual Conference*, annual. **Price:** $15.00 for nonmembers; included in membership dues ● Membership Directory, annual. **Price:** included in membership dues. **Conventions/Meetings:** annual conference, presents information on new technologies, production and marketing strategies and techniques (exhibits) - usually winter ● Summer Field - tour.

Fuel

1676 ■ American Gas Association (AGA)
400 N Capitol St. NW, Ste.400
Washington, DC 20001
Ph: (202)824-7000
Fax: (202)824-7115
E-mail: dparker@aga.org
URL: http://www.aga.org
Contact: David N. Parker, Pres./CEO
Founded: 1918. **Members:** 190. **Membership Dues:** associate, $1,000 (annual) ● international, $20,000 (annual) ● international affiliate, $5,000 (annual). **Staff:** 80. **Budget:** $23,000,000. **Description:** Advocates for local natural gas utility companies; provides a broad range of programs and services for member natural gas pipelines, marketers, gatherers, international gas companies and industry associates. **Computer Services:** Online services, gas industry information. **Committees:** Gas Employees Political Action. **Formed by Merger of:** Gas Institute and National Commercial Gas Association. **Publications:** *American Gas*, 10/year. Magazine. Describes marketing programs, new technologies, profiles of gas companies, and industry trends. Includes employee listings. **Price:** $59.00/year in U.S. and Canada; $110.00/year outside North America. ISSN: 0885-2413. **Advertising:** accepted ● *Associate*. Newsletter ● *Gas Facts*, annual. **Price:** $48.00 /year for members; $120.00 /year for nonmembers ● *Operating Section Proceedings*, annual ● Bulletins ● Catalog ● Magazines. **Conventions/Meetings:** annual Operations Conference (exhibits) - 2009 May 19-21, Pittsburgh, PA.

1677 ■ Energy Frontiers International (EFI)
1425 K St. NW, Ste.350
Washington, DC 20005
Ph: (202)587-5780
Fax: (703)995-0852
E-mail: secretariat@energyfrontiers.org
URL: http://www.energyfrontiers.org
Contact: Christopher Kidder, Pres.
Founded: 1980. **Members:** 30. **Description:** Represents private and public sector energy organizations providing members with information on emerging energy technologies. Conducts quarterly site visits to significant energy installations worldwide. Nonpolitical, non-advocacy organization with international membership. **Awards:** Walter Flowers Achievement Award. **Frequency:** annual. **Type:** recognition. **Recipient:** for significant commercial technology development. **Formerly:** (1985) National Council of Synthetic Fuels Production; (1986) Council on Synthetic Fuels. **Conventions/Meetings:** quarterly meeting.

1678 ■ Gas Technology Institute (GTI)
1700 S Mt. Prospect Rd.
Des Plaines, IL 60018-1804
Ph: (847)768-0500
Fax: (847)768-0501
E-mail: businessdevelopmentinfo@gastechnology.org
URL: http://www.gastechnology.org
Contact: David C. Carroll, Pres./CEO
Founded: 1941. **Members:** 325. **Membership Dues:** associate, $5,000 (annual). **Staff:** 340. **Budget:** $100,000,000. **Description:** Educational and research facility sponsored by companies engaged in the production, processing, transmission, and distribution of natural gas and related fuels; engineering firms; large energy consumers. Conducts contract research for government and industry in the field of non-nuclear energy technology. Offers short courses in gas production, transmission, distribution, economics, and marketing. Sponsors symposia on current topics in non-nuclear energy. **Libraries: Type:** open to the public. **Holdings:** 300,000. **Computer Services:** database, archival gas industry. **Divisions:** Education; Research. **Formed by Merger of:** (2000) Institute of Gas Technology; (2000) Gas Research Institute. **Publications:** *GasTIPS*, quarterly. Magazine. Contains overview of GTI's ongoing research on gas exploration, production, and processing. **Price:** free for qualified individuals; $149.00/year in U.S.; $99.00/year outside U.S.; $25.00 for back issues. ISSN: 1078-3954. Alternate Formats: online ● *GTI Journal*, semiannual. Magazine. Contains overview of GTI's ongoing R&D and education projects. **Price:** $100.00/year ● Proceedings, 1-2/year. Contains summaries of papers presented or panel discussions at GTI-sponsored conferences on technical subjects. **Conventions/Meetings:** annual meeting.

1679 ■ Hearth, Patio and Barbeque Association (HPBA)
1901 N Moore St., Ste.600
Arlington, VA 22209
Ph: (703)522-0086
Fax: (703)522-0548
E-mail: hpbamail@hpba.org
URL: http://www.hpba.org
Contact: Jack Goldman, Pres.
Founded: 1980. **Members:** 2,700. **Membership Dues:** manufacturer (maximum; based on annual sales), $20,500 (annual). **Staff:** 22. **Budget:** $4,500,000. **Regional Groups:** 14. **Description:** North American trade association for manufacturers, retailers, distributors, manufacturers' representatives, and service firms, along with companies having business interests related to the hearth, patio, and barbecue industries. Provides professional member services and industry support, including education, statistics, government relations, marketing, advertising, and consumer education. **Computer Services:** Mailing lists, members only. **Telecommunication Services:** electronic mail, goldman@hpba.org. **Absorbed:** (2002) Barbecue Industry Association. **Formed by Merger of:** (1980) Fireplace Institute; (1980) Wood Energy Institute. **Formerly:** (1991) Wood Heating Alliance; (2003) Hearth, Patio & Barbecue Association. **Publications:** *HPBA Directory*, annual. **Price:** $500.00 for nonmembers; $45.00 for members. **Circulation:** 2,300. **Advertising:** accepted. Alternate Formats: diskette ● *Why Does My Fireplace Smoke*. Video. **Price:** $20.00 for standard video member; $30.00 for nonmembers, looping video member; $17.50 per 5-49 copies; $15.00 per 5-10 copies. **Conventions/Meetings:** annual Hearth, Patio and Home Expo - seminar and trade show (exhibits).

1680 ■ Interstate Natural Gas Association of America (INGAA)
10 G St. NE, Ste.700
Washington, DC 20002
Ph: (202)216-5900
Fax: (202)216-0870
URL: http://www.ingaa.org
Contact: Donald F. Santa Jr., Pres.
Founded: 1944. **Members:** 40. **Staff:** 30. **Budget:** $5,000,000. **Description:** Transporters of natural gas. **Committees:** Accounting; Environment, Safety, and Operations; Government Affairs; Information Services; Legal; Policy Analysis; Public Affairs; Rate; Regulatory Affairs; State Relations; Tax. **Affiliated With:** Interstate Natural Gas Association of America. **Formerly:** (1974) Independent Natural Gas Association of America. **Conventions/Meetings:** annual meeting.

1681 ■ National Propane Gas Association (NPGA)
1150 17th St. NW, Ste.310
Washington, DC 20036-4623
Ph: (202)466-7200
Fax: (202)466-7205
E-mail: info@npga.org
URL: http://www.npga.org
Contact: Richard R. Roldan, Pres./CEO
Founded: 1931. **Members:** 3,700. **Membership Dues:** individual, $100 (annual) ● international, $250 (annual). **Staff:** 24. **Budget:** $5,000,000. **State Groups:** 39. **Description:** Represents the propane industry, including small businesses and large corporations engaged in the retail marketing of propane gas and appliances, producers and wholesalers of propane gas and equipment, manufacturers and fabricators of propane gas cylinders and tanks, propane transporters, and manufacturer's representatives. Works to promote the safe and increased use of propane; advocates in Congress and federal regulatory agencies for favorable environment for production, distributing, and marketing of propane gas. Develops safety standards and training materials for the safe use and distribution of propane gas. **Libraries: Type:** reference. **Awards:** Bill Hill Memorial Award. **Frequency:** annual. **Type:** recognition ● Distinguished Service Award. **Frequency:** annual. **Type:** recognition ● NPGA Safety. **Frequency:** annual. **Type:** recognition ● State Director of the Year. **Frequency:** annual. **Type:** recognition. **Computer Services:** Mailing lists, available to members only. **Telecommunication Services:** electronic mail, rroldan@npga.org. **Committees:** Audit; Convention; Distinguished Service Award; Education; Engine Power; Gas Check; Governmental Affairs; International; Market Development; Member Services; Research and Development; Safety; Technology and Standards. **Divisions:** Distributors; Engine Power; International; Manufacturers; Marketers; Producers; Services; Transportation and Storage. **Formed by Merger of:** (1962) Liquefied Petroleum Gas Association; National LP-Gas Council. **Publications:** *NPGA Reports*, weekly. Newsletter. Provides information on business management, federal legislation, new technologies, safe practices, and educational opportunities. **Price:** $100.00/year, available to members only. ISSN: 1549-1269. **Circulation:** 6,600 ● Booklets ● Bulletin, periodic ● Manuals ● Pamphlets ● Videos ● Also publishes marketing statistics and guidebooks for the propane gas industry. **Conventions/Meetings:** convention and trade show ● annual Pinnacle Conference - always May or June ● annual Southeastern Convention and International Trade Show - convention and trade show - always April ● workshop and convention.

1682 ■ Natural Gas Supply Association (NGSA)
805 15th St. NW, Ste.510
Washington, DC 20005

Ph: (202)326-9300
Fax: (202)326-9330
E-mail: skip.horvath@ngsa.org
URL: http://www.ngsa.org
Contact: R. Skip Horvath, Pres.
Founded: 1967. **Members:** 13. **Staff:** 10. **Budget:** $2,700,000. **Description:** Natural gas producers. Monitors legislation and economic issues affecting natural gas producers. **Committees:** Legal; Legislative; Public Affairs. **Formerly:** (1979) Natural Gas Supply Committee. **Conventions/Meetings:** annual board meeting.

1683 ■ Pellet Fuels Institute (PFI)
1901 N Moore St., Ste.600
Arlington, VA 22209-1708
Ph: (703)522-6778
Fax: (703)522-0548
E-mail: pfimail@pelletheat.org
URL: http://www.pelletheat.org
Contact: Don Kaiser, Exec. Dir.
Founded: 1982. **Members:** 90. **Membership Dues:** pellet fuel manufacturer (based on annual sales), $1,000-$12,000 (annual) ● supplier, $1,500 (annual) ● associate, $500 (annual). **Staff:** 3. **Budget:** $100,000. **Description:** Pellet and briquette manufacturers; processors of wood, and agricultural fuels; pellet burner manufacturers and distributors; combustion and handling equipment manufacturers and distributors; industry suppliers; and companies and organizations that use wood, agricultural residues, and paper as fuel. Promotes the increased use of pellets, briquettes, chips, and other renewable fiber fuels. Supports lobbying efforts promoting fiber fuels. Acts as an information clearinghouse among members. **Formerly:** (1993) Fiber Fuels Institute. **Publications:** *PFI Newsletter*, bimonthly. **Price:** $40.00/year. **Circulation:** 600. **Advertising:** accepted. **Conventions/Meetings:** quarterly board meeting ● annual meeting.

Fundraising

1684 ■ Association of Fund-Raising Distributors and Suppliers (AFRDS)
1100 Johnson Ferry Rd., Ste.300
Atlanta, GA 30342
Ph: (404)252-3663
Fax: (404)252-0774
E-mail: afrds@kellencompany.com
URL: http://www.afrds.org
Contact: Russell A. Lemieux, Exec. Dir.
Founded: 1992. **Members:** 650. **Membership Dues:** distributor, $295-$1,500 (annual) ● supplier, $800-$1,750 (annual) ● affiliate, $500 (annual). **Staff:** 4. **Description:** Distributors, suppliers, and manufacturers of products sold to fundraising organizations. Seeks to enhance the image of the product fundraising industry. Works to establish a code of ethics; conducts public relations activities and seminars. **Formed by Merger of:** (1992) National Association of Direct Sellers; National Association of Product Fund Raisers. **Formerly:** (2001) Association of Fund Raisers and Direct Sellers. **Publications:** *AFRDS Advisor*, quarterly. Newsletter. **Conventions/Meetings:** annual convention and trade show (exhibits).

1685 ■ Direct Marketing Fundraisers Association (DMFA)
224 Seventh St.
Garden City, NY 11530-5771
Ph: (516)746-6700
Fax: (516)294-8141
URL: http://www.dmfa.org
Contact: Stephanie Ceruolo, Pres.
Founded: 1972. **Members:** 280. **Membership Dues:** individual, $80 (annual) ● regular group (each person; minimum of 3 members in a group), $64 (annual). **Description:** Fundraisers and fundraising consultants; list brokers, printers, and others from closely allied businesses. Works to: help members in their professional efforts; promote and advance the direct mail fundraising industry; encourage an exchange of ideas among members; function as a clearinghouse through which trade news may be channeled, trade guidelines established, and ethical practices delineated. Maintains placement service; conducts seminars and workshops. **Awards:** Marketer of the Year. **Frequency:** annual. **Type:** recognition. **Recipient:** to the most talented, results-oriented direct marketing fundraiser from the DMFA membership roster ● Sanky Perlowin Memorial Scholarship Award. **Frequency:** annual. **Type:** scholarship. **Recipient:** for a promising newcomer in direct marketing fundraising. **Computer Services:** Mailing lists. **Formerly:** (2004) Direct Mail Fundraisers Association. **Publications:** *Forum*, quarterly. Newsletter. **Price:** free for members ● Membership Directory, annual. **Price:** free for members. **Conventions/Meetings:** monthly luncheon.

1686 ■ Giving Institute (GI)
4700 W Lake Ave.
Glenview, IL 60025
Ph: (847)375-4709
Free: (800)462-2372
Fax: (866)607-0913
E-mail: info@givinginstitute.org
URL: http://www.aafrc.org
Contact: George C. Ruotolo Jr., Chm.
Founded: 1935. **Members:** 32. **Staff:** 3. **Budget:** $400,000. **Description:** Represents fund-raising counseling firms engaged in consulting on the management and planning of campaigns for hospitals, universities, religious groups, community funds, arts organizations, social service groups and other nonprofit institutions. Conducts research in philanthropy. **Committees:** Government Affairs; Professional Ethics; Public Relations; Public Service; Research. **Affiliated With:** Giving U.S.A. Foundation. **Formerly:** (2007) American Association of Fundraising Counsel. **Publications:** *AAFRC Book on Fund-Raising Consulting 1999*, periodic. Membership Directory ● *Giving USA*, annual. Annual Report. Reports on philanthropy in the United States. **Price:** $49.95. ISSN: 0436-0257. **Circulation:** 12,000 ● *Giving USA Update*, quarterly ● *Legislative Monitor*, periodic. **Conventions/Meetings:** board meeting - 3/year.

1687 ■ The Grantsmanship Center (TGCI)
PO Box 17220
Los Angeles, CA 90017
Ph: (213)482-9860
Fax: (213)482-9863
E-mail: info@tgci.com
URL: http://www.tgci.com
Founded: 1972. **Members:** 75,000. **Membership Dues:** training program graduate, $375 (annual). **Staff:** 15. **For-Profit. Description:** Educational institution that trains individuals from nonprofit public and private agencies to develop and improve their funding and program planning skills. Offers workshops in grantsmanship, proposal writing, strategic fundraising, and business ventures for nonprofits. Conducts 200 programs annually in U.S. cities. **Libraries: Type:** not open to the public. **Holdings:** 2,000. **Computer Services:** Mailing lists, of members. **Publications:** *The Grantsmanship Center Magazine*, quarterly. Provides information on fundraising, development of new sources of revenue, and preparation of grant proposals. Includes book reviews. **Price:** free. **Circulation:** 225,000. **Advertising:** accepted. Alternate Formats: online.

1688 ■ Independent Charities of America (ICA)
1100 Larkspur Landing Cir., Ste.340
Larkspur, CA 94939
Ph: (415)924-1108
Free: (800)477-0733
Fax: (415)924-7341
URL: http://www.independentcharities.org
Contact: Mr. Bill Broughan, Dir.
Founded: 1987. **Members:** 596. **Staff:** 3. **Budget:** $323,139. **Description:** Represents 596 charitable organizations in the U.S. Coordinates workplace fund drives; areas of activity include all charitable activities. **Telecommunication Services:** additional toll-free number, (800)876-0413. **Publications:** *Affinity Mailers*, annual. Membership Directory ● Annual Report, annual. **Conventions/Meetings:** annual meeting (exhibits).

1689 ■ National Committee on Planned Giving
233 McCrea St., Ste.400
Indianapolis, IN 46225
Ph: (317)269-6274
Fax: (317)269-6276
E-mail: ncpg@ncpg.org
URL: http://www.ncpg.org
Contact: Tanya Howe Johnson, Pres./CEO
Founded: 1988. **Members:** 8,000. **Membership Dues:** individual, $90 (annual) ● federation, $140 (annual). **Staff:** 16. **Budget:** $2,200,000. **Local Groups:** 120. **Description:** Professional association of individuals from the fundraising, accounting, estate planning, insurance, and related fields. Members specialize in developing charitable gifts through bequests, trusts, annuities, life insurance, and real property. Provides education and networking opportunities. Conducts research. **Awards:** NCPG Distinguished Service Award. **Type:** recognition. **Committees:** Awards; Conference; Development; Diversity; Editorial Advisory; Education; Ethics; Finance; Government Relations; International; Membership; Outreach; Research; Technology. **Also Known As:** NCPG. **Publications:** *The Journal of Gift Planning*, quarterly. **Price:** $45.00. **Advertising:** accepted. Alternate Formats: online ● *Proceedings of the National Conference on Planned Giving*, annual. **Price:** $125.00. **Advertising:** accepted. **Conventions/Meetings:** annual National Conference on Planned Giving (exhibits) - 2008 Oct. 22-25, Denver, CO; 2009 Oct. 14-17, Potomac, MD; 2010 Oct. 13-16, Nashville, TN.

Furniture

1690 ■ American Home Furnishings Alliance (AHFA)
317 W High Ave., 10th Fl.
High Point, NC 27260
Ph: (336)884-5000
Fax: (336)884-5303
E-mail: pbowling@ahfa.us
URL: http://www.ahfa.us
Contact: Patricia Bowling, VP of Communications
Founded: 1984. **Members:** 336. **Membership Dues:** firm (minimum; under $1.5 million annual sales), $900 (annual) ● firm (maximum; over $500,000,001 annual sales), $33,060 (annual). **Description:** Furniture manufacturers seeking to provide a unified voice for the furniture industry and to aid in the development of industry personnel. Provides: market research data; industrial relations services; costs and operating statistics; transportation information; general management and information services. Compiles statistics; develops quarterly Econometric Forecast. **Affiliated With:** Summer and Casual Furniture Manufacturers Association. **Formed by Merger of:** Southern Furniture Manufacturers Association; National Association of Furniture Manufacturers. **Formerly:** (2006) American Furniture Manufacturers Association. **Publications:** Membership Directory, annual. **Conventions/Meetings:** annual meeting.

1691 ■ American Society of Furniture Designers (ASFD)
144 Woodland Dr.
New London, NC 28127
Ph: (910)576-1273
Fax: (910)576-1573
E-mail: info@asfd.com
URL: http://www.asfd.com
Contact: Christine Evans, Exec. Dir.
Founded: 1981. **Members:** 200. **Membership Dues:** professional, international professional, $225 (annual) ● corporate, international corporate, $600 (annual) ● associate, affiliate, professional (30 years old and below), $140 (annual) ● professional retired, $50 (annual) ● student, $35 (annual) ● corporate representative, $75 (annual). **Staff:** 1. **Budget:** $35,000.

Regional Groups: 1. **Multinational. Description:** Represents professional furniture designers, teachers, students, corporate suppliers of products and services; others who supply products and services related to furniture design. Seeks to promote the profession of furniture design. Conducts and cooperates in educational courses and seminars for furniture designers and persons planning to enter the field. Maintains placement service. **Awards:** Pinnacle Design Achievement Award. **Frequency:** annual. **Type:** recognition. **Recipient:** for an outstanding furniture design. **Publications:** *ASFD Bulletin*, bimonthly ● *ASFD Official Directory*, biennial. Membership Directory. **Price:** free for members; $75.00 for nonmembers. **Conventions/Meetings:** conference ● semiannual meeting, includes banquet - always April and October.

1692 ■ Business and Institutional Furniture Manufacturer's Association (BIFMA International)

2680 Horizon Dr. SE, Ste.A-1
Grand Rapids, MI 49546-7500
Ph: (616)285-3963
Fax: (616)285-3765
E-mail: email@bifma.org
URL: http://www.bifma.org
Contact: Thomas Reardon, Exec. Dir.

Founded: 1973. **Members:** 260. **Staff:** 5. **Description:** Organized group of furniture manufacturers and suppliers addressing issues of common concern to the contract furnishings industry. Works to develop, expand, and promote work environments that enhance the productivity and comfort of customers. **Committees:** Engineering Standards; Governmental; Industry Liaison; Information Systems. **Publications:** *The Download*, quarterly. Newsletter. **Circulation:** 1,440. **Advertising:** accepted ● *Standards*. Papers ● *Statistics*, monthly, quarterly, and annually. Reports. **Advertising:** accepted. Alternate Formats: online ● Membership Directory, annual. **Conventions/Meetings:** annual Management Conference, educational and networking forum - each spring ● annual meeting and breakfast.

1693 ■ Casual Furniture Retailers (CFR)

214 N Hale St.
Wheaton, IL 60187
Ph: (630)510-4562
Free: (800)956-2237
Fax: (630)510-4501
E-mail: jsvazas@integrated-solutions.com
URL: http://www.casualfurniture.org
Contact: Janet Svazas, Contact

Founded: 1981. **Members:** 300. **Membership Dues:** retailer, $300 (annual) ● associate manufacturer, $400 (annual) ● associate sales representative, $75 (annual) ● associate, $150 (annual). **Staff:** 2. **Description:** Casual furniture retailers, manufacturers, and sales representatives. Provides a forum for the exchange of ideas on the trends in casual and outdoor furniture. Seeks to maintain communication among manufacturers and retailers. **Awards:** Manufacturer Leadership Award. **Frequency:** annual. **Type:** recognition. **Programs:** CitiFinancial Financing. **Formerly:** (1998) National Association of Casual Furniture Retailers. **Publications:** *Casual Affairs*, quarterly. Newsletter ● Membership Directory. Alternate Formats: online. **Conventions/Meetings:** annual conference (exhibits) - always September in Chicago, IL.

1694 ■ Contemporary Design Group (CDG)

c/o Lawrance Furnishings
633 Univ. Ave.
San Diego, CA 92103
Ph: (619)291-1911 (858)586-7990
E-mail: sjg@contemporarydesign.com
URL: http://www.contemporarydesign.com
Contact: Sandie Garrett, Contact

Members: 23. **Description:** Promotes independent retail furniture stores. **Publications:** Brochure, quarterly, winter, spring, summer, fall. Circulars used as advertising vehicle for members. **Conventions/Meetings:** annual conference - San Diego, CA.

1695 ■ Furniture Society

111 Grovewood Rd.
Asheville, NC 28804
Ph: (828)255-1949
Fax: (828)255-1950
E-mail: info@furnituresociety.org
URL: http://www.furnituresociety.org
Contact: Rachel Fuld, Pres.

Founded: 1996. **Membership Dues:** student, trainee, apprentice, $25 (annual) ● individual, non-profit organization, $55 (annual) ● joint, $75 (annual) ● friend, business, $100 (annual) ● sustaining, $250 (annual) ● benefactor, $500 (annual) ● patron, $1,000 (annual) ● Medici, $2,000 (annual). **Staff:** 3. **Description:** Works to advance the art of furniture making; fosters understanding of furniture art and its place in society. **Awards:** Award of Distinction. **Frequency:** annual. **Type:** recognition. **Recipient:** to an individual who made a profound impact in the field of studio furniture. **Telecommunication Services:** electronic mail, president@furnituresociety.org. **Committees:** Steering. **Publications:** *Exhibition Poster: The Circle Unbroken: Continuity and Innovation in Studio Furniture* ● *Furniture Matters*, quarterly. Newsletter. Contains insights into the studio furniture field. **Price:** included in membership dues ● *Furniture Studio: The Heart of the Functional Arts*. Book ● *Furniture Studio Two: Tradition in Contemporary Furniture*. Book ● *Resource Directory*, annual. **Price:** included in membership dues. **Conventions/Meetings:** annual conference (exhibits) ● annual State of the Craft - conference (exhibits) - always June or July. 2008 June 18-21, Purchase, NY.

1696 ■ Futon Association International (FAI)

10705-7 Rocket Blvd.
Orlando, FL 32824
Ph: (407)447-1706
Fax: (866)595-1355
E-mail: b.donohoo@futon.org
URL: http://www.futon.org
Contact: Brian Donohoo, Dir.

Founded: 1984. **Members:** 450. **Membership Dues:** bronze, $350 (annual) ● silver, $500 (annual) ● gold, $1,000 (annual) ● retailer, $109 (annual) ● sales representative, $125 (annual) ● associate, $110 (annual). **Staff:** 2. **Description:** Manufacturers, suppliers, wholesalers, and retailers of futons. Facilitates contact and communication within the futon industry. Assists retailers in marketing their products. Keeps members informed of changes in the bedding industry's codes, laws, and regulations. **Libraries: Type:** reference. **Awards: Type:** recognition. **Telecommunication Services:** electronic mail, p.macmillen@futon.org. **Committees:** Futon Voluntary Compliance Program Political Action; Laws and Regulations; Marketing; Public Relations; Research. **Formerly:** (1991) Futon Association of North America. **Publications:** *Updates*, quarterly ● Bulletin, periodic ● Membership Directory, periodic. Includes updates. **Conventions/Meetings:** annual Futon EXPO - meeting.

1697 ■ Home Furnishings International Association (HFIA)

PO Box 420807
Dallas, TX 75342
Ph: (214)741-7632
Free: (800)942-4663
Fax: (214)742-9103
E-mail: info@hfia.com
URL: http://www.hfia.com
Contact: Mary Frye, Pres.

Founded: 1923. **Members:** 1,800. **Membership Dues:** associate, $320 ● affiliate, $180. **Staff:** 8. **Description:** Retailers and suppliers of home furnishings organized to protect and advance industry and member interests and increase profitability. Conducts educational seminars; makes discount bank card and group health and life insurance programs available to members. **Libraries: Type:** not open to the public. **Holdings:** books, periodicals. **Subjects:** home furnishing industry. **Telecommunication Services:** electronic mail, mary@hfia.com. **Publications:** *Home Furnishings Review*, monthly. Newsletter. **Price:** included in membership dues; $39.00 /year for nonmembers. **Circulation:** 2,000. **Advertising:** accepted. **Conventions/Meetings:** semiannual conference.

1698 ■ Independent Office Products and Furniture Dealers Association (IOPFDA)

301 N Fairfax St.
Alexandria, VA 22314
Ph: (703)549-9040
Free: (800)542-6672
Fax: (703)683-7552
E-mail: info@iopfda.org
URL: http://www.iopfda.org
Contact: Chris Bates, Pres.

Founded: 1979. **Members:** 700. **Description:** Represents and serves privately owned commercial dealers and their business partners in two divisions: National Office Products Alliance (NOPA); and Office Furniture Dealers Alliance (OFDA). Offers strategic information, government advocacy, business performance benchmarking, standards development, and management education services to members located throughout the United States and in key Canadian markets. **Formerly:** Business Products Industry Association; (1992) Contract Furnishings Forum; (2001) Office Furniture Dealers Alliance. **Publications:** *Office Furniture and Design*, bimonthly. Magazine. Highlights industry best practices, market trends and new product developments. **Advertising:** accepted ● *Office World News*, bimonthly. Magazine. Highlights industry best practices and market trends. **Advertising:** accepted. **Conventions/Meetings:** annual meeting.

1699 ■ International Furniture Rental Association (IFRA)

5229 Coll. Hill Rd.
Woodstock, VT 05091
E-mail: info@ifra.org
URL: http://www.ifra.org
Contact: Mr. Jerry Gorup, Exec. Dir.

Founded: 1967. **Members:** 60. **Membership Dues:** associate, $500 (annual) ● furniture rental company, $365-$1,450 (annual). **Staff:** 2. **Description:** Companies whose major business is the leasing and rental of home furnishings and accessories; suppliers of products and services to these companies are associate members. Dedicated in upholding ethical standards of the furniture rental industry and providing quality products and service. Conducts industry exposition and statistical surveys. Promotes industry through nationwide consumer education program. Works to safeguard against adverse legislation and regulation. **Formerly:** (1994) Furniture Rental Association of America. **Publications:** *Furniture Rental Association of America—Membership Directory*, annual. Lists member companies, main contact persons, showroom locations of voting members, and products and services offered by associated members. **Price:** free for members. **Circulation:** 60 ● *Furniture Rental Association of America—Newsletter*, bimonthly. Includes calendar of events and updates on legislation affecting furniture renters. **Price:** free for members and interested parties. **Circulation:** 250. **Advertising:** accepted. **Conventions/Meetings:** annual meeting (exhibits).

1700 ■ International Furniture Suppliers Association (IFSA)

3910 Tinsley Dr., Ste.101
High Point, NC 27265
Ph: (336)801-6130
Fax: (336)801-6102
E-mail: info@nhfa.org
URL: http://www.ifsa-info.com
Contact: Gary Chase, Chm.

Founded: 1933. **Members:** 127. **Membership Dues:** wholesale/distributor/associate, $995 (annual) ● wholesale, $650-$1,620 (annual). **Staff:** 3. **Budget:** $200,000. **Description:** Wholesalers of furniture and/or home furnishings accessories and supplier firms who manufacture products offered for sale by wholesaler-distributor members and suppliers of services utilized by wholesale furniture distributors. Maintains Distributor's Hall of Fame; conducts educational seminars. **Libraries: Type:** not open to the public. **Holdings:** 100; books, video recordings. **Subjects:** accounting, personnel management, sales. **Awards:** Industry Award. **Frequency:** annual. **Type:** recognition. **Recipient:** for service to the industry ● Man of the Year. **Frequency:** annual. **Type:** recognition. **Recipient:** for service to the industry. **Formerly:** (1992) National Wholesale Furniture Association; (2005) International Wholesale Furniture Association. **Publications:** *Distributor's Report*, quarterly. Magazine. **Circulation:** 28,000. **Advertising:** accepted ● *National Wholesale Furniture Association—Newsletter*, monthly. Contains up-to-date on current news in the home furnishings industry and IFSA community. **Price:** included in membership dues ● *Who's Who in Furniture Distribution*, annual. Membership Directory. **Price:** $42.00 for nonmembers, plus shipping and handling. **Conventions/Meetings:** semiannual banquet - always spring and fall in High Point, NC ● annual conference.

1701 ■ International Home Furnishings Market Authority (IHFMA)
PO Box 5243
High Point, NC 27262
Ph: (336)869-1000
Free: (800)874-6492
Fax: (336)869-6999
E-mail: bcasey@highpointmarket.org
URL: http://www.highpointmarket.org
Contact: Brian Casey, Pres.
Members: 4. **Description:** Furniture manufacturers and exhibition buildings working to create a cooperative business environment. **Formerly:** Furniture Factories Marketing Association of the South; (1989) Southern Furniture Market; (2003) International Home Furnishings Marketing Association. **Publications:** Brochures, semiannual. **Circulation:** 50,000 ● Pamphlets. **Conventions/Meetings:** semiannual meeting, with finished goods in case goods, upholstery, accessories, lighting, bedding, and rugs (exhibits) - always April and October. 2008 Sept. 22-28, High Point, NC; 2009 Mar. 23-29, High Point, NC.

1702 ■ International Home Furnishings Representatives Association (IHFRA)
PO Box 670
High Point, NC 27261
Ph: (336)889-3920
Free: (866)528-8634
Fax: (336)464-2125
E-mail: info@ihfra.org
URL: http://www.ihfra.org
Contact: Kathy Parks, Exec. Dir.
Founded: 1934. **Members:** 2,000. **Membership Dues:** affiliate, $160 (annual). **Staff:** 3. **Budget:** $400,000. **Regional Groups:** 32. **Description:** Local affiliated organizations of approximately 2,000 home furnishings representatives. Provides services to affiliates and individual members, including information exchange, listing manufacturers seeking representatives in all territories and representatives seeking manufacturers' lines in specific territories. Conducts certified home furnishings educational program. **Awards: Frequency:** annual. **Type:** recognition. **Formerly:** (1967) National Wholesale Furniture Salesmen's Association; (1972) National Home Furnishings Representatives Association. **Publications:** *Opportunity Center*, 10/year ● Pamphlets. **Conventions/Meetings:** annual conference.

1703 ■ National Home Furnishings Association (NHFA)
3910 Tinsley Dr., Ste.101
High Point, NC 27265-3610
Ph: (336)886-6100
Free: (800)888-9590
Fax: (336)801-6102
E-mail: info@nhfa.org
URL: http://www.nhfa.org
Contact: Steve DeHaan, Exec. VP
Founded: 1920. **Members:** 2,750. **Membership Dues:** retailer (based on total annual sales), $460-$1,670 (annual). **Staff:** 48. **Budget:** $3,500,000. **Regional Groups:** 6. **State Groups:** 5. **Multinational. Description:** Provides business services to help retailers of home furnishings grow their businesses. Provides educational programs for retail sales managers and trainers, for middle management, for owners and executives, and for family businesses. **Libraries: Type:** reference. **Awards:** Retailer of the Year. **Frequency:** annual. **Type:** recognition. **Recipient:** for contribution to industry, community service, business achievements and leadership. **Telecommunication Services:** electronic mail, sdehaan@nhfa.org. **Committees:** Education; Government Affairs; Member Services; Membership; Publications Resource. **Divisions:** Service Corporation. **Affiliated With:** Interior Design Society. **Formerly:** (1970) National Retail Furniture Association. **Publications:** *Currents*, monthly. Newsletter ● *Home Furnishings Retailer*, monthly. Magazine. **Price:** $60.00/year. ISSN: 1073-5585. **Circulation:** 14,299. **Advertising:** accepted. **Conventions/Meetings:** biennial All Industry Convention (exhibits).

1704 ■ Office Furniture Recyclers Forum
c/o Office Furniture Dealers Alliance
301 N Fairfax St.
Alexandria, VA 22314
Ph: (703)549-9040
Free: (800)542-6672
Fax: (703)683-7552
E-mail: info@ofdanet.org
Contact: Chris Bates, Pres.
Founded: 1984. **Members:** 1,220. **Description:** A division of the National Office Products Association (see separate entry). Companies that deals in and promotes mid-grade office furniture and are members of the NOPA. Encourages competition by providing a peer group for those active in the budget office furniture markets; aims to help dealers take advantage of the anticipated growth in the market. **Formerly:** (1989) Budget Furniture Forum; (1992) Retail Office Furniture Forum; (1999) Retail Office Dealer Division. **Publications:** Membership Directory, annual. **Conventions/Meetings:** annual meeting.

1705 ■ Specialty Sleep Association (SSA)
c/o Tambra Jones, Exec. Dir.
46639 Jones Ranch Rd.
Friant, CA 93626
Ph: (559)868-4187
Fax: (559)868-4185
URL: http://www.specialtysleepnet.com
Contact: Tambra Jones, Exec. Dir.
Founded: 1995. **Members:** 334. **Membership Dues:** retailer (based on number of stores), $150-$500 (annual) ● manufacturer (based on net industry sales), $300-$2,500 (annual) ● manufacturer representative, $125 (annual) ● industry associate, $110 (annual). **Staff:** 5. **Budget:** $500,000. **Description:** Manufacturers and retailers with a unified goal of expanding the waterbed industry. **Awards:** Best of Show Awards. **Frequency:** annual. **Type:** recognition. **Recipient:** for best booth set-up ● Frank Imbrie Humanitarian. **Frequency:** annual. **Type:** recognition. **Recipient:** for community service ● Hall of Fame Awards. **Frequency:** annual. **Type:** recognition. **Recipient:** for manufacturers and retailers ● Manufacturer of the Year. **Frequency:** annual. **Type:** recognition. **Recipient:** for manufacturers ● Retailer of the Year. **Frequency:** annual. **Type:** recognition. **Recipient:** for retailers ● Special Recognition. **Frequency:** annual. **Type:** recognition. **Recipient:** for advertising. **Committees:** New Markets; Product Standards and Technology; Trade Show. **Formed by Merger of:** Waterbed Manufacturers Association; National Waterbed Retailers Association. **Formerly:** (1997) Waterbed Council. **Publications:** *The Bedroom Industry*, bimonthly. Newsletter. Covers industry-related topics and association information. **Price:** free for members ● Membership Directory, annual. **Price:** free for members. **Conventions/Meetings:** annual Bedroom Show - trade show (exhibits).

1706 ■ Summer and Casual Furniture Manufacturers Association (SCFMA)
c/o Joseph P. Logan, Exec. Dir.
317 W High Ave., 10th Fl.
High Point, NC 27260
Ph: (336)884-5000
Fax: (336)884-5303
E-mail: info@ahfa.us
URL: http://www.ahfa.us
Contact: Joseph P. Logan, Exec. Dir.
Founded: 1959. **Members:** 80. **Membership Dues:** company (minimum), $1,200 (annual). **Staff:** 2. **Description:** A division of American Home Furnishings Alliance (see separate entry). Manufacturers of household summer and casual furniture. Compiles trade statistics; provides legislative, technical, management, and marketing services. Conducts technical and marketing research. **Awards:** Apollo Award. **Frequency:** annual. **Type:** recognition. **Recipient:** for excellence in casual furniture retailing ● Design Excellence Award. **Frequency:** annual. **Type:** recognition ● Lifetime Achievement Award. **Frequency:** annual. **Type:** recognition. **Telecommunication Services:** electronic mail, jlogan@ahfa.us. **Affiliated With:** American Home Furnishings Alliance. **Conventions/Meetings:** annual meeting (exhibits) - always September in Chicago, IL.

1707 ■ Unfinished Furniture Association (UFA)
15000 Commerce Pkwy., Ste.C
Mount Laurel, NJ 08054
Free: (800)487-8321
Fax: (856)439-0525
E-mail: ufa@ahint.com
URL: http://www.unfinishedfurniture.org
Contact: Michele Biordi, Exec. Dir.
Founded: 1988. **Membership Dues:** retailer (house sales representative), $100 (annual) ● retailer (associate), $200 (annual) ● retailer (independent sales representative), $300 (annual) ● retailer (based on annual sales), $230-$1,470 (annual) ● manufacturer (based on annual sales), $330-$2,585 (annual). **Staff:** 5. **Description:** Promotes the image of the unfinished furniture industry; aims to form cohesiveness and camaraderie among industry members. **Computer Services:** Information services, news and consumer education ● mailing lists, contact information of members ● online services, store finder. **Committees:** Communications/Membership; Public Relations; Steering. **Publications:** *Retailer and Manufacturer Profile*. Survey. **Price:** $10.00 for members; $25.00 for nonmembers ● *UFA Membership Directory and Buyer's Guide*, annual. **Price:** included in membership dues; $100.00 for nonmembers. **Advertising:** accepted ● *Unfinished Business*, bimonthly. Magazine. **Advertising:** accepted. **Conventions/Meetings:** annual trade show (exhibits).

1708 ■ Upholstered Furniture Action Council (UFAC)
Box 2436
High Point, NC 27261
Ph: (336)885-5065
Fax: (336)885-5072
E-mail: info@ufac.org
URL: http://www.ufac.org
Contact: Joseph Ziolkowski, Exec. Dir.
Founded: 1978. **Members:** 250. **Budget:** $500,000. **Description:** Conducts research and disseminates information regarding the development and adoption of voluntary guidelines for production of more cigarette-resistant upholstered furniture; educates the public in the safe use of smoking materials. Maintains speakers' bureau; compiles statistics. **Convention/Meeting:** none. **Committees:** Communication; Laboratory Alliance; Technical. **Formerly:** (1975) Furniture Flammability Committee. **Publications:** *UFAC: Action Guide*, annual. Serves as a guide to UFAC's voluntary program to promote cigarette-resistant upholstered furniture. Includes construction criteria and compliance. **Price:** free. **Circulation:** 5,000 ● Books ● Reports.

1709 ■ Western Home Furnishings Association (WHFA)
500 Giuseppe Ct., Ste.6
Roseville, CA 95678
Ph: (916)784-7677 (916)960-0345
Free: (800)422-3778
Fax: (916)784-7697

E-mail: kcrawford@whfa.org
URL: http://www.whfa.org
Contact: Sharron Bradley, Exec. Dir.
Founded: 1944. **Members:** 900. **Membership Dues:** manufacturer's representative, $175 (annual) ● industry consultant/industry resource/vendor, $285 (annual) ● manufacturer/wholesaler, $570 (annual) ● corporate (based on annual sales), $460-$1,670 (annual). **State Groups:** 10. **Description:** Works as industry advocate for independent home furnishings retailers. **Libraries: Type:** not open to the public. **Affiliated With:** National Home Furnishings Association. **Publications:** *Manufacturers and Service Providers Directory* ● *Western Reporter*, monthly. Journal. **Price:** included in membership dues; $35.00 /year for nonmembers. **Advertising:** accepted ● *WHFA Online Directory*. Alternate Formats: online. **Conventions/Meetings:** annual conference.

Futures

1710 ■ FINEX
c/o New York Board of Trade (NYBOT)
One North End Ave.
New York, NY 10282-1101
Ph: (212)748-4094
Free: (877)877-8890
E-mail: marketing@nybot.com
Contact: Charles H. Falk, Pres,/CEO
Founded: 1984. **Members:** 100. **Staff:** 15. **Description:** A division of the New York Cotton Exchange. Trades futures and options on the U.S. Dollar Index (USDX) and European Currency Unit (ECU). (The U.S. Dollar Index is created by the standings of ten major currencies against the U.S. dollar; each currency is "weighted" by its country's share of world trade. Thus, a given currency's value on the index is proportionate to its share of world trade. The European Currency Index used by the division is achieved similarly, but uses the ten currencies of the EEC). Trades futures on Treasury Auction Two Year and Five Year U.S. Treasury Notes. Creates and markets financial derivative products. **Telecommunication Services:** 24-hour hotline, information on prices, volume and open interest on FINEX futures and options, (212)839-9083. **Affiliated With:** New York Cotton Exchange. **Also Known As:** Financial Instrument Exchange. **Publications:** *FINEX Report*, monthly ● Brochures ● Also publishes wall charts and historical data for analysis.

1711 ■ Future 500
335 Powell St., 14th Fl.
San Francisco, CA 94102
Ph: (415)294-7775
Fax: (415)520-0830
E-mail: info@future500.org
URL: http://www.future500.org
Contact: William K. Shireman, Pres./CEO
Founded: 1995. **Members:** 300. **Membership Dues:** limited, individual, $195 (annual) ● limited, business, $395 (annual) ● full, $5,000 (annual). **Staff:** 5. **Budget:** $600,000. **Local Groups:** 3. **Description:** Resolves conflict between business and social and environmental activities. Administers an international business network founded on business as a living. **Formerly:** (2004) Global Futures Foundation. **Publications:** *What We Learned in the Rainforest - Business Lessons from Nature*. Book. **Price:** $2.50 ● Newsletter, bimonthly. **Advertising:** accepted. Alternate Formats: online. **Conventions/Meetings:** annual convention.

1712 ■ Futures Industry Association (FIA)
2001 Pennsylvania Ave. NW, Ste.600
Washington, DC 20006
Ph: (202)466-5460
Fax: (202)296-3184
E-mail: info@futuresindustry.org
URL: http://www.futuresindustry.org
Contact: Richard Berlland, Chm.
Founded: 1955. **Members:** 250. **Membership Dues:** accounting firm (based on number of partners), service organization (based on number of employees), $1,500-$3,000 (annual) ● association, $1,500 (annual) ● bank, corporation, foreign broker, institutional user, advertising agency, $2,000 (annual) ● clearing corporation (based on clearing volume in contracts), $2,000-$8,000 (annual) ● commodity trading advisor, pool operator, proprietary trading (based on futures funds), $2,000-$5,000 (annual) ● exchange (based on volume of futures and options contracts), $2,000-$15,000 (annual) ● broker, registered representative (based on number of associated persons), $1,000-$2,750 (annual) ● law firm (based on number of practicing attorney), $1,000-$3,000 (annual). **Staff:** 24. **Budget:** $2,000,000. **National Groups:** 2. **Description:** Acts as a principal spokesman for the futures and options industry. Represents all facets of the futures industry, including many international exchanges. Works to preserve the system of free and competitive markets by representing the interests of the industry in connection with legislative and regulatory issues. **Awards:** Futures Hall of Fame. **Frequency:** annual. **Type:** recognition. **Recipient:** to individuals who have made significant contributions to the futures and options industry. **Committees:** Futures Industry Political Action. **Divisions:** European Chapter; FIA Chicago; Futures Services; Information Technology; Japan Chapter; Law and Compliance. **Publications:** *eMarketBeat*, weekly. Newsletter. Delivers industry news, updates on legislative and regulatory actions affecting the industry, FIA division reports and events. **Price:** free. Alternate Formats: online ● *FIA Membership Directory*, annual ● *FIA Membership Guide*. Brochure. Alternate Formats: online ● *Futures Industry*, bimonthly. Magazine. **Price:** free to qualified individuals. **Advertising:** accepted ● *Volume Reports*, monthly ● *Weekly Bulletin*. **Conventions/Meetings:** annual Futures and Options Expo - trade show (exhibits) - every fall in Chicago, IL ● annual International Futures Industry Conference (exhibits) - always March in Boca Raton, FL.

1713 ■ National Futures Association (NFA)
200 W Madison St., No. 1600
Chicago, IL 60606-3447
Ph: (312)781-1300 (312)781-1390
Free: (800)621-3570
Fax: (312)781-1467
E-mail: information@nfa.futures.org
URL: http://www.nfa.futures.org
Contact: Daniel J. Roth, Pres./CEO
Founded: 1982. **Members:** 3,772. **Membership Dues:** commodity pool operator, commodity trading advisor, introducing broker, $750 (annual) ● futures commission merchant (exchange member), $1,500 (annual) ● futures commission merchant (non-exchange member), $5,625 (annual) ● FCM FOREX dealer (exchange member with annual FOREX revenue of $500,000 or less), $15,875 (annual) ● FCM FOREX dealer (non-exchange member with annual FOREX revenue of $500,000 or less), $20,000 (annual). **Staff:** 246. **Languages:** English, Spanish. **Description:** Futures commission merchants; commodity trading advisors; commodity pool operators; brokers and their associated persons. Works to: strengthen and expand industry self-regulation to include all segments of the futures industry; provide uniform standards to eliminate duplication of effort and conflict; remove unnecessary regulatory constraints to aid effective regulation. Conducts member qualification screening, financial surveillance, and registration. Monitors and enforces customer protection rules and uniform business standards. Maintains information center. Arbitrates customer disputes; audits non-exchange member FCM's. **Libraries: Type:** reference. **Holdings:** periodicals. **Subjects:** futures industry. **Committees:** Advisory; Appeals; Business Conduct; Discretionary Account Waiver Panel; Floor Broker; Hearing; Nominating; Telemarketing Procedures Waiver. **Publications:** *Annual Review*, annual. Booklet. **Price:** free ● *National Futures Association—News Release*, periodic. Reports group events to financial and general news media. **Price:** free. **Circulation:** 900 ● *News, Facts, Actions*, quarterly. Newsletter. Keeps businesspeople apprised of current regulations and issues affecting the operation of their commodity futures businesses. **Price:** free. **Circulation:** 4,400 ● *NFA Manual* ● Pamphlets. **Conventions/Meetings:** annual meeting - always February.

1714 ■ National Introducing Brokers Association (NIBA)
55 W Monroe St., Ste.3330
Chicago, IL 60603
Ph: (312)977-0598
Fax: (312)977-0121
E-mail: membership@theniba.com
URL: http://www.theniba.com
Contact: Melinda Schramm, Chair
Founded: 1991. **Membership Dues:** regular, $150 (annual). **Description:** Represents professionals in the futures and options industry. Aims to maximize opportunities available to its members. Strives to ensure open channels of communication among individual members and between introducing brokers, futures commissions members, and industry regulators. **Telecommunication Services:** electronic mail, volunteer@theniba.com ● electronic mail, melinda@futuresrep.com. **Publications:** Newsletter. Alternate Formats: online.

Games

1715 ■ Game Audio Network Guild (GANG)
PO Box 507
San Juan Capistrano, CA 92693-0507
Ph: (949)340-3557
E-mail: info@audiogang.org
URL: http://www.audiogang.org
Contact: Tommy Tallarico, CEO
Founded: 2002. **Members:** 461. **Membership Dues:** student, $50 (annual) ● apprentice, associate, $75 (annual) ● professional, $100 (annual). **Multinational. Description:** Promotes excellence in the interactive game audio industry. Advances the creation and development of quality sound audio. Educates the public about interactive audio. Provides information, instruction, resources, guidance and enlightenment to its members, content providers and listeners throughout the world. Addresses the issues affecting the interactive audio industry. **Awards:** G.A. N.G. Awards. **Frequency:** annual. **Type:** recognition. **Recipient:** for significant contribution to the interactive audio industry. **Publications:** Newsletter, monthly.

1716 ■ International Laser Tag Association (ILTA)
5351 E Thompson Rd., Ste.236
Indianapolis, IN 46237
Ph: (317)786-9755
Fax: (317)786-9757
E-mail: info@lasertag.org
URL: http://www.lasertag.org
Contact: Shane Zimmerman, Exec. Dir.
Founded: 1996. **Members:** 400. **Membership Dues:** developer in U.S., $495 (annual) ● developer outside U.S., $545 (annual). **Staff:** 3. **Budget:** $150,000. **Description:** Works to help operators become more efficient, to help investors learn more about the industry, to help member companies increase market share, and to promote the overall industry. **Publications:** *Data Packet*, quarterly. **Conventions/Meetings:** annual Operators and Developers Dinner.

1717 ■ Valley International Foosball Association (VIFA)
201 S Henry St.
Bay City, MI 48706
Ph: (989)893-1800
Free: (800)544-1346
Fax: (989)893-0103
E-mail: info@vifa.com
URL: http://www.vifa.com
Multinational. Description: Represents the interests of coin machine operators, foosball table manufacturers and foosball players. Promotes increased interest in the game of foosball. **Computer Services:** database, leagues around the world ● database, tournament results.

Gaming

1718 ■ American Gaming Association (AGA)
1299 Pennsylvania Ave. NW, Ste.1175
Washington, DC 20004
Ph: (202)552-2675
Fax: (202)552-2676
E-mail: info@americangaming.org
URL: http://www.americangaming.org
Contact: Frank J. Fahrenkopf Jr., Pres./CEO
Founded: 1995. **Members:** 55. **Membership Dues:** individual, $75 (annual) ● casino/gaming equipment manufacturer (maximum), $450,000 (quarterly) ● financial service, $50,000 (semiannual) ● professional service, $25,000 (semiannual) ● supplier/vendor, $1,250-$25,000 (semiannual) ● pari-mutuel operation/sport book, $10,000 (semiannual) ● association/publication/union, $5,000 (semiannual). **Staff:** 10. **Budget:** $5,000,000. **Description:** Represents the commercial casino entertainment industry by addressing federal legislative and regulatory issues affecting its members and their employees and customers; provides leadership in addressing newly emerging national issues and in developing industry-wide programs on critical issues; serves as the industry's first national information clearinghouse, providing the media, elected officials, other decision makers and the public with timely, accurate gaming industry data. **Awards:** Gaming Voice Award. **Frequency:** annual. **Type:** recognition. **Recipient:** for outstanding financial and corporate communication in gaming. **Publications:** *Inside the AGA*, bimonthly. Newsletter. **Price:** available to members only. Alternate Formats: online ● *Responsible Gaming Quarterly*. Newsletter. Alternate Formats: online. **Conventions/Meetings:** annual Global Gaming Expo - trade show and conference (exhibits) - 2008 Nov. 18-20, Las Vegas, NV; 2009 Nov. 17-19, Las Vegas, NV; 2010 Nov. 16-18, Las Vegas, NV.

1719 ■ Gaming Standards Association (GSA)
48377 Fremont Blvd., Ste.117
Fremont, CA 94538
Ph: (510)492-4060
Fax: (510)492-4001
E-mail: sec@gamingstandards.com
URL: http://www.gamingstandards.com
Contact: Peter DeRaedt, Pres.
Founded: 1998. **Members:** 37. **Membership Dues:** platinum, $80,250 (annual) ● gold, $32,100 (annual) ● silver, $21,400 (annual). **Staff:** 5. **Multinational. Description:** Gaming manufacturers, suppliers and operators. Promotes identification, definition, development, and implementation of open standards to facilitate innovation, education and communication for the gaming industry. **Committees:** Architectural Oversight; Best of Breed; GDS; Marketing; SAS Protocol; System to System; Transport. **Councils:** Operators Advisory; Regulators Advisory. **Publications:** *Gaming Standards Association Newsletter*. Alternate Formats: online ● Papers. Alternate Formats: online.

Gardening

1720 ■ Lawn and Garden Dealers Association (LGDA)
5616 S 122nd East Ave., Ste.N
Tulsa, OK 74146
Free: (800)752-5296
Fax: (918)254-0713
E-mail: info@lgda.com
URL: http://www.lgda.com
Founded: 1986. **Description:** Works to help small businesses in the outdoor industries save thousands of dollars annually by combining the buying power of thousands of companies.

Gases

1721 ■ Compressed Gas Association (CGA)
4221 Walney Rd., 5th Fl.
Chantilly, VA 20151-2923
Ph: (703)788-2700
Fax: (703)961-1831
E-mail: cga@cganet.com
URL: http://www.cganet.com
Contact: Carl T. Johnson, CEO/Pres.
Founded: 1913. **Members:** 160. **Membership Dues:** associate, $2,145-$9,360 (annual) ● active and consultant (maximum; based on revenue), $87,862 (annual). **Staff:** 12. **Budget:** $3,000,000. **Description:** Firms producing and distributing compressed, liquefied, and cryogenic gases; manufacturers of related equipment. Submits recommendations to appropriate government agencies to improve safety standards and methods of handling, transporting, and storing gases; acts as advisor to regulatory authorities and other agencies concerned with safe handling of compressed gases; collaborates with national organizations to develop specifications and standards of safety; compiles information. Maintains 25 technical committees. **Awards: Frequency:** annual. **Type:** recognition. **Recipient:** for member companies. **Telecommunication Services:** electronic mail, nflower@cganet.com. **Committees:** Atmospheric Gases and Equipment; Bulk Distribution; Carbon Dioxide; COMPGEAP; Cylinder Specifications; Cylinder Valves and Connections; Distribution and Fleet Safety; Environmental; Gas Specifications; Hazard Communication; Hazardous Material Codes; Industrial Gases Apparatus; Medical Gases and Equipment; Pressure Relief Devices; Safety and Health; Specialty Gases. **Divisions:** Canada; Safety and Environmental; Technology and Safety Standards. **Absorbed:** International Acetylene Association. **Formerly:** (1949) Compressed Gas Manufacturers Association. **Publications:** *Compressed Gas Association—Publication Catalog*, annual. **Price:** free. **Circulation:** 8,000. Alternate Formats: online ● *Compressions*, 10/year. Newsletter. Includes meeting calendar. **Price:** available to members only ● *Handbook of Compressed Gases*. Addresses the properties, safety considerations, equipment, and regulatory using compressed gas containers. **Price:** $99.00 for members (hardcopy); $179.00 for nonmembers (hardcopy) ● Bulletin, periodic ● Directory, annual. **Price:** available to members only ● Also publishes safety standards. **Conventions/Meetings:** annual meeting.

1722 ■ Gasification Technologies Council (GTC)
4301 N Fairfax Dr., Ste.300
Arlington, VA 22203
Ph: (703)276-0110
Fax: (703)276-0141
E-mail: jchildress@gasification.org
URL: http://www.gasification.org
Contact: James M. Childress, Exec. Dir.
Founded: 1995. **Members:** 31. **Membership Dues:** associate, $10,000 (annual) ● regular, $15,000 (annual). **Multinational. Description:** Corporations involved in the gasification of coal, petroleum coke, and heavy oils. Gathers and disseminates information on gasification methods and technologies. Conducts research and educational programs; compiles statistics. **Libraries: Type:** reference. **Holdings:** papers. **Conventions/Meetings:** annual conference (exhibits).

1723 ■ International Oxygen Manufacturers Association (IOMA)
1255 23rd St. NW, Ste.200
Washington, DC 20037
Ph: (202)521-9300
Fax: (202)833-3636
E-mail: ioma@iomaweb.org
URL: http://www.iomaweb.org
Contact: David A. Saunders, Exec. Dir.
Founded: 1943. **Members:** 150. **Staff:** 2. **Budget:** $500,000. **Multinational. Description:** Producers and distributors of compressed and liquefied industrial and medical gases and acetylene; manufacturers of products and equipment used by the industrial gas and cryogenics industries. **Publications:** *Broadcaster*, bimonthly. **Conventions/Meetings:** annual meeting.

Gifts

1724 ■ National Specialty Gift Association (NSGA)
7238 Bucks Ford Dr.
Riverview, FL 33569
Ph: (813)671-4757
Fax: (813)677-5075
E-mail: nsga@giftprofessionals.com
URL: http://www.nsgaonline.com/nsga
Contact: Joni Damico, Contact
Founded: 1998. **Members:** 350. **Membership Dues:** business, $150 (annual) ● professional, $100 (annual) ● affiliate vendor, $200 (annual). **Staff:** 1. **For-Profit. Description:** Gift industry association for retailers, home-based professionals, and vendors. Offers coop marketing, mentoring, vendor discounts, and international wire service. **Computer Services:** Online services, Telegift Network. **Also Known As:** Telegift Network. **Publications:** *Creative Edge*, bimonthly. Newsletter. Contains business information for specialty gift professionals. **Price:** included in membership dues. **Advertising:** accepted. Alternate Formats: online.

Glass

1725 ■ American Natural Soda Ash Corporation (ANSAC)
15 Riverside Ave., 2nd Fl.
Westport, CT 06880
Ph: (203)226-9056
Fax: (203)227-1484
E-mail: sr@ansac.com
URL: http://www.ansac.com
Contact: Sameer Rupani, Global Marketing Mgr.
Founded: 1984. **Members:** 6. **Staff:** 35. **Languages:** Chinese, English, Spanish. **Description:** Manufacturers of soda ash, a raw material used in the production of glass. Provides exportations services for member companies. (A Webb-Pomerene Act Association). **Formerly:** (1983) U.S. Soda Ash Export Association. **Conventions/Meetings:** board meeting - 3/year.

1726 ■ Art Glass Association (AGA)
PO Box 2537
Zanesville, OH 43702-2537
Ph: (740)450-6547
Free: (866)301-2421
Fax: (740)454-1194
E-mail: bbird@artglassassociation.com
URL: http://www.artglassassociation.com/mc/page.do
Contact: Bill Bird, Exec. Dir.
Founded: 1985. **Members:** 875. **Membership Dues:** associate, $35 (annual) ● professional, $125 (annual) ● patron, $300 (annual) ● benefactor (minimum donation), $500 (annual). **Staff:** 3. **Languages:** English, German, Spanish. **Description:** Manufacturers, wholesalers, importers, retailers, and others involved in the art glass industry. Promotes the industry and members' interests. Sponsors Celebrate Art Glass Month. **Awards: Type:** recognition. **Computer Services:** database, membership. **Formerly:** Art Glass Suppliers Association; (2003) Art Glass Suppliers Association International. **Publications:** *Group Report*, bimonthly. Includes show reports, association and industry news. Features articles on running a small business and other related industry topic. **Price:** free for members. **Advertising:** accepted. Alternate Formats: online ● *Official Show Directory*, annual. Lists exhibiting companies; includes membership roster. **Price:** $10.00. **Circulation:** 3,000. **Advertising:** accepted. **Conventions/Meetings:** annual The Art Glass Show - trade show, with art glass supplies, including flat glass, tools, equipment, kilns, grinders, rods, sandblasters and finished giftware items (exhibits) ● seminar ● workshop.

1727 ■ Coalition for Auto Glass Safety and Public Awareness (CASPA)
c/o National Glass Association
8200 Greensboro Dr., Ste.302
McLean, VA 22102-3881

Ph: (717)558-0939
E-mail: info@myautoglass.org
URL: http://www.myautoglass.org
Contact: Wesley Topping Jr., Chm.
Founded: 2003. **Membership Dues:** auto glass retail service company, $300 (annual) ● auto glass manufacturer/supplier (based on industry sales), $2,000-$6,000 (annual). **Description:** Promotes public understanding of auto glass as a crucial safety component in the modern vehicle's safety restraint system. Assists consumers in locating safe and reliable auto glass replacement services. Represents the professional auto glass practitioner. **Affiliated With:** National Glass Association.

1728 ■ Glass Association of North America (GANA)

2945 SW Wanamaker Dr., Ste.A
Topeka, KS 66614-5321
Ph: (785)271-0208
Fax: (785)271-0166
E-mail: gana@glasswebsite.com
URL: http://www.glasswebsite.com
Contact: Stanley L. Smith, Exec. VP
Founded: 1994. **Members:** 220. **Membership Dues:** affiliate (per individual), $160 (annual) ● individual, business (based on sales volume), $640-$7,500 (annual). **Staff:** 8. **Budget:** $1,000,000. **Description:** Independent glass distributors, contractors, and fabricators covering all flat glass products. Assists architects and the building industry. Offers educational courses on blueprint reading and labor estimating. Sponsors employee safety program. Laminated and Tempered glass fabrication. **Libraries: Type:** reference. **Holdings:** books. **Telecommunication Services:** electronic mail, stan@glasswebsite.com. **Divisions:** Building Envelope Contractors; Decorative; Flat Glass Manufacturing; Insulating; Laminating; Mirror; Tempering. **Absorbed:** Flat Glass Marketing Association; Glass Tempering Association; (1999) Laminators Safety Glass Association; (2000) North American Association of Mirror Manufacturers. **Formerly:** Flat Glass Jobbers Association. **Publications:** *FGMA Fabrication, Erection & Glazing Hours Manual (1992)*. **Price:** $10.99 for members; $19.99 for nonmembers ● *FGMA Sealant Manual (1990)*. **Price:** $17.50 for members; $25.00 for nonmembers ● *GANA Blueprint Reading & Labor Estimating Course (2003)*. Book. **Price:** $275.00 for members; $350.00 for nonmembers ● *GANA Fully Tempered Heavy Glass Door and Entrance Systems Design Guide (1999)*. Book. **Price:** $15.00 for members; $25.00 for nonmembers ● *GANA Glass Reflections*, 8/year. Newsletter. **Price:** $50.00 for nonmembers; included in membership dues. ISSN: 1077-517X. **Circulation:** 1,500 ● *GANA Glazing Manual (2004)* (in English and Spanish). **Price:** $25.00 for members; $35.00 for nonmembers; $45.00 for members (hard copy and CD version); $65.00 for nonmembers (hard copy and CD version) ● *GANA Laminating Division's Laminated Glazing Reference Manual (2003)*. **Price:** $20.00 for members; $30.00 for nonmembers; $35.00 for members (hard copy and CD version); $55.00 for nonmembers (hard copy and CD version) ● *GANA Safety*, monthly. Bulletins. **Price:** $50.00/year ● *GANA Tempering Division's Engineering Standards Manual (2002)*. **Price:** $20.00 for members; $30.00 for nonmembers. **Conventions/Meetings:** annual conference, with educational seminar and division meetings - every fall ● annual Glass Fabrication: Insulating, Laminating and Tempering - seminar ● annual Glass Week - convention.

1729 ■ Glass Manufacturing Industry Council (GMIC)

735 Ceramic Pl., Ste.101
Westerville, OH 43081
Ph: (614)818-9423
E-mail: mgreenman@gmic.org
URL: http://www.gmic.org
Contact: Michael Greenman, Exec. Dir.
Founded: 1998. **Members:** 24. **Membership Dues:** associate (based on sales), $7,000-$15,000 (annual) ● non-profit research institute, $3,000 (annual) ● university, affiliate, $500 (annual). **Description:** Promotes the interests and growth of the US glass industry through cooperation in the areas of technology, productivity and the environment. **Publications:** *Glass Industry of the Future: Resources and Tools for Energy Efficiency and Cost Reduction Now*. Manual. Contains information on innovative energy efficiency technologies and related topics. Alternate Formats: CD-ROM ● *Glass Manufacturing Issues*. Proceedings. **Price:** $25.00 for members, plus shipping and handling; $35.00 for nonmembers, plus shipping and handling. Alternate Formats: CD-ROM ● *Glass Melting Technologies of the Future*. Proceedings. **Price:** $25.00 for members, plus shipping and handling; $35.00 for nonmembers, plus shipping and handling ● Brochure. Features illustrations of the many aspects of glass, from its origins through its evolution. **Price:** $120.00/case.

1730 ■ Independent Glass Association (IGA)

385 Garrisonville Rd., Ste.116
Stafford, VA 22554
Ph: (540)720-7484
Fax: (540)720-5687
E-mail: info@iga.org
URL: http://www.iga.org
Contact: Mr. Patrick Smith, Dir. of Operations
Founded: 1995. **Members:** 900. **Membership Dues:** associate, $995 (annual) ● business (based on annual sales), $295-$995 (annual). **Staff:** 4. **Description:** Helps automotive and architectural glass retailers compete with the national chains. Unites the efforts, interests and ideas of its members. Offers marketing, billing, and purchasing programs and promotes a high standard for consumer safety, quality, service and fair trade principles. Encourages a competitive, free market environment and the independence of each member. **Libraries: Type:** reference. **Holdings:** articles. **Additional Websites:** http://www.igacertification.org. **Committees:** E-Commerce; Insurance Industry Liaison; Legislation and Legal; Nominating; Safety Standards. **Task Forces:** Convention; Ethics. **Publications:** *Beacon Bulletin*, weekly. Contains latest industry news, updates, and informative feature articles written by industry experts. Alternate Formats: online. **Conventions/Meetings:** annual Independents' Days National Convention and Spring Glass Show (exhibits).

1731 ■ Insulating Glass Certification Council (IGCC)

PO Box 9
Henderson Harbor, NY 13651
Ph: (315)646-2234
Fax: (315)646-2297
E-mail: staff@amscert.com
URL: http://www.igcc.org
Contact: Erin Ackley, Contact
Founded: 1977. **Members:** 170. **Staff:** 4. **Description:** Manufacturers of sealed insulating glass units, suppliers to the industry, consumers, and others who are responsible for, or concerned with, the quality and performance of products purchased in the public's interest. Sponsors and directs a program of laboratory testing and unannounced plant inspections to ensure continuing product performance through specified standards. **Committees:** Certification. **Publications:** *IGCC Certified Products Directory*, semiannual. **Circulation:** 2,000. **Conventions/Meetings:** semiannual meeting.

1732 ■ National Glass Association (NGA)

8200 Greensboro Dr., Ste.302
McLean, VA 22102-3881
Ph: (703)442-4890
Free: (866)DIAL-NGA
Fax: (703)442-0630
E-mail: phil@glass.org
URL: http://www.glass.org
Contact: Philip J. James CAE, Pres./CEO
Founded: 1948. **Members:** 4,700. **Membership Dues:** company (annual sales of under $1 million to $49 million), $290-$2,890 (annual) ● company (annual sales of $50 million and up), $4,620 (annual). **Staff:** 33. **Budget:** $4,000,000. **State Groups:** 17. **Description:** Manufacturers, installers, retailers, distributors, and fabricators of flat, architectural, automotive, and specialty glass and metal products, mirrors, shower and patio doors, windows, and tabletops. Provides informational, educational and technical services. **Awards:** Community Service Award. **Frequency:** annual. **Type:** recognition ● Glass Professional of the Year. **Frequency:** annual. **Type:** recognition. **Committees:** Architectural Certification; Architectural Glass Certification; Architectural Glazing; Auto Glass Certification; Glass Installer Certification; GlassBuild America Planning; Product Identification Standards; Repair of Laminated Auto Glass Standards. **Formerly:** (1948) National Auto and Flat Glass Dealers Association; (1984) National Glass Dealers Association. **Publications:** *AutoGlass Installation Guide*, annual. Magazine. Serves as a guide to installing windshields on several new model cars. **Price:** $15.95. **Advertising:** accepted ● *AutoGlass Magazine*, bimonthly. Contains information on the auto glass industry, including original equipment and after market products. **Price:** $19.95/year. **Circulation:** 7,200. **Advertising:** accepted ● *Glass Magazine*, monthly. Contains news and information on glass industry management. Topics include architectural glass, storefronts, curtainwall, skylights, and greenhouses. **Price:** $34.95/year; $5.00/issue. **Circulation:** 16,500. **Advertising:** accepted ● *Programs, Products & Services Guide*, annual. Manual ● *Window & Door Magazine*, bimonthly. Contains information on the residential window manufacturing industry. **Circulation:** 8,000. **Advertising:** accepted ● Membership Directory, annual. **Price:** available to members only ● Surveys. **Conventions/Meetings:** annual GlassBuild America: The Glass, Window & Door Expo - show ● annual National Auto Glass Conference and Expo - conference and show, features displays of autoglass and autoglass related products (exhibits) ● annual The NGA Show: America's Glass Expo (exhibits).

1733 ■ Protective Glazing Council (PGC)

2945 SW Wanamaker Dr., Ste.A
Topeka, KS 66614-5321
Ph: (785)271-0208
Fax: (785)271-0166
E-mail: stan@protectiveglazing.org
URL: http://www.protectiveglazing.org
Contact: Stanley L. Smith, Exec. Dir.
Founded: 1998. **Membership Dues:** full, $1,000 (annual) ● associate, $500 (annual) ● individual, $250 (annual). **Staff:** 5. **Description:** Manufacturers of glass with protective glazing. Seeks to advance members' economic and regulatory interests; promotes development of more effective protective glazing technologies. Facilitates communication and cooperation among members; conducts advocacy activities; serves as a clearinghouse on protective glazing. **Formerly:** (2001) Protective Glazing Association. **Publications:** *PGC E-News*, periodic. Newsletter. **Conventions/Meetings:** annual meeting - held in fall ● annual seminar.

1734 ■ Retailers of Art Glass and Supplies (RAGS)

c/o Alice Foster Zimmerman, VP
17414 Noakes Rd.
Vernonia, OR 97064
E-mail: admin@stainedglassretailers.com
URL: http://www.stainedglassretailers.com
Contact: Alice Foster Zimmerman, VP
Membership Dues: business, $75 (annual). **Multinational. Description:** Promotes and extends knowledge among retailers of all phases of operations including safety, economics, new products, processes and teaching. Acts as an agency to communicate and exchange information among retailers. Establishes communication with manufacturers, wholesalers and art glass distributors to create a better understanding of all levels of supply in the industry. **Computer Services:** Information services, stained glass resources and safety information ● mailing lists. **Publications:** Newsletter, quarterly.

1735 ■ Society of Glass and Ceramic Decorators (SGCD)

PO Box 2489
Zanesville, OH 43702
Ph: (740)588-9882

Fax: (740)588-0245
E-mail: sgcd@sgcd.org
URL: http://www.sgcd.org
Contact: Myra Smitley, Admin. Dir.
Founded: 1963. **Members:** 400. **Membership Dues:** individual, $395 (annual) ● corporate, $1,400 (annual) ● independent consultant, $140 (annual) ● student, $50 (annual). **Staff:** 2. **Budget:** $350,000. **Description:** Independent decorators of glass and ceramics, and decorating departments of glass and ceramic manufacturing firms; machinery suppliers; color and raw material suppliers; suppliers of services to the industry; purchasers of all types of decorated glass and ceramics, including architectural and automotive products. Promotes the advancement of the profession of glass and ceramic decorating; monitors legislation and regulation in the field. Advances the theory and practice of glass and ceramic decorating and the applied arts; encourages research and the preparation of papers and educational programs; stimulates interest in improvements in the mechanical, technical and manufacturing phases of the industry. **Libraries: Type:** open to the public. **Subjects:** glass, ceramics. **Awards:** Child Award. **Frequency:** annual. **Type:** recognition. **Recipient:** for major contributions to the decorating industry ● Discovery Award. **Frequency:** annual. **Type:** recognition. **Recipient:** for excellence in design and technique ● Frank S. Child Award. **Frequency:** annual. **Type:** recognition. **Recipient:** for extraordinary contributions to the decorating industry. **Computer Services:** database, corporate members ● mailing lists, rental. **Telecommunication Services:** electronic mail, andyb@sgcd.org. **Formerly:** (1984) Society of Glass Decorators. **Publications:** *Glossary of Glass and Ceramic Decorating Terminology*. **Price:** $20.00 ● *SGCD Directory*, annual. **Price:** $100.00. **Circulation:** 700. **Advertising:** accepted ● *SGCD TechNoteBook*. Manual. Contains over 100 articles for glass and ceramic decorators on decorating technology, regulations, etc. ● *Society of Glass and Ceramic Decorators Annual Program*. Lists speakers and subjects of society's annual seminar. **Price:** included in seminar registration fee. **Circulation:** 600 ● *Society of Glass and Ceramic Decorators Newsletter*, monthly. Contains news on the industry and association and legislative developments. **Price:** included in membership dues. **Circulation:** 700. **Advertising:** accepted. **Conventions/Meetings:** annual seminar (exhibits).

1736 ■ Stained Glass Association of America (SGAA)
10009 E 62nd St.
Raytown, MO 64133
Ph: (816)737-2090
Free: (800)438-9581
Fax: (816)737-2801
E-mail: headquarters@sgaaonline.com
URL: http://www.stainedglass.org
Contact: Richard Gross, Ed.
Founded: 1903. **Members:** 550. **Membership Dues:** student, $50 (annual) ● active, $300 (annual) ● affiliate, $100 (annual) ● accredited, $500 (annual) ● associate, $200 (annual). **Staff:** 3. **Budget:** $300,000. **Description:** Studios, artist designers, and craft supply associates involved in the promotion of architectural stained, leaded, or faceted glass windows; affiliate members are students of the art. Seeks to advance awareness and appreciation of the craft, and to encourage the development of innovative techniques and artistic expression. Collects and disseminates documentary information on the stained glass trade. **Libraries: Type:** not open to the public; lending. **Holdings:** video recordings. **Subjects:** ancient to contemporary stained glass, processes of manufacture, design and fabrication. **Awards:** Certificates of Competence. **Frequency:** annual. **Type:** recognition. **Recipient:** for display at annual summer meeting ● Dorothy Maddy Scholarship. **Frequency:** annual. **Type:** scholarship ● Juried Competition. **Frequency:** periodic. **Type:** monetary. **Recipient:** for winners of the competition held during annual summer meeting. **Telecommunication Services:** electronic mail, sgaa@kcnet.com. **Committees:** Apprenticeship Training; Educational; Health and Safety; Historical Studies; Marketing; Products, Process and Development; Repair and Restoration. **Formerly:** (1925) National Ornamental Glass Manufacturers Association. **Publications:** *Kaleidoscope*, semiannual. Newsletter ● *SGAA Reference and Technical Manual, 3rd Edition*. **Price:** $225.00 ● *Stained Glass*, quarterly. Magazine. Features full-color articles about historical and contemporary installations that show what others in the field are doing. **Price:** $40.00/year in U.S.; $48.00/year in Canada and Mexico; $54.00/year elsewhere. ISSN: 1067-8867. **Circulation:** 4,000. **Advertising:** accepted. **Conventions/Meetings:** annual conference and seminar ● annual conference - always June ● lecture and symposium, sponsored in cooperation with related organizations (exhibits).

Golf

1737 ■ International Association of Golf Administrators (IAGA)
3740 Cahuenga Blvd.
North Hollywood, CA 91604
Ph: (818)980-3630
Fax: (818)980-5019
E-mail: iaga@aol.com
URL: http://www.iaga.org
Contact: Kris Jonasson, Pres.
Founded: 1967. **Members:** 150. **Membership Dues:** individual, $100 (annual). **Staff:** 1. **Budget:** $50,000. **Regional Groups:** 10. **State Groups:** 50. **Local Groups:** 10. **National Groups:** 20. **Description:** Represents executive directors of golf associations united to exchange ideas and methods pertinent to golf association operations. **Awards:** IAGA Distinguished Service Award. **Frequency:** annual. **Type:** recognition. **Conventions/Meetings:** annual conference.

Gourmets

1738 ■ World Alliance of Gourmet Robustas
360 E 72nd St., Ste.C 3000
New York, NY 10021
Ph: (212)737-2548
Fax: (212)570-5947
E-mail: info@wagro.org
URL: http://www.wagro.org
Contact: Pierre E. Leblache, Founder
Founded: 2002. **Membership Dues:** individual grower, small roaster, individual retailer, individual associate (logistics/consultants/media), $75 ● small producer, $200 ● large producer, exporter, importer/trader, large roaster, multi outlet retailer, associate company (logistics/consultants/media), $400 ● trade association/institutional, $250 ● consumer, $50. **Multinational. Description:** Creates an awareness of the existence of another variety of specialty coffee with different qualities and characteristics. Promotes the few Robusta Gourmet coffees already in existence. Advertises to every link of the specialty coffee chain the advantages of producing and selling new types that can generate substantial premiums at all levels. Facilitates the development of Robusta improvement programs through consulting in the areas of production, processing and marketing.

Government

1739 ■ National Workforce Association (NWA)
810 1st St. NE, Ste.530
Washington, DC 20002
Ph: (202)842-4004 (301)562-2324
Fax: (202)842-0449
E-mail: info@nwaonline.org
URL: http://www.nwaonline.org
Contact: David A. Bradley, CEO
Founded: 2000. **Members:** 350. **Staff:** 3. **Budget:** $550,000. **Description:** Represents county elected officials; promotes the U.S. workforce development system. **Affiliated With:** National Association of Counties. **Conventions/Meetings:** conference ● Training Sessions - meeting.

Government Contracts

1740 ■ Association of Government Marketing Assistance Specialists (AGMAS)
PO Box 1607
Orange, TX 77630
Ph: (409)886-0125
Fax: (409)886-2849
E-mail: headquarters@aptac-us.org
URL: http://www.aptac-us.org
Contact: Shelia Rhoads, Contact
Founded: 1986. **Members:** 478. **Staff:** 4. **Regional Groups:** 10. **Description:** Professionals who provide technical assistance to private industry, including those involved in Federal contracting; organizations engaged in marketing or selling products or services to government agencies; interested others. Serves as an industry representative in matters of concern to members; seeks to improve and refine the stature and skills of the procurement professional. Provides networking opportunities and training programs. **Doing business as:** Association of Procurement Technical Assistance Specialists. **Publications:** *APTAC Connection*, quarterly. Newsletter. **Advertising:** accepted. **Conventions/Meetings:** semiannual conference and meeting, includes training conference and membership meeting (exhibits).

1741 ■ Coalition for Government Procurement (CGP)
1990 M St. NW, Ste.450
Washington, DC 20036
Ph: (202)331-0975
Fax: (202)822-9788
E-mail: info@thecgp.org
URL: http://www.thecgp.org
Contact: Paul Caggiano, Pres.
Founded: 1979. **Members:** 300. **Membership Dues:** company (less than $2 million government annual sales), $700 (annual) ● premier, $5,900 (annual) ● company (based on annual government sales), $1,000-$4,900 (annual). **Staff:** 5. **Budget:** $900,000. **Description:** Represents large and small businesses interested in commercial product procurement issues. Works to help protect the interests of federal government commercial product suppliers; to monitor commercial product legislation, policies, regulations, and procurement trends of federal agencies. Provides members with current information, changes, and developments in procurement policies and their impact. Conducts phone consultations. **Libraries: Type:** reference. **Telecommunication Services:** electronic mail, pjc@thecgp.org. **Committees:** Furniture; General Products and Hardware; Healthcare; Information Technology; Office and Scientific; Office Products; Security; Services. **Formerly:** (1988) Coalition for Common Sense in Government Procurement. **Publications:** *Friday Flash*, weekly. Newsletter. Abbreviated version of "Off the Shelf". **Price:** free for members ● *Off the Shelf*, monthly. Newsletter. Covers policy and regulatory developments affecting commercial businesses doing business with the federal government. **Price:** free for members ● *Official Coalition for Government Procurement Yearbook*, annual. Includes white papers written by the coalition on important policy issues of the day. **Advertising:** accepted. **Conventions/Meetings:** quarterly conference ● semiannual conference.

1742 ■ Coalition for Prompt Pay (CPP)
c/o ICIA
11242 Waples Mill Rd., Ste.200
Fairfax, VA 22030
Ph: (703)273-7200
Free: (800)659-7469
Fax: (703)278-8082
E-mail: membership@infocomm.org
URL: http://www.icia.org
Contact: Walter G. Blackwell, Exec. Dir.
Founded: 1986. **Members:** 33. **Description:** National trade associations representing companies that

sell services and products or do construction work under federal government contracts. Lobbies Congress for improvements in the Prompt Pay Act of 1982 (amended in 1988); encourages strict enforcement of the act by the Executive Branch. **Affiliated With:** InfoComm International. **Publications:** *Quick Reference Guide and Side-By-Side Explanation of Federal Prompt Pay Regulations* ● Newsletter, periodic.

1743 ■ Contract Services Association of America (CSA)
1000 Wilson Blvd., Ste.1800
Arlington, VA 22209
Ph: (703)243-2020
Fax: (703)243-3601
E-mail: info@csa-dc.org
Contact: Barry Cullen, Pres.
Founded: 1965. **Members:** 310. **Staff:** 9. **Budget:** $1,000,000. **Description:** Companies that provide, by contract, technical and support services to the federal government, particularly in defense and space programs, and to state, local and other public and international agencies. Supports reliance on the free enterprise system and improvement in the work environment for the private sector. Disseminates information on the "economies, efficiencies, and flexibility" afforded by government on use of private corporations in providing technical and support services. Corporations have contracted such services to the government as the space shuttle, the DEW Line, and National Aeronautics and Space Administration's tracking and data network. Maintains speakers' bureau. Compiles statistics. **Libraries: Type:** reference. **Telecommunication Services:** electronic mail, barry@csa-dc.org. **Committees:** Contract Services Development; Environment; Labor Relations; Legal; Legislative; PAC; Procurement; Professional Standards; Public Policy. **Formerly:** (1986) National Council of Technical Service Industries. **Publications:** *Linkage*, quarterly. Magazine ● *Service Scope*, monthly. Newsletter. Contains information on legislative and regulatory changes as they relate to the contract service industry. **Price:** free. **Conventions/Meetings:** annual board meeting - always January ● annual conference ● annual Davis-Bacon Act Training - meeting - always spring ● annual meeting - always July ● annual President's Roundtable - meeting - always May ● semiannual Service Contract Act Training Programs - meeting - usually April and November.

1744 ■ National Contract Management Association (NCMA)
21740 Beaumeade Cir., Ste.125
Ashburn, VA 20147
Ph: (571)382-0082
Free: (800)344-8096
Fax: (703)448-0939
E-mail: couture@ncmahq.org
URL: http://www.ncmahq.org
Contact: Neal J. Couture CPCM, Exec. Dir.
Founded: 1959. **Members:** 18,000. **Membership Dues:** individual, $120 (annual) ● associate, $65 (annual) ● retired, $40 (annual). **Staff:** 15. **Budget:** $3,500,000. **Local Groups:** 144. **Description:** Professional individuals concerned with administration, procurement, acquisition, negotiation and management of contracts and subcontracts. Works for the education, improvement and professional development of members and nonmembers through national and chapter programs, symposia and educational materials. Offers certification in Contract Management (CPCM, CFCM, and CCCM) designations as well as a credential program. Operates speakers' bureau. **Libraries: Type:** reference. **Awards:** James E. Cravens Membership Award. **Frequency:** annual. **Type:** recognition. **Recipient:** for outstanding membership accomplishments during the past program year ● National Achievement Award. **Frequency:** annual. **Type:** recognition. **Recipient:** for volunteers who have made notable contributions to NCMA ● Outstanding Fellow Award. **Frequency:** annual. **Type:** recognition. **Recipient:** for fellows who have made significant contributions to NCMA at the chapter or national level ● Staff Achievement Award. **Frequency:** annual. **Type:** recognition. **Recipient:** for national office staff members who have exemplified superior job performance. **Computer Services:** Mailing lists, of members ● online services, jobsite. **Committees:** Education; Specialize Topic. **Absorbed:** (1965) Government Contract Management Association of America. **Formerly:** National Association of Professional Contracts Administrators. **Publications:** *Contract Management*, monthly. Magazine. Provides information on contract procurement and management, training problems and solutions, and membership news and information. **Price:** $158.00/year. ISSN: 0190-3063. **Circulation:** 23,000. **Advertising:** accepted. Alternate Formats: online ● *Journal of Contract Management*, annual. Also Cited As: *NCMA Journal*. **Conventions/Meetings:** semiannual conference (exhibits) - always July in Los Angeles, CA and November in Washington, DC ● annual congress.

Government Relations

1745 ■ National Society of Compliance Professionals (NSCP)
22 Kent Rd.
Cornwall Bridge, CT 06754
Ph: (860)672-0843
Fax: (860)672-3005
E-mail: info@nscp.org
URL: http://www.nscp.org
Contact: Joan Hinchman, Exec. Dir.
Founded: 1987. **Members:** 1,250. **Membership Dues:** individual, $400 (annual). **Staff:** 5. **Description:** Professionals in brokerage houses, investment advisers, accounting and law firms, and banks, who are responsible for compliance with government and other regulations. Provides access to accounting and legal expertise. Provides a forum for exchange between members. Monitors new state and federal laws and regulations. Offers interpretive and practical assistance in compliance matters. Conducts educational programs. **Publications:** *NSCP Currents*, bimonthly. Journal. Includes articles on topics of special interest to compliance officials, Information Exchange Column, and Jobline. **Advertising:** accepted ● *NSCP Hotline Memo*, monthly. Bulletin. Summarizes important regulatory initiatives and tracks legislation throughout the enactment process. Includes "Jobline" listings. **Conventions/Meetings:** annual National Membership Meeting - conference (exhibits) - always fall. 2008 Oct. 20-22, Philadelphia, PA ● regional meeting - 4-5/year ● periodic workshop.

1746 ■ State Government Affairs Council (SGAC)
515 King St., Ste.325
Alexandria, VA 22314
Ph: (703)684-0967
Fax: (703)684-0968
E-mail: stategov@sgac.org
URL: http://www.sgac.org
Contact: Elizabeth A. Loudy, Exec. Dir.
Founded: 1975. **Members:** 120. **Membership Dues:** general, $5,000 (annual). **Staff:** 3. **Budget:** $500,000. **Description:** Businesses and organizations of businesses operating in multiple states. Each member has an established officer, employee or department who represents the company or organization in state legislative, regulatory or public affairs matters. Seeks to improve the state legislative process through interaction with major state governmental conferences. Acts as liaison with National Conference of State Legislatures, Council of State Governments (see separate entries) and governors' associations. Through State Government Affairs Council Foundation program, conducts educational programs on issues of public policy concern in order to further understanding between private sector business and state legislatures and agencies. **Telecommunication Services:** electronic mail, eloudy@sgac.org. **Committees:** ALEC Liaisons; CSG Liaison; NCSL Liaisons; Nominating; Programming Trends; Public Relations/Communications. **Affiliated With:** Council of State Governments; National Conference of State Legislatures. **Formerly:** (1994) State Governmental Affairs Council. **Publications:** *SGAC News*, bimonthly. Newsletter ● Also publishes member profile and roster. **Conventions/Meetings:** annual meeting.

Grain

1747 ■ American Association of Grain Inspection and Weighing Agencies (AAGIWA)
c/o Bob Peterson
20610 NE 157th St.
Kearney, MO 64060
Ph: (816)810-5000
E-mail: bob.petersen@aagiwa.org
URL: http://www.aagiwa.org
Contact: Bob Peterson, Contact
Founded: 1946. **Members:** 50. **Staff:** 4. **Budget:** $100,000. **Description:** Private and public grain inspection agencies; suppliers and groups affiliated with the industry. Provides a forum for the formulation and promotion of policies pertinent to effective grain inspection and weighing services. Promotes cooperation between members and the Federal Grain Inspection Service. Offers professional representation on issues such as training, equipment selection, laboratory monitoring, industry standardization, and new techniques. Sponsors educational programs. **Publications:** *Chaff*, quarterly. Newsletter. Includes association news and updates on the FGIS. **Price:** included in membership dues. **Circulation:** 150. Alternate Formats: online ● *Grain Gram*, biweekly. Newsletter. Alternate Formats: online. **Conventions/Meetings:** annual meeting (exhibits) - January or February, in Las Vegas, NV ● annual meeting - always summer.

1748 ■ Commodity Markets Council (CMC)
1300 L St. NW, Ste.1020
Washington, DC 20005
Ph: (202)842-0400
Fax: (202)789-7223
E-mail: ccochran@cmcmarkets.org
Contact: Christine Cochran, Dir. of Government Relations
Founded: 1936. **Members:** 40. **Staff:** 2. **Budget:** $300,000. **Description:** Represents and supports grain exchanges, boards of trade, grain companies, milling and processing companies, transportation companies, futures commission merchants, and banks. **Formerly:** (2006) National Grain Trade Council. **Publications:** *Weekly Report*. Newsletter. **Price:** free for members. **Conventions/Meetings:** semiannual conference ● annual conference.

1749 ■ Distillers Grains Technology Council (DGTC)
Univ. of Louisville
Lutz Hall, Rm. 435
Louisville, KY 40292
Ph: (502)852-1575
Free: (800)759-3448
Fax: (502)852-1577
E-mail: chstaf01@louisville.edu
URL: http://www.distillersgrains.org
Contact: Charlie Staff, Exec. Dir./CEO
Founded: 1947. **Members:** 8. **Membership Dues:** full, $5,000 (annual) ● associate, $1,000 (annual). **Staff:** 2. **Description:** Distillers who process grain and recover animal feed, pharmaceutical, and other products as by-products. **Formerly:** (1998) Distillers Feed Research Council. **Conventions/Meetings:** annual Distillers Technology Conference.

1750 ■ Grain Elevator and Processing Society (GEAPS)
PO Box 15026
Minneapolis, MN 55415-0026
Ph: (612)339-4625
Fax: (612)339-4644
E-mail: info@geaps.com
URL: http://www.geaps.com
Contact: David Krejci, Exec. VP
Founded: 1930. **Members:** 2,800. **Membership Dues:** individual, $175 (annual) ● student, $35 (annual). **Staff:** 7. **Local Groups:** 37. **Languages:**

English, Spanish. **Description:** International professional organization of operations managers of facilities used for receiving, handling, processing and storing grain and oilseeds; suppliers of equipment and services to the grain handling and processing industries. Promotes innovation, leadership and excellence in safe and efficient grain handling and processing operations. **Awards:** Industry Leader Award. **Type:** recognition ● Safety Awards. **Frequency:** annual. **Type:** recognition. **Computer Services:** Mailing lists, of members. **Committees:** Chapter Resources; Educational Programming; Grades and Weights; Membership; Safety, Health, and Environment. **Divisions:** Grain Industry Safety and Health Center. **Formerly:** Society of Grain Elevator Superintendents. **Publications:** *GEAPS DirectaSource*, annual. Membership Directory. Includes membership, products, and services; advertisers' index. **Price:** $60.00 for nonmembers. **Circulation:** 3,000. **Advertising:** accepted ● *GEAPS Exchange Proceeding*, annual. Proceedings ● *In-Grain*, monthly. Newsletter. Covers association activities and industry developments. Includes calendar of events. **Price:** $48.00 for nonmembers. ISSN: 0746-8008. **Circulation:** 3,500. Alternate Formats: online ● Also publishes grain operations safety guidebooks and training programs. **Conventions/Meetings:** annual conference and trade show, international technical conference and exposition (exhibits) - always February or March ● annual conference and board meeting, leadership conference.

1751 ■ National Barley Foods Council (NBFC)
905 W Riverside, Ste.501
Spokane, WA 99201
Ph: (509)456-4400
Fax: (509)456-2807
E-mail: mary@washingtonbarley.org
URL: http://www.barleyfoods.org
Contact: Cindy Ritter, Contact
Founded: 1989. **Members:** 6. **Membership Dues:** board (minimum), $10,001 (annual) ● advisory, $1,000-$10,000 (annual) ● associate, $500-$999 (annual). **Description:** Serves as an information clearinghouse and educational resource on behalf of the US barley industry. **Computer Services:** Information services, recipes, cooking tips, barley products, barley facts, nutrition notes. **Committees:** Barley Foods Research Steering.

1752 ■ North American Export Grain Association (NAEGA)
1250 I St. NW, Ste.1003
Washington, DC 20005
Ph: (202)682-4030
Fax: (202)682-4033
E-mail: info@naega.org
URL: http://www.naega.org
Contact: Gary C. Martin, Pres./CEO
Founded: 1920. **Members:** 40. **Membership Dues:** full, $6,000 (annual) ● associate, $5,000 (annual). **Staff:** 3. **Budget:** $700,000. **Multinational. Description:** U.S. and Canadian exporters of grain and oilseeds from the United States. **Libraries: Type:** not open to the public. **Computer Services:** Mailing lists, of members. **Committees:** Biotechnology; Contracts; Grades; Strikes. **Publications:** *Outreach*, weekly. Newsletter ● Also publishes calendar and trade lead sheets. **Conventions/Meetings:** annual meeting - always February.

1753 ■ Transportation, Elevator and Grain Merchants Association (TEGMA)
1300 L St. NW, Ste.1020
Washington, DC 20005
Ph: (202)842-0400
Fax: (202)789-7223
E-mail: ccochran@cmcmarkets.org
URL: http://www.grainnet.com
Contact: Christine Cochran, Treas.
Founded: 1918. **Members:** 46. **Budget:** $60,000. **Description:** Terminal grain elevator operators, unit train shippers, transportation companies, and others involved in grain marketing. **Additional Websites:** http://www.tegma.org. **Formerly:** (1998) Terminal Elevator Grain Association. **Conventions/Meetings:** semiannual meeting.

1754 ■ U.S.A. Rice Federation
4301 N Fairfax Dr., Ste.425
Arlington, VA 22203
Ph: (703)236-2300
Fax: (703)236-2301
E-mail: riceinfo@usarice.com
URL: http://www.usarice.com/processing
Contact: Stuart E. Proctor Jr., Pres./CEO
Founded: 1994. **Members:** 12,000. **Staff:** 35. **Budget:** $10,500,000. **Description:** Organizations comprising the U.S.A. Rice Council, U.S. Rice Producers' Group, and the Rice Millers' Association. Promotes growth and development of the U.S. rice and related industries. Coordinates members' activities; conducts lobbying and promotional activities; gathers and disseminates information. **Publications:** Annual Report, annual ● Newsletter. **Conventions/Meetings:** annual Rice Millers' Convention - always June ● annual Rice Outlook Conference - always December.

1755 ■ Wheat Foods Council (WFC)
10841 S Crossroads Dr., Ste.105
Parker, CO 80138
Ph: (303)840-8787
Fax: (303)840-6877
E-mail: wfc@wheatfoods.org
URL: http://www.wheatfoods.org
Contact: Marcia Scheideman MS, Pres.
Founded: 1972. **Members:** 50. **Membership Dues:** voting, $15,000 (annual) ● associate, $5,000 (annual) ● nonprofit, $200 (annual) ● supporter, $500 (annual). **Staff:** 3. **Budget:** $1,200,000. **Description:** Wheat producers, companies, and associations. Works to increase the demand for grain foods through nutrition education. Maintains speakers' bureau. **Publications:** *Breads: The Significant Edge* ● *Eating Well, Living Well; When You Can't Diet Anymore.* Book ● *From Wheat to Flour.* Brochure ● *Grain: Energize Your Life*, monthly. Brochure. **Price:** free for members and supporters only. **Circulation:** 1,200 ● *Grains of Wisdom*, quarterly. Newsletter. Contains current nutrition and industry information. Alternate Formats: online ● *Update*, monthly. Newsletter. **Price:** for members and supporters only. **Circulation:** 1,200. Alternate Formats: online ● Also offers posters and T-shirts. **Conventions/Meetings:** semiannual board meeting.

Graphic Arts

1756 ■ Advertising Production Club of New York (APC)
428 E State St.
Long Beach, NY 11561
Ph: (212)671-2975
Fax: (718)228-8202
E-mail: admin@apc-ny.org
URL: http://www.apc-ny.org
Contact: Vivian Cunningham, Pres.
Founded: 1932. **Members:** 500. **Membership Dues:** student, $15 (annual) ● regular, $95 (annual) ● corporate, $360 (annual) ● small business, $160 (annual). **Staff:** 1. **Description:** Production and traffic department personnel from advertising agencies, corporate or retail advertising departments, and publishing companies; college level graphic arts educators. Meetings include educational programs on graphic arts procedures and plant tours. Maintains employment service for members. **Awards:** Thomas Cochrane Sr. Scholarship Award. **Frequency:** annual. **Type:** scholarship. **Recipient:** for New York City Technical College and for study in graphic arts. **Computer Services:** database, newsletter archive ● mailing lists, of members. **Committees:** Education; Employment; Entertainment; Public Relations; Scholarship; Technical. **Formerly:** (1931) Advertising Agency Production Club of New York. **Publications:** *APC Newsletter*, quarterly. Keeps club members informed of new technology and techniques in advertising production. Includes profiles of print production persons and vendors. **Conventions/Meetings:** luncheon and seminar - 10/year.

1757 ■ American Institute of Graphic Arts (AIGA)
164 5th Ave.
New York, NY 10010
Ph: (212)807-1990 (212)710-3122
Fax: (212)807-1799
E-mail: comments@aiga.org
URL: http://www.aiga.org
Contact: Richard Grefe, Exec. Dir.
Founded: 1914. **Members:** 17,000. **Membership Dues:** professional, $295 (annual) ● associate, $210 (annual) ● student, $75 (annual) ● full-time faculty, $110 (annual) ● group, $245 (annual). **Staff:** 16. **Budget:** $5,000,000. **Regional Groups:** 47. **Description:** Graphic designers, art directors, illustrators and packaging designers. Sponsors exhibits and projects in the public interest. Sponsors traveling exhibitions. Operates gallery. Maintains library of design books and periodicals; offers slide archives. **Awards:** Gold Medal. **Frequency:** annual. **Type:** medal. **Recipient:** for distinguished achievement in the graphic arts. **Computer Services:** database, designer portfolios ● mailing lists, membership. **Telecommunication Services:** electronic mail, grefe@aiga.org. **Committees:** Education; Professional Practice. **Publications:** *365: AIGA Year in Design 24*, annual. Book. Hardbound compilation of winning graphic designs in four competitions plus AIGA Medalist and Design Leadership Award winners. **Price:** $42.00 for members; $62.00 for nonmembers. **Conventions/Meetings:** biennial BAIN: AIGA Business and Design Conference.

1758 ■ Association for Graphic Arts Training (AGAT)
c/o Albert LeBlanc
McNaughton and Gunn, Inc.
960 Woodland Dr.
Saline, MI 48176
Ph: (734)429-5411
Fax: (800)677-2665
E-mail: albertl@mcnaughton-gunn.com
URL: http://www.agatweb.org
Contact: Albert LeBlanc, Contact
Founded: 1987. **Membership Dues:** regular, $75 (annual). **Description:** Full- and part-time graphic arts trainers at printing and pre-press companies; graphic arts teachers; and other interested individuals and companies. Seeks to increase the productivity of graphic arts trainers through effective, efficient education and training with support from suppliers, educational institutions, associations, non-profit organizations, and consultants. Aims to: establish networking opportunities for trainers; share performance challenges, solutions, and resources; improve members' skills, knowledge, and professionalism; align training with corporate strategies; increase awareness of the importance of training; and create guidelines for training materials used in the industry. **Telecommunication Services:** electronic mail, d_franks@enovationgraphics.com. **Publications:** *AGAT E-Lines Newsletter*, quarterly. Alternate Formats: online. **Conventions/Meetings:** annual conference.

1759 ■ Association of Graphic Communications (AGC)
330 7th Ave., 9th Fl.
New York, NY 10001-5010
Ph: (212)279-2100
Fax: (212)279-5381
E-mail: info@agcomm.org
Contact: Susan G. Greenwood, Pres./CEO
Founded: 1865. **Members:** 650. **Membership Dues:** corporate communication (in-plant operation), $300-$500 (annual) ● consultant (individual), $300 (annual) ● consultant (2-10 companies), $500 (annual) ● consultant (over 10 companies), $1,000 (annual) ● graphic arts provider, supplier (based on sales revenue), $300-$1,000 (annual). **Staff:** 17. **Budget:** $1,900,000. **Description:** Promotes and protects the interests of member companies and their graphic capabilities. Conducts educational programs; com-

piles statistics; holds competitions; provides legislative and advocacy services. **Awards:** Franklin Award. **Frequency:** annual. **Type:** recognition ● Power of Communications. **Frequency:** annual. **Type:** recognition. **Computer Services:** database. **Publications:** *Buyers Guide*, annual. Directory. **Circulation:** 6,000. **Advertising:** accepted ● *Printout*, bimonthly. Newsletter. **Circulation:** 2,000. **Advertising:** accepted. **Conventions/Meetings:** quarterly board meeting ● bimonthly regional meeting.

1760 ■ Binding Industries Association International (BIA)
200 Deer Run Rd.
Sewickley, PA 15143
Ph: (412)259-1802 (412)741-6860
Fax: (412)259-1800
E-mail: lreynolds@piagatf.org
URL: http://www.gain.net
Contact: Laurie Reynolds, Exec. Dir.
Founded: 1955. **Members:** 325. **Membership Dues:** associate (member PIA/GATF Local), $655 (annual) ● associate (non-member PIA/GATF Local), $980 (annual) ● active (member PIA/GATF Local), $545 (annual) ● active (non-member PIA/GATF Local), $870 (annual). **Staff:** 2. **Budget:** $500,000. **Multinational. Description:** Represents trade binders and loose-leaf manufacturers united to conduct seminars, hold conventions, and formulate and maintain standards. **Awards:** Product of Excellence. **Frequency:** annual. **Type:** recognition. **Recipient:** to outstanding examples of craftsmanship. **Affiliated With:** Printing Industries of America. **Formerly:** (2000) Binding Industries of America. **Publications:** *Binders Bulletin*, monthly ● *The Binding Edge*, quarterly. **Circulation:** 15,000. **Advertising:** accepted ● Membership Directory, annual. **Price:** available to members only. **Conventions/Meetings:** annual convention, with general sessions and roundtable discussions on key technical and management topics (exhibits).

1761 ■ Book Manufacturers' Institute (BMI)
Two Armand Beach Dr., Ste.1B
Palm Coast, FL 32137-2612
Ph: (386)986-4552
Fax: (386)986-4553
E-mail: info@bmibook.com
URL: http://www.bmibook.com
Contact: Bruce W. Smith, Exec. VP
Founded: 1920. **Members:** 90. **Membership Dues:** active in U.S., $1,500-$12,500 (annual) ● active outside U.S., $1,000-$8,000 (annual) ● associate in U.S., $2,500-$5,000 (annual) ● associate outside U.S., $1,000 (annual). **Description:** Represents the trade association for manufacturers of books. **Awards:** Distinguished Master Bookman Award. **Frequency:** annual. **Type:** recognition. **Recipient:** for extraordinary contribution to the book manufacturing industry throughout a long career ● Signature Award. **Frequency:** annual. **Type:** recognition. **Recipient:** for outstanding display of superior leadership qualities on an issue of particular concern to the industry. **Formerly:** (1933) Employing Bookbinders of American. **Publications:** Bulletins ● Membership Directory, annual ● Newsletter, periodic. **Conventions/Meetings:** annual conference - always fall ● meeting - always spring.

1762 ■ California Society of Printmakers (CSP)
PO Box 475422
San Francisco, CA 94147
Ph: (415)905-4296
E-mail: info@caprintmakers.org
URL: http://www.caprintmakers.org
Contact: Barbara Milman, Pres.
Founded: 1913. **Members:** 200. **Membership Dues:** artist, $50 (annual) ● patron, $120 (annual) ● associate, $60 (annual). **Staff:** 12. **Budget:** $14,000. **Description:** Fosters the appreciation of prints and printmaking; sponsors education programs, including exhibitions. **Libraries: Type:** reference; not open to the public. **Holdings:** archival material, films. **Subjects:** slide registry contains works of current members. **Awards:** Distinguished Artist Award. **Frequency:** periodic. **Type:** recognition. **Recipient:** for lifetime dedication to printmaking. **Formed by Merger of:** (1968) Bay Area Printmakers. **Formerly:** (1913) California Society of Etchers. **Publications:** *California Printmaker*, annual. Journal. Presents a forum for dialogue and debate on printmaking and issues addressed by artists. **Price:** free, for members only. **Circulation:** 300. **Advertising:** accepted ● *Newsbrief*, 3/year. Newsletter. Contains organization's information. **Conventions/Meetings:** annual general assembly and meeting, with presentation of Distinguished Artist Award ● Membership Exhibition - meeting, includes wide range of graphic art forms (exhibits).

1763 ■ Catalog and Multichannel Marketing Council
1120 Ave. of the Americas
New York, NY 10036-6700
Ph: (212)768-7277
Free: (800)293-7279
Fax: (212)302-6714
E-mail: councils@the-dma.org
URL: http://www.the-dma.org
Contact: Donn Rappaport, Chm.
Members: 378. **Membership Dues:** direct and interactive marketing company, $1,250 (annual) ● supplier to the industry, $2,500 (annual) ● individual, $199 (annual). **Description:** Catalog houses, catalog printers, and list brokers; members of Direct Marketing Association (see separate entry). Objectives are to: keep members abreast of legislative and legal matters concerning the industry; exchange up-to-date ideas on graphics, production, and lists; share the benefits of consumer-oriented publicity projects about catalogs in newspapers and magazines. Provides representation in Congress on legislative and postal matters. Conducts workshops. **Libraries: Type:** reference. **Holdings:** 2,520; books, business records. **Subjects:** current state-of-the-art industry information. **Awards:** DMA International ECHO. **Frequency:** annual. **Type:** recognition. **Recipient:** for best direct marketing campaign ● DMFE Corporate Leadership. **Frequency:** annual. **Type:** recognition. **Recipient:** for corporations ● DMFE Educational Leadership (Edward N. Mayer, Jr.). **Frequency:** annual. **Type:** recognition. **Recipient:** for direct marketers ● DMFE Vision. **Frequency:** annual. **Type:** recognition. **Recipient:** for direct marketers. **Telecommunication Services:** electronic mail, gjm1@gjmassoc.com. **Formerly:** (2005) Direct Marketing Association Catalog Council. **Publications:** *Current and Crossroads*, monthly. Newsletter. Provides information on direct marketing in non-US markets. Alternate Formats: online ● *DMA Insider*, quarterly. Magazine. Provides DMA members with an opportunity to read articles from the beat practitioners in the industry. **Price:** included in membership dues ● Newsletter, bimonthly. **Conventions/Meetings:** annual Catalog Conference Day - meeting.

1764 ■ Digital Printing and Imaging Association (DPI)
c/o Specialty Graphic Imaging Association
10015 Main St.
Fairfax, VA 22031-3489
Ph: (703)385-1335
Free: (888)385-3588
Fax: (703)273-0456
E-mail: sgia@sgia.org
URL: http://www.sgia.org
Contact: Michael E. Robertson, Pres.
Founded: 1992. **Members:** 800. **Membership Dues:** educational institution in U.S., $25 (annual) ● active, $250 (annual). **Staff:** 4. **Languages:** English, Spanish. **Description:** Electronic printing, pre-press companies, commercial printers, service bureaus, photo labs, reprographic companies, and printer suppliers, and educational institutions. Works to advance the electronic imaging field by promoting the use of digital printing devices, responding to industry needs and concerns, and improving the industry's ability to serve its market and customers. Conducts educational programs. **Awards:** Andre Schellenberg Award. **Frequency:** annual. **Type:** recognition. **Recipient:** for winners of the print competition ● Product of the Year. **Frequency:** annual. **Type:** recognition ● Vision Award. **Frequency:** annual. **Type:** recognition. **Recipient:** for the best product introduced at the annual conference. **Computer Services:** database ● electronic publishing ● mailing lists ● online services. **Committees:** Business Development; Conference; Education; Fine Arts; Membership Development; Production; Suppliers. **Publications:** *Kwikscan*, monthly. Newsletter. **Price:** included in membership dues. **Circulation:** 1,000. Alternate Formats: online ● *RIP*, quarterly. Newsletter. **Price:** included in membership dues. **Circulation:** 1,000. **Conventions/Meetings:** annual conference (exhibits).

1765 ■ Employee Recognition Program
c/o Deena Hower
200 Deer Run Rd.
Sewickley, PA 15143
Free: (800)910-4283
Fax: (412)749-9890
E-mail: dhower@piagatf.org
URL: http://www.gain.net
Contact: Deena Hower, Contact
Founded: 1945. **Members:** 9,500. **Staff:** 3. **Description:** Serves as a division of Printing Industries of America. Supports pro-business labor law reform and modern industrial relations in plants. Conducts seminars for industrial relations directors and managers of local associations. **Libraries: Type:** reference. **Awards: Type:** recognition. **Recipient:** for craftsmanship ● Sommer/Viehman Scholarship. **Frequency:** annual. **Type:** scholarship. **Affiliated With:** Printing Industries of America. **Formerly:** (2006) Master Printers of America. **Publications:** *Master Printer*, semiannual ● Monographs. Promotes open-shop philosophy and good industrial relations. **Conventions/Meetings:** annual conference.

1766 ■ Flexographic Technical Association (FTA)
900 Marconi Ave.
Ronkonkoma, NY 11779-7212
Ph: (631)737-6020
Fax: (631)737-6813
E-mail: memberinfo@flexography.org
URL: http://www.flexography.org
Contact: Ms. Sharon Cox, Dir. of Marketing
Founded: 1958. **Members:** 1,600. **Membership Dues:** $25-$750 (annual). **Staff:** 21. **Languages:** English, Spanish. **Multinational. Description:** Firms engaged in printing by flexographic process suppliers to the industry; end users. Seeks to advance the art and science of flexographic printing and assist and recommend developments in flexography. Conducts educational activities including seminars and regional workshops for production, supervisory, and management personnel, and annual technical forum. Markets textbooks and audiovisual material for in-plant training. Sponsors the Foundation of Flexographic Technical Association. Maintains hall of fame, speakers' bureau, advisory service, and 13 committees. **Awards:** Authors' Award. **Frequency:** annual. **Type:** recognition ● Environmental Excellence Award. **Frequency:** annual. **Type:** recognition ● Excellence in Flexography. **Frequency:** annual. **Type:** recognition ● Flexography Scholarships. **Frequency:** annual. **Type:** scholarship. **Recipient:** for a high school senior or enrolled in a post-secondary institution offering a course of study in flexography; must have an overall 3.0 GPA and has demonstrated interest in a career in flexography ● Graphic Design Award. **Frequency:** annual. **Type:** recognition ● Hall of Fame. **Frequency:** annual. **Type:** recognition ● Presidents' Award. **Frequency:** annual. **Type:** recognition ● Technical Innovation Award. **Frequency:** annual. **Type:** recognition. **Additional Websites:** http://www.ftastore.com. **Publications:** *FLEXO*, monthly. Magazine. Covers all aspects of the flexographic printing and converting industry. Includes calendar of events, employment listings, and product information. **Price:** free for members; $55.00 /year for nonmembers. ISSN: 1051-7324. **Circulation:** 15,000. **Advertising:** accepted ● *SourceBook*, annual. Membership Directory ● Also publishes textbooks. **Conventions/Meetings:** annual meeting, technical programs and tabletop exhibits (exhibits) - 2009 May 3-6, Orlando, FL.

1767 ■ Graphic Arts Education and Research Foundation (GAERF)
1899 Preston White Dr.
Reston, VA 20191
Ph: (703)264-7200
Free: (866)381-9839
Fax: (703)620-3165
E-mail: gaerf@npes.org
URL: http://www.gaerf.org
Contact: Ralph Nappi, Pres.
Founded: 1983. **Description:** Promotes the printing and publishing industries. **Awards: Frequency:** annual. **Type:** grant. **Recipient:** for graphic communication projects. **Telecommunication Services:** electronic mail, ecassidy@npes.org. **Programs:** Make Your Mark In Graphic Communications; PrintED. **Affiliated With:** National Association for Printing Leadership; NPES - The Association for Suppliers of Printing, Publishing and Converting Technologies; Printing Industries of America.

1768 ■ Graphic Arts Sales Foundation (GASF)
113 E Evans St.
West Chester, PA 19380
Ph: (610)431-9780 (610)436-9778
Fax: (610)436-5238
E-mail: info@gasf.org
Contact: Judy M. Miller, Administrator
Founded: 1989. **Members:** 1,500. **Staff:** 5. **Description:** Provides one- and five-day educational programs for key management, sales, marketing, customer service, estimators, and production professionals in the graphic arts industry. Offers the designation Certified Graphic Arts Sales Representative (CGASR) in graphic arts industry. Offers custom in-house programs. **Libraries: Type:** reference. **Holdings:** articles. **Subjects:** sales, marketing, customer service, management. **Awards:** Edwin Wise Memorial Award. **Frequency:** annual. **Type:** recognition. **Recipient:** to an individual or organization who has made a unique and sustained contribution to graphic arts education ● John Dillard Award. **Frequency:** annual. **Type:** recognition. **Recipient:** for excellence in sales and marketing management and/or business development. **Publications:** *Building the Account Development Team*. **Price:** $60.00 for nonmembers; $30.00 for members ● *Company to Company Communication: Creating First-Rate Promotion Programs for Printing Companies*. **Price:** $60.00 for nonmembers; $30.00 for members ● *Evolution in Print Sales*. **Price:** $60.00 for nonmembers; $30.00 for members ● *Lessons Learned from the Current Economic Slump*, quarterly. Monographs. Includes major issues affecting print sales and management. **Price:** $60.00 for nonmembers; $30.00 for members. **Circulation:** 1,200 ● *Managing the Account Development Function*. **Price:** $60.00 for nonmembers; $30.00 for members ● *Selling the Whole Package (Distribution Services)*. **Price:** $60.00 for nonmembers; $30.00 for members ● Monographs, quarterly. Includes major issues affecting print sales and management. **Price:** included in membership dues. **Circulation:** 1,200. **Conventions/Meetings:** periodic Five-Day Business Development Institute - workshop ● monthly Five-Day Sales Institute - workshop, for sales professionals in graphic arts industry.

1769 ■ Graphic Arts Technical Foundation (GATF)
200 Deer Run Rd.
Sewickley, PA 15143-2600
Free: (800)910-GATF
Fax: (412)741-2311
E-mail: info@piagatf.org
URL: http://www.gain.net
Contact: Mr. Michael Makin, Pres./CEO
Founded: 1924. **Members:** 14,000. **Staff:** 55. **Budget:** $10,000,000. **Description:** Scientific, research, technical, and educational organization serving the international graphic communications industries. Conducts research in all graphic processes and their commercial applications. Conducts seminars, workshops, and forums on graphic arts and environmental subjects. Conducts educational programs, including the publishing of graphic arts textbooks and learning modules, videotapes and CD-ROMs and broadcast video seminars. Conducts training and certification program in sheet-fed offset press operating, Web Offset press operating, Image Assembly, and desktop publishing. Produces test images and quality control devices for the industry. Performs technical services for the graphic arts industry, including problem-solving, material evaluation, and plant audits. **Libraries: Type:** reference. **Holdings:** 5,000; archival material, books. **Subjects:** printing, graphic arts. **Computer Services:** database, library search service. **Formerly:** (1963) Lithographic Technical Foundation. **Publications:** *GATFWORLD*, bimonthly. Magazine. Includes technical and research reports. **Price:** $75.00/year in U.S.; $100.00/year outside U.S. ISSN: 1048-0293. **Circulation:** 5,000 ● *Quality Control Device Catalog*, semiannual. ISSN: 1048-0293. **Circulation:** 27,000 ● *Technology Forecast*, annual.

1770 ■ Graphic Communications Council
c/o Carol Hurlburt, Admin.
1899 Preston White Dr.
Reston, VA 20191-4367
Ph: (703)648-1768
Free: (866)381-9839
Fax: (703)620-0994
E-mail: edcouncil@npes.org
URL: http://www.gaerf.org
Contact: Carol Hurlburt, Admin.
Members: 100. **Description:** Promotes career awareness, training and a positive image for the graphic communications industry. **Additional Websites:** http://www.teched.vt.edu/gcc. **Telecommunication Services:** electronic mail, msanders@vt.edu. **Formerly:** Education Council of the Graphic Arts Industry; Graphic Communications Career Center.

1771 ■ Gravure Association of America (GAA)
1200-A Scottsville Rd.
Rochester, NY 14624
Ph: (585)436-2150
Fax: (585)436-7689
E-mail: gaa@gaa.org
URL: http://www.gaa.org
Contact: Bill Martin, Pres./CEO
Founded: 1987. **Members:** 150. **Membership Dues:** in U.S. (based on revenue from the gravure process only), $1,130-$21,800 (annual) ● international, $2,860 (annual). **Staff:** 7. **Budget:** $2,000,000. **Description:** Gravure publication, packaging and product printers; publication, packaging, and specialty engravers; publishers; suppliers of paper, film, ink, presses, and other equipment, goods and services. Cooperative organization devoted to the advancement of gravure (engraved copper plate or cylinder used as an image carrier, and the print made from it). Promotes the use of the gravure printing process for publication printing, package printing and specialty product printing. Collects, analyzes and disseminates current and historical information pertaining to gravure technology, marketing, environmental issues, government regulations, education and training. Exchanges information with the European Rotogravure Association. Compiles statistics. **Libraries: Type:** reference. **Holdings:** archival material, books. **Subjects:** gravure process. **Awards:** Golden Cylinder Award. **Frequency:** annual. **Type:** recognition. **Recipient:** for best gravure printing ● Gravure Cylinder Society Award. **Frequency:** annual. **Type:** recognition. **Recipient:** for industry leaders who have made outstanding or extraordinary contributions to the gravure industry ● Person of the Year. **Frequency:** annual. **Type:** recognition. **Recipient:** for professionals of recognized knowledge, experience and reputation in the gravure industry. **Computer Services:** database, for members only ● information services, gravure resources. **Telecommunication Services:** electronic mail, bmartin@gaa.org. **Committees:** Cylinder Preparation; Environmental; Ink; Packaging Technical; Press; Product Technical; Publication Technical; Solvent Recovery; Standards. **Councils:** Catalog and Insert; Gravure Packaging; Gravure Product; Technical Advisory. **Affiliated With:** Gravure Education Foundation. **Formed by Merger of:** Gravure Research Institute; Gravure Technical Association. **Publications:** *CONNECTIONS*, monthly. Newsletter. Published for board members. ● *GRAVURE*, bimonthly. Magazine. Provides technical, marketing, and scientific coverage of the industry. Includes information on new literature and products, and overseas news. **Price:** $67.00/year in U.S. and Canada; $145.00/year outside U.S. and Canada. ISSN: 0894-4946. **Circulation:** 3,400. **Advertising:** accepted ● *Gravure Association of America—Membership Roster*, annual. Membership Directory. Alternate Formats: online ● *Gravure Process and Technology Textbook, 2nd Edition* ● *INTERFACE*, monthly. Newsletter. Published for corporate representatives. ● Also publishes information on environmental regulations, electrostatic assist, gravure engraving, and press operations. **Conventions/Meetings:** annual Gravure Catalog and Insert Council Conference ● annual Gravure Expo - conference, with business meeting, awards ceremony (exhibits).

1772 ■ Heidelberg Digital Imaging Association (HDIA)
One Barney Rd., Ste.232
Clifton Park, NY 12065
Ph: (518)373-1225
Fax: (518)373-9205
E-mail: info@hdia.org
URL: http://www.hdia.org
Contact: Mario Assadi, Interim Pres.
Membership Dues: company, $525 (annual). **Description:** Printing, publishing, and graphic arts companies that are currently using Heidelberg Prepress (Linotype-Hell) and Direct Imaging technologies in their day-to-day operations. Represent printers, trade shops, corporate publishers, retailers, service bureaus, magazine and book publishers, multimedia agencies, and design firms.

1773 ■ IDEAlliance - International Digital Enterprise Alliance
1421 Prince St., Ste.230
Alexandria, VA 22314
Ph: (703)837-1070 (703)837-1066
Fax: (703)837-1072
E-mail: info@idealliance.org
URL: http://www.idealliance.org
Contact: David J. Steinhardt, Pres./CEO
Founded: 1966. **Members:** 250. **Membership Dues:** advertising, design agency (per office), $650 (annual) ● individual, small firm (less than 5), $850 (annual) ● firm (minimum), $2,500 (annual) ● firm (maximum), $25,000 (annual). **Staff:** 10. **Budget:** $3,000,000. **Multinational. Description:** Works to advance user-driven, cross-industry solutions for all publishing and content-related processes by developing standards fostering business alliances, and identifying best practices. **Committees:** Addressing/Distribution; B2B Paper; Canada Panel; Industry Policy and Direction; Printer Operational Issues Study Effort; Standards Architecture and Convergence. **Subcommittees:** National Magazine, Book and Film Carriers. **Subgroups:** Address Data Interchange Specification; Digital Ad Lab; Digital Image Submission Criteria; General Requirements for Applications in Commercial Offset Lithography; Independent Consultant Consortium; Information and Content Exchange; Job Instruction File Format for Industry; Mail.dat; papiNet; Production Order Specification/EDI XML; Publishing Requirements for Industry Standard Metadata; Ship.dat; Specifications for Publisher and Agency Communication Exchange XML; Women Graphic Management Technology; XML Book Industry Transaction Standards. **Task Forces:** Overages, Shortages and Damaged. **Formerly:** (2001) Graphic Communications Association. **Publications:** Proceedings. Alternate Formats: online; CD-ROM. **Conventions/Meetings:** meeting and seminar (exhibits) - 8 or more throughout the year.

1774 ■ International Association of Printing House Craftsmen (IAPHC)
7042 Brooklyn Blvd.
Minneapolis, MN 55429-1370
Ph: (763)560-1620
Free: (800)466-4274

Fax: (763)560-1350
E-mail: kkeane1069@aol.com
URL: http://www.iaphc.org
Contact: Kevin P. Keane, Pres./CEO

Founded: 1919. **Members:** 6,000. **Membership Dues:** general, $100 (annual). **Staff:** 3. **Budget:** $400,000. **Local Groups:** 107. **Description:** Individuals world-wide employed or interested in any facet of the graphic arts. Conducts field trips; maintains Speaker's Bureau; sponsors educational programs. Sponsors International Printing Week and International Gallery of Superb Printing. **Awards:** Gallery of Superb Printing Awards. **Frequency:** annual. **Type:** recognition ● **Type:** scholarship. **Computer Services:** Mailing lists, of members. **Commissions:** Public Relations. **Committees:** International Printing Week. **Publications:** *The Communicator*, monthly. Newsletter. Provides industry updates. Alternate Formats: online ● *TMN: Graphics Industry News*, monthly. Newsletter. Alternate Formats: online. **Conventions/Meetings:** annual convention and workshop - always August ● annual meeting - always February.

1775 ■ International Metal Decorators Association (IMDA)

9616 Deereco Rd.
Timonium, MD 21093
Ph: (410)252-5205
Fax: (410)628-8079
E-mail: info@metaldecorators.org
URL: http://www.nmda.org
Contact: Rick Clendenning, Pres.

Founded: 1934. **Members:** 800. **Membership Dues:** corporate, $75 (annual). **Staff:** 1. **Budget:** $275,000. **Description:** Firms decorating metal products and containers by lithography and/or roller coating processes; businesses supplying services, equipment and products to metal decorating firms. Conducts educational programs. **Awards: Frequency:** annual. **Type:** scholarship. **Recipient:** for members ● Service Award. **Frequency:** annual. **Type:** recognition. **Formerly:** (2006) National Metal Decorators Association. **Publications:** *The International Metal Decorator Magazine*, 5/year. **Price:** $65.00 ● *Waste Sheet Newsletter*, quarterly. **Conventions/Meetings:** annual conference.

1776 ■ International Publishing Management Association (IPMA)

710 Regency Dr., Ste.6
Kearney, MO 64060
Ph: (816)902-4762
Fax: (816)902-4766
E-mail: ipmainfo@ipma.org
URL: http://www.ipma.org
Contact: Mike Loyd, Pres.

Founded: 1964. **Members:** 1,500. **Membership Dues:** regular, $185 (annual) ● company (up to 5 members), $620 (annual) ● associate, $320 (annual) ● associate corporate (up to 5 members), $1,375 (annual). **Staff:** 4. **Budget:** $550,000. **Regional Groups:** 6. **Local Groups:** 35. **Description:** Managers of in-house corporate publishing or distribution activities. Offers continuing education courses and certification programs. Conducts research, surveys, and studies on industrial and technological trends. Maintains bookstore. **Libraries: Type:** reference. **Holdings:** audiovisuals, books, periodicals. **Subjects:** management, in-house publishing technology. **Awards:** In-House Promotional Excellence Award. **Frequency:** annual. **Type:** recognition. **Recipient:** for exceptional marketing/self-promotion by a corporate publishing facility ● IPMA Member of the Year Award. **Frequency:** annual. **Type:** recognition. **Recipient:** for superior attitude and contribution to the association ● James M. Brahney Scholarship. **Frequency:** annual. **Type:** scholarship. **Recipient:** for an IPMA member or any child or grandchild of an IPMA member ● Management Award. **Frequency:** annual. **Type:** recognition. **Recipient:** to an outstanding in-house corporate publishing department ● Outstanding Contributor Award. **Frequency:** annual. **Type:** recognition. **Recipient:** for members who have made extraordinary contributions ● Print on Demand. **Frequency:** annual. **Type:** recognition ● Retired Member of the Year Award. **Frequency:** annual. **Type:** recognition. **Recipient:** for superior attitude and contribution to association ● Vendor/Associate of the Year Award. **Frequency:** annual. **Type:** recognition. **Computer Services:** Mailing lists, of members. **Committees:** Advanced Technology; Awards/Honors; Bylaws; Certification/Education; Membership. **Councils:** Industry Advisory. **Formerly:** (1994) In-Plant Management Association. **Publications:** *In-House Salary and Compensation Survey*, biennial. Features salary and benefits compensation data based on shop size, industry type, and geographic area; covers management and production employees. **Price:** $50.00 for members; $150.00 for nonmembers ● *Inside Edge*. Newsletter. **Price:** $5.00 in U.S.; $6.25 outside U.S. **Advertising:** accepted. Alternate Formats: online ● *IPMA Bookstore*. Directory ● *IPMA International Directory*, annual. Contains regional and local listings of all chapter officers of the association. **Price:** available to officers only. **Circulation:** 300 ● *Perspectives*, monthly. Provides educational material, news and commentary regarding in-house publishing industry, and association activities. **Price:** included in membership dues. ISSN: 1073-0737. **Circulation:** 2,100. **Advertising:** accepted ● Manuals ● Handbooks. **Conventions/Meetings:** annual conference and seminar (exhibits) - always spring/summer ● annual regional meeting - always fall.

1777 ■ Internet Professional Publishers Association (IPPA)

c/o Digital Minute
PO Box 670446
Coral Springs, FL 33067
Ph: (954)426-3507
E-mail: info@ippa.org
URL: http://www.ippa.org
Contact: Thomas Van Hare, Chm.

Founded: 1995. **Members:** 14,000. **Membership Dues:** supporting, $29 (annual) ● professional, $49 (annual) ● studio, $95 (annual) ● charter, $249 (annual). **Description:** Fosters quality solutions for commercial applications of the Internet. Provides a forum for communication and discussions about the future of the Internet, e-commerce, e-business, and the digital revolution. **Awards:** DX Awards. **Frequency:** annual. **Type:** recognition. **Recipient:** for the most influential and cutting-edge individual designers working in the Internet and New Media.

1778 ■ Library Binding Institute (LBI)

4300 S U.S. Hwy. One, No. 203-296
Jupiter, FL 33477
Ph: (561)745-6821
Fax: (561)775-0089
E-mail: dnolan@lbibinders.org
URL: http://www.lbibinders.org
Contact: Ms. Debra Mills Nolan CAE, Exec. Dir.

Founded: 1935. **Members:** 84. **Staff:** 2. **Budget:** $150,000. **Multinational. Description:** Firms and certified library binders doing library binding in accordance with LBI Standard for Library Binding, including rebinding of worn volumes, prebinding of new volumes, initial hardcover binding of periodicals, and other binding principally for libraries and schools; associate members are suppliers and manufacturers of library binding materials and equipment. Certifies qualified binding companies after examination of work and investigation of experience, insurance for protection of customers' property, and examination of bank and library references. Conducts research on materials used in library binding. Conducts statistical surveys of unit production, operating statement data, and wage data. **Committees:** Library Liaison; Standards; Technology. **Publications:** *New Library Scene*, quarterly. Magazine. **Price:** $24.00/copy in U.S.; $26.00/copy in Canada; $27.00/copy outside North America; $4.00/back issue for members. **Advertising:** accepted ● Newsletter, monthly. **Conventions/Meetings:** annual conference - always October ● annual meeting - always spring.

1779 ■ National Association of Litho Clubs (NALC)

PO Box 6190
Shallotte, NC 28470
Ph: (910)575-0399
E-mail: nalc@graphicarts.org
URL: http://www.graphicarts.org
Contact: Edward Riggs, Exec. VP

Founded: 1945. **Members:** 3,000. **Membership Dues:** $9 (annual). **Local Groups:** 20. **Description:** Federation of technicians and supervisors for lithograph plants. Provides a forum for sharing industry information and technology. Offers educational presentations and seminars. **Libraries: Type:** reference. **Holdings:** artwork, audiovisuals, books, business records, clippings, periodicals. **Awards:** NALC Club Award. **Frequency:** annual. **Type:** recognition. **Recipient:** for an outstanding manner toward the progress and development of the litho club movement ● NALC Litho Member of the Year Award. **Frequency:** annual. **Type:** recognition. **Recipient:** for an individual who has contributed in an outstanding manner towards the progress and development of the litho club movement ● NALC/3M Award. **Frequency:** annual. **Type:** recognition ● **Frequency:** annual. **Type:** scholarship. **Committees:** Program. **Publications:** *LITHO TIPS*, 3/year. Magazine. **Price:** free. **Circulation:** 5,000. **Advertising:** accepted. **Conventions/Meetings:** annual conference ● annual convention - always June, January, or February ● meeting - always January or February.

1780 ■ National Association for Printing Leadership (NAPL)

75 W Century Rd.
Paramus, NJ 07652-1408
Ph: (201)634-9600
Free: (800)642-6275
Fax: (201)634-0324
E-mail: info@napl.org
URL: http://www.napl.org
Contact: Joseph P. Truncale CAE, Pres./CEO

Founded: 1933. **Members:** 3,600. **Staff:** 35. **Budget:** $10,000,000. **Multinational. Description:** Represents commercial printers and suppliers to the commercial printing industry. Enables those in the industry to operate their businesses for maximum profitability. Offers following management products and services: sales and marketing, customer service, financial, human resources, operations, and economic. Maintains Management Institute, which conducts Executive Certification Program. Compiles extensive economic statistics. **Awards:** Industry Award. **Frequency:** annual. **Type:** recognition. **Recipient:** for contribution to industry ● Management Plus Award. **Frequency:** annual. **Type:** recognition ● Technical Leadership Award. **Frequency:** annual. **Type:** recognition. **Recipient:** for contribution to the advancement of the graphic communications industry ● Walter E. Soderstrom Award. **Type:** recognition. **Committees:** Audit Review; Awards; Board Development; Compensation; Continuing Education; Executive; Finance; Government Relations/Safety/Environment; Graphic Arts Council of North America; Graphic Arts Education and Research Foundation; Investment; Management Services; Manufacturer/Supplier Advisory; Marketing; Nominating; President's Advisory; Publications; Show Corporation; Soderstrom Advisory; Strategic Planning. **Task Forces:** Benchmarking; Distance Learning; Trade Customs. **Formerly:** (2000) National Association of Printers and Lithographers. **Publications:** *Cost Studies*, semiannual. Books. Features studies in budgeted hourly rates on equipment. **Price:** first copy free for members; $150.00 for nonmembers ● *NAPL Business Review*, bimonthly. Magazine. Covers the following management areas: sales and marketing, operations, financial, production, human resources, customer service, and trends. Alternate Formats: online. **Conventions/Meetings:** annual Top Management Conference, strategic conference for printing executives - always February/March.

1781 ■ National Government Publishing Association (NGPA)

207 3rd Ave.
Hattiesburg, MS 39401
Ph: (601)582-3330
Fax: (601)582-3354

E-mail: info@govpublishing.com
URL: http://www.govpublishing.org
Contact: Audrey Marrocco, Pres.

Founded: 1977. **Members:** 125. **Membership Dues:** international, $225 (annual) ● full, $400 (annual) ● corporate, $750 (annual). **Staff:** 3. **Budget:** $90,000. **Regional Groups:** 4. **Description:** Members are from state government printing offices; state agency employees; industry suppliers. Universities and foreign governments are associate members. Brings members together to improve printing program management and to attain greater efficiency and economy in state government. Aids members in procuring printing products and services. Facilitates the exchange of information on printing. Compiles statistics. **Awards: Type:** recognition ● **Type:** scholarship. **Recipient:** for schools with graphic arts or printing education programs. **Affiliated With:** International Publishing Management Association. **Formerly:** (1997) National State Printing Association; (2006) National State Publishing Association. **Publications:** *NSPA Membership Directory*, annual. **Price:** included in membership dues. **Circulation:** 125 ● *NSPA Newsletter*, quarterly. Alternate Formats: online. **Conventions/Meetings:** annual conference - 2008 Oct. 19-22, Bellevue, WA ● annual meeting - usually September.

1782 ■ NPES - The Association for Suppliers of Printing, Publishing and Converting Technologies (NPES)

1899 Preston White Dr.
Reston, VA 20191-5468
Ph: (703)264-7200
Fax: (703)620-0994
E-mail: npes@npes.org
URL: http://www.npes.org
Contact: Ralph J. Nappi, Pres.

Founded: 1933. **Members:** 460. **Membership Dues:** individual, firm, corporation (based on volume of sale), $295-$5,500 (annual). **Staff:** 40. **Description:** Companies engaged in the manufacture and distribution of equipment, systems, software, and/or supplies used in the printing, publishing, and converting industries. Represents members before federal agencies and allied trade groups. Funds programs at educational institutions to train graphic arts personnel. Organizes a monthly industry statistical program that compiles and distributes data on orders and shipments. Co-owner and cosponsor of PRINT, GRAPH EXPO and CONVERTING EXPO, and the Graphic Arts Education and Research Foundation; assists members in obtaining space in overseas trade shows. **Libraries: Type:** not open to the public; reference. **Holdings:** audiovisuals, books, clippings, periodicals. **Awards:** Harold W. Gegenheimer Awards for Industry Service. **Frequency:** annual. **Type:** recognition. **Recipient:** for the leadership and commitment of the members ● Harold W. Gegenheimer Awards (Individual and Corporate) for Industry Service. **Frequency:** annual. **Type:** recognition. **Recipient:** to member company and employee; for service to the association and industry. **Computer Services:** Mailing lists, of members. **Committees:** Education; Government Affairs; International Trade; Investment; Market Research; Marketing Advisory; Product Safety; Statistics; Technical Standards. **Formerly:** (1978) National Printing Equipment Association; (1991) National Printing Equipment and Supply Association; (1998) Association for Suppliers of Printing and Publishing and Converting Technologies. **Publications:** *Directory of International Suppliers of Printing, Publishing and Converting Technologies*, annual. Contains list of member companies and their products. ● *NPES News*, monthly. Newsletter. Contains meeting schedule. **Circulation:** 1,400 ● *Vanguard*, semiannual. Newsletter. Covers the activities of the Graphic Arts Education and Research Foundation. Contains graphic arts show calendar. **Price:** free ● Also publishes legislative updates, alerts, and marketing information on overseas customers or firms wishing to represent manufacturers overseas. **Conventions/Meetings:** annual banquet and board meeting ● annual conference, economic and marketing conference - every December.

1783 ■ Pacific Printing and Imaging Association (PPI)

1400 SW 5th Ave., Ste.815
Portland, OR 97201
Free: (877)762-7742
Fax: (800)824-1911
E-mail: info@pacprinting.org
URL: http://www.pacprinting.org
Contact: Marcus Sassaman, Exec. Dir.

Membership Dues: company, $380-$6,000 (annual) ● associate (3 employees or less), $650 (annual) ● associate (more than 3 employees), $1,000 (annual) ● education, $100 (annual). **Description:** Represents graphics arts firms selling services and products to print buyers and publishers, vendors and suppliers to the industry. Works to the advancement of the printing and imaging industry in the states of Alaska, Hawaii, Idaho, Montana, Oregon, and Washington. **Programs:** Business Insurance; Classes and Seminars; Employee Discounts; Equipment Buy and Sell; Group Purchase; Health Insurance; Personnel Referral. **Subgroups:** Print Buyers. **Publications:** *Friday Notes*. Newsletter ● *InPrint*. Newsletter.

1784 ■ Packaging and Label Gravure Association Global (PLGA Global)

c/o Jim Lepp, Exec. Dir.
18481 Royal Hammock Blvd.
Naples, FL 34114
Ph: (920)217-6059
Fax: (239)775-1714
E-mail: jlepp@earthlink.net
URL: http://www.plga.com
Contact: Mr. Ed Lieb, Pres.

Founded: 1998. **Members:** 120. **Membership Dues:** printer, supplier, $800 (annual). **Multinational. Description:** Promotes the use of rotogravure printing for labels and packaging. Provides the printer/converter as well as the packaging, label and product buyer/user with information on the latest technology and operating systems available to improve pre-press and pressroom efficiency and product quality. **Awards:** Print Quality Awards. **Frequency:** annual. **Type:** recognition. **Recipient:** for outstanding design that employs the gravure process. **Computer Services:** database, member directory ● database, technical papers ● online services, member bulletin board. **Committees:** Marketing; Newsletter/Publicity; Policy; Scholarship/Education; Technical. **Publications:** Newsletter, semiannual. **Price:** included in membership dues.

1785 ■ PrintImage International

2250 E Devon Ave., Ste.245
Des Plaines, IL 60018
Ph: (847)298-8680
Free: (800)234-0040
Fax: (847)298-8705
E-mail: info@printimage.org
URL: http://www.printimage.org
Contact: Steven D. Johnson, Pres./CEO

Founded: 1975. **Members:** 1,400. **Membership Dues:** platinum, $995 (annual) ● gold, $465 (annual) ● supplier (based on number of employees), $969-$2,700 (annual) ● educational, $225 ● division, $350 ● international, $300. **Staff:** 5. **Budget:** $1,000,000. **Languages:** English, Spanish. **Multinational. Description:** Independent printers and printing franchise businesses; industry suppliers. Seeks to bring recognition, improved quality, and increased profits to the entire quick printing field. Provides services to members; works to advance the collective interests of the printing industries at the national and international levels. **Libraries: Type:** reference. **Subjects:** technical manuals. **Awards:** Honorary Lifetime Members. **Frequency:** annual. **Type:** recognition ● Industry Award of Distinction Product of the Year. **Type:** recognition ● Int'l Partnership Award. **Type:** recognition ● Printer of the Year. **Frequency:** annual. **Type:** recognition. **Recipient:** for extraordinary devotion, time and energy to the improvement of the industry ● Supplier of the Year. **Frequency:** annual. **Type:** recognition. **Computer Services:** Online services, publication. **Special Interest Groups:** Digital Imaging Applications Network; Mailing Services Group; Pxyis Network; Sales and Marketing Users Group; Young Printing Professionals. **Formerly:** (1998) National Association Quick Printers. **Publications:** *Print Image Network*, monthly. Newsletter. Covers management, production, technology, and personnel training. Includes calendar of events. **Price:** available to members only. **Circulation:** 1,500. **Advertising:** accepted ● Membership Directory, annual. Lists members alphabetically by individual name, company name, and geographically. Includes advertisers' index. **Price:** free, for members only. **Circulation:** 2,000. **Advertising:** accepted. Alternate Formats: online; CD-ROM. **Conventions/Meetings:** annual conference, for quick printer owners and top managers (exhibits) - always mid-winter ● annual Quick Print Show - trade show, for owners and employees (quick printers), sales and marketing, technical services (exhibits) - February.

1786 ■ Printing Brokerage/Buyers Association (PB/BA)

PO Box 744
Palm Beach, FL 33480
Ph: (561)546-0116
Free: (877)585-7141
Fax: (561)845-7130
E-mail: contactus@pbba.org
URL: http://www.pbba.org
Contact: Merry Francen, Pres.

Founded: 1985. **Members:** 1,100. **Membership Dues:** associate, $399 (annual) ● corporate, $599 (annual) ● print vendor, $999 (annual). **Staff:** 3. **Budget:** $475,000. **Regional Groups:** 5. **Languages:** English, French, Italian, Portuguese, Spanish. **For-Profit. Multinational. Description:** Printing buyers/brokers/distributors, printers, typographers, binders, envelope and book manufacturers, packagers, color separation houses, pre-press service organizations, and related companies in the graphic arts industry. Promotes understanding, cooperation, and interaction among members while obtaining the highest standard of professionalism in the graphic arts industry. Gathers information on current technology in the graphic communications industry. Sponsors seminars for members to learn how to work with buyers, brokers and printers; also conducts technical and management seminars. Maintains referral service; compiles statistics. Conducts charitable programs. **Libraries: Type:** reference. **Holdings:** 500; books. **Subjects:** management techniques in the graphic arts industries. **Awards:** Printing Broker of the Year. **Frequency:** annual. **Type:** recognition ● Vendor of the Year. **Frequency:** annual. **Type:** recognition. **Computer Services:** database, reprint (all buyers and sellers of printed matter). **Boards:** Broker Advisory; Buyer Advisory; Printer Advisory. **Formerly:** Printing Brokerage Association; (2001) Printing Brokerage/Buyers Association International. **Publications:** *Broker Age*, quarterly. Newsletter. Includes information on new members, schedule of events, and annual directory. **Price:** $300.00/year. **Advertising:** accepted. Alternate Formats: online ● *BrokerRatings*, quarterly. Provides information to assist printers and buyers in selecting brokers and verifying credit. ● *Corporate Print Buyer*, quarterly. Journal. **Price:** $48.00/year. **Advertising:** accepted ● *Hot Markets Annual Rankings of Buyers, Print Products and Geographies*, annual. Contains forecast of printing purchasing in each of the 25 largest buying categories by name, location, type of printing and process. **Price:** $695.00 for qualified printing industry participants ● *The Printer's Official Complete Guide to e-Everything-and How to Prevail!*. Book. Comprehensive tutorial for open end-to-end e-commerce for printing providers and buyers. ● *Printing Brokerage Directory and Sourcebook*, annual. **Price:** $395.00. **Circulation:** 5,000. **Advertising:** accepted. Alternate Formats: online. **Conventions/Meetings:** semiannual conference (exhibits).

1787 ■ Printing and Graphic Communications Association (PGCA)

Address Unknown since 2008

Founded: 1914. **Members:** 189. **Staff:** 5. **Budget:** $750,000. **Description:** Represents and promotes the printing and graphic communications industry. **Telecommunication Services:** hotline, Technical

Inquiry (412)741-6860, ext. 611 ● hotline, Environmental & Safety Inquiry (412)741-6860, ext. 606 or 608. **Affiliated With:** Printing Industries of America. **Publications:** Newsletter, biweekly.

1788 ■ Printing Industries of America (PIA)
200 Deer Run Rd.
Sewickley, PA 15143
Ph: (412)741-6860
Free: (800)910-4283
Fax: (412)741-2311
E-mail: gain@piagatf.org
URL: http://www.gain.net
Contact: Michael Makin, Pres./CEO
Founded: 1887. **Members:** 13,000. **Membership Dues:** student, educator, $49 (annual) ● international, individual, $199 (annual) ● member-at-large (minimum), $102 (annual). **Staff:** 40. **Budget:** $12,000,000. **Local Groups:** 29. **Description:** Commercial printing firms (lithography, letterpress, gravure, platemakers, typographic houses); allied firms in the graphic arts. Provides extensive management services for member companies, including government relations, industry research and statistical information, technology information and assistance, and management education and publications. Compiles statistical and economic data, including annual ratio study that provides a benchmark for printers to compare profits as a basis for improving individual member company and industry profits. Provides reporting system on provisions, rates, and other matters relating to union contracts in effect throughout the industry. Sponsors annual Premier Print Awards Competition. **Telecommunication Services:** electronic mail, piagatf@piagatf.org. **Committees:** Association Relations; Economic Research; Education; Executive; Finance and Administration; Government Affairs; Human Relations; Long Range Planning Member Service; Marketing and Member Services; Special Industry Groups. **Sections:** EPS-Digital Work Flow Group; Graphic Arts Marketing Information Service; Label Printing Industries of America; Printing Industry Financial Executives; Sales and Marketing Executives; Web Offset Association/Non-Heatset. **Affiliated With:** Association of Graphic Communications; Canadian Printing Industries Association; Pacific Printing and Imaging Association; Printing and Imaging Association Mountain States; Printing Industries of Michigan; Printing Industries of New England; Printing Industries of Virginia; Printing Industries of Wisconsin; Printing Industry Association of New York State; Printing Industry of the Carolinas. **Absorbed:** (1964) Lithographers and Printers National Association; (1990) Association of Graphic Arts Consultants. **Formerly:** (1945) United Typothetae of America; (1965) Printing Industry of America. **Publications:** *The Capital Letter*, monthly ● *DPC-Digital Impact*, quarterly ● *EBC/DPC*, monthly. Newsletter. **Price:** available to members only ● *EPS Decisions*, quarterly ● *Management Portfolio*, bimonthly. **Price:** available to members only ● *Pifelines*, quarterly ● *Ratio Studies*, annual. Booklets ● *S&ME Forum*, quarterly. Books ● Booklets ● Books ● Also publishes engineering standards for measuring productivity of machine and manual operations, proceedings of conferences, training, production, and personnel relations manuals. **Conventions/Meetings:** annual conference - usually April ● annual Presidents Conference - meeting - always February/March ● periodic regional meeting.

1789 ■ Screen Printing Technical Foundation (SPTF)
c/o Specialty Graphic Imaging Association
10015 Main St.
Fairfax, VA 22031
Ph: (703)385-1335 (703)385-1417
Free: (888)385-3588
Fax: (703)273-0456
E-mail: sptf@sgia.org
URL: http://www.sgia.org/sptf
Contact: Dawn Hohl, Technical Training Mgr.
Founded: 1986. **Staff:** 2. **Budget:** $700,000. **Languages:** English, Spanish. **Nonmembership. Multinational. Description:** Participants include corporations, institutions, and individuals interested in screen-printing. Advances the screen-printing industry. Conducts technical research and hands-on training programs to address production problems and processes. Sponsors educational programs and prepares educational materials. **Libraries: Type:** reference. **Holdings:** 1,000; articles, books, papers, periodicals, reports. **Subjects:** screen printing. **Awards:** Award of Recognition. **Frequency:** annual. **Type:** recognition. **Computer Services:** Online services, educational and technical resources. **Committees:** Education; Technical/Research. **Affiliated With:** Specialty Graphic Imaging Association. **Publications:** *Research Reports*, periodic. Alternate Formats: online ● *SPTF Update*, quarterly. Newsletter. Alternate Formats: online. **Conventions/Meetings:** annual convention (exhibits).

1790 ■ Society for Service Professionals in Printing (SSPP)
433 E Monroe Ave.
Alexandria, VA 22301
Ph: (703)684-0044
Free: (877)777-7398
Fax: (703)548-9137
E-mail: ssppinfo@sspp.org
URL: http://www.sspp.org
Contact: Peter Colaianni CAE, Exec. Dir.
Founded: 1993. **Members:** 1,400. **Membership Dues:** individual, $150 (annual). **Staff:** 2. **Budget:** $300,000. **Regional Groups:** 8. **Description:** Customer support specialists in the printing industries. Promotes professional advancement of customer service employees in industry knowledge. Makes available continuing practical, hands-on and other educational opportunities for members; conducts certification examinations and confers certification; functions as a network linking members. **Libraries: Type:** reference. **Holdings:** articles, books, periodicals. **Awards:** Management Award in Support of Customer Service. **Frequency:** annual. **Type:** recognition ● Printing Service Specialist of the Year. **Frequency:** annual. **Type:** recognition. **Affiliated With:** Document Management Industries Association; Printing Industries of America. **Publications:** *Business Printing Technologies Report*, monthly. Features technical issues affecting the industry. Alternate Formats: online ● *DMIA's E-Weekly*. Newsletter. Contains information for printing professionals. Alternate Formats: online ● *Independent Management Report*, biennial. Contains information for owners and executives of DMIA member companies. Alternate Formats: online ● *Print Solutions*, monthly. Magazine. Contains information about management, marketing and sales. **Price:** free for U.S. subscribers; $60.00 outside U.S. **Advertising:** accepted. Alternate Formats: online ● *Signature Service*, monthly. Newsletter. Features the latest and most widely used printing processes in the industry. **Price:** included in membership dues; $115.00 /year for nonmembers. ISSN: 1076-1039. **Circulation:** 3,000. Alternate Formats: online. **Conventions/Meetings:** annual board meeting.

1791 ■ Society of Typographic Aficionados (SOTA)
c/o Tamye Riggs, Dir.
3025 Alta Vista
Alameda, CA 94502
Ph: (510)748-0784
Fax: (510)748-6095
E-mail: info@typesociety.org
URL: http://www.typesociety.org
Contact: Tamye Riggs, Dir.
Founded: 1998. **Membership Dues:** corporate sustaining level, $2,000 (annual) ● individual sustaining level, $500 (annual) ● professional, $60 (annual) ● global professional level, $35 (annual) ● student level, $25 (annual). **Description:** Dedicated to promotion, study, support of type, its history and development, its use in the world of print and digital imagery and designers. **Conventions/Meetings:** annual conference - every summer.

1792 ■ Specialty Graphic Imaging Association (SGIA)
10015 Main St.
Fairfax, VA 22031-3489
Ph: (703)385-1335
Free: (888)385-3588
Fax: (703)273-0456
E-mail: sgia@sgia.org
URL: http://www.sgia.org
Contact: Michael E. Robertson, Pres./CEO
Founded: 1948. **Members:** 4,200. **Membership Dues:** corporate printer in U.S., international supplier, $300 (annual) ● supplier in U.S., $475 (annual) ● international corporate printer, $200 (annual) ● individual, $149 (annual). **Staff:** 36. **Budget:** $6,500,000. **National Groups:** 7. **Languages:** English, Spanish. **Multinational. Description:** Printers who use screen printing and/or digital printing; associate members are suppliers and manufacturers; educational institutions. Provides training and information on technical, managerial, governmental, safety, and research issues. Conducts safety, environmental, and print quality recognition programs. Compiles statistics; conducts research programs. **Libraries: Type:** reference; by appointment only; not open to the public. **Holdings:** 1,000; articles, books, periodicals. **Subjects:** screen printing, digital printing, pad printing, embroidery, sublimation, technology-related. **Awards:** Booth Award. **Frequency:** annual. **Type:** recognition. **Recipient:** for marketing effectiveness ● Certificate of Appreciation Award. **Frequency:** annual. **Type:** recognition ● Certificate of Merit. **Frequency:** annual. **Type:** recognition. **Recipient:** for service to the association ● Distinguished Service Award. **Frequency:** annual. **Type:** recognition. **Recipient:** for service to the association ● Golden Image Award. **Frequency:** annual. **Type:** recognition. **Recipient:** for print quality (44 categories) ● Key Award. **Frequency:** annual. **Type:** recognition. **Recipient:** for exceptional service to the association ● Magnus Award. **Frequency:** annual. **Type:** recognition. **Recipient:** for outstanding service in membership development ● Mentor Award. **Frequency:** annual. **Type:** recognition. **Recipient:** for an exceptional educational effort by a school and/or educator ● Outstanding Service Award. **Frequency:** annual. **Type:** recognition ● Parmele Award. **Frequency:** annual. **Type:** recognition. **Recipient:** for an outstanding contribution to the industry ● Safety Recognition Award. **Frequency:** annual. **Type:** recognition. **Recipient:** for outstanding achievement in plant safety ● Swormstedt Award. **Frequency:** annual. **Type:** recognition. **Recipient:** for author of the best technical paper on screen printing. **Computer Services:** database ● electronic publishing ● information services ● mailing lists ● online services. **Telecommunication Services:** electronic bulletin board ● information service. **Committees:** Academy of Screen Printing Technology; Convention and Exposition; Education; Environmental; Executive; Garment Decorators; Graphic Imaging; Industrial Imaging; Ink and Chemical Manufacturers; Nominating; Safety and Health; Screen Printing Industry Roundtable Exchange; Screen Printing Technical Foundation. **Councils:** Membrane Switch; Supplier's. **Affiliated With:** Digital Printing and Imaging Association. **Absorbed:** (1982) Screen Printing Association of Canada. **Formerly:** (1967) Screen Process Printing Association; (1995) Screen Printing Association International; (2004) Screenprinting and Graphic Imaging Association International. **Publications:** *Operating Rate Survey*, biennial. Contains study of industry operational ratios. **Price:** free to participants ● *SGIA Journal*, quarterly. **Price:** included in membership dues. **Circulation:** 13,000 ● *SGIA News*, monthly. Newsletter. **Price:** included in membership dues ● *Who's Who in SGIA*, annual. Directory. **Conventions/Meetings:** annual convention and trade show, includes over 2000 booths, more than 50 seminars, guest tours, golf tournament, social events, and printing awards competition (exhibits) ● annual Membrane Switch Symposium - conference - usually June ● annual Safety and Environmental Conference - spring.

1793 ■ Waterless Printing Association (WPA)
PO Box 1252
Woodstock, IL 60098
Ph: (815)337-7681
Free: (800)850-0660

Fax: (815)337-7682
URL: http://www.waterless.org
Contact: Gerald Viergever, Pres.
Founded: 1993. **Membership Dues:** printer/color separator, $250-$2,000 (annual) ● firm outside U.S., $488-$5,400 (annual) ● firm in U.S., $250-$3,000 (annual). **Multinational. Description:** Promotes the waterless printing process. **Libraries: Type:** reference. **Subjects:** waterless printing. **Publications:** *The Complete Guide to Waterless Printing*. Manual. Contains reference information for both new and experienced Waterless Printing users. **Price:** $69.00 for members; $89.00 for nonmembers ● *Waterless Currents*, monthly. Newsletter. Features news and information about waterless printing. ● Membership Directory ● Brochures.

1794 ■ Web Offset Association (WOA)
c/o Graphic Arts Information Network
PIA/GATF
200 Deer Run Rd.
Sewickley, PA 15143
Ph: (412)741-6860 (412)259-1802
Free: (800)910-4283
Fax: (412)741-2311
E-mail: lreynolds@piagatf.org
URL: http://www.gain.net
Contact: Laurie Reynolds, Asst. Dir.
Founded: 1952. **Members:** 2,000. **Staff:** 4. **Budget:** $850,000. **Description:** A section of the Printing Industries of America (see separate entry). Seeks to facilitate communication among PIA members involved in web offset printing. (Web offset printing differs from sheet printing in that the paper is fed directly onto the printing press from a roll, as opposed to arriving at the press in pre-cut sheets). **Awards:** Harry V. Quadracci Vision Award. **Frequency:** annual. **Type:** recognition. **Recipient:** for industry pioneers whose hard work and determination have created a vibrant, growing and changing industry. **Affiliated With:** Printing Industries of America. **Publications:** *Coldset/Non-Headset Directory*, biennial. Includes companies in the United States and Canada by state/province, presses by number of units and by size. **Price:** $119.95/copy. Alternate Formats: CD-ROM ● *The Effect of Certain Variables on Fluting in Heatset Web Offset Printing*, annual. Report. Features documents that was aimed at finding the means for eliminating, or at least reducing, paper deformation. **Price:** $14.95/copy ● *Heatset Web Offset*, biennial. Directory. Includes companies in United States and Canada. **Price:** $119.95/copy. Alternate Formats: CD-ROM ● *Products of Colset/Non-Heatset Web Printers*, semiannual. Catalog. Includes each company's most important products manufactured in the United States and Canada. **Price:** $79.95/copy ● *Products of Heatset Web Offset Printers*, semiannual. Catalog. Contains marketing information and lists products produced by heatset, non-heatset, and combination companies in the U.S. and Canada. **Price:** $79.95/copy ● *Web Impressions*, quarterly. Newsletter. **Advertising:** accepted ● Also publishes market outlook reports, specifications for advertising and publications. Directory available on disk. **Conventions/Meetings:** annual Management and Technical Conference - usually May.

1795 ■ Web Printing Association (WPA)
c/o PIA/GATF
200 Deer Run Rd.
Sewickley, PA 15143
Ph: (412)741-6860
Free: (800)910-4283
Fax: (412)741-2311
E-mail: gain@piagatf.org
URL: http://www.gain.net
Contact: Mary Garnett, Exec. Dir.
Founded: 1978. **Staff:** 4. **Budget:** $250,000. **Nonmembership. Description:** A special interest group of the Printing Industries of America (see separate entry). Individuals interested in the non-heatset web printing process. Advises on changing technologies, opportunities, and problems. Provides management assistance to members and supports the interests of those involved in the printing process. Sponsors competitions and research programs. **Awards:** Web Printing Association Awards Competition. **Frequency:** annual. **Type:** recognition. **Recipient:** for open/cold set web printing. **Affiliated With:** Printing Industries of America. **Formerly:** Non-Heatset Web Section; (1999) Non-Heatset Web Section. **Publications:** *Directory of Open/Cold Set Web Offset Printers and Press Installations*, biennial. **Price:** $119.00. Alternate Formats: CD-ROM ● *Open/Cold Set Product Catalog*, semiannual. Describes products manufactured. ● *SNAP (Specifications for Non-Heat Advertising Printing)*. Monographs. **Conventions/Meetings:** annual Open Web Conference - September.

1796 ■ Women in Production (WIP)
276 Bowery
New York, NY 10012
Ph: (212)334-2108 (212)334-2106
Fax: (212)431-5786
E-mail: admin@p3-ny.org
URL: http://www.p3-ny.org
Contact: Jennifer Bergin, Pres.
Founded: 1977. **Members:** 300. **Membership Dues:** individual, $125 (annual) ● non-northeast, full-time student, $25 (annual) ● bronze (6 members), $660 (annual) ● silver (7-15 members), $750 (annual) ● gold (16-49 members), $1,440 (annual) ● platinum (50-100 members), $3,500 (annual). **Staff:** 4. **Budget:** $130,000. **Description:** Persons involved in all production phases of print and graphics, web and multimedia, including those working in magazine, book, and Web publishing, agency production, conventional and digital print manufacturing, print-related vending and buying, advertising production, catalogs, direct mail; seeks to improve job performance by sharing information with members and suppliers. Sponsors placement service. **Awards:** Luminaire. **Frequency:** annual. **Type:** recognition. **Recipient:** for outstanding members of the print and production industry ● **Frequency:** annual. **Type:** scholarship. **Recipient:** for high school and college students of the graphic arts. **Committees:** Education; Employment; Luminaire; Membership; Program. **Publications:** *WIP Roster*, annual. Directory ● *WIP-WATCH*, 8-10/year. Newsletter. Includes calendar of events. **Conventions/Meetings:** Educational Luncheons - 4-6/year ● annual Luminaire Awards Dinner ● Tech Tours - 2-4/year.

1797 ■ Worldwide Printing Thermographers Association (WPT)
305 Plus Park Blvd.
Nashville, TN 37217
Free: (800)821-3138
Fax: (615)366-4192
E-mail: thermographers@earthlink.net
URL: http://www.thermographers.org
Contact: Allen Greenspan, Pres.
Founded: 1997. **Members:** 95. **Membership Dues:** regular, $850-$950 (annual) ● associate, $850 (annual) ● affiliate, $350 (annual). **Staff:** 3. **Budget:** $90,000. **Description:** Printing thermographers. Seeks to advance the practice of thermography; promotes professional development of members. Serves as a forum for the exchange of information among members; conducts educational and training programs. **Publications:** *Therm-O-Gram*, periodic.

1798 ■ Xplor International (XPLOR)
1900 Land O'Lakes Blvd., Ste.103
Lutz, FL 33549
Ph: (813)948-3171
Free: (800)669-7567
Fax: (813)948-3038
E-mail: info@xplor.org
URL: http://www.xplor.org
Contact: Skip Henk, Pres./CEO
Founded: 1981. **Members:** 5,000. **Membership Dues:** individual, $170 (annual) ● corporate, $650 (annual) ● corporate plus, $3,250 (annual) ● student, retired, and unemployed, $85 (annual). **Staff:** 50. **Budget:** $7,500,000. **Regional Groups:** 11. **Multinational. Description:** Provides organizations and individuals with learning and networking opportunities, which enhance effective use of electronic document technology to achieve business objectives. **Awards:** Innovator of the Year Award. **Frequency:** annual. **Type:** recognition. **Recipient:** for an individual, company or organization ● Technology Application of the Year Award. **Frequency:** annual. **Type:** recognition. **Recipient:** for an individual or an organization ● Xplorer of the Year Award. **Frequency:** annual. **Type:** recognition. **Recipient:** for significant service of an individual to XPLOR. **Telecommunication Services:** electronic mail, skip@xplor.org. **Committees:** Certification; Conference; Industry Awareness and Development; Member Development; Technology Interface; Vendor Affairs. **Publications:** *XPLORATION: The Journal of Electronic Document Systems*, semiannual. Includes debates and analyses on current industry issues. **Price:** $25.00 for nonmembers; free for members. ISSN: 1053-5853. **Circulation:** 6,000 ● *The Xplorer*, monthly. Newsletter. **Conventions/Meetings:** annual conference (exhibits) ● annual Euroconference - meeting (exhibits).

Graphic Arts Products

1799 ■ Art and Creative Materials Institute (ACMI)
PO Box 479
Hanson, MA 02341-0479
Ph: (781)293-4100
Fax: (781)294-0808
E-mail: debbief@acminet.org
URL: http://www.acminet.org
Contact: Deborah M. Fanning CAE, Exec. VP
Founded: 1936. **Members:** 225. **Staff:** 5. **Budget:** $1,000,000. **Description:** Manufacturers of art and creative materials; sponsors certification program to ensure that art materials are non-toxic or affixed with health warning labels where appropriate. Works with ASTM International and the American National Standards Institute to develop and maintain chronic hazard labeling standards and performance standards. Sponsors annual Youth Art Month in March to emphasize the value of art education for all children and to encourage public support for quality school art programs; publicizes value of art and art education in newspapers and magazines. **Libraries: Type:** reference. **Holdings:** 3. **Subjects:** safety of art materials, list of certified products, how to celebrate Youth Art Month. **Awards:** Claire Flanagan Memorial Grand and other Awards. **Frequency:** annual. **Type:** recognition. **Recipient:** to outstanding observances of youth art month. **Computer Services:** Information services, safety tips. **Telecommunication Services:** electronic mail, sarahs@acminet.org ● electronic mail, debbieg@acminet.org ● electronic mail, debbiem@acminet.org. **Committees:** Certification; Government Relations; International; Marketing; Membership; Technical. **Formerly:** Art and Craft Materials Institute; (1982) Crayon, Water Color and Craft Institute. **Publications:** *Institute Items*, monthly. Newsletter ● *What You Need to Know About the Safety of Art and Craft Materials*. Booklet. **Conventions/Meetings:** annual meeting ● seminar.

1800 ■ Association for Engineering Graphics and Imaging Systems (AEGIS)
c/o International Reprographic Association
401 N Michigan Ave.
Chicago, IL 60611
Ph: (312)245-1026
Fax: (312)527-6705
E-mail: sbova@irga.com
URL: http://www.irga.com
Contact: Steve Bova CAE, Exec. Dir.
Founded: 1954. **Members:** 50. **Membership Dues:** active (based on number of employees), $550-$1,495 (annual) ● active international, $425 (annual) ● associate (based on number of employees), $500-$1,495 (annual) ● associate international, $820 (annual). **Staff:** 2. **Budget:** $250,000. **Description:** Manufacturers of technical engineering graphics machines and supplies and materials. **Committees:** Design; Marketing; Recycling; Technical Practice and Standardization. **Formerly:** (1969) National Association of Blueprint and Diazotype Coaters; (1995) Association of Reproduction Materials Manufacturers. **Conventions/Meetings:** annual meeting.

1801 ■ International Reprographic Association (IRgA)
401 N Michigan Ave.
Chicago, IL 60611
Ph: (312)245-1026
Free: (800)833-4742
Fax: (312)527-6705
E-mail: info@irga.com
URL: http://www.irga.com
Contact: Steve Bova CAE, Exec. Dir.
Founded: 1927. **Members:** 985. **Membership Dues:** active, $550-$1,495 (annual) ● active (international), $425 (annual) ● associate, $500-$1,495 (annual) ● associate (international), $820 (annual). **Staff:** 7. **Budget:** $1,500,000. **Regional Groups:** 4. **Description:** Commercial blue print and photocopy firms, engineering supply stores, and materials and equipment suppliers. Conducts annual photo-tech, marketing, management, and business planning seminars. **Awards:** George K. Bukovsky Award. **Frequency:** annual. **Type:** recognition. **Recipient:** for achievement. **Telecommunication Services:** electronic mail, sbova@irga.com. **Formerly:** (1972) International Association of Blue Print and Allied Industries; (1980) International Reprographic Blueprint Association. **Publications:** *IRgA Annual Directory*, annual. **Advertising:** accepted ● *IRgA News Digest*, monthly. Newsletter. **Advertising:** accepted. Alternate Formats: online ● *Repro Report*, bimonthly. Magazine. **Price:** $150.00 /year for nonmembers; $30.00 /year for members. **Circulation:** 1,000. **Advertising:** accepted ● Surveys. Features surveys on operating ratios, compensation and benefits, and other industry issues. ● Handbooks. **Conventions/Meetings:** annual convention and trade show (exhibits) - during spring.

1802 ■ National Art Materials Trade Association (NAMTA)
15806 Brookway Dr., Ste.300
Huntersville, NC 28078
Ph: (704)892-6244
Fax: (704)892-6247
E-mail: info@namta.org
URL: http://www.namta.org
Contact: Sid Smith, Interim Exec. Dir.
Founded: 1950. **Members:** 1,200. **Membership Dues:** associate, $275 (annual) ● manufacturer's representative (domestic), $110 (annual) ● manufacturer's representative (international); supplier branch, $165 (annual) ● retailer (based on annual sales), $125-$600 (annual) ● retail branch, $75 (annual) ● retailer (international), $150 (annual) ● supplier (based on annual sales), $550-$2,200 (annual). **Staff:** 6. **Budget:** $1,200,000. **Multinational. Description:** Domestic and international retailers, distributors, manufacturers, publishers, and importers of fine art and creative materials. Provides useful business education and services, including research programs. Maintains the art materials industry's Hall of Fame. **Libraries: Type:** reference. **Awards:** NAMTA Scholarship. **Frequency:** annual. **Type:** scholarship. **Recipient:** for member or relative of member firm. **Computer Services:** Mailing lists, of members. **Telecommunication Services:** electronic mail, ssmith@namta.org. **Programs:** Youth Art Month. **Publications:** *Art Materials Retailer*, quarterly. Magazine. **Circulation:** 12,000. **Advertising:** accepted ● *NAMTA's Annual Convention Directory*. Offers a product buyer's guide to the world's largest annual gathering of the art materials industry. **Circulation:** 3,000. **Advertising:** accepted ● *National Art Materials Trade Association—News and Views*, monthly. Newsletter. Contains membership, industry, and business news. **Price:** free, for members only. **Circulation:** 1,200 ● *Who's Who in Art Materials*, annual. Directory. Includes contact and product information. **Price:** included in membership dues; $250.00 /year for nonmembers. **Advertising:** accepted. **Conventions/Meetings:** annual convention and trade show, gathering of art materials industry trade (exhibits).

1803 ■ National Association of Printing Ink Manufacturers (NAPIM)
581 Main St.
Woodbridge, NJ 07095-1148
Ph: (732)855-1525
Fax: (732)855-1838
E-mail: napim@napim.org
URL: http://www.napim.org
Contact: James E. Coleman, Exec. Dir.
Founded: 1914. **Members:** 143. **Staff:** 6. **Description:** Represents printing ink manufacturers and suppliers. Sponsors National Printing Ink Research Institute. **Awards:** Ault Award. **Frequency:** annual. **Type:** recognition. **Recipient:** for industry achievement. **Telecommunication Services:** electronic bulletin board, NAPIM NET. **Committees:** Color Standards; Conservation; Consumer Affairs; Government Relations; Health; Human Resources; Management Information; Materials Handling; Public Relations; Technical and education; Traffic. **Formerly:** (1967) National Association of Printing Ink Makers. **Publications:** *Raw Materials Data Handbooks* ● Booklets ● Bulletins ● Also publishes trade names registry. **Conventions/Meetings:** semiannual conference and convention - October and April.

1804 ■ North American Graphic Arts Suppliers Association (NAGASA)
PO Box 934483
Margate, FL 33093
Ph: (954)971-1383
Fax: (954)971-4362
E-mail: nagasa4info@nagasa.org
URL: http://www.nagasa.org
Contact: Patrick Patton, Chm.
Founded: 1992. **Members:** 125. **Membership Dues:** individual, $250 (annual) ● business, $500 (annual) ● corporate (based on sales volume), $395-$3,500 (annual). **Staff:** 1. **Budget:** $200,000. **Description:** Graphic communications dealers and manufacturers. Works to advance the interests of graphic arts dealers and manufacturers, and improve the partnership between them. Seeks to streamline costs and increase efficiency. Fosters communication between dealers and manufacturers. Produces technical and business performance information through standards, statistical, educational, and publishing services. **Libraries: Type:** reference. **Holdings:** 6. **Computer Services:** Mailing lists, provided to members. **Formed by Merger of:** (1992) National Graphic Arts Dealers Association; Graphic Arts Suppliers Association. **Publications:** *Compass*, quarterly. Newsletter. Provides information on issues of importance to graphic arts dealers. **Price:** free for members, subscribers, and the trade media ● *NAGASA—Membership Directory*, annual. Lists 400 graphic arts dealer, manufacturing companies, publishers, manufacture reps, and consultants in the U.S., Canada, and Mexico. **Price:** available to members only ● *White Paper Series*, periodic. Journal. Provides a forum for discussion and debate on the future of the graphic communications distribution channel. **Price:** free for members. **Circulation:** 400 ● Reports. **Conventions/Meetings:** annual Dealer-Manufacturer Forum - conference, covers trends and issues for print and imaging supplies and equipment ● quarterly meeting, dealer-focused training, market and technology sessions - held during industry trade shows.

Graphic Design

1805 ■ Amalgamated Printers' Association (APA)
c/o Mike O'Connor, Sec.-Treas.
PO Box 18117
Fountain Hills, AZ 85269
E-mail: mikeatfh@cox.net
URL: http://www.apa-letterpress.com
Contact: Mike O'Connor, Sec.-Treas.
Founded: 1958. **Members:** 150. **Membership Dues:** direct, $25 (annual). **Multinational. Description:** Active printers interested in the furtherance of the art and craft of printing. Encourages excellence of printing content, design, and techniques among members. Sponsors competitions. **Libraries: Type:** open to the public. **Holdings:** 600; archival material. **Subjects:** personal correspondence, printing, bibliographies of printers, typefounders, type designers, graphic arts personalities. **Awards:** Tramp Printer Award. **Frequency:** annual. **Type:** recognition. **Recipient:** for printing excellence and service to letterpress printing. **Computer Services:** database, list of members ● database, past officers. **Publications:** *Cooperative Calendar*, annual. **Price:** available to members only ● *Membership List*, annual. Membership Directory ● *Roster*, annual ● *Treasure Gems*, annual. Book. Contains works of members contributed on a voluntary basis. **Conventions/Meetings:** annual Wayzgoose - banquet and lecture (exhibits).

1806 ■ Association of Professional Design Firms (APDF)
1448 E 52nd St., No. 201
Chicago, IL 60615
Ph: (773)643-7052
Fax: (773)643-7054
E-mail: cbrownlee@apdf.org
URL: http://www.apdf.org
Contact: Cathy Brownlee, Exec. Dir.
Founded: 1985. **Members:** 90. **Membership Dues:** independent design firm, $1,595 (annual). **Staff:** 1. **Budget:** $200,000. **Description:** Independently owned design firms, industrial designers, graphic designers, and commercial interior design firms. Seeks to: increase public awareness in the field of design; improve management of design firms. Conducts educational programs, seminars, and research programs. **Awards:** APDF Wefler Scholarship. **Frequency:** annual. **Type:** scholarship. **Recipient:** to design management graduate students in North America. **Committees:** Annual Meeting/Exchange; Communications/PR; Financial Performance Survey; Forums - New Programming; Member Services. **Publications:** *Biz Brief*, monthly. Newsletter. Alternate Formats: online ● *Contract Terms and Conditions for Product Design Consultants*. Handbook ● *Design Biz*, semiannual. Newsletter. Contains association and industry news. **Circulation:** 800 ● *The Financial Handbook for Design Firms*. **Price:** $99.00 for members; $199.00 for nonmembers ● *Financial Performance Survey*, annual. **Conventions/Meetings:** annual meeting.

1807 ■ Design Management Institute (DMI)
29 Temple Pl., 2nd Fl.
Boston, MA 02111-1350
Ph: (617)338-6380
Fax: (617)338-6570
E-mail: dmistaff@dmi.org
URL: http://www.dmi.org
Contact: Thomas Lockwood, Pres.
Founded: 1975. **Members:** 1,200. **Membership Dues:** professional individual, $400 (annual) ● professional group, $1,600 (annual) ● professional organization, $3,200 (annual) ● professional forum, $6,400 (annual) ● academic student, $150 (annual) ● academic individual, $300 (annual) ● academic group, $500 (annual). **Staff:** 8. **Description:** In-house design groups and consultant design firms; individuals involved in the management of designers with in-house corporate design groups or consultant design firms. Aims to share management techniques as applied to design groups, and to facilitate better understanding by business management of the role design can play in achieving business goals. Design disciplines included are: architecture, advertising, communications, exhibit design, graphics, interior design, packaging and product design. Develops and distributes design management education materials. Sponsors seminars for design professionals. Identifies critical areas of design management study; conducts surveys and research on corporate design management. Maintains design management archive. Operates Center for Research, Center for Education, and Center for Design and Management Resources. **Libraries: Type:** by appointment only. **Holdings:** 2,000; books, periodicals. **Subjects:** design, management. **Awards:** John F. Nolan Award. **Frequency:** annual. **Type:** recognition. **Recipient:** for a senior non-design executive who has been an active champion of design for economic and cultural development ● Muriel Cooper Prize. **Frequency:** annual. **Type:** recognition. **Recipient:** for outstanding achievement in advancing design, technology and

communications in the digital environment. **Computer Services:** Mailing lists, of members. **Programs:** Certificate; Degree; Professional Development. **Publications:** *Design Management Institute Newsletter*, quarterly. Contains information about decision and management. **Price:** free. **Circulation:** 14,000. **Advertising:** accepted. Alternate Formats: online ● *Design Management Review*, quarterly. Journal. Design management practice of research. **Price:** $110.00 in U.S.; $145.00 outside U.S. **Circulation:** 7,500. **Advertising:** accepted ● Membership Directory, annual. **Conventions/Meetings:** annual International Design Management Conference, with presentations - 3-5/year.

1808 ■ National Association of Photoshop Professionals (NAPP)
333 Douglas Rd. E
Oldsmar, FL 34677
Ph: (813)433-5006
Free: (800)738-8513
Fax: (813)433-5015
E-mail: info@photoshopuser.com
URL: http://www.photoshopuser.com
Contact: Scott Kelby, Pres./CEO
Founded: 1998. **Members:** 40,000. **Membership Dues:** individual, $99 (annual) ● corporate, $279 (annual) ● educational, $89 (annual) ● individual in U.S. and Canada, $129 (annual) ● individual, international, $149 (annual). **Multinational. Description:** Serves as the trade association for Adobe Photoshop professionals and users. Enhances the expertise of members by providing education, training, and information about adobe photoshop techniques, issues, and development. **Computer Services:** Information services, photoshop resources ● online services, member gallery. **Publications:** *Newswire*, monthly. Newsletter. Contains latest Photoshop information, tips, new member discounts, deals, and new product information. Alternate Formats: online ● *Photoshop User*, 8/year. Magazine. Features step-by-step tutorials, articles, and in depth review from award winning photographers, designers, and Photoshop experts. **Price:** included in membership dues.

1809 ■ Society for Environmental Graphic Design (SEGD)
1000 Vermont Ave. NW, Ste.400
Washington, DC 20005
Ph: (202)638-5555
Fax: (202)638-0891
E-mail: segd@segd.org
URL: http://www.segd.org
Contact: Leslie Gallery Dilworth FAIA, Exec. Dir.
Founded: 1974. **Members:** 1,200. **Membership Dues:** design professional in U.S., $290 (annual) ● design professional studio (minimum), $1,160 (annual) ● design associate in U.S., $180 (annual) ● industry professional in U.S., $615 (annual) ● student in U.S., $50 (annual). **Staff:** 5. **Budget:** $750,000. **Regional Groups:** 20. **Description:** Designers and manufacturers of sign systems and environmental graphics. Establishes educational guidelines for professional development as well as governmental guidelines for environmental graphics programs; provides a forum for interaction and communication among members who are from a variety of design disciplines and with manufacturers; compiles and disseminates technical data. Offers members the opportunity to participate in government hearings, code reviews, and related proceedings regarding environmental graphic design. Conducts educational programs and develops resource materials. Maintains slide collection, library and educational materials. **Libraries: Type:** not open to the public. **Holdings:** 600. **Subjects:** design. **Awards:** Design Award. **Frequency:** annual. **Type:** recognition. **Recipient:** for a designer. **Computer Services:** Mailing lists, of members. **Formerly:** (1991) Society of Environmental Graphic Designers. **Publications:** *Environmental Graphics Sourcebooks*. **Circulation:** 1,250. Alternate Formats: online ● *Industry Directory*, annual. Includes articles, profiles, technical column, and resource listing. **Price:** free for members; $6.00/copy, for back issues. **Circulation:** 1,500. **Advertising:** accepted ● *Messages*, bimonthly. Newsletter. Includes articles, profiles, technical column, and resource listing. **Price:** free for members; $6.00/copy, for back issues. **Circulation:** 1,500. **Advertising:** accepted ● *Professional Firm Directory*, annual. Includes company profile, descriptions of professional background, representative projects, clients, and areas of expertise. ● *SEGdesign*, quarterly. Magazine. Includes project profiles, technology columns and interviews. **Price:** $200.00 in U.S.; $275.00 outside U.S. ● *You are Here, Graphics That Direct, Explain and Entertain*, bimonthly. Newsletter. **Price:** $25.00 each. **Circulation:** 1,250. **Advertising:** accepted. Alternate Formats: online ● Bulletins. **Conventions/Meetings:** annual conference, with exposition (exhibits).

1810 ■ Society of Publication Designers (SPD)
17 E 47th St., 6th Fl.
New York, NY 10017
Ph: (212)223-3332
Fax: (212)223-5880
E-mail: mail@spd.org
URL: http://www.spd.org
Contact: Bruce Ramsay, Pres.
Founded: 1965. **Members:** 1,000. **Membership Dues:** individual, $195 (annual) ● corporate, $495 (annual). **Staff:** 1. **Budget:** $600,000. **Description:** Represents art directors, designers, editors, photographers, and illustrators with the responsibility of layout and design of consumer, business, and professional publications and newspapers. Holds speakers' luncheons and auctions. **Libraries: Type:** open to the public. **Awards:** Herb Lubalin. **Type:** recognition. **Recipient:** for individual ● Magazine of the Year Award. **Frequency:** annual. **Type:** recognition. **Recipient:** for excellence in design, illustration, and photography. **Supersedes:** Society of Publication Designers. **Publications:** *GRIDS*, quarterly. Newsletter. Contains calendar of future events, or information on shows, activities, resources or products of interest to designers. **Price:** free for members ● *Publication Design Annual*, annual. Book. **Price:** $50.00/copy. **Conventions/Meetings:** annual Awards Gala - banquet (exhibits) - always May in New York City ● competition ● conference.

1811 ■ Urban Art International (UAI)
PO Box 868
Tiburon, CA 94920
Ph: (415)435-5767
Fax: (415)435-4240
E-mail: uai@hansenarchitects.com
URL: http://www.imagesite.com/compete/uai
Contact: Fani D. Hansen, Pres.
Founded: 1980. **Description:** Organizes and conducts annual US poster competition entitled "World's Most Memorable Poster". Winning posters are sent to Paris, France for international competition. Organizes US tour of international winning posters in the "World's Most Memorable Poster International Tour". **Formerly:** (1984) Women in Design International; (1991) Design International. **Publications:** *Design International Membership Directory*, annual ● *Design International Quarterly*. Newsletter. **Conventions/Meetings:** periodic conference.

Graphology

1812 ■ American Society of Professional Graphologists (ASPG)
23 South Dr.
Great Neck, NY 11021
E-mail: questions@aspghandwriting.org
URL: http://www.aspghandwriting.org
Contact: Patricia Siegel, Pres.
Membership Dues: professional, associate in New York, New Jersey, or Connecticut, $125 (annual) ● professional living outside U.S., associate elsewhere, $60 (annual). **Description:** Promotes understanding and appreciation of art and science of graphology. **Funds:** Anthony Memorial. **Publications:** *Journal of the American Society of Professional Graphologists*. **Price:** $29.00 for volume VI; $25.00 for volume V; $10.00 each, for volumes II, III, IV ● Newsletter. **Conventions/Meetings:** conference - 3/year.

Guardians

1813 ■ National Guardianship Association (NGA)
174 Crestview Dr.
Bellefonte, PA 16823
Free: (877)326-5992
Fax: (814)355-2452
E-mail: info@guardianship.org
URL: http://www.guardianship.org
Contact: Terry Hammond, Exec. Dir.
Founded: 1988. **Members:** 750. **Membership Dues:** family, volunteer, retired, $50 (annual) ● professional, allied professional (individual), $170 (annual) ● organization, $250 (annual). **Staff:** 18. **Description:** Represents guardians, conservators, fiduciaries, attorneys, social workers, bankers, advocates, representative payees, physicians and hospitals, and others interested in guardianship and surrogacy. Strives to improve services to elderly, the mentally ill, people with developmental disabilities, physical disabilities and head injuries. **Publications:** *National Guardian*, quarterly. Newsletter. Contains information on legislation, state and regional activities, issues on guardianship and related services. Provides forum about current issues. ● *NGA Membership Directory*, annual. **Conventions/Meetings:** annual conference - 2008 Oct. 4-7, Nashville, TN; 2009 Oct. 3-7, Las Vegas, NV.

Hardware

1814 ■ Aircraft Locknut Manufacturers Association (ALMA)
c/o Robert H. Ecker, Exec. Dir.
994 Old Eagle School Rd., Ste.1019
Wayne, PA 19087-1802
Ph: (610)971-4850
Fax: (610)971-4859
E-mail: info@almanet.org
URL: http://www.almanet.org
Contact: Robert H. Ecker, Exec. Dir.
Members: 10. **Staff:** 2. **Description:** Represents manufacturing companies of aerospace and aircraft locknut fasteners. Monitors standards and specifications established by customer groups such as the military, aircraft engine manufacturers, and other aircraft industry firms. Compiles statistics. **Telecommunication Services:** electronic mail, rhecker@almanet.org. **Conventions/Meetings:** semiannual meeting.

1815 ■ American Hardware Manufacturers Association (AHMA)
801 N Plaza Dr.
Schaumburg, IL 60173
Ph: (847)605-1025
Fax: (847)605-1030
E-mail: info@ahma.org
URL: http://www.ahma.org
Contact: Timothy S. Farrell, Pres./CEO
Founded: 1901. **Members:** 875. **Membership Dues:** corporate, $300 (annual). **Staff:** 22. **Description:** Represents the hardware, home improvement, lawn and garden, paint and decorating, and related industries. **Committees:** Export; Travel. **Publications:** *AHMA Eagle*, bimonthly. Newsletter ● *AHMA Employee Relations Report*, monthly. Newsletter ● *AHMA Issue Briefing*, monthly. Newsletter ● *AHMA Washington Report*, monthly. Newsletter ● Membership Directory, annual. **Conventions/Meetings:** annual AHMA Hardware Show - trade show - always April, Chicago, IL ● annual Executive Conference for the Home Improvement Industry - meeting ● annual Hardlines Technology Forum - meeting.

1816 ■ American Ladder Institute (ALI)
401 N Michigan Ave.
Chicago, IL 60611
Ph: (312)644-6610

Fax: (312)527-6705
E-mail: rpietrzak@smithbucklin.com
URL: http://www.americanladderinstitute.org
Contact: Ron Pietrzak, Exec. Dir.
Founded: 1947. **Members:** 34. **Staff:** 2. **Budget:** $200,000. **Description:** Manufacturers of wood, fiberglass, and metal ladders. Encourages adherence to voluntary standards developed by American National Standards Institute; acts as developer of the American National Standards Institute for the ANSI A14 Committee on Ladder Safety. **Committees:** Fiberglass Ladder; Material Supply; Metal Ladder; Product Liability; Safety; Statistical; Wood Ladder. **Affiliated With:** American National Standards Institute. **Publications:** *Ladderlines*, bimonthly. Newsletter. **Price:** included in membership dues. **Conventions/Meetings:** annual meeting - usually in South or Southwest in spring.

1817 ■ American Metal Detector Manufacturers Association (AMDMA)

1881 W State St.
Garland, TX 75042
Ph: (972)494-6151
Free: (800)527-4011
Fax: (972)494-1881
E-mail: sales@garrett.com
URL: http://www.garrett.com
Contact: Charles Garrett, Pres./CEO
Founded: 1977. **Members:** 6. **Description:** Metal detector manufacturers. Aims to assist members and the industry in dealing with common business problems.

1818 ■ Associated Locksmiths of America (ALOA)

3500 Easy St.
Dallas, TX 75247
Ph: (214)819-9733
Free: (800)532-2562
Fax: (214)819-9736
E-mail: charlie@aloa.org
URL: http://www.aloa.org
Contact: Robert E. Mock, Pres.
Founded: 1955. **Members:** 8,500. **Membership Dues:** outside U.S., $130 (annual) ● in U.S., $155 (annual). **Staff:** 15. **Budget:** $2,000,000. **Description:** Retail locksmiths; associate members are manufacturers and distributors of locks, keys, safes, and burglar alarms. Aims to educate and provide current information to individuals in the physical security industry. Maintains information and referral services for members; offers insurance and bonding programs. Holds annual five-day technical training classes and 3-day technical exhibit. Maintains museum. **Libraries: Type:** reference; not open to the public. **Holdings:** 2,000; books, periodicals. **Subjects:** locksmithing, locks, tools, technical procedures. **Awards:** A.L. O.A. Award. **Frequency:** annual. **Type:** recognition ● ACE Award. **Frequency:** annual. **Type:** recognition ● Don Davis Award. **Frequency:** annual. **Type:** recognition ● President's Award. **Frequency:** annual. **Type:** recognition. **Computer Services:** database, referral ● mailing lists, disk, electronic. **Publications:** *Keynotes*, monthly. Journal. Covers association and industry trade information for the physical security professional. **Price:** available to members only. **Circulation:** 10,000. **Advertising:** accepted. **Conventions/Meetings:** annual convention and conference, lock manufacturers and security products (exhibits) - usually July. 2008 June 15-21, Dallas, TX.

1819 ■ Builders Hardware Manufacturers Association (BHMA)

355 Lexington Ave., 15th Fl.
New York, NY 10017
Ph: (212)297-2122
Fax: (212)370-9047
E-mail: bhma@kellencompany.com
URL: http://www.buildershardware.com
Contact: Helen Rose, Pres.
Founded: 1925. **Members:** 75. **Membership Dues:** full (based on gross sales), $1,890-$39,000 (annual) ● associate, $3,000 (annual). **Staff:** 4. **Budget:** $500,000. **Description:** Manufacturers of builders' hardware, both contract and stock. Provides statistical services; maintains standardization program; sponsors certification programs for locks, latches, door closers, and cabinet hardware. Maintains 12 product sections. **Awards:** Circle of Excellence. **Frequency:** annual. **Type:** recognition. **Recipient:** for excellence. **Formerly:** (1961) Hardware Manufacturers Statistical Association. **Publications:** *A Guide to Builders Hardware Terminology* ● *Product Standards* ● Membership Directory, annual. **Conventions/Meetings:** annual conference ● seminar.

1820 ■ Cold Formed Parts and Machine Institute (CFPMI)

25 N Broadway
Tarrytown, NY 10591
Ph: (914)332-0040
Fax: (914)332-1541
E-mail: info@cfpmi.org
URL: http://www.cfpmi.org
Contact: Richard C. Byrne, Sec.
Founded: 1937. **Members:** 10. **Staff:** 2. **Description:** Represents manufacturers of rivets and other cold formed parts. **Committees:** Metric; Safety; Technical. **Formerly:** (1974) Tubular and Split Rivet Council; (2001) Tubular Rivet and Machine Institute. **Publications:** *Dimensional Inch and Metric Standards for General Purpose Semitubular Rivets* ● Directory, periodic. **Conventions/Meetings:** semiannual meeting.

1821 ■ Door and Hardware Institute (DHI)

14150 Newbrook Dr., Ste.200
Chantilly, VA 20151
Ph: (703)222-2010
Fax: (703)222-2410
E-mail: info@dhi.org
URL: http://www.dhi.org
Contact: Jerry Heppes CAE, CEO
Founded: 1975. **Members:** 5,500. **Membership Dues:** individual in U.S. and Canada, $225 (annual) ● distributor, manufacturer, $725 (annual) ● individual outside U.S. and Canada, $310 (annual). **Staff:** 30. **Budget:** $4,000,000. **Regional Groups:** 59. **Multinational. Description:** Commercial distributors, manufacturers and specifiers involved in doors and builders' hardware (locks, door hardware, latches, hinges, and electrified products). Works with architects, contractors, and building owners. Conducts management and technical courses and membership-related surveys. Offers certification program for the Architectural Openings Industry (AHC, CDC). **Computer Services:** Mailing lists, of members. **Committees:** Awards; Business Management; Education; Industry and Public Affairs; Industry Liaison; Industry Products; Openings Standards; Publicity and Public Relations; Technical Literature Review. **Divisions:** Board of Certification; DHI Education Foundation. **Formed by Merger of:** National Builders' Hardware Association; American Society of Architectural Hardware Consultants. **Publications:** *DHI International—Membership Directory/Buyers Guide*, annual. Lists national and international member firms and individuals by chapter. **Price:** $35.00 for members; $150.00 for nonmembers. **Circulation:** 5,500. **Advertising:** accepted ● *Doors and Hardware*, monthly. Magazine. Includes annual index, case studies, technical and informational articles, departments, and convention issues. **Price:** $69.00/year in U.S.; $109.00/year outside U.S. ISSN: 0361-5294. **Circulation:** 12,000. **Advertising:** accepted ● *The Plan Room*, quarterly. Newsletter. Covers DHI schools and their programs, industry events, DHI publications, chapter meetings, and obituaries. **Price:** free, for members only. **Circulation:** 5,500 ● Also publishes technical handbooks and reference materials. **Conventions/Meetings:** annual convention and trade show (exhibits).

1822 ■ Hand Tools Institute (HTI)

25 N Broadway
Tarrytown, NY 10591
Ph: (914)332-0040
Fax: (914)332-1541
E-mail: info@hti.org
URL: http://ww3.hti.org
Contact: Richard C. Byrne, Exec. Dir.
Founded: 1935. **Members:** 67. **Staff:** 3. **Description:** Manufacturers of hand service tools. **Committees:** Government Relations; International Trade; Products Standards and Safety; Safety Education. **Absorbed:** (1970) Machinists Vise Association. **Formerly:** (1973) Service Tools Institute. **Publications:** Books ● Directory, periodic ● Videos. **Conventions/Meetings:** semiannual meeting.

1823 ■ Industrial Fasteners Institute (IFI)

6363 Oak Tree Blvd.
Independence, OH 44131
Ph: (216)241-1482
Fax: (216)241-5901
E-mail: rharris@indfast.org
URL: http://www.industrial-fasteners.org
Contact: Robert J. Harris, Managing Dir.
Founded: 1931. **Members:** 150. **Membership Dues:** associate, $4,600 (annual) ● corporate (based on average sales of last 3 years), $4,500-$19,500 (annual). **Staff:** 6. **Budget:** $1,500,000. **Description:** Manufacturers of industrial fasteners and formed parts; associate members are suppliers of primary and secondary equipment, raw materials, and services used in the manufacture of fasteners and formed parts. Seeks to advance fastener and formed parts application engineering. Establishes standards and technical practices. **Libraries: Type:** reference. **Holdings:** 500; books. **Subjects:** fastener standards, technology. **Awards:** Industry Leadership. **Frequency:** annual. **Type:** recognition ● Special Service. **Frequency:** annual. **Type:** recognition ● Technology Development. **Frequency:** annual. **Type:** recognition. **Boards:** IFFI Trade Show Governing. **Committees:** Engineering Research and Development; Government Affairs; Quality Assurance; Standards and Technical Practices. **Divisions:** Aerospace; Automotive; Industrial Products; Suppliers. **Formerly:** American Institute of Bolt, Nut and Rivet Manufacturers. **Publications:** *Fastener Standards, 7th Edition*, quinquennial. Book. **Price:** $345.00 in U.S.; $395.00 outside U.S. **Circulation:** 10,000 ● *Metric Fastener Standards, 3rd Edition*, quinquennial. Book. **Price:** $140.00 in U.S.; $190.00 outside U.S. **Conventions/Meetings:** biennial Industrial Fastening and Farming International Expo & Conference - conference and trade show - odd years ● semiannual meeting - always spring and fall.

1824 ■ International Magnetics Association (IMA)

8 S Michigan Ave., Ste.1000
Chicago, IL 60603
Ph: (312)456-5590
Fax: (312)580-0165
E-mail: ima@gss.net
URL: http://www.intl-magnetics.org
Contact: Lowell Bosley, Pres.
Founded: 1959. **Members:** 30. **Membership Dues:** producer, distributor/fabricator, $1,000 (annual) ● supplier, user, publication/other media, university, $500 (annual) ● affiliate, $250 (annual). **Staff:** 2. **Budget:** $200,000. **Description:** Manufacturers of magnetic materials, distributors/fabricators of magnetic components and assemblies, suppliers to the magnetic industry. Affiliates include consultants, universities and publications. Promotes the worldwide growth, development and use of magnetic devices and materials. **Divisions:** Distributor/Fabrication; Permanent Magnet; Soft Ferrite. **Programs:** Benchmarking. **Formerly:** Permanent Magnet Producers Association; (2001) Magnetic Materials Producers Association. **Publications:** Manual. Contains specifications, guidelines and other technical information on permanent and soft ferrite magnets. **Conventions/Meetings:** semiannual meeting - May and November.

1825 ■ International Staple, Nail and Tool Association (ISANTA)

512 W Burlington Ave., Ste.203
La Grange, IL 60525-2245
Ph: (708)482-8138
Fax: (708)482-8186
E-mail: isanta@ameritech.net
URL: http://isanta.org
Contact: Jerry C. Koontz, VP/Gen. Mgr.
Founded: 1972. **Members:** 20. **Staff:** 2. **Description:** Firms that manufacture power driven staples,

nails, and similar fasteners and/or the tools that drive them. Works to promote and further the use of power tools and power driven staples and nails in industry and construction. Deals with engineering, safety, and other aspects of the industry. **Committees:** Public Relations; Technology. **Formerly:** (1972) Industrial Stapling Manufacturers Institute; (1982) Industrial Stapling and Nailing Technical Association. **Publications:** *Membership List*, periodic. Membership Directory. Alternate Formats: online ● *Standards*, periodic ● Books. Covers specifications. ● Brochure ● Reports. Alternate Formats: online.

1826 ■ Lighter Association (LA)
1700 Pennsylvania Ave. NW, Ste.400
Washington, DC 20036
Ph: (202)349-4190
E-mail: info@lighterassociation.org
URL: http://www.lighterassociation.org
Contact: David H. Baker, Gen. Counsel
Founded: 1986. **Members:** 15. **Membership Dues:** manufacturer, distributor (based on sales), $4,000-$48,000 (annual) ● supplier, $1,000 (annual) ● affiliated association, $3,000 (annual) ● associate, $100 (annual). **Budget:** $150,000. **Description:** Manufacturers, suppliers, and distributors; associations of manufacturers, suppliers, and distributors; research and development and consulting organizations; universities. Advances the interests of the finished lighter industry; promotes safety and encourages proper use of lighter products. Collects and disseminates information; represents members' interests before governing bodies. Provides a forum for discussing and analyzing issues such as: product liability; insurance coverage; safety standards; product transportation. Organizes public education programs. **Conventions/Meetings:** annual meeting - always October.

1827 ■ Member Insurance Association (MIA)
Address Unknown since 2007
Founded: 1972. **Description:** Retail hardware stores. Strives to provide cooperatives and associations with complete insurance solutions customized to meet specific needs.

1828 ■ National Fastener Distributors Association (NFDA)
401 N Michigan Ave.
Chicago, IL 60611
Ph: (312)527-6671
Free: (877)487-NFDA
Fax: (312)673-6740
E-mail: nfda@nfda-fastener.org
URL: http://www.nfda-fastener.org
Contact: Bryn Tuttle-Stock, Pres./Chm.
Founded: 1968. **Members:** 250. **Membership Dues:** active, associate, $1,000 (annual). **Staff:** 3. **Budget:** $600,000. **Description:** Marketers, distributors, manufacturers, and importers of the fastener industry (producers or distributors of screws, bolts, and nuts). Develops new uses for fasteners; collects and disseminates statistics and information for members; conducts membership performance surveys. Assists in the maintenance of sound and equitable relationships among members of the industry, the public, and government. Offers training and educational programs. **Awards:** NFDA Scholarship. **Frequency:** annual. **Type:** scholarship. **Recipient:** for employees of member firms or children of employees of member firms who are entering their freshman year in college. **Computer Services:** database, membership directory ● mailing lists, of members. **Committees:** Development; Education; Finance; Legislative; Scholarship; Technical Training. **Affiliated With:** American National Metric Council; American National Standards Institute; American Society of Mechanical Engineers; National Association of Wholesaler-Distributors. **Absorbed:** (1968) Southern Association of Independent Fastener Distributors. **Publications:** *Fastener Training Program*. Manual ● *Inside NFDA*, semimonthly. Newsletter. **Price:** $50.00 /year for nonmembers ● *Inside Sales Modules*. Video ● *Roster*, annual. Membership Directory ● Also produces training audiocassette and videotapes. **Conventions/Meetings:** semiannual conference (exhibits) - always March/April and September/October.

1829 ■ North American Retail Hardware Association (NRHA)
5822 W 74th St.
Indianapolis, IN 46278-1787
Ph: (317)290-0338
Free: (800)772-4424
Fax: (317)328-4354
E-mail: contact@nrha.org
URL: http://www.nrha.org
Contact: John P. Hammond, Managing Dir.
Founded: 1900. **Members:** 15,000. **Membership Dues:** regular (add $50 for each additional store branch), $195 (annual). **Staff:** 40. **Budget:** $7,000,000. **Description:** Represents independent family-owned hardware/home improvement retailers. Sponsors correspondence courses in hardware and building materials retailing; conducts annual cost-of-doing-business study. **Awards:** Young Retailer of the Year. **Frequency:** annual. **Type:** recognition. **Formerly:** (2007) National Retail Hardware Association. **Publications:** *Cost-of-Doing Business Study*, annual. Report. Details statements of accounts, balance sheets and financial ratios for retail hardware stores, home centers and consumer-oriented outlets. **Price:** $49.00 for members; $98.00 for nonmembers. ISSN: 1051-2764 ● *Do-It-Yourself Retailing*, monthly. Magazine. A how-to marketing, management, and merchandising magazine for retailers who sell do-it-yourself products. Includes new product announcements. ISSN: 8750-2569. **Circulation:** 60,000. **Advertising:** accepted. Also Cited As: *DIY Retailing*. **Conventions/Meetings:** annual convention.

1830 ■ North American Sawing Association (NASA)
1300 Sumner Ave.
Cleveland, OH 44115-2851
Ph: (216)241-7333
Fax: (216)241-0105
E-mail: nasa@sawingassociation.com
URL: http://www.sawingassociation.com
Contact: Charles M. Stockinger, Sec.-Treas.
Founded: 1959. **Members:** 9. **Staff:** 3. **Description:** Manufacturers of hack saws and metal cutting band saws from standard and high speed steel. Compiles statistics. **Divisions:** Band Saw Blade; Power Tool Accessories. **Formed by Merger of:** (1999) Hack Saw Association and Metal Cutting Band. **Formerly:** (1999) Hack and Band Saw Manufacturers Association of America. **Conventions/Meetings:** annual meeting.

1831 ■ Power Tool Institute (PTI)
1300 Sumner Ave.
Cleveland, OH 44115-2851
Ph: (216)241-7333
Fax: (216)241-0105
E-mail: pti@powertoolinstitute.com
URL: http://www.powertoolinstitute.com
Contact: Charles M. Stockinger, Exec. Mgr.
Founded: 1968. **Members:** 11. **Staff:** 5. **Description:** Represents manufacturers of portable and stationary tools, both electric and battery operated. Distributes publications and videos on power tool safety. Offers educational programs. **Committees:** Ad Hoc Global Harmonization; Engineering; Product Liability Coordinators; Public Relations and Safety. **Formerly:** (1968) Electric Tool Institute. **Publications:** Directory, annual. **Conventions/Meetings:** annual meeting - usually October.

1832 ■ Precision Machined Products Association (PMPA)
6700 W Snowville Rd.
Brecksville, OH 44141
Ph: (440)526-0300
Fax: (440)526-5803
E-mail: webmaster@pmpa.org
URL: http://www.pmpa.org
Contact: Michael B. Duffin, Exec. Dir.
Founded: 1933. **Members:** 520. **Membership Dues:** active, $600 (annual) ● associate (minimum), $700 (annual) ● technical (based on sales), $1,000-$3,000 (annual). **Staff:** 14. **Budget:** $1,000,000. **Local Groups:** 24. **Description:** Addresses the information, training, and technical needs of manufacturers of component parts to customers' order, machined from rod, bar, or tube stock, of metal, fiber, plastic, or other material, using automatic or hand screw machines, automatic bar machines, and CNC machines. **Libraries: Type:** by appointment only; not open to the public; reference. **Computer Services:** database, member's directory ● online services, e-mail Listservs: Corporate, Technical, Quality and Human Resources; Listservs are member-only forums where companies share ideas and solve problems. **Committees:** Benchmarking; Government Affairs; Human Resources; Industry Trends; Internet; Management Services; Strategic Planning. **Formerly:** (1995) National Screw Machine Products Association. **Publications:** *PMPA Reports*, bimonthly. Newsletter. **Price:** free for members ● *Production Machining Magazine*, bimonthly. **Price:** free to all companies affiliated with the industry. **Circulation:** 20,000. **Advertising:** accepted. Alternate Formats: online. **Conventions/Meetings:** annual Management Update Conference ● annual National Technical Conference (exhibits).

1833 ■ Screen Manufacturers Association (SMA)
2850 S Ocean Blvd., No. 114
Palm Beach, FL 33480-6205
Ph: (561)533-0991 (561)533-6040
Fax: (561)533-7466
E-mail: fitzgeraldfscott@bellsouth.net
URL: http://www.smacentral.org
Contact: Frank S. Fitzgerald CAE, Exec. VP
Founded: 1955. **Members:** 30. **Membership Dues:** company (based on annual sales), $1,000-$3,000 (annual). **Staff:** 2. **Budget:** $100,000. **Multinational. Description:** Manufacturers of window, patio, swimming pool, door and porch screens, and regular insect and solar screening and sections; members are also producers of aluminum, fiberglass, and hardware. Sponsors research programs; maintains speakers' bureau. **Committees:** Government Relations; Marketing; Technical. **Formerly:** (1957) Frame Screen Manufacturers Association. **Publications:** Also publishes guides to product standards and test methods. **Conventions/Meetings:** semiannual conference.

1834 ■ Security Hardware Distributors Association (SHDA)
100 N 20th St., 4th Fl.
Philadelphia, PA 19103-1443
Ph: (215)564-3484
Fax: (215)564-2175
E-mail: shda@fernley.com
URL: http://www.shda.org
Contact: Bill Silver, Pres.
Founded: 1958. **Members:** 141. **Membership Dues:** distributor (based on sales volume), $450-$1,100 (annual) ● associate, $1,200 (annual). **Staff:** 3. **Description:** Wholesalers of locksmith supplies; associate members are manufacturers of locks and locksmith supplies. **Formerly:** (1998) National Locksmith Suppliers Association. **Publications:** *SHDA Unlocked*, monthly. Newsletter. Alternate Formats: online. **Conventions/Meetings:** annual conference, general membership (exhibits).

1835 ■ Spring Manufacturers Institute (SMI)
2001 Midwest Rd., Ste.106
Oak Brook, IL 60523-1335
Ph: (630)495-8588
Fax: (630)495-8595
E-mail: info@smihq.org
URL: http://www.smihq.org
Contact: Ken Boyce, Exec. VP
Founded: 1933. **Members:** 405. **Staff:** 5. **Regional Groups:** 9. **Description:** Manufacturers of precision mechanical springs and wire forms. Sponsors educational and research programs. Compiles statistics. Offers safety and regulatory compliance assistance to members. **Committees:** Associate Member Advisory; Benchmarking; Education; Industry Relations; Magazine; Meeting Site; Membership; National and

Legal Affairs; Regulatory Compliance; Technology; Women's. **Formerly:** (1961) Spring Manufacturers Association. **Publications:** *Coiler's Gazette*, quarterly. Newsletter. Includes legislative updates. **Price:** included in membership dues. **Circulation:** 750 ● *Encyclopedia of Spring Design*. Book. **Price:** $48.00/copy; $45.00 2-10 copies; $40.00 11-25 copies; $37.50 26 or more copies ● *Handbook of Spring Design*. **Price:** $15.00/copy; $12.60 2-9 copies; $10.20 10-49 copies; $8.40 50-99 copies ● *Mechanical Springs*. Book. **Price:** $67.00/copy ● *Springs: The International Magazine of Spring Manufacture*, quarterly. Provides technical reports and management and marketing information. For upper and middle management levels of spring manufacturing firms. **Price:** free. ISSN: 0584-9667. **Circulation:** 8,000. **Advertising:** accepted. **Conventions/Meetings:** semiannual conference.

1836 ■ The Transformer Association (TTA)
1300 Sumner Ave.
Cleveland, OH 44115-2851
Ph: (216)241-7333 (860)824-5125
Fax: (216)241-0105
E-mail: info@transformer-assn.org
URL: http://www.transformer-assn.org
Contact: Peter Kent, CEO/Chm.
Founded: 1974. **Members:** 53. **Membership Dues:** industry - supplier, $950 (annual) ● manufacturer, safety agency, $850 (annual). **Staff:** 2. **Budget:** $52,000. **Description:** Represents North American transformer and other power supply manufacturers and suppliers. Serves as a voice for the industry and to provide the following services: dialogue with safety and regulatory agencies such as UL and CSA International and standards writing bodies such as the IEC; gather and disseminate industry data; monitor and present industry trends at twice yearly meetings; provide other services to support and strengthen member company business prospects. **Affiliated With:** Power Sources Manufacturers Association. **Formerly:** (1993) Power Conversion Products Council International; (2001) PCPCI-The Transformer Association. **Conventions/Meetings:** semiannual meeting, with engineering and business presentations of interest to transformer manufacturers and suppliers (exhibits) - always spring and fall.

1837 ■ U.S. Hardware Industry Association (USHIA)
7115 W North Ave., No. 272
Oak Park, IL 60302
Ph: (708)453-0080
Fax: (708)453-0083
E-mail: ushia@rentamark.com
Founded: 1975. **Members:** 96,471. **Membership Dues:** professional, $50 (annual). **Staff:** 10. **Description:** Manufacturers, distributors, and retailers of hardware and related products. Seeks to advance the U.S. hardware industries. Provides trademark licensing and product and service endorsement services to support members' activities. A major platform for the US hardware industry where buyers, sellers, employers and employees can meet online. **Libraries: Type:** not open to the public. **Holdings:** 11,671. **Awards:** US Hardware Award of the Year. **Frequency:** annual. **Type:** recognition. **Computer Services:** Mailing lists, Ad Banner (468X60 Pixol) advertising the USHI website. **Also Known As:** (2000) Hardware Association. **Publications:** *USHIA Journal*, monthly. **Price:** included in membership dues. **Circulation:** 125,678. **Advertising:** accepted. Alternate Formats: online. **Conventions/Meetings:** annual convention.

1838 ■ Valve Manufacturers Association of America (VMA)
1050 17th St. NW, Ste.280
Washington, DC 20036
Ph: (202)331-8105 (540)374-9100
Fax: (202)296-0378
E-mail: wsandler@vma.org
URL: http://www.vma.org
Contact: Bill Sandler CAE, Pres.
Founded: 1938. **Members:** 100. **Membership Dues:** business (minimum), $1,500 (annual) ● associate, $2,500 (annual). **Staff:** 6. **Budget:** $1,200,000. **Description:** Manufacturers of industrial valves and actuators including gate valves, globe valves, check valves, water works, IBBM gate valves, tapping sleeves and crosses, fire hydrants, ball valves, butterfly valves, nonmetal valves, corrosion resistant valves, thru-conduit valves, plug valves, automatic control and regulating valves, solenoid valves, and safety and relief valves; as well as suppliers to the valve and actuator industry. Compiles statistical and biographical archives. Conducts research. **Libraries: Type:** reference. **Holdings:** 300. **Subjects:** technical and industry data. **Computer Services:** database, trade statistics. **Committees:** Communications; Education; Government Affairs; Meetings and Programs; Small Manufacturers; Statistics; Technical. **Formerly:** (1985) Valve Manufacturers Association. **Publications:** *Quick Read*, weekly. Newsletter. Covers meetings and studies sponsored by the VMA, changes in the industry and individual companies, government affairs, and international trade. **Price:** included in membership dues. **Circulation:** 1,000 ● *Sourcebook of U.S. and Canadian Valves*, biennial. Directory. Lists valve and actuator manufacturers and their products and services. Includes photographs, illustrations, and descriptions of valves. **Price:** $50.00 in U.S. and Canada; free if outside U.S. and Canada. **Circulation:** 15,000. **Advertising:** accepted ● *Valve Magazine*, quarterly. Informs those outside the valve industry of the role of valves in the process and distribution industries. **Price:** $28.00 /year for nonmembers in U.S.; $50.00 /year for nonmembers outside U.S.; included in membership dues. **Circulation:** 24,000 ● *VMA Directory*, annual. Membership Directory. Includes member companies' products. **Price:** free for members. **Circulation:** 600 ● Booklets ● Videos. **Conventions/Meetings:** annual meeting.

1839 ■ Valve Repair Council (VRC)
1050 17th St. NW, Ste.280
Washington, DC 20036
Ph: (202)331-0104
Fax: (202)296-0378
E-mail: mpasternak@vma.org
URL: http://www.unitedvalve.com/vr_council.htm
Contact: Marc Pasternak, Dir.
Founded: 1989. **Members:** 30. **Staff:** 1. **Budget:** $80,000. **Description:** Represents original Equipment Manufacturers who repair valves and actuators who are members of the Valve Manufacturers Association of America; independent repair shops authorized by OEM to repair their valves. Represents the interests of members. Promotes the OEM approach to repair. **Computer Services:** database. **Affiliated With:** Valve Manufacturers Association of America. **Formerly:** Valve Remanufacturers Council. **Publications:** *VRC Review*, quarterly. Newsletter. Contains articles on industry news, meetings, and company news. **Circulation:** 24,000. Alternate Formats: online. **Conventions/Meetings:** annual meeting.

1840 ■ Wire Fabricators Association (WFA)
PO Box 304
Montgomery, IL 60538
Ph: (630)896-1469
Fax: (209)633-6265
E-mail: rhoban@wirefabricators.org
URL: http://www.wirefabricators.org
Contact: Roseanne Hoban, Exec. Dir.
Founded: 1976. **Members:** 40. **Membership Dues:** associate, $1,000 (annual) ● fabricator, $400-$500 (annual). **Staff:** 4. **Multinational. Description:** Wire fabricating companies engaged in the production of grills, store shelves, refrigerator shelves, and other wire products. Aims to promote long-term stability in the wire fabricating industry. Provides Annual Labor Review Survey and Annual Financial Information Survey to members only. **Publications:** *Financial Information Report*, annual. **Price:** available to participants ● *Labor Report*, annual ● *Productivity Survey*. **Conventions/Meetings:** annual meeting - January ● quarterly meeting.

Health and Beauty Products

1841 ■ American Health and Beauty Aids Institute (AHBAI)
PO Box 19510
Chicago, IL 60619-0510
Ph: (708)333-8740
E-mail: ahbai1@sbcglobal.net
URL: http://www.ahbai.org
Contact: Layfayette Jones, Founder/Exec. Dir.
Founded: 1981. **Members:** 18. **Membership Dues:** associate, $950 (annual). **Staff:** 2. **Description:** Minority-owned companies engaged in manufacturing and marketing health and beauty aids for the black consumer. Represents the interests of members and the industry before local, state, and federal governmental agencies. Assists with business development and economic progress within the minority community by providing informational and educational resources. Maintains speakers' bureau. Conducts annual Proud Lady Beauty Show. **Committees:** Minority Development Political Action. **Publications:** Membership Directory, annual. **Conventions/Meetings:** annual conference, proud lady beauty show - midyear.

1842 ■ Cosmetic Executive Women (CEW)
286 Madison Ave., 19th Fl.
New York, NY 10017
Ph: (212)685-5955
Fax: (212)685-3334
E-mail: cew@cew.org
URL: http://cew.org
Contact: Carlotta Jacobson, Pres.
Founded: 1954. **Members:** 1,600. **Membership Dues:** regular, $175 (annual) ● young executive, $50 (annual). **Staff:** 11. **Regional Groups:** 1. **Description:** Women in the cosmetic and allied industries. Unites women executives in the cosmetic field for industry awareness and business advancement. Promotes products, people, professional development and philanthropy. **Awards:** Beauty Awards. **Frequency:** annual. **Type:** recognition. **Recipient:** for the most innovative beauty products of the year ● Best Boss Award. **Frequency:** annual. **Type:** recognition ● Cosmetic Executive Women Achiever Award. **Frequency:** annual. **Type:** recognition. **Recipient:** for women executives in beauty ● Inner Beauty Award. **Frequency:** annual. **Type:** recognition. **Formerly:** (1981) Cosmetic Career Women. **Publications:** *Membership Roster*, periodic. Membership Directory. **Conventions/Meetings:** annual Product Demonstration - trade show, over 300 products displayed (exhibits).

1843 ■ Cosmetic Industry Buyers and Suppliers (CIBS)
c/o Elizabeth Mount, Treas.
17 Ridgedale Rd.
Scarsdale, NY 10583
Ph: (212)319-6130
E-mail: webmaster@cibsonline.com
URL: http://cibsonline.com
Contact: William Standwill Sr., Pres.
Founded: 1948. **Members:** 385. **Membership Dues:** active, associate, $75 (annual) ● sustaining, $40 (annual). **Description:** Buyers and suppliers of essential oils, chemicals, packaging, and finished goods relative to the cosmetic industry. Enhances growth, stability, prosperity, and protection of the American cosmetic industry through close personal contact and the exchange of ideas and experiences. **Awards: Frequency:** annual. **Type:** monetary. **Recipient:** for best paper presented at Cosmetic, Toiletry, and Fragrance Association meeting ● **Frequency:** annual. **Type:** scholarship. **Recipient:** for an outstanding student attending Rutgers University School of Packaging. **Committees:** Christmas Dinner Dance; Ladies Day; Special Events. **Conventions/Meetings:** monthly meeting.

1844 ■ Cosmetic Ingredient Review (CIR)
1101 17th St. NW, Ste.412
Washington, DC 20036-4702
Ph: (202)331-0651
Fax: (202)331-0088
E-mail: cirinfo@cir-safety.org
URL: http://www.cir-safety.org
Contact: Wilma F. Bergfeld MD, Chair
Founded: 1976. **Staff:** 6. **Description:** A cosmetic industry self-regulatory organization sponsored by the Cosmetic, Toiletry, and Fragrance Association.

Seeks to assure the safety of ingredients used in cosmetics. Reviews scientific data on the safety of ingredients used in cosmetics; documents validity of tests used to study ingredients. **Libraries: Type:** by appointment only. **Subjects:** unpublished safety data used in ingredient reports. **Computer Services:** database, cosmetic ingredient safety information. **Affiliated With:** Cosmetic, Toiletry and Fragrance Association. **Publications:** *CIR Annual Report*, annual. **Price:** free ● *Final Reports on Cosmetic Ingredient Safety Assessments*, quarterly. Monographs. Presents all available published and unpublished safety data and conclusions regarding the safety of cosmetic ingredients. ● *International Journal of Toxicology*, 3/year ● Also publishes CIR Compendium, Scientific Literature Reviews (monographs) and Tentative Reports (monographs). **Conventions/Meetings:** quarterly Expert Panel - meeting.

1845 ■ Cosmetic, Toiletry and Fragrance Association (CTFA)
1101 17th St. NW, Ste.300
Washington, DC 20036-4702
Ph: (202)331-1770
Fax: (202)331-1969
E-mail: membership@ctfa.org
URL: http://www.ctfa.org
Contact: Pamela G. Bailey, Pres.
Founded: 1894. **Members:** 600. **Staff:** 49. **Budget:** $11,000,000. **Description:** Manufacturers and distributors of finished cosmetics, fragrances, and personal care products; suppliers of raw materials and services. Provides scientific, legal, regulatory, and legislative services. Coordinates public service, educational, and public affairs activities. **Libraries: Type:** reference. **Computer Services:** Online services, available to members only. **Telecommunication Services:** electronic mail, international@ctfa.org. **Committees:** Political Action; Small Business Forum. **Departments:** Administration; International; Legal; Legislative; Public Affairs; Scientific Advisory. **Formerly:** Toilet Goods Association; (1921) Manufacturing Perfumers Association of the United States; (1932) American Manufacturers of Toilet Articles; (1935) Associated Manufacturers of Toilet Articles. **Publications:** *Cosmetic Ingredient Dictionary and Handbook*, biennial. **Price:** $495.00 for members; $795.00 for nonmembers. Alternate Formats: CD-ROM ● *CTFA News*, biweekly. Newsletter. Alternate Formats: online ● *International Buyer's Guide*, annual ● *International Color Handbook*. **Price:** $325.00 for members; $450.00 for nonmembers ● *International Resource Manual*. **Conventions/Meetings:** annual meeting.

1846 ■ Foragers Cosmetic Industry Associates (FCIA)
135 E 55th St., 4th Fl.
New York, NY 10022-9625
Ph: (212)759-1991
Fax: (212)755-4841
E-mail: info@rafaj.com
URL: http://www.cosmeticindex.com/ci/for
Contact: Adam Finkelstein, Pres.
Founded: 1897. **Members:** 200. **Membership Dues:** regular, $125 (annual) ● regular, $200 (biennial). **Description:** Cosmetic sales executives and cosmetic buyers. Seeks to create a forum for both retailer and manufacturer to discuss their mutual problems. Conducts buyer symposia. **Formerly:** Foragers of America. **Conventions/Meetings:** annual meeting - always in New York City, NY.

1847 ■ Independent Cosmetic Manufacturers and Distributors (ICMAD)
1220 W Northwest Hwy.
Palatine, IL 60067
Ph: (847)991-4499
Free: (800)334-2623
Fax: (847)991-8161
E-mail: info@icmad.org
URL: http://www.icmad.org
Contact: Ms. Penni Jones, Exec. Dir.
Founded: 1974. **Members:** 750. **Membership Dues:** company in U.S. and Canada (based on annual sales), $450-$1,850 (annual) ● international, $400 (annual). **Staff:** 6. **Budget:** $500,000. **Description:** Represents small cosmetic manufacturers, distributors, retailers and suppliers. Presents members' views and problems to Congress, the FDA, consumers, and the media; areas of concern includes product testing procedures, escalating costs for product liability insurance, and manufacturing practice regulations. Upholds the principle of meaningful consumer protection. Provides a group program for product liability insurance. **Awards:** ICMAD Cosmetic Entrepreneur of the Year. **Frequency:** annual. **Type:** recognition. **Recipient:** for entrepreneurs with outstanding and innovative achievements in the cosmetic industry. **Programs:** Cosmetic Legislation Workshop; FedEx Discount Shipping Service; Foreign Market Advantage; Insurance Benefits. **Publications:** *A Simplified Guide to Cosmetic Labeling*, periodic. Manual. **Price:** $35.00 for members; $50.00 for nonmembers ● *Guide to European Cosmetic Regulations*. Book. **Price:** $75.00 for nonmembers; $25.00 for members ● *ICMAD Digest: A Synopsis of Matters Current and Important to the Cosmetic Industry*, 10/year. Newsletter. **Price:** available to members only. **Circulation:** 650. **Advertising:** accepted ● *South American Trade Guide*. Directory. **Price:** $150.00 for nonmembers; $75.00 for members ● Bulletin, periodic. **Conventions/Meetings:** annual meeting - usually June, New York City ● periodic workshop, cosponsored by the federal Food and Drug Administration.

Health Care

1848 ■ Association for Benchmarking in Health Care (ABHC)
c/o The Benchmarking Network
4606 FM 1960 W, Ste.250
Houston, TX 77069-9949
Ph: (281)440-5044
Free: (800)856-8546
Fax: (281)440-6677
E-mail: abhc@ebenchmarking.com
URL: http://www.abhc.org
Contact: Mark Czarnecki, Exec. Off.
Founded: 1998. **Members:** 2,000. **Staff:** 14. **Budget:** $2,000,000. **Description:** Employees of health care corporations with an interest in benchmarking. Promotes the use of benchmarking, wherein businesses compare their processes with those of their competitors, as a means of improving corporate efficiency and profitability. Facilitates exchange of information among members; conducts target operations, procurement, development, and maintenance studies; identifies model business practices. **Conventions/Meetings:** annual meeting and roundtable.

1849 ■ National Certification Council for Activity Professionals (NCCAP)
PO Box 62589
Virginia Beach, VA 23466
Ph: (757)552-0653
E-mail: info@nccap.org
URL: http://www.nccap.org
Contact: Cindy L. Bradshaw, Exec. Dir.
Description: Activity professionals. Serves as a credentialing body setting standards and criteria to ensure that those served have optimal life experiences. Member of the National Registry of Certified Activity Professionals. **Telecommunication Services:** electronic mail, nccapexec111@aol.com. **Committees:** Appeals; Certification Review; Nominations; Personnel. **Publications:** Newsletter, quarterly. **Advertising:** accepted. Alternate Formats: online.

1850 ■ National Council of Health Facilities Finance Authorities (NCHFFA)
2211 Clermont St.
Denver, CO 80207
E-mail: information@nhhefa.com
URL: http://www.nchffa.com
Contact: Corinne Johnson, Sec.
Founded: 1990. **Description:** Serves the common interests and improves effectiveness of member authorities through communication, education, and advocacy, with emphasis on issues which directly influence the availability of or access to tax-exempt financing for healthcare facilities. **Committees:** Advocacy; Communication; Convention; Disclosure; Education; Nominating; Rating Agency/Enhancement; Strategic Planning. **Publications:** Newsletter. Alternate Formats: online. **Conventions/Meetings:** annual conference.

1851 ■ National Council on Interpreting in Health Care (NCIHC)
270 W Lawrence St.
Albany, NY 12208
Fax: (518)459-3443
E-mail: info@ncihc.org
URL: http://www.ncihc.org
Contact: Wilma Alvarado-Little MA, Co-Chair
Founded: 1998. **Membership Dues:** individual, government employee, $35 (annual) ● organization, $100 (annual). **Description:** Promotes professional health care interpreting as a means to support equal access to health care for individuals with limited English proficiency. Serves as a clearinghouse for programs and policies to improve language access to health care for limited English-proficient patients. Sponsors a national dialogue of diverse voices and interests on related issues. **Telecommunication Services:** electronic mail, interpreter@walvarado-little.net. **Publications:** Bulletin, monthly. Alternate Formats: online ● Papers. Alternate Formats: online.

1852 ■ National Organization of Life and Health Insurance Guaranty Associations (NOLHGA)
13873 Park Center Rd., Ste.329
Herndon, VA 20171
Ph: (703)481-5206
Fax: (703)481-5209
E-mail: info@nolhga.com
URL: http://www.nolhga.com
Contact: Eugene Choate RHU, Chm.
Founded: 1983. **Members:** 52. **Description:** Promotes the life and health insurance guaranty industry.

1853 ■ Paraprofessional Healthcare Institute (PHI)
349 E 149th St., 10th Fl.
Bronx, NY 10451
Ph: (718)402-7766
Free: (866)402-4138
Fax: (718)585-6852
E-mail: info@phinational.org
URL: http://www.paraprofessional.org
Contact: Steven L. Dawson, Pres.
Description: Promotes quality care through quality jobs by strengthening the direct-care workforce in nation's long-term care system. Develops and promotes client-centered caregiving practices, effective public policy, and innovative approaches to recruitment, training, and supervision. **Computer Services:** Information services, online library. **Divisions:** National Clearinghouse on the Direct Care Workforce. **Subgroups:** Practice and Policy. **Publications:** *Cooperative Home Care Associates: A Case Study of a Sectoral Development Approach*. Report. Alternate Formats: online ● *Creating a Culture of Retention: A Coaching Approach to Paraprofessionals*. Report. Alternate Formats: online ● *Federal Study Shows Missing Links in CNA Training, Education*. Report ● *Finding and Keeping Direct Care Staff*. Report. Alternate Formats: online ● *Pioneering Culture Change*. Report ● *Quality Care Partners: A Case Study*. Report. Alternate Formats: online ● *Recruiting Quality Health Care Paraprofessionals*. Report. Alternate Formats: online ● *Training Quality Home Care Workers*. Report. Alternate Formats: online ● *We Are the Roots*. Book. **Price:** $10.00/copy plus shipping and handling ● *Why Workforce Development Should Be Part of the Long-Term Care Quality Debate*. Paper. Alternate Formats: online.

1854 ■ Workgroup for Electronic Data Interchange (WEDI)
12020 Sunrise Valley Dr., Ste.100
Reston, VA 20191
Ph: (703)391-2716

Fax: (703)391-2759
E-mail: jschuping@wedi.org
URL: http://www.wedi.org
Contact: James A. Schuping CAE, Exec. VP/CEO
Membership Dues: individual, $150-$300 (annual) ● affiliate, $500 (annual) ● government, $1,000 (annual) ● not-for-profit (based on gross healthcare-related revenues), $1,000-$2,000 (annual) ● for-profit (based on gross healthcare-related revenues), $1,000-$5,000 (annual). **Description:** Promotes Electronic Commerce in the Health Care Industry. **Publications:** *WEDI Outlook*, bimonthly. Newsletter. **Price:** included in membership dues. Alternate Formats: online. **Conventions/Meetings:** annual conference - every fall. 2008 Nov. 17-20, Indian Wells, CA.

Health Care Products

1855 ■ American Orthotic and Prosthetic Association (AOPA)

330 John Carlyle St., Ste.200
Alexandria, VA 22314
Ph: (571)431-0876
Fax: (571)431-0899
E-mail: info@aopanet.org
URL: http://www.aopanet.org
Contact: Devon Bernard, Membership Asst.
Founded: 1917. **Members:** 1,580. **Membership Dues:** affiliate, $255 (annual) ● education/research, patient care facility, $1,470 (annual) ● company, $1,395 (annual) ● international company, $735 (annual) ● supplier (based on gross sales volume), $1,735-$5,510 (annual). **Staff:** 25. **Budget:** $2,600,000. **Description:** Represents more than 1,400 member companies that custom fit or manufacture componentry for patients with prostheses (artificial limbs) and orthoses (braces). **Committees:** Coding; Government Relations; Insurance Advisory; Member Services. **Formerly:** (1937) Association of Limb Manufacturers of America; (1959) Orthopedic Appliance and Limb Manufacturers Association. **Publications:** *AOPA In Advance*, biweekly. Newsletter. Provides information for O&P businesses on government relations, state issues, reimbursement, general business issues. **Price:** included in membership dues. Alternate Formats: online. Also Cited As: *AIA* ● *AOPA Yearbook*, annual. Membership Directory. Contains indices and listings of member firms and their products. **Price:** first copy included in membership dues; $29.00 each additional copy; $120.00 /year for nonmembers. **Circulation:** 2,000. **Advertising:** accepted ● *O&P Almanac*, monthly. Magazine. Provides up-to-date information on healthcare reform, government relations, reimbursement, patient management, and association activities. **Price:** $59.00 /year for nonmembers in U.S.; $99.00 /year for nonmembers outside U.S.; included in membership dues. ISSN: 1061-4621. **Circulation:** 5,900. **Advertising:** accepted. **Conventions/Meetings:** annual assembly and trade show, features business, technical, and scientific programming, health care and government issues (exhibits) - always fall.

1856 ■ Contact Lens Manufacturers Association (CLMA)

PO Box 29398
Lincoln, NE 68529
Ph: (402)465-4122
Free: (800)344-9060
Fax: (402)465-4187
E-mail: clmassociation@aol.com
URL: http://www.clma.net
Contact: Ms. Janice Schramm, Pres.
Founded: 1961. **Members:** 107. **Staff:** 2. **Budget:** $800,000. **Multinational. Description:** Represents contact lens laboratories, material, solution and equipment manufacturers in the United States and abroad. Aims to increase awareness and utilization of custom manufactured contact lenses. **Libraries: Type:** open to the public. **Holdings:** archival material. **Awards:** Creative Design and Process Award. **Frequency:** periodic. **Type:** recognition. **Recipient:** for innovation in lens design and manufacturing process for the enhancement of the contact lens industry ● Dr. Joseph Dallos Award. **Frequency:** annual. **Type:** recognition. **Recipient:** for outstanding contribution to the development and advancement of the contact lens industry and for service to humanity ● GP Lens Practitioner of the Year. **Frequency:** annual. **Type:** recognition. **Recipient:** for outstanding professional expertise in fitting gas permeable contact lenses for the benefit of the contact lens industry and corneal health ● Honorary Recognition Award. **Frequency:** annual. **Type:** recognition. **Recipient:** for lifetime dedication and service to the contact lens industry ● Industry Enhancement Award. **Frequency:** annual. **Type:** recognition. **Recipient:** for unselfish dedication to the CLMA and the contact lens industry ● Leonardo da Vinci Award. **Frequency:** periodic. **Type:** recognition. **Recipient:** for vision in establishing the focus of the CLMA and dedication to the achievement of its goal ● Trailblazers Award. **Frequency:** annual. **Type:** recognition. **Recipient:** for outstanding achievement in product development for the enhancement of the contact lens industry. **Committees:** Associate Members; Awards; Convention; Government Affairs; International; Marketing; Member Services; Nominating. **Publications:** *The Contact Report*, bimonthly. Newsletter. Contains association activities update. **Price:** included in membership dues. **Circulation:** 200. **Advertising:** accepted. **Conventions/Meetings:** annual conference (exhibits) - always fall.

1857 ■ Contact Lens Society of America (CLSA)

441 Carlisle Dr.
Herndon, VA 20170
Ph: (703)437-5100
Free: (800)296-9776
Fax: (703)437-0727
E-mail: clsa@clsa.info
URL: http://www.clsa.info
Contact: Bruce Springer, Pres.
Founded: 1955. **Members:** 1,000. **Membership Dues:** affiliate, $145 (annual) ● regular, NCLE certified, $145 (annual) ● retired, $50 (annual) ● associate, $600 (annual) ● foundation donation, $250 (annual). **Staff:** 6. **Budget:** $750,000. **Description:** Contact lens fitters; manufacturers of products associated with contact lenses. Aims to share knowledge of contact lens technology and to foster the growth and ability of the contact lens technician throughout the world. Conducts activities such as: developing improvements in instrumentation, fitting procedures, and manufacturing processes; providing a national public relations medium through which information is disseminated to governmental agencies, legislative bodies, and other professional groups. Provides Home Study Course of Contact Lens Fitters. Operates speakers' bureau. **Libraries: Type:** reference. **Holdings:** archival material. **Computer Services:** Mailing lists. **Programs:** Basic Science of Contact Lens Technology; Contact Lens Business Management; Update and Review in Contact Lens Technology. **Affiliated With:** National Contact Lens Examiners. **Publications:** *CLSA Membership Directory*, annual ● *Eyewitness*, quarterly. Magazine. **Conventions/Meetings:** annual meeting (exhibits).

1858 ■ Dental Dealers of America (DDA)

Address Unknown since 2007
Founded: 1944. **Members:** 40. **Staff:** 2. **Budget:** $40,000. **Description:** Wholesale dealers of dental instruments, equipment, and supplies. Conducts educational activities; works for better manufacturer and professional relations. Maintains information and employment services. **Committees:** Education and Training; National Affairs; Programs; Trade and Professional Relations. **Publications:** Membership Directory, biennial. **Conventions/Meetings:** annual Fall Educational Program - meeting - always October or November ● annual symposium - always February, Chicago, IL.

1859 ■ Dental Trade Alliance (DTA)

2300 Clarendon Blvd., Ste.1003
Arlington, VA 22201
Ph: (703)379-7755
Fax: (703)931-9429
E-mail: info@dentaltradealliance.org
URL: http://www.dtanews.org
Contact: Vickie Waitsman, Chair
Founded: 2004. **Members:** 210. **Membership Dues:** distributor, manufacturer, and laboratory (minimum; based on annual gross sales), $1,600 (annual) ● associate, $2,500 (annual) ● distributor, manufacturer, and laboratory (maximum; based on annual gross sales), $22,000 (annual). **Description:** Represents dental manufacturers, dental dealers, dental laboratories, dental market service providers and dental publications. **Libraries: Type:** open to the public. **Holdings:** reports. **Awards:** Distinguished Service and Chairman's Award. **Frequency:** annual. **Type:** recognition. **Recipient:** for membership service and contributions to both dental industry and community. **Subcommittees:** Annual Summer Meeting; Bylaws; Credit Management; Dental Informatics; Distributors; Domestic Strategies; Exhibits; Exports and Foreign Strategies; Fall Education; Finance; Human Resources Opportunities; Laboratories; Long Range Planning; Manufacturers; Member Retention; Mentoring Program; New Member Liaison; Nominating; Past Presidents; Professional Relations; Prospective Member Programs; Regulatory Affairs; Service Providers; Trade Relations; Web Site Development; World Dental Trade Conference. **Formed by Merger of:** (2004) Dental Manufacturers of America; (2004) American Dental Trade Association. **Publications:** *Annual Operating Ratio for Distributors*, annual. Report. Features distributors' sales report. ● *Dental Trade Newsletter*, bimonthly ● *Update*, annual. Membership Directory. **Conventions/Meetings:** annual meeting (exhibits).

1860 ■ Health Industry Distributors Association (HIDA)

310 Montgomery St.
Alexandria, VA 22314-1516
Ph: (703)549-4432 (703)838-6118
Free: (800)549-4432
Fax: (703)549-6495
E-mail: rowan@hida.org
URL: http://www.hida.org
Contact: Matthew J. Rowan, Pres./CEO
Founded: 1902. **Members:** 225. **Membership Dues:** distributor (depends on the annual sales), $22,000 (annual) ● patron (associate-manufacturer), $22,000 (annual) ● benefactor (associate-manufacturer), $11,000 (annual) ● regular (associate-manufacturer), $5,000 (annual). **Staff:** 15. **Budget:** $3,000,000. **Description:** Represents distributors of medical, laboratory, surgical, and other health care equipment and supplies to hospitals, physicians, nursing homes, and industrial medical departments. Conducts sales training, management seminars, and research through the HIDA Educational Foundation. **Libraries: Type:** open to the public. **Holdings:** archival material, reports. **Awards:** Exhibit of the Year. **Frequency:** annual. **Type:** recognition. **Recipient:** for exceptional exhibits at the HIDA MedSurg Conference and Expo ● Frank M. Rhatigan Award. **Frequency:** annual. **Type:** recognition. **Recipient:** to recognize and encourage upgrading of sales product information and packaging ● Manufacturer Excellence in Service Award. **Frequency:** annual. **Type:** recognition. **Recipient:** for medical/surgical products manufacturers who support distributor efforts by providing the highest level of service ● Product of the Year. **Frequency:** annual. **Type:** recognition. **Recipient:** for new or innovative products offered by manufacturers in the medical products distribution industry ● Repertoire/HIDA Excellence in Sales Awards. **Frequency:** annual. **Type:** recognition. **Recipient:** for a distributor and manufacturer representative who has consistently demonstrated outstanding salesmanship and customer service in the medical products industry ● Sales Promotion of the Year. **Frequency:** annual. **Type:** recognition. **Recipient:** for exceptional sales promotions created by manufacturers and suppliers in the medical products distribution industry. **Computer Services:** Mailing lists, includes market breakdowns. **Committees:** Political Action. **Councils:** Advisory. **Absorbed:** Surgical Trade Foundation. **Formerly:** (1982) American Surgical Trade Association.

Publications: *Physicians Catalog* ● Annual Report, annual ● Membership Directory, annual. Includes Buyers Guide. ● Directory, annual. **Conventions/ Meetings:** annual MedSurg - trade show and conference (exhibits) - held in fall.

1861 ■ Hearing Industries Association (HIA)
515 King St., Ste.420
Alexandria, VA 22314
Ph: (703)684-5744
Fax: (703)684-6048
E-mail: crogin@clarionmanagement.com
URL: http://www.hearing.org
Contact: Carole M. Rogin, Pres.
Founded: 1957. **Members:** 32. **Staff:** 4. **Budget:** $1,700,000. **Description:** Companies engaged in the manufacture and/or sale of electronic hearing aids, their component parts, and related products and services on a national basis. Cooperates in and contributes toward efforts to promote the number of hearing aid users; collects trade statistics; conducts market research activities, investigations, and studies in connection with hearing and hearing aids. **Telecommunication Services:** electronic mail, ehawkins@clarionmr.com. **Committees:** Statistics; Technical; Trade Show Liaison. **Formerly:** (1977) Hearing Aid Industry Conference. **Conventions/Meetings:** annual conference.

1862 ■ Independent Medical Distributors Association (IMDA)
5204 Fairmount Ave.
Downers Grove, IL 60515
Free: (866)463-2937
Fax: (630)463-0798
E-mail: imda@imda.org
URL: http://www.imda.org
Contact: Katie Swartz, Exec. Dir.
Founded: 1978. **Members:** 70. **Membership Dues:** regular (based on product sales volume), $1,200-$5,200 (annual) ● allied, $2,500 (annual). **Staff:** 7. **Budget:** $170,000. **Description:** Represents sales, marketing and distribution organizations focused on bringing innovative medical technologies to market. Employs salespeople who are technically sophisticated, and who enjoy long-standing relationships with clinicians in their territories. **Libraries: Type:** open to the public. **Holdings:** archival material. **Publications:** *IMDA Directory*, annual. Membership Directory. Lists members and their area of specialty in the industry. **Price:** $175.00 ● *IMDA—Update*, monthly. Newsletter. Covers membership activities. **Price:** available to members only. Alternate Formats: online. **Conventions/Meetings:** annual conference and workshop (exhibits) - always June.

1863 ■ International Aloe Science Council (IASC)
415 E Airport Fwy., Ste.150
Irving, TX 75062-6350
Ph: (972)258-8772
Fax: (972)258-8777
E-mail: iasc1@msn.com
URL: http://www.iasc.org
Contact: Gene Hale, Exec. Dir.
Founded: 1981. **Members:** 262. **Membership Dues:** voting, $1,100-$2,000 (annual) ● associate, $250 (annual) ● subscriber in U.S., $100 (annual) ● subscriber (international), $125 (annual). **Staff:** 2. **Budget:** $250,000. **Local Groups:** 1. **For-Profit. Multinational. Description:** Manufacturers and marketers of foods, drugs, and cosmetics containing gel of the aloe vera plant. Aims to provide scientific research for support of product claims. Educates members on the plant and its products and uses. Acts as a liaison for government agency regulations on aloe vera business. **Libraries: Type:** open to the public. **Holdings:** 500; articles. **Subjects:** research in aloe. **Awards:** Reviewed Scientific Article. **Frequency:** annual. **Type:** monetary ● Yun Ho Lee Scientific Award. **Frequency:** annual. **Type:** recognition. **Recipient:** for outstanding scientific contribution in the field of aloe research. **Computer Services:** Mailing lists, of members. **Committees:** Code of Ethics; Public Relations; Scientific and Technical Research. **Formerly:** (1989) National Aloe Science Council. **Publications:** *Inside Aloe*, monthly. Journal. **Price:** included in membership dues. **Circulation:** 1,500. **Advertising:** accepted. **Conventions/Meetings:** annual conference and seminar, scientific (exhibits).

1864 ■ Optical Laboratories Association (OLA)
11096 Lee Hwy., Ste.A-101
Fairfax, VA 22030-5039
Ph: (703)359-2830
Free: (800)477-5652
Fax: (703)359-2834
E-mail: ola@ola-labs.org
URL: http://www.ola-labs.org
Contact: Robert L. Dziuban CAE, Exec. Dir.
Founded: 1894. **Members:** 375. **Membership Dues:** associate, $513 (annual) ● HMO/vision plan lab, $513-$4,613 (annual) ● allied lab, $513-$2,392 (annual) ● retail lab, $513-$7,175 (annual) ● participating lab, $513-$61,500 (annual) ● allied lab - wholesale, $513-$20,500 (annual). **Staff:** 8. **Budget:** $1,600,000. **Multinational. Description:** Represents independent, wholesale ophthalmic laboratories and suppliers serving the ophthalmic field. **Awards:** OLA Awards of Excellence. **Frequency:** annual. **Type:** recognition. **Committees:** American National Standards Z-80 Series; Eyewear Awareness; Eyewear Dispensing; Laboratory Techniques. **Formed by Merger of:** (1963) Optical Wholesalers National Association; Association of Independent Optical Wholesalers. **Formerly:** (1977) Optical Wholesalers Association. **Publications:** *ClearVisions*, quarterly. Newsletter. **Price:** free. **Circulation:** 3,000. **Advertising:** accepted. **Conventions/Meetings:** annual The OLA - convention (exhibits).

1865 ■ Orthopedic Surgical Manufacturers Association (OSMA)
PO Box 38805
Germantown, TN 38183
Ph: (901)754-8097 (901)758-0806
Fax: (901)754-8097
E-mail: secretary@osma.cc
URL: http://www.osma.cc
Contact: Susan Krasny PhD, Pres.
Founded: 1954. **Members:** 28. **Staff:** 1. **Description:** Works to unite interested manufacturers of orthopedic surgical items in order to enhance the contributions made by the industry to orthopedic health. Cooperates with professional health associations and government agencies. Promotes the development of high standards and ethics in all phases of the industry. Maintains task forces.

1866 ■ Vision Council of America (VCA)
1700 Diagonal Rd., Ste.500
Alexandria, VA 22314
Ph: (703)548-4560
Fax: (703)548-4580
E-mail: vca@visionsite.org
URL: http://www.visionsite.org
Contact: Edward E. Greene, Board Liaison/Chm.
Founded: 1985. **Members:** 600. **Membership Dues:** full/associate (based on sales), $2,000-$25,000 (annual) ● trade media, $3,000 (annual) ● laboratory in North America, $1,000 (annual). **Staff:** 12. **Budget:** $4,000,000. **Description:** Trade association of optical industry companies that sponsor exhibits at industry trade shows. Works to serve the collective interests of the ophthalmic community; encourages the public to visit eye care practitioners regularly. Seeks to produce top quality trade shows. Conducts public educational programs. **Affiliated With:** Better Vision Institute. **Formerly:** (1990) Vision Industry Council of America. **Conventions/Meetings:** semiannual International Vision Expo - meeting, for trade only (exhibits) - always New York City (International Vision Expo East) and California (Vision Expo West).

Health Plans

1867 ■ National Association of Alternative Benefits Consultants (NAABC)
435 Pennsylvania Ave.
Glen Ellyn, IL 60137-4401
Free: (800)627-0552
Fax: (630)858-2130
E-mail: naabcx@aol.com
URL: http://www.naabc.com
Contact: Harvey Randecker, Pres.
Membership Dues: general, $100 (annual). **Description:** Provides support and education for Health Savings Account (HSA) and other consumer-driven health plan producers and practitioners. Provides members with opportunities to share HSA and self-funding prospecting and sales ideas with other members. Provides a direct link to allied lobbying and grass-roots organizations that support the type of health care reform embodied in the HSA.

Health Professionals

1868 ■ Direct Care Alliance (DCA)
c/o Paraprofessional Healthcare Institute
349 E 149th St., 10th Fl.
Bronx, NY 10451
Ph: (718)402-7766
Fax: (718)585-6852
E-mail: info@directcarealliance.org
URL: http://www.directcarealliance.org
Founded: 1998. **Description:** Ensures a stable, valued and well-trained direct-care workforce that can meet consumers' demand for high quality paraprofessional healthcare services. Improves the quality of care for consumers through the creation of higher quality jobs and working conditions for direct care paraprofessional workers. **Affiliated With:** Paraprofessional Healthcare Institute.

1869 ■ National Healthcare Collectors Association (NHCA)
1502 Williamson Rd. NE, Ste.100
Roanoke, VA 24012
Free: (888)698-8022
Fax: (540)344-1211
E-mail: mpowell@scacreditservices.com
URL: http://www.nhca1.org
Contact: Michelle A. Powell, Contact
Membership Dues: regular/associate, $300-$400 (annual) ● hospital associate, $300 (annual). **Description:** Works for the free exchange of receivables information and technology. Promotes the healthcare owned credit/collection operations through networking and leadership expectations. **Publications:** *Collection Clips*. Newsletter.

Health Services

1870 ■ International Medical Spa Association (IMSA)
310 17th St.
Union City, NJ 07087
Ph: (201)865-2065
Fax: (201)865-3961
E-mail: medspaassn@aol.com
URL: http://www.medicalspaassociation.org
Contact: Hannelore R. Leavy, Founder/Exec. Dir.
Membership Dues: sustaining, $500 (annual) ● business, $295 (annual) ● individual, $150 (annual). **Multinational. Description:** Promotes innovation and cooperation within the medical spa industry. Seeks to develop and implement programs that will help shape and enhance the future of the medical spa industry. Promotes education, communication and standards of excellence for the medical spa profession. **Publications:** *Well-Med Spa News*. Newsletter. Alternate Formats: online.

1871 ■ Medical Spa Society (MSS)
60 E 56th St., 2nd Fl.
New York, NY 10022
Free: (866)633-4772
E-mail: info@medicalspasociety.com
URL: http://www.medicalspasociety.com
Contact: Dee Deluca Mattos, Pres.
Membership Dues: regular, $300 (annual). **Description:** Seeks to raise and uphold the level of professionalism practiced throughout the medical spa industry. Promotes education, communication and

standards of excellence for the medical spa profession. Encourages exchange of information and ideas that will further enhance the image and credibility of the medical spa industry. **Publications:** Brochure. Alternate Formats: online ● Newsletter, quarterly. **Price:** included in membership dues.

Heating and Cooling

1872 ■ Air Conditioning Contractors of America (ACCA)
2800 Shirlington Rd., Ste.300
Arlington, VA 22206
Ph: (703)575-4477
Fax: (703)575-4449
E-mail: info@acca.org
URL: http://www.acca.org
Contact: Paul T. Stalknecht, Pres./CEO
Founded: 1969. **Members:** 3,800. **Membership Dues:** HVACR contractor, $355 (annual) ● associate, $480 (annual) ● vocational/professional associate/facility operator, $180 (annual) ● affiliate (associate and contractor), $130 (annual). **Staff:** 24. **Budget:** $5,000,000. **Regional Groups:** 60. **State Groups:** 60. **Local Groups:** 60. **Description:** Contractors involved in installation and service of heating, air conditioning, and refrigeration systems. Associate members are utilities, manufacturers, wholesalers, and other market-oriented businesses. Monitors utility competition and operating practices of HVAC manufacturers and wholesalers. Provides consulting services, technical training, and instructor certification program; offers management seminars. Operates annual educational institute. **Libraries: Type:** reference. **Holdings:** 13; software. **Subjects:** load calculation, HVAC system design, duct design, residential and commercial equipment selection, psychrometrics. **Awards:** Quality Contractor of the Year. **Frequency:** annual. **Type:** recognition. **Recipient:** for contributions to increased quality performance of air conditioning contractors ● Small Contractor of the Year. **Frequency:** annual. **Type:** recognition. **Committees:** Career Development; Certification; Commercial and Residential; Government Relations; Industry Relations; Insurance; Labor Relations; Management Services; Safety; Structure and Organization; Unfair Utility Competition. **Formed by Merger of:** (1946) National Warm Air Heating and Air Conditioning Association; Air Conditioning and Refrigeration Contractors of America. **Formerly:** (1978) National Environmental Systems Contractors Association. **Publications:** *ACCA News*, 10/year. Newsletter. Provides information on management and contractor relations, manufacturing guidelines, industry trends, and legislation and regulations. **Price:** free for members and instructors. **Circulation:** 1,400. **Advertising:** accepted ● *ACCA Safety Sense*, monthly. Provides information to contractors on on-the-job safety. ● *ACCA Sales Bulletin*, monthly. Provides information to contractors on selling HVAC service and replacement. ● *ACCA Technical Bulletin*, monthly ● *Air Conditioning Contractors of America Membership Directory*, annual. **Price:** included in membership dues; $50.00 for nonmembers ● *Air Conditioning Contractors of America Quality Contractor's Catalog of Products and Services*, annual. Lists of technical manuals, business management books, ACCA technical software programs, slides, and other materials available to the industry. **Price:** free. **Circulation:** 3,300 ● *HVAC Instructor News*, semiannual. Newsletter. Contains new standards, trainings, and regulations. **Conventions/Meetings:** annual conference, includes indoor air expo (exhibits) - always in February or March.

1873 ■ Air-Conditioning and Refrigeration Institute (ARI)
4100 N Fairfax Dr., Ste.200
Arlington, VA 22203
Ph: (703)524-8800
Fax: (703)528-3816
E-mail: ari@ari.org
URL: http://www.ari.org
Contact: William G. Sutton, Pres.
Founded: 1953. **Members:** 207. **Staff:** 45. **Budget:** $9,000,000. **Languages:** English, French. **Description:** Manufacturers of air conditioning, refrigeration, and heating products and components. Develops and establishes equipment and application standards and certifies performance of certain industry products; provides credit and statistical services to members. Provides representation and technical assistance to government entities in federal, state, and local legislative matters; provides public relations, consumer education, and promotional programs for the industry. **Committees:** Audit; Budget; Certification Programs and Policy; Communications; Credit; Education; Exposition Policy; General Standards; General Statistics; Government Affairs; Industry Relations; International; Nominating; Planning; Research and Technology. **Sections:** Air-Conditioning Heat Transfer; Air Control and Distribution Devices; Air Filtration and Ultraviolet Light Treatment; Air-to-Air Energy Recovery Verification; Applied Packaged Systems; Automatic Commercial Ice Makers; Automatic Controls; Chemicals and Refrigerant Reclaimers; Compressors and Condensing Units; Cooling Towers; Dehumidifiers; Fans and Blowers; Flow and Contaminant Control Products; Heat Pump Pool and Spa Heaters; Humidifiers; Industrial Refrigeration and Heat Transfer Products; Liquid Chillers; Mobile Refrigeration; Reach in Manufacturers; Thermal Storage Equipment; Unitary Large Equipment; Unitary Small Equipment; Water Coolers. **Absorbed:** Commercial Refrigerator Manufacturers Division; (1965) Manufacturers Members of the National Warm Air Heating and Air Conditioning Association; (1967) Air Filter Institute. **Formed by Merger of:** Air-Conditioning and Refrigeration Machinery Association; Refrigeration Equipment Manufacturers Association. **Publications:** *ARI Curriculum Guide*. Handbook ● *Koldfax*, monthly. Newsletter. **Price:** free. Alternate Formats: online ● *Minuteman*, monthly. Bulletin. Contains government affairs policy letter. **Price:** free, for members only. Alternate Formats: online. **Conventions/Meetings:** International Air-Conditioning, Heating, and Refrigeration Exposition - meeting ● annual meeting.

1874 ■ Air Diffusion Council (ADC)
1901 N Roselle Rd., Ste.800
Schaumburg, IL 60195
Ph: (847)706-6750
Fax: (847)706-6751
E-mail: info@flexibleduct.org
URL: http://www.flexibleduct.org
Contact: Jack Lagershausen, Exec. Dir.
Founded: 1961. **Members:** 50. **Staff:** 2. **Description:** Manufacturers and suppliers of flexible air duct. Administers industry-wide testing and rating standards for members' products. Participates in activities related to air duct performance and installation education. **Committees:** Engineering; Marketing. **Publications:** *Flexible Duct Performance and Installation Standards*, periodic. Manual. Includes installation guidelines and performance criteria. **Price:** $15.00/hardcopy or PDF file download; $10.00 CD-ROM. Alternate Formats: online; CD-ROM ● Also publishes test codes. **Conventions/Meetings:** semiannual meeting.

1875 ■ Air Distribution Institute (ADI)
4415 W Harrison St., Ste.322
Hillside, IL 60162
Ph: (708)449-2933
Fax: (708)449-0837
E-mail: info@steelduct.org
URL: http://www.steelduct.org
Contact: Patricia H. Keating, Gen. Mgr.
Founded: 1947. **Members:** 26. **Membership Dues:** regular, $2,000 (annual). **Staff:** 2. **Description:** Manufacturers of prefabricated pipes, ducts, and fittings used in the residential air distribution industry. Promotes the industry and works to improve its products. Conducts sales surveys and compiles statistics. **Telecommunication Services:** electronic mail, adi-general-manager@steelduct.org. **Committees:** Statistical; Technical. **Publications:** Bulletin, monthly.

1876 ■ Air Movement and Control Association International (AMCA International)
30 W Univ. Dr.
Arlington Heights, IL 60004-1806
Ph: (847)394-0150
Fax: (847)253-0088
E-mail: bmorrison@amca.org
URL: http://www.amca.org
Contact: Barbara L. Morrison, Exec. Dir.
Founded: 1954. **Members:** 302. **Membership Dues:** full, joint, international, $3,600 (annual). **Staff:** 22. **Regional Groups:** 6. **Multinational. Description:** Manufacturers of air movement and control equipment and related air systems equipment. Conducts research on improvement of methods of testing; develops standards for fans, louvers, dampers, shutters, and similar equipment. Operates testing laboratory and performance certification programs for fans and other devices. **Libraries: Type:** open to the public. **Holdings:** 46. **Subjects:** air systems equipment. **Divisions:** Acoustic Attenuation; Air Control; Air Movement; Airflow Measurement; Residential Ventilation. **Formed by Merger of:** (1955) National Association of Fan Manufacturers; Industrial Unit Heater Association; Power Fan Manufacturers Association. **Formerly:** (1967) Air Moving and Conditioning Association; (1999) Air Movement and Control Association. **Publications:** *AMCA International Newsletter*, quarterly. **Price:** free. Alternate Formats: online ● *Engineering Newsletter*, semiannual ● *TECHSPECS*, semiannual. Newsletter ● Also publishes standards, certification programs and application guides. **Conventions/Meetings:** annual meeting (exhibits).

1877 ■ Association of Refrigerant and Desuperheating Manufacturing (ARDM)
Addison Products Co.
ECU Div.
PO Box 607776
7050 Overland Rd.
Orlando, FL 32810
Ph: (407)290-1329 (407)292-4400
Fax: (407)290-1329
E-mail: info@addison-hvac.com
URL: http://www.addison-hvac.com
Contact: Rodney E. Weaver, Pres.
Founded: 1987. **Members:** 15. **Description:** Manufacturers of desuperheaters and heat recovery systems. Seeks to improve waste heat recovery systems. Conducts research; advocates certification of all heat recovery systems. **Publications:** *Directory of Certified Desuperheater Manufacturers*, semiannual ● *Information Guide*. **Conventions/Meetings:** annual meeting.

1878 ■ Commercial Refrigerator Manufacturers Division (CRMD)
4100 N Fairfax Dr., Ste.200
Arlington, VA 22203
Ph: (703)524-8800
Fax: (703)524-9011
E-mail: crm@ari.org
URL: http://ariadman.tempdomainname.com/crm
Contact: Stephen Yurek, Contact
Founded: 2000. **Members:** 45. **Staff:** 2. **Budget:** $140,000. **Description:** Manufacturers of refrigerated display cases and cabinets, food service refrigerators, and sectional cooling rooms. Seeks to provide a voice for manufacturers and suppliers to address industry developments and problems with companies who share common interests. Maintains a continuing presence within Congress and government agencies to monitor and respond to policies and regulations affecting the industry and represent the collective interests of members. Acts as a clearinghouse on information including foreign sales opportunities, technological developments, domestic markets, and other data of importance to the refrigeration industry. Provides technical information concerning regulations to governmental agencies. Conducts research to eliminate waste and increase efficiency of the production, distribution, and marketing of merchandise, products, or equipment related to the industry. Develops health and sanitation standard for retail food store refrigerators. Compiles statistics. **Committees:** Technical. **Publications:** *CRMA Newsbreak*, periodic. Newsletter ● *Recommended Guidelines for Retail Food Store Design*, annual ● *Recommended Guidelines for Retail Food Store Energy*

Conservation, periodic ● *Voluntary Minimum Standard for Retail Food Store Refrigerators-Health and Sanitation*, annual. **Conventions/Meetings:** semiannual meeting - always January and June in Washington, DC ● annual meeting, held in conjunction with ARI.

1879 ■ Evaporative Cooling Institute (ECI)
MSC 3ECI - NMSU
PO Box 30001
Las Cruces, NM 88003-8001
Ph: (505)646-1846
Fax: (505)646-3841
E-mail: moreinfo@evapcooling.org
URL: http://www.evapcooling.org
Contact: Robert Foster, Treas.
Founded: 1989. **Members:** 60. **Membership Dues:** voting, $300 (annual) ● associate/non-voting, $60 (annual). **Languages:** English, Portuguese, Spanish. **Description:** Represents manufacturers of evaporative apparatus; designers, specifiers, and users of heating, ventilating, and air conditioning systems; sales representatives; representatives of educational and governmental agencies; interested individuals. Seeks to advance the art and science of evaporative air cooling and air conditioning by: promoting the technology and industry; collecting and publishing information on applying, installing, operating, and maintaining evaporative systems; disseminating information on codes, standards, and certification programs; identifying and encouraging research; maintaining contact with related trade associations, professional societies, government agencies, and customers. **Libraries: Type:** reference. **Holdings:** 150; books, clippings, periodicals. **Subjects:** evaporative and desiccant coding. **Awards:** Honorary Life Membership Award. **Type:** recognition. **Recipient:** for outstanding lifetime achievements in the evaporative cooling field. **Publications:** *Cool Air News*, semiannual. Newsletter. **Circulation:** 400. **Advertising:** accepted ● *Evaporative Air-conditioning Applications for Environmentally Friendly Cooling.* Paper. **Price:** $20.00 for members; $30.00 for nonmembers ● *Membership Services Directory*, annual. Membership Directory. **Circulation:** 1,000. **Advertising:** accepted. Alternate Formats: online. **Conventions/Meetings:** semiannual meeting.

1880 ■ Hearth Education Foundation
Dept. 4045
Washington, DC 20042-4045
Ph: (703)524-8030
Fax: (703)522-0548
E-mail: info@hearthedducation.org
URL: http://www.hearthedducation.org
Contact: Caleb Woodard, Contact
Founded: 1981. **Staff:** 2. **Nonmembership. Description:** Seeks to serve the public interest in advancing the safe and efficient use of hearth appliances including wood stoves, fireplaces, pallet and gas appliances. Provides certification exams to wood stove, fireplace, pellet and gas appliance installers and inspectors. **Affiliated With:** Hearth, Patio and Barbeque Association. **Formerly:** (1993) Wood Heating Education and Research Foundation. **Publications:** *Educational Training Manual.* **Price:** $125.00 ● *Fireplace Installer.* Manual. Contains information on specific health products, venting, installation, clearances, and troubleshooting. **Price:** $125.00 ● *Gas Appliance Specialist.* Manual. Contains information on specific health products, venting, installation, clearances, and troubleshooting. **Price:** $125.00 ● *Hearth Handbook for Building Officials.* Organizes and clarifies the world of hearth. **Price:** $49.95 each; $89.95/2 copies ● *Pellet Appliance Specialist.* Manual. Contains information on specific health products, venting, installation, clearances, and troubleshooting. **Price:** $95.00 plus shipping and handling ($5) ● *Woodstove Specialist.* Manual. Contains information on specific health products, venting, installation, clearances, and troubleshooting. **Price:** $125.00. **Conventions/Meetings:** periodic board meeting.

1881 ■ Heat Exchange Institute (HEI)
1300 Sumner Ave.
Cleveland, OH 44115-2851
Ph: (216)241-7333
Fax: (216)241-0105
E-mail: hei@heatexchange.org
URL: http://www.heatexchange.org
Contact: R. Christopher Johnson, Contact
Founded: 1933. **Members:** 16. **Staff:** 3. **Description:** Represents manufacturers of steam condensers, closed feedwater heaters, steam jet ejectors, liquid ring vacuum pumps, power plant heat exchangers, and deaerators. **Sections:** Closed Feedwater Heaters; Daearators; Power Plant Heat Exchangers; Steam Surface Condensers; Vacuum Technology. **Conventions/Meetings:** semiannual meeting.

1882 ■ Heating, Airconditioning and Refrigeration Distributors International (HARDI)
1389 Dublin Rd.
Columbus, OH 43215-1084
Ph: (614)488-1835
Free: (888)253-2128
Fax: (614)488-0482
E-mail: hardimail@hardinet.org
URL: http://www.hardinet.org
Contact: Mark Faessler, Pres.
Founded: 2003. **Members:** 1,200. **Membership Dues:** corporate wholesaler and integrated wholesale distributor, $5,300 (annual) ● international wholesaler, $270 (annual) ● plan and spec distributor, $530 (annual) ● supplier (manufacturer representative supplier), $375 (annual) ● service vendor and marketing/purchasing cooperative, $430-$1,285 (annual) ● supplier (manufacturer), $530-$1,485 (annual) ● wholesaler, $590-$3,025 (annual). **Staff:** 20. **Description:** Serves as an information conduit by which companies learn about and explore trends in the industry and an educational provider that conducts meetings and publishes educational materials. **Committees:** Education and Program Planning; Executive and Finance; Industry Statistics; Insurance/Safety; Marketing Strategies; Membership Development; Technology; Young Executives. **Formed by Merger of:** (2003) Air-Conditioning and Refrigeration Wholesalers International; (2003) Northamerican Heating, Refrigeration, and Airconditioning Wholesalers Association. **Publications:** *Action Alerts*, periodic. **Advertising:** accepted ● *Counterline*, quarterly. Newsletter ● *HVAC/R Distribution Today*, quarterly. Magazine. **Price:** included in membership dues. **Advertising:** accepted ● *Key Personnel*, biennial. Directory. **Price:** free, for members only ● *Young Executives.* Directory. **Price:** free, for members only. **Circulation:** 700 ● Membership Directory. **Price:** $10.00 for members; $100.00 for nonmembers. **Advertising:** accepted. **Conventions/Meetings:** annual convention and conference (exhibits) - always in October or November. 2008 Oct. 25-28, Phoenix, AZ; 2009 Oct. 31-Nov. 3, Orlando, FL.

1883 ■ Home Ventilating Institute (HVI)
1000 N Rand Rd., Ste.214
Wauconda, IL 60084
Ph: (847)526-2010
Fax: (847)526-3993
E-mail: hvi@hvi.org
URL: http://www.hvi.org
Founded: 1955. **Members:** 34. **Membership Dues:** regular, $2,000 (annual) ● associate, $2,500 (annual). **Staff:** 2. **Description:** Aims to serve consumers and members by advancing residential ventilation. Provides a forum for industry to meet and discuss common issues. **Committees:** Continuous Ventilating Product; Engineering; Intermittent Ventilating Product; Sale and Marketing; Static Ventilating Product. **Formerly:** (1984) Home Ventilating Institute; (2006) Home Ventilating Institute Division of the Air Movement Control Association. **Publications:** *Certified Home Ventilating Products Directory*, annual. Provides information about certified ventilating devices for residences. **Price:** free ● *Home Ventilating Guide*, periodic. Brochures. Covers recommended home ventilation techniques. ● Brochures. **Conventions/Meetings:** annual meeting - always in spring.

1884 ■ Hydronics Institute Division of GAMA (HI)
PO Box 218
Berkeley Heights, NJ 07922-0218
Ph: (908)464-8200
Fax: (908)464-7818
E-mail: certification@gamanet.org
URL: http://www.gamanet.org
Contact: Lawrence Longo, Mgr. of Certification Services
Founded: 1970. **Members:** 62. **Staff:** 5. **Description:** Represents manufacturers of hydronic (hot water and steam) heating and cooling equipment. Sponsors educational programs in selected cities. Compiles statistics. **Committees:** Baseboard Technical; Boiler Technical; Burners and Components; Educational; Finned Tube Technical; Indirect Water Heaters. **Affiliated With:** Radiant Panel Association. **Absorbed:** (1989) Hydronic Radiant Heating Association. **Formed by Merger of:** Institute of Boiler and Radiator Manufacturers; Better Heating-Cooling Council. **Formerly:** (1997) Hydronics Institute. **Publications:** Distributes instruction guides and handbooks. **Conventions/Meetings:** semiannual conference.

1885 ■ Industrial Heating Equipment Association (IHEA)
PO Box 54172
Cincinnati, OH 45254
Ph: (513)231-5613
Fax: (513)624-0601
E-mail: ihea@ihea.org
URL: http://www.ihea.org
Contact: Anne Goyer, Exec. VP
Founded: 1929. **Members:** 50. **Membership Dues:** manufacturer, $2,500 (annual) ● professional service, $3,000 (annual). **Staff:** 2. **Budget:** $200,000. **Description:** Manufacturers of industrial furnaces, ovens, combustion equipment, atmosphere generators, induction and dielectric heating equipment, industrial heaters, process controls, fuel saving and heating devices, and heat recovery equipment. **Committees:** Education; Energy and Environmental; International Trade; Legislative Action; Public Relations; Safety Standards and Codes; Statistical. **Divisions:** Combustion; Industrial Heating Equipment; Oven; Process Controls; Vacuum Furnaces. **Formerly:** (1954) Industrial Furnace Manufacturers Association. **Publications:** *Annual Operating Ratio Report.* Annual Report ● *Combustion Technology Manual* ● *IHEA News*, quarterly. Newsletter. For industrial heating equipment manufacturers. ● *Membership and Information Directory.* Membership Directory ● *News Compendium*, periodic ● *Quarterly Statistical Reports.* **Conventions/Meetings:** annual Fall Business Conference ● annual meeting - always spring ● annual seminar (exhibits).

1886 ■ International Association for Cold Storage Construction (IACSC)
1500 King St., Ste.201
Alexandria, VA 22314
Ph: (703)373-4300
Fax: (703)373-4301
E-mail: email@iacsc.org
URL: http://www.iacsc.org
Contact: J. William Hudson, Pres./CEO
Founded: 1978. **Members:** 150. **Membership Dues:** in U.S., $1,825 (annual) ● outside U.S., $1,145 (annual). **Staff:** 4. **Budget:** $75,000. **Description:** Seeks to ensure high standards and professionalism in the cold storage insulation industry that involves insulating, designing, and building coolers, freight cars, industrial freezers, and other types of industrial refrigeration. Aims to improve business operations. Works to carry out insurance survey work. Acts as a clearinghouse for technical information. Compiles industry statistics. **Committees:** Government Affairs; Government Relations; Insurance; Standards of Practice; Statistics; Supplier; Technical. **Formerly:** (1985) National Association of Cold Storage Insulation Contractors; (1987) National Association of Cold Storage Contractors; (2003) International Association of Cold Storage Contractors. **Publications:** *IACSC's Design, Construction, Specification, and Fire Man-*

agement of Insulated Envelopes for Temperature Controlled Environments, 1999, semiannual. Book. **Price:** $195.00 for members; $350.00 for nonmembers. **Circulation:** 400. **Advertising:** accepted ● *International Cold Chain Directory, 2006-Membership Directory*, annual. Contains a listing of cold storage contractors and suppliers. **Price:** included in membership dues (first copy only); $18.00 per additional copy. **Circulation:** 2,000. **Advertising:** accepted. **Conventions/Meetings:** annual meeting (exhibits).

1887 ■ International Compressor Remanufacturers Association (ICRA)
PO Box 33092
Kansas City, MO 64114
Ph: (816)333-7205 (913)764-6546
Fax: (816)822-8826
E-mail: icracomp@icracomp.com
Contact: John Clark, Technical Coor.

Founded: 1965. **Members:** 60. **Membership Dues:** active, $500 (annual) ● associate, $500 (annual). **Staff:** 2. **Budget:** $30,000. **Multinational. Description:** Persons, firms, and corporations engaged in the business of remanufacturing and rebuilding refrigeration and air conditioning compressors. Seeks to foster trade, commerce, and interest of those engaged in the rebuilding, exchanging, and repairing of refrigeration and allied equipment. Promotes uniformity and certainty in the trade customs of those with an interest in the industry. Collects and disseminates information of value to members and the public; arbitrates differences among members. **Libraries: Type:** not open to the public. **Subjects:** technical information on file. **Awards:** ICRA Auxillary Scholarship. **Frequency:** annual. **Type:** scholarship. **Recipient:** for works in industry. **Formerly:** (1970) Independent Hermetic Rebuilders Association; (1988) Refrigeration Compressor Rebuilders Association. **Publications:** *ICRA Racket*, periodic. Newsletter ● Directory, annual. **Conventions/Meetings:** annual seminar and convention - fall.

1888 ■ International District Energy Association (IDEA)
125 Turnpike Rd., Ste.4
Westborough, MA 01581-2841
Ph: (508)366-9339
Fax: (508)366-0019
E-mail: idea@districtenergy.org
URL: http://www.districtenergy.org
Contact: Robert P. Thornton, Pres.

Founded: 1909. **Members:** 930. **Membership Dues:** physical plant, $645 (annual) ● manufacturer/supplier, $2,010 (annual) ● DHC association and system outside North America, $695 (annual) ● company (staff of six or more), $1,340 (annual) ● company (staff of five or fewer), $375 (annual) ● government employee/student, $95 (annual). **Staff:** 2. **Budget:** $800,000. **Multinational. Description:** Suppliers of space heating by means of steam and hot water, and air conditioning by means of steam and chilled water, via piping systems from a central station to groups of buildings. **Awards:** Environmental Champion Award. **Frequency:** annual. **Type:** recognition. **Recipient:** for longstanding commitment to sound environmental policy ● IDEA Unsung Hero Award. **Frequency:** annual. **Type:** recognition. **Recipient:** for an IDEA member who has performed above and beyond the call of duty on behalf of the industry and the Association ● Norman R. Taylor Award. **Frequency:** annual. **Type:** recognition. **Recipient:** for an individual who has contributed to the district heating and cooling industry ● System of the Year Award. **Frequency:** annual. **Type:** recognition. **Recipient:** for an exemplary district energy system providing high-level performance and service. **Committees:** College/University; Cooling; Distribution; Federal; Fuels; Legislative; Marketing; Measurement and Controls; R&D; Safety, Environment and Operations. **Formerly:** National District Heating Association; International District Heating and Cooling Association; (1984) International District Heating Association. **Publications:** *District Energy*, quarterly. Magazine. **Price:** $50.00 /year for nonmembers in U.S.; $75.00 /year for nonmembers outside U.S.; $40.00 /year for members in U.S.; $65.00 /year for members outside U.S. ISSN: 1077-6222. **Circulation:** 3,500. **Advertising:** accepted ● *District Energy Now*, quarterly. Newsletter. Available online only. **Price:** available to members only. Alternate Formats: online ● *International District Energy Association—Membership Directory*, annual. Also available online with paid membership. **Price:** available to members only. Alternate Formats: online ● *International District Energy Association—Proceedings*, annual. **Price:** $75.00/copy for members; $150.00/copy for nonmembers. **Circulation:** 600 ● *Manual of District Heating* ● *Principles of Economical Heating* ● *Unwin's Chart for Measuring Steam Flow in Piping* ● Handbook. **Conventions/Meetings:** annual conference and trade show, a vendor and manufacturer exclusive trade show - 2008 June 29-July 2, Orlando, FL; 2009 June 28-July 1, Arlington, VA ● annual conference.

1889 ■ International Ground Source Heat Pump Association (IGSHPA)
374 Cordell S
Stillwater, OK 74078-8018
Ph: (405)744-5175
Free: (800)626-4747
Fax: (405)744-5283
E-mail: igshpa@okstate.edu
URL: http://www.igshpa.okstate.edu
Contact: Lisa McArthur, Asst. Dir.

Founded: 1987. **Members:** 2,000. **Membership Dues:** student, $26 (annual) ● individual/associate, $105 (annual) ● architect, engineer, dealer, contractor, $420 (annual) ● product distributor, $525 (annual) ● association, $640 (annual) ● holding company, utility, manufacturer, foundation, $1,430 (annual) ● manufacturer 2, $905 (annual) ● manufacturer 1, foundation, $1,430 (annual). **Staff:** 11. **Budget:** $500,000. **Multinational. Description:** Manufacturers, distributors, and contractors in the ground source heat pump systems and products industry. Seeks to educate the public about ground source heat pump systems and promote their use as economical energy saving systems. (The system consists of a water source heat pump connected to a plastic pipe buried in the ground in which the earth supplies energy for space heating, domestic water heating, and a place to waste excess heat during cooling cycles.) Sponsors teleconferences, exhibits at trade show, and conducts training workshops. **Awards:** E.B. Penrod and Engineer of the Year. **Frequency:** annual. **Type:** recognition. **Recipient:** for outstanding contribution to GHP. **Councils:** Advisory. **Publications:** *Closed-Loop Ground-Source Heat Pump Systems Installation Guide*. Manual ● *Grouting Procedures for Ground Source Heat Pump Systems*. Manual. **Price:** $25.00 for members (1-27 copies); $35.00 for nonmembers (1-27 copies) ● *Installation Guide*. Manual. **Price:** $65.00 for members; $95.00 for nonmembers ● *The Source*, bimonthly. Newsletter. **Advertising:** accepted. **Conventions/Meetings:** annual May Tech - conference, includes exposition (exhibits) - May ● periodic workshop.

1890 ■ International Institute of Ammonia Refrigeration (IIAR)
1110 N Glebe Rd., Ste.250
Arlington, VA 22201
Ph: (703)312-4200
Fax: (703)312-0065
E-mail: request_info@iiar.org
URL: http://www.iiar.org
Contact: Jeff Welch, Chm.

Founded: 1971. **Members:** 1,200. **Membership Dues:** academic, affiliate, retired, $100 (annual) ● contractor, end user I, international organization, engineer, manufacturer's representative, wholesaler, $675 (annual) ● end user II, $380 (annual) ● student, $25 (annual) ● manufacturer, $975 (annual) ● associate, $260 (annual). **Staff:** 6. **Budget:** $550,000. **Languages:** English, Spanish. **Description:** Ammonia equipment manufacturers, consultants, contractors, wholesalers, and anhydrous ammonia users from 20 countries. Works to provide education, information, and standards for the proper and safe use of ammonia as a refrigerant. **Libraries: Type:** reference. **Holdings:** audiovisuals. **Committees:** Code; Education; Government Relations; Safety; Standards Review. **Affiliated With:** American National Standards Institute; American Society of Heating, Refrigerating and Air-Conditioning Engineers; Building Officials and Code Administrators International. **Publications:** *NH3 News*, quarterly. Newsletter ● Pamphlets. Contains safety procedures. **Conventions/Meetings:** annual conference and trade show (exhibits).

1891 ■ International Packaged Ice Association (IPIA)
PO Box 1199
Tampa, FL 33601-1199
Ph: (813)258-1690
Free: (800)237-8350
Fax: (813)882-3702
E-mail: cmaginnis@leerlp.com
URL: http://www.packagedice.org
Contact: Charlotte Maginnis, Sec./Asst. Treas.

Founded: 1917. **Members:** 160. **Staff:** 5. **Regional Groups:** 8. **Description:** Manufacturers and distributors of packaged ice; associate members are manufacturers of ice making equipment and supplies. Major activities are in public relations, technology, sanitation, government relations, and merchandising. Sponsors hall of fame. **Computer Services:** database, industry, associate information as well as advertising agencies and prospects ● mailing lists, can be purchased. **Committees:** Food Safety; Government Relations; Plant Operations; Research. **Formerly:** (1958) National Association of the Ice Industries; (1980) National Ice Association; (1998) Packaged Ice Association. **Publications:** *Building Packaged Ice Profits with the Highest Quality Ice*, bimonthly. Brochure ● *Ice News*, bimonthly. Newsletter ● *Ice World*, quarterly. Journal ● Bulletins. Contains management and technical information. ● Membership Directory, annual ● Also publishes management and technical bulletins. **Conventions/Meetings:** annual conference and trade show (exhibits).

1892 ■ Masonry Heater Association of North America (MHA)
c/o Richard Smith, Admin.
2180 S Flying Q Ln.
Tucson, AZ 85713
Ph: (520)883-0191
Fax: (520)883-0191
E-mail: rsmith@boreal.org
URL: http://www.mha-net.org
Contact: Richard Smith, Admin.

Founded: 1981. **Members:** 60. **Membership Dues:** associate, $100 (annual) ● voting, $250 (annual). **Staff:** 1. **Description:** Represents builders, manufacturers and retailers of masonry heaters. Seeks to promote the industry, sponsor research and development, shape regulations, standards and codes, inform and educate the public, and further the expertise and professionalism of its membership. **Computer Services:** database, ACT ● mailing lists. **Publications:** *Masonry Heaters - The Intelligent Choice*. Pamphlet. Contains brochure. ● *The Mortar Board*, periodic. Newsletter. **Conventions/Meetings:** annual meeting, with workshops for heaters and bakeovens ● annual meeting.

1893 ■ Mobile Air Conditioning Society Worldwide (MACS)
PO Box 88
Lansdale, PA 19446
Ph: (215)631-7020
Fax: (215)631-7017
E-mail: info@macsw.org
URL: http://www.macsw.org
Contact: Elvis Hoffpauir, Pres./COO

Founded: 1981. **Members:** 1,691. **Membership Dues:** manufacturer/supplier, $700 (annual) ● distributor, $400 (annual) ● servicer and installer, $200 (annual) ● educational/training facility, $140 (annual). **Staff:** 14. **Multinational. Description:** Distributors, service specialists, installers, manufacturers, and suppliers of automotive and truck air conditioners and parts. Works to disseminate information and develop specialized education. **Libraries: Type:** not open to the public. **Subjects:** automotive and truck air conditioners. **Awards:** Mobile A/C Pioneer Award. **Frequency:** annual. **Type:** recognition ● Simon Oulouhojian Achievement Award. **Frequency:** annual. **Type:** recognition. **Computer Services:** Online services, certification testing and training materials. **Formerly:** (1994) Mobile Air Conditioning Society. **Publications:** *Action*, 7/year. Magazine. Contains industry news and information. **Circulation:** 12,000. **Advertising:** accepted. Alternate Formats: online ● *Macs Service Reports*, monthly. Newsletter. Covers automotive air conditioner repair. **Conventions/Meetings:** annual convention and trade show, for manufacturers and distributors of automotive A/C (exhibits).

1894 ■ National Air Filtration Association (NAFA)

PO Box 68639
Virginia Beach, VA 23471
Ph: (757)313-7400
Fax: (757)497-1895
E-mail: nafa@nafahq.org
URL: http://www.nafahq.org
Contact: Alan C. Veeck CAFS, Exec. Dir.

Founded: 1980. **Members:** 200. **Membership Dues:** active, $520 (annual) ● associate, $920 (annual) ● supplemental, $225 (annual) ● affiliate, $100 (annual) ● professional, $150 (annual). **Staff:** 5. **Budget:** $250,000. **Regional Groups:** 6. **Description:** Companies that sell or service air filtration media to commercial and industrial users; manufacturers of air filtration media. Promotes the sale and use of air filtration media. Makes available technical education to members; conducts regional workshops. Offers certification for air filter sales/distributors and service technicians. **Libraries: Type:** open to the public. **Holdings:** books. **Subjects:** air filtration. **Awards:** Bob Bates Scholarship. **Frequency:** annual. **Type:** scholarship. **Recipient:** for students who have demonstrated outstanding personal and academic characteristics ● Clean Air Award. **Frequency:** annual. **Type:** recognition. **Publications:** *Air Media*, quarterly. Magazine. **Price:** $20.00/year. **Circulation:** 3,000. **Advertising:** accepted ● *IOM Manual*. Book. **Price:** $35.00 for members; $45.00 for nonmembers ● *NAFA Guide To Air Filtration*. Book. **Price:** $49.00 for members; $79.00 for nonmembers. **Conventions/Meetings:** annual conference.

1895 ■ National Environmental Balancing Bureau (NEBB)

8575 Grovement Cir.
Gaithersburg, MD 20877-4121
Ph: (301)977-3698
Fax: (301)977-9589
E-mail: miked@nebb.org
URL: http://www.nebb.org
Contact: Michael P. Dolim, Exec. VP

Founded: 1971. **Members:** 553. **Membership Dues:** certification, $850 (annual). **Staff:** 6. **Local Groups:** 35. **Description:** Qualified heating, ventilation, and air-conditioning contractors specializing in the fields of air and hydronic systems balancing, sound vibration measuring, testing of heating and cooling systems, building systems commissioning, and testing of cleanrooms. Seeks to establish and maintain industry standards, procedures, and specifications for testing, adjusting, and balancing work; certify those firms that meet the qualification requirements; establish educational programs to provide competent management and supervision of Testing and Balancing (TAB) work. Establishes professional qualifications for TAB supervisors. Maintains chapters in Australia and Canada. **Computer Services:** database, genealogical information. **Committees:** Building Systems Commissioning; Chapter Affairs; Cleanroom Certification; Marketing; Research and Development; Sound and Vibration; Technical Overview; Testing and Balancing. **Affiliated With:** Mechanical Contractors Association of America; Sheet Metal and Air Conditioning Contractors' National Association. **Publications:** *Environmental Systems Technology*. Book. **Price:** $160.00 for nonmembers; $80.00 for members ● *Procedural Standards for Building Systems Commissioning*. Manual. **Price:** $100.00 for nonmembers; $50.00 for members ● *Procedural Standards for Certified Testing of Cleanrooms*. Manual. **Price:** $100.00 for nonmembers; $50.00 for members ● *Procedural Standards for TAB Environmental Systems*. Manual. **Price:** $70.00 for nonmembers; $35.00 for members ● *Procedural Standards for the Measurement and Assessment of Sound and Vibration*. Manual. **Price:** $80.00 for nonmembers; $40.00 for members ● *Sound and Vibration Design and Analysis*. Manual. **Price:** $80.00 for nonmembers; $40.00 for members ● *Study Course for Certified Testing of Cleanrooms*. Manual. **Price:** $400.00 for nonmembers; $350.00 for members ● *Study Course for Measuring Sound and Vibration*. Manual. **Price:** $350.00 for nonmembers; $250.00 for members ● *Study Course for TAB Supervisors*. Manual. **Price:** $750.00 for nonmembers; $550.00 for members ● *TAB Manual for Technicians*. **Price:** $110.00 for nonmembers; $55.00 for members ● Brochures ● Manuals. **Conventions/Meetings:** annual meeting (exhibits) - always in November ● seminar, covers how to maintain standards of qualification.

1896 ■ National Kerosene Heater Association (NKHA)

Address Unknown since 2008

Founded: 1981. **Members:** 10. **Staff:** 3. **Budget:** $540,000. **Description:** Manufacturers, importers, distributors, and retailers of kerosene heaters in the U.S; associate members include those active in selling, manufacturing, or dealing in machinery, supplies, or services used by the kerosene heater industry. Objectives are: to promote the kerosene heater as a cost efficient, supplemental heating system that reduces heating expenses while conserving energy; to encourage maximum safety and efficiency in kerosene heaters marketed in the U.S; to educate the public and regulatory bodies about the safe operation and benefits of these heaters; to support member companies and their customers. Has established minimum product safety standards for members; campaigns for comprehensive product safety standards and legislation. Operates task forces. **Committees:** Consumer Advisory Panel; Public Affairs; Public Relations; Standards and Technical.

1897 ■ North American Technician Excellence (NATE)

4100 N Fairfax Dr., Ste.210
Arlington, VA 22203
Ph: (703)276-7247
Free: (877)420-NATE
Fax: (703)527-2316
E-mail: rboynton@natex.org
URL: http://www.natex.org
Contact: Rex P. Boynton, Pres.

Founded: 1997. **Members:** 30,000. **Staff:** 6. **Budget:** $2,500,000. **Multinational. Description:** Contractors, distributors, education and training providers, manufacturers, technicians, utilities, and their respective trade associations in the HVAC industry. Promotes technicians in the heating, ventilation, air-conditioning, and refrigeration (HVAC/R) industry; improves HVAC industry standards; offers testing and certification program. **Awards:** Golden Toolbox Award. **Frequency:** periodic. **Type:** recognition. **Recipient:** to field personnel for their efforts to support and promote NATE ● Ted Rees Leadership Award. **Frequency:** periodic. **Type:** recognition. **Recipient:** for leadership in promoting NATE and for showing excellence as technician.

1898 ■ Radiant Panel Association (RPA)

PO Box 717
Loveland, CO 80539
Ph: (970)613-0100
Free: (800)660-7187
Fax: (970)613-0098
E-mail: info@rpa-info.com
URL: http://www.radiantpanelassociation.org
Contact: Lawrence Drake, Exec. Dir.

Founded: 1994. **Members:** 850. **Membership Dues:** radiant equipment supplier (silver), $2,400 (annual) ● radiant equipment supplier (gold), $3,400 (annual) ● associate equipment supplier (silver), $1,200 (annual) ● associate equipment supplier (gold), $1,700 (annual) ● distributor (silver), $300 (annual) ● distributor (gold), $600 (annual) ● dealer/contractor (silver), $300 (annual) ● dealer/contractor (gold), $500 (annual) ● trade associate/architect/engineer (silver), $225 (annual) ● trade associate/architect/engineer (gold), $325 (annual) ● individual (gold), $150 (annual) ● individual (silver), $100 (annual). **Staff:** 5. **Budget:** $500,000. **Regional Groups:** 5. **Description:** Manufacturers, designers, installers, and other individuals and corporations with an interest in heating systems making use of radiators and radiating panels. Seeks to increase public awareness of the efficiency and effectiveness of radiant heating systems. Represents the interests of the radiant heating and related industries; encourages adherence to high standards in the manufacture and installation of radiant heating systems; conducts educational programs. **Awards:** System Showcase. **Frequency:** annual. **Type:** recognition. **Telecommunication Services:** electronic mail, ldrake@rpa-info.com. **Programs:** RPA Certification. **Subgroups:** Electric Radiant; Energy Efficiency; Research Liaison; Software Standardization; Standards. **Publications:** *Radiant Heating Report*. Magazine ● *Radiant Living*, quarterly. Magazine. **Circulation:** 110,000. **Advertising:** accepted. Alternate Formats: online ● *Radiant Panel Report*, monthly. Newsletter. **Conventions/Meetings:** annual REX (Radiant Expo) - conference and trade show (exhibits) - 2008 Aug. 13-15, Chicago, IL.

1899 ■ Refrigeration Service Engineers Society (RSES)

1666 Rand Rd.
Des Plaines, IL 60016-3552
Ph: (847)297-6464 (847)759-4051
Free: (800)297-5660
Fax: (847)297-5038
E-mail: general@rses.org
URL: http://www.rses.org
Contact: Mark Lowry, Exec. VP

Founded: 1933. **Members:** 30,000. **Membership Dues:** individual, $101 (annual) ● manufacturer, $300-$1,000 (annual) ● power utility, $250 (annual) ● wholesaler/distributor, training associate, industry association, $200 (annual) ● manufacturer's representative, $150 (annual) ● contractor, $150-$400 (annual). **Staff:** 38. **Budget:** $5,000,000. **Regional Groups:** 17. **State Groups:** 23. **Local Groups:** 420. **National Groups:** 2. **Languages:** English, Spanish. **Multinational. Description:** Persons engaged in refrigeration, air-conditioning and heating installation, service, sales, and maintenance. Conducts training courses and certification testing. Maintains a hall of fame and a speakers' bureau. **Libraries: Type:** reference. **Holdings:** 1,000; archival material, audiovisuals, books, clippings, periodicals. **Subjects:** heating AC programs for chapter use. **Awards:** Distinguished Service. **Frequency:** annual. **Type:** grant. **Recipient:** for members ● Educator of the Year. **Frequency:** annual. **Type:** recognition ● Rising Star Award. **Frequency:** annual. **Type:** recognition. **Recipient:** for members ● Speaker of the Year. **Frequency:** annual. **Type:** recognition. **Telecommunication Services:** electronic mail, mlowry@rses.org. **Publications:** *RSES Journal*, monthly. Magazine. **Price:** $36.00 in U.S. **Circulation:** 30,000. **Advertising:** accepted ● *Service Application Manuals*. Also Cited As: *SAM* ● Also publishes five chapter courses and twenty-two mini courses. **Conventions/Meetings:** annual conference (exhibits).

1900 ■ Sheet Metal and Air Conditioning Contractors' National Association (SMACNA)

4201 Lafayette Center Dr.
Chantilly, VA 20151-1209
Ph: (703)803-2980
Fax: (703)803-3732
E-mail: info@smacna.org
URL: http://www.smacna.org
Contact: John W. Sroka, Exec. VP

Founded: 1943. **Members:** 1,965. **Membership Dues:** regular in U.S. and Canada, state association, $200 (annual) ● international (associate), $400 (annual) ● associate (supplier/manufacturer/consultant), $500-$1,000 (annual) ● associate (manufacturer of ductwork), $1,000-$3,000 (annual). **Staff:** 42. **Budget:** $8,422,415. **Local Groups:** 99. **Description:** Ventilation, air handling, warm air heating, architectural and industrial sheet metal, kitchen equipment, testing and balancing, siding, and decking and specialty fabrication contractors. Prepares standards and codes; sponsors research and educational programs on sheet metal duct construction and fire damper (single and multi-blade) construction. Engages in legislative and labor activities; conducts business management and contractor education programs. **Libraries: Type:** reference. **Holdings:** 40; books. **Subjects:** technical and safety issues related to sheet metal and air conditioning industry. **Awards: Type:** scholarship. **Telecommunication Services:** electronic mail, jsroka@smacna.org. **Committees:** Building Services; Business Management Education; Duct Construction Standards; Duct Design; Fire and Smoke Control; Sheet Metal and Air Conditioning Contractors' Political Action. **Formerly:** (1956) Sheet Metal Contractors National Association. **Publications:** *SMACNews*, monthly. Newsletter. Alternate Formats: online ● Annual Report, annual. **Price:** free. Alternate Formats: online ● Membership Directory, annual. **Conventions/Meetings:** annual convention, includes educational training sessions (exhibits) - always in October.

1901 ■ Steamfitting Industry Promotion Fund
44 W 28th St.
New York, NY 10001
Ph: (212)481-1493
Fax: (212)447-6449
E-mail: info@nymca.org
URL: http://www.nymca.org
Contact: Raymond W. Hopkins, Exec. VP
Membership Dues: associate, $2,500 (annual). **Description:** Provides resources for the steamfitting industry. **Telecommunication Services:** electronic mail, rhopkins@nymca.org.

1902 ■ Tubular Exchanger Manufacturers Association (TEMA)
25 N Broadway
Tarrytown, NY 10591
Ph: (914)332-0040
Fax: (914)332-1541
E-mail: info@tema.org
URL: http://www.tema.org
Contact: Richard C. Byrne, Sec.
Founded: 1939. **Members:** 20. **Staff:** 2. **Description:** Manufacturers of heat exchangers and allied equipment. **Computer Services:** Online services, makes available TEMA software. **Telecommunication Services:** electronic mail, tema@tema.org. **Publications:** *TEMA Standards* ● Makes available TEMA software. **Conventions/Meetings:** semiannual meeting.

1903 ■ Used Oil Management Association (UOMA)
c/o Mary Beth Bosco
2550 M St. NW
Washington, DC 20037
Ph: (202)457-6420
Fax: (202)457-6315
URL: http://www.uoma.com
Contact: Mary Beth Bosco, Contact
Founded: 1981. **Members:** 5. **Description:** Manufacturers and distributors of appliances used to convert waste oil into heat. Serves as a forum for manufacturers to exchange information necessary to improve the quality and safety of their products. Promotes interests of the industry by providing information to public officials which will enable them to properly consider the passage of new legislation and to reexamine existing laws which the association feels unnecessarily restrict the use of waste oil burning appliances. **Formerly:** (1997) Waste Oil Heating Manufacturers Association.

Herbs

1904 ■ American Herbal Products Association (AHPA)
8484 Georgia Ave., Ste.370
Silver Spring, MD 20910-5606
Ph: (301)588-1171
Fax: (301)588-1174
E-mail: ahpa@ahpa.org
URL: http://www.ahpa.org
Contact: Michael McGuffin, Pres.
Founded: 1982. **Members:** 351. **Membership Dues:** associate, $1,000 (annual) ● active (based on herbal revenues), $1,000-$9,375 (annual). **Staff:** 4. **Budget:** $1,000,000. **Multinational. Description:** Represents growers, brokers, manufacturers, distributors, retailers, importers and related consultants of herbal products such as bulk ingredients, teas, dietary supplements, and body care products. Seeks to effectively deal with common interests and industry-related problems by acquiring, affecting and disseminating business and regulatory information. Represents industry to legislators, regulating agencies and media. Conducts trade promotion and research activities; compiles statistics. Publishes resource documents and provides educational programs. Maintains New Dietary Ingredient Database, based on FDA dockets, other databases under development. **Libraries: Type:** not open to the public. **Awards:** AHPA Herbal Hero Award. **Frequency:** annual. **Type:** recognition. **Recipient:** for individuals who made outstanding contributions to AHPA committees or initiatives; nominees must be members of AHPA ● AHPA Herbal Industry Leader Award. **Frequency:** annual. **Type:** recognition. **Recipient:** for companies that set an example of outstanding business practices or organizations that worked to move the industry forward above and beyond normal business practices; nominees must be members of AHPA ● AHPA Herbal Research Award. **Frequency:** annual. **Type:** recognition. **Recipient:** for companies, research institutions, academic facilities or programs of study that conducted outstanding research into botanicals; nominees must be nonmember of AHPA. **Publications:** *AHPA Report*, monthly. Newsletter. Keeps its members up-to-date on political and scientific news. ● *Botanical Safety Handbook*. **Price:** $54.95 for members, plus shipping and handling; $59.95 for nonmembers, plus shipping and handling ● *Guidance Documents for the Manufacture and Sale of Botanical Extracts-2001*. **Price:** $50.00 for members, plus shipping and handling; $80.00 for nonmembers, plus shipping and handling ● *Herbs of Commerce*. Manual. **Price:** $65.00 for members, plus shipping and handling; $95.00 for nonmembers, plus shipping and handling ● *Kava-Herb Safety Review*. **Price:** $60.00 plus shipping and handling ● *1999 Tonnage Survey*. **Price:** $35.00 for nonmembers, plus shipping and handling; $7.00 for members ● *St. John's Wart, Ephedra, Echinacea or Saw Palmetto*. Proceedings. **Price:** $175.00 plus shipping and handling ● *Siberian Ginseng*. **Price:** $85.00 plus shipping and handling ● *2002 International Symposium on the Role of Botanicals in Women's Health*. Proceedings. **Price:** $100.00 for members, plus shipping and handling; $125.00 for nonmembers, plus shipping and handling ● *2002 Report on Kava (Waller Report)*. **Price:** $120.00 for members, plus shipping and handling; $150.00 for nonmembers, plus shipping and handling ● Membership Directory, annual. **Price:** free for members. **Advertising:** accepted. **Conventions/Meetings:** triennial conference and board meeting ● meeting.

1905 ■ Ginseng Research Institute of America (GRIA)
c/o Ginseng Board of Wisconsin
555 N 72nd Ave., Ste.2
Wausau, WI 54401
Ph: (715)845-7300
Fax: (715)845-7300
E-mail: ginseng@ginsengboard.com
URL: http://www.ginsengboard.com
Founded: 1982. **Description:** Conducts research related to American ginseng. Coordinates health benefits studies and performs purity testing on ginseng products. Compiles statistics; conducts research programs. **Libraries: Type:** reference. **Subjects:** ginseng. **Formerly:** (1988) Ginseng Research Institute. **Publications:** *Ginseng Bibliography*. **Price:** $75.00 plus shipping and handling. **Conventions/Meetings:** periodic conference.

1906 ■ Herb Growing and Marketing Network (HGMN)
PO Box 245
Silver Spring, PA 17575-0245
Ph: (717)393-3295
Fax: (717)393-9261
E-mail: herbworld@aol.com
URL: http://www.herbworld.com
Contact: Maureen Rogers, Dir.
Founded: 1990. **Members:** 1,400. **Membership Dues:** in North America, $95 (annual) ● outside North America, $110 (annual). **Staff:** 2. **Budget:** $180,000. **For-Profit. Description:** Herb retailers, wholesalers, and growers; manufacturers of related products; serious hobbyists. Provides information on all segments of the herb industry with an emphasis on marketing and locating wholesale sources. **Libraries: Type:** reference. **Holdings:** 3,000. **Subjects:** herbs, gardening, and business. **Computer Services:** database ● online services, website design and hosting for members. **Telecommunication Services:** electronic bulletin board ● information service. **Publications:** *The Business of Herbs*, bimonthly. Journal. Alternate Formats: online ● *The Herbal Green Pages*, annual. Serves as a resource guide. **Price:** included in membership dues; $47.00 in North America (print); $57.00 outside North America. **Circulation:** 2,000. **Advertising:** accepted. Alternate Formats: CD-ROM ● *Proceedings from 5th Annual Conference*. **Price:** $25.00 in North America; $30.00 outside North America ● *Proceedings from 1st Annual Conference*. **Price:** $30.00 outside North America; $25.00 in North America ● *Proceedings from 4th Annual Conference*. **Price:** $25.00 in North America; $30.00 outside North America ● *Proceedings from 2nd Annual Conference*. **Price:** $25.00 in North America; $30.00 outside North America ● *Proceedings from 3rd Annual Conference*. **Price:** $25.00 in North America; $30.00 outside North America ● *Starting an Herb Business*. Proceedings. **Conventions/Meetings:** annual conference (exhibits).

1907 ■ International Herb Association (IHA)
PO Box 5667
Jacksonville, FL 32247-5667
Ph: (904)399-3241
Fax: (904)396-9467
E-mail: margepowell@iherb.org
URL: http://www.iherb.org
Contact: Ms. Tina Marie Wilcox, Pres.
Founded: 1985. **Members:** 100. **Membership Dues:** business, professional, individual, affiliate, $100 (annual) ● educator, small business, non-profit organization, $50 (annual) ● sponsor, $500 (annual) ● affiliate (less than 50 members), business/professional, $100 (annual) ● affiliate (more than 50 members), $200 (annual). **Budget:** $50,000. **Description:** Herb professionals. Works to unite members for growth through promotion and education. Offers help with business concerns such as the packaging and labeling of herbal products, budgets and projections, computerized business problem solving, and retail display and design. Maintains speakers' bureau. **Libraries: Type:** not open to the public. **Holdings:** business records. **Awards:** Professional Award. **Frequency:** annual. **Type:** recognition ● Service Award. **Frequency:** annual. **Type:** recognition. **Telecommunication Services:** electronic bulletin board, for members only. **Formerly:** International Herb Growers and Marketers Association. **Publications:** *Herb of The Year*, annual. Booklet. Selects a herb of the year and prepares a publication on its uses, cultivation, and other aspects of the herb. ● *IHA Membership Directory*, annual. Lists herb professionals. ● *IHA Newsletter*, quarterly. **Advertising:** accepted ● Proceedings, annual. **Advertising:** accepted. **Conventions/Meetings:** monthly board meeting ● annual conference and trade show.

Hispanic

1908 ■ National Society for Hispanic Professionals (NSHP)
1835 NE Miami Gardens Dr., No. 33
Miami, FL 33179

E-mail: creyna@nshp.org
URL: http://www.nshp.org
Contact: Carolina Reyna, Founder
Founded: 2001. **Membership Dues:** general (voting), $100 (annual) ● youth (non-voting), $25 (annual) ● educator/student (non-voting), $40 (annual). **Description:** Seeks to empower Hispanic professionals through networking and leadership opportunities. Provides information on education, careers and entrepreneurship. Fosters the civic, social and economic welfare of the Hispanic professional community. Supports a system of free individual acceptance of responsibility. Promotes Hispanic employment and advancement in the overall U.S. business picture. **Publications:** *Hispanic Professional News*, monthly. Newsletter. Contains news about other Hispanic organizations, job fairs, and other activities. **Price:** included in membership dues. Alternate Formats: online. Also Cited As: *HPN*.

Historic Preservation

1909 ■ American Historic Inns (AHI)
PO Box 669
Dana Point, CA 92629
Ph: (949)497-2232 (919)499-8070
Fax: (949)499-4022
E-mail: comments@iloveinns.com
URL: http://www.iloveinns.safeshopper.com
Founded: 1981. **Members:** 4,000. **Membership Dues:** basic, $75 (annual). **Staff:** 16. **Budget:** $1,200,000. **For-Profit. Description:** Publishers of bed and breakfast directories. Encourages the reservation of historic homes. Provides information to consumers via Bed and Breakfast guidebooks, B&B travel clubs, free night offers, Internet sites, etc. **Libraries: Type:** reference. **Holdings:** books. **Subjects:** bed and breakfasts, country inns, travel. **Awards:** Outstanding Achievement Award. **Type:** recognition. **Recipient:** for historic preservation of an inn and historic preservation community service. **Computer Services:** database, 15,000 inns ● mailing lists, 600,000 inn travellers ● online services, guidebook. **Formerly:** (1998) Association of American Historic Inns. **Publications:** *Bed and Breakfast and Country Inns*, annual. Includes information on 1600 inns. Includes certificate for a free night at a bed and breakfast listed in book. **Price:** $21.95/year. **Circulation:** 120,000 ● *Bed and Breakfast Encyclopedia*. Directory. Includes directory of 15,000 inns describing special discounts and topics of special interest. **Price:** $18.95 ● *Inn Touch*, monthly. Directory. **Advertising:** accepted ● *The Official Guide to American Historic Inns*. Provides information on 2200 historic lodging establishments in the U.S., Canada, and Puerto Rico. **Price:** $15.95. Alternate Formats: online.

Hobby Supplies

1910 ■ American Stamp Dealers Association (ASDA)
3 School St., Ste.205
Glen Cove, NY 11542-2548
Ph: (516)759-7000
Fax: (516)759-7014
E-mail: asda@asdaonline.com
URL: http://www.asdaonline.com
Contact: Eric Jackson, Pres.
Founded: 1914. **Members:** 800. **Membership Dues:** individual, $300 (annual) ● provision, $240. **Staff:** 4. **Budget:** $500,000. **Local Groups:** 14. **Description:** Dealers and wholesalers of stamps, albums, and other philatelic materials. Sponsors National Stamp Collecting Week in November. **Publications:** *American Stamp Dealers Association—Membership Directory*, annual ● *American Stamp Dealers Association—Newsletter*, monthly. **Conventions/Meetings:** annual Postage Stamp Mega Event - meeting (exhibits).

1911 ■ Craft and Hobby Association (CHA)
319 E 54th St.
Elmwood Park, NJ 07407
Ph: (201)794-1133
Fax: (201)797-0657
E-mail: info@craftandhobby.org
URL: http://www.hobby.org
Contact: Steve Berger, CEO
Founded: 1940. **Members:** 5,500. **Staff:** 23. **Budget:** $5,400,000. **Regional Groups:** 29. **Description:** Manufacturers, wholesalers, retailers, publishers, and allied firms in the craft and hobby industry. Promotes the interest of all companies engaged in the buying, selling, or manufacturing of craft and hobby merchandise; conceives, develops, and implements programs for members to achieve greater individual growth. Conducts seminars and educational workshops; sponsors national trade show. Compiles statistics. **Additional Websites:** http://www.chashow.org, http://www.craftandhobby.org. **Committees:** Awards; Education; Marketing; Member Services; Public Relations; Trade Show. **Absorbed:** Ceramic Distributors of America; National Ceramic Dealers Association; National Ceramic Manufacturers Association; National Ceramic Teachers Association; (1956) Model Industry Association; (1990) Ceramic Arts Federation International. **Formerly:** (2000) Hobby Industry Association of America; (2004) Hobby Industry Association. **Publications:** *Horizons*, quarterly. Newsletter. Covers the buying, selling, or manufacturing of hobby merchandise. Includes survey results. **Price:** free for members and selected nonmembers. **Circulation:** 4,500 ● Membership Directory, annual. Lists manufacturers, retailers, wholesalers, manufacturers' representatives, and publishers. Includes alphabetical name index. **Price:** available to members only. **Circulation:** 4,500 ● Brochure ● Bulletins ● Also publishes consumer studies and trade show book. **Conventions/Meetings:** annual trade show and convention (exhibits) - January.

1912 ■ Model Railroad Industry Association (MRIA)
Address Unknown since 2008
Founded: 1967. **Members:** 145. **Staff:** 2. **Budget:** $200,000. **Description:** Model railroad manufacturers, importers, publishers, and packagers. Purposes are: to publicize the hobby of model railroading; to provide an organized approach to any problems encountered in production of model railroad products; to provide a united voice within, and for, the model railroad industry; to keep the membership informed on all matters of interest to the industry. Assists model railroad clubs and retailers in the conduct of their "open house" or model railroad show affairs; makes available show liability insurance. Maintains hall of fame. **Publications:** *Reporter*, monthly. Newsletter. Contains industry surveys, lists of new members, and calendar of events. **Circulation:** 350 ● *Special Report*, periodic ● Pamphlet ● Reports.

1913 ■ National Plastercraft Association (NPCA)
0465 N 300 E
Albion, IN 46701
Ph: (219)636-7552
E-mail: gbkirk@ligtel.com
Contact: Barb Kirkpatrick, Contact
Founded: 1973. **Members:** 50. **Membership Dues:** professional, $50 (annual). **Staff:** 1. **Regional Groups:** 3. **Description:** Retailers, manufacturers, and distributors of plastercraft products for the hobby industry. Seeks to enhance the image of the plastercraft industry. Disseminates information; conducts seminars; sponsors painter/teacher certification program. Sponsors competitions. **Awards: Type:** recognition. **Committees:** Seminar; Teachers Certification. **Affiliated With:** Craft and Hobby Association. **Formerly:** (1978) Plastercraft Association. **Publications:** *Plastercrafter*, quarterly. Newsletter ● *So You Want to Go Into Plastercraft*. Handbook ● Membership Directory, annual. **Conventions/Meetings:** annual convention.

1914 ■ Radio Control Hobby Trade Association (RCHTA)
PO Box 315
Butler, NJ 07405-0315
Ph: (973)283-9088
Fax: (973)838-7124
E-mail: pkoziol@rchta.org
URL: http://www.ihobbyexpo.com
Contact: Pat Koziol, Exec. Dir.
Founded: 1983. **Members:** 400. **Membership Dues:** associate, $150 (annual) ● small company (under $500K), $165 (annual) ● medium company ($500K-$2M), $330 (annual) ● large company ($2M-$6M), $660 (annual) ● over $6 million, $880 (annual). **Staff:** 5. **Budget:** $1,000,000. **Description:** Brings together professionals in the radio control hobby industry involved with the manufacture, distribution, sale and promotion of products sold in hobby stores. **Libraries: Type:** not open to the public. **Holdings:** archival material. **Computer Services:** Online services, promotion of the International Model and Hobby Expo. **Telecommunication Services:** electronic mail, info@ihobbyexpo.com. **Publications:** *Faxmitter*, monthly. Bulletin ● *Transmitter*, 3/year. Newsletter. **Conventions/Meetings:** quarterly board meeting ● annual International Model & Hobby Expo - trade show (exhibits).

1915 ■ Society of Craft Designers (SCD)
Address Unknown since 2008
Founded: 1975. **Members:** 700. **Membership Dues:** individual designer, $135 (annual) ● individual international designer, $185 (annual) ● corporate, $250 (annual) ● corporate international, $300 (annual). **Description:** Designers of hobby items and consumer crafts, instructors, demonstrators, materials inventors, retailers, publishers, and writers serving the industry. Purposes are to develop creative competence in the marketplace and to upgrade the consumer craft field through member education and encouragement of a professional approach. Organizes annual educational seminar. **Publications:** *Register of Craft Designers*, periodic. Membership Directory ● *Society of Craft Designers—Newsletter*, bimonthly. **Conventions/Meetings:** annual Partners in the Creative Life - conference, for designers, manufacturers, editors and publishers (exhibits).

1916 ■ Track Owners Association (TOA)
417 Oak Pl., No. 2
Port Orange, FL 32127
Ph: (580)237-1699 (386)763-5005
Fax: (580)234-3433
E-mail: toa@slotcar.org
URL: http://www.slotcar.org
Contact: Mr. Floyd Guernsey, Exec. Dir.
Founded: 1991. **Members:** 275. **Membership Dues:** track owner, $60 (annual) ● honorary, $60-$100 (annual) ● distributor, manufacturer, publisher, $100 (annual). **Staff:** 1. **State Groups:** 3. **Multinational. Description:** Commercial slot car track owners. Provides central clearinghouse for manufacturer information, so that track owners may make informed requests of their distributors. Gives information to prospective track owners prior to opening a commercial raceway to the public. **Libraries: Type:** not open to the public. **Holdings:** 60. **Subjects:** slot car business. **Awards:** Best Show Booth. **Frequency:** annual. **Type:** recognition ● Distributor of the Year. **Frequency:** annual. **Type:** recognition ● Manufacturer of the Year. **Frequency:** annual. **Type:** recognition ● President's Award to Outstanding Individual. **Frequency:** annual. **Type:** recognition ● Publisher of the Year. **Frequency:** annual. **Type:** recognition ● Track Owner of Year. **Frequency:** annual. **Type:** recognition. **Computer Services:** database ● mailing lists ● online services. **Committees:** Executive. **Subgroups:** Budget and Finance; Competition and Rules; Convention; Marketing; Membership; Nominating; Policies and Procedures; Public Relations. **Formerly:** (2001) Track Owners Association of America. **Publications:** *All About Slot Car Racing*. Pamphlet. Provides questions and answers pertaining to model car racing. **Price:** $2.00 ● *How to Create a Business Plan* ● *How to Organize and Stage Slot Car Races*. Pamphlet ● *If You Are Thinking About Opening a Commercial Raceway*. Booklet ● *TOA Newsletter*, monthly. **Price:** included in membership dues. **Circulation:** 300. **Advertising:** accepted ● Assorted preprinted info sheets on wide variety of subjects. **Conventions/Meetings:** annual convention (exhibits).

Home Based Business

1917 ■ American Association of Home Based Businesses (AAHBB)
c/o Beverley Williams, Founder
285 Red Run Heights Rd.
Oakland, MD 21550-7907
E-mail: bevspeaks@earthlink.net
URL: http://www.smallbusinessadvocate.com/content/suites/hb_teleworking/index.shtml
Contact: Beverley Williams, Founder
Founded: 1994. **Nonmembership. For-Profit. Description:** Works to support, encourage and advocate for home-based businesses. **Publications:** TCB (Taking Care of Business), Tip Sheets, 15 topics.

1918 ■ American Home Business Association (AHBA)
965 E 4800 S, Ste.3c
Salt Lake City, UT 84117
Free: (866)396-7773
Fax: (866)396-7773
E-mail: info@homebusiness.com
URL: http://www.homebusinessworks.com
Contact: Bonnie Brijs, Pres./COO
Founded: 1994. **Members:** 25,000. **Membership Dues:** association, $29 (quarterly). **Staff:** 11. **For-Profit. Description:** Offers benefits and services dedicated to supporting the needs of home business, small business and entrepreneurs. Benefits include health-auto-home insurance, legal, low long distance and 800 numbers, business line of credit, merchant accounts, tax programs, office supply and travel discounts and more. Seeks to provide members access to the best traditional benefits and timely information that is critical to conduct a successful home, small or Internet business. **Publications:** *AHBA Hotline Newsletter*, bimonthly. Features articles and member benefits updates. **Circulation:** 25,000. **Advertising:** accepted.

1919 ■ Home Office Association of America (HOAA)
Address Unknown since 2007
Founded: 1994. **Members:** 1,000. **Membership Dues:** regular, $49 (annual). **Staff:** 3. **For-Profit. Description:** Works to support people with home-based businesses. Lobbies for changes in tax regulations to benefit home-based workers. Conducts educational programs has monthly newsletter Home Office Connections, discounts on health insurance, telephone, and travel, business insurance. Bestows Home Office Association seal of approval upon selected products. **Libraries: Type:** not open to the public. **Computer Services:** Online services, publication online. **Publications:** *Home Office Connections*, bimonthly. Newsletter. Mini business magazine for home/soho entrepreneurs reviews new products, trends, and articles on helping to grow business. **Circulation:** 2,000. **Advertising:** not accepted. Alternate Formats: online.

1920 ■ Mothers' Home Business Network (MHBN)
PO Box 423
East Meadow, NY 11554
E-mail: communicate@homeworkingmom.com
URL: http://www.homeworkingmom.com
Contact: Georganne Fiumara, Founder
Founded: 1984. **Members:** 6,000. **Membership Dues:** regular, $35 (annual). **For-Profit. Description:** Mothers choosing to work at home so they can earn income, maintain careers, and remain the primary caretakers of their children. Offers advice and support services on how to begin a successful business at home; helps members communicate with others who have chosen the same career option. Provides information on home business products and services, including home furnishings, raw materials and office supplies, and publications. Consults with corporations and manufacturers on reaching the home-based market. Refers media to potential interviewees and writers specializing in home business topics. **Computer Services:** database, Home Job Stop ● mailing lists. **Publications:** *Homeworking Mom-To-Mom*, monthly. Newsletter. Covers first person business stories, marketing advice, book reviews, excerpts, home business, and home-based employment ideas. **Price:** included in membership dues. **Circulation:** 10,000. **Advertising:** accepted. Alternate Formats: online ● *Kids and Career: New Ideas and Options for Mothers*, semiannual. **Price:** included in membership dues ● *Mothering and Managing a Mail Order Business At Home*. Booklet. **Price:** $6.50 ● *Mothering and Managing a Typing Service At Home*. Booklet. **Price:** $6.50 ● *Mothers' Home Businesspages: A Resource Guide for Home-working Mothers*, annual. **Price:** included in membership dues ● *Mothers' Money Making Manual*. Booklet. **Price:** included in membership dues ● *Selling to Home Businesses*, annual. **Price:** free upon request.

1921 ■ National Association of Home Based Businesses (NAHBB)
10451 Mill Run Cir., Ste.400
Owings Mills, MD 21117
Ph: (410)363-3698 (410)581-1373
E-mail: nahbb@msn.com
URL: http://www.usahomebusiness.com
Contact: Rudolph Lewis, Pres.
Founded: 1984. **Membership Dues:** home-based business, $99 (annual). **Staff:** 10. **Regional Groups:** 8. **Description:** Provides support and development services to home-based businesses. Offers business models and franchise development and marketing services. **Awards:** Best Home Based Business. **Frequency:** annual. **Type:** recognition. **Computer Services:** database, of home-based businesses. **Telecommunication Services:** electronic bulletin board, includes trade, national news, national register, HBB source books, how-to books, community business, business opportunity, and home business computer ● electronic mail, nahbb1@comcast.net. **Committees:** Advertising; Business Service; Education; Youth. **Publications:** *E-Mail Newsletter*, monthly. **Price:** free. **Circulation:** 10,000. **Advertising:** accepted. Alternate Formats: online ● *National Register of U.S. Home Based Business*, annual. Lists home based-businesses and indexes them by classifications. Alternate Formats: online. **Conventions/Meetings:** annual National Home Based Business Convention - banquet and meeting (exhibits).

1922 ■ National Work at Home Mom Association (NWAHMA)
Address Unknown since 2008
URL: http://nwahma.com
Membership Dues: general, $25 (annual) ● sponsorship, $150 (annual) ● partner, $325 (annual). **Multinational. Description:** Provides help and support for mothers in the United States and abroad. Increases opportunities for mothers to stay home with their children. Aims to reduce teen suicide and substance abuse rates by lobbying Congress to increase corporate opportunities for mothers to work at home. Provides mothers with continued education in financial management. **Awards: Frequency:** annual. **Type:** grant. **Recipient:** given to members of NWAHMA who have been proved to be in need. **Programs:** Certified Business Opportunity; Members Certification. **Publications:** Newsletter, monthly ● Membership Directory.

Horses

1923 ■ American Equestrian Alliance (AEA)
PO Box 6230
Scottsdale, AZ 85261
Ph: (602)992-1570
Free: (800)874-9191
Fax: (602)992-8327
E-mail: ballen@americanequestrian.com
URL: http://www.americanequestrian.com
Contact: Brent Allen, Exec. Dir.
Founded: 1989. **Membership Dues:** affiliate club/association, $15 (annual) ● individual, family, business affiliate, special event, $25 (annual) ● instructor, trainer, pony, wagon ride, outfitter, guide, stable operator, $50 (annual) ● guided trail ride, resort, guest ranch, $100 (annual). **Description:** Represents the interests of horse owners, trainers, stables, farms, ranches and equestrian-related businesses. Promotes equestrian activities, supports equine legislation and distributes educational literature. Operates as an insurance safety group for members. **Programs:** Equine Insurance Safety Group; Therapeutic Riding. **Publications:** Newsletter. **Price:** free for members.

1924 ■ American Horseman Alliance (AHA)
7550 IH-10 W, 14th Fl.
San Antonio, TX 78229
Ph: (210)541-7127
Fax: (210)298-1329
E-mail: info@ahabenefits.com
URL: http://www.ahabenefits.com
Contact: Dale Livingston, Founder
Founded: 2005. **Description:** Seeks to unite horsemen and horse associations from all disciplines to achieve "group purchasing power" for its partners. Aims to bring insurance products to market specifically designed for today's horsemen. Provides insurance products and plans for horsemen and horse association members.

1925 ■ International Association of Equine Professionals (IAEP)
Address Unknown since 2008
Members: 4,000. **Membership Dues:** $25 (annual). **Multinational. Description:** Works for the betterment of horses. Membership is made up of veterinarians, farriers, animal scientists, veterinary technicians, equine physical therapists and others who conduct professional activities in some aspect of horse care and/or management. Maintains a list of equine veterinary clinics and a farrier list. Offers web pages to members and free classified ads in the Journal. Maintenance of the home page is also available to members. **Computer Services:** Information services, professional information on all aspects of equine medicine, reproduction, nutrition, farriery, alternative medicine, equine research, animal science. **Publications:** *The Journal of Equine Veterinary Science*, monthly. **Price:** $99.00/year in U.S.; $105.00 in Canada and Mexico; $125.00 overseas.

1926 ■ North American Equine Ranching Information Council (NAERIC)
PO Box 43968
Louisville, KY 40253-0968
Ph: (502)245-0425
Fax: (502)245-0438
E-mail: carrie@naeric.org
URL: http://www.naeric.org
Contact: Carrie J. Allen, Communications Coor.
Description: Represents horse breeders and ranchers in North America engaged in collection of pregnant mares' urine used in estrogen replacement therapy. **Awards:** Wyeth Equine Ranching Scholarship. **Frequency:** annual. **Type:** scholarship. **Recipient:** to children and grandchildren of equine ranchers. **Committees:** Draft Horse Classic Sale and Futurity. **Programs:** Barrel Extravaganza; Buyers' Assistance; Incentive; North American Breeding Enhancement; Police Horse. **Projects:** Young House Development. **Publications:** *Equine Ranching*, quarterly. Magazine ● Reports. **Conventions/Meetings:** Horse Summit - conference ● Ranch Horse Classic Competition and Sale ● Super Team Competition ● annual Yearling Auction - meeting.

Hospitality Industries

1927 ■ American Hotel and Lodging Association (AH&LA)
1201 New York Ave. NW, No. 600
Washington, DC 20005-3931
Ph: (202)289-3100
Fax: (202)289-3199
E-mail: info@ahla.com
URL: http://www.ahla.com
Contact: Joseph A. McInerney CHA, Pres./CEO
Founded: 1910. **Members:** 13,000. **Membership Dues:** international (based on number of rooms),

$185-$530 (annual) ● student, $45 (annual) ● faculty (in a two-year institution), $250 (annual) ● faculty (in a four-year institution), $450 (annual) ● allied, $1,000 (annual). **Staff:** 65. **Budget:** $7,000,000. **State Groups:** 50. **Description:** Represents state lodging associations throughout the United States with some 13,000 property members worldwide, representing more than 1.7 million guest rooms. Provides its members with assistance in operations, education and communications and lobbies on Capitol Hill to provide a business climate in which the industry can continue to prosper. Individual state associations provide representation at the state level and offer many additional cost-saving benefits. **Libraries: Type:** by appointment only. **Holdings:** 5,000; articles, periodicals. **Subjects:** lodging, hospitality, travel, tourism. **Awards:** Stars of the Industry Awards. **Frequency:** annual. **Type:** recognition. **Recipient:** for outstanding achievements and quality service. **Computer Services:** Mailing lists, of members. **Committees:** AH&MA/ISHAE Liaison; Allied Member Executive; Communications; Condominium and Vacation Ownership; Copyright; Diversity and Human Resources; Engineering and Environmental; Extended Stay; Financial Management; Gaming; Governmental Affairs; Industry Real Estate Financing Advisory; Inns and Suites; International Council of Hotel/Motel Management Companies; Lodging Industry Rating Advisory; Loss Prevention and Security; Management Companies; Political Action; Quality Assurance; Resort; Risk Management; Safety and Fire Protection; Sales and Marketing; Technology. **Divisions:** American Hotel Foundation; Educational Institute of AH & MA. **Task Forces:** ADA; Experience Lodging; MORE. **Formerly:** (1962) American Hotel Association; (2001) American Hotel and Motel Association. **Publications:** *AH&LA Register*, 10/year. Newsletter. **Circulation:** 12,000 ● *Directory of Hotel and Lodging Companies*, annual. **Price:** $82.00. Alternate Formats: CD-ROM ● *Lodging*, monthly. Magazine. **Circulation:** 52,000. **Advertising:** accepted ● *Lodging Law*, monthly ● *Lodging News*, biweekly. Newsletter ● *Lodging Technology*, biweekly ● Articles ● Brochures ● Manuals ● Surveys ● Videos. **Conventions/Meetings:** annual conference, includes leadership forum (exhibits) - usually April or May ● annual meeting (exhibits) - always November in New York City.

1928 ■ American Hotel and Lodging Educational Foundation (AH&LEF)
1201 New York Ave. NW, Ste.600
Washington, DC 20005-3931
Ph: (202)289-3100
Fax: (202)289-3199
E-mail: mpoinelli@ahlef.org
URL: http://www.ahlef.org
Contact: Michelle Poinelli, Sr. VP of Foundation Programs
Founded: 2002. **Description:** Provides financial support that enhances the stability, prosperity, and growth of the lodging industry through educational and research programs. **Awards:** American Express Scholarship. **Frequency:** annual. **Type:** scholarship. **Recipient:** for lodging employees, working a minimum of 20 hours a week at AH&LA member properties and to their dependents ● Arthur J. Packard Memorial Scholarship. **Frequency:** annual. **Type:** scholarship. **Recipient:** to the most outstanding student of lodging management ● Ecolab Scholarship Program. **Frequency:** annual. **Type:** scholarship. **Recipient:** for a student who is enrolled in a U.S. baccalaureate or associate hospitality degree-granting program ● Rama Scholarship for the American Dream. **Frequency:** annual. **Type:** scholarship. **Recipient:** for students belonging to minority groups who are in need of financial aid. **Affiliated With:** American Hotel and Lodging Association. **Formerly:** (2003) American Hotel Foundation. **Publications:** *Lodging*, monthly. Magazine. **Circulation:** 40,000. **Advertising:** accepted. Alternate Formats: online.

1929 ■ American Travel Inns (ATI)
Address Unknown since 2007
Founded: 1958. **Members:** 22. **Staff:** 3. **For-Profit. Description:** Hotel/motel recommending service. Offers recognized brand-name identity without loss of individuality through national advertising program. Sponsors reservations through member-to-member referrals and group marketing. Offers reduced costs for credit card business. Sponsors training and management techniques and specific market research information to assist with individual marketing needs. Maintains strong quality control. **Convention/Meeting:** none. **Formerly:** (1977) American Travel Association. **Publications:** *Travel Guide Directory*, semiannual.

1930 ■ Asian American Hotel Owners Association (AAHOA)
66 Lenox Pointe NE
Atlanta, GA 30324-3170
Ph: (404)816-5759
Free: (800)465-5958
Fax: (404)816-6260
E-mail: info@aahoa.com
URL: http://www.aahoa.com
Contact: Fred Schwartz, Pres.
Founded: 1989. **Members:** 8,000. **Membership Dues:** regular, $125 (annual) ● spouse, $30 (annual) ● life, $3,000 ● family, $155 (annual) ● allied, regional, $1,000 (annual) ● allied, national, $1,500 (annual). **Staff:** 11. **Description:** Serves as advocacy, educational, and professional development group for Asian-American hotel owners. **Formed by Merger of:** (1994) Midsouth Indemnity Association and Asian American Hotel Owners Association. **Publications:** *AAHOA Lodging Business Magazine*, monthly. **Advertising:** accepted. **Conventions/Meetings:** annual convention and trade show (exhibits).

1931 ■ Associated Luxury Hotels International (ALHI)
1000 Connecticut Ave. NW, Ste.603
Washington, DC 20036
Ph: (202)887-7020
Fax: (202)887-0085
E-mail: meetings@alhi.com
URL: http://www.alhi.com
Contact: David G. Gabri, Pres./CEO
Founded: 1986. **Multinational. Description:** Represents four and five star hotels, resorts, and transportation companies committed to providing the finest in accommodations and meetings.

1932 ■ Association of Club Executives (ACE)
4340 Beechwood Lake Dr.
Naples, FL 34112
Ph: (216)965-7527
Fax: (239)353-7592
E-mail: angelina001@comcast.net
URL: http://www.acenational.org
Contact: Angelina Spencer, Exec. Dir.
Founded: 1999. **State Groups:** 15. **Description:** Provides information on the political and legal status of the adult nightclub industry. Protects the interests of member clubs and state club owners. **Affiliated With:** First Amendment Lawyers Association. **Publications:** Newsletter, weekly. Features legal and political developments around the US. Alternate Formats: online.

1933 ■ Association for Convention Marketing Executives (ACME)
c/o Sheila Crowley, Exec. Dir.
204 E St. NE
Washington, DC 20002
Ph: (202)547-8030 (813)342-4061
Fax: (202)547-6348
E-mail: smc@giuffrida.org
URL: http://www.acmenet.org
Contact: Sheila Crowley, Exec. Dir.
Founded: 1990. **Members:** 200. **Membership Dues:** active, associate, $225-$275 (annual) ● affiliate, $395-$495 (annual). **Staff:** 8. **Budget:** $150,000. **Description:** Convention marketing executives. Committed to the teaming of bureaus and centers, thus bringing unity and professionalism to the hospitality industry. Works as liaison between bureau marketing executives. **Awards:** Myers Award. **Frequency:** annual. **Type:** recognition. **Recipient:** for membership excellence. **Committees:** Communications; Conference Planning; Industry; Sponsorship. **Publications:** *ACMExpress*, quarterly. Newsletter. Alternate Formats: online. **Conventions/Meetings:** annual conference.

1934 ■ Association of Meeting Professionals (AMP)
2025 M St. NW, Ste.800
Washington, DC 20036
Ph: (202)973-8686
Fax: (202)973-8722
E-mail: amps@courtesyassoc.com
URL: http://www.ampsweb.org
Contact: Molly Bartkowski, Exec. Dir.
Founded: 1982. **Members:** 400. **Membership Dues:** planner, $150 (annual) ● allied, associate, $295 (annual) ● student, $25 (annual). **Staff:** 3. **Description:** Meeting planners and suppliers. Promotes professional advancement of members. Conducts educational programs; keeps members abreast of industry developments. **Awards:** Dick Noble Distinguished Service Award. **Frequency:** periodic. **Type:** recognition. **Recipient:** for consistent contribution and service rendered to the association ● Outstanding Meeting Professional Award. **Frequency:** annual. **Type:** recognition. **Recipient:** to an individual who displays commitment and dedication to AMP and the meeting industry ● Outstanding Service Professional Award. **Frequency:** annual. **Type:** recognition. **Recipient:** to an AMP supplier member who demonstrates a passion for providing service and value in the meeting industry. **Computer Services:** database ● mailing lists. **Committees:** Awards; Community Services; Nominating; Programs; Public Relations. **Publications:** *AMPS News*, monthly. Newsletter. **Price:** available to members only. **Advertising:** accepted. Alternate Formats: online. **Conventions/Meetings:** monthly meeting - every second Tuesday.

1935 ■ Association for Wedding Professionals International (AFWPI)
6700 Freeport Blvd., Ste.202
Sacramento, CA 95822
Ph: (916)392-5000
Free: (800)242-4461
Fax: (916)392-5222
E-mail: richard@afwpi.com
URL: http://www.afwpi.com
Contact: Richard Markel, Dir.
Founded: 1995. **Members:** 726. **Membership Dues:** regular, $200 (annual) ● associate, $300 (annual) ● corporate (plus $90 per division), $250 (annual). **Staff:** 5. **Regional Groups:** 3. **State Groups:** 4. **Local Groups:** 5. **For-Profit. Multinational. Description:** Professionals working in the wedding industry. Promotes adherence to high standards of ethics and practice by members; seeks to advance members' professional standing. Serves as a network linking members; offers member discounts on business services, insurance, and advertising; sponsors educational programs. **Libraries: Type:** not open to the public. **Awards:** Wedding Professional of the Year. **Frequency:** annual. **Type:** recognition. **Recipient:** voted by membership (peers). **Computer Services:** Mailing lists, brides. **Boards:** Advisory. **Committees:** Development; Education; Meeting Coordination. **Programs:** Magazine. **Publications:** *Professional Connection*, quarterly. Newsletter. Contains articles, member news, and association's announcements. **Circulation:** 500. **Advertising:** accepted ● Membership Directory. **Conventions/Meetings:** Christmas Party ● annual conference, with keynotes (exhibits) ● Monthly Networking Mixer - meeting, with featured members (exhibits) - every first Thursday.

1936 ■ Bed and Breakfast League/Sweet Dreams and Toast (BBL)
Address Unknown since 2007
Founded: 1976. **Members:** 75. **Staff:** 2. **For-Profit. Description:** A reservation service for a network of Bed and Breakfasts in Washington, DC, who welcome selected travelers into their homes. Traditionally, in a bed and breakfast (B and B) establishment, travelers are provided with overnight accommodations at reasonable prices and served breakfast the next

morning before resuming their travels. The concept has been popular in Europe for many years and the league offers the same type of accommodations in Washington, DC. A list of other B and B agencies can be obtained from the Travelers' Information Exchange, 356 Boylston St., Boston, MA 02116, (617)-536-5651, and from the Tourist House Association of America (see separate entry). **Convention/Meeting:** none. **Formed by Merger of:** (1988) Bed and Breakfast League; Sweet Dreams and Toast. **Publications:** Brochure. **Advertising:** not accepted.

1937 ■ Broker Management Council (BMC)
c/o Jake Buckner, CPFB, Pres.
5809 Reeds Rd.
Shawnee Mission, KS 66202
Ph: (913)432-9500
Free: (800)432-3877
Fax: (913)432-9565
E-mail: info@bmcsales.com
URL: http://www.bmcsales.com
Contact: Jake Buckner CPFB, Pres.

Founded: 1980. **Members:** 23. **Staff:** 2. **Budget:** $65,000. **Description:** Foodservice sales and marketing companies specializing in institutional and restaurant food and allied products. Aims to: facilitate communication and exchange of management information; increase efficiency and reduce the cost of doing business; promote a favorable image of brokers in order to enhance their acceptance. Compiles statistics; conducts specialized education program. **Publications:** *Management Letter*, monthly. **Price:** available to members only. **Conventions/Meetings:** semiannual conference.

1938 ■ Convenience Caterers and Food Manufacturers Association (CCFMA)
304 W Liberty St., Ste.201
Louisville, KY 40202
Ph: (502)583-3783
Free: (800)620-6422
Fax: (502)589-3602
E-mail: jbroom@hqtrs.com
URL: http://www.mobilecaterers.com
Contact: Joe Broom, Exec. Admin.

Founded: 1964. **Members:** 200. **Membership Dues:** regular, $300-$500 (annual) ● associate, $500 (annual). **Staff:** 4. **Budget:** $100,000. **Description:** Firms and corporations engaged in the mobile catering business and in any other business catering to industrial feeding by mobile equipment; associate members are suppliers and manufacturers. Deals with common intra-industry problems through exchange of ideas, advice on legal problems, and safety standards and licensing regulations. **Formerly:** (2004) Mobile Industrial Caterers' Association. **Publications:** *alaCARTE*, monthly. Newsletter. **Advertising:** accepted. Alternate Formats: online ● Manuals ● Membership Directory, annual ● Newsletter, 10/year ● Pamphlets. **Conventions/Meetings:** annual competition, operator's contest for various best wrapped food items ● annual conference (exhibits) - always spring ● annual convention and trade show - always fall.

1939 ■ Council of Hotel and Restaurant Trainers (CHART)
PO Box 2835
Westfield, NJ 07091
Ph: (908)389-0757
Free: (800)463-5918
Fax: (800)427-5436
E-mail: chart@chart.org
URL: http://www.chart.org
Contact: Tara Davey, Exec. Dir.

Founded: 1970. **Members:** 500. **Membership Dues:** individual, $295 (annual). **Description:** Training and development professionals working in the food and lodging industries. Promotes effective training and development as a productive element of the hospitality industry. Provides opportunities for growth in training management and program design through the sharing of ideas and networking among members. Participates in the establishment of standards in curriculum in the hospitality industry. Represents members' needs concerning legislation affecting hospitality employees. Maintains speakers' bureau. **Awards:** Commitment to People Award. **Frequency:** annual. **Type:** recognition. **Recipient:** for a President/CEO who has demonstrated commitment to training and development of people in an organization. **Computer Services:** database, members/resource directory. **Telecommunication Services:** electronic mail, tara@chart.org. **Publications:** *Flipchart*, monthly. Newsletter. Includes information on conferences and industry training topics. **Price:** available to members only. Alternate Formats: online. **Conventions/Meetings:** semiannual Hospitality Training Conference - March and August ● workshop, for skill development.

1940 ■ Dude Ranchers' Association (DRA)
1122 12th St.
PO Box 2307
Cody, WY 82414
Ph: (307)587-2339
Fax: (307)587-2776
E-mail: info@duderanch.org
URL: http://www.duderanch.org
Contact: Cheri Amos-Helmicki, Pres.

Founded: 1926. **Members:** 118. **Membership Dues:** personal, $50 (annual) ● contributing/commercial, $150 (annual) ● supporting, $250 (annual) ● life, $1,000. **Staff:** 12. **Budget:** $250,000. **Description:** Dude ranchers in 12 Western U.S. states and 2 Canadian provinces. Associate members are individuals and business firms interested in ranching. Seeks to: exchange ideas for the betterment of the ranchers and guests; publicize the advantages of a western ranch vacation; cooperate with federal land agencies; preserve and protect wildlife, parks, and forests. **Publications:** *Dude Rancher Directory*, annual. Contains descriptive listings of member ranches of the DRA. **Circulation:** 42,000. **Conventions/Meetings:** annual conference (exhibits).

1941 ■ Green Hotels Association
PO Box 420212
Houston, TX 77242-0212
Ph: (713)789-8889
Fax: (713)789-9786
E-mail: info@greenhotels.com
URL: http://www.greenhotels.com
Contact: Patricia Griffin, Pres.

Founded: 1993. **Members:** 325. **Membership Dues:** partner, $100-$750 (annual) ● ally/environmentalist, $250-$350 (annual) ● educator, $100 (annual). **Staff:** 3. **For-Profit**. **Multinational**. **Description:** Hotels, motels, inns, bed and breakfasts, and all other lodging establishments with an interest in protecting the environment. Encourages, promotes and supports ecological consciousness in the hospitality industry. **Telecommunication Services:** electronic mail, green@greenhotels.com. **Publications:** *Greening Newsletter*, bimonthly. Features in-depth information on environmental issues pertaining to the hospitality industry. **Price:** included in membership dues; $26.00 /year for nonmembers. **Advertising:** accepted ● *Membership Conservation Guidelines and Ideas*, quadrennial. Booklet. Includes conservation methods, techniques and ideas for member hotels.

1942 ■ Hospitality Asset Managers Association (HAMA)
c/o Stephanie Roy, Coor.
PO Box 381
North Scituate, MA 02060
Ph: (781)544-7330
E-mail: smroy@rcn.com
URL: http://www.hamainfo.com
Contact: Stephanie Roy, Coor.

Members: 115. **Membership Dues:** individual, $600 (annual). **Description:** Serves as a network of professionals involved in asset management, asset repositionings, operational policies, and franchise selection. Aims to improve asset management in the hospitality industry. Promotes ethical standards of conduct and mutual respect among its members and members of the hospitality industry.

1943 ■ Hospitality Institute of Technology and Management (HITM)
c/o Dr. O. Peter Snyder, Jr., Pres.
670 Transfer Rd., Ste.21A
St. Paul, MN 55114
Ph: (651)646-7077
Fax: (651)646-5984
E-mail: osnyder@hi-tm.com
URL: http://www.hi-tm.com
Contact: Dr. O. Peter Snyder Jr., Pres.

Description: Dedicated to the retail food industry. Provides education to personnel at all levels; provides consulting for the retail food industry; conducts research; assists food operators to improve customer, management, and regulatory expectations and increase operating efficiency and effectiveness. Provides consulting services, certification of HACCPO-based food safety programs and unit QA programs, certification of suppliers, development of new equipment, incorporation of nutrition into menu for the 21st century, and development of new food recipe process and ingredients to improve customer satisfaction, food quality, safety, and productivity. **Publications:** Articles.

1944 ■ Hospitality Sales and Marketing Association International (HSMAI)
8201 Greensboro Dr., Ste.300
McLean, VA 22102
Ph: (703)610-9024
Fax: (703)610-9005
E-mail: info@hsmai.org
URL: http://www.hsmai.org
Contact: Robert A. Gilbert CHME, Pres./CEO

Founded: 1927. **Members:** 7,000. **Membership Dues:** individual, $295 (annual) ● student, faculty, $60 (annual). **Staff:** 12. **Budget:** $5,000,000. **Regional Groups:** 67. **Multinational**. **Description:** Represents professional society of individuals engaged in sales and marketing in hospitality, travel and tourism. Provides and manages educational programs, recognition programs, research, marketplace events, and publications for the members and the industry. Conducts major events, meetings, trade shows, and a series of strategy conferences. **Libraries: Type:** reference. **Subjects:** sales, marketing, hospitality, travel, tourism. **Awards:** Adrian Awards Competition. **Frequency:** annual. **Type:** recognition. **Recipient:** for excellence in travel advertising, public relations, and web marketing. **Special Interest Groups:** Hotel Director of Sales and Marketing; Resort Marketing; Revenue Management; Sales and Marketing Faculty; Travel Internet Marketing. **Affiliated With:** American Hotel and Lodging Association. **Publications:** *HSMAI Marketing Review*, quarterly. Magazine. **Advertising:** accepted ● *HSMAI Update*, bimonthly. Newsletter ● Reports, periodic. Features various reports and white papers. **Advertising:** accepted. **Conventions/Meetings:** annual Affordable Meetings Mid-America - trade show (exhibits) ● annual Affordable Meetings West - trade show (exhibits).

1945 ■ Hotel Electronic Distribution Network Association (HEDNA)
1156-15th St. NW, Ste.900
Washington, DC 20005
Ph: (202)785-3232
Fax: (703)223-9741
E-mail: info@hedna.org
URL: http://www.hedna.org
Contact: Valerie Cooper CAE, Exec. Dir.

Founded: 1991. **Members:** 200. **Membership Dues:** principal, $1,000 (annual) ● allied, $1,300 (annual) ● fellowship, $250 (annual). **Multinational**. **Description:** Hotel distribution industry. Strives to increase hotel industry revenues and profitability from electronic distribution channels such as the Internet. **Libraries: Type:** reference. **Committees:** Collaboration; Distribution Management; Standards. **Formerly:** (2003) Hotel Electronic Distribution Association. **Publications:** Newsletter. Alternate Formats: online ● Books. **Conventions/Meetings:** semiannual conference (exhibits).

1946 ■ IAHI, The Owners' Association
3 Ravinia Dr., Ste.100
Atlanta, GA 30346
Ph: (770)604-5555
Free: (866)826-5808
Fax: (770)604-5684
URL: http://www.iahi.org
Contact: Eva Ferguson, Pres.
Founded: 1956. **Members:** 2,500. **Membership Dues:** associate, supplier, $950 (annual) ● regular (based on number of rooms), $350-$650 (annual). **Staff:** 5. **Budget:** $900,000. **Regional Groups:** 5. **National Groups:** 5. **Description:** Holiday Inn hotel owners and franchisees. Serves as liaison among members through owner committees. Sponsors programs in government relations and financial review; reviews corporate programs. Operates employment resume service. **Awards: Type:** scholarship. **Recipient:** for Holiday Inn local employees. **Committees:** Advertising; Capital Resources; Education; Government Affairs; INN-PAC; Marketing; Products; Reservations. **Formerly:** (2006) International Association of Holiday Inns. **Publications:** *Owner Update*, quarterly. Newsletter. **Price:** available to members only. **Conventions/Meetings:** annual meeting.

1947 ■ International Association of Conference Center Administrators (IACCA)
5976 20th St., Ste.80
Vero Beach, FL 32966
Ph: (772)562-4017
Fax: (772)562-4017
E-mail: iaccaoffice@aol.com
URL: http://www.iacca.org
Contact: Janet Begley, Exec. Dir.
Founded: 1976. **Members:** 286. **Membership Dues:** executive/business associate, $245 (annual) ● associate, $95 (annual) ● affiliate, $70 (annual) ● student, $25 (annual). **Staff:** 1. **Budget:** $65,000. **Regional Groups:** 4. **State Groups:** 1. **Description:** Provides support to conference center administrators and furthers their professional development. Conducts educational programs; compiles statistics; offers information on legislative and legal trends. Offers professional certification. **Awards:** Frank M. Washburn Award. **Frequency:** annual. **Type:** recognition. **Recipient:** for outstanding service to the field. **Computer Services:** Online services. **Committees:** Education; Membership; Publications. **Programs:** Professional Certification. **Publications:** *Association News*, quarterly. Newsletter. **Price:** included in membership dues. **Circulation:** 300 ● *IACCA Journal*, periodic. **Price:** included in membership dues. **Circulation:** 250 ● Directory. Lists members and describes centers. ● Directory. **Price:** included in membership dues; $25.00 for nonmembers. **Conventions/Meetings:** annual conference (exhibits) - always fall. 2008 Oct. 27-31, Green Lake, WI ● annual Journey of Leadership - conference (exhibits).

1948 ■ International Society of Hospitality Purchasers (ISHP)
c/o Mr. Larry Carver, Pres.
4177 NE Expy.
Atlanta, GA 30340
Ph: (770)446-2677
Fax: (770)446-6066
E-mail: lcarver@carverassoc.com
URL: http://www.ishp.org
Contact: Mr. Larry Carver, Pres.
Founded: 1999. **Membership Dues:** full, $500 (annual) ● associate, $50 (annual). **Description:** Hospitality purchasers. Works to improve member reputations. Provides forums and continued education.

1949 ■ Les Clefs d'Or U.S.A.
68 Laurie Ave.
Boston, MA 02132
Ph: (617)469-5397
Fax: (617)469-4397
E-mail: info@lcdusa.org
URL: http://www.lcdusa.org
Contact: Maurice Dancer, Pres.
Founded: 1978. **Members:** 500. **Description:** Hotel concierges of transient and resort hotels. Fosters education and networking among concierges of hotels throughout the world. **Awards:** Les Clefs d'Or USA/Penn State Hospitality School Scholarship. **Frequency:** annual. **Type:** scholarship. **Publications:** *Key Issues*, quarterly. Newsletter. **Circulation:** 200. **Conventions/Meetings:** annual congress (exhibits) ● annual international conference.

1950 ■ National Association of Black Hotel Owners, Operators and Developers (NABHOOD)
3520 W Broward Blvd., Ste.218B
Fort Lauderdale, FL 33312
Ph: (954)797-7102
Fax: (954)337-2877
E-mail: horizons@gate.net
URL: http://nabhood.com
Contact: Andy Ingraham, Pres./CEO
Membership Dues: general, $300 (annual) ● family general, $400 (annual) ● educational institute/school/faculty, $100 (annual) ● student, $10 (annual) ● allied, $1,000 (annual) ● life, $2,000 ● corporate founding sponsor, $25,000 (annual). **Description:** Enhances the stability and growth of the lodging industry. Aims to increase the number of African-Americans owning, developing, managing and operating hotels. Strives to create vendor opportunities and executive level jobs for minorities.

1951 ■ National Association of Catering Executives (NACE)
9881 Broken Land Pkwy., Ste.101
Columbia, MD 21046
Ph: (410)290-5410
Fax: (410)290-5460
E-mail: jsummers@nacenet.org
URL: http://www.nace.net
Contact: Joyce Summers, Assoc. Dir.
Founded: 1958. **Members:** 3,500. **Membership Dues:** individual, $345 (annual) ● student, $70 (annual) ● corporate (primary), $450 (annual). **Staff:** 7. **Budget:** $1,300,000. **Regional Groups:** 43. **Multinational. Description:** Professional caterers, affiliate members, the local and national suppliers and vendors in the many disciplines that impact and influence the catering business. Addresses banquet facilities, off-premise, country club, military and resort catering. Provides the most comprehensive package of continuing education, certification, networking and career support. **Awards:** Chapter of the Year Award. **Frequency:** annual. **Type:** recognition. **Recipient:** for chapters that exemplify outstanding achievement in chapter management, activity, merit and membership growth ● George Zell Spirit of NACE Award. **Frequency:** annual. **Type:** recognition. **Recipient:** for primary, affiliate or corporate members in good standing ● **Frequency:** annual. **Type:** recognition. **Recipient:** for the on and off premise catered event of the year. **Commissions:** Certification. **Committees:** Education; Foundation. **Councils:** Off-Premise Caterers. **Formerly:** (1970) Banquet Managers Guild. **Publications:** *NACE News Network*, monthly. Newsletter ● *Professional Caterer*, quarterly. Magazine. Contains current information about association activities and articles about issues and trends facing the hospitality industry. **Price:** $295.00 for members. **Circulation:** 4,000. **Advertising:** accepted. Alternate Formats: online. **Conventions/Meetings:** annual Education Conference (exhibits).

1952 ■ National Association of Condo Hotel Owners (NACHO)
8151 E Evans Rd., Ste.4
Scottsdale, AZ 85260
Ph: (480)905-2374
Fax: (480)365-8429
E-mail: info@nacho.us
URL: http://www.nacho.us
Contact: Dante Alexander, Pres./CEO
Founded: 2006. **Membership Dues:** existing/perspective unit owner, $50 (annual) ● charter counsel (voting), $150 (annual) ● business (based on annual operating budget), $350-$1,500 (annual). **Description:** Represents condo hotel owners and other individuals and companies interested in the condo hotel industry. Enhances and improves the condo hotel business segment. Fosters practices, promotion and disclosure of a standardized code of business ethics. **Publications:** *Nacho News Monitor*. Newsletter. **Price:** included in membership dues. Alternate Formats: online ● Membership Directory.

1953 ■ National Association of Pizzeria Operators (NAPO)
908 S 8th St., Ste.200
Louisville, KY 40203
Ph: (502)736-9532 (502)736-9530
Free: (800)489-8324
Fax: (502)736-9531
E-mail: jstraughan@napo.com
URL: http://www.napo.com
Contact: Joe Straughan, Exec. Dir.
Founded: 1983. **Members:** 10,396. **Membership Dues:** individual, $200 (annual) ● restaurant operator, $99 (annual) ● vendor/supplier, $1,000 (annual). **Staff:** 2. **For-Profit. Description:** Independent and franchised pizza operators; manufacturers and suppliers of pizza equipment; research organizations; schools with hotel and restaurant management programs; similar establishments in foreign countries. Promotes the advancement of marketing and product technology in the pizza industry. Provides educational references and seminars; conducts product research and development programs. Compiles statistics. **Awards:** Golden Pizza Award. **Type:** recognition ● Marketing Award. **Type:** recognition. **Computer Services:** database, sorts mailing lists ● mailing lists, members and advertisers. **Affiliated With:** American Society of Association Executives; Meeting Professionals International; National Restaurant Association. **Publications:** *Pizza Today: The Monthly Professional Guide to Pizza Profits*. Magazine. Covers industry developments as well as association activities. Features new products listing, book reviews, and directory of suppliers. **Price:** $29.95/year. **Circulation:** 40,020. **Advertising:** accepted. **Conventions/Meetings:** annual International Pizza Expo - conference (exhibits) - always in the first quarter.

1954 ■ National Bed-and-Breakfast Association (NBBA)
PO Box 332
Norwalk, CT 06852
Ph: (203)847-6196
Fax: (203)847-0469
E-mail: administrator@nbba.com
Contact: Phyllis Featherston, Pres.
Founded: 1980. **Members:** 2,000. **Staff:** 10. **Budget:** $50,000. **Description:** Innkeepers of bed and breakfast lodgings and small, family-owned and operated inns. **Divisions:** Real Estate and Management Services. **Publications:** *Bed & Breakfast Guide for the U.S., Canada, and the Caribbean, 8th Ed.* (in English, French, and Spanish), biennial. Directory. **Price:** $19.00 for nonmembers. ISSN: 0961-1298. **Circulation:** 75,000. Alternate Formats: online ● *National Relocation Directory and Magazine*, periodic ● *Official Bed and Breakfast Guide, 8th Ed.*, biennial. Directory. **Circulation:** 75,000. **Conventions/Meetings:** annual meeting.

1955 ■ National Black McDonald's Operators Association (NBMOA)
PO Box 820668
South Florida, FL 33082-0668
Ph: (954)389-4487
Fax: (954)349-5408
E-mail: nbmoa1@aol.com
URL: http://www.nbmoa.org
Contact: Ernie Adair, Chm.
Founded: 1972. **Members:** 169. **Staff:** 1. **Regional Groups:** 5. **Local Groups:** 1. **Description:** Black owners of McDonald's restaurants. Provides a forum for the exchange of ideas on the improvement of community relations and on the operation and management of restaurants. Seeks to build and improve the McDonald's restaurant image throughout the community. Sponsors training seminars on marketing, better sales practices, labor relations, and profit sharing. Conducts charitable programs. **Publications:** *Historical Highlights*. Book ● Newsletter,

quarterly. **Conventions/Meetings:** biennial convention ● biennial symposium.

1956 ■ National Concierge Association (NCA)
c/o Sara-ann G. Kasner, Pres.
2920 Idaho Ave. N
Minneapolis, MN 55427
Ph: (612)317-2932
Fax: (612)317-2910
E-mail: info@nationalconciergeassociation.com
URL: http://www.nationalconciergeassociation.com
Contact: Sara-ann G. Kasner, Pres.
Founded: 1998. **Members:** 600. **Membership Dues:** affiliated business at large, non-voting, non-specific associated chapter, $375 (annual) ● concierge voting and junior non-voting, member-at-large not associated with an NCA chapter, $165 (annual). **Staff:** 5. **Multinational**. **Description:** Represents concierges of all types and affiliated hospitality related businesses whose exceptional products and services are of benefit to concierge clientele. **Awards:** Concierge Outstanding Service. **Frequency:** annual. **Type:** recognition. **Recipient:** to NCA certified concierge professionals ● NCA Chapter of the Year. **Frequency:** annual. **Type:** recognition. **Recipient:** to an NCA chapter organization that best exemplifies the mission of the NCA ● NCA Partner of the Year. **Frequency:** annual. **Type:** recognition. **Recipient:** to 1 NCA preferred vendor/partner whose exceptional product and service is endorsed by the majority of the members. **Telecommunication Services:** electronic mail, president@nationalconciergeassociation.com. **Programs:** Certified Concierge; Preferred Partner. **Publications:** *NCA Keynotes*, biennial. Newsletter. Features news and information about the organization and its members and partners. Alternate Formats: online. **Conventions/Meetings:** annual conference and seminar, with seminars, activities and tradeshow highlighting the work of concierges (exhibits) - 2008 Aug. 11-13, Nashville, TN.

1957 ■ National Council of Chain Restaurants (NCCR)
325 7th St. NW, Ste.1100
Washington, DC 20004
Ph: (202)626-8183
Fax: (202)626-8185
E-mail: purviss@nrf.com
URL: http://www.nccr.net/newsite/index.html
Contact: Terrie M. Dort, Pres.
Founded: 1965. **Members:** 40. **Staff:** 3. **Budget:** $400,000. **Description:** Represents major multi-unit, multi-state foodservice, restaurant, and lodging companies in the U.S. Activities are directed to legislative and regulatory matters affecting members. **Committees:** Government Relations; Human Resources; Legal; Tax. **Task Forces:** Food Safety. **Formerly:** (1973) American Restaurant Institute; (1990) Foodservice and Lodging Institute. **Publications:** Newsletter. Alternate Formats: online. **Conventions/Meetings:** quarterly Membership, Tax Forum and Food Safety - meeting.

1958 ■ National Frozen Dessert and Fast Food Association
Address Unknown since 2007
URL: http://www.nfdffa.org
Founded: 1960. **Members:** 400. **Membership Dues:** operator, $90 (annual) ● supplier, $140 (annual). **Staff:** 2. **Budget:** $60,000. **Description:** Independent owners and operators of soft serve ice cream, hard ice-cream, yogurt, and fast food establishments. Objective is to gather and disseminate information and news affecting the industry. **Awards:** Chauncey "Bud" Blubaugh Scholarship Award. **Frequency:** annual. **Type:** scholarship. **Recipient:** for full-time enrollment; based on essay, sponsor, and school recommendation. **Formerly:** (1979) United Soft Serve and Fast Food Association; (1998) National Soft Serve and Fast Food Association. **Publications:** *Tid Bits*, bimonthly. Newsletter. **Price:** included in membership dues. **Circulation:** 500. **Advertising:** accepted. Alternate Formats: diskette. **Conventions/Meetings:** annual convention and seminar (exhibits) - always January, Orlando, FL.

1959 ■ National Restaurant Association (NRA)
1200 17th St. NW
Washington, DC 20036
Ph: (202)331-5900
Free: (800)424-5156
Fax: (202)331-2429
E-mail: info@dineout.org
URL: http://www.restaurant.org
Contact: Richard E. Rivere, Chm.
Founded: 1919. **Description:** Represents restaurants, cafeterias, clubs, contract foodservice management, drive-ins, caterers, institutional food services, and other members of the foodservice industry; also represents establishments belonging to non-affiliated state and local restaurant associations in governmental affairs. Supports foodservice education and research in several educational institutions. Is affiliated with the Educational Foundation of the National Restaurant Association to provide training and education for operators, food and equipment manufacturers, distributors, and educators. Has 300,000 member locations. **Libraries:** **Type:** reference. **Holdings:** 5,000; periodicals. **Subjects:** restaurant management, cookery, menus. **Awards:** Restaurant Good Neighbor Award. **Frequency:** annual. **Type:** recognition. **Recipient:** for outstanding service. **Departments:** Administration; Business Development; Communications; Federal Relations; Finance; Human Resources; Legal; Marketing; Media; Regulatory Services; Research; State Relations and Political Outreach. **Affiliated With:** National Restaurant Association Educational Foundation. **Publications:** *National Restaurant Association—Washington Report*, semimonthly, usually Monday. Newsletter. Reports on legislation and regulatory issues affecting the food service industry. Alternate Formats: online ● *Restaurant Industry Operations Report*, annual. **Conventions/Meetings:** annual National Restaurant Association Restaurant Hotel-Motel Show - trade show, largest foodservice show in North America (exhibits) - always May in Chicago, IL.

1960 ■ National Restaurant Association Educational Foundation (NRAEF)
175 W Jackson Blvd., Ste.1500
Chicago, IL 60604-2702
Ph: (312)715-1010
Free: (800)765-2122
E-mail: info@nraef.org
URL: http://www.nraef.org
Contact: Mary M. Adolf, Pres./COO
Founded: 1987. **Members:** 59,000. **Staff:** 105. **Description:** Serves as an educational foundation supported by the National Restaurant Association and all segments of the foodservice industry including restaurateurs, foodservice companies, food and equipment manufacturers, distributors, and trade associations. Advances the professional standards of the industry through education and research. Offers video training programs, management courses, and careers information. Conducts research and maintains hall of fame. **Awards:** **Type:** scholarship ● Teacher Training. **Type:** grant. **Affiliated With:** National Restaurant Association. **Formerly:** (1971) National Institute for the Foodservice Industry; (1999) Educational Foundation of the National Restaurant Association. **Publications:** *Careers in Foodservice*, *A Guide for Two-and Four-Year Hospitality Programs* ● *The Instructor*, semiannual ● Also publishes textbooks, course materials, and academic and industry product catalogs.

1961 ■ National Ski Areas Association (NSAA)
133 S Van Gordon St., Ste.300
Lakewood, CO 80228
Ph: (303)987-1111
Fax: (303)986-2345
E-mail: nsaa@nsaa.org
URL: http://www.nsaa.org
Contact: Michael Berry, Pres.
Founded: 1962. **Members:** 752. **Membership Dues:** U.S. ski area (minimum), $200 (annual) ● supplier, $350-$4,000 (annual) ● international, $400 (annual) ● affiliate/allied, $300 (annual). **Staff:** 12. **Description:** Ski area owners and operators; suppliers to the mountain resort industry. Seeks to foster, stimulate, and promote the skiing and mountain resort industries. Conducts marketing activities benefiting the sports of skiing and snowboarding; compiles industry statistics. Produces educational and training materials for ski area owners and personnel covering areas including pertinent federal safety and environmental regulations, resort operations, and guest services. **Computer Services:** database, displays all member companies and their programs. **Publications:** *NSAA Journal*, bimonthly. Features current industry trends, technologies and issues impacting the ski industry. ● *Source Book*. Alternate Formats: online ● *Sustainable Slopes: Annual Report*. Alternate Formats: online ● Newsletter, bimonthly. **Conventions/Meetings:** annual conference and trade show ● annual trade show and convention.

1962 ■ Professional Association of Innkeepers International (PAII)
207 White Horse Pike
Haddon Heights, NJ 08035
Ph: (856)310-1102
Free: (800)468-7244
Fax: (856)310-1105
E-mail: membership@paii.org
URL: http://www.paii.org
Contact: Laura Middleton, Admin. Asst.
Founded: 1988. **Members:** 3,500. **Membership Dues:** aspiring, $189 (annual) ● retired, $179 (annual) ● active, $189-$259 (annual). **Staff:** 10. **Budget:** $600,000. **For-Profit**. **Description:** Supports and serves bed and breakfast, innkeepers, and aspiring innkeepers through education, research, advocacy, and information hotline. **Libraries:** **Type:** not open to the public. **Holdings:** archival material, books, periodicals. **Subjects:** hospitality, food service, bed and breakfasts, country inn business. **Publications:** *Industry Study of Bed-and-Breakfast/Country Inns Finances, Operations and Marketing*, biennial ● *Innkeepers Library*. Catalog ● *Innkeeping*, monthly. Newsletter. Includes in-depth reporting on innkeeping issues and research, as well as studies on products, services, and industry developments. **Advertising:** accepted. **Conventions/Meetings:** biennial convention and conference (exhibits).

1963 ■ Resort Hotel Association (RHA)
2100 E Cary St., Ste.3
Richmond, VA 23223
Ph: (804)525-2020
Fax: (804)525-2021
E-mail: brooks@resorthotelinsurance.com
URL: http://www.resorthotelinsurance.com
Contact: Brooks W. Chase, Pres./CEO
Founded: 1987. **Members:** 120. **Description:** Represents resort and hotel owners. Develops and administers products and services customized for the hospitality industry. Offers both liability and property insurance programs. **Publications:** *RHA!RHA!*, quarterly. Newsletter. Contains industry news and new member updates. Alternate Formats: online. **Conventions/Meetings:** annual conference - 2008 July 11-14, Sedona, AZ.

1964 ■ Saint Croix Hotel and Tourism Association (SCHA)
PO Box 24238
Gallows Bay
St. Croix, VI 00824
Ph: (340)773-7117
Free: (800)524-2026
E-mail: info@stcroixhotelandtourism.com
URL: http://www.stcroixhotelandtourism.com
Founded: 1968. **Members:** 212. **Membership Dues:** small accommodation, $500 (annual) ● larger accommodation (per room), $3,100 (annual) ● associate (based on the number of employees), $195-$1,800 (annual). **Staff:** 2. **Description:** Hotels and tourist-related industries in St. Croix in the Virgin Islands of the United States. Strives to increase tourism in the region by providing a cleaner environment and improving security. Conducts educational programs to raise community awareness of the tourism industry and its value to St. Croix. **Affiliated With:**

American Hotel and Lodging Association; Caribbean Hotel Association. **Publications:** *Croix Destination Piece* ● *St. Croix Guide Book* ● Membership Directory, annual ● Newsletter, monthly.

1965 ■ Select Registry, Distinguished Inns of North America
PO Box 150
Marshall, MI 49068
Ph: (269)789-0393
Free: (800)344-5244
Fax: (269)789-0970
E-mail: maincontact@selectregistry.com
URL: http://www.selectregistry.com
Contact: Keith Kehlbeck, Exec. Dir.
Founded: 1968. **Members:** 404. **Staff:** 6. **Budget:** $1,500,000. **Regional Groups:** 14. **Description:** Members consist of independently owned Country Inns and Bed and Breakfasts located in the United States and Canada. The average number of rooms per inn is seventeen and all inns contain at least six or more rooms and have been in operation for a minimum of three years. A specific set of standards and criteria must be met in order to qualify for membership. Each inn is evaluated by a private evaluation firm before admission into SR and is re-evaluated at least every four years thereafter. **Publications:** *The Select Registry*, annual. Directory. Contains picture of each inn, along with description, prices and other info. Free to guests at member inns. **Price:** $15.95 plus shipping and handling. **Circulation:** 325,000. **Advertising:** accepted. Alternate Formats: online.

1966 ■ Small Luxury Hotels of the World (SLH)
370 Lexington Ave., Ste.1506
New York, NY 10017
Ph: (212)953-2064
Free: (800)525-4800
Fax: (212)953-0576
URL: http://www.slh.com
Founded: 1985. **Members:** 79. **Staff:** 3. **Description:** Independently owned and managed luxury hotels and resorts; cruise ships. Seeks to market and sell its membership to the travel industry and provide an interhotel networking system for all members. **Formerly:** (1991) Small Luxury Hotels Association; (1998) Small Luxury Hotels of the World; (2002) Small Luxury Hotels.

1967 ■ Waiters Association
c/o Vivienne J. Wildes, PhD, Founder
1100 W Beaver Ave.
State College, PA 16801
Ph: (814)238-3447
Fax: (814)238-8424
E-mail: vwildes@psu.edu
URL: http://www.personal.psu.edu/users/v/j/vjw100/contact.html
Contact: Vivienne J. Wildes PhD, Founder
Founded: 1992. **Members:** 2,500. **Membership Dues:** individual, $25 (annual) ● corporation, $500 (annual). **Staff:** 5. **Budget:** $70,000. **Description:** Hospitality professionals, educational institutions, and restaurant owners. Works to upgrade the status and public perception of wait staff to a professional level. Conducts educational programs; maintains speakers' bureau. **Awards:** Keith Hawson Scholarship. **Frequency:** annual. **Type:** scholarship. **Computer Services:** Mailing lists. **Publications:** *Generation X*, periodic. Journal. Features the demographic, societal, and psychographic influences on Generation Xers. ● *Guide to Scholarships*. Handbook ● *Hospitality*, monthly. Newsletter. Offers tips, service information, and profiles of America's waiters. **Price:** included in membership dues. **Advertising:** accepted ● *Research in Progress*, periodic. Survey. Contains the snapshot of USA Today readers' feelings about hospitality service.

Housewares

1968 ■ American Brush Manufacturers Association (ABMA)
2111 Plum St., Ste.274
Aurora, IL 60506
Ph: (630)631-5217
Fax: (630)897-9140
E-mail: info@abma.org
URL: http://www.abma.org
Contact: Barry D. Harper, Pres.
Founded: 1918. **Members:** 167. **Membership Dues:** company (based on annual sales volume), $580-$2,320 (annual) ● affiliate, supplier (based on annual sales volume), $264-$1,056 (annual). **Staff:** 3. **Budget:** $400,000. **Description:** Represents manufacturers of paint, household, industrial, personal, and other brushes, mops, and brooms; suppliers of raw materials and equipment to manufacturers. **Committees:** Convention; Education/Training; Finance; Membership; Nominating; Public Relations; Safety and Standards; Statisticals; Trade Show. **Divisions:** Broom and Mop; Industrial Maintenance; Paint Applicator; Suppliers. **Publications:** *Brush Up*, quarterly. Newsletter ● Directory, biennial. **Conventions/Meetings:** annual convention (exhibits).

1969 ■ American Innerspring Manufacturers (AIM)
1918 N Pkwy.
Memphis, TN 38112
Ph: (901)274-9030
Free: (800)882-5634
E-mail: aimy@aiminfo.org
Contact: Arthur Grehan, Exec.Dir.
Founded: 1966. **Members:** 14. **Staff:** 1. **Budget:** $140,000. **Description:** Manufacturers of steel innersprings for bedding mattresses and boxsprings (foundations). Conducts advertising, promotional, and research programs. **Formerly:** Association of Innerspring Manufacturers. **Publications:** *A Healthy Back Begins Tonight: Choosing the Proper Sleeping Surface* ● *Back to Basics: The How's and Why's of a Healthy Back* ● *Research Puts the Questions to Rest: Innersprings are Best for Your Back* ● *Support*, quarterly. Newsletter. **Circulation:** 2,500 ● *What's the Best Sleeping Surface? The Results Are Firm.* **Conventions/Meetings:** annual conference.

1970 ■ Cookware Manufacturers Association (CMA)
PO Box 531335
Birmingham, AL 35253-1335
Ph: (205)823-3448
Fax: (205)823-3449
E-mail: hrushing@usit.net
URL: http://www.cookware.org
Contact: Hugh J. Rushing, Exec. VP
Founded: 1922. **Members:** 25. **Staff:** 3. **Description:** Represents manufacturers of cooking utensils and cooking accessories. Compiles statistics. **Libraries: Type:** reference. **Holdings:** archival material, business records. **Subjects:** cookware brand name history. **Formerly:** Aluminum Wares Association; (1981) Metal Cookware Manufacturers Association. **Publications:** *Annual Statistical Report*, annual ● *Engineering Standards Guide*. **Price:** $55.00 ● *Guide to Cookware and Bakeware*. **Price:** $3.00. **Conventions/Meetings:** annual conference - always spring.

1971 ■ International Association of Dinnerware Matchers (IADM)
c/o Richard Goldberg
67 Beverly Rd.
Hawthorne, NJ 07506
E-mail: info@iadm.com
URL: http://www.iadm.com
Contact: Richard Goldberg, Contact
Founded: 1989. **Members:** 50. **Membership Dues:** general, $350 (annual). **Multinational. Description:** Assists costumers in locating hard-to-find pieces of china, crystal, and flatware. Promotes honesty, integrity and quality of service in the dinnerware matching profession. **Publications:** Directory, semiannual. **Price:** free for members. **Circulation:** 500.

1972 ■ International Housewares Association (IHA)
6400 Shafer Ct., Ste.650
Rosemont, IL 60018
Ph: (847)292-4200 (847)692-0114
Fax: (847)292-4211
E-mail: pbrandl@housewares.org
URL: http://www.housewares.org
Contact: Philip J. Brandl, Pres.
Founded: 1938. **Members:** 1,900. **Membership Dues:** regular, $350 (annual) ● associate, $450 (annual). **Staff:** 23. **Budget:** $7,000,000. **Description:** Manufacturers and distributors of housewares and small appliances. Conducts annual market research survey of the housewares industry. Manages the international housewares show. **Awards:** National Student Design Competition Award. **Frequency:** annual. **Type:** scholarship. **Recipient:** for undergraduate students in industrial design program and IDSA-sponsored school; entries are judged by a panel of housewares designers. **Computer Services:** Electronic publishing, provides online access to industry information and International Houses Show News ● electronic publishing, provides product locator and international matchmaker databases and NHMS publications. **Committees:** Retail Partnering. **Councils:** Housewares Export Council of North America; International Housewares Representatives Association; Retail Trade Show Advisory; Technology. **Formerly:** (2002) National Housewares Manufacturers Association. **Publications:** *Housewares Story* ● *January Exhibitors Directory*, annual. **Price:** $20.00/copy ● *NHMA Housewares Index*, quarterly. Newsletter. **Price:** available to members only ● *NHMA Reports Newsletter*, bimonthly. **Price:** available to members only ● *State of the Industry Report*, annual. Contains general statistics pertinent to the housewares industry. **Price:** $300.00 ● Membership Directory, annual. **Price:** $100.00/copy. **Conventions/Meetings:** annual show, showcasing thousands of new products and designs (exhibits) ● trade show.

1973 ■ International Housewares Representatives Association (IHRA)
175 N Harbor Dr., Ste.3807
Chicago, IL 60601
Ph: (312)240-0774
Free: (800)315-7430
Fax: (312)240-1005
E-mail: info@ihra.org
URL: http://www.ihra.org
Contact: Mr. Bill Weiner, Exec. Dir.
Founded: 1994. **Members:** 275. **Membership Dues:** representative, $245 (annual) ● manufacturer, $345 (annual). **Description:** Aims to promote, protect and improve the multiple-line representative function and to provide benefits and services to its members. **Publications:** *The REPorter*, monthly. Newsletter. **Advertising:** accepted. Alternate Formats: online.

1974 ■ International Sleep Products Association (ISPA)
501 Wythe St.
Alexandria, VA 22314-1917
Ph: (703)683-8371
Fax: (703)683-4503
E-mail: info@sleepproducts.org
URL: http://www.sleepproducts.org
Contact: Dick Doyle, Pres./CEO
Founded: 1915. **Members:** 750. **Membership Dues:** manufacturer (plus $43 per $100,000 of sales volume), $600 (annual) ● supplier (plus $32 per $100,000 of sales volume), $860 (annual) ● 2nd tier supplier, $2,500 (annual). **Staff:** 18. **Budget:** $3,000,000. **Description:** Represents manufacturers and suppliers of mattresses. Compiles statistics. **Formerly:** (1987) National Association of Bedding Manufacturers. **Publications:** *BEDtimes*, monthly. Magazine. Contains information for bedding manufacturers and their suppliers. Includes annual supplies directory. **Price:** free for members; $50.00 for nonmembers in U.S.; $65.00 for nonmembers outside U.S. **Circulation:** 3,600. **Advertising:** accepted. Also Cited As: *Bedding*. **Conventions/Meetings:** biennial trade show (exhibits) - always even-numbered years.

Housing

1975 ■ African American Alliance for Homeownership (AAAH)
PO Box 11531
Portland, OR 97211

Ph: (503)595-3517
Fax: (503)595-3519
E-mail: aaahownership@yahoo.com
URL: http://www.aaah.org
Contact: Cheryl L. Roberts, Exec. Dir.
Founded: 1999. **Description:** Represents the interests of housing and business professionals. Supports economic stability for African Americans through homeownership. Stimulates home buying activities and resources through homebuyer programs. Increases homeownership for African Americans by improving access, ensuring advocacy and providing awareness and education.

1976 ■ Manufactured Housing Research Alliance (MHRA)
2109 Broadway, Ste.200
New York, NY 10023
Ph: (212)496-0900
Fax: (212)496-5389
E-mail: info@research-alliance.org
URL: http://www.mhrahome.org
Contact: Emanuel Levy, Exec. Dir.
Founded: 1995. **Members:** 74. **Membership Dues:** energy-related organization, individual, factory homebuilder, supplier, supplier-related trade organization, $2,000 (annual) ● retailer, community owner/developer, lender, insurer, architect, engineer, consultant, $200 (annual). **Staff:** 16. **Description:** Works to develop new technologies to enhance the value and quality of the nations manufactured homes. Supports the industry by developing new methods for utilizing manufactured homes in a variety of housing applications. **Publications:** *Design for a Cold-Formed Steel Framing Manufactured Home: Technical Support Document*. Report. **Price:** $95.00 for members; $190.00 for nonmembers ● *Equipment Sizing Charts for Air Conditioner and Heat Pump Sizing: Technical Support Document*. Report. **Price:** $15.00 for members; $30.00 for nonmembers ● *Guidelines for Anchor System Design: Technical Support Document*. Report. **Price:** $15.00 for members; $30.00 for nonmembers ● *Manufactured Housing Fuel Switching: Field Test Study*. Report. **Price:** $15.00 for members; $30.00 for nonmembers ● *Measured Permeance Values for Selected Interior Wall Assemblies*. Report. **Price:** $15.00 for members; $30.00 for nonmembers ● *TECHNOLOGIES*, bimonthly. Newsletter. **Price:** $95.00 for nonmembers; $40.00 for retailers/community owners. Alternate Formats: online.

1977 ■ National Affordable Housing Management Association (NAHMA)
400 N Columbus St., Ste.203
Alexandria, VA 22314
Ph: (703)683-8630
Fax: (703)683-8634
E-mail: kris.cook@nahma.org
URL: http://www.nahma.org
Contact: Kris Cook CAE, Exec. Dir.
Founded: 1990. **Membership Dues:** executive, $2,900 (annual) ● associate, $1,400 (annual) ● affiliate, $900 (annual). **Description:** Companies and individuals involved with the management of affordable housing. Advocates to meet the growing need for multifamily residential affordable housing. Works with HUD, Congress, IRS, RHS, State Housing Finance Agencies, and Housing Credit Monitoring Agencies. **Awards:** Communities of Quality Awards. **Frequency:** annual. **Type:** recognition. **Recipient:** for outstanding communities.

1978 ■ National Association of Responsible Loan Officers (NARLO)
335 Beard St.
Tallahassee, FL 32303
Ph: (850)222-6000
Free: (800)761-6983
Fax: (850)222-6002
E-mail: privacy@narlo.com
URL: http://www.narlo.com
Contact: Robert Skrob, Exec. Dir.
Membership Dues: regular, $49 (monthly). **Description:** Seeks to ensure adequate consumer education commensurate with the importance of a family's home mortgage decision. Implements discount programs on insurance, recreation, food, and others. Helps improve different types of business. **Libraries: Type:** reference. **Publications:** *Consumer Education Brochure*. **Price:** included in membership dues ● *NARLO Today*, monthly. Newsletter. Features strategies to improve business income. **Price:** included in membership dues ● Directory. **Price:** included in membership dues.

Human Development

1979 ■ National Study Group on Chronic Disorganization (NSGCD)
4728 Hedgemont Dr.
St. Louis, MO 63128
Ph: (314)416-2236
Fax: (314)845-1891
E-mail: nsgcd@nsgcd.org
URL: http://www.nsgcd.org
Contact: Beth Quick-Andrews, Exec. Dir.
Membership Dues: professional organizer, professional (social worker, psychologist, psychiatrist, nurse), $150 (annual). **Staff:** 37. **Description:** Provides methods, techniques, approaches and solutions that will benefit chronically disorganized people. **Computer Services:** Information services, chronic disorganization resources. **Telecommunication Services:** electronic mail, referral@nsgcd.org ● electronic mail, info@nsgcd.org. **Programs:** Certificate. **Subgroups:** Speaker's Bureau. **Publications:** *Backsliding*. Booklet ● *Body Double Techniques*. Booklet ● *Heirs of The Chronically Disorganized*. Booklet ● *NSGCD Clutter Hoarding Scale*. Booklet ● *Working With Elderly Clients*. Booklet. Features challenges and considerations of professional organizers. ● *Working with Physically Challenged Clients*. Booklet.

Human Resources

1980 ■ Cable and Telecommunications Human Resources Association (CTHRA)
1755 Park St., Ste.260
Naperville, IL 60563
Ph: (630)416-1166
Fax: (630)416-9798
E-mail: cthra@cthra.com
URL: http://www.cthra.com
Contact: Pamela V. Williams, Exec. Dir.
Membership Dues: regular, $250 (annual). **Description:** Supports and serves cable television and telecommunication professionals. Enables the industry to maximize its potential through the development of a productive work force. Aims to help industry professionals leverage effective human resources strategies to improve organizational and industry-wide success. Provides members with human resources information and resources, networking opportunities and educational programs. **Programs:** Scouting, Selecting and Retaining Diverse Talent. **Publications:** Membership Directory. Alternate Formats: online.

1981 ■ Human Resources Outsourcing Association (HROA)
601 Pennsylvania Ave. NW, Ste.900
Washington, DC 20004
Ph: (202)220-3165
E-mail: info@hroassociation.org
URL: http://www.hroassociation.org
Contact: Mr. Adam Bleifeld, Exec. Dir.
Membership Dues: full service provider (only one user), $1,500 (annual) ● full service provider (more than one user), $15,000 (annual) ● full service provider (international; more than one user), $20,000 (annual) ● practitioner (only one user), $500 (annual) ● practitioner (more than one user), $1,000 (annual) ● practitioner (international; more than one user), $1,750 (annual). **Description:** Seeks to advance professionalism in outsourcing. Assists and encourages professionals engaged in the field of human resource outsourcing to improve their professional competence. Develops and promulgates forms, languages and standards of ethical and professional conduct within the human resources outsourcing community. **Committees:** Communications and Research; Education; Ethics; Information Technology; Legal; Nominating; Program; Public Policy.

1982 ■ National Association of African Americans in Human Resources (NAAAHR)
PO Box 11467
Washington, DC 20008
Ph: (404)346-1245
E-mail: support@naaahr.org
URL: http://www.naaahr.org
Contact: Carl C. Jefferson, Natl. Pres./CEO
Founded: 1998. **Members:** 1,000. **Membership Dues:** professional, $125 (annual) ● student, $30 (annual) ● corporate, $1,000 (annual) ● professional (life), $1,000 ● corporate elite, $5,000 (annual). **Description:** Human resource professionals. Works to provide a national forum where African Americans can share and gain information, and provide leadership on issues affecting individual careers and quality of work life for other African Americans. **Publications:** Newsletter, quarterly. Alternate Formats: online. **Conventions/Meetings:** conference.

1983 ■ National Association of Professional Background Screeners (NAPBS)
PO Box 3159
Durham, NC 27715
Ph: (919)433-0123
Free: (888)686-2727
Fax: (919)383-0035
E-mail: info@napbs.com
URL: http://www.napbs.com
Contact: David Hein, Co-Chm.
Founded: 2003. **Members:** 382. **Membership Dues:** regular, $350-$2,000 (annual) ● associate, $350 (annual) ● affiliate, $150 (annual). **Description:** Represents the interests of companies offering employment and background screening. Promotes ethical business practices. Fosters awareness of issues related to consumer protection and privacy rights. Maintains the standard of the background screening industry. **Libraries: Type:** reference. **Computer Services:** database, membership listing ● online services, discussion forum. **Committees:** Best Practices and Compliance; Ethics/Accreditation; Government Relations; Provider Advisory; Public Awareness and Communications; Resource Library; Vendor's Advisory. **Publications:** Newsletter. **Conventions/Meetings:** annual meeting, forum for members; educational programs (exhibits) - always spring.

1984 ■ Recruiting and Staffing Focus Area
c/o Society for Human Resource Management
1800 Duke St.
Alexandria, VA 22314
Ph: (703)548-3440
Free: (800)283-SHRM
Fax: (703)535-6490
E-mail: shrm@shrm.org
URL: http://www.shrm.org/ema
Members: 7,600. **Membership Dues:** general, $75 (annual). **Local Groups:** 18. **Description:** Provides employment-related programs, services and networking opportunities to members with staffing-related accountabilities. **Formerly:** (2006) Employment Management Association. **Publications:** *Global Perspectives*. Newsletter. **Price:** included in membership dues ● *iLinX Newsletter*. **Price:** included in membership dues. **Conventions/Meetings:** annual conference and lecture (exhibits).

Human Services

1985 ■ American Association of Service Coordinators (AASC)
PO Box 1178
Powell, OH 43065-1178
Ph: (614)848-5958
Fax: (614)848-5954

E-mail: info@servicecoordinator.org
URL: http://www.servicecoordinator.org
Contact: Janice C. Monks LSW, Pres.
Founded: 1999. **Membership Dues:** student, $75 (annual) ● individual, $125 (annual) ● associate, $275 (annual) ● affiliate (not-for-profit), $300 (annual) ● affiliate (for-profit), $500 (annual). **Description:** Advances the interests of the service coordinator profession. Increases awareness and understanding of service coordination and service-enriched housing. Provides guidance to members in the creation and maintenance of service-enhanced housing to families, the elderly and persons with disabilities. Strives to enhance the professionalism of its constituents through leadership, education, training, networking, and advocacy.

1986 ■ National Alliance for Direct Support Professionals (NADSP)
PO Box 13447
Minneapolis, MN 55414
Ph: (952)920-0855
Fax: (952)920-1480
E-mail: molson@nadsp.org
URL: http://nadsp.org
Contact: Mark Olson, Pres.
Membership Dues: DSP, associate, $25 (annual) ● other professional, $40 (annual) ● agency/provider affiliate, $200 (annual) ● supporting organization, $500 (annual). **Description:** Promotes the development of a highly competent human services workforce which supports individuals in achieving their life goals. Enhances the status of direct support professionals (DSP). Provides better access for all direct support professionals to high quality educational experiences and lifelong learning which enhances competency. Strengthens the working relationships and partnerships between direct support professionals, self-advocates, and other consumer groups and families. Supports the development and implementation of a national volunteer credentialling process for direct support professionals. **Publications:** *Frontline Initiative*. Newsletter. Promotes the interests of DSPs who support people with disabilities in a variety of community settings. **Price:** included in membership dues; $10.00 /year for nonmembers. Also Cited As: *FI*.

1987 ■ National Energy Assistance Directors' Association (NEADA)
1615 M St. NW, Ste.800
Washington, DC 20036
Ph: (202)237-5199
Free: (866)674-6327
Fax: (202)237-7316
E-mail: info@neada.org
URL: http://www.neada.org
Contact: Mark Wolfe, Exec. Dir.
Founded: 1983. **Description:** Represents state directors of the Low-Income Home Energy Assistance Program. Collects and disseminates information, proposes energy policy, provides program administrative advice, analyzes programs and benefits among public and private institutions, and enhances each state's capabilities and responsibilities.

Hydroponics

1988 ■ Hydroponic Merchants Association (HMA)
10210 Leatherleaf Ct.
Manassas, VA 20111-4245
Ph: (703)392-5890
Fax: (703)257-0213
E-mail: info@hydromerchants.org
URL: http://hydromerchants.org
Contact: Christine Hubbard, Pres.
Founded: 1997. **Membership Dues:** retail, allied organization, $300 (annual) ● wholesaler, distributor, manufacturer, $1,000 (annual). **Description:** Retailers, wholesalers, distributors, and manufacturers. Works to promote the international development of hydroponic education, applications, and markets. Hosts meetings, conferences, forums, seminars and lectures.

Industrial Equipment

1989 ■ Abrasive Engineering Society (AES)
144 Moore Rd.
Butler, PA 16001
Ph: (724)282-6210
Fax: (724)234-2376
E-mail: aes@abrasiveengineering.com
URL: http://www.abrasiveengineering.com
Contact: Ted Giese, Business Mgr.
Founded: 1957. **Members:** 300. **Membership Dues:** ordinary, $50 (annual). **Staff:** 1. **Budget:** $10,000. **Regional Groups:** 8. **Multinational. Description:** Promotes knowledge and understanding of abrasives (abrasive wheels, coated abrasives, media, diamonds and diamond products, dressers, dressing devices and abrasive grains) and their application in metalworking. Sponsors courses. **Libraries: Type:** not open to the public; reference. **Holdings:** archival material, books, papers, periodicals, reports. **Computer Services:** database, membership ● mailing lists. **Formerly:** (1975) American Society for Abrasive Methods. **Supersedes:** American Society for Abrasives. **Publications:** *Abrasive User's News*, biweekly. Newsletter. Contains information on new abrasives, abrasive products, and abrasive applications in metalworking. Includes industry news. **Price:** free for members; $50.00 /year for nonmembers. ISSN: 0195-0932. **Circulation:** 1,000. Alternate Formats: CD-ROM ● *Conference Proceedings*, periodic. Papers. **Price:** $35.00/copy; $45.00 Best AES Technical Papers-Coated Abrasives Technology; $45.00 Best AES Technical Paper-Superabrasive Technology. **Conventions/Meetings:** periodic regional meeting.

1990 ■ American Apparel Machinery Trade Association (AAMTA)
Address Unknown since 2007
Founded: 1933. **Members:** 14. **Description:** Firms engaged in the industrial sewing machine industry, including manufacturers of sewing machines, tables, motors, accessories, parts, and related items. **Formerly:** (1987) Sewing Machine Trade Association. **Conventions/Meetings:** annual meeting - always third Wednesday of October, New York City.

1991 ■ American Bearing Manufacturers Association (ABMA)
2025 M St. NW, Ste.800
Washington, DC 20036-2422
Ph: (202)367-1155
Fax: (202)367-2155
E-mail: info@americanbearings.org
URL: http://www.abma-dc.org
Contact: Scott Lynch, Pres./Sec.
Founded: 1933. **Members:** 35. **Membership Dues:** company (based on annual net sales), $1,200-$32,000 (annual). **Staff:** 6. **Budget:** $500,000. **Description:** Represents manufacturers of anti-friction bearings, balls, and rollers and major components used in anti-friction bearings. Promotes bearing standardization. **Committees:** Bearing Technical; Government Relations/International Trade; Industrial Relations; Statistics. **Absorbed:** Annular Bearing Engineers Committee; Roller Bearing Engineers Committee. **Formerly:** (1993) Anti-Friction Bearing Manufacturers Association. **Publications:** *ABMA Standards*. **Conventions/Meetings:** annual conference ● annual meeting.

1992 ■ American Boiler Manufacturers Association (ABMA)
8221 Old Courthouse Rd., Ste.207
Vienna, VA 22182
Ph: (703)356-7172
Fax: (703)356-4543
E-mail: randy@abma.com
URL: http://www.abma.com
Contact: W. Randall Rawson, Pres.
Founded: 1888. **Members:** 100. **Membership Dues:** associate, active, $4,635 (annual) ● institutional, $550 (annual) ● individual, $260 (annual) ● student, $55 (annual) ● international trade association, $14,000 (annual). **Staff:** 4. **Budget:** $850,000. **Description:** Represents manufacturers of boilers, combustion equipment and related products and services, as well as users and environmental systems suppliers. Compiles industry statistics. **Libraries: Type:** not open to the public. **Holdings:** 30; books. **Subjects:** technical, operational information. **Computer Services:** Mailing lists ● online services, buyer's guide for prospective customers. **Committees:** International. **Subgroups:** Aftermarket Services; Associate Members; Burner; Commercial Systems; Controls and Instrumentation; Deaerator Manufacturers; Environmental Affairs and Services; HRSG; Industrial Systems; Solid Fuel Power Generation. **Formerly:** (1960) American Manufacturers Association and Affiliated Industries. **Publications:** *ABMA Update*, periodic. Newsletter. Covers association and industry news. Includes calendar of events, and legislative and regulatory news. **Price:** available to members only. Alternate Formats: online ● *American Boiler Manufacturers Association Directory of Members' Products and Services*, annual. **Price:** free. **Advertising:** accepted. Alternate Formats: diskette ● *Handbook of Power, Utility and Boiler Terms and Phrases*. **Conventions/Meetings:** semiannual convention ● annual Manufacturers' Conference - April.

1993 ■ American Chain Association (ACA)
6724 Lone Oak Blvd.
Naples, FL 34109
Ph: (239)514-3441
Fax: (239)514-3470
E-mail: bob@americanchainassn.org
URL: http://www.americanchainassn.org
Contact: Robert A. Reinfried, Exec. Dir.
Founded: 1930. **Members:** 5. **Membership Dues:** company, $12,000 (annual). **Staff:** 2. **Budget:** $100,000. **Description:** Represents manufacturers of chain and sprockets for power transmission and the conveyance of materials. **Sections:** Engineering Steel Chain; Malleable Iron Chain; Roller Chain; Silent Chain. **Formerly:** (1971) American Sprocket Chain Manufacturers Association. **Supersedes:** Association of Roller and Silent Chain Manufacturers; Malleable Chain Manufacturers Institute. **Publications:** *American Chain Association Directory*, annual. Provides membership listing of manufacturers of chain and sprockets. **Price:** available to members only ● *Chains for Power Transmission and Material Handling*. **Conventions/Meetings:** annual meeting.

1994 ■ American Gear Manufacturers Association (AGMA)
500 Montgomery St., Ste.350
Alexandria, VA 22314-1581
Ph: (703)684-0211
Fax: (703)684-0242
E-mail: webmaster@agma.org
URL: http://www.agma.org
Contact: Joe T. Franklin Jr., Pres.
Founded: 1916. **Members:** 400. **Membership Dues:** end user, $2,000 (annual) ● supplier to the industry (based on total worldwide sales), $2,500-$9,265 (annual) ● international gear manufacturer (based on total worldwide sales), $1,500-$13,390 (annual) ● company (based on total annual sales), $1,500-$15,850 (annual) ● individual technical consultant, $750 (annual) ● academic, $50 (annual). **Staff:** 12. **Budget:** $2,500,000. **Multinational. Description:** Represents manufacturers of gears, geared speed changers, and related equipment; manufacturers of gear cutting and checking equipment; teachers of mechanical engineering and gearing. Conducts educational and research programs; compiles statistics and financial data. Develops technical standards for domestic and international industry. **Libraries: Type:** reference. **Holdings:** books, monographs, papers, periodicals. **Subjects:** art and history of gears and gearing. **Publications:** *AGMA Standards*, annual. Contains technical standards. Alternate Formats: online ● *Gear Industry Journal*, quarterly. **Advertising:** accepted ● Membership Directory, annual. **Advertising:** accepted. **Conventions/Meet-**

ings: biennial Gear Expo - trade show - always fall in odd-numbered years ● annual meeting - always spring.

1995 ■ American Machine Tool Distributors' Association (AMTDA)
1445 Res. Blvd., Ste.450
Rockville, MD 20850
Ph: (301)738-1200
Free: (800)878-2683
Fax: (301)738-9499
E-mail: jhealy@amtda.org
URL: http://www.amtda.org
Contact: John J. Healy, Pres.
Founded: 1925. **Members:** 370. **Membership Dues:** distributor (with total sales of $750,000 and below), $750-$2,500 (annual) ● distributor (with total sales of $750,001 and above), $3,000-$5,000 (annual) ● marketing associate, $1,000 (annual). **Staff:** 8. **Budget:** $2,500,000. **Description:** Distributors and builders of manufacturing technology. Offers technical training, sales training and management. Compiles statistics. **Computer Services:** database. **Publications:** *AMTDA Directory*, annual. Membership Directory. Lists members and builders for whom they distribute; contains one list of distributors with tool lines handled. **Price:** $50.00 for members; $85.00 for customers; $200.00 for foreign subscriber and nonmembers. **Advertising:** accepted ● *Tool Talk*, 10/year. Newsletter. Alternate Formats: online ● *US Machine Tool Consumption Report*, monthly. Features a statistical report containing compilation of marketing data. Also Cited As: *USMTC*. **Conventions/Meetings:** annual meeting - always April ● seminar.

1996 ■ American Mold Builders Association (AMBA)
701 E Irving Park Rd., No. 207
Roselle, IL 60172
Ph: (630)980-7667
Fax: (630)980-9714
E-mail: info@amba.org
URL: http://www.amba.org
Contact: Jeanette Bradley, Exec. Dir.
Founded: 1973. **Members:** 400. **Membership Dues:** company (15 or less employees), $100 (quarterly) ● company (16-40 employees), $150 (quarterly) ● company (41-60 employees), $250 (quarterly) ● company (over 61 employees), $400 (quarterly). **Staff:** 3. **Budget:** $800,000. **Description:** Moldmakers. Promotes the development, welfare, and expansion of businesses engaged in the manufacture of molds and related tooling. **Libraries: Type:** not open to the public. **Holdings:** periodicals. **Subjects:** moldmaking technology, management, technical, association news. **Awards:** Mold Builder of the Year. **Frequency:** annual. **Type:** recognition. **Recipient:** for outstanding contribution to the industry. **Publications:** *AMBA Membership Directory*, annual. Features member listing with services. **Price:** $50.00 for nonmembers. **Circulation:** 2,500. **Advertising:** accepted. Alternate Formats: CD-ROM; diskette ● *The American Mold Builder Publication*, quarterly. Newsletter. **Circulation:** 2,000. **Advertising:** accepted ● *The Future is Gold*. Brochure. **Price:** free first 25 copies; $20.00 for 26-75 copies; $25.00 for 76-100 copies ● *Know the True Cost of Your Molds*. Brochure. **Price:** free (up to 25 copies) ● *The Right Choice*. Video. **Price:** $25.00 single copy; $14.00 for 10 or more copies. **Conventions/Meetings:** annual convention.

1997 ■ American Textile Machinery Association (ATMA)
201 Park Washington Ct.
Falls Church, VA 22046
Ph: (703)538-1789
Fax: (703)241-5603
E-mail: info@atmanet.org
URL: http://www.atmanet.org
Contact: John M. White Jr., Chm.
Founded: 1933. **Members:** 115. **Membership Dues:** affiliate, $510 (annual). **Staff:** 12. **Budget:** $500,000. **Regional Groups:** 5. **Description:** Manufacturers of capital equipment for textile manufacture and interested individuals from academia, industry, banking, transportation, insurance, engineering, textiles, and other industries. **Formerly:** (1952) National Association of Textile Machinery Manufacturers. **Publications:** *ATMA Executive Report*, 8/year. Newsletter. **Price:** available to members only ● *Marketing Memos*, periodic ● *Membership/Product Directory*, quadrennial. Membership Directory. Includes annual updates. **Conventions/Meetings:** annual meeting and seminar, market development (exhibits) ● periodic seminar.

1998 ■ American Wire Cloth Institute (AWCI)
25 N Broadway
Tarrytown, NY 10591
Ph: (914)332-0040
Fax: (914)332-1541
E-mail: info@wireclothinstitute.org
URL: http://www.wireclothinstitute.org
Contact: Peter M. Miranda, Sec.
Founded: 1933. **Members:** 20. **Description:** Serves as a trade association of companies engaged in weaving and marketing industrial quality wire cloth and fabricated wire cloth products. Campaigns actively to promote a strong wire cloth industry. **Formerly:** (1977) Industrial Wire Cloth Institute.

1999 ■ American Wire Producers Association (AWPA)
801 N Fairfax St., Ste.211
Alexandria, VA 22314-1757
Ph: (703)299-4434
Fax: (703)299-9233
E-mail: info@awpa.org
URL: http://www.awpa.org
Contact: Kimberly A. Korbel, Exec. Dir.
Founded: 1981. **Members:** 93. **Membership Dues:** active, $500-$4,000 (quarterly) ● associate wire company and associate Canadian/Mexican wire company, $300-$1,800 (quarterly) ● associate nail committee, $437 (quarterly) ● associate rod supplier, $500-$1,375 (quarterly) ● associate supplier, $500 (quarterly). **Staff:** 4. **Budget:** $500,000. **Description:** Represents manufacturers of steel wire and wire products; suppliers of wire rods, dies, machinery, and related equipment. Assures free and fair access to a global supply of wire rod and to encourage an adequate domestic supply. **Libraries: Type:** not open to the public. **Holdings:** articles, papers, reports. **Awards:** Entrepreneurial Spirit Award. **Frequency:** annual. **Type:** recognition. **Computer Services:** database, member product directories, mailings, conference registrations, and invoices. **Formed by Merger of:** (1981) Specialty Wire Association; (1981) Independent Wire Producers Association. **Publications:** *Import Monitoring Report*, monthly. Reports. **Price:** included in membership dues; $50.00 for nonmembers. Alternate Formats: online ● *Imports Report*. Includes shipments of imported rod, wire and wire products into the US by country of origin, product and port of entry. **Price:** $50.00 each ● *Market Statistics-Rod and Wire Apparent Consumption*, monthly. Reports. **Price:** included in membership dues ● *Standards Manual*, 10/year. **Price:** $30.00 ● *WireLine*, bimonthly. Newsletter. Contains trade and legislative updates and statistics. **Price:** included in membership dues; $150.00 /year for nonmembers. **Circulation:** 600. **Conventions/Meetings:** annual conference ● annual meeting ● semiannual Operations Managers Meeting.

2000 ■ Associated Equipment Distributors (AED)
615 W 22nd St.
Oak Brook, IL 60523
Ph: (630)574-0650
Free: (800)388-0650
Fax: (630)574-0132
E-mail: info@aednet.org
URL: http://www.aednet.org
Contact: Toby Mack, Pres./CEO
Founded: 1919. **Members:** 1,250. **Membership Dues:** distributor (with gross annual revenues of up to $50 million), $850-$2,100 (annual) ● distributor, manufacturer (with gross annual revenues of $50,000,001 and above), $2,450-$4,300 (annual) ● distributor outside U.S., $650 (annual) ● manufacturer (with gross annual revenues of up to $50 million), $1,050-$2,100 (annual) ● specialized service, financial organization, $1,000 (annual) ● press, $600-$800 (annual). **Staff:** 23. **Local Groups:** 52. **Description:** Represents distributors and manufacturers of agriculture, and construction, mining, logging, forestry, public works and road maintenance equipment in the U.S., Canada, and overseas. Includes activities such as industry information and statistics, educational programs on customer service, financial management, rental management, sales management, and service and parts management program for younger executives. Maintains Washington, DC office. Oversees AED Foundation which offers industry educational programs and career/vocational services. Offers group and business insurance to members; conducts ongoing industry relations program with construction equipment manufacturers and users. Operates Market Trends Index Program, covering monthly distributor sales and inventories. **Awards:** Founders' Awards. **Frequency:** annual. **Type:** recognition. **Recipient:** for significant industry contributions and accomplishments. **Committees:** Future Leaders; Government Relations; Industry Round Table (distributors and manufacturers); Market Data. **Formerly:** National Distributors Association of Construction Equipment. **Publications:** *AED Resources Catalog*, annual. Lists publications, tapes, and services. **Price:** free ● *AEDNEWS.COM*, monthly. Newsletter. Alternate Formats: online ● *Associated Equipment Distributors—Membership Directory*, annual. **Price:** $50.00 ● *Construction Equipment Distribution*, monthly. Magazine. Contains articles aimed at making business more successful for distributors and their employees. Includes advertisers' index and convention issue. **Price:** $35.70 /year for members in U.S.; $71.40 /year for nonmembers in U.S.; $106.00 /year for members outside U.S.; $143.00 /year for nonmembers outside U.S. ISSN: 0010-6755. **Circulation:** 5,000. **Advertising:** accepted ● *Contact*, bimonthly. Newsletter. For construction equipment executives, giving news of the industry affecting distributors. **Price:** included in membership dues ● *Cost of Doing Business*, annual. Report. For construction equipment distributors covering business costs, sales, and financial data. **Price:** $75.00 for members ● Books ● Pamphlets. **Conventions/Meetings:** annual conference, executive forum ● annual meeting (exhibits) ● seminar, for salesmen.

2001 ■ Associated Wire Rope Fabricators (AWRF)
PO Box 748
Walled Lake, MI 48390-0748
Ph: (248)994-7753
Fax: (248)994-7754
E-mail: awrf@att.net
URL: http://www.awrf.org
Contact: Jeff Gilbert, Chief Exec.
Founded: 1975. **Members:** 300. **Multinational. Description:** Business firms that fabricate, manufacture, or sell lifting devices (such as wire rope, chain, or nylon) or other components of lifting, anchoring, and towing. Aims to acquire, preserve, and disseminate technical information, establish voluntary safety standards, establish product identification procedures, assist in establishing and maintaining adequate products liability insurance coverage for the industry. Conducts seminars at general meetings on such subjects as time management, economics, and banking. **Committees:** In Plant Safety; Insurance; New Products and Technology; Products Identification and Nomenclature. **Publications:** *Slingmakers*, quarterly. Newsletter ● Brochure, annual. **Conventions/Meetings:** semiannual meeting.

2002 ■ Association of Ingersoll-Rand Distributors (AIRD)
1300 Sumner Ave.
Cleveland, OH 44115-2851
Ph: (216)241-7333
Fax: (216)241-0105
E-mail: aird@aird.org
URL: http://www.aird.org
Contact: Kent Frkovich, Pres.
Members: 34. **Staff:** 2. **For-Profit. Description:** Individuals, corporations, partnerships, and other distribu-

tors of air compressors that have an Ingersoll-Rand Air Compressor Group or Full-Service Type 30 Master Distributor Agreement. Works to promote the improvement of business conditions affecting distributors of air compressors; to further a better understanding between distributors and suppliers of air compressors; to conduct research on ways and means of lowering the costs of distributing air compressors; and to collect and disseminate statistical information. **Conventions/Meetings:** conference.

2003 ■ Association of Suppliers to the Paper Industry (ASPI)
15 Tech. Pkwy. S, Ste.500
Norcross, GA 30092
Ph: (770)209-7521
Fax: (770)209-7581
E-mail: info@aspinet.org
URL: http://www.aspinet.org
Contact: Eric Fletty, Exec. Dir.
Founded: 1933. **Members:** 25. **Membership Dues:** corporation (with $10,000,000 or more in total sales), $3,407 (annual) ● corporation (with less than $10,000,000 in total sales), $2,305 (annual) ● emeritus, $450 (annual). **Staff:** 3. **Budget:** $85,000. **Description:** Represents companies engaged in supplying products and/or services to the American pulp, paper and/or board industry. **Committees:** Membership; Product Liability; Standards. **Formerly:** Pulp and Paper Machinery Association; (1989) Pulp and Paper Machinery Manufacturers Association; (2003) American Paper Machinery Association. **Publications:** Newsletter, quarterly. **Price:** included in membership dues. Alternate Formats: online. **Conventions/Meetings:** annual meeting - always January or February or March.

2004 ■ Automated Storage/Retrieval Systems (AS/RS)
8720 Red Oak Blvd., Ste.201
Charlotte, NC 28217
Ph: (704)676-1190
Fax: (704)676-1199
E-mail: rmoody@mhia.org
URL: http://www.mhia.org/psc/PSC_Products_StorageRetrieval.cfm
Contact: Dr. Richard E. Ward, Managing Exec.
Founded: 1967. **Members:** 10. **Staff:** 2. **Budget:** $80,000. **Description:** Companies manufacturing automated storage/retrieval systems. Develops and promotes standard nomenclature, codes for equipment operations, fire prevention, and personnel safety; assists and coordinates efforts of related trade associations pertaining to total systems. Develops and promotes a code of ethics; prepares and distributes publicity and educational materials. Cooperates with private and governmental groups that establish standards or safety codes. Sponsors educational programs and maintains speaker's bureau. **Libraries: Type:** reference. **Holdings:** archival material, audio recordings, books, clippings, monographs, periodicals. **Telecommunication Services:** electronic mail, dward@mhia.org. **Committees:** Communications; Engineering. **Affiliated With:** Material Handling Industry of America. **Formerly:** (1975) Controlled Mechanical Storage Systems. **Publications:** *Product Directory*, annual. **Price:** free ● *Roster of Members*, periodic. Membership Directory ● Monograph ● Also publishes case studies. **Conventions/Meetings:** semiannual conference ● trade show.

2005 ■ Automatic Guided Vehicle Systems Section of the Material Handling Institute (AGVS)
8720 Red Oak Blvd., Ste.201
Charlotte, NC 28217
Ph: (704)676-1190
Fax: (704)676-1199
E-mail: rmoody@mhia.org
URL: http://www.mhia.org/psc/PSC_Products_GuidedVehicle_agvscdrom.cfm
Contact: Dr. Richard E. Ward, Managing Dir.
Founded: 1979. **Members:** 10. **Staff:** 2. **Budget:** $80,000. **Description:** Represents manufacturers of automatic guided vehicles and systems used in manufacturing warehouses and distribution centers. Seeks to educate and promote the industry. Compiles statistics; maintains speakers' bureau. Conducts educational programs. A product section of the Material Handling Industry of America. **Libraries: Type:** reference. **Holdings:** archival material, audiovisuals, books, clippings, monographs, periodicals. **Telecommunication Services:** electronic mail, dward@mhia.org. **Affiliated With:** Material Handling Industry of America. **Formerly:** (1987) Automatic Guided Vehicle Systems. **Publications:** *AGVS Application Profile*, periodic. Book. Contains manufacturing, assembly and warehouse application case studies from 10 major manufacturers of AGV equipment. **Price:** $15.00 ● *Annual Literature Catalog*, annual. Lists current literature and educational materials. **Price:** free. **Conventions/Meetings:** semiannual meeting - always April and October.

2006 ■ AVEM International
71 Pinon Hill Pl. NE
Albuquerque, NM 87122-1914
Ph: (505)856-6924
Fax: (505)856-6716
E-mail: aveminfo@avem.org
URL: http://www.avem.org
Contact: Vivienne Harwood Mattox, Exec. Sec.
Founded: 1969. **Members:** 88. **Membership Dues:** associate, $350 (annual) ● manufacturer (based on annual sales), $520-$2,500 (annual). **Staff:** 2. **Budget:** $100,000. **Description:** Producers of vacuum equipment. Collects order receipts sales data in five categories of equipment and supplies; supports public relations efforts with users and professional societies related to the vacuum field; assists members in expanding export sales. Conducts educational programs. Compiles statistics. **Libraries: Type:** open to the public. **Subjects:** vacuum equipment and supplies. **Awards: Frequency:** annual. **Type:** recognition. **Formerly:** (1999) Association of Vacuum Equipment Manufacturers; (2002) Association of Vacuum Equipment Manufacturers International. **Publications:** *Directory of Products and Services for the Vacuum Industry*, annual. **Price:** $10.00. **Circulation:** 1,000. **Advertising:** accepted. Alternate Formats: online ● *Index of Products and Services for the Vacuum Industry*, annual. Directory ● Membership Directory, annual. **Conventions/Meetings:** annual International Spring Seminar - meeting - always spring.

2007 ■ Bearing Specialists Association (BSA)
800 Roosevelt Rd., Bldg. C, Ste.312
Glen Ellyn, IL 60137
Ph: (630)858-3838
Fax: (630)790-3095
E-mail: info@bsahome.org
URL: http://www.bsahome.org
Contact: Richard W. Church, Exec. Dir.
Founded: 1966. **Members:** 97. **Membership Dues:** regular, $863-$4,030 (annual). **Staff:** 5. **Description:** Distributors of anti-friction bearings. Promotes networking and knowledge sharing and promotes the sale of bearings through authorized distributors. **Committees:** Certification Advisory; Distributor/Manufacturer Relations; Educational Services; Information Technology and Logistics; Long Range Convention Planning. **Councils:** Bearing Industry Advisory. **Formed by Merger of:** Anti-Friction Bearing Distributors Association; Association of Bearing Specialists. **Conventions/Meetings:** annual convention ● annual meeting.

2008 ■ Cast Bronze Institute (C)
Address Unknown since 2007
Founded: 1958. **Members:** 28. **Staff:** 2. **Description:** Manufacturers of bronze sleeve bearings. Provides comprehensive technical and application aid to users and potential users of cast bronze bearings and bushings. Conducts research on materials, thrust bearing, and grease lubrication; develops standard performance tables. Has published manuals on cast bronze hydrostatic bearing design, cast bronze bearing design, cast bronze thrust bearing design and cast bronze hydrodynamic sleeve bearing. **Formerly:** Cast Bronze Bearing Institute.

2009 ■ Casting Industry Suppliers Association (CISA)
14175 W Indian School Rd., Ste.B4-504
Goodyear, AZ 85395
Ph: (623)547-0920
Fax: (623)536-1486
E-mail: info@cisa.org
URL: http://www.cisa.org
Contact: Roger A. Hayes, Exec. Dir.
Founded: 1917. **Members:** 56. **Membership Dues:** company, $3,100 (annual). **Staff:** 1. **Budget:** $400,000. **Description:** Manufacturers of foundry equipment and supplies such as molding machinery, dust control equipment and systems, blast cleaning machines, tumbling equipment, and related products. Fosters better trade practices; serves as industry representative before the government and the public. Encourages member research into new processes and methods of foundry operation and disseminates reports of progress in these fields. Compiles monthly statistics on booked and billed sales. **Committees:** Product Liability; Safety Standards; Statistics and Surveys. **Formed by Merger of:** Foundry Supply Manufacturers Group; Foundry Equipment Materials Association. **Publications:** *Buyer's Guide*, periodic ● Membership Directory, annual. **Conventions/Meetings:** conference - always March, July and November.

2010 ■ Compressed Air and Gas Institute (CAGI)
1300 Sumner Ave.
Cleveland, OH 44115-2851
Ph: (216)241-7333
Fax: (216)241-0105
E-mail: cagi@cagi.org
URL: http://www.cagi.org
Contact: John H. Addington, Sec.-Treas.
Founded: 1915. **Members:** 37. **Staff:** 3. **Description:** Represents manufacturers of air and gas compressors, pneumatic machinery, and compressed air and gas drying equipment. **Committees:** Educational and Promotional Marketing; Energy Awareness; Standards. **Sections:** Air Drying and Filtration; Blowers; Centrifugal Compressors; Home Air and Contractor; Pneumatic Tools. **Publications:** *Compressed Air and Gas Handbook* ● Also publishes charts and produces films. **Conventions/Meetings:** semiannual conference.

2011 ■ Contractors Pump Bureau (CPB)
6737 W Washington St., Ste.2400
Milwaukee, WI 53214-5647
Ph: (414)272-0943
Free: (866)236-0442
Fax: (414)272-1170
E-mail: info@aem.org
URL: http://www.aem.org/CBC/ProdSpec/CPB
Contact: Torsten Erbel, Chm.
Founded: 1938. **Members:** 20. **Description:** A bureau of the Association of Equipment Manufacturers. Manufacturers of pumping machinery and engines for the construction industry; suppliers to the manufacturers. Works toward the standardization of sizes and capacities of contractors' pumps. **Libraries: Type:** open to the public. **Committees:** Statistical; Technical. **Affiliated With:** Association of Equipment Manufacturers. **Publications:** *Asphalt Paver*. Manual. **Price:** $3.50 1-99 copies; $3.00 100 or more copies ● *Portable Pumps (Submersibles and Motor/Engine Driven)*. Manual. **Price:** $2.00 for members; $3.00 for nonmembers ● Videos ● Also publishes selection guidebook for portable dewatering pumps; pump safety video. **Conventions/Meetings:** semiannual board meeting.

2012 ■ Converting Equipment Manufacturers Association (CEMA)
201 Springs St.
Fort Mill, SC 29715
Ph: (803)802-7820
Fax: (803)802-7821

E-mail: cema@cema-converting.org
URL: http://www.cema-converting.org
Contact: Craig Sheppard, Exec. Dir.
Founded: 1984. **Members:** 70. **Membership Dues:** company, $1,000 (annual). **Budget:** $63,000. **Description:** Manufacturers of equipment used to perform a complete web converting function; company representatives who sell products and services; institutional members. Aims to promote the industry and advance the use of converting equipment; provide a forum for the exchange of ideas; cooperate and contribute to the understanding of converting equipment applications; seek new legislation and modify existing legislation regarding the industry. Conducts research on standards and guidelines. Compiles statistics. Sponsors educational programs. Maintains liaison with professional, governmental, and business organizations. **Committees:** Marketing; Safety. **Publications:** *CEMAscope*, quarterly. Newsletter. **Circulation:** 250. **Conventions/Meetings:** meeting - 3/year ● seminar.

2013 ■ Conveyor Equipment Manufacturers Association (CEMA)

6724 Lone Oak Blvd.
Naples, FL 34109
Ph: (239)514-3441
Fax: (239)514-3470
E-mail: cema@cemanet.org
URL: http://www.cemanet.org
Contact: Phil Hannigan, Contact
Founded: 1933. **Members:** 100. **Membership Dues:** manufacturing (maximum), $5,750 (annual) ● technical (based on number of people), $600-$3,000 (annual). **Staff:** 4. **Budget:** $450,000. **Description:** Manufacturers and engineers of conveyors and conveying systems, and portable and stationary machinery used in the transportation of raw materials and finished products in warehouses and on assembly line operations. Aims to standardize design, manufacture, and application of conveying machinery and component parts. **Subgroups:** Bulk Handling Components and Systems; Conveyor Controls; Palletizers; Pneumatic Conveyors; Screw Conveyors; Unit Handling Conveyors; Vibrating Equipment. **Formerly:** (1935) Association of Conveyor and Material Preparation Equipment Manufacturers; (1945) Conveyor Association. **Publications:** *Conveyor Equipment Manufacturers Association—Bulletin*, semiannual. Newsletter. Contains industry news and membership activities. **Price:** available to members only ● *Conveyor Equipment Manufacturers Association—Directory and Yearbook*. **Price:** available to members only ● *Conveyor Terms and Definitions* ● Also publishes other standards; offers film. **Conventions/Meetings:** semiannual meeting.

2014 ■ Conveyor Section of the Material Handling Institute (CS)

8720 Red Oak Blvd., Ste.201
Charlotte, NC 28217-3992
Ph: (704)676-1190
Fax: (704)676-1199
E-mail: tcarbott@mhia.org
URL: http://www.mhia.org/psc/PSC_Products_Conveyor.cfm
Contact: Ken Ruehrdanz, Chair
Founded: 1957. **Members:** 19. **Staff:** 2. **Budget:** $30,000. **Description:** Companies involved in the design, manufacture, and marketing of conveyors; publishers of magazines and periodicals that recognize and promote the best possible market for conveyors, consistent with the best interests of the user community. Seeks to foster a better understanding of conveyor equipment and its uses in government and industry. Maintains speakers' bureau; compiles statistics. Sponsors slide program. A product section of the Material Handling Institute (see separate entry). **Libraries: Type:** reference. **Committees:** Brochure; Statistical. **Publications:** *Application Guideline for Gravity Roller and Wheel Conveyors*. Book. Contains guidelines for selecting gravity roller and wheel conveyors. **Price:** $7.50 ● *Conveyor Accumulation Brochure*. **Price:** $7.00 ● *Conveyor Roster*, periodic ● *Conveyor Sortation-Equipment and Systems Design Issues*. Brochure. **Price:** $10.00 ● *Vertical Reciprocating Conveyors*. Book. **Price:** $10.00. **Conventions/Meetings:** semiannual meeting ● seminar.

2015 ■ Council of Industrial Boiler Owners (CIBO)

6035 Burke Centre Pkwy., Ste.360
Burke, VA 22015
Ph: (703)250-9042
Fax: (703)239-9042
E-mail: cibo@cibo.org
URL: http://www.cibo.org
Contact: Robert D. Bessette, Pres.
Founded: 1978. **Members:** 100. **Membership Dues:** university, $1,000 (annual) ● associate, $5,500 (annual) ● active, $11,000 (annual). **Staff:** 4. **Budget:** $700,000. **Description:** Industrial boiler owners, architect-engineers, related equipment manufacturers, and university affiliates. Works to promote the exchange of information between industry and government relating to energy and environmental policies, laws, and regulations affecting industrial boilers. Seeks to further the development of technically sound, reasonable, and cost-effective regulations for industrial boilers. **Committees:** Energy; Energy Efficiency; Environmental; Government Affairs; Technical. **Publications:** *Alternate Fuels I-IV*. Proceedings. **Price:** $25.00 each for members; $50.00 each for nonmembers ● *Boiler Life Extension I-II*. **Price:** $25.00 each for members; $50.00 each for nonmembers ● *Cogen II-III*. **Price:** $25.00 each for members; $50.00 each for nonmembers ● *Cogeneration/Energy Efficiency - 1994*. **Price:** $25.00 for members; $50.00 for nonmembers ● *Control Systems for S02 Emissions* ● *Energy Options: Cogen V and Retail Wheeling Alternatives*. Proceedings. Contains information from technical seminars and conferences. ● *Energy Options for the 1990s*. **Price:** $25.00 for members; $50.00 for nonmembers ● *Fluidized Bed I-XV*, annual. **Price:** $25.00 each for members; $50.00 each for nonmembers ● *Fuel Options-1995* ● *Industrial Power Plant Improvement - 1991 & 1993*. **Price:** $25.00 for members; $50.00 for nonmembers ● *NOx Control I-XIII*, annual. **Price:** $25.00 each for members; $35.00 each for nonmembers (volumes I-III); $50.00 each for nonmembers (volumes III-XIII) ● *Solid Fuel Combustion Systems - 1990*. **Conventions/Meetings:** annual NOx Control - conference (exhibits).

2016 ■ Crane Manufacturers Association of America (CMAA)

8720 Red Oak Blvd., Ste.201
Charlotte, NC 28217
Ph: (704)676-1190
Fax: (704)676-1199
E-mail: cmoose@mhia.org
URL: http://www.mhia.org/psc/PSC_Products_Cranes.cfm
Contact: Cathy Moose, Exec. Asst.
Founded: 1927. **Members:** 23. **Staff:** 2. **Description:** Manufacturers of electric overhead traveling cranes. Maintains speakers' bureau; compiles statistical reports. **Committees:** Engineering; Public Relations; Statistics. **Affiliated With:** Material Handling Industry of America. **Formerly:** (1968) Electric Overhead Crane Institute. **Publications:** *CMAA Specs 70 and 74* ● Publishes information and specifications on standard industrial service cranes. **Conventions/Meetings:** semiannual conference.

2017 ■ Fabricators and Manufacturers Association, International (FMA)

833 Featherstone Rd.
Rockford, IL 61107-6301
Ph: (815)399-8775 (815)227-8219
Free: (888)394-4362
Fax: (815)484-7701
E-mail: info@fmanet.org
URL: http://www.fmanet.org
Contact: Ms. Nancy Olson, Dir.
Founded: 1970. **Members:** 2,000. **Membership Dues:** individual, $150 (annual) ● advantage (one company location), $450 (annual) ● advantage plus (multiple locations), $950 (annual). **Staff:** 83. **Multinational. Description:** People involved in the metal forming and fabricating industry. Disseminates technological information on the fabrication of sheet, coil, tube, pipe, plate, and structural metal shapes. Conducts continuing education conferences. Maintains technical information center. **Libraries: Type:** by appointment only; reference. **Holdings:** 500; articles, audiovisuals, books, periodicals. **Subjects:** sheet metal fabricating, stamping, roll forming, welding, coil processing, tube and pipe producing, tube and pipe fabricating. **Computer Services:** Information services, member-only research assistance. **Councils:** Coil Processing; Plate Fabricating; Roll Forming; Safety; Sheet Metal; Stamping; Toll Processing. **Affiliated With:** Tube and Pipe Association, International. **Formerly:** (1975) Fabricating Machinery Association; (1985) Fabricating Manufacturers Association. **Publications:** *The Fabricator: Journal of Metal Forming and Fabricating Technology*, monthly. Magazine. Reports on state-of-the-art technology. Includes association and industry news, new product information, recently published literature, and reviews. **Price:** free to qualified persons; $95.00/year in Canada/Mexico; $140.00/year in all other countries. ISSN: 0192-8066. **Circulation:** 55,000. **Advertising:** accepted ● *Member Connections*, bimonthly. Newsletter. **Price:** included in membership dues ● *Practical Welding Today*, bimonthly. Magazine. Contains information on all areas of welding technology. **Price:** free to qualified subscribers; $55.00/year in Canada and Mexico; $75.00/year outside North America. **Circulation:** 40,000. **Advertising:** accepted ● *Stamping Journal*, monthly. Magazine. Contains information on metal stamping technology including presses, press feeds, coils handling equipment, tooling, and safety equipment. **Price:** free to qualified persons; $55.00/year in Canada/Mexico; $75.00/year in all other countries. **Circulation:** 34,000. **Advertising:** accepted. **Conventions/Meetings:** annual FABTECH International Exposition and Conference Series (exhibits) - odd-numbered years in November in Chicago, IL; even-numbered years in October in Cleveland, OH.

2018 ■ Fluid Controls Institute (FCI)

1300 Sumner Ave.
Cleveland, OH 44115
Ph: (216)241-7333
Fax: (216)241-0105
E-mail: fci@fluidcontrolsinstitute.org
URL: http://www.fluidcontrolsinstitute.org
Contact: J.H. Addington, Exec. Sec.
Founded: 1921. **Members:** 40. **Staff:** 3. **Description:** Works for technical advancement, promotion and understanding of a broad range of fluid control and fluid conditioning devices. Concentrates its efforts on the manufacturing and engineering aspects of control valves, solenoid valves, regulators, steam traps, pipeline strainers, secondary pressure drainers and gauges. Maintains the flexibility to adapt to changing technology by including a general products section, out of which new sections can be formed to better serve the industry and the general public. **Awards:** Past President Award. **Type:** scholarship. **Committees:** Economics; Government Relations; Industry Liaison; Standardization. **Sections:** Check Valve; Control Valve; Entrainment Separator; Gauge; General Products; Pipe Line Strainer and Filter; Regulator; Solenoid Valve; Steam Trap; Switches; Thermostatic Radiator Valves. **Formerly:** (1941) National Association of Steam and Fluid Specialty Manufacturers; (1955) National Steam Specialty Club. **Publications:** *Fluid Controls Institute—Meeting Minutes*, semiannual. **Price:** free, for members only. **Circulation:** 200 ● *Fluid Controls Institute—Membership Roster*, annual. Membership Directory ● *Fluid Controls Institute—News and Views*, quarterly. Newsletter. **Price:** free. **Circulation:** 500. **Conventions/Meetings:** semiannual meeting.

2019 ■ Fluid Power Distributors Association (FPDA)

PO Box 1420
Cherry Hill, NJ 08034-0054
Ph: (856)424-8998
Fax: (856)424-9248

E-mail: info@fpda.org
URL: http://www.fpda.org
Contact: Kathleen A. DeMarco, Exec. Dir.
Founded: 1974. **Members:** 300. **Membership Dues:** regular (based on number of employees), $600-$3,600 (annual) ● associate (based on number of employees), $1,340-$3,600 (annual). **Staff:** 8. **Budget:** $850,000. **Multinational. Description:** Represents wholesalers and manufacturers involved in the distribution of hydraulic and pneumatic equipment. Works to advance the distribution of such equipment; conducts research and educational activities. Compiles statistics. **Awards:** Tom Ralls Memorial Scholarship. **Frequency:** annual. **Type:** scholarship. **Recipient:** for young executive member. **Computer Services:** database. **Committees:** Benchmarking & Profitability; Distribution Technology; Education and Human Resources; Marketing and Public Relations; Young Executives. **Special Interest Groups:** Products and Technologies. **Publications:** *Cross-Industry Compensation Report*, biennial ● *FPDA News*, monthly. Newsletter. Provides sales and marketing tips and cost-cutting ideas submitted by members. **Price:** free. Alternate Formats: online ● *PROFIT Report*, annual. **Price:** $100.00 for members; $200.00 for nonmembers ● Membership Directory, annual. Contains list of members and their product lines; includes geographic index. **Price:** free for members; $50.00 for nonmembers. **Conventions/Meetings:** annual convention ● annual convention - always fall.

2020 ■ Fluid Sealing Association (FSA)
994 Old Eagle School Rd., No. 1019
Wayne, PA 19087
Ph: (610)971-4850
Fax: (610)971-4859
E-mail: info@fluidsealing.com
URL: http://www.fluidsealing.com
Contact: Robert H. Ecker, Exec. Dir.
Founded: 1933. **Members:** 60. **Membership Dues:** regular (based on annual sales of fluid sealing products), $3,300-$6,600 (annual) ● affiliate, $500 (annual). **Staff:** 5. **Budget:** $400,000. **Description:** Represents manufacturers of mechanical packings, sealing devices, gaskets, seals and expansion joints. **Formerly:** (1970) Mechanical Packing Association. **Publications:** *Compression Packing Handbook*. Handbooks. **Price:** $25.00 ● *Ducting Systems Non-Metallic Expansion Joints*. Handbook. **Price:** $25.00 ● *Mechanical Seals*. Handbook. **Price:** $25.00 ● *Metallic Gaskets*. Handbook. **Price:** $25.00 ● *Non-Metallic Expansion Joints and Flexible Pipe Connectors*. Handbook. **Price:** $25.00 ● *Sealing Components and Molded Packings*. Handbook. **Price:** $25.00. **Conventions/Meetings:** semiannual meeting - always April and October ● periodic symposium.

2021 ■ Gases and Welding Distributors Association (GAWDA)
100 N 20th St., 4th Fl.
Philadelphia, PA 19103
Ph: (215)564-3484 (402)964-5000
Fax: (215)963-9785
E-mail: gawda@gawda.org
URL: http://www.gawda.org
Contact: Kent Van Amburg, Exec. Dir.
Founded: 1945. **Members:** 1,200. **Membership Dues:** business (with total gross annual sales of under $1 million to $25 million), $546-$1,683 (annual) ● business (with total gross annual sales of $25 million to $250 million), $2,244-$5,304 (annual) ● business (with total gross annual sales of $250 million to over $500 million), $7,956-$16,065 (annual). **Staff:** 4. **Budget:** $200,000. **Description:** Manufacturers and distributors of welding supplies, and industrial and medical gases. Aims to promote the safe operation and economic vitality of distributors of industrial gases and welding equipment and supplies. **Telecommunication Services:** electronic mail, kvanamburg@fernley.com. **Committees:** Industry Partnering; Management Information; Safety; Training. **Formerly:** (2003) National Welding Supply Association. **Publications:** *FDA/EPA, OSHA, DOT Compliance Manual*, annual ● *Safety Organizer*, monthly ● *Spatter*, 5/year. Newsletter. Contains association and industry news. **Price:** included in membership dues ● *Welding and Gases Today*, quarterly. Journal. Contains news and announcement concerning the association. **Price:** included in membership dues; $195.00 /year for nonmembers. Alternate Formats: online. **Conventions/Meetings:** annual convention (exhibits) ● Management - conference - 3/year ● quarterly Zone Management Conference - meeting.

2022 ■ Gasket Fabricators Association (GFA)
994 Old Eagle School Rd., Ste.1019
Wayne, PA 19087
Ph: (610)971-4850
Fax: (610)971-4859
E-mail: info@gasketfab.com
URL: http://www.gasketfab.com
Contact: Robert H. Ecker, Exec. Dir.
Founded: 1979. **Members:** 120. **Membership Dues:** fabricator, $950 (annual) ● supplier, $1,500 (annual). **Staff:** 2. **Budget:** $180,000. **Description:** Represents gasket cutters and industry suppliers who are united to discuss problems and mutual solutions and to develop high standards for the gasket industry. **Publications:** *The Gasket Fabricator*, 3/year. Newsletter. Contains information on GFA meetings, member profiles and advertisements, technical articles, and general industry information. Alternate Formats: online ● *Technical Handbook*. **Price:** $12.00 plus shipping and handling ● Directory, annual. **Conventions/Meetings:** semiannual conference (exhibits) - usually March/April and September/October ● annual meeting.

2023 ■ Hoist Manufacturers Institute (HMI)
8720 Red Oak Blvd., Ste.201
Charlotte, NC 28217-3992
Ph: (704)676-1190
Fax: (704)676-1199
E-mail: cmoose@mhia.org
URL: http://www.mhia.org/psc/PSC_Products_Hoists.cfm
Contact: John Paxton, Pres.
Founded: 1968. **Members:** 17. **Staff:** 2. **Description:** Companies manufacturing various types of hoists, including overhead electric, ratchet lever, hand, and air. Compiles statistics; reviews safety codes pertaining to hoist equipment; prepares and distributes educational materials. **Committees:** Communication; Engineering. **Affiliated With:** Material Handling Industry of America. **Formerly:** Hoist Manufacturers Association. **Conventions/Meetings:** semiannual meeting.

2024 ■ Hydraulic Institute (HI)
9 Sylvan Way
Parsippany, NJ 07054
Ph: (973)267-9700
Fax: (973)267-9055
E-mail: info@pumps.org
URL: http://www.pumps.org
Contact: Robert K. Asdal, Exec. Dir.
Founded: 1917. **Members:** 90. **Staff:** 10. **Budget:** $1,600,000. **Description:** Manufacturers of pumps and products used with pumps. Compiles industry statistics, develops technical standards and meetings for pump manufacturers, creates educational programs for members and pump users worldwide and focuses on energy-savings with pumps and pumping systems through its Pump Systems Matter market transformation initiative. Provides education and tools for the effective application, testing, installation, operation and maintenance of pumps and pumping systems. **Additional Websites:** http://www.pumplearning.org, http://www.pumpsystemsmatter.org. **Telecommunication Services:** electronic mail, membership@pumps.org. **Committees:** Associate Member Technical. **Sections:** Air Operated Pump; Centrifugal Pump; Controlled Volume Metering Pump; Reciprocating Pump; Rotary Pump; Vertical Pump. **Publications:** *ANSI/HI Pump Standards for All Major Pump Types*. Books ● *Engineering Data Book* ● *Life Cycle Costs Guideline*. Book ● *Seal Guideline, Pump Systems Efficiency Guide, Technical White Papers and Educational Products*. Books ● *Variable Speed Pumping Guideline*. Book. **Conventions/Meetings:** annual Fall Management Conference and Technical Meeting, held for industry management and technical staff ● annual meeting - 2009 Feb. 20-24, Marco Island, FL; 2010 Feb. 19-23, Marco Island, FL ● annual Spring Technical Meeting.

2025 ■ Hydraulic Tool Manufacturers Association (HTMA)
PO Box 5416
Glendale Heights, IL 60139-5416
Ph: (630)893-7755
Fax: (630)790-2626
E-mail: kpolifka@wachsco.com
URL: http://www.htma.net
Contact: Tom Itrich, Contact
Founded: 1974. **Members:** 12. **Membership Dues:** manufacturer, $400 (annual). **Staff:** 2. **Budget:** $3,000. **Description:** Manufacturers of hydraulic tools. Seeks to promote the use of portable hydraulic tools through market education, tool classification, and standardization. Has established a system for the classification of hydraulic tools based on rate of flow. Cooperates with related industry groups and standards committees; represents members to appropriate agencies or officials of the federal government. Develops research and educational programs; conducts demonstrations. **Libraries: Type:** reference. **Holdings:** papers, reports. **Committees:** Engineering Standards. **Publications:** *HTMA Flush-Faced Quick-Connect Coupler Requirements*. Paper ● *Membership List*, periodic. Membership Directory ● *Recommended Standards for Hydraulic Tool Operation the Hydraulic Systems (Power Sources) on Construction, Utility, Farm, and Similar Equipment*. Paper ● Brochure, 2-3/year. Describes the mission, history, major accomplishments, publications, projects, membership policies, and objectives of the association. **Price:** free ● Also publishes industry standards. **Conventions/Meetings:** semiannual meeting - April and October.

2026 ■ Industrial Diamond Association (IDA)
PO Box 29460
Columbus, OH 43229
Ph: (614)797-2265
Fax: (614)797-2264
E-mail: tkane-ida@insight.rr.com
URL: http://www.superabrasives.org
Contact: Mr. Terry M. Kane, Exec. Dir.
Founded: 1946. **Members:** 210. **Membership Dues:** regular, associate, international, $500-$2,500 (annual) ● education, research, $125 (annual). **Staff:** 2. **Multinational. Description:** Represents industrial diamond, CBN, CVD diamond and polycrystalline and other superabrasive manufacturers, toolmakers, end users, contractors, machine tool builders and related suppliers. **Libraries: Type:** reference. **Holdings:** 4. **Subjects:** grinding machine, CNC machines, diamonds, cubic baron nitride, applications. **Awards:** Lifetime Membership Award. **Frequency:** periodic. **Type:** recognition. **Recipient:** for a major contribution to the association and/or industry over their lifetime of service ● President's Award for Distinguished Service. **Frequency:** annual. **Type:** recognition. **Recipient:** for outstanding contribution to the association and the industry. **Committees:** Communications; Education; Finance; Membership; Outreach; Standards. **Formerly:** (1946) Industrial Diamond Association of America. **Publications:** *Finer Points*, quarterly. Magazine. Serves as a trade magazine for superabrasives industry. **Price:** free for members; $10.00 for nonmembers; $75.00 for overseas subscribers. **Circulation:** 5,000. **Advertising:** accepted. Alternate Formats: online ● *Superabrasives Resource Directory*, annual. Lists superabrasive product, tool and service suppliers. ● *Technical Symposia Proceedings* ● Also publishes application information, standards, descriptive data, and technical data sheets. **Conventions/Meetings:** annual convention and conference ● biennial INTERTECH - international conference, dedicated to education and growth of the superabrasive industry through technical and practical application presentations (exhibits).

2027 ■ Industrial Supply Association (ISA)
100 N 20th St., 4th Fl.
Philadelphia, PA 19103
Ph: (215)320-3862
Free: (866)460-2360

Fax: (877)460-2365
E-mail: info@isapartners.org
URL: http://www.isapartners.org
Contact: Mr. John Buckley, Exec. VP
Membership Dues: affiliate, $750 (annual) ● associate, $249 (annual) ● manufacturer (based on annual sales volume), $239-$2,500 (annual) ● distributor (based on annual sales volume), $199-$2,500 (annual). **Staff:** 2. **Description:** Represents manufacturers of industrial machinery, maintenance, repair, operating and production supplies sold through industrial distributors. **Awards:** American Eagle. **Frequency:** annual. **Type:** recognition. **Recipient:** for ISA members ● Gary L. Buffington Memorial Scholarship. **Frequency:** annual. **Type:** scholarship. **Recipient:** to a rising senior in a qualified undergraduate industrial distribution program. **Telecommunication Services:** electronic mail, jbuckley@isapartners.org. **Formed by Merger of:** Industrial Supply Manufacturers Association; Industrial Distribution Association. **Formerly:** (2002) American Supply and Machinery Manufacturers Association; (2003) Industrial Supply and Machinery Manufacturers Association. **Conventions/Meetings:** annual meeting.

2028 ■ Institute of Caster Manufacturers (ICM)
Address Unknown since 2008
Founded: 1933. **Members:** 30. **Staff:** 2. **Budget:** $62,000,000. **Description:** Trade association representing manufacturers of casters and wheels for material handling equipment. **Libraries:** **Type:** reference. **Subjects:** caster hand truck guidelines. **Formerly:** (1990) Caster and Floor Truck Manufacturers Association.

2029 ■ International Association of Diecutting and Diemaking (IADD)
651 W Terra Cotta Ave., Ste.132
Crystal Lake, IL 60014
Ph: (815)455-7519
Free: (800)828-4233
Fax: (815)455-7510
E-mail: cccrouse@iadd.org
URL: http://www.iadd.org
Contact: Cindy C. Crouse CAE, CEO
Founded: 1972. **Members:** 900. **Membership Dues:** patron, $755 (annual) ● company, $425 (annual) ● associate, $120 (annual) ● affiliate, $295 (annual) ● individual, $195 (annual). **Staff:** 3. **Budget:** $500,000. **Regional Groups:** 7. **Multinational. Description:** Serves as international association for all companies involved in the diemaking and diecutting process. Provides conferences, educational and training programs, networking opportunities, monthly magazine, technical articles, regional chapter meetings, publications and training manuals, recommended specifications, safety guide, tech tips, and surveys. Strives to serve as a catalyst in inspiring industry success and the ultimate benefits to society that the industry provides. Aims to be the pivotal force in the diecutting converting industry, bringing together and serving people who convert soft to semi-rigid materials into various cut parts. **Awards:** Lifetime Achievement Award. **Frequency:** periodic. **Type:** recognition. **Recipient:** for exceptional, long term, and consistent contributions to the industry and the association ● Package Printing and Converting's Diecutter/Diemaker of the Year Award. **Frequency:** annual. **Type:** recognition. **Recipient:** to members who have demonstrated a significant contribution to the diecutting and diemaking process ● Presidential Award. **Frequency:** annual. **Type:** recognition. **Recipient:** for exceptional leadership, active support of association programs and activities, significant contributions to the association, and achievement in the industry ● S. Ray Miller International Award. **Frequency:** periodic. **Type:** recognition. **Recipient:** to members who are instrumental in advancing diecutting or diemaking on an international basis ● Safety Award. **Frequency:** annual. **Type:** recognition. **Recipient:** to companies with the lowest incidence rates of accidents per hours worked. **Computer Services:** Mailing lists. **Formerly:** (1980) Diemakers and Diecutters Association; (1991) National Association of Diemakers and Diecutters. **Publications:** *The Cutting Edge*, monthly. Magazine. Includes trends and technical information relevant to commercial and inplant diecutters and diemakers. **Price:** $99.00 for nonmembers; included in membership dues; $149.00 for nonmembers outside U.S. **Circulation:** 2,000. **Advertising:** accepted. Alternate Formats: CD-ROM; online ● *Glossary of Terms*. Booklets. **Price:** $10.00 for members; $15.00 for nonmembers ● *Membership Roster*, annual. Annual Report. **Price:** $25.00 plus shipping and handling ● *Recommended Specifications and Standards*. Manual. **Price:** $100.00 for members; $145.00 for nonmembers ● *Safety Guide*. Manual. **Price:** $95.00 for members; $145.00 for nonmembers ● *Tech Notes - Eliminating Flaking*. Papers. Includes white papers. **Price:** $30.00 for members; $45.00 for nonmembers ● *Training Guide for Bending Steel Rule*. Manual. **Price:** $150.00 for members; $275.00 for nonmembers. **Conventions/Meetings:** semiannual meeting, leadership seminars - always March and September ● Midyear Leadership Conference, chapter meetings - 1-4/year ● seminar, technical - 2-4/year ● trade show, chapter meetings - 1-4/year.

2030 ■ International Glove Association (IGA)
PO Box 146
Brookville, PA 15825
Ph: (814)328-5208 (763)416-2129
Fax: (814)328-2308
E-mail: gloves@alltel.net
URL: http://www.iga-online.com
Contact: David Burdge, Exec. Dir.
Founded: 1902. **Members:** 64. **Staff:** 2. **Multinational. Description:** Represents manufacturers, distributors, and the material suppliers of fabric, leather, coated, and liquid proof gloves and mittens for hand and arm protection. Seeks to expand the worldwide market and sales opportunities for work gloves. **Committees:** Communications; Program Development. **Formerly:** National Association of Cotton Cloth Glove Manufacturers; (1968) Work Glove Institute; (1991) Work Glove Manufacturers Association; (2003) International Hand Protection Association. **Publications:** *IGA Newsletter*, 11/year. Alternate Formats: online. **Conventions/Meetings:** annual conference (exhibits) ● annual seminar.

2031 ■ International Special Tooling and Machining Association (ISTMA)
c/o Mr. Egon Jaeggin, VP
2200 Foster Ave.
Wheeling, IL 60090
Ph: (847)394-3610
Fax: (847)394-3962
E-mail: ejaeggin@numericalprecision.com
URL: http://www.istma.org
Contact: Mr. Egon Jaeggin, VP
Founded: 1973. **Members:** 24. **Staff:** 1. **Languages:** English, French, German. **Multinational. Description:** Represents associations of tool, die, and mold manufacturers. Works to facilitate the exchange of business and technical information on a permanent basis. Compiles statistics. **Libraries:** **Type:** reference. **Subjects:** nomenclature, terminology, professional education. **Committees:** Business Management; Personnel Activities within the Industry; Standardization; Technical. **Divisions:** ISTA America; ISTA Asia; ISTA Europe. **Formerly:** (1960) National Tool and Die Manufacturers Association; (1980) National Tool, Die and Precision Machining Association; (1997) International Special Tooling Association. **Publications:** *Abstract Services*, periodic ● *Special Bulletins*, periodic ● Also publishes study papers; is compiling a glossary of technical terms. **Conventions/Meetings:** triennial conference ● periodic conference.

2032 ■ Investment Casting Institute (ICI)
136 Summit Ave.
Montvale, NJ 07645-1745
Ph: (201)573-9770
Fax: (201)573-9771
E-mail: ici@investmentcasting.org
URL: http://www.investmentcasting.org
Contact: Michael C. Perry, Exec. Dir.
Founded: 1953. **Members:** 200. **Membership Dues:** casting regular, $950-$5,700 (annual) ● casting associate, $850-$5,100 (annual) ● supplier regular, $475-$1,663 (annual) ● supplier associate, $425-$1,487 (annual) ● university/school (regular), $475 (annual) ● university/school (associate), $425 (annual). **Staff:** 4. **Budget:** $1,000,000. **Description:** Comprised of manufacturers of precision castings for industrial use made by the investment (or lost wax) process and suppliers to such manufacturers. Provides training courses and other specialized education programs. **Libraries:** **Type:** reference. **Awards:** **Type:** recognition. **Committees:** Publications; Strategic Review. **Publications:** *Catalogue of Publication* ● *Incast*, monthly. Magazine. Includes industry news and case studies. **Price:** $60.00/year in U.S. and Canada; $90.00/year outside U.S. and Canada. ISSN: 1045-5779. **Circulation:** 1,800. **Advertising:** accepted ● Bibliography, annual. **Price:** available to members only ● Membership Directory. **Price:** free for members; $25.00 for nonmembers ● Proceedings, annual ● Books ● Videos ● Booklets. **Conventions/Meetings:** annual Technical Conference and Expo (exhibits) - always September or October ● annual World Conference on Investment Casting - meeting and conference - 2008 Oct. 19-22, Dallas, TX.

2033 ■ Iron Casting Research Institute (ICRI)
2802 Fisher Rd.
Columbus, OH 43204
Ph: (614)275-4201
Fax: (614)275-4203
E-mail: webmaster@ironcasting.com
URL: http://www.ironcasting.org
Contact: Bruce T. Blatzer, Exec. Dir.
Founded: 1939. **Members:** 20. **Membership Dues:** regular, $20,000 (annual). **Staff:** 3. **Budget:** $510,000. **Description:** Iron castings companies and plants united to stay abreast of technical and operating developments in the industry. Arranges plant visits; conducts research and surveys on members' technical and operating practices; compiles statistics. Organizes in-plant seminars; holds operators and task force meetings and workshops; maintains library on metal casting and related fields. **Committees:** Research. **Formerly:** (1984) Gray Iron Research Institute. **Publications:** Newsletter, periodic ● Also publishes reports and technical abstracts.

2034 ■ Lift Manufacturers Product Section - Material Handling Industry of America (LMPS)
8720 Red Oak Blvd., Ste.201
Charlotte, NC 28217-3996
Ph: (704)676-1190
Fax: (704)676-1199
E-mail: jnofsinger@mhia.org
URL: http://www.mhia.org/psc/PSC_Products_Lifts.cfm
Contact: Louis Coleman, Acting Chm.
Founded: 1990. **Members:** 14. **Staff:** 2. **Budget:** $15,000. **Description:** Manufacturers of lift equipment, such as lift tables, dock lifts, die tables, and manually propelled stackers, designed to raise, lower, and position industrial materials. Promotes the advancement of the industry. Conducts educational programs; maintains speakers' bureau. **Libraries:** **Type:** reference. **Holdings:** audio recordings, books, periodicals, video recordings. **Publications:** Papers. Alternate Formats: online.

2035 ■ Loading Dock Equipment Manufacturers (LODEM)
8720 Red Oak Blvd., Ste.201
Charlotte, NC 28217
Ph: (704)676-1190
Fax: (704)676-1199
E-mail: rniemeyer@mhia.org
URL: http://www.mhia.org
Contact: Norbert Hahn, Chm.
Members: 8. **Staff:** 2. **Description:** Manufacturers of qualifying loading dock equipment. Promotes the loading dock equipment market by participating in trade shows and distributing informational materials on the industry. A product section of the Material Handling Institute. **Committees:** Engineering. **Conventions/Meetings:** meeting - 3/year.

2036 ■ Machine Knife Association (MKA)
30200 Detroit Rd.
Cleveland, OH 44145-1967
Ph: (440)899-0010
Fax: (440)892-1404
E-mail: djh@wherryassoc.com
URL: http://www.mka.org
Contact: Jeffery Wherry, Exec. Sec.
Founded: 1933. **Members:** 7. **Staff:** 2. **Description:** Manufacturers of woodworking and metal cutting knives for machinery. Represents the industry and compiles statistics. **Absorbed:** (1984) Metal Cutting Knife Association. **Formerly:** (1983) Machine Knife Manufacturers Association. **Conventions/Meetings:** semiannual meeting.

2037 ■ Machinery Dealers National Association (MDNA)
315 S Patrick St.
Alexandria, VA 22314-3501
Ph: (703)836-9300
Free: (800)872-7807
Fax: (703)836-9303
E-mail: office@mdna.org
URL: http://www.mdna.org
Contact: Joseph R. Kraemer CAE, Pres.
Founded: 1941. **Members:** 450. **Membership Dues:** company, $900 (annual). **Staff:** 5. **Regional Groups:** 14. **Multinational. Description:** Dealers in used, rebuilt, and reconditioned industrial machinery. **Libraries: Type:** reference. **Subjects:** parts manuals for industrial machine tools. **Committees:** Government Affairs; Public and Industry Relations. **Publications:** *Buyer's Guide*, annual. Contains listing of dealers. ● *News*, bimonthly. Newsletter. Contains events and programs. ● *Truckers and Riggers*. Directory. **Conventions/Meetings:** annual convention (exhibits) - always April or May.

2038 ■ Manufacturers of Aerial Devices and Digger-Derricks Council (MADDDC)
6737 W Washington St., Ste.2400
Milwaukee, WI 53214-5647
Ph: (414)272-0943 (414)298-4149
Fax: (414)272-1170
E-mail: aem@aem.org
URL: http://www.aem.org/CBC/ProdSpec/MADDDC
Contact: Dan Moss, Contact
Founded: 1975. **Members:** 21. **Description:** A council of the Association of Equipment Manufacturers (see separate entry). Corporations actively engaged in the manufacture and national marketing of vehicle-mounted aerial devices and digger-derricks. Works on issues in governmental/legislative relations, specification/definitions, and technical standards required to comply with federal and state regulations. **Conventions/Meetings:** semiannual meeting.

2039 ■ Manufacturers Alliance/MAPI
1600 Wilson Blvd., Ste.1100
Arlington, VA 22209-2594
Ph: (703)841-9000
Fax: (703)841-9514
E-mail: info@mapi.net
URL: http://www.mapi.net
Contact: Mr. Thomas J. Duesterberg, Pres./CEO
Founded: 1933. **Members:** 450. **Staff:** 38. **Budget:** $5,000,000. **Description:** Manufacturing and related business service companies. Membership concentrated in the following sectors: aerospace; automotive; scientific instruments; electronics; computers and telecommunication equipment; high technology; chemicals/pharmaceuticals; oil and oil-related equipment; electrical equipment farm, construction, food, material handling, and other machinery; primary and fabricated metals. Provides member services through councils and research programs. Produces a variety of research, including economic, policy, and benchmark work to assist members in their planning, compliance, and process improvement efforts. **Formerly:** (1989) Machinery and Allied Products Institute; (2000) Manufacturers Alliance for Productivity and Innovation. **Publications:** *Economic Report*, periodic ● *MAPI Policy Review*, periodic ● Also publishes legislative and regulatory analyses, books, manuals, pamphlets, and economic briefs on capital formation and investment, government contracts, export financing, business investment management, risk management, product liability, and other management problems.

2040 ■ Manufacturers Standardization Society of the Valve and Fittings Industry (MSS)
127 Park St. NE
Vienna, VA 22180-4602
Ph: (703)281-6613
Fax: (703)281-6671
E-mail: info@mss-hq.org
URL: http://www.mss-hq.com
Contact: Robert O'Neill, Exec. Dir.
Founded: 1924. **Members:** 98. **Membership Dues:** corporate, $1,800 (annual). **Staff:** 4. **Budget:** $300,000. **Multinational. Description:** Manufacturers of valves, valve actuators, flanges, pipe fittings, pipe hangers, and associated seals. Engineering society for the valve and fittings industry devoted to the development and publication of standards, specifications, and related engineering matters. Issues numerous publications on standards and specifications. **Libraries: Type:** reference. **Awards: Frequency:** annual. **Type:** recognition. **Recipient:** for outstanding service. **Committees:** Iron Flanged and Flanged Fittings; Marking and Terminology; Non-Ferrous Fittings and Flanges; Non-Ferrous Industrial Valves; Packings and Gaskets; Pipe Hangers; Quality Standards; Valve Actuators. **Publications:** Standards for products in the valve and fittings industry. **Conventions/Meetings:** annual meeting, for MSS membership and all technical committees - 2009 Apr. 28-May 8, Marco Island, FL.

2041 ■ Manufacturers of Telescoping and Articulated Cranes Council (MOTACC)
c/o Association of Equipment Manufacturers
6737 W Washington St., Ste.2400
Milwaukee, WI 53214-5647
Ph: (414)298-4132 (414)272-0943
Fax: (414)272-1170
E-mail: info@aem.org
URL: http://www.aem.org/cbc/prodspec/motacc
Contact: Scott Rolston, Chm.
Founded: 1975. **Members:** 15. **Description:** A council of the Association of Equipment Manufacturers (see separate entry). Manufacturers and/or national distributors of truck and stationary-mounted telescoping and articulating cranes. Promotes the proper and mutual interests of members. Develops proposals for engineering, safety, and specifications; generates proprietary sales and inventory statistics for members. **Computer Services:** Mailing lists, of members. **Conventions/Meetings:** semiannual meeting, held in conjunction with Equipment Manufacturers Institute.

2042 ■ Material Handling Accessory Manufacturers, Production Section of the Material Handling Industry
8720 Red Oak Blvd., Ste.201
Charlotte, NC 28217-3992
Ph: (704)676-1190
Free: (800)345-1815
Fax: (704)676-1199
E-mail: jnofsinger@mhia.org
URL: http://www.mhia.org
Contact: Mr. Alan Howie, Dir. of Professional Development
Founded: 1970. **Members:** 10. **Staff:** 2. **Description:** A product section of the Material Handling Institute. Companies that are members of the MHI and actively engaged in the manufacture and marketing of overhead component devices. Attempts to promote the largest possible market for members and to protect the interests of users. **Affiliated With:** Material Handling Industry of America. **Formerly:** (1990) Below/Hook Lifters Section of the Material Handling Institute; (1993) Overhead Components Manufacturers Product Section of the Material Handling Institute; (1999) Overhead Components Manufacturers Production Section of the Material Handling Institute of America. **Publications:** Manual. Contains guidelines for the safe operation of close proximity and remotely operated lifting magnets. **Conventions/Meetings:** annual meeting.

2043 ■ Material Handling Equipment Distributors Association (MHEDA)
201 U.S. Hwy. 45
Vernon Hills, IL 60061-2398
Ph: (847)680-3500
Fax: (847)362-6989
E-mail: connect@mheda.org
URL: http://www.mheda.org
Contact: Liz Richards, Exec. VP
Founded: 1954. **Members:** 700. **Membership Dues:** distributor, factory-owned branch/manufacturing representative (based on company's gross annual sales volume), $615-$2,660 (annual) ● supplier/associate (based on company's gross annual sales volume), $1,050-$2,650 (annual). **Staff:** 9. **Budget:** $1,000,000. **Description:** Distributors and manufacturers of material handling equipment. Aims to improve the proficiency of independent material handling distributors. **Publications:** *MHEDA Journal*, quarterly. Contains articles pertaining to the material handling industry. **Price:** $129.00 for nonmembers; free for members. **Circulation:** 3,500. **Advertising:** accepted. Alternate Formats: online ● Membership Directory, annual. **Price:** $50.00 for members; $950.00 for nonmembers. **Conventions/Meetings:** annual convention (exhibits) - 2009 May 2-6, Palm Desert, CA.

2044 ■ Material Handling Industry of America (MHIA)
8720 Red Oak Blvd., Ste.201
Charlotte, NC 28217-3992
Ph: (704)676-1190
Fax: (704)676-1199
E-mail: miemeyer@mhia.org
URL: http://www.mhia.org
Contact: J.B. Nofsinger, CEO
Founded: 1945. **Members:** 750. **Membership Dues:** regular, $2,000 (annual). **Staff:** 30. **Budget:** $12,000,000. **Description:** Consultants, integrators, publishers, 3PL providers and manufacturers of industrial material handling equipment and systems. Promotes education in the use of material handling equipment. Compiles, distributes, and exchanges information; supports and finances technical education; promotes industry standards; informs users of the advantages of integrated material handling systems. Maintains 18 product sections. Conducts trade shows and educational conferences. **Libraries: Type:** reference; open to the public. **Holdings:** periodicals, reports. **Subjects:** engineering. **Awards:** Material Handling Education Foundation Scholarship. **Frequency:** annual. **Type:** scholarship. **Committees:** Communications; Education; Statistical Information. **Councils:** Ergonomics Assist Systems and Equipment; Integrated Systems and Controls; Order Fulfillment. **Sections:** AGVS Product; AS/RS Product; Conveyor Product; Industrial Controls and Components Manufacturers Product; Loading Dock Manufacturers Product; Reusable Plastic Pallet and Container Product. **Subgroups:** Crane Manufacturers Association of America; Hoist Manufacturers Institute; Industrial Caster and Wheel Association; Monorail Manufacturers Association. **Affiliated With:** Automated Storage/Retrieval Systems; Automatic Guided Vehicle Systems Section of the Material Handling Institute; Conveyor Section of the Material Handling Institute; Crane Manufacturers Association of America; Hoist Manufacturers Institute; Industrial Metal Containers and Wire Decking, a Product Section of the Material Handling Industry; Lift Manufacturers Product Section - Material Handling Industry of America; Loading Dock Equipment Manufacturers; Monorail Manufacturers Association; Rack Manufacturers Institute; Storage Equipment Manufacturers Association. **Formerly:** (1991) Material Handling Institute; (2002) Material Handling Industry. **Publications:** *E-On The Move*, monthly. Newsletter. Alternate Formats: online ● *The Exhibitor*, quarterly. Newsletter. Contains information on exhibiting in trade shows. **Price:** free ● *MHI Literature Catalog*, annual. Lists publications available from the institute and other

sources of information. **Price:** free ● *On-The-Move*, bimonthly. Newsletter. Includes information on member activities. **Conventions/Meetings:** annual meeting - 2008 Sept. 7-11, Scottsdale, AZ ● annual Spring Membership - meeting (exhibits).

2045 ■ Mechanical Power Transmission Association (MPTA)
6724 Lone Oak Blvd.
Naples, FL 34109
Ph: (239)514-3441
Fax: (239)514-3470
E-mail: bob@mpta.org
URL: http://www.mpta.org
Contact: Robert A. Reinfried, Exec. Dir.
Founded: 1933. **Members:** 21. **Membership Dues:** maximum, $3,850 (annual). **Staff:** 2. **Budget:** $100,000. **Description:** Manufacturers of multiple V-belt drive sheaves and elastomeric couplings for mechanical power transmission machinery. **Formerly:** Multiple V-Belt Drive and Mechanical Power Transmission Association. **Conventions/Meetings:** meeting.

2046 ■ Monorail Manufacturers Association (MMA)
8720 Red Oak Blvd., Ste.201
Charlotte, NC 28217
Ph: (704)676-1190
Fax: (704)676-1199
E-mail: cmoose@mhia.org
URL: http://www.mhia.org/psc/PSC_Products_Monorail.cfm
Contact: David Butwid, Pres.
Founded: 1933. **Members:** 17. **Staff:** 2. **Description:** Manufacturers of overhead/under hung material-handling equipment monorails, stacker cranes, and under hung traveling cranes. Prepares and distributes training inspection and maintenance recommendations that are available to all users. **Committees:** Engineering. **Affiliated With:** Material Handling Industry of America. **Publications:** Brochures. **Conventions/Meetings:** semiannual meeting, business.

2047 ■ National Association of Hose and Accessories Distribution (NAHAD)
105 Eastern Ave., Ste.104
Annapolis, MD 21403-3300
Ph: (410)263-1014
Free: (800)624-2227
Fax: (410)263-1659
E-mail: info@nahad.org
URL: http://www.nahad.org
Contact: Joseph M. Thompson Jr., Exec. VP
Founded: 1985. **Members:** 540. **Staff:** 5. **Budget:** $800,000. **Description:** Manufacturers and distributors of industrial hose products and accessories such as rubber, metal, and hydraulic hoses. Fosters and improves communication among manufacturers and distributors in the industrial hose and accessories industry. Offers educational programs. **Libraries: Type:** reference. **Holdings:** 80; books, reports, video recordings. **Subjects:** management, sales, human resources, technical issues. **Awards:** Annual College Scholarships. **Frequency:** annual. **Type:** scholarship. **Recipient:** to four students with financial need. **Computer Services:** Online services. **Committees:** Communications; Education and Training; International; Management Information; Membership; Standards; Technology. **Publications:** *NAHAD Membership Directory*, annual. **Price:** $50.00 for members; $250.00 for nonmembers. **Advertising:** accepted ● *NAHAD News*, bimonthly. Newsletter. Alternate Formats: online. **Conventions/Meetings:** annual meeting and convention (exhibits) - always March, April or May.

2048 ■ National Association of Vertical Transportation Professionals (NAVTP)
c/o Curtis E. Forney, Exec. Dir.
2107 Pounge Ave.
Cincinnati, OH 45208-3267
Ph: (513)533-3500
Fax: (513)871-3504
E-mail: forneyce@fuse.net
URL: http://www.navtp.org
Contact: Curtis E. Forney, Exec. Dir.
Founded: 1990. **Members:** 82. **Membership Dues:** professional, $200 (annual). **Staff:** 1. **Regional Groups:** 4. **Description:** Independent elevator consultants and engineers. Seeks to enhance elevator and escalator safety. Offers safety awareness programs. Provides a forum for exchange among members. **Telecommunication Services:** electronic mail, curtisnavtp@fuse.net. **Publications:** Newsletter, bimonthly. **Conventions/Meetings:** annual workshop, with educational programs and seminars, present topics and products of interest to the association (exhibits) - always held in spring; usually May. 2010 May, Nashville, TN.

2049 ■ National Elevator Industry, Inc. (NEII)
1677 County Rte. 64
PO Box 838
Salem, NY 12865-0838
Ph: (518)854-3100
Fax: (518)854-3257
E-mail: info@neii.org
URL: http://www.neii.org
Contact: Edward A. Donoghue, Admin.
Founded: 1934. **Members:** 40. **Staff:** 1. **Budget:** $900,000. **National Groups:** 10. **Description:** Serves as a trade association of the building transportation industry. Promotes safe building transportation for new and existing products and technologies, and adoption of the current codes by local government agencies. **Libraries: Type:** not open to the public. **Holdings:** books, business records, reports. **Computer Services:** database ● mailing lists. **Committees:** National and Area Codes; Performance Standards; Safety. **Formerly:** (1969) National Elevator Manufacturing Industry. **Publications:** *Building Transportation Standards and Guidelines - NEII-1-2000*, quinquennial ● Yearbook, annual. **Conventions/Meetings:** annual conference.

2050 ■ National Fluid Power Association (NFPA)
3333 N Mayfair Rd., Ste.211
Milwaukee, WI 53222-3219
Ph: (414)778-3344 (414)778-3351
Fax: (414)778-3361
E-mail: nfpa@nfpa.com
URL: http://www.nfpa.com
Contact: Eric Lanke, Exec. Dir.
Founded: 1953. **Members:** 250. **Membership Dues:** regular, distributor (minimum), $1,100 (annual) ● international (minimum), $5,500 (annual) ● associate, $2,750 (annual). **Staff:** 10. **Budget:** $1,500,000. **Languages:** English, French, German, Spanish. **Description:** Manufacturers of components such as fittings used in transmitting power by hydraulic and pneumatic pumps, valves, cylinders, filters, seals; the components are used in industrial and mobile machinery in the material-handling, automotive, railway, aircraft, marine, aerospace, construction, agricultural, and other industries. Works to develop: American National Standards Institute and International Organization for Standardization (see separate entries); fluid power technical standards; fluid power index (industry sales); management and marketing studies. Compiles statistics. Administers and serves as secretariat to several international project groups and other fluid power organizations. **Libraries: Type:** reference. **Holdings:** papers, reports. **Awards:** Standards Development Award. **Frequency:** annual. **Type:** recognition. **Committees:** Management Services; Marketing; Performance Standards Development; Technical. **Affiliated With:** American National Standards Institute; International Organization for Standardization. **Publications:** *Fluid Power Publications Catalog*, annual. Bibliography. Lists fluid power standards, marketing, management, and technical publication offered by the Association. **Price:** free. **Circulation:** 5,000 ● *Fluid Power Standards*, periodic. Contains both design and performance standards for fluid power products and systems. Individual volumes available separately. **Price:** $300.00. Alternate Formats: microform ● *National Fluid Power Association—Directory and Membership Guide*, annual. **Price:** $100.00 for nonmembers. **Circulation:** 1,800 ● *National Fluid Power Association—Reporter*, bimonthly. Newsletter. Includes articles on the fluid power market, manufacturing, people, meetings, and statistics. **Price:** included in membership dues; $50.00 for nonmembers. **Circulation:** 2,000 ● *Statistical Handbook* ● Books ● Brochures ● Reports ● Videos. **Conventions/Meetings:** semiannual conference - always spring and fall ● annual Economic Outlook Conference - meeting - always fall ● quadrennial International Fluid Power Exposition - meeting ● annual meeting and conference - always spring. 2009 Feb. 19-22, Tucson, AZ.

2051 ■ National Industrial Belting Association (NIBA)
N19 W24400 Riverwood Dr.
Waukesha, WI 53188
Ph: (262)523-9090
Free: (800)488-4845
Fax: (262)523-9091
E-mail: support@niba.org
URL: http://www.niba.org
Contact: Rene Morf, Pres.
Founded: 1927. **Members:** 300. **Membership Dues:** regular (based on annual sales volume), $90-$725 (annual). **Staff:** 2. **Description:** Manufacturers and fabricator-distributors of all types of flat belting, including rubber, PVC, and leather belting used for power transmission and conveying. Sponsors educational programs. **Libraries: Type:** reference. **Holdings:** articles, video recordings. **Awards:** NIBA Scholarship Foundation. **Frequency:** annual. **Type:** scholarship ● Ray Snow Memorial Scholarship. **Frequency:** annual. **Type:** scholarship. **Recipient:** for candidates pursuing a minimum 2-year course of study at an accredited college, university or technical who have demonstrated exceptional qualifications in the areas of scholarship and scholastic achievement, leadership, and community service. **Computer Services:** Mailing lists, of members. **Also Known As:** (2002) NIBA - The Belting Association. **Formerly:** (1926) American Leather Belting Association; (1976) National Industrial Leather Association. **Publications:** *Belt Line*, 5/year. Newsletter. **Conventions/Meetings:** annual convention (exhibits).

2052 ■ National New England Lead Burning Association
c/o Karl Weiss, CEO
800 W Cummings Park, Ste.3950
Woburn, MA 01801
Ph: (781)933-1940
Free: (800)635-2613
Fax: (781)932-8647
URL: http://www.nelco-usa.com
Contact: Karl Weiss, CEO
Founded: 1945. **Members:** 10. **Description:** Lead burning contractors engaged in fabrication and installation in shop and field of lead-lined equipment for handling corrosive chemicals, and for radiation shielding in atomic energy plants and X-ray rooms. **Formerly:** (1997) National Lead Burning Association. **Conventions/Meetings:** semiannual meeting.

2053 ■ Non-Ferrous Founders' Society (NFFS)
1480 Renaissance Dr., Ste.310
Park Ridge, IL 60068
Ph: (847)299-0950
Fax: (847)299-3598
E-mail: nffstaff@nffs.org
URL: http://www.nffs.org
Contact: James L. Mallory CAE, Exec. Dir.
Founded: 1943. **Members:** 150. **Membership Dues:** company (with 1-10 employees), $825 (annual) ● company (with 11-25 employees), $1,550 (annual) ● company (with 26-50 employees), $2,275 (annual) ● company (with 50-100 employees), $2,750 (annual) ● company (with 101 and up employees), $3,825 (annual). **Staff:** 4. **Budget:** $675,000. **Description:** Manufacturers of brass, bronze, aluminum, and other nonferrous castings. **Committees:** Government Relations; Insurance; Management Conference; Planning; Quality; Technical Research. **Absorbed:** (1988) Cast Bronze Bearings Institute. **Publications:** *The Cru-*

cible, bimonthly. Magazine. Features articles relevant to the day-to-day management of aluminum, brass, bronze, and other non-ferrous foundries. **Price:** free for members. **Circulation:** 1,500. **Advertising:** accepted. **Conventions/Meetings:** annual meeting (exhibits).

2054 ■ North American Die Casting Association (NADCA)
241 Holbrook Dr.
Wheeling, IL 60090-5809
Ph: (847)279-0001
Fax: (847)279-0002
E-mail: nadca@diecasting.org
URL: http://www.diecasting.org
Contact: Daniel Twarog CAE, Pres.
Founded: 1989. **Members:** 3,200. **Membership Dues:** corporate die caster/corporate supplier (minimum), $1,975 (annual) ● corporate affiliate, $500 (annual) ● individual, $80 (annual) ● corporate individual, $80 (annual) ● student, $25 (annual) ● associate individual, $150 (annual) ● corporate die caster/corporate supplier (maximum), $11,300 (annual). **Staff:** 17. **Budget:** $3,000,000. **Regional Groups:** 7. **Local Groups:** 23. **Description:** Represents producers of die castings and suppliers to the industry, product and die designers, metallurgists, and students. Develops product standards; compiles trade statistics on metal consumption trends; conducts promotional activities; provides information on chemistry, mechanics, engineering, and other arts and sciences related to die casting. Provides training materials and short, intensive courses in die casting. Maintains speakers' bureau. **Libraries: Type:** reference. **Holdings:** 300; archival material. **Awards:** Doehler, Gullo and Treiber Award. **Type:** recognition ● Edward A. Kruszynski Achievement Award. **Frequency:** biennial. **Type:** recognition ● Lilligren Award. **Type:** recognition ● Nysellius Award. **Type:** recognition. **Committees:** Awards; DCE Editorial Advisory Harvill Foundation; Die Materials; Industry; Industry Relations; Member Services; National Affairs; Operating Tech; Research and Development. **Councils:** International Technical; Technical. **Absorbed:** (1987) Die Casting Research Foundation. **Formed by Merger of:** American Die Casting Institute; Society of Die Casting Engineers. **Publications:** *A Guide to Reducing and Treating Dross*. Book. Focuses on dross formation, the influence of furnace type and operational procedures on dross and fluxing. ● *Die Casting Engineer*. Magazine. For die casting engineers and executives; includes information on new products and literature, chapter news, and calendar of events. **Price:** included in membership dues. ISSN: 0012-253X. **Advertising:** accepted ● *Financial Survey*, annual. Provides a snapshot view of the financial performance expected from a company in the die casting industry. ● *Introduction to Die Casting*. Book ● *LINKS*, bimonthly. Magazine. Provides a unique insight into economic trends within industry and external influences. ● *Product Standards for Die Casting*. Book ● Also publishes technical books, indices, engineering aids, and various technical films. **Conventions/Meetings:** competition ● periodic conference (exhibits) ● biennial congress (exhibits) ● periodic seminar.

2055 ■ North American Punch Manufacturers Association (NAPMA)
21 Turquoise Ave.
Naples, FL 34114
Ph: (239)775-7245
E-mail: bobjanmay@aol.com
URL: http://www.napma.org
Contact: Robert May, Contact
Founded: 1963. **Members:** 18. **Membership Dues:** full, $1,000 (annual) ● associate, $350 (annual). **Staff:** 1. **Budget:** $25,000. **Description:** Punch manufacturing companies. Promotes use of standards for punches, die buttons, and related products. **Formerly:** National Association of Punch Manufacturers. **Conventions/Meetings:** annual conference - always March.

2056 ■ Paper Machine Clothing Council
Address Unknown since 2007
Founded: 1924. **Description:** Manufacturers of machine clothing for fourdrinier machines used for manufacturing paper in an endless web. **Formerly:** Fourdrinier Wire Council; (1965) Paper Mill Fourdrinier Wire Cloth Manufacturers Association.

2057 ■ Powder Actuated Tool Manufacturers' Institute (PATMI)
136 S Main St., Ste.2E
St. Charles, MO 63301
Ph: (314)889-7117
Fax: (314)725-6592
E-mail: info@patmi.org
URL: http://www.patmi.org
Contact: James A. Borchers, Exec. Dir.
Founded: 1952. **Members:** 7. **Staff:** 2. **Budget:** $42,000. **Description:** Manufacturers of fastening tools powered by an energy source called a power load; associate members include suppliers of expendable goods related to the industry who are not directly involved in the manufacture of powder actuated tools. Serves as a common voice for manufacturers of powder actuated fastening systems. Promotes safety in use, operation, and application of such tools; participates in adoption of American National Standard Safety Requirements for Powder Actuated Fastening Systems. Monitors federal and state legislation pertinent to the industry. Conducts proactive safety awareness program; distributes posters, press releases, and trade ads. **Libraries: Type:** not open to the public. **Holdings:** articles, books, business records, video recordings. **Committees:** Technical. **Publications:** *PATMI Education/Instruction Video*. Provides brief history and proper use of powder-actuated fastening systems. **Price:** $10.00 each ● *Powder Actuated Fastening Systems Basic Training Manual*, periodic. Provides information/instruction on the proper use of powder-actuated fastening systems. **Price:** $2.50 each ● Brochure. **Conventions/Meetings:** quarterly board meeting and meeting.

2058 ■ Power Crane and Shovel Association (PCSA)
c/o Association of Equipment Manufacturers
6737 W Washington St., Ste.2400
Milwaukee, WI 53214-5647
Ph: (414)272-0943 (414)298-4132
Fax: (414)272-1170
URL: http://www.aem.org/CBC/ProdSpec/PCSA
Contact: Richard Dressler PE, Contact
Founded: 1945. **Members:** 10. **Staff:** 2. **Description:** A bureau of the Association of Equipment Manufacturers (see separate entry). Represents manufacturers of mobile cranes, hydraulic excavators, and similar equipment. **Committees:** Crane Technical; Statistical. **Publications:** Publishes technical bulletins and standards. **Conventions/Meetings:** semiannual meeting.

2059 ■ Power-Motion Technology Representatives Association (PTRA)
One Spectrum Pointe, Ste.150
Lake Forest, CA 92630
Ph: (949)859-2885
Free: (888)817-PTRA
Fax: (949)855-2973
E-mail: info@ptra.org
URL: http://www.ptra.org
Contact: Jay Ownby, Exec. Dir.
Founded: 1972. **Members:** 300. **Membership Dues:** active, $350 (annual) ● allied (based upon the sales volume), $289-$701 (annual). **Staff:** 3. **Budget:** $250,000. **Description:** Manufacturers and independent manufacturers representatives in the power transmission industry. Seeks to provide a channel of communication between manufacturers' independent representatives and their principals, and other manufacturers within the industry by allowing interchange of sound business management ideas and by offering consultation on solving operational problems. Provides information and referral; compiles surveys. Offers training programs that include panels, table talk discussions, and seminars on special topics. **Computer Services:** Mailing lists, fee based. **Formerly:** Power Transmission Representatives Association. **Publications:** *Focus*, quarterly. Newsletter ● Reports ● Also publishes special studies. **Conventions/Meetings:** annual conference, for prospective members only.

2060 ■ Power Transmission Distributors Association (PTDA)
230 W Monroe, Ste.1410
Chicago, IL 60606-4703
Ph: (312)516-2100
Fax: (312)516-2101
E-mail: ptda@ptda.org
URL: http://www.ptda.org
Contact: Mary Sue Lyon, Exec. VP
Founded: 1960. **Members:** 425. **Staff:** 6. **Budget:** $1,500,000. **Multinational. Description:** Distributors and manufacturers of power transmission/motion and position control equipment. Maintains business management and continuing education resources; conducts educational programs; compiles statistics; sponsors industry summit; conducts research; co-sponsors industry tradeshows. **Telecommunication Services:** electronic mail, mslyon@ptda.org. **Committees:** Business Process; Employee Development; Industry Relations; Marketing; Technical Education. **Councils:** Manufacturers. **Formerly:** (1966) Mechanical Power Transmission Equipment Distributors Association. **Publications:** *Business Planning Manuals* ● *Human Resources Manuals* ● *Market Trend Report*, monthly ● *Product Training Handbook* ● *Transmissions*, quarterly. Newsletter. **Price:** $79.00/year. **Circulation:** 1,100. **Advertising:** accepted. Alternate Formats: online ● Also publishes distribution financial performance report, compensation surveys, and employee training materials. **Conventions/Meetings:** annual Industry Summit - conference (exhibits).

2061 ■ Pressure Vessel Manufacturers Association (PVMA)
800 Roosevelt Rd., Bldg. C, Ste.312
Glen Ellyn, IL 60137
Ph: (630)942-6590 (609)294-2686
Fax: (630)790-3095
E-mail: info@pvma.org
URL: http://www.pvma.org
Contact: Barry A. Berquist, Pres.
Founded: 1975. **Members:** 33. **Membership Dues:** associate, $1,500 (annual) ● fabricating company (based on annual sales volume), $1,500-$4,500 (annual). **Staff:** 3. **Description:** Represents manufacturers of pressure vessels made in accordance with the ASME Boiler and Pressure Vessel Code, Section VIII, Division 1 and Division 2, and suppliers of materials and services to the pressure vessel fabricating industry. Member companies produce the major share of ASME-Code, Section VIII pressure vessels manufactured in the United States. Associate members are pressure vessel fabricating industry suppliers. Exchanges information on technical and manufacturing problems, and on the impact of regulations and standards on industry operations. **Conventions/Meetings:** annual meeting.

2062 ■ Pressure Washer Manufacturers Association (PWMA)
1300 Sumner Ave.
Cleveland, OH 44115-2851
Ph: (216)241-7333
Fax: (216)241-0105
E-mail: pwma@pwma.org
URL: http://www.pwma.org
Founded: 1997. **Members:** 3. **Description:** Manufacturers of pressure washers. Promotes the interests of the pressure washer industry; seeks to increase the understanding of pressure washers. Formulates standards of quality and performance for pressure washers; represents members' commercial and regulatory interests. **Publications:** *PWMA Certified Products Directory*. Alternate Formats: online ● Membership Directory. Alternate Formats: online.

2063 ■ Process Equipment Manufacturers Association (PEMA)
201 Park Washington Ct.
Falls Church, VA 22046-4527
Ph: (703)538-1796
Fax: (703)241-5603

E-mail: info@pemanet.org
URL: http://www.pemanet.org
Contact: Susan A. Denston, Exec. Dir.
Founded: 1960. **Members:** 45. **Membership Dues:** single entity, $1,775-$4,845 (annual). **Budget:** $100,000. **Description:** Represents North American process equipment companies. Maintains an organization of capital equipment manufacturers. Provides a social/business base where members can meet to share and exchange views on common interests. **Telecommunication Services:** electronic mail, sdenston@pemanet.org. **Publications:** *PEMA PRESS*, bimonthly. Newsletter. **Price:** free. **Circulation:** 100. Alternate Formats: online ● Membership Directory, annual. Alternate Formats: online. **Conventions/Meetings:** annual meeting - 3/year, always February, May, and October.

2064 ■ Rack Manufacturers Institute
c/o John B. Nofsinger, Sr., Managing Dir.
8720 Red Oak Blvd., Ste.201
Charlotte, NC 28217-3992
Ph: (704)676-1190
Fax: (704)676-1199
E-mail: jnofsinger@mhia.org
URL: http://www.mhia.org/rmi
Contact: Gary Slater, Pres.
Founded: 1957. **Members:** 28. **Membership Dues:** business, $6,000 (annual). **Staff:** 2. **Budget:** $120,000. **Multinational. Description:** Represents manufacturers of industrial steel storage racks and directly related structural decking products; programs include compiling statistics, development of standards and nomenclature, engineering research and education. **Libraries: Type:** reference. **Holdings:** books. **Subjects:** specifications, design, testing, utilization of industrial steel storage racks. **Awards:** Material Handling Education Foundation Scholarship. **Frequency:** annual. **Type:** scholarship. **Computer Services:** Bibliographic search, Material Handling Industry Data Acquisition Services. **Boards:** Communications. **Committees:** Engineering; Statistical Information. **Affiliated With:** Material Handling Industry of America. **Publications:** *ANSI MH16.1-2004: Specification for the Design/Testing/Utilization of Industrial Steel Storage Racks (Formerly RMI-2002 Edition)*, 5/year. Manual. **Price:** $18.00. Alternate Formats: CD-ROM ● *ANSI MH26.2 - Specification for the Design, Testing and Utilization of Welded - Wire Rack Decking*, 5/year. Manuals. **Price:** $18.00. Alternate Formats: CD-ROM ● *Portable Rack Guidelines*. Brochure ● *Specification for the Use of Industrial and Commercial Steel Storage Racks, Manual of Safety Practices/A Code of Safety Practices*, 5/year. Booklet. **Price:** $20.00 ● *Stacker Rack Nomenclature*. Brochure ● Also publishes specification commentary with illustrations, industrial storage racks brochure, and safety manual. **Conventions/Meetings:** annual meeting.

2065 ■ Resistance Welding Manufacturing Alliance (RWMA)
550 NW Lejeune Rd.
Miami, FL 33126
Ph: (305)443-9353 (616)257-8700
Fax: (305)442-7451
E-mail: rwma@aws.org
URL: http://www.aws.org/rwma
Contact: Michael Simmons, Chm.
Founded: 1935. **Members:** 50. **Membership Dues:** regular, $425 (annual). **Budget:** $160,000. **Description:** Manufacturers, suppliers, and users of resistance welding equipment and supplies. Conducts Resistance Welding School, an annual educational program. Compiles statistics. Offers VHS tape program on basics of resistance welding. **Awards:** Elihu Thompson Resistance Welding Award. **Frequency:** annual. **Type:** monetary. **Recipient:** for contributions to the technology and advancement of resistance welding ● RWMA Scholarship. **Frequency:** annual. **Type:** scholarship. **Recipient:** for students pursuing a career or degree in resistance welding. **Committees:** Controls; Education; Electrical; Electrode and Alloy; Manual Rewrite; Marketing; Mechanical; Membership; Safety; Technical; Welding School. **Formerly:** (2006) Resistance Welder Manufacturers Association. **Publications:** *News*, quarterly. Newsletter. Includes member promotions, lists personnel changes, and association activities. **Price:** free ● *Resistance Welder Manufacturers Association—Membership Directory*, annual. **Price:** free ● *Resistance Welding Manual, 4th Edition*. **Price:** $95.00 each ● Bulletins, periodic. **Conventions/Meetings:** semiannual meeting.

2066 ■ Secondary Materials and Recycled Textiles (SMART)
131 E Broad St., Ste.206
Falls Church, VA 22046
Ph: (703)538-1000
Fax: (703)538-6305
E-mail: bernie@smartasn.org
URL: http://www.smartasn.org
Contact: Bill Schapiro, Pres.
Founded: 1932. **Members:** 215. **Membership Dues:** regular, $1,600 (annual) ● overseas, associate, emerging business, $1,200 (annual). **Staff:** 3. **Description:** Manufacturers and distributors of industrial wiping materials, recycled clothing, recycled textile products, fibers and other cloth products. Monitors international trade activities, recycling and environmental issues. **Awards:** Distinguished Service. **Type:** recognition ● President's Award. **Type:** recognition. **Computer Services:** Mailing lists, of members. **Telecommunication Services:** electronic mail, maryann@smartasn.org. **Committees:** Convention Continuing Education Advisory; Long Range Planning; Women of SMART. **Formerly:** International Association of Wiping Cloth Manufacturers; Sanitary Institute of America. **Publications:** *SMARTTalk*, monthly. Newsletter. **Price:** included in membership dues. **Advertising:** accepted. **Conventions/Meetings:** annual convention - usually during February, March or early April.

2067 ■ Sewn Products Equipment and Suppliers of the Americas (SPESA)
9650 Strickland Rd., Ste.103-324
Raleigh, NC 27615
Ph: (919)872-8909
Fax: (919)872-1915
E-mail: spesa@spesa.org
URL: http://www.spesa.org
Contact: Benton Gardner, Exec. VP/Sec.
Founded: 1990. **Members:** 100. **Membership Dues:** associate, affiliate, $750 (annual) ● regular (based on gross revenues of up to 9.999 million), $850-$2,500 (annual) ● regular (based on gross revenues between 10 million to 20 million), $3,500-$5,000 (annual). **Staff:** 10. **Budget:** $300,000. **Description:** Suppliers to the sewn products industry. Promotes and protects members' interests. Gathers and disseminates industry information; facilitates communication and cooperation among members. Conducts educational programs. Owns and produces SPESA EXPO, a triennial exhibition for the sewn products industry that focuses on the Western Hemisphere. **Computer Services:** Online services. **Formerly:** (2004) Sewn Products Equipment Suppliers Association of the Americas. **Publications:** *Behind the Seams*, biweekly. Newsletter. **Price:** free. **Circulation:** 11,000. **Advertising:** accepted. Alternate Formats: online ● *SPESA Products and Services Directory* (in English and Spanish), annual. **Price:** free ● *SPESA Speaks*, bimonthly. Newsletter. **Price:** free. Alternate Formats: online. **Conventions/Meetings:** periodic board meeting (exhibits) ● periodic conference ● triennial Sewn Products Industry Expo - trade show (exhibits).

2068 ■ Society of Professional Rope Access Technicians (SPRAT)
994 Old Eagle School Rd., Ste.1019
Wayne, PA 19087-1802
Ph: (610)971-4850
Fax: (610)971-4859
E-mail: info@sprat.org
URL: http://www.sprat.org
Contact: Mike Soderstrom, Pres.
Membership Dues: sustaining, $350 (annual) ● corporate, $850 (annual) ● associate, $75 (annual) ● subscribing, $45 (annual). **Description:** Aims to develop safe and practical industry standards for rope access techniques. Provides resources for information, networking, and support for companies and workers who use on-the-job rope access techniques. Promotes the interests of its members. **Telecommunication Services:** electronic mail, msoderstrom@sprat.org.

2069 ■ Specialty Tools and Fasteners Distributors Association (STAFDA)
PO Box 44
Elm Grove, WI 53122
Ph: (262)784-4774
Free: (800)352-2981
Fax: (262)784-5059
E-mail: info@stafda.org
URL: http://www.stafda.org
Contact: Georgia H. Foley, Exec. Dir.
Founded: 1976. **Members:** 2,600. **Membership Dues:** company, $350 (annual). **Staff:** 4. **Budget:** $1,500,000. **Description:** Distributors and suppliers of power tools, power-actuated tools, anchors, fastening systems, diamond drilling, and related construction equipment. Encourages legal, ethical, and friendly business relations within the industry. Collects and disseminates information pertinent to the industry; develops more effective, economical, and profitable distribution. **Telecommunication Services:** electronic mail, ghfoley@stafda.org. **Publications:** *Trade News*, monthly. Newsletter ● Membership Directory, annual. **Conventions/Meetings:** annual convention (exhibits) - always November. 2008 Nov. 9-11, Denver, CO; 2009 Nov. 8-10, New Orleans, LA; 2010 Nov. 7-9, Phoenix, AZ.

2070 ■ Steel Founders' Society of America (SFSA)
780 McArdle Dr., Unit G
Crystal Lake, IL 60014-8155
Ph: (815)455-8240
Fax: (815)455-8241
E-mail: monroe@sfsa.org
URL: http://www.sfsa.org
Contact: Raymond W. Monroe, Exec. VP
Founded: 1902. **Members:** 82. **Membership Dues:** regular/associate, $250-$4,040 (quarterly) ● regular/associate, $6,000 (annual). **Staff:** 5. **Budget:** $500,000. **Regional Groups:** 4. **Multinational. Description:** Represents manufacturers of steel castings. Provides technical support and research. **Telecommunication Services:** electronic mail, blairr@sfsa.org. **Committees:** Marketing; Specifications; Technical Research. **Absorbed:** (1970) Alloy Casting Institute. **Publications:** *Directory of Steel Foundries*, biennial. Lists steel foundries in the United States, Canada, and Mexico. **Price:** $45.00 for members; $95.00 for nonmembers. **Circulation:** 2,000 ● *Steel Castings*. Handbook. **Price:** $168.00 for members; $210.00 for nonmembers ● Booklets. Covers technical aspects and specifications of steel castings. **Conventions/Meetings:** annual conference - always September in Chicago, IL.

2071 ■ Storage Equipment Manufacturers Association (SMA)
8720 Red Oak Blvd., Ste.201
Charlotte, NC 28217
Ph: (704)676-1190
Fax: (704)676-1199
E-mail: vwheeler@mhia.org
URL: http://www.mhia.org/psc/PSC_Products_Storage.cfm
Contact: Doug Edwards, Chm.
Founded: 1974. **Members:** 18. **Membership Dues:** business, $2 (annual). **Staff:** 2. **Budget:** $50,000. **Description:** Manufacturers of steel shelving, industrial mezzanines, and related industrial storage equipment. Works to promote the largest possible market consistent with the users' best interests. Encourages production of high quality shelving and storage products. Collects and disseminates statistical, legislative, and international trade information; develops and promotes standard nomenclature of shelving items, quality codes, and a code of ethics. Fosters communication and serves as liaison among members, user groups, related product associations,

and private and governmental groups. Participates in educational events and trade expositions; prepares and distributes publicity and educational materials; coordinates shelving testing. Conducts research programs. **Libraries: Type:** reference. **Subjects:** industrial shelving, industrial mezzanines. **Awards:** Material Handling Education Foundation Scholarship. **Frequency:** annual. **Type:** scholarship. **Computer Services:** database, material handling industry Data Acquisition Services. **Committees:** Engineering; Statistical Information. **Affiliated With:** Material Handling Industry of America; Order Selection, Staging and Storage Council of the Material Handling Industry of America. **Absorbed:** (1999) Association of Mezzanine Manufacturers. **Formerly:** (1998) Shelving Manufacturers Association. **Publications:** *Mezzanine Users Guide*. Brochures ● *Multi-Level Shelving Systems*. Book ● *Nomenclature for Industrial Grade Steel Shelving*. Book ● *Shelving Applications Brochure* ● *Shelving Manufacturers Association—Membership Roster*, periodic. Membership Directory ● *Shelving Users Guide*. Book ● *Specification for Design/Testing/Utilization of Industrial Steel Shelving*. Brochure ● *Specifications for Design & Testing of Metal Wood Shelving*. Book ● *Standard Practices Guidelines - Mezzanines*. Brochures ● *Storage Equipment Bracing Considerations*. **Conventions/Meetings:** semiannual Engineering and Business Conference - meeting.

2072 ■ Surface Mount Technology Association (SMTA)

5200 Willson Rd., Ste.215
Edina, MN 55424
Ph: (952)920-7682
Fax: (952)926-1819
E-mail: joann@smta.org
URL: http://www.smta.org
Contact: JoAnn Stromberg, Exec. Admin.

Founded: 1984. **Members:** 4,000. **Membership Dues:** user/supplier corporate in U.S. and Canada, $450 (annual) ● individual, $75 (annual) ● participating in U.S. and Canada, $50 (annual) ● associate, $5 (annual) ● international user/supplier corporate, $550 (annual) ● international chapter affiliate, $25 (annual) ● user global/supplier global, $1,495 (annual). **Staff:** 8. **Budget:** $1,000,000. **Local Groups:** 35. **Description:** Users and suppliers of surface mount technology (SMT) and those interested in SMT. (SMT is used to place components on circuit boards.) Seeks to: accelerate the growth of SMT worldwide; mediate the collection and dissemination of information and publications; provide a forum for industry representatives. **Awards:** Charles Hutchins Educational Grant. **Frequency:** annual. **Type:** grant. **Recipient:** for thesis research in electronic assembly or a related field ● Founder's Award. **Frequency:** annual. **Type:** recognition. **Recipient:** for exceptional contribution to the industry as well as support and service to SMTA ● Member of Distinction Award. **Frequency:** annual. **Type:** recognition. **Recipient:** for significant contribution over a period of at least 3 years ● SMTA Corporate Award. **Frequency:** annual. **Type:** recognition. **Recipient:** to a corporate member company that has shown exceptional support. **Computer Services:** database ● mailing lists ● online services. **Committees:** Awards; Grant Technical; International Chapter Development; Student Membership; Testability. **Publications:** *Proceedings of the Technical Conference*, annual ● *Technical Journal*, quarterly. Contains technical papers on surface mount technology. **Price:** free, for members only ● Membership Directory, annual. Includes product information. **Price:** free, for members only ● Newsletter, monthly. Contains technical papers and local chapter news. **Price:** included in membership dues ● Also publishes test guidelines. **Conventions/Meetings:** annual conference ● annual conference and trade show (exhibits).

2073 ■ Tooling, Manufacturing and Technologies Association (TMTA)

PO Box 9151
Farmington Hills, MI 48333-9151
Ph: (248)488-0300
Free: (800)969-9MTA
Fax: (248)488-0500
E-mail: rob@themta.com
URL: http://www.mtaonline.com
Contact: Robert J. Dumont, Pres./CEO

Founded: 1933. **Members:** 730. **Membership Dues:** corporation (1 to over 400 employees), $75-$690 (quarterly). **Staff:** 8. **Budget:** $1,200,000. **For-Profit. Description:** Manufacturers of dies, jigs, fixtures, molds, gages, tools, special machinery, and related products; suppliers of die tryout, machining, and experimental and designing service. **Formerly:** (1990) Detroit Tooling Association; (2007) Michigan Tooling Association. **Publications:** *Tool Talk*, monthly. Newsletter. **Price:** included in membership dues. **Circulation:** 1,250. Alternate Formats: online.

2074 ■ Unified Abrasives Manufacturers' Association - Grain Division (UAMA)

30200 Detroit Rd.
Cleveland, OH 44145-1967
Ph: (440)899-0010
Fax: (440)892-1404
E-mail: contact@uama.org
URL: http://www.uama.org
Contact: J.J. Wherry, Sec.

Founded: 1934. **Members:** 6. **Staff:** 2. **Description:** Manufacturers of bonded, coated and super abrasive products and abrasive grains. **Committees:** Abrasive Micrgrits; Analytical Procedures; Standards. **Departments:** Public Relations. **Formerly:** (1999) Abrasive Grain Association. **Publications:** *ANSI Standards*. **Conventions/Meetings:** semiannual meeting - always spring and fall.

2075 ■ Unified Abrasives Manufacturers' Association - Superabrasives Division (UAMA)

30200 Detroit Rd.
Cleveland, OH 44145-1967
Ph: (440)899-0010
Fax: (440)892-1404
E-mail: contact@uama.org
URL: http://www.uama.org
Contact: Jeff Wherry, Exec. Dir.

Founded: 1999. **Members:** 10. **Staff:** 3. **Description:** Represents companies that manufacture diamond, CBN abrasive wheels. **Committees:** Safety, Standards and Health. **Divisions:** Bonded; Coated; Grain. **Formerly:** (1999) Diamond Wheel Manufacturers Institute; (2003) United Abrasives Manufacturers' Association - Superabrasives Division. **Publications:** *ANSI Standards* ● *Technical Bulletins*. **Conventions/Meetings:** semiannual meeting.

2076 ■ United States Cutting Tool Institute (USCTI)

1300 Sumner Ave.
Cleveland, OH 44115-2851
Ph: (216)241-7333
Fax: (216)241-0105
E-mail: uscti@taol.com
URL: http://www.uscti.com
Contact: Gary A. Vanderpol, Pres.

Founded: 1988. **Members:** 98. **Staff:** 3. **Description:** Manufacturers of rotary metal cutting tools. Objectives are to: promote the manufacture and sale of rotary metal cutting tools in the U.S. and in foreign markets; promote the standardization of sizes, dimensions, and tolerances in cooperation with the American National Standards Institute, American Society of Mechanical Engineers (see separate entries), and other engineering organizations; increase the use of metal cutting tools and allied products. **Divisions:** Carbide Tooling; Diamond and CBN; Drill and Reamer; Milling Cutter; Tap and Die; Tool Holders. **Projects:** Environmental Concerns; Governmental Affairs; Labor Relations; Standards; Technical Information. **Affiliated With:** American National Standards Institute; American Society of Mechanical Engineers. **Formed by Merger of:** Metal Cutting Tool Institute; Cutting Tool Manufacturers of America. **Formerly:** (1983) Cutting Tool Manufacturers Association. **Publications:** *Cutting Tool Informer*. Newsletter. Alternate Formats: online ● *Drilled Holes for Tapping*. Booklet. **Price:** $5.00 for members; $10.00 for nonmembers ● *Metal Cutting Tool Handbook*. **Price:** $42.95 for members; $48.90 for nonmembers ● *Standards and Dimensions for Ground Thread Taps*. Booklet. **Price:** $5.00 for members; $10.00 for nonmembers ● *Tolerances for Twist Drill and Reamers*. Booklet. **Price:** $5.00 for members; $10.00 for nonmembers ● Membership Directory, periodic. Includes product and trade name listings. **Conventions/Meetings:** semiannual conference.

2077 ■ Water and Wastewater Equipment Manufacturers Association (WWEMA)

PO Box 17402
Washington, DC 20041
Ph: (703)444-1777
Fax: (703)444-1779
E-mail: info@wwema.org
URL: http://www.wwema.org
Contact: Dawn Kristof Champney, Pres.

Founded: 1908. **Members:** 70. **Staff:** 3. **Budget:** $450,000. **Description:** Manufacturers of equipment for water works, wastewater, and industrial wastes disposal plants. Sponsors public relations, public affairs, and marketing programs. Conducts research; compiles statistics. Maintains placement service. **Awards:** Member of the Year. **Frequency:** annual. **Type:** recognition. **Recipient:** for service to the association. **Committees:** Global Competitiveness; Government Affairs; Membership. **Formerly:** Water Works Manufacturers Association; (1965) Water and Sewage Works Manufacturers Association. **Publications:** *Membership Directory and Product Guide*, annual ● *Washington Analysis Newsletter*, bimonthly. **Conventions/Meetings:** annual meeting - always November ● annual Washington Forum - meeting.

2078 ■ Web Sling and Tie Down Association (WSTDA)

2105 Laurel Bush Rd., Ste.200
Bel Air, MD 21015
Ph: (443)640-1070 (905)545-5025
Fax: (443)640-1031
E-mail: wstda@ksgroup.org
URL: http://www.wstda.com
Contact: John Walsh, Pres.

Founded: 1973. **Members:** 85. **Membership Dues:** regular (based on annual synthetic product sales), $1,000-$2,200 (annual) ● associate, $1,300 (annual) ● affiliate, $1,000 (annual). **Staff:** 3. **Budget:** $200,000. **Description:** Manufacturers of web slings and web tie downs and major components for web slings and web tie downs. (Web slings are used for hoisting, lifting and lowering applications in general industrial and specified operations. Web tie downs are used for cargo restraint applications, tensioning devices, and/or end fitting devices in transportation and industrial operations. The webbing for these products is woven from synthetic fibers.) Works to foster and further the common interests of the web sling industry; promote a spirit of cooperation among members for the improved production, proper use, and increased distribution of web slings; increase the amount and improve the quality of service to the public, develop and publish recommended standard specifications for industry products. **Formerly:** (1988) Web Sling Association. **Publications:** *Uplifting News*, semiannual. Newsletter. **Advertising:** accepted. Alternate Formats: online. **Conventions/Meetings:** annual meeting - usually fall. 2008 Oct. 5-7, St. Louis, MO ● annual meeting.

2079 ■ Wire Industry Suppliers Association (WISA)

Address Unknown since 2007

Founded: 1923. **Members:** 35. **Budget:** $40,000. **Description:** Firms engaged in the designing, building, and selling of machinery and equipment for use in plants producing wire or wire products. Includes wire and rod drawing machinery and accessories, shaping and flattening mills, stranding, cabling cutting off, pointing straightening, armoring, bending, forming, and cold heading equipment. **Formerly:** (1987) Wire Machinery Builders Association. **Publications:** *Executive Newsletter*, annual. **Conventions/Meetings:** annual meeting.

2080 ■ Wood Machinery Manufacturers of America (WMMA)
100 N 20th St., 4th Fl.
Philadelphia, PA 19103-1443
Ph: (215)564-3484
Free: (800)BUY-WMMA
Fax: (215)963-9785
E-mail: wmma@fernley.com
URL: http://www.wmma.org
Contact: Bill Norton, Exec. VP
Founded: 1899. **Members:** 250. **Membership Dues:** regular associate, $550 (annual) ● individual associate, $100 (annual). **Staff:** 5. **Budget:** $1,000,000. **Description:** Manufacturers of industrial woodworking machinery, cutting tools, and supplies for use in furniture factories, woodworking plants, veneer mills, saw and planning mills. Promotes more widespread use of wood and its derivatives; seeks to develop better high-speed, high-precision production equipment and assist the user in its selection. Conducts research programs on labor, sales, and service policies and machinery safeguards. Maintains speakers' bureau; compiles statistics. **Awards:** Ralph E. Baldwin Award. **Frequency:** annual. **Type:** recognition. **Recipient:** for individuals who have made outstanding contributions to the industry. **Committees:** Education and Scholarship; Export Development; Industry Marketing; Leadership Development; Long Range Planning; Management Information; Membership; Product and Engineering Standards; Public Policy. **Formerly:** Association of Manufacturers of Woodworking Machinery; (1969) Woodworking Machinery Manufacturers Association; (1983) Woodworking Machinery Manufacturers of America. **Publications:** *The Cutting Edge*, monthly. Newsletter. **Price:** free. **Circulation:** 800. Alternate Formats: online ● *Export Brochure* ● *International Distributor Directory* ● *Marketing Brochures* ● *Wood Machinery Manufacturers of America—Buyers Guide and Directory*, biennial. Membership Directory. Lists manufacturers and member companies; contains cross-reference index listing machines, manufacturers, and customer aids. **Price:** free. **Conventions/Meetings:** International Woodworking Fair - meeting, held in conjunction with Woodworking Machinery Industry Association and American Furniture Manufacturers Association (exhibits) - even-numbered years in August, Atlanta, GA ● annual Woodworking Industry Conference - convention.

2081 ■ Woodworking Machinery Industry Association (WMIA)
3313 Paper Mill Rd., Ste.202
Phoenix, MD 21131
Ph: (410)628-1970
Fax: (410)628-1972
E-mail: info@wmia.org
URL: http://www.wmia.org
Contact: Giordano Checchi, Pres.
Founded: 1978. **Members:** 170. **Membership Dues:** importer, distributor, associate, $600 (annual). **Staff:** 5. **Description:** Woodworking machinery import and distribution firms. Pursues members' common interests and goals in such areas as sales terms and conditions, safety regulations, and insurance. Maintains code of ethics. **Awards:** Educator of the Year. **Frequency:** annual. **Type:** recognition. **Recipient:** for excellence within the woodworking industry ● Exporter of the Year Award. **Frequency:** annual. **Type:** recognition ● Global Marketer of the Year. **Frequency:** annual. **Type:** recognition. **Recipient:** for excellence within the woodworking industry ● Innovator of the Year. **Frequency:** annual. **Type:** recognition. **Recipient:** for excellence within the woodworking industry ● Partner of the Year Award. **Frequency:** annual. **Type:** recognition. **Recipient:** for a manufacturer or importer of woodworking machinery or tooling deemed to have done the most outstanding job, over the past year in partnering with distributors. **Formerly:** (1998) Woodworking Machinery Importers Association of America. **Publications:** *1999 Sourcebook*, biennial. Directory. **Price:** free. **Circulation:** 15,000. **Advertising:** accepted ● *WMIA Bulletin*, quarterly. Newsletter ● Newsletter, monthly ● Bulletins. **Conventions/Meetings:** biennial International Woodworking Machinery and Furniture Supply Fair - trade show (exhibits) ● annual Woodworking Industry Conference - convention.

2082 ■ Woven Wire Products Association (WWPA)
PO Box 610280
Birmingham, AL 35261-0280
Ph: (517)542-2501
Free: (800)783-0341
Fax: (205)592-3725
E-mail: robin@millerwireworks.com
URL: http://www.wovenwire.org
Contact: Bonny DesJardin, VP/Membership Chm.
Founded: 1942. **Members:** 30. **Staff:** 1. **Description:** Represents manufacturers of woven wire products united to promote the use of their products. **Conventions/Meetings:** semiannual meeting - always April and October.

Industrial Security

2083 ■ ASIS International
1625 Prince St.
Alexandria, VA 22314-2818
Ph: (703)519-6200
Fax: (703)519-1501
E-mail: asis@asisonline.org
URL: http://www.asisonline.org
Contact: Michael J. Stack, Exec. Dir.
Founded: 1955. **Members:** 33,000. **Membership Dues:** regular, associate, $170 (annual) ● student, $25 (annual). **Staff:** 75. **Regional Groups:** 26. **Local Groups:** 204. **Multinational. Description:** Security professionals responsible for loss prevention, asset protection and security for businesses, government, or public organizations and institutions. Sponsors educational programs on security principles (basic through advanced levels) and current security issues. Administers professional certification programs (CPP, PCI, PSP). Offers networking opportunities to professionals; provides an online service for employment and resumes, publishes books, directories, and other resources. **Libraries: Type:** reference. **Subjects:** security and asset protection. **Awards:** Allan J. Cross, CPP, Award. **Frequency:** annual. **Type:** scholarship. **Recipient:** for outstanding ASIS members ● Chapter Matching Scholarship. **Frequency:** annual. **Type:** scholarship. **Recipient:** for outstanding ASIS members and other students of merit who are interested in the security profession. **Telecommunication Services:** electronic mail, pr@asisonline.org. **Formerly:** (1998) American Society for Industrial Security. **Publications:** *ASIS Security Industry Buyers Guide*, annual. Directory. Lists security products and service providers. **Price:** $179.00. **Advertising:** accepted ● *Dynamics*, bimonthly. Newsletter. Covers membership and legislative news. **Price:** available to members only. **Circulation:** 31,000. **Advertising:** accepted ● *Security Journal*, quarterly. **Price:** $240.00 for members; $480.00 for nonmembers ● *Security Management*, monthly. Magazine. Serves those who are concerned with security and loss prevention of assets, people, and data in industrial, commercial, and private organizations. **Price:** $48.00/year. ISSN: 0145-9406. **Circulation:** 38,000. **Advertising:** accepted. Alternate Formats: microform. **Conventions/Meetings:** annual conference and trade show, with seminars (exhibits) - always September ● monthly meeting.

2084 ■ Association of Certified Fraud Examiners (ACFE)
The Gregor Bldg.
716 West Ave.
Austin, TX 78701-2727
Ph: (512)478-9000
Free: (800)245-3321
Fax: (512)478-9297
E-mail: memberservices@acfe.com
URL: http://www.acfe.com
Contact: James D. Ratley, Pres.
Founded: 1988. **Members:** 27,000. **Membership Dues:** certified fraud examiner, $120 (annual) ● associate, $95 (annual). **Staff:** 40. **Local Groups:** 105. **Multinational. Description:** Represents corporate managers, executives, auditors, trainers, security directors, and others employed in financial institutions; business, law enforcement, and social science professionals. Works to classify and examine financial crimes such as white-collar embezzlement, forgery, and fraud as well as their frequency and methodology to develop effective preventive plans and policies for businesses. Provides lectures on topics including fraud prevention, detection, auditing, security, and management awareness. Sponsors training seminars on fraud and loss prevention and administers credentialing program for Certified Fraud Examiners. Conducts research programs. Offers placement service. **Libraries: Type:** reference. **Holdings:** 500; books, periodicals. **Subjects:** government, trade, research on white-collar crime. **Awards:** Cliff Robertson Sentinel Award. **Frequency:** annual. **Type:** recognition. **Recipient:** to a person who has publicly disclosed wrongdoing in business or government ● Donald R. Cressey Memorial Award. **Frequency:** annual. **Type:** recognition. **Recipient:** for outstanding contribution to white-collar crime prevention ● Morris R. Walker Award. **Frequency:** annual. **Type:** recognition. **Recipient:** to a person with the highest score on CFE examination. **Formerly:** (1985) Institute for Financial Crime Prevention; (1993) National Association of Certified Fraud Examiners. **Publications:** *Beyond the Numbers*. Handbook. Includes a workbook. **Price:** $125.00 for members, print only; $139.00 for nonmembers, print only; $159.00 for members, package (video/DVD plus workbook); $179.00 for nonmembers, package (video/DVD plus workbook). Alternate Formats: CD-ROM ● *Cooking the Books: What Every Accountant Should Know About Fraud*. Video. Includes a workbook. **Price:** $59.00 for members; $79.00 for nonmembers. Alternate Formats: CD-ROM ● *The Corporate Con: Internal Fraud and the Auditor*. Video. Includes a workbook. ● *Encyclopedia of Fraud*. Book. **Price:** $59.00 for members; $79.00 for nonmembers. Alternate Formats: CD-ROM ● *Frankensteins of Fraud*. Book. **Price:** $25.00 for members; $39.00 for nonmembers ● *Fraud Examiners Manual, Third Edition*. Book. **Price:** $159.00 for members, print; $249.00 for nonmembers, print. Alternate Formats: CD-ROM ● *Introduction to Fraud*. Video. Includes a workbook. ● *Occupational Fraud and Abuse*. Book ● *Using Benford's Law to Detect Fraud*. Handbook. **Price:** $125.00 for members; $139.00 for nonmembers ● *The White Paper: Topical Issues on White Collar Crime*, bimonthly. Magazine. **Price:** included in membership dues; $55.00 for nonmembers in North America; $75.00 for nonmembers elsewhere. **Circulation:** 27,000. **Advertising:** accepted. **Conventions/Meetings:** annual conference (exhibits) - 2008 July 13-18, Boston, MA ● semiannual symposium - always in Austin, TX.

2085 ■ Association of Certified Fraud Specialists (ACFS)
PO Box 348777
Sacramento, CA 95834-8777
Ph: (916)419-6319
Free: (866)HEY-ACFS
Fax: (916)419-6318
E-mail: headquarters@acfsnet.org
URL: http://acfsnet.org
Contact: Charles W. Raborn Jr., Exec. Dir.
Founded: 1993. **Membership Dues:** regular, $150 (annual) ● associate, $75 (annual) ● corporate (emerald), $4,500 (annual) ● corporate (sapphire), $3,000 (annual) ● corporate (ruby), $1,500 (annual). **Description:** Works to combat financial crimes caused by fraudulent activities. Fosters a national forum and governing body for the affiliation of anti-fraud professionals. Advocates for the advancement of the anti-fraud profession through development and promulgation of fraud detection, prevention and investigation principles. Promotes the observance of professional standards and ethics in the anti-fraud profession. **Awards:** Distinguished Service Award. **Frequency:** annual. **Type:** recognition. **Recipient:** to chapter members or officers who have rendered quality service to the community ● Edwin H. Sutherland Award. **Frequency:** annual. **Type:** recognition. **Recipient:** for outstanding service to the public or

outstanding contribution to the advancement of the anti-fraud profession ● Founders Award. **Frequency:** annual. **Type:** recognition. **Recipient:** to a certified fraud specialist whose work embodies the purpose and objectives of the association ● Sentinel Award. **Frequency:** annual. **Type:** recognition. **Recipient:** to anti-fraud professionals who have demonstrated vigilance in the performance of their duties.

2086 ■ Business Espionage Controls and Countermeasures Association (BECCA)
PO Box 55582
Shoreline, WA 98155-0582
E-mail: office@becca-online.org
URL: http://www.becca-online.org
Contact: William M. Johnson, Exec. Dir.
Founded: 1990. **Multinational. Description:** Management consultants, law enforcement officials, investigators, information specialists, and other professionals involved in business espionage controls and countermeasures. Promotes awareness of the growing concern of espionage in the business community. Seeks to establish and maintain ethical practices and high standards of professional conduct in the field. Collects, disseminates, and exchanges statistical and other data and information to keep members abreast of new technologies. Offers a referral and inquiry service which acts as a problem-solving resource. Offers a Certified Confidentiality Officer (CCO) certification program. **Libraries: Type:** not open to the public; reference. **Holdings:** 1,000; archival material, articles, books, papers, periodicals, reports. **Subjects:** business espionage controls and countermeasures. **Computer Services:** Online services. **Subgroups:** Controls and Countermeasures. **Publications:** *BECCA Security Survey Guide*. Book ● *The Business Espionage Report and BECCA Resource Bulletin*, monthly. Newsletter. ISSN: 1054-4216. Alternate Formats: online ● *Introduction to Business Espionage*. Booklet ● *101 Q&A About Business Espionage*. Book ● *What Every Manager Needs To Know About Business Espionage*. Booklet.

2087 ■ Communications Fraud Control Association (CFCA)
4 Becker Farm Rd., 4th Fl.
PO Box 954
Roseland, NJ 07068
Ph: (973)871-4032
Fax: (973)871-4075
E-mail: fraud@cfca.org
URL: http://www.cfca.org
Contact: Dana Bruce Berry CCSP, Pres.
Founded: 1985. **Members:** 225. **Membership Dues:** corporate carrier, $350-$2,600 (annual) ● corporate industry, $350-$2,500 (annual) ● law enforcement, $75 (annual) ● retired, $50 (annual). **Staff:** 4. **Budget:** $300,000. **Multinational. Description:** Telecommunications companies, long distance and local exchange companies, law enforcement agencies, and end-user companies (owners of CPE, hotels, hospitals, universities, etc.). Promotes fraud control and prevention in the telecommunications industry. Provides a forum for the discussion of fraud control problems and solutions. Works with the industry and law enforcement agencies to conduct training workshops and seminars on fraud detection, prevention, and investigative techniques. **Awards:** Law Enforcement. **Frequency:** annual. **Type:** recognition. **Computer Services:** database, Amcrin CrimeDex (available to corporate regular and law enforcement members only, upon approval by Amcrin), fraudulent checks. **Publications:** *CFCA Communicator*, quarterly. Journal. **Advertising:** accepted ● *Communications Fraud - The Bottom Line*. Handbook ● *Weekly Fraud Alert*. Alternate Formats: online ● Membership Directory. **Conventions/Meetings:** annual conference and trade show - always June.

2088 ■ Computer Security Institute (CSI)
600 Harrison St.
San Francisco, CA 94107
Ph: (415)947-6320
Free: (800)250-2429
Fax: (847)763-9606
E-mail: csi@cmp.com
URL: http://www.gocsi.com
Contact: Chris Keating, VP, Security Media Group
Founded: 1973. **Members:** 5,000. **Membership Dues:** in U.S., Canada, and Mexico, $224 (annual) ● international, $264 (annual) ● student (in U.S. only), $99 (annual). **Staff:** 13. **For-Profit. Description:** Serves the information security professional. **Computer Services:** Mailing lists, of members. **Telecommunication Services:** electronic mail, ckeating@cmp.com. **Publications:** *Computer Security Alert*, monthly. Newsletter. **Price:** included in membership dues. Alternate Formats: online ● *Computer Security Buyers Guide*, annual. **Price:** included in membership dues. **Advertising:** accepted ● *Computer Security Journal*, quarterly. **Price:** included in membership dues ● *CSI/FBI Computer Crime and Security Survey*, annual ● *Frontline*, quarterly. Newsletter. **Price:** $1,860.00/year ● *Topline*, quarterly. Newsletter. **Conventions/Meetings:** annual Computer Security Conference and Exhibition, computer and information security (exhibits) ● seminar, regional ● annual Technical Dimensions in Network Security - conference (exhibits) ● workshop.

2089 ■ Energy Security Council (ESC)
10701 Corporate Dr., Ste.250
Stafford, TX 77477
Ph: (281)565-6677
Fax: (281)565-6682
E-mail: info@energysecuritycouncil.org
URL: http://www.energysecuritycouncil.org
Contact: John J. Covert, Exec. Dir.
Founded: 1982. **Members:** 350. **Membership Dues:** corporate, $1,250 (annual) ● company, $500 (annual) ● individual, $150 (annual). **Staff:** 2. **Languages:** English, Russian. **Description:** Represents individuals, companies, and corporations in the field of energy security. Identifies current issues and concerns. **Computer Services:** database, crime information. **Formerly:** (1999) Petroleum Industry Security Council. **Publications:** *Corporate Security Directory*, annual ● *Security Report*, quarterly. Newsletter ● Brochures ● Pamphlets. **Conventions/Meetings:** annual conference (exhibits) ● annual Investigative Audit Forum - conference, retail forum (exhibits) ● seminar, for theft prevention.

2090 ■ Information Systems Security Association (ISSA)
9220 SW Barbur Blvd., No. 119-333
Portland, OR 97219
Ph: (206)388-4584
Free: (866)349-5818
Fax: (206)299-3366
E-mail: customercare@issa.org
URL: http://www.issa.org
Contact: Mr. Howard Schmidt, Pres.
Founded: 1984. **Members:** 8,000. **Membership Dues:** individual, $95 (annual). **Staff:** 16. **Budget:** $380,000. **Regional Groups:** 5. **State Groups:** 55. **Local Groups:** 56. **Multinational. Description:** Computer security practitioners whose primary responsibility is to ensure protection of information assets on a hands-on basis; electronic data processing auditors, contingency planners, consultants, and individuals in related fields; membership represents banking, retail, insurance, aerospace, and publishing industries. Aims to increase knowledge about information security; to sponsor educational programs, research, discussion, and dissemination of information; to provide criteria for specific levels of expertise within the field of information security and protection. **Awards:** Chapter of the Year. **Frequency:** annual. **Type:** trophy ● Hall of Fame. **Frequency:** annual. **Type:** trophy ● Honor Roll. **Frequency:** annual. **Type:** trophy ● Outstanding Organization of the Year. **Frequency:** annual. **Type:** trophy ● Presidents' Award for Communication Program of the Year. **Frequency:** annual. **Type:** trophy ● Presidents' Award for Public Service. **Frequency:** annual. **Type:** trophy ● Security Professional of the Year. **Frequency:** annual. **Type:** trophy. **Committees:** Awards; Ethics; GAISP; International Development; Nominations. **Publications:** *The ISSA Journal*, monthly. Magazine. **Price:** included in membership dues. **Circulation:** 20,000. **Advertising:** accepted. Alternate Formats: CD-ROM; online.

2091 ■ National Center for Computer Crime Data (NCCCD)
Address Unknown since 2007
Founded: 1978. **Staff:** 3. **Description:** Individuals and organizations in the security, law enforcement, legal, business, accounting, and computing professions. Facilitates the prevention, investigation, and prosecution of computer crime by disseminating documents and other data to those in need of this information. (Computer crime is defined broadly by the center as all crime perpetrated through the use of computers and all crimes where damage is done to computers.) Sponsors speakers and publications for the education of both the professional communities and the public. Conducts research; compiles statistics. Maintains speakers' bureau. **Libraries: Type:** reference. **Subjects:** Computer Crimes. **Awards: Type:** recognition. **Computer Services:** database. **Formerly:** (1979) National Computer Crime Data Center. **Publications:** *Computer Crime Law Reporter*, annual. Reference updating service that contains compilation of state and federal computer-crime laws, texts of pending bills, and legislation history. **Price:** $140.00 for basic copy ● *Computer Crime Laws* ● *Introduction to Computer Crime* ● *Spectacular Computer Crimes*. **Conventions/Meetings:** seminar.

2092 ■ NCMS — Society of Industrial Security Professionals
994 Old Eagle School Rd., Ste.1019
Wayne, PA 19087-1866
Ph: (610)971-4856
Fax: (610)971-4859
E-mail: info@classmgmt.com
URL: http://www.classmgmt.com
Contact: Mrs. Sharon K. Tannahill, Exec. Dir.
Founded: 1964. **Members:** 2,000. **Membership Dues:** individual, $75 (annual). **Budget:** $150,000. **Local Groups:** 29. **Description:** Contractor and government employees, including military personnel, whose principal duty is managing, supervising, or performing in a security classification management capacity in industry, government, the military services, or an educational institution. Seeks to: establish systems and techniques for identifying information or materials requiring protection in the national interests; determine levels of defense security classifications and identify restricted or formerly restricted data; establish procedures and practices for regrading and for management of classified material inventory and company private and proprietary information; indoctrinate and train personnel in the application of procedures. Maintains placement service. **Awards:** Woodbridge Award for Excellence. **Frequency:** annual. **Type:** recognition. **Recipient:** for excellence in the field of security. **Telecommunication Services:** electronic mail, sharont@mmco1.com. **Formerly:** (2005) National Classification Management Society. **Publications:** *Classification Management Bulletin*, bimonthly. **Price:** $30.00 for nonmembers; free for members. **Circulation:** 2,000 ● *National Classification Management Society—Membership Directory*, semiannual. **Price:** included in membership dues. **Circulation:** 2,000. **Conventions/Meetings:** annual seminar - always June and July.

Informatics

2093 ■ International Association of Information Technology Asset Managers (IAITAM)
1915A Gingerich St. NW
Hartville, OH 44632
Ph: (330)877-1437
Free: (866)942-4826
E-mail: info@iaitam.org
URL: http://www.iaitam.org
Contact: Barbara Rembiesa, Pres./Founder
Founded: 1998. **Membership Dues:** individual, $295 (annual) ● corporate, $1,790 (annual) ● provider,

$2,390 (annual). **Multinational. Description:** Represents the interests of individuals involved in any aspect of the life cycle processes for IT assets in organizations. Seeks to provide a centralized "real world" based skills development for the IT professional. Promulgates an understanding of IT asset management best practices and their value to the organization. **Telecommunication Services:** electronic mail, barb@iaitam.org. **Programs:** CAPc; Employee Awareness; ISCS; Provider Member; Recertification. **Publications:** *ITAK*, bimonthly. Magazine. **Price:** included in membership dues. **Circulation:** 50,000. **Conventions/Meetings:** annual conference (exhibits).

2094 ■ International Society for Computational Biology (ISCB)
c/o San Diego Supercomputer Ctr., UC San Diego
9500 Gilman Dr., MC 0505
La Jolla, CA 92093-0505
Ph: (858)822-0852
Fax: (760)888-0313
E-mail: admin@iscb.org
URL: http://www.iscb.org
Contact: Michael Gribskov PhD, Pres.
Founded: 1997. **Members:** 1,300. **Membership Dues:** professional (PH dues category), $99 (annual) ● professional (PM dues category), $40 (annual) ● professional (PL dues category), student/trainee - SM dues category, $20 (annual) ● student/trainee (SH dues category), $49 (annual) ● student/trainee (SL dues category), $10 (annual). **Multinational. Description:** Promotes the application of computational methods to problems of biological significance. Facilitates basic and applied research, scientific communication, education and international cooperation in computational biology. Funds research and educational projects in computational biology. **Awards:** Overton Prize. **Frequency:** annual. **Type:** recognition. **Recipient:** for outstanding accomplishment in computational biology by a scientist in the early or mid-stage of his/her career ● Senior Scientist Accomplishment Award. **Frequency:** annual. **Type:** recognition. **Recipient:** for outstanding accomplishment in computational biology by a scientist who is more than 12 to 15 years post-degree. **Telecommunication Services:** electronic mail, mgribsko@purdue.edu. **Committees:** Affiliates and SIGs; Awards; Conferences; Education; Governance; Nominations; Public Affairs and Policies; Publications.

Information Management

2095 ■ AIIM - The Enterprise Content Management Association
1100 Wayne Ave., Ste.1100
Silver Spring, MD 20910
Ph: (301)587-8202
Free: (800)477-2446
Fax: (301)587-2711
E-mail: aiim@aiim.org
URL: http://www.aiim.org
Contact: Jan Andersson, Chm.
Founded: 1943. **Members:** 10,000. **Membership Dues:** professional, $125 (annual) ● trade, $1,000 (annual) ● channel connection, $500 (annual). **Staff:** 50. **Budget:** $5,000,000. **Regional Groups:** 50. **Description:** Manufacturers, vendors, and individual users of information and image management equipment, products, and services. Holds special meetings for trade members and companies. Maintains Speaker's Bureau. Operates resource center. Compiles statistics. **Libraries: Type:** reference. **Holdings:** 26,000; audiovisuals, books, clippings, monographs, periodicals. **Subjects:** micrographics, optical imaging and peripheral technologies, video, multimedia, networks. **Awards:** Award of Merit. **Type:** recognition. **Recipient:** for distinguished service to the industry ● **Type:** fellowship ● Pioneer Medal. **Type:** medal. **Computer Services:** database, bibliographic ● database, resource center. **Boards:** Advisory Trade Member. **Committees:** Awards; Board of Directors Nominating; Document Management Service Providers Advisory; MIT/LIT Accreditation; Standards. **Councils:** Professional Advisory. **Subgroups:** Emerging Technologies Advisory. **Formerly:** National Microfilm Association; National Micrographics Association; (2002) Association for Information and Image Management. **Publications:** *E-Doc*, bimonthly. Magazine. Alternate Formats: online ● *INFORM*, 10/year. Magazine. Covers document imaging topics. **Price:** included in membership dues; $89.00 for nonmembers. **Advertising:** accepted. Alternate Formats: online. Also Cited As: *FYI Inform* ● Also publishes technical books and standards. **Conventions/Meetings:** annual trade show (exhibits).

2096 ■ ARMA International - The Association of Information Management Professionals
13725 W 109th St., Ste.101
Lenexa, KS 66215
Ph: (913)341-3808
Free: (800)422-2762
Fax: (913)341-3742
E-mail: hq@arma.org
URL: http://www.arma.org
Contact: Marilyn Bier, Exec. Dir.
Founded: 1975. **Members:** 10,500. **Membership Dues:** basic, $150 (annual) ● student/retired, $25 (annual). **Staff:** 29. **Budget:** $5,000,000. **Regional Groups:** 10. **Local Groups:** 130. **Multinational. Description:** Provides education, research, and networking opportunities to information professionals to enable them to use their skills and experience to leverage the value of records, information and knowledge as corporate assets and as contributors to organizational success. **Libraries: Type:** reference. **Holdings:** 50; films. **Awards:** Britt Literary Award. **Type:** recognition. **Recipient:** for an outstanding article in the professional journal ● Chapter Member of the Year. **Frequency:** annual. **Type:** recognition ● Chapter Newsletter of the Year. **Frequency:** annual. **Type:** recognition ● Chapter of the Year. **Frequency:** annual. **Type:** recognition ● Company of Fellows. **Frequency:** annual. **Type:** recognition. **Recipient:** for outstanding achievements and contributions to the profession ● Special Projects Award. **Type:** recognition. **Recipient:** for innovative special projects that promote records and information management. **Committees:** Canadian Legislative and Regulatory Affairs; Conference Program; Education Development; Electronic Records; International Issues; Professional Issues; Standards; Technical Publications and Education; U.S. Government Relations. **Formed by Merger of:** (1982) Association of Records Executives and Administrators; American Records Management Association. **Publications:** *The Information Management Journal*, bimonthly. Includes articles on research and issues in the field of records and information management. **Price:** $90.00/year. ISSN: 1050-2343. **Circulation:** 13,000. **Advertising:** accepted. **Conventions/Meetings:** annual conference (exhibits) - usually October. 2008 Oct. 20-23, Las Vegas, NV; 2009 Oct. 15-18, Orlando, FL.

2097 ■ Association of Independent Information Professionals (AIIP)
8550 United Plaza Blvd., Ste.1001
Baton Rouge, LA 70809
Ph: (225)408-4400
Fax: (225)408-4422
E-mail: info@aiip.org
URL: http://www.aiip.org
Contact: Jane John, Pres.
Founded: 1987. **Members:** 800. **Membership Dues:** full, associate, $200 (annual) ● student, $50 (annual) ● supporting, $500 (annual) ● retired, $75 (annual). **Multinational. Description:** Independent information professionals involved in computer and manual organization, retrieval, and dissemination of information. Organized to further the professionalism of the information field and to educate members and the public about independent information professionals. Encourages high standards of practice. **Awards:** AIIP Technology Award. **Frequency:** annual. **Type:** recognition ● Myra T. Grenier Award. **Frequency:** annual. **Type:** recognition ● President's Award. **Frequency:** annual. **Type:** recognition ● Sue Rugge Memorial Award. **Frequency:** annual. **Type:** recognition. **Telecommunication Services:** electronic mail, jjohn@onpointresearch.com ● information service, electronic discussion list, private forum. **Formerly:** (1987) International Association of Independent Information Brokers. **Publications:** *Connections*, quarterly. Newsletter. Alternate Formats: online ● *Professional Paper Series*, periodic. Papers ● Membership Directory, annual. ISSN: 1524-9468. **Circulation:** 800. **Advertising:** accepted. **Conventions/Meetings:** annual conference (exhibits) - always spring.

2098 ■ College of Healthcare Information Management Executives (CHIME)
3300 Washtenaw Ave., Ste.225
Ann Arbor, MI 48104-5184
Ph: (734)665-0000
Fax: (734)665-4922
E-mail: staff@cio-chime.org
URL: http://www.cio-chime.org
Contact: Richard A. Correll, Pres./CEO
Founded: 1992. **Members:** 750. **Membership Dues:** joint CHIME-HIMSS in U.S., $475 (annual) ● individual in U.S., $335 (annual) ● joint CHIME-HIMSS outside U.S., $525 (annual) ● individual outside U.S., $385 (annual). **Staff:** 11. **Description:** Healthcare chief information officers. Works to advance the use of innovative technology in healthcare. **Awards:** CHIME Collaboration Award. **Frequency:** annual. **Type:** recognition. **Recipient:** for the best collaborative effort ● Innovator of the Year Award. **Frequency:** annual. **Type:** recognition. **Recipient:** to a CIO who has demonstrated value to his/her organization through the creative application of technology ● John Gall CIO of the Year. **Frequency:** annual. **Type:** recognition. **Recipient:** to a CIO who has best demonstrated the qualities of leadership in healthcare ● John Glasser Scholarship. **Frequency:** annual. **Type:** scholarship. **Recipient:** for IT staff. **Computer Services:** database. **Committees:** Awards; Planning. **Programs:** Fellow. **Publications:** *The Connection*, monthly. Newsletter. Features Gartner research on relevant IT topics. **Price:** included in membership dues. **Conventions/Meetings:** semiannual CIO Forum - meeting, members only.

2099 ■ DSL Forum
48377 Fremont Blvd., Ste.117
Fremont, CA 94538
Ph: (510)492-4020 (510)492-4023
Fax: (510)492-4001
E-mail: info@dslforum.org
URL: http://www.dslforum.org/index.shtml
Contact: Christine Freytag, Exec. Dir.
Founded: 1994. **Members:** 200. **Membership Dues:** principal, $7,500 (annual) ● small company principal, $3,500 (annual) ● auditing, $2,500 (annual) ● associate, $500 (annual). **Staff:** 3. **Description:** Increases the knowledge of potential market for DSL by offering technical and marketing programs. Maintains speakers' bureau. **Publications:** *DSL Forum Report*, quarterly. Newsletter. Contains current issues and activities of the forum. Alternate Formats: online ● Annual Report, annual. Includes committee achievements, financial report progress, membership list, staff information, and membership statistics. Alternate Formats: online. **Conventions/Meetings:** quarterly meeting.

2100 ■ Electronic Document Systems Foundation (EDSF)
1845 Precinct Line Rd., Ste.212
Hurst, TX 76054
Ph: (817)849-1145
Fax: (817)849-1185
E-mail: info@edsf.org
URL: http://www.edsf.org
Contact: Jeanne Mowlds, Exec. Dir.
Founded: 1996. **Staff:** 2. **Multinational. Description:** Supports the industry's future by granting academic scholarships, providing research/mentoring grants, creating an awareness of career opportunities, and recognizing innovative educators and educational programs. Serves vendors and users who design and implement document solutions for business applications; this includes the enterprise content management field-records management, document management, workflow management, web

content management and electronic imaging. **Awards:** Educator of the Year Award. **Frequency:** annual. **Type:** recognition. **Recipient:** for an academic representative ● Innovation in Continuing Education. **Frequency:** annual. **Type:** recognition ● Innovation in Distance Education and Training. **Frequency:** annual. **Type:** recognition ● Innovation in Higher Education. **Frequency:** annual. **Type:** recognition. **Recipient:** for a degree granting institute or organization at the undergraduate, graduate, or post graduate level. **Telecommunication Services:** electronic mail, jmowlds@edsf.org. **Affiliated With:** Xplor International. **Publications:** *Defining the Document Industry - Economic Impact and Future Growth Trends* ● *Document Communications Industry Trends: 2004 Survey Results* ● *EDSF REPORT*, bimonthly. Newsletter ● *Network, Screen and Page: The Future of Reading and Writing in the Digital Age* ● *Printing in the Age of WEB and Beyond* ● *Reaching Clients Through Cross Media Communications: Strategies for Financial Services.* **Conventions/Meetings:** semiannual board meeting, in conjunction with the Xplor International annual conference.

2101 ■ Information Resources Management Association (IRMA)
701 E Chocolate Ave., Ste.200
Hershey, PA 17033
Ph: (717)533-8879
Fax: (717)533-8661
E-mail: member@irma-international.org
URL: http://www.irma-international.org
Contact: Dr. Mehdi Khosrow-Pour, Pres.
Membership Dues: individual, $85 (annual) ● organization, $205 (annual) ● corporate, $500 (annual) ● student, $35 (annual) ● life, $800. **Multinational. Description:** Promotes the understanding, development and practice of managing information resources as key enterprise assets among IT professionals. Promotes the association to individuals with an interest in the field of management of information resources. Provides resources, assistance, encouragement and incentives to individuals either engaged in or planning to become engaged in the field of information resource management. **Computer Services:** Mailing lists, IRMA-L ● online services, shopping; IRM press catalogue. **Programs:** Fellow; Worldwide Representatives. **Subgroups:** Professional Development Institute. **Publications:** *International Journal of Business Data Communications and Networking*, quarterly. Covers guided and wireless communications of voice, data, images and video. **Price:** $90.00 /year for individuals; $225.00 /year for institutions; $30.00/year for students. ISSN: 1548-0631 ● *International Journal of Web Services Research*, quarterly. Features research findings and industry solutions dealing with all aspects of web services technology. **Price:** $95.00 /year for individuals; $255.00 /year for institutions. ISSN: 1545-7362 ● *International Journal on Semantic Web and Information Systems*, quarterly. Features information about Semantic Web technology in Information Systems. **Price:** $90.00 /year for individuals; $225.00 /year for institutions. ISSN: 1552-6283 ● *Mobile Services in the Networked Economy.* Book. Provides new insights into the structure and dynamics of the mobile services industry. **Price:** $71.96 for nonmembers; $35.98 for members ● *Wireless Information Highways.* Book. Contains methodologies to support data management in asymmetric communication environments. **Price:** $76.46 for nonmembers; $38.23 for members. **Conventions/Meetings:** annual international conference.

2102 ■ Information Technology Solution Provider Alliance (ITSPA)
PO Box 10641
Portland, OR 97296
Ph: (503)231-3086
E-mail: rmorgan@itspa.net
URL: http://www.itspa.net
Contact: Russell Morgan, Pres./Founder
Founded: 2003. **Description:** Provides advice and recommends technology solutions to business problems. Helps small and medium-sized businesses adopt new technology to solve day-to-day business challenges. Helps small business executives understand how using local technology consultants can enable them to boost their companies' productivity, increase efficiency and provide a higher return on investment.

2103 ■ Institute of Certified Records Managers (ICRM)
5818 Molloy Rd.
Syracuse, NY 13211
Ph: (315)234-1904
Free: (877)244-3128
Fax: (315)474-1784
E-mail: admin@icrm.org
URL: http://www.icrm.org
Contact: Linda J. Cusimano CRM, Pres.
Founded: 1975. **Members:** 875. **Membership Dues:** active, $150 (annual) ● inactive, $25 (annual) ● retired, $10 (annual). **Staff:** 11. **Budget:** $30,000. **Description:** Certified records managers united to develop a program for the maintenance of certification for members of the Institute; promote the value of certification of records managers to the various national, state, and local governments and the private sector; develop and administer a program for the professional certification of records managers, including the granting of appropriate recognition; develop and administer certification examinations in records management with complete responsibility for the scope, complexity, and integrity of such examinations. **Awards:** Emmett Leahy Award. **Frequency:** annual. **Type:** recognition. **Recipient:** for outstanding contributions. **Telecommunication Services:** electronic mail, ljcusim@sandia.gov. **Committees:** Certification by Examination. **Publications:** *Institute of Certified Records Managers—Membership Directory*, annual. **Price:** free for members ● *Preparing for the CRM Examination: A Handbook* ● *ProfessioNotes*, quarterly. Newsletter. Contains information for certified records managers. **Price:** free for members and candidates preparing for CRM. Alternate Formats: online. **Conventions/Meetings:** semiannual board meeting ● annual meeting, held in conjunction with the ARMA conference - usually fall.

2104 ■ International Association of Privacy Professionals (IAPP)
266 York St.
York, ME 03909
Ph: (207)351-1500
Free: (800)266-6501
Fax: (207)351-1501
E-mail: information@privacyassociation.org
URL: http://www.privacyassociation.org
Contact: J. Trevor Hughes CIPP, Exec. Dir.
Founded: 2001. **Members:** 3,000. **Membership Dues:** student, $50 (annual) ● academic/government/not-for-profit, $100 (annual) ● professional, $250 (annual) ● business, $495 (annual) ● corporate, $3,000 (annual) ● silver, $5,000 (annual) ● gold, $10,000 (annual) ● platinum, $20,000 (annual). **Multinational. Description:** Seeks to define, promote and improve the privacy profession globally. Provides a forum for privacy professionals to share practices and track trends. Advances privacy management issues and standardizes the designations for privacy professionals. Provides education and guidance on opportunities in the field of privacy. **Awards:** IAPP/Deloitte and Touche Vanguard Award. **Frequency:** annual. **Type:** recognition. **Recipient:** to the single privacy professional who demonstrates exemplary leadership, knowledge, creativity and innovation in privacy ● IAPP Privacy Innovation Award. **Frequency:** annual. **Type:** recognition. **Recipient:** for private sector and public sector organizations. **Publications:** *The Daily Dashboard.* Newsletter. **Price:** free. Alternate Formats: online ● *The Privacy Advisor*, monthly. Newsletter. Provides in-depth and timely coverage of the most relevant privacy issues. **Price:** included in membership dues. Alternate Formats: online.

2105 ■ Management Information Systems Group (MISG)
10 Lab. Dr.
Research Triangle Park, NC 27709-3966
Ph: (919)406-8829
Fax: (919)549-8733
E-mail: info@misg.com
URL: http://www.misg.com
Contact: Al Jones, Pres.
Description: Trading partners in the automotive, heavy duty, industrial part, Christian retailing, publishing, plumbing, heating, cooling and piping. Strives to serve as a forum for industry interaction, education and idea exchange regarding matters of common interest to MIS managers and related executives in the automotive manufacturing companies. Develops and manages E-commerce and EDI programs for members.

2106 ■ National Association for Information Destruction (NAID)
3420 E Shea Blvd., Ste.115
Phoenix, AZ 85028
Ph: (602)788-6243
Fax: (602)788-4144
E-mail: rjohnson@naidonline.org
URL: http://www.naidonline.org
Contact: Robert Johnson, Exec. Dir.
Membership Dues: individual, active/franchise (in U.S.), $545 (annual) ● active/franchise (in Canada), $545 (annual) ● associate, vendor, $600 (annual). **Multinational. Description:** Companies providing information destruction services, and their suppliers of products, equipment and services. Promotes the information destruction industry and the standards and ethics of its member firms. **Publications:** *NAIDnews.* Journal.

2107 ■ National Public Records Research Association (NPRRA)
2501 Aerial Center Pkwy., Ste.103
Morrisville, NC 27560
Ph: (919)459-2078
Fax: (919)459-2075
E-mail: info@nprra.org
URL: http://www.nprra.org
Contact: Kevin Roberts, Pres.
Members: 264. **Membership Dues:** associate, $250 (annual) ● company (based on number of employees), $250-$600 (annual). **Staff:** 1. **Description:** Companies that provide research and information from public records. **Publications:** *The Record*, quarterly. Newsletter ● Membership Directory, annual. **Conventions/Meetings:** annual board meeting - always March ● annual conference (exhibits).

2108 ■ The Open Group
44 Montgomery St., Ste.960
San Francisco, CA 94104-4704
Ph: (415)374-8280
Fax: (415)374-8293
E-mail: memnews-feedback@opengroup.org
URL: http://www.opengroup.org
Contact: Allen Brown, Pres./CEO
Membership Dues: IT supplier (below $25M revenues), $2,500 ● IT supplier ($25M-$100M), $12,500 ● IT supplier ($100M above), $20,000 ● IT customer (below $25M), $2,500 ● IT Customer ($25-$100), $7,500 ● IT customer ($100 above), $12,500 ● government (200 staff below), $2,500 ● government (200 staff or more), $7,500 ● academia faculty, $1,000. **Multinational. Description:** Promotes boundary-less information flow through global interoperability in a secure, reliable and timely manner. **Councils:** Customer; Supplier. **Sections:** Active Loss Prevention Initiative; Architecture Forum; Directory Interoperability Forum; Enterprise Management Forum; Messaging Forum; Mobile Management Forum; Platform Forum; Quality of Service Forum; Real-Time and Embedded Systems Forum; Security Forum. **Publications:** *Architecture.* Newsletter ● *Conference and Member Meetings Proceedings* ● Catalog. **Conventions/Meetings:** quarterly conference - 2008 July 20-25, Chicago, IL; 2008 Oct. 19-24, Munich, Germany.

2109 ■ PRISM International - Professional Records and Information Services Management (PRISM)
131 US 70 W
Garner, NC 27529
Ph: (919)771-0657
Free: (800)336-9793

Fax: (919)771-0457
E-mail: staff@prismintl.org
URL: http://www.prismintl.org
Contact: Jim Booth, Exec. Dir.
Founded: 1980. **Members:** 600. **Membership Dues:** company, $765 (annual) ● corporate partner, $770 (annual) ● affiliate, associate, $215 (annual). **Staff:** 4. **Budget:** $1,200,000. **Multinational. Description:** Represents owners and operators of commercial information management facilities, which include: commercial record centers, media vaults, imaging service bureaus, confidential destruction vendors, digital archiving operations, vendors to the industry, self-vended records and data repositories, government records repositories and educators. Seeks to provide operating guidelines, education, and research in the industry. Promotes professional quality of services offered by commercial and non-commercial information management organizations; facilitates exchange of technical and management information; provides conferences and educational events in the United States, Europe and Asia; works to advocate for and improve public image of commercial information management industry. **Telecommunication Services:** electronic mail, jim@prismintl.org. **Absorbed:** (1994) National Association of Security and Data Vaults. **Formerly:** (1997) Association of Commercial Records Centers. **Publications:** *InFocus*, quarterly. Magazine. **Price:** free for members. **Advertising:** accepted. Alternate Formats: online. **Conventions/Meetings:** annual conference (exhibits).

2110 ■ SCSI Trade Association (STA)
Presidio of San Francisco
Bldg. 572B, Ruger St.
PO Box 29920
San Francisco, CA 94129
Ph: (415)561-6273
Fax: (415)561-6120
E-mail: info@scsita.org
URL: http://www.scsita.org
Contact: Chris Lyon, Exec. Dir.
Founded: 1996. **Membership Dues:** sponsorship, $25,000 (annual) ● principal, $10,000 (annual) ● promotional, interop, $4,500 (annual). **Description:** Aims to help educate OEM's, resellers, and information technology professionals. **Programs:** SAS Plugfest. **Publications:** *Buyer's Guide* ● *Serial Storage Wire*. Newsletter. Alternate Formats: online ● Papers. Alternate Formats: online. **Conventions/Meetings:** annual meeting ● seminar (exhibits) ● trade show.

2111 ■ Supply-Chain Council (SCC)
1400 Eye St. NW, Ste.1050
Washington, DC 20005
Ph: (202)962-0440
Fax: (202)962-3939
E-mail: info@supply-chain.org
URL: http://www.supply-chain.org/cs/root/home
Contact: Sean Simmons, Exec. Dir.
Founded: 1996. **Members:** 800. **Membership Dues:** end user/practitioner/enabling technology company/ software vendor/consultant/analyst, $3,000 (annual) ● non-profit (academic/consortium/association/ government agency), $600 (annual) ● global/ multinational, $5,000 (annual) ● small/medium enterprise, $1,500 (annual). **Staff:** 8. **National Groups:** 8. **Languages:** English, French, German, Japanese, Korean. **Multinational. Description:** Expands knowledge about the SCOR-model around the globe. Promotes research and thought leadership in the supply chain management area. Sponsors and supports educational programs including conferences, retreats, benchmarking studies and development of the Supply-Chain Operations Reference-model (SCOR), the process reference model designed to improve users' efficiency and productivity. **Awards:** Supply-Chain Excellence. **Frequency:** annual. **Type:** recognition. **Recipient:** to an organization that made the greatest contribution to demonstrating or advancing the supply chain management body of knowledge. **Computer Services:** Online services, publication. **Publications:** Newsletter, periodic. **Price:** free. Alternate Formats: online. **Conventions/Meetings:** periodic seminar ● annual Supply-Chain World-North America - conference.

2112 ■ U.S. Product Data Association (US PRO)
5300 Intl. Blvd., Ste.204
North Charleston, SC 29418
Ph: (843)760-3293 (843)760-3545
Fax: (843)760-3349
E-mail: uspro-info@aticorp.org
Contact: Lynn Crane, Program Dir.
Membership Dues: organization (based on number of employees), $1,000-$5,000 (annual) ● academic organization, $1,000 (annual). **Description:** Provides the management functions for the IGES/PDES Organization (IPO) and its related activities. Supports the development, publication and distribution of the Initial Graphics Exchange Specification (IGES) and Product Data Exchange using STEP (PDES) standards in the US. Helps remove barriers that inhibit the exchange of product data and its flow across the supply chain linked to product design, manufacture and support. Ensures that critical requirements for business or industry will be addressed in order to meet PDE needs. **Awards:** International William J. Conroy Standards Professional Award. **Frequency:** annual. **Type:** recognition. **Recipient:** to an individual who has shown exceptional leadership in the development or implementation of Product Data Exchange standards. **Publications:** Catalogs. Includes standards developed by the IGES/PDES Organization and other documents available from the U.S. Product Data Association (US PRO). Alternate Formats: online ● Newsletter. Alternate Formats: online.

2113 ■ Usability Professionals' Association (UPA)
140 N Bloomingdale Rd.
Bloomingdale, IL 60108-1017
Ph: (630)980-4997
Fax: (630)351-8490
E-mail: office@usabilityprofessionals.org
URL: http://www.upassoc.org
Contact: John E. Kasper PhD, Exec. Dir.
Founded: 1991. **Members:** 1,700. **Membership Dues:** professional, $100 (annual) ● student, $35 (annual). **Staff:** 4. **Budget:** $750,000. **Regional Groups:** 5. **Multinational. Description:** Usability professionals and other individuals with an interest in the application of information technology and design to make products more usable. **Committees:** Chapters; Conference; Outreach; Professional Development; Publications. **Projects:** Developing the Profession; Usability in E-Government; Voting and Usability. **Publications:** *Journal of Usability Studies*. Promotes and enhances the practice, research, and education of usability engineering. Alternate Formats: online ● *UPA Monthly* (in English, French, German, Hebrew, Italian, Portuguese, and Spanish). Newsletter. Features announcements, chapter news, and links to a few good articles on usability. Alternate Formats: online ● *User Experience*, quarterly. Magazine. Features articles dealing with the broad field of usability and the user experience. **Price:** $12.00/copy for members; $18.00/copy for nonmembers. **Circulation:** 1,700. **Advertising:** accepted ● *The Voice*. Newsletter. Alternate Formats: online. **Conventions/Meetings:** annual conference (exhibits).

2114 ■ World Organization of Webmasters (WOW)
PO Box 143
Folsom, CA 95630
Ph: (916)989-2933
Fax: (916)987-3022
E-mail: info@joinwow.org
URL: http://www.joinwow.org
Contact: Bill Cullifer, Exec. Dir.
Founded: 1996. **Membership Dues:** student, $49 (annual) ● government/educational, $69 (annual) ● individual, $89 (annual) ● community college, $295 (annual) ● university, $495 (annual) ● small business, $595 (annual) ● high school, $195 (annual). **Description:** Individuals who create, manage, market, or maintain websites. Seeks to advance the profession of website creation and management; promotes the online industries. Represents members' interests; facilitates communication and cooperation among members. **Awards:** Web Professional Awards. **Frequency:** annual. **Type:** recognition. **Recipient:** for web professionals. **Committees:** Web Design Technical; Web Professional Award. **Programs:** Members Advantage; Mentoring; Web Professional Certification. **Formerly:** (2001) National Association of Webmasters. **Publications:** Newsletter, monthly.

Innovation

2115 ■ Innovation Network
c/o Joyce Wycoff, Co-Founder
8200 Kroll Way, No. 72
Bakersfield, CA 93311
Ph: (870)656-4141
E-mail: staff@thinksmart.com
URL: http://www.thinksmart.com
Contact: Joyce Wycoff, Co-Founder
Founded: 1993. **Members:** 50. **Description:** Individuals and companies. Committed to innovative thinking and processes. **Awards:** George Land Award. **Frequency:** annual. **Type:** recognition. **Subgroups:** Innovation Associates. **Publications:** *Mind-Play*, weekly. Newsletter. **Price:** free for members. Alternate Formats: online. **Conventions/Meetings:** annual Convergence - conference.

Inspectors

2116 ■ American Institute of Inspectors (AII)
PO Box 248
Lower Lake, CA 95457
Free: (800)877-4770
Fax: (707)277-7852
E-mail: execdir@inspection.org
URL: http://www.inspection.org
Contact: Sylvia Duerksen, Exec. Dir.
Founded: 1989. **Members:** 280. **Description:** Certified home inspectors. Works to set standards for impartial evaluations of residential properties. Certifies members in four areas: residential homes, mobile homes, mechanics, and earthquake hazard reduction. Maintains speakers' bureau. **Libraries: Type:** not open to the public. **Holdings:** books, video recordings. **Subjects:** electromagnetic fields, construction materials. **Publications:** *AII Newsletter*, monthly. **Price:** free for members. **Circulation:** 280. **Conventions/Meetings:** semiannual conference - spring and fall ● annual meeting.

2117 ■ Association of Construction Inspectors (ACI)
21640 N 19th Ave., Suite C-2
Phoenix, AZ 85027
Ph: (623)580-4646
Fax: (623)580-9656
E-mail: info@aci-assoc.org
URL: http://www.aci-assoc.org
Contact: Robert Johnson, Exec. Dir.
Founded: 1978. **Members:** 3,200. **Membership Dues:** CCI/CCPM/CCC designation, $195 (annual). **Staff:** 8. **Budget:** $2,000,000. **Description:** Works to provide education, training, standards and professional recognition to construction inspectors and project managers. Offers the professional designation of CCI (certified construction inspector) and CCPM-certified construction project manager. Provides networking opportunities and educational programs. **Awards:** President's Club. **Frequency:** annual. **Type:** scholarship. **Computer Services:** database ● mailing lists ● online services. **Publications:** *Conspect*, monthly. Newsletter ● *Construction Management of Major Commercial Projects*. Booklet. **Price:** $10.00 ● *Directory of Designated Members*, annual. Membership Directory ● *Industrializing the Residential Construction Site*. Report. **Price:** $35.00. **Conventions/Meetings:** annual conference (exhibits) ● annual seminar.

2118 ■ Examination Board of Professional Home Inspectors (EBPHI)
800 E Northwest Hwy., Ste.700
Palatine, IL 60074
Ph: (847)298-7750
Free: (877)543-5222

E-mail: info@homeinspectionexam.org
URL: http://www.homeinspectionexam.org
Contact: Noel Zak, Exec. Dir.
Founded: 1999. **Nonmembership. Description:** Home inspectors. Provides information on exams and testing locations.

2119 ■ Housing Inspection Foundation (HIF)
21640 N 23rd Dr., Ste.C-2
Phoenix, AZ 85027
Ph: (623)580-4646
Fax: (623)580-9656
E-mail: info@hif-assoc.org
URL: http://www.hif-assoc.org
Contact: Robert G. Johnson, Exec. Dir.
Membership Dues: registered home inspector (at least 1 year of experience), $195 (annual) ● certified home inspector (at least 3 years of experience), $225 (annual). **Description:** Appraisers, environmental specialists, real estate professionals and construction professionals. Dedicated to the promotion and development of housing inspection. Provides educational programs, information, and ethical standards. Offers Registered Home Inspector designation. **Computer Services:** Mailing lists. **Formerly:** (2003) Housing Inspection Foundation/Association of Home Inspectors. **Publications:** *How to Perform Home Inspections*. Video. **Price:** $35.00 ● *Inspection*, quarterly. Newsletter ● Booklets ● Articles. Alternate Formats: online. **Conventions/Meetings:** annual How to Perform a Home Inspection - seminar, fundamentals and information on performing home inspections.

2120 ■ International Federation of Inspection Agencies-Americas Committee (IFIA AC)
3942 N Upland St.
Arlington, VA 22207
Ph: (703)533-9539
Fax: (703)533-1612
E-mail: info@ifia-ac.org
URL: http://www.ifia-ac.org
Contact: Graham Lees, Chm.
Membership Dues: general, $2,750 (annual). **Description:** Inspection agencies located in the United States. Represents the interests of the majority of the inspection industry in the Americas. Promotes internationally accepted standards in methods, documentation and qualification of companies and personnel. **Subcommittees:** Consumer Products; Laboratory; Legal; Petroleum. **Publications:** *Technical Bulletin*, periodic. Alternate Formats: online.

2121 ■ National Association of Certified Home Inspectors (NACHI)
1750 30th St.
Boulder, CO 80301
Fax: (650)429-2057
E-mail: fastreply@nachi.org
URL: http://www.nachi.org
Contact: Blaine Wiley, Pres.
Membership Dues: general, $289 (annual). **Multinational. Description:** Helps home inspectors achieve financial success and maintain inspection excellence. Ensures that each member recognizes changes within the home inspection industry. Promotes high standards of professionalism, business ethics and inspection procedures. **Computer Services:** database, inspector lists ● online services, inspector examination ● online services, message board. **Telecommunication Services:** hotline, consumer complaint line, (610)917-8000. **Publications:** *The Inspector*, monthly. Magazine ● *Inspector's Quarterly*, 3/year. Newspaper. **Circulation:** 64,000. Alternate Formats: online.

2122 ■ National Association of Home Inspectors (NAHI)
4248 Park Glen Rd.
Minneapolis, MN 55416
Ph: (952)928-4641
Free: (800)448-3942
Fax: (952)929-1318
E-mail: info@nahi.org
URL: http://www.nahi.org
Contact: Mallory C. Anderson, Exec. Dir.
Founded: 1987. **Members:** 1,335. **Membership Dues:** associate, regular, $295 (annual) ● Certified Real Estate Inspector, $345 (annual). **Staff:** 4. **State Groups:** 13. **Description:** Promotes and develops the home inspection industry and furthers the professionalism of members. Conducts educational programs. Develops public policy and industry practices guidelines. Operates a national referral service. Provides public relations support and materials. **Telecommunication Services:** electronic mail, mallory@nahi.org. **Publications:** *Most Important Visitor*. Brochure ● *NAHI Forum*, bimonthly. Newsletter. **Circulation:** 1,400. **Advertising:** accepted ● *Standards of Practice Guidelines and Code of Ethics*. Book. **Conventions/Meetings:** seminar, includes a 4-day West Caribbean cruise (exhibits) - February, June and September.

2123 ■ National Association of Property Inspectors (NAPI)
303 W Cypress St.
San Antonio, TX 78212
Free: (800)486-3676
Fax: (210)225-8450
URL: http://napi.lincoln-grad.org
Founded: 1992. **Members:** 500. **Membership Dues:** associate, $50 (annual) ● candidate, $60 (annual) ● certified senior inspector, $125 (annual). **Staff:** 5. **Description:** Property inspectors throughout North America wishing to be certified. Provides certification and recognition for real estate professionals who have completed specialized educational courses, demonstrated competence, and agreed to abide by a code of ethics. Works with Lincoln Graduate Center to offer educational courses and programs. Plans to offer seminars throughout the country. **Libraries: Type:** reference; not open to the public. **Holdings:** articles, books, business records, periodicals. **Awards:** Certified Senior Inspector. **Type:** recognition. **Publications:** *Property Inspector News*, quarterly. Newsletter. Contains latest information on legal matters, research findings and industry advancements. **Price:** included in membership dues ● Membership Directory, annual. Contains a list of Real Estate Professionals. **Conventions/Meetings:** annual meeting.

Instrumentation

2124 ■ Instrumentation Testing Association (ITA)
631 N Stephanie St., No. 279
Henderson, NV 89014
Ph: (702)568-1445
Free: (877)236-1256
Fax: (702)568-1446
E-mail: ita@instrument.org
URL: http://www.instrument.org
Contact: Steven J. Gluck, Pres.
Founded: 1984. **Members:** 75. **Membership Dues:** individual, $95 (annual) ● regulatory agency, $1,100 (annual) ● academic/non-profit organization, $275 (annual) ● public/private utility (based on the utility service population), $255-$3,800 (annual) ● industry facility (based on the number of corporate treatment facility), $820-$1,580 (annual) ● consultant/manufacturer representative (based on corporate size), $315-$2,530 (annual) ● manufacturer (based on annual gross sales), $950-$8,855 (annual). **Staff:** 2. **Budget:** $250,000. **Multinational. Description:** Manufacturers, end-users of instrumentation (public works and regulatory agencies, industrial firms design and consulting firms, non-profit educational/professional scientific organizations and academic/research institutes). Promotes the understanding, selection, improvement and cost-effective use of instrumentation and automation applications used for monitoring and controlling water, wastewater and industrial systems. **Libraries: Type:** not open to the public. **Holdings:** 35. **Subjects:** water, wastewater. **Computer Services:** database, instruments; water/wastewater instruments. **Committees:** Manufacturer; Technical. **Subcommittees:** Maintenance; Program. **Formerly:** (2005) Water and Wastewater Instrumentation Testing Association of North America. **Publications:** *eNews*, quarterly. Newsletter. **Price:** included in membership dues. **Circulation:** 100. **Advertising:** accepted. Alternate Formats: online. **Conventions/Meetings:** annual Flow Measurement - workshop ● annual meeting.

Insurance

2125 ■ ACORD
2 Blue Hill Plz., 3rd Fl.
PO Box 1529
Pearl River, NY 10965-8529
Ph: (845)620-1700
Fax: (845)620-3600
E-mail: memberservices@acord.org
URL: http://www.acord.org
Contact: Gregory A. Maciag, Pres./CEO
Founded: 1970. **Members:** 30,000. **Staff:** 50. **Budget:** $10,000,000. **Description:** Facilitates the development and use of standards for the insurance, reinsurance and related financial services industries. Accomplishes its mission by remaining an objective, independent advocate for sharing information among diverse platforms. **Awards:** ACORD Implementation Award. **Frequency:** annual. **Type:** monetary. **Recipient:** for growth, level of standards implementation. **Telecommunication Services:** electronic mail, gmaciag@acord.org. **Committees:** ACORD Standards. **Publications:** *@ACORD eNewsletter*, periodic. Alternate Formats: online ● *In ACORD*, quarterly. Magazine. **Price:** included in membership dues. Alternate Formats: online. **Conventions/Meetings:** annual conference (exhibits) ● workshop.

2126 ■ Alliance of Claims Assistance Professionals (ACAP)
c/o Lisa Norris, ACAP, Pres.
25500 Hawthorne Blvd., Ste.1158
Torrance, CA 90505
Free: (888)394-5163
Fax: (630)690-0377
E-mail: info@claims.org
URL: http://www.claims.org
Contact: Lisa Norris ACAP, Pres.
Membership Dues: individual, $25 (annual). **Description:** Health insurance claims assistance professionals working for insurance providers and patients. Promotes the "effective management of health insurance claims." Develops standards of practice for health insurance claims assistance; makes available referral services; sponsors educational programs. **Publications:** *Health Claims Update*, quarterly. Newsletter. **Price:** included in membership dues.

2127 ■ American Academy of Actuaries
1100 17th St. NW, 7th Fl.
Washington, DC 20036
Ph: (202)223-8196 (212)785-7871
Fax: (202)872-1948
E-mail: cronin@actuary.org
URL: http://www.actuary.org
Contact: Kevin Cronin, Exec. Dir.
Founded: 1965. **Members:** 13,000. **Membership Dues:** individual, $555 (annual). **Staff:** 44. **Budget:** $6,000. **Description:** Ensures that the American public recognizes and benefits from the independent expertise of the actuarial profession in the formulation of public policy and the adherence of actuaries to high professional standards in discharging their responsibilities. Represents the entire profession: Casualty Actuarial Society; Conference of Consulting Actuaries; Society of Actuaries; Fraternal Actuarial Association (now defunct). Maintains speakers' bureau. **Libraries: Type:** reference. **Awards:** Jarvis Farley Service Award. **Frequency:** annual. **Type:** recognition. **Recipient:** for exceptional contributions to the actuarial profession ● Robert J. Myers Public Service Award. **Frequency:** annual. **Type:** recognition. **Recipient:** for exceptional contributions to the common good. **Committees:** Communications;

Health Insurance; Life Insurance; Litigation Review; Pensions; Personnel and Compensation; Property/Casualty Insurance; Qualifications and Standards of Practice. **Publications:** *Actuarial Update*, monthly. Newsletter. Reports on developing actuarial issues, legislative and regulatory activity, and standards proposals in progress. **Price:** available to members only ● *American Academy of Actuaries Yearbook*. **Price:** free for members; $25.00 for nonmembers ● *Contingencies*, bimonthly. Magazine. Provides actuarial perspective on a range of major social issues. Contains research. **Price:** free for members; $24.00 for nonmembers ● *Directory of Actuarial Memberships*, annual. **Price:** free for members; $100.00 for nonmembers ● *Enrolled Actuaries Report*, quarterly. Newsletter. Includes legislative and regulatory news. **Price:** included in membership dues. **Conventions/Meetings:** annual Enrolled Actuaries Meeting (exhibits).

2128 ■ American Agents Association (AAA)

Address Unknown since 2007

Founded: 1980. **Members:** 250. **Membership Dues:** $25 (annual). **Staff:** 2. **Local Groups:** 2. **National Groups:** 4. **Description:** Licensed insurance agents. Purpose is to provide programs to enhance the security of insurance agents and their families and to take advantage of programs designed for insurance agents. Offers placement services; compiles statistics. Plans to establish a scholarship program for members' children. Conducts seminars and classes on markets and marketing. Maintains hall of fame. **Libraries: Type:** reference. **Holdings:** 2,500. **Subjects:** life and health insurance. **Awards: Type:** recognition. **Computer Services:** database ● mailing lists. **Publications:** *American Eagle*, bimonthly. Newsletter. **Price:** free. **Circulation:** 300. **Advertising:** not accepted. **Conventions/Meetings:** annual conference (exhibits).

2129 ■ American Association of Crop Insurers (AACI)

1 Massachusetts Ave. NW, Ste.800
Washington, DC 20001
Ph: (202)789-4100
Fax: (202)408-7763
E-mail: aaci@mwmlaw.com
URL: http://www.cropinsurers.com
Contact: Mike McLeod, Exec. Dir.

Founded: 1981. **Members:** 18. **Membership Dues:** standard, $100-$1,000 (annual) ● advisor, associate, $2,500 (annual) ● affiliate, $5 (annual). **Staff:** 3. **Budget:** $485,000. **Description:** Represents private sector companies, agencies, and individual agents that sell multiple-peril crop insurance. Aims to educate Congress on crop insurance issues. Monitors crop insurance legislation, and to inform members about these activities. **Committees:** Government Relations; Grassroots; Political Action. **Publications:** *Crop Insurance Insider*, quarterly. Newsletter. Monitors crop insurance legislation and reports on efforts to educate the U.S. Congress on crop insurance issues. Includes new product information. **Price:** included in membership dues. **Circulation:** 5,000 ● Newsletter, quarterly. Contains information for affiliate members. **Conventions/Meetings:** annual Crop Insurance Industry Meeting ● seminar, for agents.

2130 ■ American Association of Dental Consultants (AADC)

10032 Wind Hill Dr.
Greenville, IN 47124
Ph: (812)923-2600
Free: (800)896-0707
Fax: (812)923-2900
E-mail: info@aadc.org
URL: http://www.aadc.org
Contact: Ms. Judith Salisbury, Exec. Dir.

Founded: 1979. **Members:** 422. **Membership Dues:** active, associate, $225 (annual) ● affiliate, $112 (annual). **Staff:** 1. **Budget:** $120,000. **Description:** Dental insurance consultants and others concerned with dental insurance plans from administrative and design perspectives. Works to increase knowledge in the area of dental insurance plans, including the interrelationship between insurance carriers, the dental profession, and the insured. Operates certification program. **Libraries: Type:** reference. **Holdings:** articles. **Awards:** Sonnie Shulman Meritorious Service Award. **Frequency:** periodic. **Type:** recognition. **Recipient:** for meritorious service. **Publications:** *Beacon*, triennial. Newsletter. **Price:** included in membership dues. **Circulation:** 422. **Conventions/Meetings:** annual workshop, held in conjunction with American Dental Association - every spring. 2009 May 7-9, Scottsdale, AZ; 2010 May 6-8, San Diego, CA.

2131 ■ American Association of Insurance Services (AAIS)

1745 S Naperville Rd.
Wheaton, IL 60187-8132
Ph: (630)681-8347 (630)681-8045
Free: (800)564-AAIS
Fax: (630)681-8356
E-mail: info@aaisonline.com
URL: http://www.aaisonline.com
Contact: Mr. Paul Baiocchi, Pres./CEO

Founded: 1975. **Members:** 500. **Staff:** 50. **Description:** Property and casualty insurance companies; mutual, stock, and reciprocal companies. Develops loss costs, rules, forms, and statistical services for property and casualty insurance. Licensed in all states, the District of Columbia, and the Commonwealth of Puerto Rico. **Libraries: Type:** reference. **Holdings:** articles, reports. **Formed by Merger of:** Mutual Aircraft Conference; Mutual Marine Conference. **Formerly:** (1975) Transportation Insurance Rating Bureau. **Publications:** *AAIS Viewpoint*, quarterly. Magazine. Contains PC issues. **Price:** free ● *Press Release*, periodic ● Bulletin, periodic. **Conventions/Meetings:** annual conference.

2132 ■ American Association for Long-Term Care Insurance (AALTCI)

3835 E Thousand Oaks Blvd., Ste.336
Westlake Village, CA 91362
Ph: (818)597-3227
Fax: (818)597-3206
E-mail: info@aaltci.org
URL: http://www.aaltci.org
Contact: Mickey Batsell MBA, Contact

Founded: 1998. **Membership Dues:** regular, $49 (annual) ● regular, $79 (biennial) ● regular, $99 (triennial). **Description:** Serves insurance and financial professionals who provide Long-Term Care (LTC) financing solutions. Promotes the importance of planning for long-term care needs. Creates heightened awareness among consumers for the need and benefits of owning individual and employer sponsored LTC insurance. Provides support and information to agents, brokers, financial professionals and insurers involved in the long-term care insurance marketplace. **Publications:** *LTCi Sales Strategies*, quarterly. Magazine. **Price:** included in membership dues.

2133 ■ American Association of Managing General Agents (AAMGA)

150 S Warner Rd., Ste.156
King of Prussia, PA 19406
Ph: (610)225-1999
Fax: (610)225-1996
E-mail: bernie.heinze@aamga.org
URL: http://www.aamga.org
Contact: Bernd G. Heinze Esq., Exec. Dir.

Founded: 1926. **Members:** 450. **Membership Dues:** active, $850 (annual) ● associate, $2,500 (annual) ● business service, $2,000 (annual). **Staff:** 10. **Budget:** $750,000. **Regional Groups:** 3. **Description:** Managing general agents of insurance companies. Conducts specialized education programs; compiles statistics. **Awards:** Achievement Award. **Type:** recognition. **Committees:** Archives; Automation; Communications; Foreign Seminar; Government Affairs; Inter-Association Liaison; Member Services and Benefits; University Foundation Finance. **Councils:** University Administrative. **Publications:** *Communique*, quarterly. Newsletter. **Price:** available to members only ● Yearbook. **Price:** available to members only. **Conventions/Meetings:** annual meeting (exhibits).

2134 ■ American Association of State Compensation Insurance Funds (AASCIF)

7501 E Lowry Blvd.
Denver, CO 80230
Ph: (303)361-4890
Fax: (303)361-5892
E-mail: info@aascif.org
URL: http://www.aascif.org
Contact: Mr. Ken Ross, Pres.

Membership Dues: associate, $300 (annual). **Multinational. Description:** Aims to improve, refine, and preserve state workers' compensation systems. Facilitates an effective and efficient operation of its member funds to provide an assured market for employers to secure workers' compensation coverage, adequate and equitable benefits to injured workers and their dependents, and service and assistance in the prevention of accidents and occupational disease. Provides resources and support for the adoption and establishment of state funds in those states not currently served by funds. **Awards:** Communications Award. **Frequency:** annual. **Type:** recognition. **Recipient:** for excellence in presenting information concerning topics relating to state compensation insurance funds by using different forms of media. **Publications:** *AASCIF News*, quarterly. Newsletter. **Price:** included in membership dues. Alternate Formats: online. **Conventions/Meetings:** annual conference - 2008 Aug. 17-20, Midway, UT - **Avg. Attendance:** 500.

2135 ■ American Council of Life Insurers (ACLI)

101 Constitution Ave. NW
Washington, DC 20001-2133
Ph: (202)624-2000 (202)624-2434
Free: (877)674-4659
Fax: (202)624-2319
E-mail: media@acli.com
URL: http://www.acli.com
Contact: Frank Keating, Pres./CEO

Founded: 1976. **Members:** 377. **Staff:** 130. **Budget:** $28,000,000. **Description:** Represents the interests of legal reserve life insurance companies in legislative, regulatory and judicial matters at the federal, state and municipal levels of government and at the NAIC. Member companies hold majority of the life insurance in force in the United States. **Libraries: Type:** not open to the public. **Holdings:** books, papers, periodicals. **Subjects:** disability insurance, annuities, financial services, pension, retirement, insurance laws and regulations. **Sections:** Compliance; Forum 500; Investment; Legal; Medical. **Publications:** *ACLI Digest*, biweekly. Newsletter ● *Investment Bulletins*, quarterly. Booklet. Alternate Formats: online ● *Life Insurance Fact Book*, annual. Booklet. Reports on U.S. life insurance companies and their products. **Circulation:** 25,000. Alternate Formats: online. **Conventions/Meetings:** annual conference (exhibits) - always October. 2008 Oct. 19-21, Boston, MA.

2136 ■ American Hull Insurance Syndicate (AHIS)

30 Broad St.
New York, NY 10004
Ph: (212)405-2803 (212)405-2816
Fax: (212)344-1667
URL: http://www.amhull.com
Contact: Fred Robertie, Pres./CEO

Founded: 1920. **Members:** 15. **Membership Dues:** individual, $50 (annual). **Description:** Insurance firms in the United States and foreign countries acting as a syndicate for the writing of insurance on ocean-going and Great Lakes vessels, foreign hulls, and builders risks. Purposes are to assist the development and success of the American Merchant Marine and the foreign trade and commerce of the United States and to offer protection to ship owners, shipbuilders, and maritime interests worldwide. Negotiates rates and terms with brokers, issues subscription policy, collects and remits premiums, and effects claim settlements. **Formerly:** (1943) American Marine Insurance Syndicate; (1956) American Marine Hull Insurance Syndicate. **Conventions/Meetings:** annual meeting - always fourth Thursday in March.

2137 ■ American Institute for CPCU (AICPCU)
720 Providence Rd., Ste.100
PO Box 3016
Malvern, PA 19355-0716
Ph: (610)644-2100
Free: (800)644-2101
Fax: (610)640-9576
E-mail: customersupport@cpcuiia.org
URL: http://www.aicpcu.org
Contact: Peter L. Miller MBA, Pres./CEO
Founded: 1942. **Members:** 900. **Staff:** 140. **Budget:** $20,000,000. **Description:** Determines qualifications for professional certification of insurance personnel; conducts examinations and awards designation of Chartered Property Casualty Underwriter (CPCU). **Libraries: Type:** open to the public. **Holdings:** 9,000; periodicals. **Subjects:** insurance, business, law, finance, risk management, economics. **Awards:** Awards for Academic Excellence. **Frequency:** annual. **Type:** monetary. **Recipient:** for outstanding performance on examinations ● Distinguished Graduate Awards. **Frequency:** annual. **Type:** monetary. **Recipient:** for outstanding performance on examinations. **Telecommunication Services:** electronic mail, cserv@cpcuiia.org. **Committees:** Ethical Inquiry. **Departments:** Administrative Services; Curriculum; Educational Services; Examinations; Finance; Information Technology; Marketing; Personnel and Training; Publications. **Affiliated With:** Insurance Institute of America. **Formerly:** American Institute for Chartered Property Casualty Underwriters; (1991) American Institute for Property and Liability Underwriters. **Publications:** *CPCU Course Guides*, annual. Contains study guides for each of the CPCU courses. ● *CPCU/IIA Catalogue*, annual ● *Key Information*, annual ● *Malvern Examiner*, annual. Newsletter. Contains program updates, new study material listings, news items, and more. **Price:** free. **Circulation:** 160,000 ● Also publishes CPCU/IIA textbooks. **Conventions/Meetings:** annual Conferment Ceremony - meeting, held in conjunction with CPCU Society (exhibits).

2138 ■ American Institute of Marine Underwriters (AIMU)
14 Wall St.
New York, NY 10005
Ph: (212)233-0550
Fax: (212)227-5102
E-mail: aimu@aimu.org
URL: http://www.aimu.org
Contact: James M. Craig, Pres.
Founded: 1898. **Members:** 105. **Membership Dues:** associate, $1,500 (annual) ● corporate (minimum fee), $5,000 (annual) ● subscriber, $2,500 (annual). **Staff:** 5. **Description:** Marine insurance companies authorized to conduct business in one or more states of the U.S. Services to members includes: referral information on legislative and regulatory questions; training and educational programs; analysis of international conventions and agreements affecting the business of marine insurance; access to offices of correspondents worldwide; development of forms and clauses to meet changing maritime requirements; information-gathering assistance. Sponsors educational programs. **Libraries: Type:** reference. **Holdings:** archival material, papers, reports. **Awards:** Distinguished Service Award. **Frequency:** annual. **Type:** recognition. **Recipient:** for significant individual contributions to the American Ocean Marine Industry through one or more activities of AIMU. **Committees:** Cargo Loss Prevention; Cargoes; Claims Services; Correspondents; Forms and Clauses; Liability; Ocean Hull; Reinsurance; Technical Services. **Publications:** Bulletin, weekly. **Conventions/Meetings:** annual meeting - always November in New York City ● seminar, training and educational.

2139 ■ American Insurance Association (AIA)
1130 Connecticut Ave. NW, Ste.1000
Washington, DC 20036
Ph: (202)828-7100 (202)828-7183
Free: (800)242-2302
Fax: (202)293-1219
E-mail: info@aiadc.org
URL: http://www.aiadc.org/aiadotnet
Contact: Marc Racicot, Pres.
Founded: 1964. **Members:** 430. **Staff:** 150. **Budget:** $45,000,000. **Description:** Represents companies providing property and casualty insurance and suretyship. Monitors and reports on economic, political, and social trends; serves as a clearinghouse for ideas, advice, and technical information. Represents members' interests before state and federal legislative and regulatory bodies; coordinates members' litigation. **Libraries: Type:** reference. **Holdings:** 30,000; archival material, books, clippings, monographs, papers, periodicals. **Subjects:** property/causality law, legislation, theory, general law, legal and insurance treatises, all state codes and regulations. **Computer Services:** Online services, Lexis/Nexis, Westlaw, Dialog, AIAccess ESIN. **Committees:** Political Action. **Departments:** Business Development; Claims Administration; Federal Affairs; Government Affairs (State); Law; Legislative Reporting; Policy Development and Research; Public Affairs. **Formed by Merger of:** (1964) National Board of Fire Underwriters; (1964) Association of Casualty and Surety Companies; American Insurance Association. **Publications:** *Adjuster's Digest*. Book ● *Automobile Insurance Laws*. Book ● *Claims Administration Digest*. Book ● *Digest of Statutes Relating to Agents*. Book ● *Environmental Liability Laws*. Book ● *Guide to Campaign Laws*. Book ● *State Rating Guide*. Book ● *State Taxation Manual*. Book ● *Summary of States Regulations and Laws Affecting General Contractors*. Book ● *Surety*. Newsletter ● *Termination and Renewal of Property/Casualty Insurance Policies*. Book ● *Worker's Compensation Laws*. Book. Alternate Formats: CD-ROM. **Conventions/Meetings:** annual meeting.

2140 ■ American Insurance Marketing and Sales Society (AIMS)
PO Box 35718
Richmond, VA 23235
Ph: (804)674-6466
Free: (877)674-CPIA
Fax: (804)915-9435
E-mail: info@cpia.com
URL: http://www.aimssociety.com
Contact: Kitty Ambers, Exec. Dir.
Founded: 1968. **Members:** 500. **Membership Dues:** individual, $225 (annual) ● agency, $750 (annual) ● producer, $1,175 (annual) ● e-ssociate, $95 (annual). **Staff:** 3. **Budget:** $225,000. **Description:** Serves as preeminent national organization dedicated to provide sales training, networking, and marketing innovation to property/casualty insurance professionals. **Telecommunication Services:** electronic mail, k.ambers@comcast.net. **Formerly:** (2004) Certified Professional Insurance Agents Society. **Publications:** *Agency Ideas*, bimonthly. Newsletter ● *Bright Ideas from CPIA*, monthly. Via broadcast fax and e-mail. Alternate Formats: online ● *Quick Sales Tip*, biweekly. Via broadcast and e-mail. Alternate Formats: online. **Conventions/Meetings:** annual National Sales and Marketing Education Conference - convention.

2141 ■ Americas Association of Cooperative/Mutual Insurance Societies (AAC/MIS)
8201 Greensboro Dr., Ste.300
McLean, VA 22102
Ph: (703)245-8077
Fax: (703)610-9005
E-mail: info@aacmis.org
URL: http://www.aacmis.org
Contact: Mr. Edward Potter CAE, Exec. Dir.
Founded: 1979. **Members:** 55. **Staff:** 1. **Budget:** $1,221,000. **Multinational. Description:** Supports and develops effective and viable cooperative and mutual insurance organizations throughout North, South, Central America and the Caribbean. Organizes annual conference, seminars, and international development projects. Issues publications. **Libraries: Type:** not open to the public. **Holdings:** 3; monographs, reports. **Affiliated With:** International Cooperative and Mutual Insurance Federation. **Formed by Merger of:** (1992) North American Association of the International Cooperative Insurance Federation; (1992) American Hemisphere Association of the International Cooperative Insurance Federation. **Conventions/Meetings:** annual conference.

2142 ■ APIW
c/o Maryanne Sherman, Pres.
Sherman Think Tank
15 Hopkins Dr.
Lawrenceville, NJ 08648
Ph: (609)896-2280 (212)867-0228
Fax: (609)896-0063
E-mail: info@apiw.org
URL: http://www.apiw.org
Contact: Maryanne Sherman, Pres.
Founded: 1976. **Members:** 170. **Membership Dues:** individual, $125 (annual). **Description:** Professional women from the insurance/reinsurance industry. Promotes cooperation and understanding among members; maintains high professional standards in the insurance industry; provides a strong network of professional contacts and educational aid; recognizes the contributions of women to insurance; encourages women to seek employment in the insurance community. **Awards:** Lang James Memorial Scholarship. **Frequency:** annual. **Type:** scholarship. **Recipient:** for an insurance student ● Woman of the Year Award. **Frequency:** annual. **Type:** recognition. **Recipient:** for a woman who has achieved prominence in the insurance industry. **Telecommunication Services:** electronic mail, msherman@shermanthinktank.com. **Committees:** Communications and Public Relations; Corporate Sponsorship; Job Bank; Member Events and Professional Development; Web Site; Woman of the Year. **Formerly:** (1982) Association of Professional Insurance Women. **Publications:** *APIW News*, 3/year. Newsletter ● Membership Directory. **Conventions/Meetings:** lecture and luncheon.

2143 ■ Applied Systems Client Network (ASCNET)
801 Douglas Ave., Ste.205
Altamonte Springs, FL 32714
Ph: (407)869-0404
Free: (800)605-1045
Fax: (407)869-0418
E-mail: info@ascnet.org
URL: http://www.ascnet.org
Contact: Linn Wheeling CAE, CEO
Founded: 1987. **Members:** 5,000. **Membership Dues:** insurance carrier, $110-$525 (annual) ● TAM, Vision, and Doris user, $210-$310 (annual) ● associate, consultant, $525 (annual) ● agency/brokerage, $110-$310 (annual). **Staff:** 11. **Budget:** $2,400,000. **Local Groups:** 73. **For-Profit. Description:** Insurance agents and brokers all using the Agency Manager software. Seeks to provide educational services and products and to represent members' interests in automation, especially in regards to the Agency Manager software. **Awards:** Interface Partner. **Frequency:** annual. **Type:** trophy. **Recipient:** chosen by Interface Committee based on number of transactions and percentage increase. **Computer Services:** Online services, newsgroups. **Formerly:** (1998) NAUGAS. **Publications:** *The Accounting*. Manual. **Price:** $69.95 for members in U.S.; $89.95 for members in Canada; $212.95 for nonmembers in U.S.; $272.64 for nonmembers in Canada ● *ASCnet Quarterly*. Magazine. Contains technical information, association news, and industry information. **Price:** included in membership dues. **Circulation:** 5,000. **Advertising:** accepted. Alternate Formats: online. **Conventions/Meetings:** annual conference and trade show, industry related (exhibits).

2144 ■ Association for Advanced Life Underwriting (AALU)
2901 Telestar Ct.
Falls Church, VA 22042
Ph: (703)641-9400 (703)641-8114
Free: (888)275-0092
Fax: (703)641-9885

E-mail: stertzer@aalu.org
URL: http://www.aalu.org
Contact: David Stertzer FLMI, CEO
Founded: 1957. **Members:** 2,000. **Membership Dues:** active, associate, retired, $1,700 (annual). **Budget:** $1,200,000. **Description:** Represents advanced life underwriters who specialize in the more complex fields of estate analysis, business insurance, pension planning, employee benefit plans, and other subjects related to the sale and service of large volumes of life insurance. Serves as conference of the National Association of Life Underwriters. **Committees:** Federal Law and Legislation. **Publications:** *Quarterly Update*. Newsletter. Alternate Formats: online ● *Roster*, annual. Membership Directory ● *Washington Report*, weekly. **Conventions/Meetings:** annual meeting (exhibits) - always in Washington, DC.

2145 ■ Association of Average Adjusters of the United States (AAAUS)
126 Midwood Ave.
Farmingdale, NY 11735
E-mail: averageadjusters@aol.com
URL: http://www.usaverageadjusters.org
Contact: John Woods, Chm.
Founded: 1879. **Members:** 800. **Membership Dues:** full, $175 ● junior, $110 ● resident, $90 ● foreign, $75. **Staff:** 1. **Description:** Marine insurance adjusters, marine insurers, admiralty lawyers, and appraisers of ships and cargoes. Promotes correct principles in the Adjustment of Marine Hull Claims and uniformity of practice among Average Adjusters. **Libraries: Type:** reference. **Holdings:** 500; archival material, books, papers. **Subjects:** marine insurance. **Publications:** *Report of Annual Meeting*. Annual Report ● Bulletin, periodic. **Conventions/Meetings:** annual meeting - always first Thursday in October, New York City.

2146 ■ Association of Finance and Insurance Professionals (AFIP)
PO Box 1933
Colleyville, TX 76034
Ph: (817)428-2434
E-mail: david.robertson@afip.com
URL: http://www.afip.com
Contact: David N. Robertson, Exec. Dir.
Founded: 1989. **Members:** 8,000. **Membership Dues:** industry level, $3,500 (annual) ● general agent, $1,750 (annual) ● F&I manager, $670 (annual). **Staff:** 2. **Languages:** English, French. **For-Profit. Description:** Provides state and federal regulatory information and ethical-practice standards to franchised automobile, RV, motorcycle and watercraft dealers. Represents the interests of Industry Members and the F&I practitioners in matters of government legislation and policy. Offers the NADA-recommended F&I Professional Certification to establish a mastery of federal and state laws that govern the F&I industry process; AFIP-Certified F&I professionals must sign and abide by an enforceable code of ethical conduct. Provides or co-provides regulatory compliance and best-practices products for the motor vehicle and recreational vehicle industries. **Libraries: Type:** reference; not open to the public. **Subjects:** insurance dealership; finance and insurance products, people, industry. **Awards:** AFIP Man/Woman of the Year. **Frequency:** annual. **Type:** recognition. **Publications:** *Management and Technology*, bimonthly. Magazine. **Circulation:** 30,000.

2147 ■ Association of Financial Guaranty Insurers (AFGI)
c/o Mackin and Company
139 Lancaster St.
Albany, NY 12210-1903
Ph: (518)449-4698
Fax: (518)432-5651
E-mail: bmackin@mackinco.com
URL: http://www.afgi.org
Contact: Mr. Robert Mackin, Exec. Dir.
Founded: 1986. **Members:** 10. **Description:** Insurers and reinsurers of municipal bonds and asset-backed securities that play a major role in the global capital markets. Promotes investment in guaranteed bonds and securities by providing an irrevocable pledge of guaranteeing timely payment of principal and interest; facilitates exchange of information among members. **Committees:** Government Affairs; Industry Affairs; Information Technology.

2148 ■ Association of Home Office Underwriters (AHOU)
2300 Windy Ridge Pkwy., Ste.600
Atlanta, GA 30339
Ph: (770)984-3715
Fax: (770)984-6419
E-mail: ahou@loma.org
URL: http://www.ahou.org
Contact: Nazir Damji FLMI, Pres.
Founded: 2002. **Members:** 1,400. **Membership Dues:** individual, $100 (annual). **Multinational. Description:** Underwriters of legal reserve life insurance companies. Offers educational program, through the Academy Life Underwriting, designed specifically for professional home office life underwriters. **Committees:** Life Underwriting Education. **Formerly:** (2001) Home Office Life Underwriters Association. **Publications:** Proceedings, annual ● Papers. **Conventions/Meetings:** annual conference.

2149 ■ Association of Online Insurance Agents (AOIA)
1440 N Harbor Blvd., Ste.725
Fullerton, CA 92835
Free: (888)223-4773
E-mail: aoia@agentquote.com
URL: http://www.aoia.com
Membership Dues: general, $99 (biennial). **Description:** Provides insurance consumers Internet resources for making informed purchasing decisions for life, health, property or business coverage. **Computer Services:** database, online insurance agents.

2150 ■ Aviation Insurance Association (AIA)
14 W 3rd St., Ste.200
Kansas City, MO 64105
Ph: (816)221-8488
Fax: (816)472-7765
E-mail: mandie@aiaweb.org
URL: http://www.aiaweb.org
Contact: Mandy Bannwarth, Exec. Dir.
Founded: 1976. **Members:** 900. **Membership Dues:** corporate, $150 (annual) ● individual, $95 (annual) ● student, $45 (annual). **Staff:** 2. **Budget:** $500,000. **Description:** Individuals engaged in providing aviation insurance; related professionals including attorneys and risk managers. Promotes high standards of ethics and practice in the provision of aviation insurance. Conducts educational programs. **Awards:** Annual College Scholarship. **Frequency:** annual. **Type:** monetary. **Recipient:** for aviation studies ● Pinnacle Award. **Frequency:** annual. **Type:** recognition. **Recipient:** for an individual who exemplifies the standards and goals of the AIA. **Publications:** *The Binder*, quarterly. Newsletter ● *Conference Proceedings*, annual ● Membership Directory, annual. **Conventions/Meetings:** annual Educational Conference (exhibits) - always May.

2151 ■ Bank Insurance and Securities Association (BISA)
303 W Lancaster Ave., Ste.2D
Wayne, PA 19087
Ph: (610)989-9047
Fax: (610)989-9102
E-mail: bisa@bisanet.org
URL: http://www.bisanet.org
Contact: John Vaughan, Pres.
Founded: 2002. **Members:** 400. **Membership Dues:** bank basic, $750-$2,500 (annual) ● bank participating, $2,500-$5,000 (annual) ● bank leadership, $5,000-$9,500 (annual). **Staff:** 8. **Description:** Represents financial institutions of all sizes, their broker/dealer, insurance, and mutual fund subsidiaries, and firms providing products and/or services to support these operations. Works to serve the needs of those responsible for marketing securities, insurance and other investment and risk management products through commercial banks, trust companies, savings institutions and credit unions. **Awards:** Community Based Program of the Year. **Frequency:** annual. **Type:** recognition. **Recipient:** to the outstanding bank securities, insurance or investment program in the community based institution category ● Executive of the Year. **Frequency:** annual. **Type:** recognition. **Recipient:** to an executive who has made extraordinary contributions during the year to his/her institution ● Large Bank Program of the Year. **Frequency:** annual. **Type:** recognition. **Recipient:** to the outstanding bank securities, insurance or investment programs in the larger or international bank category ● Raiken-Sender Lifetime Achievement. **Frequency:** annual. **Type:** recognition. **Recipient:** for an individual whose lifetime achievement is worthy of industry recognition ● Regional Bank Program of the Year. **Frequency:** annual. **Type:** recognition. **Recipient:** to the outstanding bank securities, insurance or investment program in the regional bank category. **Computer Services:** database ● electronic publishing. **Committees:** Communications; Legislative and Regulatory; Marketing and Productivity; Program; Research. **Formerly:** Bank Securities Association; (2003) Financial Institutions Insurance Association. **Publications:** *Bank Insurance and Securities Marketing*, quarterly. Magazine. **Price:** included in membership dues. **Circulation:** 22,000. **Advertising:** accepted. Alternate Formats: online ● *Bank Insurance and Securities Marketing - Online*, biweekly. Magazine. **Circulation:** 11,750. Alternate Formats: online. Also Cited As: *BISM-Online* ● *BISA Daily News Service*. Newsletter. Alternate Formats: online. **Conventions/Meetings:** annual BISA Technology and Operations Conference (exhibits) - always November ● annual Community and Regional Bank Forum - symposium (exhibits) - always September ● annual convention (exhibits) - March ● annual Legislative Regulatory and Compliance Conference - always June ● quarterly Regional Sales Management Workshops.

2152 ■ Captive Insurance Companies Association (CICA)
4248 Park Glen Rd.
Minneapolis, MN 55416
Ph: (952)928-4655 (727)374-7146
Fax: (952)929-1318
E-mail: cica@cicaworld.com
URL: http://www.captiveassociation.com
Contact: Dennis P. Harwick, Pres.
Founded: 1972. **Members:** 200. **Membership Dues:** captive, $700 (annual) ● service provider, $2,000 (annual) ● additional, $300 (annual). **Budget:** $400,000. **Description:** Insurance companies originally formed for the purpose of providing coverage for the sponsoring organization (businesses and employers). Seeks to promote captive insurance companies, regardless of domicile or structure, as viable alternatives available to optimize risk transfer and risk funding. Purposes are to preserve and disseminate information useful to firms utilizing the captive insurance company concept to solve corporate insurance problems; to study, advise, and recommend the enactment of legislation in the interest of the industry; to promote closer contact among those engaged in the industry; to cooperate for the improvement and stabilization of the industry. **Committees:** Conference; Education; Risk Sharing/Fronting; Technology/Web. **Publications:** *CICA Membership Directory*, annual. **Advertising:** accepted. Alternate Formats: online. **Conventions/Meetings:** annual international conference (exhibits).

2153 ■ Casualty Actuarial Society (CAS)
4350 N Fairfax Dr., Ste.250
Arlington, VA 22203
Ph: (703)276-3100
Fax: (703)276-3108
E-mail: office@casact.org
URL: http://www.casact.org
Contact: Cynthia R. Ziegler, Exec. Dir.
Founded: 1914. **Members:** 4,100. **Membership Dues:** fellow/associate/affiliate, $375 (annual). **Staff:** 24. **Budget:** $4,500,000. **Regional Groups:** 15. **Description:** Professional society of property/casualty actuaries. Seeks to advance the body of knowledge of actuarial science applied to property, casualty and similar risk exposures, to maintain qualification standards, promote high standards of conduct and

competence, and increase awareness of actuarial science. Examinations required for membership. **Libraries: Type:** reference. **Holdings:** papers, reports. **Telecommunication Services:** electronic mail, ziegler@casact.org. **Committees:** Audit; Continuing Education; Discipline; Dynamic Financial Analysis; Dynamic Financial Analysis Advisory; Editorial; Education Policy; Examinations; External Communications; Finance; International Relations; Long Range Planning; Management Data and Information; Minority Recruiting; Online Services; Principles; Professionalism Education; Program Planning; Ratemaking; Reinsurance Research; Reserves; Review of Papers; Seminar Planning; Student Liaison; Syllabus; Theory of Risk; Valuation, Finance and Investments; Volunteer Resources. **Publications:** *The Actuarial Review*, quarterly. Newsletter. **Price:** $10.00. **Circulation:** 6,500 ● *Casualty Actuarial Society Yearbook*, annual ● *Forum*, quarterly. Journal ● *Future Fellows*, quarterly. Newsletter. **Price:** free to candidates ● *Proceedings of the Casualty Actuarial Society*, annual ● *Syllabus of Examinations*, annual. **Conventions/Meetings:** annual Casualty Loss Reserve - seminar, for members only - always September. 2008 Sept. 18-19, Washington, DC ● annual meeting - always November. 2008 Nov. 16-19, Seattle, WA ● annual Seminar on Ratemaking, with continuing education programs - always March ● annual Seminar on Reinsurance - always June.

2154 ■ Claims Support Professional Association (CSP)

6451 N Fed. Hwy., Ste.121
Fort Lauderdale, FL 33308
Free: (800)523-3680
Fax: (954)537-4942
E-mail: info@claimssupport.com
URL: http://www.claimssupport.com
Contact: James R. Hogge, CEO

Founded: 1990. **Members:** 250. **For-Profit. Description:** Serves the challenging needs of today's insurance claims handling process. Consists of specialty firms and noted individuals who provide consultation, mitigation, and the restoration of property which is subject to coverage as a result of insurance-covered losses. **Libraries: Type:** not open to the public. **Holdings:** archival material. **Subjects:** forensic engineering. **Computer Services:** Online services, discussion forums. **Publications:** *Claims Support News: Insurance Claims Bulletin*, quarterly.

2155 ■ Coalition Against Insurance Fraud

1012 14th St. NW, Ste.200
Washington, DC 20005
Ph: (202)393-7330 (202)393-7331
Fax: (202)318-9189
E-mail: info@insurancefraud.org
URL: http://www.insurancefraud.org
Contact: Dennis Jay, Exec. Dir.

Founded: 1993. **Membership Dues:** insurer (based on premium volume or number of policies in force), $7,500-$27,500 (annual) ● association, $5,500 (annual) ● associate, $6,000 (annual). **Languages:** English, Spanish. **Description:** Works to combat insurance fraud by advocating for the enactment of new anti-fraud laws and regulations. Raises awareness on all aspects of insurance fraud and how the public can fight back. Serves as a national clearinghouse of fraud information. **Telecommunication Services:** electronic mail, dj@insurancefraud.org. **Publications:** *Fraud Focus*, quarterly. Newsletter. Covers new trends in fraud and related issues affecting the insurance industry. Alternate Formats: online ● *Insurance Fraud Weekly ePort*. Report. Compiles the latest fraud news from around the US. Alternate Formats: online.

2156 ■ Committee of Annuity Insurers (CAI)

c/o Davis and Harman LLP
1455 Pennsylvania Ave. NW, Ste.1200
Washington, DC 20004
Ph: (202)347-2230
Fax: (202)393-3310
E-mail: jfmckeever@davis-harman.com
URL: http://www.annuity-insurers.org
Contact: Joseph F. McKeevek III, Contact

Founded: 1982. **Members:** 40. **Description:** Life insurance companies selling annuities. Seeks to increase public awareness of annuities and current issues affecting them. Serves as a clearinghouse on annuities and related issues; facilitates networking among members. **Libraries: Type:** reference. **Holdings:** articles. **Subjects:** annuities.

2157 ■ Conference of Consulting Actuaries (CCA)

3880 Salem Lake Dr., Ste.H
Long Grove, IL 60047-6400
Ph: (847)719-6500
Fax: (847)719-6506
E-mail: conference@ccactuaries.org
URL: http://www.ccactuaries.org
Contact: Thomas S. Terry, Pres.

Founded: 1950. **Members:** 1,100. **Membership Dues:** regular, $375 (annual). **Staff:** 6. **Description:** Full-time consulting actuaries or governmental actuaries. Develops and maintains structure and programs to reinforce, enhance, or add to members' knowledge and skills; this includes continuing education, through diverse delivery methods, for all practice areas and for consulting and business skills. **Awards:** John Hanson Memorial Prize. **Frequency:** annual. **Type:** recognition. **Recipient:** for the best paper on an employee benefits topic ● Lifetime Achievement Award. **Frequency:** annual. **Type:** recognition. **Recipient:** to a volunteer for contributions made to the Conference of Consulting Actuaries ● Most Valuable Volunteer Award. **Frequency:** annual. **Type:** recognition. **Recipient:** to a volunteer for contributions made to the Conference of Consulting Actuaries ● Wynn Kent Public Communication Award. **Frequency:** annual. **Type:** recognition. **Recipient:** for a member of the actuarial profession who has contributed to the communication of financial risk and the work product of the actuarial profession. **Committees:** Disciplinary; Professionalism; Publications; Strategic Planning. **Task Forces:** Member Value Equation; Seminar Marketing; Small Firms; Volunteer. **Affiliated With:** American Academy of Actuaries; Society of Actuaries. **Formerly:** (1991) Conference of Actuaries in Public Practice. **Publications:** *Consulting Actuary*, 3/year. Newsletter. **Price:** included in membership dues ● *The Proceedings*, annual. Journal. Contains papers presented at annual conference and includes views of specialists in related fields. ● Yearbook, annual. Contains contact and practice area information of conference members. Includes policies, programs and historical information. **Price:** $100.00/copy for non-actuaries; free for actuaries. **Conventions/Meetings:** annual conference - always fall. 2008 Oct. 26-29, Bonita Springs, FL.

2158 ■ Consumer Credit Industry Association (CCIA)

c/o William F. Burfeind, Exec. VP
542 S Dearborn St., Ste.400
Chicago, IL 60605
Fax: (312)939-2242
E-mail: webmaster@cciaonline.com
URL: http://www.cciaonline.com
Contact: Barbara Hollonquest, Chair

Founded: 1951. **Members:** 140. **Staff:** 5. **Budget:** $1,000,000. **Description:** Insurance companies underwriting consumer credit insurance in areas of life insurance, accident and health insurance, and property insurance. **Awards:** Arthur J. Morris Award. **Frequency:** periodic. **Type:** recognition. **Recipient:** for outstanding contributions to the consumer credit insurance industry. **Publications:** *Consumer Credit Insurance Association—Annual Meeting Proceedings* ● *Consumer Credit Insurance Association—Digest Bulletin*, periodic. Includes summaries of pending state legislation affecting the credit insurance industry. ● *Consumer Credit Insurance Association—Information Bulletin*, periodic ● *Consumer Credit Insurance Association—Legislative Bulletin*, periodic. Includes full texts of significant legislation affecting the credit insurance industry. ● Newsletter, monthly. **Conventions/Meetings:** annual meeting, for members (exhibits) - always spring ● annual meeting.

2159 ■ Council of Insurance Agents and Brokers

701 Pennsylvania Ave. NW, Ste.750
Washington, DC 20004-2608
Ph: (202)783-4400
Fax: (202)783-4410
E-mail: ciab@ciab.com
URL: http://www.ciab.com
Contact: Ken A. Crerar, Pres.

Founded: 1913. **Members:** 100. **Staff:** 18. **Budget:** $3,000,000. **Description:** Represents the interests of the leading commercial property and casualty insurance agencies and brokerage firms in the U.S. and around the world. **Libraries: Type:** reference. **Holdings:** periodicals. **Subjects:** insurance/risk management. **Committees:** Political Action. **Formerly:** National Association of Casualty and Surety Agents. **Publications:** *Council Advocate*, monthly. Newsletter ● *Leader's Edge*, bimonthly. Magazine. **Price:** included in membership dues; $100.00 for nonmembers in U.S.; $175.00 for nonmembers outside U.S. **Advertising:** accepted ● Annual Report, annual. Alternate Formats: online. **Conventions/Meetings:** board meeting ● conference, for legislative issues ● Executive Leadership at the Wharton School - meeting ● annual Insurance Leadership Forum at the Greenbrier - conference - always in White Sulphur Springs, WV ● Management - seminar ● Sales Management Seminar ● workshop.

2160 ■ CPCU Society

720 Providence Rd.
Malvern, PA 19355-3402
Ph: (610)251-2727
Free: (800)932-2728
Fax: (610)251-2780
E-mail: membercenter@cpcusociety.org
URL: http://www.cpcusociety.org
Contact: James R. Marks CAE, Exec. VP

Founded: 1944. **Members:** 28,000. **Membership Dues:** national, $140 (annual) ● section, $30 (annual). **Staff:** 35. **Budget:** $6,000,000. **Local Groups:** 154. **Description:** Serves as a professional society of individuals who have passed national examinations of the American Institute for Chartered Property Casualty Underwriters (see separate entry), have 3 years of work experience, have agreed to be bound by a code of ethics, and have been awarded CPCU designation. Promotes education, research, social responsibility, and professionalism in the field. Holds seminars, symposia, and workshops. **Libraries: Type:** reference. **Holdings:** archival material. **Awards:** Circle of Excellence Recognition Program. **Frequency:** annual. **Type:** recognition. **Recipient:** for outstanding chapter performance ● **Type:** recognition. **Recipient:** for excellence in the areas of education, public relations, continuing professional and candidate development. **Computer Services:** Mailing lists. **Telecommunication Services:** electronic mail, jmarks@cpcusociety.org. **Committees:** Budget and Finance; Ethics; Nominating. **Sections:** Agent and Broker; Claims; Consulting, Litigation and Expert Witness; Excess/Surplus/Specialty Lines; Information Technology; International Insurance; Loss Control; Personal Lines; Regulatory and Legislative; Reinsurance; Risk Management; Senior CPCU; Total Quality; Underwriting. **Also Known As:** Chartered Property Casualty Underwriter Society. **Formerly:** (1993) Society of Chartered Property and Casualty Underwriters. **Publications:** *CPCU eJournal*, monthly. Alternate Formats: online ● *CPCU News*, 5/year. Newsletter. Covers membership activities. **Price:** included in membership dues; $9.00 /year for nonmembers. ISSN: 0007-8883. Alternate Formats: online ● *CPCU Yearbook*, annual. **Price:** free to annual meeting attendees. **Circulation:** 5,000. **Advertising:** accepted. **Conventions/Meetings:** annual meeting and seminar (exhibits).

2161 ■ Crop Insurance Research Bureau (CIRB)

10800 Farley, Ste.330
Overland Park, KS 66210

Ph: (913)338-0470
Free: (888)274-2472
Fax: (913)339-9336
E-mail: denicec@cropinsurance.org
URL: http://www.cropinsurance.org
Contact: Paul L. Horel, Pres.
Founded: 1964. **Members:** 33. **Staff:** 3. **Budget:** $300,000. **Description:** Promotes improvement in the industry and supports research through joint sponsorship of programs to increase the accuracy of hail loss settlements. Encourages continuing education and training of crop adjusters and others in the field. Provides funding for agricultural college and university research on crops, adjusting procedures, and simulated hail damage to crops; cosponsors educational programs on public relations and management development. Monitors the Federal Crop Insurance Program; acts as liaison between members and the U.S. Dept. of Agriculture. Seeks to develop strategies for private crop insurers to successfully market and issue all-risk coverage to farmers. Works to protect members' interests by lobbying at the federal level, offering campaign contributions to supportive legislators, and by testifying before congressional committees and field meetings across the country. Keeps members informed of legislative and industry developments; issues news releases. Sponsors industry and public affairs programs. **Libraries: Type:** reference. **Holdings:** audiovisuals, business records. **Telecommunication Services:** electronic mail, paulh@cropinsurance.org. **Committees:** Compliance, Policy and Program; Government Affairs; Public Relations; Research and Development. **Affiliated With:** National Association of Mutual Insurance Companies. **Publications:** *CIRB Notes*, quarterly. Newsletter. **Price:** free for members. **Circulation:** 200. Alternate Formats: online ● *Crop Insurance Research Bureau—Annual Statistical Report*. Annual Report. Includes premium and loss statistics. **Price:** available to members only ● *Legislative Bulletin*, periodic. Alternate Formats: online ● *Member Bulletin*, periodic. **Conventions/Meetings:** annual meeting - every 1st quarter.

2162 ■ Direct Marketing Insurance and Financial Services Council (IFSC)
c/o Direct Marketing Association
1120 Ave. of the Americas, 13th Fl.
New York, NY 10036-6700
Ph: (212)768-7277
Fax: (212)302-6714
E-mail: hr@the-dma.org
URL: http://www.the-dma.org
Contact: John A. Greco Jr., Pres./CEO
Members: 300. **Staff:** 3. **Description:** Direct response divisions of insurance companies; service companies that works with direct response divisions. Conducts educational programs. **Awards:** Direct Marketing Company of the Year Award. **Frequency:** annual. **Type:** recognition ● Direct Marketing Insurance and Financial Services Executive of the Year Award. **Frequency:** annual. **Type:** recognition. **Affiliated With:** Direct Marketing Association. **Formerly:** (1994) Direct Marketing Insurance Council. **Publications:** *IFSC Newsletter*, quarterly. **Advertising:** accepted ● *IFSC Roster*, quarterly. Directory. **Conventions/Meetings:** annual meeting and seminar (exhibits) ● semiannual regional meeting ● quarterly symposium.

2163 ■ Eastern Claims Conference (ECC)
PO Box 2730
Stamford, CT 06906-0730
Ph: (203)352-3074
Free: (866)452-4542
Fax: (203)328-5859
E-mail: stash312@optonline.net
URL: http://www.easternclaimsconference.com
Contact: Stanley Brzozowski, Contact
Founded: 1977. **Members:** 1,100. **Staff:** 40. **Budget:** $40,000. **Description:** Participants include claim examiners of life, health, disability, and group claims of the insurance industry. Provides education and training to examiners, managers, and officers who review medical and disability claims for financial support in the form of disability, death benefits, or pensions. Sponsors charitable and educational programs. Maintains speakers' bureau. **Computer Services:** Mailing lists, of members. **Committees:** Accommodations; Conference; Exhibitor Liaison; Program; Promotion; Registration; Treasurer. **Publications:** *Letter of Invitation*, annual. Journal. Contains membership list plus ad journal. **Price:** included in membership dues. **Circulation:** 1,200. **Advertising:** accepted ● Brochure, annual. **Price:** free. **Circulation:** 1,200. **Advertising:** accepted. Alternate Formats: online ● Directory, annual ● Monographs ● Also publishes research papers. **Conventions/Meetings:** annual Insurance Claim Conference, travel, investigators, data base, consulting (exhibits) - always in New York City, NY ● seminar, for life, health, and disability insurance companies.

2164 ■ Foreign Credit Insurance Association (FCIA)
125 Park Ave., 14th Fl.
New York, NY 10017
Ph: (212)885-1500
Fax: (212)885-1535
E-mail: service@fcia.org
URL: http://www.fcia.com
Contact: Lindley M. Franklin, Pres./CEO
Founded: 1991. **Members:** 2. **Description:** Represents marine, property, and casualty insurance companies. Insures companies against the risks of nonpayment by buyers for commercial and/or political reasons. Facilitates the financing of term credit sales, thus providing companies with support to meet competitive terms of payment offered by others. **Publications:** *FCIA Country Update*. Newsletter ● Brochures.

2165 ■ Fraternal Field Managers' Association (FFMA)
c/o Eugene McBride, Sec.-Treas.
PO Box 100
Temple, TX 76503-0100
Ph: (254)773-1575
E-mail: genemc@spjst.com
URL: http://www.ffma.info
Contact: Eugene McBride, Sec.-Treas.
Founded: 1935. **Members:** 70. **Membership Dues:** society ($10 billion or more worth of assets), $1,000 (annual) ● society ($5 billion - $10 billion worth of assets), $750 (annual) ● society ($1 billion - $5 billion worth of assets), $500 (annual) ● society ($100 million - $1 billion worth of assets), $250 (annual) ● society ($25 million - $100 million worth of assets), $100 (annual) ● society (under $25 million worth of assets), $50 (annual). **Staff:** 1. **Budget:** $20,000. **Description:** A section of the National Fraternal Congress of America (see separate entry). Sales managers for fraternal life insurance societies. Sponsors designation of Fraternal Insurance Counselor for representatives meeting education and production standards. Sponsors the National Association of Fraternal Insurance Counselors (see separate entry). **Awards:** Agency Builder of the Year. **Frequency:** annual. **Type:** recognition ● FIC of the Year. **Frequency:** annual. **Type:** recognition. **Affiliated With:** National Fraternal Congress of America. **Conventions/Meetings:** annual conference.

2166 ■ GAMA International
2901 Telestar Ct., Ste.140
Falls Church, VA 22042-1205
Ph: (703)770-8184
Free: (800)345-2687
Fax: (703)770-8182
E-mail: gamamail@gama.naifa.org
URL: http://www.gamaweb.com
Contact: Jeff Hughes, CEO
Founded: 1951. **Members:** 5,000. **Membership Dues:** PMG silver, functional specialist, $150 (annual) ● PMG partner, non-PMG, $300 (annual). **Staff:** 16. **Budget:** $3,700,000. **Multinational. Description:** Provides world-class education and training resources for individuals, companies and organizations involved with the recruitment and development of field managers, representatives and staff in the life insurance and financial services industry; advocates of the value-added role of field management and representatives in the ethical distribution of life insurance and financial products and services industry. **Libraries: Type:** not open to the public. **Awards:** Career Development Award. **Frequency:** annual. **Type:** recognition ● International Management Award. **Frequency:** annual. **Type:** recognition ● Master Agency Award. **Frequency:** annual. **Type:** recognition. **Programs:** The Essentials of Management Development; Field Leaders Forum Teleconferences; Leading Practices Self-Study Workshop. **Affiliated With:** National Association of Insurance and Financial Advisors. **Formerly:** (1991) General Agents and Managers Conference of NALU; (1998) General Agents and Managers Association. **Publications:** *GAMA International Journal*, bimonthly. Provides solutions for the leaders in the insurance and financial services industry. **Price:** $30.00 for members (in addition to annual dues); $150.00 for nonmembers; $175.00 for international subscriptions. ISSN: 1095-7367. **Circulation:** 5,000. **Advertising:** accepted. Also Cited As: *GIJ* ● *Showcase*. Book. Alternate Formats: CD-ROM; online. **Conventions/Meetings:** annual conference, with speaker presentations and networking opportunities with peers (exhibits).

2167 ■ Group Underwriters Association of America (GUAA)
c/o Curt Zepeda, Treas.
PO Box 581933
Minneapolis, MN 55458-1933
Ph: (612)342-3558
Fax: (612)342-7179
E-mail: curtis.zepeda@ing-re.com
URL: http://www.guaa.com
Contact: Curt Zepeda, Treas.
Membership Dues: regular, $200 (annual). **Description:** Promotes the study, analysis, and discussion pertaining to all matters of mutual interest in underwriting group products. Seeks to uphold the standards of practices within the group insurance industry. Provides its members the opportunities for professional development, networking and information gathering. **Publications:** *Risk Review*. Newsletter. Keeps members updated with the latest news concerning the association and its activities. Alternate Formats: online.

2168 ■ Highway Loss Data Institute (HLDI)
1005 N Glebe Rd., Ste.700
Arlington, VA 22201
Ph: (703)247-1600
Fax: (703)247-1595
E-mail: bodonnell@iihs.org
URL: http://www.iihs.org
Contact: Brenda O'Donnell, Dir. of Insurer Relations
Founded: 1972. **Members:** 20. **Staff:** 15. **Description:** Motor vehicle property and casualty companies. Aims to gather, process, and provide the public with insurance industry data concerning human and economic losses resulting from highway crashes. **Computer Services:** database, insurance losses by make and model of vehicle. **Committees:** Technical Resource. **Affiliated With:** Insurance Institute for Highway Safety. **Publications:** *Insurance Loss Reports*, annual. Lists insurance losses for injury, collision, and theft. **Price:** free. Alternate Formats: diskette.

2169 ■ Independent Insurance Agents and Brokers of America (IIABA)
127 S Peyton St.
Alexandria, VA 22314
Ph: (703)683-4422
Free: (800)221-7917
Fax: (703)683-7556
E-mail: info@iiaba.org
URL: http://www.iiaba.net
Contact: Mr. Alex Soto, Pres.
Founded: 1896. **Members:** 34,000. **Staff:** 68. **State Groups:** 51. **Local Groups:** 1,200. **Description:** Sales agencies handling property, fire, casualty, and surety insurance. Organizes technical and sales courses for new and established agents. Sponsors Independent Insurance Agent Junior Classic Golf Tournament. **Committees:** Board Steering/Election; Government Affairs; Technical Affairs; Young Agents.

Councils: Agents Council for Technology. **Task Forces:** Co-Branded Website Oversight; Curriculum & Research; Diversity. **Formerly:** (1975) National Association of Insurance Agents; (2003) Independent Insurance Agents of America. **Publications:** *Independent Agent*, monthly. Magazine ● *Insurance News and Views*, weekly. Newsletter ● Books ● Handbooks. **Conventions/Meetings:** annual convention and conference (exhibits).

2170 ■ Inland Marine Underwriters Association (IMUA)
14 Wall St., 8th Fl.
New York, NY 10005
Ph: (212)233-0550
Fax: (212)227-5102
E-mail: rthornton@imua.org
URL: http://www.imua.org
Contact: Ronald G. Thornton CPCU, Pres./CEO
Founded: 1930. **Members:** 1,500. **Membership Dues:** regular (minimum), $3,200 (annual) ● associate, $1,750 (annual). **Staff:** 3. **Budget:** $600,000. **Regional Groups:** 5. **Description:** Insurance companies transacting commercial inland marine insurance in the U.S. Purposes are to provide a forum for the discussion of insurance problems of common concern; to develop underwriting and loss prevention guidelines for the protection of property; to advise with respect to legislation affecting the business. Conducts specialized education programs nationwide. **Libraries: Type:** reference. **Awards:** Committee Person of the Year Award. **Frequency:** annual. **Type:** monetary. **Recipient:** for panel review of entries. **Computer Services:** Mailing lists, of members. **Committees:** Arts and Records; Claims/Loss Control; Construction and Contractors Equipment; Education; Information Technology; Legislative and Regulatory Affairs; Manufacturers and Dealers; Natural Disasters; Transportation. **Publications:** *IMUA Advantage*, quarterly. Newsletter. Reports industry trends and association news. **Price:** included in membership dues. **Circulation:** 1,250. Alternate Formats: online ● *Inland Marine Trends and Developments*, annual. Contains reviews of statistical, legal, technological, and regulatory trends. **Circulation:** 1,500 ● Also publishes bulletins & reports. **Conventions/Meetings:** annual meeting (exhibits) ● trade show.

2171 ■ Institute for Business and Home Safety (IBHS)
4775 E Fowler Ave.
Tampa, FL 33617
Ph: (813)286-3400
Fax: (813)286-9960
E-mail: info@ibhs.org
URL: http://www.ibhs.org
Contact: Harvey G. Ryland, Pres./CEO
Founded: 1971. **Members:** 210. **Membership Dues:** associate (class 2/all other entity, institution, organization not included in classes 1 or 2), $750 (annual) ● associate (class 1/individual), $200 (annual). **Staff:** 22. **Description:** Aims to reduce the social and economic effects of natural disasters and other property losses by conducting research and advocating improved construction, maintenance and preparation. **Computer Services:** Online services, publication. **Formerly:** (1994) National Committee on Property Insurance; (1998) Insurance Institute for Property Loss Reduction. **Publications:** *Disaster Safety Review*, quarterly. Journal. **Price:** free. **Circulation:** 3,000. Alternate Formats: online. **Conventions/Meetings:** annual Conference on Property Loss Reduction (exhibits).

2172 ■ Insurance Accounting and Systems Association (IASA)
PO Box 51340
Durham, NC 27717
Ph: (919)489-0991
Fax: (919)489-1994
E-mail: info@iasa.org
URL: http://www.iasa.org
Contact: Joseph P. Pomilia, Exec. Dir.
Founded: 1928. **Members:** 1,700. **Membership Dues:** associate, $500 (annual) ● regular, $500 (annual). **Staff:** 8. **Local Groups:** 28. **Languages:** Chinese, English. **Multinational. Description:** Insurance companies writing all lines of insurance. Associate members are independent public accountants, actuarial consultants, management consultants, statisticians, statistical organizations, and other organizations related to the insurance industry that is not eligible for active membership. Maintains research files. **Awards: Frequency:** annual. **Type:** recognition. **Recipient:** for the best paper submitted. **Committees:** Communications; Housing; Interpreter; Marketing; Research; Seminars; Site Advisory; Textbook. **Divisions:** Life/Health/Group; Property/Liability; Technology. **Formerly:** (1983) Insurance Accounting and Statistical Association. **Publications:** *The Interpreter*, quarterly. Magazine. Includes interviews with business leaders, reports on industry trends, and information about association's activities. **Price:** $25.00 for members; $35.00 for nonmembers. **Circulation:** 6,000. Alternate Formats: online ● *Life Accident and Health Insurance Accounting Textbook* ● *Property and Liability Insurance Accounting Textbook* ● *Systems Project Management*, as needed-available anytime. Book. **Conventions/Meetings:** annual conference and show (exhibits) - 2009 June 7-10, Orlando, FL; 2010 June 5-8, Nashville, TN; 2011 June 5-8, San Diego, CA.

2173 ■ Insurance Brokers and Agents of the West (IBA West)
7041 Koll Center Pkwy., Ste.290
Pleasanton, CA 94566-3128
Free: (800)772-8998
Fax: (818)888-1757
E-mail: cpayan@ibawest.com
URL: http://www.ibawest.com/cgi-bin/default.asp
Contact: Clark Payan AAI, CEO
Description: Promotes insurance brokers and agents in the western U.S.

2174 ■ Insurance Consumer Affairs Exchange (ICAE)
PO Box 746
Lake Zurich, IL 60047
Ph: (847)991-8454
E-mail: info@icae.com
URL: http://icae.com
Contact: Nancy Brebner, Exec. Dir.
Founded: 1976. **Members:** 115. **Membership Dues:** individual, $250 (annual) ● organization, $500 (annual). **Budget:** $50,000. **Description:** Voluntary, professional group of consumer affairs specialists from insurance companies, insurance regulators, and consumer information centers. Provides opportunities to exchange ideas for improving communication between insurers, consumers, and regulators. **Telecommunication Services:** electronic mail, nbrebner@icae.com. **Publications:** *Catalyst*, semiannual. Newsletter. Informs members on news and consumer issues. Alternate Formats: online ● *Resource Manual*. Contains resources for consumer complaint processing. **Price:** free for members; $100.00 for nonmembers. **Conventions/Meetings:** annual Winds of Change: Steering Customer Relations - conference.

2175 ■ Insurance Data Management Association (IDMA)
c/o Richard Penberthy, Exec. Dir.
545 Washington Blvd., 22-16
Jersey City, NJ 07310-1686
Ph: (201)469-3069
Fax: (201)748-1690
E-mail: rpenberthy@idma.org
URL: http://www.idma.org
Contact: Richard Penberthy, Exec. Dir.
Founded: 1984. **Membership Dues:** organizational, $3,500-$20,000 (annual) ● individual-private sector, $500 (annual) ● individual-public sector, $250 (annual). **Description:** Promotes professionalism on the data management discipline in the insurance industry. **Awards:** Fellow in Insurance Data Management (FIDM). **Frequency:** annual. **Type:** recognition. **Recipient:** for long-term and meaningful contribution to the discipline of insurance data management. **Publications:** *Executive Data Management Information Service*, monthly. Bulletin. Contains up-to-date information on data management and reporting issues. ● *IDM Quarterly*. Newsletter. **Price:** free for members. Alternate Formats: online ● *IDMA Inventory of Carrier Reports*, semiannual. Provides means of scheduling and tracking internal performance and response. Alternate Formats: online. **Conventions/Meetings:** annual meeting - April or May ● seminar ● symposium.

2176 ■ Insurance Information Institute (III)
110 William St.
New York, NY 10038
Ph: (212)346-5500
Free: (800)331-9146
E-mail: johns@iii.org
URL: http://www.iii.org
Contact: Dr. Robert P. Hartwig CPCU, Pres./Chief Economist
Founded: 1959. **Members:** 300. **Staff:** 50. **Budget:** $7,000,000. **Languages:** English, Spanish. **Description:** Property and casualty insurance companies. Provides information and educational services to mass media, educational institutions, trade associations, businesses, government agencies, and the public. **Libraries: Type:** reference. **Holdings:** 1,400; books, periodicals. **Subjects:** property and casualty insurance and related topics. **Telecommunication Services:** electronic mail, media@iii.org ● hotline, National Insurance Consumer Helpline, (800)942-4242. **Committees:** Commercial Lines; Communications; Personal Lines. **Departments:** Consumer Communications; Information Services; Issues Analysis; National Media; Subscriber Services; Technical Services; Washington Media. **Divisions:** Communications; Finance and Administration; Planning and Issues Analysis; Programs and Operations. **Publications:** *I.I.I. Insurance Daily*, 5/week. Newsletter. Includes electronic news abstracts of insurance related articles. **Price:** free for members; $7.00/day, for nonmembers ● *I.I.I. Insurance Fact Book*. **Price:** $6.00 for members; $39.50 for nonmembers, plus shipping and handling ● *Insurance Issues Update*, monthly. Report ● Handbook. Includes a glossary of over 300 insurance and other financial services terms. **Price:** $12.50 for nonmembers, plus shipping and handling; $5.00 for members. **Conventions/Meetings:** annual Property/Casualty Insurance Joint Industry Forum - conference - always winter.

2177 ■ Insurance Institute of America (IIA)
720 Providence Rd., Ste.100
Malvern, PA 19355
Ph: (610)644-2100
Free: (800)644-2101
Fax: (610)640-9576
E-mail: customersupport@cpcuiia.org
URL: http://www.aicpcu.org
Contact: Peter L. Miller, Pres./CEO
Founded: 1909. **Staff:** 143. **Budget:** $20,000,000. **Description:** Sponsors educational programs for property and liability insurance personnel. Conducts exams and awards certificates and diplomas. **Libraries: Type:** open to the public. **Holdings:** 9,500; periodicals. **Subjects:** ethics, general insurance management, risk management, general property and liability insurance, information resources, insurer operations, insurer finances, public policy, quality improvement, regulation. **Awards:** Award for Academic Excellence and Distinguished Graduate Award. **Frequency:** annual. **Type:** monetary. **Recipient:** for outstanding performance on examinations. **Affiliated With:** American Institute for CPCU. **Publications:** *Course Guides*, annual ● *Succeed*, annual. Booklet. Describes educational programs and materials provided by institutes. Includes information on obtaining materials and registering for national exams. **Price:** free. **Circulation:** 160,000. Also Cited As: *CPCU/IIA Catalog or Key Information* ● Also publishes textbooks. **Conventions/Meetings:** Annual Conferment - convention and meeting, held in conjunction with the American Institute for CPCU (exhibits) ● annual meeting.

2178 ■ Insurance Loss Control Association (ILCA)
118 Treetops Dr.
Lancaster, PA 17601-1790
Ph: (440)946-8397

Fax: (800)736-7026
E-mail: administration@insurancelosscontrol.org
URL: http://www.insurancelosscontrol.org
Contact: Barry Reutter ALCM, Pres.

Founded: 1931. **Members:** 300. **Membership Dues:** general, $65 (annual). **Staff:** 1. **Description:** Represents loss prevention specialists for property and casualty insurance companies. Conducts an educational program on loss prevention techniques. **Affiliated With:** National Association of Mutual Insurance Companies. **Formerly:** (1958) Association of Mutual Fire Insurance Engineers; (1980) Association of Mutual Insurance Engineers. **Publications:** *Hazard Evaluation and Loss Prevention Bulletin*, quarterly. Covers current issues in the loss control and risk management fields. **Price:** free for members. **Circulation:** 450. Also Cited As: *HELP*. **Conventions/Meetings:** annual conference - usually October.

2179 ■ Insurance Marketing Communications Association (IMCA)

4916 Point Fosdick Dr. NW, No. 180
Gig Harbor, WA 98335
Ph: (206)219-9811
Fax: (866)210-2481
E-mail: tseibert@imcanet.com
URL: http://www.imcanet.com
Contact: September J. Seibert, Exec. Dir.

Founded: 1923. **Members:** 156. **Membership Dues:** corporate, $750 (annual) ● individual, $300 (annual). **Staff:** 1. **Budget:** $150,000. **Description:** Advertising, marketing, public relations, and sales promotion executives of property and casualty insurance companies. Provides members with a forum for enhancing their knowledge of marketing and communications techniques and strategies, so that they can attain the highest standards of professional excellence in serving the information needs of their policyholders, employees, producers and the general public. **Awards:** Golden Torch Award. **Frequency:** annual. **Type:** recognition. **Recipient:** for organization or individual for outstanding achievement in insurance communications ● Sammy Award. **Frequency:** annual. **Type:** recognition. **Recipient:** for the year's overall best in show ● Showcase Awards. **Frequency:** annual. **Type:** recognition. **Recipient:** for members who have shown excellence in advertising, sales promotion, public relations, and employee communications. **Formerly:** (1984) Insurance Advertising Conference. **Publications:** *Membership Roster*, annual. Directory ● *UPDATE*, quarterly. Newsletter. ISSN: 1048-0889. **Conventions/Meetings:** annual conference.

2180 ■ Insurance Marketplace Standards Association (IMSA)

4550 Montgomery Ave., Ste.700N
Bethesda, MD 20814
Ph: (240)744-3030
Fax: (240)744-3031
E-mail: contact@imsaethics.org
URL: http://www.imsaethics.org
Contact: Brian K. Atchinson, Pres./CEO

Founded: 1996. **Description:** Aims to strengthen consumer trust and confidence in the marketplace for individually sold life insurance, long-term care insurance, and annuities. Develops and maintains policies and procedures to promote ethical business practices. Maintains a system of supervision and review to achieve compliance with its principles of ethical marketing conduct. **Publications:** *IMSA Assessment Handbook*. Alternate Formats: online ● *IMSA Independent Assessment Manual*. Alternate Formats: online ● Brochures. Provides helpful information about the association and the importance of dealing with insurance companies that practice proper market conduct. Alternate Formats: online.

2181 ■ Insurance Premium Finance Association (IPFA)

2890 Niagara Falls Blvd.
PO Box 726
Amherst, NY 14226
Ph: (716)695-8757
Fax: (716)695-8758
Contact: Eric Bouskill, Pres.

Founded: 1961. **Staff:** 1. **Description:** Represents firms licensed by New York state to finance automobile, personal property, and liability insurance premiums on an installment basis. **Committees:** Legislative; Statistical. **Conventions/Meetings:** annual conference - always November, New York City.

2182 ■ Insurance Regulatory Examiners Society (IRES)

12710 S Pflumm Rd., Ste.200
Olathe, KS 66062
Ph: (913)768-4700
Fax: (913)768-4900
E-mail: ireshq@swbell.net
URL: http://www.go-ires.org
Contact: Douglas A. Freeman CIE, Pres.

Founded: 1987. **Members:** 1,000. **Membership Dues:** general, $75 (annual) ● AIE, $100 (annual) ● CIE, $110 (annual) ● sustaining, $285 (annual) ● retired, $45 (annual). **Staff:** 5. **State Groups:** 50. **Description:** Works to enhance efforts of state regulators who serve with state or federal insurance regulatory bodies. **Awards:** Al Greer Membership Award. **Frequency:** annual. **Type:** recognition. **Recipient:** to an examiner ● IRES President's Award. **Frequency:** annual. **Type:** recognition. **Recipient:** for a significant contribution to the society and the regulatory profession ● Paul DeAngelo Memorial Teaching Award. **Type:** recognition. **Recipient:** to those who have distinguished themselves in the field of insurance education and training ● Schrader-Nelson Publications Award. **Type:** recognition. **Recipient:** for outstanding original contribution to the society's newsletter. **Publications:** *The Regulator*, bimonthly. Newsletter. Contains informative articles on topics of interest to regulators. **Price:** included in membership dues. Alternate Formats: online. **Conventions/Meetings:** annual Career Development Seminar.

2183 ■ Insurance Research Council (IRC)

PO Box 3025
Malvern, PA 19355-0725
Ph: (610)644-2212
Fax: (610)640-5388
E-mail: irc@cpcuiia.org
URL: http://www.ircweb.org
Contact: Ms. Elizabeth A. Sprinkel, Sr. VP

Founded: 1977. **Members:** 9. **Staff:** 7. **Budget:** $1,200,000. **Description:** Serves as a division of the American Institute for Chartered Property Casualty Underwriters and the Insurance Institute of America. Aims to provide educational programs, professional certification, and research for the property-casualty insurance business. Seeks to provide timely and reliable research to all parties involved in public policy issues affecting risk and insurance, but does not lobby or take legislative positions; is supported by leading property-casualty insurance organizations. **Computer Services:** database, research links ● information services, public policy issues ● online services, library. **Affiliated With:** American Institute for CPCU. **Formerly:** (1991) All-Industry Research Advisory Council. **Publications:** *Public Attitude Monitor*, annual. **Price:** $10.00 ● Books ● Monographs ● Reports ● Surveys ● Also publishes research studies. **Conventions/Meetings:** board meeting.

2184 ■ Insurance Society of New York (ISNY)

c/o School of Risk Management
101 Murray St.
New York, NY 10007-2165
Ph: (212)341-9346 (212)277-5136
Fax: (212)277-5123
E-mail: wallerr@stjohns.edu
URL: http://new.stjohns.edu/academics/graduate/tobin/srm/isny
Contact: Ricky Waller, Contact

Founded: 1901. **Members:** 480. **Membership Dues:** corporate sponsorship (based on number of employees), $1,500-$12,500 (annual) ● company (single location), $500 (annual) ● individual, not-for-profit association, government agency, $200 (annual) ● alumnus/alumna of the College of Insurance, $125 (annual) ● retiree, $75 (annual). **Staff:** 70. **Budget:** $10,100,000. **Description:** Parent organization of the College of Insurance, a fully accredited, undergraduate and graduate degree-granting educational institution located in New York City. Offers courses in risk management, actuarial science, and insurance and financial services. Sponsors lectures. **Libraries:** **Type:** reference. **Holdings:** 100,000; books, periodicals. **Subjects:** insurance, actuarial science, risk management. **Publications:** *General Bulletin*, annual ● *The Insurance Connection!*, quarterly. Newsletter. **Conventions/Meetings:** annual meeting.

2185 ■ Intermediaries and Reinsurance Underwriters Association (IRU)

971 Rte. 202 N
Branchburg, NJ 08876
Ph: (908)203-0211
Fax: (908)203-0213
E-mail: info@irua.com
URL: http://www.irua.com
Contact: Amy Barra, Exec. Dir.

Founded: 1967. **Membership Dues:** regular, affiliate, $4,500 (annual). **Description:** Reinsurance underwriters and intermediaries. Promotes "professionalism and educational advancement" of members. Serves as a forum "for the useful exchange of ideas among member companies;" maintains liaison with other segments of the insurance industry; works to improve understanding of reinsurance among the public and academic communities; functions as a clearinghouse on reinsurance; sponsors educational programs for members.

2186 ■ International Association of Black Actuaries (IABA)

c/o Mosher and Associates
19 S LaSalle St., Ste.1400
Chicago, IL 60603
Ph: (919)317-4105
Fax: (919)317-4105
E-mail: iaba@blackactuaries.org
URL: http://www.blackactuaries.org
Contact: Stafford L. Thompson Jr., Pres./Dir.

Founded: 1992. **Membership Dues:** college student, professor, unemployed, $45 (annual) ● actuarial student, retiree, actuarial professional no longer practicing, $90 (annual) ● actuarial professional (more than 5 years of experience), fellow, associate, recruiter, other correspondent, $175 (annual). **Multinational. Description:** Works to contribute to an increase in the number of black actuaries. Provides support to black students and professionals pursuing an actuarial career. Promotes and enhances the career development, civic growth and achievement of black actuaries. Provides networking opportunities and continuing education and development to actuarial students and professionals. **Awards:** IABA Scholarship. **Frequency:** annual. **Type:** scholarship. **Recipient:** to black students and professionals pursuing an actuarial career. **Publications:** *The Voice of IABA*, quarterly. Newsletter. Alternate Formats: online.

2187 ■ International Association of Insurance Receivers (IAIR)

c/o Paula Keyes, CPCU, Exec. Dir.
174 Grace Blvd.
Altamonte Springs, FL 32714
Ph: (407)682-4513
Fax: (407)682-3175
E-mail: info@iair.org
URL: http://www.iair.org
Contact: Paula Keyes CPCU, Exec. Dir.

Founded: 1991. **Members:** 370. **Membership Dues:** ordinary, $275 (annual). **Staff:** 3. **Budget:** $100,000. **Multinational. Description:** Professional insurance receivers. Promotes adherence to high standards of ethics and professional practice in the administration of insurance receiverships. Seeks to raise public awareness of insurance receivership services. Formulates standards of professional practice; conducts continuing professional development programs; makes available benefits to organizations pursuing related goals; represents members' interests before government agencies, industry organizations, and the public. **Computer Services:** Mailing lists, of members. **Committees:** Accreditation and Ethics; Accreditation Education; Achievements; Amicus; International; Marketing; Nominations, Elections and Meetings; Publications. **Publications:** *The Insurance Receiver*, quarterly. Newsletter. **Advertising:** accepted. Alternate Formats: online. **Conventions/ Meetings:** quarterly conference ● quarterly roundtable.

2188 ■ International Association of Special Investigation Units (IASIU)
c/o The Management Alliance
8015 Corporate Dr., Ste.A
Baltimore, MD 21236
Ph: (410)931-3332
Fax: (410)931-2060
E-mail: iasiu@managementalliance.com
URL: http://www.iasiu.org
Contact: David Rioux, Pres.
Founded: 1984. **Membership Dues:** regular, associate, $50 (annual) ● retiree, $25 (annual) ● state police/local, $30 (annual). **State Groups:** 42. **Multinational. Description:** Works on combating insurance industry fraud, providing education, creating awareness of insurance fraud, and supporting legislation that deters the crime of insurance fraud. **Awards:** Analyst Award. **Frequency:** annual. **Type:** recognition ● Investigator of the Year. **Frequency:** annual. **Type:** recognition ● Outstanding Service Award. **Frequency:** annual. **Type:** recognition ● Public Service Award. **Frequency:** annual. **Type:** recognition. **Publications:** *IASIU Online Membership Directory*, weekly. **Price:** included in membership dues. **Advertising:** accepted. Alternate Formats: online ● *SIU Today*, quarterly. Magazine. **Price:** $50.00 for nonmembers; free for members. **Circulation:** 5,000. **Advertising:** accepted. Alternate Formats: online. **Conventions/ Meetings:** annual convention (exhibits) - 2008 Sept. 7-10, Atlanta, GA - **Avg. Attendance:** 1200.

2189 ■ International Claim Association (ICA)
1155 15th St. NW, Ste.500
Washington, DC 20005
Ph: (202)452-0143
Fax: (202)530-0659
E-mail: pmccarter@claim.org
URL: http://www.claim.org
Contact: Rebecca L. Huerta FLHC, Pres.
Founded: 1909. **Members:** 302. **Membership Dues:** corporate, $800 (annual) ● individual, $600 (annual). **Staff:** 2. **Description:** Claim executives and administrators representing companies writing life, health, or accident insurance. Promotes efficiency, effectiveness and high standards of performance in claim administration by member companies. Provides a forum for research, education and the exchange of ideas relating to various aspects of claim administration. **Awards:** Outstanding Claim Achievement Award. **Frequency:** annual. **Type:** recognition ● Student of the Year. **Frequency:** annual. **Type:** monetary. **Recipient:** for student with the best grades. **Committees:** Administrative Management; Annual Meeting Team; Disability; Education; Executive; Fraud and Claim Abuse; Future Directions; Health; Law; Life; Marketing; Membership Development; Nominating; Oversight; Strategic Planning; Workshop Coordinator. **Publications:** *Claim Administration: Principles and Practices*. **Price:** $65.00 ● *Dentistry and Dental Insurance Claims* ● *The Human Body - Its Function in Health and Disease* ● *ICA News*, quarterly. Newsletter. Focuses on Annual Meeting, Claim Abuse, Health Problems, Law, etc. **Price:** free for members. **Circulation:** 2,000 ● *International Claim Association—Annual Report*. **Price:** $15.00 ● *Life and Health Insurance Law*. **Price:** $65.00 ● *Managing Claim Department Operations*. **Price:** $75.00. **Conventions/Meetings:** annual meeting (exhibits) - 2008 Sept. 21-24, Palm Desert, CA; 2009 Oct. 4-7, Marco Island, FL.

2190 ■ International Insurance Society (IIS)
101 Murray St.
New York, NY 10007-2165
Ph: (212)815-9291
Fax: (212)815-9297
E-mail: jeastmond@iisonline.org
URL: http://www.iisonline.org
Contact: Mr. Patrick W. Kenny, Pres./CEO
Founded: 1965. **Members:** 1,000. **Membership Dues:** individual, $150 (annual) ● corporate, $2,000 (annual) ● global, $7,000 (annual). **Multinational. Description:** Facilitates international understanding and the transfer of ideas and innovations among insurance markets through a joint effort of leading executives and academics on a worldwide basis. Maintains museum; administers Insurance Hall of Fame. **Libraries: Type:** reference. **Holdings:** archival material. **Awards:** Founders Award for Excellence. **Frequency:** annual. **Type:** recognition ● The Insurance Hall of Fame. **Frequency:** annual. **Type:** recognition ● Research Round Table. **Frequency:** annual. **Type:** recognition. **Committees:** Honors. **Formerly:** (1986) International Insurance Seminars. **Publications:** *The Geneva Papers on Risk and Insurance Issues and Practice - Special Issue*, annual. **Conventions/Meetings:** annual meeting and seminar - always July.

2191 ■ Intersure - Singer Nelson Charlmers
PO Box 16
Teaneck, NJ 07666
Ph: (201)837-1100 (212)826-9744
Fax: (201)837-5050
URL: http://www.singernelson.com
Contact: Al Singer, Pres.
Founded: 1966. **Members:** 35. **Staff:** 3. **Budget:** $50,000. **Description:** Commercial lines insurance agencies that have revenues of at least three million dollars annually, have a separate life department and a risk management and consulting department, and are regarded as highly professional organizations among insurance companies and clients. Promotes the exchange of experience, knowledge, techniques, and on-the-spot assistance among members. Brings together "a highly sophisticated, versatile and knowledgeable group of firms" which perform functions in their areas for each other, including risk evaluation, claims, and other problems that require specialized knowledge of the risk and the area involved. **Committees:** Computer Update; London Market; Mass Merchandising; Risk Management. **Formerly:** (1980) Association of International Insurance Agents; (2001) Intersure. **Publications:** Membership Directory, annual. **Conventions/Meetings:** semiannual conference - always May and November.

2192 ■ Liability Insurance Research Bureau (LIRB)
3025 Highland Pkwy., Ste.800
Downers Grove, IL 60515-1291
Ph: (630)724-2250
Free: (800)711-LIRB
Fax: (630)724-2260
URL: http://www.lirb.org
Contact: Nancy Aufrecht, Contact
Founded: 1990. **Description:** Represents insurance companies, stock companies, mutuals, and reciprocals. Strives to achieve and maintain competence among those representing member insurers in insurance adjustment claims, reduce legal and training costs, and promote clarity in insurance policy language.

2193 ■ Life Insurance Settlement Association (LISA)
1011 E Colonial Dr., Ste.500
Orlando, FL 32803
Ph: (407)894-3797
Fax: (407)897-1325
E-mail: support@lisassociation.org
URL: http://www.lisassociation.org
Contact: Ramiro Rencurrell, Pres.
Founded: 1995. **Members:** 150. **Membership Dues:** voting, associate, $6,000 (annual). **Description:** Promotes the development, integrity and reputation of the life settlement industry. Strives to create a competitive market for the people it serves. Provides information for the consumer, member companies, regulators, legislators and all interested parties.

2194 ■ Life Insurers Council (LIC)
2300 Windy Ridge Pkwy., Ste.600
Atlanta, GA 30339-8443
Ph: (770)951-1770 (770)984-3724
Free: (800)275-5662
Fax: (770)984-3780
E-mail: lic@loma.org
URL: http://www.loma.org/IndexPage-LIC.asp
Contact: Michael H. Sims, Exec. Dir.
Founded: 1910. **Members:** 110. **Membership Dues:** international associate, $1,800-$6,000 (annual) ● international affiliate, $1,650 (annual) ● international academic, $750 (annual) ● full (minimum), $1,000 (annual) ● affiliate (based on total revenues), $2,100-$4,675 (annual). **Staff:** 2. **Budget:** $330,000. **Description:** Represents the interests of insurance companies. Serves the basic insurance needs of the general public including the underserved markets by providing products and services that are on the cutting edge of the industry. **Committees:** Actuarial; Advisory; Agency; Auditors; Business Standards; Credit-related Products; Federal Issues; Laws and Legislation. **Formerly:** (1917) Southern Casualty and Surety Conference; (1925) Southern Industrial Insurers' Conference; (1948) Industrial Insurers' Conference. **Publications:** *Home Service Insurance*. Brochure ● *Home Service Insurance, An Annotated Bibliography 1970-1990*. Brochure ● *Life Insurers Council—Directory*, periodic. Contains listing of member companies alphabetically and by state. Includes convention schedule. **Conventions/Meetings:** annual meeting.

2195 ■ LIMRA International
300 Day Hill Rd.
Windsor, CT 06095
Ph: (860)688-3358
Free: (800)235-4672
Fax: (860)298-9555
E-mail: webmaster@limra.com
URL: http://www.limra.com
Contact: Robert A. Kerzner CLU, Pres./CEO
Founded: 1916. **Members:** 850. **Staff:** 250. **Budget:** $38,000,000. **Languages:** English, Spanish. **Multinational. Description:** Life insurance and financial services companies. Conducts market, consumer, economic, financial, and human resources research; monitors industry distribution systems and product and service developments. Provides executive and field management development schools and seminars. Offers human resource development consulting services, including needs analysis and program design, evaluation, and implementation. **Libraries: Type:** reference. **Holdings:** 6,000; archival material, books, periodicals. **Subjects:** insurance and financial services, marketing, industrial psychology, management. **Computer Services:** Online services, forum for members. **Formed by Merger of:** (1945) Association of Life Agency Officers; (1945) Life Insurance Sales Research Bureau. **Formerly:** (1974) Life Insurance Agency Management Association; (1995) Life Insurance Marketing and Research Association. **Publications:** *LIMRA's MarketFacts*, quarterly. Magazine. **Advertising:** accepted ● Also publishes research reports and management aids. **Conventions/Meetings:** annual meeting and conference (exhibits) - usually October.

2196 ■ LOMA
2300 Windy Ridge Pkwy., Ste.600
Atlanta, GA 30339-8443
Ph: (770)951-1770
Free: (800)275-5662
Fax: (770)984-0441
E-mail: askloma@loma.org
URL: http://www.loma.org
Contact: Thomas P. Donaldson FLMI, Pres./CEO
Founded: 1924. **Members:** 1,200. **Membership Dues:** full in U.S. and Canada, $1,075 (annual) ● affiliate in U.S. and Canada (based on total revenues), $2,100-$4,675 (annual) ● associate outside U.S. and Canada (based on life premium income), $1,800-$6,000 (annual) ● affiliate outside U.S. and Canada, $1,650 (annual) ● academic outside U.S. and Canada, $750 (annual). **Staff:** 180. **Budget:** $20,000,000. **Multinational. Description:** Life and

health insurance companies and financial services in the U.S. and Canada; and overseas in 45 countries; affiliate members are firms that provide professional support to member companies. Provides research, information, training, and educational activities in areas of operations and systems, human resources, financial planning and employee development. Administers FLMI Insurance Education Program, which awards FLMI (Fellow, Life Management Institute) designation to those who complete the ten-examination program. **Libraries: Type:** reference. **Subjects:** company operations. **Committees:** Human Resources; Operations; Technology. **Divisions:** e-Business and Member Services; Education; International; Management Services; Research. **Formerly:** (2001) Life Office Management Association. **Publications:** *Research Reports*. Includes issues on life insurance and financial service industries. **Price:** $125.00 for members; $375.00 for nonmembers ● *Resource*, monthly. Magazine. Covers topics of interest to insurance company management including systems, human resources, corporate planning, and financial management. **Price:** $48.00 for nonmembers in U.S.; $60.00 for nonmembers in Canada. **Circulation:** 27,000. **Advertising:** accepted ● Manuals ● Proceedings ● Reports ● Surveys ● Videos ● Also publishes index of publications, and products and services catalog. **Conventions/Meetings:** annual conference.

2197 ■ Loss Executives Association (LEA)
PO Box 37
Tenafly, NJ 07670
Ph: (201)569-3346 (212)384-6205
Free: (800)877-0600
E-mail: info@lossexecutives.com
URL: http://www.lossexecutivesassoc.org
Contact: Thomas N. Leidell, Dir.
Founded: 1921. **Members:** 400. **Description:** Works to further the advancement and education of the property loss profession and provide a means by which current issues can be discussed. **Committees:** Forms; Industry; Liaison with Independent Adjusters. **Conventions/Meetings:** annual meeting.

2198 ■ Mass Marketing Insurance Institute (M12)
14 W 3rd St., Ste.200
Kansas City, MO 64105
Ph: (816)221-7575
Fax: (816)472-7765
E-mail: kenb@robstan.com
URL: http://www.mi2.org
Contact: Ken Bowman, Exec. Dir.
Founded: 1969. **Members:** 250. **Membership Dues:** administrator, vendor, $495 (annual) ● broker, producer, marketer, $149 (annual) ● manufacturer, $749 (annual). **Staff:** 2. **Budget:** $250,000. **Description:** Independent brokers, carriers, and companies active in worksite marketing of employee benefit products. Disseminates information to members. **Awards:** Harlan Sher Member of the Year Award. **Frequency:** annual. **Type:** recognition. **Recipient:** upon determination by board of directors ● Richard A. Ancy Summit Award. **Frequency:** annual. **Type:** recognition. **Recipient:** upon determination by board of directors. **Publications:** *Worksite Insights*, bimonthly. Newsletter. **Advertising:** accepted. **Conventions/Meetings:** annual conference, includes exposition (exhibits).

2199 ■ Million Dollar Round Table (MDRT)
325 W Touhy Ave.
Park Ridge, IL 60068-4265
Ph: (847)692-6378 (847)993-4911
Fax: (847)518-8921
E-mail: info@mdrt.org
URL: http://www.mdrt.org
Contact: John J. Prast CAE, Exec. VP
Founded: 1927. **Members:** 32,981. **Membership Dues:** individual, $350 (annual) ● life, $115. **Staff:** 60. **Budget:** $10,000,000. **Description:** Life insurance agents who earn $60,000 in eligible commissions, at least 60&percent; in life insurance annuities, or disability income up to 40&percent; from health coverage, long-term care or mutual funds. Members from the U.S. must belong to the National Association of Life Underwriters and must requalify for membership annually. Conducts Cost of Doing Business and Membership Profile surveys. Markets motivational and educational products for life insurance agents. **Libraries: Type:** by appointment only. **Holdings:** books, periodicals. **Subjects:** insurance, association management. **Awards:** Quality of Life. **Frequency:** annual. **Type:** grant. **Boards:** Top of the Table Advisory. **Divisions:** Business and Educational Services; Communications; Special Projects. **Publications:** *Annuity Advisor*. Newsletter ● *Information Retrieval Index* ● *Mentoring Message*. Newsletter ● *Million Dollar Round Table—Proceedings*, annual. Includes information on insurance sales and motivational speeches. **Price:** $35.00/issue. **Circulation:** 25,000 ● *Round the Table*, bimonthly. Magazine. Contains texts of speeches and presentations on life insurance sales ideas. Provides news of members and the association. **Price:** included in membership dues; $14.00 /year for nonmembers in U.S.; $16.00 /year for nonmembers outside U.S. ISSN: 0161-7125. **Circulation:** 25,000. Also Cited As: *RTT* ● *Sales Ideas Concept*. Newsletter ● Audiotapes ● Manuals ● Reprints. **Conventions/Meetings:** annual meeting, with speakers (exhibits) - 2008 June 22-26, Toronto, ON, Canada.

2200 ■ Mortgage Insurance Companies of America (MICA)
1425 K St. NW, Ste.210
Washington, DC 20005
Ph: (202)682-2683 (202)393-5566
Fax: (202)842-9252
E-mail: info@privatemi.com
URL: http://www.privatemi.com
Contact: Jeff Lubar, Dir. of Communications
Founded: 1973. **Members:** 10. **Staff:** 6. **Description:** U.S. and Australian mortgage insurance companies united to provide a forum for discussion of industrywide standards, and for representation before Congress and federal and state regulatory agencies that reviews housing-related legislation. Compiles statistics. **Additional Websites:** http://www.micanews.com. **Telecommunication Services:** electronic mail, jeff@micadc.org. **Subcommittees:** Accounting and Finance; House Counsel; Loss Management; Research; Risk Management; State Government Relations. **Publications:** *Fact Book and Directory*, annual ● Also publishes press releases and consumer booklets. **Conventions/Meetings:** annual meeting.

2201 ■ Mutual Atomic Energy Liability Underwriters (MAELU)
Address Unknown since 2007
Founded: 1956. **Members:** 4. **Description:** Underwriting syndicate of 4 mutual casualty insurance companies writing nuclear energy liability policies. **Conventions/Meetings:** annual meeting - always March.

2202 ■ National African-American Insurance Association (NAAIA)
1718 M St. NW, Box No. 1110
Washington, DC 20036
Free: (866)566-2242
E-mail: info@naaia.org
URL: http://www.naaia.org
Contact: Charmaine R. Davis, Chair
Membership Dues: general, $100 (annual) ● chapter (per member), $50 (annual) ● associate, $35 (annual) ● affiliate, $300 (annual). **Description:** Seeks to empower African American insurance professionals. Promotes the interest of minorities in the expanding marketplace of the insurance industry. Provides networking opportunities for its members. **Telecommunication Services:** electronic mail, cdavis@naaia.org. **Publications:** Newsletter, quarterly.

2203 ■ National Alliance for Insurance Education and Research
PO Box 27027
Austin, TX 78755-2027
Free: (800)633-2165
Fax: (512)349-6194
E-mail: alliance@scic.com
URL: http://www.scic.com
Contact: William T. Hold PhD, Pres.
Founded: 1969. **Membership Dues:** Society of Certified Insurance Counselor, $85 (annual). **Description:** Provides insurance and risk management professionals with continuing education and research. **Divisions:** Professional and Personal Development; Technical and Practical Education. **Publications:** *Resources*. Magazine. **Conventions/Meetings:** seminar.

2204 ■ National Association of Bar-Related Title Insurers (NABRTI)
1430 Lee St.
Des Plaines, IL 60018
Ph: (847)298-8300
Fax: (847)298-8388
E-mail: joanne@elliottlaw.com
URL: http://www.nabrti.com
Contact: Joanne P. Elliott, Exec. VP/Exec. Ed.
Founded: 1965. **Members:** 10. **Description:** Title insurance companies identified as "bar-related", a registered trademark term of the association. Aims to express the common interests of the industry; to act as a center for the exchange of information and ideas among member companies; to foster the growth of the bar-related title insurance industry; and to promote the image of bar-related title insurance as an acceptable, safe, and reliable consumer product available through practicing attorneys. **Committees:** Forms; Governmental Relations; Reinsurance. **Formerly:** (1980) National Conference of Bar-Related Title Insurers. **Publications:** *National Association of Bar-Related Title Insurers—Newsletter*, bimonthly. Covers national legislation and real estate and title insurance cases. **Price:** free to lawyer-associate members; $25.00 /year for nonmembers. **Conventions/Meetings:** executive committee meeting - 3/year.

2205 ■ National Association of Catastrophe Adjusters (NACA)
PO Box 821864
North Richland Hills, TX 76182
Ph: (817)498-3466
Fax: (817)498-0480
E-mail: naca@nacatadj.org
URL: http://www.nacatadj.org
Contact: Woody Britton AIC, Pres.
Founded: 1976. **Members:** 200. **Membership Dues:** regular, associate, associate business, apprentice, $100 (annual). **Staff:** 1. **Description:** Insurance catastrophe claims adjusters. (Catastrophe is defined here as wind, hail, flood, tornado, earthquake, and other disastrous conditions.) Promotes the welfare of members and maintains the highest ethical and professional standards. Conducts continuing education classes in all lines of losses. **Publications:** *NACA News*, quarterly. Newsletter. Alternate Formats: online ● Membership Directory, annual. **Price:** free. **Advertising:** accepted. **Conventions/Meetings:** annual convention (exhibits) - always January.

2206 ■ National Association of Fire Investigators (NAFI)
857 Tallevast Rd.
Sarasota, FL 34243
Ph: (941)359-2800
Free: (877)506-NAFI
Fax: (941)351-5849
E-mail: info@nafi.org
URL: http://www.nafi.org
Contact: Heather Kennedy, Dir. of Membership Services
Founded: 1961. **Members:** 5,000. **Membership Dues:** regular, $45 (annual) ● certified, $55 (annual). **Budget:** $125,000. **Description:** Seeks to increase the knowledge and improve the skills of persons engaged in the investigation and analysis of fires, explosions, or in the litigation that ensures from such investigations; has also originated and implemented the National Certification Board. Each year, the Board certifies Fire and Explosion Investigators, Fire Investigation Instructors and Vehicle Fire Investigators. Through this program, those certified are

recognized for their knowledge, training, and experience and accepted for their expertise. **Awards:** Member of the Year Award. **Frequency:** annual. **Type:** recognition. **Publications:** *National Fire Investigator*, quarterly. Newsletter. **Price:** free with membership. **Circulation:** 5,000. **Conventions/Meetings:** biennial International Symposium on Fire Investigation Science and Technology ● annual National Fire, Arson and Explosion Investigation Training Program - seminar - usually August in Sarasota, FL.

2207 ■ National Association of Fraternal Insurance Counsellors (NAFIC)
c/o Anna Maenner, Exec. Sec.
211 Canal Rd.
Waterloo, WI 53594
Free: (866)478-3880
Fax: (920)478-9586
E-mail: office@nafic.org
URL: http://www.nafic.com
Contact: Ellsworth L. Stout FICF, Pres.

Founded: 1950. **Members:** 3,100. **Membership Dues:** regular, $95 (annual). **Staff:** 1. **State Groups:** 32. **Description:** Professional organization of sales personnel for fraternal benefit life insurance societies. Promotes and educates the sales force in fraternal life insurance. **Awards:** Production Awards. **Frequency:** annual. **Type:** recognition. **Recipient:** for production awards ● Quality Service Award. **Frequency:** annual. **Type:** recognition. **Committees:** Awards; Education; Publicity. **Affiliated With:** Fraternal Field Managers' Association. **Formerly:** (1966) Fraternal Insurance Counsellors Association. **Publications:** *FIC Perspective*, bimonthly. Magazine. Contains news and information about the association. ● *The Fraternal Monitor*, monthly. **Conventions/Meetings:** annual convention.

2208 ■ National Association of Health Underwriters (NAHU)
2000 N 14th St., Ste.450
Arlington, VA 22201
Ph: (703)276-0220 (703)276-3806
Fax: (703)841-7797
E-mail: info@nahu.org
URL: http://www.nahu.org
Contact: Janet Trautwein, Exec. VP/CEO

Founded: 1930. **Members:** 18,500. **Membership Dues:** individual, $145 (annual). **Staff:** 21. **Budget:** $4,300,000. **Regional Groups:** 7. **Local Groups:** 162. **Description:** Insurance agents and brokers engaged in the promotion, sale, and administration of disability income and health insurance. Sponsors advanced health insurance underwriting and research seminars. Testifies before federal and state committees on pending health insurance legislation. Sponsors Leading Producers Roundtable Awards for leading salesmen. Maintains a speakers' bureau and a political action committee. **Awards:** Harold R. Gordon Memorial Award. **Frequency:** annual. **Type:** recognition. **Recipient:** to health insurance industry person of the year ● Leading Producers' Round Table. **Frequency:** annual. **Type:** recognition. **Recipient:** to top sales producers of health insurance and related benefits products. **Computer Services:** Mailing lists, of members; available for one-time rental. **Committees:** Awards; Health Underwriters Political Action; Media Relations. **Roundtables:** Leading Producers. **Formerly:** National Association of Accident and Health Underwriters; (1961) International Association of Accident and Health Underwriters; (1978) International Association of Health Underwriters. **Publications:** *Health Insurance Underwriter*, monthly. Journal. **Price:** $40.00/year. ISSN: 0017-9019. **Circulation:** 30,000. **Advertising:** accepted. Alternate Formats: diskette; online. **Conventions/Meetings:** annual Capital Conference (exhibits) - 2009 Mar. 30-Apr. 1, Washington, DC; 2010 Mar. 8-10, Washington, DC ● annual convention and symposium, with regional meetings, award luncheon, Town Hall meeting, educational workshops and House of Delegates (exhibits) - always June. 2008 June 29-July 2, San Diego, CA; 2009 June 28-July 1, New York, NY; 2010 June 27-30, Las Vegas, NV; 2011 June 26-29, San Antonio, TX.

2209 ■ National Association of Independent Insurance Adjusters (NAIIA)
c/o Mr. Dave Mehren, Exec. VP
825 W State St., Ste.117 C and B
Geneva, IL 60134
Ph: (630)397-5012 (312)315-2305
Fax: (630)397-5013
E-mail: assist@naiia.com
URL: http://www.naiia.com
Contact: Mr. Dave Mehren, Exec. VP

Founded: 1937. **Members:** 500. **Description:** Claims adjusters and firms operating independently on a fee basis for all insurance companies. Originator of adjusters educational program administered by Insurance Institute of America. **Awards:** NAIIA Award. **Frequency:** annual. **Type:** recognition. **Committees:** Catastrophe; Educational; "Help" Service; Legislative. **Councils:** Advisory. **Publications:** *Blue Book of Adjusters*, annual ● *Independent Adjuster*, quarterly ● *Status Report*, quarterly. **Conventions/Meetings:** annual convention.

2210 ■ National Association of Independent Insurance Auditors and Engineers (NAIIAE)
PO Box 794
Clifton Park, NY 12065
Free: (800)243-0337
Fax: (518)373-8658
E-mail: service@c-hock.com
URL: http://www.naiiae.com
Contact: Mr. Chris Wikinson, Pres.

Founded: 1963. **Description:** Independent companies providing audits, underwriting surveys, loss control services and other related services to the insurance industry, limited to organizations in the audit, inspection, engineering and related fields. Seeks to improve the quality of audits and inspections; provides forum for exchange of professional ideas and solutions to industry issues; distributes educational information to members. **Publications:** *Code of Ethics*. Serves as a guide to the insurance industry. ● Newsletter, periodic. Contains insurance related articles submitted by members. **Conventions/Meetings:** convention and seminar, with guest speakers ● annual meeting, for membership companies, with speakers from the insurance industry.

2211 ■ National Association of Independent Life Brokerage Agencies (NAILBA)
12150 Monument Dr., Ste.125
Fairfax, VA 22033
Ph: (703)383-3081
Fax: (703)383-6942
E-mail: jnormandy@nailba.org
URL: http://www.nailba.org
Contact: John Felton, Chm.

Founded: 1982. **Members:** 351. **Membership Dues:** regular, provisional, associate, $1,195 (annual). **Staff:** 6. **Budget:** $1,195. **Description:** Represents at least 3 insurance companies that are made up of licensed independent life brokerage agencies. Aims to foster the growth and effectiveness of life insurance distribution and related financial services for consumers, agents, and companies. Seeks to further the education of member agency principals in efficient, lawful, and profitable applications of technology. Sponsors research and other activities that will lead to the development of computer applications and the like which will benefit the procedures of member agencies, such as maximizing potential profits, advertising, and promotion. Promotes legislation, regulation, and practices that will affect members as well as the financial services industry. **Awards:** Douglas Mooers Award for Excellence. **Frequency:** annual. **Type:** recognition. **Recipient:** for an individual involved in furthering the independent life brokerage enterprise. **Committees:** Charitable Foundation; Communications; Education; Long-Range Planning; Marketing; Meetings; Public Affairs; Technology. **Publications:** Magazine, 5/year. **Advertising:** accepted. **Conventions/Meetings:** annual conference (exhibits) - early November. 2008 Nov. 13-15, San Diego, CA; 2009 Nov. 12-14, Hollywood, FL; 2010 Nov. 18-20, Dallas, TX.

2212 ■ National Association of Insurance and Financial Advisors (NAIFA)
PO Box 12012
Falls Church, VA 22042-1205
Ph: (703)770-8100 (703)770-8112
Free: (877)866-2432
Fax: (877)508-9842
E-mail: membersupport@naifa.org
URL: http://www.naifa.org
Contact: David F. Woods, CEO

Founded: 1890. **Members:** 75,000. **Membership Dues:** regular, $141 (annual). **Staff:** 90. **Budget:** $14,000,000. **State Groups:** 52. **Local Groups:** 806. **Description:** Federation of states and local associations representing 75,000 financial planners, life insurance agents, general agents, and managers; associate members are independent insurance agents, general managers of life companies and other life and health insurance professionals. Supports and maintains the highest principles and standards of life and health insurance. Promotes high ethical standards. Informs the public, render community service, and promotes public goodwill. Sponsors public service programs. Offers educational programs. **Libraries: Type:** reference. **Holdings:** archival material, books, periodicals. **Subjects:** life and health insurance. **Awards: Frequency:** annual. **Type:** recognition. **Committees:** Associations; Community Service; Company Field Relations; Education; Federal Law and Legislation; Field Practices; Life Underwriters Political Action; Public Relations; Recognition of Quality and Achievement; State Law, Legislation, and Political Involvement. **Departments:** Law and Government Affairs; Marketing and Membership Services; Public Relations. **Affiliated With:** Association for Advanced Life Underwriting; GAMA International. **Formerly:** (2000) National Association of Life Underwriters. **Publications:** *Advisor Today*, monthly. Magazine. Features industry news and instructional articles on sales techniques and business management. Includes book and legislative reviews. **Price:** free for members; $7.00 for nonmembers. ISSN: 0024-3078. **Circulation:** 100,000. **Advertising:** accepted. Alternate Formats: microform. **Conventions/Meetings:** annual meeting (exhibits) - always September.

2213 ■ National Association of Insurance Women International (NAIW)
6528 E 101st St., Ste.D-1
PMB No. 750
Tulsa, OK 74133
Free: (800)766-6249
Fax: (918)743-1968
E-mail: joinnaiw@naiw.org
URL: http://www.naiw.org
Contact: L. King, Natl. Exec. VP

Founded: 1940. **Members:** 12,000. **Membership Dues:** member-at-large, $96 (annual) ● local, $68 (annual). **Staff:** 6. **Regional Groups:** 9. **State Groups:** 50. **Local Groups:** 350. **Multinational. Description:** Insurance industry professionals. Promotes continuing education and networking for the professional advancement of its members. Offers education programs, meetings, services, and leadership opportunities. Provides a forum to learn about other disciplines in the insurance industry. **Awards:** Certified Professional Insurance Woman/Man. **Type:** recognition. **Recipient:** for qualified members who have passed one of several national examinations ● Diversified Advanced Education CDAE. **Type:** recognition. **Programs:** Communicate with Confidence; Drinking and Driving Awareness; Grass Roots Political Participation; Health and Life Insurance and Basic Estate Planning; How To Be a Best Seller; Insurance: What is It? Do I Really Need It?; Leadership Development; Mentors and Proteges: Sharing for Mutual Rewards; Rules of the Road; Successful Negotiations for the Insurance Professional; Underwriting for the Non-Underwriter. **Formerly:** National Association of Insurance Women. **Publications:** *The Connections*. Newsletter. Contains information on association news and opportunities. ● *Today's Insurance Professionals*, bimonthly. Magazine. Presents articles on industry issues, association news, and member accomplishments. **Price:** included in membership dues; $15.00 /year for nonmembers in U.S.; $25.00 /year for nonmembers outside U.S. ISSN: 0892-4414. **Circulation:** 12,000. **Advertising:** accepted. **Conventions/Meetings:** annual convention (exhibits).

2214 ■ National Association of Mutual Insurance Companies (NAMIC)
3601 Vincennes Rd.
Indianapolis, IN 46268
Ph: (317)875-5250
Fax: (317)879-8408
E-mail: service@namic.org
URL: http://www.namic.org
Contact: Chuck Chamness, Pres./CEO

Founded: 1895. **Members:** 1,480. **Staff:** 50. **State Groups:** 48. **Description:** Underwrites 43 percent of the property/casualty insurance premium in the United States. Strengthens and supports its members and the property/casualty insurance industry by providing effective and high value advocacy, member services and public policy development. **Libraries: Type:** reference. **Holdings:** 300. **Subjects:** insurance. **Awards:** Service Award. **Frequency:** annual. **Type:** recognition. **Recipient:** for merit and service within the industry. **Committees:** Accounting; Arson; Claims Education; Environmental Impairment Liability; Farm Conference; Farm Underwriting; Federal Tax; Financial Analysis; Investment; Legislative; Loss Control; Merit Society; PAC; Pension Administrative; Property Casualty Conference; Public Affairs; Special Services; Urban Issues. **Task Forces:** Guaranty Fund. **Affiliated With:** Crop Insurance Research Bureau; Insurance Loss Control Association. **Publications:** *The Farm Mutual Forum*, monthly. Newsletter. Covers safety and underwriting statistics, legislative updates, research findings, trends, and tort reform; includes member and association news. **Price:** free. **Circulation:** 1,400 ● *IN Magazine*, quarterly. Reports on current industry issues, legislation, and regulation. Includes educational articles to assist managers. **Price:** included in membership dues. **Circulation:** 2,300. **Advertising:** accepted ● Brochures ● Bulletin ● Also issues press releases. **Conventions/Meetings:** annual regional meeting and workshop.

2215 ■ National Association of Professional Insurance Agents (PIA)
400 N Washington St.
Alexandria, VA 22314
Ph: (703)836-9340
Fax: (703)836-1279
E-mail: piaweb@pianet.org
URL: http://www.pianet.com
Contact: Leonard Brevik, Exec. VP

Founded: 1931. **Regional Groups:** 41. **Description:** Represents independent agents in all 50 states, Puerto Rico and the District of Columbia. Represents members' interests in government and industry; provides educational programs; compiles statistics; conducts research programs; develops products/services unique to independent agencies; provides information and networking opportunities. **Libraries: Type:** reference. **Holdings:** 600. **Subjects:** insurance. **Awards:** Agent of the Year. **Frequency:** annual. **Type:** recognition. **Recipient:** for excellence in the insurance field. **Committees:** Business Technology; Communications; Company Relations; Education; Federal and State Government Affairs; Industry and Research; Marketing and Advertising; Political Action; Public Relations. **Also Known As:** PIA National. **Formerly:** (1976) National Association of Mutual Insurance Agents. **Publications:** *PIA Connection*, monthly. Newsletter. **Price:** included in membership dues; $24.00 for nonmembers. **Advertising:** accepted. **Conventions/Meetings:** annual meeting (exhibits).

2216 ■ National Association of Professional Surplus Lines Offices (NAPSLO)
200 NE 54th St., No. 200
Kansas City, MO 64118
Ph: (816)741-3910
Fax: (816)741-5409
E-mail: info@napslo.org
URL: http://www.napslo.org
Contact: Richard Bouhan, Exec. Dir.

Founded: 1975. **Members:** 800. **Membership Dues:** wholesale broker, $925 (annual) ● company/associate (based on annual premium volume), $3,300-$6,600 (annual) ● underwriting manager (based on annual premium volume), $1,325-$6,600 (annual) ● intermediary firm, $3,300 (annual). **Staff:** 5. **Budget:** $1,800,000. **Description:** Wholesale insurance brokers and agents. Develops standards for the surplus lines industry. Offers educational and internship programs. Conducts midyear educational seminar and workshops. Maintains speakers' bureau. **Libraries: Type:** reference. **Subjects:** legislative issues. **Awards:** Charles A. McAlear/NAPSLO Industry Award. **Frequency:** annual. **Type:** recognition ● President's Award. **Frequency:** annual. **Type:** recognition ● **Type:** scholarship. **Committees:** Budget, Finance and Audit; Education; Industry and Public Relations; Information Systems and Technology; Internship; Legislative; Members' Forum; Membership. **Publications:** *Income and Expense Survey of Brokers*, annual. Report. Alternate Formats: online ● *NAPSLO News*, bimonthly. Newsletter. **Price:** free. **Circulation:** 1,100. Alternate Formats: online ● *Security and Review Analysis of Specialty Insurance Companies*, semiannual ● Directory, annual. **Conventions/Meetings:** annual meeting and convention - always September. 2008 Sept. 10-13, San Diego, CA.

2217 ■ National Association of Public Insurance Adjusters (NAPIA)
21165 Whitfield Pl., No. 105
Potomac Falls, VA 20165
Ph: (703)433-9217
Fax: (703)433-0369
E-mail: info@napia.com
URL: http://www.napia.com
Contact: David W. Barrack, Exec. Dir.

Founded: 1951. **Members:** 500. **Membership Dues:** regular, $765 (annual) ● associate, $325 (annual) ● independent contractor, $150 (annual). **Staff:** 2. **State Groups:** 7. **Description:** Professional society of public insurance adjusters. Sponsors certification and professional education programs. **Awards:** Person of the Year. **Frequency:** annual. **Type:** recognition. **Recipient:** for individual as determined by committee. **Committees:** Legal; Legislative; Professional Education; Professional Ethics; Public Relations. **Publications:** *NAPIA Bulletin*, quarterly. **Price:** free for members. **Circulation:** 700. **Advertising:** accepted ● *The Professional Public Insurance Adjuster-Working For You.On Your Side!*. Brochures ● Directory, annual. **Advertising:** accepted ● Also publishes charts. **Conventions/Meetings:** semiannual meeting (exhibits) - always June and December.

2218 ■ National Association of State Farm Agents (NASFA)
8015 Corporate Dr., Ste.A
Baltimore, MD 21236
Ph: (410)931-3332
Fax: (410)931-2060
E-mail: info@nasfa.com
URL: http://www.nasfa.com
Contact: Mr. Ronald Sohn, Exec. Dir.

Founded: 1973. **Membership Dues:** regular, $300 (annual) ● regular, $160 (semiannual) ● gold, retired gold, $348 (annual) ● gold, retired gold, $184 (semiannual) ● platinum, $540 (annual) ● platinum, $280 (semiannual) ● retired, $126 (annual) ● retired, $63 (semiannual) ● regular, $25 (monthly) ● retired, $10 (monthly) ● gold, retired gold, $29 (monthly) ● platinum, $45 (monthly). **Description:** Dedicated to the individual State Farm contractor agent. Provides information to members. Fosters a spirit of camaraderie and professional fellowship. **Funds:** Legal. **Publications:** *The Mirror*, quarterly. Magazine. Reflects the latest information on legislation, company issues and best ideas for running profitable agency. **Price:** included in membership dues. Alternate Formats: online ● *NASFAX*. **Conventions/Meetings:** annual general assembly.

2219 ■ National Association of Surety Bond Producers (NASBP)
1828 L St. NW, Ste.720
Washington, DC 20036-5104
Ph: (202)686-3700
Fax: (202)686-3656
E-mail: info@nasbp.org
URL: http://www.nasbp.org
Contact: Richard A. Foss, Exec. VP

Founded: 1942. **Members:** 600. **Staff:** 10. **Budget:** $2,500,000. **Description:** Insurance agents and brokers writing surety bonds. Strengthens professionalism, expertise and innovation in surety and advocates its use worldwide. **Telecommunication Services:** electronic mail, dfoss@nasbp.org. **Committees:** Annual Meeting Program; Automation and Technology; Commercial Surety; Government Relations; Industry Relations; Professional Development and Education; Professional Standards; Surety Information Office Policy. **Publications:** *National Association of Surety Bond Producers—Membership Directory*, annual. Contains alphabetical and geographic access. **Price:** available to members only ● *Pipeline*, monthly. Newsletter. Contains news for the surety industry. **Price:** available to members and surety company personnel. **Conventions/Meetings:** annual conference (exhibits) - always spring.

2220 ■ National Association for Variable Annuities (NAVA)
11710 Plaza Am. Dr., Ste.100
Reston, VA 20190
Ph: (703)707-8830
Fax: (703)707-8831
E-mail: nava@navanet.org
URL: http://www.navanet.org
Contact: Mark J. Mackey, Pres./CEO

Founded: 1991. **Members:** 300. **Membership Dues:** insurance company/company managing variable annuity asset, $6,667-$33,333 (annual) ● other company, $1,000-$4,000 (annual) ● affiliate, $1,000 (annual). **Staff:** 7. **Budget:** $2,000,000. **Description:** Seeks to promote knowledge of variable annuities and variable life insurance products among members and the public. **Awards:** John D. Marsh Memorial Award. **Frequency:** annual. **Type:** recognition. **Computer Services:** database. **Committees:** Education; Marketing Practices; Membership; Operations; Regulatory Affairs; Research; Tax; Variable Life Insurance. **Publications:** *NAVA Outlook*, monthly. Newsletter. Contains articles on variable insurance products. **Price:** free for members; $26.00 /year for nonmembers. Alternate Formats: online ● Pamphlets ● Books. **Conventions/Meetings:** annual Compliance Conference ● annual Marketing Conference - conference and meeting (exhibits) - 2009 Feb. 22-25, Palm Desert, CA ● annual meeting - 2008 Oct. 5-7, Philadelphia, PA; 2009 Sept. 19-22, Boston, MA ● annual Operations Conference, focuses on latest marketing compliance legal and operations issues for variable annuities (exhibits) - 2009 June 28-July 1, Boston, MA ● annual Variable Life Conference (exhibits).

2221 ■ National Council on Compensation Insurance (NCCI)
901 Peninsula Corporate Cir.
Boca Raton, FL 33487
Ph: (561)893-1000
Free: (800)622-4123
Fax: (561)893-1191
URL: http://www.ncci.com
Contact: Stephen J. Klingel, Pres./CEO

Founded: 1919. **Members:** 700. **Staff:** 1,200. **Budget:** $60,000,000. **Regional Groups:** 3. **State Groups:** 15. **Description:** Insurance providers of all types writing workers' compensation insurance. Conducts ratemaking, research, and statistical programs. **Committees:** Actuarial; Claims; Occupational Diseases; Policy Forms; Premium Audit; Rates; Research; Underwriting. **Formerly:** (1922) National Council on Workmen's Compensation Insurance. **Publications:** *Annual Statistical Bulletin*, annual. **Price:** $125.00 ● *Digest*, quarterly. Journal. **Price:** free for members. **Circulation:** 7,000 ● *Legislation Update Service*, periodic ● Booklets ● Monographs. **Conventions/Meetings:** annual meeting - always first Thursday of April.

2222 ■ National Council of Self-Insurers (NCSI)
1253 Springfield Ave.
PMB 345
New Providence, NJ 07974
Ph: (908)665-2152
Fax: (908)665-4020
E-mail: natcouncil@aol.com
URL: http://www.natcouncil.com
Contact: Max Koonce, Pres.
Founded: 1946. **Members:** 350. **Membership Dues:** individual company (over 10,000 employees), $600 (annual) ● individual company (5,000-9,999 employees), $500 (annual) ● individual company (3,000-4,999 employees), $400 (annual) ● individual company (under 3,000 employees), $300 (annual) ● group self-insurer, state self-insurer, $475 (annual) ● professional serving self-insurer, $400 (annual). **State Groups:** 34. **Description:** State associations, individual companies, associate members, and professional members concerned with self-insurance under the workmen's compensation laws. Promotes and protects, at all governmental levels, the interests of self-insurers or legally non-insured employers and their employees in matters of legislative and administrative activity affecting workmen's compensation; assists, advises, and uses its resources in developing and implementing common objectives among self-insurers. Current goals are: a workmen's compensation program that is just, both to the individual and to the employer; equitable distribution of the compensation dollar; strong vocational rehabilitation incentives for the injured employee. **Telecommunication Services:** electronic mail, max.koonce@cmiw.com. **Formerly:** (1972) National Council of State Self-Insurers' Associations. **Publications:** *Officers, Membership, and By-Laws*, bimonthly. Newsletter ● *Self-Insurance Requirements of the States*, periodic. Newsletter ● Also publishes self-insurance requirements of all states. **Conventions/Meetings:** annual meeting - always May ● annual meeting, held in conjunction with International Association of Industrial Accidents Boards and Commissions - always September.

2223 ■ National Crop Insurance Services (NCIS)
8900 Indian Creek Pkwy., Ste.600
Overland Park, KS 66210-1567
Ph: (913)685-2767
Free: (800)951-2647
Fax: (913)685-3080
E-mail: danaf@ag-risk.org
URL: http://www.ag-risk.org
Contact: Robert Parkerson, Pres.
Founded: 1989. **Members:** 142. **Staff:** 45. **Budget:** $3,900,000. **Regional Groups:** 18. **Description:** Serves the crop insurance industry, in one form or another, since 1915. Gathers and analyzes crop statistics. Promotes standard policy terms and conditions so that agents and consumers need to understand only a few basic program options. Develops loss adjustment methods and adjuster training to support the appraisal of crop damage so that losses can be settled fairly. Helps insurance companies position themselves to meet the needs of the farm community and gives the public more options for better supporting agriculture. Reduces the vulnerability of rural communities as a result of crop failure. **Awards:** Industry Leadership Award. **Frequency:** periodic. **Type:** recognition. **Recipient:** for an individual who is directly involved in the crop insurance industry by providing outstanding leadership ● Outstanding Service Award. **Frequency:** periodic. **Type:** recognition. **Recipient:** for an individual who has demonstrated outstanding service and outreach in a positive way. **Committees:** Crop-Hail Actuarial and Statistics; Crop-Hail Policy, Procedure, and Loss Adjustment; MPCI Actuarial and Statistics; MPCI Policy, Procedure, and Loss Adjustment; Program Development; Public Relations and Education; Technology and Information Processing; Training. **Formed by Merger of:** (1989) Crop-Hail Insurance Actuarial Association; National Crop Insurance Association. **Publications:** *Crop Insurance Today*, quarterly. Magazine. **Price:** $13.00/year in U.S.; $25.00/year outside U.S. **Circulation:** 5,000. **Advertising:** accepted. **Conventions/Meetings:** annual convention.

2224 ■ National Insurance Crime Bureau (NICB)
1111 E Touhy Ave., Ste.400
Des Plaines, IL 60018
Ph: (847)544-7000 (703)222-6250
Free: (800)447-6282
E-mail: csg@nicb.org
URL: http://www.nicb.org
Contact: Robert M. Bryant, Pres./CEO
Founded: 1912. **Members:** 1,000. **Staff:** 300. **Budget:** $27,000,000. **Description:** Property-casualty insurance companies; self-insured firms, works in detecting, preventing and deterring insurance-related crime. Assists authorities in recovering stolen vehicles and detecting insurance fraud. Conducts investigations; research and educational programs; maintains Speaker's Bureau; compiles statistics. **Formerly:** National Automobile Theft Bureau; Insurance Crime Prevention Institute. **Publications:** *Spotlight on Insurance Crime*, biennial. Magazines. Contains investigative techniques and case studies. **Circulation:** 13,000 ● *UpClose*. Newsletter. Alternate Formats: online. **Conventions/Meetings:** annual conference.

2225 ■ National Risk Retention Association (NRRA)
4248 Park Glen Rd.
Minneapolis, MN 55416
Ph: (952)928-4656
Free: (800)999-4505
Fax: (952)929-1318
E-mail: dbarnes@nrra-usa.org
URL: http://www.nrra-usa.org
Contact: Douglas K. Barnes, Assoc. Dir.
Founded: 1987. **Members:** 85. **Membership Dues:** RRG or PG (less than $10 million in premiums), $1,000 (annual) ● RRG or PG ($10 million or more in premiums), $1,500 (annual) ● service provider, organization, individual, $1,200 (annual) ● affiliate, associate, $200 (annual). **Description:** Lawyers, insurance companies, reinsurance companies, consultants, and representatives of risk retention and reinsurance purchasing groups. Supports the Federal Risk Retention Act allowing insurance companies to organize risk retention groups, pool their insurance buying power, and cover their own liability risks. Provides a forum for information exchange on industry issues; establishes and monitors standards for risk retention and purchasing groups; conducts educational programs. **Publications:** *NRRA News*, quarterly. Newsletter. **Circulation:** 100. **Advertising:** accepted. **Conventions/Meetings:** annual meeting (exhibits).

2226 ■ National Society of Insurance Premium Auditors (NSIPA)
PO Box 1896
Columbus, OH 43216-1896
Free: (888)846-7472
Fax: (614)221-2335
E-mail: nsipa@nsipa.org
URL: http://www.nsipa.org
Contact: Mario Fiel, Pres.
Founded: 1975. **Members:** 600. **Membership Dues:** individual, $95 (annual) ● life, $15. **Budget:** $90,000. **Regional Groups:** 5. **Description:** Employees of insurance companies or fee service companies who are engaged in field, administrative, or support service policy auditing to determine insurance premiums. Develops study and proficiency testing procedures. Acts as forum for exchange, development, and dissemination of technical information. Contributes premium auditing information to the insurance industry. Establishes uniform standards for auditing. Promotes and conducts research and holds seminars. In conjunction with Insurance Institute of America (see separate entry), sponsors technical education program leading to designation as Associate in Premium Auditing. Maintains library. **Libraries: Type:** lending. **Holdings:** video recordings. **Subjects:** premium auditing and professional enhancement skills. **Awards:** Certified Insurance Premium Auditor Award. **Type:** recognition ● Distinguished Graduate Award. **Type:** monetary ● Distinguished Service Award. **Type:** recognition. **Telecommunication Services:** electronic mail, mario.fiel@olsi.net. **Committees:** CIPA; Educational and Technical Development; Honors and Awards; Industry Research. **Publications:** *Newsline*, quarterly. Newsletter. **Price:** free, for members only. ISSN: 0748-3961. **Advertising:** accepted. Alternate Formats: online. **Conventions/Meetings:** annual seminar (exhibits).

2227 ■ National Society of Professional Insurance Investigators (NSPII)
PO Box 88
Delaware, OH 43015
Free: (888)677-4498
Fax: (740)369-7155
E-mail: nspii@columbus.rr.com
URL: http://www.nspii.com
Contact: Stephen W. Miller, Pres.
Membership Dues: auxiliary, $20 (annual). **Description:** Promotes professionalism in conducting insurance investigation. **Awards:** F. Lee Brininger Award. **Frequency:** annual. **Type:** recognition. **Recipient:** for outstanding contribution to the fight against insurance fraud ● Outstanding Achievement Award. **Frequency:** annual. **Type:** recognition. **Recipient:** for outstanding achievement in the fight against fraudulent insurance claims ● President's Award. **Frequency:** annual. **Type:** recognition. **Recipient:** for member ● Public Service Award. **Frequency:** annual. **Type:** recognition. **Recipient:** for professionalism, dedication, and accomplishment in the fight against fraudulent insurance claims and/or arson. **Publications:** Newsletter. **Conventions/Meetings:** annual seminar ● workshop.

2228 ■ National Truck and Heavy Equipment Claims Council (NTHECC)
c/o Tom Fergus, Admin.
PO Box 27
Wolfeboro Falls, NH 03896-0027
Ph: (603)569-8910
Fax: (603)569-8920
E-mail: admin@nthecc.org
URL: http://www.nthecc.org
Contact: Tom Fergus, Admin.
Founded: 1961. **Members:** 125. **Local Groups:** 1. **Description:** Insurance companies, manufacturing and repair facilities, and individual adjusters concerned with the insuring of trucks and heavy equipment. Seeks to: promote safety and study causes of highway accidents; combat crime; promote and develop a high standard of ethics in the handling of insurance claims and to expedite the servicing of claims; bring about wider public recognition and acceptance of the functions of insurance. Sponsors scholarships. **Formerly:** Truck and Heavy Equipment Claims Council. **Publications:** Directory, annual. **Conventions/Meetings:** semiannual meeting.

2229 ■ Organized Flying Adjusters (OFA)
c/o Donald H. Hendricks, Exec. Sec.
1501 Bluff Dr.
Round Rock, TX 78681
Ph: (512)255-2740 (512)246-1066
E-mail: larryofa95@compuserve.com
URL: http://www.ofainc.com
Contact: Donald H. Hendricks, Exec. Sec.
Founded: 1958. **Members:** 60. **Description:** Aircraft insurance adjusters; rated pilots and/or pilots with equivalent aircraft experience; associate members include company claims personnel, manufacturers, and general insurance members. Promotes high standards in the processing of aviation insurance claims; aims to objectively investigate causes of aircraft accidents; promotes air safety. Conducts crash investigation courses and provides information on legal implications involved in aircraft investigations. **Telecommunication Services:** electronic mail, wlhall@jshaw.com. **Publications:** *OFA Newsletter*, quarterly. **Price:** free for members. **Circulation:** 600 ● *Organization of Flying Adjusters—Membership Directory*, annual. **Price:** free for members. **Circula-**

tion: 600. **Conventions/Meetings:** annual conference ● annual seminar, for company claims personnel, manufacturers' representatives, and aircraft-oriented suppliers.

2230 ■ Professional Insurance Marketing Association (PIMA)
230 E Ohio St., Ste.400
Chicago, IL 60611
Ph: (817)569-7462
Fax: (312)644-8557
E-mail: george.bode@pearlins.com
URL: http://www.pima-assn.org
Contact: George Bode, Pres.
Founded: 1975. **Members:** 500. **Staff:** 4. **Budget:** $700,000. **Description:** Insurance companies, agencies, and others servicing the insurance industry. Promotes the mass marketing of insurance; encourages favorable legislation and regulation in the industry; furthers professional education. Has established code of ethics. Sponsors annual marketing methods competition. **Awards:** The Best of PIMA Award for Excellence in Mass Marketing. **Frequency:** annual. **Type:** recognition. **Formerly:** (1982) Professional Independent Mass Marketing Administrators; (1997) Professional Insurance Mass-Marketing Association. **Publications:** *PIMA Membership Directory and Buyer's Resource Guide*, annual. **Price:** free, for members only ● *PIMAnews*, quarterly. Newsletter. Keeps members informed of industry news, the Association's activities and upcoming events. **Price:** included in membership dues. **Circulation:** 600. **Advertising:** accepted. **Conventions/Meetings:** conference ● annual MarketTech Conference - conference and competition (exhibits) - late October or early November ● annual meeting - January or February.

2231 ■ Professional Liability Underwriting Society (PLUS)
c/o Derek B. Hazeltine, Exec. Dir.
5353 Wayzata Blvd., Ste.600
Minneapolis, MN 55416
Ph: (952)746-2580
Free: (800)845-0778
Fax: (952)746-2599
E-mail: info@plusweb.org
URL: http://www.plusweb.org
Contact: Derek B. Hazeltine, Exec. Dir.
Founded: 1986. **Members:** 6,000. **Membership Dues:** individual, $150 (annual) ● corporate sponsor, $1,000 (annual) ● corporate affiliate, $100 (annual). **Staff:** 9. **Regional Groups:** 14. **Multinational. Description:** Represents individuals interested in the promotion and development of the professional liability industry. Seeks to enhance professionalism through education and other activities and to address issues related to professional liability. **Libraries: Type:** reference. **Holdings:** 300; articles. **Subjects:** professional liability. **Awards:** Gilmartin Scholarship. **Frequency:** annual. **Type:** scholarship. **Recipient:** to a child of plus member. **Publications:** *Journal*, monthly. Newsletter. Contains industry articles and news about PLUS. **Price:** free for members. Alternate Formats: online. **Conventions/Meetings:** annual international conference - 2008 Nov. 12-14, San Francisco, CA.

2232 ■ Property Casualty Insurers Association of America (PCI)
2600 S River Rd.
Des Plaines, IL 60018-3286
Ph: (847)297-7800 (847)553-3604
Fax: (847)297-5064
E-mail: joseph.annotti@pciaa.net
URL: http://www.pciaa.net
Contact: Joseph Annotti, Sr. VP for Public Affairs
Founded: 2004. **Members:** 1,000. **Staff:** 140. **Budget:** $30,500,000. **Description:** Independent property and casualty insurance companies. Provides advocacy and technical information. Maintains 32 committees, including political action. Conducts educational programs; compiles statistics. **Libraries: Type:** reference. **Holdings:** audiovisuals, books, business records, periodicals. **Subjects:** law, insurance. **Computer Services:** database, legislative for all states and congress. **Formed by Merger of:** (2004) National Association of Independent Insurers; (2004) Alliance of American Insurers. **Publications:** *Greenbook*, annual ● *Individual State Profile*, annual. Directory ● *Legislative Reporter*, biweekly ● *NAIC Reporter*, quarterly. Bulletin ● *State Filing Guide*, annual ● *State Insurance Department Directory*, annual ● *Weekly Digest*. Newsletter ● Also publishes studies and compilations and quarterly bulletins for personal lines, commercial lines and workers' compensation coverages. **Conventions/Meetings:** annual meeting.

2233 ■ Property Loss Research Bureau (PLRB)
3025 Highland Pkwy., Ste.800
Downers Grove, IL 60515-1291
Ph: (630)724-2200
Free: (888)711-PLRB
Fax: (630)724-2260
E-mail: tmallin@plrb.org
URL: http://www.plrb.org
Contact: Thomas Mallin, Pres./COO
Founded: 1947. **Members:** 900. **Staff:** 22. **Budget:** $5,258,300. **Description:** Insurance companies. Sponsored by mutual and stock insurance companies. Promotes education and new and beneficial developments within the property and casualty insurance industry. Encourages productivity and efficiency in the property and liability loss and claim adjustment processes of members and the industry as a whole. **Formerly:** Mutual Loss Research Bureau. **Conventions/Meetings:** annual Claims Conference (exhibits).

2234 ■ Reinsurance Association of America (RAA)
1301 Pennsylvania Ave. NW, Ste.900
Washington, DC 20004-1701
Ph: (202)638-3690
Free: (800)638-3651
Fax: (202)638-0936
E-mail: infobox@reinsurance.org
URL: http://www.reinsurance.org
Contact: Franklin W. Nutter, Pres.
Founded: 1968. **Members:** 36. **Staff:** 24. **Budget:** $5,500,000. **Description:** Represents reinsurers and reinsurance brokers. Advances the issues of the US property and casualty industry by influencing the legal, regulatory and economic environment. Produces a variety of legal, statistical and educational products for the benefit of its members and affiliates. **Formerly:** (1970) National Association of Property and Casualty Reinsurers. **Publications:** *Arbitrators Directory*, annual. Provides background information on each arbitrator and mediator in a clear and concise manner. **Price:** $95.00. Alternate Formats: online ● *Digest of Reinsurance Caselaw*, semiannual. Book. **Price:** $395.00/year ● *Fundamentals of Property-Casualty Reinsurance* ● *Manual for the Resolution of Reinsurance Disputes*, annual. Offers a "how to" approach, with sample forms, a directory of services and recommendations for improving the practice of arbitration. **Price:** $195.00/year. **Conventions/Meetings:** annual meeting.

2235 ■ Risk and Insurance Management Society (RIMS)
1065 Ave. of the Americas, 13th Fl.
New York, NY 10018
Ph: (212)286-9292 (212)655-6032
Fax: (212)655-7423
E-mail: membership@rims.org
URL: http://www.rims.org
Contact: Mary Roth, Exec. Dir.
Founded: 1950. **Members:** 10,000. **Membership Dues:** corporate, $465 (annual) ● associate, $485 (annual) ● educational/retired, $100 (annual) ● affiliate, $75 (annual) ● student, $50 (annual). **Staff:** 70. **Budget:** $14,000,000. **Local Groups:** 81. **Description:** Business association serving corporate risk and insurance managers. Dedicated to advancing the practice of risk management, a discipline that protects physical, financial, and human resources. **Awards:** Arthur Quern Quality Award. **Frequency:** annual. **Type:** recognition. **Recipient:** for activities and programs that have significant contributions within the field of risk management ● Chapter Recognition Award. **Frequency:** annual. **Type:** recognition. **Recipient:** for outstanding chapter achievement ● Harry & Dorothy Goodell Award. **Frequency:** annual. **Type:** recognition. **Recipient:** for outstanding lifetime achievement in the field of risk management ● Richard W. Bland Memorial Award. **Frequency:** annual. **Type:** recognition. **Recipient:** to a member with outstanding performance in the area of legislation and/or regulation related to risk and insurance ● Ron Judd Heart of RIMS Award. **Frequency:** annual. **Type:** recognition. **Recipient:** to a deputy member who exhibits qualities that advance risk management at his/her local chapter. **Computer Services:** Mailing lists, conference registrants. **Committees:** Conference Programming; Editorial Advisory; Education; Exhibits Advisory; International; Member and Chapter Services; Research; Risk Management Roundtable; Student Involvement. **Formerly:** (1954) National Insurance Buyers Association; (1975) American Society of Insurance Management. **Publications:** *Annual Risk Management Buyers Guide*, annual. Directory. Contains a directory of risk management service providers. **Price:** $65.00 for nonmembers; free for members. **Circulation:** 10,000. **Advertising:** accepted ● *Compensation and Benefits Survey*. Contains salary and prerequisites for risk managers. **Price:** $75.00 for members; $100.00 for nonmembers ● *RIMSCANADA* (in English and French), quarterly. Newsletter. Provides information on members with Canadian operations. **Circulation:** 1,000 ● *RIMSCOPE*, monthly. Newsletter. Provides brief notes on legal, government, and current events, including industry news, educational courses, seminars, and publications. **Circulation:** 8,000. Alternate Formats: online ● *Risk Management*, monthly. Magazine. **Price:** $64.00/year; $74.00/year in Canada. **Circulation:** 15,000. **Advertising:** accepted. **Conventions/Meetings:** annual conference (exhibits) - always April.

2236 ■ Securities and Insurance Licensing Association (SILA)
c/o Beth McGuire, Exec. Dir.
PO Box 68203
Indianapolis, IN 46268-0203
Free: (800)428-8329
Fax: (800)876-SILA
E-mail: bmcguire@sila.org
URL: http://www.sila.org
Contact: Beth McGuire, Exec. Dir.
Founded: 1990. **Membership Dues:** regular, $150 (annual). **Description:** Provides better understanding of the financial services industry. Promotes and improves communication between licensing experts. Provides professional and technical education opportunities. Discusses solutions to common licensing and registration problems. Seeks to develop relationships with industry organizations, associations, licensing and registration departments and related organizations. **Awards:** Licensing/Registration Administrator of the Year. **Frequency:** annual. **Type:** recognition. **Recipient:** to an insurance licensing or securities registration professional ● Organization Appreciation Award. **Frequency:** annual. **Type:** recognition. **Recipient:** for dedication and continuous support and service to the association ● Regulatory Unit Recognition Award. **Frequency:** annual. **Type:** recognition. **Recipient:** for fostering harmonious relationship between the insurance department and the companies and agencies ● Richard P. Andersen Scholarship. **Frequency:** annual. **Type:** scholarship. **Recipient:** to a SILA member ● Robert C. Kennedy Appreciation Award. **Frequency:** annual. **Type:** recognition. **Recipient:** for dedication and continuous volunteering and service to the association ● Securities Regulator Recognition Award. **Frequency:** annual. **Type:** recognition. **Recipient:** for fostering harmonious relationship between the insurance department and the companies and agencies ● Special Achievement Award. **Frequency:** annual. **Type:** recognition. **Recipient:** for dedication and continuous volunteering and service to the association ● Warren E. Spruill Regulator Recognition Award. **Frequency:** annual. **Type:** recognition. **Recipient:** for fostering harmonious relationship between the insurance department and the companies and agen-

cies. **Publications:** *SILA Quarterly*. Newsletter. Contains articles written by SILA members and regulators, journal updates, chapter meeting notes, and licensing survey results. **Price:** included in membership dues. Alternate Formats: online ● Journal, annual. **Price:** included in membership dues ● Membership Directory. **Price:** included in membership dues.

2237 ■ Self-Insurance Institute of America (SIIA)
PO Box 1237
Simpsonville, SC 29681
Free: (800)851-7789
Fax: (864)962-2483
E-mail: jkinder@siia.org
URL: http://www.siia.org
Contact: James A. Kinder, CEO

Founded: 1981. **Members:** 1,200. **Membership Dues:** regular corporate, $1,295 (annual) ● self-insured employer (minimum), $250 (annual) ● contributing corporate, $2,500 (annual) ● supporting corporate, $5,000 (annual) ● sustaining corporate, $10,000 (annual) ● premier corporate, $25,000 (annual). **Staff:** 17. **Budget:** $2,500,000. **Description:** Represents actuaries, attorneys, claims adjusters, consultants, corporations, employers, insurance companies, risk managers, third party administrators, and others involved or interested in self-insurance. Aims to foster and promote alternative methods of risk protection as opposed to conventional insurance. Seeks to advance the concept of self-insurance characterized by the transfer of risk from an insurance company to the individual employer. Seeks to improve the quality and efficiency of self-insurance plans, thereby increasing their acceptance among the business community and general public. Protects the industry from adverse legislation and regulation. Advocates greater professionalism in the industry; encourages quality public service. Offers educational programs in areas such as educational certification. Disseminates information on topics including human resources, workers' compensation and legislation at state and federal levels, and plans to implement a speakers' bureau. **Committees:** Electronic Commerce; Government Relations/Public Affairs; National Conference; Promotion; Publications; Workers' Compensation. **Publications:** *The Self Insurer*, monthly. Journal. Includes management articles on self-insurance issues, systems, procedures, and legislation. **Price:** included in membership dues; $195.50 /year for nonmembers in U.S. and Canada; $225.00 /year for nonmembers outside U.S. and Canada. **Circulation:** 1,500. **Advertising:** accepted ● *Who's Who in Self-Insurance Services*, annual ● Also publishes position papers and contributes news releases and feature articles to public press and trade publications. **Conventions/Meetings:** annual conference (exhibits) - always between September and November.

2238 ■ Shipowners Claims Bureau (SCB)
1 Battery Park Plz., 31st Fl.
New York, NY 10004
Ph: (212)847-4500
Fax: (212)847-4599
E-mail: info@american-club.com
URL: http://www.american-club.com
Contact: Joseph Hughes, Chm.

Description: Represents protection and indemnity insurance management and claims advisers. **Telecommunication Services:** electronic mail, joe.hughes@american-club.com.

2239 ■ Society of Actuaries (SOA)
475 N Martingale Rd., No. 600
Schaumburg, IL 60173
Ph: (847)706-3500 (847)706-3510
Fax: (847)706-3599
E-mail: membership@soa.org
URL: http://www.soa.org
Contact: Edward L. Robbins, Pres.

Founded: 1949. **Members:** 16,353. **Membership Dues:** associate (of less than 5 years), $305 ● fellow, associate (of 5 years or over), $555. **Staff:** 90. **Budget:** $17,229,000. **Description:** Serves as a professional organization of individuals trained in the application of mathematical probabilities to the design of insurance, pension, and employee benefit programs. Sponsors series of examinations leading to designation of fellow or associate in the society. Maintains speakers' bureau; conducts educational and research programs. **Libraries:** **Type:** reference; lending; by appointment only. **Holdings:** 2,800; archival material, audiovisuals, books, business records, monographs, periodicals. **Subjects:** actuarial science, insurance. **Awards:** AERF Practitioners Award. **Frequency:** annual. **Type:** recognition. **Recipient:** for considerable research in non-academic settings; research should be practical and innovative ● Annual Prize. **Frequency:** annual. **Type:** recognition ● Everett Curtis Huntington Prize. **Type:** recognition. **Recipient:** for best research paper; must be receiving associateship or fellowship credit under the society's education program ● Halmstad Prize. **Frequency:** annual. **Type:** recognition. **Recipient:** for papers on actuarial research ● L. Ronald Hill Memorial Prize. **Frequency:** annual. **Type:** recognition ● Triennial Prize. **Frequency:** triennial. **Type:** recognition. **Committees:** Communication and Publications; Continuing Education and International Relations; Examination and Basic Education; Financial, Investment Management and Emerging Practice Areas; Health Benefit Systems Practice Area; International Issues; Life Insurance Practice Area; Presidential; Research; Retirement. **Formed by Merger of:** (1949) Actuarial Society of America; (1949) American Institute of Actuaries. **Publications:** *The Actuary*, bimonthly. Magazine. Alternate Formats: online ● *Directory of Actuarial Memberships*, annual. Membership Directory. Contains a list of 6 organizations representing actuaries in the U.S. and Canada, arranged by name and business affiliation. **Price:** $100.00 ● *The Future Actuary*, quarterly. Newsletter. **Price:** $15.00 in U.S. **Advertising:** accepted ● *Index to Publications*, annual. Indexes all serials, reports, proceedings, books, and study notes published by SOA through previous year. ● *North American Actuarial Journal*, quarterly. **Price:** $95.00 ● *Society of Actuaries—Record*. Includes convention transcripts; annual index. Alternate Formats: online ● *Society of Actuaries Yearbook*, annual. Contains constitution, bylaws, committee rosters, membership statistics, and history. **Price:** $25.00 ● *Statistics for Pension Actuaries*, annual. **Price:** $15.00. **Conventions/Meetings:** annual conference ● semiannual meeting (exhibits).

2240 ■ Society of Financial Service Professionals (SFSP)
17 Campus Blvd., Ste.201
Newtown Square, PA 19073-3230
Ph: (215)321-9662 (610)526-2500
Free: (800)927-2427
Fax: (610)527-1499
E-mail: mpepe@financialpro.org
URL: http://www.financialpro.org
Contact: Joseph E. Frack, CEO

Founded: 1928. **Members:** 23,000. **Membership Dues:** regular, $224 (annual) ● associate, $112 (annual) ● student, $56 (annual). **Staff:** 47. **Budget:** $7,500,000. **Local Groups:** 196. **Multinational. Description:** Represents the interests of financial advisers. Fosters the development of professional responsibility. Assists clients to achieve personal and business-related financial goals. Offers educational programs, online professional resources and networking opportunities. **Awards:** American Business Ethics Award. **Frequency:** annual. **Type:** recognition. **Recipient:** for businesses that demonstrate high standards of business ethics in everyday activities and in crisis situations ● Kenneth Black, Jr. Journal Author Awards. **Frequency:** annual. **Type:** recognition. **Recipient:** to authors of journal articles. **Computer Services:** Bibliographic search, society publications ● online services, professional tools. **Telecommunication Services:** electronic mail, rmacdona@financialpro.org. **Special Interest Groups:** Business and Compensation Planning; Employee Benefits; Estate Planning; Financial Planning; Leadership and Management; Life, Health and Disability; Multiple Risk Management; Qualified Plans. **Formerly:** (1998) American Society of CLU and ChFC. **Publications:** *Journal of Financial Service Professionals*, bimonthly. Provides information on insurance and financial services. **Price:** $86.00 /year for nonmembers. ISSN: 1537-1816. **Circulation:** 25,000. **Advertising:** accepted. **Conventions/Meetings:** annual Financial Service Forum - conference, with speakers, networking events, continuing education, professional resource center and practice-building seminars (exhibits).

2241 ■ Society of Insurance Research (SIR)
c/o Ed Budd, Exec. Dir.
631 Eastpointe Dr.
Shelbyville, IN 46176
Ph: (317)398-3684
Fax: (317)642-0535
E-mail: sir.mail@comcast.net
URL: http://www.sirnet.org
Contact: Ed Budd, Exec. Dir.

Founded: 1970. **Members:** 400. **Membership Dues:** individual, $195 (annual) ● corporate, associate corporate, $2,000 (annual). **Staff:** 2. **Budget:** $100,000. **Description:** Represents individuals or companies interested or actively involved in insurance research and planning. Stimulates insurance research through the interchange of ideas on research methodology and developments in technology. **Libraries:** **Type:** open to the public. **Holdings:** 40; articles. **Subjects:** insurance research. **Committees:** Annual Conference; Audit; Marketing; Research; Workshops. **Publications:** *Insurance Organization Sourcebook*, annual. Alternate Formats: online ● *SIR News*, quarterly. Newsletter. Includes schedule of events and member news. ISSN: 0899-5060. Alternate Formats: online ● Membership Directory, annual. **Conventions/Meetings:** annual conference (exhibits) - always November ● seminar - 3/year ● annual Summer Workshop Series.

2242 ■ Society of Registered Professional Adjusters (RPA)
PO Box 3810
Napa, CA 94558
Ph: (707)226-5762
Free: (800)949-5272
Fax: (707)226-5746
E-mail: info@rpa-adjuster.com
URL: http://www.rpa-adjuster.com
Contact: Susan K. Sunny, Exec. Dir.

Founded: 1996. **Members:** 1,300. **Membership Dues:** associate RPA program, $85 (annual) ● Registered Professional Adjuster, $200 (annual) ● retiree, $25 (annual). **Multinational. Description:** Aims to establish and promote rigorous professional standards for continuing education, ethics and experience among adjusters worldwide. Promotes the Registered Professional Adjuster (RPA) designation as the global standard of excellence for claims adjusters. Grants recognition and accreditation to adjusters who meet the RPA standards and requirements. **Telecommunication Services:** electronic mail, susanksunny@rpa-adjuster.com. **Publications:** *RPA Exam Study Guide*. Brochure. Alternate Formats: online ● Newsletter, quarterly. Alternate Formats: online.

2243 ■ Society for Risk Analysis (SRA)
1313 Dolley Madison Blvd., Ste.402
McLean, VA 22101
Ph: (703)790-1745
Fax: (703)790-2672
E-mail: sra@burkinc.com
URL: http://www.sra.org
Contact: Richard J. Burk Jr., Exec. Sec.

Founded: 1981. **Members:** 2,000. **Membership Dues:** full, fellow, $105 (annual) ● editor fellow, retired, editor, student, individual (with salary of below $30,000), $55 (annual) ● student (without journal), $10 (annual) ● supporting, $155 (annual). **Staff:** 10. **Description:** Represents risk assessment professionals from varied areas. Studies scientifically the risks posed by technological development; gathers and disseminates information. **Awards:** Chauncy Starr. **Frequency:** annual. **Type:** recognition. **Recipient:** for young analysts ● Distinguished Achievement Award. **Frequency:** annual. **Type:** recognition. **Re-**

cipient: for outstanding career in risk analysis ● Outstanding Practitioner. **Frequency:** annual. **Type:** recognition ● Outstanding Service Award. **Frequency:** annual. **Type:** recognition. **Recipient:** for service to Society for Risk Analysis. **Telecommunication Services:** electronic mail, rburk@burkinc.com. **Publications:** *Risk Analysis*, bimonthly. Journal. Covers topics of great interest to regulators, researchers, and scientific administrators. ● *RISK Newsletter*, quarterly. **Price:** included in membership dues. **Conventions/Meetings:** annual conference and meeting (exhibits).

2244 ■ Society of Risk Management Consultants (SRMC)
330 S Executive Dr., Ste.301
Brookfield, WI 53005-4275
Free: (800)765-SRMC
E-mail: webmaster@srmcsociety.org
URL: http://www.srmcsociety.org
Contact: Thomas J. Krzys CPCU, Membership Chm.

Founded: 1984. **Members:** 150. **Multinational. Description:** Independent risk management and insurance consultants who do not sell insurance. Aims to ensure high ethical standards, professional competence, and independence among risk management and insurance consultants. Maintains speakers' bureau. **Awards:** Award of Academic Excellence. **Type:** recognition ● **Type:** recognition. **Recipient:** for a graduate student in the field. **Formed by Merger of:** Insurance Consultants Society; Institute of Risk Management. **Publications:** *SRMC Journal*, 2-3/year ● Membership Directory, periodic. **Conventions/Meetings:** periodic conference ● semiannual seminar - always spring and fall.

2245 ■ Surety and Fidelity Association of America (SFAA)
1101 Connecticut Ave. NW, Ste.800
Washington, DC 20036
Ph: (202)463-0600 (202)778-3621
Fax: (202)463-0606
E-mail: lschubert@surety.org
URL: http://www.surety.org
Contact: Lynn M. Schubert, Pres.

Founded: 1908. **Members:** 650. **Staff:** 16. **Description:** Represents insurance companies engaged in fidelity, surety, and forgery bond underwriting. Classifies risks; prepares forms, provisions, terms, and riders; secures statistical and other data; files with regulatory authorities for members upon request. Provides a forum for discussion of problems of common interest to members; acts as information clearinghouse. **Absorbed:** (1947) Towner Rating Bureau. **Formerly:** (2006) Surety Association of America. **Publications:** Newsletter, bimonthly. **Price:** free for members; $65.00 for nonmembers ● Booklets. **Conventions/Meetings:** annual meeting.

2246 ■ Water Quality Insurance Syndicate (WQIS)
80 Broad St., 21st Fl.
New York, NY 10004
Ph: (212)292-8700
Free: (800)736-5750
Fax: (212)292-8716
E-mail: rhobbie@wqis.com
URL: http://www.wqis.com
Contact: Richard H. Hobbie III, Pres.

Founded: 1971. **Members:** 17. **Staff:** 12. **For-Profit. Description:** Represents companies that insure vessel owners and operators against statutory and third party pollution liability. **Publications:** none. **Convention/Meeting:** none.

2247 ■ Women in Insurance and Financial Services (WIFS)
6748 Wauconda Dr.
Larkspur, CO 80118
Ph: (303)681-9777
Free: (866)264-9437
Fax: (303)681-3221
E-mail: office@w-wifs.com
URL: http://www.w-wifs.org
Contact: Laura J. LaTourette CFP, Pres.

Founded: 1936. **Members:** 600. **Membership Dues:** full-national, $150 (annual). **Staff:** 2. **Budget:** $175,000. **Regional Groups:** 14. **Languages:** English, Japanese, Spanish. **Multinational. Description:** Represents women in the insurance and financial services industry. Supports and encourages relationships and activities that enhance the success of women in the insurance and financial services industry. **Awards:** Chapter Achievement Award. **Frequency:** annual. **Type:** recognition. **Recipient:** for local chapters ● Leaders Recognition Society Award. **Frequency:** annual. **Type:** recognition. **Recipient:** for members who have achieved significant income levels in the insurance and financial services industry ● Woman of the Year Award. **Frequency:** annual. **Type:** recognition. **Telecommunication Services:** electronic mail, lauralatourette@windstream.net. **Committees:** Education; Mentor. **Formerly:** (1998) Women Life Underwriters Confederation. **Supersedes:** Women Life Underwriters Conference of the National Association of Life Underwriters. **Publications:** *Membership*. Brochure ● *Roster*, bimonthly. Directory ● *WIFS News*, quarterly. Newsletter. **Price:** included in membership dues. **Advertising:** accepted. **Conventions/Meetings:** semiannual Leadership Forum - meeting, educational ● annual New Horizons - convention (exhibits) - usually September/October.

2248 ■ Workers Compensation Insurance Organizations (WCIO)
Pennsylvania Compensation Rating Bur.
Widener Bldg., 6th Fl., One S Penn Sq.
Philadelphia, PA 19107-3577
Ph: (215)568-2371
E-mail: bpiacentino@pcrb.com
URL: http://www.iisprojects.com/WCIO
Contact: Bonnie Piacentino, EDI Committee Chm.

Description: Represents statutorily authorized or licensed rating, advisory, or data service organizations that collect workers compensation insurance information in one or more states. Provides a forum for the exchange of information about workers compensation insurance. Develops and publishes specifications and guidelines to assist insurers and Data Collection Organizations (DCOs) reporting workers compensation data. **Publications:** *Workers Compensation Data Reporting Handbook*. Serves as a guideline and reference for industry professionals. Alternate Formats: online ● *Workers Compensation Data Specifications Manual*. Contains compilation of electronic and hard copy specifications developed under the direction of the managers of DCOs. Alternate Formats: online ● Bulletin. Alternate Formats: online ● Paper. Alternate Formats: online.

Interior Design

2249 ■ Allied Board of Trade
Address Unknown since 2007

Founded: 1925. **Members:** 3,500. **Membership Dues:** $115 (annual). **Staff:** 10. **For-Profit. Description:** Interior decorators and designers and design firms. For a fee, provides business services including arbitration and collection assistance, source information and credit reports, and trade information on manufacturers and jobbers nationwide. Operates membership reference service and source reference library. Makes available to members discounts on trade magazines, hotel accomodations, and car rentals; assists members in obtaining passes to major trade shows; offers group rates on medical and term life insurance. **Convention/Meeting:** none. **Computer Services:** Mailing lists. **Publications:** *Interior Designer Classification Directory* ● *National Directory of Professional Interior Decorators and Designers*, annual. Membership Directory. Also Cited As: *Green Book* ● Brochure ● Bulletin, bimonthly. Supplements the membership directory.

2250 ■ American Floorcovering Alliance (AFA)
210 W Cuyler St.
Dalton, GA 30720
Ph: (706)278-4101
Free: (800)288-4101
Fax: (706)278-5323
E-mail: afa@americanfloor.org
URL: http://www.americanfloor.org
Contact: Eric Brown, Pres.

Founded: 1979. **Members:** 180. **Membership Dues:** regular, $400 (annual). **Staff:** 2. **Budget:** $140,000. **Description:** Floorcovering manufacturers and companies providing services or supplies to the floor covering industry. Promotes the floor covering industry. Provides insurance programs for members. **Awards: Type:** recognition. **Additional Websites:** http://www.Floor-Tek.com. **Telecommunication Services:** electronic mail, eric.brown@colbond.com. **Committees:** Advertising; Entertainment; Marketing. **Formerly:** (2003) Dalton Floor Covering Market Association. **Publications:** *AFA News & Updates*, quarterly. Newsletter ● *Floor Tek Source Guide*, biennial. Directory. Includes convention exhibition guide. **Price:** free for members and convention visitors. **Circulation:** 5,000. **Advertising:** accepted ● *Industry Profile*, quarterly. Directory ● AFA Membership directory-A complete list of all members with information on each company. **Conventions/Meetings:** biennial Floor-Tek - trade show, machinery, equipment, suppliers and services for the floor covering industry (exhibits).

2251 ■ American Society of Interior Designers (ASID)
608 Massachusetts Ave. NE
Washington, DC 20002-6006
Ph: (202)546-3480
Fax: (202)546-3240
E-mail: asid@asid.org
URL: http://www.interiors.org
Contact: Susan Globus, Pres.

Founded: 1975. **Members:** 34,500. **Membership Dues:** professional, $415 (annual) ● professional education, allied, $255 (annual) ● allied international, $275 (annual) ● student, $40 (annual). **Staff:** 35. **Budget:** $9,000,000. **Local Groups:** 48. **Description:** Represents practicing professional interior designers, students, and industry partners. ASID Educational Foundation sponsors scholarship competitions, finances educational research, and awards special grants. **Computer Services:** Mailing lists. **Additional Websites:** http://www.asid.org. **Programs:** ASID Advantage; Communications and Knowledge Resources; Education; Government and Public Affairs; Industry Partners; Member Services; Special Projects. **Affiliated With:** International Federation of Interior Architects/Designers. **Formed by Merger of:** American Institute of Decorators; National Society of Interior Designers. **Publications:** *ASID Icon*, quarterly. Magazine. **Price:** available to members only. **Advertising:** accepted ● *ASID Resource Guide and Industry Partner Directory*, annual. **Price:** available to members only. **Advertising:** accepted ● Brochures ● Papers. **Conventions/Meetings:** annual conference (exhibits).

2252 ■ Association of University Interior Designers (AUID)
c/o Jo Morrisson, Second VP/Membership Chair
WMU Campus Architecture and Design
1201 Oliver St.
Kalamazoo, MI 49008-5313
E-mail: webmaster@auid.org
URL: http://www.auid.org
Contact: Cindy Howe, Pres.

Founded: 1976. **Members:** 85. **Membership Dues:** professional, $35 (annual). **Description:** In-house interior designers associated with universities. Serves as an educational forum to share ideas and concerns of interior design relating to universities and colleges. **Awards:** Scholarship Award. **Frequency:** annual. **Type:** recognition. **Recipient:** for design students. **Committees:** Design Competition. **Publications:** *Clearstory*, annual. Newsletter. Contains information on previous year's annual conference. Includes list of officials. **Circulation:** 100. **Conventions/Meetings:** periodic competition ● annual conference and seminar - always fall.

2253 ■ Carpet Cushion Council (CCC)
23 Courtney Cir.
Bryn Mawr, PA 19010
Ph: (610)527-3880
Fax: (610)527-8535
E-mail: carpetcushion@msn.com
URL: http://www.carpetcushion.org
Contact: G. William Haines, Exec. Dir.

Founded: 1969. **Members:** 30. **Membership Dues:** manufacturing (maximum), $22,500 (annual) ● associate (with $2.5 - $15 million net sales), $2,250-$7,500 (annual) ● associate (above $15 million net sales), $18,000 (annual). **Budget:** $200,000. **Description:** Works to promote the sale and use of separate carpet cushions; to act as public relations counsel for the industry; to maintain contact with various government agencies; to establish quality and performance standards. Compiles statistics; maintains speakers' bureau. **Awards: Type:** recognition. **Committees:** Forecast; Public Relations; Technical. **Publications:** *Fact Sheet*. Newsletter. Addresses specific concerns. **Price:** included in membership dues ● Pamphlets. **Conventions/Meetings:** semiannual conference.

2254 ■ Carpet and Rug Institute (CRI)
PO Box 2048
Dalton, GA 30722-2048
Ph: (706)278-3176
Free: (800)882-8846
Fax: (706)278-8835
URL: http://www.carpet-rug.com
Contact: Werner Braun, Pres.

Founded: 1968. **Members:** 200. **Membership Dues:** manufacturer, associate supplier, $5,000 ● associate, $2,000-$7,000 ● insurance, accounting, transportation, utility, bank, factor, financial, $2,000. **Staff:** 24. **Description:** Represents the carpet and rug industry; sources of extensive carpet information for consumers, writers, interior designers, specifiers, facility managers, architects, builders, and building owners and managers. **Libraries: Type:** reference. **Subjects:** functional and financial benefits of carpet, selection, installation, construction, fiber characteristics, maintenance, technical, environment and carpet. **Committees:** Customer Satisfaction; Environmental; Financial; Government Relations; Health; Technical Issues. **Formed by Merger of:** (1969) American Carpet Institute; Tufted Textile Manufacturers Association. **Publications:** *Carpet and Rug Industry Review*, annual. Report. Presents a seven-year summary of industry shipments in square yards and dollars; includes statistics, graphs, charts and tables. ● *Carpet and Rug Manufacturing Plants and Corporate Locations in the U.S. and Canada*, annual. Directory. Identifies commission tufters and mills and provides a cross-reference of company names with parent names. ● *Carpet Primer*. Manual. Serves as a guide to carpet construction. ● *Myths and Truths about Carpet*. Brochure. Identifies the myths surrounding carpet and dispels them with the truth through references of scientific information. **Price:** $32.00 ● Books. Covers various aspects of the carpet industry. **Conventions/Meetings:** annual meeting and conference.

2255 ■ Certified Interior Decorators International (CID)
649 SE Central Pkwy.
Stuart, FL 34994
Ph: (772)287-1855
Free: (800)624-0093
Fax: (772)287-0398
E-mail: info@cidinternational.org
URL: http://www.cidinternational.org
Contact: Ron Renner, Founder/Dir.

Founded: 1997. **Membership Dues:** professional, $295 (annual) ● student, $150 (annual) ● trade partner/educational partner, $195 (annual). **Multinational. Description:** Promotes the interior decorator as a professional; works to enhance business image and earnings of decorating consultants. **Publications:** Newsletter, quarterly.

2256 ■ Contractors Co-Op Council (IDA)
Address Unknown since 2008
Founded: 1973. **Members:** 662. **Staff:** 11. **Budget:** $350,000. **Local Groups:** 26. **Description:** Custom drapery merchants. Organizes cooperative advertising, warehousing, and purchasing. Sponsors workshops on computers, bookkeeping, sales, and manufacturing. Compiles statistics. **Formerly:** (1970) White Front Drapery Concessionaires; (1997) International Drapery Association. **Publications:** *Basic Operation Manual* ● Newsletter, quarterly. **Conventions/Meetings:** quarterly conference.

2257 ■ Council for Qualification of Residential Interior Designers (CQRID)
PO Box 16028
High Point, NC 27261
Ph: (336)886-6100 (336)883-1680
Fax: (336)801-6110
E-mail: info@cqrid.org
URL: http://www.cqrid.org
Contact: Pamela White, Exec. Dir.
Description: Works to ensure that an appropriate and fair testing vehicle is available to residential interior designers to attain certification, registration, or licensure credentials. **Publications:** *Home Study Workbook*. Handbook. **Price:** $235.00 plus shipping and handling. **Conventions/Meetings:** Professional Designer's Advanced Training - workshop - 3-day program.

2258 ■ Home Fashion Products Association (HFPA)
355 Lexington Ave.
New York, NY 10017-6603
Ph: (212)297-2155
Fax: (212)297-2127
E-mail: cjennings@kellencompany.com
URL: http://downandfeathercouncil.com
Contact: Carolynn Jennings, Exec. Dir.
Founded: 1968. **Members:** 65. **Staff:** 3. **Description:** Manufacturers of curtains, draperies, bedding, rugs and related products. Sponsors annual scholarship for students attending accredited schools in home textiles. **Awards:** Scholarship. **Frequency:** annual. **Type:** recognition. **Recipient:** for college student in home textile surface design, and home textile marketing and development, excluding freshmen. **Sections:** American Down; Feather. **Absorbed:** (2002) American Down Association. **Conventions/Meetings:** annual general assembly - always in New York City.

2259 ■ Institute of Inspection, Cleaning and Restoration Certification (IICRC)
2715 E Mill Plain Blvd.
Vancouver, WA 98661
Ph: (360)693-5675
Free: (800)835-4624
Fax: (360)693-4858
E-mail: info@iicrc.org
URL: http://www.iicrc.org
Contact: Tom Hill, Exec. Admin.
Founded: 1972. **Members:** 2,000. **Description:** Fabric restoration firms and technicians. Sets standards of skill and ethics in the fabric restoration industry; works with regulatory bodies to establish proficiency standards. Certifies technicians, firms, and inspectors. **Formerly:** (1993) International Institute of Carpet and Upholstery Certification. **Publications:** *International Directory of Certified Professionals*, annual. **Conventions/Meetings:** semiannual board meeting.

2260 ■ Interior Design Society (IDS)
3910 Tinsley Dr., Ste.101
High Point, NC 27265
Free: (800)888-9590
Fax: (336)801-6110
E-mail: info@interiordesignsociety.org
URL: http://www.interiordesignsociety.org
Contact: Andrew Limone, Pres.
Founded: 1973. **Members:** 3,500. **Membership Dues:** affiliate, $150 (annual) ● associate, affiliate partner, $175 (annual) ● professional, $250 (annual) ● studio, $275 (annual) ● sponsor store, $400 (annual) ● home furnishing sales specialist, $75 (annual) ● trade partner, $300 (annual) ● sales/manufacturer representative, $60 (annual) ● student, $35 (annual) ● certified home furnishings consultant, $125 (annual) ● partner in design, $500 (annual). **Staff:** 3. **Local Groups:** 60. **Description:** Represents independent designers and decorators, retail designers and sales people, design-oriented firms, and manufacturers. Grants accreditation and recognition to qualified residential interior designers and retail home furnishing stores. Conducts educational seminars in design, sales training, and marketing. Offers products and publications for designers and a correspondence course for home furnishing sales people. **Awards: Type:** recognition. **Committees:** Professional Qualifications and Ethics. **Councils:** Trade. **Divisions:** Trade Member. **Affiliated With:** National Home Furnishings Association. **Publications:** *Design for Success*, monthly. Newsletter. **Price:** included in membership dues ● *Portfolio*, quarterly. Newsletter. Reports on society activities and news of the design industry. **Price:** free for members. **Circulation:** 3,000. **Advertising:** accepted ● *Residential Interior Design Books and Designer Tools*. **Conventions/Meetings:** monthly Regional Chapter & National Events - meeting.

2261 ■ International Association of Home Staging Professionals (IAHSP)
4807 Clayton Rd., Ste.200
Concord, CA 94521
Ph: (925)686-2413
Fax: (925)686-6386
E-mail: directorofoperations@iahsp.com
URL: http://www.iahsp.com
Contact: Barb Schwarz, CEO/Founder
Membership Dues: regular, $150 (annual). **Multinational. Description:** Advances the art and education of professional stagers who prepare homes for sale. Seeks to enhance the home staging skills of its members. Facilitates home stager business development opportunities. **Publications:** Newsletter. **Price:** included in membership dues.

2262 ■ International Association of Lighting Designers (IALD)
Merchandise Mart, Ste.9-104
200 World Trade Ctr.
Chicago, IL 60654
Ph: (312)527-3677
Fax: (312)527-3680
E-mail: marsha@iald.org
URL: http://www.iald.org
Contact: Marsha L. Turner CAE, Exec. VP
Founded: 1969. **Members:** 700. **Membership Dues:** professional, $250 (annual) ● associate, practicing/commercial affiliate, $150 (annual) ● press affiliate, $75 (annual) ● educator, $50 (annual) ● student, $20 (annual). **Staff:** 4. **Budget:** $1,000,000. **Regional Groups:** 20. **National Groups:** 2. **Description:** Represents professionals, educators, students, and others working in the field of lighting design worldwide. Promotes the benefits of quality lighting design and emphasizes the potential impact of lighting on architectural design and environmental quality. Furthers professional standards of lighting designers and seeks to increase their function in the interior design industry. Sponsors national awards program, summer intern program for qualified college students interested in lighting design as a profession, and career development lectures and seminars. **Libraries: Type:** not open to the public. **Holdings:** periodicals. **Subjects:** lighting. **Awards:** IALD Award. **Frequency:** annual. **Type:** recognition. **Recipient:** for a lighting designer ● IALD Scholarship. **Frequency:** annual. **Type:** scholarship. **Recipient:** for students pursuing architectural lighting design as a course of study. **Computer Services:** database, list of member lighting designers ● mailing lists. **Committees:** Awards; Business Standards; Education; Energy; Intern; Marketing; Metrics of Quality; Professional Development; Scholarship/Grant. **Publications:** *e-Reflections*, monthly. Newsletter. Covers association and industry news; includes calendar of events. **Price:** free for members. **Circulation:** 1,000. Alternate Formats: online ● *International Association of*

Lighting Designers—Membership Directory, annual. Alternate Formats: online ● *Why Hire an IALD Lighting Designer?*. Brochure. **Conventions/Meetings:** annual Lightfair International - trade show (exhibits).

2263 ■ International Design Guild (IDG)
670 Commercial St.
Manchester, NH 03101
Free: (800)205-4345
E-mail: info@design-guild.com
URL: http://www.design-guild.com
Contact: Terry L. Gissell, VP of Membership
Founded: 1992. **Multinational. Description:** Brings together interior designers to share and gain insight for business development and networking. Provides members with customizable marketing, merchandising, educational and operational tools. Aims to help members operate their businesses more profitably. **Awards:** Designer Showcase Awards. **Frequency:** annual. **Type:** recognition. **Recipient:** for interior designers.

2264 ■ International Furnishings and Design Association (IFDA)
150 S Warner Rd., Ste.156
King of Prussia, PA 19406
Ph: (610)535-6422
Fax: (610)535-6423
E-mail: info@ifda.com
URL: http://www.ifda.com
Contact: Judith Clark-Janofsky, Pres.
Founded: 1947. **Members:** 2,000. **Membership Dues:** professional, $250 (annual) ● student, $25 (annual). **Staff:** 2. **Budget:** $250,000. **Regional Groups:** 15. **Local Groups:** 15. **Description:** Represents individuals engaged in design, production, distribution, education, promotion, and editorial phases of the interior furnishings industry and related fields. Founded IFDA Educational Foundation in 1968. Conducts charitable programs; maintains speakers' bureau. **Awards:** IFDA Fellow. **Frequency:** annual. **Type:** fellowship. **Recipient:** to members for service to the association, industry and community ● National Honorary Recognition Award. **Frequency:** annual. **Type:** recognition. **Recipient:** for members who have made notable contributions to the industry or to socio-environmental improvement on the national level ● Trailblazer Award. **Frequency:** annual. **Type:** recognition. **Recipient:** for a person of outstanding achievement in the industry. **Computer Services:** Mailing lists, for a fee. **Telecommunication Services:** electronic mail, judith@delements.com. **Formerly:** (1953) Home Fashions League; (1987) National Home Fashions League. **Publications:** *IFDA Directory*, annual. Contains a list of members arranged by chapter. **Price:** free for members; $225.00 for nonmembers. **Circulation:** 5,000. **Advertising:** accepted ● *IFDA Network*, quarterly. Newsletter. Provides industrial, national, and chapter news. Alternate Formats: online. **Conventions/Meetings:** annual conference and symposium.

2265 ■ International Interior Design Association (IIDA)
222 Merchandise Mart Plz., Ste.1540
Chicago, IL 60654
Ph: (312)467-1950
Free: (888)799-4432
Fax: (312)467-0779
E-mail: iidahq@iida.org
URL: http://www.iida.org
Contact: Cheryl S. Durst, Exec. VP/CEO
Founded: 1994. **Members:** 10,000. **Membership Dues:** professional, affiliate, $434 (annual) ● associate, $245 (annual). **Staff:** 16. **Budget:** $2,000,000. **Regional Groups:** 9. **Local Groups:** 34. **Multinational. Description:** Represents professional interior designers, including designers of commercial, healthcare, hospitality, government, retail, residential facilities; educators; researchers; representatives of allied manufacturing sources. Conducts research, student programs, and continuing education programs for members. Has developed a code of ethics for the professional design membership. **Awards: Frequency:** annual. **Type:** recognition. **Recipient:** for product design, contract interiors, professional recognition, residential interiors. **Telecommunication Services:** electronic mail, cdurst@iida.org. **Committees:** College of Fellows; Continuing Education; Design Research; Government and Regulatory Affairs. **Formed by Merger of:** (1994) Institute of Business Designers, Council for Federal Interior Designers; (1994) International Society of Interior Designer. **Publications:** *DesignMatters*, biweekly. Newsletter. Contains information on design research, chapter, and forum activities. ● *Perspective*, quarterly. Magazine. Covers industry news and issues. Includes a calendar of events. **Advertising:** accepted. **Conventions/Meetings:** annual meeting - always June in Chicago, IL.

2266 ■ Jute Carpet Backing Council and Burlap and Jute Association (JCBC)
c/o Dayton National Sales Office and Plant
322 Davis Ave.
Dayton, OH 45403
Ph: (937)258-8000
Free: (800)543-3400
Fax: (937)258-0029
E-mail: bcouch@daybag.com
URL: http://www.daybag.com
Contact: Bob Couch, Contact
Founded: 1960. **Members:** 8. **Membership Dues:** individual, $250 (annual). **Budget:** $5,000. **Description:** U.S. importers of India and Bangladesh jute carpet backing. Promotes jute carpet backing for use by U.S. domestic carpet mills in the manufacturing of tufted carpeting. **Publications:** none. **Committees:** Arbitration. **Affiliated With:** Burlap and Jute Association. **Formerly:** (2000) Jute Carpet Backing Council. **Conventions/Meetings:** annual conference - always November or December, New York City.

2267 ■ Kitchen Cabinet Manufacturers Association (KCMA)
1899 Preston White Dr.
Reston, VA 20191-5435
Ph: (703)264-1690
Fax: (703)620-6530
E-mail: info@kcma.org
URL: http://www.kcma.org
Contact: C. Richard Titus, Exec. VP
Founded: 1955. **Members:** 350. **Staff:** 4. **Budget:** $1,000,000. **Description:** Serves as a national trade association representing cabinet and countertop manufacturers and suppliers to the industry. Promotes the cabinet manufacturing industry, develops standards for the industry, administers a testing and certification program, conducts education programs and meetings, provides management information and industry data, and engages in activities on behalf of members on legislative and regulatory issues. **Telecommunication Services:** electronic mail, dtitus@kcma.org. **Committees:** Government and Regulatory Affairs; Marketing; Standards and Certification. **Formerly:** (1962) National Institute of Wood Kitchen Cabinets; (1990) National Kitchen Cabinet Association. **Publications:** *Cabinet News*, bimonthly. Newsletter. Includes lists of companies added or dropped from KCMA, legislative updates, management update, and information on new products. ● *Directory of Certified Cabinet Manufacturers*, annual ● *Kitchen Cabinet Manufacturers Association—Income and Expense Study*, annual. **Price:** available to members only ● *Kitchen Cabinet Manufacturers Association—Wage and Labor Study*, annual. **Price:** available to members only ● *Recommended Performance and Construction Standards for Kitchen and Vanity Cabinets* ● Also publishes materials requirements. **Conventions/Meetings:** annual conference - always spring ● seminar, educational and management ● tour, for members.

2268 ■ National Candle Association (NCA)
1156 15th St., Ste.900
Washington, DC 20005
Ph: (202)393-2210
Fax: (202)331-2714
E-mail: info@candles.org
URL: http://www.candles.org
Contact: Valerie Cooper CAE, Exec. VP
Founded: 1974. **Members:** 180. **Membership Dues:** regular (based on annual sales volume), $2,100-$44,100 (annual) ● associate, affiliate (based on annual sales volume), $2,625-$10,500 (annual). **Staff:** 7. **Budget:** $1,500,000. **Description:** Represents manufacturers and distributors of candles and candle accessories in the United States at the wholesale level; suppliers and retailers to the Industry worldwide. Aims to: maintain high quality standards for the industry; foster goodwill between the candle industry and the public; strengthen and support the candle business. **Libraries: Type:** reference. **Holdings:** papers. **Committees:** Membership; Public Relations; Regulatory/Trade; Technical. **Formerly:** (1974) Candle Manufacturers Association. **Publications:** *Illuminations*, quarterly. Newsletter. **Conventions/Meetings:** semiannual meeting, supplier exhibits (exhibits).

2269 ■ National Council for Interior Design Qualification (NCIDQ)
1200 18th St. NW, Ste.1001
Washington, DC 20036-2506
Ph: (202)721-0220
Fax: (202)721-0221
E-mail: info@ncidq.org
URL: http://www.ncidq.org
Contact: Jeffrey F. Kenney, Exec. Dir.
Founded: 1974. **Members:** 19. **Membership Dues:** corporate, $2,750 (annual). **Staff:** 9. **Budget:** $1,800,000. **Languages:** English, French. **Description:** Independent organization of state and provincial regulatory bodies. Provides the public with the means to identify those interior designers who have demonstrated the minimum level of competence needed to practice in this profession. Provides a professional examination in interior design. Endeavors to maintain the most advanced examining procedures, and to update continually the examination to reflect expanding professional knowledge and design development techniques to protect the health, safety and welfare of the public. Seeks acceptance of the NCIDQ examination as a universal standard by which to measure the competency of interior designers practicing as professionals. **Libraries: Type:** reference. **Subjects:** interior design. **Awards:** Louis S. Tregre Award. **Frequency:** annual. **Type:** recognition. **Recipient:** for individuals involved in grassroots and volunteer work within the organization. **Publications:** *QLetter*, semiannual. Newsletter. Alternate Formats: online.

2270 ■ National Guild of Professional Paperhangers (NGPP)
136 S Keowee St.
Dayton, OH 45402
Ph: (937)222-6477
Free: (800)254-6477
Fax: (937)222-5794
E-mail: ngpp@ngpp.org
URL: http://www.ngpp.org
Contact: David DiBacco, Pres.
Founded: 1974. **Members:** 860. **Membership Dues:** associate (chapter affiliation), $150 (annual) ● associate (national affiliation), $360 (annual). **Staff:** 9. **Budget:** $250,000. **Regional Groups:** 8. **Local Groups:** 39. **Description:** Paperhangers united to: promote use of wallcoverings; upgrade the skills of paperhangers and the quality of materials; foster unity among members; encourage good business practices and ethics in the industry. Conducts charitable programs. Sponsors educational programs. **Libraries: Type:** reference. **Holdings:** 110; books, video recordings. **Subjects:** wallcovering installation. **Awards: Frequency:** annual. **Type:** recognition. **Computer Services:** database ● mailing lists. **Telecommunication Services:** electronic mail, dadwpr@frontiernet.net. **Committees:** Communications; Education; Ethics; Membership Services; Problem Reporting; Technical. **Formerly:** (1980) Guild of Professional Paperhangers. **Publications:** *Wallcovering Installer*, bimonthly. Newsletter. Covers association and industry news. **Price:** included in membership dues. **Advertising:** accepted ● Membership Directory, annual. **Price:** included in membership dues. **Advertising:** accepted ● Brochures. **Conventions/Meetings:** annual meeting, tech tour ● annual

National Paperhangers Forum - convention and trade show (exhibits) - always September.

2271 ■ National Kitchen and Bath Association (NKBA)
687 Willow Grove St.
Hackettstown, NJ 07840
Ph: (908)852-0033
Free: (800)843-6522
Fax: (908)852-1695
E-mail: feedback@nkba.org
URL: http://www.nkba.org
Contact: Larry R. Spangler, CEO
Founded: 1963. **Members:** 25,000. **Membership Dues:** associate (business), $750 (annual) ● associate (individual employee), $150 (annual) ● associate (educational institution), $300 (annual). **Staff:** 44. **Budget:** $10,000,000. **Regional Groups:** 64. **Description:** Manufacturers and firms engaged in retail kitchen sales; manufacturers' representatives and wholesale distributors; utilities, publications, and other firms supplying products or services to the kitchen and bathroom industry. Protects and promotes the interest and welfare of members by fostering a better business climate in the industry. Awards titles of Certified Kitchen Designer and Certified Bathroom Designer to individuals with proven knowledge, ability, and experience in the design, planning, and installation supervision of residential kitchens. Conducts kitchen and bathroom training schools throughout the country. Sponsors business management and consumer awareness programs. Maintains speakers' bureau and Hall of Fame. **Boards:** Dealers; Decorative Plumbing and Hardware; Designers; Manufacturers; Manufacturers' Representatives; Multi-Branch Retailers; Wholesale Distributors. **Formerly:** (1982) American Institute of Kitchen Dealers. **Publications:** *Profiles*, bimonthly. Magazine. **Price:** available to members only. **Advertising:** accepted. **Conventions/Meetings:** annual conference (exhibits) ● annual National Design Competition.

2272 ■ Oriental Rug Importers Association (ORIA)
100 Park Plaza Dr.
Secaucus, NJ 07094
Ph: (201)866-5054
Fax: (201)866-6169
E-mail: oria@oria.org
URL: http://www.oria.org
Contact: Andrew Peykar, Pres.
Founded: 1931. **Members:** 81. **Description:** Represents wholesalers and importers of Oriental rugs. Fosters ethical business practices and promotes the best interests of the Oriental Rug Trade in the United States and in countries that produce Oriental rugs. **Publications:** *AREA Magazine*, quarterly. **Price:** free for members. **Advertising:** accepted. **Conventions/Meetings:** annual National Oriental Rug Show (exhibits).

2273 ■ Oriental Rug Retailers of America (ORRA)
c/o Elizabeth Arnold, Exec. Dir.
PO Box 71831
Richmond, VA 23255
Ph: (804)270-3195
Fax: (804)270-3196
E-mail: orra@orrainc.com
URL: http://www.orrainc.com
Contact: Elizabeth Arnold, Exec. Dir.
Founded: 1969. **Members:** 325. **Membership Dues:** regular, $250 (annual). **Budget:** $642,000. **Description:** Represents professional Oriental rug retailers. Conducts workshops, seminars, and annual examination for Oriental rug appraiser certification. Disseminates information. Maintains hall of fame. **Awards: Type:** grant ● **Frequency:** annual. **Type:** recognition. **Computer Services:** Mailing lists, consumer. **Committees:** Advertising; Consumer Protection; Education and Appraisal; Grievance; Public Relations; Recognition; Research; Theft Information; Trade Fair. **Publications:** *ORRA Directory* ● *ORRA Newsletter*, biennial. **Advertising:** accepted ● *Theft Information Kit Manual*. **Conventions/Meetings:** annual conference (exhibits) ● annual conference and convention.

2274 ■ Paint and Decorating Retailers Association (PDRA)
403 Axminister Dr.
Fenton, MO 63026-2941
Ph: (636)326-2636
Free: (800)737-0107
Fax: (636)326-1823
E-mail: r.mueller@benjaminmoorecalgary.com
URL: http://www.pdra.org
Contact: Robert Mueller, Pres.
Founded: 1947. **Members:** 3,000. **Membership Dues:** business, $139 (annual). **Staff:** 12. **Budget:** $6,000,000. **State Groups:** 4. **Local Groups:** 3. **Multinational. Description:** Serves as a trade association of locally owned paint and decorating stores in the U.S., Canada, and around the world. Offers professional advice, personal service and quality products for every paint, wall covering, window treatment, and floor covering project. **Computer Services:** Mailing lists. **Absorbed:** Southern Paint and Wallcovering Dealers Association; Canadian Decorating Products Association. **Formerly:** Retail Paint and Wallpaper Distributors of America; Paint and Wallpaper Association of America; (1997) National Decorating Products Association. **Publications:** *Decorating Registry*, annual. Directory. Includes product listings, brand and trade names, manufacturers' representatives, testing laboratories, and company listings. **Price:** free. **Circulation:** 27,000. **Advertising:** accepted ● *Gold Book*, annual. Directory. Lists wallcovering collections and their distributors, manufacturers, and their lines. **Price:** free for members. ISSN: 0011-7404. **Circulation:** 22,000. **Advertising:** accepted ● *Paint and Decorating Retailer*, monthly. Magazine. Includes information on legislation and regulation affecting the industry. For paint and wallpaper, window and floor covering and paint retailers. **Price:** free. ISSN: 0011-7404. **Circulation:** 27,000. **Advertising:** accepted ● Newsletter, bimonthly. **Conventions/Meetings:** annual Paint and Decorating Show - convention and trade show, exhibits include paint, wallpaper, sundries, window treatments and equipment (exhibits).

2275 ■ Residential Space Planners International (RSPI)
20 Ardmore Dr.
Minneapolis, MN 55422
Free: (800)548-0945
Fax: (612)377-8189
E-mail: maryfisherdesigns1@cox.net
Contact: Mary Knott, Exec. Dir.
Founded: 1985. **Membership Dues:** professional/general, $80 (annual). **Description:** Interior designers and architects who specialize in planning residential interiors, primarily kitchens and bathrooms. **Libraries: Type:** not open to the public.

2276 ■ Set Decorators Society of America (SDSA)
1646 N Cherokee Ave.
Hollywood, CA 90028
Ph: (323)462-3060
Fax: (323)462-3099
E-mail: sdsa@setdecorators.org
URL: http://www.setdecorators.org
Contact: Tara Stephenson, Pres.
Founded: 1993. **Membership Dues:** set decorator, $225 (annual) ● set decorator retiree/sustaining/friend, $100 (annual) ● associate, $150 (annual) ● student/apprentice, $50 (annual). **Description:** Promotes and supports the profession of set decorating. Fosters fellowship and networking opportunities for its members. Offers internships to interested students and apprentices. **Awards:** SDSA Chair Award. **Frequency:** annual. **Type:** recognition. **Recipient:** for outstanding volunteer work done in support of the organization ● SDSA Lifetime Achievement Award. **Frequency:** annual. **Type:** recognition. **Recipient:** to a set decorator who has made a significant contribution in the field of set decorating. **Publications:** *Set Decor*, quarterly. Magazine. Covers news and articles pertaining to the art of set decorating. **Price:** $24.00/year; $10.00/issue. **Advertising:** accepted. Alternate Formats: online.

2277 ■ Society of Certified Kitchen Designers (SCKD)
c/o Sean Ruck
687 Willow Grove St.
Hackettstown, NJ 07840
Ph: (908)813-3792
Free: (800)843-6522
Fax: (908)852-1695
E-mail: sruck@nkba.org
URL: http://www.nkba.org
Contact: Larry Spangler, CEO
Founded: 1969. **Members:** 2,500. **Membership Dues:** individual, $300 (annual). **Staff:** 3. **Description:** A project of National Kitchen and Bath Association. Residential kitchen designers whose design abilities are certified by means of experience, work samples, professional and consumer references, and examination. Aims to establish within the industry, and for consumers, professional standards for residential kitchen design, and to identify designers who have met those standards. Conducts educational, business management, and consumer awareness programs. **Libraries: Type:** open to the public. **Holdings:** 35; books. **Subjects:** kitchen/bath design, installation, business management. **Affiliated With:** National Kitchen and Bath Association. **Conventions/Meetings:** annual competition, held in conjunction with National Kitchen and Bath Association ● annual conference.

2278 ■ Wallcoverings Association (WA)
401 N Michigan Ave., Ste.2200
Chicago, IL 60611
Ph: (312)644-6610 (312)673-5793
Fax: (312)527-6705
E-mail: rpietrzak@smithbucklin.com
URL: http://www.wallcoverings.org
Contact: Ron Pietrzak, Exec. Dir.
Founded: 1920. **Members:** 140. **Staff:** 3. **Budget:** $600,000. **Description:** Manufacturers, converters, distributors, and suppliers in the wallcoverings industry. **Awards:** Allman Award. **Frequency:** annual. **Type:** recognition. **Computer Services:** database ● mailing lists. **Programs:** Contract; Government Affairs; International; Marketing; Membership; Statistical and Technical. **Formerly:** National Wallpaper Wholesalers Association; (1959) Wallpaper Wholesalers Association; (1974) Wallcovering Manufacturers Association; (1992) Wallcovering Distributors Association. **Publications:** Membership Directory, annual. Contains listing of members by membership type. **Price:** free for members. **Conventions/Meetings:** annual convention (exhibits) ● annual meeting - always mid-year.

2279 ■ Window Covering Manufacturers Association (WCMA)
355 Lexington Ave., 17th Fl.
New York, NY 10017
Ph: (212)297-2122
Fax: (212)370-9047
URL: http://www.wcmanet.org
Founded: 1979. **Members:** 22. **Budget:** $100,000. **Description:** Represents corporations engaged in the manufacture or assembly of Venetian blinds, vertical blinds, pleated shades, or their components. Promotes the use, utility, image, and attractiveness of the products and services offered by the window covering industry. **Awards:** Product Innovation Awards. **Frequency:** annual. **Type:** recognition. **Recipient:** for companies with significant product advancements in the window covering industry. **Committees:** Marketing; Technical. **Councils:** Window Covering Safety. **Formerly:** (1985) U.S. Venetian Blind Association; (1991) American Window Covering Manufacturers Association. **Publications:** *ANSI/WCMA A100.1-2002 American National Standard for Safety of Corded Window Covering Products*. **Price:** $9.00 for members; $18.00 for nonmembers. **Conventions/Meetings:** annual meeting.

2280 ■ Window Coverings Association of America (WCAA)
2646 Hwy. 109, Ste.205
Wildwood, MO 63040
Ph: (636)273-4090
Free: (888)298-9222
Fax: (636)273-4439
E-mail: info@wcaa.org
URL: http://www.wcaa.org
Contact: Mark Nortman, Exec. Dir.
Founded: 1987. **Members:** 1,500. **Membership Dues:** regular, $135 (annual) ● regular, $240 (biennial). **Staff:** 2. **Budget:** $500,000. **Regional Groups:** 29. **Description:** Trade association for independent workrooms, retail dealers, decorators, and designers of window coverings and other interior fashion products. Provides benefits and services in line with goals of making available educational opportunities, encouraging a code of ethics for fair business practices and working for the betterment of the interior fashion industry. Sponsors the Certified Window Treatment Consultant Program and the Certified Workroom Professional Program. **Committees:** Education. **Publications:** *WCAA Cover Story*, bimonthly. Newsletter. Features articles geared towards the window covering retailer and workroom. **Price:** free for members. Alternate Formats: online.

International Standards

2281 ■ Council for International Tax Education (CITE)
PO Box 1012
White Plains, NY 10602
Ph: (914)328-5656
Fax: (914)328-5757
E-mail: info@citeusa.org
URL: http://www.citeusa.org
Contact: William H. Green, Exec. Dir.
Founded: 1982. **Members:** 400. **Membership Dues:** individual, $295 (annual) ● corporate (up to three persons), $595 (annual). **Staff:** 6. **Budget:** $1,000,000. **Description:** Corporations, professional firms, and individual tax advisors. Works to maximize members' understanding of U.S. tax incentives and other offshore benefits available to exporters. Conducts educational programs for companies that generate tax incentives for the export of U.S. goods. Holds seminars on international tax, export and cross-border lease finance, and incentives offered companies that set up manufacturing or operating sites abroad. **Formerly:** FSC/DISC Tax Club; (2002) FSC/DISC Tax Association. **Publications:** *International Tax News*, quarterly. Newsletter. **Price:** $345.00 for members. **Circulation:** 400. **Conventions/Meetings:** annual conference and seminar (exhibits).

2282 ■ FCIB-NACM Corp.
8840 Columbia 100 Pkwy.
Columbia, MD 21045-2158
Ph: (410)423-1840
Free: (888)256-3242
Fax: (410)423-1845
E-mail: fcib_info@fcibglobal.com
URL: http://www.fcibglobal.com
Contact: Ms. Aneta Spilman, Pres./COO
Founded: 1919. **Members:** 730. **Membership Dues:** full, $840 (annual) ● affiliate, $420 (annual) ● associate, $100 (annual). **Staff:** 6. **Multinational. Description:** Provides services to international credit and trade finance professionals, including international receivables management education, products, services and networking. Offers roundtable discussions, international trade surveys, industry groups, conferences, credit hotline, workshops and research services. **Libraries: Type:** reference. **Holdings:** books, clippings, periodicals, reports. **Subjects:** global trade materials. **Committees:** Global; International Credit Executives; Round Table Agenda. **Formerly:** (1970) Foreign Credit Interchange Bureau. **Publications:** *Country Report*. Contains credit rating and political and economic conditions of a specific country. **Price:** $100.00 for members; $125.00 for nonmembers ● *Credit and Collection Survey*, quarterly. **Price:** free for members ● *International Credit Reports* ● *U.S. and Europe Round Table Minutes*. Covers panelist and participant discussion of international trade, credit issues, and economic conditions of various nations. **Price:** free for members and attendees only ● Bulletin, quarterly. **Price:** free for members ● Membership Directory, annual. **Price:** free for members ● Newsletter, quarterly. **Price:** free for members.

2283 ■ Federation of International Trade Associations (FITA)
1900 Campus Commons Dr., Ste.340
Reston, VA 20191
Ph: (703)620-1588
Free: (800)969-3482
Fax: (703)620-4922
E-mail: info@fita.org
URL: http://www.fita.org
Contact: Mr. Nelson T. Joyner, Chm.
Founded: 1984. **Members:** 450. **Staff:** 10. **Budget:** $300,000. **Languages:** Chinese, English, Spanish. **Multinational. Description:** Fosters international trade by strengthening the role of local, regional, and national associations throughout the United States, Mexico, and Canada that have an international mission; affiliates are 450 independent international associations. **Libraries: Type:** reference. **Awards:** Really Useful Sites Award. **Frequency:** biweekly. **Type:** recognition. **Recipient:** for websites determined to be of value to professionals in international trade. **Computer Services:** database ● mailing lists. **Publications:** *Directory of North American Trade Association*, annual. Membership Directory. Includes geographical and alphabetical listing of member organizations. **Price:** $50.00. **Circulation:** 4,500. Alternate Formats: online ● *FITA's Really Useful Sites*, biweekly. Newsletter. Alternate Formats: online.

2284 ■ International Trade Club of Chicago (ITCC)
134 N LaSalle St., Ste.1300
Chicago, IL 60602
Ph: (312)368-9197
Fax: (312)553-1470
E-mail: president@itcc.org
URL: http://www.itcc.org
Contact: Sidney Salvadori, Pres.
Founded: 1919. **Members:** 500. **Membership Dues:** individual, $95 (annual) ● corporate, $245 (annual) ● diplomatic, $85 (annual) ● academic, not-for-profit, $75 (annual) ● full-time student, $50 (annual). **Staff:** 1. **Description:** Individuals who are involved in international export and import operations for their firms; representatives of allied service fields. Fosters and seeks to expand international business by removing barriers that may interfere with its development and by providing members with a medium for the discussion of problems and sharing of experience. Promotes a better understanding of U.S. foreign policy and its impact on international business. Conducts trade development and professional training programs, including the monthly ITCC Import Workshop series and the Global Manufacturing Series; conducts seminars on current trade issues, industry sectors, world markets; holds business networking events 4-5 times a year. **Telecommunication Services:** electronic mail, execdir@itcc.org. **Committees:** Export Expansion; Import; International Finance; International Liaison; Publications; Transportation. **Councils:** Export Managers. **Formerly:** (1957) Export Managers Club of Chicago; (1980) International Trade Club of Chicago; (1981) International Business Council; (1987) International Business Council Midamerica. **Publications:** *ITCC Trade News*, annual. Membership Directory. **Price:** $75.00 ● *ITCC Trade Report*, monthly. Newsletter. Explores trade issues, spotlighting specific industries, regions, upcoming events and member companies. **Price:** included in membership dues. Alternate Formats: online ● Membership Directory. **Price:** $75.00. Alternate Formats: online. **Conventions/Meetings:** annual Chicago World Trade Conference - meeting.

2285 ■ International Trade Council (ITC)
Address Unknown since 2007
Founded: 1976. **Members:** 850. **Membership Dues:** regular, $10,000 (annual) ● associate, $1,000 (annual). **Staff:** 35. **Budget:** $1,250,000. **National Groups:** 1. **Languages:** Danish, French, German, Spanish, Swedish. **Description:** Companies and organizations that import and export products, commodities, and services in 300 major industries including agricultural commodities, livestock, food, farm implements, and food machinery; agencies dealing with health and medicine, housing, energy, communications, transportation, forestry, water, and sanitation. Promotes free trade and the elimination of trade barriers and facilitates logistics, research, and marketing for members. Maintains legislative and educational services to develop world trade. Conducts management, technical, and educational programs; conducts financial studies of export banking, insurance, performance bonds, and transportation costs to enable exporters to be more competitive; offers speakers' bureau. Sponsors International Development Institute; offers Opportunity/Risk Analysis Service to help members find new or expandable overseas markets for their commodities, products, services, and investments. **Libraries: Type:** reference. **Holdings:** 8,000; books, clippings, monographs, periodicals. **Subjects:** trade policy, fiscal and monetary policy, economic forecasting and opportunity/risk analysis in 230 countries and territories. **Awards:** Exporter of the Year. **Frequency:** annual. **Type:** recognition. **Recipient:** innovation in opening new markets. **Computer Services:** database, producers in the US and globally ● database, trade regulations, tariff barriers, transportations costs, insurance, and banking for international trade. **Committees:** Government Relations; International Advisory Board; International Trade Policy. **Divisions:** Agricultural Trade Council. **Formerly:** (1976) Agricultural Trade Council. **Publications:** *Geo Economic Review*, quarterly. **Advertising:** accepted ● *Research Report*, monthly. Opportunity Risk Analysis reports on each of 250 countries and territories plus market studies. **Price:** $450.00. Alternate Formats: CD-ROM; magnetic tape ● *World Opportunity/Risk Review*, quarterly ● *World Source Directory*, annual ● *World Trade Directory*, periodic ● *World Trade Review*, quarterly ● *Worldbusiness Directory*, annual ● *Worldbusiness Review*, quarterly ● *Worldbusiness Weekly*. Newsletter. Covers international business news, governmental regulations, and bid listings. ● Membership Directory, annual. **Advertising:** accepted. **Conventions/Meetings:** Outlook Conference & Trade Development Conference, legislative review (exhibits) - April, May, June, September, October, November ● quarterly Trade Development Conference & Geo Political Outlook Conference - meeting and seminar (exhibits) ● annual Trade Methodology - conference - always April.

2286 ■ Iranian Trade Association (ITA)
PO Box 927743
San Diego, CA 92192
Ph: (619)368-6790
Fax: (858)547-0823
E-mail: info@iraniantrade.org
URL: http://www.iraniantrade.org
Contact: Shahriar Afshar, Pres.
Membership Dues: corporate bronze, $250 (annual) ● corporate silver, $500 (annual) ● corporate gold, $1,000 (annual) ● corporate patron, $5,000 (annual). **Description:** International enterprises active in global trade that have specific interests in Iran. Promotes increased trade between the United States and Iran. Works to expand international investment in Iran; sponsors trade missions; conducts promotional events. **Councils:** U.S.-Iran Business. **Publications:** *Onward*, monthly. Newsletter. Features Iranian foreign trade news, trade leads, current events, member profiles and policy development. **Price:** $49.00/year. **Advertising:** accepted ● Reports. **Price:** $100.00 for members; $125.00 for nonmembers. **Conventions/Meetings:** quarterly conference.

2287 ■ Moroccan American Business Council (MABC)
1085 Commonwealth Ave., Ste.194
Boston, MA 02215

Ph: (508)230-9943 (508)230-5985
Fax: (508)230-9943
E-mail: mission@usa-morocco.org
URL: http://www.usa-morocco.org
Contact: Ron Leavell, Contact

Founded: 1995. **Members:** 500. **Staff:** 16. **Budget:** $100,000. **Regional Groups:** 3. **Local Groups:** 1. **Languages:** Arabic, English, French. **Description:** Promotes commerce and business between Morocco and the United States. **Publications:** Newsletter. **Price:** free for members. Alternate Formats: online.

2288 ■ National Council on International Trade Development (NCITD)
1707 L St. NW, Ste.570
Washington, DC 20036
Ph: (202)872-9280
Fax: (202)293-0495
URL: http://www.ncitd.org
Contact: Kevin Byrne, Contact

Founded: 1967. **Membership Dues:** corporate (based on gross sales), $500-$3,000 (annual). **Description:** Exporters, importers, freight forwarders and brokers, ocean and airline carriers, banks, attorneys, trade groups, and consulting firms. Aims to identify impediments to all aspects of international commerce and to provide solutions to facilitating the global trade process. **Conventions/Meetings:** monthly TRAD Compliance Committee Meeting.

2289 ■ National Foreign Trade Council (NFTC)
1625 K St. NW, Ste.200
Washington, DC 20006
Ph: (202)887-0278
Fax: (202)452-8160
E-mail: nftcinformation@nftc.org
URL: http://www.nftc.org
Contact: William A. Reinsch, Pres.

Founded: 1914. **Members:** 300. **Staff:** 14. **Description:** Manufacturers, exporters, importers, foreign investors, banks, transportation lines, and insurance, communication, law, accounting, service, and publishing firms. Works to promote and protect American foreign trade and investment. Areas of concern include the removal of arbitrary barriers to expansion of international trade and investment; a greater awareness by the government that this expansion is essential to the economic growth of the U.S; the formation of a cohesive, consistent international economic policy. **Libraries: Type:** not open to the public. **Subjects:** trade, human resources, general business in over 150 countries. **Awards:** NFTC Trade Award. **Frequency:** annual. **Type:** recognition. **Telecommunication Services:** electronic mail, breinsch@nftc.org. **Committees:** China Human Resources; Expatriate Management; Export Finance; Global Compensation; International Benefits; International Trade and Investment; International Training and Education; Iran Working Group; Management Resources; Taxation; Trade and Investment. **Absorbed:** Council for Inter-American Cooperation. **Publications:** *Council Highlights*, bimonthly. Newsletter. **Price:** free, for members only. Alternate Formats: online ● Bulletin, periodic ● Also publishes memoranda and texts of laws, regulations, and treaties. **Conventions/Meetings:** periodic board meeting and conference.

2290 ■ Organization of Women in International Trade (OWIT)
Address Unknown since 2007
URL: http://www.owit.org

Founded: 1987. **Members:** 750. **Description:** International trade organizations in the United States. Seeks to enhance "the visibility of and opportunities for women in the field of international trade." Makes available educational and networking opportunities for women pursuing careers in international trade. **Formerly:** (2002) Women in International Trade. **Conventions/Meetings:** weekly lecture, brownbag lunch ● monthly lecture, with lunch.

2291 ■ Society of International Business Fellows (SIBF)
One Georgia Ctr.
600 W Peachtree St., Ste.490
Atlanta, GA 30308
Ph: (404)525-7423
Fax: (404)525-5331
E-mail: info@sibf.org
URL: http://www.sibf.org/swghome.asp?ID=2
Contact: Nancy Haselden, Exec. Dir.

Founded: 1981. **Members:** 450. **Staff:** 8. **Multinational. Description:** Businesspeople active or with an interest in international trade. Promotes "enhancement of the international competitiveness and prosperity of its members and the growth of the South as a vital region for global business." Works to strengthen personal and professional relations among members; conducts educational programs in international business and trade. **Programs:** New Member. **Conventions/Meetings:** annual meeting - every fall.

2292 ■ U.S. Business Council for Southeastern Europe (USBCSEE)
Address Unknown since 2007

Founded: 1974. **Members:** 150. **Staff:** 4. **Budget:** $100,000. **Regional Groups:** 5. **Description:** Industrial, financial, and commercial firms. Represents firms in the U.S. in development of trade and investment with southeastern Europe. Conducts meetings on current topics of interest. **Libraries: Type:** not open to the public. **Holdings:** 7; books. **Subjects:** tourism, banking, economics. **Computer Services:** database ● mailing lists. **Councils:** U.S.-Bosnia and Herzegovina Business Council; U.S.-Croatia Business Council; U.S.-Macedonia Business Council; U.S.-Slovenia Business Council; U.S.-Yugoslavia Business Council. **Formerly:** (1992) U.S. Yugoslav Economic Council. **Publications:** *U.S. Business Council for Southeastern Europe—Business News*, monthly. Newsletter. Covers southeastern economic trends including laws and regulations, business opportunities for U.S. firms, and trends in trade. **Price:** available to members only. **Circulation:** 300. **Advertising:** not accepted. **Conventions/Meetings:** annual Government Agency Conference - meeting ● annual luncheon - always New York City or Washington, DC.

2293 ■ U.S.-Russia Business Council (USRBC)
1701 Pennsylvania Ave. NW, Ste.520
Washington, DC 20006
Ph: (202)739-9180
Fax: (202)659-5920
E-mail: lawson@usrbc.org
URL: http://www.usrbc.org
Contact: Eugene K. Lawson, Pres.

Founded: 1933. **Members:** 300. **Membership Dues:** company, $1,500-$12,500 (annual) ● non-profit organization, $1,250 (annual). **Staff:** 9. **Multinational. Description:** U.S. corporations doing business in Russia. Promotes adoption of public policies conducive to international trade in both the United States and Russia. Conducts lobbying activities; facilitates establishment of joint ventures involving U.S. and Russian companies; maintains bank of job listings; compiles trade statistics. Gathers and disseminates information on political, economic, and social issues affecting trade with Russia. **Libraries: Type:** reference. **Holdings:** books, periodicals. **Subjects:** Russia, international trade. **Committees:** Agribusiness; Energy; Legal. **Working Groups:** Aerospace/Aviation; IT/E-Commerce; WTO. **Publications:** *Event Transcript*, periodic. Proceedings ● *Russia Business Watch*, quarterly. Magazine. Covers the latest commercial and political developments in U.S.-Russian relations. **Advertising:** accepted. Alternate Formats: online. **Conventions/Meetings:** annual conference.

2294 ■ US-Taiwan Business Council (USTBC)
1700 N Moore St., Ste.1703
Arlington, VA 22209
Ph: (703)465-2930
Fax: (703)465-2937
E-mail: council@us-taiwan.org
URL: http://www.us-taiwan.org
Contact: Rupert J. Hammond-Chambers, Pres.

Founded: 1976. **Members:** 250. **Membership Dues:** corporate, $5,000 (annual) ● Chairman's Circle, $15,000 (annual). **Staff:** 4. **Budget:** $700,000. **Languages:** Chinese, English. **Description:** Promotes business relations between the United States and Taiwan. Holds conferences and seminars to promote understanding of business climate and opportunities, government policies, and laws and regulations. Acts to improve regulations; and fosters the development of business communications and contacts. Maintains information on Taiwan of importance to U.S. business. Publishes weekly news updates and quarterly analysis reports on the business climate in Taiwan. **Libraries: Type:** not open to the public. **Subjects:** business. **Formerly:** U.S.A.-Republic of China Economic Council; (1998) U.S.A-ROC Economic Council; (2003) U.S.-ROC (Taiwan) Business Council. **Publications:** *Business eBulletin*, weekly. Report. Alternate Formats: online ● *Defense and Security Report*, quarterly ● *Occasional Paper Series*, periodic. Papers. Alternate Formats: online ● *Sector eBulletins*, weekly. Alternate Formats: online ● *Semiconductor Report*, quarterly ● Also publishes conference papers; distributes material on the laws and regulations of Taiwan and a variety of Taiwan business publications. **Conventions/Meetings:** annual Defense Industry Conference (exhibits) ● semiannual Sector-Specific Conference ● annual Taiwan China Semiconductor Industry Outlook Conference.

2295 ■ World Trade Center of New Orleans (WTCNO)
2 Canal St., Ste.2900
New Orleans, LA 70130
Ph: (504)529-1601
Fax: (504)529-1691
E-mail: wtc-info@wtcno.org
URL: http://www.wtcno.org
Contact: April Gonzalez, Membership Mgr.

Founded: 1985. **Members:** 2,100. **Membership Dues:** corporate, $2,500 (annual) ● sustaining, $400 (annual) ● small business, $300 (annual) ● special, $175 (annual). **Staff:** 60. **Description:** U.S. and foreign business leaders united for the promotion of international trade, friendship, and understanding. Programs visits for foreign VIPs; sends trade and cultural missions of business and civic leaders abroad each year. Offers instruction in foreign languages. Houses library with volumes on world trade, travel, and international relations. Offers seminars and luncheon briefings. **Awards: Frequency:** annual. **Type:** recognition. **Telecommunication Services:** electronic bulletin board, WTCA Online. **Departments:** International Business. **Affiliated With:** World Trade Centers Association. **Formed by Merger of:** International House - World Trade Center; International Trade Mart. **Publications:** *Louisiana International Trade*. Bulletin. Contains many important articles about the activities of the WTC and other Louisiana organizations. **Price:** free ● *Louisiana International Trade Directory*, biennial. Contains company name, contact person, address, telephone and fax numbers, e-mail and Internet addresses and products handled. **Price:** $40.00 for nonmembers; $20.00 for members. Alternate Formats: online ● *Trade Winds*, periodic. **Conventions/Meetings:** annual meeting.

International Trade

2296 ■ America-Georgia Business Council (AGBC)
2300 M St. NW, Ste.800
Washington, DC 20037
Ph: (202)416-1606
Fax: (202)416-3083
E-mail: agbdc@agbdc.com
URL: http://www.agbdc.com
Contact: S. Enders Wimbush, Pres.

Founded: 1998. **Membership Dues:** founding, $8,500 (annual) ● regular, $4,500 (annual) ● non-profit, $950 (annual). **Multinational. Description:** Promotes investment, trade, political and cultural cooperation between America and Georgia. Seeks to raise Georgia's visibility in North America as a place to invest and do business. Increases understanding of Georgian political and business landscape. Fosters business to business relationships between American and Georgian entrepreneurs. **Publications:** *America-Georgia Business Outlook*. Newsletter. Alternate Formats: online.

2297 ■ American Association of Exporters and Importers (AAEI)
1050 17th St. NW, Ste.810
Washington, DC 20036
Ph: (202)857-8009
Fax: (202)857-7843
E-mail: hq@aaei.org
URL: http://www.aaei.org
Contact: Hallock Northcott, Pres./CEO

Founded: 1921. **Members:** 450. **Membership Dues:** importer/exporter (based on US dollar value of volume of imports and exports), $525-$5,550 (annual) ● broker/forwarder (based on number of employees), $525-$3,600 (annual) ● law firm (based on attorneys in firm handling trade), $525-$2,000 (annual) ● trade service (based on number of employees handling trade), $550-$2,700 (annual) ● port authority, trade association, $500 (annual) ● student, $50 (annual). **Staff:** 4. **Description:** Exporters and importers of goods, products, and raw materials; wholesalers and retailers; customs brokers and forwarders; banks; insurance underwriters; steamship companies; customs attorneys and others engaged directly or indirectly in dealing with exports and imports. Seeks fair and equitable conditions for world trade. Anticipates problems of interpretation of laws and regulations affecting members' businesses; gathers and disseminates data on world trade; supports and creates legislation promoting balanced international trade; works for fair administration of policy. Maintains liaison with government committees, agencies, and other trade policy groups. Testifies for exporters and importers before government and other official bodies. Studies problems concerning export and import; offers advice and support to members facing problems in their businesses; conducts forums and workshops on timely topics and developments; holds exporting and importing seminars. Operates extensive library of research information and government data, and records legal precedents. **Awards:** Lifetime Achievement. **Frequency:** annual. **Type:** recognition. **Recipient:** for members ● Trade Warrior. **Frequency:** annual. **Type:** recognition. **Recipient:** for contributions to the global trade. **Computer Services:** Electronic publishing, International Trade Alert. **Telecommunication Services:** electronic mail, hnorthcott@aaei.org. **Committees:** Chemicals and Bulk; Chemicals and Bulk Commodities; Customs Policy and Procedures; Drawback; Export Barriers and Restrictions; Export Compliance and Facilitation; Land Border Operations; Membership Services and Education; Regulated Industries; Textiles, Apparel and Footwear; Trade Policy; Western Regional. **Formerly:** (1967) National Council of American Importers; (1981) American Importers Association. **Publications:** *International Trade Alert*, weekly. Newsletter. Reports on government and trade issues as they affect importers and exporters. Includes news of the status of various imported and exported products. **Price:** free for members; $625.00/year for those not qualified for membership ● Newsletter, weekly ● Newsletter, quarterly ● Also publishes broad range of import/export-related documents. **Conventions/Meetings:** semiannual Trade Conference and Exhibition for Exporters and Importers - conference and workshop (exhibits) - always fall/winter.

2298 ■ American Importers Association of the United States (AIAUS)
214 7th St. N
Safety Harbor, FL 34695
Ph: (727)204-8500
Fax: (727)726-0166
E-mail: info@americanimporters.org
URL: http://www.americanimporters.org
Contact: Phillip W. Byrd, Dir. Gen.

Founded: 1999. **Members:** 13,000. **Description:** Brings exporters worldwide together with American importers and buying agents. **Computer Services:** Online services, publication. **Publications:** *AIA E-Newsletter*, monthly. Offers news, advice and tips on exporting to the United States. **Price:** free. **Circulation:** 100,000. Alternate Formats: online.

2299 ■ American-Kuwaiti Alliance (AKA)
2550 M St. NW
Washington, DC 20037
Ph: (202)429-4999
Fax: (202)429-4994
E-mail: kpulley@american-kuwaitialliance.org
URL: http://www.american-kuwaitialliance.org
Contact: Jim LeBlanc, Exec. Dir.

Founded: 2003. **Membership Dues:** founding, $100,000 ● corporate, $50,000 ● individual, non-profit company, $5,000 (annual). **Multinational. Description:** Aims to expand and deepen the political, commercial and cultural ties between the U.S. and Kuwait. Fosters the existing U.S.-Kuwaiti relations by facilitating expanded political relationships and policies. Promotes increased trade and commerce, and creates opportunities for American and Kuwaiti citizens to exchange cultural experiences. **Publications:** *AKAlliance News*, quarterly. Newsletter. Alternate Formats: online.

2300 ■ Business Association Italy America (BAIA)
199 Fremont St., 21st Fl.
San Francisco, CA 94105
Ph: (415)992-7454
E-mail: info@baia-network.org
URL: http://www.baia-network.org
Contact: Giorgio Ghersi, Co-Founder/Exec. Dir.

Founded: 2005. **Membership Dues:** individual, $100 (annual) ● student, $25 (annual) ● basic corporate, $250 (annual) ● bronze corporate, $500 (annual) ● silver corporate, $1,000 (annual) ● gold corporate, $3,000 (annual). **Multinational. Description:** Aims to create tangible business value between the business communities operating in the United States and Italian business interests. Provides a forum for businesses and professionals operating in the United States and in Italy. Brings open source governance to business networking based on an Open Source Governance model. **Publications:** Newsletter. **Price:** included in membership dues.

2301 ■ Canada-United States Business Association (CUSBA)
600 Renaissance Ctr., Ste.1100
Detroit, MI 48243
Ph: (313)446-7013
Fax: (313)567-2164
E-mail: cheryl.clark@international.gc.ca
URL: http://www.dfait-maeci.gc.ca/can-am/detroit/home_page/cusba-en.asp
Contact: Cheryl Clark, Coor.

Founded: 1992. **Members:** 1,000. **Staff:** 2. **Description:** Consists of supporters of business such as labor, banking, consulting, government, and academia. Promotes stronger business and trading lineages between the U.S. and Canada by providing a forum to exchange information and ideas and to build relationships. Conducts educational programs; maintains speakers' bureau, panels, and special events. **Publications:** Newsletter. **Conventions/Meetings:** quarterly meeting and lecture.

2302 ■ Czech and Slovak-U.S. Business Council
c/o Chamber of Commerce of the U.S.
1615 H St. NW
Washington, DC 20062-2000
Ph: (202)659-6000
Free: (800)638-6582
Fax: (202)463-3114
E-mail: eurasia@uschamber.com
URL: http://www.uschamber.com
Contact: Thomas J. Donohue, Pres./CEO

Founded: 1975. **Members:** 30. **Membership Dues:** regular, $5,000 (annual). **Staff:** 6. **Description:** Executives of firms having significant actual or potential trade involvement with the Czech Republic and Slovakia. Trilateral council of U.S., Czech, and Slovak companies. Provides a forum for discussing trade and investment issues and formulation of policy issues to promote and expand economic relations between the U.S., the Czech Republic, and Slovakia. **Libraries: Type:** not open to the public. **Holdings:** articles, books, periodicals. **Subjects:** international trade, investment. **Formerly:** (1993) Czechoslovak-U.S. Economic Council; (1998) Czech and Slovak-U.S. Economic Council. **Conventions/Meetings:** periodic conference and convention.

2303 ■ Emergency Committee for American Trade (ECAT)
1211 Connecticut Ave. NW, Ste.801
Washington, DC 20036
Ph: (202)659-5147
Fax: (202)659-1347
E-mail: info@ecattrade.com
URL: http://www.ecattrade.com
Contact: Calman J. Cohen, Pres.

Founded: 1967. **Members:** 60. **Membership Dues:** U.S. international firm, $12,500 (annual). **Staff:** 4. **Description:** Represents major United States corporations. Supports liberal international trade and investment policies and opposes legislation restricting trade and investment, such as import quotas and capital controls. **Publications:** *Membership List*, periodic. Membership Directory. **Conventions/Meetings:** annual meeting - always March.

2304 ■ Engineering Export Promotion Council of India (EEPCI)
Kensington Bus. Center
1601 Feehanville Dr., Ste.200
Mount Prospect, IL 60056
Ph: (312)236-2162
Fax: (312)236-4625
E-mail: eepcchicago@worldnet.att.net
Contact: Mr. Ashish Mehra, Dir.

Founded: 1968. **Members:** 7,000. **Description:** Manufacturers of engineering products in India. Aids members in sales and product promotion, marketing research, advertising, and importation of engineering products into the Canadian and American markets. Provides service to importers in the U.S. on the selection and choice of products from India. **Formerly:** (1998) Engineering Export Promotion Council. **Publications:** *Directory of Indian Engineering Exporters*, triennial. Lists companies in India involved in the export of engineering goods. **Price:** $25.00/copy ● *Indian Engineering Exporter*, quarterly. Journal ● *Turnkey Offers From India*, biennial. Directory. Lists companies in India involved in international projects. **Price:** free.

2305 ■ Global Offset and Countertrade Association (GOCA)
818 Connecticut Ave. NW, 12th Fl.
Washington, DC 20006
Ph: (202)887-9011
Fax: (202)872-8324
E-mail: goca@globaloffset.org
URL: http://www.globaloffset.org
Contact: Mary O. Fromyer, Exec. Dir.

Founded: 1986. **Members:** 100. **Membership Dues:** regular, associate, $450 (annual). **Multinational. Description:** Promotes trade and commerce between companies and their foreign customers who engage in reciprocal trade, including offset and countertrade, as a form of doing business. **Formerly:** (2005) American Countertrade Association. **Publications:** *ACA Newsletter*, periodic. Includes calendar of events. **Price:** included in membership dues. **Conventions/Meetings:** annual convention ● semiannual meeting - always spring and fall in various locations.

2306 ■ Joint Industry Group (JIG)
1620 I St. NW, Ste.615
Washington, DC 20006
Ph: (202)466-5490
Fax: (202)463-8498
E-mail: jig@moinc.com
URL: http://www.jig.org
Contact: James B. Clawson, Sec.
Founded: 1976. **Members:** 160. **Membership Dues:** primary, $700 (annual). **Staff:** 3. **Budget:** $60,000. **National Groups:** 6. **Description:** Trade associations and business and professional firms engaged in international trade. Seeks to influence administration of customs and related trade laws to facilitate trade and encourage compliance. **Awards:** Excellence in Government Award. **Frequency:** annual. **Type:** recognition. **Recipient:** to a government employee working in customs trade area who displays excellence in government service. **Publications:** *JIG News*, monthly. Newsletter. **Price:** free. **Circulation:** 160 ● Newsletter, weekly. **Price:** free for members. **Conventions/Meetings:** annual meeting.

2307 ■ National Association of Export Companies (NEXCO)
c/o Ms. Gerri Cristantiello, Exec. Dir.
P.O Box 3949
Grand Central Sta.
New York, NY 10163
Free: (877)291-4901
Fax: (646)349-9628
E-mail: director@nexco.org
URL: http://www.cmiregistration.com/user/splash.jxp?org=191
Contact: Ms. Gerri Cristantiello, Exec. Dir.
Founded: 1963. **Members:** 300. **Membership Dues:** basic, $95 (annual) ● corporate, $395 (annual) ● sponsor, $1,000 (annual). **Staff:** 2. **Languages:** English, French, Spanish. **Description:** Established independent international trade firms, bilateral chambers of commerce, banks, law firms, accounting firms, trade associations, insurance companies, and product/service providers; export trading companies; export management companies. Promotes expansion of U.S. trade. Promotes the participation of members in international trade. Conducts educational programs. **Computer Services:** database, exporters and importers internationally. **Committees:** Curriculum; Membership. **Conventions/Meetings:** monthly seminar.

2308 ■ National Association of Foreign-Trade Zones (NAFTZ)
1001 Connecticut Ave. NW, Ste.350
Washington, DC 20036
Ph: (202)331-1950
Fax: (202)331-1994
E-mail: info@naftz.org
URL: http://www.naftz.org
Contact: Sam Aucoin, Dir.
Founded: 1973. **Members:** 700. **Membership Dues:** active, $1,150 (annual) ● inactive, $650 (annual) ● sustaining and educational, $250 (annual). **Staff:** 4. **Budget:** $600,000. **Description:** Foreign-trade zone grantees, operators, and users; law firms, automobile manufacturers, port authorities, customs brokers, industrial firms, chambers of commerce, magazine and newspaper firms, development corporations, and concerned individuals. Aims to promote, stimulate, and improve foreign-trade zones and their utilization as integral and valuable tools in the international commerce of the U.S; to encourage the establishment of foreign-trade zones to foster investment and the creation of jobs in the US. Sponsors seminars. **Publications:** *FTZs: A Positive Force in Trade and Economic Development*. Booklet. Provides answers to commonly asked questions about FTZs. **Price:** $3.00 for members; $4.00 for nonmembers ● *The Impact of Foreign Trade Zones on the 50 States and Puerto Rico*. Report. Provides a state-by-state breakdown of foreign trade zone activity. **Price:** $50.00/copy ● *U.S. Foreign Trade Zones*. Brochure. Contains information on the many advantages of FTZs. **Price:** $1.00 for members; $2.00 for nonmembers ● *Zones Report*, periodic. Newsletter. **Conventions/Meetings:** annual conference and seminar (exhibits).

2309 ■ National Customs Brokers and Forwarders Association of America (NCBFAA)
1200 18th St. NW, No. 901
Washington, DC 20036
Ph: (202)466-0222
Fax: (202)466-0226
E-mail: staff@ncbfaa.org
URL: http://www.ncbfaa.org
Contact: Barbara Reilly, Exec. VP
Founded: 1897. **Members:** 700. **Membership Dues:** regular, $36-$57 (annual) ● affiliate (based on number of employees), $550-$1,650 (annual) ● associate, $220 (annual). **Staff:** 5. **Budget:** $1,100,000. **Regional Groups:** 34. **Description:** Treasury-licensed customs brokers, FMC-licensed independent ocean freight forwarders, and CNS-registered air cargo agents; associate members in 25 foreign countries. Seeks to maintain high standards of business practice throughout the industry. Monitors legislative and regulatory issues affecting customs brokers and forwarders; conducts seminars on new developments and techniques in the industry; provides forum for exchange among brokers and forwarders. Conducts educational programs. **Awards: Frequency:** annual. **Type:** scholarship. **Telecommunication Services:** electronic mail, br@ncbfaa.org. **Committees:** Freight Forwarding; Legislative; Regulatory Agencies. **Formerly:** (1922) Customs Clerks Association of the Port of New York; (1948) New York Customs Brokers Association; (1962) Customs Brokers and Forwarders Association of America. **Publications:** *NCBFAA Bulletin*, quarterly. Newsletter. Reports on legislation, regulation, and tax codes affecting the industry. **Price:** available to members only. **Advertising:** accepted ● *NCBFAA Membership Directory: The Who's Who of American Customs Brokers and International Freight Forwarders*, annual. **Price:** $30.00 for members in U.S.; $35.00 in Canada; $15.00 additional copy for members. **Advertising:** accepted. **Conventions/Meetings:** annual conference (exhibits) - always in April ● annual Government Affairs Conference - meeting - always September in Washington, DC.

2310 ■ North America-Mongolia Business Council (NAMBC)
1015 Duke St.
Alexandria, VA 22314
Ph: (703)549-8444
Fax: (703)549-6526
E-mail: hqinfo@nambc.org
URL: http://www.nambc.org
Contact: Steve Saunders, Pres.
Founded: 1990. **Membership Dues:** corporate (based on annual revenue), $750-$4,000 (annual) ● individual US or Canadian citizen in North America, $750 (annual) ● not-for-profit organization, $600 (annual) ● Mongolian corporate (based on annual revenue), $450-$12,000 (annual) ● individual Mongolian citizen, $450 (annual) ● Mongolian not-for-profit organization, $300 (annual) ● Mongolian associate, $150 (annual). **Multinational. Description:** Aims to promote business, trade, investment and technical cooperation between Mongolia and North America. Serves as a source of information for U.S. legislators and policy-makers influencing the direction of policy affecting Mongolia. Encourages and assists in the formation of joint ventures involving North American and Mongolian companies.

2311 ■ North American Importers Association (NAIA)
Empire State Bldg.
350 5th Ave., Manhattan
New York, NY 10118
Ph: (716)989-4234
Fax: (209)436-3820
E-mail: info@usacan.org
URL: http://www.usacan.org
Contact: Angela Wylie, Contact
Members: 47,500. **Multinational. Description:** Serves as a sales representation program for importer members. Enhances the flow of quality merchandise allowing consumers to sample for themselves the different levels of quality among diverse cultures. Facilitates communication and cooperation among members.

2312 ■ Overseas Sales and Marketing Association of America (OSMA)
1S132 Summit Ave., Ste.202D
Oakbrook Terrace, IL 60181-3940
Ph: (630)424-0600
Fax: (630)424-0605
E-mail: cfexport@yahoo.com
Founded: 1964. **Members:** 35. **Staff:** 2. **Description:** Export management and export trading companies. Serves the common interests of independent exporters. Seeks to uphold high standards of professional conduct in the field. Serves as forum for the exchange of views and concerns; acts as clearinghouse for contacts with manufacturers, industry groups, overseas buyers, and government agencies. **Publications:** Membership Directory, periodic. **Conventions/Meetings:** periodic meeting.

2313 ■ Small Business Exporters Association of the United States (SBEA)
c/o James Morrison, Pres.
1156 15th St. NW, Ste.1100
Washington, DC 20005
Ph: (202)659-9320
Free: (800)345-6728
Fax: (202)872-8543
E-mail: info@sbea.org
URL: http://www.sbea.org
Contact: James Morrison, Pres.
Founded: 1937. **Members:** 150,000. **Membership Dues:** company (1-5 employees), $200 (annual) ● company (6-10 employees), $250 (annual) ● company (11-20 employees), $500 (annual) ● company (21-50 employees), $800 (annual) ● company (51-100 employees), $1,300 (annual) ● company (101-250 employees), $2,500 (annual) ● company (251-500 employees), $5,500 (annual). **Staff:** 2. **Description:** Exporters with fewer than 500 employees, banks, insurance underwriters, carriers, custom brokers, trade associations, trade clubs, researchers, students, and individuals employed by federal or state agencies. Promotes interests of small and mid-size export companies. Informs public and governmental agencies of small business concerns and issues. Disseminates information to members on legislation that influences small export companies. Offers information on marketplace opportunities. Conducts educational and research programs. Operates extensive, interactive website. **Libraries: Type:** not open to the public. **Awards:** Export Enhancement Awards. **Frequency:** annual. **Type:** recognition. **Computer Services:** database ● online services. **Committees:** Banking and Finance; Electronic Data; Export Regulations; Government Affairs; Marketing; Research. **Formerly:** (2004) Small Business Exporters Association. **Publications:** *SBEA Update*, periodic. Newsletter. Contains news for exporters. **Price:** available to members only. Alternate Formats: online ● Brochure. Alternate Formats: online. **Conventions/Meetings:** annual meeting ● periodic seminar ● periodic trade show.

2314 ■ Swiss-American Business Council (SABC)
PO Box 641724
Chicago, IL 60601
Ph: (312)498-7285
E-mail: director@sabcnow.com
URL: http://www.sabcnow.com
Contact: Andre C. Frieden, Exec. Dir.
Founded: 1999. **Membership Dues:** corporate, $300 (annual) ● individual, $110 (annual) ● full-time student, $45 (annual). **Multinational. Description:** Focuses on strengthening transatlantic business and technology partnerships. Assists companies, trade groups, entrepreneurs and professionals to expand opportunities in regional, national and transatlantic commerce. Provides information resources and networking opportunities designed to enhance business partnerships, trade and research collaboration.

Publications: *SABC Business & Technology Directory*. **Price:** included in membership dues. **Advertising:** accepted ● Newsletter, quarterly. **Price:** included in membership dues.

2315 ■ U.S.-Bahrain Business Council (USBBC)
c/o Selma Habib, Exec. Dir.
1615 H St. NW
Washington, DC 20062
Ph: (202)463-5401
Fax: (202)463-3114
E-mail: info@usbahrainbusiness.org
URL: http://www.usbahrainbusiness.org
Contact: Selma Habib, Exec. Dir.
Founded: 2006. **Membership Dues:** corporate, $5,000 (annual) ● associate corporate, $3,000 (annual) ● affiliate, $1,000 (annual). **Multinational. Description:** Serves as a platform for fostering business to business relationships between American and Bahraini entrepreneurs. Advances the bilateral commercial relations between the United States and the Kingdom of Bahrain. Provides an international forum where public and private sector stockholders can address bilateral business relations.

2316 ■ U.S.-Cuba Trade Association (USCTA)
2300 M St. NW, Ste.800
Washington, DC 20037
Ph: (202)530-5236
Fax: (202)293-3083
E-mail: kjones@uscuba.org
URL: http://www.uscuba.org
Contact: Kirby Jones, Pres./Founder
Membership Dues: corporate, $1,500-$2,000 (annual) ● state government agency, trade association, $1,000 (annual) ● educational, non-profit, $500 (annual). **Multinational. Description:** Works on behalf of U.S. business members to protect the current trade and to expand and increase the potential for future business between the United States and Cuba. Provides the U.S. business community with information on all issues surrounding trade and business between the United States and Cuba. Promotes the full normalization of commercial relations between the United States and Cuba. Helps U.S. companies understand and know how to undertake business in Cuba. **Telecommunication Services:** electronic mail, info@uscuba.org. **Publications:** Newsletter, monthly. Includes business and political events related to Cuba. **Price:** included in membership dues.

2317 ■ U.S.-Kazakhstan Business Association (USKBA)
1200 G St. NW, Ste.827
Washington, DC 20005
Ph: (202)434-8791
Fax: (202)638-3040
E-mail: exdir@uskba.net
URL: http://www.uskba.net
Contact: William C. Veale, Exec. Dir.
Founded: 1999. **Multinational. Description:** Maintains an ongoing liaison with Kazakhstani government officials in the U.S. and in Kazakhstan to provide the appropriate forum for visiting Kazakhstani officials. Facilitates a forum for the exchange of views and information on business matters between the business and government leaders of both the United States and Kazakhstan. Provides communications to all members regarding business opportunities and business conditions in Kazakhstan. **Publications:** *The Snow Leopard*, quarterly. Newsletter. Alternate Formats: online.

2318 ■ United States-New Zealand Council (USNZC)
DACOR Bacon House
1801 F St. NW
Washington, DC 20006
Ph: (202)842-0772
Fax: (202)842-0749
E-mail: info@usnzcouncil.org
URL: http://www.usnzcouncil.org
Contact: John E. Mullen, Pres.
Founded: 1986. **Staff:** 2. **Description:** Corporations, nonprofit organizations, trade groups, and individuals interested in strengthening economic ties and improving communication between the U.S. and New Zealand. Seeks to enhance the climate for trade and investment, research, and public understanding. Serves as clearinghouse for information. Conducts educational and research programs. Sponsors briefings and social events. Maintains Friends of New Zealand (subsidiary). Compiles statistics; operates speakers' bureau. **Awards: Type:** recognition ● US-NZ Torchbearer Awards. **Frequency:** periodic. **Type:** recognition. **Recipient:** for Americans and New Zealanders who promoted the relationship between the two countries. **Councils:** Joint Economic. **Publications:** *Council Snapshot* ● *New Zealand in the News*, monthly. Contains news summaries and analysis. ● *President's Report*. **Conventions/Meetings:** periodic Council Roundtable - meeting ● meeting.

2319 ■ US-China Business Council (USCBC)
1818 N St. NW, Ste.200
Washington, DC 20036-2470
Ph: (202)429-0340
Fax: (202)775-2476
E-mail: info@uschina.org
URL: http://www.uschina.org
Contact: Mr. John Frisbie, Pres.
Founded: 1973. **Members:** 220. **Staff:** 21. **Description:** Represents American companies trading with and investing in the People's Republic of China (PRC). Established to facilitate the development of U.S.-China business relations. Provides representation, practical assistance, and up-to-date information to members. Provides business advisory services and sponsors briefings on China trade and investment subjects for member firms. Maintains offices in Washington, DC, in Beijing, and Shanghai. **Telecommunication Services:** electronic mail, jfrisbie@uschina.org. **Formerly:** (1988) National Council for US-China Trade. **Publications:** *China Business Review*, bimonthly. Magazine. Provides information and statistics on the development of China's economy, international trade, business practices, planning, and regulations. **Price:** $149.00/year in U.S. and Canada; $199.00/year, international airmail. ISSN: 0163-7169. **Circulation:** 4,000. **Advertising:** accepted. Alternate Formats: microform; online ● *China Market Intelligence*, weekly. Newsletter. Covers current business and legislative developments in the U.S. and China; includes market opportunities and calendar of events. **Price:** free, for members only. **Circulation:** 2,200. Alternate Formats: online.

Internet

2320 ■ Virtual Private Network Consortium (VPNC)
127 Segre Pl.
Santa Cruz, CA 95060
Ph: (831)426-9827
E-mail: paul.hoffman@vpnc.org
URL: http://www.vpnc.org
Contact: Paul Hoffman, Contact
Founded: 1999. **Members:** 30. **Membership Dues:** corporate, $4,000 (annual). **Multinational. Description:** Promotes the products of its members to the press and to potential customers through publicity and support for interoperability testing events. Increases interoperability between members by demonstrating where the products interoperate. Serves as a forum for the manufacturers and service providers throughout the world. Helps the press and potential customers understand VPN technologies and standards. **Computer Services:** database, documentation profiles ● information services, downloadable certification software, VPN protocols ● mailing lists, of members and working group. **Working Groups:** IKEv2 Mobility and Multihoming; IP Security; IP Security Policy; Layer 3 Virtual Private Networks; Layer 2 Virtual Private Networks; Profiling Use of PKI in IPsec; Pseudo Wire Emulation Edge to Edge. **Publications:** Reports. Serves as a product documentation profile for members. Alternate Formats: online ● Papers. Alternate Formats: online.

2321 ■ VON Coalition
c/o Beverly Orr, Exec. Admin.
1718 M St. NW
PMB No. 336
Washington, DC 20036
Ph: (202)387-5282
Fax: (202)387-5319
E-mail: beverly321@gmail.com
URL: http://www.von.org
Contact: Beverly Orr, Exec. Admin.
Founded: 1996. **Membership Dues:** smaller company with annual sales less than $500 million, $10,000 (annual) ● company with sales of more than $500 million but less than $1 billion, $15,000 (annual) ● larger company with annual sales of $1 billion or more, $25,000 (annual) ● sponsor, $20,000 (annual) ● participating, $6,000 (annual). **Description:** Represents service and software providers and equipment manufacturers. Educates policy makers, regulators and the media about net opportunities, technologies, products, benefits and practices. Recommends actions on regulation and legislation that affects the interests of voice on the net industry. Provides a forum and encourages exchange of ideas on matters relevant to voice on the net industry. **Telecommunication Services:** electronic mail, beverly@essential.org. **Publications:** Magazine. Contains news and other articles about VoIP technology. **Price:** free in U.S. and Canada; $49.00/year for outside U.S. and Canada. Alternate Formats: online.

Investigation

2322 ■ Council of International Investigators (CII)
2150 N 107th St., Ste.205
Seattle, WA 98133-9009
Ph: (206)361-8889
Free: (888)759-8884
Fax: (206)367-8777
E-mail: office@cii2.org
URL: http://www.cii2.org
Contact: Jay L. Groob, Chm.
Founded: 1955. **Members:** 300. **Membership Dues:** certified, associate, affiliate, qualified, $100 (annual). **Staff:** 1. **Budget:** $30,000. **Multinational. Description:** Represents licensed and accredited professional private investigators and detectives in 28 countries. Conducts seminars on investigation, security work, criminology, and lie detection. **Awards:** International Investigator of the Year Award. **Frequency:** annual. **Type:** recognition ● Malcolm Thomson Memorial Medal. **Frequency:** annual. **Type:** recognition. **Telecommunication Services:** electronic mail, information@cii2.org ● electronic mail, aisjlg@aol.com. **Committees:** Audit & Finance; Education/Conference; Historian; International Investigator of the Year; Legislative; Membership; Parliamentary; Public Relations Nominating; Publications; Research and Development; Strategic Plan. **Publications:** *Focus International*, 3/year. Newsletter. **Circulation:** 450. **Advertising:** accepted ● *International Councilor*, bimonthly. Newsletter. **Price:** available to members only. Alternate Formats: online ● *Roster/Membership*, annual. Membership Directory. **Price:** available to members only. **Conventions/Meetings:** semiannual conference and seminar (exhibits).

2323 ■ International Security and Detective Alliance (ISDA)
Address Unknown since 2007
Founded: 1984. **Members:** 600. **Membership Dues:** lifetime, $250. **Staff:** 1. **Multinational. Description:** Honors society for private investigation and security professionals, and is also open to writers, researchers, military personnel, and related professions. **Computer Services:** Information services ● mailing lists. **Absorbed:** (1988) United States Private Security and Detective Association. **Conventions/Meetings:** periodic meeting.

2324 ■ ION
4548 Jones Rd.
Oak Harbor, WA 98277
Ph: (360)279-8343
Free: (800)338-3463

Fax: (360)279-8343
E-mail: webreq@ioninc.com
URL: http://www.ioninc.com
Contact: Leroy E. Cook, Pres.
Founded: 1987. **Members:** 400. **Membership Dues:** individual, $150 (annual). **Staff:** 3. **Languages:** English, French. **For-Profit. Description:** Private investigators, insurance claims investigators, information vendors, and journalists. Provides international referral service for hiring. **Additional Websites:** http://www.investigatorsanywhere.com. **Also Known As:** Investigators Anywhere Resource Line. **Formerly:** Investigative Open Network. **Publications:** *IONIQUE*, bimonthly. Newsletter. **Conventions/Meetings:** annual meeting, focus group.

2325 ■ National Association of Investigative Specialists (NAIS)
PO Box 82148
Austin, TX 78708
Ph: (512)719-3595
Fax: (512)719-3594
E-mail: rthomas007@aol.com
URL: http://www.pimall.com/nais
Contact: Ralph D. Thomas, Dir.
Founded: 1984. **Members:** 4,000. **Membership Dues:** regular, $85 (biennial). **Staff:** 5. **Languages:** English, Spanish. **For-Profit. Description:** Private investigators, automobile repossessors, bounty hunters, and law enforcement officers. Promotes professionalism and provides for information exchange among private investigators. Lobbies for investigative regulations. Offers training programs and issues certificates of completion. Sponsors charitable programs; compiles statistics; maintains speakers' bureau and placement service. Operates Investigators' Hall of Fame of Private Investigators. Offers seminars on cassette tape. **Libraries: Type:** reference. **Holdings:** 700; archival material, biographical archives. **Awards: Type:** recognition. **Recipient:** to outstanding investigators. **Computer Services:** database, members, sources, and research services ● mailing lists. **Committees:** Bounty Hunting; Computer/Database Records; Computer Research; Insurance Fraud; Legal Investigation; Licensing; Physical Surveillance; Skip Trace Missing Persons. **Formerly:** (1984) International Association Private Investigators. **Publications:** *How to Find Anyone Anywhere: Secret Sources and Techniques for Locating Missing Persons*, annual. Manual. Contains statistics, book reviews, directory of computer banks, and lists of organizations. **Price:** $35.00/issue. **Circulation:** 10,000. Alternate Formats: CD-ROM ● *How to Investigate by Computer* ● *Physical Surveillance Training Manual*, annual. Reports on conducting physical surveillance, writing a legally correct surveillance report, obtaining legal evidence, presenting evidence in court. **Price:** $35.00. **Circulation:** 7,000 ● *Private Investigator's Catalog*, bimonthly. Lists books, services, and products available through the association. **Price:** $5.00/copy. **Circulation:** 30,000. **Advertising:** accepted ● *Private Investigator's Connection*, bimonthly. Newsletter. Includes trends, sources, services, and business opportunities for private investigative/security professionals; also contains membership news. **Price:** included in membership dues. **Circulation:** 4,000. **Advertising:** accepted. Alternate Formats: online. **Conventions/Meetings:** annual PI Super Conference - convention (exhibits).

2326 ■ National Association of Legal Search Consultants (NALSC)
1525 N Park Dr., Ste.102
Weston, FL 33326
Ph: (954)349-4428
Free: (866)902-6587
Fax: (954)349-1979
E-mail: info@nalsc.org
URL: http://www.nalsc.org
Contact: Marina Sirras, Pres.
Founded: 1984. **Members:** 181. **Membership Dues:** firm ($150 per year for additional office), $595 (annual) ● affiliate, $395 (annual) ● supporting, $500 (annual). **Staff:** 2. **Description:** Legal search firms. Promotes and represents members' interests. Conducts educational programs; maintains speakers' bureau. **Computer Services:** Mailing lists, of members. **Committees:** Ethics. **Publications:** *NALSC Code of Ethics*. Alternate Formats: online ● Brochure ● Directory, annual. **Price:** included in membership dues ● Newsletter, quarterly. **Price:** included in membership dues. Alternate Formats: online. **Conventions/Meetings:** annual board meeting and conference.

2327 ■ World Investigators Network
c/o Mrs. Carolyn Ward, Exec. Dir.
7501 Sparrows Point Blvd.
Baltimore, MD 21219
Ph: (410)477-8879
Free: (888)946-6389
Fax: (410)388-0846
E-mail: worldinvestigators@comcast.net
URL: http://worldinvestigatorsnetwork.com
Contact: Mrs. Carolyn Ward, Exec. Dir.
Founded: 1996. **Members:** 350. **Membership Dues:** regular, $175 (annual). **Staff:** 1. **Budget:** $50,000. **Multinational. Description:** Investigators and security professionals. Seeks to promote cooperation of those in the profession. Conducts educational programs. Maintains speakers' bureau. **Awards:** Area Governor of the Year Award. **Frequency:** annual. **Type:** recognition. **Recipient:** for area governors ● Investigator of the Year. **Frequency:** annual. **Type:** recognition. **Recipient:** for investigators ● The Jack Henebry Professional of the Year Award. **Frequency:** annual. **Type:** recognition. **Recipient:** for members ● Security Professional of the Year. **Frequency:** annual. **Type:** recognition. **Recipient:** for security professionals. **Publications:** *The W.I.N. Communicator*, bimonthly. Newsletter. **Price:** included in membership dues. **Circulation:** 900. **Advertising:** accepted. Alternate Formats: CD-ROM; online; magnetic tape ● Membership Directory. **Price:** included in membership dues. **Conventions/Meetings:** annual conference ● annual Mid-Year Meeting.

Investments

2328 ■ Association of Foreign Investors in Real Estate (AFIRE)
Ronald Reagan Bldg.
1300 Pennsylvania Ave. NW
Washington, DC 20004
Ph: (202)312-1400
Fax: (202)312-1401
E-mail: afireinfo@afire.org
URL: http://www.afire.org
Contact: James A. Fetgatter, Chief Exec.
Founded: 1988. **Members:** 150. **Membership Dues:** associate, supporting, $9,000 (annual) ● institutional, $7,500 (annual). **Staff:** 3. **Budget:** $1,000,000. **Multinational. Description:** Foreign institutions with investment interests in the U.S; domestic firms that manage and advise real estate investment accounts of foreign investors; accounting and law firms with offices overseas. Encourages foreign real estate investment in the U.S. Informs the public of the benefits of foreign investment; disseminates information. **Formerly:** (2000) Association of Foreign Investors in U.S. Real Estate. **Publications:** *AFIRE News*, bimonthly. Newsletter. Includes articles on real estate investing, market trends and tax and legal issues. **Price:** available to members only. Alternate Formats: online ● *Annual Meeting Digest*, annual. Report ● Membership Directory. **Conventions/Meetings:** annual conference - every winter ● annual conference - every spring ● annual European Conference ● annual meeting and seminar.

2329 ■ Association of Investment Management Sales Executives (AIMSE)
1320 19th St. NW, Ste.300
Washington, DC 20036-1636
Ph: (202)296-3560
Free: (800)343-5659
Fax: (202)371-8977
E-mail: nkraich@tkgllc.org
URL: http://www.aimse.com
Contact: Norbert Kraich, Exec. Dir.
Founded: 1977. **Members:** 1,414. **Membership Dues:** active, $250 (annual) ● associate, $350 (annual). **Staff:** 3. **Budget:** $1,100,000. **Description:** Represents investment management sales executives. Aims to foster professionalism of the investment sales industry. Educates members to improve skills that will change the marketplace. **Publications:** *Advisor*, quarterly. Newsletter. Contains current issues and activities. Alternate Formats: online.

2330 ■ Center for Venture Research (CVR)
Univ. of New Hampshire
Whittemore School of Bus. and Economics
15 Coll. Rd.
Durham, NH 03824-3593
Ph: (603)862-3885
Fax: (603)862-4468
E-mail: jeff.sohl@unh.edu
URL: http://wsbe2.unh.edu/center-venture-research
Contact: Jeffrey E. Sohl, Dir.
Founded: 1986. **Description:** Encourages and conducts research into methods of financing new technology-based industries and firms.

2331 ■ CFA Institute
560 Ray C. Hunt Dr.
Charlottesville, VA 22903-2981
Ph: (434)951-5499
Free: (800)247-8132
Fax: (434)951-5262
E-mail: info@cfainstitute.org
URL: http://www.cfainstitute.org
Contact: Jeffrey J. Diermeier CFA, Pres./CEO
Founded: 1990. **Members:** 68,500. **Membership Dues:** charterholder, regular, affiliate (membership activated between July 1 to December 31), $225 (annual) ● charterholder, regular, affiliate (membership activated between January 1 to March 31), $113 (annual). **Staff:** 230. **Multinational. Description:** Security and financial analyst association whose members are practicing investment analysts. Includes private, voluntary self-regulation program in which members are enrolled. Internationally renowned for its rigorous Chartered Financial Analyst curriculum and examination program, which has more than 86,000 candidates from 143 countries enrolled for exams. In addition, it is internationally recognized for its investment performance standards, which investment firms use to document and report investment results, as well as for its Code of Ethics and Standards of Professional Conduct. **Awards:** Society Leader Award. **Frequency:** annual. **Type:** recognition. **Recipient:** for a member who has served the investment community by using innovative ideas to advance the interests of CFA Institute Member Societies. **Computer Services:** Mailing lists, of members. **Committees:** Candidate Curriculum. **Councils:** Examiners. **Divisions:** Advocacy; Curriculum and Examinations; Educational Programs; Finance Operations; Member: Candidate Services; Standard Setting. **Formed by Merger of:** (1990) Institute of Chartered Financial Analysts; (1990) Financial Analysts Federation. **Formerly:** (2004) Association for Investment Management and Research. **Publications:** *AIMR Annual Report*. **Price:** free. Alternate Formats: online ● *AIMR Exchange*, bimonthly. Newsletter. **Price:** $25.00 ● *AIMR Membership Directory*, annual. **Price:** $150.00/year ● *AIMR Standards of Practice Handbook* ● *CFA Candidate Study and Examination Program Brochure* ● *CFA Digest*, quarterly. **Price:** $40.00. Alternate Formats: online ● *CFA Magazine*, bimonthly. **Price:** free for members; $75.00 /year for nonmembers ● *Financial Analysts Journal*, bimonthly. **Price:** $150.00/year; $25.00/issue. **Advertising:** accepted ● *Research Foundation Monographs*, 5/year. **Price:** $75.00/year; $20.00 each ● *Seminar Proceedings*, 4-6/year. **Price:** $100.00/year ● *Society Programs*, quarterly. **Price:** $45.00/year. **Conventions/Meetings:** annual conference.

2332 ■ Chartered Alternative Investment Analyst Association (CAIA)
29 S Pleasant St.
Amherst, MA 01002

Ph: (413)253-7373
Fax: (413)253-4494
E-mail: info@caia.org
URL: http://www.caia.org
Contact: E. Craig Asche, Exec. Dir.
Founded: 2002. **Multinational. Description:** Seeks to establish the Chartered Alternative Investment Analyst designation as the educational standard for the alternative investment industry. Advocates for high standards of professional conduct in the field of alternative investment analysis. Promotes professional development through continuous education. Facilitates communication among industry professionals. **Publications:** *Journal of Alternative Investments*. Covers topics on asset allocation, risk management, indexing, regulation and taxation. Also Cited As: *JAI* ● Bibliography. Contains a compilation of alternative investment research abstracts. Alternate Formats: online.

2333 ■ Hedge Fund Association (HFA)
2875 NE 191st St., Ste.900
Aventura, FL 33180
Ph: (202)478-2000
Fax: (202)478-1999
E-mail: info@thehfa.org
URL: http://www.thehfa.org
Contact: David Friedland, Pres.
Founded: 1996. **Membership Dues:** individual, $1,000 (annual) ● manager, $100 (annual). **Multinational. Description:** Hedge fund managers, service providers, and investors. Strives to promote awareness and opportunities in hedge funds. Lobbies to ensure all investors have access to hedge funds. **Formerly:** (1998) Fund of Funds Association.

2334 ■ Independent Investor Protective League (IIPL)
PO Box 5031
Fort Lauderdale, FL 33310
Ph: (954)749-1551
Fax: (954)749-1553
Contact: Merrill Sands, Exec. VP
Founded: 1970. **Members:** 3,000. **Membership Dues:** open, $5 (annual). **Description:** Seeks to protect small investors by referring them to proper agencies or by taking independent action on their behalf. **Conventions/Meetings:** annual meeting.

2335 ■ International Swaps and Derivatives Association (ISDA)
360 Madison Ave., 16th Fl.
New York, NY 10017
Ph: (212)901-6000
Fax: (212)901-6001
E-mail: isda@isda.org
URL: http://www.isda.org
Contact: Jonathan P. Moulds, Chm.
Founded: 1985. **Members:** 650. **Multinational. Description:** Providers and users of privately negotiated derivatives. Encourages "prudent and efficient" investment in derivatives; promotes sound risk management practices. Formulates standards of commercial conduct for the derivatives business; conducts educational programs to raise public awareness of derivatives as an investment option; serves as a forum for the discussion and analysis of derivatives investments. Makes available accounting and market practice advisory services; conducts market surveys. **Committees:** Accounting and Disclosure; Asia Pacific; Collateral; Commodity Derivatives; Documentation; Emerging Markets; Equity Derivatives; Euro; Regulatory; Risk Management; Tax; Trading Practices. **Publications:** *A Retrospective of ISDA's Activities*, annual. Annual Report. Alternate Formats: online ● *Market Survey*, periodic. Report. Alternate Formats: online. **Conventions/Meetings:** annual international conference and meeting ● annual meeting - always March ● annual meeting - always September/October ● periodic regional meeting.

2336 ■ Investment Management Consultants Association (IMCA)
5619 DTC Pkwy., Ste.500
Greenwood Village, CO 80111
Ph: (303)770-3377
Fax: (303)770-1812
E-mail: epahl@imca.org
URL: http://www.imca.org
Contact: Edythe McClatchy Pahl, Exec. Dir.
Founded: 1985. **Members:** 6,000. **Membership Dues:** individual, $395 (annual). **Staff:** 20. **Budget:** $5,000,000. **Multinational. Description:** Consultants, money managers, and others in the investment management consultant business. Purposes are to increase public awareness of investment management consultants, provide educational programs to members, and encourage high business standards. Operates consulting industry certification program. Maintains a legislative network with state and federal legislative information affecting the industry. **Awards:** IMCA Journalism Award. **Frequency:** annual. **Type:** recognition. **Recipient:** for best article in industry which impacts consultants ● Kessler Award. **Frequency:** annual. **Type:** recognition. **Recipient:** for an article written for The Monitor which best helps consultants ● The Richard J. Davis Ethics Award. **Frequency:** annual. **Type:** recognition. **Recipient:** to the author of an article that has made a significant contribution to advancing the understanding and knowledge of the investment management consulting profession in the area of ethics. **Computer Services:** Online services, publishing and education programs. **Absorbed:** (2003) Institute for Certified Investment Management Consultants. **Publications:** *Essentials of Investment Consulting*. Brochure. Contains information about investment consulting. **Price:** $600.00 for members; $700.00 for nonmembers. Alternate Formats: online ● *Ethical Considerations for Consultants*. **Price:** $12.00 for members; $22.00 for nonmembers ● *The Facts About Investing*. Booklet. **Price:** $65.00/25 copies for members; $77.00/25 copies for nonmembers; $129.00/50 copies for members; $150.00/50 copies for nonmembers ● *IMCA Practice Management Standards* ● *IMCA Reporting Standards*, semiannual ● *The Journal of Investment Consulting*, semiannual. Newsletter. **Price:** $160.00 ● *The Monitor*, bimonthly. Newsletter. Alternate Formats: online ● *Wealth Management Course*. **Price:** $39.00. Alternate Formats: online. **Conventions/Meetings:** annual conference and general assembly, for 3 days (exhibits) - spring ● annual Fall Investment Management Expo - general assembly and workshop ● quarterly Regional Consultants Conferences - regional meeting and general assembly - plus one in Canada.

2337 ■ Investment Program Association (IPA)
1140 Connecticut Ave. NW, Ste.1040
Washington, DC 20036
Ph: (202)775-9750
Fax: (202)331-8446
E-mail: contact@ipa-dc.org
URL: http://www.ipa-dc.org
Contact: John White, Exec. Dir.
Founded: 1985. **Members:** 150. **Membership Dues:** associate, $5,000 (annual). **Staff:** 5. **Budget:** $1,500,000. **Description:** Partnership sponsors and investors in energy, leasing, research and development, real estate, and communications. Aims to promote and preserve the investment partnership as a vehicle for capital formation. Compiles statistics. **Formerly:** (1990) Investment Partnership Program. **Publications:** *Technical Bulletin*, periodic. **Conventions/Meetings:** annual conference - always fall, Washington, DC ● annual convention - always spring ● seminar ● workshop.

2338 ■ Investorside Research Association (IRA)
1050 Connecticut Ave. NW, Ste.1000
Washington, DC 20036
Ph: (202)223-2769
Fax: (202)223-8647
E-mail: info@investorside.org
URL: http://www.investorside.org
Contact: John Eade, Co-Founder/Chm.
Membership Dues: associate, $200 (annual) ● certified provider, $1,000 (annual) ● founding, $7,500 (annual). **Description:** Works to increase investor and pensioner trust in U.S. capital markets system through investment research aligned with investor interests.

2339 ■ MicroComputer Investors Association (MCIA)
264 Anderson Dr.
Fredericksburg, VA 22405
Ph: (703)371-5474
E-mail: jwillie2@cox.net
URL: http://members.cox.net/jwillie2
Contact: Dr. Jack M. Williams, Admin.
Founded: 1976. **Description:** Investors utilizing microcomputers. Seeks to: share data relating to personal computer use to aid in portfolio management; assist personal computer users in examining, selecting, and keeping track of financial investments. Sponsors speakers' bureau. Compiles statistics. **Libraries: Type:** reference. **Holdings:** software. **Computer Services:** database. **Telecommunication Services:** electronic bulletin board. **Publications:** *MicroComputer Investor*, semiannual. Journal. **Conventions/Meetings:** periodic meeting ● seminar.

2340 ■ National Association of Government Defined Contribution Administrators (NAGDCA)
201 E Main St., Ste.1405
Lexington, KY 40507
Ph: (859)514-9161
Fax: (859)514-9188
E-mail: infonagdca@amrms.com
URL: http://www.nagdca.org
Contact: Mindy Harris, Pres.
Founded: 1979. **Members:** 206. **Membership Dues:** government, $600 (annual) ● industry, $900 (annual) ● associate industry, $400 (annual). **Staff:** 2. **Budget:** $160,000. **Description:** Deferred compensation administrators representing states, cities and counties; vendor firms. (Deferred compensation is payment that, usually for tax reasons, is postponed by an individual until another tax year; such payments include dividends on stocks, insurance settlements, and cash.) Encourages the exchange of information within the industry. Monitors legislation; sponsors educational programs. **Formerly:** (2003) National Association of Government Deferred Compensation Administrators. **Conventions/Meetings:** annual conference - 2008 Sept. 15-19, Baltimore, MD; 2009 Sept. 12-16, Austin, TX.

2341 ■ National Association of Investment Professionals (NAIP)
12664 Emmer Pl., Ste.201
St. Paul, MN 55124
Ph: (952)322-4322
E-mail: tokeefe@naip.com
URL: http://www.naip.com
Contact: Thomas S. O'Keefe, Founder/Pres.
Membership Dues: individual, $150 (annual). **Description:** Represents investment professionals. Enhances the image of investment professionals and promote their interests with regulators, and helps businesses grow.

2342 ■ National Association of Investors Corporation (NAIC)
PO Box 220
Royal Oak, MI 48068
Ph: (248)583-6242
Free: (877)275-6242
Fax: (248)583-4880
E-mail: service@betterinvesting.org
URL: http://www.betterinvesting.org
Contact: Bonnie Reyes, Pres./CEO
Founded: 1951. **Members:** 550,000. **Membership Dues:** individual, $50-$80 (annual) ● club, $25-$40 (annual) ● youth, $20 (annual) ● life, $875. **Staff:** 81. **Budget:** $20,000,000. **Regional Groups:** 102. **Description:** Federation of independent investment clubs ranging from 10 to 20 members each; interested individuals. Members contribute 20 dollars or more per month, which is invested in securities as a group. Has councils staffed by volunteers in 65 cities to counsel and teach investing techniques and sound

investment procedures to interested people. Operates National Association of Individual Investors to provide services and publications to individual investors who do not belong to investment clubs. Sponsors Investment Education Institute (see separate entry). Compiles annual statistics on amount of investment per month and on rate of earnings of members. Conducts educational programs regionally and nationally. **Libraries: Type:** not open to the public. **Holdings:** 300. **Subjects:** finance. **Awards:** Nicholson Award. **Frequency:** annual. **Type:** recognition. **Recipient:** for Corporation Annual Reports from the viewpoint of the individual investor. **Computer Services:** database, of programs for analysis of individual stocks. **Boards:** Computer Group Advisory; National Investors Association. **Affiliated With:** Investment Education Institute. **Formerly:** (1983) National Association of Investment Clubs. **Publications:** *Better Investing*, monthly. Magazine. Contains educational information regarding stock investing. **Price:** $24.00 /year for nonmembers; $3.00/issue for nonmembers; included in membership dues. ISSN: 0006-016X. **Circulation:** 386,000. **Advertising:** accepted ● *Better Investing Bits*, 10/year. Magazine ● *The Official Guide to Starting and Running a Profitable Investment Club*, periodic. Manual. **Conventions/Meetings:** annual competition - always August ● annual convention (exhibits).

2343 ■ National Association of Publicly Traded Partnerships (NAPTP)
1801 K St. NW, Ste.500
Washington, DC 20006
Ph: (202)973-3150 (202)973-4515
Fax: (202)973-3101
E-mail: lyman@navigantconsulting.com
URL: http://www.naptp.org
Contact: Ms. Mary Lyman, Exec. Dir.
Founded: 1983. **Members:** 65. **Membership Dues:** small PTP (with less than $400 million assets and $200 million revenue), $12,000 (annual) ● large PTP (with more than $400 million assets and $200 million revenue), $16,000 (annual) ● national investment banking firm, $11,000 (annual) ● regional investment firm (banking/law/accounting/other service firm), $6,000 (annual). **Budget:** $450,000. **Description:** Promotes the interests of publicly traded ("master") limited partnerships (PTPs or MLPs) and those who work with them. Consists of PTPs and their corporate sponsors; investment banking firms, law firms, accounting firms, other financial and service firms. Monitors congress, state legislatures, and federal and state agencies for actions and proposals affecting PTPs; lobbies on federal and state legislation related to PTPs; provides information on PTPs to investors, the press, and the general public; promotes PTPs as an investment. **Committees:** Federal Legislative; Federal Regulatory; Public Relations; State Legislative. **Formerly:** (1986) Coalition for the Equitable Treatment of Publicly Traded Limited Partnerships; (1987) Coalition of Publicly Traded Limited Partnerships; (2007) Coalition of Publicly Traded Partnerships. **Conventions/Meetings:** annual MLP Investor - conference, features presentations by PTPs to interested investors.

2344 ■ National Council of Real Estate Investment Fiduciaries (NCREIF)
2 Prudential Plz.
180 N Stetson Ave., Ste.2515
Chicago, IL 60601
Ph: (312)819-5890
Fax: (312)819-5891
E-mail: bleagle@ncreif.org
URL: http://www.ncreif.com
Contact: Anne Pfeiffer, Pres.
Founded: 1982. **Members:** 225. **Membership Dues:** voting, $20,000 (annual). **Staff:** 7. **Budget:** $1,000,000. **Description:** Promotes real estate as a viable investment vehicle for institutional investors. Formed Real Estate Research Institute, that identifies major research issues relevant to performance analysis, asset allocation, and institutional investment in real estate. Maintains a Property Index that measures institutional real estate performance. Acts as a clearinghouse for new research ideas of interest to institutional investors and investment advisors. Sponsors data submission and portfolio strategy seminars. Compiles statistics. **Libraries: Type:** not open to the public. **Holdings:** 500. **Computer Services:** database, index data. **Committees:** Accounting; Information Management; Performance Measurement; Portfolio Strategy; Research; Risk Management; Timberland; Valuation. **Publications:** *NCREIF Real Estate Performance Report*, quarterly. Provides quantitative analysis of real estate performance data. **Price:** included in membership dues; $1,000.00 /year for nonmembers ● *NCREIF Source Book*, annual. Membership Directory. **Price:** available to members only. **Conventions/Meetings:** conference - 3/year. 2008 June 18-20, Washington, DC.

2345 ■ National Investment Company Service Association (NICSA)
2 Mt. Royal Ave., 3rd Fl.
Marlborough, MA 01752
Ph: (508)485-1500
Fax: (508)485-1500
E-mail: info@nicsa.org
URL: http://www.nicsa.org
Contact: Peggy C. Schooley, Pres.
Founded: 1962. **Members:** 400. **Membership Dues:** national corporate, $3,000 (annual) ● global leader, $10,000 (annual) ● primary corporate location, $1,250 (annual) ● international corporate location, $500 (annual). **Staff:** 7. **Budget:** $2,000,000. **Description:** Mutual fund investment managers, distributors, custodians, transfer agents, accounting and legal firms, broker/dealers, and general providers of services and products to the mutual fund industry. Seeks to address future service needs and trends by providing a forum on operational and technological developments. **Awards:** NICSA/William T. Blackwell Scholarship. **Frequency:** annual. **Type:** scholarship. **Recipient:** for academic excellence ● PricewaterhouseCoopers Award. **Frequency:** annual. **Type:** recognition. **Recipient:** for service to National Investment Company Service Association ● Robert L. Gould Award. **Frequency:** annual. **Type:** recognition. **Recipient:** for service to the investment management industry. **Committees:** Alternative Investment; Annual Conference; Compliance and Risk Management; Distribution Channels; East Coast; Educational and Program Content; Fund Administration/Custody; Ireland International; Luxembourg International; Midwest; Retirement Plan Issues; Tax; Technology; Transfer Agent; West Coast. **Publications:** *Inside NICSA*, quarterly. Newsletter ● *NICSA News*, quarterly. Newsletter. Alternate Formats: online ● Annual Report, annual. **Circulation:** 4,000 ● Membership Directory, annual ● Surveys. **Conventions/Meetings:** annual conference ● annual conference ● seminar ● workshop.

2346 ■ National Investor Relations Institute (NIRI)
8020 Towers Crescent Dr., Ste.250
Vienna, VA 22182
Ph: (703)506-3570
Fax: (703)506-3571
E-mail: info@niri.org
URL: http://www.niri.org
Contact: Matthew Stroud, Chm.
Founded: 1969. **Members:** 4,900. **Membership Dues:** corporate, counselor, service provider, affiliated profession, $475 (annual) ● academic, $100 (annual). **Staff:** 21. **Budget:** $2,500,000. **Regional Groups:** 31. **Description:** Executives engaged in investor relations. Identifies the role of the investor relations practitioner; protects a free and open market with equity and access to investors of all kinds; improves communication between corporate management and shareholders, present and future. Holds professional development seminars and conducts research programs. Maintains placement service and speakers' bureau; compiles statistics. **Telecommunication Services:** electronic mail, mstroud@darden.com. **Committees:** Communications; Education; Government and Securities; Industry Affairs. **Publications:** *Executive Alert*, periodic. Bulletin ● *Investor Relations Quarterly (IRQ)*. Journal ● *IR Update*, monthly. Newsletter ● *Roster*, annual. Membership Directory ● *Standards of Practice for Investor Relations*, periodic. Booklet. **Conventions/Meetings:** annual conference (exhibits) - always June.

2347 ■ National Real Estate Investors Association (NREIA)
525 W 5th St., Ste.230
Covington, KY 41011
Ph: (859)261-3335
Free: (888)762-7342
Fax: (859)581-5993
E-mail: info@nationalreia.com
URL: http://www.nationalreia.com
Contact: Rebecca McLean, Exec. Dir.
Founded: 1986. **Members:** 40,000. **Membership Dues:** group (1 to 24 members), $125 (annual) ● group (25 to 99 members), $150 (annual) ● group (100 to 199 members), $200 (annual) ● group (200 to 299 members), $350 (annual) ● group (300 to 499 members), $500 (annual) ● group (500 to 749 members), $750 (annual) ● group (750 to 999 members), $1,000 (annual) ● group (1000 or more members), $1,500 (annual). **Staff:** 3. **Local Groups:** 230. **Description:** Local associations of real estate investors. Works to educate and support the leaders of real estate associations through training, networking, motivation and provision of benefits to their associations. Conducts educational programs; publishes resource manuals and quarterly newsletter, facilitates discussion among local REIAs. **Awards:** Award of Excellence. **Frequency:** annual. **Type:** recognition. **Recipient:** for the association that has demonstrated paramount achievement ● Honor of Merit: Community Service. **Frequency:** annual. **Type:** recognition ● Honor of Merit: Convention and Trade Show. **Frequency:** annual. **Type:** recognition ● Honor of Merit: Education. **Frequency:** annual. **Type:** recognition ● Honor of Merit: Electronic Communications. **Frequency:** annual. **Type:** recognition ● Honor of Merit: Finance. **Frequency:** annual. **Type:** recognition ● Honor of Merit: Government Affairs. **Frequency:** annual. **Type:** recognition ● Honor of Merit: Membership Development. **Frequency:** annual. **Type:** recognition ● Honor of Merit: Print Communications. **Frequency:** annual. **Type:** recognition. **Publications:** *Leader's Edge*, quarterly. Newsletter. **Advertising:** accepted. **Conventions/Meetings:** annual Mid-year - conference, three days of networking and education with the associations' proven leaders ● annual Winter Cruise - conference and trade show.

2348 ■ National Venture Capital Association (NVCA)
1655 N Ft. Myer Dr., Ste.850
Arlington, VA 22209
Ph: (703)524-2549
Fax: (703)524-3940
E-mail: mheesen@nvca.org
URL: http://www.nvca.org
Contact: Mark G. Heesen, Pres.
Founded: 1973. **Members:** 335. **Membership Dues:** organization, $1,000-$26,000 (annual). **Staff:** 10. **Budget:** $2,000,000. **Description:** Venture capital organizations, corporate financiers, and individual venture capitalists who are responsible for investing private capital in young companies on a professional basis. Fosters a broader understanding of the importance of venture capital to the vitality of the U.S. economy and to stimulate the free flow of capital to young companies. Seeks to improve communications among venture capitalists throughout the country and to improve the general level of knowledge of the venturing process in government, universities, and the business community. **Awards:** Steiger Award. **Frequency:** annual. **Type:** recognition. **Recipient:** for a person who has contributed outstanding service to the nation in the area of economic growth. **Computer Services:** Mailing lists. **Telecommunication Services:** electronic mail, gwendolyn.taylor@nvca.org. **Committees:** Incentives; Industry; International Relations; Markets; Political Action; Professional Standards; SEC. **Publications:** *National Venture Capital Association—Annual Membership Directory*. Alternate Formats: CD-ROM ● *NVCA Today*, quarterly. Provides information on current legislative and regulatory issues. **Price:** free ● *The Venture Capital*

Review, semiannual. Magazine. Includes in-depth articles analyzing meaningful trends important to the NVCA membership. **Price:** free ● Yearbook, annual. Details the state of the venture capital industry. **Price:** free for members; $225.00 for nonmembers ● Report, annual. Includes articles on the state on the venture capital industry and the accomplishments of the association during the year. **Price:** free. Alternate Formats: online. **Conventions/Meetings:** annual conference.

2349 ■ Professional Association for Investment Communications Resources (PAICR)
191 Clarksville Rd.
Princeton Junction, NJ 08550
Ph: (609)799-4382
Free: (800)562-0751
Fax: (609)799-7032
E-mail: michael.kay@paulsonco.com
URL: http://www.paicr.org
Contact: Michael Kay, Pres.
Founded: 1997. **Members:** 700. **Membership Dues:** individual, $200 (annual). **Multinational. Description:** Strives to enhance the investment industry communications through empowerment and education. **Publications:** *Points*. Newsletter. Alternate Formats: online. **Conventions/Meetings:** annual conference - 2008 Sept. 18-19, New York, NY.

2350 ■ Resourceful Women (RW)
Address Unknown since 2008
Founded: 1983. **Members:** 200. **Membership Dues:** individual, $225 (annual). **Staff:** 2. **Description:** Individuals and organizations. Promotes "positive social change by empowering and educating women to make informed choices about investing.". **Libraries: Type:** not open to the public. **Holdings:** articles, books, business records, periodicals. **Subjects:** investments, women.

2351 ■ Stable Value Investment Association (SVIA)
1025 Connecticut Ave. NW, Ste.1000
Washington, DC 20036
Ph: (202)580-7620
Fax: (202)580-7621
E-mail: info@stablevalue.org
URL: http://www.stablevalue.org
Contact: Richard Cook, Chm.
Founded: 1990. **Members:** 350. **Membership Dues:** corporate plan sponsor, $195 (annual) ● service firm, $6,000 (annual). **Staff:** 2. **Budget:** $750,000. **Description:** Pension plan sponsors, investment managers, banks, life insurance companies and consultants. Promotes retirement savings and educates individuals on the role that stable value funds can play in achieving a financially secure retirement. **Libraries: Type:** reference; not open to the public. **Holdings:** archival material, articles, clippings, monographs, periodicals. **Subjects:** stable-value asset management. **Formerly:** (1999) Stable Value Association. **Publications:** *Member Alert*, monthly. Newsletter ● Brochure ● Directory ● Monographs. **Conventions/Meetings:** annual meeting and convention ● periodic regional meeting.

Iranian

2352 ■ Iranian American Technology Council (IATC)
PO Box 123
Sterling, VA 20167-0123
Free: (800)788-7824
E-mail: info@iatc.us
Contact: Fred Korangy, Contact
Founded: 2004. **Membership Dues:** individual - student, $50 (annual) ● individual - general, $200 (annual) ● corporate, $2,500 (annual) ● corporate - premier, $15,000 (annual) ● corporate - premier plus, $35,000 (annual). **Description:** Seeks to provide Iranian American students and young professionals access to the experience, opportunities, resources and guidance of a network of well-seasoned professionals.

Islamic

2353 ■ Islamic Food and Nutrition Council of America (IFANCA)
5901 N Cicero Ave., Ste.309
Chicago, IL 60646
Ph: (773)283-3708
Fax: (773)283-3973
URL: http://www.ifanca.org
Contact: Dr. Muhammad Munir Chaudry, Pres.
Languages: English, French. **Multinational. Description:** Promotes Halal food and the institution of Halal. Certifies products in all food industries, cosmetics, meat and poultry slaughter, packaging materials and chemicals. Provides consulting on product development, marketing and quality assurance to help consumers choose authentic Halal products. **Publications:** *Halal Digest*. Newsletter. Contains articles, relevant news, recipes and other related information about Halal topics. ISSN: 1533-3361. Alternate Formats: online.

Jewelry

2354 ■ Accredited Gemologists Association (AGA)
c/o G-Force Services
3315 Juanita St.
San Diego, CA 92105
Ph: (619)501-5444
Fax: (619)286-7541
E-mail: info@accreditedgemologists.org
URL: http://accreditedgemologists.org
Contact: Joseph DuMouchelle GG, Pres.
Founded: 1974. **Members:** 143. **Membership Dues:** voting, $100 (annual) ● associate, $75 (annual) ● student, $50 (annual) ● supplier, $150 (annual). **Staff:** 2. **Budget:** $25,000. **Regional Groups:** 4. **Description:** Gemologists. Promotes the advancement of the science of gemology. Conducts research and educational programs. **Awards:** Accredited Gemologist - Antonio C. Bonnano Award. **Frequency:** annual. **Type:** monetary. **Recipient:** for outstanding achievement and contribution to gemological science. **Computer Services:** Mailing lists. **Committees:** Accredited Laboratory; Education; Ethics and Grievances; Historian; Standards and Disclosure; Website. **Publications:** *AGA Newswire*, monthly. Newsletter ● *Certified Gemological Lab Directory*, annual ● *Cornerstone*, annual. Journal. Includes timely reports on new gemstone enhancements and detection issues. **Price:** included in membership dues. Alternate Formats: online. **Conventions/Meetings:** annual conference and seminar - always February, Tucson, AZ.

2355 ■ American Diamond Industry Association (ADIA)
Address Unknown since 2008
Founded: 1982. **Members:** 3,000. **Description:** Diamond brokers, dealers, distributors, importers, and manufacturers. Purpose is to establish a continuing source of current, reliable information on diamonds in the U.S. for the press and public. Maintains speakers' bureau; compiles statistics. **Awards: Type:** recognition. **Affiliated With:** Diamond Dealers Club; Diamond Manufacturers and Importers Association of America; Diamond Trade and Precious Stone Association of America. **Publications:** *ADIA Newsletter*, 2-3/year. Discusses the American diamond industry and sources for diamonds worldwide. Includes statistics.

2356 ■ American Gem Society (AGS)
8881 W Sahara Ave.
Las Vegas, NV 89117
Ph: (702)255-6500
Free: (866)805-6500
Fax: (702)255-7420
E-mail: info@ags.org
URL: http://www.americangemsociety.org
Contact: Ruth Batson, Exec. Dir./CEO
Founded: 1934. **Members:** 4,400. **Staff:** 20. **Budget:** $5,000,000. **Regional Groups:** 23. **Description:** Represents 1,600 retail and manufacturer jewelry firms in North America dedicated to proven ethics, knowledge and consumer protection. Encourages members to pursue studies in gemology; confers titles of Registered Jeweler, Registered Supplier, Certified Gemologist, and Certified Gemologist Appraiser upon those taking recognized courses and passing extensive examinations. Sponsors national promotional programs. Conducts educational programs. **Awards:** Lifetime Achievement. **Type:** recognition ● Richard T. Liddicoat Journalism Award. **Type:** recognition ● Robert Shipley Award. **Frequency:** annual. **Type:** recognition ● Triple Zero. **Type:** recognition. **Committees:** Appraisal; Conclave; Diamond Standards; Education; Ethics; Finance; Grievance and Review; Marketing; Membership. **Publications:** *Spectra*, bimonthly. **Price:** free, for members only. **Circulation:** 4,400. **Advertising:** accepted ● Booklets ● Brochures ● Also publishes appraisal guidelines. **Conventions/Meetings:** annual International Conclave - meeting (exhibits) - April.

2357 ■ American Gem Trade Association (AGTA)
3030 LBJ Fwy., Ste.840
Dallas, TX 75234
Ph: (214)742-4367
Free: (800)972-1162
Fax: (214)742-7334
E-mail: info@agta.org
URL: http://www.agta.org
Contact: Douglas K. Hucker, CEO
Founded: 1981. **Members:** 700. **Membership Dues:** firm, $1,000 (annual) ● affiliate, $350 (annual). **Staff:** 7. **Description:** Represents suppliers of natural colored gemstones; retail jewelers and jewelry manufacturers. Promotes natural colored gemstones; encourages high ethical standards among members and within the industry. Seeks to establish closer communication within the industry; works to protect consumers from fraud and to create a greater awareness of natural colored gemstones. Conducts seminars; maintains speakers' bureau. **Awards: Type:** recognition. **Committees:** Ethics and Grievance; Industry Rules; Nomenclature; Promotion; Spectrum Awards. **Publications:** *AGTA Newsletter*, quarterly ● *AGTA Source Directory*, biennial ● Also publishes promotional and educational literature and materials. **Conventions/Meetings:** annual Design Competition ● annual Gem Fair - trade show (exhibits) - always February, in Tucson, AZ.

2358 ■ American Watch Association (AWA)
Address Unknown since 2007
Founded: 1933. **Members:** 40. **Staff:** 1. **Budget:** $150,000. **Description:** Importers of watch movements, watches, and clocks; assemblers of watches, using imported or domestic movements and cases; domestic manufacturers of watch products; suppliers of goods and services. **Committees:** Anti-Counterfeiting; CAB; FTC Warrantee; Tariff and Customs. **Formerly:** (1951) American Watch Assemblers Association. **Conventions/Meetings:** semiannual conference.

2359 ■ American Watchmakers-Clockmakers Institute (AWI)
701 Enterprise Dr.
Harrison, OH 45030
Ph: (513)367-9800
Free: (866)367-2924
Fax: (513)367-1414
E-mail: jlubic@awci.com
URL: http://www.awci.com
Contact: James E. Lubic CMW, Exec. Dir.
Founded: 1960. **Members:** 6,000. **Membership Dues:** individual, $84 (annual). **Staff:** 11. **Budget:** $1,100,000. **State Groups:** 32. **Description:** Jewelers, watchmakers, clockmakers, watch and clock engineers, scientists, repairmen, and others in the watch, clock, and jewelry industry. Examines and

certifies master watchmakers and clockmakers. Maintains a museum displaying horological items, and the National Watch Mark Identification Bureau. Conducts home study course in clock repairing and bench courses for watchmakers in most major U.S. cities. Disseminates career information to vocational counselors in the form of brochures and filmstrips. **Libraries: Type:** reference. **Holdings:** 4,500; books, periodicals. **Subjects:** horology, tools, repair and construction of watches and clocks, technical and parts information. **Computer Services:** Information services, answers request via email for members and consumers. **Telecommunication Services:** electronic bulletin board. **Committees:** Industry Advisory; Research and Educational; Technical. **Formed by Merger of:** United Horological Association of America; Horological Institute. **Formerly:** American Watchmaker Institute; (2003) American Watchmakers Institute. **Publications:** *Horological Times*, monthly. Magazine. Professional, technical journal for watchmakers, clockmakers, and jewelers; includes AWI news. **Price:** available to members only. ISSN: 0145-9546. **Circulation:** 7,500. **Advertising:** accepted. Alternate Formats: CD-ROM; online. **Conventions/Meetings:** annual meeting, for suppliers (exhibits).

2360 ■ Diamond Council of America (DCA)
3212 W End Ave., Ste.202
Nashville, TN 37203
Ph: (615)385-5301
Free: (877)283-5669
Fax: (615)385-4955
URL: http://www.diamondcouncil.org
Contact: Terry Chandler, Pres./CEO
Founded: 1944. **Members:** 14,514. **Staff:** 10. **Description:** Retail jewelry firms and suppliers of gemstones. Firms operating approximately 4900 retail jewelry stores; associated manufacturers and importers. Offers courses in "gemology" and "diamontology" to employees of member firms; bestows titles of Certified Diamontologist and Guild Gemologist upon those completing courses and examinations. Supplies members with advertising and educational materials, sales tools, displays, ad copy, radio and television scripts, and merchandise plans. **Libraries: Type:** reference. **Subjects:** gemstones, minerals, diamonds, jewelry. **Awards:** Barr Award. **Frequency:** annual. **Type:** recognition ● Lode-Van-Bercken Award. **Frequency:** biennial. **Type:** recognition ● Storm Award. **Frequency:** annual. **Type:** recognition. **Publications:** *DCA Jeweler*. Newsletter. Contains information on the activities of the association. Alternate Formats: online ● *Diamond Council of America—Directory*, annual. **Price:** available to members only ● *Diamontologist*, bimonthly. Newsletter. Contains association and industry news. **Price:** available to members only. **Conventions/Meetings:** semiannual meeting.

2361 ■ Diamond Dealers Club (DDC)
580 5th Ave., 47th St.
New York, NY 10036
Ph: (212)869-9777
Fax: (212)869-5164
E-mail: mhochbaum@ddcny.com
URL: http://www.nyddc.com
Contact: Dr. Martin Hochbaum, Managing Dir.
Founded: 1931. **Members:** 2,000. **Membership Dues:** full, $1,325 (annual) ● retail e-trader, $500 (annual) ● industry e-trader, $1,020 (annual) ● bourse e-trader, $850 (annual). **Staff:** 40. **Budget:** $2,500,000. **Description:** Seeks to foster the interests of the diamond industry, promote equitable trade principles, eliminate abuses and unfair trade practices, disseminate accurate and reliable information concerning the industry, establish uniform business ethics, and cooperate with other persons and organizations for the advancement of the trade. Maintains active trading floor for all categories of wholesale diamonds and offers all members arbitration tribunals for dispute settlement. Operates charitable program. **Committees:** Banking Relations; Charity; Creditors Protection; Gemological Services; Marketing and Promotion; Public Relations; Security. **Publications:** *A 50 Year History - The Diamond Dealers' Club* ● *Connections: A Profile of Diamond People and Their History* ● *New York Diamonds*, quarterly. Journal. Includes analysis on the jewelry business, precious stones, manufacturing, and trading activities. **Price:** $36.00/year. **Circulation:** 18,000. **Advertising:** accepted ● *News*, quarterly. Newsletter. **Conventions/Meetings:** annual general assembly - always January in New York City.

2362 ■ Diamond Manufacturers and Importers Association of America (DMIAA)
PO Box 5297
New York, NY 10185-5297
Ph: (212)944-2066
Fax: (212)202-7525
E-mail: info@dmia.net
URL: http://www.dmia.net
Contact: Ronald J. Friedman, Pres.
Founded: 1932. **Members:** 180. **Membership Dues:** regular, $500 (annual). **Staff:** 2. **Description:** Represents importers, cutters, and polishers of gem diamonds. **Formerly:** Diamond Manufacturers Association. **Publications:** Yearbook, annual.

2363 ■ Diamond Trade and Precious Stone Association of America (DTPSAA)
Address Unknown since 2008
Founded: 1941. **Members:** 700. **Membership Dues:** $1,200 (annual). **Staff:** 15. **Budget:** $2,000,000. **Regional Groups:** 1. **State Groups:** 1. **Local Groups:** 1. **National Groups:** 19. **Multinational**. **Description:** Dealers, brokers, and manufacturers of diamonds and colored stones. **Formerly:** (1988) Diamond Trade Association of America. **Conventions/Meetings:** annual meeting - always January.

2364 ■ Gem and Lapidary Dealers Association (GLDA)
PO Box 2391
Tucson, AZ 85702-2391
Ph: (520)792-9431
Fax: (520)882-2836
E-mail: info@glda.com
URL: http://www.glda.com
Contact: Tanna Wyatt, Pres.
Description: Wholesale gem and jewelry show promotion organization. **Conventions/Meetings:** annual Las Vegas Gem and Jewelry Trade Show, with wholesalers and exhibitors from around the world (exhibits) ● annual specialty show, gem show (exhibits) - held in February.

2365 ■ Gemological Institute of America (GIA)
5345 Armada Dr.
The Robert Mouawad Campus
Carlsbad, CA 92008
Ph: (760)603-4000
Free: (800)421-7250
Fax: (760)603-4003
E-mail: donna.baker@gia.edu
URL: http://www.gia.edu
Contact: Donna M. Baker, Pres.
Founded: 1931. **Staff:** 1,100. **Description:** Works to ensure the public trust in gems and jewelry by upholding the highest standards of integrity, academics, science, and professionalism through research, education, gemological laboratory services, and instrument development; alumni are sustaining members. Conducts home study programs, resident courses, online classes and traveling seminars in identification and quality analysis of diamonds and other gemstones and pearls, and in jewelry making and repair, jewelry designing, and jewelry sales. Manufactures and sells gem testing, diamond grading equipment and audiovisual gemstone presentations through subsidiaries. Maintains gem testing and research laboratories in Carlsbad, CA and New York City. Offers job placement service; organizes gemological study tours. Awards diplomas and operates speakers' bureau. **Libraries: Type:** reference. **Holdings:** 14,000. **Awards: Type:** scholarship. **Computer Services:** Online services, classes and courses. **Publications:** *Alumni Directory*, annual ● *Gems & Gemology*, quarterly. Journal. Features articles on gemstone localities, synthetics, treatments, instrumentation, identification and history. Includes annual index and book reviews. **Price:** $69.95/year. ISSN: 0016-626X. **Circulation:** 12,000 ● *GIA Diamond Dictionary*. Book. **Price:** $39.95. Alternate Formats: CD-ROM ● *The GIA Insider*, biweekly. Newsletter. For members, the industry and the general public. Alternate Formats: online ● *GIA Jeweler's Manual* ● *Handbook of GEM Identification*. **Price:** $37.50 ● *In Focus* ● *Loupe*.

2366 ■ Independent Jewelers Organization (IJO)
25 Seir Hill Rd.
Norwalk, CT 06850
Ph: (203)846-4215
Free: (800)624-9252
Fax: (203)846-8571
E-mail: ijo@ijo.com
URL: http://www.ijo.com
Contact: Jeffrey Roberts, Pres./CEO
Founded: 1972. **Members:** 850. **Staff:** 10. **Budget:** $3,000,000. **For-Profit**. **Description:** Works to aid independent jewelers in competing in local markets through advertising, promotion, and buyers' assistance. Sponsors international buying trip to foreign countries; conducts semiannual buying show; maintains speakers' bureau. **Awards:** Bill Roberts GIA Scholarship. **Frequency:** annual. **Type:** scholarship. **Recipient:** to member applicant. **Publications:** *IJO Observer*, semiannual. Newsletter ● *Retailer and Manufacturing Directory*, semiannual. **Conventions/Meetings:** semiannual congress (exhibits).

2367 ■ Indian Diamond and Colorstone Association (IDCA)
56 W 45th St., No. 705
New York, NY 10036
Ph: (212)921-4488 (212)755-3232
Fax: (212)768-7935
E-mail: idca@verizon.net
URL: http://www.idcany.org
Contact: Rajesh Bhagat, Pres.
Founded: 1984. **Members:** 276. **Membership Dues:** regular, $450 (annual). **Staff:** 1. **Budget:** $300,000. **Description:** Diamond and colorstone dealers of Indian descent and others who work with diamonds and gemstones from India. Promotes the growth and awareness of the Indian gem industry in the U.S. **Awards:** Manufacturer of the Year. **Frequency:** annual. **Type:** recognition ● Retailer of the Year. **Frequency:** annual. **Type:** recognition. **Subgroups:** Colorstone; Diamond. **Publications:** *Business Directory*, annual ● *IDCA By-Laws Directory*, annual ● *IDCA Pocket Directory*, periodic ● Newsletter, quarterly ● Membership Directory, annual. **Conventions/Meetings:** annual seminar.

2368 ■ International Jewelry Design Guild (IJDG)
c/o Stacy Blackshaw, Exec. Dir.
19 Mantua Rd.
Mount Royal, NJ 08061
Ph: (856)423-7222
Fax: (856)423-3420
E-mail: info@ijdg.com
Contact: Stacy Blackshaw, Exec. Dir.
Founded: 1998. **Members:** 70. **Membership Dues:** regular, $2,050 (annual). **Multinational**. **Description:** Raises worldwide awareness of fine designer jewelry. Promotes design as one of the most important elements in the value of fine jewelry. Provides structure and leadership for trade shows, charity and fundraising events, community and academic projects. Conducts business networking, public relations, marketing communication services, and lobbying within the jewelry and fashion industry. **Telecommunication Services:** electronic mail, sblackshaw@talley.com.

2369 ■ Jeweler's Advisory Group (JAG)
PO Box 17241
Richmond, VA 23226
Ph: (804)673-9046
Fax: (804)282-1274

E-mail: 3030@polygon.net
URL: http://jag.polygon.net
Contact: Ms. Michelle Voecks, Sec.-Treas.
Founded: 1995. **Membership Dues:** regular, $75 (annual). **Description:** Aims to uphold, nurture and protect the ethical integrity, professional fundamentals, and public image of the jewelry industry. Assists and encourages its members to improve their professional expertise and competence through continuing education. Raises awareness of management processes and technological change concerning the jewelry industry. **Publications:** *JAG Phoenix*, quarterly. Newsletter.

2370 ■ Jewelers of America (JA)
52 Vanderbilt Ave., 19th Fl.
New York, NY 10017-3827
Ph: (646)658-0246
Free: (800)223-0673
Fax: (646)658-0256
E-mail: info@jewelers.org
URL: http://www.jewelers.org
Contact: Matthew A. Runci, Pres./CEO
Founded: 1957. **Members:** 11,000. **Staff:** 16. **Budget:** $5,000,000. **Regional Groups:** 4. **State Groups:** 38. **Description:** Retailers of jewelry, watches, silver, and allied merchandise. Conducts surveys and compiles statistics. Conducts educational programs. Provides information to consumers. **Awards:** Affiliate Design Competition. **Frequency:** annual. **Type:** recognition. **Recipient:** to members and their employees ● GIA Scholarship. **Frequency:** annual. **Type:** scholarship. **Recipient:** to an employee of a member firm. **Telecommunication Services:** electronic mail, contactus@jewelers.org. **Formerly:** Retail Jewelers of America. **Publications:** Manuals. **Conventions/Meetings:** workshop, co-sponsored with state affiliates to bring management information to retail jeweler members.

2371 ■ Jewelers Board of Trade (JBT)
PO Box 6928
Providence, RI 02940
Ph: (401)467-0055
Fax: (401)467-1199
E-mail: info@jewelersboard.com
URL: http://www.jewelersboard.com
Contact: Diane D. Kenyon, Pres.
Founded: 1884. **Members:** 3,300. **Membership Dues:** domestic firm, $850 (semiannual) ● international firm, $995 (annual). **Staff:** 60. **Budget:** $4,000,000. **Description:** Serves as a credit reporting agency for manufacturers, wholesalers, and importers of jewelry. Maintains branch offices in New York City, Chicago, IL, and Los Angeles, CA. **Computer Services:** Mailing lists, of members ● online services, credit reports (for members). **Departments:** Adjustment; Collection; Reporting; Research. **Publications:** *Confidential Reference Book*, semiannual ● *New Name Bulletin*, weekly ● *Service*, weekly ● Also publishes credit reports on manufacturers, wholesalers, and retailers of jewelry; collections services offered.

2372 ■ Jewelers' Security Alliance (JSA)
6 E 45th St.
New York, NY 10017
Free: (800)537-0067
Fax: (212)808-9168
E-mail: jsa2@jewelerssecurity.org
URL: http://www.jewelerssecurity.org
Contact: John J. Kennedy, Pres.
Founded: 1883. **Members:** 21,000. **Membership Dues:** associate (non-jeweler), $600 (annual) ● regular (based on number of employees), $180-$830 (annual) ● retail chain (plus $50 per branch; maximum of $2750), $250 (annual). **Staff:** 6. **Description:** Advocates for crime prevention in the jewelry industry. Provides crime information and assistance to the jewelry industry and law enforcement. **Libraries: Type:** not open to the public. **Awards:** Gold and Silver Shield Awards. **Frequency:** annual. **Type:** recognition. **Recipient:** for contribution to crime prevention ● James B. White JSA Award. **Frequency:** annual. **Type:** recognition. **Recipient:** to a law enforcement person. **Formerly:** (2000) Jewelers Security Alliance of the U.S. **Publications:** *Annual Report on Crime Against the Jewelry Industry in U.S.*, annual ● *JSA Manual of Jewelry Security*, biennial. **Price:** $29.95 for members; $49.95 for nonmembers. **Circulation:** 18,000. **Advertising:** accepted ● *JSA Newsletter*, quarterly. **Price:** free for members. **Advertising:** accepted. Alternate Formats: online ● Bulletins, periodic. Features advisories on crime prevention. **Price:** included in membership dues. **Circulation:** 13,000. **Conventions/Meetings:** annual Security Seminar and Expo for Retail Jewelry Chains, two-day event with seminars and exhibits (exhibits).

2373 ■ Jewelers Shipping Association (JSA)
125 Carlsbad St.
Cranston, RI 02920
Ph: (401)943-6020 (401)943-6490
Free: (800)688-4572
Fax: (401)943-1490
E-mail: eturenne@jewelersshipping.com
URL: http://www.jewelersshipping.com
Contact: David Roche, Managing Dir.
Founded: 1962. **Members:** 170. **Staff:** 35. **Description:** Represents primarily jewelry and silverware manufacturers; others whose freight complements jewelry-type freight. Provides surface and air freight shipping services for members. **Committees:** Rate. **Conventions/Meetings:** annual meeting - always December, Providence, RI.

2374 ■ Jewelers Vigilance Committee (JVC)
25 W 45th St., Ste.1406
New York, NY 10036
Ph: (212)997-2002
Fax: (212)997-9148
E-mail: clgjvc@aol.com
URL: http://www.jvclegal.org
Contact: Cecilia L. Gardner Esq., Pres./CEO/Gen. Counsel
Founded: 1917. **Members:** 1,200. **Membership Dues:** retailer/individual proprietor (based on number of employees), $175-$6,500 (annual) ● distributor/manufacturer/wholesaler (based on number of employees), $395-$6,000 (annual). **Staff:** 5. **Description:** Represents manufacturers, importers, wholesalers, and retailers. Combats deceptive trade practices and misleading advertising. Aims to develop and maintain high trade standards. Provides advice on markings and assists in prosecution of violations of marking, advertising, and related jewelry industry laws. **Libraries: Type:** reference. **Absorbed:** (1943) American Jewelers Protective Association. **Publications:** *The Complete Consumer Guide to Purchasing Fine Jewelry*. Brochure. Covers general terms of sale questions and basic questions about most product categories. **Price:** $25.00 per 200 brochures, for members; $35.00 per 200 brochures, for nonmembers ● *Guide to Jewelry Markings and Descriptions* ● *Manufacturers' Legal Handbook*. Covers information for jewelry manufacturers, suppliers, wholesalers and designers. **Price:** $19.95 for members; $39.95 for nonmembers ● *News and Views*, quarterly. Newsletter. Alternate Formats: online. **Conventions/Meetings:** semiannual meeting - always in New York City and Las Vegas, NV.

2375 ■ Jewelry Industry Distributors Association (JIDA)
701 Enterprise Dr.
Harrison, OH 45030
Ph: (513)367-2357
Fax: (513)367-1414
E-mail: lfuleki@jida.info
URL: http://www.jida.info
Contact: Harvey Cobrin, Pres.
Founded: 1946. **Members:** 75. **Membership Dues:** active, $405 (annual) ● associate (initiation fee), $150 ● associate, $505 (annual). **Staff:** 2. **Description:** Distributors of watch material, jewelers' tools, watchmakers' equipment, jewelry, and related commodities; suppliers. Seeks to: raise service standards in the industry; act as a forum for exchange of information; promote and stimulate business relationships among all elements of the watch and jewelry industry. Conducts studies on methods of improving efficiency in areas such as computer installation. Discusses topics including merchandising, management, and vendor relations. Sponsors annual tour of member firms. **Formerly:** (1969) Watch Material Distributors Association of America; (1984) Watch Material and Jewelry Distributors Association. **Publications:** *JIDA News*. Newsletter. **Advertising:** accepted ● Bulletins, periodic ● Directory, annual. **Conventions/Meetings:** annual meeting and convention (exhibits).

2376 ■ Jewelry Information Center (JIC)
52 Vanderbilt Ave., 19th Fl.
New York, NY 10017
Ph: (646)658-0240
Free: (800)459-0130
Fax: (646)658-0245
E-mail: info@jic.org
URL: http://www.jic.org
Contact: Myriam Gumuchian, Chair
Founded: 1946. **Members:** 2,300. **Membership Dues:** manufacturer (based on annual sales volume), $250-$10,000 (annual) ● retailer (based on annual sales volume), $65-$10,000 (annual) ● special category, $10,000 (annual). **Staff:** 4. **Description:** Represents retailers, wholesalers, and manufacturers of fine jewelry products. Conducts industry-wide promotional and educational programs; sponsors marketing seminars and consumer-oriented programs on radio, television, and print media. **Libraries: Type:** not open to the public. **Holdings:** 100. **Subjects:** fine jewelry, history, design, manufacturing info. **Divisions:** Jewelry; Tabletop; Watches; Writing Instruments. **Formerly:** (1993) Jewelry Industry Council. **Publications:** *LINK*, 3/year. Newsletter. Includes marketing information. **Price:** included in membership dues. **Circulation:** 1,500.

2377 ■ Leading Jewelers of the World (LJW)
500 7th Ave., 12th Fl.
New York, NY 10018
Ph: (212)768-2744
Fax: (212)768-2748
E-mail: info@ljotw.com
URL: http://www.ljotw.com
Contact: Jack Gredinger, Exec. Dir.
Members: 44. **Multinational. Description:** Selects leaders in high-end retail jewelry for membership in an exclusive market area basis within the United States. Provides customers with "ultimate jewelry buying experience" by continually meeting the highest standards and practices required by the association by conducting routine inspections, personnel training and exacting compliance requirements mandated by the association. **Computer Services:** Information services, diamond facts ● online services, member exclusive page.

2378 ■ Manufacturing Jewelers and Suppliers of America (MJSA)
45 Royal Little Dr.
Providence, RI 02904
Ph: (401)274-3840
Free: (800)444-MJSA
Fax: (401)274-0265
E-mail: info@mjsa.org
URL: http://www.mjsa.org
Contact: Alan Bell, Chm.
Founded: 1903. **Members:** 1,600. **Staff:** 25. **Budget:** $4,000,000. **Description:** Represents American manufacturers and suppliers within the jewelry industry. Seeks to foster long-term stability and prosperity of the jewelry industry. Provides leadership in government affairs and industry education. **Awards:** American Vision Award. **Frequency:** annual. **Type:** recognition. **Recipient:** to designers whose works are influencing the future design trends of the jewelry industry ● Education Foundation Scholarship Award. **Frequency:** annual. **Type:** scholarship. **Recipient:** for a student who intends to pursue a career in the jewelry industry. **Committees:** Education; Government Affairs; Membership. **Programs:** Cost-Saving Business. **Formerly:** (1998) Manufacturing Jewelers and Silversmiths of America. **Publications:** *AJM: The Authority on Jewelry Manufacturing*, monthly. Magazine. Provides informative articles addressing the latest in jewelry repair,

manufacturing, and business trends. **Price:** $47.00/ year in U.S.; $60.00/year in Canada; $99.00/year outside U.S. and Canada. ISSN: 0193-0931. **Circulation:** 8,000. **Advertising:** accepted ● *Buyers Guide*, biennial. **Price:** $125.00 for nonmembers; free for members. **Circulation:** 4,500. **Advertising:** accepted. **Conventions/Meetings:** annual meeting.

2379 ■ Metal Findings Manufacturers Association (MFMA)

Address Unknown since 2008
URL: http://www.mfma.net

Founded: 1929. **Members:** 65. **Membership Dues:** manufacturer, $150 (annual). **Description:** Manufacturers of findings (stamped, fabricated) for jewelry. **Publications:** Membership Directory, biennial. **Conventions/Meetings:** bimonthly meeting.

2380 ■ National Association of Jewelry Appraisers (NAJA)

PO Box 18
Rego Park, NY 11374-0018
Ph: (718)896-1536
Fax: (718)997-9057
E-mail: naja.appraisers@netzero.net
URL: http://www.najaappraisers.com
Contact: Ms. Gail Brett Levine GG, Exec. Dir.

Founded: 1981. **Members:** 700. **Membership Dues:** individual in U.S., $175 (annual) ● individual outside U.S. and Canada (plus 25 processing fee; nonrefundable), $215 (annual). **Staff:** 3. **Budget:** $110,000. **For-Profit. Multinational. Description:** Gem and jewelry appraisers, jewelers, importers, brokers, manufacturers, gemological students, and others professionally interested in jewelry appraisal. Seeks to recognize and make available to the public the services of highly qualified, experienced, independent, and reliable jewelry appraisers. Conducts seminars on jewelry appraisal techniques, methods, and pricing for members and the public. Supports legislation to establish minimum standards of competency and licensing of jewelry appraisers; maintains code of professional ethics. Operates appraiser referral program; sponsors ongoing public relations campaign. Offers equipment discounts, new appraisal forms, travel discounts, insurance, and professional aids for members only. Compiles statistics. **Libraries: Type:** not open to the public. **Holdings:** books. **Publications:** *Jewelry Appraiser*, quarterly. Newsletter. Includes information on new products, chart of wholesale diamond prices per carat, calendar of events, and listing of new applicants for membership. **Price:** free for members. **Circulation:** 750. **Advertising:** accepted ● *National Association of Jewelry Appraisers—Membership Directory*, annual. Lists international members by state and country. Includes alphabetical index to members. **Price:** free for members. **Conventions/Meetings:** semiannual conference (exhibits) - always February and 1st week in August.

2381 ■ Platinum Guild International USA (PGI)

620 Newport Center Dr., Ste.800
Newport Beach, CA 92660
Ph: (714)760-8279
Free: (800)207-PLAT
Fax: (714)760-8780
E-mail: usainfo@pgiglobal.com
URL: http://www.preciousplatinum.com

Founded: 1992. **Members:** 25,000. **Description:** Promotes the use of platinum metal. **Publications:** *This Week in Platinum*. Newsletter. Alternate Formats: online ● *Today in Platinum*. Newsletter. Alternate Formats: online ● Reports.

2382 ■ Rocky Mountain Jewelers Association (RMJA)

c/o Terrence J. Zebarth, Exec. Dir.
PO Box 1704
Colorado Springs, CO 80901-1704
Ph: (719)632-8171
Fax: (719)635-8963
E-mail: lbtyman@aol.com
Contact: Terrence J. Zebarth, Exec. Dir.

Members: 100. **Membership Dues:** single store, $100 (annual) ● each additional store, $50 (annual). **Description:** Strives to increase knowledge and professionalism of jewelers in the Rocky Mountain region; aims to combat unscrupulous treatment of consumers by unethical merchants. Provides legislative representation. **Libraries: Type:** reference. **Holdings:** video recordings. **Publications:** Newsletter. **Conventions/Meetings:** annual convention ● seminar.

2383 ■ Twenty-Four Karat Club of the City of New York

c/o John J. Kennedy, Sec.
Jewelers Security Alliance of the U.S.
6 E 45th St., No. 1005
New York, NY 10017
Ph: (212)687-0328
Fax: (212)808-9168
Contact: John J. Kennedy, Sec.

Founded: 1902. **Members:** 200. **Description:** Limited to 200 U.S. citizens leading the concerns in the manufacturing or wholesaling of jewelry or kindred products; individuals in allied industries. **Conventions/Meetings:** bimonthly meeting ● meeting.

2384 ■ Women's Jewelry Association (WJA)

19 Mantua Rd.
Mount Royal, NJ 08061-1006
Ph: (856)423-3156
Fax: (856)423-3420
E-mail: info@womensjewelry.org
URL: http://www.womensjewelry.org
Contact: Ann S. Arnold, Pres.

Founded: 1983. **Members:** 1,500. **Membership Dues:** regular (initial), $150 ● student, $75 (annual) ● regular, $125 (annual). **Staff:** 1. **Regional Groups:** 10. **Description:** Represents those involved in jewelry design, manufacture, retail, and advertising. Aims to: enhance the status of women in the jewelry industry; make known the contribution of women to the industry; provide a network for women involved with fine jewelry. Maintains hall of fame. **Awards:** Grant Program. **Frequency:** annual. **Type:** grant. **Recipient:** for members ● Hall of Fame Lifetime Achievement Award. **Frequency:** annual. **Type:** recognition. **Recipient:** for outstanding women in the jewelry and watch industry ● Scholarship Program. **Frequency:** annual. **Type:** scholarship. **Recipient:** for students studying fine jewelry and watch design. **Committees:** Awards Dinner; Chapter Affairs; Event Planning; Fundraising; Publicity/Marketing; Scholarship. **Publications:** *Jewelry Association Newsletter*, semiannual ● Membership Directory.

Juvenile

2385 ■ American Specialty Toy Retailing Association (ASTRA)

116 W Illinois St., Ste.5E
Chicago, IL 60610
Ph: (312)222-0984
Free: (800)591-0490
Fax: (312)222-0986
E-mail: info@astratoy.org
URL: http://www.astratoy.org
Contact: Kathleen McHugh, Exec. Dir.

Founded: 1992. **Members:** 800. **Membership Dues:** manufacturer representative, $115 (annual) ● affiliate, $230 (annual) ● manufacturer - minimum (based on gross sales), $290 (annual) ● manufacturer - maximum (based on gross sales), $7,500 (annual) ● retailer - minimum (based on gross sales), $195 (annual) ● retailer - maximum (based on gross sales), $5,000 (annual). **Budget:** $500,000. **Description:** Specialty manufacturers and retailers, sales representatives, and industry-related members of the specialty toy industry. Works to secure the "right of all children to achieve their full potential through fun and positive play." Serves as a forum for discussion of issues facing the specialty toy industry; provides a unified voice for the industry. Conducts programs to educate parents about the importance of specialty toys in child development. Provides resources to specialty toy and related businesses; conducts market research; makes available to members discount credit card services. Compiles statistics. **Computer Services:** Mailing lists, of members. **Telecommunication Services:** electronic mail, kmchugh@astratoy.org. **Publications:** *Convention Program*, annual ● *Manufacturer's Savings Coupon Book* ● *Toys, Tips, and Topics - Your Tools For Competent Customer Service*. Video ● Membership Directory, annual ● Newsletter, 5/year. **Price:** included in membership dues. **Conventions/Meetings:** annual convention ● periodic regional meeting.

2386 ■ Diaper Service Accreditation Council (DSAC)

994 Old Eagle School Rd., Ste.1019
Wayne, PA 19087-1802
Ph: (610)971-4850
Fax: (610)971-4859
E-mail: nads@diapernet.org
URL: http://www.diapernet.org
Contact: Jack Shiffert, Exec. Dir.

Founded: 1970. **Staff:** 3. **Description:** Acts as a certification organization of the National Association Diaper Services (see separate entry) for diaper services that meet the council's standards after self-evaluation and site inspection. Has established standards in operation, marketing, and quality control. **Affiliated With:** National Association of Diaper Services.

2387 ■ International Formula Council (IFC)

5775 Peachtree-Dunwoody Rd., Bldg. G, Ste.500
Atlanta, GA 30342-1558
Ph: (404)252-3663
Fax: (404)252-0774
URL: http://www.infantformula.org

Founded: 1970. **Members:** 6. **Staff:** 5. **Description:** Is a U.S.-based international association of manufacturers and marketers of formulated nutrition products such as infant formulas and adult nutritionals. Supports scientific research regarding the characteristics, qualities, and uses of infant formula products. Collects scientific information on such products for dissemination to the public. Keeps members informed of regulatory and legislative matters. Provides communication between infant formula manufacturers and government and regulatory bodies. **Formerly:** (1998) Infant Formula Council. **Publications:** *Infant Feeding and Nutrition*. Brochure ● *Infant Formula: Questions and Answers*. Brochure. **Conventions/Meetings:** annual meeting.

2388 ■ Juvenile Products Manufacturers Association (JPMA)

15000 Commerce Pkwy., Ste.C
Mount Laurel, NJ 08054
Ph: (856)638-0420
Fax: (856)439-0525
E-mail: jpma@ahint.com
URL: http://www.jpma.org
Contact: Robert B. Waller Jr., Pres.

Founded: 1962. **Members:** 400. **Membership Dues:** company (minimum), $865 (annual) ● company (maximum), $16,400 (annual). **Staff:** 10. **Budget:** $2,500,000. **Description:** Manufacturers of infants' furniture, baby carriages, strollers, chairs, and related products. Exchanges credit information. Conducts annual trade show, research, and surveys. Active in product safety and standardization. **Publications:** *Connections*, bimonthly. Newsletter ● *Retail Rattle*, quarterly. Newsletter. **Price:** included in membership dues. Alternate Formats: online. **Conventions/Meetings:** annual International Juvenile Products Show - trade show (exhibits).

2389 ■ National Association of Diaper Services (NADS)

994 Old Eagle School Rd., Ste.1019
Wayne, PA 19087
Ph: (610)971-4850
Fax: (610)971-4859

E-mail: nads@diapernet.com
URL: http://www.diapernet.org
Contact: John A. Shiffert, Exec. Dir.
Founded: 1938. **Members:** 190. **Staff:** 7. **Description:** Owners of diaper rental and laundry services and industry suppliers. Supports research on stain prevention formulas, softening agents, antiseptics, market and motivation studies of customers and automation. Maintains information bureau on management problems and industrial relations; offers statistical service. Conducts laboratory tests to measure washroom efficiency, soil removal, and whiteness retention and grants certification to members meeting quality standards. Maintains Diaper Service Accreditation Council (see separate entry). **Formerly:** (1960) Diaper Service Institute of America; (1971) Diaper Service Industry Association; (1984) National Institute of Infant Services. **Publications:** *Research Report*, monthly ● Newsletter, monthly. **Conventions/Meetings:** semiannual meeting.

Knives

2390 ■ International Saw and Knife Association (ISKA)
c/o Mr. Kirk M. Wethey, Membership Chm.
Ideal Saw Works
351 O St.
Fresno, CA 93721
Ph: (559)237-0809 (419)589-2727
Fax: (559)237-8879
E-mail: kirk@idealsaw.com
URL: http://www.iska.org
Contact: John Mabee, Pres.
Founded: 1968. **Members:** 145. **Membership Dues:** regular, $125 (annual) ● associate, $225 (annual). **Staff:** 7. **Description:** Independent shops that repair circular and wide band saws, paper knives, shear blades, and slitters for the wood, metal, plastics, and paper trades. Encourages better relationships between saw shops, saw and knife grinding manufacturers, sawmill equipment manufacturers and sawmill operators, paper knife and shear blade manufacturers, and machinery dealers and manufacturers. Conducts specialized education programs. **Formerly:** (1983) National Association of Saw Shops. **Publications:** *Cutting Times*, quarterly. Newsletter. Alternate Formats: online ● Membership Directory, annual. **Conventions/Meetings:** semiannual meeting ● annual meeting.

Laboratory

2391 ■ Independent Laboratories Institute (ILI)
c/o American Council of Independent Laboratories
1629 K St. NW, Ste.400
Washington, DC 20006-1633
Ph: (202)887-5872
Fax: (202)887-0021
E-mail: jcassedy@acil.org
URL: http://www.acil.org/displaycommon.cfm?an=1&subarticlenbr=15
Contact: Joan Walsh Cassedy CAE, Dir.
Founded: 1992. **Description:** Provides quality training for the laboratory community.

Lamps

2392 ■ Association of Stained Glass Lamp Artists (ASGLA)
5070 Cromwell Dr. NW
Gig Harbor, WA 98335
E-mail: wskyrnr21@comcast.net
URL: http://www.asgla.com
Contact: Kevin Hendon, Contact
Founded: 1991. **Membership Dues:** individual, $10 (annual). **Description:** Promotes the art and craft of stained glass lamp construction. **Publications:** *2002 Calendar* ● Video. Shows video of the Tiffany exhibit at the Queens Museum. **Price:** free for members. **Conventions/Meetings:** seminar.

Landscaping

2393 ■ Association of Professional Landscape Designers (APLD)
4305 N Sixth St., Ste.A
Harrisburg, PA 17110
Ph: (717)238-9780
Fax: (717)238-9985
E-mail: admin@apld.org
URL: http://www.apld.org
Contact: Patrick Bones, Pres.
Founded: 1989. **Members:** 800. **Membership Dues:** associate, $200 (annual) ● allied, $300 (annual) ● student, $50 (annual) ● educator, $125 (annual). **Staff:** 2. **Multinational. Description:** Landscape design professionals, students; and interested others. Works to improve status and establish professional credentials for landscape designers. International and regional continuing education opportunities. Offers certification programs. **Awards:** Award of Distinction. **Type:** recognition. **Recipient:** for a landscape designer ● Harry Schuster Award. **Frequency:** annual. **Type:** recognition. **Recipient:** for a person who reflects the enthusiasm of Harry Schuster for APLD ● Landscape Design Award - Residential Designs. **Frequency:** annual. **Type:** recognition. **Recipient:** for a landscape designer. **Computer Services:** Mailing lists, of members. **Publications:** *APLD Designer*, quarterly. Newsletter. **Circulation:** 800. **Advertising:** accepted. **Conventions/Meetings:** annual conference.

2394 ■ Independent Turf and Ornamental Distributors Association (ITODA)
174 Crestview Dr.
Bellefonte, PA 16823-8516
Ph: (814)326-5995
Free: (877)326-5995
Fax: (814)335-2542
E-mail: info@itoda.org
URL: http://www.itoda.org
Contact: Patricia E. Heuser, Exec. Dir.
Founded: 1990. **Members:** 70. **Membership Dues:** associate, premiere distributor, $850 (annual) ● training distributor, $250 (annual). **Budget:** $75,000. **Description:** Wholesale suppliers of lawn and turf chemicals, fertilizers, and equipment. Represents members' interests. Conducts educational programs. Provides consulting services. Maintains speakers' bureau; compiles statistics. **Publications:** *The Independent Gazette*, quarterly. Newsletter. **Price:** available to members only. **Circulation:** 125. **Advertising:** accepted. **Conventions/Meetings:** annual meeting (exhibits) - June or October. 2008 Oct. 22-24, Charleston, SC ● seminar.

2395 ■ Lawn and Garden Marketing and Distribution Association (LGMDA)
2105 Laurel Bush Rd., Ste.200
Bel Air, MD 21015
Ph: (443)640-1080
Fax: (443)640-1031
E-mail: lgmda@ksgroup.org
URL: http://www.lgmda.org
Contact: Steve Wise, Pres.
Founded: 1969. **Members:** 300. **Membership Dues:** manufacturer/distributor, $1,000 (annual) ● affiliate, $500 (annual). **Staff:** 3. **Budget:** $250,000. **Description:** Distributor members are persons or firms engaged in the wholesale distribution of lawn and garden supplies; manufacturer members are manufacturers and producers; affiliate members are groups or individuals with an interest in lawn and garden distribution, such as manufacturers' representatives. Promotes the lawn and garden industry nationally; provides sales and training aids to improve selling techniques and standardize policy; seeks to create a prestigious position for the lawn and garden distributor in the marketplace. **Awards:** Product and Package Awards. **Frequency:** annual. **Type:** recognition. **Telecommunication Services:** electronic mail, lgmda@fernley.com. **Formerly:** National Lawn and Garden Distributors Association; (1979) Lawn and Garden Distributors Association. **Publications:** *Grassroots*, quarterly. Newsletter. Alternate Formats: online ● Membership Directory, annual. Provides information on membership activities. **Price:** $500.00 for nonmembers. **Advertising:** accepted. **Conventions/Meetings:** annual conference ● annual convention (exhibits) ● periodic seminar.

2396 ■ National Landscape Association (NLA)
c/o American Nursery and Landscape Association
1000 Vermont Ave. NW, Ste.300
Washington, DC 20005-4914
Ph: (202)789-2900
Fax: (202)789-1893
E-mail: leagle@anla.org
URL: http://www.anla.org/about/nla/nla.htm
Contact: Lindsay Eagle, Contact
Founded: 1939. **Members:** 700. **Staff:** 2. **Description:** Landscape firms. Works to: enhance the professionalism of its member firms in designing, building, and maintaining quality landscapes in a profitable and environmentally responsible manner; represent the landscape perspective within the industry. Sponsors annual landscape tour in conjunction with American Association of Nurserymen (see separate entry). **Awards:** Landscape Design Awards. **Frequency:** annual. **Type:** recognition. **Formerly:** (1970) National Landscape Nurserymen's Association. **Publications:** *NLA Landscape News*, quarterly. Newsletter. **Price:** included in membership dues ● Also publishes reports. **Conventions/Meetings:** annual Convention and Learning Retreat ● annual Landscape Operations Tour ● annual Management Clinic - symposium ● annual workshop.

2397 ■ New York State Turf and Landscape Association (NYSTLA)
1 Prospect Ave.
White Plains, NY 10607
Ph: (914)993-9455
Fax: (914)993-9051
E-mail: nystla@aol.com
URL: http://www.nystla.com
Contact: Joseph Tinelli, Pres.
Founded: 1968. **Members:** 250. **Membership Dues:** associate, $200 (annual) ● individual, $175 (annual) ● organization, $150 (annual) ● retired, student, $25 (annual) ● business, $375 (annual). **Staff:** 3. **Description:** Landscaping and grounds keeping professionals. Promotes the landscaping industry. **Awards:** Louis Squobbo Scholarship Award. **Frequency:** annual. **Type:** scholarship ● Person of the Year Award. **Frequency:** annual. **Type:** recognition. **Formerly:** (1998) Professional Turf and Landscape Conference. **Publications:** *The Grapevine*, monthly. Magazine. **Circulation:** 500. **Advertising:** accepted ● *How To Hire A Landscaper*. Pamphlet. **Conventions/Meetings:** annual Professional Turf and Landscape Conference (exhibits).

2398 ■ Professional Landcare Network (PLANET)
950 Herndon Pkwy., Ste.450
Herndon, VA 20170
Ph: (703)736-9666
Free: (800)395-2522
Fax: (703)736-9668
E-mail: info@landcarenetwork.org
URL: http://www.landcarenetwork.org
Contact: Jim Martin CLP, Pres.
Founded: 1961. **Members:** 2,400. **Membership Dues:** green industry service provider (based on annual sales volume), $299-$5,700 (annual) ● green industry supplier (based on annual sales volume), $505-$1,700 (annual) ● state and allied regional association, $110 (annual) ● affiliate, $85 (annual) ● student, $25 (annual) ● student chapter, $130 (annual). **Staff:** 15. **Budget:** $3,000,000. **State Groups:** 40. **Description:** Landscape contractors. Works to represent, lead, and unify the interior and exterior landscape industry by working together on a national basis; addressing environmental and legislative issues; and creating increased opportunities in busi-

ness. Provides forum to encourage members' profitability, personal growth, and professional advancement. **Libraries: Type:** reference. **Holdings:** 150; books, video recordings. **Subjects:** technical, business management, training, marketing. **Awards:** ALCA Environmental Improvement Award. **Frequency:** annual. **Type:** recognition. **Telecommunication Services:** electronic mail, j.martin@jamesmartinassociates.com. **Committees:** Awards; Crystal Ball; Education; Employee Recruitment; Government Affairs; Green Industry Conference; Leadership Development; Marketing. **Formed by Merger of:** (2005) Associated Landscape Contractors of America and Professional Lawn Care Association of America. **Publications:** *Landscape Contractor News*, monthly. Newsletter. Covers association and industry news. **Price:** free for members. **Circulation:** 2,500. **Advertising:** accepted ● *Who's Who in Landscape Contracting*, annual. Membership Directory ● Manuals ● Reports. **Conventions/Meetings:** annual Executive Forum - conference, business forum for owners and top managers - always February ● annual Green Industry Conference - conference and trade show (exhibits) - always November.

2399 ■ Sports Turf Managers Association (STMA)
805 New Hampshire St., Ste.E
Lawrence, KS 66044
Free: (800)323-3875
Fax: (800)366-0391
E-mail: stmainfo@tma.org
URL: http://www.stma.org
Contact: Mike Andersen, Pres.
Founded: 1981. **Members:** 2,400. **Membership Dues:** commercial, $295 (annual) ● commercial associate, $75 (annual) ● individual, $110 (annual) ● affiliate, $50 (annual) ● student, $25 (annual). **Staff:** 8. **Budget:** $975,000. **Regional Groups:** 26. **Multinational. Description:** Represents sports turf managers (sports turf managers are individuals who take care of athletic surfaces), educators in turf and soil related fields, manufacturers and service providers that offer goods and services related to the sports turf field. **Awards:** Dick Ericson Award. **Frequency:** annual. **Type:** recognition. **Recipient:** for an individual who has made significant contributions to the STMA ● Dr. William H. Daniel Award. **Frequency:** annual. **Type:** recognition. **Recipient:** for individuals with significant contribution to the sports turf industry through research, teaching and extension outreach ● Field of the Year. **Frequency:** annual. **Type:** recognition. **Recipient:** for contributions to the sports field ● George Toma Golden Rake Award. **Frequency:** annual. **Type:** recognition. **Recipient:** for individuals with strong work ethics and job performance ● Harry C. Gill Memorial Award. **Frequency:** annual. **Type:** recognition. **Recipient:** to individuals for their hard work in the sports turf industry ● **Frequency:** annual. **Type:** scholarship. **Recipient:** for students interested in sports turf management. **Computer Services:** Online services. **Committees:** Awards; Bylaws; Certification; Chapter Relations; Communications; Education; Ethics; Marketing. **Publications:** *E-Digest*. Newsletter. Alternate Formats: online ● *Sportsturf*, monthly. Magazine. **Conventions/Meetings:** annual conference (exhibits) - always January. 2009 Jan., San Jose, CA; 2010 Jan. 13-17, Orlando, FL.

2400 ■ Turf and Ornamental Communicators Association (TOCA)
PO Box 156
New Prague, MN 56071
Ph: (952)758-6340
Fax: (952)758-5813
E-mail: tocaassociation@aol.com
URL: http://www.toca.org
Contact: Den Gardner, Exec. Dir.
Founded: 1989. **Members:** 210. **Membership Dues:** individual, $115 (annual). **Staff:** 3. **Budget:** $100,000. **Description:** Editors, writers, photographers, public relations and advertising practitioners involved in green industry communications (turf and ornamental). Promotes communications excellence within trade and consumer media. Maintains speakers' bureau. **Awards:** Photography/Design Award. **Frequency:** annual. **Type:** recognition. **Recipient:** for members ● TOCA Scholarship. **Frequency:** annual. **Type:** scholarship. **Recipient:** for students majoring in horticulture or related field with an interest in communications ● Writing Award. **Frequency:** annual. **Type:** recognition. **Recipient:** for members. **Computer Services:** Electronic publishing, quarterly newsletter ● mailing lists, of members. **Publications:** *TOCA Talk*, quarterly. Newsletter. **Circulation:** 125. Alternate Formats: online. **Conventions/Meetings:** annual meeting - always May.

Laundry

2401 ■ Association for Linen Management (ALM)
2161 Lexington Rd., Ste.2
Richmond, KY 40475
Ph: (859)624-0177
Free: (800)669-0863
Fax: (859)624-3580
E-mail: admin@nlmnet.org
URL: http://www.nlmnet.org
Contact: Jim Thacker, Exec. Dir.
Founded: 1939. **Members:** 1,600. **Membership Dues:** regular, $130 (annual) ● retired, $20 (annual) ● facility, $200 (annual) ● chapter affiliation, $10-$70 (annual) ● associate (national level), $500 (annual) ● associate (regional level), $325 (annual). **Staff:** 6. **Budget:** $500,000. **Regional Groups:** 47. **Description:** Managers of laundries serving institutions such as hospitals, nursing homes, hotels, schools, and correctional facilities. Seeks improvement of laundry technology and management through exchange of information and educational programs. Conducts formal schools and confers Registered Laundry and Linen Director (RLLD) and Certified Laundry/Linen Manager (CLLM) designations. Provides wash test piece service. Operates the American Laundry and Linen College. Maintains Speaker's Bureau. **Awards:** Allied Tradesman of the Year Citation. **Frequency:** annual. **Type:** recognition ● American Laundry/Linen College Scholarship. **Frequency:** annual. **Type:** scholarship. **Recipient:** to NAILM member ● NAILM Manager of the Year Citation. **Frequency:** annual. **Type:** recognition. **Computer Services:** database, membership. **Telecommunication Services:** electronic mail, jim@nlmnet.org. **Committees:** Bylaws; Conference; Credentials; Educational Affairs; Nominating. **Subcommittees:** ALLC; CLLM. **Formerly:** (1985) National Association of Institutional Laundry Managers; (2007) National Association of Institutional Linen Management. **Publications:** *Accounting*. Manual. For certification. ● *AIDS/HIV Guide* ● *ALM Journal*, bimonthly. **Price:** included in membership dues. **Circulation:** 3,000. **Advertising:** accepted ● *Chemistry*. Manual. For certification. ● *Equipment*. Manual. For certification. ● *Glossary*. Manual. For certification. ● *Infection Control*. Manual. For certification. ● *Linen Management*. Manual. For certification. ● *Management*. Manual. For certification. ● *Membership Survey* ● *Procedures for Infection Control* ● *Production*. Manual. For certification. ● *Roster*, annual. Membership Directory ● *Textiles*. Manual. For certification. ● *What Is a Professional Laundry Manager?*. Brochure. **Conventions/Meetings:** biennial Clean Show, held in conjunction with other laundry/drycleaning associations (exhibits) - always during odd years ● seminar.

2402 ■ Coin Laundry Association (CLA)
1315 Butterfield Rd., Ste.212
Downers Grove, IL 60515
Ph: (630)963-5547
Free: (877)CLA-IDEA
Fax: (630)963-5864
E-mail: info@coinlaundry.org
URL: http://www.coinlaundry.org
Contact: Brian Wallace, Pres./CEO
Founded: 1960. **Members:** 2,700. **Membership Dues:** single-store owner, $230 (annual) ● multiple-store owner, $260 (annual) ● distributor, $649 (annual) ● manufacturer (up to 2 million annual sales), $795 (annual) ● manufacturer (2,000,001 to 4 million annual sales), $1,795 (annual) ● manufacturer (4,000,001 to 6 million annual sales), $2,795 (annual) ● manufacturer (6,000,001 to 10 million annual sales), $3,995 (annual) ● potential investor, $230 (annual). **Staff:** 10. **Budget:** $1,200,000. **Regional Groups:** 17. **Description:** Manufacturers of equipment or supplies used in self-service (coin-operated) laundry or dry cleaning establishments; distributors of equipment services and supplies; owners and operators of self-service laundry and/or dry cleaning stores. Compiles statistics. **Libraries: Type:** reference. **Holdings:** archival material, business records, monographs, periodicals, video recordings. **Subjects:** management. **Committees:** Awards; Distributor Services; Long Range Planning; Manufacturer Services; Owners Services; Public Relations; Statistical Reports. **Councils:** Leadership. **Formerly:** (1983) National Automatic Laundry and Cleaning Council. **Publications:** *CLA Management Guidelines*, quarterly. Bulletin. **Price:** free, for members only. **Circulation:** 2,700 ● *CLA Member News*, quarterly. Newsletter. **Price:** free, for members only. **Circulation:** 2,700 ● *The Journal of the Coin Laundry Industry*, monthly. Magazine. Includes legislative alerts, owner/store profiles, and industry forum. **Price:** $36.00/year. **Circulation:** 25,500. **Advertising:** accepted ● *The Record*. **Price:** $5.95 for members; $9.95 for nonmembers ● *Today's Coin Laundry: A Comprehensive Guide to Entering the Self-Service Laundry Industry*. **Price:** $249.00 plus shipping and handling ● Directory, annual. Serves as a guide to manufacturers and distributors of coin-operated laundering and drycleaning equipment, services and supplies. **Price:** free for members; $25.00/issue for nonmembers. **Circulation:** 28,000. **Conventions/Meetings:** annual convention, educational seminars ● biennial trade show (exhibits) ● annual workshop, regional educational workshops - always spring.

2403 ■ Healthcare Laundry Accreditation Council (HLAC)
c/o Chris Isely, Exec. Dir.
2123 McDaniel Ave.
Evanston, IL 60201-2126
Ph: (847)328-3700
Fax: (847)328-3761
E-mail: info@hlacnet.org
URL: http://www.hlacnet.org
Contact: Chris Isely, Exec. Dir.
Founded: 2005. **Description:** Operates a voluntary inspection and accreditation program for healthcare laundry operators. Conducts an inspection of laundries that process healthcare textiles for hospitals, nursing homes, and other healthcare facilities. Grants accreditation to laundry operators who meet or exceed the high standards of processing healthcare textiles. **Telecommunication Services:** electronic mail, chris.isely@hlacnet.org.

2404 ■ International Drycleaners Congress (IDC)
c/o Carolyn Portwood, Exec. Sec.
PO Box 261
West College Corner, IN 47003
Ph: (403)685-4755
Fax: (403)265-9565
URL: http://www.idcnews.org
Contact: Mr. Chris Tebbs, Exec. Dir.
Founded: 1959. **Members:** 1,070. **Membership Dues:** regular, $150 (annual) ● Silver Club, $200 (annual) ● Platinum Club, $250 (annual) ● Benefactors' Club, $500 (annual). **Staff:** 3. **Budget:** $45,000. **Description:** Drycleaners, launderers, and allied tradesmen. Serves as a clearinghouse for the exchange of information and ideas among members. Organizes study groups on textile care and periodic international tour; offers international exchange and training programs. Maintains small library, biographical archives, and hall of fame. Bestows travel scholarships and awards. **Awards:** International Drycleaner of the Year. **Frequency:** annual. **Type:** recognition. **Recipient:** for outstanding service in the industry. **Committees:** International Traveling Scholarship. **Councils:** Japan Productivity Cleaning. **Publications:** *International Drycleaners Congress—Member-*

ship List, annual. Directory. **Price:** $10.00/copy. **Conventions/Meetings:** annual convention.

2405 ■ International Fabricare Institute (IFI)
14700 Sweitzer Ln.
Laurel, MD 20707
Ph: (301)622-1900
Free: (800)638-2627
Fax: (240)295-0685
E-mail: techline@ifi.org
URL: http://www.ifi.org
Contact: William E. Fisher, CEO/Corporate Sec.
Founded: 1972. **Members:** 6,000. **Membership Dues:** drycleaner in non-affiliated state, $316-$898 (annual) ● drycleaner in affiliated state, $401-$1,385 (annual) ● drycleaner in affiliated state (additional location), $125 (annual) ● drop store, $175 (annual) ● national manufacturer/supplier, $1,950 (annual) ● regional manufacturer/supplier, $995 (annual) ● local manufacturer/supplier, $550 (annual) ● consultant, $365 (annual) ● apparel manufacturer/institutional (up to 300 beds), $295 (annual) ● institutional (over 300 beds), $395 (annual) ● international cleaner, $200 (annual) ● retailer, $190 (annual) ● educator, $45 (annual). **Staff:** 32. **State Groups:** 17. **Languages:** English, Korean. **Description:** Retail and industrial drycleaners, hospital laundries, linen supply and drapery services, distributors and manufacturers of supplies and machinery, dry-cleaning and laundry associations, and individual launders in 43 countries. Provides washability and dry-cleanability testing for manufacturers of fabrics and related products; offers quality testing and consulting services; conducts research for members. Organizes courses in dry-cleaning, laundering, management, and maintenance. Maintains consulting service, speakers' bureau, research facilities, and library. **Programs:** Caring for the Future Now. **Formed by Merger of:** American Institute of Laundering; National Institute of Drycleaning. **Publications:** *Fabricare News*, monthly. Newsletter. Includes calendar of events. **Price:** $65.00/year. ISSN: 0161-8040. **Circulation:** 13,000. **Advertising:** accepted ● *International Fabricare Institute—Bulletins*, periodic. Serves as a supplement to *Fabricare News*. Each series covers a specific aspect of the dry-cleaning or laundering industry. **Price:** available to members only. **Circulation:** 13,000 ● *International Fabricare Institute—Industry FOCUS*, 4-5/year. Bulletin. **Price:** available to members only. **Circulation:** 13,000. **Conventions/Meetings:** annual meeting (exhibits).

2406 ■ Multi-Housing Laundry Association (MLA)
1500 Sunday Dr., Ste.102
Raleigh, NC 27607
Ph: (919)861-5579
Free: (800)380-3652
Fax: (919)787-4916
E-mail: nshore@mla-online.com
URL: http://www.mla-online.com
Contact: David J. Feild, Exec. Dir.
Founded: 1959. **Members:** 65. **Staff:** 3. **Budget:** $450,000. **Regional Groups:** 1. **Description:** Operating and supplier companies. Strives to provide tenants with professionally operated laundry facilities. Sponsors annual convention and trade show. **Committees:** Building Codes; Ethics; Government Relations; Industry Promotion; Information Exchange; Local Associations; Standards; Workers Comp/Polygraph. **Formerly:** (1982) National Association of Coin Laundry Equipment Operators. **Publications:** *MLA News*, bimonthly. Newsletter. Keeps route operators and manufacturers abreast of industry matters and events. **Circulation:** 250. **Advertising:** accepted. Alternate Formats: online. **Conventions/Meetings:** annual convention and trade show, educational offerings (exhibits).

2407 ■ Textile Care Allied Trades Association (TCATA)
271 Rte. 46 W, No. D203
Fairfield, NJ 07004
Ph: (973)244-1790
Fax: (973)244-4455
E-mail: info@tcata.org
URL: http://www.tcata.org
Contact: David H. Cotter, CEO
Founded: 1920. **Members:** 275. **Membership Dues:** North American supply, machinery manufacturer (minimum; based on sales volume), $630 (annual) ● North American supply, machinery manufacturer (maximum; based on sales volume), $2,430 (annual) ● distributor (minimum; based on sales volume), international company, trade journal, manufacturer (representative and niche), $525 (annual) ● North American distributor (maximum; based on sales volume), $2,200 (annual). **Staff:** 2. **Description:** Represents Manufacturers and distributors of laundry and dry-cleaning machinery, and supplies. **Awards:** Dean Allen College Tuition Scholarships. **Type:** scholarship. **Divisions:** Distributors; Machinery Manufacturers; Supply Manufacturers. **Absorbed:** Laundry and Dry Cleaners Machinery Manufacturers Association; National Laundry Allied Trades Association. **Formerly:** Laundry and Cleaners Allied Trades Association. **Publications:** *Allied Activities*, bimonthly ● *Convention Calendar*, quarterly ● *Roster and Buyers Guide*, annual. **Conventions/Meetings:** annual conference.

2408 ■ Uniform and Textile Service Association (UTSA)
1501 Lee Hwy., Ste.304
Arlington, VA 22209
Ph: (703)247-2600 (703)247-2601
Free: (800)486-6745
Fax: (703)841-4750
E-mail: info@utsa.com
URL: http://www.utsa.com
Contact: David F. Hobson, Pres./CEO
Founded: 1933. **Members:** 75. **Staff:** 10. **Budget:** $3,500,000. **Multinational. Description:** Industrial laundry and cleaning plants specializing in rental of work uniforms, table linens, napkins, gloves, wiping towels, dust control and entrance mats, and other items to industry, commerce, and government. Conducts research in improved processes, materials, and marketing practices. Maintains placement service; compiles statistics. **Additional Websites:** http://www.uniforminfo.com. **Telecommunication Services:** electronic mail, hobson@utsa.com. **Committees:** Customer Service; Environmental; Marketing; National Affairs; Plant Operations. **Programs:** Laundry Environmental Stewardship. **Formerly:** (1993) Institute of Industrial Launderers. **Publications:** *Industrial Launderer*, monthly. Magazine. Covers industry-specific customer service issues as well as general customer service principles. **Circulation:** 5,000. **Advertising:** accepted ● *Uniform and Textile Service Association—Buyers' Guide*, annual. **Conventions/Meetings:** Clean Show - trade show ● annual conference ● annual convention - always September/October.

Law

2409 ■ National Association of Legal Fee Analysis (NALFA)
10275 W. Higgins Rd., Ste.420
Rosemont, IL 60018
Ph: (312)907-7275
E-mail: info@thenalfa.org
URL: http://www.thenalfa.org
Founded: 2006. **Members:** 25. **Membership Dues:** general, $2,500 (annual). **Staff:** 1. **Budget:** $65,000. **Description:** Law firms, attorney fee experts, legal cost consultants, and qualifying legal audit services. Review, analyze, evaluate, and counsel on attorney fees or legal costs. Strive to provide integrity and reliability to the legal fee analysis profession. **Publications:** *NALFA Best Practices*.

Law Enforcement

2410 ■ International Association of Accident Reconstruction Specialists (IAARS)
PO Box 534
Grand Ledge, MI 48837-0534
Ph: (517)622-3135
E-mail: brandtb@benchmarktrafficservices.com
URL: http://www.iaars.org
Contact: Bill Brandt, Sec.-Treas.
Founded: 1980. **Members:** 160. **Membership Dues:** individual, $75 (annual). **Multinational. Description:** Represents law enforcement and private sector involved in accident reconstruction. Supports high standards of ethics, integrity, credibility and honor in the field of accident reconstruction; promotes traffic safety; communicates on matters of mutual interest; establishes high standards and professionalism in the investigation of traffic crashes and the presentation of testimony in a court of law; encourages training programs relating to accident investigation; and cherishes a spirit of brotherhood among members and associates. **Publications:** Newsletter, quarterly. **Conventions/Meetings:** annual seminar, includes training sessions - 2008 July 6-13, Vancouver, BC, Canada.

Leadership

2411 ■ National Association of Latina Leaders (NALL)
1230 6th Ave., Ste.700
New York, NY 10020
E-mail: info@latinaleaders.org
URL: http://www.latinaleaders.org
Contact: Rosario Marin, Chair
Description: Represents Latina leaders from major cities across the U.S. Promotes the advancement of Hispanic women in all aspects American life. Addresses issues of concern to all Latinas, including workplace and economic equality.

2412 ■ National Institute for Leadership Development (NILD)
1202 W Thomas Rd.
Phoenix, AZ 85013
Ph: (602)285-7727
Fax: (602)285-7728
E-mail: nild@nildleaders.org
URL: http://www.pc.maricopa.edu/nild
Contact: Carrole A. Wolin, Pres.
Members: 4,000. **Membership Dues:** sustaining, $1,000 (annual) ● sponsoring, $750 (annual) ● contributing, $500 (annual). **Description:** Provides leadership development opportunities for women and men in higher education, public service agencies and private businesses. **Programs:** Leaders Institute. **Conventions/Meetings:** conference ● symposium.

Leather

2413 ■ International Federation of Leather Guilds (IFLG)
c/o Ernie Wayman, Exec. Dir.
3117 Babette Dr.
Southport, IN 46227
Ph: (317)787-2586
E-mail: executivedirector@leatherguilds.org
URL: http://www.ifolg.org
Contact: Ernie Wayman, Exec. Dir.
Founded: 1966. **Members:** 600. **Staff:** 4. **Local Groups:** 30. **Multinational. Description:** Leather artists who foster, promote interest in, and teach leathercraft art. Offers instruction and addresses questions in the field; brings together members to acknowledge outstanding craftsmen. Sponsors competitions. Plans to establish educational programs. **Computer Services:** by-laws information on local groups ● membership list and activities information. **Divisions:** Master; Open. **Formerly:** (1988) Federation of Leather Guilds. **Publications:** Newsletter, quarterly. **Conventions/Meetings:** annual meeting.

2414 ■ International Internet Leather Crafters' Guild (IILG)
c/o Pat Hay, Treas.
PO Box 98
Cary, MS 39054

E-mail: president@iilg.net
URL: http://iilg.net
Contact: Ron Ross, Pres.
Founded: 1996. **Members:** 300. **Membership Dues:** individual, family, $10 (annual) ● life, $150. **Staff:** 4. **Description:** Promotes the art and craft of leather; brings leather workers together via the Internet. **Telecommunication Services:** electronic mail, treasurer@iilg.net. **Divisions:** Leather Crafts Knowledge Base Database. **Conventions/Meetings:** periodic Members Only Carving Contest - competition.

2415 ■ Leather Apparel Association (LAA)
19 W 21st St., Ste.403
New York, NY 10010
Ph: (212)727-1210
Fax: (212)727-1218
E-mail: info@leatherapparelassociation.com
URL: http://www.leatherapparelassociation.com
Contact: Richard Harrow, Exec. Dir.
Founded: 1990. **Members:** 93. **Staff:** 1. **Description:** Manufacturers, retailers, tanners, cleaners, and other individuals involved in the leather garment industry. Seeks to increase the sales of leather clothing through public relations, consumer education, and business support services. Marketing programs focus on fashion videos, media tours, press kits, brochures, hangtags, manufacturing and cleaning guidelines, and market research. Conducts seminars. **Publications:** Newsletter, bimonthly. **Price:** included in membership dues. **Conventions/Meetings:** semiannual meeting - always March/October.

2416 ■ Leather Industries of America (LIA)
3050 K St. NW, Ste.400
Washington, DC 20007
Ph: (202)342-8497
Fax: (202)342-8583
E-mail: info@leatherusa.com
URL: http://www.leatherusa.com
Contact: Mr. John L. Wittenborn, Pres.
Founded: 1917. **Members:** 75. **Staff:** 3. **Budget:** $1,500,000. **Description:** Represents the interests of the American tanner and leather suppliers. Provides environmental, technical, education, statistical and marketing services. **Formed by Merger of:** Morocco Manufacturers National Association; National Association of Tanners; Patent and Enamelled Leather Manufacturers Association. **Formerly:** (1985) Tanners' Council of America. **Publications:** *Dictionary of Leather Terminology*, periodic. **Price:** $6.00 ● *Leather Facts*. Book. Contains information about manufacturing process. **Price:** $15.00 ● *Leather Industries of America's Member Directory and Buyer's Guide*, annual. Membership Directory. **Price:** free for members and select others ● *Technical Bulletin*, periodic. Newsletter. Reports on environmental and technical issues affecting the leather industry. **Price:** free for members. **Circulation:** 300 ● *U.S. Leather Industries Statistics*, annual. Book. Presents the following data: leather production, livestock population and slaughter, footwear production and foreign trade activities. **Price:** free for members; $18.00/copy for nonmembers. **Conventions/Meetings:** annual Asia Pacific Leather Fair - trade show ● annual meeting, for members, in late summer or early fall.

2417 ■ Leathercraft Guild (LG)
c/o Robert Ambriz
1434 S Pine Ave.
Ontario, CA 91762
Ph: (909)983-9544 (818)342-9120
E-mail: leatherguild@email.com
URL: http://www.theleathercraftguild.com
Contact: Robert Ambriz, Contact
Founded: 1949. **Members:** 60. **Membership Dues:** individual, $20 (annual) ● family, $30 (annual). **Regional Groups:** 1. **State Groups:** 1. **Local Groups:** 1. **Description:** Works to preserve and promote the art of leather carving and stamping. Seeks to improve the skills of members, raise the standards of the craft, and promote the appreciation of handcrafted leatherwork. Produces designs. Keeps a collection of carved works by expert leather carvers. **Libraries: Type:** reference. **Awards: Type:** recognition. **Publications:** Newsletter, monthly. **Price:** included in membership dues. **Advertising:** accepted. Alternate Formats: CD-ROM; diskette. **Conventions/Meetings:** annual Leather Show and Demonstration ● monthly Leathercraft Meeting - competition and workshop, with show - every 3rd Sunday.

2418 ■ National Luggage Dealers Association (NLDA)
1817 Elmdale Ave.
Glenview, IL 60025-1355
Ph: (847)998-6869
Fax: (847)998-6884
E-mail: inquiry@nlda.com
URL: http://www.nlda.com
Contact: M. Howard Kaplan, Exec. Dir.
Founded: 1925. **Members:** 110. **Staff:** 14. **Description:** Represents retailers of luggage, leather goods, gifts, and handbags. Buying group producing promotional materials. **Committees:** Catalog; Gift; Luggage; Personal Leather Goods and Handbags. **Also Known As:** NLDA Associates. **Publications:** *Christmas Catalog*, annual. Features gifts and luggage for resale and consumer catalog. **Price:** free. **Advertising:** accepted ● Membership Directory, annual. **Conventions/Meetings:** annual convention ● annual meeting (exhibits) - usually March or June.

2419 ■ Saddle, Harness and Allied Trades Association (SHATA)
c/o Proleptic, Inc.
PO Box 818
Harrisonburg, VA 22803
Ph: (540)434-9845
Fax: (540)434-5298
E-mail: shoptalk@proleptic.net
URL: http://www.proleptic.net
Contact: Daniel S. Preston PhD, Dir.
Founded: 1994. **Members:** 320. **Membership Dues:** individual, $38 (annual) ● supplier, $75 (annual). **Staff:** 4. **Description:** Leather and nylon workers; suppliers of leather and textile fibers for the manufacture of saddles and harnesses. Promotes growth and development of the saddle and harness industries. Serves as a clearinghouse on the saddle, harness, and allied trades. Sponsors training programs for craftspeople; conducts research and educational programs; compiles statistics. **Libraries: Type:** reference; not open to the public. **Holdings:** books, periodicals. **Subjects:** leather and nylon fabrics, leather and nylon equipment. **Publications:** *Shop Talk!*, monthly. Journal. Contains information for the professional leather and nylon worker. **Price:** $26.00. ISSN: 1076-996X. **Circulation:** 3,200. **Advertising:** accepted ● *Trade Directory and The New Big Book*, semiannual. **Conventions/Meetings:** periodic seminar.

2420 ■ Sponge and Chamois Institute (SCI)
c/o Jules Schwimmer, Exec. Sec.
117 Wilmot Cir., No. 2
Scarsdale, NY 10583-6761
Ph: (914)725-4646
Fax: (914)725-1183
E-mail: bjschwimm@att.net
Contact: Jules Schwimmer, Exec. Sec.
Founded: 1933. **Members:** 10. **Staff:** 2. **Description:** Represents dealers and suppliers of natural sponges and genuine chamois. **Conventions/Meetings:** annual meeting.

2421 ■ U.S. Hide, Skin and Leather Association (USHSLA)
1150 Connecticut Ave. NW, 12th Fl.
Washington, DC 20036
Ph: (202)587-4261 (202)587-4244
Fax: (202)587-4303
E-mail: jreddington@meatami.com
URL: http://www.ushsla.org
Contact: John Reddington, Pres.
Founded: 1980. **Members:** 125. **Membership Dues:** regular, $1,200-$4,200 (annual) ● associate, $1,000 (annual). **Staff:** 2. **Description:** A division of the American Meat Institute. Producers, processors, exporters, brokers, dealers, and meat packers handling hides and skins; associate members are renderers, tanners, and others in allied trades. Aims to promote good relations within the industry. Conducts training course; engages in market development missions overseas. Sponsors biennial hide school. **Affiliated With:** American Meat Institute. **Formed by Merger of:** (1979) American Association of Hide, Skin and Leather Merchants; National Hide Association. **Publications:** *Hides and Skins*. Book ● *Modern Cattlehide Processing*. Video. Covers modern cattlehide processing. ● *Trade Practices for Proper Packer Cattlehide Delivery* ● *U.S. Hide, Skin and Leather Association—Letter to the Membership*, monthly. Newsletter. Includes trade statistics and business opportunities. **Price:** free, for members only ● Membership Directory, annual. **Conventions/Meetings:** annual convention ● Hide Training School - meeting.

Lending

2422 ■ American Financial Services Association (AFSA)
919 18th St. NW, Ste.300
Washington, DC 20006-5517
Ph: (202)296-5544
Fax: (202)223-0321
E-mail: cstinebert@afsamail.org
URL: http://www.afsaonline.org
Contact: Chris Stinebert, Pres./CEO
Founded: 1916. **Members:** 569. **Membership Dues:** industrial bank (based on the assets), $50,000 (annual) ● affiliate, $225 (annual) ● associate, $2,000 (annual) ● foreign, $1,000 (annual). **Staff:** 30. **Budget:** $4,300,000. **State Groups:** 55. **Description:** Represents companies whose business is primarily direct credit lending to consumers and/or the purchase of sales finance paper on consumer goods. Has members that have insurance and retail subsidiaries; some are themselves subsidiaries of highly diversified parent corporations. Encourages the business of financing individuals and families for necessary and useful purposes at reasonable charges, including interest; promotes consumer understanding of basic money management principles as well as constructive uses of consumer credit. Includes educational services such as films, textbooks, and study units for the classroom and budgeting guides for individuals and families. Compiles statistical reports; offers seminars. **Awards:** Distinguished Service Award. **Frequency:** annual. **Type:** recognition. **Computer Services:** Online services, legislative tracking service. **Telecommunication Services:** electronic mail, pmanuel@afsamail.org. **Committees:** Accounting; Financial Relations; Human Resources; Information Systems; Law; Marketing; Operations; Political Action; Public Communications; State Government Relations; Tax. **Divisions:** Communication; Legislative Affairs; Research. **Sections:** American HomEquity; Independent Operations. **Absorbed:** (1971) American Industrial Bankers Association. **Formerly:** (1983) National Consumer Finance Association. **Publications:** *Credit*, bimonthly. Newsletter. Alternate Formats: online ● *Independent Credit Operations*, quarterly. Newsletter. Alternate Formats: online ● *Spotlight*, monthly. Newsletter. Alternate Formats: online. **Conventions/Meetings:** annual Independents Conference (exhibits).

2423 ■ Commercial Finance Association (CFA)
225 W 34th St., Ste.1815
New York, NY 10122
Ph: (212)594-3490
Fax: (212)564-6053
E-mail: info@cfa.com
URL: http://www.cfa.com
Contact: Bruce H. Jones, Exec. Dir.
Founded: 1944. **Members:** 240. **Membership Dues:** company (up to 100 million in assets), $2,000 (annual) ● company (100-500 million in assets), $4,000 (annual) ● company (over 500 million to 1 billion in assets), $7,000 (annual) ● company (over 1 billion in assets), $9,000 (annual). **Staff:** 15. **Budget:** $4,000,000. **Regional Groups:** 16. **Multinational. Description:** Organizations engaged in asset-based

financial services including commercial financing and factoring and lending money on a secured basis to small- and medium-sized business firms. Acts as a forum for information and consideration about ideas, opportunities, and legislation concerning asset-based financial services. Seeks to improve the industry's legal and operational procedures. Offers job placement and reference services for members. Sponsors School for Field Examiners and other educational programs. Compiles statistics; conducts seminars and surveys; maintains Speaker's Bureau and 21 committees. **Computer Services:** Mailing lists, of members. **Absorbed:** (1975) Association of Commercial Finance Companies of New York. **Formerly:** (1953) National Conference of Commercial Receivable Companies; (1983) National Commercial Finance Conference; (1990) National Commercial Finance Association. **Publications:** *Secured Lender: Magazine of the Asset-Based Financial Services Industry*, bimonthly. Includes advertising index, annual index, federal and state legislative review, and calendar of events. **Price:** $28.00 /year for members; $56.00 /year for nonmembers. **Circulation:** 7,200. **Advertising:** accepted. **Conventions/Meetings:** annual convention (exhibits) - always fall.

2424 ■ Consumer Mortgage Coalition (CMC)
101 Constitution Ave. NW, 9th Fl. W
Washington, DC 20001
Ph: (202)742-4366
Fax: (202)403-3926
E-mail: anne@canfieldassoc.com
Contact: Anne C. Canfield, Exec. Dir.
Founded: 1995. **Members:** 8. **Description:** Financial institutions making consumer mortgage loans. Seeks to advance the consumer mortgage lending industry. Facilitates communication and cooperation among members; represents the interests of the consumer mortgage industry before banking and financial organizations and regulatory bodies. **Libraries: Type:** not open to the public. **Holdings:** archival material, business records, periodicals. **Subjects:** housing finance, lending regulations and compliance.

2425 ■ National Aircraft Finance Association (NAFA)
PO Box 1570
Edgewater, MD 21037
Ph: (410)571-1740
E-mail: info@nafa.aero
URL: http://www.nafa.aero
Contact: Karen Griggs, Treas./Exec. Dir.
Founded: 1969. **Members:** 70. **Membership Dues:** full, associate, $600 (annual). **Description:** Banks, finance companies, and other lending institutions involved in aircraft financing. Provides a forum where interests and problems concerning matters such as credit reporting, collateral evaluation, titling, and insurance may be expressed. Provides speakers; offers credit reporting facilities and collateral seizure assistance; proposes and supports legislation. **Publications:** Newsletter. Alternate Formats: online. **Conventions/Meetings:** annual conference ● seminar.

2426 ■ National Association of Church and Institutional Financing Organizations (NACIFO)
c/o Ms. Kerrie Bernardo, Sec.-Treas.
Reliance Financial Corp.
1100 Abernathy Rd.
500 Northpark
Atlanta, GA 30328
Ph: (404)266-0663
Fax: (404)365-7055
E-mail: kbernardo@relico.com
Contact: Ms. Kerrie Bernardo, Sec.-Treas.
Founded: 1967. **Members:** 22. **Membership Dues:** $400 (annual). **Budget:** $25,000. **Description:** Firms engaged in church and nonprofit institutional financing. Aims to coordinate trade practices and standards and establish rules of fair practice and self-discipline among its members. Provides consultation to governmental, church, and other agencies in dealing with problems affecting investors, the public, and financial organizations. **Conventions/Meetings:** annual meeting - always fall ● annual meeting - always midyear.

2427 ■ National Association of Development Companies (NADCO)
6764 Old McLean Village Dr.
McLean, VA 22101
Ph: (703)748-2575
Fax: (703)748-2582
E-mail: merril@nadco.org
URL: http://www.nadco.org
Contact: Christopher L. Crawford, Pres./CEO
Founded: 1981. **Members:** 450. **Membership Dues:** regular, $250-$3,000 (annual) ● affiliate, $300 (annual). **Staff:** 6. **Description:** Small Business Administration Section 504 certified development companies. Provides long-term financing to small and medium-sized businesses. Represents membership in negotiations with the SBA, Congress, and congressional staff members; negotiates changes in legislation, regulations, operation procedures, and other matters such as prepayments problems, reporting requirements, and loan servicing procedures. Provides technical assistance and information regarding special training programs, marketing techniques, audit checklists, and loan closing and processing procedures. Compiles statistics. **Awards: Type:** recognition. **Committees:** Colson User; Congressional Relations; House Appropriations; House Small Business; Portfolio Standards; Technical Advisory Services; Technical Issues; Zions Advisory. **Publications:** *NADCO News*, monthly. Newsletter. Includes issues affecting Section 503 of the Small Business Act. **Price:** free to association members. **Circulation:** 750 ● Also publishes information packages. **Conventions/Meetings:** annual meeting.

2428 ■ National Foundation for Credit Counseling (NFCC)
801 Roeder Rd., Ste.900
Silver Spring, MD 20910
Ph: (301)589-5600
Free: (800)388-2227
Fax: (301)495-5623
E-mail: press@nfcc.org
Contact: Susan C. Keating, Pres./CEO
Founded: 1951. **Members:** 178. **Staff:** 1. **Budget:** $5,800,000. **Regional Groups:** 5. **Languages:** English, Spanish. **Description:** Umbrella group for 200 member services operating over 1,500 offices throughout the United States and Canada. Promotes the wise use of credit through education, counseling, and debt repayment programs. Member agencies provide teaching units and other money management educational materials to high schools, universities, employee assistance programs, and community groups. Sponsors confidential credit and budget and homeownership counseling. **Libraries: Type:** reference. **Holdings:** articles. **Subjects:** consumer credit. **Awards:** Pace Awards. **Frequency:** annual. **Type:** recognition. **Committees:** Monitoring and Compliance. **Supersedes:** (1951) Retail Credit Institute of America. **Publications:** *Directory of Member Agencies*, annual. **Price:** $1.00/copy. **Circulation:** 5,000 ● *Money and You*, quarterly. Newsletter. **Circulation:** 60,000 ● *Synergy*, bimonthly. Newsletter. **Circulation:** 3,000 ● Pamphlets ● Also publishes plans and working suggestions for local counseling service organizations. **Conventions/Meetings:** annual conference (exhibits) - always September.

2429 ■ National Pawnbrokers Association (NPA)
PO Box 1040
Roanoke, TX 76262-1040
Ph: (817)491-4554
Fax: (817)491-8770
E-mail: info@nationalpawnbrokers.org
URL: http://www.nationalpawnbrokers.org
Contact: Dave Adelman, Pres.
Founded: 1989. **Members:** 2,450. **Membership Dues:** pawnbroker in U.S., student, $250 (annual) ● pawnbroker outside U.S., associate, $300 (annual). **Staff:** 3. **Budget:** $875,000. **For-Profit. Description:** Pawnbrokers and interested others. Seeks to educate and inform the public on the pawnbroking industry. Provides continuing education on technological changes. **Committees:** Communications; Convention; Ethics and Qualifications; Government Relations; Legal; Planning; Public Relations; State Action. **Publications:** *Buyers Guide*, periodic. Book ● *National Pawnbroker*, quarterly. Magazine. Contains articles on industry trends, legal issues, and other items of interest. **Circulation:** 9,000. **Advertising:** accepted ● *Pawnbroker News*, periodic. Newsletter. Alternate Formats: online. **Conventions/Meetings:** annual convention, for those interested in serving the Pawnbrokers (exhibits) - usually June. 2008 July 8-10, Las Vegas, NV.

2430 ■ National Reverse Mortgage Lenders Association (NRMLA)
1400 16th St. NW, Ste.420
Washington, DC 20036
Ph: (202)939-1760 (202)939-1741
Fax: (202)265-4435
E-mail: pbell@dworbell.com
URL: http://www.nrmlaonline.org
Contact: Peter H. Bell, Pres.
Founded: 1997. **Membership Dues:** firm (based on the number of reverse mortgages), $1,000-$2,750 (annual) ● associate (per firm), $1,500 (annual) ● public (per firm), $350 (annual) ● GSE/investor (per firm), $10,000 (annual) ● additional delegate (per person), $50 (annual). **Description:** Aims to enhance the professionalism in the reverse mortgage business. Serves as an educational resource, policy advocate and public affairs center for reverse mortgage lenders and related professionals. Promotes the reverse mortgage as an important financial option for senior homeowners. Educates consumers and lenders about the varied applications of reverse mortgage. **Publications:** *Just the FAQs: Answers to Common Questions About Reverse Mortgages*. Booklet. Contains lists of common questions asked by consumers about reverse mortgages; also includes answers to questions. Alternate Formats: online ● *The NRMLA Guide to Aging in Place*. Booklet. Alternate Formats: online ● *NRMLA Washington Update*, monthly. Newsletter. Covers market trends, senior issues, legislative and regulatory updates, and other NRMLA activities. Alternate Formats: online ● *Reverse Mortgage Advisor*, quarterly. Newsletter. Contains in-depth stories on management and marketing topics, business trends and borrower profiles. ● *Using Reverse Mortgages for Health Care: A NRMLA Guide for Consumers*. Booklet. Alternate Formats: online.

Lighting

2431 ■ American Lighting Association (ALA)
PO Box 420288
Dallas, TX 75342-0288
Ph: (214)698-9898
Free: (800)274-4448
Fax: (214)698-9899
E-mail: webmaster@americanlightingassoc.com
URL: http://www.americanlightingassoc.com
Contact: Richard D. Upton, Pres.
Founded: 1942. **Members:** 1,100. **Membership Dues:** associate, designer, $400 (annual) ● showroom, distributor, $480-$3,015 (annual) ● manufacturers' representative, $400-$610 (annual) ● manufacturer (with less than $5 million-$15 million annual sales), $3,070-$6,140 (annual) ● manufacturer (with $15,000,001 and above annual sales), $20,920 (annual) ● component manufacturer, $610 (annual). **Staff:** 10. **Budget:** $1,700,000. **Description:** Manufacturers, manufacturers' representatives, distributors, and retailers of residential lighting fixtures, portable lamps, component parts, accessories, and bulbs. Trains and certifies lighting consultants; conducts showroom sales seminars; disseminates marketing and merchandising information. Compiles statistics. **Awards:** Hall of Fame Award. **Type:** recognition ● Lighting Person of the Year. **Frequency:** annual. **Type:** recognition. **Committees:** Convention; Education; Engineering; Governance; PR; Standards/Engineering. **Subgroups:** Component Part Manufacturers; Manufacturers; Manufacturers' Sales Representatives; Retail Lighting Showroom. **Formerly:** (1988) American Home Lighting Associa-

tion. **Publications:** *American Lighting Association Membership Directory*, annual. Includes program of work. **Price:** free for members; $100.00/copy for nonmembers. **Advertising:** accepted ● *Ceiling Fans* ● *Energy Efficiency*. Brochure ● *Light Up Your Kitchen and Bath*. Brochure. **Price:** $5.00 ● *Light Up Your Landscape*. Brochure. **Price:** $5.00 ● *Lighting Your Life*. Brochure. **Price:** $5.00 ● *Lightrays*, bimonthly. Newsletter. **Price:** available to members only. Alternate Formats: online. **Conventions/Meetings:** annual convention and workshop (exhibits) - always fall.

2432 ■ International Association of Lighting Management Companies (NALMCO)
East Grand Office Park
100 E Grand Ave., Ste.330
Des Moines, IA 50309-1835
Ph: (515)243-2360
Fax: (515)243-2049
E-mail: director@nalmco.org
URL: http://www.nalmco.org
Contact: Molly Lopez CAE, Exec. Dir.
Founded: 1953. **Members:** 125. **Membership Dues:** associate, manufacturer, utility, distributor, $1,000 (annual) ● company (based on annual sales), $750-$4,200 (annual). **Staff:** 2. **Description:** Independent lighting management contractors that manage, clean, repair, relamp, and retrofit commercial and industrial lighting installations on a contract basis. Individual members usually operate within 50 to 100 miles of their offices. Compiles statistics; conducts specialized education programs and seminars. **Committees:** Certification; Member Services. **Publications:** *Lighting Management and Maintenance*, quarterly. Magazine. Includes collection of articles and information pertaining to current issues and technology facing the lighting industry. **Price:** $75.00 /year for members; $100.00 /year for nonmembers. **Circulation:** 250. **Advertising:** accepted ● Directory. **Conventions/Meetings:** annual convention and trade show (exhibits) - 2008 Oct. 12-15, Scottsdale, AZ.

2433 ■ Lighting Controls Association (LCA)
c/o NEMA
1300 N 17th St., Ste.1847
Rosslyn, VA 22209
Ph: (703)841-3226
Fax: (703)841-3374
E-mail: info@aboutlightingcontrols.org
URL: http://www.aboutlightingcontrols.org
Contact: Kurt Riesenberg, Exec. Dir.
Members: 13. **Membership Dues:** control/ballast manufacturer, $6,000 (annual). **Description:** Educates the professional building design and construction and management communities about the benefits and operations of automatic switching and dimming controls. **Telecommunication Services:** electronic mail, kur_riesenberg@nema.org. **Affiliated With:** National Electrical Manufacturers Association.

2434 ■ National Association of Independent Lighting Distributors (NAILD)
2207 Elmwood Ave.
Buffalo, NY 14216-1009
Ph: (716)875-3670
Fax: (716)875-0734
E-mail: info@naild.org
URL: http://www.naild.org
Contact: Linda Daniel, Admin.
Founded: 1977. **Members:** 150. **Membership Dues:** distributor, $790 (annual) ● vendor, $3,800 (annual). **Staff:** 2. **Description:** Distributors of specialized lighting products; vendor members are manufacturers and suppliers of lighting goods. Increases effectiveness and profitability through educational programs. Makes available information on the distribution of lighting products develop marketing techniques through an exchange of ideas. Develops methods of exchanging slow-moving inventory among members. Shares solutions to supply and distribution problems. Sponsors educational programs in the areas of accounting, finance, inventory control, general management, personnel training, and product cost analysis. **Libraries: Type:** reference. **Subjects:** motivational materials. **Telecommunication Services:** electronic mail, lmd@naild.org. **Publications:** *Today's Lighting Distributor*, bimonthly. Magazine. **Advertising:** accepted ● Membership Directory, annual. **Advertising:** accepted. **Conventions/Meetings:** annual trade show and seminar (exhibits).

2435 ■ National Council on Qualifications for the Lighting Professions (NCQLP)
PO Box 142729
Austin, TX 78714-2729
Ph: (512)973-0042
Fax: (512)973-0043
E-mail: info@ncqlp.org
URL: http://www.ncqlp.org
Contact: Mary Jane Kolar CAE, Exec. Dir.
Founded: 1991. **Description:** Works to serve and protect the public through effective and efficient lighting practice. Through a peer-review process, establishes the education, experience and examination requirements for baseline certification across the lighting professions. **Publications:** *LC Candidate Handbook*. Alternate Formats: online ● *NCQLP Brochure*.

2436 ■ National Lighting Bureau (NLB)
8811 Colesville Rd., Ste.G106
Silver Spring, MD 20910
Ph: (301)587-9572
Fax: (301)589-2107
E-mail: info@nlb.org
URL: http://www.nlb.org
Contact: John P. Bachner, Communications Dir.
Founded: 1976. **Staff:** 3. **Budget:** $100,000. **Multinational. Description:** Information source sponsored by trade associations, professional societies, manufacturers, utilities, and agencies of the federal government. Focuses on High-Benefit lighting (tm). Does not promote any specific form of lighting or brand name component. **Awards:** Lighting Awards. **Frequency:** annual. **Type:** recognition. **Recipient:** to lighting achievements that demonstrate electric illumination's ability to enhance human performance and well-being. **Publications:** Directory, periodic ● Handbooks.

Linguistics

2437 ■ Linguistic Data Consortium (LDC)
3600 Market St., Ste.810
Philadelphia, PA 19104-2653
Ph: (215)898-0464 (215)573-5489
Fax: (215)573-2175
E-mail: ldc@ldc.upenn.edu
URL: http://www.ldc.upenn.edu
Contact: Christopher Cieri, Exec. Dir.
Founded: 1992. **Membership Dues:** standard commercial, $20,000 (annual) ● standard non-profit, government entity, $2,000 (annual) ● subscription commercial, $25,000 (annual) ● subscription non-profit, government entity, $3,500 (annual). **Staff:** 41. **Multinational. Description:** Supports language-related education, research, and technology development by creating and sharing linguistic resources, data, tools and standards. Creates, collects and distributes speech and text databases, lexicons, and other resources for research and development purposes. **Computer Services:** Online services, access to corpora, resources. **Programs:** Automatic Content Extraction. **Projects:** American National Corpus; Annotation Graph Toolkit; Data Annotations for Socio Linguistics; Effective, Affordable, Reusable Speech-to-Text; Querying Linguistic Databases; TalkBank; Translingual Information Detection, Extraction and Summarization. **Publications:** Catalog. Contains hundreds of corpora of language data. Alternate Formats: online ● Papers. Alternate Formats: online.

Livestock

2438 ■ American Grassfed Association (AGA)
1648 Gaylord St.
Denver, CO 80206
Free: (877)774-7277
E-mail: aga@americangrassfed.org
URL: http://americangrassfed.com
Contact: Carrie Balkcom, Exec. Dir.
Founded: 2003. **Membership Dues:** producers, $100 (annual) ● professionals, $50 (annual) ● personal, $30 (annual). **Description:** Represents the interests of producers of all types of grassfed livestock, professionals in education, health, food service and other related industries, and consumers. Promotes the grassfed industry through government relations, research, concept marketing and public education. Works to establish a legal definition for grassfed and to implement a labeling program that benefits producers. Protects and promotes true grassfed producers and grassfed products through national communication and marketing efforts. **Publications:** Newsletter. Alternate Formats: online.

Luggage

2439 ■ American Luggage Dealers Cooperative (ALDC)
20 First Plaza Ctr. NW, Ste.310
Albuquerque, NM 87102
Ph: (505)246-0087
Fax: (505)246-0096
E-mail: frank@luggagedealers.com
URL: http://www.luggagedealers.com
Contact: Frank Fine, Exec. Dir.
Founded: 1970. **Members:** 50. **Staff:** 4. **Budget:** $2,000,000. **For-Profit. Description:** Retail luggage stores united to develop progressive merchandise and marketing programs for its members. **Publications:** *ALDA Line*, semiannual. Newsletter ● *Christmas Catalog*, annual. **Circulation:** 2,000,000 ● *Corporate Catalog*, periodic ● *Fall Flyer*, annual ● *Membership Roster*, annual. Membership Directory ● *Spring Flyer*, annual. **Conventions/Meetings:** annual meeting (exhibits) - usually held in February or March ● annual meeting - held in June.

2440 ■ International Luggage Repair Association (ILRA)
5102 Mayfield Rd.
Mayfield Heights, OH 44124
Ph: (440)442-5910
Fax: (440)442-5325
E-mail: lyndhurstluggage@aol.com
Contact: Jim Prikryl, Owner
Membership Dues: regular, $100 (annual). **Multinational. Description:** Committed to quality and timely luggage repair; promotes networking opportunities to provide ideas and techniques of repair for consumers, manufacturers and the airlines. **Publications:** *ILRA Direct Repair Guide*. Handbook. Contains a membership listing that is mailed to airline and luggage industry representatives. **Price:** included in membership dues ● Newsletter. Contains updated industry information. **Price:** included in membership dues. **Conventions/Meetings:** annual meeting.

2441 ■ Travel Goods Association (TGA)
5 Vaughn Dr., Ste.105
Princeton, NJ 08540
Ph: (609)720-1200
Fax: (609)720-0620
E-mail: michele@travel-goods.org
URL: http://travel-goods.org
Contact: Michele Marini Pittenger, Pres.
Members: 375. **Membership Dues:** independent sales representative, $250 (annual) ● subsidiary, $1,500 (annual) ● retailer (based on total sales), $100-$1,000 (annual) ● manufacturer/affiliate (maximum; based on total sales), $6,200 (annual). **Description:** Travel goods industry advocacy; provides statistical research, including textile luggage producer survey, China quota fill rates, and U.S. imports for consumption of luggage and flat goods. Offers services such as merchant card processing, business insurance, employee benefit plan, trademark registry, employment advertising, magazine advertising, education, 24-hour access, ground freight program, air express and air freight program, press kit, travel and office products discounts. Serves as an

information clearinghouse. **Libraries: Type:** reference. **Holdings:** photographs. **Subjects:** industry products, people, events. **Awards:** Community Service Award. **Frequency:** annual. **Type:** recognition. **Recipient:** for companies that have distinguished themselves by engaging in meaningful community service activities ● Product Innovation Award. **Frequency:** annual. **Type:** recognition. **Recipient:** for outstanding achievement in new products and in finding creative ways to meet the demands of today's travelers ● The TGA Award. **Frequency:** annual. **Type:** recognition. **Recipient:** for an individual or company that makes an outstanding contribution to the association or to the community. **Computer Services:** Electronic publishing, TGA news, monthly e-letter to membership ● online services, industry search. **Publications:** *Travel Goods Showcase*, 5/year. Magazine. Contains information on latest consumer trends, marketing tips and tactics, people in the industry, travel factoids, product news and more. **Price:** $40.00. ISSN: 1535-5756. **Circulation:** 45,000. **Advertising:** accepted. Alternate Formats: online ● Membership Directory. **Conventions/Meetings:** annual Travel Goods Show - trade show, over 250 exhibitors featuring more than 40,000 products (exhibits).

Machinery

2442 ■ Association of Equipment Management Professionals (AEMP)

PO Box 1368
Glenwood Springs, CO 81602-1368
Ph: (970)384-0510
Fax: (970)384-0512
E-mail: info@aemp.org
URL: http://www.aemp.org
Contact: Stan D. Orr CAE, Exec. Dir.

Founded: 1980. **Members:** 1,000. **Membership Dues:** organization, $700 (annual) ● individual or trade press, university, trade school, $200 (annual) ● associate, $545-$1,550 (annual). **Staff:** 2. **Budget:** $350,000. **Regional Groups:** 7. **Multinational. Description:** Persons who select, maintain, or manage the operations of heavy equipment and components, editorial members of the trade press, and representatives of educational institutions; individuals or companies that manufacture, sell, or service mobile heavy equipment. Seeks to: represent and provide a forum for personnel concerned with the selection, application, management, and maintenance of heavy equipment used in mobile operations; provide training and continuing education programs; establish better working relationships with equipment manufacturers, suppliers, federal and state agencies, equipment dealerships, universities, technical colleges, and other maintenance groups affecting the design, knowledge, and service of mobile heavy equipment. Maintains speakers' bureau; offers placement service. Conducts seminars and workshops. Compiles statistics on equipment use. **Libraries: Type:** reference; not open to the public. **Holdings:** 250; articles, books. **Subjects:** equipment, maintenance, service. **Awards:** Outstanding Associates. **Frequency:** annual. **Type:** recognition. **Recipient:** for associate member company/corporation/firm which through past efforts has significantly enhanced or promoted the association ● Richard Hawkins Award. **Frequency:** annual. **Type:** recognition. **Recipient:** for outstanding associate who best exemplifies the dedication of Richard Hawkins ● Silver Wrench. **Frequency:** annual. **Type:** recognition ● Technician of the Year Award. **Frequency:** annual. **Type:** recognition. **Recipient:** for exemplary contributions to the equipment technician profession. **Divisions:** Aviation Ground Service Equipment; Construction; Educational; Governmental; Large Commercial Farms; Logging and Forestry; Manufacturer, Dealer and Distributor; Mining; Oil Field, Exploration and Drilling; Solid Waste; Utilities. **Formerly:** (2003) Equipment Maintenance Council. **Publications:** *Up and Running*, bimonthly. Newsletter. **Price:** included in membership dues. **Circulation:** 1,500. **Advertising:** accepted. Alternate Formats: online ● Directory. Alternate Formats: online ● Membership Directory, annual. Alternate Formats: online. **Conventions/Meetings:** annual meeting (exhibits).

Magazines

2443 ■ International Regional Magazine Association (IRMA)

c/o Herman Kelly, Exec. Dir.
1320 E Univ. Ave.
Georgetown, TX 78626
Ph: (512)819-9500
E-mail: us002848@earthlink.net
URL: http://www.regionalmagazines.org/heart.htm
Contact: Herman Kelly, Exec. Dir.

Founded: 1960. **Membership Dues:** regional magazine, $450 (annual) ● associate, $3,500 (annual) ● major sponsor, $7,900 (annual). **Multinational. Description:** Magazine publishers. Improves magazines through free and open communication among members. **Awards:** Award of Merit. **Frequency:** annual. **Type:** recognition. **Recipient:** for active member ● Bronze Plaque. **Frequency:** annual. **Type:** recognition. **Recipient:** for active member ● Gold Plaque. **Frequency:** annual. **Type:** recognition. **Recipient:** for active member ● Magazine of the Year. **Frequency:** annual. **Type:** trophy. **Recipient:** for active member ● Silver Plaque. **Frequency:** annual. **Type:** recognition. **Recipient:** for active member. **Publications:** *eSignature*. Newsletter. **Price:** included in membership dues. Alternate Formats: online. **Conventions/Meetings:** annual conference.

Mail

2444 ■ Airforwarders Association (AfA)

1156 15th St. NW, Ste.900
Washington, DC 20005
Ph: (202)393-2818
Fax: (202)223-9741
E-mail: bfried@airforwarders.org
URL: http://www.airforwarders.org
Contact: Brandon Fried, Exec. Dir.

Founded: 1991. **Members:** 250. **Membership Dues:** regular (based on the number of employees), $625-$2,350 (annual) ● associate (based on the number of employees), $945-$1,420 (annual). **Staff:** 2. **Budget:** $300,000. **Description:** Provides educational programs and a voice for the industry. **Computer Services:** database ● mailing lists. **Telecommunication Services:** electronic mail, mlancaster@stanton-comm.com. **Boards:** Airline Advisory; Motor Carriers Advisory. **Committees:** Education; Strategic Planning. **Publications:** *AirMail*, weekly. Newsletter. Alternate Formats: online ● *Forward*, quarterly. Newsletter. **Circulation:** 3,200. **Advertising:** accepted ● *Membership Directory and Buyers Guide*, annual. **Conventions/Meetings:** Air Cargo - conference ● annual Air Freight Management Conference and Exposition - conference and board meeting (exhibits).

2445 ■ Alliance of Nonprofit Mailers (ANM)

1211 Connecticut Ave. NW, Ste.620
Washington, DC 20036-2701
Ph: (202)462-5132
Fax: (202)462-0423
E-mail: alliance@nonprofitmailers.org
URL: http://www.nonprofitmailers.org
Contact: Anthony W. Conway, Exec. Dir.

Founded: 1980. **Members:** 250. **Membership Dues:** mailer (based upon the annual nonprofit mail volume), $375-$17,250 (annual). **Staff:** 3. **Budget:** $500,000. **Description:** Relies on preferred postal rate mailings for raising funds and disseminating information; businesses concerned with non-profit postal rates. Seeks to stabilize rates for non-profit mail. Represents non-profit mailers in rate and mail classification cases before the Postal Rate Commission; testifies before congressional committees. Informs nonprofit organizations of postal developments affecting them. Maintains speakers' bureau; compiles statistics. **Formerly:** (1983) Alliance of Third-Class Nonprofit Mailers. **Publications:** *Alliance Report*, weekly. Newsletter. Reports on U.S. Postal Service actions, the Postal Rate Commission, changes in non-profit postal rates and regulations, and government action. **Price:** available to members only. **Conventions/Meetings:** semiannual meeting.

2446 ■ Associated Mail and Parcel Centers (AMPC)

950 Glenn Dr., Ste.150
Folsom, CA 95630
Ph: (707)226-9384
Free: (800)365-2672
Fax: (800)390-2672
E-mail: lowell.fennie@ampc.org
URL: http://www.ampc.org
Contact: Lowell Fennie, CEO

Founded: 1982. **Members:** 2,350. **Membership Dues:** regular, $240 (annual) ● additional location, $25 (annual). **Staff:** 4. **Budget:** $500,000. **For-Profit. Description:** Mail and parcel centers that offer communication services such as mailbox rental, facsimile service, parcel shipping, copying, and secretarial services; individuals working to establish a center in the industry; vendors who supply products or services to the industry. Works to improve business profitability and assists members in successfully establishing a center by disseminating business information. Provides networking opportunities. Offers health care and insurance benefits, discounts on supplies, and assistance with local and national publicity. Conducts educational programs addressing concerns such as location, interior design, profit forecasting, capitalization, and supply sources. **Publications:** *AMPC News and Ideas*, monthly. Newsletter. Compiles current industry information, news, and ideas. **Price:** included in membership dues. **Advertising:** accepted. **Conventions/Meetings:** annual convention and trade show (exhibits) ● workshop (exhibits) - 10/year.

2447 ■ Association of Alternate Postal Systems (AAPS)

1725 Oaks Way
Oklahoma City, OK 73131
Ph: (405)478-0161
E-mail: aaps@cox.net
URL: http://www.aapsinc.org
Contact: Mike Lynch, Pres.

Founded: 1975. **Members:** 130. **Staff:** 1. **Budget:** $130,000. **Description:** Companies in the business of delivering private postal advertising material to residences. Seeks to improve industry credibility and increase the public's awareness of the private postal industry. **Awards:** Award of Excellence. **Frequency:** annual. **Type:** recognition. **Recipient:** for quality delivery statistics and management. **Committees:** Education; Ethics; Marketing; Postal Affairs. **Formerly:** (1990) Association of Private Postal Systems. **Publications:** *Association of Alternate Postal Systems—Member Directory*, annual. Membership Directory. **Price:** $25.00/issue. **Circulation:** 1,000. Alternate Formats: online ● *Association of Alternate Postal Systems—Update*, 8/year. Newsletter. **Price:** free for members, clients, and industry observers. **Circulation:** 300. **Conventions/Meetings:** annual Alternative Delivery Conference (exhibits) ● annual conference.

2448 ■ Association of Mailing, Shipping, and Office Automation Specialists (AIMED)

949 Winding Brook Ln.
Walnut, CA 91789
Free: (888)750-6245
Fax: (909)594-9743
E-mail: barbara@aimedweb.org
URL: http://www.aimedweb.org
Contact: Barbara Price, Exec. Dir.

Founded: 1977. **Members:** 300. **Membership Dues:** dealer (based on the number of employees), $275-$325 (annual). **Staff:** 1. **Budget:** $100,000. **Regional Groups:** 4. **Description:** Independent dealers of mail-related products and services; manufacturers of mailing equipment. Keeps members informed about industry changes and new products. Maintains speakers' bureau, hall of fame; conducts educational programs. **Libraries: Type:** reference. **Holdings:**

archival material, artwork, books, business records. **Awards:** Murray Keating Award. **Frequency:** annual. **Type:** recognition. **Recipient:** to member who contributes the most to further the mission of the association. **Computer Services:** database ● mailing lists. **Telecommunication Services:** electronic bulletin board ● electronic mail, dcampbell@campbell-busmach.com. **Formerly:** (2003) Association of Independent Mailing Equipment Dealers. **Publications:** *AIMED Hotline*, bimonthly. Newsletter. Contains educational articles and classified ads. **Price:** included in membership dues. **Circulation:** 500. **Advertising:** accepted. **Conventions/Meetings:** semiannual conference and seminar (exhibits) ● annual meeting (exhibits).

2449 ■ Association for Postal Commerce (PostCom)
1901 N Ft. Myer Dr., Ste.401
Arlington, VA 22209-1609
Ph: (703)524-0096
Fax: (703)524-1871
E-mail: info@postcom.org
URL: http://www.postcom.org
Contact: Gene A. Del Polito PhD, Pres.

Founded: 1947. **Members:** 228. **Staff:** 4. **Budget:** $1,200,000. **Description:** Represents supporters and users of mail as an advertising, marketing, and fundraising medium. Seeks to protect interests of members with respect to postal rates and services before Congress, the U.S. Postal Service, and the Postal Rate Commission. **Awards:** J. Edward Day Award. **Frequency:** annual. **Type:** recognition ● Lee Epstein Award. **Frequency:** annual. **Type:** recognition ● Stan Woodruff Award. **Frequency:** annual. **Type:** recognition. **Telecommunication Services:** electronic mail, genedp@postcom.org. **Committees:** Postal Operations; Postal Policy; Public Affairs. **Formerly:** Associated Third Class Mail Users; (1992) Third Class Mail Association; (2000) Advertising Mail Marketing Association. **Publications:** *Post Ops Update*, published when events warrant. Newsletter. Contains news and information on postal operation issues. ● *Postal Issue Summary*, semiannual. Membership Directory ● *PostCom Bulletin*, weekly. Newsletter. Considered the most comprehensive source of both national and international postal news. **Advertising:** accepted. Alternate Formats: online ● Membership Directory, annual. Includes a listing of members, Congress, the Senate and the U.S. Postal Service. **Advertising:** accepted. **Conventions/Meetings:** board meeting - 3/year.

2450 ■ Mail Systems Management Association (MSMA)
PO Box 1145
North Riverside, IL 60546-1145
Ph: (708)853-0471
Free: (800)714-6762
E-mail: fahyb@aol.com
URL: http://www.msmanational.org
Contact: Ronald J. Goglia, Pres.

Founded: 1981. **Members:** 2,000. **Membership Dues:** individual, $75 (annual) ● corporate (up to three), $175 (annual). **Budget:** $110,000. **Local Groups:** 18. **Description:** Mail management executives. Provides training, through the development of management skills, in reducing costs, improving services, and reducing employee turnover. Organizes meetings to discuss topics such as presort discounts, scheduling, and recruiting and training personnel. Conducts certification program, training programs for mail distribution clerks, and management programs for mail managers and supervisors. Maintains placement service. Conducts research; operates speakers' bureau and consulting service. **Awards:** Distinguished Service Award. **Frequency:** annual. **Type:** recognition ● Mail Manager Award. **Frequency:** annual. **Type:** recognition. **Telecommunication Services:** electronic mail, ron.goglia@cigna.com. **Publications:** *Postscript*, quarterly. Newsletter. Alternate Formats: online ● Newsletter. For chapters. **Conventions/Meetings:** annual conference and seminar (exhibits).

2451 ■ Mailers Council
c/o Robert E. McLean, Exec. Dir.
2001 Jefferson Davis Hwy., Ste.1004
Arlington, VA 22202-3617
Ph: (703)418-0390
Fax: (703)416-0014
E-mail: bmclean@mailers.org
URL: http://www.mailers.org
Contact: Robert E. McLean, Exec. Dir.

Founded: 1988. **Members:** 50. **Description:** Represents corporations, organizations, and associations using the U.S. Postal Service to deliver mail; works to improve the postal system. **Conventions/Meetings:** meeting.

2452 ■ National Association of Presort Mailers (NAPM)
c/o Joel J. Thomas, Exec. Dir./CEO
PO Box 3295
Annapolis, MD 21403-0295
Free: (877)620-6276
Fax: (410)990-1182
E-mail: napmasst@cs.com
URL: http://www.napmweb.org
Contact: Sue Herdrich, Admin. Asst.

Founded: 1984. **Members:** 130. **Membership Dues:** vendor, $1,000-$5,000 (annual) ● contributing, $300 (annual). **Staff:** 2. **Description:** Trade association representing the interests of presort mailers. **Telecommunication Services:** electronic mail, napmexec@aol.com. **Conventions/Meetings:** semiannual meeting.

2453 ■ National Star Route Mail Contractors Association (NSRMCA)
324 E Capitol St.
Washington, DC 20003-3897
Ph: (202)543-1661
Fax: (202)543-8863
E-mail: info@starroutecontractors.org
URL: http://www.starroutecontractors.org
Contact: Cliff Blackburn, Pres.

Founded: 1933. **Members:** 5,000. **Membership Dues:** associate, $20 (annual) ● affiliate, $100 (annual) ● contractor (maximum), $7,500 (annual). **Staff:** 4. **Regional Groups:** 5. **State Groups:** 48. **Description:** Highway mail contractors with the U.S. Postal Service transporting mail over the highway on authorized schedules. **Committees:** Political Action. **Formerly:** (1982) National Star Route Mail Carriers Association. **Publications:** *Star Carrier*, monthly. **Conventions/Meetings:** annual meeting (exhibits) ● regional meeting - 5/year.

2454 ■ Parcel Shippers Association (PSA)
1211 Connecticut Ave. NW, Ste.620
Washington, DC 20036-2701
Ph: (202)296-3690
Fax: (202)331-8318
E-mail: psa@parcelshippers.org
URL: http://www.parcelshippers.org
Contact: Don Cato, Chm.

Founded: 1953. **Members:** 200. **Membership Dues:** regular (based upon the annual shipment expense), $2,000-$15,000 (annual) ● associate, $3,000 (annual). **Staff:** 2. **Budget:** $350,000. **Description:** Wholesalers, retailers, mail order houses, and other firms using parcel post service for distribution of products. Promotes the efficient and economical distribution of small package shipments. **Committees:** Parcel Shippers Association Political Action. **Formerly:** (1977) Parcel Post Association. **Conventions/Meetings:** biennial meeting.

2455 ■ Periodical Publications Association
c/o Kimberly Scott, Exec. Dir.
PO Box 10669
Rockville, MD 20849-0669
Ph: (301)260-0929
Fax: (301)260-1647
E-mail: periodicalpubs@yahoo.com
Contact: Kimberly Scott, Exec. Dir.

Founded: 1964. **Members:** 23. **Membership Dues:** publisher, $1,800-$3,000 (annual) ● associate, $1,200 (annual). **Staff:** 1. **Budget:** $25,000. **Description:** Business publications, magazines, and newspapers qualifying for periodical postage rates. Protects periodical mail rates by appropriate activity in Washington, DC. Endeavors to find solutions to postal problems of concern to members. Follows postal issues in Congress and regulation changes at United States Postal Service headquarters. **Committees:** Postal Affairs. **Formerly:** (1964) Paid Circulation Committee; (1965) Paid Circulation Council; (1974) Second Class Mail Publications; (1979) Association of Second Class Mail Publications; (1982) Association of Second Class Mail Publishers; (2001) Association of Paid Circulation Publications. **Publications:** *PPA Washington Report*, monthly. Newsletter. **Conventions/Meetings:** quarterly Postal Roundtable - seminar, on paid circulation publishing.

2456 ■ Red Tag News Publications Association (RTNPA)
c/o Lindsey Klingele
1415 N Dayton St.
Chicago, IL 60622
Ph: (312)274-2000 (312)274-2215
Free: (877)RED1TAG
Fax: (312)266-3363
E-mail: jim@redtag.org
URL: http://www.redtag.org
Contact: Jim Franklin, Exec. Dir.

Founded: 1971. **Members:** 35. **Membership Dues:** full, $2,000-$6,000 (annual) ● associate, $1,250 (annual). **Staff:** 3. **Description:** Seeks to achieve optimum mail delivery for members. Compiles statistics. **Committees:** Traffic. **Formerly:** Red Tag News Publications. **Publications:** Bulletin, periodic ● Newsletter, monthly. **Conventions/Meetings:** biennial symposium - always September, Washington, DC.

Mail Order

2457 ■ American Mailorder Association (AMOA)
2272 Colorado Blvd., No. 1228
Los Angeles, CA 90041
Fax: (323)344-8594
E-mail: jamkraut@earthlink.net
Contact: J. Pequod, Dir.

Founded: 1982. **Staff:** 3. **Budget:** $280,000. **Description:** Individuals, firms, and organizations that use mail-order or direct mail marketing. Disseminates information and news on related events and activities; reviews computer programs used in mail order and direct mail marketing, books, products, and other materials; issues warnings about mail order frauds; provides expertise to legislators. **Convention/Meeting:** none. **Libraries: Type:** not open to the public. **Holdings:** 600. **Subjects:** mail order. **Awards: Type:** recognition. **Publications:** Booklets ● Books ● Manuals.

Maintenance

2458 ■ American Homeowners Association (AHA)
PO Box 16817
Stamford, CT 06905
Ph: (203)323-7715
Free: (800)470-2242
Fax: (203)323-4558
E-mail: memberservices@ahamembership.com
URL: http://www.ahahome.com/index.cfm
Contact: Richard J. Roll, Pres./Founder

Founded: 1994. **For-Profit. Description:** Represents homeowners and cooperative, townhouse, and condominium dwellers. Provides contractor referral service to members for emergency and non-emergency home repair or replacement work. Collects performance rating information from members upon completion of work. Provides insurance counseling and other assistance to members.

2459 ■ Building Service Contractors Association International (BSCAI)
401 N Michigan Ave., Ste.2200
Chicago, IL 60611-4267
Ph: (312)321-5167
Free: (800)368-3414
Fax: (312)673-6735
E-mail: info@bscai.org
URL: http://www.bscai.org
Contact: Oliver Yandle, Exec. VP

Founded: 1965. **Members:** 2,000. **Membership Dues:** professional contractor in U.S. (based upon the company's sales volume), $145-$2,650 (annual) ● professional contractor outside U.S. (based upon the company's sales volume), $250-$5,000 (annual) ● allied/affiliate, $75 (annual) ● franchisor, $1,650 (annual) ● franchise affiliate, associate affiliate, $75 (annual) ● security company, $250-$550 (annual) ● in-house professional, subscribing, $145 (annual) ● association, $250 (annual) ● manufacturer, $600 (annual) ● consultant, $400 (annual) ● distributor, $200 (annual). **Staff:** 20. **Budget:** $3,000,000. **Multinational. Description:** Firms and corporations in 40 countries engaged in contracting building maintenance services including the provision of labor, purchasing materials, and janitorial cleaning and maintenance of a building or its surroundings; associate members are manufacturers of cleaning supplies and equipment. Seeks to provide a unified voice for building service contractors and to promote increased recognition by government, property owners, and the general business and professional public. Conducts continuing study and action, through committees and special task groups on areas such as public affairs, costs and ratios, uniform accounting, industrial relations and personnel, marketing and sales, contract improvement, research and planning, materials and supplies sources, group insurance, management training, statistics collection, safety, and insurance costs. Has developed a certification program for building service executives, and a registration program for building service managers. **Formerly:** (1974) National Association of Building Service Contractors. **Publications:** *Building Service Contractors Association International—Services*, monthly. Magazine. Includes calendar of events, classified ads, new product information, new members, industry promotions and appointments, and new literature. **Price:** included in membership dues; $30.00 /year for nonmembers. ISSN: 0279-0548. **Circulation:** 20,000. **Advertising:** accepted ● *Information Central Guide*, annual ● *Who's Who in Building Service Contracting*, annual. Membership Directory. Lists companies and contains buyer's guide. **Price:** included in membership dues; $30.00 for nonmembers. **Circulation:** 3,000. **Advertising:** accepted. Also Cited As: *Building Service Contractors Association International—Membership Directory* ● Monographs. Contains management and technical information. ● Videos. **Conventions/Meetings:** annual convention and trade show (exhibits) ● annual seminar.

2460 ■ Chimney Safety Institute of America (CSIA)
2155 Commercial Dr.
Plainfield, IN 46168
Ph: (317)837-5362
Free: (800)536-0118
Fax: (317)837-5365
E-mail: mmcsweeney@csia.org
URL: http://www.csia.org
Contact: Mark McSweeney, Exec. Dir.

Founded: 1983. **Staff:** 6. **Budget:** $200,000. **Description:** Provides information on proper and safe installation, maintenance, and operation of chimneys, fireplaces, vents, and solid fuel burning appliances to chimney service companies and the general public. Sponsors National Chimney Sweep Training School and training seminars; provides sweep training study materials; conducts certification exam. Sponsors research programs. Compiles statistics. **Affiliated With:** National Chimney Sweep Guild. **Publications:** Brochures ● Bulletins ● Newsletter. Alternate Formats: online. **Conventions/Meetings:** quarterly board meeting ● Certification Study Seminar ● Chimney Sweep School - workshop.

2461 ■ Cleaning Equipment Trade Association (CETA)
968 Lake St. S, Ste.202
Forest Lake, MN 55025
Ph: (651)982-0010
Free: (800)441-0111
Fax: (651)982-0030
E-mail: carol@ceta.org
URL: http://www.ceta.org
Contact: Ms. Carol Wasieleski, Exec. Dir.

Founded: 1980. **Members:** 300. **Membership Dues:** manufacturer, $1,000 (annual) ● supplier, $775 (annual) ● distributor, $325 (annual). **Staff:** 3. **Multinational. Description:** Manufacturers, suppliers, and distributors of pressure washer, self-serve car wash, and powered floor care systems; manufacturers of component parts for pressure washer systems. Promotes the powered cleaning systems and components industry. Acts as a voice for the industry; maintains national media relations. Promotes certified educational advancement of members through programs on current industry topics such as finance, marketing, and sales. Maintains Speaker's Bureau; compiles statistics; conducts educational programs. **Committees:** Communications and Public Relations; Government Relations; Marketing Research and Statistics; Member Benefits; Product Standards; Professionalism and Ethics; Regional Educational Seminars; Technical. **Publications:** *News Bulletins*, monthly ● Newsletter, monthly. **Price:** free. **Advertising:** accepted. Alternate Formats: online ● Annual Report, annual. Includes membership directory. **Price:** $25.00. **Advertising:** accepted. **Conventions/Meetings:** annual Power Clean - trade show and convention (exhibits).

2462 ■ Cleaning Management Institute (CMI)
13 Century Hill Dr.
Latham, NY 12110
Ph: (518)783-1281
Fax: (518)783-1386
E-mail: cmi@ntpmedia.com
URL: http://www.cminstitute.net
Contact: Ms. Kitty Finn, Admin.

Founded: 1958. **Members:** 2,000. **Membership Dues:** regular, in U.S., Canada and Mexico, $129 (annual) ● international, $200 (annual). **Staff:** 65. **Budget:** $400,000. **For-Profit. Description:** Represents individuals and organizations active in cleaning maintenance and management, including contract cleaner firms. Develops home study educational courses and publications to promote professional certification, self-improvement, and efficient work methods. **Libraries: Type:** reference. **Holdings:** 120; articles, books, software, video recordings. **Subjects:** building maintenance. **Formerly:** (1985) American Institute of Maintenance. **Publications:** *Cleanfax*, monthly. Magazine. Features carpet cleaning. **Price:** $49.00. **Advertising:** accepted. Alternate Formats: CD-ROM; online. Also Cited As: *CF* ● *Cleaning and Maintenance Management Magazine*, monthly. **Price:** free for members. **Circulation:** 43,000. **Advertising:** accepted. Alternate Formats: CD-ROM; magnetic tape ● *Custodial Technician Handbook - Basic and Advanced Levels* ● *Networking*, monthly. Newsletter. **Price:** included in membership dues. **Circulation:** 2,000 ● *Professional Car Washing and Detailing*, monthly. Magazine. Alternate Formats: online. **Conventions/Meetings:** annual Cleaning and Maintenance Conference and Exposition - conference and seminar (exhibits).

2463 ■ Environmental Management Association (EMA)
c/o Bill Doetsch, Pres.
PO Box 610548
Port Huron, MI 48061
Ph: (810)982-7271
Fax: (313)475-9229
E-mail: bdoetsch@emaweb.org
URL: http://www.emaweb.org
Contact: Bill Doetsch, Pres.

Founded: 1957. **Members:** 100. **Membership Dues:** corporate, $295 (annual). **Staff:** 2. **Budget:** $35,000. **Regional Groups:** 1. **State Groups:** 1. **Description:** Individuals administering environmental sanitation maintenance programs in industrial plants, commercial and public buildings, institutions, and governmental agencies. Conducts educational programs; operates placement service; compiles statistics. **Awards:** Chapter Awards. **Frequency:** annual. **Type:** recognition. **Recipient:** by nomination ● Honorary Awards. **Frequency:** annual. **Type:** recognition ● J. Lloyd Barron. **Frequency:** annual. **Type:** recognition. **Recipient:** by nomination ● Subsidiary Awards. **Frequency:** annual. **Type:** recognition. **Formed by Merger of:** (1956) National Association of Bakery Sanitarians; (1956) Industrial Sanitation Management Association; Association of Food Industry Sanitarians. **Formerly:** Institute of Sanitation Management. **Publications:** *EMA News*, quarterly. Newsletter. Includes planning and design, waste management and recycling, and facilities management, service, systems, and trends. **Price:** included in membership dues. ISSN: 1051-2837. **Circulation:** 1,000. **Advertising:** accepted. Alternate Formats: online. **Conventions/Meetings:** annual conference (exhibits).

2464 ■ International Executive Housekeepers Association (IEHA)
1001 Eastwind Dr., Ste.301
Westerville, OH 43081-3361
Ph: (614)895-7166
Free: (800)200-6342
Fax: (614)895-1248
E-mail: excel@ieha.org
URL: http://www.ieha.org
Contact: J. Darrel Hicks, Pres.

Founded: 1930. **Members:** 4,000. **Membership Dues:** regular, $135 (annual) ● joint in-house service provider, $250 (annual) ● joint building service contractor, $380 (annual). **Staff:** 5. **Budget:** $900,000. **Regional Groups:** 15. **Local Groups:** 105. **Multinational. Description:** Persons engaged in facility housekeeping management in hospitals, hotels and motels, schools, and industrial establishments. Established educational standards. Sponsors certificate and collegiate degree programs. Holds annual International Housekeepers Week celebration. **Libraries: Type:** reference. **Holdings:** archival material, books, video recordings. **Awards: Type:** scholarship. **Computer Services:** Mailing lists. **Telecommunication Services:** electronic mail, darrel.hicks@stlukes-stl.com. **Committees:** Convention; Education; Ethics; Focus and Awards; Information and Resources; Policy and Procedure; Publicity and Public Relations Development; Trade Show. **Formerly:** (1996) National Executive Housekeepers Association. **Publications:** *Executive Housekeeping Today*, monthly. Magazine. Primarily for management executives of the health care and hospitality industries; also includes association news. **Price:** free for members; $40.00 /year for nonmembers in U.S.; $50.00 /year for nonmembers outside U.S. **Circulation:** 8,000. **Advertising:** accepted. **Conventions/Meetings:** biennial congress and convention (exhibits).

2465 ■ International Maintenance Institute (IMI)
PO Box 751896
Houston, TX 77275-1896
Ph: (281)481-0869
Free: (888)207-1773
Fax: (281)481-8337
E-mail: iminst@swbell.net
URL: http://www.imionline.org
Contact: Joyce Rhoden, Exec. Sec.

Founded: 1961. **Members:** 2,700. **Membership Dues:** senior/technical, $50 (annual) ● associate, $100 (annual) ● student, $10 (annual) ● corporate, $750 (annual). **Staff:** 2. **Regional Groups:** 4. **Local Groups:** 25. **Description:** Persons directly engaged in maintenance in a key position (superintendent, supervisor, foreman, or manager) for chemical refineries, manufacturing firms, government agencies, institutions, and other organizations; associate members are persons indirectly engaged in maintenance in sales, service, consulting, or publications capacities. Seeks to promote the professionalism of maintenance personnel and keep members informed of developments in the field. Assembles and disseminates maintenance information related to modern cost-saving methods, processes, and equipment. Conducts plant tours; local chapters sponsor monthly meetings, lectures, and discussions on such topics as preventive maintenance, electrical specification and maintenance, purchasing procedures, painting, heating, and grounds maintenance. Maintains hall of fame. **Awards: Type:** scholarship. **Publications:** *The IMI News*, bimonthly. Newsletter. Features news and upcoming events from chapters, along with informative technical articles written by authors from around the country. ● *Maintenance Journal*, bimonthly. Provides association news and technical articles. Includes calendar of events. **Circulation:** 4,000. **Advertising:** accepted. **Conventions/Meetings:** annual meeting (exhibits).

2466 ■ International Sanitary Supply Association (ISSA)
7373 N Lincoln Ave.
Lincolnwood, IL 60712-1799
Ph: (847)982-0800
Free: (800)225-4772
Fax: (847)982-1012
E-mail: info@issa.com
URL: http://www.issa.com
Contact: John Garfinkel, Exec. Dir.
Founded: 1923. **Members:** 4,700. **Membership Dues:** building service contractor (based on sales volume), $275-$550 (annual) ● in-house service provider, $150 (annual) ● associate, $395-$625 (annual) ● wholesaler/distributor (based on sales volume), $430-$3,285 (annual) ● manufacturer/associate (based on sales volume), $575-$3,285 (annual) ● manufacturer representative (based on number of employees), $365-$475 (annual) ● joint in-house service provider, $250 (annual) ● corporate in-house service provider, $275 (annual). **Staff:** 26. **Languages:** English, Spanish. **Multinational. Description:** Manufacturers, distributors, wholesalers, manufacturer representatives, publishers, and associate members of cleaning and maintenance supplies, chemicals, and equipment used by janitors, custodians, and maintenance workers in all types of industrial, commercial, and institutional buildings. Represents members in 83 countries. Produces videos and other educational materials. Offers specialized education seminars. **Libraries: Type:** reference. **Holdings:** audio recordings, books, video recordings. **Subjects:** application techniques to general management and sales training. **Computer Services:** Mailing lists, of members and member classification type. **Additional Websites:** http://www.issafoundation.org. **Telecommunication Services:** electronic mail, info@issafoundation.org. **Boards:** Directors; European Representatives; Foundation; Mexican Representatives; South American Representatives. **Formerly:** National Sanitary Supply Association. **Publications:** *ISSA Today* (in English and Spanish), bimonthly. Magazine. Covers business topics geared to the janitorial/sanitation industry. **Price:** $20.00; C$30.00; EUR 25.00. **Advertising:** accepted. Alternate Formats: online ● *Legislative and Regulatory Update*, monthly. Newsletter. Alternate Formats: online ● Booklets. Covers maintenance subjects. ● Membership Directory, annual ● Newsletters. Alternate Formats: online. **Conventions/Meetings:** periodic INTERCLEAN - convention and seminar, show for member and non-member companies, with training seminars (exhibits) ● trade show.

2467 ■ International Society of Facilities Executives (ISFE)
c/o INSITE
200 Corporate Pl., Ste.6B
Peabody, MA 01960-3840
Ph: (978)536-0100
Fax: (978)536-0199
E-mail: insite@insite.org
URL: http://www.isfe.org
Contact: Kreon L. Cyros, Chm.
Founded: 1989. **Members:** 300. **Membership Dues:** associate, $175 (annual) ● professional or subscribing, $290 (annual). **Staff:** 2. **Budget:** $200,000. **Description:** Senior facilities executives with "ultimate responsibilities for their corporate and institutional assets". Promotes professional advancement of members. Facilitates exchange of information among facilities executives; serves as a clearinghouse on facilities management; conducts research and educational programs. Develops and distributes educational materials. **Libraries: Type:** reference. **Holdings:** archival material, audio recordings, monographs, video recordings. **Subjects:** facilities management. **Publications:** *Executive Briefs*, quarterly. Newsletter ● *Executive Updates*, monthly. Newsletter ● Membership Directory, annual. **Conventions/Meetings:** periodic board meeting and conference ● periodic seminar ● periodic trade show.

2468 ■ International Window Cleaning Association (IWCA)
14 W 3rd St., Ste.200
Kansas City, MO 64105
Ph: (816)471-4922
Free: (800)875-4922
Fax: (816)472-7765
E-mail: iwca@robstan.com
URL: http://www.iwca.org
Contact: Jack Pitzer, Exec. Dir.
Founded: 1989. **Members:** 750. **Membership Dues:** professional (based on gross sales), $225-$750 (annual) ● corresponding, $225 (annual) ● associate (based on gross sales), $500-$1,000 (annual). **Staff:** 2. **Budget:** $400,000. **Multinational. Description:** Commercial and residential window cleaning companies. Dedicated to raising the standards of professionalism within the industry. Promotes upgraded safety standards by setting safety guidelines; informs members of code and regulation changes; provides networking opportunities. **Libraries: Type:** not open to the public; by appointment only. **Awards:** Window Cleaner of the Year. **Frequency:** annual. **Type:** recognition. **Computer Services:** database ● mailing lists. **Publications:** *Professional Window Cleaner Magazine*, quarterly. **Price:** $35.00. **Advertising:** accepted ● Membership Directory. **Conventions/Meetings:** annual convention and trade show (exhibits) - 2009 Feb. 18-21, Atlanta, GA ● regional meeting.

2469 ■ Master Window Cleaners of America (MWCoA)
PO Box 495
Cumberland, MD 21501
E-mail: director@mwcoa.com
URL: http://www.mwcoa.com
Contact: Jack Nelson, Exec. Dir.
Membership Dues: professional, $50 (annual). **Description:** Seeks to improve opportunities for professional residential and route window cleaners. Gathers and provides information to its members in all aspects of window cleaning. Maintains the highest professional standards of management and service to members. Promotes and uplifts the image of the window cleaning industry as a whole. **Awards:** Thread of the Month Award. **Frequency:** monthly. **Type:** recognition. **Recipient:** to the person who starts a thread that creates the most responses, is of special interest or concern to window cleaners or the person that answers a thread with the best response ● Window Cleaner of the Month. **Frequency:** monthly. **Type:** recognition. **Recipient:** for outstanding contributions to the improvement and promotion of the Association and the professional window cleaning industry ● Window Cleaner of the Year. **Frequency:** annual. **Type:** recognition. **Recipient:** for outstanding contributions to the improvement and promotion of the Association and the professional window cleaning industry. **Publications:** Membership Directory. Alternate Formats: online.

2470 ■ National Air Duct Cleaners Association (NADCA)
1518 K St. NW, Ste.503
Washington, DC 20005
Ph: (202)737-2926
Fax: (202)347-8847
E-mail: info@nadca.com
URL: http://www.nadca.com
Contact: Kenneth M. Sufka, Exec. VP
Founded: 1989. **Members:** 650. **Membership Dues:** certified regular/associate, $825 (annual) ● affiliate, $175 (annual) ● supplemental (per location), $250 (annual). **Staff:** 5. **Budget:** $1,100,000. **Regional Groups:** 9. **Description:** Conducts educational programs on the air duct industry; promotes the ventilation system cleaning industry. **Libraries: Type:** not open to the public. **Holdings:** artwork, books, periodicals. **Computer Services:** database ● online services. **Telecommunication Services:** electronic mail, membership@nadca.com. **Publications:** *DucTales*, bimonthly. Journal. **Price:** included in membership dues; $50.00 for nonmembers. **Advertising:** accepted. **Conventions/Meetings:** annual convention and board meeting (exhibits) ● annual Technical Seminar - fall.

2471 ■ National Chimney Sweep Guild (NCSG)
2155 Commercial Dr.
Plainfield, IN 46168
Ph: (317)837-1500
Fax: (317)837-5365
E-mail: mmcsweeney@ncsg.org
URL: http://www.ncsg.org
Contact: Mark McSweeney, Exec. Dir.
Founded: 1977. **Members:** 1,000. **Membership Dues:** voting, $420 (annual) ● associate (supplier), dual, $625 (annual) ● affiliate, senior, in Canada, $210 (annual) ● foreign, $460 (annual). **Staff:** 6. **Budget:** $700,000. **Description:** Individuals in the chimney service profession. Provides an opportunity for chimney service professionals to learn about technical aspects of trade and new equipment, and to share ideas for building strong businesses and promoting chimney safety. Conducts training and certification seminars. **Computer Services:** Mailing lists. **Committees:** Certification; Codes and Standards; Technical. **Formerly:** (1979) Chimney Sweep Guild. **Publications:** *News/Link*, monthly. Bulletin. Features legislative updates and industry news. **Circulation:** 1,100 ● *Successful Chimney Sweeping Manual* ● *Sweeping*, monthly. Magazine. Provides latest information on tools, products, industry trends, and safety measures. **Price:** included in membership dues. **Advertising:** accepted. **Conventions/Meetings:** annual convention and trade show, educational (exhibits).

2472 ■ National Uniform Certification of Building Operators (NUCBO)
Address Unknown since 2007
Founded: 1983. **Staff:** 1. **Description:** Building operators, managers, plumbers, and electricians; boiler operators; others involved in building maintenance. Encourages members' compliance with national, state, and local standards, laws, and codes that are designed to protect health, life, and property. Works to establish, maintain, and update uniform qualifications, standards, and terms. Acts as an adviser to educational institutions that teach building operation and technology. Grants and issues commissions to examining agencies; sponsors examinations to test operator competency and provide NUCBO certification. Maintains NUCBO certification registry. **Awards: Type:** recognition. **Computer Services:** Mailing lists. **Publications:** Publishes standard curriculum. **Conventions/Meetings:** annual conference.

2473 ■ North American Power Sweeping Association (naPSa)
PO Box 2114
Kalamazoo, MI 49003-2114
Ph: (269)383-6993
Fax: (269)383-6994
E-mail: info@napsaonline.com
URL: http://www.napsaonline.com
Contact: Rachel Gornowicz, Pres.
Founded: 2000. **Membership Dues:** contractor/dealer/professional service provider, $275 (annual) ● municipal, $100 (annual) ● sterling, $1,000 (annual) ● premier, $3,000 (annual). **Description:** Represents contract sweepers, sweeping equipment dealers, service providers, municipalities, sweeping equipment manufacturers and sweeping industry suppliers dedicated to providing beneficial support to members, consolidating and enhancing services to the sweep-

ing industry. Provides sweeping industry information and resources to members. **Programs:** Mentoring. **Publications:** Newsletter, quarterly. **Price:** for members.

2474 ■ Power Washers of North America (PWNA)

PO Box 668
Quakertown, PA 18951
Free: (800)393-7962
E-mail: pwnahq@pwna.org
URL: http://www.pwna.org
Contact: Michael Beaudry, Exec. Off.

Founded: 1992. **Members:** 700. **Membership Dues:** professional (based on gross sales), $195-$350 (annual) ● associate, $399 (annual) ● corresponding, $195 (annual). **Staff:** 12. **Budget:** $1,000,000. **Regional Groups:** 4. **Multinational. Description:** Manufacturers and distributors of power washers; power washing contractors; suppliers to the power washing industries. Promotes use of power washing equipment and services. Serves as a clearinghouse on the industry; conducts educational programs. **Publications:** *Water Works*, quarterly. Newsletter. **Price:** included in membership dues. **Advertising:** accepted. **Conventions/Meetings:** semiannual conference and board meeting (exhibits) - always March and October ● annual convention (exhibits).

2475 ■ Restoration Industry Association (RIA)

9810 Patuxent Woods Dr., Ste.K
Columbia, MD 21046-1595
Ph: (443)878-1000
Free: (800)272-7012
Fax: (443)878-1010
E-mail: gdooner@duallservices.com
URL: http://www.ascr.org
Contact: Gary Dooner CR, Pres.

Founded: 1947. **Members:** 1,350. **Membership Dues:** general, associate, $650 (annual) ● franchisor (must be registered with FTC as a Franchisor), $1,600 (annual). **Staff:** 6. **Budget:** $1,750,000. **Regional Groups:** 2. **Description:** Companies engaged in the cleaning and restoration of carpet, upholstery, and draperies; those providing fire, flood, and other disaster restoration services; suppliers to the industry. Gathers and disseminates information on cleaning and restoration; assists members in finding solutions to specific cleaning and restoration problems. Conducts educational programs and seminars; operates laboratory. Maintains certification program. **Libraries: Type:** not open to the public. **Holdings:** articles, periodicals. **Awards:** Distinguished Service Award. **Frequency:** annual. **Type:** recognition. **Recipient:** for innovation and contribution to the industry. **Councils:** Environmental; Restoration; Textile. **Subgroups:** Water Loss Institute. **Affiliated With:** World Floor Covering Association. **Formerly:** (1984) AIDS International; (2007) Association of Specialists in Cleaning and Restoration. **Publications:** *Cleaning and Restoration*, monthly. Magazine. **Price:** $69.00 /year for nonmembers in U.S.; $79.00 /year for nonmembers in Canada; $99.00 /year for nonmembers outside U.S. and Canada; $49.00 /year for members in U.S. ISSN: 0886-9901. **Circulation:** 2,600. **Advertising:** accepted ● Membership Directory, annual. **Advertising:** accepted ● Brochures ● Pamphlets. **Conventions/Meetings:** annual Ahead of the Curve - convention (exhibits) ● annual convention (exhibits) ● annual Solutions - convention (exhibits) ● annual State of the Art - convention.

2476 ■ Sanitary Supply Wholesaling Association (SSWA)

PO Box 98
Swanton, OH 43558
Ph: (419)825-3055
Fax: (419)825-1815
E-mail: info@sswa.com
URL: http://www.sswa.com
Contact: Donna R. Frendt, Exec. Dir.

Founded: 1981. **Members:** 70. **Membership Dues:** associate, $695 (annual) ● wholesaler, manufacturer, $795 (annual). **Staff:** 1. **Budget:** $100,000. **Description:** Wholesalers and manufacturers of janitorial supplies and/or paper products. Seeks to create integrity and recognition of wholesale distribution in the sanitary supply industry. **Affiliated With:** International Sanitary Supply Association; National Association of Wholesaler-Distributors. **Publications:** *The Wholesaler*, quarterly. Newsletter. **Advertising:** accepted. Alternate Formats: online ● Membership Directory, annual. **Conventions/Meetings:** annual conference, for executives (exhibits) - usually June.

2477 ■ Society of Cleaning and Restoration Technicians (SCRT)

200 Vantage Way
Franklin, TN 37067
Ph: (615)591-9610
Free: (800)949-4728
Fax: (615)591-6920
E-mail: info@scrt.org
URL: http://www.scrthq.org
Contact: Gary Glenn, Pres.

Founded: 1970. **Members:** 324. **Membership Dues:** regular, $275 (annual) ● associate, $395 (annual). **Staff:** 5. **Budget:** $90,000. **Regional Groups:** 12. **For-Profit. Description:** Professional on-site carpet and upholstery cleaners, firms, and suppliers. Provides a forum for the exchange of technical and procedural information, including catastrophe restoration data, updates on new chemicals and processes, and technical, management, sales, and production materials. Monitors and reports on events affecting the carpet cleaning industry. Conducts workshops. **Libraries: Type:** reference. **Holdings:** 7. **Subjects:** fibers, fabrics, production, sales, marketing, janitorial, inspections. **Awards:** Niles Fletcher Award. **Frequency:** annual. **Type:** recognition. **Recipient:** for professionalism and sharing time to help the cleaning industry. **Telecommunication Services:** electronic mail, whyscrt@scrt.org ● electronic mail, garyg@scrt.org. **Formerly:** Society of Cleaning Technicians; (2004) International Society of Cleaning Technicians. **Publications:** *The Monitor*, 10/year. Newsletter. **Advertising:** accepted ● *Pro-Pak*, 10/year. **Advertising:** accepted ● *Read Book*, annual. Directory. **Conventions/Meetings:** annual conference and trade show (exhibits).

2478 ■ Society for Maintenance and Reliability Professionals (SMRP)

8201 Greensboro Dr., Ste.300
McLean, VA 22102
Ph: (703)245-8011
Free: (800)950-7354
Fax: (703)610-9005
E-mail: pwinters@smrp.org
URL: http://www.smrp.org
Contact: Patrick Winters CAE, Exec. Dir.

Members: 1,992. **Membership Dues:** student, $25 (annual) ● individual, $125 (annual) ● executive, $1,250 (annual) ● academic, $250 (annual) ● sustaining, $1,000 (annual). **Staff:** 10. **Budget:** $1,000,000. **Description:** Maintenance and reliability professionals in the manufacturing industries. Seeks to improve the quality and delivery of manufacturing maintenance and reliability services. Serves as a clearinghouse on manufacturing maintenance and reliability services; facilitates communication and cooperation among members; sponsors educational and training programs. Conducts industry surveys. **Subgroups:** Certifying Organization. **Publications:** *SMPR Solutions*, quarterly. Newsletter. **Circulation:** 2,000. **Advertising:** accepted. Alternate Formats: online. **Conventions/Meetings:** annual conference (exhibits).

2479 ■ World Federation of Building Service Contractors (WFBSC)

10201 Lee Hwy., Ste.225
Fairfax, VA 22030
Ph: (703)359-7090
Fax: (703)352-0493
E-mail: cdean@wfbsc.org
URL: http://www.wfbsc.org
Contact: Carol A. Dean, Exec. VP

Founded: 1978. **Members:** 25. **Membership Dues:** association, corporation (manufacturing and consulting), $900-$10,000 (annual) ● associate in U.S., affiliate, subscribing, $500 (annual) ● associate outside U.S., $1,000 (annual). **Staff:** 1. **Budget:** $80,000. **Multinational. Description:** Represents approximately 12,000 companies engaged in the business of building service contracting as well as suppliers to the industry. Operates as an active international platform giving its members the opportunity to consult information sources and establish important contacts which will aid them in the continuing professionalism of the associations in their own countries. **Libraries: Type:** reference. **Holdings:** 1; articles. **Committees:** Strategic Planning/Nominating. **Task Forces:** Financial Strategy Development. **Working Groups:** Executive Management. **Affiliated With:** Building Service Contractors Association International. **Publications:** *International Dimensions*, monthly. Newsletter. **Price:** free. **Circulation:** 8,000. **Advertising:** accepted. Alternate Formats: online. **Conventions/Meetings:** biennial World Congress - convention (exhibits).

Management

2480 ■ American Association of Industrial Management (AAIM)

PO Box 924
Agawam, MA 01001
Ph: (413)737-8766
Fax: (413)737-1976
E-mail: aaimnmta@aol.com
Contact: Christy Karr, Pres.

Founded: 1899. **Members:** 50. **Staff:** 4. **Languages:** English, Greek. **Description:** Provides management consulting services with products focusing on wage and salary administration. **Libraries: Type:** reference. **Holdings:** 2,640. **Subjects:** manufacturing management, labor relations. **Formerly:** (1964) National Metal Trades Association. **Publications:** *Consumer Price Index*. Newsletter ● *Executive Manager*, periodic. Manuals ● *Job Evaluation Manuals*, annual ● *Signs of the Times*, periodic. **Conventions/Meetings:** periodic Conference on Job Evaluation, regional training.

2481 ■ American Management Association (AMA)

1601 Broadway
New York, NY 10019-7420
Ph: (212)586-8100
Free: (800)262-9699
Fax: (212)903-8168
E-mail: membership@amanet.org
URL: http://www.amanet.org
Contact: Roger Kelleher, Public Relations Mgr.

Founded: 1923. **Members:** 80,000. **Membership Dues:** corporate, small business, $1,800 (annual) ● individual, $225 (annual) ● student, $95 (annual). **Staff:** 1,000. **Multinational. Description:** Provides educational forums worldwide where members and their colleagues learn superior, practical business skills and explore best practices of world-class organizations through interaction with each other and expert faculty practitioners. Maintains a publishing program providing tools individuals use to extend learning beyond the classroom in a process of lifelong professional growth and development through education. **Absorbed:** (1925) National Association of Sales Managers; (1973) American Foundation for Management Research. **Formed by Merger of:** (1920) National Association of Corporation Schools; (1920) National Association of Employment Managers. **Formerly:** (1923) National Personnel Association. **Publications:** *HR Focus*, monthly. Keeps HR managers abreast of the progressive personnel practices and developments in the field. ISSN: 1509-6038. **Circulation:** 6,500. Also Cited As: *Personnel* ● *Management Review*, monthly. Magazine. Provides information on management trends and techniques. Includes book reviews and case studies. ISSN: 0025-1895. **Circulation:** 85,000. **Advertising:** accepted ● *Organizational Dynamics: A Quarterly Review of Organizational Behavior for Professional Managers*. Includes annual index. ISSN: 0090-2616. **Circulation:** 6,000 ● *The Take-Charge Assistant*, monthly. Newsletter. Provides information for executive secretaries and administrative assistants. Contains tips on computer use, interpersonal skills and general trends. ISSN: 0010-4248. **Circulation:** 4,000 ● Audiotapes ● Books ● Reports ● Videos. **Conventions/Meetings:** annual Conference for Executive Secretaries and Administrative Assistants (exhibits) ● periodic seminar.

2482 ■ APQC
123 N Post Oak Ln., 3rd Fl.
Houston, TX 77024
Ph: (713)681-4020
Free: (800)776-9676
Fax: (713)681-8578
E-mail: apqcinfo@apqc.org
URL: http://www.apqc.org/portal/apqc/site
Contact: Carla O'Dell PhD, Pres.
Founded: 1977. **Members:** 500. **Membership Dues:** corporate (based upon the annual sales revenues), $6,000-$15,000 (annual) ● professional, $25,000 (annual) ● government, $15,000 (annual). **Staff:** 100. **Budget:** $15,000,000. **Multinational. Description:** Resource for process and performance improvement. Helps organizations adapt to rapidly changing environments, build new and better ways to work, and succeed in a competitive marketplace. Focuses on productivity, knowledge management, benchmarking, and quality improvement initiatives. Works with member organizations to identify best practices, discover effective methods of improvement, broadly disseminate findings, and connect individuals with one another and the knowledge and tools they need to succeed. Serves approximately 500 organizations worldwide in all sectors of business, education, and government. **Libraries: Type:** reference. **Holdings:** 1,800; books. **Subjects:** productivity, quality, quality of work life, benchmarking, measurement, reengineering, human resources, knowledge management, customer relationships. **Computer Services:** Online services, Knowledge Sharing Network, with more than 8,500 documents dealing with a wide variety of business processes. **Subgroups:** International Benchmarking Clearinghouse. **Formerly:** (1988) American Productivity Center; (2004) American Productivity & Quality Center. **Publications:** *APQC Center View*, monthly. Newsletter. **Price:** free. **Circulation:** 25,000. Alternate Formats: online ● *Best Practice*, 10-15/year. Reports. Features findings from multiclient benchmarking studies. ● Bibliographies ● Monographs ● Also publishes case studies, conference proceedings, Passport to Success series. **Conventions/Meetings:** semiannual conference and workshop, with presentations and activities targeted to all levels of bench markers and process owners.

2483 ■ Association of Certified Adizes Practitioners International (ACAPI)
6404 Via Real
Carpinteria, CA 93013
Ph: (805)565-2901
Fax: (805)565-0741
E-mail: paula@adizes.com
URL: http://www.adizes.com
Contact: Paula Gray, Contact
Founded: 1981. **Members:** 115. **Languages:** English, Hebrew, Slovak, Spanish. **Multinational. Description:** Professional management consultants who are certified to practice the Adizes Method of management. (The Adizes method, devised by Dr. Ichak Adizes, is a comprehensive approach to creating and managing healthy change within a company.) Promotes organizational transformation (consulting) as a profession. Facilitates discussion of ideas and exchange of information among members. Conducts research and educational programs. **Libraries: Type:** reference. **Formerly:** (1991) Adizes Network International. **Publications:** *Adizes News*, quarterly. Newsletter ● *Insights*, monthly. Newsletter ● Membership Directory, annual. **Conventions/Meetings:** annual convention - always July ● lecture ● seminar.

2484 ■ Association of Internal Management Consultants (AIMC)
824 Caribbean Ct.
Marco Island, FL 34145
Ph: (239)642-0580
Fax: (239)642-1119
E-mail: info@aimc.org
URL: http://www.aimc.org
Contact: Dr. William Trotter, Pres.
Founded: 1971. **Members:** 150. **Membership Dues:** individual, $250 (annual) ● corporate, $750 (annual) ● additional corporate, $200 (annual) ● student, $50 (annual). **Multinational. Description:** Internal management consultants. Seeks to develop and encourage the professional practice of internal management-consulting; establish high standards of professional performance; serve as a forum for the exchange of information and the sharing of professional methods and techniques; cooperate with commercial, educational, and governmental bodies on matters of common interest. Conducts educational seminars. **Computer Services:** database, industry information, for members only. **Committees:** Chapters; Education; Ethics; Public Relations. **Subgroups:** Functional; Industry. **Publications:** Brochure ● Newsletter, quarterly. **Conventions/Meetings:** annual conference.

2485 ■ Association of Management Consulting Firms (AMCF)
380 Lexington Ave., Ste.1700
New York, NY 10168
Ph: (212)551-7887
Fax: (212)551-7934
E-mail: info@amcf.org
URL: http://www.amcf.org
Contact: Elizabeth Ann Kovacs, Pres./CEO
Founded: 1929. **Members:** 60. **Membership Dues:** category A, $5,000 (annual) ● category B, $7,500 (annual) ● category C, $10,000 (annual) ● category D, $15,000 (annual) ● category E, $20,000 (annual) ● category F, $30,000 (annual) ● category G, $45,000 (annual). **Staff:** 6. **Budget:** $1,000,000. **Description:** Trade association for consulting organizations that provide a broad range of managerial services to commercial, industrial, governmental, and other organizations and individuals. Seeks to unite management-consulting firms in order to develop and improve professional standards and practice in the field. Offers information and referral services on management consultants; administers public relations program. Conducts research. Monitors regulatory environment. **Committees:** Education; Governmental Relations; International Advisory; Management Practices; Public Relations; University Relations. **Councils:** Chief Financial Officers; Communications Directors; Human Resource Directors; Legal Directors; Professional Development Directors. **Formerly:** (1982) Association of Consulting Management Engineers. **Publications:** *15th Annual Operating Ratios for Management Consulting Firms: A Resource for Benchmarking*, annual. **Price:** $495.00 /year for members; $695.00 /year for nonmembers; $300.00 /year for libraries ● *Research Findings*, annual. **Conventions/Meetings:** quarterly Affinity Groups - meeting ● annual meeting, with speakers and panels - multi-day ● quarterly roundtable, with seminars and workshops.

2486 ■ Association of Productivity Specialists (APS)
521 5th Ave., Ste.1700
New York, NY 10175
Ph: (212)286-0943
URL: http://www.a-p-s.org
Contact: Elaine Clarke, Sec.
Founded: 1976. **Members:** 2,500. **Membership Dues:** local company, $1,500 (annual) ● regional company, $2,500 (annual) ● global company, $4,000 (annual). **Staff:** 3. **Multinational. Description:** Firms and individuals engaged in the Productivity Specialist segment of the management consultant profession. Seeks to promote greater public knowledge of the productivity specialist profession (productivity specialists develop management systems to achieve business objectives in numerous areas, including production levels, quality performance, inventory costs, operating costs, and manufacturing lead times); to improve professional capabilities of member firms by promoting educational and research and development programs; to cooperate with federal, state, and local government agencies on matters of interest to members; to help member firms improve, develop, and review skills of their professional employees. Has established standards of ethics and competence for productivity specialists. **Libraries: Type:** reference. **Awards:** Advanced Productivity Specialist Award. **Type:** recognition ● Certified Productivity Specialist Award. **Type:** recognition. **Recipient:** for test, peer review board ● Master Productivity Specialist Award. **Type:** recognition. **Computer Services:** Mailing lists, educational. **Publications:** *APS Quarterly*. Newsletter. **Price:** free. **Circulation:** 1,000. Alternate Formats: online ● *APSReview*, quarterly. **Price:** free. **Circulation:** 1,000. Alternate Formats: online ● *Readers Advisory Service—A Bibliography of Suggested Readings on Productivity Improvement*, periodic ● *Salary and Fringe Benefit Survey*, annual. Newsletter. Covers association and industry news. Includes book reviews. **Price:** free, for members only ● *The Spokesman*, quarterly. Newsletter. Covers association and industry news. Includes book reviews. **Price:** free, for members only. **Conventions/Meetings:** semiannual conference.

2487 ■ Association of Proposal Management Professionals (APMP)
PO Box 668
Dana Point, CA 92629-0668
Ph: (949)493-9398
Fax: (949)240-4844
E-mail: apmpinfo@apmp.org
URL: http://www.apmp.org
Contact: David L. Winton, Exec. Dir.
Founded: 1989. **Members:** 1,700. **Membership Dues:** individual, $125 (annual). **Staff:** 2. **Budget:** $250,000. **Local Groups:** 16. **Description:** Proposal managers, proposal planners, proposal writers, consultants, desktop publishers, and marketing managers. Encourages unity and cooperation among industry professionals. Seeks to broaden member knowledge and skills through developmental, educational, and social activities. Maintains speakers' bureau. Provides current information and developments in the field. **Awards:** APMP Fellows Award. **Frequency:** annual. **Type:** recognition. **Recipient:** for individuals who have made substantial contributions to the profession. **Publications:** *APMP Professional Journal*, semiannual ● *Perspective*, quarterly. Newsletter. **Price:** included in membership dues. **Circulation:** 1,700. **Advertising:** accepted ● Proceedings, annual. **Conventions/Meetings:** annual conference (exhibits) - always May or June.

2488 ■ Center for Creative Leadership (CCL)
PO Box 26300
Greensboro, NC 27438-6300
Ph: (336)545-2810
Fax: (336)282-3284
E-mail: info@leaders.ccl.org
URL: http://www.ccl.org
Contact: John Alexander, Pres.
Founded: 1970. **Staff:** 500. **Budget:** $55,000,000. **Multinational. Description:** Promotes behavioral science research and leadership education. **Libraries: Type:** reference. **Holdings:** 6,000. **Subjects:** management development, industrial and organizational psychology. **Awards:** Distinguished Alumni Award. **Frequency:** annual. **Type:** recognition. **Recipient:** for accomplishments and continuing growth and development of individuals who have participated in CCL leadership development programs ● Kenneth Clark Award. **Type:** monetary. **Recipient:** for outstanding unpublished papers by undergraduate and graduate students ● Walter Ulmer Award, Jr. Applied Research Award. **Type:** monetary. **Recipient:** to an individual whose research career exemplifies the Center's value of integrating science and practice. **Divisions:** Client Services/Registration; Education and Nonprofit Sector; Information Services; Leadership; Marketing; Research; Training. **Publications:** *Center for Creative Leadership Catalog*, annual. Includes training programs, assessment tools, and publications. **Price:** free. **Circulation:** 35,000. Alternate Formats: online ● *Leadership in Action*, bimonthly. Newsletter. Highlights CCL research. Includes book reviews and upcoming CCL training

programs. **Price:** $189.00 in U.S. and Canada, Mexico; $225.00 other countries. **Circulation:** 35,000 ● *Research Reports*, periodic ● Bibliographies ● Books ● Reports. **Conventions/Meetings:** annual Friends of the Century Leadership - conference, for CCL alumni, partners, colleagues, and thought leaders.

2489 ■ Center for Management Effectiveness (CME)
15332 Antioch St., Ste.46
Pacific Palisades, CA 90272
Ph: (310)459-6052 (310)459-6502
Free: (888)819-0200
Fax: (310)459-9307
E-mail: info@cmeinc.com
URL: http://www.cmeinc.org
Contact: Eric L. Herzog PhD, Pres.

Founded: 1981. **Staff:** 6. **For-Profit. Description:** Participants are directors of training and management development from industry, government, and nonprofit organizations. Conducts programs for management trainers on topics such as stress management, resolution of disagreements, risk-taking, problem solving, strategic decision-making and managing change. **Publications:** *Managing Conflict and Disagreement.* Manual. Contains training materials. **Price:** $25.00 for participant workbook; $8.95 for self-assessment; $12.95 for book; $1,225.00/package ● *Managing Stress.* Manual. **Price:** $25.00 for participant's workbook; $8.95 for self-assessment; $15.95 for book; $1,045.00/package ● *Risk Taking.* Manual. **Price:** $25.00 for participant's workbook; $8.95 for self-assessments; $12.95 for book; $1,030.00/package. **Conventions/Meetings:** periodic meeting and workshop, on managing disagreements and conflict, managing stress, and leading change ● periodic Training Trainers in Managing Conflict and Disagreement, Managing Stress, and Risk Taking and Managing Change - seminar and workshop.

2490 ■ Center for Management Technology (CMT)
16 E 96th St., Apt. 4A
New York, NY 10128-0784
Ph: (212)730-5430
Fax: (212)730-5434
Contact: William D. Greenspan, Managing Dir.

Founded: 1965. **For-Profit. Description:** Management consultants who help organizations improve business operations and profitability.

2491 ■ College of Performance Management (CPM)
101 S Whiting St., Ste.320
Alexandria, VA 22304
Ph: (703)370-7885
Fax: (703)370-1757
E-mail: execadmin@pmi-cpm.org
URL: http://www.pmi-cpm.org
Contact: Gaile Argiro, Exec. Admin.

Founded: 1985. **Members:** 1,750. **Membership Dues:** individual, $119 (annual) ● student, $30 (annual) ● retiree, $60 (annual). **Staff:** 1. **Regional Groups:** 4. **Local Groups:** 18. **Description:** Serves as a forum for the exchange of information on project management and performance measurement in business. Conducts educational programs. **Libraries: Type:** reference. **Awards:** Chapter Growth Award. **Frequency:** annual. **Type:** recognition ● Outstanding Chapter Member. **Frequency:** annual. **Type:** recognition ● Whitey Preissnack Award. **Frequency:** annual. **Type:** recognition. **Computer Services:** database, of membership. **Affiliated With:** Society of Cost Estimating and Analysis. **Formerly:** (2000) Performance Management Association. **Publications:** *The Measurable News*, quarterly. Newsletter. **Price:** included in membership dues. **Circulation:** 1,300. **Advertising:** accepted. Alternate Formats: online ● Annual Report, annual. Alternate Formats: online. **Conventions/Meetings:** annual conference (exhibits).

2492 ■ Construction Management Association of America (CMAA)
7926 Jones Branch Dr., Ste.800
McLean, VA 22102
Ph: (703)356-2622 (703)677-3368
Fax: (703)356-6388
E-mail: info@cmaanet.org
URL: http://www.cmaanet.org
Contact: Bruce D'Agostino, Pres./CEO

Founded: 1981. **Members:** 1,850. **Membership Dues:** large corporation, $6,000 (annual) ● mid-size corporation, $3,000 (annual) ● small corporation, $1,500 (annual) ● sole proprietor, $450 (annual) ● CM practitioner, $350 (annual) ● owner organization, $1,200 (annual) ● owner individual, faculty, $120 (annual) ● associate, $500 (annual) ● student, $25 (annual). **Staff:** 8. **Budget:** $1,700,000. **Regional Groups:** 16. **Description:** Promotes the growth and development of construction management as a professional service; encourages high professional standards. Conducts conferences and forums on construction management topics. Sponsors a professional certification program. **Libraries: Type:** reference. **Awards:** Person of the Year Award. **Frequency:** annual. **Type:** recognition. **Recipient:** for an industry leader who has made a significant contribution on behalf of the construction management industry ● Project Achievement Awards. **Frequency:** annual. **Type:** recognition. **Recipient:** for project excellence. **Telecommunication Services:** electronic mail, bdagostino@cmaanet.org. **Committees:** Certification Program; Contract Documents; Standards of Practice; Technical. **Publications:** *CM Advisor*, bimonthly. Newsletter. Covers association activities; provides legal, legislative, and industry news concerning construction management. Includes calendar of events. **Price:** free, for members only. **Circulation:** 2,200. **Advertising:** accepted ● *CMAA Documents: Standard CM Services and Practice*, annual. Manual. **Circulation:** 500. Also Cited As: *CMAA Manual: Standards of Practice* ● *Owners Guide to Construction Management*, annual ● *Time Management Procedures*, annual ● Also publishes contract documents. **Conventions/Meetings:** annual conference and trade show (exhibits) - 2008 Oct. 12-14, San Francisco, CA ● annual seminar.

2493 ■ Cost Management Group (CMG)
c/o Institute of Management Accountants
10 Paragon Dr.
Montvale, NJ 07645-1773
Ph: (201)573-9000
Free: (800)638-4427
Fax: (201)474-1600
E-mail: ima@imanet.org
URL: http://www.imanet.org/membership_communities_cost_management.asp
Contact: Paul A. Sharman ACMA, Pres./CEO

Founded: 1991. **Members:** 1,500. **Staff:** 2. **Description:** A group within the Institute of Management Accountants. Seeks to improve the quality of corporate cost management systems. Educates business professionals about decision-making and productivity improvement. Provides a means of exchanging opinions and experiences about cost management systems. Conducts surveys; compiles statistics. **Affiliated With:** Institute of Management Accountants. **Publications:** Reprints.

2494 ■ Employers Group
1150 S Olive St., Ste.2300
Los Angeles, CA 90015
Ph: (213)748-0421
Free: (800)748-8484
Fax: (213)742-0301
E-mail: customeradvocate@employersgroup.com
URL: http://www.employersgroup.com
Contact: Mark Wilbur, Pres./CEO

Founded: 1896. **Members:** 4,000. **Staff:** 79. **Budget:** $10,000,000. **Regional Groups:** 3. **For-Profit. Description:** Provides human resources management services including wage, salary, and benefit surveys; personnel practices surveys; management counseling; management education programs; litigation surveillance; government relations; and research library service. Provides customized human resources services including employee opinion surveys and employee communications programs through its subsidiary, The Employers Group Service Corp. Offers unemployment insurance services, workers' compensation programs, and in-house management training programs. Conducts research and educational programs; maintains speakers' bureau. **Libraries: Type:** reference. **Formed by Merger of:** (1993) Federated Employers; Merchants and Manufacturers Association. **Publications:** *California Employment Law*, annual. Includes reference work covering California laws governing employment in the private sector. ● *California Wage and Hour GuideAL*, annual. Includes reference work covering California wage and hour laws and workplace regulations. ● Newsletter, monthly ● Manuals ● Monographs ● Papers.

2495 ■ Governance Institute (TGI)
6333 Greenwich Dr., Ste.200
San Diego, CA 92122
Ph: (858)909-0811
Free: (877)712-8778
Fax: (858)909-0813
E-mail: info@governanceinstitute.com
URL: http://www.governanceinstitute.com
Contact: Jona Raasch, Pres.

Founded: 1986. **Members:** 11,000. **Description:** Provides essential knowledge and solutions to achieve excellence in governance. **Libraries: Type:** reference. **Subjects:** governance. **Publications:** *Annual Governance Trends and Practices* ● *BoardRoom Press*, bimonthly. Newsletter. Includes current issues, Board leader profiles, and topics from conferences. ● *Directory of Speakers* ● *8 Minute Quarterly Videos for Boards*. Features topics on Board effectiveness and important healthcare issues. ● Papers, quarterly. Includes latest topics of interest to hospital and health system Boards. **Conventions/Meetings:** annual Chairperson and CEO Conference ● conference - 5/year.

2496 ■ Human Resource Planning Society (HRPS)
317 Madison Ave., Ste.1509
New York, NY 10017
Ph: (212)490-6387
Fax: (212)682-6851
E-mail: info@hrps.org
URL: http://www.hrps.org
Contact: Walter J. Cleaver, Pres./CEO

Founded: 1977. **Members:** 3,500. **Membership Dues:** individual, $395 ● corporate (bronze), $5,000 ● corporate (silver), $10,000 ● corporate (gold), $20,000 ● corporate (platinum), $30,000. **Staff:** 7. **Budget:** $1,700,000. **Regional Groups:** 14. **Description:** Human resource planning professionals representing 160 corporations and 3000 individual members, including strategic human resources planning and development specialists, staffing analysts, business planners, line managers, and others who function as business partners in the application of strategic human resource management practices. Seeks to increase the impact of human resource planning and management on business and organizational performance. Sponsors program of professional development in human resource planning concepts, techniques, and practices. Offers networking opportunities. **Committees:** Professional Development; Research. **Publications:** *Human Resource Planning*, quarterly. Journal. Provides surveys, case studies, analysis techniques, research reports, and articles regarding human resource planning. **Price:** included in membership dues; $150.00 for nonmembers. **Circulation:** 3,600. **Advertising:** accepted ● *Human Resource Planning Society—Membership Directory*, annual. Lists individual members alphabetically, geographically, and by company. Includes calendar of events. **Circulation:** 2,200 ● Also publishes educational materials on best practices. **Conventions/Meetings:** annual conference ● annual meeting, forum for sponsors only ● biennial symposium ● monthly workshop.

2497 ■ Institute of Certified Professional Managers (ICPM)
James Madison Univ.
MSC 5504
Harrisonburg, VA 22807

Ph: (540)568-3247
Free: (800)568-4120
Fax: (540)801-8650
E-mail: icpmcm@jmu.edu
URL: http://cob.jmu.edu/icpm
Contact: Lynn S. Powell CM, Dir.
Founded: 1974. **Members:** 10,000. **Membership Dues:** professional, $50 (annual). **Staff:** 4. **Budget:** $350,000. **Multinational. Description:** Seeks to raise competency and professionalism in the field of management through training and certification of individuals, management chapters, and corporate groups. Sets performance standards for managers worldwide, offers services in the areas of management education, academic assessment, and certification. **Libraries: Type:** not open to the public. **Holdings:** articles. **Awards:** Certified Manager. **Type:** recognition. **Recipient:** for an individual passing 3 management exams, meeting education, and experience criteria. **Computer Services:** Online services, CM Directory. **Publications:** *Certified Letter*, semiannual. Newsletter. Features information for and about Certified Managers. Alternate Formats: online ● *Management World*, monthly. Journal. Features articles on a variety of management topics. Alternate Formats: online. **Conventions/Meetings:** board meeting.

2498 ■ Institute for Health and Productivity Management (IHPM)
4435 Waterfront Dr., Ste.101
Glen Allen, VA 23060
Ph: (804)527-1905
Fax: (804)747-5316
E-mail: bill@ihpm.org
URL: http://www.ihpm.org
Contact: Dr. W.C. Williams III, Sr. VP/Co-Founder
Founded: 1997. **Membership Dues:** individual, $195 (annual) ● advisory council, $25,000 (annual) ● advisory committee, $5,000 (annual) ● affiliate, $2,500 (annual) ● employer group, $1,500 (annual). **Description:** Health and productivity managers. Seeks to advance the professional status of members; works to improve management techniques. Conducts research and educational programs; compiles statistics. **Awards:** Corporate Health and Productivity Management Awards. **Frequency:** annual. **Type:** recognition. **Recipient:** for health corporations. **Committees:** Consultant Advisory; Health Plan/Insurer Advisory; Provider Advisory. **Councils:** Advisory; Business Leadership; Health Management Strategic Advisory. **Publications:** *Health and Productivity Management*, quarterly. Magazine. **Price:** $95.00/year; $155.00 for 2 years; $30.00/issue. **Circulation:** 12,000. **Advertising:** accepted. Alternate Formats: online ● *Measuring Employee Productivity: A Guide to Self-Assessment Tools - The Gold Book.* **Price:** $49.00 for members; $59.00 for nonmembers. Alternate Formats: online ● *Platinum Book: Practical Applications of the Health and Productivity Management Model.* **Price:** $85.00 for members; $95.00 for nonmembers ● Bulletin. Alternate Formats: online ● Reports. **Price:** $34.95 for members; $49.95 for nonmembers. **Conventions/Meetings:** annual conference - always fall ● periodic conference.

2499 ■ Institute of Management Consultants USA (IMC USA)
2025 M St. NW, Ste.800
Washington, DC 20036-3309
Ph: (202)367-1134
Free: (800)221-2557
Fax: (202)367-2134
E-mail: office@imcusa.org
URL: http://www.imcusa.org
Contact: Megan Renner, Acting Exec. Dir.
Founded: 1968. **Members:** 2,800. **Membership Dues:** professional, $295 (annual) ● affiliate, $175 (annual) ● student, $50 (annual). **Staff:** 7. **Budget:** $500,000. **National Groups:** 28. **Description:** Individual management consultants who work privately or in consulting firms. Sets standards of professionalism and ethics for the management consulting profession. **Awards:** Fellow Certified Management Consultant. **Frequency:** annual. **Type:** recognition. **Recipient:** for exemplary service to IMC & The Management. **Affiliated With:** Association of Management Consulting Firms. **Absorbed:** Society of Professional Management Consultants; Association of Management Consultants. **Publications:** *Connector*, monthly. Newsletter. **Price:** included in membership dues. Alternate Formats: online ● *Management Consultants Resource Guide*, annual. Membership Directory. **Price:** $95.00. **Conventions/Meetings:** annual conference (exhibits) ● Consultants' Western Confab - conference ● Management Consulting - workshop, for professionals.

2500 ■ Institute for Operations Research and the Management Sciences (INFORMS)
7240 Parkway Dr., Ste.310
Hanover, MD 21076-1310
Ph: (443)757-3500
Free: (800)446-3676
Fax: (443)757-3515
E-mail: informs@informs.org
URL: http://www.informs.org
Contact: Mark G. Doherty, Exec. Dir.
Founded: 1995. **Members:** 10,500. **Membership Dues:** regular, $130 (annual) ● student, retired, $32 (annual). **Staff:** 34. **Budget:** $6,000,000. **Regional Groups:** 9. **State Groups:** 4. **Local Groups:** 27. **National Groups:** 36. **Multinational. Description:** International scientific society dedicated to improving operational processes, decision-making and management through the application of methods from science and mathematics. Represents operations researchers, management scientists, and those working in related fields within engineering and the information, decision, mathematical, and social sciences. **Libraries: Type:** reference. **Holdings:** archival material. **Awards:** Franz Edelman Award for Management Science Achievement. **Type:** monetary. **Recipient:** to OR/MS practitioners for outstanding examples of management science and operations research practice ● George B. Dantzig Dissertation Award. **Frequency:** annual. **Type:** recognition. **Recipient:** for the best dissertation that is innovative and relevant to the practice of operations research and management sciences ● George E. Kimball Medal. **Type:** medal. **Recipient:** for distinguished service to the institute and profession of operations research and management sciences ● George Nicholson Student Paper Competition. **Frequency:** annual. **Type:** monetary. **Recipient:** for outstanding papers in the field of operations research and management sciences written by a student ● INFORMS Expository Writing Award. **Frequency:** annual. **Type:** monetary. **Recipient:** to an operations research/management scientist whose publications demonstrate consistently high standard of expository writing ● INFORMS President's Award. **Frequency:** annual. **Type:** recognition. **Recipient:** for contributions to the welfare of society by members ● INFORMS Prize. **Frequency:** annual. **Type:** recognition. **Recipient:** for effective integration of Operations Research/Management Science (OR/MS) into organizational decision making ● INFORMS Prize for the Teaching of OR/MS Practice. **Frequency:** annual. **Type:** recognition. **Recipient:** to a university or college teacher for excellence in teaching the practice of OR/MS ● John von Neumann Theory Prize. **Frequency:** annual. **Type:** monetary. **Recipient:** for fundamental, sustained contributions to theory in operations research and management sciences ● Lanchester Prize. **Frequency:** annual. **Type:** recognition. **Recipient:** for the best paper in field ● Philip McCord Morse Lectureship Award. **Type:** monetary. **Recipient:** to a distinguished member who has exemplified the true spirit of Dr. Morse and is an outstanding spokesperson for OR/MS profession. **Computer Services:** Mailing lists, of members. **Committees:** Academic/Practitioner Interface; Bylaws, Policies and Procedures; Case Study Prize; Dantzig Dissertation. **Formerly:** (1998) The Institute of Management Sciences. **Publications:** *Information Systems Research*, quarterly. Journal. Contains theory, research, and intellectual development, focusing on information systems in organizations, institutions, the economy and society. **Price:** $132.00 for nonmembers in U.S.; $172.00 for nonmembers outside U.S.; free for members. ISSN: 1047-7047. **Advertising:** accepted. Alternate Formats: online ● *INFORMS Journal on Computing*, quarterly. Publishes papers on the intersection of operations research and computer science. **Price:** $132.00 for nonmembers in U.S.; $172.00 for nonmembers outside U.S.; free for members. ISSN: 0899-1499. Alternate Formats: online ● *Informs Transactions on Education*, periodic. Journal. Committed to publishing the best in scholarly articles on the topic of education in Operations Research and Management Sciences. **Price:** free for members ● *Interfaces*, bimonthly. Journal. Seeks to improve communications between managers and professionals in OR/MS and to inform the academic community. Published in conjunction with ORSA. **Price:** $142.00 for nonmembers in U.S.; $184.00 for nonmembers outside U.S.; free for members. ISSN: 0092-2102. **Advertising:** accepted ● *Management Science*, monthly. Journal. Published to scientifically address problems, interests, and concerns of organizational decision-makers. **Price:** $160.00 for nonmembers in U.S.; $208.00 for nonmembers outside U.S.; free for members. ISSN: 0025-1909. **Advertising:** accepted. Alternate Formats: online ● *Manufacturing and Service Operations Management*, quarterly. Journal. Publishes state of the art theory and practice oriented articles related to managing all aspects of the production of goods and services. **Price:** $132.00 for nonmembers in U.S.; $172.00 for nonmembers outside U.S.; free for members. ISSN: 1523-4614 ● *Marketing Science*, quarterly. Journal. Published in conjunction with ORSA. **Price:** $132.00 for nonmembers in U.S.; $172.00 for nonmembers outside U.S.; free for members. ISSN: 0732-2399. **Advertising:** accepted ● *Mathematics of Operations Research*, quarterly. Journal. Publishes significant research and reviews papers with relevance to operations research and management science. **Price:** $142.00 for nonmembers in U.S.; $184.00 for nonmembers outside U.S.; free for members. ISSN: 0364-765X. Alternate Formats: online ● *Operations Research*, bimonthly. Journal. Serves the entire Operations Research community, including practitioners, researchers, educators, and students. **Price:** $142.00 for nonmembers in U.S.; $184.00 for nonmembers outside U.S.; free for members. ISSN: 0030-364X. Alternate Formats: online ● *OR/MS Today*, bimonthly. Magazine. Provides comprehensive look at OR and MS through news stories, features articles, case studies, software reviews, and surveys. **Price:** included in membership dues; $38.00 /year for nonmembers; $58.00 /year for institutions ● *Organization Science*, bimonthly. Journal. Publishes research from all over the world. **Price:** $142.00 for nonmembers in U.S.; $184.00 for nonmembers outside U.S.; free for members. ISSN: 1047-7039. Alternate Formats: online ● *PubsOnLine Suite*, 54 updates per year (total of all journal updates). Includes all 10 online journals. Alternate Formats: online ● *Transportation Science*, quarterly. Journal. Publishes original contributions and surveys on phenomena associated with all modes of transportation, present, and prospective. **Price:** $142.00 for nonmembers in U.S.; $184.00 for nonmembers outside U.S.; free for members. ISSN: 0041-1655. Alternate Formats: online ● Also publishes marketing management models. **Conventions/Meetings:** semiannual Analyzing and Enhancing the Extended Enterprise: INFORMS Conference on Practice - competition, for student papers on successful applications of management science ● semiannual conference, sponsored by Society on Manufacturing and Service Operations Management (MSOM) (exhibits) ● INFORMS Telecommunications Conference ● Marketing Science Conference ● annual meeting - 2008 Oct. 12-15, Washington, DC; 2009 Oct. 11-14, San Diego, CA; 2010 Nov. 7-10, Austin, TX.

2501 ■ Issue Management Council (IMC)
207 Loudoun St. SE
Leesburg, VA 20175-3115
Ph: (703)777-8450
Fax: (703)777-8484
E-mail: info@issuemanagement.org
URL: http://www.issuemanagement.org
Contact: Teresa Yancey Crane, Pres.
Founded: 1988. **Members:** 150. **Membership Dues:** regular, $640 (annual) ● associate, $195 (annual) ●

provider, $1,000 (annual) ● corporate, $2,500 (annual). **Staff:** 3. **Multinational. Description:** Issue managers, primarily those employed by corporations. Works to enhance members' skills, contribute to their knowledge of issues, and maximize organizational effectiveness through the application of issue management. Facilitates exchange of information among members on matters of mutual concern. Conducts educational programs and workshops. **Awards:** W. Howard Chase Award. **Frequency:** annual. **Type:** recognition. **Recipient:** for organizational excellence in issue management. **Formerly:** The Issue Exchange. **Publications:** *Corporate Public Issues and Their Management*, monthly. Newsletter. **Price:** $288.00/year. ISSN: 0730-5192 ● *The Issue Barometer*, monthly. Newsletter. **Price:** $257.00/year. **Conventions/Meetings:** annual conference.

2502 ■ MRA-The Management Association
PO Box 911
Pewaukee, WI 53072-0911
Ph: (262)523-9090
Free: (800)488-4845
Fax: (262)523-9091
E-mail: infonow@mranet.org
URL: http://www.mranet.org
Contact: Susan Fronk, Pres./CEO
Founded: 1901. **Members:** 2,400. **Staff:** 140. **Description:** Aims to maximize performance of organizations and employees. Provides information and communications, training, transactional HR solutions, and high-level business and human resource consulting; members range in size from two employees to 10,000 and represent manufacturing service, healthcare, and finance. **Publications:** *COBRA Guide*, annual. **Price:** $195.00 for members; $275.00 for nonmembers ● *The Human Resource Digest*, monthly. **Price:** available to members only ● *Illinois Law Guide*, annual. **Price:** $175.00 for members (print); $220.00 for nonmembers (print); $150.00 for members (CD); $195.00 for nonmembers (CD). Alternate Formats: CD-ROM ● *IM Journal*, quarterly. **Price:** available to members only ● *Wisconsin Law Guide*, annual. **Price:** $175.00 for members (print); $150.00 for members (CD); $220.00 for nonmembers (print); $195.00 for nonmembers (CD). Alternate Formats: CD-ROM ● Surveys. **Conventions/Meetings:** annual HR Conference ● annual Safety Conference.

2503 ■ NAED Education and Research Foundation (NERF)
c/o National Association of Electrical Distributors
1100 Corporate Square Dr., Ste.100
St. Louis, MO 63132
Ph: (314)991-9000
Free: (888)791-2512
Fax: (314)991-3060
E-mail: info@naed.org
URL: http://www.naed.org
Contact: Michelle Jaworowski, Exec. Dir.
Founded: 1969. **Staff:** 4. **Budget:** $1,000,000. **Description:** Established by the National Association of Electrical Distributors (see separate entry) to provide electrical distributor and distributor-oriented manufacturers with the opportunity to become better business people by expanding their managerial skills. Designs and conducts seminars, workshops, conferences, and home study materials covering all aspects of professional management in the electrical supply industry. **Affiliated With:** National Association of Electrical Distributors. **Publications:** Annual Report, annual. Alternate Formats: online.

2504 ■ National Association of Corporate Directors (NACD)
2 Lafayette Centre
1133 21st St. NW, Ste.700
Washington, DC 20036
Ph: (202)775-0509
Fax: (202)775-4857
E-mail: info@nacdonline.org
URL: http://www.nacdonline.org
Contact: Kenneth Daly, Pres./CEO
Founded: 1977. **Members:** 3,000. **Membership Dues:** individual, $475 (annual) ● corporate, $2,800 (annual) ● associate, $2,500 (annual). **Staff:** 10. **Regional Groups:** 7. **State Groups:** 10. **Description:** Corporate directors and boards of directors; chief executive officers, presidents, accountants, lawyers, consultants, and other executives are members. Conducts research, surveys, and seminars. **Libraries: Type:** reference. **Holdings:** books, clippings, monographs, periodicals. **Subjects:** corporate governance. **Awards:** Director of the Year. **Frequency:** annual. **Type:** recognition. **Recipient:** for a person who possesses an excellent leadership reputation, especially in ethics and governance and is recognized by peers and the business community as a "role model" in promoting high professional standards for board and director performance. **Computer Services:** Online services, director matching service. **Publications:** *Blue Ribbon Commission Reports*, annual. **Price:** $50.00 for members; $100.00 for nonmembers ● *Board Building Series* ● *Directors Monthly*. Newsletter. **Price:** included in membership dues ● *Governance Surveys*. **Conventions/Meetings:** annual Corporate Governance - meeting - always late October ● seminar and symposium.

2505 ■ National Bureau of Certified Consultants (NBCC)
c/o Peter A. Land Associates
4210 Lomac St.
Montgomery, AL 36106
Ph: (334)271-2639
E-mail: nationalbureau@att.net
URL: http://www.peteland.com/cpcm.htm
Founded: 1989. **Members:** 2,200. **Membership Dues:** professional, $125 (annual) ● certified professional consultant to management (CPCM), $225 (annual). **Staff:** 4. **Regional Groups:** 14. **Languages:** English, Italian. **Description:** Management consultants. Promotes adherence to high standards of ethics and practice in the field of management consulting. Works to improve management consulting curricula. Promulgates and enforces standards of conduct; Conducts research and educational programs; maintains speakers' bureau. **Libraries: Type:** reference; not open to the public. **Holdings:** 300; articles, books, business records, clippings, periodicals. **Subjects:** business, management. **Awards:** Award for Excellence. **Type:** recognition ● Intern Consultant Awards. **Frequency:** annual. **Type:** recognition. **Recipient:** for university students enrolled in MBA/consultancy programs and certificate/consultancy programs. **Computer Services:** database ● mailing lists ● online services, publication. **Committees:** National Committee for Legislative Certification. **Affiliated With:** Association of Professional Consultants. **Formerly:** (1998) National Bureau of Professional Management Consultants. **Publications:** *Consultants Bulletin*, bimonthly. Newsletter. **Circulation:** 5,000 ● *Observation and Comments*. **Conventions/Meetings:** annual North American Conference of Professional Consultants.

2506 ■ National Conference of Executives of the Arc (NCE)
1010 Wayne Ave., Ste.650
Silver Spring, MD 20910
Ph: (301)565-5475
Fax: (301)565-3843
E-mail: pterhune@arcoftstanlync.org
URL: http://www.ncearc.org
Contact: Peggy Terhune, Pres.
Founded: 1953. **Members:** 400. **Membership Dues:** regular (based on agency budget), $99-$199 (annual) ● associate, affiliate, multiple regular, $99 (annual). **Description:** Executives of the Arc. Promotes professional development of members; seeks to enhance the lives of people with mental retardation. Provides educational opportunities and professional support to Arc executives. **Awards: Frequency:** periodic. **Type:** recognition. **Telecommunication Services:** electronic mail, ncearc@thearc.org. **Publications:** *The Executive*, bimonthly. Newsletter ● *NCE Employment Registry*, periodic. Directory ● *Salary and Benefits Survey*, periodic. Report. **Conventions/Meetings:** annual conference ● annual convention.

2507 ■ National Grants Management Association (NGMA)
11654 Plaza Am. Dr., No. 609
Reston, VA 20190-4700
Ph: (703)648-9023
Fax: (703)648-9024
E-mail: info@ngma.org
URL: http://www.ngma-grants.org
Contact: Torryn P. Brazell, Exec. Dir.
Founded: 1978. **Members:** 400. **Membership Dues:** individual, $95 (annual). **Staff:** 2. **Budget:** $200,000. **Description:** Strengthens the relationship between grant-making agencies and grant recipients by empowering both sides with knowledge through training, seminars, workshops, and conferences. Focuses on federal, state, and local governments and private foundations that provide grants, grants-in-aid, cooperative agreements, and subsidies. **Formerly:** (1992) National Assistance Management Association. **Publications:** *NGMA eBulletin*, 8/year. Includes short, informative announcements, including new grants and other NGMA-related programs. **Advertising:** accepted. Alternate Formats: online ● *NGMA Grants Management Journal*, semiannual. **Price:** included in membership dues ● *NGMA News Brief*, quarterly. Newsletter. **Price:** included in membership dues. Alternate Formats: online ● *Who's Who in Grants Management*, annual. Membership Directory. **Advertising:** accepted. **Conventions/Meetings:** annual Grants Management Training Conference (exhibits) - every April/May in Washington, DC area ● Luncheon Training Series, one-hour training luncheons on a specific topic in the grants management industry - 8/year.

2508 ■ National Institute of Management Counsellors (NIMC)
Address Unknown since 2008
Founded: 1954. **Members:** 250. **Staff:** 3. **Description:** Management and industrial engineers and counsellors. Conducts research to improve standards and industry studies. **Divisions:** Industrial; Retail; Service. **Sections:** Referral; Research.

2509 ■ National Management Association (NMA)
2210 Arbor Blvd.
Dayton, OH 45439
Ph: (937)294-0421
Fax: (937)294-2374
E-mail: nma@nma1.org
URL: http://www.nma1.org
Contact: K. Stephen Bailey CM, Pres.
Founded: 1925. **Members:** 60,000. **Membership Dues:** individual, $40 (annual). **Staff:** 29. **Regional Groups:** 6. **Local Groups:** 255. **Description:** Business and industrial management personnel; membership comes from supervisory level, with the remainder from middle management and above. Seeks to develop and recognize management as a profession and to promote the free enterprise system. Prepares chapter programs on basic management, management policy and practice, communications, human behavior, industrial relations, economics, political education, and liberal education. Maintains speakers' bureau and hall of fame. Maintains educational, charitable, and research programs. Sponsors charitable programs. **Awards:** American Enterprise Speech Contest Award. **Frequency:** annual. **Type:** monetary. **Recipient:** for high school students who have won local, regional, and finalist competitions ● Executive of the Year Award. **Frequency:** annual. **Type:** recognition. **Recipient:** to an outstanding executive in the U.S. who has made a contribution of leadership towards the preservation and advancement of the American Enterprise System. **Committees:** Free Enterprise; Industry/Government Activities; Management Certification; Management Development; Productivity. **Absorbed:** (2004) International Management Council of the YMCA. **Formerly:** (1956) National Association of Foremen. **Publications:** *Board of Directors' Directory*, annual ● *Manage*, quarterly. Magazine ● *National Speakers' Directory*, periodic. **Conventions/Meetings:** competition ● annual conference - usually September or October.

2510 ■ Organization Design Forum (ODF)
5713 Carriage House Ct.
Apex, NC 27539
Ph: (919)662-8548
Fax: (919)662-9751
E-mail: info@organizationdesignforum.org
URL: http://www.organizationdesignforum.org
Contact: Brenda Price, Admin.

Founded: 1989. **Members:** 100. **Membership Dues:** individual, $110 (annual) ● student, $20 (annual). **Staff:** 1. **Budget:** $50,000. **Multinational. Description:** Academics, practitioners, consultants, and human resource professionals. Works to promote the knowledge and practice of organizational design. Focuses on the effect organization structure and processes have on the performance of individuals, groups, and the organization itself. Offers basic and advanced training in organization design techniques. **Libraries: Type:** not open to the public. **Holdings:** 3; video recordings. **Subjects:** recipients of Crystal Apple Award presentation. **Awards:** Crystal Apple. **Frequency:** annual. **Type:** recognition. **Recipient:** for long term contribution in the field of organization design. **Computer Services:** database ● mailing lists. **Formerly:** (2003) Association for the Management of Organization Design. **Publications:** *Designer's Forum*, quarterly. Newsletter. Alternate Formats: online ● *Organization Design*. Bibliography ● Membership Directory, annual ● Also publishes monographs on organization design. **Conventions/Meetings:** annual conference (exhibits).

2511 ■ Product Development and Management Association (PDMA)
15000 Commerce Pkwy., Ste.C
Mount Laurel, NJ 08054
Ph: (856)439-9052
Free: (800)232-5241
Fax: (856)439-0525
E-mail: pdma@pdma.org
URL: http://www.pdma.org
Contact: Dr. Robin Karol, CEO

Founded: 1976. **Members:** 2,900. **Membership Dues:** individual, $225 (annual) ● individual (working for a non-profit organization), $135 (annual) ● individual, $400 (biennial) ● individual (working for a non-profit organization), $250 (biennial) ● student, $30 (annual) ● individual, $595 (triennial) ● individual (working for a non-profit organization), $375 (triennial). **Staff:** 4. **Budget:** $1,200,000. **Regional Groups:** 24. **Multinational. Description:** Managers working in product innovation; teachers and researchers in the areas of product innovation management, product planning and development, and new product marketing; government regulators and facilitators involved in the product development process; product innovation consultants; market research firms; new product institutes; advertising agencies and media; testing companies; trade associations. Promotes improved product innovation management by drawing upon members' resources. Encourages research designed to make product innovation management more effective and efficient; Provides forum for the exchange of ideas and findings among universities, industry, government, and related sectors. **Awards:** Corporate Innovator Award. **Frequency:** annual. **Type:** recognition ● Student Dissertation Award. **Frequency:** annual. **Type:** monetary. **Recipient:** for the best student dissertation relating to new product development. **Computer Services:** database ● online services. **Committees:** Research. **Publications:** *Journal of Product Innovation Management: An International Publication of the Product Development and Management Association*, bimonthly. Presents research, experiences, and insights of academics, consultants, practicing managers, economists, scientists, lawyers, and sociologists. **Price:** included in membership dues. ISSN: 0737-6782. **Circulation:** 2,900. **Advertising:** accepted. Alternate Formats: online ● *The PDMA Handbook of New Product Development*. Offers information on the stages of the product development process from generation to delivery. **Price:** $95.00 ● *PDMA Toolbooks 1 and 2 for New Product Development* ● *Visions: PDMA Practitioner Magazine*, quarterly. Includes information on new members, research reports, table of contents of the next issue of the *Journal of Product Innovation Management*. **Price:** included in membership dues. **Circulation:** 2,900. **Advertising:** accepted. Alternate Formats: online ● Membership Directory, annual. Includes company and geographic index. **Price:** included in membership dues. **Circulation:** 2,900. **Conventions/Meetings:** annual international conference (exhibits).

2512 ■ Production and Operations Management Society (POMS)
c/o Dr. Sushil K. Gupta, Exec. Dir.
Coll. of Bus.
Florida Intl. Univ.
Miami, FL 33174
Ph: (305)348-1413
Fax: (305)348-6890
E-mail: poms@fiu.edu
URL: http://www.poms.org
Contact: Dr. Sushil K. Gupta, Exec. Dir.

Founded: 1989. **Members:** 1,100. **Membership Dues:** regular, $95 (annual) ● student, retired, college, $20 (annual). **Staff:** 3. **Budget:** $250,000. **Multinational. Description:** Production and operations management (POM) professionals and academics. Works to advance POM technology and practice. Provides a forum for interaction between business and engineering schools, corporations, and government. Encourages the development of production and operation curriculums. **Computer Services:** Online services, placement service. **Publications:** *POM Chronicle*, quarterly. Newsletter. **Advertising:** accepted ● *Productions and Operations Management*, quarterly. Journal. Includes papers on various POM topics. ISSN: 1059-1478. Alternate Formats: online. **Conventions/Meetings:** annual meeting (exhibits) ● periodic seminar ● periodic workshop.

2513 ■ Professional Services Management Association (PSMA)
99 Canal Center Plz., Ste.330
Alexandria, VA 22314
Ph: (703)739-0277
Free: (866)739-0277
Fax: (703)549-2498
E-mail: info@psmanet.org
URL: http://www.psmanet.org
Contact: Ronald D. Worth CPSM, Exec. VP

Founded: 1975. **Members:** 350. **Membership Dues:** professional, $450 (annual) ● affiliate, $500 (annual) ● sustaining, $1,500 (annual). **Staff:** 12. **Budget:** $350,000. **Local Groups:** 1. **Description:** Individuals responsible for any or all aspects of business management in a professional design firm. Aims to improve the effectiveness of professional design firms through the growth and development of business management skills. Seeks to: provide a forum for the exchange of ideas and information and discussion and resolution of common problems and issues; establish guidelines for approaches to common management concerns; initiate and maintain professional relationships among members; improve recognition and practice of management as a science in professional design firms; advance and improve reputable service to clients; offer a variety of comprehensive educational programs and opportunities. Maintains speakers' bureau and placement service. Holds seminars. Conducts surveys and research programs. Compiles statistics. **Awards:** Management Achievement Award. **Frequency:** annual. **Type:** recognition. **Recipient:** for management. **Computer Services:** Online services, listserv. **Committees:** Education and Research; National Conference; Public Relations. **Formerly:** (1979) Professional Services Business Management Association. **Publications:** *PSMA Authority*, bimonthly. Newsletter. Covers management, finance, marketing, operations, and human resources information for design and engineering firm personnel. **Price:** $100.00/year. **Circulation:** 500. **Conventions/Meetings:** annual The Next Wave - conference, 2 1/2 days of educational and networking opportunities for design industry leaders (exhibits).

2514 ■ Project Management Institute (PMI)
4 Campus Blvd.
Newtown Square, PA 19073-3299
Ph: (610)356-4600
Fax: (610)356-4647
E-mail: customercare@pmi.org
URL: http://www.pmi.org
Contact: Gregory Balestrero, CEO

Founded: 1969. **Members:** 100,000. **Membership Dues:** individual, $119 (annual) ● student, $30 (annual) ● retiree, $60 (annual). **Staff:** 120. **Budget:** $27,400,000. **Local Groups:** 200. **Multinational. Description:** Corporations and individuals engaged in the practice of project management; project management students and educators. Seeks to advance the study, teaching, and practice of project management. Establishes project management standards; conducts educational and professional certification courses; bestows Project Management Professional credential upon qualified individuals. Offers educational seminars and global congresses. **Libraries: Type:** reference; open to the public. **Holdings:** 3,800; archival material, articles, audiovisuals, books, monographs, periodicals. **Subjects:** project management. **Awards:** PMI Professional Awards. **Frequency:** annual. **Type:** recognition ● PMI Project of the Year Award. **Frequency:** annual. **Type:** recognition. **Recipient:** for a project whose team members have demonstrated superior performance in application of project management principles and techniques. **Computer Services:** Mailing lists, project management professionals. **Telecommunication Services:** electronic mail, gregory.balestrero@pmi.org. **Committees:** Certification; Education; Research; Standards. **Publications:** *PM Network*, monthly. Magazine. Covers industry applications and practical issues in managing projects. **Price:** included in membership dues. ISSN: 1040-8754. **Circulation:** 100,000. **Advertising:** accepted ● *PM Network's Career Track*, semiannual. Magazine. Contains news and information on career-related PMI programs and services. Alternate Formats: online ● *PMI Today*, monthly. Newsletter. Serves as a supplement to PM Network. ● *Project Management Institute—Annual Proceedings*. Contains proceedings of annual conference, global congresses. ● *Project Management Journal*, quarterly. Features peer-reviewed articles devoted to theory and practice in field of project management. **Price:** included in membership dues. ISSN: 8756-9728. **Circulation:** 100,000. **Advertising:** accepted ● Also publishes abstracts, books, papers presented at past seminars, and special research reports. **Conventions/Meetings:** annual Global Congress - Europe - spring/summer ● annual Global Congress North America, with symposium (exhibits) - always fall.

2515 ■ Society for Advancement of Management (SAM)
6300 Ocean Dr. - FC 111
Corpus Christi, TX 78412
Ph: (361)825-6045
Free: (888)827-6077
Fax: (361)825-2725
E-mail: moustafa.abdelsamad@tamucc.edu
URL: http://www.cob.tamucc.edu/sam
Contact: Dr. Moustafa H. Abdelsamad, Pres./CEO

Founded: 1912. **Members:** 5,050. **Membership Dues:** professional, $75 (annual) ● student in U.S., $25 (annual) ● student outside U.S., retired, $40 (annual) ● associate in U.S., $35 (annual) ● associate outside U.S., academic in U.S., $50 (annual) ● academic outside U.S., $60 (annual). **Staff:** 1. **Description:** Represents management executives in industry commerce, government, and education. Fields of interest include management education, policy and strategy, MIS, international management, administration, budgeting, collective bargaining, distribution, incentives, materials handling, quality control, and training. **Awards: Type:** recognition. **Recipient:** for various aspects of management. **Divisions:** University. **Absorbed:** (1964) Industrial Methods Society. **Formed by Merger of:** (1936) Taylor Society; Society of Industrial Engineers. **Publications:** *Management in Practice*, quarterly. Monograph. Covers current topics that have practical applications. **Price:** $25.00/year in U.S.; $69.00/year outside U.S. ISSN: 0036-0805. **Circulation:** 5,000 ● *SAM Advanced Management Journal*, quarterly. Covers current topics that have practical applications. **Price:** $64.00/year, plus shipping and handling ● *The SAM News International*, quarterly. Newspaper. **Advertising:** accepted ● *Society for Advancement of Management—International Management Conference Proceedings*, annual. Alternate Formats: CD-ROM ● Proceedings. **Conventions/Meetings:** annual meeting (exhibits) - always March or April.

2516 ■ Society for Information Management (SIM)
401 N Michigan Ave.
Chicago, IL 60611-4267
Ph: (312)527-6734
E-mail: sim@simnet.org
URL: http://www.simnet.org
Contact: Jim Luisi, Exec. Dir.
Founded: 1968. **Members:** 2,500. **Membership Dues:** individual, $285 (annual) ● corporate enterprise, $420 (annual) ● academic institution, $1,500 (annual) ● joint academic institution, $2,500 (annual). **Staff:** 17. **Budget:** $3,500,000. **Local Groups:** 30. **Description:** Provides a diverse membership with a sound infrastructure to pool insights resulting to access to international IT perspectives, continuing education opportunities and an elite network of peer resources through programs designed exclusively for the information management executive. Aims to support IT leaders by increasing the knowledge base of members and associates; giving back to local communities; being the voice of the IT community on critical issues and developing the next generation of effective IT leaders. **Formerly:** (1983) Society for Management Information Systems. **Publications:** *Executive Briefs*, quarterly ● *MIS Quarterly*. Journal ● *Network*, monthly. Newsletter ● *Network Online*, monthly. Newsletter. Alternate Formats: online ● *Special Reports*, semiannual. Newsletter. **Conventions/Meetings:** annual convention ● annual Interchange - conference.

2517 ■ Turnaround Management Association (TMA)
150 S Wacker Dr., Ste.900
Chicago, IL 60606
Ph: (312)578-6900
Fax: (312)578-8336
E-mail: info@turnaround.org
URL: http://www.turnaround.org
Contact: Linda Delgadillo CAE, Exec. Dir.
Founded: 1988. **Members:** 4,300. **Membership Dues:** individual, $375 (annual) ● academic, government, $150 (annual) ● student, $85 (annual). **Staff:** 9. **Budget:** $1,500,000. **Regional Groups:** 32. **Description:** Practitioners (interim managers, consultants, corporate managers, and professional advisors), academics, students, attorneys and judges, commercial lenders, and legislative personnel. Promotes the image and credibility of the turnaround profession; fosters professional development and networking opportunities for turnaround executives; serves as a clearinghouse of information and research pertinent to the profession. Conducts networking forums; offers educational and credentialing programs. **Awards:** Turnaround of the Year. **Frequency:** annual. **Type:** recognition. **Recipient:** for best turnaround in 4 categories: large company, small company, international, and pro bono. **Computer Services:** database ● mailing lists. **Councils:** Academic Advisory. **Affiliated With:** American Bankers Association; American Bankruptcy Institute; American Institute of Certified Public Accountants; Association of Insolvency and Restructuring Advisors; Institute of Management Accountants; National Association of Bankruptcy Trustees. **Publications:** *The Journal of Corporate Renewal*, monthly. **Price:** free for members; $75.00 /year for nonmembers. **Circulation:** 5,000. **Advertising:** accepted ● *Professional Fees in Bankruptcy Handbook*. **Price:** $50.00 ● *TMA Directory of Members and Services*, annual. **Price:** $150.00 for nonmembers; free for members. **Circulation:** 5,000. **Advertising:** accepted. **Conventions/Meetings:** Leadership Conference ● seminar ● annual Spring Leadership Meeting - conference - always spring ● annual conference (exhibits) - always fall. 2008 Oct. 27-30, New Orleans, LA; 2009 Oct. 5-9, Phoenix, AZ; 2010 Oct. 5-8, Orlando, FL.

2518 ■ Women in Management (WIM)
PO Box 1032
Dundee, IL 60118-7032
Ph: (708)386-0496
Free: (877)946-6285
Fax: (847)683-3751
E-mail: nationalwim@wimonline.org
URL: http://www.wimonline.org
Contact: K.L. Robertson Daly, Pres.
Founded: 1976. **Members:** 1,700. **Staff:** 2. **Budget:** $75,000. **Description:** Supports network of women in professional and management positions that facilitate the exchange of experience and ideas. Promotes self-growth in management; provides speakers who are successful in management; sponsors workshops and special interest groups to discuss problems and share job experiences. **Awards: Type:** recognition. **Telecommunication Services:** electronic mail, klrobertsondaly@msn.com ● electronic mail, tcarlstedt@firstfedsavingsbank.com. **Committees:** Awards; Career Development; Hospitality; Speakers' Bureau; Special Events. **Publications:** *WIM National Newsletter*, quarterly. Includes chapter contacts. **Price:** free, for members only ● *Women in Management—National Directory*, annual. **Price:** included in membership dues. **Advertising:** accepted. **Conventions/Meetings:** annual meeting - always June.

Managers

2519 ■ American Society for the Advancement of Project Management (ASAPM)
6547 N Acad., No. 404
Colorado Springs, CO 80918
Ph: (931)647-7373
Fax: (719)487-0673
E-mail: info@asapm.org
URL: http://www.asapm.org
Contact: Lew Ireland, Pres.
Membership Dues: student, $15 (annual) ● affiliate, retired, $30 (annual) ● regular, $60 (annual) ● life, $500. **Multinational**. **Description:** Promotes the mainstreaming of project management as a profession and as a way to improve human welfare. Advances project management methods, standards, and practical application techniques. Seeks to improve understanding and practice of the profession. **Affiliated With:** International Project Management Association. **Publications:** Newsletter. Alternate Formats: online.

2520 ■ Association of Call Center Managers (ACCM)
2505 Living Rock Ave.
Las Vegas, NV 89106
Ph: (702)367-2288
E-mail: info@callcentermanagers.org
Contact: Robert Garcia, Pres.
Membership Dues: distinguished, $209 (annual) ● vendor, $450 (annual). **Description:** Represents call center managers and leaders dedicated to advancing the profession of call center management. Provides networking, peer mentoring, research, education and other resources that elevate the role and value of a call center leader. Strives to raise awareness of the call center profession and to heighten awareness of the strategic and economic value of call/contact centers. **Telecommunication Services:** electronic mail, rgarcia@sound-tele.com. **Publications:** *Call Center Leadership*, monthly. Newsletter. Contains information on call center best practices and emerging technologies. **Price:** included in membership dues. Alternate Formats: online.

2521 ■ Association for Strategic Alliance Professionals (ASAP)
31 Washington St.
Wellesley, MA 02481
Ph: (781)972-1346
Fax: (781)927-5425
E-mail: blundberg@strategic-alliances.org
URL: http://www.strategic-alliances.org
Contact: Bill Lundberg, Exec. Dir./Founding Pres.
Founded: 1999. **Membership Dues:** full, $550 (annual) ● basic, $195 (annual) ● associate/student, $95 (annual). **Multinational**. **Description:** Seeks to create a distinct professional identity for executives and managers of strategic alliances. Sets standards of professional performance in the formation and management of strategic alliances. Creates awareness of the contributions of strategic alliances and strategic alliance professionals among corporate managers and executives and among the general public. **Awards:** Alliance Program Excellence Award. **Frequency:** annual. **Type:** recognition. **Recipient:** for effective management of major alliances ● Individual Alliance Excellence Award. **Frequency:** annual. **Type:** recognition. **Recipient:** for companies with successful alliance relationships. **Publications:** *Best Practices*, monthly. Bulletin. Contains news and other important information. **Price:** included in membership dues. Alternate Formats: online.

2522 ■ Location Managers Guild of America (LMGA)
8033 Sunset Blvd., Ste.1017
West Hollywood, CA 90046
Ph: (310)967-2007
E-mail: boardofdirectors@locationmanagers.org
URL: http://www.locationmanagers.org
Contact: Kayla Thames-Berge, Pres.
Founded: 2004. **Membership Dues:** location manager/scout, $100 (annual) ● Associate, $50 (annual) ● business/industry partner, $250-$5,000 (annual). **Description:** Enhances recognition and respect for members within the entertainment and related industries. Strengthens their ability to develop meaningful and credible careers. Strives to serve the public and the production industries through philanthropic and educational programs. Identifies, improves, exchanges and encourages the mutual benefits of location filming among the entertainment industries and the communities.

2523 ■ National Association of Senior Move Managers (NASMM)
911 N Elm St., Ste.228
Hinsdale, IL 60521
Free: (877)606-2766
Fax: (630)325-0749
E-mail: nasmm@lsni.org
URL: http://www.nasmm.com
Contact: Peg Guild, Pres.
Founded: 2002. **Membership Dues:** organization, $295 (annual) ● affiliate, $385 (annual). **Description:** Promotes senior move management services. Facilitates the physical and emotional aspects of relocation for older adults and their families. Increases industry awareness of relocation. Establishes a national referral network for senior move managers. **Publications:** Newsletter, monthly. **Price:** included in membership dues.

Manufactured Housing

2524 ■ Building Systems Councils of NAHB (BSC-NAHB)
c/o National Association of Home Builders
1201 15th St. NW
Washington, DC 20005
Ph: (202)266-8200
Free: (800)368-5242
Fax: (202)266-8400
E-mail: efulton@nahb.com
URL: http://www.nahb.org
Contact: Eric Fulton, Contact
Founded: 1943. **Members:** 275. **Membership Dues:** manufacturer, associate (based on annual sales), $450-$1,750 (annual). **Staff:** 4. **Description:** Serves as a council of the National Association of Home Builders of the U.S. Home manufacturers; suppliers of building materials and associations and industry service oriented companies. Works to improve the

design, engineering, production, and marketing of pre-cut, panelized, modular, log and dome homes. Sponsors plant tours in various geographic locations. **Awards:** S.A. Walters Chairman's Award. **Frequency:** annual. **Type:** recognition. **Recipient:** to a member who has made significant contribution to the industry. **Computer Services:** Information services, consumer lead service for members. **Councils:** Associate Members; Log Homes; Modular Building Systems; National Dome; Panelized Building Systems. **Affiliated With:** National Association of Home Builders. **Formerly:** Prefabricated Home Manufacturers Institute; (1971) Home Manufacturers Association; (1976) National Association of Building Manufacturers; (1982) National Association of Home Manufacturers; (1987) Home Manufacturers Councils of NAHB. **Publications:** *The American Dream.The Log Home* ● *Building Systems Review*, monthly. **Price:** included in membership dues. **Circulation:** 600 ● *Building Your Dreams (Modular)* ● *Most Frequently Asked Questions (Modular)* ● *Welcome to the World of Building Systems (Panel)*. **Conventions/Meetings:** trade show and convention, operational or technical.

2525 ■ Log Homes Council (LHC)
c/o National Association of Home Builders
1201 15th St. NW
Washington, DC 20005
Ph: (202)266-8577
Free: (800)368-5242
Fax: (202)266-8141
E-mail: cklein@nahb.com
URL: http://www.loghomes.org
Contact: David Kauffman, Exec. Dir.
Founded: 1977. **Members:** 51. **Staff:** 4. **Description:** Represents companies that manufacture and handcraft log homes. Works to develop thermal, log grading, and fire rating standards for log homes; promotes the industry to the public, building regulatory officials, and regulatory agencies. **Affiliated With:** Building Systems Councils of NAHB. **Formerly:** (1985) Log Homes Council; (1991) American Log Homes Council. **Publications:** *An American Dream, The Log Home*. Alternate Formats: online ● *Tradition of Excellence*. Video. **Conventions/Meetings:** annual President's Tour - tour and conference, offers tours of log home production facilities and industry roundtable meetings for log home builders and manufacturers - always March.

2526 ■ Manufactured Housing Association for Regulatory Reform (MHARR)
c/o Manufactured Housing Institute
2101 Wilson Blvd., Ste.610
Arlington, VA 22201
Ph: (703)558-0400
Fax: (703)558-0401
E-mail: info@mfghome.org
URL: http://www.manufacturedhousing.org
Contact: Gail Cardwell, Pres.
Founded: 1985. **Members:** 60. **Staff:** 4. **Budget:** $500,000. **Description:** Producers of manufactured housing. Represents the interests of members by seeking reform of federal regulations affecting manufactured housing. Works to improve relations with the federal government and congress and to promote reasonable regulations, with the goal of reducing industry costs. Areas of concern include contemplated changes to HUD Construction and Safety Standards, proposed Federal Trade Commission rules affecting manufactured housing, and regulations initiated by Congress and federal agencies that may adversely affect manufactured housing. **Telecommunication Services:** electronic mail, gcardwell@mfghome.org. **Formerly:** (1998) Association for Regulatory Reform. **Publications:** *MHARR News*, periodic. Newsletter ● *MHARR Washington Update*, quarterly ● Papers. Covers regulatory and deregulatory and legislative issues. **Conventions/Meetings:** annual meeting - usually in Washington, DC.

2527 ■ Manufactured Housing Institute (MHI)
2101 Wilson Blvd., Ste.610
Arlington, VA 22201-3062
Ph: (703)558-0400
Fax: (703)558-0401
E-mail: info@mfghome.org
URL: http://www.manufacturedhousing.org
Contact: Michael O'Brien CAE, Exec. VP
Founded: 1936. **Members:** 450. **Membership Dues:** manufacturer, $17 (annual) ● wholesale supplier (based on annual sales), $625-$6,250 (annual) ● after market supplier (based on number of states), $500-$3,000 (annual) ● retail/mortgage lending (based on number of states), $2,000-$10,000 (annual) ● owner/manager, developer, $500 (annual) ● affiliate (based on the annual sales volume), $625-$2,125 (annual) ● floor planning lending, insurance service (based on number of states), $2,000-$6,000 (annual) ● loan brokerage/appraisal (based on number of states), $1,000-$5,000 (annual) ● consulting service (based on number of states), $1,000-$3,000 (annual). **Staff:** 18. **Budget:** $3,000,000. **State Groups:** 49. **Description:** Manufacturers of manufactured homes; suppliers of equipment, components, furnishings and services, financial services companies, state association organizations, retailers and community owners. Promotes sales of manufactured homes through programs and services in six key areas: government relations, technical activities, financing, public relations, site development, and community operations. Conducts research and educational programs; provides statistics. **Telecommunication Services:** electronic mail, mobrien@mfghome.org. **Absorbed:** National Manufactured Housing Federation; Southeastern Manufactured Housing Institute; (1975) Trailer Coach Association. **Formerly:** Trailer Coach Manufacturers Association; (1975) Mobile Home Manufacturers Association. **Publications:** *Developer Video*. Videos ● *How to Buy a Manufactured Home Booklet*. Reports ● *Manufacturing Report*, monthly. Provides monthly statistics tracking the manufactured housing industry. **Price:** $150.00/year. ISSN: 1090-1345 ● *Modern Homes*, bimonthly. Magazine. Contains news on industry issues. ● *Quick Facts*, annual. Brochure. **Conventions/Meetings:** meeting - 3/year ● annual National Congress & Expo for Manufactured & Modular Housing, largest convention for manufactured housing industry (exhibits) - 2009 Apr. 14-16, Las Vegas, NV ● annual show.

2528 ■ Metal Building Contractors and Erectors Association (MBCEA)
PO Box 499
Shawnee Mission, KS 66201
Ph: (913)432-3800
Free: (800)866-6722
Fax: (913)432-3803
E-mail: mbcea@kc.rr.com
URL: http://www.mbcea.org
Contact: Angela M. Cruse, Exec. Dir.
Founded: 1968. **Members:** 300. **Membership Dues:** contractor, $365 (annual) ● national, regional industry, $495 (annual) ● in North and South Carolina, $500 (annual). **Staff:** 1. **Budget:** $500,000. **Regional Groups:** 1. **State Groups:** 4. **Description:** Firms engaged in marketing metal buildings; suppliers and manufacturers. Promotes increased use of metal buildings and better relations among members and owners, public bodies, architects, engineers, and associated manufacturers. Provides information on business practices, new markets, and sales techniques. **Awards:** Buildings of the Year Award. **Frequency:** annual. **Type:** recognition. **Recipient:** for eight categories. **Telecommunication Services:** electronic mail, angela@mbcea.org. **Committees:** Conference; Education/Training/Certification; Membership Networking/Services. **Programs:** Certification; Erector Resource Center; Mentoring; Quality & Craftsmanship Training Series. **Formerly:** (1983) Metal Building Dealers Association; (2003) Systems Builders Association. **Publications:** *Employee Safety Handbook* (in English and Spanish). **Price:** $3.00 for members; $4.00 for nonmembers ● *MBCEAtoday*, monthly. Newsletter. **Price:** free for members. Alternate Formats: online. **Conventions/Meetings:** annual conference, with programs and seminars (exhibits).

2529 ■ Modular Building Systems Council (MBSC)
c/o National Association of Home Builders
1201 15th St. NW
Washington, DC 20005
Ph: (202)266-8200
Free: (800)368-5242
Fax: (202)266-8400
E-mail: efulton@nahb.com
URL: http://www.nahb.org
Contact: Jerry M. Howard, Exec. VP/CEO
Founded: 1942. **Members:** 60. **Staff:** 4. **Description:** Operates under the Building Systems Council of NAHB. Modular building manufacturers. Monitors state and federal housing legislation that impacts the building industry. Provides a forum for communication, networking, and recruiting for those involved in manufacturing modular building systems. Addresses and solves problems specific to the council; offers consumer leads service. **Affiliated With:** Building Systems Councils of NAHB. **Publications:** *Building Systems Review*, monthly. Includes industry news updates. Published in conjunction with the NAHB. ● *Building Your Dreams* ● *The Most Frequently Asked Questions about Modular Homes*. **Conventions/Meetings:** annual convention and trade show (exhibits) - always fall.

2530 ■ National Dome Council (NDC)
c/o Building Systems Councils of NAHB
1201 15th St. NW
Washington, DC 20005
Ph: (202)266-8200
Free: (800)368-8242
Fax: (202)266-8400
E-mail: efulton@nahb.com
URL: http://www.nahb.org
Contact: David Kauffman, Exec. Dir.
Founded: 1976. **Staff:** 3. **Description:** Manufacturers of panelized geodesic dome components. Objectives include: helping the dome housing industry achieve acceptance by building and zoning officials; acquainting lending institutions with the potential of this energy-efficient, economical, and durable form of housing; maintaining a code of ethics for the industry. Promotes dome homes to consumers; represents the industry's views before government organizations and business and financial institutions. Serves as an information clearinghouse. **Formerly:** (1980) National Association of Dome Home Manufacturers; (1982) National Dome Association; (1985) Dome Committee of the Home Manufacturers Council of NAHB; (1989) National Dome Council; (2002) National Dome Committee. **Publications:** *Energy White Paper*, periodic ● *Home Mortgage White Paper*, periodic.

2531 ■ Panelized Building Systems Council (PBSC)
c/o National Association of Home Builders
1201 15th St. NW
Washington, DC 20005
Ph: (202)266-8200
Free: (800)368-5242
Fax: (202)266-8400
E-mail: info@nahb.com
URL: http://www.nahb.org
Contact: David L. Pressly Jr., Pres.
Founded: 1942. **Members:** 40. **Staff:** 4. **Description:** A council of the Building Systems Councils of NAHB. Corporations that manufacture pre-cut, panelized, geodesic dome and component buildings. (Precut, panelized, and component buildings are prefabricated factory-produced housing components and packages that can be quickly assembled to form a dwelling). Offers educational programs for builders in use of component and panelized construction. Promotes use of components as building and construction method. **Affiliated With:** Building Systems Councils of NAHB. **Publications:** *Building Systems Review*, monthly. Newsletter. **Price:** included in membership dues. **Circulation:** 700 ● *Welcome to the World of Building Systems*. **Conventions/Meetings:** competition ● annual trade show - always fall.

2532 ■ Western Manufactured Housing Communities Association (WMA)
455 Capitol Mall, Ste.800
Sacramento, CA 95814
Ph: (916)448-7002
Fax: (916)448-7085

E-mail: info@wma.org
URL: http://www.wma.org
Contact: Sheila Dey, Exec. Dir.
Founded: 1945. **Membership Dues:** community, $500 (annual) ● individual, $295 (annual) ● service, industry, $900 (annual). **Description:** Manufactured housing community owners, operators, and developers. Promotes and represents the interests, rights and image of its members by taking an assertive role in advocating positions at state and local level, through education and public relations, and by enhancing communications and relations with home owners and providing professional services. **Formerly:** (2002) Western Mobilehome Parkowners Association. **Publications:** *Newsline*, monthly. Newsletter ● *WMA Reporter*, monthly. Magazine. **Conventions/Meetings:** annual convention ● Renaissance Committee Meeting.

Manufacturers Representatives

2533 ■ Agricultural and Industrial Manufacturers Representatives Association (AIMRA)

c/o Jim Manke, Exec. Dir.
7500 Flying Cloud Dr., Ste.900
Eden Prairie, MN 55344
Ph: (952)253-6230 (901)683-5005
Fax: (952)835-4774
E-mail: jrmanke@associationsolutionsinc.com
URL: http://www.aimrareps.org
Contact: Jim Manke, Exec. Dir.
Membership Dues: associate, $275 (annual) ● representative, $495 (annual). **Description:** Manufacturers' representatives employed by agricultural and industrial firms. Promotes continuing professional development of members. Serves as a clearinghouse on the manufacturers' representative profession; facilitates exchange of information among members; conducts educational and training programs; and provides support and services to members. **Publications:** *AIMRA E-Newsline*. Newsletter. Alternate Formats: online ● *The Locator*. Membership Directory ● Directory, annual.

2534 ■ Association of Independent Manufacturers'/Representatives (AIM/R)

One Spectrum Pointe, Ste.150
Lake Forest, CA 92630-2283
Ph: (949)859-2884
Free: (866)729-0975
Fax: (949)855-2973
E-mail: info@aimr.net
URL: http://www.aimr.net
Contact: Richard Banner CPMR, Pres.
Founded: 1972. **Members:** 320. **Membership Dues:** representative, $375 (annual) ● associate, $250 (annual). **Staff:** 4. **Budget:** $175,000. **Regional Groups:** 11. **Description:** Manufacturers' representative companies in the plumbing-heating-cooling-piping industry promoting the use of independent sales representatives. Conducts educational programs and establishes a code of ethics between members and customers. **Awards:** National Manufacturer of the Year. **Frequency:** annual. **Type:** recognition ● National Wholesaler of the Year. **Frequency:** annual. **Type:** recognition. **Committees:** Executive; Regional Officers; State Directors. **Formerly:** (2004) Association of Industry Manufacturers Representatives. **Publications:** *AIM/R News and Views*, quarterly. Newsletter. Covers business operation of manufacturers' representatives' agencies. **Price:** available to members only. **Circulation:** 350. Alternate Formats: online ● *Representatives—Membership Directory*, annual. **Price:** $100.00 for nonmembers; free for members. **Conventions/Meetings:** annual Management Conference - conference and workshop - always spring.

2535 ■ Association of Visual Merchandise Representatives (AVMR)

c/o Tom Raguse, Pres.
307 Cove Creek Ln.
Houston, TX 77042-1023
Ph: (713)782-5533
Fax: (713)785-1114
E-mail: raguse@attglobal.net
Contact: Tom Raguse, Pres.
Founded: 1983. **Members:** 45. **Membership Dues:** independent sales representative, $150 (annual). **Staff:** 4. **Description:** Sales representatives from manufacturers of visual merchandise. (Visual merchandise are items such as mannequins, decorative trim, and other equipment used in department store displays.) Seeks to increase the communication link among retailers, manufacturers, and educators within the visual merchandise industry; organize and communicate with the sales force in the U.S. and Canada; provide benefits and better working conditions for sales representatives; support established industry principles and code of ethics. Conducts educational and research programs; offers placement services. **Libraries: Type:** not open to the public. **Awards:** Salesperson of the Year. **Frequency:** annual. **Type:** recognition. **Committees:** Political Action. **Publications:** Newsletter, quarterly. **Price:** free. **Circulation:** 60. **Conventions/Meetings:** biennial trade show, held in conjunction with the National Association of Display Industries (exhibits) - always May and December, in New York City; always April, in Chicago.

2536 ■ Incentive Manufacturers and Representatives Alliance (IMRA)

1601 N Bond St., Ste.303
Naperville, IL 60563
Ph: (630)369-7786
Fax: (630)369-3773
E-mail: tom@incentivemarketing.org
URL: http://www.imraorg.net
Contact: Thomas F. Renk, Exec. Dir.
Founded: 1963. **Members:** 225. **Membership Dues:** corporate, not-for-profit organization, $225 (annual). **Staff:** 2. **Budget:** $250,000. **Description:** Manufacturers' representatives and manufacturers specializing in sales in the premium and incentive market and associated manufacturers' sales executives who sell their products for premium use through specialized premium representatives. Conducts information and educational programs to improve understanding of the function of the direct factory representative in the premium and incentive market. **Libraries: Type:** reference. **Telecommunication Services:** information service, list of IMRA member representatives. **Committees:** Annual Marketing Conference; New York Show Liaison; Strategic Planning. **Formerly:** National Premium Manufacturers Representatives; (2002) Incentive Manufacturers and Representatives Association. **Publications:** *Incentive Managers Handbook*. Contains information on how to organize and manage an incentive department. **Price:** $250.00 each for nonmembers; included in membership dues ● *Inside IMRA*, bimonthly. Newsletter. Contains both industry and association news to keep members informed about activities and networking opportunities. ● Membership Directory, annual. Alternate Formats: online. **Conventions/Meetings:** annual conference, marketing education and sales meetings - every spring.

2537 ■ Manufacturers' Agents National Association (MANA)

1 Spectrum Pointe, Ste.150
Lake Forest, CA 92630-2283
Ph: (949)859-4040
Free: (877)626-2776
Fax: (949)855-2973
E-mail: mana@manaonline.org
URL: http://www.manaonline.org
Contact: Bryan Shirley, Pres./CEO
Founded: 1947. **Members:** 6,000. **Membership Dues:** regular in U.S. and Canada (manufacturer's agent), $229 (annual) ● regular outside U.S. and Canada (manufacturer's agent), $339 (annual) ● associate (manufacturer), $329 (annual). **Staff:** 16. **Description:** Manufacturers' agents in all fields representing two or more manufacturers on a commission basis; associate members are manufacturers and others interested in improving the agent-principal relationship. Maintains code of ethics and rules of business and professional conduct; issues model standard form of agreement. **Telecommunication Services:** electronic mail, bryan@manaonline.org. **Committees:** Education; Speakers' Bureau. **Publications:** *Agency Sales*, monthly. Magazine. Contains how-to articles for manufacturers' agents and manufacturers. Includes book reviews and manufacturer's corner. **Price:** $54.00/year in U.S. ISSN: 0749-2332. **Circulation:** 9,000. **Advertising:** accepted ● *MANA Matters*, monthly. Newsletter. Alternate Formats: online ● *MANA Online Directory of Manufacturers' Sales Agencies*, updated daily. Membership Directory. Contains list of manufacturers' sales agencies. **Price:** free to agent members; $199.00 for nonmembers. **Circulation:** 25,000. **Advertising:** accepted. Alternate Formats: online ● *Manufacturers' Agents National Association—Special Report*, periodic. Monograph. Includes problem-solving reports on issues recurrent in a manufacturer-agency relationship. ● Also publishes special reports and bulletins. **Conventions/Meetings:** quarterly seminar - usually February, May, September, and November.

2538 ■ Manufacturers for Fair Trade (MFT)

PO Box 310
Cranesville, PA 16410
Ph: (814)756-5765 (724)355-4637
Fax: (814)756-5765
E-mail: dfrengel@mftcoalition.org
Contact: Dave Frengel, Exec. Dir.
Founded: 2002. **Membership Dues:** manufacturing company (based on the number of employees), $250-$1,000 (annual) ● state/regional/community-based manufacturing organization, $500 (annual) ● statewide/national manufacturing organization, $1,000 (annual) ● associate (non-manufacturing company), $250 (annual) ● associate (non-manufacturing organization), $500 (annual). **Description:** Works to identify and promote trade policies that advance U.S. manufacturing. Supports the expansion of U.S. involvement in international trade. Supports efficient measures to maintain a safe and clean workplace and environment.

2539 ■ Manufacturers Representatives Educational Research Foundation (MRERF)

8329 Cole St.
Arvada, CO 80005
Ph: (303)463-1801
Fax: (303)463-3198
E-mail: info@mrerf.org
URL: http://www.mrerf.org
Contact: Ms. Susannah L. Hart, Admin. Dir.
Founded: 1984. **Members:** 35. **Staff:** 3. **Budget:** $1,000,000. **National Groups:** 35. **Description:** Sponsored by 35 national and state associations of manufacturers' representatives, distributors, and manufacturers. Promotes the profession of outsourced field sales through academic research and publication; disseminates research findings on the role of manufacturers' representatives to academic institutions; provides a forum for the exchange of information. Operates professional certification program for agency owners and sales people. Also provides educational programs for manufacturers who outsource field sales. **Libraries: Type:** not open to the public. **Holdings:** 450; video recordings. **Awards: Type:** grant. **Recipient:** for research. **Telecommunication Services:** electronic mail, susannah@mrerf.org. **Publications:** *New Directions in Inside Sales*. Video. Includes video, leaders guide, and participant workbook. **Price:** $249.00 ● *Operations Manual for Manufacturers' Representatives*. Manuals. **Price:** $60.00. Alternate Formats: CD-ROM ● *Outsourcing Field Sales*. **Price:** $16.00 ● *Synergistic Selling for the 21st Century*, periodic. Book. **Price:** $89.00. **Conventions/Meetings:** semiannual Certified Professional Manufacturers' Representatives - seminar ● Certified Sales Professional - seminar, with exam - 3/year ● Managing Your Manufacturer's Representative Network - seminar - 3/year.

2540 ■ Mechanical Equipment Manufacturers Representatives Association (MEMRA)

c/o Engineering Center
11 W Mt. Vernon Pl.
Baltimore, MD 21201

Ph: (410)793-0202 (410)732-1000
Fax: (410)732-9842
E-mail: jeff@uepsales.com
URL: http://www.memra.org
Contact: Jeff Smollon, Pres.
Founded: 1960. **Members:** 40. **Description:** Manufacturers' representatives united to seek better ways to serve the industry and to help members improve the efficiency of their business operations. Sponsors expositions. Membership presently concentrated in the Baltimore, MD area, but new chapters in other cities may be formed. **Awards:** Marano Scholarship Fund. **Frequency:** annual. **Type:** scholarship. **Recipient:** to Poly students ● **Frequency:** annual. **Type:** scholarship. **Recipient:** to either a Hopkins or U.M. B.C. engineering student. **Publications:** Directory, annual.

2541 ■ NAGMR
c/o Ron Otto
1421 Ridgetree Trails
St. Louis, MO 63021-5944
Ph: (636)527-7115
Fax: (636)527-2116
E-mail: rotto@nationalsalessolutions.com
URL: http://www.nagmr.com
Contact: Carlton Swan, Pres.
Founded: 1948. **Members:** 40. **Membership Dues:** broker, $500 (annual). **Staff:** 1. **Budget:** $100,000. **Description:** Consumer products brokers specializing in selling drug, health, beauty aids, and nonfood products to food chains and the same products and grocery items to the nonfood market. **Awards:** NAGMR Award of Excellence. **Frequency:** annual. **Type:** monetary. **Recipient:** to a member or dependent of NAGMR firm. **Computer Services:** database, member. **Formerly:** National Association of Drug Manufacturers Representatives; (1978) National Association of Diversified Manufacturers Representatives; (1999) National Association General Merchandise Representatives Consumer Product Brokers; (2001) NAGMR Consumer Products Broker; (2002) NAGMR Consumer Products Sales Agencies. **Conventions/Meetings:** annual convention, table tops for new products looking for representation (exhibits) - always August/September.

2542 ■ National Mobility Equipment Dealers Association (NMEDA)
3327 W Bearss Ave.
Tampa, FL 33618
Ph: (813)264-2697
Free: (800)833-0427
Fax: (813)962-8970
E-mail: nmeda@aol.com
URL: http://www.nmeda.org
Contact: Ms. Dana Roeling, Exec. Dir.
Founded: 1987. **Members:** 650. **Membership Dues:** dealer, associate, manufacturer, $525-$1,050 (annual) ● professional, $52 (annual). **Staff:** 5. **Budget:** $500,000. **Regional Groups:** 5. **State Groups:** 50. **Description:** Automobile manufacturers, adaptive equipment dealers and manufacturers, driver evaluator/trainers for the disabled, doctors, lawyers, insurance adjusters, and government officials from U.S., Canada and England. Assists dealers regarding equipment, problem-solving, and updated information regarding the industry. Maintains the Quality Assurance Program. **Computer Services:** Online services, used equipment listing. **Publications:** *Circuit Breaker*, quarterly. Journal. **Advertising:** accepted. Alternate Formats: online. **Conventions/Meetings:** annual conference (exhibits) - 2009 Feb. 4-7, Daytona Beach, FL.

2543 ■ North American Industrial Representatives Association (NIRA)
Address Unknown since 2008
URL: http://www.nira.org
Founded: 1986. **Members:** 275. **Membership Dues:** manufacturer, salesperson, $395-$595 (annual) ● manufacturer, $495 (annual). **Budget:** $100,000. **Description:** Industrial products representatives. Seeks to further the function and professionalism of manufacturers' representatives. Serves as a conduit linking manufacturers and representatives; sponsors continuing professional development courses for members; conducts educational programs to raise awareness among industrial firms of the advantages of working with manufacturers' representatives. **Publications:** *NIRA Locator Membership Directory*, annual. Contains a listing of member companies. ● *NIRA News*, bimonthly. Newsletter. Contains articles affecting the industry and the association. Alternate Formats: online.

2544 ■ United Association Manufacturers Representatives (UAMR)
PO Box 986
Dana Point, CA 92629
Ph: (949)240-4966
Fax: (949)240-7001
E-mail: info@uamr.com
URL: http://www.uamr.com
Contact: Karen Mazzola, Exec. Dir.
Founded: 1965. **Members:** 1,500. **Membership Dues:** associate, $850 (annual) ● foreign, $950 (annual). **Staff:** 5. **Budget:** $150,000. **For-Profit. Description:** Manufacturers and manufacturers' representatives. Offers consulting services; connects manufacturers with representatives; sponsors seminars. Provides services such as: auto rental discounts; insurance and employee retirement system plans; profile and travel services; aid in commission collection and contract preparation; advertising and advertising discounts; subscription discounts; import/export services. Monitors federal legislation. **Publications:** *UAMR Confidential Bulletin*, monthly. Contains employment listing for manufacturers' representatives. Includes company, address, product line, and territories available. **Price:** free for members; $63.00 /year for nonmembers. **Circulation:** 1,500. **Advertising:** accepted ● *UAMR Health of the Rep Newsletter*, monthly. Contains health tips of general interest. **Price:** free for members. **Circulation:** 1,500 ● *UAMR Newsletter*, monthly. Contains information for manufacturers' representatives and manufacturers. **Price:** free, for members only ● *UAMR Travel Newsletter*, monthly. **Price:** free for members. **Circulation:** 1,500 ● Directory, periodic ●. Also publishes education portfolio. **Conventions/Meetings:** meeting - 3/year.

Manufacturing

2545 ■ Agile Manufacturing Benchmarking Consortium (AMBC)
4606 FM 1960 W, Ste.250
Houston, TX 77069
Ph: (281)440-5044
Fax: (281)440-6677
URL: http://www.ambcbenchmarking.org
Description: Promotes the use of benchmarking to facilitate process improvement and to achieve total quality. Facilitates exchange of information among members, conducts target operations, procurement, development and maintenance studies, and identifies model business practices.

2546 ■ American Industrial Extension Alliance (AIEA)
c/o Dr. Ronald A. Cox, Pres.
Center for Indus. Res. and Ser.
2272 Howe Hall, Ste.2620
Ames, IA 50011-2272
Ph: (515)294-9592
Fax: (515)294-4925
E-mail: rcox@iastate.edu
URL: http://www.ciras.iastate.edu/aiea
Contact: Dr. Ronald A. Cox, Pres.
Founded: 1992. **Membership Dues:** regular, $250 (annual). **Description:** Promotes the modernization of American manufacturing. Aims to raise the visibility of state industrial/technology programs. Develops information on best practices and establishes criteria for evaluation of the effectiveness of industrial/technology extension programs.

2547 ■ American Manufacturing Trade Action Coalition (AMTAC)
910 16th St. NW, Ste.760
Washington, DC 20006
Ph: (202)452-0866
Fax: (202)452-0739
E-mail: lwood@amtacdc.org
URL: http://www.amtacdc.org
Contact: Augustine D. Tantillo, Exec. Dir.
Description: Preserves and creates American manufacturing jobs through the establishment of trade policy and other measures necessary for the U.S. manufacturing sector to stabilize and grow. Ensures that the interests of the domestic industry and workers are upheld as part of major trade negotiations. Develops proactive legislative and administrative remedies, including an examination of the value of existing trade laws to U.S. manufacturing.

2548 ■ Association for Manufacturing Excellence (AME)
3115 N Wilke Rd., Ste.G
Arlington Heights, IL 60004
Ph: (224)232-5980
Fax: (224)232-5981
E-mail: info@ame.org
URL: http://www.ame.org
Contact: Ralph L. Keller, Pres.
Founded: 1985. **Members:** 4,000. **Membership Dues:** individual in U.S., $150 (annual) ● student in U.S., $25 (annual) ● international (outside U.S. and Canada, outside UK and Australia), $190 (annual). **Staff:** 5. **Regional Groups:** 10. **State Groups:** 9. **National Groups:** 9. **Multinational. Description:** Professional manufacturing executives united in the pursuit of excellence in manufacturing. Works to foster the understanding, analysis, and exchange of world-class productivity methods in an effort to achieve manufacturing excellence. **Libraries: Type:** reference. **Holdings:** archival material. **Publications:** *Target*, bimonthly. Magazine. Contains "how-to" information on productivity improvements; sequence, mistakes and results from specific companies. **Price:** included in membership dues. **Advertising:** accepted. **Conventions/Meetings:** annual conference (exhibits) - 2008 Oct. 20-24, Toronto, ON, Canada.

2549 ■ Association of Needle-Free Injection Manufacturers (ANFIM)
c/o Linda D'Antonio
6308 Fly Rd.
East Syracuse, NY 13057
Ph: (315)463-4999
Fax: (315)463-5267
E-mail: linda@dantonioconsultants.com
URL: http://www.anfim.com
Contact: Linda D'Antonio, Contact
Founded: 1997. **Membership Dues:** needle-free device manufacturer, $500 (annual) ● needle-free developer (no sales), $300 (annual) ● related industry, $250 (annual) ● observer (public health), $25 (annual). **Description:** Promotes and protects the public health through the advancement of needle-free injection technology. Provides exposure, education, and information to the healthcare, pharmaceutical, and health insurance industries and to consumers. Provides members with access to information relevant to the industry.

2550 ■ Aviation Suppliers Association (ASA)
2233 Wisconsin Ave. NW, Ste.503
Washington, DC 20007
Ph: (202)347-6899
Fax: (202)347-6894
E-mail: info@aviationsuppliers.org
URL: http://www.aviationsuppliers.org
Contact: Michele Dickstein, Pres.
Founded: 1993. **Members:** 300. **Membership Dues:** regular (based on number of employees), $1,200-$3,000 (annual) ● associate, $600 (annual). **Staff:** 7. **Multinational. Description:** Suppliers, distributors, manufacturers, and airline surplus sales organizations. Works to promote safety and ethical business practices; address the concerns of the aviation supply business; represent the interests of members on legislative and regulatory matters. **Awards:** Edward J. Glueckler Award. **Frequency:** annual. **Type:** recognition. **Recipient:** for outstanding commitment, dedication, and contribution to the association and the aviation industry. **Committees:** Quality Assur-

ance. **Formerly:** (2002) Airline Suppliers Association. **Publications:** *Update Report*, monthly. Newsletter. Contains information related to the aviation parts industry, events, and announcements. ● Reports, monthly. **Circulation:** 1,000. **Advertising:** accepted ● Videos. **Conventions/Meetings:** annual conference (exhibits) ● workshop.

2551 ■ CAMUS International
505 Beach St., Ste.130
San Francisco, CA 94133
Ph: (415)647-4503
Fax: (415)647-4539
E-mail: info@camus.org
URL: http://www.camus.org
Contact: Jeffrey L. Milde, Exec. Dir.
Membership Dues: regular, $450 (annual) ● associate, $550 (annual). **Multinational. Description:** Provides forum for manufacturing application users to interact with and learn from each other. **Working Groups:** Common Interest; Regional User. **Publications:** Newsletter. Alternate Formats: online. **Conventions/Meetings:** conference.

2552 ■ Composites Manufacturing Association of the Society of Manufacturing Engineers (CMA/SME)
PO Box 930
Dearborn, MI 48121-0930
Ph: (313)425-3000
Free: (800)733-4763
Fax: (313)425-3400
E-mail: leadership@sme.org
URL: http://www.sme.org/cgi-bin/communities.pl?/communities/cma/cmahome.htm&&&SME&
Contact: Mark Tomlinson, Exec. Dir./Gen. Mgr.
Founded: 1990. **Members:** 1,100. **Membership Dues:** individual, $125 (annual). **Staff:** 1. **Multinational. Description:** A division of the Society of Manufacturing Engineers. Composites manufacturing professionals and students in 21 countries. Addresses design, tooling, assembly, producibility, supportability, and future trends of composites materials and hardware; promotes advanced composites technology. Analyzes industry trends; evaluates composites usage. Conducts educational programs; facilitates exchange of information among members; operates placement service. **Affiliated With:** Society of Manufacturing Engineers. **Publications:** *Composite Materials and Manufacturing*. Video. Explains the basics of composite materials and manufacturing. **Price:** $229.00 for members; $255.00 for nonmembers ● *Composites in Manufacturing*, quarterly. Video. **Price:** free for members; $110.00 for nonmembers. **Circulation:** 1,100 ● *Composites in Manufacturing*, quarterly. Newsletter. Covers methods, processes and industry news. **Price:** $85.00/issue. Alternate Formats: online ● *Fundamental Manufacturing Processes, Composite Materials and Manufacturing*. Video. Highlights 22 of the most important manufacturing processes. **Price:** $50.00 for members; $60.00 for nonmembers ● *Fundamental Manufacturing Processes, Plastics Machining and Assembly*. Video. Focuses on the primary machining and assembly processes used for plastics. **Price:** $229.00 for members; $255.00 for nonmembers ● *Fundamentals of Composites Manufacturing: Materials, Methods and Applications*. Book. **Price:** $59.00 for members; $70.00 for nonmembers ● *Introduction to Composites Technology* ● *Manufacturing Engineering*, 10/year. Magazine. Contains information for job shop owners and other manufacturing professional. **Price:** free for members. **Circulation:** 120,000. **Advertising:** accepted. Alternate Formats: online ● *Tool and Manufacturing Engineers Handbook, Vol. 8: Plastic Part Manufacturing* ● Papers ● Reprints. **Conventions/Meetings:** annual Manufacturing Large Plants with Plastics and Composites - conference, technical forum (exhibits).

2553 ■ Consortium for Advanced Manufacturing International (CAM-I)
6832 Bee Cave, Ste.256
Austin, TX 78746
Ph: (512)617-6428
Fax: (817)426-5799
E-mail: ashok@cam-i.org
URL: http://www.cam-i.org
Contact: Ashok Vadgama, Pres.
Founded: 1972. **Members:** 100. **Membership Dues:** CMS program, $25,000 (annual) ● PBM program, $15,000 (annual) ● CMS/PBM program, $35,000 (annual). **Staff:** 20. **Description:** Companies, consultancies and academics. Working cooperatively in a precompetitive environment to solve problems that are common to the group. **Committees:** Advanced Technical Planning; Standards. **Programs:** Cost Management Systems; Process Based Management. **Projects:** Advanced Numerical Control; CIM Enterprise; Factory Management; Process Planning; Product Modelings; Quality Assurance. **Publications:** *Cameos*, quarterly. Newsletter. Provides information on activities of the organization. **Price:** included in membership dues ● *Membership and Representative Directory*, annual ● *Project and Committee Proceedings*, 20/year ● Books. **Conventions/Meetings:** semiannual trade show.

2554 ■ Door and Access Systems Manufacturers Association International (DASMA)
1300 Sumner Ave.
Cleveland, OH 44115-2851
Ph: (216)241-7333
Fax: (216)241-0105
E-mail: dasma@dasma.com
URL: http://www.dasma.com
Contact: John H. Addington, Exec. Dir.
Founded: 1996. **Members:** 101. **Staff:** 3. **Multinational. Description:** Members are prime manufacturers of upward-acting residential and commercial garage doors; operating devices for garage doors and gates, sensing devices, and electronic remote controls for garage doors and gate operators; and rolling doors, fire doors, grilles, counter shutters, sheet doors, and related products. **Telecommunication Services:** electronic mail, jaddington@dasma.com. **Publications:** *Door & Access Systems*, quarterly. Magazine. **Price:** free. **Circulation:** 15,000. **Advertising:** accepted ● Publishes steel gauge charts. **Conventions/Meetings:** annual conference.

2555 ■ Employer Association Group (EAG)
c/o National Association of Manufacturers
1331 Pennsylvania Ave. NW
Washington, DC 20004
Ph: (202)637-3000 (202)637-3052
Fax: (202)637-3182
E-mail: mstuart@nam.org
URL: http://www.nam.org/eag
Contact: Mark Stuart, Exec. Dir.
Founded: 1907. **Members:** 124. **Membership Dues:** organization (based on operating budget), $600-$2,200 (annual). **Budget:** $250,000. **Regional Groups:** 2. **State Groups:** 46. **Local Groups:** 75. **Description:** Network of 70 local associations that provide human resource services to the employer community. Based at the National Association of Manufacturers' local industrial and business associations. **Libraries: Type:** reference. **Holdings:** books, periodicals. **Subjects:** Labor/Employment Law. **Telecommunication Services:** electronic mail, ccataldo@nam.org. **Affiliated With:** National Association of Manufacturers. **Formerly:** (2000) National Industrial Council. **Publications:** *EAG Network Notes*, bimonthly. Newsletter. Alternate Formats: online ● *Executive Compensation Survey*, annual ● *Speakers' Survey*, periodic ● *Successful Programs/Services Survey*, annual ● Directory, annual. **Conventions/Meetings:** semiannual conference.

2556 ■ Entertainment Services and Technology Association (ESTA)
875 6th Ave., Ste.1005
New York, NY 10001
Ph: (212)244-1505
Fax: (212)244-1502
E-mail: info@esta.org
URL: http://www.esta.org
Contact: Lori Rubinstein, Exec. Dir.
Founded: 1987. **Members:** 470. **Membership Dues:** branch office (minimum), $60 (annual) ● individual, non-profit organization, $125 (annual) ● international, $495 (annual) ● full (based on number of full time employees), $450-$2,610 (annual). **Staff:** 7. **Budget:** $1,200,000. **Multinational. Description:** Represents broad spectrum of companies supplying the live entertainment industry; creates standards and recommended practices for the industry through the ANSI accredited Technical Standards Program; develops certification programs for personnel in the technical entertainment field; provides quarterly data on market size and share for specific product categories through Market Research Program for Manufacturers. Offers education and information exchange and promotion of members. **Awards:** Dealers' Choice Customer Service. **Frequency:** annual. **Type:** recognition. **Recipient:** for manufacturers who provide good customer service ● Dealers' Choice Product. **Frequency:** annual. **Type:** recognition. **Recipient:** for outstanding new entertainment technology product ● Eva Swan. **Frequency:** annual. **Type:** recognition. **Recipient:** for ESTA member with major contribution to the association ● Manufacturers' Choice Dealer of the Year. **Frequency:** annual. **Type:** recognition. **Recipient:** for dealers with superior performance. **Telecommunication Services:** electronic mail, lrubinstein@esta.org. **Committees:** Business Education; Communications and Publications; Risk Management. **Programs:** Essential Skills Certificate; Market Research; Technical Education; Technical Standards. **Projects:** Industry History. **Formerly:** (1995) Theatrical Dealers Association. **Publications:** *ANSI E.2-2000 Design, Manufacture and Use of Aluminum Trusses and Towers* ● *ANSI E1.14-2001, Recommendations for Inclusions in Fog Equipment Manuals* ● *ANSI E1.9-2001, Reporting Photometric Performance Data for Luminaires Used in Entertainment Lighting* ● *ANSI E1.1-1999 Construction and Use of Wire Rope Ladders* ● *ANSI E1.16 2002, Configuration Standard for Metal-Halide Ballast Power Cable* ● *ANSI E1.3-2001, Lighting Control Systems 0 to 10V Analog Control Specification* ● *Introduction to Modern Atmospheric Effects, 3rd Edition* ● *Protocol*, quarterly. Journal. **Circulation:** 6,000. **Advertising:** accepted ● *Recommended Practice for Ethernet Cabling Systems in Entertainment* ● *Supplement to Recommended Practice for Ethernet Cabling Systems in Entertainment Lighting Applications* ● Membership Directory, annual. Contains listing of all members with brief description of their business. **Circulation:** 10,000. **Advertising:** accepted. **Conventions/Meetings:** quarterly board meeting.

2557 ■ Heavy Duty Manufacturers Association (HDMA)
10 Lab. Dr.
PO Box 13966
Research Triangle Park, NC 27709-3966
Ph: (919)549-4800 (919)406-8808
Fax: (919)549-4824
E-mail: info@hdma.org
URL: http://www.hdma.org
Contact: Tim Krause, Exec. Dir.
Founded: 1983. **Members:** 120. **Membership Dues:** general (based on sales volume), $900-$17,000 (annual) ● affiliate, $2,000 (annual) ● divisional, $1,000 (annual) ● publication, $500 (annual). **Staff:** 3. **Description:** Promotes North American manufacturers of all types of components and equipment (both and aftermarket) for classes 6, 7, and 8 trucks. Provides extensive market research, state and federal government legislative and regulatory monitoring and reporting economic forecasts, industry information, and executive conferences. **Telecommunication Services:** electronic mail, tkraus@hdma.org. **Affiliated With:** Motor and Equipment Manufacturers Association. **Publications:** *Diesel Download*, biweekly. Newsletter. Features the latest news from the heavy duty sector. Alternate Formats: online ● *Heavy Duty Directions*, bimonthly. Newsletter. Contains news and trends affecting the heavy duty sector. Alternate Formats: online. **Conventions/Meetings:** biennial Heavy Duty Dialogue - conference.

2558 ■ International Society of Agile Manufacturing (ISAM)
c/o Suren Dwivedi, PhD, IJAMS Chief Ed.
2851 Johnston St., PMB No. 325
Lafayette, LA 70503

Ph: (337)989-7262
Fax: (337)989-7272
E-mail: dwivedi@louisiana.edu
URL: http://www.soberit.hut.fi/ISAM
Contact: Suren Dwivedi PhD, IJAMS Chief Ed.

Founded: 1995. **Multinational**. **Description:** Seeks to accelerate the international exchange of ideas and scientific knowledge with no barriers of either discipline domain or field of technological application. Fosters the cross-fertilization of technology, strategy and 4M resources (Manpower, Machine, Money and Management). Enhances productivity, competitive advantage and improves general quality of life. Emphasizes on the cross-fertilization of emerging innovative technologies and their effective utilization of 4M resources. Develops a community of researchers interested in Productivity Enhancement within the Extended Enterprise. **Publications:** *International Journal of Advanced Manufacturing Systems*. Addresses the utilization of Agile and Advanced Manufacturing systems. **Price:** $100.00 per year. Alternate Formats: online. Also Cited As: *IJAMS* ● *International Journal of Agile Manufacturing*, semiannual. Addresses the utilization of Agile and Advanced Manufacturing systems. **Price:** $100.00 per year. Alternate Formats: online. Also Cited As: *IJAM* ● Newsletter ● Proceedings. **Conventions/Meetings:** annual conference (exhibits).

2559 ■ International Solid Surface Fabricators Association (ISSFA)

975 Amer. Pacific Dr., Ste.102
Henderson, NV 89014-7823
Ph: (702)567-8150
Free: (877)GO-ISSFA
Fax: (702)567-8145
E-mail: oxley@issfa.org
URL: http://www.issfa.org
Contact: Robert Oxley, Exec. Dir.

Founded: 1997. **Members:** 1,000. **Membership Dues:** surfacing manufacturer (with revenue up to $20 million), $2,000-$7,500 (annual) ● surfacing distributor, supplier, $499 (annual) ● student, $50 (annual) ● fabricator, subscriber, industry partner, $400 (annual). **Staff:** 5. **Budget:** $1,000,000. **Regional Groups:** 7. **State Groups:** 50. **Languages:** English, French, German, Spanish. **Multinational**. **Description:** Fabricators of solid surfaces. Promotes growth and development of members' operations. Facilitates communication and cooperation among members; represents the collective commercial and regulatory interests of solid surface fabricators. **Libraries: Type:** reference. **Holdings:** periodicals. **Subjects:** solid surface. **Awards:** The Associate of the Year. **Frequency:** annual. **Type:** recognition. **Recipient:** for the manufacturer, distributor or supplier ● The Fabricator of the Year Award. **Frequency:** annual. **Type:** recognition. **Recipient:** for outstanding member of the year ● The Hall of Fame Award. **Frequency:** annual. **Type:** recognition. **Recipient:** for very unique individual who has served the industry in a lasting way over many years ● The Innovation Award. **Frequency:** annual. **Type:** recognition. **Recipient:** for individual who creates a unique product or use of product ● The Invision Award. **Frequency:** annual. **Type:** recognition. **Recipient:** for uniqueness in application, business development, design or leadership in the industry ● The ISSFA Champions. **Frequency:** annual. **Type:** recognition. **Recipient:** for outstanding volunteers who have served the membership in an exceptional way. **Publications:** *The ISSFA Business Journal*, bimonthly. Journals. Includes best practices: management, fabrication, product application and business strategies and tactics. **Price:** included in membership dues. **Circulation:** 1,200. **Conventions/Meetings:** annual Solid Surface - trade show (exhibits).

2560 ■ Machinery Information Management Open Systems Alliance (MIMOSA)

2704 8th St.
Tuscaloosa, AL 35401
Ph: (949)625-8616
Fax: (949)625-8616
E-mail: info@mimosa.org
URL: http://www.mimosa.org
Contact: Alan T. Johnston, Pres.

Members: 60. **Membership Dues:** corporate sponsor, $5,000 (annual) ● corporate, $500-$1,000 (annual) ● academic, $250 (annual). **Description:** Develops and encourages the adoption of open information standards for Operations and Maintenance and Collaborative Asset Lifecycle Management in commercial and military applications. Provides a forum for the members, bringing together subject matter experts in cross disciplinary technologies, to enable complex solutions for Equipment Operators, Maintainers and Fleet Managers. **Computer Services:** database, specification download area ● electronic publishing ● information services.

2561 ■ National Association of Manufacturers (NAM)

1331 Pennsylvania Ave. NW
Washington, DC 20004-1790
Ph: (202)637-3000
Free: (800)248-6626
Fax: (202)637-3182
E-mail: manufacturing@nam.org
URL: http://www.nam.org
Contact: Mr. John Engler, Pres./CEO

Founded: 1895. **Members:** 12,000. **Membership Dues:** general (based on annual expense budget), $600-$2,300 (annual). **Staff:** 180. **Budget:** $5,000,000. **Description:** Manufacturers and cooperating non-manufacturers having a direct interest in or relationship to manufacturing. Represents industry's views on national and international problems to government. Maintains public affairs and public relations programs. Reviews current and proposed legislation, administrative rulings, and interpretations, judicial decisions, and legal matters affecting industry. Maintains numerous policy groups: Human Resources Policy; Small and Medium Manufacturers; Tax Policy; Resources & Environmental Policy; Regulation and Legal Reform Policy; International Economic Affairs. Affiliated with 150 local and state trade associations of manufacturers through National Industrial Council and 250 manufacturing trade associations through the Associations Council. **Awards:** Excellence in Manufacturing Leadership Award. **Frequency:** annual. **Type:** recognition. **Recipient:** for an outstanding manufacturing leader ● Manufacturing Achievement Award. **Frequency:** annual. **Type:** recognition. **Computer Services:** Online services, NAMNET. **Telecommunication Services:** electronic bulletin board, daily legislative news brief. **Publications:** *Directory of Officers, Directors and Committees*, annual ● *Just in Time*, monthly. Newsletter. Alternate Formats: online ● *NAM Member Focus*, monthly. Newsletter. Alternate Formats: online ● *Small and Medium Manufacturers NewsLine*, monthly. Newsletter. Available by fax. Alternate Formats: online ● *Washington 1000* ● *Winning at Public Affairs* ● Bulletin, periodic ● Reports ● Also publishes legal studies, issue briefs, and specialized publications. **Conventions/Meetings:** annual National Manufacturing Week - trade show (exhibits).

2562 ■ National Association of Manufacturers Council of Manufacturing Associations (NAM/CMA)

1331 Pennsylvania Ave. NW
Washington, DC 20004-1790
Ph: (202)637-3000
Free: (800)814-8468
Fax: (202)637-3182
E-mail: manufacturing@nam.org
URL: http://www.nam.org/council
Contact: David Asselin, Exec. Dir.

Founded: 1907. **Members:** 220. **Membership Dues:** association (based on operating budget), $600-$2,300 (annual). **Staff:** 3. **Budget:** $450,000. **Description:** Represents national manufacturing trade associations. Fosters national legislative, regulatory and judicial policies beneficial to the manufacturing sector and the trade associations that represent it. Facilitates educational forums and other networking opportunities for association executives representing the manufacturing sector. **Affiliated With:** National Association of Manufacturers. **Formerly:** (1993) Associations Council of the National Association of Manufacturers. **Publications:** *Council Update*, semiweekly. Newsletter. Contains association activities; carries meeting, legislative, and council news. Includes calendar of council and member association events. **Price:** included in membership dues. **Circulation:** 250 ● *Manufacturing Association Practices*, biennial. Survey. Covers management and governance trends among manufacturing trade associations. **Price:** $150.00/copy for nonmembers. **Circulation:** 300 ● *Membership Directory of the Council of Manufacturing Associations*, annual. **Price:** included in membership dues; $25.00/copy for nonmembers. **Circulation:** 250. **Advertising:** accepted ● *Mission Statement Reference Guide* ● Brochures. **Conventions/Meetings:** semiannual Leadership Conference, for chief staff officers of manufacturing associations ● workshop - 3/year.

2563 ■ National Council for Advanced Manufacturing (NACFAM)

2000 L St. NW, Ste.807
Washington, DC 20036
Ph: (202)429-2220
Fax: (202)429-2422
E-mail: nacfam@nacfam.org
URL: http://www.nacfam.org
Contact: Eric Mittelstadt, CEO

Founded: 1989. **Members:** 1,200. **Membership Dues:** advanced manufacturing leader with sales of over 10 billion, $50,000 (annual) ● advanced manufacturing leader with sales of 500 million to 10 billion, $25,000 (annual) ● advanced manufacturing leader with sales of below 100 million, non-profit organization, $5,000 (annual) ● alliance, $1,000 (annual). **Staff:** 12. **Budget:** $2,000,000. **Description:** Companies, university centers, laboratories, and manufacturing extension services, national trade associations, and national technical education associations. Seeks to "enhance the productivity, quality and competitiveness of all tiers of the U.S. domestic industrial base." Organizes public and private technology research and development projects; serves as a network linking members; conducts workforce skills standards development programs. **Councils:** Advanced Manufacturing Leadership Forum. **Formerly:** (2004) National Coalition for Advanced Manufacturing. **Publications:** *NACFAM Weekly*. Newsletter. **Price:** $395.00/year. Alternate Formats: online ● Reports. Alternate Formats: online ● Papers.

2564 ■ The Remanufacturing Institute (TRI)

c/o Ron Giuntini, Exec. Dir.
PO Box 48
Lewisburg, PA 17837
Ph: (570)523-0992
E-mail: rgiuntini@reman.org
URL: http://www.reman.org
Contact: Ron Giuntini, Exec. Dir.

Multinational. **Description:** Represents all segments of the remanufacturing industry. **Divisions:** Remanufacturing Tax Credit Center. **Publications:** *Reman E-News*, periodic. Newsletter. Covers the remanufacturing industry. **Price:** $50.00. Alternate Formats: online.

2565 ■ SEAMS Association

4921-C Broad River Rd.
Columbia, SC 29212
Ph: (803)772-5861
Fax: (803)731-7709
E-mail: sarah@seams.org
URL: http://www.seams.org
Contact: Sarah Friedman, Exec. Dir.

Founded: 1967. **Members:** 175. **Membership Dues:** contractor, manufacturer, $440-$770 (annual) ● supplier, $605 (annual). **Staff:** 2. **Description:** Represents manufacturing and contract manufacturing companies in the sewn products industry. Strives to enhance and support sound economic growth in the apparel and sewn products industry. Offers benefits packages to members. **Formerly:** (2003) SEAMS. **Publications:** *SEAMS Important*, bimonthly. Newsletter. Alternate Formats: online. **Conventions/Meet-**

ings: semiannual Networking Conference - usually spring and fall.

2566 ■ Tooling and Manufacturing Association (TMA)
1177 S Dee Rd.
Park Ridge, IL 60068
Ph: (847)825-1120
Fax: (847)825-0041
E-mail: charan@tmanet.com
URL: http://www.tmanet.com
Contact: Bruce Braker, Pres.

Founded: 1925. **Members:** 1,600. **Membership Dues:** regular, $250 (quarterly). **Staff:** 20. **Budget:** $3,000,000. **Description:** Precision metalworking, plastic molding, and supplier companies. Established to provide programs and services to help businesses grow and prosper, train employees, and provide medical benefits. **Programs:** Apprentice Training. **Publications:** *Metalworking Opportunities*. Newsletter. Alternate Formats: online ● Bulletin, semimonthly. Alternate Formats: online.

2567 ■ Unified Abrasives Manufacturers' Association (UAMA)
30200 Detroit Rd.
Cleveland, OH 44145-1967
Ph: (440)899-0010
Fax: (440)892-1404
E-mail: contact@uama.org
URL: http://www.uama.org
Contact: Mr. Jerry Wherry, Managing Dir.

Founded: 1999. **Members:** 30. **Description:** Represents manufacturers of bonded, coated and super abrasive products and abrasive grains. **Committees:** ANSI Accredited Standards B7/B74; Education, Conference and Workshop; Environmental and Occupational Safety; Human Resources; Industrial Information; Meeting Arrangements; Public Relations. **Formerly:** (1999) Grinding Wheel Institute; (1999) Abrasive Grain Association; (1999) Coated Abrasives Manufacturers Institute; (1999) Diamond Wheel Manufacturers Institute. **Publications:** *Vision*. Newsletter. **Conventions/Meetings:** semiannual conference and lecture, includes educational workshops and a social and recreational forum.

Marine

2568 ■ American Boat Builders and Repairers Association (ABBRA)
50 Water St.
Warren, RI 02885
Ph: (401)247-0318
Fax: (401)247-0074
E-mail: mamaral@abbra.org
URL: http://www.abbra.org
Contact: Mark Amaral, Managing Dir.

Founded: 1943. **Members:** 350. **Membership Dues:** professional, $230 (annual) ● active (based on number of employees), $290-$525 (annual) ● associate, $530 (annual) ● international, $345 (annual) ● student, $75 (annual). **Staff:** 2. **Budget:** $150,000. **Description:** Boat yards, marinas, and sailmakers. Seeks to: develop and encourage high standards of service and conduct within the industry; foster and promote the common business and professional interests of members; provide a forum for the discussion of problems and the exchange of experiences and ideas. **Awards:** President's Award. **Frequency:** annual. **Type:** recognition. **Recipient:** for outstanding service from a member to the organization ● Star Membership Award. **Frequency:** annual. **Type:** recognition. **Telecommunication Services:** electronic mail, rquigley@abbra.org. **Formerly:** (1955) Atlantic Coast Boat Builders and Repairers Association. **Publications:** *American Boat Builders and Repairers Association—Newsletter*, monthly. **Price:** available to members only. **Circulation:** 500. **Advertising:** accepted ● *Boatyard and Marinas Operators Manual* ● *Capstan*, monthly. **Price:** free for members. **Circulation:** 500 ● *Environmental Briefing*. Manual ● *Gel Coat Blister Repair*. Manual. **Conventions/Meetings:** semiannual conference (exhibits) - always fall and winter ● seminar.

2569 ■ American Boat and Yacht Council (ABYC)
613 Third St., Ste.10
Annapolis, MD 21403
Ph: (410)990-4460
Fax: (410)990-4466
E-mail: info@abycinc.org
URL: http://www.abycinc.org
Contact: Mr. Skip Burdon, Pres./CEO

Founded: 1954. **Members:** 4,700. **Membership Dues:** business, $175 (annual) ● sustaining, $250 (annual) ● manufacturer, $300 (annual) ● participating, $500 (annual) ● silver, $1,000 (annual) ● silver Plus, $1,500 (annual) ● gold, $2,500 (annual) ● platinum, $5,000 (annual). **Staff:** 16. **Budget:** $1,500,000. **Description:** Consists of boatbuilders, boat owners, boat yards, dealerships, educational institutions, equipment and accessory manufacturers, government agencies, insurance companies, law firms, marinas, marine retailers, service technicians, surveyors and trade associations. Develops the consensus-based safety standards for the design, construction, equipage, maintenance and repair of small craft and their systems through 18 project technical committees. **Libraries: Type:** reference. **Holdings:** 2,000. **Subjects:** boating safety. **Awards:** ABYC Service Award. **Frequency:** annual. **Type:** recognition. **Recipient:** for outstanding service to the ABYC and for furthering boating safety. **Divisions:** Electrical; Equipment; Hull; Propulsion and Auxiliary Machinery; Technical Information Standards. **Publications:** *ABYC Roster of Members*, 11/year. Directory. Currently available online, only to members. **Price:** available to members only. Alternate Formats: online ● *American Boat and Yacht Council—News*, quarterly. Newsletters. Provides notices and articles of interest to members of the marine community. **Price:** available to members only. **Circulation:** 4,300. Alternate Formats: online ● *Rules and Regulations for Recreational Boats*, periodic. Book. Contains excerpts from the CFR listing laws and rules governing the U.S. Coast guard boating safety program for the marine industry. **Price:** $24.95 for members, plus shipping and handling; $32.95 for nonmembers, plus shipping and handling ● *Standards and Technical Information Reports for Small Craft*, annual. Articles. Contains compendium of safety standards developed in conjunction with members of the marine industry for manufacturing, repairing, and surveying. **Price:** $219.00 for members, plus shipping and handling. Alternate Formats: CD-ROM ● *USCG Compliance Guidelines*, periodic, revised January 2002. Book. Contains explanatory CFR information prepared in conjunction with the USCG. Commonly known as the "How To's" of the Rules and Regulations book. **Price:** $25.00 plus shipping and handling. Alternate Formats: CD-ROM. **Conventions/Meetings:** periodic seminar (exhibits) ● workshop.

2570 ■ American Maritime Safety, Inc. (AMS)
445 Hamilton Ave., Ste.1204
White Plains, NY 10601-1833
Ph: (914)997-2916
Fax: (914)997-6959
E-mail: ams@maritimesafety.org
URL: http://www.maritimesafety.org
Contact: Louis Meltz Esq., Pres.

Founded: 1987. **Description:** Works to facilitate the maritime industry's compliance with U.S. Coast Guard regulations and international protocols. **Conventions/Meetings:** Training and Education Seminars.

2571 ■ American Pilots' Association (APA)
499 S Capitol St. SW, Ste.409
Washington, DC 20003
Ph: (202)484-0700
Fax: (202)484-9320
E-mail: contact@americanpilots.org
URL: http://www.americanpilots.org
Contact: Paul G. Kirchner, Exec. Dir./Gen. Counsel

Founded: 1884. **Members:** 60. **Membership Dues:** individual, $120 (monthly). **Staff:** 4. **Description:** State associations of licensed state marine pilots representing 1200 members. Seeks to improve pilotage services. **Telecommunication Services:** electronic mail, captwatson@americanpilots.org. **Committees:** Political Action. **Publications:** *On Station*, quarterly. Newsletter. **Conventions/Meetings:** biennial convention (exhibits) - 2008 Oct. 18-25, Koloa, HI.

2572 ■ Association of Certified Marine Surveyors (ACMS)
209/241 Nooseneck Hill Rd.
West Greenwich, RI 02817
Ph: (401)397-1888
E-mail: membership@acms-usa.com
URL: http://acms-usa.com

Founded: 1999. **Description:** Promotes the marine surveying industry through communication and cooperation through individuals.

2573 ■ Association of Marine Technicians (AMTECH)
513 River Estates Pkwy.
Canton, GA 30114-9419
Ph: (770)720-4234
Free: (800)467-0982
Fax: (770)720-4329
E-mail: jdemarco@am-tech.org
URL: http://www.am-tech.org
Contact: Joseph J. DeMarco, Pres./Founder

Founded: 1999. **Members:** 750. **Membership Dues:** manufacturer, $500 (annual) ● associate, distributor, association, business gold level, individual gold level, $250 (annual) ● individual silver level, $125 (annual) ● business basic, $150 (annual) ● school, $100 (annual) ● individual basic, $75 (annual). **Staff:** 4. **Description:** Marine dealers, educators, engine and boat manufacturers, technicians. Work to improve skills and productivity for marine technicians. **Computer Services:** Online services, marine engine diagnostics. **Publications:** *Service Writer*, quarterly. Newsletter. **Price:** free. Alternate Formats: online. **Conventions/Meetings:** annual National Marine Service Expo - trade show and workshop (exhibits).

2574 ■ Committee for Private Offshore Rescue and Towing (C-PORT)
PO Box 4070
Annapolis, MD 21403
Free: (866)847-3609
Fax: (410)263-3186
E-mail: info@c-port.org
Contact: Terry Hill, Chair

Founded: 1986. **Members:** 190. **Membership Dues:** associate, company (1 vessel), $300 (annual) ● company (2 vessels), $350 (annual) ● company (3 vessels), $400 (annual) ● company (4 vessels), $500 (annual) ● company (5 vessels), $600 (annual) ● company (6 vessels), $700 (annual). **Staff:** 3. **Regional Groups:** 4. **Local Groups:** 2. **Description:** Small boat-towing and salvage companies. Seeks to provide members with a coordinated voice and promote their interests; acts as a regulatory body for the industry. Administers certification program for accrediting commercial assistance and professional towing. Sponsors a group insurance program. Compiles statistics. **Committees:** Coast Guard; Government Affairs; Industry Certification; Public Affairs. **Publications:** *C-PORT News*, monthly. Newsletter. Contains vital industry news, information on rules and regulations, new member benefits and much more. Alternate Formats: online ● *Washington Update*, periodic. Newsletter. **Conventions/Meetings:** semiannual meeting (exhibits) - always April, Washington, DC, and November, mid-Atlantic region.

2575 ■ Council of American Master Mariners (CAMM)
c/o Capt. Donald Moore, Sec.-Treas.
PO Box 5034
Lynnwood, WA 98046-5034
Ph: (425)775-2331

E-mail: captmoore@mastermariner.org
URL: http://www.mastermariner.org
Contact: Capt. Donald Moore, Sec.-Treas.
Founded: 1936. **Members:** 1,300. **Membership Dues:** regular, special, associate, honorary, $60 (annual). **Staff:** 1. **Budget:** $63,000. **Regional Groups:** 8. **State Groups:** 12. **Description:** Master mariners who serve or have served on ocean-going vessels. Serves as a voice for master mariners on professional issues. **Telecommunication Services:** electronic mail, captbradley@mastermariner.org. **Publications:** *Membership Roster*, annual. Directory. **Circulation:** 1,300. **Advertising:** accepted. Alternate Formats: diskette ● *Sidelights*, quarterly. Newsletter. **Circulation:** 1,300. **Advertising:** accepted. Alternate Formats: online. **Conventions/Meetings:** annual meeting - usually April or May.

2576 ■ Dredging Contractors of America (DCA)

503 D St. NW, Ste.150
Washington, DC 20001
Ph: (202)737-2674
Fax: (202)737-2677
E-mail: jimrausch@dredgingcontractors.org
URL: http://www.dredgingcontractors.org
Contact: Jim Rausch, Exec. Dir.
Founded: 1948. **Members:** 28. **Staff:** 2. **Budget:** $600,000. **Description:** Chief executive officers of small dredging companies united to enable these companies to compete with large dredging operations. (Dredging involves widening and deepening waterways.) Seeks to upgrade industry standards; works with the Army Corps of Engineers and other governmental agencies; engages in environmental and ecological issues. Compiles statistics. **Libraries: Type:** reference. **Holdings:** 300; reports. **Telecommunication Services:** electronic mail, barryholliday@dredgingcontractors.org. **Formed by Merger of:** American Association for Small Dredging and Marine Construction Companies; National Association of Dredging Contractors. **Conventions/Meetings:** annual meeting - always spring.

2577 ■ Inland Seas Education Association (ISEA)

100 Dame St.
Suttons Bay, MI 49682
Ph: (231)271-3077
Fax: (231)271-3088
E-mail: isea@schoolship.org
URL: http://www.greatlakeseducation.org
Contact: Christine Diana, Education Dir.
Founded: 1989. **Members:** 500. **Membership Dues:** patron, $1,000 (annual) ● sustaining, $500 (annual) ● contributing, $100 (annual) ● family, $40 (annual) ● supporting, $60 (annual) ● individual, $25 (annual). **Staff:** 12. **Description:** Individuals concerned with the stewardship of the Great Lakes. Develops leadership, understanding, and commitment needed for long-term stewardship of the Great Lakes. Provides shipboard educational programs where people of all ages can gain first-hand training and experience in the Great Lakes ecosystem. Offers aquatic science, environmental awareness, and sail training classes. **Computer Services:** database ● mailing lists ● online services. **Programs:** Schoolship; Volunteer Instructor Training. **Publications:** *Schoolship Log*, quarterly. Newsletter. **Price:** free for members. **Circulation:** 1,400 ● Also publishes schoolship instructor's manual, program manuals.

2578 ■ International Association of Marine Investigators (IAMI)

711 Medford Ctr., No. 419
Medford, OR 97504
Ph: (541)776-8601
Free: (866)844-4264
Fax: (541)857-8498
E-mail: iamimarine@aol.com
URL: http://www.iamimarine.org
Contact: Samuel Bean, Pres.
Founded: 1986. **Members:** 2,000. **Membership Dues:** law enforcement, $30 (annual) ● non-law enforcement, $60 (annual) ● permanently retired, $20 (annual) ● law enforcement agency, $100 (annual). **Budget:** $100,000. **Multinational. Description:** Works to combat marine theft and insurance fraud. **Publications:** *Exchange*. Newsletter. Alternate Formats: online. **Conventions/Meetings:** annual meeting, with 3-day training seminar.

2579 ■ International Ship Masters' Association (ISMA)

c/o ISMA-Toledo Lodge No. 9
PO Box 167820
Oregon, OH 43616
Ph: (440)933-4376
Fax: (440)930-2869
E-mail: ismalodge3@yahoo.com
URL: http://www.shipmaster.org
Contact: Russell Brohl, Grand Pres.
Founded: 1890. **Members:** 750. **Regional Groups:** 15. **Description:** Represents licensed marine officers operating on the Great Lakes. Promotes legislation to increase greater safety, health, and welfare of Great Lakes transportation and navigation. **Committees:** Convention Feasibility; Navigation; Navigation, Engineering and Legislative; Public Relations. **Formerly:** (1984) International Shipmasters Association of the Great Lakes. **Publications:** *ISMA Letter*, bimonthly. Newsletter ● *Minutes of Convention*, annual. **Conventions/Meetings:** annual meeting (exhibits).

2580 ■ Marine Retailers Association of America (MRAA)

PO Box 1127
Oak Park, IL 60304
Ph: (708)763-9210
Fax: (708)763-9236
E-mail: mraa@mraa.com
URL: http://www.mraa.com
Contact: Phil Keeter, Pres.
Founded: 1971. **Members:** 3,000. **Membership Dues:** retailer (based on volume sales), $200-$750 (annual) ● retail patron, $1,200 (annual) ● associate (based on volume sales), $300-$1,200 (annual) ● silver patron, $2,500 (annual) ● gold patron, $5,000 (annual) ● platinum patron, $10,000 (annual) ● diamond patron, $15,000 (annual) ● patron, $1,200 (annual). **Staff:** 5. **Budget:** $700,000. **State Groups:** 12. **Description:** Marine retail dealers, marine manufacturers and accessory distributors, and marine services. Disseminates information and promotes activities and programs for the betterment of recreational boating. Co-sponsors dealer management seminars to improve professional management skills. Maintains speakers' bureau; compiles statistics. **Awards:** Excellence in Business Award. **Frequency:** annual. **Type:** recognition. **Recipient:** to outstanding manufacturers in business practice, community relations and the general promotion of boating. **Computer Services:** Mailing lists, of members. **Telecommunication Services:** electronic mail, pkeeter@mraa.com ● electronic mail, larryinnis@aol.com. **Committees:** Education; Government Relations; Insurance; Internet; Long-Range Planning; Marketing. **Programs:** Financial Planning; Seal of Approval. **Publications:** *Boating Industry Supplement*, annual ● *Brarings*, monthly. Newsletter. Reports association activities and developments in the recreational boating industry and sport. **Price:** included in membership dues. **Circulation:** 3,000. **Advertising:** accepted ● *Washington Watch*. Newsletter. Contains updates and important issues in Washington DC. **Conventions/Meetings:** annual meeting (exhibits) - always fall.

2581 ■ Marine Society of the City of New York (MSCNY)

17 Battery Pl., Ste.714
New York, NY 10004
Ph: (212)425-0448
Fax: (212)425-1117
E-mail: info@marinesocietyny.org
URL: http://www.marinesocietyny.org
Contact: Capt. Timothy Ferrie, Pres.
Founded: 1769. **Members:** 300. **Membership Dues:** life, $200. **Staff:** 1. **Budget:** $100,000. **Description:** Ship masters. Promotes advancement of maritime knowledge. Supports charitable program for children and widows of deceased members. Membership concentrated in New York City. **Libraries: Type:** reference. **Holdings:** 1,000. **Subjects:** maritime, history. **Awards: Frequency:** annual. **Type:** scholarship. **Recipient:** for relatives of members. **Telecommunication Services:** electronic mail, webmaster@marinesocietyny.org. **Publications:** *Captains Quarters*, quarterly. Newsletter. Includes minutes of meetings and obituaries. **Circulation:** 400. Alternate Formats: online. **Conventions/Meetings:** annual dinner - always April ● quarterly meeting - always second Monday in January, April, July, and third Monday in October.

2582 ■ National Association of Charterboat Operators (NACO)

PO Box 2990
Orange Beach, AL 36561
Ph: (251)981-5136
Free: (866)981-5136
Fax: (251)981-8191
E-mail: info@nacocharters.org
URL: http://www.nacocharters.org
Contact: Mrs. Bobbi Walker, Exec. Dir.
Founded: 1991. **Members:** 4,000. **Membership Dues:** regular, $35 (annual). **Description:** Represents charterboat captains. Serves as industry representative to the federal government. Provides a forum for the discussion of industry issues. Offers insurance and drug testing consortium. **Telecommunication Services:** electronic mail, bobbi.walker@nacocharters.org. **Publications:** *NACO Report*, bimonthly. Newsletter. **Advertising:** accepted. **Conventions/Meetings:** annual meeting.

2583 ■ National Association of Marine Products and Services (NAMPS)

200 E Randolph Dr., Ste.5100
Chicago, IL 60601
Ph: (312)946-6200
Fax: (312)946-0388
E-mail: webmaster@nmma.org
URL: http://www.nmma.org
Contact: Thomas Dammrich, Pres.
Founded: 1972. **Members:** 950. **Staff:** 111. **Description:** Represents manufacturers of recreational marine equipment. Promotes the growth of pleasure boating and the industry which serves it. Conducts specialized education and research programs. Compiles statistics. **Affiliated With:** National Marine Manufacturers Association. **Absorbed:** (1979) Trailer Manufacturers Association. **Formerly:** (1979) Marine Accessories and Services Association. **Conventions/Meetings:** annual meeting, held in conjunction with the Marine Trade Exhibition (exhibits) - always in Chicago, IL.

2584 ■ National Association of Marine Services (NAMS)

5458 Wagon Master Dr.
Colorado Springs, CO 80917
Ph: (719)573-5946
Fax: (719)573-5952
E-mail: nams@namsshipchandler.com
URL: http://www.namsshipchandler.com
Contact: William L. Robinson, Exec. Dir.
Founded: 1950. **Members:** 70. **Staff:** 2. **Budget:** $80,000. **Description:** Ship chandlers; wholesalers and manufacturers of marine supplies and equipment for commercial vessels. **Affiliated With:** International Ship Suppliers Association. **Formerly:** (1951) Associated Ship Chandlers; (1969) National Associated Marine Suppliers. **Publications:** *Directory of American Ship Services*, annual. Contains a listing of ship supplies and associate members. ● *ISSA Register*, annual ● *NAMS News*, quarterly. Newsletter. **Conventions/Meetings:** annual meeting (exhibits).

2585 ■ National Marine Distributors Association (NMDA)

37 Pratt St.
Essex, CT 06426-1159
Ph: (860)767-7898
Fax: (860)767-7932

E-mail: info@nmdaonline.com
URL: http://www.nmdaonline.com
Contact: Nancy Cueroni, Exec. Dir.
Founded: 1965. **Members:** 300. **Staff:** 1. **Budget:** $350,000. **Description:** Wholesale distributors of marine accessories and hardware to the Pleasure Boating Industry. **Libraries: Type:** not open to the public. **Telecommunication Services:** electronic mail, executivedirector@nmdaonline.com. **Publications:** Journal, bimonthly. **Conventions/Meetings:** annual conference (exhibits) ● annual executive committee meeting ● annual S.T.E.P. Conference.

2586 ■ National Marine Electronics Association (NMEA)
Seven Riggs Ave.
Severna Park, MD 21146
Ph: (410)975-9425
Free: (800)808-6632
Fax: (410)975-9450
E-mail: info@nmea.org
URL: http://www.nmea.org
Contact: David J. Hayden, Pres./Exec. Dir.
Founded: 1957. **Members:** 425. **Membership Dues:** manufacturer, $595-$1,395 (annual) ● boat builder, $595-$1,395 (annual) ● dealer/trade, $325 (annual) ● associate, $145 (annual). **Staff:** 3. **Budget:** $250,000. **Regional Groups:** 9. **Description:** Manufacturers, retail service dealers, distributors, educational institutions, and organizations associated with sales and service of marine electronics. Promotes the education and advancement of the marine electronics industry and the market which it serves. **Awards:** NMEA Product Awards. **Frequency:** annual. **Type:** recognition. **Telecommunication Services:** electronic mail, dhayden@nmea.org. **Committees:** Awards; Dealer Education; Standards; Technician Certification. **Programs:** Certified Marine Electronics Technicians; Marine Electronics Installer. **Publications:** *Marine Electronics*, bimonthly. Journal. **Price:** $18.00 in U.S.; $28.00 in Canada; $38.00 others. **Advertising:** accepted. **Conventions/Meetings:** annual conference and convention (exhibits) - every November or October.

2587 ■ National Marine Manufacturers Association (NMMA)
200 E Randolph Dr., Ste.5100
Chicago, IL 60601
Ph: (312)946-6200 (312)946-6220
E-mail: webmaster@nmma.org
URL: http://www.nmma.org
Contact: Thomas J. Dammrich, Pres.
Founded: 1979. **Members:** 1,700. **Membership Dues:** manufacturer (based on sales volume), $300,000 (annual) ● associate, $650 (annual). **Description:** Members of Association of Marine Engine Manufacturers, National Association of Boat Manufacturers, and National Association of Marine Products and Services; manufacturers of pleasure boats, marine engines, outboard motors, and boating products. Compiles statistics and provides specialized training for designers of yachts. Sponsors consumer boat shows. Maintains 14 committees including: Aluminum Boat; Boat Shows; Canoe; Engineering; Government Relations; Insurance; Sales Promotion; Statistics. **Formed by Merger of:** National Association of Engine and Boat Manufacturers; Boating Industry Associations; Boat Manufacturers Association. **Formerly:** (1978) Outboard Motor Manufacturers Association; (2001) Marine Engine Manufacturers Association. **Publications:** *Film Directory*, periodic ● *Inter/Port*, weekly. Newsletter. Provides news, views, and trends for recreational boat manufacturers. **Price:** available to members only ● *Monthly Statistical Report* ● *Show Calendar*, annual ● Booklets. Covers boating safety, marinas and statistics. ● Also publishes boating writer's information guide and state boating laws. **Conventions/Meetings:** annual conference ● annual conference, in conjunction with Chicago Trade Show - usually September.

2588 ■ National Marine Representatives Association (NMRA)
PO Box 360
Gurnee, IL 60031
Ph: (847)662-3167
Fax: (847)336-7126
E-mail: info@nmraonline.org
URL: http://www.nmraonline.org
Contact: Mr. Jay Sanders, Pres.
Founded: 1960. **Members:** 400. **Membership Dues:** representative, $300 (annual) ● affiliate, manufacturer, $125 (annual). **Staff:** 1. **Budget:** $80,000. **Description:** Works to serve the marine industry independent sales representatives and the manufacturers selling through representatives. Serves as industry voice, networking tool and information source promoting benefits of utilizing independent marine representatives for sales. Aims to assist manufacturers find the right marine sales reps for product lines. **Awards:** Mel Barr Award. **Frequency:** annual. **Type:** recognition. **Recipient:** to an individual who has made significant contributions to the marine industry. **Computer Services:** Mailing lists. **Publications:** *Tidings*, quarterly. Newsletter. Contains articles written to help manufacturers develop sound and profitable relationships with independent sales representatives. **Price:** included in membership dues. **Circulation:** 400. **Advertising:** accepted ● Membership Directory, annual. Lists independent sales representatives of pleasure boats and boating accessories. Provides territories covered and the primary customers. **Price:** available to members only. **Circulation:** 400. **Advertising:** accepted. **Conventions/Meetings:** annual general assembly.

2589 ■ Northwest Marine Trade Association (NMTA)
1900 N Northlake Way, No. 233
Seattle, WA 98103-9087
Ph: (206)634-0911
Fax: (206)632-0078
E-mail: info@nmta.net
URL: http://www.nmta.net
Contact: Michael Campbell, Pres.
Founded: 1947. **Members:** 1,000. **Membership Dues:** active, affiliate, $445 (annual) ● individual, $50 (annual). **Staff:** 9. **Description:** Sole proprietorships, firms, partnerships, or corporations engaged in the sales, service, distribution, and construction of boats, engines, and accessories; allied businesses. Seeks to further the interests of members; to promote public interest in boating; to cooperate with similar organizations; to develop local and state legislation beneficial to the industry and the boating public. Produces and sponsors boat shows; serves as legislative consultant and watchdog for the industry; conducts seminars and management and sales workshops; maintains advertising and public relations programs for the industry; commissions special studies and reports; conducts social activities. **Telecommunication Services:** electronic mail, michael@nmta.net. **Committees:** Boat Show; Boatyard; Fish; Government Affairs; Marine Technicians; Political Action; Promotion. **Programs:** Grow Boating. **Formerly:** (1974) Northwest Marine Industries. **Publications:** *Northwest Marine Trade Association—Membership Directory*, annual. **Price:** free, for members only ● *Water Life*, monthly. Newsletter. Covers association and industry news. Includes calendar of events and new members. **Circulation:** 1,500. Alternate Formats: online. **Conventions/Meetings:** semiannual Seattle Boat Show - always in Seattle, WA.

2590 ■ Offshore Marine Service Association (OMSA)
990 N Corporate Dr., Ste.210
Harahan, LA 70123
Ph: (504)734-7622
Fax: (504)734-7134
E-mail: kenwells@offshoremarine.org
URL: http://www.offshoremarine.org
Contact: Ken Wells, Pres.
Founded: 1957. **Members:** 285. **Membership Dues:** associate (based on annual gross revenue), $189-$990 (annual) ● regular (based on number of vessels and barges), $1,060-$2,805 (annual). **Staff:** 4. **Budget:** $650,000. **Description:** Owners, operators, suppliers and crews of vessels servicing offshore oil and mineral installations. Seeks to advance the industry worldwide; monitors legislation and governmental regulations affecting the construction of offshore oil marine equipment and the operation of these specialized vessels, used primarily to supply and service offshore oil and gas operations worldwide. Conducts educational and personnel development and training programs; disseminates information on insurance and legal issues affecting offshore vessel operations. Maintains numerous committees representing all types of vessels engaged in the support of offshore installations. **Computer Services:** database ● mailing lists. **Committees:** Associate Member Business Development; Crew and Utility Vessel; Liftboat; Offshore Supply Vessel; Offshore Tug and Barge; Safety, Health and Environmental. **Subcommittees:** Legal; OMSA/ABS. **Affiliated With:** International Association of Drilling Contractors. **Formerly:** (1969) Gulf Offshore Marine Service Association. **Publications:** *OMSA Newsletter*, quarterly. Covers offshore marine operations and management, legislative and judicial matters, and government regulatory activity affecting the industry. **Price:** free. **Circulation:** 575. Alternate Formats: online ● Membership Directory, annual. Includes information on government agencies with jurisdiction over aspects of offshore marine operations. **Price:** $25.00 for members. **Circulation:** 575. **Conventions/Meetings:** quarterly meeting - usually in New Orleans, LA.

2591 ■ Passenger Vessel Association (PVA)
901 N Pitt St., Ste.100
Alexandria, VA 22314
Ph: (703)518-5005
Free: (800)807-8360
Fax: (703)518-5151
E-mail: pvainfo@passengervessel.com
URL: http://www.passengervessel.com
Contact: John Groundwater, Exec. Dir.
Founded: 1971. **Members:** 500. **Membership Dues:** national associate, $860 (annual) ● regional associate, $650 (annual) ● vessel (based on passenger capacity), $375-$3,255 (annual) ● gold, $8,250 (annual) ● silver, $6,525 (annual) ● bronze, $4,575 (annual) ● individual, retired, $110 (annual). **Staff:** 6. **Budget:** $800,000. **Regional Groups:** 5. **Description:** Owners, operators, and suppliers of U.S. and Canadian flagged passenger vessels, including dinner vessels, private charter, tour, and excursion boats, casino gambling boats, overnight cruise vessels, and whale watching and eco-tourism operators. Monitors and disseminates information on current and proposed federal regulation and legislation affecting passenger ship owners; represents the industry's views to legislative and regulatory bodies. **Awards: Type:** recognition. **Committees:** High Speed; Insurance; Legislative; Regulatory; Safety. **Councils:** Ferry; Overnight Cruise. **Formerly:** (1993) National Association of Passenger Vessel Owners. **Publications:** *Foghorn*, monthly. Newsletter. **Advertising:** accepted ● *PVA Passenger Vessel Directory*, annual. **Conventions/Meetings:** annual Maritrends - convention.

2592 ■ Shipbuilders Council of America (SCA)
1455 F St. NW, Ste.225
Washington, DC 20005
Ph: (202)347-5462
Fax: (202)347-5464
E-mail: ibennitt@dc.bjllp.com
URL: http://www.shipbuilders.org
Contact: Ian Bennitt, Contact
Founded: 1921. **Members:** 121. **Membership Dues:** corporate (based on number of assessable employees), $5,000-$40,000 (annual) ● allied (based on sales to the industry), $1,550-$5,150 (annual). **Staff:** 2. **Description:** Companies engaged in the construction and repair of vessels and other marine craft; manufacturers of all types of propelling machinery, boilers, marine auxiliaries, marine equipment and supplies; dry-dock operators. Promotes and maintains sound private shipbuilding and ship repairing industries; develops and maintains adequate mobilization potential of shipbuilding and ship repairing facilities, organizations, and skilled personnel in time of national emergency. Compiles statistical data on shipbuilding and repair. **Absorbed:** Atlantic and Gulf

Coasts Dry Dock Association. **Formerly:** National Council of American Shipbuilders; National Shipyard Association. **Publications:** *Shipyard Chronicle*, monthly. Newsletter. **Conventions/Meetings:** annual meeting - always March in Washington, DC.

2593 ■ Society of Small Craft Designers (SSCD)
Address Unknown since 2007
Founded: 1949. **Members:** 300. **Membership Dues:** professional and associate, $20 (annual). **Local Groups:** 5. **National Groups:** 1. **Description:** Boat designers, builders, and manufacturers. To stimulate the study of mutual problems; to foster exchange of information and sponsor research; to advance the status and recognition of qualified small craft designers, engineers, and technicians. Members present technical papers on design, construction, and other marine-related subjects at meetings. **Committees:** Industry Liaison; Legal and Government Relations; Technical. **Publications:** *The Log*. Newsletter. **Advertising:** not accepted ● *Planimeter*, annual. Journal. **Advertising:** not accepted ● *"Planimeter" Technical Journal*, annual. **Advertising:** not accepted. **Conventions/Meetings:** annual meeting - always fall, Chicago, IL.

2594 ■ United States Maritime Alliance (USMX)
485 Rte. 1 S, Bldg. C, Ste.100
Iselin, NJ 08830
Ph: (732)404-2960
Fax: (732)750-0587
E-mail: info@usmx.com
URL: http://www.usmx.com
Contact: James A. Capo, Chm./CEO
Founded: 1997. **Description:** Works to preserve and protect the interests of management groups in labor relations issues affecting longshore and related maritime activities. **Telecommunication Services:** electronic mail, jcapo@usmx.com.

2595 ■ West Gulf Maritime Association (WGMA)
1717 E Loop
Portway Plz., Ste.200
Houston, TX 77029
Ph: (713)678-7655
Free: (800)435-5038
Fax: (713)672-7452
E-mail: barbara@wgma.org
URL: http://www.wgma.org
Contact: Walter Niemand, Pres.
Founded: 1968. **Members:** 76. **Description:** Ship owners, agents and independent stevedores serving Texas ports and the port of Lake Charles, LA. Handles industry-wide problems arising with port authorities, governmental agencies, and associations of pilots and other maritime service groups; negotiates and administers the deep sea long shore labor agreements in the West Gulf area. Seeks to: decrease the risks and improve the methods of handling ocean cargoes moving through these ports; solve other industry problems. **Telecommunication Services:** electronic mail, waniemand@wgma.org. **Formed by Merger of:** Brownsville Maritime Association; Galveston Maritime Association; Houston Maritime Association. **Publications:** *Maritime Bulletins*. Alternate Formats: online ● Membership Directory, biennial. **Conventions/Meetings:** annual meeting.

2596 ■ Western Dredging Association (WEDA)
c/o Lawrence M. Patella, Exec. Dir.
PO Box 5797
Vancouver, WA 98668-5797
Ph: (360)750-0209
Fax: (360)750-1445
E-mail: weda@comcast.net
URL: http://www.westerndredging.org
Contact: Lawrence M. Patella, Exec. Dir.
Founded: 1978. **Members:** 3,300. **Membership Dues:** student, $25 (annual) ● regular, $100 (annual) ● sustaining, $8,000. **Staff:** 2. **Budget:** $100,000. **Regional Groups:** 5. **Local Groups:** 5. **Description:** A division of the World Organization of Dredging Associations. Encompasses North, Central, and South America. Executives, engineers, and others who, by degree and/or experience, have four years or more in the dredging industry (full members); student members. Seeks to develop professionalism and stature for those involved in the dredging industry and to advance dredging technology. Cosponsors a research program on dredging and marine ecology. **Libraries: Type:** reference. **Holdings:** 16; books, business records, clippings, periodicals. **Subjects:** dredging. **Awards:** Dredger of the Year. **Frequency:** annual. **Type:** recognition. **Recipient:** for exceptional service to the dredging industry ● Lifetime Achievement Award. **Frequency:** annual. **Type:** recognition. **Recipient:** for contributions to the dredging industry ● Most Outstanding Paper. **Frequency:** annual. **Type:** recognition ● William R. Murden Scholarship (Texas A&M). **Frequency:** annual. **Type:** scholarship. **Recipient:** for Texas A&M students studying dredging technology. **Computer Services:** Online services, forums. **Commissions:** Environmental; Safety. **Affiliated With:** Central Dredging Association. **Publications:** *Proceedings of World Dredging Congress*, triennial. Contains technical papers presented at the Congress; covers subjects in dredging and related marine engineering and construction. **Price:** $125.00. Also Cited As: *World Dredging Congress—Proceedings* ● *Western Dredging Association—Membership Directory*, annual. **Price:** free, for members only. **Circulation:** 3,300 ● *Western Dredging Association—Newsletter*, 3/year. Includes calendar of events. **Price:** free, for members only. **Circulation:** 3,300. Alternate Formats: online. **Conventions/Meetings:** annual congress, technical sessions (exhibits) - always May/June.

2597 ■ World Organization of Dredging Associations (WODA)
c/o Western Dredging Association
PO Box 5797
Vancouver, WA 98668-5797
Ph: (360)750-0209
Fax: (360)750-1445
E-mail: weda@comcast.com
URL: http://www.woda.org
Contact: Mr. Lawrence M. Patella, Exec. Dir.
Founded: 1967. **Members:** 1,500. **Multinational. Description:** Serves as a forum for developing professionalism in individuals involved in the dredging industry. Representatives from the Western Dredging Association, the Central Dredging Association (see separate entries), and the Eastern Dredging Association serve on the board. **Publications:** none. **Affiliated With:** Western Dredging Association. **Formerly:** World Dredging Association. **Conventions/Meetings:** triennial World Dredging Congress (exhibits).

2598 ■ Yacht Brokers Association of America (YBAA)
105 Eastern Ave., Ste.104
Annapolis, MD 21403-3366
Ph: (410)263-1014
Fax: (410)263-1659
E-mail: info@ybaa.com
URL: http://www.ybaa.com
Contact: Joseph Thompson, Exec. Dir.
Founded: 1920. **Members:** 827. **Membership Dues:** corporate (1 broker), $325 (annual) ● corporate (2-3 brokers), $400 (annual) ● corporate (4-6 brokers), $525 (annual) ● corporate (7-14 brokers), $675 (annual) ● corporate (15 or more brokers), $800 (annual). **Staff:** 7. **Budget:** $140,000. **Description:** Yacht brokers. Seeks to protect and further the common interests of members; encourages wider interest in the sport of yachting. Collects and disseminates information; provides standard business forms to members; conducts educational programs at meetings. **Awards: Type:** recognition ● YBAA Presidents Award. **Frequency:** annual. **Type:** recognition. **Recipient:** to an industry leader recognized for outstanding service to the yacht brokerage profession. **Computer Services:** Mailing lists. **Telecommunication Services:** electronic mail, jthompson@ybaa.com. **Committees:** Communications; Ethics; Executive; Membership Development; Membership Services; Professional Development. **Formerly:** (1999) Yacht Architects and Brokers Association. **Publications:** *Annual Industry Guide*, annual. Directory. Contains the annual directory of members, association Code of Ethics, and committees. ● *Yacht Broker News*, quarterly. **Price:** free for members. **Advertising:** accepted. Alternate Formats: online. **Conventions/Meetings:** annual conference (exhibits) - January ● annual regional meeting (exhibits).

Marine Corps

2599 ■ USMC Motor Transport Association (USMC MTA)
PO Box 1372
Jacksonville, NC 28541-1372
E-mail: secretary@usmcmta.org
URL: http://www.usmcmta.org
Contact: Terry Hightower, Natl. Sec.
Founded: 1997. **Membership Dues:** general, $20 (annual). **Description:** Serves as a forum for all retired, former, active duty and reserve individuals who have served in or with the USMC Motor Transport Occupational Field. Organizes reunions for members. **Computer Services:** Information services, MTA resources ● online services, message board.

Marine Industries

2600 ■ American Bureau of Shipping (ABS)
16855 Northchase Dr.
Houston, TX 77060
Ph: (281)877-5800
Fax: (281)877-5803
E-mail: abs-worldhq@eagle.org
URL: http://www.eagle.org
Contact: Robert D. Somerville, Pres./CEO
Founded: 1862. **Members:** 565. **Staff:** 1,400. **Description:** Shipowners, shipbuilders, naval architects, marine underwriters, and others associated with the international marine industry. Works to determine mechanical and structural fitness of vessels, drilling units, and other marine structures for intended services. Establishes universal standards by which ships, mobile offshore drilling units, and other marine structures are designed, built, and maintained. Maintains 160 offices on 6 continents. **Committees:** Cargo Containers; Cargo Gear; Chemical Cargoes; Electrical Engineering; Fixed Offshore Installations; Materials; Ocean Thermal Energy Conversions; Offshore Mobile Drilling Units; Reinforced Plastic Vessels; Ship Operations; Single Point Moorings; Underwater Vehicles, Systems, and Hyperbaric Facilities; Welding. **Subgroups:** Floating Dry Docks; Gears; Propellers. **Publications:** *ABS Activity Report*, monthly ● *Activities*, quarterly. Magazine. Alternate Formats: online ● *The Record*, annual. Contains ship register. ● *Rules and Guides for Construction and Classification of Various Types of Marine Vessels*, periodic ● *Surveyor*, quarterly. Magazine. Alternate Formats: online ● Annual Report, annual. Alternate Formats: online ● Brochures ● Report, annual. Alternate Formats: online. **Conventions/Meetings:** annual meeting - always April, New York.

2601 ■ American Waterways Operators (AWO)
801 N Quincy St., Ste.200
Arlington, VA 22203
Ph: (703)841-9300
Fax: (703)841-0389
E-mail: tallegretti@vesselalliance.com
URL: http://www.americanwaterways.com
Contact: Thomas A. Allegretti, Pres./CEO
Founded: 1944. **Members:** 375. **Membership Dues:** carrier/corporate business or partnership, $4,000 (annual) ● affiliate, $1,350 (annual) ● affiliate associate, $540 (annual). **Staff:** 20. **Budget:** $2,800,000. **Description:** Bulk commodities transporters, shipdocking and harbor services operators, fueling, bunkering and lightering services operators, shipyards and affiliated service members. Represents the inland and

coastal tugboat, towboat and barge industry. Promotes an understanding of the domestic waterborne transportation industry's contribution to the U.S. economy. **Telecommunication Services:** electronic mail, kreddington@vesselalliance.com. **Publications:** *AWO Letter*, biweekly. Newsletter.

2602 ■ Association of Marina Industries (AMI)
50 Water St.
Warren, RI 02885
Ph: (401)737-9775
Free: (866)367-6622
Fax: (401)247-0074
E-mail: info@marinaassociation.org
URL: http://www.marinaassociation.org
Contact: James Frye, Pres.

Founded: 1986. **Members:** 1,500. **Membership Dues:** supplier, $500 (annual) ● marina, $275 (annual). **Staff:** 5. **Description:** Marinas and other boat storage facilities. Promotes growth and professional development among members and their employees. Gathers and disseminates business and technical information of interest to members. Conducts continuing professional education courses for marina personnel in areas including management, facilities maintenance, and environmental protection. **Libraries: Type:** not open to the public. **Holdings:** 40; books. **Subjects:** marina education. **Awards:** Outstanding Achievement Award. **Frequency:** periodic. **Type:** recognition. **Computer Services:** database ● information services, classified ads. **Formerly:** (2005) International Marina Institute. **Publications:** *Dock Lines*, biweekly. Newsletter ● *International Marina Institute*, annual. Catalog. Includes membership directory and publications list. ● *Practices and Products for Clean Marinas*. Handbook ● Books ● Pamphlets. **Conventions/Meetings:** annual conference (exhibits) ● annual National Marina Conference and Trade Show (exhibits) ● periodic seminar ● periodic workshop.

2603 ■ Association of Ship Brokers and Agents - U.S.A. (ASBA)
510 Sylvan Ave., Ste.201
Englewood Cliffs, NJ 07632
Ph: (201)569-2882
Fax: (201)569-9082
E-mail: asba@asba.org
URL: http://www.asba.org
Contact: James Ford, Pres.

Founded: 1934. **Members:** 130. **Membership Dues:** company (with 3 or more brokers/agents), $800 (annual) ● company (with 1 or 2 brokers/agents), $450 (annual). **Staff:** 2. **Description:** Represents ship brokers and agents in industry and government affairs. Revises, and makes available to the trade, various Charter Parties. Offers online and correspondence courses on Basic Principles of Chartering; awards certificates for completion of courses. Sponsors a course on Advanced Chartering Problems given by the State University of New York, Maritime College. Assists the American tanker community through maintenance of nominal freight rates used for reference purposes. Sponsors an annual cargo conference. **Committees:** Agency Affairs; Charter Party; Education; Entertainment; Ethics; Government Activities Liaison; Tanker. **Affiliated With:** Federation of National Associations of Shipbrokers and Agents. **Publications:** *American Tanker Rate Schedule*, biennial. Contains nominal freight rates. **Price:** $2,250.00. **Circulation:** 100 ● *Basic Principles of Chartering*, annual. Book. Serves as a correspondence course text book. **Price:** $800.00 for members; $1,000.00 for nonmembers in U.S.; $1,200.00 for nonmembers in other locations. **Circulation:** 150 ● *Commercial Trade Transactions*, annual. **Price:** $750.00 for members; $1,000.00 for nonmembers ● *Maritime Law*, semiannual. Features online course. **Price:** $900.00 for members; $1,250.00 for nonmembers ● *Shipbroking and Chartered Vessel Operations*, semiannual. Features online course. **Price:** $1,800.00 for members; $2,250.00 for nonmembers. **Conventions/Meetings:** annual Cargo Conference - always second Tuesday of January, in New York City.

2604 ■ Inland Rivers Ports and Terminals (IRPT)
316 Bd. of Trade Pl.
New Orleans, LA 70130
Ph: (504)585-0715
Fax: (504)525-8197
E-mail: admin@irpt.net
URL: http://www.irpt.net
Contact: Deirdre McGowan, Exec. Dir.

Founded: 1974. **Members:** 165. **Membership Dues:** corporate, $300 (annual) ● associate, $100 (annual) ● individual government, $50 (annual). **Staff:** 1. **Regional Groups:** 5. **Description:** Port and terminal owners and operators of inland waterway facilities; suppliers of related services and equipment; port commissions and authorities; interested individuals and groups. Objectives are to: support the specific needs and objectives peculiar to inland waterway interests; promote river- and port-related commercial and industrial development; encourage foreign and domestic commerce on inland waterways; develop improved services to shippers; encourage the development of waterborne transportation. Supports the proposition that the most economical, efficient, and energy conserving transportation system is one which brings cargo as close as possible to the shipper and receiver by water. Keeps abreast of related economic matters; represents members' interests and takes action at every level of government. Makes available audio presentation. **Computer Services:** database, list of members. **Committees:** Annual Meeting; Communications; Legislative; Market Development; Planning and Development. **Publications:** *Membership Roster*, annual. Membership Directory ● *News Bulletin*, bimonthly. **Conventions/Meetings:** annual meeting (exhibits).

2605 ■ Inlandboatman's Union of the Pacific (IBU)
1711 W Nickerson St., Ste.D
Seattle, WA 98119
Ph: (206)284-6001
Fax: (206)284-5043
E-mail: alan.ibu@mindspring.com
URL: http://www.ibu.org
Contact: Alan Cote, Pres.

Founded: 1918. **Members:** 4,000. **Description:** Marine Division of the International Longshore and Warehouse Union (ILWU). Represents maritime workers in seven 'regions' on passenger carrying (e.g. Washington State Ferries) and commercial vessels (towing industry) on the Pacific coastline (Alaska, Washington, Oregon, and California) and to Hawaii; marine freight (casuals/lashers); marine environmental cleanup; as well as Alaska non-resident seafood processing workers. Works solely for the betterment of its members. **Publications:** *IBU Lookout*. Newspaper. Alternate Formats: online.

2606 ■ Lake Carriers' Association (LCA)
614 W Superior Ave.
Cleveland, OH 44113-1383
Ph: (216)621-1107 (216)861-0592
Fax: (216)241-8262
E-mail: info@lcaships.com
URL: http://www.lcaships.com
Contact: James H.I. Weakley, Pres.

Founded: 1880. **Members:** 12. **Staff:** 4. **Budget:** $700,000. **Description:** Represents operators of U.S.-Flag Great Lakes bulk carriers before federal and state agencies. **Computer Services:** database, marketing contacts. **Committees:** Advisory; Captains; Fleet Engineers; International Joint Conference; Navigation; Vessel Personnel and Safety. **Absorbed:** (1892) Cleveland Vessel Owners Association. **Publications:** *Great Lakes Shipping and Michigan: Partners in Commerce*. Brochure ● *Great Lakes Shipping: The Vital Link for Ohio Industry*. Brochure ● *Tonnage Statistics*, monthly ● *US-Flag Shipping on the Great Lakes*. Brochures ● Annual Report, annual. **Price:** $10.00 for individuals (not involved with industry) ● Videos. Features benefits of Great Lakes shipping. **Conventions/Meetings:** annual International Joint Conference - alternates between U.S. and Canada.

2607 ■ Liberian Shipowners' Council (LSC)
99 Park Ave., Ste.1700
New York, NY 10016
Ph: (212)973-3896
Fax: (212)217-3869
Contact: Richard J. Deely, Gen.Sec.

Founded: 1974. **Members:** 80. **Membership Dues:** auxiliary, $1,500 (annual) ● company, $3,000 (annual). **Staff:** 3. **Description:** International shipowners and operators whose ships fly the Liberian flag; banks, law firms, and other organizations connected with shipping. Promotes the technical, political, and labor interests of members. Supports a strong ship safety inspection program. **Publications:** none. **Conventions/Meetings:** annual meeting - usually October or November.

2608 ■ Marine Machinery Association (MMA)
8665 Sudley Rd., Ste.270
Manassas, VA 20110-4588
Ph: (703)791-4800
Fax: (703)791-4808
E-mail: admin@marmach.org
URL: http://www.marmach.org
Contact: Jack P. Janetatos, Chm.

Founded: 1984. **Members:** 45. **Membership Dues:** manufacturing company, $2,000-$4,000 (annual) ● non-manufacturing company, $2,000 (annual). **Staff:** 2. **Description:** Represents the interests of the American machinery and equipment manufacturers to the world's shipyards. **Awards:** Jack Flannigan Award. **Frequency:** periodic. **Type:** recognition. **Recipient:** for individuals who have made contributions to the quality of shipboard machinery and equipment. **Conventions/Meetings:** annual conference.

2609 ■ National Association of Waterfront Employers (NAWE)
Address Unknown since 2007

Founded: 1933. **Members:** 34. **Staff:** 3. **Description:** Firms engaged in ship loading and unloading and marine terminal operations and other waterfront related employers. Promotes the interests of the private stevedoring and marine terminal industries. **Formerly:** (1993) National Association of Stevedoes. **Publications:** *Legal Report*, quarterly ● *Legislative Update*. Report ● Bulletin, periodic ● Newsletter, monthly. **Conventions/Meetings:** annual meeting.

2610 ■ National Marine Charter Association (NMCA)
1600 Duke St., Ste.400
Alexandria, VA 22314
Free: (800)745-6094
Fax: (703)519-1716
E-mail: info@marinecharter.org
URL: http://www.marinecharter.org
Contact: John Kanaskie, Exec. Dir.

Membership Dues: basic, $40 (annual) ● professional, $80 (annual) ● sponsor, $250 (annual). **Description:** Serves as the national voice for the marine charter industry on regulatory and legislative matters. Promotes standards for the marine charter industry through self regulatory programs. Offers group benefits and services to lower the cost of operating a charter business. Cooperates with marine firms, associations and organizations on common interests and concerns. **Telecommunication Services:** electronic mail, nmca@wpa.org. **Publications:** *NMCA E-News*, monthly. Newsletter. Contains key industry news and information. **Price:** included in membership dues. Alternate Formats: online.

Marketing

2611 ■ ABA Marketing Network
1120 Connecticut Ave. NW
Washington, DC 20036
Free: (800)BANKERS
Fax: (202)828-4540

E-mail: marketingnetwork@aba.com
URL: http://www.aba.com/MarketingNetwork/default.htm
Contact: J. Douglas Adamson, Exec. Dir.
Founded: 1915. **Members:** 2,300. **Membership Dues:** employee of an ABA Bank, $295 (annual) ● employee of a non-ABA Bank/other organization, $395 (annual). **Staff:** 17. **Local Groups:** 23. **Description:** Marketing and public relations executives for commercial and savings banks, credit unions, and savings and loans associations, and related groups such as advertising agencies and research firms. Provides marketing education, information, and services to the financial services industry. Conducts research; cosponsors summer sessions of fundamentals and advanced courses in marketing at the University of Colorado at Boulder; compiles statistics. **Libraries: Type:** reference. **Holdings:** 4,000. **Subjects:** public relations, marketing, advertising, business development, special promotions. **Awards:** Advertising Awards. **Frequency:** annual. **Type:** recognition. **Recipient:** for best ads in print, on radio, and on television ● Golden Coin Award. **Frequency:** annual. **Type:** recognition. **Recipient:** for marketing and communications efforts. **Computer Services:** database, financial industry information service online bibliographic ● mailing lists, for service members only. **Affiliated With:** American Bankers Association. **Formerly:** (1947) Financial Advertisers Association; (1965) Financial Public Relations Association; (1970) Bank Public Relations and Marketing Association; (2001) Bank Marketing Association. **Publications:** *Bank Marketing*, monthly. Magazine. Covers the financial marketing field. **Price:** included in membership dues; $120.00 /year for nonmembers. ISSN: 0888-3149. **Circulation:** 4,500. **Advertising:** accepted. Alternate Formats: microform ● *Bank Marketing Association—Membership Directory*, annual ● *Information Center Newsletter*, semiannual. Abstracts School of Banking books and papers; lists Golden Coin awards available. ISSN: 0741-2185. **Circulation:** 5,000 ● *Marketing Edge*. Newsletter. Focuses on issues and challenges that marketers face from day-to-day. **Price:** included in membership dues. Alternate Formats: online. **Conventions/Meetings:** periodic competition ● annual conference (exhibits) ● periodic seminar ● periodic workshop.

2612 ■ Alliance for Healthcare Strategy and Marketing (The Alliance)

Address Unknown since 2007
Founded: 1984. **Members:** 1,400. **Membership Dues:** professional, $175 (annual). **Staff:** 1. **Budget:** $1,100,000. **Regional Groups:** 2. **Description:** Marketing professionals in the health care field; vice presidents and directors of hospitals, health maintenance organizations, nursing homes, and other health care institutions. Promotes the marketing of health services; sponsors continuing education for and professional development of members to this end. Conducts seminars; offers placement service. **Awards:** Frank J. Weaver Leadership Award. **Frequency:** annual. **Type:** recognition ● Trevor Fisk Young Marketer of the Year Award. **Frequency:** annual. **Type:** recognition. **Also Known As:** (1995) Academy for Health Services Marketing. **Publications:** *Alliance Report*, bimonthly. Newsletter. Includes strategies and case studies in healthcare marketing. **Price:** included in membership dues; $175.00/year. **Advertising:** accepted ● *Marketing Best Practices*, quarterly ● *Resource Guide and Membership Directory*, monthly. Alternate Formats: online ● *Trendwatch*, quarterly. **Conventions/Meetings:** annual Conference on Healthcare Strategy and Marketing (exhibits) - always March ● annual Internet and Healthcare Conference.

2613 ■ American Marketing Association (AMA)

311 S Wacker Dr., Ste.5800
Chicago, IL 60606
Ph: (312)542-9000
Free: (800)262-1150
Fax: (312)542-9001
E-mail: info@ama.org
URL: http://www.marketingpower.com
Contact: Debra Ringold, Chair
Founded: 1937. **Members:** 38,000. **Membership Dues:** professional practitioner/academic, $185 (annual) ● collegiate, $39 (annual) ● bridge, $75 (annual) ● doctoral student, $95 (annual). **Staff:** 70. **Regional Groups:** 500. **Description:** Serves as a professional society of marketing and market research executives, sales and promotion managers, advertising specialists, academics, and others interested in marketing. Fosters research; sponsors seminars, conferences, and student marketing clubs; provides educational placement service and doctoral consortium. **Libraries: Type:** lending; reference; not open to the public. **Holdings:** 6,000; archival material, books, clippings, monographs, periodicals. **Subjects:** marketing, marketing research. **Awards: Type:** recognition. **Special Interest Groups:** Academic; Practitioner. **Formed by Merger of:** (1934) American Marketing Society; National Association of Marketing Teachers. **Publications:** *American Marketing Association—Proceedings*, annual. Includes author indexes. Alternate Formats: microform ● *Journal of Marketing*, quarterly. Provides information on marketing discoveries, trends, and techniques. Includes legal developments, literature and book reviews, and annual index. **Price:** $45.00 /year for members; $80.00 /year for nonmembers; $200.00 /year for institutions; $25.00/year for student members. ISSN: 0022-2429. **Circulation:** 9,000. **Advertising:** accepted. Alternate Formats: microform ● *Journal of Marketing Research*, quarterly. Deals with philosophical, conceptual, or technical aspects of fundamental research in marketing. Includes research notes and book reviews. **Price:** $45.00 /year for members; $25.00/year for student members; $200.00 /year for institutions and corporations; $80.00 /year for nonmembers. ISSN: 0022-2437. **Circulation:** 6,000. **Advertising:** accepted. Alternate Formats: microform ● *Journal of Public Policy and Marketing*, semiannual. Covers issues such as the effects of legislation and regulation on the industry and marketing techniques used by public policy makers. **Price:** $45.00 /year for members; $70.00 /year for nonmembers; $100.00 /year for institutions; $25.00/year for student members. ISSN: 0743-9156. **Circulation:** 675 ● *The M Guide*, annual. Membership Directory. **Advertising:** accepted ● *Marketing Academics at AMA*, bimonthly. Newsletter. Provides news and information about upcoming events and receive updates on what's new at the academic resource center. Alternate Formats: online ● *Marketing Health Service*, quarterly. Magazine. Includes book reviews, Health Care Marketing Abstracts, and case studies. **Price:** $53.00 for members; $90.00 for institutions; $75.00 for individual nonmember. ISSN: 1094-1304. **Circulation:** 2,000. **Advertising:** accepted. Alternate Formats: microform ● *Marketing Management*, bimonthly. Magazine. Provides treatment of cutting edge marketing issues facing senior marketing managers. **Price:** $45.00 /year for members; $70.00 /year for nonmembers; $90.00 /year for institutions and corporations; $25.00/year for student members. ISSN: 1061-3846. **Circulation:** 4,500. **Advertising:** accepted ● *Marketing Matters*, biweekly. Newsletter. Contains information on the latest happenings in the marketing profession and how it can affect business. **Price:** free for members. Alternate Formats: online ● *Marketing News: Reporting on the Marketing Professional and Its Association*, biennial. Magazine. Reports on marketing news and trends. Includes calendar of events, book reviews and chapter news. **Price:** included in membership dues; $130.00 /year for institutions and corporations; $100.00 /year for nonmembers. ISSN: 0025-3790. **Circulation:** 26,815. **Advertising:** accepted. Alternate Formats: microform ● *Marketing Power Personalized*, biweekly. Newsletter. **Price:** free. Alternate Formats: online ● *Marketing Research*, quarterly. Magazine. Explores market research techniques and related legal and ethical issues. **Price:** $45.00 /year for members; $24.00/year for students; $70.00 /year for nonmembers; $120.00 /year for institutions and corporations. **Circulation:** 4,000. **Advertising:** accepted ● Bibliographies ● Books ● Pamphlets. **Conventions/Meetings:** annual Advanced Research Methods - conference ● annual Executive Insights - conference (exhibits) ● annual Frontiers in Services Marketing - conference, research and theory in service quality, customer satisfaction, and services marketing ● annual Institute for Marketing Communications and Strategy - meeting, strategy development, media planning and buying, direct marketing, sales promotion, budgeting, program evaluation ● annual International Collegiate Conference ● annual Marketing Research Conference, latest developments in qualitative and quantitative research (exhibits) ● annual Marketing Workshop ● annual Summer Marketing Educator's Conference, competitive papers addressing the most recent marketing theories and strategies (exhibits) ● Symposium for the Marketing of Higher Education, marketing the colleges and universities of America ● annual Winter Marketing Educators Conference (exhibits).

2614 ■ American Teleservices Association (ATA)

3815 River Crossing Pkwy., Ste.20
Indianapolis, IN 46240
Ph: (317)816-9336
Free: (877)779-3974
Fax: (317)218-0323
E-mail: contact@ataconnect.org
URL: http://www.ataconnect.org
Contact: Tim Searcy, CEO
Founded: 1983. **Members:** 3,500. **Membership Dues:** small business, $695 (annual) ● corporate, $1,795-$2,895 (annual) ● platinum, $5,000 (annual) ● non-profit, $195 (annual) ● academic, $150 (annual). **Staff:** 12. **Budget:** $1,000,000. **Regional Groups:** 10. **Languages:** Dutch, English, French, German, Portuguese, Russian, Spanish. **Multinational. Description:** Businesses involved in teleservices, telephone marketing sales, including suppliers, distributors, users, and hardware and software manufacturers; educators and teleservice businesses. Provides for the specific needs of the total telephone services community; assists in understanding and using telephone communications for marketing purposes; sponsors educational programs. **Libraries: Type:** reference. **Holdings:** articles, audiovisuals, monographs. **Awards:** Board of Directors. **Frequency:** annual. **Type:** recognition. **Computer Services:** Mailing lists, of members. **Committees:** Compliance Officers Forum; Government Affairs; International; Non Profit and Charities; Technology. **Subcommittees:** Federal Legislative; State Legislative. **Formerly:** (1998) American Telemarketing Association. **Publications:** *Compendium of State Laws and Regulations*, annual. Journal ● *E-Connections*, biweekly. Newsletter. Covers industry issues and association news. **Price:** included in membership dues. **Circulation:** 3,500. **Advertising:** accepted. Alternate Formats: online ● *Holding the Line*. Newsletter. **Price:** free. Alternate Formats: online ● *Membership Directory and Buyers Guide*. Continuously updated online. **Advertising:** accepted. Alternate Formats: online ● Also produces recordings of seminars. **Conventions/Meetings:** semiannual convention, includes compliance seminars (exhibits) ● annual Legislative Conference - meeting - always spring.

2615 ■ Association for Accounting Marketing (AAM)

14 W Third St., Ste.200
Kansas City, MO 64105
Ph: (816)221-1296
Fax: (816)472-7765
E-mail: info@accountingmarketing.org
URL: http://www.accountingmarketing.org
Contact: Granville Loar, Exec. Dir.
Founded: 1989. **Members:** 600. **Membership Dues:** executive, affiliate, associate, $250 (annual) ● educator, student, $150 (annual). **Staff:** 3. **Budget:** $250,000. **Regional Groups:** 6. **Description:** Professional marketers and marketing departments serving accounting firms. Seeks to advance the practice of accounting marketing; promotes professional development of members. Facilitates communication among accounting marketers; conducts continuing professional education; serves as a resource for members and accounting firms. **Awards:** AAM-MAA Marketing Achievement Awards. **Frequency:** annual. **Type:** recognition ● Volunteer of the Year. **Frequency:** annual. **Type:** recognition. **Publications:** *MarkeTrends*, bimonthly. Newsletter. **Price:** available to members only. **Advertising:** accepted ● Member-

ship Directory, annual. **Price:** available to members only. Alternate Formats: online. **Conventions/Meetings:** annual conference (exhibits).

2616 ■ Association of Directory Marketing (ADM)
1187 Thorn Run Rd., Ste.630
Moon Township, PA 15108-3198
Ph: (412)269-0663
Fax: (412)269-0655
E-mail: adm@admworks.org
URL: http://www.admworks.org
Contact: Herb Gordon, Pres./CEO

Founded: 1990. **Members:** 107. **Membership Dues:** agency, $2,000 (annual) ● major publisher, $10,000 (annual) ● small publisher, supplier, $3,000 (annual). **Staff:** 9. **Description:** Certified marketing representatives and agencies; directory publishers; suppliers. Promotes use of telephone directories in marketing. Provides support and services to marketers wishing to make use of print and internet directories, telephone directories. **Publications:** *Flash*, monthly. Newsletter. **Price:** included in membership dues. **Circulation:** 1,700. Alternate Formats: online. **Conventions/Meetings:** annual conference.

2617 ■ Association for Rehabilitation Marketing (ARM)
118 Julian Pl.
PMB 105
Syracuse, NY 13210
Fax: (315)598-8937
E-mail: info@rehabmarketing.org
URL: http://www.rehabmarketing.org
Contact: Ms. Mary Ann C. Benkoski, Contact

Founded: 1986. **Membership Dues:** agency, organization, $200 (annual). **Description:** Represents rehabilitation sales and marketing professionals. Provides a forum to facilitate the exchange of information supporting the development of work opportunities for adults with developmental disabilities; members handle all types of labor-intensive projects to give their customers an affordable solution to jobs they do not wish to handle in-house. **Conventions/Meetings:** annual conference.

2618 ■ Calendar Marketing Association (CMA)
214 N Hale St.
Wheaton, IL 60187
Ph: (630)510-4564
Fax: (630)510-4501
E-mail: info@calendarassociation.org
URL: http://www.calendarassociation.org
Contact: Allan Togliatti, Contact

Founded: 1989. **Members:** 200. **Membership Dues:** corporate, $350 (annual) ● individual, $150 (annual). **Staff:** 4. **For-Profit. Description:** Calendar designers, marketers, printers, publishers, suppliers and all others involved in the calendar industry. Represents industry interests. Sponsors Calendar Marketplace at Book Expo America. **Convention/Meeting:** none. **Libraries: Type:** reference; lending. **Holdings:** 6; articles. **Subjects:** calendars. **Awards:** National Calendar Award. **Frequency:** annual. **Type:** recognition ● World Calendar Award. **Frequency:** annual. **Type:** recognition. **Computer Services:** database, serves as a resource for both the calendar industry and its customers ● mailing lists, of prospect information. **Publications:** *Calendar News*, quarterly. Newsletter. Contains information on the calendar industry and trends. **Circulation:** 5,000. **Advertising:** accepted ● *Publishing and Marketing Your Calendar*. Book. **Price:** $34.95 soft copy. **Advertising:** accepted. Alternate Formats: online ● *State of the Calendar*, annual. Report. Intended for national media.

2619 ■ CCNG International
PO Box 92790
Southlake, TX 76092
Free: (800)840-2264
Fax: (972)692-8985
E-mail: membership@ccng.com
URL: http://www.ccng.com
Contact: Michelle Porterfield, Mgr.

Founded: 1982. **Members:** 125. **Membership Dues:** individual, $250 (annual) ● corporate, $2,600 (annual) ● industry sponsor, $9,500 (annual). **Staff:** 1. **Budget:** $10,000. **State Groups:** 1. **Description:** Managers of telemarketing operations. Promotes professional advancement of members. Represents members' interests; conducts educational programs. **Libraries: Type:** lending; not open to the public. **Holdings:** articles, audio recordings, books, periodicals, video recordings. **Subjects:** telemarketing. **Awards:** Certified Telemarketing Representative. **Frequency:** annual. **Type:** recognition. **Recipient:** for student who passed course offered by association. **Computer Services:** Mailing lists, of members. **Formerly:** Contact Center Associates; (1998) Telemarketing Managers Association; (2004) Teleprofessional Managers Association. **Publications:** *Connections Magazine*, monthly. **Price:** included in membership dues; $25.00 for nonmembers in U.S.; $49.00 for nonmembers in Canada; $75.00 for nonmembers outside U.S. and Canada ● Newsletter, quarterly. **Advertising:** accepted. **Conventions/Meetings:** annual Expo - convention, held in conjunction with ICCM (exhibits) - October.

2620 ■ Circulation Council of DMA
1120 Ave. of the Americas
New York, NY 10036-6700
Ph: (212)768-7277
Fax: (212)302-6714
E-mail: membership@the-dma.org
URL: http://www.the-dma.org/councils/circulation-council
Contact: Lori Magill-Cook, Co-Chair

Founded: 1977. **Members:** 250. **Membership Dues:** marketing company (base), $1,300 (annual) ● agency/supplier (base), $2,950 (annual) ● organization (base), $600 (annual). **Staff:** 3. **Description:** A division of the Direct Marketing Association. Publishers, suppliers, and circulation directors. Seeks to advance the field of circulation management; provides educational programs. Promotes annual Circulation Day. Operates hall of fame. **Libraries: Type:** reference. **Awards:** Circulation Hall of Fame. **Frequency:** annual. **Type:** recognition. **Recipient:** to an individual who has contributed significantly to circulation of the industry. **Computer Services:** Mailing lists, of members. **Committees:** Operating; Programming; Sponsorship. **Affiliated With:** Direct Marketing Association. **Publications:** *Circulation Council Newsletter*, 3/year. Contains case histories and technique oriented articles written by industry professionals. **Price:** free for members. **Circulation:** 1,000. **Advertising:** accepted ● *Circulation Handbook* ● *Industry Trend Surveys: Renewals, Billings, Gifts, Customer Service, and Direct Mail*. **Conventions/Meetings:** annual Circulation Day - conference, exclusively for circulators of consumer publications (exhibits) ● luncheon - 6-8/year.

2621 ■ Corporate Event Marketing Association (CEMA)
1512 Weiskopf Loop
Round Rock, TX 78664
Ph: (512)310-8330
Fax: (512)682-0555
E-mail: ebrunke@cemaonline.com
URL: http://www.cemaonline.com
Contact: Mitch Ahiers, Pres.

Founded: 1990. **Members:** 300. **Membership Dues:** corporate, $795 (annual) ● individual, $295 (annual). **Staff:** 2. **Description:** Serves marketing communications professionals in the information technology industry. Provides a series of interactive forums, councils, and information exchange sessions. **Awards:** Pinnacle Award. **Frequency:** annual. **Type:** recognition. **Recipient:** to individuals who have made significant contributions to the association as well as companies that have excelled in the IT event industry. **Computer Services:** database, membership directory. **Formerly:** (2006) Computer Event Marketing Association. **Publications:** *TechEvents*, quarterly. Magazine. Focuses on event and experiential marketing in the technology sector. ● *Technology Meetings*. Magazine. Dedicated to IT Event Marketing needs. **Price:** included in membership dues.

2622 ■ Council for Marketing and Opinion Research (CMOR)
110 Natl. Dr., 2nd Fl.
Glastonbury, CT 06033
Ph: (860)657-1881
Fax: (860)682-1010
E-mail: information@cmor.org
URL: http://www.cmor.org
Contact: Donna Gillin, Dir. of Operations

Founded: 1992. **Members:** 160. **Membership Dues:** academic (patron level), $525 (annual) ● academic (leadership level), $760 (annual) ● provider (patron level; based on company revenues), $22,050 (annual) ● provider (leadership level; based on company revenues), $26,250 (annual) ● purchaser (patron level; based on company expenditures), $1,050-$5,250 (annual) ● purchaser (leadership level; based on company expenditures), $1,365-$6,825 (annual) ● government, $495 (annual). **Staff:** 4. **Budget:** $800,000. **Description:** Represents the marketing and opinion research industry. Addresses government affairs and respondent cooperation issues. **Computer Services:** database, issues regarding government affairs and respondent cooperation ● mailing lists. **Publications:** *Industry Watch*, quarterly. Newsletter. Includes updates of issues in the industry. **Price:** included in membership dues. Alternate Formats: online ● *Legislative Watch*, monthly. Newsletter. Contains updates on legislative arena. Alternate Formats: online.

2623 ■ CUES Financial Suppliers Forum (FSF)
5510 Res. Park Dr.
Madison, WI 53711-5377
Ph: (608)271-2664
Free: (800)252-2664
Fax: (608)271-2303
E-mail: sales@cues.org
URL: http://www.cues.org
Contact: Karin Weiss CEM, Advertising and Sales Dir.

Founded: 1983. **Members:** 100. **Membership Dues:** full, $895 (annual). **Description:** A division of the Credit Union Executives Society (see separate entry). Represents suppliers interested in marketing products and services to financial institutions, specifically credit unions. **Awards:** Chairman's Club. **Type:** recognition. **Recipient:** for members who have sponsored other executives for membership ● CUES Future Leader Award. **Frequency:** annual. **Type:** recognition. **Recipient:** for leaders ● CUES Hall of Fame. **Frequency:** annual. **Type:** recognition. **Recipient:** for lifetime achievement and contributions to the credit union movement ● CUES Rising 100. **Frequency:** biennial. **Type:** recognition ● DEF Director of the Year. **Frequency:** annual. **Type:** recognition. **Recipient:** to a DEF member for extraordinary leadership in the credit union movement and the community ● Executive of the Year. **Frequency:** annual. **Type:** recognition. **Recipient:** for outstanding CEO leadership contributions to CUES, its councils and the community at large ● FSF Supplier of the Year. **Frequency:** annual. **Type:** recognition. **Recipient:** for suppliers ● Golden Mirror Awards. **Frequency:** annual. **Type:** recognition. **Recipient:** for the most outstanding and successful credit union marketing efforts of the year ● Outstanding Councils. **Frequency:** annual. **Type:** recognition. **Recipient:** for CUES Councils that have exhibited outstanding programming and involvement for the year. **Formerly:** (1988) Financial Suppliers Association; (1997) Financial Suppliers Forum. **Publications:** *Credit Union Management*, monthly. Magazine. **Price:** included in membership dues. **Advertising:** accepted ● *FSF Connection*, quarterly. Newsletter. Includes exhibits and sponsor information and schedule of CUES council meetings. **Price:** included in membership dues. Alternate Formats: online. **Conventions/Meetings:** annual CEO Institute I: Strategic Planning - meeting ● annual CEO Institute II: Organizational Effectiveness - meeting ● annual CEO Institute III:

Strategic Leadership Development - meeting ● CEO Network - conference ● annual CUES Symposium: CEO/Chairman Exchange ● Directors Conference ● Directors Leadership Institute - meeting ● Executive Summit - meeting ● annual Executive Technology Forum - meeting ● annual Marketing and Technology for Credit Union Directors - convention ● annual Nexus Conference.

2624 ■ Diagnostic Marketing Association (DxMA)
10293 N Meridian St., Ste.175
Indianapolis, IN 46290
Ph: (317)816-1640
Free: (800)278-7886
Fax: (317)816-1633
E-mail: info@dxma.org
URL: http://dxma.org
Contact: John Sperzel, Pres.
Members: 350,000. **Membership Dues:** regular, $300 (annual). **Staff:** 9. **Description:** Diagnostic marketers in the biomedical field. Compiles statistics. **Awards:** Dx Awards of Excellence. **Frequency:** annual. **Type:** recognition. **Recipient:** to the finest communications efforts in diagnostics marketing. **Programs:** Executive Educational. **Formerly:** (2006) Biomedical Marketing Association. **Publications:** *Biomedical Marketing Association—Directory*, annual ● *Conjoint Measurement Monograph and Salary Survey* ● *Diagnostic Insight*, quarterly. Magazine. Provides information on industry changes and marketing techniques. **Price:** included in membership dues. Alternate Formats: online ● *The Messenger*, bimonthly. Newsletter. Includes listing of job promotions and appointments. **Advertising:** accepted. **Conventions/Meetings:** annual conference ● seminar, research and educational.

2625 ■ Direct Marketing Association (DMA)
1120 Ave. of the Americas
New York, NY 10036-6700
Ph: (212)768-7277
Fax: (212)302-6714
E-mail: presiden@the-dma.org
URL: http://www.the-dma.org
Contact: John A. Greco Jr., Pres./CEO
Founded: 1917. **Members:** 5,200. **Membership Dues:** marketing company, $1,300 (annual) ● supplier, $2,950 (annual) ● non-profit, $600 (annual). **Staff:** 136. **Description:** Manufacturers, wholesalers, public utilities, retailers, mail order firms, publishers, schools, clubs, insurance companies, financial organizations, business equipment manufacturers, paper and envelope manufacturers, list brokers, compilers, managers, owners, computer service bureaus, advertising agencies, letter shops, research organizations, printers, lithographers, creators, and producers of direct mail and direct response advertising. Studies consumer and business attitudes toward direct mail and related direct marketing statistics. Offers Mail Preference Service for consumers who wish to receive less mail advertising, Mail Order Action Line to help resolve difficulties with mail order purchases, and Telephone Preference Service for people who wish to receive fewer telephone sales calls. Maintains hall of fame; offers placement service; compiles statistics. Sponsors several three-day Basic Direct Marketing Institutes, Advanced Direct Marketing Institutes, and special interest seminars and workshops. Maintains Government Affairs office in Washington, DC. Operates Direct Marketing Educational Foundation. **Libraries:** **Type:** open to the public. **Holdings:** 700; articles, books, periodicals. **Subjects:** direct marketing. **Awards:** DMA Hall of Fame. **Frequency:** annual. **Type:** recognition. **Recipient:** to individuals who have contributed significantly to the field of direct/interactive marketing ● International ECHO Awards. **Frequency:** annual. **Type:** recognition. **Recipient:** to the best direct marketing campaigns. **Computer Services:** Online services, library. **Committees:** Analytics; Broadcast; Government Affairs. **Councils:** Alternate Response Media; Business-to-Business; Catalog and Multichannel Marketing; Circulation; Customer Relationship Management; Direct Marketing Agency; Directo (Hispanic); Financial Services; Insert Media; International; List and Database; Marketing Technology and Internet; Pharmaceutical Marketing; Retail Marketing; Search Engine Marketing; Teleservices; Travel and Hospitality. **Affiliated With:** Direct Marketing Educational Foundation. **Absorbed:** Business Mail Foundation; Direct Marketing Computer Association; (2001) Association of Direct Marketing Agencies. **Formerly:** Direct Mail Advertising Association; (1983) Direct Mail/Marketing Association. **Publications:** *Business Review*, quarterly. Journal. Provides up-to-date economic performance, indicators, and business trends. Alternate Formats: online ● *Council Newsletter*, quarterly ● *Dateline: DMA* (in English, French, Japanese, and Spanish), quarterly. Newsletter ● *Direct Line: The DMA Newsletter Serving the Direct Marketing Industry*, monthly. Reports on association activities and matters relevant to direct marketers. **Price:** free for members. ISSN: 0743-7625. **Circulation:** 7,500 ● *The DMA Insider*, quarterly. Magazine. Covers industry innovations, trends and emerging technologies. **Price:** available to members only ● *DMA Washington Report: Federal and State Regulatory Issues of Concern*, monthly. Newsletter. Reviews federal and state regulations affecting direct mail marketing, such as cable privacy laws, and trade rule violations. **Price:** free for members. **Circulation:** 7,500 ● *Fact Book on Direct Marketing*, annual. Includes charts and graphs on every aspect of the DM industry from more than 100 different sources. **Price:** $79.95 for members; $104.95 for nonmembers ● *Membership Roster*, annual. Membership Directory ● *MyDMA*. Newsletter. **Price:** free. Alternate Formats: online ● *Washington Alert* ● Annual Report, annual. Provides an overview of association's yearly goals, activities, and budget. **Conventions/Meetings:** annual conference, opportunities for education and networking (exhibits) ● annual convention (exhibits) ● annual international conference, about big league strategies for fundraising.

2626 ■ Electronic Retailing Association (ERA)
2000 N 14th St., Ste.300
Arlington, VA 22201
Ph: (703)841-1751
Free: (800)987-6462
Fax: (703)841-1860
E-mail: contact@retailing.org
URL: http://www.retailing.org
Contact: Ms. Barbara Tulipane CAE, Pres./CEO
Founded: 1990. **Members:** 400. **Membership Dues:** company in U.S. (based on annual revenues), $3,400-$26,750 (annual) ● company in Europe and Middle East (based on annual revenues), EUR 3,000-EUR 25,000 (annual) ● company in Latin America, $1,500 (annual) ● company in rest of the world, $3,000-$25,000 (annual). **Staff:** 12. **Budget:** $2,500,000. **Multinational. Description:** Serves companies that use the power of electronic media to sell goods and services to the public. Its global membership includes television, radio and Internet retailers, along with expert back-end suppliers. **Libraries:** **Type:** not open to the public; reference. **Awards:** ERA Awards. **Frequency:** annual. **Type:** recognition. **Recipient:** for programs and personalities. **Computer Services:** Online services. **Telecommunication Services:** electronic mail, btulipane@retailing.org. **Committees:** Ethics; Government Affairs; Meeting and Convention; New Product; Policy and Bylaw Review; Strategic Planning. **Councils:** Technology. **Programs:** Electronic Retailing Self-Regulation. **Formerly:** (1990) National Infomercial Marketing Association; (1994) NIMA International. **Publications:** *E-News Weekly*, every Thursday. Newsletter. **Advertising:** accepted. Alternate Formats: online ● *Electronic Retailer*, monthly. Magazine. **Price:** $59.95/year. **Circulation:** 18,000 ● *Marketing, Meetings and Membership*, monthly. Newsletter. Highlights upcoming programs and events, membership promotions, exhibition opportunities and advertising news. **Advertising:** accepted. Alternate Formats: online ● *Retailing.org*, bimonthly. Magazine. Explores the new world of electronic direct marketing. **Price:** free. **Circulation:** 20,000. **Advertising:** accepted ● *Retailing.org Daily*. Newsletter. Provides industry news and association information. **Advertising:** accepted ● Annual Report. Alternate Formats: online. **Conventions/Meetings:** annual Access - conference ● annual Asia Meeting - conference (exhibits) ● annual European Conference - meeting and trade show, with awards ceremony (exhibits) ● annual Spring Conference - meeting (exhibits).

2627 ■ Health Industry Representatives Association (HIRA)
7315 E 5th Ave.
Denver, CO 80230
Ph: (303)756-8115
Fax: (303)341-0282
E-mail: hira@mgmtoffice.com
URL: http://www.hira.org
Contact: Lyn Dee Rankin CPMR, Pres.
Founded: 1978. **Members:** 375. **Membership Dues:** allied, $350 (annual) ● representative, $300 (annual). **Staff:** 5. **Budget:** $200,000. **Description:** Represents manufacturers who operate independent marketing firms under contract to manufacturers of non-competing lines and manufacturers within the health-care industry who market through independent marketing firms. Conducts special surveys at regular intervals for members. Provides panel discussions and special discounts for member firms on advertising and reference publications. **Awards:** Allied Member Annual Distinction Award. **Frequency:** annual. **Type:** recognition. **Recipient:** to an allied member who best meets the criteria approved by HIRA members ● Lee Walters Award. **Frequency:** periodic. **Type:** recognition. **Recipient:** to an individual for personal contribution to the healthcare industry. **Formerly:** (1986) Health Associated Representatives. **Publications:** *Health Industry Representatives Association—Membership Directory*, annual. **Price:** $245.00/year. Alternate Formats: online ● *Health Industry Representatives Association—Serial Publications*, monthly. Brochures ● *Health Industry Representatives Association—The Communicator*, monthly. Newsletter. Alternate Formats: online. **Conventions/Meetings:** annual conference and roundtable ● seminar and workshop, roundtable discussions.

2628 ■ Hispanic Marketing and Communication Association (HMCA)
PO Box 565891
Miami, FL 33256-5891
Ph: (305)648-2848
E-mail: hmca@hmca.org
URL: http://www.hmca.org
Contact: Elena del Valle, Pres.
Membership Dues: individual, $75 (annual) ● corporate (up to 4 representatives), $225 (annual). **Multinational. Description:** Represents individuals of diverse backgrounds with a common interest in the Hispanic market in the United States, Latin America and the Caribbean. Promotes excellence in Hispanic marketing. Encourages professional development. Provides opportunities to network among practitioners who practice or have an interest in the Hispanic Market. **Publications:** *Interaccion*, quarterly. Newsletter. Includes updates on Hispanic marketing, news and events. **Price:** included in membership dues. Alternate Formats: online.

2629 ■ Incentive Federation
5008 Castlerock Way
Naples, FL 34112-7926
Ph: (239)775-7527
Fax: (239)775-7537
E-mail: incentivefed@aol.com
URL: http://www.incentivecentral.org
Contact: Howard Henry CAE, Exec. Dir.
Founded: 1985. **Members:** 100. **Membership Dues:** professional, $5,000 (annual). **Staff:** 2. **Description:** Represents motivational companies on the state and federal level. Acts as the government affairs voice of the premium and incentive industry. Conducts research programs. Compiles statistics. Manages the incentive industry's media relations program. **Computer Services:** database ● mailing lists. **Publications:** *Washington Update*, quarterly. Newsletter.

Conventions/Meetings: quarterly board meeting - always January, May, September and October.

2630 ■ International Collegiate Licensing Association (ICLA)

c/o NACDA
PO Box 16428
Cleveland, OH 44116
Ph: (440)892-4000
Fax: (440)892-4007
E-mail: jgalaska@nacda.com
URL: http://nacda.cstv.com/icla/nacda-icla.html
Contact: Jason Galaska, Admin./Liaison

Members: 265. **Membership Dues:** college/university, $195 (annual) ● bowl/conference, $295 (annual) ● affiliate, $395 (annual) ● student, $50 (annual). **Staff:** 2. **Description:** Administrators of licensing at colleges and universities. Promotes protection of the copyrights of colleges and universities; seeks to insure that institutions of higher learning receive just royalties from sales of memorabilia and clothing bearing university or college logo. Facilitates communication and cooperation among members. **Awards:** ICLA Corporate Service Award. **Frequency:** annual. **Type:** recognition. **Recipient:** for an affiliate member who has shown commitment to parties involved in the collegiate licensing process either local, regional or national level ● ICLA Distinguished Service Award. **Frequency:** annual. **Type:** recognition. **Recipient:** for a retired licensing administrator or currently employed member who has demonstrated a history of solid contributions to the field as a pioneer/innovator in the collegiate licensing industry ● ICLA Gold Star Awards. **Frequency:** annual. **Type:** recognition. **Recipient:** for current members who have made contributions to an individual in the collegiate licensing industry through innovation or new ideas during the current academic year ● ICLA Synergy Award: Collegiate Licensing Program of the Year. **Frequency:** annual. **Type:** recognition. **Recipient:** for members who have demonstrated extraordinary commitment to the collegiate licensing that has directly contributed to the betterment of the industry. **Formed by Merger of:** (2003) Association of Collegiate Licensing Administrators; (2003) National Collegiate Licensing Association. **Publications:** Newsletter, periodic ● Directory, periodic. **Conventions/Meetings:** annual convention, in conjunction with the NACDA, NACMA and NAADD (exhibits) ● periodic regional meeting ● annual symposium - winter.

2631 ■ International Experiential Marketing Association (IXMA)

380 Alabama St., No. 10
San Francisco, CA 94110
Ph: (415)355-1586
E-mail: director@ixma.org
URL: http://www.ixma.org
Contact: Erik Hauser, Dir.

Membership Dues: charter, $1,000-$25,000 (annual). **Multinational. Description:** Represents the interests of individuals and organizations formed for the advancement of experiential marketing (XM). Acts as the voice of the XM industry by improving the understanding of XM by marketers, agencies, academics and students. Plans, develops and implements formal and informal education programs. Develops best industry practice and facilitates active collaboration between members. **Publications:** *IXMA ExMark*, quarterly. Newsletter. **Price:** included in membership dues.

2632 ■ Legal Marketing Association (LMA)

1926 Waukegan Rd., Ste.1
Glenview, IL 60025
Ph: (847)657-6717
Free: (888)562-9494
Fax: (847)657-6819
E-mail: lma-hq@tcag.com
URL: http://www.legalmarketing.org
Contact: Nat Slavin, Pres.

Founded: 1986. **Members:** 2,300. **Membership Dues:** full in U.S., $350 (annual) ● full outside U.S., $175 (annual) ● affiliate/limited, $125 (annual) ● student, $35 (annual). **Staff:** 10. **Local Groups:** 15. **Multinational. Description:** Professional organization serving the needs and maintaining the standards of those engaged in developing and implementing marketing programs for law firms. Compiles statistics. Operates speakers' bureau and job bank. Conducts surveys. **Awards:** Your Honor Awards. **Frequency:** annual. **Type:** recognition. **Recipient:** for creativity, effectiveness, quality of execution, return on investment, and overall excellence in legal marketing. **Formerly:** (1990) National Association of Law Firm Marketing Administrators; (2002) National Law Firm Marketing Association. **Publications:** *Salary Survey*, biennial ● *Strategies*, monthly. Newsletter. Includes reports on association activities and law marketing developments. **Price:** available to members only ● Membership Directory, annual. **Conventions/Meetings:** annual competition and conference (exhibits) - 2009 Mar. 31-Apr. 4, Washington, DC; 2010 Mar. 9-13, Denver, CO ● annual meeting.

2633 ■ Marketing Executive Networking Group (MENG)

15 Bond St.
East Norwalk, CT 06855
E-mail: admin@mengonline.com
URL: http://www.mengonline.com
Contact: Ruth Bardos, Admin.

Founded: 1995. **Members:** 1,500. **Membership Dues:** regular, $150 (annual). **Regional Groups:** 12. **Description:** Promotes enhancement of professional skills, relationships, and knowledge. **Computer Services:** database, members, resources ● online services, bulletin board. **Committees:** Benefits; Recruiter Relations; Screening/Admissions. **Special Interest Groups:** B2B; Consulting; Consumer Packaged Goods; Cosmetics; Direct Marketing; Finance; Media; Online Marketing; Pharma; Sales; Startups. **Working Groups:** Regional Chapters (numerous). **Publications:** *Welcome Guide for New Members*, periodic. Pamphlet.

2634 ■ Marketing Research Association (MRA)

110 Natl. Dr., 2nd Fl.
Glastonbury, CT 06033-1212
Ph: (860)682-1000
Fax: (860)682-1010
E-mail: larry.brownell@mra-net.org
URL: http://www.mra-net.org
Contact: Larry Brownell, Exec. Dir.

Founded: 1954. **Members:** 2,600. **Membership Dues:** educator, $75 (annual) ● government, $200 (annual) ● student, $55 (annual) ● level H (maximum), $11,625 (annual) ● level A (minimum), $650 (annual). **Staff:** 13. **Budget:** $1,000,000. **Regional Groups:** 12. **Description:** Companies and individuals involved in any area of opinion and marketing research, such as data collection, research, or as an end-user. **Computer Services:** Mailing lists, of members. **Committees:** Conference; Legislative; Marketing; Memberships; Professional Standards; Publication. **Councils:** Consumer Advocacy. **Formerly:** (1971) Marketing Research Trade Association. **Publications:** *Alert*, monthly. Magazine. Provides marketing researchers with the insights, technologies and tools they need to succeed in today's profession. **Price:** included in membership dues; $85.00 /year for nonmembers. **Circulation:** 2,600. **Advertising:** accepted ● *Blue Books Research Service Directory*, annual. Lists research and data collection companies. **Price:** $99.95 for members, plus shipping and handling; $169.95 for nonmembers, plus shipping and handling. **Advertising:** accepted ● *Communication Responsibilities During Data Collection Process Guidelines*. **Price:** $19.95 for members; $29.95 for nonmembers ● *The Connector*, annual. Membership Directory. **Price:** free for members; $85.00 for nonmembers. **Circulation:** 2,600. Alternate Formats: online ● *Field Auditor Recommended Practices Quality Control Series*. **Price:** $19.95 for members; $29.95 for nonmembers ● *Guidelines and Practices to Promote Respondent Cooperation* ● *Incidence Guideline* ● *Interviewer Training*. Video ● *MRA News and Events*, monthly. Newsletter. **Price:** free. Alternate Formats: online ● *MRA Student Focus*, monthly. Newsletter. **Price:** free. Alternate Formats: online ● *Recruiting and Facility Management Qualitative Handbook*. **Conventions/Meetings:** annual conference and symposium - every spring ● semiannual meeting - every May/June and October/November.

2635 ■ Marketing Science Institute (MSI)

1000 Massachusetts Ave.
Cambridge, MA 02138-5396
Ph: (617)491-2060
Fax: (617)491-2065
E-mail: msi@msi.org
URL: http://www.msi.org
Contact: Russell Winer, Exec. Dir.

Founded: 1961. **Members:** 64. **Membership Dues:** corporate, $33,000 (annual). **Staff:** 10. **Description:** Seeks to improve marketing practice and education by developing theories and techniques that can be applied to understanding and solving current marketing problems. Conducts research and brings together researchers from different universities and schools of business. **Libraries: Type:** reference. **Holdings:** 500; papers, reports. **Subjects:** marketing topics. **Awards:** H. Paul Root Award. **Frequency:** annual. **Type:** recognition. **Recipient:** to the article chosen by the JM editorial review board for its significant contribution to marketing practice ● Paul Green Award. **Frequency:** annual. **Type:** recognition. **Recipient:** to the Journal of Marketing Research articles that have contributed to the practice of marketing research ● Robert D. Buzzell Best Paper Award. **Frequency:** annual. **Type:** recognition. **Recipient:** to the authors of MSI working papers that have made the most significant contribution to marketing practice. **Programs:** Research. **Publications:** *Catalog of Publications*, annual ● *Insights from MSI*. Newsletter. Features new ideas on topics such as innovation, marketing metrics and customer relationship management. ● *MSI Reports*, quarterly. Includes reading lists, MSI working paper "classics" and other articles. ● *MSI Review*. Newsletter. Features news from the MSI community, including interviews, highlights from recent conferences and research initiatives. ● Monographs ● Newsletter, periodic ● Papers. **Conventions/Meetings:** periodic competition ● periodic conference and workshop.

2636 ■ Materials Marketing Associates (MMA)

136 S Keowee St.
Dayton, OH 45402
Ph: (937)222-1024
Fax: (937)222-5794
E-mail: email@mma4u.com
URL: http://www.mma4u.com
Contact: Kimberly Fantaci, Exec. Dir.

Founded: 1963. **Members:** 16. **Staff:** 4. **Budget:** $100,000. **Description:** Distributors and manufacturers' representatives who market chemical raw material specialties, containers, and equipment. Provides a forum for the exchange of technical and marketing information. Arranges distribution for suppliers to the chemical industry. **Conventions/Meetings:** annual conference, technical ● seminar.

2637 ■ Medical Marketing Association (MMA)

1525 Valley Center Pkwy., Ste.150
Bethlehem, PA 18017
Ph: (610)868-8530
Free: (800)551-2173
Fax: (610)868-8387
E-mail: mma@mmanet.org
URL: http://www.mmanet.org
Contact: Deb Bronstein, Pres.

Founded: 1965. **Members:** 1,000. **Membership Dues:** individual, $199 (annual) ● group or corporate (per person), $175 (annual) ● student, $65 (annual) ● retired, $45 (annual). **Budget:** $600,000. **Regional Groups:** 6. **Description:** Individuals and corporations engaged in the marketing of pharmaceuticals, diagnostics, medical devices, and biologics. Promotes excellence in the practice of medical marketing; facilitates professional advancement of members. Conducts educational programs; sponsors competitions; maintains speakers' bureau. **Awards:** Gold Obelisk. **Frequency:** annual. **Type:** recognition. **Recipient:** for most successful medical marketers ● IN-AWE Awards. **Frequency:** annual. **Type:** recognition.

Recipient: for creators of medical marketing campaigns and materials ● Medical Marketer of the Year. **Frequency:** annual. **Type:** recognition. **Recipient:** for individuals and teams who have made exceptional contributions to outstanding results-oriented marketing programs. **Computer Services:** Mailing lists, of members ● online services, publication. **Publications:** *Marketplace*, semiannual. Newsletter. **Circulation:** 1,200. **Advertising:** accepted. Alternate Formats: online. **Conventions/Meetings:** annual conference (exhibits) ● periodic regional meeting.

2638 ■ Multi-Level Marketing International Association (MLMIA)
119 Stanford Ct.
Irvine, CA 92612
Ph: (949)854-0484
Fax: (949)854-7687
E-mail: info@mlmia.com
URL: http://www.mlmia.com
Contact: Doris Wood, Chair
Founded: 1985. **Members:** 5,000. **Membership Dues:** corporate (based on number of distributor), $1,200-$12,000 (annual) ● individual, $60 (annual) ● 2 people at same address, $90 (annual) ● support (based on yearly industry billing), $600-$1,000 (annual). **Staff:** 2. **Budget:** $250,000. **Multinational. Description:** Companies, support groups, and distributors. Seeks to strengthen and improve the Multi-Level Marketing (also known as Network Marketing) industry in the U.S. and abroad. (Multi-Level Marketing is a method of selling products directly, independently, and usually out of the home, without the medium of a retail outlet.) Provides educational services to consumers and law enforcement agencies. Serves as an information source for the industry. Offers recommendations for start-up companies; maintains speakers' bureau; conducts training programs. **Libraries: Type:** reference. **Holdings:** 100. **Subjects:** MLM industry, self-improvement. **Awards:** Distributor of the Year. **Frequency:** annual. **Type:** recognition ● Hall of Fame. **Frequency:** periodic. **Type:** recognition ● International Company. **Frequency:** periodic. **Type:** recognition ● MLM Company of the Year. **Frequency:** annual. **Type:** recognition ● Supplier of the Year. **Frequency:** annual. **Type:** recognition ● Support Company of the Year. **Frequency:** annual. **Type:** recognition. **Computer Services:** database. **Telecommunication Services:** electronic mail, doriswood@mlmia.com. **Boards:** Directors. **Committees:** Government Relations. **Councils:** Corporate; Distribution; Support. **Working Groups:** Government Liaison. **Publications:** *Connecting Point*. Newsletter. **Price:** included in membership dues. Alternate Formats: online ● *Corporate Directory - Support Directory*, quarterly. **Price:** free for members only. Alternate Formats: online ● Articles. **Conventions/Meetings:** semiannual conference and convention (exhibits) - April and October ● quarterly convention and trade show, regional meetings for corporate and distributor members.

2639 ■ Mystery Shopping Providers Association (MSPA)
12300 Ford Rd., Ste.135
Dallas, TX 75234
Ph: (972)406-1104
Fax: (972)755-2561
E-mail: info@mysteryshop.org
URL: http://www.mysteryshop.org
Contact: David Rich, Pres.
Founded: 1998. **Members:** 150. **Membership Dues:** regular, $495 (annual) ● associate, $695 (annual). **Staff:** 4. **Description:** Marketing research and merchandising companies, private investigation firms, training organizations and companies specializing in mystery shopping services. Work to enhance service levels.

2640 ■ National Agri-Marketing Association (NAMA)
11020 King St., Ste.205
Overland Park, KS 66210
Ph: (913)491-6500
Fax: (913)491-6502
E-mail: agrimktg@nama.org
URL: http://www.nama.org
Contact: Stephanie Gable, Pres.
Founded: 1965. **Members:** 2,500. **Membership Dues:** regular, $140-$170 (annual) ● Agri Broadcast Management Council, Commodity Promotion Council, $170 (annual) ● Agri Broadcast Management Council (associate), $75 (annual) ● Commodity Promotion Council (associate), $25 (annual). **Staff:** 10. **Budget:** $1,500,000. **State Groups:** 50. **Description:** Persons engaged in agricultural marketing for manufacturers, advertising agencies, and the media. Promotes the highest standards of agricultural marketing; provides for the exchange of ideas; encourages the study and better understanding of agricultural advertising, selling, and marketing; works to broaden understanding of the economic importance of agriculture; encourages careers in agricultural marketing. Provides agri-marketing short courses. **Awards:** Agribusiness Leader of the Year. **Frequency:** annual. **Type:** recognition. **Recipient:** to an outstanding leader in agribusiness, education, government service or other agribusiness related area ● NAMA Marketer of the Year. **Frequency:** annual. **Type:** recognition. **Recipient:** for active members with senior management of marketing and/or sales responsibilities. **Telecommunication Services:** electronic mail, eldonw@nama.org. **Formerly:** (1957) Chicago Area Agricultural Advertising Association; (1965) National Agricultural Advertising and Marketing Association. **Publications:** *Agri Marketing*, 10/year. Magazine. Reports on membership activities. Includes calendar of events, and employment referral service. **Price:** free. **Circulation:** 10,000 ● *NAMA Directory of Members*, annual. Membership Directory. **Price:** $150.00. **Circulation:** 3,000. **Advertising:** accepted. Alternate Formats: online. **Conventions/Meetings:** annual conference and trade show, for agri-marketing (exhibits) - 2009 Apr., Atlanta, GA; 2010 Apr., Kansas City, MO.

2641 ■ National Alliance of Market Developers (NAMD)
c/o Clyde C. Allen, Exec. Dir.
620 Sheridan Ave.
Plainfield, NJ 07060
Ph: (908)561-4062
Fax: (908)561-6827
E-mail: allenpartner@earthlink.net
URL: http://www.namdntl.org
Contact: Clyde C. Allen, Exec. Dir.
Founded: 1953. **Members:** 700. **Membership Dues:** corporate, $500 ● professional, $125 ● student, $80. **Staff:** 2. **Local Groups:** 18. **Description:** Professionals engaged in marketing, sales, sales promotion, advertising, or public relations who are concerned with the delivery of goods and services to the minority consumer market. **Formerly:** (2002) National Association of Market Developers. **Publications:** *Briefcase*, bimonthly. Contains articles about the social position of African-Americans, convention reports, and job opportunity listings. ● *EMPHASIS*, annual. Magazine. Includes chapter news, convention reports, and articles about minority markets in the U.S. ● *President's Report*, bimonthly ● Brochure. **Conventions/Meetings:** annual conference - always May.

2642 ■ National Association of Display Industries (NADI)
4651 Sheridan St., Ste.470
Hollywood, FL 33021
Ph: (954)893-7300
Fax: (954)893-7500
E-mail: nadi@nadi-global.com
URL: http://www.nadi-global.com
Contact: Klein Merriman, Exec. Dir.
Founded: 1942. **Members:** 350. **Membership Dues:** company, $450 (annual) ● retail, $250 (annual) ● student, $25 (annual). **Staff:** 3. **Description:** Represents and promotes the visual merchandising profession. **Publications:** *NADIrect to You*, bimonthly. Newsletter. Alternate Formats: online ● *NADI's Visual Merchandising/Store Planning Design Directory*, periodic. **Conventions/Meetings:** annual general assembly (exhibits) ● annual show, targets retailers looking for design inspiration and innovation.

2643 ■ National Mail Order Association (NMOA)
2807 Polk St. NE
Minneapolis, MN 55418-2954
Ph: (612)788-1673
Fax: (612)788-1147
E-mail: info@nmoa.org
URL: http://www.nmoa.org
Contact: John D. Schulte, Chm./Chief Mgr.
Founded: 1972. **Members:** 4,000. **Membership Dues:** manufacturer/reseller/service provider, $365 (annual) ● individual/entrepreneur, $199 (annual) ● manufacturer/reseller/service provider - international, $410 (annual) ● individual/entrepreneur - international, $234 (annual). **Staff:** 4. **National Groups:** 2. **Description:** Provides education, information, and business contacts to those involved in direct marketing and mail order. Reports new and established product sources, ideas, techniques, developments, and services of value to mail marketers. Reviews and disseminates information on reports, government findings, new books and directories, mailing lists, and general data relating to developing maximum mail order sales. **Libraries: Type:** not open to the public. **Holdings:** 1,000. **Subjects:** mail order, direct mail, catalog marketing, database marketing, event marketing, tradeshows. **Awards:** Hot Products Awards. **Frequency:** annual. **Type:** recognition. **Recipient:** for the most unique and interesting products made in America. **Computer Services:** Online services, info library. **Telecommunication Services:** electronic mail, schulte@nmoa.org. **Publications:** *Direct Marketing Digest*, monthly. Newsletter. Provides unique direct marketing information to entrepreneurial-minded executives and companies. **Price:** included in membership dues; $10.00 for nonmembers; $99.00 /year for nonmembers. Alternate Formats: online ● *Mail Order Digest*, monthly. Newsletter. Provides information on new product sources, promotional ideas, merchandising developments, direct mail techniques, and mail marketing opportunities. **Price:** included in membership dues. **Circulation:** 2,500. **Advertising:** accepted. Alternate Formats: online ● *Washington Newsletter*, monthly. Covers federal regulations pertinent to the mail order business. Provides information on changes in rates, and postal service procedures. **Price:** included in membership dues. **Conventions/Meetings:** trade show, one stop connecting point for mail marketers.

2644 ■ National Organization for Diversity in Sales and Marketing (NODSM)
PO Box 61118
Raleigh, NC 27661
Free: (888)689-8896
Fax: (919)573-9584
E-mail: info@minoritymarketshare.com
URL: http://www.minoritymarketshare.com
Contact: Toure Claiborne, Contact
Founded: 2003. **Membership Dues:** student, $35 (annual) ● professional, $99 (annual) ● small business, $595 (annual) ● corporate, $2,595 (annual). **Description:** Provides a national platform with an approach to diversity of thought, race, gender, sexual orientation, physical ability, age and lifestyle. Approaches sales professionalism and multicultural marketing as a discipline. Offers solutions that address the problems and opportunities of diversity and multiculturalism in corporate America.

2645 ■ Paper and Plastic Representatives Management Council (PPRMC)
PO Box 150229
Arlington, TX 76015
Ph: (682)518-6008
Fax: (682)518-6476
E-mail: assnhqtrs@aol.com
URL: http://www.pprmc.com
Contact: Pamela L. Bess, Exec. Dir.
Founded: 1995. **Members:** 20. **Membership Dues:** company, $150 (monthly). **Budget:** $50,000. **Description:** National networking group of manufacturer representative firms. Conducts educational programs.

Computer Services: Mailing lists, of members. **Publications:** *Cost of Business Report* ● *Management Report*, monthly. **Conventions/Meetings:** semiannual conference - always May and November.

2646 ■ Private Label Manufacturers Association (PLMA)
630 Third Ave., 4th Fl.
New York, NY 10017
Ph: (212)972-3131
Fax: (212)983-1382
E-mail: info@plma.com
URL: http://www.plma.com
Contact: Ms. Debra Best, Trade Show Sales Dir.
Founded: 1979. **Members:** 2,500. **Staff:** 40. **Description:** Membership consists of manufacturers, brokers, suppliers, and consultants. Educates consumers on the quality and value of private label or store brand products; promotes private label industry. Compiles statistics; conducts research programs for members. **Awards:** Salute to Excellence. **Type:** recognition. **Recipient:** for outstanding merchandising and marketing of store brands by retailers. **Publications:** *Scanner*, bimonthly. Newsletter. **Price:** available to members only. Alternate Formats: online. **Conventions/Meetings:** annual Domestic Trade Show ● annual International Trade Show - trade show and international conference (exhibits).

2647 ■ Promotion Marketing Association (PMA)
257 Park Ave. S, 11th Fl.
New York, NY 10010-7304
Ph: (212)420-1100
Fax: (212)533-7622
E-mail: pma@pmalink.org
URL: http://www.pmalink.org
Contact: Mark Mears, Chm.
Founded: 1911. **Members:** 700. **Membership Dues:** academic, $250 (annual) ● legal, marketer, supplier, $1,000 (annual) ● corporate affiliate, $100 (annual) ● student, $50 (annual) ● associate, $150 (annual) ● primary corporate, $2,500 (annual). **Staff:** 12. **Budget:** $1,900,000. **Description:** Fortune 500 marketer companies, promotion agencies, and companies using promotion programs; supplier members are manufacturers of package goods, cosmetics, and pharmaceuticals, consultants, and advertising agencies. Conducts surveys and studies of industry issues. **Libraries: Type:** reference. **Awards:** Promotion Marketer of the Year. **Frequency:** annual. **Type:** recognition. **Recipient:** for organizations ● Reggie Awards. **Frequency:** annual. **Type:** recognition. **Recipient:** for 10 best promotions of the year. **Committees:** Audit; Cause Related Marketing; Diversity Marketing; Education; Government and Legal Affairs; Promotion Law/Marketing Conference; Sweepstakes. **Formerly:** (1977) Premium Advertising Association of America; (1998) Promotion Marketing Association of America. **Publications:** *Outlook*, 5/year. Newsletter. **Price:** included in membership dues. **Circulation:** 750. **Advertising:** accepted ● Membership Directory, annual. **Conventions/Meetings:** Basics of Promotion Marketing - seminar, three-day intensive course for entry-level/junior-level personnel requiring fundamentals of promotion marketing ● annual Promotion Law Conference - always November ● annual Promotion Update Conference - always March.

2648 ■ Search Engine Marketing Professional Organization (SEMPO)
401 Edgewater Pl., Ste.600
Wakefield, MA 01880
Ph: (781)876-8866
URL: http://www.sempo.org
Contact: Jeffrey Pruitt, Pres.
Founded: 2003. **Membership Dues:** corporate (circle), $5,000 (annual) ● corporate (general), $1,000 (annual) ● individual, $299 (annual). **Multinational. Description:** Develops, promotes, and advances the search engine marketing industry. Increases awareness and understanding of the value of search engine marketing worldwide. Provides a foundation for industry growth through education and research. **Publications:** Newsletter.

2649 ■ Society for Marketing Professional Services (SMPS)
99 Canal Center Plz., Ste.330
Alexandria, VA 22314
Ph: (703)549-6117
Free: (800)292-7677
Fax: (703)549-2498
E-mail: info@smps.org
URL: http://www.smps.org
Contact: Ronald D. Worth CAE, CEO
Founded: 1973. **Members:** 5,600. **Membership Dues:** individual, $295 (annual) ● interim, $50 (annual) ● student, $25 (annual) ● emeritus, $30 (annual). **Staff:** 14. **Budget:** $2,500,000. **Local Groups:** 51. **Description:** Marketing employees of architectural, engineering, planning, interior design, landscape architectural, and construction management firms who are responsible for the new business development of their companies. Compiles statistics. Offers local and national educational programs; maintains certification program. **Libraries: Type:** reference. **Awards:** Chapter President of the Year Award. **Frequency:** annual. **Type:** recognition. **Recipient:** for excellence in leadership ● Marketing Achievement Award. **Frequency:** annual. **Type:** recognition. **Recipient:** to professionals who have exemplary achievements and lasting contributions to the field ● Marketing Communications Award. **Frequency:** annual. **Type:** recognition. **Recipient:** for excellence in marketing communications by professional service firms in the design and building industry ● Striving for Excellence Award. **Frequency:** annual. **Type:** recognition. **Recipient:** to chapters, for excellence in management and service to members. **Computer Services:** Mailing lists, of members. **Programs:** Certified Professional Services Marketer; Fellows Recognition. **Special Interest Groups:** Business Development Institute. **Task Forces:** Diversity; Emerging Leaders. **Publications:** *Marketer*, bimonthly. Journal. Includes market trends, marketing techniques and technology, membership profiles, employment opportunities, book reviews, and calendar of events. **Price:** included in membership dues. ISSN: 0199-3690. **Circulation:** 5,500. **Advertising:** accepted ● *SMPS News*, monthly. Newsletter. **Advertising:** accepted. Alternate Formats: online. **Conventions/Meetings:** annual The Next Wave - conference (exhibits) - always August or September ● regional meeting, provides specialized education.

2650 ■ Strategic Account Management Association (SAMA)
150 N Wacker Dr., Ste.2222
Chicago, IL 60606
Ph: (312)251-3131
Fax: (312)251-3132
E-mail: sama@strategicaccounts.org
URL: http://www.strategicaccounts.org
Contact: Bernard Quancard, Pres./CEO
Founded: 1964. **Members:** 3,000. **Membership Dues:** individual, corporate, $450 (annual) ● one time initiation fee, $100. **Staff:** 20. **Budget:** $2,000,000. **Multinational. Description:** Corporation sales executives concerned with strategic account sales. Holds seminars on strategic account management. Serves as an information provider on strategic customer-supplier relationship resources. **Libraries: Type:** reference. **Holdings:** 500; archival material, audio recordings, books, clippings, monographs, periodicals. **Subjects:** account management, cross-functional teams, strategic partnering and alliances, channel conflict, national and global account management programs, supply chain management, value-added selling. **Awards:** Executive of the Year Award. **Frequency:** annual. **Type:** recognition. **Recipient:** for demonstrated executive-level leaders in sales and marketing who have supported the concept of major account/strategic relationships with key customers ● SAMA Performance Award. **Frequency:** annual. **Type:** recognition. **Recipient:** for best practices in strategic account management programs. **Committees:** Annual Conference; Growth; International; Knowledge; Strategic Sales Leadership. **Formerly:** (1993) National Account Marketing Association; (2000) National Account Management Association. **Publications:** *Annual Compensation Survey of Strategic Account Managers and Directors/VPs*, annual. **Price:** $125.00 for members; $250.00 for nonmembers ● *Focus: Account Manager*, semiannual. Newsletter. Contains information specific to the account manager. Alternate Formats: online ● *Focus: Teams*, semiannual. Newsletter. Contains information specific to team issues. Alternate Formats: online ● *Velocity*, quarterly. Magazine. Includes association news and articles about strategic account programs, best practices and research findings. **Price:** included in membership dues; $95.00 for nonmembers. **Circulation:** 5,000. **Advertising:** accepted. **Conventions/Meetings:** annual conference (exhibits) - always April or May.

2651 ■ Trial Lawyers Marketing (TLMA)
Address Unknown since 2007
Founded: 1986. **Members:** 300. **Staff:** 6. **For-Profit. Description:** Lawyers, marketing directors, office administrators, and trial firms. Provides legal marketing information and the opportunity to exchange ideas with colleagues in different geographic areas. Bestows Golden Gavel Awards for marketing communications developed by or for law firms marketing to customers. **Computer Services:** prospect list available for rental. **Formerly:** (1991) Trial Lawyer Marketing Association. **Publications:** *Marketing Ideas That Work*, periodic. Includes case studies. ● *Trial Lawyers Marketing Briefs*, periodic. Includes ideas, tips, and advice in firm marketing and management. ● *Trial Lawyers Marketing News*, semiannual. Includes articles on marketing tools; also contains rules, tips, and techniques on legal marketing, calendar of events, and member news. **Price:** available to members only. **Advertising:** not accepted ● Membership Directory, periodic. **Conventions/Meetings:** annual conference (exhibits) ● roundtable.

2652 ■ Women in Direct Marketing International (WDMI)
c/o Berenice Ladden, Pres.
200 Circle Dr. N
Piscataway, NJ 08854
Ph: (732)469-8414 (718)792-0839
E-mail: bladden@directmaildepot.com
URL: http://www.wdmi.org
Contact: Berenice Ladden, Pres.
Founded: 1970. **Members:** 125. **Membership Dues:** individual, $95 (annual) ● associate, student, $45 (annual). **Budget:** $110,000. **Regional Groups:** 4. **Local Groups:** 3. **National Groups:** 2. **Description:** Direct marketing professionals. Seeks to: advance the interests and influence of women in the direct response industry; provide for communication and career education; assist in advancement of personal career objectives; serve as professional network to develop business contacts and foster mutual goals. Maintains career talent bank. Distributes information nationally; maintains other chapters in Chicago, IL, Los Angeles, CA, Dallas, TX, Japan, UK, and Belgium. **Awards:** Direct Marketing Woman of the Year Award. **Frequency:** annual. **Type:** recognition. **Recipient:** for 10 years in industry; for significant professional and personal contributions to industry. **Committees:** Advertising Sales; Education; Membership; Newsletter; Night of the Roundtables; Programming; Publicity; Research; Special Seminar Series; Talent Bank; Woman of the Year Award. **Formerly:** Women's Direct Marketing International. **Publications:** *Women in Direct Marketing International-Membership Roster*, annual. Membership Directory. **Price:** included in membership dues. **Circulation:** 400. **Advertising:** accepted ● Newsletter, quarterly. Contains information on career developments. Includes calendar of events and profiles of new members. **Price:** included in membership dues. **Circulation:** 400. **Advertising:** accepted. **Conventions/Meetings:** annual meeting - always June ● monthly seminar and workshop.

2653 ■ Word of Mouth Marketing Association (WOMMA)
333 W North Ave., No. 500
Chicago, IL 60610
Ph: (312)853-4400
Fax: (312)275-7687

E-mail: info@womma.com
URL: http://www.womma.org
Contact: Susan L. Tibbits, Exec. Dir.
Membership Dues: governing, $10,000 (annual) ● standard, $3,000 (annual) ● small business, $1,000 (annual). **Description:** Represents companies pioneering the art and science of amplifying genuine consumer enthusiasm. Seeks to promote and improve word of mouth (WOM) marketing. Improves the profession through standards and best practices. Encourages the use of WOM as an effective marketing tool. **Publications:** Newsletters. Alternate Formats: online.

Marriage

2654 ■ American Association of Wedding Planners
c/o Weddings Beautiful Worldwide
1004 N Thompson St., Ste.205
Richmond, VA 23230
Ph: (804)342-6061
Fax: (804)342-6062
E-mail: info@weddingsbeautiful.com
URL: http://www.weddingsbeautiful.com
Contact: Nancy Tucker, Contact
Founded: 1954. **Members:** 600. **Membership Dues:** $119 (semiannual). **Budget:** $5,000,000. **Languages:** English, Japanese. **Multinational. Description:** Provides Certified Wedding Specialist training for independent wedding consultants, planners, coordinators. Members receive bimonthly newsletters, website advertising, bridal leads and much more. **Publications:** *The Groom's Corner* ● *One Perfect Day*. **Conventions/Meetings:** semiannual seminar.

Martial Arts

2655 ■ Martial Arts Industry Association (MAIA)
1000 Century Blvd.
Oklahoma City, OK 73110
Free: (866)626-7481
E-mail: memberservices@masuccess.com
URL: http://www.masuccess.com
Contact: Frank Silverman, Exec. Dir.
Membership Dues: value, $19 (monthly) ● success, $99 (annual). **Multinational. Description:** Promotes the martial arts industry. Provides martial art teachers with tools needed for the advancement of martial arts. **Computer Services:** Information services, martial arts resources ● online services, discussion boards. **Publications:** *Martial Arts Success*, annual. Magazine. Alternate Formats: online.

Meat

2656 ■ American Association of Meat Processors (AAMP)
PO Box 269
Elizabethtown, PA 17022
Ph: (717)367-1168
Free: (877)877-0168
Fax: (717)367-9096
E-mail: info@aamp.com
URL: http://www.aamp.com
Contact: Jay Wenther PhD, Exec. Dir.
Founded: 1939. **Members:** 1,800. **Membership Dues:** supplier, $325 (annual) ● operator, $175 (annual) ● allied, international, $75 (annual) ● associate, $50 (annual) ● operator in Canada, $100 (annual). **Staff:** 7. **Budget:** $600,000. **Regional Groups:** 2. **State Groups:** 34. **Description:** Represents small and mid-sized packers, processors, wholesalers, home food service businesses, meat retailers, deli, mail order businesses and catering operators and their suppliers. Represents its members at the federal level of government. Provides education, insurance options and business management assistance to the independent segment of the meat industry. **Libraries: Type:** not open to the public. **Holdings:** 600. **Subjects:** processing, marketing, training, equipment. **Awards:** Accomplishment Award. **Frequency:** annual. **Type:** recognition. **Recipient:** for members who have made strides in the meat industry ● Achievement Award. **Frequency:** annual. **Type:** recognition. **Recipient:** for continuing service to the meat industry ● American Cured Meat Championship Award. **Frequency:** annual. **Type:** recognition. **Recipient:** for the winner of the annual competition ● Best Booth Awards. **Frequency:** annual. **Type:** recognition. **Recipient:** for AAMP supplier firm ● Clarence Knebel Best of Show Memorial Award. **Frequency:** annual. **Type:** recognition. **Recipient:** for the best award-winning product entered in the annual American Cured Meat Championships ● Cured Meat Hall of Fame Award. **Frequency:** annual. **Type:** recognition. **Recipient:** for individuals who have shown a long-standing excellence in the production of cured meats ● F.W. Witt Supplier Award. **Frequency:** annual. **Type:** recognition. **Recipient:** for a person and/or supplier member who has devoted much of his or her career to the meat and poultry industry ● Golden Cleaver Trophy. **Frequency:** annual. **Type:** trophy. **Recipient:** for a member who recruited the highest number of new members ● Outstanding Service Award. **Frequency:** annual. **Type:** recognition. **Recipient:** for affiliated associations, officers, secretaries or leaders whose dedication and enthusiasm have elevated the association to an outstanding degree ● Package Wrapping Award. **Frequency:** annual. **Type:** recognition. **Recipient:** for recognition of an AAMP members' skill of wrapping objects ● Sharpest Knife in North America. **Frequency:** annual. **Type:** recognition. **Recipient:** for recognition of a members' skill in sharpening a knife ● Stephen Krut Scholarship Award. **Frequency:** annual. **Type:** scholarship. **Recipient:** to a deserving university or technical school student who anticipates a career in animal, meat, or food science, agricultural engineering or any related field. **Computer Services:** Mailing lists, information services. **Committees:** Accomplishment Award; Code of Ethics; Convention; Cured Meat Competition Advisory; Cured Meats Hall of Fame; Education and Training; Executive; Food Safety and Science; Meat Inspection/Governmental Affairs; Nominating; Outstanding Service Award; Property Management; Scholarship; Strategic Planning. **Affiliated With:** Missouri Association of Meat Processors; National Country Ham Association; Ohio Association of Meat Processors; Pennsylvania Association of Meat Processors. **Formerly:** Frozen Food Locker Institute; National Frozen Food Locker Association; National Frozen Food Locker Institute; (1973) National Institute of Locker and Freezer Provisioners. **Publications:** *AAMPlifier*, semimonthly. Newsletter. Contains association and industry newsletter. **Price:** included in membership dues; $50.00 /year for nonmembers. **Circulation:** 2,000 ● *Capitol Line-Up*, semimonthly. Newsletter. Covers regulatory and legislative affairs. **Price:** included in membership dues; $50.00 /year for nonmembers ● *The Membership Directory and Buyers' Guide of the American Association of Meat Processors*, biennial. Lists AAMP members and their products/services. **Price:** free for members; $300.00/issue for nonmembers. **Circulation:** 2,000. **Conventions/Meetings:** annual meeting and convention, with educational sessions and exhibits (exhibits).

2657 ■ American Meat Goat Association (AMGA)
PO Box 676
Sonora, TX 76950
Ph: (325)387-6100 (830)895-5886
Fax: (325)387-5814
E-mail: marvin@sonoratx.net
URL: http://www.meatgoats.com
Contact: Marvin F. Shurley, Pres.
Founded: 1992. **Members:** 504. **Membership Dues:** associate, $30 (annual) ● breeder, $100 (annual) ● active, $50 (annual). **Staff:** 6. **Description:** Producers and others interested in meat goats. Promotes meat goats as a viable source of long-term, stable income in agricultural operations. Seeks to establish group breeding plans for the improvement of meat goats and to enhance consumer demand at the retail level. **Awards:** Willie B. Whitehead, Jr. Scholarship. **Frequency:** annual. **Type:** scholarship. **Recipient:** to a graduating senior for the best 300-350 words essay. **Publications:** *Meat Goat Monthly News*. Magazine. Contains information about meat goat raising and showing. **Price:** included in membership dues. **Circulation:** 3,000. **Advertising:** accepted. **Conventions/Meetings:** annual Premium Buck & Doe Sale - conference.

2658 ■ American Meat Institute (AMI)
1150 Connecticut Ave. NW, 12th Fl.
Washington, DC 20036
Ph: (202)587-4200
Fax: (202)587-4300
E-mail: memberservices@meatami.com
URL: http://www.meatami.com
Contact: J. Patrick Boyle, Pres./CEO
Founded: 1906. **Members:** 1,100. **Membership Dues:** associate, $1,000 (annual) ● general (minimum; based on number of employees), $1,200 (annual) ● supplier, $1,125-$15,000 (annual). **Staff:** 31. **Budget:** $10,000,000. **Description:** Represents the interests of packers and processors of beef, pork, lamb, veal, and turkey products and their suppliers throughout North America. Provides legislative, regulatory, and public relations services. Conducts scientific research. Offers marketing and technical assistance. Sponsors educational programs. **Libraries: Type:** reference. **Holdings:** books, periodicals. **Committees:** Allied Products; Animal Welfare; Beef; Environmental; Foodservice/Retail; Human Resources; Inspection; International Trade; Lamb; Pork; Poultry; Prepared Meats; Scientific Affairs; Strategic Affairs; Supplier; Turkey; Worker Safety and Health. **Absorbed:** (1984) National Meat Association. **Formerly:** (1919) American Meat Packers Association; (1941) Institute of American Meat Packers. **Publications:** *Meat and Poultry Facts*, annual. Contains statistical review. ● *Weekly Trade Alert*. Newsletter. **Conventions/Meetings:** annual convention (exhibits) ● annual International Meat, Poultry, and Seafood Convention and Exposition - meeting and convention, part of the Worldwide Food Expo (exhibits).

2659 ■ International Natural Sausage Casing Association (INSCA)
c/o North American Natural Casing Association
494 Eight Ave., Ste.805
New York, NY 10001
Ph: (206)682-6845 (212)695-7153
Free: (800)682-6845
Fax: (206)382-0883
E-mail: insca@insca.org
URL: http://www.insca.org
Contact: Mr. Michael Mayo, Treas.
Founded: 1965. **Members:** 275. **Membership Dues:** regular, $1,500 (annual) ● associate, $500 (annual) ● association, affiliate, $750 (annual). **Staff:** 5. **Budget:** $400,000. **Multinational. Description:** Represents importers and processors of natural sausage casings in 40 countries. **Libraries: Type:** reference. **Telecommunication Services:** electronic mail, info@overseacasing.com. **Supersedes:** Natural Casing Institute. **Publications:** *INSCA Newsletter*, periodic. **Price:** free. **Circulation:** 200 ● *National Link*. **Price:** free for members. **Circulation:** 250. **Advertising:** accepted. **Conventions/Meetings:** annual meeting - usually May or June ● semiannual meeting - always September, October, or November.

2660 ■ Meat Importers Council of America (MICA)
1901 N Ft. Myer Dr.
Arlington, VA 22209
Ph: (703)522-1910
Free: (800)522-1910
Fax: (703)524-6039
E-mail: lauriebryant@micausa.org
URL: http://www.micausa.org
Contact: Mr. Laurie I. Bryant, Exec. Dir./Sec.
Founded: 1962. **Members:** 170. **Membership Dues:** regular, $2,000 (annual) ● associate, $1,000 (annual) ● affiliate, $1,250 (annual). **Staff:** 1. **Description:** Importers of fresh, chilled, and frozen meats and oth-

ers indirectly associated with such importation. Promulgates industry guidelines and standards; circulates information to the industry. **Formerly:** Meat Importers' Council. **Publications:** *Membership List*, periodic. Membership Directory. **Conventions/Meetings:** annual convention.

2661 ■ Meat Industry Suppliers Association (MISA)
201 Park Washington Ct.
Falls Church, VA 22046-4527
Ph: (703)533-0251
Fax: (703)241-5603
E-mail: mbittle@asmii.com
URL: http://www.asmii.com
Contact: Clay D. Tyeryar, Staff Exec.
Founded: 1948. **Members:** 2. **Staff:** 17. **Budget:** $50,000. **Description:** Firms supplying products and services to the meat, poultry, and seafood processing industries. Members include manufacturers and distributors of machinery, casings, seasonings, material handling and packaging equipment and materials, and other items used in slaughterhouses, packaging plants, processing plants, and supermarkets. **Committees:** Exhibitions; Foundation; Import/Export; Industry/Trade Relations; Program. **Divisions:** Food Machinery Service Institute; Meat Machinery Manufacturers Institute. **Absorbed:** (1991) Meat Machinery Manufacturers Institute. **Formerly:** (1982) Meat Industry Supply and Equipment Association. **Publications:** *Organizations Manual*, periodic ● Membership Directory, periodic. **Conventions/Meetings:** annual meeting - always spring ● annual workshop - always fall.

2662 ■ National Meat Association (NMA)
c/o NMA West
1970 Broadway, Ste.825
Oakland, CA 94612
Ph: (510)763-1533
Fax: (510)763-6186
E-mail: staff@nmaonline.org
URL: http://www.nmaonline.org
Contact: Rosemary Mucklow, Dir. Emeritus
Founded: 1982. **Members:** 600. **Staff:** 12. **Budget:** $1,000,000. **Description:** Meat packers, processors, slaughterers, and jobbers. Promotes interests of independent meat packers in all states. Conducts group purchasing activities and administers group insurance program. Provides legal, freight rate, and contract advisory services. Offers research programs; compiles statistics. **Awards:** E. Floyd Forbes Award. **Frequency:** annual. **Type:** recognition. **Recipient:** for outstanding contribution to the meat industry ● Supplier of the Year. **Frequency:** annual. **Type:** recognition. **Recipient:** for an individual who made outstanding contribution to the meat and poultry industry. **Committees:** Associate Advisory; Beef; Education; Food Safety; Nomination; Processed Meats; Small Stock; Workplace Issues. **Formed by Merger of:** Western States Meat Packers Association; Pacific Coast Meat Association. **Formerly:** (1995) Western States Meat Association. **Publications:** *Lean Trimmings*, weekly. Newsletter. Covers inspection issues, labor relations, and other developments regarding the red meat industry. **Price:** available to members only. **Circulation:** 1,100. Alternate Formats: online ● Membership Directory, annual. **Price:** available to members only. **Advertising:** accepted. **Conventions/Meetings:** biennial competition, equipment exposition ● annual convention.

2663 ■ North American Meat Processors Association (NAMP)
1910 Assn. Dr.
Reston, VA 20191
Ph: (703)758-1900
Free: (800)368-3043
Fax: (703)758-8001
E-mail: info@namp.com
URL: http://www.namp.com
Contact: Philip Kimball, Exec. Dir.
Founded: 1942. **Members:** 325. **Membership Dues:** regular (based on annual sales volume), $675-$2,500 (annual) ● associate, $750 (annual). **Staff:** 4. **Multinational. Description:** Represents wholesalers of meats and meat products to hotels, restaurants, schools, hospitals, and institutions. Conducts technical seminars. **Awards:** Educator's Award. **Frequency:** annual. **Type:** recognition. **Telecommunication Services:** electronic mail, pkimball@namp.com. **Formerly:** National Association of Hotel and Restaurant Meat Purveyors; (1997) National Association of Meat Purveyors. **Publications:** *Meat Buyers Guide*. Serves as an industry meat cutting, buying and identification reference. **Price:** $49.00. Alternate Formats: CD-ROM ● *NAMP Science Letter*, monthly. Highlights industry science needs. ● *North American Meat Processors Association Newsfax*, weekly. Informs member companies of industry developments, particularly federal legislation affecting the industry; also covers association news. **Conventions/Meetings:** annual convention ● annual Management Conference.

2664 ■ Shelf-Stable Food Processors Association (SFPA)
1150 Connecticut Ave. NW, 12th Fl.
Washington, DC 20036
Ph: (202)587-4273
Fax: (202)587-4303
E-mail: sfpa@meatami.com
Contact: James Hodges, Exec. Sec.
Founded: 1923. **Members:** 40. **Membership Dues:** regular, $2,000 (annual) ● associate, $1,500 (annual). **Staff:** 3. **Description:** Serves the shelf-stable prepared food industry. Represents the interests of shelf-stable food processors and their suppliers on issues affecting the industry. Members include companies of all sizes, from regional processors to large multi-plant operations. **Committees:** Government Relations; Scientific. **Affiliated With:** American Meat Institute. **Formerly:** (2007) National Meat Canners Association. **Conventions/Meetings:** annual meeting - 2009 Mar. 8-10, Longboat Key, FL.

2665 ■ United States Meat Export Federation (USMEF)
1050 17th St., Ste.2200
Denver, CO 80265
Ph: (303)623-6328
Fax: (303)623-0297
E-mail: info@usmef.org
URL: http://www.usmef.org
Contact: Lynn Heinze, VP, Information Services
Founded: 1976. **Members:** 183. **Staff:** 70. **Budget:** $22,000,000. **Languages:** Chinese, English, French, Japanese, Korean, Russian. **Multinational. Description:** Represents meat producers, packers, purveyors, exporters, and processors; livestock breeding associations; manufacturers of meat industry equipment and supplies; others related to the industry. Seeks to develop and identify overseas markets for U.S. beef, pork, lamb, and other meats. Participates in overseas trade shows and foreign market survey trips; disseminates information; coordinates product demonstrations and menu promotions; sponsors seminars for U.S. exporters and foreign importers; compiles statistics. **Committees:** Communications; Industry Relations; International Programs; Research; Technical. **Publications:** *Directory of U.S. Meat Suppliers*, annual. Lists U.S. packers, processors, purveyors, and exporters of red meat and red meat products. **Price:** included in membership dues ● *USMEF Export Newsline*, weekly. Newsletter. Details USMEF market development activities and red meat trade news. Includes statistics. **Conventions/Meetings:** semiannual International Buyers Conference - meeting and board meeting (exhibits) - always May or June and November.

Media

2666 ■ Association for Applied Interactive Multimedia (AAIM)
PO Box 182
Charleston, SC 29402-0182
E-mail: seayj@cofc.edu
URL: http://www.aaim.org
Contact: Jared A. Seay, Exec. Dir./Acting Pres.
Founded: 1992. **Membership Dues:** regular, $40 (annual). **Multinational. Description:** Works to support professionals using and developing interactive multimedia for education and training. **Computer Services:** Online services, AAIMforum. **Committees:** Conference; Elections; Publications. **Publications:** Articles. Alternate Formats: online ● Membership Directory. **Price:** included in membership dues. **Conventions/Meetings:** workshop and conference.

2667 ■ International Webcasting Association (IWA)
4206 F Tech. Ct.
Chantilly, VA 20151
E-mail: info@webcasters.org
URL: http://www.webcasters.org
Contact: Roger Dean, Chm.
Founded: 1996. **Membership Dues:** regular, $500 (annual) ● associate - company/institution, $250 (annual) ● associate - individual, $100 (annual). **Multinational. Description:** Represents the interests of webcasters, streaming media companies, entrepreneurs, individuals and academics throughout the United States, Europe, Asia, Canada and Australia. Serves as a forum for the ideas, people and issues shaping the future of the webcasting industry.

2668 ■ Media Guilds International (MGI)
10020 Benjamin Nicholas Pl., No. 103
Las Vegas, NV 89144
Ph: (702)255-1179
Free: (888)898-4298
E-mail: info@mediaguilds.com
URL: http://www.mediaguilds.com
Contact: Betty I. Lougaris, Exec. Dir.
Founded: 1995. **Members:** 200. **Membership Dues:** premium, $700 (annual) ● renewal, $50 (annual). **Staff:** 2. **Regional Groups:** 1. **State Groups:** 1. **Languages:** English, Greek, Spanish. **Description:** Represents media professionals. Provides referrals, networking, and discounts. **Computer Services:** Mailing lists. **Conventions/Meetings:** weekly meeting.

2669 ■ National Association of Media and Technology Centers (NAMTC)
PO Box 9844
Cedar Rapids, IA 52409-9844
Ph: (319)654-0608
Fax: (319)654-0609
E-mail: bettyge@mchsi.com
URL: http://www.namtc.org
Contact: Betty D. Gorsegner Ehlinger, Exec. Dir.
Membership Dues: institutional, $100 (annual) ● retired, $20 (annual) ● individual, $80 (annual) ● corporate, $300 (annual). **Description:** Regional K-12 and higher education media centers which serve K-12 students as well as commercial media and technology companies. Committed to promoting leadership among its membership through networking, advocacy and support activities; strives to enhance equitable access to media, technology and information services to educational communities. **Publications:** Newsletter. Contains current issues, products and events related to the institutional media. Alternate Formats: online. **Conventions/Meetings:** conference.

Medical Records

2670 ■ Medical Transcription Industry Association (MTIA)
4230 Kiernan Ave., Ste.130
Modesto, CA 95356
Ph: (209)527-9620
Free: (800)543-MTIA
Fax: (209)527-9633
E-mail: mtia@mtia.com
URL: http://www.mtia.com
Contact: Jay Cannon, Pres.
Founded: 1989. **Membership Dues:** general, $325-$4,000 (annual) ● supporting, $2,000 (annual) ● vendor, $600 (annual) ● associate, $250 (annual) ● affiliate, $100 (annual). **Description:** Works as a source of useful, up-to-date information on managing a transcription business. **Formerly:** (2006) Medical

Transcription Industry Alliance. **Publications:** Newsletter. Alternate Formats: online. **Conventions/Meetings:** annual conference.

Meeting Places

2671 ■ International Association of Assembly Managers (IAAM)
635 Fritz Dr., Ste.100
Coppell, TX 75019-4442
Ph: (972)906-7441
Free: (800)935-4226
Fax: (972)906-7418
E-mail: dexter.king@iaam.org
URL: http://www.iaam.org
Contact: Dexter King CFE, Exec. Dir.
Founded: 1924. **Members:** 3,250. **Membership Dues:** active/allied-extra, $365 (annual) ● allied, $500 (annual) ● student, $55 (annual) ● faculty, $105 (annual). **Staff:** 20. **Budget:** $2,800,000. **Regional Groups:** 7. **Description:** Represents auditorium, arena, stadium, convention center, theatre, amphitheatre, and exhibit hall managers. Conducts seminars in auditorium, arena, and performing arts facility management. Maintains databank of documents pertaining to the industry. Sponsors 23 committees. **Libraries: Type:** reference. **Holdings:** 600; articles, audio recordings, books, video recordings. **Subjects:** public assembly facility management. **Awards:** Charles McElravy Award. **Frequency:** annual. **Type:** recognition. **Recipient:** to members for exceptional service. **Computer Services:** database, venue resources. **Formerly:** Auditorium Managers Association; (1996) International Association of Auditorium Managers. **Publications:** *Arena Salaries Survey - 2002*. **Price:** $40.00 for members; $65.00 for nonmembers ● *Facility Manager*, bimonthly. Magazine. Contains information for the facility management industry. Includes new product and legislative information. **Price:** free for members; $55.00 for nonmembers in North America; $110.00 for nonmembers outside North America. **Circulation:** 3,550. **Advertising:** accepted ● *IAAM News*. Newsletter. Contains association and industry news. Includes employment listings. **Price:** free for members. **Circulation:** 3,575. **Advertising:** accepted ● *International Association of Assembly Managers—Directory*, annual. Membership Directory. **Price:** free for members (initial copy); $30.00 extra copy for members; $200.00 /year for nonmembers. **Circulation:** 3,000. **Advertising:** accepted ● *International Association of Assembly Managers—Industry Profile*, periodic. Survey. **Price:** $200.00 /year for nonmembers; $50.00 /year for members ● *Performing Arts Venue Salaries/Personnel*, annual. Survey. **Price:** $40.00 for members; $65.00 for nonmembers ● *Public Assembly Facility Management: Principles*. Book. **Price:** $49.95 for members; $59.95 for nonmembers ● Also publishes reference guide to descriptions and statistics on public assembly facilities. **Conventions/Meetings:** annual International Crowd Conference Management (exhibits).

2672 ■ International Association of Conference Centers (IACC)
243 N Lindbergh Blvd.
St. Louis, MO 63141
Ph: (314)993-8575
Fax: (314)993-8919
E-mail: info@iacconline.org
URL: http://www.iacconline.org
Contact: Tom Bolman CAE, Exec. VP
Founded: 1981. **Members:** 500. **Staff:** 5. **Budget:** $1,200,000. **National Groups:** 5. **Multinational. Description:** Executive, resort, corporate, college/university, and nonresidential conference centers in 13 countries; firms providing products and services to conference centers; conference center personnel. Promotes members' interests and disseminates marketing information. Provides educational programs, speakers, and trainers within the industry; conducts public relations campaign. Maintains Internet site with searchable database of all members. **Additional Websites:** http://www.iaccnorthamerica.org. **Committees:** Continuing Education. **Publications:** *Center Lines*, quarterly. Newsletter ● *Conference Center Concept*. Brochure ● Membership Directory, annual. **Conventions/Meetings:** annual conference (exhibits).

Meeting Planners

2673 ■ Association of Collegiate Conference and Events Directors-International (ACCED-I)
Colorado State Univ.
8037 Campus Delivery
Fort Collins, CO 80523-8037
Ph: (970)491-3772 (970)491-5151
Free: (877)50-ACCED
Fax: (970)491-0667
E-mail: acced@colostate.edu
URL: http://www.acced-i.org
Contact: Deborah Blom, Exec. Dir.
Founded: 1980. **Members:** 1,500. **Membership Dues:** institution, $625 (annual) ● individual, $290 (annual) ● associate, $460 (annual) ● student, $85 (annual) ● corporate, $795 (annual). **Staff:** 3. **Budget:** $400,000. **Regional Groups:** 11. **Description:** University conference and special events directors; professionals who design, coordinate, and market conferences and special events on college and university campuses. Dedicated to the professional development of the members; promotes the growth and distinction of the profession by uniting personnel and encouraging camaraderie. Promotes high standards of business and ethical conduct; works to foster communication, cooperation, and information sharing. Conducts research programs; collaborates with sister associations. Provides leadership opportunities through committee and board participation. Acts as an information clearinghouse; compiles statistics. **Libraries: Type:** reference. **Holdings:** archival material, audio recordings, books, periodicals. **Subjects:** conference and events information. **Awards:** Jack Thornton Distinguished Service Award. **Frequency:** annual. **Type:** recognition. **Telecommunication Services:** electronic mail, deborah.blom@colostate.edu. **Publications:** *ACCEDEye*, quarterly. Newsletter. Contains examination of the trends that could affect collegiate conferences and events. **Circulation:** 1,600. Alternate Formats: online ● *e-Communique*, 5/year. Newsletters. Contains collegiate conference and events management articles, association information, and annual conference information. **Advertising:** accepted. Alternate Formats: online. **Conventions/Meetings:** annual conference (exhibits) - always spring. 2009 Mar. 22-25, Boston, MA; 2010 Mar. 21-24, Louisville, KY.

2674 ■ Association for Convention Operations Management (ACOM)
191 Clarksville Rd.
Princeton Junction, NJ 08550
Ph: (609)799-3712
Fax: (609)799-7032
E-mail: info@acomonline.org
URL: http://www.acomonline.org
Contact: Lynn McCullough, Exec. Dir.
Founded: 1988. **Members:** 550. **Membership Dues:** student, educational institution, $25 (annual) ● allied, $175 (annual) ● active, meeting professional, $225 (annual). **Staff:** 3. **Budget:** $250,000. **State Groups:** 3. **Multinational. Description:** Convention service directors and managers of hotels, convention centers, and convention bureaus; suppliers of services and products to the convention and meetings industry are affiliate members. Works to increase the effectiveness, productivity, and quality of meetings, conventions, and exhibitions. Works to establish high ethical standards, improve professional management techniques, and increase awareness of client, employer, and provider needs. Maintains speakers' bureau, resource center, and placement services; compiles statistics. Conducts research and educational programs. **Libraries: Type:** reference. **Awards:** Convention Service Manager of the Year. **Type:** recognition ● Executive Excellence Award. **Frequency:** annual. **Type:** recognition ● Meeting Professional of the Year Award. **Frequency:** annual. **Type:** recognition. **Recipient:** for exhibiting professional characteristics ● Member of the Year Award. **Frequency:** annual. **Type:** recognition. **Recipient:** for outstanding member. **Computer Services:** database ● mailing lists, of members. **Publications:** *ACOMmodate*, quarterly. Newsletter. Includes news, networking ideas and association news. Alternate Formats: online ● *Convention Proceedings*, annual ● Membership Directory, weekly. Alternate Formats: online. **Conventions/Meetings:** annual conference.

2675 ■ Association of International Meeting Planners (AIMP)
Address Unknown since 2007
Founded: 1986. **Members:** 36. **Budget:** $1,000,000. **Description:** Trade and professional associations organized for the exchange of information on meeting locations. Negotiates meetings and incentive travel. **Publications:** Newsletter, monthly. **Conventions/Meetings:** bimonthly board meeting.

2676 ■ Connected International Meeting Professionals Association (CIMPA)
9200 Bayard Pl.
Fairfax, VA 22032
Ph: (512)684-0889
Fax: (267)390-5193
E-mail: susan2@cimpa.org
URL: http://www.cimpa.org
Contact: Andrea Sigler PhD, Pres./CEO
Founded: 1984. **Members:** 8,200. **Membership Dues:** gold planner, $295 (annual) ● gold supplier, $495 (annual) ● ruby planner, $1,895 ● ruby supplier, $2,895. **Staff:** 15. **Budget:** $1,000,000. **National Groups:** 7. **For-Profit. Description:** Meeting planners, incentive organizers, travel agents, tour operators, and seminar organizers in 42 countries. Works to improve the skills of professional conference and convention planners. Serves as a clearinghouse of information on new travel destinations and planning technologies, techniques, and strategies. Facilitates exchange of information among Internet professionals. Produces a television program on travel and meetings. Conducts educational courses and awards Certified Internet Meeting Professional designation. Conducts research programs and placement service. Sponsors training courses on the Internet. **Libraries: Type:** not open to the public. **Awards:** Tech-Savvy Hotels Award. **Frequency:** annual. **Type:** recognition. **Recipient:** for hotels that have the most up to date technology. **Computer Services:** Mailing lists ● online services, register of certified international internet meeting professionals. **Projects:** Friendship Corps. **Formerly:** International Institute of Conference Management; (1998) International Institute of Convention Management. **Publications:** *Course Catalog*, quarterly. **Price:** free for members. **Advertising:** accepted. Alternate Formats: online ● *How to Comply with the American Disability Act*. Video ● *How To Plan Meetings on the Internet* ● *Job Leads*, monthly. Newsletter ● *Journal of Technology, Meetings and Incentives* ● *Marketing to Meeting Planners*. Video ● *Meeting Checklists*. Handbook ● *Organizing Meetings on the Internet* ● *Tech-Savvy Meeting Professional*, bimonthly. Newsletter. **Advertising:** accepted. **Conventions/Meetings:** annual International Technology Meetings and Incentives Conference, meeting planners and suppliers (exhibits).

2677 ■ Council of Protocol Executives (COPE)
101 W 12th St., Ste.PH-H
New York, NY 10011
Ph: (212)633-6934
Fax: (212)633-6934
E-mail: copeorg@aol.com
URL: http://www.councilofprotocolexecutives.org
Contact: Felice F. Axelrod, Pres.
Founded: 1988. **Members:** 300. **Membership Dues:** general, $200 (annual). **Description:** Persons who coordinate executive level meetings and special events for governments, corporations, and professional and nonprofit organizations; dedicated to increasing the level of professionalism in the field. Works to develop new ideas in all areas of meeting

planning and identify trends in the industry. Reviews and recommends new and existing facilities and suppliers; conducts educational programs covering topics such as invitations, sports marketing, wines, entertainment of foreign guests, and speakers and entertainers; facilitates networking among members. **Publications:** *Protocol*, annual. Directory. Contains all the resources needed to put on an upscale event for 55 cities worldwide. **Price:** $48.00 plus shipping and handling ● Newsletter, quarterly. Features interviews with and profiles of people in the industry; includes information on resources. **Price:** free. **Conventions/Meetings:** biennial conference.

2678 ■ Destination Marketing Association International (DMAI)
2025 M St. NW, Ste.500
Washington, DC 20036
Ph: (202)296-7888
Free: (888)275-3140
Fax: (202)296-7889
E-mail: info@destinationmarketing.org
URL: http://www.iacvb.org
Contact: Michael D. Gehrisch, Pres./CEO
Founded: 1914. **Members:** 1,300. **Membership Dues:** bureau (minimum; based on annual operating budget), professional staff, $250 (annual) ● bureau (maximum; based on annual operating budget), $6,200 (annual) ● state and regional CVB association, $1,000 (annual) ● educator, $100 (annual) ● student, $40 (annual). **Staff:** 22. **Budget:** $2,700,000. **Description:** Aims to promote sound professional practices in the solicitation and servicing of meetings and conventions. Enhances the professionalism through employees and maintains good image of destination in terms of marketing organization worldwide. **Telecommunication Services:** electronic mail, mgehrisch@destinationmarketing.org. **Formerly:** (2006) International Association of Convention and Visitor Bureaus. **Publications:** *IACVB News*, monthly. Newsletter. **Price:** $49.00/year. **Circulation:** 1,200. **Advertising:** accepted. **Conventions/Meetings:** annual convention (exhibits) - always July ● annual convention - always July. 2008 July 27-30, Las Vegas, NV ● annual Mid-Winter Management and Education Conference - seminar.

2679 ■ Exposition Service Contractors Association (ESCA)
2340 E Trinity Mills Rd., Ste.100
Carrollton, TX 75006
Ph: (469)574-0698
Free: (877)792-3722
Fax: (469)574-0697
E-mail: info@esca.org
URL: http://www.esca.org
Contact: Larry Arnaudet, Exec. Dir.
Founded: 1970. **Members:** 160. **Membership Dues:** general service contractor, $400-$9,000 (annual) ● specialty contractor, $300-$5,000 (annual) ● associate, $800 (annual) ● labor organization, $500 (annual) ● facility, $300 (annual) ● individual, $200 (annual). **Staff:** 5. **Budget:** $300,000. **Description:** Engages in the provision of material and/or services normally furnished for trade shows, conventions, exhibitions, and corporate meetings. Serves as a clearinghouse for the exchange of information among members and all other entities of the trade show and convention field. Seeks to promote and maintain progressive business and professional standards; advances better show techniques; improves the efficiency of material handling and on-site organization; enhances the use of manpower. **Committees:** Education; Governmental Affairs; Public Relations. **Formerly:** (2003) Exhibition Services and Contractors Association. **Publications:** *ESCA Post*, monthly. Newsletter. **Circulation:** 1,200. **Advertising:** accepted. Alternate Formats: online ● *Guide to Exposition Service*, annual. Directory. Contains rules and regulations of various exhibit facilities. **Advertising:** accepted ● *Membership Directory and Roster*, annual. **Conventions/Meetings:** annual Summer Educational Conference - meeting.

2680 ■ Foundation for International Meetings (FIM)
c/o International Meeting Network Solutions
1110 N Glebe Rd., Ste.580
Arlington, VA 22201
Ph: (703)908-0707
Fax: (703)908-0709
Contact: Michael Wilson, Contact
Founded: 1983. **Members:** 300. **Membership Dues:** professional, $475 (annual). **Staff:** 3. **Budget:** $100,000. **Description:** Chief executive officers of associations or corporations that conduct international meetings. Promotes improved professionalism in the conduct of international meetings, study missions, and conventions. Seeks to develop better liaison with international suppliers and executives of organizations actively engaged in international meetings. Conducts international inspection visits. **Awards:** Frank Martineau Industry Executive of the Year. **Frequency:** annual. **Type:** recognition. **Publications:** *The Globe*, quarterly. Newsletter. Keeps members, suppliers and colleagues on the cutting edge of developments within the international meeting industry. **Price:** included in membership dues ● *International Meetings*, quarterly. Newsletter. **Conventions/Meetings:** annual meeting (exhibits).

2681 ■ Green Meeting Industry Council (GMIC)
6220 NE Glisan
Portland, OR 97213
Ph: (503)731-8971
Fax: (503)261-0964
E-mail: amy@greenmeetings.info
URL: http://www.greenmeetings.info
Contact: Amy Spatrisano, Chair
Membership Dues: individual, $125 (annual) ● supporting business, $2,500-$10,000 (annual) ● founding, $35,000 (biennial). **Description:** Seeks to improve meeting management practices by promoting environmentally responsible strategies through the collaborative efforts of the hospitality industry, corporations, government and community organizations. Promotes green practices globally by offering educational programs in the form of training workshops and online resources. **Telecommunication Services:** electronic mail, nancy@greenmeetings.info.

2682 ■ International Association of Exhibitions and Events (IAEE)
PO Box 802425
Dallas, TX 75380
Ph: (972)458-8002
Fax: (972)458-8119
E-mail: news@iaee.com
URL: http://www.iaem.org
Contact: Steven Hacker, Pres.
Founded: 1928. **Members:** 7,500. **Membership Dues:** exhibition manager, $325 (annual) ● associate, $425 (annual) ● student, $35 (annual) ● educator, $160 (annual) ● retired, $60 (annual) ● chapter, $35 (annual) ● auxiliary, $250 (annual) ● industry outside North America, $440 (annual). **Staff:** 22. **Regional Groups:** 18. **Description:** Managers and executives of shows, exhibits, and expositions; suppliers are associate members. Sponsors seminars to educate show managers. Conducts surveys, compiles statistics, and maintains placement service. Works to promote the exhibition industry throughout the world and to provide for the education and professional growth of its members. **Libraries:** **Type:** open to the public. **Holdings:** audio recordings, books, video recordings. **Subjects:** exposition management. **Awards:** Distinguished Service Merit. **Frequency:** annual. **Type:** recognition. **Computer Services:** database, management for chapters of IAEE ● mailing lists, registration through CompuServe. **Committees:** Audit; Awards; CEM; Dues Review; Editorial Advisory; Education; Executive; Expo! Expo! Advisory; Finance. **Councils:** Asia Exhibition. **Formerly:** National Association of Exposition Managers; (2000) International Association for Exposition Management; (2007) International Association for Exhibition Management. **Publications:** *Art of the Show Textbook*, annual ● *E2: Exhibitions and Events*, monthly. Magazine. Digital e-zine with tools and best practices for the exhibition/event industry. **Circulation:** 50,000. **Advertising:** accepted. Alternate Formats: online ● *Guidelines for Display Rules and Regulations.* Handbook ● *Hotel/Client Agreement Guidelines and Information.* Brochure ● *IAEM Industry News & Report*, weekly. Newsletter. **Price:** included in membership dues. **Circulation:** 3,800. **Advertising:** accepted ● Annual Report, annual. Includes financial statement. ● Also publishes Fact Files on various exposition management topics and Pocket Card tips on how-to's for exhibitors. **Conventions/Meetings:** annual meeting - always summer ● annual meeting (exhibits).

2683 ■ International Association of Fairs and Expositions (IAFE)
PO Box 985
Springfield, MO 65801
Ph: (417)862-5771
Free: (800)516-0313
Fax: (417)862-0156
E-mail: iafe@fairsandexpos.com
URL: http://www.fairsandexpos.com
Contact: Jim Tucker, Pres./CEO
Founded: 1885. **Members:** 3,000. **Membership Dues:** associate, $195 (annual) ● fair, $100-$1,350 (annual) ● alumni association/affiliate, $50 (annual). **Staff:** 14. **Budget:** $2,000,000. **Regional Groups:** 8. **State Groups:** 52. **Languages:** English, Spanish. **Multinational. Description:** Represents state associations of fairs that comprises 3,200 states, district, and county agricultural fairs. Includes 1,300 individual fairs. **Libraries:** **Type:** reference. **Holdings:** 5,000. **Subjects:** fair management. **Awards:** Agricultural Awards. **Frequency:** annual. **Type:** recognition ● Hall of Fame Award. **Frequency:** annual. **Type:** grant ● Hall of Honor Communications Awards. **Frequency:** annual. **Type:** recognition ● Heritage Award. **Frequency:** annual. **Type:** monetary. **Computer Services:** Online services, listserv, email blast, membership and convention registration. **Committees:** Advertising-Promotions and Public Relations; Agriculture; Awards; Certification; Commercial Exhibits and Concessions; Competitive Exhibits-Non Commercial; County Fairs-Federation of Fairs; Facility Usage and Off-Season Usage; Industry Relations; International Convention; International Development; Nominating; Past Officers and Directors Program; Physical Plant-Operations; Professional Improvement; Sponsorship; Spring Conference; Web Site and Technology. **Publications:** *Fairs and Expositions* (in English and Spanish), 10/year. Magazine. Includes calendar of events. **Price:** free for members; $30.00 /year for nonmembers. ISSN: 0194-4649. **Circulation:** 3,400. **Advertising:** accepted ● *IAFE Directory*, annual. Lists all member fairs, names of services and suppliers, and state and provincial fair associations. **Price:** free for members; $125.00/copy for nonmembers. **Circulation:** 3,400. **Advertising:** accepted ● *Statistical Report*, annual. **Conventions/Meetings:** annual meeting and trade show (exhibits) - always first week after Thanksgiving in Las Vegas, NV.

2684 ■ International Association of Hispanic Meeting Professionals (IAHMP)
1120 NASA Rd. 1, Ste.405
Houston, TX 77058
Ph: (281)333-1552
Fax: (281)333-1996
E-mail: membership@iahmp.org
URL: http://www.hispanicmeetingprofessionals.com
Contact: Margaret Gonzalez, Founder/Pres.
Founded: 1995. **Membership Dues:** student, $50 (annual) ● planner, $175 (annual) ● supplier, $325 (annual) ● industry advisory council, $500 (annual). **Multinational. Description:** Seeks to develop the leadership and professional skills of Hispanic Meeting Professionals. Stimulates interest in the Hispanic culture and its potential for enhancing the meeting experience. Quantifies and publicizes the economic impact of Hispanic meetings and conventions. Furthers industry and public recognition of the unique contribution of Hispanic meeting professionals. Assists hospitality industry-related companies marketing to Hispanics. **Awards:** IAHMP Diversity Awards. **Frequency:** annual. **Type:** recognition. **Recipient:** for outstanding achievement in addressing diversity issues. **Telecommunication Services:** electronic mail, mgonzalez@iahmp.org. **Publications:** *Hoy*. Newsletter. Alternate Formats: online.

2685 ■ International Society of Meeting Planners (ISMP)
1224 N Nokomis NE
Alexandria, MN 56308-5072
Ph: (320)763-4919
Fax: (320)763-9290
E-mail: ismp@iami.org
URL: http://ismp-assoc.org
Contact: Robert G. Johnson, Exec. Dir.
Founded: 1966. **Members:** 2,486. **Membership Dues:** designated/affiliate, $195 (annual) ● corporate, $1,200 (annual). **Staff:** 14. **Regional Groups:** 8. **Description:** Meeting planners and related industries. Works to improve professionalism and competency in the industry as well as create new business opportunities for members. Provides networking opportunities. Offers professional designations: the RMP - Registered Meeting Planner, CDS - Certified Destination Specialist, ITS - Incentive Travel Specialist, and CEP - Certified Event Planner. **Libraries: Type:** reference. **Holdings:** 86; articles, books, periodicals. **Subjects:** meeting planning. **Awards:** Meeting Facility of the Year. **Frequency:** annual. **Type:** recognition. **Recipient:** for service to ISMP. **Computer Services:** Mailing lists. **Publications:** *Directory of Designated Members*, annual. Membership Directory ● *Global Connections*, quarterly. Newsletter. **Conventions/Meetings:** annual congress - always in May.

2686 ■ Meeting Professionals International (MPI)
3030 Lyndon B. Johnson Fwy., Ste.1700
Dallas, TX 75234-2759
Ph: (972)702-3000
Fax: (972)702-3070
E-mail: feedback@mpiweb.org
URL: http://www.mpiweb.org
Contact: Angie Pfeifer, Chair
Founded: 1972. **Members:** 17,000. **Membership Dues:** planner/supplier, $375 (annual) ● student, $40 (annual) ● faculty, $195 (annual). **Staff:** 74. **Budget:** $16,200,000. **Regional Groups:** 64. **Description:** Meeting planners, full meeting consultants, and suppliers of goods and services. Works to: improve meeting method education; create an "open platform" for research and experimentation. Provides survey results, statistics, supply sources, and technical information; offers members assistance with specific problems; encourages information and idea exchange. Maintains professional code; standardizes terminology; monitors legislation affecting the industry. Maintains resource center. Conducts educational, charitable, and research programs. **Libraries: Type:** reference; open to the public. **Holdings:** 2,500; articles, books, periodicals. **Subjects:** meetings industry. **Awards:** Chapters of the Year. **Frequency:** annual. **Type:** recognition. **Recipient:** to outstanding chapters ● Global Paragon Award. **Frequency:** annual. **Type:** recognition. **Recipient:** for members/nonmembers ● Industry Award. **Frequency:** annual. **Type:** recognition. **Recipient:** for distinguished service to meetings industry ● Meeting Professional Award-Marion N. Kershner Memorial Chapter Leader. **Frequency:** annual. **Type:** recognition. **Recipient:** to an outstanding chapter leader ● Meeting Professional Awards-Planner/Supplier of the Year Award. **Frequency:** annual. **Type:** recognition. **Recipient:** to an outstanding planner and supplier ● President's Award. **Frequency:** annual. **Type:** recognition. **Recipient:** for outstanding contributions to MPI. **Computer Services:** database, membership list. **Committees:** Awards; Chapter Relations; Education; Global Strategy; Government Affairs; International Development; International Development Leadership; Marketing; Nominating. **Councils:** Canadian; European. **Formerly:** (1994) Meeting Planners International. **Publications:** *The Meeting Professional*, monthly. Magazine. Provides membership and industry information and articles. **Price:** free for members; $99.00 for nonmembers in U.S.; $129.00 for nonmembers in Canada; $129.00 for nonmembers outside U.S. and Canada. ISSN: 8750-7218. **Circulation:** 12,000. **Advertising:** accepted ● *Meeting Professionals International—Membership Directory*, annual. Includes member profiles. **Price:** free for members; $155.00/copy for nonmembers. **Circulation:** 14,200. **Advertising:** accepted. **Conventions/Meetings:** annual Professional Education Conference - North America (exhibits) ● annual World Education Congress - convention (exhibits).

2687 ■ National Coalition of Black Meeting Planners (NCBMP)
8630 Fenton St., Ste.126
Silver Spring, MD 20910
Ph: (202)628-3952
Fax: (301)588-0011
E-mail: jmardis.richards@yahoo.com
URL: http://www.ncbmp.com
Contact: Janice Mardis-Richards, Pres.
Founded: 1983. **Members:** 800. **Membership Dues:** regular, $175 (annual) ● associate, $325 (annual). **Staff:** 6. **Budget:** $250,000. **Description:** Black meeting planners. Purposes are to: act as liaison with hotels, airlines, convention centers, and bureaus in an effort to assess the impact of minorities in these fields; assess the needs of the convention industry and how best to meet these needs; enhance members' sophistication in planning meetings; maximize employment of minorities in the convention industry. Maintains speakers' bureau. Conducts educational and research programs and compiles statistics on demographic employment of minorities in the convention industry. Maintains placement service. **Libraries: Type:** reference. **Holdings:** books, periodicals. **Awards: Frequency:** annual. **Type:** scholarship. **Recipient:** for students majoring in hospitality. **Formerly:** (1984) National Black Meeting Planners Coalition. **Publications:** *People On the Move*, quarterly. Newsletter. **Price:** included in membership dues. **Circulation:** 1,000. **Advertising:** accepted ● Directory, annual. Lists all members, associates and meeting planners. **Price:** included in membership dues. **Conventions/Meetings:** semiannual conference (exhibits) - always April and November.

2688 ■ National Convention Association (NCA)
1560 Broadway, 46th St.
Times Sq.
New York, NY 10036-1518
Ph: (212)555-8665
Fax: (212)555-3873
URL: http://underscore-collective.net/nca
Founded: 2004. **Description:** Serves the academic discipline of convention and conventioning. Strengthens the conventioning profession. Contributes to the greater good of the educational enterprise and society.

2689 ■ Professional Convention Management Association (PCMA)
2301 S Lake Shore Dr., Ste.1001
Chicago, IL 60616-1419
Ph: (312)423-7262
Free: (877)827-7262
Fax: (312)423-7222
E-mail: president@pcma.org
URL: http://www.pcma.org
Contact: Deborah Sexton, Pres./CEO
Founded: 1957. **Members:** 5,800. **Membership Dues:** supplier partner, $475 (annual) ● professional, $350 (annual) ● associate supplier partner, $250 (annual) ● faculty, $195 (annual) ● student, $40 (annual). **Staff:** 40. **Budget:** $10,000,000. **Regional Groups:** 16. **Multinational. Description:** Represents the interests of meeting management executives from associations, non-profit organizations, corporations, independent meeting planning companies, and multi-management firms who recognize the importance of meetings to their organization. Provides education, research and advocacy to advance the meetings and hospitality industry. Empowers members with the tools they need to succeed as meeting professionals and to promote the value of the industry to their organizations and the general public. **Libraries: Type:** reference. **Awards:** Achievement Award. **Frequency:** annual. **Type:** recognition. **Recipient:** to individuals and organizations for outstanding contribution to PCMA or to the meetings and convention industry ● Distinguished Convention Service Manager Award. **Frequency:** annual. **Type:** recognition. **Recipient:** to a convention service manager or convention coordinator ● Distinguished Member Award. **Frequency:** annual. **Type:** recognition. **Recipient:** for members who have made exemplary contributions to PCMA of chapters ● Educator of the Year Award. **Frequency:** annual. **Type:** recognition. **Recipient:** to speakers, educators and college/university faculty for great contributions to meetings and conventions industry ● Outstanding Service to a Chapter Award. **Frequency:** annual. **Type:** recognition. **Recipient:** to a member who has made an exemplary contribution to PCMA through its network of chapter ● Spirit Award. **Frequency:** annual. **Type:** recognition. **Recipient:** for an organization that significantly affected lives in a charitable/humanitarian way through the meetings and conventions industry. **Telecommunication Services:** electronic mail, administration@pcma.org. **Publications:** *Convene*, 11/year. Journal. Covers membership and industry news, meeting information, and president's message. Includes advertisers index and new member information. **Price:** free for members; $50.00 /year for nonmembers in U.S.; $75.00 /year for nonmembers outside U.S. **Circulation:** 35,000. **Advertising:** accepted ● *Professional Convention Management Association—Membership Directory*, annual. Includes classified section of suppliers to the association meetings industry. **Circulation:** 5,000. **Conventions/Meetings:** annual meeting - always in January.

2690 ■ Religious Conference Management Association (RCMA)
1 RCA Dome, Ste.120
Indianapolis, IN 46225
Ph: (317)632-1888
Fax: (317)632-7909
E-mail: rcma@rcmaweb.org
URL: http://www.rcmaweb.org
Contact: Dr. DeWayne S. Woodring CMP, CEO/Exec. Dir.
Founded: 1972. **Members:** 3,400. **Membership Dues:** individual, $50 (annual) ● associate, $100 (annual). **Staff:** 5. **Budget:** $949,000. **Multinational. Description:** Represents persons responsible for planning and/or managing religious conventions, meetings, and assemblies; associate members are individuals who directly support the logistics of religious meetings. Promotes professional excellence through exchange of ideas, techniques, and methods of management. **Awards:** Award of Excellence. **Frequency:** annual. **Type:** recognition ● President's Award. **Frequency:** annual. **Type:** recognition. **Formerly:** (1982) Religious Convention Managers Association. **Publications:** *RCMA Highlights*, periodic. Newspaper. **Advertising:** accepted ● *Religious Conference Manager*, bimonthly. Magazine. Contains news and educational articles on religious meeting planning. **Price:** included in membership dues. **Circulation:** 4,000. **Advertising:** accepted. Alternate Formats: online ● *Who's Who in Religious Conference Management*, annual. Membership Directory. **Circulation:** 3,200. **Advertising:** accepted. **Conventions/Meetings:** annual conference (exhibits) - 2009 Jan. 27-30, Grand Rapids, MI.

2691 ■ Society of Government Meeting Professionals (SGMP)
908 King St., Lower Level
Alexandria, VA 22314
Ph: (703)549-0892
Free: (800)827-8916
Fax: (703)549-0708
E-mail: carl.c.thompson@sgmp.org
URL: http://www.sgmp.org
Contact: Melody Kebe CGMP, Natl. Pres.
Founded: 1981. **Members:** 4,000. **Membership Dues:** government planner, $50 (annual) ● contract planner, $125 (annual) ● associate supplier, $225 (annual) ● supplier, $300 (annual) ● educator/student, retiree, $25 (annual). **Staff:** 9. **Budget:** $1,000,000. **Description:** Individuals involved in planning government meetings on a full- or part-time basis; suppliers of services to government planners. Provides education in basic and advanced areas of meeting planning and facilitates professional contact

with other government planners and suppliers knowledgeable in government contracting. Maintains referral network of planning resources, information on latest techniques, and opportunities to inspect conference facilities. **Awards:** Sam Gilmer Award. **Frequency:** annual. **Type:** recognition ● Sam Gilmer Partnership Award. **Frequency:** annual. **Type:** recognition. **Recipient:** for corporations, contributors. **Publications:** *Government Meeting Professional*, monthly. Newsletter. **Price:** free for members ● *Government Meetings Advantage Magazine*, quarterly. **Advertising:** accepted ● Membership Directory, annual. **Price:** free for members. **Conventions/Meetings:** annual convention (exhibits).

Metal

2692 ■ Aluminum Association (AAI)
1525 Wilson Blvd., Ste.600
Arlington, VA 22209
Ph: (703)358-2960 (703)358-2965
Fax: (703)358-2961
E-mail: slarkin@aluminum.org
URL: http://www.aluminum.org
Contact: J. Stephen Larkin, Pres.
Founded: 1933. **Members:** 200. **Membership Dues:** associate (based on sales to North American Aluminum Producers), $2,500-$10,000 (annual). **Staff:** 21. **Budget:** $7,200,000. **Description:** Producers of aluminum and manufacturers of semi-fabricated aluminum products. Represents members' interests in legislative activity. Conducts seminars and workshops. Provides publications on aluminum technology and the aluminum industry. Sponsors competition; compiles statistics. **Awards: Type:** recognition. **Divisions:** Electrical; Extruded Products; Foil; Forgings and Impacts; Master Alloy and Additives; Pigments and Powder; Primary Aluminum; Recycling; Sheet and Plate. **Publications:** *Aluminum Now*, bimonthly. Magazine. **Advertising:** accepted ● *Aluminum Situation*, monthly. Survey ● *Aluminum Standards and Data*, biennial ● *Aluminum Statistical Review*, annual. **Conventions/Meetings:** semiannual conference and meeting (exhibits) - always spring and September/October in Washington, DC.

2693 ■ Aluminum Extruders Council (AEC)
1000 N Rand Rd., Ste.214
Wauconda, IL 60084
Ph: (847)526-2010
Fax: (847)526-3993
E-mail: mail@aec.org
URL: http://www.aec.org
Contact: Rand A. Baldwin CAE, Pres.
Founded: 1950. **Members:** 152. **Staff:** 6. **Budget:** $1,000,000. **Multinational. Description:** Manufacturers of extruded aluminum shapes and their suppliers. Compiles statistics; provides technical assistance and develops markets. Conducts workshops for management, sales, and plant personnel. **Committees:** Business Information; Die; Finishing; Marketing; Technical Service. **Publications:** *Aluminum Extrusion*. Manual. Contains extensive information on the process of aluminum extrusion as well as more in-depth data about dies, alloys, and geometric tolerances. **Price:** $25.00 for members; $55.00 for nonmembers. Alternate Formats: CD-ROM ● *Buyer's Guide*. Brochure. Contains detailed AEC member information, including plant locations, press sizes, production capabilities and services offered. ● *Executive Report*, bimonthly. Bulletins. **Circulation:** 550 ● *Publications Catalog*. Brochure. **Conventions/Meetings:** annual conference - always spring ● annual Management Conference - always September.

2694 ■ American Copper Council (ACC)
2 S End Ave., No. 4C
New York, NY 10280
Ph: (212)945-4990
Fax: (212)945-4992
E-mail: mcb@americancopper.org
URL: http://www.americancopper.org
Contact: Mary C. Boland, Exec. Dir.
Founded: 1975. **Members:** 120. **Membership Dues:** producer, scrap dealer, merchant, broker, trader, warehouse, transportation service, $1,000 ● copper fabricator; distributor of copper, refinery, foundry, wire, brass, tube; cable manufacturer, service center, $500 ● consumer, consultant, service, $250. **Staff:** 2. **Budget:** $300,000. **Description:** Copper producers, fabricators, merchants, consumers, and traders. Provides a forum for the exchange of news and opinions between copper industry executives and government officials. Maintains liaison with national metal trade press and contributes news data and background information related to copper industry events. Maintains speakers' bureau available for academic, industry, and government meetings. Conducts quarterly seminar and holds biennial Copper College, a week-long program of economic reviews of the national and international copper industry by experts representing all copper industry sectors. **Awards: Type:** scholarship. **Recipient:** for metals study student at Major Eastern University. **Formerly:** (1974) Committee to Release Stockpile. **Publications:** Directory, annual ● Newsletter, quarterly. **Conventions/Meetings:** biennial meeting.

2695 ■ American Institute for International Steel (AIIS)
8201 Greensboro Dr., Ste.300
McLean, VA 22102
Ph: (703)245-8075
Fax: (703)610-9005
E-mail: phelps@aiis.org
URL: http://www.aiis.org
Contact: David H. Phelps, Pres.
Founded: 1990. **Members:** 200. **Membership Dues:** regular, steel mill, non-sales mill representative, $6,500 (annual) ● associate, $1,150 (annual). **Staff:** 3. **Budget:** $950,000. **Regional Groups:** 4. **Description:** Importers and exporters of steel produced worldwide. Represent also port authorities, ocean carriers, stevedoring firms, customs brokers, steel distributors, steel mills. Promotes free trade in steel for members. **Publications:** *Steel News*, monthly. Newsletter. Alternate Formats: online. **Conventions/Meetings:** annual conference and dinner - Monday following Thanksgiving.

2696 ■ American Iron Ore Association (AIOA)
614 Superior Ave. W, Ste.915
Cleveland, OH 44113-1383
Ph: (216)241-8261
URL: http://www.aioa.org
Contact: Frank Ongaro, Contact
Founded: 1882. **Members:** 8. **Staff:** 2. **Budget:** $90,000. **Description:** Iron ore producing companies in the U.S. and Canada. Goals are: to compile and disseminate statistics concerning the iron ore industry; to provide a forum for the discussion of industry problems. Conducts in-house statistic compilation. **Committees:** Environmental; Public Relations; Safety and Health; Statistics. **Formerly:** (1895) Western Iron Ore Association; (1957) Lake Superior Iron Ore Association. **Publications:** *Iron Ore*, annual. Features tables of iron ore statistics primarily in the United States and Canada; grade names and analyses; average analyses and tonnage. **Price:** $15.00; $17.00/year outside U.S. and Canada; free to librarians and educators ● *Iron Ore Report U.S. and Canada*, monthly. Includes single sheet of tables of receipts, consumption, and inventory of iron ore at U.S. and Canadian steel plants. **Price:** free to librarians and educators; $18.00; $20.00/year ouc ● *Shipments of U.S. and Canadian Iron Ore from Loading Docks Destined to the U.S. and Canada*, monthly. Includes single sheet of tables; statistics of iron ore vessel shipments from upper lake ports to the U.S. and Canada; also lists rail shipments. **Price:** $18.00/year; $20.00/year outside U.S. and Canada; free to librarians and educators. **Conventions/Meetings:** annual meeting.

2697 ■ American Iron and Steel Institute (AISI)
1140 Connecticut Ave. NW, Ste.705
Washington, DC 20036
Ph: (202)452-7100
Fax: (202)463-6573
E-mail: sbridgewater@steel.org
URL: http://www.steel.org
Contact: Andrew G. Sharkey III, Pres./CEO
Founded: 1908. **Members:** 157. **Membership Dues:** regular (based on annual sales volume), $1,000-$5,000 (annual) ● customer, academic institution, publisher, trade association, non-profit organization, $1,000 (annual). **Staff:** 50. **Budget:** $30,000,000. **Description:** Represents basic manufacturers in the steel industry. Operates steel mills, blast furnaces, finishing mills, and iron ore mines. Includes products such as pig iron, steel ingots, sheets, plates, bars, shapes, strips, tin plate, nails, pipe and tubes, railroad rails, wire products, and other basic forms of ferrous metals. Conducts extensive research programs on manufacturing technology, basic materials, environmental quality control, energy, and fuels consumption. Compiles statistics. **Awards:** American Iron and Steel Institute Medal Awards. **Frequency:** annual. **Type:** medal. **Recipient:** for a technical paper having special merit ● Richard S. Fountain Award. **Frequency:** annual. **Type:** recognition. **Recipient:** to a member of the AISI Steel Bridge Task Force and AASHTO Technical Committee for Structural Design. **Computer Services:** database, steel industry suppliers. **Committees:** Ironmaking; Maintenance; Manufacturing Technology; Metallic Coated Sheet Practice; Metallurgy of Tin Mill Practice; Metallurgy - Steelmaking and Casting; Packaging, Shipping and Transportation Methods; Plates. **Absorbed:** (1912) American Iron and Steel Association. **Publications:** *American Iron and Steel Institute—Annual Statistical Report*. **Price:** $250.00. Alternate Formats: CD-ROM; diskette ● *eNews*. Newsletter. Alternate Formats: online ● Membership Directory. **Price:** included in membership dues ● Annual Report, annual. Alternate Formats: online ● Papers. Alternate Formats: online. **Conventions/Meetings:** annual conference ● annual Great Designs in Steel - seminar.

2698 ■ American Tin Trade Association (ATTA)
Address Unknown since 2007
Founded: 1928. **Members:** 60. **Membership Dues:** $350 (annual). **Staff:** 1. **Budget:** $15,000. **Description:** Tin brokers, importers, and firms consuming tin in manufacturing operations. **Conventions/Meetings:** semiannual meeting - always May and November, New York City.

2699 ■ American Zinc Association (AZA)
2025 M St. NW, Ste.800
Washington, DC 20036
Ph: (202)367-1151
Fax: (202)367-2232
E-mail: zincinfo@zinc.org
URL: http://www.zinc.org
Contact: George F. Vary, Exec. Dir.
Founded: 1991. **Members:** 18. **Staff:** 1. **Budget:** $300,000. **Description:** Producers of zinc metal, oxide and dust selling in the U.S. Promotes the zinc industry; represents members' interests with government, media, and the public. **Libraries: Type:** reference. **Publications:** Videos. **Conventions/Meetings:** annual International Zinc Conference - meeting.

2700 ■ Association of Steel Distributors (ASD)
401 N Michigan Ave.
Chicago, IL 60611
Ph: (312)644-6610
Fax: (312)527-6705
E-mail: asd@smithbucklin.com
URL: http://www.steeldistributors.org
Contact: Ron Pietrzak, Exec. Dir.
Founded: 1943. **Members:** 180. **Membership Dues:** regular, associate, mill associate, allied, $1,900 (annual) ● corporate, $5,000 (annual). **Staff:** 2. **Budget:** $500,000. **Regional Groups:** 3. **Description:** Represents wholesalers of steel and steel products. Provides the steel distribution industry a forum for ideas exchange and market information. **Awards:** President's Award of Merit. **Frequency:** annual. **Type:** recognition. **Recipient:** for outstanding service ● Steel Distributor of the Year Award. **Frequency:**

annual. **Type:** recognition. **Recipient:** to individuals who have made lasting contributions to the industry over a significant period of time. **Committees:** Bylaws; Central Region Nominating; Conference; Government Relations; Long Range Planning; Nominating; Site Selection; Steelman. **Publications:** *ASD Directory*, annual. Membership Directory. **Price:** free, for members only. **Circulation:** 180 ● *News and Views*, quarterly. Newsletter. Includes statistics. **Price:** included in membership dues. **Circulation:** 200. Alternate Formats: online. **Conventions/Meetings:** annual convention and meeting ● semiannual seminar.

2701 ■ Brass and Bronze Ingot Industry (BBII)
Address Unknown since 2007
Founded: 2001. **Members:** 12. **Description:** Manufacturers of brass and bronze ingots. **Committees:** Technical. **Formed by Merger of:** (1989) Association of Brass and Bronze Ingot Manufacturers; Brass and Bronze Ingot Institute. **Formerly:** (2002) Brass and Bronze Ingot Manufacturers. **Conventions/Meetings:** meeting - 4/year.

2702 ■ Cemented Carbide Producers Association (CCPA)
30200 Detroit Rd.
Cleveland, OH 44145-1967
Ph: (440)899-0010
Fax: (440)892-1404
E-mail: leh@wherryassoc.com
URL: http://www.ccpa.org
Contact: Linda Hamill, Contact
Founded: 1954. **Members:** 23. **Staff:** 7. **Description:** Represents manufacturers of sintered carbide containing tungsten. **Committees:** Accredited Standards ANSI/ASC B212. **Conventions/Meetings:** annual meeting.

2703 ■ Cold Finished Steel Bar Institute (CFSBI)
c/o Kevin Van de Ven, Chm.
LMP Steel Wire and Co.
20000 E First St.
Maryville, MO 64468
Ph: (660)582-3127
Fax: (660)582-7730
E-mail: kvandeven@lmpsteel.com
URL: http://www.cfsbi.com
Contact: Kevin Van de Ven, Chm.
Founded: 1971. **Members:** 22. **Staff:** 1. **Description:** Represents producers of cold finished steel bar products in North America. Promotes growth and development of the industry and fosters awareness of matters affecting the industry. Compiles statistics and is active in governmental affairs. **Awards:** Man of Steel. **Frequency:** annual. **Type:** recognition. **Committees:** Education; Government Affairs; Industrial Relations; Industry Technical; Meeting and Seminars; Product Promotion and Member Education; Public Relations. **Publications:** *Extensive Manual on Product Quality* ● *Monthly Import Analysis*. Contains import analysis of cold finished steel bars from various countries. **Price:** available to members only ● Books ● Audiotapes ● Videos. **Conventions/Meetings:** semiannual meeting - always June and December, Washington, DC.

2704 ■ Copper and Brass Fabricators Council (CBFC)
1050 17th St. NW, Ste.440
Washington, DC 20036
Ph: (202)833-8575
Fax: (202)331-8267
E-mail: copbrass@aol.com
Contact: Joseph L. Mayer, Pres.
Founded: 1966. **Members:** 20. **Staff:** 4. **Budget:** $600,000. **Description:** Copper and brass fabricators. Activities involve foreign trade in copper and brass fabricated products, and federal regulatory matters including legislation, regulations, rules, controls, stockpiling, and other similar measures affecting domestic fabricators of copper and brass products. **Formerly:** (1966) Copper and Brass Fabricators Foreign Trade Association.

2705 ■ Copper and Brass Servicenter Association (CBSA)
994 Old Eagle School Rd., Ste.1019
Wayne, PA 19087-1802
Ph: (610)971-4850
Fax: (610)971-4859
E-mail: diana@cbsa.copper-brass.org
URL: http://www.cbsa.copper-brass.org
Contact: Denis Brady, Pres.
Founded: 1950. **Members:** 73. **Staff:** 2. **Description:** Represents wholesalers of copper and brass sheet, tubing, pipe, and related products; supplier members are copper mills, metal strip platters and re-rollers. Compiles statistics. **Awards: Frequency:** annual. **Type:** scholarship. **Recipient:** for college student children of employees of member companies. **Committees:** Education; Government Regulations; Members' Operations; Public Relations and Marketing; Supplier Relations; Website Oversight. **Publications:** *CBSA Capsules*, monthly. Newsletter. Includes reports on legislative and governmental actions and covers member and association activities. **Price:** free for members; $35.00 for nonmembers. **Circulation:** 200 ● *Copper and Brass Servicenter Association—Membership Directory*, annual. **Price:** $35.00 ● *Guide for Marketing—Copper, Brass, Bronze*. Book. **Price:** $35.00 ● *Guide to Brass Mills, Metal Strip Platters and Industry Associations*, quinquennial. Handbook. **Price:** $20.00 ● *Shipment Report*, monthly. **Price:** $50.00/year ● *Sources Handbook*, quadrennial. Lists products stocked and metals process capabilities of copper and brass servicenters. **Price:** $30.00. **Circulation:** 500. **Conventions/Meetings:** annual convention - March or April.

2706 ■ Custom Roll Forming Institute (CRFI)
6363 Oak Tree Blvd.
Independence, OH 44131-2500
Ph: (216)901-8800
Fax: (216)901-9190
E-mail: pma@pma.org
URL: http://www.pma.org/division
Contact: Bob Stephenson, Division Dir.
Founded: 1972. **Members:** 30. **Staff:** 2. **Description:** Represents Manufacturing companies that produce nonproprietary, or custom roll formed sections. Works to: make available to users information common to fabricators of roll formed sections; advance and encourage engineering knowledge and practices; exchange ideas of precise and economical methods of production; keep abreast of consumer requirements and engineering practices; expand proven uses for roll formed sections and stimulate acceptance of new applications. **Publications:** *Know Your Custom Roll Former*.

2707 ■ Foil Stamping and Embossing Association (FSEA)
2150 SW Westport Dr., Ste.101
Topeka, KS 66614
Ph: (785)271-5816
Fax: (785)271-6404
E-mail: jeff@fsea.com
URL: http://www.fsea.com
Contact: Jeff Peterson, Exec. Dir.
Founded: 1992. **Members:** 350. **Membership Dues:** active, $175-$500 (annual) ● associate, $250-$750 (annual). **Staff:** 3. **Budget:** $500,000. **Description:** Foil stampers, embossers, die cutters and industry suppliers working together for the advancement of the industry. **Awards:** Gold Leaf Award. **Frequency:** annual. **Type:** recognition. **Telecommunication Services:** electronic mail, gayla@petersonpublications.com. **Committees:** Nominating. **Programs:** Employee Recognition. **Publications:** *A Different Breed: The Designers Guide to Foil Stamping and Embossing*. Book. **Price:** $15.00 for members; $20.00 for nonmembers ● *FSEA Operations and Wage Survey*. **Price:** $60.00 for members; $250.00 for nonmembers ● *Inside Finishing*, quarterly. Magazine. **Price:** free for members; $44.00 for nonmembers in Canada, plus shipping and handling; $50.00 for nonmembers foreign. **Circulation:** 6,000. **Advertising:** accepted ● Membership Directory. **Price:** $5.00 in U.S.; $10.00 in Canada, Mexico; $15.00 international. **Conventions/Meetings:** annual convention (exhibits).

2708 ■ Forging Industry Association (FIA)
Landmark Off. Towers
25 Prospect Ave. W, Ste.300
Cleveland, OH 44115
Ph: (216)781-6260
Fax: (216)781-0102
E-mail: info@forging.org
URL: http://www.forging.org
Contact: Charles H. Hageman, Exec. VP
Founded: 1913. **Members:** 210. **Staff:** 11. **Budget:** $1,100,000. **Description:** North American manufacturers of forgings and worldwide suppliers of raw materials, equipment, or major technical services used by the forging industry. Industry specific services include: statistics, technical information, education and training, common voice on legislation and regulation. **Awards:** Human Resource Award. **Frequency:** annual. **Type:** recognition ● Safety Award. **Frequency:** annual. **Type:** recognition. **Divisions:** Government Affairs; Marketing; Open Die and Rolled Ring; Plant Engineering; Safety and Health; Technical. **Formerly:** Drop Forging Association. **Publications:** *Forging Capability Guide*, periodic. Assists purchasing agents in locating suppliers of forgings. Summarizes abilities of seamless rolled ring, open, impression die and cold forgers. **Price:** free to buyers in Mexico, Canada, and U.S. **Circulation:** 10,000 ● *Forging Handbook*. **Price:** $60.00 for nonmembers; $42.50 for members ● *Open Die Forging Technology*. **Price:** $49.00 for nonmembers; $35.00 for members. **Conventions/Meetings:** triennial Forge Fair Trade Show, with equipment and products used by forging producers (exhibits) ● annual meeting, for members - always May ● annual meeting - every fall.

2709 ■ Industrial Perforators Association (IPA)
5157 Deerhurst Crescent Cir.
Boca Raton, FL 33486
Ph: (561)447-7511
Fax: (561)447-7511
E-mail: info@iperf.org
URL: http://www.iperf.org
Contact: Delores M. Morris, Exec. Sec.
Founded: 1961. **Members:** 15. **Budget:** $75,000. **Description:** Manufacturers of perforated products. Promotes increased use of perforated metal; establishes industry standards; develops new and improved products and methods; provides technical services. **Additional Websites:** http://www.perforatingdesigns.com. **Telecommunication Services:** electronic mail, info@perforatingdesigns.com. **Publications:** *Acoustical Uses for Perforated Metals*. Handbook. Contains information on acoustical uses for perforated metals. Alternate Formats: online; CD-ROM ● *Challenge Your Imagination*. Video ● *Designers, Specifiers, and Buyers Handbook for Perforated Metals* (in English and Spanish). Contains information on perforated metals. Alternate Formats: online; CD-ROM ● *Formability II Handbook*. Alternate Formats: online; CD-ROM ● *Riverbank Studies*. Handbook. Alternate Formats: online; CD-ROM ● Brochure.

2710 ■ International Hard Anodizing Association (IHAA)
PO Box 579
Moorestown, NJ 08057-0579
Ph: (856)234-0330
Fax: (856)727-9504
E-mail: denise.downing@comcast.net
URL: http://www.ihanodizing.com
Contact: Denise Downing, Sec./Exec. Dir.
Founded: 1988. **Members:** 40. **Membership Dues:** regular, $400 (annual) ● associate, $500 (annual). **Staff:** 5. **Budget:** $15,000. **Description:** Represents companies engaged in the production of hard anodized finishes on aluminum components and the suppliers to those companies to promote their common interests, advance the process of hard anodizing and to develop technical and general information about hard anodizing. **Publications:** Newsletter, quarterly. **Conventions/Meetings:** biennial Technical Symposium - conference and symposium - always even numbered years.

2711 ■ International Magnesium Association (IMA)
1000 N Rand Rd., Ste.214
Wauconda, IL 60084
Ph: (847)526-2010
Fax: (847)526-3993
E-mail: info@intlmag.org
URL: http://www.intlmag.org
Contact: Greg Patzer, Exec. VP

Founded: 1943. **Members:** 124. **Membership Dues:** producer, distributor, trader (minimum), $2,000 (annual) ● user, diecaster, recycler, casting user, $2,000-$3,950 (annual) ● associate, $1,950 (annual) ● producer, distributor, trader (maximum), $15,000 (annual) ● university, $500 (annual) ● student, $25 (annual). **Staff:** 3. **Budget:** $560,000. **Multinational. Description:** Represents manufacturers, processors, users, suppliers, and recyclers of magnesium. Works to promote the magnesium industry; develops and increases the use of magnesium and its alloys; publicizes and promotes new uses of the metal to end-use markets. Conducts research programs, compiles statistics and offers educational programs. **Awards:** IMA Awards of Excellence. **Frequency:** annual. **Type:** recognition. **Recipient:** for design, process and application. **Telecommunication Services:** electronic mail, gpatzer@tso.net. **Boards:** Directors. **Committees:** Auto; Awards; Communications; Die Casting; European; Executive; Health and Safety; Technical. **Formerly:** (1973) Magnesium Association. **Publications:** *Desulfurization of Hot Metal by Magnesium*. Book. Contains work in the field of iron desulfurization through magnesium powder infusion. **Price:** $30.00 for members; $60.00 for nonmembers ● *Electrolytic Production of Magnesium*. Book. Talks about electrolytic production of magnesium. **Price:** $50.00 for members; $100.00 for nonmembers ● *Magnesium Buyer's Guide*. Directory. Lists member firms. Designed to assist organizations that use or wish to use magnesium. Includes product/service and geographic indexes. **Advertising:** accepted. Alternate Formats: online ● *Magnesium: Safe Handling for Manufacturing, Storage and Use* (in English, French, German, and Italian). Video. Reviews proper procedures for handling magnesium on a daily basis and in emergency situations. **Price:** $60.00 ● *Weekly Update*. Newsletter. Includes membership news and magnesium events worldwide. **Price:** free, for members only. **Circulation:** 400. **Advertising:** accepted. Alternate Formats: online ● *World Magnesium Statistics*, quarterly. Compilation of primary shipment, production, and year-end inventory numbers from 1983 to date; more current stats include imports from CIS and PRC. **Conventions/Meetings:** annual Automotive Educational Seminar, die cast automotive parts (exhibits) ● biennial workshop ● annual World Magnesium Conference.

2712 ■ International Titanium Association (ITA)
2655 W Midway Blvd., Ste.300
Broomfield, CO 80020-7187
Ph: (303)404-2221
Fax: (303)404-9111
E-mail: ita@titanium.org
URL: http://www.titanium.org
Contact: Jennifer Simpson, Exec. Dir.

Founded: 1986. **Members:** 2,500. **Membership Dues:** supplier, $4,500 (annual) ● non-profit, $1,000 (annual) ● vendor, consultant, $800 (annual) ● university, $500 (annual). **Staff:** 2. **Multinational. Description:** Represents producers, fabricators, extruders, and users of titanium (a metallic element used especially in alloys); companies performing some value-added function to titanium. Works to expand existing market, increase awareness and understanding of titanium in engineering and academic communities, and maintain an appropriate and meaningful statistics program. Maintains speakers' bureau; answers technical questions; provides application committees; sponsors educational programs. **Libraries: Type:** reference. **Holdings:** 30; archival material, articles, artwork, books, clippings, periodicals. **Subjects:** titanium metal. **Awards:** Titanium Achievement Award. **Frequency:** annual. **Type:** recognition. **Computer Services:** database ● online services. **Committees:** Aerospace; Applications; Chemical Processing; Conference and Trade Shows; Consumer/Sporting Goods; Education; Marine; Marine Applications; Medical; Medical Applications; Membership; Safety; Specifications; Sporting/Consumer Products; Statistics; VAR Melt Safety. **Formerly:** (1995) Titanium Development Association. **Publications:** *Buyer's Guide*, annual. Describes the member company's activities and listing of the major offices, technical representatives, sales and marketing personnel. ● *Conference Proceedings*, annual. Contains papers presented at annual conference. **Price:** $150.00. Alternate Formats: CD-ROM ● *Products and Services Guide of Member Companies*, annual. Directory. **Price:** free ● *Ti, The Choice*, annual. Contains basic primer in Ti. **Price:** $10.00. **Circulation:** 10,000 ● *Titanium Facts*. Booklet. **Price:** $1.00 for members; $4.00 for nonmembers. Alternate Formats: online ● *Titanium Statistical Review*, annual. Reports statistics internationally. **Price:** $75.00 for nonmembers ● *Titanium Update Newsletter*, monthly. Contains updated information on the titanium industry. **Price:** free. **Circulation:** 4,000. **Advertising:** accepted. Alternate Formats: online ● Brochure. Alternate Formats: online ● Books ● Handbooks. **Conventions/Meetings:** annual Titanium - international conference (exhibits) - 2008 Sept. 21-23, Las Vegas, NV.

2713 ■ Metal Injection Molding Association (MIMA)
c/o Metal Powder Industries Federation
105 Coll. Rd. E
Princeton, NJ 08540-6692
Ph: (609)452-7700
Fax: (609)987-8523
E-mail: info@mpif.org
URL: http://www.mpif.org
Contact: Matthew Bulger, Pres.

Staff: 15. **Description:** Represents the metal injection-molding business, including injection molded products utilizing metal or other particulate materials, including ceramics, as the basic starting constituent. Strives to improve and promote the product of the metal injection molding industry; collects and disseminates quarterly statistics, including MIM shipments (pieces, parts, and pounds) to various market sectors, tracks marketing trends; develops materials standards and test methods for industry products; provides customer leads to members; offers educational short courses. **Boards:** Industry Development; Technical. **Publications:** *Buyers Guide*, annual. **Conventions/Meetings:** conference ● annual Part-of-the-Year Design Competition, for members and their customers ● seminar ● symposium.

2714 ■ Metal Powder Industries Federation (MPIF)
105 Coll. Rd. E
Princeton, NJ 08540-6692
Ph: (609)452-7700
Fax: (609)987-8523
E-mail: info@mpif.org
URL: http://www.mpif.org
Contact: C. James Trombino CAE, Exec. Dir./CEO

Founded: 1944. **Members:** 260. **Staff:** 14. **Budget:** $3,600,000. **Multinational. Description:** Manufacturers of metal powders, powder metallurgy processing equipment and tools, powder metallurgy products, and refractory and reactive metals. Member associations are: Metal Injection Molding Association; Metal Powder Producers Association; Advanced Particulate Materials Association; Powder Metallurgy Equipment Association; Powder Metallurgy Parts Association; Refractory Metals Association. Promotes the science and industry of powder metallurgy and metal powder application through: sponsorship of technical meetings, seminars, and exhibits; establishment of standards; compilation of statistics; public relations; publications. Maintains speakers' bureau and placement service; conducts research. **Libraries: Type:** reference. **Holdings:** 1,500. **Subjects:** powder metallurgy technology and particulate materials. **Awards:** Pioneer Award. **Frequency:** quadrennial. **Type:** recognition. **Recipient:** for distinguished service to powder metallurgy. **Boards:** Industry Development; Standards Development; Technical. **Affiliated With:** APMI International. **Formerly:** (1957) Metal Powder Association. **Publications:** *Advances in Powder Metallurgy and Particulate Materials*, annual. Proceedings. Contains proceedings of MPIF annual conferences. Alternate Formats: CD-ROM ● *Powder Metallurgy in Defense Technology*, periodic. Proceedings. Contains proceedings of seminars on applications of powder metallurgy in military defense. ISSN: 0149-3922 ● Monographs ● Authored books on Powder Metallurgy Industry Standards. **Conventions/Meetings:** annual International Conference of Powder Metallurgy and Particulate Materials (exhibits) ● World Congress on Powder Metallurgy and Particulate Materials - conference (exhibits) - every six years.

2715 ■ Metal Powder Producers Association (MPPA)
c/o Metal Powder Industries Federation
105 Coll. Rd. E
Princeton, NJ 08540-6692
Ph: (609)452-7700
Fax: (609)987-8523
E-mail: info@mpif.org
URL: http://www.mpif.org/AboutMPIF/mppa.asp?linkid=31
Contact: Michael E. Lutheran, Pres.

Staff: 23. **Description:** Corporations (and any divisions thereof), and firms commercially engaged for more than a year in the production and sale of metal powders, metal flakes, metal fibers or non-metallic powder additives used with these materials, such as graphite or lubricants. Strives to improve and promote the products of the industry; promotes research and investigation, and information exchange; dedicated to education in the science, practice and application of metal powders; disseminates information to the industry. Provides the MPPA Statistics Program; supports P/M Parts Marketing Program and active standards development program. **Computer Services:** Online services, directory. **Publications:** *Metal Powder Directory*, annual. Features answers to inquiries about leading powder suppliers. ● *Suppliers Directory*. Contains lists of 154 companies and organizations that produce ferrous and non ferrous metal powders. ● Proceedings. **Conventions/Meetings:** annual conference and seminar.

2716 ■ Metal Roofing Alliance (MRA)
E 4142 Hwy. 302
Belfair, WA 98528
Ph: (360)275-6164
E-mail: info@metalroofing.com
URL: http://www.metalroofing.com
Contact: Tom Black, Exec. Dir.

Founded: 1998. **Description:** Represents manufacturers, paint suppliers and coaters, dealers, associations and roofing contractors in the metal roofing industry. **Computer Services:** Mailing lists. **Publications:** *Metal Roofing eNewsletter*, periodic.

2717 ■ Metal Treating Institute (MTI)
1550 Roberts Dr.
Jacksonville Beach, FL 32250-3222
Ph: (904)249-0448
Fax: (904)249-0459
E-mail: info@metaltreat.com
URL: http://www.metaltreat.com
Contact: M. Lance Miller CAE, CEO

Founded: 1933. **Members:** 475. **Membership Dues:** regular, international (depends on sales range), $1,200-$42,000 (annual) ● supplier, education, technology, $3,000 (annual) ● captive, $243 (quarterly). **Staff:** 3. **Budget:** $750,000. **Regional Groups:** 7. **Multinational. Description:** Firms engaged in commercial and in-house heat-treating of metals, tools, and other metal products and suppliers thereto; members are represented by an officer, partner, or other top management person. Facilitates exchange of information among members; represents members before government agencies and in national affairs affecting the industry. Activities include: technical and financial research, statistics, studies and surveys, labor relations, cost accounting, and public and customer relations. Provides extensive training programs online via MTI Academy. **Additional Websites:** http://www.heattreatonline.com. **Telecommunication Services:** electronic mail, lance@heattreatonline.com. **Conventions/Meetings:** semiannual Furnaces North America - convention (exhibits) - always spring and fall.

2718 ■ Metals Service Center Institute (MSCI)
4201 Euclid Ave.
Rolling Meadows, IL 60008-2025
Ph: (847)485-3000 (847)485-3002
Fax: (847)485-3001
E-mail: info@msci.org
URL: http://www.msci.org
Contact: M. Robert Weidner III, Pres./CEO
Founded: 1909. **Members:** 350. **Staff:** 12. **Budget:** $5,000,000. **Local Groups:** 28. **Description:** Wholesalers of industrial steel products; associate members include companies manufacturing these products. Seeks to improve distribution and management performance standards of member companies through research, statistical, promotional, and public relations activities. **Committees:** Chapter Leadership Development; Nominating. **Divisions:** Bar Products; Canadian; Flat Rolled Products; Plates and Shapes; Specialty Metals; Tubular Products. **Subcommittees:** Benchmarking; Education; Market Information; Supply Chain. **Absorbed:** (2003) National Association of Purchasing Management. **Formerly:** (2002) Steel Service Center Institute. **Publications:** *Center Lines*, monthly ● *Forward*, bimonthly. Magazine. **Price:** $1.00 for nonmembers; free for members. **Advertising:** accepted ● *Roster of Members*, semiannual. Directory. **Conventions/Meetings:** annual convention.

2719 ■ National Association of Architectural Metal Manufacturers (NAAMM)
800 Roosevelt Rd., Bldg. C, Ste.312
Glen Ellyn, IL 60137
Ph: (630)942-6591
Fax: (630)790-3095
URL: http://www.naamm.org
Contact: C. John Wiley, Pres.
Founded: 1938. **Members:** 105. **Membership Dues:** associate (based on sales volume), $1,145-$3,430 (annual). **Staff:** 3. **Budget:** $250,000. **Description:** Manufacturers of metal products for building construction; stairs, railings, flagpoles, doors/frames, steel/aluminum bar grating, metal lath and furring, modular steel cells and related facilities. **Divisions:** Architectural Metal Products; Expanded Metal Manufacturers Association; Flagpole; Hollow Metal Manufacturers Association; Metal Bar Grating; Metal Lath/Steel Framing; Modular Steel Cell. **Absorbed:** (1962) National Steel Door and Frame Association. **Formerly:** National Association of Ornamental Metal Manufacturers. **Publications:** *Metal Stairs Manual*. **Price:** $35.00 ● *Pipe Railing Manual*. Covers finishes, grating, hollow metal doors, metal stairs, metal flagpoles, railings, lightweight steel framing, and metal lathing and furring. **Price:** $22.00. **Conventions/Meetings:** semiannual meeting - every spring and fall.

2720 ■ National Association of Graphic and Product Identification Manufacturers (GPI)
1300 Sumner Ave.
Cleveland, OH 44115-2851
Ph: (216)241-7333
Fax: (216)241-0105
E-mail: gpi@gpionline.org
URL: http://www.gpionline.org
Contact: David Clarkson, Pres.
Founded: 1951. **Members:** 80. **Membership Dues:** associate, $828 (biennial) ● corporate (maximum), $971 (annual) ● corporate (minimum), $510 (annual). **Staff:** 5. **Budget:** $185,000. **Description:** Manufacturers of name plates, labels, and decorative metal and plastic parts. **Formerly:** American Metal Etching Manufacturers Trade Association; National Association of Nameplate Manufacturers; (1969) Metal Etching and Fabricating Association; (1979) National Association of Metal Name Plate Manufacturers. **Publications:** *Name Newsletter*, 3/year. **Price:** included in membership dues. **Circulation:** 200. **Advertising:** accepted. Alternate Formats: online ● *Name Plate Industry Standards and Practices*, annual. Book. **Price:** included in membership dues. **Advertising:** accepted. Alternate Formats: online ● Membership Directory, annual. **Price:** free for members. **Advertising:** accepted. Alternate Formats: online. **Conventions/Meetings:** semiannual conference (exhibits) - always March/April and September/October.

2721 ■ National Institute of Steel Detailing (NISD)
7700 Edgewater Dr., Ste.670
Oakland, CA 94621-3022
Ph: (510)568-3741
Fax: (510)568-3781
E-mail: nisd@sbcglobal.net
URL: http://www.nisd.org
Contact: Robert Beauchamp, Pres.
Founded: 1969. **Members:** 375. **Membership Dues:** regular (based on annual gross income), $290-$450 (annual) ● associate/overseas, $360 (annual) ● individual associate, $65 (annual) ● emeritus, $100 (annual). **Staff:** 1. **Budget:** $160,000. **Regional Groups:** 15. **Multinational**. **Description:** Enhances structural steel detailing. Promotes and serves the interest of the steel detailing industry. **Awards:** Man of the Year Award. **Frequency:** annual. **Type:** recognition. **Recipient:** to a person who has volunteered his or her time in a special way, often on a committee working on special projects. **Committees:** The Connections; Constitution and By-Laws; Education; Erector Liaison; Individual Detailer Certification; Industry Standards; Liaison; Marketing; Membership; NASCC Planning; Nominating; Publications; Quality Procedures Program; Web Site. **Publications:** *The Connection*, quarterly. Newsletter. Covers membership activities. **Price:** free, for members only. ISSN: 1076-5522. **Circulation:** 500. **Advertising:** accepted. Alternate Formats: online ● *National Institute of Steel Detailing—Membership Directory*, annual. **Price:** $10.00 for members; $20.00 for nonmembers ● *NISD Industry Standard Manual*. **Price:** $20.00 for members; $35.00 for nonmembers ● Reports ● Videos. **Conventions/Meetings:** annual conference (exhibits) ● seminar.

2722 ■ National Ornamental and Miscellaneous Metals Association (NOMMA)
1535 Pennsylvania Ave.
McDonough, GA 30253
Ph: (770)288-2004
Free: (888)516-8585
Fax: (770)288-2006
E-mail: nommainfo@nomma.org
URL: http://www.nomma.org
Contact: Barbara H. Cook, Exec. Dir.
Founded: 1958. **Members:** 1,000. **Membership Dues:** fabricator, $415 (annual) ● nationwide supplier, $585 (annual) ● regional supplier, $455 (annual) ● local supplier, $365 (annual) ● affiliate (teacher, school, non-profit organization), $300 (annual). **Staff:** 6. **Budget:** $1,000,000. **Local Groups:** 4. **Description:** Represents fabricators of ornamental and miscellaneous metal products; firms supplying equipment, products, and services to fabricators on a local, regional, or national basis. Purposes are to promote greater recognition, use, and sales of ornamental and miscellaneous metal fabricators; to educate craftsmen, designers, and managers through support of and participation in educational and training programs; to encourage quality production by suggesting voluntary guidelines for fabrication to meet building codes and other regulations; to foster friendly relations among members of the industry and to keep them informed. Conducts seminars. Sponsors insurance programs; organizes competitions. **Awards:** Ernest Wiemann Top Job Award. **Frequency:** annual. **Type:** recognition. **Recipient:** for superior job fabrication. **Computer Services:** Online services, technical support. **Committees:** Education; Insurance. **Divisions:** Technical Affairs. **Formerly:** (1962) National Ornamental Iron Manufacturers Association; (1977) National Ornamental Metal Manufacturers Association. **Publications:** *Fabricator's Journal*, bimonthly. Bulletin. **Price:** included in membership dues. **Circulation:** 1,000 ● *Ornamental and Miscellaneous Metal Fabricator*, bimonthly. Magazine. **Price:** $30.00/year in U.S., Canada and Mexico; $44.00/year all other countries. **Circulation:** 10,000. **Advertising:** accepted ● *TechNotes*, bimonthly. Newsletter. **Price:** free, for members only. **Circulation:** 1,000 ● Videos ● Brochure. **Conventions/Meetings:** annual METALfab - convention and trade show (exhibits).

2723 ■ Non-Ferrous Metals Producers Committee (NFMPC)
2030 M St. NW, Ste.800
Washington, DC 20036
Ph: (202)466-7720
Fax: (202)466-2710
URL: http://www.arcat.com/arcatcos/cos37/arc37679.cfm
Contact: Kenneth R. Button, VP
Founded: 1975. **Description:** Represents domestic copper, lead, and zinc producers. Promotes the interests of copper, lead, and zinc mining and metal industries in the U.S. with emphasis on tariffs, laws, regulations, and government policies affecting international trade and foreign imports. **Formerly:** (1987) Lead-Zinc Producers Committee. **Supersedes:** Emergency Lead-Zinc Producers Committee; Lead-Zinc Producers.

2724 ■ North American Steel Alliance (NASA)
2266 N State College Blvd.
Fullerton, CA 92831
Ph: (714)256-8707
Fax: (714)256-8716
URL: http://www.steelalliance.com
Contact: Tom Harrington, Chm.
Founded: 1996. **Members:** 90. **Description:** Provides the platform to link the highest quality independent member-owners with superior suppliers. Creates a participatory environment that promotes the transaction of business that is professional, ethical and accountable. Creates and shares increased profitability and opportunities for members. **Computer Services:** Online services, message board.

2725 ■ Photo-Chemical Machining Institute (PCMI)
PO Box 739
38 Strawberry Ln.
East Dennis, MA 02641-0739
Ph: (508)385-0085
Fax: (508)385-0086
E-mail: info@pcmi.org
URL: http://www.pcmi.org
Contact: Ms. Betty Berndt-Brown, Exec. Dir.
Founded: 1967. **Members:** 520. **Membership Dues:** regular, allied, associate, $750 (annual) ● associate (artwork only), $500 (annual) ● senior, $65 (annual). **Staff:** 2. **Budget:** $95,000. **Regional Groups:** 3. **Multinational**. **Description:** Represents Companies connected with industries producing metal parts by photochemical machining, such as photo etching. Maintains speakers' bureau; conducts research. **Libraries: Type:** reference. **Holdings:** articles, papers, periodicals, reports. **Awards:** PCMI Grant. **Frequency:** annual. **Type:** grant. **Computer Services:** Mailing lists, of members. **Telecommunication Services:** electronic mail, photomach@aol.com. **Committees:** Education; Environmental Effects; Industry Trends; Phototooling; Promotion and Publications; Quality Assurance; Raw Materials and Process Effects; Seminars and Meetings. **Publications:** *DXF Etch Data Test Pattern*. **Price:** $10.00 each. Alternate Formats: diskette ● *Master Listing of PCMI Journal Articles July 1980-Current*, annual. **Price:** $2.00 each ● *PCMI Journal: Member's Only Edition*, quarterly. Offers technical papers and marketing updates to the photo chemical market. **Price:** $5.00 ● *Photo Chemical Machining. Metal Parts Without Stamping Dies*, quarterly. Journal. Contains original research, reports on committee findings, meeting summaries, and pertinent reprints from other trade magazines. **Price:** $5.00 each - back issues for members; $10.00 each - back issues for nonmembers. **Circulation:** 600. **Advertising:** accepted ● *Photo Chemical Machining Institute—Journal*, quar-

terly. Contains original research, reports on committee findings, meeting summaries, and pertinent reprints from other trade magazines. **Price:** $50.00 for nonmembers. **Circulation:** 600. **Advertising:** accepted ● *Photo Chemical Machining Institute—Membership Directory*, annual. Articles. Lists members with descriptions of products, services, or job shop involvement with industry; includes midyear update. **Price:** $5.00 for nonmembers; free for members ● *Photo Resist in Photo Chemical Machining Applications.* Book. Provides valuable and useful data pertinent to the problems encountered in the application of photo chemical machinery principles. **Price:** $10.00 ● *Phototool Design Guide.* Book. **Price:** $5.00 ● *Spray Etching of Stainless Steel.* Journal. Describes the fundamental research work on the photochemical manufacture of stainless steel parts. **Price:** $25.00 ● *Terms & Definitions in Photo Chemical Machining.* Book. **Price:** $5.00 each. **Conventions/Meetings:** semiannual conference - usually April and September.

2726 ■ Precision Metalforming Association (PMA)

6363 Oak Tree Blvd.
Independence, OH 44131-2556
Ph: (216)901-8800
Fax: (216)901-9190
E-mail: pma@pma.org
URL: http://www.metalforming.com
Contact: William E. Gaskin CAE, Pres./Sec.

Founded: 1942. **Members:** 1,200. **Membership Dues:** contract manufacturer in U.S., $950-$5,675 (annual) ● end product manufacturer in U.S., $750-$2,800 (annual) ● associate supplier in U.S., $625-$2,300 (annual) ● contract manufacturer in Canada, $620-$3,036 (annual) ● end product manufacturer in Canada, $520-$1,932 (annual) ● associate supplier in Canada, $416-$1,518 (annual) ● manufacturer in Mexico, $450-$1,575 (annual) ● associate supplier in Mexico, $375-$1,200 (annual) ● international, $175 (annual). **Staff:** 40. **Budget:** $10,000,000. **Regional Groups:** 20. **Multinational. Description:** Represents the metalforming industry of North America; the industry that creates precision metal products using stamping, fabricating and other value-added processes. Its member companies include metal stampers, fabricators, spinners, slide formers and roll formers, as well as suppliers of equipment, materials and services to the industry. Members are located in 30 countries, with the majority found in North America; in 41 states of the United States as well as Canada and Mexico. Conducts technical and educational programs, compiles statistics, offers training systems, and provides legislative and regulatory assistance to members. **Awards:** A.R. Hedberg Training and Education Award. **Frequency:** annual. **Type:** recognition. **Recipient:** to a PMA member company, for notable efforts to technically train and educate its employees by instituting a total training program throughout the company ● Parkview Metal Products Award for Excellence in Quality Assurance. **Frequency:** annual. **Type:** recognition. **Recipient:** to a PMA manufacturing member, for outstanding achievement in the development and implementation of a company-wide quality assurance system that effectively uses continuous improvement ● Pitcher Insurance Agency Award for Safety. **Frequency:** annual. **Type:** recognition. **Recipient:** for effective comprehensive safety program or a specific innovative idea in the context of an effective safety program ● R.D. Pritchard-Higgins Award for Design. **Frequency:** annual. **Type:** recognition. **Recipient:** to an innovative metalforming company, for creative and effective product design ● Signature Technologies Process Control Award. **Type:** recognition. **Recipient:** for innovative electronic solutions implemented by any manufacturing company ● SKD Automotive Group Award for Productivity. **Frequency:** annual. **Type:** recognition. **Recipient:** for outstanding achievement by a PMA manufacturing member in the development and implementation of programs, processes and utilization of assets that lead to significant improvements in productivity ● Ulbrich Award for Competitive Excellence in Product Development. **Type:** recognition. **Recipient:** for a metalforming company that develops and manufactures a product which best utilizes metal in place of a competitive material. **Additional Websites:** http://www.metalform.com, http://www.metalformingmagazine.com. **Committees:** Awards; Government Relations; International; Management Information; Nominating; Quality Technical Seminar; Safety and Environment; Sales and Marketing; Technical Research; Training and Education. **Divisions:** Custom Roll Forming; Metal Fabricating; Metal Spinning; Metal Stamping; Slide Forming; Small Lot; Tool and Die; Washer. **Formerly:** (1961) Pressed Metal Institute; (1987) American Metal Stamping Association. **Publications:** *MetalForming*, monthly. Magazine. Covers materials and equipment, electronics in metal forming and assembly, taxes, legal issues, and management. **Price:** $25.00/year in U.S. and Canada; $175.00/year outside U.S. and Canada. ISSN: 0026-069X. **Circulation:** 60,000. **Advertising:** accepted. Alternate Formats: online; CD-ROM ● *PMA Update.* Newsletter. Alternate Formats: online ● Reports. **Price:** included in membership dues ● Brochure. Alternate Formats: online. **Conventions/Meetings:** biennial METALFORM Exhibition - conference and trade show (exhibits).

2727 ■ Silver Institute (SI)

1200 G St. NW, Ste.800
Washington, DC 20005
Ph: (202)835-0185
Fax: (202)835-0155
E-mail: info@silverinstitute.org
URL: http://www.silverinstitute.org
Contact: Mr. Michael DiRienzo, Exec. Dir./Sec.

Founded: 1971. **Members:** 54. **Staff:** 8. **Description:** Companies that mine, refine, and manufacture silver-containing products; silver bullion suppliers. Seeks to encourage the development and use of silver and silver products. Helps develop markets. Fosters research on present and prospective uses of silver. Collects and publishes statistics and other information regarding production, distribution, marketing consumption, and uses of silver and silver products. **Libraries: Type:** reference. **Holdings:** articles, books. **Subjects:** silver. **Publications:** *Get the Skinny on Silver Investing.* Book. Features silver as the best investment. **Price:** $9.95 print/electronic copy; $25.00 signed copy. Alternate Formats: online ● *Silver News*, quarterly. Newsletter. Features articles on new uses of silver in industry, the arts, and coinage. Includes statistics and information on new members. **Price:** free ● *Silver the Indispensable Metal.* Brochures ● *World Silver Survey*, annual. **Price:** $195.00.

2728 ■ Silver Users Association (SUA)

11240 Waples Mill Rd., No. 200
Fairfax, VA 22030
Ph: (703)930-7790
Fax: (703)359-7562
E-mail: pmiller@mwcapitol.com
URL: http://www.silverusersassociation.org
Contact: Jon Potts, Pres.

Founded: 1947. **Members:** 30. **Staff:** 1. **Budget:** $109,000. **Description:** Represents companies that make, sell and distribute products and services in which silver is an essential component. Informs members, government and the public on all the facets of the silver market in a timely manner. **Libraries: Type:** by appointment only. **Holdings:** 150. **Subjects:** silver statistics, executive branch policies and legislative proposals affecting silver. **Committees:** Goals and Objectives; Legislative; Web Site. **Affiliated With:** American League of Lobbyists; International Imaging Industry Association; International Precious Metals Institute; National Association of Manufacturers; National Economists Club; Society for Mining, Metallurgy, and Exploration; U.S. Chamber of Commerce. **Publications:** *Silver Users Association — Speeches*, periodic. Contains text of speeches by association officials in loose leaf form. **Price:** free ● *Washington Report*, monthly. Newsletter. Reviews supply, demand, and price of silver of the previous year, as well as major news events and outlook for the upcoming year. **Price:** free. **Circulation:** 375. Alternate Formats: online. **Conventions/Meetings:** semiannual conference and seminar - always April/May and October/November in Washington, DC.

2729 ■ Specialty Steel Industry of North America (SSINA)

3050 K St. NW
Washington, DC 20007
Ph: (202)342-8630
Free: (800)982-0355
Fax: (202)342-8631
E-mail: ssina@colliershannon.com
URL: http://www.ssina.com
Contact: Jack W. Shilling, Chm.

Founded: 1964. **Members:** 15. **Staff:** 1. **Description:** Facilitates the fomentation of the Specialty Steel Industry. Promotes the use of stainless steel. **Formerly:** Specialty Steel Industry of the United States; (1982) Tool and Stainless Steel Industry Committee. **Conventions/Meetings:** bimonthly meeting - alternately in Washington, DC and Pittsburgh, PA.

2730 ■ Steel Alliance

Address Unknown since 2007

Description: Working to help consumers, the people who buy automobiles, appliances, houses, canned food or any of the may products made with steel recognize the material's attributes.

2731 ■ Steel Framing Alliance (SFA)

1201 15th St. NW, Ste.320
Washington, DC 20005
Ph: (202)785-2022
Free: (800)797-8335
Fax: (202)785-3856
E-mail: lwilliams@steelframing.org
URL: http://www.steelframingalliance.com
Contact: Larry Williams, Pres.

Membership Dues: steel manufacturer, $50,000 (annual) ● steel association, $35,000 (annual) ● zinc producer/coil coater, $25,000 (annual) ● stud manufacturer, $1,000-$12,500 (annual) ● non-SSMA/non-CSSBI rollformer, $12,500 (annual) ● specialty product manufacturer, $2,500 (annual) ● equipment manufacturer, $7,500 (annual) ● association (other), $1,000 (annual) ● individual, $100 (annual). **Multinational. Description:** Seeks to advance the iron and steel industries. Enables and encourages the practical and economic use of and preference for cold-formed steel framing in residential construction. Fosters the use of steel framing as a load bearing element in commercial construction. **Publications:** *Framework*, bimonthly. Journal ● Annual Report, annual. **Price:** included in membership dues.

2732 ■ Steel Manufacturers Association (SMA)

1150 Connecticut Ave. NW, Ste.715
Washington, DC 20036-4131
Ph: (202)296-1515
Fax: (202)296-2506
E-mail: stuart@steelnet.org
URL: http://www.steelnet.org
Contact: Thomas A. Danjczek, Pres.

Founded: 1988. **Members:** 170. **Membership Dues:** associate, $1,000 (annual). **Staff:** 4. **Budget:** $850,000. **Multinational. Description:** Steel producers, mainly mini-mills. Stimulates cooperation among its members in the study of administrative and production problems and the exchange of related information. Operates an office to administer cooperative interests in public affairs, education, technology, and research. Conducts seminars and semiannual plant tours. **Awards:** Achievement in Community Involvement Award. **Frequency:** annual. **Type:** recognition. **Recipient:** for individuals with strong commitment to community involvement and social responsibility ● Distinguished Recycler Award. **Frequency:** annual. **Type:** recognition. **Recipient:** for outstanding achievement. **Committees:** Energy; Environment; Human Resources; Safety. **Divisions:** Plant Operations. **Formed by Merger of:** Steel Bar Mills; National Steel Producers Association. **Publications:** *The Refrigerator Door.* Video. Alternate Formats: online ● Membership Directory, annual. **Price:** $100.00. Alternate Formats: online ● Articles. Alternate Formats: online ● Also publishes an annual public policy statement. **Conventions/Meetings:** annual board meeting ● annual conference.

2733 ■ Steel Truss and Component Association (STCA)
6300 Enterprise Ln., Ste.300
Madison, WI 53719
Ph: (608)217-3712
Fax: (608)271-7006
E-mail: info@steeltruss.org
URL: http://www.steeltruss.org
Contact: Mr. Michael Noonan, Pres./Treas.
Membership Dues: regular (based on annual gross sales of steel components), $1,000-$3,000 (annual) ● supplier, $1,000-$4,000 (annual) ● associate, $200 (annual). **Description:** Promotes the use of cold formed steel trusses and components. Advances the standards of conduct and operation for the industry, including manufacturing and quality control standards. Fosters the safe, economic, and structurally sound use of steel trusses and related components. Supports research, development and testing of cold formed steel trusses and components. **Telecommunication Services:** electronic mail, stca@steeltruss.org.

2734 ■ Vanadium Producers and Reclaimers Association (VPRA)
900 2nd St. NE, Ste.201
Washington, DC 20002
Ph: (202)842-0219 (202)842-3204
Fax: (202)842-0439
E-mail: jhilbert@khaconsultants.com
URL: http://www.vanadiumproducers.com
Contact: John W. Hilbert III, Pres.
Founded: 2003. **Members:** 5. **Description:** Represents ferroalloy producers. Serves the interests of ferroalloy producers before governmental agencies and congress. **Formerly:** (2003) The Ferroalloys Association.

Microscopy

2735 ■ Optical Imaging Association (OPIA)
225 Reinekers Ln., Ste.625
Alexandria, VA 22314
Ph: (703)836-1360
Fax: (703)836-6644
E-mail: cmulligan@opia.org
URL: http://www.opia.org
Members: 25. **Description:** Represents companies that manufacture or distribute microscopes and/or products, components and peripherals for microscopy and the microscopy imaging industry. **Sections:** Electronic Imaging Detector Manufacturers; Imaging and Software Manufacturers; Peripheral Components Manufacturers.

Military

2736 ■ Logistics Officer Association (LOA)
PO Box 2264
Arlington, VA 22202
Ph: (703)693-8395
Fax: (703)693-8554
E-mail: president@loanational.org
URL: http://www.loanational.org
Contact: Col. Rick Matthews, Pres.
Founded: 1982. **Members:** 3,500. **Membership Dues:** general, $25 (annual) ● student, $15 (annual). **Multinational. Description:** Strives to enhance the military logistics profession. Provides an open forum to promote quality logistical support and logistics officer professional development. **Awards:** Chapter Distinguished Services Award. **Frequency:** annual. **Type:** recognition. **Recipient:** for member who made the greatest contribution in support of his/her local chapter ● Chapter of the Year Award. **Frequency:** annual. **Type:** recognition. **Recipient:** for the best chapter of the year ● General George T. Babbitt Award. **Frequency:** annual. **Type:** recognition. **Recipient:** for member with the greatest contribution to the furthering of the association's goals and objectives ● Lifetime Achievement Award. **Frequency:** annual. **Type:** recognition. **Recipient:** for member who demonstrated sustained superior leadership service. **Computer Services:** Information services, chapters resources. **Programs:** Scholarship. **Publications:** *Exceptional Release*, quarterly. Journal. Contains articles and editorials on the latest topics from all logistics disciplines.

Millers

2737 ■ International Association of Operative Millers (AOM)
5001 Coll. Blvd., Ste.104
Leawood, KS 66211
Ph: (913)338-3377
Fax: (913)338-3553
E-mail: info@iaom.info
URL: http://www.aomillers.org
Contact: Melinda Farris, Interim Exec. VP
Founded: 1895. **Members:** 1,800. **Membership Dues:** active, associate, $195 (annual) ● junior, $30 (annual). **Staff:** 3. **Budget:** $500,000. **Regional Groups:** 14. **Languages:** English, French, Spanish. **Multinational. Description:** Represents operation managers, plant managers, superintendents, grinders, bolters, engineers, and others engaged in the production of flour, feeds and cereal products through processing of wheat, corn, oats, rice, seeds, and spices. **Libraries: Type:** not open to the public. **Subjects:** previous technical bulletins covering all aspects of milling. **Committees:** Allied Trades Advisory; Education; Food Protection; Technical. **Formerly:** (2003) Association of Operative Millers. **Publications:** *Association of Operative Millers—Annual Program Book and Directory*. Lists members; includes summary of annual technical conference and trade show. **Circulation:** 1,700. **Advertising:** accepted ● *Association of Operative Millers—Technical Bulletin*, monthly. Provides articles about grain milling research reports and statistics, and association and industry news. **Price:** $20.00 for members; $30.00 for nonmembers ● *Cereal Millers*. Handbook. **Price:** $65.00 for members; $95.00 for nonmembers. **Conventions/Meetings:** annual conference and trade show (exhibits).

2738 ■ North American Millers' Association (NAMA)
600 Maryland Ave. SW, Ste.825 W
Washington, DC 20024
Ph: (202)484-2200
Fax: (202)488-7416
E-mail: generalinfo@namamillers.org
URL: http://www.namamillers.org
Contact: Betsy Faga, Pres.
Founded: 1902. **Members:** 72. **Membership Dues:** associate, $1,000 (annual). **Staff:** 6. **Budget:** $1,000,000. **Description:** Millers of wheat, corn, oats, durum, and rye flour; members mill 95 percent of total U.S. capacity. **Telecommunication Services:** electronic mail, bfaga@namamillers.org. **Absorbed:** (1976) National Soft Wheat Association; (1982) Durum Wheat Institute; (1986) Wheat Flour Institute; (1998) American Corn Millers' Federation; (1998) American Oat Association; (1998) Protein Grain Products International. **Formerly:** (1999) Millers' National Federation. **Publications:** *NAMA News*, monthly. Newsletter. Alternate Formats: online ● Membership Directory, annual. **Price:** available to members only. **Conventions/Meetings:** annual meeting.

2739 ■ Rice Millers' Association (RMA)
c/o USA Rice Federation
4301 N Fairfax Dr., Ste.425
Arlington, VA 22203
Ph: (703)236-2300
Fax: (703)236-2301
E-mail: riceinfo@usarice.com
URL: http://www.usarice.com
Contact: Mike LaGrande, Chm.
Founded: 1899. **Members:** 58. **Membership Dues:** trader, $9,000 (annual) ● broker, merchandiser, user, $5,000 (annual) ● allied server, $1,500 (annual). **Description:** Represents Independent and farmer-cooperative rice milling operators. Provides economic and statistical information on production, milling, and distribution of rice. Promotes research aimed at new uses for rice products and improvements in processing, packaging, storing, and distributing rice. Maintains liaison with U.S. and foreign government agencies, congress, and foreign buyers of U.S. rice. **Telecommunication Services:** electronic mail, tsomers@usarice.com. **Publications:** *Rice Millers' Association—Roster of Members*, periodic. Membership Directory. **Conventions/Meetings:** annual convention (exhibits).

Minerals

2740 ■ Asbestos Information Association/North America (AIA/NA)
PMB 114
1235 Jefferson Davis Hwy.
Arlington, VA 22202-3283
Ph: (703)560-2980
Fax: (703)560-2981
E-mail: aiabjpigg@aol.com
Contact: B.J. Pigg, Pres.
Founded: 1970. **Members:** 6. **Staff:** 1. **Budget:** $64,000. **Description:** Manufacturers, processors, and miners/millers of asbestos or products containing asbestos. Purposes are: to provide industry wide information on asbestos and health and on industry efforts to eliminate existing hazards; to cooperate with government agencies in developing and implementing industry wide standards for exposure to asbestos dust and for the control of asbestos dust emissions into community air and water; to exchange information on methods and techniques of asbestos dust control; to assist in the solution of problems arising from the health effects of asbestos; to increase public knowledge of the unique benefits and importance of asbestos products. Acts as central agency for the collection and dissemination of medical and technical information on asbestos-related disease, asbestos dust control, and other asbestos-related ecological considerations. **Libraries: Type:** reference. **Committees:** Technical. **Publications:** Also publishes informational/technical materials.

2741 ■ Gypsum Association (GA)
810 1st St. NE, Ste.510
Washington, DC 20002
Ph: (202)289-5440
Fax: (202)289-3707
E-mail: info@gypsum.org
URL: http://www.gypsum.org
Contact: Michael Gardner, Exec. Dir.
Founded: 1930. **Members:** 9. **Staff:** 10. **Budget:** $1,001,000. **Description:** Miners and manufacturers of gypsum and gypsum products. Sponsors basic and applied research programs at educational institutions and commercial testing laboratories on fire resistant assemblies, structural assemblies, wallboard application techniques, and new uses for gypsum products. Compiles statistics. **Awards:** Drywall Construction Competition. **Frequency:** annual. **Type:** monetary. **Recipient:** for creative, quality application of gypsum board. **Committees:** Building Codes; Operations and Regulatory Offices; Promotion; Technical. **Publications:** *Fire Resistance Design*. Manual. Depicts over 340 systems that may be used for fire-rated walls and partitions. **Price:** $30.00 17th edition; $30.00 15th-16th edition; $18.00 18th edition; $45.00 14th edition ● Bulletins. Provides information about gypsum products and its building codes. ● Newsletter ● Also makes available programs on gypsum products, and educational and training materials. **Conventions/Meetings:** semiannual conference - always October.

2742 ■ Industrial Minerals Association - North America (IMA-NA)
2011 Pennsylvania Ave. NW, Ste.301
Washington, DC 20006
Ph: (202)457-0200

Fax: (202)457-0287
E-mail: info@ima-na.org
URL: http://www.ima-na.org
Contact: Mark Ellis, Pres.

Founded: 2002. **Multinational. Description:** Advances the interests of North American companies that mine or process minerals used throughout the manufacturing and agricultural industries. Provides industrial minerals information and services to members and to the public. Addresses issues that are particular to each industrial mineral's needs, characteristics and interests. **Affiliated With:** European Industrial Minerals Association. **Conventions/Meetings:** annual meeting.

2743 ■ National Industrial Sand Association (NISA)

2011 Pennsylvania Ave., Ste.301
Washington, DC 20006
Ph: (202)457-0200
Fax: (202)457-0287
E-mail: info@sand.org
URL: http://www.sand.org
Contact: Robert E. Glenn, Pres.

Founded: 1936. **Members:** 38. **Staff:** 3. **Budget:** $600,000. **Description:** Represents processors and miners of sand for purposes other than construction. **Conventions/Meetings:** annual meeting - always October ● annual meeting - always spring ● annual workshop (exhibits) - always spring.

2744 ■ Salt Institute (SI)

700 N Fairfax St.
Fairfax Plz., Ste.600
Alexandria, VA 22314-2040
Ph: (703)549-4648
Fax: (703)548-2194
E-mail: dick@saltinstitute.org
URL: http://www.saltinstitute.org
Contact: Richard L. Hanneman, Pres.

Founded: 1914. **Members:** 34. **Staff:** 4. **Budget:** $1,500,000. **Multinational. Description:** Works to increase public awareness of the benefits of salt and salt products. Promotes participation in public policy as it relates to salt production, salt distribution and salt products. Fosters research in ice and snow control, agricultural feeding practices, water treatment, and salt in nutrition. Conducts public information program. Maintains Tech Data Center on salt-related materials. Sponsors industry safety contest. Compiles sales statistics. **Libraries: Type:** reference. **Holdings:** 22,000; books, papers, periodicals, photographs, reports, video recordings. **Subjects:** every aspect of salt production and use including diet and health. **Awards:** Excellence in Storage Award. **Frequency:** annual. **Type:** recognition. **Recipient:** for excellent salt storage programs. **Computer Services:** Electronic publishing, about two dozen RSS web feeds of new information about salt. **Formerly:** (1963) Salt Producers Association. **Publications:** *Salt and Health*, quarterly. Newsletters. Discusses public health issues related to salt (e.g. critical need for outcomes studies and reliance on evidence-based policy process). **Price:** $1.00. Alternate Formats: online ● *Salt and Highway Deicing*, quarterly. Newsletters. Includes news and commentary for public works officials and private contractors with winter maintenance responsibilities. **Price:** $1.00. Alternate Formats: online ● *Salt and Trace Minerals*, quarterly. Newsletter. Covers use of salt and trace minerals as a food supplement for livestock and other animals. **Price:** free. **Circulation:** 2,600 ● *SI Report*, monthly. Newsletter. Covers general salt industry news. **Price:** free to snow and ice control professionals. **Circulation:** 8,000. **Conventions/Meetings:** annual meeting.

2745 ■ Sorptive Minerals Institute (SMI)

1155 15th St. NW, Ste.500
Washington, DC 20005
Ph: (202)289-2760
Fax: (202)530-0659
E-mail: lcoogan@navista.net
URL: http://www.sorptive.org
Contact: Lee Coogan, Exec. Dir.

Founded: 1970. **Members:** 15. **Staff:** 2. **Description:** Miners and processors of absorbent clays used for pet litter, oil, grease, absorbents, and agricultural absorbents. Works to promote and protect the absorbent clay industry and find solutions for industry problems. **Committees:** Technical. **Conventions/Meetings:** annual Industrial Minerals Forum - conference.

2746 ■ World Gold Council (WGC)

444 Madison Ave.
New York, NY 10022
Ph: (212)317-3800
Fax: (212)688-0410
E-mail: info@gold.org
URL: http://www.gold.org
Contact: Pierre Lassonde, Chm.

Founded: 1987. **Multinational. Description:** Promotes the growth potential of investing in gold as a portfolio diversifier for investment funds. **Publications:** *Gold Bulletin*, quarterly. Journal. Alternate Formats: online ● Magazine.

Mining

2747 ■ ADSC: International Association of Foundation Drilling

Pacific Center I
14180 Dallas Pkwy., Ste.510
Dallas, TX 75254
Ph: (214)343-2091
Fax: (214)343-2384
E-mail: adsc@adsc-iafd.com
URL: http://www.adsc-iafd.com
Contact: S. Scot Litke, Exec. Dir.

Founded: 1972. **Members:** 850. **Membership Dues:** corporate associate, $350-$875 (annual) ● individual in U.S., $95 (annual) ● individual outside U.S., $115 (annual). **Staff:** 9. **Budget:** $1,600,000. **Regional Groups:** 6. **National Groups:** 7. **Description:** Represents the foundation drilling and anchored geo-support industries. Conducts educational and research programs, trade shows, and state federal government liaison. **Libraries: Type:** reference. **Holdings:** 200; articles, audiovisuals, books, monographs. **Subjects:** drilled shaft, earth retention. **Awards: Type:** scholarship ● **Frequency:** annual. **Type:** scholarship. **Computer Services:** Mailing lists, of members. **Publications:** *Foundation Drilling*, 8/year. Magazine. **Price:** $75.00 in U.S.; $95.00 outside U.S. ISSN: 0274-186. **Circulation:** 2,000. **Advertising:** accepted. **Conventions/Meetings:** Equipment EXPO - convention (exhibits) ● annual meeting.

2748 ■ China Clay Producers Association (CCPA)

113 Arkwright Landing
Macon, GA 31210
Ph: (478)757-1211
Fax: (478)757-1949
E-mail: info@georgiamining.org
URL: http://www.kaolin.com
Contact: Lee Lemke, Exec. VP

Founded: 1978. **Members:** 4. **Description:** Works to: educate producers of China clay concerning federal and state governmental activities, which could affect the industry; promote the exchange of information between producers and legislators and government officials; influence the development of laws, regulations, and governmental policies to improve business conditions for producers in the China clay mining industry. Operates charitable program. **Committees:** Political Action. **Formerly:** (2002) China Clay Producers Trade Association. **Conventions/Meetings:** semiannual meeting.

2749 ■ Colorado Mining Association (CMA)

216 16th St., Ste.1250
Denver, CO 80202
Ph: (303)575-9199
Fax: (303)575-9194
E-mail: colomine@coloradomining.org
URL: http://www.coloradomining.org
Contact: Stuart A. Sanderson, Pres.

Founded: 1876. **Members:** 700. **Membership Dues:** individual, $80 (annual). **Staff:** 2. **Budget:** $350,000. **Regional Groups:** 1. **Description:** Mining companies, coal companies, operators, mining engineers, geologists, geological engineers, supply and equipment houses, and manufacturers. Maintains Colorado Mining Association Educational Foundation which conducts 4-week summer school for teachers and counselors. **Libraries: Type:** reference. **Holdings:** archival material, reports. **Awards:** Health and Safety: Reclamation. **Frequency:** annual. **Type:** recognition. **Committees:** Air Quality; Coal; Hard Rock; Health and Safety; International; Legislative; Mining Law; Nominating; Partnership; Public Lands; Small Operators. **Publications:** *CMA Directory*, annual. **Price:** $25.00/copy. **Advertising:** accepted ● *CMA Rock and Coal*, monthly. Newsletter. Contains information on mining activity, regulatory issues, and personnel changes within the mining community. **Price:** included in membership dues. **Advertising:** accepted ● *Colorado Mining: Today and Tomorrow*, annual. Magazine. **Advertising:** accepted ● Bulletins. **Conventions/Meetings:** annual National Western Mining Conference (exhibits) - always in Denver or Colorado Springs, CO.

2750 ■ Copper Development Association (CDA)

260 Madison Ave.
New York, NY 10016
Ph: (212)251-7200 (212)251-7223
Free: (800)CDA-DATA
Fax: (212)251-7234
E-mail: questions@cda.copper.org
URL: http://www.copper.org
Contact: Andrew G. Kireta Sr., Pres./CEO

Founded: 1962. **Members:** 70. **Staff:** 30. **Budget:** $9,000,000. **Description:** Represents U.S. and foreign copper mining, smelting and refining companies, U.S. fabricating companies such as brass and wire mills, foundries, and ingot makers. Seeks to expand the uses and applications and to broaden the markets of copper and copper products. Functions in groups or divisions corresponding to principal market areas such as transportation, building construction, electrical and electronic products, industrial machinery and equipment, and consumer and general products. Provides technical service to users of copper and copper alloy products. Has industrywide responsibility for market statistics and research. Maintains 10 field offices in the U.S. **Libraries: Type:** not open to the public. **Holdings:** archival material. **Subjects:** copper metal metallurgy. **Computer Services:** Information services, typical uses of copper and copper alloys ● online services, Copper Data Center. **Additional Websites:** http://www.copperinyourhome.org. **Supersedes:** Copper and Brass Research Association. **Publications:** *Cast Bronze Bearing Design*. Manual ● *Copper Topics*, semiannual. Bulletins. Alternate Formats: online ● *Innovations*. Magazine ● Handbooks ● Reports. Includes technical materials. ● Annual Report, annual ● Videos. **Conventions/Meetings:** semiannual meeting - always June and December.

2751 ■ Mining Electrical Maintenance and Safety Association (MEMSA)

c/o Bill Collins, Sec.-Treas.
PO Box 7163
Lakeland, FL 33807
Fax: (863)644-5531
E-mail: memsa@tampabay.rr.com
URL: http://www.miningelectrical.org
Contact: Mike Casson, Pres.

Founded: 1945. **Members:** 300. **Membership Dues:** regular, $45 (annual). **Description:** Represents mining industry electrical management, electrical suppliers, machine manufacturers, utilities, cable manufacturers, universities, and governmental employees. Seeks to advance uniform standards of applied electricity in connection with open-pit mining and to promote the development of necessary safety devices for protection of personnel and equipment. Regulates major spare parts pool. Makes available engineers from participating manufacturers for informal discussions with coal company electrical personnel on subjects of mutual interest, with emphasis on new technology and developments. **Committees:** Mine Safety; Parts. **Formerly:** (1999) Open Pit Mining Association. **Publications:** Papers. Alternate Formats: online. **Conventions/Meetings:** annual meeting.

2752 ■ Mining Foundation of the Southwest (MFSW)
PO Box 42317
Tucson, AZ 85733
Ph: (520)577-7519
Fax: (520)577-7073
E-mail: admin@miningfoundationsw.org
URL: http://www.miningfoundationsw.org
Contact: Ms. Jean Austin, Exec. Office Mgr.
Founded: 1973. **Members:** 100. **Membership Dues:** voting, associate, silver, gold, $100 (annual). **Staff:** 1. **Local Groups:** 1. **Description:** International group of persons professionally involved with the mining industry. Advances the science of mining and related industries, educates members and the public and functions as a social club. **Libraries: Type:** reference. **Holdings:** articles, books, periodicals. **Subjects:** mining. **Awards:** American Mining Hall of Fame. **Frequency:** annual. **Type:** recognition. **Committees:** Foresight. **Formerly:** (1993) Mining Club of the Southwest. **Publications:** *Concentrates*, monthly. Newsletter. Contains member news and foundation events. **Price:** included in membership dues ● *History of Mining in Arizona - 3 Volumes*. Booklets. **Conventions/Meetings:** annual American Mining Hall of Fame - meeting, with dinner and featured speakers - every first Saturday of December.

2753 ■ Northwest Mining Association (NWMA)
10 N Post St., Ste.220
Spokane, WA 99201
Ph: (509)624-1158
Fax: (509)623-1241
E-mail: nwma_info@nwma.org
URL: http://www.nwma.org
Contact: Laura Skaer, Exec. Dir.
Founded: 1895. **Members:** 1,500. **Membership Dues:** active, $95 (annual) ● retired, senior, spouse, full-time student, $25 (annual) ● corporate (minimum), $500 (annual) ● corporate (maximum), $25,000 (annual). **Staff:** 4. **Budget:** $900,000. **State Groups:** 35. **Multinational. Description:** Seeks to support and advance the mineral resource and related industries, to represent and inform members on technical, legislative and regulatory issues. Disseminates educational materials related to mining, and to foster and promote economic opportunity and environmentally responsible mining. **Libraries: Type:** reference. **Subjects:** mining and mineral resource topics. **Computer Services:** Mailing lists, sold to members only. **Telecommunication Services:** electronic mail, info@nwma.org. **Committees:** Abandoned Mine Lands; Environmental Issues; Mining Law; Public Lands. **Publications:** *Mineral Industry Costs* ● *Practical Geophysics for the Exploration Geologist* ● *Service Directory*, annual ● *Short Course Volumes* ● Newsletter, monthly ● Bulletin, bimonthly. Alternate Formats: online. **Conventions/Meetings:** annual convention (exhibits) - always first week of December.

2754 ■ Perlite Institute (PI)
4305 N 6th St., Ste.A
Harrisburg, PA 17110
Ph: (717)238-9723
Fax: (717)238-9985
E-mail: info@perlite.org
URL: http://www.perlite.org
Contact: Roger Smith, Pres.
Founded: 1949. **Members:** 51. **Membership Dues:** furnace producer, $2,000 (annual) ● associate, $500 (annual) ● ore producer, $10,000 (annual). **Staff:** 3. **Budget:** $400,000. **Multinational. Description:** Mining firms, processors (expanding), and applicators of perlite, a volcanic rock used for insulation, plaster and concrete aggregate, and other purposes in chemical, foundry, and horticultural industries. Conducts and sponsors research on physical properties of masonry insulation, perlite-gypsum and perlite-portland cement mixes, and floor fills and curtain walls; designs and specifications for perlite plaster construction and concrete roof decks; fire resistance of perlite plaster and concrete construction; horticultural applications. Develops standards for quality and the application of perlite as aggregate. **Libraries: Type:** reference. **Holdings:** archival material. **Awards:** Honorary Member. **Frequency:** annual. **Type:** recognition ● Louis Lloyd Award. **Frequency:** annual. **Type:** recognition. **Recipient:** for an individual who has contributed substantially to the perlite industry and to the institute. **Telecommunication Services:** electronic mail, rsmith9179@aol.com. **Committees:** Communications; Fines/Waste; Fuels/Ores/Furnace Suppliers; Marketing/Promotion/New Markets; Standards; Technical. **Publications:** *Perlite Today*, quarterly. Newsletter. **Price:** included in membership dues. **Conventions/Meetings:** annual meeting - held every spring.

2755 ■ Solution Mining Research Institute (SMRI)
105 Apple Valley Cir.
Clarks Summit, PA 18411
Ph: (570)585-8092
Fax: (570)585-8091
E-mail: smri@solutionmining.org
URL: http://www.solutionmining.org
Contact: John O. Voigt, Exec. Dir.
Founded: 1958. **Members:** 100. **Staff:** 2. **Description:** Salt and chemical companies; companies developing and operating salt caverns for oil and gas storage; companies providing services to the industry; consultants. Identifies and supports research programs, acts as technical clearinghouse, and monitors and disseminates information on related environmental areas. Deals with subjects such as dissolution theory, rock mechanics, salt cavity utilization, subsidence, drilling, fracing, completion, and logging. Sponsors technical conferences. **Libraries: Type:** reference. **Holdings:** 800; books, papers, reports. **Subjects:** solution mining. **Formerly:** (1962) Brine Cavity Research Group. **Conventions/Meetings:** semiannual conference - usually April and October.

2756 ■ Women in Mining (WIM)
PO Box 260246
Lakewood, CO 80226-0246
Ph: (303)298-1535
E-mail: wim@womeninmining.org
URL: http://www.womeninmining.org
Contact: Scotty Norman, Pres.
Founded: 1981. **Members:** 500. **Membership Dues:** individual, $20 (annual) ● sustaining, $300-$5,000 (annual). **Budget:** $10,000. **Regional Groups:** 7. **Description:** Individuals employed or interested in the mining and mineral resource industry. Provides technical education and scientific programs fostering public awareness of economic and technical interrelationships between mineral production and the national economy. Monitors and participates in related legislative activities. Provides speakers at monthly meeting; conducts field trips and seminars; holds legislative receptions; participates in career days at local schools. Encourages the growth of additional chapters. Sponsors competitions and minerals education workshops at regional National Science Teacher Association conventions; maintains hall of fame. **Computer Services:** Information services, list of officers, location of chapters. **Boards:** Education Foundation. **Committees:** National Quarterly; Public Relations. **Formerly:** Women in Mining. **Publications:** *Minerals Activity Booklets*. Contains information about earth science for classroom demonstration of educators. Alternate Formats: online ● *National Quarterly*. Newsletter. **Price:** $10.00 ● *Women in Mining National—Membership Directory*, annual. **Price:** available to members only. **Conventions/Meetings:** annual meeting (exhibits).

Minorities

2757 ■ National Association for Multi-Ethnicity in Communications (NAMIC)
336 W 37th St., Ste.302
New York, NY 10018
Ph: (212)594-5985
Fax: (212)594-8391
E-mail: info@namic.com
URL: http://www.namic.com
Contact: Kathy A. Johnson, Pres.
Founded: 1980. **Members:** 1,500. **Membership Dues:** platinum (president, vice president, director and general manager), $275 (annual) ● gold (manager, supervisor and professional not defined in platinum), $150 (annual) ● silver (professional in customer contact in non-exempt positions), $75 (annual) ● student (full-time student enrolled in an accredited college or university), $40 (annual). **Staff:** 8. **Local Groups:** 17. **National Groups:** 16. **Description:** Minority cable and telecommunications professionals. Strives to raise awareness, expand opportunity and shape the future for minorities in the communications industry through education, advocacy, and empowerment. Provides access to a national job bank and industry white papers. **Awards:** NAMIC Vision Awards. **Frequency:** annual. **Type:** recognition. **Recipient:** for cable television entities that have demonstrated a commitment to producing quality, multi-ethnic and cross-cultural programming content. **Formerly:** (2005) National Association of Minorities in Communications. **Publications:** *In Touch*, bimonthly. Newsletter. Discusses issues of national interest and upcoming events. Alternate Formats: online ● Membership Directory. Alternate Formats: online. **Conventions/Meetings:** annual Awards Breakfast ● annual conference - 2008 Sept. 14-16, New York, NY.

Minority Business

2758 ■ Airport Minority Advisory Council (AMAC)
Ronald Reagan Washington Natl. Airport
Washington, DC 20001
Ph: (703)417-2622
Fax: (703)417-2620
E-mail: amac.info@amac-org.com
URL: http://www.amac-org.com
Contact: Gene Roth, Exec. Dir.
Founded: 1998. **Membership Dues:** student, $7-$25 (annual) ● associate, $38-$150 (annual) ● government, $56-$225 (annual) ● business, $125-$500 (annual) ● airport, $375-$1,500 (annual) ● corporate, $500-$2,000 (annual). **Description:** Advocates for equal opportunity for minorities and women in airport contracting and employment. **Telecommunication Services:** electronic mail, amacoffice@verizon.net. **Affiliated With:** Airports Council International - North America; American Association of Airport Executives. **Publications:** *AMAC Informational Brochure and Membership*. Alternate Formats: online ● *AMACESP Informational Brochure*. Alternate Formats: online ● Membership Directory. Alternate Formats: online.

2759 ■ Alliance of Minority Women for Business and Political Development
c/o Brenda Alford, Pres.
1316 Fenwick, Ste.908
Silver Spring, MD 20910
Ph: (301)585-8051
Fax: (301)681-3681
Contact: Brenda Alford, Pres.
Founded: 1988. **Members:** 210. **Membership Dues:** organization, $500 (annual). **Staff:** 2. **Budget:** $50,000. **Description:** Organizations in support of minority women in business and politics. Seeks to increase number of minority women business owners as elected officials, especially on the state level. Political action committee supports candidates through fundraising, endorsements, and training. **Publications:** *Power in Color and Gender*, quarterly.

2760 ■ American Association of Minority Businesses (AAMB)
c/o Charles L. Kelly, Pres./CEO
PO Box 35432
Charlotte, NC 28235
Ph: (704)596-1870

Fax: (704)599-6146
E-mail: ckelly@aambnet.com
URL: http://www.aambnet.com
Contact: Charles L. Kelly, Pres./CEO
Founded: 1992. **Members:** 17,000. **Membership Dues:** general, $60 (annual) ● associate, $100 (annual) ● corporate, $1,000 (annual). **Staff:** 5. **Budget:** $500,000. **Description:** Businesses in the United States that are owned or operated by individuals belonging to a racial or ethnic minority. Promotes effective, ethical, and profitable operation of minority-owned businesses. Conducts educational programs for members and their staff; makes available management, personnel, operational, technical, customer service, and financial support to members. **Awards:** AAMB Entrepreneur of the Year. **Frequency:** annual. **Type:** recognition. **Computer Services:** database ● online services. **Publications:** *Business Partner*, quarterly. Newsletter. **Conventions/Meetings:** periodic board meeting ● monthly meeting.

2761 ■ Diversity Information Resources (DIR)

2105 Central Ave. NE
Minneapolis, MN 55418
Ph: (612)781-6819
Fax: (612)781-0109
E-mail: info@diversityinforesources.com
URL: http://www.diversityinforesources.com
Contact: Leslie Bonds, Exec. Dir.
Founded: 1968. **Members:** 20. **Staff:** 4. **Description:** Promotes businesses with minority, women, veteran, service-disabled veteran and HUBZone ownership. Compiles and publishes minority and women-owned business directories to acquaint major corporations and government purchasing agents with the products and services of minority and women-owned firms. Sponsors national supplier diversity seminars. **Libraries: Type:** open to the public. **Holdings:** books. **Computer Services:** database, of buyers ● database, of suppliers. **Telecommunication Services:** electronic mail, lbonds@diversityinforesources.com. **Formerly:** (1970) National Buy-Black Campaign; (1984) National Minority Business Campaign; (1991) National Minority Business Directories; (2000) Try Us Resources. **Publications:** *National Minority and Women-Owned Business Directory*, annual. Lists approximately 7000 minority-owned firms, arranged by product/service and state; includes business description for each entry. **Price:** $120.00/year (print version); $125.00/year (disk version). **Advertising:** accepted ● *Purchasing People in Major Corporations*, annual. Directory. Lists corporate purchasing locations. Includes names of minority business program administrator, if that position exists. **Price:** $60.00/year (print version); $85.00/year (disk version). **Advertising:** accepted. Alternate Formats: CD-ROM ● *Supplier Diversity Information Resource Guide*, annual. Directory. Lists public and private sector minority business resources. **Price:** $70.00/year. **Conventions/Meetings:** board meeting - 3/year.

2762 ■ Executive Leadership Council (ELC)

1001 N Fairfax St., Ste.300
Alexandria, VA 22314
Ph: (703)706-5200
Fax: (703)535-6830
E-mail: elc_info@elcinfo.com
URL: http://www.elcinfo.com
Contact: Carl Brooks, Pres./CEO
Founded: 1986. **Members:** 400. **Staff:** 8. **Budget:** $3,200,000. **Description:** Provides senior African-American corporate executives with a network and leadership forum that adds perspective and direction to the achievement of excellence in business, economic and public policies for the African-American community and its corporations, and the community at large. Conducts educational and research programs. **Awards:** Achievement Award. **Frequency:** annual. **Type:** recognition. **Recipient:** for excellence in business related to corporate efforts to advance diversity and achievements of African American executives ● Corporate Award. **Frequency:** annual. **Type:** recognition. **Recipient:** for excellence in business related to corporate efforts to advance diversity and achievements of African American executives ● Heritage Award. **Frequency:** annual. **Type:** recognition. **Recipient:** for excellence in business related to corporate efforts to advance diversity and achievements of African American executives. **Publications:** *Contact*, quarterly. Newsletter. **Circulation:** 2,000. Alternate Formats: online. **Conventions/Meetings:** annual CEO Diversity Leadership Summit - conference ● annual Mid-Level Manager's Symposium ● annual Recognition Dinner - always October ● annual Spring Meeting - always June ● annual Winter Meeting - always February.

2763 ■ Minority Business Enterprise Legal Defense and Education Fund (MBELDEF)

1100 Mercantile Ln., Ste.115-A
Largo, MD 20774
Ph: (301)583-4648
Fax: (301)772-8392
E-mail: info@mbeldef.org
URL: http://www.mbeldef.org
Contact: Kimberly A. Pumphrey, Special Asst.
Founded: 1980. **Membership Dues:** student, $35 (annual) ● individual, $125 (annual) ● non-profit organization, $250 (annual) ● corporate, $500 (annual) ● bronze, $1,000 (annual) ● silver, $2,500 (annual) ● gold, $5,000 (annual) ● platinum, $10,000 (annual). **Description:** Minority businesspersons united to defend, enhance, and expand minority business. Acts as advocate and legal representative for the minority business community, offering legal representation in matters of national or regional importance. **Publications:** *New Vanguard*, quarterly. Newsletter. Alternate Formats: online. **Conventions/Meetings:** annual meeting - always June, in Washington, DC.

2764 ■ National Association of Investment Companies (NAIC)

1300 Pennsylvania Ave. NW, Ste.700
Washington, DC 20004
Ph: (202)204-3001
Fax: (202)204-3022
E-mail: inquiries@naicvc.com
URL: http://www.naicvc.com
Contact: Samuel J. Boyd Jr., Pres./CEO
Founded: 1971. **Members:** 150. **Membership Dues:** corporate, $4,000-$12,000 (annual) ● affiliate, $5,000 (annual). **Staff:** 5. **Description:** Aims to: represent the minority small business investment company industry in the public sector; provide industry education; develop research material on the activities of the industry; promote the growth of minority-owned small businesses by informing the public of their contribution to the vitality of the nation's economy; collect and disseminate relevant business and trade information to members; facilitate the exchange of new ideas and financing strategies; assist organizing groups attempting to form or acquire minority enterprise small business investment companies; provide management and technical assistance to members; monitor regulatory agency actions. Conducts three professional seminars; sponsors research; compiles statistics. **Committees:** Education; Fundraising; Legislative; Practices; Regulatory. **Formerly:** (1987) American Association of Minority Enterprise Small Business Investment Companies. **Publications:** *NAIC Membership Directory*, annual. **Price:** $30.00 ● *National Association of Investment Companies—Perspective*, monthly. Newsletter. Presents issues, events, and trends of interest to the small business investment company industry and to the minority small business entrepreneurs. **Price:** $36.00/year ● Bibliographies ● Handbooks. **Conventions/Meetings:** annual convention - always October.

2765 ■ National Association of Minority Automobile Dealers (NAMAD)

8201 Corporate Dr., Ste.190
Lanham, MD 20785
Ph: (301)306-1614
Fax: (301)306-1493
URL: http://www.namad.org
Contact: Damon Lester, Pres.
Founded: 1980. **Members:** 500. **Membership Dues:** premier, associate, friend, $500 (annual) ● regular, corporate, $5,000 (annual) ● dealer, $150 (annual) ● affiliate, $200 (annual) ● automobile manufacturer, $25,000 (annual). **Staff:** 4. **Budget:** $1,000,000. **Languages:** English, Spanish. **Description:** Automobile dealers. Acts as liaison between membership, the federal government, the community, and industry representatives; seeks to better the business conditions of its members on an ongoing basis. Serves as a confidential spokesperson for dealers. Offers business analysis, financial counseling, and short- and long-term management planning. Conducts research programs; compiles statistics. **Publications:** *NAMAD Newsletter*, bimonthly. **Price:** free for members. **Circulation:** 1,000. **Advertising:** accepted. Alternate Formats: online ● *Resource Guide*, annual. **Advertising:** accepted. **Conventions/Meetings:** quarterly board meeting ● annual conference (exhibits).

2766 ■ National Association of Minority Women in Business (NAMWIB)

Address Unknown since 2007
Founded: 1972. **Members:** 5,000. **Description:** Minority women in business ownership and management positions; college students. Serves as a network for the exchange of ideas and information on business opportunities for minority women in the public and private sectors. Conducts research; sponsors workshops, conferences, seminars, and luncheons. Maintains speakers' bureau, hall of fame, and placement service; compiles statistics. **Awards: Type:** recognition. **Recipient:** to women who have made significant contributions to the field. **Publications:** *Today*, bimonthly. Newsletter. **Advertising:** accepted ● Brochures. **Conventions/Meetings:** annual conference (exhibits) ● semiannual conference.

2767 ■ National Business League (NBL)

Address Unknown since 2007
URL: http://www.thenationalbusinessleague.com/
Founded: 1900. **Members:** 10,000. **Staff:** 12. **Budget:** $500,000. **Local Groups:** 127. **Description:** Organizational vehicle for minority businesspeople. Promotes the economic development of minorities. Encourages minority ownership and management of small businesses and supports full minority participation within the free enterprise system. Maintains file of minority vendors and corporate procurement and purchasing agents. Conducts special projects. **Awards: Type:** recognition. **Formerly:** National Negro Business League. **Publications:** *Corporate Guide for Minority Vendors*, annual ● *National Memo*, monthly. Membership Directory ● *President's Briefs*, monthly. Bulletin. **Conventions/Meetings:** annual conference (exhibits) - usually fall.

2768 ■ National Minority Business Council (NMBC)

120 Broadway, 19th Fl.
New York, NY 10271
Ph: (212)693-5050
Fax: (212)693-5048
E-mail: nmbc@msn.com
URL: http://www.nmbc.org
Contact: John F. Robinson, Pres./CEO
Founded: 1972. **Members:** 400. **Membership Dues:** small/minority business, women-owned business, $375 (annual). **Staff:** 5. **Budget:** $350,000. **Description:** Represents minority businesses in all areas of industry and commerce. Seeks to increase profitability by developing marketing, sales, and management skills in minority businesses. Acts as an informational source for the national minority business community. Includes programs such as: legal services plan that provides free legal services to members in such areas as sales contracts, copyrights, estate planning, and investment agreement; business referral service that develops potential customer leads; international trade assistance program that provides technical assistance in developing foreign markets; executive banking program that teaches members how to package a business loan for bank approval; procurement outreach program for minority and women business owners. Conducts continuing management education and provides assistance in teaching youth the free enterprise system. **Awards:** Luncheon Award. **Frequency:** annual. **Type:** recognition. **Recipient:** for minority and corporate leaders who have distin-

guished themselves in their respective industries. **Committees:** Women's Business. **Programs:** BizDev; International Trade; SBA (8a) Certification. **Publications:** *Corporate Minority Vendor Directory*, annual ● *Corporate Purchasing Directory*, annual ● *NMBC Business Report*, biennial. Alternate Formats: online.

2769 ■ National Minority Supplier Development Council (NMSDC)
1040 Ave. of the Americas, 2nd Fl.
New York, NY 10018
Ph: (212)944-2430
Fax: (212)719-9611
E-mail: nmsdc1@aol.com
URL: http://www.nmsdcus.org
Contact: Harriet R. Michel, Pres.

Founded: 1972. **Members:** 455. **Staff:** 20. **Budget:** $14,222,337. **Regional Groups:** 39. **Description:** Provides a direct link between its 3,500 corporate members and minority-owned businesses (Black, Hispanic, Asian and Native American) and increases procurement and business opportunities for minority businesses of all sizes. **Libraries: Type:** not open to the public; reference. **Subjects:** business. **Awards:** Corporation of the Year. **Frequency:** annual. **Type:** recognition. **Computer Services:** database, certified minority suppliers ● online services, certified minority-owned businesses. **Additional Websites:** http://www.nmsdc.org. **Programs:** Advanced Management Education; Centers of Excellence; Corporate Plus; Regional Seminars and Supplier Diversity Online course. **Formerly:** (1980) National Minority Purchasing Council. **Publications:** *Minority Supplier News*, quarterly. Newsletter. **Price:** free for members. Alternate Formats: online ● *National Minority Supplier Development Council—Annual Report*. Reports financial data of the organization. **Conventions/Meetings:** annual Conference and Business Opportunity Fair - conference and trade show (exhibits) - always October. 2008 Oct. 26-29, Las Vegas, NV; 2009 Oct. 25-28, New Orleans, LA; 2010 Oct. 24-27, Phoenix, AZ.

2770 ■ NuBian Exchange News
Address Unknown since 2008
URL: http://nubian_exchange.tripod.com/newsltr.html

Founded: 1994. **Members:** 200. **Membership Dues:** individual, $9. **Staff:** 1. **For-Profit. Description:** Seeks to assist consumers in locating African-American businesses, products, services, and organizations nationally. **Computer Services:** database.

Mortuary Services

2771 ■ American Institute of Commemorative Art (AICA)
11003 Fellswood Ct.
Louisville, KY 40243-0602
Ph: (502)254-1375
Fax: (502)254-1375
E-mail: lelandb@monuments-aica.com
URL: http://www.monuments-aica.com
Contact: Leland B. Longstreth, Exec. Dir.

Founded: 1951. **Members:** 120. **Staff:** 2. **Budget:** $80,000. **Description:** Retailers of memorials and cemetery monuments. **Libraries: Type:** reference. **Holdings:** artwork. **Subjects:** cemetery memorials. **Committees:** Awards; Business Procedures and New Technology; Design; Ideas and Standards; Sales Ideas Techniques; Scholarship. **Publications:** *AICA Directory*, annual ● *Milestone*, quarterly. **Conventions/Meetings:** annual conference ● annual meeting.

2772 ■ American Monument Association (AMA)
c/o Pennie Sabel, Exec. Dir.
30 Eden Alley, Ste.301
Columbus, OH 43215
Ph: (614)461-5852
Fax: (614)461-1497
URL: http://www.imsa-online.com/ammonas.htm
Contact: Pennie Sabel, Exec. Dir.

Founded: 1904. **Members:** 70. **Staff:** 1. **Budget:** $220,000. **Regional Groups:** 2. **Description:** Quarriers, manufacturers, and wholesalers of granite and marble used in the fabrication of memorials. **Computer Services:** Mailing lists. **Formerly:** (1914) National Association of American Granite Producers; (1946) American Granite Association. **Publications:** *Red Book*, annual ● *Stone in America*, monthly. Magazine. Includes information for retail monument dealers, with emphasis on marketing and promotion of the concept of upright memorials. **Price:** $30.00/year in U.S.; $36.00/year in Canada; $37.00/year outside U.S. and Canada. ISSN: 0160-7243. **Circulation:** 2,100. **Advertising:** accepted ● Pamphlets. Includes information for retail merchants. **Conventions/Meetings:** annual meeting.

2773 ■ American Society of Embalmers (ASE)
PO Box 0685
Forest Park, IL 60130-0685
Free: (800)728-9185
Fax: (800)815-6610
E-mail: amsocembalmers@sbcglobal.net
URL: http://www.amsocembalmers.org
Contact: Melissa Johnson Williams CFSP, Exec. Dir./Co-Founder

Founded: 2004. **Members:** 250. **Membership Dues:** individual, $35 (annual) ● associate, $150 (annual). **Description:** Establishes and promotes embalming education standards. Promotes ethical practice standards in the fields of embalming and restorative art. Works for public awareness and better understanding of the preservative processes. Promotes a better understanding of the real and potential health issues of the embalmer. **Publications:** *The Embalmers Quarterly Journal*. Newsletter. **Price:** included in membership dues. Alternate Formats: online ● Membership Directory. **Price:** included in membership dues. Alternate Formats: online.

2774 ■ Associated Funeral Directors International (AFDSI)
PO Box 1089
Hammonton, NJ 08037-5089
Ph: (423)392-1985
Free: (800)346-7151
Fax: (423)392-1179
Contact: Richard A. Santore, Exec. Off.

Founded: 1939. **Members:** 1,000. **Staff:** 3. **Budget:** $89,000. **Description:** Funeral homes and mortuaries; franchise-membership granted to one establishment in a community. Services other funeral directors in the shipping of human remains. Provides members with business and professional aids, including public relations and advertising programs, booklets and leaflets, and cooperative buying of products. **Libraries: Type:** reference. **Holdings:** artwork, periodicals. **Awards: Type:** recognition. **Computer Services:** database ● mailing lists. **Formerly:** (1986) Associated Funeral Directors Service; (1992) Associated Funeral Directors Service International. **Publications:** *AFDS Today*, bimonthly. Magazine. **Price:** $29.95/year. **Circulation:** 20,000. **Advertising:** accepted. Alternate Formats: online ● *Associated Funeral Directors Service International—Shipping Directory*, annual. Journal. Covers the funeral service field. Includes obituaries, directory and member list. **Price:** free for funeral homes, suppliers, and libraries. **Circulation:** 10,000. **Advertising:** accepted. **Conventions/Meetings:** annual conference ● annual seminar.

2775 ■ Casket and Funeral Supply Association of America (CFSA)
49 Sherwood Terr., Ste.Y
Lake Bluff, IL 60044-2231
Ph: (847)295-6630
Fax: (847)295-6647
E-mail: mallen@cfsaa.org
URL: http://www.cfsaa.org
Contact: Mark B. Allen, Exec. Dir.

Founded: 1913. **Members:** 170. **Membership Dues:** firm (minimum), $500 (annual) ● firm (maximum), $15,000 (annual). **Staff:** 3. **Budget:** $450,000. **Description:** Manufacturers and distributors of burial caskets and other funeral supplies. **Telecommunication Services:** electronic mail, brussell@cfsaa.org. **Formerly:** Casket Manufacturers Association of America. **Publications:** Newsletter, monthly. Keeps members abreast of the changing trends in the industry. **Circulation:** 500.

2776 ■ Catholic Cemetery Conference (CCC)
1400 S Wolf Rd., Bldg. No. 3
Hillside, IL 60162-2197
Ph: (708)202-1242
Free: (888)850-8131
Fax: (708)202-1255
E-mail: info@ntriplec.com
URL: http://www.ntriplec.com
Contact: Ms. Sidney Cristol, Exec. Dir.

Founded: 1949. **Members:** 1,400. **Staff:** 5. **Multinational. Description:** Archdiocesan and diocesan directors of Catholic cemeteries; associate members are administrators of Catholic cemeteries. **Libraries: Type:** reference. **Subjects:** cemetery monuments, shrines. **Committees:** Design and Construction; Environment; Future; Law and Legislation; Liturgy; Management; Marketing; Membership; Public Relations; Smaller Parish Cemetery. **Formerly:** (2006) National Catholic Cemetery Conference. **Publications:** *The Catholic Cemetery*, monthly. Magazine. Includes advertisers' index. **Price:** available to members only. **Circulation:** 2,000. **Advertising:** accepted ● *The Catholic Cemetery: A Vision for the Millennium*. Book. **Price:** $5.00 plus shipping and handling ● *Design and Construction Manual*. Handbook ● *Field Operation Manual*. Handbook ● *Guidelines for Christian Burial* ● *Mausoleum Maintenance Manual*. Handbook ● *National Catholic Cemetery Conference—Membership and Resource Directory*, annual. Membership Directory. **Price:** available to members only. **Circulation:** 2,000. **Advertising:** accepted ● *Parish Cemetery Handbook*. **Conventions/Meetings:** annual convention (exhibits).

2777 ■ Cremation Association of North America (CANA)
401 N Michigan Ave.
Chicago, IL 60611
Ph: (312)245-1077 (312)321-6806
Fax: (312)321-4098
E-mail: cana@smithbucklin.com
URL: http://www.cremationassociation.org
Contact: Kevin Hacke, Exec. Dir.

Founded: 1913. **Members:** 1,500. **Membership Dues:** regular/supplier/consultant/association, $350 (annual) ● affiliate, $175 (annual). **Staff:** 4. **Budget:** $700,000. **Multinational. Description:** Cemeteries, crematories, funeral directors, and manufacturers. Seeks to increase public awareness and knowledge of cremation and memorialization. Conducts research; compiles statistics. Holds certification programs and trade show. **Telecommunication Services:** electronic mail, khacke@smithbucklin.com. **Affiliated With:** International Cremation Federation. **Formerly:** (1975) Cremation Association of America. **Publications:** *Cremationist*, quarterly. Magazine. **Price:** $24.00/year; $36.00/2 years. **Circulation:** 1,700. **Advertising:** accepted ● *Newsletter Update*, bimonthly. **Conventions/Meetings:** annual convention, tabletop exhibits (exhibits) - always August ● annual Cremation Marketing - seminar.

2778 ■ Federated Funeral Directors of America (FFDA)
PO Box 19244
Springfield, IL 62794-9244
Ph: (217)525-1712
Fax: (217)525-2104
E-mail: info@ffda.com
URL: http://www.ffda.com
Contact: John R. Rodenburg, Pres.

Founded: 1925. **For-Profit. Description:** Provides management counsel, accounting, and business services to member funeral homes. Compiles statistics on funeral services and funeral costs. **Publications:** *FFDA Comments*, bimonthly. Newsletter.

2779 ■ Flying Funeral Directors of America (FFDA)
Address Unknown since 2007

Founded: 1960. **Members:** 130. **Description:** Funeral directors who own planes, have a pilot's license, or are interested in flying; persons associated with allied funeral industries who are licensed pilots. Purposes are: to create and further a common interest in flying and funeral service; to join together in case of mass disaster; to improve flying safety. **Awards: Type:** recognition. **Publications:** *Crosswinds*, quarterly ● *Membership Roster*, biennial. **Conventions/Meetings:** annual meeting, held in conjunction with the National Funeral Directors Association ● annual meeting - usually April or May.

2780 ■ Funeral Consumers Alliance (FCA)
33 Patchen Rd.
South Burlington, VT 05403
Ph: (802)865-8300
Free: (800)765-0107
Fax: (802)865-2626
E-mail: fca@funerals.org
URL: http://www.funerals.org
Contact: Joshua Slocum, Exec. Dir.

Founded: 1963. **Members:** 500,000. **Membership Dues:** individual, representative of other organization, $25 (annual). **Staff:** 3. **Budget:** $265,000. **Local Groups:** 120. **Description:** Promotes a consumer's right to choose a dignified, meaningful, affordable funeral. Provides educational material to the public and affiliates. Monitors the funeral and cemetery industry for consumers nationwide. Responds to consumer complaints. Maintains speakers' bureau. **Libraries: Type:** reference. **Holdings:** 50; books. **Subjects:** death, dying, grief, burials, cremation. **Telecommunication Services:** electronic mail, joshua@funerals.org. **Formerly:** The Leader; (1994) Continental Association of Funeral and Memorial Societies; (2001) Funeral and Memorial Societies of America. **Publications:** *The FCA Newsletter*, quarterly. **Price:** $10.00/year ● Membership Directory, periodic. Includes U.S. members. **Price:** free ● Also publishes informational materials. **Conventions/Meetings:** biennial meeting, attended by board members of each society.

2781 ■ International Cemetery and Funeral Association (ICFA)
107 Carpenter Dr., Ste.100
Sterling, VA 20164
Ph: (703)391-8400
Free: (800)645-7700
Fax: (703)391-8416
E-mail: gen4@icfa.org
URL: http://www.icfa.org
Contact: Robert Fells, External COO/Gen. Counsel

Founded: 1887. **Members:** 6,200. **Membership Dues:** regular/supplier, $195 (annual) ● music licensing, $238 (annual) ● associate, $75 (annual) ● professional, $135 (annual) ● mortuary school faculty/student/trainee, $25 (annual). **Staff:** 15. **Description:** Owners and managers of cemeteries and funeral homes; related suppliers and professional service firms. **Formed by Merger of:** (1997) American Cemetery Association; (1997) National Association of Cemeteries. **Publications:** *ICFA Buyer's Guide and Membership Directory*, annual ● *International Cemetery and Funeral Management*, 10/year. Journal. **Price:** $29.95/year. ISSN: 0270-5281. **Circulation:** 6,100. **Advertising:** accepted. **Conventions/Meetings:** annual convention (exhibits) ● annual Management Conference - always fall ● Sales Management and Marketing Conference ● seminar, educational ● Small Cemetery and Funeral Management Conference.

2782 ■ International Memorialization Supply Association (IMSA)
PO Box 663
Export, PA 15632
Free: (800)864-4174
E-mail: info@imsa-online.com
URL: http://www.imsa-online.com
Contact: David A. Beck, Sec.

Founded: 1955. **Members:** 110. **Membership Dues:** ordinary, $75 (annual). **Description:** Suppliers to the death care industry. **Formerly:** (1979) Cemetery Supply Association; (1994) International Cemetery Supply Association.

2783 ■ International Order of the Golden Rule (IOGR)
PO Box 28689
St. Louis, MO 63146-1189
Ph: (314)209-7142
Free: (800)637-8030
Fax: (314)209-1289
E-mail: info@ogr.org
URL: http://www.ogr.org
Contact: William A. Edmunds, Exec. Dir.

Founded: 1926. **Members:** 1,200. **Staff:** 18. **Multinational. Description:** Service organization comprising independent funeral directors united for public relations, advertising, continuing professional educational purposes, and as a resource guide to the public on death care issues. Motto is "service measured not by gold but by the Golden Rule". Sponsors business support services and educational programs. **Libraries: Type:** reference. **Holdings:** artwork, books, clippings, periodicals. **Awards:** Exemplary Service Award. **Frequency:** annual. **Type:** recognition. **Recipient:** to a member for excellence in service to families ● Golden Light Award. **Frequency:** annual. **Type:** recognition. **Recipient:** to members for professional achievement ● OGR Award of Excellence. **Frequency:** annual. **Type:** monetary. **Recipient:** for mortuary students who have demonstrated excellence in the study of mortuary science. **Telecommunication Services:** electronic mail, bedmunds@ogr.org. **Also Known As:** OGR. **Publications:** *The Independent*, bimonthly. Magazine. Features funeral service news and information. **Price:** free for members; $30.00 for nonmembers. **Circulation:** 1,500. **Advertising:** accepted. Alternate Formats: diskette. **Conventions/Meetings:** annual conference (exhibits) - always spring ● triennial seminar, 2-day educational meeting/seminar (exhibits).

2784 ■ Jewish Funeral Directors of America (JFDA)
150 Lynnway, Ste.506
Seaport Landing
Lynn, MA 01902
Ph: (781)477-9300
Fax: (781)477-9393
E-mail: info@jfda.org
URL: http://www.jfda.org
Contact: Florence Pressman CAE, Exec. Dir.

Founded: 1927. **Members:** 200. **Staff:** 1. **Description:** Predominantly serves members of the Jewish faith. Assists people of the Jewish faith arrange meaningful and affordable funerals in the Jewish tradition. **Telecommunication Services:** electronic mail, jfdamer@aol.com. **Publications:** *Funeral Etiquette*, 3/year. Newsletter. **Circulation:** 200. **Advertising:** accepted ● *How to Explain Death to Children*, 3/year. Newsletter. **Circulation:** 200. **Advertising:** accepted ● *If You Will Lift the Load*, annual. Newsletter ● *Jewish Funeral Director*, annual. Newsletter. **Price:** $30.00/copy ● *Jewish Funeral Guide* (in English and Russian) ● *Jewish Funeral in Contemporary Life* ● *Suicide in the Young*. **Conventions/Meetings:** semiannual board meeting ● annual meeting.

2785 ■ Monument Builders of North America (MBNA)
PO Box 917525
Longwood, FL 32791
Free: (800)233-4472
Fax: (407)774-6751
E-mail: info@monumentbuilders.org
URL: http://www.monumentbuilders.org
Contact: Paul A. DiMatteo CM, Pres.

Founded: 1906. **Members:** 900. **Membership Dues:** regular, $435 (annual) ● branch, $120 (annual) ● associate, $195 (annual) ● regular, in Canada, $370 (annual). **Staff:** 6. **Budget:** $1,000,000. **Languages:** English, French. **Description:** Monument retailers, manufacturers, and wholesalers; bronze manufacturers and suppliers. Provides sales, advertising, and management materials to members. Develops modern and religious memorial designs. Provides Affinity Programs such as discounts and low-cost credit card processing. Opposes "restrictive business practices and unfair competition". Compiles statistics; conducts specialized education and certification programs; maintains speakers' bureau. **Libraries: Type:** not open to the public. **Holdings:** 10; video recordings. **Subjects:** monument design and production. **Awards:** ASPIRE Awards. **Frequency:** annual. **Type:** recognition. **Committees:** Certification; Industry Action. **Absorbed:** American Historic Monument Society. **Formed by Merger of:** Monument Builders of America; Monument Builders of Canada. **Publications:** *Membership Roster and Buyer's Guide*, annual. Membership Directory. **Price:** $250.00. **Advertising:** accepted. Alternate Formats: online; CD-ROM ● *Monument Builders News*, monthly. **Conventions/Meetings:** annual convention (exhibits) - usually end of January or first week of February ● annual Monument Industry Convention and Show - convention and trade show (exhibits).

2786 ■ National Casket Retailers Association (NCRA)
c/o Dean Magliocca, Chm.
403 E Hallandale Beach Blvd.
Hallandale, FL 33009
Ph: (954)454-7474
E-mail: dean@funeraldepot.com
URL: http://www.casketstores.com
Contact: Dean Magliocca, Chm.

Founded: 1997. **Membership Dues:** regular, $95 (annual). **Description:** Represents and promotes the retail casket industry. **Publications:** *Casket Retailing*. Newsletter. **Price:** included in membership dues. Alternate Formats: online ● *Casket Store National Directory*. **Price:** included in membership dues; $40.00 for nonmembers. **Advertising:** accepted ● *NCRA Consumer Survey*. **Conventions/Meetings:** annual meeting.

2787 ■ National Concrete Burial Vault Association (NCBVA)
PO Box 917525
Longwood, FL 32791-7525
Ph: (407)788-1996
Free: (800)538-1423
Fax: (321)226-9007
E-mail: tom@camco.biz
URL: http://ncbva.org
Contact: Mr. Thomas A. Monahan CAE, Exec. Dir.

Founded: 1929. **Members:** 301. **Membership Dues:** regular, $170-$525 (annual) ● affiliate, $600 (annual) ● associate, $150 (annual). **Staff:** 2. **Budget:** $150,000. **Description:** Manufacturers of concrete burial vaults. Provides a unified voice for the concrete burial vault industry regardless of product affiliation, brand recognition or location. **Publications:** *The Bulletin*, bimonthly ● Directory, annual. **Conventions/Meetings:** annual conference (exhibits) - always June.

2788 ■ National Funeral Directors Association (NFDA)
13625 Bishop's Dr.
Brookfield, WI 53005-6607
Ph: (262)789-1880 (262)814-1527
Free: (800)228-6332
Fax: (262)789-6977
E-mail: nfda@nfda.org
URL: http://www.nfda.org
Contact: Christine Pepper CAE, CEO

Founded: 1882. **Members:** 15,000. **Membership Dues:** individual, $295 (annual) ● retired licensee, apprentice/intern, $55-$65 (annual) ● life, $888. **Staff:** 44. **Budget:** $9,100,000. **State Groups:** 50. **Description:** Federation of state funeral directors' associations with individual membership of funeral directors. Seeks to enhance the funeral service profession and promote quality services to the consumers. Conducts professional education seminars and home study courses. Compiles statistics.

Libraries: Type: reference. **Holdings:** 1,000; audio recordings, books, video recordings. **Subjects:** dying, death, bereavement. **Awards:** Pursuit of Excellence. **Frequency:** annual. **Type:** recognition. **Recipient:** for meeting the criteria for community relations programming and professional accomplishment. **Committees:** Communications; Education; Government Relations; Operations. **Publications:** *The Director*, monthly. Magazine. Contains articles regarding funeral service. Includes advertisers' index, calendar of events, and book reviews. **Price:** included in membership dues; $30.00 /year for nonmembers; $36.00 for nonmembers (foreign). ISSN: 0199-3186. **Circulation:** 15,000. **Advertising:** accepted ● *National Funeral Directors Association—Directory of Members*, annual. **Price:** free for members; $75.00/ issue for others. **Circulation:** 15,000 ● Brochures. Contains consumer information about death, dying, and bereavement. **Price:** free for individuals. **Conventions/Meetings:** annual conference ● annual convention - usually October.

2789 ■ National Funeral Directors and Morticians Association (NFDMA)
3951 Snapfinger Pkwy., Ste.570
Omega World Center
Decatur, GA 30035
Free: (800)434-0958
Fax: (404)286-6573
E-mail: info@nfdma.com
URL: http://www.nfdma.com
Contact: Sharon L. Seay CMP, Exec. Dir.
Founded: 1924. **Members:** 1,600. **Membership Dues:** professional, $200 (annual) ● apprentice, $75 (annual) ● student, $25 (annual). **Staff:** 4. **Budget:** $450,000. **Regional Groups:** 9. **State Groups:** 27. **Description:** State, district, and local funeral directors and embalmers associations and their members. Promotes ethical practices; encourages just and uniform laws pertaining to funeral directing and embalming industry. **Libraries: Type:** reference. **Holdings:** periodicals. **Subjects:** training and development, industry updates, CEU credits. **Awards:** NFDM Scholarship. **Frequency:** annual. **Type:** scholarship. **Formed by Merger of:** (1957) National Negro Funeral Directors and Morticians Association. **Publications:** *The Mini Scope*, quarterly. Newsletter. **Price:** included in membership dues. **Circulation:** 2,000. **Advertising:** accepted. Alternate Formats: CD-ROM; online; magnetic tape. **Conventions/Meetings:** annual meeting (exhibits) - every first week of August.

2790 ■ Preferred Funeral Directors International (PFDI)
PO Box 335
Indian Rocks Beach, FL 33785
Free: (888)655-1566
E-mail: info@pfdi.org
URL: http://www.pfdi.org
Contact: F. Daniel Moloney Jr., Pres.
Founded: 1937. **Members:** 90. **Staff:** 1. **Budget:** $150,000. **Description:** Funeral firms (consisting of more than one home) and individual homes. Selects members based on the continued utilization of innovative management practices over a period of years. Seeks to increase public awareness of the funeral home industry. **Awards: Type:** recognition. **Formerly:** Advertising Funeral Directors of America. **Publications:** *Preferred Directories*, quarterly. Directory ● Newsletter. Alternate Formats: online. **Conventions/Meetings:** semiannual meeting - always spring and fall.

2791 ■ Selected Independent Funeral Homes
500 Lake Cook Rd., Ste.205
Deerfield, IL 60015
Ph: (847)236-9401
Free: (800)323-4219
Fax: (847)236-9968
E-mail: info@selectedfuneralhomes.org
URL: http://www.selectedfuneralhomes.org
Contact: Porter Loring III, Pres.
Founded: 1917. **Members:** 965. **Staff:** 11. **Description:** Funeral directors. Aims to study, develop, and establish a standard of service for the benefit of its consumers. Provides a continuing forum for the exchange, development and dissemination of knowledge and information beneficial to members and the public. **Committees:** Insurance Trust. **Formerly:** (2001) National Selected Morticians. **Publications:** *The Bulletin*, bimonthly. Newsletter ● *Membership Roster*, annual. Membership Directory ● Brochure. Alternate Formats: online. **Conventions/Meetings:** annual meeting.

2792 ■ Telophase Society (TS)
c/o Stewart Enterprises, Inc.
1333 S Clearview Pkwy.
Jefferson, LA 70121
Ph: (619)299-0805 (504)729-1400
Free: (800)520-5146
Fax: (619)299-8417
E-mail: klocantr@stei.com
URL: http://www.stewartenterprises.com
Founded: 1971. **Members:** 55,000. **Membership Dues:** life, $20. **Regional Groups:** 3. **Local Groups:** 4. **For-Profit. Description:** Provides services for cremation and burial at sea. Counselors offer assistance to families with financial arrangements, death certificate needs, and Veteran arrangements for burial or reimbursements after death. **Also Known As:** Sentinel Cremation Societies.

Motion Picture

2793 ■ Production Equipment Rental Association (PERA)
PO Box 77327
San Francisco, CA 94107-0327
Ph: (415)552-2094
E-mail: info@peraonline.org
URL: http://peraonline.org/cgi-bin/WebObjects/PERA
Contact: Kay Baker, Pres.
Multinational. Description: Represents suppliers of production equipment, including film cameras, broadcast and professional video cameras and equipment, lighting equipment, grip equipment, support equipment, studio space and production facilities to motion picture/film, broadcast television, corporate/ promotional video and commercial productions, also insurance brokers, trade show producers, magazine and directory publishers, business systems and management consultants and other companies. Promotes the production equipment industry. Maintains an equipment database. **Telecommunication Services:** electronic bulletin board, postings of missing equipment and product announcements from member companies, industry related messages, and used equipment sales notices. **Publications:** *Rental Resource Guide* ● Membership Directory.

2794 ■ United Drive-In Theatre Owners Association (UDITOA)
PO Box 24771
Middle River, MD 21220
E-mail: mail@uditoa.org
URL: http://www.uditoa.org
Contact: Walt Effinger, Pres.
Founded: 1999. **Members:** 202. **Membership Dues:** full (voting), $50 (annual) ● corporate associate, $100 (annual) ● individual associate (non-voting), $30 (annual) ● temporary - limit of 2 years, reviewable yearly (non-voting), $1,000. **Multinational. Description:** Serves drive-in theatre owners. Promotes commercial motion picture exhibition at drive-in theatres worldwide. Ensures that drive-in theatres remain a viable and competitive part of the motion picture industry. Forms a strong membership of drive-in owners who can help one another with problems, assists others in getting into the business, and educates the public, the media, and association members. Produces a benchmark to the industry. **Publications:** Newsletter, bimonthly. **Price:** included in membership dues. **Conventions/Meetings:** annual convention.

Motorcycle

2795 ■ Motorcycle Industry Council (MIC)
2 Jenner St., Ste.150
Irvine, CA 92618-3806
Ph: (949)727-4211
Fax: (949)727-3313
E-mail: aftmgr@mic.org
URL: http://www.mic.org
Contact: Tim Buche, Pres.
Founded: 1914. **Members:** 310. **Staff:** 20. **Budget:** $3,500,000. **Description:** Manufacturers and distributors of motorcycles and allied industries. Maintains liaison with state and federal governments. Operates collection of research documents, federal and state government documents, and trade publications. Compiles statistics. **Libraries: Type:** reference. **Holdings:** 1,000. **Committees:** Aftermarket; Industry Relations; Land Use; Public Relations; Statistics; Technical. **Formerly:** Motorcycle and Allied Trades Association; Motorcycle, Scooter and Allied Trades Association. **Publications:** *Membership Mailing*, monthly. Pamphlets. **Conventions/Meetings:** annual meeting.

Music

2796 ■ American Disc Jockey Association (ADJA)
20118 N 67th Ave., Ste.300-605
Glendale, AZ 85308
Ph: (623)882-8048
Free: (888)723-5776
Fax: (623)362-9537
E-mail: office@adja.org
URL: http://www.adja.org
Contact: Peter Merry, Pres.
Founded: 1992. **Members:** 1,500. **Membership Dues:** full, $525-$825 (triennial) ● full, $200-$300 (annual) ● affiliate, $500 (annual) ● limited to liability insurance (access only), $99 (annual) ● Canadian DJ listing, $25 (annual) ● Club DJ listing, $25 (annual). **Staff:** 8. **Regional Groups:** 6. **State Groups:** 27. **Local Groups:** 47. **Description:** Mobile and night club disc jockeys. Seeks to promote the disc jockey as a professional form of entertainment; improves the industry by establishing standards, procedures, and benefits. Assists and trains members; provides forums for professional disc jockeys; conducts educational, charitable, and research programs. **Libraries: Type:** by appointment only; lending; reference. **Holdings:** 36; archival material, articles, audiovisuals, business records, periodicals, video recordings. **Subjects:** scripting, networking, wedding ceremonies, taxes, contracts, Latin music, ballroom dancing, country music, multi system operations, internet marketing, digital DJ technologies content requests. **Awards:** Chapter of the Year. **Frequency:** annual. **Type:** trophy. **Recipient:** to the best chapter, the one that most exemplified the spirit of the ADJA ● Michael Butler Humanitarian Award. **Frequency:** annual. **Type:** trophy. **Recipient:** to the member whose service to others most exemplifies that of Michael Butler, a member, who as a paramedic died while saving the lives of others ● Peter Merry Leadership Award. **Frequency:** annual. **Type:** trophy. **Recipient:** to the member who most embodies the qualities of leadership that the past president Peter Merry exemplified in his leadership. **Computer Services:** database ● electronic publishing, newsletter ● mailing lists. **Publications:** *ADJA Newsletter*, quarterly. **Circulation:** 10,000. **Advertising:** accepted ● *Mobile Beat*, annual. Magazine. **Price:** $25.00. **Advertising:** accepted ● Brochures, annual. **Price:** $25.00. **Conventions/Meetings:** annual meeting - every February in Las Vegas, NV.

2797 ■ American Federation of Violin and Bow Makers (AFVBM)
321 Columbus Ave.
Boston, MA 02116
E-mail: creuning@reuning.com
URL: http://www.afvbm.com
Contact: John Montgomery, Governor
Founded: 1980. **Members:** 120. **Membership Dues:** regular, $300 (annual). **Description:** Professionals who make, restore, and repair violins and bows. Aims to elevate professional standards of craftsmanship and ethical conduct among members. Designs

programs to develop members' technical skills and knowledge; aims to establish internship programs for individuals who wish to become violin makers or repair persons. Conducts competitions and annual exhibition. Grants journeyman and master status in the field. Maintains speakers' bureau, museum, and biographical archives. Holds seminars. **Libraries: Type:** not open to the public. **Awards: Type:** recognition. **Recipient:** for the best instruments displayed. **Committees:** Ethics; Exhibition Guidelines; Master's Examination; Pernambuco Conservation; Publicity. **Publications:** Membership Directory, annual. **Price:** free. Alternate Formats: online ● Also publishes materials on lectures, symposia, competitions, and exhibits. **Conventions/Meetings:** annual Players Meet Makers - meeting, exhibits include violins, violas, cellos, and bows made by members (exhibits).

2798 ■ American Institute of Organbuilders (AIO)
PO Box 130982
Houston, TX 77219
Ph: (713)529-2212
Fax: (713)529-2212
E-mail: execsec@pipeorgan.org
URL: http://www.pipeorgan.org
Contact: Howard Maple, Exec. Sec.
Founded: 1974. **Members:** 370. **Membership Dues:** regular, $80 (annual). **Staff:** 1. **Budget:** $70,000. **Description:** Professional builders and service technicians of pipe organs. Advances the art of pipe organ building by encouraging discussion, inquiry, and research; furthers knowledge regarding pipe organ building through lectures and the exchange of information. Conducts examinations and small-group training seminars. **Libraries: Type:** reference. **Holdings:** archival material. **Awards:** AIO Scholarship. **Frequency:** annual. **Type:** scholarship. **Recipient:** for organbuilders or maintenance technicians with more than one year of full-time experience. **Committees:** Audit; Convention Overview; Education; Ethics; Examination; Nominating. **Affiliated With:** American Guild of Organists; American Theatre Organ Society; Associated Pipe Organ Builders of America; International Society of Organbuilders; Organ Historical Society. **Publications:** *AIO Service Manual.* Alternate Formats: online ● *Apprenticeship and Training Policy Manual* ● *Journal of American Organbuilding*, quarterly. Contains technical articles and notices of membership nominations. **Price:** $5.00/back issue; $12.00 /year for nonmembers; included in membership dues. ISSN: 1048-2482. **Circulation:** 600. **Advertising:** accepted ● *Membership List*, annual. Membership Directory ● Video. **Price:** $10.00 for members; $20.00 for nonmembers. **Conventions/Meetings:** annual convention, with booths for industry suppliers (exhibits) - always October.

2799 ■ Associated Pipe Organ Builders of America (APOBA)
PO Box 155
Chicago Ridge, IL 60415
Free: (800)473-5270
E-mail: qpo1@earthlink.net
URL: http://www.apoba.com
Contact: Michael Quimby, Pres.
Founded: 1941. **Members:** 27. **Description:** Manufacturers of pipe organs and pipe organ parts. Aims to expand and perfect the art of pipe organ building in the U.S. Sponsors educational programs and speakers' bureau. Compiles marketing statistics. **Computer Services:** database, Encyclopedia Organica. **Affiliated With:** American Guild of Organists; American Institute of Organbuilders; Organ Historical Society. **Publications:** *The American Organist*, monthly. Journal ● *Organ Building in America: 200 Years of Craftsmanship* ● *Planning Space for Pipe Organ.* Booklet. **Price:** free. Alternate Formats: online ● *Success Stories: Five Pipe Organ Projects Summarized.* Booklet. **Price:** free. Alternate Formats: online. **Conventions/Meetings:** annual meeting ● annual meeting.

2800 ■ Association of Independent Music Publishers (AIMP)
PO Box 69473
Los Angeles, CA 90069
Ph: (818)771-7301
E-mail: lainfo@aimp.org
URL: http://www.aimp.org
Contact: Cathy Merenda, Pres.
Founded: 1977. **Members:** 266. **Membership Dues:** regular, $75 (annual). **Description:** Individuals involved in the music publishing business. Provides a forum for the discussion of issues and problems facing independent publishers. Seeks to inform members as to how new and existing copyrights may be exploited; serves as the voice of independent publishers before societies, agencies, and the copyright office in Washington, DC, in regard to matters affecting publishers. **Conventions/Meetings:** bimonthly luncheon (exhibits) - always Los Angeles, CA.

2801 ■ Association of Music Producers (AMP)
3 W 18th St., 5th Fl.
New York, NY 10011
Ph: (212)924-4100
Fax: (212)675-0102
E-mail: info@ampnow.com
URL: http://www.ampnow.com
Contact: Jan Horowitz, Pres.
Founded: 1998. **Membership Dues:** individual, $250 (annual) ● corporate (based on billings), $500-$1,500 (annual) ● associate, $500 (annual). **Local Groups:** 4. **Description:** Represents the interests and concerns of producers, composers and music professionals. Gathers and shares information on music production and music business. **Awards:** AMP Mixer of the Year. **Frequency:** annual. **Type:** recognition. **Recipient:** for the best TV commercials of the year. **Computer Services:** Information services, music production ● online services, discussion group. **Committees:** Agency Issues; Public Relations; Union Issues; Writer's Royalties. **Publications:** Membership Directory. Alternate Formats: online.

2802 ■ Blues Music Association (BMA)
Address Unknown since 2008
Founded: 1998. **Membership Dues:** company or individual with gross income of $50000 to above $25 million, $200-$3,000 (annual) ● professional musician or musical group, $100 (annual). **Description:** Blues musicians and music lovers. Working toward increasing the blues audience. Holds monthly committee meetings and annual board meetings. **Publications:** Reports.

2803 ■ Downhill Battle
c/o Nicholas Reville, Dir.
28 Monadnock Rd.
Worcester, MA 01609
Ph: (508)963-7832
Fax: (508)963-5645
E-mail: contact@downhillbattle.org
URL: http://www.downhillbattle.org
Contact: Nicholas Reville, Dir.
Description: Seeks to bring change to the music industry, including the end to the monopoly of the five major record labels. **Telecommunication Services:** electronic mail, npr@downhillbattle.org. **Funds:** Peer-to-Peer Legal Defense.

2804 ■ Guild of American Luthiers (GAL)
8222 S Park Ave.
Tacoma, WA 98408-5226
Ph: (253)472-7853
Fax: (253)472-7853
E-mail: dale@luth.org
URL: http://www.luth.org
Contact: Timothy L. Olsen, Pres.
Founded: 1972. **Members:** 3,300. **Membership Dues:** in U.S., $48 (annual) ● in Canada and Mexico, $52 (annual) ● international, $58 (annual). **Staff:** 6. **Budget:** $200,000. **Multinational. Description:** Luthiers (makers and repairers of stringed instruments such as guitars, violins, lutes, harpsichords, banjos and dulcimers); suppliers; luthier schools; interested musicians, musicologists and aficionados. Disseminates information on instrument building and repair. Seeks to create and sustain an active community of luthiers. **Publications:** *American Lutherie*, quarterly. Journal. Contains news, interviews, research and technical how-to information. **Price:** included in membership dues. ISSN: 0104-7176. **Circulation:** 3,300. **Advertising:** accepted ● *The Big Red Book of American Lutherie, Volume One.* **Price:** $40.00 for members; $45.00 for nonmembers, plus shipping and handling ● *The Big Red Book of American Lutherie, Volume Two.* **Price:** $40.00 for members; $45.00 for nonmembers, plus shipping and handling ● *Historical Lute Construction.* Book. **Price:** $60.00 for members; $65.00 for nonmembers, plus shipping and handling ● *Lutherie Tools.* Book. **Price:** $25.00 for members; $30.00 for nonmembers, plus shipping and handling ● *Lutherie Woods and Steel String Guitar.* Book. **Price:** $25.00 for members; $30.00 for nonmembers, plus shipping and handling. **Conventions/Meetings:** quadrennial lecture and convention, with demonstrations (exhibits).

2805 ■ Guitar and Accessories Marketing Association (GAMA)
PO Box 757
New York, NY 10033
Ph: (212)795-3630
Fax: (212)795-3630
E-mail: assnhdqs@earthlink.net
URL: http://www.discoverguitar.com
Contact: Jerome Hershman, Exec. VP
Founded: 1924. **Members:** 45. **Membership Dues:** supporting, $250 (annual) ● regular, $500-$3,000 (annual). **Staff:** 2. **Budget:** $100,000. **Description:** Manufacturers of stringed musical instruments and accessories, other than piano and band instruments. Works for the promotion of musical instruments, primarily the guitar, and musical education. Supports the American Music Conference (see separate entry). **Committees:** Promotion. **Affiliated With:** American Music Conference. **Formerly:** (1963) National Association of Musical Merchandise Manufacturers; (1982) Guitar and Accessory Manufacturers Association; (1992) Guitar and Accessories Music Marketing Association. **Publications:** *Statistical Sales Data Report on Guitar and Bass Sales*, quarterly. Contains information to help analyze the trends in sales. **Price:** included in membership dues ● Newsletter, quarterly. **Conventions/Meetings:** semiannual meeting, held in conjunction with National Association of Music Merchants - always January, Anaheim, CA and July, Nashville, TN.

2806 ■ Independent Music Retailers Association (IMRA)
912 Carlton Rd.
Tarpon Springs, FL 34689
Ph: (727)938-0571
URL: http://masj.com/imra.html
Contact: Don Kulak, Contact
Founded: 1989. **Members:** 1,000. **Membership Dues:** music retailer, $65 (annual). **Description:** Independent record retailers. Seeks to provide independent music stores with money-making marketing information. Aims to create better working relationships between record labels and independent stores. Maintains speakers' bureau and museum; compiles statistics. Bulk purchasing discounts on industry products and services. **Libraries: Type:** reference. **Holdings:** archival material, business records, clippings, monographs, periodicals. **Subjects:** music business. **Computer Services:** Online services, custom database searches. **Committees:** Political Action. **Publications:** *Journal of the Independent Music Retailers Association*, bimonthly. Includes music marketing information and co-op marketing opportunities. **Price:** $75.00/year for music stores. ISSN: 1042-0649. **Circulation:** 11,000. **Advertising:** accepted ● *Marketing Strategies - A Guide to Distribution.* Book. Music retailing-outselling the major chains. **Price:** $65.00. **Conventions/Meetings:** semiannual convention, with music marketing seminars (exhibits).

2807 ■ Interactive Audio Special Interest Group (IASIG)
c/o MIDI Manufacturers Association
PO Box 3173
La Habra, CA 90632-3173
Ph: (714)736-9774

Fax: (714)736-9775
E-mail: info@iasig.org
URL: http://www.iasig.org
Contact: Kurt Heiden, Chm.
Founded: 1994. **Members:** 200. **Membership Dues:** individual, $50 (annual) ● corporate sponsor (with revenue under $1 million to over $500 million), $250-$2,500 (annual). **Description:** Represents persons involved in the interactive audio development industry. **Working Groups:** Game Audio Education; Interactive XMF; Mobile Audio Technologies. **Publications:** *The Interactive Audio Journal*, periodic. Newsletter. Alternate Formats: online. **Conventions/Meetings:** annual meeting.

2808 ■ International Association of Electronic Keyboard Manufacturers (IAEKM)
c/o Korg USA
316 S Ser. Rd.
Melville, NY 11747
Ph: (631)390-6500
Fax: (631)390-6501
E-mail: mikek@korgusa.com
URL: http://www.iaekm.org
Founded: 1960. **Members:** 20. **Description:** Manufacturers and distributors of electronic keyboards in the U.S. Compiles statistics on industry unit and dollar sales. **Publications:** none. **Affiliated With:** American Music Conference. **Formerly:** (1983) National Association of Electronic Organ Manufacturers; (1988) National Association of Electronic Keyboard Manufacturers. **Conventions/Meetings:** semiannual meeting, held in conjunction with National Association of Music Merchants.

2809 ■ International Association of Piano Builders and Technicians (IAPBT)
c/o Piano Technicians Guild
4444 Forest Ave.
Kansas City, KS 66106
Ph: (913)432-9975
Fax: (913)432-9986
E-mail: iapbt@ptg.org
URL: http://www.ptg.org/iapbt
Contact: Barbara Cassaday, Exec. Dir.
Founded: 1979. **Languages:** Chinese, English, German, Japanese, Korean. **Multinational. Description:** Works as worldwide association of piano service organizations and individuals. Seeks to form and maintain a worldwide fellowship of piano technicians and rebuilders. Provides a means of exchange of technical information and related subjects and for cooperation in scientific research to improve the quality of pianos. Exchange of information is on a voluntary basis. **Telecommunication Services:** electronic mail, exec@ptg.org. **Publications:** *IAPBT Bulletin*, quarterly. Newsletter. Concerned with association activities and technical questions. **Price:** free for members. **Conventions/Meetings:** biennial meeting.

2810 ■ International Band and Orchestral Products Association (NABIM)
PO Box 757
New York, NY 10033
Ph: (212)795-3630
Fax: (212)795-3630
E-mail: assnhdqs@earthlink.net
URL: http://www.nabim.org
Contact: Robert Sulkow, Contact
Founded: 1933. **Members:** 33. **Membership Dues:** regular, $500-$3,000 (annual). **Staff:** 2. **Budget:** $250,000. **Description:** Represents domestic manufacturers and importers of band instruments and accessories. **Formerly:** (2003) National Association of Band Instrument Manufacturers. **Publications:** Newsletter, quarterly. **Conventions/Meetings:** annual meeting - always spring.

2811 ■ International Computer Music Association (ICMA)
1819 Polk St., Ste.330
San Francisco, CA 94109
Fax: (734)878-3031
E-mail: icma@umich.edu
URL: http://www.computermusic.org
Contact: Perry Cook, Pres.
Founded: 1974. **Members:** 500. **Membership Dues:** individual, $60 (annual) ● student, $25 (annual) ● corporation, $300 (annual) ● sustaining, $100 (annual) ● senior, $35 (annual) ● institutional, $200 (annual). **Staff:** 2. **Regional Groups:** 3. **Multinational. Description:** Composers, computer software and hardware developers, researchers, and musicians. Works to advance individuals and institutions involved in the technical, creative, and performance aspects of computer music. Provides networking opportunities; sponsors research and projects; holds competitions. **Libraries: Type:** reference. **Holdings:** archival material, articles. **Subjects:** computer music. **Awards:** Best Presentation Award. **Type:** recognition. **Recipient:** for outstanding research presentation ● Eric Siday Musical Creativity Award. **Frequency:** annual. **Type:** recognition. **Recipient:** for composers up to age of 40 ● International Computer Music Commission Awards. **Frequency:** annual. **Type:** monetary. **Recipient:** for computer composers ● Swets & Zeitlinger Distinguished Paper Award. **Frequency:** annual. **Type:** monetary. **Recipient:** for outstanding research paper. **Computer Services:** database ● mailing lists. **Publications:** *ARRAY*, 3/year. Newsletter. **Advertising:** accepted. Alternate Formats: online. **Conventions/Meetings:** annual International Computer Music Conference.

2812 ■ International DJ Guild (IDJG)
c/o Rembrandt, Turner and Griswold
395 Lockwood Dr.
Shirley, NY 11967
Ph: (631)772-2020
E-mail: webmaster@internationaldjguild.org
Contact: Mr. Michael Rura, Pres.
Multinational. Description: Seeks to uphold professional standards within the trade of disc jockeying. Represents the interests of the professional and the semi-professional DJs. Supports the needs and concerns of members. Advances the knowledge of members in areas of equipment, techniques, business and numerous other factors relating to the trade of disc jockeying. **Publications:** Newsletter. Alternate Formats: online.

2813 ■ MIDI Manufacturers Association (MMA)
PO Box 3173
La Habra, CA 90632-3173
E-mail: info@midi.org
URL: http://www.midi.org
Contact: Athan Billias, Contact
Founded: 1984. **Membership Dues:** company/individual (sales under $1 million), $475 (annual) ● company/individual (sales between $1-$10 million), $950 (annual) ● company/individual (sales between $10-$100 million), $1,900 (annual) ● company/individual (sales over $100 million), $3,000 (annual) ● company/individual (sales over $1 billion), $6,000 (annual). **Description:** Company or individual involved in the commercial development or manufacturing of MIDI hardware or software. Maintains the MIDI specification as an open standard. Provides forums for proposal discussions and sponsors the Interactive Audio Special Interest Group (IA-SIG).

2814 ■ Music Distributors Association (MDA)
1026 Northwood Dr.
Effingham, IL 62401
Ph: (217)347-6699
Fax: (217)347-6699
E-mail: geobev@consolidated.net
URL: http://www.musicdistributors.org
Founded: 1939. **Members:** 140. **Membership Dues:** domestic, $675 (annual) ● international, $350 (annual). **Staff:** 2. **Budget:** $75,000. **Multinational. Description:** International distributors and suppliers of musical instruments, sheet music, and allied merchandise; manufacturers of musical merchandise. **Computer Services:** database, list of members. **Formerly:** (1977) National Association of Musical Merchandise Wholesalers. **Publications:** Newsletter, bimonthly. **Conventions/Meetings:** annual convention - always January.

2815 ■ Music Publishers' Association of the United States (MPA)
243 5th Ave., Ste.236
New York, NY 10016
Ph: (212)327-4044
Fax: (212)327-4044
E-mail: admin@mpa.org
URL: http://www.mpa.org
Contact: Lauren Keiser, Pres.
Founded: 1895. **Members:** 70. **Staff:** 1. **Description:** Publishers of music intended for educational and concert purposes. Promotes trade and commerce; encourages understanding of and compliance with copyright laws to protect musical works against piracy and infringement. **Awards:** Paul Revere Awards for Graphic Excellence. **Frequency:** annual. **Type:** recognition. **Recipient:** examination of recent publications by panel of judges. **Computer Services:** database, directory of music publishers. **Committees:** ACDA Liaison; Annual Meeting; Archive; Awards and Production; Copyright and Licensing; Educational Contracts and Trade Relations; Engraving; International Contacts. **Affiliated With:** American Choral Directors Association; American Society of Composers, Authors and Publishers; Broadcast Music, Inc.; MENC: The National Association for Music Education; Music Library Association; National Music Publishers' Association. **Conventions/Meetings:** annual meeting (exhibits).

2816 ■ Musical Instrument Technicians Association, International (MITA)
c/o Fran Hellmann, Treas./Office Mgr.
376 Old Woodbury Rd.
Southbury, CT 06488
E-mail: president@mitatechs.com
URL: http://www.mitatechs.com
Contact: Ken Gerler, Pres.
Membership Dues: basic, $150 (annual). **Multinational. Description:** Seeks to advance the electronic musical instrument service industry. Promotes music and the use of electronic musical instruments. Develops ongoing programs of technical and professional development. Provides a vehicle for exchange of ideas and communications between the members and between the members and manufacturers. **Telecommunication Services:** electronic mail, treasurer@mitatechs.com. **Publications:** *MITA-TECH*, quarterly. Journal. Features technical articles and service information on a wide variety of old and new electronic instruments. **Advertising:** accepted.

2817 ■ NAMM, the International Music Products Association (NAMM)
5790 Armada Dr.
Carlsbad, CA 92008
Ph: (760)438-8001
Free: (800)767-6266
Fax: (760)438-7327
E-mail: info@namm.com
URL: http://www.namm.com
Contact: Joe Lamond, Pres./CEO
Founded: 1901. **Members:** 9,000. **Membership Dues:** retail, affiliate retail, commercial, and affiliate commercial, $195 (annual) ● manufacturer representative, $100 (annual). **Staff:** 25. **Multinational. Description:** Retailers of musical instruments and allied products, manufacturers, distributors, jobbers, wholesalers and publishers of print music. Holds several professional development seminars in various locations around the country and 2 major trade shows. **Libraries: Type:** open to the public. **Holdings:** books, video recordings. **Subjects:** statistics, retailing, professional development. **Awards:** William R. Gard Memorial Scholarship. **Frequency:** annual. **Type:** scholarship. **Recipient:** for a college student. **Telecommunication Services:** electronic mail, scottr@namm.com. **Affiliated With:** American Music Conference. **Formerly:** (2002) National Association of Music Merchants. **Publications:** *Cost of Doing Business Survey*, annual. Book. Includes operating statistics for music stores. ● *Music USA*, annual. Report. Features a statistical report of the music

products industry. **Price:** $5.00 for members; $10.00 for nonmembers ● *Playback*, bimonthly. Newsletter. Focuses on marketing and economic topics for the music products industry. Covers association trade shows and industry developments. **Price:** available to members only. **Conventions/Meetings:** annual The NAMM Show - international conference and trade show (exhibits) - 2009 Jan. 15-18, Anaheim, CA.

2818 ■ National Association of Professional Band Instrument Repair Technicians (NAPBIRT)
PO Box 51
Normal, IL 61761
Ph: (309)452-4257
Fax: (309)452-4825
E-mail: napbirt@napbirt.org
URL: http://www.napbirt.org

Founded: 1976. **Members:** 1,300. **Membership Dues:** regular, $95 (annual). **Staff:** 1. **Budget:** $150,000. **Regional Groups:** 9. **State Groups:** 45. **Description:** Aims to offer continuing education in the field of band instrument repair. Promotes technical integrity in the craft. Conducts self-evaluation programs, local parts and services exchange programs, and problem solution services. Surveys tools and procedures to improve work quality. Serves as liaison between manufacturers/suppliers and technicians by providing a technical audience for the introduction and evaluation of new products and policies. Has established a code of ethics. Provides placement service. Holds hands-on training sessions per year. **Libraries: Type:** not open to the public; reference. **Holdings:** 500; archival material, articles, audiovisuals, books, periodicals, video recordings. **Subjects:** construction, repair, restoration of band instruments. **Publications:** *TechniCom*, bimonthly. Journal. **Price:** included in membership dues. **Advertising:** accepted. **Conventions/Meetings:** annual conference (exhibits) - always April.

2819 ■ National Association of School Music Dealers (NASMD)
14070 Proton Rd., Ste.100
Dallas, TX 75244-3601
Ph: (972)233-9107
Fax: (972)490-4219
E-mail: office@nasmd.com
URL: http://www.nasmd.com
Contact: Scott Summerhays, Pres.

Founded: 1962. **Members:** 280. **Membership Dues:** dealer, $225-$325 (annual) ● associate, $325 (annual). **Budget:** $80,000. **Description:** Retail music stores and companies engaged in sales, service and repair of band and orchestra instruments to elementary and secondary schools and colleges. **Publications:** *NASMD Membership Directory*, annual ● *NASMD Newsletter*, quarterly. Alternate Formats: online. **Conventions/Meetings:** annual convention.

2820 ■ National Music Publishers' Association (NMPA)
101 Constitution Ave. NW, Ste.705 E
Washington, DC 20001
Ph: (202)742-4375
Fax: (202)742-4377
E-mail: pr@nmpa.org
URL: http://www.nmpa.org
Contact: David M. Israelite, Pres./CEO

Founded: 1917. **Members:** 800. **Membership Dues:** general, $100 (annual). **Staff:** 5. **Description:** Represents music publishers. **Formerly:** (1966) Music Publishers Protective Association. **Publications:** *NMPA News and Views*, quarterly. Newsletter. Advises music publishers and songwriters on recent legislative, judicial and regulatory hearings, findings and rules. **Price:** free. **Circulation:** 6,000. Alternate Formats: online ● Pamphlets. **Conventions/Meetings:** annual meeting - always June or July; even-numbered years in Los Angeles, CA; odd-numbered years in New York City.

2821 ■ Piano Manufacturers Association International (PMAI)
c/o Donald W. Dillon, Exec. Dir.
5960 W Parker Rd., Ste.278, No. 233
Plano, TX 75093-7792
Ph: (972)625-0110
Fax: (972)625-0110
E-mail: don@dondillon.com
URL: http://www.pianonet.com
Contact: Donald W. Dillon, Exec. Dir.

Founded: 1881. **Members:** 20. **Description:** Manufacturers of pianos and parts suppliers. Compiles monthly unit shipment and dollar volume reports. Supports National Piano Foundation. **Formerly:** (1986) National Piano Manufacturers Association of America. **Conventions/Meetings:** annual trade show, held in conjunction with National Association of Music Merchants.

2822 ■ Piano Technicians Guild (PTG)
4444 Forest Ave.
Kansas City, KS 66106-3750
Ph: (913)432-9975
Fax: (913)432-9986
E-mail: ptg@ptg.org
URL: http://www.ptg.org
Contact: Dale E. Probst RPT, Pres.

Founded: 1958. **Members:** 4,100. **Membership Dues:** individual, $147 (annual). **Staff:** 7. **Budget:** $950,000. **Multinational. Description:** Piano tuners and technicians. Conducts technical institutes at conventions, seminars and local chapter meetings. Promotes public education in piano care; maintains liaison with piano manufacturers and teachers. Maintains hall of fame. **Telecommunication Services:** electronic mail, pres@ptg.org ● electronic mail, board@ptg.org. **Commissions:** Delegates. **Committees:** Awards; Chapter Management; Editor Advisory; Ethics; Examination and Test Standards; Institute; International Relations; Trade and Teacher Relations; University and College Technicians; Visually Impaired. **Affiliated With:** International Association of Piano Builders and Technicians. **Formed by Merger of:** American Society of Piano Technicians; National Association of Piano Tuners. **Publications:** *Piano Action Handbook* ● *Piano Parts and Their Functions, Illustrated*. Journal ● *Piano Technicians Journal*, monthly. Covers tuning, maintenance, repair, rebuilding, and restoration of pianos; includes calendar of events. **Price:** $104.50/year; $181.50 for 2 years. ISSN: 0031-9562. **Circulation:** 4,000. **Advertising:** accepted. **Conventions/Meetings:** annual convention ● annual meeting (exhibits) - always July.

2823 ■ Retail Print Music Dealers Association (RPMDA)
14070 Proton Rd., Ste.100
Dallas, TX 75244
Ph: (972)233-9107
Fax: (972)490-4219
E-mail: office@printmusic.org
URL: http://www.printmusic.org
Contact: Madeleine Crouch, Exec. Dir.

Founded: 1976. **Members:** 300. **Membership Dues:** general, $225 (annual). **Staff:** 8. **Budget:** $80,000. **Description:** Retailers of printed music. Seeks to advance the print music industry; promotes improved relations between members and music publishers. Represents members' collective interests in areas including intellectual property rights and arts advocacy. Serves as a forum for the exchange of information among members; promotes music education; formulates standards of ethics and practice for print music retailers; conducts educational and training programs. **Awards: Frequency:** annual. **Type:** scholarship. **Recipient:** to individuals in the print music industry to further their education. **Publications:** *The Measure*, quarterly. Newsletter. **Conventions/Meetings:** annual convention - every spring.

2824 ■ Southern Songwriters Guild
PO Box 52656
Shreveport, LA 71135-2656
E-mail: songguild@aol.com
URL: http://members.aol.com/songguild
Contact: Ray Horton, Exec. Dir.

Founded: 1984. **Members:** 38. **Membership Dues:** individual, $30 (annual). **Staff:** 2. **Description:** Provides services to members in the art and craft of songwriting. **Awards:** Song of the Year. **Frequency:** biennial. **Type:** monetary. **Publications:** *The Hook*, bimonthly. Newsletter. **Circulation:** 500. **Advertising:** accepted. Alternate Formats: online.

2825 ■ United States Online Disc Jockey Association (USODJA)
209 S 4th St.
West Branch, MI 48661
E-mail: president@usodja.com
URL: http://www.usodja.com
Contact: Dave Yantz, Pres.

Description: Represents the interests of professional disc jockeys across the United States. Promotes professionalism and maintains the highest standards in the mobile disc jockey industry. Ensures that its members provide quality services to all clients. **Telecommunication Services:** electronic mail, membership@usodja.com.

Musicians

2826 ■ Accordian Professionals International
3964 Calculus
Dallas, TX 75244
Ph: (972)247-0071
Free: (800)966-5190
Fax: (972)241-9454
Contact: Nick R. Ballarini, Contact

Founded: 1978. **Members:** 36. **Membership Dues:** full, $50 (annual). **Staff:** 3. **Local Groups:** 1. **Description:** Promotes professionalism amongst accordionists. Works to overcome the stereotype of the accordionist as a polka-only player. Promotes the distinction of the professional performers over amateur contest winners. **Libraries: Type:** reference; not open to the public. **Subjects:** ethnic, American, Celtic music.

2827 ■ Creative Musicians Coalition (CMC)
PO Box 6205
Peoria, IL 61601-6205
Ph: (309)685-4843
Free: (800)882-4262
Fax: (309)685-4879
E-mail: aimcmc@aol.com
URL: http://www.creativemusicianscoalition.com
Contact: Ronald A. Wallace, Pres.

Founded: 1984. **Members:** 1,000. **For-Profit. Description:** Members come from all walks of life, but have the same desire to experience, appreciate, and participate in the advancement of independent music composition, production, arrangement, performance, promotion, and distribution. Seeks to advance independent music and the success of independent musicians. Promotes and distributes independent music to the general public. **Additional Websites:** http://www.musicdiscoveries.com. **Formerly:** (1988) Association of Independent Microdealers; (1989) Computer Musicians Cooperative; (1993) Computer Musician Coalition. **Publications:** *AfterTouch-New Music Discoveries*, annual. Catalog. Includes original music compositions and articles relating to the industry. **Price:** $5.00/year. **Circulation:** 7,500. **Advertising:** accepted. Alternate Formats: online ● *Music Discovery Experience Interactive CD-Rom*, annual. Catalog. **Circulation:** 1,800. Alternate Formats: CD-ROM.

2828 ■ International Songwriters Guild (ISG)
c/o Russ Robinson, Pres.
5108 Louvre Ave.
Orlando, FL 32812-1028
Ph: (407)851-5328 (407)679-4017

E-mail: isgorl@cfl.rr.com
URL: http://www.isgorlando.org
Contact: Russ Robinson, Pres.
Founded: 1973. **Members:** 362,000. **Membership Dues:** individual, $35 (annual). **Staff:** 6. **Description:** Beginning and experienced musicians. Strives to help members with songwriting process. Critiques songs and offers feedback. Helps in collaboration and demo tape preparation. Offers hotline regarding publishing and recording contracts. **Libraries: Type:** reference; not open to the public. **Holdings:** articles, books, business records, clippings. **Subjects:** the art and business of songwriting. **Awards:** Best Song of the Year. **Frequency:** periodic. **Type:** recognition. **Publications:** *Guild Tidings*, monthly. Newsletter. **Price:** $10.00/copy.

2829 ■ Just Plain Folks Songwriting/Musician Networking Organization
5327 Kit Dr.
Indianapolis, IN 46237
E-mail: justplainfolks@aol.com
URL: http://www.jpfolks.com
Contact: Brian Austin Whitney, Founder
Members: 25,000. **State Groups:** 50. **National Groups:** 70. **Multinational. Description:** Promotes and represents songwriters, recording artists, music publishers, record labels, performing arts societies, educational institutions, recording studios and engineers, producers, legal professionals, publicists and journalists, publications, music manufacturers and retailers and other members of the music industry. **Awards:** Album Awards. **Type:** recognition ● Founders Awards. **Type:** recognition ● Just Plain Folks Music Awards. **Type:** recognition. **Computer Services:** database, awards and member music ● online services, survey. **Telecommunication Services:** electronic bulletin board, message boards ● electronic mail, jpnotes@aol.com. **Conventions/Meetings:** Just Plain Folks Music Awards Ceremony and Showcase.

Native American

2830 ■ American Indian Business Leaders (AIBL)
c/o Tina Begay, Exec. Dir.
Gallagher Bus. Bldg., Ste.366
Missoula, MT 59812
Ph: (406)243-4879
Free: (877)245-2425
Fax: (406)243-2086
E-mail: tina.begay@aibl.org
URL: http://www.aibl.org
Contact: Dave Archambault, Chm.
Founded: 1995. **Local Groups:** 52. **Description:** Provides a support system for American Indian students interested in learning the skills necessary to acquire a job, design their own business, raise capital, and network with successful American Indian business people. Provides career development opportunities for members as well as opportunities to develop strong work ethics and gain professional experience. **Publications:** *Student Chapter Handbook*. Alternate Formats: online ● Newsletter.

Natural Disasters

2831 ■ National Storm Shelter Association (NSSA)
PO Box 41023
Lubbock, TX 79409
Ph: (806)742-6773
Free: (877)700-6772
E-mail: info@nssa.cc
URL: http://www.nssa.cc
Contact: Dr. Ernst W. Kiesling, Exec. Dir.
Membership Dues: associate, professional, $200 (annual) ● corporate sponsor, $500-$10,000 (annual) ● individual sponsor, $100 (annual) ● regular, $500 (annual). **Description:** Ensures the quality of manufactured and constructed storm shelters for protecting people from injury or loss of life from the effects of natural disasters. Seeks to maintain public confidence and respect for the storm shelter industry. **Computer Services:** database, members ● information services, shelter quality checklists ● information services, shelter quality verification.

Navy

2832 ■ Navy Nurse Corps Association (NNCA)
PO Box 1229
Oak Harbor, WA 98277-1229
Ph: (360)678-0825
Free: (866)662-2674
E-mail: mike@nnca.org
URL: http://www.nnca.org
Contact: Mr. Michael W. Benway, Exec. Dir.
Founded: 1987. **Members:** 2,500. **Membership Dues:** individual, $20 (annual). **Staff:** 1. **Regional Groups:** 11. **Description:** Navy nurses. Works to preserve the history of the Navy Nurse Corps, develop locator files and personnel information, and identify needs of members and eligible nonmembers. **Computer Services:** Online services, forum. **Publications:** Newsletter, 3/year. **Price:** included in membership dues.

Needlework

2833 ■ Charted Designers Association (CDA)
c/o Designs with TLC
7310 W Roosevelt St., Ste.6
Phoenix, AZ 85043
Ph: (623)936-9900
Fax: (623)936-9981
E-mail: dwtlc@att.net
URL: http://www.stitching.com/CDA
Contact: Stew Capps, Pres.
Founded: 1979. **Membership Dues:** regular, sustaining, $75 (annual). **Description:** Represents design companies, designers, and suppliers specializing in the field of printed needlework charts, kits, and patterns. Strives to standardize and promote the charted design industry. **Awards:** Ginnie Awards. **Frequency:** periodic. **Type:** recognition. **Recipient:** for excellence in charted needlework design. **Formerly:** (2002) Charted Designers of America.

Networking

2834 ■ Benchmarking Network
4606 FM 1960 W, Ste.250
Houston, TX 77069
Ph: (281)440-5044
Free: (888)323-6246
Fax: (281)440-6677
E-mail: additional@benchmarkingnetwork.com
URL: http://www.benchmarkingnetwork.com
Contact: Mark T. Czarnecki, Pres.
Founded: 1992. **Members:** 120,000. **Staff:** 14. **Budget:** $2,000,000. **Languages:** English, Spanish. **Description:** Works to promote benchmarking among members. Provides networking services and information. **Computer Services:** database ● mailing lists. **Publications:** *eBenchmarking*. Newsletter. Alternate Formats: online. **Conventions/Meetings:** annual conference.

New Age

2835 ■ Coalition of Visionary Resources (COVR)
194 Main St.
Butler, NJ 07405
Ph: (973)838-2280
Fax: (973)838-2270
E-mail: info@covr.net
URL: http://www.covr.org
Contact: Michelle Payton, Pres.
Founded: 1996. **Membership Dues:** regular, $80 (annual). **Description:** Retailers, wholesalers, distributors, manufacturers, publishers. Dedicated to supporting independent retailers of New Age and metaphysical products, books, music and more. **Telecommunication Services:** electronic mail, michelle@covr.net. **Formerly:** (2003) Coalition of Visionary Retailers. **Publications:** *Inside COVR*, quarterly. Newsletter. Features articles on improving profitability and survivability of visionary businesses.

Notions

2836 ■ Belt and Button Association
Address Unknown since 2008
Founded: 1941. **Members:** 18. **Staff:** 7. **Description:** Manufacturers of covered buttons and buckles. Principal activity is a labor relations program. **Formerly:** Covered Button and Buckle Association of New York; (1997) Covered Button Association of New York.

2837 ■ Graphic Products Association (GPA)
c/o Veda Communications Co.
4709 N El Capitan Ave., Ste.103
Fresno, CA 93722
Ph: (559)276-8494
Free: (800)276-8428
Fax: (559)276-8496
E-mail: info@graphicspro.org
URL: http://www.graphicspro.org
Contact: Michael Neer, Exec. Dir.
Founded: 1994. **Members:** 1,500. **Membership Dues:** producer, $120 (annual) ● supplier, $240 (annual). **For-Profit. Description:** Represents and promotes full service, professional business owners who put graphics onto products, including awards, decorated apparel, custom gifts, promotional items, signs, and stamps. **Libraries: Type:** reference. **Holdings:** articles, books, periodicals. **Subjects:** personalized products. **Computer Services:** database, of industry suppliers and products ● mailing lists, of members. **Formerly:** (2003) Personalization and Identification Association; (2003) Personalized and ID Products Association. **Publications:** *Graphics Pro*, monthly. Magazine. **Circulation:** 7,500. **Advertising:** accepted ● *Graphics Products Source Book*, annual. Directory. Serves as a buyers guide for equipment, tools, materials, services, and blank products for all types of businesses that put graphics onto products. **Price:** $80.00. **Circulation:** 1,500. **Advertising:** accepted. Alternate Formats: online. **Conventions/Meetings:** quarterly Graphix Guild Conference and Expo - trade show, educational and training conferences for some exhibits (exhibits).

Nursing

2838 ■ American Nurses Credentialing Center (ANCC)
8515 Georgia Ave., Ste.400
Silver Spring, MD 20910-3492
Ph: (301)628-5250
Free: (800)284-2378
E-mail: ancccomm@ana.org
URL: http://www.nursecredentialing.org
Contact: Ms. Jeanne M. Floyd PhD, Exec. Dir.
Founded: 1991. **Members:** 150,000. **Description:** Offers specialty and advanced nursing certification in five areas: gerontology, medical-surgical, pediatrics, perinatal, psychiatric and mental health. **Programs:** Accreditation; Certification; Credentialing International; Institute for Credentialing Innovation; Magnet Recognition; Research. **Publications:** *Credentialing News*. Newsletter. Alternate Formats: online ● *Magnet: Best Practices in Today's Challenging Health Care Environment*. Book. **Price:** $35.00 ● Annual Report, annual ● Catalogs ● Manuals.

2839 ■ National Association of Independent Nurses (NAIN)
1125 E Broadway Rd., Ste.116
Tempe, AZ 85282
Ph: (480)894-6060
Free: (800)338-5105
Fax: (480)557-9459
E-mail: nurse@independentrn.com
URL: http://www.independentrn.com
Contact: Mary A. Egel, Exec. Dir.
Founded: 2001. **Members:** 1,500. **Membership Dues:** individual, $95 (annual) ● individual life, $500. **Staff:** 3. **Budget:** $100,000. **Description:** Represents independent nurses; serves as educational and networking association for nurses; promotes nurses working independently as opposed to an employee of healthcare providers; assists nurses to form professional practice groups which are staffing registries owned by the practicing nurses. **Publications:** *Nurses Notes*, quarterly. Newsletter.

2840 ■ Philippine Nurses Association of America (PNAA)
333 E 14th St., Apt. 8G
New York, NY 10003-4212
Ph: (212)677-2261
E-mail: pnaapres0608@aol.com
URL: http://www.philippinenursesaa.org
Contact: Rosario May P. Mayor MA, Pres.
Description: Facilitates the cultural and professional adjustment of Filipino nurses in the United States. Promotes activities that will unify Filipino American nurses in the United States and its territories. Seeks to influence legislation and public policies that directly and indirectly affect nursing. **Awards:** PNAA Nursing Scholarship Award. **Frequency:** annual. **Type:** scholarship. **Recipient:** graduate student currently pursuing a Master's Degree in Nursing, a Post Master's program or Doctoral Program. **Computer Services:** Information services, professional resources ● online services, forum.

Nutrition

2841 ■ Council for Responsible Nutrition (CRN)
1828 L St. NW, Ste.900
Washington, DC 20036-5114
Ph: (202)776-7929
Fax: (202)204-7980
E-mail: webmaster@crnusa.org
URL: http://www.crnusa.org
Contact: Steven M. Mister Esq., Pres./CEO
Founded: 1973. **Members:** 100. **Membership Dues:** associate, $3,000 (annual) ● international, $2,500 (annual) ● voting (minimum; based on sales), $4,000 ● voting (maximum; based on sales), $150,000. **Staff:** 11. **Budget:** $3,200,000. **Description:** Manufacturers, distributors, and other companies involved in the production and sale of nutritional supplements, including vitamins, minerals and herbal products. Seeks an improvement in the general health of the U.S. population through responsible nutrition, including the appropriate use of nutritional supplements. Acts as a liaison between vitamin and mineral products manufacturers and government regulatory agencies, such as the Food and Drug Administration, the Federal Trade Commission, and the U.S. Congress. Keeps members informed of relevant legislative developments. Provides a forum to review governmental actions and evaluate current nutrition information. Acts as a clearinghouse to keep members informed of new scientific developments in nutrient safety, health, and nutrition. **Publications:** *CRN News*, monthly. Newsletter. **Price:** free, for members only ● Reports. Alternate Formats: online. **Conventions/Meetings:** annual conference.

Nuts

2842 ■ Northern Nut Growers Association (NNGA)
c/o Mr. Thomas Molnar, PhD, Sec.
59 Dudley Rd.
Foran Hall
New Brunswick, NJ 08901
Ph: (732)932-9711
Fax: (732)932-9441
E-mail: molnar@aesop.rutgers.edu
URL: http://www.northernnutgrowers.org
Contact: Mr. Thomas Molnar PhD, Sec.
Founded: 1911. **Members:** 850. **Membership Dues:** individual in U.S., $25 (annual) ● individual in Canada, $27 (annual) ● individual outside U.S. and Canada, $30 (annual) ● family in U.S., $30 (annual) ● contributing, $35 (annual) ● sustaining, $50 (annual) ● life, $400. **Multinational. Description:** Consists of nut tree culturists, farmers, amateur and commercial nut tree growers, experiment station workers, horticultural teachers, scientists, nut tree breeders, nursery people, and foresters. Conducts visits to amateur and commercial orchards, experimental and research sites, nurseries and nut processing plants. **Libraries: Type:** reference; not open to the public. **Holdings:** 1,000; articles, books, papers, periodicals. **Subjects:** nut tree culture. **Awards:** Big Nut. **Frequency:** annual. **Type:** recognition. **Recipient:** for use of crown and necklace both made of nuts for one year ● Merit. **Frequency:** annual. **Type:** medal ● Merit and Service: A Big Nut. **Frequency:** annual. **Type:** recognition. **Recipient:** selected by last year's Big Nut ● Research Grants. **Frequency:** annual. **Type:** monetary ● Service. **Frequency:** annual. **Type:** medal. **Publications:** *A Guide to Nut Tree Culture in North America, Vol. 1*. Book. Contains information on nuts and nut tree culture. ● *The Hazel Book*. Contains information on nuts and nut tree culture. ● *The Nutshell*, quarterly. Newsletter. Contains articles on nut tree growing, reports and current information of interest to members. **Price:** included in membership dues; $5.00/copy. Alternate Formats: online ● Membership Directory, annual. Includes contacts with U.S. authorities on culture of nut bearing trees, commercial growers, horticultural experts, and top-ranking authorities. **Price:** included in membership dues. **Circulation:** 1,000. **Advertising:** accepted ● Annual Report, annual. Contains proceedings of the latest annual meeting, and current data and authoritative information on all phases of nut tree growing. **Price:** included in membership dues; $15. 00/copy. **Conventions/Meetings:** annual banquet - usually August ● board meeting ● meeting.

Occupational Safety and Health

2843 ■ National Truckdrivers Safety Association (NTSA)
Address Unknown since 2008
Founded: 1997. **Membership Dues:** general, $100 (annual). **Description:** Represents the interests of truckdrivers. Fosters communication between truckers and non-truckers. Promotes public awareness of the problems that truckdrivers face everyday. Gets discounts for members on prices of insurance, fuel, oil, equipment, parts and services. **Computer Services:** Information services, unsafe and unfair practices ● online services, non-member chatrooms ● online services, public message board ● online services, truckers chat. **Programs:** Affiliate.

Office Equipment

2844 ■ Business Technology Association (BTA)
12411 Wornall Rd., Ste.200
Kansas City, MO 64145-1212
Ph: (816)941-3100
Free: (800)505-2821
Fax: (816)941-4838
E-mail: info@bta.org
URL: http://www.bta.org
Contact: Shannon Oliver, Pres.
Founded: 1926. **Members:** 1,000. **Membership Dues:** dealer/value added reseller, $430 (annual) ● branch dealer, $125 (annual) ● keylink (dealer and vendor), $100 (annual) ● publications associate, $150 (annual) ● vendor associate, $1,500-$2,500 (annual) ● service associate, $500-$950 (annual). **Staff:** 6. **Budget:** $1,000,000. **Regional Groups:** 4. **Local Groups:** 86. **Description:** Dealers and resellers of office equipment and networking products and services. Offers 60 seminars on management, service, technology, and business systems. Conducts research, provides business-supporting services and benefits, including insurance, and legal counsel. **Libraries: Type:** lending. **Holdings:** books. **Awards:** Channel Choice Award. **Frequency:** annual. **Type:** recognition. **Recipient:** for an outstanding provider in the imaging solutions industry ● Manufacturer/Supplier Award. **Frequency:** annual. **Type:** trophy. **Recipient:** for business equipment, computer manufacturer and supplier ● Reseller of the Year. **Frequency:** annual. **Type:** recognition. **Recipient:** for outstanding performance in the BTA member reseller community. **Computer Services:** Online services, industry data, news, and information. **Formerly:** National Typewriter and Office Machine Dealers Association; National Office Machine Dealers Association. **Publications:** *Annual Audit Report*, annual. Alternate Formats: online ● *BTA Membership Directory*, annual. Features an alphabetical/geographical listing of all BTA member companies. **Price:** $125.00 for members; $995.00 for nonmembers. **Circulation:** 1,500. Alternate Formats: CD-ROM; online ● *Business Owner*, bimonthly. Newsletter. Delivers valuable information containing ideas, advisories, case studies and reports provided for members. **Advertising:** accepted. Alternate Formats: online ● *Channel Benchmarking Report*. **Price:** $200.00/copy, for nonmembers ● *Custom Employee Policy and Procedure Manual*. Handbook. **Price:** $795.00. Alternate Formats: online ● *Office Technology*, monthly. Magazine. **Advertising:** accepted. Alternate Formats: online ● Papers. Alternate Formats: online.

2845 ■ Copier Dealers Association (CDA)
c/o Jeff Elkin, Dir.
PO Box 627
Cockeysville, MD 21030-0627
Ph: (954)917-5510
E-mail: jeffe@advancestuff.com
URL: http://www.cdainfo.org
Contact: Jeff Elkin, Dir.
Founded: 1977. **Members:** 80. **Multinational. Description:** Consists of companies within the copier industry. Works to exchange business ideas and techniques for the continuous progress of the industry. **Telecommunication Services:** electronic mail, rickz@rabbitoa.com. **Conventions/Meetings:** meeting - 3/year, usually March, June and October.

2846 ■ Dvorak International (DI)
PO Box 44
Poultney, VT 05764-0044
Ph: (802)287-2343
E-mail: dvorakint@aol.com
URL: http://www.extremespin.com/dvorak/dvorakint
Contact: Steve Ingram, Pres./Ed.
Founded: 1978. **Members:** 300. **Staff:** 1. **Description:** Promotes use of the Dvorak two-hand and one-hand layouts. (The Dvorak keyboard was patented in 1936 by August Dvorak, professor and pioneer of ergonomics, to improve speed, comfort, and efficiency in typing. Dvorak's design "allows a much faster 2-handed rhythm and the arrangement of letters on the home row - AOEUIDHTNS - eliminates frequent movement from row to row"). Provides assistance to schools, businesses, and individuals who wish to convert to the Dvorak layout. **Libraries: Type:** reference. **Holdings:** archival material. **Formerly:** (1987) Dvorak International Federation. **Publications:** *Striking Home*, quarterly. Newsletter. Latest Dvorak news, product reviews, personal accounts. **Price:** $15.00/year. ISSN: 1093-8923. **Circulation:** 1,000. **Advertising:** accepted. Alternate Formats: online ● Software: Dvorak conversion software for the Macintosh. Costs $5 for shipping and handling.

2847 ■ ISDA - Association of Storage and Retrieval Professionals
4060 Pike Ln.
Concord, CA 94520
Ph: (925)687-3100
Fax: (925)687-3108

E-mail: sales@advancedofficesystems.com
URL: http://www.isdanet.net
Contact: Gary Hatfield, Contact
Founded: 1973. **Members:** 125. **Staff:** 5. **Budget:** $500,000. **For-Profit. Description:** Independent dealers of office filing systems and microfilm equipment. Aims to promote the development of the filing systems industry, and to maintain a high standard of ethics among members. Distributes information, encourages better business methods, and promotes the services of members to consumers. Sponsors dealer management and sales training programs. **Telecommunication Services:** electronic mail, glhatfield@advancedofficesystems.com. **Committees:** Microfilm Products; Product Selection; Systems Products. **Formerly:** (1981) International Systems Dealers Association; (2004) ISDA - The Office Systems Cooperative. **Publications:** *Office Systems Management*, quarterly. **Advertising:** accepted. **Conventions/Meetings:** annual meeting, for shareholders (exhibits).

2848 ■ Modular Building Institute (MBI)
944 Glenwood Sta. Ln., Ste.204
Charlottesville, VA 22901-1480
Ph: (434)296-3288
Free: (888)811-3288
Fax: (434)296-3361
E-mail: info@mbinet.org
URL: http://www.mbinet.org
Contact: Tom Hardiman CAE, Exec. Dir.
Founded: 1983. **Members:** 257. **Membership Dues:** regular (with gross revenues of $500000 to over $50 million), $500-$9,500 (annual) ● associate (with gross revenues of $5 to over $20 million), $500-$3,500 (annual). **Staff:** 5. **Budget:** $445,000. **Multinational. Description:** Manufacturers and dealers of mobile and modular commercial units. Serves as a national structure for dealing with regulations. Enhances the future growth and capabilities of the industry by encouraging innovation and quality among its members. Conducts surveys of the industry. Compiles statistics from industry and government surveys. Operates educational programs. **Awards:** Award of Distinction. **Frequency:** annual. **Type:** recognition. **Recipient:** for commercial buildings and marketing pieces ● Hall of Fame. **Frequency:** annual. **Type:** recognition. **Recipient:** for contributions of those whose careers are dedicated to the industry ● Outstanding Achievement Award. **Frequency:** annual. **Type:** recognition. **Recipient:** for an individual who has made exemplary contribution and service to the commercial modular buildings industry. **Formerly:** (1993) Mobile Modular Office Association. **Publications:** *Commercial Modular Construction*, bimonthly. Magazine. **Advertising:** accepted. Alternate Formats: online ● *State of the Industry Report*, annual. Survey. **Circulation:** 300 ● Membership Directory, annual. **Advertising:** accepted. **Conventions/Meetings:** annual competition (exhibits) ● regional meeting and board meeting - 3/year ● annual trade show and convention (exhibits).

2849 ■ School and Home Office Products Association (SHOPA)
3131 Elbee Rd.
Dayton, OH 45439
Ph: (937)297-2250
Free: (800)854-7467
Fax: (937)297-2254
E-mail: info@shopa.org
URL: http://www.shopa.org
Contact: Dee Dee Hunt, Sec.
Founded: 1991. **Members:** 2,100. **Membership Dues:** domestic/international, $300 (annual). **Staff:** 18. **Budget:** $4,000,000. **Languages:** English, German, Spanish. **Description:** Manufacturers, wholesaler and service merchandisers, importers, retailers, commercial/contract stationers, manufacturers' representatives, and associated individuals. Promotes the advancement of the school, office, and home office product industry through an annual trade show, research initiations and other benefits and services. **Awards:** Life Member Recognition. **Frequency:** annual. **Type:** recognition. **Recipient:** for unique contributions to the industry, and/or significant dedication to the association. **Computer Services:** database. **Telecommunication Services:** electronic mail, stevej@shopa.org. **Committees:** Educate; Steering. **Councils:** Trade. **Roundtables:** President's. **Publications:** *ShopTalk*, monthly. Newsletter. Contains news on association's events, member company, and industry news. **Circulation:** 7,400. Alternate Formats: online. **Conventions/Meetings:** annual International Show - trade show, school, office, and home office products/supplies (exhibits) ● biennial Learning Curve Conference, includes guest speakers, industry experts, and research analysts discussing trends in office products.

Oils and Fats

2850 ■ Fats and Proteins Research Foundation (FPRF)
c/o Sergio Nates, PhD, Pres./Dir. of Technical Services
801 N Fairfax St., Ste.205
Alexandria, VA 22314-1776
Ph: (703)683-2914
Fax: (703)683-2626
E-mail: info@fprf.org
URL: http://www.fprf.org
Contact: Sergio Nates PhD, Pres./Dir. of Technical Services
Founded: 1962. **Members:** 250. **Budget:** $400,000. **Multinational. Description:** Members of the rendering industry, meat packers-renderers, individual renderers, and related industry companies. Works to expand use of animal fats and proteins produced by the rendering industry through financing grants and contract research carried on by university, government, and private laboratories. **Libraries: Type:** reference. **Holdings:** books, periodicals. **Subjects:** fats, proteins, animal by-product origin. **Awards: Frequency:** semiannual. **Type:** recognition. **Recipient:** for individual project proposals with merit. **Boards:** Biodiesel Technical Advisory; Non Feed/Non Food Projects Advisory. **Committees:** Animal Co-Products Research and Education Center Steering; By Laws; Education and Awareness; Liaison; Research; Search and Transition. **Affiliated With:** National Renderers Association. **Publications:** *Director's Digest*, quarterly. Newsletter. **Price:** available to members only. **Circulation:** 250 ● *Fat Manual* ● *President's Report*. Alternate Formats: online ● *Protein Manual* ● *Technical Services Bulletins*. Alternate Formats: online ● Also publishes research project reports, analyses, and evaluations. **Conventions/Meetings:** semiannual meeting.

2851 ■ Institute of Shortening and Edible Oils (ISEO)
1750 New York Ave. NW, Ste.120
Washington, DC 20006-5301
Ph: (202)783-7960
Fax: (202)393-1367
E-mail: info@iseo.org
URL: http://www.iseo.org
Contact: Robert M. Reeves, Pres.
Founded: 1932. **Members:** 18. **Staff:** 2. **Description:** Refiners of edible vegetable oils and animal fats. **Libraries: Type:** reference. **Committees:** Ecology and Environment; Energy; Occupational Safety; Public Relations; Statistics; Technical; Transportation. **Formerly:** Institute of Shortening Manufacturers. **Publications:** *Directory of Edible Oil Industry in the U.S.*, quinquennial. Includes edible oil refiner company names and addresses, plant locations, types of processing capabilities and index of brand names. Alternate Formats: online ● *Food Fats and Oils*. Booklet. Contains technical issues associated with fats and oils. Alternate Formats: online ● *Treatment of Wastewaters from Food Oil Processing Plants in Municipal Facilities*. Alternate Formats: online. **Conventions/Meetings:** semiannual board meeting.

2852 ■ International Castor Oil Association (ICOA)
521 Pomona Rd.
Cinnaminson, NJ 08077-4225
Ph: (856)786-2893
Fax: (215)717-1220
E-mail: icoa@icoa.org
URL: http://www.icoa.org
Contact: Ms. Marjorie Klayman, Pres.
Founded: 1957. **Members:** 35. **Membership Dues:** ordinary, $700 (annual). **Budget:** $40,000. **Multinational. Description:** Processors, distributors, supporting services, and consumers of bulk castor oil in nine countries. **Computer Services:** database, of members ● mailing lists, of members. **Committees:** Promotion; Technical. **Formerly:** Linseed Castor Seed Association of New York. **Publications:** *The Chemistry of Castor Oil and Its Derivatives and Their Applications*. Bulletin. **Price:** $40.00 for nonmembers, in U.S.; $45.00 for nonmembers, outside U.S. Also Cited As: *Technical Bulletin No. 2* ● *The Processing of Castor Meal Detoxification and Deallergination*. Bulletin. **Price:** $17.00 for nonmembers, in U.S.; $22.00 for nonmembers, outside U.S. Also Cited As: *Technical Bulletin No. 1* ● Membership Directory. Alternate Formats: online. **Conventions/Meetings:** annual conference.

2853 ■ National Association of Margarine Manufacturers (NAMM)
1156 15th St. NW, Ste.900
Washington, DC 20005
Ph: (202)785-3232
Fax: (202)223-9741
E-mail: namm@kellencompany.com
URL: http://www.margarine.org
Contact: Keith Keeney, Contact
Founded: 1936. **Members:** 30. **Description:** Margarine manufacturers, distributors and industry suppliers. Represents members' legislative and regulatory interests. Develops and disseminates information about margarine and margarine products to the public. **Publications:** *The Advocate*, quarterly. Newsletter. **Conventions/Meetings:** annual convention.

2854 ■ National Cottonseed Products Association (NCPA)
104 Timber Creek Dr., Ste.200
PO Box 172267
Cordova, TN 38018-4234
Ph: (901)682-0800
Fax: (901)682-2856
E-mail: info@cottonseed.com
URL: http://www.cottonseed.com
Contact: Danny W. Brown, Pres.
Founded: 1897. **Members:** 200. **Membership Dues:** regular, $300 (annual). **Staff:** 2. **Budget:** $1,000,000. **Languages:** English, Spanish. **Description:** Oil mills, refiners, dealers, brokers, chemists, and others interested in margarine, cooking fats, soaps, lubricants, cattle feed, and fertilizer. Maintains uniform trading rules covering the buying, selling, weighing, sampling, and analysis of cottonseed and its products; supports extensive research program to increase processing efficiency and to improve the quality and usefulness of cottonseed products. Conducts research programs and market development activities. **Libraries: Type:** reference. **Committees:** Chemists; Investment; Rules; Seed Grading. **Divisions:** Research. **Formerly:** (1929) Interstate Cotton Seed Crushers' Association. **Publications:** *Cottonseed and Its Products*, periodic. Booklet ● *Directory of Manufacturers and Suppliers of Cottonseed Products*, annual ● *Statistical Handbook of the Cottonseed Processing Industry* ● *Trading Rules*, annual ● Newsletter, bimonthly. **Conventions/Meetings:** annual convention.

2855 ■ National Fish Meal and Oil Association (NFMOA)
c/o National Fisheries Institute
7918 Jones Br. Dr., Ste.700
McLean, VA 22102-3319
Ph: (703)524-8884 (703)752-8880
Fax: (703)524-4619
E-mail: contact@nfi.org
URL: http://www.aboutseafood.com
Founded: 1965. **Staff:** 2. **Budget:** $150,000. **Description:** A division of the National Fisheries Institute (see separate entry). **Affiliated With:** Na-

tional Fisheries Institute. **Conventions/Meetings:** annual meeting.

2856 ■ National Institute of Oilseed Products (NIOP)
1156 15th St. NW, Ste.900
Washington, DC 20005-1717
Ph: (202)785-8450
Fax: (202)223-9741
E-mail: niop@kellencompany.com
URL: http://www.oilseed.org
Contact: Carol Freysinger, Exec. Dir.
Founded: 1934. **Members:** 200. **Membership Dues:** regular, $950 (annual). **Multinational. Description:** Shippers, brokers, growers, manufacturers, refiners, transportation, end users—anything to do with oilseeds. Establishes and maintains trading rules. **Telecommunication Services:** electronic mail, cfreysinger@kellencompany.com. **Committees:** Convention; Nominating; Rules; Settlement Price; Technical. **Publications:** *National Institute of Oilseed Products—Washington Correspondence*, semimonthly. Newsletter. **Price:** included in membership dues; $250.00 /year for nonmembers. **Circulation:** 400 ● *Trading Rules*, annual. Book. Provides a list of certified chemists, samplers, weighers and various guidelines. ● Membership Directory. **Conventions/Meetings:** annual convention - usually March.

2857 ■ National Oilseed Processors Association (NOPA)
1300 L St. NW, Ste.1020
Washington, DC 20005-4168
Ph: (202)842-0463
Fax: (202)842-9126
E-mail: nopa@nopa.org
URL: http://www.nopa.org
Contact: Thomas A. Hammer, Pres.
Founded: 1929. **Members:** 13. **Staff:** 6. **Budget:** $1,800,000. **Description:** Represents processors of oilseeds. **Telecommunication Services:** electronic mail, thammer@nopa.org. **Formerly:** (1990) National Soybean Processors Association. **Publications:** *National Oilseed Processors Association Statistical Report*. Alternate Formats: online ● *National Oilseed Processors Association—Yearbook and Trading Rules*, annual. **Price:** $50.00. **Conventions/Meetings:** annual meeting.

2858 ■ National Renderers Association (NRA)
801 N Fairfax St., Ste.205
Alexandria, VA 22314-1776
Ph: (703)683-0155
Fax: (703)683-2626
E-mail: renderers@nationalrenderers.com
URL: http://www.renderers.org
Contact: Tom Cook, Pres.
Founded: 1933. **Members:** 300. **Staff:** 5. **Budget:** $2,000,000. **Regional Groups:** 3. **Multinational. Description:** Producers of tallow and grease products (for use in soap and lubricants), and meat meal (for use in animal feeds), obtained as by-products of the meat-packing industry. Conducts research and educational programs; provides international and domestic market development services and legislative representation. **Additional Websites:** http://www.rendermagazine.com. **Committees:** International Marketing; Legislative Action. **Affiliated With:** Fats and Proteins Research Foundation. **Publications:** *National Renderers Association Bulletin*, quarterly. Alternate Formats: online ● *Render*, bimonthly. Magazine. **Price:** free. **Advertising:** accepted ● *Renditions*, monthly. Newsletter ● Membership Directory. Alternate Formats: online. **Conventions/Meetings:** annual convention (exhibits) - always October or November.

2859 ■ North American Olive Oil Association (NAOOA)
3301 Rte. 66, Bldg. C, Ste.205
Neptune, NJ 07753-2705
Ph: (732)922-3008
Fax: (732)922-3590
E-mail: info@afius.org
URL: http://naooa.mytradeassociation.org
Contact: Bob Bauer, Pres.
Founded: 1917. **Members:** 75. **Membership Dues:** associate/overseas, $495 (annual) ● regular (based on olive oil sales), $1,040-$2,685 (annual). **Multinational. Description:** A division of Association of Food Industries. Represents importers, processors, and distributors of olive oil. **Affiliated With:** Association of Food Industries. **Formerly:** (1989) Olive Oil Group; (1993) Olive Oil Association; (1997) American Olive Oil Association. **Publications:** *AFI Newsletter*, bimonthly ● *Association of Food Industries*, annual. Directory. **Price:** $45.00 ● *Import Report*, monthly. **Conventions/Meetings:** annual conference and meeting.

Optical Equipment

2860 ■ Optical Storage Technology Association (OSTA)
19925 Stevens Creek Blvd.
Cupertino, CA 95014
Ph: (408)253-3695
Fax: (408)253-9938
E-mail: questions@osta.org
URL: http://www.osta.org
Contact: Bob Zollo, Chm.
Founded: 1992. **Membership Dues:** associate/affiliate, $3,000-$4,500 (quarterly) ● individual, $300 (annual). **Multinational. Description:** Promotes market demand for optical recording products. Provides forum for resolution of issues that inhibit industry growth. Develops solutions that make optical recording products easier to use. Defines and enables advances that will meet market needs. Promotes industry understanding of market expectations and opportunities for optical recording products. **Publications:** *Optical Storage News*. Newsletter. Alternate Formats: online.

2861 ■ Optoelectronics Industry Development Association (OIDA)
1133 Connecticut Ave. NW, Ste.600
Washington, DC 20036
Ph: (202)785-4426
Fax: (202)785-4428
E-mail: lebby@oida.org
URL: http://www.oida.org
Contact: Michael Lebby, Pres./CEO
Founded: 1991. **Members:** 50. **Membership Dues:** voting, $40,000 (annual) ● associate/foreign, $15,000 (annual) ● university affiliate, $3,000 (annual). **Multinational. Description:** Encourages the expansion of the optoelectronics industry. Enhances the skills of its member companies. Provides a network for the exchange of ideas and information within the industry. **Programs:** Infrastructure Development; New Business Development; Technology Advancement; Unified Voice of the Industry. **Publications:** *OIDA News*, quarterly. Newsletter. **Price:** included in membership dues ● *Workshop*. Reports. **Price:** $75.00 for members. **Conventions/Meetings:** annual meeting ● monthly workshop.

Optics

2862 ■ International Photonics Commercialization Alliance (IPCA)
c/o David A. Gottfried, Operations Mgr.
The Javelin Gp. Inc.
5450 Campus Dr.
Canandaigua, NY 14424
Ph: (585)919-3081
Fax: (585)919-3041
E-mail: info@ipcalliance.org
URL: http://www.ipcalliance.com
Contact: David A. Gottfried, Operations Mgr.
Multinational. Description: Provides international leadership and support for the commercialization of photonic enabled technologies. Offers member assistance in all aspects of commercialization. Cultivates opportunities and provides an environment where entrepreneurs, investors and researchers meet and exchange ideas. Facilitates the commercialization of photonic enabled ideas. **Telecommunication Services:** electronic mail, davidg@ipcalliance.com ● electronic mail, davidg@javelin-group.com. **Publications:** *LightNEWS*, bimonthly. Newsletter. Highlights recent IPCA activities. Alternate Formats: online.

2863 ■ Plastic Optical Fiber Trade Organization (POFTO)
c/o Richard Beach, Dir.
Beach Communications
674 High St.
Santa Cruz, CA 95060
Ph: (831)426-1424
E-mail: rbeach@standfordalumni.org
URL: http://www.pofto.com
Contact: Richard Beach, Dir.
Membership Dues: corporate, $750 (annual) ● small business, $250 (annual) ● individual, $125 (annual) ● educational, $50 (annual). **Description:** Seeks to promote the high-bandwidth Plastic Optical Fiber (POF) systems serving data communication markets. Promotes industry awareness, acceptance, and advancement of POF. Accelerates the adoption and usage of POF products and services. Encourages the application of POF and component systems in the data communications markets. Promotes the advancement and acceptance of standards incorporating POF. **Publications:** Newsletter. **Price:** included in membership dues. **Conventions/Meetings:** annual conference - 2008 Sept., Cambridge, MA.

Organic Farming

2864 ■ Organic Exchange
5332 Coll. Ave., Ste.203
Oakland, CA 94618
Ph: (510)597-9949
Fax: (510)597-9944
E-mail: terry@organicexchange.org
URL: http://www.organicexchange.org
Contact: Rebecca Calahan Klein, Pres.
Founded: 2002. **Description:** Focuses on creating environmental and social benefits through the expansion of organic agriculture. Brings together brands and retailers to learn more about the social and environmental benefits of organic agriculture and to develop new business models and tools that support greater use of organic inputs such as organic cotton. Works to help increase consumer awareness of the organic cotton products. **Publications:** *Organic Cotton Market Report*, semiannual ● *Organic Cotton Sourcing Directory*. Alternate Formats: online ● *Organic Exchange Update*, quarterly. Newsletter. Alternate Formats: online.

Organization Development

2865 ■ International Registry of Organization Development Professionals (IRODP)
c/o The Organization Development Institute
11234 Walnut Ridge Rd.
Chesterland, OH 44026
Ph: (440)729-7419
Fax: (440)729-9319
E-mail: donwcole@aol.com
URL: http://members.aol.com/odinst
Contact: Dr. Donald W. Cole RODC, Pres.
Founded: 1968. **Members:** 430. **Membership Dues:** regular, $110 (annual) ● professional consultant, $150 (annual) ● full-time student (not working full-time), $80 (annual). **Staff:** 1. **Multinational. Description:** Educational subsidiary of the Organization Development Institute. Organization development professionals, students, and persons interested in improving the way organizations function. Promotes a better understanding of and disseminates information about organization development. Maintains job placement service. Conducts specialized education. **Libraries: Type:** reference. **Holdings:** 100; biographical archives. **Subjects:** organization development. **Awards:** Jack Gibb Award. **Frequency:** an-

nual. **Type:** monetary. **Recipient:** for best presentation at the National Conference by a full time student ● Outstanding O.D. Article of the Year Award. **Frequency:** annual. **Type:** monetary ● Outstanding O.D. Project of the Year Award. **Frequency:** annual. **Type:** recognition ● Outstanding Organization Development Consultant of the Year Award. **Frequency:** annual. **Type:** recognition ● Outstanding Presentation Award. **Frequency:** annual. **Type:** recognition. **Recipient:** for best presentation by full time student who is working full-time ● Silver Bowl Awards. **Frequency:** annual. **Type:** recognition. **Additional Websites:** http://www.odinstitute.org. **Boards:** International Advisory. **Committees:** Accreditation of OD/OB Academic Programs; Define O.D.'s Body of Knowledge and Skill; Ethics: To Investigate Complaints of Ethics; The Future of O.D.; Liaison with Other O.D. Networks Worldwide; Marketing the O.D. Journal; More Effective Marketing of O.D. Services; O.D. in Electronic Mail and Electronic Conferencing; O.D. in Federal, State and City Government; O.D. in Higher Education; O.D. in Medical Settings; O.D. in the Financial Services Industry; O.D. in the Nuclear Power Industry; O.D. in Voluntary Organizations; The O.D. Journal Peer Review Panel-International; The O.D. Journal Peer Review Panel-USA; O.D. Looks at the Future of Government; O.D. Research; Public Relations; Recognize Outstanding O.D. Projects; Refine the RODP and RODC Requirements; Research of Organizational Evil; Research/Study Team on Nonviolent Large Systems Change. **Affiliated With:** Organization Development Institute. **Publications:** *Conflict Resolution Technology*. Book. **Price:** $20.00 ● *Improving Profits Through O.D.*. Book. **Price:** $10.00 ● *Improving Profits Through Organization Development*. Book. **Price:** $10.00 ● *International Registry of Organization Development Professionals/OD Handbook*, annual. **Price:** $25.00 ● *Organization and Change*, monthly ● *Organization Development: A Straightforward Reference Guide for Executives Seeking to Improve their Organizations*. Book. **Price:** $10.00 ● *Organization Development Journal*, quarterly. Includes articles on what is new in Organization Development, book reviews, research column, and calendar of events. **Price:** $80.00 /year for members, corporations, organizations, and libraries; $20.00 for single issue. ISSN: 0889-6402. **Circulation:** 1,000. **Advertising:** accepted ● *Professional Suicide*. Book. **Price:** $20.00 ● *What is New in Organization Development*. Book. **Price:** $20.00. **Conventions/Meetings:** annual Information Exchange - conference (exhibits) - usually May ● annual O.D. World Congress (exhibits) - always outside U.S.

2866 ■ Organization Development Institute
11234 Walnut Ridge Rd.
Chesterland, OH 44026
Ph: (440)729-7419
Fax: (440)729-9319
E-mail: donwcole@aol.com
URL: http://www.odinstitute.org
Contact: Dr. Donald W. Cole RODC, Pres.

Founded: 1968. **Members:** 488. **Membership Dues:** student, $80 (annual) ● regular, $110 (annual) ● professional consultant, $150 (annual). **Staff:** 1. **Regional Groups:** 172. **Multinational. Description:** Professionals, students, and individuals interested in organization development. Disseminates information on and promotes a better understanding of organization development worldwide. Conducts specialized education programs. Develops the International O.D. Code of Ethics and a competency test for individuals wishing to qualify as a Registered Organization Development Consultant and a statement on the knowledge and skill necessary to be competent in organization development and criteria for the accreditation of OD/OB academic programs. Maintains job and consultant information service. Sponsors International Registry of Organization Development Professionals and Research/Study Team on Nonviolent Large Systems Change. Maintains 18 committees including an International Advisory Board. **Libraries: Type:** not open to the public. **Holdings:** 100. **Awards:** Jack Gibb Award. **Frequency:** annual. **Type:** monetary. **Recipient:** to the best presentation at the Annual Information Exchange by a full time student who is not working full time ● Outstanding O.D. Consultant of the Year Award. **Frequency:** annual. **Type:** recognition. **Recipient:** for outstanding organization development consultant ● Outstanding O.D. Project of the Year Award. **Frequency:** annual. **Type:** recognition. **Recipient:** to an outstanding O.D. project ● Outstanding OD Article of the Year Award. **Frequency:** annual. **Type:** monetary. **Recipient:** to an outstanding OD article. **Computer Services:** Mailing lists. **Affiliated With:** International Registry of Organization Development Professionals. **Formerly:** (1968) Ohio Organization Development Network; (1974) Midwest Organization Development Network. **Publications:** *Improving Profits Through Organization Development*. Book. **Price:** $10.00 ● *International Registry of Organization Development Professionals and Organization Development Handbook*, annual. Available for the purpose of networking and obtaining consulting assignments; includes geographical and language capabilities listings. **Price:** $30.00/year. **Circulation:** 600 ● *Organization Development: A Straight Forward Reference Guide for Executives Seeking to Improve Their Organizations*, monthly. Newsletter. **Price:** $10.00 ● *Organization Development Journal*, quarterly. Includes book reviews, calendar of events, research column, and listings of outstanding professionals and projects in the field. **Price:** $80.00/year, in U.S.; $20.00 for single copy. ISSN: 0889-6402. **Circulation:** 1,000. **Advertising:** accepted ● *Organizations and Change*, monthly. Newsletter. Includes employment listings, consulting opportunities, and conference schedule for organizational development professionals. **Price:** free for members; $110.00 /year for nonmembers. **Circulation:** 600 ● *Professional Suicide or Organizational Murder*. Book. **Price:** $20.00 ● *What Is New in Organization Development*. Book. **Price:** $20.00. **Conventions/Meetings:** annual Information Exchange - conference, with awards presentation (exhibits) ● annual Organization Development World Congress.

2867 ■ Organization Development Network (ODN)
71 Valley St., Ste.301
South Orange, NJ 07079-2825
Ph: (973)763-7337
Fax: (973)763-7448
E-mail: odnetwork@odnetwork.org
URL: http://www.odnetwork.org
Contact: Margaret Franks Hoyer, Exec. Dir.

Founded: 1964. **Members:** 4,200. **Membership Dues:** individual in U.S., $160 (annual) ● individual in Canada and Mexico, $180 (annual) ● online outside U.S. and Canada, $145 (annual) ● student in U.S., $85 (annual) ● senior, $85 (annual). **Staff:** 5. **Budget:** $1,000,000. **Regional Groups:** 51. **Description:** Represents practitioners, academics, managers, and students employed or interested in organization development. Works to enhance and provide opportunities for colleagueship and professional development. **Awards:** Larry Porter Award. **Frequency:** annual. **Type:** recognition. **Recipient:** for excellence in writing ● OD Network Annual Conference Scholarship. **Frequency:** annual. **Type:** scholarship. **Recipient:** to OD Practitioners and full time students who are financially unable to cover the conference registration fee. **Telecommunication Services:** hotline, ODN Job Exchange, (707)865-2495. **Formerly:** (1966) Industrial Network. **Publications:** *Conference Proceedings* ● *OD Education Directory*. Alternate Formats: online ● *OD Practitioner*, quarterly. Journal. **Price:** included in membership dues. ISSN: 1086-2609. **Circulation:** 3,700. Alternate Formats: online ● *OD Resources Directory*. Alternate Formats: online ● *OD Seasonings*, quarterly. Journal. Alternate Formats: online ● *Practicing OD*. Magazine. Alternate Formats: online ● *Roster*, annual. Membership Directory. **Conventions/Meetings:** annual conference, special interest (exhibits).

2868 ■ Society for Organizational Learning (SoL)
25 First St., Ste.414
Cambridge, MA 02141-1802
Ph: (617)300-9500 (617)300-9540
Fax: (617)354-2093
E-mail: info@solonline.org
URL: http://www.solonline.org
Contact: Sherry Immediato, Pres./Managing Dir.

Founded: 1997. **Membership Dues:** researcher, consultant, $275 (annual) ● student, $125 (annual) ● online (up to 20 members), $1,000 (annual). **Multinational. Description:** Provides a forum for corporations, organizations, researchers and consultants to generate knowledge and capacity for fundamental innovation and change. Generates business and social systems results, new intellectual capital and personal and professional networks. **Computer Services:** Information services, organizational learning resources. **Telecommunication Services:** electronic mail, immediato@solonline.org. **Committees:** Capacity Building; Global Steering; Research; Strategic Integration. **Subgroups:** Hex Chrome; Leather; Packaging; Polypropylene. **Publications:** *Reflections*. Journal. Alternate Formats: online.

Outdoor Recreation

2869 ■ Association for Challenge Course Technology (ACCT)
c/o Sylvia Dresser, Exec. Dir.
496 Castlewood Ln.
Deerfield, IL 60015
Ph: (847)945-0829
Fax: (847)317-0155
E-mail: info@acctinfo.org
URL: http://www.acctinfo.org
Contact: Sylvia Dresser, Exec. Dir.

Founded: 1993. **Members:** 1,500. **Membership Dues:** associate in U.S., $65 (annual) ● associate outside U.S., $75 (annual) ● institutional in U.S., $225 (annual) ● institutional outside U.S., $250 (annual). **Description:** Establishes and promotes the standard of care and measure of excellence that defines professional practice and effective challenge course programs. Seeks to identify, refine and publish standards for installing, maintaining and managing challenge courses. Provides leadership in the promotion and use of challenge course programs. Provides forums for education and professional development and advocates for the challenge course industry. **Telecommunication Services:** electronic mail, sylvia@acctinfo.org. **Conventions/Meetings:** annual symposium and conference, for challenge course technology industry practitioners and individuals.

2870 ■ Outdoor Industry Association (OIA)
4909 Pearl East Cir., Ste.200
Boulder, CO 80301
Ph: (303)444-3353
Fax: (303)444-3284
E-mail: info@outdoorindustry.org
URL: http://www.outdoorindustry.org
Contact: Frank Hugelmeyer, Pres.

Founded: 1989. **Members:** 1,200. **Membership Dues:** company - minimum (based on annual revenue), $250 (annual) ● company - maximum (based on annual revenue), $1,000 (annual) ● associate, $500 (annual). **Staff:** 12. **Description:** Supports the business of outdoor recreation, focusing on government affairs, market research, member benefits, education, marketing, and communication. **Awards:** Outdoor Leadership Awards. **Frequency:** annual. **Type:** recognition. **Formerly:** (2002) Outdoor Recreation Coalition of America. **Publications:** *Distribution Study: The Outdoor Market in the U.S.* ● *Outdoor Recreation Business News*, weekly. Bulletin. Alternate Formats: online ● *The Outdoor Recreation Participation Study*, annual ● *State of the Industry Report*, annual. **Conventions/Meetings:** annual Outdoor Industry Rendezvous - conference - 2008 Sept. 30-Oct. 2, Boston, MA.

Outsourcing

2871 ■ International Association of Outsourcing Professionals (IAOP)
c/o Christina L. Powers, Exec. Dir.
2600 South Rd., Ste.44-240
Poughkeepsie, NY 12601

Ph: (845)452-0600
Fax: (845)452-6988
E-mail: memberservices@outsourcingprofessional.org
URL: http://www.outsourcingprofessional.org
Contact: Michael F. Corbett, Founder/Chm.

Founded: 2005. **Members:** 40,000. **Membership Dues:** customer corporate, $3,500 (annual) ● provider/advisor corporate, $18,500 (annual) ● professional, $345 (annual). **Multinational. Description:** Promotes outsourcing as a management practice, as a profession and as an industry. Strives to lead the effort to transform the world of business through outsourcing. Helps organizations to increase outsourcing success rate, improve outsourcing Return on Investment (ROI) and expand outsourcing opportunities across the organization. **Awards:** The Outsourcing Hall of Fame. **Frequency:** annual. **Type:** recognition. **Recipient:** to individuals working in the field of outsourcing. **Telecommunication Services:** electronic mail, michael.corbett@outsourcingprofessional.org. **Publications:** *IAOP: Launching a New Breed of Outsourcing Professionals.* Paper. Alternate Formats: online ● *Outsourcing Insights*, monthly. Newsletters. Alternate Formats: online ● Brochure. Alternate Formats: online.

Packaging

2872 ■ Aseptic Packaging Council (APC)

2120 L St. NW, Ste.400
Washington, DC 20037
Ph: (202)478-6158
Free: (800)277-8088
Fax: (202)478-0104
E-mail: jlofton@mrss.com
URL: http://www.aseptic.org
Contact: Jeff Lofton, Dir./Admin.

Founded: 1989. **Members:** 2. **Staff:** 3. **Description:** Represents the major U.S. manufacturers of drink boxes — Tetra Pak Inc. of Vernon Hills, Illinois, and SIG Combibloc Inc., of Columbus, Ohio. Works to inform the American public about the product benefits and environmental attributes of aseptic packaging. Promotes recycling programs. **Convention/Meeting:** none. **Publications:** *Drink Box Recycling.* Brochure. **Price:** free (through email request only) ● *Packaging for a Healthy Lifestyle.* Brochure. **Price:** free (through email request only) ● *Wastewise*, triennial. Contains primary and secondary school curriculum guide. **Price:** free.

2873 ■ Contract Packaging Association (CPA)

1601 N Bond St., Ste.101
Naperville, IL 60563
Ph: (630)544-5053
Fax: (630)544-5055
E-mail: info@contractpackaging.org
URL: http://www.contractpackaging.org
Contact: James Ellis, Pres.

Founded: 1992. **Members:** 70. **Membership Dues:** contract packager, $1,500 (annual) ● associate, $2,500 (annual). **Staff:** 10. **Budget:** $300,000. **Description:** Represents interests of members and brings together contract packagers, suppliers and end-users. **Computer Services:** Mailing lists. **Formerly:** (1999) Contract Packagers Association; (2001) Contract Packaging Association; (2005) Contract Manufacturing and Packaging Association. **Publications:** *Contract Packaging*, semiannual. Magazine. **Advertising:** accepted. Alternate Formats: online ● *CPA Quarterly Report Newsletter.* Alternate Formats: online ● Brochure. **Conventions/Meetings:** semiannual meeting and board meeting ● annual meeting ● annual Packaging Services Expo - conference (exhibits).

2874 ■ Corrugated Packaging Council (CPC)

25 Northwest Point Blvd., Ste.510
Elk Grove Village, IL 60007
Ph: (847)364-9600
Fax: (847)364-9639
E-mail: hmarshall@fibrebox.org
URL: http://oldcpc.corrugated.org
Contact: Rachel K. Kenyon, Chair

Description: Develops programs to promote the performance and environmental benefits of corrugated packaging. Aims to produce long-term benefits to the corrugated industry by developing communications to support the industry's objectives. **Additional Websites:** http://cpc.corrugated.org.

2875 ■ Flexible Packaging Association (FPA)

971 Corporate Blvd., Ste.403
Linthicum, MD 21090-2253
Ph: (410)694-0800
Fax: (410)694-0900
E-mail: fpa@flexpack.org
URL: http://www.flexpack.org
Contact: Marla Donahue, Pres.

Founded: 1950. **Members:** 150. **Staff:** 20. **Budget:** $2,000,000. **Description:** Converters of paper, foil, and plastic packaging materials; associate members are industry suppliers. Promotes the welfare of the flexible packaging industry by: communicating with federal and state governments and the public on subjects of concern to the industry; promoting the use of flexible packaging; conducting technical, manufacturing, and statistical programs; establishing standards and specifications. Offers six lesson plans on packaging for grades 5-9. Sponsors children's services; compiles statistics. **Libraries: Type:** reference. **Holdings:** periodicals. **Subjects:** flexible packaging. **Awards:** Green Globe Award for Environmental Achievement. **Frequency:** annual. **Type:** recognition ● **Type:** scholarship ● Top Packaging Awards. **Frequency:** annual. **Type:** recognition. **Committees:** Business and Economic Research; Government Relations; Membership; Program Development; Public Relations and Marketing; Technology and Regulatory Affairs. **Councils:** Sterilization Packaging Manufacturers. **Absorbed:** Industrial Bag and Cover Association; Waxed Paper Institute. **Formerly:** (1979) National Flexible Packaging Association. **Publications:** *FPA Update*, monthly. Newsletter. **Circulation:** 1,500 ● *Right-to-Know Compliance Manual* ● *State of the Industry Report.* **Price:** $25.00 for members; $3,500.00 for nonmembers ● Manual ● Reports ● Surveys ● Also publishes technical specifications and special studies. **Conventions/Meetings:** annual competition ● annual Management Leadership Conference.

2876 ■ Packaging Machinery Manufacturers Institute (PMMI)

4350 N Fairfax Dr., Ste.600
Arlington, VA 22203-1632
Ph: (703)243-8555
Free: (888)275-7664
Fax: (703)243-8556
E-mail: pmmiwebhelp@pmmi.org
URL: http://www.pmmi.org
Contact: Charles D. Yuska, Pres.

Founded: 1932. **Members:** 500. **Membership Dues:** regular, $1,500 (annual) ● supplier, $2,000 (annual). **Staff:** 18. **Languages:** English, Spanish. **Description:** Represents manufacturers of machinery used for all packaging operations including filling, capping, labeling, wrapping, cartoning, case loading, blister packaging, aerosol, check weighing, coding, counting, form-fill-seal, and bagging. **Telecommunication Services:** electronic mail, cyuska@pmmi.org. **Committees:** Education; Global Marketing; Show, Industry Relations; Statistics; Surveys; Technical Information; Trade Liaison. **Publications:** *American National Standard.* Covers safety requirements. ● *Handbook for Writing Operation and Maintenance Manuals* ● *Just In Time*, weekly. Newsletter. Contains upcoming programs and services of the association. **Price:** available to members only ● *MarketTrends Newsletter*, monthly. Features top packaging headlines from around the world. Alternate Formats: online ● *Packaging Machinery Directory*, biennial. Lists member firms by machine functions and by trade names; includes descriptions of the types of machines offered by each firm. **Price:** $25.00. **Circulation:** 55,000 ● *Packaging Machinery Technology Magazine*, bimonthly. Alternate Formats: online ● *PMMI News Latinoamerica* (in English and Spanish), monthly. Newsletter. Alternate Formats: online ● *PMMI Reports*, monthly. Newsletter. **Circulation:** 700. Alternate Formats: online ● *Tech Notes.* Newsletter. Contains European Union and EN directives and safety codes being promulgated around the world. Alternate Formats: online ● Manuals. **Conventions/Meetings:** annual conference - 2008 Nov. 10-12, Chicago, IL ● biennial trade show (exhibits) - 2008 Nov. 9-13, Chicago, IL.

2877 ■ Paperboard Packaging Council (PPC)

201 N Union St., Ste.220
Alexandria, VA 22314-2651
Ph: (703)836-3300
Fax: (703)836-3290
E-mail: paperboardpackaging@ppcnet.org
URL: http://www.ppcnet.org
Contact: Jerome T. Van de Water, Pres.

Founded: 1964. **Members:** 68. **Membership Dues:** principal (maximum), $70,000 (annual) ● principal (minimum), $1,000 (annual). **Staff:** 6. **Budget:** $1,500,000. **Description:** Represents manufacturers of paperboard packaging. Sponsors public relations activities, safety programs, and biannual human resource seminars. Conducts overall industry statistical studies, marketing surveys, product reviews, and labor relations and bargaining agreement studies. Provides active technical and production service. **Libraries: Type:** reference. **Awards:** Carton Competition Award. **Frequency:** annual. **Type:** recognition. **Recipient:** for the outstanding design and technology in paperboard packaging ● Robert Grair Award. **Frequency:** annual. **Type:** recognition. **Recipient:** for outstanding individual member ● Safety Awards. **Frequency:** annual. **Type:** recognition. **Recipient:** for member plants that demonstrate proactive approaches to safety. **Formed by Merger of:** Institute for Better Packaging; Folding Paper Box Association of America. **Publications:** *Ideas and Innovation Handbook.* Serves as a reference guide, highlighting more than 700 carton styles. **Price:** $65.00 for members and students; $95.00 for nonmembers ● *National Paperboard Packaging Competition Awards Booklet 2006*, annual. Contains photos and information about the winning packages in the annual carton competition. **Price:** $3.00 for members; $5.00 for nonmembers ● *PPC Directory* ● *PPC Live!.* Newsletter. Alternate Formats: online ● *PPC Today*, quarterly. Newsletter. **Price:** free. **Circulation:** 2,000. Alternate Formats: online ● *T&P Forum Booklet.* Contains a compilation of presentations and handouts from the PPC's biannual forum. **Price:** free to participating member; $25.00 for non-participants; $75.00 for nonmembers ● *Trends Report*, annual ● Reports.

2878 ■ Petroleum Packaging Council (PPC)

c/o ATD Management Inc.
1219 Ganado
San Clemente, CA 92673
Ph: (949)369-7102
Fax: (949)366-1056
E-mail: ppc@atdmanagement.com
URL: http://www.ppcouncil.org
Contact: Mr. Andrew Rapp, Pres.

Founded: 1950. **Members:** 400. **Membership Dues:** individual (regular), $525 (annual) ● individual (associate), $575 (annual) ● corporate (regular), $2,000 (annual) ● corporate (associate), $2,200 (annual). **Description:** Individuals and companies involved in the packaging of automotive or industrial lubricants and fluids. Works to provide technical support and education to the petroleum industry. Provides a forum for exchange of information and works with related groups and trade associations. **Libraries: Type:** not open to the public. **Holdings:** archival material, business records. **Awards:** PPC Scholarship. **Frequency:** annual. **Type:** scholarship. **Recipient:** for a junior or senior in packaging school, maintaining a 3.0 grade point average in all courses, requiring financial assistance as recommended by schools faculty; awarded through Michigan State University, Clemson University and California Polytechnic University. **Committees:** Communications; Industry Liaisons; Long Range Planning; Packaging-Containers and Components; Plant Operations-

Blending and Packaging; Regulation and Legislation; Safety, Health and Environment; Supply Chain Management (Warehousing/Shipping). **Publications:** *NewsFlash*, monthly. Newsletter. **Price:** included in membership dues ● Membership Directory, annual. **Conventions/Meetings:** quarterly board meeting ● semiannual conference ● biennial trade show.

2879 ■ Plastics Foodservice Packaging Group (PFPG)
c/o American Chemistry Council
1300 Wilson Blvd., 8th Fl.
Arlington, VA 22209
Ph: (703)741-5000
Fax: (703)741-6050
URL: http://www.americanchemistry.com/pfpg
Contact: Michael H. Levy, Dir.

Founded: 1988. **Members:** 11. **Membership Dues:** polystyrene resin supplier, $500 (annual) ● foam polystyrene fabricator, $250 (annual) ● solid oriented polystyrene (OPS) fabricator, $125 (annual) ● company outside U.S., association, $5,000 (annual) ● non-polystyrene resin supplier, $155 (annual). **Staff:** 3. **Description:** Promotes the effective use and disposal of polystyrene. Works to provide accurate and reliable information about environmentally-sound, solid waste disposal practices. Offers technical information to public officials, consumers, and local businesses. **Computer Services:** database, recycling and grass roots. **Formerly:** (2007) Polystyrene Packaging Council. **Publications:** *How Plastic Make It Possible*. Brochure. Includes physical properties and performance benefits of plastics in wide variety of applications. **Price:** free. Alternate Formats: online ● *Plastic Packaging: Opportunities and Challenges*. Booklet. Provides information about the benefits of plastics. **Price:** free ● *Plastics in Perspective*. Booklet. Provides answers to the most frequently asked questions about plastics in the environment. **Price:** free. Alternate Formats: online ● *Plastics in the Microwave: A Common Sense Approach*. Brochure. Contains tips and guidance on proper and safe use of plastic containers and wraps in the microwave oven. **Price:** free. Alternate Formats: online ● *The Waste That Wasn't*. Report. Contains information on all types of packaging. **Conventions/Meetings:** annual meeting.

2880 ■ Retail Packaging Association (RPA)
PO Box 17656
Covington, KY 41017
Ph: (859)341-9623
Fax: (859)341-6211
E-mail: info@retailpackaging.org
URL: http://www.retailpackaging.org
Contact: Ron Watson, Pres.

Founded: 1989. **Members:** 1,000. **Membership Dues:** company (based on the number of employees), $350-$500 (annual). **Staff:** 3. **Description:** Retail packaging professionals. Advances the retail packaging industry through educational programs, services and forums. **Awards:** Dave Haber Merit Scholarship. **Frequency:** annual. **Type:** scholarship. **Recipient:** for high school seniors and college freshmen, sophomores and juniors who are dependents and/or dependent sons and daughters of full time employees of any member firm ● RPA Scholarship. **Frequency:** annual. **Type:** scholarship. **Recipient:** for high school seniors and college freshmen, sophomores and juniors who are dependents and/or dependent sons and daughters of full time employees of any member firm. **Computer Services:** database, membership directory ● electronic publishing, ENews. **Formerly:** (2005) Retail Packaging Manufacturers Association. **Conventions/Meetings:** annual convention and seminar (exhibits) ● annual trade show (exhibits).

2881 ■ Tube Council of North America (TCNA)
87 West St., Ste.101
Walpole, MA 02081
Ph: (508)850-5179
Fax: (508)850-5178
E-mail: cdw@thefillingstation.net
URL: http://www.tube.org
Contact: Patrick Farrey, Exec. Dir.

Founded: 1937. **Members:** 12. **Membership Dues:** tube manufacturer in North America, $3,000 (annual) ● tube manufacturer outside North America, $2,000 (annual) ● associate, $1,200 (annual). **Staff:** 2. **Description:** Represents manufacturers of squeeze tubes (such as toothpaste tubes) united to further the use of metal, laminate, and plastic tubes. Maintains speakers' bureau; sponsors competitions; compiles statistics. **Awards:** Tube of the Year Award. **Frequency:** annual. **Type:** recognition. **Recipient:** for the best tube innovations, technologies, components, processes and designs of the year. **Telecommunication Services:** electronic mail, pfarrey@landon-farrey.com. **Formerly:** (1966) Collapsible Metal Tube Association; (1982) Metal Tube Packaging Council of North America. **Publications:** *E-NEWS*, quarterly. Newsletter. **Price:** free. **Circulation:** 4,000 ● *List of Member and Associate Member Companies*, periodic. **Conventions/Meetings:** semiannual meeting.

2882 ■ Women in Packaging (WMPKG)
4290 Bells Ferry Rd., Ste.106-17
Kennesaw, GA 30144-1300
Ph: (770)924-3563 (678)594-6872
Fax: (770)928-2338
E-mail: wpstaff@womeninpackaging.org
URL: http://womeninpackaging.org
Contact: JoAnn R. Hines, Founder

Founded: 1993. **Members:** 800. **Membership Dues:** professional, $150 (annual) ● corporate, $175-$575 (annual) ● student, $35 (annual). **Staff:** 35. **Budget:** $100,000. **Regional Groups:** 3. **Local Groups:** 13. **Description:** Works to promote and encourage women in the packaging industry. Educates the packaging industry about the contributions of women to the industry; helps to eliminate stereotypes and discrimination in the profession; offers networking opportunities; conducts career enhancement programs; compiles statistics; maintains speakers' bureau. **Libraries: Type:** reference. **Holdings:** biographical archives. **Computer Services:** Online services, job resource. **Committees:** Communications; Membership; Program. **Publications:** *Career Hotline*, monthly. Contains job listings. **Price:** $200.00. **Advertising:** accepted ● *Packaging Horizons*. Magazine. **Advertising:** accepted. Alternate Formats: online ● *Update*. Newsletter. **Conventions/Meetings:** annual meeting ● quarterly regional meeting ● periodic seminar ● periodic Training Programs - luncheon and dinner (exhibits).

Paints and Finishes

2883 ■ Color Guild Associates
Address Unknown since 2007
URL: http://www.colorguild.com

Founded: 1978. **Members:** 42. **Staff:** 3. **Description:** Paint manufacturers. Sponsors cooperative buying program for paint ingredients, raw materials, and sundries. **Formerly:** Guild CPO. **Conventions/Meetings:** semiannual conference - always spring and fall.

2884 ■ National Paint and Coatings Association (NPCA)
1500 Rhode Island Ave. NW
Washington, DC 20005
Ph: (202)462-6272
Fax: (202)462-8549
E-mail: npca@paint.org
URL: http://www.paint.org
Contact: J. Andrew Doyle, Pres.

Founded: 1933. **Members:** 350. **Membership Dues:** associate/subscriber, $1,700. **Staff:** 40. **Budget:** $6,000,000. **Local Groups:** 26. **Description:** Manufacturers of paints and chemical coatings; suppliers of raw materials and equipment. Conducts: statistical surveys; research, government, and public relations programs. Provides management information programs and management and technician development programs. Compiles statistics. **Awards:** George Baugh Heckel Award. **Frequency:** annual. **Type:** recognition. **Recipient:** for outstanding achievement and initiative toward the advancement of NPCA's goals ● Industry Statesman Awards. **Frequency:** annual. **Type:** recognition. **Recipient:** for long and devoted service to the paint and coatings industry. **Telecommunication Services:** electronic mail, members@paint.org. **Committees:** Air Quality; Architectural Coatings; Communications; Industrial Coatings; Industry Suppliers; Labeling and Product Safety; Management Information; Manufacturing Management; Marine Coatings; Spray Paint; Transportation and Distribution; Water Quality/Waste Management. **Formed by Merger of:** (1933) American Paint Manufacturers Association; (1933) National Paint, Oil and Varnish Association. **Formerly:** National Paint, Varnish and Lacquer Association. **Publications:** *eCoatings*, periodic. Newsletter ● *Guide to U.S. Government Paint Specifications* ● *Insider News*. Newsletters. Alternate Formats: online ● *Member Services Directory*. **Advertising:** accepted ● *Paint Industry Labeling Guide* ● *Raw Materials Indexes* ● *Technical Bulletin* ● *Trademark Directory*, periodic ● *2002 e-Business Company Survey*. Report. **Price:** $100.00 for members; $300.00 for nonmembers ● Annual Report, annual ● Bulletins ● Pamphlets ● Brochures. Alternate Formats: online. **Conventions/Meetings:** annual convention.

2885 ■ SSPC: The Society for Protective Coatings (SSPC)
40 24th St., 6th Fl.
Pittsburgh, PA 15222-4656
Ph: (412)281-2331
Free: (877)281-7772
Fax: (412)281-9992
E-mail: liston@sspc.org
URL: http://www.sspc.org
Contact: William L. Shoup, Exec. Dir.

Founded: 1950. **Members:** 7,500. **Membership Dues:** individual in North America, $95 (annual) ● individual outside North America, $120 (annual) ● patron, $700 (annual) ● sustaining, $1,750-$1,800 (annual) ● affiliate, $5,500-$10,500 (annual). **Staff:** 30. **Budget:** $3,750,000. **Regional Groups:** 30. **Multinational. Description:** Seeks to advance the technology and promote the use of protective coatings to preserve industrial, marine and commercial structures, components and substrates. **Libraries: Type:** reference. **Holdings:** 100; archival material, articles, books, papers. **Subjects:** coatings, chemistry, steel, certification, concrete, protective coatings, shop painting, paint, systems and specifications, inspection, standards, paint application, surface preparation, surface profile, weathering steel, marine coatings, lead paint, paint removal. **Telecommunication Services:** electronic mail, shoup@sspc.org ● electronic mail, kline@sspc.org. **Committees:** Application, Inspection, and Quality Control; Coating Materials; Education and Certification; Improved Performance of Coatings; Safety and Health; Surface Preparation. **Formerly:** (1998) Steel Structures Painting Council. **Publications:** *Cleaning and Coating Concrete*. Manual. Presents a thorough examination of concrete's physical and chemical properties. **Price:** $105.00 for members; $150.00 for nonmembers. Alternate Formats: CD-ROM ● *Good Painting Practice, Vol. 1 and 2*. Manual. Features a comprehensive overview of procedures for preparation and coating. **Price:** $123.00 for members; $175.00 for nonmembers ● *Journal of Protective Coatings and Linings*, monthly. Reports on association activities, research, products and equipment, and regulations. Includes service directory, calendar, and maintenance tips. **Price:** $80.00. ISSN: 8755-1985. **Advertising:** accepted. Alternate Formats: online ● *Shop Painting of Steel*. Manual. Discusses shop painting versus painting in the field. **Price:** $67.00 for members; $95.00 for nonmembers ● *SSPC Membership Directory*, annual. **Price:** free for members; $85.00/copy for nonmembers ● *Systems and Specifications*. Manual. Alternate Formats: CD-ROM. **Conventions/Meetings:** annual The Industrial Protective Coatings Conference and Exhibit - conference and seminar, with tutorials (exhibits) ● annual Paint and Coatings Expo - meeting.

Paper

2886 ■ 100% Recycled Paperboard Alliance
1331 F St. NW, Ste.800
Washington, DC 20004
Ph: (202)347-8000
Free: (877)772-6200
E-mail: info@rpa100.com
URL: http://www.rpa100.com
Contact: Paul J. Schutes, Exec. Dir.
Description: Works to increase the use and labeling of 100 percent recycled paperboard packaging.

2887 ■ Fibre Box Association (FBA)
25 NW Point Blvd., Ste.510
Elk Grove Village, IL 60007
Ph: (847)364-9600
Fax: (847)364-9639
E-mail: fba@fibrebox.org
URL: http://www.fibrebox.org
Contact: Dwight Schmidt, Pres.
Founded: 1940. **Members:** 156. **Staff:** 7. **Description:** Works to bring together North American manufacturers of corrugated paperboard products to provide comprehensive services for the industry. Compiles statistical reports and industry forecasts; disseminates information on labor negotiations and settlements; presents industry positions to government agencies; develops performance test methods, standards and requirements; monitors environmental issues and/or regulations. **Awards:** Safety and Health Statistics. **Frequency:** annual. **Type:** recognition. **Recipient:** for company with the best safety performance. **Committees:** Data Services; Environment; Human Resources; Safety/Health. **Publications:** *Corrugated Economic Trends and Forecast*, quarterly. Report. **Price:** free for members. Alternate Formats: online ● *Corrugated Industry Statistics*, monthly. Report. **Price:** free for members ● *Corrugated Plant Lists*, annual. Directory. **Price:** free for members; $200.00 for nonmembers ● *Fibre Box Handbook*. **Price:** $25.00 for members; $50.00 for nonmembers ● *Publications and Reports*. Catalog. Lists publications issued by the FBA. **Conventions/Meetings:** annual Independent Corrugator Executive Conference ● annual meeting - always spring ● annual Sheet Plant Owner/Operator Workshop.

2888 ■ International Molded Pulp Environmental Packaging Association (IMPEPA)
1425 W Mequon Rd., Ste.A
Mequon, WI 53092
Ph: (262)241-0522
Fax: (262)241-3766
E-mail: info@impepa.org
URL: http://www.impepa.org
Contact: Joseph Grygny, Chm.
Founded: 1997. **Members:** 70. **Membership Dues:** individual, $75 (annual) ● corporate, $850 (annual). **Staff:** 3. **Budget:** $150,000. **Languages:** English, French, German. **Description:** Promotes the use of waste paper as a means to produce molded product pulp for the packaging materials market. **Libraries: Type:** reference. **Holdings:** articles, audiovisuals, business records, monographs. **Subjects:** molded pulp machinery, manufacturing and uses. **Awards:** Best Molded Pulp Packaging Design (AMSTAR Award through IOPP). **Frequency:** annual. **Type:** scholarship. **Recipient:** for students in packaging engineering programs. **Committees:** Seminars. **Publications:** *IMPEPA Newsletter*, 3/year. Contains molded pulp industry news and advice for users and manufacturers. **Price:** included in membership dues. **Circulation:** 700. **Conventions/Meetings:** semiannual Molded Pulp Manufacturing - seminar, for members and non-members.

2889 ■ International Thermographers Association (ITA)
Address Unknown since 2008
Founded: 1973. **Members:** 78. **Staff:** 1. **Description:** Special industry group of Printing Industries of America whose members specialize in thermographic printing, foilstamping and embossing. (Thermography is a printing process involving the use of heat in conjunction with powder to produce raised lettering.) Works to provide technical information on thermography and networking opportunities for members. Sponsors annual Thermographic Product Excellence Contest. **Awards:** Thermographic Product Excellence. **Frequency:** annual. **Type:** recognition. **Publications:** *Thermogram*, quarterly. Membership Directory. Contains technical thermography and membership activities information. **Price:** free for members ● Membership Directory, annual. **Price:** free. **Conventions/Meetings:** annual convention and regional meeting (exhibits) - always fall.

2890 ■ National Association of Paperstock Women (NAPW)
PO Box 826
Williamsville, NY 14221
Ph: (630)585-7604
E-mail: jenniferj.smith@awin.com
URL: http://www.napw.org
Contact: Jennifer Smith, Membership Committee Chair
Founded: 1988. **Membership Dues:** individual, $50 (annual) ● corporate (plus $25 for each additional corporate member), $100 (annual). **Description:** Represents and promotes professionals within the paper industry and related fields. **Awards: Frequency:** annual. **Type:** scholarship. **Computer Services:** database, membership directory ● electronic publishing, e-newsletter. **Programs:** Scholarship.

2891 ■ NPTA Alliance
500 Bi-County Blvd., Ste.200E
Farmingdale, NY 11735
Ph: (631)777-2223
Free: (800)355-6782
Fax: (631)777-2224
E-mail: bill@gonpta.com
URL: http://gonpta.com
Contact: William H. Frohlich, Pres.
Founded: 1903. **Members:** 2,200. **Staff:** 12. **Description:** Represents wholesale distributors and suppliers of paper, plastics, and allied products. **Telecommunication Services:** electronic mail, linda@gonpta.com. **Divisions:** Business Imaging; Commercial Printing; Disposables; E-Commerce; International; Jan/San; Packaging; Publishing; Young Leaders. **Formerly:** (2004) National Paper Trade Association. **Publications:** *Distribution Sales and Management*, monthly. Magazine. **Advertising:** accepted. **Conventions/Meetings:** annual meeting and convention.

2892 ■ Paper Distribution Council (PDC)
c/o NPTA Alliance
500 Bi-County Blvd., Ste.200E
Farmingdale, NY 11735
Ph: (631)777-2223
Free: (800)355-NPTA
Fax: (631)777-2224
E-mail: bill@gonpta.com
URL: http://gonpta.com
Contact: William H. Frohlich, Pres.
Founded: 1958. **Members:** 35. **Membership Dues:** distributor, $420 (annual) ● supplier, $1,200 (annual). **Description:** Represents paper manufacturers and paper merchants. Seeks to study and discuss wholesale paper distribution with the purpose of improving service and efficiency for the mutual benefit of the manufacturers, paper merchants, and consumers. **Affiliated With:** NPTA Alliance. **Conventions/Meetings:** semiannual conference.

2893 ■ Paper Industry Management Association (PIMA)
15 Tech. Pkwy. S
Norcross, GA 30092
Ph: (770)209-7230
Fax: (770)209-7359
E-mail: tcampbell@pimaweb.com
URL: http://www.pimaweb.org
Contact: Tammi Campbell, Contact
Founded: 1919. **Members:** 1,500. **Membership Dues:** individual, $150 (annual) ● corporate, $400 (annual) ● affiliate firm, $400 (annual) ● future leader/student, $15 (annual) ● retired, $35 (annual) ● couch pit university, $150 (annual). **Staff:** 10. **Regional Groups:** 10. **Description:** Professional organization of pulp, paper mill, and paper converting production executives. **Awards:** Brookshire Moore Superintendent of the Year. **Frequency:** annual. **Type:** recognition. **Recipient:** for a mill superintendent ● Delano L. Boutin Division Service. **Frequency:** annual. **Type:** recognition. **Recipient:** for an affiliate member ● Executive of the Year. **Frequency:** annual. **Type:** recognition. **Recipient:** for a senior level executive ● Glen T. Renegar. **Frequency:** annual. **Type:** recognition. **Recipient:** for individuals ● Mill Manager of the Year. **Frequency:** annual. **Type:** recognition. **Recipient:** for a mill manager ● Ray H. Cross Community Service. **Frequency:** annual. **Type:** recognition. **Recipient:** for a person in the pulp and paper industry ● Student of the Year. **Frequency:** annual. **Type:** recognition. **Recipient:** for an outstanding student ● Thomas F. Sheerin, Sr. Service. **Frequency:** annual. **Type:** recognition. **Recipient:** for a supplier. **Telecommunication Services:** electronic mail, sblevins@pimaweb.org. **Subgroups:** Information Systems; Manufacturing Reliability; Purchasing and Affiliates. **Formerly:** (1960) American Pulp and Paper Mill Superintendents Association. **Publications:** *PIMA Buyers Guide*, annual. Directory. Contains reference source for pulp and paper mill operating management. **Price:** free for members. **Circulation:** 1,500. **Advertising:** accepted. Alternate Formats: online. **Conventions/Meetings:** annual international conference ● annual Leadership Conference (exhibits).

2894 ■ Sales Association of the Paper Industry (SAPI)
500 Bi-County Blvd., Ste.200E
Farmingdale, NY 11735
Free: (866)307-7274
Fax: (631)777-2224
E-mail: news@sapi1.org
Contact: Sheila Borgese, Exec. Dir.
Founded: 1919. **Members:** 150. **Membership Dues:** company, $125 (annual). **Staff:** 2. **Budget:** $125,000. **Description:** Represents sales, marketing, advertising, and sales promotion personnel of primary producers of pulp, paper, and paperboard. **Awards:** Scholarship Award. **Frequency:** annual. **Type:** scholarship. **Recipient:** to a high school student whose parents are employed by the sales department of a paper company affiliated with SAPI. **Formerly:** (1972) Salesmen's Association of the Paper Industry. **Publications:** *Monthly Sales Report*. Newsletter. Alternate Formats: online ● *Sales Report*, monthly. Bulletin. **Advertising:** accepted. **Conventions/Meetings:** semiannual conference and meeting - always in New York City, NY ● annual luncheon - always March during Paper Week.

2895 ■ TAPPI - Technical Association of the Pulp and Paper Industry
15 Tech. Pkwy. S
Norcross, GA 30092
Ph: (770)446-1400
Free: (800)332-8686
Fax: (770)446-6947
E-mail: memberconnection@tappi.org
URL: http://www.tappi.org
Contact: Mark R. McCollister Jr., Chm.
Founded: 1915. **Members:** 34,000. **Staff:** 95. **Budget:** $16,000. **Local Groups:** 27. **Description:** Executives, managers, engineers, research scientists, superintendents, and technologists in the pulp, packaging, converting, paper, non-wovens, and allied industries. Conducts conferences on coating, pulp manufacturing, engineering, non-wovens, process and product quality, polymers, laminations and coatings, paper and board manufacturing, corrugated containers, packaging, forest biology, printing, research and development, environment, finishing, and converting. Develops testing methods for laboratory analyses and process control. Sponsors Paper Express program to interest students in math, science, and careers in the paper and related industries. **Awards:** Gunnar Nicholson Gold Medal. **Frequency:**

annual. **Type:** monetary ● Herman Joachim Distinguished Service. **Type:** monetary. **Computer Services:** Online services, press catalogue, some CD ROM products, fax on demand. **Telecommunication Services:** additional toll-free number, in Canada, (800)446-9431. **Divisions:** Coating and Graphic Arts; Corrugated Containers; Engineering; Environmental; Finishing and Converting; Nonwovens; Paper and Board Manufacture; Polymers, Laminations, and Coatings; Process and Product Quality; Process Control Electronics and Information; Pulp Manufacture; Research and Development. **Publications:** *Tappi Journal*, monthly. **Price:** free with membership. **Circulation:** 44,000. **Advertising:** accepted. Alternate Formats: online ● *TAPPI PRESS*. Books ● Catalog. Contains information on pulp and paper industries. ● Membership Directory, annual ● Proceedings ● Also publishes test methods, technical information papers, training aids, and home study courses. **Conventions/Meetings:** triennial Industry Exhibit - meeting (exhibits) ● periodic symposium (exhibits).

Paranormal

2896 ■ American Association of Paranormal Investigators (AAPI)

13973 E Utah Cir.
Aurora, CO 80012
Ph: (303)482-6897
E-mail: stephen@ghostpi.com
URL: http://www.ghostpi.com
Contact: Stephen Weidner, Founder

Description: Promotes the use of scientific method as well as psychic ability in documenting paranormal phenomena. Assists individuals who are unable to deem or understand things that lie beyond the normal senses. Aims to build a laboratory that will further assist the association in studying paranormal activity with the aid of science. **Awards:** Paranormal Excellence Award. **Frequency:** annual. **Type:** recognition. **Recipient:** for outstanding paranormal research by a paranormal investigator. **Computer Services:** Information services, tools, glossary of terms, research findings, links ● online services, forum, photo gallery, store. **Publications:** *Dowsing/Divining Rods*. Article. Alternate Formats: online ● *Energy Flux As An Indication of Paranormal Activity*. Article. Alternate Formats: online ● *Tools Report*. Article. Alternate Formats: online ● *Understanding Orbs*. Article. Alternate Formats: online ● Reports. Contains summaries of paranormal investigations. Alternate Formats: online.

2897 ■ International Society for Paranormal Research (ISPR)

4712 Admiralty Way, No. 541
Marina del Rey, CA 90292
Ph: (323)644-8866
E-mail: investigationrequests@ispr.net
URL: http://www.ispr.net
Contact: Dr. Larry Montz, Founder

Founded: 1972. **Multinational. Description:** Offers professional parapsychological services including paranormal field investigations, psychic testing, Ghost Expeditions and various research studies. Assists government agencies in resolving missing persons and homicide cases. Creates and produces original paranormal reality documentaries, media consultants and on-air talent. **Computer Services:** Online services, psi test, press room. **Publications:** *ISPR Investigates: The Ghosts of New Orleans*. Book. Features studies and information about the haunted places in New Orleans. **Price:** $14.95 plus shipping and handling.

2898 ■ Paranormal Solutions

Address Unknown since 2007

Founded: 1993. **Staff:** 1. **Nonmembership. Multinational. Description:** Promotes understanding of the paranormal; provides expert investigations, clearings, and exorcisms.

Parking

2899 ■ International Parking Institute (IPI)

701 Kenmore Ave., Ste.200
Fredericksburg, VA 22401
Ph: (540)371-7535
Fax: (540)371-8022
E-mail: ipi@parking.org
URL: http://www.parking.org
Contact: Aisha Duckworth, Receptionist

Founded: 1962. **Members:** 1,300. **Membership Dues:** academic, $520 (annual) ● consultant, $735 (annual) ● commercial, $775 (annual) ● associate, $150 (annual) ● student, $50 (annual). **Staff:** 8. **Budget:** $2,500,000. **Regional Groups:** 4. **State Groups:** 16. **Description:** Parking, transit, transportation, public works, and security departments of cities, airports, civic centers, port authorities, colleges, universities, and hospitals; individuals within these departments; engineers, architects, planners, and suppliers to the parking industry. Provides information on developments in the parking field in the areas of management, construction, planning, and technical advancements. Conducts regional seminars on such topics as hospital parking, residential permit parking programs, enforcement, airport parking, garage deterioration, computers, and security. Sponsors technical sessions and research programs. Compiles statistics; maintains Speaker's Bureau; operates placement service. Has established the International Parking Clearinghouse Foundation, and a professional certification program with the University of Virginia Certified Administrator of Public Parking (CAPP). **Libraries: Type:** reference. **Holdings:** 1,200; articles, audio recordings, books, video recordings. **Subjects:** parking. **Awards:** Award for Excellence. **Frequency:** annual. **Type:** recognition. **Recipient:** for design consultants, engineers, planners, and facility owners. **Committees:** Americans with Disabilities; Diversity Enhancement; International Outreach; Parking Technology; Professional Certification; State/Regional Parking Association; Strategic Long Range Planning. **Formerly:** (1976) International Municipal Parking Congress; (1995) Institutional and Municipal Parking Congress. **Publications:** *Parking Buyer's Guide*, annual. Catalog. Lists of parking equipment and suppliers. Includes advertisers' index. **Price:** $29.95/copy. **Circulation:** 4,000. **Advertising:** accepted ● *Parking Management: The Next Level*. Book. **Price:** $250.00 ● *Parking 101: A Parking primer*. Book. **Price:** $195.00 ● *The Parking Professional*, monthly. Journal. Covers the parking industry. Includes calendar of events, new products, features, and statistics. **Price:** included in membership dues; $60.00 /year for nonmembers. ISSN: 0896-2324. **Circulation:** 10,000. **Advertising:** accepted ● *Who's Who in Parking*, annual. Membership Directory. Includes data book. **Circulation:** 1,270. **Conventions/Meetings:** annual International Parking Conference and Exposition (exhibits) - always May or June.

2900 ■ National Parking Association (NPA)

1112 16th St. NW, Ste.300
Washington, DC 20036
Ph: (202)296-4336
Free: (800)647-PARK
Fax: (202)331-8523
E-mail: info@npapark.org
URL: http://www.npapark.org
Contact: Martin L. Stein, Exec. Dir.

Founded: 1951. **Members:** 1,200. **Membership Dues:** regular (1 to 3 locations), $395 (annual) ● regular (4 to 249 locations), $4,200-$5,775 (annual) ● regular (250 to 749 locations), $7,350-$8,925 (annual) ● regular (750 and above locations), $10,500 (annual) ● Parking Consultant Council, $725 (annual) ● allied, $595 (annual) ● student, $50 (annual) ● governmental, institutional, and non-profit, $395 (annual) ● international, $525 (annual) ● associate, $310 (annual) ● affiliate, $500 (annual). **Staff:** 6. **Budget:** $6,000,000. **Description:** Owners and operators of off-street parking facilities; architects, traffic engineers, equipment suppliers and manufacturers, colleges, universities, municipalities, airport authorities; others with an interest in downtown parking. Provides specialized education programs; offers scholarship program through the Parking Industry Institute. **Awards:** Parking Industry Institute Program. **Frequency:** annual. **Type:** scholarship. **Recipient:** to employees of member organizations, their spouses or children. **Telecommunication Services:** electronic mail, mstein@npapark.org ● electronic mail, plangfeld@npapark.org. **Committees:** Political Action. **Councils:** NPA Parking Consultants. **Publications:** *Parking Magazine*, 10/year. Includes government affairs reports and industry news. **Price:** $95.00/year in U.S.; $125.00/year outside U.S. **Circulation:** 5,000. **Advertising:** accepted. Alternate Formats: CD-ROM; online; magnetic tape ● *Parking Products and Services Directory*, annual, usually December ● Also publishes information on design, construction and maintenance of parking facilities. **Conventions/Meetings:** annual International Convention and Exposition (exhibits).

Personnel

2901 ■ Black Human Resources Network (BHRN)

Address Unknown since 2007
URL: http://www.bhrn.org/

Founded: 1988. **Members:** 250. **Membership Dues:** regular, $125 (annual) ● affiliate, $300 (annual) ● corporate, $900 (annual) ● student, $30 (annual). **Description:** Human resources professionals and practitioners. Promotes the welfare of African American human resource practitioners; encourages development and information exchange among members. Monitors legislation pertaining to human resources; conducts seminars and charitable programs. **Libraries: Type:** reference. **Holdings:** business records. **Awards: Frequency:** annual. **Type:** scholarship. **Recipient:** for student in good standing majoring in human resources or personnel management. **Publications:** *Annual Awards Dinner and Gala Program* ● *Annual Conference Program*. **Conventions/Meetings:** annual Awards Dinner and Gala - conference ● annual Job Fair ● bimonthly meeting, for membership.

2902 ■ Human Resource Certification Institute (HRCI)

1800 Duke St.
Alexandria, VA 22314
Ph: (703)548-3440
Free: (866)898-4724
E-mail: info@hrci.org
URL: http://www.hrci.org
Contact: Cornelia Springer CAE, Exec. Dir.

Founded: 1976. **Staff:** 10. **Description:** Promotes the establishment of standards for the profession. Recognizes human resource professionals who have met, through demonstrated professional experience and the passing of a comprehensive written examination, the Institute's requirements for mastering the codified HR body of knowledge. Offers three professional certifications: Professional in Human Resources (PHR), Senior Professional in Human Resources (SPHR), and Global Professional in Human Resources (GPHR). **Affiliated With:** Society for Human Resource Management. **Formerly:** (1977) ASPA Accreditation Institute; (1991) Personnel Accreditation Institute. **Publications:** *Certification Study Guide* ● *PHR SPHR GPHR Certification Handbook*. Alternate Formats: online. **Conventions/Meetings:** semiannual meeting - always first Saturday of May and December.

2903 ■ Media Human Resources Association (MHRA)

c/o Society for Human Resource Management
1800 Duke St.
Alexandria, VA 22314
Ph: (703)548-3440 (703)548-6999
Free: (800)283-SHRM
Fax: (703)535-6490

E-mail: shrm@shrm.org
URL: http://www.shrm.org
Contact: Janet N. Parker, Chair
Founded: 1949. **Members:** 830. **Membership Dues:** full, $160 (annual) ● outside U.S. (internet-only), $95 (annual) ● student, $35 (annual). **Staff:** 3. **Budget:** $200,000. **Description:** Acts as a professional emphasis group within the Society for Human Resource Management (see separate entry). International media human resources and labor relations executives; media executives whose companies do not have human resources departments; associate members' suppliers. Seeks to advance human resources and industrial relations by seeking ways for management to make more effective use of people and by educating members in basic methods and techniques. Conducts research on human resource issues in the media industry. **Awards:** Blodger Diversity Award. **Frequency:** annual. **Type:** recognition. **Recipient:** for advancing the concept of diversity within the media industry ● Catalyst Award. **Frequency:** annual. **Type:** recognition. **Recipient:** for career dedication to human resources in media industry. **Telecommunication Services:** electronic mail, janetn.parker@regions.com. **Affiliated With:** Society for Human Resource Management. **Formerly:** (1998) Newspaper Personnel Relations Association. **Publications:** *MHRA News*, bimonthly. Newsletter. Covers trends in human resources and labor, management, training, and legal updates. **Price:** available to members only ● Directory, annual. **Advertising:** accepted. **Conventions/Meetings:** annual conference, held in conjunction with Society for Human Resource Management (exhibits).

2904 ■ National Association for Government Training and Development (NAGTAD)

2516 Wertherson Ln.
Raleigh, NC 27613-1700
Ph: (919)306-1787
Fax: (919)845-6922
E-mail: go2nagtad@aol.com
URL: http://www.nagtad.org
Contact: Jack Lemons, Admin.
Founded: 1980. **Members:** 94. **Membership Dues:** entity, $400 (annual) ● professional, $125 (annual). **Staff:** 1. **Budget:** $38,000. **Regional Groups:** 10. **State Groups:** 50. **Description:** Training and development administrators and practitioners employed by governmental jurisdictions (local, state and federal). Seeks to advance the study and practice of public sector human resource training and development. Promotes growth and development of members. Encourages increased public understanding of the importance of training and development programs for public service employees. Facilitates networking and exchange of information among members; serves as a clearinghouse on public sector human resources development; provides research and technical support to public sector training and development programs. **Awards:** Program of the Year. **Frequency:** annual. **Type:** recognition. **Computer Services:** Mailing lists. **Conventions/Meetings:** annual meeting (exhibits) ● annual Professional Development Conference - 2008 Oct. 26-29, Columbia, SC.

2905 ■ National Human Resources Association (NHRA)

PO Box 7326
Nashua, NH 03060-7326
Free: (866)523-4417
Fax: (603)891-5760
E-mail: info@humanresources.org
URL: http://www.humanresources.org
Contact: Brian Barry, Pres.
Founded: 1951. **Members:** 1,500. **Local Groups:** 16. **Description:** Represents human resource executives in business, industry, education, and government. Established to expand and improve the professionalism of those in human resource management. **Committees:** Communications; Professional Development; Professional Issues. **Formerly:** (1993) International Association for Personnel Women. **Publications:** *Connections*, bimonthly. Newsletter. **Price:** $25.00 /year for members; $30.00 /year for nonmembers. **Circulation:** 1,600. **Advertising:** accepted ● *Membership Roster*, annual. Membership Directory. **Conventions/Meetings:** annual conference (exhibits).

2906 ■ North American Trucking Industrial Relations Association (NTIRA)

Address Unknown since 2007
Founded: 1987. **Members:** 150. **Membership Dues:** individual, $150 (annual). **Staff:** 2. **Budget:** $50,000. **Regional Groups:** 5. **Description:** Labor and personnel executives, CEOs, and attorneys involved in the trucking industry. Conducts and promotes educational activities relative to the areas of industrial relations and human resources. **Formerly:** (2000) National Trucking Industrial Relations Association. **Publications:** Newsletter, quarterly. **Conventions/Meetings:** annual conference.

2907 ■ SHRM Global Forum

1800 Duke St.
Alexandria, VA 22314
Ph: (703)548-3440
Free: (800)283-SHRM
Fax: (703)535-6490
E-mail: shrm@shrm.org
URL: http://www.shrm.org/global
Contact: Janet N. Parker SPHR, Chair
Founded: 1977. **Members:** 6,400. **Membership Dues:** general/associate/professional, $160 (annual) ● global internet, $95 (annual) ● student, $35 (annual). **Staff:** 4. **Budget:** $1,100,000. **Description:** Executives responsible for international human resource management. Acts as an information clearinghouse on international concerns and issues; provides a forum for networking. Maintains information center of publications and periodicals on international human resources management. A division of the Society for Human Resource Management (SHRM). **Libraries:** **Type:** reference. **Holdings:** 400,000; articles. **Affiliated With:** Society for Human Resource Management. **Formerly:** (1989) American Society for Personnel Administration International; (2000) Institute for International Human Resources. **Publications:** *HRMagazine*, monthly. **Price:** $70.00/year in U.S.; $90.00/year in Canada; $125.00/year outside U.S. and Canada. Alternate Formats: online ● *SHRM Global Perspectives*, monthly. Newsletter. Covers current topics of interest, member news, calendar of events, and publications and resources. Includes book reviews. **Price:** included in membership dues. **Circulation:** 7,000. Alternate Formats: online ● *Staff Management*, quarterly. Magazine. **Price:** $35.00/year in U.S.; $55.00/year in Canada; $85.00/year outside U.S. and Canada. **Conventions/Meetings:** annual Global HR Forum - meeting and conference, human resources management (exhibits) ● biennial World Congress on Personnel Management - meeting.

2908 ■ Society for Human Resource Management (SHRM)

1800 Duke St.
Alexandria, VA 22314-3499
Ph: (703)548-3440 (703)535-6078
Free: (800)283-7476
Fax: (703)535-6490
E-mail: shrm@shrm.org
URL: http://www.shrm.org
Contact: Susan R. Meisinger SPHR, Pres./CEO
Founded: 1948. **Members:** 63,000. **Membership Dues:** associate, professional, general (national), $160 (annual) ● global Internet, $95 (annual). **Staff:** 1. **Budget:** $25,000,000. **Regional Groups:** 7. **State Groups:** 53. **Local Groups:** 433. **Description:** Professional organization of human resource, personnel, and industrial relations professionals and executives. Promotes the advancement of human resource management. Sponsors SHRM Foundation. Offers certification through the Human Resource Certification Institute. **Libraries:** **Type:** reference. **Holdings:** 3,500; books, clippings, monographs, periodicals. **Subjects:** human resource management. **Awards:** Award for Professional Excellence. **Frequency:** annual. **Type:** recognition. **Recipient:** for excellence in human resources ● Creative Excellence Award for Recruitment Advertising. **Frequency:** annual. **Type:** recognition. **Recipient:** to agencies with highest achievements in creative recruitment advertising ● EMA Foundation. **Frequency:** annual. **Type:** scholarship. **Recipient:** for an HR major ● Pericles Achievement Award. **Type:** recognition. **Recipient:** to an employment executive for achievement in the field of employment and human resources. **Computer Services:** Mailing lists, rental. **Committees:** College Relations; Compensation and Benefits; Education; Employee and Labor Relations; Employment Practices; HR Information Systems; Legislative Affairs; Research; Training and Development; Workplace Diversity; Workplace Health and Safety. **Programs:** Issues Management. **Affiliated With:** Human Resource Certification Institute; Media Human Resources Association; SHRM Global Forum. **Formerly:** (1989) American Society for Personnel Administration. **Publications:** *HR Magazine*, monthly. Covers new ideas emerging in the personnel/industrial relations' field. Includes book reviews and listing of microcomputer software and vendors. **Price:** free for members; $60.00 /year for nonmembers. ISSN: 0031-5729. **Circulation:** 73,000. **Advertising:** accepted. Alternate Formats: microform; online. Also Cited As: *Personnel Administrator: The Magazine of Human Resource Management* ● *HR News*, monthly. Includes employment listings and a section monitoring legislative activities; tabloid for professionals. **Price:** free for members; $44.00 /year for nonmembers. ISSN: 0746-7850. **Circulation:** 63,000. **Advertising:** accepted. Also Cited As: *American Society for Personnel Administration—Resource: Monthly News on Human Resource Management* ● *Issues in HR*, bimonthly ● *Speakers Directory*, periodic ● Books ● Monographs ● Reports ● Surveys. **Conventions/Meetings:** annual conference and convention (exhibits) ● seminar.

Pest Control

2909 ■ Interstate Professional Applicators Association (IPAA)

PO Box 13262
Salem, OR 97309
Ph: (503)363-7205
Fax: (503)378-0864
E-mail: ipaa2002@hotmail.com
Contact: Debbie Ego, Sec.
Founded: 1953. **Members:** 100. **Membership Dues:** $250 (annual). **State Groups:** 2. **Local Groups:** 1. **Description:** Companies engaged in the application of horticultural spraying. Aims to insure a healthy and safe environment through proper pesticide usage. Works to acquire and disseminate technological information regarding the safe application of pesticides. Contributes to state research facilities. Sponsors seminars on entomology, pathology, safety, soils, business management, and employee relations. **Awards:** **Type:** recognition. **Formerly:** (1989) International Pesticide Applicators Association. **Conventions/Meetings:** annual conference and trade show (exhibits).

2910 ■ National Pest Management Association International (NPMA)

9300 Lee Hwy., Ste.301
Fairfax, VA 22031
Ph: (703)352-6762
Free: (800)678-6722
Fax: (703)352-3031
E-mail: info@pestworld.org
URL: http://www.pestworld.org
Contact: Mr. Robert F. Lederer, Exec. VP
Founded: 1933. **Members:** 5,500. **Staff:** 17. **Budget:** $4,000,000. **State Groups:** 36. **Multinational. Description:** Represents firms engaged in control of insects, rodents, birds, and other pests, in or around structures, through use of insecticides, rodenticides, miticides, fumigants, and non-chemical methods. Provides advisory services on control procedures, new products, and safety and business administration practices. Promotes June as National Pest Control Month. Sponsors research, periodic technical and management seminars. **Awards:** Committee of

the Year Award. **Frequency:** annual. **Type:** recognition. **Additional Websites:** http://www.npmapestworld.org. **Telecommunication Services:** electronic mail, lederer@pestworld.org, **Committees:** Chemical and Chemical Safety; Education; Financial Management; Food Protection; Fumigation; Government Affairs; Insect Control; Marketing Management; Operations; Personnel Management; Political Action; Public Relations; Vertebrate Control; Wood Destroying Organisms. **Formerly:** (1937) National Association of Exterminators and Fumigators; (2001) National Pest Control Association. **Publications:** *National Pest Control Association—Technical Release*, monthly. Newsletter. Provides information on the various technical problems associated with biological habits and control of pests. **Circulation:** 5,000 ● *National Pest Management Association—Series of Management Reports*, periodic. Newsletter. Reports on current management topics. **Circulation:** 5,000 ● *NPCA Newsletter*, monthly. **Price:** free, for members only ● *Who's Who in Professional Pest Management*, annual. Arranged geographically; includes resource catalog. **Price:** free for members; $50.00/copy for nonmembers. **Circulation:** 5,500. **Advertising:** accepted ● Also publishes technical releases, manuals, videos and reports; distributes business aids, filmstrips, and slides. **Conventions/Meetings:** annual PestWorld - meeting (exhibits) - always October.

2911 ■ Pesticide Applicators Professional Association (PAPA)

PO Box 80095
Salinas, CA 93912-0095
Ph: (831)442-3536
Fax: (831)442-2351
E-mail: stephanie@papaseminars.com
URL: http://www.papaseminars.com

Founded: 1985. **Members:** 6,500. **Membership Dues:** regular, $40 (annual). **Staff:** 6. **Budget:** $750,000. **Description:** Seeks to provide continuing education for members to be able to renew state licenses. **Computer Services:** database. **Publications:** *Pesticide Applicators News*, quarterly. Newsletter. **Circulation:** 6,000. **Conventions/Meetings:** weekly regional meeting.

2912 ■ Responsible Industry for a Sound Environment (RISE)

1156 15th St. NW, Ste.400
Washington, DC 20005
Ph: (202)872-3860
Fax: (202)355-1467
E-mail: margulies@bluepumpkingroup.com
URL: http://www.pestfacts.org
Contact: Angela B. Jamison, Pres.

Founded: 1991. **Members:** 160. **Staff:** 3. **Budget:** $1,000,000. **Description:** Manufacturers, formulators, distributors, and representatives of the specialty pesticides industry. Promotes the environmental, health, and safety benefits of the proper use of specialty pesticides. **Also Known As:** RISE. **Publications:** *Newslines*, bimonthly. Newsletter. **Price:** free for members. **Circulation:** 300. **Conventions/Meetings:** annual meeting.

Petroleum

2913 ■ American Association of Professional Landmen (AAPL)

4100 Fossil Creek Blvd.
Fort Worth, TX 76137-2723
Ph: (817)847-7700
Fax: (817)847-7704
E-mail: aapl@landman.org
URL: http://www.landman.org
Contact: Robin Forte, Exec. VP

Founded: 1955. **Members:** 8,500. **Membership Dues:** active/associate, $100 (annual) ● life, $2,500. **Staff:** 8. **Budget:** $2,000,000. **Regional Groups:** 10. **Local Groups:** 48. **Multinational. Description:** Professional society of petroleum landmen, independent lease brokers, oil operators, and company exploration managers. Supports a four-year college curriculum developed by AAPL and a trust fund granting scholarships to students. Sponsors annual local and national institutes; approves industry forms. Operates landman certification program; maintains placement service; operates speakers' bureau. **Telecommunication Services:** electronic mail, rforte@landman.org. **Committees:** Annual Meeting; Awards; Certification; Education; Educational Foundation Fund Raising; Ethics; Field Landman; Forms; Industry/Public Relations; Legislative/Regulatory; Public Lands; Publications. **Formerly:** (1992) American Association of Petroleum Landmen. **Publications:** *The Landman*, bimonthly. Magazine. Reports industry, association, and member news; includes listing of educational opportunities, bulletin board, tax topics, and annual index. **Price:** $25.00 for members; $100.00 for nonmembers. ISSN: 0457-088X. **Circulation:** 8,000. **Advertising:** accepted ● *Landman 2*, bimonthly. Newsletter ● *Landmen's Directory*, annual. ISSN: 0272-8370. **Advertising:** accepted ● *Update*, bimonthly. Newsletter ● Annual Report, annual. **Conventions/Meetings:** quarterly board meeting ● annual international conference (exhibits) - usually June ● annual meeting.

2914 ■ American Exploration and Production Council (AXPC)

101 Constitution Ave. NW, Ste.800
Washington, DC 20001-2133
Ph: (202)742-4300
E-mail: info@dpcusa.org
URL: http://www.dpcusa.org
Contact: William F. Whitsitt, Pres.

Description: Represents large United States independent natural gas and crude oil exploration and production companies. Works constructively for sound energy, environmental and related public policies. **Conventions/Meetings:** annual meeting.

2915 ■ American Oil and Gas Historical Society (AOGHS)

1201 15th St. NW, Ste.300
Washington, DC 20005
Ph: (202)857-4785
Fax: (202)857-4799
E-mail: bawells@aoghs.org
URL: http://www.aoghs.org
Contact: Bruce Wells, Founder/Exec. Dir.

Founded: 2003. **Membership Dues:** student, $50 (annual) ● sustaining, $75 (annual) ● patron, $200-$999 (annual) ● benefactor, $1,000 (annual). **Description:** Aims to preserve the history of U.S. oil and natural gas exploration and production. Provides advocacy for organizations that work to preserve that history through exhibition, material preservation, and educational programming. Maintains a communication network of community oil and gas museums, education programs, historical societies, and individuals committed to energy education. **Awards:** Oil Patch Preservationist Award. **Frequency:** annual. **Type:** recognition. **Recipient:** for dedication in preserving the heritage of the oil and natural gas industry. **Publications:** *American Oil and Gas Families*. Booklet. Describes historic discoveries, communities and individuals. ● *The Petroleum Age*, quarterly. Newsletter. Contains news and exhibit information from U.S. oil and natural gas museums, historical societies, and related organizations. **Price:** included in membership dues. Alternate Formats: online. **Conventions/Meetings:** annual conference (exhibits).

2916 ■ American Petroleum Institute (API)

1220 L St. NW
Washington, DC 20005-4070
Ph: (202)682-8000 (202)682-8120
Fax: (202)682-8033
E-mail: mediacenter@api.org
URL: http://api-ec.api.org/newsplashpage/index.cfm
Contact: Jim Craig, VP/Dir.

Founded: 1919. **Members:** 400. **Staff:** 270. **Budget:** $42,000,000. **State Groups:** 33. **Description:** Corporations in the petroleum and allied industries, including producers, refiners, marketers, and transporters of crude oil, lubricating oil, gasoline and natural gas. Provides public policy development, advocacy, research, and technical services to enhance the ability of the petroleum industry to fulfill its mission: meeting the nation's energy needs; enhancing the environmental, health, and safety performance of the industry; conducting research to advance petroleum technology, equipment, and standards; Consensus policies and collective action on issues impacting its members; and works collaboratively with all industry oil and gas associations, and other organizations, to enhance industry unity and effectiveness in its advocacy. Also provides the opportunity for standards development, technical cooperation and other activities to improve the industry's competitiveness through sponsorship of self-supporting programs. **Awards:** Gold Medal. **Frequency:** annual. **Type:** medal. **Recipient:** for contributions or advancements to the industry ● Outstanding Safety and Environmental Performance. **Frequency:** annual. **Type:** recognition. **Recipient:** for safety performances and operations. **Computer Services:** database, statistical and bibliographical information. **Divisions:** Downstream; General Membership; Marine; Pipeline; Upstream. **Publications:** *American Petroleum Institute—Publications and Materials*, annual. Catalog. Lists publications and audiovisual materials available through API. **Circulation:** 200,000. Alternate Formats: CD-ROM; online ● *Basic Petroleum Data Book*, semiannual. Contains statistical background data on energy, reserves, exploration and drilling, production, finance, prices, demand, and refining. **Price:** $650.00 printed; $3,500.00 online with continuous updates. Alternate Formats: online ● *Imported Crude Oil and Petroleum Products*, monthly. Contains data on crude oil imports and major products detailing the importer, port of entry, country of origin, recipient, and destination. **Price:** $2,000.00 printed; $7,000.00 online. Alternate Formats: online ● *Inventories of Natural Gas Liquids and Liquefied Refinery Gases*, monthly. Geographical listing of inventories of liquefied petroleum and liquefied refinery gases at plants and refineries, and in underground storage. **Price:** $700.00 printed; $2,350.00 online. Alternate Formats: online ● *Joint Association Survey on Drilling Costs*, annual. Reports the estimated cost of drilling oil wells, gas wells, and dry holes by depth range for regions in the U.S. **Price:** $850.00 printed; $1,850.00 online ● *Monthly Statistical Report.* Summarizes the estimated U.S. petroleum balance with analyses of the trends reflected in the Weekly Statistical Bulletin. **Price:** $300.00 printed; $2,050.00 online ● *Weekly Statistical Bulletin and Monthly Statistical Report.* Presents data on U.S. refinery activity and principal inventories, crude oil and product imports, and crude oil production. **Price:** $450.00 printed; $7,000.00 online. Alternate Formats: online ● *Well Completion Report*, quarterly. Includes a regional report by quarter of completion for total wells drilled and by depth intervals. Provides annual summary table on total wells. **Price:** $600.00 printed; $1,850.00 online. Alternate Formats: online ● Also publishes several hundred manuals, booklets, and other materials on production, refining, marketing, transportation, research, safety and fire protection, standards and codes, and related areas. **Conventions/Meetings:** annual meeting and conference.

2917 ■ Association of Desk and Derrick Clubs (ADDC)

5153 E 51st St., Ste.107
Tulsa, OK 74135-7442
Ph: (918)622-1749
Fax: (918)622-1675
E-mail: adotulsa@swbell.net
URL: http://www.addc.org
Contact: Ms. Bonnie Fish, Pres.

Founded: 1951. **Members:** 2,500. **Membership Dues:** regular, $35 (annual). **Staff:** 1. **Regional Groups:** 7. **Local Groups:** 70. **Description:** Employers or employees in the petroleum, energy, and allied industries. Conducts educational meetings and field trips. Operates the Desk and Derrick Educational Trust. Operates ADDC Foundation. **Libraries: Type:** reference. **Holdings:** archival material, video recordings. **Awards:** Desk and Derrick Educational Trust. **Type:** scholarship. **Recipient:** for women pursuing degrees in the petroleum and allied industries ● **Type:** recognition. **Formerly:** (1978) Association of Desk and Derrick Clubs of North America. **Publications:** *Desk and Derrick Journal*, quarterly. **Price:** included in membership dues (available to members only). **Advertising:** accepted. **Conventions/Meetings:** annual convention ● convention.

2918 ■ Association of Energy Service Companies (AESC)
10200 Richmond Ave., Ste.275
Houston, TX 77042-4140
Ph: (713)781-0758
Free: (800)692-0771
Fax: (713)781-7542
E-mail: kjordan@aesc.net
URL: http://www.aesc.net
Contact: Kenny Jordan, Exec. Dir.
Founded: 1956. **Members:** 600. **Membership Dues:** sustaining (base), $600 (annual) ● associate/producer (class I), $700 (annual) ● associate/producer (class II), $500 (annual) ● individual, $150 (annual). **Staff:** 5. **Budget:** $1,200,000. **Regional Groups:** 17. **Languages:** English, Spanish. **For-Profit. Description:** Oil-well servicing and workover contractors, manufacturers, engineers, consultants, Rental Tool Companies, Wireline Well loggers, Trucking Service Companies, Water Hauling and Vacuum Trucks, Production Testing Companies, Drilling Units, Pump Units, Coil Tubing Companies, Insurance, production, and Financial Institutions. Promotes the interests of the energy service industry to its customers, employees, governmental agencies and the public. **Libraries: Type:** open to the public. **Holdings:** books, video recordings, video recordings. **Subjects:** oil and gas well servicing, rig driving and safety, H25, ADA, DOT, Haz Com, basic data/safety, hand and finger accident prevention, fall prevention. **Awards:** AESC Safety Award. **Frequency:** annual. **Type:** recognition. **Recipient:** for best record in hours worked vs. number of recordable accidents ● **Type:** scholarship. **Recipient:** for members and/or their dependents. **Computer Services:** Mailing lists, in house mailing service. **Committees:** Associate/Allied; Business Analysis; Health, Safety, and Environmental; Human Relations; Oilfield Trucking/Fluid Hauling; Political Affairs; Small Business Issues; Technical. **Formerly:** (2000) Association of Oilwell Servicing Contractors. **Publications:** *AESC Directory*, annual. Lists energy service company members and the products and services they offer; includes data on number of rigs, horsepower ratings, and equipment. **Price:** $45.00 for members; $90.00 for nonmembers. **Circulation:** 3,000. **Advertising:** accepted ● *Field Reports*, quarterly. Newsletter. Includes association and industry news, calendar of events, rig activity newsletter, and legislative updates. **Price:** free for members. **Circulation:** 1,400. **Advertising:** accepted ● *Well Servicing*, bimonthly. Magazine. Includes articles on industry events, new technology, equipment, and products, rig activity reports, personality profiles. **Price:** free. ISSN: 0043-2393. **Circulation:** 11,000. **Advertising:** accepted ● Manuals. Contains basic data and information on management rights, accident prevention, drug testing, insurance, and a various safety-related topics. **Conventions/Meetings:** semiannual conference.

2919 ■ Association of Oil Pipe Lines (AOPL)
1808 Eye St. NW
Washington, DC 20006
Ph: (202)408-7970
Fax: (202)208-1949
E-mail: rdobre@aopl.org
URL: http://www.aopl.org
Contact: Shirley J Neff, Pres./CEO
Founded: 1947. **Members:** 49. **Staff:** 3. **Budget:** $2,000,000. **Description:** Oil pipeline companies, most of which are regulated common carriers. Assembles statistical and other data relating to the pipeline industry for presentation to congress, governmental departments, agencies and commissions, trade associations, and the public. **Affiliated With:** American Petroleum Institute. **Formerly:** (1956) Committee for Pipe Line Companies; (1960) Committee for Oil Pipe Lines. **Publications:** *In the Pipe*, monthly. Newsletter. Covers issues about new industry initiative, day to day operations, government oversight and other related matters. **Price:** free ● *Shifts in Petroleum Transportation*, annual. Report. Shows movement in ton-miles of crude oil and petroleum products by pipelines, water carriers, motor carriers, and railroads. **Price:** free ● Papers, periodic. Defines industry views on regulatory matters. **Price:** free ● Reports, periodic. Provides information about the pipeline industry. **Price:** free. **Conventions/Meetings:** annual Accounting and Finance Workshop - always May ● annual meeting - usually summer or winter.

2920 ■ BP Amoco Marketers Association (BPAMA)
15 Lake St., Ste.280
Savannah, GA 31411-2971
Ph: (912)598-7939
Fax: (912)598-7949
E-mail: jkleine@bpama.com
URL: http://www.bpama.com
Contact: John Kleine, Exec. Dir.
Founded: 1974. **Members:** 500. **Membership Dues:** jobber (based on light oil volume), $300-$1,600 (annual) ● vendor, $500 (annual). **Staff:** 2. **Budget:** $300,000. **Regional Groups:** 4. **Description:** Wholesale jobber marketers under the BP Amoco trademarks. Provides a forum for communication between refiner-supplier, BP Amoco, and its marketers. **Awards:** Marketer of the Year. **Frequency:** annual. **Type:** recognition. **Recipient:** nomination and selection by membership. **Computer Services:** Mailing lists, of members. **Formerly:** (1990) Gulf Oil Wholesale Marketers Association; (1999) BP and Amoco Oil Marketers Association. **Publications:** *BPAMA Bulletin*, quarterly ● *BPAMA News*, monthly. Newsletter. **Conventions/Meetings:** biennial convention (exhibits) ● biennial convention (exhibits) - usually in fall ● periodic meeting, special call meetings ● periodic seminar, skills improvement - locations vary.

2921 ■ Coordinating Research Council (CRC)
3650 Mansell Rd., Ste.140
Alpharetta, GA 30022
Ph: (678)795-0506
Fax: (678)795-0509
E-mail: bkbailey@crcao.org
URL: http://www.crcao.org
Contact: Mr. Brent Bailey, Exec. Dir.
Founded: 1942. **Members:** 12. **Staff:** 6. **National Groups:** 5. **Multinational. Description:** Coordinates research activities among petroleum, equipment, and transportation industries in cooperation with other stakeholders and government organizations. **Committees:** Air Pollution Research Advisory; Automotive Vehicle Fuel, Lubricant, and Equipment Research; Aviation Fuel, Lubricant and Equipment Research. **Publications:** Papers, periodic ● Manual, periodic. **Conventions/Meetings:** On-Road Vehicle Emissions Workshop, workshop format reporting of current research on the emissions of in-use vehicles (exhibits).

2922 ■ Drilling Engineering Association (DEA)
c/o Morris Keene, Chm.
Occidental Oil and Gas Corp.
5 Greenway Plz., Ste.2400
Houston, TX 77046
Ph: (713)215-7118
Fax: (713)215-7517
URL: http://www.dea-global.org
Contact: Morris Keene, Chm.
Membership Dues: full, $500 ● associate, $200. **Description:** Promotes advancement of new technologies related to drilling wells. Provides a forum for presenting proposals for industry-drilling related projects.

2923 ■ Energy Traffic Association (ETA)
3303 Main St. Corridor
Houston, TX 77002-9321
Ph: (713)528-2868
Fax: (713)464-0702
E-mail: russell@energytraffic.org
URL: http://www.energytraffic.org
Contact: Ernest M. Powell, Exec. Dir.
Founded: 1942. **Members:** 53. **Membership Dues:** individual, $75 (annual) ● company, $150 (annual). **Staff:** 1. **Budget:** $50,000. **Description:** Major oil companies, pipelines, shippers, and oil field equipment companies. Provides specialized education programs. **Formerly:** (1998) Shippers Oil Field Traffic Association. **Publications:** *SOFTA Newsletter*, monthly ● Bulletin, periodic ● Membership Directory, annual. **Conventions/Meetings:** semiannual conference and seminar.

2924 ■ Gas Processors Association (GPA)
6526 E 60th St.
Tulsa, OK 74145-9202
Ph: (918)493-3872
Fax: (918)493-3875
E-mail: gpa@gasprocessors.com
URL: http://gasprocessors.com
Contact: Gene Thomas, Pres.
Founded: 1921. **Members:** 120. **Membership Dues:** production (minimum; based on average daily production during the first 6 months), associate, $895 (annual) ● further processor, $2,663 (annual) ● international, $1,318 (annual). **Staff:** 7. **Budget:** $1,000,000. **Regional Groups:** 6. **State Groups:** 1. **Multinational. Description:** Firms producing, processing, and handling natural gas liquids, and other hydrocarbon products (such as liquefied petroleum gases) at gas-processing plants. Develops technical standards and specifications for products; compiles basic data on hydrocarbon behavior, testing procedures, laboratory analysis, and plant safety practices. Cooperates with educational institutions on specific research projects. Compiles statistics. **Awards: Type:** recognition. **Committees:** Legislative and Regulatory Affairs; Liquefied Natural Gas; Operational; Plant Control; Research; Safety; Statistics; Technical; Volunteer Benefits. **Formerly:** (1922) Association of Natural Gasoline Manufacturers; (1961) Natural Gasoline Association of America; (1974) Natural Gas Processors Association. **Publications:** *Annual Convention Proceedings*, annual. Alternate Formats: online ● *E-Brief*, quarterly. Newsletter. Alternate Formats: online ● Papers. **Price:** $15.00 for sponsors; $500.00 for nonsponsors; $30.00 for university libraries. Alternate Formats: online ● Also publishes technical standards. **Conventions/Meetings:** annual meeting and convention, three-day technical session.

2925 ■ Gas Processors Suppliers Association (GPSA)
6526 E 60th St.
Tulsa, OK 74145-9202
Ph: (918)493-3872
Fax: (918)493-3875
E-mail: msutton@gasprocessors.com
URL: http://gpsa.gasprocessors.com
Contact: Mark Sutton, Exec. Dir.
Founded: 1928. **Members:** 350. **Membership Dues:** general, $300 (annual). **Staff:** 7. **Budget:** $500,000. **Description:** Manufacturers and wholesalers of natural gas processing equipment and supplies. Furnishes technical data to plant operators and engineers. **Committees:** Editorial; Technical. **Formerly:** Natural Gasoline Supply Men's Association; (1974) Natural Gas Processors Supplier's Association. **Publications:** *Engineering Data Book*, periodic. Contains the designs and operations for the gas processing and other related industries. **Price:** $72.00 for members and students; $162.00 for nonmembers; $122.00 for booksellers and universities. **Conventions/Meetings:** annual meeting - always March.

2926 ■ Gasoline Pump Manufacturers Association (GPMA)
Address Unknown since 2007
Members: 3. **Description:** Manufacturers of gasoline pumps. Conducts technical activities.

2927 ■ Independent Lubricant Manufacturers Association (ILMA)
400 N Columbus St., Ste.201
Alexandria, VA 22314-2264
Ph: (703)684-5574

Fax: (703)836-8503
E-mail: ilma@ilma.org
URL: http://www.ilma.org
Contact: Greg T. Julian, Pres.
Founded: 1948. **Members:** 300. **Membership Dues:** regular, $875 (annual). **Staff:** 7. **Budget:** $2,000,000. **Multinational. Description:** Independent compounders and blenders of automotive and industrial lubricants and greases in the United States; supplier members are base stock suppliers and additive and equipment manufacturers; international members are independent compounders outside the United States; marketing members are compounders and blenders as well as lubricant distributors. Conducts educational programs. Represents industry before Congress and federal regulatory agencies. Compiles statistics. **Awards:** Distinguished Service Award. **Frequency:** annual. **Type:** recognition. **Recipient:** for a member who has made significant contributions to the association ● ILMA Scholarship. **Frequency:** annual. **Type:** scholarship. **Recipient:** for college students. **Committees:** Engine and Transmission Lubricants; Grease; Industrial Lubricants; Metalworking Lubricants; Safety, Health, Environmental and Regulatory Affairs. **Formerly:** (1980) Independent Oil Compounders Association. **Publications:** *Compoundings*, monthly. Magazine. For owners and managers of independent lubricant manufacturing companies. **Price:** included in membership dues. **Circulation:** 2,500. **Advertising:** accepted. Alternate Formats: online ● *Flashpoint*, weekly. Newsletter. Contains interim news flashes between issues of compoundings. ● *Independent Lubricant Manufacturers Association—Membership Directory*, annual. Lists companies and detailed product information. **Price:** $75.00 for members; $175.00 for nonmembers. **Circulation:** 500. **Advertising:** accepted. **Conventions/Meetings:** annual Management Forum - meeting - usually March or April ● annual meeting - always October. 2008 Oct. 11-14, Scottsdale, AZ.

2928 ■ Independent Petroleum Association of America (IPAA)

1201 15th St. NW, Ste.300
Washington, DC 20005
Ph: (202)857-4722
Fax: (202)857-4799
E-mail: rcarter@ipaa.org
URL: http://www.ipaa.org
Contact: Mike Linn, Chm.
Founded: 1929. **Members:** 30,000. **Membership Dues:** regular, $420 (annual) ● partner, $840 (annual) ● scout, $1,680 (annual) ● roustabout, $3,400 (annual). **Staff:** 27. **State Groups:** 33. **Description:** Small, individually owned oil and gas exploration and production enterprises to the largest independent oil and gas companies, as well as exploration and production service and supply companies, providers of financial and other capital services, land and mineral owners, providers of consulting services, etc. Advocates the administration, and federal agencies. Works to ensure a strong, viable domestic oil and natural gas industry. Recognizes that an adequate and secure supply of energy is essential to the national economy. Provides opportunities to access capital markets; creates networking and educational opportunities; represents the industry to the media; develops economic and statistical information on the industry. **Committees:** Capital Markets; Communications; Crude Oil; Environment and Safety; International; Land and Royalty; Law; Natural Gas; Offshore; Supply and Demand; Tax; Wildcatters PAC. **Publications:** *America's Independent/Hart's E&P*, bimonthly. Magazine. **Price:** included in membership dues. **Circulation:** 30,000. **Advertising:** accepted ● *IPAA Washington Report*, weekly. Newsletter. Contains Washington legislative and regulatory activities information. **Price:** available to members only. Alternate Formats: online ● Papers, annual. Contains information about oil and natural gas industry. **Price:** included in membership dues. **Conventions/Meetings:** monthly Leadership Training Program For Executives - meeting (exhibits).

2929 ■ Independent Terminal Operators Association (ITOA)

1150 Connecticut NW, 9th Fl.
Washington, DC 20036
Ph: (202)828-4100 (202)828-4300
Fax: (202)828-4130
E-mail: wbode@bode.com
Contact: William H. Bode, Gen. Counsel
Founded: 1969. **Members:** 14. **Description:** Consists of independent terminal operators concerned with national policies affecting foreign oil imports and other matters affecting the independent sectors of the oil industry.

2930 ■ International Association of Drilling Contractors (IADC)

PO Box 4287
Houston, TX 77210-4287
Ph: (713)292-1945
Fax: (713)292-1946
E-mail: info@iadc.org
URL: http://www.iadc.org
Contact: Robert L. Long, Chm.
Founded: 1940. **Members:** 980. **Staff:** 21. **Regional Groups:** 10. **Description:** Represents oil, natural gas, and geothermal contract drilling firms. **Committees:** Contracts and Risk Management; Drilling Technology; Environmental Affairs; Government Affairs; Human Resources; Offshore. **Formerly:** (1972) American Association of Oilwell Drilling Contractors. **Publications:** *Drilling Contractor*, bimonthly. Magazine. Provides political and technological information of interest to oil-related businesses. **Price:** included in membership dues. **Advertising:** accepted ● Membership Directory, annual. Alternate Formats: online ● Newsletters, monthly. Alternate Formats: online ● Also publishes personnel training study courses. **Conventions/Meetings:** annual conference - always September ● Drilling Conference.

2931 ■ International Association of Geophysical Contractors (IAGC)

2550 N Loop W, Ste.104
Houston, TX 77092
Ph: (713)957-8080
Fax: (713)957-0008
E-mail: iagc@iagc.org
URL: http://www.iagc.org
Contact: Chip Gill, Pres.
Founded: 1971. **Members:** 189. **Membership Dues:** self employed, $275 (annual) ● supporting (based on annual revenue), $775-$27,500 (annual). **Budget:** $286,000. **Regional Groups:** 8. **Multinational. Description:** Independent service companies performing geophysical petroleum exploration in 60 countries; geophysical equipment manufacturers and suppliers; data processing, brokerage, and exchange companies; geophysical consultants and geophysical departments of major oil companies. Fosters the continued development of geophysics as a profession; cooperates with other segments of the petroleum exploration industry. Works to establish guidelines for operating efficiency, growth, safety standards, and procedures, and promotes safe practices and environmental sensitivity in the geophysical industry. Conducts research programs. Serves as a clearinghouse on geophysical field operations. **Libraries: Type:** reference. **Holdings:** articles, reports. **Subjects:** environmental effects of geophysical operations. **Committees:** Data Licensing; HSE Steering; Human Resources; Marine Mammals; Public and Governmental Affairs; Safety; Step Change Steering; Tax. **Publications:** *Environmental Impacts from Geophysical Operation.* Manual. Contains research studies, special technical reports, articles, and other literature on the possible environmental effects of geophysical operations. Alternate Formats: CD-ROM ● *Land Geophysical Safety*, periodic. Manual. Contains the highlight areas of concern in seismic operations. Alternate Formats: online ● *Marine Geophysical Safety*, periodic. Manual. Contains the highlight areas of concern in geophysical operations. Alternate Formats: online. **Conventions/Meetings:** annual meeting - always May in Houston, TX.

2932 ■ International Oil Scouts Association (IOSA)

PO Box 940310
Houston, TX 77094-7310
Ph: (512)472-7173
E-mail: kamora@statoilhydro.com
URL: http://www.oilscouts.com
Contact: Karen Morales, Pres.
Founded: 1924. **Members:** 200. **Membership Dues:** general, $100 (annual). **Staff:** 8. **Budget:** $20,000. **Description:** Federation of 13 United States district associations of oil scouts. Compiles statistics on exploratory and development wells in the U.S. (since 1930) and in the "Free World" (since 1959) and on production in oil and gas fields. Offers continuing professional development and scholarship programs. Maintains collection of yearbooks. **Formerly:** (1960) National Oil Scouts and Landmen's Association. **Publications:** *International Oil and Gas Development*, annual. Yearbook ● Membership Directory, annual ● Newsletter, weekly. **Conventions/Meetings:** annual meeting.

2933 ■ Liaison Committee of Cooperating Oil and Gas Associations (LCCOGA)

c/o Texas Independent Producers and Royalty Owners Association
919 Cong. Ave., Ste.1000
Austin, TX 78701
Ph: (512)477-4452
Fax: (512)476-8070
E-mail: info@tipro.org
URL: http://www.tipro.org
Contact: Adam P. Haynes, Exec. VP
Founded: 1957. **Members:** 34. **Description:** Comprises of oil and gas producers and royalty owners. Provides for informal exchange among members. **Telecommunication Services:** electronic mail, ahaynes@tipro.org. **Publications:** Newsletter, periodic. **Conventions/Meetings:** annual meeting (exhibits) - always August or September.

2934 ■ National Association of Division Order Analysts (NADOA)

2805 Oak Trail Ct., No. 6312
Arlington, TX 76016
Ph: (405)749-6601
E-mail: nadoa_org@hotmail.com
URL: http://www.nadoa.org
Contact: Pamela Parrish, Pres.
Founded: 1971. **Members:** 910. **Membership Dues:** associate, active, $50 (annual). **Local Groups:** 9. **Description:** Individuals employed by companies in oil, gas, or energy-related fields who deal with oil and gas revenue payments from the sale of energy-related products. Division Order Analysts are generally responsible for the payment of such royalties related to division orders, the instrument on which shares of oil and gas production are set out. Analyzes all types of land title documents, energy leases, unitization agreements, applying state and federal laws concerning energy accounting, and real property, heirship, and escheat. **Awards:** Corporate Award. **Frequency:** annual. **Type:** recognition ● Education Award. **Frequency:** annual. **Type:** recognition ● Lifetime Achievement. **Frequency:** annual. **Type:** recognition. **Computer Services:** Mailing lists, of members. **Committees:** Annual Institute; Certification of Division Order Analysts; Education; Ethics; Interaction. **Publications:** *Institute Journal*, annual ● *Pictorial Directory of Members*, annual ● Newsletter, bimonthly. **Conventions/Meetings:** annual meeting and seminar, for educational institute.

2935 ■ National Association of Royalty Owners (NARO)

15 W 6th St., Ste.2626
Tulsa, OK 74119
Ph: (918)794-1660
Free: (800)558-0557
Fax: (918)794-1662
E-mail: naro@naro-us.org
URL: http://www.naro-us.org
Contact: Mr. Jeff Miller, Dir.
Founded: 1980. **Members:** 5,000. **Membership Dues:** basic, $105 (annual) ● family/trust, $200 (annual) ● business/corporate/institutional, $300 (annual). **Staff:** 3. **Budget:** $200,000. **Regional Groups:** 3. **State Groups:** 3. **Description:** Owners of mineral properties and oil and gas royalties, industry professionals, bank trust officers, attorneys, and oil tax

advisers. Assists mineral and royalty owners in the effective management of their mineral properties and provides information on tax, regulatory, and legislative matters that affect their mineral interests. Provides information to Congress and the states on legislation. Conducts mineral management seminars; maintains hall of fame. Compiles statistics. **Awards: Type:** recognition. **Computer Services:** database. **Councils:** Inter-Industry Council National Legislative. **Publications:** *A Royalty Owners Guide to the Oklahoma Corporation Commission.* Book. Contains helpful tips on getting information, appearing at hearings; knowing what questions to ask. **Price:** $10.00 ● *Am I Being Shorted?: Analyzing Your Run Check Stub.* Booklet. Outlines some typical payment problems and how to deal with them. **Price:** $5.00 ● *How to Survive Force Pooling in Oklahoma.* Book. Includes simplified explanation of current force pooling procedures at the Oil and Gas Conservation Division. **Price:** $15.00 ● *Look Before You Lease.* Book. Includes basics of leasing from the small mineral owner's perspective. **Price:** $18.00 for nonmembers; $6.50 for members ● *Mineral Management Library.* Pamphlet. Lists all of the NARO publications and audiocassette tape recordings. **Price:** free ● *NARO's Great Texas Lease Mark-Up Handbook.* A mineral owner's guide to amending standard printed Texas Oil and Gas Lease forms like the pros. **Price:** $20.00 ● *Royalty Owners Action Report*, monthly. Newsletter. Provides legislative, legal, oil and gas explorations. **Price:** $105.00 for nonmembers; included in membership dues. **Conventions/Meetings:** annual convention (exhibits).

2936 ■ National Association of Shell Marketers (NASM)
6551 Loisdale Ct., Ste.100
Springfield, VA 22150
Ph: (703)922-9784 (703)922-9785
Fax: (703)971-9526
E-mail: dks@nasmonline.com
URL: http://www.nasmonline.com
Contact: Darrell Smith, Pres.
Founded: 1974. **Members:** 650. **Staff:** 3. **Budget:** $500,000. **Description:** Provides a forum for members to network and solve Shell-specific issues and mutual problems pertaining to the petroleum industry. Aims to improve communications between marketers and Shell/Motiva, federal agencies, the US Congress, and other petroleum industry associations for the purpose of attaining mutually satisfactory solutions to the problems facing petroleum marketers; to enhance the marketing capabilities of individual marketers; to assist marketers in understanding and complying with legislative and regulatory requirements of the federal government and policies of Shell/Motiva; to assure marketers are provided a fair, equitable, and competitive market in which to distribute petroleum products; to assist Shell/Motiva and their marketers to grow the Shell brand; and to facilitate Shell/Motiva being the supplier of choice for among members. **Formerly:** (1976) National Association of Texaco Consignees; (1999) National Association of Texaco Wholesalers; (2003) National Association of Texaco and Shell Marketers. **Publications:** Newsletter, monthly. Alternate Formats: online. **Conventions/Meetings:** biennial convention and seminar (exhibits).

2937 ■ National Lubricating Grease Institute (NLGI)
4635 Wyandotte St.
Kansas City, MO 64112-1509
Ph: (816)931-9480
Fax: (816)753-5026
E-mail: nlgi@nlgi.com
URL: http://www.nlgi.com
Contact: Kimberly Bott, Exec. Dir.
Founded: 1933. **Members:** 300. **Staff:** 2. **Multinational. Description:** Companies manufacturing or selling all types of lubricating greases; suppliers to such companies; technical and educational organizations. Promotes research and testing for the development of better lubricating greases and improved grease lubrication engineering service to industry. Collects and disseminates technical data; conducts forums and educational program. Operates the National Lubricating Grease Institute Research Fund. **Awards: Type:** recognition. **Additional Websites:** http://www.nlgi.org. **Committees:** Technical. **Affiliated With:** American Petroleum Institute; Independent Lubricant Manufacturers Association; National Petrochemical and Refiners Association. **Publications:** *Lubricating Grease Guide.* Handbook. Contains basic information on lubricating grease. **Price:** $25.00 for members; $35.00 for nonmembers ● *NLGI Spokesman*, monthly. Magazine. Provides readers with information and test results on lubricants. Also includes information on the industry and new plants. **Price:** $18.00/year. **Circulation:** 2,500. **Advertising:** accepted. Alternate Formats: microform. **Conventions/Meetings:** annual meeting - usually last week of October.

2938 ■ National Oil Recyclers Association (NORA)
c/o Scott D. Parker, Exec. Dir.
5965 Amber Ridge Rd.
Haymarket, VA 20169
Ph: (703)753-4277
Fax: (703)753-2445
E-mail: sparker@noranews.org
URL: http://www.noranews.org
Contact: Scott D. Parker, Exec. Dir.
Founded: 1984. **Members:** 220. **Membership Dues:** associate, $1,000 (annual) ● affiliate, $500-$1,000 (annual) ● collector, multiple service provider, processor, marketer, chemical recycler, $750-$6,000 (annual) ● transporter, $500-$1,500 (annual) ● parts cleaner, $750-$4,000 (annual) ● filter recycler, $750-$2,500 (annual). **Staff:** 5. **Budget:** $600,000. **Description:** Recycling companies, plant managers, environmental engineers, laboratory managers, environmental consultants, and other individuals and firms with an interest in the recycling of oil. Promotes reduction of emissions and pollution associated with the production and use of oil. Conducts research and analysis of separation technologies, ash and metals reduction procedures, oil filter recovery systems, and other topics relevant to the recycling of oil, antifreeze, wastewater, filters, re-refiners, and parts cleaners. Sponsors educational programs. **Publications:** *Liquid Recycling*, quarterly. Newsletter. **Price:** free for members; $20.00/issue for nonmembers. **Advertising:** accepted. Alternate Formats: online ● *Membership Directory of Products.* **Conventions/Meetings:** annual conference and meeting (exhibits) - late October or early November.

2939 ■ National Petrochemical and Refiners Association (NPRA)
1899 L St. NW, Ste.1000
Washington, DC 20036-3810
Ph: (202)457-0480
Fax: (202)457-0486
E-mail: info@npra.org
URL: http://www.npra.org
Contact: James Mahoney, Chm.
Founded: 1902. **Members:** 450. **Staff:** 31. **Budget:** $3,000,000. **Description:** Petroleum, refining and petrochemical manufacturers. Seeks to inform policymakers and the public on how the industries help improve their lives, strengthen the economy, protect the environment and promote national security. **Committees:** Computer; Environmental; Fire and Accident Prevention; Fuels and Lubricants; Industrial Relations; Issues; Maintenance; Manufacturing; Petrochemical; Security. **Formed by Merger of:** National Petroleum Association; Western Petroleum Refiners Association. **Formerly:** (1998) National Petroleum Refiners Association. **Publications:** Papers, annual. Includes formal written papers of presentations made at NPRA conferences. **Price:** $25.00/copy, for nonmembers. **Conventions/Meetings:** biennial Cat Cracker Seminar - conference ● biennial Clean Fuels Conference ● annual Environmental Conference ● annual International Lubricants and Waxes Meeting - conference ● annual International Petrochemical Conference, with sessions covering political, economic and environmental issues affecting the petroleum industry ● annual Labor Relations/Human Resources Conference, with speakers, panel discussions, and breakout sessions ● annual meeting, with speakers ● annual National Safety Conference, with overview of safety challenges and issues affecting refineries and petrochemical plants ● annual Reliability and Maintenance Conference and Exhibition, with presentation and discussion (exhibits) ● annual Technology Q&A Session - conference.

2940 ■ National Stripper Well Association (NSWA)
Address Unknown since 2007
Founded: 1934. **Staff:** 2. **Description:** Federation of regional and state associations of producers of crude petroleum from small wells. **Publications:** *National Stripper Well Association—Annual Report* ● *National Stripper Well Survey*, annual ● Also publishes statistical material and distributes petroleum material relating to the stripper well segment of the petroleum industry. **Conventions/Meetings:** semiannual meeting, held in conjunction with Independent Petroleum Association of America.

2941 ■ Petroleum Equipment Institute (PEI)
PO Box 2380
Tulsa, OK 74101-2380
Ph: (918)494-9696
Fax: (918)491-9895
E-mail: info@pei.org
URL: http://www.pei.org
Contact: Robert N. Renkes, Exec. VP
Founded: 1951. **Members:** 1,659. **Membership Dues:** company (based on annual gross sales), $350-$1,000 (annual) ● operations/engineering division, $150 (annual). **Staff:** 11. **Budget:** $2,100,000. **Multinational. Description:** Distributors and manufacturers of equipment used in service stations, bulk plants, and other petroleum marketing operations. **Libraries: Type:** lending. **Holdings:** audiovisuals. **Committees:** Aboveground Tank Installation; Education; Election; Electrical Continuity Testing; Exhibitor/Convention Advisory; Fuel Dispensing Equipment; Insurance; Safety. **Formerly:** (1966) National Association of Oil Equipment Jobbers. **Publications:** *Petroleum Equipment Directory*, annual. Contains information in geographic arrangement on distributors and manufacturers, including officers, lines handled, and products manufactured. **Price:** $40.00 for members; $120.00 retail. **Circulation:** 3,000. **Advertising:** accepted. Alternate Formats: CD-ROM ● *TulsaLetter*, 2-3/month. Covers regulations and technology related to petroleum marketing equipment. Includes annual index, calendar of events, and obituaries. **Price:** $72.00/year. ISSN: 0193-9467 ● Newsletters. Alternate Formats: online. **Conventions/Meetings:** annual convention (exhibits) - always September/October.

2942 ■ Petroleum Equipment Suppliers Association (PESA)
9225 Katy Fwy., Ste.310
Houston, TX 77024-1510
Ph: (713)932-0168
Fax: (713)932-0497
E-mail: webmaster@pesa.org
URL: http://www.pesa.org
Contact: Galen Cobb, Chm.
Founded: 1933. **Members:** 200. **Staff:** 6. **Description:** Promotes improvement of the petroleum equipment, service, and supply industries. Represents members' interests; cooperates with the federal government in matters of national concern; gathers and disseminates information. Conducts educational programs. **Committees:** Corporate Counsel Advisory; E-Business; Explorers of Houston; Health, Safety and Environment; Human Resources; International Operations; Lien Law; Manufacturers; Public Affairs; Quality; Service; Supply Company; Tax. **Divisions:** Credit Interchange. **Formerly:** American Petroleum Equipment Suppliers. **Publications:** *PESA News*, monthly. Newsletter. **Price:** free ● *Service Point Directory*, biennial ● Report. **Conventions/Meetings:** annual meeting - usually April.

2943 ■ Petroleum Marketers Association of America (PMAA)
1901 N Ft. Myer Dr., Ste.500
Arlington, VA 22209-1604
Ph: (703)351-8000

Fax: (703)351-9160
E-mail: info@pmaa.org
URL: http://www.pmaa.org
Contact: Daniel F. Gilligan, Pres.
Founded: 1941. **Members:** 45. **Staff:** 18. **Description:** Federation of state and regional petroleum marketing associations with approximately 11,000 independent wholesale petroleum marketers (jobbers) and retail fuel oil dealers as members. Preserves the private enterprise risk-reward system. Prevents undue economic concentration. Ensures a favorable competitive climate in petroleum distribution. Encourages an adequate supply of petroleum products in order to best serve the customer. Sponsors management institutes for jobbers. **Awards:** Distinguished Service Award. **Frequency:** annual. **Type:** recognition. **Recipient:** for a jobber. **Committees:** Heating Fuels; Motor Fuels; Operations and Engineering; Small Businessmen's Political Action. **Absorbed:** National Oil Fuel Institute; Oil Heat Institute of America. **Formerly:** (1942) Council of Independent Petroleum Marketers; (1948) National Council of Independent Petroleum Association; (1984) National Jobbers Council. **Publications:** *Journal of Petroleum Marketing*, monthly ● *Petroleum Marketing Databook*, semiannual ● *PMAA Directory*, annual ● *PMAA Journal*, quarterly. **Circulation:** 60,000. **Advertising:** accepted. Alternate Formats: online ● *PMAA Weekly Review* ● Also publishes independent petroleum marketer and industry operating results surveys. **Conventions/Meetings:** annual convention and trade show - always fall.

2944 ■ Petroleum Technology Transfer Council (PTTC)
c/o E. Lance Cole, Exec. Dir.
PO Box 246
Sand Springs, OK 74063
Ph: (918)241-5801 (703)620-4797
Fax: (918)241-5728
E-mail: hq@pttc.org
URL: http://www.pttc.org
Contact: E. Lance Cole, Exec. Dir.
Founded: 1993. **Staff:** 3. **Budget:** $800,000. **Regional Groups:** 10. **Description:** Promotes transfer of petroleum and natural gas exploration and production technologies from the research community to independent companies. Maintains resource centers; conducts educational programs. **Computer Services:** database. **Publications:** *Case Study*, periodic. Report. **Advertising:** accepted. Alternate Formats: CD-ROM ● *Network News*, quarterly. Newsletter. **Price:** free. Alternate Formats: online ● *Technical Report*, periodic. **Conventions/Meetings:** annual Emerging Technologies Energy Conference.

2945 ■ Pipe Line Contractors Association (PLCA)
1700 Pacific Ave., Ste.4100
Dallas, TX 75201-4675
Ph: (214)969-2700 (817)337-7115
Fax: (214)969-2705
E-mail: plca@plca.org
URL: http://www.plca.org
Contact: J. Patrick Tielborg, Managing Dir.
Founded: 1948. **Members:** 120. **Membership Dues:** regular (gross volume of work performed), $2,500-$15,000 (annual) ● associate, $1,500 (annual). **Staff:** 5. **Description:** Contractors of mainline cross-country pipeline. Associate members are equipment manufacturers, suppliers, and dealers. Represents the industry in labor negotiations. **Telecommunication Services:** electronic mail, jptielborg@plca.org. **Funds:** International Union of Operating Engineers and Pipe Line Contractors Association Training. **Programs:** Operator Qualification. **Publications:** *Labor Agreements Manual* ● *Primer of Pipe Line Construction* ● *Safety Manual for Pipe Line Construction* ● *Safety Newsletter*, monthly ● Newsletter, weekly. **Conventions/Meetings:** annual meeting.

2946 ■ Service Station Dealers of America/National Coalition of Petroleum Retailers and Allied Trades (SSDA/NCPR-AT)
1532 Pointer Ridge Pl., Ste.E
Bowie, MD 20716-1883
Ph: (301)390-4405
Fax: (301)390-3161
E-mail: pfiore@wmda.net
URL: http://www.ssda-at.org
Contact: Mr. Paul Fiore, Exec. VP
Founded: 1947. **Members:** 27. **Membership Dues:** regular, $99 (annual) ● associate, $300 (annual). **Staff:** 8. **Budget:** $1,000,000. **State Groups:** 22. **Description:** Service station operators and affiliated state and local associations. Works for the betterment of its members as a voice on Capitol Hill, with federal regulators, with the media, in the courts, and with suppliers. **Awards:** Friend of the Industry. **Frequency:** annual. **Type:** recognition. **Recipient:** for anyone outside of the industry who promotes the welfare of the dealer/shop-owner community ● Golden Nozzle. **Frequency:** annual. **Type:** recognition. **Recipient:** for committee selection ● Hall of Fame. **Frequency:** annual. **Type:** recognition. **Recipient:** for committee selection. **Committees:** Government Affairs; Political Action. **Formerly:** (1980) National Congress of Petroleum Retailers; (2003) Service Station Dealers of America; (2006) Service Station Dealers of America and Allied Trades. **Publications:** *SSDA/NCPR-AT News*, monthly. Newsletter. **Conventions/Meetings:** annual convention (exhibits).

2947 ■ Society of Independent Gasoline Marketers of America (SIGMA)
11495 Sunset Hills Rd., Ste.215
Reston, VA 20190-5213
Ph: (703)709-7000
Fax: (703)709-7007
E-mail: sigma@sigma.org
URL: http://www.sigma.org
Contact: Kenneth A. Doyle CAE, Exec. VP
Founded: 1958. **Members:** 350. **Membership Dues:** regular (minimum), $60 (monthly) ● associate (fleet card and financial services), $5,000 (annual) ● fuel supplier associate, $250-$1,333 (monthly) ● fuel transport associate, $3,000-$5,000 (annual). **Staff:** 9. **Budget:** $2,000,000. **Description:** Represents chain gasoline marketers, wholesale and retail. Works to inform members of current governmental and legislative activities; represents the marketers' interests before government and legislative and regulatory agencies; and provides statistical data on industry. **Telecommunication Services:** electronic mail, kdoyle@sigma.org. **Committees:** Communications; Education; Financial Services; Fleet Fueling; Fuel Suppliers Relations; Legislative; Long Range Planning; Marketer Operations. **Publications:** *Independent Gasoline Marketing*, bimonthly. Magazine. Contains member profiles, legislative issues, and topical issues. **Price:** included in membership dues; $35.00 /year for nonmembers in U.S.; $50.00 /year for nonmembers outside U.S. **Circulation:** 3,200. **Advertising:** accepted. Alternate Formats: online. Also Cited As: *IGM* ● *Society of Independent Gasoline Marketers Membership Directory*, annual. **Price:** available to members only ● *Society of Independent Gasoline Marketers of America—Weekly Report*. Newsletter ● *Statistical Report*, annual. Alternate Formats: online ● Also publishes news releases and information on industry issues. **Conventions/Meetings:** annual convention - always spring ● annual meeting ● annual Winter Management Conference (exhibits).

2948 ■ Society of Professional Women in Petroleum (SPWP)
PO Box 550788
Houston, TX 77255-0788
Ph: (713)939-2263
E-mail: mcampana@spwp.org
URL: http://www.spwp.org
Contact: Mary Campana, Pres.
Founded: 1981. **Members:** 60. **Membership Dues:** active, $75 (annual). **Local Groups:** 1. **Description:** Women employed by the petroleum industry. Promotes professional development of members. Facilitates exchange of information among members; represents members' interests; conducts educational programs; participates in charitable activities. **Awards:** Woman of Excellence. **Frequency:** annual. **Type:** scholarship. **Recipient:** for female high school graduates planning to attend universities in Texas. **Programs:** Scholarship. **Publications:** *SPWP News*, monthly. Newsletter. Alternate Formats: online.

2949 ■ Texas Independent Producers and Royalty Owners Association (TIPRO)
919 Cong. Ave., Ste.1000
Austin, TX 78701
Ph: (512)477-4452
Fax: (512)476-8070
E-mail: info@tipro.org
URL: http://www.tipro.org
Contact: Adam P. Haynes, Exec. VP
Founded: 1946. **Members:** 2,400. **Membership Dues:** regular, $275-$824 (annual) ● executive, $825-$2,499 (annual) ● explorer (base), $2,500 (annual). **Staff:** 4. **Description:** Independent oil and gas producers, royalty owners, and others concerned with this segment of the petroleum industry. Promotes economic and government principles that increase political accountability and free-market transparency. **Awards:** Hat's Off Award. **Frequency:** annual. **Type:** recognition. **Recipient:** for special service to the oil and gas industry. **Committees:** Audit; Environmental; National Issues; Nominating; Programs; State Issues; Technical Information Services. **Publications:** *Register Membership Directory*, annual. **Advertising:** accepted ● *TIPRO's Legislative Report*. Alternate Formats: online ● *Tuesday Target*, weekly. Newsletter. **Advertising:** accepted. Alternate Formats: online. **Conventions/Meetings:** annual convention, with products and software for energy industry (exhibits) - always in February; also summer policy meeting in August.

2950 ■ U.S. Oil and Gas Association (USOGA)
217 W Capitol St., Ste.201
Jackson, MS 39201
Ph: (601)948-8903
Fax: (601)948-8919
E-mail: usoil@usoga.com
URL: http://www.usoga.com
Contact: Wayne Gibbens, Pres.
Founded: 1944. **Members:** 7,500. **Staff:** 5. **State Groups:** 4. **Description:** Oil and gas producers, royalty owners, refiners, gasoline manufacturers, transporters, drilling contractors, supply and equipment dealers and wholesalers, bankers, and other individuals interested in oil business. Companies do not hold membership. Works to establish and maintain reasonable statewide public policy that have a significant impact on the industry. **Formerly:** (1998) Mid-Continent Oil and Gas Association. **Conventions/Meetings:** annual board meeting and executive committee meeting (exhibits).

2951 ■ Western States Petroleum Association (WSPA)
1415 L St., Ste.600
Sacramento, CA 95814-3964
Ph: (916)498-7750
Fax: (916)444-5745
E-mail: elaine@wspa.org
URL: http://www.wspa.org
Contact: Joe Sparano, Pres.
Founded: 1907. **Members:** 35. **Membership Dues:** associate, $100 (annual) ● chapter, $50 (annual). **Staff:** 32. **Regional Groups:** 4. **Description:** Represents petroleum exploration, production, refining, transportation, and wholesale marketing companies in Arizona, California, Hawaii, Nevada, Oregon, and Washington. Offers advisory services for industry members. **Libraries: Type:** reference. **Holdings:** books, clippings, periodicals. **Subjects:** research projects, energy, oil and gas, environmental. **Computer Services:** database, news clippings. **Committees:** Downstream; Environmental Health and Safety; Environmental Marketing; Excise Tax; External Affairs; Fire and Safety; Fuels Policy; Income Tax; Land and Exploration; Legal; Marine; Pipeline; Property Tax; Road; State Government Affairs; Tax; Toxic Policy; Transportation; Upstream; Waste Management. **Formerly:** (1988) Western Oil and Gas Association. **Publications:** *Directory of Officers, Directors, Committees and Staff of WSPA*, annual ● *WSPA*

Annual Report, annual ● *WSPA News*, monthly. Newsletter. **Circulation:** 5,000 ● Also issues fact sheets and news releases. **Conventions/Meetings:** annual meeting.

2952 ■ World Federation of Pipe Line Contractors Associations (WFPLCA)
c/o Pipe Line Contractors Association
1700 Pacific Ave., Ste.4100
Dallas, TX 75201-4675
Ph: (214)969-2700
Fax: (214)969-2705
E-mail: plca@plca.org
URL: http://www.plca.org
Contact: J. Patrick Tielborg, Managing Dir./Gen. Counsel
Founded: 1977. **Members:** 5. **Description:** Represents worldwide pipeline contractors. Supports the update and exchange of information of mutual interest including equipment depreciation, tax structure, and union issues. **Telecommunication Services:** electronic mail, jptielborg@plca.org. **Conventions/Meetings:** quarterly meeting.

Pets

2953 ■ Accredited Pet Cemetery Society (APCS)
c/o Angie Pavone, Pres.
Paws Awhile Pet Memorial Park
3426 Brush Rd.
Richfield, OH 44286
Ph: (330)659-4270
Fax: (330)659-4254
E-mail: apcsangiepavone@aol.com
URL: http://www.olatheplaces.com/apcs
Contact: Angie Pavone, Pres.
Founded: 1993. **Members:** 15. **Membership Dues:** pet cemetery owner, $150 (annual). **Budget:** $10,000. **Description:** Pet cemeterians. Promotes highest standards of professionalism. Endorses deed restriction of pet cemetery property and meaningful pet cemetery legislation. Offers educational programs on pet bereavement, support groups, and professional business management. **Awards: Frequency:** annual. **Type:** recognition. **Committees:** Care Fund Guidelines; Code of Ethics; Education and Program; Standards and Methods to Implement. **Publications:** *APCS Bulletin*, quarterly. **Price:** included in membership dues. **Circulation:** 70. **Conventions/Meetings:** annual conference (exhibits).

2954 ■ American Boarding Kennels Association (ABKA)
1702 E Pikes Peak Ave.
Colorado Springs, CO 80909-5717
Ph: (719)667-1600
Free: (877)570-7788
Fax: (719)667-0116
E-mail: info@abka.com
URL: http://www.abka.com
Contact: James Krack CAE, CEO/Exec. Dir.
Founded: 1977. **Members:** 3,000. **Membership Dues:** active/auxiliary, $225 (annual) ● associate/industry supplier, $265 (annual). **Staff:** 13. **Budget:** $1,000,000. **Regional Groups:** 11. **Description:** Persons or firms that board pets; kennel suppliers; others interested in the facility boarding kennel industry. Seeks to upgrade the industry through accreditation educational programs, seminars and conventions. Provides insurance resources for members and supplies pet care information to the public. Promotes code of ethics and accreditation program for recognition and training of superior kennel operators. Compiles boarding facility statistics. **Libraries: Type:** reference. **Holdings:** periodicals. **Subjects:** how to select a boarding kennel, pet services. **Awards: Frequency:** annual. **Type:** recognition. **Committees:** Education; Ethics; Facilities Accreditation. **Affiliated With:** Delta Society; Morris Animal Foundation. **Publications:** *Boarderline Newsletter*, monthly. **Price:** included in membership dues. **Circulation:** 3,000. **Advertising:** accepted. Alternate Formats: online ● *Pet Services Journal*, bimonthly. Magazine. Covers animal care and business management, with statistics and association news. Includes kennel profiles. **Price:** included in membership dues. **Circulation:** 3,000. **Advertising:** accepted ● Booklets ● Books ● Brochures. **Conventions/Meetings:** annual convention and trade show, for the pet care industry (exhibits) - during fall.

2955 ■ American Mobile Groomers Association (AMGA)
c/o Barkleigh Management Group, Inc.
970 W Trindle Rd.
Mechanicsburg, PA 17055
Ph: (717)691-3388
Fax: (717)691-3381
E-mail: info@amgroomers.com
URL: http://www.amgroomers.com
Contact: Frank Weag III, Dir.
Membership Dues: regular - new, $125 ● regular, $100 (annual). **Description:** Supports and promotes the professional mobile groomer. Promotes the welfare of animals. Seeks to improve and expand the industry of professional grooming as a whole. Serves as a network for the exchange of ideas and information on all aspects of mobile grooming, including current industry practices. Educates the pet-owning public to the advantages of mobile grooming. **Publications:** *Groomer to Groomer*, 9/year. Magazine. **Price:** included in membership dues ● *Mobile Groomer*, annual. Magazine. **Price:** included in membership dues ● Newsletter, quarterly. Contains helpful tips and useful information. **Price:** included in membership dues.

2956 ■ American Pet Products Manufacturers Association (APPMA)
255 Glenville Rd.
Greenwich, CT 06831
Ph: (203)532-0000
Free: (800)452-1225
Fax: (203)532-0551
E-mail: info@appma.org
URL: http://www.appma.org
Contact: Robert L. Vetere, Pres.
Founded: 1958. **Members:** 900. **Membership Dues:** active/domestic livestock, $500-$10,000 (annual) ● associate/international livestock, $700-$11,000 (annual) ● manufacturers' representative, $350 (annual). **Staff:** 14. **Budget:** $3,000,000. **Multinational. Description:** U.S. Manufacturers and importers of pet products. Provides public relations program to promote pet ownership and pet care. Sponsors the annual APPMA National Pet Products Trade Show, publishes APPMA's National Pet Owner's Survey, the most comprehensive market research study in the pet industry. **Awards:** APPMA Jules Schwimmer Scholarship Program. **Frequency:** annual. **Type:** scholarship. **Recipient:** for a full-time student, or child of an employee of an APPMA member ● New Product and Point-of-Purchase Award. **Frequency:** annual. **Type:** recognition. **Recipient:** for best new products exhibited at trade show. **Committees:** Industry Liaison; Long Range Planning; Member Services; National Trade Show; Product Issues; Public Relations; Trade Show. **Publications:** *APPMA Advisor*, quarterly. Newsletter. Deals with pet-related issues. **Circulation:** 830. **Advertising:** accepted ● *National Pet Owners Survey*, biennial. Book. Survey of pet owners in all pet categories. **Price:** $595.00 for members and students; $895.00 for nonmembers ● Membership Directory. Alternate Formats: online. **Conventions/Meetings:** annual trade show (exhibits).

2957 ■ American Veterinary Distributors Association (AVDA)
2105 Laurel Bush Rd., Ste.200
Bel Air, MD 21015
Ph: (443)640-1040
Fax: (443)640-1086
E-mail: kaymie@ksgroup.org
URL: http://www.avda.net
Contact: Jackwelyn King, Exec. Dir.
Founded: 1976. **Members:** 72. **Membership Dues:** associate, $1,500 (annual) ● active (based on annual sales volume), $1,500-$5,000 (annual) ● affiliate, $1,500 (annual). **Staff:** 4. **Description:** Companies that distribute animal health products; manufacturers of animal health products. Promotes mutually beneficial relationship between the distributing and manufacturing sectors of the animal health industry; facilitates exchange of information among members; promotes use of wholesale distributors; fosters application of sound business principles in the distribution of animal health products. Encourages research; operates continuing education program for sales representatives. **Libraries: Type:** reference. **Committees:** Government Relations. **Publications:** *Animal Health Distributor*, quarterly. Newsletter. Contains news on industry and association activities. Alternate Formats: online ● *Veterinary Compounding Brochure*. Contains veterinary supply channel with regulations that apply to compounding. **Price:** free for members. **Conventions/Meetings:** annual conference.

2958 ■ Independent Pet and Animal Transportation Association International (IPATA)
745 Winding Trail
Holly Lake Ranch, TX 75765-7148
Ph: (903)769-2267
Fax: (903)769-2867
E-mail: inquiries@ipata.com
URL: http://www.ipata.com
Contact: Gay O'Brien, Pres.
Founded: 1979. **Members:** 110. **Membership Dues:** active/associate, $225 (annual). **Staff:** 1. **Budget:** $100,000. **Multinational. Description:** Companies providing complete domestic and international animal relocation services to corporate relocation personnel, commercial movers, individual shippers, boarding kennel operators, veterinarians, and pet owners. Studies, evaluates, and disseminates information on the practices and procedures involved in animal relocation in order to arrange transfers that are efficient and that pose minimal disruption to the animal owner and provide maximum comfort to the animal. Typical services include provisions for boarding, grooming, flight reservations, health certification, and domestic and international documentation. Allows for reciprocal services among companies; provides liaison with federal and local government officials concerned with animal transportation. **Publications:** *Locator Brochure*, annual. Brochures ● *Paw Prints*, bimonthly. Newsletter ● Membership Directory, annual. **Price:** free, for members only. **Conventions/Meetings:** annual conference (exhibits) ● annual international conference (exhibits).

2959 ■ International Association of Pet Cemeteries and Crematories (IAOPCC)
PO Box 163
5055 Rte. 11
Ellenburg Depot, NY 12935-0163
Ph: (518)594-3000
Fax: (518)594-8801
E-mail: iaopc@aol.com
URL: http://www.iaopc.com
Contact: Stephen Drown, Exec. Dir.
Founded: 1971. **Members:** 180. **Membership Dues:** affiliate, regular, $200 (annual) ● supplier, $250 (annual). **Staff:** 1. **Budget:** $75,000. **Regional Groups:** 3. **State Groups:** 15. **Description:** Individuals who own or operate pet cemeteries and who sell products to pet cemeteries; interested others. Educates the public on pet burials and the disposal of sick and diseased animals to eliminate contamination and pollution of the ground and water. Facilitates exchange of information among members. Revitalizes inactive and unkept cemeteries. Conducts workshops and research and specialized education programs; sponsors the Pet Loss Foundation. Establishes minimum standards for member pet cemeteries. Promotes recognition of Pet Memorial Day, the second Sunday of September. **Awards:** President Award. **Type:** recognition. **Committees:** Care Fund; Education and Program; Evaluation and Certification; Human Companion/Animal Bond; Job Descriptions; Legislative; National Pet Memorial Day; Scholarship Fund; Standards; Veterinary Liaison. **Formerly:** (1979) National Association of Pet Cemeteries; (2006)

International Association of Pet Cemeteries. **Publications:** *News and Views*, bimonthly. Features articles about pet cemeteries and crematories and their problems and triumphs and events of the association. **Price:** included in membership dues. **Advertising:** accepted ● Membership Directory, annual ● Videos. **Conventions/Meetings:** annual conference (exhibits) ● semiannual Prospective Pet Cemeterian Seminars - symposium ● periodic symposium.

2960 ■ International Professional Groomers (IPG)
120 Turner Ave.
Elk Grove Village, IL 60007
Ph: (847)758-1938
Fax: (847)758-8031
E-mail: ipgroom@aol.com
URL: http://ipgcmg.org
Contact: Judy Kurpiel, Pres.
Founded: 1988. **Members:** 400. **Membership Dues:** associate, $25 (annual) ● groomer, $50 (annual). **Staff:** 5. **Budget:** $40,000. **Description:** Professional pet groomers. Promotes adherence to high standards of ethics and practice among members. Conducts certification examinations and continuing professional development courses for pet groomers; sponsors consumer awareness programs; maintains speakers' bureau. **Publications:** Newsletter, quarterly.

2961 ■ National Association of Professional Pet Sitters (NAPPS)
15000 Commerce Pkwy., Ste.C
Mount Laurel, NJ 08054
Ph: (856)439-0324
Fax: (856)439-0525
E-mail: napps@ahint.com
URL: http://www.petsitters.org
Contact: Felicia Lembesis, Exec. Dir.
Founded: 1989. **Members:** 1,600. **Membership Dues:** company, $140 (annual) ● individual, $95 (annual) ● individual (associate), $100 (annual) ● nonprofit (associate), $100 (annual) ● professional (associate), $500 (annual) ● corporate (associate), $2,000 (annual). **Staff:** 5. **Budget:** $300,000. **Description:** Owners or employees of pet-sitting services; professionals or businesses in related fields. Promotes professional and ethical standards in pet sitting and fosters cooperation among members of the pet-care industry. Serves as a network for the exchange of ideas and information on pet sitting and current industry practices. Disseminates information educating the pet-owning public on the advantages of leaving pets in a home environment and how to choose a reliable sitter. **Libraries: Type:** reference. **Subjects:** pet-sitting. **Awards:** Pet Sitters Hall of Fame. **Frequency:** annual. **Type:** recognition. **Committees:** Benefits; Marketing; Membership. **Subcommittees:** Annual Conference; Newsletter. **Formerly:** National Association of Pet Sitters. **Publications:** *The NAPPS Network*, quarterly. Newsletter. Includes articles and tips useful to pet sitters, new product updates and reviews, industry statistics and business information. **Price:** included in membership dues. **Circulation:** 2,500. **Advertising:** accepted. **Conventions/Meetings:** annual meeting and conference (exhibits).

2962 ■ National Dog Groomers Association of America (NDGAA)
PO Box 101
Clark, PA 16113-0101
Ph: (724)962-2711
Fax: (724)962-1919
E-mail: ndga@nationaldoggroomers.com
URL: http://www.nationaldoggroomers.com
Contact: Jeffrey L. Reynolds, Exec. Dir.
Founded: 1969. **Members:** 2,500. **Membership Dues:** general, $85 (annual) ● outside U.S., $91 (annual). **Staff:** 2. **Budget:** $200,000. **For-Profit. Description:** Dog groomers and supply distributors organized to upgrade the profession. Conducts state and local workshops; sponsors competitions and certification testing. Makes groomer referrals. **Computer Services:** Mailing lists, of members. **Publications:** *Convention Manual*, annual ● *Groomers Voice*, quarterly. Newsletter. Includes information on shows, new grooming techniques, and new products. Contains workshop and certification test sites and dates. **Price:** included in membership dues. **Circulation:** 3,000. **Advertising:** accepted ● Membership Directory, semiannual. Contains names and addresses of Registered and Certified members. **Conventions/Meetings:** annual convention and trade show - always June or October ● annual meeting and seminar (exhibits).

2963 ■ Pet Food Institute (PFI)
2025 M St. NW, Ste.800
Washington, DC 20036-2422
Ph: (202)367-1120
Fax: (202)367-2120
E-mail: info@petfoodinstitute.org
URL: http://www.petfoodinstitute.org
Contact: Duane H. Ekedahl, Exec. Dir.
Founded: 1958. **Members:** 120. **Staff:** 5. **Description:** Represents the manufacturers of 97&percent; of the commercial pet food produced in the United States. Serves as the voice of the industry before legislative and regulatory bodies at both the federal and state levels. **Additional Websites:** http://www.petfoodreport.com. **Committees:** Export Development; Public Affairs; Regulatory Affairs. **Publications:** Membership Directory, annual. **Conventions/Meetings:** annual Suppliers Mart - meeting and trade show, includes tabletop exhibits of industry suppliers (exhibits).

2964 ■ Pet Industry Distributors Association (PIDA)
2105 Laurel Bush Rd., Ste.200
Bel Air, MD 21015-5200
Ph: (443)640-1060
Fax: (443)640-1031
E-mail: pida@ksgroup.org
URL: http://www.pida.org
Contact: Steven T. King, Pres.
Founded: 1969. **Members:** 250. **Staff:** 5. **Budget:** $800,000. **Description:** Strives to enhance the well-being of the pet product wholesaler-distributor. Promotes partnerships between suppliers and customers. Fosters the human-companion animal bond. **Awards:** Lifetime Achievement Award. **Type:** recognition. **Recipient:** for outstanding contribution to the pet industry ● Supplier of the Year. **Frequency:** annual. **Type:** recognition. **Computer Services:** Mailing lists. **Committees:** Awards; Education/Program; Finance; Livestock; Long Range Planning; Marketing; Membership; Nominating; Technology; Trade Show. **Affiliated With:** National Association of Wholesaler-Distributors; Pet Industry Joint Advisory Council. **Publications:** *PIDA Bulletin*, bimonthly. Includes calendar of events, new member information, and annual membership directory. **Price:** free for members only. **Circulation:** 650 ● *Roster*, annual. Directory. **Conventions/Meetings:** annual conference, for leading pet product distributors and manufacturers ● annual Global Pet Expo - trade show (exhibits) - always spring ● seminar and trade show.

2965 ■ Pet Industry Joint Advisory Council (PIJAC)
1220 19th St. NW, Ste.400
Washington, DC 20036-2438
Ph: (202)452-1525
Free: (800)553-7387
Fax: (202)293-4377
E-mail: info@pijac.org
URL: http://www.pijac.org
Contact: Marshall Meyers Esq., Exec. VP
Founded: 1971. **Members:** 2,000. **Membership Dues:** manufacturer (maximum; based on annual gross sales), $25,000 (annual) ● supplier (maximum; based on annual gross sales), $3,000 (annual) ● retailer (based on annual gross sales), $55-$750 (annual) ● distributor (maximum; based on annual gross sales), $20,000 (annual) ● individual/salesperson, $50 (annual) ● hobbyist, $35 (annual). **Staff:** 5. **Budget:** $1,400,000. **Description:** Pet retailers, manufacturers, and distributors; companion animal suppliers; pet industry trade associations. Works to monitor federal and state regulations and legislation affecting the industry. Sponsors research projects and industry-related educational programs. **Telecommunication Services:** electronic mail, mmeyers@pijac.org. **Committees:** Education; Governmental Affairs; Research. **Publications:** *Animal Reference Manuals*. Includes reference source books on basic animal care. Books available in Avian, Canine, Feline, freshwater fish, reptile, and Small Animals Care. **Price:** $65.00/copy ● *Pet Alert*, periodic. Newsletter. Alerts members to proposed legislation and regulations affecting the industry. ● *PetLetter*, periodic. Newsletter. Reports on federal and state legislative and regulatory issues and providing information on research and companion animals. **Price:** free, for members only. **Circulation:** 2,500 ● Also publishes regulatory alerts and public awareness materials and reference manuals in continuing education program. **Conventions/Meetings:** annual meeting - usually March.

2966 ■ Pet Lovers Association (PLA)
PO Box 145
Joppa, MD 21085
Ph: (410)679-0978
Contact: Elden Harrison, Pres.
Founded: 1983. **Members:** 350. **Description:** Pet lovers and interested companies. Informs pet owners of available options for the disposition of their dead pets. Works to eliminate indifference toward grieving pet lovers and to establish rights and obligations owed them. Acts as a liaison between pet owners and companies and organizations offering assistance, including groomers, pet shops, and funeral homes. Offers children's services; conducts charitable and educational programs. Operates hall of fame. **Awards: Type:** recognition. **Publications:** Books ● Brochures ● Pamphlets. **Conventions/Meetings:** annual meeting (exhibits) - always July.

2967 ■ Pet Sitters International
201 E King St.
King, NC 27021
Ph: (336)983-9222
E-mail: info@petsit.com
URL: http://www.petsit.com
Contact: Patti Moran, Pres.
Founded: 1994. **Members:** 7,600. **Membership Dues:** regular, $129 (annual). **Staff:** 8. **For-Profit. Multinational. Description:** Represents professional pet sitters. Serves as an educational organization for professional pet sitters and advocates of at-home pet care. Promotes, recognizes and supports excellence in pet sitting. Provides a forum of communication for members who share a common vision of excellence in at-home pet care. **Libraries: Type:** reference. **Holdings:** clippings, periodicals. **Subjects:** pet sitting. **Awards:** Pet Sitter of the Year. **Frequency:** annual. **Type:** monetary. **Recipient:** for pet sitters who have exemplified the standards of professionalism recommended by PSI ● PSIs "First Canine" Award. **Frequency:** annual. **Type:** monetary. **Recipient:** to the writer of the best fictional story written from the perspective of a dog. **Computer Services:** database ● mailing lists. **Programs:** Accreditation; Ambassador Bureau. **Publications:** *A Funny Thing Happened While Pet Sitting*. Book. Features true stories submitted by members. **Price:** $10.95 ● *Pet Owner's World*, biennial. Magazine. **Price:** included in membership dues; $36.00 for nonmembers. **Circulation:** 30,000. **Advertising:** accepted ● *The World of Professional Pet Sitting*, bimonthly. Magazine. **Price:** included in membership dues. **Circulation:** 8,000. **Advertising:** accepted. Alternate Formats: online. **Conventions/Meetings:** annual Quest for Excellence - conference and trade show, educational and networking opportunities for professional pet sitters (exhibits) - always mid-September or mid-October.

2968 ■ World Wide Pet Industry Association (WWPIA)
135 W Lemon Ave.
Monrovia, CA 91016-2809
Ph: (626)447-2222
Free: (800)999-7295
Fax: (626)447-8350

E-mail: info@wwpia.org
URL: http://www.wwpia.org
Contact: Doug Poindexter CAE, Exec. VP

Founded: 1951. **Members:** 550. **Membership Dues:** corporate, $550 (annual). **Staff:** 6. **Budget:** $2,100,000. **Multinational. Description:** Manufacturers, retailers, and distributors of pet food and services and of avian, aquarium, and companion animal care products, equipment, and services. Seeks to advance the economic interests of members; promotes responsible pet ownership. Conducts trade shows, certificate training courses, and seminars for pet shop retailers, grooming establishments, and veterinary clinics. **Computer Services:** Mailing lists, of members. **Telecommunication Services:** electronic mail, doug.poindexter@wwpia.org. **Committees:** Education; Grants; Legislative. **Absorbed:** (1992) California Association of Pet Professionals. **Formerly:** (1978) Western Wholesale Pet Supply Association; (1994) Western World Pet Supply Association; (2005) World Wide Pet Supply Association. **Publications:** *Super-Zoo*, annual. Includes show program. **Conventions/Meetings:** annual Super Zoo Trade Show, includes demonstrations, speakers, product exhibits, hobbyist shows and rides for children, and contests (exhibits) - 2008 Sept. 24-26, Las Vegas, NV; 2009 Sept. 23-25, Las Vegas, NV.

Pharmaceuticals

2969 ■ American Society for Automation in Pharmacy (ASAP)

492 Norristown Rd., Ste.160
Blue Bell, PA 19422
Ph: (610)825-7783
Fax: (610)825-7641
E-mail: will@computertalk.com
URL: http://www.asapnet.org
Contact: Bill Lockwood, Exec. Dir.

Founded: 1989. **Members:** 350. **Membership Dues:** corporate, $1,000 (annual) ● individual, $495 (annual). **Staff:** 4. **Description:** Pharmacy software developers; pharmacy and insurance companies; related organizations. Addresses issues related to computer use in the pharmacy industry. **Conventions/Meetings:** annual meeting, with table-top exhibits (exhibits) - 2009 Jan. 15-17, St. Pete Beach, FL ● meeting - mid-year. 2010 June 18-20, Palm Beach, FL.

2970 ■ Animal Health Institute (AHI)

c/o Ron Phillips, VP, Legislative and Public Affairs
1325 G St. NW, Ste.700
Washington, DC 20005-3127
Ph: (202)637-2440
Fax: (202)393-1667
E-mail: rphillips@ahi.org
URL: http://www.ahi.org
Contact: Alexander S. Mathews, Pres./CEO

Founded: 1941. **Members:** 22. **Staff:** 13. **Budget:** $2,500,000. **Description:** Represents manufacturers of animal health products (vaccines, pharmaceuticals, and feed additives used in modern food production; and medicines for household pets). Works with government agencies and legislators; prepares position papers; and compiles and disseminates information. Sponsors AHI Foundation. **Committees:** Government Relations; Law; Market Research; Public Information. **Sections:** Animal Drug; International; Veterinary Biologicals. **Publications:** *AHI Quarterly*. Newsletter. Covers developments of significance to animal health, livestock, and veterinary industries. Includes legislative and regulatory updates and research. **Price:** free. **Circulation:** 2,500 ● *Net Sales Survey*, annual ● *Source Book*, annual. Provides information on members, governmental agencies, and allied organizations. ● Directory, annual. Provides information on membership activities. ● Report, annual ● Surveys. Provides information on research and development. **Conventions/Meetings:** annual conference - always May ● periodic meeting and symposium.

2971 ■ Aspirin Foundation of America (AFA)

807 Natl. Press Bldg.
Washington, DC 20045-1801
Free: (800)432-3247
Fax: (202)737-8406
E-mail: info@aspirin.org
URL: http://www.aspirin.org
Contact: Caroline Perrin, Contact

Founded: 1981. **Members:** 8. **Staff:** 3. **Budget:** $1,250,000. **Description:** Represents manufacturers, producers, distributors, and processors of aspirin and aspirin products. Works to facilitate and encourage an understanding of the potential health benefits of aspirin and to collect and disseminate that information. **Computer Services:** Mailing lists, of members. **Committees:** Legal and Legislative Affairs; Medical and Scientific; Public Relations. **Affiliated With:** Synthetic Organic Chemical Manufacturers Association. **Publications:** *Aspirin Advocate*, quarterly ● *Aspirin Foundation of America—Annual Report*. **Conventions/Meetings:** annual meeting ● biennial symposium.

2972 ■ Chain Drug Marketing Association (CDMA)

43157 W Nine Mile Rd.
PO Box 995
Novi, MI 48376-0995
Ph: (248)449-9300
Free: (800)935-2362
Fax: (248)449-4634
E-mail: devine@chaindrug.com
URL: http://www.chaindrug.com
Contact: James Devine, Pres.

Founded: 1926. **Members:** 104. **Membership Dues:** retail/wholesale store, $3,000 (annual). **Staff:** 15. **Budget:** $2,500,000. **Description:** Drug store chains located throughout the world. Represents members in the market for merchandises; keeps them abreast of trends in relevant fields. **Libraries: Type:** not open to the public. **Formed by Merger of:** Associated Chain Drug Stores; Affiliated Drug Stores. **Formerly:** Chain Drug Marketing Associates; (1992) Affiliated/Associated Drug Stores. **Publications:** *Front End Focus*, quarterly. Newsletter. **Circulation:** 800. **Conventions/Meetings:** quarterly conference (exhibits).

2973 ■ Consumer Healthcare Product Association (CHPA)

900 19th St. NW, Ste.700
Washington, DC 20006
Ph: (202)429-9260
Fax: (202)223-6835
E-mail: lsuydam@chpa-info.org
URL: http://www.chpa-info.org
Contact: Linda A. Suydam DPA, Pres.

Founded: 1881. **Members:** 210. **Staff:** 35. **Budget:** $9,000,000. **Description:** Marketers of nonprescription medicines and dietary supplements, which are packaged and available over-the-counter; associate members include suppliers, consultants, research and testing laboratories, advertising agencies, and media. Obtains and disseminates business, legislative, regulatory, and scientific information; conducts voluntary labeling review service to assist members in complying with laws and regulations. **Libraries: Type:** reference. **Holdings:** 600; archival material, audiovisuals, books, clippings, monographs, periodicals. **Subjects:** state and federal codes covering foods, drugs, cosmetics, and related laws; nonprescription drug industry; FDA OTC Review process; bill history; federal regulatory files. **Committees:** Business Development; Dietary Supplements; Dietary Supplements Methods and Standards; Government Affairs; International Affairs; Legislative Advisory; Logistics; Manufacturing Controls; Public Affairs; Scientific Affairs. **Formerly:** (1989) The Proprietary Association; (1999) Nonprescription Drug Manufacturers Association. **Publications:** *Executive Newsletter*, biweekly ● *State Legislative News Bulletin*, periodic ● *Who's Who in the Nonprescription Drug and Dietary Supplement Industries*, weekly. Directory. Alternate Formats: online ● Pamphlets. Subjects include self-medication and the safe use of over-the-counter medications and dietary supplements. **Conventions/Meetings:** annual meeting and conference.

2974 ■ Drug, Chemical and Associated Technologies Association (DCAT)

1 Washington Blvd., Ste.7
Robbinsville, NJ 08691-3162
Ph: (609)448-1000
Free: (800)640-3228
Fax: (609)448-1944
E-mail: mtimony@dcat.org
URL: http://www.dcat.org
Contact: Margaret M. Timony, Exec. Dir.

Founded: 1890. **Members:** 375. **Membership Dues:** corporate (based on number of employees), $650-$1,995 (annual) ● retiree, $50 (annual). **Staff:** 5. **Budget:** $1,500,000. **Regional Groups:** 3. **Description:** Business development organization for manufacturers of drugs, chemicals, and related products (packaging, cosmetics, essential oils); publications, advertising agencies, agents, brokers, and importers. **Awards:** DCAT Making a Difference Award for NSTA. **Frequency:** annual. **Type:** grant. **Recipient:** for innovative middle school programs in science ● DCAT Scholarships. **Frequency:** annual. **Type:** scholarship. **Recipient:** to graduating high school seniors who are children of employees of member firms. **Telecommunication Services:** electronic mail, info@dcat.org. **Committees:** Nutrition and Health; Packaging; Supply Management. **Formerly:** (1959) Drug, Chemical and Allied Trades Section of the New York Board of Trade; (2004) Drug, Chemical and Allied Trades Association. **Publications:** *DCAT Digest*, quarterly. Newsletter. Contains member news and organizational updates. **Price:** free, for members only. **Circulation:** 2,000. Alternate Formats: online ● Directory, annual. Provides information about members. **Price:** available to members only. **Conventions/Meetings:** annual dinner - in March.

2975 ■ Generic Pharmaceutical Association (GPhA)

2300 Clarendon Blvd., Ste.400
Arlington, VA 22201
Ph: (703)647-2480
Fax: (703)647-2481
E-mail: info@gphaonline.org
URL: http://www.gphaonline.org
Contact: Kathleen Jaeger, Pres./CEO

Founded: 2000. **Description:** Promotes the common interests of the members and the general welfare of the pharmaceutical industry; prepares and disseminates among members and others, accurate and reliable information concerning the industry, products, needs and requirements; participates in international, federal, state and municipal legislative, regulatory and administrative proceedings with respect to law, rules and orders affecting the pharmaceutical industry; participates in scientific research and product development with intent to increase consumer access to generic products; and raises awareness and visibility of the significant benefits and value of generic drugs to the consumers. **Telecommunication Services:** electronic mail, kjaeger@gphaonline.org. **Formed by Merger of:** (2002) Generic Pharmaceutical Industry Association; (2002) National Pharmaceutical Alliance. **Publications:** *GPhA eDigest*. Alternate Formats: online ● Pamphlets ● Videos. **Conventions/Meetings:** periodic Educational Conference.

2976 ■ International Federation of Pharmaceutical Wholesalers (IFPW)

10569 Crestwood Dr.
Manassas, VA 20109
Ph: (703)331-3714
Fax: (703)331-3715
E-mail: info@ifpw.com
URL: http://www.ifpw.com
Contact: William G. Goetz, Pres.

Multinational. Description: Wholesalers and distributors of pharmaceutical products. Promotes efficient delivery of pharmaceuticals to hospitals, physicians, and pharmacists; seeks to increase public awareness of the role played by members in the health care system. Facilitates cooperation and exchange of information among members; represents members' commercial and regulatory interests; sponsors educational and promotional programs. **Publica-**

tions: *Focus* (in English, German, and Spanish), semimonthly. Newsletter. Alternate Formats: online. **Conventions/Meetings:** annual meeting ● annual roundtable.

2977 ■ International Pharmaceutical Excipients Council of the Americas (IPEC-AMERICAS)

1655 N Ft. Myer Dr., Ste.700
Arlington, VA 22209
Ph: (703)875-2127
Fax: (703)525-5157
E-mail: info@ipecamericas.org
URL: http://www.ipecamericas.org
Contact: Alan W. Mercill, Sec.-Treas.

Founded: 1991. **Members:** 42. **Membership Dues:** full, affiliate (based on previous year's sales), $8,000-$20,000 (annual) ● academic associate, nonprofit scientific organization, $100 (annual) ● individual consultant, company with no more than 2 employees, pharmaceutical industry, $250 (annual) ● supplier of specialized services, $1,000 (annual). **Staff:** 3. **Budget:** $550,000. **National Groups:** 4. **Multinational. Description:** Pharmaceutical and excipient manufacturing companies. Promotes good manufacturing practice standards for bulk pharmaceutical excipients; establishes guidelines for GMP assessment auditing of excipient suppliers; promotes harmonized pharmacopoeial standards for quality, purity, and identity; new excipient safety evaluation criteria; industry codes of conduct; and formal national regulatory approval procedures for pharmaceutical excipients. Develops safety guidelines and good manufacturing practices guidelines. Provides expertise and information to the U.S. Food and Drug Administration, U.S. Pharmacopoeia and equivalents in Europe and Japan. **Committees:** Compendial Review/Harmonization: Carboxymethylcellulose; Compendial Review/Harmonization: Cellulose Derivatives; Compendial Review/Harmonization: Ethyl Cellulose; Compendial Review/Harmonization: Gelatin; Compendial Review/Harmonization: Glycerin; Compendial Review/Harmonization: Heavy Metals; Compendial Review/Harmonization: Hydroxyethylcellulose; Compendial Review/Harmonization: Hydroxypropylcellulose & Low Viscosity HPC; Compendial Review/Harmonization: Hydroxypropylmethylcellulose & Methyl Cellulose; Compendial Review/Harmonization: Magnesium Stearate; Compendial Review/Harmonization: Method Validation; Compendial Review/Harmonization: Polyethylene Glycol; Compendial Review/Harmonization: Polyols; Compendial Review/Harmonization: Starches, Potato, Wheat & Tapioca; Compendial Review/Harmonization: Titanium Dioxide; Good Manufacturing Practices; Membership; Microbiological; Nominating; Safety; Science and Regulatory Policy; Science and Regulatory Policy: Dietary Supplements; Science and Regulatory Policy: Regulatory Affairs; Supplier Assessment and Qualification; Supplier Assessment and Qualification: Auditor Training and Certification; Supplier Assessment and Qualification: Certificates of Analysis; Supplier Assessment and Qualification: Distributors GMP Audit; Supplier Assessment and Qualification: GMP Audit; Supplier Assessment and Qualification: Significant Change Reporting; Supplier Assessment and Qualification: Specifications Development; Supplier Assessment and Qualification: 3rd Party Auditing Program. **Formerly:** (2001) International Pharmaceutical Excipients Council. **Publications:** *Certificate of Analysis Guide* ● *GMP Audit Guide for Distributors* ● *GMP Audit Guide for Producers* ● *GMP Guide for Bulk Pharmaceutical Excipients*. **Price:** $10.00 ● *GMP Guide for Bulk Pharmaceutical Excipients 2001* (in English and Spanish) ● *IPEC Newsletter*, monthly. **Price:** free, for members only ● *New Excipient Safety Guidelines* ● *Significant Change Guide*. **Conventions/Meetings:** annual conference (exhibits).

2978 ■ National Pharmaceutical Council (NPC)

1894 Preston White Dr.
Reston, VA 20191-5433
Ph: (703)620-6390 (703)715-2759
Fax: (703)476-0904
E-mail: info@npcnow.com
URL: http://www.npcnow.org
Contact: Karen Williams, Pres.

Founded: 1953. **Members:** 29. **Staff:** 16. **Budget:** $5,000,000. **Description:** Pharmaceutical manufacturers producing high quality prescription medication and other pharmaceutical products. Generates research; conducts specialized educational programs, and forums. **Libraries: Type:** reference. **Telecommunication Services:** electronic mail, kwilliams@npcnow.com. **Publications:** Directory, annual ● Also publishes educational materials. **Conventions/Meetings:** periodic board meeting and executive committee meeting ● periodic seminar and symposium.

2979 ■ PDA

4350 E West Hwy., Ste.200
Bethesda, MD 20814-4426
Ph: (301)656-5900
Fax: (301)986-1093
E-mail: info@pda.org
URL: http://www.pda.org
Contact: Robert Myers, Pres.

Founded: 1946. **Members:** 10,000. **Membership Dues:** standard, $195 (annual) ● developing economy, $100 (annual) ● government/health authority, academic, $80 (annual) ● student, $30 (annual). **Staff:** 21. **Budget:** $5,500,000. **Regional Groups:** 22. **Multinational. Description:** Individuals working in the research, development, or manufacture of parenteral (injectable) drugs and sterile products. Promotes the advance of parenteral science and technology in the interest of public health. Encourages the exchange of information and technical expertise. Conducts open forums for manufacturers, suppliers, users, regulatory agencies, and academia; sponsors research and educational programs; and operates placement service and speakers' bureau. **Awards:** Personeus, Carleton, Korczynski Lecture. **Frequency:** annual. **Type:** recognition. **Computer Services:** database, membership ● mailing lists, of members. **Committees:** Awards; Regulatory Affairs; Science and Technology. **Formerly:** (2000) Parenteral Drug Association. **Publications:** *PDA Journal of Pharmaceutical Science and Technology*, bimonthly. Covers pharmaceutical science research, production, and development. **Price:** $135.00/year in U.S.; $90.00/year outside U.S. **Circulation:** 10,500. **Advertising:** accepted ● *PDA Letter*, monthly. Newsletter. Covers governmental and industrial developments relating to pharmaceutical manufacturing and quality control. **Price:** included in membership dues. **Circulation:** 10,000. **Advertising:** accepted ● Membership Directory, annual. Alternate Formats: online ● Annual Report, annual. Alternate Formats: online ● Reports. Alternate Formats: CD-ROM ● Books ● Proceedings ● Booklets ● Also publishes technical materials. **Conventions/Meetings:** semiannual meeting, held in conjunction with the Food and Drug Administration ● annual Science Driven Manufacturing: The Application of Emerging Technologies - meeting and workshop (exhibits).

2980 ■ Pharmaceutical Research and Manufacturers of America (PhRMA)

950 F St. NW
Washington, DC 20004
Ph: (202)835-3400
Fax: (202)835-3414
URL: http://www.phrma.org
Contact: Kevin Sharer, Pres./CEO

Founded: 1958. **Members:** 63. **Staff:** 80. **Description:** Research based manufacturers of ethical pharmaceutical and biological products that are distributed under their own labels. Encourages high standards for quality control and good manufacturing practices; researches toward the development of new and better medical products; enactment of uniform and reasonable drug legislation for the protection of public health. Disseminates information on governmental regulations and policies, but does not maintain or supply information on specific products, prices, distribution, promotion, or sales policies of its individual members. Has established the Pharmaceutical Manufacturers Association Foundation to promote public health through scientific and medical research. **Libraries: Type:** reference. **Holdings:** 1,600; books, periodicals. **Subjects:** scientific, legislative, business, economic aspects of the pharmaceutical industry. **Sections:** Financial; International; Law; Public Affairs; Science and Regulatory Affairs; State Government Affairs; Washington Representatives. **Formed by Merger of:** American Drug Manufacturers Association; American Pharmaceutical Manufacturers Association. **Formerly:** Pharmaceutical Manufacturers Association. **Publications:** *Fact Book*, annual ● *Trademarks Listed with the Pharmaceutical Manufacturers Association*, periodic. Includes monthly supplements. **Price:** $25.00/year ● Annual Report, annual. Alternate Formats: online ● Newsletter, weekly.

2981 ■ Returns Industry Association (RIA)

Address Unknown since 2007

Membership Dues: associate and voting, $2,500 (annual). **Description:** Pharmaceutical reverse distributors. Provide help to pharmacies and drug wholesalers in returning pharmaceutical products which have become outdated. **Publications:** *RIA Guidelines for Minimum Federal Regulatory Standards for Reverse Distributors*. Report. Lists federal regulatory standards and interpretations to aid reverse distributors in meeting terms pertinent to federal regulations.

2982 ■ Society For Clinical Data Management (SCDM)

555 E Wells St., Ste.1100
Milwaukee, WI 53202-3823
Ph: (414)226-0362
Fax: (414)276-3349
E-mail: info@scdm.org
URL: http://www.scdm.org
Contact: Ms. Kim Breitbach, Exec. Dir.

Founded: 1994. **Members:** 1,600. **Membership Dues:** individual, $90 (annual). **Staff:** 4. **Description:** Strives to advance the discipline of Clinical Data Management as profession in the pharmaceutical and health care industries, to support educational opportunities, to promote standards of good practice within Clinical Data Management, to enhance communication across a discipline-wide network for introduction and management of innovation among related groups involved in Clinical Data Management and to promote global harmony of the pharmaceutical discipline. **Publications:** *Data Basics*, quarterly. Newsletter. **Advertising:** accepted ● *Data Connections*, monthly. Newsletter. Alternate Formats: online. **Conventions/Meetings:** annual convention.

Pharmacy

2983 ■ AARP Pharmacy Services

PO Box 1087
Bensalem, PA 19020-9956
Free: (800)289-8849
Fax: (800)530-5014
URL: http://www.aarppharmacy.com

Founded: 1959. **Description:** Serves as a mail service pharmacy for members of the American Association of Retired Persons (see separate entry). Provides prescription and nonprescription drugs, vitamins, and other health care items through mail service and walk-in facilities in California, Texas, Missouri, Oregon, Indiana, Connecticut, Florida, Pennsylvania, Nevada, Virginia, and Washington, DC. Encourages consumer awareness, comparison-shopping, and use of generic drugs. **Telecommunication Services:** additional toll-free number, (800)933-4327. **Affiliated With:** AARP. **Formerly:** (2004) Retired Persons Services.

2984 ■ Healthcare Distribution Management Association (HDMA)

901 N Glebe Rd., Ste.1000
Arlington, VA 22203
Ph: (703)787-0000
Fax: (703)935-3200

E-mail: info@hdmanet.org
URL: http://www.healthcaredistribution.org
Contact: John M. Gray, Pres./CEO
Founded: 1876. **Members:** 314. **Staff:** 41. **Description:** Wholesalers and manufacturers of drug and health care products and industry service providers. Seeks to secure safe and effective distribution of health care products, create and exchange industry knowledge affecting the future of distribution management, and influence standards and business processes that produce efficient health care commerce. Compiles statistics; sponsors research and specialized education programs. **Libraries: Type:** not open to the public. **Holdings:** 1,000. **Subjects:** distribution, logistics, pharmacy, wholesale marketing. **Awards:** Diana Award. **Frequency:** annual. **Type:** recognition. **Recipient:** for supplier with excellence in working with wholesaler ● Nexus Award. **Frequency:** annual. **Type:** recognition. **Recipient:** to a member who has consistently demonstrated exemplary service to the industry and community, leadership qualities, and professional excellence ● NWDA Innovation for Success Awards. **Frequency:** annual. **Type:** recognition. **Recipient:** for an individual who has implemented an effective new process ● NWDA Technology Award. **Frequency:** annual. **Type:** recognition. **Recipient:** for effective use of technology to improve operations. **Committees:** Logistics and Operations. **Councils:** Government and Public Policy; Industry Relations. **Absorbed:** (1984) Drug Wholesalers Association. **Formerly:** (1881) Western Wholesale Druggists; (2003) National Wholesale Druggists' Association. **Publications:** *Industry Profile and Healthcare Factbook*, annual. Report. **Price:** $200.00 for members; $400.00 for nonmembers ● Membership Directory, annual. **Price:** $50.00 for members; $295.00 for nonmembers. **Conventions/Meetings:** annual Business Partners Exchange - meeting - usually March ● annual Distribution Management and Expo - meeting (exhibits) ● annual Leadership Forum - meeting, with CEOs and industry representatives.

2985 ■ National Association of Chain Drug Stores (NACDS)
413 N Lee St.
Alexandria, VA 22314
Ph: (703)549-3001
Fax: (703)836-4869
URL: http://www.nacds.org
Contact: Steven C. Anderson, Pres./CEO
Founded: 1933. **Membership Dues:** manufacturer's representative/publisher, $2,760 (annual) ● associate, $2,880-$9,960 (annual) ● international chain retailer (based on annual sales), $1,500-$2,500 (annual) ● international chain (Canada/Mexico), $1,500-$7,425 (annual) ● international associate, $2,500 (annual). **Staff:** 100. **Budget:** $30,000,000. **Description:** Represents the concerns of community pharmacies in Washington, in state capitals, and across the country. Members are more than 210 chain community pharmacy companies. Collectively, community pharmacy comprises the largest component of pharmacy practice with over 107,000 FTE pharmacists. Membership also includes more than 1000 suppliers of goods and services to chain community pharmacies. International membership consists of almost 100 members from 30 countries. **Libraries: Type:** by appointment only. **Holdings:** 10,000; audio recordings, books, periodicals, reports, video recordings. **Subjects:** industry history, trends, statistics, pharmacy and OTC statistics, pharmacy and retail management, managed care. **Awards:** Harold W. Pratt Award. **Frequency:** annual. **Type:** recognition. **Recipient:** for contributions and support within the chain drug industry ● Robert B. Begley Award. **Frequency:** annual. **Type:** recognition. **Recipient:** to an individual who possesses qualities of great personal warmth, generous spirit, and good humor ● Sheldon W. Fantle Lifetime Achievement Honor Award. **Frequency:** annual. **Type:** recognition. **Recipient:** to an individual with exceptional accomplishments and contributions to the chain pharmacy industry. **Divisions:** Finance and Administration; Government Affairs; Member Programs and Services; Office of the President and Communications; Pharmacy Operations; Regulatory and Legal Affairs; Strategic Alliances and Development. **Conventions/Meetings:** annual Marketplace - conference (exhibits) ● annual meeting ● annual Pharmacy Conference and Managed Care Forum.

2986 ■ National Community Pharmacists Association (NCPA)
100 Daingerfield Rd.
Alexandria, VA 22314
Ph: (703)683-8200
Free: (800)544-7447
Fax: (703)683-3619
E-mail: info@ncpanet.org
URL: http://www.ncpanet.org
Contact: Bruce Roberts RPh, Exec. VP/CEO
Founded: 1898. **Members:** 25,000. **Membership Dues:** active, sustaining, $295 (annual) ● life, $2,500 ● active spouse, $95 (annual) ● pharmacist, $175 (annual) ● recent graduate, $30 (annual) ● pharmacy student, $25 (annual) ● affiliate, retired pharmacist, $100 (annual) ● pharmacy technician, $75 (annual) ● corporate, $3,500-$9,500 (annual). **Staff:** 41. **State Groups:** 50. **Description:** Owners and managers of independent drugstores and pharmacists employed in community pharmacies offering pharmacy service. Provides support for undergraduate pharmacy education through National Community Pharmacists Association Foundation. **Committees:** Home Health Care Pharmacy Services; Long-Term Care Pharmacy Services; Multiple Locations; Third-Party Payment Programs. **Departments:** Legal; Legislative; Long Term Care; Management Institute; Professional; Student Loans. **Formerly:** (1988) National Association of Retail Druggists. **Publications:** *America's Pharmacist*, monthly. Magazine. Contains continuing education series, updates, and news from Washington. **Price:** included in membership dues; $50.00 /year for nonmembers in U.S.; $70.00 /year for nonmembers outside U.S. ISSN: 0027-5972. **Circulation:** 25,000. **Advertising:** accepted ● *Good Health Calendar*, annual ● *NCPA Newsletter*, semimonthly. Contains legislative information related to pharmaceutical field. **Price:** included in membership dues; $50.00 for nonmembers in U.S.; $70.00 for nonmembers outside U.S. ISSN: 0162-1602. Alternate Formats: online ● *NCPA/Pharmacia Digest* ● Newsletters. Alternate Formats: online. **Conventions/Meetings:** annual show and trade show (exhibits).

2987 ■ National Council for Prescription Drug Programs (NCPDP)
9240 E Raintree Dr.
Scottsdale, AZ 85260-7518
Ph: (480)477-1000
Fax: (480)767-1042
E-mail: ncpdp@ncpdp.org
URL: http://www.ncpdp.org
Contact: Lee Ann C. Stember, Pres.
Founded: 1977. **Members:** 1,300. **Membership Dues:** individual, $650 (annual). **Staff:** 19. **Budget:** $1,500,000. **Description:** Works to create and promote data interchange and processing standards to the pharmacy services sector of the health care industry; and to provide a continuing source of accurate and reliable information that supports the diverse needs of its membership. **Computer Services:** Mailing lists, of members. **Telecommunication Services:** electronic mail, lstember@ncpdp.org. **Working Groups:** Enrollment Standard; Government Programs; Maintenance and Control; Manufacturer Rebates; Payment Reconciliation; Pharmacist/ Prescriber Interface; Product Identification; Professional Pharmacy Services; Standard Identifiers; Telecommunication. **Publications:** *Council Connection*, bimonthly. Newsletter. Communicates the latest developments and trends in the pharmacy services sector of health care. **Price:** $42.00/year; $8.00/ issue. **Circulation:** 1,500. **Advertising:** accepted. Alternate Formats: online. **Conventions/Meetings:** annual Building New Technologies - conference, with speakers, educational session and tradeshow (exhibits) - always early spring ● annual meeting, educational forum.

2988 ■ Pharmaceutical Care Management Association (PCMA)
601 Pennsylvania Ave. NW, 7th Fl.
Washington, DC 20004-2601
Ph: (202)207-3610
Fax: (202)207-3623
E-mail: info@pcmanet.org
URL: http://www.pcmanet.org
Contact: Mark Merritt, Pres./CEO
Founded: 1975. **Members:** 147. **Membership Dues:** affiliate industry, service company, $12,000 (annual) ● service company (revenue under $100 million), $1,500 (annual) ● academic/governmental institution, $250 (annual). **Staff:** 16. **Budget:** $2,000,000. **Description:** Represents managed care pharmacy, Pharmaceutical Benefits Management companies (PBMs) and their healthcare partners in pharmaceutical care. Promotes education, legislation, practice standards, and research to foster quality, affordable pharmaceutical care. **Libraries: Type:** reference. **Awards:** Excellence in Pharmaceutical Care. **Frequency:** annual. **Type:** recognition ● Latiolais Honor Medal. **Frequency:** annual. **Type:** medal. **Recipient:** for exemplary service in the managed healthcare arena ● Outstanding Individual and Company. **Frequency:** annual. **Type:** recognition. **Computer Services:** Mailing lists, of members. **Formed by Merger of:** (1997) American Managed Care Pharmacy Association. **Formerly:** (1989) National Association of Mail Service Pharmacies. **Publications:** *The Journal of Managed Pharmaceutical Care* ● Annual Report, annual. Includes Directory of Managed Care Pharmacy Providers. ● Newsletters. Alternate Formats: online ● Also publishes booklets, directories, and speech resource references. **Conventions/Meetings:** annual meeting and conference.

Photography

2989 ■ Advertising Photographers of America (APA)
PO Box 250
White Plains, NY 10605
Free: (800)272-6264
Fax: (888)889-7190
E-mail: president@apanational.com
URL: http://www.apanational.org
Contact: Don Dormeyer, Pres.
Founded: 1981. **Members:** 500. **Membership Dues:** photographer assistant, affiliate/member emeritus, $125 (annual) ● emerging photographer, international, $225 (annual) ● professional photographer, $350 (annual) ● benefactor, $700 (annual) ● student, $45 (annual) ● educator, $75 (annual) ● educational institution, $500 (annual). **Staff:** 5. **Budget:** $150,000. **Description:** Enhances dialogue among advertising photographers and their clients. Suggests standards and business practices to improve the quality of advertising photography; and acts as a forum for discussion of problems and solutions. Conducts discussion groups. **Publications:** *APA Business Manual*. Alternate Formats: online ● *1999 APA National Photographer's Survey Report*. Alternate Formats: online. **Conventions/Meetings:** bimonthly lecture ● monthly seminar ● tour.

2990 ■ American Photographic Artists Guild (APAG)
c/o D. John McCarthy, Pres.
568 Main St.
Wilbraham, MA 01095-1604
Ph: (413)596-8752
Fax: (413)599-0043
E-mail: djohnmccarthy@mac.com
URL: http://apag.net
Contact: D. John McCarthy, Pres.
Founded: 1966. **Members:** 200. **Membership Dues:** individual, corporate, $55 (annual) ● retired, $20 (annual). **Budget:** $12,000. **Description:** Photographic color artists, retouchers, airbrush artists, color correctors, laboratory technicians, receptionists, and professional photographers working for a photographic business. Encourages a better understanding between the photographer and the color artist and retoucher.

Conducts educational programs on all types of work on color and black and white photographs (including industrial and commercial). **Affiliated With:** Professional Photographers of America. **Formerly:** National Professional Colorists of America; (1976) American Photographic Artists Guild; (2004) American Photographic Artisans Guild. **Publications:** *Palette Page*, semiannual. Newsletter. **Advertising:** accepted. **Conventions/Meetings:** lecture, on methods and tools used in retouching, restoration, and creation of photographs including color applied by hand.

2991 ■ American Professional Wedding Photographers Association (APWPA)
1155 Sherman St., No. 203
Denver, CO 80203
Free: (800)725-1650
Fax: (800)909-5890
E-mail: info@apwpa.com
URL: http://www.apwpa.com
Contact: Andrew Clark, Pres.
Founded: 2004. **Description:** Represents the interests of professional wedding photographers in the United States. Promotes high artistic and technical standards in wedding photography. Works for the further development of its members' craft. **Telecommunication Services:** electronic mail, andrew@andrewclarkphotography.com.

2992 ■ American Society of Media Photographers (ASMP)
150 N 2nd St.
Philadelphia, PA 19106
Ph: (215)451-2767
Fax: (215)451-0880
E-mail: mopsik@asmp.org
URL: http://www.asmp.org
Contact: Eugene Mopsik, Exec. Dir.
Founded: 1944. **Members:** 5,500. **Membership Dues:** general (full voting), $300 (annual) ● associate, affiliate, $200 (annual) ● emerging associate, $125 (annual) ● student, $55 (annual). **Staff:** 6. **Budget:** $1,500,000. **Regional Groups:** 38. **Description:** Professional society of freelance photographers. Works to evolve trade practices for photographers in communications fields. Provides business information to photographers and their potential clients; promotes ethics and rights of members. Holds educational programs and seminars. Compiles statistics. **Convention/Meeting:** none. **Computer Services:** Mailing lists, of members. **Special Interest Groups:** Architecture; Fine Arts; Nature; Underwater Photography. **Formerly:** (1944) Society of Magazine Photographers; (1970) ASMP - The Society of Photographers in Communications; (1993) American Society of Magazine Photographers. **Publications:** *ASMP Bulletin*, quarterly. **Advertising:** accepted. Alternate Formats: online ● *Copyright Guide for Photographers* ● *Professional Business Practices*. Serves as a guide for professional media photographers. ● *Rights and Values* ● *Valuation of Lost or Damaged Transparencies*.

2993 ■ American Society of Picture Professionals (ASPP)
117 S St. Asaph St.
Alexandria, VA 22314
Ph: (703)299-0219
Fax: (703)299-9910
E-mail: cathy@aspp.com
URL: http://www.aspp.com
Contact: Cathy Sachs, Exec. Dir.
Founded: 1966. **Members:** 800. **Membership Dues:** general, $125 (annual) ● senior, $95 (annual) ● overseas (general), $135 (annual) ● overseas (senior), $105 (annual) ● student, $25 (annual). **Staff:** 4. **Budget:** $100,000. **Regional Groups:** 5. **Description:** Composes of image experts committed to sharing their experience and knowledge throughout the industry. Provides professional networking and educational opportunities for those who create, edit, research, license, manage or publish pictures. Individuals having at least four years' professional experience with still pictures including picture editors, researchers, graphic designers, picture librarians and curators, and photographers and their agents. Members work in publishing, advertising, design, educational organizations, filmstrips, and television. Promotes recognition of the various distinct professions in the picture field and encourages high professional standards. Offers a forum where professional problems and practices, such as rights and permissions, can be discussed. **Awards:** Picture Professional of the Year. **Frequency:** annual. **Type:** recognition. **Recipient:** for a member who has demonstrated one or more of the following qualities: significant contributions to photography, a single outstanding achievement, long-time service to the association. **Publications:** *eNews*, monthly. Newsletter. Alternate Formats: online ● *The Picture Professional*, quarterly. Magazine. Includes technical book reviews, and articles on professional practices. **Price:** free for members; $20.00/issue for nonmembers. **Circulation:** 1,000. **Advertising:** accepted. **Conventions/Meetings:** monthly meeting, chapter meetings for special programs and events - always Washington, DC; Seattle, WA; Boston, MA; Chicago, IL; and New York, NY.

2994 ■ Antique and Amusement Photographers International (AAPI)
PO Box 150
Eureka Springs, AR 72632
Ph: (479)253-8554
Fax: (479)253-8225
E-mail: gail@oldtimephotos.org
URL: http://www.oldtimephotos.org
Contact: Gail P. Larimer, Exec. Dir.
Founded: 1993. **Members:** 150. **Membership Dues:** studio photography company, $140 (annual) ● supplier or vendor, $175 (annual). **Staff:** 2. **Budget:** $50,000. **Multinational. Description:** Represents professional antique and amusement, costume, event and historical reenactment photographers; vendors and suppliers of equipment and supplies used by antique and amusement photographers. Promotes high standards of professional practice and ethics among members. Conducts research and educational programs. Sponsors competitions. **Libraries: Type:** reference. **Holdings:** articles, periodicals, photographs. **Subjects:** antique and amusement, costume, event and historical reenactment photography. **Awards:** Photography Awards. **Frequency:** annual. **Type:** recognition. **Recipient:** for proficiency in photographic arts ● Service Awards. **Frequency:** annual. **Type:** recognition. **Recipient:** for service to association and industry. **Telecommunication Services:** electronic bulletin board, online information exchange for members. **Publications:** *Flash Newsletter*, quarterly. **Circulation:** 750. **Advertising:** accepted. **Conventions/Meetings:** annual convention, educational seminars, industry trade show, photographic competitions, social and networking events (exhibits).

2995 ■ Commercial Photographers International (CPI)
229 Peachtree St. NE, Ste.2200
Atlanta, GA 30303-1608
Free: (866)886-4989
E-mail: kevin@amesphoto.com
URL: http://www.mycpi.com
Contact: Kevin Ames, Contact
Membership Dues: photographer, $273 (annual) ● assistant, $58 (annual). **Multinational. Description:** Serves as a venue for commercial photographers to promote their work and excel in their field. Provides guidance and solutions in all aspects of commercial photography. Conducts online discussion forums.

2996 ■ Editorial Photographers (EP)
PO Box 591811
San Francisco, CA 94159-1811
E-mail: info@editorialphoto.com
URL: http://www.editorialphoto.com
Contact: Brian Smith, Pres.
Founded: 1999. **Membership Dues:** editorial photographer, $50 (annual) ● student, assistant, $25 (annual). **Description:** Aims to improve the health and profitability of editorial photography. Seeks to educate photographers and photography buyers about business issues affecting the industry, and to raise the level of business practices in the profession. Promotes healthy relationships between photographers and publishers.

2997 ■ Glamour Photographers International (GPI)
PO Box 84374
San Diego, CA 92138
Ph: (619)575-0100
E-mail: info@glamourphotonet.com
URL: http://www.glamourphotonet.com
Founded: 1984. **Members:** 21. **Membership Dues:** individual, $45 (annual) ● international, $65 (annual) ● business, $85 (annual) ● sponsor, $95 (annual). **Local Groups:** 1. **Multinational. Description:** Promotes high quality photographic fashion, glamour, pin-up, figure photo shoots, and workshops. Provides amateur and professional glamour photographers the opportunity to work with beautiful models and meet with other photographers with the same interests. **Awards:** GPI Photo Days. **Type:** recognition. **Recipient:** for the best entry submitted in the Photo Day competition ● International Glamour Photography Awards. **Type:** recognition. **Computer Services:** database, members website directory, models registry and directory ● mailing lists, of members ● online services, message board, photo gallery. **Publications:** *The Glamour Photographer*. Journal. **Price:** included in membership dues. **Advertising:** accepted. **Conventions/Meetings:** monthly Lingerie and Lace Photo Shoot - workshop ● monthly Marina Village Photo Day - workshop ● monthly Outdoor Glamour Figure Shoot - workshop.

2998 ■ Independent Photo Imagers (IPI)
2510 Anthem Village Pkwy., Ste.110
Henderson, NV 89052
Ph: (702)617-1141
Fax: (702)617-1181
E-mail: trena@ipiphoto.com
URL: http://www.ipiphoto.com
Contact: Brent D. Bowyer, Pres./Exec. Dir.
Founded: 1982. **Membership Dues:** general, $300 (quarterly). **Staff:** 5. **Description:** Independent photo finishing laboratories and imaging business owners. Promotes increased efficiency in photographic laboratory processes; seeks to advance the photographic industries. Serves as a clearinghouse on photo finishing; encourages exchange of information among members; conducts educational programs. **Telecommunication Services:** electronic mail, brent@ipiphoto.com. **Committees:** Color Paper; Employee Practices and Liability; Insurance, Safety and Health; Marketing; Photography; Portrait Studios. **Subgroups:** Framers; Professional.

2999 ■ International Association of Architectural Photographers (IAAP)
2901 136th St. NW
Gig Harbor, WA 98332-9111
Free: (877)845-4783
E-mail: admin@architecturalphotographers.org
URL: http://www.architecturalphotographers.org
Founded: 2003. **Membership Dues:** associate, $10 (monthly) ● associate, $100 (annual). **Multinational. Description:** Provides a voice and valuable resources for the development of the architectural photographer. Provides those in need of architectural photography services a means to make an educated decision on the choice of a professional photographer. Creates an interactive community of professional architectural photographers. Promotes the exchange of ideas and resources. **Awards:** Featured Photographer. **Frequency:** monthly. **Type:** recognition. **Computer Services:** database, member directory ● information services, services, resources ● mailing lists, of members ● online services, forums, request for proposals.

3000 ■ International Association of Panoramic Photographers (IAPP)
PO Box 3371
New York, NY 10008
E-mail: gs1060@yahoo.com
URL: http://www.panoramicassociation.org
Contact: Dan Rose, Pres.
Membership Dues: regular, in North America, $50 (annual) ● regular, outside North America, $60 (an-

nual). **Staff:** 10. **Multinational. Description:** Represents the interests of amateur and professional photographers. Promotes the art of panoramic photography. **Computer Services:** Information services, panoramic cameras resources ● online services, discussion forum. **Programs:** Qualified Panoramic Photographer. **Affiliated With:** Professional Photographers of America. **Publications:** *Panorama*. Magazine. Features articles and news regarding panoramic photography. **Conventions/Meetings:** conference ● convention ● meeting ● workshop.

3001 ■ International Fire Photographers Association (IFPA)

c/o David Sassaman, Membership Coor.
146 W Caracas Ave.
Hershey, PA 17033-1510
Ph: (717)533-4133
E-mail: membership@ifpaonline.com
Contact: David Sassaman, Membership Coor.

Founded: 1964. **Members:** 300. **Membership Dues:** in U.S., $35 (annual) ● in Canada, $37 (annual) ● outside U.S. and Canada, $40 (annual) ● life, $525 ● corporate, $100 (annual). **Staff:** 5. **Budget:** $10,000. **Regional Groups:** 9. **Description:** Photographers in 7 countries interested in fire photography. Promotes the use of photography in the fire service. **Libraries: Type:** open to the public. **Awards:** Man or Woman of the Year Award. **Frequency:** annual. **Type:** recognition ● **Frequency:** annual. **Type:** recognition. **Recipient:** for special contributions to the association ● **Frequency:** annual. **Type:** recognition. **Recipient:** for winners of photo contest. **Committees:** Public Relations; Seminar; Training. **Programs:** Levels of Photographer Certification; Master Photographer Certification. **Publications:** *IFPA Photography Journal*, quarterly. Magazine. Provides information on new products, public education photography, and fire and arson photography and video taping. **Price:** included in registration fee. **Circulation:** 700. **Advertising:** accepted. **Conventions/Meetings:** annual conference (exhibits) - October, September, August ● annual Fire-Rescue International - competition, photo contest (exhibits) ● seminar, training on basic fire photography and arson investigation.

3002 ■ International Imaging Industry Association (I3A)

701 Westchester Ave., Ste.317W
White Plains, NY 10604-3018
Ph: (914)285-4933
Fax: (914)285-4937
E-mail: i3amembership@i3a.org
URL: http://www.i3a.org
Contact: Lisa A. Walker, Pres.

Founded: 1946. **Members:** 50. **Membership Dues:** associate (up to $500 million total annual revenue), $1,500-$5,000 (annual) ● associate ($500,000,001 and above total annual revenue), $6,500-$9,500 (annual) ● participating (minimum), $5,000 (annual) ● participating (maximum), $32,500 (annual) ● strategic (minimum), $25,000 (annual) ● strategic (maximum), $80,000 (annual). **Staff:** 4. **Budget:** $500,000. **Multinational. Description:** Develops and promotes the adoption of open industry standards, addressing environmental issues and providing a voice for the industry that will benefit all users. Promotes environment, health and safety concerns; works with various government agencies including the EPA, TSA, and WTO to ensure the best interests of the imaging industry are represented. **Libraries: Type:** not open to the public. **Holdings:** periodicals, reports. **Awards:** Leadership Award. **Frequency:** annual. **Type:** recognition. **Recipient:** for individuals in the international imaging community who have exhibited exemplary qualities and innovative vision of a leader ● Safety Excellence Award. **Frequency:** annual. **Type:** recognition. **Recipient:** for company sites that demonstrate the best levels of safety performance and leadership. **Telecommunication Services:** electronic mail, i3ainfo@i3a.org. **Committees:** AV Systems; Digital Photography; Films and Papers; Image Evaluation; Image Permanence; Photochemicals; Photofinishing. **Working Groups:** PFAS. **Affiliated With:** PMA - The Worldwide Community of Imaging Associations. **Formerly:** (1997) National Association of Photographic Manufacturers; (2002) Photographic and Imaging Manufacturers Association. **Publications:** *Future Image Report* ● *13A Eye on Imaging*, bimonthly. Newsletter. **Price:** free for members. Alternate Formats: online ● *13A Eye on Standards*, bimonthly. Newsletter. **Price:** free for members. Alternate Formats: online. **Conventions/Meetings:** annual meeting (exhibits).

3003 ■ International Institute of Photographic Arts (IIPA)

1690 Frontage Rd.
Chula Vista, CA 91911
Ph: (619)628-1466
Fax: (619)575-9090
E-mail: lgiddens@iipa.org
URL: http://www.iipa.org
Contact: Lorena Giddens, Contact

Founded: 1972. **Multinational. Description:** Committed to bring photographers the means to print limited editions of fine art photographs with current archival methods.

3004 ■ National Association of Photographic Equipment Technicians (NAPET)

c/o PMA - The Worldwide Community of Imaging Associations
3000 Picture Pl.
Jackson, MI 49201
Ph: (517)788-8100
Free: (800)762-9287
Fax: (517)788-8371
URL: http://napet.pmai.org
Contact: Allen McEver, Pres.

Founded: 1957. **Members:** 210. **Description:** A division of Photo Marketing Association International (see separate entry). Provides photo/video repair services. **Awards:** George LaCroix Award. **Frequency:** semiannual. **Type:** recognition. **Recipient:** for a member displaying outstanding service to the photo/video repair industry. **Affiliated With:** PMA - The Worldwide Community of Imaging Associations. **Publications:** *NAPET News*, quarterly. Newsletter ● *Who's Who in Photographic Management*, semiannual ● Surveys. **Conventions/Meetings:** annual meeting and trade show.

3005 ■ National Press Photographers Association (NPPA)

3200 Croasdaile Dr., Ste.306
Durham, NC 27705-2588
Ph: (919)383-7246
Fax: (919)383-7261
E-mail: info@nppa.org
URL: http://www.nppa.org
Contact: Jim Straight, Exec. Dir.

Founded: 1946. **Members:** 10,000. **Membership Dues:** professional, $110 (annual) ● student, retired professional, $65 (annual) ● family, $60 (annual) ● outside U.S. (air mail), $180 (annual). **Staff:** 5. **Budget:** $1,400,000. **Regional Groups:** 11. **Local Groups:** 29. **National Groups:** 2. **Description:** Professional news photographers and others whose occupation has a direct professional relationship with photojournalism, the art of news communication by photographic image through publication, television film, or theater screen. Sponsors annual television-news film workshop and annual cross-country (five locations) short course. Conducts annual competition for news photos and for television-news film, and monthly contest for still clipping and television-news film. **Libraries: Type:** reference. **Holdings:** audio recordings, audiovisuals. **Subjects:** photojournalism. **Awards:** J. Winton Lemen Fellowship Award. **Frequency:** annual. **Type:** recognition. **Recipient:** for outstanding technical achievement in photography ● Joseph Acosta Award. **Frequency:** annual. **Type:** recognition. **Recipient:** for outstanding initiative, leadership, and service ● Josephine A. Sprague Memorial Award. **Frequency:** annual. **Type:** recognition. **Recipient:** to a working photojournalist ● NPPA Special Citation. **Frequency:** annual. **Type:** recognition. **Recipient:** for significant contributions that advance the interests of photojournalism ● Outstanding Publication Award. **Frequency:** annual. **Type:** recognition. **Recipient:** for outstanding regional or chapter publication ● Robin F. Garland Educator Award. **Frequency:** annual. **Type:** recognition. **Recipient:** for outstanding service as a photojournalism educator ● Samuel Mellor Award. **Frequency:** annual. **Type:** recognition. **Recipient:** to the regional associate director ● **Frequency:** annual. **Type:** scholarship. **Computer Services:** Mailing lists, of members. **Committees:** ACEJ Representative; Admissions; Careers; Education; Freedom of Information; Historian; Honorary Recognitions; Job Placement; Joint Media; Judiciary; Lecture Distribution; National Student Intern Program; National Student Program; NPPA-KAM Liaison; Pictures of the Year Exhibit; Police-Fire-Press; Sports; Television Newsfilm Education. **Subcommittees:** Audio-Visual. **Publications:** *National Press Photographers Association, Inc.—Membership Directory*, annual. Contains resource information, member listings, and information manual. **Price:** $40.00. **Circulation:** 11,000. **Advertising:** accepted ● *News Photographer Magazine*, monthly. Journal. Covers photojournalism. **Price:** $38.00/year. **Circulation:** 11,000. **Advertising:** accepted ● Newsletter, quarterly ● Annual Report, annual. Alternate Formats: online. **Conventions/Meetings:** annual Business and Education Seminar and Convention - seminar and convention (exhibits).

3006 ■ North American Nature Photography Association (NANPA)

10200 W 44th Ave., Ste.304
Wheat Ridge, CO 80033-2840
Ph: (303)422-8527
Fax: (303)422-8894
E-mail: info@nanpa.org
URL: http://www.nanpa.org
Contact: Francine Butler, Exec. Dir.

Founded: 1994. **Members:** 2,500. **Membership Dues:** student, $25 (annual) ● general, $90 (annual) ● joint, $120 (annual) ● friend, $250-$999 (annual) ● bronze, $1,000-$2,499 (annual) ● silver, $2,500-$4,999 (annual) ● gold (minimum), $5,000 (annual). **Staff:** 3. **Budget:** $600,000. **Description:** Wildlife photographers and other individuals with an interest in outdoor photography, environmental education and protection, including educators, government workers, biologists, and editors and publishers. Seeks to insure professionalism and ethical conduct in the photographing of wildlife; promotes wildlife photography as an art form and educational tool. Represents the professional interests of wildlife photographers. Serves as a forum for the discussion of issues in wildlife photography and for the exchange of information among members. Serves as liaison between wildlife photographers and environmental protection agencies and organizations. Develops guidelines for environmentally and ethically responsible wildlife photography. **Awards:** Fellows Award. **Frequency:** annual. **Type:** recognition. **Recipient:** for individuals contributing to the profession of wildlife photography for at least twenty years ● Industry Recognition Award. **Frequency:** annual. **Type:** recognition. **Recipient:** for supplier of products or services to the photo industry ● Lifetime Achievement in Nature Photography. **Frequency:** periodic. **Type:** recognition ● NANPA Recognition Award. **Frequency:** annual. **Type:** recognition. **Recipient:** for individuals whose photography helped deter environmentally destructive development ● Outstanding Nature Photographer Award. **Frequency:** annual. **Type:** recognition. **Recipient:** for nature photographers ● Outstanding Service Award. **Frequency:** annual. **Type:** recognition. **Recipient:** for members with outstanding services to the association. **Committees:** Awards; Communications; Education; Environment; Ethics; History; International; Nominations and Elections; Publications and Products; Refuge Blind; Regional Events; Resource Relations; Summit; Youth Action. **Programs:** College Scholarship; High School Scholarship. **Publications:** *American Photo*, bimonthly. Magazine. Features masters of photography. **Price:** $11.00 in U.S.; $19.00 in Canada; $25.00 international ● *Currents*, bimonthly. Newsletter. Contains articles about the association and its members. **Price:** included in membership dues. **Advertising:** accepted. Alternate Formats: online ● *Membership Brochure* ● *Nature Photographer*, quarterly. Magazine.

Contains articles on nature photography. **Price:** $15.00 in U.S.; $23.00 in Canada; $27.00 international ● *Nature's Best*, quarterly. Magazine. Features winning images from the annual Nature's Best Photography Awards. **Price:** $21.00 in U.S.; $31.00 in Canada; $56.00 international ● *Outdoor Photographer*, monthly. Magazine. Contains information on how to improve one's own photography. **Price:** $11.00 in U.S.; $21.00 in Canada; $21.00 international ● *Popular Photography*, monthly. Magazine. Features advice on how to improve one's own photography. **Price:** $10.00 in U.S.; $18.00 in Canada; $18.00 international ● Membership Directory, annual. Includes information on the association. **Advertising:** accepted. **Conventions/Meetings:** quarterly board meeting ● periodic regional meeting ● annual seminar (exhibits) ● annual trade show.

3007 ■ Photoimaging Manufacturers and Distributors Association (PMDA)

109 White Oak Ln., Ste.72F
Old Bridge, NJ 08857-1981
Ph: (732)679-3460
Fax: (732)679-2294
E-mail: nunn@pmda.com
URL: http://www.pmda.com
Contact: Robert H. Nunn, Exec. Dir.

Founded: 1939. **Members:** 85. **Membership Dues:** full, $1,500 (annual) ● associate (non-voting), $750 (annual). **Staff:** 2. **Description:** Represents manufacturers, wholesalers, distributors, and importers of photographic equipment. Holds lecture meetings presenting programs on topics facing the photographic industry. Helps to further the consumer's interest in photography through its website and a traveling information booth. **Awards:** Person of the Year Award. **Frequency:** annual. **Type:** recognition ● Professional Photographer Award. **Frequency:** annual. **Type:** recognition ● Technical Achievement Award. **Frequency:** annual. **Type:** recognition. **Committees:** International Relations; Standardization. **Programs:** Education. **Formerly:** (1947) Photographic Merchandising and Distributing Association; (1998) Photographic Manufacturers and Distributors Association. **Publications:** *PMDA Today*, bimonthly. Newsletter. **Conventions/Meetings:** periodic symposium.

3008 ■ Picture Archive Council of America (PACA)

c/o Cathy Aron, Exec. Dir.
23046 Avenida de la Carlota, Ste.600
Laguna Hills, CA 92653-1537
Ph: (949)282-5065
Fax: (949)282-5066
E-mail: execdirector@pacaoffice.org
URL: http://www.pacaoffice.org
Contact: Cathy Aron, Exec. Dir.

Founded: 1975. **Members:** 170. **Membership Dues:** affiliate outside U.S., $500 (annual) ● friend, $375 (annual) ● general (1-64 employees), $700-$5,000 (annual) ● general (65-499 employees), $5,250-$10,000 (annual) ● general (1000 and above employees), $22,500 (annual) ● corporate sponsor, $1,750 (annual). **Staff:** 1. **Budget:** $200,000. **Description:** Agencies engaged in the sale or rental and licensing of photographs and illustrations for purposes of reproduction in any communication form. Aims to unite the picture agencies of America into a cohesive organization and foster common business and financial interests. Achieves uniformity in business practices. Establishes moral and ethical business standards. Collects, compiles, and disseminates information pertinent to the improvement and protection of members' businesses and to the business of the photographic industry as a whole; attempts to reform and eliminate all unethical practices in the trade. **Formerly:** (2003) Picture Agency Council of America. **Publications:** *PACA Update*, bimonthly. Newsletters. Contains industry and association news and information. **Circulation:** 300. Alternate Formats: online.

3009 ■ PMA - The Worldwide Community of Imaging Associations

3000 Picture Pl.
Jackson, MI 49201-8853
Ph: (517)788-8100
Free: (800)762-9287
Fax: (517)788-8371
E-mail: pma_membership@pmai.org
URL: http://www.pmai.org
Contact: Ken Strawbridge, Pres.

Founded: 1924. **Members:** 20,000. **Staff:** 100. **Budget:** $10,000,000. **Regional Groups:** 21. **Local Groups:** 13. **Languages:** Czech, English, French, German, Italian, Spanish. **Description:** Retailers of photo and video equipment, film, and supplies; firms developing and printing film. Maintains hall of fame. Compiles statistics; conducts research and educational programs. **Libraries: Type:** reference. **Holdings:** 200; periodicals. **Subjects:** photo finishing, retailing. **Computer Services:** Mailing lists. **Divisions:** Communications; Environmental; Industry Relations; Marketing Research; Trade Exhibits. **Formed by Merger of:** Master Photo Finishers and Dealers Association; National Photographic Dealers Association. **Formerly:** (1974) Master Photo Dealers' and Finishers' Association; (2006) Photo Marketing Association International. **Publications:** *Mini Lab Focus*, monthly. Newsletter. Provides association mini lab members with information on industry trends and activities, and advertising and marketing techniques. **Price:** $18.00 /year for members. **Circulation:** 3,820 ● *NAPET News*, bimonthly. Newsletter. Provides information on association activities, trends in photo/video field, manufacturers' training programs for repair people, and new products. **Circulation:** 1,008 ● *Photo Marketing Association International—Newsline*, semimonthly. Newsletter. Provides a digest of pertinent information about the photo industry. Includes surveys of industry leaders on current topics and people profiles. **Price:** $36.00/year, for those in the photographic industry only. **Circulation:** 12,307 ● *Photo Marketing Magazine*, monthly. Features articles examining industry issues, product innovations, business management, and interviews with leading industry experts. **Price:** $15.00/year, for those in the photo industry only. **Circulation:** 22,000. **Advertising:** accepted ● *Sales Counter*, monthly. Newsletter. Contains articles on techniques of selling photographic products, market trends and innovations, and other consumer information. **Price:** available to those who have passed qualifying exam. **Circulation:** 1,194 ● *Specialty Lab Update*, monthly. Newsletter. Provides information on marketing techniques, business financing and management, government regulations, technical developments in the industry. **Price:** $18.00/year, for those in the photo industry only. **Circulation:** 2,500 ● *SPFE Newsletter*, bimonthly. Covers society activities, technical developments, and EPA guidelines. Contains information on APFT titles awarded and new products. **Price:** available to those who pass an exam. **Circulation:** 1,034 ● *Who's Who in Photographic Management*, annual. Directory. **Advertising:** accepted. Alternate Formats: online. **Conventions/Meetings:** annual seminar (exhibits) - always fall ● annual trade show (exhibits).

3010 ■ Professional Aerial Photographers Association (PAPA)

c/o Office of the Sec.
4910 Willowbend, Ste.E
Houston, TX 77035
Ph: (713)721-6593
Fax: (713)721-6586
E-mail: julie@the111th.com
URL: http://www.papainternational.org
Contact: Julie Belanger, Exec. Dir.

Founded: 1974. **Membership Dues:** general, $125 (annual) ● associate, $75 (annual) ● corporate sponsor, $500 (annual). **Multinational. Description:** Serves a worldwide community of aerial photographers by providing safety tips, professional business practices, new technologies, and practical training. **Awards:** Best of Show Artistic. **Frequency:** annual. **Type:** recognition ● Best of Show Commercial. **Frequency:** annual. **Type:** recognition ● Judges' Choice. **Frequency:** annual. **Type:** recognition ● People's Choice Awards-Best Commercial-Digital. **Frequency:** annual. **Type:** recognition ● People's Choice Awards-Best Commercial-Photo. **Frequency:** annual. **Type:** recognition ● People's Choice-Best Artistic-Digital. **Frequency:** annual. **Type:** recognition ● People's Choice-Best Artistic-Photo. **Frequency:** annual. **Type:** recognition. **Computer Services:** database, directory of aerial photographers ● information services, copyright law ● mailing lists, e-mail discussion list ● online services, bulletin board, photo gallery. **Publications:** Newsletter, quarterly. Alternate Formats: online. **Conventions/Meetings:** annual convention (exhibits).

3011 ■ Professional Photographers of America (PPA)

229 Peachtree St. NE, Ste.2200
Atlanta, GA 30303-1608
Ph: (404)522-8600
Free: (800)786-6277
Fax: (404)614-6400
E-mail: csc@ppa.com
URL: http://www.ppa.com
Contact: Jack Reznicki, Pres.

Founded: 1880. **Members:** 14,000. **Membership Dues:** professional active (with malpractice protection), $323 (annual) ● professional active (without malpractice protection), $273 (annual) ● aspiring photographer (with malpractice protection), $194 (annual) ● aspiring photographer (without malpractice protection), $144 (annual) ● additional associate, $246 (annual) ● corporate, $500-$5,000 (annual) ● in Canada, $170-$220 (annual) ● outside U.S. and Canada, $170 (annual). **Staff:** 40. **Budget:** $7,500,000. **Regional Groups:** 9. **State Groups:** 52. **Local Groups:** 120. **National Groups:** 15. **Description:** Strives to create a global perspective that promotes business first, creativity foremost and excellence always. Aims to be the leader in the dissemination of knowledge in the areas of professional business practices and creative image-making, and to define and maintain the industry's standards of excellence. Represents portrait, wedding, commercial, industrial, and specialized photographers. Sponsors PPA International School of Professional Photography. Maintains speakers' bureau. **Libraries: Type:** reference. **Awards:** Craftsman Degree. **Type:** recognition ● Master Artists Business and Marketing Degree. **Type:** recognition ● Master Electronic Imaging Degree. **Type:** recognition ● Masters Degree. **Type:** recognition. **Computer Services:** Mailing lists, rental. **Committees:** Certification; Education; Electronic Imaging; Ethics; Fine Arts; Marketing; Photographic Exhibitions; Public Relations; Technical Standards. **Sections:** Commercial Advertising; Digital Imaging; Portrait; Video; Wedding. **Formerly:** (1958) Photographers' Association of America. **Publications:** *Directory of Professional Photography*, annual ● *Photo Electronic Imaging*, monthly. Magazine. **Price:** $20.00. **Circulation:** 45,000. **Advertising:** accepted ● *PP of A Today*, monthly. Newsletter. Provides information on the association and the photographic industry. Includes calendar of events. **Price:** included in membership dues. ISSN: 0886-0289. Also Cited As: *Professional Photographers of America—Today* ● *Professional Photographer*, monthly. Magazine. Covers the business and artistic aspects of photography. Includes book reviews and new product information. **Price:** included in membership dues; $27.00 /year for nonmembers. ISSN: 0033-0167. **Advertising:** accepted. Alternate Formats: microform ● *Who's Who in Professional Photography*, annual ● Bulletin, periodic ● Reprints. **Conventions/Meetings:** annual conference, on marketing and management - always January ● annual trade show (exhibits).

3012 ■ Professional School Photographers Association International (PSPA)

c/o Robert W. Kerr, Pres.
26 W Broad St.
Bethlehem, PA 18018-5732
Ph: (610)694-8825
Fax: (610)694-0930
E-mail: royal@schoolportraits.com
URL: http://pspa.pmai.org
Contact: Robert W. Kerr, Pres.

Founded: 1951. **Members:** 331. **Description:** A section of the Photo Marketing Association International (see separate entry). Firms engaged in the photographing and/or processing of school photographs. Purposes are: to encourage the exchange of production ideas and economies; to cooperate in the overall promotion of photography; to work for better relations and understanding with schools; to act as a group in making manufacturers of sensitized goods and photographic equipment aware of the specialized needs of school photography; to maintain a close watch on any legislation that may affect school photography; to promote career possibilities and personnel training and recruitment for school photography; to foster the well-being of the member firms by providing some of the advantages of a large-scale operation. **Affiliated With:** PMA - The Worldwide Community of Imaging Associations. **Formerly:** (1977) American Association of School Photographers; (2004) Professional School Photographers of America. **Publications:** *School Photographer*, monthly. Newsletter. Covers association activities, market trends, and legislative developments affecting the relationship among school photographers. **Price:** included in membership dues. **Conventions/Meetings:** annual meeting (exhibits) - always spring.

3013 ■ Professional Women Photographers (PWP)
511 Ave. of the Americas, No. 138
New York, NY 10011
Ph: (212)726-8292
E-mail: info@pwponline.org
URL: http://www.pwponline.org
Contact: Fran Dickson, Pres.
Founded: 1975. **Members:** 200. **Membership Dues:** individual, $95 (annual) ● student, $35 (annual) ● institutional (up to 2 individuals), $125 (annual) ● subscriber, $40 (annual) ● international subscriber, $50 (annual). **Local Groups:** 1. **Description:** Women professional photographers; other interested individuals. Supports and promotes the work of women photographers through the sharing of ideas, resources, and experience. Provides educational forums to encourage artistic growth and photographic development. Stimulates public interest and support for the art of photography. **Libraries: Type:** reference. **Holdings:** archival material. **Awards:** High School Student Awards for Photography. **Frequency:** annual. **Type:** scholarship. **Recipient:** for a female junior or senior student at a NYC public school demonstrating financial need. **Computer Services:** Mailing lists. **Committees:** Developments; Exhibitions; Programs. **Special Interest Groups:** Digital; Salons. **Publications:** *PWP Newsletter*, 3/year. Includes meeting schedule and selected biographies. **Circulation:** 1,000. **Advertising:** accepted. Alternate Formats: CD-ROM ● Brochure. Alternate Formats: CD-ROM.

3014 ■ Society of Photo-Technologists (SPT)
11112 S Spotted Rd.
Cheney, WA 99004-9038
Ph: (509)624-9621
Free: (888)662-7678
Fax: (509)624-5320
E-mail: cc5@earthlink.net
URL: http://www.spt.info
Contact: Chuck Bertone, Exec. Dir.
Founded: 1959. **Members:** 1,200. **Membership Dues:** class A (under $50,000 in gross annual repair/part sales), $175 (annual) ● class B ($50,000-$100,000 in gross annual repair/part sales), $205 (annual) ● class C ($100,000-$250,000 in gross annual repair/part sales), $225 (annual) ● sustaining, $335 (annual) ● technician, student, associate, $105 (annual). **Staff:** 1. **Regional Groups:** 11. **Multinational**. **Description:** International, professional society of camera repair technicians. Member of the American National Standards Institute (see separate entry). Official channel through which the Japan Camera Industry Association communicates with U.S. camera repairmen. Updates the *National Standards for Apprenticeship* in Photographic Equipment Repair for the U.S. Department of Labor. Maintains placement service; compiles statistics; offers credit service. **Libraries: Type:** reference. **Holdings:** 200. **Subjects:** camera repair. **Awards:** Manufacturers Award. **Frequency:** biennial. **Type:** recognition. **Recipient:** for service to the industry ● Zimmerman Award. **Type:** recognition. **Committees:** Parts Availability. **Affiliated With:** American National Standards Institute. **Publications:** *Annual Parts and Service Manual Directory*. **Advertising:** accepted ● *Journal and Service Notes*, bimonthly ● Newsletter, monthly. Alternate Formats: online ● Also publishes technical, industrial, and career information. **Conventions/Meetings:** annual meeting.

3015 ■ Society of Sport and Event Photographers (SEP)
229 Peachtree St. NE, Ste.2200
Atlanta, GA 30303-1608
Free: (877)427-3778
Fax: (301)604-0158
E-mail: csc@sepsociety.com
URL: http://www.iapep.com
Contact: Jim Roshan, Pres.
Founded: 2001. **Membership Dues:** professional, $100 (annual) ● multi-association professional, $50 (annual). **Description:** Provides education and networking opportunities for sports and event photographers by creating an online information portal focused exclusively on the needs of member photographers. Promotes copyright protection. **Computer Services:** database, member directory ● online services, forum, downloadable files, classifieds, calendar. **Formerly:** (2006) International Association of Professional Event Photographers. **Publications:** *Action News*, quarterly. Newsletter. Contains association and industry news. **Circulation:** 6,000. **Advertising:** accepted. Alternate Formats: online ● Brochure. Alternate Formats: online.

3016 ■ United States Senate Press Photographers Gallery (USSPPG)
U.S. Capitol
S-317
Washington, DC 20510
Ph: (202)224-6548
URL: http://www.senate.gov/galleries/photo
Contact: Jeffrey Kent, Dir.
Members: 300. **Description:** Press photographers assigned to United States Senate and House of Representatives. **Libraries: Type:** reference. **Holdings:** photographs.

3017 ■ Wedding and Portrait Photographers International (WPPI)
1312 Lincoln Blvd.
PO Box 2003
Santa Monica, CA 90406-2003
Ph: (310)451-0090
Fax: (310)395-9058
URL: http://www.wppinow.com/index2.tml
Contact: Jennifer O'Brien, Contact
Founded: 1973. **Members:** 4,000. **Membership Dues:** regular, in U.S., $99 (annual) ● regular, in Canada, $109 (annual) ● regular, outside U.S. and Canada, $139 (annual). **Staff:** 15. **Budget:** $250,000. **Multinational**. **Description:** Represents wedding portrait and digital photographers and photographers employed at general photography studios. Promotes high artistic and technical standards in wedding photography. Serves as a forum for the exchange of technical knowledge and experience; makes available the expertise of top professionals in the field of photographic arts and technology, advertising, sales promotion, marketing, public relations, accounting, business management, tax, and profit planning. Members are offered the opportunity to purchase special products and services. **Libraries: Type:** open to the public. **Holdings:** books, video recordings. **Awards:** Accolade Program. **Frequency:** semiannual. **Type:** recognition ● Print Competitions. **Frequency:** annual. **Type:** recognition. **Formerly:** (1977) Wedding Photographers of America; (1998) Wedding Photographers International. **Publications:** *Marketing and Technical Manual*, quarterly. Newsletter. Includes supplements. ● *Rangefinder*. Magazine. **Price:** included in membership dues ● *Wedding Photographer*, monthly. Newsletter. Covers market trends, management guidelines, photographic techniques, and other industry news for professional wedding photographers. **Price:** free for members. **Circulation:** 4,000 ● *WPPI Photography Monthly*. Newsletter. Alternate Formats: online ● Video. **Price:** $37.95/tape; $204.90/six tapes; $443.95/thirteen tapes. **Conventions/Meetings:** semiannual competition and seminar, for prints and albums (exhibits) ● annual trade show (exhibits).

3018 ■ White House News Photographers Association (WHNPA)
7119 Ben Franklin Sta.
Washington, DC 20044-7119
Ph: (202)785-5230
E-mail: info@whnpa.org
URL: http://www.whnpa.org
Contact: Dennis Brack, Pres.
Founded: 1921. **Members:** 500. **Membership Dues:** active, $85 (annual) ● associate, $60 (annual) ● student, $25 (annual). **Staff:** 12. **Budget:** $200,000. **Description:** Professional news photographers (still and electronic/videotape) who cover the White House, government agencies, and Congress for wire services, newspapers, television stations and national weekly news networks, and magazines. Maintains speakers' bureau. **Awards: Frequency:** annual. **Type:** grant. **Recipient:** for members ● **Type:** scholarship. **Computer Services:** Mailing lists, for a fee. **Publications:** *The Report*, quarterly. Newsletter ● *White House News Photographer Awards Book*, annual. **Conventions/Meetings:** annual competition, news photo contest for members ● annual dinner, includes award presentation - always April or May in Washington, DC ● annual seminar, for high school students on photojournalism.

3019 ■ Women in Photography International (WIPI)
569 N Rossmore Ave., No. 604
Los Angeles, CA 90004
Ph: (303)462-1444
E-mail: info@womeninphotography.org
URL: http://www.womeninphotography.org
Contact: Jean Ferro, Pres./Interim Exec. Dir.
Founded: 1981. **Membership Dues:** charter (life), $1,000 ● charter (in memory of), $500 ● professional, $150 (annual) ● general, $50 (annual) ● student, $35 (annual). **Multinational**. **Description:** Promotes the visibility of women photographers and their work through a variety of programs, exhibitions, juried competitions and publications. **Awards:** Distinguished Photographer's Award. **Frequency:** annual. **Type:** recognition. **Recipient:** to an artist for significant contribution to the world of photography ● Membership Award. **Frequency:** monthly. **Type:** recognition. **Recipient:** for women photographers. **Publications:** *F2 eZine*, quarterly. Magazine. Contains member profiles and portfolios, interviews, book reviews, product information and gallery listings. Alternate Formats: online. **Conventions/Meetings:** competition, juried competitions ● conference ● New Photographers Lecture Series, to honor emerging talent, features discussion and slide presentation ● workshop, for working photographers, students and photo enthusiasts.

Physical Fitness

3020 ■ Fitness Industry Suppliers Association - North America (FISA N.A.)
3525 Del Mar Heights Rd.
Box 381
San Diego, CA 92130
Ph: (858)509-0034
Fax: (858)792-1251
E-mail: info@fisana.org
URL: http://www.fisana.org
Contact: David Dinerman, Exec. Dir.
Founded: 2004. **Membership Dues:** company (based on annual sales), $900-$2,500 (annual). **Multinational**. **Description:** Provides market intelligence that enables its members to design, manufacture, and deliver products and services to meet the needs of commercial and retail fitness purchasers. Improves business conditions within the commercial fitness

sector. Promotes the adoption of a healthy lifestyle and the improvement of health for everyone. **Telecommunication Services:** electronic mail, dinerman@san.rr.com. **Publications:** *Commercial Market Trend Report*, annual. Tracks the global sale of commercial fitness equipment. ● *Fitness Specialty Market Trend Report*, annual. Tracks the domestic sale of fitness equipment sold through the fitness specialty channel.

3021 ■ International Health, Racquet and Sportsclub Association (IHRSA)
263 Summer St.
Boston, MA 02210
Ph: (617)951-0055
Free: (800)228-4772
Fax: (617)951-0056
E-mail: info@ihrsa.org
URL: http://cms.ihrsa.org
Contact: Joe Moore, Pres./CEO
Founded: 1981. **Members:** 6,500. **Staff:** 50. **Budget:** $10,500,000. **Regional Groups:** 8. **Multinational. Description:** Health, racquet, and sport clubs; racquet sports manufacturers and suppliers. Promotes the continued growth of the health, racquet, and sports club industry in 70 countries. Aids member clubs in making educated business decisions. Sets standards for club management; offers group purchasing program. Organizes management training seminars. Compiles statistics; disseminates information. Conducts market research and educational programs; conducts sponsored membership promotion programs. Provides government relations and public relations services. **Libraries: Type:** not open to the public. **Subjects:** government relations, club operations. **Awards: Type:** recognition. **Computer Services:** database ● mailing lists. **Formed by Merger of:** National Tennis Association; Indoor Tennis Association; National Indoor Tennis Association; National Court Clubs Association. **Formerly:** (1988) International Racquet Sports Association; (1994) IRSA, The Association of Quality Clubs. **Publications:** *Club Business International*, monthly. Magazine. Concerned with the quality and profitability of commercial health, racquet, and sports clubs. **Price:** free for members. **Circulation:** 25,000. **Advertising:** accepted. Also Cited As: *IRSA Club Business* ● Also publishes industry studies. **Conventions/Meetings:** annual trade show and international conference, seminars and networking opportunities to improve members' business (exhibits) - 2009 Mar. 18-21, San Francisco, CA; 2010 Mar. 10-13, San Diego, CA.

Physicians

3022 ■ The IPA Association of America (TIPAAA)
17120 Jami Lynn Ln.
Village of Loch Lloyd, MO 64012
Ph: (816)322-7906
Fax: (816)322-7900
E-mail: info@tipaaa.com
URL: http://www.tipaaa.com
Contact: Allecia Holloway, Founder/Pres./CEO
Founded: 1994. **Members:** 300,000. **Membership Dues:** group with risk contracts (99999 or below covered lives), $550-$3,000 (annual) ● group with risk contracts (100000 to more than 200000 covered lives), $5,000-$10,000 (annual) ● individual associate, $285 (annual) ● corporate associate, $5,000 (annual) ● key corporate associate, $20,000 (annual) ● key market associate, $25,000 (annual). **Description:** Represents independent/integrated physician associations. Offers products to improve organization and contract structure and to manage risks. **Computer Services:** Mailing lists. **Publications:** *TIPS On Managed Care*, bimonthly. Magazine. Alternate Formats: online. **Conventions/Meetings:** annual conference, for vendors, IPA executives, medical directors and staff members.

Pipes

3023 ■ American Concrete Pipe Association (ACPA)
1303 W Walnut Hill Ln., Ste.305
Irving, TX 75038-3008
Ph: (972)506-7216
Fax: (972)506-7682
E-mail: info@concrete-pipe.org
URL: http://www.concrete-pipe.org
Contact: Matt Childs, Pres.
Founded: 1907. **Members:** 200. **Staff:** 12. **Budget:** $2,400,000. **Description:** Companies and individuals actively engaged in the manufacture of concrete pipe, those interested in the expansion of the concrete pipe industry, and those contributing professionally to the welfare of the industry. Holds joint membership in Concrete Pipe Associations (see separate entry). Gathers and disseminates information about concrete pipe, its engineering properties, manufacture, and installation. Sponsors Technical School sessions in February. Conducts specialized education and research programs; compiles statistics. **Libraries: Type:** reference. **Holdings:** archival material. **Awards: Type:** recognition. **Telecommunication Services:** electronic mail, mchilds@concrete-pipe.org. **Publications:** *Concrete Pipe News*, quarterly. Magazine ● *NewsCast*, monthly. Newsletter. **Price:** free for members. **Advertising:** accepted ● Brochures. **Price:** $37.50 for members (per package of 25); $75.00 for nonmembers (per package of 25) ● Also publishes technical literature dealing with the design and installation of concrete pipe. **Conventions/Meetings:** annual convention - always February ● annual Educational Meeting Short Course School - workshop and meeting - always February ● annual meeting.

3024 ■ American Concrete Pressure Pipe Association (ACPPA)
11800 Sunrise Valley Dr., Ste.309
Reston, VA 20191-5302
Ph: (703)391-9135
Fax: (703)391-9136
E-mail: americanconcretepressurepipe@erols.com
URL: http://www.acppa.org
Contact: David P. Prosser, Pres.
Founded: 1949. **Members:** 7. **Staff:** 2. **Description:** International trade association of the concrete pressure pipe industry. Represents companies actively engaged in the manufacture of concrete pressure pipe. Gathers and disseminates information about concrete pressure pipe, its engineering properties, manufacture, and installation. **Committees:** Government Affairs; Marketing; Technical. **Publications:** *Concrete Pressure Pipe Digest*, quarterly ● Directory, periodic ● Also publishes technical literature. **Conventions/Meetings:** annual conference.

3025 ■ American Pipe Fittings Association (APFA)
Address Unknown since 2007
Founded: 1938. **Members:** 45. **Staff:** 2. **Budget:** $140,000. **Description:** Manufacturers of cast and malleable iron pipe fittings and flanges, malleable iron unions, brass fittings and unions, cast brass solder fittings, pipe hangers and supports, pipe nipples, steel pipe couplings, forged steel fittings and unions, butt weld fittings, plastic lined pipes and fittings, forged steel flanges, and welding outlet fittings. Conducts meetings, seminars, and panel discussions. Compiles statistics. **Awards: Type:** recognition. **Absorbed:** (1990) National Association of Pipe Nipple Manufacturers. **Formerly:** Pipe Fittings Manufacturers Association. **Publications:** *American Pipe Fittings Association—Membership and Product Directory*, annual. **Price:** $10.00. **Advertising:** not accepted. **Conventions/Meetings:** semiannual conference ● annual meeting.

3026 ■ Association of Asbestos Cement Product Producers (AACPP)
1235 Jefferson Davis Hwy.
PMB 114
Arlington, VA 22202-3283
Ph: (514)861-1153
Fax: (514)861-1152
E-mail: aia@chrysotile.com
URL: http://www.chrysotile.com
Contact: B.J. Pigg, Dir. Gen.
Founded: 1972. **Members:** 10. **Staff:** 1. **Budget:** $20,000. **Description:** Manufacturers of asbestos cement products. Promotes the worldwide acceptance of and confidence in asbestos cement products. Maintains liaison with major segments of the international asbestos cement products industry. **Committees:** International Affairs. **Formerly:** (2001) Association of Asbestos Cement Pipe Producers. **Publications:** Publishes informational and educational materials, regulatory bulletins, and technical reports. **Conventions/Meetings:** annual conference.

3027 ■ Cast Iron Soil Pipe Institute (CISPI)
5959 Shallowford Rd., Ste.419
Chattanooga, TN 37421
Ph: (423)892-0137
Fax: (423)892-0817
E-mail: blevan@mindspring.com
URL: http://www.cispi.org
Contact: William H. LeVan, Exec. Dir.
Founded: 1949. **Members:** 5. **Staff:** 8. **Description:** Manufacturers of cast iron soil pipe and fittings. Seeks to aid and improve the plumbing industry. Develops promotional, advertising, and standardization programs; assists plumbing apprentice schools. **Committees:** Market Development; Quality Control; Technical. **Publications:** *Cast Iron Soil Pipe and Fittings Handbook*. Alternate Formats: online ● *Recommendations — Deep Burial of Cast Iron Soil Pipe* ● Directory, annual ● Reports. **Conventions/Meetings:** annual meeting.

3028 ■ Concrete Pipe Associations (CPA)
1303 W Walnut Hill Ln., Ste.305
Irving, TX 75038-3008
Ph: (972)506-7216
Fax: (972)506-7682
E-mail: info@concrete-pipe.org
URL: http://www.concrete-pipe.org
Contact: Matt Childs PE, Pres.
Founded: 1907. **Description:** Represents American Concrete Pipe Association and American Concrete Pressure Pipe Association (see separate entries). **Affiliated With:** American Concrete Pipe Association; American Concrete Pressure Pipe Association.

3029 ■ Ductile Iron Pipe Research Association (DIPRA)
245 Riverchase Pkwy. E, Ste.O
Birmingham, AL 35244
Ph: (205)402-8700 (205)402-8702
Fax: (205)402-8730
E-mail: info@dipra.org
URL: http://www.dipra.org
Contact: L. Gregg Horn PE, Pres.
Founded: 1915. **Members:** 7. **Staff:** 22. **Description:** Provides engineering information about cast iron and ductile iron pipe to utility and construction engineers. **Committees:** Advertising. **Formerly:** (1915) Cast Iron Pipe Publicity Bureau; (1928) Cast Iron Pipe Institute; (1980) Cast Iron Pipe Research Association. **Publications:** *Bridge Crossings with Ductile Iron Pipe* ● *Cement-Mortar Linings for Ductile Iron Pipe* ● *Design of Ductile Iron Pipe* ● *Design of Ductile Iron Pipe on Supports*. Brochure ● *DIPRA Computer Programs*. Brochure. Alternate Formats: online ● *Direct Tapping of 6-Inch Pressure Class 350 Ductile Iron Pipe* ● *Ductile Iron Pipe* ● *Ductile Iron Pipe for Wastewater Applications* ● *Ductile Iron Pipe Subaqueous Crossings* ● *Ductile Iron Pipe Versus HDPE Pipe* ● *Ductile Iron Pipe Versus PVC* ● *Ductile Iron Pipe Versus PVCO* ● *Ductile Iron Pipe Versus Steel Pipe* ● *The Effect of Overhead AC Power Lines Paralleling Ductile Iron Pipelines* ● *Field Welding and Cutting Ductile Iron Pipe* ● *Flanged Ductile Iron Pipe* ● *Gasket Materials Used for Ductile Iron Pipe In Water and Sewage Service* ● *Hydraulic Analysis of Ductile Iron Pipe* ● *Installation Guide for Ductile Iron Pipe*.

3030 ■ Expansion Joint Manufacturers Association (EJMA)
25 N Broadway
Tarrytown, NY 10591
Ph: (914)332-0040
Fax: (914)332-1541

E-mail: inquiries@ejma.org
URL: http://www.ejma.org
Contact: Richard C. Byrne, Sec.

Founded: 1955. **Members:** 12. **Staff:** 2. **Description:** Represents manufacturers of expansion joints for piping systems. **Committees:** Technical. **Publications:** *Standards of the Expansion Joint Manufacturers Association.* **Conventions/Meetings:** semiannual meeting.

3031 ■ National Association of Pipe Fabricators (NAPF)

1901 NW 161st St.
Edmond, OK 73013
Free: (888)798-1924
Fax: (800)860-5700
E-mail: info@napf.com
URL: http://www.napf.com
Contact: Ted Wright, Pres./Exec. Dir.

Founded: 1977. **Members:** 40. **Description:** Manufacturers of ductile pipe. Promotes production of quality pipes by independent fabricators. Formulates performance and manufacturing standards for ductile pipes; creates and distributes technical manuals; represents members' commercial and regulatory interests. **Publications:** *The Pipeline*, quarterly. Newsletter. Alternate Formats: online ● Membership Directory. Alternate Formats: online.

3032 ■ National Association of Steel Pipe Distributors (NASPD)

1501 E Mockingbird Ln., Ste.307
Victoria, TX 77904
Ph: (361)574-7878
Fax: (832)201-9479
E-mail: info@naspd.com
URL: http://www.naspd.com
Contact: Dianne Burger, Pres.

Founded: 1975. **Members:** 165. **Membership Dues:** regular, $950-$1,200 (annual) ● associate/professional affiliate, $1,050-$1,300 (annual) ● continuing, $100 (annual). **Staff:** 4. **Budget:** $250,000. **Regional Groups:** 3. **Description:** Distributors of steel pipe and tubing whose principals are experienced physical plant operators who have a sales volume of $1 million or more; associate members are companies that manufacture steel pipe or pipe-related products, equipment, or fabricating used in the steel pipe distribution industry. Fosters and promotes the interests of members; works to develop increased efficiency and economy in the business; encourages harmony and cooperation among members; defines and sets forth standards of ethical practices throughout the industry; procures uniformity in the customs and usages of trade in the industry and related business; secures freedom from unjust and unlawful exactions. Conducts educational and research programs. **Libraries: Type:** reference. **Holdings:** video recordings. **Subjects:** safety, OSHA. **Computer Services:** database, company profiles ● mailing lists, of members. **Programs:** Employee Assistance; Safety. **Publications:** *National Association of Steel Pipe Distributors—Membership Directory*, annual. Provides information on personnel, product line and description, transportation sources, services, and number of employees. **Price:** included in membership dues; $185.00 /year for nonmembers. **Circulation:** 1,000. **Advertising:** accepted. Alternate Formats: online ● *Pipeline*, monthly. Magazine. Covers all subjects regarding the distribution, manufacturing, and inventory of steel pipe. Includes calendar of events and new member information. **Price:** included in membership dues; $55.00 /year for nonmembers. **Circulation:** 1,000. **Advertising:** accepted. Alternate Formats: online ● *Tubular Products Manual: A Steel Pipe and Tubing Text Book*, annual. Contains information on tabular products. **Price:** $40.00 for members; $50.00 for nonmembers ● Also distributes videotapes on safety procedures; provides consulting services for safety inspections and quality procedures training. **Conventions/Meetings:** semiannual conference and seminar, with speakers and social functions - 2008 Oct. 9-11, Boston, MA ● annual convention, with industry related speakers, motivational, and entertainment speakers (exhibits) - usually early spring.

3033 ■ National Certified Pipe Welding Bureau (NCPWB)

1385 Piccard Dr.
Rockville, MD 20850
Ph: (301)869-5800
Free: (800)556-3653
Fax: (301)990-9690
E-mail: nnikpourfard@mcaa.org
URL: http://www.mcaa.org/ncpwb
Contact: Nick Nikpourfard, Exec. Dir.

Founded: 1944. **Members:** 650. **Membership Dues:** contractor, $475 (semiannual) ● initiation fee, $750. **Staff:** 2. **Budget:** $340,000. **Local Groups:** 42. **Description:** Contractors in the piping field. Conducts research on development in the field of certified welding for the piping industry; establishes uniform welding procedures for pipe welding; provides for interchange of records of qualified welders. **Committees:** Technical. **Publications:** *An Explanation of Certified Welding.* **Price:** $2.00 for members; $4.00 for nonmembers ● *By-Laws of the NCPWB.* **Price:** $4.00 for members; $8.00 for nonmembers ● *General Brazing Guidelines.* **Price:** $4.00 for members; $8.00 for nonmembers ● *General Instructions for Testing Pipefitters/Welders*, semiannual. Newsletter. **Price:** $5.25 for members; $11.00 for nonmembers ● *General Welding Guidelines.* Video. Covers inspection during welding. **Price:** $4.00 for members; $8.00 for nonmembers ● *Instruction Manual for Completing Welder/Operator Qualification Test.* **Price:** $40.00 for members; $80.00 for nonmembers ● *MCAA Reporter*, monthly. Newsletter. Alternate Formats: online ● *NCPWB Quality Weld Video.* Covers inspection during welding. **Price:** $200.00 for nonmembers ● *NCPWB Video.* **Price:** $35.00 for members; $70.00 for nonmembers ● *NCPWB Welding Talks.* **Price:** $5.00 for members; $10.00 for nonmembers. **Conventions/Meetings:** annual meeting.

3034 ■ National Clay Pipe Institute (NCPI)

PO Box 759
Lake Geneva, WI 53147
Ph: (262)248-9094
Fax: (262)248-1564
E-mail: info@ncpi.org
URL: http://www.ncpi.org
Contact: E.J. Sikora, Pres.

Founded: 1942. **Members:** 6. **Staff:** 5. **Description:** Manufacturers of vitrified clay sewer pipe and fittings. Promotes use of clay pipe for sanitary sewer systems. Provides engineering advisory services; conducts scientific research; acts as government liaison. **Committees:** Government Relations; Technical Services. **Formerly:** National Clay Pipe Manufacturers. **Publications:** *Clay Pipe Installation.* Handbook. **Price:** free ● *Sewer Sense*, quarterly ● Brochures. Provides technical information. ● Manuals ● Also produces computer design programs. **Conventions/Meetings:** semiannual meeting.

3035 ■ National Corrugated Steel Pipe Association (NCSPA)

14070 Proton Rd., Ste.100, LB 9
Dallas, TX 75244
Ph: (972)850-1907
Fax: (972)490-4219
E-mail: info@ncspa.org
URL: http://www.ncspa.org
Contact: Dwight Thompson, Pres.

Founded: 1956. **Members:** 75. **Staff:** 3. **Budget:** $500,000. **Description:** Represents firms fabricating corrugated steel drainage pipe and structures; steel mills; allied industries. Provides engineering service in design and installation of drainage products and systems. Conducts research programs. **Libraries: Type:** reference. **Holdings:** 1,000; books. **Committees:** Mill Producers; Product Promotion; Technical Advisory. **Councils:** Regional. **Formerly:** (1959) Corrugated Metal Pipe Association; (1964) National Corrugated Metal Pipe Association. **Publications:** *Condition Survey of Corrugated Steel Pipe Detention Systems: An Interim Report* ● *Field Performance Evaluation of Polymer Coated CSP Structures in New York.* Report. **Price:** $5.00 ● *Handbook of Steel Drainage and Highway Construction Products.* Contains discussion of storm drainage applications and special drainage problems. **Price:** $30.00 ● *Installation Manual for Corrugated Steel Drainage Structures.* **Price:** $2.50 ● *Modern Sewer Design.* Manual. **Price:** $17.00. Alternate Formats: CD-ROM ● *NCSPA News*, quarterly. Newsletter ● *Pipeline*, quarterly. Newsletter. **Price:** free ● Videos. **Conventions/Meetings:** annual meeting ● periodic Underground Detention Design for Stormwater Management - seminar, for engineering, sales, and production personnel.

3036 ■ Pipe Fabrication Institute (PFI)

511 Ave. of the Americas, No. 601
New York, NY 10011
Ph: (514)634-3434
Free: (866)913-3434
Fax: (514)634-9736
E-mail: pfi@pfi-institute.org
URL: http://www.pfi-institute.org
Contact: Guy Fortin, Exec. Dir.

Founded: 1913. **Members:** 57. **Membership Dues:** charter, $1,800 (annual) ● contractor, $600 (annual) ● associate, $1,200 (annual) ● affiliate, $600 (annual). **Multinational. Description:** Promotes the pipe fabrication industry; initiates engineering, research and studies; maintains industry standards. **Affiliated With:** United Association of Journeymen and Apprentices of the Plumbing, Pipe Fitting, Sprinkler Fitting Industry of the U.S. and Canada. **Publications:** Bulletins. **Conventions/Meetings:** quarterly meeting, for members.

3037 ■ Plastic Pipe and Fittings Association (PPFA)

800 Roosevelt Rd.
Bldg. C, Ste.312
Glen Ellyn, IL 60137
Ph: (630)858-6540
Fax: (630)790-3095
E-mail: info@ppfahome.org
URL: http://www.ppfahome.org
Contact: Richard W. Church, Exec. Dir.

Founded: 1978. **Members:** 76. **Staff:** 4. **Budget:** $1,000,000. **Description:** Raw material suppliers and processors of plastic pipe and fittings. Seeks to: provide a forum for exchange of information and ideas; see that existing code approvals for use of plastic pipe and fittings are retained; obtain additional code approvals and develop new markets for products; provide leadership and continuity for the industry; seek liaison and involvement with other organizations within the industry. **Libraries: Type:** reference. **Publications:** Newsletter, biweekly. **Conventions/Meetings:** semiannual meeting - always spring and fall.

3038 ■ Plastics Pipe Institute (PPI)

105 Decker Ct., Ste.825
Irving, TX 75062
Ph: (469)499-1044 (469)499-1046
Fax: (469)499-1063
E-mail: info@plasticpipe.org
URL: http://www.plasticpipe.org
Contact: Tony Radoszewski, Exec. Dir.

Founded: 1950. **Members:** 120. **Staff:** 8. **Budget:** $2,500,000. **Multinational. Description:** Manufacturers of plastic pipe and fittings and suppliers of plastic pipe raw materials. Develops technical reports and promotes trade and user acceptance. Compiles statistics; offers research programs. Conducts periodic training seminar on plastic piping. **Telecommunication Services:** electronic mail, tonyr@plasticpipe.org. **Committees:** Technical. **Divisions:** Fuel Gas; Hydrostatic Stress; Municipal and Industrial. **Formerly:** Thermoplastic Pipe Division of the Society of the Plastics Industry. **Publications:** *Handbook of PE Pipe.* Alternate Formats: CD-ROM ● *Plastics Pipe Institute—Literature List*, annual. Directory. Contains technical and marketing information for engineers, designers, specifiers, and users of thermoplastic piping systems. **Price:** free ● Brochures. Alternate Formats: online. **Conventions/Meetings:** semiannual meeting, for members only ● annual meeting.

3039 ■ Pressure Vessel Research Council (PVRC)
PO Box 1942
New York, NY 10156
Ph: (216)658-3847
Fax: (216)658-3854
E-mail: mprager@forengineers.org
URL: http://www.forengineers.org/pvrc
Contact: Dr. Martin Prager, Contact

Founded: 1945. **Membership Dues:** company, $1,250 (annual) ● individual, $775 (annual). **Description:** Works to encourage, promote, and conduct research in the field of pressure vessels and related pressure equipment technologies, including evaluation of materials, design, fabrication, inspection, and testing. **Committees:** Bolted Flanged Connections and Gasket Technology; Continued Operation of Equipment; Cyclic Life and Environmental Effects; Dynamic Analysis and Testing; Elevated Temperature Design; Failure Modes of Components; Fatigue and Fracture; Flaw Evaluation; NDE; Nondestructive Examination; Piping, Nozzles and Vessels, Plastic Analysis; Polymer Pressure Components; Thermal and Mechanical Effects on Materials; Weld Metals and Welding Procedures. **Divisions:** Design; Materials and Fabrication. **Task Forces:** Continued Modernization of Codes. **Working Groups:** Flange Joints. **Publications:** *Progress Reports*. **Price:** included in membership dues ● *The Welding Journal* ● *Welding Research Abroad*, 8-12/year ● *Welding Research Council Bulletins*, 10/year. Contains reference documents on technical issues and/or Codes Criteria. **Price:** included in membership dues ● *Welding Research News*, quarterly ● Newsletter. **Price:** included in membership dues. **Conventions/Meetings:** conference ● meeting ● workshop.

3040 ■ Tube and Pipe Association, International (TPA)
833 Featherstone Rd.
Rockford, IL 61107-6301
Ph: (815)399-8775
Fax: (815)484-7701
E-mail: info@tpatube.org
URL: http://www.tpatube.org
Contact: Paul Russo, Chm.

Founded: 1996. **Members:** 500. **Membership Dues:** individual, $150 (annual) ● company, $450 (annual) ● student, $25 (annual) ● advantage plus, $950 (annual). **Staff:** 83. **Multinational. Description:** Educational Association serving the tube and pipe fabricating and producing industry. Offers products and services that include technical conferences, in-plant training, bookstore products, the industry's largest research library, industry surveys, coordinate scholarship and award programs. **Libraries: Type:** not open to the public; by appointment only. **Holdings:** 500. **Subjects:** tube, pipe fabricating, producing, end forming, welding, finishing processes, material handling. **Computer Services:** Information services. **Councils:** Extrusion, Drawing and Tube Reducing; Tube Fabricating; Tube Producing. **Affiliated With:** Fabricators and Manufacturers Association, International. **Formed by Merger of:** (1996) American Tube Association and Tube and Pipe Fabricators Association, International. **Publications:** *Member Connections*, bimonthly. Newsletter. **Price:** included in membership dues. **Circulation:** 1,600 ● *TPJ - The Tube and Pipe Journal*, 8/year. Magazine. **Price:** free to qualified persons; $65.00/year in Canada and Mexico; $85.00/year, all other countries. **Circulation:** 25,000. **Advertising:** accepted ● *Who's Who in Metal Forming and Fabricating*, annual. Membership Directory. **Price:** $200.00 for nonmembers; included in membership dues. **Advertising:** accepted. **Conventions/Meetings:** annual FABTECH International Exposition and Conference (exhibits) - October.

3041 ■ Uni-Bell PVC Pipe Association (UNI-BELL)
2711 LBJ Fwy., Ste.1000
Dallas, TX 75234
Ph: (972)243-3902
Fax: (972)243-3907
E-mail: info@uni-bell.org
URL: http://www.uni-bell.org
Contact: Robert P. Walker, Exec. Dir.

Founded: 1971. **Members:** 55. **Staff:** 7. **Languages:** English, French. **Multinational. Description:** Manufacturers of Polyvinyl Chloride (PVC) pipe with gasket joints and other industry stakeholders. Educates market through seminars and symposia on topics including water pipes, sewer pipes, and irrigation. **Libraries: Type:** reference. **Holdings:** 7,000; articles, books, video recordings. **Subjects:** pipe, pipe products design. **Committees:** Operating. **Formerly:** Uni-Bell Plastic Pipe Association. **Publications:** *Handbook of PVC Pipe - Design and Construction*. **Price:** $40.00. **Circulation:** 50,000. Alternate Formats: CD-ROM; diskette ● *PVC News*, semiannual. Newspaper. Provides up-to-date technical information on the design and installation of PVC pipe. Features association and member news. **Price:** free. **Circulation:** 45,000 ● *Recommended Standards and Practices* ● Reports. **Conventions/Meetings:** annual conference - usually in April.

Planning

3042 ■ Association for Strategic Planning (ASP)
12021 Wilshire Blvd., Ste.286
Los Angeles, CA 90025-1200
Free: (877)816-2080
Fax: (323)954-0507
E-mail: executivedirector@strategyplus.org
URL: http://www.strategyplus.org
Contact: James A. McComb, Pres.

Founded: 1999. **Membership Dues:** student, $90 (annual) ● individual, $195 (annual) ● corporate, $5,000 (annual). **Description:** Advances thought and practice in strategy development and deployment for business, non-profit and government organizations. Provides opportunities to explore strategy principles and practices that enhance organizational success and enhance members' and organizations' knowledge, capability and capacity for innovation and professionalism. **Awards:** Richard Goodman Strategic Planning Award. **Frequency:** annual. **Type:** recognition. **Recipient:** for distinction in the practice of strategy.

Plaster

3043 ■ National Plasterers Council (NPC)
2811-D Tamiami Trail
Port Charlotte, FL 33952
Ph: (941)766-0634
Free: (866)483-4672
Fax: (941)764-6050
E-mail: npconline@comcast.net
URL: http://www.npconline.org
Contact: Mitch Brooks, Exec. Dir.

Founded: 1988. **Membership Dues:** active, $400 (annual) ● associate, $600 (annual) ● auxiliary, $200 (annual). **Description:** Provides a forum for swimming pool plasterers. Offers publications to assist swimming pool plasterers, test pools, field surveys, and laboratory research.

Plastics

3044 ■ American Plastics Council (APC)
1300 Wilson Blvd.
Arlington, VA 22209
Ph: (703)741-5000 (703)741-5626
Free: (800)2-HELP-90
Fax: (703)741-6626
E-mail: rob_krebs@americanchemistry.com
URL: http://www.americanplasticscouncil.org
Contact: Robert Krebs, Dir. of Communications

Founded: 1996. **Description:** Plastics Industry. Focuses on resource conservation and related environmental issues to demonstrate the use of plastic for a safer and cleaner environment for the future. Sponsors programs to emphasize contributions of the plastics industry to U.S. society. **Committees:** Transportation and Logistics. **Publications:** *How Plastics Make It Possible*. Brochure. **Price:** free. Alternate Formats: online ● *Plastics in the Microwave: Revolutionizing American Mealtime*. Brochure. Contains tips and guidance on proper and safe use of plastic containers and wraps in the microwave oven. Alternate Formats: online ● Reports. Highlights the role of plastics in the society. Alternate Formats: online.

3045 ■ Association of Postconsumer Plastic Recyclers (APR)
2000 L St. NW, Ste.835
Washington, DC 20006
Ph: (202)316-3046
E-mail: info@plasticsrecycling.org
URL: http://plasticsrecycling.org
Contact: Robin Cotchan, Exec. Dir.

Description: Works to increase the post-consumer plastics recycling industry. **Committees:** Market Development; Technical. **Affiliated With:** American Plastics Council; National Association for PET Container Resources; National Recycling Coalition. **Conventions/Meetings:** seminar.

3046 ■ Association of Rotational Molders International (ARM International)
800 Roosevelt Rd., Bldg. C, Ste.312
Glen Ellyn, IL 60137
Ph: (630)571-0611 (630)942-6589
Fax: (630)571-0616
E-mail: info@rotomolding.org
URL: http://www.rotomolding.org
Contact: Jeffrey S. Arnold CAE, Exec. Dir./CEO

Founded: 1976. **Members:** 460. **Membership Dues:** regular (based on annual sales volume), $870-$1,680 (annual) ● supplier (based on total annual sales volume), $1,160-$3,260 (annual) ● designer, consultant, $525 (annual). **Staff:** 5. **Budget:** $1,000,000. **Regional Groups:** 2. **Languages:** English, Spanish. **Multinational. Description:** Plastic processors who use the rotational molding process; their suppliers; overseas molders. Purposes are to increase awareness of rotomolding, exchange technical information, provide education, and standardize production guidelines. Conducts research; produces seminars and educational video and slide programs. Sponsors product contest and Student Design Competition. **Libraries: Type:** reference. **Holdings:** audiovisuals. **Awards: Frequency:** annual. **Type:** recognition. **Computer Services:** database, membership. **Committees:** Education; Forums and Programs; Membership Development; Moldmakers; Polyolefin; Processes, Equipment, and Tooling; Public Relations; Special Materials. **Subcommittees:** International Development. **Formerly:** (2005) Association of Rotational Molders. **Publications:** *ARM International Directory*, annual. Membership Directory. Contains geographic index; arranged by company. **Price:** one copy free for members ● *Engineers Guide* ● *Glossary of Terms* ● *Machinery* ● *Resin Properties*. **Conventions/Meetings:** annual meeting (exhibits) - always fall.

3047 ■ Center for the Polyurethanes Industry (CPI)
1300 Wilson Blvd.
Arlington, VA 22209
Ph: (703)741-5656 (703)741-5654
Free: (800)243-5790
Fax: (703)741-5655
E-mail: api@plastics.org
URL: http://www.polyurethane.org
Contact: Ms. Neeva-Gayle Candelori, Dir.

Founded: 1962. **Members:** 39. **Membership Dues:** basic, $1,000 (annual) ● Steering Committee, $7,500 (annual). **Staff:** 6. **Budget:** $2,000,000. **Description:** A business unit of the American Plastics Council. Members are U.S. producers or distributors of chemicals and equipment used to make polyurethanes, or are manufacturers of polyurethane products. Promotes the health and vigor of the industry by identifying and managing issues that could adversely affect the industry. **Awards:** Polyurethane

Hall of Fame Award. **Frequency:** periodic. **Type:** recognition ● Polyurethane Innovation Award. **Frequency:** annual. **Type:** recognition. **Recipient:** for companies and/or individuals whose visions and perseverance bring new products and technologies to the marketplace. **Formerly:** (1974) Urethane Institute, Society of the Plastics Industry Polyurethane Division; (2000) Polyurethane Division, Society of the Plastics Industry; (2007) Alliance for the Polyurethanes Industry (A Business Unit of the American Plastics Council). **Publications:** *Polyurethane News*. Newsletter. Includes calendar of events. **Conventions/Meetings:** annual Polyurethanes Expo - conference (exhibits) - always fall. 2008 Sept. 29-Oct. 1, San Antonio, TX - **Avg. Attendance:** 1500; 2009 Oct. 5-7, Fort Washington, MD - **Avg. Attendance:** 1200.

3048 ■ Chemical Fabrics and Film Association (CFFA)

1300 Sumner Ave.
Cleveland, OH 44115-2851
Ph: (216)241-7333
Fax: (216)241-0105
E-mail: cffa@chemicalfabricsandfilm.com
URL: http://www.chemicalfabricsandfilm.com
Contact: Robert Kahn, Pres.

Founded: 1927. **Members:** 40. **Staff:** 3. **Multinational. Description:** Represents manufacturers of chemically coated materials, supported and unsupported vinyl, and urethane materials; associate member are raw suppliers. **Committees:** Environmental; Human Resources; Marketing Communications; Technical. **Divisions:** Automotive/Transportation; Decorative Products; Industrial Products. **Formerly:** Plastic Coatings and Film Association; (1972) Vinyl Fabrics Institute. **Publications:** *Commercial Wallcoverings - An Excellent Decorating Choice*. **Price:** $2.50 for nonmembers ● *Decorative Building Components - Fact Sheet on Mold* ● *Environmental Profile: Vinyl Roofing Membranes* ● *Environmental Profile: Vinyl Wallcovering* ● *Fitness for Use* ● *Glossary of Terms for the Chemical Fabrics and Film Industry*. **Price:** $1.25 each ● *Heavy Metal Free* ● *Layflat of Plastic Film - Definition and Causes* ● *Mold and Mildew - An Overview/Marine Upholstery* ● *Mold and Mildew - An Overview/Wallcovering* ● *Mold - Cause, Effect and Response* ● *PPAP (Production Part Approval Process) Standard - 1998 Edition* ● *PPM - (Parts per Million) Standard - 1998 Edition* ● *Quality Standard for Vinyl Coated Fabric Wallcoverings - 2000 Edition* ● *Recommended Performance Standards for Vinyl-Coated and Other Chemical Coated Upholstery Fabrics - Indoor - 1998 Edition* ● *Recommended Performance Standards for Vinyl-Coated and Other Chemical Coated Upholstery Fabrics - Marine - 1998 Edition* ● *Recommended Performance Standards for Vinyl Swimming Pool Liners In-Ground - 2003 Edition* ● *SPEC-DATA Unit - Vinyl coated Fabric Wallcovering - 1996 Edition*. **Price:** free ● *Standard Test Methods*. Pamphlet. **Price:** $5.00 each ● *Vinyl's Health, Safety and Environmental Performance Q&A*. **Price:** $1.00 each. **Conventions/Meetings:** annual meeting.

3049 ■ Corrugated Polyethylene Pipe Association (CPPA)

c/o Plastics Pipe Institute
1825 Connecticut Ave. NW, Ste.680
Washington, DC 20009
Ph: (202)462-9607
Free: (800)510-2772
Fax: (866)768-2995
E-mail: rgottwald@plasticpipe.org
URL: http://www.plasticpipe.org/intro.html
Contact: Rich Gottwald, Exec. Dir.

Multinational. Description: Manufacturers, raw materials suppliers, equipment distributors, designers. Works to provide its members with information about the technology, design, specification, and installation of corrugated polyethylene pipe. Sponsors research.

3050 ■ EPS Molders Association (EPSMA)

1298 Cronson Blvd., Ste.201
Crofton, MD 21114
Ph: (410)451-8341
Free: (800)607-3772
Fax: (410)451-8343
E-mail: info@epsmolders.org
URL: http://www.epsmolders.org
Contact: Betsy Steiner, Exec. Dir.

Founded: 1995. **Members:** 45. **Staff:** 5. **Budget:** $500,000. **Description:** Works to promote the use of block molded polystyrene products. **Conventions/Meetings:** annual EPS Expo - convention and conference (exhibits) - always March/April.

3051 ■ International Association of Plastics Distributors (IAPD)

4707 Coll. Blvd., Ste.105
Leawood, KS 66211
Ph: (913)345-1005
Fax: (913)345-1006
E-mail: iapd@iapd.org
URL: http://www.iapd.org
Contact: Susan E. Avery CAE, Exec. Dir.

Founded: 1956. **Members:** 415. **Membership Dues:** company, $575 (annual). **Staff:** 7. **Budget:** $1,500,000. **Description:** Represents manufacturers and distributors of plastics materials, piping, and resins. Aims to promote the distribution channel, and the education and training of plastics distributors. Maintains liaison with associated organizations. Compiles statistics. **Libraries: Type:** reference. **Awards:** Award of Merit. **Frequency:** annual. **Type:** recognition ● PaceSetter Award. **Frequency:** annual. **Type:** recognition. **Committees:** Canadian; Education; Manufacturers; Manufacturers' Representatives; Pipe, Valves & Fittings; Scholarship; Young Executives' Society. **Affiliated With:** National Association of Wholesaler-Distributors. **Formerly:** (1966) United Plastics Distributors Association; (1991) National Association of Plastics Distributors. **Publications:** *IAPD Distributor Profit Report*, annual. Survey ● *IAPD Magazine*, bimonthly ● *The IAPD Membership Directory*, annual. **Price:** $155.50 for nonmembers in North America; $35.50 for members in North America; $162.00 for nonmembers outside North America; $42.00 for members outside North America ● *Introduction to Plastics*. Manuals. Includes the plastics training manual. **Price:** $50.00 for nonmembers ● Also publishes charts and other materials. **Conventions/Meetings:** annual convention (exhibits).

3052 ■ International Association of Used Equipment Dealers (IAUED)

214 Edgewood Dr., Ste.100
Wilmington, DE 19809
Ph: (302)765-3571
Fax: (302)765-3571
E-mail: info@iaued.org
URL: http://iauedadmin.bluestep.net
Contact: Mr. Darryl McEwen, Pres.

Founded: 2001. **Members:** 50. **Membership Dues:** general, $250 (annual). **Staff:** 1. **Budget:** $100,000. **Multinational. Description:** Represents used capital equipment dealers. **Publications:** *IAUEDispatch*, monthly. Newsletter.

3053 ■ International Card Manufacturers Association (ICMA)

PO Box 727
Princeton Junction, NJ 08550
Ph: (609)799-4900
Fax: (609)799-7032
E-mail: info@icma.com
URL: http://www.icma.com
Contact: Jeffrey E. Barnhart, Co-Founder/Exec. Dir.

Founded: 1990. **Members:** 230. **Membership Dues:** principal/personalizer, $2,200 (annual) ● associate, $3,000 (annual) ● manufacturer representative/sales agent, $1,650 (annual) ● contributing, $1,100 (annual) ● branch, $1,000 (annual). **Staff:** 8. **Budget:** $800,000. **Multinational. Description:** Manufacturers, industry suppliers and personalizers of plastic cards ranging from non-secure ID and access cards to secure credit cards. Includes cards with smart card chips and magnetic stripes. **Awards:** Elan Awards. **Frequency:** annual. **Type:** recognition. **Recipient:** for card manufacturing excellence and community service ● Spiritus Awards. **Frequency:** annual. **Type:** recognition. **Recipient:** to member companies for outstanding programs that have had a significant impact on the society. **Publications:** *Card Flash*, monthly. Newsletter. **Price:** included in membership dues ● *Card Manufacturing*, 8/year. Magazine. Features information on card manufacturing technology and industry trends. **Price:** $75.00 in U.S. and Canada; included in membership dues; $100.00 outside U.S. and Canada. **Circulation:** 3,000. **Advertising:** accepted. Alternate Formats: online ● *ICMA's Card Manufacturer Product/Service Buyer's Guide*. Membership Directory. **Price:** $500.00 for nonmembers; included in membership dues. Alternate Formats: online. **Conventions/Meetings:** annual Card Manufacturing Expo - show (exhibits).

3054 ■ PET Resin Association (PETRA)

355 Lexington Ave., Ste.1500
New York, NY 10017-6603
Ph: (212)297-2125
E-mail: rvasami@kellencompany.com
URL: http://www.petresin.org
Contact: Ralph Vasami Esq., Exec. Dir.

Founded: 2005. **Multinational. Description:** Represents North American PET (Polyethylene Terephthalate) resin manufacturers. Promotes the growth of PET products. Seeks to educate the public on the benefits and values of PET resin products.

3055 ■ Plastic Lumber Trade Association (PLTA)

PO Box 211
Worthington, MN 56187
Ph: (507)372-5558
Fax: (507)372-5726
E-mail: blarsen@bedfordtech.com
URL: http://www.plasticlumber.org
Contact: Brian Larsen PE, Pres.

Membership Dues: student (non-voting), $50 (annual) ● individual, $250 (annual) ● corporate, $500 (annual). **Description:** Represents and promotes plastic lumber industry; promotes use of recycled plastics.

3056 ■ Plastic and Metal Products Manufacturers Association (PMPMA)

145 W 45th St., Ste.800
New York, NY 10036
Ph: (212)398-5400
Fax: (212)398-7818
Contact: Sheldon M. Edelman, Exec. Dir.

Founded: 1937. **Members:** 120. **Staff:** 7. **Description:** Manufacturers of housewares, toys, handbag accessories and parts, costume jewelry, and optical frames. **Formerly:** Plastic Products Manufacturers Association.

3057 ■ Polyurethane Foam Association (PFA)

c/o Robert J. Luedeka, Exec. Dir.
9724 Kingston Pike, Ste.503
Knoxville, TN 37922
Ph: (865)690-4648
Fax: (865)690-4649
E-mail: rluedeka@pfa.org
URL: http://www.pfa.org
Contact: Robert J. Luedeka, Exec. Dir.

Founded: 1980. **Members:** 51. **Membership Dues:** manufacturing, associate supplier, $1,750 (annual). **Staff:** 2. **Description:** Represents manufacturers of flexible polyurethane foam and suppliers of goods and services to the industry. Provides a forum for discussion of industry issues and makes current information available to members. Monitors legal and regulatory issues. Conducts technical research with other organizations on subjects including test procedures and standards. Compiles volume statistics. **Libraries: Type:** not open to the public. **Holdings:** archival material, audiovisuals, papers. **Awards:** Hall of Fame. **Frequency:** annual. **Type:** recognition. **Computer Services:** Online services, access to archives. **Committees:** Technical. **Absorbed:** (1985) Bureau of Urethane. **Formerly:** (1981) Flexible Polyurethane Foam Manufacturers Association. **Publications:** *INTOUCH*, 1-2/year. Bulletin ● Newsletter. **Price:** free for members. Alternate Formats: online. **Conventions/Meetings:** semiannual conference and executive committee meeting, with technical program and business meetings.

3058 ■ Polyurethane Manufacturers Association (PMA)
6737 W Washington Ave., Ste.1420
Milwaukee, WI 53214
Ph: (414)431-3094
Fax: (414)276-7704
E-mail: info@pmahome.org
URL: http://www.pmahome.org
Contact: Corey D. Barge, Pres.
Founded: 1971. **Members:** 120. **Membership Dues:** processor, $750 (annual) ● supplier (based on annual sales), $1,000-$5,000 (annual) ● academic/research laboratory/consultant, $150 (annual) ● associate, $50 (annual). **Staff:** 4. **Description:** Represents manufacturing companies whose products are primarily of polyurethane raw materials; suppliers to these manufacturers. Aims to improve conditions in the industry and exchange information. Maintains Speaker's Bureau. **Libraries: Type:** reference. **Holdings:** books. **Awards:** Best Paper Award. **Frequency:** semiannual. **Type:** recognition. **Telecommunication Services:** electronic mail, cbarge9199@aol.com. **Divisions:** Marketing; Member Services; Regulatory Affairs; Technology. **Publications:** *Dynamic Solutions*. Brochure. **Price:** free ● *PolyTopics*, bimonthly. Newsletter. **Price:** $40.00. **Conventions/Meetings:** annual meeting (exhibits) ● seminar, covers regulatory compliance and processing techniques.

3059 ■ Society of the Plastics Industry (SPI)
1667 K St. NW, Ste.1000
Washington, DC 20006
Ph: (202)974-5200 (202)974-5222
Fax: (202)296-7005
E-mail: feedback@socplas.org
URL: http://www.plasticsindustry.org
Contact: William R. Carteaux, Pres.
Founded: 1937. **Members:** 1,000. **Staff:** 50. **Regional Groups:** 4. **Description:** Represents manufacturers and processors of molded, extruded, fabricated, laminated, calendared, and reinforced plastics; manufacturers of raw materials, machinery, tools, dies, and molds; testing laboratories; consultants. Serves as the voice of the broad-based plastics industry locally, nationally and internationally, with emphasis on influencing public policy on issues of concern to the industry. Increases global awareness and competitiveness by providing resources to members, while fostering growth of the plastics industry worldwide. Supports research; proposes standards for plastics materials, machinery and products; compiles statistics; sponsors trade shows and organizes competitions. **Awards: Type:** recognition. **Telecommunication Services:** electronic mail, wcarteaux@plasticsindustry.org. **Publications:** *Financial and Operating Ratios*, annual. Survey. Measures significant financial and operating ratios affecting plastics processing firms. Includes survey questionnaire and glossary. **Price:** $150.00 for members; $300.00 for nonmembers ● *Society of the Plastics Industry—Membership and Buyers' Guide*. Membership Directory. Contains list of member companies, their products and services. **Conventions/Meetings:** triennial National Plastics Exposition - trade show (exhibits) ● triennial Plastics USA - trade show.

Play

3060 ■ International Play Equipment Manufacturers Association (IPEMA)
4305 N 6th St., Ste.A
Harrisburg, PA 17110
Ph: (717)238-1744
Free: (888)944-7362
Fax: (717)238-9985
E-mail: info@ipema.org
URL: http://www.ipema.org
Contact: Denise Calabrese, Exec. Dir.
Membership Dues: firm (based on gross annual sales), $750-$1,100 (annual). **Multinational. Description:** Represents and promotes an open market for manufacturers of play equipment. Promotes the importance of play in the development of children. Encourages the creation of safer play environments. Provides a voluntary third party certification program to validate conformance to the ASTM 1487 Playground Equipment Standard and the ASTM 1292 Playground Surfacing Standard. **Telecommunication Services:** electronic mail, admin@ipema.org. **Publications:** *Value of Play*. Brochure. Alternate Formats: online.

Plumbing

3061 ■ American Supply Association (ASA)
222 Merchandise Mart Plz., Ste.1400
Chicago, IL 60654
Ph: (312)464-0090
Fax: (312)464-0091
E-mail: info@asa.net
URL: http://www.asa.net
Contact: Joel Becker, Pres.
Founded: 1969. **Members:** 1,050. **Membership Dues:** wholesale distributor (less than $1 million up to $500 million sales), $550-$11,025 (annual) ● wholesale distributor ($501 million or more sales), $17,640 (annual) ● vendor (based on sales), $880-$4,700 (annual) ● manufacturer representative (based on annual commission), $295-$590 (annual). **Staff:** 22. **Budget:** $8,000,000. **Regional Groups:** 13. **Description:** Represents wholesale, distributors, and manufacturers of plumbing and heating, cooling, pipes, valves, and fittings. Compiles statistics on operating costs and makes occasional studies of compensation, fringe benefits, wages, and salaries. Conducts research studies and forecasting surveys. Offers group insurance. Maintains management institutes, home study courses under the ASA Education Foundation and Endowment program, provides technology and produces a CD-ROM and internet catalogue of manufacturers. **Committees:** Intra Industry Relations; Member Services; Political Action; Technology. **Councils:** PVF Manufactures. **Divisions:** ASA Education Foundation; Associate Member; Industrial Piping; Partners of ASA; Young Executive. **Programs:** Management Institutes; Product Pro CD-ROM Training; Self-Instruction Training; Showroom Video Training. **Formed by Merger of:** Central Supply Association; American Institute of Supply Associations. **Publications:** *Action Plan 2003: Industry Futures Study*. Features annual forecasting survey. **Price:** $25.00 ● *American Supply Association—Membership Directory*, annual. Contains complete list of all members, branches, cross-referenced by city, state, region and division or special interest groups. **Price:** $85.00. **Circulation:** 5,000. **Advertising:** accepted ● *ASA Convention Daily*, 3/year. Published in conjunction with annual convention. **Advertising:** accepted ● *ASA News*, bimonthly. Newsletter. **Circulation:** 25,000. **Advertising:** accepted ● *Report of Operating Performance*, annual ● *Training Manuals*. Features on-sales training and operation. **Conventions/Meetings:** annual convention, conference booth program (exhibits) ● biennial North American Exposition - conference (exhibits) - always even-numbered years ● seminar.

3062 ■ Bath Enclosure Manufacturers Association (BEMA)
c/o Christopher E. Birch, Exec. Dir.
PO Box 4730
Topeka, KS 66604
Ph: (785)273-0393
Fax: (785)273-0393
E-mail: info@bathenclosures.org
URL: http://www.bathenclosures.org
Contact: Christopher E. Birch, Exec. Dir.
Founded: 1992. **Membership Dues:** associate, $600 (annual) ● dealer, $300 (annual) ● active (based on annual sales volume), $500-$1,500 (annual). **Description:** Manufacturers of bath enclosures. Seeks to raise consumer awareness of bath enclosures as an alternative to a traditional shower with shower curtains. Conducts promotional campaigns; facilitates communication and cooperation among members. **Awards:** BEMA Design Awards. **Frequency:** annual. **Type:** recognition. **Recipient:** for excellence in bath enclosure design. **Publications:** *Today's Bath Enclosure*. Brochure.

3063 ■ National Association of Plumbing Specialty Distributors (NAPSD)
Address Unknown since 2007
URL: http://www.napsd.org
Founded: 1983. **Membership Dues:** $350 (annual). **Description:** Represents plumbing specialty distributors. Provides a forum for exchange of ideas; promotes professional relationships. **Computer Services:** Mailing lists. **Publications:** *Newsleak*, QRT. Newsletter. **Circulation:** 150. **Advertising:** not accepted. **Conventions/Meetings:** annual conference (exhibits).

3064 ■ North Central Wholesalers Association (NCWA)
3271 Springcrest Dr.
Hamilton, OH 45011
Ph: (513)895-0695
Free: (800)537-6585
Fax: (513)895-1739
E-mail: dan310@earthlink.net
URL: http://www.asa4.org
Contact: Jim Wilson, Pres.
Founded: 1974. **Members:** 75. **Staff:** 1. **Description:** Wholesale distributors of plumbing, heating, and cooling supplies. Provides a forum for the exchange of ideas and information pertaining to the industry. Conducts surveys; sponsors seminars and educational programs. Compiles statistics; reports on wages and business conditions. **Affiliated With:** American Supply Association. **Formerly:** (2003) Central Wholesalers Association. **Publications:** Newsletter, monthly. **Conventions/Meetings:** annual trade show - always May, in Columbus, OH.

3065 ■ Plumbing and Drainage Institute (PDI)
800 Turnpike St., Ste.300
North Andover, MA 01845
Ph: (978)557-0720
Free: (800)589-8956
Fax: (978)557-0721
E-mail: pdi@pdionline.org
URL: http://www.pdionline.org
Contact: William C. Whitehead, Exec. Dir.
Founded: 1928. **Members:** 15. **Staff:** 1. **Description:** Represents manufacturers of engineered plumbing and drainage products. Promotes the advancement of engineered plumbing products through publicity, public relations, research, and standardization of plumbing requirements. Works on codes and standards for plumbing drainage products. **Awards: Frequency:** annual. **Type:** recognition. **Formerly:** (1949) Plumbing and Drainage Manufacturers Association. **Publications:** *Code Guide 302 and Glossary of Industry Terms*. Alternate Formats: online ● *Guide to Grease Interceptors*. Alternate Formats: online ● *Minimum Space Requirements for Fixture Support*. Alternate Formats: online ● *Testing and Rating Procedure for Grease Interceptor, PDI-G101* ● *Water Hammer Arrestor Standard, WH-201*. **Conventions/Meetings:** annual board meeting.

3066 ■ Plumbing Manufacturers Institute (PMI)
1921 Rohlwing Rd., Unit G
Rolling Meadows, IL 60008
Ph: (847)481-5500
Fax: (847)481-5501
E-mail: pmiadmin@pmihome.org
URL: http://www.pmihome.org
Contact: Ken Martin, Pres.
Founded: 1956. **Members:** 40. **Membership Dues:** regular (based on sales level), $67,500 (annual). **Staff:** 4. **Multinational. Description:** Manufacturers of plumbing products. **Committees:** Codes; Government Affairs; Intra Industry; Standards; Statistics. **Sections:** Non-Residential; Residential. **Formerly:** Brass Gas Stop Institute; Sanitary Brass Institute; Tubular Brass Institute; (1975) Plumbing Brass Institute. **Publications:** *PMI News*. Newsletter. **Conventions/Meetings:** semiannual meeting.

3067 ■ Wholesale Distributors Association (WDA)
10935 Estate Ln., Ste.110
Dallas, TX 75238
Ph: (972)513-1134
Fax: (214)349-7946
URL: http://www.wdainc.com
Contact: Gina Bollinger, Exec. Dir.
Founded: 1929. **Members:** 140. **Staff:** 3. **Description:** Wholesalers representing the plumbing, heating, piping, and cooling industries. Provides a forum for the exchange of information and ideas among members. Represents members in Washington, DC on legislative and regulatory issues. Maintains Wholesale Distributors Association Educational Foundation, which provides scholarships to students pursuing careers in the industry. Conducts seminars and research programs; compiles statistics. **Awards:** Service Excellence Award. **Type:** recognition. **Affiliated With:** American Supply Association. **Publications:** *Framing Supply*. Catalog. Alternate Formats: online ● *WDA News and Views*, bimonthly. Newsletter ● Directory, periodic. **Price:** $50.00. **Conventions/Meetings:** annual meeting.

Police

3068 ■ Community Policing Consortium
1726 M St. NW, Ste.801
Washington, DC 20036
Free: (800)833-3085
Fax: (202)833-9295
E-mail: cpc@communitypolicing.org
URL: http://www.communitypolicing.org
Contact: William Matthews, Exec. Dir.
Founded: 1993. **Description:** Works to deliver community policing training and technical assistance to police departments and sheriff's offices that are designated COPS grantees. **Affiliated With:** International Association of Chiefs of Police; National Organization of Black Law Enforcement Executives; National Sheriffs' Association; Police Executive Research Forum; Police Foundation. **Publications:** *Community Links*. Newsletter. Reports how to make progress through partnerships from the civilian perspective. Alternate Formats: online ● *Community Policing Exchange*. Newsletter. Alternate Formats: online ● *Sheriff Times*. Newsletter. Alternate Formats: online ● *Understanding Community Policing: A Framework for Action*. Monograph. Describes the historical evolution of community policing and its potential for the future. Alternate Formats: online.

Political Products

3069 ■ Political Products Manufacturers Association (PPMA)
Address Unknown since 2007
Founded: 1972. **Members:** 14. **Staff:** 1. **Regional Groups:** 3. **Description:** Manufacturers interested in the political products field. Monitors laws related to campaign spending and practices as they affect the political products field; aids in the marketing of political products. Compiles statistics; conducts research programs. **Committees:** Research.

Pollution Control

3070 ■ Clean Harbors Cooperative (CHC)
4601 Tremley Point Rd.
Linden, NJ 07036
Ph: (908)862-7500
Fax: (908)862-7560
E-mail: chcllc@aol.com
Contact: Dennis McCarthy, Mgr.
Founded: 1977. **Staff:** 4. **Description:** A joint venture of petroleum and energy companies including Amoco, British Petroleum, Chevron, Citgo, Con Edison, Exxon, Mobil, New York Power Authority, Northville, Royal, Shell Oil, Stolt Terminals, Sun Oil, Bayway Refining Co, GATX, Star Enterprise, PSE&G, and Sea River Maritime. Makes available oil spill clean-up equipment and trained equipment operators to member companies in the greater New York Harbor area. Assists nonmember companies for a rental fee at the request of the U.S. Coast Guard.

3071 ■ Institute of Clean Air Companies (ICAC)
1730 M St. NW, Ste.206
Washington, DC 20036
Ph: (202)457-0911
Fax: (202)331-1388
E-mail: dfoerter@icac.com
URL: http://www.icac.com
Contact: Mr. David C. Foerter, Exec. Dir.
Founded: 1960. **Members:** 75. **Membership Dues:** associate (based on sales revenue), $1,500-$5,000 (annual) ● one-time initiation fee, $500 ● regular (based on sales revenue), $52,000 (annual). **Staff:** 4. **Budget:** $600,000. **Description:** Represents air pollution control and measurement equipment manufacturers and service providers for the stationary industrial and electric power generation sources. Promotes accurate and effective communication on air pollution control and measurement technologies between the air pollution control and measurement vendors and environmental regulators, customers and other stakeholders. Promotes the application of these technologies in the market place. **Awards:** Outstanding Service Award. **Frequency:** annual. **Type:** recognition ● President's Award. **Frequency:** annual. **Type:** recognition. **Telecommunication Services:** electronic mail, icacinfo@icac.com. **Divisions:** Emission Measuring; Industrial Source Controls; Mercury Control; NOX Control; Particulate Control; SO2 Control; VOC and HAP Control. **Affiliated With:** American Coal Council. **Formerly:** (1992) Industrial Gas Cleaning Institute. **Publications:** *Clean Air Technology News*, semiannual. Newsletter ● *Executive Update*, weekly. Updates current events of interest to the air pollution control industry. Provided with membership. ● *ICAC—Organization Directory*, annual. Membership Directory ● Also publishes technical guidelines for each division and an annual market study. **Conventions/Meetings:** annual conference (exhibits) ● meeting and conference, product division and technical - 6-8/year.

3072 ■ Manufacturers of Emission Controls Association (MECA)
1730 M St. NW, Ste.206
Washington, DC 20036
Ph: (202)296-4797
Fax: (202)331-1388
E-mail: info@meca.org
URL: http://www.meca.org
Contact: Dale L. McKinnon, Exec. Dir.
Founded: 1976. **Members:** 44. **Description:** Manufacturers of automobile exhaust and evaporative control devices and stationary source catalytic controls. Represents the emission controls industry before all levels of government; maintains close contact with policy planners and technical experts of governmental agencies worldwide concerned with environmental issues and regulations. Acts as a central source of information on emission technology and industry capabilities and views. Monitors and reports on congressional actions that affect industry; provides technical and industry information to congressional committees involved in environmental and related legislation. Consults with other industry organizations concerned with national environmental issues. Provides the media with background, corrective, and explanatory data. Undertakes special studies on issues of major importance to the industry. **Conventions/Meetings:** bimonthly meeting.

3073 ■ Spill Control Association of America (SCAA)
2105 Laurel Bush Rd., Ste.200
Bel Air, MD 21015
Ph: (443)640-1085
Fax: (443)640-1086
E-mail: info@scaa-spill.org
URL: http://www.scaa-spill.org
Contact: John Parker, Pres.
Founded: 1973. **Members:** 150. **Membership Dues:** full, $1,250 (annual) ● associate, $500 (annual) ● governmental, educational, $250 (annual). **Description:** Third party contractors; manufacturers or suppliers of pollution control and containment equipment; individuals in private or governmental capacities involved with spill clean-up and containment operations; associate companies. Aims to provide information on the oil and hazardous material emergency response and remediation industry's practices, trends, and achievements; to establish liaison with local, state, and federal government agencies responsible for laws and regulations regarding pollution caused by oil and hazardous materials; to cooperate in the development of industry programs and efforts so that pollutants are properly controlled and removed from land and water. Provides certification for hazardous material technicians. Maintains Spill Control Institute, Technical Services Division; collects and disseminates educational and technical information. Operates speakers' bureau; conducts research. Maintains placement service. **Libraries:** **Type:** reference. **Formerly:** (1978) Oil Spill Control Association of American. **Publications:** *Analysis of Federal Standard for Hazardous Waste Worker Training* ● *Spill Briefs*, weekly. Newsletter. Provides current information, issues, and regulation regarding hazardous materials, oil spill cleanup, and the response industry. **Price:** free for members ● Papers ● Reports ● Videos. **Conventions/Meetings:** annual Homeland Environmental Security Conference (exhibits) ● seminar.

Postcards

3074 ■ Post Card and Souvenir Distributors Association (PCSDA)
2105 Laurel Bush Rd., Ste.200
Bel Air, MD 21015
Ph: (443)640-1055
Fax: (443)640-1031
E-mail: steve@ksgroup.org
URL: http://www.postcardcentral.org
Contact: Steven T. King CAE, Exec. VP
Founded: 1973. **Members:** 200. **Membership Dues:** principal, $350 (annual) ● associate, $50 (annual) ● affiliate, $200 (annual). **Staff:** 2. **Description:** Represents distributors and manufacturers of post cards, souvenirs, and novelty items. **Awards:** Distributor of the Year. **Frequency:** annual. **Type:** recognition. **Recipient:** for the best postcard and souvenir designs ● Industry Awards. **Frequency:** annual. **Type:** recognition. **Recipient:** for the best postcard and souvenir designs ● Printer of the Year. **Frequency:** annual. **Type:** recognition. **Recipient:** for the best postcard and souvenir designs ● Souvenir Supplier of the Year. **Frequency:** annual. **Type:** recognition. **Recipient:** for the best postcard and souvenir designs. **Formerly:** (2000) Post Card Distributors Association of North America. **Publications:** *Post Card Letter*, quarterly. Newsletter. Keeps members informed about association events, legal and legislative issues, and trends affecting the distribution and manufacturing industries. **Price:** included in membership dues. **Advertising:** accepted ● Surveys. **Conventions/Meetings:** annual convention and trade show (exhibits) - 2008 Sept. 14-17, Portland, OR - **Avg. Attendance:** 350.

Power

3075 ■ Power Sources Manufacturers Association (PSMA)
PO Box 418
Mendham, NJ 07945-0418
Ph: (973)543-9660
Fax: (973)543-6207
E-mail: power@psma.com
URL: http://www.psma.com
Contact: Mr. Joseph Horzepa, Exec. Dir.
Founded: 1984. **Members:** 155. **Membership Dues:** regular, $650-$2,250 (annual) ● associate, $600 (an-

nual) ● affiliate, $125 (annual). **Staff:** 2. **Budget:** $100,000. **Multinational. Description:** Manufacturers and users of power sources and conversion equipment, organizations involved in serving the power industry, individuals, universities and other organizations involved in education or instruction in power related subjects. Conducts research and educational programs. **Awards:** PSMA APEC Attendance Education Grant. **Frequency:** annual. **Type:** monetary. **Recipient:** for undergraduate or graduate students to reimburse some of the expenses related to attending the APEC conference ● PSMA Education Award. **Frequency:** annual. **Type:** monetary. **Recipient:** to individuals and companies that foster awareness of the power electronics industry, especially in the kindergarten through undergraduate years of education. **Committees:** Alternative Energy; Battery; BMPS; Capacitor; Energy Efficiency; Executive Event; Industry-Education; Magnetics; Manufacturing; Marketing; Power Electronics Packaging; Semiconductor. **Publications:** *Power Technology Roadmap From APEC*, triennial. Report. **Price:** $1,995.00 for nonmembers; $495.00 for members. Alternate Formats: CD-ROM ● *Technical Reports*, periodic. Contains technical reports and studies. ● *Update*, quarterly. Newsletter. Includes news on the association, members, publications and meetings. **Price:** free. **Circulation:** 700. Alternate Formats: online. **Conventions/Meetings:** Applied Power Electronics Conference & Exposition - international conference, technical papers presented (exhibits).

Press

3076 ■ American Agricultural Editors' Association (AAEA)
PO Box 156
New Prague, MN 56071
Ph: (952)758-6502
Fax: (952)758-5813
E-mail: ageditors@aol.com
URL: http://www.ageditors.com
Contact: Den Gardner, Exec. Dir.
Founded: 1921. **Members:** 380. **Membership Dues:** student, $25 (annual) ● active, affiliate, $165 (annual) ● retired, $80 (annual) ● life, $525. **Staff:** 2. **Budget:** $125,000. **Description:** Editors and editorial staff members of farm publications; affiliate members are agricultural public relations and advertising personnel, and state and national agricultural officials. Maintains the AAEA Professional Improvement Foundation. Conducts educational programs. **Awards:** AAEA Design Awards. **Frequency:** annual. **Type:** recognition. **Recipient:** for members ● AAEA Photography Awards. **Frequency:** annual. **Type:** recognition. **Recipient:** for members ● AAEA Writing Awards. **Frequency:** annual. **Type:** recognition. **Recipient:** for members ● Distinguished Service Award. **Frequency:** annual. **Type:** recognition. **Recipient:** for an individual with significant contributions to the agriculture industry ● Lifetime Achievement Award. **Frequency:** annual. **Type:** recognition. **Recipient:** to a member or former member providing outstanding service to the organization over a sustained period of time. **Computer Services:** Mailing lists, of members. **Boards:** Advisory. **Committees:** ByLine; Design Contest; Distinguished Service Award; International; Member Services; Photo Contest; Sponsorship; Writing Contest. **Publications:** *American Agricultural Editors' Association—Directory of Members*, annual. Membership Directory. **Price:** $125.00 for nonmembers ● *The Byline*, 10/year. Newsletter. Includes membership activities. **Price:** included in membership dues. **Circulation:** 560. **Conventions/Meetings:** annual Agricultural Media Summit - meeting (exhibits) - every last week of July or first week of August.

3077 ■ American Association of Dental Editors (AADE)
750 N Lincoln Memorial Dr., Ste.422
Milwaukee, WI 53202
Ph: (414)272-2759
Fax: (414)272-2754
E-mail: aade@dentaleditors.org
URL: http://www.dentaleditors.org
Contact: Detlef B. Moore, Exec. Dir.
Founded: 1931. **Members:** 400. **Membership Dues:** publication, $145 (annual) ● publication associate, individual, $50 (annual) ● student publication associate, $30 (annual) ● student publication, $40 (annual) ● affiliate/international, $55 (annual). **Staff:** 2. **Budget:** $35,000. **Description:** Seeks to promote and advance dental journalism. **Libraries: Type:** reference. **Holdings:** archival material, artwork. **Subjects:** dental. **Awards:** Distinguished Service Award. **Frequency:** annual. **Type:** recognition. **Recipient:** for outstanding individual. **Programs:** Certified Dental Editor. **Projects:** Internet Education Information. **Publications:** *Editors' Newsletter*, quarterly. Covers new developments in dental journalism. **Price:** included in membership dues; $40.00 /year for nonmembers. **Circulation:** 350. Alternate Formats: online. **Conventions/Meetings:** annual Editors' Conference, held in conjunction with the American Dental Association's annual session.

3078 ■ American Association of Independent News Distributors (AAIND)
c/o Erik Zenhausern, Exec. Dir.
93 Second St.
Harrison, NY 10528
Free: (877)GO-AAIND
Fax: (914)777-0406
E-mail: erikz@aaind.org
URL: http://aaind.org
Contact: Erik Zenhausern, Exec. Dir.
Founded: 1971. **Members:** 700. **Membership Dues:** associate, $400 (annual) ● sponsor, $2,000 (annual) ● distributor (based on annual sales and total distribution), $400-$600 (annual). **Staff:** 5. **Regional Groups:** 8. **Description:** Represents independent newspaper distributors and dealers. Conducts seminars. **Awards:** Lifetime Achievement. **Frequency:** biennial. **Type:** recognition. **Programs:** Bonding. **Publications:** *American Association of Independent News Distributors—News*, quarterly. Newsletter. Contains association and industry news. **Price:** available to members only. **Circulation:** 1,500. **Advertising:** accepted. Alternate Formats: online. **Conventions/Meetings:** semiannual meeting (exhibits).

3079 ■ American Association of Sunday and Feature Editors (AASFE)
c/o Kalyani Chadha, Exec. Dir.
Coll. of Journalism
Univ. of Maryland
1117 Journalism Bldg.
College Park, MD 20742-7111
Ph: (301)314-2631
E-mail: kchadha@jmail.umd.edu
URL: http://www.aasfe.org
Contact: Kalyani Chadha, Exec. Dir.
Founded: 1947. **Members:** 250. **Membership Dues:** active (for papers with 300,000 circulation), $150 (annual) ● active (for papers with 75,001-299,999 circulation), $125 (annual) ● active (for papers with 75,000 and under circulation), $75 (annual). **Staff:** 1. **Description:** Represents Sunday and feature newspaper editors. **Awards:** Excellence in Feature Writing Contest. **Frequency:** annual. **Type:** monetary ● Minority Scholarships. **Type:** scholarship. **Publications:** *Feedback*, quarterly. Newsletter ● *Style*, semiannual. Magazine. **Conventions/Meetings:** annual Excellence in Feature Writing Contest - competition ● annual meeting - always fall.

3080 ■ American Copy Editors Society (ACES)
c/o Carol DeMasters, Admin.
7 Avenida Vista Grande, Ste.B7, No. 467
Santa Fe, NM 87508
E-mail: carolafj@execpc.com
URL: http://www.copydesk.org
Contact: Chris Wienandt, Pres.
Founded: 1997. **Membership Dues:** full, associate, $55 (annual) ● student, $35 (annual) ● scholastic, $10 (annual) ● life, $1,000. **Description:** Dedicated to improving quality of journalism and working standards of journalists. **Awards:** Aubespin Scholarship. **Frequency:** annual. **Type:** scholarship. **Recipient:** for students ● Robinson Prize. **Frequency:** annual. **Type:** recognition. **Recipient:** to a person whose exemplary work upholds the craft. **Computer Services:** Online services, job postings. **Committees:** Conference; Contest; Planning. **Publications:** Membership Directory. **Price:** included in membership dues ● Newsletter, quarterly. **Price:** included in membership dues. **Conventions/Meetings:** annual conference.

3081 ■ American Jewish Press Association (AJPA)
PO Box 19121
Washington, DC 20036
Ph: (202)250-6144
Fax: (202)250-6151
E-mail: info@ajpa.org
URL: http://www.ajpa.org
Contact: Toby Dershowitz, Exec. Dir.
Founded: 1943. **Members:** 250. **Membership Dues:** full (based upon the circulation), $465-$645 (annual) ● associate, $275 (annual) ● individual, $150 (annual) ● affiliate, $300 (annual). **Staff:** 2. **Budget:** $80,000. **Description:** Seeks to raise and maintain the standards of professional Jewish journalism. Creates instruments of information for the American Jewish community and provides a forum for the exchange of ideas and information among Jewish publications and journalists in the U.S. and Canada. **Awards:** Simon Rockower Memorial Awards. **Frequency:** annual. **Type:** recognition. **Recipient:** for excellence in Jewish journalism; for members only. **Computer Services:** Online services, member directory. **Telecommunication Services:** electronic mail, toby@ajpa.org. **Committees:** Advertising; Awards; Editorial. **Formerly:** American Association of English Jewish Newspapers. **Publications:** *Advisories*, periodic ● *Roster*, annual. Membership Directory. **Price:** $10.00. **Conventions/Meetings:** biennial Editorial, Freelance, and Business - meeting and workshop ● annual meeting and conference.

3082 ■ American Medical Writers Association (AMWA)
40 W Gude Dr., No. 101
Rockville, MD 20850-1192
Ph: (301)294-5303
Fax: (301)294-9006
E-mail: amwa@amwa.org
URL: http://www.amwa.org
Contact: Ms. Donna Munari, Exec. Dir.
Founded: 1940. **Members:** 5,300. **Membership Dues:** individual, $135 (annual) ● student, $45 (annual). **Staff:** 8. **Budget:** $1,300,000. **Regional Groups:** 19. **Description:** Medical writers, editors, marketing and public relations specialists, pharmaceutical personnel, educators, publishers, researchers, translators, physicians and other health care professionals, scriptwriters, and others concerned with communication in medicine and allied health professions and sciences. Provides educational programming and other resources for medical communicators. Conducts annual conference with more than 100 open sessions and workshops; an educational certificate program; chapter conferences with educational programs; on-site education offered at pharmaceutical and other large companies; quarterly journal; job services. **Awards:** Eric W. Martin Award for Excellence in Medical Writing. **Frequency:** annual. **Type:** trophy. **Recipient:** for article, brochure, or monograph on a topic related to pharmaceutical sciences ● John P. McGovern Medal. **Frequency:** annual. **Type:** medal. **Recipient:** for distinctive contributions to the association ● Medical Book Awards. **Frequency:** annual. **Type:** recognition. **Recipient:** for medical books ● Walter C. Alvarez Award. **Frequency:** annual. **Type:** recognition. **Recipient:** for excellence in communicating health care development and concepts to the public. **Formerly:** (1948) Mississippi Valley Medical Editors' Association. **Publications:** *American Medical Writers Association Journal*, quarterly. Includes calendar of events, book reviews, obituaries, and member news. **Price:** included in membership dues; $35.00 /year for nonmembers. ISSN: 0090-046X. **Advertising:** ac-

cepted. Also Cited As: *AMWA Journal* ● *American Medical Writers Association—Membership Directory*, annual. Arranged alphabetically, by chapter, and by primary section affiliation. **Price:** included in membership dues; $100.00/copy for nonmembers. **Circulation:** 4,500 ● *Biomedical Communication: Selected AMWA Workshops*. Book. Includes 24 manuscripts of AMWA's workshop program, written by the workshop leaders. **Price:** $35.00 for members; $75.00 for nonmembers. **Conventions/Meetings:** annual conference (exhibits) - 2008 Oct. 23-25, Louisville, KY - **Avg. Attendance:** 900.

3083 ■ American News Women's Club (ANWC)
1607 22nd St. NW
Washington, DC 20008
Ph: (202)332-6770
Fax: (202)265-6092
E-mail: anwclub@covad.net
URL: http://www.anwc.org
Contact: Theresa Werner, Pres.
Founded: 1932. **Members:** 300. **Membership Dues:** professional (26-36 years old), $75 (annual) ● affiliate, associate, $165 (annual) ● full-time student, $25 (annual) ● out of state, retired, professional (25 years old and below), $50 (annual) ● professional (37 years and above), $140 (annual). **Staff:** 1. **Description:** Promotes professional pursuits and good fellowship among members; provides access to newsmakers and a place for members to find helpful assistance and encouragement in their professional development. **Libraries: Type:** open to the public. **Holdings:** 1,500. **Subjects:** biography, journalism. **Awards:** American News Women's Club Newsperson of the Year Award. **Frequency:** annual. **Type:** recognition. **Computer Services:** Online services, message board. **Telecommunication Services:** electronic mail, theresa_werner@hotmail.com. **Committees:** Authors; Congressional Liaison; Development; Education; Embassy; Professional Activities; Special Events. **Formerly:** (1981) American Newspaper Women's Club. **Publications:** *American News Women's Club Directory*, annual. **Price:** $10.00. **Advertising:** accepted ● *Shop Talk*, monthly. Newsletter. **Conventions/Meetings:** monthly Program Series - meeting, with lectures, discussions, and presentations by speakers in fields of literature, communications, politics, government, and journalism ● annual Roast and Toast - dinner, benefits scholarship fund.

3084 ■ American Society of Business Publication Editors (ASBPE)
214 N Hale St.
Wheaton, IL 60187
Ph: (630)510-4588
Fax: (630)510-4501
E-mail: info@asbpe.org
URL: http://www.asbpe.org
Contact: Janet Svazas, Exec. Dir.
Founded: 1964. **Members:** 750. **Membership Dues:** regular, freelancers, affiliate, $75 (annual). **Staff:** 3. **Local Groups:** 14. **Description:** Represents editors and writers working for business, trade, association, professional, technical print magazines and newsletters and Internet publications. Serves to enhance editorial standards and quality and raise the level of publication management skills of its members. **Libraries: Type:** not open to the public. **Holdings:** articles, reports. **Subjects:** information to help editorial members. **Awards:** Best Blog. **Frequency:** annual. **Type:** recognition ● Best Digital Magazine. **Frequency:** annual. **Type:** recognition ● Best E-Newsletter. **Frequency:** annual. **Type:** recognition ● Design Excellence. **Frequency:** annual. **Type:** recognition ● Editorial Excellence. **Frequency:** annual. **Type:** recognition ● Lifetime Achievement Award. **Frequency:** annual. **Type:** recognition ● Magazine of the Year. **Frequency:** annual. **Type:** recognition ● Stephen Barr Award. **Frequency:** annual. **Type:** monetary. **Recipient:** for best feature writer ● Web Site of the Year. **Frequency:** annual. **Type:** recognition ● Young Leaders Scholarship. **Frequency:** annual. **Type:** scholarship. **Computer Services:** Online services, discussion forum, members database, original editorial research. **Committees:** Awards; Conference; Marketing; Research. **Formerly:** (1965) Society of Business Magazine Editors; (2000) American Society of Business Press Editors. **Publications:** *Area Chapter Meetings from Around the Country*, periodic ● *Editor's Notes*, bimonthly. Newsletter. **Price:** free for members. **Circulation:** 700. **Advertising:** accepted. Alternate Formats: online ● *Online Membership Directory*, periodic. **Price:** free for members. Alternate Formats: online. **Conventions/Meetings:** annual National Awards of Excellence Banquet - banquet and competition, for business magazine and web editorial and design excellence (exhibits) ● annual National Editorial Conference - conference and luncheon, educational and networking conference with workshops and seminars (exhibits) ● periodic regional meeting, city chapter meetings with speakers (exhibits).

3085 ■ American Society of Magazine Editors (ASME)
810 7th Ave., 24th Fl.
New York, NY 10019
Ph: (212)872-3700
Fax: (212)906-0128
E-mail: asme@magazine.org
URL: http://www.magazine.org/Editorial
Contact: Marlene Kahan, Exec. Dir.
Founded: 1963. **Members:** 900. **Membership Dues:** regular, $375 (annual) ● associate, $175 (annual). **Staff:** 43. **Description:** Represents magazine editors. Sponsors annual editorial internship program for college juniors and the National Magazine Awards. **Publications:** none. **Awards:** Lifetime Achievement. **Frequency:** annual. **Type:** recognition. **Recipient:** for individual ● Magazine Editor's Hall of Fame. **Frequency:** annual. **Type:** recognition. **Recipient:** for a select group of magazine editor ● National Magazine Award. **Frequency:** annual. **Type:** recognition. **Affiliated With:** Magazine Publishers of America. **Conventions/Meetings:** annual meeting.

3086 ■ American Society of Newspaper Editors (ASNE)
11690B Sunrise Valley Dr.
Reston, VA 20191-1409
Ph: (703)453-1122 (703)453-1120
Fax: (703)453-1133
E-mail: asne@asne.org
URL: http://www.asne.org
Contact: Scott Bosley, Exec. Dir.
Founded: 1922. **Members:** 800. **Membership Dues:** retired, $155 (annual) ● group executive/news service executive, $675 (annual) ● regular (based on circulation), $195-$675 (annual). **Staff:** 10. **Budget:** $1,264,500. **Description:** Directs editors who determine editorial and news policies of daily newspapers and news gathering operations of daily newspapers. **Libraries: Type:** by appointment only. **Holdings:** books, periodicals, reports. **Awards:** Distinguished Writing, Jesse Laventhol Prizes, Community Service Photojournalism. **Frequency:** annual. **Type:** monetary. **Recipient:** for outstanding writers in various categories; community service photojournalism ● Editorial Leadership. **Frequency:** annual. **Type:** recognition. **Telecommunication Services:** electronic mail, sbosley@asne.org. **Committees:** American Editor; Awards; Convention Program; Craft Development; Diversity; Education for Journalism; Ethics and Values; Freedom of Information; High School Journalism; International; Membership; Multimedia; Nominations; Readership Issues; Small Newspapers; Writing Awards. **Publications:** *The American Editor*, semimonthly, except July-August. Magazine. Covers major press controversies, newspaper editing and writing, ethics, management, and minority recruitment. **Price:** $29.00/year. ISSN: 1083-5210. **Circulation:** 1,600. Alternate Formats: online ● *ASNE Proceedings*, annual. Covers controversies concerning journalism education, ethics, and credibility. Includes committee reports and membership roster. **Price:** $25.00/year. **Conventions/Meetings:** annual convention.

3087 ■ Arab-American Press Guild (AAPG)
13313 Debell St.
Arleta, CA 91331
Ph: (818)896-5860
Fax: (818)896-5860
E-mail: yhaddad29@hotmail.com
Contact: Yousef Elia Haddad, Pres.
Founded: 1985. **Members:** 124. **Membership Dues:** active, $50 (annual) ● in-active, $25 (annual). **Description:** Arab-American members of the press, public relations, and related journalistic services community united to promote Arab-American understanding. Purposes are to: serve Arab-American journalists; coordinate the media of the Arab-American community; bridge the understanding to the Arab world press in America. Operates speakers' bureau; compiles statistics. Conducts seminars on the role of the Arab-American press in the U.S. and ways to enhance it. Maintains data on all Arab-American presses in the U.S. **Awards: Frequency:** annual. **Type:** scholarship. **Recipient:** for Arab-American students majoring in journalism. **Committees:** Public Relations; Research; Scholarship. **Publications:** *Arab-American Press Guide*, biennial. Directory. **Advertising:** accepted ● *Arab-American Press Guild News Letter*, bimonthly. **Conventions/Meetings:** annual convention (exhibits) ● monthly meeting.

3088 ■ Asian American Journalists Association (AAJA)
1182 Market St., Ste.320
San Francisco, CA 94102
Ph: (415)346-2051
Fax: (415)346-6343
E-mail: national@aaja.org
URL: http://www.aaja.org
Contact: Jeanne Mariani-Belding, Pres.
Founded: 1981. **Members:** 2,000. **Membership Dues:** full, working journalist/associate, working nonjournalist, $55 (annual) ● gold full/gold associate, $80 (annual) ● student/retired, $20 (annual) ● full, option/associate, $100 (biennial) ● corporate, news media only, $1,500 (annual). **Staff:** 8. **Budget:** $1,200,000. **Regional Groups:** 19. **Local Groups:** 19. **Description:** Represents more than 2,000 members. Serves Asian Americans and Pacific Islanders by encouraging young people to consider journalism as a career, developing managers in the media industry, and promoting fair and accurate news coverage. Serves as an alliance partner in UNITY Journalists of Color, along with the Native American Journalists Association, National Association of Hispanic Journalists, and National Association of Black Journalists. **Awards:** Award of Excellence. **Frequency:** annual. **Type:** recognition. **Recipient:** for journalistic achievement ● Student Scholarships. **Frequency:** annual. **Type:** scholarship. **Publications:** *All American: How to Cover Asian America*. Handbook. Alternate Formats: online ● *Dateline*, quarterly. Newsletter. Alternate Formats: online ● Booklets. **Conventions/Meetings:** annual convention, includes job fair (exhibits) ● annual Journalism Opportunities Conference ● periodic workshop.

3089 ■ Associated Press (AP)
450 W 33rd St.
New York, NY 10001
Ph: (212)621-1500
Fax: (212)621-1955
E-mail: info@ap.org
URL: http://www.ap.org
Contact: William Dean Singleton, Chm.
Founded: 1846. **Members:** 1,716. **Staff:** 3,374. **Budget:** $417,964. **State Groups:** 50. **Languages:** Danish, English, French, German, Spanish, Swedish. **Description:** News cooperative that gathers and disseminates world, national, regional, and state news, pictures, and audio reports. Information travels via satellites and landlines to 1,500 newspapers and 5,700 radio and television stations in the United States, and to more than 10,000 newspapers and broadcast stations worldwide. **Publications:** *The AP World*, quarterly. **Conventions/Meetings:** annual meeting.

3090 ■ Associated Press Managing Editors (APME)
19 Commerce Ct. W
Cranbury, NJ 08512-2416
Ph: (212)621-1838

Fax: (212)506-6102
E-mail: apme@ap.org
URL: http://www.apme.com
Contact: Karen Magnuson, Pres.

Founded: 1933. **Members:** 1,850. **Membership Dues:** supporting, retiree, educator, associate, $100 (annual) ● Editor's Circle, $250 (annual). **Description:** Represents managing editors or executives on the news or editorial staff of The Associated Press newspapers. Aims to: advance the journalism profession; examine the news and other services of the Associated Press in order to provide member newspapers with services that best suit their needs; provide a means of cooperation between the management and the editorial representatives of the members of the Associated Press. Maintains committees dealing with newspapers and news services. **Awards:** Freedom of Information Award. **Type:** recognition ● Public Service Award. **Type:** recognition. **Recipient:** to Associated or Canadian Press member newspapers for meritorious service to the community, state or nation ● **Type:** recognition. **Recipient:** for top performance. **Telecommunication Services:** electronic mail, kmagnuso@democratandchronicle.com. **Publications:** *APME News*, bimonthly. Newsletter ● Reports. **Conventions/Meetings:** annual conference.

3091 ■ Association of Alternative Newsweeklies (AAN)
1250 Eye St. NW, Ste.804
Washington, DC 20005
Ph: (202)289-8484
Fax: (202)289-2004
E-mail: web@aan.org
URL: http://www.aan.org
Contact: Mr. Richard Karpel, Exec. Dir.

Founded: 1978. **Members:** 126. **Membership Dues:** associate, $300 (annual). **Staff:** 6. **Budget:** $1,300,000. **Description:** Members include Village Voice, L.A. Weekly, Chicago Reader, and Washington City Paper. Provides members with information and communication relevant to the business of publishing an alternative newspaper. Holds annual convention. Compiles financial standards report, publishes monthly newsletter, and administers annual editorial awards contest. **Libraries: Type:** reference; not open to the public; by appointment only. **Holdings:** clippings, periodicals. **Subjects:** member publications. **Awards:** Alternative Newsweekly Awards. **Frequency:** annual. **Type:** recognition. **Recipient:** for editorial excellence ● Diversity Internship Grant. **Frequency:** semiannual. **Type:** grant. **Recipient:** to minority journalists. **Additional Websites:** http://www.altweeklies.com. **Telecommunication Services:** electronic mail, rkarpel@aan.org. **Publications:** *AAN Annual Directory*, annual. **Price:** $25.00. **Circulation:** 2,500 ● Newsletters, 1-7/week. Features headlines and links from different sections to its website. Alternate Formats: online. **Conventions/Meetings:** annual convention (exhibits).

3092 ■ Association of American Editorial Cartoonists (AAEC)
3899 N Front St.
Harrisburg, PA 17110
Ph: (717)703-3069
Fax: (717)703-3001
URL: http://www.editorialcartoonists.com
Contact: Rob Rogers, Pres.

Founded: 1957. **Members:** 300. **Membership Dues:** regular/associate, $150 (annual) ● retired, $60 (annual) ● student, $65 (annual). **Staff:** 1. **Budget:** $60,000. **Description:** Active and retired editorial cartoonists for newspapers, magazines, and syndicates. Promotes and encourages the art of editorial cartooning nationally. **Computer Services:** Mailing lists. **Publications:** *Association of American Editorial Cartoonists—Notebook*, quarterly. Newsletter. Contains membership activities. **Price:** included in membership dues; $40.00 for nonmembers. **Circulation:** 400. **Advertising:** accepted. Alternate Formats: online ● *Best Editorial Cartoons of the Year*, annual ● Membership Directory, biennial. **Conventions/Meetings:** annual convention.

3093 ■ Association of Earth Science Editors (AESE)
c/o Mary Ann Schmidt
554 Chess St.
Pittsburgh, PA 15205
E-mail: llindsay@sunbeltpub.com
URL: http://www.aese.org
Contact: Lowell Lindsay, Treas.

Founded: 1967. **Members:** 250. **Membership Dues:** individual, $35 (annual) ● student, $15 (annual). **Staff:** 1. **Budget:** $10,000. **Multinational. Description:** Editors, managing editors, and others in editorial management positions in the field of earth science publications; interested individuals. Seeks to provide efficient means for cooperation among earth science editors and to promote effective publishing of journals, reviews, monograph series, maps, abstract journals and services, indexes, micro cards, and other publications that disseminate information on the earth sciences. **Awards:** Outstanding Editorial or Publishing Contributions Award. **Frequency:** annual. **Type:** recognition. **Recipient:** for individuals ● Outstanding Publication Award. **Frequency:** annual. **Type:** recognition. **Recipient:** for publishers. **Affiliated With:** American Association for the Advancement of Science; American Geological Institute; Council of Science Editors; Geological Society of America. **Publications:** *AESE Directory*, annual. Membership Directory. **Price:** included in membership dues. **Circulation:** 400 ● *Blueline*, quarterly. Newsletter. Includes member news, book reviews, and calendar of events. **Price:** included in membership dues. **Circulation:** 400. **Advertising:** accepted. Alternate Formats: online. **Conventions/Meetings:** annual conference (exhibits) - in October.

3094 ■ Association of Food Journalists (AFJ)
c/o Carol DeMasters, Exec. Dir.
7 Avienda Vista Grande, Ste.B7 467
Santa Fe, NM 87508-9199
E-mail: caroldemasters@yahoo.com
URL: http://www.afjonline.com
Contact: Carol DeMasters, Exec. Dir.

Founded: 1974. **Members:** 300. **Membership Dues:** active/associate, $75 (annual) ● retired, $37 (annual). **Staff:** 1. **Regional Groups:** 5. **Multinational. Description:** Represents individuals employed as food journalists by newspapers, magazines, internet services, and broadcasters; freelance food journalists. Aims to encourage communication and professional development among food journalists and to increase members' knowledge of food and food-related issues. Promotes professional ethical standards. **Awards:** AFJ Awards Competition. **Frequency:** annual. **Type:** monetary. **Recipient:** for excellence in reporting, writing, and photography in all media. **Formerly:** Newspaper Food Editors and Writers Association. **Publications:** Newsletter, monthly. **Price:** included in membership dues. **Conventions/Meetings:** annual conference and symposium - usually autumn.

3095 ■ Association of Health Care Journalists (AHCJ)
10 Neff Hall
Columbia, MO 65211
Ph: (573)884-5606
Fax: (573)884-5609
E-mail: info@healthjournalism.org
URL: http://www.healthjournalism.org
Contact: Trudy Lieberman, Pres.

Membership Dues: active, $60 (annual) ● active, $108 (biennial) ● active, $162 (triennial) ● associate, $90 (annual) ● student in U.S., $30 (annual) ● active corporate, $54 (annual). **Multinational. Description:** Represents and supports journalists who cover health, medicine, and business of health care. **Awards:** AHCJ Excellence in Health Care Journalism Award. **Frequency:** annual. **Type:** recognition. **Computer Services:** Online services, listserv. **Committees:** Conference Program; Freedom of Information; Freelance Affairs. **Also Known As:** (2004) Center for Excellence in Health Care Journalism. **Publications:** Membership Directory ● Newsletter, quarterly. **Conventions/Meetings:** annual conference (exhibits).

3096 ■ Association for Women Journalists (AWJ)
PO Box 2199
Fort Worth, TX 76113
Ph: (817)685-3876
E-mail: jessamybrown@star-telegram.com
URL: http://www.awjdfw.org
Contact: Jessamy Brown, Co-Pres.

Founded: 1988. **Members:** 150. **Membership Dues:** journalist, $30 (annual) ● student, $20 (annual). **Description:** Men and women in the print and broadcast media, newsroom support personnel, freelance journalists, and journalism students and academics. Seeks to support women in journalism and promote respectful treatment of women by the news media. Facilitates communication and cooperation among members; conducts educational and continuing professional development programs. **Publications:** *Notebook*. Newsletter.

3097 ■ Association for Women in Sports Media (AWSM)
3899 N Front St.
Harrisburg, PA 17110
Ph: (717)703-3086
E-mail: needalede@comcast.net
URL: http://www.awsmonline.org
Contact: Vicki Michaelis, Pres.

Founded: 1987. **Members:** 450. **Membership Dues:** professional, $50 (annual) ● student, $25 (annual). **Multinational. Description:** Women sportswriters, copy editors, broadcasters and media relations directors; interested men and women. Supports and fosters advancement of women involved in sports media. Sponsors internship/scholarship program. Maintains job bank. **Awards:** Broadcasting Scholarship/Internship. **Frequency:** annual. **Type:** scholarship. **Recipient:** for female college students ● Copy Editing Scholarship/Internship. **Frequency:** annual. **Type:** scholarship. **Recipient:** for female college students ● Mary Garber Scholarship/Internship (Sportswriting). **Frequency:** annual. **Type:** scholarship. **Recipient:** for female college students ● Pioneer Award. **Frequency:** annual. **Type:** recognition. **Recipient:** for an individual in sports media ● Public Relations Scholarship/Internships. **Type:** scholarship. **Publications:** *AWSM Newsletter*, quarterly. **Price:** included in membership dues. **Circulation:** 600 ● Directory, annual. **Price:** included in membership dues. **Conventions/Meetings:** annual convention, job fair (exhibits) ● annual convention.

3098 ■ Association of Young Journalists (AYJ)
1117 Journalism Bldg.
Univ. of Maryland
Philip Merrill Coll. of Journalism
College Park, MD 20742-7111
E-mail: youngjournos@comcast.net
Contact: Jenny Medina, Pres.-Elect

Founded: 2003. **Members:** 900. **State Groups:** 21. **Multinational. Description:** Creates and formalizes a community of young journalists of all backgrounds. Promotes and facilitates opportunities for the professional development and growth of journalists in their first decade in the journalism career. Provides a voice for young journalists. Upholds the high standards and ethics in the practice of journalism and the free flow of information.

3099 ■ Baseball Writers Association of America (BBWAA)
PO Box 610611
Bayside, NY 11361
Ph: (718)767-2582 (631)236-2648
Fax: (718)767-2583
E-mail: bbwaa@aol.com
URL: http://baseballwriters.org
Contact: Jack O'Connell, Sec.-Treas.

Founded: 1908. **Members:** 800. **Membership Dues:** regular, $65 (annual). **Description:** Membership restricted to sports writers on direct assignment to major league baseball. Maintains a chapter in each major league city. **Convention/Meeting:** none.

3100 ■ Boating Writers International (BWI)
108 9th St.
Wilmette, IL 60091
Ph: (847)736-4142
E-mail: info@bwi.org
URL: http://www.bwi.org
Contact: Greg Proteau, Exec. Dir.
Founded: 1970. **Members:** 500. **Membership Dues:** active, $35 (annual) ● associate, $40 (annual) ● supporting, $150 (annual). **Staff:** 1. **Multinational. Description:** Individuals in numerous countries including newspaper, magazine, radio, and television writers and photographers covering boating, fishing, and outdoor recreation and public relations. Seeks to: cover boating as a competitive as well as recreational sport; promote boating safety; encourage enjoyment of other outdoor water sports. **Awards:** BWI Writing Awards. **Frequency:** annual. **Type:** monetary. **Recipient:** for writers. **Publications:** *BWI Journal*, 11/year. Includes calendar of events and member news; lists employment opportunities and new publications. **Price:** included in membership dues. **Circulation:** 500 ● Directory, annual. Details work and specialties used by magazines, communication firms, manufacturers and others to find writers. **Conventions/Meetings:** annual meeting, held in conjunction with Miami Boat Show - always in mid-February.

3101 ■ Bowling Writers Association of America (BWAA)
8501 N Manor Ln.
Fox Point, WI 53217-2348
Ph: (414)351-6085
E-mail: sjames2652@wi.rr.com
URL: http://www.bowlingwriters.com
Contact: Steve James, Exec. Dir.
Founded: 1937. **Members:** 300. **Membership Dues:** regular, $20 (annual). **Staff:** 1. **Budget:** $10,000. **Regional Groups:** 4. **Description:** Reporters of bowling news. **Awards:** Chuck Pezzano Scholarships. **Frequency:** annual. **Type:** scholarship. **Formed by Merger of:** (2007) Bowling Writers Association of America and National Women Bowling Writers Association. **Formerly:** (1931) National Bowling Writer's Association. **Publications:** *BWAA Newsletter*, semiannual. **Conventions/Meetings:** annual conference, held in conjunction with American Bowling Congress Tournament - always March.

3102 ■ Capital Press Club (CPC)
PO Box 19403
Washington, DC 20036-9403
Ph: (202)628-1122
Fax: (301)588-7739
E-mail: cpc1944@aol.com
URL: http://www.cpcomm.org
Contact: Derrick Kenny, Pres.
Founded: 1944. **Members:** 250. **Membership Dues:** professional, $85 (annual) ● student, $25 (annual) ● corporate, $400 (annual). **State Groups:** 3. **Description:** Supports the presence and role of African-Americans in communications. Strives to be a networking resource for members, encourages and supports entrepreneurship, provides professional opportunities to increase skills and knowledge, exposes members to leaders in government, politics, business and communications, creates alliances with public and private sector companies and organizations in order to be an employment resource, provides a forum for the discussion and exchange of ideas, experiences and opinions, strengthens relationships with local, regional and national organizations that share the common goals of supporting and increasing the number of African Americans in the communications profession, gather, archive and disseminate communications information and research data for the benefit of members and interested audiences, promote and recognize professional excellence through competitions and award events for outstanding achievements, and provide scholarships and opportunities for internships to African Americans. **Awards: Frequency:** annual. **Type:** recognition ● **Frequency:** annual. **Type:** scholarship. **Telecommunication Services:** electronic mail, dkenny@wallscomm.com ● electronic mail, dkenny@bamgood.com. **Committees:** Chapter Development; Community and Student Outreach; Conference; Finance; Fund Raising/Development; Membership; Program; Public Relations; Publications; Website. **Publications:** *CPComm*, quarterly. Newsletter. **Advertising:** accepted. Alternate Formats: online. **Conventions/Meetings:** annual conference ● bimonthly NewsMaker Forums - meeting.

3103 ■ Catholic News Service (CNS)
3211 4th St. NE
Washington, DC 20017
Ph: (202)541-3250 (202)541-3293
Fax: (202)541-3255
E-mail: cns@catholicnews.com
URL: http://www.catholicnews.com
Contact: Tony Spence, Dir.
Founded: 1920. **Staff:** 30. **Multinational. Description:** A division of the United States Conference of Catholic Bishops (see separate entry). Aims to provide information, photographs, and news stories of interest to Catholics, Catholic publications and general interest news organizations. **Libraries: Type:** by appointment only. **Holdings:** 1,000; archival material. **Subjects:** U.S. Catholicism, world religions. **Additional Websites:** http://www.originsonline.com. **Formerly:** National Catholic News Service. **Publications:** *Catholic Trends*, biweekly. Newsletter. Includes commentary on current trends in Catholicism. **Price:** $36.00/year ● *Movie Guide Monthly*. Newsletter. Includes capsule film reviews. **Price:** $12.00/year ● *Origins CNS Documentary Service*, periodic. Magazine. Documentary service of the church. **Price:** $99.00/year. Alternate Formats: online.

3104 ■ Chess Journalists of America (CJA)
c/o Jerry Hanken, Pres.
2012 Yosemite Dr., No. 1
Los Angeles, CA 90041
Ph: (323)257-9839
E-mail: president@chessjournalism.org
URL: http://chessjournalism.org
Contact: Jerry Hanken, Pres.
Founded: 1972. **Members:** 100. **Membership Dues:** regular/associate, $10 (annual) ● foreign, $15 (annual). **Description:** Chess journalists and editors. Encourages the improvement of chess writing, including adherence to a code of ethics, and seeks to popularize the game of chess. Presents merit awards. Holds workshop at U.S. Open Tournament. **Libraries: Type:** reference. **Holdings:** archival material. **Formerly:** (1980) Association of U.S. Chess Journalists. **Publications:** *Chess Journalist*, quarterly. Alternate Formats: online. **Conventions/Meetings:** annual meeting - always August.

3105 ■ Committee of Concerned Journalists (CCJ)
Natl. Press Bldg.
529 14th St. NW, Ste.450
Washington, DC 20045
Ph: (202)662-7155
E-mail: ccj@concernedjournalists.org
URL: http://www.concernedjournalists.org
Contact: Bill Kovach, Chm.
Founded: 1997. **Staff:** 11. **Budget:** $4,000,000. **Nonmembership. Description:** Committed to securing the future of journalism. **Publications:** *The Elements of Journalism: What Newspeople Should Know and the Public Should Expect*. Book ● *journalrnalism.org*, quarterly. Newsletter. Alternate Formats: online ● Surveys. **Conventions/Meetings:** workshop.

3106 ■ Construction Writers Association
c/o Sheila Wertz, Exec. Dir.
PO Box 5586
Buffalo Grove, IL 60089-5586
Ph: (847)398-7756
Fax: (847)590-5241
E-mail: office@constructionwriters.org
URL: http://www.constructionwriters.org
Contact: Sheila Wertz, Exec. Dir.
Founded: 1958. **Members:** 280. **Membership Dues:** individual, $100 (annual). **Staff:** 1. **Budget:** $50,000. **Multinational. Description:** Writers and editors for media, public relations, and marketing in the construction field. **Awards:** Gordon B. Wright Photojournalism. **Frequency:** annual. **Type:** recognition. **Recipient:** for excellence in communication through the use of photography ● Kneeland Godfrey Award. **Frequency:** annual. **Type:** recognition. **Recipient:** for editorial body of work ● Marketing Communications Award. **Frequency:** annual. **Type:** recognition. **Recipient:** for excellence in construction related marketing and communications, public relations, and advertising ● Robert F. Boger Award. **Frequency:** annual. **Type:** recognition. **Recipient:** for excellence in magazine writing editorials ● Silver Hardhat Award. **Frequency:** annual. **Type:** recognition. **Recipient:** for individual(s) making a significant contribution to the construction industry or the association ● T. Randolph Russell Award. **Frequency:** annual. **Type:** recognition. **Recipient:** for outstanding newsletter ● Website Award. **Frequency:** annual. **Type:** recognition. **Recipient:** for excellence in website design and information delivery. **Publications:** *CWA News*, quarterly. Newsletter. **Advertising:** accepted. **Conventions/Meetings:** semiannual meeting - spring, Washington, DC; fall, Chicago, IL.

3107 ■ Council for the Advancement of Science Writing (CASW)
PO Box 910
Hedgesville, WV 25427
Ph: (304)754-5077
Fax: (304)754-5076
E-mail: diane@nasw.org
URL: http://www.casw.org
Contact: Ben Patrusky, Exec. Dir.
Founded: 1959. **Staff:** 2. **Budget:** $100,000. **Nonmembership. Description:** Operated by a council of 19 science writers, editors, television executives, scientists, and physicians. Works to increase public understanding of science by upgrading the quality and quantity of science writing and improving the relationship between scientists and the press. Conducts seminars, workshops, and conferences; sponsors programs to train minority journalists in science and medical writing. **Awards:** Alton Blakespee Fellowship. **Frequency:** annual. **Type:** fellowship ● Medical Writing Fellowship. **Frequency:** annual. **Type:** fellowship ● Rennie Taylor Fellowship. **Frequency:** annual. **Type:** fellowship. **Publications:** *A Guide to Careers in Science Writing*. Booklet. **Price:** free with SASE. **Conventions/Meetings:** annual New Horizon Press Briefing - seminar - always November.

3108 ■ Council of Science Editors (CSE)
c/o Drohan Management Group
12100 Sunset Hills Rd., Ste.130
Reston, VA 20190
Ph: (703)437-4377
Fax: (703)435-4390
E-mail: cse@councilscienceeditors.org
URL: http://www.councilscienceeditors.org
Contact: Kathy Hoskins, Exec. Dir.
Founded: 1957. **Members:** 1,289. **Membership Dues:** international, $185 (annual) ● in North America, Mexico, $156 (annual) ● student, $41 (annual). **Budget:** $250,000. **Description:** Active and former editors of primary and secondary journals in the life sciences and those in scientific publishing and editing. Through study and discussion groups, panels, and committees, considers all aspects of communication in the life sciences with emphasis on publication, especially in primary journals and retrieval in secondary media. **Awards:** Award for Meritorious Achievement. **Frequency:** annual. **Type:** recognition. **Recipient:** for excellence in scientific communication ● Distinguished Service Award. **Frequency:** annual. **Type:** recognition. **Recipient:** for outstanding contribution to CBE. **Computer Services:** Mailing lists, with rental fee ($250). **Committees:** Author's Editors; Awards and Honors; Editorial Policy; Education; Information Management; Publications; Style Manual. **Programs:** Annual Meeting. **Formerly:** Conference of Biological Editors; (2002) Council of Biology Editors. **Publications:** *CBE Views*, bimonthly. Newsletter. Provides forum for the exchange of information among authors, editors, and publishers in the life sciences. **Price:** included in membership dues; $38.00 /year for nonmembers. ISSN: 0164-5609. **Circulation:** 1,200. **Advertising:**

accepted. Also Cited As: *CBE Newsletter* ● *Council of Biology Editors—Membership Directory*, annual. **Price:** included in membership dues. **Circulation:** 1,200. **Advertising:** accepted ● *Editorial Forms: A Guide to Journal Management* ● *Ethics and Policy in Scientific Publication* ● *Financial Management of Scientific Journals* ● *Illustrating Science: Standards for Publication* ● *Latin American Research Libraries in Natural History: A Survey, Second Edition* ● *Peer Review in Scientific Publishing* ● *Scientific Style and Format, 6th edition.* **Conventions/Meetings:** annual conference (exhibits).

3109 ■ Deadline Club
15 Gramercy Park S
New York, NY 10003
Ph: (212)353-9598
E-mail: info@deadlineclub.org
URL: http://deadlineclub.org
Contact: Mr. Tim Paradis, Pres.
Members: 450. **Membership Dues:** professional, $30 (annual) ● associate, $35 (annual) ● national, $72 (annual). **Description:** New York City chapter of the Society of Professional Journalists. **Awards:** Deadline Club Awards. **Frequency:** annual. **Type:** recognition. **Recipient:** to the top journalists in New York. **Publications:** *Deadliner*, quarterly. Magazine. **Conventions/Meetings:** monthly board meeting.

3110 ■ Dog Writers' Association of America (DWAA)
c/o Ms. Pat Santi, Sec.
173 Union Rd.
Coatesville, PA 19320
Ph: (610)384-2436
Fax: (610)384-2471
E-mail: dwaa@dwaa.org
URL: http://www.dwaa.org
Contact: Amy Fernandez, Pres.
Founded: 1935. **Members:** 530. **Membership Dues:** professional/associate (initial), $75 ● professional/associate, $40 (annual). **Description:** Represents persons who write professionally about dogs for magazines, newspapers, or other publications; editors and publishers of magazines devoted to dogs. Promotes interests of dog owners; provides medium for the exchange of ideas, methods, and professional courtesies among members; maintains high standard of ethics in the collection and dissemination of dog news. Sponsors Dog Writers' Educational Trust. **Awards:** Dog Writers Contest. **Frequency:** annual. **Type:** recognition. **Recipient:** for outstanding writing. **Telecommunication Services:** electronic mail, flappy666@aol.com. **Publications:** *DWAA Newsletter*, monthly, except February ● *Members Bulletin*, annual ● *The Write Dog*, 10/year. Newsletter. **Price:** included in membership dues ● Membership Directory, annual. **Conventions/Meetings:** annual Writing Contest - competition and banquet, with awards ceremony - 2nd weekend of February, New York City, NY.

3111 ■ Editorial Freelancers Association (EFA)
71 W 23rd St., 4th Fl.
New York, NY 10010-4181
Ph: (212)929-5400
Free: (866)929-5400
Fax: (212)929-5439
E-mail: office@the-efa.org
URL: http://www.the-efa.org
Contact: J.P. Partland, Co-Exec.
Founded: 1970. **Members:** 1,500. **Membership Dues:** resident, $125 (annual) ● non-resident, $105 (annual). **Staff:** 1. **Budget:** $150,000. **Description:** Represents persons who work full or part-time as freelance writers or editorial freelancers. Promotes professionalism and facilitates the exchange of information and support. Conducts professional training seminars; and offers job listings. **Computer Services:** Mailing lists. **Telecommunication Services:** electronic mail, mugwump@panix.com. **Committees:** Benefits; Education; Job Phone; Programs; Publicity; Rates. **Absorbed:** (2001) Freelance Editorial Association. **Publications:** *The Freelancer*, bimonthly. Newsletter. **Price:** included in membership dues; $20.00 /year for nonmembers. **Circulation:** 1,500. **Advertising:** accepted. Alternate Formats: online ● Also publishes Tips for Successful Freelancing, The Freelancers Bookshelf, Grammatical Gleanings, and Resumes for Freelancers. **Conventions/Meetings:** seminar - 10/year, in New York and other local chapter locations.

3112 ■ Education Writers Association (EWA)
2122 P St. NW, Ste.201
Washington, DC 20037
Ph: (202)452-9830
Fax: (202)452-9837
E-mail: ewa@ewa.org
URL: http://www.ewa.org
Contact: Lisa J. Walker, Exec. Dir.
Founded: 1947. **Members:** 1,000. **Membership Dues:** active, associate, $65 (annual) ● student, $30 (annual) ● foundation, $250 (annual) ● institutional, group, $195 (annual). **Staff:** 6. **Description:** Education writers and reporters of daily and weekly newspapers, national magazines of general circulation, and radio and television stations; associate members are school and college public relations personnel and others with a serious interest in education writing. Improves the quality of education reporting and interpretation; encourages the development of education coverage by the press; to help attract top-notch writers and reporters to the education field. Sponsors regional and special workshops. Provides job referral/bank services. **Awards:** National Awards for Education Reporting. **Frequency:** annual. **Type:** recognition. **Recipient:** for individuals in the field of education writing. **Computer Services:** Mailing lists, labels. **Telecommunication Services:** electronic mail, lwalker@ewa.org. **Absorbed:** (1975) National Council for the Advancement of Education Writing. **Publications:** *Covering the Education Beat*, annual. Book. Serves as a source book for education reporters. **Price:** included in membership dues; $60.00 for nonmembers. Alternate Formats: online ● *Education Reporter*, bimonthly. Newsletter ● *ReformBrief*, quarterly. **Conventions/Meetings:** annual seminar, display of materials for education reporters (exhibits).

3113 ■ Foreign Press Association (FPA)
c/o Suzanne Adams, Exec. Dir.
333 E 46th St., Ste.1K
New York, NY 10017-7425
Ph: (212)370-1054
Fax: (212)370-1058
E-mail: fpanewyork@aol.com
URL: http://www.nyforeignpress.org
Contact: Suzanne Adams, Exec. Dir.
Founded: 1918. **Members:** 500. **Membership Dues:** active, associate, $95 (annual). **Multinational. Description:** Represents foreign print and broadcast correspondents stationed in the U.S. **Awards:** FPA Scholarship Award. **Frequency:** annual. **Type:** scholarship. **Recipient:** to foreign students at graduate schools of journalism in the U.S. **Publications:** *Foreign Press Association—Directory of Members*, annual. Membership Directory. Lists aims, offices, and members of FPA, their countries, affiliations, and addresses. Sent to members, consulates, missions, and embassies. **Price:** free for members and contributors. **Circulation:** 1,000. **Advertising:** accepted ● *FPA News*, bimonthly. Newsletter. Reports news and events pertinent to foreign press correspondents throughout the world. Includes obituaries and information on new members. **Price:** free. **Circulation:** 1,000. **Conventions/Meetings:** annual meeting.

3114 ■ Gridiron Club of Washington, DC (GCW)
Address Unknown since 2008
Founded: 1885. **Members:** 183. **Staff:** 1. **Description:** Daily newspaper reporters, editors, columnists, and cartoonists employed in Washington, DC (60); retired editors, reporters, columnists, and cartoonists are associate members. Social organization sponsoring annual dinner and program of songs and skits that satirize top government officials, celebrities, and current news events. The Washington, DC club is not affiliated with organizations of similar names in other cities. **Conventions/Meetings:** annual dinner - always Washington, DC; **Avg. Attendance:** 600.

3115 ■ Hollywood Foreign Press Association (HFPA)
646 N Robertson Blvd.
West Hollywood, CA 90069
Ph: (310)657-1731
Fax: (310)657-5576
E-mail: info@hfpa.org
URL: http://www.hfpa.org
Contact: Chantal Dinnage, Managing Dir.
Founded: 1942. **Members:** 107. **Staff:** 3. **Description:** Represents foreign correspondents covering Hollywood and the entertainment industry for newspapers, magazines, and radio and television around the world. Establishes favorable relations and cultural ties between foreign countries and the United States through dissemination of information about the U.S. as depicted in motion pictures, television, and other media. **Awards:** Golden Globe Awards. **Frequency:** annual. **Type:** recognition. **Recipient:** for the film and television industry and outstanding entertainment personalities. **Committees:** Foreign Language Films; Public Relations; Television. **Publications:** Membership Directory, annual. **Conventions/Meetings:** annual dinner - always January in Beverly Hills, CA.

3116 ■ Independent Press Association (IPA)
65 Battery, 2nd Fl.
San Francisco, CA 94111
Ph: (415)445-0230
Fax: (415)445-0231
E-mail: members@indypress.org
Contact: Richard Landry, Exec. Dir.
Founded: 1996. **Members:** 200. **Description:** Works to promote and support independent publications committed to social justice and a free press. Provides technical assistance to member publications. Advocates for the independent press. **Publications:** *Ink Reader*, quarterly. Newsletter. **Circulation:** 4,500. **Advertising:** accepted. Alternate Formats: online.

3117 ■ International Center for Journalists (ICFJ)
1616 H St. NW, 3rd Fl.
Washington, DC 20006
Ph: (202)737-3700
Fax: (202)737-0530
E-mail: editor@icfj.org
URL: http://www.icfj.org
Contact: James F. Hoge Jr., Chm.
Founded: 1984. **Staff:** 30. **Languages:** English, French, Russian, Spanish. **Multinational. Description:** Conducts training programs for journalists from developed and developing nations. Provides consulting services to foreign news organizations; offers fellowships and exchange programs for foreign and American journalists. **Libraries: Type:** reference. **Awards:** Arthur F. Burns Fellowship. **Frequency:** annual. **Type:** fellowship. **Recipient:** for young German and American journalists ● Knight International Press Fellowship. **Frequency:** semiannual. **Type:** fellowship. **Recipient:** for media professionals ● McGee Journalism Fellowship in Southern Africa. **Frequency:** annual. **Type:** fellowship. **Recipient:** for print and broadcast professionals or journalism educators. **Formerly:** (1996) Center for Foreign Journalists. **Publications:** *The International Journalist*, semiannual. Newsletter. Reports on journalism and journalism training worldwide. **Price:** free. **Circulation:** 14,000 ● *Knightline*, semiannual. Magazine ● Also makes available training manuals and videos. **Conventions/Meetings:** periodic seminar ● periodic workshop.

3118 ■ International Food, Wine and Travel Writers Association (IFWTWA)
1142 S Diamond Bar Blvd., No. 177
Diamond Bar, CA 91765-2203
Ph: (909)860-6914
Free: (877)439-8929
Fax: (877)439-8929

E-mail: admin@ifwtwa.org
URL: http://www.ifwtwa.org
Contact: Ms. Patricia A. Anis, Exec. Dir.
Founded: 1954. **Members:** 350. **Membership Dues:** regular, $120 (annual) ● associate, $235 (annual) ● student, $75 (annual). **Staff:** 3. **Budget:** $125,000. **Regional Groups:** 9. **Description:** Professional food, wine, and travel journalists, photographers, broadcasters and industry professionals in 28 countries; associate members are organizations in the hospitality industries. Seeks to bring recognition to those in the food, wine, and travel industry who have met the association's criteria. Offers scholarships in culinary arts and sciences journalism (food-wine-travel). **Computer Services:** database. **Additional Websites:** http://www.global-writes.com. **Committees:** Awards; By-Laws; Conferences & Media Trips; Ethics & Long Range Planning; Membership; Publications; Publicity. **Publications:** *Global Writes*, quarterly. Magazine. Includes members' articles. **Advertising:** accepted. Alternate Formats: online ● *International Food, Wine and Travel Writers Association—Membership Roster*, annual. Membership Directory. **Price:** included in membership dues; $150.00 for nonmembers ● *New Asian Cuisine: Fabulous Recipes from Celebrity Chefs*. Book. **Price:** $14.95 ● *Press Pass*, monthly. Newsletter. Covers association and industry news. Includes book reviews and updates of new members and address changes. **Price:** included in membership dues; $100.00 for nonmembers. **Advertising:** accepted. Alternate Formats: online ● Brochures. **Price:** $14.95. **Conventions/Meetings:** annual Board Retreat - conference ● annual international conference.

3119 ■ International Foodservice Editorial Council (IFEC)

PO Box 491
Hyde Park, NY 12538-0491
Ph: (845)229-6973
Fax: (845)229-6993
E-mail: info@ifeconline.com
URL: http://www.ifec-is-us.com
Contact: Carol Lally, Exec. Dir.
Founded: 1956. **Members:** 250. **Membership Dues:** individual, $275 (annual). **Staff:** 2. **Budget:** $140,000. **Description:** Key communicators within the U.S. foodservice industry, including top editors and marketing and public relations personnel for leading food companies and foodservice educational institutions. Organized to sound the marketing directions of the industry on all levels; seeks to improve communications. **Awards:** IFEC Foodservice Communications Scholarships. **Frequency:** annual. **Type:** scholarship. **Recipient:** for students preparing for food service communications careers. **Programs:** Scholarship. **Formerly:** (1975) Institutional Food Editorial Council. **Publications:** Newsletter, monthly. **Price:** included in membership dues. Alternate Formats: online ● Membership Directory, annual. Lists names, addresses, and business categories of members. **Price:** available to members only. **Conventions/Meetings:** annual conference - always fall.

3120 ■ International Motor Press Association (IMPA)

4 Park St.
Harrington Park, NJ 07640
Ph: (201)750-3533
Fax: (201)750-2010
E-mail: fred.chieco@abc.com
URL: http://www.impa.org
Contact: Fred Chieco, Pres.
Founded: 1962. **Members:** 500. **Membership Dues:** individual, $60 (annual). **Staff:** 21. **Regional Groups:** 1. **Description:** Represents automotive press members and individuals from 5 countries working in public relations, primarily those concerned with the automotive industry. **Awards:** Ken Purdy Award. **Frequency:** annual. **Type:** recognition. **Recipient:** for excellence in automotive writing. **Telecommunication Services:** electronic mail, rnewman@usanews.com. **Publications:** *Impact*, monthly. Newsletter. Contains monthly meeting details. **Circulation:** 500. Alternate Formats: online ● *Membership Roster and Contact List*, annual. Membership Directory. **Conventions/Meetings:** monthly meeting.

3121 ■ International Newspaper Group (ING)

c/o Marty Donner, Sec.-Treas.
64 Spyglass Dr.
Jackson, NJ 08527
E-mail: marty.donner@comcast.net
URL: http://www.azcentral.com/advert/ing
Contact: Marty Donner, Sec.-Treas.
Founded: 1975. **Staff:** 1. **Description:** Individuals employed in the newspaper publishing industry; sales representatives of suppliers and manufacturers of newspaper-related products. Seeks to improve efficiency of newspaper production. Offers assistance in solving newspaper production problems; encourages the exchange of information on new techniques and processes. **Awards:** ING Scholarships. **Frequency:** annual. **Type:** scholarship. **Recipient:** to a student at an accredited graphic arts college. **Publications:** Newsletter, semiannual. **Circulation:** 2,000. **Conventions/Meetings:** annual conference.

3122 ■ International Pentecostal Press Association (IPPA)

c/o Homer Rhea
PO Box 12609
Oklahoma City, OK 73157
Ph: (405)787-7110
Fax: (405)789-3957
E-mail: sspencer@iphc.org
Contact: John Maempa, Pres.
Founded: 1970. **Members:** 150. **Membership Dues:** individual, $25 (annual). **Description:** Editors, writers, publishers, and publishing houses. Gathers and syndicates news of the Pentecostal movement, including books and articles about Pentecostal history, practice, and doctrine; improve the journalistic quality and content of members' publications. Organizes seminars for editors and writers with the Pentecostal World Conference. **Awards: Frequency:** annual. **Type:** scholarship. **Recipient:** for journalism. **Publications:** *Pentecostal International Report*, quarterly ● *World Directory of Pentecostal Periodicals*. **Conventions/Meetings:** triennial conference, world writers and editors.

3123 ■ International Press Institute, American Committee (IPI)

c/o IPI Global Journalist
Missouri Scholarship of Journalism
132A Neff Annex
Columbia, MO 65211
Ph: (573)884-1599 (573)884-7542
Fax: (573)884-1699
E-mail: ipi@freemedia.at
URL: http://www.freemedia.at/cms/ipi
Contact: Prof. Johann P. Fritz, Dir.
Founded: 1951. **Members:** 170. **Multinational. Description:** Editors and editorial directors of newspapers, magazines, and news agencies and broadcasting system staff members who control or contribute to news policy in the press and broadcasting systems; educators, foreign correspondents, and others interested in journalism. Works to improve the flow of news and journalism practices. Seeks to protect freedom of the press and increase contacts and exchanges within the profession. Conducts research on news sources and presentation, foreign news reporting, and flow of news. **Publications:** *IPI Annual World Congress Report*, annual. Covers problems of international journalism and press laws. Alternate Formats: online ● *IPI Global Journalist*, quarterly. Magazine. **Price:** $180.00/year; $19.95 for individual. **Conventions/Meetings:** annual meeting (exhibits).

3124 ■ International Science Writers Association (ISWA)

c/o James C. Cornell, Pres.
6666 N Mesa View Terr.
Tucson, AZ 85718
Ph: (520)529-6835
E-mail: cornelljc@earthlink.net
URL: http://www.internationalsciencewriters.org
Contact: James C. Cornell, Pres.
Founded: 1965. **Members:** 250. **Membership Dues:** individual, $25 (annual). **Description:** Science writers. Seeks to insure a free press and maximize access to printed scientific information worldwide. Represents members' interests; conducts continuing professional development courses; gathers and disseminates information. **Publications:** Newsletter.

3125 ■ International Society of Weekly Newspaper Editors (ISWNE)

c/o Dr. Chad Stebbins, Exec. Dir.
Inst. of Intl. Stud.
Missouri Southern State Univ.
3950 E Newman Rd.
Joplin, MO 64801-1512
Ph: (417)625-9736
Fax: (417)659-4445
E-mail: stebbins-c@mssu.edu
URL: http://www.iswne.org
Contact: Dr. Chad Stebbins, Exec. Dir.
Founded: 1955. **Members:** 275. **Membership Dues:** individual, $50 (annual). **Staff:** 2. **Description:** Represents editors and writers of editorial comment in weekly newspapers. Promotes wise and independent editorial comments, news content and leadership in community newspapers throughout the world. Facilitates the exchange of ideas and viewpoints of community editors. Helps in the development of the community newspaper press as an instrument of mutual understanding and world peace and fosters freedom of the press in all nations. **Awards:** Eugene Cervi Award. **Frequency:** annual. **Type:** recognition. **Recipient:** for aggressive local reporting and community service over a number of years ● Golden Quill Editorial Award. **Frequency:** annual. **Type:** recognition. **Recipient:** for outstanding non-daily editorials. **Formerly:** International Conference of Weekly Newspaper Editors. **Publications:** *Grassroots Editor*, quarterly. Journal. Provides information for those concerned with community journalism. **Price:** included in membership dues. ISSN: 0017-3541. **Circulation:** 1,000. Alternate Formats: microform ● *ISWNE Newsletter*, monthly. Provides membership activity information. **Price:** included in membership dues. **Circulation:** 300. **Conventions/Meetings:** annual conference - 2008 June 25-29, Santa Fe, NM; 2009 June 24-28, Charlottetown, PE, Canada.

3126 ■ Investigative Reporters and Editors (IRE)

Missouri School of Journalism
138 Neff Annex
Columbia, MO 65211
Ph: (573)882-2042
Fax: (573)882-5431
E-mail: info@ire.org
URL: http://www.ire.org
Contact: Brant Houston, Exec. Dir.
Founded: 1975. **Members:** 4,500. **Membership Dues:** student, $25 (annual) ● professional/academic/associate/retiree; international with journal (electronic), $60 (annual) ● international student, $30 (annual) ● international (with journal sent through mail), $80 (annual). **Staff:** 12. **Budget:** $1,000,000. **Multinational. Description:** Persons who report or edit in-depth journalism; journalism educators and students. Provides educational services, including computer-assisted reporting through its National Institute for Computer-Assisted Reporting. **Libraries: Type:** reference. **Holdings:** 20,000; clippings, video recordings. **Subjects:** investigative reporting. **Awards:** FOI Award. **Frequency:** annual. **Type:** recognition. **Recipient:** for open records reporting ● IRE Award. **Frequency:** annual. **Type:** recognition. **Recipient:** for investigative work in newspapers, broadcast journalism, books, and magazines ● Tom Renner Award. **Frequency:** annual. **Type:** recognition. **Recipient:** for organized crime reporting. **Computer Services:** database. **Publications:** *Beat Book Series*, quarterly. Handbook. Contains individual report topics including aviation, safety, crime statistics, and non-profits. **Price:** $20.00 for nonmembers; $15.00 for members ● *The Best of IRE, Vols. 1-6.*

Journal ● *IRE Journal*, bimonthly. Magazine. Features articles on how to investigate individuals, governments, businesses, and other institutions. Includes annual index and book reviews. **Price:** free for members; $70.00 /year for nonmembers. ISSN: 0164-7016. **Circulation:** 5,000. **Advertising:** accepted ● *IRE Members Directory*, annual. Membership Directory ● *Reporter's Handbook* ● *Uplink*, bimonthly. Newsletter. Features tips and articles on computer-assisted reporting. **Price:** $40.00 for members; $60.00 for nonmembers; $70.00 for institutions and overseas. **Advertising:** accepted. **Conventions/Meetings:** periodic Computer-Assisted Reporting Boot Camp - seminar, topics include investigative reporting and computer-assisted journalism ● annual conference, with panels, workshops, classes (exhibits) ● workshop - 4-8/year.

3127 ■ Jazz Journalists Association (JJA)
c/o Arnold Jay Smith
436 State St.
Brooklyn, NY 11217
URL: http://www.jazzhouse.org
Contact: Howard Mandel, Pres.

Founded: 1986. **Members:** 300. **Membership Dues:** working journalist, $75 (annual) ● industry associate, supporting, $300 (annual) ● student, $25 (annual). **Multinational. Description:** Promotes high standards and respect for jazz works. Creates a professional network of writers, editors, photographers, broadcasters, filmmakers, educators, and media professionals to increase general interest in jazz. **Computer Services:** database, member list. **Publications:** *Jazz Notes*, quarterly. Newsletter.

3128 ■ National Academy of Television Journalists (NATJ)
PO Box 31
Salisbury, MD 21803
Ph: (410)546-9333 (410)251-2511
E-mail: info@thenationalacademyoftelevisionjournalists.com
URL: http://www.angelfire.com/md/NATJ
Contact: Neil F. Bayne, Exec. Dir.

Founded: 1985. **Members:** 400. **Membership Dues:** active professional, $50 (annual) ● retired/student, $15 (annual) ● associate professional, $75 (annual). **Staff:** 6. **For-Profit. Description:** Promotes professional advancement of members. Makes available employment services; conducts educational programs; sponsors competitions. **Awards:** Golden Viddy Award. **Frequency:** annual. **Type:** recognition. **Recipient:** for professional television journalists and television journalism students. **Computer Services:** database ● mailing lists. **Additional Websites:** http://www.thenationalacademyoftelevisionjournalists.com. **Conventions/Meetings:** annual Awards Ceremony - meeting - always second Saturday in May.

3129 ■ National Association of Black Journalists (NABJ)
Univ. of Maryland
8701-A Adelphi Rd.
Adelphi, MD 20783-1716
Ph: (301)445-7100
Free: (866)479-NABJ
Fax: (301)445-7101
E-mail: nabj@nabj.org
URL: http://www.nabj.org
Contact: Karen Wynn Freeman, Exec. Dir.

Founded: 1975. **Members:** 4,700. **Membership Dues:** student, $40 (annual) ● associate, $75 (annual) ● full, $100 (annual) ● premium, $150 (annual) ● high school, $35 (annual) ● emeritus, retired, $79 (annual) ● life, $1,500. **Staff:** 8. **Budget:** $1,500,000. **Regional Groups:** 40. **Description:** Persons employed in the production, dissemination, and distribution of news by newspapers, magazines, and radio and television stations. Strengthens the ties between blacks in the black media and blacks in the white media. Sensitizes the white media to the "institutional racism in its coverage". Expands the white media's coverage and "balanced reporting" of the black community. Honors excellence and outstanding achievement among black journalists. Works with high schools to identify potential journalists. Awards scholarships to journalism programs that especially support minorities. Acts as a national clearinghouse for job information. Maintains biographical archives. Sponsors competitions. **Awards:** Ida B. Wells Award. **Frequency:** annual. **Type:** recognition. **Recipient:** to a media executive or manager who has made outstanding efforts to make newsrooms and news coverage more accurately reflect the diversity of the communities they serve ● NABJ Hall of Fame. **Frequency:** annual. **Type:** recognition. **Recipient:** to black journalists who have made outstanding contributions to the journalism profession ● Salute to Excellence Awards. **Frequency:** annual. **Type:** recognition. **Recipient:** to exemplary coverage of people or issues in the African Diaspora ● Special Honors Awards. **Frequency:** annual. **Type:** recognition. **Recipient:** for outstanding work in journalism. **Telecommunication Services:** electronic mail, kfreeman@nabj.org. **Committees:** Constitution and Operating Procedures; Elections; Hall of Fame; Investigative Journalism; Media Entrepreneurism; Media Mentoring; Special Honors. **Councils:** Presidents. **Publications:** *NABJ Journal*, quarterly. **Price:** included in membership dues; $3.50/issue for nonmembers. Alternate Formats: online. **Conventions/Meetings:** annual conference, with workshops, plenary sessions and a career expo (exhibits).

3130 ■ National Association of Hispanic Journalists (NAHJ)
1000 Natl. Press Bldg.
529 14th St. NW
Washington, DC 20045-2001
Ph: (202)662-7145
Free: (888)346-NAHJ
Fax: (202)662-7144
E-mail: nahj@nahj.org
URL: http://www.nahj.org
Contact: Ivan Roman, Exec. Dir.

Founded: 1984. **Members:** 1,700. **Membership Dues:** regular, associate, academic, $55 (annual) ● student, $25 (annual) ● individual, $110 (annual) ● corporate, $1,100 (annual). **Staff:** 7. **Budget:** $1,500,000. **Regional Groups:** 8. **Languages:** English, Spanish. **Description:** Aims to organize and support Hispanics involved in news gathering and dissemination. Encourages journalism and communications study and practice by Hispanics. Seeks recognition for Hispanic members of the profession regarding their skills and achievements. Promotes fair and accurate media treatment of Hispanics; opposes job discrimination and demeaning stereotypes. Works to increase educational and career opportunities and development for Hispanics in the field. Seeks to foster greater awareness of members' cultural identity, interests, and concerns. Provides a united voice for Hispanic journalists with the aim of achieving national visibility. Offers placement services to Hispanic students. Activities include: a census of Hispanic media professionals nationwide; writing contest for Hispanic students. Offers scholarships, seminars, and training workshops. **Awards:** Professional Journalism Awards. **Frequency:** annual. **Type:** monetary. **Recipient:** for journalists ● Ruben Salazar Scholarship Fund. **Frequency:** annual. **Type:** monetary. **Recipient:** for academic excellence and an interest in a journalism career and financial need ● **Frequency:** annual. **Type:** scholarship. **Recipient:** for excellence in the study of journalism. **Computer Services:** database, Hispanic news media professional job opportunities. **Boards:** Unity '99. **Affiliated With:** American Society of Association Executives. **Publications:** *Latinos in the United States: A Resource Guide for Journalists*. Book. **Price:** $8.50 shipping included ● *Manual de Estilo* (in Spanish). Book. **Price:** $14.95 plus shipping and handling ● *NAHJ Newsletter*, quarterly. **Price:** free for members. **Circulation:** 3,000. **Advertising:** accepted. **Conventions/Meetings:** annual convention (exhibits).

3131 ■ National Association of Home and Workshop Writers (NAHWW)
PO Box 12
Baker, NV 89311
Ph: (847)255-0210
Free: (866)457-2582
E-mail: dstowe@arkansas.net
URL: http://www.nahww.org
Contact: Doug Stowe, Pres.

Founded: 1973. **Members:** 90. **Membership Dues:** active, associate, $36 (annual) ● supporting, $220 (annual). **Description:** Writers and illustrators of materials on home maintenance and improvement projects, manual skills, woodworking, and do-it-yourself projects and techniques. Aims to promote communication among colleagues by sharing information on publishers, marketing conditions, and mutual problems. **Libraries: Type:** not open to the public. **Awards:** Vaughan and Bushnell Awards. **Frequency:** annual. **Type:** monetary. **Recipient:** for home and workshop writers ● Vaughan and Bushnell Scholarship. **Frequency:** annual. **Type:** scholarship. **Recipient:** for promising student writers. **Computer Services:** Mailing lists. **Telecommunication Services:** electronic bulletin board. **Publications:** *NAHWW Newsletter*, quarterly. **Price:** included in membership dues. **Circulation:** 90. Alternate Formats: online ● Membership Directory, annual. Contains a listing of all members with their professional specialties. **Circulation:** 400. **Conventions/Meetings:** annual meeting, in conjunction with the National Hardware Show (exhibits).

3132 ■ National Association of Real Estate Editors (NAREE)
1003 NW 6th Terr.
Boca Raton, FL 33486-3455
Ph: (561)391-3599
Fax: (561)391-0099
E-mail: madkimba@aol.com
URL: http://www.naree.org
Contact: Mary Doyle-Kimball, Exec. Dir.

Founded: 1929. **Members:** 700. **Membership Dues:** active, $75 (annual) ● associate, $150 (annual). **Staff:** 1. **Budget:** $100,000. **Description:** Print and broadcast journalists, and associated publicists specializing in real estate, building design, mortgage finance, and commercial real estate. Sponsors conferences and contests to study common problems and exchange ideas. Reviews prize-winning real estate and home news sections. **Awards:** Real Estate Journalism Award. **Frequency:** annual. **Type:** monetary. **Recipient:** for independent publications and web producers. **Computer Services:** Mailing lists. **Formerly:** (1936) National Conference of Real Estate Editors. **Publications:** *NAREE News*, bimonthly. Newsletter. Includes industry updates, professional tips, member profiles and job opportunities. **Price:** available to members only. **Circulation:** 800. **Advertising:** accepted. Alternate Formats: online ● *NAREE Source Book*, biennial. Lists of national real estate contacts for real estate and housing journalists. **Price:** free for members; $175.00 for nonmembers. **Circulation:** 1,500 ● *NAREE Sourcebook*. Directory ● *National Association of Real Estate Editors—Roster: NAREE Network*, annual. Membership Directory. Contains list of members, cross-indexed to show affiliation. **Price:** available to members only. **Circulation:** 800. **Conventions/Meetings:** annual conference.

3133 ■ National Association of Science Writers (NASW)
PO Box 890
Hedgesville, WV 25427
Ph: (304)754-5077
Fax: (304)754-5076
E-mail: director@nasw.org
URL: http://www.nasw.org
Contact: Diane McGurgan, Exec. Dir.

Founded: 1934. **Members:** 2,450. **Membership Dues:** individual in U.S., $75 (annual) ● student, $25 (annual) ● student outside U.S., $30 (annual) ● individual in Canada, $80 (annual) ● individual outside U.S. and Canada, $90 (annual). **Staff:** 1. **Budget:** $100,000. **Regional Groups:** 5. **Local Groups:** 4. **Multinational. Description:** Writers and editors engaged in the preparation and interpretation of science news for the public. **Awards:** Science in Society Journalism Award. **Frequency:** annual. **Type:** recognition. **Committees:** Science Liaison; TV-Press Relations; Vocational. **Affiliated With:** Council for the

Advancement of Science Writing. **Publications:** *Awards*, annual. **Advertising:** accepted ● *Field Guide For Science Writers.* **Price:** $15.00 for members ● *Guide to Careers in Science Writing.* **Price:** free with SASE ● *Roster of Members*, annual. Directory. **Price:** available to members only ● *Science Writer*, quarterly. Newsletter. Includes employment opportunity information. **Price:** included in membership dues. **Advertising:** accepted. Also Cited As: *NASW Newsletter.* **Conventions/Meetings:** annual meeting, held in conjunction with American Association for the Advancement of Science - always February.

3134 ■ National Catalog Managers Association (NCMA)
c/o Automotive Aftermarket Industry Association
7101 Wisconsin Ave., Ste.1300
Bethesda, MD 20814-3415
Ph: (301)654-6664
Fax: (301)654-3299
E-mail: ncma@aftermarket.org
URL: http://www.ncmacat.org
Contact: Chris Nierintz, Pres.
Founded: 1974. **Members:** 156. **Membership Dues:** regular, $200. **Description:** Individuals actively engaged in the management, preparation, production, and distribution of automotive product catalogs. Purposes are to: exchange practical and useful ideas in the creation, compilation, production, and distribution of catalogs; raise standards of catalogs in automotive and related industries; create a better understanding of the current developments in the field of graphics; establish a professional and fraternal relationship with colleagues; improve professional recognition of the catalog specialist; promote high standards of ethics in the cataloging industry. Operates placement service. **Awards:** Catalog Excellence Award. **Type:** recognition. **Recipient:** for five companies with the best catalogs, as judged by NCMA in CD-ROM and web categories. **Publications:** Newsletter, semiannual ● Membership Directory. Alternate Formats: online. **Conventions/Meetings:** annual conference - always April or May.

3135 ■ National Collegiate Baseball Writers Association (NCBWA)
c/o Russell Anderson, Assoc. Exec. Dir.
Conf. USA
5201 N O'Connor, Ste.300
Irving, TX 75039
Ph: (214)774-1351 (214)418-6132
E-mail: rdanderson@c-usa.org
URL: http://www.sportswriters.net/ncbwa
Contact: Bo Carter, Exec. Dir.
Founded: 1962. **Members:** 250. **Description:** Sportswriters, sportscasters, publicity directors, and others interested in college baseball. Upgrades and improves the media coverage of intercollegiate baseball. Cosponsors annual baseball brochure contest. **Awards:** Pro-Line Cap Players of the Week. **Frequency:** weekly. **Type:** recognition. **Recipient:** for the top hitter and pitcher ● Stopper of the Year. **Frequency:** annual. **Type:** recognition. **Recipient:** for the top relief pitcher ● Wilbur Snypp Award. **Frequency:** annual. **Type:** recognition. **Recipient:** for contributions to college baseball ● Xanthus Dick Howser Trophy. **Frequency:** annual. **Type:** recognition. **Recipient:** for top collegiate of the year. **Publications:** *National Collegiate Baseball Records Book*, annual ● Newsletter, monthly. **Conventions/Meetings:** annual meeting, held in conjunction with College Sports Information Directors of America - usually in June.

3136 ■ National Conference of Editorial Writers (NCEW)
3899 N Front St.
Harrisburg, PA 17110
Ph: (717)703-3015
Fax: (717)703-3014
E-mail: ncew@pa-news.org
URL: http://www.ncew.org
Contact: Ms. Sherid Virnig, Dir. of Admin.
Founded: 1947. **Members:** 550. **Membership Dues:** newspaper (with circulation of over 100,000/top 10 markets), $200 (annual) ● newspaper (with circulation of 50,000-100,000/markets 11-50), columnist/commentator, online journalist, $180 (annual) ● newspaper (with circulation of 20,000-50,000/markets 51-100), $140 (annual) ● newspaper (with circulation of under 20,000/markets below the top 100), associate, $90 (annual) ● academic (journalism educator), $100 (annual) ● retired, $50 (annual) ● college student, $25 (annual) ● broadcast, $90-$200 (annual). **Staff:** 1. **Budget:** $100,000. **Multinational. Description:** Represents professional editorial writers who prepare institutional opinion on a regular basis for newspapers or magazines of general circulation or radio or television stations, or online outlets; columnists; teachers of journalism; college students who profess a serious interest in editorial writing; others who play an active role in editorial operations. Aims to stimulate the conscience and the quality of editorials. **Awards:** Barry Bingham Senior Fellowship. **Frequency:** annual. **Type:** fellowship. **Recipient:** to a journalism educator who has shown distinction in preparing minority students for careers in journalism ● Ida B. Wells Award. **Frequency:** annual. **Type:** recognition. **Recipient:** for minorities in the field of journalism; in conjunction with the National Association of Black Journalists (see separate entry). **Computer Services:** Mailing lists. **Committees:** Broadcast/New Media; Development; Diversity; Ethics; Exhibit Fair; Futures; Innovations; International Relations; Journalism Education; Member Services (offering critique services); New Technology; Open Government; Regional Conferences; Site Selection. **Absorbed:** (1992) National Broadcast Editorial Association. **Publications:** *Beyond Argument: A Handbook for Editorial Writers.* Provides solid advice on practical matters of editorial writing and a glimpse of the future of opinion writing. ● *The Masthead*, quarterly. Journal. Covers all aspects of the work of a professional editorial writer in any medium. Includes conference news and broadcast editorial coverage. **Price:** $35.00/year. ISSN: 0025-5122. **Circulation:** 1,000 ● *NCEW E-Newsletter*, monthly. **Price:** available to members only. Alternate Formats: online ● Membership Directory, annual. **Conventions/Meetings:** annual convention and workshop, syndicates (by invitation) plus fee (exhibits).

3137 ■ National Federation of Press Women (NFPW)
PO Box 5556
Arlington, VA 22205
Ph: (703)812-9487
Free: (800)780-2715
Fax: (703)812-4555
E-mail: presswomen@aol.com
URL: http://www.nfpw.org
Contact: Ms. Carol Pierce, Exec. Dir.
Founded: 1937. **Members:** 2,000. **Membership Dues:** professional (plus state dues), $51 (annual) ● student (plus state dues), $10 (annual) ● retired (plus state dues), $20 (annual). **Budget:** $180,000. **State Groups:** 50. **Description:** Serves as federal of state associations of professional women and men in all phases of communications on a full-time or freelance basis. Seeks to: encourage the highest standards of professionalism in journalism; provide for exchange of ideas, knowledge, and experience. Offers specialized education programs. **Awards:** Achievement Award. **Frequency:** annual. **Type:** recognition. **Recipient:** for significant contributions to the field of communications. **Committees:** Communications Contest; Communicator of Achievement; Youth Projects. **Publications:** *Agenda*, quarterly. Newsletter. **Circulation:** 3,500. **Advertising:** accepted. Alternate Formats: online. **Conventions/Meetings:** annual Communications Conference (exhibits) ● annual conference (exhibits) - always fall.

3138 ■ National Lesbian and Gay Journalists Association (NLGJA)
1420 K St. NW, Ste.910
Washington, DC 20005
Ph: (202)588-9888
Fax: (202)588-1818
E-mail: info@nlgja.org
URL: http://www.nlgja.org
Contact: Eric Hegedus, Pres.
Founded: 1990. **Members:** 1,300. **Membership Dues:** basic, associate, supporting individual, $75 (annual) ● student, retiree, international, $25 (annual) ● LGBT media, $45 (annual) ● nonprofit institution, $320 (annual) ● corporate, $960 (annual) ● couple, $135 (annual). **Staff:** 5. **Budget:** $650,000. **Regional Groups:** 19. **Description:** Represents journalists, online media professionals, and students that works from within the journalism industry to foster fair and accurate coverage of lesbian, gay, bisexual and transgender issues. Opposes workplace bias against all minorities and provides professional development for its members. **Awards:** Excellence in Journalism Awards. **Frequency:** annual. **Type:** monetary. **Recipient:** for NLGJA members who have made exceptional work in the field of journalism on issues related to the LGBT community ● LGBT Journalists Hall of Fame. **Frequency:** annual. **Type:** recognition. **Recipient:** for individuals who have made exemplary contributions through their careers to NLGJA's mission ● Women's Distinguished Service Award. **Frequency:** annual. **Type:** recognition. **Recipient:** to a dedicated NLGJA member who has demonstrated a commitment to issues focusing on women in journalism. **Computer Services:** Online services. **Publications:** *Directory of News Media Companies/Unions with Domestic Partner Benefits.* Booklet ● *National Convention Program Book*, annual ● *NLGJA Outlook*, quarterly. Magazine. **Price:** free for members. **Circulation:** 3,500. **Advertising:** accepted. Alternate Formats: online ● *Stylebook Addenda Gay/Lesbian Terminology* (in English and Spanish). Pamphlet. Alternate Formats: online. **Conventions/Meetings:** annual convention and workshop, includes a job fair, panels (exhibits).

3139 ■ National News Bureau (NNB)
PO Box 43039
Philadelphia, PA 19129
Ph: (215)849-9016
Fax: (215)893-5394
E-mail: nnbfeature@aol.com
URL: http://www.nationalnewsbureau.com
Contact: Harry Jay Katz, Publisher/Ed.-in-Chief
Founded: 1979. **Members:** 385. **Staff:** 14. **For-Profit. Description:** Sells syndicated feature stories to 308 magazines, newspapers, and other periodicals. Conducts internship program for college students. **Libraries: Type:** not open to the public. **Subjects:** travel, entertainment, fashion, beauty, new products, film, video, food, wine. **Conventions/Meetings:** semiannual Editorial Conference - always June and December.

3140 ■ National Newspaper Association (NNA)
PO Box 7540
Columbia, MO 65205-7540
Ph: (573)882-5800 (573)882-5680
Free: (800)829-4662
Fax: (573)884-5490
E-mail: briansteffens@nna.org
URL: http://www.nna.org
Contact: Brian Steffens, Exec. Dir.
Founded: 1885. **Members:** 2,500. **Membership Dues:** newspaper (based on circulation level), $141-$1,168 (annual) ● individual, $95 (annual) ● retired publisher, student, $50 (annual). **Staff:** 5. **Budget:** $1,600,000. **Description:** Aims to protect, promote, and enhance community newspapers. Represents community newspapers across America; represents the industry before legislators, agencies and departments in Washington, D.C. that enact laws, rules and regulations, or conduct business, and that affect community newspapers. Promotes quality journalism and business practices at its annual convention, through its various contests and awards, and various other educational programs. **Awards:** Amos and McKinney Award. **Frequency:** annual. **Type:** recognition. **Recipient:** to a working newspaperman/woman ● Best of Newspaper In Education Contest. **Frequency:** annual. **Type:** recognition. **Recipient:** for excellence and achievement in newspaper in education pro-

grams in community newspapers ● Better Newspaper Advertising Contest. **Frequency:** annual. **Type:** recognition. **Recipient:** for the best in community newspaper advertising ● Better Newspaper Contest. **Frequency:** annual. **Type:** recognition. **Committees:** Annual Convention; Contests and Awards; Continuing Education; Government Relations; Postal; Publishers' Auxiliary. **Formerly:** (1956) National Editorial Association. **Publications:** *Publishers' Auxiliary*, monthly. Newspaper. Covers issues important to community newspapers. **Price:** $85.00/year. ISSN: 0048-5942. **Circulation:** 5,800. **Advertising:** accepted. **Conventions/Meetings:** annual convention and trade show (exhibits) - always September/October. 2008 Sept. 25-28, St. Paul, MN ● annual Government Affairs Conference.

3141 ■ National Press Club (NPC)
Natl. Press Bldg.
529 14th St. NW, 13th Fl.
Washington, DC 20045
Ph: (202)662-7500 (202)662-7505
Fax: (202)662-7512
E-mail: info@press.org
URL: http://www.press.org
Contact: Jerry Zremski, Pres.

Founded: 1908. **Members:** 4,350. **Membership Dues:** active, $163-$527 (annual) ● affiliate, $163-$669 (annual) ● associate, $553-$797 (annual) ● provisional, $180-$514 (annual) ● graduate student, $169 (annual). **Staff:** 100. **For-Profit. Description:** Reporters, writers, and news people employed by newspapers, wire services, magazines, radio and television stations, and other forms of news media; former news people and associates of news people are nonvoting members. Sponsors sports, travel, and cultural events, rap sessions with news figures and authors, and newsmaker breakfasts and luncheons. Offers monthly training. **Libraries: Type:** reference. **Holdings:** 4,000; archival material, books, periodicals, photographs. **Subjects:** journalism, media, politics. **Awards:** Consumer Journalism Award. **Frequency:** annual. **Type:** recognition ● Diplomatic Correspondence Award. **Frequency:** annual. **Type:** recognition ● Environmental Reporting Award. **Frequency:** annual. **Type:** recognition ● Freedom of the Press Award. **Frequency:** annual. **Type:** recognition ● Newsletter Journalism Award. **Frequency:** annual. **Type:** recognition ● Online Journalism Award. **Frequency:** annual. **Type:** recognition ● Political Journalism Award. **Frequency:** annual. **Type:** recognition ● Press Criticism Award. **Frequency:** annual. **Type:** recognition ● Regional Reporting Award. **Frequency:** annual. **Type:** recognition ● Washington Correspondence Award. **Frequency:** annual. **Type:** recognition ● Writing on Problems of Geriatrics. **Frequency:** annual. **Type:** recognition. **Computer Services:** database. **Additional Websites:** http://npc.press.org. **Telecommunication Services:** hotline, (202)879-6795 ● 24-hour hotline, (202)662-7595. **Committees:** Awards; Book and Author; Book Fair; Cartoons and Cocktails; Chess; Employment; Entertainment; Events; Exhibits; Fellowship; Fitness Center; 5k Run; Forums; Fourth Estate Award; Fourth Estate Dinner; Freedom of the Press; Golf; High Tech; House; International Correspondents; Lawmakers of the Club; Library, Archives; Morning Newsmakers; Oral History; Professional Affairs; Public Relations; Publications; Scholarships; Silver Owls; Speakers; Tennis; Travel; Young Members. **Absorbed:** (1985) Washington Press Club. **Publications:** *National Press Club Directory*, annual. Membership Directory. **Price:** available to members only. **Advertising:** accepted ● *The Record*, weekly. Newsletter. Contains membership activities. Includes calendar of events, job announcements, and information on new members. **Price:** included in membership dues. ISSN: 0027-9927. Alternate Formats: online. **Conventions/Meetings:** seminar, on Washington reporting ● annual WebFest - trade show, technology/internet trade show (exhibits) - always August.

3142 ■ National Press Foundation (NPF)
1211 Connecticut Ave. NW, Ste.310
Washington, DC 20036
Ph: (202)663-7280
Fax: (202)530-2855
E-mail: bob@nationalpress.org
URL: http://www.nationalpress.org
Contact: Bob Meyers, Pres.

Founded: 1975. **Staff:** 5. **Budget:** $716,000. **Description:** Individuals, corporations, and foundations. Promotes excellence in American journalism. Conducts public forums. Funds the National Press Club (see separate entry) Library and Reference Center. Issues the NPC journalism awards. Administers the Washington Journalism Center. **Awards:** Berryman Award. **Frequency:** annual. **Type:** recognition. **Recipient:** for editorial cartooning ● Distinguished Contributions to Journalism Award. **Frequency:** annual. **Type:** recognition. **Recipient:** for lifetime achievement ● Editor of the Year Award. **Frequency:** annual. **Type:** recognition. **Recipient:** for excellence in journalism ● Excellence in Online Journalism. **Frequency:** annual. **Type:** recognition. **Recipient:** for achievement in the rapidly changing field of internet journalism ● **Frequency:** annual. **Type:** fellowship ● **Frequency:** annual. **Type:** fellowship. **Recipient:** to active journalists for Spanish language, management, and banking ● **Frequency:** annual. **Type:** grant ● Sol Taishoff Award. **Frequency:** annual. **Type:** recognition. **Recipient:** for excellence in broadcast journalism. **Telecommunication Services:** electronic mail, npf@nationalpress.org. **Committees:** Audit; Development; Editor of the Year; Hall of Journalism; Library; Minority Programs; National Press Forums; Program Development; Strategic Intent; Taishoff Award; Washington Journalism Center. **Programs:** Journalist-to-Journalist. **Publications:** *Update Newsletter*, quarterly ● Annual Report, annual ● Video. **Conventions/Meetings:** annual dinner, includes awards (exhibits) ● workshop, for reporters.

3143 ■ National Society of Newspaper Columnists (NSNC)
PO Box 411532
San Francisco, CA 94141
Ph: (415)722-7030
Free: (866)440-6762
Fax: (866)635-5759
E-mail: director@columnists.com
URL: http://www.columnists.com
Contact: Luenna H. Kim, Exec. Dir.

Founded: 1979. **Members:** 550. **Membership Dues:** regular, $50 (annual) ● life, $500 ● student, $35 (annual). **Staff:** 3. **Budget:** $25,000. **Description:** Serves as professional society for newspaper columnists. **Awards:** Writing Contest. **Frequency:** annual. **Type:** recognition. **Computer Services:** database ● mailing lists. **Publications:** *The Columnist*, bimonthly. Newsletter. Alternate Formats: online ● *Guide to Syndication, 2nd Edition.* **Conventions/Meetings:** annual conference, with panel discussions by famous writers and awards.

3144 ■ National Sportscasters and Sportswriters Association (NSSA)
PO Box 1545
Salisbury, NC 28145
Ph: (704)633-4275 (704)223-0385
Fax: (704)633-2027
E-mail: nssahalloffame@aol.com
URL: http://www.nssahalloffame.com
Contact: Glenn Hudson, Exec. Dir.

Founded: 1959. **Members:** 1,000. **Membership Dues:** regular, $30 (annual). **Staff:** 1. **Budget:** $80,000. **Description:** Sportscasters and sportswriters. Pursues matters of common interest to members. Elects charter members to U.S. Olympic Hall of Fame. **Libraries: Type:** not open to the public. **Awards:** Hall of Fame. **Type:** recognition ● National Caster Writer. **Frequency:** annual. **Type:** recognition ● NSSA Sportscasters and Sportswriters. **Frequency:** annual. **Type:** recognition. **Recipient:** for outstanding sportscasters and sportswriters. **Publications:** *NSSA News*, quarterly. Newsletter. Provides members with excerpts from the published articles and statements of other members along with professional information on the member. **Price:** free for members. **Circulation:** 1,000. **Conventions/Meetings:** annual National Sportscasters and Sportswriters Award Program - meeting and seminar - always April in Salisbury, NC.

3145 ■ National Turf Writers Association (NTWA)
3920 Grassy Creek Dr.
Lexington, KY 40514
Ph: (859)219-9437
Fax: (859)223-8338
E-mail: info@turfwriters.org
URL: http://www.turfwriters.org
Contact: Jill Williams, Sec.-Treas.

Founded: 1960. **Members:** 225. **Membership Dues:** regular, associate, $40 (annual). **Staff:** 1. **Description:** Newspaper and magazine writers, sports editors, and columnists who regularly write about or publish news of Thoroughbred horse racing and breeding. Improves the working conditions of its members. **Libraries: Type:** not open to the public. **Awards:** Joe Palmer Award. **Frequency:** annual. **Type:** recognition. **Recipient:** for typifying the spirit of racing ● Mr. Fitz Award. **Frequency:** annual. **Type:** recognition. **Recipient:** for meritorious service to the racing industry ● Walter Haight Award. **Frequency:** annual. **Type:** recognition. **Recipient:** for lifetime achievement in turf writing. **Publications:** *Awards Dinner Program*, annual. Booklet ● Membership Directory, annual ● Newsletter, monthly. **Conventions/Meetings:** semiannual meeting - during the week of the Kentucky Derby, Louisville, KY.

3146 ■ National Writers Association (NWA)
10940 S Parker Rd., No. 508
Parker, CO 80134
Ph: (303)841-0246
Fax: (303)841-2607
E-mail: anitaedits@aol.com
URL: http://www.nationalwriters.com
Contact: Sandy Whelchel, Exec. Dir.

Founded: 1945. **Members:** 150. **Staff:** 1. **Description:** Professional full- or part-time freelance writers who specialize in business writing. Aims to serve as a marketplace whereby business editors can easily locate competent writing talent. Establishes communication among editors and writers. **Formerly:** (1999) Associated Business Writers of America. **Publications:** *Authorship*, quarterly. Magazine. Contains news of the literary and publishing world, hot Hollywood inside information and marketing tips. ● Directory, quarterly ● Newsletter, quarterly. Alternate Formats: online. **Conventions/Meetings:** annual conference - usually second weekend of June.

3147 ■ Native American Journalists Association (NAJA)
Univ. of Oklahoma
Gaylord Coll.
Norman, OK 73019-0001
Ph: (405)436-3744
Fax: (405)325-7565
E-mail: info@naja.com
URL: http://www.naja.com
Contact: Jeff Harjo, Exec. Dir.

Founded: 1984. **Members:** 600. **Membership Dues:** corporate, $500 (annual) ● nonprofit/academic, $300 (annual) ● tribal media, $250 (annual) ● associate, individual, $55 (annual) ● student, $20 (annual) ● high school, $10 (annual). **Staff:** 3. **Multinational. Description:** Journalists of Native American descent. Seeks to serve and empower Native communicators. Conducts educational programs in areas including journalism, Native American culture, politics and history, and free speech and expression. Represents members' professional interests; sponsors lobbying activities. **Awards: Type:** fellowship. **Recipient:** for an enrolled member of a federal or state recognized tribe ● **Type:** scholarship. **Recipient:** for an enrolled member of a federal or state recognized tribe. **Computer Services:** database, membership/Native media lists. **Also Known As:** (2000) Native American Press Association. **Publications:** *The American Indian and the Media.* Book. **Price:** $10.00 for members; $15.00 for nonmembers ● *NAJA News*, 8/year. Newsletter. **Price:** free for members. **Circulation:** 600. Alternate Formats: online. **Conventions/Meetings:** annual convention (exhibits) - 2008 July 23-27, Chicago, IL.

3148 ■ New York Financial Writers' Association (NYFWA)
PO Box 338
Ridgewood, NJ 07451-0338
Ph: (201)612-0100
Fax: (201)612-9915
E-mail: info@nyfwa.org
URL: http://www.nyfwa.org
Contact: Sheila Mulan, Pres.

Founded: 1938. **Members:** 350. **Membership Dues:** professional, $50 (annual) ● student, $10 (annual). **Staff:** 1. **Budget:** $300,000. **Description:** Financial and business editors and reporters whose publications are located in metropolitan New York. **Awards:** NYFWA Scholarships. **Frequency:** annual. **Type:** scholarship. **Recipient:** for college students who are interested in the field of financial journalism. **Publications:** Directory, annual. **Conventions/Meetings:** annual Awards Dinner - banquet ● annual Financial Follies - dinner ● annual meeting - always fourth Wednesday in January, New York City ● seminar, for college students interested in the financial journalism field.

3149 ■ Newspaper Association Managers (NAM)
70 Washington St., Ste.214
Salem, MA 01970
Ph: (978)744-8940
Fax: (978)744-0333
URL: http://www.nammanagers.com
Contact: Morley L. Piper, Clerk

Founded: 1923. **Members:** 65. **Description:** Represents full-time executives of national, state, and regional newspaper associations. Sponsors National Newspaper Week. **Publications:** *The Roundtable*, bimonthly. **Conventions/Meetings:** annual conference - always December ● annual meeting - always August.

3150 ■ Newswomen's Club of New York (NCNY)
15 Gramercy Park S
New York, NY 10003
Ph: (212)777-1610
E-mail: lyonsc29@aol.com
URL: http://www.newswomensclubnewyork.com
Contact: Jeanne King, Pres.

Founded: 1922. **Members:** 275. **Membership Dues:** professional, $75 (annual). **Description:** Women journalists working full-time or freelancing for New York City and metropolitan daily newspapers, wire services, syndicates, national news and news/feature magazines published in New York City, and radio and television stations or networks whose broadcasts originate in New York City; associate members are former actives who have left the media business. Sponsors professional, educational, social, and charitable activities; arranges for speeches by news headliners; invites journalism students to various events to learn about the field from professionals. Honors the best work by women journalists in the Metro NY area with its annual front page awards. Gives graduate scholarships to women students at Columbia University Graduate School of Journalism through its Anne O'Hare McCormick Scholarship Fund. **Awards:** Anne O'Hare McCormick Scholarship Fund. **Frequency:** annual. **Type:** scholarship. **Recipient:** for aspiring women journalists ● Front Page Awards. **Frequency:** annual. **Type:** recognition. **Recipient:** for best stories of the year by women journalists. **Committees:** Front Page Awards; Publicity. **Formerly:** New York Newspaper Women's Club; Newspaper Women's Club of New York. **Publications:** Bulletin, monthly. **Circulation:** 260 ● Membership Directory, biennial. **Conventions/Meetings:** annual Front Page Awards - dinner (exhibits) - always November, in New York City.

3151 ■ Online News Association (ONA)
PO Box 2022
New York, NY 10101
Ph: (646)290-7900
E-mail: lschwab@journalists.org
URL: http://www.onlinenewsassociation.org
Contact: Lori Schwab, Exec. Dir.

Founded: 1999. **Members:** 900. **Membership Dues:** professional, academic faculty, associate, $50 (annual) ● student, $25 (annual). **Staff:** 1. **Description:** Promotes the Internet as powerful communications medium and represents online journalists and professionals associated with producing news for digital presentation. **Awards:** Online Journalism Awards. **Frequency:** annual. **Type:** recognition. **Recipient:** for excellence in online journalism. **Publications:** Newsletter, monthly. **Price:** free, for members only. **Conventions/Meetings:** annual conference and banquet, with keynote speaker - 2008 Sept. 11-13, Washington, DC.

3152 ■ Organization of News Ombudsmen (ONO)
c/o Gina Lubrano, Exec. Sec.
PO Box 120191
San Diego, CA 92123
Ph: (858)292-1594
E-mail: ono@uniontrib.com
URL: http://www.newsombudsmen.org
Contact: Gina Lubrano, Exec. Sec.

Founded: 1980. **Members:** 80. **Membership Dues:** regular, associate, $150 (annual). **Multinational. Description:** Newspaper and broadcast ombudsmen; reader advocates. (An ombudsman is an individual who investigates reported complaints, reports findings, and assists in settling disagreements.) Seeks to improve communications between the media and their readers and viewers. Many ombudsmen give speeches for community and professional groups. **Formerly:** (1983) Organization of Newspaper Ombudsmen. **Publications:** *News from ONO*, monthly. Newsletter. **Price:** free for members. **Conventions/Meetings:** annual conference (exhibits).

3153 ■ Outdoor Writers Association of America (OWAA)
121 Hickory St., Ste.1
Missoula, MT 59801
Ph: (406)728-7434
Free: (800)692-2477
Fax: (406)728-7445
E-mail: owaa@montana.com
URL: http://www.owaa.org
Contact: Kevin Rhoades, Exec. Dir.

Founded: 1927. **Members:** 2,200. **Membership Dues:** active, associate, apprentice, $125 (annual) ● supporting, business, agency, $375 (annual) ● student, $30 (annual) ● government natural resource agency, $162 (annual) ● sustaining, $1,000 (annual). **Staff:** 6. **Budget:** $450,000. **Description:** Professional organization of newspaper, magazine, radio, television and motion picture writers and photographers (both staff and free-lance) concerned with outdoor recreation and conservation. Conducts surveys for educational and industrial organizations; compiles market data for writer members and offers liaison aid in writer assignments. **Libraries: Type:** reference. **Awards:** Bodie McDowell Scholarship. **Frequency:** annual. **Type:** scholarship. **Recipient:** to college students with career goals in outdoor communications ● John Madson Fellowship. **Frequency:** annual. **Type:** fellowship. **Recipient:** to members who attend the wild branch writing workshop, annual conference, college courses or professional seminars - virtually any opportunity to enhance communications skills. **Committees:** Awards; Educational and Scholarship; Ethics. **Publications:** *Outdoors Unlimited*, monthly. Newsletter. Includes craft improvement stories, industry news tips, letters to the editor, jobs, conservation news, new technology tidbits and more. **Price:** included in membership dues. **Circulation:** 2,000. **Conventions/Meetings:** annual conference.

3154 ■ Overseas Press Club of America (OPC)
40 W 45 St.
New York, NY 10036
Ph: (212)626-9220
Fax: (212)626-9210
E-mail: sonya@opcofamerica.org
URL: http://www.opcofamerica.org
Contact: Sonya Fry, Exec. Dir.

Founded: 1939. **Members:** 600. **Membership Dues:** active/associate (resident), $375 (annual) ● active/associate (non-resident/overseas), $175 (annual) ● active (young), $100 (annual). **Staff:** 2. **Multinational. Description:** Professional association of international journalists with overseas experience including correspondents, editors, reporters, photographers, freelance writers, and authors of published books on foreign affairs. Maintains reciprocal privileges with numerous press clubs in the U.S. and globally. **Awards:** Overseas Press Club Awards. **Frequency:** annual. **Type:** recognition. **Recipient:** for excellence in newspaper, wire service, radio, television, magazine, cartoon and photographic reporting from abroad. **Telecommunication Services:** electronic mail, admin@opcofamerica.org. **Committees:** Awards; Freedom of the Press. **Publications:** *Dateline*, annual. Magazine. Contains information awards and winners listings as well as articles on international topics. **Price:** free. **Advertising:** accepted ● *OPC of America - Directory*, periodic. Membership Directory ● Newsletter, monthly. **Price:** free for members. **Conventions/Meetings:** annual dinner, with awards - always April, in New York City.

3155 ■ People's News Agency (PNA)
c/o Proutist Universal New York Sector
6310 Tilden Ln.
Rockville, MD 20852
Ph: (301)231-0110 (202)468-3004
Fax: (202)829-0462
E-mail: nysector@prout.org
URL: http://www.prout.org/pna
Contact: Dada Shubhacetanananda, Contact

Founded: 1972. **Members:** 968. **Staff:** 17. **Languages:** Bengali, Danish, English, French, German, Hindi, Mandarin, Portuguese, Spanish. **Description:** Writers, artists, and journalists; news publications. Provides alternative news stories to the international, national, regional, and local press. Serves as a clearinghouse of information; provides certification of agency correspondents. **Telecommunication Services:** electronic mail, pna-news@igc.org. **Publications:** *Global Times*, semimonthly. Newspaper ● *PROUT Journal*, quarterly. Features topics on alternative socio-economic ideas, holistic living and spirituality. **Price:** $12.00/year. **Circulation:** 10,000. Alternate Formats: online ● *Prout Magazine*, weekly ● *Prout Times*, weekly ● *Tara Magazine*, quarterly ● Catalog ● Newspapers. **Conventions/Meetings:** annual meeting.

3156 ■ Professional Hockey Writers' Association (PHWA)
c/o Sherry L. Ross, Sec.-Treas.
1480 Pleasant Valley Way, No. 44
West Orange, NJ 07052
Ph: (973)669-8607
Contact: Sherry L. Ross, Sec.-Treas.

Founded: 1967. **Members:** 400. **Membership Dues:** $15 (annual). **Regional Groups:** 26. **Description:** Writers who cover member teams of the National Hockey League (see separate entry). Encourages high standards among professional hockey writers. Seeks to assure writers are provided adequate facilities at arenas. Promotes good working relations between writers and club management, especially concerning access to players and coaches. Contributes to the William Masterton Scholarship Fund, based in Bloomington, MN. Nominates members for writers wing of NHL Hall of Fame. Maintains hall of fame. **Awards:** All-Star Team. **Frequency:** annual. **Type:** recognition ● Bill Masterton Memorial Trophy. **Frequency:** annual. **Type:** recognition. **Recipient:** for the player who shows the most perseverance, sportsmanship, and dedication to hockey ● Dick Dillman Press Box and Press Guide Awards. **Frequency:** annual. **Type:** recognition ● Most Valuable Player of the Year. **Type:** recognition ● Rookie of the Year. **Frequency:** annual. **Type:** recognition. **Committees:** Hall of Fame Media Recognition. **Formerly:** (1971) National Hockey League Writers' Association.

Publications: *PHWA Newsletter*, quarterly. **Price:** free for members. **Conventions/Meetings:** annual congress.

3157 ■ Regional Reporters Association (RRA)
PO Box 254
Ben Franklin Sta.
Washington, DC 20044
Ph: (202)408-2705
E-mail: president@rra.org
URL: http://www.rra.org
Contact: Suzanne Strunglinski, Pres.
Founded: 1987. **Members:** 200. **Membership Dues:** regular, $20 (annual). **Description:** Correspondents for newspapers and electronic media in the United States. Promotes responsible journalism; seeks to ensure freedom of the press. Facilitates exchange of information among members; sponsors educational programs. **Publications:** *Regional Reporter*, monthly. Newsletter. Alternate Formats: online.

3158 ■ Religion News Service (RNS)
1101 Connecticut Ave. NW, Ste.350
Washington, DC 20036
Ph: (202)463-8777
Free: (800)767-6781
Fax: (202)463-0033
E-mail: info@religionnews.com
URL: http://www.religionnews.com
Contact: Kevin Eckstrom, Ed.
Founded: 1934. **Staff:** 6. **For-Profit. Multinational. Description:** Daily newspapers, religious publications of all denominations, radio and television stations, and religious agencies. Disseminates news of interest to the entire religious constituency. Provides daily and weekly news reports, features, and photo service. **Telecommunication Services:** electronic mail, kevin.eckstrom@religionnews.com. **Formerly:** (1994) Religious News Service.

3159 ■ Religion Newswriters Association (RNA)
PO Box 2037
Westerville, OH 43086-2037
Ph: (614)891-9001
Fax: (614)891-9774
E-mail: mason@rna.org
URL: http://www.rna.org
Contact: Debra L. Mason, Exec. Dir.
Founded: 1949. **Members:** 250. **Membership Dues:** active print (more than 50,000 circulation), freelancer, international print, broadcast, affiliate, associate, educator, $50 (annual) ● student, retired, active print (under 50,000 circulation), $25 (annual). **Staff:** 3. **Description:** Provides support and educational services for religion news editors and reporters on secular daily and weekly newspapers, news services, newsmagazines, and broadcasting outlets. **Awards:** Cassels Award. **Frequency:** annual. **Type:** monetary. **Recipient:** for publications with circulations below 50,000 ● Chandler Award. **Frequency:** annual. **Type:** monetary. **Recipient:** for excellence in writing with emphasis on reporting skill and grasp of religion issues that is fair, balanced and in accordance with journalistic standards ● Cornell Award. **Frequency:** annual. **Type:** monetary. **Recipient:** for publications with circulations between 50,000-150,000 ● Schachern Award. **Frequency:** annual. **Type:** recognition. **Recipient:** for religion sections or pages in the secular press ● Supple Award. **Frequency:** annual. **Type:** monetary. **Recipient:** for religion writer of the year ● Templeton Reporter of the Year Award. **Frequency:** annual. **Type:** monetary. **Recipient:** for best religion reporter of the year ● Templeton Story of the Year Award. **Frequency:** annual. **Type:** monetary. **Recipient:** for religion story of the year. **Computer Services:** database, members only and newsletter subscribers ● information services, training, resources for journalists ● mailing lists ● online services, dues payments, membership application, conference registration. **Additional Websites:** http://www.religionlink.org. **Committees:** Contest; Mentoring; Nominating. **Formerly:** (1970) Religious Newswriters Association. **Publications:** *RNA Annual Program Guide*, annual. **Circulation:** 500. **Advertising:** accepted ● *RNA Extra Online*, bimonthly. Newsletter. **Price:** included in membership dues; $100.00 /year for nonmembers. **Circulation:** 450. **Advertising:** accepted. **Conventions/Meetings:** annual conference (exhibits) - 2008 Sept. 25-28, Washington, DC; 2009 Sept. 10-13, Chicago, IL.

3160 ■ Reporters Network
c/o Criminal Justice Journalists
Jerry Lee Center of Criminology
720 7th St. NW, 3rd Fl.
Washington, DC 20001
Ph: (202)448-1717
E-mail: cjj@reporters.net
URL: http://www.reporters.net
Contact: Ted Gest, Pres.
Founded: 1995. **Membership Dues:** working journalist, $40 (annual) ● associate, $60 (annual) ● student, $20 (annual). **Description:** Promotes the Internet as a research and communications medium for working journalists. **Publications:** *Crime and Justice News*, daily. Report. Contains summaries of major print and broadcast stories on crime and justice subjects.

3161 ■ Society of American Business Editors and Writers (SABEW)
c/o Missouri Scholarship of Journalism
385 McReynolds
Columbia, MO 65211-1200
Ph: (573)882-7862 (573)882-8985
Fax: (573)884-1372
E-mail: sabew@missouri.edu
URL: http://www.sabew.org
Contact: Carrie M. Paden, Exec. Dir.
Founded: 1964. **Members:** 3,200. **Membership Dues:** business journalist, associate, $50 (annual) ● student, $20 (annual) ● institutional (traditional), $115-$335 (annual) ● institutional (electronic), $95-$315 (annual). **Staff:** 5. **Budget:** $250,000. **Description:** Active business, economic, and financial news writers and editors for newspapers, magazines, and other publications; broadcasters of business news; teachers of business or journalism at colleges and universities. Plans periodic seminars on problems and techniques in business news coverage and occasional special meetings with business, financial, government and labor leaders, and other experts. Maintains the Resume Bank, a service that keeps resumes of members on file; editors looking for job candidates can request the resumes of candidates that meet their requirements. **Libraries: Type:** open to the public. **Holdings:** 30; periodicals. **Subjects:** business journalism. **Awards:** Distinguished Achievement Award. **Frequency:** annual. **Type:** recognition. **Recipient:** for individuals who have made a significant impact on the field of business journalism. **Telecommunication Services:** electronic mail, padenc@missouri.edu. **Committees:** Annual Conference; Best In Business Contest; Communications; Development; Distinguished Achievement Award; Education; Nominations; Pre-Audit. **Affiliated With:** Association for Education in Journalism and Mass Communication. **Formerly:** (1976) Society of American Business Writers; (1986) Society of American Business and Economic Writers. **Publications:** *The Business Journalist*, bimonthly. Newsletter. Informs members about industry trends. **Price:** included in membership dues; $65.00 for nonmembers. ISSN: 1527-7321. **Circulation:** 3,500. **Advertising:** accepted. Alternate Formats: online. Also Cited As: *TBJ* ● Membership Directory, annual. **Advertising:** accepted. **Conventions/Meetings:** annual conference (exhibits) - always in late April or early May.

3162 ■ Society of American Travel Writers (SATW)
7044 S 13th St.
Oak Creek, WI 53154
Ph: (414)908-4949
Fax: (414)768-8001
E-mail: satw@satw.org
URL: http://www.satw.org
Contact: Nancy Short, Exec. Dir.
Founded: 1956. **Members:** 1,305. **Membership Dues:** active, $130 (annual) ● associate, $250 (annual). **Staff:** 2. **Budget:** $230,000. **Regional Groups:** 5. **Local Groups:** 5. **Description:** Represents editors, writers, broadcasters, photographers, and public relations representatives. Strives to provide travelers with accurate reports on destinations, facilities, and services; "seeks to guard the right of freedom to travel"; encourages preservation of historic sites and conservation of nature. **Awards:** Lowell Thomas Awards. **Frequency:** annual. **Type:** recognition. **Recipient:** for North American journalists ● Phoenix Awards. **Frequency:** annual. **Type:** recognition. **Recipient:** for individuals, organizations, or communities championing the cause of conservation, preservation, and beautification of America ● SATW Photographer of the Year. **Frequency:** annual. **Type:** recognition. **Recipient:** for photographers. **Councils:** Associates; Editors; Freelance; Past Presidents; Seniors. **Publications:** *Society of American Travel Writers—Annual Directory of Members*. Membership Directory. Includes specialties and affiliations. **Price:** $250.00 book form or disk; $400.00 book form and disk. **Circulation:** 1,700. **Advertising:** accepted. Alternate Formats: CD-ROM ● *Travel Writer*, monthly. Newsletter. Details important industry trends. Includes listing of new members, book reviews, calendar of events, and obituaries. **Price:** free for members. **Circulation:** 950. **Advertising:** accepted. Alternate Formats: online. **Conventions/Meetings:** annual convention - 2008 Oct. 17-22, Houston, TX ● annual SATW Institute for Travel Writing and Photography - workshop, intensive real-world professional travel writing training session.

3163 ■ Society for News Design (SND)
1130 Ten Rod Rd., Ste.D 202
North Kingstown, RI 02852-4180
Ph: (401)294-5233 (401)294-5234
Fax: (401)294-5238
E-mail: snd@snd.org
URL: http://www.snd.org
Contact: Elise Burroughs, Exec. Dir.
Founded: 1979. **Members:** 2,500. **Membership Dues:** professional in U.S., $105 (annual) ● small paper in U.S., educator in U.S., $95 (annual) ● student in U.S., $55 (annual) ● student chapter in U.S., $45 (annual) ● professional outside U.S., $125 (annual) ● small paper outside U.S., $115 (annual). **Staff:** 3. **Budget:** $850,000. **Regional Groups:** 20. **Multinational. Description:** Editors, publishers, artists, photographers, copy editors, online journalists and designers employed by news organizations or related businesses; high school and college journalism students and educators. Works to improve journalism through good design. Serves as a forum for news professionals interested in visual journalism and web design. Seeks to strengthen journalism design as a profession and newspaper publishing as a business. Offers materials and seminars on newspaper design and graphics. Sponsors annual international design competition and annual workshop and exhibition. **Libraries: Type:** open to the public. **Holdings:** 23. **Subjects:** newspaper design. **Awards:** Best of Newspaper Design Creative Competition. **Frequency:** annual. **Type:** recognition. **Recipient:** for excellence ● **Frequency:** monthly. **Type:** recognition. **Recipient:** for excellence in design of online journalism projects. **Computer Services:** Mailing lists, of members for a fee ● online services, bibliographies, consultants, bookstore. **Committees:** Advertising Design; Competition; Diversity; Education; Information Graphics; Membership and Marketing; New Media; Publications; Quick Course; Technology; Workshop. **Formerly:** (1982) Society of Newspaper Design. **Publications:** *Best of Newspaper Design TM* (in English and Spanish), annual. Book. Features best newspaper designs, graphics and photo. **Price:** included in membership dues; $35.00 for nonmembers. ISSN: 1520-4251. Alternate Formats: online. Also Cited As: *Awards Annual* ● *Design, The Journal of the Society for News Design*, quarterly. Magazine. Covers the scholarship and craftsmanship of news design. **Price:** included in membership dues; $10.00/copy. ISSN: 1520-4243. **Advertising:** accepted ● *SND Update*, 8/year. Newsletter. **Price:** available to members only. ISSN: 1520-426X ● *World's Best-Designed Newspapers*, annual. Video. Contains images of winners of the SND Award for World's Best-

Designed newspapers. **Price:** $25.00. Alternate Formats: CD-ROM. **Conventions/Meetings:** annual Infographics - workshop and convention (exhibits) - 2-3/year ● annual international conference, visual journalists from around the world gather for workshops and general sessions (exhibits) ● New Media Workshop, international workshops - 2-3/year ● SND Quick Course - regional meeting and workshop, regional one-day workshops that cover graphics, design, and newspapers - 12-18/year.

3164 ■ Society of Professional Journalists (SPJ)
3909 N Meridian St.
Indianapolis, IN 46208-4011
Ph: (317)927-8000
Fax: (317)920-4789
E-mail: tharper@spj.org
URL: http://www.spj.org
Contact: Clint Brewer, Pres.

Founded: 1909. **Members:** 9,900. **Membership Dues:** professional, $72 (annual) ● retired, household, student, $36 (annual) ● associate, $90 (annual). **Staff:** 12. **Budget:** $1,700,000. **Regional Groups:** 12. **State Groups:** 287. **Description:** Professional society - journalism. Promotes a free and unfettered press; high professional standards and ethical behavior; journalism as a career. Conducts lobbying activities; maintains legal defense fund. Sponsors Pulliam/Kilgore Freedom of Information Internships in Washington, DC, and Indianapolis, IN. Holds forums on the free press. **Awards:** Distinguished Teaching in Journalism Award. **Type:** recognition. **Recipient:** for an outstanding journalism educator who made a significant contribution to journalism education ● Eugene C. Pulliam Editorial Writing Fellowship. **Frequency:** annual. **Type:** fellowship ● Helen Thomas Lifetime Achievement Award. **Frequency:** annual. **Type:** recognition. **Recipient:** for lifetime service to the journalism profession ● Outstanding Graduate Citations. **Type:** recognition ● Sigma Delta Chi Award. **Type:** recognition. **Recipient:** for outstanding achievement in all forms of journalism ● Wells Memorial Key. **Frequency:** annual. **Type:** recognition. **Recipient:** for outstanding service to the society. **Computer Services:** Online services, active forums. **Committees:** Awards and Honors; Diversity; Ethics; Freedom of Information; Freelance; Legal Defense Fund; Professional Development; Project Watchdog. **Affiliated With:** Sigma Delta Chi Foundation. **Absorbed:** (1985) Economics News Broadcasters Association. **Formerly:** (1973) Sigma Delta Chi; (1988) Society of Professional Journalists, Sigma Delta Chi. **Publications:** *Quill*, 9/year. Magazine. **Price:** $72.00/year. ISSN: 0480-7898. **Advertising:** accepted. **Conventions/Meetings:** annual Convention and National Journalism Conference - conference and seminar (exhibits).

3165 ■ Society of the Silurians
PO Box 1195
Madison Square Sta.
New York, NY 10159
Ph: (212)532-0887
E-mail: silurians@aol.com
URL: http://www.silurians.com
Contact: Eve Berliner, Ed.

Founded: 1924. **Members:** 500. **Membership Dues:** individual, $55 (annual). **Description:** Veteran journalists who worked for 12 or more years on the staffs of New York City and metropolitan area newspapers, magazines, television media and other media groups as reporters, editors, columnists, photographers, artists, and illustrators. Sponsors major journalism awards and other charitable activity. **Awards:** Excellence in Journalism Award. **Frequency:** annual. **Type:** recognition. **Recipient:** for outstanding achievement in all major categories including investigative, feature writing, editorial commentary, and community service ● Lifetime Achievement Award. **Frequency:** annual. **Type:** recognition. **Recipient:** for distinguished lifetime work of highest achieving journalists in the field. **Publications:** *Directory and Handbook*, biennial ● *Shoeleather and Printers' Ink* ● *Silurian News*, semiannual. **Conventions/Meetings:** semiannual banquet and reunion - always New York City.

3166 ■ South Asian Journalists Association (SAJA)
c/o Prof. Sreenath Sreenivasan
Columbia Graduate School of Journalism
2950 Broadway
New York, NY 10027
Ph: (212)854-5979
E-mail: saja@columbia.edu
URL: http://www.saja.org
Contact: Ms. Deepti Hajela, Pres.

Founded: 1994. **Members:** 800. **Membership Dues:** full, $20 (annual) ● student, $10 (annual) ● associate, $40 (annual). **Local Groups:** 10. **Description:** Provides a networking and resource forum for journalists of South Asian origin and journalists covering South Asia or the South Asian Diaspora for North American news organizations. Acts as a resource to facilitate and promote accurate coverage of South Asia and South Asians in North America. **Awards:** SAJA Journalism Awards. **Frequency:** annual. **Type:** recognition. **Recipient:** for excellence in coverage of South Asia and outstanding reporting by South Asian journalists and students in U.S. and Canada ● SAJA Journalism Scholarships. **Frequency:** annual. **Type:** scholarship. **Recipient:** for high school, college, and graduate students with financial hardship. **Computer Services:** Mailing lists, open to the public ● online services, publication. **Telecommunication Services:** electronic mail, sree@sree.net ● electronic mail, sajadeepti@yahoo.com. **Committees:** Awards; Chapters; Convention; Governance; Mediawatch; Special Programs; Student Affairs and Scholarship. **Publications:** *SAJA Directory*, periodic. Alternate Formats: online ● *SAJA Stylebook*. Handbook ● Newsletter, periodic. Alternate Formats: online. **Conventions/Meetings:** annual convention (exhibits) - each summer in New York City; June or July at Columbia University.

3167 ■ Travel Journalists Guild (TJG)
PO Box 10643
Chicago, IL 60610
Ph: (312)664-9279
Fax: (312)664-9701
E-mail: pdhoffman32@msn.com
URL: http://www.tjgonline.com
Contact: Philip D. Hoffman, Exec. Sec.

Founded: 1980. **Members:** 75. **Membership Dues:** individual, $150 (annual). **Staff:** 1. **Budget:** $25,000. **Description:** Independent travel writers who earn a substantial portion of their income by writing travel articles or books, selling travel photographs, or by lecturing and presenting travel films. Aims to improve working conditions for travel writers with regard to financial compensation for their work, retention of rights to published pieces, and travel opportunities for the purpose of research. Sponsors four to six research and writing trips per year.

3168 ■ United Nations Correspondents Association (UNCA)
United Nations
405 E 42nd St., Rm. S-326
New York, NY 10017
Ph: (212)963-7137
E-mail: contactus@unca.com
URL: http://www.unca.com
Contact: J. Tuyet Nguyen, Pres.

Founded: 1948. **Members:** 250. **Membership Dues:** professional, $65 (annual). **Budget:** $20,000. **Description:** Accredited United Nations press, radio, and television correspondents. Seeks to maintain the freedom and prestige of press, radio, and television correspondents in their relations with the UN. Protects the rights of bonafide correspondents to secure accreditation and unhindered access to the UN headquarters or regional offices, and to their normally available facilities, without discrimination. **Libraries: Type:** not open to the public. **Holdings:** 200; books, periodicals. **Awards:** Dag Hammarskjold Memorial Scholarship Fund. **Frequency:** annual. **Type:** scholarship. **Recipient:** for journalists in developing countries ● UNCA Prize for UN Coverage. **Frequency:** annual. **Type:** monetary. **Recipient:** for excellence in media coverage of UN worldwide availability. **Affiliated With:** United Nations. **Publications:** Membership Directory, annual. Lists all members and affiliations, and UN mission press officers. **Price:** $5.00. **Circulation:** 4,000. **Advertising:** accepted. **Conventions/Meetings:** annual meeting - always January in New York City.

3169 ■ United Press International (UPI)
1510 H St. NW
Washington, DC 20005
Ph: (202)898-8188 (202)898-8000
Free: (800)796-4874
Fax: (202)898-8048
E-mail: hguerra@upi.com
URL: http://www.upi.com
Contact: Dr. Christopher Ching, VP of Finance

Founded: 1907. **For-Profit. Multinational. Description:** Gathers news and photographs of current events to distribute to newspapers, periodicals, cable systems, and radio and television stations throughout the world; maintains 204 local news bureaus in 79 countries. Provides speakers. **Boards:** Broadcast Advisory; Newspaper Advisory. **Formed by Merger of:** United Press Associations; International News Service. **Publications:** *The Iraq War: As Witnessed by the Correspondents and Photographers of UPI*. Book ● *UPI Stylebook and Guide to Newswriting*.

3170 ■ United States Harness Writers' Association (USHWA)
c/o Jerry Connors, Sec.
Box 1314
Mechanicsburg, PA 17055
Ph: (717)766-3219
E-mail: ushwa@paonline.com
URL: http://www.ustrotting.com/absolutenm/anmviewer.asp?a=6793&z=30
Contact: Gordon Waterstone, Pres.

Founded: 1947. **Members:** 335. **Membership Dues:** in U.S., $40 (annual) ● associate, $25 (annual). **Staff:** 1. **Local Groups:** 12. **Description:** Writers, reporters, editors, broadcasters, columnists, and cartoonists who cover harness racing for the press. Seeks to further the interests of light harness racing. Maintains hall of fame and charitable program. Votes on national awards. **Publications:** *U.S. Harness Writers' Association—Newsletter*, quarterly. **Conventions/Meetings:** annual conference, includes awards presentation ● annual dinner, includes awards presentation.

3171 ■ U.S. Marine Corps Combat Correspondents Association (USMCCCA)
110 Fox Ct.
Wildwood, FL 34785-9081
Ph: (352)748-4698
Fax: (352)748-4698
E-mail: usmccca@cfl.rr.com
URL: http://www.usmccca.org
Contact: Don H. Gee, Exec. Dir.

Founded: 1941. **Members:** 700. **Membership Dues:** sergeant, $15 (annual) ● regular, associate, affiliate, $30 (annual) ● life, $175-$350. **Staff:** 1. **Budget:** $70,000. **Regional Groups:** 20. **Local Groups:** 20. **Description:** Active duty, reserve, retired, and former Marines who served or are serving as reporters, still and motion picture photographers, radio and TV newscasters, TV and broadcast production people, artists and illustrators, and public relations and advertising practitioners or have similar civilian occupations in mass communications. **Libraries: Type:** reference. **Holdings:** articles, biographical archives, photographs. **Awards:** Brigadier General Robert L. Denig Distinguished Service. **Frequency:** annual. **Type:** recognition. **Recipient:** for a civilian communicator ● Donald L. Dickenson Memorial. **Frequency:** annual. **Type:** recognition. **Recipient:** for members ● USMCCCA Merit Awards. **Frequency:** annual. **Type:** recognition. **Recipient:** for excellence in a variety of mass communication areas. **Computer Services:** database ● mailing lists ● online services. **Affiliated With:** U.S. Marine Corps Combat Correspondents Association. **Publications:** *CC Newsletter*, quarterly. Contains obituaries, organization related news. **Price:** included in membership dues. **Circulation:** 1,000. Alternate Formats: online ● *Last to Know, First to Go.* Book ● *U.S. Marine Corps Combat Correspondents Association—Annual Conference Journal.* Presents award winners recognized at annual conference for distinguished performance for the preceding year. **Price:** included in membership dues. **Circulation:** 2,000. **Advertising:** accepted. Also Cited As: *MCCCA Journal* ● Membership Directory, annual. **Circulation:** 1,100. Alternate Formats: diskette. **Conventions/Meetings:** annual competition and conference, gathering of members for seminars, awards ceremony, business meeting, elections and camaraderie ● annual conference - always September ● seminar.

3172 ■ UNITY: Journalists of Color
7950 Jones Br. Dr.
McLean, VA 22107
Ph: (703)854-3585
Fax: (703)854-3586
E-mail: info@unityjournalists.org
URL: http://www.unityjournalists.org
Contact: Onica Makwakwa, Exec. Dir.

Description: Comprised of the Asian American Journalists Association, the National Association of Black Journalists, the National Association of Hispanic Journalists, and the Native American Journalists Association. Advocates for fair and accurate news coverage about people of color. Raises awareness and participation of the media industry in understanding the diverse cultures represented by the UNITY alliance members. Increases representation of people of color at all levels in the nation's newsrooms.

3173 ■ White House Correspondents' Association (WHCA)
1920 N St. NW, Ste.300
Washington, DC 20036
Ph: (202)452-4836
E-mail: shearer@northwestern.edu
URL: http://www.whca.net
Contact: Julia Whiston, Exec. Dir.

Founded: 1914. **Members:** 600. **Description:** Washington, DC, newspaper, magazine, and television-radio correspondents engaged exclusively in news work. **Awards:** Aldo Beckman Award. **Frequency:** annual. **Type:** monetary. **Recipient:** for repeated excellence in White House coverage ● Edgar A. Poe Award. **Frequency:** annual. **Type:** monetary. **Recipient:** for excellence in coverage of news of national or regional significance ● Merriman Smith Award. **Frequency:** annual. **Type:** monetary. **Recipient:** for presidential news coverage under deadline pressure ● WHCA Frank Cormier Scholarship Award. **Frequency:** annual. **Type:** scholarship. **Recipient:** for achievements and potential of a selected college-bound senior. **Conventions/Meetings:** competition ● annual dinner (exhibits).

3174 ■ Women's National Book Association (WNBA)
c/o Susannah Greenberg, Public Relations Mgr.
PO Box 237
New York, NY 10150
Ph: (212)208-4629
Fax: (212)208-4629
E-mail: publicity@bookbuzz.com
URL: http://www.wnba-books.org
Contact: Susannah Greenberg, Public Relations Mgr.

Founded: 1917. **Members:** 1,000. **Membership Dues:** sustaining (based on annual sales), $500-$2,500 (annual). **Budget:** $16,000. **Local Groups:** 10. **Description:** Women and men who work with and value books. Exists to promote reading and to support the role of women in the book community. **Awards:** Ann Heidbreder Eastman Grant. **Frequency:** annual. **Type:** scholarship. **Recipient:** for a librarian who wishes to study publishing ● Lucile Micheels Pannell Award. **Frequency:** annual. **Type:** recognition. **Recipient:** for creative use of books with children ● The WNBA Award. **Frequency:** biennial. **Type:** recognition. **Recipient:** for a woman who has made outstanding contributions to society through books. **Committees:** Ann Eastman Grant; Pannell Award; WNBA Award. **Publications:** *The Bookwoman*, 3/year. Covers association activities and women's issues in the publishing industry; includes book reviews and member profile. **Price:** free for members; $15.00 /year for nonmembers in U.S.; $20.00 /year for nonmembers outside U.S. ISSN: 0163-1128. **Circulation:** 1,500. **Advertising:** accepted. Alternate Formats: online.

3175 ■ World Bowling Writers (WBW)
122 S Michigan Ave., Ste.1506
Chicago, IL 60603
Ph: (312)341-1110
Fax: (312)341-1469
E-mail: keithhale679@aol.com
URL: http://www.worldbowlingwriters.com
Contact: Hazel McLeary, Pres.

Founded: 1977. **Members:** 390. **Membership Dues:** regular, $30 (annual). **Staff:** 1. **Multinational. Description:** Individuals involved in the communications media who cover the bowling industry. Seeks to: inform members of developments in the sport of bowling worldwide; improve media coverage of bowling. Maintains hall of fame. **Awards:** Distinguished Service. **Frequency:** annual. **Type:** recognition. **Recipient:** for service to the bowling industry ● Gosta Zellen Golden Quill. **Type:** recognition. **Recipient:** for outstanding bowling journalist ● Male and Female Bowler of the Year. **Frequency:** annual. **Type:** recognition. **Recipient:** for performance in international competitions. **Publications:** *Worldletter*, monthly. Newsletter. Contains wrap-up of bowling events, brief stories, and notices. **Price:** included in membership dues ● *Worldletter Plus*, periodic. Newsletter. Contains in-depth information, such as tournament standings, opinion pieces, etc. **Conventions/Meetings:** annual general assembly - usually November.

Privatization

3176 ■ Privacy Rights Clearinghouse (PRC)
3100 5th Ave., Ste.B
San Diego, CA 92103
Ph: (619)298-3396
Fax: (619)298-5681
E-mail: bgivens@privacyrights.org
URL: http://www.privacyrights.org
Contact: Beth Givens, Founder/Dir.

Founded: 1992. **Staff:** 3. **Description:** Advocates for consumers in Internet privacy, identity theft, telemarketing, junk mail, medical records, workplace privacy and more. **Publications:** *Fact Sheets* (in English and Spanish). Contains information on privacy issues. Alternate Formats: online.

Product Testing

3177 ■ International Association for Product Development (IAPD)
PO Box 998
New Canaan, CT 06840
Ph: (203)254-3677
Fax: (203)254-3679
E-mail: info@iapdonline.com
URL: http://www.iapdonline.com
Contact: Kemp V. Dwenger, Founder/Dir.

Founded: 1990. **Membership Dues:** company, $20 (annual). **Multinational. Description:** Facilitates the understanding and implementation of cultural and process change that will enable member companies to sustain growth and enhance global competitiveness through product innovation. Enables member companies to continually improve their management of product development and innovation. Provides an environment in which hands-on experience is shared among members, practitioners and presenters. Emphasizes continuous improvement. **Telecommunication Services:** electronic mail, kemp@iapdonline.com.

3178 ■ International Consumer Product Health and Safety Organization (ICPHSO)
PO Box 1785
Germantown, MD 20875-1785
Ph: (301)528-0310
Fax: (301)601-3543
E-mail: icphso@aol.com
URL: http://www.icphso.org
Contact: Jack Walsh, Pres.

Founded: 1993. **Multinational. Description:** Resolves health and safety issues related to consumer products manufactured and marketed worldwide. **Publications:** *Update*, quarterly. Newsletter. Provides news and information on health and safety. Alternate Formats: online.

Professionals

3179 ■ Alliance for Work-Life Progress (AWLP)
14040 N Northsight Blvd.
Scottsdale, AZ 85260-3601
Ph: (480)922-2007
Free: (800)874-9383
Fax: (480)603-0791
E-mail: awlp@worldatwork.org
URL: http://www.awlp.org
Contact: Kathie Lingle, Dir.

Founded: 1996. **Description:** Committed in developing workplaces that encourage people to achieve success in their personal and work lives. Works to identify and advance practical ways of reducing work-life conflict and fostering the integration of work and personal goals, in the knowledge that this creates better performing workplaces, healthier and more productive employees, and more stable communities. Works to bring work-life issues to the forefront through publications, forums, education, and an annual conference. **Affiliated With:** WorldatWork.

3180 ■ American Association of Electronic Reporters and Transcribers (AAERT)
23812 Rock Cir.
Bothell, WA 98021-8573
Free: (800)233-5306
E-mail: aaert@blarg.net
URL: http://www.aaert.org
Contact: Gillian Lawrence, Pres.

Founded: 1994. **Membership Dues:** general, $85 (annual) ● apprentice/intern/learner, $55 (annual) ● vendor, $325 (annual) ● corporate (based on number of employees), $125-$325 (annual). **Description:** Provides education and certification for professional individuals engaged in electronic reporting, transcribing and other related field. Advocates for public awareness and acceptance of the electronic reporting industry. **Awards:** Reporter of the Year. **Frequency:** annual. **Type:** recognition. **Recipient:** to outstanding reporter for his/her achievements and contributions to the association ● Transcriber of the Year. **Frequency:** annual. **Type:** recognition. **Recipient:** to outstanding transcriber for his/her achievements and contributions to the association. **Publications:** *Certification Test Study Guide.* Manual. Contains electronic reporting information. ● *The Court Reporter*, quarterly. Newsletter. Contains latest legislative issues and industry news. Alternate Formats: online ● Membership Directory, annual.

3181 ■ American Business Association of Russian Professionals (AmBAR)
1290 Oakmead Pkwy., Ste.118
Sunnyvale, CA 94085
E-mail: advornikova@ambarclub.org
URL: http://www.ambarclub.com
Contact: Alexei Andreev PhD, Exec. VP

Description: Provides a forum for the professional community of Russian expatriates in the US. Enhances cooperation between the United States and Russia in high technology areas. Provides recruitment resources to members. **Computer Services:** Online services, discussion forum ● online services, job postings.

3182 ■ American Society for Training and Development (ASTD)
1640 King St.
Box 1443
Alexandria, VA 22313-2043
Ph: (703)683-8100
Free: (800)628-2783
Fax: (703)683-8103
E-mail: memberservices@astd.org
URL: http://www.astd.org
Contact: Kimo Kippen, Chm.
Founded: 1944. **Members:** 70,000. **Membership Dues:** classic (individual), $180 (annual) ● classic (Canada and Mexico), $205 (annual) ● classic (all other country), $250 (annual) ● senior, $90 (annual) ● student, $59 (annual). **Regional Groups:** 150. **National Groups:** 100. **Multinational. Description:** Promotes workplace learning and performance; represents the field to U.S. federal and state policy-makers through education, policy development, grassroots support and work in coalitions with other national organizations in business, education and labor. Offers the Human Performance Improvement Certificate Program. **Councils:** Policy. **Subgroups:** Benchmarking Forum. **Publications:** *ASTD Buyer's Guide and Consultants Directory*. Contains a listing of training suppliers in the field of workplace learning and performance. Alternate Formats: online ● *Info-line Plus*, monthly. Book. **Price:** $89.00/year in U.S.; $114.00/year in Canada and Mexico; $169.00/year in all other countries ● *TD Magazine*. Features industry news and professional guidance. **Advertising:** accepted ● Annual Report, annual ● Newsletter, monthly. **Price:** free. Alternate Formats: online. **Conventions/Meetings:** international conference, presents and discusses new issues and practices in learning and performance (exhibits) ● seminar ● annual TechKnowledge Conference and Exposition (exhibits).

3183 ■ International Association of Facilitators (IAF)
14985 Glazier Ave., Ste.550
St. Paul, MN 55124
Ph: (952)891-3541
Free: (800)281-9948
Fax: (952)891-1800
E-mail: office@iaf-world.org
URL: http://www.iaf-world.org
Contact: Betty J. Kjellberg CAE, Exec. Dir.
Founded: 1994. **Members:** 1,300. **Membership Dues:** regular, $125 (annual) ● affiliate, $115 (annual) ● group, $100 (annual) ● student/individual residing in a developing country, $50 (annual). **Multinational. Description:** Promotes, supports and advances the art and practice of professional facilitation through methods exchange, professional growth, practical research, collegial networking and support services. Develops the appropriate opportunities, methodologies, models, tools and modes that support the practice of exemplary participatory facilitation. Provides a network to foster interchange between professional practitioners in the field. **Publications:** *Global Flipchart*, monthly. Newsletter. Alternate Formats: online ● *Group Facilitation: A Research and Applications Journal*, semiannual. Alternate Formats: online.

3184 ■ National Association of Reunion Managers (NARM)
PO Box 59713
Renton, WA 98058-2713
Free: (800)654-2776
E-mail: info@reunions.com
URL: http://www.reunions.com
Contact: Wanda Diroll, Pres.
Founded: 1986. **Members:** 55. **Membership Dues:** reunion manager, $395 (annual) ● satellite office, $100 (annual). **Staff:** 1. **Description:** Professional reunion managers. Strives for excellence in all aspects of reunion management using only legal and ethical means in all reunion management activities. **Computer Services:** Online services, directory lists. **Conventions/Meetings:** annual convention, for members and vendors - every January.

3185 ■ National Association of Subrogation Professionals (NASP)
PO Box 390197
Edina, MN 55439-0197
Ph: (952)835-8700
Free: (800)574-9961
Fax: (952)835-8708
E-mail: gloria@subrogation.org
URL: http://www.subrogation.org
Contact: Gloria Isackson, Exec. Dir.
Founded: 1999. **Members:** 1,900. **Membership Dues:** professional, $125 (annual) ● service provider, $300 (annual) ● silver, $550 (annual) ● gold, $850 (annual) ● platinum, $1,150 (annual) ● diamond sponsor, $2,200 (annual). **Staff:** 5. **Regional Groups:** 7. **Local Groups:** 24. **Description:** Broker, program administrator, reinsurance intermediary, producer, attorney insurance subrogation, professional, collector, independent agent and subrogation manager. Provides a national forum for education, training, networking and information sharing. Promotes effectiveness of the subrogation industry. **Publications:** *Subrogator*, 3/year. Magazine. Dedicated to the art of subrogation. **Price:** included in membership dues. **Advertising:** accepted. Alternate Formats: CD-ROM; diskette. **Conventions/Meetings:** annual conference, with keynote speaker (exhibits) - 2008 Nov. 2-5, Hollywood, FL; 2009 Nov. 1-4, Colorado Springs, CO.

3186 ■ Upwardly Global
San Francisco Off.
582 Market St., Ste.1207
San Francisco, CA 94104
Ph: (415)834-9901
Fax: (415)840-0334
E-mail: jane@upwardlyglobal.org
URL: http://www.upwardlyglobal.org
Contact: Jane Leu, Founder/Exec. Dir.
Membership Dues: life - refugee/asylee, $40 ● life - immigrant, $100. **Description:** Helps refugees, asylees, and immigrants develop professional networks. Helps businesses put the right people in the right jobs. Provides help in writing resumes and sharpening interviewing skills.

Property

3187 ■ Property Records Industry Association (PRIA)
PO Box 3159
Durham, NC 27715-3159
Ph: (919)433-0121
Fax: (919)383-0035
E-mail: coordinator@pria.us
URL: http://www.pria.us
Contact: Stevie Hughes, Admin. Mgr.
Membership Dues: corporate (president's circle/ambassador/platinum/gold/silver/bronze), $500-$10,000 (annual) ● individual, $500 (annual) ● associate, $50 (annual) ● affiliate association/organization, $5,000 (annual). **Description:** Identifies problems, opportunities and solutions that will make property records systems more efficient, effective and responsive to the public. Provides a clearinghouse for information about property records practices, systems, procedures and legislation. Educates legislators and the public about the organization, role and functions of the property records industry. **Computer Services:** Mailing lists. **Committees:** Education; Legislative and Public Policy; Publicity; Real Property Law; Records Access Policy Advisory; Standards; State Advisory; Technology. **Publications:** *For The Record*. Newsletter.

Property Management

3188 ■ International Facility Management Association (IFMA)
1 E Greenway Plz., Ste.1100
Houston, TX 77046-0104
Ph: (713)623-4362
Fax: (713)623-6124
E-mail: ifma@ifma.org
URL: http://www.ifma.org
Contact: David Brady, Pres./CEO
Founded: 1980. **Members:** 18,000. **Membership Dues:** professional/associate (premium membership package), $368 (annual) ● retired (premium membership package), $299 (annual) ● student (basic membership package), $35 (annual). **Staff:** 44. **Budget:** $9,000,000. **Local Groups:** 130. **Multinational. Description:** Facility managers worldwide representing all types of organizations including banks, insurance companies, hospitals, colleges and universities, utility companies, electronic equipment manufacturers, petroleum companies, museums, auditoriums, and federal, state, provincial, and local governments. Purposes are to enhance the professional goals of persons involved or interested in the field of facility management (the planning, designing, and managing of workplaces); to cultivate cooperation, foster understanding, and create interest among firms, individuals, and other associations and professions as they may affect facility management; to engage in the interchange of views regarding legislation, regulation, and procedures that affect facility management. Offers job placement assistance; sponsors academic research; certifies facility managers; compiles statistics; sells books. Conducts educational and research programs. **Libraries: Type:** reference. **Holdings:** 500; books, periodicals. **Subjects:** facility management, workplace management, real estate, ergonomics, outsourcing, telecommuting. **Awards:** IFMA Award of Excellence. **Frequency:** annual. **Type:** recognition ● IFMA Fellows. **Type:** recognition. **Computer Services:** Online services, JOBnet. **Telecommunication Services:** electronic mail, membership@ifma.org ● electronic mail, webmaster@ifma.org. **Committees:** Awards; Codes and Regulations; Program; Research; Standards. **Councils:** Academic Facilities; Airport Facilities; Banking Institutions and Credit Unions; Call Centers; Corporate Headquarters; Corporate Real Estate; Environmental Health and Safety; FM Consultants; Health Care; Information Technology; Legal Industry; Manufacturing; Museums/Cultural Institutions; Public Sector Facilities; Religious Facilities; Research and Development Facilities; Utilities. **Special Interest Groups:** European. **Formerly:** (1982) National Facility Management Association. **Publications:** *Annual Conference Proceedings*, annual. Contains world workplace proceedings. **Price:** $75.00. **Circulation:** 4,000. Alternate Formats: CD-ROM ● *Facility Management Journal*, bimonthly. Includes recommended reading list. **Price:** $36.00 /year for members; $75.00 /year for nonmembers. ISSN: 1059-3667. **Circulation:** 18,000. **Advertising:** accepted. Alternate Formats: online ● *FM Buyers Guide*, annual. Contains an insert in Facility Management Journal and on Web site. Alternate Formats: online ● *Operations and Maintenance Benchmarks Survey*. Alternate Formats: online ● Membership Directory. Alternate Formats: online. **Conventions/Meetings:** periodic World Workplace - conference and workshop, with expositions (exhibits) ● annual World Workplace - Europe - conference and trade show (exhibits) - held in Europe.

3189 ■ National Association of Residential Property Managers (NARPM)
638 Independence Pkwy.
Chesapeake, VA 23320
Free: (800)782-3452
Fax: (866)466-2776
E-mail: info@narpm.org
URL: http://www.narpm.org
Contact: Sylvia L. Hill MPM, Pres.
Founded: 1988. **Members:** 1,200. **Membership Dues:** professional, affiliate, $245 (annual) ● support specialist, $100 (annual). **Staff:** 8. **Description:** Sponsors educational programs. Supports the professional and ethical practices of rental home management through networking, education and certification. **Computer Services:** database ● mailing lists. **Publications:** *Residential Resource*, monthly. Newsletter. **Advertising:** accepted. **Conventions/Meetings:** annual convention and trade show (exhibits).

3190 ■ National Property Management Association (NPMA)
28100 US Hwy. 19 N, Ste.400
Clearwater, FL 33761

Ph: (727)736-3788
Fax: (727)736-6707
E-mail: hq@npma.org
URL: http://www.npma.org
Contact: Paul Nesbitt, Exec. Dir.
Founded: 1970. **Members:** 4,100. **Membership Dues:** individual, $75 (annual) ● level I group (dues per member), $67 (annual) ● level II group (dues per member), $60 (annual). **Staff:** 4. **Budget:** $1,000,000. **Regional Groups:** 3. **Local Groups:** 56. **Description:** Aims to build leadership by educating, training and promoting standards of competency and ethical behavior in the asset management of personal property. Serves property professionals throughout the United States; members represent companies and organizations in both the public and private sectors, including scientific laboratories, universities, hospitals, public school systems, and local, state and federal government agencies. **Libraries: Type:** reference. **Holdings:** 6; archival material, articles, books, papers, periodicals, reports. **Subjects:** asset and government property management. **Awards:** Chapter of the Year. **Frequency:** annual. **Type:** recognition ● Federal Property Person of the Year. **Frequency:** annual. **Type:** recognition ● Property Person of the Year. **Frequency:** annual. **Type:** recognition ● **Type:** scholarship. **Computer Services:** database ● mailing lists. **Formed by Merger of:** National Industrial Property Management Association; Property Administration Association. **Publications:** *Certification Handbook* ● *Conference Planning Guide* ● *NPMA Survey* ● *Property Manual*. Manuals. **Price:** $50.00 for members; $60.00 for nonmembers ● *Property Professional*, bimonthly. **Price:** $35.00/year. **Circulation:** 2,500. **Advertising:** accepted ● Videos. **Conventions/Meetings:** annual meeting and symposium (exhibits) ● regional meeting (exhibits) - 3/year ● annual seminar.

Public Lands

3191 ■ National Brownfield Association (NBA)
5440 N Cumberland Ave., Ste.155
Chicago, IL 60656
Ph: (773)714-0407
Fax: (773)714-0989
E-mail: ken.cornell@aig.com
URL: http://www.brownfieldassociation.org
Contact: Kenneth Cornell, Pres.
Founded: 1999. **Membership Dues:** government employee in U.S., $200 (annual) ● professional in U.S., $300 (annual) ● professional in Canada, $374 (annual) ● student in U.S., $25-$75 (annual) ● corporate in U.S., $2,500 (annual) ● corporate in Canada, C$3,745 (annual). **Multinational. Description:** Represents brownfield stakeholders, property owners, developers, investors, service professionals and government representatives. Stimulates the responsible redevelopment of brownfields. Provides a forum for networking with peers and learning about best practices. Keeps members informed of changing market conditions, policy and legislation. **Publications:** *Brownfield News*, bimonthly. Magazine. **Price:** included in membership dues; $79.95 /year for nonmembers; $94.95 /year for nonmembers outside U.S. **Advertising:** accepted. Alternate Formats: online ● Brochure. Alternate Formats: online.

Public Relations

3192 ■ Agricultural Relations Council (ARC)
62768 N Star Dr.
Montrose, CO 81401
Ph: (970)249-1465
Fax: (970)249-4385
E-mail: jmo@rmmc.biz
URL: http://www.agrelationscouncil.org
Contact: Bob Giblin, Pres.
Founded: 1953. **Members:** 250. **Membership Dues:** individual, $170 (annual). **Staff:** 4. **Budget:** $80,000. **Description:** Professional society of agricultural public relations executives employed by private business firms, associations, publications, and government agencies. Operates placement service. **Awards:** Golden ARC Award. **Frequency:** annual. **Type:** recognition. **Publications:** *Agricultural Relations Council—Directory of Members*, annual. Lists of persons engaged in agricultural public relations. **Price:** $50.00 for nonmembers. **Circulation:** 350. **Advertising:** accepted ● *ARClight*, monthly. Newsletter. Includes employment opportunities; for council members who are engaged in agricultural public relations. **Price:** available to members only. **Circulation:** 300. **Conventions/Meetings:** annual meeting - usually in February ● annual seminar - always summer.

3193 ■ IPREX
2861 Kingsland Ct.
Atlanta, GA 30339
Ph: (770)433-9084
Fax: (770)433-9318
E-mail: experts@iprex.com
URL: http://www.iprex.com
Contact: Jim Walsh, Pres.
Founded: 1983. **Members:** 45. **Budget:** $70,000. **Description:** Independent public relations firms. Offers forum for sharing business ideas and opportunities; provides services to member firms. **Libraries: Type:** reference. **Holdings:** articles. **Computer Services:** database. **Divisions:** Asia; Canada; Europe; Pacific Rim. **Formerly:** Public Relations Exchange; PRX International. **Publications:** *InterChange*, periodic. Newsletter. **Conventions/Meetings:** conference (exhibits) - 3/year.

3194 ■ National Black Public Relations Society (NBPRS)
4929 Wilshire Blvd., Ste.245
Los Angeles, CA 90010
Ph: (323)857-1171
Fax: (323)857-7210
URL: http://www.nbprs.org
Contact: Wynona Redmond, Pres.
Founded: 1981. **Members:** 100. **Membership Dues:** professional, $100 (annual) ● associate, $60 (annual) ● student, $25 (annual). **Description:** Black public relations professionals who are either self-employed or employed by advertising agencies, radio and television stations, businesses, or nonprofit organizations. Provides a forum for discussion of topics related to public relations; holds professional development workshops; conducts seminars; maintains speakers' bureau to promote the image of blacks in business. **Affiliated With:** National Association of Black Journalists. **Publications:** Newsletter, quarterly ● Also publishes instructional brochures; plans to publish a directory of black public relations professionals. **Conventions/Meetings:** quarterly meeting.

3195 ■ Public Relations Society of America (PRSA)
33 Maiden Ln., 11th Fl.
New York, NY 10038-5150
Ph: (212)460-1400 (212)460-1401
Fax: (212)995-0757
E-mail: exec@prsa.org
URL: http://www.prsa.org
Contact: William Murray, Pres.
Founded: 1947. **Members:** 20,000. **Membership Dues:** individual (full), $225 (annual) ● associate, $115-$155 (annual) ● associate (graduate student and PRSSA graduate), $60 (annual). **Staff:** 54. **Budget:** $11,000,000. **Local Groups:** 121. **Description:** Professional society of public relations practitioners in business and industry, counseling firms, government, associations, hospitals, schools, and nonprofit organizations. Conducts professional development programs. Maintains a Professional Resource Center. Offers accreditation program. **Libraries: Type:** reference; open to the public. **Holdings:** 1,000; archival material. **Subjects:** public relations. **Awards:** Bronze Anvil Awards. **Frequency:** annual. **Type:** recognition. **Recipient:** for outstanding public relations tools and tactics ● Gold Anvil Award. **Frequency:** annual. **Type:** recognition. **Recipient:** for a PRSA member whose accomplishments have made a major contribution to the profession ● Outstanding Educator Award. **Frequency:** annual. **Type:** recognition. **Recipient:** for significant contributions to the advancement of public relations education through college or university teaching ● Paul M. Lund Public Service Award. **Frequency:** annual. **Type:** recognition. **Recipient:** for a member whose participation as a volunteer in important public activities has increased the common good and reflected credit to the society ● Silver Anvil Awards. **Frequency:** annual. **Type:** recognition. **Recipient:** for outstanding public relations programs. **Telecommunication Services:** electronic mail, membership@prsa.org ● TDD, (212)254-3464. **Committees:** Educational Affairs; Honors and Awards; National Conference; Public Relations; Women in PR. **Sections:** Association; Corporate; Counselors Academy; Counselors in Higher Education; Educators Academy; Employee Communications; Environment; Financial Communications; Food and Beverage; Health Academy; International; Multicultural Communications; Professional Services; Public Affairs and Government; Technology; Travel and Tourism. **Subgroups:** Accreditation; Body of Knowledge; Continuing Education; Eligibility and Orientation; Ethics and Professional Standards. **Absorbed:** (1961) American Public Relations Association; (1977) National Communication Council for Human Services. **Formed by Merger of:** American Council on Public Relations; National Association of Public Relations Counsel. **Publications:** *The Public Relations Strategist*, quarterly. Magazine. Addresses executive-level public relations practitioners. **Price:** $150.00 /year for nonmembers in U.S.; included in membership dues; $160.00 /year for nonmembers in Canada; $170.00 /year for nonmembers outside U.S. and Canada ● *Public Relations Tactics*, monthly. Newspaper. Helps PR practitioners improve their job skills and stay competitive. **Price:** included in membership dues; $100.00 /year for nonmembers in U.S.; $110.00 /year for nonmembers in Canada; $120.00 /year for nonmembers outside U.S. and Canada ● Monographs ● Directories, annual. Features PRSA organizational and leadership information, the Society's Member Code of Ethics, and the PRSA Bylaws. **Price:** included in membership dues; $75.00 additional copy for nonmembers; $275.00 for libraries and educational institution; $400.00 for nonmembers ● Newsletter, monthly. **Price:** free for members. Alternate Formats: online ● Also publishes research studies, and abstracts. **Conventions/Meetings:** annual conference (exhibits).

3196 ■ Society of Consumer Affairs Professionals in Business (SOCAP)
675 N Washington St., Ste.200
Alexandria, VA 22314
Ph: (703)519-3700 (415)501-7953
Fax: (703)549-4886
E-mail: socap@socap.org
URL: http://www.socap.org
Contact: Mr. Matthew D'Uva, Pres.
Founded: 1973. **Members:** 2,000. **Membership Dues:** student, $50 (annual) ● regular, $295 (annual) ● affiliate, $135 (annual) ● associate, $130 (annual). **Staff:** 8. **Budget:** $2,000,000. **Regional Groups:** 21. **Multinational. Description:** Individuals engaged in the management of consumer affairs/customer service divisions of businesses. Fosters the integrity of business in its dealings with consumers. Promotes harmonious relationships among business, government, and consumers. Advances the consumer affairs profession. Seeks to provide a means for businesses to compare their successes and failures in consumer affairs. Conducts research and educational programs; maintains speakers' bureau; operates placement service. **Libraries: Type:** reference. **Holdings:** archival material, papers, reports. **Awards:** Mobius Award. **Frequency:** annual. **Type:** recognition. **Computer Services:** Mailing lists. **Committees:** Brand Marketing; Chapter Relations; Conference; Organization and Governance; Product and Services Innovation; Publication; Research; Resource Management. **Publications:** *Customer Relationship Management*, quarterly. Journal. **Price:** available to members only. **Circulation:** 3,000. **Advertising:** accepted ● *Society of Consumer Affairs Professionals in Business—Membership Directory*, annual ● *Up-*

date, monthly. Newsletter. Contains information of interest to members. Alternate Formats: online ● Resource Center Library. **Conventions/Meetings:** annual conference (exhibits) - 2008 Oct. 5-8, Miami, FL ● annual symposium - 2009 May 3-6, Tucson, AZ.

3197 ■ Women Executives in Public Relations (WEPR)
PO Box 7657, FDR Sta.
New York, NY 10150-7657
Ph: (212)859-7375
Fax: (212)859-7375
E-mail: info@wepr.org
URL: http://www.wepr.org
Contact: Barbara Coen, Admin.
Founded: 1946. **Members:** 100. **Membership Dues:** individual, $150 (annual) ● non-resident, associate, $60 (annual). **Staff:** 1. **Local Groups:** 1. **Description:** Public relations organization for senior level women in the field. Provides a forum for the exchange of career, management and practitioner issues among peers. **Awards: Frequency:** semiannual. **Type:** grant. **Recipient:** for students enrolled in public relations courses ● WEPR Foundation Crystal Obelisk Awards for Social Responsibility. **Frequency:** annual. **Type:** recognition. **Recipient:** to honor campaigns that effectively address social problems. **Computer Services:** Mailing lists. **Formerly:** (1971) Committee on Women in Public Relations. **Publications:** *Network*, quarterly. Newsletter. **Circulation:** 600. **Conventions/Meetings:** monthly meeting.

Publishing

3198 ■ About Books, Inc. (ABI)
1618 W Colorado Ave.
Colorado Springs, CO 80904
Ph: (719)632-8226
Fax: (719)471-2182
E-mail: info@about-books.com
URL: http://www.about-books.com
Contact: Debi Flora, Pres./Co-Owner
Founded: 1979. **Staff:** 5. **Description:** Information clearinghouse on self-publishing and marketing of books. Provides educational programs; maintains speakers' bureau. Provides audiotape programs and books on the subject. **Libraries: Type:** reference. **Conventions/Meetings:** periodic seminar.

3199 ■ Alliance of Area Business Publications (AABP)
c/o C. James Dowden, Exec. Dir.
4929 Wilshire Blvd., Ste.428
Los Angeles, CA 90010
Ph: (323)937-5514
Fax: (323)937-0959
E-mail: administrator@bizpubs.org
URL: http://www.bizpubs.org
Contact: C. James Dowden, Exec. Dir.
Founded: 1979. **Members:** 74. **Membership Dues:** publication, vendor, $1,000 (annual) ● associate, $1,350 (annual). **Staff:** 10. **Budget:** $250,000. **Description:** Local area business publications. Encourages high journalistic standards among area business publications. Acts as a forum for the exchange of ideas and information, especially on common issues such as editorial excellence, postal regulations, government regulations, and advertising. Compiles statistics of business patterns in markets of members; has engaged in cooperative member market research. **Awards:** Editorial and Design Award. **Frequency:** annual. **Type:** recognition. **Recipient:** for editorial content and design of member publications. **Formerly:** (2005) Association of Area Business Publications. **Publications:** Newsletter, monthly. Provides publishers with news and analysis of local area businesses; includes awards and employment listings. **Price:** included in membership dues ● Directory, annual. Lists member publishers including each publication's key personnel, format, frequency, circulation, and page rates. **Price:** included in membership dues; $25.00 for nonmembers. **Conventions/Meetings:** annual Editorial and Design Awards Banquet - competition, for editorial excellence of member publications (exhibits) - always summer ● annual Editors and Publishers Convention - always June or July ● annual Publishers Convention - always January ● workshop, covers sales management, circulation, and production.

3200 ■ American Book Producers Association (ABPA)
381 Park Ave.
New York, NY 10016
Ph: (212)645-2368
Free: (800)209-4575
Fax: (212)802-2893
E-mail: office@abpaonline.org
URL: http://www.abpaonline.org
Contact: Dan Tucker, Pres.
Founded: 1980. **Members:** 60. **Membership Dues:** general, $575 (annual). **Budget:** $30,000. **Description:** Book producing companies that develop the concepts for books and, based on a contractual agreement with a publisher, may produce finished books or production-ready film, camera-ready mechanicals, finished manuscripts, art, and layouts. Aims to increase the book industry's awareness of members' capabilities and the state of the book producers' art. Facilitates exchange of information for the purpose of improving business and establishing trade standards. **Publications:** *American Book Producers Association—Directory of Members*, annual. Membership Directory. Includes services offered and books produced. **Price:** free ● *American Book Producers Association—Newsletter*, monthly. **Price:** free for members. **Conventions/Meetings:** monthly luncheon ● annual seminar.

3201 ■ American Business Media
675 3rd Ave.
New York, NY 10017-5704
Ph: (212)661-6360
Fax: (212)370-0736
E-mail: info@abmmail.com
URL: http://www.americanbusinessmedia.com
Contact: Gordon T. Hughes II, Pres./CEO
Founded: 1906. **Members:** 239. **Staff:** 15. **Budget:** $3,500,000. **Regional Groups:** 4. **Description:** Represents global business-to-business information providers. Members include producers of print and online magazines, newsletters and databases, as well as trade shows, conferences, seminars and other ancillary media. Exists to advance the common interests of business-to-business media organizations. Focuses on governmental affairs, promotion of the industry, best practices, and ethical standards. Its 200 plus member companies represent upwards of 1200 print publications, 1350 web sites, and 850 trade shows, serving 181 industries and reaching 90 million readers. **Libraries: Type:** reference. **Awards:** Neal Awards. **Frequency:** annual. **Type:** recognition. **Recipient:** for those who achieved editorial excellence in business media. **Committees:** Advertising and Marketing; Continuing Education; Custom Media; Publishers; Publishing Management; Specialized Periodical Political Action; Standards; Washington Legal. **Formed by Merger of:** (1985) American Business Press; (1985) National Business Publications; Associated Business Publications. **Formerly:** (1990) Association of Business Publishers. **Publications:** *Business Media Matters*, monthly. Newsletter ● *E-News*, weekly. Newsletter. Alternate Formats: online. **Conventions/Meetings:** annual conference - usually spring/May ● annual Top Management Meeting - conference (exhibits) - usually in late November.

3202 ■ American Court and Commercial Newspapers (ACCN)
c/o Public Notice Resource Center
PO Box 5337
Arlington, VA 22205
Ph: (703)812-0561 (703)534-5579
Fax: (703)812-4555
E-mail: information@pnrc.net
URL: http://www.pnrc.net
Contact: Richard Gard, Pres.
Founded: 1930. **Members:** 80. **Staff:** 1. **Budget:** $50,000. **Description:** Newspapers of general circulation devoted to lawyers and courts, financial and real estate professionals, contractors, and business interests. Functions as an advertising medium for business and legal vendors, marketers, advertising agencies, and related businesses. Operates Speaker's Bureau; conducts research reports. Compiles statistics. **Formerly:** (1979) Associated Court and Commercial Newspapers. **Publications:** *ACCN Bulletin*, quarterly. Newsletter. **Price:** included in membership dues. **Conventions/Meetings:** semiannual conference.

3203 ■ American Horse Publications
49 Spinnaker Cir.
South Daytona, FL 32119
Ph: (386)760-7743
Fax: (386)760-7728
E-mail: ahorsepubs@aol.com
URL: http://www.americanhorsepubs.org
Contact: Christine W. Brune, Exec. Dir.
Founded: 1970. **Members:** 450. **Membership Dues:** business, $250-$350 (annual) ● publication, $100-$200 (annual) ● individual, $100 (annual) ● student, $25 (annual). **Staff:** 1. **Description:** Members are horse-oriented publications, professionals and businesses. Aims to improve the horse publication field and network within the equine publishing industry. **Awards:** Equine Industry Vision Award. **Frequency:** annual. **Type:** recognition. **Conventions/Meetings:** annual conference and seminar.

3204 ■ American Medical Publishers' Association (AMPA)
308 E Lancaster Ave., Ste.110
Wynnewood, PA 19096
Ph: (610)642-2810
Fax: (610)642-0628
E-mail: ampa@association-cba.org
URL: http://www.ampaonline.org/fr_welcome.htm
Contact: Robin B. Bartlett, Pres.-Elect
Founded: 1961. **Members:** 70. **Membership Dues:** individual, $295 (annual) ● sustaining, $1,250 (annual) ● regular (based on annual income), $500-$5,000 (annual). **Staff:** 1. **Budget:** $50,000. **Description:** U.S. medical publishing companies. Objectives are: to exchange information among members; to improve the creation, distribution, and sale of medical books and journals; to facilitate communication with medical organizations, schools, and the medical community. Recent educational program topics include: panel discussions on copyright protection; computer fulfillment; export sales; the creative editorial process. **Awards:** Lifetime Achievement Award. **Frequency:** annual. **Type:** recognition. **Committees:** Annual Meeting; Coalition for Healthcare Communication; Copyright; Industry Relations; Luncheon Seminars; Philanthropy; Statistics; Website. **Formerly:** (1974) Association of American Medical Book Publishers. **Publications:** *American Medical Publishers' Association—Newsletter*, quarterly. Covers information regarding copyright laws and other matters. Includes lists of job promotions and changes and company profiles. **Price:** $50.00 for nonmembers; included in membership dues. **Circulation:** 400. **Advertising:** accepted. Alternate Formats: online ● Bulletin, periodic ● Directory, annual. **Conventions/Meetings:** annual Convergence - convention and seminar (exhibits) - usually end of February/early March, in Philadelphia, PA ● annual seminar.

3205 ■ Associated Church Press (ACP)
PO Box 621001
Oviedo, FL 32762-1001
Ph: (407)341-6615
Fax: (407)386-3236
E-mail: contactacp@aol.com
URL: http://www.theacp.org
Contact: Jerry Van Marter, Pres.
Founded: 1916. **Members:** 178. **Membership Dues:** former ACP editor, $30 (annual) ● student, $25 (annual) ● individual, $40 (annual) ● affiliate, $125 (annual) ● publication (based on circulation), $139-$792 (annual) ● newsletter (based on circulation), $70-$396 (annual). **Staff:** 2. **Budget:** $100,000. **Description:** Publishers of Protestant, Orthodox, Roman Catholic, Anglican, and independent church periodicals, with a combined circulation in excess of 29 mil-

lion. Works to share ideas and concerns in religious publishing, stimulate higher standards of religious journalism, and enable member publications to exert a more positive influence on contemporary civilization. Sponsors research in Christian journalism. Offers consultative services. **Awards:** Best of the Christian Press. **Frequency:** annual. **Type:** recognition. **Recipient:** to members with professional excellence ● Citation of Honor. **Frequency:** periodic. **Type:** recognition. **Recipient:** for individuals with outstanding contributions in the field of religious journalism ● William B. Lipphard Award. **Frequency:** periodic. **Type:** recognition. **Recipient:** for distinguished service to religious journalism ● Writing and Design Awards. **Frequency:** annual. **Type:** recognition. **Recipient:** for excellence in content, makeup and typography. **Computer Services:** database, freelancers directory ● mailing lists. **Formerly:** (1937) Editorial Council of the Religious Press. **Publications:** *ACPwire*, monthly. Newsletter. Contains timely and helpful information and resources. **Advertising:** accepted. Alternate Formats: online ● *Associated Church Press—Newslog*, quarterly. Newsletter. Includes awards and news about member publications. **Advertising:** accepted. **Conventions/Meetings:** annual convention - in April or May ● periodic workshop.

3206 ■ Association of American Publishers (AAP)
71 5th Ave., 2nd Fl.
New York, NY 10003-3004
Ph: (212)255-0200
Fax: (212)255-7007
E-mail: pschroeder@publishers.org
URL: http://www.publishers.org
Contact: Patricia S. Schroeder, Pres./CEO
Founded: 1970. **Members:** 310. **Staff:** 23. **Budget:** $5,000,000. **Description:** Represents the producers of: hardbound and softbound general, educational, trade, reference, religious, scientific, technical, and medical books; instructional materials; classroom periodicals; maps, globes, tests, and software. Conducts seminars and workshops on various publishing topics including rights and permission, sales, and educational publishing. Sponsors Publishers Forum, an informal discussion group. Compiles statistics. **Awards:** Curtis G. Benjamin Award. **Frequency:** annual. **Type:** recognition. **Recipient:** for creative publishing ● Miriam Bass Award for Creativity in Independent Publishing. **Frequency:** annual. **Type:** recognition. **Recipient:** for creativity in independent publishing ● School Division Education Research Award. **Frequency:** annual. **Type:** recognition. **Computer Services:** Bibliographic search, PubNet. **Committees:** Copyright; Electronic Publishing; Freedom to Read; International Freedom to Publish; Postal; Statistics. **Divisions:** General Publishing; Higher Education; International; Paperback Publishing; Professional and Scholarly; School. **Formed by Merger of:** American Educational Publishers Institute; American Book Publishers Council. **Publications:** *AAP Exhibits Directory*, annual ● *AAP Monthly Report*. Alternate Formats: online ● Annual Report, annual. Alternate Formats: online. **Conventions/Meetings:** annual meeting and conference ● annual Professional and Scholarly Publishers Meeting - conference ● annual School Division - meeting ● annual Smaller and Independent Publishers Meeting - conference.

3207 ■ Association of Art Editors (AAE)
c/o Phil Freshman, Pres.
3912 Natchez Ave. S
St. Louis Park, MN 55416
Ph: (952)922-1374
Fax: (952)922-1374
E-mail: pfreshman@mm.com
URL: http://www.artedit.org
Contact: Phil Freshman, Pres.
Membership Dues: general, $20 (annual). **Description:** Seeks to advance and set standards for the profession of art editors. Provides a forum for the exchange of information among art editors and other individuals involved in art-related publications. Provides authors with information about editing and publication procedures. **Computer Services:** database, members' information ● database, skills index of members. **Affiliated With:** College Art Association.

3208 ■ Association of Directory Publishers (ADP)
116 Cass St.
PO Box 1929
Traverse City, MI 49685-1929
Free: (800)267-9002
Fax: (231)486-2182
E-mail: hq@adp.org
URL: http://www.adp.org
Contact: R. Lawrence Angove, Pres./CEO
Founded: 1898. **Members:** 274. **Membership Dues:** publisher, associate publisher (based on annual gross sales), $900-$25,000 (annual) ● partner, $1,750 (annual) ● international publisher, $3,000 (annual) ● agency, $350 (annual). **Staff:** 6. **Budget:** $800,000. **Description:** Represents publishers of printed and electronic telephone, city, and special interest directories. **Libraries: Type:** reference. **Subjects:** directories. **Awards:** Gold Book Awards. **Frequency:** semiannual. **Type:** recognition. **Recipient:** for directory publishers. **Computer Services:** database ● mailing lists, directory of publishers and advertising agencies handling the yellow pages. **Telecommunication Services:** electronic mail, larry.angove@adp.org. **Committees:** Carrier Relations; Executive; Finance; Gold Book Awards; Internet Yellow Pages; National Relations; Nominations; Political Action; Programs; Public Policy; Strategic Planning; Supplier Relations. **Formerly:** (1992) Association of North American Directory Publishers. **Publications:** *ADP Roster*, annual. Membership Directory. **Price:** included in membership dues. **Advertising:** accepted ● *theExtra*. Newsletter. **Price:** included in membership dues. **Advertising:** accepted. Alternate Formats: online. **Conventions/Meetings:** semiannual conference and trade show, suppliers of products and services to directory publishers (exhibits) - always spring and fall ● annual conference ● annual convention ● annual Mid-Year Convention and Publishers Trade Show.

3209 ■ Association of Medical Publications (AMP)
c/o Cheryl L. Pizor, Exec. Dir.
231 N Ave. W, No. 335
Westfield, NJ 07090
Ph: (908)233-8147
Fax: (908)233-8305
E-mail: amp-office@att.net
URL: http://www.amponline.org/AMP/AMP.html
Contact: Cheryl L. Pizor, Exec. Dir.
Membership Dues: full (minimum), $2,500 (annual) ● international affiliate, $2,500 (annual) ● associate, $500-$1,000 (annual) ● independent representative, firm, $250 (annual). **Description:** Promotes publishing firms in the medical field. **Awards:** Doctors' Choice Award. **Frequency:** annual. **Type:** recognition. **Recipient:** for effective journal advertising ● Nexus Representatives of the Year Award. **Frequency:** annual. **Type:** recognition. **Recipient:** for outstanding sales professionals. **Committees:** Advertising Research, Marketing and Promotion; Editorial and Electronic Publishing; Government and Industry Relations; Long-Range Planning.

3210 ■ Association of Test Publishers (ATP)
1201 Pennsylvania Ave. NW, Ste.900
Washington, DC 20004
Free: (866)240-7909
Fax: (717)755-8962
E-mail: wgh.atp@att.net
URL: http://www.testpublishers.org
Contact: William G. Harris PhD, Exec. Dir.
Founded: 1992. **Members:** 125. **Membership Dues:** regular (based on annual gross sales), $750-$20,000 (annual) ● associate (based on annual revenues), $1,100-$5,500 (annual) ● subscriber, $75 (annual). **Staff:** 1. **Budget:** $1,000,000. **Description:** Companies and organizations that develop, market, score, interpret or provide psychological tests. Works to promote and advance assessment services and products and their value to society. Represents the interests of test publishers; educates the public and government about the benefits of tests; promotes awareness of and compliance with copyright and trademark laws; develops industry standards and guidelines; compiles statistics. **Awards:** Career Achievement. **Frequency:** annual. **Type:** recognition. **Computer Services:** database, member products and services. **Publications:** *Answers to Questions About Tests*. Booklet. **Price:** free (single copy) ● *Copyright Questions and Answers for the Test Purchasers* ● *Copyright Questions and Business for the Test Publishing Industry* ● *Guidelines for Computer Based Testing* ● *Journal of Applied Testing Technology*, annual. Alternate Formats: online. Also Cited As: *JATT* ● *Model Guidelines for Pre-Employment Integrity Testing, Second Edition*. Booklet ● *Test Publisher*, semiannual, every spring and fall. Newsletter. Alternate Formats: online. **Conventions/Meetings:** annual Innovations in Testing - conference and meeting, includes content sessions, keynote speakers (exhibits) ● meeting.

3211 ■ Authors and Publishers Association (APA)
8919 Friendship Rd.
Houston, TX 77080-4111
E-mail: info@authorsandpublishers.org
URL: http://www.authorsandpublishers.org
Contact: Ron Kaye, Interim Pres.
Membership Dues: individual, $50 (annual) ● in continental US, $25 (annual) ● outside continental US, $30 (annual) ● corporate, family, $50 (annual). **Description:** Authors, aspiring authors, editors, artists, printers and publishers, marketers, distributors, booksellers, and other corporations and individuals with an interest in the book trade. Seeks to assist writers, authors, and publishers to "keep the literary craft alive". Serves as a clearinghouse on the book publishing industry; provides employment and other information to writers; facilitates networking among members. **Telecommunication Services:** electronic mail, moonshad@swbell.net. **Publications:** Newsletter, periodic.

3212 ■ Bay Area Independent Publishers Association (BAIPA)
PO Box E
Corte Madera, CA 94976
Ph: (415)456-0247
E-mail: books4women@yahoo.com
URL: http://www.baipa.net
Contact: Margaret Speaker Yuan, Exec. Dir.
Founded: 1979. **Members:** 250. **Membership Dues:** general, $40 (annual). **Budget:** $20,000. **Local Groups:** 1. **Description:** Promotes authors interested in independent publishing as an alternative to the commercial publishing system; printers, artists, typists, and others in allied fields. Aims to become a comprehensive source of self-publishing information and to develop knowledge and expertise to better assist members in promoting, marketing, and publishing their works. Acts as a liaison and clearinghouse of information and provides guidance in all aspects of self-publishing, including copy preparation, book production, and marketing and sales. **Awards:** Jack Mason Award. **Frequency:** annual. **Type:** recognition. **Recipient:** for outstanding contributions on the field of self publishing. **Formerly:** Marin Self-Publishers Association; (1998) Marin Small-Publishers Association. **Publications:** *SPEX*, monthly. Newsletter. Alternate Formats: online ● Booklets ● Brochures ● Catalog ● Pamphlets. **Conventions/Meetings:** monthly meeting - every 2nd Saturday ● annual seminar.

3213 ■ Book Industry Study Group (BISG)
370 Lexington Ave., Ste.900
New York, NY 10017
Ph: (646)336-7141
Fax: (646)336-6214
E-mail: info@bisg.org
URL: http://www.bisg.org
Contact: Sara Raffel, Office Mgr.
Founded: 1976. **Members:** 200. **Membership Dues:** individual, independent consultant (revenue under $500,000), $550 (annual) ● commercial ($500,000-$1

million), $950 (annual) ● commercial ($1-$5 million), $1,950 (annual) ● commercial ($5-$10 million), $2,950 (annual) ● commercial ($10-$50 million), $5,950 (annual) ● commercial ($50-$100 million), $7,950 (annual) ● commercial ($100 million-$1 billion), $9,950 (annual) ● commercial ($1 billion and up), $14,950 (annual) ● gold sponsor (optional), $25,000 (annual) ● public library, $550 (annual) ● nonprofit ($1 million and under), $950 (annual) ● nonprofit ($1 million-$5 million), $1,250 (annual) ● nonprofit ($5 million and up), $1,450 (annual). **Staff:** 3. **Multinational. Description:** Represents publishers, manufacturers, suppliers, wholesalers, retailers, librarians, and other engaged in the business of print and electronic media. **Publications:** *Book Industry Trends 2004*, annual. Eleven-year (1999-2009) review and forecast of book sales in dollars and units, arranged by market segment and product classification. **Price:** free for members (level B or above); $750.00 /year for nonmembers. **Circulation:** 800 ● *2002 Consumer Research Study on Book Purchasing*, annual. **Price:** $500.00 for nonmembers; free for members.

3214 ■ Catholic Book Publishers Association (CBPA)

8404 Jamesport Dr.
Rockford, IL 61108-7030
Ph: (815)332-3245
Fax: (815)332-3476
E-mail: cbpa3@aol.com
URL: http://www.cbpa.org
Contact: Terry Wessels, Exec. Dir.

Founded: 1987. **Members:** 80. **Membership Dues:** publisher, $250-$750 (annual) ● service company, $200 (annual) ● individual, $100 (annual). **Staff:** 1. **Budget:** $65,000. **Multinational. Description:** Facilitates the sharing of professional information, networking, cooperation, and friendship among those involved in Catholic book publishing in the United States and abroad. **Awards:** Catholic Publishers Sponsors Writers' Scholarship. **Frequency:** annual. **Type:** scholarship. **Recipient:** for a writer who attends the annual Catholic Writers' Conference and Retreat ● Outstanding Service Award. **Frequency:** annual. **Type:** recognition. **Computer Services:** Mailing lists, Catholic bookstores. **Additional Websites:** http://www.CatholicsRead.org. **Publications:** *The Catholic Book Publishers Association Directory*, annual. **Price:** $35.00. ISSN: 1077-6656. **Circulation:** 2,200. **Advertising:** accepted. Alternate Formats: online ● *The Spirit of Books*, semiannual. Catalog. ISSN: 1077-6648. **Circulation:** 275,000. **Advertising:** accepted. **Conventions/Meetings:** workshop, professional skills techniques - 3/year in New York City, Los Angeles, and Chicago.

3215 ■ Catholic Press Association (CPA)

3555 Veterans Memorial Hwy., Unit O
Ronkonkoma, NY 11779
Ph: (631)471-4730
Fax: (631)471-4804
E-mail: cathjourn@catholicpress.org
URL: http://www.catholicpress.org
Contact: Tom Conway, Exec. Dir.

Founded: 1911. **Members:** 725. **Staff:** 325. **Budget:** $500,000. **Regional Groups:** 4. **Description:** Consists of Catholic writers and publishers of Catholic newspapers, magazines, newsletters and books. Maintains 25 committees, including Freedom of Information, Fair Publishing Practices Code, Catholic News Service Liaison. **Libraries: Type:** reference. **Awards:** Bishop John England Award. **Frequency:** annual. **Type:** recognition. **Recipient:** for outstanding publishers ● Book Award. **Frequency:** annual. **Type:** recognition ● Journalism Award. **Frequency:** annual. **Type:** recognition ● St. Francis DeSales Award. **Frequency:** annual. **Type:** recognition. **Recipient:** for contributions to Catholic Journalism. **Computer Services:** Mailing lists, of members and nonmembers. **Telecommunication Services:** electronic mail, tconway@catholicpress.org. **Affiliated With:** International Catholic Union of the Press. **Publications:** *Catholic Journalist*, monthly. Covers Catholic publishing and individuals in the field. Includes book reviews, calendar of events, and obituaries. **Price:** $12.00/year. **Circulation:** 2,700. **Advertising:** accepted ● *Catholic Press Directory*, annual. Lists Catholic newspapers, magazines, and publishers in the U.S. and Canada. **Price:** $50.00 for nonmembers; $25.00 for members. **Conventions/Meetings:** annual convention (exhibits) - always May.

3216 ■ The Christian Science Publishing Society (TCSPS)

Jour., Sentinel, and Herald Editorial Dept. C04-10
1 Norway St.
Boston, MA 02115
Ph: (617)450-2000
Free: (800)288-7090
Fax: (617)450-2317
E-mail: geslert@csps.com
URL: http://www.spirituality.com
Contact: M. Victor Westberg, Dir.

Founded: 1898. **Description:** Publishes and distributes daily newspaper, religious magazines and books. Produces and distributes religious programs for shortwave radio. **Publications:** *The Christian Science Journal*, monthly. Contains instructive articles and verified reports of Christian healing to give the reader a working understanding of the divine Principle. **Price:** $49.00/year ● *The Christian Science Monitor*, daily. Newsletter. Available in daily U.S. edition and weekly international edition. **Price:** $164.00/year ● *Christian Science Quarterly*. Journal. Available in full text, study, and regular size editions in 17 languages including English and Braille. **Price:** $20.00/year ● *Christian Science Sentinel*, weekly. Magazine. **Price:** $78.00/year ● *The Herald of Christian Science* (in Danish, English, Finnish, French, German, Italian, Japanese, Norwegian, Portuguese, Spanish, Swedish, and Turkish), 4-12/year. Monthly in German, French, Spanish and Portuguese, and quarterly in eight other languages. **Conventions/Meetings:** annual meeting (exhibits) - always 1st Monday of June in Boston, MA.

3217 ■ Christian Small Publishers Association (CSPA)

PO Box 481022
Charlotte, NC 28269
Ph: (704)277-7194
Fax: (704)717-2928
E-mail: cspa@christianpublishers.net
URL: http://www.christianpublishers.net
Contact: Sarah Bolme, Dir.

Founded: 2004. **Membership Dues:** regular, $75 (annual). **Multinational. Description:** Represents small publishers producing materials for the Christian marketplace. Promotes and strengthens the small publishing industry for the Christian marketplace. Provides networking opportunities with other Christian small publishers. **Awards:** Christian Small Publisher Book of the Year. **Frequency:** annual. **Type:** recognition. **Recipient:** to honor books produced by small publishers for outstanding contribution to Christian life. **Publications:** *CSPA Circular*, bimonthly. Newsletter. **Price:** included in membership dues. Alternate Formats: online.

3218 ■ City and Regional Magazine Association (CRMA)

4929 Wilshire Blvd., Ste.428
Los Angeles, CA 90010
Ph: (323)937-5514
Fax: (323)937-0959
E-mail: administrator@citymag.org
URL: http://www.citymag.org
Contact: C. James Dowden, Exec. Dir.

Founded: 1978. **Members:** 96. **Membership Dues:** associate, $1,750 (annual) ● active/affiliate, $1,000-$6,120 (annual). **Staff:** 10. **Budget:** $250,000. **Description:** City and regional consumer-oriented magazines; related businesses involved in printing, advertising, and circulation. Strives to gain presence in the marketplace and command an increased following among national advertisers. Serves as a channel of communication between city and regional consumer magazines and coordinates research projects. Distributes information; creates press materials. Compiles statistics. **Awards:** National City and Regional Magazine Awards. **Frequency:** annual. **Type:** recognition. **Recipient:** for winning publications, writers, and art directors. **Publications:** *Communicator*, monthly. Newsletter. Features news and developments affecting city magazines. **Price:** included in membership dues. **Circulation:** 100 ● Membership Directory. Alternate Formats: online ● Also publishes news releases and survey results. **Conventions/Meetings:** annual conference (exhibits) - always spring ● semiannual seminar, for professional development - September-October and January.

3219 ■ Comics Magazine Association of America (CMAA)

Address Unknown since 2008

Founded: 1954. **Members:** 8. **Staff:** 3. **Budget:** $100,000. **Description:** Publishers, distributors, printers, and engravers of comic magazines. Operates Comics Code Authority, a self-regulation program for the industry to maintain high standards of decency and good taste and eliminate objectionable material in comics magazines. **Publications:** *Code of the Comics Magazine Association*, periodic. **Conventions/Meetings:** annual meeting - usually December, New York City.

3220 ■ CrossRef

40 Salem St.
Lynnfield, MA 01940
Ph: (781)295-0072
Fax: (781)295-0077
E-mail: info@crossref.org
URL: http://www.crossref.org
Contact: Julie Surette, Admin. Asst.

Founded: 2000. **Membership Dues:** publisher (based on total publishing revenue), $250-$30,000 (annual) ● affiliate (based on study query account), $500-$10,000 (annual) ● affiliate agent, $2,000 (annual) ● affiliate linking solutions partner, $5,000 (annual). **Multinational. Description:** Promotes the development and cooperative use of new and innovative technologies to speed and facilitate scholarly research. Serves as the official Digital Object Identifiers (DOI) registration agency for scholarly and professional publications. Enables easy identification and use of trustworthy electronic content. **Publications:** Newsletter. Alternate Formats: online ● Annual Report, annual. Alternate Formats: online.

3221 ■ Educational Paperback Association

c/o Marilyn Abel, Exec. Sec.
PO Box 1399
East Hampton, NY 11937
Ph: (631)329-3315
E-mail: edupaperback@aol.com
URL: http://www.edupaperback.org
Contact: Marilyn Abel, Exec. Sec.

Founded: 1975. **Members:** 90. **Membership Dues:** associate, $700 (annual) ● book wholesaler, publisher, $600 (annual). **Staff:** 2. **Description:** Paperback book publishers and wholesalers involved in the educational book market. Aims to develop and maintain high professional standards in serving schools, colleges, and libraries. Encourages the use of trade books in schools and libraries. **Awards:** Jeremiah Ludington Memorial Award. **Frequency:** annual. **Type:** recognition. **Recipient:** for a significant contribution to the educational paperback business. **Computer Services:** Online services, information on paperbacks for young readers and sources of supply. **Telecommunication Services:** electronic mail, bcombs@edupaperback.org. **Publications:** *Annual Survey of K-12 Sales*, annual. Report. **Price:** $495.00/copy ● *Impact of Trade Books on Reading Achievement*. Report. Alternate Formats: online. **Conventions/Meetings:** annual meeting - always January.

3222 ■ Engineering College Magazines Associated (ECMA)

Address Unknown since 2008

Founded: 1920. **Members:** 13. **Membership Dues:** $200 (annual). **Staff:** 1. **Budget:** $5,000. **Description:** Engineering colleges publishing technical magazines for students. Promotes improvement of engineering journalism, simplification of solicitation of national advertising, and standardization of size and format of publications. **Awards: Frequency:** annual. **Type:** recognition. **Recipient:** for outstanding work in 15 categories, best article, best layout, etc. **Computer Services:** Mailing lists. **Conventions/Meetings:** annual conference and workshop.

3223 ■ Evangelical Christian Publishers Association (ECPA)
9633 S 48th St., Ste.140
Phoenix, AZ 85044
Ph: (480)966-3998
Fax: (480)966-1944
E-mail: info@ecpa.org
URL: http://www.ecpa.org
Contact: Mark W. Kuyper, Pres./CEO
Founded: 1974. **Members:** 280. **Membership Dues:** voting, $1,512-$15,000 (annual) ● small press associate, professional service affiliate, $600 (annual) ● international associate, $75-$300 (annual) ● industry affiliate, $1,300 (annual) ● individual, $125 (annual) ● alumni, $25 (annual). **Staff:** 12. **Budget:** $1,100,000. **Multinational. Description:** Companies that primarily publish Christian religious literature. Conducts annual sales and operation survey, and a series of educational seminars and trade shows. **Awards:** Gold Medallion Book Awards. **Frequency:** annual. **Type:** medal. **Recipient:** for literary quality content, design and significance of contribution ● Platinum Book Award. **Frequency:** periodic. **Type:** recognition. **Recipient:** for an outstanding sales achievement in the publication of Christian literature. **Committees:** Membership; Recognition; Training. **Task Forces:** ECPA Trade Shows Advisory; General Principles and Practices. **Affiliated With:** Evangelical Christian Publishers Association. **Publications:** *Footprints*, monthly. Newsletter. **Price:** free for members. **Circulation:** 900. **Advertising:** accepted ● *Monday Rush*, weekly. Newsletter. **Price:** free for members. Alternate Formats: online ● Directory, annual. **Conventions/Meetings:** ECPA Publishing University - seminar - usually November ● Introducing ECPA Publishing University - seminar ● semiannual seminar, for management - always April and November ● Spring Management Seminar ● annual trade show - January.

3224 ■ Fulfillment Management Association (FMA)
60 E 42nd St., Ste.1166
New York, NY 10165
Ph: (303)604-7362
Fax: (303)604-7840
E-mail: info@fmanational.org
URL: http://www.fmanational.org
Contact: John Hang, Pres.
Founded: 1948. **Members:** 400. **Membership Dues:** individual, $140 (annual). **Staff:** 5. **Budget:** $100,000. **Regional Groups:** 1. **Description:** Fulfillment executives, direct mail marketing management, publishing, circulation, and fundraising executives. Educates, updates, and maintains high standards of service in operations management and customer service. Offers monthly luncheon Programs, Annual Fulfillment Day in New York; sponsors three seminars per year. Maintains job advisory service. **Awards:** Fulfillment Hall of Fame Award. **Frequency:** annual. **Type:** recognition. **Recipient:** to an individual who, through innovative and strategic thinking, has made significant contributions to the fulfillment industry ● Fulfillment Manager of the Year Award. **Frequency:** annual. **Type:** recognition. **Recipient:** to an individual who has demonstrated excellence in providing customer service through the fulfillment process ● Lee C. Williams Award. **Frequency:** annual. **Type:** recognition. **Recipient:** to an individual who has made an outstanding contribution to the periodical publishing circulation field. **Committees:** Art Director/Membership Directory; Audiolibrary; Career Guidance; Facilities; Fulfillment; Mailers Technical Advisory; Membership; On-line Service; Programming; Publicity; Registration; Sponsor Relations; Training and Education. **Formerly:** (1972) Subscription Fulfillment Managers Association. **Publications:** *Postal Briefings*, periodic ● Membership Directory, annual ● Brochure. **Conventions/Meetings:** annual Fulfillment Day in New York - seminar and luncheon ● luncheon and seminar - always New York City.

3225 ■ Great Lakes Booksellers Association (GLBA)
PO Box 901
208 Franklin St.
Grand Haven, MI 49417
Ph: (616)847-2460
Free: (800)745-2460
Fax: (616)842-0051
E-mail: info@books-glba.org
URL: http://www.books-glba.org
Contact: Jim Dana, Exec. Dir.
Founded: 1989. **Members:** 575. **Membership Dues:** bookstore business, $100 (annual) ● affiliate (wholesaler, publisher, rep group, service and sideline company), $150 (annual) ● employee of a bookstore business or affiliate business, $30 (annual) ● independent industry professional (author, librarian, illustrator), $75 (annual) ● multiple store, $50 (annual). **Staff:** 3. **Budget:** $450,000. **Description:** Booksellers. Supports bookstores and promotes excellence in publishing, distribution, promotion, and selling of books. Provides a forum for information exchange; fosters a sense of community among booksellers; provides information and services for the advancement of members; promotes literacy; and supports the First Amendment rights of members. **Awards:** Great Lakes Book Awards. **Frequency:** annual. **Type:** recognition. **Recipient:** for excellence in writing and publishing of books that capture the spirit and enhance awareness of the Great Lakes region. **Computer Services:** Mailing lists, labels. **Publications:** *Books for Holiday Giving*, annual. Catalog ● *Directory and Handbook*, annual. Lists member bookstores and representatives, wholesalers and publishers in the Great Lakes region, and monitors regional First Amendment challenges. **Price:** $10.00 for members; $25.00 for nonmembers. **Circulation:** 700. **Advertising:** accepted. Alternate Formats: online ● *Great Lakes Bookseller*, bimonthly. Newsletter. Covers association news, member news, trade shows, and important dates. Alternate Formats: online. **Conventions/Meetings:** annual convention and trade show, includes presentations from sales representatives on lead books, readings and autographs from authors, workshops on the practical aspects of bookselling, and a silent auction (exhibits).

3226 ■ Independent Free Papers of America (IFPA)
107 Hemlock Dr.
Rio Grande, NJ 08242
Ph: (609)408-8000
Fax: (609)889-8359
E-mail: gary@ifpa.com
URL: http://www.ifpa.com
Contact: Gary Rudy, Exec. Dir.
Founded: 1980. **Members:** 287. **Membership Dues:** regular, associate, $150 (annual). **Budget:** $50,000. **Description:** Publishers of locally distributed, independently owned, free circulation shopping guides and community newspapers; interested businesses. Compiles statistics. **Awards:** Distinguished Service Award. **Frequency:** annual. **Type:** recognition. **Computer Services:** Mailing lists, of members. **Telecommunication Services:** electronic mail, paperman@gbpnews.com. **Also Known As:** National Classified Network. **Publications:** *Independent Publisher*, monthly. Magazine. **Price:** available to members only. **Circulation:** 1,000. **Advertising:** accepted. **Conventions/Meetings:** annual conference (exhibits) - always fall.

3227 ■ Inland Press Association
701 Lee St., Ste.925
Des Plaines, IL 60016
Ph: (847)795-0380
Fax: (847)795-0385
E-mail: inland@inlandpress.org
URL: http://www.inlandpress.org
Contact: Ray Carlsen, Exec. Dir.
Founded: 1885. **Members:** 1,200. **Membership Dues:** daily newspaper (based on circulation), $100-$2,000 (annual) ● non-daily newspaper (with less than 5 issues a week), $125 (annual). **Staff:** 11. **Description:** Provides newspaper-specific training programs and research. **Programs:** Awards and Contests. **Publications:** *The Inlander*, biweekly. Magazine. Features operational advice for the newspaper industry. **Circulation:** 4,100. **Advertising:** accepted. Alternate Formats: online ● *National Cost and Revenue Study for Daily Newspapers*, annual. Report. Features industry standard in newspaper cost and revenue benchmarks. Also Cited As: *Cost and Revenue Study* ● *Newspaper Industry Compensation Survey*, annual. Features industry standard in planning, explaining newspaper compensation decisions. Also Cited As: *NICS*. **Conventions/Meetings:** annual Key Executives Conference, for newspaper departments - mid-winter ● annual meeting, opportunity for obtaining new operational ideas and networking with top newspaper executives - October.

3228 ■ International Association of Cross-Reference Directory Publishers (IACRDP)
c/o Bresser Co.
684 W Baltimore St.
Detroit, MI 48202-2902
Ph: (313)874-0570
Fax: (313)874-3510
E-mail: information@bressers.com
URL: http://www.bressers.com
Founded: 1948. **Members:** 10. **Description:** Cross-reference directory publishers. Aims to keep members aware of advances in the field of cross-reference publishing. Offers opportunities for the exchange of information among members. **Libraries: Type:** reference. **Holdings:** 500. **Committees:** Sales. **Publications:** *Catalog of Directories*, annual ● *President's Letter*, periodic. **Conventions/Meetings:** annual meeting.

3229 ■ International Labor Communications Association, AFL-CIO/CLC (ILCA)
815 16th St. NW
Washington, DC 20006
Ph: (202)637-5068 (202)637-5015
Fax: (202)637-5069
E-mail: ilca@aflcio.org
URL: http://www.ilcaonline.org
Contact: Mr. Steve Stallone, Pres.
Founded: 1955. **Members:** 672. **Membership Dues:** media production, $150-$275 (annual) ● affiliate, $225 (annual) ● associate, $50-$1,000 (annual). **Staff:** 2. **Regional Groups:** 12. **State Groups:** 60. **Local Groups:** 600. **National Groups:** 50. **Description:** A professional support organization for labor communicators in North America, especially those of the AFL-CIO and the CLC. Works to strengthen and expand labor communications and to improve the professional and technical quality of member publications, websites, and media productions; it also maintains a Code of Ethics governing promotion and sale of advertising space. Holds a convention every two years immediately preceding each regular AFL-CIO convention. Officers are elected for two-year terms by convention delegates. **Awards:** ILCA Media Contest Awards. **Frequency:** annual. **Type:** recognition. **Recipient:** for member publications, websites, film and video, and broadcast productions. **Telecommunication Services:** electronic mail, steve.stallone@ilwu.org. **Affiliated With:** AFL-CIO. **Formed by Merger of:** (1955) CIO Editors and Public Relations Conference; International Labor Press of America. **Formerly:** International Labor Press Association. **Publications:** *The ILCA Reporter*, bimonthly. Newsletter. **Conventions/Meetings:** biennial convention.

3230 ■ International Newspaper Marketing Association (INMA)
10300 N Central Expy., Ste.467
Dallas, TX 75231-8654
Ph: (214)373-9111
Fax: (214)373-9112

E-mail: broke.bode@inma.org
URL: http://www.inma.org
Contact: Earl J. Wilkinson, Exec. Dir./CEO
Founded: 1930. **Members:** 1,282. **Membership Dues:** individual, $595 (annual). **Staff:** 15. **Regional Groups:** 6. **Multinational. Description:** Represents individuals engaged in marketing, circulation, research, and public relations of newspapers. Conducts conferences; holds newspaper executives marketing and strategic planning seminars. **Libraries: Type:** reference. **Awards:** Silver Shovel. **Frequency:** annual. **Type:** recognition. **Recipient:** for an outstanding INMA member. **Formerly:** (1969) Newspaper Promotion Association; (1987) International Newspaper Promotion Association. **Publications:** *IDEAS Magazine*, monthly. Covers promotion ideas, advertising, circulation, research, marketing, public relations, and association news. **Price:** available to members only. **Circulation:** 1,300. **Advertising:** accepted ● Also publishes winning entries of annual print, television, and radio contests. **Conventions/Meetings:** annual international conference and competition ● annual World Congress - conference and trade show (exhibits) - always April/May/June.

3231 ■ The International Publication Planning Association (TIPPA)
1840 41st Ave., Stes. 102-132
Capitola, CA 95010
Ph: (704)889-1288
E-mail: ellen@publicationplanningassociation.org
URL: http://www.publicationplanningassociation.org
Contact: Ellen Wofford, Contact
Multinational. Description: Fosters excellence in medical publications and communications within the biopharmaceutical industry. Provides a foundation from which industry can stand together to organize thoughts and present recommendations and ethical guidance. Gives practical strategies for developing, implementing and executing an effective publication and communication plan. Helps biopharmaceutical communication executives and their agencies to produce ethical and targeted publications and clinical data throughout the product lifecycle. **Awards:** TIPPA Award. **Frequency:** annual. **Type:** recognition. **Recipient:** for professionals who have made a significant contribution in publication planning development and ethical guidance. **Telecommunication Services:** electronic mail, tippamembership@publicationplanningassociation.org. **Publications:** *TIPPA News*. Newsletter. Alternate Formats: online.

3232 ■ Literary Source
Address Unknown since 2008
URL: http://www.literarysource.com
Founded: 2004. **Membership Dues:** aspiring author, $100 (annual) ● published author, $150 (annual). **Description:** Provides industry knowledge, support and inspiration to aspiring and new self-published as well as mainstream authors. Provides marketing and promotion tips to writers. **Computer Services:** database, writer's organizations ● information services, copyright information.

3233 ■ Livestock Publications Council (LPC)
910 Currie St.
Fort Worth, TX 76107
Ph: (817)336-1130
Fax: (817)232-4820
E-mail: dianej@flash.net
URL: http://www.livestockpublications.com
Contact: Diane E. Johnson, Exec. Dir.
Founded: 1974. **Members:** 180. **Membership Dues:** service, $150 (annual) ● publication, $175 (annual) ● student, $35 (annual). **Staff:** 1. **Budget:** $105,000. **Description:** Represents livestock industry magazines, newspapers, and newsletters in the United States and Canada. Service members are allied firms and individuals. Promotes improvement of the editorial and advertising content, visual appeal, industry impact, and financial well-being of livestock publications; enhances productivity of allied individuals and of the livestock industry. Sponsors workshops, panel discussions, and tours to publishing enterprises. **Awards:** CME Scholarship Award. **Frequency:** annual. **Type:** scholarship ● Forrest Bassford Student Award. **Frequency:** annual. **Type:** scholarship. **Recipient:** for winning contestant between college sophomore and junior agricultural journalism majors ● Hall of Fame Award. **Frequency:** annual. **Type:** recognition. **Recipient:** for livestock publishing leadership ● Headliner Award. **Frequency:** annual. **Type:** recognition. **Recipient:** for livestock industry leadership. **Committees:** Awards; Education; Peer Review; Site Selection; Sponsorship; Student Award. **Publications:** *Actiongram*, monthly. Newsletter. Includes employment listings. **Price:** included in membership dues. **Circulation:** 620 ● Membership Directory, annual. **Conventions/Meetings:** annual breakfast and competition, in conjunction with National Cattlemen's Association - usually February ● annual meeting and seminar, in design, art, writing, advertising layout and copy, and photography (exhibits) ● workshop.

3234 ■ Macrocosm USA
PO Box 185
Cambria, CA 93428
Ph: (805)927-2515
E-mail: brockway@macronet.org
URL: http://www.macronet.org
Contact: Sandi Brockway, Pres./Founder
Founded: 1989. **Members:** 300. **Budget:** $15,000. **Description:** Publishes reader/directories for educators, journalists, students, and activists. Compiles and edits materials into utilitarian formats such as handbooks, databases, a databank, and newsletters. Networks people, projects, and organizations. Self-serve, searchable directory, calendar, and forums online. **Libraries: Type:** not open to the public; by appointment only. **Holdings:** articles, books, clippings, periodicals. **Computer Services:** database, 6,000 organizations, periodicals, publishers, businesses, media contacts, resource guides. **Publications:** *Macrocosm USA: Possibilities For A New Progressive Era*. Handbook. **Price:** free to educators and libraries; $24.95 for nonmembers. Alternate Formats: online ● Handbooks.

3235 ■ Magazine Publishers of America (MPA)
810 7th Ave., 24th Fl.
New York, NY 10019
Ph: (212)872-3700
Fax: (212)888-4217
E-mail: mpa@magazine.org
URL: http://www.magazine.org
Contact: Nina Link, Pres./CEO
Founded: 1919. **Members:** 200. **Staff:** 37. **Budget:** $10,000,000. **Description:** Publishers of more than 1000 consumer and other magazines issued not less than four times a year. Activities include: Advertising Marketing Department to promote magazines as an advertising medium; Washington office to report on federal legislation and postal rates and regulations; Consumer Marketing Department to provide information services and assistance to members in all areas of circulation marketing. Conducts member surveys on magazine finance, paper usage, and compensation. Administers Publishers Information Bureau and Media Credit Association. **Libraries: Type:** reference. **Holdings:** periodicals. **Subjects:** magazine publishing. **Awards: Type:** recognition. **Committees:** Advertising Marketing; Circulation Marketing; Distribution; Government Affairs; Human Resources; International Affairs; Legal Affairs; Paper; Political Action; Postal Services/Private Delivery; Production; Professional Development; Tax. **Affiliated With:** American Society of Magazine Editors; Media Credit Association; Publishers Information Bureau. **Formerly:** (1920) National Association of Periodical Publishers; (1947) National Publishers Association; (1952) National Association of Magazine Publishers; (1987) Magazine Publishers Association. **Publications:** *Newsletter of International Publishing*. Magazine ● *Washington Newsletter*. Magazine. **Conventions/Meetings:** annual American Magazine Conference - always fall ● seminar.

3236 ■ Midwest Free Community Papers (MFCP)
PO Box 1350
Iowa City, IA 52244-1350
Ph: (319)341-4352
Free: (800)248-4061
Fax: (319)341-4358
E-mail: mfcp@mchsi.com
URL: http://www.mypaper.com
Contact: Brian Gay, Exec. Dir.
Founded: 1955. **Members:** 142. **Membership Dues:** regular, $100 (annual). **Staff:** 2. **Regional Groups:** 12. **Description:** Works to improve member publications through education, idea exchange and information. **Awards:** Merle Been Scholarship. **Frequency:** annual. **Type:** scholarship. **Telecommunication Services:** electronic mail, briangay@mchsi.com. **Affiliated With:** Association of Free Community Papers; Independent Free Papers of America. **Publications:** Newsletter, monthly. **Circulation:** 250. **Advertising:** accepted. **Conventions/Meetings:** quarterly meeting.

3237 ■ National Association of Hispanic Publications (NAHP)
8201 Greensboro Dr., Ste.300
McLean, VA 22102
Ph: (703)610-0205
Fax: (703)610-9005
E-mail: kstockpole@nahp.org
URL: http://www.nahp.org
Contact: Kerry C. Stackpole CAE, Interim Exec. Dir.
Founded: 1982. **Members:** 184. **Staff:** 5. **Regional Groups:** 7. **Languages:** English, Spanish. **Description:** Newspapers, magazines, and other periodicals published in Spanish (or bilingually in English and Spanish) in the United States. Promotes adherence to high standards of ethical and professional standards by members; advocates continuing professional development of Hispanic journalists and publishers. Provides technical assistance to members in areas including writing and editing skills, circulation and distribution methods, attracting advertisers, obtaining financing, design and layout, and graphic arts. Conducts public service programs including voter registration drives. **Libraries: Type:** open to the public. **Holdings:** books. **Subjects:** Hispanic scholarship. **Awards:** Amigo Awards. **Frequency:** annual. **Type:** recognition. **Recipient:** selected by NAHP Board or industry committee ● Corporate Recognition Awards. **Frequency:** annual. **Type:** recognition. **Recipient:** selected by NAHP Board or industry committee ● Hispanic Print Awards. **Frequency:** annual. **Type:** recognition. **Recipient:** selected by NAHP Board or industry committee. **Publications:** *The Hispanic Press* (in English and Spanish), quarterly. Newsletter. Contains articles on industry, events and notices. **Price:** free. **Circulation:** 2,000. **Advertising:** accepted. Alternate Formats: online. **Conventions/Meetings:** annual convention, promotes industry and services (exhibits).

3238 ■ National Association of Independent Publishers (NAIP)
PO Box 430
Highland City, FL 33846-0430
Ph: (813)648-4420
Fax: (813)648-4420
E-mail: naip@aol.com
URL: http://www.loc.gov/loc/cfbook/coborg/nai.html
Contact: Betsy Lampe, Exec. Dir.
Founded: 1985. **Members:** 500. **Membership Dues:** publisher/author, $75 (annual) ● vendor, $75 (annual). **Staff:** 3. **State Groups:** 1. **For-Profit. Description:** Independent and small publishing companies; vendors and interested individuals. Purpose is to assist and educate small publishing companies. Collects and disseminates information on book production, promotion and distribution. Concentrates on small presses. **Libraries: Type:** reference. **Holdings:** archival material. **Publications:** *Publisher's Report*, weekly. Newsletter. Provides production, marketing, and other information. **Price:** included in membership dues; $40.00 /year for nonmembers. ISSN: 0884-3090. **Circulation:** 500. **Advertising:** accepted. **Conventions/Meetings:** semiannual conference, held in conjunction with Florida Publishers Association (exhibits) - spring and fall ● seminar, on marketing strategies, selection of target audiences, and techniques of book distribution.

3239 ■ National Association of Independent Publishers Representatives (NAIPR)
PMB 157
111 E 14th St.
New York, NY 10003-4103
Ph: (646)414-2993
Free: (888)624-7779
Fax: (800)416-2586
E-mail: greatblue2@rcn.com
URL: http://www.naipr.org
Contact: Mr. Paul Williams, Exec. Dir.
Founded: 1989. **Members:** 700. **Membership Dues:** sales representative, $50 (annual) ● associate, $50 (annual). **Staff:** 1. **Description:** Promotes the welfare and interests of its members. Educates publishers to the advantages of independent sales representation. Fosters closer relationships among publishers, wholesalers, sales representatives, and booksellers. Exchanges information, ideas, plans, and programs helpful to the members. Educates the publishing community at large about sales issues and practices related to field sales promotion and independent bookselling. **Publications:** *The Call Report*, quarterly. Newsletters. Features news and information for associate members. **Circulation:** 400 ● *NAIPR News Online*, monthly. Newsletters. Features news and information for sales representative members. **Circulation:** 300 ● *Selling On Commission: Guidelines For Publishers.* Pamphlet. Guides publishers on how to sell their books to booksellers, wholesalers, and appropriate special markets through commissioned book sales reps.

3240 ■ National Federation of Hispanic Owned Newspapers (NFHON)
20 W 22nd St., Ste.808
New York, NY 10010-5804
Ph: (708)652-6397
E-mail: eldinews@eldinews.com
Contact: Carlos Carrilio, Pres.
Founded: 1992. **Members:** 70. **Membership Dues:** active/associated, $125 (annual) ● allied, $500. **Staff:** 6. **Budget:** $40,000. **Regional Groups:** 10. **Languages:** English, Spanish. **Description:** Publishers and editors representing 70 Hispanic newspapers printed in the U.S. and Puerto Rico. Promotes the Hispanic print media as a valuable means of communication; encourages recruitment and training of Hispanics as print journalists. Serves as clearinghouse providing information on current Hispanic newspapers and those out of print. Works to ensure that member newspapers are listed in national media directories. Seeks to increase advertiser awareness and use of Hispanic print media. Conducts research and compiles statistics on the Hispanic reading market. Sponsors speakers' bureau. Conducts educational and research programs; operates placement service. **Libraries: Type:** reference. **Holdings:** 170; books, monographs, periodicals. **Subjects:** journalism. **Awards:** Hispanic Print Media Awards. **Frequency:** annual. **Type:** recognition. **Computer Services:** Mailing lists. **Committees:** Convention; Ethics; Group Advertising Sales; Membership. **Formerly:** (1992) National Federation of Hispanic Publications. **Publications:** *National Hispanic Media Directory*, annual. **Price:** $30.00 plus shipping and handling. **Advertising:** accepted ● *National Rate Book*, annual. **Price:** $30.00 plus shipping and handling. **Circulation:** 1,000. **Advertising:** accepted ● *Ultima Hora*, quarterly. Newsletter. **Price:** free. **Circulation:** 1,000. **Advertising:** accepted. **Conventions/Meetings:** competition ● annual International Hispanic Media Conference (exhibits) ● annual National Hispanic Newspaper Week - meeting.

3241 ■ National Newspaper Publishers Association (NNPA)
3200 13th St. NW
Washington, DC 20010
Ph: (202)588-8764
Fax: (202)588-5302
E-mail: chairman@nnpa.org
URL: http://www.nnpa.org
Contact: John B. Smith Sr., Chm.
Founded: 1940. **Members:** 215. **Budget:** $450,000. **State Groups:** 38. **Description:** Represents publishers of daily and weekly newspapers. Maintains Hall of Fame. **Libraries: Type:** open to the public. **Holdings:** books. **Subjects:** information on the black press of America. **Awards:** Distinguished Service Award. **Frequency:** annual. **Type:** recognition. **Recipient:** for a black leader who has made the most significant contribution to black advancement during the previous year. **Committees:** Advertising; Awards; Circulation; Editorial; Foundation; Scholarship. **Also Known As:** (2006) Black Press of America. **Formerly:** (1956) National Negro Newspaper Publishers Association. **Publications:** *Convention Journal*, biennial. **Advertising:** accepted ● Quarterly Publication "The Torch light". **Conventions/Meetings:** annual conference (exhibits) - always summer ● annual workshop and conference - usually mid-winter.

3242 ■ National Trade Circulation Foundation, Inc. (NTCFI)
c/o JoAnn Binz
PO Box 515
Swiftwater, PA 18370-0515
Ph: (570)839-2708
E-mail: joann@qcs1989.com
URL: http://www.ntcfi.org
Contact: Philip Scarano III, Pres.
Founded: 1948. **Members:** 200. **Membership Dues:** corporate, $195 (annual). **Description:** Professional circulators in the business and special publications field. Seeks to: keep members abreast of new developments, trends, and techniques in the field of circulation; promote the professional status of the circulation manager in publishing. **Awards:** Angelo Venezian Award. **Frequency:** annual. **Type:** recognition. **Recipient:** for a member advancing professionalism in the field. **Formerly:** (1999) National Business Circulation Association. **Publications:** *Qualified Source*, quarterly. Newsletter. **Price:** included in membership dues. **Advertising:** accepted ● Membership Directory, annual. **Price:** included in membership dues. **Advertising:** accepted. **Conventions/Meetings:** meeting - 10/year, usually second Wednesday, September through June.

3243 ■ Networking Alternatives for Publishers, Retailers and Artists (NAPRA)
c/o Marilyn McGuire, Founder
PO Box 9
Eastsound, WA 98245-0009
Ph: (360)376-2001
E-mail: marilyn@marilynmcguire.com
URL: http://www.napra.com
Contact: Marilyn McGuire, Founder
Founded: 1987. **Members:** 690. **Staff:** 8. **Budget:** $700,000. **For-Profit. Description:** Publishers, producers, manufacturers, distributors, retailers, authors, and others in 15 countries involved with New Age and/or New Consciousness materials, including books, CD's, gift items, periodicals, and audio- and videocassettes. Encourages the distribution of information that supports spiritual growth and positive social change. Serves as a clearinghouse for New Age information; provides opportunities for members to interact. Rents mailing list of publishers and New Age bookstores; presents educational programs at annual BEA/ABA convention. **Committees:** Educational Outreach for Booksellers; Educational Outreach for Libraries; Educational Outreach for Publishers. **Formerly:** Publishers Information Foundation; (1998) New Age Publishing and Retailing Alliance. **Publications:** *Membership and Networking Directory*, annual. Membership Directory ● *NAPRA ReView*, bimonthly. Journal. Features reviews and news releases. **Price:** $75.00 in U.S.; $125.00 outside U.S. **Circulation:** 12,000. **Advertising:** accepted ● Journal. **Advertising:** accepted. **Conventions/Meetings:** annual workshop and convention, held in conjunction with American Booksellers Association Convention (exhibits).

3244 ■ Newspaper Association of America (NAA)
4401 Wilson Blvd., Ste.900
Arlington, VA 22203-1867
Ph: (571)366-1000
Free: (800)656-4622
Fax: (571)366-1195
E-mail: katie.woodward@naa.org
URL: http://www.naa.org
Contact: Susan Clark-Johnson, Chair
Founded: 1992. **Members:** 2,000. **Staff:** 180. **Description:** Promotes the interests of the newspaper business. **Libraries: Type:** by appointment only. **Holdings:** 5,000; artwork, books, periodicals, video recordings. **Subjects:** newspaper publishing, history, advertising, journalism. **Awards:** Display Federation Advertising Agency of the Year. **Frequency:** annual. **Type:** recognition. **Recipient:** for advertising agency ● Display Federation John Maione. **Frequency:** annual. **Type:** recognition. **Recipient:** for individuals ● Display Federation Newspaper Advertising Educator of the Year. **Frequency:** annual. **Type:** recognition. **Recipient:** for individual educator ● Display Federation Sales and Marketing Leadership. **Frequency:** annual. **Type:** recognition. **Recipient:** for newspaper advertiser ● Katharine Graham Lifetime Achievement. **Frequency:** annual. **Type:** recognition. **Recipient:** for individuals ● Research Federation Award of Merit. **Frequency:** annual. **Type:** recognition. **Recipient:** for a professional researcher. **Telecommunication Services:** electronic mail, sheila.owens@naa.org. **Formed by Merger of:** (1992) American Newspaper Publishers Association; (1992) International Circulation Managers Association; (1992) International Newspaper Advertising and Marketing Executives; (1992) Newspaper Advertising Bureau; (1992) Association of Newspaper Classified Advertising Managers; (1992) Newspaper Advertising Co-Op Network; (1992) Newspaper Research Council. **Publications:** *Facts About Newspapers*, annual. Booklet ● *Presstime*, monthly. Journal ● *TechNews*, bimonthly. Journal. **Price:** included in membership dues; $210.00/year subscription in Canada and overseas (surface); $265.00 overseas (airmail); $165.00/2 years. **Advertising:** accepted ● *Update*, quarterly. Newsletter. **Conventions/Meetings:** annual conference (exhibits) ● annual NEXPO - conference and convention (exhibits) - usually April.

3245 ■ Online Publishers Association (OPA)
249 W 17th St.
New York, NY 10011
Ph: (212)204-1488
Fax: (212)204-1514
E-mail: info@online-publishers.org
URL: http://www.online-publishers.org
Contact: Debora Wilson, Chair
Founded: 2001. **Membership Dues:** organization (with annual revenues greater than $50 million), $63,000 (annual) ● organization (with annual revenues less than $50 million), $26,250 (annual). **Description:** Online publishers. Seeks to advance the interests of online publishers to the advertising community, the press, the government and the public. **Publications:** *OPA Intelligence Report*, biweekly. Newsletter. Alternate Formats: online.

3246 ■ Parenting Publications of America (PPA)
4929 Wilshire Blvd., Ste.428
Los Angeles, CA 90010
Ph: (323)937-5514
Fax: (323)937-0959
E-mail: jdowden@prodigy.net
URL: http://www.parentingpublications.org
Contact: C. James Dowden, Exec. Dir.
Founded: 1988. **Members:** 120. **Membership Dues:** regular (with publication circulation of 1-40000), $700-$935 (annual) ● associate, $1,400 (annual) ● regular (with publication circulation of 40001-150000), $1,020-$1,740 (annual) ● regular (with publication circulation of 150001-750000), $2,170-$5,785 (annual) ● regular (with publication circulation 750001 up), $7,230 (annual). **Staff:** 3. **Budget:** $200,000. **Description:** Publishers of parenting publications. Promotes publications for and about parents. Sponsors competitions; compiles statistics. **Awards:** Design Award. **Frequency:** annual. **Type:** recognition ● Editorial Award. **Frequency:** annual. **Type:** recognition. **Computer Services:** database ● mailing lists. **Publications:** Newsletter, quarterly. **Price:** available to members only ● Directory, annual. **Conventions/**

Meetings: semiannual board meeting ● annual convention ● annual trade show.

3247 ■ Periodical and Book Association of America (PBAA)
481 8th Ave., Ste.826
New York, NY 10001
Ph: (212)563-6502
Fax: (212)563-4098
E-mail: lisawscott@hotmail.com
URL: http://www.pbaa.net
Contact: Lisa W. Scott, Exec. Dir.

Founded: 1966. **Members:** 75. **Staff:** 1. **Description:** Magazine and paperback publishers concerned with single copy or newsstand sales. Carries out concerted action in areas of publishing, production, and sales. **Awards:** Publishing Leader of the Year. **Frequency:** annual. **Type:** recognition. **Telecommunication Services:** electronic mail, lscott@pbaa.net. **Publications:** *PBAA News*, quarterly. Newsletter. **Conventions/Meetings:** annual convention.

3248 ■ PMA - Independent Book Publishers Association
627 Aviation Way
Manhattan Beach, CA 90266
Ph: (310)372-2732
Fax: (310)374-3342
E-mail: info@pma-online.org
URL: http://www.pma-online.org
Contact: Jan Nathan, Exec. Dir.

Founded: 1983. **Members:** 4,000. **Membership Dues:** publisher, $109-$415 (annual) ● non-publisher, $160-$590 (annual). **Description:** Entrepreneurial publishers of trade books and video and audio cassette tapes. Aims to assist independent publishers in the marketing and sale of their titles to bookstores, libraries, and specialty markets. Holds marketing and educational programs. **Libraries: Type:** open to the public. **Holdings:** 2,000; books. **Awards:** Benjamin Franklin Award. **Frequency:** annual. **Type:** recognition. **Recipient:** for previous years copyright. **Computer Services:** Online services, members and U.S. publisher's lists. **Telecommunication Services:** electronic mail, terry@pma-online.org. **Formerly:** (2006) Publishers Marketing Association. **Publications:** *PMA Resource Directory*, annual ● Newsletter, monthly. ISSN: 1058-4102. **Circulation:** 7,000. **Advertising:** accepted. **Conventions/Meetings:** annual Publishing University - conference (exhibits) - always 3 days prior to BEA convention.

3249 ■ Protestant Church-Owned Publishers Association (PCPA)
2850 Kalamazoo Ave. SE
Grand Rapids, MI 49560
Ph: (616)224-0831 (616)224-0795
Fax: (616)224-0834
E-mail: mulder@pcpaonline.org
URL: http://www.pcpanews.org
Contact: Gary Mulder, Dir.

Founded: 1951. **Members:** 32. **Staff:** 2. **Budget:** $70,000. **Description:** Official publishing houses of 32 Protestant denominations. **Committees:** Armed Forces Curriculum; Education; Projects. **Publications:** *PCPA Round Table*, quarterly. Newsletter. **Price:** available to members only. **Circulation:** 600. Alternate Formats: online. **Conventions/Meetings:** biennial convention.

3250 ■ Reader's Digest Association (RDA)
Reader's Digest Rd.
Pleasantville, NY 10570-7000
Ph: (914)244-5425
Free: (800)310-6261
E-mail: rdservice@custhelp.com
URL: http://www.rd.com
Contact: Thomas O. Ryder, Chm./CEO

Founded: 1922. **For-Profit. Description:** Publishes *Reader's Digest*, a monthly magazine. **Publications:** *Reader's Digest*, monthly. Magazine. **Price:** $24.98/year.

3251 ■ Singles Press Association (SPA)
PO Box 2139
Sioux Falls, SD 57101
Free: (800)825-6632
Fax: (605)335-6649
E-mail: harlanjacobsen@webtv.net
URL: http://www.countrysingles.com/contactus.html
Contact: Harlan Jacobsen, Publisher

Founded: 1986. **Members:** 12. **Membership Dues:** individual, $35 (annual). **Description:** Publishers of periodicals for adult singles. Promotes a positive image of single life and works to enhance the image of singles publications. Compiles statistics. **Publications:** *SPA Newsletter*, quarterly. Covers the business aspects of producing a singles publication, and association news. **Circulation:** 12. **Conventions/Meetings:** annual conference.

3252 ■ Small Press Center for Independent Publishing
20 W 44th St.
New York, NY 10036
Ph: (212)764-7021
Fax: (212)840-2046
E-mail: info@smallpress.org
URL: http://www.smallpress.org
Contact: Karin Taylor, Exec. Dir.

Founded: 1984. **Membership Dues:** individual, $50 (annual) ● dual/family/publisher, $75 (annual) ● contributing friend, $100 (annual) ● literary benefactor, $250 (annual) ● corporate/supporting sponsor, $300 (annual) ● patron, $500 (annual). **Description:** Represents cultural and educational institution committed to promoting interaction between the public and small independent book publishers. Works as an educational program of the General Society of Mechanics & Tradesmen of the City of New York. **Libraries: Type:** reference. **Holdings:** 2,000; books. **Awards:** Poor Richard Award. **Frequency:** annual. **Type:** recognition. **Publications:** *Small Press Center Newsletter*, quarterly. Contains news for small and independent presses. **Price:** included in membership dues. **Conventions/Meetings:** annual conference ● annual Independent and Small Press Book Fair - trade show - every December ● workshop.

3253 ■ Small Publishers, Artists and Writers Network (SPAWN)
PMB 123
323 E Matilija St., Ste.110
Ojai, CA 93023
Ph: (818)886-4281
Fax: (818)886-3320
E-mail: execdir@spawn.org
URL: http://www.spawn.org
Contact: Patricia Fry, Pres.

Founded: 1996. **Membership Dues:** regular, $45 (annual) ● partner program, $35 (annual) ● spouse or business partner at same address, $22 (annual). **Multinational. Description:** Publishers, editors, designers, authors, book manufacturers, distributors, illustrators, printers, artists, photographers, booksellers, and publicists. Provides opportunities for those involved in the process of publishing to exchange ideas and information; promotes an interest in art and literature to encourage creative expression and to help those interested in the arts connect with others for educational purposes and mutual support. **Publications:** *SPAWNews*, monthly. Newsletter. Presents a forum for ideas and information on subjects of interest to members. **Price:** free. **Circulation:** 2,000. Alternate Formats: online ● Catalogs. Alternate Formats: online. **Conventions/Meetings:** periodic festival, book fair of members' books (exhibits) ● monthly meeting, for networking (exhibits) ● workshop and seminar - 2008 July 12-19, Chautauqua, NY.

3254 ■ Small Publishers Association of North America (SPAN)
1618 W Colorado Ave.
Colorado Springs, CO 80904
Ph: (719)475-1726
Fax: (719)471-2182
E-mail: info@spannet.org
URL: http://www.spannet.org
Contact: Scott Flora, Exec. Dir.

Founded: 1996. **Members:** 1,400. **Membership Dues:** regular, $105 (annual) ● associate, $135 (annual) ● partner program, $70 (annual) ● universe customer, $50 (annual). **Staff:** 8. **Description:** For self-publishers, authors, and small presses. Works to advance the image and profits of independent publishers through education and marketing. Offers continuing education, co-op buying power, and sales and networking opportunities, plus discounts on many products and services. Publishes monthly newsletter. **Publications:** *Publisher's Weekly*. Magazine. **Price:** $214.00/year ● *SPAN's Marketing Plan Workbook, 2005 Edition* ● Handbook, annual. **Conventions/Meetings:** annual conference (exhibits).

3255 ■ Society for the Promotion of Science and Scholarship (SPOSS)
4139 El Camino Way
PO Box 10139
Palo Alto, CA 94303-0139
Ph: (650)853-0111
Fax: (650)853-0102
URL: http://www.sposs.org
Contact: Dr. Janet V.P. Gardiner, Exec. Off.

Founded: 1976. **Members:** 9. **Staff:** 2. **Description:** Works to promote science and scholarship books. **Publications:** *Ancestral Houses: Virginia Woolf and the Aristocracy*. Book. **Price:** $35.00 in U.S.; $38.00 outside U.S. ● *Art and Society: The New Art Movement in Vienna, 1897-1914*. Book. **Price:** $27.50 in U.S.; $29.50 outside U.S. ● *Austrian Expressionism: The Formative Years*. Book. **Price:** $49.50 hardcover; $24.95 paperback ● *Drink and the Politics of Social Reform: Anti-alcoholism in France since 1870*. Book. **Price:** $36.00 in U.S.; $38.00 outside U.S. ● *Egon Schiele: Art, Sexuality, and Viennese Modernism*. Book. **Price:** $37.50 hardcover; $22.50 paperback ● *From William Morris to Sergeant Pepper: Studies in the Radical Domestic*. Book. **Price:** $49.50 hardcover; $22.50 paperback ● *History of Switzerland: From Before the Beginning to the Days of the Present*. Book. **Price:** $40.00 in U.S.; $45.00 outside U.S. ● *Modern Austria*. Book. **Price:** $26.00 in U.S.; $28.00 outside U.S. ● *Modern Belgium*. Book. **Price:** $45.00 in U.S.; $48.00 outside U.S. ● *Modern Portugal*. Book. **Price:** $39.50 hardcover; $22.50 paperback ● *The New Switzerland: Problems and Policies*. Book. **Price:** $39.50 in U.S.; $42.50 outside U.S. ● *Pigeon Holes of Memory: The Life and Times of Dr. John Mackenzie, 1803-1886*. Book. **Price:** $24.00 in U.S. ● *Politics and Culture in Modern Germany: Essays from The New York Review of Books*. **Price:** $49.50 hardcover; $24.50 paperback ● *Population Pressures: Emigration and Government in Late Nineteenth-Century Britain*. Book. **Price:** $18.00 in U.S.; $20.00 outside U.S. ● *Poverty, Migration, and Settlement in the Industrial Revolution: Sojourners' Narratives*. Book. **Price:** $28.00 in U.S.; $30.00 outside U.S. ● *Redesigning the World: William Morris, the 1880s, and the Arts and Crafts*. Book. **Price:** $17.95 paperback ● *Tradition and Innovation in Contemporary Austria*. Book. **Price:** $15.00 in U.S.; $16.00 outside U.S.

3256 ■ Society for Scholarly Publishing (SSP)
10200 W 44th Ave., Ste.304
Wheat Ridge, CO 80033-2840
Ph: (303)422-3914
Fax: (303)422-8894
E-mail: info@sspnet.org
URL: http://www.sspnet.org
Contact: Francine Butler PhD, Exec. Dir.

Founded: 1978. **Members:** 750. **Membership Dues:** student, $25 (annual) ● librarian, early career, $57 (annual) ● individual, $125 (annual) ● friend, independent professional, $275 (annual) ● supporting, $1,200 (annual) ● sustaining, $2,900 (annual). **Staff:** 2. **Budget:** $500,000. **Description:** Individuals, including librarians, booksellers, publishers, printers, authors, and editors interested in scholarly publication; organizations. Serves as an educational forum. **Committees:** Annual Meeting Program; Communications; Development; Editorial; Education; Publications. **Publications:** Directory, annual. **Conventions/Meetings:** annual meeting (exhibits) ● seminar, on academic and professional publishing.

3257 ■ Southern Newspaper Publishers Association (SNPA)
3680 N Peachtree Rd., Ste.300
Atlanta, GA 30341
Ph: (404)256-0444
Fax: (404)252-9135
E-mail: edward@snpa.org
URL: http://www.snpa.org
Contact: Edward VanHorn, Exec. Dir.
Founded: 1903. **Members:** 400. **Regional. Description:** Works as regional association of daily newspaper publishers that specializes in educational programming. **Committees:** Audience Development; Education for Journalists; First Amendment; Human Resources; Literacy; Marketing; Smaller Newspapers. **Programs:** Traveling Campus. **Publications:** Newsletters, weekly. Contains up-to-date news and information about the newspaper industry. **Circulation:** 6,000. **Advertising:** accepted. Alternate Formats: online. **Conventions/Meetings:** annual Audience Development Conference ● annual convention ● annual Key Executives Conference (exhibits).

3258 ■ Specialized Information Publishers Association (SIPA)
8201 Greensboro Dr., Ste.300
McLean, VA 22102
Ph: (703)610-0260
Free: (800)356-9302
Fax: (703)610-9005
E-mail: info@sipaonline.com
URL: http://www.sipaonline.com
Contact: Janine Hergesell, Assoc. Dir.
Founded: 1977. **Members:** 600. **Membership Dues:** publisher (minimum; depends upon the annual gross revenues), $295 (annual) ● industry supplier/vendor (depends upon the annual gross revenues), $445-$1,195 (annual) ● publisher (maximum; depends upon the annual gross revenues), $4,395 (annual). **Staff:** 5. **Budget:** $1,000,000. **Local Groups:** 9. **Multinational. Description:** Represents firms that publish for-profit, subscription-based newsletters and specialized information products and suppliers of goods and services to the newsletter publishing industry. Aims to further the professional, economic, and organizational interest of members and their employees. Plans include: conducting research and preparing reports; representing members before federal agencies and monitoring legislation; holding seminars and workshops for members. **Libraries: Type:** open to the public. **Holdings:** books, periodicals. **Subjects:** newsletter publishing. **Awards:** Newsletter Journalism Awards. **Frequency:** annual. **Type:** recognition. **Recipient:** for editorial excellence in newsletter journalism. **Working Groups:** Customer Service; Editorial; Electronic Publishing; Marketing; New-Product Development; Small Publishers. **Absorbed:** (1979) National Association of the Investment Advisory Publishers. **Formerly:** (1983) Newsletter Association of America; (1991) Newsletter Association; (2000) Newsletter Publishers Association; (2006) Newsletter and Electronic Publishers Association. **Publications:** *Directory of Members and Industry Suppliers*. Membership Directory ● *Hotline*, biweekly. Newsletter. **Advertising:** accepted ● *How To Launch A Newsletter*. Report ● *Newsletter Publishers' Guidebook* ● *The Ultimate Guide to Newsletter Publishing*. Book. **Conventions/Meetings:** annual International Newsletter and Specialized-Information Conference (exhibits) - always in Washington, DC ● annual Reality Marketing - conference.

3259 ■ Suburban Newspapers of America (SNA)
116 Cass St.
Traverse City, MI 49684
Ph: (843)390-1531
Free: (888)486-2466
Fax: (231)932-2985
E-mail: sna@suburban-news.org
URL: http://www.suburban-news.org
Contact: Nancy Lane, Pres.
Founded: 1971. **Members:** 200. **Staff:** 6. **Budget:** $1,000,000. **Description:** Represents publishing firms or individual community-oriented newspapers in suburban or urban areas (regular members) and companies in related professions and industries (associate and professional members). Services the trade, research, and marketing needs of its members. Holds annual advertising, circulation, editorial, and management seminars. Sponsors advertising and editorial contests. **Awards:** Dean S. Lesher Recipient. **Frequency:** annual. **Type:** recognition. **Recipient:** for outstanding industry leadership and contributions ● General Excellence/Newspaper of the Year. **Frequency:** annual. **Type:** recognition. **Recipient:** for top newspapers in the country in six different circulation classes ● Suburban Advertising Director of the Year. **Frequency:** annual. **Type:** recognition ● Suburban Journalist of the Year. **Frequency:** annual. **Type:** recognition. **Telecommunication Services:** electronic mail, nancylanesna@aol.com. **Absorbed:** (1971) National Advertising Newspaper Association. **Formed by Merger of:** Accredited Home Newspapers of America; Suburban Section of the National Newspaper Association. **Publications:** *Suburban Publisher*, monthly. Newsletter. **Circulation:** 4,000. Alternate Formats: online ● Membership Directory, annual ● Also publishes advertising sales training materials. **Conventions/Meetings:** annual Circulation Managers and Classified Managers - conference (exhibits) ● annual Classified Advertising Conference ● annual Fall Publishers and Advertising Directors' Conference (exhibits).

3260 ■ Women in Scholarly Publishing (WISP)
c/o Susan Worst, Treas.
1070 Beacon St., Apt. 6D
Brookline, MA 02446-3951
E-mail: sworst@comcast.net
Contact: Maria Coughlin, Pres.
Founded: 1979. **Members:** 350. **Description:** Women involved in scholarly publishing and men who support the organization's goals. Promotes professional development and advancement, management skills, and opportunities for women in scholarly publishing. Concerns include career development, job-sharing information, and surveys of salaries and job opportunities for women, and practical workshops or other training opportunities. Provides a forum and network for communication among women in presses throughout the U.S. Sponsors educational workshops, programs, and seminars, in conjunction with the Association of American University Presses (see separate entry). Compiles statistics. **Awards:** Career Development Fund. **Type:** monetary. **Recipient:** for members who attended the workshops and seminars for professional development. **Computer Services:** Mailing lists. **Publications:** *WISP Newsletter*, quarterly. Includes association news, columns on benefit issues, calendar of events, and job openings; lists award recipients. **Circulation:** 350. **Conventions/Meetings:** annual conference.

3261 ■ Yellow Pages Association (YPA)
200 Connell Dr., Ste.1700
Berkeley Heights, NJ 07922-2747
Ph: (908)286-2380
Fax: (908)286-0620
E-mail: kimberly.enik@ypassociation.org
URL: http://www.ypassociation.org
Contact: Kimberly Enik, Exec. Asst.
Founded: 1975. **Members:** 344. **Staff:** 40. **Budget:** $13,000,000. **Description:** Mission is to lead, serve and grow the yellow pages industry. Publishing companies producing Yellow Pages telephone directories. Purposes are to facilitate the buying and selling of Yellow Pages advertising; encourage the use of Yellow Pages by consumers and advertisers and to establish and promote a cooperative advertising program. Represents members before other bodies; acts as a forum for discussion and resolution of members' common problems. Conducts market research and directory usage studies; compiles statistics; maintains speakers' bureau. **Libraries: Type:** reference. **Holdings:** 6,600. **Subjects:** yellow pages directories. **Awards:** Industry Excellence Awards. **Frequency:** annual. **Type:** recognition. **Committees:** CO-OP; Communication/PR; Department of Homeland Security Steering; Distribution; Electronic Yellow Pages; Elite Executive Steering; Elite Metrics Steering; Graphics. **Formed by Merger of:** (1988) National Yellow Pages Service Association; (1988) American Association of Yellow Pages Publishers. **Formerly:** (2002) Yellow Pages Publishers Association; (2005) Yellow Pages Integrated Media Association. **Publications:** *The 2001 YPPA Industry Usage Study*. Booklet ● *Yellow Pages Facts and Media Guide 2001*. Booklet ● *Yellow Pages IMA Membership Roster and Industry Guide*. Membership Directory. Alternate Formats: online; CD-ROM ● Also publishes materials concerning rates, research, promotion, and training. **Conventions/Meetings:** annual New Tools, New World - conference, geared towards yellow pages executives and suppliers to the industry (exhibits).

Purchasing

3262 ■ American Purchasing Society
PO Box 256
Aurora, IL 60506
Ph: (630)859-0250
Fax: (630)859-0270
E-mail: support@american-purchasing.com
URL: http://www.american-purchasing.com
Contact: Dr. Harry E. Hough, Pres./CEO
Founded: 1969. **Members:** 4,500. **Membership Dues:** individual, $174 (annual) ● company, $339 (annual). **Staff:** 6. **Budget:** $450,000. **For-Profit. Description:** Seeks to certify qualified purchasing personnel. Maintains speakers' bureau and placement service. Conducts research programs; compiles statistics including salary surveys. Provides consulting service for purchasing, materials management, and marketing. Conducts seminars and online courses. **Libraries: Type:** reference. **Holdings:** 1,500; articles, audio recordings, books. **Subjects:** purchasing, materials management. **Awards:** Certified Purchasing Professional. **Frequency:** periodic. **Type:** recognition. **Recipient:** for experience, education, examination and recognition ● Excellent Supplier Award. **Frequency:** annual. **Type:** recognition. **Computer Services:** database, contains price and supplier information. **Publications:** *Annual Report of Purchasing Salaries and Employment Trends*, annual. Provides information for buyers and purchasing managers. **Price:** included in membership dues ● *Benchmarking Purchasing*, annual. Journal ● *Contemporary Management*. Book. **Price:** $115.00 for members; $120.00 for nonmembers ● *50 Tips for Outstanding Purchasing* ● *Handbook of Buying and Purchasing Management*. **Price:** $81.00 for members; $89.00 for nonmembers ● *How to Become a Smart MRO Buyer* ● *How To Get the Best Results from your Purchasing Department*, biennial. Handbook ● *Policies and Procedures Manual for Purchasing with Job Descriptions*. Book. **Price:** $195.00 for members; $295.00 for nonmembers ● *Professional Purchasing*, monthly. Newsletter. **Circulation:** 15,000 ● *Purchasing Fundamentals for Today's Buyer*. Book. **Price:** $69.95 for members; $75.00 for nonmembers ● *The Resume Handbook*. **Price:** $8.95 for members; $9.95 for nonmembers ● *The Search of How to Get a Higher Salary* ● *10 Checklists for Buyers and Purchasing Managers* ● *25 Cost Saving Tips for Businesses* ● *What a Salesperson Should Know about the Law* ● Reports. Provides information for buyers and purchasing managers. **Conventions/Meetings:** meeting ● seminar (exhibits).

3263 ■ Institute for Supply Management (ISM)
PO Box 22160
Tempe, AZ 85285-2160
Ph: (480)752-6276 (212)733-7874
Free: (800)888-6276
Fax: (480)752-7890

E-mail: ashaw@ism.ws
URL: http://www.ism.ws
Contact: Lisa Martin CPM, Chair
Founded: 1915. **Members:** 46,000. **Staff:** 90. **Budget:** $11,000,000. **Regional Groups:** 181. **Description:** Represents industrial, commercial, and utility firms; educational institutions and government agencies. Disseminates information on procurement. Works to develop more efficient supply management methods. Conducts program for certification as a supply manager. Cosponsors executive purchasing management institutes at Michigan State University and Arizona State University. Provides in-company training. Maintains Speaker's Bureau and reference service. **Libraries: Type:** reference. **Holdings:** 700; archival material, reports. **Subjects:** purchasing, supply management. **Awards:** J. Shipman Gold Medal. **Frequency:** annual. **Type:** medal. **Recipient:** for individuals with modest, unselfish, sincere, and persistent efforts made for the advancement of the supply management field ● R. Gene Richter Awards for Leadership and Innovation in Supply Management. **Frequency:** annual. **Type:** recognition. **Recipient:** for individuals and organizations embracing leadership and creativity to manage complexity and risk. **Committees:** International; Nonferrous Metals; Packaging; Paper; Textiles; Wood Products. **Subgroups:** Chemical; Educational and Institutional; Electronics; Environmental; Federal Acquisition and Subcontract Management; Materials Management; Medical Industry; Minority Business Development; Multi-Division Purchasing; Petroleum Industry; Rail Industry; Steel. **Formerly:** (1968) National Association of Purchasing Agents; (2003) National Association of Purchasing Management. **Publications:** *InfoEdge*, 3/year. Alternate Formats: online ● *The Journal of Supply Chain Management*, quarterly. **Price:** $59.00 for members in U.S.; $69.00 for members outside U.S.; $79.00 for nonmembers in U.S.; $89.00 for nonmembers outside U.S. ISSN: 0094-8594. **Circulation:** 3,500. Alternate Formats: microform ● *Purchasing Today*, monthly. ISSN: 1047-7470. **Circulation:** 46,000. **Advertising:** accepted. Alternate Formats: microform ● *Report on Business*, monthly. **Conventions/Meetings:** annual conference (exhibits) ● annual International Purchasing - conference (exhibits) - always May. 2009 May 3-6, Charlotte, NC.

3264 ■ National Association of Purchasing Card Professionals (NAPCP)
10520 Wayzata Blvd.
Minnetonka, MN 55305
Ph: (952)546-1880
Fax: (952)546-1857
E-mail: napcp@napcp.org
URL: http://www.napcp.org
Contact: Diane McGuire, Managing Dir.
Founded: 1999. **Membership Dues:** individual, $495 (annual) ● associate, $149 (annual). **Description:** Seeks to advance purchasing card professionals and practices. Provides an organized forum for networking, and direction for the purchasing card industry. Establishes and communicates industry standards. **Computer Services:** Information services, purchasing card resources ● online services, career center ● online services, message board. **Telecommunication Services:** electronic mail, diane_mcguire@napcp.org. **Committees:** Best Practices; Data Capture and Accuracy; E-Commerce; Events; International Initiatives; Professional Certification; Sales and Use Tax; Standardizing Supplier Processes. **Publications:** *NAPCP E-News*. Newsletter. **Price:** included in membership dues. **Advertising:** accepted. Alternate Formats: online.

3265 ■ National Association of Purchasing and Payables (NAPP)
c/o Larry Kreider, Treas.
1570 Doxee Terr.
Marco Island, FL 34145
E-mail: davidelko@comcast.net
URL: http://www.nappconference.com
Contact: Dave Elko, Chm.
Membership Dues: regular, $195 (annual). **Description:** Aims to advance the concept of the entire requisition to payment and reconciliation process. Provides purchasing and payables professionals and their technical colleagues with new and innovative ideas. Seeks to enhance the critical interaction between the purchasing and payables disciplines. **Publications:** *NAPP News & Notes*, quarterly. Newsletter. **Price:** included in membership dues.

3266 ■ National Purchasing Institute (NPI)
PO Box 370192
Las Vegas, NV 89137-0192
Ph: (702)989-8095 (972)744-4132
Free: (866)877-7641
Fax: (702)967-0744
E-mail: info@npiconnection.com
URL: http://www.npiconnection.org
Contact: Craig Rowley, Exec. Dir.
Founded: 1968. **Members:** 400. **Membership Dues:** dual, $90 (annual) ● regular, $210 (annual). **Staff:** 1. **Budget:** $110,000. **Regional Groups:** 3. **Description:** Purchasing agents, directors of purchasing and procurement, buyers, and others employed by governmental, educational, or other tax-supported agencies. Seeks to improve the field through development of simplified standards of specifications, improved communication, and promotion of uniform purchasing laws. Compiles statistics. **Libraries: Type:** reference. **Subjects:** purchasing specifications. **Awards:** Achievement of Excellence in Procurement. **Frequency:** annual. **Type:** recognition. **Recipient:** for organizational excellence in public procurement ● Carlton N. Parker Award for Outstanding Service. **Frequency:** annual. **Type:** recognition. **Recipient:** for outstanding contributions to the development and progress of NPI. **Telecommunication Services:** electronic mail, executivedirector@npiconnection.com. **Committees:** Professional Development; Public Relations. **Affiliated With:** Institute for Supply Management. **Formerly:** (1973) Southern Purchasing Institute. **Publications:** *Annual Conference Program*, annual. Newsletter. **Circulation:** 300 ● *Membership Roster*, annual. Membership Directory. **Price:** available to members only ● *Public Purchasing Review*, bimonthly. Newsletter. Includes calendar of events and listings of job opportunities and new members and articles of significance to purchasing professionals. **Price:** free for members. **Circulation:** 750. **Advertising:** accepted. **Conventions/Meetings:** annual conference, products expo (exhibits) ● annual conference (exhibits).

Pyrotechnics

3267 ■ American Pyrotechnics Association (APA)
PO Box 30438
Bethesda, MD 20824
Ph: (301)907-8181
Fax: (301)907-9148
E-mail: jheckman@americanpyro.com
URL: http://www.americanpyro.com
Contact: Ms. Julie L. Heckman, Exec. Dir.
Founded: 1948. **Members:** 242. **Membership Dues:** full (based on annual sales), $1,300-$8,300 (annual) ● foreign manufacturer/exporter (based on annual sales), $1,300-$5,700 (annual) ● supplier, $1,000 (annual). **Staff:** 3. **Description:** Manufacturers, importers, and distributors of pyrotechnic products (primarily commercial and public display fireworks). Purposes are: to promote safety in the manufacture, transportation, and use of pyrotechnics through information and education programs; to keep members informed of activities of federal agencies that pertain to the pyrotechnics industry. Conducts safety education programs annually. **Absorbed:** (1980) National Pyrotechnic Distributors Association. **Publications:** *APA Report*, quarterly. Newsletter ● *Directory of State Laws*. Alternate Formats: online ● *2004 Convention Ad Book*. **Price:** $10.00 for members ● Brochure. **Conventions/Meetings:** annual convention and trade show (exhibits).

3268 ■ Pyrotechnics Guild International (PGI)
c/o Bill Bahr, Pres.
19 Yellowbrook Rd.
Freehold, NJ 07728
Ph: (732)919-1120
E-mail: gabamort@aol.com
URL: http://www.pgi.org
Contact: Bill Bahr, Pres.
Founded: 1969. **Members:** 3,881. **Membership Dues:** full, junior (without bulletin), $35 (annual) ● full, junior (with bulletin), $50 (annual) ● life (without bulletin), $875 ● life (with bulletin), $1,500. **Staff:** 5. **Budget:** $300,000. **Regional Groups:** 12. **State Groups:** 4. **Local Groups:** 6. **Multinational. Description:** Promotes the safe and legal use of fireworks worldwide. Produces public service announcements encouraging safe fireworks usage; conducts research programs and fireworks safety training course for those who fire professional displays. **Awards:** Max P. Vander Horch Circle of Excellence. **Frequency:** annual. **Type:** recognition. **Recipient:** to a person who has made exceptional contributions that reflect PGI's origin and values. **Computer Services:** Mailing lists, of members only. **Committees:** Display Operator Training Programs; Fire-Medical; Safety; Security. **Publications:** *PGI Convention Competition Rules*. Book. Alternate Formats: online ● *Pyrotechnics Guild International Bulletin*, 5/year. Covers fireworks manufacturing, safety, education, insurance, and regulations. Includes updating service and fireworks. **Price:** included in membership dues. **Circulation:** 4,000. **Advertising:** accepted ● Brochures ● Directories. Alternate Formats: online. **Conventions/Meetings:** annual competition, with fireworks (exhibits) ● annual meeting and symposium (exhibits).

Quality Assurance

3269 ■ International Association of Service Evaluators (IASE)
c/o Evelyn Arnette
815 Pavilion Ct.
McDonough, GA 30253
Ph: (770)288-2717
Fax: (404)795-0535
E-mail: getshopped@acpview.com
URL: http://www.iasemysteryshop.com
Contact: Evelyn Arnette, Contact
Founded: 1998. **Membership Dues:** full, $125 (annual) ● associate, $75 (annual). **Multinational. Description:** Improves the quality of service evaluation reports. Promotes high ethical standards in the service evaluation industry. Increases efficiency and profitability of the industry. Provides networking, mentoring and educational programs. **Telecommunication Services:** electronic mail, iase@acpview.com. **Publications:** Newsletter, quarterly. Contains articles about running a mystery shopping business. **Price:** included in membership dues. Alternate Formats: online.

3270 ■ Society of Quality Assurance (SQA)
2365 Hunters Way
Charlottesville, VA 22911
Ph: (434)297-4772
Fax: (434)977-1856
E-mail: sqa@sqa.org
URL: http://www.sqa.org
Contact: Barbara A. Foy, Pres.
Founded: 1984. **Members:** 2,000. **Membership Dues:** active, affiliate, $130 (annual). **Staff:** 4. **Regional Groups:** 8. **Multinational. Description:** Represents professionals involved in scientific research regulated by GCPs, GLPs, or GMPs; provides opportunities for interaction with regulatory officials, colleagues, and consultants, and specialized training; provides contact hours for clinical CEUs. **Computer Services:** Online services, for members only. **Boards:** Publications; Strategic Advisory. **Committees:** Articles of Incorporation and Bylaws; Corporate Relations; Education; Ethics and Membership Credentials; Historical; International Relations; Liaison; Membership Retention and Development; Program; Regional Chapter Presidents; Regulatory Forum; Tellers. **Councils:** Professional Registration. **Sections:** Animal Health; Beyond Compliance; Bioanalytical; Biotechnology; Clinical; Computer Validation Initia-

tive; EPA-GLP; FDA-GLP; Good Manufacturing Practices; Medical Device; Scientific Archiving; University. **Affiliated With:** American Association for Laboratory Animal Science; American Association of Pharmaceutical Scientists; American Association of Veterinary Laboratory Diagnosticians; American Chemical Society; American College of Toxicology; American Society for Quality; Animal Health Institute; Association of Clinical Research Professionals; CropLife America; Drug Information Association; National Alliance of Independent Crop Consultants; Pharmaceutical Research and Manufacturers of America; Regulatory Affairs Professionals Society; Society of Environmental Toxicology and Chemistry; Society of Toxicologic Pathology; Society of Toxicology. **Publications:** *Quality Assurance*, quarterly. Journal ● Newsletter, quarterly. **Price:** included in membership dues. **Circulation:** 2,000. **Advertising:** accepted. Alternate Formats: online. **Conventions/Meetings:** annual Fall Training - meeting - September ● annual meeting (exhibits) - 2009 Apr. 19-24, San Diego, CA.

Radiation

3271 ■ Association for Directors of Radiation Oncology Programs (ADROP)
c/o Steven Smith, Membership Dir.
8280 Willow Oaks Corporate Dr., Ste.500
Fairfax, VA 22031
Ph: (703)502-1550
Free: (800)962-7876
Fax: (703)502-7852
E-mail: stevens@astro.org
URL: http://www.adrop.org
Contact: Steven Smith, Membership Dir.
Membership Dues: regular, $100 (annual). **Description:** Seeks to advance the quality of residency training and education in radiation oncology.

Radio

3272 ■ Public Radio Programmer's Association (PRPD)
517 Ocean Front Walk, Ste.10
Venice, CA 90291
Ph: (310)664-1591
Fax: (310)664-1592
E-mail: info@prpd.org
URL: http://www.prpd.org
Contact: Marcia Alvar, Co-Founder
Founded: 1987. **Members:** 200. **Membership Dues:** radio station, $385-$3,000 (annual) ● institution, $750-$3,250 (annual) ● individual, $330 (annual). **Description:** Radio stations. Strives to lead, train, and provide resources to public radio programmers; acts as a clearinghouse for current information in public radio and broadcasting industry; promotes program directors and their perspective on public radio issues. Co-sponsors The Pledge Drive Workshop; hosts web-based Discussion Forum for members only. **Committees:** CPB Program Fund Guidelines Advisory Panel. **Working Groups:** PRPD-NPR Live Events/Special Coverage. **Publications:** *NewsWrap*, monthly. Newsletter. Contains news and features about radio in general and public radio in particular. **Price:** free, free, for members only. Alternate Formats: online ● *The Public Radio Program Directors Handbook*. Alternate Formats: online. **Conventions/Meetings:** annual conference, devoted to programming issues - 2008 Sept. 17-20, Hollywood, CA ● annual workshop.

3273 ■ Western Public Radio (WPR)
Fort Mason Center, Bldg. D
San Francisco, CA 94123
Ph: (415)771-1160
E-mail: wprsf@aol.com
URL: http://www.nfcb.org/services/wpr.jsp
Contact: Dr. K.L. Van Putten, Pres./CEO
Founded: 1978. **Staff:** 2. **Budget:** $50,000. **Description:** Supports public radio production; provides training, technical and production support for the public radio system, including station-based professionals, independents, and novices. **Computer Services:** Mailing lists. **Affiliated With:** National Federation of Community Broadcasters. **Conventions/Meetings:** workshop, for intro, mid-level and advanced, including digital training.

Railroads

3274 ■ Air Brake Association (ABA)
c/o Joe Faust, Sec.-Treas.
2098 E 10140 S
Sandy, UT 84092
Ph: (801)944-5270
Fax: (801)944-2916
E-mail: joefaust@comcast.net
Contact: Joe Faust, Sec.-Treas.
Founded: 1893. **Membership Dues:** in U.S., Canada, Mexico, $50 (annual) ● other foreign, $60 (annual). **Staff:** 1. **Budget:** $25,000. **Description:** Railway air brake engineers, suppliers, supervisors, and air brake manufacturing engineers. **Libraries: Type:** reference. **Holdings:** 100; archival material, papers. **Subjects:** matters related to railway air brakes. **Awards: Type:** scholarship. **Publications:** Books, annual. Includes railway brake information. **Price:** included in membership dues. **Circulation:** 700. **Advertising:** accepted ● Proceedings, annual. **Conventions/Meetings:** annual convention - always September.

3275 ■ Alliance for Rail Competition (ARC)
101 Constitution Ave. NW, Ste.800
Washington, DC 20001
Ph: (202)742-4435
Fax: (202)742-4435
E-mail: info@railcompetition.org
URL: http://www.railcompetition.org
Contact: Mr. Michael Snovitch, Exec. Dir.
Founded: 1987. **Members:** 60. **Staff:** 1. **Budget:** $1,000,000. **Description:** Shippers and other businesses making use of rail transportation. Seeks to ensure the availability of efficient and cost-effective rail freight services. Participates in public policy debates impacting railroad services; conducts research and serves as a clearinghouse on rail rates and services; seeks to raise public awareness of the social and environmental benefits of rail freight transportation.

3276 ■ American Association of Private Railroad Car Owners (AAPRCO)
630 Constitution Ave. NE, Ste.B
Washington, DC 20002-6036
Ph: (202)547-5696
Free: (800)856-6876
Fax: (202)547-5623
E-mail: execdirector@aaprco.com
URL: http://www.aaprco.com
Contact: Diane Elliott, Exec. Dir.
Founded: 1977. **Members:** 550. **Membership Dues:** car owner, non-Amtrak, $350 (annual) ● car owner, Amtrak, $500 (annual) ● associate, $90 (annual) ● trade, $150 (annual). **Staff:** 1. **Budget:** $100,000. **Description:** Private railroad passenger car owners (individuals, partnerships, and corporations), suppliers, and interested parties. Represents interests of private car owners before Amtrak and rail carriers. Encourages private passenger car operation; provides mechanical and operational seminars and information services; compiles register of private passenger cars. **Telecommunication Services:** electronic mail, patrick@phcp.com. **Committees:** Insurance; Mechanical; Private Car Roster; Public Relations; Safety; Tour and Charter. **Publications:** *Charter Referral Directory*, annual. Lists and describes private railroad passenger cars available for charter. **Price:** $5.00. **Advertising:** accepted ● *Directory of Private Railroad Car Facilities and Services*, periodic. Provides information on the availability of electricity, water, sanitation, and other services used in private railroad cars. **Price:** available to members only ● *Directory of Station Facilities and Services*, periodic. **Price:** available to members only ● *Membership Roster*, biennial. Membership Directory ● *Private Varnish*, quarterly. Magazine. Provides information on private railroad activities; includes Amtrak news and "Classified Mart" ads. **Price:** $30.00/year in U.S.; $33.00/year outside U.S.; $5.50/issue. **Circulation:** 3,000. **Advertising:** accepted ● *PV News Briefs*, 4-6/year. Newsletter. **Price:** available to members only ● *Rider Certification Manual*. **Price:** $10.00 for associates and public. **Conventions/Meetings:** annual conference (exhibits) - usually September or October.

3277 ■ American Association of Railroad Superintendents (AARS)
PO Box 456
Tinley Park, IL 60477-0456
Ph: (708)342-0210
Fax: (708)342-0257
E-mail: aars@railroadsuperintendents.org
URL: http://www.railroadsuperintendents.org
Contact: Pat Weissmann, Admin. Mgr.
Founded: 1896. **Members:** 600. **Membership Dues:** individual, $75 (annual). **Staff:** 1. **Description:** Represents operating department officers of railroads such as superintendents, trainmasters, signal engineers, and road foremen. **Libraries: Type:** not open to the public. **Awards:** Frank J. Richter Scholarship. **Frequency:** annual. **Type:** scholarship. **Publications:** *AARS News*, quarterly. Newsletter. Contains membership activities news; includes calendar of events, information on new members. **Price:** $50.00. **Circulation:** 1,100. **Advertising:** accepted ● *American Association of Railroad Superintendents—Proceedings*, annual. Contains the transcript of annual and winter meetings. **Price:** free for members; $60.00 for nonmembers. **Circulation:** 700. **Advertising:** accepted. **Conventions/Meetings:** semiannual conference (exhibits) - every winter and summer.

3278 ■ American Railway Car Institute (ARCI)
29W 140 Butterfield Rd., Ste.103-A
Warrenville, IL 60555
Ph: (630)393-0106
Free: (888)393-0107
Fax: (630)393-0108
E-mail: rpi@rpi.org
URL: http://www.rsiweb.org/committees/com_arci.aspx
Contact: Martin Graham, Chm.
Founded: 1915. **Members:** 22. **Staff:** 2. **Description:** Independent manufacturers of railroad and freight cars. Conducts research and standardization activities, particularly in freight car design and container standards. Provides for exchange of data on new devices used in freight cars. Compiles statistics on orders, deliveries, and backlogs of railroad cars with Association of American Railroads (see separate entry). Maintains historical files. **Committees:** Freight Car Design; Market Forecasting. **Formerly:** (1926) Railway Car Manufacturers Association.

3279 ■ American Railway Development Association (ARDA)
PO Box 1025
Paoli, PA 19301
Ph: (484)467-1414 (785)272-2252
Fax: (785)228-6298
URL: http://www.amraildev.com
Contact: Mr. William F. Krupinski, Exec. Dir.
Founded: 1906. **Members:** 205. **Staff:** 1. **Budget:** $20,000. **Multinational. Description:** Professional organization of railroad marketing, industrial development, and real estate executives. Fosters marketing and development activities and exchange of ideas among North American railroads. Presents Distinguished Service Award annually. **Publications:** Newsletter, periodic. **Conventions/Meetings:** annual conference - usually May.

3280 ■ American Railway Engineering and Maintenance of Way Association (AREMA)
10003 Derekwood Ln., Ste.210
Lanham, MD 20706-4875
Ph: (301)459-3200
Fax: (301)459-8077

E-mail: chemely@arema.org
URL: http://www.arema.org
Contact: Dr. Charles H. Emely, Exec. Dir./CEO
Founded: 1891. **Members:** 5,000. **Membership Dues:** full and associate, $125 (annual) ● student, $20 (annual). **Staff:** 9. **Budget:** $2,000,000. **Multinational. Description:** Professional organization of railway and transit officials concerned with design, construction, and maintenance of bridges, buildings, water service facilities, communications and signals systems, and other railway structures; engineering professors, editors, and government and private timber specialists. **Libraries: Type:** not open to the public. **Awards:** Arema Scholarship. **Frequency:** annual. **Type:** scholarship. **Recipient:** for college students studying railway engineering. **Formerly:** (1898) American Railway Engineering and Maintenance Association; (1899) American Railway Bridge and Building Association. **Publications:** *American Railway Engineering and Maintenance of Way Association—Annual Proceedings*. Provides complete texts of all conference events and papers presented, and a complete membership list. **Price:** $75.00. **Advertising:** accepted ● *AREMA News*, quarterly. Newsletter. Includes book reviews. ● *Communications and Signals Manual*, annual. **Price:** $595.00 for members; $945.00 for nonmembers ● *Manual for Railway Engineering*, annual. **Price:** $595.00 for members; $945.00 for nonmembers ● *Portfolio of Track Work Plans*, annual. Manual ● *Practical Guide to Railway Engineering*. Book. **Price:** $134.95 for members; $179.95 for nonmembers. **Conventions/Meetings:** annual conference (exhibits) - always September. 2008 Sept. 21-24, Salt Lake City, UT; 2009 Sept. 13-16, Chicago, IL ● periodic seminar, on bridge inspection and repair and railway engineering.

3281 ■ American Short Line and Regional Railroad Association (ASLRRA)
50 F St. NW, Ste.7020
Washington, DC 20001-1507
Ph: (202)628-4500 (202)585-3442
Fax: (202)628-6430
E-mail: aslrra@aslrra.org
URL: http://www.aslrra.org
Contact: Richard F. Timmons, Pres./Treas.
Founded: 1913. **Members:** 700. **Membership Dues:** railroad, $1,325-$7,185 (annual) ● associate, $1,430 (annual) ● sustaining, $1,000 (annual). **Staff:** 8. **Budget:** $1,800,000. **Regional Groups:** 4. **Description:** Independently owned short line (usually less than 100 miles) railroads. Monitors and reports on related legislative and regulatory activities. **Committees:** Legislative Policy; Operating Maintenance. **Formerly:** (1998) American Short Line Railroad Association. **Publications:** *American Short Line and Regional Railroad Association—Views and News*, biweekly. Newsletter. Includes summaries of current transportation, regulatory, and legislative issues. **Price:** free for members. Alternate Formats: online ● *Safety Bulletin*. Alternate Formats: online. **Conventions/Meetings:** annual convention (exhibits).

3282 ■ Association of American Railroads (AAR)
50 F St. NW
Washington, DC 20001-1564
Ph: (202)639-2100 (202)639-2555
Fax: (202)639-2286
E-mail: ehamberger@aar.org
URL: http://www.aar.org
Contact: Mr. Edward R. Hamberger, Pres./CEO
Founded: 1934. **Members:** 7. **Membership Dues:** gold associate, $7,500 (annual) ● silver associate, $15,000 (annual) ● non-class I railroad affiliate (based on revenue), $5,000-$20,000 (annual). **Staff:** 70. **Description:** Coordinating and research agency of the American freight railway industry. Fields of interest include railroad operation and maintenance, statistics, research, public relations, communications, signals, car exchange rules, safety, police and security matters, and testing and standards of railroad equipment. Operates Transportation Technology Center in Pueblo, CO and Railinc in Cary, NC. **Libraries: Type:** reference. **Holdings:** 2,000; periodicals. **Subjects:** rail and transportation policy. **Computer Services:** database, Universal Machine Language Equipment Register on all railcars, trailers, and containers used in North America. **Departments:** Administration; Communication; Law; Operations; Policy. **Publications:** *Analysis of Class I Railroads*, annual ● *Railroad Facts*, annual ● *Ten Year Trends*, annual ● *TRAIN-IT*, biweekly. Newsletter ● Also publishes statistical codes, statistical reports, technical research, and information publications.

3283 ■ Locomotive Maintenance Officers' Association (LMOA)
c/o Ron Pondel, Sec.-Treas.
701 Maple Ln.
Bensenville, IL 60106
Ph: (630)860-5511 (708)229-8827
Fax: (630)238-4654
E-mail: rpondel@stdcar.com
Contact: Ron Pondel, Sec.-Treas.
Founded: 1905. **Members:** 400. **Membership Dues:** railroad associate in U.S., $30 (annual) ● retired railroad associate, $10 (annual) ● railroad associate outside U.S., $40 (annual). **Staff:** 1. **Budget:** $25,000. **Description:** Represents presidents, chief operating officers, general purchasing agents, chief mechanical officers, and other railroad and supply company personnel concerned with diesel locomotive maintenance. **Committees:** Diesel Electrical; Diesel Material Control; Diesel-Mechanical Maintenance; Fuel, Lube, and Environmental; New Technologies; Shop Equipment and Processes. **Absorbed:** (1955) Master Boilermakers' Association. **Formerly:** (1938) International Railway General Foremen's Association. **Publications:** *LMOA Annual Proceedings*, annual. Journal. Contains technical papers on locomotive maintenance. **Price:** included in membership dues. **Circulation:** 600. **Advertising:** accepted. **Conventions/Meetings:** annual conference (exhibits) - always September.

3284 ■ National Association of Railroad Passengers (NARP)
900-2nd St. NE, Ste.308
Washington, DC 20002
Ph: (202)408-8362
Fax: (202)408-8287
E-mail: narp@narprail.org
URL: http://www.narprail.org
Contact: Ross B. Capon, Exec. Dir.
Founded: 1967. **Members:** 15,000. **Membership Dues:** individual, $35 (annual) ● student, $20 (annual) ● family, $45 (annual) ● donor, $50 (annual) ● sponsor, $75 (annual) ● sustaining, $125 (annual). **Staff:** 5. **Budget:** $500,000. **Description:** Users of rail passenger service, other concerned individuals, and organizations wishing to improve and expand rail passenger service. Seeks to increase public awareness and understanding of rail passenger service and its benefits. Works for fair and equal treatment for rail passenger service by government, in relation to other forms of transportation, and in the areas of defense transportation, mail transportation, taxation and user charges, and research and development expenditures. Seeks the establishment of a national transportation policy that includes rail passenger service as an essential element; initiates specific rail passenger improvements with appropriate government and transportation officials. **Libraries: Type:** reference. **Holdings:** archival material. **Awards:** George Falcon Golden Spike. **Frequency:** annual. **Type:** recognition. **Committees:** Amtrak Revitalization; Consists and Equipment; Editorial Response; Mail and Express; Membership and Grievance; Rail Finance; Routes and Schedules; Service Quality and Customer Relations. **Publications:** *NARP News*, 11/year. Newsletter. Reports on legislative and executive actions affecting railroad passenger service, mass transit, and general transportation. **Price:** included in membership dues. ISSN: 0739-3490. **Circulation:** 15,000. **Conventions/Meetings:** semiannual conference - always April and October.

3285 ■ National Association of Railway Business Women (NARBW)
c/o Cynthia Chandler, Natl. 3rd VP
16507 Hilo Cir.
Papillion, NE 68046-5602
Ph: (610)328-2975
E-mail: narbwinfo@narbw.org
URL: http://www.narbw.org
Contact: Cynthia Chandler, Natl. 3rd VP
Founded: 1921. **Members:** 900. **Membership Dues:** chapter, $20-$25 (annual) ● individual (member-at-large), $25 (annual). **Staff:** 14. **Regional Groups:** 3. **State Groups:** 32. **Description:** Women who work for railroads. Stimulates interest in the railroad industry. Fosters cooperation and understanding among members and people in related fields; promote good public relations for the railroad industry. Further the educational, social, and professional interests of members. Conducts charitable, benevolent, educational, children's service, and social welfare projects. Maintains a residence for retired members at Green Valley, AZ. Sponsors seminars and competitions. **Awards:** Benevolent Grant. **Type:** grant. **Recipient:** for members in need of financial assistance ● Railroad Woman of the Year. **Type:** recognition ● **Frequency:** annual. **Type:** scholarship. **Telecommunication Services:** electronic mail, tharper@railporttc.com. **Councils:** Emeritus. **Formerly:** (1954) Railway Business Women's Association. **Publications:** *Capsule*, quarterly. Newsletter. Alternate Formats: online ● Newsletter, monthly. **Price:** free for members. **Advertising:** accepted ● Brochures. **Conventions/Meetings:** annual conference and regional meeting - every fall ● annual convention - always May.

3286 ■ National Association of Retired and Veteran Railway Employees (NARVRE)
300 Cedar Blvd., Ste.201-A
Pittsburgh, PA 15228-1155
Ph: (763)757-1501
Free: (877)668-3864
Fax: (763)767-5794
E-mail: narvre@cs.com
URL: http://www.narvre.com
Contact: Whitey Westphal, Natl. Pres.
Founded: 1937. **Members:** 27,000. **Membership Dues:** individual, $12 (annual) ● couple, $19 (annual). **Staff:** 5. **Budget:** $200,000. **Regional Groups:** 8. **State Groups:** 4. **Local Groups:** 168. **Description:** Active and retired railroad men and women with at least 10 years of service; widows and widowers of railroad personnel; individuals with less than 10 years of service are associate members. Unites to advance the rights of members, primarily through legislative action. Works to retain pension benefits for railway employees and their families under the revised Railroad Retirement Act of 1974. **Libraries: Type:** not open to the public. **Holdings:** books. **Subjects:** history of NARVRE. **Computer Services:** database. **Telecommunication Services:** additional toll-free number, (877)668-3866. **Committees:** National Legislative. **Formerly:** National Association of Retired and Veteran Railway Employees. **Publications:** *NARVRE News*, monthly. Newsletter. Covers legislation affecting railroad retirees. **Price:** included in membership dues. **Circulation:** 16,000 ● Directory, biennial. Lists officers. **Price:** included in membership dues. **Conventions/Meetings:** biennial convention - every 1st week of May in even-numbered years.

3287 ■ National Railroad Construction and Maintenance Association (NRC)
500 New Jersey Ave. NW, Ste.400
Washington, DC 20001
Ph: (202)715-2920 (202)715-2919
Free: (800)883-1557
Fax: (202)318-0867
E-mail: info@nrcma.org
URL: http://www.nrcma.org
Contact: Chuck Baker, Exec. Dir./VP
Founded: 1978. **Members:** 150. **Membership Dues:** associate, $630 (annual) ● supplier, affiliate, $787 (annual) ● contractor (based on annual revenues), $630-$2,625 (annual). **Staff:** 2. **Budget:** $400,000. **Description:** Contractors who build public and private passenger and freight railroads and metropolitan rapid transit systems; suppliers to these contractors. Handles labor negotiations with unions, maintains liaison with government agencies, acts as information clearinghouse, encourages sound busi-

ness methods, and fosters good public relations. **Awards:** Certificate of Commendation. **Type:** recognition ● Safe Contractor of the Year Award. **Frequency:** annual. **Type:** recognition. **Recipient:** for a contractor member with active safety program. **Computer Services:** database, membership directory ● online services, railroad construction buyers' service. **Committees:** Government Affairs; Labor; Rail Safety Advisory; Safety and Education. **Formerly:** (1978) Railroad Construction and Maintenance Association. **Publications:** *Government Affairs*. Bulletin. Alternate Formats: online ● *Membership Directory and Railroad and Transit Buyers' Guide*, annual. **Advertising:** accepted ● *Rail Transportation and Operation Agreement*, annual. Videos ● *Safety and Education*. Videos. Alternate Formats: online. **Conventions/Meetings:** annual conference and trade show (exhibits) - always January.

3288 ■ National Railway Labor Conference (NRLC)
1901 L St. NW, Ste.500
Washington, DC 20036
Ph: (202)862-7200
Fax: (202)862-7230
E-mail: gevans@rrnlc.org
Founded: 1963. **Members:** 60. **Staff:** 18. **Budget:** $6,000,000. **Description:** Railroads, switching and terminal companies. Serves as a management collective bargaining agency for the freight railroad industry. Conducts bargaining with unions on a national level in connection with rates of pay, rules, and working conditions. Compiles statistics. **Libraries: Type:** reference. **Holdings:** archival material, business records, papers. **Committees:** National Carriers Conference.

3289 ■ Railway Engineering-Maintenance Suppliers Association (REMSA)
417 W Broad St., Ste.203
Falls Church, VA 22046
Ph: (703)241-8514
Fax: (703)241-8589
E-mail: contact@remsa.org
URL: http://www.remsa.org
Contact: Judi Meyerhoeffer, Exec. Dir.
Founded: 1965. **Members:** 200. **Membership Dues:** ordinary, $675 (annual). **Staff:** 2. **Budget:** $374,000. **Multinational. Description:** Provides global business development opportunities to members. Works to transfer knowledge about markets, products and the industry to members and their customers. Supports government initiatives that advance the North American railroad industry. **Computer Services:** Mailing lists ● online services, member directory and buyer's guide. **Committees:** Exhibit; Government Affairs; Nominating; Scholarship. **Formed by Merger of:** (1958) Association of Track and Structures Suppliers; (1965) Railway Engineering-Maintenance Suppliers Association. **Publications:** *Mainline*, quarterly. Newsletter. **Price:** free. **Circulation:** 1,700. Alternate Formats: online. **Conventions/Meetings:** biennial World Rail Expo - conference and trade show, informational showplace for railroad maintenance of way products, equipment, and services pertaining to rail track, track products, and track maintenance machinery (exhibits).

3290 ■ Railway Supply Institute (RSI)
29W 140 Butterfield Rd., Ste.103-A
Warrenville, IL 60555
Ph: (630)393-0106 (202)347-4664
Free: (888)393-0107
Fax: (630)393-0108
E-mail: rsupply@aol.com
URL: http://www.rsiweb.org
Contact: Howard E. Tonn, Exec. Dir.
Founded: 1908. **Members:** 150. **Membership Dues:** income class is 10.9 million or less and special, $1,000 (annual) ● income class is 11 to 49.9 million, $6,000 (annual) ● income class is 50 to 99.9 million, $12,000 (annual) ● income class is 100 to 349.9 million, $18,000 (annual) ● income class is 350 million and up, $24,000 (annual). **Staff:** 6. **Description:** Railway and rapid transit rail equipment and supply companies. Functions as the voice and promotional arm of the railway and rail rapid transit supply industry. Believes that the railway equipment and supply industry can prosper only as the American railroads prosper. Represents members before committees of the U.S. Congress and the executive branch. **Libraries: Type:** reference. **Holdings:** articles. **Committees:** Engineering and Maintenance; Equipment Leasing; Grade Crossing Safety; Intermodalism; Legislative Affairs; Passenger Transportation; Public Relations; State Tax; Tank Car; Train Control Technologies. **Formed by Merger of:** (2003) Railway Progress Institute. **Formerly:** (1956) Railway Business Association; (2003) Railway Supply Association. **Publications:** *Railway Progress Institute*, annual. Annual Report. **Price:** free ● *Railway Progress News*, bimonthly. Newsletter. Reports on industry events. Includes membership update and list of new member companies. **Price:** free. **Circulation:** 1,500. **Conventions/Meetings:** annual convention.

3291 ■ Railway Systems Suppliers, Inc. (RSSI)
9304 New LaGrange Rd., Ste.200
Louisville, KY 40242-3671
Ph: (502)327-7774
Fax: (502)327-0541
E-mail: rssi@rssi.org
URL: http://www.rssi.org
Contact: Donald F. Remaley, Exec. Dir.
Founded: 1960. **Members:** 225. **Membership Dues:** active or associate, $350 (annual). **Staff:** 2. **Budget:** $450,000. **Description:** Corporations, partnerships, and individuals engaged in the manufacture, sale, and service of products, appliances, apparatus, and devices used in railway signals, controls, and communications; engineers and contractors engaged in construction or maintenance of any such product. Collects and disseminates information of interest to members. **Formed by Merger of:** Railway Communications Suppliers Association; Signal Appliance Association. **Formerly:** (1971) Railway Signal and Communications Suppliers Association. **Publications:** Newsletter, quarterly. Alternate Formats: online. **Conventions/Meetings:** annual meeting (exhibits) - 2009 May 19-21, Nashville, TN.

3292 ■ Railway Tie Association (RTA)
115 Commerce Dr., Ste.C
Fayetteville, GA 30214-7335
Ph: (770)460-5553
Fax: (770)460-5573
E-mail: ties@rta.org
URL: http://www.rta.org
Contact: Jim Gauntt, Exec. Dir.
Founded: 1919. **Members:** 2,600. **Membership Dues:** producer, $350 (annual) ● preservation supplier, $2,500 (annual) ● non-preservative supplier, $525 (annual) ● contractor, global associate, recycling management, and timberland-owner, $150 (annual) ● associate, $50 (annual) ● railroad corporate, $150-$350 (annual). **Staff:** 2. **Budget:** $250,000. **Description:** Cross tie producers, sawmill owners, wood preservation companies, railroad maintenance engineers, purchasing officials, and others interested in the manufacture and procurement of wood railroad ties. Cooperates with government agencies in conservation of forests and forest products, planting trees, and reforestation. Collects statistics and promotes standardization of cross ties. **Libraries: Type:** reference. **Holdings:** articles, papers, reports. **Awards:** Branding Hammer Award. **Frequency:** annual. **Type:** recognition. **Recipient:** for a railroader ● Broad Axe Award. **Type:** recognition ● John Mabry RTA Scholarship. **Frequency:** annual. **Type:** scholarship. **Recipient:** for forestry ● Silver Saw Award. **Frequency:** annual. **Type:** recognition. **Recipient:** for indirect producer member. **Computer Services:** Mailing lists. **Telecommunication Services:** electronic mail, jgauntt@rta.org. **Committees:** Accident Prevention; Education and Information; Environmental Affairs; Legislative and Environmental Affairs Response; Manufacturing and Handling; Marketing; National Affairs; Research and Development; Strategic Planning; Timber Resources. **Formerly:** National Association of Railroad Tie Producers. **Publications:** *Crossties*, bimonthly. Magazine. Covers the wood crosstie industry, as concerned with today's railroad track systems. Includes advertisers' index and production reports. **Price:** $35.00/year. **Circulation:** 2,500. **Advertising:** accepted. Alternate Formats: magnetic tape; online ● *RTA Specification and Visual Guide to Tie Defects*. Booklet. **Price:** $18.00 for members; $35.00 for nonmembers. Alternate Formats: online ● *Tie Guide*. Handbook. **Price:** $8.00 for members; $15.00 for nonmembers ● Membership Directory. Includes contacts, phone/fax numbers, and producer map. Alternate Formats: online ● Papers. Alternate Formats: online. **Conventions/Meetings:** annual convention ● annual Crosstie Grading Seminar.

3293 ■ Tourist Railway Association (TRAIN)
c/o Dan Ranger, Exec. Dir.
PO Box 1245
Chama, NM 87520-1245
Ph: (505)756-1240
Free: (800)678-7246
Fax: (505)756-1238
E-mail: train@valornet.com
URL: http://traininc.org
Contact: Dan Ranger, Exec. Dir.
Founded: 1972. **Members:** 225. **Membership Dues:** full ($100000-$500000 gross operating revenues), $175-$460 (annual) ● full (greater than $500000 gross operating revenues), $575 (annual) ● vendor, $250 (annual) ● associate, non-voting, $115 (annual). **Staff:** 5. **Multinational. Description:** Tourist railways and static railroad museums; railroad equipment and service suppliers; gift shop suppliers; interested others. Informs members of laws, regulations, and other actions and events that affect the industry; provides for the exchange of technical data and the pooling of purchasing power among members; seeks to establish safety program and standards within the industry. Represents members before federal agencies and legislative bodies. **Awards:** Crook-Freeman Award. **Frequency:** annual. **Type:** recognition. **Recipient:** for outstanding service to the industry ● Distinguished Service Award. **Type:** recognition. **Recipient:** for work within the association. **Committees:** Diesel Locomotive; Gift Shop; Passenger Cars; Regulations; Safety; Steam Locomotives; Streetcars; Track and Structures. **Publications:** *Educational/Technical Materials*, periodic. Manuals ● *Safety Training Tape*. Videos. Covers safety and training. ● *Trainline*, bimonthly. Newsletter. Includes list of new members and information on upcoming meetings. **Price:** $12.00 /year for nonmembers. **Advertising:** accepted. Alternate Formats: online ● Brochure ● Directory, annual. **Conventions/Meetings:** annual meeting and seminar (exhibits) - always fall.

Rangeland

3294 ■ Working Ranch Cowboys Association (WRCA)
PO Box 7765
Amarillo, TX 79114
Ph: (806)374-9722
Fax: (806)374-9724
E-mail: wrca@arn.net
URL: http://www.wrca.org
Contact: Gary Morton, Dir.
Founded: 1995. **Membership Dues:** cowboy, $25 (annual) ● cowboy collectible, $75 (annual) ● corporate, $300 (annual) ● Riding for the Brand, $500 (quinquennial) ● Jigger Boss (10-year membership), $1,000 ● Cowboy Boss (life), $2,500. **Description:** Seeks to preserve the heritage and lifestyle of the working ranch cowboy, as well as ranching. **Awards:** WRCF Scholarship. **Frequency:** annual. **Type:** scholarship. **Recipient:** to working ranch cowboys and their family showing interest in continuing their education. **Funds:** Cowboy Crisis. **Publications:** *Hungry Loop*. Newsletter. **Price:** included in membership dues. **Conventions/Meetings:** Ranch Horse Show ● Wild Horse Prairie Days - show ● World Championship Ranch Rodeo - competition.

Real Estate

3295 ■ AIR Commercial Real Estate Association (AIR)
800 W 6th St., Ste.800
Los Angeles, CA 90017-2741
Ph: (213)687-8777 (949)608-2027
Fax: (213)687-8616
E-mail: thayes@airea.com
URL: http://www.airea.com
Contact: Tim Hayes, Exec. Dir.
Founded: 1960. **Members:** 1,600. **Staff:** 16. **Budget:** $2,700,000. **Description:** Real estate men and women specializing in industrial and commercial properties; affiliate members are title companies, mortgage loan companies, public utilities, and developers. Membership concentrated in Southern California. Encourages high professional standards. Sponsors a course on industrial real estate, in cooperation with the University of California. Develops industrial multiple listing system and standard lease forms. Supports the Industrial Multiple, a clearinghouse for information on industrial listings. Maintains a computerized multiple listing system. **Committees:** Budget and Finance; Computer; Education; Ethics and Arbitration; Governmental Affairs; Marketing; Membership; Orientation. **Publications:** *Air News Bulletin*, monthly. Contains information for members only. **Circulation:** 1,000. Alternate Formats: online ● *AirWaves*, bimonthly. Newsletter. Alternate Formats: online ● *The Multiple*, weekly. **Conventions/Meetings:** annual meeting and seminar, with planning seminar.

3296 ■ American Homeowners Foundation (AHF)
6776 Little Falls Rd.
Arlington, VA 22213-1213
Free: (800)489-7776
Fax: (703)536-7079
E-mail: amerhome@americanhomeowners.org
URL: http://www.americanhomeowners.org
Contact: Mr. Bruce Hahn, Pres.
Founded: 1984. **Members:** 5,000. **Staff:** 2. **Budget:** $200,000. **Description:** Homeowners and prospective homeowners. Serves as an educational and research organization; publishes books, model contracts, videos and other educational materials acts as a unified voice for American homeowners. **Publications:** *The Complete Home Buyers Guide*. Book. **Price:** $12.95 ● *How To Sell Your Home Fast!*. Book. **Price:** $12.95 ● *Mortgage Tips and Payment Tables*. Book. **Price:** $7.95 ● Reports. Includes topics in time-sharing properties, homeownership in resort areas, and the effects of tax bills on homeowners. ● Also publishes model contracts for remodeling of homes, construction of new homes, purchase or sale of home, and leases.

3297 ■ American Land Title Association (ALTA)
1828 L St. NW, Ste.705
Washington, DC 20036-5182
Ph: (202)296-3671
Free: (800)787-ALTA
Fax: (202)223-5843
E-mail: service@alta.org
URL: http://www.alta.org
Contact: James R. Maher, Exec. VP
Founded: 1907. **Members:** 2,400. **Membership Dues:** associate, $460 (annual). **Staff:** 17. **Budget:** $3,700,000. **State Groups:** 40. **Description:** Represents the abstracters, title insurance companies, and attorneys specializing in real property law. **Libraries: Type:** reference. **Holdings:** archival material, reports. **Telecommunication Services:** electronic mail, jim_maher@alta.org. **Committees:** Title Industry Political Action. **Sections:** Abstracters and Title Insurance Agents; Title Insurance and Underwriters. **Formerly:** American Title Association. **Publications:** *ALTA Abstracter and Title Agents Annual Technology Survey*, annual. Surveys. **Price:** $130.00 for members; $255.00 for nonmembers ● *ALTA Directory*, annual. **Price:** $50.00 for members; $125.00 for nonmembers ● *ALTA Policy Forms Handbook*. **Price:** $60.00 for members; $160.00 for nonmembers ● *Title News*, bimonthly. Magazine. **Price:** $30.00 for members; $48.00 for nonmembers ● *2006-2007 ALTA Membership Directory*, annual. **Price:** $55.00 for members; $130.00 for nonmembers. **Conventions/Meetings:** annual convention (exhibits) - 2008 Oct. 15-18, Koloa, HI ● annual Federal Conference ● annual Tech Forum - meeting (exhibits).

3298 ■ American Resort Development Association (ARDA)
1201 15th St. NW, No. 400
Washington, DC 20005-2842
Ph: (202)371-6700 (202)207-1076
Fax: (202)289-8544
E-mail: webmaster@arda.org
URL: http://www.arda.org
Contact: Howard C. Nusbaum, Pres./CEO
Founded: 1969. **Members:** 850. **Membership Dues:** active (based on annual revenues), $1,875-$13,500 (annual) ● home owner/property owner association, $300 (annual) ● public agency/public official/public interest group/school/library, $260 (annual) ● international, $615 (annual) ● associate, $1,650 (annual). **Staff:** 30. **Budget:** $7,000,000. **Description:** Represents developers of timeshare resort and recreational communities; suppliers to the resort development industries. Advocates legislative and regulatory issues. Offers seminars; conducts research and surveys; annual convention and trade show; legislative and regulatory advocacy. **Libraries: Type:** reference. **Holdings:** reports. **Awards: Frequency:** annual. **Type:** recognition. **Recipient:** for productivity, professionalism, creativity, and leadership. **Telecommunication Services:** electronic mail, rgoodhope@arda.org. **Committees:** International; International Foundation; Membership; Political Action; Property Management; Technology. **Formerly:** (1985) American Land Development Association; (1990) American Resort and Residential Development Association. **Publications:** *Developments*, 10/year. Magazine. Includes regulatory and legislative news; for those concerned with resort and community development. **Price:** included in membership dues. **Circulation:** 3,400. **Advertising:** accepted. **Conventions/Meetings:** periodic conference and workshop (exhibits) ● annual convention (exhibits).

3299 ■ Asian American Real Estate Association (AAREA)
6600 Sands Point, Ste.210
Houston, TX 77074
Ph: (281)275-4419 (281)788-7870
Fax: (713)777-4828
E-mail: info@aarea.us
URL: http://www.aarea.us
Contact: Lauris Tam, Pres.
Founded: 2003. **Membership Dues:** regular, $60 (annual) ● affiliate, $120 (annual). **Description:** Strengthens the image of Asian American real estate agents. Promotes real estate business through cooperation from every business enterprise and small business owner. Provides market research and development for Asian American real estate businesses. **Publications:** Newsletter.

3300 ■ Association of Real Estate Women (AREW)
322 Eighth Ave., Ste.501
New York, NY 10001
Ph: (212)599-6181
Fax: (212)645-1147
E-mail: info@arew.org
URL: http://www.arew.org
Contact: Frances Ann Delgorio, Pres.
Founded: 1978. **Members:** 300. **Membership Dues:** individual, $575 (annual). **Staff:** 3. **Description:** Women and men in real estate. Conducts luncheons, networking, community outreach and educational programs. **Awards:** Founders' Award. **Frequency:** annual. **Type:** recognition. **Recipient:** for an AREW member who personifies excellence in representing AREW. **Publications:** *AREW News*, monthly. Newsletter.

3301 ■ Building Owners and Managers Association International (BOMA)
1201 New York Ave. NW, Ste.300
Washington, DC 20005-3966
Ph: (202)408-2662
Fax: (202)326-6377
E-mail: info@boma.org
URL: http://www.boma.org
Contact: Henry Chamberlain, Pres./COO
Founded: 1908. **Members:** 18,000. **Membership Dues:** member-at-large, $400 (annual) ● national associate, $1,195 (annual). **Staff:** 35. **Budget:** $7,000,000. **Regional Groups:** 10. **State Groups:** 6. **Local Groups:** 106. **Description:** Building owners, managers, developers, leasing professionals, facility managers, asset managers and the providers of goods and services. Represents all facets of the commercial real estate industry. **Libraries: Type:** reference. **Awards:** Earth Awards. **Frequency:** annual. **Type:** recognition. **Recipient:** for excellence in environmentally sound office building management ● Office Building of the Year Earth Award. **Frequency:** annual. **Type:** recognition. **Recipient:** for excellence in operations management and for environmentally conscious buildings. **Computer Services:** Mailing lists. **Committees:** Energy; State Government Affairs. **Councils:** Agency Management; Associate Member and Exhibitor; Building Review Service; Suburban Buildings. **Divisions:** Building Operations; Financial Information and Reporting; Government Affairs; Marketing; Special Purpose Buildings. **Special Interest Groups:** Government Buildings. **Formerly:** (1966) National Association of Building Owners and Managers. **Publications:** *BOMA/Cushman and Wakefield Market Intelligence Report*, quarterly. Newsletter. Provides trends, analysis, and forecasts. ● *BOMA Magazine*, monthly. **Price:** $50.00 for members; $75.00 for nonmembers. **Advertising:** accepted ● *BOMA Office Market Review*, annual. Report ● *Cleaning Study* ● *Experience Exchange Report for Downtown and Suburban Office Buildings*, annual. Provides economic statistics. ● *Functional Accounting Guide and Chart of Accounts* ● *Office Tenant Satisfaction Survey*. Magazine ● *Who's Who in the Commercial Real Estate Industry?*, annual. Directory ● Also publishes educational texts, workbooks, and analyses. **Conventions/Meetings:** annual The Office Building Show and Convention - convention and trade show, with keynote sessions (exhibits).

3302 ■ CCIM Institute
430 N Michigan Ave., Ste.800
Chicago, IL 60611-4092
Ph: (312)321-4460
Free: (800)621-7027
Fax: (312)321-4530
E-mail: info@ccim.com
URL: http://www.ccim.com
Contact: Susan Groeneveld CAE, Exec. VP
Founded: 1969. **Members:** 15,000. **Membership Dues:** designee, candidate, $450 (annual) ● individual, $485 (annual). **Staff:** 40. **Budget:** $10,000,000. **Regional Groups:** 12. **Local Groups:** 61. **Languages:** Chinese, English, French, German, Japanese, Spanish. **Multinational. Description:** Commercial investment real estate brokers, developers, asset managers, and others involved in commercial investment properties. Seeks to enhance the professional competence of commercial real estate practitioners. Represents interests of members through legislative advocacy, technology products, and networking opportunities; provides research in the field of commercial investment real estate; conducts educational programs and awards certification. **Programs:** Certified Commercial Investment Member Designation. **Affiliated With:** National Association of Realtors. **Publications:** *Commercial Investment Real Estate Magazine*, bimonthly. Provides articles and features on brokering, financing, taxation, technology, marketing, legal, and other aspects of commercial real estate. **Price:** free for members; $38.00 /year for nonmembers. ISSN: 0744-6446. **Circulation:** 18,000. **Advertising:** accepted. **Conventions/Meetings:** annual symposium, two-day program designed to give real estate management

and brokerage professionals an opportunity to network and learn (exhibits).

3303 ■ Certified Exchangors (CE)
c/o Doris Grutzmacher, Exec. Officer
PO Box 12490
Scottsdale, AZ 85267-2490
Ph: (480)860-8838
Fax: (480)614-8303
E-mail: grutzmachr@aol.com
Contact: Doris Grutzmacher, Exec. Officer
Founded: 1977. **Members:** 120. **Description:** Real estate exchanging professionals. Serves as a forum for the promotion of high standards and information exchange in the field. Awards Certified Exchanger designation to members who have demonstrated competency in the field and passed a comprehensive testing certification program. Sponsors educational seminars and marketing sessions. **Publications:** Brochure ● Newsletter, periodic. **Conventions/Meetings:** semiannual meeting.

3304 ■ Commercial Mortgage Securities Association (CMSA)
30 Broad St., 28th Fl.
New York, NY 10004
Ph: (212)509-1844
Fax: (212)509-1895
E-mail: info1@cmbs.org
URL: http://www.cmbs.org
Contact: Dottie Cunningham, CEO
Founded: 1994. **Members:** 389. **Membership Dues:** principal, professional, $4,500 (annual) ● associate, investor, $1,500 (annual) ● academic, $100 (annual). **Staff:** 19. **Multinational. Description:** Securities professionals. Promotes the ongoing strength, liquidity and viability of commercial real estate capital market finance worldwide. Sponsors annual meetings, seminars, and regional roundtables. **Publications:** *CMBS World*, quarterly. Magazine. Contains articles focused exclusively on commercial mortgage-backed securities. **Price:** $100.00. **Advertising:** accepted. Alternate Formats: online. **Conventions/Meetings:** annual conference, for investors - 2009 Jan. 11-13, Miami Beach, FL ● annual convention.

3305 ■ CoreNet Global
260 Peachtree St., Ste.1500
Atlanta, GA 30303-1237
Ph: (404)589-3200 (416)921-9088
Free: (800)726-8111
Fax: (404)589-3201
E-mail: jclarke@corenetglobal.org
URL: http://www.corenetglobal.org
Contact: David M. Harris MCR, Chm.
Founded: 1969. **Members:** 3,000. **Membership Dues:** end user, $595 (annual) ● service and economic provider, $750 (annual) ● academic, student, journalist, retired, $95 (annual). **Staff:** 18. **Budget:** $3,000,000. **Local Groups:** 35. **Multinational. Description:** Executives, attorneys, real estate department heads, architects, engineers, analysts, researchers, and anyone responsible for the management, administration, and operation of national and regional real estate departments of national and international corporations. Encourages professionalism within corporate real estate through education and communication; protects the interests of corporate realty in dealing with adversaries, public or private; maintains contact with other real estate organizations; publicizes the availability of fully qualified members to the job market. Conducts seminars, including concentrated workshops on the corporate real estate field. Compiles statistics; sponsors competitions; maintains biographical archives and placement service. **Libraries: Type:** reference. **Holdings:** archival material, reports. **Awards:** Global Innovators Award. **Frequency:** annual. **Type:** recognition. **Recipient:** for excellence in the strategic management of corporate real estate ● Sustainable Leadership Award. **Frequency:** annual. **Type:** recognition. **Recipient:** for individuals who have been patiently leading by example in the design and business communities. **Computer Services:** database, membership. **Divisions:** Educational Services; Professional Liaison; Public and Professional Policy. **Formed by Merger of:** (2002) NACORE International; (2002) International Development Research Council. **Formerly:** (1973) National Association of Location Analysts and Negotiators; (1983) National Association of Corporate Real Estate Executives; (1987) International Association of Corporate Real Estate Executives. **Publications:** *Corporate Real Estate Leader*, bimonthly. Journal. Provides educational and informative articles on all aspects of corporate real estate. **Price:** included in membership dues; $75.00 /year for nonmembers. ISSN: 1042-9115. **Circulation:** 3,200. **Advertising:** accepted ● *Welcome! Program*, annual ● *Who's Who in Corporate Real Estate*. Directory ● Newsletter, quarterly. **Conventions/Meetings:** annual conference and symposium, exposition (exhibits) - always fall ● annual symposium (exhibits).

3306 ■ Council of Real Estate Brokerage Managers (CRB)
430 N Michigan Ave.
Chicago, IL 60611-4011
Free: (800)621-8738
Fax: (312)329-8882
E-mail: info@crb.com
URL: http://www.crb.com
Contact: Ginny Shipe CAE, CEO
Founded: 1968. **Members:** 7,000. **Membership Dues:** regular, $125 (annual) ● candidate, $185 (annual). **Staff:** 8. **Budget:** $2,000,000. **Multinational. Description:** Represents managers, brokers and owners, serving nearly 7,000 members through superior educational programming, products and publications. Exemplifies professional achievement and recognition in real estate brokerage management. Bestows CRB (Certified Real Estate Brokerage Manager) designation on members who have completed courses conducted by REBMC. **Awards:** Hall of Leaders Award. **Frequency:** annual. **Type:** recognition. **Recipient:** for CRB designees whose significant contributions continue to shape and impact the real estate industry locally and nationally. **Telecommunication Services:** electronic mail, gshipe@crb.com. **Affiliated With:** Council of Residential Specialists; National Association of Realtors. **Formerly:** (1985) Marketing Management Council; (1991) Real Estate Brokerage Council; (2002) Real Estate Brokerage Managers Council. **Publications:** *e-Connections Newsletter*, monthly. Alternate Formats: online ● *Issues and Trends*, quarterly. Newsletter. Alternate Formats: online ● *Real Estate Business Magazine*, bimonthly. **Price:** $24.99 for nonmembers. ISSN: 0744-642X. **Circulation:** 10,000. **Advertising:** accepted. **Conventions/Meetings:** annual meeting, held in conjunction with National Association of Realtors.

3307 ■ Council of Residential Specialists (CRS)
430 N Michigan Ave., 3rd Fl.
Chicago, IL 60611
Ph: (312)321-4400
Free: (800)462-8841
Fax: (312)329-8851
E-mail: crshelp@crs.com
URL: http://www.crs.com
Contact: Kay L. West, Chair
Founded: 1977. **Members:** 42,000. **Membership Dues:** individual, $120 (annual). **Staff:** 40. **Budget:** $9,000,000. **Regional Groups:** 16. **State Groups:** 50. **Description:** Serves the country's top-producing residential real estate agents. Certified Residential Specialist designation (CRS) to experienced realtors who complete advanced training in listing and selling. **Awards:** Realtor Designation - Certified Residential Specialist. **Type:** recognition. **Committees:** Conflict of Interest; Education; Membership Development; Nominating; Product Review; Strategic Planning. **Subcommittees:** Faculty Administration. **Affiliated With:** National Association of Realtors. **Formerly:** (1999) Residential Sales Council. **Publications:** *CRS Membership Referral Directory*, annual. **Advertising:** accepted ● *CRS Online Update*, monthly. Newsletter. Alternate Formats: online ● *The Residential Specialist*, bimonthly. Magazine. Contains real estate information for residential sales agents and brokerage managers. **Price:** free for members; $29.95 /year for nonmembers; $54.95/2 years for nonmembers; $12.95 /year for nonmembers (online). **Circulation:** 40,000. **Advertising:** accepted. Alternate Formats: online. **Conventions/Meetings:** annual Sell-a-bration - rally and trade show, educational sessions and networking (exhibits).

3308 ■ Counselors of Real Estate (CRE)
430 N Michigan Ave.
Chicago, IL 60611-4011
Ph: (312)329-8427 (312)329-8429
Fax: (312)329-8456
E-mail: info@cre.org
URL: http://www.cre.org
Contact: Mary Walker Fleischmann, Pres.
Founded: 1953. **Members:** 1,100. **Membership Dues:** regular, $1,500 (annual). **Staff:** 10. **Budget:** $1,200,000. **Local Groups:** 26. **Multinational. Description:** Professional society of individuals with extensive experience in all phases of real estate who provide a counseling service. Members are entitled to use the Professional Designation CRE (Counselor of Real Estate). Conducts educational programs during three national meetings. **Awards:** James D. Landauer/John R. White Award. **Frequency:** annual. **Type:** recognition. **Recipient:** for demonstrating outstanding professionalism in real estate ● James Felt Creative Counseling Award. **Frequency:** annual. **Type:** recognition. **Recipient:** for counseling work exemplifying excellence and integrity. **Computer Services:** Mailing lists. **Committees:** Alternative Dispute Resolution; Counselors' Consulting Corps; Education; Ethics; Public Policy; Public Relations; Publications; Regional and Chapter Activities; Technology. **Affiliated With:** National Association of Realtors. **Formerly:** (1993) American Society of Real Estate Counselors. **Publications:** *The Counselor*, quarterly. Newsletter. **Price:** free. **Circulation:** 1,100. Alternate Formats: online ● *CRE Member Directory*, annual. **Price:** free. Also Cited As: *The Counselors of Real Estate—Directory* ● *New Statistical Primer for Real Estate Problem Solving*. Book ● *The Office Building From Concept to Investment Reality*. Book ● *Opportunities in Single Tenant Retail Properties* ● *Real Estate and the Money Markets*. Book ● *Real Estate Counseling*. Book ● *Real Estate Counseling in a Plain Brown Wrapper*. Journal ● *Real Estate Issues*, 3/year. Journal. Contains articles covering divestiture, syndication, brokerage, tax appraisal, market research, investments, and cap rates and yields. **Price:** $48.00 /year for nonmembers. **Circulation:** 1,800. **Advertising:** accepted. **Conventions/Meetings:** A Clash of Cultures: Examining Life in the Global Village - conference ● annual conference and meeting - always mid-year ● semiannual meeting.

3309 ■ CREW Network
1201 Wakarusa Dr., Ste.C3
Lawrence, KS 66049
Ph: (785)832-1808
Fax: (785)832-1551
E-mail: gaila@crewnetwork.org
URL: http://www.crewnetwork.org
Contact: Ms. Gail Ayers PhD, CEO
Founded: 1989. **Members:** 7,000. **Membership Dues:** individual, $140 (annual). **Staff:** 17. **State Groups:** 61. **Description:** Women employed in the commercial real estate industry. Aims to advance the success of women in commercial real estate. Fosters productive and supportive relationships among members; conducts industry research; provides services to members; sponsors educational courses; facilitates civic involvement of members. **Awards:** Community Impact Award. **Frequency:** annual. **Type:** recognition. **Recipient:** for significant contributions of a CREW Network chapter to the local community ● Deal of the Year Award. **Frequency:** annual. **Type:** recognition. **Recipient:** to an exceptional real estate transaction involving two or more members of CREW Network ● Networking Story of the Year. **Frequency:** annual. **Type:** recognition. **Recipient:** to an outstanding networking experience between two or more members of CREW Network ● Organization of the Year. **Frequency:** annual. **Type:** recognition. **Recipient:** to a company with outstanding involvement and

exemplary support to the network. **Boards:** Directors. **Committees:** Audit; Development; Industry Research; Member Education; Recognition. **Task Forces:** Technology. **Formerly:** (2001) National Network of Commercial Real Estate Women.

3310 ■ FIABCI-U.S.A. - U.S. Chapter, International Real Estate Federation
2000 N 15th St.
Arlington, VA 22201
Ph: (703)524-4279
Fax: (703)991-6256
E-mail: info@fiabci-usa.com
URL: http://www.fiabci-usa.com
Contact: Susan Newman, Sec. Gen.

Founded: 1956. **Members:** 1,000,000. **Membership Dues:** regular, $845 (annual) ● special, $895 (annual). **Staff:** 2. **Local Groups:** 20. **Description:** Brings together nearly 1,000,000 members in 57 countries; members represent all specializations in real estate, including brokerage, development, counseling, management, appraisal, and financing. Conducts discussion among members in global real estate trends, emerging markets, case studies of international real estate transactions, and refer business to each other. **Awards:** FIABCI-USA International Property Consultant (FIPC). **Type:** recognition. **Computer Services:** database ● online services. **Formerly:** (1984) American Chapter, International Real Estate Federation. **Publications:** *FIABCI Press*, 5/year. Newsletter. Includes reports on international chapters and worldwide real estate information. **Price:** free. **Circulation:** 7,000. **Advertising:** accepted. Alternate Formats: online ● *World Directory*, annual. Lists the 5000 members in 57 countries with their specializations. **Advertising:** accepted. **Conventions/Meetings:** annual congress, international (exhibits) - always May ● annual meeting - in the fall ● annual meeting - always March.

3311 ■ Hotel Brokers International (HBI)
1420 NW Vivion Rd., Ste.111
Kansas City, MO 64118
Ph: (816)505-4315
Fax: (816)505-4319
E-mail: contact@hbihotels.com
URL: http://www.hbihotels.com
Contact: Charles H. Fritsch, Pres.

Founded: 1959. **Members:** 80. **Membership Dues:** individual, $550 (annual). **Staff:** 2. **Regional Groups:** 31. **Multinational. Description:** Real estate brokers specializing in sales of and investments in hotel and motel properties. Members cooperate in the interchange of listings and data by computer, so the buying public will have information concerning all hotels available through the members of the association. Maintains speakers' bureau. **Awards:** Broker of the Year Award. **Frequency:** annual. **Type:** recognition. **Recipient:** for sales volume. **Computer Services:** database, hotel real estate comparable data. **Affiliated With:** American Hotel and Lodging Association; Asian American Hotel Owners Association; FIABCI-U.S.A. - U.S. Chapter, International Real Estate Federation. **Formerly:** (1984) Motel Brokers Association of America; (1985) American Hotel and Motel Brokers; (2002) Hotel Motel Brokers of America. **Publications:** *Innside Issues*, quarterly. Newsletter. Covers the lodging industry for real estate brokers specializing in the sale, exchange, and syndication of hotel and motel properties. **Price:** free. **Circulation:** 30,000. Alternate Formats: online ● *TransActions Recap*, annual. Report. **Conventions/Meetings:** annual meeting.

3312 ■ Institute of Real Estate Management (IREM)
430 N Michigan Ave.
Chicago, IL 60611-3900
Ph: (312)329-6000
Free: (800)837-0706
Fax: (800)338-4736
E-mail: custserv@irem.org
URL: http://www.irem.org
Contact: Robert B. Toothaker, Pres.

Founded: 1933. **Members:** 16,530. **Membership Dues:** CPM emeritus, $150 (annual) ● ARM (service fee), $195 (annual) ● CPM candidate (service fee), $470 (annual) ● AMO, $405 (annual) ● CPM, $525 (annual). **Staff:** 68. **Budget:** $10,600,000. **Regional Groups:** 13. **Local Groups:** 89. **Languages:** English, French, German, Italian, Japanese, Korean, Polish, Portuguese, Russian, Spanish. **Multinational. Description:** Professional organization of real property and asset managers. Awards professional designation Certified Property Manager (CPM) to qualifying individuals, Accredited Management Organization (AMO) to qualifying management firms and also awards Accredited Residential Manager (ARM) accreditation to qualifying individuals who are primarily residential site managers. Monitors legislation affecting real estate management. Offers management courses and seminars; conducts research and educational programs, publishes books and reports; maintains formal code of ethics; compiles statistics; maintains employment Website for real estate management industry. **Awards:** Academy of Authors Award. **Frequency:** annual. **Type:** recognition. **Recipient:** to IREM members only ● ARM of the Year Award. **Frequency:** annual. **Type:** recognition ● Certified Property Manager of the Year Award. **Frequency:** annual. **Type:** recognition. **Recipient:** to top professionals in the real estate management industry ● Chapter of the Year Award. **Frequency:** annual. **Type:** recognition. **Recipient:** for an individual who has made a significant contribution to the field of real estate management ● Donald M. Furbush Scholarship. **Frequency:** annual. **Type:** scholarship. **Recipient:** to IREM members only ● George M. Brooker Collegiate Scholarships for Minorities. **Frequency:** annual. **Type:** scholarship. **Recipient:** for minority students who are interested in pursuing a career in property management ● IREM Foundation Scholarship. **Frequency:** annual. **Type:** scholarship ● J. Wallace Paletou Award. **Frequency:** annual. **Type:** recognition. **Recipient:** for an individual who has made a significant contribution to the field of real estate management ● JPM Articles of the Year Award. **Frequency:** annual. **Type:** recognition ● Lloyd D. Hanford Sr. Distinguished Faculty Award. **Frequency:** annual. **Type:** recognition. **Recipient:** for excellence by members of IREM's national faculty ● Louise L. and Y.T. Lum Award. **Frequency:** annual. **Type:** recognition. **Recipient:** for financial need, academic performance, commitment to real estate management as a career ● Minority Outreach Scholarship. **Frequency:** quarterly. **Type:** scholarship ● Paul H. Rittle Sr. Memorial Scholarship Award. **Frequency:** quarterly. **Type:** scholarship. **Recipient:** for financial need, academic performance, commitment to real estate management as a career. **Computer Services:** Mailing lists. **Committees:** Bylaws and Internal Policy; Education; Ethics and Discipline; Executive; International Affairs; Legislative; Membership; Nominating; Regional Vice Presidents. **Affiliated With:** National Association of Realtors. **Publications:** *Apartment Building, Office Building, Condominium/Cooperative, Shopping Center, and Federally-Assisted Apartment Income/Expense Analyses*, annual. Books. Contains statistical analysis of property income and expenses. ● *Before Disaster Strikes: Developing an Emergency Procedures Manual* ● *Catalogs of Courses and Publications*, annual ● *CPM, AMO, and ARM Profiles/Compensation Studies*, triennial ● *IREM Key Reports-A Practical Guide to Energy Management*, periodic. Monographs. Includes a series on industry issues. **Price:** $29.95 each ● *IREM Your Professional Advantage*. Brochures ● *Journal of Property Management*, bimonthly. **Price:** $56.95/year. **Circulation:** 17,369. **Advertising:** accepted ● *Principles of Real Estate Management and many other titles*. Books ● *Your Real Estate Investment Deserves a CPM*. Brochure ● Audiotapes. **Conventions/Meetings:** annual convention ● annual Education Conference - always April ● annual Leadership and Legislative Summit - conference, for real estate property management professionals (exhibits).

3313 ■ International Accrediting Commission for Real Estate and Appraisal Education and Training (IACREAET)
c/o Robert G. Johnson, Exec. Dir.
1224 N Nokomis NE
Alexandria, MN 56308-5072
Ph: (320)763-7626
Fax: (320)763-9290
Contact: Robert G. Johnson, Exec. Dir.

Founded: 1989. **Membership Dues:** program (with less than 30 days' duration), $500 (annual) ● program (with more than 30 days' duration), $750 (annual) ● program (with more than 240 days' duration), $1,000 (annual). **Staff:** 12. **Budget:** $1,500,000. **Description:** Real estate and appraisal training programs and institutions. Promotes advancement of real estate and appraisal education and training. Conducts research and educational programs; maintains speakers' bureau; compiles statistics. **Awards:** Global Accreditation Award. **Frequency:** annual. **Type:** recognition. **Publications:** *Global Accreditation Newsletter*, quarterly. **Circulation:** 2,000. **Advertising:** accepted. **Conventions/Meetings:** periodic board meeting ● periodic conference ● annual convention.

3314 ■ International Association of Attorneys and Executives in Corporate Real Estate (AECRE)
c/o Lisa V. Carreras, Exec. VP/Dir.
20106 S Sycamore Dr.
Frankfort, IL 60423
Ph: (815)464-6019
Fax: (815)464-8334
E-mail: lcarreras@aecre.org
URL: http://www.aecre.org
Contact: Lisa V. Carreras, Exec. VP/Dir.

Founded: 1990. **Members:** 250. **Membership Dues:** regular, $360 (annual) ● nonprofit, academic, $180 (annual) ● reduced, $125 (annual). **Staff:** 3. **Multinational. Description:** Attorneys and executives active in the sale and purchase of corporate real estate. Seeks to "provide a collegial forum for real estate executives and attorneys to explore corporate real estate issues of common interest." Promotes professional advancement of members. Facilitates communication and cooperation among members; gathers and disseminates information on legislation and legal developments affecting corporate real estate; creates codes of training, conduct, and practice for members; sponsors educational programs. **Publications:** *Corporate Real Estate and The Law*, quarterly. Newsletter. **Price:** included in membership dues. **Advertising:** accepted ● *Lease Negotiation*. Handbook. **Price:** $134.50 for members; $177.50 for nonmembers. **Conventions/Meetings:** annual conference - held in spring ● annual meeting - held in fall.

3315 ■ International Business Brokers Association (IBBA)
401 N Michigan Ave., Ste.2200
Chicago, IL 60611-4267
Ph: (703)453-2226 (571)217-0845
Free: (888)686-4222
Fax: (312)673-6599
E-mail: admin@ibba.org
URL: http://www.ibba.org
Contact: Pat Appelhans, Pres.

Founded: 1982. **Members:** 1,250. **Membership Dues:** regular, associate, $395 (annual). **Staff:** 13. **Description:** Business brokerage firms. Serves the interests of brokers and brokerages whose specialty is bringing together the buyers and sellers of businesses. Develops a code of ethics for the field. Disseminates industry information. Encourages growth of sales; assists in new industry developments. Represents members in legislative matters and lobbies for recognition of the industry. Coordinates activity among business brokerages and cooperates with other types of brokerages. Conducts educational and promotional programs for members. Holds seminars. Maintains library on legal aspects of business brokerage. **Committees:** Administrative Hearing Com Charter and Responsibilities; Affiliates Charter; Conference Planning Charter; Credentialing Charter; Data Management Charter; Education Steering; Ethics; Strategic Issues Task Force Charter. **Publications:** *IBBA News*, periodic. Newsletter ● Bulletin, periodic. **Conventions/Meetings:** semiannual convention and workshop, with speakers, educational classes and professional workshops - every June and November.

3316 ■ International Real Estate Institute (IREI)
1224 N Nokomis NE
Alexandria, MN 56308-5072
Ph: (320)763-4648
Fax: (320)763-9290
E-mail: irei@iami.org
URL: http://irei-assoc.org
Contact: Robert G. Johnson, Exec. Dir.

Founded: 1975. **Members:** 6,500. **Membership Dues:** professional, $195 (annual). **Staff:** 10. **Budget:** $1,250,000. **Description:** Professionals in 120 countries specializing in the development, finance, investment, and valuation of real estate. Conducts educational seminars and regional programs; operates speakers' bureau and placement service. Compiles statistics, consults United Nations on property issues. **Libraries: Type:** reference. **Awards:** Lifetime Achievement. **Frequency:** annual. **Type:** recognition. **Boards:** Advisory. **Publications:** *International Real Estate Investor*, monthly. Newspaper. Covers real estate development and sales worldwide. ● *International Real Estate Journal*, semiannual. **Price:** $75.00/year. **Circulation:** 40,000. **Advertising:** accepted ● *International Real Estate Newsletter*, quarterly. Covers real estate developments in major nations. **Price:** free. **Circulation:** 20,000. **Advertising:** accepted ● Monographs. **Conventions/Meetings:** annual Caribbean Basin Real Estate Congress (exhibits) ● annual World Real Estate Congress.

3317 ■ National Apartment Association (NAA)
4300 Wilson Blvd., Ste.400
Arlington, VA 22203-4168
Ph: (703)518-6141
Fax: (703)248-9440
E-mail: webmaster@naahq.com
URL: http://www.naahq.org
Contact: Doug Culkin CAE, Pres.

Founded: 1939. **Members:** 26,000. **Membership Dues:** regular, associate, $125 (annual). **Staff:** 42. **Budget:** $3,800,000. **Regional Groups:** 9. **State Groups:** 37. **Local Groups:** 130. **Description:** Federation of 155 state and local associations of industry professionals engaged in all aspects of the multifamily housing industry, including owners, builders, investors, developers, managers, and allied service representatives. Provides education and certification for property management executives, on-site property managers, maintenance personnel, property supervisors, and leasing agents. Offers a nationwide legislative network concerned with governmental decisions at the federal, state, and local levels. **Libraries: Type:** reference. **Holdings:** archival material, clippings, periodicals. **Awards: Frequency:** annual. **Type:** scholarship ● Victor Awards. **Frequency:** annual. **Type:** recognition. **Recipient:** for membership growth, education and building design. **Committees:** Budget and Finance; Convention; Education; Government Relations; Membership/Affiliate Services. **Councils:** Association Executives; Independent Rental Owner; National Suppliers. **Programs:** Certified Apartment Maintenance Technician; Certified Apartment Manager; Certified Apartment Property Supervisor; National Apartment Leasing Professional; Rental Owners Course. **Formerly:** National Apartment Owners Association. **Publications:** *NAA Leadership Directory*, annual ● *UNITS*, 9/year. Magazine. Includes information on building and development, taxes, maintenance, legislation, insurance, property management, economics, marketing, interviews. **Price:** $28.00/year. **Circulation:** 32,000. **Advertising:** accepted ● Also publishes books. **Conventions/Meetings:** annual conference and seminar (exhibits) - always June. 2008 June 26-28, Orlando, FL.

3318 ■ National Association of Counselors (NAC)
303 W Cypress St.
PO Box 12528
San Antonio, TX 78212-0528
Ph: (210)271-0781
Free: (800)486-3676
Fax: (210)225-8450
URL: http://nac.lincoln-grad.org

Founded: 1982. **Members:** 250. **Membership Dues:** individual (initial), $40 ● candidate, $45 (annual) ● designated, $100 (annual). **Staff:** 18. **Description:** Real estate counselors. Promotes the advancement of real estate counseling. Monitors legislation in the field; develops new counseling forms; conducts educational programs. **Convention/Meeting:** none. **Libraries: Type:** reference. **Holdings:** books, periodicals. **Awards:** Senior Realty Counselor (SRC). **Type:** recognition. **Publications:** *Advise and Counsel*. Newsletter. **Circulation:** 2,000 ● *Registry of Real Estate Counselors*, annual. Directory ● Brochure.

3319 ■ National Association of Hispanic Real Estate Professionals (NAHREP)
1150 17th St. NW, Ste.504
Washington, DC 20036
Free: (800)964-5373
Fax: (202)263-4636
URL: http://www.nahrep.org
Contact: Felix De Herrera, Chm.

Founded: 1999. **Members:** 5,201. **Membership Dues:** full, $99 (annual) ● corporate, $395 (annual). **Staff:** 3. **Budget:** $490,000. **Regional Groups:** 12. **State Groups:** 32. **Languages:** English, Spanish. **Description:** Real estate professionals of Hispanic descent. Promotes professional advancement of members; seeks to improve real estate service and practice. Serves as a forum for the exchange of information among members; sponsors continuing professional development courses. **Libraries: Type:** reference. **Holdings:** archival material, business records. **Subjects:** real estate. **Publications:** *Real Voices*, 3/year. Magazine. **Advertising:** accepted. Alternate Formats: online. **Conventions/Meetings:** annual conference.

3320 ■ National Association of Industrial and Office Properties (NAIOP)
2201 Cooperative Way, 3rd Fl.
Herndon, VA 20171-3034
Ph: (703)904-7100
Free: (800)666-6780
Fax: (703)904-7942
E-mail: bisacquino@naiop.org
URL: http://www.naiop.org
Contact: Thomas J. Bisacquino, Pres.

Founded: 1967. **Members:** 11,000. **Membership Dues:** full principal, $590 (annual). **Staff:** 30. **Budget:** $6,000,000. **Local Groups:** 49. **Description:** Owners and developers of industrial, office, and related properties; others interested in commercial and industrial real estate are admitted as associate members. Seeks to stimulate the growth of the commercial real estate industry and to help improve prospects and profits of members. Promotes exchange of information; speaks on behalf of members concerning legislation and taxation problems affecting the industry; fosters establishment and maintenance of standards for the operation of industrial/office properties; seeks liaison and cooperation with other groups. Has established an information center for members, and disseminates information to the public. Compiles statistics. Maintains political development fund. **Libraries: Type:** reference. **Subjects:** real estate development. **Awards:** Developer of the Year. **Frequency:** annual. **Type:** recognition. **Recipient:** for leadership and active support in the industry ● Green Development Award. **Frequency:** annual. **Type:** recognition. **Recipient:** for outstanding work in the area of green development. **Telecommunication Services:** electronic mail, membership@naiop.org ● additional toll-free number, (800)456-4144. **Committees:** Chapter Relations; Communications; Education; Government Affairs; Industry Trends; Political Action; Technology. **Programs:** National Forums; Project Analysis; Public Relations. **Formerly:** National Association of Industrial Parks; (1992) National Association of Industrial and Office Parks; (1994) NAIOP - The Association for Commercial Real Estate. **Publications:** *Development Magazine*, quarterly. Includes information on architecture, finance, commercial real estate, marketing, public affairs, and related topics. **Price:** included in membership dues; $65.00 /year for nonmembers. ISSN: 0888-6067. **Circulation:** 16,000. **Advertising:** accepted. Alternate Formats: online ● *Legislative News*, biweekly. Newsletter. **Advertising:** accepted ● *NAIOP News Online*, biweekly. Newsletter. **Advertising:** accepted. Alternate Formats: online ● Also publishes resource books and issues cassette tapes. **Conventions/Meetings:** annual conference (exhibits) - always October. 2008 Oct. 20-23, Las Vegas, NV ● annual seminar and workshop, executive symposium.

3321 ■ National Association of Master Appraisers (NAMA)
303 W Cypress St.
San Antonio, TX 78212
Free: (800)229-6262
Fax: (210)225-8450
E-mail: maitca@bellsouth.net
URL: http://www.masterappraisers.org
Contact: Timothy C. Andersen MSA, Pres.

Founded: 1982. **Members:** 2,350. **Membership Dues:** candidate, $120 (annual) ● associate, $60 (annual) ● master appraiser, $180 (annual). **Staff:** 18. **State Groups:** 15. **Description:** Appraisers, analysts, assessors, brokers, salespersons, and others involved in real estate appraisal. Works to enhance competency in the appraisal industry through education. Provides basic and advanced courses and educational meetings in techniques, management practices, and marketing strategies. Offers certification. Areas of interest include: residential, commercial, and rural property; review appraisal; condemnation proceedings; tax assessing. Keeps members apprised of new legislation and legal changes in policy. Sponsors Lender Awareness Program to increase awareness among banks and savings association officers. Provides referral services and speakers' bureau. **Libraries: Type:** reference. **Subjects:** appraisal industry. **Awards:** Master Senior Appraiser. **Type:** recognition. **Recipient:** for appraisers. **Computer Services:** database ● mailing lists. **Publications:** *The Master Appraiser*, monthly. Newsletter. Contains information on new license acts, regulations, and rules. **Circulation:** 3,000. Alternate Formats: online ● *NAMA Alert*, periodic. Bulletin. Contains industry information. ● *NAMA Educational Catalog*, periodic. Includes course descriptions and membership information. **Circulation:** 3,000 ● Brochures ● Membership Directory, annual. **Circulation:** 5,000. **Advertising:** accepted ● Also publishes textbooks. **Conventions/Meetings:** annual conference (exhibits).

3322 ■ National Association of Media Brokers (NAMB)
5074 Dorsey Hall Dr., Ste.205
Ellicott City, MD 21042-7793
Ph: (410)740-0250
Fax: (410)740-7222
E-mail: exline@pacbell.net
URL: http://www.nambonline.com
Contact: Andrew P. McClure, Pres.

Founded: 1979. **Members:** 100. **Description:** Media brokerage firms. Seeks to share information on activities of mutual interest. (Media brokers deal in newspaper, cable TV, radio, and television properties.) Compiles statistics. **Formerly:** (1980) National Association of Business Brokers. **Publications:** Membership Directory, annual. **Conventions/Meetings:** semiannual conference - always spring and fall.

3323 ■ National Association of Real Estate Brokers (NAREB)
c/o Clifford Turner, Pres.
225 S 42nd St., Ste.303-A
Louisville, KY 40212
Ph: (502)774-8909
Fax: (502)774-5678
E-mail: chturner1@usa.net
URL: http://www.nareb.com
Contact: Clifford Turner, Pres.

Founded: 1947. **Members:** 7,500. **Staff:** 3. **Budget:** $285,000. **Regional Groups:** 15. **State Groups:** 6. **Local Groups:** 58. **Description:** Members of the real estate industry. Research, educational, and certification programs include: Real Estate Management Brokers Institute; National Society of Real Estate Appraisers; Real Estate Brokerage Institute; United Developers Council. Encourages unity among those who are engaged in real estate. Promotes and maintains high standards of conduct. Protects the public against unethical, improper, or fraudulent practices connected with the real estate business. Conducts research; compiles statistics on productivity, marketing, and development. Gives members license to use "Realtist" symbol. Sponsors educational seminars. Maintains Willis E. Carson Library. **Awards:** Realtist of the Year Award. **Frequency:** annual. **Type:** recognition. **Committees:** Education; HUD-VA Liaison; Industry Franchise; NARELLO; Public Affairs; Resolution. **Councils:** Historical Preservation; Personnel; Women's. **Divisions:** Contractors. **Task Forces:** Funding. **Publications:** *Catalog of NAREB's Real Estate* ● *Exhibitors Prospectus* ● *Realtist Communicator*, quarterly ● *Realtist Membership Directory*, annual ● *Souvenir Journal*. **Conventions/Meetings:** annual conference ● annual convention (exhibits) - always midwinter.

3324 ■ National Association of Real Estate Buyer Brokers (NAREBB)

2704 Wemberly Dr.
Belmont, CA 94002
Ph: (650)655-2500
Fax: (650)591-6807
E-mail: raymond@raymondstoklosa.com
URL: http://www.raymondstoklosa.com
Contact: Raymond J. Stoklosa, Exec. Dir.

Founded: 1982. **Membership Dues:** life (individual), $99. **Staff:** 3. **Description:** Real estate licensees. Promotes buyer representation in real estate transactions. Informs consumers and professionals of the advantages and benefits of retaining a buyer's agent specialist when buying property. Conducts seminars and workshops to facilitate professionalism and enhance consumer awareness. Presents educational programs leading to a designation as a Certified Real Estate Buyer's Broker (CREBB). Manages free referral program for home buyers seeking representation. **Libraries: Type:** reference. **Holdings:** artwork, audiovisuals, books, clippings, periodicals. **Telecommunication Services:** 24-hour hotline, referral hotline, (800)503-1512. **Publications:** *Who Represents You When You Buy a Home?*. Book ● Newsletter, quarterly. **Conventions/Meetings:** periodic The Art and Craft of Buyer Representation - seminar.

3325 ■ National Association of Real Estate Companies (NAREC)

216 W Jackson Blvd., Ste.625
Chicago, IL 60606
Ph: (312)263-1755
Fax: (312)750-1203
E-mail: info@narec.org
URL: http://www.narec.org
Contact: Michael Heiken, Pres.

Founded: 1977. **Members:** 200. **Membership Dues:** company, $575 (annual) ● individual, $225 (annual). **Staff:** 1. **Local Groups:** 4. **Description:** Individuals associated with companies involved in the financial management of real estate development companies. Seeks to formulate positions and inform members on current accounting and financial reporting issues relating to real estate companies and to voice these positions to appropriate accounting rule-making bodies. Cooperates with such bodies in order to establish accounting and financial guidelines; provides a forum for members dealing with issues faced in managing the financial affairs of real estate companies such as financial reporting, financial management, tax planning, and information technology. **Committees:** Financial Accounting Standards; Financial Management; Information Technology; Tax. **Publications:** Newsletter, quarterly. Alternate Formats: online. **Conventions/Meetings:** annual conference ● annual Tax Conference - 2008 June 17-20, Williamsburg, VA.

3326 ■ National Association of Real Estate Investment Managers (NAREIM)

11755 Wilshire Blvd., Ste.1380
Los Angeles, CA 90025-1539
Ph: (310)479-2219
Fax: (310)445-2565
E-mail: fredhalperin@nareim.org
URL: http://www.nareim.org
Contact: Fredric Halperin, Pres.

Founded: 1990. **Members:** 77. **Membership Dues:** initiation (one-time charge), $2,500 ● corporate, $7,000 (annual). **Staff:** 2. **Budget:** $750,000. **Description:** Represents corporate real estate firms. Seeks to provide knowledge and insight into the real estate industry. Hosts 12 forums and 7 regional roundtable discussions. **Conventions/Meetings:** annual Senior Executive Officer Strategic Issues Discussion Forum - meeting - 2008 June 23-24, Boston, MA ● annual symposium - every January.

3327 ■ National Association of Real Estate Investment Trusts (NAREIT)

1875 I St. NW, Ste.600
Washington, DC 20006-5413
Ph: (202)739-9400
Free: (800)3NAREIT
Fax: (202)739-9401
E-mail: info@nareit.com
URL: http://www.nareit.com
Contact: Steven A. Wechsler, Pres./CEO

Founded: 1960. **Members:** 1,800. **Membership Dues:** primary, $1,045 (annual) ● additional, $605 (annual) ● tax-exempt institutional, $330 (annual) ● academic, $220 (annual). **Staff:** 34. **Budget:** $11,000,000. **Description:** Real estate investment trusts; corporations, partnerships, or individuals (other than trusts) that manage multiple-owned real estate, or that have a business or professional interest in real estate trusts, associations, corporations, and funds. Compiles statistics. **Telecommunication Services:** electronic mail, swechsler@nareit.com. **Committees:** Accounting; Government Relations; Institutional Investors; Insurance; Public Relations. **Formerly:** National Association of Real Estate Investment Funds. **Publications:** *Compendium on IRS Rulings*, annual. Book. Compiles federal legislation, Treasury Department regulations and ruling affecting REITs. **Price:** $350.00 for members; $500.00 for nonmembers ● *NAREIT Quick Member Guide*, annual. Directory. **Advertising:** accepted ● *Real Estate Portfolio*, bimonthly. Magazine. **Advertising:** accepted ● *REIT Watch*, monthly. **Conventions/Meetings:** annual convention - always fall ● annual Institutional Investor Forum - conference ● annual Law and Accounting Conference - always spring.

3328 ■ National Association of Realtors (NAR)

430 N Michigan Ave.
Chicago, IL 60611-4088
Free: (800)874-6500
Fax: (312)329-5960
E-mail: infocentral@realtors.org
URL: http://www.realtor.org
Contact: Dale Stinton, Exec. VP/CEO

Founded: 1908. **Members:** 1,038,371. **Membership Dues:** real estate broker, agent, $64 (annual). **State Groups:** 54. **Local Groups:** 1,860. **Description:** Federation of 54 state and territory associations and 1,860 local real estate boards whose members are real estate brokers and agents; terms are registered by the association in the U.S. Patent and Trademark Office and in the states. Promotes education, high professional standards, and modern techniques in specialized real estate work such as brokerage, appraisal, property management, land development, industrial real estate, farm brokerage, and counseling. Conducts research programs. **Libraries: Type:** reference. **Subjects:** real estate. **Additional Websites:** http://www.realtor.com. **Divisions:** Communications; Economics and Research; Education; Forecasting; Governmental Affairs; Legal Affairs; Political Affairs; Research. **Affiliated With:** CCIM Institute; Counselors of Real Estate; Institute of Real Estate Management; Realtors Land Institute; Society of Industrial and Office Realtors; Women's Council of Realtors. **Formerly:** (1915) National Association of Real Estate Exchanges; (1973) National Association of Real Estate Boards. **Publications:** *Real Estate Outlook*, monthly. Magazine. **Price:** $95.00 for members; $200.00 /year for nonmembers. Alternate Formats: online ● *Realtor Magazine*, monthly. Provides information and ideas for those in residential, brokerage, management, and commercial investment real estate. **Price:** included in membership dues; $56.00 /year for nonmembers. **Circulation:** 715,000. **Advertising:** accepted. Alternate Formats: microform; online. **Conventions/Meetings:** annual Realtors Conference and Expo - convention and trade show (exhibits) - 2008 Nov. 7-10, Orlando, FL; 2009 Nov. 13-16, San Diego, CA; 2010 Nov. 5-8, New Orleans, LA.

3329 ■ National Association of Review Appraisers and Mortgage Underwriters (NARA/MU)

1224 N Nokomis NE
Alexandria, MN 56308-5072
Ph: (320)763-6870
Fax: (320)763-9290
E-mail: nara@iami.org
URL: http://www.iami.org/nara
Contact: Robert G. Johnson, Exec. Dir.

Founded: 1975. **Members:** 8,000. **Membership Dues:** associate/CRA/RMU/CVC, $215 (annual). **Staff:** 12. **Budget:** $2,100,000. **Languages:** English, Spanish. **Description:** Real estate professionals and mortgage underwriters who aid in determining value of property. Acts as umbrella group for real estate appraisers. Conducts educational seminars; maintains speakers' bureau; operates placement service. **Libraries: Type:** reference. **Holdings:** 3,211; books, periodicals. **Awards:** Reviewer of the Year. **Frequency:** annual. **Type:** recognition. **Computer Services:** database ● mailing lists ● online services. **Publications:** *Appraisal Review Journal*, quarterly. Includes instructional articles on reviewing property appraisals and underwriting real estate mortgages. **Price:** $45.00/year. **Circulation:** 10,000. **Advertising:** accepted. Alternate Formats: magnetic tape ● *Reviews*, quarterly. Newsletter. Provides information on reviewing property appraisals and mortgage underwriting. **Price:** $60.00/year. **Circulation:** 28,000. **Advertising:** accepted ● Directory, annual. **Price:** $65.00/copy ● Books ● Monographs. **Conventions/Meetings:** annual conference (exhibits).

3330 ■ National Association of Screening Agencies (NASA)

3337 Duke St.
Alexandria, VA 22314
Ph: (703)370-7436
Fax: (703)370-7437
E-mail: nasahq@n-a-s-a.com
URL: http://www.n-a-s-a.com
Contact: Barbara Tucci, Pres.

Membership Dues: regular, $500 (annual). **Description:** Companies that provide tenant screening services. Monitors state and federal legislation related to the industry. Promotes ethical standards for tenant screening firms. Serves as an information clearinghouse for member companies. Offers educational programs.

3331 ■ National Council of Exchangors (NCE)

PO Box 668
Morro Bay, CA 93443-0668
Free: (800)324-1031
Fax: (800)324-1031
E-mail: nce@infoville.com
URL: http://www.infoville.com/nce
Contact: Tom Van Erp, Pres.

Founded: 1977. **Members:** 386. **Membership Dues:** real estate exchanger, $150 (annual). **Staff:** 2. **Description:** Real estate professionals who possess specialized training in the fields of real estate exchanging, real estate tax law, investment analysis, client counseling, and equity marketing. Promotes educational programs. Provides a forum for member exchanges. **Publications:** *NCE News*, periodic. Magazine. Includes association updates. **Price:** included in membership dues; $20.00 /year for nonmembers. **Advertising:** accepted. **Conventions/Meetings:** semiannual Marketing Conference (exhibits) - October and February.

3332 ■ National Multi Housing Council (NMHC)
1850 M St. NW, Ste.540
Washington, DC 20036-5803
Ph: (202)974-2300
Fax: (202)775-0112
E-mail: info@nmhc.org
URL: http://www.nmhc.org
Contact: Doug Bibby, Pres.
Founded: 1978. **Members:** 900. **Membership Dues:** associate, $2,500 (annual) ● board of director, $20,000 (annual) ● advisory committee, $5,000 (annual). **Staff:** 28. **Budget:** $5,000,000. **Description:** Builders, developers, owners, financiers, and managers of multifamily housing developments, and interested multifamily housing organizations. Monitors and responds to federal legislative and regulatory actions and issues affecting multifamily housing. Serves as clearinghouse and coordinator for other associations. **Committees:** Multifamily Finance; Political Action; Property Management; State and Local Issues; Tax. **Formerly:** (1981) National Rental Housing Council. **Publications:** *Building Codes Update*, semiannual. Newsletter ● *Environmental Update*, 3/year. Newsletter ● *Market Trends*, quarterly. Newsletter ● *Political Update*, periodic. Newsletter ● *Property Management Update*, 3/year. Newsletter ● *Research Notes*, quarterly. Newsletter ● *Tax Update*, quarterly. Newsletter ● *Technology Update*, quarterly. Newsletter ● *Washington Update*, semimonthly. Newsletter. Includes information on legislative and regulatory developments. **Price:** included in membership dues. **Circulation:** 3,000. **Conventions/Meetings:** quarterly conference ● annual meeting.

3333 ■ National Residential Appraisers Institute (NRAI)
2001 Cooper Foster Park Rd.
Amherst, OH 44001
Ph: (440)282-7925
Free: (800)331-2732
Fax: (440)282-7925
E-mail: questions@nraiappraisers.com
URL: http://www.nraiappraisers.com
Contact: Ade J. Schreiber, Pres.
Founded: 1977. **Members:** 600. **Membership Dues:** individual, $95 (annual). **Staff:** 3. **For-Profit. Description:** Promotes professionalism in the evaluation of residential real estate. Requires demonstration appraisals and testing for the professional designations of Certified Market Data Analyst (CMDA), Graduate Senior Appraiser (GSA), Senior Certified Appraiser (SCA), and Senior Licensed Appraiser (SLA). Provides continuing education courses and public relations services. Maintains speakers' bureau. **Publications:** *Appraisers News Network*, quarterly. Newsletter. **Price:** included in membership dues. **Conventions/Meetings:** annual meeting.

3334 ■ National Society of Environmental Consultants (NSEC)
PO Box 12528
San Antonio, TX 78212-0528
Ph: (210)271-0781
Free: (800)486-3676
Fax: (210)225-8450
URL: http://nsec.lincoln-grad.org
Founded: 1992. **Members:** 600. **Membership Dues:** associate, $50 (annual) ● candidate, $75 (annual) ● designated EAC, ESC and ELC, $150 (annual). **Staff:** 3. **For-Profit. Description:** Environmental consulting professionals and others interested in the environmentally responsible use of real estate. Encourages an awareness of environmental risks and regulations regarding their impact on real property value; promotes the development of ethics and standards of professional practice for environmental consultants. Conducts educational programs. Bestows the Environmental Assessment Consultant (EAC) designation, the Environmental Screening Consultant (ESC) designation, and the Environmental Lead Consultant (ELC) designation. **Libraries: Type:** reference. **Holdings:** 800. **Subjects:** real estate, appraisal, environmental. **Telecommunication Services:** hotline, (210)271-0741. **Publications:** *Environmental Consultant*, quarterly. Newsletter. **Circulation:** 3,650 ● Membership Directory, annual ● Also publishes numerous informational pieces. **Conventions/Meetings:** annual National Real Estate Environmental Conference (exhibits).

3335 ■ Pension Real Estate Association (PREA)
100 Pearl St., 13th Fl.
Hartford, CT 06103
Ph: (860)692-6341
Fax: (860)692-6351
E-mail: prea@prea.org
URL: http://www.prea.org
Contact: Mary Ludgin, Chm.
Founded: 1979. **Members:** 1,710. **Membership Dues:** full (corporate), $5,990 (annual) ● standard (corporate), $3,570 (annual) ● basic (corporate), $2,845 (annual) ● institutional investor (not for profit)/ academic, $330 (annual) ● institutional investor (for profit), $1,950 (annual). **Staff:** 7. **Budget:** $3,000,000. **Description:** Tax-exempt pension and endowment fund plan sponsors who invest or plan to invest plan assets in real estate; real estate investment management firms; and lawyers, appraisers, accountants, and others who provide services to the industry. Informs and educates members on recent developments relating to pension plan investment in real estate. **Libraries: Type:** reference. **Holdings:** periodicals. **Subjects:** real estate investment and finance. **Awards:** Graaskamp Award for Research Excellence. **Frequency:** biennial. **Type:** scholarship. **Committees:** Conference; Government Affairs; Institute; Publications; Reporting and Valuation; Research. **Councils:** Plan Sponsor. **Publications:** *PREA Quarterly*. Magazine. **Circulation:** 2,000. **Advertising:** accepted. Alternate Formats: online ● *Research Review*, semiannual. Magazine. Abstracts of Research Articles published in various magazines and journals. Alternate Formats: online. **Conventions/Meetings:** semiannual conference - every spring and fall. 2009 Mar. 25-26, Washington, DC ● annual Plan Sponsor Real Estate Conference - meeting - 2008 Oct. 1-3, Chicago, IL.

3336 ■ Property Management Association (PMA)
7900 Wisconsin Ave., Ste.305
Bethesda, MD 20814
Ph: (301)657-9200
Fax: (301)907-9326
E-mail: info@pma-dc.org
URL: http://www.pma-dc.org
Contact: Tricia Culpepper, Pres.
Founded: 1952. **Members:** 1,100. **Membership Dues:** full, $155 (annual) ● associate, $720 (annual). **Staff:** 4. **Budget:** $1,300,000. **Regional Groups:** 1. **Description:** Property management professionals who own and operate multifamily residential, commercial, retail, industrial and other income-producing properties and firms that provide goods and services used in real property management. Works to enhance the interests and welfare of property owners, managers, supervisory employees, and contractors involved in the management of multifamily residential and commercial property. Provides education and a forum for exchange of ideas on efficient methods of operation and progressive policies of management. **Committees:** August Social; Community Service; Holiday Ball; PMEXPO; Program and Seminar; Spring Break. **Councils:** Associate; Tax Credit and Low Income Housing. **Formerly:** (1991) Property Management Association of America. **Publications:** *Property Management Association—Bulletin*, monthly. For property managers and vendors. Includes methods of operation and policies, tax tips, employee relations, and monthly meeting previews. **Price:** included in membership dues; $100.00 /year for nonmembers. **Advertising:** accepted ● *Property Management Association—Membership Directory*, annual. Includes name and firm affiliation of PMA members, Services/ Products Directory, and Emergency Housing Reference Guide. **Price:** free for members; $50.00/copy for nonmembers. **Circulation:** 1,500. **Conventions/ Meetings:** annual Property Management Exposition - meeting (exhibits).

3337 ■ Real Estate Buyer's Agent Council (REBAC)
430 N Michigan Ave.
Chicago, IL 60611
Ph: (312)329-8656
Free: (800)648-6224
Fax: (312)329-8632
E-mail: rebac@realtors.org
URL: http://www.rebac.net
Contact: Marc Gould, Exec. Dir.
Founded: 1988. **Members:** 40,000. **Membership Dues:** full, $16 (annual). **Description:** Real estate professionals. Represents the real estate buyers. Keeps members informed of developments in buyer representation. Assists members improve their business. **Awards:** Distinguished Service Award. **Frequency:** annual. **Type:** recognition. **Recipient:** for outstanding accredited buyers' representative designees. **Publications:** *The Real Estate Professional*, bimonthly. Magazine. **Price:** included in membership dues ● *TBR HotSheet*, weekly. Newsletter. **Price:** included in membership dues. Alternate Formats: online ● *Today's Buyer's Rep*, monthly. Newsletter. Contains information about events, legislation, and education important to buyers' representatives. **Price:** included in membership dues. ISSN: 1526-4289. Alternate Formats: online. **Conventions/Meetings:** annual conference.

3338 ■ Real Estate Educators Association (REEA)
19 Mantua Rd.
Mount Royal, NJ 08061
Ph: (856)423-3215
Fax: (856)423-3420
E-mail: info@reea.org
URL: http://www.reea.org
Contact: Meridyth Senes, Exec. Dir.
Founded: 1979. **Members:** 1,200. **Membership Dues:** individual, institution, $129 (annual) ● institutional, $329 (annual) ● sustaining, $549 (annual) ● patron, $1,099 (annual). **Staff:** 7. **Budget:** $325,000. **Description:** Individuals involved in real estate education and training. Encourages the establishment of criteria for consistency and excellence in real estate education; works for the standardization of content in real estate training programs. Offers Distinguished Real Estate Instructor certification program. Sponsors instructor assessment examination to evaluate the field knowledge of instructors. **Awards: Frequency:** annual. **Type:** recognition ● **Frequency:** annual. **Type:** scholarship. **Recipient:** to a student or students studying real estate courses in an accredited college and university. **Computer Services:** Mailing lists, rental to members only. **Telecommunication Services:** electronic mail, msenes@talley.com. **Publications:** *Real Estate Educators Association—Directory*, annual. **Price:** available to members only ● *Real Estate Educators Association—Proceedings*, annual. Includes academic papers presented at conference. ● Journal, quarterly. Includes articles of interest to real estate educators and other association and industry news. **Price:** free for members. **Advertising:** accepted. **Conventions/ Meetings:** annual conference (exhibits) - always May or June.

3339 ■ Real Estate Information Professionals Association (REIPA)
c/o InfoMarketing Inc.
PO Box 3159
Durham, NC 27715-3159
Ph: (919)383-0044
Fax: (919)383-0035
E-mail: reipa@reipa.org
URL: http://www.reipa.org
Contact: Sarah Carlton, Exec. Dir.
Founded: 1995. **Membership Dues:** corporate representative (plus $295 per representative), $550 (annual). **Description:** Providers of real estate information or information technology related to the real estate industry. Seeks to ensure free and open access to public real estate information. Serves as a clearinghouse on real estate and real estate information technologies; works to ensure responsible use of real estate information; conducts educational pro-

grams for policy makers and the public; facilitates exchange of information among members. **Committees:** Collateral Assessment and Technologies; Communications; Conference; Government Relations. **Formerly:** (2001) Real Estate Information Providers Association. **Publications:** *The Friday Letter*, semimonthly. Newsletter. Provides news within the real estate industry. Alternate Formats: online ● Directory, periodic. **Conventions/Meetings:** annual meeting.

3340 ■ Real Estate Roundtable
801 Pennsylvania Ave. NW, Ste.720
Washington, DC 20004
Ph: (202)639-8400
Fax: (202)639-8442
E-mail: info@rer.org
URL: http://www.rer.org
Contact: Jeffrey D. DeBoer, Pres./CEO
Founded: 1969. **Members:** 200. **Membership Dues:** roundtable, $27,500 (annual) ● President's Council, $12,500 (annual). **Staff:** 10. **Budget:** $2,500,000. **Description:** An organization where leaders of the nation's top public and privately held real estate ownership, development, lending and management firms work together with the leaders of major national real estate trade associations to jointly address key national policy issues relating to real estate and the overall economy. Identifies, analyzes and coordinates policy positions to ensure that a cohesive industry voice is heard by government officials and the public about real estate and its important role in the global economy. Collectively, Roundtable members hold portfolios containing over 2.5 billion square feet of developed property valued at more than $250 billion. Participating trade associations represent more than one million people involved in virtually every aspect of the real estate business. **Telecommunication Services:** electronic mail, meetings@rer.org. **Committees:** Environmental Policy Advisory; Real Estate Capital Policy Advisory; Tax Policy Advisory; Technology and Buildings. **Task Forces:** Infrastructure. **Also Known As:** Real Estate's Roundtable. **Publications:** *America's Real Estate: Annual National Policy Agenda*, annual. Book. Provides information on real estate ownership, financing public services, foreign ownership, nonresidential buildings, and real estate values. ● *Cornerstone*, bimonthly. Newsletter. **Conventions/Meetings:** annual State of the Industry Meeting - always June, Washington, DC.

3341 ■ Real Estate Services Providers Council (RESPRO)
2000 L St. NW, Ste.522
Washington, DC 20036
Ph: (202)862-2051
Fax: (202)862-2052
E-mail: info@respro.org
URL: http://www.respro.org
Contact: Brian Levy, Chm.
Membership Dues: general (based on gross revenues under 12 million to over 2 billion), $1,100-$33,000 (annual) ● associate, $1,100 (annual) ● state, $550 (annual). **Description:** Promotes the efforts of settlement service providers to deliver innovative and cost-effective services to home buyers and home owners through business alliances across industry lines. Enables members to share ideas and develop successful business relationships across industry lines. **Publications:** Newsletter. **Price:** for members.

3342 ■ Realtors Land Institute (RLI)
430 N Michigan Ave.
Chicago, IL 60611
Free: (800)441-5263
Fax: (312)329-8633
E-mail: rli@realtors.org
URL: http://www.rliland.com
Contact: John A. McAllister, Pres.
Founded: 1944. **Members:** 1,500. **Membership Dues:** individual, $295 (annual). **Staff:** 3. **State Groups:** 48. **Description:** Real estate brokers and salespersons selling, managing, appraising, or developing all types of land. Maintains educational programs for real estate brokers; promotes competence and accredits members. Sponsors courses for realtors and others seeking professional excellence on Land Brokerage, Agricultural Land Brokerage, Exchanging Properties, Estate Planning, Subdivision Development, and Financial Analysis of Land Investment. **Awards:** Realtor of the Year. **Frequency:** annual. **Type:** recognition. **Committees:** Agri Land; Communications; Designations; Education; Electronic Services; Marketing Sessions; Regional VPs; Strategic Planning; Urban Land. **Councils:** Chapter Services; Education Services; Marketing Services. **Affiliated With:** National Association of Realtors. **Formerly:** Institute of Farm Brokers; National Institute of Farm and Land Brokers; (1986) Farm and Land Institute. **Publications:** *Realtors Land Institute—Roster of Members*, annual. Membership Directory. **Price:** $50.00. **Advertising:** accepted ● Newsletter, bimonthly. **Price:** $24.00/year. **Circulation:** 2,000. **Advertising:** accepted. **Conventions/Meetings:** annual National Land - conference.

3343 ■ Society of Industrial and Office Realtors (SIOR)
1201 New York Ave. NW, Ste.350
Washington, DC 20005
Ph: (202)449-8200
Fax: (202)216-9325
E-mail: admin@sior.com
URL: http://www.sior.com
Contact: Richard Hollander, Exec. VP
Founded: 1941. **Members:** 2,000. **Membership Dues:** active, in U.S., $985 (annual) ● active, in Canada, $610 (annual) ● active outside U.S. and Canada, educator associate in U.S., $300 (annual) ● corporate associate in U.S., developer associate outside U.S. and Canada, general associate outside U.S. and Canada, $500 (annual) ● corporate associate in Canada, $350 (annual) ● corporate associate outside U.S. and Canada, $250 (annual) ● developer associate in U.S., general associate in U.S., $1,500 (annual) ● developer associate in Canada, $1,030 (annual) ● educator associate in Canada, retired in Canada, $210 (annual) ● educator associate outside U.S. and Canada, candidate in U.S., $200 (annual) ● general associate in Canada, $1,025 (annual) ● retired in U.S., $65-$300 (annual) ● retired outside U.S. and Canada, candidate outside U.S. and Canada, $100 (annual) ● candidate in Canada, $125 (annual) ● chapter, $50-$350 (annual). **Staff:** 17. **Budget:** $3,000,000. **Regional Groups:** 10. **Local Groups:** 39. **Description:** Real estate brokers specializing in industrial and office properties; representatives of utilities, financial institutions, corporations, and industrial park developments. Conducts studies on special problems of industrial development, development of sale-lease back techniques, surveys of plants or site locations, and availability. Conducts six educational courses and eight seminars annually. Sponsors SIOR Educational Foundation. Compiles statistics. **Awards:** Cooperative Transaction Awards. **Frequency:** annual. **Type:** recognition. **Telecommunication Services:** electronic mail, rhollander@sior.com. **Committees:** Admissions; Advertising and Public Relations; Education; Grievance and Professional Standards; Membership Development and Retention; Membership Evaluation; New Member Welcoming and Orientation; Nominating; Research and Publications. **Affiliated With:** National Association of Realtors. **Formerly:** (1986) Society of Industrial Realtors. **Publications:** *Comparative Statistics of Industrial and Office Real Estate Markets*, annual. Book. Features a summary of SIOR's survey of industrial and office real estate activity in the U.S., Canada, Mexico, and Western Europe. **Price:** $60.00 for members; $135.00 for nonmembers in U.S.; $155.00 for nonmembers outside U.S. Alternate Formats: online ● *Executive Guide to Specialists in Industrial and Office Real Estate*, annual. Membership Directory. Lists industrial and office real estate brokers, developers, consultants, park developers, and corporate associates, including retired members. **Price:** free for members; $70.00 for nonmembers, in U.S.; $80.00 for nonmembers, outside U.S. **Circulation:** 9,000 ● *Industrial Real Estate*. Book. **Price:** $25.00 for members; $40.00 for nonmembers, in U.S.; $50.00 for nonmembers, outside U.S. ● *Professional Report of Industrial and Office Real Estate*, bimonthly. Magazine. Includes articles on industry trends, cooperative real estate transactions, tax and legislative developments affecting the industry, and member news. **Price:** included in membership dues; $25.00 /year for nonmembers in U.S.; $50.00 /year for nonmembers outside U.S. **Circulation:** 3,000. **Advertising:** accepted ● Also publishes guides and studies. **Conventions/Meetings:** seminar.

3344 ■ Vacation Rental Managers Association (VRMA)
PO Box 1202
Santa Cruz, CA 95061-1202
Ph: (831)426-8762
Free: (800)871-8762
Fax: (831)458-3637
E-mail: info@vrma.com
URL: http://www.vrma.com
Contact: Michael Sarka, Exec. Dir.
Founded: 1985. **Members:** 600. **Membership Dues:** vacation rental manager, $400 (annual). **Staff:** 3. **Budget:** $750,000. **State Groups:** 3. **Description:** Companies that rent and manage vacation properties, resorts, townhomes, and condominiums on a short-term basis. Promotes the interests of the vacation rental industry to the public. **Awards:** North American Marketing Awards. **Frequency:** annual. **Type:** recognition ● Regional Marketing Awards. **Type:** recognition. **Committees:** Annual Conference Planning; Membership; Standards and Ethics. **Formerly:** Association of Vacation Home Rental Managers. **Publications:** *VRMA Review*, quarterly. Newsletter. **Circulation:** 700. **Advertising:** accepted. **Conventions/Meetings:** biennial conference and seminar (exhibits) - every spring.

3345 ■ Women's Council of Realtors (WCR)
430 N Michigan Ave.
Chicago, IL 60611
Ph: (312)329-8481
Free: (800)245-8512
Fax: (312)329-3290
E-mail: info@wcr.org
URL: http://www.wcr.org
Contact: Judy Moses ABR, Pres.
Founded: 1938. **Members:** 14,000. **Membership Dues:** international affiliate, $140 (annual). **Staff:** 9. **Budget:** $2,000,000. **Regional Groups:** 9. **State Groups:** 34. **Local Groups:** 250. **Description:** Women and men real estate brokers and salespeople. Provides opportunity for real estate professionals to participate at local, state, and national levels. Makes programs available for personal and career growth. Offers courses in leadership training, referral and relocation business. Members may earn the Leadership Training Graduate (LTG) designation. **Awards:** Pinnacle Awards. **Frequency:** annual. **Type:** monetary. **Telecommunication Services:** electronic mail, wcr@wcr.org. **Formerly:** (1992) Women's Council of Realtors of the National Association of Realtors. **Publications:** *Women's Council of Realtors—Connections*, bimonthly. Magazine. **Price:** free for members; $25.00 /year for nonmembers. ISSN: 0199-9028. **Circulation:** 15,000. **Advertising:** accepted ● *Women's Council of Realtors—Referral Roster*, annual. Membership Directory. **Price:** free for members. **Circulation:** 15,000. **Advertising:** accepted. **Conventions/Meetings:** annual convention - 2008 Nov. 5-9, Orlando, FL.

Recording Industry

3346 ■ Alliance of Artists and Recording Companies (AARC)
700 N Fairfax St., Ste.601
Alexandria, VA 22314
Ph: (703)535-8101
Fax: (703)535-8105
E-mail: contact@aaroyalties.com
URL: http://aarcroyalties.com
Contact: Linda R. Bocchi, Exec. Dir.
Founded: 1993. **Multinational**. **Description:** Protects the rights of featured artists and recording

companies in the areas of hometaping and rental rights. Collects and distributes Audio Home Recording Act of 1992 (AHRA) royalties to featured recording artists and sound recording copyright owners. Ensures the proper compensation of artist community and recording industry. **Publications:** Brochure. Alternate Formats: online.

Recordings

3347 ■ Audio Publishers Association (APA)
191 Clarksville Rd.
Princeton Junction, NJ 08550
Ph: (609)799-6327
Fax: (609)799-7032
E-mail: info@audiopub.org
URL: http://www.audiopub.org
Contact: JoAnna Laskas, Exec. Dir.
Founded: 1986. **Members:** 231. **Membership Dues:** regular (based upon the annual gross), $250-$6,000 (annual) ● large retailer, $500 (annual) ● small retailer, small supplier, media, $250 (annual) ● large supplier, $1,500 (annual) ● medium supplier, $750 (annual) ● individual (industry professional), $200 (annual) ● librarian, $50 (annual) ● voice talent, $100 (annual). **Staff:** 2. **Description:** Advocates high production value; advises on industry-specific technical standards; serves as a networking, educational and information forum for members; delivers programs and services that serve the common business interests of members; promotes policies and activities that accelerate audiobook industry growth. **Awards:** Audie Award. **Frequency:** annual. **Type:** recognition. **Recipient:** for the best titles in audio publishing. **Publications:** *APA E-Newsletter*, monthly. **Price:** free for members. Alternate Formats: online. **Conventions/Meetings:** annual conference.

3348 ■ National Association of Record Industry Professionals (NARIP)
PO Box 2446
Toluca Lake, CA 91610-2446
Ph: (818)769-7007
Fax: (818)769-6191
E-mail: info@narip.com
URL: http://www.narip.com
Contact: Tess Taylor, Pres.
Membership Dues: regular (add $20 for overseas airmail), $120 (annual). **Description:** Promotes education, career advancement, and collegiality among record executives. **Computer Services:** database, member resume for employers. **Publications:** Newsletter. **Conventions/Meetings:** Incredible Shrinking Profit Margin - meeting ● Independent Distribution Solution: Getting Records from Concept to Consumer - workshop ● lecture ● meeting.

3349 ■ National Association of Recording Merchandisers (NARM)
9 Eves Dr., Ste.120
Marlton, NJ 08053
Ph: (856)596-2221
Fax: (856)596-3268
E-mail: donio@narm.com
URL: http://www.narm.com
Contact: Jim Donio, Pres.
Founded: 1958. **Members:** 500. **Membership Dues:** individual, $135 (annual) ● company (with gross sales volume of under $499999), $165 (annual) ● company (with gross sales volume of over $2 billion), $32,445 (annual) ● entertainment service provider, $7,500-$15,000 (annual). **Staff:** 10. **Budget:** $3,000,000. **Description:** Serves the music and other prerecorded entertainment software industry as a forum for insight and dialogue; members include retailers, wholesalers, distributors, entertainment software suppliers, and suppliers of related products and services. **Libraries:** **Type:** not open to the public. **Subjects:** merchandising, loss prevention, classical music, EDI. **Awards:** Advertising Awards. **Frequency:** annual. **Type:** recognition. **Recipient:** for advertising excellence ● Merchandiser of the Year. **Frequency:** annual. **Type:** recognition. **Recipient:** for excellence in music retailing ● Supplier of the Year. **Frequency:** annual. **Type:** recognition. **Recipient:** for excellence in music retailing. **Computer Services:** database, proprietary industry catalogs and promotional files. **Committees:** Classical Music; Entertainment Software Suppliers; Loss Prevention; Merchandising; Operations; Retail; Scholarship; Suppliers of Related Products and Services; Wholesale/Distribution. **Formerly:** National Association of Record Merchandisers. **Publications:** *NARM Convention Official Guide*, annual. Directory. Contains convention programming information, maps, and attendees listings. **Price:** free. **Circulation:** 1,500. **Advertising:** accepted ● *NARM Membership Directory and Buyer's Guide*, annual. Contains names, addresses, and primary contacts of NARM members. **Price:** free. **Circulation:** 1,500. **Advertising:** accepted ● *NARM News Bits*, monthly. Newsletter. Contains industry and association news; profiles of members. **Price:** free. **Circulation:** 8,000. Alternate Formats: online ● *NARM Research Briefs*, monthly. Newsletter. Alternate Formats: online. **Conventions/Meetings:** annual Insights and Sounds - convention (exhibits).

3350 ■ Recording Industry Association of America (RIAA)
Address Unknown since 2008
Founded: 1952. **Members:** 250. **Staff:** 60. **Description:** Promotes the mutual interests of recording companies, manufacturers and distributors, as well as the music industry through government relations, intellectual property protection, anti-piracy activities, research and public relations. Creates, markets and distributes approximately 90 percent of all legitimate sound recordings produced and sold in the United States. Acts as the official certification agency for gold, platinum and multi-platinum awards. **Awards:** Cultural Award. **Frequency:** annual. **Type:** recognition. **Recipient:** for an individual or institution that has encouraged cultural activities in the U.S. **Computer Services:** database. **Committees:** Engineering; International; Labor Relations; Legal; Market Research; Marketing; Operations and Systems; Postal; Public Relations; Tax; Traffic/Freight; Video. **Formerly:** (1970) Record Industry Association of America. **Publications:** *Fast Tracks*, biweekly. Newsletter ● Brochures ● Report, annual ● Also publishes list of Gold and Platinum Record Award Winners. **Conventions/Meetings:** annual Anti-Piracy Investigators' Conference.

3351 ■ Society of Professional Audio Recording Services (SPARS)
9 Music Sq. S, Ste.222
Nashville, TN 37203
Free: (800)771-7727
Fax: (615)296-0386
E-mail: spars@spars.com
URL: http://www.spars.com
Contact: Ms. Marcia Kautz, Exec. Dir.
Founded: 1978. **Members:** 200. **Membership Dues:** active, $425 (annual) ● associate, $175 (annual) ● educational, $350 (annual) ● sustaining (manufacturer), $1,500 (annual) ● sustaining (service provider), $500 (annual). **Staff:** 1. **Description:** Recording and video studio owners; suppliers, manufacturers, producers, engineers, and recording service users involved with audio commercial facilities. Works to improve every phase of business operations and to provide members with the opportunity to play an effective role in shaping the future of their industry. Acts as a forum for the industry; maintains a high technical cultural standard; addresses interested parties on issues confronting the industry's present and future equipment needs. Analyzes, evaluates, and comments upon the use of professional audio equipment; fosters the dissemination of information concerning techniques of studio management and technical innovation; conducts educational activities. Assists in the development of projects, undertakings, and studies related to the industry; considers and deals with intratrade problems; attempts to reform abuses and inculcate principles of justice and equity in the audio recording industry. **Formerly:** (1987) Society of Professional Audio Recording Studios. **Publications:** *Time Code Primer*. Handbook. Contains information that deals with time code. **Price:** $16.95 for members, plus shipping and handling; $24.95 for nonmembers, plus shipping and handling.

Recreation

3352 ■ American Spa and Health Resort Association (ASHRA)
PO Box 585
Lake Forest, IL 60045
Ph: (847)234-8851
Fax: (847)295-7790
Contact: Melanie Ruehle, Dir.
Founded: 1982. **Members:** 25. **Description:** Health spa owners and operators. Seeks to establish and maintain high standards of quality in U.S. health spas. Plans to conduct inspections and confer certification on qualifying facilities. Negotiates with health insurance professionals who will set standards for insurance recognition. **Publications:** none. **Convention/Meeting:** none.

3353 ■ Association of Pool and Spa Professionals (APSP)
2111 Eisenhower Ave., Ste.500
Alexandria, VA 22314
Ph: (703)838-0083
Fax: (703)549-0493
E-mail: memberservices@theapsp.org
URL: http://www.theapsp.org
Contact: Bill Weber, Pres./CEO
Founded: 1956. **Members:** 5,000. **Membership Dues:** manufacturer (with $599,999 - 19,999,999 annual sales volume), $800-$8,800 (annual) ● manufacturer (with $20,999,999 - 99,999,999 annual sales volume - maximum), $25,400 (annual) ● manufacturer (with $100,000,000 - 199,999,999 annual sales volume maximum), $36,500 (annual) ● distributor (based on annual sales volume), $1,300-$7,600 (annual) ● builder, retailer, service company (based on annual sales volume), $200-$950 (annual). **Staff:** 30. **Budget:** $7,000,000. **Regional Groups:** 11. **Local Groups:** 80. **Multinational. Description:** Builders, dealers, designers, service companies, retail stores, engineers, manufacturers, distributors, public officials, suppliers, and service persons concerned with public and residential swimming pools, spas, and hot tubs. Aims to raise spa and pool industry standards; expand interest and use of swimming pools, spas, and hot tubs; seeks to achieve uniformity in federal, state, and local regulations affecting swimming pool, spa, and hot tub operations. Promotes the industry to the consumer; protects interests of the industry through government relations and technical programs. Establishes voluntary standards for the design and construction of swimming pools and spas. Compiles cost of doing business data and other statistics. **Awards:** Swimming Pool, Spa, and Hot Tub Awards of Excellence. **Frequency:** annual. **Type:** recognition. **Recipient:** for members in good standing. **Committees:** Consumer Awareness; Government Relations; Industry, Growth, and Promotion; Technical. **Councils:** Builders; Distributors; Manufacturers; Manufacturers' Agents; Retailers; Service; Spa and Tub. **Formerly:** (1980) National Swimming Pool Institute; (2005) National Spa and Pool Institute. **Publications:** *National Member News*, monthly. Newsletter. Reports on the pool and spa industry. **Price:** included in membership dues. **Circulation:** 4,400. **Advertising:** accepted. Alternate Formats: online ● *Standards for Public and Residential Pools and Spas* ● *Swimming Pool and Spa Industry Market Report*, annual ● Brochures. **Conventions/Meetings:** annual International Expo - convention, deals with business and products (exhibits) ● annual trade show (exhibits).

3354 ■ Best Holiday Trav-L-Park Association (BHTPA)
545 Lonely Cottage Dr.
Upper Black Eddy, PA 18972
Free: (866)665-5448

E-mail: info@bestholiday.org
URL: http://www.bestholiday.org
Founded: 1981. **Members:** 70. **Membership Dues:** active, $595 (annual). **Staff:** 3. **Description:** Independently owned campgrounds. Seeks to increase business of members through networking and the establishment of a common logo. **Publications:** *Best Holiday Directory*, annual. Contains directory of members. **Price:** free for members. **Circulation:** 175,000. **Conventions/Meetings:** annual conference.

3355 ■ International Spa Association (ISPA)
2365 Harrodsburg Rd., Ste.A325
Lexington, KY 40504
Ph: (859)226-4326
Free: (888)651-4772
Fax: (859)226-4445
E-mail: ispa@ispastaff.com
URL: http://www.experienceispa.com
Contact: Lynne Walker McNees, Pres.
Founded: 1991. **Members:** 1,450. **Staff:** 8. **Regional Groups:** 2. **Multinational. Description:** Professional association and voice of the spa industry. Forms and maintains alliances that educate, set standards, provide resources, influence policy and build coalitions for the industry. Raises awareness of the spa industry and educates the public and industry professionals about the benefits of the spa experience. **Publications:** *Pulse*, bimonthly. Magazine. **Conventions/Meetings:** annual conference and seminar, geared toward education and business (exhibits).

3356 ■ KampGround Owners Association (KOA)
3416 Primm Ln.
Birmingham, AL 35216
Ph: (205)824-0022
Free: (800)678-9976
Fax: (205)823-2760
E-mail: info@koaowners.org
URL: http://www.koaowners.org
Contact: William Ranieri, Exec. Dir.
Founded: 1964. **Members:** 400. **Membership Dues:** regular, $50 (annual). **Staff:** 4. **State Groups:** 30. **Description:** Represents KOA franchisees. Offers seminars and workshops. Compiles statistics; maintains speakers' bureau, charitable program, and several committees. **Publications:** *Kampground Owners News*, bimonthly. **Conventions/Meetings:** annual meeting.

3357 ■ National Association of RV Parks and Campgrounds (National ARVC)
113 Park Ave.
Falls Church, VA 22046
Ph: (703)241-8801
Fax: (703)241-1004
E-mail: lprofaizer@arvc.org
URL: http://www.arvc.org
Contact: Linda Profaizer, Pres./CEO
Founded: 1966. **Members:** 3,700. **Membership Dues:** associate, individual, $75 (annual) ● corporation, $500 (annual) ● supplier, $575 (annual). **Staff:** 8. **Budget:** $950,000. **State Groups:** 31. **Description:** Regular members are commercial campground owners and operators; associate members are manufacturers and suppliers of campground products and services. Promotes and protects the interests of the commercial campground industry, with government officials and agencies, campers, the press, and the general public. Represents the campground industry in contact with RV manufacturers, RV dealers, and other branches of the camping business. Offers specialized education. Works to develop better, more efficient, more profitable campground management and business methods. Compiles statistics. Operates National RV Park and Campground Industry Education Foundation and a Certified Park Operators program. **Awards:** Park of the Year. **Frequency:** annual. **Type:** recognition. **Recipient:** for involvement in RV park/campground ● RV Park Operator of the Year. **Frequency:** annual. **Type:** recognition. **Recipient:** to park operator for involvement in RV park/campground ● Stan Martin Memorial Award. **Frequency:** annual. **Type:** recognition. **Recipient:** for involvement in RV park/campground. **Formerly:** (1993) National Campground Owners Association. **Publications:** *ARVC Report*, monthly. Newsletter. Contains association news and industry information. **Circulation:** 4,100. **Advertising:** accepted ● *Biennial National Operations Survey of the Campground Industry* ● *Direct Line*, monthly. Newsletter ● *Membership Directory and Buyer's Guide*, annual ● Directory. **Conventions/Meetings:** annual Insites - National Parks & Paddles Convention & Expo - convention and trade show, for suppliers of campground/RV park products and services (exhibits) - always November.

3358 ■ National Forest Recreation Association (NFRA)
PO Box 488
Woodlake, CA 93286
Ph: (559)564-2365
Fax: (559)564-2048
E-mail: info@nfra.org
URL: http://www.nfra.org
Contact: Marily Reese, Exec. Dir.
Founded: 1948. **Members:** 250. **Membership Dues:** general (based on annual revenues), $250-$2,500 (annual) ● associate/supplier, $500 (annual) ● supporting, $100 (annual). **Staff:** 1. **Budget:** $100,000. **Description:** Owners and operators of resorts, winter sports areas, marinas, campgrounds, stores, river trip outfitters, packer-outfitters, restaurants, and motels located on or adjacent to federal land. Participates in trade and public relations matters that is of interest to members, including legislation and relationships with U.S. agencies; state and local officials in matters of taxation, insurance, finance, health, and building requirements; and employment. **Awards:** Distinguished Service Award. **Type:** recognition ● Ranger of the Year Award. **Frequency:** annual. **Type:** recognition. **Recipient:** to individuals who have made outstanding contributions to the forest service and recreation field. **Divisions:** Campgrounds; Marinas; Packer Outfitters; Resorts; Retail; River Outfitters; Ski Areas; Winter Sports. **Publications:** *NFRA Report*, quarterly. Newsletter. Covers membership activities and issues of interest/importance to members. **Price:** available to members and by request. **Circulation:** 6,000. **Advertising:** accepted. Alternate Formats: online. **Conventions/Meetings:** annual conference and trade show (exhibits).

3359 ■ National Party Boat Owners Alliance (NPBOA)
181 Thames St.
Groton, CT 06340
Ph: (860)535-2066
Fax: (860)535-8389
Contact: Capt. Bradley J. Glas, Pres./Exec. Dir.
Founded: 1952. **Members:** 500. **Description:** Owners and operators of passenger carrying vessels, including party fishing, charter fishing, sightseeing, and ferry boats. Promotes safe operation of passenger carrying vessels; advises members of changes in regulations. Opposes what the group considers restrictive and unwarranted industry regulations. **Publications:** *NPBOA Newsletter*, periodic.

3360 ■ National Swimming Pool Foundation (NSPF)
4775 Granby Cir.
Colorado Springs, CO 80919-3131
Ph: (719)540-9119
Fax: (719)540-2787
E-mail: margaret.smith@nspf.com
URL: http://www.nspf.org
Contact: Ms. Margaret Smith, Dir. of Operations
Founded: 1965. **Staff:** 7. **Description:** Aims to improve public health by creating a safer aquatic environment through education and research, and to attract more people to aquatic exercise. Works toward its mission with educational products like the Aquatic Safety Compendium, Certified Pool-Spa Operator training, Certified Pool-Spa Inspector training and the World Aquatic Health Conference. Provides program for pool and spa operators and health officials, certifying over 180,000 from 45 countries. **Awards:** Board of Directors Scholarship. **Frequency:** annual. **Type:** scholarship ● **Frequency:** biennial. **Type:** fellowship. **Recipient:** for graduate students and/or post doctoral researchers who investigate important topics related to swimming pools and spas ● **Frequency:** biennial. **Type:** grant ● Ray B. Essick Scholarship. **Frequency:** annual. **Type:** scholarship ● **Frequency:** annual. **Type:** scholarship. **Publications:** *Certified Pool-Spa Operator Handbook* (in English and Spanish). Contains professional training to operate pools and spas and reduce risks to people and the facility. **Price:** $59.95 ● *Math Workbook*, periodic. Booklet. **Price:** $20.00 ● *Official Swimming Pool Design Compendium*, periodic. Book. **Price:** $65.00.

3361 ■ Resort and Commercial Recreation Association (RCRA)
PO Box 1564
Dubuque, IA 52004
Fax: (563)690-3296
E-mail: bruce.boliver@sru.edu
URL: http://www.r-c-r-a.org
Contact: Bruce Boliver, Pres.
Founded: 1981. **Members:** 700. **Membership Dues:** professional, $115 (annual) ● associate, $130 (annual) ● student, $50 (annual) ● agency, $230 (annual) ● educational institution, $230 (annual) ● affiliated student, $40 (annual). **Staff:** 1. **Budget:** $150,000. **Regional Groups:** 12. **State Groups:** 20. **Local Groups:** 1. **Description:** Professionals, agencies, vendors, educators, and students involved in the resort and commercial recreation field. Seeks to advance the resort and commercial recreation industries; increase the profitability of commercial recreation enterprises; foster communication among members; promote professionalism within the industry; provide opportunities for continuing education. Acts as a vehicle for networking; offers program exchange and job placement services. Holds specialized educational presentations; operates student chapters; encourages and facilitates internships. Provides car rental discount program. **Awards:** Achievement Award. **Frequency:** annual. **Type:** recognition. **Recipient:** for a member's significant contribution and dedicated service to RCRA ● Debbie Regnone Service Award. **Frequency:** annual. **Type:** recognition. **Recipient:** for a member's commitment and excellent service to RCRA ● Excellence in Programming Award. **Frequency:** annual. **Type:** recognition. **Recipient:** for professional(s) or student(s) who have created and implemented a special, unique, and innovative program ● Excellence in Research Award. **Frequency:** annual. **Type:** recognition. **Recipient:** for the valuable contribution of a selected piece of research that is presented at the RCRA Research Symposium ● Fellow Award. **Frequency:** annual. **Type:** recognition. **Recipient:** for a distinguished member ● Outstanding Professor Award. **Frequency:** annual. **Type:** recognition. **Recipient:** for a member who has made a significant impact at his/her College or University ● Outstanding Student Award. **Frequency:** annual. **Type:** recognition. **Recipient:** for a student or intern member ● Premiere Recreation Operation Award. **Frequency:** annual. **Type:** recognition. **Recipient:** for recreation operations/departments with outstanding leadership in the development and promotion of quality recreation programs and services. **Computer Services:** Online services, intern directory preference selection ● online services, job placement service. **Publications:** *Job Placement Bulletin*, monthly ● *Management Strategy and Member Services Update*, quarterly ● *Noah's Art*. Books ● *RCRA Newsletter*, bimonthly. Alternate Formats: online ● *RCRA Update*, 8/year. Journal. **Price:** included in membership dues. **Circulation:** 1,500. **Advertising:** accepted ● *Recipe of Programs*. Brochure ● Bulletin, quarterly ● Membership Directory, annual. Alternate Formats: online. **Conventions/Meetings:** competition ● annual conference ● periodic regional meeting ● annual seminar.

3362 ■ Sauna Society of America (SSA)
PO Box 19001
Washington, DC 20036-9001

Ph: (202)331-1363
Contact: V.S. Choslowsky, Exec. Dir.
Founded: 1965. **Members:** 32. **Staff:** 4. **Description:** Importers, manufacturers, builders, and suppliers of saunas. Provides information about the construction and use of the authentic Finnish sauna. Conducts program in cooperation with the International Sauna Society in Helsinki, Finland to assist in medical documentation of the use of and research into the sauna. Maintains information and referral service. **Publications:** *Sauna*. Brochure. **Price:** $3.00 ● *Sauna - and Your Health*. **Price:** $17.50 ● *Sauna Studies*. **Price:** $19.50 ● Also publishes Let's Have a Sauna $5. **Conventions/Meetings:** quadrennial International Sauna Congress - conference, in conjunction with the International Sauna Society.

3363 ■ Society of Recreation Executives (SRE)
Box 520
Gonzalez, FL 32560-0520
Ph: (850)937-8354
Free: (800)281-9186
E-mail: rltresoource@spydee.net
Contact: K.W. Stephens, Pres.
Founded: 1986. **Members:** 3,897. **Membership Dues:** individual, $99 (annual). **Staff:** 12. **Budget:** $140,000. **Regional Groups:** 2. **State Groups:** 3. **Local Groups:** 8. **Description:** Corporate executives in the recreation, leisure, and travel industry. To obtain individual and collective recognition for recreation executives. Works to: provide a perspective on needs, trends, and changes within the industry; provide opportunities for the exchange of ideas and expertise among members; inform, train, and instruct members in industry principles and practices. Supports favorable legislation. Sponsors continuing education and selfhelp programs. Operates placement service and speakers' bureau. **Libraries: Type:** reference. **Holdings:** archival material. **Committees:** Management Advisory; Publicity. **Publications:** *The Recreation Executive*, bimonthly. Newsletter. Contains statistics and research reports on recreation, leisure, and travel. Includes information on employment opportunities. **Price:** included in membership dues. **Circulation:** 24,000. **Advertising:** accepted ● *Who's Who In Recreation*, annual. **Conventions/Meetings:** annual rally (exhibits) - always June ● seminar ● workshop.

3364 ■ Suntanning Association for Education (SAE)
PO Box 1181
Gulf Breeze, FL 32562
Free: (800)536-8255
Fax: (850)436-7695
E-mail: suntanningedu@gmail.com
URL: http://www.suntanningedu.com
Contact: Joe Schuster, Contact
Founded: 1986. **Members:** 1,760. **Membership Dues:** $90 (annual). **Staff:** 2. **Budget:** $300,000. **State Groups:** 1. **Description:** Companies and individuals involved in the indoor tanning industry. Educates members and the public about indoor tanning. Conducts educational and training program for salon operators; sponsors research. **Libraries: Type:** not open to the public. **Committees:** Development; Education; Legal Affairs; Public Relations. **Publications:** *Tanning Talk*, quarterly. Newsletter. Contains business and marketing articles and information on association's trade show and seminars. **Price:** included in membership dues. **Circulation:** 1,750. **Advertising:** accepted. **Conventions/Meetings:** annual trade show and convention (exhibits).

3365 ■ United Franchise Benefits Association (UFBA)
Address Unknown since 2007
Founded: 1979. **Members:** 97,019. **Membership Dues:** $315 (annual). **Staff:** 12. **Regional Groups:** 216. **National Groups:** 18. **Description:** Provides discount buying, including health insurance for franchisors, franchisees, licensees, licensors, dealerships etc. **Libraries: Type:** not open to the public. **Holdings:** 958; audio recordings. **Subjects:** franchising globally and U.S. **Publications:** *Franchise News*, monthly. Magazine. **Price:** free for members. **Circulation:** 100,000. **Advertising:** accepted. **Conventions/Meetings:** annual conference.

3366 ■ Wood Tank Manufacturers Association (WTMA)
Address Unknown since 2007
Founded: 1983. **Members:** 12. **Membership Dues:** $100 (annual). **Budget:** $82,000. **Description:** Manufacturers of wooden tanks used as hot tubs. Seeks to promote the safe use of wooden tanks, and to counter what the group describes as common myths about wooden hot tubs such as they leak and cannot be repaired, are more susceptible to bacterial contamination, and less comfortable than other types of tanks or spas. Conducts laboratory research on the use of wooden tanks. Operates speakers' bureau. Plans to launch a consumer education program on wooden hot tubs. Maintains Hall of Fame. **Libraries: Type:** reference. **Awards: Type:** scholarship. **Computer Services:** database. **Publications:** *Wood Tank Manufacturers Association—Membership Directory*, annual. **Price:** free. **Circulation:** 20,000. **Advertising:** accepted. **Conventions/Meetings:** annual conference (exhibits).

Recreational Vehicles

3367 ■ Delta Houseboat Rental Association (DHRA)
Address Unknown since 2007
Founded: 1977. **Members:** 5. **Description:** Houseboat rental companies. Works to: stimulate national interest in houseboating on the California Delta; provide historical and advisory information on the Delta. (The California Delta consists of nearly 700,000 acres of rich, agricultural land featuring a network of over 1000 miles of navigable waterways.) Presently inactive. **Publications:** *Let's Go Houseboating the Delta*.

3368 ■ International Snowmobile Manufacturers Association (ISMA)
1640 Haslett Rd., Ste.170
Haslett, MI 48840
Ph: (517)339-7788
Fax: (517)339-7798
URL: http://www.gosnowmobiling.org
Contact: Edward Klim, Pres.
Founded: 1995. **Members:** 4. **Staff:** 2. **Budget:** $300,000. **Description:** Manufacturers of snowmobiles. Seeks to promote the "welfare of the industry" and the "safe and proper use of snowmobiles as a family recreational vehicle". Encourages optimum development of trail systems and formation of local snowmobile clubs; advocates multi-use of public lands. **Awards:** International Award of Merit. **Frequency:** annual. **Type:** recognition. **Recipient:** for government officials. **Publications:** Booklets ● Handbook. **Conventions/Meetings:** annual congress - always June.

3369 ■ Personal Watercraft Industry Association (PWIA)
444 N Capitol St., Ste.645
Washington, DC 20001
Ph: (202)737-9768 (202)737-9750
Fax: (202)628-4716
E-mail: info@pwia.org
URL: http://www.pwia.org
Contact: Maureen Healey, Exec. Dir.
Founded: 1987. **Members:** 4. **Staff:** 3. **Description:** Represents the four U.S. personal watercraft manufacturers. Works to ensure that personal watercraft (PWC) and personal watercraft users are treated fairly when local, state, and federal government officials consider boating regulations; supports and actively advocates for reasonable regulations, strong enforcement of boating and navigation laws, and mandatory boating safety education for all PWC operators. **Affiliated With:** National Marine Manufacturers Association. **Publications:** *An Environmental Guide for Personal Watercraft Operators*. Pamphlet. **Price:** free ● *Riding Rules for Personal Watercraft*. Pamphlet. **Price:** free ● Also distributes safety training package for rental operations.

3370 ■ Recreation Vehicle Dealers Association of America (RVDA)
3930 Univ. Dr.
Fairfax, VA 22030-2515
Ph: (703)591-7130
Fax: (703)359-0152
E-mail: info@rvda.org
URL: http://www.rvda.org
Contact: Michael A. Molino CAE, Pres.
Founded: 1970. **Members:** 1,500. **Membership Dues:** RV dealer, $440 ● rental association (RV rental only; add $120 for dealer member), $200 ● aftermarket (RV service, parts, and accessories retailers only), $195. **Staff:** 15. **Budget:** $2,300,000. **Description:** Firms that have as their principal business the retail sale of recreation vehicles (commonly known as travel trailers, camping trailers, truck campers, and motor homes) and who maintain a permanent business establishment open for business and service on what they sell year-round. Provides information and liaison on government regulation of safety, trade, warranty, and franchising; fosters improved dealer-manufacturer relations; encourages communications among dealers and state and local RV associations. Offers education programs and training, advertising, sales, and service information. Provides public relations and publicity among the RV dealers and the rest of the industry, the public, and the government; works to improve standards of service to the consumer; sponsors local retail RV shows and dealer seminars. Supports improved availability and quality of campgrounds. Maintains speakers' bureau; compiles statistics; sponsors educational programs. Maintains the Recreation Vehicle Rental Association (see separate entry) and Recreation Vehicle Aftermarket Division to help improve the professional quality of rental and service businesses. **Committees:** Convention/Expo; Industry and Government Affairs; Market Expansion. **Publications:** *RV Executive Today*, monthly. Magazine. Covers topics of concern to recreation vehicle dealers and suppliers, including industry and government trends and association's news. **Price:** included in membership dues; $30.00 /year for nonmembers. **Circulation:** 2,000. **Advertising:** accepted ● *RV Service Management Guide*, periodic ● *Stolen RV Bulletin*, periodic ● Brochures ● Membership Directory, annual ● Books. **Conventions/Meetings:** annual RV Dealers International Convention/Expo (exhibits) - always fall.

3371 ■ Recreation Vehicle Industry Association (RVIA)
1896 Preston White Dr.
Reston, VA 20191
Ph: (703)620-6003
Fax: (703)620-5071
E-mail: rparsons@rvia.org
URL: http://www.rvia.org
Contact: Rachel Parsons, Public Relations Mgr.
Founded: 1973. **Members:** 550. **Staff:** 56. **Budget:** $11,500,000. **Description:** Recreation vehicle manufacturers, manufacturers' representatives, and suppliers of accessories and equipment used by manufacturers. Seeks to provide a unified recreation vehicle organization for manufacturers and component parts suppliers of motor homes, travel trailers, truck campers, folding camping trailers, and conversion vehicles. Promotes and represents the growth and concerns of the industry to federal and state government departments, the media, and the public. Collects shipment statistics, technical data, and consumer and media information. Monitors industry compliance with safety standards and the activities of federal and state governments that affect the RV industry. Provides legal and public relations services. Sponsors market research. **Awards:** Distinguished Achievement in RV Standards Award. **Frequency:** annual. **Type:** recognition. **Recipient:** for outstanding contributions towards the advancement of standards in the industry ● Distinguished Service to the RV Industry Award. **Frequency:** annual. **Type:** recognition. **Recipient:** for individuals in the industry who have distinguished themselves through outstanding service ● National

Service Award. **Frequency:** periodic. **Type:** recognition. **Recipient:** for individuals, corporations, or organizations outside of the recreation vehicle industry who have contributed in an outstanding way to the industry. **Committees:** Conversion Vehicle; Industry Education; Lawyers; Market Information; Membership; National Show; Public and Legislative Affairs; Public Relations; Standards Steering and Enforcement; Supplier. **Formed by Merger of:** (1974) Recreational Vehicle Institute; Recreational Vehicle Division of the Trailer Coach Association. **Publications:** *Recreation Vehicle Industry Association—Industry Profile Report*, annual. Contains statistical abstract of industry production. **Price:** $25.00 ● *Recreation Vehicle Industry Association—Membership Directory and Industry Buyers' Guide*, annual ● *Recreation Vehicle Industry Association—Year End Review*, annual ● *RV Road Signs*, quarterly ● *RVIA Monitor*, monthly. Features state and federal administrative and legislative report. ● *RVIA Today*, monthly. Newsletter ● *State Guide for RV Manufacturers*, biennial ● *Survey of RV Financing*, annual ● Also publishes standards data, consumer booklets and other pamphlets, and materials relating to the industry. **Conventions/Meetings:** annual California RV Show - trade show, trade and public retail RV show.

3372 ■ Recreation Vehicle Rental Association (RVRA)
3930 Univ. Dr.
Fairfax, VA 22030
Ph: (703)591-7130
Fax: (703)591-0734
E-mail: info@rvda.org
URL: http://www.rvamerica.com/rvra
Contact: Michael A. Molino CAE, Pres.
Founded: 1982. **Members:** 247. **Membership Dues:** corporate, $180 (annual) ● individual, $193 (annual) ● additional payment for dealer, $111 (annual). **Description:** Dealers involved in the rental of recreation vehicles such as folding trailers, travel trailers, and motor homes. Works to improve the professionalism of the RV rental dealer through educational programs and promote the use of rentals by disseminating information. Compiles statistics; conducts seminars. **Affiliated With:** Recreation Vehicle Dealers Association of America. **Conventions/Meetings:** annual convention (exhibits) - usually September.

3373 ■ Recreational Park Trailer Industry Association (RPTIA)
30 Greenville St., 2nd Fl.
Newnan, GA 30263-2602
Ph: (770)251-2672
Fax: (770)251-0025
E-mail: info@rptia.org
URL: http://www.rptia.com
Contact: William R. Garpow, Exec. Dir.
Founded: 1993. **Members:** 100. **Membership Dues:** supplier, service firm, $600 (annual) ● associate RV dealer and park, $75 (annual) ● manufacturer, $375 (quarterly). **Staff:** 3. **Budget:** $400,000. **Description:** Represents the interests of manufacturers of recreational park trailer vehicles, original equipment producers as well as the service providers, RV dealers and RV parks. Maintains statistical information on sales and compiles demographic profiles of owners; offers educational programs and training. Serves as the industry voice with government media and consumers. Maintains the National Safety Standard for Recreational Park Trailers ANSI A119.5 and assists its member manufacturers with adherence to a pledge they made. Provides assistance to RV parks and dealerships in the development of a profitable investment in recreational park trailers. Works to provide them with assistance to overcome any obstacles or resistance to the legal and appropriate use of units. **Libraries: Type:** reference; not open to the public; by appointment only. **Holdings:** 100; archival material, articles, audiovisuals, business records, clippings, periodicals. **Subjects:** recreational park trailers, park models. **Computer Services:** database, cemographic profile of park trailer buyers ● information services ● mailing lists ● online services. **Committees:** Executive; Public Relations; Show; Standards. **Affiliated With:** American Recreation Coalition; National Association of RV Parks and Campgrounds; Recreation Vehicle Industry Association. **Publications:** *ANSI A119.5 Standard for Recreational Park Trailers*, quadrennial. Book. Contains national safety standards for recreational park trailers. **Price:** $27.00 includes priority mail postage and handling ● *Recreational Park Trailers: A History of Product Undergoing Positive Changes*. Brochure. **Price:** free. Alternate Formats: online ● *RPTIA Flash Watch*. Newsletter. **Circulation:** 600. Alternate Formats: online ● *RPTIA Membership Directory*. **Conventions/Meetings:** quarterly board meeting - January, April, July and October.

Religious Supplies

3374 ■ National Church Goods Association (NCGA)
800 Roosevelt Rd., Bldg. C, Ste.312
Glen Ellyn, IL 60137
Ph: (630)942-6599
Fax: (630)790-3095
E-mail: ncga@ncgaweb.com
URL: http://www.ncgaweb.com
Contact: Richard Tonini, Pres.
Founded: 1907. **Members:** 300. **Staff:** 1. **Description:** Represents firms that manufacture, import, and/or sell religious items, books, or church supplies. Concerns itself with the business and social welfare of members. **Libraries: Type:** reference. **Publications:** Newsletter, 3/year. **Conventions/Meetings:** annual convention - always January ● annual meeting, catalog publishers - always May.

Renting and Leasing

3375 ■ American Automotive Leasing Association (AALA)
675 N Washington St., Ste.410
Alexandria, VA 22314
Ph: (703)548-0777
Fax: (703)548-1925
E-mail: peters@aalafleet.com
URL: http://www.aalafleet.com
Contact: Pamela Sederholm, Exec. Dir.
Founded: 1955. **Members:** 35. **Budget:** $400,000. **Description:** Represents the commercial automotive fleet leasing and management industry. **Telecommunication Services:** electronic mail, sederholm@aalafleet.com. **Publications:** Brochures. Alternate Formats: online. **Conventions/Meetings:** annual meeting - always September or October.

3376 ■ American Car Rental Association (ACRA)
12324 E 86th St. N, No. 130
Owasso, OK 74055-2543
Free: (888)200-2795
E-mail: seanbusking@acraorg.com
URL: http://acraorg.com
Contact: Dick Radzis, Pres.
Founded: 1996. **Members:** 350. **Membership Dues:** independent rental operator (based on fleet size), $150-$2,500 (annual) ● affiliate independent rental operator, $3,000 (annual) ● single brand, $25,000 (annual) ● dual brand, $40,000 (annual). **Description:** Independent automobile and truck renting and leasing firms. Seeks to promote, improve, and enhance the vehicle rental industry. Facilitates communication and cooperation among members; represents members' commercial and regulatory interests. **Awards:** President's Award. **Frequency:** annual. **Type:** recognition. **Formerly:** (2005) Association for Car and Truck Rental Independents and Franchisees. **Conventions/Meetings:** annual Car Rental Show ● convention (exhibits).

3377 ■ American Rental Association (ARA)
1900 19th St.
Moline, IL 61265
Free: (800)334-2177
Fax: (309)764-1533
E-mail: ara@ararental.org
URL: http://www.ararental.org
Contact: Christine L. Wehrman, CEO
Founded: 1956. **Members:** 8,562. **Membership Dues:** associate, $500 (annual) ● company (minimum; based on gross rental revenues), $365 (annual) ● company (maximum; based on gross rental revenues), $3,120 (annual). **Staff:** 37. **Budget:** $10,000,000. **Regional Groups:** 11. **State Groups:** 39. **Local Groups:** 56. **Description:** Firms engaged in the rental of event and party equipment, tools, machinery, and other products; includes independent, franchised, and chain store operators. Associates are suppliers of equipment, merchandise, and other items. Seeks to foster better business methods; promote study of economic trends in the rental industry. **Libraries: Type:** reference. **Holdings:** video recordings. **Subjects:** management, products, training. **Awards:** Distinguished Service Award. **Frequency:** annual. **Type:** recognition. **Recipient:** for an outstanding ARA member ● Meritorious Service Award. **Frequency:** annual. **Type:** recognition. **Recipient:** for an ARA general member ● Outstanding Leadership Award. **Frequency:** annual. **Type:** recognition. **Recipient:** for an outstanding ARA member ● Regional Person of the Year Award. **Frequency:** annual. **Type:** recognition. **Recipient:** for an outstanding ARA member ● Rental E-Web Image Award. **Frequency:** annual. **Type:** recognition. **Recipient:** for a business in the rental industry ● Rental Hall of Fame. **Frequency:** annual. **Type:** recognition. **Recipient:** for the rental industry ● Special Service Award. **Frequency:** annual. **Type:** recognition. **Recipient:** for an individual who is not into the rental business. **Committees:** Business Development; Education; Governmental Affairs; Local and State Association; Manufacturers Relations; Marketing and Advertising; Political Action. **Special Interest Groups:** Construction and Industrial; General Tool; Next Generation; Party and Events. **Absorbed:** (1986) National Rental Service Association. **Formerly:** (1961) American Associated Rental Operators. **Publications:** *Cost of Doing Business Report* ● *Rental Management*, monthly. Magazine. **Conventions/Meetings:** annual The Rental Show - trade show and convention, marketplace for the equipment rental industry (exhibits).

3378 ■ Amtralease
Address Unknown since 2008
Founded: 1978. **Members:** 80. **Description:** Independent truck rental and leasing companies. Members offer reciprocal maintenance and other services to other members. Engages in group purchasing and encourages the exchange of ideas. Holds seminars on administration, finances, maintenance and operations, and sales. **Conventions/Meetings:** annual meeting.

3379 ■ Association of Progressive Rental Organizations (APRO)
1504 Robin Hood Trail
Austin, TX 78703
Free: (800)204-2776
Fax: (512)794-0097
E-mail: bkeese@aprovision.org
URL: http://www.rtohq.org
Contact: Larry Carrico, Pres.
Founded: 1980. **Members:** 4,500. **Membership Dues:** RTO dealer (based on number of stores), $225-$375 (annual) ● associate (RTO vendor), $600 (annual). **Staff:** 9. **Budget:** $1,500,000. **Description:** Represents dealer and industry suppliers. Serves rental dealers in the home appliance, furniture, and consumer electronics industry who market their products with a rental-purchase plan. Purposes are to: foster trade and commerce; collect and disseminate information; represent members before legislative committees, government bureaus, and other bodies in matters affecting the industry. Encourages competition among members and increased use of industry services; establishes advertising standards to prevent misleading and false advertising; considers and deals with common problems of management, including those involving production, distribution, employment, and financial functions

within the rental industry. Sponsors workshops and seminars in accounting, sales, customer satisfaction and relations, personnel, inventory management, management development, and legal issues; makes available training materials. Conducts government relations program; compiles statistics. **Awards:** Buddy Awards. **Frequency:** annual. **Type:** recognition. **Recipient:** for outstanding individuals and organizations that have raised the level of what can be done to better the industry for everyone. **Publications:** *Progressive Rentals Magazine*, bimonthly. **Price:** included in membership dues; $30.00 /year for nonmembers. **Circulation:** 6,400. **Advertising:** accepted ● *Rental-To-Own Almanac*, annual. Membership Directory. **Advertising:** accepted ● *Rental Viewpoint Online*, biweekly. Newsletter. **Price:** free. **Circulation:** 2,800. **Advertising:** accepted. Alternate Formats: online ● Brochures ● Manuals. **Conventions/Meetings:** annual Convention/Buying Show - trade show (exhibits) - always summer.

3380 ■ Avis Licensee Association (ALA)

300 Old Country Rd., Ste.341
Mineola, NY 11501
Ph: (516)747-4951
Fax: (516)747-0195
Contact: Robert Klein, Exec. Dir.

Founded: 1981. **Members:** 80. **Staff:** 5. **Description:** Owners of licensed Avis Rent-A-Car franchises. Disseminates information concerning the daily operation of a car rental business; assists member businesses in finding ways to operate more efficiently. **Publications:** *The Access*, periodic. Newsletter ● Membership Directory. **Conventions/Meetings:** convention - every 18 months ● regional meeting.

3381 ■ Equipment Leasing and Finance Association (ELFA)

1825 K St. NW, Ste.900
Washington, DC 20006
Ph: (202)238-3400
Fax: (202)238-3401
E-mail: rscoggins@elfaonline.org
URL: http://www.elfaonline.org
Contact: Kenneth E. Bentsen Jr., Pres.

Founded: 1961. **Members:** 850. **Membership Dues:** regular, $2,300-$7,500 (annual) ● associate, $2,500-$5,500 (annual) ● arranger, $2,500-$12,000 (annual) ● international (flat), $2,500 (annual) ● business unit (10&percent; of parent company), $2,300 (annual) ● transitioning individual (flat), $600 (annual). **Staff:** 25. **Budget:** $8,000,000. **Multinational. Description:** Individuals, companies, divisions, or subsidiaries whose principal activity is the leasing of equipment to other commercial users. Includes companies that function or operate in the capacity of brokers and that do not write leases on their own forms, as well as bank-related lessors. Promotes understanding of problems involved in equipment leasing; works to advance the interests of members so they may better serve the public. Compiles statistics. **Libraries: Type:** reference. **Formerly:** (1961) Association of Equipment Lessors; (1974) American Association of Equipment Lessors; (1992) Equipment Leasing Association; (2007) Equipment Leasing Association of America. **Publications:** *Compensation*, annual. Survey ● *Equipment Leasing Today*, 10/year. Magazine. Includes information on accounting, finance, legal, and tax matters. **Price:** $100.00 /year for nonmembers. ISSN: 1046-6665. **Circulation:** 11,000. **Advertising:** accepted. Alternate Formats: online ● *Survey of Industry Activity* ● Catalog. **Conventions/Meetings:** annual meeting (exhibits) ● roundtable ● seminar ● workshop, includes sessions on leasing, credit, and finance.

3382 ■ National Association of Equipment Leasing Brokers (NAELB)

455 S Fourth St., Ste.650
Louisville, KY 40202
Ph: (502)583-3783
Free: (800)996-2352
Fax: (877)875-4750
E-mail: info@naelb.org
URL: http://www.naelb.org
Contact: Ms. Monica Harper, Exec. Admin.

Founded: 1990. **Members:** 850. **Membership Dues:** broker, $295 (annual) ● associate, $600 (annual) ● funding source, $750 (annual). **Staff:** 3. **Description:** Seeks to advance the professional practice of equipment leasing. Represents members' interests before government agencies, industry associations, and the public. Facilitates exchange of information among members; conducts continuing professional development programs; links members with potential funding sources. **Libraries: Type:** reference. **Awards:** Membership Award. **Frequency:** annual. **Type:** recognition. **Recipient:** for individuals working to increase NAELB membership ● **Frequency:** quinquennial. **Type:** recognition. **Recipient:** for companies maintaining their membership for five consecutive years. **Committees:** Communications; Education; Ethics; Funder/Sponsorship; Meetings; Member Benefits. **Task Forces:** Distance Learning. **Publications:** *Leasing Logic*, quarterly. Newsletter. **Circulation:** 4,000. **Conventions/Meetings:** annual conference, pipe and drape displays (exhibits) - spring ● quarterly workshop - fall.

3383 ■ National Retail Tenants Association (NRTA)

60 Shaker Rd.
East Longmeadow, MA 01028-2760
Ph: (413)525-4565
Fax: (413)525-4590
E-mail: nrta@retailtenants.org
URL: http://www.retailtenants.org
Contact: Paul T. Kinney, Exec. Dir.

Founded: 1997. **Membership Dues:** regular, additional affiliate, $150 (annual) ● affiliate, $375 (annual). **Description:** Fosters the principles of education for the personal, professional and economic development of its members. Helps its members to properly execute their responsibilities under commercial leases. Develops and conducts programs dedicated to furthering the education of its members. Collects, analyzes, and disseminates information with respect to existing and proposed legislation, regulations, and administrative action. **Libraries: Type:** reference. **Holdings:** articles, papers. **Awards: Frequency:** annual. **Type:** scholarship. **Recipient:** to children of NRTA members. **Publications:** *Tenants In-Common*. Newsletter. **Price:** included in membership dues ● Membership Directory. **Price:** included in membership dues. **Conventions/Meetings:** annual Trailblazing for Changing Times - conference, for lease administration professionals (exhibits).

3384 ■ National Truck Leasing System (NTLS)

1S450 Summit Ave., Ste.300
Oakbrook Terrace, IL 60181
Free: (800)729-6857
Fax: (630)953-0040
E-mail: info@nationalease.com
URL: http://www.ntls.com
Contact: John Grainger, Pres.

Founded: 1944. **Members:** 120. **Staff:** 20. **Description:** Franchiser of independent companies. Provides full-service truck leasing. Promotes simplification of operating practices. Sponsors seminars. **Committees:** Advertising; Fuel; Group Purchasing; Maintenance Directors; Management Study. **Formerly:** (1995) NationaLease. **Publications:** *NationaLease Newsletter*, weekly ● Booklets ● Manuals. **Conventions/Meetings:** annual meeting, for owners only - always September in Chicago, IL.

3385 ■ National Vehicle Leasing Association (NVLA)

1199 N Fairfax St., Ste.400
Alexandria, VA 22314
Free: (800)225-NVLA
Fax: (703)548-8536
E-mail: info@nvla.org
URL: http://www.nvla.org
Contact: Tarry Shebesta, Pres.

Founded: 1968. **Members:** 313. **Membership Dues:** regular (based on number of employees), $695-$2,495 (annual) ● associate (single location), $695 (annual) ● associate (multiple location), $1,295 (annual). **Staff:** 4. **Budget:** $1,000,000. **Regional Groups:** 9. **Description:** Companies that lease vehicles. Provides education and information services. Lobbies on behalf of members. Maintains speakers' bureau; offers placement services; compiles statistics. **Computer Services:** database, members and prospective members (for member firms only). **Committees:** Conference; Educational; Electronic Communications; Ethics; Industry Relations; Legislative; Membership; Publications/PR. **Formerly:** (1981) California Vehicle Leasing Association; (1984) Western Vehicle Leasing Association. **Publications:** *Lifeline*, bimonthly. Newsletter. Provides updates on industry issues, events and legislative highlights. ● *Vehicle Leasing Today*, quarterly. Magazine. **Price:** included in membership dues; $39.00 /year for nonmembers. **Advertising:** accepted. **Conventions/Meetings:** annual conference, includes auto show, with exposition (exhibits) ● semiannual seminar.

3386 ■ Textile Rental Services Association of America (TRSA)

1800 Diagonal Rd., Ste.200
Alexandria, VA 22314
Ph: (703)519-0029
Free: (877)770-9274
Fax: (703)519-0026
E-mail: trsa@trsa.org
URL: http://www.trsa.org
Contact: Roger F. Cocivera, Pres./CEO

Founded: 1913. **Members:** 1,400. **Membership Dues:** in U.S. (up to $14,999,999 total revenue), $845-$7,050 (annual) ● in U.S. ($15 million and more total revenue), $48,000 (annual) ● outside U.S. and Canada, $845-$3,000 (annual) ● supplier, $845-$7,780 (annual). **Staff:** 23. **Budget:** $4,000,000. **Description:** Industrial laundering, linen supply, dust control, commercial laundering, and other for-profit textile maintenance and rental services, and allied companies. Conducts seminars in customer contracts, customer service and retention, delivery management, energy conservation, health care laundering, industrial marketing, laundering technology, management development, marketing, preventive maintenance, production management, profitability analysis, sales, strategic planning, supervisory training, and textile management. Compiles statistics. **Libraries: Type:** reference. **Holdings:** 230; archival material, periodicals, video recordings. **Awards:** Centennial Recognition and Hourly Employee Recognition Programs. **Frequency:** annual. **Type:** recognition. **Recipient:** for companies with 100 years and hourly employees with 25 years of service ● Service Awards. **Frequency:** annual. **Type:** recognition. **Recipient:** for executives and managers with 25 or more years of experience. **Computer Services:** Mailing lists, of members and subscriber listings. **Committees:** Associate; Budget; Environmental; Government; Healthcare; Human Resources; Insurance; Long Range Planning; Marketing; Meetings; Membership; Nominating; Plant; Strategic Management; Technology; Textile Management; Textile Specification. **Formerly:** (1979) Linen Supply Association of America. **Publications:** *Sales Tips*, monthly. Newsletter. Contains a monthly bulletin written especially for route representatives. **Price:** $60.00 for 5 copies; $24.00 poster (for set of 2) ● *Textile Control Tips*, monthly ● *Textile Rental Magazine*, monthly. Journal. Covers management information for the linen and uniform rental executive. **Price:** $110.00/year. **Circulation:** 6,000. **Advertising:** accepted ● *TRSA Roster/Buyers' Guide*, annual ● Manuals ● Videos ● Also issues periodical advertising materials. **Conventions/Meetings:** annual convention.

3387 ■ Truck Renting and Leasing Association (TRALA)

675 N Washington St., Ste.410
Alexandria, VA 22314-1939
Ph: (703)299-9120
Fax: (703)299-9115

E-mail: pvroom@trala.org
URL: http://www.trala.org
Contact: Peter J. Vroom, Pres./CEO
Founded: 1978. **Members:** 700. **Membership Dues:** associate, $1,495-$5,980 (annual) ● Industry Council, $2,500-$10,000 (annual) ● regular (minimum), $300 (annual) ● regular (maximum), $195,000 (annual). **Staff:** 6. **Budget:** $2,000,000. **Description:** Truck and trailer rental and leasing companies and systems; suppliers to the industry. Seeks to encourage and promote a favorable climate and sound environment conducive to the renting and leasing of trucks, tractors, and trailers, and dedicated contract carriage. **Awards:** Larry Miller Memorial Scholarship. **Frequency:** annual. **Type:** scholarship. **Recipient:** for dependent children of employees of TRALA member companies. **Committees:** Annual Meeting; Government Relations; Membership; Planning. **Councils:** Associate Member Advisory; Consumer Truck Rental. **Working Groups:** Federal Tax Policy; Operating Tax and Registration. **Publications:** *Inside Trala*, quarterly. Newsletter. Alternate Formats: online ● *TRALA Vehicle*, annual. Membership Directory. **Price:** available to members only. **Circulation:** 3,000. **Advertising:** accepted ● *TRALA Weekly Wire*. Newsletter. Provides a summary of federal and state laws and regulations that affect truck renting and leasing. Includes industry and supplier news. **Price:** available to members only. Alternate Formats: online ● *Truck Renting and Leasing Association—News Digest*, quarterly. Newsletter. **Price:** available to members only. **Conventions/Meetings:** annual National Leadership Conference - meeting (exhibits).

3388 ■ United Association of Equipment Leasing (UAEL)
78120 Calle Estado, Ste.201
La Quinta, CA 92253
Ph: (760)564-2227
Fax: (760)564-2206
E-mail: jwoodley@uael.org
URL: http://www.uael.org
Contact: Joe Woodley, Exec. Dir.
Founded: 1975. **Membership Dues:** broker/lessor (based on annual funded volume by equipment cost), $595-$1,295 (annual) ● funder, $1,995 (annual) ● service provider (based on number of employees), $795-$1,495 (annual). **Description:** Works to foster exchange of information and ideas on transacting business within the equipment leasing and commercial finance industry.

Repair

3389 ■ National Association of Service Dealers (NASD)
c/o North American Retail Dealers Association
4700 W Lake Ave.
Glenview, IL 60025
Ph: (847)375-4713
Free: (800)621-0298
Fax: (866)879-7505
E-mail: tdrake@narda.com
URL: http://www.narda.com
Contact: Tom Drake, Pres./CEO
Founded: 1984. **Members:** 1,200. **Membership Dues:** individual, $295 (annual). **Staff:** 3. **Budget:** $500,000. **Description:** Firms and the service divisions of retail companies that repair home appliances, consumer electronics, and computers. Promotes good relations and mutually profitable affiliation between service companies and manufacturers. Provides business and management information. Sponsors annual School of Service Management. Represents interests of service companies before legislative bodies. Compiles statistics; a division of North American Retail Dealers Association. **Libraries: Type:** reference. **Holdings:** audio recordings, books. **Subjects:** service management. **Awards:** Master of Service Marketing. **Frequency:** annual. **Type:** recognition. **Publications:** *NASD News*, monthly. **Advertising:** accepted. **Conventions/Meetings:** annual conference ● seminar, on service management.

Research

3390 ■ Alliance in Support of Independent Research
c/o Lee A. Pickard, Counsel
1990 M St. NW, Ste.660
Washington, DC 20036
Ph: (202)223-4418
E-mail: alliance@pickdjin.com
URL: http://www.alliance-research.org
Contact: Lee A. Pickard, Counsel
Description: Represents brokers-dealers who furnish independent research and other support services to investment managers. Promotes a regulatory environment in which independent research services and products may be furnished to the money management community for the benefit of investors. Promotes the observance of proper standards under the securities laws for disseminating research of portfolio transactions for managed accounts. **Publications:** Papers. Alternate Formats: online.

3391 ■ Shareholders Research Alliance (SRA)
PO Box 750471
Forest Hills, NY 11375-0471
Ph: (718)896-5060
Fax: (718)896-5326
E-mail: info@shareholdersresearch.com
URL: http://www.shareholdersresearch.com
Contact: Gayle Essary, Admin.
Founded: 2005. **Description:** Develops programs and processes that result in the increased availability of independent financial research on small companies whose shares are publicly traded in the U.S. market. Develops standards that define independent research and independent research providers. Encourages small public companies to commission ongoing independent research.

Restaurant

3392 ■ Council of International Restaurant Real Estate Brokers (CIRB)
c/o William M. Kotis III, Pres.
PO Box 9296
Greensboro, NC 27429
Free: (866)247-2123
Fax: (866)247-2329
E-mail: cirbhq@cirb.net
URL: http://www.cirb.net
Contact: William M. Kotis III, Pres.
Founded: 1991. **Membership Dues:** full, $5,000 (annual). **Multinational. Description:** Represents independent real estate brokers who specialize solely in restaurant and related real estate. Provides assistance to restaurateurs, developers, landlords, and lenders with restaurant real estate brokerage and consulting services. Raises awareness of the specialized area of brokerage and consulting that deals with all phases of the restaurant industry. **Publications:** Newsletter. Alternate Formats: online.

3393 ■ Federation of Dining Room Professionals (FDRP)
1417 Sadler Rd., No. 100
Fernandina Beach, FL 32034
Ph: (904)491-6690
Free: (877)264-FDRP
Fax: (904)491-6689
E-mail: info@fdrp.com
URL: http://www.fdrp.com
Contact: Bernard Martinage, Pres./Founder/Chm.
Founded: 1998. **Members:** 1,000. **Membership Dues:** corporation/institution - life, $375 ● individual - life, $65. **Staff:** 5. **Regional Groups:** 4. **Languages:** English, Spanish. **For-Profit. Multinational. Description:** Offers professional support, development and training material to dining room staff, host-proprietors, and chef-owners. **Libraries: Type:** reference. **Holdings:** 12. **Subjects:** restaurants. **Computer Services:** database, pro-success information resource. **Programs:** FDRP Service Certification. **Publications:** *Dining Room Essentials Manual*. Includes self-study guide for certified associates. **Price:** $22.00 for nonmembers; $17.60 for members ● *Pro-Success*. Newsletter. Alternate Formats: online ● *Professional Service Guide*. Book. **Price:** $65.00 for nonmembers; $52.00 for members. **Conventions/Meetings:** annual American Culinary Federation Convention.

3394 ■ International Society of Restaurant Association Executives (ISRAE)
5024-R Campbell Blvd.
Baltimore, MD 21236
Ph: (410)931-8100 (410)933-3454
Fax: (410)931-8111
E-mail: cristac@clemonsmgmt.com
URL: http://www.israe.org
Contact: Crista LeGrand CMP, Exec. Dir.
Founded: 1936. **Members:** 183. **Membership Dues:** executive, CEO, $125 (annual) ● associate, $75 (annual). **Staff:** 1. **State Groups:** 51. **Multinational. Description:** Restaurant executives and professional staff. Provides an international medium for the exchange of ideas relative to restaurant association management, education to improve the association management skills of its members, a network of cooperation among restaurant associations and restaurant association executives, and public relations to promote the purpose and importance of restaurant associations. **Conventions/Meetings:** semiannual conference - usually summer and fall ● annual meeting.

3395 ■ McDonald's Hispanic Operators Association (MHOA)
c/o Ronald McDonald House Charities
One Kroc Dr.
Oak Brook, IL 60523
Ph: (630)623-7048
Fax: (630)623-7488
URL: http://www.rmhc.org
Founded: 1977. **Members:** 195. **State Groups:** 31. **Description:** Represents Hispanic owners/operators; committed to assuring McDonald's maintains position as preferred QSR within Hispanic Consumer Market. **Awards:** RMHC/HACER Scholarship. **Type:** scholarship. **Recipient:** for Hispanic high school students. **Committees:** Awards; Communications; External Relations; Franchise Relations; Government Relations; Marketing; Operations; Purchasing. **Conventions/Meetings:** annual meeting - usually October in Oak Brook.

Retailing

3396 ■ American Booksellers Association (ABA)
200 White Plains Rd.
Tarrytown, NY 10591
Free: (800)637-0037
Fax: (914)591-2720
E-mail: info@bookweb.org
URL: http://www.bookweb.org
Contact: Avin Mark Domnitz, CEO
Founded: 1900. **Members:** 2,500. **Membership Dues:** regular, provisional, associate, $350 (annual) ● auxiliary, $200 (annual). **Staff:** 175. **Regional Groups:** 10. **Description:** Seeks to meet the needs of members, independently owned bookstores with storefront locations, through education, information dissemination, and advocacy. Supports free speech, literacy, and programs that encourage reading. **Awards:** Book Sense Book of the Year Award. **Frequency:** annual. **Type:** recognition. **Recipient:** for the book that booksellers enjoy selling the most. **Computer Services:** Mailing lists. **Telecommunication Services:** electronic mail, avin@bookweb.org. **Publications:** *ABA Electronic Book Buyer's Handbook*. Lists trade, discount, and return policies of publishers for booksellers. **Price:** free for members. Alternate Formats: online ● *ABACUS*, annual. Survey. Financial survey of member bookstores. ● *Bookselling this Week*, weekly. Newsletter. Covers industry mergers, censorship legislation, market trends, and other topics of interest to booksellers.

Includes book reviews. **Price:** free for members. **Circulation:** 10,500. **Advertising:** accepted. Alternate Formats: online ● *Censorship and First Amendment Rights: A Primer.* **Price:** free ● *Operating a Bookstore: Practical Details for Improving Profit.* **Price:** free. **Conventions/Meetings:** annual BookExpo America - meeting, for bookseller members with exhibit portion owned and managed by Reed Expositions (exhibits).

3397 ■ American Truck Stop Owners Association (ATSOA)
PO Box 4949
Winston-Salem, NC 27115-4949
Ph: (336)744-5555
Fax: (336)744-1184
E-mail: salem1@triad.rr.com
Contact: Lloyd L. Golding, Pres.
Founded: 1981. **Members:** 755. **Membership Dues:** owner, $1,000 (annual). **Staff:** 7. **Budget:** $1,600,000. **Regional Groups:** 8. **State Groups:** 51. **Description:** Truck stop operators and suppliers united to promote and improve the truck stop industry. **Committees:** Advertising; Credit; Government Affairs; Industrial Relations; Marketing; Public Relations. **Conventions/Meetings:** semiannual conference (exhibits) - always Nashville, TN.

3398 ■ American Wholesale Booksellers Association (AWBA)
c/o Patty Walsh, Exec. Sec.
702 S Michigan
South Bend, IN 46601
Ph: (574)288-4141 (574)232-8500
Fax: (303)265-9292
E-mail: info@awba.com
URL: http://www.awba.com
Contact: Patty Walsh, Exec. Sec.
Founded: 1984. **Members:** 40. **Staff:** 1. **Description:** Wholesale booksellers. Aims to: promote and develop the sale and distribution of books; educate customers and publishers about the role of the wholesale sector; develop and advance industry standards; exchange ideas on industry-wide topics such as credit management, industry relations, and methods of distribution. **Publications:** *Publishers: Why Use A Wholesaler?*. Booklet. Alternate Formats: online ● Pamphlet, annual. Lists members' terms, policies, fields of specialization, and services. **Price:** free for bookstores; $15.00 for non-bookstores. **Conventions/Meetings:** annual Membership Meeting - every spring/fall/winter.

3399 ■ Association of Coupon Professionals (ACP)
200 E Howard St., Ste.280
Des Plaines, IL 60018
Ph: (847)297-7773
Fax: (847)297-8428
E-mail: acphq@aol.com
URL: http://www.couponpros.org
Contact: Ron Fischer, Pres.
Founded: 1987. **Members:** 40. **Membership Dues:** category 1, $3,200 (annual) ● category 2, $2,200 (annual) ● category 3, $1,700 (annual). **Staff:** 2. **Description:** Retail clearinghouses, manufacturer redemption agents, and sorting agents that process manufacturers' coupons for retail stores; retailers using commercial coupon processors, state associations and wholesalers with coupon programs, and other companies that process coupons as a by-product of their operations. Seeks to improve business conditions for the coupon industry; promotes use of coupons as a sales and marketing tactic. Works to improve the development, distribution, and redemption of coupons. **Awards:** Industry Impact Award. **Frequency:** annual. **Type:** recognition. **Recipient:** for individuals who have displayed outstanding achievement within an annual period ● William B. Vargill Award. **Frequency:** annual. **Type:** recognition. **Recipient:** for professionals who have succeeded within their own organization. **Publications:** *ACP Coupon Exchange E-zine*, quarterly. Newsletter. Alternate Formats: online ● *Membership Brochure.* Alternate Formats: online ● Reports. Alternate Formats: online. **Conventions/Meetings:** semiannual meeting.

3400 ■ Association for Retail Technology Standards (ARTS)
325 7th St. NW, Ste.1100
Washington, DC 20004-2818
Ph: (202)626-8140
Free: (800)673-4692
Fax: (202)783-6520
E-mail: arts@nrf.com
URL: http://www.nrf-arts.org
Contact: Richard Mader, Exec. Dir.
Founded: 1993. **Members:** 250. **Membership Dues:** retailer (up to $50 million annual sales), $1,500 (annual) ● retailer (between $50 and $500 million annual sales), $2,000 (annual) ● retailer (over $500 million annual sales), $3,000 (annual) ● vendor (up to $50 million annual revenues), $2,500 (annual) ● vendor (between $50 and $500 million annual revenues), $4,000 (annual) ● vendor (over $500 million annual revenues), $5,000 (annual). **Staff:** 3. **Budget:** $500,000. **Description:** Retailers and retail systems/service suppliers. Seeks to provide cost-effective, integrated application solutions that protect retailer's current investment; allows hardware and software components to function together without modifications; provides a common interface for problem determination. Develops standards that allow integration of cross-industry applications; provides compliance certification of hardware and software. EPOS administration standard data model for all retail segments. **Publications:** *Software Distribution in Retail-Workbook*, monthly. Article. **Price:** free for members. Alternate Formats: online. **Conventions/Meetings:** annual trade show (exhibits).

3401 ■ Black Retail Action Group (BRAG)
c/o Rockefeller Center Station
PO Box 1192
New York, NY 10185
Ph: (212)319-7751
Fax: (212)997-5102
E-mail: info@bragusa.org
URL: http://www.bragusa.org
Contact: Gail Monroe-Perry, Pres.
Founded: 1970. **Members:** 300. **Membership Dues:** professional, $50 (annual) ● college student, $25 (annual) ● high school student, $15 (annual). **Staff:** 1. **Description:** Represents minorities dedicated to the inclusion of all groups in the mainstream of the American economy. Promotes the professional development and leadership skills of its members. Assists major retail corporations in the selection, development, and advancement of diverse persons of color. **Committees:** Communication; Community Service; Employment Referral; Fundraising; Gala; Newsletter; Workshops and Seminars. **Publications:** *Brag On.* Newsletter. **Price:** included in membership dues. **Conventions/Meetings:** conference and workshop, minority issues in the 21st Century.

3402 ■ Board Retailers Association (BRA)
PO Box 1170
Wrightsville Beach, NC 28480
Ph: (910)509-0109 (910)509-7475
Fax: (910)509-3181
E-mail: info@boardretailers.org
URL: http://www.boardretailers.org
Contact: Ms. Melissa Clary, Exec. Dir.
Founded: 2001. **Members:** 500. **Membership Dues:** retail, $125 (annual) ● associate bronze (with annual sales of less than $5 million), $500 (annual) ● associate silver (with annual sales between $5 million and $19 million), $1,000 (annual) ● associate gold (with annual sales between $20 million and $99 million), $2,000 (annual) ● associate platinum (with annual sales of more than $100 million), $4,000 (annual). **Staff:** 2. **Description:** Represents over 500 independently owned board sport retailers. Serves as the preeminent voice, for independent retailers of surf, skate, snow and wake products, on a grass-roots level with manufacturers, trade show representatives, and other associations. Provides educational resources, exclusive discounts and savings from vendors on the day-to-day costs of business via the Associate Membership Program. **Telecommunication Services:** electronic mail, melissa@boardretailers.org ● electronic mail, mike@boardretailers.org. **Publications:** Newsletter, annual. **Price:** free. Alternate Formats: online.

3403 ■ CBA
PO Box 62000
Colorado Springs, CO 80962-2000
Ph: (719)265-9895
Free: (800)252-1950
Fax: (719)272-3510
E-mail: info@cbaonline.org
URL: http://www.cbaonline.org
Contact: William R. Anderson, Pres./CEO
Founded: 1950. **Members:** 3,400. **Staff:** 43. **Multinational. Description:** Serves as trade association for retail stores selling Christian books, Bibles, gifts, and Sunday school and church supplies. Compiles statistics; conducts specialized education programs. **Awards:** Store of the Year. **Frequency:** annual. **Type:** recognition ● Supplier of the Year. **Frequency:** annual. **Type:** recognition. **Telecommunication Services:** electronic mail, banderson@cbaonline.org. **Formerly:** (1998) Christian Booksellers Association. **Publications:** *Aspiring Retail.* Magazine. **Price:** $49.95 /year for members; $59.95 /year for nonmembers; $7.50/issue for members; $9.50/issue for nonmembers. Alternate Formats: online ● *CBA Marketplace*, monthly. Magazines. Provides information on business and ministry for Christian retailers and suppliers. **Price:** $7.50 for members; $9.50 for nonmembers. ISSN: 0006-7563. **Circulation:** 8,500. **Advertising:** accepted ● *Suppliers Directory*, annual. **Price:** $50.00 /year for members; $90.00 /year for nonmembers. **Advertising:** accepted. Alternate Formats: CD-ROM. **Conventions/Meetings:** annual International Christian Retail Show - convention (exhibits) - usually July. 2008 July 13-17, Orlando, FL; 2009 July 12-16, Denver, CO.

3404 ■ CIES, Food Business Forum
8455 Colesville Rd., Ste.705
Silver Spring, MD 20910
Ph: (301)563-3383
Fax: (301)563-3386
E-mail: us.office@ciesnet.com
URL: http://www.ciesnet.com
Contact: Alan McClay, CEO
Founded: 1953. **Members:** 369. **Regional Groups:** 5. **Languages:** English, French, German, Japanese, Spanish. **Multinational. Description:** Membership in 44 countries includes: food industry chain store firms with combined outlets of over 100,000; associations; firms supplying articles and services to chain food stores. Fosters cooperation between chain store organizations and their suppliers. Serves as a liaison between members. Assists in the exchange of trainees among member firms. Conducts studies on methods, technical progress, and the growth rate of chain store organizations throughout the world. **Telecommunication Services:** electronic mail, a.mcclay@ciesnet.com. **Committees:** IT; Merchandising; Warehousing, Transportation and Central Distribution; Young Executives. **Formerly:** Food Business Forum; (1989) International Association of Chain Stores. **Publications:** *CIES Yearbook* (in English, French, German, and Spanish), annual. Provides a list of all members by country. ● *Food Business News* (in English and French), monthly. Journal. **Price:** $120.00 for members; $240.00 for nonmembers ● Annual Report, annual. Alternate Formats: online. **Conventions/Meetings:** annual World Food Business Summit - meeting - always June. 2008 June 18-20, Munich, Germany; 2009 June 17-19, New York, NY.

3405 ■ Food Industry Association Executives (FIAE)
PO Box 2510
Flemington, NJ 08822
Ph: (908)782-7833
Fax: (908)782-6907

E-mail: bmcconnell@fiae.net
URL: http://www.fiae.net
Contact: Barbara McConnell, Pres.
Founded: 1927. **Members:** 155. **Membership Dues:** active (based on annual gross revenue), $175-$1,000 (annual) ● affiliate, $500 (annual). **Budget:** $102,000. **Description:** Professional executives of local, state, and national retail grocers associations. **Libraries: Type:** reference. **Awards: Type:** recognition. **Computer Services:** Mailing lists, listserv. **Formerly:** (1959) National Retail Grocers Secretaries Association. **Publications:** *ExecuNews*, bimonthly. Newsletter. Alternate Formats: online ● Membership Directory, annual ● Reports ● Brochure. Alternate Formats: online ● Surveys. Alternate Formats: online. **Conventions/Meetings:** annual convention.

3406 ■ Food Marketing Institute (FMI)
2345 Crystal Dr., Ste.800
Arlington, VA 22202-4801
Ph: (202)452-8444
Fax: (202)429-4519
E-mail: fmi@fmi.org
URL: http://www.fmi.org
Contact: Timothy M. Hammonds, Pres.
Founded: 1977. **Members:** 1,500. **Membership Dues:** associate (tier 1), $2,500 (annual) ● associate (tier 2), $10,000 (annual) ● associate (tier 3), $25,000 (annual) ● associate (tier 4), $50,000 (annual) ● international (based on total sales), $1,000-$3,000 (annual). **Staff:** 130. **Description:** Grocery retailers and wholesalers. Maintains liaison with government and consumers. Conducts 30 educational conferences and seminars per year. Conducts research programs; compiles statistics. **Libraries: Type:** reference. **Awards: Type:** recognition. **Formed by Merger of:** (1977) Supermarket Institute; National Association of Food Chains. **Publications:** *Advantage*, monthly. Magazine. ISSN: 1542-247X. **Advertising:** accepted. Alternate Formats: online ● *Facts About Supermarket Development*, annual. Report ● *Food Marketing Industry Speaks*, annual. Report ● Also publishes guidebooks and training aids. **Conventions/Meetings:** annual show (exhibits).

3407 ■ Home Center Institute (HCI)
c/o North American Retail Hardware Association
5822 W 74th St.
Indianapolis, IN 46278-1787
Ph: (317)290-0338
Free: (800)772-4424
Fax: (317)328-4354
E-mail: contact@nrha.org
URL: http://www.nrha.org
Contact: Kevin Hohman, VP
Founded: 1971. **Members:** 300. **Description:** Chain and independent home center retailers. Conducts research and educational programs on loss prevention, safety, training managers, and executive training. **Libraries: Type:** reference. **Publications:** *The Bottom Line: Cost of Doing Business Survey*, annual. Contains financial operating data for retail home centers and consumer-oriented lumberyards. **Price:** $24.95 for members; $54.95 for nonmembers. ISSN: 1051-2756 ● Report, monthly. **Circulation:** 300. **Conventions/Meetings:** annual Loss Prevention/Safety/Risk Management - conference (exhibits) ● periodic meeting.

3408 ■ Institute of Store Planners (ISP)
25 N Broadway
Tarrytown, NY 10591-3221
Ph: (914)332-0040
Fax: (914)332-1541
E-mail: info@ispo.org
URL: http://ww3.ispo.org
Contact: Andrew R. McQuilkin ISP, Pres.
Founded: 1961. **Members:** 865. **Membership Dues:** student, $10 (annual) ● professional, $200 (annual) ● primary trade (initiation), $500 ● primary trade, $335 (annual) ● educator, $25 (annual) ● life, $25 ● associate, $100 (annual). **Local Groups:** 14. **Multinational. Description:** Persons active in store planning and design; visual merchandisers, students, and educators; contractors and suppliers to the industry; dedicated to the professional growth of members while providing service to the public through improvement of the retail environment. Provides forum for debate and discussion by store design experts, retailers, and public figures. Makes available speakers for store planning and design courses at the college level; develops programs for store planning courses. Sponsors student design competitions and annual international store design competition with awards in 10 categories. Maintains placement service. **Awards:** ISP/VMSD Store of the Year. **Frequency:** annual. **Type:** trophy. **Committees:** Education. **Publications:** *Directory of Store Planners and Consultants*, periodic. Directories. Contains detailed description of 50 member design firms. **Price:** $250.00. Alternate Formats: online ● *ISP International News*, quarterly. Newsletter. Includes committee reports, news of institute activities, and competition results. **Advertising:** accepted. **Conventions/Meetings:** annual conference.

3409 ■ International Association of Airport Duty Free Stores (IAADFS)
2025 M St. NW, Ste.800
Washington, DC 20036-3309
Ph: (202)367-1184
Fax: (202)429-5154
E-mail: iaadfs@iaadfs.org
URL: http://www.iaadfs.org
Contact: Michael L. Payne, Exec. Dir.
Founded: 1970. **Members:** 500. **Membership Dues:** concessionaire/supplier, $450 (annual). **Staff:** 6. **Budget:** $1,000,000. **Languages:** English, Spanish. **Description:** Operators, owners, and suppliers of airport duty-free concessions. Maintains contact with the U.S. Customs Service in order to keep members informed of changes in duty-free and customs regulations. Operates an extensive promotional campaign highlighting the duty-free industry through magazine advertising. **Publications:** *IAADFS Membership Directory and Brand Profile*, annual. **Price:** included in membership dues. **Circulation:** 3,200. **Advertising:** accepted ● *IAADFS Show Guide*, annual. Directory. Contains information about general show, schedule of events, list of exhibitors, and points of interest in the local venue. **Circulation:** 3,200. **Advertising:** accepted. **Conventions/Meetings:** annual Duty Free Show of the Americas - trade show, features active social program (exhibits).

3410 ■ International Council of Shopping Centers (ICSC)
1221 Ave. of the Americas, 41st Fl.
New York, NY 10020-1099
Ph: (646)728-3800
Fax: (732)694-1755
E-mail: icsc@icsc.org
URL: http://www.icsc.org
Contact: Michael P. Kercheval, Pres./CEO
Founded: 1957. **Members:** 35,000. **Membership Dues:** public and academic affiliate, $50 (annual) ● public/academic, $100 (annual) ● regular/associate, $800 (annual) ● student, $50 (annual). **Staff:** 100. **Budget:** $35,000,000. **Description:** Owners, developers, retailers, and managers of shopping centers; architects, engineers, contractors, leasing brokers, promotion agencies, and others who provide services and products for shopping center owners, shopping center merchant associations, retailers, and public and academic organizations. Promotes professional standards of performance in the development, construction, financing, leasing, management, and operation of shopping centers throughout the world. Engages in research and data gathering on all aspects of shopping centers; compiles statistics. Sponsors school for professional development annually, offering courses in all areas of the industry; leading to the designations CSM (Certified Shopping Center Manager) and CMD (Certified Marketing Director), and CLS (Certified Leasing Specialist). Holds 200 seminars and conferences annually. **Libraries: Type:** reference. **Holdings:** 1,000; audiovisuals, books, clippings, periodicals. **Subjects:** retailing, real estate. **Awards:** International Design and Development Awards. **Frequency:** annual. **Type:** recognition. **Recipient:** for the best shopping center design ● Maxi Award. **Frequency:** annual. **Type:** recognition. **Recipient:** for shopping center promotions. **Computer Services:** Mailing lists, of members. **Committees:** Political Action. **Publications:** *Directory of Products and Services*, annual. Lists suppliers of products and securities to the shopping center industry. **Price:** $24.95 for members; $49.95 for nonmembers. **Circulation:** 6,000. **Advertising:** accepted. Alternate Formats: online ● *Government Affairs Report*, quarterly ● *ICSC Membership Directory*, annual ● *ICSC Research Quarterly* ● *Journal of Shopping Center Research*, semiannual. **Price:** $24.95 for members; $49.95 for nonmembers and institutions ● *Legal Update*, triennial ● *Monthly Mall Merchandise Indy* ● *Retail Challenge*, quarterly ● *Shopping Centers Today* (in English and Spanish), monthly. Magazine. **Advertising:** accepted. **Conventions/Meetings:** annual convention.

3411 ■ International League of Antiquarian Booksellers (ILAB)
c/o Tom Congalton
35 W Maple Ave.
Merchantville, NJ 08109-5141
Ph: (856)665-2284
Fax: (856)665-3639
E-mail: info@ilab.org
URL: http://www.ilab-lila.com
Contact: Michael Steinbach, Pres.
Founded: 1947. **Members:** 2,000. **National Groups:** 20. **Languages:** English, French. **Description:** Represents national associations of antiquarian booksellers around the world. Organizes professional training courses for members. Sponsors book fairs. **Awards:** Bibliographic Award. **Frequency:** periodic. **Type:** recognition. **Affiliated With:** Antiquarian Booksellers Association of America. **Publications:** Directory ● Newsletter. Alternate Formats: online. **Conventions/Meetings:** biennial congress, with bookfair (exhibits).

3412 ■ International Mystery Shopping Alliance (IMSA)
c/o Arcadio Roselli
210 Crossways Park Dr.
Woodbury, NY 11797
Ph: (516)576-1188
Fax: (516)576-1195
E-mail: aroselli@serviceevaluation.com
URL: http://www.theimsa.com
Contact: Jeff Hall, Pres.
Founded: 2003. **Multinational. Description:** Improves the quality of mystery shopping services. Promotes high quality standards in service evaluation. Provides technical and communication platforms for mystery shopping.

3413 ■ Mailorder Gardening Association (MGA)
5836 Rockburn Woods Way
Elkridge, MD 21075
Ph: (410)540-9830
Fax: (410)540-9827
E-mail: info@mailordergardening.com
URL: http://www.mailordergardening.com
Contact: Don Zeider, Pres.
Founded: 1934. **Membership Dues:** regular, $300-$1,250 (annual) ● subsidiary/wholesale/allied, $375 (annual). **Description:** Mailorder gardening catalog companies and gardening magazine publishers. Promotes growth and development of the mailorder gardening industries. Facilitates exchange of information among members. Formulates standards of business practice and ethics for the industry. Monitors legislation and business practices of interest to members. Provides services to members including marketing and statistical data, supply source referrals, and consumer awareness campaigns. Makes available children's services; sponsors competitions. **Awards:** Kids Growing With Dutch Bulbs Awards. **Frequency:** annual. **Type:** recognition. **Recipient:** for schools and youth groups using bulb flowers to beautify public spaces. **Telecommunication Services:** electronic mail, consumer@mailordergardening.com. **Committees:** Education and Training; Industry Cooperation; Legislative; Public Relations; Research and Evaluation; USPS Mailers Technical Advisory. **Affiliated With:** Direct Marketing Associa-

tion; Parcel Shippers Association. **Publications:** *MGA Messenger*. Newsletter. Alternate Formats: online. **Conventions/Meetings:** annual convention ● semiannual meeting - always winter and summer.

3414 ■ Museum Store Association (MSA)
4100 E Mississippi Ave., Ste.800
Denver, CO 80246-3055
Ph: (303)504-9223
Fax: (303)504-9585
E-mail: rherman@msaweb.org
URL: http://www.museumdistrict.com
Contact: Beverly J. Barsook, Exec. Dir.
Founded: 1955. **Members:** 2,375. **Membership Dues:** exhibitor affiliate, $275 (annual) ● corporate sponsor, $775 (annual) ● exhibitor affiliate/corporate sponsor, $1,050 (annual) ● museum (based on annual gross income), $145-$385 (annual) ● commercial affiliate, $550 (annual). **Staff:** 10. **Regional Groups:** 10. **Description:** Provides education, buying, and sales information and education for staff in museum stores, including museums of fine arts, history, ethnography, and science. Encourages dialogue and assistance among members. **Awards:** Annual Meeting Scholarship. **Frequency:** annual. **Type:** scholarship. **Recipient:** for members only. **Publications:** *Manager's Guide*. Book. **Price:** $49.95 for members; $69.95 for nonmembers. Alternate Formats: CD-ROM ● *MSA Directory* ● *Museum Retail Industry Report*. Book. **Price:** $245.00 for members; $349.00 for nonmembers ● *Museum Retailing*, bimonthly. Newsletter ● *Museum Store*, quarterly. Magazine. Provides information on museum store management; includes information on new products and calendar of events. **Price:** included in membership dues; $34.00 for nonmembers in U.S.; $59.00 for nonmembers outside U.S. **Circulation:** 2,700 ● *New Store Workbook*. **Price:** $49.95 for members; $69.95 for nonmembers ● *Product News*, quarterly. Newsletter. **Conventions/Meetings:** annual Museum Retail Conference and Expo - conference and trade show, with educational sessions and vendors (exhibits) - usually April/May.

3415 ■ National Association of College Stores (NACS)
500 E Lorain St.
Oberlin, OH 44074
Ph: (440)775-7777
Free: (800)622-7498
Fax: (440)775-4769
E-mail: membership@nacs.org
URL: http://www.nacs.org
Contact: Brian E. Cartier CAE, CEO
Founded: 1923. **Members:** 4,100. **Membership Dues:** individual/professional, $50 (annual) ● affiliate and full store (minimum), $200 (annual) ● associate (plus initiation fee of $250), $425 (annual) ● full store (maximum), $2,300 (annual). **Staff:** 350. **Budget:** $135,000,000. **State Groups:** 29. **Description:** Institutional, private, leased, and cooperative college stores (2,800) selling books, supplies, and other merchandise to college students, faculty, and staff; associate members include publishers and suppliers (1,200). Seeks to effectively serve higher education by providing educational research, advocacy and other to college stores and their suppliers. Maintains NACSCORP, Inc., a wholly owned subsidiary corporation, which distributes trade and mass market books and educational software. Sponsors seminars. Conducts manager certification, specialized education, and research programs. Maintains College Stores Research and Educational Foundation which provides grants for educational programs and conducts research. **Telecommunication Services:** electronic mail, bcartier@nacs.org. **Committees:** Annual Meeting Program; Associate Advisory; Education; Financial Survey; General Book; Health Science Stores; Large Stores Group; Merchandising; Nominating; Privately Owned Stores; Smaller Stores; Textbook/Course Materials. **Subgroups:** Campus Computer Resellers Alliance. **Task Forces:** Book Donations; Disabilities; Environmental Concerns; Store Activities. **Formerly:** (1931) College Bookstore Association. **Publications:** *Campus Marketplace*, weekly. Newsletter. Includes news of interest to college store managers. **Advertising:** accepted ● *The College Store*, bimonthly. Magazine. Includes annual *NACS Buyer's Guide* listing member vendors by product category and alphabetically. ● *College Store Monthly Planner*, annual. Serves as a guide to college store industry events; includes operational checklists and a 16-month calendar. ● *NACS Book Buyers Manual*, annual. Provides list of textbook publishers and their policies. ● *NACS Directory of Colleges and College Stores*, annual ● *NACS Directory of Publishers*, biennial. Lists textbook publishers who provide free copies to faculty members. ● *NACS Schedule of College and University Dates*, annual. **Conventions/Meetings:** annual CAMEX - meeting, college retailing (exhibits).

3416 ■ National Association of Convenience Stores (NACS)
1600 Duke St.
Alexandria, VA 22314
Ph: (703)684-3600
Free: (800)966-6227
Fax: (703)836-4564
E-mail: nacs@nacsonline.com
URL: http://www.nacsonline.com
Contact: Henry Armour, Pres./CEO
Founded: 1961. **Members:** 4,000. **Membership Dues:** supplier, $600 (annual) ● domestic retailer (based on sales), $200-$10,000 (annual) ● international retailer (based on number of stores and/or stores owned and/or franchised), $750-$2,500 (annual). **Staff:** 55. **Multinational. Description:** Retail stores that sell gasoline, fast foods, soft drinks, dairy products, beer, cigarettes, publications, grocery items, snacks, and nonfood items and are usually open seven days per week for longer hours than conventional supermarkets. Convenience stores generally stock 1,500 to 3,000 items, compared to 7,000 or more in most supermarkets. Estimates there are some 140,000 convenience stores. Conducts educational and legislative activities; sponsors management seminars. Maintains task forces; compiles statistics. **Libraries: Type:** reference. **Holdings:** 500; periodicals, reports, video recordings. **Subjects:** convenience store industry. **Awards:** Global Scholarship. **Frequency:** annual. **Type:** scholarship ● Jim Yates Scholarship. **Frequency:** annual. **Type:** scholarship. **Recipient:** for college students. **Computer Services:** database, of convenience store industry and membership ● mailing lists, of daily news or industry events. **Telecommunication Services:** hotline, show hotline and administration services, (877)684-3600. **Committees:** Audit; Government Relations; Member Services; Research and Development; Supplier. **Publications:** *Compensation Survey*, annual. **Price:** $75.00 for members; $150.00 for nonmembers ● *NACS Magazine*, monthly. **Price:** included in membership dues; $70.00 /year for nonmembers. **Advertising:** accepted. Alternate Formats: online ● *National Association of Convenience Stores—Membership and Services Directory*, annual. Membership Directory. **Price:** included in membership dues; $200.00 for nonmembers. **Circulation:** 4,000 ● *State of the Industry Report/Fact Book*, annual. **Price:** $450.00 for nonmembers; $150.00 for members. Alternate Formats: CD-ROM. **Conventions/Meetings:** annual convention, convenience store and petroleum marketing industry event with more than 1,700 exhibitors (exhibits) ● annual show - 2008 Oct. 4-7, Chicago, IL.

3417 ■ National Association of Resale and Thrift Shops (NARTS)
PO Box 80707
St. Clair Shores, MI 48080-5707
Ph: (586)294-6700
Free: (800)544-0751
Fax: (586)294-6776
E-mail: info@narts.org
URL: http://www.narts.org
Contact: Chris Cowman, Pres.
Founded: 1984. **Members:** 1,100. **Membership Dues:** primary, $120 (annual) ● secondary, $84 (annual) ● association, $36 (annual) ● provisional, $120 (annual) ● affiliate, $165 (annual). **Staff:** 2. **Budget:** $250,000. **Description:** Owners, managers, professionals, and other individuals involved in the resale and thrift shop industry. Works for the exchange of ideas and information among members, develops public recognition and knowledge of the field, and promotes professionalism in the industry. Helps members to become more professional and to increase profits. Offers educational materials. **Libraries: Type:** not open to the public. **Holdings:** audio recordings, books. **Subjects:** resale, advertising, marketing. **Awards:** Affiliate Member Award. **Frequency:** annual. **Type:** recognition. **Recipient:** to an affiliate member for outstanding support and participation in the association ● Educational Service Award. **Frequency:** annual. **Type:** recognition. **Recipient:** for member in recognition of significant commitment to enhance and enrich educational opportunities for the membership ● Outstanding Service Award. **Frequency:** annual. **Type:** recognition. **Recipient:** for a member with exceptional involvement, distinctive commitment, and outstanding service to the association ● Renee River Award. **Type:** recognition. **Recipient:** to a past board member for outstanding service and contributions to the association. **Computer Services:** database ● mailing lists ● online services. **Committees:** Conference. **Publications:** *A Guide to Opening A Resale Shop*. Book. **Price:** $30.00 for members; $45.00 for nonmembers ● *Operating Survey 2005*. Book. Presents a statistical survey for the resale industry. **Price:** $45.00 for members; $85.00 for nonmembers ● *Your NARTS Network*, monthly. Newsletter. **Price:** included in membership dues. **Advertising:** accepted. **Conventions/Meetings:** annual conference (exhibits) - usually last week in June. 2008 June 27-30, Indianapolis, IN ● quarterly regional meeting ● quarterly workshop.

3418 ■ National Association for Retail Marketing Services (NARMS)
PO Box 906
Plover, WI 54467-0906
Ph: (715)342-0948
Free: (888)52N-ARMS
Fax: (715)342-1943
E-mail: admin@narms.com
URL: http://www.narms.com
Contact: Daniel C. Borschke CAE, Pres./CEO
Founded: 1995. **Members:** 498. **Membership Dues:** merchandising/marketing company (based on total company revenue), $595-$6,000 (annual) ● divisional, $250 (annual) ● manufacturer, associate, retailer, $1,500 (annual). **Staff:** 3. **Budget:** $500,000. **Description:** Individuals and businesses providing retail merchandising services. Seeks to advance the retail merchandising industries. Represents members' collective interests; facilitates communication and cooperation among members. **Absorbed:** (2003) Field Marketing Services Association. **Formerly:** (2003) National Association for Retail Merchandising Services. **Publications:** *NARMS Today*, quarterly. Newsletter. Alternate Formats: online. **Conventions/Meetings:** annual conference - 2009 Apr. 4-7, Colorado Springs, CO; 2011 Apr. 9-12, Monterey, CA ● annual meeting (exhibits).

3419 ■ National Confectionery Sales Association (NCSA)
c/o Teresa M. Tarantino, Co-Exec. Dir.
10225 Berea Rd., Ste.B
Cleveland, OH 44102
Ph: (216)631-8200
Fax: (216)631-8210
E-mail: ttarantino@mail.propressinc.com
URL: http://www.candyhalloffame.com
Contact: Teresa M. Tarantino, Co-Exec. Dir.
Founded: 1899. **Members:** 375. **Membership Dues:** individual, $100 (annual). **Staff:** 2. **Regional Groups:** 6. **Description:** Salespersons, brokers, sales managers, wholesalers, and manufacturers in the candy industry. Maintains Candy Hall of Fame. **Awards:** Candy Hall of Fame Award. **Frequency:** annual. **Type:** recognition. **Recipient:** for years in industry and community service. **Formerly:** (2000) National Confectionery Sales Association of America. **Publications:** *National Confectionery Sales Association of America-Journal*, annual. Includes directory of members and obituaries. **Price:** free. **Circulation:**

1,000. **Advertising:** accepted. **Conventions/Meetings:** annual meeting and convention, with Candy Hall of Fame inductions.

3420 ■ National Convenience Store Advisory Group (NCSAG)
2063 Oak St.
Jacksonville, FL 32204
Ph: (904)384-1010
Free: (877)466-2724
Fax: (904)387-3362
URL: http://www.csdecisions.com
Contact: Joseph H. Howton, Exec. VP/CEO

Founded: 1983. **Members:** 500. **Membership Dues:** retail, $300 (annual) ● associate, $350 (annual). **Staff:** 4. **Budget:** $500,000. **For-Profit. Description:** Top-level management of retail companies organized to enhance buying power, utilization of merchandising programs, and exchange of ideas. Offers volume discounts on equipment, products, and services. Provides information on the latest equipment, marketing trends, and business methods. Implements a national program to test new products for resale in the convenience store/petroleum market industry. **Libraries: Type:** not open to the public. **Awards:** NCSAG Scholarship Fund. **Frequency:** annual. **Type:** scholarship. **Recipient:** for members with a 2.7 or higher GPA. **Subgroups:** Young Executive Organization. **Formerly:** (1987) National Advisory Group, Convenience Stores/Petroleum Companies; (2000) National Advisory Group, Convenience Stores/ Petroleum Marketers Association. **Publications:** *Buying Guide*, quarterly. Newsletter. **Price:** free for members ● *NCSAG Bulletin*, quarterly. **Conventions/ Meetings:** semiannual meeting and symposium (exhibits) - always spring and fall.

3421 ■ National Grocers Association (NGA)
1005 N Glebe Rd., Ste.250
Arlington, VA 22201-5758
Ph: (703)516-0700
Fax: (703)516-0115
E-mail: info@nationalgrocers.org
URL: http://www.nationalgrocers.org
Contact: Thomas K. Zaucha, Pres./CEO

Founded: 1982. **Members:** 2,060. **Staff:** 30. **Budget:** $5,000,000. **State Groups:** 50. **Local Groups:** 10. **Description:** Independent food retailers; wholesale food distributors servicing 29,000 food stores. Promotes industry interests and works to advance understanding, trade, and cooperation among all sectors of the food industry. Represents members' interests before the government. Aids in the development of programs designed to improve the productivity and efficiency of the food distribution industry. Offers services in areas such as store planning and engineering, personnel selection and training, operations, and advertising. Sponsors seminars and inhouse training. Maintains liaison with Women Grocers of America (see separate entry), which serves as an advisory arm. **Libraries: Type:** reference. **Holdings:** 500. **Awards:** Clarence G. Adamy Great American Award. **Type:** recognition ● Spirit of America Award. **Type:** recognition. **Recipient:** for leadership and distinction in the areas of community and government affairs for the food distribution industry. **Departments:** Communications; Public Affairs; Research and Education. **Formed by Merger of:** National Association of Retail Grocers of the United States; Cooperative Food Distributors of America. **Publications:** *Action Alert*, periodic ● *Advocate*. Newsletter ● *Bit by Bit Technology Newsletter* ● *Congressional or Regulatory Update*, periodic. Newsletter. Contains report of current congressional and regulatory affairs. **Price:** included in membership dues ● *Employee and Labor Relations*, quarterly. Newsletter. **Price:** included in membership dues ● *Express Lane*, weekly or biweekly. Newsletter. Contains news and information about the activities of the association and its staff. **Price:** included in membership dues ● *National Grocer*, quarterly ● *Retail Operations White Papers*, periodic. **Conventions/Meetings:** monthly conference ● annual Supermarket Synergy Showcase - convention (exhibits).

3422 ■ National Piggly Wiggly Operators Association (NPWOA)
Piggly Wiggly, LLC
2605 Sagebrush Dr., Ste.200
Flower Mound, TX 75028-2739
Ph: (972)906-7191
Free: (800)800-8215
E-mail: mrpig@pigglywiggly.com
URL: http://www.pigglywiggly.com
Contact: Jim Garrison, Pres.

Founded: 1916. **Members:** 2,500. **Staff:** 2. **Budget:** $450,000. **Description:** Owners and personnel of independently owned food stores that operate under Piggly Wiggly franchises. Shares experiences and provides a forum for Piggly Wiggly owners and personnel and the manufacturers, processors, and suppliers. **Awards:** Clarence Saunders Operator of the Year. **Frequency:** annual. **Type:** recognition. **Publications:** *Turnstile*, monthly. Newspaper. **Conventions/Meetings:** annual meeting and lecture, includes demonstrations (exhibits).

3423 ■ National Retail Federation (NRF)
325 7th St. NW, Ste.1100
Washington, DC 20004
Ph: (202)783-7971
Free: (800)673-4692
Fax: (202)737-2849
E-mail: mullint@nrf.com
URL: http://www.nrf.com
Contact: Tracy Mullin, Pres./CEO

Founded: 1990. **Membership Dues:** retailer (minimum), $175 (annual) ● retailer (maximum), $2,970 (annual) ● international retailer, $195-$1,250 (annual) ● national association, $400-$1,000 (annual) ● company (minimum), $500 (annual) ● company (maximum), $8,000 (annual) ● university and educational institution, $150 (annual) ● local association and chamber of commerce, $100 (annual). **Staff:** 70. **State Groups:** 50. **Description:** Represents state retail associations, several dozen national retail associations, as well as large and small corporate members representing the breadth and diversity of the retail industry's establishment and employees. Conducts informational and educational conferences related to all phases of retailing including financial planning and cash management, taxation, economic forecasting, expense planning, shortage control, credit, electronic data processing, telecommunications, merchandise management, buying, traffic, security, supply, materials handling, store planning and construction, personnel administration, recruitment and training, and advertising and display. **Libraries: Type:** reference. **Holdings:** 1,000. **Subjects:** retail management, fashion merchandising. **Awards:** American Spirit Award. **Frequency:** annual. **Type:** recognition ● Gold Medal in Retailing. **Frequency:** annual. **Type:** recognition ● Leadership/ Public Service Award. **Frequency:** annual. **Type:** recognition. **Committees:** Credit Management; Employee Benefits; Employment Law; Environmental Affairs; Financial Executives; Foreign Trade; Government and Legal Affairs; Human Resources; Information Systems; Internal Audit; International Credit; Investor Relations; Lawyers; Logistics; Loss Prevention; Marketing; Political Action; Public Relations; Retail Accounting Principles; Skills Standards; Small Stores Sales Promotion; Taxation; Technical; Transportation. **Task Forces:** Bank Check. **Absorbed:** (1995) Apparel Retailers of America. **Formed by Merger of:** American Retail Federation; National Retail Merchants Association. **Publications:** *NRF Foundation Focus*, quarterly. Newsletter. Alternate Formats: online ● *NRF Update*. Newsletter. Alternate Formats: online ● *STORES Magazine*, monthly. Provides retail executives and other retail personnel with information on current trends, concepts, and promotional innovations in retail. **Price:** $120.00/year. ISSN: 0039-1867. **Circulation:** 35,000. **Advertising:** accepted ● *Washington Retail Report*, weekly. Newsletter. Covers federal legislative and regulatory issues. **Price:** included in membership dues. **Conventions/Meetings:** annual Human Resources Summit - roundtable ● annual Retail's Big Show - convention.

3424 ■ NATSO
1737 King St., Ste.200
Alexandria, VA 22314
Ph: (703)549-2100
Free: (888)275-6287
Fax: (703)684-4525
E-mail: acarle@natso.com
URL: http://www.natso.com
Contact: Lisa J. Mullings, Pres./CEO

Founded: 1960. **Members:** 1,140. **Membership Dues:** strategic partner, $1,300 (annual) ● preferred partner, $6,000 (annual) ● Chairman's Circle, $14,000 (annual). **Staff:** 20. **Budget:** $3,000,000. **Description:** Owners and operators of travel plazas and truck stops that can facilitate professional truckers and all highway travelers; allied members include oil companies and other product and service vendors. Seeks to elevate the image of the industry by encouraging superior service and facilities. Provides credit information, government affairs representation, public relations services, and educational training programs. **Libraries: Type:** reference. **Subjects:** transportation industries. **Awards:** Distinguished Member Award. **Frequency:** annual. **Type:** recognition. **Recipient:** for community/industry service ● The NATSO Foundation Bill Moon Memorial Scholarship. **Frequency:** annual. **Type:** scholarship. **Recipient:** for academics, essay. **Computer Services:** Online services, check verification updated throughout the day with good and bad check information for truck stops and travel plazas. **Telecommunication Services:** electronic mail, lmullings@natso.com. **Committees:** Allied Advisory; Conventions; Education; Government Affairs/PAC; Information and Research; Membership and Member Services; Public Awareness; Strategic Planning; Technology and Systems. **Formerly:** (1993) National Association of Truck Stop Operators; (2000) NATSO, Representing the Travel Plaza and Truckstop Industry. **Publications:** *Membership Directory and Buyers' Guide*, annual. **Price:** free for members; $1,100.00 for nonmembers. **Circulation:** 3,000. **Advertising:** accepted. Alternate Formats: diskette ● *NATSO News Weekly*. Newsletter. Includes legislative and industry news. **Advertising:** accepted. Alternate Formats: online ● *Stop Watch*, bimonthly. Magazine. **Circulation:** 2,500. **Advertising:** accepted ● *Truckers News*, monthly. Magazine. ISSN: 1040-2284. **Circulation:** 225,000. **Advertising:** accepted. **Conventions/Meetings:** annual Government Affairs Conference (exhibits) ● annual show (exhibits).

3425 ■ Natural Products Association
2112 E 4th St., Ste.200
Santa Ana, CA 92705
Ph: (714)460-7732
Free: (800)966-6632
Fax: (714)460-7444
E-mail: natural@naturalproductsassoc.org
URL: http://www.naturalproductsassoc.org
Contact: David Taylor, Pres.

Founded: 1936. **Members:** 8,000. **Membership Dues:** retailer, $30 (annual). **Staff:** 16. **Budget:** $4,000,000. **Regional Groups:** 7. **Description:** Represents retailers, wholesalers, brokers, distributors and manufacturers of natural, nutritional, dietetic foods, supplements, and natural body care products. **Committees:** Advocacy Action; Association Governance; Communications; ComPLI; Conventions; Education; History and Archives. **Formerly:** (1970) National Dietary Foods Association; (2006) National Nutritional Foods Association. **Publications:** *NNFA Today*, 11/year. Newsletter. Provides information on industry business practices, legislative issues, scientific updates and certification programs. **Price:** free for members. **Circulation:** 7,000. Alternate Formats: online ● Reports, annual. Alternate Formats: online. **Conventions/Meetings:** annual convention and trade show (exhibits) - always July.

3426 ■ Planning and Visual Education Partnership (PAVE)
4651 Sheridan St., Ste.470
Hollywood, FL 33021
Ph: (954)893-7225
Fax: (954)893-8375

E-mail: pave@paveinfo.org
URL: http://p-a-v-e.info
Contact: Richard Stolls, Pres.
Founded: 1992. **Members:** 106. **Staff:** 6. **Description:** Retail executives, visual merchandisers, store planners, architects, specifiers, students. Seeks to educate and motivate members and encourage interaction among their related fields. Holds annual design competition; offers an internship program; donates proceeds of shows toward financial aid for students. **Awards:** Student Design Competition. **Frequency:** annual. **Type:** scholarship. **Recipient:** to student selected by PAVE board members. **Committees:** Curriculum; Field Studies; Gala Student Support; Industry Auction; Internship; Student Design Competition Guidelines; Vision. **Conventions/Meetings:** annual competition, with student design competition - December, New York City ● annual seminar.

3427 ■ Retail Industry Leaders Association (RILA)
1700 N Moore St., Ste.2250
Arlington, VA 22209
Ph: (703)841-2300
Fax: (703)841-1184
E-mail: erin.dimuzio@retail-leaders.org
URL: http://www.retail-leaders.org
Contact: Ms. Sandy Kennedy, Pres.
Founded: 1969. **Members:** 400. **Staff:** 25. **Description:** Mass discount retailing chains and suppliers to the mass retail industry. Aims to conduct research and educational programs on every phase of mass retailing. Conducts studies on industry practices and procedures and generates information on all areas of the business. Maintains public affairs program for liaison with government at the state and federal levels. Compiles statistics. **Libraries: Type:** reference. **Committees:** Financial and Technology Executives; Governmental Affairs Executives; Human Resources and Store Operations Executives; Logistics; Loss Prevention, Auditing, and Safety Executives; Supply Chain Security; Tax Executives. **Absorbed:** (1986) Association of General Merchandise Chains. **Formerly:** (1970) Mass Merchandising Research Foundation; (1977) Mass Retailing Institute; (1987) National Mass Retailing Institute.

3428 ■ Retail Marketing Coalition (RMC)
Address Unknown since 2008
Members: 6. **Multinational. Description:** Works as comprehensive source of retail-based brand marketing information available to the public. **Telecommunication Services:** electronic mail, dblatt@popai.com. **Affiliated With:** Association of Independent Corrugated Converters; International Sign Association; National Association for Retail Marketing Services; National Association of Store Fixture Manufacturers; Point-of-Purchase Advertising International; Promotion Marketing Association. **Conventions/Meetings:** conference.

3429 ■ Retail Tobacco Dealers of America (RTDA)
4 Bradley Park Ct., Ste.2-H
Columbus, GA 31904-3637
Ph: (706)494-1143
Fax: (706)494-1893
E-mail: info@rtda.org
URL: http://www.rtda.org
Contact: Mr. Joseph Rowe Jr., Exec. Dir.
Founded: 1932. **Members:** 2,100. **Membership Dues:** retailer (international and domestic), broker, $125 (annual) ● associate, $500 (annual) ● international distributor, $200 (annual). **Staff:** 4. **State Groups:** 2. **Local Groups:** 7. **Description:** Retailers of legal tobacco products and related items. Conducts marketing and merchandising programs. **Publications:** *Tobacco Retailers' Almanac*, annual. Directory. **Advertising:** accepted ● Newsletter, quarterly. **Conventions/Meetings:** annual convention (exhibits).

3430 ■ Women Grocers of America (WGA)
c/o National Grocers Association
1005 N Glebe Rd., Ste.250
Arlington, VA 22201-5758
Ph: (703)516-0700
Fax: (703)516-0115
E-mail: wga@nationalgrocers.org
URL: http://www.nationalgrocers.org
Contact: Kristen Comley, Liaison
Founded: 1983. **Members:** 100. **Membership Dues:** segment of the grocery industry, $15 (annual). **Staff:** 1. **Description:** Serves as an information and advisory arm to the National Grocers Association (see separate entry). Supports and encourages the education of students pursuing grocery industry-related careers in the independent segment of the industry through its scholarship program. Encourages all segments of the food industry to promote breast cancer awareness and prevention. Participates in and supports the programs offered by the National Grocers Association. **Awards:** Mary Macey Scholarship. **Frequency:** annual. **Type:** scholarship. **Recipient:** for planning a career in the independent sector of the grocery industry ● Woman of the Year. **Frequency:** annual. **Type:** recognition. **Recipient:** for industry retail or wholesale woman. **Telecommunication Services:** electronic mail, kcomley@nationalgrocers.org. **Publications:** *Exchange*, 3/year. Newsletter ● Brochure. **Conventions/Meetings:** annual meeting, held in conjunction with the NGA.

3431 ■ World Floor Covering Association (WFCA)
2211 E Howell Ave.
Anaheim, CA 92806
Ph: (714)978-6440
Free: (800)624-6880
Fax: (714)978-6066
E-mail: wfca@wfca.org
URL: http://www.wfca.org
Contact: D. Christopher Davis, Pres./CEO
Founded: 1995. **Members:** 3,000. **Membership Dues:** regular, $275 (annual) ● associate, $525-$1,050 (annual). **Staff:** 10. **Budget:** $6,000,000. **Description:** Retail floorcovering store owners and managers; floorcovering distributors and manufacturers. Provides liaison, through a Washington, DC lobbyist, between the membership and government organizations that affect the business. Conducts seminars promoting professional development and increased profits; compiles business activity statistics; sponsors research. **Libraries: Type:** reference. **Awards:** Hall of Fame. **Frequency:** annual. **Type:** recognition. **Additional Websites:** http://wfca-pro.org. **Committees:** Education; Executive. **Councils:** Advisory. **Formed by Merger of:** (1995) American Floorcovering Association; Western Floor Covering Association. **Publications:** *World Floor Covering Association—Annual Management Report*. Annual Report. **Price:** $75.00 for members; $150.00 for nonmembers. **Conventions/Meetings:** annual Surfaces - conference (exhibits) ● annual symposium.

Rubber

3432 ■ International Institute of Synthetic Rubber Producers (IISRP)
2077 S Gessner Rd., Ste.133
Houston, TX 77063
Ph: (713)783-7511
Fax: (713)783-7253
E-mail: info@iisrp.com
URL: http://www.iisrp.com
Contact: James L. McGraw, CEO/Managing Dir.
Founded: 1960. **Members:** 42. **Membership Dues:** corporate, $20,000 (annual). **Staff:** 4. **Budget:** $1,000,000. **Multinational. Description:** Synthetic rubber manufacturers in 21 countries. Promotes standardization of synthetic rubber polymers; cooperates with governmental departments and agencies in matters affecting the industry; compiles statistics. Has made research grants to universities and institutes in Japan, United States, France, United Kingdom, Germany, and the Netherlands. Maintains European office in Milan, Italy and Far Eastern Office in Tokyo, Japan. **Libraries: Type:** not open to the public. **Awards:** Institute Annual Award. **Frequency:** annual. **Type:** recognition. **Recipient:** for technical and/or general contributions to the synthetic rubber industry. **Telecommunication Services:** electronic mail, jlmcgraw@iisrp.com. **Committees:** Environmental Health; Statistical; Technical and Operating. **Formerly:** IISRP. **Publications:** *Butadiene Popcorn Polymer Resource Book*. **Price:** $100.00 for members ● *Proceedings of the IISRP Annual Meeting*, annual. Includes a complete, verbatim report of each conference. **Price:** $250.00 for members ● *The Story of an Industry*. Report. **Price:** $20.00/copy in North America, plus $5 shipping; $40.00/copy outside North America, plus $20 shipping ● *Synthetic Rubber Manual*, 3/year. Lists all synthetic rubbers manufactured, including the technical and quality criteria for each individual brand. **Price:** $250.00 for members ● *Worldwide Rubber Statistics*, annual. Lists all synthetic rubber producers' names, addresses, and locations; includes 10-year production figures by type and area and 5-year forecasts. **Price:** $1,050.00/issue in North America, plus $5 shipping; $1,050.00/issue outside North America, plus $15 shipping. **Conventions/Meetings:** annual meeting - usually in May.

3433 ■ Rubber Division, American Chemical Society
PO Box 499
Akron, OH 44309-0499
Ph: (330)972-7814
Fax: (330)972-5269
E-mail: office@rubber.org
URL: http://www.rubber.org
Contact: Edward L. Miller, Exec. Dir.
Founded: 1909. **Members:** 3,300. **Membership Dues:** regular in North America, $55 (annual) ● regular outside North America, $70 (annual). **Staff:** 9. **Local Groups:** 27. **Description:** Polymer scientists, engineers, chemists, technicians. Advances the professionalism of members. Provides continuing education and training in rubber science and technology. **Libraries: Type:** lending; reference; open to the public. **Holdings:** archival material, books, business records, clippings, monographs, periodicals. **Subjects:** rubber. **Awards:** Charles Goodyear Award. **Type:** recognition. **Recipient:** for outstanding invention or innovation in the rubber industry ● Chemistry of Thermoplastic Elastomers Award. **Type:** recognition. **Recipient:** for contributions to the advancement of the chemistry of TPEs ● Fernley H. Banbury Award. **Type:** recognition. **Recipient:** for innovators of commercial production equipment ● George Stafford Whitby Award for Distinguished Teaching and Research. **Type:** recognition. **Recipient:** for outstanding teachers of chemistry and polymer science ● John D. Ferry Fellowship. **Type:** fellowship. **Recipient:** for a postgraduate student working toward a doctoral degree in polymer science education ● Melvin Mooney Distinguished Technology Award. **Type:** recognition. **Recipient:** for members and affiliates of exceptional technical competence ● Paul J. Flory Fellowship. **Type:** fellowship. **Recipient:** for a doctoral level student ● Rubber Technology Training Award. **Frequency:** annual. **Type:** scholarship. **Recipient:** for workers who want to further their education in the polymer and rubber industries ● Sparks-Thomas Award. **Type:** recognition. **Recipient:** for outstanding contributions in the field of elastomers by younger scientists. **Computer Services:** Record retrieval services. **Additional Websites:** http://www.rubberdivision.org. **Publications:** *Rubber Chemistry and Technology*, 5/year. Journal. Contains major technical papers. **Price:** $290.00 for members; $425.00 /year for institutions; $390.00 for nonmembers. ISSN: 0035-9475. **Advertising:** accepted. Alternate Formats: microform ● *Rubber Reviews*, annual. Features major scientific advances in polymer chemistry. **Price:** included in membership dues. **Conventions/Meetings:** biennial Rubber Expo - trade show, latest developments in rubber and chemistry industry (exhibits) - every fall in odd-numbered years ● biennial Rubber Mini Expo - trade show (exhibits) - even-numbered years.

3434 ■ Rubber Manufacturers Association (RMA)
1400 K St. NW, Ste.900
Washington, DC 20005
Ph: (202)682-4800

Fax: (202)682-4854
E-mail: info@rma.org
URL: http://www.rma.org
Contact: Donald B. Shea CAE, Pres./CEO

Founded: 1915. **Members:** 120. **Membership Dues:** supplier, $3,450-$11,500 (annual) ● manufacturer, $3,000-$45,000 (annual). **Staff:** 25. **Budget:** $4,000,000. **Description:** Manufacturers of tires, tubes, mechanical and industrial products, roofing, sporting goods, and other rubber products. **Awards:** S.H.I.P. **Frequency:** annual. **Type:** recognition. **Recipient:** for safety, health award. **Committees:** Environment; Federal Excise; Flat Belt; Governmental Relations; GPG Management; Hose Market Analysis; Hose Technical; Human Resources; Molded and Extruded Market Analysis; Natural Rubber; Oil Seal Market Analysis; Oil Seal Technology; OSHA; Passenger Tire Engineering; Power Transmission Belt Analysis; Power Transmission Technology; Public Relations; Retread and Repair Materials; Rubber Market Analysis; Scrap Tire Steering; Statistics; Technical; Tire Engineering Policy; Tire Management; Transportation. **Divisions:** General Products Group. **Programs:** Environmental; Safety and Health; Scrap Tires; Statistical; Technical. **Formerly:** (1909) New England Rubber Club; (1917) Rubber Club of America; (1929) Rubber Association of America. **Publications:** *Recreational Vehicle Tire Care and Safety Guide*. **Price:** free ● *Safety Specifications for Mills and Calendars in the Rubber Society*. **Price:** $30.00 for members; $60.00 for nonmembers ● Membership Directory.

3435 ■ Rubber Trade Association of North America (RTA)

220 Maple Ave.
PO Box 196
Rockville Centre, NY 11571
Ph: (516)536-7228
Fax: (516)536-3771
Contact: Fred B. Finley, Sec.

Founded: 1914. **Members:** 43. **Staff:** 2. **Budget:** $100,000. **Description:** Dealers' group: importers of crude natural rubber from the Far East and exporters of synthetic rubber. Brokers' and agents' group: representatives of Far Eastern shippers. Associate members' group: suppliers of services to the rubber trade, such as steamship companies and banks. **Formerly:** (1993) Rubber Trade Association of New York. **Conventions/Meetings:** annual seminar and dinner - always second Tuesday in December, New York City.

Safety

3436 ■ American Biological Safety Association (ABSA)

1200 Allanson Rd.
Mundelein, IL 60060-3808
Ph: (847)949-1517
Fax: (847)566-4580
E-mail: absa@covad.net
URL: http://www.absa.org
Contact: Bob Hawley PhD, Pres.

Founded: 1984. **Members:** 800. **Membership Dues:** student, $25 (annual) ● individual, $175 (annual) ● corporate, $650 (annual). **Description:** Promotes biosafety as a scientific discipline and serves the growing needs of biosafety professionals throughout the world. Seeks to provide a professional association that represents the interests and needs of practitioners of biological safety, and to provide a forum for the continued and timely exchange of biosafety information. **Awards:** Arnold G. Wedum Distinguished Achievement Award. **Frequency:** annual. **Type:** recognition. **Recipient:** to a member for outstanding contributions to biological safety accomplished through teaching, research or leadership ● Everett Hanel, Jr. Presidential Award. **Frequency:** annual. **Type:** recognition. **Recipient:** for outstanding contributions by promoting biological safety and fostering the high professional standards of its membership ● John H. Richardson Special Recognition Award. **Frequency:** annual. **Type:** recognition. **Recipient:** to an individual for a specific contribution that has enhanced the profession of biosafety. **Computer Services:** Mailing lists, of members. **Committees:** Affiliate Relations; Arrangements; Awards; Bylaws; Marketing; Nominating; Scientific Program; Website. **Publications:** *Applied Biosafety: Journal of the American Biological Safety Association*, quarterly. **Price:** included in membership dues; $92.00 /year for nonmembers; $122.00 /year for libraries; $18.00/ issue for nonmembers. ISSN: 1535-6760. **Circulation:** 720. **Advertising:** accepted. Alternate Formats: online ● Books. **Price:** $3.00 in U.S.; $5.00 in Canada; $15.00 outside U.S. and Canada. **Conventions/Meetings:** annual Biological Safety - conference (exhibits) - always October. 2008 Oct. 19-22, Reno, NV; 2009 Oct. 18-21, Miami, FL.

3437 ■ American Fire Sprinkler Association (AFSA)

12750 Merit Dr., Ste.350
Dallas, TX 75251
Ph: (214)349-5965
Fax: (214)343-8898
E-mail: afsainfo@firesprinkler.org
URL: http://www.sprinklernet.org
Contact: Steve A. Muncy, Pres.

Founded: 1981. **Members:** 784. **Membership Dues:** contractor/associate (minimum), $600 (annual) ● contractor/associate (maximum), $20,000 (annual) ● Authority Having Jurisdiction (AHJ) category, $100 (annual) ● designer category, $200 (annual). **Staff:** 16. **Multinational. Description:** Fire sprinkler contractors, manufacturers, and national and local suppliers devoted to serving the educational and training needs of the open shop contractors (contractors employing non-union craftsmen) and promoting the use of automatic sprinklers. Aims to encourage and maintain high standards of service to the public; to provide leadership training and professional development programs through regional chapters. Offers courses and training for sprinkler designers and fitters, and in skills that are in short supply in the fire sprinkler industry. Compiles statistics. Establishes National Apprenticeship Training Standards as guidelines for state and local apprenticeship programs. Conducts charitable activities. **Libraries: Type:** not open to the public. **Holdings:** clippings. **Committees:** Apprenticeship; Education; Legislative. **Publications:** *Buyer's Guide*, annual. Includes magazine. ● *Contractors Network*, quarterly. Newsletter. Focuses on construction-related issues, especially open shops. **Price:** free. **Circulation:** 1,300 ● *Sprinkler Designer*. Book ● *Tech Update*, monthly. Newsletter ● *TechTalk*. Newsletter ● *Training for Excellence*. Features a series of correspondence courses for fire sprinkler contracts. **Conventions/Meetings:** annual convention and trade show (exhibits) - 2008 Oct. 15-19, Washington, DC; 2009 Oct. 14-18, San Diego, CA.

3438 ■ American Traffic Safety Services Association (ATSSA)

15 Riverside Pkwy., Ste.100
Fredericksburg, VA 22406-1077
Ph: (540)368-1701
Free: (800)272-8772
Fax: (540)368-1717
E-mail: hross@usa-sign.com
URL: http://www.atssa.com
Contact: Roger Wentz, Exec. Dir.

Founded: 1966. **Members:** 1,600. **Membership Dues:** full/affiliate (based on annual revenue), $670-$2,832 (annual) ● transportation agency official, $66 (annual) ● manufacturers' representative, $180 (annual) ● associate, $114 (annual) ● international, $618 (annual) ● individual consultant, supplemental division representative, $237 (annual) ● traffic engineering, design firm, $603-$894 (annual) ● instructor, $124 (annual). **Staff:** 28. **Budget:** $5,000,000. **State Groups:** 20. **Description:** Individuals and firms engaged in the renting, leasing, and/or selling of highway signs, pavement markings, and traffic control devices for construction and repair areas; suppliers to the industry. Distributes technical information; promotes safety; compiles statistics; promotes uniform use of lights, signs, pavement markings, and barricades. Sponsors training courses for Worksite Traffic Supervisors and Pavement Marking technicians annually. Conducts research programs. **Libraries: Type:** reference. **Awards:** National Safety Award. **Type:** recognition ● Pioneer Achievement Award. **Frequency:** annual. **Type:** recognition. **Committees:** Environmental; Government Relations; Guardrail; Legislative; Manufacturers and Suppliers; Pavement Marking; Safety and Public Awareness; Sign; Temporary Traffic Control. **Councils:** ITS. **Formerly:** American Traffic Safety Control Devices Association; (1985) American Traffic Services Association. **Publications:** *American Traffic Safety Services Association—Membership Directory*, annual. **Price:** free for members. **Circulation:** 6,000. **Advertising:** accepted ● *ATSSA Flash*, biweekly. Newsletter. Covers the transportation safety industry. Includes membership directory updates and legislative news. **Price:** free for members. **Circulation:** 1,050 ● *ATSSA Signal*, quarterly. Newsletter. Covers transportation and traffic control specifications and standards; for members and federal, state, and city engineers. **Price:** free for members and public officials. **Circulation:** 6,000 ● *Flagging Handbook*, annual. Features equipment, positioning, rules of conduct, and how to handle emergency situations for highway flaggers. **Price:** $2.50 first copy for members and public agencies; $3.75 first copy for nonmembers. **Circulation:** 10,000 ● *Work Zone Standards*, annual. Reprint. Features the part VI of federal manual on traffic control devices. **Price:** $8.50 first copy for members. **Conventions/Meetings:** annual convention and trade show (exhibits).

3439 ■ Automatic Fire Alarm Association (AFAA)

PO Box 951807
Lake Mary, FL 32795-1807
Ph: (407)833-9133
Fax: (407)833-9131
E-mail: fire-alarm@afaa.org
URL: http://www.afaa.org
Contact: Robert Boyer, Chm.

Founded: 1953. **Membership Dues:** manufacturing, $1,500-$8,000 (annual) ● distribution, $200-$1,000 (annual) ● auxiliary, $50-$100 (annual). **Staff:** 4. **Budget:** $830,000. **Regional Groups:** 4. **Description:** Represents automatic fire detection and fire alarm systems industry. Membership is made up of state and regional member associations, manufacturers, installing distributors, authorities having jurisdiction, and end users. Promotes Life Safety in America through involvement in the codes and standards making process and by providing training seminars on a national basis. **Awards:** Person-of-the-Year Award. **Frequency:** annual. **Type:** recognition. **Telecommunication Services:** electronic mail, bob.boyer@ge.com. **Committees:** Chapter Growth; Codes and Standards; Training. **Publications:** *Signifire*, quarterly. Newsletter. Includes membership activities and technical industry information. **Price:** included in membership dues; $24.00 /year for nonmembers ● Manuals. **Conventions/Meetings:** quarterly board meeting ● annual meeting (exhibits) ● seminar - over 100/year.

3440 ■ Board of Certified Hazard Control Management (BCHCM)

PO Box 1662
Pelham, AL 35124
Ph: (202)987-9836
Fax: (205)987-9916
E-mail: info@chcm-chsp.org
URL: http://www.chcm-chsp.org
Contact: Harold M. Gordon, Exec. Dir.

Founded: 1976. **Members:** 2,000. **Staff:** 1. **Description:** Safety managers dedicated to the establishment of professional standards and refinements in the industry. Evaluates and certifies individuals involved primarily in the administration of safety and health programs. Levels of certification are senior and master, with master being the highest attainable status indicating that the individual possesses the skill and knowledge necessary to effectively manage comprehensive safety and health programs. Provides advice and assistance to those who wish to improve their status in the profession by acquiring skills in administration and combining them with technical safety abilities. Establishes curricula in conjunction with colleges, universities, and other training institutions to better prepare hazard control managers for their duties. **Formerly:** (1980) International Hazard Control Manager Certification Board. **Publications:** *Directory of Certified Hazard Control Managers*, biennial. Includes membership list and geographic index. ● *Management Approach to Hazard Control*. Newsletter. Provides a concise and meaningful presentation of the management principles, concepts and techniques. **Price:** $8.95 postage not included; $7.25 for diplomats ● Brochure. **Conventions/Meetings:** annual meeting.

3441 ■ Board of Certified Product Safety Management (BCPSM)

PO Box 1662
Pelham, AL 35124
Ph: (205)987-9836
Fax: (205)987-9916
E-mail: info@chcm-chsp.org
URL: http://www.chcm-chsp.org
Contact: Harold M. Gordon, Exec. Dir.

Founded: 1979. **Description:** Professional managers and engineers involved in product safety and liability. Evaluates qualifications of persons in the administration of product safety management programs or those whose responsibilities encompass broad aspects of product safety. Certifies individuals as competent in the field and seeks to increase their competence and continued development. Maintains an academy for the exchange of ideas and information in product safety management. Conducts training conferences and research; offers placement service. **Formerly:** International Product Safety Management Certification Board. **Publications:** *Board of Certified Product Safety Management—Membership Directory*, annual. Includes geographic index. ● *Certification Update*.

3442 ■ Central Station Alarm Association (CSAA)

440 Maple Ave., Ste.201
Vienna, VA 22180-4723
Ph: (703)242-4670
Fax: (703)242-4675
E-mail: communications@csaaul.org
URL: http://www.csaaul.org
Contact: Stephen Doyle, Exec. VP

Founded: 1950. **Members:** 150. **Staff:** 5. **Budget:** $1,000,000. **Languages:** English, French, Spanish. **Multinational. Description:** Individuals, firms, associations, and burglar and fire alarm corporations engaged primarily in the operation of central station burglar and fire alarm businesses. Aims to foster and improve the relationship between sellers, users, bureaus, and other agencies for the advancement of the central station electrical protection services industry. **Awards:** Central Station Excellence Awards. **Frequency:** annual. **Type:** trophy. **Recipient:** for excellence in central station, manager and operator categories ● Stanley C. Lott Award. **Frequency:** annual. **Type:** recognition. **Recipient:** for significant contributions for the betterment of the association and the industry. **Additional Websites:** http://www.csaaforum.com. **Telecommunication Services:** electronic mail, director@csaaul.org. **Committees:** Alarm Industry Communications. **Formerly:** (1990) Central Station Electrical Protection Association. **Publications:** *CSAA Directory*, annual. **Advertising:** accepted ● *CSAA Dispatch*, quarterly. Newsletter. **Advertising:** accepted ● *CSAA Signals*, periodic. Newsletter. **Conventions/Meetings:** annual Electronic Security Forum and Exposition - meeting (exhibits) - always spring ● annual meeting - usually October.

3443 ■ Fire Equipment Manufacturers' Association (FEMA)

1300 Sumner Ave.
Cleveland, OH 44115
Ph: (216)241-7333
Fax: (216)241-0105
E-mail: fema@taol.com
URL: http://www.yourfirstdefense.com
Contact: John H. Addington, Exec. Dir.

Founded: 1925. **Members:** 27. **Staff:** 3. **Description:** Represents companies of manufacturing devices that control or extinguish fires, including portable fire extinguishers; fire hose, engineered and pre-engineered systems, and interior fire protection devices used in high-rise and special hazard occupancies. Promotes proper installation and use of equipment; assists in promulgating standards. **Divisions:** Fire Hose; Interior Equipment; Portable Extinguisher; Systems. **Publications:** *Balanced Fire Protection*. Brochure ● *Everyone's Nightmare*. Video ● *Fire Hose Stations*. Video ● *Restaurant Fire Protection Changes - UL300*. Video. **Conventions/Meetings:** semiannual conference.

3444 ■ Fire Suppression Systems Association (FSSA)

5024-R Campbell Blvd.
Baltimore, MD 21236-5943
Ph: (410)931-8100 (410)933-3454
Fax: (410)931-8111
E-mail: fssa@clemonsmgmt.com
URL: http://www.fssa.net
Contact: Crista LeGrand CMP, Exec. Dir.

Founded: 1982. **Members:** 118. **Membership Dues:** designer, installer, $980 (annual) ● manufacturer, supplier, $4,000-$5,500 (annual). **Staff:** 3. **Description:** Firms that design, manufacture, sell, install, or repair and maintain fire suppression systems. Facilitates discussion and exchange of information among members. Seeks to strengthen group's position within the fire protection industry. **Publications:** *FSSA Pipe Design Handbook*. **Price:** $50.00 for members; $75.00 for nonmembers ● *FYI*, bimonthly. Newsletter ● *Technical Bulletin*, periodic ● Membership Directory, annual. **Conventions/Meetings:** annual meeting ● seminar.

3445 ■ International Safety Equipment Association (ISEA)

1901 N Moore St.
Arlington, VA 22209-1762
Ph: (703)525-1695
Fax: (703)528-2148
E-mail: isea@safetyequipment.org
URL: http://www.safetyequipment.org
Contact: William M. Lambert, Chm.

Founded: 1934. **Members:** 80. **Membership Dues:** supplier/testing laboratory, $4,250 (annual) ● service/publisher/distributor, $2,650 (annual) ● educational institution, $1,000 (annual). **Staff:** 7. **Budget:** $1,000,000. **Multinational. Description:** Manufacturers of personal protective clothing and equipment for workers. Supports its members in manufacturing and marketing the highest quality safety and health products. **Awards:** Legislative Leadership Award. **Frequency:** annual. **Type:** recognition. **Recipient:** for a member of Congress who has given significant efforts to promote worker's safety and health ● Lincoln C. Bailey Memorial Scholarship. **Frequency:** annual. **Type:** scholarship. **Recipient:** to college junior or senior whose parent is employed by a member company in the association ● Robert G. Hurley Distinguished Service Award. **Frequency:** annual. **Type:** recognition. **Recipient:** for a person who has made a significant impact on worker's safety and health. **Subgroups:** Clean Room; Emergency Eyewash and Shower; Ergonomic Products; Eye and Face Protection; Fall Protection; Hand Protection; Head Protection; Hearing Protection; High Visibility Products; Industrial First Aid; Industrial Warning Devices; Instruments; Marketing and Distribution; Protective Apparel; Respiratory Protection; Respiratory Protective Escape Devices. **Formerly:** (1998) Industrial Safety Equipment Association. **Publications:** *Buyers Guide*, annual. Catalog. **Price:** free. **Circulation:** 800. Alternate Formats: online ● *ISEA Safety Signals*, quarterly. Newsletter. **Price:** free for members. **Circulation:** 800 ● *ISEA Washington Report*, monthly. **Price:** free for members ● *Protection Update*, quarterly. Newsletter. Contains information for PPE users in construction industries. **Price:** free. **Circulation:** 65,000. **Advertising:** accepted. Alternate Formats: online. **Conventions/Meetings:** annual assembly and conference, for safety equipment industry - usually April/May ● annual Fall Meeting - assembly and conference - always November.

3446 ■ Lightning Protection Institute (LPI)

PO Box 99
Maryville, MO 64468
Ph: (804)314-8955
Free: (800)488-6864
E-mail: lpi@lightning.org
URL: http://www.lightning.org
Contact: Harold VanSickle III, Exec. Dir.

Founded: 1955. **Members:** 200. **Staff:** 4. **Description:** Manufacturers and installers of LPI certified lightning protection equipment; professional members. Offers course for installers; provides testing for certification of LPI Certified Master Installers, LPI Certified Professional Designers, and LPI Certified Inspectors of lightning protection systems. **Awards: Type:** recognition. **Recipient:** for contributions to lighting safety. **Committees:** Certification; Codes and Specifications; Education; Public Relations. **Publications:** *Standard of Practice LPI-175*, quadrennial. Manual. Consists of basic lightning protection requirements found to be essential to the safety of ordinary structures. **Price:** $10.00 includes shipping and handling within U.S. **Conventions/Meetings:** annual Contractor Division Conference ● annual Membership Meeting ● annual Professional Division Conference.

3447 ■ Motorcycle Safety Foundation (MSF)

2 Jenner St., Ste.150
Irvine, CA 92618-3806
Ph: (949)727-3227
Free: (800)446-9227
Fax: (949)727-4217
E-mail: msf@msf-usa.org
URL: http://www.msf-usa.org
Contact: Tim Buche, Pres.

Founded: 1973. **Members:** 10. **Staff:** 20. **Budget:** $5,500,000. **Description:** Promotes the safety of motorcyclists with programs in rider training, operator licensing and public information. Sponsored by the U.S. manufacturers and distributors of BMW, Ducati, Harley-Davidson, Honda, Kawasaki, KTM, Piaggio/Vespa, Suzuki, Victory, and Yamaha motorcycles. **Libraries: Type:** reference. **Holdings:** audiovisuals. **Subjects:** motorcycle safety, motorist awareness, driving under the influence. **Divisions:** Communications; Program Services; Training Programs. **Formerly:** (1973) Motorcycle Industry Council Safety and Education Foundation. **Publications:** *Safe Cycling*, quarterly. Newsletter. Covers foundation activities and developments in the motorcycle safety field. **Price:** free for members; $15.00 /year for nonmembers. **Circulation:** 6,000 ● Also publishes instructional, licensing, research/data, and consumer safety materials. See the Library/Safety Tips page on www.msf-usa.org.

3448 ■ National Association of Fire Equipment Distributors (NAFED)

104 S Michigan Ave., Ste.300
Chicago, IL 60603
Ph: (312)263-8100
Fax: (312)263-8111
E-mail: dharris@nafed.org
URL: http://www.nafed.org
Contact: Danny Harris, Exec. Dir. of Operations

Founded: 1963. **Members:** 1,200. **Membership Dues:** distributor, $395 (annual) ● supplier, $550 (annual) ● affiliate, $250 (annual). **Staff:** 6. **Budget:** $1,100,000. **Description:** Distributors of fire and safety equipment. Promotes better use of equipment; seeks to raise standards of recharge and service. Participates on national fire standards committees and councils with regard to regulating the service of fire protection equipment. Conducts service training program. **Affiliated With:** National Fire Protection Association. **Publications:** *Checklist for Fire Extinguisher Applications* ● *Federal Regulations*, quarterly ● *Fire Wire*, quarterly. Newsletter ● *Firewatch*, quarterly. Magazine. Contains articles on fire protection equipment companies, personnel, and products;

provides industry reports as well as surveys. **Price:** $40.00/year (2-year minimum order). **Circulation:** 2,500. **Advertising:** accepted ● *Portable Fire Extinguishers Selection Guide* ● *Technical Report*, quarterly ● Membership Directory, annual. Alternate Formats: online. **Conventions/Meetings:** annual conference (exhibits) ● seminar, on business management.

3449 ■ National Fire Sprinkler Association (NFSA)
40 Jon Barret Rd.
Patterson, NY 12563
Ph: (845)878-4200
Fax: (845)878-4215
E-mail: info@nfsa.org
URL: http://www.nfsa.org
Contact: John A. Viniello, Pres.
Founded: 1914. **Members:** 1,000. **Membership Dues:** subscriber, $85 (annual) ● professional, $165 (annual) ● supplier and manufacturer (base on annual sales), $20,000 (annual). **Staff:** 30. **Budget:** $2,500,000. **Regional Groups:** 20. **Description:** Manufacturers, suppliers, contractors, and installers of fire sprinklers and related products and services. Conducts labor negotiations for the industry with 19 local unions. Conducts educational programs to promote the concept of automatic fire sprinkler protection. Acts as liaison for the industry and participates in fire test research with insurance organizations and fire services. Acts as consultant for building codes; has developed model fire protection codes. Conducts research; compiles statistics. Maintains speakers' bureau and hall of fame. **Libraries: Type:** reference. **Awards:** Golden Sprinkler Award. **Frequency:** annual. **Type:** recognition. **Recipient:** for service to the fire sprinkler industry. **Computer Services:** Mailing lists, of members. **Committees:** Awards; Building Code; Education; Engineering and Standards; Insurance, Loss Control, and Safety; Labor Relations; Legislative; Marketing; Seminar and Exhibition. **Councils:** Contractors; Manufacturers; Suppliers. **Formerly:** National Automatic Sprinkler Association; (1983) National Automatic Sprinkler and Fire Control Association. **Publications:** *Codewatch*, quarterly. Newsletter. Lists of changes in model codes and state and local laws and regulations, and amendments to building codes and local ordinances. **Price:** included in membership dues. **Circulation:** 2,500. Alternate Formats: online ● *Grass Roots*, monthly. Newsletter. **Price:** included in membership dues. **Circulation:** 2,500. Alternate Formats: online ● *Labor Line*, bimonthly. Newsletter. Reports to unionized contractors on federal and state labor laws. **Price:** included in membership dues. **Circulation:** 400 ● *Membership List*, annual. Membership Directory ● *Regional Report*, monthly. Newsletter. **Price:** included in membership dues. Also Cited As: *Regional Manager Newsletter* ● *Sprinkler Quarterly*. Journal. Provides information on fire sprinkler protection; includes features and technical information for and about the industry. Covers association news. **Price:** included in membership dues. ISSN: 1050-4958. **Circulation:** 2,500. **Advertising:** accepted ● *Sprinkler Technotes*, bimonthly. Newsletter. Lists of proposed changes to fire sprinkler codes and standards; also covers developing fire protection technology. **Price:** included in membership dues. **Circulation:** 2,500. Alternate Formats: online ● Pamphlets ● Also publishes technical guides. **Conventions/Meetings:** periodic international conference (exhibits) ● annual seminar (exhibits) - always fall.

3450 ■ National Floor Safety Institute (NFSI)
PO Box 92607
Southlake, TX 76092
Ph: (817)749-1700
Fax: (817)749-1702
E-mail: info@nfsi.org
URL: http://www.nfsi.org
Contact: Russell J. Kendzior, Exec. Dir./Founder
Founded: 1997. **Members:** 500. **Membership Dues:** individual, $99 (annual) ● associate, $500 (annual) ● corporate, $2,500 (annual). **Staff:** 1. **Description:** Product manufacturers, insurance companies, and independent contractors. Aims to aid in the prevention of slip and fall accidents through education, training, and research. **Libraries: Type:** reference. **Holdings:** 3. **Subjects:** slip and fall injury claim data. **Computer Services:** database. **Publications:** *A World of Safety*. Brochure. Alternate Formats: online ● *Slip and Fall Prevention Made Easy*. Book. **Price:** $60.00 ● Newsletter. Alternate Formats: online. **Conventions/Meetings:** periodic Slip and Fall Prevention Made Easy - meeting.

3451 ■ National Operating Committee on Standards for Athletic Equipment (NOCSAE)
11020 King St., Ste.215
Overland Park, KS 66210
Ph: (913)888-1340
Fax: (913)498-8817
E-mail: mike.oliver@nocsae.org
URL: http://www.nocsae.org
Contact: Mike Oliver, Exec. Dir.
Founded: 1969. **Members:** 21. **Staff:** 3. **Budget:** $500,000. **Description:** Board consists of representatives from manufacturers, reconditioners, consumers, medical specialties, collegiate sports, athletic trainers, equipment managers, and other organizations interested in reducing athletic injuries through the improvement and the establishment of standards for athletic equipment. Commissions research. Conducts research on head and neck injuries sustained in football, baseball, and other sports; has established football, baseball, lacrosse helmet, and football faceguard standards and is currently researching protective body padding. **Awards: Frequency:** annual. **Type:** grant. **Recipient:** for independent research. **Publications:** *Report*, semiannual. Newsletter ● *Standards*, biennial. Manual. **Price:** free. **Conventions/Meetings:** semiannual board meeting - always January and June.

3452 ■ The Product Liability Alliance (TPLA)
c/o National Association of Wholesaler-Distributors
1725 K St. NW, Ste.300
Washington, DC 20006-1419
Ph: (202)872-0885
Fax: (202)785-0586
E-mail: naw@nawd.org
URL: http://www.naw.org
Contact: James A. Anderson Jr., VP for Government Relations
Founded: 1981. **Members:** 325. **Membership Dues:** direct, $690 (annual) ● associate, $950 (annual). **Staff:** 35. **Description:** Coalition of trade associations, manufacturers, and nonmanufacturing product sellers. Seeks enactment of federal product liability tort reform legislation. Supports and coordinates members' efforts in gaining passage of a product liability law. Works with the business community to develop suggestions and guidelines for such a law. **Telecommunication Services:** electronic mail, janderson@nawd.org.

3453 ■ Product Liability Prevention and Defense (PLPD)
201 Park Washington Ct.
Falls Church, VA 22046-4513
Ph: (703)538-1797
Fax: (703)241-5603
E-mail: plpdhq@aol.com
Contact: Clay D. Tyeryar, Exec. Dir.
Founded: 1984. **Members:** 52. **Staff:** 2. **Description:** Trade associations of factory machinery manufacturers. Seeks to achieve more effective and efficient litigation defense by individual association members. Collects and disseminates information; offers rosters of expert witnesses. **Computer Services:** database, literature abstracts (for use in product liability suits). **Formerly:** (1989) Product Liability Common Defense. **Publications:** *The Gavel*. Newsletter. Covers past litigation issues. **Circulation:** 500. **Conventions/Meetings:** semiannual workshop - usually Midwest and Northeast areas.

3454 ■ Safety Equipment Distributors Association (SEDA)
2105 Laurel Bush Rd., Ste.200
Bel Air, MD 21015
Ph: (443)640-1065
Fax: (443)640-1086
E-mail: seda@ksgroup.org
URL: http://www.safetycentral.org
Contact: Ms. Jackie King, Exec. Dir.
Founded: 1968. **Members:** 250. **Staff:** 4. **Description:** Represents distributors and manufacturers of safety equipment for industrial workers. Supports the interests of members before all external bodies. **Libraries: Type:** reference. **Holdings:** audiovisuals. **Awards: Type:** recognition. **Telecommunication Services:** electronic mail, jackie@ksgroup.org. **Committees:** Catalog; Distributor Operations; Government Relations; Market Research; Sales and Marketing. **Publications:** *Compensation Survey Report*, biennial. Provides information concerning compensation and benefits. Alternate Formats: CD-ROM ● *Profit Report*, annual. Contains benchmarking ratio studies. ● *SEDA Roster and Resource Manual*, annual ● *SEDA Scene*, bimonthly. Newsletter. Covers association activities, programs and news. Includes calendar of events. **Price:** free for members, staff, and trade press. **Circulation:** 350. Alternate Formats: online. **Conventions/Meetings:** semiannual Qualified Safety Sales Professional Course - seminar, technical and regulatory training for safety sales professionals ● annual Safety Week - conference.

3455 ■ Safety Equipment Institute (SEI)
1307 Dolley Madison Blvd., Ste.3A
McLean, VA 22101
Ph: (703)442-5732
Fax: (703)442-5756
E-mail: info@seinet.org
URL: http://www.seinet.org
Contact: Patricia A. Gleason, Pres.
Founded: 1981. **Members:** 70. **Staff:** 6. **Budget:** $500,000. **Languages:** English, French. **Multinational. Description:** Works to foster and advance public interest in safety and protective equipment, and to assist the safety equipment industry and government agencies in their mutual goal of providing workers with the best possible protective equipment. Recognizes products that are certified to meet appropriate standards; manages a third-party certification program. Convention/Meeting: none. **Publications:** *SEI Certified Product List*, quarterly. Directory. **Price:** free. **Circulation:** 3,000. Alternate Formats: online.

3456 ■ SEMAA - The Safety Affiliate of NIRA (SEMAA/NIRA)
105 Eastern Ave., Ste.104
Annapolis, MD 21403
Ph: (410)263-1014
Free: (800)315-7429
Fax: (410)263-1659
E-mail: info@semaa.org
Contact: Joseph Thompson, Exec. Dir.
Founded: 1986. **Members:** 90. **Membership Dues:** representative, salesperson, $395-$595 (annual) ● manufacturer, $495 (annual) ● regular, $75 (annual). **Staff:** 2. **Budget:** $35,000. **Description:** Safety equipment multiple-line manufacturers' representatives and agencies organized to improve the industrial safety equipment business. Works to inform members of developments in the field. **Also Known As:** (2003) Safety Equipment Manufacturers' Agents Association. **Publications:** *The Locator*, annual. Membership Directory. **Price:** $50.00 /year for nonmembers ● *The Reporter*, quarterly. Newsletter. Features articles and reports impacting the representative function. **Price:** included in membership dues ● Bulletins. Alternate Formats: online. **Conventions/Meetings:** annual convention and conference, in conjunction with NIRA (exhibits) ● semiannual meeting - always spring and fall.

3457 ■ System Safety Society (SSS)
PO Box 70
Unionville, VA 22567-0070
Ph: (540)854-8630
E-mail: systemsafety@system-safety.org
URL: http://www.system-safety.org
Contact: Cathy Carter, Contact
Founded: 1963. **Members:** 1,000. **Membership Dues:** student, $35 (annual) ● affiliate (in U.S. and

Canada and Mexico), $65 (annual) ● other, $75 (annual). **Staff:** 5. **Budget:** $65,000. **Local Groups:** 17. **Description:** Professionals engaged in a practice related to the fields of safety in products, systems and services, or in work that contributes to the advancement of system safety concepts, techniques, and approaches. Advances the art of system safety. Contributes to a meaningful scientific and technological understanding of system safety. Disseminates newly acquired information to interested groups and individuals. Sponsors professional development seminars and symposia. Supports other related professional organizations in joint meetings and activities. **Awards:** Chapter of the Year Award. **Type:** recognition ● Professional Development Award. **Type:** recognition. **Computer Services:** database, keyworded reference of all technical articles appearing in publications ● online services, JOBNET, a placement service. **Committees:** Education; Governmental and Inter-Society Affairs; Historian; Policy and Issues; Professional Development; Professional Registration; Research; Software System Safety; Special Projects; Standards. **Formerly:** (1966) Aerospace System Safety Society. **Publications:** *Assurance Technologies; Principles and Practice: A Product, Process, and System Safety Perspective*. Book. **Price:** $70.00 each ● *Consultants' Directory*, periodic. Lists each consultant alphabetically in the first section; second section contains sort lists to help in locating consultants. **Price:** $20.00. Also Cited As: *System Safety Society Directory of Consultants* ● *Hazard Prevention*, quarterly. Journal. Contains articles of topical interest; includes news of the society, calendar of events, book reviews, and listing of local chapters. ISSN: 0743-8826. **Circulation:** 2,500. **Advertising:** accepted ● *Journal of System Safety*, bimonthly. Contains technical information, industry reports, expert opinions, book reviews and conference previews. **Price:** included in membership dues; $55.00 /year for nonmembers (USA, Canada and Mexico); $70.00 /year for nonmembers (international); $15.00/back issue, for members. **Circulation:** 1,750. **Advertising:** accepted. Alternate Formats: online ● *System Safety Analysis Handbook*. **Price:** $80.00 for members; $100.00 for nonmembers ● *System Safety Engineering and Management 2nd Edition*. Book. **Price:** $150.00 each ● *System Safety for the 21st Century*. Book. **Price:** $89.95 each ● *System Safety Society Proceedings of International Conferences*, biennial. Includes compilation of technical paper. ● Membership Directory, periodic ● Newsletter, periodic. **Conventions/Meetings:** annual conference.

3458 ■ Transportation Safety Equipment Institute (TSEI)

10 Lab. Dr.
Research Triangle Park, NC 27709
Ph: (919)406-8841
Fax: (919)406-1306
E-mail: tsei@mema.org
URL: http://www.tsei.org
Contact: Dominic Grote, Pres.

Founded: 1962. **Members:** 28. **Staff:** 5. **Budget:** $80,000. **Languages:** English, French, Russian. **Description:** Manufacturers of automotive and truck lighting and associated devices, mirrors and reflectors, and emergency products for OEM (original equipment manufacturer) and aftermarket applications. Seeks improved highway safety and enforcement legislation. Provides a technical forum to resolve industry problems, government representation, and monitoring services of proposed and enacted legislation and regulations. **Committees:** Driver Information; Engineering (Emergency Products, Lights, Mirrors); Government Relations; Marketing; Vehicle Conspicuity Technology. **Subcommittees:** Communications; Standards. **Affiliated With:** Motor and Equipment Manufacturers Association. **Formerly:** (1986) Truck Safety Equipment Institute. **Publications:** Membership Directory, periodic ● Report, periodic. **Price:** available to members only.

3459 ■ Underwriters Laboratories (UL)

333 Pfingsten Rd.
Northbrook, IL 60062-2096
Ph: (847)272-8800
Free: (877)854-3577
Fax: (847)272-8129
E-mail: cec@us.ul.com
URL: http://www.ul.com
Contact: Loring Knoblauch, Pres./CEO

Founded: 1894. **Staff:** 3,900. **Multinational. Description:** Establishes and operates product safety certification programs to ascertain that items produced under the service are safeguarded against reasonably foreseeable risks. Maintains a worldwide network of field representatives who make visits to factories to monitor products bearing the UL Mark. **Convention/Meeting:** none. **Councils:** Environmental and Public Health; Management System Advisory. **Departments:** Burglary Protection and Signaling; Casualty and Chemical Hazards; Electrical; Fire Protection; Follow-Up Services; Heating, Air Conditioning and Refrigeration; Marine. **Publications:** *Catalog of Standards for Safety*, semiannual ● *EPH RegULator*, quarterly. Newsletter. Alternate Formats: online ● *Lab Data*, quarterly ● *Trends*, quarterly ● Brochures ● Directories, annual.

3460 ■ United Fire Equipment Service Association (UFESA)

500 Telcer Rd.
Lake Zurich, IL 60047
Ph: (847)438-2343
Fax: (847)438-1869
E-mail: ifec@mc.net

Founded: 1954. **Members:** 28. **Membership Dues:** active, $150 (annual). **Staff:** 3. **Description:** State associations of firms engaged in the sales and servicing of fire extinguishers. Sponsors a college program for service technicians in the University of Illinois. **Publications:** *Information Bulletin*, periodic. **Conventions/Meetings:** monthly meeting.

3461 ■ United Lightning Protection Association (ULPA)

426 North Ave.
Libertyville, IL 60048
Free: (800)668-8572
Fax: (847)362-6443
E-mail: info@ulpa.org
URL: http://www.ulpa.org
Contact: Kim Loehr, Pres.

Founded: 1932. **Members:** 93. **Membership Dues:** regular, $200 (annual) ● affiliate, $50 (annual). **Staff:** 1. **Description:** Individuals involved in the manufacture, sale, or installation of lightning protection systems. Works to increase public interest in and awareness of the lightning protection industry; encourage and extend the use of lightning protection; promote public education on the merits and economy of lightning protection systems; educate members on the technical and commercial features of these systems in order to aid the public in securing safe, dependable, and attractive installations. Collects and disseminates information related to the industry. **Committees:** Publicity; Technical. **Publications:** *More Static*, periodic. Newsletter. Alternate Formats: online. **Conventions/Meetings:** annual conference ● periodic convention.

Sales

3462 ■ American Association of Professional Sales Engineers

Address Unknown since 2007

Founded: 1983. **Members:** 600. **Membership Dues:** student, $25 (annual) ● certified sales engineer, $125 (annual) ● certified senior sales engineer, $125 (annual) ● certified master sales engineer, $125 (annual). **Staff:** 2. **Description:** Professional sales engineers. Objectives are to promote the profession and provide continuing education (technical, commercial, ethical, and legal) via affiliation with a major research/teaching university (currently under negotiation). **Libraries:** **Type:** reference; not open to the public. **Holdings:** books, business records, clippings, periodicals. **Subjects:** economics. **Computer Services:** Mailing lists ● online services. **Publications:** Newsletter, quarterly. **Advertising:** not accepted. **Conventions/Meetings:** quarterly conference and board meeting.

3463 ■ Association of Retail Marketing Services (ARMS)

10 Drs. James Parker Blvd., Ste.103
Red Bank, NJ 07701-1500
Ph: (732)842-5070
Fax: (732)219-1938
E-mail: info@goarms.com
Contact: Gerri Hopkins, Exec.Dir.

Founded: 1957. **Members:** 150. **Membership Dues:** regular, $500 (annual) ● independent sales representative, $300 (annual). **Staff:** 4. **Budget:** $325,000. **Description:** Devoted to the promotional needs of the retail industry. Recommends incentive promotion at the retail level. Offers legal and legislative services and public relations programs. Conducts research programs; compiles statistics. Publishes newsletter and sponsors a tradeshow. **Awards:** Management Achievement Award. **Frequency:** periodic. **Type:** recognition. **Recipient:** for retail incentive marketing. **Computer Services:** Mailing lists, of members. **Committees:** Planning; Trade Show Membership. **Formerly:** (1982) Trading Stamp Institute of America; (1983) TSIA—The Association of Retail Marketing Services. **Publications:** *Creative Marketing*, quarterly. Newsletter. For retail executives planning consumer and employee incentives promotions. **Price:** free for members. **Circulation:** 6,500. **Advertising:** accepted ● Membership Directory, annual. Lists members and their products and services. **Price:** free. **Circulation:** 4,300 ● Also publishes mailing lists and case studies. **Conventions/Meetings:** annual Supermarket Promotion Show (exhibits) - always March, Chicago, IL.

3464 ■ Association of Sales Administration Managers (ASAM)

c/o Bill Martin, Sec.-Treas.
Box 1356
Laurence Harbor, NJ 08879
Ph: (732)264-7722
E-mail: asamnet@aol.com
Contact: Bill Martin, Sec.-Treas.

Founded: 1981. **Members:** 100. **Description:** Independent consultants providing sales and marketing services, including establishing broker and rep sales networks, field sales management, and marketing and branch office administrative services. Primary expertise is in the consumer packaged goods field, both private label and branded. Offers consulting services. **Conventions/Meetings:** quarterly conference ● annual meeting.

3465 ■ Direct Selling Association (DSA)

1667 K St. NW, Ste.1100
Washington, DC 20006
Ph: (202)452-8866
Fax: (202)452-9010
E-mail: info@dsa.org
URL: http://www.dsa.org
Contact: Mr. Neil H. Offen, Pres.

Founded: 1910. **Members:** 200. **Membership Dues:** supplier, $2,500 (annual) ● global associate, $3,000 (annual). **Staff:** 22. **Budget:** $4,000,000. **Description:** Manufacturers and distributors selling consumer products through person-to-person sales, by appointment, and through home-party plans. Products include food, gifts, house wares, dietary supplements, cosmetics, apparel, jewelry, decorative accessories, reference books, and telecommunications products and services. Offers specialized education; conducts research programs; compiles statistics. Maintains hall of fame. Sponsors Direct Selling Education Foundation (see separate entry). **Libraries:** **Type:** reference. **Holdings:** archival material, audiovisuals, books, clippings, monographs, periodicals. **Subjects:** direct selling. **Awards:** Hall of Fame. **Frequency:** annual. **Type:** recognition ● Innovation. **Frequency:** annual. **Type:** recognition ● Vision for Tomorrow. **Frequency:** annual. **Type:** recognition. **Committees:** Direct Selling Association Political Action; Government Relations. **Councils:** International; Lawyers. **Affiliated With:** Direct Selling Education Foundation; World

Federation of Direct Selling Associations. **Formerly:** (1970) National Association of Direct Selling Companies. **Publications:** *Data Tracker*, quarterly. **Circulation:** 1,000 ● *News from Neil*, monthly ● *State Status Sheet*, weekly. Report. **Circulation:** 1,200 ● Annual Report, annual. **Conventions/Meetings:** annual conference and meeting (exhibits).

3466 ■ Direct Selling Education Foundation (DSEF)

1667 K St. NW, Ste.1100
Washington, DC 20006-1660
Ph: (202)452-8866
Fax: (202)452-9015
E-mail: info@dsef.org
URL: http://www.dsef.org
Contact: Ms. Judith A. Cranford, Exec. Dir.

Founded: 1973. **Staff:** 4. **Budget:** $1,000,000. **Multinational. Description:** Serves the public interest with education, information, and research, thereby enhancing acceptance and public awareness of direct selling in the global marketplace. **Libraries: Type:** reference. **Holdings:** archival material, books. **Subjects:** direct selling. **Awards:** Circle of Honor. **Frequency:** annual. **Type:** recognition. **Recipient:** for outstanding services to the Direct Selling Education Foundation ● **Type:** grant. **Recipient:** for recognized consumer and academic organizations. **Telecommunication Services:** electronic mail, jcranford@dsef.org. **Committees:** Academic Program; Capital Campaign; Consumer and Community Program; Development; Global Outreach; International; Strategic Marketing Plan. **Affiliated With:** Direct Selling Association. **Publications:** *DSEF: A Foundation That Works*. Article. Highlights the DSEF contributions to the academic community and consumer advocacy with a variety of programs. ● *Moral Suasion*. Monograph. Describes how the member companies of the Direct Selling Association developed and enacted a code of ethics. **Conventions/Meetings:** seminar, for professors on direct selling, operation policy issues, and possible areas of research.

3467 ■ Foodservice Group (FSG)

630 Village Trace, Bldg. 15, Ste.A
Marietta, GA 30067
Ph: (770)989-0049
Fax: (770)956-7498
E-mail: info@fsgroup.com
URL: http://www.fsgroup.com
Contact: Kenneth W. Reynolds, Exec. Dir.

Founded: 1964. **Members:** 42. **Staff:** 2. **Budget:** $100,000. **Description:** Independent food service brokers and brokerage companies. Seeks to serve the sales and marketing needs of food service producers in the U.S. and Canada. **Formerly:** (1978) National Foodservice Marketing Associates. **Conventions/Meetings:** annual meeting, for sales and marketing.

3468 ■ Marketing Agencies Association Worldwide (MAA)

460 Summer St., 4th Fl.
Stamford, CT 06901
Ph: (203)978-1590
Fax: (203)969-1499
E-mail: keith.mccracken@maaw.org
URL: http://www.maaw.org
Contact: Mr. Keith McCracken, Exec. Dir.

Founded: 1969. **Members:** 60. **Membership Dues:** individual company, $3,700 (annual) ● individual company (initial), $4,700 ● group/network company (based on number of office), $6,200-$11,250 (annual). **Staff:** 9. **Budget:** $350,000. **Regional Groups:** 5. **Multinational. Description:** Represents the interests of CEOs, presidents, managing directors and principals of top marketing services agencies. Provides opportunity for marketing professionals to meet with peers, raise company profile on both a national and a global platform, and influence the future of industry. Fosters networking through conferences. **Awards:** MAA Worldwide Awards - The Globes. **Frequency:** annual. **Type:** recognition. **Recipient:** for best marketing campaigns from around the world. **Committees:** Administration; Communications; Ethics and Trade Practices; Professional Development; Professional Recognition; Public Affairs; Seminars; Student. **Formerly:** (1995) Council of Sales Promotion Agencies; (2003) Association of Promotion Marketing Agencies Worldwide. **Conventions/Meetings:** semiannual conference, for professional development - always spring and fall.

3469 ■ National Alliance of Black Salesmen and Black Saleswomen

Address Unknown since 2007

Founded: 1983. **Description:** Promotes and represents professional Black salesmen and saleswomen.

3470 ■ National Association of Sales Professionals (NASP)

8300 N Hayden Rd., Ste.207
Scottsdale, AZ 85258
Ph: (480)951-4311
Free: (877)800-7192
Fax: (480)626-4436
E-mail: info@nasp.com
URL: http://www.nasp.com
Contact: Aaron Bare, CEO

Founded: 1991. **Members:** 3,000. **Membership Dues:** life professional, $495. **Staff:** 4. **Budget:** $200,000. **Description:** Professional salespersons. Serves the training, educational and developmental needs of men and women in sales to earn designation as a Certified Professional Sales Person (CPSP). **Libraries: Type:** reference. **Holdings:** 450; books. **Subjects:** sales. **Computer Services:** database. **Publications:** *EduMart*, monthly. Catalog. Lists current books and cassette albums spanning a wide range of sales related topics. Alternate Formats: online. **Conventions/Meetings:** annual convention (exhibits).

3471 ■ National Field Selling Association (NFSA)

100 N 20th St., 4th Fl.
Philadelphia, PA 19103-1443
Ph: (215)564-1627 (215)564-3484
Fax: (215)564-2175
E-mail: nfsa@fernley.com
URL: http://www.nfsa.com
Contact: Vincent R. Pitts, Pres.

Founded: 1987. **Members:** 300. **Staff:** 3. **Description:** Individuals and businesses engaged in direct sales. Promotes direct sales as a profession and a method of doing business; seeks to improve the public image of direct sales. Formulates standards of ethics and practice for direct sales personnel. **Publications:** *Direct Seller*, quarterly. Newsletter. **Price:** free. Alternate Formats: online. **Conventions/Meetings:** annual convention and meeting.

3472 ■ Professional Society for Sales and Marketing Training (SMT)

5905 NW 54th Cir.
Coral Springs, FL 33067
Free: (800)219-0096
Fax: (800)219-0096
URL: http://www.smt.org
Contact: Joel Cataldo, Pres.

Founded: 1940. **Members:** 150. **Membership Dues:** individual, $350 (annual). **Staff:** 3. **Description:** Directors of training. Seeks to improve sales, marketing, and customer relations through training. Conducts educational conferences and sales training clinics. **Formerly:** National Society of Sales Training Executives. **Publications:** *Trainer Talk*, bimonthly. Newsletter. Provides current and highly applicable information to sales and marketing training executives. **Circulation:** 5,500. Alternate Formats: online. **Conventions/Meetings:** annual meeting (exhibits).

3473 ■ Sales and Marketing Executives International (SMEI)

PO Box 1390
Sumas, WA 98295-1390
Ph: (312)893-0751
Free: (800)999-1414
Fax: (604)855-0165
E-mail: admin@smei.org
URL: http://www.smei.org
Contact: Willis Turner CSE, Pres./CEO

Founded: 1935. **Members:** 10,000. **Membership Dues:** e-chapter, $195 (annual) ● regional, special interest, $150-$500 (annual). **Regional Groups:** 29. **Multinational. Description:** Executives concerned with sales and marketing management, research, training, and other managerial aspects of distribution; members' control activities of 3,000,000 salespersons. Undertakes studies in the field of selling and sales management; sponsors sales workshops, rallies, clinics, and seminars. Conducts career education programs, working with teachers, establishing sales clubs and fraternities, and cooperating with Junior Achievement and Distributive Education Clubs of America to interest young people in sales careers. Offers Graduate School of Sales Management and Marketing at Syracuse University, NY. Seeks to make overseas markets more accessible by interchange of selling information and marketing techniques with executives in other countries; affiliated associations are located in 49 countries. Maintains hall of fame and speakers' bureau; sponsors competitions. **Libraries: Type:** not open to the public. **Holdings:** 500; articles. **Subjects:** sales and marketing. **Awards:** International Marketing Executive of the Year. **Frequency:** annual. **Type:** recognition. **Recipient:** for marketing business executives and educators ● International Sales Executive of the Year. **Frequency:** annual. **Type:** recognition. **Recipient:** for sales business executives and educators. **Computer Services:** Mailing lists. **Committees:** Affiliate Services; Executive Management Conference; Foundation; Government Relations; International; International Marketing Convention; Junior Achievement; Member Services; Membership Development; Professional Development; PSE Marketing Fraternities in Colleges and Universities; Public Relations; Student Education. **Publications:** *Marketing Times*, quarterly. Newsletter. **Price:** free for members. **Circulation:** 6,000. **Advertising:** accepted. Alternate Formats: online. **Conventions/Meetings:** annual Leadership Conference (exhibits) - usually September.

3474 ■ Sales Professionals USA (SP)

PO Box 149
Arvada, CO 80001
Ph: (303)433-1051
Free: (888)763-7767
E-mail: salespro@salesprofessionals-usa.com
URL: http://www.salesprofessionals-usa.com
Contact: Jay Berg, Natl. Pres.

Founded: 1955. **Members:** 200. **Membership Dues:** general, $75 (annual). **Staff:** 1. **Budget:** $25,000. **State Groups:** 3. **Local Groups:** 5. **Description:** Salespersons, owners of small businesses, and those interested in free enterprise from Australia, Singapore, New Zealand, and the United States. Endeavors to increase an individual's effectiveness and earning power in any field of salesmanship, in particular creative salesmanship. Fosters the interchange of ideas, techniques, philosophies, and concepts relative to salesmanship; encourages high standards and ethical behavior for those in selling; maintains a good relation between business and the buying public; educates and increases the abilities of those currently engaged in selling; promotes the profession to youth. Conducts in-class sales training for high school and college students; sponsors symposia and workshops. Maintains speakers' bureau. **Awards: Frequency:** annual. **Type:** recognition. **Recipient:** for outstanding salesperson, sales manager, booster, or service person, and entrepreneur. **Committees:** Chartering; Free Enterprise; Youth Involvement. **Also Known As:** Salesman With a Purpose. **Publications:** *Wired for Sales*, quarterly. Newsletter. Contains local club news plus articles on selling skills, motivation, etc. **Circulation:** 350. **Advertising:** accepted. **Conventions/Meetings:** annual convention and meeting.

3475 ■ Society of Pharmaceutical and Biotech Trainers (SPBT)

4423 Pheasant Ridge Rd., Ste.100
Roanoke, VA 24014-5274
Ph: (540)725-3859

Fax: (540)989-7482
E-mail: info@spbt.org
URL: http://www.spbt.org
Contact: Brian Fagan, Exec. Dir.
Founded: 1971. **Members:** 1,050. **Membership Dues:** individual, trainer (within a pharmaceutical and biotech company), $175 (annual). **Staff:** 5. **Budget:** $500,000. **Languages:** English, French. **Description:** Sales training directors and sales training personnel of healthcare companies. Seeks to improve professionalism within the field by raising standards of development and training programs. Encourages members' self-development by facilitating information exchange. Works to improve client relations. **Awards:** Anne Walsh Service Award. **Frequency:** annual. **Type:** recognition. **Recipient:** for service to the society ● Outstanding Member of the Year. **Frequency:** annual. **Type:** recognition. **Recipient:** for excellence in pharmaceutical training and service to the society. **Boards:** Advisory. **Committees:** Annual Conference Workshop; Industry Partners; Publicity. **Formerly:** (2000) National Society of Pharmaceutical Sales Trainers. **Publications:** *Focus*, quarterly. Journal. Articles on subjects relating to sales training procedures. **Price:** $100.00/year; free for members. **Circulation:** 1,050. **Advertising:** accepted ● Also issues conference summaries and consultant service updates. **Conventions/Meetings:** annual conference, limited exhibit space by design and policy (exhibits) ● annual meeting (exhibits) - always May or June.

3476 ■ United Professional Sales Association (UPSA)
1700 Pennsylvania Ave. NW, Ste.400
Washington, DC 20006
Free: (877)694-8262
Fax: (866)685-2550
E-mail: hq@upsa-intl.org
URL: http://www.upsa-intl.org
Contact: Brian Lambert, Chm.
Founded: 2002. **Membership Dues:** professional in U.S., $55 (annual) ● international, $70 (annual). **Multinational. Description:** Represents and promotes sales professionals. **Publications:** *Compendium of Professional Selling*. **Price:** included in membership dues ● *Dynamic Transactions*, monthly. Newsletter. **Price:** included in membership dues ● *Selling Power*. Magazine. **Price:** $15.00/year. **Conventions/Meetings:** annual conference ● CRSP Certification Prep Course - meeting ● seminar ● annual symposium.

3477 ■ World Federation of Direct Selling Associations (WFDSA)
1667 K St. NW, Ste.1100
Washington, DC 20006
Ph: (202)452-8866
Fax: (202)452-9010
E-mail: info@wfdsa.org
URL: http://www.wfdsa.org
Contact: Neil H. Offen, Chm.
Founded: 1978. **Members:** 53. **Membership Dues:** business (minimum; based on retail sales), $15,000 (annual) ● business (maximum; based on retail sales), $40,000 (annual). **Staff:** 6. **Budget:** $500,000. **Regional Groups:** 10. **National Groups:** 53. **Multinational. Description:** Organized for the purpose of promoting the common business interests of its members. Exchanges information among members. Fosters highest standards of direct selling practices, consumer protection and ethics in the marketplace, by adoption and promotion of the Codes of Conduct for Direct Selling. Improves communications through sponsorship of World Congress of direct selling. Encourages personal relationships and cooperation among people in direct selling. Promotes education internationally through programs and funding, relying on the United States Direct Selling Education Foundation (USDSEF) to help it towards this objective. **Awards:** Outstanding Service Award. **Frequency:** triennial. **Type:** recognition. **Committees:** Advocacy; Association Services; Ethics; Regulatory/Legislative Affairs. **Affiliated With:** Direct Selling Association; Federation of European Direct Selling Associations. **Publications:** *WFDSA Directory of Members*, annual. Membership Directory ● *World Federation News*, bimonthly. Newsletter. **Price:** included in membership dues. **Circulation:** 2,000. **Conventions/Meetings:** triennial congress.

School Services

3478 ■ National Association of College Auxiliary Services (NACAS)
7 Boar's Head Ln.
Charlottesville, VA 22903-4610
Ph: (434)245-8425
Fax: (434)245-8453
E-mail: info@nacas.org
URL: http://www.nacas.org
Contact: Dr. Bob Hassmiller CAE, CEO
Founded: 1969. **Members:** 1,400. **Membership Dues:** subscribers, $125 (annual) ● business partner, $525 (annual) ● institution (based on full time enrollment), $245-$945 (annual) ● overseas institutional, $430 (annual) ● business partner (additional individual), $95 (annual). **Staff:** 11. **Budget:** $1,500,000. **Regional Groups:** 4. **Description:** Directors of college auxiliary services (vending, food services, bookstores, laundries, printing, and housing). Promotes standards, communication, information sharing, and industry improvement. Encourages professional development. **Libraries: Type:** reference. **Holdings:** papers. **Awards:** The Golden Award. **Frequency:** annual. **Type:** recognition. **Recipient:** for outstanding campus leadership, activities and/or programs promoting cultural awareness and inclusion ● The Outstanding Business Partner Award. **Frequency:** annual. **Type:** recognition. **Recipient:** to the companies, which have made particularly noteworthy contributions to NACAS member institutions and to the auxiliary services profession ● Robert F. Newton Award for Distinguished Service. **Frequency:** annual. **Type:** recognition. **Recipient:** for extraordinary and outstanding service to NACAS and to the profession ● Silver Torch Award. **Frequency:** annual. **Type:** recognition. **Recipient:** for continuing positive influence on the Association and on the profession. **Computer Services:** database, lists of members. **Committees:** Awards; Business Partner; Cultural Diversity; Media Services; Membership; Nominating; Professional Development; Strategic Planning. **Formerly:** (1973) Association of College Auxiliary Services. **Publications:** *College Services*, bimonthly. Journal. **Circulation:** 2,300. **Advertising:** accepted ● *NACAS Quarterly*. Newsletter. Contains news and updates on issues important to the Association and the profession. Alternate Formats: online ● Membership Directory, annual ● Papers ● Also publishes position openings. **Conventions/Meetings:** annual conference (exhibits) - always October or November. 2008 Nov. 2-5, Chicago, IL; 2009 Nov. 8-11, Honolulu, HI ● workshop.

3479 ■ National School Supply and Equipment Association (NSSEA)
8380 Colesville Rd., Ste.250
Silver Spring, MD 20910
Ph: (301)495-0240
Free: (800)395-5550
Fax: (301)495-7362
E-mail: nssea@nssea.org
URL: http://www.nssea.org
Contact: Tim Holt, Pres./CEO
Founded: 1916. **Members:** 1,500. **Membership Dues:** dealer, $175-$350 (annual) ● supplier, service provider (based on gross annual sales), $700-$1,700 (annual) ● independent representative, $310 (annual). **Staff:** 14. **Budget:** $3,000,000. **Languages:** English, Spanish. **Description:** Manufacturers, dealers, retailers, and independent manufacturers' representatives of school equipment, instructional materials, and supplies. **Libraries: Type:** not open to the public. **Holdings:** 500; articles, books, periodicals, video recordings. **Subjects:** federal grants, education regulation, bar coding, school market. **Awards:** David McCurrach Distinguished Service Award. **Frequency:** annual. **Type:** recognition. **Recipient:** for a distinguished long-time member ● Education Excellence Awards. **Frequency:** annual. **Type:** recognition. **Recipient:** for involvement with local schools. **Computer Services:** Online services, available to members only. **Telecommunication Services:** electronic mail, tholt@nssea.org. **Committees:** Business Technology; Independent Manufacturers Representatives; Paper Manufacturers/Converters; Young Executives. **Councils:** Distributors; Equipment; Manufacturers; Retail Store. **Sections:** Auditorium Seating; Bleacher; Classroom Seating; Instructional Materials Group; Operable Partitions; Playground Equipment. **Absorbed:** (1978) Education Industries Association. **Formerly:** (1958) National School Service Institute. **Publications:** *Essentials*, bimonthly. Magazine. Includes the latest industry news, regular columns by recognized experts, association happenings, and school market profiles. **Price:** included in membership dues; $75.00 for nonmembers. **Circulation:** 3,200. **Advertising:** accepted ● Directory, annual. Features a complete alphabetical listing of all members by category, with geographic, personnel, and product group indexes. ● Also publishes special reports. **Conventions/Meetings:** annual convention and meeting (exhibits) - every fall ● annual Ed Expo - trade show, back to school show for educational products (exhibits) - always spring. 2009 Mar. 5-7, Dallas, TX.

Scientific Products

3480 ■ American Precision Optics Manufacturers Association (APOMA)
PO Box 20001
Rochester, NY 14602
Ph: (585)292-2676 (585)346-9513
Fax: (585)346-9513
E-mail: info@apoma.org
URL: http://www.apoma.org
Contact: Jim Sydor, Pres.
Founded: 1986. **Members:** 146. **Membership Dues:** corporate, $200-$1,200 (annual) ● associate, $250 (annual) ● affiliate, $1,200 (annual). **Description:** Precision optics manufacturers, glass manufacturers, and producers of optical materials. (Precision optics are ground and polished surfaces that are used in instrumentation panels to transmit, refract, and reflect radiation.) Seeks to increase members' share of precision optics markets in the U.S; works to inform users of optical components on the availability of domestic materials. Conducts research and educational programs; compiles statistics. Includes plan such as: disseminating information on federal regulatory policies affecting the industry; conducting surveys; developing and coordinating standards; developing a training program for precision optical manufacturing technicians. **Awards:** Student Support. **Frequency:** annual. **Type:** grant. **Publications:** *Communications*, quarterly. Newsletter. **Price:** free. **Conventions/Meetings:** quarterly conference (exhibits).

3481 ■ American Scientific Glassblowers Society (ASGS)
PO Box 778
Madison, NC 27025
Ph: (336)427-2406
Fax: (336)427-2496
E-mail: natl-office@asgs-glass.org
URL: http://www.asgs-glass.org
Contact: Jack Korfage, Pres.-Elect
Founded: 1952. **Members:** 700. **Membership Dues:** regular/associate, $75 (annual) ● junior, $60 (annual) ● student, $20 (annual) ● international, $85 (annual). **Regional Groups:** 11. **Description:** Glassblowers with more than 5 years' experience in making scientific glass apparatus (condensers, distillation apparatus, glass-to-metal seals, and vacuum devices); junior members are glassblowers with less than 5 years' professional experience; associates are persons connected with the manufacture or use of glass or glassblowing equipment in scientific work. Seeks to gather and disseminate information concerning scientific glassblowing, apparatus, equipment, and materials. **Libraries: Type:** not open to the public. **Holdings:** audiovisuals. **Awards:** Helmut

Drechsel Achievement Award. **Frequency:** annual. **Type:** recognition. **Recipient:** for outstanding contributions in promoting the society and scientific glassblowing at the section level ● J. Allen Alexander Award. **Frequency:** annual. **Type:** recognition. **Recipient:** for outstanding contributions in furthering the aims and ideals of the organization. **Committees:** Awards; Computer; Education; Elections; International Liaison; Methods and Materials; Outreach; Questions and Answers; References and Abstracts; Safety and Hazards; Section Liaison; Visual-Audio Education. **Publications:** *Fusion*, quarterly. Journal. Contains educational or informative articles on the business of scientific glass. Includes committee reports and news from overseas. **Price:** included in membership dues; $40.00 /year for nonmembers. **Circulation:** 800. **Advertising:** accepted ● *Proceedings of Symposium*, annual. **Price:** $33.00 each (hard cover); $25.00 each (soft cover). **Conventions/Meetings:** annual symposium (exhibits) - usually June.

3482 ■ Association of Medical Diagnostics Manufacturers (AMDM)

555 13th St. NW, Ste.7W-404
Washington, DC 20004
Ph: (202)637-6837 (202)637-8647
Fax: (202)637-5910
E-mail: amdm_secretary@sbcglobal.net
URL: http://www.amdm.org
Contact: Judi Smith, Pres.

Founded: 1973. **Members:** 75. **Membership Dues:** company with 500 or more employees (multiple sites), $2,200 (annual) ● company with 500 or more employees, $1,550 (annual) ● company with 101-500 employees, $850 (annual) ● company with 11-100 employees, $600 (annual) ● company with 1-10 employees, $300 (annual). **Budget:** $100,000. **Description:** Medical device manufacturers, distributors, and users. Informs members of regulatory policies and government legislation affecting the microbiological diagnostic equipment manufacturing industry. Represents members at legislative hearings. **Formerly:** (1984) Association for Microbiological Media Manufacturers; (2000) Association of Microbiological Diagnostic Manufacturers. **Publications:** *AMDM Newsletter*, biennial. **Price:** free for members. **Circulation:** 150. Alternate Formats: online. **Conventions/Meetings:** annual Focus Meeting ● annual meeting (exhibits) ● periodic seminar.

3483 ■ Independent Laboratory Distributors Association (ILDA)

PO Box 1464
Fairplay, CO 80440
Ph: (719)836-9091
Free: (888)878-4532
Fax: (719)836-9112
E-mail: kbretcko@ilda.org
URL: http://www.ilda.org
Contact: Bob Davison, Chm.

Founded: 1988. **Members:** 70. **Membership Dues:** distributor, manufacturer's representative, $750 (annual) ● associate (based on annual sales volume), $2,000-$3,000 (annual). **Staff:** 1. **Description:** Laboratory product distributors and suppliers. Works to provide a forum for networking and educating its members. Hosts annual meetings. **Telecommunication Services:** electronic mail, bdavison@bvascientific.com.

3484 ■ Laboratory Products Association (LPA)

225 Reinekers Ln., Ste.625
Alexandria, VA 22314
Ph: (703)836-1360
Fax: (703)836-6644
E-mail: membershipservices@lpanet.org
URL: http://www.lpanet.org
Contact: Jim Orcutt, Pres.

Founded: 1918. **Members:** 125. **Staff:** 2. **Budget:** $700,000. **Description:** Manufacturers and distributors of scientific research equipment and supplies. Conducts educational programs; compiles statistics. **Publications:** *LPA Reporter*, periodic. Newsletter. Alternate Formats: online. **Conventions/Meetings:** annual conference and board meeting - always November.

3485 ■ Measurement, Control, and Automation Association (MCAA)

PO Box 3698
Williamsburg, VA 23187-3698
Ph: (757)258-3100
Fax: (757)258-3100
E-mail: mcaa@measure.org
URL: http://www.measure.org
Contact: Cynthia A. Esher, Pres.

Founded: 1918. **Members:** 135. **Membership Dues:** manufacturer (based on annual sales), $1,560-$10,345 (annual) ● corporate group (based on aggregate sales), $7,210-$13,370 (annual) ● press and major consultancy, $2,400 (annual) ● independent consultant, $1,305 (annual) ● corporate (participating division), $1,925 (annual) ● representative/distributor, systems integrator (based on annual sales), $1,110-$1,775 (annual). **Staff:** 3. **Budget:** $400,000. **Description:** Manufacturers and distributors of instrumentation and systems. Seeks to expand members' share of the instrumentation and systems market through networking and education. Conducts management surveys on bookings, financial ratios, and salaries. **Formerly:** PMC Section of the Scientific Apparatus Makers Association. **Publications:** *Measuring Markets*, quarterly. Newsletter. Covers general economic indicators as well as specific industry trends. **Price:** included in membership dues; $250.00 /year for nonmembers. **Circulation:** 600. Alternate Formats: online. **Conventions/Meetings:** annual Executive Forum - conference, senior management education and networking - always spring ● annual Industry Breakfast - breakfast and meeting, in conjunction with Society for Instrumentation, Systems & Automation Exhibit - fall.

3486 ■ Medical Device Manufacturers Association (MDMA)

1350 I St. NW, Ste.540
Washington, DC 20005
Ph: (202)354-7171 (202)354-7174
E-mail: mleahey@medicaldevices.org
URL: http://www.medicaldevices.org
Contact: Mark B. Leahey Esq., Exec. Dir.

Founded: 1992. **Members:** 130. **Membership Dues:** active, $520 (annual). **Staff:** 4. **Description:** Represents and serves the innovators and entrepreneurs in the medical technology industry. **Telecommunication Services:** electronic mail, mdmainfo@medicaldevices.org. **Formerly:** Smaller Manufacturers Medical Device Association. **Publications:** *The MDMA Biweekly*. Newsletter. **Price:** included in membership dues ● Has also published the book Do Less Better, an analysis of the book Less Than the Sum of Its Parts by the House Energy and Commerce Committee, April 1994. **Conventions/Meetings:** annual meeting and conference (exhibits).

3487 ■ National Association of Scientific Materials Managers (NAOSMM)

c/o Amy Aldrige, Treas.
Florida State Univ.
Chemistry Dept.
106 DLC
Tallahassee, FL 32306
E-mail: aldridge@chem.fsu.edu
URL: http://www.naosmm.org
Contact: Joanne Brown CSMM, Pres.

Founded: 1974. **Members:** 500. **Membership Dues:** regular, $50 (annual) ● associate, $75 (annual) ● corporate, $150 (annual). **Description:** Stockroom managers and supervisors of federal, state, university, and commercial research facilities who are involved in the purchase and supply of scientific chemicals and scientific apparatus; associate members are manufacturing companies and scientific supply companies. Seeks to: provide safer handling of chemicals and equipment involved in scientific research; encourage recycling; provide information on safety and organization of storage areas. **Awards:** Nalge Nunc International Professional Training Fund. **Frequency:** annual. **Type:** monetary. **Recipient:** for regular members who receive little or no financial assistance from their employer ● NAOSMM Seminar & Trade Show Attendance Award. **Frequency:** annual. **Type:** monetary. **Recipient:** to members who do not have financial support to attend the yearly Conference and Trade Show ● Outstanding Scientific Materials Manager of the Year. **Frequency:** annual. **Type:** recognition. **Recipient:** for members. **Computer Services:** database, members, vendors, and trade show exhibitors ● mailing lists. **Telecommunication Services:** electronic mail, jcbrown@haverford.edu. **Committees:** Certification Program; Service Awards. **Publications:** *NAOSMM Newsline*, quarterly. Newsletter. Covers waste disposal, the relationship between exposure to chemicals and cancer, and the U.S. Occupational Safety and Health Administration. **Price:** included in membership dues. **Circulation:** 350. **Advertising:** accepted ● Directory, annual. Lists of individual and corporate members as well as vendors and exhibitors at the NAOSMM annual meeting. **Price:** included in membership dues. **Circulation:** 300. **Conventions/Meetings:** annual meeting, with symposium and exhibits (exhibits) - always July or August ● seminar and workshop, topics include safety, waste disposal, computerization of stock, and inventory control.

3488 ■ SAMA Group of Associations (SAMA)

c/o Laboratory Products Association
225 Reinekers Ln., Ste.625
Alexandria, VA 22314
Ph: (703)836-1360
Fax: (703)836-6644
E-mail: membershipservices@lpanet.org
URL: http://www.lpanet.org
Contact: Rick Moore, Chm.

Founded: 1918. **Members:** 200. **Staff:** 5. **Budget:** $1,500,000. **Description:** Umbrella organization of trade associations including the Analytical Life Science Systems Association, the Laboratory Products Association, and the Opto-Precision Instruments Association. Member companies include manufacturers and distributors of analytical, biomolecular, and optical instrumentation, laboratory equipment, and related products and services. Compiles industry statistics; conducts market research and industry surveys. Provides executive education. **Formerly:** Scientific Apparatus Makers Association; (1948) Apparatus Makers Association of America. **Publications:** *A/A News*, quarterly. Newsletter. **Price:** included in membership dues ● *LPA Business Report*, quarterly. Newsletter. **Price:** included in membership dues. **Conventions/Meetings:** seminar, on topics including distribution, exporting, and marketing.

3489 ■ Scientific Equipment and Furniture Association (SEFA)

c/o David J. Sutton, CAE, Exec. Dir.
1205 Franklin Ave., Ste.320
Garden City, NY 11530
Ph: (516)294-5424
Free: (877)294-5424
Fax: (516)294-2765
E-mail: sefalabs@aol.com
URL: http://www.sefalabs.com
Contact: David J. Sutton CAE, Exec. Dir.

Founded: 1988. **Members:** 80. **Membership Dues:** executive (based on annual revenue), $2,000-$3,800 (annual) ● associate, $700 (annual) ● sustaining (based on annual revenue), $1,500-$3,000 (annual). **Staff:** 2. **Multinational. Description:** Manufacturers of scientific and laboratory equipment, furniture, and fixtures and designers of the labs. Promotes growth and development of the scientific equipment industries. Works to improve the quality, safety, and timeliness of completion of laboratories and related facilities; conducts educational programs; represents members' interests before government agencies, industrial organizations, and the public. **Libraries: Type:** reference. **Holdings:** periodicals. **Subjects:** laboratories, scientific equipment, standards. **Awards:** Lab of the Year. **Frequency:** annual. **Type:** recognition. **Recipient:** for research laboratories, quality assurance laboratories, software development facilities, and testing and standards labs. **Computer Services:** Online services, publications on products.

Committees: Casework; Ductless Enclosure; Fixtures; Fume Hoods; Installation; Laboratory of Work Surfaces; Scope of Work; Standards. **Publications:** *SEFA Desk Reference Manual*. **Price:** $79.95/copy. Alternate Formats: online; CD-ROM ● *SEFAScope*. Newsletter. Alternate Formats: online. **Conventions/ Meetings:** semiannual conference ● semiannual meeting, educational ● annual meeting and conference.

3490 ■ Ultrasonic Industry Association (UIA)
PO Box 2307
Dayton, OH 45401-2307
Ph: (937)586-3725
Fax: (937)586-3699
E-mail: uia@ultrasonics.org
URL: http://www.ultrasonics.org
Contact: Foster Stulen, Pres.
Founded: 1973. **Members:** 98. **Membership Dues:** sustaining, $765 (annual) ● corporate, $305 (annual) ● individual, $115 (annual) ● student, $40 (annual). **Staff:** 2. **Budget:** $60,000. **Description:** Manufacturers and users of ultrasonic equipment and component parts for ultrasonic equipment. Promotes the ultrasonic industry; cooperation with government on legislation and relations affecting ultrasonic equipment; collection and dissemination of information; research into use and safety of ultrasonic products; establishment of liaison with other organizations in the field. **Libraries: Type:** not open to the public. **Holdings:** 1; articles. **Awards:** Graduate Research Award. **Frequency:** annual. **Type:** recognition. **Recipient:** to an individual who has made a significant contribution to the ultrasonic industry ● Outstanding New Ultrasonic Product. **Frequency:** annual. **Type:** recognition. **Recipient:** to a company that has introduced the most significant new ultrasonic product ● Outstanding Ultrasonic Application. **Frequency:** annual. **Type:** recognition. **Recipient:** to a company with the most significant ultrasonic application in the past year. **Councils:** High Frequency Ultrasonic. **Subcommittees:** Ultrasonic Products Classification. **Formed by Merger of:** Ultrasonic Manufacturers Association; Ultrasonic Industry Council. **Publications:** *Vibrations*, quarterly. Newsletter. **Advertising:** accepted. Alternate Formats: online ● Directory, annual. **Conventions/Meetings:** annual symposium and workshop (exhibits).

Seafood

3491 ■ American Scallop Association (ASA)
c/o Harvey Mickelson, Gen. Counsel
30 Cornell St.
New Bedford, MA 02740
Ph: (508)993-8800
Fax: (508)992-8031
Contact: Harvey Mickelson, Gen. Counsel
Founded: 1991. **Members:** 40. **Membership Dues:** voting, $3,000 (annual). **Description:** Promotes consumption of scallops. Represents the interests of scallop processors and fishermen before government agencies and the public. **Publications:** *American Scallop Association Newsletter*, monthly. **Conventions/Meetings:** monthly meeting.

3492 ■ Maine Lobstermen's Association (MLA)
21C Western Ave., Box 1
Kennebunk, ME 04043
Ph: (207)967-4555
Fax: (866)407-3770
E-mail: info@mainelobstermen.org
URL: http://www.mainelobstermen.org
Contact: Patrice McCarron, Exec. Dir.
Founded: 1954. **Members:** 1,200. **Membership Dues:** harvester voting (over 65/under 18), $50 (annual) ● harvester voting (highliner), $175 (annual) ● harvester voting (regular), associate non-voting (friend, sternman/apprentice), $100 (annual) ● harvester voting (family), $150 (annual) ● business highliner (non-voting), $250 (annual) ● business (non-voting), $125 (annual). **Staff:** 3. **Description:** Licensed lobstermen and supporting business. Gives Maine's lobstermen a voice and influence at the highest levels of government. **Computer Services:** database, business directory. **Publications:** Newsletter, monthly. **Price:** free for members. **Circulation:** 2,000.

3493 ■ Middle Atlantic Fisheries Association (MAFA)
Address Unknown since 2008
Founded: 1928. **Members:** 125. **Staff:** 2. **Description:** Wholesalers and boat owners in Middle Atlantic area.

3494 ■ Molluscan Shellfish Institute
c/o National Fisheries Institute
7918 Jones Br. Dr., Ste.700
McLean, VA 22102
Ph: (703)752-8880
Fax: (703)752-7583
E-mail: contact@nfi.org
URL: http://www.aboutseafood.com
Contact: Bob Collette, Contact
Founded: 1908. **Members:** 100. **Staff:** 2. **Description:** A division of the National Fisheries Institute (see separate entry). Shellfish producers, processors, distributors, growers, and suppliers to the industry. Works to promote, protect, and advance the interests of the shellfish industry. Cooperates with federal, state, and municipal authorities in matters of legislation, sanitation standards, controls, and conservation. **Affiliated With:** National Fisheries Institute. **Formerly:** Shellfish Institute of North America; (1970) Oyster Institute of North America. **Conventions/Meetings:** annual convention.

3495 ■ National Blue Crab Industry Association (NBCIA)
Address Unknown since 2007
Members: 25. **Staff:** 2. **Description:** Harvesters and processors of blue crabs. A division of National Fisheries Institute (see separate entry). **Affiliated With:** National Fisheries Institute. **Conventions/ Meetings:** annual meeting.

3496 ■ National Fisheries Institute (NFI)
7918 Jones Br. Dr., Ste.700
McLean, VA 22102
Ph: (703)752-8880
Fax: (703)752-4619
E-mail: contact@nfi.org
URL: http://aboutseafood.com
Contact: John Connelly, Pres.
Founded: 1945. **Members:** 700. **Membership Dues:** general restaurant (based on number of restaurant), $1,000-$10,000 (annual) ● trade association (based on budget), $1,000-$5,000 (annual). **Staff:** 15. **Budget:** $2,300,000. **Regional Groups:** 8. **Description:** Producers (boat owners), distributors, processors, wholesalers, importers and exporters and canners of fish and shellfish. **Libraries: Type:** not open to the public. **Subjects:** technical, regulatory. **Awards:** NFI Person of the Year. **Frequency:** annual. **Type:** recognition. **Computer Services:** Information services, fish and seafood industry resources. **Additional Websites:** http://icfa.net. **Telecommunication Services:** electronic mail, jconnelly@nfi.org. **Committees:** National Fisheries Political Action. **Divisions:** Fisheries Scholarship Fund; National Blue Crab Industry Annual (see separate entry); National Fish Meal and Oil Association Works for complete equality and integration of the blind in society. Provides support and information services.; Shellfish Institute of North America Works for complete equality and integration of the blind in society. Provides support and information services. **Publications:** *Buyers Guide*, annual. Membership Directory. Includes membership list and suppliers guide. **Price:** free for members; $200.00 for nonmembers. **Circulation:** 1,300. **Advertising:** accepted ● *NFI Insider*, weekly. Newsletter. Reports on legislation and regulation affecting the industry; industry and institute news; membership updates; new member news. **Price:** free, for members only. **Circulation:** 2,000. **Conventions/Meetings:** annual conference and convention (exhibits) - always October or November.

3497 ■ National Seafood Educators (NSE)
PO Box 60006
Seattle, WA 98160
Ph: (206)546-6410
Free: (800)348-0010
Fax: (206)546-6411
E-mail: informationnse@seafoodeducators.com
URL: http://www.seafoodeducators.com
Contact: Evie Hansen, Dir./Founder
Founded: 1982. **Staff:** 3. **Budget:** $500,000. **Description:** Promotes the consumption of seafood. Seeks to educate the public about nutrition and seafood. Maintains speakers' bureau; conducts educational programs; operates training seminars. **Libraries: Type:** reference. **Holdings:** artwork, audiovisuals, books, clippings, periodicals. **Subjects:** seafood. **Awards:** Seafood Business Award. **Type:** recognition. **Publications:** *Light-Hearted Seafood*. Book. **Price:** $10.95/copy ● *Seafood*, biweekly. Article ● *Seafood: A Collection of Heart-Healthy Recipes*. Book. **Price:** $13.95/copy ● *Seafood Grilling Twice a Week*. Book. **Price:** $14.95/copy ● *Seafood Twice A Week*. Book. **Price:** $14.95/copy.

3498 ■ National Shrimp Industry Association (NSIA)
c/o Beth Dancy
1520 Berkeley Rd.
Highland Park, IL 60035
Ph: (847)831-2030
Fax: (847)831-2343
E-mail: info@nsiaonline.org
Contact: Beth Dancy, Contact
Founded: 1957. **Members:** 40. **Membership Dues:** individual, $500 (annual). **Staff:** 1. **Description:** Producers and processors of breaded, cooked, peeled, and quick frozen shrimp; industry suppliers of ingredients and services. **Formerly:** (1984) National Shrimp Breaders and Processors Association; (2000) National Shrimp Processors Association. **Conventions/Meetings:** annual conference - always spring.

3499 ■ New England Fisheries Development Association (NEFDA)
c/o Kenelm W. Coons, Exec. Dir.
PO Box 5307
Annapolis, MD 21403-0702
Ph: (443)482-9889
Fax: (443)482-9420
E-mail: kencoons@comcast.net
Contact: Kenelm W. Coons, Exec. Dir.
Founded: 1980. **Members:** 180. **Staff:** 2. **State Groups:** 4. **Local Groups:** 8. **Description:** Fishermen, processors, retailers, and suppliers united to: expand regional efforts to upgrade fish quality; develop new domestic and overseas markets; work with shippers and handlers to improve quality protection; develop new market forms and products. Acts as information source for the industry and provide services, including sales leads and referrals, technical assistance and media information. **Formerly:** (1989) New England Fisheries Development Foundation. **Publications:** Publishes consumer education materials and operating guides for seafood packers and vessel operators.

3500 ■ Northwest Fisheries Association (NWFA)
2208 NW Market St., Ste.318
Seattle, WA 98107
Ph: (206)789-6197
Fax: (206)789-8147
E-mail: marilyn@northwestfisheries.org
URL: http://www.northwestfisheries.org
Contact: Marilyn Klansnic, Business Mgr.
Founded: 1951. **Members:** 165. **Staff:** 1. **Description:** Primary and secondary seafood processors, seafood brokers, distributors, and direct support industries. Provides a positive business climate for members and enhances the flow of information throughout the Pacific fishing and seafood industry. **Affiliated With:** National Fisheries Institute. **Publications:** Brochure.

3501 ■ Pacific Coast Shellfish Growers Association (PCSGA)
120 State Ave. NE, PMB No. 142
Olympia, WA 98501
Ph: (360)754-2744
Fax: (360)754-2743
E-mail: pcsga@pcsga.org
URL: http://www.pcsga.org
Contact: Robin Downey, Exec. Dir.
Founded: 1930. **Members:** 170. **Membership Dues:** grower (maximum; based on annual sales), $59,000 (annual) ● subscriber, $40 (annual) ● friend, $125 (annual) ● associate, $275 (annual) ● sustaining, $600 (annual) ● corporate, $1,200 (annual) ● patron, $5,000 (annual). **Staff:** 3. **Budget:** $310,000. **Description:** Oyster, clam, mussel, scallop, geoduck growers, openers, packers and shippers in Alaska, California, Oregon, Washington, Hawaii, and Mexico. **Libraries: Type:** reference. **Telecommunication Services:** electronic mail, robindowney@pcsga.org. **Committees:** Administration/Fundraising; Annual Conference Planning; Government Relations; Marketing and Public Relations. **Formerly:** (1999) Pacific Coast Oyster Growers Association. **Publications:** *Longlines PCSGA*, bimonthly. Newsletter. **Price:** $35.00 for nonmembers; free for members. **Advertising:** accepted. Alternate Formats: online. **Conventions/Meetings:** annual conference and general assembly, includes trade show (exhibits) - always fall, September-October.

3502 ■ Pacific Seafood Processors Association (PSPA)
1900 W Emerson Pl., No. 205
Seattle, WA 98119
Ph: (206)281-1667
Fax: (206)283-2387
E-mail: info@pspafish.net
URL: http://www.pspafish.net
Contact: Glenn E. Reed, Pres.
Founded: 1914. **Members:** 16. **Staff:** 4. **Description:** Represents processors of canned and frozen seafood of Alaska, Oregon, and Washington. Aims to foster a better public understanding of the importance of the seafood industry and its value to the regional and national economies. **Libraries: Type:** not open to the public. **Formerly:** (1978) Association of Pacific Fisheries. **Conventions/Meetings:** annual meeting.

3503 ■ Seafood Choices Alliance (SCA)
8401 Colesville Rd., Ste.500
Silver Spring, MD 20910
Ph: (301)495-9570
Fax: (301)495-4846
E-mail: info@seafoodchoices.com
URL: http://www.seafoodchoices.com
Contact: Mike Boots, Dir.
Founded: 2001. **Members:** 2,400. **Multinational. Description:** Represents seafood professionals. Seeks to inform, connect and mobilize the nation's "leading voices" in support of a sustainable supply of seafood choices. Enables members to advance actions that reflect their shared concern for the long term supply of seafood and the long term health of the ocean environment. Provides the seafood sector, including fishermen, chefs and other purveyors with the information needed to make better choices about seafood. **Computer Services:** database, list of members ● database, SeaSense ● information services, seafood resources. **Publications:** *Afishianado*. Newsletter. Details the current trends in sustainable seafood, current market research and listings of upcoming seafood events nationwide.

3504 ■ Southeastern Fisheries Association (SFA)
1118-B Thomasville Rd.
Tallahassee, FL 32303
Ph: (850)224-0612
Fax: (850)222-3663
E-mail: bobfish@aol.com
URL: http://www.southeasternfish.org
Contact: Robert P. Jones, Exec. Dir./Ed.
Founded: 1952. **Members:** 400. **Membership Dues:** boat captain, $50 (annual) ● friend of fishermen, $100 (annual) ● retail, HACCP, seafood restaurant, $200 (annual) ● associate, $500 (annual) ● full corporate, $800 (annual). **Staff:** 3. **Description:** Producers, distributors and suppliers of seafood in the South Atlantic and Gulf of Mexico areas. Disseminates information on legislation, both proposed and implemented, which affects fishermen in that area. Promotes and represents commercial fishermen's interests in legislative, industrial and environmental matters. Provides HAACP training onsite. **Computer Services:** Online services, America. **Telecommunication Services:** electronic mail, bobfish@southeasternfish.org. **Publications:** *Hot Lines*, monthly. Newsletter. Alternate Formats: online ● *Importing Seafood - A Buyer's Guide*. Book. **Price:** $3.70 for members; $20.00 for nonmembers ● *International Conference on Shrimp Bycatch*. Proceedings. **Price:** $10.00 for members; $55.00 for nonmembers. **Conventions/Meetings:** annual meeting (exhibits) - every June.

3505 ■ United States Freshwater Prawn and Shrimp Growers Association (USFPSGA)
655 Napanee Rd.
Leland, MS 38756
Ph: (662)686-2894 (662)390-3528
Fax: (662)686-2894
E-mail: usprawngrowers@yahoo.com
URL: http://www.freshwaterprawn.org
Contact: Dolores Fratesi, Pres.
Founded: 2002. **Membership Dues:** producer, $50 (annual) ● allied tradesman, $100 (annual) ● education and research personnel, federal/state agency or organization, $10 (annual) ● friend, $25 (annual). **Description:** Assimilates and disseminates information on the production, management and marketing of farm-raised prawn and shrimp. Encourages and promotes educational programs pertaining to farm-raised prawn and shrimp production and management. Fosters the development of farm-raised prawn and shrimp production as a thriving commercial business that will benefit its members and the public. **Telecommunication Services:** electronic mail, aquaculture@tecinfo.com. **Publications:** Newsletter, quarterly. Alternate Formats: online ● Brochure. Alternate Formats: online.

3506 ■ United States Tuna Foundation (USTF)
c/o National Fisheries Institute
7918 Jones Br. Dr., Ste.700
McLean, VA 22102
Ph: (703)752-8880
E-mail: info@tunafoundation.org
URL: http://www.tunafacts.com
Contact: Mary Anne Hansan, VP
Founded: 1976. **Members:** 77. **Description:** Represents tuna boat owners, fishermen, processors, fishermen's unions, and cannery workers' unions. Analyzes all matters related to or affecting the industry as a whole. **Councils:** Tuna Nutrition. **Absorbed:** (1987) Tuna Research Foundation.

Securities

3507 ■ American Stock Exchange (AMEX)
86 Trinity Pl.
New York, NY 10006
Ph: (212)306-1000
Free: (866)422-2639
Fax: (212)306-1218
E-mail: amexfeedback@amex.com
URL: http://www.amex.com
Contact: Neal L. Wolkoff, Chm./CEO
Members: 864. **Staff:** 777. **Description:** Represents domestic and international equities and derivative securities market. Provides an auction marketplace that integrates service and information programs for its listed companies. **Divisions:** Administration and Finance; Derivative Securities; Equities; Legal and Regulatory; Member Firm and Trading Floor Services. **Formerly:** (1908) New York Curb Agency; (1911) New York Curb Market Association; (1921) New York Curb Market; (1929) New York Curb Exchange. **Publications:** *American Stock Exchange—Annual Report*. Includes review of previous year's activities of the association with financial statement. **Price:** free ● *AMEX Fact Book*, annual. Features a statistical reference work covering equities and derivatives; includes directories of company trading statistics and corporate addresses. **Price:** $12.50/copy, plus tax. **Conventions/Meetings:** annual meeting - every second Monday in April, New York City.

3508 ■ Association of Securities and Exchange Commission Alumni (ASECA)
PO Box 5767
Washington, DC 20016
Ph: (202)462-1211
E-mail: info@secalumni.org
URL: http://www.secalumni.org
Contact: Cecile Srodes, Exec. Dir.
Founded: 1990. **Members:** 1,000. **Membership Dues:** individual, $50 (annual). **Staff:** 4. **Regional Groups:** 9. **Description:** Former employees of the Securities and Exchange Commission. Sponsors educational programs; maintains speakers' bureau. **Awards:** William O. Douglas Award. **Frequency:** annual. **Type:** recognition. **Recipient:** for outstanding contribution to growth and development of federal securities laws. **Publications:** *ASECA Newsletter*, quarterly. **Circulation:** 780. **Conventions/Meetings:** semiannual meeting and convention.

3509 ■ Chicago Board Options Exchange (CBOE)
400 S LaSalle St.
Chicago, IL 60605
Ph: (312)786-5600
Free: (877)THE-CBOE
Fax: (312)786-7409
E-mail: help@cboe.com
URL: http://www.cboe.com
Contact: Ms. Janice Calvin, Contact
Founded: 1973. **Description:** Individuals, institutions and firms engaged in the buying and selling of various products including stock options, cash-settled index options, options on HOLDRs, options on Exchange Traded Funds and Structured Products. **Telecommunication Services:** electronic mail, calvinj@cboe.com. **Publications:** Also publishes rule book (revised as needed), and product brochures.

3510 ■ Chicago Stock Exchange (CHX)
One Financial Pl.
440 S LaSalle St.
Chicago, IL 60605
Ph: (312)663-2222
E-mail: info@chx.com
URL: http://www.chx.com
Contact: David A. Herron, CEO
Founded: 1882. **Members:** 446. **Description:** Brokers and dealers in local and national securities. Wholly-owned subsidiaries: Midwest Securities Trust Company; Midwest Clearing Corp; Mortgage Backed Securities Clearing Corporation. Provides an auction market for purchase and sale of equity securities. **Formerly:** (1993) Midwest Stock Exchange. **Publications:** Report, annual. **Conventions/Meetings:** annual meeting - always April, Chicago, IL.

3511 ■ Consolidated Tape Association (CTA)
c/o Brian McNelis, Vendor Rep.
Reuters Am., Inc.
The Reuters Bldg.
3 Times Sq., 22nd Fl.
New York, NY 10036
Ph: (646)223-4439
Fax: (862)266-4176
E-mail: brian.mcnelis@reuters.com
URL: http://www.nysedata.com/cta
Contact: Brian McNelis, Vendor Rep.
Founded: 1974. **Members:** 9. **Description:** American, Boston, Cincinnati, Chicago, New York, Pacific, and Philadelphia Stock Exchanges, the Chicago Board Options Exchange, and the National Association of Securities Dealers (see separate entry). Administers the real time collection, reporting, processing, and dissemination of stock transaction information. **Convention/Meeting:** none. **Publications:** *Activity Report*, monthly.

3512 ■ Council of Institutional Investors (CII)
888 17th St. NW, Ste.500
Washington, DC 20006
Ph: (202)822-0800
Fax: (202)822-0801
E-mail: info@cii.org
URL: http://www.cii.org
Contact: Ann Yerger, Exec. Dir.
Founded: 1985. **Members:** 294. **Staff:** 8. **Description:** Representatives of public and union pension funds and nonprofit foundations and endowment funds. Primary concern is to encourage pension fund trustees to take an active role in assuring that corporate actions are not taken at the expense of shareholders. Objectives are to: help members increase return on their investments and satisfy their fiduciary obligations; study, on a nonpartisan basis, issues of corporate governance, policies, or practices affecting the well-being and financial security of participants and beneficiaries covered under benefit plans; observe existing or proposed federal, state, or local legislation or regulations affecting institutional investors and their beneficiaries; recommend positions on legislative, administrative, and regulatory actions affecting institutional investors and their beneficiaries, and corporate actions affecting the value of members' investments. Plans to provide members with information on a variety of nontraditional investments and, where appropriate, assist members in acting jointly to take advantage of some of these investments. **Libraries: Type:** not open to the public. **Publications:** *Alert*, weekly ● Newsletter, monthly. **Conventions/Meetings:** semiannual conference.

3513 ■ EMTA
360 Madison Ave., 18th Fl.
New York, NY 10017
Ph: (646)637-9100
Fax: (646)637-9128
E-mail: sortiz@emta.org
URL: http://www.emta.org
Contact: Suzette Ortiz, Office Mgr.
Founded: 1990. **Members:** 110. **Membership Dues:** full, $30,000 (annual) ● associate, $15,000 (annual) ● affiliate, buy-side (2) (under $1B EM assets under management), $5,000 (annual) ● buy-side (1) (with $1B or more EM assets under management), $10,000 (annual). **Staff:** 10. **Budget:** $3,000,000. **Multinational. Description:** Represents Emerging Markets trading and investment community. Promotes the orderly development of fair, efficient and transparent trading markets for Emerging Markets instruments and to helping integrate the Emerging Markets into the global capital markets. **Formerly:** (2004) Emerging Markets Traders Association. **Publications:** *Debt Trading Volume Survey*, quarterly. **Price:** $250.00 ● Bulletin, quarterly. **Price:** free for members. **Conventions/Meetings:** annual Fall Forum - meeting - in New York City ● annual Spring Forum - meeting - New York City ● annual Summer Forum - meeting - in United Kingdom ● annual Winter Forum - meeting - in United Kingdom.

3514 ■ Investment Adviser Association (IAA)
1050 17th St. NW, Ste.725
Washington, DC 20036-5503
Ph: (202)293-4222
Fax: (202)293-4223
E-mail: iaa@investmentadviser.org
URL: http://www.icaa.org
Contact: Mr. David G. Tittsworth, Exec. Dir./VP
Founded: 1937. **Members:** 300. **Membership Dues:** firm (based on assets under management), $2,500-$15,000 (annual). **Staff:** 8. **Description:** Federally registered investment adviser firms. Represents the interests of the investment management profession before legislative and regulatory bodies. **Additional Websites:** http://www.investmentadviser.org. **Telecommunication Services:** electronic mail, david.tittsworth@investmentadviser.org. **Committees:** Legal and Regulatory; Performance Advertising; Technology. **Formerly:** (2005) Investment Counsel Association of America. **Publications:** *Directory of Member Firms*, annual. Lists member firms, telephone numbers, addresses, types of accounts. **Price:** free ● *Standards of Practice* ● Newsletter, monthly. **Conventions/Meetings:** annual conference (exhibits).

3515 ■ Investment Company Institute (ICI)
1401 H St. NW, 12th Fl.
Washington, DC 20005
Ph: (202)326-5800
Fax: (202)326-8309
E-mail: memberservices@ici.org
URL: http://www.ici.org
Contact: Paul Schott Stevens, Pres.
Founded: 1940. **Members:** 8,518. **Staff:** 180. **Budget:** $44,000,000. **Description:** Represents open-end and closed-end investment companies registered under Investment Company Act of 1940; investment advisers to, and underwriters of, such companies; unit investment trust sponsors; interested others. Represents members in matters of legislation, taxation, regulation, economic research marketing, and public information. Provides a clearinghouse for information on the mutual fund industry. Compiles statistics. **Libraries: Type:** reference; not open to the public. **Subjects:** economic, financial, legal. **Awards:** Financial Writers Award. **Frequency:** annual. **Type:** recognition ● Journalism Award. **Frequency:** annual. **Type:** recognition. **Committees:** Accounting/Treasurers; Closed-End Investment Company; Federal Legislation; Industry Statistics; International; Investment Advisers; Operations; Pension; Public Information; Research; SEC Rules; Shareholder Communications; Small Funds; Tax. **Absorbed:** (1973) Association of Mutual Fund Plan Sponsors; (1987) Association of Publicly Traded Investment Funds. **Formerly:** (1961) National Association of Investment Companies. **Publications:** *Investment Company Service Directory*, annual. Contains lists of service type providers to the investment company industry. **Price:** $35.00. **Advertising:** accepted ● *Mutual Fund Fact Book*, annual. Lists facts and figures on the U.S. mutual fund industry; articles on sales and performance trends, and history and growth. **Price:** $25.00 ● *Trends in Mutual Fund Activity*, monthly. Features tables of statistics showing the following: industry sales, exchanges, redemptions, assets, cash holdings, and portfolio transactions. **Price:** free for members; $400.00 /year for nonmembers ● Annual Report. Summarizes the mutual fund industry's events and accomplishments over the preceding year. **Price:** free. **Conventions/Meetings:** annual meeting, general membership (exhibits) - always spring, Washington, DC.

3516 ■ Mutual Fund Education Alliance (MFEA)
100 NW Englewood Rd., Ste.130
Kansas City, MO 64118
Ph: (816)454-9422
Fax: (816)454-9322
E-mail: info@mfea.com
URL: http://www.mfea.info
Contact: Michelle A. Smith, Managing Dir.
Founded: 1971. **Members:** 39. **Staff:** 5. **Description:** Represents mutual fund marketers and distributors. Helps investors understand mutual funds and the benefits of long-term investing; members are America's leading mutual fund companies who collectively serve over eighty million shareholders and manage nearly 3 trillion in assets; approximately one half of all assets invested in mutual funds today. Maintains Mutual Fund Investor's Center, designed to serve as a resource for investors who want to use mutual funds to reach their financial goals; here investors can find "the largest collection of mutual fund companies, website links, fund listings and exclusive planning, tracking and monitoring tools available on the Internet". **Awards:** STAR Shareholder Communication's Awards Program. **Frequency:** annual. **Type:** recognition. **Telecommunication Services:** electronic mail, masmith@mfea.com. **Councils:** E-Commerce; Intermediary Distribution; Marketing and Communications. **Formerly:** (1988) No-Load Mutual Fund Association. **Conventions/Meetings:** annual conference.

3517 ■ NASD
1735 K St. NW
Washington, DC 20006-1500
Ph: (301)590-6500 (646)625-6541
Fax: (240)386-5443
URL: http://www.nasd.com
Contact: Mary L. Schapiro, Chair/CEO
Founded: 1939. **Members:** 5,500. **Staff:** 2,000. **Budget:** $185,000,000. **Description:** Represents the interests of securities firms doing business with the public. Engages in financial regulatory services, dedicated to "bringing integrity to the markets and confidence to investors through effective and efficient regulation and complementary compliance, and technology-based services. Touches virtually every aspect of the securities business - from registering and educating all industry participants, to examining securities firms, enforcing both NASD rules and the federal securities laws, and administering the largest dispute resolution forum for investors and member firms". **Formerly:** (1936) Investment Bankers Conference; (2003) National Association of Securities Dealers. **Publications:** *NASD Notices to Members*, monthly. Report. Reports on NASD board actions, market-related developments, and disciplinary actions taken against member firms. **Price:** $225.00/year; $25.00/copy. **Circulation:** 17,000 ● Annual Report, annual. **Price:** free. **Circulation:** 18,000. Alternate Formats: online. **Conventions/Meetings:** semiannual conference ● bimonthly meeting.

3518 ■ National Association of Securities Professionals (NASP)
1212 New York Ave. NW, Ste.950
Washington, DC 20005-3987
Ph: (202)371-5535
Fax: (202)371-5536
E-mail: info@nasphq.com
URL: http://www.nasphq.org
Contact: Cheryl Marrow, Chair
Founded: 1985. **Members:** 300. **Membership Dues:** individual (based on years in the industry), $125-$325 (annual) ● associate, $75 (annual) ● student, $25 (annual). **Staff:** 2. **Description:** Individuals and organizations engaging in a job function dealing with taxable or tax-exempt debt or equity instruments. Seeks to represent the interests of minorities and women in the securities industry. Maintains business records. **Awards:** Joyce Johnson Award. **Frequency:** annual. **Type:** recognition ● Joyce Johnson Scholarship Fund. **Type:** scholarship ● Travers J. Bell, Jr. Award. **Frequency:** annual. **Type:** recognition. **Recipient:** for above average business success and standard for excellence, achievement, and enlightened leadership in the finance industry. **Computer Services:** database, jobs ● database, membership directory ● mailing lists. **Telecommunication Services:** electronic mail, cmarrow@koried.com. **Publications:** *Bull's Eye*, periodic. Newsletter ● Brochure. **Conventions/Meetings:** annual luncheon - mid-March ● annual meeting (exhibits) - September ● annual Pension and Financial Services - conference - June.

3519 ■ New York Society of Security Analysts (NYSSA)
1177 Ave. of the Americas, 2nd Fl.
New York, NY 10036-2714
Ph: (212)541-4530
Free: (800)248-0108
Fax: (212)541-4677
E-mail: staff@nyssa.org
URL: http://www.nyssa.org
Contact: Dodge O. Dorland, Pres.
Founded: 1937. **Members:** 8,000. **Membership Dues:** regular, affiliate, non-primary and friend, $200 (annual) ● student and retired, $60 (annual). **Staff:** 16. **Budget:** $4,000,000. **Description:** Security analysts and portfolio managers employed primarily in New York by brokerage houses, banks, insurance companies, mutual funds, and other financial institutions. Conducts educational forums on topics relating to the securities markets. Maintains placement service. **Libraries: Type:** reference. **Holdings:** audio recordings, video recordings. **Subjects:** corporate meetings, other investment topics. **Telecommunication Services:** electronic mail, dodge@nyssa.org. **Committees:** Alternative Investments; Career Development; Corporate Governance and Shareholder

Rights; Education; High Net Worth Individual; International; Investment Strategy; Membership; New Media; Scholarship/Mentoring; Seminar and Portfolio Management; Value Investing. **Publications:** *Corporate Governance Handbook*. **Price:** $5.00 for members; $10.00 for nonmembers ● *Executive Recruiters Directory for Investment Professionals*. **Price:** $20.00/copy ● *NYSSA News*, monthly. Newsletter. Includes program meeting announcements, career development bulletin, and new member listings. **Price:** free for members; $100.00 /year for nonmembers ● Membership Directory. **Price:** $100.00. **Conventions/Meetings:** luncheon and seminar, for executives of nationally and internationally known firms.

3520 ■ New York Stock Exchange (NYSE)

c/o The Corporate Secretary
11 Wall St.
New York, NY 10005
Ph: (212)656-3000 (212)656-2062
Fax: (212)656-3939
E-mail: boardofdirectors@nyse.com
URL: http://www.nyse.com
Contact: John A. Thain, CEO/Dir.

Founded: 1792. **Description:** Aims to "add value to the capital-raising and asset-management process by providing the highest-quality and most cost-effective self-regulated marketplace for the trading of financial instruments, promote confidence in and understanding of that process, and serve as a forum for discussion of relevant national and international policy issues". **Publications:** *The Exchange*, monthly. Newsletter. Alternate Formats: online ● *New York Stock Exchange: Another Century*. Book. **Price:** $75.00 each ● *The New York Stock Exchange: The First 200 Years*. Book. **Price:** $49.95 each ● *Weekly Bulletin*. Alternate Formats: online ● Magazine, bimonthly.

3521 ■ North American Securities Administrators Association (NASAA)

750 1st St. NE, Ste.1140
Washington, DC 20002-8034
Ph: (202)737-0900
Free: (800)84-NASAA
Fax: (202)783-3571
E-mail: info@nasaa.org
URL: http://www.nasaa.org
Contact: Russ Iuculano, Exec. Dir.

Founded: 1919. **Members:** 66. **Staff:** 15. **Description:** Represents the interests of the state, provincial and territorial securities administrators in the U.S., Canada, Mexico and Puerto Rico. Provides support to its members in government relations and with federal regulators, industry SROs and other groups. **Committees:** Communications; CRD/IARD Forms and Process; CRD/IARD Steering; Federal Legislation; International; Legal Services; NASAA Corporate Governance; Standards, Certification and Training. **Sections:** Broker/Dealer; Corporate Finance; Enforcement; Investor Education. **Formerly:** (1945) National Association of Securities Commissioners. **Publications:** *NASAA Reports in CCH*, monthly. **Conventions/Meetings:** annual conference - usually fall ● annual Public Policy Spring Conference.

3522 ■ Pacific Stock Exchange (PSE)

Address Unknown since 2008

Founded: 1957. **Members:** 551. **Staff:** 376. **Budget:** $47,000,000. **Description:** Maintains markets in nearly 1800 equity issues and 300 options in San Francisco and Los Angeles, CA. **Committees:** Political Action. **Formerly:** Pacific Coast Stock Exchange. **Publications:** *Directory of Securities*, quarterly ● Annual Report, annual ● Newsletter, quarterly ● Also publishes marketing related materials. **Conventions/Meetings:** annual board meeting - always California.

3523 ■ Securities Industry and Financial Markets Association (SIFMA)

120 Broadway, 35th Fl.
New York, NY 10271-0080
Ph: (212)608-1500
Fax: (212)968-0703
E-mail: rbrockhaus@sifma.org
URL: http://www.sifma.org
Contact: Marc E. Lackritz, Pres./CEO

Founded: 1972. **Members:** 600. **Staff:** 120. **Regional Groups:** 8. **State Groups:** 13. **Multinational. Description:** Represents more than 650 member firms of all sizes, in all financial markets in the U.S. and around the world. Enhances the public's trust and confidence in the markets, delivering an efficient, enhanced member network of access and forward-looking services, as well as premiere educational resources for the professionals in the industry and the investors whom they serve. Maintains offices in New York City and Washington, DC. **Committees:** Capital Markets; Clearing Firms; Securities Industry Political Action; Trading. **Divisions:** Compliance and Legal; Credit; Customer Account Transfer; Data Management; Dividend; Financial Management; Internal Auditors; International Operations; Proxy; Reorganization; Securities Lending; Securities Operations. **Absorbed:** Glass-Steagall Act Study Committee. **Formed by Merger of:** (2007) Securities Industry Association and The Bond Market Association; Investment Bankers Association of America; Association of Stock Exchange Firms. **Publications:** *Research Reports*, monthly ● *Securities Industry Association—Directory and Guide*, annual ● *Securities Industry Association—Foreign Activity Report*, quarterly. Covers purchases and sales of U.S. securities by foreign investors; includes statistics and graphs. **Price:** $50.00 /year for members; $75.00 /year for nonmembers ● *Securities Industry Association—Yearbook*. Contains detailed information on individual firms, including key personnel and department heads, number of accounts, and capital. **Price:** $110.00 for members; $150.00 for nonmembers ● *Securities Industry Trends*, quarterly. Report. Covers trends within the securities industry and on economic developments affecting securities firms; includes statistics. **Price:** $75.00 /year for members; $125.00 /year for nonmembers. **Conventions/Meetings:** annual Compliance and Legal Seminar ● annual Internet Conference ● annual Small Firms Conference (exhibits).

3524 ■ Securities Transfer Association (STA)

PO Box 5220
Hazlet, NJ 07730
Ph: (732)888-6040
Fax: (732)888-2121
E-mail: cgaffney@stai.org
URL: http://www.stai.org
Contact: Carol A. Gaffney, Admin.

Founded: 1911. **Members:** 200. **Membership Dues:** commercial transfer agent, $500-$1,500 (annual) ● mutual fund transfer agent, $1,000-$1,500 (annual) ● in-house TA and corporate, $1,000 (annual) ● non-agent, $2,000 (annual). **Staff:** 2. **Budget:** $600,000. **Multinational. Description:** Commercial transfer agents, banks, corporations; and vendors. Aims to transmit information and exchange ideas in the securities industry as it pertains to securities transfer. **Formerly:** New York Stock Transfer Association; (1987) Stock Transfer Association. **Publications:** Newsletter, quarterly. **Conventions/Meetings:** annual meeting - usually October.

3525 ■ Security Traders Association (STA)

420 Lexington Ave., Ste.2334
New York, NY 10170
Ph: (212)867-7002
Fax: (212)867-7030
E-mail: traders@securitytraders.org
URL: http://www.securitytraders.org
Contact: Mr. John Giesea, Pres./CEO

Founded: 1934. **Members:** 7,000. **Staff:** 4. **Regional Groups:** 33. **Local Groups:** 35. **Multinational. Description:** Brokers and dealers handling listed and OTC securities, stocks, and bonds, and all securities. Conducts educational programs. Promotes the interests of members throughout the global financial markets. Provides representation of these interests in the legislative, regulatory and technological processes. Fosters goodwill and high standards of integrity in accord with the Association's founding principle. **Telecommunication Services:** electronic mail, jgiesea@securitytraders.org. **Formerly:** (1989) National Security Traders Association. **Publications:** *Traders Annual*. Contains convention information. **Advertising:** accepted. **Conventions/Meetings:** annual meeting (exhibits) - always October/November.

Security

3526 ■ American Society for Amusement Park Safety and Security (ASAPSS)

c/o George Hull, Treas.
Brookfield Zoo
3300 Golf Rd.
Brookfield, IL 60513
Ph: (708)485-0023
E-mail: gehull@brookfieldzoo.org
URL: http://www.asapss.com
Contact: George Hull, Treas.

Founded: 1972. **Members:** 100. **Description:** Security and safety supervisors of amusement parks in the U.S. and Canada. Provides forum for discussion of safety and security problems. **Publications:** Newsletter, semiannual. **Conventions/Meetings:** annual conference.

3527 ■ International Association of Home Safety and Security Professionals (IAHSSP)

Address Unknown since 2008

Founded: 1992. **Membership Dues:** professional, $150 (annual) ● allied, $250 (annual) ● associate, $125 (annual). **Description:** Locksmiths, security consultants, security guards, alarm system and home automation installers, researchers, writers, educators, manufacturers, retailer suppliers, and other safety and security professionals. Provides information on personal, home, and auto safety to journalists, educators, students, and other laypersons. Promotes and represents the interests of members. **Libraries: Type:** reference. **Holdings:** archival material, artwork, audiovisuals, books, clippings, periodicals. **Computer Services:** database ● online services. **Telecommunication Services:** electronic mail, director@iahssp.org. **Publications:** *The Home Protector*, monthly. Newsletter. Includes technical articles, interviews, and product reviews. **Price:** free, for members only. Alternate Formats: online.

3528 ■ International Association of Investigative Locksmiths (IAIL)

1507 Whitmarsh Cir.
Severn, MD 21144
E-mail: mail@iail.org
URL: http://www.iail.org
Contact: James Bickers CFL, Pres.

Membership Dues: individual, $35 (annual). **Multinational. Description:** Seeks to improve the safety and security of the public in general. Educates locksmiths, police officers, insurance investigators and security professionals in the capabilities and techniques used in the field of investigative locksmithing. Offers technical, professional advice, and investigative services to the community, insurance companies, and law enforcement officials. Educates the public in the field of investigative locksmithing through seminars and meetings. **Telecommunication Services:** electronic mail, bickersj@msn.com.

3529 ■ International Association of Professional Security Consultants (IAPSC)

525 SW 5th St., Ste.A
Des Moines, IA 50309-4501
Ph: (515)282-8192
Fax: (515)282-9117
E-mail: iapsc@iapsc.org
URL: http://www.iapsc.org
Contact: Elliot A. Boxerbaum, Pres.

Founded: 1984. **Members:** 72. **Membership Dues:** active/associate/internal consultant, $500 (annual). **Budget:** $30,000. **Description:** Security management, technical, training, and forensic consultants. Promotes understanding and cooperation among members and industries or individuals requiring such services. Seeks to enhance members' knowledge through seminars, training programs, and educational materials. Works to foster public awareness of the security consulting industry; serves as a clearinghouse for consultants' requirements. Maintains code of conduct, ethics, and professional standards. Offers consultant referral service; operates speakers' bureau. **Awards:** Charles A. Sennewald Distinguished Service Accolade. **Frequency:** annual. **Type:** recognition. **Recipient:** for significant contributions to the profession. **Computer Services:** database, members. **Telecommunication Services:** phone referral service, Consultant Referral Service, (202)-466-7212. **Committees:** Ethics. **Publications:** *Consultants Directory*, annual ● *Independent Consultant*, bimonthly. Newsletter ● Also publishes registry. **Conventions/Meetings:** annual convention, educational and practice management ● How to Succeed as a Professional Security Consultant - seminar, precedes the Annual Conference and Business Meeting.

3530 ■ International Cargo Security Council (ICSC)
1400 Eye St. NW, Ste.1050
Washington, DC 20005
Ph: (202)962-0190
Fax: (202)962-3939
E-mail: admin@cargosecurity.com
URL: http://www.cargosecurity.com
Contact: Graham Hauck, Exec. Dir.
Founded: 1975. **Members:** 1,100. **Membership Dues:** individual, $300 (annual) ● affiliate, $40 (annual) ● corporate, $2,000-$4,000 (annual) ● affiliate (unit), $200 (annual). **Staff:** 4. **Regional Groups:** 7. **Description:** Cargo transportation and security professionals. Unites to improve cargo transportation security, serves as a central clearinghouse for collection and distribution of information, provides a platform to address transportation industry matters relating to cargo theft, and assists and supports voluntary and self-help initiatives by government, transportation centers, and industry cargo security interests to develop programs to combat cargo loss. **Awards:** Government Leadership. **Frequency:** annual. **Type:** recognition ● Industry Leadership Award. **Frequency:** annual. **Type:** recognition ● Law Enforcement Award. **Frequency:** annual. **Type:** recognition ● Media Leadership. **Frequency:** annual. **Type:** recognition ● National Leadership Award. **Frequency:** annual. **Type:** recognition. **Publications:** *Cargo Security Report*, quarterly. Newsletter. Contains information regarding cargo security. **Price:** free for members; $60.00 for nonmembers ● *Guidelines for Cargo Security and Loss Control*, triennial. Book. **Price:** free for members; $30.00 additional copy for members; $35.00 for nonmembers ● *Who's Who in Cargo Security*, annual. Membership Directory. **Price:** free for members; $30.00 additional copy for members; $75.00 for nonmembers. **Conventions/Meetings:** annual conference (exhibits) ● annual meeting, membership ● roundtable - 3/year ● seminar - 3/year.

3531 ■ International Foundation for Protection Officers (IFPO)
PO Box 771329
Naples, FL 34107-1329
Ph: (239)430-0534
Fax: (239)430-0533
E-mail: sandi@ifpo.com
URL: http://www.ifpo.org
Contact: Sandi Davies, Exec. Dir.
Founded: 1988. **Members:** 5,000. **Membership Dues:** associate, $45 (annual). **Staff:** 15. **Description:** Seeks to provide for the education, training, and certification of protection officers worldwide. Maintains and improves standards of excellence and establish ethical standards within the industry. Improves the public perception of protection officers. Interacts with colleges, universities, and other post-secondary educational institutions to facilitate education and certification; conducts research. Maintains Certified Protections Officer program, that provides professional designation and consists of training in patrols, report writing, crime scenes, interviewing, investigations, public relations, stress management, physical security, VIP protection, and first aid. **Publications:** *Protection Officer News*, quarterly. Newsletter. **Price:** $18.00. **Circulation:** 5,000. **Advertising:** accepted. **Conventions/Meetings:** seminar.

3532 ■ International Intelligence Network (INTELNET)
PO Box 350
Gladwyne, PA 19035
Ph: (610)520-9222
Free: (800)784-2020
E-mail: intelnet@bellatlantic.net
URL: http://www.intelnetwork.org
Contact: James P. Carino Jr., Exec. Dir.
Members: 400. **Membership Dues:** regular, $100 (annual). **Multinational. Description:** Serves as a network of investigators and security consultants. Provides a means of identifying qualified, reliable individuals who have the particular skills needed to accomplish assignments related to the private investigation and security fields. Provides an assortment of services to corporations, law firms, families, individuals and foreign allies. **Awards:** Lifetime Membership Award. **Frequency:** annual. **Type:** recognition. **Recipient:** to INTELNET member for recognition of outstanding service to the association. **Publications:** *Intelnet News*. Newsletter. Alternate Formats: online ● Articles. Alternate Formats: online.

3533 ■ International Organization of Black Security Executives (IOBSE)
PO Box 92
Fairfield, CA 94533
Free: (888)884-6273
Fax: (301)352-7807
E-mail: earl_watson@gap.com
URL: http://www.iobse.com
Contact: Earl Watson, Pres.
Founded: 1982. **Multinational. Description:** Creates an international network for minority security professionals. Promotes the security industry by providing professional resources. Educates minorities on the careers and opportunities in security management. Encourages members to promote the exchange of information, ideas, experience and knowledge about the process and techniques relating to security. **Special Interest Groups:** Consultant; Executive Protection; Healthcare; Investigations; Retail Assets Protection. **Publications:** *Insight*, monthly. Newsletter.

3534 ■ International Security Management Association (ISMA)
PO Box 623
Buffalo, IA 52728
Free: (800)368-1894
Fax: (563)381-4283
E-mail: isma3@aol.com
URL: http://www.ismanet.com
Contact: Margaret Levine, Sec.
Founded: 1983. **Members:** 420. **Membership Dues:** active, $700 (annual) ● life, $700. **Staff:** 1. **Multinational. Description:** Senior security executives of multinational business firms and chief executive officers of full service security services companies. Aims to assist senior security executives in coordinating and exchanging information about security management and to establish high business and professional standards. **Publications:** Membership Directory, periodic. **Price:** available to members only ● Also publishes in-house information letter. **Conventions/Meetings:** semiannual conference - always June and January ● annual workshop.

3535 ■ International Security, Trust and Privacy Alliance (ISTPA)
3525 Del Mar Heights Rd., Ste.327
San Diego, CA 92130-2122
Ph: (703)478-7600
E-mail: director@istpa.org
URL: http://www.istpa.org
Contact: John Sabo, Pres.
Membership Dues: corporate, $1,000-$4,000 (annual) ● university, government, $1,000 (annual) ● individual, $250 (annual). **Multinational. Description:** Promotes the protection of personal information. Works to clarify and resolve existing and revolving issues related to security, trusts and privacy. Develops a framework for the protection of personal and organizational data. Creates understanding of the usability, manageability and cost implications of technologies in data protection. Conducts research, demonstration and inter operatibility projects. **Awards:** Distinguished Service Award. **Type:** recognition. **Recipient:** for exceptional contributions to the ISTPA.

3536 ■ National Alarm Association of America (NAAA)
PO Box 3409
Dayton, OH 45401
Ph: (937)461-2208
Free: (800)283-6285
Fax: (937)461-4759
E-mail: info@naaa.org
URL: http://www.naaa.org
Contact: Gene D. Riddlebaugh, Pres.
Founded: 1984. **Members:** 400. **Membership Dues:** regular, associate, $100 (annual). **Description:** Individuals, partnerships, and corporations that sell, install, or maintain alarm systems, or provide alarm service; manufacturers that supply equipment and services to members. Seeks to: develop an educational program on the need for and use of professionally installed and maintained alarm systems; promote a code of business ethics in the security industry; support legislation affecting the industry; open regular channels of communication between members and manufacturers of security products. **Awards:** Robert J. Bargert Award. **Frequency:** annual. **Type:** recognition. **Recipient:** making the industry better. **Publications:** *Alarm Installer Training Course and Manual*. **Price:** $850.00 for nonmembers; $679.00 for members ● *Alarm Installer Training Manual*. Book. **Price:** $231.00 for nonmembers; $181.00 for members ● *Counterforce*, semiannual. Newsletter ● *Fire Alarm Handbook - NICET Level 1 and 2*. **Price:** $100.00 for nonmembers; $90.00 for members ● *Video Tape Installer Training Program*. Manual. Includes a *Manual on Testing Program*, lessons, and tapes. **Conventions/Meetings:** annual Northwest Security Show - general assembly, electronic security of all types (exhibits) - end of July ● regional meeting.

3537 ■ National Association of Security Companies (NASCO)
1625 Prince St., Ste.225-B
Alexandria, VA 22314
Ph: (703)519-0912
Fax: (703)519-0915
E-mail: information@nasco.org
URL: http://www.nasco.org
Contact: Joseph Ricci, Exec. Dir.
Founded: 1972. **Members:** 16. **Staff:** 2. **Description:** Major security guard companies. Monitors legislation affecting the industry. **Awards:** Colonel Edgar B. Watson Award. **Frequency:** annual. **Type:** recognition. **Formerly:** (1994) Committee of National Security Companies. **Conventions/Meetings:** meeting - 3/year.

3538 ■ National Burglar and Fire Alarm Association (NBFAA)
2300 Valley View Ln., Ste.230
Irving, TX 75062
Ph: (214)260-5970
Free: (888)447-1689
Fax: (214)260-5979
E-mail: webmaster@alarm.org
URL: http://www.alarm.org
Contact: Merlin Guilbeau, Exec. Dir.
Founded: 1948. **Members:** 2,600. **Staff:** 14. **Budget:** $1,500,000. **State Groups:** 42. **Description:** Represents electronic safety, security and systems professionals. **Awards:** Morris F. Weinstock Memorial Award. **Frequency:** annual. **Type:** recognition ● Sara Jackson Award. **Frequency:** annual. **Type:** recognition. **Recipient:** for member in good standing. **Telecommunication Services:** electronic mail, merling@alarm.org. **Committees:** Alarm Industry Research and Education Foundation; Training and Education. **Publications:** *Considerations When Purchasing Home Burglar Alarm System*. Brochures ● *Model False Alarm Ordinance* ● *National Burglar and Fire*

Alarm Association—Membership Directory, annual. Includes personnel index. **Price:** first copy free for members. **Circulation:** 3,500. **Advertising:** accepted. Also Cited As: *NBFAA Roster* ● *National Newsline*, monthly. **Price:** $150.00 /year for nonmembers ● *Weekly E-Zines*. Magazine. Alternate Formats: online ● NBFAA Resource Center Publications. **Conventions/Meetings:** annual conference and trade show, with suppliers (exhibits) ● annual meeting.

3539 ■ National Council of Investigation and Security Services (NCISS)

7501 Sparrows Point Blvd.
Baltimore, MD 21219-1927
Free: (800)445-8408
Fax: (410)388-9746
E-mail: nciss@comcast.net
URL: http://www.nciss.org
Contact: Carolyn Ward, Exec. Dir.

Founded: 1975. **Members:** 877. **Membership Dues:** regular, $125 (annual) ● associate, $75 (annual) ● service, $250 (annual) ● association, $100 (annual). **Staff:** 1. **Budget:** $35,000. **Description:** Monitors national and state legislative and regulatory activities. Develops and encourages the practice of high standards of personal and professional conduct. Acquires, preserves, and disseminates data and valuable information; promotes the purpose of investigation and guard companies. Provides information about state legislation and regulatory activities that could have an impact on a particular firm or on the industry in general; acts as spokesman for the industry before legislative and regulatory bodies at both federal and state levels. **Awards:** John J. Duffy Award. **Frequency:** annual. **Type:** recognition. **Recipient:** to an individual who brought credit to NCISS ● Wayne Wonder Award. **Frequency:** annual. **Type:** recognition. **Recipient:** to members of NCISS. **Telecommunication Services:** electronic mail, eferraro@businesscontrols.com. **Committees:** Advertising; Audit; Awards; Education and Training; Ethics; Insurance; Legislative. **Publications:** *NCISS Report*, quarterly. Newsletter. **Price:** included in membership dues. **Circulation:** 1,050. **Advertising:** accepted ● Directory published annually. **Conventions/Meetings:** annual conference (exhibits) - always spring ● annual meeting.

3540 ■ Nine Lives Associates (NLA)

Executive Protection Inst.
PO Box 802
Berryville, VA 22611-0802
Ph: (540)554-2540 (540)554-2547
Fax: (540)554-2558
E-mail: info@personalprotection.com
URL: http://www.personalprotection.com
Contact: Dr. Richard W. Kobetz, Dir.

Founded: 1978. **Members:** 2,500. **Membership Dues:** regular, $45 (annual). **Staff:** 1. **Budget:** $20,000. **Multinational. Description:** Law enforcement, correctional, military, and security professionals who have been granted Personal Protection Specialist Certification through completion of the protective services program offered by the Executive Protection Institute; conducts research; EPI programs emphasize personal survival skills and techniques for the protection of others. Provides professional recognition for qualified individuals engaged in executive protection assignments. Maintains placement service. Operates speakers' bureau; compiles statistics. **Libraries: Type:** reference. **Holdings:** 1,000. **Subjects:** law enforcement and security subjects. **Awards:** N.L.A. Achievement Award. **Frequency:** annual. **Type:** recognition. **Recipient:** for heroism and outstanding achievements in executive protection. **Committees:** Awards; Training. **Affiliated With:** Academy of Security Educators and Trainers. **Publications:** *Business Intelligence - A Primer*. Book. **Price:** $22.00 each ● *Executive Protection Specialist*. Handbook. Aids the learning process in the field of providing protective services. **Price:** $25.00 each ● *Nine Lives Associates—Network*, quarterly. Newsletter. Includes obituaries, training information, and book lists. **Price:** available to members or by request ● *Providing Executive Protection*. Book. Features photographs, charts, guidelines, checklists, appendices and resource information. **Price:** $29.00 each; $49.00 combined (volume 1 and 2) ● Membership Directory, annual. **Price:** available to members only ● Providing executive protection, Volume II. **Conventions/Meetings:** annual conference, for training.

3541 ■ Safe and Vault Technicians Association (SAVTA)

3500 Easy St.
Dallas, TX 75247
Ph: (214)819-9771
Fax: (214)819-9736
E-mail: mary@aloa.org
URL: http://www.savta.org
Contact: Ron Snively CPS, Pres.

Founded: 1986. **Members:** 2,000. **Membership Dues:** individual in U.S., $161 (annual) ● individual in Canada, $176 (annual) ● individual outside U.S. and Canada, $218 (annual). **Staff:** 3. **Budget:** $500,000. **For-Profit. Description:** Retail safe techs; associate members are manufacturers and distributors of safes and vaults. Aims to educate and provide current information to individuals in the physical security industry. Maintains information and referral services for members; offers insurance and bonding programs. Conducts annual three-day technical training courses. **Libraries: Type:** reference; not open to the public. **Holdings:** 2,000; books, periodicals. **Subjects:** locksmithing, vaults, safes, technical procedures. **Awards:** Hall of Fame. **Frequency:** annual. **Type:** recognition. **Recipient:** for support in industry. **Computer Services:** database ● online services, Safe-Tech forum. **Committees:** Education; Proficiency Registration. **Publications:** *Safe and Vault Technicians Association Directory*, annual. Membership Directory. **Price:** included in membership dues. **Circulation:** 3,000. **Advertising:** accepted ● *Safe and Vault Technology*, monthly. Journal. Covers association and industry information for the physical security professional. **Price:** included in membership dues; $96.00 /year for nonmembers. **Circulation:** 3,000. **Advertising:** accepted ● *Technical Bulletins*, annual. **Conventions/Meetings:** annual SAFETECH - convention and trade show (exhibits) - always April/May.

3542 ■ Security Industry Association (SIA)

635 Slaters Ln., Ste.110
Alexandria, VA 22314
Ph: (703)683-2075
Free: (866)817-8888
Fax: (703)683-2469
E-mail: info@siaonline.org
URL: http://www.siaonline.org
Contact: Richard Chace, Exec. Dir.

Founded: 1969. **Members:** 220. **Membership Dues:** regular (based on annual sales), $500-$30,000 (annual) ● division/subsidiary of regular and associate (based on annual sales), $250-$5,000 (annual) ● correspondent, $250 (annual). **Staff:** 10. **Description:** Security equipment manufacturers and distributors. Seeks for the advancement of companies in the security products industry. Promotes the export of American security products. Conducts research programs, educational programs, technical seminars, communications with related industries, and other activities. Maintains speakers' bureau; compiles statistics. **Libraries: Type:** not open to the public. **Holdings:** 100. **Subjects:** security. **Awards:** George R. Lippert. **Frequency:** annual. **Type:** recognition ● Gold Circle. **Frequency:** annual. **Type:** recognition ● New Product Showcase. **Frequency:** semiannual. **Type:** recognition. **Computer Services:** Mailing lists, of members. **Telecommunication Services:** electronic mail, webmaster@siaonline.org. **Committees:** Education; Global Marketing; Government Relations; Industry Relations; Management Conference. **Special Interest Groups:** Access Control; Biometrics; CCTV; Contract Monitoring; Distributors; Fire Detection; Sensors. **Formerly:** Security Equipment Manufacturers Association; (1988) Security Equipment Industry Association. **Publications:** *Quarterly Research Update*. Reports. Features a compilation of news briefs reporting electronic security and related industry business and technology trends and information. **Price:** $250.00 for nonmembers; free for members. **Circulation:** 2,500. Alternate Formats: online. Also Cited As: *QRU* ● Also publishes ANSI-accredited technical standards. **Conventions/Meetings:** annual Management Conference - meeting - always fall ● annual meeting (exhibits).

3543 ■ United States Contract Security Association (USCSA)

PO Box 54244
Atlanta, GA 30308
Ph: (770)486-3425 (770)486-3436
Free: (866)92-USCSA
Fax: (770)486-4894
E-mail: info@uscsa.org
URL: http://www.uscsa.org
Contact: Billy Ray Jackson, Pres.

Membership Dues: regular, $500 (annual) ● associate, $250 (annual). **Description:** Promotes performance through empowerment. Serves the Security Association community by enhancing the effectiveness of communications and improving the awareness of security issues and concerns. Develops professionalism in the private security industry. **Telecommunication Services:** additional toll-free number, (866)89-USCSA ● additional toll-free number, (866)91-USCSA.

Self Defense

3544 ■ Association of Defensive Spray Manufacturers (ADSM)

906 Olive St., Ste.1200
St. Louis, MO 63101-1434
Ph: (314)241-1445
Fax: (314)241-1449
E-mail: adsm@pepperspray.org
URL: http://www.pepperspray.org
Contact: Kevin Dallett, Pres.

Founded: 1992. **Membership Dues:** filler, supplier, distributor, $1,000 (annual). **Description:** Dedicated to manufacturers of defensive aerosol sprays. Facilitates the cooperation of its members to their mutual advantage and protection in matters relating to the manufacture of non-lethal chemical weapons. **Libraries: Type:** reference. **Holdings:** clippings. **Subjects:** defensive sprays, including studies.

Service

3545 ■ Association for Services Management International (AFSMI)

1342 Colonial Blvd., Ste.25D
Fort Myers, FL 33907
Ph: (239)275-7887
Free: (800)333-9786
Fax: (239)275-0794
E-mail: sfern@afsmi.org
URL: http://www.afsmi.org
Contact: J.B. Wood, CEO

Founded: 1975. **Members:** 5,000. **Membership Dues:** individual (new), $375 (annual) ● individual, $650 (biennial). **Staff:** 15. **Budget:** $3,000,000. **Multinational. Description:** Provides networking, market research, education and certification opportunities to professions in the industry sectors of professional services, e-service, hardware, services, software support, and marketing and business development. Publishes and sponsors studies and market research covering best practices, professional services, benchmarking, online databases, personnel compensation, healthcare, the state of the industry, and future trends. **Libraries: Type:** reference. **Holdings:** articles, books. **Awards:** George Harmen Award. **Frequency:** annual. **Type:** recognition. **Committees:** Education Summit. **Special Interest Groups:** Healthcare. **Formerly:** (1990) Association of Field Service Managers, International. **Publications:** *Sbusiness: The Journal For Executives and Managers of the High Technology Service Industry*, bimonthly. Lists chapter meeting locations and dates and AFSMI award winners; includes advertisers index, information, research, and case studies for s-business. **Price:** $65.00/year. ISSN: 1049-2135. **Circulation:** 5,000.

Advertising: accepted. **Conventions/Meetings:** annual S-Business Education Summit & Expo - international conference.

3546 ■ Association of Support Professionals (ASP)
122 Barnard Ave.
Watertown, MA 02472-3414
Ph: (617)924-3944
Fax: (617)924-7288
E-mail: jfarber@asponline.com
URL: http://www.asponline.com
Contact: Jane Farber, Contact
Members: 1,200. **Membership Dues:** individual, $80 (annual) ● corporate, $500 (annual). **Multinational. Description:** Publishes research reports on a wide range of support topics, including support compensation and fee-based support. Provides members with career development services. **Libraries: Type:** open to the public. **Holdings:** articles, reports. **Subjects:** tech support, outsourcing, call center, management, quality. **Awards:** Ten Best Web Support Sites. **Frequency:** annual. **Type:** recognition. **Recipient:** for excellence in online service and support. **Publications:** *CAN-SPAM Guidelines for Tech Support E-mail.* Report. Offers a detailed look at what support organizations must do to comply with new Federal Anti-Spam Law. **Price:** $60.00 for nonmembers; included in membership dues ● *Tech Support Cost Ratio Survey.* Provides benchmark data for revenue and headcount ratios, labor and overhead costs, productivity, escalation, and other useful metrics. **Price:** $60.00 for nonmembers; included in membership dues ● *Technical Support Salary Survey*, annual. Provides compensation data for senior support executives, department managers, and project managers. **Price:** $60.00 for nonmembers; included in membership dues ● *Technical Support Training Metrics.* Report. Provides benchmarks and guidance for best practices in in-house training. **Price:** $60.00 for nonmembers; included in membership dues ● *Training Salary Survey.* Contains new survey data on compensation benchmarks for instructor, trainers, and content developers. **Price:** $60.00 for nonmembers; included in membership dues.

3547 ■ Coalition of Service Industries (CSI)
1090 Vermont Ave. NW, Ste.420
Washington, DC 20005
Ph: (202)289-7460
Fax: (202)775-1726
URL: http://www.uscsi.org
Contact: J. Robert Vastine, Pres.
Founded: 1982. **Members:** 60. **Staff:** 5. **Description:** Increases attention to measurement of productivity in services and revises national economic indicators to account for services. Represents US service sector in multilateral trade negotiations. Works with interested groups internationally. **Computer Services:** Mailing lists, of members. **Committees:** Data Collection; Tax; Trade. **Publications:** *CSI Reports*, quarterly. Newsletter. Reports on coalition activities and legislation affecting the service industries. Includes tax and conference news, bibliography file, media update. **Price:** free ● *The Service Economy*, quarterly ● Brochure. **Conventions/Meetings:** annual meeting.

3548 ■ Custom Electronic Design Installation Association (CEDIA)
7150 Winton Dr., Ste.300
Indianapolis, IN 46268
Ph: (317)328-4336
Free: (800)669-5329
Fax: (317)280-8527
E-mail: member@cedia.org
URL: http://www.cedia.net
Contact: Utz Baldwin, Pres.
Founded: 1989. **Members:** 3,501. **Membership Dues:** residential electronic systems professional (provisional), $400 (annual) ● residential electronic systems professional (full), affiliate, $500 (annual) ● manufacturer (based on annual revenues), $1,000-$10,000 (annual) ● consultant, sales representative, $300 (annual) ● distributor (based on annual revenues), $500-$2,000 (annual). **Staff:** 5. **Multinational. Description:** Develops and encourages high standards of conduct and service from installers of electronic systems for the home. Compiles statistics related to the custom installation business; conducts educational programs. **Libraries: Type:** reference. **Holdings:** artwork, audio recordings, books, clippings, periodicals, video recordings. **Subjects:** custom design installation. **Awards:** Designer. **Frequency:** annual. **Type:** recognition ● Electronic Systems Contractor of the Year. **Frequency:** annual. **Type:** recognition ● Lifetime Achievement. **Frequency:** annual. **Type:** recognition ● Manufacturer's Excellence. **Frequency:** annual. **Type:** recognition. **Publications:** *Electronic Lifestyles*, quarterly. Magazine. **Conventions/Meetings:** annual Exposition, Educational Conference, and Trade Show - convention (exhibits) - 2008 Sept. 3-7, Denver, CO.

3549 ■ Equipment Service Association (ESA)
c/o Kathleen A. DeMarco, Exec. Dir.
PO Box 1420
Cherry Hill, NJ 08034
Ph: (856)489-0753
Free: (866)372-3155
Fax: (856)424-9248
E-mail: esa@2esa.org
URL: http://www.2esa.org
Contact: Kathleen A. DeMarco, Exec. Dir.
Founded: 1959. **Members:** 180. **Membership Dues:** regular, $260 (annual) ● supporting, $460 (annual). **Staff:** 1. **Budget:** $100,000. **Multinational. Description:** Independent businessmen whose companies repair and rebuild tools and equipment. Promotes good relations with equipment managers; improves the status and image of the equipment service industry; encourages the use of advanced management techniques among members; improves profitability among members and promote new business for the industry. Sponsors business and technical workshops. Maintains library. **Computer Services:** database ● mailing lists. **Publications:** *ESA Bulletin*, monthly. Newsletter. Includes computer corner, new members, parts and equipment buy/sell, president's letter, and shop talk. **Price:** included in membership dues. **Circulation:** 400. **Advertising:** accepted ● Directory, annual. Includes membership information. **Price:** included in membership dues. **Circulation:** 225. **Advertising:** accepted. **Conventions/Meetings:** annual convention (exhibits).

3550 ■ Help Desk Institute (HDI)
102 S Tejon, Ste.1200
Colorado Springs, CO 80903
Ph: (719)268-0174
Free: (800)248-5667
Fax: (719)268-0184
E-mail: support@thinkhdi.com
URL: http://www.thinkhdi.com
Contact: Sophie Klossner, Board Admin.
Founded: 1989. **Members:** 7,500. **Membership Dues:** platinum plus, $1,295 (annual) ● platinum plus - international, $1,395 (annual) ● platinum, $560 (annual) ● platinum - international, $660 (annual) ● gold, $340 (annual) ● gold - international, $440 (annual) ● silver, $115 (annual) ● bronze, $75 (annual). **Staff:** 26. **For-Profit. Multinational. Description:** Corporations, organizations, and agencies offering help desks or other customer or user information services. Promotes effective operation of help desks and related services. Facilitates exchange of information among members; evaluates and certifies support centers; conducts research and educational programs. **Awards:** HDI All Star Award. **Frequency:** monthly. **Type:** recognition. **Recipient:** for the outstanding performance of nominated professionals in the help desk and support services industry ● Help Desk Analyst of the Year Award. **Frequency:** annual. **Type:** recognition. **Recipient:** to the industry's best first level support analysts ● Help Desk Hero Award. **Frequency:** quarterly. **Type:** recognition. **Recipient:** to professionals who are exemplary role models for their team, their organization and the industry ● Team Excellence Award. **Frequency:** annual. **Type:** recognition. **Recipient:** to a team that enhances the image of the help desk profession. **Computer Services:** Online services, discussion room. **Publications:** *Focus Book Series* ● *HDI Industry Insider*, biweekly. Newsletter. Delivers industry news and trends to service and support professionals around the world. Alternate Formats: online ● *Support and Service Suppliers Directory*, periodic ● *SupportWorld.* Magazine. **Advertising:** accepted ● Reports, annual. **Conventions/Meetings:** annual conference.

3551 ■ International Customer Service Association (ICSA)
401 N Michigan Ave.
Chicago, IL 60611
Ph: (312)321-6800
Free: (800)360-4272
E-mail: icsa@smithbucklin.com
URL: http://www.icsa.com
Contact: Kimberly Mims, Pres.
Founded: 1981. **Members:** 3,000. **Membership Dues:** professional, affiliate, $245 (annual). **Staff:** 7. **Budget:** $1,250,000. **Local Groups:** 25. **Description:** Customer service professionals in public and private sectors united to develop the theory and understanding of customer service and management. Goals are to: promote professional development; standardize terminology and phrases; provide career counseling and placement services; establish hiring guidelines, performance standards, and job descriptions. Provides a forum for shared problems and solutions. Compiles statistics. **Awards:** Award of Excellence. **Frequency:** annual. **Type:** recognition. **Computer Services:** Mailing lists, of members. **Telecommunication Services:** electronic mail, kbarksdale@manpowerutah.com. **Publications:** *Customer Service Management Guide.* **Price:** $75.00 for members; $95.00 for nonmembers ● *ICSA Journal*, semiannual. **Price:** included in membership dues ● *ICSA News*, bimonthly. Newsletter. Reports customer service innovations and practices implemented by ICSA members and lists new members. **Price:** included in membership dues. **Circulation:** 3,000. **Advertising:** accepted ● *1995 Compensation Study.* **Price:** $45.00 for members; $75.00 for nonmembers ● *1996 Benchmarking Study.* **Price:** $95.00 for members; $145.00 for nonmembers ● Membership Directory, annual. **Conventions/Meetings:** annual conference (exhibits).

3552 ■ National Association of Service Managers (NASM)
PO Box 250796
Milwaukee, WI 53225
Ph: (414)466-6060 (414)847-1200
Fax: (414)466-0840
E-mail: kenc@kencook.com
URL: http://www.nasm.com
Contact: Mr. Ken Cook, Treas.
Founded: 1955. **Members:** 200. **Membership Dues:** regular/associate, $225 (annual) ● chapter, $112 (annual). **Staff:** 1. **Budget:** $20,000. **Description:** Business executives concerned with product service. Supports companies in all segments of the economy by providing professional development education to their service executives; communicates the impact of technological innovations on service management methods; establishes and promulgates principles of effective products service management. Co-sponsors Service Management Institute with University of Wisconsin at Madison, and University of Texas at Arlington, TX. Offers placement services; compiles statistics. **Awards:** Certificate of Appreciation. **Frequency:** annual. **Type:** recognition ● Certified Service Executive. **Frequency:** 5/year. **Type:** recognition. **Recipient:** for certification in the service, parts and warranty business similar to CPA or CPM for the accounting and purchasing professions. **Computer Services:** Mailing lists ● online services, registration, educational program, member's only area. **Programs:** Educational. **Absorbed:** (1972) Service Managers of America. **Publications:** *NASM Directory*, annual. Alternate Formats: online ● *Salary Survey*, annual ● *Service Management*, quarterly. Newsletter. Alternate Formats: online ● Membership Directory, annual. **Advertising:** accepted. Alternate Formats: online. **Conventions/Meetings:** annual conference (exhibits) ● conference - always mid-year.

3553 ■ Professional Service Association (PSA)
71 Columbia St.
Cohoes, NY 12047
Ph: (518)237-7777
Free: (888)777-8851
Fax: (518)237-0418
E-mail: psaworld@aol.com
URL: http://www.psaworld.com
Contact: Ron Sawyer, Exec. Dir.
Founded: 1989. **Members:** 680. **Membership Dues:** full, $150 (annual). **Staff:** 2. **Budget:** $125,000. **Description:** Appliance and electronics service companies. Promotes the service and repair industry. Facilitates communication and cooperation between manufacturers and member companies. Provides information exchange. **Publications:** *Professional Service Association News*, quarterly. Newspaper. Contains trade information for the appliance and electronics service and repair industry. **Price:** $35.00 /year for nonmembers; included in membership dues. **Circulation:** 20,000. **Advertising:** accepted ● *PSA Member Update*, monthly. **Price:** included in membership dues. **Circulation:** 1,200. **Advertising:** accepted. **Conventions/Meetings:** annual National All Service Convention (exhibits).

3554 ■ Service Contract Industry Council (SCIC)
c/o Timothy J. Meenan, Gen. Counsel/Exec. Dir.
204 S Monroe St.
Tallahassee, FL 32301
Ph: (850)681-1058
Fax: (850)681-6713
E-mail: info@go-scic.com
URL: http://www.go-scic.com
Contact: Timothy J. Meenan, Gen. Counsel/Exec. Dir.
Founded: 1991. **Membership Dues:** service contract company, manufacturer, self-insuring major retailer, $8,000 (annual). **Description:** Manufacturers, insurers, retailers, and administrators. Represents the interests of the service contract industry. Monitors state and national legislative and regulatory activities; lobbies for standards beneficial to consumers and the industry; works with lawmakers and regulators to develop regulations. **Telecommunication Services:** electronic mail, membership@go-scic.com. **Conventions/Meetings:** annual meeting.

3555 ■ Service Industry Association (SIA)
c/o Claudia J. Betzner, Exec. Dir.
2164 Historic Decatur Rd., Villa 19
San Diego, CA 92106
Ph: (619)221-9200
Fax: (619)221-8201
E-mail: cbetzner@servicenetwork.org
URL: http://www.servicenetwork.org
Contact: Claudia J. Betzner, Exec. Dir.
Members: 20,200. **Membership Dues:** regular company, associate, $375-$1,250 (annual) ● corporate sponsorship, $2,250-$20,000. **Description:** Technology service and support organizations, including manufacturers, independent service providers, resellers, and all other related entities. Provides a forum for information exchange; strives to enhance the high-technology industry through an open environment of interdependence and cooperation between manufacturers, independent service organizations and users by providing solutions for customers. **Conventions/Meetings:** annual Executive Summit for Service Leaders - conference, for top executives (exhibits).

3556 ■ Service and Support Professionals Association (SSPA)
11031 Via Frontera, Ste.A
San Diego, CA 92127
Ph: (858)674-5491
Fax: (858)674-6794
E-mail: info@thesspa.com
URL: http://www.thesspa.com
Contact: Mr. Stephen Smith, Exec. Dir.
Founded: 1989. **Multinational. Description:** Focuses on the specific needs of service executives who are responsible for support centers and overall customer relations. Provides a reliable and comprehensive resource for news, research, benchmarking, standards and collaboration. **Awards:** Hall of Fame. **Type:** recognition ● Star Awards. **Type:** recognition. **Publications:** *SSPA News*, weekly. Newsletter. Contains articles about the service and support industry.

Shipping

3557 ■ American Import Shippers Association (AISA)
662 Main St.
New Rochelle, NY 10801
Ph: (914)633-3770
Fax: (914)633-4041
E-mail: info@aisaship.com
URL: http://www.aisaship.com
Contact: Hubert Wiesenmaier, Exec. Dir.
Founded: 1987. **Members:** 300. **Membership Dues:** regular, $250 (annual). **Staff:** 4. **Description:** Negotiates discounted ocean freight rates for its 300 member companies importing apparel, footwear, and fashion accessories. Represents members' interests to freight transportation companies and government agencies. **Computer Services:** database. **Publications:** *ATTN - Apparel Trade and Transportation News*, monthly. **Price:** included in membership dues; $225.00 /year for nonmembers. **Circulation:** 600. Alternate Formats: online. **Conventions/Meetings:** annual Apparel Trade and Transportation Conference (exhibits) ● monthly seminar ● monthly workshop.

3558 ■ American Institute for Shippers' Associations (AISA)
PO Box 33457
Washington, DC 20033-0457
Ph: (202)628-0933
Fax: (202)296-7374
E-mail: info@shippers.org
URL: http://www.shippers.org
Contact: Bill Clark, Pres.
Founded: 1961. **Members:** 50. **Staff:** 2. **Budget:** $60,000. **Description:** Comprises of shippers that consolidate and distribute freight on a non-profit basis for the purpose of securing the benefits of volume rates; carriers serving and shippers utilizing services of these associations; others who work with and are interested in the continued existence of cooperative shipping. Serves as spokesman for members in various activities including representation before Congress, the Federal Maritime Commission, the Department of Commerce and the Department of Transportation. Offers public relations and legal services. **Publications:** *American Institute for Shippers' Associations—News*, monthly. Newsletter ● *Guide to Shipping Cooperatives*, annual. **Conventions/Meetings:** annual conference.

3559 ■ American Moving and Storage Association (AMSA)
1611 Duke St.
Alexandria, VA 22314-3406
Ph: (703)683-7410
Fax: (703)683-7527
E-mail: info@moving.org
URL: http://www.moving.org
Contact: Linda Bauer Darr, Pres./CEO
Founded: 1936. **Members:** 3,400. **Membership Dues:** tariff (minimum; based on total moving and storage revenue), $475 (annual) ● tariff (maximum; based on total moving and storage revenue), $2,275 (annual). **Staff:** 27. **Budget:** $4,800,000. **State Groups:** 29. **Local Groups:** 6. **Multinational. Description:** Local, intrastate, interstate, and international movers who transport household goods, office and institutional equipment, and high-value products. Sponsors Household Goods Dispute Settlement Program which handles consumer complaints between consumers and interstate moving companies. **Awards:** Safety Awards. **Frequency:** annual. **Type:** recognition. **Recipient:** for best safety records ● Super Driver Awards. **Frequency:** annual. **Type:** recognition. **Additional Websites:** http://www.promover.org. **Committees:** Regulatory Affairs; Safety; Small Business and Agent Affairs; Tariff Research and Restructure; Tax and Legislative Affairs. **Programs:** Household Goods Dispute Settlement. **Affiliated With:** American Trucking Associations. **Formed by Merger of:** (1994) Household Goods Carriers' Bureau; (1994) National Moving and Storage Association; (1994) American Movers Conference; (2000) American Movers Institute. **Formerly:** (1998) American Moving and Storage Technical Foundation. **Publications:** *AMSA Membership Directory*, annual. Lists members in the household goods moving industry, with addresses; also provides information about carrier affiliation. **Price:** free for members; $600.00 for nonmembers. **Circulation:** 3,400. **Advertising:** accepted. Also Cited As: *Professional Movers Sourcebook* ● *Direction*, monthly. Magazine. **Price:** $35.00/year. ISSN: 0886-9707. **Circulation:** 3,500. **Advertising:** accepted ● *Government Traffic News*, monthly. Newsletter. Emphasizes information and issues concerning the moving of household goods for military personnel. **Price:** free for members (upon request). **Circulation:** 1,000 ● *Household Goods Carriers' Bureau Mileage Guide*, triennial ● *Moving Industry Financial Statistics*, annual ● *The Moving World*, biweekly. Newspaper. Covers issues affecting movers. **Price:** $35.00/year. **Circulation:** 3,500. **Advertising:** accepted ● *Scale Directory*, periodic ● *Transportation Fact Book*, annual ● Manuals. Reference and training. **Conventions/Meetings:** semiannual GSA Household Goods and Freight Conference - meeting and conference ● annual Management Conference and Trade Show (exhibits) - always spring.

3560 ■ Armored Transportation Institute (ATI)
c/o James L. Dunbar, Chm.
50 Schilling Rd.
Hunt Valley, MD 21031
Ph: (410)229-1929 (410)584-9800
Free: (800)888-2129
Fax: (410)229-1930
URL: http://www.dunbararmored.com
Contact: James L. Dunbar, Chm.
Founded: 1977. **Members:** 50. **Description:** Independent armored carriers who transport valuables. Acts as forum for the industry; stays abreast of current trends. Monitors federal legislation relating to the industry. Collects and disseminates information. Conducts seminars. **Publications:** Newsletter, 3/year. **Conventions/Meetings:** annual conference.

3561 ■ Boston Shipping Association (BSA)
Address Unknown since 2008
Founded: 1946. **Members:** 17. **Staff:** 5. **Description:** Shipping owners and agents; contracting stevedores; individuals, firms, and corporations engaged in or affiliated with maritime interests in Boston, MA and vicinity. Objectives are to negotiate and carry out labor agreements between employers and employees and to improve working conditions in the shipping industry. Promotes the growth of maritime trade through the port of Boston. Assists federal, state, and local government in promoting Massachusetts as a maritime state. Conducts safety programs; compiles labor and maritime statistics. **Convention/Meeting:** none. **Also Known As:** Martime Association of Greater Boston. **Publications:** *Port of Boston Handbook*, periodic. Directory. **Advertising:** accepted ● Also publishes special studies on port facilities and labor costs.

3562 ■ Conference on Safe Transportation of Hazardous Articles (COSTHA)
7803 Hill House Ct.
Fairfax Station, VA 22039-2043
Ph: (703)451-4031
Fax: (703)451-4207
E-mail: mail@costha.com
URL: http://www.costha.com
Contact: William Duff, Pres.
Founded: 1972. **Members:** 194. **Membership Dues:** company (based on annual revenue), $1,000-$3,550 (annual) ● trade association (based on number of members), $1,000-$3,000 (annual). **Staff:** 3. **Description:** Participates in international harmonization efforts. Promotes regulatory compliance and safety in

the hazardous materials transportation industry. Promotes the growth and development of its members as Hazardous Materials Professionals. **Formerly:** (1985) Council on the Safe Transportation of Hazardous Articles. **Publications:** *Abstracts of Regulations*, monthly ● Bulletins. **Conventions/Meetings:** annual meeting (exhibits) ● annual seminar.

3563 ■ Dangerous Goods Advisory Council (DGAC)
1100 H St. NW, Ste.740
Washington, DC 20005-5484
Ph: (202)289-4550
Fax: (202)289-4074
E-mail: info@dgac.org
URL: http://www.dgac.org
Contact: Mr. Michael Morrissette, Pres.

Founded: 1978. **Members:** 300. **Membership Dues:** company (based on the gross annual sales or revenues), $1,100-$4,300 (annual). **Staff:** 10. **Budget:** $2,000,000. **Description:** Represents shippers, carriers, and container manufacturers of hazardous materials, substances, and wastes, shipper and carrier associations. Works to promote safe transportation of these materials; provides assistance in answering regulatory questions, guidance to appropriate governmental resources, and advice in establishing corporate compliance and safety programs. Conducts seminars on domestic and international hazardous materials packaging and transporting; sponsors educational programs. Provides training courses. **Awards:** George L. Wilson Memorial Award. **Frequency:** annual. **Type:** recognition. **Recipient:** for outstanding achievements in hazardous materials transportation safety by a person or company. **Committees:** Education and Training; International Regulations; North American Regulatory and Legislative Affairs. **Also Known As:** (2002) Hazardous Materials Advisory Council. **Formerly:** (1978) Hazardous Materials Advisory Committee. **Publications:** *Federal Register Extract Service (FRES)*, semimonthly. Provides the full text of items appearing in the Federal Register that affect businesses involved in the hazardous materials transportation industry. ● Directory, annual. **Conventions/Meetings:** annual conference (exhibits) - usually October/November. 2008 Nov. 5-7, Savannah, GA ● annual conference and meeting - usually March/April.

3564 ■ Distribution and LTL Carriers Association (DLTLCA)
4218 Roanoke Rd., Ste.200
Kansas City, MO 64111-4735
Ph: (816)753-0411
Fax: (816)931-4339
E-mail: info@dltl.org
URL: http://www.dltlca.com
Contact: Jeff Michalson, Pres./Sec.

Founded: 1938. **Members:** 200. **Membership Dues:** associate, $400-$500 (annual). **Staff:** 3. **Description:** Represents for-hire motor common carriers of general freight who specialize in less-than-truckload shipments throughout the U.S. Provides government relations, networking, business development programs, and publications. **Computer Services:** database, economic data and LTL carrier. **Committees:** Policy; Program and Education. **Affiliated With:** American Trucking Associations. **Formerly:** Regional and Distribution Carriers Conference; (1997) Regular Common Carrier Conference. **Publications:** *Highway Common Carrier Newsletter*, bimonthly. Reports on economic and business trends and political issues affecting the trucking industry. Includes statistics. **Price:** $50.00/year. **Advertising:** accepted. **Conventions/Meetings:** semiannual meeting.

3565 ■ Express Delivery and Logistics Association (XLA)
14 W Third St., No. 200
Kansas City, MO 64105
Ph: (816)221-0254
Free: (888)838-0761
Fax: (816)472-7765
E-mail: info@expressassociation.org
URL: http://www.expressassociation.org
Contact: Ms. Kristy McKibben, Exec. Dir.

Founded: 1976. **Members:** 75. **Membership Dues:** industry (based on sales), $683-$4,247 (annual) ● associate, $1,139 (annual) ● airline, $4,200 (annual). **Staff:** 5. **Budget:** $300,000. **Multinational. Description:** Represents air couriers, small package express delivery companies, airlines and associated industry members (75); supports companies and facilities such as airlines and airports. Seeks to: provide industry forum for ideas, educate members about new technologies within the industry; represent air couriers before governmental bodies; inform members of legislation affecting the industry; develop and maintain relationships among members. Conducts seminars and workshops. **Libraries: Type:** not open to the public. **Holdings:** articles. **Committees:** Air Liaison; Education; Government Affairs; Strategic Planning. **Subcommittees:** Customs; International Trade; Postal; Security. **Formerly:** (2005) Air Courier Conference of America. **Publications:** *XLA Alert*, periodic. Bulletins. Features breaking news about the industry. **Advertising:** accepted. Alternate Formats: online ● *XLA Express*, quarterly. Newsletter. Includes reports on association activities, industry news, and other issues that affect express and logistics operators. **Advertising:** accepted. Alternate Formats: online ● *XLA Extra*, periodic. Bulletins. **Advertising:** accepted. Alternate Formats: online. **Conventions/Meetings:** annual meeting (exhibits).

3566 ■ Freight Transportation Consultants Association (FTCA)
c/o William J. Augello, Esq., Exec. Dir./Gen. Counsel
8683 W Sahara Ave., Ste.240
Las Vegas, NV 89117
E-mail: williamaugello@comcast.net
URL: http://www.transportpros.org
Contact: William J. Augello Esq., Exec. Dir./Gen. Counsel

Founded: 1959. **Members:** 100. **Membership Dues:** business (with 1-2 employees), $175 (annual) ● business (with 3-10 employees), $300 (annual) ● business (with 11 or more employees), $450 (annual). **Description:** Represents businesses and individuals providing freight bill payment and audit services and transportation consulting services to freight shippers, carriers, and others. Seeks to enhance the profession through educational programs, information exchange, and communication. **Publications:** *The FTCA Report*, monthly. Newsletter. Alternate Formats: online ● *Supplement*, monthly. Newsletter. **Conventions/Meetings:** annual conference.

3567 ■ Household Goods Forwarders Association of America (HHGFAA)
5904 Richmond Hwy., Ste.404
Alexandria, VA 22303-1864
Ph: (703)317-9950
Fax: (703)317-9960
E-mail: info@hhgfaa.org
URL: http://www.hhgfaa.org
Contact: Terry R. Head, Pres.

Founded: 1962. **Members:** 1,800. **Membership Dues:** young professional (age 35 and below), $100 (annual) ● industry veteran, $150 (annual) ● student, $25 (annual). **Staff:** 4. **Budget:** $3,000,000. **Multinational. Description:** Represents carriers engaged in the movement of household goods by the door-to-door container method. **Publications:** *The Portal Magazine*, bimonthly. **Price:** included in membership dues. **Circulation:** 2,350. **Advertising:** accepted. **Conventions/Meetings:** annual meeting (exhibits).

3568 ■ Independent Armored Car Operators Association (IACOA)
7101 N Mesa St., No. 518
El Paso, TX 79912-3613
Ph: (661)726-9864
Fax: (661)949-7877
E-mail: jmiacoa@yahoo.com
URL: http://www.iacoa.com
Contact: John Margaritis, Exec. Sec.

Founded: 1971. **Members:** 127. **Membership Dues:** regular, $450 (annual) ● associate/international, $500 (annual). **Staff:** 1. **Description:** Advances and promotes interests of independent individuals, firms, or corporations engaged in the business of furnishing armored car services. Brings together armored service operators from throughout the world to pool knowledge, attack problems faced by the industry and to develop minimum standards for armored services operations. **Awards:** Heroism Award. **Frequency:** annual. **Type:** recognition. **Committees:** Heroism; Insurance; Legislative; Loss and Prevention. **Publications:** *IACOA Newsletter*, quarterly. **Circulation:** 500. **Conventions/Meetings:** annual convention ● semiannual meeting.

3569 ■ International Association of Structural Movers (IASM)
PO Box 2637
Lexington, SC 29071-2637
Ph: (803)951-9304
Fax: (803)951-9314
E-mail: gbrymer@alltel.net
URL: http://www.iasm.org
Contact: N. Eugene Brymer, Staff Exec.

Founded: 1982. **Members:** 350. **Membership Dues:** company (based on revenues), $275-$750 (annual) ● additional company representative, retired, $150 (annual). **Staff:** 2. **Budget:** $250,000. **Multinational. Description:** Movers of heavy structural equipment, trusses, buildings, and machinery. Seeks to unify professionals in the field and to improve relations with the public. Promotes high standards in the field. Conducts seminars; compiles statistics. **Awards:** Best Time Saving Device. **Frequency:** annual. **Type:** recognition. **Recipient:** for members in good standing both the year the project was finished and the year of the conference ● Heaviest Structure Moved Not On Rubber Tired Dollies. **Frequency:** annual. **Type:** recognition. **Recipient:** for members in good standing both the year the project was finished and the year of the conference ● Heaviest Structure Moved on Dollies Under $30000. **Frequency:** annual. **Type:** recognition. **Recipient:** for members in good standing both the year the project was finished and the year of the conference ● Heaviest Structure Moved On Rubber Tired Dollies. **Frequency:** annual. **Type:** recognition. **Recipient:** for members in good standing both the year the project was finished and the year of the conference ● Heaviest Structure Moved Under $30000. **Frequency:** annual. **Type:** recognition. **Recipient:** for members in good standing both the year the project was finished and the year of the conference ● Longest Structure Moved. **Frequency:** annual. **Type:** recognition. **Recipient:** for members in good standing both the year the project was finished and the year of the conference ● Longest Structure Moved Under $30000. **Frequency:** annual. **Type:** recognition. **Recipient:** for members in good standing both the year the project was finished and the year of the conference ● Most Innovative Move. **Frequency:** annual. **Type:** recognition. **Recipient:** for members in good standing both the year the project was finished and the year of the conference ● Most Unusual Move. **Frequency:** annual. **Type:** recognition. **Recipient:** for members in good standing both the year the project was finished and the year of the conference ● **Frequency:** annual. **Type:** scholarship. **Recipient:** for child of employee of member or for child of member ● Structure Moved the Longest Distance on Land. **Frequency:** annual. **Type:** recognition. **Recipient:** for members in good standing both the year the project was finished and the year of the conference ● Structure Moved with the Most Square Footage on One Floor. **Frequency:** annual. **Type:** recognition. **Recipient:** for members in good standing both the year the project was finished and the year of the conference ● Tallest Structure Moved. **Frequency:** annual. **Type:** recognition. **Recipient:** for members in good standing both the year the project was finished and the year of the conference ● Tallest Structure Moved Under $30000. **Frequency:** annual. **Type:** recognition. **Recipient:** for members in good standing both the year the project was finished and the year of the conference ● Widest Structure Moved. **Frequency:** annual. **Type:** recognition. **Recipient:** for members in good standing both the year the project was finished and the year of the conference ● Widest Structure Moved Under $30000. **Frequency:** annual. **Type:** recognition. **Recipient:** for members in good standing both the year the project was finished and the year of the conference. **Committees:** Awards; Education; Legal/Utilities Elevation; Scholarship; Vendors. **Publications:** *IASM Newsletter*, bimonthly ● *Structural Mover Magazine*, quarterly. Covers current or historic moves of interest. **Price:** included in membership dues; $65.00/year for non-movers. ISSN: 1054-1195. **Circulation:** 2,000. **Advertising:** accepted ● Brochure ● Membership Directory, annual. **Conventions/Meetings:** annual conference, equipment and services used by members, educational sessions, awards, recognition dinner (exhibits) ● semiannual Director's Meeting.

3570 ■ International Furniture and Transportation Logistics Council (IFTLC)

PO Box 889
Gardner, MA 01440-0889
Ph: (978)632-1913
Fax: (978)630-2917
E-mail: raybohman@aol.com
URL: http://www.iftlc.org
Contact: Raynard F. Bohman Jr., Managing Dir.

Founded: 1926. **Members:** 1,156. **Membership Dues:** ordinary, $150 (annual). **Staff:** 2. **Multinational.** **Description:** Represents and promotes furniture transportation logistics professionals. **Libraries: Type:** reference. **Holdings:** 500; articles, books, periodicals. **Subjects:** transportation and law. **Telecommunication Services:** electronic mail, jsears@iftlc.org. **Formerly:** (2000) National Furniture Traffic Conference. **Publications:** *The Furniture Transporter*, monthly. Newsletter. **Price:** included in membership dues. **Circulation:** 150. Alternate Formats: online ● *Ocean Shipping News Summary*, monthly. Newsletter. **Price:** included in membership dues. **Circulation:** 150 ● *Traffic Newsletter*, monthly. **Price:** included in membership dues. **Circulation:** 150. **Conventions/Meetings:** annual International Conference of Furniture Transportation and Logistics Managers.

3571 ■ International Safe Transit Association (ISTA)

1400 Abbott Rd., Ste.160
East Lansing, MI 48823-1900
Ph: (517)333-3437
Free: (888)FOR-ISTA
Fax: (517)333-3813
E-mail: echurch@ista.org
URL: http://www.ista.org
Contact: Edward A. Church, Exec. Dir.

Founded: 1948. **Members:** 780. **Membership Dues:** primary location, $525-$650 (annual) ● additional shipper location, $100-$250 (annual) ● associate, $100 (annual) ● individual, $150 (annual). **Staff:** 6. **Budget:** $300,000. **Multinational.** **Description:** Shippers, carriers, manufacturers, testing laboratories, and packagers. Seeks to help manufacturers of any product reduce transit and handling damage. Has established standard pre-shipment testing procedures for assessing the viability of packaging. Small packages and heavy freight packagings, which pass the test, qualify to carry the association's seal. Maintains a committee to monitor changes in the shipping environment and modify test procedures accordingly. Certifies testing laboratories to ensure that they meet requirements. Serves as forum for the exchange of ideas. **Telecommunication Services:** electronic mail, bkipp@ista.org. **Committees:** Operations; Technical Steering. **Councils:** Asian-South Pacific Advisory; European Advisory; Technical. **Divisions:** Carrier; International; Shipper; Technical. **Programs:** Transit Tested. **Formerly:** (1974) National Safe Transit Committee; (1992) National Safe Transit Association; (1994) National/International Safe Transit Association. **Publications:** *ISTA Resource Book*, annual. Directory. **Price:** $175.00 for nonmembers; $75.00 for members. **Circulation:** 2,000. **Advertising:** accepted. Alternate Formats: CD-ROM ● *PreShipment Testing News*, quarterly. Newsletter. **Circulation:** 1,800. **Advertising:** accepted. Also Cited As: *PST* ● Proceedings. **Conventions/Meetings:** annual Dimensions - conference, international forum on transport packaging (exhibits) - usually March.

3572 ■ Maritime Association of the Port of New York/New Jersey (MAPONY/NJ)

17 Battery Pl., Ste.913
New York, NY 10004
Ph: (212)425-5704
Fax: (212)635-9498
E-mail: themaritimeassoc@erols.com
URL: http://www.nymaritime.org
Contact: Edward J. Kelly, Exec. Dir.

Founded: 1873. **Members:** 500. **Staff:** 10. **Description:** Represents steamship companies, towing and transportation companies, shipbuilders and drydocks, warehouses, marine sales and service companies, banks, and admiralty attorneys. Provides complete statistical review of vessel activities. **Telecommunication Services:** electronic mail, op24@verizon.net. **Formerly:** (1985) Maritime Association of the Port of New York. **Publications:** *The Maritime Newsletter*, monthly ● *Port Handbook of the Tri-States*, annual. Directory ● *Ship Agents/Owners/Operators Directory*, periodic.

3573 ■ Messenger Courier Association of the Americas (MCAA)

1156 15th St. NW, Ste.900
Washington, DC 20005
Ph: (202)785-3298
Fax: (202)223-9741
E-mail: bdecaprio@kellencompany.com
URL: http://www.mcaa.com
Contact: Rob Slack, Pres.

Founded: 1987. **Members:** 400. **Membership Dues:** regular, $650-$3,499 (annual) ● affiliate, $400 (annual) ● international, $250 (annual). **Staff:** 5. **Budget:** $300,000. **Description:** Trade organization of local and international messenger courier companies. Addresses issues facing the industry, including municipal traffic ordinances that impede industry operations. Works to establish driver pools and to develop centralized core computer service bureaus for smaller courier companies. Provides training, discount purchasing programs, and legislative and regulatory issue monitoring. Conducts educational and research programs; compiles statistics. **Formerly:** (1990) Messenger Courier Association of America. **Publications:** *Courier Magazine*, quarterly. Contains industry news, developments, and activities. **Circulation:** 4,000. **Advertising:** accepted. Alternate Formats: online ● *Who's Who in the Messenger Courier Industry*, annual. Directory. Lists all U.S. courier companies who do on-call and contractual delivery work, arranged alphabetically by airport city. **Price:** $18.50. **Advertising:** accepted. **Conventions/Meetings:** competition ● annual meeting (exhibits).

3574 ■ NASSTRAC

9382 Oak Ave.
Waconia, MN 55387
Ph: (952)442-8850
Fax: (952)442-3941
E-mail: brian07@nasstrac.org
URL: http://www.nasstrac.org
Contact: Brian Everett, Exec. Dir.

Founded: 1952. **Members:** 500. **Membership Dues:** regular/associate (based on gross global sales), $550-$2,000 (annual) ● additional individual, academic, press, association and civic organization, $150 (quarterly). **Staff:** 3. **Budget:** $320,000. **Description:** Protects the interests of firms making minimum or small, individual shipments (less than 10,000 pounds) by rail, motor, or air. Conducts seminars and workshops; offers printed materials to help members deal with the economic environment and fluctuating distribution. **Awards:** Member and Associate Member of the Year Award. **Frequency:** annual. **Type:** recognition. **Recipient:** for two members selected as having contributed the most time, support and innovation to other members ● NASSTRAC LTL Carrier of the Year Award-Multi-Regional. **Frequency:** annual. **Type:** recognition ● NASSTRAC LTL Carrier of the Year Award-Nationwide. **Frequency:** annual. **Type:** recognition. **Recipient:** for carrier providing the best LTL services to members ● NASSTRAC LTL Carrier of the Year Award-Regional. **Frequency:** annual. **Type:** recognition ● Shipper of the Year Award. **Frequency:** annual. **Type:** recognition. **Recipient:** for company with the most cost-effective innovative distribution program. **Formerly:** (1982) National Small Shipments Traffic Conference. **Publications:** *The NASSTRAC Newslink*, monthly. Newsletter. **Circulation:** 400. **Advertising:** accepted ● Brochures ● Pamphlets. **Conventions/Meetings:** semiannual meeting (exhibits) - usually April/September.

3575 ■ National Armored Car Association (NACA)

c/o Larry Sabbath, Exec. Dir.
9532 Stevebrook Rd.
Fairfax, VA 22032
Ph: (703)426-1976
Fax: (703)978-2399
E-mail: lsabbath@nationalarmoredcar.com
URL: http://www.nationalarmoredcar.com
Contact: Larry Sabbath, Exec. Dir.

Founded: 1929. **Members:** 5. **Staff:** 1. **Budget:** $180,000. **Description:** Represents companies engaged in the secure transportation, storage, and processing of valuables. **Committees:** Banking and Legislative; Driver Safety; Insurance; Labor Contracts; Legal; Loss Prevention; Merit Awards; Operating Standards and Security. **Publications:** Newsletter, quarterly.

3576 ■ National Cargo Bureau (NCB)

17 Battery Pl., Ste.1232
New York, NY 10004-1110
Ph: (212)785-8300
Fax: (212)785-8333
E-mail: ncbnyk@natcargo.org
Contact: Capt. James J. McNamara, Pres.

Founded: 1952. **Members:** 320. **Staff:** 105. **Budget:** $10,000,000. **Description:** Representatives of the maritime industry, marine underwriters, and government departments closely associated with the maritime industry. Recommends regulations to the government for the safe and uniform stowage of dangerous cargo and grain in bulk. Provides cargo inspection service to American and foreign flag merchant ships, inspection and certification of shipboard cargo handling gear, and complete container loading inspection service. Seeks uniform safety standards and regulations. Offers courses. **Awards:** S. Fraser Sammis Award. **Frequency:** annual. **Type:** recognition. **Formed by Merger of:** (1952) Bureau of Inspection of Board of Underwriters of New York; Board of Marine Underwriters of San Francisco. **Publications:** *General Information for Grain Loading*. Includes ships stability & stability for fisherman correspondence courses. ● *Self Study Course in Hazardous Materials* ● *Self Study Course in Ship's Stability* ● *Self Study Course in Stability for Fishermen*. **Conventions/Meetings:** annual meeting - always March, New York City.

3577 ■ National Motor Freight Traffic Association (NMFTA)

1001 N Fairfax, Ste.600
Alexandria, VA 22314
Ph: (703)838-1810
Free: (866)411-6632
Fax: (703)683-1094
E-mail: membership@nmfta.org
URL: http://www.nmfta.org
Contact: Bill Pugh, Exec. Dir.

Founded: 1956. **Members:** 2,000. **Staff:** 33. **Budget:** $2,500,000. **Regional Groups:** 100. **Description:** Motor common carriers of general commodities. Represents interests of membership before the Surface Transportation Board, the Congress, the courts and state regulatory agencies. **Telecommunication Services:** electronic mail, director@nmfta.org. **Committees:** National Classification. **Publications:** *Classification Matters*. Newsletter. Alternate Formats: online ● *National Motor Freight Classification*, annual. Book. Contains industry standard guide. **Price:** $135.00 plus shipping and handling. **Circulation:** 10,000. Alternate Formats: magnetic tape. Also

Cited As: *NMFC* ● *Standard Carrier Alpha Codes.* Directory. Provides listing of transportation-providing firms and their standard carrier alpha codes. **Price:** $168.00 printed form; $790.00 in CD. Alternate Formats: CD-ROM ● *Standard Point Location Code.* Directory. Provides each point originating freight and each point receiving freight in North America. **Price:** $166.00 printed form; $790.00 CD. Alternate Formats: CD-ROM. Also Cited As: *SPLC.* **Conventions/Meetings:** meeting, private ● quarterly National Classification Committee and Panel Meetings, includes public and private meetings - every February, May, August and November.

3578 ■ National Shippers Strategic Transportation Council (NASSTRAC)
9382 Oak Ave.
Waconia, MN 55387
Ph: (952)442-8850
Fax: (952)442-3941
E-mail: brian@nasstrac.org
URL: http://www.nasstrac.org
Contact: Brian Everett, Exec. Dir.
Founded: 1952. **Membership Dues:** regular, associate (based on gross global sales of parent company), $550-$2,000 (annual) ● academic, press, association, civic organization, $150 (annual). **Description:** Acts as shipper's association focusing on essential transportation and supply chain activities. **Formerly:** (2006) National Small Shipments Traffic Conference.

3579 ■ National Solid Wastes Management Association (NSWMA)
4301 Connecticut Ave. NW, Ste.300
Washington, DC 20008-2304
Ph: (202)244-4700
Fax: (202)364-3792
E-mail: membership@envasns.org
URL: http://www.nswma.org
Contact: Bruce J. Parker, Pres./CEO
Members: 700. **Staff:** 32. **Budget:** $200,000. **Regional Groups:** 3. **State Groups:** 32. **National Groups:** 3. **Description:** Commercial firms that collect and dispose solid wastes. Acts as a forum for the discussion of specific aspects of hazardous waste transport. Promotes professionalism in the industry to minimize the risks to public health and safety. Aids in the development of industry laws and regulations. Fosters public understanding of waste transport and disposal through educational programs. Urges members to: comply with federal liability insurance requirements; employ drivers who have completed a comprehensive training program and obtained their Department of Transportation commercial vehicle operator's license and medical evaluation certificate; set limits on drivers' hours of service; and maintain transport vehicles in accordance with federal motor carrier safety regulations. **Awards:** Distinguished Service Awards. **Frequency:** annual. **Type:** recognition. **Recipient:** for outstanding service to NSWMA ● Member of the Year. **Frequency:** annual. **Type:** recognition. **Recipient:** for extraordinary service to NSWMA and the industry over the last 12 months ● Special Governors Awards. **Frequency:** annual. **Type:** recognition. **Recipient:** for meritorious contributions to a chapter over a period of time. **Telecommunication Services:** electronic mail, bparker@envasns.org. **Affiliated With:** Environmental Industry Associations; Waste Equipment Technology Association. **Formerly:** (1997) Chemical Waste Transportation Institute. **Publications:** *Legal Bulletin*, monthly. **Price:** $295.00/year ● *Manual of Recommended Safety Practices.* **Price:** $60.00 for members; $175.00 for nonmembers ● *Waste Industry News*, monthly. Newsletter. **Conventions/Meetings:** annual Waste-Expo - conference (exhibits).

3580 ■ National Tank Truck Carriers (NTTC)
2200 Mill Rd.
Alexandria, VA 22314
Ph: (703)838-1960
Fax: (703)684-5753
E-mail: inquiries@tanktruck.org
URL: http://www.tanktruck.org
Contact: Clifford J. Harvison, Exec.
Founded: 1945. **Members:** 260. **Membership Dues:** associate, $700 (annual) ● carrier (minimum; based on annual gross revenue), $275 (annual) ● carrier (annual gross revenue of $50 million to $200 million), $10,500 (annual). **Staff:** 7. **Budget:** $1,000,000. **Description:** Common or contract "for-hire" tank truck carriers transporting liquid and dry bulk commodities, chemicals, food processing commodities, petroleum, and related products; allied industry suppliers. Promotes federal standards of construction, design, operation, and use of tank trucks and equipment. Coordinates truck transportation system for shippers of bulk commodities. Secures improvements in tank specifications. Sponsors annual schools; conducts research. **Awards:** Safety Award. **Frequency:** annual. **Type:** recognition. **Recipient:** for premier Hazmat safety program in the country. **Committees:** Industry Education; International Carriers; Management Systems. **Councils:** Tank Cleaning; Tank Truck Safety. **Publications:** *Board of Directors Minutes*, periodic. Bulletin. **Price:** included in membership dues ● *Cargo Tank Hazardous Materials Regulations*, annual. Book. **Price:** $65.00 for members; $85.00 for nonmembers ● *Cargo Tank Maintenance Manual*, periodic. **Price:** $325.00 for members; $450.00 for nonmembers ● *National Tank Truck Directory*, annual. **Price:** $54.00 for members; $80.00 for nonmembers ● *Tank Truck Driver's Guide to Transporting Hazmat.* Pamphlets ● *Washington Newsletter*, monthly. Covers a wide range of bulk transport/hazardous material issues. **Price:** included in membership dues. Alternate Formats: online ● Books. **Conventions/Meetings:** annual Cargo Tank Maintenance Seminar (exhibits) ● annual conference and seminar (exhibits) - always May.

3581 ■ National Waterways Conference (NWC)
4650 Washington Blvd., No. 608
Arlington, VA 22201
Ph: (703)243-4090
Fax: (703)243-4155
E-mail: worth@waterways.org
URL: http://www.waterways.org
Contact: Worth Hager, Pres.
Founded: 1960. **Members:** 350. **Membership Dues:** carrier, shipper, waterway services, $1,000 (annual) ● association, $700 (annual) ● public, $870 (annual). **Staff:** 3. **Budget:** $400,000. **Description:** Petroleum, coal, chemical, electric power, building materials, iron and steel, and grain companies; industrial development agencies, port authorities, and other governmental bodies; water carriers; companies which build, repair, service, or insure vessels; water resource development associations, banks, chambers of commerce, and individuals. Seeks to promote a better understanding of the public value of the American waterways system. Conducts research on the economics of water transportation; sponsors an educational program to point up the diverse benefits of efficient water transport; keeps members and other waterway proponents posted on developments affecting national waterways policy. **Libraries: Type:** not open to the public. **Holdings:** 500; articles, books, periodicals. **Subjects:** navigation, flood control, hydropower, water supply, environmental restoration. **Awards:** Waterways Literature and Promotional Materials Competition. **Frequency:** annual. **Type:** trophy. **Recipient:** for excellence in literature. **Computer Services:** Electronic publishing ● information services. **Telecommunication Services:** electronic bulletin board ● electronic mail, connie@waterways.org ● information service. **Publications:** *Washington Watch*, monthly. Covers water transportation and water resources policy issues. **Price:** included in membership dues; $100.00 /year for nonmembers. **Circulation:** 1,500 ● Reports. **Conventions/Meetings:** annual meeting (exhibits) - always September.

3582 ■ New York/New Jersey Foreign Freight Forwarders and Brokers Association (NY/NJFFFB)
PO Box 8217
Red Bank, NJ 07701
Ph: (732)747-1936
Fax: (732)747-1161
E-mail: info@nynjfffb.org
URL: http://www.nynjforwarders-brokers.org
Contact: Stewart B. Hauser, Chm.
Founded: 1917. **Members:** 124. **Membership Dues:** full (based on number of employees), $350-$700 (annual) ● non-resident, $250 (annual) ● affiliated, $425 (annual). **Staff:** 2. **Description:** Freight forwarders and brokers serving import-export trade in New York area. Meets periodically to discuss traffic matters and mutual problems and to hear reports of counsel on existing or proposed legislation. Makes recommendations to Federal Maritime Commission and other government bodies; intervenes as an interested party in legal proceedings affecting the industry. **Awards:** Person of the Year Award. **Frequency:** annual. **Type:** recognition. **Committees:** Public Affairs. **Affiliated With:** International Federation of Freight Forwarders Associations. **Formerly:** New York Foreign Freight Forwarders and Brokers Association. **Publications:** *New York/New Jersey Foreign Freight Forwarders and Brokers Association Directory*, annual ● Bulletin, periodic. **Conventions/Meetings:** annual dinner - always January in New York City, NY.

3583 ■ New York Shipping Association (NYSA)
100 Wood Ave. S, Ste.304
Iselin, NJ 08830-2716
Ph: (732)452-7800 (732)452-7824
Fax: (732)452-6315
E-mail: bfedorko@nysanet.org
URL: http://www.nysanet.org
Contact: Frank M. McDonough, Pres.
Founded: 1932. **Members:** 80. **Description:** Steamship lines, contracting stevedores and other shipping-related waterfront employers in the bi-state port of New York and New Jersey. Negotiates and administers, on behalf of employer members, waterfront labor contracts with the International Longshoremen's Association and the Port Police and Guard Union. **Awards:** NYSA Safety Award. **Frequency:** annual. **Type:** recognition. **Recipient:** for terminal operators and longshoremen. **Computer Services:** Information services, issues and initiatives. **Telecommunication Services:** electronic mail, fmcdonough@nysanet.org. **Publications:** Annual Report. **Conventions/Meetings:** annual meeting - always April.

3584 ■ North American Shippers Association (NASA)
1600 St. Georges Ave.
PO Box 249
Rahway, NJ 07065
Ph: (732)680-4535
Fax: (732)388-6580
E-mail: j.barrett@jfhillebrand.com
URL: http://www.nasaships.com
Contact: Joan Barrett, Insurance Admin.
Founded: 1987. **Members:** 550. **Membership Dues:** regular, $75 (annual). **Staff:** 2. **Description:** Shippers of wine and spirits. Seeks to advance the industry. Offers members discount benefits on ocean freight and marine insurance coverage. **Publications:** *NASA News*, quarterly. Newsletter. Alternate Formats: online. **Conventions/Meetings:** annual board meeting.

3585 ■ Pacific Maritime Association (PMA)
555 Market St.
San Francisco, CA 94105-2800
Ph: (415)576-3200 (206)298-3434
Fax: (415)348-8392
URL: http://www.pmanet.org
Contact: James C. McKenna, Pres./CEO
Founded: 1949. **Members:** 95. **Staff:** 135. **Description:** Provides industrial relations services for the shipping industry on the West Coast. **Computer Services:** Online services, information about cargo handling in ports in California, Oregon and Washington: publications and labor agreements ● online services, safety bulletins. **Publications:** *PMA Update*, monthly. Newsletter. Contains articles related to West Coast waterborne cargo handling industry. **Price:** included in membership dues. ISSN: 1062-6484. **Cir-**

culation: 1,500. Alternate Formats: online ● Annual Report, annual. ISSN: 8756-3622. Alternate Formats: online.

3586 ■ Propeller Club of the U.S. (PCUS)
3927 Old Lee Hwy., No. 101A
Fairfax, VA 22030
Ph: (703)691-2777
Fax: (703)691-4173
E-mail: info@propellerclubhq.com
URL: http://www.propellerclubhq.com
Contact: Bart Goedhard, COO
Founded: 1927. **Members:** 11,000. **Staff:** 4. **Budget:** $375,000. **Regional Groups:** 13. **Local Groups:** 60. **National Groups:** 20. **Description:** Promotes and supports the American Merchant Marine and aids in the development of Great Lakes, inland waterway, and harbor improvement. Activities include: National Maritime Essay Contests; Adopt-a-Ship Plan, Student Port Program. **Awards:** American Merchant Marine Writers Award. **Type:** recognition ● Pi Sigma Phi Award. **Type:** recognition. **Recipient:** for outstanding scholarship in maritime subjects. **Computer Services:** database, port addresses. **Telecommunication Services:** electronic mail, bart@propellerclubhq.com ● electronic mail, greelongeal@bellsouth.net. **Committees:** Position and Resolutions. **Projects:** Adopt-A-Ship. **Publications:** *Proceedings of the American Merchant Marine and Maritime Industry Conference*, annual. **Price:** free ● *Propeller Club Quarterly*. Magazine. **Circulation:** 12,000. Alternate Formats: online. **Conventions/Meetings:** annual conference (exhibits) ● annual Salute to Congress - dinner.

3587 ■ Shippers of Recycled Textiles (SORT)
7131 E Broad St., Ste.206
Falls Church, VA 22046
Ph: (703)538-1000
Fax: (703)538-6305
E-mail: maryann@smartasn.org
URL: http://www.smartasn.org
Contact: Eric Stubin, Pres.
Founded: 1988. **Members:** 100. **Membership Dues:** general, $200 (annual). **Description:** Firms and corporations engaged in the shipment and distribution of used clothing, wiping cloth materials, recycled textiles, textile products, fibers, and nonwoven and paper products. Promotes high standards and ethics within the shipping industry. Collects, distributes, and makes available information and economic data pertaining to the shipment and distribution of textiles and related products. Negotiates discount transportation rates based on volume commitments to the carrier, which are generally lower than individual firms can arrange. Initiates activities relating to technical research and development in transportation. Presents members' views to legislative and governmental bodies and agencies. **Additional Websites:** http://www.sorti.com. **Conventions/Meetings:** semiannual meeting, in conjunction with International Association of Wiping Cloth Manufacturers.

3588 ■ Society of Marine Port Engineers (SMPE)
PO Box 369
Eatontown, NJ 07724
Ph: (732)389-2009
Fax: (732)389-2264
E-mail: dmoore@smpe.org
URL: http://www.smpe.org
Contact: Paul Hormann, Sec.
Founded: 1946. **Members:** 560. **Membership Dues:** full/associate, $75 (annual). **Staff:** 2. **Description:** Superintendent engineers, port engineers or equivalent positions in marine management of organizations engaged in oceangoing transportation operations. Must hold valid, unlimited ocean licenses as chief engineer of steam or motor vessels, or an engineering degree from a university. **Awards:** SMPE Scholarship Loan. **Frequency:** annual. **Type:** scholarship. **Recipient:** for children of society members. **Committees:** Computer and Office Equipment; Dinner Dance; Golf Outing; Information Technology; Journal; Papers and Technical; Retention; Welfare and Relief. **Publications:** *The De-Air-Ator*, quarterly. Newsletter. **Circulation:** 550. Alternate Formats: online. **Conventions/Meetings:** annual dinner, formal dinner dance ● annual meeting ● annual meeting - always May in New York City.

3589 ■ Specialized Carriers and Rigging Association (SC&RA)
2750 Prosperity Ave., Ste.620
Fairfax, VA 22031-4312
Ph: (703)698-0291
Fax: (703)698-0297
E-mail: info@scranet.org
URL: http://www.scranet.org
Contact: Joel M. Dandrea, Exec. VP
Founded: 1947. **Members:** 1,100. **Membership Dues:** first-time, $395 ● international, $600 (annual) ● A to K (depending on the gross revenue range), $615-$3,200 (annual). **Staff:** 11. **Budget:** $2,750,000. **Multinational. Description:** Common carriers, crane and rigging companies, and millwright contractors engaged in the transportation of heavy and specialized articles, machinery, iron and steel, construction, and military traffic. Operates Heavy and Specialized Carriers Tariff Bureau. Conducts Fleet Safety and Outstanding Hauling, Rigging, and Millwright Job of the Year contests. Compiles statistics. **Awards:** Crane and Rigging Safety Awards. **Frequency:** annual. **Type:** recognition. **Recipient:** for members ● Million Miler Award for Safety Excellence. **Type:** recognition ● President's Award. **Frequency:** annual. **Type:** recognition. **Recipient:** for members ● SC&R Foundation Scholarship. **Frequency:** annual. **Type:** scholarship. **Recipient:** to students preparing for a career related to transportation or construction management ● SC&RA Hauling Job of the Year Awards. **Frequency:** annual. **Type:** recognition. **Recipient:** for transportation projects ● Transportation Safety Awards. **Frequency:** annual. **Type:** recognition. **Recipient:** for member companies. **Telecommunication Services:** electronic mail, jdandrea@scranet.org. **Programs:** Endorsed Insurance. **Formerly:** (1943) Heavy Specialized Carriers Section - Local Cartage National Conference; (1959) Heavy Specialized Carriers Conference. **Publications:** *Lifting and Transportation International Magazine*, 9/year. Contains advertisers index and calendar of events; concerned with technical activities in the industry. **Price:** included in membership dues. **Circulation:** 21,500. **Advertising:** accepted. Also Cited As: *Transportation Engineer Magazine* ● *Moving the World*. Video. **Price:** $29.00 ● *Safety, Industrial Relations, and Government Affairs Special Reports*, periodic ● *Specialized Carriers and Rigging Association-Membership Directory*, annual. **Price:** included in membership dues; $95.00 for nonmembers ● *Specialized Carriers and Rigging Association-Newsletter*, weekly. Features a review of current events affecting specialized transportation and crane, millwright, and rigging companies. **Price:** free for members ● Books ● Manuals ● Booklets. **Conventions/Meetings:** annual conference.

3590 ■ Sporting Goods Shippers Association (SGSA)
9237 Dove Ct.
Gilroy, CA 95020
Ph: (408)846-9592
Fax: (408)846-9213
E-mail: info@sgsa.net
URL: http://www.sgsa.net
Contact: Angela Munson, Managing Dir.
Membership Dues: customer, $20-$80. **Multinational. Description:** Provides services for exercise equipment and sporting goods importers and distributors. Negotiates ocean freight rates and contracts with steamship carriers that would be favorable to customers. Assists and advises customer companies on individual shipping problems, requirements and procedures. **Programs:** Domestic Airfreight; International Airfreight; Ocean.

3591 ■ Steamship Association of Louisiana (SALA)
2217 World Trade Center
2 Canal St.
New Orleans, LA 70130-1407
Ph: (504)522-9392
Fax: (504)523-2140
E-mail: steamship@sshipla.org
URL: http://www.sshipla.org
Contact: Paul Clancey, Chm.
Founded: 1912. **Members:** 40. **Staff:** 10. **Local Groups:** 1. **Description:** Steamship agents, owners, operators and stevedores. Represents shipping interests in matters of industry-wide concern including navigational safety, deep-draft anchorage areas and channels and entrance passes. Acts as liaison with governmental agencies and port authorities. Negotiates and administers labor contracts. **Libraries: Type:** reference. **Subjects:** labor law, industrial relations, maritime topics. **Computer Services:** database, steamship agents ● database, summary of past circulars. **Divisions:** General; Labor Relations. **Formerly:** (1997) New Orleans Steamship Association.

3592 ■ Trans-Atlantic American Flag Liner Operators/Trans-Pacific American Flag Berth Operators (TAAFLO/TPAFBO)
80 Wall St., Ste.1117
New York, NY 10005-3688
Ph: (212)269-2415
Fax: (212)269-2418
E-mail: halevy1@attglobal.net
URL: http://www.taaflo-tpafbo.com
Contact: Howard A. Levy, Admin.
Description: Provides current and future TAAFLO/TPAFBO rates to members. Operates U.S. flag vessels in ocean common service between ports in the U.S. and ports in Europe and elsewhere; provides transportation by sea for general commercial cargo as well as cargo reserved by law for such transport to vessels of U.S. flag registry.

3593 ■ Transportation Institute (TI)
5201 Auth Way
Camp Springs, MD 20746
Ph: (301)423-3335 (202)347-2590
E-mail: info@trans-inst.org
URL: http://www.trans-inst.org
Contact: James L. Henry, Chm./Pres.
Founded: 1967. **Members:** 140. **Staff:** 25. **Description:** U.S. deep-sea and inland waters shipping, towing and dredging companies devoted to research and education on a broad range of transportation problems, with emphasis on problems related to the nation's citizen-owned and citizen-manned Merchant Marine. Addresses the need for halting the decline of deep-sea commerce aboard vessels flying the American flag and the need for full development of waterborne commerce on the Great Lakes. Supports utilizing America's 25,000-mile long network of inland waterways to meet the domestic transportation needs of a growing nation and the need for revitalizing the American fishing industry to halt the incursion of foreign fishing fleets on U.S. spawning grounds. Supports the need for a national oceanographic policy to ensure maximum exploitation of the wealth of the sea. Conducts ongoing research. **Libraries: Type:** reference. **Computer Services:** database, member companies ● information services, industry profile ● online services, resource aids. **Formerly:** (1968) Andrew Furuseth Foundation for Maritime Research. **Publications:** *Currents*, monthly. Newsletter ● Also publishes legislative and research reports, special studies, and analyses of maritime issues and actions.

3594 ■ Transportation Intermediaries Association (TIA)
1625 Prince St., Ste.200
Alexandria, VA 22314
Ph: (703)299-5700
Fax: (703)836-0123
E-mail: info@tianet.org
URL: http://www.tianet.org
Contact: Robert A. Voltmann, Pres./CEO
Founded: 1978. **Members:** 750. **Membership Dues:** regular/associate (both based on annual gross revenue), $468-$2,460 (annual) ● branch, $100 (annual). **Staff:** 11. **Budget:** $700,000. **Description:** Leading organization for North American transportation intermediaries. Members include property brokers, domestic freight forwarders, consolidators,

ocean and air forwarders, NVOCCs, intermodal marketing companies, agricultural and refrigerated brokers, and logistics management firms. Associate members include shippers, suppliers, computer software developers/providers, and other companies in third party transportation. Represents members of all disciplines doing business in domestic and international commerce. Serves as a voice of transportation intermediaries to shippers, carriers, government officials, and international organizations. **Awards:** Lund/Sooy Scholarship. **Frequency:** annual. **Type:** scholarship. **Computer Services:** database, list of members ● mailing lists, of members. **Telecommunication Services:** electronic mail, voltmann@tianet.org. **Committees:** Education; Programs; Public Relations/Publications. **Formerly:** (1995) Transportation Brokers Conference of America. **Publications:** *The Logistics Journal*, monthly. Covers the latest industry news and association business. **Advertising:** accepted ● *TIA Membership Directory and Handbook*, annual. Contains member information. ● *TIA Update*, monthly. Newsletter. Contains info concerning third parties. **Price:** included in membership dues. **Advertising:** accepted. **Conventions/Meetings:** annual convention and trade show, for educational/networking and exhibiting (exhibits) - usually late February or early March ● periodic symposium.

3595 ■ Transportation and Logistics Council (TLC)

120 Main St.
Huntington, NY 11743
Ph: (631)549-8988
Fax: (631)549-8962
E-mail: tlc@transportlaw.com
URL: http://www.tlcouncil.org
Contact: John L. Burke, Sec.-Treas.

Founded: 1974. **Members:** 400. **Membership Dues:** regular, $395 (annual) ● associate, $345 (annual) ● multiple subscriber, $200 (annual). **Staff:** 8. **Regional Groups:** 7. **Description:** Aims to serve the shipping public by providing high quality educational programs and materials, promoting and representing the interests of the entire shipping community in issues relating to transportation of goods in today's deregulated environment. **Libraries: Type:** not open to the public. **Holdings:** books. **Subjects:** transportation law, government regulations, loss and damage, freight change liability, cargo insurance, contracting. **Awards:** Transportation Professional of the Year. **Frequency:** annual. **Type:** recognition. **Telecommunication Services:** electronic mail, burke@uniprofoodservice.com. **Formerly:** (1990) Shippers National Freight Claim Council, Inc.; (1996) Transportation Claims and Prevention Council; (2005) Transportation Consumer Protection Council. **Publications:** *A Guide to Transportation After the Sunsetting of the ICC*. **Price:** $65.00 for members; $75.00 for nonmembers ● *Contracting for Transportation and Logistics Services*. **Price:** $40.00 for members; $48.00 for nonmembers ● *Corporate Procedures for Shipping and Receiving*. **Price:** $80.00 for members; $95.00 for nonmembers ● *Freight Claims in Plain English (3rd ed., 1995)*, annual. **Price:** $85.00 for members; $100.00 for nonmembers ● *How to Read Tariffs to Avoid Surprises*. **Price:** $17.00 for members; $20.00 for nonmembers ● *Protecting Shippers' Interests*. **Price:** $65.00 for members; $75.00 for nonmembers ● *Shippers Domestic Truck Bill of Lading (C) and Common Carrier Rate Agreement Kit*. **Price:** $43.00 for members; $50.00 for nonmembers ● *TransDigest*, monthly. Newsletter. Contains current transportation, issues, laws, etc. **Price:** included in membership dues; $150.00 /year for nonmembers. **Circulation:** 400. **Advertising:** accepted. Alternate Formats: online ● *Transportation Protection Council*, annual. Membership Directory. **Conventions/Meetings:** annual Claim Conference - board meeting and conference, with discussions of freight transportation problems and solutions (exhibits) ● semiannual seminar - always spring and fall.

3596 ■ Unishippers Association

746 E Winchester St., Ste.200
Salt Lake City, UT 84107
Ph: (801)487-0600
Free: (800)999-8721
Fax: (801)487-0920
E-mail: contact@unishippers.com
URL: http://www.unishippers.com
Contact: Steve Nelson, CEO

Founded: 1987. **Members:** 305. **Staff:** 58. **For-Profit. Description:** For-profit shipping company. Not an association. **Publications:** *Update*, quarterly. Newsletter. Gives shipping information to readers. Alternate Formats: online. **Conventions/Meetings:** annual convention, for Unishippers Association Franchisees (exhibits).

3597 ■ West African Discussion Agreement (WADA)

Address Unknown since 2007

Founded: 1995. **Members:** 7. **Staff:** 1. **Budget:** $20,000. **Description:** Steamship companies flying the flags of 6 countries and serving West African ports, U.S. North Atlantic and Gulf. Promotes trade and freight rates, charges and practices relating to the transportation of cargo by sea to and from the U.S. and 18 nations of West Africa. The Discussion Agreement is unusual among the agreements approved by the Federal Maritime Commission in that its scope is both eastbound and westbound, serving U.S. and West African ports. **Formerly:** (1945) American West African Freight Conference. **Publications:** Publishes ocean freight rate tariffs. **Conventions/Meetings:** annual conference - always May.

3598 ■ Women's International Shipping and Trading Association (WISTA)

c/o Jeanne M. Grasso, Recording Sec.
Blank Rome, LLP
600 New Hampshire Ave. NW
Washington, DC 20037
E-mail: grasso@blankrome.com
URL: http://www.wista.net
Contact: Jeanne M. Grasso, Recording Sec.

Founded: 1974. **Members:** 500. **Membership Dues:** $75 (annual). **National Groups:** 22. **Multinational. Description:** Seeks to advance the interests of women engaged in shipping and trading-related business throughout the world. **Conventions/Meetings:** annual international conference - 2008 Oct. 15-19, New Orleans, LA ● annual international conference and lecture, 3-days with excursions.

Shooting

3599 ■ National Association of Shooting Ranges (NASR)

c/o Richard Patterson, Exec. Dir.
Flintlock Ridge Off. Ctr.
11 Mile Hill Rd.
Newtown, CT 06470-2359
Ph: (203)426-1320
Fax: (203)426-1087
E-mail: nasr@nssf.org
URL: http://www.rangeinfo.org
Contact: Richard Patterson, Exec. Dir.

Membership Dues: shooting range developer/not-for-profit shooting range, $75 (annual) ● for profit range/firearm retailer, $75-$250 (annual). **Description:** Promotes the development of state-of-the-art target shooting facilities as safety education and entertainment centers. Promotes and protects target shooting facilities by providing leadership in information, communication and partnerships between ranges, industry and community. **Affiliated With:** National Shooting Sports Foundation. **Publications:** Catalog.

Skating

3600 ■ Ice Skating Institute (ISI)

17120 N Dallas Pkwy., Ste.140
Dallas, TX 75248-1187
Ph: (972)735-8800
Fax: (972)735-8815
E-mail: isi@skateisi.org
URL: http://www.skateisi.org
Contact: Peter Martell, Exec. Dir.

Founded: 1959. **Members:** 55,000. **Membership Dues:** individual in U.S., $13 (annual) ● individual outside U.S., $15 (annual) ● professional/affiliate in U.S., $65 (annual) ● professional/affiliate outside U.S., $75 (annual) ● administrative in U.S., $325 (annual) ● administrative outside U.S., $350 (annual) ● builder, supplier, $425 (annual). **Staff:** 12. **Budget:** $1,500,000. **Regional Groups:** 18. **Multinational. Description:** Represents ice rink owners and managers; builders and suppliers for the industry; skaters; ice skating instructors. Seeks to educate ice arena owners, operators, and instructors and to increase public interest in ice skating. Provides information on building ice facilities. Provides recreational ice skater class programs, and a national test registration program to identify and record skating skill development in-free-style, couple and pair skating, ice dancing, figures, hockey, and speed skating. Sponsors Ice Skating Hall of Fame, annual conference and trade show and annual recreational ice skating competitions. Offers professional certification courses through ISI's Ice Arena Institute of Management. **Awards:** ISIA Education Foundation Scholarship. **Frequency:** annual. **Type:** scholarship. **Computer Services:** Mailing lists. **Telecommunication Services:** electronic mail, pmartell@skateisi.org. **Sections:** Builders and Suppliers; Commercial Rinks; Hockey; Instructors; Publicly Owned Rinks; Schools and Colleges. **Formerly:** (1998) Ice Skating Institute of America. **Publications:** *ISI EDGE*, bimonthly. Journal. Provides information for rink owners, operators, and instructors. Includes calendar of events and employment listings. **Price:** included in membership dues. **Circulation:** 5,000. **Advertising:** accepted ● *Recreational Ice Skater Team Competition Standards*. Handbook. Contains instructions and rules for running ISI team competitions. **Price:** $50.00 for administrative members only. **Circulation:** 750 ● *Recreational Ice Skating*, quarterly. Magazine. For figure, hockey, and speed skaters. Includes print and photo coverage of championship events, competitions and shows, profiles of skaters. **Price:** $12.00 /year for nonmembers. **Circulation:** 60,000. **Advertising:** accepted ● *Skaters and Coaches Handbook*. **Circulation:** 75,000 ● Membership Directory, annual. **Price:** free. **Circulation:** 5,000. **Advertising:** accepted ● Also publishes hockey test standards, competition standards, technical papers, and promotional materials. **Conventions/Meetings:** annual Adult Championships - competition, for ice skaters 21 years and older ● annual conference and trade show, includes ice skating industry builders and suppliers (exhibits) ● annual Synchronized Skating Championships - competition ● annual World Recreational Team Championship - competition.

3601 ■ Roller Skating Association International (RSA)

6905 Corporate Dr.
Indianapolis, IN 46278
Ph: (317)347-2626
Fax: (317)347-2636
E-mail: jcline@rollerskating.com
URL: http://www.rollerskating.com
Contact: Jason A. Cline, Contact

Founded: 1937. **Members:** 1,100. **Membership Dues:** basic, $360 (annual). **Staff:** 10. **Budget:** $1,200,000. **Regional Groups:** 13. **State Groups:** 24. **Multinational. Description:** Independent roller skating rink operators; associate members are rink managers, teachers, and suppliers and manufacturers. Promotes the business and recreational sport of roller skating. Provides business and marketing information to skating center owners. **Libraries: Type:** reference. **Holdings:** 100; archival material, artwork, audiovisuals, books, clippings, periodicals. **Subjects:** roller skating. **Awards:** Rink Operator of the Year (Life Member). **Frequency:** annual. **Type:** recognition ● Teacher/Coach of the Year. **Frequency:** annual. **Type:** recognition. **Additional Websites:** http://www.rollerskating.org. **Divisions:** Roller Hockey Coaches Association; Society of Roller Skating Teachers of America (see separate entry); Speed

Coaches Association. **Formerly:** (1982) Roller Skating Operators Association of America; (1992) Roller Skating Rink Operators Association. **Publications:** *Coaching Roller Skating*. Book. Features instructions on all phases of the sport including roller skate dancing, figure and free skating, speed, hockey, and scoring. **Price:** $29.95 ● *Roller Skating Business*, bimonthly. Magazine. Includes calendar of events, profiles of members, and reviews of products and services. **Price:** $45.00 for nonmembers; free for members. **Circulation:** 2,000. **Advertising:** accepted ● *Roller Skating Industry Guide*. Book. Contains information on starting a roller skating rink. **Price:** $250.00 ● *Roller Skating Manufacturer's Newsletter* ● *RSA Today*, monthly. Newsletter. Contains association news. **Advertising:** accepted ● *RSA Today—Coaches Edition*, bimonthly. **Price:** $60.00/year. **Circulation:** 1,000. **Advertising:** accepted. **Conventions/Meetings:** annual convention and trade show (exhibits) - always May.

Small Business

3602 ■ American Independent Business Alliance (AMIBA)
222 S Black Ave.
Bozeman, MT 59715
Ph: (406)582-1255
E-mail: info@amiba.net
URL: http://www.amiba.net
Contact: Jennifer Rockne, Co-Founder/Dir.
Founded: 1997. **Description:** Represents small business owners. Works to fill the professional needs of small and home-based business owners. Hosts conferences. **Formerly:** (2003) Independent Business Alliance. **Conventions/Meetings:** workshop.

3603 ■ American Small Businesses Association (ASBA)
206 E Coll. St., Ste.201
Grapevine, TX 76051
Free: (800)942-2722
Fax: (817)251-8578
E-mail: rsawyer@utaic.com
URL: http://www.asbaonline.org
Contact: James C. Musser, Contact
Founded: 1975. **Members:** 5,000. **Membership Dues:** individual, $60 (annual). **Staff:** 4. **Description:** Represents small business owners. Supports legislation favorable to the small business enterprise; organizes members to collectively oppose unfavorable legislation. Informs members of proposed legislation affecting small businesses; conducts business education programs. Operates scholarship program. **Awards: Frequency:** annual. **Type:** scholarship. **Recipient:** to dependents and grandchildren of ASBA members. **Formerly:** American Small Business Association. **Publications:** *ASBA Benefits Guide*, annual. Catalog ● *ASBA Today*, bimonthly. Newsletter. **Price:** free for members.

3604 ■ American Woman's Economic Development Corporation (AWED)
216 E 45th St., 10th Fl.
New York, NY 10017
Ph: (917)368-6100
E-mail: info@awed.org
URL: http://www.awed.org
Contact: Roseanne Antonucci, Exec. Dir.
Founded: 1976. **Members:** 300. **Membership Dues:** regular, $55 (annual) ● supporting, $65 (annual) ● contributing, $85 (annual) ● associate, $29 (annual). **Staff:** 15. **Budget:** $1,500,000. **Description:** Entrepreneurs and executives from the private sector. Seeks to help entrepreneurial women start and grow their own businesses. Provides formal course instruction, one-on-one business counseling, seminars, special events, and peer group support. Seeks to increase the start-up, survival and expansion rates of small businesses. Represents women from all socioeconomic levels, including formerly employed women and women from low-income communities. **Publications:** *AWED's in Business*, bimonthly. Newsletter. **Advertising:** accepted.

3605 ■ Association for Enterprise Opportunity (AEO)
1601 N Kent St., Ste.1101
Arlington, VA 22209
Ph: (703)841-7760
Fax: (703)841-7748
E-mail: aeo@assoceo.org
URL: http://www.microenterpriseworks.org
Contact: Amy McKenna Luz, Pres./CEO
Founded: 1991. **Members:** 475. **Membership Dues:** practitioner, $200-$400 (annual) ● individual, $100 (annual) ● consultant/training firm, government agency, $250 (annual) ● university/educational institution, $300 (annual) ● national organization, $500 (annual) ● bank/financial institution/corporation/foundation, $1,000 (annual) ● underwriting, $5,000 (annual). **Staff:** 16. **Description:** Represents microenterprise development organizations serving economically disadvantaged areas across the United States. Promotes improved economic opportunity for aspiring entrepreneurs with limited access to financial resources. Facilitates networking among members; provides training and technical assistance to members; develops and distributes educational materials; conducts advocacy. **Awards:** Innovation Awards. **Frequency:** annual. **Type:** recognition. **Recipient:** to members for innovative work in microenterprise development program design and for innovative use of technology ● Maria Padilla-Orasel Scholarship Fund. **Frequency:** annual. **Type:** scholarship. **Recipient:** to minority women new to the microenterprise development field. **Committees:** Conference; Fund Development and Strategic Alliances; Governance; Policy; Rural; SBA Microloan; Standards and Accreditation/Research; Training and Education. **Publications:** *AEO Exchange*, quarterly. Newsletter. Alternate Formats: online. **Conventions/Meetings:** annual conference, training and networking conference for members and those interested in microenterprise development (exhibits).

3606 ■ Association of Small Business Development Centers (ASBDC)
8990 Burke Lake Rd.
Burke, VA 22015
Ph: (703)764-9850
Fax: (703)764-1234
E-mail: info@asbdc-us.org
URL: http://www.asbdc-us.org
Contact: Donald T. Wilson, Pres./CEO
Founded: 1980. **Members:** 58. **Staff:** 5. **National Groups:** 950. **Description:** Local centers providing advice for those planning to establish a small business. Aims to facilitate information exchange among members and to represent their interests before the federal government. Informs the Small Business Administration on issues of interest to the small business community. **Committees:** Certification; Education; International Trade; New Resources. **Publications:** *Business Plan for Special Use Permits Training Manual*. Alternate Formats: online ● *Business Plan Workbook for Special Use Permits*. Alternate Formats: online ● Proceedings. Alternate Formats: online. **Conventions/Meetings:** Professional Development Conference ● annual conference (exhibits) - always spring or fall, Washington, DC. 2008 Sept. 2-5, Chicago, IL; 2010 Sept. 21-25, San Antonio, TX; 2011 Sept. 6-9, San Diego, CA.

3607 ■ BEST Employers Association (BEA)
2505 McCabe Way
Irvine, CA 92614
Ph: (949)253-4080
Free: (800)433-0088
Fax: (949)222-1004
E-mail: info@bestlife.com
URL: http://www.bestlife.com
Contact: Donald R. Lawrenz, Owner/Chm./Pres./CEO
Founded: 1980. **Members:** 25,000. **Staff:** 3. **Languages:** English, Spanish. **Description:** Provides small independent businesses with managerial, economic, financial, and sales information helpful for business improvement. Organizes and sponsors healthcare alliances for small employers. (The acronym BEST stands for Beneficial Employees Security Trust). **Computer Services:** Mailing lists. **Publications:** *Newsbeat*, quarterly. Newsletter. Features business updates and healthcare issues for small employer groups.

3608 ■ Employers of America (EofA)
c/o Mr. Jim Collison, Pres.
PO Box 1874
Mason City, IA 50402-1874
Ph: (641)424-3187
E-mail: employer@employerhelp.org
URL: http://www.employerhelp.org
Contact: Mr. Jim Collison, Pres.
Founded: 1976. **Members:** 600. **Membership Dues:** participating, $149 (annual). **Staff:** 6. **Budget:** $250,000. **Description:** Assists employers, managers, and supervisors in keeping their businesses profitable by maintaining the best possible workplace policies and practices, and to deal safely, effectively, and profitably with employees. Publishes e-Letter to help members achieve more with their employees. **Formerly:** (1998) ISBE Employers of America. **Publications:** *HRmadeEasy*, weekly. Newsletter. Includes recommendations to deal safely and effectively with employees. **Price:** $149.00/year. **Circulation:** 1,000. Alternate Formats: online.

3609 ■ Family Firm Institute (FFI)
200 Lincoln St., Ste.201
Boston, MA 02111
Ph: (617)482-3045
Fax: (617)482-3049
E-mail: ffi@ffi.org
URL: http://www.ffi.org
Contact: Judy L. Green PhD, Exec. Dir.
Founded: 1986. **Members:** 1,100. **Membership Dues:** non-consulting educator, researcher (individual), $300 (annual) ● professional (individual), $580 (annual) ● student (individual), $80 (annual) ● professional (organizational), $2,000 (annual) ● educational (organizational), $1,200 (annual) ● benefactor, $3,000 (annual) ● patron, $7,500 (annual). **Staff:** 4. **Budget:** $850,000. **State Groups:** 2. **Local Groups:** 16. **National Groups:** 2. **Multinational. Description:** Works to assist family firms by increasing the interdisciplinary skills of family business advisors, educators, researchers and consultants. **Libraries: Type:** reference. **Holdings:** archival material, books, periodicals. **Subjects:** family business. **Awards:** Barbara Hollander Award. **Frequency:** annual. **Type:** recognition. **Recipient:** to an individual who exemplifies Hollander's love for education ● Best Doctoral Dissertation. **Frequency:** annual. **Type:** monetary. **Recipient:** for outstanding academic achievement ● Best Unpublished Research Paper. **Frequency:** annual. **Type:** monetary. **Recipient:** for unpublished research in the field of family business study ● Interdisciplinary Award. **Frequency:** annual. **Type:** recognition. **Recipient:** for advancement made in interdisciplinary service ● International Award. **Frequency:** annual. **Type:** recognition. **Recipient:** to an individual or organization ● Richard Beckhard Practice Award. **Frequency:** annual. **Type:** recognition. **Recipient:** for outstanding contributions in family business practice. **Computer Services:** Mailing lists ● online services. **Committees:** Awards; Body of Knowledge; Certificate Program; Educators Task Force; Networking; Nominating; Student Liaison. **Subcommittees:** Study Group. **Publications:** *Family Business Review*, quarterly. Journal. **Price:** $95.00 in U.S. ISSN: 0894-4865. **Circulation:** 2,000. **Advertising:** accepted ● *FFI Conference Proceedings* ● *FFI Yellow Pages*. Directory. **Conventions/Meetings:** annual conference (exhibits).

3610 ■ International Association for Business Organizations (INAFBO)
3 Woodthorn Ct., Ste.12
Owings Mills, MD 21117
Ph: (410)581-1373
E-mail: nahbb@msn.com
Contact: Rudolph Lewis, Exec. Off.
Founded: 1986. **Description:** Business organizations that develop and support small businesses that have the capability to provide their products or services on an international level. Establishes

international business training institutions; promotes a business code of ethics for members. Conducts market studies; supplies member organizations with management assistance. Encourages joint marketing services and international trade assistance among members. Certifies international trader. **Affiliated With:** National Association for Business Organizations; National Association of Home Based Businesses. **Publications:** Newsletter, periodic. **Conventions/Meetings:** annual convention (exhibits).

3611 ■ International Council for Small Business (ICSB)
The George Washington Univ.
Scholarship of Bus.
Dept. of Mgt.
2201 G St. NW, Funger 315
Washington, DC 20052
Ph: (202)994-0704
Fax: (202)994-4930
E-mail: icsb@gwu.edu
URL: http://www.icsb.org
Contact: Rob Van der Horst, Pres.

Founded: 1957. **Members:** 1,900. **Staff:** 1. **Regional Groups:** 11. **Multinational**. **Description:** Management educators, researchers, government officials, and professionals in 80 countries. Fosters discussion of topics pertaining to the development and improvement of small business management. **Telecommunication Services:** electronic mail, rvh@eim.nl. **Formerly:** (1978) National Committee for Small Business Management Development. **Publications:** *ICSB Bulletin*, quarterly. Newsletter. Includes information about member activities and upcoming entrepreneurship conferences. ● *Journal of Small Business Management*, quarterly. Features topics related to small business financing. Also Cited As: *JSBM* ● Membership Directory, annual. Alternate Formats: online ● Proceedings, annual. **Conventions/Meetings:** annual conference - always in June. 2008 June 22-25, Halifax, NS, Canada ● annual seminar and international conference.

3612 ■ International Small Business Consortium (ISBC)
3309 Windjammer St.
Norman, OK 73072
E-mail: sb@isbc.com
URL: http://www.isbc.com
Contact: Nick Baker, Contact

Members: 33,000. **State Groups:** 140. **Multinational**. **Description:** Works to assist small businesses in maximizing the Internet in the most cost-efficient manner. Aims to improve the image and credibility of the SME community, to help promote SMEs in general and to provide a means for SMEs to be better known internationally. Helps small businesses apply the Internet to further their business goals and to help them find support and answers in dealing with all business aspects.

3613 ■ National Alliance for Fair Competition (NAFC)
3 Bethesda Metro Center, Ste.1100
Bethesda, MD 20814
Ph: (410)235-7116
Fax: (410)235-7116
E-mail: ampesq@aol.com
Contact: Tony Ponticelli, Exec. Dir.

Founded: 1982. **Members:** 20. **Membership Dues:** organization, $2,500 (annual). **Staff:** 1. **Budget:** $50,000. **State Groups:** 10. **National Groups:** 20. **Description:** National trade groups representing 4.5 million small businesses. Aims to: combat anticompetitive and unfair trade practices by utilities through legislation, litigation, and public service/utility commissions; develop clearinghouses for examples and case studies aiding those involved with assisting state and local associations and small businesses; work with Congress and federal agencies to facilitate action dealing with unfair trade practices. **Formerly:** Alliance for Fair Competition. **Conventions/Meetings:** biennial meeting.

3614 ■ National Association of Business Leaders (NABL)
Address Unknown since 2007

Founded: 1986. **Members:** 40,000. **Membership Dues:** $695 (annual). **Staff:** 39. **Languages:** English, Spanish. **For-Profit**. **Description:** Provides support for small businesses. Offers services such as a guaranteed $30,000 line of credit, mentoring, educational assistance, discounts on business products and services, and free member advertising. **Libraries: Type:** reference. **Holdings:** audio recordings, video recordings. **Subjects:** Small business. **Publications:** *Structure*, quarterly. Magazine ● Newsletter, periodic ● Directory, periodic. **Conventions/Meetings:** annual conference ● annual convention ● periodic seminar ● annual Winter Institute - meeting.

3615 ■ National Association for Business Organizations (NAFBO)
3 Woodthorne Ct., No. 12
Owings Mills, MD 21117
Ph: (410)363-3698
E-mail: nahbb@msn.com
URL: http://www.ameribizs.com/global
Contact: Rudolph Lewis, Pres.

Founded: 1986. **Description:** Business organizations that develop and support small businesses that have the capability to provide their products or services on a national level. Promotes small business in a free market system; represents the interests of small businesses to government and community organizations on small business affairs; monitors and reviews laws that affect small businesses; promotes a business code of ethics. Supplies members with marketing and management assistance; encourages joint marketing services between members. Operates a Home Based Business Television Network that provides an affordable audio/visual media for small and home based businesses. **Awards:** Entrepreneur Certificate. **Type:** recognition. **Recipient:** to members of affiliate organizations, colleges and business institutions that offer noncredit business courses. **Computer Services:** Online services. **Affiliated With:** International Association for Business Organizations; National Association of Home Based Businesses. **Publications:** Newsletter, periodic. **Conventions/Meetings:** annual convention (exhibits).

3616 ■ National Association of Private Enterprise (NAPE)
Address Unknown since 2008

Founded: 1983. **Members:** 5,000. **Membership Dues:** $120 (annual). **Description:** Employers and employees of small businesses; self-employed individuals. Seeks to ensure the continued growth of private enterprise through education, benefits programs such as health insurance, and legislation. Promotes the common interest of members. **Convention/Meeting:** none. **Awards:** Seminar Scholarships. **Frequency:** quarterly. **Type:** scholarship. **Recipient:** for member, directly related to business. **Publications:** *NAPE News*, quarterly. Newsletter. **Price:** included in membership dues. **Advertising:** accepted. Alternate Formats: online.

3617 ■ National Association for the Self-Employed (NASE)
PO Box 612067
DFW Airport
Dallas, TX 75261-2067
Free: (800)232-6273
Fax: (800)551-4446
E-mail: mpetron@nase.org
URL: http://www.nase.org
Contact: Robert Hughes, Pres.

Founded: 1981. **Members:** 250,000. **Membership Dues:** access level, $120 (annual) ● premiere resource level, $480 (annual). **Budget:** $20,000,000. **Description:** Self-employed and small independent businesspersons. Acts as an advocate at the state and federal levels for self-employed people. Provides discounts on products and services important to self-employed and small business owners. **Awards:** Future Entrepreneur. **Frequency:** annual. **Type:** scholarship. **Recipient:** for a legal dependent of member. **Subgroups:** Small Business Crusader. **Publications:** *Get Connected*, biweekly. Newsletter. **Price:** free ● *NASE Annual Report*, annual. Features updates on the success of NASE and its members. Alternate Formats: online ● *Self-Employed America*, bimonthly. Magazine. Includes business and association news. **Price:** included in membership dues; $12.00 for nonmembers. ISSN: 1041-8741. **Circulation:** 350,000. **Advertising:** accepted ● *Washington Watch*, weekly. Newsletter. Contains information concerning legislative issues that affect small entrepreneurs. **Price:** free. Alternate Formats: online. **Conventions/Meetings:** annual conference.

3618 ■ National Association of Small Business Investment Companies (NASBIC)
666 11th St. NW, Ste.750
Washington, DC 20001
Ph: (202)628-5055
Fax: (202)628-5080
E-mail: nasbic@nasbic.org
URL: http://www.nasbic.org
Contact: Lee W. Mercer, Pres.

Founded: 1958. **Members:** 300. **Staff:** 6. **Budget:** $1,500,000. **Regional Groups:** 4. **Description:** Firms licensed as Small Business Investment Companies (SBICs) under the Small Business Investment Act of 1958. **Awards:** Portfolio Company of the Year Award. **Frequency:** annual. **Type:** recognition. **Recipient:** for portfolio company of a member. **Computer Services:** database. **Telecommunication Services:** electronic mail, lmercer@nasbic.org. **Committees:** Education; Ethics; Legislation; Political Action; Public Relations. **Affiliated With:** Small Business Legislative Council. **Publications:** *Layman's Guide to the Legal Aspects of Venture Investments*. Paper. Serves as a legal guide. **Price:** free for members; $250.00 for nonmembers ● *NASBIC Membership Directory*, annual. Lists members by state. **Price:** $35.00 for nonmembers ● *NASBIC News*, quarterly. Newsletter. Covers association activities and legislative developments affecting SBICs and small business in general. **Price:** free for members; $125.00 /year for nonmembers. ISSN: 1089-7321 ● *Today's SBICs: Investing in America's Future*. Brochure. Includes information on the new SBIC program and examples. **Price:** free. **Conventions/Meetings:** annual convention and meeting (exhibits) ● seminar ● annual Venture Capital Institute for Entrepreneurs - meeting ● annual Venture Capital Institute Graduate Program - meeting.

3619 ■ National Business Association (NBA)
PO Box 700728
Dallas, TX 75370
Ph: (972)458-0900
Free: (800)456-0440
Fax: (972)960-9149
E-mail: info@nationalbusiness.org
URL: http://www.nationalbusiness.org
Contact: Raj Nisankarao, Pres.

Founded: 1982. **Members:** 50,000. **Membership Dues:** individual, $180 (annual). **Staff:** 10. **Languages:** English, Spanish. **Description:** Employed owners of small businesses. Promotes and assists the growth and development of small businesses. Aids members in obtaining government small business and education loans; makes available insurance policies and software in conjunction with the U.S. Small Business Administration. Maintains career, educational institution, and scholarship information program for members and their dependents. Offers over 100 benefits, services and programs in the areas of Business, Health, Lifestyle and Education. **Publications:** *Biz Corner*, weekly. Newsletter. Alternate Formats: online ● *NBA boss*, bimonthly. Magazine. **Price:** included in membership dues. **Circulation:** 50,000. Alternate Formats: online ● Booklets. Contains business, training and motivational information. **Circulation:** 52,000 ● Brochures. **Conventions/Meetings:** seminar ● trade show.

3620 ■ National Business Owners Association (NBOA)
PO Box 111
Stuart, VA 24171-0111

Ph: (276)251-7500
Free: (866)251-7505
Fax: (276)251-2217
E-mail: membershipservices@nboa.org
URL: http://www.rvmdb.com/nboa
Contact: Paul LaBarr, Exec. Dir.

Founded: 1987. **Members:** 4,200. **Membership Dues:** small business (based on revenue and employee size), $200-$1,000 (annual) ● vendor, partner (based on target market), $1,000-$10,000 (annual). **Staff:** 4. **Budget:** $1,600,000. **State Groups:** 3. **Description:** Small business owners. Promotes the interests of small business. Provides government relations services, educational information, and member benefit programs. Disseminates information. **Convention/Meeting:** none. **Computer Services:** database. **Publications:** *Numbers Talk*, monthly. Newsletter.

3621 ■ National Center for Fair Competition
Address Unknown since 2008

Founded: 1997. **Members:** 25. **Membership Dues:** company CEO, state and local small business trade association CEO, and elected leader, $500 (annual). **Staff:** 1. **Budget:** $12,000. **For-Profit. Description:** Coalition of small firms against competition from governments and nonprofit organizations. Seeks to eliminate unfair advantages of tax-exempt organizations that produce, sell or lease products and services. Helps small businesses fight government and tax-favored organizations which convert their special privileges into competitive advantages in the commercial marketplace. **Formerly:** (1998) Business Coalition for Fair Competition. **Publications:** Newsletter, periodic. **Price:** $100.00/year. **Circulation:** 300. **Conventions/Meetings:** annual Washington Conference on Commercial Non-Profits & Government Commercial Enterprises.

3622 ■ National Federation of Independent Business (NFIB)
53 Century Blvd., Ste.250
Nashville, TN 37214
Ph: (615)872-5800
Free: (800)NFIBNOW
Fax: (615)232-4035
Contact: Todd Stottlemyer, Pres./CEO

Founded: 1943. **Members:** 607,000. **Staff:** 225. **Budget:** $65,000,000. **Description:** Independent business and professional people. Presents opinions of small and independent business to state and national legislative bodies. Conducts surveys at the state level with area directors and government affairs representatives working with state legislatures. Maintains 50 person legislative, research, and public affairs office in Washington, DC. Compiles statistics. **Libraries: Type:** reference. **Holdings:** books, clippings, monographs, periodicals. **Subjects:** small business. **Committees:** Political Action. **Publications:** *Independent Business*, bimonthly ● *NFIB Mandate*, bimonthly ● Also prepares and disseminates weekly press releases to daily papers, trade associations, and chambers of commerce nationwide, and monthly materials to high schools, colleges, and universities throughout the U.S. **Conventions/Meetings:** quadrennial meeting.

3623 ■ National Small Business Association (NSBA)
1156 15th St. NW, Ste.1100
Washington, DC 20005
Ph: (202)293-8830
Free: (800)345-6728
Fax: (202)872-8543
E-mail: press@nsba.biz
URL: http://www.nsba.biz
Contact: Mr. Grafton Willey, Chm.

Founded: 1937. **Members:** 150,000. **Staff:** 24. **Regional Groups:** 11. **State Groups:** 3. **Description:** Small businesses including manufacturing, wholesale, retail, service, and other firms. Works to advocate at the federal level on behalf of smaller businesses. **Committees:** Economic Development; Health Care Policy; Membership Services; Regulatory; Taxation. **Councils:** Small Business Technology. **Formed by Merger of:** (1988) National Small Business Association; Small Business United. **Formerly:** National Small Business United. **Publications:** *Advocate*, bimonthly. Newsletter. Provides members with information on updates, issues, resource guides and survey results. **Price:** included in membership dues. **Circulation:** 12,000. **Advertising:** accepted. Alternate Formats: online. **Conventions/Meetings:** monthly Small Business Meetup Day - meeting, networking opportunity.

3624 ■ Research Institute for Small and Emerging Business (RISEbusiness)
722 12th St. NW
Washington, DC 20005
Ph: (202)628-8382
Fax: (202)628-8392
E-mail: info@riseb.org
URL: http://www.riseb.org
Contact: Allan Neece Jr., Chm.

Founded: 1976. **Staff:** 3. **Budget:** $400,000. **Description:** Conducts and publishes research on small, entrepreneurial and emerging business. **Formerly:** (1998) Small Business Foundation of America; (1998) Research Institute for Small and Engineering Business. **Publications:** *Exportise - A Handbook on Exporting, Planning for Technology, and Job Generation through High Technology* ● *Is the Independent Entrepreneurial Firm a Valuable Organizational Form?*. Paper ● *Twenty Years of Job Creation Research: What Have We Learned?*. Paper.

3625 ■ SCORE
409 3rd St. SW, 6th Fl.
Washington, DC 20024
Ph: (202)205-6762
Free: (800)634-0245
Fax: (202)205-7636
E-mail: media@score.org
URL: http://www.score.org
Contact: W. Kenneth Yancey Jr., CEO

Founded: 1964. **Members:** 11,200. **Staff:** 15. **Budget:** $5,000,000. **State Groups:** 68. **Local Groups:** 389. **Description:** Serves as volunteer program sponsored by U.S. Small Business Administration in which working and retired business management professionals provide free business counseling to men and women who are considering starting a small business, encountering problems with their business, or expanding their business. Offers free one-on-one counseling, online counseling and low cost workshops on a variety of business topics. **Libraries: Type:** reference. **Holdings:** books, clippings, periodicals. **Subjects:** business. **Awards:** SCORE Chapter of the Year Award. **Frequency:** annual. **Type:** recognition. **Recipient:** for chapters whose expert counselors have exceeded high standards for counseling small business clients. **Formerly:** (1980) Service Corps of Retired Executives. **Publications:** *SCORE eNews*, monthly. Newsletter. Offers latest trends and resources for small business. **Price:** free. Alternate Formats: online ● *SCORE Expert Answers*, monthly. Newsletter. Brings marketplace trends and advice from small business experts and industry leaders. **Price:** free. Alternate Formats: online ● *SCORE Today*, monthly. Newsletter. Covers association activities. **Price:** free for members. **Circulation:** 16,000 ● Annual Report, annual. Includes SCORE client success stories. Alternate Formats: online.

3626 ■ Small Business and Entrepreneurship Council (SBEC)
2944 Hunter Mill Rd., Ste.204
Oakton, VA 22124
Ph: (703)242-5840
Fax: (703)242-5841
E-mail: membership@sbsc.org
URL: http://www.sbecouncil.org
Contact: Karen Kerrigan, Pres./CEO

Founded: 1994. **Members:** 70,000. **Membership Dues:** business start-up, $50 (annual) ● General Council, $100 (annual) ● Entrepreneur Council, $500 (annual) ● CEO Council, $1,000 (annual). **Staff:** 5. **Budget:** $1,200,000. **Description:** Works to protect small business and sustain entrepreneurship. **Formerly:** (2004) Small Business Survival Committee. **Publications:** *SBEC Council Weekly Brief*, every Friday. Newsletter. Includes member activities and the key issues and trends in business. **Price:** included in membership dues. Alternate Formats: online. **Conventions/Meetings:** annual conference.

3627 ■ Small Business Legislative Council (SBLC)
1100 H St. NW, Ste.540
Washington, DC 20005
Ph: (202)639-8500
Fax: (202)296-5333
E-mail: email@sblc.org
URL: http://www.sblc.org
Contact: John Satagaj, Pres./Gen. Counsel

Founded: 1976. **Members:** 106. **Membership Dues:** association (based on the potential member's total association budget), $650-$3,500. **Staff:** 2. **Description:** Serves as an independent coalition of trade and professional associations that share a common commitment to the future of small business. Represents the interests of small businesses in such diverse economic sectors as manufacturing, retailing, distribution, professional and technical services, construction, transportation, and agriculture. **Awards: Type:** recognition. **Committees:** Anti-Trust; Capital Formation; Employment Issues and Pension Laws; Environment; Government Procurement; Tax Policy. **Task Forces:** Liability Insurance/Tort Reform. **Publications:** Brochure ● Newsletter, monthly. **Conventions/Meetings:** meeting - always in Washington, DC ● seminar.

3628 ■ Small Business Service Bureau (SBSB)
554 Main St.
PO Box 15014
Worcester, MA 01615-0014
Ph: (508)756-3513
Free: (800)343-0939
Fax: (508)770-0528
E-mail: membership@sbsb.com
URL: http://www.sbsb.com
Contact: Francis R. Carroll, Founder/CEO

Founded: 1968. **Members:** 50,000. **For-Profit. Description:** Represents businesses with less than 100 employees. Offers planning and strategy programs to aid businesspersons in starting, improving, or expanding small businesses. Disseminates guides, manuals, and other materials on small business operations. Offers trade assistance to the People's Republic of China. **Convention/Meeting:** none. **Formerly:** (2001) Small Business Assistance Center. **Publications:** *Legislative News*, bimonthly. Newsletter ● Bulletin, bimonthly, every January, March, May, July, September, and November. Updates members on small business issues currently before the U.S. Congress, which affect the reader's business. **Price:** $5.00/year. ISSN: 0893-8326. Alternate Formats: online.

3629 ■ Small Business in Telecommunications (SBT)
Address Unknown since 2008
URL: http://www.sbthome.org

Membership Dues: general, $300. **Description:** Represents the interests of small businesses in the global telecommunications marketplace. Seeks to serve the public's demand for service from local operators while maintaining the competitive strength of its members. **Publications:** Newsletter, monthly. Alternate Formats: online.

3630 ■ SOHO America
PO Box 941
Hurst, TX 76053-0941
Free: (800)495-SOHO
Fax: (800)841-4445
E-mail: soho@1sas.com
URL: http://www.soho.org

Description: Provides virtual community for small business and home office professionals with information pertaining to small and home-based businesses.

3631 ■ Support Services Alliance (SSA)
PO Box 130
Schoharie, NY 12157
Free: (800)836-4772
E-mail: info@ssamembers.com
URL: http://smallbizgrowth.com
Contact: Steve Cole, Pres.
Founded: 1977. **Members:** 15,000. **Membership Dues:** general, $50 (annual). **Staff:** 70. **For-Profit. Description:** Represents small businesses (less than 50 employees), the self-employed, and associations of such individuals. Provides services and programs such as group purchasing discounts, health coverage, legislative advocacy, and business and financial support services. **Telecommunication Services:** electronic mail, comments@ssamembers.com ● additional toll-free number, (800)909-2772. **Councils:** Member Advisory. **Publications:** *Capital Crier*. Newsletter. Contains issues affecting business. **Price:** included in membership dues. Alternate Formats: online ● *Small-Biz Growth*, monthly. Magazine. Contains articles on management practice, wellness and other issues related to small business. **Price:** available to members only and their employees. **Circulation:** 30,000. **Advertising:** accepted. **Conventions/Meetings:** annual Small Biz - conference and workshop, with speakers dealing with small business issues (exhibits).

3632 ■ United States Association for Small Business and Entrepreneurship (USASBE)
c/o Joan Gillman, Exec. Dir.
975 Univ. Ave., No. 3260
Madison, WI 53706
Ph: (608)262-9982
Fax: (608)263-0818
E-mail: jgillman@wisc.edu
URL: http://www.usasbe.org
Contact: Joan Gillman, Exec. Dir.
Founded: 1981. **Membership Dues:** regular, $95 (annual) ● student, $55 (annual) ● organization, $250 (annual). **Staff:** 2. **Description:** Fosters business development through entrepreneurship education and research. Improves management knowledge, techniques and skills of small business owners and entrepreneurs. Develops an understanding of small businesses and entrepreneurship to promote a continuing exchange of expertise. **Awards:** USASBE Entrepreneurship Educator of the Year Award. **Frequency:** annual. **Type:** recognition. **Recipient:** for distinguished leadership in the field of entrepreneurship education ● USASBE Fellows. **Frequency:** annual. **Type:** fellowship. **Recipient:** for outstanding contribution to the organization ● USASBE National Model Entrepreneurship Program of the Year. **Frequency:** annual. **Type:** recognition. **Recipient:** for exemplary programs that reflect innovation, quality and impact ● USASBE Pedagogy Award. **Frequency:** annual. **Type:** recognition. **Recipient:** for a truly state of the art entrepreneurship course. **Computer Services:** Information services, small business and entrepreneurship resources. **Divisions:** Corporate Entrepreneurship; Entrepreneurship Education; Entrepreneurship in the Arts; Entrepreneurship Support Organizations; Family Business; Individual Entrepreneurship; International Entrepreneurship; Small Business. **Affiliated With:** International Council for Small Business. **Publications:** *Liaison*, 3/year. Newsletter ● Membership Directory ● Proceedings. **Conventions/Meetings:** annual conference, with paper presentation.

Social Change

3633 ■ Social Enterprise Alliance (SEA)
c/o Jim McClung, Pres.
19341 8th Ave. NW
Shoreline, WA 98177
Ph: (206)407-3630
E-mail: jim@se-alliance.org
URL: http://www.se-alliance.org
Contact: Jim McClung, Pres.
Founded: 2002. **Membership Dues:** individual, $150 (annual) ● affiliate, $75 (annual) ● student, $50 (annual) ● sustainer, $500 (annual) ● investor, $1,000 (annual) ● builder, $2,500 (annual) ● angel, $5,000 (annual) ● group (up to 3 people), $350 (annual). **Description:** Seeks to build stronger, more effective nonprofit organizations by mobilizing a community of practitioners and investors to advance earned income strategies. Links nonprofit executives who have operated in isolation with an ongoing forum for addressing the needs and concerns of the enterprising nonprofit. Connects entrepreneurial nonprofits with learning opportunities, technical assistance and resources to further their efforts. **Publications:** *Enterprising Voice*, biweekly. Bulletin. **Price:** included in membership dues. Alternate Formats: online.

Space

3634 ■ International Association of Space Entrepreneurs (IASE)
206 Stoneledge Pl. NE
Leesburg, VA 20176
Ph: (703)386-9737
Free: (800)701-0828
E-mail: info@spaceentrepreneurs.org
URL: http://www.spaceentrepreneurs.org
Contact: Guillermo Sohnlein, Founder/Chm.
Founded: 2003. **Multinational. Description:** Promotes global entrepreneurship in the space industry through concerted efforts in business, public policy, and education. Fosters space-related ventures by enabling valuable business connections and supporting professional development efforts. Provides networking opportunities, tools, resources and services to its members. **Publications:** Newsletter, quarterly.

Sporting Goods

3635 ■ American Fly-Fishing Trade Association (AFFTA)
940 Hill St.
Athens, GA 30606
Ph: (706)355-3804
Fax: (706)353-2390
E-mail: robert@affta.com
URL: http://www.affta.com
Contact: Robert Ramsay, Pres.
Members: 400. **Membership Dues:** general (based on annual revenue), $75-$4,000 (annual). **Staff:** 16. **Description:** Manufacturers and retailers of fly-fishing equipment. Promotes increased participation in fly-fishing; and seeks to advance members' commercial and regulatory interests. Represents members before government agencies and industrial organizations. **Committees:** Consumer Recruitment; Government and Alliances; Trade Development. **Publications:** *AFFTA Connects*, bimonthly. Newsletter. **Advertising:** accepted. Alternate Formats: online ● *The Fly Fishing Market in the U.S. (97-02)* ● *Fly Fishing Tactics*, bimonthly. Newsletter. **Advertising:** accepted. Alternate Formats: online. **Conventions/Meetings:** annual Fly Fishing Retailer World Trade Expo - trade show (exhibits).

3636 ■ American Recreational Golf Association (ARGA)
7300 W Fullerton Ave.
PO Box 35215
Chicago, IL 60707-0215
Ph: (708)453-0080
Fax: (708)453-0083
E-mail: concido@concido.com
Founded: 1974. **Members:** 79,074. **Membership Dues:** individual, $25 (annual) ● business, $100 (annual) ● corporate sponsor, $250 (annual). **Staff:** 10. **Description:** Initiated by the American Recreational Sports Association. Evaluates golf equipment for the sporting goods industry and offers equipment certification program. Studies trends in the golf industry. Maintains a hall of fame; sponsors competitions; conducts charitable and educational programs. **Libraries: Type:** reference; not open to the public. **Awards:** Best Buyer Award. **Frequency:** annual. **Type:** recognition ● Best Manufacturer Award. **Type:** recognition ● Best Player Award. **Frequency:** annual. **Type:** recognition. **Computer Services:** Mailing lists. **Committees:** Political Action.

3637 ■ American Recreational Racket Sports Association (ARRSA)
7115 W North Ave., Ste.272
Oak Park, IL 60302
Ph: (708)453-0080
Fax: (708)453-0083
E-mail: arras@rentamark.com
Contact: L. David Stoller, Chm.
Founded: 1975. **Members:** 53,429. **Membership Dues:** individual, $49 (annual) ● corporate, $250 (annual). **Staff:** 25. **Description:** Initiated by the American Recreational Sports Association. Evaluates tennis and other racket sport equipment for the sporting goods industry and offers equipment certification program. Maintains speakers' bureau and hall of fame; sponsors competitions; provides education for members through selection of books; conducts educational and charitable programs. Studies trends dealing with racket sports. Provides licensing of it's logo for product and service endorsements, to support members' activities. **Libraries: Type:** reference. **Awards:** Best Buyer Award. **Frequency:** monthly. **Type:** recognition ● Best Manufacturer Award. **Frequency:** monthly. **Type:** recognition. **Computer Services:** Mailing lists. **Committees:** Political Action. **Affiliated With:** American Recreational Golf Association. **Publications:** *ARGSA Golf Equipment Recommendations*, quarterly. Newsletter. **Price:** $2.95. **Circulation:** 50,000. **Advertising:** accepted. Alternate Formats: online ● *ARRSA Tennis Racket Guide*, quarterly. **Price:** $2.95. **Circulation:** 50,000. **Advertising:** accepted. Alternate Formats: online. **Conventions/Meetings:** annual convention (exhibits) - always September, Chicago, IL.

3638 ■ Archery Trade Association (ATA)
Bus. and Trade Show Off.
860 E 4500 S, Ste.No. 310
Salt Lake City, UT 84107
Ph: (801)261-2380
Free: (866)266-2776
Fax: (801)261-2389
E-mail: info@archerytrade.org
URL: http://www.archerytrade.org
Contact: Jay McAninch, CEO/Pres.
Founded: 1954. **Members:** 1,500. **Staff:** 6. **Multinational. Description:** Manufacturers, distributors, dealers, and suppliers of bows, arrows, and other archery and bowhunting products; sales representatives and the archery and bowhunting media. Seeks to promote and protect the sport of archery. Assists in establishing standards for the industry. **Computer Services:** Information services. **Formerly:** Archery Manufacturers and Dealers Association; (1965) Archery Manufacturers Association; (1994) Archery Manufacturers Organization; (2003) Archery Manufacturers and Merchants Organization. **Publications:** Also publishes standards and distributes promotional films. **Conventions/Meetings:** annual trade show (exhibits).

3639 ■ Association of Golf Merchandisers (AGM)
PO Box 7247
Phoenix, AZ 85011-7247
Ph: (602)604-8250
Fax: (602)604-8251
E-mail: info@agmgolf.org
URL: http://www.agmgolf.org
Contact: Desane Blaney, Exec. Dir.
Founded: 1989. **Members:** 700. **Membership Dues:** merchandiser, $225 (annual) ● associate, student, $100 (annual) ● affiliate, $450 (annual). **Staff:** 3. **Budget:** $250,000. **Regional Groups:** 11. **Description:** Golf buyers and vendors. Dedicated to maximizing members' learning and earning capabilities. Conducts continuing educational programs; provides networking opportunities, scholarships and a forum for communication; compiles statistics. **Libraries: Type:** lending; not open to the public. **Awards:** AGM Scholarship Fund. **Frequency:** annual. **Type:** schol-

arship. **Recipient:** for college student pursuing careers in golf merchandising. **Publications:** *AGM E-tailer*, monthly. Newsletter. **Circulation:** 1,000. Alternate Formats: online ● *AGM Merchandise Manual* ● *The Merchandiser*, monthly. Newsletter. **Conventions/Meetings:** semiannual conference - held during January and September.

3640 ■ Bicycle Product Suppliers Association (BPSA)
PO Box 187
Montgomeryville, PA 18936
Ph: (215)393-3144
Fax: (215)893-4872
E-mail: bpsa@bpsa.org
URL: http://www.bpsa.org
Contact: Maureen Waddington, Exec. Dir.
Founded: 1912. **Members:** 130. **Membership Dues:** company (based on sales), $350-$3,000 (annual). **Staff:** 3. **Budget:** $100,000. **Description:** Wholesalers of bicycles, bicycle parts, and accessories; vendor members are manufacturers and suppliers. Affiliate members supply services and products to bicycle retailers. Offers educational programs; compiles statistics and safety information. **Committees:** Barcoding; Conference; Long Range Planning; Membership; Nominating; Partnership Development Project; Safety; Statistical. **Formerly:** (1960) Cycle Jobbers Association; (1997) Bicycle Wholesale Distributors Association. **Publications:** *Statistical Report*, annual ● *U.S. Tariff Schedules*, annual ● Newsletter, quarterly. **Price:** free. **Circulation:** 150. Alternate Formats: online. **Conventions/Meetings:** annual conference, for members only (exhibits).

3641 ■ Billiard and Bowling Institute of America (BBIA)
PO Box 6573
Arlington, TX 76005
Free: (800)343-1329
Fax: (817)633-2940
E-mail: answer@billiardandbowling.org
URL: http://www.billiardandbowling.org
Contact: Lori Tessmar, Pres.
Founded: 1940. **Members:** 95. **Membership Dues:** manufacturer, $650 (annual) ● distributor, $425 (annual) ● retailer, $325 (annual) ● associate, $425 (annual). **Staff:** 2. **Budget:** $85,000. **Description:** Represents distributors and manufacturers of billiard and bowling equipment. **Awards:** Industry Service Award. **Frequency:** annual. **Type:** recognition. **Publications:** *BBIA Membership and Product Information Guide*, annual. Directory. Lists BBIA members, their products, and brand names. **Price:** free. **Circulation:** 2,000 ● *BBIA Newsline*, quarterly. Newsletter. Covers membership activities. **Price:** free. **Circulation:** 1,000. Alternate Formats: online ● *Bowling for Everyone — Fundamentals of the Game*. **Conventions/Meetings:** annual conference and seminar (exhibits) ● annual convention, with popular keynote speakers.

3642 ■ Diving Equipment and Marketing Association (DEMA)
3750 Convoy St., Ste.310
San Diego, CA 92111-3741
Ph: (858)616-6408
Free: (800)862-3483
Fax: (858)616-6495
E-mail: info@dema.org
URL: http://www.dema.org
Contact: Tom Ingram, Exec. Dir.
Founded: 1972. **Members:** 1,500. **Membership Dues:** category A (based on gross income), $100-$2,500 (annual) ● category B, $100 (annual). **Staff:** 7. **Budget:** $2,500,000. **Description:** International recreational scuba diving and snorkeling organizations and associations promoting or reporting diving activities, individuals or organizations providing educational, retail, travel, media or other services in the field. Aims to promote advancement within the diving equipment industry, encourage the growth of diving activities, and enhance public enjoyment of recreational diving. Cooperates with domestic governmental and private agencies that develop standards or are involved in regulating activities affecting the diving industry and related products. Seeks to establish continuing education programs to instruct and assist industry members in business, quality control and the marketing of diving products. Organizes conferences dealing with topics such as governmental regulations, product standards, quality control, and standardized bookkeeping methods. **Libraries: Type:** not open to the public. **Subjects:** scuba diving, snorkeling. **Awards:** Reaching Out Award - Diving Hall of Fame. **Frequency:** annual. **Type:** recognition. **Recipient:** nominated by past recipients and board of directors. **Computer Services:** database. **Telecommunication Services:** electronic mail, tingram@dema.org. **Committees:** Membership; Trade Show. **Formerly:** (1995) Diving Equipment Manufacturers Association. **Publications:** *DEMA News & Industry Report*, monthly. Newsletter. Contains DEMA and industry news. **Price:** included in membership dues. **Circulation:** 2,500. Alternate Formats: online. **Conventions/Meetings:** annual trade show, trade only (exhibits).

3643 ■ Kite Trade Association International (KTAI)
PO Box 443
Otis, OR 97368
Ph: (541)994-9647
Free: (800)243-8548
Fax: (626)657-2792
E-mail: exdir@kitetrade.org
URL: http://www.kitetrade.org
Contact: Maggie Vohs, Exec. Dir.
Founded: 1983. **Members:** 300. **Membership Dues:** manufacturer, wholesaler, retailer (based on annual gross sales), $150-$450 (annual) ● non-profit, $75 (annual). **Budget:** $145,000. **Description:** Represents manufacturers, retailers, and wholesalers of kites; persons providing services to the kite industry. Promotes the kite industry. Maintains statistics pertinent to the kite trade. **Awards:** Excellence in Manufacturing Award. **Frequency:** annual. **Type:** recognition. **Recipient:** for kite manufacturers ● Retailer of the Year. **Frequency:** annual. **Type:** recognition. **Recipient:** for kite retailers. **Computer Services:** database ● mailing lists. **Telecommunication Services:** electronic mail, info@kitetrade.org. **Publications:** *Attendee Brochure*. Alternate Formats: online ● *Tradewinds*, quarterly. Newsletter. Contains industry news, trade announcements and success stories of members. **Price:** included in membership dues. **Advertising:** accepted ● Membership Directory, annual. Includes listing of members and their business information. Alternate Formats: online. **Conventions/Meetings:** annual conference and trade show (exhibits) - January.

3644 ■ National Association of Sporting Goods Wholesalers (NASGW)
c/o Wayne Smith, Pres.
PO Box 881525
Port St. Lucie, FL 34988-1525
Ph: (772)621-7162
Fax: (772)264-3233
E-mail: wsmith@nasgw.org
URL: http://www.nasgw.org
Contact: Wayne Smith, Pres.
Founded: 1954. **Members:** 350. **Membership Dues:** regular wholesaler, $500 (annual) ● associate manufacturer, $300 (annual) ● associate representative, $150 (annual). **Staff:** 1. **Description:** Represents wholesalers and manufacturers of primarily fishing tackle and shooting equipment. **Awards:** College Scholarship Program. **Frequency:** annual. **Type:** scholarship. **Recipient:** for deserving children of full-time employees from member companies. **Publications:** *NASGW News*, quarterly. Newsletter ● Membership Directory, annual. **Price:** $25.00 available to members only. **Conventions/Meetings:** annual trade show.

3645 ■ National Bicycle Dealers Association (NBDA)
777 W 19th St., Ste.O
Costa Mesa, CA 92627
Ph: (949)722-6909
Fax: (949)722-1747
E-mail: info@nbda.com
URL: http://www.nbda.com
Contact: Fred Clements, Exec. Dir.
Founded: 1946. **Members:** 1,600. **Membership Dues:** dealer, category C associate, $125 (annual) ● associate, $300 (annual) ● category I information, $40 (annual). **Staff:** 2. **State Groups:** 15. **Description:** Represents independent retail dealers who sell and service bicycles. Sponsors workshops and provides programs. **Publications:** *Outspokin'*, monthly. Newsletter ● *So You Want to Start A Bike Shop* ● Brochure. **Conventions/Meetings:** annual conference - always February.

3646 ■ National Ski and Snowboard Retailers Association (NSSRA)
1601 Feehanville Dr., Ste.300
Mount Prospect, IL 60056-6035
Ph: (847)391-9825
Fax: (847)391-9827
E-mail: info@nssra.com
URL: http://www.nssra.com
Contact: Brad Nelson, Chm.
Founded: 1987. **Members:** 250. **Membership Dues:** retailer (1-3 stores), $115 (annual) ● retailer (4-10 stores), $175 (annual) ● retailer (more than 10 stores), $300 (annual). **Staff:** 2. **Description:** Ski & snowboard stores. Represents the interests of members and provides services beneficial to their businesses. Compiles statistics. **Formerly:** National Ski Retailers Asso. **Publications:** *Cost-of-Doing-Business Survey for Ski and Snowboard Shops*, biennial. Provides key profitability, productivity & financial performance indicators, balance sheets and income statements for 9 types of retailers. **Price:** free for members; $125.00 for nonmembers. **Advertising:** accepted ● *NSSRA Newsletter*, quarterly. **Conventions/Meetings:** annual meeting - always Las Vegas, NV.

3647 ■ National Sporting Goods Association (NSGA)
1601 Feehanville Dr., Ste.300
Mount Prospect, IL 60056
Ph: (847)296-6742
Free: (800)815-5422
Fax: (847)391-9827
E-mail: info@nsga.org
URL: http://www.nsga.org
Contact: James L. Faltinek, Pres./CEO
Founded: 1929. **Members:** 3,000. **Membership Dues:** retailer, dealer, wholesaler (based on annual sales volume), $125-$370 (annual) ● manufacturer, $535 (annual) ● industry associate, $335 (annual). **Staff:** 18. **Description:** Provides services, education and information to assist member to profit in a competitive marketplace. **Computer Services:** Mailing lists. **Divisions:** Independent Retailer; Specialty Fitness Dealer; Specialty Golf Retailer; Team Dealer. **Publications:** *NSGA Buying Guide*, annual. Directory. Contains lists of over 8,000 sporting goods suppliers. **Price:** available to members only. **Advertising:** accepted ● *NSGA Retail Focus*, bimonthly. Magazine. Provides information on recent research, retail management, store design, and sales management for sporting goods dealers. **Price:** free for members; $50.00 for nonmembers ● *Sporting Goods Market*, annual. Contains results of annual consumer survey provided to membership in the sports equipment, footwear, and clothing fields. **Price:** $235.00/copy for members; $325.00/copy for nonmembers ● *Sports Participation-Series I & II*, annual. Features a research study, in two series, on sports participation. **Price:** $395.00 for members; $475.00 for nonmembers ● Also publishes research and statistical studies. **Conventions/Meetings:** annual Management Conference and Team Dealer Summit - meeting.

3648 ■ NSGA Team Dealer Division
1601 Feehanville Dr., Ste.300
Mount Prospect, IL 60056-6042
Ph: (847)296-6742
Fax: (847)391-9827

E-mail: info@nsga.org
URL: http://www.nsga.org
Contact: Larry Weindruch, Dir. of Communications
Founded: 1970. **Members:** 1,900. **Staff:** 1. **Description:** A division of the National Sporting Goods Association. Aims to keep athletic team dealers informed of rule changes that affect equipment sales and to relay other information concerning team sales. **Computer Services:** Online services, access to Original Market Research published by the association ● online services, new products' directory ● online services, sporting goods buying guide. **Telecommunication Services:** electronic mail, lweindruch@nsga.org. **Affiliated With:** National Sporting Goods Association. **Formerly:** (1998) Non Profit Association for Sporting Goods; (2006) Athletic Goods Team Distributors. **Publications:** *Team Lineup*, quarterly. Newsletter. **Price:** available to members only. **Circulation:** 1,900. **Conventions/Meetings:** annual NSGA Team Dealer Summit - convention - every May.

3649 ■ Professional Clubmakers' Society (PCS)
70 Persimmon Ridge Dr.
Louisville, KY 40245
Ph: (502)241-2816
Free: (800)548-6094
Fax: (502)241-2817
E-mail: pcs@proclubmakers.org
URL: http://www.proclubmakers.org
Contact: Barry J. Palm, Exec. Dir.
Founded: 1989. **Members:** 1,100. **Membership Dues:** regular, $208 (annual) ● initial, $95 ● junior, $75 (annual) ● life, $75 ● certification level, $267 (annual). **Staff:** 6. **Budget:** $500,000. **Multinational. Description:** Works to foster, promote and elevate the profession of custom fitting, building and repair of golf clubs and promote the game of golf. Conducts educational and research programs, certification program; maintains Hall of Fame. Supports clubmakers worldwide. **Awards:** Clubmaker of the Year. **Frequency:** annual. **Type:** recognition. **Recipient:** for excellence in clubmaking and in the clubmaking business ● Clubmakers Hall of Fame. **Frequency:** annual. **Type:** recognition. **Recipient:** for those who have greatly contributed to the art and business of clubmaking ● Elmore A. Just Award. **Frequency:** annual. **Type:** recognition. **Recipient:** to an individual who has gone above and beyond the call of duty with PCS ● Top Shop. **Frequency:** annual. **Type:** recognition. **Recipient:** to the most professional retail shop and a homebased shop. **Computer Services:** database ● mailing lists ● online services. **Telecommunication Services:** electronic mail, bob@proclubmakers.org. **Publications:** *E-Newsletter*, monthly. Alternate Formats: online ● *PCS Expo Directory*, annual. Contains guides to the expo. **Price:** $15.00. **Circulation:** 2,500. **Advertising:** accepted ● *PCS Journal*, bimonthly. Contains technical, business, marketing and industry articles. **Circulation:** 2,500. **Advertising:** accepted ● *PCS Membership Directory*, annual. **Circulation:** 2,500. **Advertising:** accepted. **Conventions/Meetings:** annual Membership Conference, educational seminars/workshops; exhibits of over 70 components, equipment and supply companies; social/networking events (exhibits).

3650 ■ Professional Paddlesports Association (PPA)
7432 Alban Sta. Blvd., Ste.B-232
Springfield, VA 22150
Ph: (703)451-3864
Free: (800)789-2202
Fax: (703)451-1015
E-mail: staff@paddlesportsindustry.org
URL: http://www.propaddle.com
Contact: Mathew E. Menashes, Exec. Dir.
Founded: 1978. **Members:** 500. **Membership Dues:** renter, retailer, instruction school, sales representative, $230 (annual) ● manufacturer, industry service provider (per brand), $300 (annual). **Staff:** 2. **Budget:** $200,000. **Regional Groups:** 5. **State Groups:** 12. **Description:** Renters and outfitters of canoes, kayaks, and rafts; manufacturers and distributors of equipment and products. Promotes safety in non-power watercraft; seeks to protect the nation's waterways and the rights of the public to use them. Provides members with legislative representation; on-water liability insurance; member service programs; certification courses; and professional development. **Awards:** Environmental Excellence. **Frequency:** annual. **Type:** recognition ● Frank A. Jones Memorial. **Frequency:** annual. **Type:** recognition. **Computer Services:** Mailing lists. **Telecommunication Services:** electronic mail, matt@paddlesportsindustry.org. **Formerly:** National Associations of Canoe Liveries and Outfitters. **Publications:** Also publishes standards guide and code of ethics. **Conventions/Meetings:** annual National Waterways - conference and trade show (exhibits) ● seminar.

3651 ■ Soccer Industry Council of America (SICA)
c/o Sporting Goods Manufacturers Association
1150 17th St. NW, Ste.850
Washington, DC 20036
Ph: (202)775-1762 (202)349-9412
Fax: (202)296-7462
E-mail: info@sgma.com
URL: http://www.sgma.com
Contact: Tom Cove, Pres./CEO
Founded: 1985. **Members:** 120. **Staff:** 2. **Budget:** $130,000. **Description:** Subsidiary organization of the Sporting Goods Manufacturers Association. Manufacturers, suppliers, and retailers of soccer apparel, footwear and equipment; others involved in the soccer industry. Promotes the growth of soccer in the U.S. Supports grassroots programs that offer playing opportunities to economically-disadvantaged youth, as well as the physically and mentally handicapped. Publishes statistical abstract and overview of the American soccer marketplace. **Awards:** Simon Sherman Leadership Award. **Frequency:** annual. **Type:** recognition. **Recipient:** for significant contribution to the development of soccer in the USA. **Affiliated With:** Sporting Goods Manufacturers Association International; US Soccer. **Publications:** *National Soccer Participation Survey*, annual. Demographic analysis of U.S. soccer participation. **Price:** $150.00 ● *Retail Soccer USA*. Directory. Contains listings of soccer equipment dealers. ● *Soccer in the USA*. Contains an overview of the American soccer market. **Conventions/Meetings:** annual Leadership Conference - congress, with focus on strategic planning ● seminar, provides information for dealers attending the Super Show.

3652 ■ Sporting Goods Manufacturers Association International (SGMA)
1150 17th St. NW, Ste.850
Washington, DC 20036
Ph: (202)775-1762
Fax: (202)296-7462
E-mail: info@sgma.com
URL: http://www.sgma.com
Contact: Tom Cove, Pres./CEO
Founded: 1906. **Members:** 2,000. **Membership Dues:** corporate (based on annual sales volume), $700-$7,000 (annual) ● corporate (based on annual sales volume), $9,000-$35,000 (annual) ● youth, trade, university, sports-related organization, exempt organization, $200 (annual) ● advertising, consultant, independent sales agency, non-athletic goods manufacturer, $700 (annual). **Staff:** 25. **Budget:** $3,000,000. **Description:** Manufacturers of athletic clothing, footwear, and sporting goods. Seeks to increase sports participation and create growth in the sporting goods industry. Owns and operates the largest sports products trade show in the world. **Computer Services:** Mailing lists, of members. **Committees:** Product Standards; Soccer. **Divisions:** Communications; Government Relations; International Trade; Market Research; Member Services; Trade Show. **Affiliated With:** National Golf Foundation; Tennis Industry Association. **Formerly:** Athletic Goods Manufacturers Association; (2003) Sporting Goods Manufacturers Association. **Publications:** *American Sports Data Analysis Participation Summary Report*, periodic. Provides demographic data and participation growth for 30 sport activities. ● *Financial Performance Study*, annual. Features financial ratios on profitability, productivity, expenses to sales, asset control, and risk by company size and major product line. ● *Import/Export Rates* ● *SGMA Recreation Market Report*, periodic ● *SGMA Trademark Enforcement Manual* ● *Sporting Goods Manufacturers Association—Executive Compensation Study*, annual ● *Sports Edge*, monthly ● *Sports Edge NewsWire*, semiweekly. Newsletter. Alternate Formats: online ● Videos. **Conventions/Meetings:** annual Retail Summit - meeting, for CEOs/VPs of sales and marketing to discuss industry trends and issues - always March ● The Super Show - trade show.

3653 ■ Tennis Industry Association (TIA)
117 Executive Ctr.
Hilton Head Island, SC 29928
Ph: (843)686-3036
Free: (866)686-3036
Fax: (843)686-3078
E-mail: info@tennisindustry.org
URL: http://www.tennisindustry.org
Contact: Jolyn deBoer, Exec. Dir.
Founded: 1987. **Members:** 130. **Staff:** 2. **Budget:** $2,500,000. **Description:** Represents manufacturers of tennis equipment, apparel, and footwear; court builders and architects; accessory manufacturers; suppliers and distributors. Aims to promote and encourage participation in recreational tennis and to work for the betterment of the game. Represents members' interests in Washington, DC; supports implementation of recreational tennis programs. Compiles statistics. **Libraries: Type:** reference. **Holdings:** archival material. **Committees:** Credit; Government Relations; Membership and Member Services; Trade Relations. **Programs:** Racket Donation. **Affiliated With:** Sporting Goods Manufacturers Association International. **Formed by Merger of:** Tennis Foundation of North America; Tennis Manufacturers Association. **Formerly:** American Tennis Industry Federation. **Publications:** *Tennis Participation*, periodic. Includes demographic information on tennis-playing population. **Price:** $1,000.00 ● Brochures. Covers history of tennis racquets and research projects. **Conventions/Meetings:** annual The Super Show - trade show (exhibits) - always February.

3654 ■ Trade Association of Paddlesports (TAPS)
PO Box 6353
Olympia, WA 98507
Ph: (360)352-0764
Free: (800)755-5228
Fax: (360)352-0784
E-mail: info@gopaddle.org
URL: http://www.gopaddle.org
Contact: Mr. Michael Pardy, Exec. Dir.
Founded: 1998. **Members:** 350. **Membership Dues:** manufacturer, $300 (annual) ● associate/outfitter/retailer, $100 (annual). **Staff:** 4. **Budget:** $200,000. **Description:** Manufacturers, retailers, outfitters, importers and liveries of paddlesports equipment. Seeks to support, encourage and promote the paddlesports trade in North America. Provides information and referrals on sources of insurance for paddlesports businesses; undertakes research projects; develops and maintains safety, warning and product performance standards; conducts statistical surveys; co-organized the National River Cleanup Week; conducts educational programs; lobbies on behalf of the industry. **Publications:** Journal, quarterly. **Price:** free with membership. Alternate Formats: online ● Membership Directory, annual. Contains lists of members by state with codes describing their type of business. **Advertising:** accepted. **Conventions/Meetings:** annual Paddlesports Symposia - meeting.

3655 ■ Water Sports Industry Association (WSIA)
PO Box 568512
Orlando, FL 32856-8512
Ph: (407)251-9039
Fax: (407)251-9039
E-mail: wsiaheadquarters@earthlink.net
URL: http://www.watersportsindustry.com
Contact: Larry Meddock, Exec. Dir.
Founded: 1986. **Members:** 170. **Membership Dues:** regular (gross sales up to $1 million), $300 (annual)

● regular (gross sales $1-5 million), associate (gross sales over $5 million), $600 (annual) ● regular (gross sales $5-10 million), $900 (annual) ● regular (gross sales over $10 million), $1,200 (annual) ● associate (gross sales up to $1 million), $180 (annual) ● associate (gross sales $1-5 million), $350 (annual) ● dealer, sales representative, friend, school, $100 (annual). **Staff:** 2. **Description:** Manufacturers and distributors of water sports equipment including skis, boats, wet suits, and towlines. Regular members are manufacturers and importers whose revenues are primarily derived from the water sports industry; associate members are firms with sales and manufacturing interests not primarily directed towards watersports. Monitors legislation affecting the water sports industry and keeps manufacturers and distributors informed of such action. Promotes the sports of water skiing, wakeboarding, kneeboarding, tubing and riding personal watercraft. **Awards:** Dealer of the Year. **Frequency:** annual. **Type:** recognition. **Recipient:** to an outstanding dealer/ambassador. **Computer Services:** Mailing lists, water sports equipment dealers. **Committees:** Grassroots; Industry Summit; Wakeboarding/Wake Surfing; Warnings. **Affiliated With:** Sporting Goods Manufacturers Association International. **Formerly:** (1990) Water Ski Industry Association. **Publications:** *Boating Bob Guidebook for Inboard Tournament Towboats*. Pamphlet. **Conventions/Meetings:** semiannual trade show (exhibits).

Sports

3656 ■ American Sports Association (ASA)

2 Sarah Ln.
Monroe, NJ 08831
Ph: (732)446-8794
E-mail: asa_today@aol.com
URL: http://www.americansportsassociation.org
Contact: Thomas Paulikas, Contact

Founded: 1975. **Members:** 96,781. **Membership Dues:** individual, $25 (annual) ● business, $100 (annual) ● corporate sponsor, $250 (annual). **Description:** Manufacturers of sports equipment; providers of sports services. Seeks to advance the U.S. sports industries. Provides trademark licensing and product and service endorsement to support members' activities. **Computer Services:** Mailing lists.

3657 ■ Archery Range and Retailers Organization (ARRO)

156 N Main, Ste.D
Oregon, WI 53575
Ph: (608)835-9060
Free: (800)234-7499
Fax: (608)835-9360
E-mail: lynn@archeryretailers.com
URL: http://www.archeryretailers.com
Contact: Lynn Stiklestad, Exec. Sec./Admin. Dir.

Founded: 1981. **Members:** 90. **Membership Dues:** individual, $400 (annual). **Staff:** 2. **Description:** Owners of archery retail shops and/or indoor archery lanes. Functions as a cooperative buying group. Sanctions indoor archery leagues; provides national cash awards. **Formerly:** (1980) Archery Lane Operators Association. **Conventions/Meetings:** Bowhunting Show ● Shot Show.

3658 ■ Athletic Institute (AI)

c/o Sporting Goods Manufacturers Association
1150 17th St. NW, Ste.850
Washington, DC 20036
Ph: (202)775-1762
Fax: (202)296-7462
E-mail: info@sgma.com
URL: http://www.sgma.com
Contact: Mike May, Dir. of Media Relations

Founded: 1936. **Staff:** 2. **Description:** Aims to help increase participation in sports, fitness, health, and recreation. Promotes and supports local sports boosters' clubs through American Sports Education Institute. **Telecommunication Services:** electronic mail, mmay@sgma.com. **Publications:** Videos.

3659 ■ Bowling Proprietors' Association of America (BPAA)

615 Six Flags Dr.
Arlington, TX 76011
Free: (800)343-1329
Fax: (817)633-2940
E-mail: john@bpaa.com
URL: http://www.bpaa.com
Contact: John Berglund CAE, Exec. Dir.

Founded: 1932. **Members:** 3,300. **Membership Dues:** regular (per lane for tenpin establishment), $29 (annual) ● regular (per lane for non-tenpin establishment), $14 (annual) ● allied, $495 (annual). **Staff:** 25. **Budget:** $4,500,000. **State Groups:** 35. **Local Groups:** 151. **Description:** Represents proprietors of bowling establishments. **Committees:** Audits; Awards; Constitution & Bylaws; Education; Executive Evaluation; International Bowl Expo; International Growth; Legislative; Military Relations; Nominating; Tournament; Youth. **Publications:** *Bowling Center Management*, monthly. Magazine. Covers promotions, business practices, equipment, and other information of interest to the bowling proprietor. Includes advertisers' index. **Price:** free for members; $30.00 /year for nonmembers. ISSN: 0006-8446. **Circulation:** 5,200. **Advertising:** accepted. Also Cited As: *BCM* ● *Talking Human Resources*. Newsletter. Alternate Formats: online. **Conventions/Meetings:** annual International Bowl Expo - convention (exhibits) - always June.

3660 ■ Cross Country Ski Areas Association (CCSAA)

259 Bolton Rd.
Winchester, NH 03470
Ph: (603)239-4341
Free: (877)779-2754
Fax: (603)239-6387
E-mail: ccsaa@xcski.org
URL: http://www.xcski.org
Contact: Ms. Chris Frado, Pres./Exec. Dir.

Founded: 1976. **Members:** 350. **Membership Dues:** ski area, product supplier, $475 (annual). **Staff:** 2. **Budget:** $130,000. **Description:** Owners and operators of cross country ski facilities; suppliers to the industry; individuals engaged in businesses related to cross-country skiing. Objectives are: to foster, stimulate, and promote cross country skiing in North America; to protect the legitimate interests of the cross-country ski area. Serves as a clearinghouse for cross-country ski areas of all sizes. Compiles and distributes information concerning ongoing developments in the cross country ski industry. Provides trail signs for ski areas to adequately inform or instruct the skier. Works with national groups such as the SnowSports Industries America, National Ski Patrol System, Professional Ski Instructors of America, and Canadian Ski Council. Compiles statistics on the ski industry. **Computer Services:** database, membership. **Committees:** Government Relations; Marketing. **Affiliated With:** National Ski Patrol System; SnowSports Industries America. **Formerly:** National Ski Touring Operators' Association; (1988) Cross Country Ski Areas of America. **Publications:** *The Best of Cross Country Skiing and Snowshoeing*, annual. Membership Directory. Serves as a guide for consumers of where to XC ski in the U.S. and Canada. **Price:** $3.00 ● *Cross Country Close to Home: A Ski Area Development Manual*. Provides information on how to set up and operate a cross-country ski area. **Price:** $100.00 ● *Nordic Network*, quarterly. Newsletter. Contains information for operators of cross-country ski areas. **Price:** $25.00 for nonmembers in U.S.; $12.00 for members in U.S. **Circulation:** 390. **Advertising:** accepted ● *XC Ski Area Visit Study*, annual. **Conventions/Meetings:** annual conference and trade show (exhibits) - always April.

3661 ■ Eastern Winter Sports Representatives Association (EWSRA)

5142 State St.
White Haven, PA 18661
Ph: (570)443-7180
Fax: (570)443-0388
E-mail: ewsra@uplink.net
URL: http://www.ewsra.org
Contact: Chris Bremer, Board Member

Founded: 1971. **Members:** 265. **Membership Dues:** regular, $300 (annual). **Staff:** 1. **Description:** Independent company sales representatives for firms associated with the snow-ski industry. Conducts preview showings of hard and soft goods for retailers. **Telecommunication Services:** electronic mail, cbremer@us.head.com. **Formerly:** (1998) Eastern Ski Representatives Association. **Publications:** *Buyer's Guide*, annual ● *Retail Guide*, annual ● Newsletter, periodic. **Conventions/Meetings:** Market Week - show, includes demonstrations ● annual trade show.

3662 ■ Golf Course Builders Association of America (GCBAA)

727 O St.
Lincoln, NE 68508
Ph: (402)476-4444
Fax: (402)476-4489
E-mail: paul_gcbaa@alltel.net
URL: http://www.gcbaa.org
Contact: Paul Foley, Exec. Dir.

Founded: 1972. **Members:** 700. **Staff:** 2. **Description:** Golf course builders, suppliers, consultants, manufacturers. Endeavors to provide comprehensive services and programs to contractors and specialists in golf course construction. **Formerly:** Golf Course Builders of America; (1992) Golf Course Builders Association. **Publications:** *Earth-Shaping News*, quarterly. Newsletter. Features industry and member news and activities. **Price:** free. **Circulation:** 800. **Advertising:** accepted ● *Guide to Estimating Cost for Golf Course Construction*. **Price:** $50.00. Alternate Formats: CD-ROM ● Membership Directory, annual. Contains company profiles of member companies. **Price:** $15.00. **Circulation:** 3,500. **Advertising:** accepted. **Conventions/Meetings:** meeting, with cocktail reception and golf tournament ● annual meeting, for members - February.

3663 ■ Golf Course Superintendents Association of America (GCSAA)

1421 Res. Park Dr.
Lawrence, KS 66049-3859
Ph: (785)841-2240 (785)832-4430
Free: (800)472-7878
Fax: (785)832-4488
E-mail: infobox@gcsaa.org
URL: http://www.gcsaa.org
Contact: Stephen F. Mona CAE, CEO

Founded: 1926. **Members:** 21,000. **Membership Dues:** superintendent, $300 (annual) ● assistant superintendent, associate, $150 (annual). **Staff:** 125. **Budget:** $20,000,000. **Local Groups:** 102. **Description:** Golf course superintendents, agronomists, and research and commercial interests concerned with golf course maintenance and improvement. Sponsors Scholarship and Research Fund; operates Speaker's Bureau and placement service for members; Conducts certification program; sponsors seminars. **Libraries: Type:** reference. **Holdings:** audiovisuals, books. **Subjects:** golf. **Awards: Type:** recognition. **Computer Services:** Mailing lists ● online services, events listing. **Committees:** Certification; Conference and Show; Election; Magazine; Scholarship; Standards; Technical Resource Advisory. **Councils:** Industrial Advisory. **Formerly:** National Greenkeeping Superintendents Association. **Publications:** *GCSAA Directory and Source Book*, annual. Membership Directory. **Price:** available to members only ● *Golf Course Management*, monthly. Magazine. Contains information on turfgrass management practices including course design, construction, and maintenance. Also includes product news. **Price:** included in membership dues; $48.00 /year for nonmembers. **Circulation:** 40,000. **Advertising:** accepted. Also Cited As: *Golf Course Superintendent* ● *Golf Course Superintendents Association of America—Newsline*, monthly. Newsletter. **Price:** available to members only ● *Government Relations Briefings*, monthly. Newsletter ● Brochures ● Also publishes reference material list. **Conventions/Meetings:** annual conference and trade show (exhibits) - always February.

3664 ■ Golf Range Association of America (GRAA)
c/o Mr. Steve J. di Costanzo, Founder/Pres.
PO Box 240
Georgetown, CT 06829
Ph: (203)938-2720
Fax: (203)938-2721
E-mail: steve@golfrange.org
URL: http://www.golfrange.org
Contact: Mr. Steve J. di Costanzo, Founder/Pres.
Founded: 1992. **Members:** 750. **Membership Dues:** golf range/short course, $299 (annual) ● 18-hole golf course (plus $100 for food and beverage), $620 (annual) ● supplier, $899 (annual) ● developer, $199 (annual). **Staff:** 3. **For-Profit. Description:** Owners of golf driving ranges and other practice facilities; suppliers to the golf practice industry. Promotes growth and development of the golf industry. Gathers and disseminates information on economic and social trends affecting the golf industries; conducts educational programs. **Awards:** Top 50 Golf Range Instructors. **Frequency:** annual. **Type:** recognition ● Top 100 Ranges in America. **Frequency:** annual. **Type:** recognition ● Top Short Courses in America. **Frequency:** annual. **Type:** recognition. **Computer Services:** Mailing lists ● online services, Range Finder link. **Publications:** *Golf Range Development and Operations*. Manual. **Price:** $299.00 each; $375.00 with Golf Range Magazine ● *Golf Range Magazine*, bimonthly. **Price:** included in membership dues. **Circulation:** 9,200. **Advertising:** accepted ● *Profile of Golf Practice Facility Operations 2003*. Report. **Price:** $150.00 for nonmembers; $100.00 for members; $799.00 combo package. **Conventions/Meetings:** semiannual Golf Range Industry Conference & Exhibition - workshop, in conjunction with the PGA Merchandise Show and PGA International Show (exhibits) - always in January and September.

3665 ■ International Physical Fitness Association (IPFA)
415 W Court St.
Flint, MI 48503
Ph: (810)239-2166
Free: (877)520-IPFA
Fax: (810)239-9390
E-mail: contact@ipfa.us
URL: http://www.ipfa.us
Contact: Jerome B. Kahn, Pres.
Founded: 1960. **Members:** 2,000. **Description:** Physical fitness centers. Facilitates the transfer of individual memberships from one member club to another. **Formerly:** (1975) Universal Gym Affiliates. **Publications:** *IPFA Membership Roster*, annual. Membership Directory. **Price:** $5.00.

3666 ■ Midwest Winter Sports Representatives Association (MWSRA)
PO Box 76
Hazelhurst, WI 54531
Ph: (715)358-6262
Fax: (715)358-6126
E-mail: mwsragayle@aol.com
URL: http://www.midwestwinterreps.com
Contact: Bruce Marsh, Pres.
Founded: 1966. **Members:** 120. **Membership Dues:** regular, $150 (annual). **Staff:** 1. **Regional Groups:** 1. **Description:** Manufacturers' representatives serving the U.S. Midwest ski industry. Coordinates buying shows. **Telecommunication Services:** electronic mail, brmreps@aol.com. **Affiliated With:** SnowSports Industries America. **Formerly:** Midwest Ski Representatives Association; (1998) Midwest Winter Ski Representative Association. **Publications:** *Buyers Guide*, annual. Directory. **Conventions/Meetings:** Buying Show (exhibits) - always spring in Wisconsin.

3667 ■ National Association of Bankshot Operators (NABO)
785F Rockville Pike
PMB 504
Rockville, MD 20852
Ph: (301)309-0260
Free: (800)933-0140
Fax: (301)309-0263
E-mail: info@bankshot.com
URL: http://www.nabo-assn.com
Contact: Dr. Reeve Robert Brenner, Pres./Founder
Founded: 1980. **Members:** 200. **Staff:** 6. **Regional Groups:** 1. **State Groups:** 1. **Local Groups:** 200. **National Groups:** 200. **Multinational. Description:** Operators of bankshot basketball courts. (Bankshot basketball does not require running or jumping, consisting instead of a series of shooting opportunities involving bank shots off multi-sided backboards.) Promotes the sport of bankshot basketball, which can be played simultaneously and enjoyably by people of varying ages and physical abilities. Facilitates communication and cooperation among members; encourages establishment of new bankshot basketball courts. **Awards:** National Tournament of Champions. **Frequency:** annual. **Type:** recognition. **Recipient:** for winning a Bankshot National Tournament. **Computer Services:** Mailing lists. **Also Known As:** Bankshot Sports. **Publications:** *Court Report*. Brochure. **Price:** free. **Circulation:** 2,000. **Advertising:** accepted. Alternate Formats: online. **Conventions/Meetings:** annual competition, celebrates persons of all abilities enjoying sports.

3668 ■ National Golf Course Owners Association (NGCOA)
291 Seven Farms Dr.
Charleston, SC 29492
Ph: (843)881-9956
Free: (800)933-4262
Fax: (843)881-9958
E-mail: info@ngcoa.org
URL: http://www.ngcoa.org
Contact: Henry DeLozier, Pres.
Founded: 1979. **Members:** 2,100. **Membership Dues:** 9 holes/Par 3, $190 (annual) ● 18 holes, $355 (annual) ● driving range, $190 (annual) ● 18 holes plus, $380 (annual) ● 27 holes to 5 courses, $550 (annual) ● allied, $350 (annual). **Staff:** 13. **Description:** Owners and operators of privately owned golf courses. Assist members to develop more productive, efficient, and profitable golf operations. Provides information on taxation, destination golf, community relations, environmental regulations, and marketing. Offers group purchasing opportunities. Conducts educational seminars. Compiles statistics. **Awards:** Award of Merit. **Frequency:** annual. **Type:** recognition ● Course of the Year. **Frequency:** annual. **Type:** recognition ● Don Rossi Award. **Frequency:** annual. **Type:** recognition. **Boards:** Advisory; Directors. **Publications:** *Golf Business*, monthly. Magazine. Contains issues related to golf industry legislative, management, marketing, and membership news. **Circulation:** 17,000. **Advertising:** accepted. Alternate Formats: online ● *Various-Marketing, Hiring, Operations*. Manuals ● Membership Directory. **Conventions/Meetings:** annual Golf Industry Show - conference and trade show, product displays and educational sessions for golf course owners and managers (exhibits) ● annual Solutions Summit - conference.

3669 ■ National Golf Foundation (NGF)
1150 S U.S. Hwy. 1, Ste.401
Jupiter, FL 33477
Ph: (561)744-6006
Free: (888)275-4643
Fax: (561)744-6107
E-mail: general@ngf.org
URL: http://www.ngf.org
Contact: Dr. Joseph F. Beditz, Pres./CEO
Founded: 1936. **Members:** 4,500. **Staff:** 25. **Budget:** $4,000,000. **Description:** Golf-oriented businesses including: equipment and apparel companies; golf facilities; golf publications; golf course architects, developers and builders; companies offering specialized services to the golf industry; golf associations; teachers, coaches and instructors and other interested individuals. Serves as a market research and strategic planning organization for the golf industry and promotes public golf course development in the U.S. Provides information and consulting services for golf course planning, construction, and operation. Conducts golf course development and operations seminars including the National Institute of Golf Management. **Awards:** Graffis Award. **Frequency:** annual. **Type:** recognition. **Recipient:** for outstanding contributions to the game of golf. **Computer Services:** database, golf facilities, golf retailing, golf companies in the U.S. ● mailing lists, golf facilities, golf retailers, golf companies in the U.S. **Departments:** Membership Services; NGF Consulting; Research. **Publications:** *Golf Facilities in the U.S.*, annual. Book ● *Golf Industry Report*, bimonthly. Newsletter ● *Golf Participation in the U.S.*, annual ● Books ● Reports ● Also issues executive summaries and instructional materials.

3670 ■ National Health Club Association (NHCA)
640 Plaza Dr., Ste.300
Highlands Ranch, CO 80129
Free: (800)765-6422
Fax: (303)980-8006
URL: http://www.nhcainsurance.com
Contact: Susie Schmitz, Dir.
Founded: 1988. **Members:** 3,000. **Staff:** 3. **For-Profit. Description:** Fitness centers and health clubs. Provides insurance and financial services to the fitness center/health club industry nationwide. Awards strength and aerobic certification. **Absorbed:** (1990) Fitness Trade Association. **Formerly:** (1987) National Fitness Association. **Conventions/Meetings:** annual meeting (exhibits) - always fall.

3671 ■ SnowSports Industries America (SIA)
8377-B Greensboro Dr.
McLean, VA 22102-3587
Ph: (703)556-9020
Fax: (703)821-8276
E-mail: siamail@snowsports.org
URL: http://www.snowsports.org
Contact: David Ingemie, Pres.
Founded: 1954. **Members:** 1,178. **Membership Dues:** standard, exhibiting supporting, $1,200 (annual) ● non-exhibiting supporting, $500 (annual) ● professional supporting, $250 (annual). **Staff:** 25. **Budget:** $4,000,000. **Description:** Manufacturers, distributors, and suppliers of ski, snowboard, on-snow, and outdoor action sports apparel, equipment, footwear, and accessories. Monitors activities at the federal level to protect the interest of on-snow product manufacturers and distributors. Provides information on the on-snow industry to the media. Promotes snow sports through market development programs. Conducts research programs. Operates 14 committees. **Libraries: Type:** reference. **Holdings:** archival material, artwork, books, business records, clippings, periodicals. **Subjects:** skiing, outdoor action sports. **Computer Services:** database ● mailing lists. **Formerly:** (1998) Ski Industries Association. **Publications:** *Retailer/Rep Advisor*, biennial. Report ● *SIA Member Update*, semimonthly. Report. Contains industry and association news coverage. **Price:** included in membership dues. **Circulation:** 1,500 ● *SIA Trade Show Directory*, annual ● Also publishes research reports. **Conventions/Meetings:** annual Ski, Snowboard, and Outdoor Sports Show - trade show (exhibits) ● annual Snowsports Show - trade show (exhibits).

3672 ■ Sport Marketing Association (SMA)
The Univ. of Memphis
Bur. of Sport and Leisure Commerce
Dept. of Human and Sport Sciences
101 Wilder Tower
Memphis, TN 38152
E-mail: webmaster@sportmarketingassociation.com
URL: http://www.sportmarketingassociation.com
Contact: Richard Irwin, Pres.
Founded: 2002. **Membership Dues:** professional (in U.S.), $100 (annual) ● professional (overseas), $125 (annual) ● student, $50 (annual). **Description:** Develops a mutually beneficial relationship between professional practitioners and academicians engaged in the business of sport marketing. Provides a forum for professional interaction among practicing sport marketers, sport marketing academicians and students of the sport industry. Seeks to impact future developments within the academic discipline and the

field of sport marketing. **Computer Services:** Online services, discussion board.

3673 ■ United States Association of Independent Gymnastic Clubs (USAIGC)
c/o Paul Spadaro, VP
450 N End Ave., Ste.20F
New York, NY 10282
Ph: (212)227-9792
Free: (800)480-0201
Fax: (212)227-9793
E-mail: usaigcpsny2@aol.com
URL: http://www.usaigc.com
Contact: Paul Spadaro, VP
Founded: 1972. **Members:** 1,000. **Membership Dues:** club (location), $135 (annual) ● club (faxed/mailed), $130 (annual) ● club (online), $125 (annual) ● athlete (mailed/faxed), $25 (annual) ● athlete (online), $20 (annual). **Staff:** 3. **State Groups:** 30. **Description:** Gymnastic clubs and independent gymnastic club businesses (725) offering professional class instruction and coaching; manufacturers (25) of gymnastic equipment, apparel, and supplies. Aims to provide services, programs, and business advice to help gymnastic businesses to grow and prosper; locate organizations and individuals that will provide needed services for members' clientele; further coaching knowledge; advance the U.S. in gymnastic competitions throughout the world. Offers certification for coaches and developmental-training programs for gymnasts to prepare for international competitions. Provides placement service; conducts research programs. Maintains Medical Advisory Board and hall of fame. **Libraries: Type:** open to the public. **Holdings:** audiovisuals, video recordings. **Subjects:** gymnastics. **Awards:** Individual and Club Awards. **Type:** recognition. **Publications:** *ClubNews*, quarterly. Newsletter ● *Trends*, monthly. Newsletter. **Conventions/Meetings:** annual National Club Owners Meeting (exhibits).

3674 ■ United States Racquet Stringers Association (USRSA)
330 Main St.
Vista, CA 92084
Ph: (760)536-1177
Fax: (760)536-1171
E-mail: usrsa@racquettech.com
URL: http://racquettech.com
Contact: David Bone, Exec. Dir.
Founded: 1975. **Members:** 7,000. **Membership Dues:** regular, in U.S., $99 (annual) ● regular, in Canada, $119 (annual) ● regular (other country), $135 (annual) ● regular in Mexico, $124 (annual). **Staff:** 9. **For-Profit. Description:** Racquet stringers; individuals interested in learning about the stringing of racquets and new patterns on the market. Conducts experiments with new racquets and patterns. Provides free stringing business consulting service. Offers Certification Program. Offers instruction-workshops and video instruction. **Additional Websites:** http://www.usrsa.com. **Telecommunication Services:** electronic mail, dave@racquettech.com. **Publications:** *Racquet Sports Industry*. Magazine. **Price:** $25.00/year in U.S.; $35.00/year in Canada; $40.00/year in Mexico; $51.00/year (other country). **Advertising:** accepted. Alternate Formats: online ● *Racquet Tech Magazine*, monthly. Newsletter. Provides product updates, string techniques, and industry trends; includes updates of USRSA's racquet stringing guide. **Price:** included in membership dues. **Circulation:** 7,500. **Advertising:** accepted. Alternate Formats: online ● *The Stringer's Digest*, annual. Manual. Provides stringing instructions for all racquets. **Price:** available to members only. **Circulation:** 7,500. **Advertising:** accepted ● *Total Racquet Service*. Video. **Price:** $24.95 for members; $34.95 for nonmembers. **Conventions/Meetings:** workshop.

3675 ■ Western Winter Sports Representatives Association (WWSRA)
726 Tenacity Dr., Unit B
Longmont, CO 80504
Ph: (303)532-4002
Fax: (303)512-6162
E-mail: info@wwsra.com
URL: http://www.wwsra.com
Contact: Cami Garrison, Contact
Founded: 1949. **Members:** 908. **Membership Dues:** regular, $75 (annual). **Staff:** 3. **Description:** Representatives in the ski industry. Sponsors buyers' shows in the Eastern U.S. Membership and activities are focused in the western part of the U.S. **Publications:** *Ski Show Directory-Sporting Goods Directory*, semiannual ● Newsletter, quarterly.

Sports Facilities

3676 ■ Association of Luxury Suite Directors (ALSD)
135 Merchant St., Ste.145
Cincinnati, OH 45246
Ph: (513)674-0555
Fax: (513)674-0577
E-mail: feedback@alsd.com
URL: http://www.alsd.com
Contact: Matt Pietsch, Pres./Founder
Founded: 1990. **Membership Dues:** associate, $500 (annual) ● charter, $345 (annual) ● affiliate, $115 (annual) ● introductory, $250 (annual). **Description:** Establishes a clearinghouse of information to advance effective decision-making, policies and professional excellence in the premium seating industry. Supports a network of individuals to share information, ideas and values that will enhance the stability of premium seating industry. **Computer Services:** database, membership directories ● mailing lists ● online services, message board. **Publications:** *Premium Seat Source Book*, annual. Manual. Includes information from the leagues, racing venues and colleges. **Price:** $100.00 for members; $150.00 for nonmembers. Alternate Formats: online ● *SEAT*, quarterly. Magazine. Contains articles about the current trends and changes in the industry. **Advertising:** accepted.

Stationery

3677 ■ Business Forms Management Association (BFMA)
319 SW Washington, No. 710
Portland, OR 97204-2618
Ph: (503)227-3393
Fax: (503)274-7667
E-mail: bfma@bfma.org
URL: http://www.bfma.org
Contact: Mr. Andy Palatka, Exec. Dir.
Founded: 1958. **Members:** 600. **Membership Dues:** individual/chapter, $175 (annual). **Staff:** 2. **Budget:** $360,000. **Local Groups:** 26. **Multinational. Description:** Persons engaged in forms management work, forms procedures analysis, forms design, or in education in this field; customer service firms selling, manufacturing, or servicing forms and supplies. Provides leadership and education to businesses in areas where the forms profession has demonstrated its special competence; promotes a broader function as a component of effective management; encourages, establishes, and maintains high standards of professional education, competence, and performance; provides a means for the sharing of information through study, programs, and research. **Libraries: Type:** reference. **Subjects:** forms and information management. **Awards:** Award of Excellence. **Frequency:** annual. **Type:** recognition ● Jo Warner Award. **Frequency:** annual. **Type:** recognition ● Member of the Year. **Frequency:** annual. **Type:** recognition. **Telecommunication Services:** electronic mail, andy@bfma.org. **Boards:** Professional Certification. **Publications:** *Annual Report and Directory*, annual. Cross-referenced member listing. **Price:** available to members only. Alternate Formats: online ● *Infocus*, bimonthly. Newsletter. Covers products, services, and trends in information resources management. Includes career information, and calendar of classes and events. **Price:** included in membership dues; $50.00 /year for nonmembers. ISSN: 1040-2179. **Advertising:** accepted. **Conventions/Meetings:** annual International Symposium on Forms and Business Processes - meeting (exhibits) - always May ● seminar.

3678 ■ Check Payment Systems Association (CPSA)
2025 M St. NW, Ste.800
Washington, DC 20036
Ph: (202)367-1144
Fax: (202)367-2144
E-mail: info@cpsa-checks.org
URL: http://www.cpsa-checks.org
Contact: Steven Antolick, Exec. Dir.
Founded: 1952. **Members:** 52. **Membership Dues:** affiliate, $650 (annual) ● associate, $3,000 (annual) ● regular (based on company's annual sales), $650-$53,900 (annual). **Staff:** 3. **Budget:** $250,000. **Description:** Firms that print bank checks and related items; firms that participate in the check payment system. Conducts management and technical workshops and surveys. **Formerly:** (1985) Bank Stationers Association; (1999) Financial Stationers Association. **Publications:** *CheckUp*, quarterly. Newsletter. **Price:** included in membership dues ● *FSA Facts*, 8/year. **Conventions/Meetings:** quarterly board meeting ● annual meeting.

3679 ■ Document Management Industries Association (DMIA)
433 E Monroe Ave.
Alexandria, VA 22301-1645
Ph: (703)836-6232
Fax: (703)836-2241
E-mail: dmia@dmia.org
URL: http://www.dmia.org
Contact: Mr. Peter Colaianni CAE, Exec. VP
Founded: 1946. **Members:** 2,000. **Membership Dues:** international, $700 (annual) ● company (minimum; based on sales volume), $575 (annual) ● company (maximum; based on sales volume), $18,545 (annual). **Staff:** 45. **Budget:** $6,900,000. **Multinational. Description:** Independent distributors, manufacturers, and suppliers to the forms, business printing and document management industries. Sponsors educational and channel marketing programs. Compiles statistics. **Libraries: Type:** not open to the public. **Holdings:** articles, books, periodicals. **Subjects:** business printing, document management, home study courses. **Awards:** Manufacturer Award. **Frequency:** annual. **Type:** recognition. **Recipient:** for members only ● Member of the Year. **Frequency:** annual. **Type:** recognition. **Recipient:** for members only ● Presidents' Award. **Frequency:** annual. **Type:** recognition. **Recipient:** for members only ● Print Excellence and Knowledge (PEAK) Awards. **Frequency:** annual. **Type:** recognition. **Recipient:** for companies that meet and exceed customers' printing needs. **Computer Services:** Mailing lists, of members. **Telecommunication Services:** electronic mail, pcolaianni@dmia.org. **Affiliated With:** Society for Service Professionals in Printing. **Absorbed:** IADT, The International Association for Document Technologies. **Formerly:** (1995) National Business Forms Association. **Publications:** *Business Printing Technologies Report*, monthly. Features technology and product design. **Price:** included in membership dues; $1.00 for nonmembers. **Circulation:** 11,000. Alternate Formats: online ● *E-Weekly*. Newsletter. Contains weekly news for DMIA members. **Price:** $1.00 for nonmembers; free for members. **Circulation:** 12,000. **Advertising:** accepted. Alternate Formats: online ● *Independent Management Report*, biweekly. Newsletter. Provides management news and information for company executives. **Price:** included in membership dues; $1.00 for nonmembers. **Circulation:** 2,500. **Advertising:** accepted. Alternate Formats: online ● *Print Solutions Magazine*, monthly. Focuses on management and marketing education. **Price:** $19.00 /year for members; $29.00 /year for nonmembers. ISSN: 0532-1700. **Circulation:** 13,000. **Advertising:** accepted. Alternate Formats: online ● *Who's Who in the Business Printing and Document Management Industry*, annual. Membership Directory. **Price:** $1.00 for nonmembers; free for members. **Circulation:** 2,300. **Advertising:** accepted. Alternate Formats: online. **Conventions/Meetings:** annual Print Solutions Conference and Expo - convention,

with 450 booths and conference seminars ● annual trade show and meeting.

3680 ■ Engraved Stationery Manufacturers Association (ESMA)
305 Plus Park Blvd.
Nashville, TN 37217-1005
Ph: (615)366-1094
Fax: (615)366-4192
URL: http://www.pias.org
Contact: Harris Griggs, Mgr.
Founded: 1911. **Members:** 520. **Description:** Manufacturers of engraved stationery products such as letterheads, envelopes, business cards, greeting cards, invitations, announcements, and diplomas. Associate members are suppliers of paper, ink, machinery, and chemicals. Sponsors Engraved Stationery Manufacturers Research Institute. **Formerly:** (1938) National Association of Steel and Copper Plate Engravers. **Publications:** *Employee Handbook Guidelines* ● *Positive Employee Relations Manual.* Provides legal information to employees. ● *Printsouth*, monthly. Magazine. Provides timely information to area printers. ● Newsletter, bimonthly ● Directory, annual. **Conventions/Meetings:** annual competition ● annual conference - usually June or early July.

3681 ■ Envelope Manufacturers Association (EMA)
500 Montgomery St., Ste.550
Alexandria, VA 22314
Ph: (703)739-2200
Fax: (703)739-2209
E-mail: mhbenjamin@envelope.org
URL: http://www.envelope.org
Contact: Maynard H. Benjamin CAE, Pres./CEO
Founded: 1933. **Members:** 175. **Staff:** 7. **Budget:** $1,750,000. **Description:** Represents envelope manufacturers and their suppliers. **Computer Services:** database, envelope manufacturers ● information services, manufacturing management ● information services, postal learning. **Telecommunication Services:** electronic mail, aseaton@envelope.org. **Formed by Merger of:** American Envelope Manufacturers Association; Bureau of Envelope Manufacturers of America. **Formerly:** (1962) Envelope Manufacturers Association of America. **Publications:** *Envelope Report*, monthly. Newsletter. **Price:** available to members only ● *Family Album*, annual. Directory. **Price:** available to members only. **Conventions/Meetings:** semiannual meeting.

3682 ■ Greeting Card Association (GCA)
1156 15th St. NW, Ste.900
Washington, DC 20005
Ph: (202)393-1778
Fax: (202)331-2714
E-mail: info@greetingcard.org
URL: http://www.greetingcard.org
Contact: Clancy Delbarre, Exec. Dir.
Founded: 1941. **Members:** 190. **Membership Dues:** regular or affiliate (less than $500,000 previous year sales), $250 (annual) ● regular or affiliate ($500,000-$999,999 previous year sales), $825 (annual) ● regular or affiliate ($1M-$1,999,999 previous year sales), $1,750 (annual) ● regular or affiliate ($2M-$4,999,999 previous year sales), $3,500 (annual) ● regular or affiliate ($5M-$14,999,999 previous year sales), $8,000 (annual) ● regular or affiliate ($15M-$49,999,999 previous year sales), $11,000 (annual) ● regular or affiliate ($50M-$99,999,999 previous year sales), $17,500 (annual) ● regular or affiliate ($100M-$250M previous year sales), $23,000 (annual) ● regular or affiliate (more than $250M previous year sales), $75,000 (annual) ● regular subsidiary, $5,000 (annual) ● associate, $1,000-$3,125 (annual) ● international, $350 (annual). **Staff:** 6. **Budget:** $500,000. **Description:** Publishers of greeting cards and suppliers of materials. **Awards:** International Greeting Card Awards. **Frequency:** annual. **Type:** recognition. **Recipient:** for winners in 80 categories ● Lifetime Achievement Award. **Frequency:** annual. **Type:** recognition. **Recipient:** for those who have made lifetime contributions to the greeting card industry ● LOUIE Awards. **Frequency:** annual. **Type:** recognition. **Recipient:** for designers, illustrators and writers of the greeting card industry. **Committees:** Awards; Convention; Government Relations; Public Relations. **Formerly:** (1983) National Association of Greeting Card Publishers. **Publications:** *Basics of Copyright and Trademark Law for the Greeting Card Publisher.* Book. **Price:** $25.00 for members; $45.00 for nonmembers. ISSN: 0938-3692 ● *Basics of Starting a Small Business.* **Price:** $20.00 for members; $35.00 for nonmembers ● *Changing World of International Trade.* Audiotape. **Price:** $30.00 for members; $45.00 for nonmembers ● *Color Trends into the 1990's and the Psychological Appeal of Color.* Audiotape. **Price:** $20.00 for members; $30.00 for nonmembers ● *Competitive Excellence—Only the Best Survive.* Audiotape. **Price:** $25.00 for members; $35.00 for nonmembers ● *Directory of Greeting Card Sales Representatives*, biennial. Lists U.S. companies that represent greeting cards. **Price:** $50.00 for members; $95.00 for nonmembers. ISSN: 0938-3693 ● *Electronic Data Interchange—Impacting the Way Greeting Card Publishers Do Business.* Audiotape. **Price:** $20.00 for members; $35.00 for nonmembers ● *Emerging Changes in the Relationship Between Employers and Employees in the 1990's.* Audiotape. **Price:** $20.00 for members; $30.00 for nonmembers ● *Facts, Figures, Findings—Staying in Touch with Industry Change.* Audiotape. **Price:** $20.00 for members; $35.00 for nonmembers ● *Greeting Card Industry Directory*, biennial. Lists over 12000 publishing companies and suppliers to the industry. **Price:** $75.00 for members; $95.00 for nonmembers. ISSN: 0938-3693. Alternate Formats: CD-ROM ● *Guide to Handling Your Own Publicity*, biennial. Directory. Lists over 1800 publishing companies and suppliers to the industry including US and international companies. **Price:** $10.00 for members; $20.00 for nonmembers. ISSN: 0938-3693. Alternate Formats: CD-ROM ● *How to Open and Operate a Card and Gift Shop.* **Price:** $20.00 for members; $50.00 for nonmembers ● *Is it Legal?—A Presentation on Leading Legal Issues Affecting Business and Personnel Policy Today.* Audiotape. **Price:** $20.00 for members; $35.00 for nonmembers ● *Making Your Rep Organization a Full Partner.* Audiotape. **Price:** $10.00 for members; $30.00 for nonmembers ● *Selecting the Transaction Format that Suits You.* Audiotape. **Price:** $20.00 for members; $35.00 for nonmembers. **Conventions/Meetings:** annual convention (exhibits).

3683 ■ International Marking and Identification Association (IMIA)
655 Rockland Rd., Ste.5
Lake Bluff, IL 60044
Ph: (847)283-9810
Fax: (847)283-9808
E-mail: office@marking-id.org
URL: http://www.marking-id.org
Contact: Steve Hewitt, Exec. Dir.
Founded: 1910. **Members:** 300. **Membership Dues:** business/regular, $375 (annual) ● international, $99 (annual). **Staff:** 1. **Budget:** $200,000. **Regional Groups:** 10. **Languages:** English, German. **Multinational. Description:** Represents manufacturers and suppliers of marking identification products including rubber and metal stamps, nameplates, seals, and other identification products. **Libraries: Type:** not open to the public. **Holdings:** archival material, articles, business records, periodicals, reports, software. **Computer Services:** Information services, industry news and technical information about product manufacturing, sources and seal formats. **Formerly:** International Stamp Manufacturers Association; (1988) Marking Device Association; (2002) Marking Device Association International. **Publications:** *IMIA E-Newsletter*, biweekly. Newsletters. Contains current news particularly of notary seals and engineers, architects, land surveyors, landscape architects and geologists seals. **Circulation:** 350. **Advertising:** accepted ● *MDAI Membership Directory*, annual. **Price:** free for members. **Circulation:** 400. Alternate Formats: online ● *Mr. Marking's Compendium*, bimonthly. Manual. Serves as a source for hard-to-find marking and identification products. **Price:** $375.00 ● *Seal Manual*, annual. **Advertising:** accepted ● *Update*, semimonthly. Newsletter. Includes articles on technical and management subjects. **Price:** included in membership dues. **Circulation:** 600. **Advertising:** accepted. **Conventions/Meetings:** annual trade show, for owners of companies that manufacture rubber stamps and embossing seals, and other hand held marking devices and identification products (exhibits).

3684 ■ Label Printing Industries of America (LPIA)
200 Deer Run Rd.
Sewickley, PA 15143-2600
Ph: (412)741-6860 (412)259-1802
Free: (800)910-4283
Fax: (412)259-1800
E-mail: lreynolds@piagatf.org
URL: http://www.gain.net
Contact: Laurie M. Reynolds, Exec. Dir.
Founded: 1976. **Members:** 68. **Membership Dues:** associate, $1,500 (annual) ● active (based on sales volume), $750-$5,500 (annual). **Staff:** 1. **Description:** Companies that print labels for items including food, cosmetics, drugs, beverages, and household products. Disseminates information and services of special interest and benefit to label printers; is a special industry group of the Printing Industries of America (see separate entry). **Affiliated With:** Printing Industries of America. **Publications:** *Label Industry Facts and Guidelines 2nd Edition.* Book ● *Labelgram*, bimonthly. Newsletter ● *PIA Ratios-Label Edition*, annual. **Conventions/Meetings:** annual conference, fall management conference - always October/September ● seminar, spring technical seminars - always April.

3685 ■ National Office Products Alliance (NOPA)
301 N Fairfax St.
Alexandria, VA 22314
Ph: (703)549-9040
Free: (800)542-6672
Fax: (703)683-7552
E-mail: info@nopanet.org
URL: http://www.nopanet.org
Contact: Chris Bates, Pres.
Founded: 1904. **Members:** 1,200. **Membership Dues:** dealer, $495 (annual) ● service provider, $850 (annual) ● wholesaler, manufacturer (based on annual sales volume), $850-$4,000 (annual) ● manufacturer representative (based on annual sales volume), $350-$550 (annual). **Staff:** 5. **Description:** Dealers who sell office supplies to commercial accounts and through retail stores. Seeks to provide members with the information, tools, and knowledge needed to be profitable in an evolving business environment. **Computer Services:** Electronic publishing, for members ● information services, for members. **Formerly:** (1994) Contract Stationers Forum; (1999) Office Products of the Business Products Industry Association Dealers Alliance. **Publications:** *Office Products Industry Report*, monthly. Newsletter. **Circulation:** 1,000. **Advertising:** accepted. Alternate Formats: online.

3686 ■ Office Products Wholesalers Association (OPWA)
5024 Campbell Blvd., Ste.R
Baltimore, MD 21236-5943
Ph: (410)931-8100
Fax: (410)931-8111
E-mail: calc@clemonsmgmt.com
URL: http://www.opwa.org
Contact: Calvin K. Clemons CAE, Exec. VP
Founded: 1995. **Members:** 170. **Membership Dues:** wholesaler, $650-$2,500 (annual) ● manufacturer, $750-$4,000 (annual). **Multinational. Description:** Firms that specialize in the wholesale distribution of office products. Promotes the office products industry. Operates charitable program. **Awards:** OPWA Manufacturer of the Year Award. **Frequency:** annual. **Type:** recognition. **Recipient:** to a manufacturer ● **Frequency:** annual. **Type:** scholarship. **Recipient:** to a talented and worthy young people within the office products industry. **Committees:** Awards; Conference; Manufacturers; Standards. **Formerly:** (1991) National Association of Writing Instrument Distributors; (1994) National Association of Wholesale Independent

Distributors. **Publications:** *Office Products Executive Summit Magazine*, annual. **Advertising:** accepted. Alternate Formats: online ● *OPWA Membership Directory and Facilities Guide*, annual. **Price:** free for members; $100.00 for nonmembers. Alternate Formats: online ● *OPWA Record*, quarterly. Newsletter. **Conventions/Meetings:** annual conference.

3687 ■ Tag and Label Manufacturers Institute (TLMI)
40 Shuman Blvd., Ste.295
Naperville, IL 60563-8251
Ph: (630)357-9222
Free: (800)533-8564
Fax: (630)357-0192
E-mail: fas@tlmi.com
URL: http://www.tlmi.com
Contact: Frank A. Sablone, Pres.
Founded: 1933. **Members:** 325. **Membership Dues:** international, $300 (annual) ● supplier, $2,500 (annual) ● converter, $800-$4,000 (annual). **Staff:** 5. **Budget:** $870,000. **Multinational. Description:** North American manufacturers of pressure-sensitive labels for merchandising and industrial use and tags including shipping, marking, merchandising, and pricing tags; manufacturers of allied products; suppliers of equipment, base stock, adhesives, and ink. Sponsors liner recycling program and competitions; compiles statistics. **Libraries: Type:** reference. **Awards:** Converter of the Year. **Frequency:** annual. **Type:** recognition. **Recipient:** for a member who has made significant contributions to the industry or to the association ● Supplier of the Year Award. **Frequency:** annual. **Type:** recognition. **Recipient:** for an individual who has given voluntary service and dedication to TLMI and the industry ● TLMI Eugene Singer Award. **Frequency:** annual. **Type:** recognition. **Recipient:** for excellence in business management ● TLMI Scholarship. **Frequency:** annual. **Type:** scholarship. **Recipient:** to a junior or senior in the field of printing or graphic arts. **Telecommunication Services:** electronic mail, office@tlmi.com. **Boards:** Directors. **Committees:** Communications; Environmental; Industry Trends; Scholarship/Internship; Statistical; Technical. **Formerly:** Tag Manufacturers Institute. **Publications:** *Illuminator*, bimonthly. Newsletter. Contains industry news. ● *TLMI Glossary of Terms*. Book. **Price:** $11.95 ● *TLMI Manual of Recommended Standards Specifications*. **Price:** $49.00 for members; $149.00 for nonmembers ● *TLMI North American Label Study*, annual. Report. **Price:** $495.00 for members; $4,000.00 for nonmembers; $750.00 for FINAT members. Alternate Formats: CD-ROM ● *TLMI Products and Services Guide*, annual. **Price:** free for members ● Reports. Alternate Formats: online. **Conventions/Meetings:** biennial conference - always August or September ● annual meeting and board meeting - always fall.

3688 ■ Writing Instrument Manufacturers Association (WIMA)
15000 Commerce Pkwy., Ste.C
Mount Laurel, NJ 08054-2212
Ph: (856)638-0426
Fax: (856)439-0525
E-mail: wima@ahint.com
URL: http://www.wima.org
Contact: Jeff Green, Pres.
Founded: 1943. **Members:** 70. **Staff:** 4. **Multinational. Description:** Manufacturers of handwriting and marking instruments and parts; industry suppliers. Conducts activities in government and public relations; offers product certification program. Compiles import and export statistics, annual total industry sales, and quarterly industry product sales with detailed breakdowns. Collects information on trademarks. **Committees:** Employee Relations; International Trade; Marketing Research and Statistical; Pencil Section; Product Safety and Technical Standards. **Programs:** Ink Certification; Pencil Certification; Program and Exhibits. **Absorbed:** (1998) Pencil Makers Association. **Formerly:** (1965) Fountain Pen and Mechanical Pencil Manufacturers Association. **Publications:** *Directory of Manufacturers and Products*. Membership Directory. Alternate Formats: online ● *Write Notes*, semiannual. Newsletter. Lists manufacturers, suppliers, and products of the writing instrument industry. **Price:** $50.00. **Conventions/Meetings:** annual meeting - always fall.

Stone

3689 ■ Allied Stone Industries (ASI)
c/o Gary Weller, Pres.
40 Rolling Rock Rd.
Boyertown, PA 19512
Ph: (610)987-6226
Fax: (610)987-3284
E-mail: gweller@rollrock.com
URL: http://www.alliedstone.com
Contact: Gary Weller, Pres.
Founded: 1958. **Members:** 75. **Membership Dues:** regular, $500 (annual). **Description:** Quarriers and fabricators of natural stone. Promotes the interests of members. **Computer Services:** database, membership directory. **Conventions/Meetings:** semiannual convention.

3690 ■ American Rock Mechanics Association (ARMA)
c/o Peter H. Smeallie, Exec. Dir.
600 Woodland Terr.
Alexandria, VA 22302
Ph: (703)683-1808
Fax: (703)683-1815
E-mail: smeallie@armarocks.org
URL: http://www.armarocks.org
Contact: Peter H. Smeallie, Exec. Dir.
Founded: 1994. **Members:** 450. **Membership Dues:** student, $15 (annual) ● individual, $65 (annual) ● individual (life), $1,000 ● individual (charter), $100 (annual) ● individual (non-US), $85 (annual) ● nonprofit corporation, $500 (annual) ● igneous corporation, $1,000 (annual) ● metamorphic corporation, $2,500 (annual) ● sedimentary corporation, $5,000 (annual). **Staff:** 1. **Budget:** $200,000. **Multinational. Description:** Corporations and individuals engaged in rock mechanics and rock engineering. Seeks to keep members abreast of developments in the fields of rock mechanics and rock engineering. Serves as liaison between members and government agencies, industry and scientific organizations, and other institutions with an interest in rock mechanics. Conducts research and educational programs; facilitates communication and cooperation among members. **Libraries: Type:** open to the public. **Holdings:** 10,000; papers, photographs, reports. **Subjects:** rock mechanics. **Publications:** *ARMA Update*, periodic. Newsletter. **Price:** included in membership dues. **Conventions/Meetings:** annual U.S. Rock Mechanics Symposium (exhibits).

3691 ■ Barre Granite Association (BGA)
PO Box 481
Barre, VT 05641
Ph: (802)476-4131
Fax: (802)476-4765
E-mail: bga@barregranite.org
URL: http://www.barregranite.org
Contact: Mr. John P. Castaldo, Exec. Dir.
Founded: 1889. **Members:** 81. **Staff:** 3. **For-Profit. Description:** Quarriers and manufacturers of building granite, cemetery monuments, markers, and mausoleums. Negotiates with labor unions on behalf of members; conducts trade and national advertising programs. Promotes purchase of memorials and other granite products. **Libraries: Type:** open to the public. **Holdings:** 200. **Subjects:** memorials, monuments, death, mourning. **Publications:** *Barre Life*, quarterly. Magazine. Contains news on member firms and their products. **Price:** free to customers and allied organizations. **Circulation:** 8,500 ● *BGA Advisor*, quarterly. Newsletter ● Also publishes sales aids. **Conventions/Meetings:** periodic seminar.

3692 ■ Building Stone Institute (BSI)
551 Tollgate Rd., Ste.C
Elgin, IL 60123
Ph: (847)695-0170
Free: (866)786-6313
Fax: (847)695-0174
E-mail: jeff@buildingstoneinstitute.org
URL: http://www.buildingstoneinstitute.org
Contact: Jeff Buczkiewicz, Exec. VP
Founded: 1919. **Members:** 400. **Membership Dues:** regular, $1,000 (annual) ● professional, $200 (annual). **Staff:** 3. **Budget:** $750,000. **Description:** Represents Natural Stone quarriers, fabricators, installers, dealers, importers, expo and restorers. Serves as a clearinghouse of information for architects, contractors, decorstors, and masons. Promotes the use of Natural Stone. **Awards:** Tucker Architecture Award. **Frequency:** biennial. **Type:** recognition. **Recipient:** for architects with outstanding design work. **Telecommunication Services:** electronic mail, maggie@buildingstoneinstitute.org. **Committees:** Advertising; Marble and Stone Care; Stone Dealers; Technical Advancement; Wholesalers and Distributors. **Formerly:** (1945) International Cut Stone Quarrymen's Association. **Publications:** *BSI News Update*, monthly. **Price:** $55.00. **Advertising:** accepted ● *Building Stone Magazine*, quarterly. **Price:** $65.00/year. **Circulation:** 14,000. **Advertising:** accepted ● *Stone Information Manual* ● *Who's Who in the Stone Business*, annual. Directory. **Circulation:** 10,000 ● Brochures. **Conventions/Meetings:** annual convention - every 1st week of March ● annual Study Tour - conference and tour, for member operations - every September.

3693 ■ Elberton Granite Association (EGA)
PO Box 640
Elberton, GA 30635
Ph: (706)283-2551
Fax: (706)283-6380
E-mail: granite@egaonline.com
URL: http://www.egaonline.com
Founded: 1951. **Members:** 150. **Staff:** 11. **Budget:** $1,000,000. **Description:** Represents granite quarriers and manufacturers; dedicated to traditional memorialization, high quality standards, and maintains a voice in both national and international granite technology and development. **Publications:** *The Graniteer Magazine*, quarterly. Features news on the memorial industry with a focus on Elberton firms. **Price:** free for members. **Circulation:** 11,000.

3694 ■ Indiana Limestone Institute of America (ILIA)
400 Stone City Bank Bldg.
Bedford, IN 47421
Ph: (812)275-4426
Fax: (812)279-8682
E-mail: jim@iliai.com
URL: http://www.iliai.com
Contact: James P. Owens, Exec. Dir.
Founded: 1928. **Members:** 90. **Staff:** 3. **Description:** Conducts promotional and technical services for the Indiana limestone industry; sponsors research; establishes standards; offers technical service in product use to architects, builders, and owners. Maintains speakers' bureau; conducts specialized education. **Absorbed:** National Association for Indiana Limestone. **Publications:** *Indiana Limestone Handbook*, biennial ● Pamphlets. **Conventions/Meetings:** semiannual meeting.

3695 ■ International Colored Gemstone Association (ICGA)
19 W 21st St., Ste.705
New York, NY 10010-6805
Ph: (212)620-0900
Fax: (212)352-9054
E-mail: ica@gemstones.org
URL: http://www.gemstone.org
Contact: Joseph M. Menzie, Pres.
Founded: 1983. **Members:** 30. **Membership Dues:** regular, associate, $600 (annual) ● junior, $300 (annual). **Multinational. Description:** Represents the international gemstone industry. Promotes understanding, appreciation and sales of colored gemstones worldwide. Aims to build closer international cooperation between all levels of the gemstone trade. Works in developing a common language and consistent standards to improve communication between gemstone producing countries and gemstone con-

suming countries. **Computer Services:** Information services, gems resources. **Publications:** *ICA Gazette*, bimonthly. Newsletter. Contains updated news and information about gems.

3696 ■ Marble Institute of America (MIA)
28901 Clemens Rd., Ste.100
Cleveland, OH 44145
Ph: (440)250-9222
Fax: (440)250-9223
E-mail: miainfo@marble-institute.com
URL: http://www.marble-institute.com
Contact: Garis F. Distelhorst CAE, Exec. VP
Founded: 1944. **Members:** 1,200. **Membership Dues:** regular/associate, in North America, $750 (annual) ● regular/associate (foreign), $825 (annual) ● branch, $125 (annual) ● affiliate, $95 (annual). **Staff:** 6. **Budget:** $1,350,000. **Multinational. Description:** Quarriers, exporters, fabricators, importers, wholesalers, finishers, suppliers and installing contractors of dimension stone for interior and exterior application; persons involved in the refinishing and restoration of dimension stone. Promotes the uses of dimension stone to architects, engineers, designers and other specifying authorities. Sponsors visual aid projects; works with ASTM in developing standard specifications for the use of dimension stone in construction. Compiles statistics. Distributes consumer information. Publishes technical guidelines, advisories and manuals. **Libraries: Type:** reference. **Holdings:** artwork, audiovisuals, books, clippings, monographs, periodicals. **Subjects:** dimension stone, stone sources, stone in design. **Awards:** Advertising Awards. **Frequency:** annual. **Type:** recognition. **Recipient:** for stone industry companies ● Migliore Award for Lifetime Achievement. **Frequency:** annual. **Type:** recognition. **Recipient:** for individual who has made extraordinary contribution to the natural stone industry ● Pinnacle Awards. **Frequency:** annual. **Type:** recognition. **Recipient:** for projects that exemplify professional mastery in the use of natural stone in commercial and residential environments ● Prism Awards. **Frequency:** annual. **Type:** recognition. **Recipient:** for outstanding examples of architectural achievement in the use of natural stone. **Computer Services:** Online services, consumer resources ● online services, industry and professional resources. **Committees:** Education; Technical. **Programs:** Accreditation. **Absorbed:** (1972) National Association of Marble Dealers. **Publications:** *A List of the World's Marbles*. Directory. **Price:** $50.00/copy ● *Care and Cleaning Brochure for Natural Stone Surfaces*. **Price:** $20.00/package, plus shipping and handling ● *Cutting Edge*, monthly. Newsletter. Alternate Formats: online ● *Dimension Stone - Design Manual, Version VI*. **Price:** $175.00 ● *Marble Institute of America—Membership Products and Services Directory*, semiannual. **Price:** $25.00 in U.S.; $40.00 outside U.S. **Conventions/Meetings:** annual convention (exhibits) ● seminar.

3697 ■ National Building Granite Quarries Association (NBGQA)
1220 L St. NW, Ste.100-167
Washington, DC 20005
Free: (800)557-2848
URL: http://www.nbgqa.com
Founded: 1916. **Members:** 9. **Budget:** $25,000. **Description:** Represents quarriers and manufacturers of building granites. Provides specifications for designers. **Publications:** *Specifications for Architectural Granite*, annual ● *Sweets Catalog*, annual. **Conventions/Meetings:** annual conference - always April, Washington, DC.

3698 ■ National Quartz Producers Council (NQPC)
PO Box 1719
Wheat Ridge, CO 80034
Ph: (303)432-0044
Fax: (303)467-0107
Contact: M.R. Busley, Pres.
Founded: 1967. **Members:** 6. **Description:** Represents plants producing decorative crushed stone. Establishes uniform standards of sizing and quality control on quartz, quartzite, and other hard aggregates used in exposed architectural concrete work. Promotes the use of these materials by concrete contractors and architects. **Committees:** Advertising and Promotion; Quality Control. **Conventions/Meetings:** periodic meeting.

3699 ■ National Stone, Sand and Gravel Association (NSSGA)
1605 King St.
Alexandria, VA 22314
Ph: (703)525-8788
Free: (800)342-1415
Fax: (703)525-7782
E-mail: info@nssga.org
URL: http://www.nssga.org
Contact: Jennifer Joy Wilson, Pres./CEO
Founded: 2000. **Members:** 850. **Staff:** 29. **Budget:** $6,500,000. **Description:** Provides information to the construction aggregates industry and represents producers of sand, gravel, crushed and broken stone before legislative, regulatory, and technical organizations. **Libraries: Type:** reference. **Subjects:** construction materials and highway construction. **Awards:** Quarry engineering. **Frequency:** annual. **Type:** scholarship. **Recipient:** for engineering students pursuing a career in aggregates. **Telecommunication Services:** electronic mail, jwilson@nssga.org. **Committees:** Communications & Community Relations; Education; Engineering and Research; Environment, Safety and Health; Government Affairs; Market Development; Operations. **Divisions:** Manufacturers and Services. **Absorbed:** (1990) Pulverized Limestone Association. **Formed by Merger of:** (1985) National Crushed Stone Association; (1985) National Limestone Institute; (2001) National Aggregates Association; (2001) National Stone Association. **Publications:** *Digest*, biweekly. Newsletter. Covers developments on legislation/regulations and aggregate industry news. **Price:** included in membership dues. Alternate Formats: online ● *Stone, Sand & Gravel Review*, bimonthly. Magazine. Provides information on industry technology, trends, developments, and concerns. **Price:** included in membership dues; $48.00 /year for nonmembers. ISSN: 8750-9210. **Circulation:** 6,000. **Advertising:** accepted. **Conventions/Meetings:** triennial Conexpo-Con/Agg Show - convention (exhibits).

Sugar

3700 ■ American Society of Sugar Cane Technologists (ASSCT)
c/o Dr. Denver T. Loupe, Gen. Sec.-Treas.
PO Box 25100
Baton Rouge, LA 70894-5100
Ph: (225)578-6930
Fax: (225)578-1403
E-mail: assct@assct.org
URL: http://www.assct.org
Contact: Dr. Denver T. Loupe, Gen. Sec.-Treas.
Membership Dues: active, $10-$20 (annual) ● foreign, $20 (annual) ● associate, $25 (annual) ● supporting, $50 (annual). **Local Groups:** 2. **Description:** Represents the interests of individuals dedicated to the advancement of the mainland sugarcane industry in the United States. Focuses on the general study of the sugarcane industry in the United States. Disseminates information to members through meetings and publications. **Publications:** *Journal of the American Society of Sugar Cane Technologists*, annual. Includes articles covering agricultural and manufacturing research. **Price:** $10.00 in U.S.; $15.00 outside U.S. Alternate Formats: online. Also Cited As: *JASSCT*. **Conventions/Meetings:** annual meeting - usually held in June.

Surplus

3701 ■ Associated Surplus Dealers (ASD)
c/o ASD/AMD Trade Shows
11835 W Olympic Blvd., Ste.550E
Los Angeles, CA 90064-5810
Ph: (310)481-7300
Free: (800)421-4511
Fax: (310)481-1900
E-mail: custserv@merchandisegroup.com
URL: http://www.merchandisegroup.com
Contact: Sam Bundy, Exec. Dir.
Founded: 1950. **Members:** 600. **Staff:** 30. **Description:** Represents surplus, general merchandise, and close-out dealers, manufacturers, manufacturers' representatives, and others. Promotes trade shows; provides liaison with government agencies; offers group life insurance coverage. **Awards: Type:** recognition. **Divisions:** Associated Merchandise Dealers. **Publications:** *ASD/AMD Trade News*, monthly ● *Buyers' Guide*, annual. **Conventions/Meetings:** bimonthly trade show.

3702 ■ Investment Recovery Association (IRA)
638 W 39th St.
Kansas City, MO 64111
Ph: (816)561-5323
Free: (800)728-2272
Fax: (816)561-1991
E-mail: info@invrecovery.org
URL: http://www.invrecovery.org
Contact: Jane Male CAE, Exec. Dir.
Founded: 1980. **Members:** 341. **Membership Dues:** regular, $400 (annual) ● one time initiation fee, $200 ● associate, $550 (annual). **Staff:** 8. **Budget:** $250,000. **Description:** Utility, chemical, petroleum, steel, food, aerospace, textile, and other companies that have surplus assets to sell, yet are not primarily involved in sales. Promotes the study, development, and implementation of techniques to improve disposition of surplus assets in an effort to reduce costs, improve asset utilization and return on investment, and reduce exposure risk from government regulation and product warranty/liability. Members share knowledge in areas including product liability dismantlement methods and establishing an Investment Recovery Department. Holds panel discussions. **Publications:** *IRA News Journal*, bimonthly. Covers membership activities. **Price:** available to members only. **Circulation:** 600. **Advertising:** accepted ● Directory, annual. **Price:** included in membership dues; $300.00 for nonmembers. **Circulation:** 500. **Advertising:** accepted. **Conventions/Meetings:** semiannual conference (exhibits) - always spring and fall ● workshop and seminar.

Surveying

3703 ■ Council of Professional Surveyors (COPS)
1015 15th St. NW, 8th Fl.
Washington, DC 20005-2605
Ph: (202)347-7474
Fax: (202)898-0068
E-mail: dbixby@acec.org
URL: http://www.acec.org/coalitions/COPS/index.cfm
Contact: David C. Bixby, Contact
Founded: 1999. **Members:** 180. **Membership Dues:** $250 (annual). **Staff:** 2. **Description:** Represents and supports the business interests of professional surveying services. **Publications:** Membership Directory.

Systems Integrators

3704 ■ Control and Information Systems Integrators Association (CSIA)
640 Rice Blvd.
Exton, PA 19341
Free: (800)661-4914
Fax: (888)581-3666
E-mail: execdir@controlsys.org
URL: http://www.controlsys.org
Contact: Norman F. O'Leary, Exec. Dir.
Founded: 1994. **Membership Dues:** integrator, $750 ● partner, $875. **Description:** Serves as the organization for established systems integrators specializing in automating industrial and manufacturing ap-

plications. Provides insights into the effective business, marketing, and project management practices for the automation and IT domains. **Publications:** Articles. Alternate Formats: online.

3705 ■ LonMark International
550 Meridian Ave.
San Jose, CA 95126
Ph: (408)938-5266
Fax: (408)790-3838
E-mail: info@lonmark.org
URL: http://www.lonmark.org
Contact: Barry Haaser, Exec. Dir.
Founded: 1994. **Members:** 300. **Membership Dues:** sponsor, $20,000 (annual) ● partner, $5,000 (annual) ● associate, $1,000 (annual) ● individual, $200 (annual). **Staff:** 5. **Multinational. Description:** Aims to promote and advance the business of efficient and effective integration of open, multi-vendor control systems utilizing ANSI/EIA 709 ("open systems") and related standards. **Formerly:** (2004) LonMark Interoperability Association. **Publications:** *Interoperable News*, monthly. Newsletter. **Price:** free. Alternate Formats: online ● *LonMark Magazine*, quarterly. Promotes LonMark open systems and other solutions based on the ANSI/CEA 709.1 and EN14908 protocol standards. **Circulation:** 12,000. **Advertising:** accepted. Alternate Formats: online. **Conventions/Meetings:** annual LonWorld - convention (exhibits).

3706 ■ NASBA - The Association of System Builders and Integrators (NASBA)
19 Corporate Plz., Ste.200
Newport Beach, CA 92660
Ph: (949)729-2259 (949)500-4815
Fax: (949)729-0789
E-mail: robert@nasba.com
URL: http://www.nasba.com
Contact: Robert Danese, Exec. Dir.
Founded: 2001. **Description:** Represents system builders. Works to enhance communication within the system integrator industry. **Additional Websites:** http://www.nasbadigitalhome.com. **Formerly:** (2002) North American System Builders Association.

3707 ■ National Association of Campus Card Users (NACCU)
9201 N 25th Ave., Ste.188
Phoenix, AZ 85021
Ph: (602)395-8989
Fax: (602)395-9090
E-mail: naccu@naccu.org
URL: http://naccu.org
Contact: Lowell Adkins, Exec. Dir.
Founded: 1993. **Membership Dues:** institutional (based on FTE enrollment), $400-$700 (annual) ● business campus, $625 (annual) ● corporate associate (bronze), $750 (annual) ● corporate associate (silver), $2,500 (annual) ● corporate associate (gold), $5,000 (annual). **Description:** Works to provide learning and networking opportunities for campus ID card and card industry professionals. **Telecommunication Services:** electronic mail, lowell@naccu.org. **Publications:** *CardTalk*, monthly. Newsletter. **Conventions/Meetings:** annual conference ● seminar ● workshop.

Tableware

3708 ■ American Edged Products Manufacturers Association (AEPMA)
21165 Whitfield Pl., No. 105
Potomac Falls, VA 20165
Ph: (703)433-9281
Fax: (703)433-0369
E-mail: info@aepma.org
URL: http://www.aepma.org
Contact: David W. Barrack, Exec. Dir.
Founded: 1947. **Members:** 30. **Membership Dues:** manufacturer (based on total cutlery sales for previous year), $1,605-$4,245 (annual) ● associate (based on sales level to the cutlery industry), $840-$1,680 (annual). **Staff:** 2. **Description:** Represents manufacturers of knives, scissors, and edged hand tools; suppliers to the industry. Works for the promotion of the edged products industry. Conducts seminars and educational programs. Sponsors research; compiles statistics. **Formerly:** (2000) American Cutlery Manufacturers Association. **Publications:** *Cutting Edge*, quarterly. Newsletter. Alternate Formats: online ● Membership Directory, annual. **Advertising:** accepted. **Conventions/Meetings:** annual meeting - spring.

3709 ■ Associated Glass and Pottery Manufacturers (AGPM)
520 Westchester Dr.
Greensburg, PA 15601
Ph: (724)837-2332
Contact: Mr. Robert Gonze, Pres.
Founded: 1923. **Members:** 20. **Membership Dues:** regular, $75 (annual). **Description:** Manufacturers of ceramic dinnerware (vitrified and semivitrified) and glass. Conducts activities for the benefit and improvement of business conditions in the industry. Sponsors research projects in educational institutions and other research organizations. Gathers and disseminates industry news and information. **Conventions/Meetings:** annual meeting.

3710 ■ Gift Associates Interchange Network (GAIN)
c/o ABC-Amega, Inc.
1100 Main St.
Buffalo, NY 14209-2356
Ph: (716)887-9508 (716)887-9515
Free: (800)746-9428
Fax: (716)887-9599
E-mail: info@gaingroup.com
URL: http://www.gaingroup.com
Contact: Jeff Markley, VP for Credit Information
Founded: 1974. **Members:** 200. **Description:** Represents manufacturers and importers of giftware, tabletop accessories, china, greeting cards, silk and floral products, book publishers, desk and wall calendar manufacturers. Collects, computes, and exchanges factual ledger information on mutual customers. Conducts seminars. **Telecommunication Services:** electronic mail, jeff.markley@abc-amega.com. **Formerly:** Giftware Associate Interchange Network; (1997) Giftware Manufacturers Credit Interchange. **Publications:** *Credit Sense*. Newsletter. Alternate Formats: online ● Directory, periodic. **Conventions/Meetings:** semiannual conference.

3711 ■ National Tabletop and Giftware Association (NTGA)
112 Adrossan Ct.
Deptford, NJ 08096
Ph: (856)227-6802
E-mail: demasi@nationaltabletop.org
URL: http://www.nationaltabletop.org
Contact: Tony DeMasi, Exec. Dir.
Founded: 1979. **Members:** 80. **Staff:** 1. **Budget:** $100,000. **Description:** Manufacturers, distributors, and publication and service organizations involved in the tabletop and decorative gift accessory industry. (Tabletop refers to decorative pieces commonly displayed on tables, such as crystal, ceramics, flatware, and china.) Serves as a forum and a unified voice for the tabletop and gift industry. Conducts educational programs. **Committees:** Executive Conference; Logistics; Marketing and Bridal. **Affiliated With:** Points of Light Foundation. **Formerly:** National Tabletop Association. **Publications:** *Bridal Registrars*, periodic. Directory. **Price:** $50.00 for nonmembers. **Conventions/Meetings:** semiannual conference - every April and October ● semiannual Executive Conference - meeting (exhibits) - spring, fall in New York City.

3712 ■ Society of American Silversmiths (SAS)
PO Box 72839
Providence, RI 02907
Ph: (401)461-6840
Fax: (401)461-6841
E-mail: sas@silversmithing.com
URL: http://www.silversmithing.com
Contact: Jeffrey Herman, Founder/Exec. Dir.
Founded: 1989. **Members:** 280. **Membership Dues:** associate, $20 (annual) ● supporting (foreign and non full-time student), $45 (annual) ● supporting, $40 (annual). **Staff:** 1. **For-Profit. Description:** Silversmiths both practicing and retired, who now or used to smith as a livelihood, are provided with support, networking, and greater access to the market. Professional organization solely devoted to the preservation and promotion of contemporary silversmithing. Artisans are silversmiths who have been juried into the Society based on their outstanding technical skill. Educates the public in demystifying silversmithing techniques, silver care, restoration and conservation, and the aesthetic values of this art form through its free consulting service. Seeks to assist those students who have a strong interest in becoming silver craftsmen. Offers workshops throughout the school year. Maintains an extensive library and a referral service that commission's work from its Artisans and archives. Also maintains the world's largest website totally devoted to the silversmiths' art. **Libraries: Type:** reference. **Holdings:** archival material, books, periodicals, photographs. **Subjects:** artisan work, silver history, techniques, restoration, maker's marks, other silver-related subjects. **Awards:** Hans Christensen Sterling Silversmiths Award. **Frequency:** annual. **Type:** recognition. **Recipient:** to outstanding silversmiths residing in the United States. **Computer Services:** Mailing lists, of members. **Publications:** Newsletter. Alternate Formats: online. **Conventions/Meetings:** annual SilverWorks - meeting (exhibits).

Tangible Assets

3713 ■ Industry Council for Tangible Assets (ICTA)
PO Box 1365
Severna Park, MD 21146-8365
Ph: (410)626-7005
Fax: (410)626-7007
E-mail: eloiseullman@comcast.net
URL: http://ictaonline.org
Contact: Eloise A. Ullman, Exec. Dir.
Founded: 1983. **Members:** 400. **Membership Dues:** firm (based on annual sales volume), $300-$25,000 (annual) ● associate, patron, $100 (annual) ● supporter, $50 (annual). **Staff:** 2. **Budget:** $240,000. **Description:** Individuals and firms engaged in the fabrication, manufacture, importation, wholesale distribution, or retail sale of any tangible asset (precious or other metals, coins, antiques, stamps, or art objects). Cooperates in maintaining an appropriate and favorable regulatory climate in the U.S; serves as liaison with governmental and other agencies. **Computer Services:** database ● mailing lists. **Publications:** *ICTA Washington Wire*, quarterly. Newsletter. Covers federal and state legislation affecting the industry. **Price:** included in membership dues. **Circulation:** 400 ● Brochures.

Tattooing

3714 ■ Alliance of Professional Tattooists (APT)
9210 S Hwy. 17-92
Maitland, FL 32751
Ph: (407)831-5549
E-mail: info@safe-tattoos.com
URL: http://www.safe-tattoos.com
Founded: 1992. **Members:** 2,500. **Membership Dues:** supporting, $50 (annual) ● associate non-artist, $75 (annual) ● associate tattooist, $100 (annual) ● cosmetic tattooist, $125 (annual) ● professional, $150 (annual). **Description:** Seeks to address the health and safety issues facing the tattoo industry. Strives to educate lawmakers, dispel myths and counter misinformation with researched facts about tattooing. **Publications:** *Basic Guidelines for Getting a Tattoo*. Pamphlet. Provides answers to the most often asked questions about tattooing. ● *Skin Scribe*.

Newsletter. Contains updates on issues that affect the tattoo business practices.

3715 ■ Association of Professional Piercers (APP)
PO Box 1287
Lawrence, KS 66044
Ph: (785)841-6060
Free: (888)888-1277
Fax: (785)841-6060
E-mail: info@safepiercing.org
URL: http://www.safepiercing.org
Contact: Ms. Caitlin McDiarmid, Admin.

Founded: 1994. **Membership Dues:** corporate associate, $200 (annual) ● professional business, patron, associate, $50 (annual). **Multinational. Description:** Piercing professionals. Promotes safety and proper hygiene. Provides members with up to date information and materials. Distributes educational materials to piercers, piercees, the general public, educators, health inspectors and healthcare personnel on body piercing. Holds Annual Educational Conference for body piercers, studio owners, and health inspectors. Participates in National Health Conferences: American Public Health Assoc., American College Health Assoc., American Dental Hygienists Assoc., and others. Provides telephone/email question and answer service on body piercing. Assists legislators and piercers to establish good fair comprehensive legislation governing body piercing. Offer annual educational seminars in Mexico for spanish-speaking piercers. **Awards:** Al D. Scholarship. **Frequency:** annual. **Type:** scholarship. **Recipient:** for volunteers ● President's Award. **Frequency:** annual. **Type:** recognition. **Recipient:** to individuals for contribution to the piercing industry. **Publications:** *APP Procedure Manual*. Alternate Formats: CD-ROM ● *Body and Facial Piercing Aftercare Guidelines*. Brochure ● *Body Piercing Troubleshooting*. Brochure ● *Oral Piercing Aftercare Guidelines*. Brochure ● *Oral Piercing Risks and Safety Measures*. Brochure ● *Picking Your Piercer - A Consumer's Guide*. Brochure. **Price:** $15.00 per 100 copies for nonmembers ● *The Point*. Magazine. **Price:** $10.00 for nonmembers; free for members. Alternate Formats: online ● *What is the APP?*. Brochure. Outlines the mission of the organization, services provided, membership categories, etc. **Price:** $20.00/100 copies. **Conventions/Meetings:** annual conference, piercing procedures and training - always in Las Vegas, NV.

3716 ■ Professional Tattoo Artists Guild (PTAG)
Address Unknown since 2008
URL: http://www.tattooequipment.com

Members: 2,000. **Description:** Professional tattoo artists.

Taxation

3717 ■ Federation of Exchange Accommodators (FEA)
100 N 20th St., 4th Fl.
Philadelphia, PA 19103-1443
Ph: (215)320-3881
Fax: (215)564-2175
E-mail: fea@fernley.com
URL: http://www.1031.org
Contact: Kathryn E. Gifford, Assoc. Dir.

Founded: 1989. **Members:** 245. **Membership Dues:** regular, affiliate, $975 (annual). **Staff:** 3. **Budget:** $500,000. **Regional Groups:** 7. **Description:** Promotes ideas and innovations, as well as standards, for exchange accommodator profession and exchange industry. **Councils:** Certification Council for Certified Exchange Specialist. **Publications:** Newsletter, quarterly. Contains current information of interest to members. Alternate Formats: online. **Conventions/Meetings:** annual conference and lecture ● annual meeting and conference - October. 2008 Oct. 10-11, Las Vegas, NV ● regional meeting.

Taxidermy

3718 ■ National Taxidermists Association (NTA)
108 Br. Dr.
Slidell, LA 70461
Ph: (985)641-4682
Free: (866)662-9054
Fax: (985)641-9463
E-mail: ntahq@aol.com
URL: http://www.nationaltaxidermists.com
Contact: Bill Haynes, Pres.

Founded: 1973. **Members:** 2,400. **Membership Dues:** individual in U.S., $50 (annual) ● individual in Canada and Mexico, family, $70 (annual) ● individual (foreign non-North American), $90 (annual) ● judge, $10 (annual) ● life (individual), $500 ● life (family), $750 ● life (judge), $50. **Staff:** 3. **Budget:** $100,000. **Description:** Professional and amateur taxidermists. Seeks to promote and teach better taxidermy methods. Holds educational seminars and maintains hall of fame and museum. **Awards:** Charlie Fleming Educational Scholarship. **Frequency:** annual. **Type:** scholarship. **Recipient:** for members and/or their children. **Telecommunication Services:** electronic mail, bhay@numail.org. **Committees:** Competition and Judging; Ethics; Insurance; Seminars. **Publications:** *Membership List*, bimonthly. Magazine. **Circulation:** 2,500. **Advertising:** accepted ● *National Taxidermists Association—Outlook*, bimonthly. Newsletter. Provides information on legislation and regulation affecting the industry; also includes association news. **Price:** free for members. **Circulation:** 2,400 ● Annual Report. Includes membership directory, arranged geographically. **Price:** free for members. **Conventions/Meetings:** annual convention ● annual meeting (exhibits).

Technical Consulting

3719 ■ SAE Service Technology Program Office (STPO)
c/o Society of Automotive Engineers
400 Commonwealth Dr.
Warrendale, PA 15096-0001
Ph: (724)776-4841
Free: (877)606-7323
Fax: (724)774-0790
E-mail: stpo@sae.org
URL: http://www.sae.org/about/programoffices/stpo.htm
Contact: Wayne Juchno, Managing Dir.

Founded: 1996. **Members:** 6,000. **Membership Dues:** individual, $29 (annual). **Staff:** 2. **Budget:** $1,000,000. **Local Groups:** 14. **Multinational. Description:** Aims to advance the knowledge, skills and image of service technicians. Fosters communication and cooperation among service technicians and other professionals. **Libraries: Type:** not open to the public. **Holdings:** 600; audiovisuals. **Computer Services:** Mailing lists, of members. **Formerly:** (2003) Service Technicians Society. **Publications:** *Service Tech*, bimonthly. Magazine. **Circulation:** 10,500. **Advertising:** accepted. Alternate Formats: online.

Technology

3720 ■ 1394 High Performance Serial Bus Trade Association (1394 TA)
1560 E Southlake Blvd., Ste.242
Southlake, TX 76092
Ph: (817)416-2200
Fax: (817)416-2256
E-mail: jsnider@1394ta.org
URL: http://www.1394ta.org
Contact: James Snider, Exec. Dir.

Founded: 1994. **Membership Dues:** company (based on company's gross revenue), $500-$10,000 (annual) ● non-profit organization, $1,000 (annual) ● custom home network installer, $500 (annual). **Description:** Promotes the proliferation of the IEEE 1394 Serial Bus standard technology into the computer, consumer, peripheral and industrial markets. Fosters industry awareness, acceptance and advancement of the IEEE 1394 High Performance Serial Bus. Accelerates the adoption and usage of 1394 products and services. Encourages the bridging of the consumer electronics and computer markets.

3721 ■ Advanced Media Workflow Association (AMWA)
436 N Westfield Rd.
Madison, WI 53717
Ph: (770)414-9952
Fax: (608)833-0508
E-mail: info@amwa.tv
URL: http://www.aafassociation.org
Contact: Brad Gilmer, Exec. Dir.

Founded: 2000. **Membership Dues:** individual, $175 (annual) ● associate, $1,500 (annual) ● general, $5,000 (annual) ● principal, $10,000 (annual). **Description:** Seeks to promote the development and adoption of advanced authoring format technology throughout the media industry. Intends to help deliver the full benefits of digital media to content creators including film, television, internet and post-production professionals. **Telecommunication Services:** electronic mail, brad_gilmer@amwa.tv. **Formerly:** (2007) Advanced Authoring Format Association.

3722 ■ Application Service Provider Industry Consortium (ASP)
c/o Computing Technology Industry Association
1815 S Meyers Rd., Ste.300
Oakbrook Terrace, IL 60181-5228
Ph: (630)678-8300
Fax: (630)678-8384
URL: http://www.comptia.org

Founded: 1999. **Members:** 500. **National Groups:** 21. **Description:** A section of The Computing Technology Industry Association. Independent software vendors, network service providers, application service providers, and emerging business models and other sectors supporting the industry. Advocates the application service provider industry by sponsoring research and articulating the strategic and measurable benefits of this evolving delivery model. **Awards:** ASPire. **Frequency:** periodic. **Type:** recognition. **Affiliated With:** Computing Technology Industry Association.

3723 ■ Association for Competitive Technology (ACT)
1401 K St. NW, Ste.502
Washington, DC 20005
Ph: (202)331-2130
E-mail: info@actonline.org
URL: http://www.actonline.org
Contact: Jonathan Zuck, Pres.

Founded: 1998. **Members:** 3,000. **Membership Dues:** corporate, affiliate, $100 (annual). **Staff:** 6. **Description:** Technology executives and organizations. Strives to preserve and enhance the innovation, competition, and entrepreneurial spirit of the technology industry. **Publications:** *Tech Environmental Quality Index*, periodic. Report. Alternate Formats: online.

3724 ■ Geekcorps
901 15th St. NW, Ste.1010
Washington, DC 20005
Ph: (202)326-0280
Fax: (202)326-0289
E-mail: geekcorps@iesc.org
URL: http://www.geekcorps.org

Nonmembership. Multinational. Description: Promotes economic growth in the developing world by sending highly skilled technology volunteers to teach communities how to use innovative and affordable information and communication technologies to solve development problems. **Affiliated With:** International Executive Service Corps; International Executive Service Corps.

3725 ■ Novell Users International (NUI)
c/o Brent Sharp, Exec. Dir.
1800 S Novell Pl.
MS/H-811
Provo, UT 84606
Free: (800)228-4684
E-mail: bsharp@novell.com
URL: http://www.nuinet.com
Contact: Brent Sharp, Exec. Dir.
Founded: 1986. **Members:** 90,000. **Multinational. Description:** Novell/Linux professionals. Aims to bring technical resources from Novell departments, including technical services, consulting and education; provides direct contact with technical experts from Novell and its vendor partners; helps Novell and Linux professionals work more efficiently in complex, multi-platform environments; and provides certification opportunities. **Formerly:** (2002) NetWare Users International. **Publications:** Newsletter. Alternate Formats: online.

3726 ■ Optical Internetworking Forum (OIF)
48377 Fremont Blvd., Ste.117
Fremont, CA 94538
Ph: (510)492-4040 (510)492-4043
Fax: (510)492-4001
E-mail: info@oiforum.com
URL: http://www.oiforum.com
Contact: Andria Kosich, Exec. Dir.
Membership Dues: principal, $8,000 (annual) ● principal, company (with less than $10 million annual revenues), $4,000 (annual) ● auditing, $3,000 (annual) ● academic, $1,000 (annual). **Multinational. Description:** Promotes global development of optical internetworking products, fosters development and deployment of interoperable products and services for data switching and routing using optical networking. **Telecommunication Services:** electronic mail, akosich@oiforum.com. **Programs:** Speakers' Bureau. **Publications:** Articles. **Conventions/Meetings:** meeting, for committee and principal members only ● annual meeting.

3727 ■ PC/104 Consortium
1712 Devonshire Rd.
Sacramento, CA 95864
Ph: (916)270-2016
Fax: (866)746-3815
E-mail: info@pc104.org
URL: http://www.pc104.org
Contact: Jeffrey L. Milde, Exec. Dir.
Founded: 1992. **Members:** 83. **Membership Dues:** executive, $5,000 (annual) ● associate, $1,750 (annual) ● affiliate, $750 (annual). **Multinational. Description:** Strives to disseminate information about PC/104 and to provide a liaison function between PC/104 and standard organizations.

3728 ■ SSA Global Users - North America (SSAU)
401 N Michigan Ave.
Chicago, IL 60611
Ph: (312)527-6651
Free: (888)839-9020
Fax: (312)673-6682
E-mail: info@ssaglobalusers.org
URL: http://www.ssaglobalusers.org
Contact: Ms. Karen Zader, Admin.
Membership Dues: customer, $595 (annual) ● alliance, $2,000 (annual). **Multinational. Description:** Provides SSA Global customers and vendors with a forum for networking, sharing information and helping each other address their current and future SSA Global-related business needs. **Formerly:** (2005) Infinium UserNet. **Publications:** *UserNet News*, quarterly. Newsletter. Alternate Formats: online. **Conventions/Meetings:** annual conference, with participation from Infinium and associate members providing education and training - always fall ● annual conference.

3729 ■ United States Display Consortium (USDC)
84 W Santa Clara St., Ste.790
San Jose, CA 95113
Ph: (408)993-8111
Fax: (408)993-8121
E-mail: usdc@usdc.org
URL: http://www.usdc.org
Contact: Michael Ciesinski, Pres./CEO
Founded: 1993. **Membership Dues:** voting, associate (maximum, based on number of employees), $40,000 (annual) ● general, $10,000 (annual) ● sustaining (based on number of employees), $2,000-$10,000 (annual) ● military and avionics user group, commercial user group, $5,000-$10,000 (annual) ● associate (minimum; based on number of employees), $10,000 (annual) ● associate (maximum; based on number of employees), $40,000 (annual). **Description:** Represents and promotes flat panel manufacturers, developers, users, equipment and material supplies in the display industry. **Publications:** *Display Trends*, semiannual. Newsletter. Alternate Formats: online. **Conventions/Meetings:** conference.

Technology Education

3730 ■ Internet Business Alliance (IBA)
PO Box 11518
Seattle, WA 98110-5518
E-mail: iba@alliance.org
URL: http://www.alliance.org
Contact: Guy R. Cook, Dir./Pres.
Founded: 1994. **Membership Dues:** general, $100 (annual). **Staff:** 6. **Description:** Represents professionals. Works to serve the needs of professionals who use, or want to learn to use, the Internet for business applications. Conducts seminars and forums.

Telecommunications

3731 ■ Alliance for Telecommunications Industry Solutions (ATIS)
1200 G St. NW, Ste.500
Washington, DC 20005
Ph: (202)628-6380 (202)434-8828
Fax: (202)393-5453
E-mail: smiller@atis.org
URL: http://www.atis.org
Contact: Susan Miller, Pres./CEO
Founded: 1984. **Members:** 250. **Membership Dues:** business (class A - maximum; based on total annual revenues), $259,000 (annual) ● business (class B - maximum; based on total annual revenues), $46,700 (annual) ● business (class C - based on total annual revenues), $2,200-$10,200 (annual) ● business (class D - based on total annual revenues), $1,000-$1,500 (annual) ● affiliate, $1,000 (annual). **Description:** A member company organization that is the leader for standards and operating procedures for the telecommunications industry. More than 1,500 experts from over 400 telecommunications companies participate in the organization's 19 committees, forums, and Incubator Solutions programs, where work focus includes network interconnection standards, number portability, improved data transmission, wireless communications, Internet telephony, toll-free access, and order and billing issues. **Councils:** Technology and Operations. **Subgroups:** Industry Numbering; Network Interconnection/Interoperability Forum; Ordering and Billing Forum; Tall Fraud Prevention. **Formerly:** (2000) Carrier Liaison Committee. **Publications:** *ATIS e-Report*, quarterly. Newsletter ● *ATIS News*, quarterly. Newsletter ● Annual Report, annual ● Also publishes resolution documents and operational guidelines.

3732 ■ American Facsimile Association (AFaxA)
2200 Benjamin Franklin Pkwy., Ste.E105A
Philadelphia, PA 19130
Ph: (215)981-0292
Fax: (215)981-0295
E-mail: faxinfo@afaxa.com
URL: http://2world.com/staging/afaxa
Contact: Jerry Brodsky, Pres.
Founded: 1986. **Membership Dues:** corporate, $5,000 (annual) ● individual, $900 (annual). **Staff:** 10. **Description:** Hardware/software manufacturers, fax service providers, and others interested in messaging. Works to serve as main resource for fax information; to promote the use of fax as the primary document and message delivery system; promote communication among members; to represent members' legislative interests. Operates placement service; compiles statistics. **Computer Services:** database, fax dictionary ● information services, fax resources, for members only. **Working Groups:** Advertising and Marketing; Banking and Finance; Engineering and Architecture; Fax Marketing and Distribution; Fax Technologies; Government and Law Enforcement; Health and Medical Care; Insurance; Law; Library and Information Science; Publishing; Real Estate; Retailing and Wholesaling. **Publications:** *AFaxA Journal*, quarterly ● *Fax Focus*, weekly. Newspaper. **Price:** $300.00/year in U.S.; $400.00/year in Canada; $600.00/year, rest of the world. **Circulation:** 5,000. **Advertising:** accepted ● *FaxPro*, periodic. Serves as a comparison guide.

3733 ■ American Public Communications Council (APCC)
625 Slaters Ln., Ste.104
Alexandria, VA 22314
Ph: (703)739-1322
Free: (800)868-2722
Fax: (703)739-1324
E-mail: apcc@apcc.net
URL: http://www.apcc.net
Contact: Willard R. Nichols, Pres.
Founded: 1988. **Members:** 12. **Membership Dues:** consultant, $500 (annual) ● international, $1,000 (annual) ● service provider, $3,000-$50,000. **Staff:** 11. **State Groups:** 30. **Description:** Manufacturers, suppliers, distributors, and operators involved in the sale, lease, installation, and maintenance of pay telephone equipment. Goals are to protect and expand domestic and foreign markets for public communications, and to provide services that will improve business opportunities for members. Provides members with market strategies, legal assistance, networking opportunities, and guidance in international distribution. Represents the interests of members in legislative and regulatory concerns. **Supersedes:** National Payphone Association. **Publications:** *Perspectives on Public Communication*, monthly. Magazine. **Price:** $40.00/year in Canada and Mexico; $120.00/year, rest of the world. **Circulation:** 11,500. **Advertising:** accepted. **Conventions/Meetings:** annual show (exhibits) - always spring, in Western U.S.

3734 ■ Association for Interactive Marketing (AIM)
1430 Broadway, 8th Fl.
New York, NY 10018
Free: (888)337-0008
Fax: (212)391-9233
URL: http://www.kingproc.com/examples/imarketing.html
Contact: Kevin M. Nooman, Exec. Dir.
Founded: 1992. **Members:** 550. **Membership Dues:** governing, $5,000 (annual) ● corporate standard, $1,000 (annual) ● standard (for DMA members only), $750 (annual). **Staff:** 15. **Budget:** $1,000,000. **Description:** Organizations, corporations, and individuals interested in the interactive television industry. Promotes the interests and image of the interactive television industry through political action and press releases. Provides reporters with research assistance, expert opinions, and contact information. Works to keep members updated on issues affecting the industry. Maintains speakers' bureau; conducts research and educational programs; offers placement service. Hosts networking events around the country, seminars, and conferences. **Libraries: Type:** not open to the public. **Holdings:** archival material, audiovisuals, books, clippings, monographs, periodicals. **Subjects:** interactive television, telecommunications. **Councils:** Search Engine Marketing. **Formerly:** (1998) Interactive Television Association; (2003) Association for Interactive Media. **Publications:** *AIM Membership Directory*, annual. **Price:** included in membership dues. **Advertising:** accepted. Alternate Formats: online ● Newsletters, four weekly and vari-

ous bi-weekly and monthly newsletters. **Price:** free. Alternate Formats: online. **Conventions/Meetings:** monthly Dinner and a Deal - conference and seminar ● annual meeting ● periodic seminar.

3735 ■ Association of TeleServices International (ATSI)
12 Acad. Ave.
Atkinson, NH 03811
Free: (866)896-ATSI
Fax: (603)362-9486
E-mail: admin@atsi.org
URL: http://www.atsi.org
Contact: Lori Jenkins, Pres.

Founded: 1942. **Members:** 350. **Membership Dues:** company (based on annual revenue; with 50 percent discount for new members), $550-$1,200 (annual). **Staff:** 3. **Budget:** $300,000. **State Groups:** 16. **Description:** Telephone answering and voice message service providers. Seeks to foster growth and development in the industry. Represents the industry before Congress and regulatory agencies; negotiates with telephone companies. Holds seminars and workshops on the latest telecommunications technology; compiles statistics. Maintains hall of fame. **Libraries: Type:** reference. **Holdings:** archival material. **Awards:** Award of Excellence. **Frequency:** annual. **Type:** recognition. **Recipient:** to member organizations for providing the best service to the public. **Computer Services:** Online services, e-mail discussion forum. **Telecommunication Services:** electronic mail, help@atsi.org. **Committees:** Education; Industry Relations; Research and Development; Technical. **Formerly:** (1959) Associated Telephone Exchanges; (1987) Associated Telephone Answering Exchanges; (1999) Association of Telemessaging Services International. **Publications:** *Summer Buyer's Guide*, annual ● *TeleCommunicator*, bi-weekly. Newsletter. Contains information on telephone answering and voice technology, association programs, marketing, sales, and new equipment technology. **Price:** included in membership dues. **Circulation:** 1,200. Alternate Formats: online ● Membership Directory, annual. **Conventions/Meetings:** annual convention (exhibits) - usually May or June.

3736 ■ BICSI
World HQ
8610 Hidden River Pkwy.
Tampa, FL 33637-1000
Ph: (813)979-1991
Free: (800)242-7405
Fax: (813)971-4311
E-mail: bicsi@bicsi.org
URL: http://www.bicsi.org
Contact: David C. Cranmer, Exec. Dir.

Founded: 1977. **Membership Dues:** individual, $150 (annual) ● corporate, $300 (annual) ● active-duty military, retired individual, $75 (annual). **Staff:** 52. **Multinational. Description:** Telecommunications professionals. Provides education, a library, worldwide conferences, and registration programs. **Publications:** *BICSI News*, bimonthly. Newsletter. **Price:** free for members. Alternate Formats: online ● *Sounds and Communications*. Magazine. **Price:** free for members. Alternate Formats: online.

3737 ■ Broadband Services Forum (BSF)
48377 Fremont Blvd., Ste.117
Fremont, CA 94538
Ph: (510)492-4025 (510)492-4029
Fax: (510)492-4001
E-mail: info@broadbandservicesforum.org
URL: http://www.broadbandservicesforum.org
Contact: Florencia Dazzi, Exec. Dir.

Members: 20. **Membership Dues:** principal, $10,000 (annual) ● principal (small business), $7,500 (annual) ● principal (business with less than $2 million in annual revenue), $4,500 (annual) ● associate, $3,000 (annual). **Multinational. Description:** Addresses issues affecting end-to-end delivery of broadband content and services to consumers and businesses. **Libraries: Type:** reference. **Holdings:** articles, papers. **Subjects:** broadband industry. **Computer Services:** Mailing lists, of non-member companies ● online services, webinar series. **Formerly:** (2005) Broadband Content Delivery Forum.

3738 ■ Communications Marketing Association (CMA)
PO Box 36275
Denver, CO 80236
Ph: (303)988-3515
Fax: (303)988-3517
E-mail: mercycontreras@comcast.net
URL: http://www.cma-cmc.org
Contact: Steve Rahn, Pres.

Founded: 1974. **Members:** 400. **Membership Dues:** manufacturer, $325 (annual) ● representative and distributor, $200 (annual). **Staff:** 1. **Budget:** $50,000. **Description:** Manufacturers, independent manufacturers' representatives, and distributors who deal in two-way radio and wireless communication equipment and associated products. Promotes effective marketing and ensures professional industry standards. **Awards:** Foundation Award. **Frequency:** annual. **Type:** recognition. **Recipient:** to a CMA Board member, or past Board member, who gives above and beyond of his/her time, energy and talent to CMA. **Telecommunication Services:** electronic mail, srahn01@earthlink.net. **Formerly:** (1994) Communications Market Association. **Publications:** *CMA Newsletter*, quarterly. **Circulation:** 500. **Conventions/Meetings:** annual Communications Marketing Conference - meeting - always second week before Thanksgiving.

3739 ■ Computer and Communications Industry Association (CCIA)
900 17th St. NW, Ste.1100
Washington, DC 20006
Ph: (202)783-0070
Fax: (202)783-0534
E-mail: ccia@ccianet.org
URL: http://www.ccianet.org
Contact: Edward J. Black, Pres./CEO

Founded: 1972. **Members:** 60. **Staff:** 10. **Budget:** $2,500,000. **Description:** Manufacturers and providers of computer, information processing, and telecommunications-related products and services. Represents interests of members in domestic and foreign trade, capital formation and tax policy, federal procurement policy and telecommunications policy before Congress, federal agencies, and the courts. Keeps members advised of policy, political, technological, market, and economic developments and trends. Conducts workshops. Hosts policy briefings on legislative and regulatory matters. **Telecommunication Services:** electronic mail, eblack@ccianet.org. **Formerly:** (1976) Computer Industry Association. **Publications:** *CyberInsecurity: The Cost of Monopoly*. Report. Alternate Formats: online. **Conventions/Meetings:** annual Washington Caucus - general assembly.

3740 ■ Council for Electronic Revenue Communication Advancement (CERCA)
600 Cameron St., Ste.309
Alexandria, VA 22314
Ph: (703)340-1655
E-mail: cerca@cerca.org
URL: http://www.cerca.org
Contact: Mike Cavanagh, Exec. Dir.

Founded: 1994. **Membership Dues:** corporate (based on annual revenues), $600-$4,800 (annual) ● government agency, $250 (annual) ● company (with industry revenues above $100 million), $7,500 (annual) ● subsidiary company of full CERCA member, $1,200 (annual). **Description:** Private sector companies and government agencies. Committed to expand acceptance of electronic filing and electronic revenue communication. Works closely with Internal Revenue Service (IRS) Electronic Tax Administration leaders to provide stakeholder input on key issues. **Committees:** Business E-Filing; Electronic Commerce; Electronic Filing; Electronic Government; Systems Modernization. **Conventions/Meetings:** annual conference ● meeting - usually spring.

3741 ■ CTIA - The Wireless Association (CTIA)
1400 16th St. NW, Ste.600
Washington, DC 20036
Ph: (202)785-0081
Fax: (202)785-0721
E-mail: memberservices@ctia.org
URL: http://www.ctia.org
Contact: Steve Largent, Pres./CEO

Founded: 1984. **Members:** 450. **Membership Dues:** associate, $6,000 (annual) ● carrier, supplier, $5,000 (annual). **Staff:** 25. **Budget:** $9,000,000. **Description:** Individuals and organizations actively engaged in cellular radiotelephone communications, including: telephone companies and corporations providing radio communications; lay firms; engineering firms; consultants and manufacturers. (A cellular radiotelephone is a mobile communications device. An area is geographically divided into low frequency cells monitored by a computer that switches callers from one frequency to another as they move from cell to cell.) Objectives are to: promote, educate, and facilitate the professional interests, needs, and concerns of members with respect to the development and commercial applications of cellular technology; provide an opportunity for exchanging experience and concerns; broaden the understanding and importance of cellular communication technology. Conducts discussions, studies, and courses. **Awards:** VITA Award. **Frequency:** annual. **Type:** recognition. **Recipient:** for individuals who demonstrate the life-saving potential of cellular communications systems. **Committees:** Legislative/Regulatory; Roamer; Safety; Small Market and Finance; Technology. **Absorbed:** (1984) Cellular Radio Communications Association. **Formed by Merger of:** (2007) CTIA - The Wireless Association and Wireless Data Forum. **Formerly:** (1985) Cellular Communications Industry Association; (2004) Cellular Telecommunications Industry Association. **Publications:** *Cellular Industry Report*, monthly. **Price:** $200.00/year ● *Cellular Market Maps* ● *Cellular Technology Report*, monthly. **Price:** available to participants only ● *Industry Data Survey*, semiannual ● *Roamer Review*, quarterly. **Price:** available to members only ● *State of Cellular Industry*, annual. **Price:** $50.00/copy. **Conventions/Meetings:** annual conference (exhibits) - 2009 Mar. 24-26, Orlando, FL; 2010 Mar. 23-25, Las Vegas, NV.

3742 ■ Enterprise Wireless Alliance (EWA)
8484 Westpark Dr., Ste.630
McLean, VA 22102-3590
Ph: (703)528-5115 (703)797-5114
Free: (800)886-4222
Fax: (703)524-1074
E-mail: customerservice@enterprisewireless.org
URL: http://www.ita-relay.com
Contact: Mark E. Crosby, Pres./CEO

Founded: 1953. **Members:** 3,500. **Membership Dues:** business enterprise user (based on number of units), $155-$3,000 (annual) ● communications service provider (based on number of units), $395-$10,000 (annual) ● radio dealer, trade association, $395 (annual) ● technology manufacturer (vertically integrated), $10,000 (annual) ● other manufacturer, $1,500 (annual). **Staff:** 25. **Budget:** $3,000,000. **Description:** Private land mobile radio licensees and independent radio sales and service organizations. Represents members before the FCC and U.S. Congress. Provides frequency coordination, licensing, education, communications engineering, license data, and FCC research. **Computer Services:** database, FCC licenses in the industrial business and 421-430, 800/900 MHZ frequency pools, and 929 MHz paging ● online services, NetLicense2. **Telecommunication Services:** additional toll-free number, (800)482-8282. **Committees:** Government Affairs; Telephone Maintenance Frequency Advisory. **Councils:** Independent Communication Suppliers; Member Advisory. **Affiliated With:** Alliance of Motion Picture and Television Producers; Land Mobile Communications Council. **Formed by Merger of:** (2005) Industrial Telecommunications Association; (2005) American Mobile Telecommunications Association. **Formerly:** (1992) Special Industrial Radio Service Association. **Publications:** *Enterprise Wireless*, quarterly. Magazine. Reports on legislation and FCC regulation, new products, and interference solutions. Features annual membership reports. **Price:** included in membership dues; $37.00 for nonmembers. **Circulation:** 3,500. **Advertising:** accepted. Alternate Formats: online ● *EWA 800 MHz Transition Report*. **Conventions/Meetings:** annual conference (exhibits).

3743 ■ Fibre Channel Industry Association (FCIA)

PO Box 29920
San Francisco, CA 94129-0920
Ph: (415)561-6270
Fax: (415)561-6120
E-mail: info@fibrechannel.org
URL: http://www.fibrechannel.org
Contact: Chris Lyon, Exec. Dir.

Founded: 1999. **Members:** 150. **Membership Dues:** sponsor, $20,000 (annual) ● principal, $12,000 (annual) ● associate, $8,000 (annual) ● observer, $2,500 (annual) ● individual observer, $475 (annual). **Description:** Electronics manufacturers and other corporations with an interest in fibre channel technology. Seeks to "nurture and help develop the broadest market for fibre channel products." Conducts market development programs; monitors industry standards; sponsors educational courses; fosters interoperability among members' products. **Formerly:** (2001) Fibre Channel Associates.

3744 ■ Inter-American Telecommunication Commission (CITEL)

1889 F St. NW
Washington, DC 20006
Ph: (202)458-3004
Fax: (202)458-6854
E-mail: citel@oas.org
URL: http://www.citel.oas.org
Contact: Mr. Clovis Baptista, Exec. Sec.

Founded: 1923. **Members:** 34. **Languages:** English, Spanish. **Description:** Representatives of countries organized to facilitate the advancement of telecommunications industries in the Americas. Promotes the study and implementation of new regulations governing technological developments in the field. Fosters the expansion of shared services among members such as launching and maintaining communications satellites. Disseminates information to members on technological developments. **Computer Services:** Online services, electronic forum. **Committees:** Radio Communications including Broadcasting; Steering; Telecommunications Public Services. **Working Groups:** Conference Preparatory. **Formerly:** Inter-American Electrical Communication Commission; Inter-American Telecommunication Conference. **Publications:** *CITEL Bulletin*, semiannual ● *Tele-Education in the Americas*. Book. Alternate Formats: online ● *Universal Service in the Americas* (in English and Spanish). Book. **Conventions/Meetings:** annual meeting.

3745 ■ International Alliance of Avaya Users (INAAU)

c/o Renee Seay, CEO
Bldg. 960, 2nd Fl.
1 Franklin Pkwy.
San Mateo, CA 94403
Ph: (781)251-7857 (650)312-3722
Free: (800)334-6489
E-mail: inaau@experient-inc.com
URL: http://www.inaau.org
Contact: Renee Seay, CEO

Membership Dues: regular, $250 (annual) ● non-voting, $500 (annual). **Description:** Serves as the user group for customers of Avaya products and services. Encourages and provides a forum for the dissemination of information about Avaya Inc. and their business partners' products and services globally. Strives to provide value-added services to members. **Telecommunication Services:** electronic mail, rseay@frk.com. **Publications:** Brochure. Alternate Formats: online.

3746 ■ International Association of Satellite Users and Suppliers (IASUS)

Address Unknown since 2007

Founded: 1980. **Members:** 60. **Staff:** 4. **Languages:** English, French, German, Spanish. **Description:** Satellite suppliers, users, and related organizations. Seeks to interpret, report on, and raise user awareness of current developments in satellite communications. Provides guidance to persons wishing to use satellite technology. Promotes market development and professional networking within the industry. Provides catalog of new and used telecommunications equipment. **Formerly:** (1984) International Association of Satellite Users. **Publications:** *Telecommunications Equipment Catalog*, bimonthly. **Price:** $55.00/year; $10.00/issue. **Advertising:** accepted.

3747 ■ International BBSing and Electronic Communications Corporation (IBECC)

PO Box 21766
Denver, CO 80221-0766
Ph: (303)426-1847
E-mail: ibecc@ibecc.org
URL: http://www.ibecc.org
Contact: Marshall Barry, Contact

Founded: 1991. **Description:** Electronic communications professionals and users. Promotes the field of electronic communications, including bulletin board services (BBS). Works to advance and improve telecommunications, teleconferencing, and communications between electronic networks. Works to educate users in the uses, requirements, and security of online systems. Serves as a clearinghouse of information on electronic communications. **Publications:** *IBECC Newsletter*, periodic.

3748 ■ International Communication Association (ICA)

1500 21st St. NW
Washington, DC 20036
Ph: (202)955-1444
Fax: (202)955-1448
E-mail: icahdq@icahdq.org
URL: http://www.icahdq.org
Contact: Sonia Livingstone, Pres.

Founded: 1950. **Members:** 600. **Membership Dues:** student, $60 (annual) ● regular, $130 (annual) ● affiliate educator, $100 (annual) ● corporate, $975 (annual) ● sustaining, $290 (annual) ● association, $225 (annual). **Staff:** 2. **Budget:** $4,000,000. **Description:** Represents thousands of Information Technology (IT) professionals in commercial, government and educational organizations. Facilitates the professional development and growth of its members through education, networking and involvement in association projects and committees. Has working relationships with major universities that offer degree programs in IT. Strives to provide best in class services and programs, whether by producing events on its own or in strategic partnership with other leading organizations. Membership is corporate; each membership includes voting privilege for the primary representative and includes four alternate members. All IT professionals are included in corporate membership. Membership is open to all end users and includes leading companies in every industry sector. **Awards:** Aubrey Fisher Mentorship Award. **Frequency:** annual. **Type:** recognition. **Recipient:** for outstanding scholars, teachers, and advisors who have served as role models in the field of communication ● ICA/UN Foundation Award. **Frequency:** annual. **Type:** monetary. **Recipient:** for the meritorious accomplishment of an original study of international communication ● Steven H. Chaffee Career Productivity Award. **Frequency:** annual. **Type:** monetary. **Recipient:** to a scholar or small group of collaborating scholars for sustained work on a communication research problem over an extended period ● Young Scholar Award. **Frequency:** annual. **Type:** scholarship. **Recipient:** for outstanding contribution in the field of communication. **Telecommunication Services:** electronic mail, rrice@comm.ucsb.edu. **Committees:** Academic Development; Technical Program; Telecommunications Public Policy. **Councils:** Communication Libraries. **Divisions:** Communication and Technology; Communication Law and Policy; Feminist Scholarship; Gay, Lesbian and Bisexual Studies; Health Communication; Information Systems; Instructional and Developmental Communication; Intercultural and Development Communication; Interpersonal Communication; Language and Social Interaction; Mass Communication; Organizational Communication; Philosophy of Communication; Political Communication; Popular Communication; Public Relations; Visual Communication. **Formerly:** (1953) National Committee of Communications Supervisors; (1966) Industrial Communications Association; (1969) National Society for the Study of Communication. **Publications:** *Annual Survey of North American Telecommunications Issues*, annual ● *Communication Theory*, quarterly. Journal. Contains research studies, theoretical essays, and reviews. **Price:** $15.00 ● *Communication Yearbook*, annual ● *Guide to Publishing in Scholarly Communication Journals* ● *Human Communication Research*, quarterly. **Price:** $15.00 ● *International Communications Association—IMPACT Newsletter*, quarterly. Contains association and industry news. Includes calendar of events, new members listings, and job listings. **Price:** included in membership dues. **Circulation:** 2,500 ● *Journal of Communication*, quarterly. **Price:** $15.00 ● Annual Report, annual. **Price:** free ● Membership Directory, annual ● Newsletter, 10/year. **Conventions/Meetings:** annual conference and trade show (exhibits) ● seminar.

3749 ■ International Telecommunications Society (ITS)

c/o Leland W. Schmidt, Treas./Finance Committee Chm.
33 Alpine Dr.
Gilford, NH 03249
Ph: (603)293-4094
Fax: (603)293-4095
E-mail: lschmidt@metrocast.net
URL: http://www.itsworld.org
Contact: Leland W. Schmidt, Treas./Finance Committee Chm.

Founded: 1986. **Members:** 400. **Membership Dues:** corporate global, $6,000 (annual) ● corporate international, $3,000 (annual) ● corporate society, $1,500 (annual) ● individual, $100 (annual) ● nonprofit, government, $500 (annual). **Multinational. Description:** Represents telecommunications professionals in consultancy, telephone operating companies, government agencies, and academic institutions. Concerned with telecommunications planning, policy formation, and economic analysis. Provides a forum for industry analysis and problem solving. **Awards:** Best Student Paper. **Frequency:** biennial. **Type:** grant. **Recipient:** for quality paper. **Publications:** *Communications and Strategies*, quarterly. Journal. Features academic journal on telecommunications. **Price:** included in membership dues. ISSN: 0167-6245 ● *Interconnect*. Newsletter. **Advertising:** accepted. Alternate Formats: online. **Conventions/Meetings:** biennial conference - 2008 June 24-27, Montreal, QC, Canada.

3750 ■ International Telework Association and Council (ITAC)

14040 N Northsight Blvd.
Scottsdale, AZ 85260
Ph: (480)348-7285
Free: (877)951-9191
E-mail: knowledgecenter@worldatwork.org
URL: http://www.workingfromanywhere.org
Contact: Marcia Rhodes, Contact

Founded: 1993. **Members:** 250. **Membership Dues:** sole proprietor/education/non-profit, $250 (annual) ● user, government agency, $500 (annual) ● vendor, $1,000-$3,000 (annual). **Staff:** 1. **Budget:** $175,000. **Regional Groups:** 20. **Description:** Individuals, corporations, government agencies, educators, consultants and vendors. Promotes the economic, social and environmental benefits of telecommuting and telework. Disseminates information on the design and implementation of telecommuting programs, the development of the U.S. telecommuting sector, the virtual office and telecommuting research. **Libraries: Type:** by appointment only. **Holdings:** audiovisuals, books, clippings, monographs, periodicals, reports. **Computer Services:** database ● electronic publishing, e-newsletter. **Committees:** Agency Special Interest; Research. **Formerly:** (1998) Telecommuting Advisory Council/International Telework Association. **Publications:** *TeleTrends*, quarterly. Newsletter. **Circulation:** 500. **Advertising:** accepted. **Conventions/Meetings:** annual conference (exhibits).

3751 ■ Land Mobile Communications Council (LMCC)
8484 Westpark Dr., Ste.630
McLean, VA 22102-5117
Ph: (703)528-5115
Fax: (703)524-1074
E-mail: donald.vasek@enterprisewireless.org
URL: http://www.lmcc.org
Contact: Ralph Haller, Pres.
Founded: 1967. **Members:** 22. **Description:** Professional communications associations. Ensures that the Land Mobile Radio Services are allocated a sufficient portion of the radio spectrum to meet their frequency needs. **Committees:** Drafting; FCC Liaison. **Conventions/Meetings:** annual meeting - usually March or April, Washington, DC.

3752 ■ PCIA - The Wireless Infrastructure Association (PCIA)
500 Montgomery St., Ste.700
Alexandria, VA 22314-1560
Ph: (703)535-7447 (703)535-7409
Free: (800)759-0300
Fax: (703)836-1608
E-mail: kevin.kelly@pcia.com
URL: http://www.pcia.com
Contact: Michael T.N. Fitch, Pres./CEO
Founded: 1965. **Members:** 200. **Staff:** 22. **Multinational. Description:** Promotes the wireless infrastructure, tower and siting industry through advocacy, education, programs, a trade show and other marketplace initiatives. **Libraries: Type:** reference. **Holdings:** books, papers, periodicals, reports. **Subjects:** personal communications services. **Awards:** Eugene C. Bowler Award. **Frequency:** annual. **Type:** recognition ● Eugene C. Bowler Scholarship. **Frequency:** annual. **Type:** scholarship. **Recipient:** for students in telecommunications field at Boston University Law School ● PCIA Industry Awards. **Frequency:** annual. **Type:** recognition. **Recipient:** for outstanding contributions to the development and advancement of the industry ● PCIA Marketing Awards. **Frequency:** annual. **Type:** recognition. **Recipient:** for outstanding achievements in the marketing of mobile communications products and services. **Computer Services:** Mailing lists. **Committees:** Advocacy; Interconnection; Legislative and Regulatory; Paging Technical; PCS Legislative and Regulatory; PCS Marketing and Consumer Affairs; PCS Technical and Engineering; Program and Education. **Formed by Merger of:** (1999) National Association of Business and Educational Radio and Association of Communications Technicians. **Formerly:** Telocator, The Personal Communications Industry; (1977) National Association of Radio Telephone Systems; (1988) Telocator Network of America; (1994) National Mobile Radio System; (2003) Personal Communications Industry Association. **Publications:** *PCIA Global Wireless Portfolio*, annual. Book. **Price:** $250.00 plus shipping and handling ● *PCIA Zoning Field Guide: Information and Resources for Tower Siting*. Book. **Price:** $99.00. Alternate Formats: online ● Brochure. Alternate Formats: online. **Conventions/Meetings:** Hot Topic Seminar Series - 3-4/year ● annual PCIA Wireless Infrastructure Conference and Expo - trade show (exhibits).

3753 ■ Radio Technical Commission for Maritime Services (RTCM)
1800 N Kent St., Ste.1060
Arlington, VA 22209-2109
Ph: (703)527-2000 (703)283-2266
Fax: (703)351-9932
E-mail: information@rtcm.org
URL: http://www.rtcm.org
Contact: R.L. Markle, Pres.
Founded: 1947. **Members:** 140. **Membership Dues:** regular, $960 (annual). **Staff:** 2. **Budget:** $200,000. **Multinational. Description:** International organization involved with maritime telecommunications including inland and high seas shipping lines, equipment manufacturers, electronic sales and services companies and other service providers, common carriers, recreational boating and professional maritime associations, maritime labor unions and publications, offshore industries, and educational organizations. Aims to advance the technical quality and professional application of maritime telecommunications for the benefit of all concerned. Facilitates development and exchange of information on a national and international basis between governments, private industry, and the public; analyzes maritime telecommunications practices; makes recommendations and advises national and international governmental agencies. Formed originally as a government/industry organization under the auspices of the U.S. State Department. **Telecommunication Services:** electronic mail, membership@rtcm.org. **Committees:** Special Committee 104: Differential Global Navigation Satellite Systems; Special Committee 109: Electronic Charts; Special Committee 119: Maritime Survivor Locating Devices; Special Committee 110: Emergency Beacons. **Formerly:** (1947) RTCM; (1982) Radio Technical Commission for Marine Service. **Publications:** *Reports and Standards*, periodic ● *Symposium Papers*, annual ● Also publishes recommended standards. **Conventions/Meetings:** annual meeting and conference, covers current developments in marine radio communications and electronic navigation (exhibits).

3754 ■ Satellite Broadcasting and Communications Association (SBCA)
1730 M St. NW, Ste.600
Washington, DC 20036
Ph: (202)349-3620
Free: (800)541-5981
Fax: (202)349-3621
E-mail: info@sbca.org
URL: http://www.sbca.com
Contact: Patricia A. Sumler, Exec. Dir.
Founded: 1986. **Members:** 1,100. **Membership Dues:** satellite provider (executive), $7,500 (annual) ● satellite provider (affiliate), $100,000 (annual) ● installation provider, manufacturer, $1,000 (annual) ● broadband provider, $2,500 (annual) ● distributor, $3,000 (annual) ● technical school, $1,000-$5,000 (annual) ● retailer, $320 (annual) ● programmer, $10,000 (annual) ● professional associate, $500 (annual). **Staff:** 26. **Budget:** $5,800,000. **Description:** Represents all segments of the home satellite industry and is committed to expanding the utilization of satellite technology for the broadcast delivery of entertainment, news, information, and educational programming. Works with the Federal Communications Commission, Congress, and the White House to ensure private earth station development. Conducts educational and research programs. Maintains speakers' bureau; compiles statistics. **Awards:** Arthur C. Clarke Award. **Frequency:** annual. **Type:** recognition ● Chairman's Award. **Frequency:** annual. **Type:** recognition ● Retailer of the Year Award. **Frequency:** annual. **Type:** recognition. **Computer Services:** Mailing lists. **Committees:** Government Affairs and Public Policy; Information and Education; Marketing; Public Affairs; Technical. **Divisions:** DBS Service Providers; Equipment Manufacturers; Programmers; Retail/Distributor; Satellite System Operators. **Formed by Merger of:** (1993) Direct Broadcast Satellite Association; Satellite Television Industry Association. **Conventions/Meetings:** annual Satellite Show - trade show (exhibits).

3755 ■ Society of Satellite Professionals International (SSPI)
The New York Info. Tech. Center
55 Broad St., 14th Fl.
New York, NY 10004
Ph: (212)809-5199
Fax: (212)825-0075
E-mail: rbell@sspi.org
URL: http://www.sspi.org
Contact: Robert Bell, Exec. Dir.
Founded: 1983. **Members:** 1,000. **Membership Dues:** professional, $100 (annual) ● emerging markets professional, $50 (annual). **Staff:** 2. **Budget:** $200,000. **Regional Groups:** 9. **State Groups:** 8. **Multinational. Description:** Professional membership organization for individuals in the satellite industry, with emphasis on communication satellite construction, launch, and services. Creates opportunities for member education and interaction, while honoring achievements and recognizing potential. Has chapters in the Mid-Atlantic, Northeast, Upper Midwest, Southern California, Canada, United Kingdom, and Tokyo. **Awards: Type:** scholarship. **Committees:** Awards; Human Resources; Scholarship; Sponsorship. **Councils:** Academic. **Formerly:** (1989) Society of Satellite Professionals. **Publications:** *ORBITER*, bimonthly. Newsletter. Provides information on the industry. **Price:** available to members only. **Circulation:** 1,000. **Advertising:** accepted ● *Society of Satellite Professionals International-Membership Directory*, annual. **Price:** included in membership dues. **Conventions/Meetings:** annual meeting.

3756 ■ Society of Telecommunications Consultants (STC)
PO Box 70
Old Station, CA 96071-0070
Ph: (530)335-7313
Free: (800)STC-7670
Fax: (530)335-7360
E-mail: stchdq@stcconsultants.org
URL: http://www.stcconsultants.org
Contact: Byron Battles, Pres.
Founded: 1976. **Members:** 275. **Membership Dues:** consultant/associate, $450 (annual) ● affiliate, $325 (annual) ● vendor, $850 (annual) ● student, $50 (annual). **Staff:** 3. **Description:** Telecommunications consultants. Purposes are to: promote telecommunications consulting as a recognized profession; uphold high ethical and professional standards; foster a better understanding of the role, function, and contribution of telecommunications consultants. Cooperates with other industrial, technical, educational, professional, and governmental bodies on matters of mutual interest and concern. Promotes high level skills and technological advances; cooperates with educational institutions in the development of telecommunications curricula. Promotes the continuing education of telecommunication consultants through semi-annual conferences and electronic and print media. **Awards:** STC Memorial Scholarship. **Frequency:** annual. **Type:** scholarship. **Computer Services:** database. **Committees:** Conference Planning; Education; Membership; Membership Benefits; Public Relations; Special Projects. **Councils:** Vendor Advisory. **Publications:** *Membership Roster*, semiannual. Directory ● *STC Consultant Directory*, daily. Profiles areas of individual consultant expertise. **Price:** $250.00 hard copy and diskette; $225.00 hard copy only ● *STC Lines*, quarterly. Newsletter. Contains general information for telecommunications consultants. Includes STC news and consultant profile. **Price:** free. **Circulation:** 600. Alternate Formats: online. **Conventions/Meetings:** semiannual conference (exhibits).

3757 ■ Society of Wireless Pioneers (SOWP)
PO Box 86
Geyserville, CA 95441-0086
E-mail: k6dzy@sonic.net
URL: http://www.sowp.org
Contact: Waldo T. Boyd, Exec. Sec.
Founded: 1968. **Members:** 5,700. **Membership Dues:** individual, $15 (annual). **Staff:** 3. **Local Groups:** 4. **Description:** Individuals who have earned their living as professional wireless/radio telegraphers; persons who have contributed to the growth and efficacy of wireless; government and military personnel; teachers and other professionals are technical associates. Promotes continued use of Morse Code as an emergency means of communication. Preserves and records the history of wireless telegraphy, especially with regard to marine communication. Maintains museum of early communication memorabilia and equipment and hall of fame to honor those who have lost their lives at sea in the line of duty. Compiles personal accounts of ship-

wrecks and aircraft disasters where wireless/radio was involved. **Libraries: Type:** open to the public. **Holdings:** 3,000. **Subjects:** wireless. **Awards:** SOS Certificate of Participation. **Type:** recognition. **Recipient:** for persons who have performed outstanding service in the communications field and to those historic men who have stuck to their key in time of disaster, and whose SOS calls sent under great stress have resulted in saving lives and property. **Committees:** Curator; Historian; Roundup. **Formerly:** American Society of Wireless Pioneers of the Seven Seas; Society of Professional Wireless Pioneers. **Publications:** *The Wireless Almanac*. Book. **Price:** $14.50 ● *The Wireless Register*, quinquennial. Membership Directory ● *The World Wireless Beacon*, quarterly. Bulletin. Includes news, articles, and member letters. **Price:** included in membership dues. **Circulation:** 1,500 ● Also publishes special information bulletins. **Conventions/Meetings:** weekly Amateur Radio Net - meeting, on the air using Morse Code ● periodic meeting, via Internet chat room, keyboard or voice.

3758 ■ Telecommunications Benchmarking International Group (TBIG)
4606 FM 1960 W, Ste.250
Houston, TX 77069
Ph: (281)440-5044
Fax: (281)440-6677
URL: http://www.tbig.org
Contact: Mark T. Czarnecki MBA, Pres.
Founded: 1995. **Members:** 3,500. **Staff:** 14. **Budget:** $2,000,000. **Description:** Works to identify the business processes to assist members in delivering excellent services to their customers. Supports the use of benchmarking; collects data; provides networking opportunities. Members must produce and/or distribute telecommunication services. **Publications:** Newsletter. **Conventions/Meetings:** annual meeting.

3759 ■ Telecommunications Industry Association (TIA)
2500 Wilson Blvd., Ste.300
Arlington, VA 22201-3834
Ph: (703)907-7700 (703)907-7701
Fax: (703)907-7727
E-mail: gseiffert@tiaonline.org
URL: http://www.tiaonline.org
Contact: Grant Seiffert, Pres.
Founded: 1988. **Members:** 700. **Membership Dues:** general, $1,200-$72,000 (annual) ● associate, foreign agent/distributor, $1,200-$6,000 (annual). **Staff:** 100. **Description:** Serves the communications and IT industry, with proven strengths in standards development, domestic and international public policy, and trade shows. Facilitates business development and opportunities and a competitive market environment; provides a forum for member companies, the manufacturers and suppliers of products and services used in global communications. Represents the communications sector of the Electronic Industries Alliance. **Computer Services:** database ● mailing lists. **Telecommunication Services:** electronic mail, mflanigan@tiaonline.org. **Committees:** Grassroots Action; International Affairs; Public Policy; Small Business Development. **Divisions:** Fiber Optic; Satellite; User Premises Equipment; Wireless. **Affiliated With:** Electronic Industries Alliance. **Formed by Merger of:** U.S. Telecommunications Suppliers Association; Information and Telecommunications Technologies Group of Electronic Industries Association. **Publications:** *Channel Intelligence Report*. Newsletter. Alternate Formats: online ● *Industry Beat*, weekly. Bulletin. Provides an online bulletin to the membership. **Price:** included in membership dues. Alternate Formats: online ● *Market Development White Papers*. **Price:** free ● *PulseOnline*, monthly. Newsletter. Contains statistics, calendar of events, listing of new members, and legislative and regulatory updates. **Price:** included in membership dues. **Circulation:** 8,005. Alternate Formats: online ● *Telecommunications Market Review and Forecast*, annual. Report. **Price:** $650.00 for members, hard copy; $1,495.00 for nonmembers, hard copy; $950.00 for members, PDF on CD; $1,795.00 for nonmembers, PDF on CD. Alternate Formats: CD-ROM; online ● *TIA's TechTrends*. Newsletter. Alternate Formats: online ● *World Network Equipment Industry Recovery Survey*. **Price:** $495.00 for members; $595.00 for nonmembers ● Annual Report, annual. Alternate Formats: online. **Conventions/Meetings:** annual NX-Tcomm - trade show (exhibits).

3760 ■ Telecommunications Industry Forum (TCIF)
c/o Alliance for Telecommunications Industry Solutions
1200 G St. NW, Ste.500
Washington, DC 20005
Ph: (202)628-6380
Fax: (202)393-5453
E-mail: smiller@atis.org
URL: http://www.atis.org/index.shtml
Contact: Susan Miller, Pres./CEO
Founded: 1986. **Members:** 60. **Description:** A committee of the Alliance for Telecommunications Industry Solutions. Purchasers, manufacturers, and suppliers of telecommunications equipment, products, and services. Works to develop guidelines for use by the telecommunications industry that facilitate effective information exchange among trading partners. Reviews and analyzes standards, reports, and other materials. Develops positions on existing standards and subjects under consideration in national and international standards bodies. Advises members of industry developments. **Committees:** Bar-Code/Standard Coding; Electronic Communications Interchange; Electronic Data Interchange; Information Products Interchange. **Publications:** *Preliminary Guideline No. 4, Product Change Notices, Engineering Complaints*. **Price:** $60.00/copy. Alternate Formats: online ● *Preliminary Guideline No. 3, Quality Assurance Reporting*. **Price:** $64.00/copy ● *Preliminary Guideline No. 2, Service Request Applications*. **Price:** $110.00/copy. **Conventions/Meetings:** semiannual convention.

3761 ■ Telecommunications Risk Management Association (TRMA)
4 Becker Farm Rd.
Roseland, NJ 07068
Ph: (973)871-4080
Fax: (973)871-4075
E-mail: info@trmanet.org
URL: http://www.trmanet.org
Contact: Roberta Aronoff, Exec. Dir.
Founded: 1997. **Members:** 302. **Membership Dues:** vendor affiliate, $8,000 (annual) ● regular, $1,200-$8,000 (annual). **Staff:** 3. **Budget:** $500,000. **Description:** Telecommunications carriers. Brings professionals together to reduce fraud and debt related to credit and collection risk management. **Libraries: Type:** not open to the public. **Subjects:** telecommunications, credit and collection, risk management. **Special Interest Groups:** Fraud and ID Theft. **Conventions/Meetings:** conference - 3/year - February, June, October.

3762 ■ United Telecom Council (UTC)
1901 Pennsylvania Ave. NW, 5th Fl.
Washington, DC 20006-3405
Ph: (202)872-0030
Fax: (202)872-1331
E-mail: utcadmin@utc.org
URL: http://www.utc.org
Contact: William R. Moroney, Pres./CEO
Founded: 1948. **Members:** 750. **Membership Dues:** associate (minimum; based on annual revenue), $850 (annual) ● core (minimum; based on annual revenue), $365 (annual) ● associate (maximum; based on annual revenue), $11,500 (annual) ● core (maximum; based on annual revenue), $21,300 (annual). **Staff:** 17. **Regional Groups:** 10. **Multinational. Description:** Represents the telecommunications and information technology interests of electric, gas and water utilities, energy companies, natural gas pipelines and other critical infrastructure companies and their strategic business partners. **Libraries: Type:** reference. **Holdings:** papers. **Subjects:** technical. **Awards:** Dondonville Award. **Frequency:** annual. **Type:** recognition. **Recipient:** to member who exhibits active and effective participation. **Computer Services:** database, power line carrier ● mailing lists, for newsletters subscription. **Committees:** Automation Technology; Fiber Communications; Forward Planning; Frequency Coordination; Information Technology; Member Services; Wireless. **Divisions:** Business Developments; International; Public Policy; Support Services; Technical. **Sections:** Finance; Rural Users Forum; Wireline. **Formerly:** (1962) National Committee for Utilities Radio; (1994) Utilities Telecommunications Council. **Publications:** *Information Bulletin: Legislative Update*, monthly. Newsletter ● *UTC Alert*, weekly. Bulletin. Contains news and information about the members. Alternate Formats: online ● *UTC Industry Intelligence*. Newsletter. Alternate Formats: online ● *UTC Journal*, quarterly. **Conventions/Meetings:** annual conference (exhibits) ● annual regional meeting (exhibits) - always fall ● annual workshop and seminar.

3763 ■ Veteran Wireless Operators Association (VWOA)
PO Box 1003
Peck Slip
New York, NY 10272-1003
E-mail: wenben@nyc.rr.com
URL: http://www.vwoa.org
Contact: Alan Ehrlich, Pres.
Founded: 1925. **Members:** 300. **Membership Dues:** individual, $10 (annual) ● individual, $25 (triennial). **Description:** Individuals in the radio-telegraph and radio-telephone commercial communications field. Maintains Wireless Operators Monument. **Libraries: Type:** reference. **Holdings:** books. **Awards:** David Kintzer Memorial Award Plaque. **Frequency:** annual. **Type:** recognition. **Recipient:** to individuals for outstanding service to the organization ● DeForest Audion Gold Medal Award. **Frequency:** annual. **Type:** medal. **Recipient:** to individuals for significant contributions to the world of technology ● DeForest Audion Gold Medal of Dedication. **Frequency:** annual. **Type:** medal. **Recipient:** to individuals for significant contributions to the organization. **Committees:** Amateur Net; Battery Park, New York City; Memorial-Monument. **Publications:** *Veteran Wireless Operators Association—Annual Yearbook* ● Newsletter, quarterly ● Bulletin, quarterly. Contains information about historical as well as current radio communications. **Conventions/Meetings:** annual banquet.

3764 ■ Wireless Communications Association International (WCA)
1333 H St. NW, Ste.700 W
Washington, DC 20005-4754
Ph: (202)452-7823
Fax: (202)452-0041
E-mail: president@wcai.com
URL: http://www.wcai.com
Contact: Andrew Kreig, Pres.
Founded: 1988. **Members:** 500. **Membership Dues:** affiliate, $400-$450 (annual) ● supplier, financial/professional consultant, $1,200-$5,000 (annual) ● licensee, $650 (annual). **Staff:** 10. **Budget:** $2,400,000. **Languages:** English, French, German, Spanish. **Description:** Represents the wireless broadband industry. Membership includes the wireless broadband industry's leading carriers, vendors, and consultants. Seeks to advance the interests of the wireless carriers that provide high-speed data, Internet, voice and video services on broadband spectrum through land-based towers to fixed reception/transmit devices in all broadband spectrum bands. Advocates for issues vital to the industry including auction rules, regulatory filings for flexible use, technical standards, protection against interference, and pro-competitive rules for inside wiring, roof rights, and interconnection. Organizes semi-annual business conferences and exhibitions devoted exclusively to fixed wireless broadband access, which includes data, voice, and video communications experts from around the world who discuss market strategies, emerging technologies, new applications, and financing and regulatory options. **Libraries: Type:** by appointment only. **Holdings:** 5,000; books, periodicals. **Subjects:** communications, telecommunications. **Awards:** Wemmies and Golden Eagles.

Frequency: annual. **Type:** recognition. **Computer Services:** database ● mailing lists ● online services. **Committees:** Engineering; Government Relations; License Exempt; Nominations and Elections. **Task Forces:** Fixed Wireless Millimeter Wave Alliance. **Absorbed:** (1986) MDS Industry Association. **Formerly:** (1987) Microwave Communications Association. **Publications:** *Member Bulletin*, weekly. Newsletter. Reports on current events in the wireless communications industry. **Price:** available to members only. **Circulation:** 3,000. **Conventions/Meetings:** annual conference (exhibits) ● annual Global Symposium and Business Expo - conference (exhibits).

3765 ■ Wireless Dealers Association (WDA)
9746 Tappenbeck Dr.
Houston, TX 77055-4102
Ph: (713)467-0077
Free: (800)624-6918
E-mail: topbox@wirelessindustry.com
URL: http://www.wirelessdealers.com
Contact: Bob Hutchinson, Pres.
Founded: 1987. **Description:** Individuals involved in the cellular mobile telephone industry including agents, carriers, dealers, distributors, manufacturers, and consultants. Works to: foster members' financial and professional success in the cellular industry; make available skills improvement and educational materials necessary for professional growth; develop a more professional structure conducive to career success. Promotes benefits of cellular telephones and services to current and prospective cellular users. Conducts marketing and sales training seminars. Offers customized primary training materials. **Formerly:** (1997) National Association of Cellular Agents. **Publications:** *Cellular Agent*, bimonthly. Newsletter. **Price:** included in membership dues. **Circulation:** 3,000 ● *NACA Agent/Reseller Bulletin*, quarterly ● *Paging Reseller Profits Manual*. **Conventions/Meetings:** annual meeting.

3766 ■ World Teleport Association (WTA)
55 Broad St., 14th Fl.
New York, NY 10004
Ph: (212)825-0218
Fax: (212)825-0075
E-mail: wta@worldteleport.org
URL: http://www.worldteleport.org
Contact: Robert Bell, Exec. Dir.
Founded: 1985. **Members:** 125. **Membership Dues:** government, $700 (annual) ● company, $850-$3,250 (annual) ● industry patron, $8,000 (annual) ● industry leader, $17,000 (annual). **Staff:** 5. **Budget:** $400,000. **Regional Groups:** 3. **Languages:** English, German. **Multinational. Description:** Works to benefit members in two ways: by expanding markets through activities that promote the understanding, use and development of teleports; and by helping members meet their business development or economic development goals. **Libraries: Type:** not open to the public. **Holdings:** audiovisuals, books, periodicals. **Subjects:** teleports. **Awards:** Intelligent Community Awards. **Frequency:** annual. **Type:** recognition. **Recipient:** for outstanding examples of teleport development and operation, executive leadership, intelligent cities and intelligent buildings ● Teleport Awards for Excellence. **Frequency:** annual. **Type:** recognition. **Recipient:** for outstanding examples of teleport development and operation, executive leadership, intelligent cities and intelligent buildings. **Publications:** *Business Development News*, bimonthly. Newsletter. Contains information on business opportunities in the teleport industry. ● *Update*, quarterly. Newsletter. **Conventions/Meetings:** annual general assembly and workshop, with plenary sessions and tours of teleports (exhibits).

Telephone Service

3767 ■ International Prepaid Communications Association
Address Unknown since 2007
Founded: 1995. **Members:** 240. **Staff:** 3. **Budget:** $500,000. **Description:** Works to promote and protect the prepaid telecom industry. Educates consumers regarding pre-paid phone cards and prepaid wireless. Protects consumers from phone card fraud. **Awards:** Prepaid Communications of the Year. **Frequency:** annual. **Type:** recognition. **Formerly:** (2001) International Telecard Association.

Textiles

3768 ■ Acrylic Council
1285 Ave. of the Americas, 35th Fl.
New York, NY 10019
Ph: (212)554-4040
Fax: (212)554-4042
Contact: Lynn Misiak, Exec.Dir.
Founded: 1988. **Members:** 13. **Staff:** 1. **Budget:** $1,000,000. **Description:** Acrylic fiber producers, yarn spinners, and ingredient suppliers. Seeks to promote awareness and increased use of acrylic fiber and yarn. Conducts educational and research programs. **Awards:** Excellence in Acrylic. **Frequency:** annual. **Type:** recognition. **Computer Services:** Mailing lists, of members. **Publications:** *Accent on Acrylic*, quarterly. Newsletter ● *If You Wear Clothes Take This Test*. Brochure ● *What Do Professional Feet Know?*. Brochure.

3769 ■ American Fiber Manufacturers Association (AFMA)
1530 Wilson Blvd., Ste.690
Arlington, VA 22209
Ph: (703)875-0432
Fax: (703)875-0907
E-mail: afma@afma.org
URL: http://www.fibersource.com
Contact: Ms. Gina Stewart, Corporate Sec./Office Mgr.
Founded: 1933. **Members:** 34. **Staff:** 7. **Description:** Producers of manufactured fibers used in apparel, household goods, industrial materials, and other types of products. Represents the industry in educational, governmental, and foreign trade matters. Distributes a video depicting production and end uses of manufactured fibers. **Committees:** Legislative; Technical; Trade and Statistics. **Publications:** *Manufactured Fiber Fact Book* ● *Manufactured Fiber Guide*, periodic. Also Cited As: *Man-Made Fiber Guide*. **Conventions/Meetings:** annual meeting.

3770 ■ American Flock Association (AFA)
6 Beacon St., Ste.1125
Boston, MA 02108
Ph: (617)303-6288
Fax: (617)542-2199
E-mail: info@flocking.org
URL: http://www.flocking.org
Contact: Thomas Witham, Chm.
Founded: 1985. **Members:** 65. **Staff:** 2. **Budget:** $100,000. **Description:** Manufacturers, suppliers, and users of flocked products; consultants to the flocking industry. (Flocked products are made from very short or pulverized fibers which, when attached to cloth or paper, form a velvet-like surface and are used in the textile, furniture, and packaging industries, as well as for protective coatings for metal and plastic.) Aims to foster the use of flocked products. Strives to improve the flocking industry and to advance flocking technology. Represents interests of members in economic, legal, technical, and scientific affairs. Serves as a forum for the exchange of information. Conducts educational and research programs; maintains speakers' bureau and museum. **Telecommunication Services:** electronic mail, jcarmel@flocking.org. **Affiliated With:** National Textile Association. **Publications:** *AFA Directory*, biennial. Lists members and services. **Price:** free. **Advertising:** accepted ● *Design with Flock in Mind*. Brochure. Covers the flocking process. **Conventions/Meetings:** annual convention (exhibits) - always fall.

3771 ■ American Reusable Textile Association (ARTA)
PO Box 1053
Mulberry, FL 33860-1053
Ph: (863)660-5350
E-mail: njenkins@arta1.com
URL: http://www.arta1.com
Contact: Nancy Jenkins, Exec. Dir.
Founded: 1982. **Members:** 70. **Membership Dues:** general, $650 (annual). **Staff:** 1. **Budget:** $35,000. **Description:** Fiber producers and mills; textile fabricators, distributors and processors; manufacturers of laundry equipment, chemicals and supplies. Protects and promotes members' interests by convincing consumers, especially hospitals and industrial users, that reusable textiles cost less per use, are safer and environmental friendly. **Committees:** Political Action; Public Relations; Research. **Publications:** *The Responsible Choice*, periodic. Brochures. **Price:** $1.00 for nonmembers. **Circulation:** 20,000 ● *Reusable Textiles - A Prescription for Change*. Brochure. Alternate Formats: online. **Conventions/Meetings:** conference - 3/year.

3772 ■ American Textile Manufacturers Institute (ATMI)
1130 Connecticut Ave. NW
Washington, DC 20036-3954
Ph: (202)862-0500
Fax: (202)862-0570
E-mail: info@textileweb.com
URL: http://www.textileweb.com/storefronts/amertextile.html
Contact: James W. Chesnutt, Chm.
Founded: 1949. **Staff:** 30. **Description:** Textile mill firms operating machinery for manufacturing and processing cotton, man-made, wool, and silk textile products; includes spinning, weaving, bleaching, finishing, knitting, and allied plants; does not include manufacturers of hosiery or firms that produce man-made fibers and yarn by a chemical process. Operates public relations program for the industry, government relations program, textile market program, and statistical and economic information service. Holds seminars and meetings. Sponsors safety contest among textile mills. **Libraries: Type:** reference. **Holdings:** 1,200. **Computer Services:** database, textile, apparel, import, export. **Committees:** Carpet; Communications; Consumer Affairs; Cotton; Economic Affairs; Environmental Preservation; Finishers; International Trade; Safety and Health; Textile Market; Upholstery Fabrics; Wool. **Divisions:** Economic Information; Government Relations; Market. **Absorbed:** (1958) National Federation of Textiles; (1964) Association of Cotton Textile Merchants of New York; (1965) National Association of Finishers of Textile Fabrics; (1969) Textile Data Processing Association; (1971) National Association of Wool Manufacturers. **Formed by Merger of:** American Cotton Manufacturers Association; Cotton Textile Institute. **Formerly:** (1962) American Cotton Manufacturers Institute. **Publications:** *ATMI Member Product Directory*, periodic. Contains information about textile products made in the U.S. by ATMI member companies. **Price:** $8.00/copy ● *Official Directory*, annual ● *Textile Hi-Lights*, quarterly. Includes monthly supplements. ● *Textile Trends*, weekly ● Annual Report, annual ● Bulletin, periodic. **Conventions/Meetings:** annual meeting.

3773 ■ American Wool Council (AWC)
c/o American Sheep Industry Association
9785 Maroon Cir., Ste.360
Englewood, CO 80112
Ph: (303)771-3500
Fax: (303)771-8200
E-mail: info@sheepusa.org
URL: http://www.sheepusa.org
Contact: Jim Bristol, Chm.
Founded: 1980. **Description:** A division of the American Sheep Industry Association. Promotes the use of wool and wool products. **Affiliated With:** American Sheep Industry Association.

3774 ■ American Yarn Spinners Association (AYSA)
2500 Lowell Rd.
Gastonia, NC 28053
Ph: (704)824-3522

Fax: (704)824-0630
URL: http://www.textileweb.com/storefronts/aysa.html
Contact: Michael S. Hubbard, Exec. VP
Founded: 1967. **Members:** 120. **Staff:** 4. **Description:** Manufacturers of combed cotton sales yarn and carded yarns spun from cotton, wool, and/or synthetics. Provides full service to the sales yarn industry. **Affiliated With:** Craft Yarn Council of America; Southern Textile Association; Synthetic Yarn and Fiber Association. **Absorbed:** (1974) Long Staple Yarn Association; (1976) Yarn Dyers Association; (1982) Carpet Yarn Association; (1988) Association of Synthetic Yarn Manufacturers. **Formed by Merger of:** Combed Yarn Spinners Association; Carded Yarn Association. **Publications:** *American Yarn Directory* ● Newsletter, monthly. **Conventions/Meetings:** annual convention.

3775 ■ Association for Contract Textiles (ACT)
PO Box 101981
Fort Worth, TX 76185
Ph: (817)924-8048
Fax: (817)924-8050
E-mail: janan@contracttextiles.org
URL: http://www.contracttextiles.org
Contact: Janan Rabiah, Exec. Dir.
Founded: 1985. **Description:** Promotes the design, manufacture and sale of textiles used or associated with commercial interior furnishings. **Awards:** ACT Scholarship. **Type:** scholarship. **Publications:** Membership Directory. **Conventions/Meetings:** annual Scholarship Quilt Auction - meeting.

3776 ■ Association of Yarn Distributors (AYD)
Address Unknown since 2007
URL: http://www.knowships.org
Founded: 1915. **Members:** 50. **Description:** Brokers, agents, and representatives of processors, spinners, and dyers of yarns. **Formerly:** Association of Cotton Yarn Distributors. **Conventions/Meetings:** annual meeting - usually October, New York City ● biennial meeting - usually April, New York City.

3777 ■ Boston Wool Trade Association (BWTA)
Address Unknown since 2007
Founded: 1911. **Members:** 130. **Staff:** 1. **Description:** Wool dealers, brokers, and topmakers. **Committees:** Arbitration; Domestic Wool; Imports; Technical; Transportation; Waste; Wool Trade Relief Fund. **Conventions/Meetings:** annual meeting and luncheon - always November, Boston, MA.

3778 ■ Burlap and Jute Association (BJA)
c/o Susan Spiegel
PO Box 8
Dayton, OH 45401
Ph: (937)258-8000
Free: (800)543-3400
Fax: (937)258-0029
Contact: Susan Spiegel, Contact
Founded: 1923. **Members:** 8. **Membership Dues:** individual, $250 (annual). **Staff:** 1. **Budget:** $5,000. **Description:** Represents U.S. importers, brokers, and agents of burlap and jute products and raw jute. **Committees:** Arbitration. **Affiliated With:** Jute Carpet Backing Council and Burlap and Jute Association; Textile Bag and Packaging Association. **Publications:** *Grabbag*, 3/year. Newsletter. **Advertising:** accepted. **Conventions/Meetings:** semiannual meeting (exhibits).

3779 ■ Cashmere and Camel Hair Manufacturers Institute (CCMI)
6 Beacon St., Ste.1125
Boston, MA 02108
Ph: (617)542-7481
Fax: (617)542-2199
E-mail: info@cashmere.org
URL: http://www.cashmere.org
Contact: Karl H. Spilhaus, Pres.
Founded: 1984. **Members:** 15. **Languages:** English, German, Italian. **Description:** Promotes the use of cashmere and camel hair products. **Libraries: Type:** not open to the public.

3780 ■ Elastic Fabric Manufacturers Council of the National Textile Association (EFMC)
6 Beacon St., Ste.1125
Boston, MA 02108
Ph: (617)542-8220
Fax: (617)542-2199
E-mail: info@nationaltextile.org
URL: http://www.nationaltextile.org
Contact: Karl Spilhaus, Pres.
Founded: 1915. **Members:** 12. **Staff:** 4. **Description:** A council of the Northern Textile Association (see separate entry). Provides exchange and management services, trade promotion, statistical programs, and informative bulletins. **Divisions:** Elastic Braid; Warp Knit; Woven Elastic. **Affiliated With:** National Textile Association. **Absorbed:** American Power Net Association; Braided Trimming Manufacturers Association; Elastic Braid Manufacturers Association; Woven Elastic Manufacturers Association. **Formerly:** (1970) Elastic Fabric Manufacturers Institute; (1999) Elastic Fabric Manufacturers Association of the Northern Textile Association; (2004) Elastric Fabric Manufacturers Council of the National Textile Association. **Conventions/Meetings:** annual meeting.

3781 ■ Embroidery Trade Association (ETA)
12300 Ford Rd., Ste.135
Dallas, TX 75234
Free: (888)628-2545
Fax: (972)755-2561
E-mail: info@embroiderytrade.org
URL: http://www.embroiderytrade.org
Contact: John Swinburn CAE, Exec. Dir.
Founded: 1990. **Members:** 1,200. **Membership Dues:** corporate (based on annual sales), $195-$315 ● pro-plus (digitizer), $315 ● new special, $329. **Staff:** 5. **Budget:** $250,000. **For-Profit. Description:** Commercial embroidery professionals; manufacturers, marketers, and interested others. Promotes communication among members; assists those who are new to the industry. Conducts research and educational programs; operates speakers' bureau. Offers purchasing programs. Conducts educational seminars and training in embroidery and digitizing. **Publications:** *ETA Member Minute*, weekly. Newsletter. Features tips, marketing concepts, business operations recommendations, etc. **Price:** free. **Circulation:** 1,200. **Advertising:** accepted. Alternate Formats: online. **Conventions/Meetings:** annual Embroidery Lab - conference, industry techniques on sourcing, digitizing, embroidery, business/marketing, machine maintenance, educating the industry with hands-on user sessions (exhibits).

3782 ■ Fabric Salesmen's Association (FSA)
Address Unknown since 2007
Founded: 1982. **Members:** 375. **Description:** Persons who have worked in the apparel and textile industry for one year or more, particularly salesmen. Provides information and health and unemployment benefits; serves as sounding board for complaints and problems. Membership currently concentrated in New York City area. **Awards: Frequency:** annual. **Type:** recognition. **Recipient:** for one person in textiles ● **Frequency:** annual. **Type:** recognition. **Recipient:** for one person in fashion. **Formed by Merger of:** Fabric Salesmen's Guild; Piece Goods Salesmen's Association. **Publications:** Journal, annual. **Conventions/Meetings:** annual meeting.

3783 ■ Hemp Industries Association (HIA)
PO Box 1571
Brattleboro, VT 05302
Ph: (707)874-3648
Fax: (707)874-3648
E-mail: info@thehia.org
URL: http://www.testpledge.com
Contact: Eric Steenstra, Exec. Dir.
Founded: 1992. **Members:** 300. **Membership Dues:** full (with $100000 or less annual revenue), $200 (annual) ● supporting, $35 (annual) ● full (with less than $50000 annual revenue), $100 (annual) ● full (with $250000 or less annual revenue), $300 (annual) ● full (with above $250000 annual revenue), $400 (annual). **Staff:** 10. **Multinational. Description:** Companies trading in legal hemp products, including textiles, food, body care, paper, building materials, and seed oil products. Seeks "to expand the existing markets and to protect the reputation of the hemp industries." Facilitates the association's lobbying and voter outreach. **Awards:** Honorary Membership Award. **Frequency:** annual. **Type:** monetary. **Recipient:** for service to the industry. **Additional Websites:** http://www.thehia.org, http://www.HempStores.com, http://www.votehemp.com. **Councils:** Food and Oil; International; Public Policy; Resolution; Retail; Textiles. **Publications:** *HIA Hemp News*, quarterly. Newsletter. **Price:** included in membership dues. **Circulation:** 300. Alternate Formats: online ● *Journal of Industrial Hemp*. Contains information on agronomy, taxonomy, breeding, crop physiology, and modeling. **Price:** $40.80 for members. **Conventions/Meetings:** periodic board meeting ● annual convention and seminar, with networking activities, hemp foods (exhibits).

3784 ■ Home Sewing Association (HSA)
PO Box 1312
Monroeville, PA 15146
Ph: (412)372-5950
Fax: (412)372-5953
E-mail: info@sewing.org
URL: http://www.sewing.org
Contact: Joyce Perhac, Exec. Dir.
Founded: 1978. **Members:** 800. **Membership Dues:** associate/retailer, $250 (annual) ● supplier (based on sales volume), $750-$5,400 (annual) ● educator, $50 (annual). **Staff:** 3. **Budget:** $975,000. **Description:** Manufacturers and retailers of home sewing merchandise, including fabrics, patterns, sewing machines, sewing notions, needlework, and crafts. **Libraries: Type:** reference. **Holdings:** 400; books, periodicals. **Subjects:** home sewing, crafts, quilting. **Committees:** Consumer Education; Membership; Public Relations; Show and Convention; Strategy; Technology. **Absorbed:** (1996) International Sewing Machine Association. **Formed by Merger of:** National Home Sewing Association; American Home Sewing Council. **Formerly:** (1998) American Home Sewing and Craft Association. **Publications:** *Advertising Brochure*. Alternate Formats: online ● *Guidelines*. Papers. Contains sewing product information. **Price:** free ● *HSA Connections*, quarterly. Newsletter. Alternate Formats: online ● *Inside HSA*. Newsletter. **Price:** free for members ● Also distributes sewing month publicity kits. **Conventions/Meetings:** annual National Sewing Show - convention and trade show (exhibits).

3785 ■ INDA, Association of the Nonwoven Fabrics Industry (INDA)
PO Box 1288
Cary, NC 27512-1288
Ph: (919)233-1210
Free: (800)716-9001
Fax: (919)233-1282
E-mail: rholmes@inda.org
URL: http://www.inda.org
Contact: Rory Holmes, Pres.
Founded: 1968. **Members:** 290. **Membership Dues:** corporate (sales up to and including $4,800,000), $1,300 (annual) ● corporate (sales of $87,000,000 or greater), $23,500 (annual) ● academic, $120 (annual) ● associate consultant, $500 (annual) ● research agency, $1,000 (annual) ● association, $500 (annual). **Staff:** 20. **Budget:** $4,000,000. **Description:** Primary and secondary manufacturers and marketers of non-woven fabrics, suppliers of raw materials, institutions, and manufacturers of machinery. Funds research. **Computer Services:** Mailing lists, of members. **Committees:** Disposability; Government Relations; Health and Safety; International Trade; Marketing; Needlepunch; Standard Test Methods; Technical. **Councils:** Universities. **Formerly:** Disposables Association; (1977) International Nonwovens and Disposables Association. **Publications:** *Analysis: North American Wipes Industry 2005-2010*, triennial. Survey. Contains estimated sales and

volumes of consumer and industrial wiping segment in North America and forecasts for 2010. **Price:** $2,200.00 for members; $3,000.00 for nonmembers ● *Analysis of the Nonwoven Industry in North America*, triennial. Survey. Includes statistical report on technologies and applications of nonwoven fabrics in North America and forecasts for 2010. Alternate Formats: CD-ROM ● *Analysis of the Nonwovens Industry: Asia Pacific*, triennial. Survey. Contains estimated nonwoven fabric production and growth rates from 2004-2009. **Price:** $2,200.00 for members; $3,000.00 for nonmembers ● *e-Filter*, monthly. Newsletter. **Price:** free. Alternate Formats: online ● *INDA Newsletter*, quarterly. **Price:** free. Alternate Formats: online ● *International Nonwovens Directory*, annual. Alternate Formats: online ● *Journal of Engineered Fibers & Fabrics*, quarterly. **Price:** free. Alternate Formats: online ● *Nonwoven Fabrics Handbook*. **Price:** $65.00 for members; $85.00 for nonmembers ● *Small Business*, monthly. Newsletter. **Price:** free. Alternate Formats: online ● *Spunbond and Meltblown Technology Handbook*. **Price:** $55.00 for members; $70.00 for nonmembers ● *Vision*, monthly. Newsletter. **Price:** free. Alternate Formats: online ● *Worldwide Outlook of the Nonwovens Industry 2004-2009*, triennial. Survey. Includes worldwide production data and regional economic analyses. **Conventions/Meetings:** annual Filtration - trade show (exhibits) ● triennial IDEA - trade show ● annual International Nonwovens and Technical Conference ● annual The Link - convention (exhibits) ● quarterly Nonwovens Training Course - conference ● annual Vision - conference.

3786 ■ Independent Textile Rental Association (ITRA)
PO Box 190
Hogansville, GA 30230
Free: (800)477-7843
Fax: (706)637-8875
E-mail: info@itra.us
URL: http://www.itra.us
Contact: Ron Evans, Exec. Dir./Convention Coor.
Membership Dues: associate, $1,200 (annual) ● active (based on total number of routes for all plants), $500-$1,250 (annual). **Multinational. Description:** Promotes and develops independent textile rental operators. Seeks to create a wider recognition for independent textile rental operators. Aims to increase the efficiency of independent textile rental operators through an interchange of technical ideas and operating methods. Provides education and business solutions for its member companies and their personnel. **Publications:** *The ITRA Press*, quarterly. Newsletter. Provides information on upcoming meetings, new programs and other matters pertaining to the activities of the association. **Price:** included in membership dues. Alternate Formats: online. **Conventions/Meetings:** annual convention.

3787 ■ Industrial Fabrics Association International (IFAI)
1801 County Rd. B W
Roseville, MN 55113-4061
Ph: (651)225-2508 (651)225-6909
Free: (800)225-4324
Fax: (651)225-6966
E-mail: generalinfo@ifai.com
URL: http://www.ifai.com
Contact: Stephen M. Warner CAE, Pres.
Founded: 1912. **Members:** 2,000. **Staff:** 75. **Budget:** $9,000,000. **Description:** Fiber producers, weavers, non-woven producers, coaters, laminators, finishers, and producers and manufacturers of canvas and specialty fabric end products in more than 36 countries. Provides technical, marketing, production, governmental and public relations services. **Awards:** International Achievement Awards. **Frequency:** annual. **Type:** recognition. **Recipient:** for excellence in fabrics in 29 categories. **Telecommunication Services:** electronic mail, smwarner@ifai.com. **Divisions:** Automotive Materials Association; Banner, Flag and Graphics Association; The Casual Furniture Fabrics Association; Geosynthetic Materials Association; Inflatable Recreational Products; Lightweight Structures Association; Marine Fabricators Association; Narrow Fabrics Institute; Professional Awning Manufacturers Association; Safety and Protective Products; Tent Rental; Truck Cover and Tarp Association; United States Industrial Fabrics Institute. **Sections:** IFAI Canada; IFAI Japan. **Formerly:** (1956) National Canvas Goods Manufacturers Association; (1980) Canvas Products International. **Publications:** *Fabric Architecture*, bimonthly. Magazine. Provides design and specifying information on industrial fabrics used in architectural projects. **Price:** $39.00/year; $43.00/year in Canada and Mexico; $55.00/year in all other countries. ISSN: 1045-0483. **Circulation:** 13,000. **Advertising:** accepted ● *GFR*, 9/year. Magazine. Supports the geotextile, geomembrane, and related products industry, especially in relation to geotechnical and civil engineering. **Price:** $47.00/year; $59.00/year in Canada and Mexico; $69.00/year in all other countries. ISSN: 0882-4983. **Circulation:** 16,000. **Advertising:** accepted ● *Industrial Fabric Products Review*, monthly. Magazine. Features articles on developing technology and market trends. Contains listings of new products and publications, and calendar of events. **Price:** $52.00/year in U.S.; $65.00/year in Canada and Mexico; $131.00/year outside U.S. ISSN: 0019-8307. **Circulation:** 11,000. **Advertising:** accepted ● *Industrial Fabric Products Review Buyer's Guide*, annual. Directory. Lists companies, products, and trade names of the industrial fabrics industry. **Price:** included in membership dues; $20.00 for nonmembers. ISSN: 0019-8307. **Circulation:** 10,500. **Advertising:** accepted ● *InTents*, quarterly. Magazine. Promotes use of tents and accessories to special events and hospitality industry professionals. Covers use of tents at fairs/festivals, etc. **Price:** $31.00 in U.S.; $39.00 in Canada and Mexico; $49.00 outside U.S. **Circulation:** 15,000. **Advertising:** accepted ● *Marine Fabricator*, quarterly. Magazine. Features cut and sew techniques and technology. Photo showcases of fabricator craftsmanship and business management articles. **Price:** $31.00 in U.S.; $39.00 in Canada and Mexico; $49.00 outside U.S. ISSN: 1079-8250. **Circulation:** 5,000. **Advertising:** accepted ● *Upholstery Journal*. **Conventions/Meetings:** annual conference, features displays of fibers, fabrics, film, hardware, findings, webbing, equipment and other products related to the specialty fabrics industry (exhibits) ● biennial Geosynthetics - conference, features innovation, design trends, manufacturing, and construction in geosynthetics (exhibits).

3788 ■ Institutional and Service Textile Distributors Association (ISTDA)
1609 Connecticut Ave. NW, Ste.200
Washington, DC 20009
Ph: (202)986-0105
Fax: (202)986-0448
E-mail: istdatextiles@aol.com
URL: http://www.istdatextiles.org
Contact: Kathleen Ewing, Exec. Sec.
Founded: 1944. **Members:** 33. **Membership Dues:** $3,000 (annual). **Staff:** 2. **Budget:** $100,000. **Description:** Wholesale distributors and manufacturers of textile products to hotels, restaurants, hospitals, and similar institutions. Maintains guidelines for marking and packing institutional textile products; compiles statistics on members' sales. **Committees:** Hall of Fame Award; Standards and Guidelines. **Publications:** *Institutional and Service Textile Distributors Association-Membership Directory*, annual. Contains company name, address, shipping address, phone and fax numbers, and contact person. **Conventions/Meetings:** annual meeting, for membership - always November in New York City, NY ● annual Mill Conference - always April in New York City, NY.

3789 ■ International Silk Association - U.S.A. (ISA)
c/o Seritex
One Madison St.
East Rutherford, NJ 07073
Ph: (973)472-4200
Fax: (973)472-0222
Contact: Bill Kattermann, Pres.
Founded: 1950. **Members:** 28. **Description:** Firms engaged in various phases of the silk industry. Promotes the use of silk in all its forms. **Conventions/Meetings:** annual meeting.

3790 ■ International Society of Industrial Fabric Manufacturers (ISIFM)
Address Unknown since 2007
Founded: 1974. **Members:** 300. **Description:** Engineers, technical service representatives, company executive officers, and salespersons. Purposes are: to coordinate technical efforts and facilitate solutions to such problems as noise, vibration, and process improvements; to promote research and development within the industry. **Formerly:** International Society of Industrial Yarns Manufacturers. **Publications:** *American Textile Reporter*, monthly ● *Textile Industries*, monthly ● *Textile World*, monthly. **Conventions/Meetings:** semiannual seminar and workshop.

3791 ■ International Textile and Apparel Association (ITAA)
6060 Sunrise Vista Dr., Ste.1300
Citrus Heights, CA 95610
Ph: (916)723-1628
Fax: (916)722-8149
E-mail: info@itaaonline.org
URL: http://www.itaaonline.org
Contact: Kim J.P. Johnson, Pres.-Elect
Founded: 1944. **Members:** 950. **Membership Dues:** active and associate in U.S., $115 (annual) ● emeritus and reserve in U.S., $95 (annual) ● graduate and undergraduate in U.S., $55 (annual) ● corporate, $300 (annual) ● sector, $20 (annual) ● active and associate (in Canada and Mexico), $130 (annual) ● emeritus and reserve (in Canada and Mexico), $110 (annual) ● graduate and undergraduate (in Canada and Mexico), $70 (annual) ● active and associate (outside U.S.), $135 (annual) ● emeritus and reserve (outside U.S.), $115 (annual) ● graduate and undergraduate (outside U.S.), $75 (annual). **Budget:** $150,000. **Description:** Textile, design, and apparel professors and associates. Disseminates information about clothing and textiles. Maintains speakers' bureau. **Libraries: Type:** reference. **Awards: Type:** fellowship. **Recipient:** for graduate students. **Computer Services:** database ● mailing lists. **Formerly:** (1991) Association of College Professors of Textiles and Clothing. **Publications:** *Clothing and Textiles Research Journal*, quarterly. **Price:** included in membership dues; $140.00 /year for libraries; $155.00 /year for libraries in Canada; $160.00 /year for libraries outside North America. ISSN: 0887-302X. **Circulation:** 1,400. Alternate Formats: online ● *ITAA Membership Directory*, periodic. **Price:** included in membership dues ● *ITAA Newsletter*, bimonthly. Covers association activities nationally, regionally, and at universities. Includes calendar of events and lists employment opportunities. **Price:** included in membership dues. **Circulation:** 1,200 ● *ITAA Proceedings*, annual. Contains abstracts of research presentations at regional and national meetings. **Price:** included in membership dues. **Circulation:** 950. Alternate Formats: online. **Conventions/Meetings:** annual competition (exhibits) ● annual conference (exhibits).

3792 ■ Narrow Fabrics Institute (NFI)
1801 County Rd. B W
Roseville, MN 55113-4061
Ph: (651)222-2508
Free: (800)225-4324
Fax: (651)631-9334
E-mail: tjohnson@ribbonwebbing.com
URL: http://www.narrowfabrics.org
Contact: Tim Johnson, Pres.
Founded: 1956. **Members:** 36. **Membership Dues:** corporate, $100 (annual). **Staff:** 1. **Multinational. Description:** Division of Industrial Fabrics Association International (see separate entry). Manufacturers of woven narrow fabrics products. Clearinghouse of narrow fabric information. **Committees:** Military Specifications; Research. **Sections:** Tape; Trimmings and Ribbon; Webbing. **Absorbed:** Woven Fabric Belting Manufacturers Association. **Publications:** Newsletter, quarterly. **Conventions/Meetings:** annual Outlook Conference.

3793 ■ National Association of Decorative Fabric Distributors (NADFD)
1 Windsor Cove, Ste.305
Columbia, SC 29223-1833
Free: (800)445-8629
Fax: (803)765-0860
E-mail: info@nadfd.com
URL: http://www.nadfd.com
Contact: Harvey Giberson, Pres.
Founded: 1969. **Members:** 130. **Membership Dues:** regular, associate, $750 (annual). **Staff:** 10. **Description:** Wholesalers and distributors of drapery and upholstery fabric; suppliers to the industry are associate members. Encourages ethical trade practices and clean competition throughout the industry. Studies industry problems and, where necessary, recommends industry standards. Acts as a forum for members and industry consumers, dealers, distributors, and suppliers. Promotes industry interests. **Committees:** Education and Training; Legal and Legislative; Marketing; Publicity and Publications; Statistical and Industry Information. **Formerly:** (1974) National Association of Upholstery Fabric Distributors. **Conventions/Meetings:** annual meeting (exhibits).

3794 ■ The National Needle Arts Association (TNNA)
1100-H Brandywine Blvd.
Zanesville, OH 43701-7303
Ph: (740)455-6773
Free: (800)889-8662
Fax: (740)452-2552
E-mail: tnna.info@offinger.com
URL: http://www.tnna.org
Contact: Marilyn Murphy, Pres.
Founded: 1975. **Members:** 2,358. **Membership Dues:** wholesale (based on annual sales), $275-$850 (annual) ● retail/affiliate, $60 (annual) ● yarn group, $50 (annual) ● needlepoint group, $25 (annual) ● counted thread and embroidery group, $30 (annual). **Staff:** 4. **Description:** Manufacturers, retailers, and distributors of upscale needle art products (needlepoint, embroidery, cross stitch, crochet, knitting, books, and accessories). Advances its community of professional businesses by encouraging the passion for needle arts though education, industry knowledge exchange, and a strong marketplace. **Awards:** Excellence in Needlework Award. **Frequency:** annual. **Type:** recognition. **Recipient:** for contributions to the needle arts. **Subgroups:** Counted Thread and Embroidery; Needlepoint; Yarn. **Formerly:** (2004) The National Needlework Association. **Publications:** *Directory of Exhibitors*, semiannual ● *TNNA Today*, quarterly. Newsletter ● Membership Directory, annual. **Conventions/Meetings:** semiannual trade show, upscale specialty needlework (exhibits) ● annual trade show (exhibits).

3795 ■ National Textile Association (NTA)
6 Beacon St., Ste.1125
Boston, MA 02108
Ph: (617)542-8220
Fax: (617)542-2199
E-mail: info@nationaltextile.org
URL: http://www.nationaltextile.org
Contact: James F. Robbins, Chm.
Founded: 1854. **Members:** 275. **Staff:** 4. **Description:** Cotton, synthetic, wool, and elastic fabric textile mills (including felt), located principally in the U.S. **Committees:** Government Procurement; Intellectual Property Right; Promotions; Technical; Upholstery. **Councils:** Cotton and Synthetic; Elastic Manufacturers; Felt Manufacturers; Knitted Textile Manufacturers; Wool Manufacturers. **Formed by Merger of:** (2003) Northern Textile Association; (2003) Knitted Textile Association. **Formerly:** (1956) National Association of Cotton Manufacturers. **Conventions/Meetings:** annual meeting ● annual seminar.

3796 ■ Schiffli Embroidery Manufacturers Promotion Fund (SEMPB)
22 Indus. Ave.
Fairview, NJ 07022
Ph: (201)943-7757
Fax: (201)943-7793
E-mail: info@schiffli.org
URL: http://www.schiffli.org
Contact: Larry Squiccimari, Pres.
Founded: 1968. **Members:** 30. **Staff:** 2. **Description:** Represents embroidery firms contributing to promotional activities to increase demand for laces, embroideries, emblems, and motifs manufactured on Schiffli embroidery machines. Serves as promotional arm of the Schiffli lace and embroidery industry. **Formerly:** Schiffli Embroidery Institute; Schiffli Embroidery Manufacturers Promotion Fund; Schiffli Embroidery Promotion Council; Schiffli Manufacturers Promotion Fund; (1982) Embroidery Manufacturers Promotion Board; (1995) Schiffli Embroidery Manufacturers Promotion Foundation. **Publications:** *Laces and Embroideries*. Video.

3797 ■ Schiffli Lace and Embroidery Manufacturers Association (SLEMA)
22 Indus. Ave.
Fairview, NJ 07022
Ph: (201)943-7757 (201)867-1442
Fax: (201)943-7793
E-mail: info@schiffli.org
URL: http://www.schiffli.org
Contact: Larry Squiccimari, Pres.
Founded: 1937. **Members:** 100. **Staff:** 2. **Description:** Represents manufacturers of machine-produced embroidery and lace; allied trades. The embroidery industry is highly concentrated in Northern New Jersey and New York City. **Formerly:** Embroidery Manufacturers Bureau. **Publications:** *Embroidery News*, bimonthly. Newsletter. Contains information for embroidery and lace manufacturers and allied trades. **Circulation:** 400. **Advertising:** accepted ● *Lace and Embroideries Directory*, annual. Includes lace and embroidery patterns, resource list, and report on annual convention. **Price:** $5.00/issue, plus postage. **Circulation:** 1,500. **Advertising:** accepted. **Conventions/Meetings:** annual convention - usually October or November.

3798 ■ Southeastern Fabric, Notions and Crafts Association (SEFNCA)
2724 2nd Ave.
Des Moines, IA 50313
Ph: (515)282-9101
Free: (800)367-5651
Fax: (515)282-4483
URL: http://www.sefabrics.com
Contact: Judy Patterson, Pres.
Founded: 1967. **Regional Groups:** 1. **Description:** Serves as a wholesale market for fabrics, notions and crafts by wholesalers selling to manufacturers of sewn products and accessories, retail stores, equipment dealers, interior decorators, and costumers. Encourages and enables credentialed buyers to make seasonal and immediate delivery purchases. **Also Known As:** Southeastern Fabric Show. **Publications:** *Attendee List*, semiannual. **Price:** included in booth fee (for exhibitors only) ● *Market Directory*, semiannual. **Price:** for registered attendees and exhibitors only. **Conventions/Meetings:** semiannual show, wholesale buyers' market (exhibits) - always March/April and September/October in Atlanta, GA.

3799 ■ Southern Textile Association (STA)
PO Box 66
Gastonia, NC 28053
Ph: (704)824-3522
Fax: (704)824-0630
E-mail: info@southerntextile.org
URL: http://www.southerntextile.org
Contact: Lillian G. Link, Sec.-Treas.
Founded: 1908. **Members:** 450. **Membership Dues:** active/associate, $75 (annual). **Staff:** 1. **State Groups:** 4. **Description:** Professional society of textile operating executives. **Affiliated With:** American Yarn Spinners Association. **Conventions/Meetings:** semiannual Division Meeting - always spring and fall ● annual meeting - always summer ● annual seminar - always winter.

3800 ■ Surface Design Association (SDA)
PO Box 360
Sebastopol, CA 95473-0360
Ph: (707)829-3110
Fax: (707)829-3285
E-mail: surfacedesign@mail.com
URL: http://www.surfacedesign.org
Contact: Joy Stocksdale, Exec. Dir.
Founded: 1976. **Members:** 3,700. **Membership Dues:** individual, supporting, $50 (annual) ● student, $30 (annual) ● sponsor, professional, $200 (annual) ● business, benefactor, $500 (annual) ● fellow, $1,000 (annual). **Staff:** 4. **Regional Groups:** 7. **State Groups:** 46. **Local Groups:** 5. **Description:** Individuals involved in surface design on fiber surfaces. Aims to improve communication among artists, designers, and teachers working in surface design on textiles and other media. Seeks to encourage members and their work. Conducts educational programs. **Computer Services:** Mailing lists. **Publications:** *SDA Newsletter*, quarterly. Contains president's report, announcements, and reports from regional chapters; back issues available. **Price:** included in membership dues. **Circulation:** 4,000 ● *Surface Design Journal*, quarterly. Contains book reviews and articles on contemporary textiles artist/designers. **Price:** included in membership dues; $10.00/copy for nonmembers. ISSN: 0197-4483. **Circulation:** 5,000. **Advertising:** accepted ● Manual. **Conventions/Meetings:** biennial National Surface Design - competition and lecture, includes panels (exhibits) ● semiannual National Surface Design Conference, gallery/museum shows (exhibits) ● workshop.

3801 ■ Synthetic Yarn and Fiber Association (SYFA)
PO Box 66
Gastonia, NC 28053-0066
Ph: (704)824-3522
Fax: (704)824-0630
E-mail: info@tyaa.org
URL: http://www.thesyfa.org
Contact: Jerry N. King, Exec. Sec.
Founded: 1971. **Members:** 380. **Membership Dues:** regular, $140 (annual). **Description:** Individuals affiliated with the textured yarn industry as a fiber producer, throwster, knitter, weaver, dyer, and finisher, or in the manufacture or research of dyes, chemicals, processes, or fibers for use in the industry, or in the testing of such products; students, corporations, and other interested individuals. Conducts research and educational programs. **Formerly:** (2006) Textured Yarn Association of America. **Publications:** Newsletter, 3-4 per copy ● Papers, biennial. Contains transcript of papers presented at association meetings. **Conventions/Meetings:** semiannual conference - always last weekend in July and February, Myrtle Beach, SC.

3802 ■ Textile Distributors Association (TDA)
980 Ave. of the Americas
New York, NY 10018-3617
Ph: (212)868-2210
Fax: (212)868-2214
E-mail: tda104@msn.com
Contact: Bruce Roberts, Exec. Dir.
Founded: 1938. **Members:** 150. **Staff:** 3. **Description:** Distributors or converters of fabrics made predominantly of man-made and natural fibers and blends for all end uses. Member services include routing assistance and Trademark and Copyright Bureau. **Formerly:** Textile Distributors Institute; (1965) Textile Fabric Distributors Association. **Publications:** Newsletter, monthly. **Conventions/Meetings:** annual meeting - usually June.

3803 ■ Textile Fibers and By-Products Association (TFBPA)
PO Box D
1531 Indus. Dr.
Griffin, GA 30224
Ph: (770)412-2325
Fax: (770)227-6321

E-mail: info@tfbpa.org
URL: http://www.tfbpa.org
Contact: C.E. Williams Jr., Exec. Sec.
Founded: 1931. **Members:** 98. **Staff:** 1. **Budget:** $30,000. **Description:** Firms purchasing and marketing textile fiber by-products, commonly designated as textile waste. **Formerly:** (1959) Textile Waste Exchange; (1966) Textile Waste Association. **Publications:** *General Communiques*, periodic. **Conventions/Meetings:** annual meeting ● semiannual meeting.

3804 ■ Textile Information Users Council (TIUC)
c/o Philadelphia College of Textiles and Science
4201 Henry Ave.
Philadelphia, PA 19144
Ph: (215)951-2842
Fax: (215)951-2574
E-mail: lowryb@philau.edu
URL: http://www.philau.edu
Contact: Barbara Lowry, Coor.
Founded: 1969. **Members:** 30. **Description:** Represents fiber producers, textile manufacturers, dyestuff manufacturers, chemical suppliers, and affiliated companies. Acts as a forum for the exchange of ideas, needs, and experiences in the field of textile documentation; suggests guidelines to information suppliers; acts as an advisory council for evaluation of proposed or existing services. Does not provide information service to the public. **Awards:** Stan Backer Award. **Type:** recognition. **Recipient:** for outstanding contributions in the field of textile information science. **Conventions/Meetings:** annual conference.

3805 ■ Textile Society of America (TSA)
PO Box 70
Earleville, MD 21919-0070
Ph: (410)275-2329
Fax: (410)275-8936
E-mail: tsa@textilesociety.org
URL: http://www.textilesociety.org
Contact: Carol Bier, Pres.
Founded: 1987. **Members:** 500. **Membership Dues:** individual in U.S. and Canada, $55 (annual) ● indvidual outside U.S. and Canada, $65 (annual) ● student in U.S. and Canada, $30 (annual) ● student outside U.S. and Canada, $40 (annual) ● institutional in U.S. and Canada, $70 (annual) ● institutional outside U.S. and Canada, $80 (annual) ● supporting, in U.S. and Canada, $135 (annual) ● supporting, outside U.S. and Canada, $145 (annual) ● corporate, $1,000 (annual). **Multinational. Description:** Represents the interests of textile specialists and enthusiasts. Provides an international forum for the exchange and dissemination of information about textiles worldwide, from artistic, cultural, economic, historic, political, social, and technical perspectives. **Awards:** R.L. Shep Book Award. **Frequency:** annual. **Type:** recognition. **Recipient:** for best book of the year in ethnic textile studies. **Publications:** *Textile Society of America Newsletter*, 3/year. **Price:** included in membership dues ● Membership Directory, annual. **Price:** included in membership dues ● Bibliography, annual. **Price:** included in membership dues ● Proceedings. **Price:** free for members. **Conventions/Meetings:** biennial Textile as Cultural Expressions - symposium - 2008 Sept. 24-27, Honolulu, HI.

3806 ■ TRI/Princeton
PO Box 625
Princeton, NJ 08542
Ph: (609)430-4820
Fax: (609)683-7836
E-mail: info@triprinceton.org
URL: http://www.triprinceton.org
Contact: Dr. Gail R. Eaton, Pres.
Founded: 1930. **Members:** 80. **Membership Dues:** individual, $60 (annual). **Staff:** 25. **Budget:** $3,000,000. **Multinational. Description:** Conducts scientific research in support of the fiber and allied industries. Conducts fiber-related pre-doctoral, post-doctoral, and continuing professional education in the physical and engineering sciences. **Libraries: Type:** not open to the public; reference. **Holdings:** 4,550. **Subjects:** textile-related topics. **Formerly:** United States Institute for Textile Research; Textile Research Institute. **Conventions/Meetings:** annual Human Hair/Cosmetic Interactions: Fundamentals and Methodology - seminar ● annual Porous Materials Characterization - seminar and meeting.

3807 ■ United States Association of Importers of Textiles and Apparel (USA-ITA)
13 E 16th St., 6th Fl.
New York, NY 10003
Ph: (212)463-0089
Fax: (212)463-0583
E-mail: quota@aol.com
URL: http://www.usaita.com
Contact: Laura E. Jones, Exec. Dir.
Founded: 1989. **Members:** 250. **Membership Dues:** importer/retailer, $1,100-$16,500 (annual) ● associate, $1,100-$5,000 (annual). **Staff:** 3. **Description:** Importers and retailers of textiles and apparel in the U.S. Represents members' interests before the federal government, the business community, and the public. Disseminates information on changes in federal regulations and legislation, customs laws, and import quotas affecting members. **Computer Services:** database ● mailing lists ● online services, quota bulletin board service. **Publications:** *ATTN Magazine*, bimonthly ● *Customs Update*, monthly. Newsletter. **Price:** included in membership dues ● *Illegal-Transshipment Manual*. **Price:** $50.00 for members; $40.00 additional copy for members; $85.00 for nonmembers ● *International Property Newsletter*, periodic ● *Monthly Washington Report* ● Videos. Features videos for sale on variety of industry related topics. **Conventions/Meetings:** annual Textile and Apparel Trade and Transportation Conference - seminar, hosted jointly with American Import Shippers Association ● annual Trade and Transportation Conference.

3808 ■ United States Industrial Fabrics Institute (USIFI)
1801 County Rd. B.W.
Roseville, MN 55113-4061
Ph: (651)222-2508
Free: (800)225-4324
Fax: (651)631-9334
E-mail: generalinfo@ifai.com
URL: http://www.usifi.com
Contact: Ms. Ruth Stephens, Exec. Dir.
Founded: 1986. **Members:** 40. **Membership Dues:** company (engaged in manufacturing and use of specialty fabrics), $1,200 (annual). **Staff:** 1. **Budget:** $350,000. **Description:** U.S. specialty fabric manufacturers and users. Works to represent the interests of the industry. **Committees:** Events and Conferences; Government/Legislative; Military Shelters; Military Specifications; Outlook Conference. **Affiliated With:** Industrial Fabrics Association International. **Publications:** *Electronic Newsletter*, semiweekly. **Price:** included in membership dues. **Conventions/Meetings:** annual Outlook Conference, legislative, political and economic topics and forecasts - usually spring.

3809 ■ Wool Manufacturers Council (WMC)
c/o Northern Textile Association
6 Beacon St., Ste.1125
Boston, MA 02108-3812
Ph: (617)542-8220
Fax: (617)542-2199
E-mail: info@nationaltextile.org
URL: http://www.nationaltextile.org
Contact: Karl Spilhaus, Dir.
Founded: 1956. **Members:** 23. **Description:** Represents wool textile mills. Autonomous part of Northern Textile Association (see separate entry). **Affiliated With:** National Textile Association. **Conventions/Meetings:** annual meeting ● annual seminar.

3810 ■ Woolmark Company
1230 Ave. of the Americas, 7th Fl.
New York, NY 10020
Ph: (646)756-2535
Free: (800)986-WOOL
Fax: (646)756-2538
E-mail: carl_brescia@wool.com
URL: http://www.woolmark.com
Contact: Carl Brescia, Business Mgr.
Founded: 1949. **Staff:** 5. **Languages:** English, Spanish. **Multinational. Description:** Sponsored by the wool growers of Australia to carry out global promotional and research programs. Works with American mills, apparel, upholstery fabric, carpet, and other end-product manufacturers and retailers at promotional and technical levels; conducts programs of product and market development; provides wool industry with marketing and statistical information; offers technical advice to increase manufacturing efficiency and assist in the introduction at the commercial level of new processes and products. Maintains Technical Services Center that tests and evaluates chemical and finishing processes developed to add new performance characteristics to wool products and to create new market outlets. **Convention/Meeting:** none. **Divisions:** Apparel Promotion; Market Research; Merchandising; Public Relations; Statistics; Technical Services; Woolmark Quality Control. **Formerly:** (1998) Wool Bureau.

Theatre

3811 ■ International Cinema Technology Association (ICTA)
770 Broadway, 5th Fl.
New York, NY 10003-9522
Ph: (646)654-7680
Fax: (646)654-7694
E-mail: info@itea.com
URL: http://www.itea.com
Contact: Robert H. Sunshine, Exec. Dir.
Founded: 1971. **Members:** 225. **Membership Dues:** active, $375 (annual) ● associate, $200 (annual). **Staff:** 1. **Description:** Individuals in the theatre equipment industry. **Awards:** Teddy and Rodney Awards. **Frequency:** annual. **Type:** recognition. **Absorbed:** (1999) Theatre Equipment Association. **Formerly:** (2006) International Theatre Equipment Association. **Publications:** Newsletter. **Price:** included in membership dues. Alternate Formats: online ● Membership Directory. **Conventions/Meetings:** annual convention.

Time Equipment

3812 ■ National Time Equipment Association (NTEA)
PO Box 27399
Memphis, TN 38167-0399
Free: (800)235-6832
E-mail: ntea2000@aol.com
URL: http://www.thentea.com
Contact: Janet Gage, Exec. Sec.
Founded: 1978. **Members:** 300. **Membership Dues:** direct, affiliate, $149 (annual) ● associate, $349 (annual) ● subscription, $69 (annual). **Staff:** 1. **Budget:** $50,000. **Description:** Represents time equipment dealers and manufacturers; products include time clocks, parking equipment, and computerized time equipment. Serves as a communications center for members and as a liaison between members and other dealers. Conducts technical workshop on training and repair of time equipment. **Libraries: Type:** reference. **Publications:** *Marking Time*, quarterly. Newsletter. Contains news and views that are of interest to members. ● *NTEA Members Handbook*, annual ● *The Times*, monthly. Newsletter. Covers new products and members. **Price:** free for members. **Circulation:** 350. **Conventions/Meetings:** annual conference (exhibits) ● semiannual symposium.

Tires

3813 ■ International Tire Association (ITA)
Address Unknown since 2008
Founded: 1985. **Members:** 1,000. **Membership Dues:** $100 (annual). **Staff:** 2. **For-Profit. Multina-**

tional. **Description:** Individuals working in the tire industry. Promotes international goodwill and communication in the industry. Bestows membership and achievement awards. Sponsors seminars on tire industry issues. **Libraries: Type:** reference. **Computer Services:** Mailing lists, labels. **Formerly:** (1963) Central States Retreaders' Association; (1966) American Retreaders Association.

3814 ■ Tire Industry Association (TIA)
1532 Pointer Ridge Pl., Ste.G
Bowie, MD 20716-1883
Ph: (301)430-7280
Free: (800)876-8372
Fax: (301)430-7283
E-mail: info@tireindustry.org
URL: http://www.tireindustry.org
Contact: Paul Hyatt, Pres.
Founded: 1921. **Members:** 4,500. **Membership Dues:** business (with annual sales volume of zero to less than 5 million), $250-$750 (annual) ● business (with annual sales volume of 5 to 20 million), $1,000-$2,000 (annual) ● business (with annual sales volume of over 20 million), $3,000 (annual). **Staff:** 6. **Budget:** $1,200,000. **State Groups:** 25. **Description:** Corporations engaged in all sectors of the replacement tire industry. Seeks to advance members' interests. Serves as a clearinghouse on economic and regulatory issues affecting the replacement tire industry; conducts educational programs; sponsors lobbying activities. **Absorbed:** (1978) Tire Retreading Institute. **Formed by Merger of:** (2002) Tire Association of North America; (2002) International Tire and Rubber Association. **Formerly:** National Association of Independent Tire Dealers; (2001) National Tire Dealers and Retreaders Association. **Publications:** *TANA—Who's Who Membership Directory*, annual. **Price:** included in membership dues; $50.00 for nonmembers ● *Video Training Network Directory* ● Magazine, quarterly. **Price:** $20.00/year ● Newsletter, monthly. **Conventions/Meetings:** annual meeting.

3815 ■ Tire Retread Information Bureau (TRIB)
900 Weldon Grove Pl.
Pacific Grove, CA 93950
Ph: (831)372-1917
Free: (888)473-8732
Fax: (831)372-9210
E-mail: info@retread.org
URL: http://www.retread.org
Contact: Mr. Harvey Brodsky, Managing Dir.
Founded: 1974. **Members:** 479. **Membership Dues:** retreader/tire dealer, supplier/casing dealer, international, $350 (annual) ● individual, $150 (annual) ● consulting/investment company, $300 (annual) ● new tire manufacturer, $1,000 (annual) ● trucking company, $200 (annual). **Staff:** 2. **Budget:** $200,000. **Languages:** English, French, Spanish. **Multinational. Description:** Retreaders, tire repair information, suppliers to the retread industry. Serves as information resource for the retread industry. Receives logistical support from industry associations, suppliers, and retreaders. Operates speakers' bureau. **Libraries: Type:** reference. **Holdings:** articles. **Subjects:** retreaded tires/repair of tires/importance of proper tire inflation. **Publications:** *Information Packet*, annual. Articles. Features news releases and articles about retreading. **Price:** free. Alternate Formats: diskette ● Also publishes pamphlets and information packets, audio CDs, and videos/DVDs. **Conventions/Meetings:** workshop.

3816 ■ Tire and Rim Association (TRA)
175 Montrose W Ave., Ste.150
Copley, OH 44321
Ph: (330)666-8121
Fax: (330)666-8340
E-mail: tra@us-tra.org
URL: http://www.us-tra.org
Contact: J.F. Pacuit, Exec. VP
Founded: 1903. **Members:** 123. **Staff:** 3. **Description:** Manufacturers of tires, rims, wheels, and related parts. Establishes standards (primarily dimensional) for the interchangeability of tires, rim contours, tubes, valves, and flaps for passenger cars, motorcycles, trucks, buses, airplanes, and for earth moving, road building, agricultural, and industrial vehicles. **Committees:** Standards and Technical Advisory. **Subcommittees:** Agricultural Tire and Rim; Aircraft Tire and Rim; Cycle Tire and Rim; Industrial Tire and Rim; Off-the-Road Tire and Rim; Passenger Car Tire and Rim; Rim; Truck-Bus Tire and Rim; Tube and Valve. **Publications:** *Engineering Design Information for Aircraft Tires and Rims*, periodic. Book. **Price:** $37.00 each, main edition; $32.00/year for revisions ● *Engineering Design Information for Ground Vehicle Tires and Rims*, periodic. Book. **Price:** $117.50 each, main edition; $70.00/year for revisions ● *Military Supplement*. Provides standards on dimensions and tire load ratings for military applications. **Price:** $65.00 each ● *Tire and Rim Association-Aircraft Year Book*, annual. Yearbook. Provides standards on dimensions and tire load ratings for aircraft. **Price:** $120.00 each, plus shipping and handling ● *Tire and Rim Association-Year Book*, annual. Yearbook. Provides standards on dimensions and tire load ratings for the purpose of interchangeability. **Price:** $80.00 each, plus shipping and handling. Alternate Formats: CD-ROM. **Conventions/Meetings:** meeting - 3/year.

Tobacco

3817 ■ Association of Dark Leaf Tobacco Dealers and Exporters (ADLTDE)
c/o Hail and Cotton, Inc.
PO Box 638
Springfield, TN 37172-0638
Ph: (615)384-9576
Fax: (615)384-6461
URL: http://www.hailcotton.com
Contact: Tom Wilks, Pres.
Founded: 1947. **Members:** 22. **Description:** Dealers and exporters of dark fire-cured and dark air-cured leaf tobacco. Develops, protects, and expands domestic and foreign markets for dark leaf tobacco; advises growers of leaf tobacco on requirements of the tobacco manufacturing industry in the U.S. and abroad. **Conventions/Meetings:** semiannual meeting - always spring and fall.

3818 ■ Burley Marketing Association
620 S Broadway St.
Lexington, KY 40508-3126
Ph: (859)255-4504
Fax: (859)255-4534
E-mail: bawa@gte.net
Contact: Donna Graves, Exec. Dir.
Founded: 1946. **Members:** 220. **Staff:** 2. **Description:** Warehouse companies selling burley tobacco at auction in the eight burley-producing states (Indiana, Kentucky, Missouri, North Carolina, Ohio, Tennessee, Virginia, and West Virginia). Works with farmers to increase exports of tobacco; encourages fair trade practices in the auction system and supports continuation of the production control program. **Publications:** none. **Formerly:** (2003) Burley Auction Warehouse Association. **Conventions/Meetings:** annual meeting (exhibits) - always June.

3819 ■ Cigar Association of America (CAA)
Address Unknown since 2008
Founded: 1937. **Members:** 68. **Staff:** 5. **Budget:** $3,000,000. **Description:** Manufacturers of cigars (machine- and handmade); suppliers, and importers. Collects and disseminates statistics on cigar removals, exports and imports, and production. Provides government relations services. **Publications:** *Cigar Association Statistical Record*, annual ● *Imports of Cigars by Country of Origin*, monthly ● *Monthly Statistical Bulletin* ● *Trademark Bulletin*, monthly ● Also publishes reports to the cigar industry. **Conventions/Meetings:** annual meeting - always September/October; **Avg. Attendance:** 200.

3820 ■ National Association of Tobacco Outlets (NATO)
15560 Boulder Pointe Rd.
Minneapolis, MN 55437
Free: (866)869-8888
Fax: (952)934-7442
E-mail: info@natocentral.org
URL: http://www.natocentral.org
Contact: Thomas A. Briant, Exec. Dir.
Founded: 2001. **Membership Dues:** tobacco retailer, associate retailer (based on number of stores), $100-$475 (annual) ● wholesaler/distributor (based on number of warehouses), $600-$1,650 (annual) ● manufacturer/importer (based on annual sales volume), $1,150-$14,000 (annual) ● associate, $750 (annual). **Description:** Works to protect the freedom to sell and use tobacco products. Encourages the expansion of the tobacco outlet marketplace segment of the tobacco industry in a responsible and law-abiding manner. Educates members about the issues affecting the tobacco outlet industry. **Publications:** *NATO Monitor*. Newsletter. **Price:** free for members. Alternate Formats: online.

3821 ■ Pipe Tobacco Council (PTC)
1707 H St. NW, Ste.800
Washington, DC 20006
Ph: (202)223-8207
Fax: (202)833-0379
Contact: Norman F. Sharp, Pres.
Founded: 1988. **Members:** 17. **Staff:** 3. **Budget:** $280,000. **Description:** Importers and manufacturers of pipe and "roll-your-own" tobaccos. Provides governmental relations services; compiles statistics. **Conventions/Meetings:** annual meeting - always November.

3822 ■ Smokeless Tobacco Council (STC)
Address Unknown since 2007
Founded: 1970. **Members:** 5. **Staff:** 8. **Description:** Major domestic producers of smokeless tobacco products including snuff and chewing tobacco. Acts as information bureau and media and legislative source. **Convention/Meeting:** none. **Formerly:** (1970) Snuff Producers Council.

3823 ■ Tobacco Associates
8452 Holly Leaf Dr.
McLean, VA 22102
Ph: (703)821-1255
Fax: (703)821-1511
E-mail: taw@tobaccoassociatesinc.org
URL: http://www.tobaccoassociatesinc.org
Contact: Ms. Veronica Martins, Office Mgr.
Founded: 1947. **Staff:** 6. **Nonmembership. Multinational. Description:** Represents U.S. flue-cured producers in export promotion and market development. **Publications:** Annual Report, annual. **Conventions/Meetings:** annual meeting - always March.

3824 ■ Tobacco Merchants Association (TMA)
PO Box 8019
Princeton, NJ 08543-8019
Ph: (609)275-4900
Fax: (609)275-8379
E-mail: tma@tma.org
URL: http://www.tma.org
Contact: Farrell Delman, Pres.
Founded: 1915. **Members:** 182. **Membership Dues:** manufacturer in U.S. (per billion units of manufactured cigarette), $2,348 (annual) ● manufacturer outside U.S. (per billion units of manufactured cigarette), $480 (annual) ● non-manufacturer, $1,500-$9,000 (annual). **Staff:** 20. **Description:** Manufacturers of tobacco products, leaf dealers, suppliers, distributors, and others related to the tobacco industry. Maintains records of trademarks. **Libraries: Type:** reference. **Holdings:** 2,000. **Awards:** TMA Award. **Frequency:** semiannual. **Type:** recognition. **Recipient:** for outstanding contribution to the field of tobacco economics. **Computer Services:** Online services, economic, statistical, media-tracking, legislative and regulatory information. **Publications:** *Executive Summary*, weekly. Newsletter. Summarizes industry developments worldwide. Serves as an index to other TMA publications. **Circulation:** 1,200 ● *Issues Monitor*, biennial. Newsletter. Tracks issues and trends affecting the tobacco industry worldwide. Covers import and export news, related legislation, production and marketing. **Price:** free for members. **Circulation:** 935

• *Leaf Bulletin*, weekly, July-April. Reports tobacco auction market statistics. Analyzes developments and trends and compares current statistics to those of the previous year. **Price:** free for members. **Circulation:** 678 • *Legislative Bulletin*, biweekly. Analyzes Congressional and State legislative activity on all issues affecting tobacco products and summarizes key provisions of these bills and laws. **Price:** free for members. **Circulation:** 495 • *Tobacco Barometer*, monthly. Newsletter. Reports on manufactured production, taxable removals, and tax-exempt removals for cigarettes, cigars, chewing tobacco, snuff, and pipe tobacco. **Price:** free for members. **Circulation:** 876 • *Tobacco Barometer: Smoking, Chewing, and Snuff*, quarterly. Newsletter. Contains statistics on quarterly and cumulative production and sales of smoking tobacco, chewing tobacco, and snuff. Provides seasonal adjustments. **Price:** free for members. **Circulation:** 775 • *Tobacco Trade Barometer*, monthly. Newsletter. Details all imports and exports of all tobacco leaf products, including tobacco sundries, by product and country. **Price:** free for members. **Circulation:** 273 • *Tobacco Weekly*. Newsletter. Summarizes key domestic industry issues as they unfold at the Federal, State, and Local levels. • *World Alert*, weekly. Newsletter. Contains country by country description of industry and corporate developments including corporate finance, excise taxes, and distribution issues. **Price:** free for members. **Circulation:** 1,257. **Conventions/Meetings:** annual Tobacco International - trade show and conference.

3825 ■ Tobacconists' Association of America (TAA)
1211 N Tutor Ln.
Evansville, IN 47715-9115
Ph: (812)479-8070
Fax: (812)479-5939
E-mail: t-a-a@t-a-a.us
URL: http://www.t-a-a.com
Contact: Ted Clark, Exec. Dir.
Founded: 1968. **Members:** 150. **Description:** Retail tobacco merchants, usually one firm to an area or city, selling quality pipes, lighters, cigars, smokers, requisites, and personally blended tobaccos. **Libraries: Type:** reference. **Publications:** *Smoke Signals*, quarterly • Brochure • Catalog, annual • Directory, annual. Provides membership information. **Conventions/Meetings:** semiannual meeting.

Tourism

3826 ■ Association for the Promotion of Tourism to Africa (APTA)
c/o Nancy Decker-Davidson, Exec. Dir.
21761 Via Del Lago
Trabuco Canyon, CA 92679
Ph: (949)400-9989
Fax: (949)635-0110
E-mail: info@apta.biz
URL: http://www.apta.biz
Contact: Nancy Decker-Davidson, Exec. Dir.
Founded: 1980. **Membership Dues:** individual, $35 (annual) • corporate, $300 (annual) • associate, $30 (annual) • multi-line company representative, $500 (annual). **Multinational. Description:** Promotes tourism to the African continent and its islands. Seeks to improve tourism to Africa through the education of its members. Educates and informs the travel agents about available products. Provides networking opportunities with Africa specialists. **Telecommunication Services:** electronic mail, nancy.dd@cox.net • electronic mail, corporate@apta.biz. **Publications:** *APTA News*, quarterly. Newsletter. Contains information and updates from suppliers and members, and other related articles. **Price:** included in membership dues.

3827 ■ Convention Industry Council (CIC)
1620 Eye St. NW, Ste.615
Washington, DC 20006
Ph: (202)429-8634
Free: (877)429-8634
Fax: (202)463-8498
E-mail: jason@moinc.com
URL: http://www.conventionindustry.org
Contact: Jason Clawson, Pres./CEO
Founded: 1949. **Members:** 31. **Staff:** 6. **Budget:** $1,500,000. **Description:** Convention, meeting and exhibition, and travel and tourism industry. Provides a focal point for the industry to work collectively to exchange information, recommends solutions to industry problems, develops programs to serve the industry and the public, and creates an awareness of the magnitude of the industry. **Publications:** *2004 Economic Impact Study: The Economic Impact of Conventions, Exhibitions, Meetings and Incentive Travel*. Report. Provides the most current findings of the economic impact of the meetings, conventions, exhibitions, and incentive travel industry in the United States. **Price:** $95.00 • Manual. Serves as a reference to prepare for the Certified Meeting Professional (CMP) examination. **Price:** $60.00 each.

3828 ■ International Association of Reservation Executives (IARE)
7400 E Arapahoe Rd., Ste.211
Centennial, CO 80112
Ph: (303)694-4728
Fax: (303)694-4869
E-mail: iare@assnoffice.com
URL: http://www.iare.com
Contact: Michele Rowan, Pres.
Founded: 1985. **Members:** 140. **Membership Dues:** associate center (based on the number of employees), $100-$200 (annual) • principal center (based on the number of employees), $200-$400 (annual) • allied, $300 (annual). **Description:** Representatives from call centers throughout the travel and hospitality industry. Established to create a network for sharing ideas and opportunities relevant to the profession. **Awards:** IARE Spirit Award. **Frequency:** annual. **Type:** recognition. **Recipient:** for those who have served on an IARE Committee and displayed the highest level of IARE support and spirit • Manager Excellence Award. **Frequency:** annual. **Type:** recognition. **Recipient:** for those who manage a department or a function at a strategic level • Representative Excellence Award. **Frequency:** annual. **Type:** recognition. **Recipient:** for those who deal directly with the customer in a sales or service capacity • Staff Excellence Award. **Frequency:** annual. **Type:** recognition. **Recipient:** for those in an administrative or support role • Supervisor Excellence Award. **Frequency:** annual. **Type:** recognition. **Recipient:** for those who have direct responsibility to employees. **Publications:** Newsletter, quarterly. Stimulates creativity and improves business performance. **Price:** included in membership dues. Alternate Formats: online. **Conventions/Meetings:** annual conference (exhibits).

3829 ■ The International Ecotourism Society (TIES)
1333 H St. NW, Ste.300
East Tower
Washington, DC 20005
Ph: (202)347-9203
Fax: (202)789-7279
E-mail: info@ecotourism.org
URL: http://www.ecotourism.org
Contact: David Sollitt, Exec. Dir.
Founded: 1990. **Members:** 1,600. **Membership Dues:** professional, $75 (annual) • business/institution, $150 (annual) • sponsor, $1,000 (annual) • traveler, $35 (annual). **Staff:** 6. **National Groups:** 110. **Multinational. Description:** Works to generate and disseminate information about ecotourism. Represents members from academics, consultants, conservation professionals and organizations, governments, architects, tour operators, lodge owners and managers, general development experts, and ecotourists in more than 80 countries. Provides guidelines and standards, training, technical assistance, research and publications to foster sound ecotourism development. **Libraries: Type:** open to the public; by appointment only. **Holdings:** books, clippings. **Computer Services:** database • mailing lists • online services. **Formerly:** (2000) Ecotourism Society. **Publications:** *The Ecolodge Sourcebook for Planners and Developers*. **Price:** $19.00 for members; $21.50 for nonmembers • *Ecotourism: A Guide for Planners and Managers*. **Price:** $19.00 for members; $22.00 for nonmembers • *Ecotourism: An Annotated Bibliography for Planners and Managers*. **Price:** $15.00 for members; $18.00 for nonmembers • *Ecotourism Guidelines for Nature Tour Operations*. **Price:** $5.00 for members; $6.00 for nonmembers • *The Environmental Tourist: An Ecotourism Revolution*. Video. **Price:** $65.00 for members; $70.00 for nonmembers • *Tourism, Ecotourism, and Protected Areas*. Book. **Price:** $30.00 for members; $35.00 for nonmembers • Membership Directory, annual. **Price:** $15.00 for members. **Conventions/Meetings:** biennial board meeting • seminar • workshop.

3830 ■ United States Air Tour Association (USATA)
c/o Steve Bassett, Pres.
9626 Hadleigh Ct., Ste.101
Laurel, MD 20723
Ph: (301)483-0158 (410)340-2787
Fax: (443)583-0761
E-mail: srbassett-tcw@comcast.net
URL: http://www.usata-dc.com
Contact: Steve Bassett, Pres.
Founded: 1995. **Members:** 55. **Membership Dues:** regular, $1,000 (annual) • associate, $500 (annual). **Description:** Represents air tour operators and associated companies in the US.

Toys

3831 ■ International Council of Toy Industries (ICTI)
1115 Broadway, 4th Fl.
New York, NY 10010
Ph: (212)675-1141
E-mail: icti@toy-tia.org
URL: http://www.toy-icti.org
Contact: Mr. T.S. Wong, Pres.
Founded: 1975. **Members:** 18. **Multinational. Description:** Acts as a forum for discussion and the exchange of information to improve communications on important toy industry issues and trends. Promotes ethical and safe practices in toy factories. Promotes toy safety standards. Fosters relationships with those interested in the design and educational value of toys. **Computer Services:** Information services, toy industry resources • mailing lists, for members. **Publications:** *Care Process*, bimonthly. Newsletter. Alternate Formats: online • *Vinyl Toys Are Safe*. Article. Alternate Formats: online • *World Toy Facts and Figures*. Survey. Alternate Formats: online.

3832 ■ Toy Industry Association (TIA)
1115 Broadway, Ste.400
New York, NY 10010
Ph: (212)675-1141
Fax: (212)633-1429
E-mail: info@toy-tia.org
URL: http://www.toy-tia.org
Contact: Daniel Grossman, Chm.
Founded: 1916. **Members:** 350. **Membership Dues:** regular (under 1 million annual net sales), $1,500 (annual) • regular (over 1 billion annual net sales), $75,000 (annual) • sales representative firm (based on current no. in firm), $1,000-$2,200 (annual) • designer/inventor (based on current no. in firm), $550-$2,200 (annual) • testing laboratory, $2,200 (annual) • promotion firm, trade/consumer toy magazine, licensor, $1,000 (annual) • consultant, $550 (annual) • retired industry executive, $275 (annual). **Staff:** 31. **Budget:** $10,000,000. **Description:** Provides business services to U.S. manufacturers and importers of toys. Manages American International Toy Fair; represents the industry before Federal, State and Local government on issues of importance; provides legal and legislative counsel; conducts educational programs; compiles industry statistics. **Awards:** Toy of the Year Awards. **Frequency:** annual. **Type:** recognition. **Recipient:** for the best toys developed by the international toy

industry. **Formerly:** (2002) Toy Manufacturers of America. **Publications:** *American International Toy Fair Official Directory*, annual ● *Children with Special Needs* ● *Fun Play, Safe Play.* **Conventions/Meetings:** annual American International Toy Fair - trade show, toys, games, holiday decorations (exhibits) - always second Monday of February, New York City ● annual TOYCON - conference.

3833 ■ United League Toy Representatives Associations (ULTRA)
1107 Broadway, Rm. 1204
New York, NY 10010
Ph: (212)691-3030
E-mail: mgrill@ustoyreps.com
URL: http://www.ultratoyreps.com
Contact: Mark Grill, Co-Pres.
Membership Dues: general, $200 (annual) ● initiation fee, $200. **Description:** Informs, promotes, protects and preserves the interests and welfare of manufacturer representatives in the toy, hobby and seasonal industry. Elevates and improves the moral and commercial standards of independent representatives. Educates potential manufacturers and current manufacturers of the advantages of doing business with independent sales representatives. **Telecommunication Services:** electronic mail, astern@bsareps.com ● electronic mail, matt@almistsales.com ● electronic mail, fmwsales@aol.com.

3834 ■ Women in Toys (WIT)
c/o Toy Industry Association
1115 Broadway, Ste.1000
New York, NY 10010
E-mail: info@womenintoys.com
URL: http://www.womenintoys.com
Contact: Anne Pitrone, Pres./Co-Founder
Founded: 1991. **Membership Dues:** individual, $100 (annual) ● student, $25 (annual) ● corporation, $75-$90 (annual) ● individual, $180 (biennial). **Description:** Provides a professional networking base for women working within the toy, entertainment and licensing industries. Acknowledges and promotes the achievements of these women. **Computer Services:** Online services, bulletin board. **Publications:** *WIT News*, quarterly. Newsletter. Alternate Formats: online.

Trade

3835 ■ Aftermarket Council on Electronic Commerce (ACEC)
c/o Alan Jones
Motor and Equip. Mfrs. Assn.
10 Lab. Dr.
Research Triangle Park, NC 27709-3966
Ph: (919)549-4800
Fax: (919)549-8733
E-mail: ajones@mema.org
URL: http://www.aceconline.org
Contact: Alan Jones, Contact
Description: Promotes the coordination of electronic commerce standardization activities between all industry segments. **Telecommunication Services:** electronic mail, cgardner@misg.com. **Conventions/Meetings:** meeting.

3836 ■ Alliance for Responsible Trade (ART)
PO Box 5206
Hyattsville, MD 20782
Ph: (301)699-0042
Fax: (301)864-2182
URL: http://www.art-us.org
Contact: Tom Loudon, Coor.
Multinational. Description: Represents the interests of labor, family-farm, religious, women's, environmental, development and research organizations. Promotes equitable and sustainable trade and development. Focuses primarily on trade issues. Supports efforts of groups in countries where the Central American Free Trade Agreement (CAFTA) has not yet been ratified.

3837 ■ America Council for Trade in Services (ACTS)
Address Unknown since 2007
URL: http://www.acts-talks.com
Founded: 1994. **Members:** 22. **Membership Dues:** active, $6,000 (annual) ● associate, $3,000 (annual) ● friends of ACTS, $600 (annual). **Staff:** 4. **Description:** United to promote the export interests of the U.S. service sector; organize forums, seminars, and discussion sessions on international trade in services; and inform and educate government officials on services industry issues and concerns. **Libraries: Type:** reference. **Holdings:** archival material, articles, books, clippings, periodicals. **Subjects:** international trade in services. **Publications:** *ACTS-Talks*, monthly. Newsletter. Alternate Formats: online.

3838 ■ Canadian/American Border Trade Alliance (Can/Am BTA)
PO Box 929
Lewiston, NY 14092
Ph: (716)754-8824
Fax: (716)754-8824
E-mail: canambta@aol.com
URL: http://www.canambta.org
Contact: James D. Phillips, Pres./CEO
Membership Dues: basic (1 to 50 employees), city/local government association, $250 ● mid size corporation/organization (51 to 200 employees), $500 ● large size corporation/organization (above 200 employees), state/province government association, $1,000 ● sponsor, $2,500 ● patron, $5,000 ● grand patron (one-time), $15,000 ● founding patron (one-time), $25,000. **Multinational. Description:** Works to collaborate with and integrate interests of Canadian and U.S. organizations to resolve border-wide issues, problems, and needs. Provides a unified voice committed to ensuring continued growth of two-way cross border trade along the US/Canada border. Enhances two-way commerce, transportation, and tourism activities between the U.S. and Canada. **Publications:** Brochure. Alternate Formats: online ● Report. Alternate Formats: online.

3839 ■ Council on Competitiveness (CoC)
1500 K St. NW, Ste.850
Washington, DC 20005
Ph: (202)682-4292
Fax: (202)682-5150
E-mail: dwince-smith@compete.org
URL: http://www.compete.org
Contact: Deborah L. Wince-Smith, Pres.
Founded: 1986. **Members:** 150. **Staff:** 16. **Budget:** $2,000,000. **Description:** Chief Executive Officers of corporate, educational, and labor organizations. Works to increase public awareness and develop a consensus among public and private sector leadership regarding the best way to maintain and improve U.S. competitiveness. Views U.S. economic competitiveness as a reflection of developments in all sectors of society. Has established agenda of issues crucial to U.S. competitiveness including: capital formation policies that encourage investment; development of an educated and skilled workforce; maintenance of a solid scientific and technological infrastructure; formulation of international economic and trade policies that better reflect the prevailing world economic order. Provides assistance to other organizations engaged in competitiveness activities; holds consultations with members of Congress and the Executive Branch; provides testimony at congressional hearings; issues appraisals of national budgets and other assessments of the effects of government policies on U.S. international competitiveness. Conducts media education campaign for U.S. and foreign journalists and commentators. **Publications:** *Breaking the Barriers to the National Information Infrastructure.* Report. **Price:** $25.00 plus shipping and handling ● *Building on Baldridge: American Quality for the 21st Century (1995).* Report. **Price:** $15.00 ● *Capital Choices: Changing the Way America Invests In Industry (1992).* Report. **Price:** $40.00 ● *Challenges*, 10/year. Newsletter. Covers U.S. competitiveness issues. **Price:** $50.00 sign up fee; $150.00 outside U.S. ● *Competition Policy: Unlocking the National Information Infrastructure (1993).* Report. **Price:** $25.00 ● *Competitiveness Index*, annual. Report. **Price:** $25.00 print; $10.00 download; $30.00 print and download ● *Critical Technologies Update 1994.* Report. **Price:** $10.00 ● *Economic Security: The Dollars and Sense of U.S. Foreign Policy (1994).* Report. **Price:** $25.00 ● *Endless Frontier, Limited Resources: U.S. R&D Policy for Competitiveness (1996).* Report. **Price:** $25.00 ● *Gaining New Ground: Technology Priorities for America's Future (1991).* Report. **Price:** $40.00 ● *Going Global: The New Shape of American Innovation (1998).* Report ● *Highway to Health: Transforming U.S. Health Care in the Information Age (1996).* Report. **Price:** $25.00 ● *Human Resources Competitiveness Index (1995).* Report. **Price:** $15.00 ● *The New Challenge to America's Prosperity: Findings from the Innovation Index (1999).* Report. **Price:** $38.50 in U.S.; $47.50 outside U.S. ● *Winning The Skills Race (1998).* Report. **Price:** $28.00. **Conventions/Meetings:** annual meeting, closed meeting for members and invited guests.

3840 ■ Export Institute of the United States (EXUSA)
6901 W 84th St., Ste.317
Minneapolis, MN 55438
Ph: (952)943-1505
Free: (800)943-3171
E-mail: jrj@exportinstitute.com
URL: http://www.exportinstitute.com
Contact: Mr. John R. Jagoe, Managing Dir.
Founded: 1964. **Budget:** $800,000. **Nonmembership. For-Profit. Multinational. Description:** Educates potential and active exporters on how to enter foreign markets or to expand their current international sales and profits. Offers online classes in exporting leading to a Certificate in Export Management. **Publications:** *Export Sales and Marketing Manual*, annual. Book. **Price:** $295.00. **Circulation:** 3,000. Alternate Formats: CD-ROM; online ● *How to Become a Successful Export Agent.* Report.

3841 ■ International Reciprocal Trade Association (IRTA)
140 Metro Park Dr.
Rochester, NY 14623-2641
Ph: (585)424-2940
Fax: (585)424-2964
E-mail: krista@irta.com
URL: http://www.irta.com
Contact: Krista Vardabash, Exec. Dir.
Founded: 1979. **Members:** 200. **Membership Dues:** applicant exchange, $500 (annual) ● certified, $1,250 (annual) ● trade exchange franchiser, $5,000 (annual) ● associate/service provider/licensor headquarter/standard, $1,000 (annual). **Staff:** 2. **Budget:** $150,000. **Multinational. Description:** Individuals, partnerships, corporations, and firms that engage in the commercial barter industry worldwide, including local trade exchanges which act as clearinghouses, and corporate trade companies which arrange domestic and international barter transactions. Works to foster and promote the interests of the commercial barter industry through the establishment of ethical standards and self-regulation; to represent members before government agencies in matters affecting the industry; to introduce firms engaged in bartering activities; to resolve disputes between members; influence public laws and regulations affecting the industry; disseminate information and conduct public relations programs. Serves as a clearinghouse for industry and public inquiries. Compiles statistics on the segment of commercial barter accounted for by organized trade exchanges and corporate trade companies. Conducts consumer protection, educational, and training programs. Operates Corporate Barter Council as a self-governing body for the corporate trade sector. Awards professional accreditation; operates referral and placement services; maintains Speaker's Bureau; supports charitable programs. **Libraries: Type:** reference. **Holdings:** clippings, papers. **Subjects:** commercial barter. **Awards:** Distinguished Service Award. **Frequency:** annual. **Type:** recognition ● IRTA Hall of Fame. **Frequency:** annual. **Type:** recognition ● Outstanding Achievement Award. **Frequency:** annual. **Type:**

recognition. **Computer Services:** Mailing lists, provided on disk. **Committees:** Accreditation; Barter Political Action; Ethics; Government Relations; Public Relations. **Formerly:** (1984) International Association of Trade Exchanges. **Publications:** *IRTA Dialogue*, quarterly. Newsletter. Covers association events and activities, industry news. **Conventions/Meetings:** annual Barter Congress - convention (exhibits) - always fall ● annual convention - always spring, New York City, NY.

3842 ■ LTD Shippers Association (LTD)
1230 Pottstown Pike, Ste.6
Glenmoore, PA 19343
Ph: (610)458-3636
Fax: (610)458-8039
URL: http://www.ltdmgmt.com
Contact: Tom Craig, Pres.
Founded: 1994. **Members:** 200. **Multinational. Description:** Works to leverage the buying power of the members for lower ocean freight prices. Has scope that includes ocean rates from Asia to United States, to Canada, Mexico, Puerto Rico and many other destinations; also rates to the US and Canada from Brazil, the Mediterranean, India and other origins. Aims to design, develop, negotiate, implement and manage logistics or transportation programs for members. **Conventions/Meetings:** annual meeting.

3843 ■ Morocco-United States Council on Trade and Investment
Address Unknown since 2007
Founded: 1995. **Members:** 60. **Membership Dues:** board, $10,000 (annual) ● corporate, $5,000 (annual) ● leadership, $1,000 (annual). **Description:** Strives to incorporate private sector views into the development of Moroccan trade policy. Works to eliminate costly impediments to trade between the United States and Morocco.

3844 ■ National Association of Trade Exchanges (NATE)
c/o Tom McDowell, Exec. Dir.
8836 Tyler Blvd.
Mentor, OH 44060
Ph: (440)205-5378
Fax: (440)205-5379
E-mail: bartertrainer@aol.com
URL: http://www.nate.org
Contact: Tom McDowell, Exec. Dir.
Founded: 1984. **Membership Dues:** regular, $495 (annual). **Description:** Trade exchange owners. Operates accreditation programs. **Awards:** Monkman-Crumpton Award. **Frequency:** annual. **Type:** recognition. **Recipient:** for an individual who exemplifies the same energy and tireless dedication to NATE. **Computer Services:** Mailing lists. **Committees:** Awards; By-Laws; Convention; Government; Newsletter; Program; Technology; Training. **Publications:** *NATE Update*. Newsletter. **Price:** included in membership dues.

3845 ■ New York Board of Trade (NYBOT)
World Financial Center
1 N End Ave., 13th Fl.
New York, NY 10282-1101
Ph: (212)748-4000 (212)748-4107
Free: (877)877-8890
E-mail: webmaster@nybot.com
Contact: Thomas W. Farley, Pres./COO
Founded: 1873. **Membership Dues:** individual, $750. **Description:** Corporations and professional people. Promotes trade and commerce. **Telecommunication Services:** additional toll-free number, (800)HEDGE-IT. **Conventions/Meetings:** annual meeting - always New York City, NY.

3846 ■ Sales Exchange for Refugee Rehabilitation and Vocation (SERRV)
PO Box 365
New Windsor, MD 21776-0365
Ph: (608)255-0440
Free: (800)423-0071
Fax: (608)255-0451
E-mail: servdirector@aol.com
URL: http://www.agreatergift.org
Contact: Robert Chase, Pres.
Founded: 1949. **Multinational. Description:** Promotes the social and economic progress of people in developing regions of the world by marketing their products in a just and direct manner. Seeks to alleviate poverty and empower low-income people through trade, training and other forms of community support. **Computer Services:** database, artisans and farmers ● online services, catalog. **Publications:** *Partnerships*. Newsletter. Alternate Formats: online.

3847 ■ Swedish Trade Council
150 N Michigan Ave., Ste.1950
Chicago, IL 60601
Ph: (312)781-6222
Free: (888)275-7933
Fax: (312)276-8606
E-mail: usa@swedishtrade.se
URL: http://www.swedishtrade.com/usa
Contact: Mr. Hakan Dahlfors, Sr. Proj. Leader
Founded: 1972. **Staff:** 25. **Languages:** English, Swedish. **Nonmembership. Description:** Promotes Swedish exports and assists American companies in contacting Swedish suppliers. Performs market developments studies and research, partner searches, and project management. **Formerly:** (1979) Swedish Trade Commission; (1995) Swedish Trade Council- North America; (2005) Swedish Trade Council - United States. **Publications:** *Swedish Export Directory*, annual. Contains Swedish exporting companies. Alternate Formats: online.

3848 ■ U.S. - ASEAN Business Council
1101 17th St. NW, Ste.411
Washington, DC 20036
Ph: (202)289-1911
Fax: (202)289-0519
E-mail: mail@usasean.org
URL: http://www.us-asean.org
Contact: Mr. Martin J. Sullivan, Pres./CEO
Founded: 1983. **Members:** 500. **Membership Dues:** corporate, $7,500 (annual). **Staff:** 15. **Budget:** $3,500,000. **Description:** Promotes increased trade and investment between the United States and the countries comprising the Association of South East Asian Nations. **Computer Services:** database ● mailing lists. **Committees:** Food and Agriculture. **Projects:** Center for Technology Cooperation. **Working Groups:** Auto Sector; Defense and Security; Information and Communication Technology; Life Sciences. **Formerly:** (1997) U.S. - ASEAN Council for Business and Technology. **Publications:** *U.S. - ASEAN Business Report*, quarterly. Newsletter. **Circulation:** 5,000 ● Brochure. Alternate Formats: online. **Conventions/Meetings:** periodic board meeting ● periodic conference ● periodic regional meeting.

3849 ■ World Economic Processing Zones Association (WEPZA)
PO Box 3808
Evergreen, CO 80437-3808
Ph: (303)679-0980
Fax: (303)679-0985
E-mail: director@wepza.org
URL: http://www.wepza.org
Contact: Robert Haywood, Dir.
Founded: 1978. **Members:** 50. **Membership Dues;** regular, $5,000 (annual). **Staff:** 5. **Budget:** $250,000. **Regional Groups:** 2. **National Groups:** 35. **Description:** Attracts enterprise investment to all countries. Comprise many types of free zones, special economic zones, export processing zones, foreign trade zones, free ports, and logistics zones. Provides sites and infrastructure which attract firms assembling and manufacturing products, warehousing, financing, and servicing clients to add speed and efficiency to global marketing. **Computer Services:** database, world trade manufactured goods from 224 countries to USA and the European Union. **Affiliated With:** United Nations Industrial Development Organization. **Formerly:** (1999) World Export Processing Zones Association. **Publications:** *The Changing World of Free Zones*. Book. **Price:** $40.00 ● *The Dynamic Transformation of Economic Zones*. Book. **Price:** $40.00/copy, soft cover ● *Export Processing Zones Move to High Technology*. Book. **Price:** $40.00/copy, soft cover ● *Free Zones and Export Processing Zones in Central*. Book. **Price:** $40.00/copy, soft cover ● *The Global Network of Free Zones in the 21st Century*. Book. **Price:** $40.00/copy, soft cover ● *The Impact of 57 New EPZs in Mercosur*. Book. **Price:** $40.00/copy, soft cover ● *Journal of The Flagstaff Institute*, semiannual. Discusses free trade zones, free economic zones, development of a global market, and investment attraction in developing countries. **Price:** $150.00/year for corporations and government agencies; $50.00/year for individuals and nonprofit institutions; $40.00/back issue. ISSN: 0146-1958. **Circulation:** 150. Alternate Formats: online ● *Mainline Free Zones: Mediterranean, Gulf*. Book. **Price:** $40.00/copy, soft cover ● *WEPZA International Directory*. **Price:** $25.00/copy, soft cover ● *The World Impact of NAFTA*. Book. **Price:** $40.00/copy, soft cover ● Publishes various books. **Conventions/Meetings:** annual conference (exhibits).

3850 ■ World Trade Centers Association (WTCA)
420 Lexington Ave., Ste.518
New York, NY 10170
Ph: (212)432-2626 (212)432-2604
Free: (800)937-8886
Fax: (212)488-0064
E-mail: wtca@wtca.org
URL: http://world.wtca.org/portal/site/wtcaonline
Contact: Guy F. Tozzoli, Pres.
Founded: 1970. **Members:** 287. **Membership Dues:** 1st year (plus $200,000 initial fee), $10,000. **Staff:** 20. **Budget:** $5,500,000. **Description:** Regular members are organizations involved in the development or operation of a World Trade Center (WTC). Affiliate members are Chambers of Commerce, clubs, exhibit facilities or other international trade related organizations. Encourages expansion of world trade and international business relationships. **Computer Services:** database, listings of World Trade Centers ● mailing lists ● online services, catalog ● online services, Trade Flow Pricing Service ● online services, WTC Network. **Committees:** Facilities; Industrializing Nations; Information and Communications; Planning and Finance; Standards and Reciprocity; Trade Education; Trade Fairs and Marts; Trade Policy. **Publications:** *World Trade Centers Association—Proceedings of the General Assembly*, annual. **Price:** available to members only ● *WTCA News*, monthly. Newsletter. Covers membership activities online. **Price:** free for members (in limited quantity) ● *WTCA Services Directory*, annual. **Price:** free for members (in limited quantity); $10.00/copy for nonmembers ● Membership Directory, annual ● Brochures. **Conventions/Meetings:** annual general assembly (exhibits) ● annual meeting (exhibits).

Trainers

3851 ■ American Dog Trainers Network (ADTN)
Address Unknown since 2007
URL: http://www.inch.com/~dogs
Description: Dog trainers. Promotes humane education, responsible pet care, and the use of positive motivation in dog training. Serves as "a comprehensive, one-stop resource for dog owners, dog trainers, and the media." Conducts educational programs for dog trainers and the public; maintains list of reputable dog trainers.

Translation

3852 ■ American Association of Language Specialists (TAALS)
PO Box 39339
Washington, DC 20016-9339
Ph: (301)365-9088 (202)580-5587
E-mail: admin@taals.net
URL: http://www.taals.net
Contact: Ms. M. Teresa G. Willett, Pres.
Founded: 1957. **Members:** 150. **Membership Dues:** interpreter and translator, $100 (annual). **Multina-**

tional. **Description:** Professional association of conference interpreters, translators, revisers and precis-writers. **Computer Services:** database, list of members with working language combinations. **Councils:** Executive Secretariat. **Publications:** Yearbook, annual. **Conventions/Meetings:** annual general assembly - always December.

3853 ■ American Translators Association (ATA)
225 Reinekers Ln., Ste.590
Alexandria, VA 22314-2875
Ph: (703)683-6100
Fax: (703)683-6122
E-mail: ata@atanet.org
URL: http://www.atanet.org
Contact: Mr. Walter W. Bacak Jr., Exec. Dir.
Founded: 1959. **Members:** 9,000. **Membership Dues:** joint, $380 (annual) ● corporate, $450 (annual) ● institutional, $270 (annual) ● associate, $217 (annual) ● student, $120 (annual). **Staff:** 10. **Budget:** $2,100,000. **Regional Groups:** 13. **Description:** Fosters the professional development of translators and interpreters and promotes the translation and interpretation professions. **Libraries: Type:** reference. **Awards:** Alexander Gold Medal. **Frequency:** annual. **Type:** recognition. **Recipient:** for lifelong service to the translation profession ● Ungar German Translation Award. **Frequency:** biennial. **Type:** recognition. **Recipient:** for distinguished literary translation from German to English published in the United States. **Computer Services:** Mailing lists, rental of list. **Divisions:** Chinese Language; French Language; German Language; Interpreters; Italian Language; Japanese Language; Literary; Medical; Nordic; Portuguese Language; Slavic Languages; Spanish Language; Translation Company. **Affiliated With:** International Federation of Translators. **Publications:** *ATA Chronicle*, monthly. Magazine. Reports on professional translator/interpreter activities. Contains book reviews, association news, and listing of translating opportunities. **Price:** included in membership dues; $50.00 /year for nonmembers. ISSN: 1078-6457. **Circulation:** 9,000. **Advertising:** accepted ● *ATA Translator Series (Vols. 1-11)* ● *Translation and Interpretation Services Survey*, biennial ● *Translator and Interpreter Programs in North America*. Survey. **Conventions/Meetings:** annual conference (exhibits) - usually fall. 2008 Nov. 5-8, Orlando, FL; 2009 Oct. 28-31, New York, NY; 2010 Oct. 27-30, Denver, CO.

3854 ■ National Alliance of Black Interpreters (NAOBI)
PO Box 2777
North Canton, OH 44720-0777
E-mail: correspondingsecretary@naobi.org
URL: http://www.naobi.org
Contact: Leandra Williams, Pres.
Founded: 1987. **Membership Dues:** full/individual supporting, $40 (annual) ● student, $25 (annual) ● organization supporting, $100 (annual). **State Groups:** 4. **Local Groups:** 6. **Description:** Promotes excellence and empowerment among African Americans/Blacks in the field of sign language interpreting. Fosters growth and development of sign language interpretation through education and latest technology. **Computer Services:** Information services, interpreter ● information services, technology. **Telecommunication Services:** electronic mail, webmaster@naobi.org. **Publications:** Newsletter, quarterly.

3855 ■ Translators and Interpreters Guild (TTIG)
962 Wayne Ave., No. 500
Silver Spring, MD 20910
Ph: (301)563-6450
Free: (800)992-0367
Fax: (301)563-6020
E-mail: info@ttig.org
Contact: Joseph B. Coblentz, Pres.
Founded: 1991. **Members:** 300. **Membership Dues:** regular, $120 (annual) ● associate (full time student), affiliate (TNG-CWA local member), $60 (annual). **Staff:** 1. **Budget:** $40,000. **Local Groups:** 4. **Description:** Organization of independent linguists, not a traditional translation or interpretation agency. Aims to improve the quality of language services provided to the public and the working conditions of translators and interpreters. Provides a referral service that puts translators and interpreters in direct contact with clients. **Affiliated With:** Communications Workers of America; The Newspaper Guild. **Publications:** *The Voice*, quarterly. Newsletter. Features updates on the latest member's activities, issues and benefits. **Circulation:** 400. Alternate Formats: online. **Conventions/Meetings:** bimonthly board meeting.

Transportation

3856 ■ Agricultural and Food Transporters Conference (AFTC)
c/o Russell Laird, Exec. Dir.
950 N Glebe Rd., Ste.210
Arlington, VA 22203-4181
Ph: (703)838-7964
Fax: (703)519-1866
E-mail: rlaird@trucking.org
URL: http://www.truckline.com/aboutata/affiliates/aftc
Contact: Russell Laird, Exec. Dir.
Founded: 1995. **Members:** 80. **Staff:** 1. **Budget:** $150,000. **Description:** Transporters of agricultural commodities and forest and mineral products. Seeks to increase the profitability of members' businesses. Represents members before government and judicial agencies; facilitates exchange of information among members; serves as a clearinghouse on federal regulations affecting the agricultural transport industry. Conducts educational programs. **Formerly:** (2003) Agricultural Transporters Conference. **Publications:** *Horizons*, monthly. Newsletter. Reports information of interest to commercial agricultural transporters. **Advertising:** accepted. Alternate Formats: online. **Conventions/Meetings:** annual conference, held in conjunction with the annual meeting of American Trucking Associations (exhibits).

3857 ■ Air Courier Association (ACA)
PO Box 2036
Cherry Hill, NJ 08034
Free: (877)303-4258
URL: http://www.aircourier.org
Membership Dues: regular, $39 (annual). **Description:** Represents and promotes air couriers and customers interested in discounted flights to travelers. **Publications:** Newsletter. Alternate Formats: online.

3858 ■ Airport Ground Transportation Association (AGTA)
c/o USML Center for Transportation Studies
154 Univ. Ctr.
8001 Natural Bridge Rd.
St. Louis, MO 63121-4499
Ph: (314)516-7271
Fax: (314)516-7272
E-mail: admin@agtaweb.org
URL: http://www.agtaweb.org
Contact: Farouq Massoud, Pres.
Founded: 1945. **Membership Dues:** operator/airport/associate/allied, $350 (annual). **Staff:** 2. **Budget:** $75,000. **Description:** Airport ground transportation operators, suppliers, and related government agencies. Promotes improved airport ground transportation services. Conducts studies; collects data; compiles statistics. **Computer Services:** database, airport regulation of ground transportation. **Formerly:** (1975) Airline Ground Transportation Association. **Publications:** *AGTA Membership Directory*, annual ● *AGTA Newsletter*, bimonthly. **Conventions/Meetings:** semiannual conference and workshop (exhibits) - usually March and September.

3859 ■ American Bus Association (ABA)
700 13th St. NW, Ste.575
Washington, DC 20005-5934
Ph: (202)842-1645
Free: (800)283-2877
Fax: (202)842-0850
E-mail: abainfo@buses.org
URL: http://www.buses.org
Contact: Doug Anderson, Chm.
Founded: 1926. **Members:** 3,000. **Membership Dues:** hardware/service supplier, $350 (annual) ● manufacturer (based on the number of buses), $350-$1,800 (annual) ● motorcoach operator (minimum), tour operator, $400 (annual) ● management group, corporate chains (based on the number of location), $650-$1,000 (annual). **Staff:** 23. **Budget:** $5,000,000. **Description:** Privately owned bus-operating firms engaged in intercity, local, charter, and tour service; state associations; motor bus manufacturers; oil, gas and tire distributors and other suppliers; travel/tourism industry destinations, attractions and organizations. Represents almost 900 motorcoach and tour operators in the United States and Canada. Its members operate charter, tour, regular route, airport express, special operations and some contract services (commuter, school transit). Another 2,400 member organizations represent the travel and tourism industry and supplies of bus products and services that work in partnership with the North American motorcoach industry. Delineates the business concerns of both U.S. and Canadian, privately owned motorcoach and tour operators. Serves the U.S. bus industry in Washington, DC and supports the government affairs activities of its Canadian members and counterpart associations. Facilitates relationships between the North American motorcoach industry and all related segments of the travel and supplier industry. In addition, it creates awareness of the motorcoach industry among consumers in North America (USA, Canada and Mexico), and communicates publicly on important issues like motorcoach and highway safety. **Libraries: Type:** reference. **Holdings:** archival material, audiovisuals, books, business records, periodicals. **Awards:** Driver and Mechanic Competitions and the Coach Classic Final. **Type:** recognition ● George T. Snyder Jr. Scholarship Program. **Frequency:** annual. **Type:** scholarship. **Recipient:** for ABA member company employees and immediate families whose course of study is motorcoach, tour, travel and related industries ● Guide Awards. **Frequency:** annual. **Type:** recognition. **Recipient:** for destination marketing organizations that submit tourism promotional materials ● Top 100 Events in North America. **Frequency:** annual. **Type:** recognition. **Recipient:** nomination by ABA member convention and visitors bureaus, regional promotional organizations and state/provincial tourism offices. **Committees:** BUSPAC; Marketplace. **Councils:** Safety. **Formerly:** Motor Bus Division of American Automobile Association; National Motor Bus Division of American Automobile Association; (1960) National Association of Motor Bus Operators; (1977) National Association of Motor Bus Owners. **Publications:** *ABA Express*, quarterly. Newsletter ● *ABA Motorcoach Marketer*, annual. Directory. Contains information about the group tour industry. **Advertising:** accepted ● *Destinations*, monthly. Magazine. **Price:** $25.00 in U.S.; $30.00 in Canada. **Circulation:** 6,000. **Advertising:** accepted ● *Digest*, biweekly. Bulletin ● *The Report*, weekly. Newsletter. Contains legislative and regulatory news for the motorcoach industry, as well as marketing tips, travel and tourism news. **Advertising:** accepted. **Conventions/Meetings:** annual The American Bus Marketplace - meeting ● annual Business and Education Conference - meeting, business, marketing, safety and technical seminars (exhibits).

3860 ■ American Public Transportation Association (APTA)
1666 K St. NW, Ste.1100
Washington, DC 20006
Ph: (202)496-4800
Fax: (202)496-4321
E-mail: info@apta.com
URL: http://www.apta.com
Contact: William W. Millar, Pres.
Founded: 1882. **Members:** 1,550. **Membership Dues:** transit (based on the operating expenses), $50,794 (annual) ● transit management company (minimum), $1,132 (annual) ● business (based on the annual gross transit sales), $39,225 (annual) ●

governmental agency (based on the population), $997-$5,307 (annual) ● affiliate, $483-$604 (annual) ● retiree, $104 (annual). **Staff:** 80. **Multinational. Description:** Motor bus and rapid transit systems; organizations responsible for planning, designing, constructing, financing, and operating transit systems; business organizations which supply products and services to transit, academic institutions, and state associations and departments of transportation. Represents the public interest in improving transit. Encourages cooperation among its members, their employees, the general public and compliance with the letter and spirit of equal opportunity principles. Seeks to: collect information relative to public transit; assist in the training, education, and professional development of all persons involved in public transit; and engage in activities which promote public transit. Provides a medium for exchange of experiences, discussion, and a comparative study of public transit affairs; Promotes research. **Libraries: Type:** by appointment only; reference. **Holdings:** 10,000; archival material, articles, books, papers, periodicals, reports. **Subjects:** urban transportation and related fields. **Awards:** Awards Program. **Frequency:** annual. **Type:** recognition. **Recipient:** for outstanding achievement in many categories ● Safety Awards. **Frequency:** annual. **Type:** recognition. **Recipient:** for safety recognition. **Computer Services:** database, restricted only to members. **Formed by Merger of:** (1974) American Transit Association. **Formerly:** (2000) American Public Transit Association. **Publications:** *Passenger Transport: The Weekly Newspaper of the Transit Industry*. Covers news, events, policies, and people that shape transit; such as: Federal funding, administrative, and regulatory actions, and new products. **Price:** $65.00/year. ISSN: 0364-345X. **Circulation:** 5,000. **Advertising:** accepted ● *Public Transportation Fact Book*, annual. Annual Reports. Breaks down the trends of transit finances and operations by modes of travel. Contains glossary of transit terms. **Price:** free for a single copy. **Conventions/Meetings:** annual conference (exhibits) ● triennial EXPO - meeting, held in conjunction with annual meeting (exhibits) ● triennial international conference, held in conjunction with annual meeting (exhibits).

3861 ■ American Society of Transportation and Logistics (AST&L)

1400 Eye St. NW, Ste.1050
Washington, DC 20005
Ph: (202)580-7270
Fax: (202)962-3939
E-mail: ldenham@astl.org
URL: http://www.astl.org
Contact: Laurie Denham PLS, Exec. Dir.

Founded: 1946. **Members:** 900. **Membership Dues:** certified, $175 (annual) ● associate, $145 (annual) ● educator, $75 (annual) ● student, $25 (annual) ● distinguish logistic professional, $500 (annual). **Staff:** 1. **Budget:** $190,000. **State Groups:** 4. **Description:** Persons engaged in transportation, traffic, logistics, or physical distribution management. Works to establish standards of knowledge, technical training, experience, conduct, and ethics, and to encourage high standards of education and technical training requisite for the proper performance of traffic, transportation, logistics, and physical distribution management. Conducts extensive educational programs. **Awards:** Honorary Distinguished Logistics Professional. **Frequency:** annual. **Type:** recognition. **Affiliated With:** National Industrial Transportation League. **Formerly:** (1983) American Society of Traffic and Transportation. **Publications:** *Membership Roster*, annual. Membership Directory. **Advertising:** accepted ● *Transportation Journal*, quarterly. **Price:** $95.00 for members in U.S.; $130.00 for nonmembers outside U.S.; $105.00 for nonmembers in U.S. ISSN: 0041-1612 ● Also publishes study guides and exams. **Conventions/Meetings:** annual conference (exhibits) - usually mid-November.

3862 ■ American Truck Dealers (ATD)

c/o National Automobile Dealers Association
8400 Westpark Dr.
McLean, VA 22102
Ph: (703)821-7000
Free: (800)252-6232
Fax: (703)749-4700
E-mail: nadainfo@nada.org
URL: http://www.nada.org
Contact: James H. Westlake, Exec. Dir.

Founded: 1970. **Members:** 2,400. **Membership Dues:** dealer, $165-$390 (annual) ● affiliate, $100 (annual). **Staff:** 5. **Description:** A division of the National Automobile Dealers Association (see separate entry). Represents franchised retail medium- and heavy-duty truck dealers' interests before government, industry, and concerned organizations. Informs members of legislative activities in Washington, DC; and maintains liaison with congressional members and key regulatory individuals and apprises them of truck dealers' attitudes and concerns. Provides analytical, legal, and technical services. Works for repeal of the truck excise tax and advocates fairness in the passage of truck taxation laws. Gives concern to the truck-related aspects of safety and the environment. Seeks to develop management guides, bulletins, and seminars on topics such as tax law changes, dealership operations, cash management, and product liability. **Awards:** Truck Dealer of the Year. **Frequency:** annual. **Type:** recognition. **Recipient:** for an outstanding truck dealer. **Affiliated With:** National Automobile Dealers Association. **Publications:** Newsletter, monthly. **Circulation:** 2,800 ● Bulletins. **Conventions/Meetings:** annual convention, includes equipment and services (exhibits).

3863 ■ American Trucking Associations (ATA)

950 N Glebe Rd., Ste.210
Arlington, VA 22203-4181
Ph: (703)838-1700
Free: (888)333-1759
Fax: (703)684-5720
E-mail: atamembership@trucking.org
URL: http://www.truckline.com
Contact: Hon. Bill Graves, Pres./CEO

Founded: 1933. **Members:** 2,200. **Staff:** 200. **Budget:** $36,000,000. **State Groups:** 51. **Description:** Motor carriers, suppliers, state trucking associations, and national conferences of trucking companies. Works to influence the decisions of federal, state, and local government bodies; promotes increased efficiency, productivity, and competitiveness in the trucking industries; sponsors American Trucking Associations Foundation. Provides quarterly financial and operating statistics service. Offers comprehensive accounting service for all sizes of carriers. Promotes highway and driver safety; supports highway research projects; and studies technical and regulatory problems of the trucking industry. Sponsors competitions; compiles statistics. Maintains numerous programs and services including: Management Information Systems Directory; Compensation Survey; Electronic Data Interchange Standards. **Libraries: Type:** not open to the public. **Holdings:** 28,000. **Subjects:** trucking, transportation. **Departments:** Customer Services; Engineering; Environmental Policy; Federation Relations; Highway Policy; Human Resources; Information Services; International Affairs; Law; Legislative and Intergovernmental Affairs; Office of Public Affairs; Safety Policy; Statistics; Tax and Economic Policy. **Affiliated With:** Agricultural and Food Transporters Conference; Distribution and LTL Carriers Association; National Tank Truck Carriers; Truckload Carriers Association. **Formed by Merger of:** American Highway Freight Association; Federation Truck Associations of America. **Publications:** *ATA Catalog*, quarterly. Lists publications. ● *North American Truck Fleet Directory*, annual ● *Transport Topics*, weekly. ISSN: 0041-1558. **Circulation:** 30,000. **Advertising:** accepted. **Conventions/Meetings:** annual Management Conference and Exhibition - meeting (exhibits).

3864 ■ Buses International Association (BIA)

PO Box 9337
Spokane, WA 99209
Ph: (509)328-2494
Fax: (509)325-5396
E-mail: billluke@ztc.net
Contact: William A. Luke, Exec.Dir.

Founded: 1981. **Members:** 100. **Membership Dues:** sustaining, $40 (annual) ● regular, $25 (annual). **Description:** Individuals from 20 countries professionally employed in the bus industry and related businesses interested in the development and progress of bus transportation worldwide. Promotes the exchange of information and ideas for the improvement of buses and bus transportation services; organizes and promotes tours enabling members to visit bus operating and manufacturing facilities; encourages education for the purpose of promoting careers in bus transportation. Plans to establish an information source for documents, books, photographs, films, recorded tapes, and other materials. **Convention/Meeting:** none. **Publications:** *Buses International*, quarterly. Newsletter. Provides information on international bus systems and companies. Contains calendar of events and reading list. **Price:** available to members only. **Circulation:** 100.

3865 ■ Certified Claims Professional Accreditation Council (CCPAC)

PO Box 550922
Jacksonville, FL 32255-0922
Ph: (904)390-1506
Fax: (904)390-1244
E-mail: jodell@landstar.com
URL: http://www.ccpac.com
Contact: John O'Dell, Exec. Dir.

Founded: 1980. **Members:** 300. **Membership Dues:** regular, $50 (annual) ● associate, $40 (annual) ● cosponsor, $200 (annual) ● corporate sponsor, $250 (annual). **Budget:** $30,000. **State Groups:** 2. **Local Groups:** 2. **Description:** Certifies freight claims management personnel in all levels of the domestic and international transportation industry and individuals who have achieved a degree of expertise in freight claims management through testing programs and procedures. Gives special recognition to those who, by passing an examination and fulfilling prescribed standards of performance and conduct, have demonstrated a high level of competence and ethical fitness. **Libraries: Type:** open to the public. **Subjects:** cargo claims. **Computer Services:** database, claims personnel ● mailing lists, of claims professionals. **Publications:** *Passport to Claims Professionalism*, biennial. Directory. Provides information on membership activities. **Price:** included in membership dues ● *Proclaim*, quarterly. Newsletter. Provides information on transportation freight claims and losses. **Price:** $75.00/year; $25.00/issue. **Advertising:** accepted ● Also issues reprints of essays submitted in Certification Programs. **Conventions/Meetings:** annual conference, held in conjunction with Shippers National Freight Claim Council.

3866 ■ Conference of Minority Transportation Officials (COMTO)

818 18th St. NW, Ste.850
Washington, DC 20006
Ph: (202)530-0551
Fax: (202)530-0617
E-mail: comto@comto.org
URL: http://www.comto.org
Contact: Julie A. Cunningham, Pres./CEO

Founded: 1971. **Members:** 2,000. **Membership Dues:** undergraduate student, $25 (annual) ● individual, professor/administrator, $58-$100 (annual) ● elected official, $250 (annual) ● transportation system (based on operating expenses), $1,500-$15,000 (annual) ● business (based on annual gross sales), $1,200-$5,000 (annual) ● nonprofit organization, $500 (annual) ● university/college, $1,000 (annual) ● Historically Underutilized Business, $250-$2,000 (annual). **Staff:** 4. **Local Groups:** 20. **Description:** Committed to insuring positive end benefits for minority community at large. **Committees:** Advanced Technology; Bylaws; Fundraising; International Initiative; Program Planning. **Councils:** Academic Advisory; Corporate Advisory; Multimodal Advisory. **Publications:** *Cable Express*, bimonthly. Newsletter. Contains information on members, national trends and events of the organization. Alternate Formats: online. **Conventions/Meetings:** annual meeting and conference.

3867 ■ Driver Employer Council of America (DECA)
1150 17th St. NW, Ste.900
Washington, DC 20036
Ph: (202)842-3400
Fax: (202)842-0011
E-mail: dking@transportdrivers.com
URL: http://www.decausa.org
Contact: Mr. Dexter King, Pres.
Founded: 1967. **Members:** 35. **Staff:** 1. **Description:** Represents companies engaged in recruiting and screening qualified truck drivers, whose services are then leased to commercial motor carriers (typically "private" carriers). Represents interests of members before federal government agencies that regulate the trucking industry. **Formerly:** (1998) Driver Leasing Council of America. **Conventions/Meetings:** annual seminar.

3868 ■ Gray Line Sightseeing Association (GLSA)
c/o Gray Line Worldwide
1835 Gaylord St.
Denver, CO 80206
Ph: (303)394-6920
Fax: (303)394-6950
E-mail: info@grayline.com
URL: http://www.grayline.com
Contact: Brad Webber, Pres./CEO
Founded: 1910. **Members:** 150. **Staff:** 15. **Description:** Independent and autonomous sightseeing tour companies. Members are licensed to use Gray Line name and trademark to sell sightseeing tours, packages, charters and transportation services. **Publications:** *Grayline Express*, monthly. Newsletter. **Price:** available to members only ● *Travel Guide*, annual. Directory. Lists all tours worldwide. **Price:** free. **Advertising:** accepted. Alternate Formats: online. **Conventions/Meetings:** annual convention (exhibits) - always held in the fall.

3869 ■ Greek National Tourist Organization (GNTO)
Olympic Tower
645 5th Ave., Ste.903
New York, NY 10022
Ph: (212)421-5777
Fax: (212)826-6940
E-mail: info@greektourism.com
URL: http://www.gnto.gr
Contact: Athanasios Oikonomou, Sec. Gen.
Staff: 10. **Languages:** English, Greek. **Description:** Promotes tourism to Greece. **Libraries: Type:** reference. **Holdings:** books. **Subjects:** Greece as a tourist destination. **Additional Websites:** http://www.greektourism.com. **Telecommunication Services:** electronic mail, info@gnto.gr. **Formerly:** (2001) Greek National Tourist Organization; (2003) Greek National Tourism Organization. **Publications:** Brochures. **Price:** free. **Advertising:** accepted. **Conventions/Meetings:** annual International Tourism Exhibition - meeting (exhibits) ● seminar, for travel agents.

3870 ■ Independent Truckers and Drivers Association (ITDA)
1109 Plover Dr.
Baltimore, MD 21227
Ph: (410)242-0507
E-mail: rbontz@comcast.net
Contact: Rita Bontz, Pres.
Founded: 1974. **Description:** Independent truckers, drivers, and others involved in the trucking industry. Purposes are to: keep truckers informed of current events, issues, and legislation; conduct information campaigns to help the public understand the role of independent truckers in the surface transportation industry; work with legislators and other government officials to bring about changes and improvements that ensure the effectiveness of the trucking industry. **Formerly:** (1988) Maryland Independent Truckers and Drivers Association. **Publications:** *Truckers Newsletter*, monthly. **Conventions/Meetings:** quarterly meeting.

3871 ■ Intelligent Transportation Society of America (ITSA)
1100 17th St. NW, Ste.1200
Washington, DC 20036
Ph: (202)484-4847
Free: (800)374-8472
Fax: (202)484-3483
E-mail: info@itsa.org
URL: http://www.itsa.org
Contact: Scott Belcher, Pres./CEO
Founded: 1991. **Members:** 500. **Membership Dues:** federal, state agency, turnpike, bridge or tunnel authority, $2,625 (annual) ● transit authority, nonprofit trade/professional association, public interest group, college or university, $1,050 (annual) ● city/county agency, metropolitan planning organization, public safety agency, $750 (annual) ● private industry (based on the total gross annual revenue of the parent corporation), $750-$15,750 (annual). **Staff:** 20. **Budget:** $9,000,000. **State Groups:** 22. **Description:** Strives to provide its more than 500 member organizations a voice "at the table" when public policy, regulations, standards and other matters are discussed relating to intelligent transportation systems. Works to raise awareness of the value of ITS among consumers, legislators, and media; increase federal funding through transportation reauthorization; and works to expand the use of technology solutions where people and goods are transported without delay, injury or fatality by integrated systems that are built and operated to be safe, cost-efficient, and secure. Also provides numerous membership services and programs to assist its member organizations in stimulating the market for ITS and the achievement of their ITS deployment and business objectives. **Publications:** *ITS America News*, monthly. Newsletter. **Price:** available to members only. Alternate Formats: online. **Conventions/Meetings:** annual meeting - 2008 Nov. 16-20, New York, NY; 2009 June 1-3, Washington, DC; 2010 May 17-19, Houston, TX; 2011 Oct. 16-20, Orlando, FL.

3872 ■ Intermodal Association of North America (IANA)
11785 Beltsville Dr., Ste.1100
Calverton, MD 20705-4049
Ph: (301)982-3400
Fax: (301)982-4815
E-mail: iana@intermodal.org
URL: http://www.intermodal.org
Contact: Joanne F. Casey, Pres./CEO
Founded: 1991. **Members:** 660. **Membership Dues:** voting (minimum), $350 (annual) ● non-voting, at-large, associate, $125 (annual) ● voting (maximum), $15,000 (annual). **Staff:** 21. **Budget:** $3,000,000. **Description:** Companies involved in intermodal freight transportation domestically and/or internationally within North America, including railroad, ocean carrier/stack train operator, intermodal truck/highway carrier, intermodal marketing, and supplier companies; associate members are companies which have an interest in the well-being and development of the intermodal industry. Aims to promote the benefits of intermodal freight transportation and encourage its growth through innovation and dialogue. Goals are: to promote the benefits of the shipping community; to provide members a forum to discuss common issues and innovations; to foster members professional development; to participate in governmental proceedings impacting the industry; to inform and educate lawmakers and other government representatives about the industry. **Divisions:** Foundation for Intermodal Research and Education. **Formerly:** IANA. **Publications:** *IMC Market Activity Report*, monthly. **Price:** $150.00 /year for members; $300.00 /year for nonmembers ● *Intermodal Freight Transportation, 4th Edition*. Book. **Price:** $45.00 for members; $75.00 for nonmembers ● *Intermodal Insights*, monthly. Newsletter. **Price:** included in membership dues; $375.00 for nonmembers. **Advertising:** accepted ● *Intermodal Product and Supplier Directory*, annual. **Price:** free ● *Intermodal Trucker Database*, daily ● *Membership Handbook*, annual. **Price:** free for members ● *Rail Traffic Report*, monthly. **Price:** $395.00 /year for members; $595.00 /year for nonmembers. **Conventions/Meetings:** annual Intermodal Conference and Membership Meeting - conference and meeting, held in conjunction with the National Industrial Transportation League and the Transportation Intermediaries Association ● periodic Intermodal Operations and Maintenance Seminar ● periodic International Intermodal Expo - meeting, held at Georgia World Congress Center (exhibits).

3873 ■ The International Air Cargo Association (TIACA)
PO Box 661510
Miami, FL 33266-1510
Ph: (786)265-7011
Fax: (786)265-7012
E-mail: secgen@tiaca.org
URL: http://www.tiaca.org
Contact: Daniel C. Fernandez, Sec. Gen.
Membership Dues: affiliate, $100 (annual) ● corporate, trustee, $1,000 (annual). **Multinational. Description:** Firms, individuals, and institutions engaged in the air logistics industries, including air and surface freight carriers, forwarders, shippers, service vendors, manufacturers, airports, government agencies, financial institutions, and consultants. Promotes growth and development of the global air logistics industries. Serves as a "single, dynamic force for progress and growth in the ever-expanding arena of world trade and economic development." Represents members before labor and international trade organizations and government agencies. **Awards:** Hall of Fame. **Frequency:** annual. **Type:** recognition. **Recipient:** to individuals who made significant and lasting contributions to the air cargo industry. **Committees:** Education; Galaxy; Industry Affairs; Nominations; Operations; Program; Site Selections. **Publications:** *TIACA Times*, quarterly. Newsletter. Contains summary of TIACA events and the air cargo industry. **Price:** free, for members only. Alternate Formats: online. **Conventions/Meetings:** biennial conference (exhibits).

3874 ■ International Road Federation (IRF)
500 Montgomery St., 5th Fl.
Alexandria, VA 22314-1565
Ph: (703)535-1001
Fax: (703)535-1007
E-mail: info@internationalroadfederation.org
URL: http://www.irfnet.org
Contact: Peter J. Boyd, Chm.
Founded: 1948. **Members:** 750. **Staff:** 7. **Languages:** English, French, German, Spanish, Vietnamese. **Description:** Road associations, private sector firms, and public sector firms in 70 countries. Encourages the development and improvement of highways and highway transportation and the exchange of technologies. Provides educational grants to select countries for graduate training through the International Road Educational Foundation. **Libraries: Type:** reference. **Holdings:** books, periodicals. **Awards:** Man of the Year. **Frequency:** annual. **Type:** recognition. **Additional Websites:** http://www.irfnews.org. **Publications:** *World Highways*, 8/year. **Circulation:** 25,000. **Advertising:** accepted ● *World Road Statistic*, annual ● Also produces videotape training aids and reports. **Conventions/Meetings:** meeting (exhibits).

3875 ■ Mid-West Truckers Association (MTA)
2727 N Dirksen Pkwy.
Springfield, IL 62702
Ph: (217)525-0310
Fax: (217)525-0342
E-mail: info@mid-westtruckers.com
URL: http://www.mid-westtruckers.com
Contact: Donald Schaefer, Exec. VP
Founded: 1961. **Members:** 2,616. **Membership Dues:** regular, $230 (annual). **Staff:** 10. **Budget:** $12,000,000. **Regional Groups:** 3. **State Groups:** 3. **For-Profit. Description:** Owners and operators of trucking companies. Serves as a unified voice for truckers nationwide; conducts lobbying. Sponsors services to members including: mass purchasing program, whereby members may purchase parts at

wholesale rates; drug and alcohol testing program; assistance with international registration; license plate procurement; group insurance programs self-funded worker's Compensation Program. Conducts seminars and educational programs; maintains speakers' bureau. **Libraries: Type:** reference. **Holdings:** 102; video recordings. **Subjects:** safety, drugs, alcohol, truck and trailer maintenance. **Awards:** Safe and Courteous Driver Award. **Frequency:** annual. **Type:** recognition. **Recipient:** for most miles driven without accidents or violations ● Truck of the Year Award. **Frequency:** annual. **Type:** recognition. **Computer Services:** database, internal ● mailing lists, for associate business members. **Telecommunication Services:** electronic mail, truckers@iname.com. **Committees:** Political Action (TRK-PAC). **Publications:** *Cost Summary Booklet*. Contains cost summaries. ● *Keep on Truckin' News*, monthly. Magazine. Includes legislative developments, safety issues, and equipment news. Contains semiannual associate business member listing. **Price:** $5.00/year, for members only. **Circulation:** 4,000. **Advertising:** accepted ● Also publishes rate tariffs, designated highway map, safety programs, videos, books and pamphlets. **Conventions/Meetings:** annual Mid-West Truck Show, trucking industry services and supplies (exhibits).

3876 ■ National Accounting and Finance Council (NAFC)

950 N Glebe Rd., Ste.210
Arlington, VA 22203-4181
Ph: (703)838-1700 (703)838-1915
Fax: (703)836-0751
E-mail: nafc@trucking.org
URL: http://www.truckline.com/aboutata/councils/nafc
Contact: David Hershey, Exec. Dir.

Founded: 1954. **Members:** 1,100. **Membership Dues:** motor carrier (with annual revenues of more than $250 million), $125-$370 (annual) ● motor carrier (with annual revenues of $250 million or less), $115-$330 (annual) ● associate, $165-$420 (annual). **Staff:** 7. **Budget:** $650,000. **Local Groups:** 10. **Description:** Chief financial and executive officers of trucking companies; bankers, security analysts, CPAs, insurance agents, and software companies affiliated with the trucking industry. Works to advance standards in the motor carrier field and provide means for member self-improvement through interaction with other members and regulatory agencies, committee work, and educational activities. Conducts seminars. **Libraries: Type:** reference. **Holdings:** 1,500; papers. **Awards:** J. Frank Dixon Award. **Type:** recognition. **Recipient:** for the most outstanding affiliated council ● James E. Roelker Award. **Type:** recognition. **Recipient:** for an individual with distinguished service to the council. **Telecommunication Services:** electronic mail, dhershey@trucking.org ● electronic mail, dsalerno@trucking.org. **Committees:** Accounting Principles; Credit Collection Practices; Financial Relations; Independent Contractors; Risk Management; Taxation. **Affiliated With:** American Trucking Associations. **Formerly:** (1954) National Committee on Accounting. **Publications:** *Another Bulletin Newsletter*, periodic. **Price:** included in membership dues ● *ATA Accounting Service*, periodic. Assists Class I and Class II motor carriers in complying with Interstate Commerce Commission regulations. **Price:** $95.00 for members; $125.00 for nonmembers ● *Motor Carrier Credit and Collection Practices Manual*, annual. Deals with credit and collection concerns of motor carriers such as tariff rules. **Price:** $115.00 for members; $145.00 for nonmembers ● *Motor Freight Controller*, bimonthly. Magazine. Covers technical developments, financial topics, and association news for chief financial officers of trucking companies. **Price:** included in membership dues. **Circulation:** 1,100. **Advertising:** accepted ● *NAFC Federal Excise Tax Guide*, semiannual. Provides coverage of key excise tax areas including: heavy vehicle use tax, communication, fuel and tire taxes. **Price:** $95.00 /year for members; $125.00 /year for nonmembers ● *NAFC Membership Directory*, annual ● *NAFC Risk Management Manual for Motor Carriers*, periodic. Serves as a reference for motor carrier managers, which seeks to help them deal with the current insurance market. **Price:** $135.00 for members; $175.00 for nonmembers ● *NAFC Sales Tax Service*, quarterly. Contains current information related to sales and use taxes. **Price:** $120.00 for members; $145.00 for nonmembers ● *NAFC State Tax Guide*, bimonthly. Contains information from each of the 50 states on corporate organization, qualification fees, and annual reports. **Price:** $275.00 /year for members; $295.00 /year for nonmembers ● *NAFC Tax Information Service*, monthly. Gives information for motor carrier managers on developments in taxation on the federal and state levels. **Price:** $95.00 /year for members; $125.00 /year for nonmembers ● *Workers Compensation Manual*, quarterly. Tracks coverage of laws on a state-by-state basis, including owner-operator statutes and self-insurance requirements. **Price:** $130.00 for members; $160.00 for nonmembers. **Conventions/Meetings:** annual conference (exhibits) - always June.

3877 ■ National Association of Publicly Funded Truck Driving Schools (NAPFTDS)

c/o Chuck Collins, Exec. Dir.
1109 E Park Ridge Ave.
Appleton, WI 54911
Ph: (920)739-9786 (570)839-2778
Fax: (920)997-1777
E-mail: katchuckco@aol.com
URL: http://www.napftds.org
Contact: Chuck Collins, Exec. Dir.

Founded: 1990. **Membership Dues:** full, $175 (annual) ● associate, $350 (annual) ● affiliate, $250 (annual). **Staff:** 16. **Description:** Promotes public education for the transportation industry; provides network of public institutional and transportation-related industries. **Publications:** *Learning Curve*. Newsletter. Alternate Formats: online. **Conventions/Meetings:** annual convention.

3878 ■ National Bus Traffic Association (NBTA)

700 13th St. NW, Ste.575
Washington, DC 20005-5923
Ph: (202)898-2700
Fax: (202)842-0850
E-mail: kmusiime@buses.org
URL: http://www.bustraffic.org
Contact: Peter J. Pantuso, Pres.

Founded: 1933. **Members:** 270. **Membership Dues:** carrier, $500 (annual) ● associate, $100 (annual). **Staff:** 3. **Description:** Establishes by the intercity regular route bus carriers. Serves as tariff publisher for its industry. **Publications:** *Bus Passenger Tariffs*, periodic ● *National Mileage Guides*, periodic. **Conventions/Meetings:** annual conference and meeting.

3879 ■ National Industrial Transportation League (NITL)

1700 N Moore St., Ste.1900
Arlington, VA 22209
Ph: (703)524-5011
Fax: (703)524-5017
E-mail: info@nitl.org
URL: http://www.nitl.org
Contact: John Ficker, Pres.

Founded: 1907. **Members:** 1,400. **Membership Dues:** corporation, firm, sole proprietorship, agent, $690-$4,760 (annual) ● organization (based on annual budget), $690-$1,030 (annual) ● affiliate, $350 (annual). **Staff:** 12. **Budget:** $2,200,000. **Description:** Seeks to promote adequate national and international transportation; encourages the exchange of ideas and information concerning traffic and transportation; and cooperates with regulatory agencies and other transportation companies in developing an understanding of legislation. **Telecommunication Services:** electronic mail, ficker@nitl.org ● electronic mail, gilanshah@nitl.org. **Committees:** Air Transportation; Highway Transportation; Information and Technology Advancement. **Formerly:** (1982) National Industrial Traffic League. **Publications:** *Annual Meeting and TransComp Guide*, annual ● *The Notice*, weekly. Newsletter. Covers recent developments in transportation legislation, regulatory and court proceedings, and industry innovations. **Price:** included in membership dues. **Circulation:** 1,400. **Advertising:** accepted ● *Reference Manual*, quarterly. Handbook. **Conventions/Meetings:** annual TransCamp - trade show and meeting, for transportation service providers (exhibits).

3880 ■ National Limousine Association (NLA)

49 S Maple Ave.
Marlton, NJ 08053
Ph: (856)596-3344
Free: (800)652-7007
Fax: (856)596-2145
E-mail: info@limo.org
URL: http://www.limo.org
Contact: Ms. Patricia Nelson, Exec. Dir.

Founded: 1985. **Members:** 1,600. **Membership Dues:** state and regional limousine association, $360 (annual) ● supplier, $505 (annual) ● manufacturer, $1,015 (annual) ● limousine operator (based on number of vehicles), $200-$1,530 (annual). **Staff:** 3. **Budget:** $500,000. **State Groups:** 31. **Description:** Limousine owners and operators; limousine manufacturers and suppliers to the industry. Seeks to: promote and advance industry professionalism and the common interests of members; increase use of limousines in both business and public sectors. Monitors legislation and organizes lobbying activities. Sponsors seminars on safety/regulatory issues and management techniques. Operates speakers' bureau; compiles statistics; offers insurance plans. **Computer Services:** Mailing lists. **Additional Websites:** http://www.nlaride.com. **Publications:** *Limo Scene*, bimonthly. Newsletter. Includes reports on federal and state legislation, industry trends, member features, seminars and trade shows, and new marketing techniques. **Price:** included in membership dues. **Circulation:** 1,600. **Advertising:** accepted. Alternate Formats: online ● Membership Directory, periodic. **Conventions/Meetings:** annual show (exhibits).

3881 ■ National Private Truck Council (NPTC)

950 N Gelebe Rd., Ste.530
Arlington, VA 22203-4183
Ph: (703)683-1300
Fax: (703)683-1217
E-mail: info@nptc.org
URL: http://www.nptc.org
Contact: Mr. George Mundell, Sr. VP

Founded: 1988. **Members:** 570. **Membership Dues:** fleet, $685-$950 (annual) ● allied (small volume supplier), $695-$1,040 (annual) ● allied (large volume supplier), $1,445-$8,665 (annual) ● third-party provider, $1,155-$5,775 (annual). **Staff:** 6. **Budget:** $1,850,000. **Multinational. Description:** Represents private motor carrier truck fleets and their suppliers. **Libraries: Type:** not open to the public. **Holdings:** 12. **Subjects:** fleet management, finance, safety, legal and regulatory, equipment. **Awards:** CTP Scholarship. **Frequency:** annual. **Type:** scholarship. **Recipient:** to CTP candidates who are NPTC member private fleet and transportation managers ● Dodi Reagan Humanitarian Award. **Frequency:** annual. **Type:** recognition. **Recipient:** to a driver or ex-driver with a similar outstanding commitment to the improvement of the condition of fellow human beings ● Driver Hall of Fame. **Frequency:** annual. **Type:** recognition. **Recipient:** for drivers ● Fleet Awards. **Frequency:** annual. **Type:** recognition. **Recipient:** for individuals who have made significant contributions to the organization, their profession and the private trucking community ● Fleet Safety Awards. **Frequency:** annual. **Type:** recognition. **Recipient:** to fleets for outstanding and/or improved safety records based on their crash rates. **Computer Services:** Online services, Fleet Learning Center. **Telecommunication Services:** electronic mail, gmundell@nptc.org. **Committees:** Conference Planning; Legislative and Regulatory; Public Relations/Marketing; Safety. **Formed by Merger of:** (1988) Private Truck Council of America; (1988) National Private Trucking Association. **Publications:** *Membership Directory & Buyers' Guide*, annual. **Price:** included in membership dues. **Circulation:** 3,500. **Advertising:** accepted ● *Private Fleet Directory/FleetSeek*. Alternate Formats: online ● *Weekly Update*. Newsletter. **Price:** included in membership dues. **Circulation:** 800. Alternate Formats: online ● Yearbook, annual. **Circulation:**

15,000. **Advertising:** accepted. **Conventions/Meetings:** annual Education Management & Exhibition - conference (exhibits).

3882 ■ National School Transportation Association (NSTA)

113 S West St., 4th Fl.
Alexandria, VA 22314
Ph: (703)684-3200
Free: (800)222-NSTA
Fax: (703)684-3212
E-mail: info@yellowbuses.org
URL: http://www.yellowbuses.org
Contact: Barry Stock, Pres.-Elect

Founded: 1964. **Members:** 3,000. **Membership Dues:** contractor, $150 (annual) ● manufacturer, $4,000 (annual) ● supplier, $2,000 (annual) ● public, $250 (annual). **Staff:** 5. **Budget:** $350,000. **State Groups:** 22. **Description:** Private owners and operators of school buses, manufacturers of school buses, and allied industries. (Members represent 40&percent; of the school buses operated for school functions.) Aims to provide safe pupil transportation, foster safety, and provide an atmosphere conducive to private enterprise. Conducts ongoing school bus safety research. Operates speakers' bureau; sponsors School Bus Driver International Safety Competition for driver skill awareness. **Libraries: Type:** reference. **Awards:** Contractor of the Year. **Frequency:** annual. **Type:** recognition. **Recipient:** for contractors ● Distinguished Service Award. **Frequency:** annual. **Type:** recognition. **Recipient:** for contractors who offer excellence of service ● Golden Merit Award. **Frequency:** annual. **Type:** recognition. **Recipient:** for contractors who offer excellence of service ● Hall of Fame Award. **Frequency:** annual. **Type:** recognition. **Recipient:** for members ● Outstanding Driver Service Award. **Frequency:** annual. **Type:** recognition. **Recipient:** to men and women who have done an exemplary job as drivers and role models for their communities ● Outstanding School Transportation Administrative Award. **Frequency:** annual. **Type:** recognition. **Recipient:** to drivers who have done their best in terms of school transportation. **Committees:** Association and Industry Development; Government Relations; Human Resources; Marketing/Communications; Nominating; Railroad; Safety; Security; Special Education; Sponsor and Associates; Strategic Planning; Technology Planning. **Formerly:** (1975) National Association of School Bus Contract Operators. **Publications:** *Awards Booklet*. Alternate Formats: online ● *National School Transportation Association-Newsletter*, biweekly. Provides information on federal legislation and regulation affecting the association and school bus contracts. **Price:** free for members. **Circulation:** 1,100. Alternate Formats: online. **Conventions/Meetings:** annual competition ● annual convention (exhibits) - always July.

3883 ■ National Trailer Dealers Association (NTDA)

37400 Hills Tech Dr.
Farmington Hills, MI 48331
Free: (800)800-4552
Fax: (248)489-8590
E-mail: info@ntda.org
URL: http://www.ntda.org
Contact: Steve Carey, Exec. Dir.

Founded: 1990. **Membership Dues:** dealer, $175 (annual) ● allied, $200 (annual). **Description:** Companies concerned with all aspects of the semi-trailer industry, including: licensed dealers; manufacturers; parts and accessories manufacturers and suppliers; rental and leasing firms; trailer repair and maintenance shop suppliers; consultants to dealers; trade publications; insurance and finance companies. Strives to promote goodwill and public relations of independent semi-trailer dealers. Advocates high standards of service and conduct within the industry, encourages public highway safety, and educates members on industry relevant matters. Offers assistance to members in areas such as financial analysis, advertising, sales promotion, graphics, and publishing. **Awards: Frequency:** annual. **Type:** scholarship. **Publications:** Newsletter. **Price:** included in membership dues. **Conventions/Meetings:** annual convention, with networking opportunities - always fall. 2008 Oct. 9-11, Orlando, FL.

3884 ■ National Truckers Association (NTA)

3131 Turtle Creek Blvd., Ste.910
Dallas, TX 75219
Free: (800)823-8454
E-mail: info@nationaltruckers.com
URL: http://www.nationaltruckers.com

Membership Dues: affiliate, $120 (annual). **Description:** Aims to develop membership programs and products for industries, independent contractors, owner operators and motor carriers. Protects the interests of independent truck drivers. **Publications:** *National Truckers' Headlines*, quarterly. Newsletter. Contains current issues and latest developments. Alternate Formats: online.

3885 ■ North American Rail Shippers Association (NARS)

2115 Portsmouth Dr.
Richardson, TX 75082-4839
Ph: (972)690-4740 (973)541-8076
Fax: (972)644-8208
E-mail: nars@railshippers.com
URL: http://www.railshippers.com
Contact: E. Leo Mountjoy, Exec. Dir.

Founded: 1937. **Members:** 2,000. **Budget:** $86,000. **Regional Groups:** 6. **Description:** Federation of six regional associations of rail shippers; membership includes shippers and receivers of rail freight. Cooperates with railroads in development of a sound transportation system. **Awards:** NARS Person of the Year. **Frequency:** annual. **Type:** recognition. **Computer Services:** Mailing lists. **Formerly:** (1983) National Association of Shippers Advisory Boards; (1985) National Association of Rail Shippers Advisory Boards; (2001) National Association of Rail Shippers. **Publications:** Newsletter, semiannual. **Conventions/Meetings:** annual meeting and seminar.

3886 ■ North American Railcar Operators Association (NARCOA)

c/o Joel Williams, Sec.
PO Box 802
Lock Haven, PA 17745
Ph: (570)893-1610
E-mail: joel.williams@earthlink.net
URL: http://www.narcoa.org
Contact: Pat Coleman, Pres.

Founded: 1980. **Members:** 1,800. **Membership Dues:** general, $24 (annual). **Description:** Works for safe and legal operation of railroad equipment historically used for maintenance of way. Increases awareness of motorcars and railroads. Promotes motorcar operational safety. **Computer Services:** Mailing lists, of members ● online services, forum. **Committees:** Rail Preservation. **Publications:** *The Set Off*. Newsletter.

3887 ■ North America's SuperCorridor Coalition (NASCO)

901 Main St., Ste.4400
Dallas, TX 75202
Ph: (214)744-1042
Fax: (214)744-1043
E-mail: tiffany@nascocorridor.com
URL: http://www.nascocorridor.com
Contact: Tiffany Melvin JD, Exec. Dir.

Founded: 1994. **Membership Dues:** private sector - individual, $500 ● private sector - associate, $1,000 ● private sector - educational institution/investor, $2,500 ● private sector - patron, $5,000 ● private sector - benefactor, public sector - patron, $10,000 ● public sector - benefactor, $25,000. **Multinational. Description:** Seeks to improve the trade competitiveness and quality of life in North America through advocacy, strategic planning, infrastructure and non-infrastructure improvements, trade facilitation, technology applications and solutions, and education. Serves as an advocacy and lobby group for transportation and related issues and interests of the jurisdictions along the corridor. Facilitates and supports any corridor related projects or initiatives that focus on enhancing the security, safety and efficiency of transportation, trade processing and logistics systems along the corridor.

3888 ■ Owner-Operator Independent Drivers Association (OOIDA)

1 NW OOIDA Dr.
Grain Valley, MO 64029-7903
Ph: (816)229-5791
Free: (800)444-5791
Fax: (816)229-0518
E-mail: ooida@ooida.com
URL: http://www.ooida.com
Contact: Jim Johnston, Pres.

Founded: 1973. **Members:** 152,338. **Membership Dues:** regular, $45 (annual) ● basic corporate, $250 (annual) ● silver corporate, $2,500 (annual) ● gold corporate, $5,000 (annual). **Staff:** 230. **Budget:** $2,000,000. **Description:** Truck owner-operators, small fleet operators, and drivers. Lobbying association seeking to improve owner-operator working conditions. Provides national recognition and a channel for members to voice interests and concerns on changes that affect the trucking business. Addresses issues including: freight rates commensurate with costs; rules guaranteeing prompt payment for owner-operators; flexible hours of operation; taxes; safety initiatives. Offers medical, truck, dental, and accident programs. Sponsors research programs; compiles statistics; maintains speakers' bureau. **Libraries: Type:** reference. **Holdings:** periodicals. **Awards:** OOIDA Scholarship. **Frequency:** annual. **Type:** scholarship. **Recipient:** for child or grandchild of member; submit essay on trucking topic assigned by review committee ● Safe Driving Award. **Frequency:** annual. **Type:** recognition. **Recipient:** to OOIDA members, for their safe, accident-free operation of a commercial vehicle. **Additional Websites:** http://www.landlinemag.com. **Telecommunication Services:** electronic mail, webmaster@ooida.com ● electronic mail, jjohnston@ooida.com. **Programs:** Business Services; Drug and Alcohol Testing Consortium; Health and Life; Retirement Plan; Safe Driving Award; Telecommunications; Truck and Trailing Financing; Truck Insurance. **Publications:** *Land Line*, 10/year. Magazine. Serves owners and operators of class-8 heavy trucks. **Price:** included in membership dues; free to any trucker. ISSN: 0279-6503. **Circulation:** 204,941. **Advertising:** accepted. Alternate Formats: CD-ROM; diskette; online ● *Owner-Operator News*, quarterly. Newsletter. Covers legislative, economic, and general news of interest to small business truckers. **Price:** included in membership dues. **Circulation:** 100,000 ● Videos. **Conventions/Meetings:** semiannual board meeting.

3889 ■ Professional Truck Driver Institute (PTDI)

555 E Braddock Rd.
Alexandria, VA 22314-2182
Ph: (703)647-7015
Fax: (703)836-6610
E-mail: ptdi@truckload.org
URL; http://www.ptdi.org
Contact: Chris Burruss, Pres.

Founded: 1985. **Staff:** 2. **Nonmembership. Description:** Stakeholders include carriers, schools, trade associations, manufacturers, insurance companies, regulatory bodies, funding organizations, and suppliers to the trucking industry. Develops skill and curriculum standards for truck driver training and standards for the certification of truck driver training courses; certifies commercial truck driver training courses and driver finishing programs. **Awards:** Lee J. Crittenden Memorial Award. **Frequency:** annual. **Type:** recognition. **Recipient:** to an individual who has made a noteworthy contribution to further the organization. **Committees:** Certification. **Formerly:** (1998) Professional Truck Driver Institute of America. **Publications:** *Certification Standards and Requirements for Entry-Level Tractor-Trailer Driver Courses*. Manual ● *Certification Standards and Requirements for Tractor-Trailer Driver Finishing Programs*. Manual ● *Curriculum Standard Guidelines for Entry-Level Tractor-Trailer Driver Courses*. Manual ● *Skill Standards for Entry-Level Tractor-Trailer Drivers*. Manual

• *Skill Standards for Professional Solo Tractor-Trailer Drivers*. Manual.

3890 ■ Professional Trucking Services Association (PTSA)

c/o Anthony L. Keenan, Pres.
United Truckers Ser.
1385 Iris Dr.
Conyers, GA 30013
Ph: (770)922-6200
Fax: (770)929-3201
Contact: Anthony L. Keenan, Pres.

Founded: 1984. **Members:** 56. **Description:** Seeks to provide reputable service bureaus to assist businesses involved in the licensing and acquiring of permits for the trucking industry. **Publications:** Newsletters, periodic. **Conventions/Meetings:** annual meeting and symposium (exhibits).

3891 ■ Railway Industrial Clearance Association (RICA)

c/o Michael R. Scott, Sec.-Treas.
6119 Hampton Way Ct.
Spring, TX 77389
Ph: (832)585-3854
Fax: (832)585-3854
E-mail: secretarytreasurer@rica.org
URL: http://www.rica.org
Contact: Michael R. Scott, Sec.-Treas.

Founded: 1969. **Members:** 500. **Membership Dues:** active, $50 (annual). **Description:** Railroads, port authorities, riggers, heavy haulers, expediters, marine operators, consultants, manufacturers of industrial equipment that is "dimensional" (bigger than a boxcar or extremely heavy) and which is therefore unsuited for regular rail shipment and requires shipping clearance from railroads. Facilitates communication among members. **Libraries: Type:** not open to the public. **Holdings:** video recordings. **Subjects:** dimensional shipping. **Computer Services:** Mailing lists. **Committees:** Clearance; Electronic Data Interchange; Equipment; Publicity; Service. **Formerly:** (2000) Railway Industry Clearance Association. **Publications:** *RICA Business to Business Survey*, periodic. Includes updated company's information. • Newsletter, quarterly. **Conventions/Meetings:** annual meeting (exhibits) - always June.

3892 ■ The Road Information Program (TRIP)

1726 M St. NW, Ste.401
Washington, DC 20036-4521
Ph: (202)466-6706
Fax: (202)785-4722
E-mail: trip@tripnet.org
URL: http://www.tripnet.org
Contact: William M. Wilkins, Exec. Dir.

Founded: 1971. **Members:** 300. **Staff:** 6. **Budget:** $800,000. **Description:** Conducts public education programs for the highway industry. Promotes transportation policies that relieve traffic congestion, improve air quality, make highway travel safer and enhance economic productivity. **Telecommunication Services:** electronic mail, wilkins@tipnet.org. **Publications:** *State Highway Funding Methods*, annual • *Trip Update*, quarterly. **Conventions/Meetings:** quarterly board meeting.

3893 ■ Society of Professional Drivers (SPD)

5235 Mission Oaks Blvd., Ste.200
Camarillo, CA 93012
Ph: (818)774-3889
Fax: (805)491-0708
E-mail: wally@stuntplayers.com
URL: http://www.stuntplayers.com
Contact: Wally Crowder, Founder/CEO

Founded: 1957. **For-Profit. Description:** Encourages professionalism among truck, school bus, and passenger car drivers. Focuses on safe driving, energy efficiency, and increasing vehicle longevity through better driving techniques. **Publications:** *Traffilert*, bimonthly. Newsletter • Manual, periodic.

3894 ■ Taxicab, Limousine and Paratransit Association (TLPA)

3849 Farragut Ave.
Kensington, MD 20895-2004
Ph: (301)946-5701
Fax: (301)946-4641
E-mail: info@tlpa.org
URL: http://www.tlpa.org
Contact: Alfred B. LaGasse III, Exec. VP

Founded: 1917. **Members:** 1,100. **Membership Dues:** vehicle, $18 (annual) • fleet operator/international fleet operator, $144 (annual) • associate, $500-$788 (annual) • public sector/trade association, $250-$538 (annual). **Staff:** 5. **Multinational. Description:** Ground transportation fleet owners operating 108,000 passenger vehicles including taxicabs, limousines, sedans, airport shuttles, paratransit, and non-emergency medical. **Awards:** Driver of the Year. **Frequency:** annual. **Type:** recognition • Operator of the Year. **Frequency:** annual. **Type:** recognition. **Telecommunication Services:** electronic mail, alagasse@tlpa.org. **Committees:** Political Action. **Formed by Merger of:** National Association of Taxicab Owners; Cab Research Bureau; American Taxicab Association. **Formerly:** (1991) International Taxicab Association; (2001) International Taxicab and Livery Association. **Publications:** *Dispatch: The Business Report the For-Hire Vehicle Industry*, bimonthly. Newsletter. **Price:** free for members. ISSN: 0743-7269. **Circulation:** 1,100. **Advertising:** accepted • *Limousine*, bimonthly. Newsletter • *Paratransit*, bimonthly. Newsletter • *Taxicab*, bimonthly. Newsletter • *Transportation Leader*, quarterly. Magazine. Contains advertisers' index, legal column, and buyer's guide. **Price:** $4.00/issue; $16.00/year in U.S.; $26.00/year international. ISSN: 0040-0426. **Circulation:** 5,700. **Advertising:** accepted. **Conventions/Meetings:** annual convention and trade show (exhibits) - always October or November • annual convention and trade show (exhibits) - always March/April • annual convention and trade show (exhibits) - always July.

3895 ■ Technology and Maintenance Council of the American Trucking Associations (TMC/ATA)

950 N Glebe Rd., Ste.210
Arlington, VA 22203-4181
Ph: (703)838-1763 (703)838-1700
Free: (800)ATA-LINE
Fax: (703)684-4328
E-mail: tmc@trucking.org
URL: http://www.truckline.com/aboutata/councils/tmc
Contact: Carl T. Kirk, Exec. Dir.

Founded: 1979. **Members:** 3,200. **Membership Dues:** fleet manager or executive (non-ATA) and full manager/executive level, $395 (annual) • service/dealer corporate and associate, $460 (annual) • fleet educational, additional fleet or IT manager, IT executive, manager and owner/operator, $150 (annual) • fleet manager or executive (ATA member), $340 (annual) • fleet (non-ATA), additional associate, and additional service-dealer, $175 (annual) • technician, $75 (annual) • student technician, $30 (annual). **Staff:** 200. **Budget:** $4,500,000. **Languages:** English, Spanish. **Description:** Dedicated to the improvement of trucking equipment and its maintenance. Cooperates in mutual exchange of information among vehicle designers, manufacturers, users, and equipment and maintenance specialists. Maintains liaison with appropriate federal agencies. Conducts studies on vehicle design and operation, more efficient maintenance procedures, and other areas pertaining to vehicle/fleet maintenance. Sponsors maintenance management product exhibition. **Computer Services:** database, coding conventions for equipment cost accounting. **Formerly:** (2002) The Maintenance Council of the American Trucking Associations. **Publications:** *Fleet Advisor*, monthly. Newsletter. Provides in-depth articles on industry news. • *Fleet Maintenance and Technology*, quarterly. Magazine. Offers coverage of Council news and features in-depth articles on topics important to trucking professionals. • *Recommenced Maintenance Practices Manual* • *Trailblazer*. Journal. **Price:** $60.00 for members; $100.00 for nonmembers • *Transport Topics*, weekly. Newspaper. Covers current industry events. • Manuals • Membership Directory, annual. Contains name, title, company affiliation, address and phone numbers of all TMC members. **Price:** included in membership dues. **Conventions/Meetings:** annual Transportation Equipment Exhibition - meeting (exhibits) - always March.

3896 ■ Transportation Clubs International (TCI)

PO Box 2223
Ocean Shores, WA 98569
Free: (877)858-8627
Fax: (360)289-3188
E-mail: info@transportationclubsinternational.com
URL: http://www.transportationclubsinternational.com
Contact: Katie DeJonge, Exec. Dir.

Founded: 1921. **Members:** 10,000. **Membership Dues:** resident, $4 (annual) • sustaining, $15 (annual) • regular (based on number of members), $50-$1,000 (annual). **Staff:** 3. **Local Groups:** 155. **Description:** Men and women in the traffic and transportation fields, including railroads, bus lines, trucking firms, and traffic managers of industrial firms. Sponsors National Transportation Week. **Awards:** TCI Scholarship Awards. **Frequency:** annual. **Type:** scholarship. **Recipient:** to students enrolled in accredited institutions of higher learning in a vocational or degree program in the fields of Transportation Logistics or Traffic Management • Transportation Person of the Year. **Frequency:** annual. **Type:** fellowship. **Computer Services:** Online services, club help desk. **Telecommunication Services:** electronic mail, dtam@transportationclubsinternational.com • additional toll-free number, (877)858-8628. **Committees:** Advertising; Awards/TCI Person of the Year; Bylaws; Club Publications; Club Services; Credentials; Education; National Transportation Week; Public Relations; Scholarship Trustees; Speakers; Special Projects. **Formerly:** (1973) Associated Traffic Clubs; (1983) Traffic Clubs International. **Publications:** *Transportation Education Magazine*, annual • Membership Directory, annual • Newsletters. Alternate Formats: online • Reports. **Price:** included in membership dues. **Conventions/Meetings:** annual Transportation Education Symposium - meeting (exhibits) - always September/October.

3897 ■ Trucking Industry Defense Association (TIDA)

6201 W Howard St., Ste.201
Niles, IL 60714
Ph: (847)647-7226
Fax: (847)647-8940
E-mail: terrir@tida.org
URL: http://www.tida.org/tida
Contact: Terri Ryan, Admin.

Founded: 1993. **Members:** 500. **Membership Dues:** industry, $125 (annual) • corporate, attorney, $425 (annual). **Description:** Professionals in all aspects of the trucking industry. Seeks to provide economies of scale to members in handling of individual claims; assists in loss prevention; and obtains information regarding expert witnesses, legal theories, and solutions to common problems. Benefits include a Desk Reference, State Law Summary, and seminars. **Publications:** Newsletter, quarterly. **Conventions/Meetings:** annual seminar, for industry - 2008 Oct. 1-3, San Diego, CA.

3898 ■ Trucking Management, Inc. (TMI)

566 El Dorado St., Ste.101
Pasadena, CA 91101
Ph: (626)792-9621
Fax: (626)628-3049
E-mail: lbarber@motor-freight.com
URL: http://www.mfca.org
Contact: Jim Roberts, Pres.

Founded: 1963. **Members:** 6. **Staff:** 5. **Budget:** $2,500,000. **Description:** Less-Than-Truckload (LTL) motor carriers. Promotes economic interests of unionized LTL motor carriers. Represents members' interests in public policy and economic issues. Works as the primary multi-employer bargaining arm of the unionized general freight trucking industry. **Committees:** Communications; General Counsel; Safety and

Health. **Divisions:** Government Affairs. **Affiliated With:** American Highway Users Alliance; Commercial Vehicle Safety Alliance; National Safety Council. **Formerly:** (1963) Trucking Employers; (1978) Trucking Management, Inc.; (2005) Motor Freight Carriers Association. **Conventions/Meetings:** annual meeting.

3899 ■ Truckload Carriers Association (TCA)
555 E Braddock Rd.
Alexandria, VA 22314-2182
Ph: (703)838-1950
Fax: (703)836-6610
E-mail: tca@truckload.org
URL: http://www.truckload.org
Contact: Jim O'Neal, Chm.
Founded: 1938. **Members:** 1,000. **Membership Dues:** carrier (based on company's annual gross revenue), $350-$2,600 (annual) ● associate, $750 (annual). **Staff:** 16. **Budget:** $3,800,000. **Description:** Engages in the truckload segment of the motor carrier industry. Represents dry van, refrigerated, flatbed, and intermodel container carriers operating in the 48 contiguous states as well as Alaska, Mexico, and Canada. Represents operators of over 200,000 trucks. **Awards:** Past Chairmen's Award. **Frequency:** annual. **Type:** recognition. **Recipient:** for an industry leader who has significant contribution to the truckload industry through the association ● TCA Scholarship. **Frequency:** annual. **Type:** scholarship. **Recipient:** for deserving students affiliated with the trucking industry. **Boards:** Benchmarking; Driver Recruitment and Retention; Next Generation; Shipper/Receiver. **Committees:** Operating Practices. **Divisions:** Independent Contractors; Industry Supplier; Refrigerated. **Affiliated With:** American Trucking Associations. **Formed by Merger of:** Contract Carrier Conference; Common Carrier Conference -Irregular Route. **Formerly:** (1988) Interstate Carriers Conference; (1998) Interstate Truckload Carriers Conference. **Publications:** *Preview Magazine for Annual Meeting*, annual. **Advertising:** accepted ● *Truckload Carrier Report*, weekly. Newsletter ● Membership Directory, annual. **Advertising:** accepted. **Conventions/Meetings:** annual convention and meeting (exhibits).

3900 ■ United Motorcoach Association (UMA)
113 S West St., 4th Fl.
Alexandria, VA 22314-2824
Ph: (703)838-2929
Free: (800)424-8262
Fax: (703)838-2950
E-mail: info@uma.org
URL: http://www.uma.org
Contact: Brian Scott, Chm.
Founded: 1971. **Members:** 2,000. **Membership Dues:** motorcoach operator (active), $225-$1,125 (annual) ● motorcoach vendor and travel partner (associate), $395-$1,700 (annual). **Staff:** 5. **Budget:** $750,000. **Description:** Represents bus and motorcoach companies. Concerns itself with issues related to buses such as safety standards and regulations. **Additional Websites:** http://www.motorcoachexpo.com. **Committees:** Legislative and Regulatory; Marketing; Meetings; Risk Management. **Programs:** Discount Wireless Services; Health Insurance; Workers Compensation Insurance; Wright Express. **Formerly:** (1997) United Bus Owners of America. **Publications:** *The Docket*, bimonthly. Newsletter. Reports on association activities and federal and state government activity. Includes obituaries. **Price:** free for members. **Circulation:** 1,500 ● *Operating Ratio Study*. Survey. **Price:** $125.00 for members; $200.00 for nonmembers ● *Safety and Courtesy Video*. **Price:** $20.00 for members; $25.00 for nonmembers ● Membership Directory, annual. **Price:** $20.00 for members; $100.00 for nonmembers ● Report. **Price:** $5.00 for members; $25.00 for nonmembers. **Conventions/Meetings:** annual Bus Show (exhibits).

3901 ■ Women's Transportation Seminar (WTS)
1701 K St. NW, Ste.800
Washington, DC 20006
Ph: (202)955-5085
Fax: (202)955-5088
E-mail: membership@wtsinternational.org
URL: http://wtsinternational.org
Contact: Diane James CAE, Exec. Dir.
Founded: 1977. **Members:** 3,600. **Membership Dues:** professional, $95-$210 (annual) ● student, $50 (annual) ● retired, $90 (annual) ● member-at-large, $140 (annual). **Staff:** 4. **Budget:** $1,000,000. **Regional Groups:** 38. **Multinational. Description:** Represents the interests of transportation professionals, both women and men, who lead the way in the professional development of women in transportation. Fosters interaction and communication among members in the transportation industry through an extensive program of meetings, programs, conferences and chapter development. Provides a forum for the exchange of information and a vehicle for professional development. **Awards:** Employer of the Year. **Frequency:** annual. **Type:** recognition. **Recipient:** for employers who have excelled in the field ● Helene M. Overly Memorial Graduate Scholarship. **Frequency:** annual. **Type:** scholarship. **Recipient:** for outstanding female graduate students majoring in transportation related fields ● Louise Moritz Molitoris Leadership Award. **Frequency:** annual. **Type:** recognition. **Recipient:** to women pursuing undergraduate studies in transportation or a related field who demonstrate leadership skills, ability and interest ● Member of the Year. **Frequency:** annual. **Type:** recognition. **Recipient:** for outstanding member in the field of transportation ● Sharon D. Banks Memorial Undergraduate Scholarship. **Frequency:** annual. **Type:** recognition. **Recipient:** for outstanding female undergraduate and students majoring in transportation ● Woman of the Year. **Frequency:** annual. **Type:** recognition. **Recipient:** for women and employers who have excelled in the field. **Committees:** Appointments; Chapter Development; Communications; Conference Site Selection; Corporate Relations; Diversity; Historian; Job Bank; Leadership Series; Legal Affairs and Bylaws; Membership; Newsletter; Professional Development; Public Relations; Recognitions; Scholarship; Speakers Bureau; TRB Reception; Web Site; WMDBE. **Publications:** *TranScript*, quarterly. Newsletter. Covers current transportation issues, board meetings, and association activities. **Price:** included in membership dues. **Circulation:** 4,200. Alternate Formats: online. **Conventions/Meetings:** quarterly board meeting ● annual conference (exhibits) - always May.

Travel

3902 ■ Adventure Travel Trade Association
601 Union St., 42nd Fl.
Seattle, WA 98101
Ph: (360)805-3131
Fax: (360)805-0649
E-mail: info@adventuretravel.biz
URL: http://www.adventuretravel.biz
Contact: Mr. Shannon Stowell, Pres.
Founded: 1990. **Members:** 350. **Membership Dues:** operator, agency, accommodation, $500 (annual) ● individual, $100 (annual) ● industry partner, city/county DMO, $750 (annual) ● national DMO, $1,500 (annual) ● state, province, territory DMO, $1,000 (annual). **For-Profit. Multinational. Description:** Serves the adventure travel industry as a membership organization. Aims to grow the adventure travel industry overall and to help build up its member organizations. Provides exposure, marketing expertise, education, research, and discount to its members. **Libraries: Type:** not open to the public. **Holdings:** 4. **Computer Services:** database. **Publications:** Newsletter. **Advertising:** accepted. **Conventions/Meetings:** annual Adventure Travel World Summit - conference (exhibits).

3903 ■ Africa Travel Association (ATA)
166 Madison Ave., 5th Fl.
New York, NY 10016
Ph: (212)447-1357
Fax: (212)725-8253
E-mail: info@africatravelassociation.com
URL: http://www.africa-ata.org
Contact: Hon. Jake Obetsebi-Lamptey MP, Pres.
Founded: 1975. **Members:** 760. **Membership Dues:** government tourism ministry/government department, $1,500 (annual) ● airline, international and regional carrier, cruise line, sea/ocean carrier, and hotel chain, $1,000 (annual) ● individual hotel, travel agency, wholesaler, tour operator, local ground operator, $300 (annual) ● allied, $200 (annual) ● associate, $100 (annual) ● student, $50 (annual). **Staff:** 3. **Budget:** $250,000. **Regional Groups:** 16. **Languages:** English, French. **Multinational. Description:** Represents individuals and travel industry agencies involved in the development of tourism to Africa. Conducts trade show exhibitions. Sponsors Africa Guild (see separate entry) to help develop a general interest in Africa. **Libraries: Type:** reference. **Awards:** ATA Awards. **Frequency:** annual. **Type:** recognition. **Recipient:** for individuals with outstanding service to the organization. **Telecommunication Services:** electronic mail, africa@dowco.com. **Affiliated With:** American Society of Travel Agents. **Formerly:** (1977) American Federation of Representatives of International Companies in Africa; (1985) Africa - The African Travel Association. **Publications:** *Africa Memo*, periodic ● *African Travel*, quarterly. Magazine. **Advertising:** accepted ● *Annual Congress Journal*, annual ● *Membership List*, annual. Membership Directory ● Yearbook, annual. Alternate Formats: online. **Conventions/Meetings:** conference, on ecotourism ● annual International Congress on African Tourism - meeting (exhibits) - always April/May.

3904 ■ American Association of Premium Incentive, Travel Suppliers and Agents (AAPITSA)
PO Box 35189
Chicago, IL 60707-0189
Ph: (708)453-0080
Fax: (708)453-0083
Founded: 1975. **Description:** Travel and premium incentive suppliers and travel agents. Seeks to increase members' public visibility and professional influence. Provides trademark licensing and product and service endorsement services to support members' activities. **Computer Services:** Mailing lists.

3905 ■ American Automobile Touring Alliance (AATA)
c/o National Automobile Club
1151 E Hillsdale Blvd.
Foster City, CA 94404
Ph: (650)294-7000
Free: (800)622-2136
Fax: (650)294-7040
URL: http://www.nationalautoclub.com
Founded: 1932. **Members:** 200,000. **Description:** Promotes and facilitates touring between nations. **Conventions/Meetings:** annual meeting.

3906 ■ American Small Business Travel Alliance (ASBTA)
PO Box 270543
Flower Mound, TX 75027-0543
Ph: (469)648-0190
E-mail: info@asbta.com
URL: http://www.asbta.com
Contact: Chuck Sharp, Pres.
Membership Dues: travel agency, $50 (annual). **Description:** Serves small business travelers by providing information and resources. Works with airlines, lodging, technology companies, travel agencies, and other companies that serve small business travelers. Offers travel information, education, networking and services to help meet the needs of the small business traveler. **Publications:** Newsletter, quarterly. **Price:** included in membership dues ● Newsletter, monthly. **Price:** included in membership dues ● Survey, quarterly. **Price:** included in membership dues.

3907 ■ American Society of Travel Agents (ASTA)
1101 King St., Ste.200
Alexandria, VA 22314
Ph: (703)739-2782
Free: (800)440-2782
Fax: (703)684-8319

E-mail: askasta@astahq.com
URL: http://www.astanet.com
Contact: William A. Maloney CTC, Exec. VP/COO
Founded: 1931. **Members:** 28,600. **Membership Dues:** travel agency company, international company, travel school, $365 (annual) ● travel professional, $189 (annual) ● allied company associate, travel school (affiliated with an ASTA member travel company), $85 (annual) ● international company associate, $99 (annual) ● allied company, $499 (annual) ● future travel professional, $75 (annual) ● future travel professional (student of an ASTA Member Travel School), $50 (annual) ● multiple chapter, $20 (annual). **Staff:** 95. **Budget:** $11,500,000. **Local Groups:** 31. **Multinational. Description:** Travel agents; allied members are representatives of carriers, hotels, resorts, sightseeing and car rental companies, official tourist organizations, and other travel interests. Aims to: promote and encourage travel among people of all nations and the use of professional travel agents worldwide; serve as an information resource for the travel industry worldwide; promote and represent the views and interests of travel agents to all levels of government and industry; promote professional and ethical conduct in the travel agency industry worldwide; facilitate consumer protection and safety for the traveling public. Maintains biographical archives and travel hall of fame. Conducts research and education programs. **Awards:** Allied Member Award. **Frequency:** annual. **Type:** recognition. **Recipient:** based on review and decision by awards committee ● Environmental Award. **Frequency:** annual. **Type:** recognition. **Recipient:** to an individual, company or country that has made a significant impact in preserving and protecting the environment ● International Travel Agent of the Year. **Frequency:** annual. **Type:** recognition. **Recipient:** to a travel agent who has made the greatest contribution to the travel industry ● Lifetime Achievement Award. **Frequency:** periodic. **Type:** recognition. **Recipient:** to a travel industry luminary whose creativity, dedication and inspiration has advanced the travel and tourism industry ● **Frequency:** periodic. **Type:** scholarship. **Recipient:** for the most qualified students in a bachelor's degree, master's degree, doctoral, community college, or travel school program, and to travel professionals seeking to further their education ● Travel Agent of the Year. **Frequency:** annual. **Type:** recognition. **Recipient:** based on review and decision by awards committee ● Travel Hall of Fame Award. **Frequency:** annual. **Type:** recognition. **Recipient:** based on nomination by members ● Travel Journalist of the Year Award. **Frequency:** annual. **Type:** recognition. **Recipient:** to individuals for extraordinary journalistic achievement in the field of travel. **Computer Services:** database, Agency Specialization. **Committees:** Consumer Awareness; Future Planning; Government Representation; Member Communication and Services; Member Education; Special Project; Supplier Relations; World Travel Congress. **Councils:** Chapter Presidents. **Programs:** Model Agency; Tour Operator. **Formerly:** (1944) American Steamship and Tourist Agents Association. **Publications:** *ASTA Network*, quarterly. Magazine. **Price:** included in membership dues. **Advertising:** accepted ● *ASTA Officials Directory*, annual. Lists information on committee, council, and task force activities and members. Includes antitrust compliance guidelines, code of ethics, and bylaws. ● *Dateline ASTA*, weekly. Newsletter. **Price:** included in membership dues. **Advertising:** accepted. Alternate Formats: online ● *Travel Industry Honors*, periodic ● Membership Directory, annual. **Price:** included in membership dues ● Pamphlets. **Conventions/Meetings:** annual trade show (exhibits).

3908 ■ Assist Card International (ACI)
1001 Brickell Bay Dr., Ste.2302
Miami, FL 33131
Ph: (305)381-9959
Free: (800)874-2223
Fax: (305)375-8135
E-mail: usa@assist-card.com
URL: http://www.assist-card.com
Contact: Dr. Omar Cadreche, Gen. Mgr.
Founded: 1972. **Languages:** Bahasa Indonesia, English, French, Hungarian, Portuguese, Spanish, Turkish. **For-Profit. Description:** Provides medical, legal, financial, and personal assistance to travelers in 56 countries.

3909 ■ Association of Corporate Travel Executives (ACTE)
515 King St., Ste.440
Alexandria, VA 22314
Ph: (703)683-5322
Fax: (703)683-2720
E-mail: info@acte.org
URL: http://www.acte.org
Contact: Richard Crum, Pres.
Founded: 1988. **Members:** 2,400. **Membership Dues:** general, $425 (annual). **Budget:** $4,000,000. **Description:** Corporate travel managers, meeting planners, and purchasing managers; travel agencies, hotels, and resorts; airlines, car rental companies, and limousine services; other individuals and groups involved in the travel industry. Provides a forum for the discussion of ideas and information related to the travel industry. Conducts charitable and educational programs. **Awards: Frequency:** annual. **Type:** recognition. **Recipient:** for individuals' positive impact on the business travel profession. **Publications:** *ACTE Quarterly*. Magazine. **Price:** included in membership dues. **Circulation:** 4,000. **Advertising:** accepted ● Membership Directory, annual ● Newsletter, 8/year. **Conventions/Meetings:** annual international conference ● semiannual meeting - always November and May.

3910 ■ Association of Destination Management Executives (ADME)
PO Box 2307
Dayton, OH 45401-2307
Ph: (937)586-3727
Fax: (937)586-3699
E-mail: info@adme.org
URL: http://www.adme.org
Contact: Fran Rickenbach CAE, Exec. VP
Founded: 1995. **Members:** 210. **Membership Dues:** executive, $425 (annual) ● active, $325 (annual) ● affiliate, $625 (annual) ● associate, $225 (annual) ● faculty, $150 (annual) ● student, $75 (annual). **Staff:** 3. **Budget:** $2,000,000. **Multinational. Description:** Works to increase the professionalism of owners, CEOs and employees of destination management companies. Conducts educational conferences and meetings. **Awards:** Best Innovative Event. **Frequency:** annual. **Type:** recognition ● Best Logistics. **Frequency:** annual. **Type:** recognition. **Recipient:** for best transportation logistics ● Best Overall Program. **Frequency:** annual. **Type:** recognition. **Recipient:** to a DMC who has provided at least three different services for a multi-day program ● Destination Management Professional of the Year. **Frequency:** annual. **Type:** recognition. **Recipient:** to a DM professional who made significant contributions to the profession ● Destination Management Rising Star. **Frequency:** annual. **Type:** recognition. **Recipient:** to an outstanding DM professional with less than five years experience. **Computer Services:** Online services, find a DMC by geographical location. **Publications:** *ADME Xpressions*, quarterly. Newsletter. **Circulation:** 551. **Advertising:** accepted. Alternate Formats: online. **Conventions/Meetings:** annual The Best is Yet to Come - conference, educational sessions, presentation of achievement awards, exhibits (exhibits) ● annual conference.

3911 ■ Association of Retail Travel Agents (ARTA)
4320 N Miller Rd.
Scottsdale, AZ 85251
Free: (800)969-6069
Fax: (615)985-0600
E-mail: info@artaonline.com
URL: http://www.artaonline.com
Contact: Nancy Linares, Chm.
Founded: 1963. **Members:** 4,000. **Membership Dues:** agency, $250 (annual) ● individual/associate, $75 (annual). **Staff:** 4. **Budget:** $400,000. **Description:** Represents retail travel agents and agencies in North America. Promotes the interests of retail travel agents through representation on industry councils, testimony before Congress, and participation government proceedings. Conducts joint marketing and educational programs; sponsors work-study program. **Computer Services:** database, destinations. **Publications:** *ARTAFACTS*, weekly. Newsletter. Includes calendar of events, advice to travel agents, industry news. Distributed weekly by fax or daily by email. **Circulation:** 3,500. **Advertising:** accepted. Alternate Formats: online. **Conventions/Meetings:** annual conference (exhibits) ● international conference ● seminar.

3912 ■ Association of Travel Marketing Executives (ATME)
c/o Kristin Zern, Exec. Dir.
331 W 57th St., Ste.482
New York, NY 10019
Ph: (212)765-0625
Fax: (212)765-0624
E-mail: admin@atme.org
URL: http://www.atme.org
Contact: Kristin Zern, Exec. Dir.
Founded: 1980. **Members:** 750. **Membership Dues:** active travel marketer, marketing solution provider, $295 (annual) ● media, $395 (annual) ● educator, $195 (annual). **Staff:** 2. **Budget:** $500,000. **Description:** Travel marketing executives working in an executive or managerial capacity related to marketing a travel product or service including airlines, cruise lines, hotels, and convention and visitors' bureaus. Prepares special reports; conducts Certified Travel Marketing Executive educational program; honors travel marketing executives. **Libraries: Type:** reference. **Holdings:** archival material. **Awards:** ATME Atlas Awards. **Frequency:** annual. **Type:** recognition. **Recipient:** for outstanding travel marketing executive ● **Type:** recognition. **Recipient:** for career achievement and innovation. **Committees:** ATLAS Awards; Marketing; Programming and Education. **Publications:** *ATMES Travel Marketing Newsletter - Market Flash*, 6-8/year ● *Directory of ATME Members*, annual. **Price:** $75.00 for nonmembers. **Advertising:** accepted ● *Travel Marketing Decisions*, quarterly. Magazine. **Price:** included in membership dues; $95.00 for nonmembers. **Circulation:** 14,000. **Advertising:** accepted. **Conventions/Meetings:** seminar and workshop, addresses marketing issues related to the travel industry ● annual Travel Marketing Conference, for tabletops (exhibits).

3913 ■ Caribbean Hotel Association (CHA)
1000 Ponce de Leon Ave., 5th Fl.
San Juan, PR 00907-3668
Ph: (787)725-9139
Fax: (787)725-9108
E-mail: asanguinetti@chahotels.com
URL: http://www.caribbeanhotelassociation.com
Contact: Alec Sanguinetti, Dir. Gen./CEO
Founded: 1962. **Members:** 1,500. **Staff:** 20. **Budget:** $2,000,000. **National Groups:** 35. **Languages:** English, French, Spanish. **Multinational. Description:** Hotels and hotel associations throughout the Caribbean region; allied members are companies selling related products and services. Promotes the continuing improvement and expansion of the Caribbean hospitality industry. Maintains Caribbean Hospitality Training Institute, Caribbean Hotel Foundation, Caribbean Alliance for Sustainable Tourism CHA Reservation Management System and Caribbean Culinary Federation. **Libraries: Type:** reference. **Awards:** Caribbean Hotelier of the Year. **Frequency:** annual. **Type:** recognition ● Employee of the Year. **Frequency:** annual. **Type:** recognition ● Environmental Awards. **Frequency:** annual. **Type:** recognition ● Supervisor of the Year. **Frequency:** annual. **Type:** recognition. **Committees:** Caribbean Society of Hotel Association Executives; Finance; Government Affairs; Marketing; Membership; Product Development. **Formerly:** (1962) Caribbean Hotel Council of the Caribbean Travel Association. **Publications:** *Caribbean Gold Book*, semiannual. Directory. Lists hotel properties throughout the Caribbean; including information such as number of rooms, location, and distance to island attractions. **Price:** free to certified travel agencies. **Circulation:** 40,000. **Advertising:** accepted ● *The Caribbean Travel Planner*,

semiannual. Magazine. Guides the leisure traveler planning a Caribbean vacation, showcases 36 Caribbean destinations falling within the CHA and CTO footprint. **Price:** $4.99 plus shipping and handling ● *CHA Construction Report*, quarterly. **Price:** included in membership dues ● *CHAdvance*, biweekly. Newsletter. Contains industry news and happenings. **Price:** included in membership dues. **Circulation:** 2,300. **Advertising:** accepted. Alternate Formats: online ● *Small Hotels Reference Manual* ● Membership Directory, annual. Lists member hotels; includes property name, mailing address, number of rooms, manager's name, and member discount availability. **Price:** free for members. **Circulation:** 1,500. **Advertising:** accepted ● Handbook, annual. Includes CHA membership listing. Comprises of purchasing index, tourist board information, and featured articles. **Price:** free for members. **Advertising:** accepted. **Conventions/Meetings:** annual Caribbean Hotel and Tourism Investment Conference - trade show ● annual Caribbean Hotel Industry Conference (exhibits) ● annual Caribbean Marketplace - meeting, buyers and suppliers are matched through a computerized program of appointments ● annual Leadership Conference for Association Executives.

3914 ■ Cruise Club of America (CCOA)

PO Box 318
North Pembroke, MA 02358
Free: (800)982-2276
Fax: (781)826-6156
E-mail: cruises@cruise-club.com
URL: http://www.cruise-club.com
Contact: Bill Kraus, Founder
Founded: 1997. **Membership Dues:** basic, $35 (annual) ● life gold, $299 ● life platinum, $399. **Multinational**. **Description:** Represents all major cruise lines. Aims to participate in the regulatory and policy development process and promote all measures that foster a safe, secure and healthy cruise ship environment. Advocates industry positions to key domestic and international regulatory organizations, policymakers and other industry partners.

3915 ■ Cruise Lines International Association (CLIA)

910 SE 17th St., Ste.400
Fort Lauderdale, FL 33316
Ph: (754)224-2200
Fax: (754)224-2250
E-mail: info@cruising.org
URL: http://www.cruising.org
Contact: Terry Dale, Pres.
Founded: 1975. **Members:** 33. **Staff:** 21. **Description:** Represents 20,000 travel agents, united for promotional and training activities. Conducts agency training programs. **Formed by Merger of:** International Passenger Ship Association; Pacific Cruise Conference. **Publications:** Manual, annual.

3916 ■ European Travel Commission (ETC)

c/o Spring, O'Brien and Co.
50 W 23rd St., 11th Fl.
New York, NY 10010
E-mail: etc@spring-obrien.com
URL: http://www.VisitEurope.com
Contact: Robert K. Franklin, Exec. Dir.
Founded: 1948. **Members:** 33. **Staff:** 6. **Multinational**. **Description:** Represents government tourism organizations cooperating to promote travel to Europe and further international goodwill and economic prosperity. **Awards:** Europa Award. **Frequency:** annual. **Type:** recognition. **Recipient:** for contribution to marketing Europe in the US. **Publications:** *VisitEurope*, monthly. Newsletter. Serves as a supplement to major newspapers. **Price:** free. **Circulation:** 3,300,000. **Advertising:** accepted. **Conventions/Meetings:** annual Trans-Atlantic Travel Marketing Conference, for review of tourism prospects for the coming year - fall.

3917 ■ German National Tourist Board (GNTB)

German Natl. Tourist Off.
122 E 42nd St., 52nd Fl.
New York, NY 10168-0072
Ph: (212)661-7200
Free: (800)651-7010
Fax: (212)661-7174
E-mail: germanyinfo@d-z-t.com
URL: http://visits-to-germany.com
Contact: Ursula Schoeicher, Chm.
Founded: 1948. **Members:** 26. **Staff:** 159. **Budget:** DM 50,900,000. **Languages:** English, German. **Description:** Encourages and promotes tourism to Germany. **Additional Websites:** http://www.cometogermany.com, http://www.germany-tourism.de. **Affiliated With:** World Association of Travel Agencies.

3918 ■ Institute of Certified Travel Agents

148 Linden St., Ste.305
Wellesley, MA 02482
Ph: (781)237-0280
Free: (800)542-4282
Fax: (781)237-3860
E-mail: info@thetravelinstitute.com
URL: http://www.thetravelinstitute.com
Contact: Scott Ahlsmith CTC, Chm.
Founded: 1964. **Members:** 16,000. **Membership Dues:** regular, $95 (annual). **Staff:** 9. **Budget:** $4,000,000. **Description:** Individuals who have been accredited as Certified Travel Counselors (CTC) or Certified Travel Associates (CTA) must meet the institute's testing and experience requirements. Seeks to increase the level of competence in the travel industry. Provides continuing education, and examination and certification programs; conducts workshops and professional management seminars. Operates Travel Career Development Program to increase professional skills and Destination Specialist Programs to enhance the geographical knowledge of sales agents. Organizes study groups of instruction with enrolled student bodies in most major cities. **Committees:** Seminar. **Funds:** Terry Lee Scholarship. **Programs:** Certified Travel Associate; Certified Travel Counselor; Certified Travel Industry Executive. **Also Known As:** The Travel Institute. **Publications:** *Sales Skills Development*. Video. Includes workbook. Used for in-house training at agencies. ● *Travel Counselor*, bimonthly. Newsletter. Offers travel management tips and information on ICTA educational programs. **Price:** available to members only. **Circulation:** 25,000. **Advertising:** accepted ● *Travel Professional*, bimonthly. Magazine. Provides information to career travel agents. **Price:** included in membership dues. **Circulation:** 25,000. **Advertising:** accepted. Alternate Formats: online ● Books. **Conventions/Meetings:** annual meeting - always November/December.

3919 ■ Inter-American Travel Congress (IATC)

c/o Organization of American States
1889 F St. NW
Washington, DC 20006
Ph: (202)458-3221
Fax: (202)458-3190
E-mail: dperna@oas.org
URL: http://www.oas.org/TOURISM/tr_inte.htm
Contact: Daniel Perna, Contact
Founded: 1939. **Members:** 34. **Languages:** English, Spanish. **Multinational**. **Description:** Promotes the sustainable development of tourism in the Americans through the organization of a series of hemispheric congresses dealing with relevant technical matters and developing inter-American cooperation in the tourism industry. Fosters the dissemination of best practices for small tourism enterprises. Sponsors the adoption of official agreements among American governments relating to tourist travel; disseminates information on congress decisions. Encourages comparative studies and technical projects focusing on tourism development in the hemisphere. Coordinates activities of intergovernmental and private organizations in the area of tourism development. **Affiliated With:** Organization of American States; United Nations. **Publications:** *Final Acts of Congress*, quadrennial ● *Final Acts of Permanent Executive Committee Meetings*, annual ● *Final Reports of Meeting of Experts*, periodic. **Conventions/Meetings:** triennial congress, tourism trade show (exhibits).

3920 ■ InterAmerican Travel Agents Society (ITAS)

c/o Jackie Alton, CTC, Board Member
CWT/Almeda Travel
450 Meyerland Plz.
Houston, TX 77096
Ph: (713)592-8000
Fax: (713)592-8080
URL: http://itas.travelasp.com
Contact: Jackie Alton CTC, Board Member
Founded: 1953. **Members:** 300. **Membership Dues:** active, travel professional, $200 (annual) ● independent contractor, $150 (annual) ● allied (large company), $500 (annual) ● allied (small company), $250 (annual). **Staff:** 2. **Description:** Represents African-American travel agents and agencies. Provides contracting information on corporate, military and government travel management services. **Formerly:** (2001) Inter-America Travel Agents Society. **Publications:** Newsletter, quarterly. **Advertising:** accepted. **Conventions/Meetings:** semiannual conference and convention (exhibits) - always in spring and fall.

3921 ■ International Association of Antarctica Tour Operators (IAATO)

c/o Denise Landau, Exec. Dir.
PO Box 2178
Basalt, CO 81621
Ph: (970)704-1047
Fax: (970)704-9660
E-mail: iaato@iaato.org
URL: http://www.iaato.org
Contact: Denise Landau, Exec. Dir.
Founded: 1991. **Members:** 97. **Membership Dues:** full, provisional, probational, $1,500 (annual) ● associate, sailing vessel (under 12 passengers), $750 (annual) ● provisional (1st year), $2,000. **Multinational**. **Description:** Advocates, promotes, and practices safe and environmentally responsible private-sector travel to the Antarctic. Represents Antarctic tour operators and others organizing and conducting travel to the Antarctic. Fosters continued cooperation among members. Monitors programs, including the pattern and frequency of visits to specific sites within the Antarctic. **Computer Services:** Information services, statistics, Antarctic tourism, science and research overview ● online services, member directory. **Publications:** *Passenger Briefing Kits*. Handbook. **Price:** $75.00. Alternate Formats: CD-ROM.

3922 ■ International Association of Tour Managers - North American Region (IATM North America)

24 Blevins Rd.
Kerhonkson, NY 12446-1302
Ph: (212)208-6800
Fax: (212)208-6800
E-mail: chairman@tourmanager.org
URL: http://www.tourmanager.org
Contact: Mr. Scott Mcgraw CTM, Chm.
Founded: 1962. **Members:** 1,500. **Membership Dues:** active/professional tour manager, $125 (annual) ● affiliate/student tour manager, $65 (annual) ● associate, educator, tour operator, guide association, and hotel, EUR 220 (annual). **Staff:** 2. **Budget:** $105,000. **Multinational**. **Description:** Works to maintain the highest possible standards of tour management; guarantee excellence of performance; educate the travel world on the role of the tour manager (also referred to as tour director, tour escort, or tour leader) in the successful completion of the tour itinerary and in bringing business to related industries. Represents members in influencing legislation and advising on travel policy. Trains tour managers to plan, research, and lead tours to specific domestic and foreign destinations; operates Advisory Board in Professional Tour Management; offers placement service; conducts Professional travel agents, travel wholesalers, airlines, hotel associations, shipping lines, tourist organizations, restaurants, shops, and entertainment organizations Tour Management International Certificate Program. **Computer Services:** database, list of tour managers available on the internet. **Committees:** European Community Liaison. **Affiliated With:** American Society of Travel

Agents. **Publications:** *International Association of Tour Managers—Membership Directory*, annual. **Price:** free, for members only ● *The Professional Tour Manager*, quarterly. Magazine. **Conventions/Meetings:** semiannual congress (exhibits).

3923 ■ International Council of Cruise Lines (ICCL)

2111 Wilson Blvd., 8th Fl.
Arlington, VA 22201
Ph: (703)522-8463
Free: (800)595-9338
Fax: (703)522-3811
E-mail: info@cruising.org
URL: http://www.cruising.org
Contact: J. Michael Crye, Pres.

Founded: 1990. **Members:** 17. **Membership Dues:** associate, $10,000 (annual). **Staff:** 9. **Description:** Represents cruise ship operators. Aims to participate in the regulatory and policy development process and promote all measures that foster a safe, secure and healthy cruise ship environment. Advocates industry positions to key domestic and international regulatory organizations, policymakers and other industry partners. **Libraries: Type:** not open to the public. **Holdings:** books, business records, clippings, periodicals. **Subjects:** cruise lines, travel industries. **Computer Services:** database ● online services. **Publications:** *Even Keel*, 3/year. Newsletter. Alternate Formats: online.

3924 ■ International Gay and Lesbian Travel Association (IGLTA)

4331 N Fed. Hwy., No. 304
Fort Lauderdale, FL 33308
Ph: (954)776-2626
Free: (800)448-8550
Fax: (954)776-3303
E-mail: iglta@iglta.org
URL: http://www.iglta.org
Contact: John Tanzella, Exec. Dir.

Founded: 1983. **Members:** 1,500. **Membership Dues:** associate, $75 (annual). **Staff:** 2. **Multinational. Description:** Travel agents, tour operators, hoteliers, guesthouse and resort owners, travel clubs, and allied businesses interested in promoting travel services to the gay community. Works to: enhance member businesses; inform travel agents and consumers about properties, businesses, and destinations welcoming gay clientele; provide a networking opportunity for members. Offers familiarization trips to promote member businesses in locations of special appeal to gay travelers. Operates public awareness campaign. **Awards:** Award of Merit. **Type:** recognition ● IGGY Award. **Frequency:** annual. **Type:** recognition. **Recipient:** for best advertising. **Publications:** *IGTA Connections*, quarterly. Membership Directory. **Advertising:** accepted ● *IGTA Today*, quarterly. Newsletter. **Circulation:** 2,500. **Advertising:** accepted. Alternate Formats: online ● *Marketing Mailing*, quarterly. **Price:** included in membership dues. **Advertising:** accepted. **Conventions/Meetings:** annual conference and workshop, includes tour (exhibits) - always May.

3925 ■ International Society of Travel and Tourism Educators (ISTTE)

23220 Edgewater
St. Clair Shores, MI 48082-2037
Ph: (586)294-0208
Fax: (586)294-0208
E-mail: joannb@istte.org
URL: http://www.istte.org
Contact: Michael Sabitoni, Pres.

Founded: 1980. **Members:** 250. **Membership Dues:** active, $150 (annual) ● associate, $175 (annual) ● allied, $200 (annual) ● graduate student, $95 (annual) ● emeritus, $75 (annual). **Staff:** 1. **Budget:** $100,000. **Description:** Teachers, administrators, and researchers employed by institutions offering courses or degrees in the travel and tourism fields. Associate members are corporate trainers and consultants. Allied members include people in supporting industries, such as vendors of educational materials and employers of travel and tourism graduates. Works to promote the development and exchange of information related to travel and tourism education and research; serve as a forum and clearinghouse of ideas and information; provides guidance in formulation of public policy on matters of curricula, vocational and technical training programs, and professional preparation programs; encourages greater interaction among educators and practicing professionals through internships, lectureships, fieldwork experiences, and industrial training; and identifies and supports efforts to develop knowledge and skill areas in the travel and tourism professions. Conducts seminars and forums. **Libraries: Type:** open to the public. **Holdings:** 12. **Subjects:** research paper. **Awards:** ISTTE Four-Year University and College Achievement Award. **Frequency:** biennial. **Type:** recognition. **Recipient:** to an individual who has made significant lifetime contributions to the field of travel and tourism at the 4-year level course ● ISTTE High School and Proprietary School Achievement Award. **Frequency:** biennial. **Type:** recognition. **Recipient:** to an individual who has made significant lifetime contributions to the field of travel and tourism at the high school or proprietary school educational institutions ● ISTTE Institutional Achievement Award. **Frequency:** biennial. **Type:** recognition. **Recipient:** to an institute that has made significant long term contributions to the field of travel and tourism education ● ISTTE John C. Kesler Memorial Community College Achievement Award. **Frequency:** biennial. **Type:** recognition. **Recipient:** to an individual who has made significant lifetime contributions to the field of travel and tourism at the 2-year level educational institutions ● ISTTE Martin Opperman Memorial Award for Lifetime Achievement. **Frequency:** triennial. **Type:** recognition. **Recipient:** to an individual who has provided significant service to the society. **Committees:** Conference; Scholarship. **Formerly:** (1997) Society of Travel and Tourism Educators. **Publications:** *Conference Proceedings*, annual. **Price:** $79.00 for members; $99.00 for nonmembers. Alternate Formats: CD-ROM ● *International Travel and Tourism Books in Print*. Monograph ● *The Journal of Teaching in Travel and Tourism*. **Price:** included in membership dues ● *News and Views*, quarterly. Newsletter. **Price:** included in membership dues. **Advertising:** accepted. Alternate Formats: online ● *World Directory*, annual ● Brochure. Alternate Formats: online.

3926 ■ International Travel Writers and Editors Association (ITWEA)

1224 N Nolcomis NE
Alexandria, MN 56308
Ph: (320)763-7626
Fax: (320)763-9290
E-mail: iami@iami.org
URL: http://iami.org
Contact: Robert G. Johnson, Contact

Founded: 1982. **Members:** 1,650. **Membership Dues:** travel writers, editors, $175 (annual). **Staff:** 12. **Budget:** $1,500,000. **Description:** Conducts educational programs; maintains Speaker's Bureau. **Computer Services:** database ● mailing lists. **Publications:** Brochure ● Directory ● Newsletter. **Advertising:** accepted. **Conventions/Meetings:** board meeting ● annual convention (exhibits).

3927 ■ National Association of Commissioned Travel Agents (NACTA)

1101 King St., Ste.200
Alexandria, VA 22314
Ph: (703)739-6826
Fax: (703)739-6861
E-mail: nacta@aol.com
URL: http://www.nacta.com
Contact: Joanie Ogg CTC, Pres.

Founded: 1986. **Membership Dues:** individual, $95 (annual) ● agency, $145 (annual) ● allied supplier, $495 (annual) ● host agency, $395 (annual). **Description:** Home based, independent, outside sales, cruise oriented travel professionals. Conducts numerous cruise seminars, land based seminars and regional workshops. **Publications:** *Jax Fax*, periodic. Magazine.

3928 ■ National Association of Cruise-Oriented Agencies (NACOA)

7378 Atlantic Blvd., No. 115
Margate, FL 33063
Ph: (305)663-5626
Fax: (866)816-7143
E-mail: nacoafl@aol.com
URL: http://www.nacoaonline.com
Contact: Donna Esposito, Pres.

Founded: 1985. **Members:** 800. **Membership Dues:** voting, $75 (annual) ● individual agent, $75 (annual). **Staff:** 2. **Description:** Professional association of travel agencies dedicated to the cruise vacation product. Provides educational and training programs, including Seminars-At-Sea, and Ship Inspection weekends. Offers Safe Sail insurances and Errors and Omissions insurance. **Affiliated With:** American Society of Travel Agents; Association of Retail Travel Agents. **Formerly:** (2001) National Association of Cruise Only Agencies. **Publications:** *Now Hear This!*, bimonthly. Newsletter. Contains updates on industry news and issues. **Price:** free, for members only. **Circulation:** 1,500. **Advertising:** accepted. **Conventions/Meetings:** semiannual convention (exhibits) - summer and winter.

3929 ■ National Business Travel Association (NBTA)

110 N Royal St., 4th Fl.
Alexandria, VA 22314
Ph: (703)684-0836
Fax: (703)684-0263
E-mail: info@nbta.org
URL: http://www.nbta.org
Contact: Bill Connors CTC, Pres./Chief Operating Off.

Founded: 1968. **Members:** 2,400. **Membership Dues:** direct/allied umbrella, $345 (annual) ● government travel group, $245 (annual) ● allied, $1,295 (annual). **Budget:** $5,100,000. **Local Groups:** 45. **Description:** Travel managers and providers. Works to enhance the educational advancement and image of the profession and membership; enhance the value of the travel manager in meeting corporate travel needs and financial goals; provide education to members about industry matters, issues, and technology; cultivate a positive public image of the corporate travel industry; advocate and protect the interests of members and their corporations on legislative and regulatory matters; promote safety, security, efficiency and quality travel; and enhance professionalism and recognition of the industry and individual members. Provides a forum for the constructive exchange of information and ideas among members. **Libraries: Type:** reference. **Awards:** Appreciation for Services. **Frequency:** annual. **Type:** recognition ● Mike Kabo Scholarship. **Frequency:** annual. **Type:** scholarship. **Recipient:** for members/individuals. **Committees:** Aviation; Data Protection; Global Risk Management; Government Contractors; Ground Transportation; Groups and Meetings; Hotel; Technology. **Councils:** Allied Leadership; Chapter Presidents; Legislative Advisory. **Programs:** Direct Referral. **Formerly:** (1989) National Passenger Traffic Association. **Publications:** *Conference Journal*, annual. **Advertising:** accepted ● Membership Directory, annual. **Advertising:** accepted ● Papers. Alternate Formats: online. **Conventions/Meetings:** annual convention and trade show (exhibits).

3930 ■ National Tour Association (NTA)

546 E Main St.
Lexington, KY 40508
Ph: (859)226-4444
Free: (800)682-8886
Fax: (859)226-4414
E-mail: questions@ntastaff.com
URL: http://www.ntaonline.com
Contact: Randy Julian, Chm./CEO

Founded: 1951. **Members:** 4,000. **Membership Dues:** tour operator, $460 (annual) ● individual tour supplier, destination marketing organization, $625 (annual) ● multiple tour supplier, $975 (annual) ● corporate tour supplier, $1,700 (annual) ● associate, $335 (annual) ● educator, $135 (annual) ● dual - tour operator/individual tour supplier, $785 (annual) ●

dual - tour operator/multiple tour supplier, $1,135 (annual) ● dual - tour operator/corporate tour supplier, $1,860 (annual). **Staff:** 45. **Multinational. Description:** Operators of group tours and packaged travel; travel industry-related companies providing services/ facilities to tour operators (hotels, attractions, restaurants); and destination marketing organizations such as convention and visitor bureaus, and state tourism departments. Seeks to: maintain a code of ethical standards within the tour industry; develop and increase public interest in packaged travel. Represents members before governmental bodies and agencies. Conducts research and educational programs. **Libraries: Type:** reference. **Holdings:** archival material, reports. **Subjects:** travel and tour. **Awards:** National Tourism Foundation Awards. **Frequency:** annual. **Type:** scholarship. **Recipient:** for students in the tour and travel industry study areas. **Computer Services:** Online services, for tour operators. **Committees:** Communications; Consumer Protection Plan; Convention; Education; Industry and Government Relations; International Relations; Marketing; Member Services; Operations; Past Presidents; Strategic Planning; Technology Advisory Team. **Councils:** Canadian; Destination Marketing Organization; Tour Supplier. **Formerly:** (1984) National Tour Brokers Association; (2005) CrossSphere: the Global Association for Packaged Travel. **Publications:** *Courier*, monthly. Magazine. Features destination snapshots, tips on tour business and other industry and association information. **Circulation:** 5,200. **Advertising:** accepted ● *Tuesday*, monthly. Newsletter ● Directory, annual. Contains a comprehensive list of all the association's members. **Conventions/Meetings:** annual convention and meeting (exhibits) ● annual Tour Operator Spring Meets - meeting - 2009 June 4-6, Monterey, CA.

3931 ■ National Travel Club (NTC)
Address Unknown since 2008
Founded: 1901. **Members:** 130,000. **For-Profit. Description:** Provides services that offer subscribers travel insurance, car rental discounts, trip routing and local area services, dining benefits, information, and magazines. **Absorbed:** (1980) National Association of Consumers and Travelers.

3932 ■ Opening Door
8049 Ormesby Ln.
Woodford, VA 22580
Ph: (804)633-6752
Fax: (804)633-6752
E-mail: dukefamily@travelguides.org
URL: http://www.travelguides.org
Contact: William A. Duke, Pres.
Founded: 1987. **Description:** Acts as clearinghouse and consultant to the travel and lodging industry for disabled travelers. Sponsors seminars on disability etiquette and the effect of the Americans with Disabilities Act on public accommodations. Maintains speakers' bureau. Conducts activities internationally. Publishes travel and access guides. **Awards:** Beverly Chapman Award. **Frequency:** annual. **Type:** recognition. **Recipient:** for outstanding customer service to persons with disabilities. **Telecommunication Services:** electronic mail, suggestions@travelguides.org. **Affiliated With:** American Council of the Blind. **Publications:** *Enabled RVer*, monthly. Magazine. Covers topics such as accessible trails and parks. Alternate Formats: online ● *Virginia Travel Guide for Persons with Disabilities*, biennial. Includes detailed information on accessibility to Virginia lodging and attractions. **Price:** free. **Circulation:** 75,000. **Advertising:** accepted. **Conventions/Meetings:** periodic meeting (exhibits).

3933 ■ Pacific Asia Travel Association (PATA)
Latham Square Bldg.
1611 Telegraph Ave., Ste.550
Oakland, CA 94612
Ph: (510)625-2055
Fax: (510)625-2044
E-mail: americas@pata.org
URL: http://www.pata.org
Contact: Mr. Peter de Jong, Pres./CEO
Founded: 1951. **Members:** 2,000. **Membership Dues:** government/destination/carrier (level 2), $2,400 (annual) ● government/destination (level 3), $1,500 (annual) ● corporate, $4,000 (annual) ● corporate affiliate/education, $500 (annual) ● young tourism professional, $25 (annual) ● industry, associate, media, $1,000 (annual). **Staff:** 25. **Budget:** $2,500,000. **Multinational. Description:** Represents Government tourist bureaus; cruise companies, airlines, railroads, commercial travel bureaus, hotels, tour operators, and hotel associations throughout the world. Conducts marketing program to promote travel to the countries and islands of the Greater Pacific region; works to facilitate and unify entry and exit procedures in members' countries; provides travel information service to the industry disseminates travel news to the press and other media; coordinates market research to determine potential markets and the future impact of overseas travelers. Develops destination development task forces. Compiles statistics. **Libraries: Type:** reference. **Holdings:** 2,000; books, films, periodicals, video recordings. **Subjects:** tourism, Asia. **Awards:** Chapter Awards. **Frequency:** annual. **Type:** recognition. **Recipient:** for PATA chapters ● Face of the Future Award. **Frequency:** annual. **Type:** recognition. **Recipient:** for exceptional young leaders of the travel and tourism industry ● Honorary Life Membership. **Frequency:** annual. **Type:** recognition. **Recipient:** for members ● Merit of Award. **Frequency:** annual. **Type:** recognition. **Recipient:** to individuals who demonstrate exceptional service and leadership to PATA ● PATA Gold Awards. **Frequency:** annual. **Type:** recognition. **Recipient:** for travel writers, photographers, and poster, travel brochure, film, CD-ROM, website, publication, and advertisement producers. **Formerly:** (1986) Pacific Area Travel Association. **Publications:** *Compass*, monthly. Magazine. **Price:** included in membership dues. **Circulation:** 2,000. **Advertising:** accepted ● *Conference Proceedings*. **Price:** $30.00 for members; $50.00 for nonmembers ● *Market Intelligence*. Reports. **Price:** included in membership dues ● *Market Research*. Reports. Alternate Formats: online ● *Pacific Asia Travel Association—Annual Report*. **Price:** included in membership dues. **Circulation:** 5,000 ● *Pacific Asia Travel Association—Annual Statistical Report*. Presents visitor arrival statistics for each of 30 member countries, outbound travel data, and tourism information such as visitor expenditures. **Price:** $250.00 for members; $350.00 for nonmembers. ISSN: 1066-0356 ● *PATA Quarterly Statistical Report*. **Price:** $200.00 for members; $275.00 for nonmembers. ISSN: 1066-0356 ● *PATA Worldwide Chapter Directory*, annual. Lists officers and executive committee members of 66 PATA chapters worldwide. **Price:** included in membership dues; $50.00/ copy for nonmembers. **Circulation:** 1,000. **Advertising:** accepted ● *Task Force Reports*. Alternate Formats: online ● *YTP Voice*. Newsletter. Alternate Formats: online ● Membership Directory, annual. Lists member organizations alphabetically by country and category of membership. Includes member services and PATA publications list. **Price:** $25.00/ copy for members; $250.00/copy for nonmembers. **Circulation:** 12,000. **Advertising:** accepted ● Papers. Alternate Formats: online ● Videos. **Conventions/Meetings:** annual conference.

3934 ■ Romanian National Tourist Office (RoNTO)
355 Lexington Ave., 19th Fl.
New York, NY 10017
Ph: (212)545-8484
Fax: (212)251-0429
E-mail: infous@romaniatourism.com
URL: http://www.romaniatourism.com
Contact: Simion Alb, Dir.
Founded: 1968. **Members:** 20. **Staff:** 21. **Languages:** English, French. **Description:** Provides free travel literature and tourist information, films, and slides on Romania. Assists travel agencies in producing and selling Romanian tourism programs to groups and individuals. **Awards: Type:** recognition. **Formerly:** (2003) Romanian Tourist Board. **Publications:** *Holidays in Romania* (in English, French, and German), quarterly. Magazine. **Price:** free. **Circulation:** 200,000. Alternate Formats: online ● *Romania-Natural and Cultural*, periodic. Newsletter ● *Tour Romania*. **Conventions/Meetings:** annual Romania International Travel Show - trade show, travel and tourism (exhibits) - end of October.

3935 ■ Society of Incentive and Travel Executives (SITE)
401 N Michigan Ave.
Chicago, IL 60611
Ph: (312)321-5148 (312)673-4902
Fax: (312)527-6783
E-mail: brenda_anderson@site-intl.org
URL: http://www.site-intl.org
Contact: Brenda Anderson, CEO
Founded: 1973. **Members:** 2,100. **Membership Dues:** regular, $395 (annual). **Staff:** 8. **Budget:** $1,700,000. **Regional Groups:** 12. **National Groups:** 24. **Multinational. Description:** Represents individuals responsible for the administration or sale of incentive programs including corporate users, incentive marketing companies, cruise lines, hotel chains, resort operators, airlines, and tourist boards. Unites individuals in the incentive industry and facilitates information exchange and problem solving on a personal and professional basis. Supports expansion of incentive programs through public relations, promotion, and speakers' bureau activities. Contributes to the continuing professional education of members through meetings, publications, and research services. Helps upgrade standards through educational services to nonmembers. Compiles statistics; provides placement service. **Awards:** SITE Crystal Award. **Frequency:** annual. **Type:** recognition. **Recipient:** for outstanding and world-class programs. **Computer Services:** Mailing lists, of members. **Committees:** Academic Relations; Awards; Chapter Services; Education; Ethics; Member Services. **Formerly:** Society of Incentive Travel Executives. **Publications:** *In-Site*, bimonthly. Journal. Covers trends and developments affecting the incentive travel industry. Includes surveys and European and Asian reports. **Price:** included in membership dues. **Circulation:** 2,500 ● *Incentive Travel Factbook*, annual ● Membership Directory, annual ● Pamphlets ● Reports ● Reports. **Conventions/Meetings:** annual Crystal Awards - competition, for outstanding incentive travel accomplishments ● annual international conference ● seminar - 3/year.

3936 ■ Society of Polish-American Travel Agents (SPATA)
74 Nassau Ave.
Brooklyn, NY 11222
Ph: (718)383-7211
Fax: (718)349-1767
E-mail: info@spata.org
URL: http://www.spata.org
Contact: Peter Pachacz, Pres.
Founded: 1959. **Members:** 150. **Description:** Promotes interest in tourism to Poland and among Polish communities in the U.S. and abroad. Encourages development of ethical standards within the industry; stresses cooperation and solidarity among members; promotes activities contributing to the betterment of the travel industry. **Telecommunication Services:** electronic mail, albatravel@aol.com. **Publications:** *SPATA Bulletin*, quarterly. Newsletter. Alternate Formats: online. **Conventions/Meetings:** annual meeting ● annual regional meeting.

3937 ■ South American Explorers (SAE)
126 Indian Creek Rd.
Ithaca, NY 14850
Ph: (607)277-0488
Free: (800)274-0568
Fax: (607)277-6122
E-mail: explorer@saexplorers.org
URL: http://www.saexplorers.org
Contact: Don Montague, Pres.
Founded: 1977. **Members:** 10,000. **Membership Dues:** regular, $50 (annual) ● couple, contributing, $80 (annual) ● supporting, $150 (annual) ● life, $600 ● contributing couple, $125 (annual) ● supporting couple, $225 (annual) ● couple - life, $1,150 ● afterlife, $6,000 ● afterlife couple, $10,000. **Staff:** 5. **Budget:** $200,000. **Regional Groups:** 1. **National Groups:** 3. **Languages:** English, Portuguese, Span-

ish. **Multinational. Description:** Seeks to further the exchange of information among scientists, adventurers, and travelers of all nations with the purpose of encouraging exploration throughout Latin America. Supports all forms of scientific field exploration in such areas as biology, geography, anthropology, and archaeology as well as field sports, including backpacking, hiking, mountaineering, and whitewater rafting. Provides volunteer opportunities for travelers. Focuses attention on environmental and ecological concerns. Collects and makes available reliable information on all organizations in Latin America that offer services to travelers, scientists, and outdoorsmen. Maintains speakers' bureau. **Convention/Meeting:** none. **Libraries: Type:** not open to the public. **Holdings:** 2,000; biographical archives. **Subjects:** Latin American history, travel, ethnobotany, fiction. **Computer Services:** database ● mailing lists ● online services. **Telecommunication Services:** electronic mail, admin@saexplorers.org. **Formerly:** (2002) South American Explorers Club. **Publications:** *SAE Newsletter*, monthly. **Advertising:** accepted. Alternate Formats: online ● *South American Explorer*, quarterly. Magazine. Covers Latin American exploration. Contains book reviews and club news. **Price:** included in membership dues; $22.00 /year for nonmembers. ISSN: 0889-7891. **Circulation:** 7,000. **Advertising:** accepted. Alternate Formats: online ● *South American Explorers Club Catalogue*, annual. **Circulation:** 10,000. **Advertising:** accepted ● Also publishes maps and trip reports written by members.

3938 ■ Student and Youth Travel Association (SYTA)
3048 Clarkston Rd.
Lake Orion, MI 48362
Ph: (248)814-7982
Free: (800)509-7982
Fax: (248)814-7150
E-mail: info@syta.org
URL: http://www.syta.org
Contact: Michael Palmer, Exec. Dir.
Membership Dues: active, international affiliate, $500 (annual) ● wholly-owned subsidiary, $200 (annual) ● associate, $750 (annual). **Multinational. Description:** Promotes student and youth travel. Aims to foster integrity and professionalism among student and youth travel service providers. Seeks to create positive awareness of and desire for student and youth travel. Fosters financial stability and credibility in the student and youth travel marketplace. Promotes a professional code of ethics for companies operating in the student and youth travel business. **Telecommunication Services:** electronic mail, mpalmer@syta.org. **Publications:** *SYTA On The Move*, quarterly. Newsletter. Alternate Formats: online. **Conventions/Meetings:** annual conference - 2008 Sept. 5-9, San Antonio, TX; 2009 Aug. 28-Sept. 1, Norfolk, VA.

3939 ■ Swedish Travel and Tourism Council
PO Box 4649
Grand Central Sta.
New York, NY 10163-4649
Ph: (212)885-9700
Fax: (212)885-9710
E-mail: usa@visitsweden.com
URL: http://www.visitsweden.com
Contact: Linda Ericsson, Contact
Languages: Danish, English, Estonian, Finnish, French, German, Italian, Norwegian, Russian, Spanish, Swedish. **Description:** Promotes Sweden as a travel destination. **Publications:** *Sweden 2003*. Features a travel guide on Sweden, containing travel facts, maps and FAQ's on the country.

3940 ■ Taiwan Visitors Association
c/o Taipei Economic and Cultural Office in New York
1 E 42 St., 9th Fl.
New York, NY 10017
Ph: (212)867-1632
Fax: (212)317-7398
E-mail: tbrocnyc@aol.com
URL: http://www.tva.org.tw/eng/e_company.php
Contact: Ambassador Andrew L.Y. Hsia, Contact
Languages: Chinese, English. **Description:** Individuals and corporations engaged in the travel and tourism industries. Promotes Taiwan as a destination for travelers. Gathers and disseminates tourist information; provides services to tourists; conducts promotional activities.

3941 ■ Travel Industry Association of America (TIAA)
1100 New York Ave. NW, Ste.450
Washington, DC 20005-3934
Ph: (202)408-8422
Fax: (202)408-1255
E-mail: feedback@tia.org
URL: http://www.tia.org
Contact: Roger Dow, Pres./CEO
Founded: 1941. **Members:** 2,400. **Membership Dues:** regular, $350 (annual) ● associate, $320 (annual). **Staff:** 52. **Description:** Corporations engaged in the hospitality and travel industries. Promotes increased profitability within the travel industries. Serves as a clearinghouse on the hospitality, travel, and related industries; represents members' interests on the national level; conducts industry research and surveys. Facilitates communication and cooperation among members. **Publications:** *e-Newsline*, semimonthly. Newsletter. Alternate Formats: online. **Conventions/Meetings:** annual conference.

3942 ■ Travel and Tourism Research Association (TTRA)
PO Box 2133
Boise, ID 83701
Ph: (208)429-9511
Fax: (208)429-9512
E-mail: admin@randymorgan.com
URL: http://www.ttra.com
Contact: Patty Morgan, Exec. Dir.
Founded: 1970. **Members:** 800. **Membership Dues:** student, $45 (annual) ● standard, $125 (annual) ● premier, $295 (annual) ● professional organization, $495 (annual). **Multinational. Description:** Professional providers and users of travel and tourism research. Advocates standards and promotes the application of quality travel and tourism research and marketing information. **Computer Services:** database, research articles ● mailing lists, members' contact information. **Publications:** *Journal of Travel Research*, quarterly ● *TTRA Annual Conference Proceedings*, annual. Features selected research and marketing papers from industry experts. ● Membership Directory, annual. **Conventions/Meetings:** annual conference.

3943 ■ United States Tour Operators Association (USTOA)
275 Madison Ave., Ste.2014
New York, NY 10016-1101
Ph: (212)599-6599
Fax: (212)599-6744
E-mail: information@ustoa.com
URL: http://www.ustoa.com
Contact: Linda Kundell, Contact
Founded: 1972. **Members:** 524. **Membership Dues:** active, $1,150-$5,750 (annual) ● associate, $750 (annual) ● allied, $350 (annual). **Staff:** 4. **Budget:** $930,000. **Description:** Represents wholesale tour operators, common carriers, associations, government agencies, suppliers, purveyors of travel services, trade press, communications media, and public relations and advertising representatives. Encourages and supports professional and financial integrity in tourism. Protects the legitimate interests of the consumer and the retail agent from financial loss from business conducted with members. Provides tour operators with an opportunity to formulate and express an independent industry voice on matters of common interest and self-regulation. Strives to facilitate and develop travel on a worldwide basis. **Awards: Type:** recognition. **Telecommunication Services:** electronic mail, kundellcom@nyc.rr.com ● electronic mail, lrkpr@aol.com. **Publications:** *USTOA World Tour*, annual. Membership Directory. **Price:** free. **Advertising:** accepted ● Newsletter, quarterly. **Conventions/Meetings:** annual conference, for members only ● seminar.

3944 ■ U.S. Travel Data Center (USTDC)
c/o Travel Industry Association of America
1100 New York Ave. NW, Ste.450
Washington, DC 20005-3934
Ph: (202)408-8422
Fax: (202)408-1255
E-mail: feedback@tia.org
URL: http://www.tia.org
Contact: William Norman, Pres.
Founded: 1973. **Staff:** 10. **Budget:** $1,000,000. **Description:** Conducts statistical, economic, and market research concerning travel; encourages standardized travel research terminology and techniques. Monitors trends in travel activity and the travel industry. Measures the economic impact of travel on geographic areas and the cost of travel in the U.S. Evaluates the effect of government programs on travel and the travel industry. Forecasts travel activity and expenditures. **Publications:** *Economic Review of Travel in America*, annual ● *Impact of Travel on State Economies*, annual ● *National Travel Survey*, quarterly ● *Survey of State Travel Offices*, annual ● *Travel Printout*, monthly ● Also publishes guide to publications and research services. **Conventions/Meetings:** annual Travel Outlook Forum - meeting.

3945 ■ Venezuelan Tourism Association
PO Box 3010
Sausalito, CA 94966-3010
Ph: (415)331-0100
E-mail: vtajb@hotmail.com
URL: http://www.venezuelanadventures.com
Contact: John Benus, Dir./Founder
Founded: 1990. **Members:** 350. **Membership Dues:** tourism related, $450 (biennial). **Staff:** 2. **Languages:** English, Spanish. **Multinational. Description:** Individuals and corporations engaged in the travel and tourism industries. Promotes Venezuela as a destination for travelers. Gathers and disseminates tourist information; provides services to tourists; conducts promotional activities. **Publications:** *Travel Planner for Venezuela*, biennial. Book. Provides details and contacts for Venezuela. **Price:** $20.00. **Circulation:** 5,000. **Advertising:** accepted. Alternate Formats: CD-ROM; online; magnetic tape.

Travel Services

3946 ■ Interactive Travel Services Association (ITSA)
1156 15th St. NW, Ste.900
Washington, DC 20005
Ph: (202)955-0089
Fax: (202)223-9741
E-mail: execdir@interactivetravel.org
URL: http://www.interactivetravel.org
Contact: Art Sackler, Exec. Dir.
Founded: 1998. **Description:** Promotes consumer choice, access, confidence, protection, and information pertaining to online travel. Seeks to develop a consensus among industry, consumer organizations and policy makers on issues concerning consumer use of the internet to meet their travel needs. Keeps its members informed about legislative and regulatory actions that affect the online travel industry.

Trees

3947 ■ Pacific Northwest Christmas Tree Association (PNWCTA)
PO Box 3366
Salem, OR 97302
Ph: (503)364-2942
Fax: (503)581-6819
URL: http://www.nwtrees.com
Founded: 1955. **Membership Dues:** associate, $120 (annual) ● retailer/pre-harvest grower/choose and cut only grower, $175 (annual) ● industrial, $275 (annual) ● grower (1-100 acres), $225-$420 (annual) ● grower (100 to over 300 acres), $620-$1,025 (annual). **Description:** Provides guidance and assistance to Christmas tree growers in the Northwest. **Computer Services:** Mailing lists, potential buyers.

Committees: Research; Retailer. **Programs:** Tree Industry Partnership. **Publications:** *Buy-Sell Directory*, annual, April. Contains information on the Christmas tree seller's name and contact information. **Price:** free. **Circulation:** 8,000. **Advertising:** accepted ● *Christmas Tree Lookout*, 3/year. Magazine. Contains articles on all aspects of the Christmas tree industry. **Price:** free for members in Oregon and Washington; $25.00/year. **Circulation:** 1,500. **Advertising:** accepted ● Membership Directory, annual. Contains information on the types of trees and services that their fellow member provides. **Price:** included in membership dues. **Circulation:** 1,100. **Advertising:** accepted. **Conventions/Meetings:** annual meeting and tour, includes farm tour - always June ● annual Short Course - seminar - always February ● annual Tree Fair - trade show - always September.

Underwriters

3948 ■ American Nuclear Insurers (ANI)
95 Glastonbury Blvd.
Glastonbury, CT 06033-4438
Ph: (860)682-1301
Fax: (860)659-0002
E-mail: info@nuclearinsurance.com
URL: http://www.amnucins.com
Contact: John Quattrocchi, Sr. VP
Founded: 1957. **Description:** Domestic property/casualty nuclear insurance companies. Strives to ensure safe and secure insurance capacity for customers. Audits financial performance of all member companies annually, ensures compliance with guidelines. **Additional Websites:** http://www.nuclearinsurance.com. **Publications:** Newsletters, periodic.

Unions

3949 ■ Council on Union-Free Environment (CUE)
825 W Bitters Rd., Ste.103
San Antonio, TX 78216
Free: (866)409-4283
Fax: (210)545-4284
E-mail: info@cueinc.com
URL: http://www.cueinc.com
Founded: 1977. **Members:** 300. **Description:** Dedicated to assisting companies desiring to remain union-free through positive employee relations. **Committees:** Labor Lawyers Advisory. **Publications:** *Employment and Labor Law Audit*. Manual. **Price:** $145.00 for members; $185.00 for nonmembers ● *Ending Employment Relationships, Without Ending Up In Court*. Book. **Price:** $17.95 for members; $19.95 for nonmembers ● *Legal Alert*, quarterly. Newsletter. **Price:** included in membership dues. Alternate Formats: online ● *Network News*, monthly. Newsletter. **Price:** included in membership dues. Alternate Formats: online ● *Remaining Union-Free: A Supervisor's Guide*. Handbook. **Price:** $35.00 for members; $45.00 for nonmembers. **Conventions/Meetings:** semiannual conference.

Utilities

3950 ■ 1-800 American Free Trade Association
PO Box 1049
Burlington, VT 05402-1049
Ph: (802)383-0816
Fax: (802)860-4821
E-mail: info@1800afta.org
URL: http://1800afta.org
Contact: Stephanie Perrotte, Contact
Membership Dues: founding/full, $2,500 (annual) ● associate, $1,000 (annual) ● vendor, $3,500 (annual). **Description:** Advocates for the advancement of sound business practices within the toll-free telephone services number industry. Creates a positive regulatory and market environment for 1-800 service companies and their customers. Provides interaction to open new market opportunities. Delivers vital information on industry and regulatory developments. **Publications:** Newsletter, periodic. Alternate Formats: online.

3951 ■ American Public Gas Association (APGA)
201 Massachusetts Ave. NE, Ste.C-4
Washington, DC 20002
Ph: (202)464-2742
Free: (800)927-4204
Fax: (202)464-0246
E-mail: bkalisch@apga.org
URL: http://www.apga.org
Contact: Bert Kalisch, Pres./CEO
Founded: 1961. **Members:** 595. **Staff:** 6. **Budget:** $1,000,000. **Description:** Publicly owned gas systems; private corporations, persons or firms dealing with public gas systems are associate members. Promotes efficiency among public gas systems and protects the interests of the gas consumer. Provides information service on federal developments affecting natural gas; surveys municipal systems. **Awards:** Service Awards. **Frequency:** annual. **Type:** recognition. **Telecommunication Services:** electronic mail, lwillsdudich@apga.org. **Committees:** Awards; Gas Supply; Marketing; Membership; Operations; Regulatory and Legislative. **Publications:** *American Public Gas Association—Directory*, annual. Presents a list of publicly owned natural gas systems. **Price:** $50.00 ● *American Public Gas Association—Newsletter*, biweekly. **Conventions/Meetings:** annual conference (exhibits) - always July or August ● seminar and workshop.

3952 ■ Association of Edison Illuminating Companies (AEIC)
c/o Earl B. Parsons, Jr., Exec. Dir./Sec.-Treas.
PO Box 2641
Birmingham, AL 35291
Ph: (205)257-2530
Fax: (205)257-2540
E-mail: aeicdir@bellsouth.net
URL: http://www.aeic.org
Contact: Earl B. Parsons Jr., Exec. Dir./Sec.-Treas.
Founded: 1885. **Members:** 157. **Staff:** 3. **Multinational. Description:** Represents the interests of investor-owned public utilities, generating and transmitting or distributing companies. **Committees:** Cable Engineering; Electric Power Apparatus; Load Research; Meter and Services; Power Delivery; Power Generation. **Publications:** *Annual Report of the Load Research Committee*, annual. **Price:** $35.00/copy ● *Biennial Directory of Load Research Projects*. **Price:** $50.00/copy ● *Cumulative Index of Subjects Load Research Committee Reports 1959-1989* ● *Load Research Manual 1990* ● Also publishes cable specifications, guides, and committee reports. **Conventions/Meetings:** annual meeting - 2008 Oct. 16-18, White Sulphur Springs, WV.

3953 ■ Automatic Meter Reading Association (AMRA)
60 Revere Dr., Ste.500
Northbrook, IL 60062
Ph: (847)480-9628
Fax: (847)480-9282
E-mail: amra@amra-intl.org
URL: http://www.amra-intl.org
Contact: Brian Pugliese, Exec. Dir.
Founded: 1987. **Members:** 900. **Membership Dues:** individual (utility), $325 (annual) ● all access (based on number of members), $950-$1,400 (annual) ● individual (non-utility), $350 (annual). **Staff:** 4. **Budget:** $1,040,000. **Description:** Gas, water and electric utilities, telephone companies, equipment vendors and manufacturers, installation companies, and consultants. Promotes the use of automation technology for meter reading and energy management. Fosters deployment of technology by providing a forum for research and development of standards, guidelines, and practices. Keeps members informed of developments in the field. **Committees:** Exhibitor; Program; Publications; Standards. **Publications:** *AMRA Newsletter*, periodic. **Advertising:** accepted ● *Trials and Installations*, semiannual. Report. **Price:** $75.00. **Conventions/Meetings:** annual symposium, includes educational programs (exhibits).

3954 ■ Communications Supply Service Association (CSSA)
5700 Murray St.
Little Rock, AR 72209
Ph: (501)562-7666
Free: (800)252-2772
Fax: (501)562-7616
E-mail: cdavis@cssa.net
URL: http://www.cssa.net
Contact: Larry W. Hoaglan, Pres./CEO
Founded: 1976. **Members:** 293. **Staff:** 27. **Budget:** $18,000,000. **Description:** Small, independent, cooperative or commercial telephone companies. Coordinates group purchases of telecommunications equipment and supplies providing firms with savings commensurate with the size of the company. Offers assistance in technical matters. **Libraries: Type:** reference. **Holdings:** audiovisuals. **Computer Services:** database. **Committees:** Standards. **Publications:** *The Member Link*, bimonthly. Newsletter. **Price:** free for members. **Circulation:** 900. **Advertising:** accepted. Alternate Formats: online. **Conventions/Meetings:** annual meeting, in conjunction with National Telephone Cooperative Association (exhibits).

3955 ■ CompTel/ALTS
900 17th St. NW, Ste.400
Washington, DC 20006
Ph: (202)296-6650
Fax: (202)296-7585
E-mail: ecomstock@comptel.org
URL: http://www.comptelascent.org
Contact: Earl Comstock, Pres./CEO
Founded: 2003. **Members:** 400. **Membership Dues:** service provider (voting; based on annual revenue), $3,450-$74,250 (annual) ● supplier associate (based on annual revenue), $3,000-$16,500 (annual) ● international associate (based on annual revenue), $2,500-$7,000 (annual) ● professional associate, $2,500 (annual). **Staff:** 16. **Budget:** $4,000,000. **Description:** Represents competitive facilities-based telecommunications service providers, emerging VoIP providers, integrated communications companies and their supplier partners, and companies of all sizes and profiles that provide voice, data and video services in the U.S. and around the world. Aims to create and sustain true competition in the telecommunications industry. **Telecommunication Services:** electronic mail, mboles@comptel.org. **Committees:** International Communications; Legislative; Regulatory. **Councils:** Meetings; Supplier Advisory. **Task Forces:** Public Relations. **Formed by Merger of:** (2003) Association of Communications Enterprises; (2003) Competitive Telecommunications Association; (2005) CompTel/ASCENT Alliance and Association for Local Telecommunications Services; American Council for Competitive Telecommunications; Association of Long Distance Telephone Companies. **Publications:** *The Connection*, weekly. Newsletter. Alternate Formats: online ● Annual Report, annual. Contains summary of the association's accomplishments for the previous year. Alternate Formats: online. **Conventions/Meetings:** semiannual Convention and Expo - conference and trade show (exhibits).

3956 ■ Edison Electric Institute (EEI)
701 Pennsylvania Ave. NW
Washington, DC 20004-2696
Ph: (202)508-5000 (202)508-5649
Free: (800)334-4688
Fax: (202)508-5360
E-mail: bfarrell@eei.org
URL: http://www.eei.org
Contact: Brian Farrell, Dir. of Assoc. Services
Founded: 1933. **Members:** 200. **Membership Dues:** associate (with less than $50 million annual revenues), $4,000 (annual) ● associate (with more than $50 million annual revenues), $6,000 (annual). **Staff:** 200. **Budget:** $50,000,000. **Multinational. Description:** Shareholder-owned electric utility companies operating in the U.S; international affiliates and as-

sociates worldwide. **Libraries: Type:** reference; by appointment only. **Holdings:** 22,000; books, periodicals, reports. **Subjects:** electric industry, energy, regulation, legislation. **Awards:** Edison Award. **Frequency:** annual. **Type:** recognition. **Recipient:** for distinguished leadership innovation and contribution to the advancement of the electric industry for the benefit of all ● Index of Investor-Owned Electric Utilities Award. **Frequency:** annual. **Type:** recognition. **Recipient:** for outstanding corporate financial performance. **Computer Services:** database, electric utility news on the Internet. **Committees:** POWERPAC. **Absorbed:** (1975) Electric Energy Association; (1978) National Association of Electric Companies. **Publications:** *Electric Perspectives*, bimonthly. Magazine. Provides valuable insight into the issues, trends, and developments of concern to electric utility executives. **Price:** $50.00/year. ISSN: 0364-474X. **Circulation:** 17,000. **Advertising:** accepted ● *Statistical Reports*, quarterly ● *Statistical Yearbook*, annual. **Conventions/Meetings:** annual convention (exhibits) - every June.

3957 ■ Electricity Storage Association (ESA)

830 Claremont Dr.
Morgan Hill, CA 95037
Ph: (614)716-1269
E-mail: info@electricitystorage.org
URL: http://www.energystorage.org
Contact: Brad Roberts, Contact

Membership Dues: general, $750 (annual) ● sponsor, $1,750 (annual). **Multinational. Description:** Promotes the development and commercialization of energy storage technologies. Coordinates and attracts international interest and involvement in energy storage. Provides a forum for technical and commercial information exchange between suppliers, customers and researchers. **Publications:** Newsletter. Alternate Formats: online. **Conventions/Meetings:** annual meeting - every spring.

3958 ■ Institute of Public Utilities (IPU)

Michigan State Univ.
W157 Owen Graduate Hall
East Lansing, MI 48825-1109
Ph: (517)355-1876
Fax: (517)355-1854
E-mail: ipu@msu.edu
URL: http://www.ipu.msu.edu
Contact: Janice A. Beecher PhD, Dir.

Founded: 1965. **Members:** 30. **Membership Dues:** Corporate Advisory Board, $12,000 (annual). **Staff:** 10. **Budget:** $250,000. **Languages:** English, German, Spanish. **Description:** Represents the interests of privately and publicly owned utility companies in energy, telecommunications and water. Facilitates research and discussion of problems currently faced by public utility industry. Conducts educational programs in conjunction with National Association of Regulatory Utility Commissioners. Holds periodic seminars and special training programs. **Libraries: Type:** not open to the public. **Holdings:** 2,000; books, periodicals. **Subjects:** electricity, natural gas, telecommunications, energy, regulation. **Awards:** IPU Annual Award. **Frequency:** annual. **Type:** recognition. **Computer Services:** Online services, discussion forum ● online services, library. **Telecommunication Services:** electronic mail, beecher@msu.edu. **Committees:** Corporate Advisory; Regulatory Advisory. **Publications:** *Working Paper Series*, 6-12/year. Books. Covers topics in utility regulation. ● Books. Covers topics in utility regulation. **Circulation:** 1,000. Alternate Formats: CD-ROM; online; diskette. **Conventions/Meetings:** annual Advanced Regulatory Studies Program - workshop ● annual conference - always first week of December in Williamsburg, VA.

3959 ■ NASSCO - Setting the Industry Standards for the Rehabilitation of Underground Utilities

1314 Bedford Ave., Ste.201
Baltimore, MD 21208
Ph: (410)486-3500
Fax: (410)486-6838
URL: http://www.nassco.org
Contact: Rod Thornhill, Pres.

Founded: 1975. **Members:** 250. **Membership Dues:** contractor, manufacturer, $450 (annual) ● contractor, manufacturer, dealer (sustaining), $650 (annual) ● professional, $250 (annual). **Staff:** 3. **Budget:** $140,000. **Description:** Companies providing services including sewer evaluation, cleaning, inspection, and rehabilitation; manufacturers and suppliers of sewer service equipment; consulting engineers and municipal government officials. Serves as a forum for discussion of needs, ideas, and information among members. Works to: improve standards and procedures for sewer evaluation, maintenance, rehabilitation, and worker safety; promote members' services and assist in marketing sewer service of equipment, materials, and supplies; educate owners, engineers, and inspectors about sewer rehabilitation methods and procedures. Conducts training seminars in maintenance and rehabilitation, inspection, and safety. Provides referral services. **Awards:** Scholarship. **Frequency:** annual. **Type:** scholarship. **Computer Services:** Mailing lists, of members. **Formerly:** (2001) National Association of Sewer Service Companies. **Publications:** *Inspector Handbook for Sewer Collection System Rehabilitation*. **Price:** $75.00 for nonmembers; $25.00 for members. Alternate Formats: CD-ROM ● *Manual of Practices*. Book. **Price:** $75.00 for nonmembers; $25.00 for members. Alternate Formats: CD-ROM ● *Sewer Worker Safety Training*. Video. **Price:** $75.00 for nonmembers; $50.00 for members ● *Specifications Guidelines*. Contains specifications for sewer rehab processes, TV inspection, and cleaning. **Price:** $45.00 for members. Alternate Formats: CD-ROM ● Directory, annual. **Advertising:** accepted. Alternate Formats: CD-ROM. **Conventions/Meetings:** annual meeting (exhibits) - February.

3960 ■ National Exchange Carrier Association (NECA)

80 S Jefferson Rd.
Whippany, NJ 07981-1009
Free: (800)228-8597
Fax: (973)884-8469
E-mail: necainfo@neca.org
URL: http://www.neca.org
Contact: Mr. Nolan Moulle, Vice Chm.

Founded: 1983. **Members:** 1,000. **Staff:** 500. **Regional Groups:** 7. **Description:** All local telephone companies in the continental U.S., Puerto Rico, Virgin Islands, Hawaii, and Alaska. Prepares and files interstate access charges and administers revenue pools created by those charges. Compiles statistics. **Libraries: Type:** reference. **Computer Services:** database. **Formerly:** (1983) Exchange Carrier Association. **Publications:** *ACCESS*, bimonthly. Newsletter. **Circulation:** 1,600. **Conventions/Meetings:** annual meeting.

3961 ■ National Submetering and Utility Allocation Association (NSUAA)

6757 Arapaho Rd., Ste.711-145
Dallas, TX 75248-4005
Ph: (972)392-9619
Free: (866)225-1668
Fax: (972)392-0759
E-mail: nsuaa@nsuaa.org
URL: http://www.nsuaa.org
Contact: Suzanne Perry, Exec. Dir.

Founded: 1998. **Members:** 60. **Membership Dues:** general, $2,600 (annual) ● associate, individual, $500 (annual) ● owner/manager, $1,000 (annual). **Staff:** 5. **Multinational. Description:** Manufacturers, service providers, and property owners. Represents and serves the submetering and utility allocation industry. Facilitates communication among members; disseminates information; promotes the public policy interests of the Utility Allocation Industry. **Libraries: Type:** reference. **Holdings:** articles. **Subjects:** utility submetering and allocation. **Awards:** Groundbreaker Award. **Frequency:** annual. **Type:** recognition. **Recipient:** for innovation in areas related to a submerged utility billing program ● Property Choice Award. **Frequency:** annual. **Type:** recognition. **Recipient:** for excellence in managing the utility billing program ● Ultimate Challenge Award. **Frequency:** annual. **Type:** recognition. **Recipient:** to a property manager, management company, or owner who faced and solved the greatest resident complaint related to utility billing. **Publications:** Newsletter, quarterly. **Conventions/Meetings:** annual meeting.

3962 ■ National Telecommunications Cooperative Association (NTCA)

4121 Wilson Blvd., Ste.1000
Arlington, VA 22203
Ph: (703)351-2000 (703)351-2048
Fax: (703)351-2001
E-mail: mbrunner@ntca.org
URL: http://www.ntca.org
Contact: Michael E. Brunner, CEO

Founded: 1954. **Members:** 1,153. **Membership Dues:** associate (with benefits), subsidiary, $400-$1,000 (annual) ● international, $500 (annual). **Staff:** 130. **Budget:** $8,000,000. **Regional Groups:** 10. **State Groups:** 62. **Description:** Represents the 600 locally owned and controlled telecommunications cooperatives and companies throughout rural and small-town of America. Provides members with aggressive legislative representation on Capital Hill, and regulatory representation at the Federal Communications Commission and in the courts. Holds more than fifty educational seminars, workshops and round tables, regional meetings, and a national Annual Meeting and Expo. Maintains a comprehensive benefits program including health insurance; retirement and savings programs; and directors' and officers' insurance. **Libraries: Type:** reference. **Holdings:** 800; audiovisuals, books, business records, periodicals. **Subjects:** telecommunications, America. **Awards:** Best Subscriber Communications. **Frequency:** annual. **Type:** recognition ● Director - Life Achievement. **Frequency:** annual. **Type:** recognition ● Manager Achievement. **Frequency:** annual. **Type:** recognition ● Manager-Life Achievement. **Frequency:** annual. **Type:** recognition ● Marketing Achievement. **Frequency:** annual. **Type:** recognition. **Computer Services:** Online services, BBS for members, offering updated news of the rural telecommunications industry, as well as association news and information. **Committees:** Association Services; Awards; Business and Technology; Commercial Company; Futures; Government Affairs; Industry; Legal; Marketing; Program Planning; Resolutions; Task Force; Television; Wireless. **Councils:** Associate Member Advisory. **Formerly:** (2003) National Telephone Cooperative Association. **Publications:** *Book on Telephone History*. **Price:** $30.00/copy; $60.00 for nonmembers ● *Compensation and Benefits Survey*. **Price:** $50.00 for participants; $75.00 for additional copies; $150.00 for members, nonparticipants; $299.00 for nonmembers. Also Cited As: *C and B Survey* ● *The Competitor*, bimonthly. Newsletter. **Price:** free, for members only ● *ePapers*. **Price:** free, for members only. Alternate Formats: online ● *The Exchange*, bimonthly. Newsletter. Contains news and information for cooperative and commercial telephone company managers, directors, and owners. **Price:** $15.00 ● *Marketing and Benchmark Survey*. **Price:** $695.00 for members (participants); $950.00 for nonmembers (participants); $1,500.00 for non-participants ● *National Telecommunications Cooperative Association—Membership Directory*, annual. Arranged geographically; contains company name, phone, fax, address contact person, and advertisers' indexes. **Price:** $30.00 for members; $150.00 for nonmembers; $495.00 for company member (electronic edition); $695.00 for company nonmember (electronic edition). **Advertising:** accepted ● *The New Edge*, bimonthly. Newsletter. **Price:** free, for members only ● *PRNetworkings*, monthly. Newsletter. **Price:** free, for members only ● *Rural Telecommunications*, bimonthly. Magazine. Monitors legislative, regulative, and legal issues affecting the industry. Shares expertise on management, marketing, trends and technology. **Price:** $25.00 /year for members; $125.00 /year for nonmembers. ISSN: 0744-2548. **Advertising:** accepted ● *Telephone Cooperatives*. Brochure ● *Washington Report*, weekly. Provides information on current federal and state legislation and regulation affecting the industry. **Price:** $75.00 /year for members; $225.00 /year for nonmembers. **Conventions/Meetings:** annual Legislative and Policy Conference - convention, on legislation (exhibits) - 2009 Mar. 23-25, Washington, DC ● annual meeting - 2009 Feb. 8-11, Long Beach, CA; 2010 Jan. 31-Feb. 3, Tampa, FL ● periodic Pre-Retirement Planning - seminar ● biennial workshop - 2009 Aug. 24-30, Asheville, NC; 2011 Aug. 8-14, Asheville, NC; 2013 Aug. 5-11, Asheville, NC ● annual Fall Conference - 2008 Sept. 21-24, Indian Wells, CA; 2009 Sept. 12-15, New York, NY; 2010 Sept. 19-22, St. Louis, MO.

3963 ■ National Utility Training and Safety Education Association (NUTSEA)
c/o Melissa Robokoff
8240 Resurrection Dr.
Anchorage, AK 99504
Ph: (907)563-2551
Fax: (907)561-5547
E-mail: mrobokoff@alaskapower.org
URL: http://www.nutsea.org
Contact: Melissa Robokoff, Contact
Founded: 1976. **Membership Dues:** individual, $100 (annual). **Description:** Utility professionals. Promotes professionalism in the fields of safety and training. Works to assist job training and safety instructors. Promotes exchange of information among members of the association to increase professional competence. Conducts research to benefit job training. **Conventions/Meetings:** annual conference.

3964 ■ Organization for the Promotion and Advancement of Small Telecommunications Companies (OPASTCO)
21 Dupont Cir. NW, Ste.700
Washington, DC 20036
Ph: (202)659-5990
Fax: (202)659-4619
E-mail: mks@opastco.org
URL: http://www.opastco.org
Contact: Martha Silver, Dir. of Public Relations
Founded: 1963. **Members:** 590. **Membership Dues:** associate (based on number of employees), $300-$1,300 (annual) ● telecommunications company (based on number of customers), $500-$5,500 (annual). **Staff:** 18. **Description:** Small, independent telephone companies and cooperatives serving rural areas (560); associate members are telephone equipment and service suppliers (165). Seeks to promote and advance small, independent telephone companies and provide a forum for the exchange of ideas and discussion of mutual problems. Represents rural companies' interests before Congress and regulatory bodies. Provides clearinghouse for the compilation, publication, and distribution of information of interest to members. Offers guidance to members on matters of industry-wide importance. Encourages recognition of the contribution made to the telephone industry by members. **Awards: Type:** recognition. **Committees:** Education; Legislative and Regulatory Affairs; Marketing; Public Relations; Technical. **Formerly:** (1999) Organization for the Protection and Advancement of Small Telephone Companies. **Publications:** *Advocate*, monthly. Magazine ● *OPASTCO 411*, biweekly. Report. Contains information on federal regulations, legislation, and events affecting the independent telephone industry. ● *OPASTCO Online Membership Directory*, annual. **Price:** free, for members only. Alternate Formats: online ● *OPASTCO Roundtable: The Magazine of Ideas for Small Telephone Companies*, quarterly. Provides how-to information on various aspects of the independent telephone industry, including business ventures and technology. **Price:** included in membership dues; $14.00/year for additional subscriptions; $27.00 /year for nonmembers. **Circulation:** 3,000. **Advertising:** accepted. **Conventions/Meetings:** annual conference ● semiannual convention (exhibits) - always January and July.

3965 ■ United States Telecom Association (USTA)
607 14th St. NW, Ste.400
Washington, DC 20005
Ph: (202)326-7300 (202)326-7370
Fax: (202)326-7333
E-mail: membership@ustelecom.org
URL: http://www.usta.org
Contact: Walter B. McCormick Jr., Pres./CEO
Founded: 1897. **Members:** 1,200. **Membership Dues:** carrier (minimum), $250 (annual) ● supplier, $2,000 (annual) ● partner supplier, $10,000 (annual) ● international (based on revenue), $5,000-$25,000 (annual). **Staff:** 55. **Budget:** $16,000,000. **Description:** Local operating telephone companies or telephone holding companies. Members represent a total of 114 million access lines. Conducts educational and training programs. Maintains 21 committees. **Libraries: Type:** by appointment only. **Holdings:** books, periodicals. **Subjects:** telecommunications. **Awards:** Distinguished Service Award. **Type:** recognition. **Recipient:** to outstanding leaders in industry and other fields ● Pacesetter Award. **Type:** recognition. **Formerly:** Independent Telephone Association of America; National Independent Telephone Association; (1983) United States Independent Telephone Association; (2000) United States Telephone Association. **Publications:** *Holding Company Report*, annual ● *Phonefacts*, annual ● *Statistical Volumes*, annual ● *Teletimes*, bimonthly. Booklets ● Brochures ● Membership Directory, annual. **Conventions/Meetings:** annual NXTcomm - conference and trade show (exhibits).

3966 ■ Utilities Service Alliance (USA)
9200 Indian Creek Pkwy., Ste.201
Overland Park, KS 66210
Ph: (913)451-5641
Fax: (913)451-3893
E-mail: info@usainc.org
URL: http://www.usainc.org
Contact: Carl Parry, Pres.
Founded: 1994. **Description:** Improves individual plant and fleet performance. Reduces operating and maintenance costs. Provides world-class resources and business opportunities to participants in the most cost-effective manner possible. **Programs:** Air Operated Valve; Operator Performance Improvement; Radiation Protection. **Conventions/Meetings:** annual Nuclear Generator and Supplier Executive Summit - conference.

3967 ■ Utility Shareholders Association
52 Woods Rd.
Little Falls, NJ 07424-2051
Ph: (973)785-1609
Contact: Mr. John R. Moscinski, Contact
Founded: 1991. **Members:** 12. **Staff:** 1. **Description:** Utility shareholders. United to discourage utility participation in nuclear energy. Argues that peak energy requirement is only needed during daylight hours or 9:00 am to 4:00 pm and that this time period is suited admirably for collecting the sun's energy thereby eliminating the need for "billion dollar excess energy generation for just one-third of the day energy requirement." Believes that capitol construction costs for a generating plant only used for a third of the day is "wasteful, polluting, dangerous and costly to the environment and economy." Presents proposals at annual shareholder meetings. **Libraries: Type:** reference. **Holdings:** articles, books, clippings, periodicals. **Subjects:** solar energy, nuclear generation, utilities. **Affiliated With:** National Association of Civilian Conservation Corps Alumni. **Conventions/Meetings:** annual meeting - always April, Poughkeepsie, NY.

3968 ■ Water and Sewer Distributors of America (WASDA)
100 N 20th St., 4th Fl.
Philadelphia, PA 19103-1443
Ph: (215)564-3484
Fax: (215)963-9785
E-mail: wasda@fernley.com
URL: http://www.wasda.com
Contact: Lindsay Groff, Exec. Dir.
Founded: 1979. **Members:** 62. **Membership Dues:** distributor (based on annual sales volume), $600-$6,600 (annual) ● associate, $1,000 (annual). **Budget:** $350,000. **Description:** Owners of distributorships that provide products to municipal water and sewer markets. Seeks to: promote the municipal water and sewer supply industry; provide education to members; and act as liaison to related interest groups. **Libraries: Type:** open to the public. **Holdings:** archival material. **Awards:** Matt Stager Memorial Scholarship. **Frequency:** annual. **Type:** scholarship. **Recipient:** for students. **Committees:** Education; Leadership; Marketing. **Publications:** *Connections*, quarterly. Newsletter. Covers association and industry news for water and sewer distributors. **Price:** free for members. **Circulation:** 100. Alternate Formats: online. **Conventions/Meetings:** semiannual convention ● annual meeting.

Vegetables

3969 ■ Canned Vegetable Council (CVC)
Address Unknown since 2008
Founded: 1977. **Description:** Works to increase consumption of vegetables in cans. **Computer Services:** Information services. **Publications:** *A Dozen Reasons Why You Should Use Vegetables In Cans*. Brochure ● *Delicious & Nutritious Recipes Using Vegetables in Cans*. Booklet ● *Posters*. Suitable for classroom and lunchroom use. **Conventions/Meetings:** board meeting.

Vending

3970 ■ International Association of Ice Cream Vendors (IAICV)
100 N 20th St., 4th Fl.
Philadelphia, PA 19103-1443
Ph: (215)564-3484
Fax: (215)564-2175
E-mail: iaicv@fernley.com
URL: http://www.iaicv.org
Contact: Lindsay Groff, Exec. Dir.
Founded: 1969. **Members:** 140. **Membership Dues:** vendor, $500 (annual) ● supplier, $900 (annual) ● associate vendor, $300 (annual) ● broker, distributor, $700 (annual). **Staff:** 3. **Multinational. Description:** Ice cream vendors, manufacturers of ice cream vending equipment, and suppliers to the industry. Promotes responsible and ethical practice in the ice cream vending industry; seeks to maintain a positive public image of ice cream vendors; works to insure ongoing profitability in the industry. Serves as a clearinghouse on the ice cream vending industry; facilitates exchange of information among members; conducts safety education programs. **Awards:** Al Reynold Scholarship. **Frequency:** annual. **Type:** scholarship ● Doc Abernathy Memorial Scholarship. **Frequency:** annual. **Type:** scholarship ● IAICV Safety Award. **Frequency:** annual. **Type:** recognition ● IAICV Scholarship. **Frequency:** annual. **Type:** scholarship ● Jim Roberts Scholarship. **Frequency:** annual. **Type:** scholarship ● Manny Ginsberg Scholarship. **Frequency:** annual. **Type:** scholarship. **Committees:** Awards; Legislative; Membership; Safety; Scholarship. **Publications:** *Chimes*, 3/year. Newsletter. Alternate Formats: online. **Conventions/Meetings:** annual convention (exhibits).

3971 ■ National Automatic Merchandising Association (NAMA)
20 N Wacker Dr., Ste.3500
Chicago, IL 60606-3102
Ph: (312)346-0370
Free: (888)337-VEND
Fax: (312)704-4140
E-mail: rgeerdes@vending.org
URL: http://www.vending.org
Contact: Richard M. Geerdes, Pres./CEO
Founded: 1936. **Members:** 2,500. **Membership Dues:** vending, coffee service, foodservice operator, $325 (annual) ● supplier, $700-$12,000 (annual) ● machine manufacturer, $1,800-$25,000 (annual) ● distributor, broker, $525-$1,800 (annual) ● sustaining, $400 (annual). **Staff:** 25. **Budget:** $5,000,000. **State Groups:** 30. **Description:** Manufacturing and operating companies in the automatic vending machine industry; food service management firms; office coffee machine operators; suppliers of products

and services. Compiles industry statistics. **Committees:** Ad Hoc Certification; Automatic Merchandising; Coffee Service; Image; Operating Statistics; Vending. **Absorbed:** (2001) National Coffee Service Association. **Publications:** *Food Service Manual.* Contains daily solutions for long-time productivity, management and profit. **Price:** $125.00 ● *National Automatic Merchandising Association—Directory of Members*, annual. Membership Directory. Includes service firms, alphabetically by state; machine manufacturers, alphabetically by company name; suppliers, alphabetically by name. **Price:** included in membership dues; $150.00 for nonmembers. **Advertising:** accepted ● *National Automatic Merchandising Association-In Touch*, quarterly. Newsletter. **Price:** included in membership dues ● *National Automatic Merchandising Association—State Legislative Review*, periodic. Newsletter. Contains state legislation affecting the vending/foodservice management industry. **Price:** free for members ● *Quarterly Labor Relations Comprehensive Bulletin.* Newsletter. Concerned with technical-legal aspects of employee relation's policies in the vending/foodservice management industry. **Price:** free for members. **Conventions/Meetings:** annual National Expo - convention and trade show ● annual Spring Expo - meeting and trade show.

3972 ■ National Bulk Vendors Association (NBVA)
191 N Wacker Dr., Ste.1800
Chicago, IL 60606-1615
Ph: (312)521-2400
Fax: (312)521-2300
E-mail: nbva@muchshelist.com
URL: http://www.nbva.org
Contact: Morrie Much, Counsel
Founded: 1950. **Members:** 300. **Membership Dues:** operator (based on number of machines), $100-$1,000 (annual) ● supplier, manufacturer, distributor, $750 (annual). **Staff:** 2. **Budget:** $300,000. **Description:** Manufacturers, distributors, and operators of bulk vending merchandise and equipment. **Awards:** Operator of the Year. **Frequency:** annual. **Type:** recognition. **Recipient:** for outstanding achievement ● **Type:** scholarship. **Telecommunication Services:** electronic mail, mmuch@muchshelist.com. **Formerly:** (1973) National Vendors Association. **Publications:** *National Bulk Vendors Association—Bulletin*, every 6 weeks. Provides legislative, tax, convention, and membership news. **Price:** free for members. **Circulation:** 400. **Conventions/Meetings:** annual convention and workshop (exhibits) - always March, April, or May.

3973 ■ Randolph-Sheppard Vendors of America (RSVA)
1808 Faith Pl., Ste.B
Terrytown, LA 70056-4104
Ph: (504)368-7785
Free: (800)467-5299
Fax: (504)368-7739
E-mail: rsva@juno.com
URL: http://www.acb.org/rsva
Contact: Kim M. Venable, Treas.
Founded: 1968. **Members:** 1,000. **Membership Dues:** general, $10 (annual). **State Groups:** 20. **Description:** Vending facility managers united for promotion, education, and legislative activities. Attempts to upgrade the vending facility program for the blind in the U.S. **Affiliated With:** American Council of the Blind. **Publications:** *Vendorscope*, quarterly. Newsletter. **Conventions/Meetings:** annual meeting, held in conjunction with American Council for the Blind (exhibits).

Warehousing

3974 ■ Affiliated Warehouse Companies (AWC)
PO Box 295
Hazlet, NJ 07730-0295
Ph: (732)739-2323
Fax: (732)739-4154
E-mail: sales@awco.com
URL: http://www.awco.com
Contact: Mr. James McBride III, Pres.
Founded: 1953. **Members:** 120. **Staff:** 8. **For-Profit. Description:** Represents franchised public merchandise warehouse companies united for national sales work, advertising, and public relations. Assists in gathering rates and data pertaining to warehousing and distribution. Offers free consultation services to industry. Maintains placement service; compiles statistics. **Computer Services:** database, public warehouse users ● online services, quote. **Publications:** *Affiliated Warehouse Companies—Directory*, biennial. Membership Directory. Arranged by state and city. Includes facilities and services offered by members. **Price:** free. **Circulation:** 16,000. Alternate Formats: diskette ● *Newsletter and Summary of Sales Work*, biweekly. Provides information on the public warehousing industry, industry meetings advertising information, sales calls, and member news. **Price:** included in membership dues. **Circulation:** 110 ● Technical Paper "Selecting a Public Warehouse as your Third Party Provider".

3975 ■ Allied Distribution, Inc. (ADI)
PO Box 607
Eagle River, WI 54521
Ph: (715)479-3530
Fax: (715)479-3551
E-mail: info@warehousenetwork.com
URL: http://www.warehousenetwork.com
Contact: Ernest B. Brunswick, Pres.
Founded: 1933. **Members:** 50. **Staff:** 3. **For-Profit. Description:** Represents public and contract warehouses and distribution centers. Maintains an associated network of public warehouse and distribution centers throughout the U.S., Canada, Mexico, and other areas. Not affiliated with Allied Van Lines. **Convention/Meeting:** none. **Publications:** *Warehousing and Distribution Centers Membership Directory*, biennial.

3976 ■ American Chain of Warehouses (ACW)
156 Flamingo Dr.
Beecher, IL 60401-9725
Ph: (708)946-9792
Fax: (708)946-9793
E-mail: bjurus@acwi.org
URL: http://www.acwi.org
Contact: William L. Jurus, VP, Sales and Marketing
Founded: 1911. **Members:** 51. **Staff:** 2. **For-Profit. Description:** Represents commercial warehouses. Provides national sales representation. Disseminates information. **Publications:** Membership Directory, periodic. Lists financial data, types of storage, floor space, general facilities, insurance contents rate, and other services.

3977 ■ Independent Liquid Terminals Association (ILTA)
1444 I St. NW, No. 400
Washington, DC 20005
Ph: (202)842-9200
Fax: (202)326-8660
E-mail: info@ilta.org
URL: http://www.ilta.org
Contact: E. David Doane, Pres.
Founded: 1974. **Members:** 75. **Membership Dues:** for-hire (terminal), $3,395-$8,327 (annual) ● proprietary (terminal), $2,547-$6,455 (annual) ● international (terminal), $1,698-$4,164 (annual) ● supplier, $415 (annual). **Staff:** 6. **Budget:** $1,250,000. **Regional Groups:** 4. **Description:** Independent terminal companies that provide services to handle, transfer, and store bulk liquid commodities. Members operate deep water and barge terminals for the storage of chemicals, petroleum, fertilizers, and basic bulk liquid food products such as animal fats and vegetable oils, molasses, and spirits. Objectives are to advise members of pending legislation and regulations and to respond to these proposals; to provide and facilitate the exchange of information among operators; to promote the safe and efficient handling of an increasing variety of liquid products. Maintains speakers' bureau and placement services. **Additional Websites:** http://www.tankfarm-ilta.com. **Task Forces:** Environmental; Safety; Training. **Publications:** *ILTA Newsletter*, monthly. Provides information on federal and state legislation and regulations affecting the liquid terminal and related industries. **Price:** $120.00 /year for nonmembers; included in membership dues. **Circulation:** 1,200 ● *ILTA Supplier Member Directory*, annual. Membership Directory. Lists over 400 member companies, contacts, and goods and services available to the terminal and tank farm industry. Contains keyword index. **Price:** $30.00. **Circulation:** 750 ● *ILTA Terminal Member Directory*, annual. Membership Directory. Lists terminals and tank farms, contact, capacity, products handled, transportation modes served, and other facilities and services. **Price:** $95.00/year. **Circulation:** 900 ● Brochures. **Conventions/Meetings:** annual International Operating Conference and Trade Show - conference and trade show (exhibits) ● annual trade show.

3978 ■ International Association of Refrigerated Warehouses (IARW)
1500 King St., Ste.201
Alexandria, VA 22314
Ph: (703)373-4300
Fax: (703)373-4301
E-mail: email@iarw.org
URL: http://www.iarw.org
Contact: J. William Hudson, Pres./CEO
Founded: 1891. **Members:** 1,000. **Membership Dues:** active, $1,200 (annual) ● associate in U.S. and Canada, $1,050 (annual) ● regular, $400 (annual) ● sustaining, $1,000 (annual) ● sponsoring, $2,000 (annual). **Staff:** 10. **Budget:** $2,800,000. **Regional Groups:** 7. **Description:** Public refrigerated warehouses storing all types of perishable foods and other perishable products; associate members are industry suppliers. **Committees:** Construction Codes; Education/Standards; Finance and Administration; Government Affairs; Insurance and Risk Management; Refrigeration Technology and Energy Services; Technical; Trends; Warehouse Operations. **Publications:** *Cold Facts*, bimonthly. Newsletter. Covers industry events, meetings, and legislative/regulatory developments. Contains book reviews, statistics, and management reports. **Price:** free for members and selected others. **Circulation:** 1,300 ● *Crisis Management Manual*, periodic ● *Directory of Public Refrigerated Warehouses*, annual. Lists locations, descriptions of facilities, and services of public refrigerated warehouses in 50 countries. **Price:** free to qualified businesses; $150.00 for nonmembers. **Circulation:** 5,000. **Advertising:** accepted ● *Energy Conservation Manual* ● *Maintenance and Modernization Manual* ● *Operations Manual* ● Bulletin, periodic. **Conventions/Meetings:** annual trade show and convention (exhibits) - 2009 Apr. 18-23, San Antonio, TX.

3979 ■ International Warehouse Logistics Association (IWLA)
2800 S River Rd., Ste.260
Des Plaines, IL 60018-6003
Ph: (847)813-4699
Free: (800)525-0165
Fax: (847)813-0115
E-mail: email@iwla.com
URL: http://www.iwla.com
Contact: Joel D. Anderson, Pres./CEO
Founded: 1891. **Members:** 550. **Staff:** 10. **Budget:** $2,500,000. **Description:** Fosters and promotes the growth and success of public and contract warehousing and related logistics services. Serves as the unified voice of the global outsourced warehouse logistics industry, representing 3PLs (third party logistics providers), 4PLs (fourth party logistics providers), public and contract warehouse logistics companies and their suppliers, setting standards, legal frameworks and best practices for the warehousing logistics industry for 110 years. Members of the Association receive services including legal assistance, marketing assistance and group buying programs. Owns its own insurance company (passing cost savings to members), holds an annual convention each year, and produces educational

programs. **Libraries: Type:** reference. **Holdings:** archival material, artwork, audiovisuals, books, clippings, periodicals. **Committees:** Convention Planning; Education Advisory; Government Affairs; Industry Marketing; Insurance; Membership; Operating Technology; Political Actions; Procurement Advisory. **Councils:** Information Technology. **Formerly:** (1992) American Warehousemen's Association; (1998) American Warehouse Association. **Publications:** *NewsGram*, quarterly. Newsletter. **Circulation:** 15,000 ● *Resource Guide for Logistics Professionals*, annual ● *The 3PL Executive Week*, quarterly. Magazine. Alternate Formats: online. **Conventions/ Meetings:** annual The Quest for Excellence - conference (exhibits).

3980 ■ Order Selection, Staging and Storage Council of the Material Handling Industry of America
8720 Red Oak Blvd., Ste.201
Charlotte, NC 28217-3992
Ph: (704)676-1190
Fax: (704)676-1199
E-mail: jnofsinger@mhia.org
URL: http://www.mhia.org
Contact: John B. Nofsinger, CEO
Founded: 1986. **Members:** 48. **Membership Dues:** business, $800 (annual). **Staff:** 1. **Budget:** $75,000. **Description:** Trade associations comprising storage industries. Compiles statistics; sponsors research and educational programs. **Libraries: Type:** reference. **Holdings:** books, video recordings. **Awards:** Material Handling Education Foundation Annual Scholarship. **Frequency:** annual. **Type:** scholarship. **Affiliated With:** Material Handling Industry of America. **Formerly:** (1997) Storage Council. **Publications:** *Adding Value With Traditional Material Handling Solutions*. Video ● *Storage and Handling Idea Book*. **Conventions/Meetings:** semiannual congress.

3981 ■ Performance Warehouse Association (PWA)
41-701 Corporate Way, Ste.1
Palm Desert, CA 92260
Ph: (760)346-5647
Fax: (760)346-5847
E-mail: glight@speedwarehouse.com
URL: http://www.pwa-par.org
Contact: Gary Light, Pres.
Founded: 1971. **Members:** 1,000. **Staff:** 2. **Description:** Advises members on intra-industry problems involving management, distribution, employment, and finances. Provides supplies; sponsors seminars and conferences. **Awards:** Honorary. **Frequency:** annual. **Type:** recognition. **Recipient:** for individual and company's conscientious efforts and valuable contributions to the growth and progress of the organization ● Manufacturer of the Year. **Frequency:** annual. **Type:** recognition. **Recipient:** for outstanding contributions to the specialty equipment industry and in appreciation of conscientious efforts in support of the warehouse distributor concept of merchandise distribution ● Person of the Year. **Frequency:** annual. **Type:** recognition. **Recipient:** to an outstanding member, in appreciation of his/her conscientious dedication to the specialty equipment industry ● Pioneer Award. **Frequency:** annual. **Type:** recognition. **Recipient:** for outstanding contributions to the development of the warehouse distributor in the specialty equipment industry. **Committees:** Sales Aid. **Publications:** *Performance Warehouse Association—Membership Directory*, periodic ● *PWA Fax Directory*, annual. Lists companies in the automotive industry with fax machines. Cites company, contact, address, phone number, fax number, email and website. **Price:** $50.00. **Advertising:** accepted ● *PWA Newsletter*, monthly. **Price:** available to members only. **Advertising:** accepted ● *PWA Newsline*, quarterly. Newsletter. **Advertising:** accepted. Alternate Formats: online. **Conventions/Meetings:** annual conference.

3982 ■ Recreational Vehicle Aftermarket Association (RVAA)
c/o Karl J. Etshied, Exec. Dir.
54 Westerly Rd.
Camp Hill, PA 17011
Ph: (717)730-0300
Fax: (717)730-0544
E-mail: karl@rvaahq.com
URL: http://www.rvaftermarket.org
Contact: Karl J. Etshied, Exec. Dir.
Founded: 1969. **Members:** 125. **Membership Dues:** distributor, supplier, manufacturer agent, press, $875 (annual). **Staff:** 2. **Budget:** $350,000. **Description:** Distributors, suppliers, and manufacturer's agents in the RV aftermarket industry. **Awards:** Agent of the Year. **Frequency:** annual. **Type:** recognition ● Best of the Year. **Frequency:** annual. **Type:** recognition ● Catalog of the Year. **Frequency:** annual. **Type:** recognition ● Suppliers of the Year. **Frequency:** annual. **Type:** recognition. **Affiliated With:** National Association of Wholesaler-Distributors. **Formerly:** (2001) Warehouse Distributors Association; (2002) WDA: The RV Aftermarket Association. **Publications:** *Communicator*, quarterly. Magazine. Contains industry news and promotions. **Circulation:** 1,000. **Conventions/Meetings:** board meeting - 3/year ● annual Executive Conference.

3983 ■ Self Storage Association (SSA)
1900 N Beauregard St., Ste.110
Alexandria, VA 22311
Ph: (703)575-8000
Free: (888)735-3784
Fax: (703)575-8901
E-mail: ssa@selfstorage.org
URL: http://www.selfstorage.org
Contact: Michael T. Scanlon Jr., Pres./CEO
Founded: 1975. **Members:** 3,000. **Membership Dues:** regular, management firm, prospective owner, $395 (annual) ● vendor, $725 (annual) ● small facility (less than 20,000 sq. ft. of storage space), $195 (annual) ● associate, $100 (annual). **Staff:** 19. **Budget:** $3,000,000. **Regional Groups:** 4. **Description:** Represents owners and operators of self-storage facilities. Improves the quality of management, customer service, facilities; promotes public awareness of the self-storage industry. Conducts educational meetings on management, marketing, security, and related topics. Lobbies for state legislation protecting and recognizing self-storage owners and operators. **Libraries: Type:** reference. **Holdings:** 1,000; archival material, audiovisuals, books, periodicals. **Subjects:** self storage. **Formerly:** (1989) Self-Service Storage Association. **Publications:** *Membership Directory and Resource Guide*, annual. **Advertising:** accepted ● *SSA Globe Magazine*, monthly. **Price:** $50.00/year, available to members only. **Circulation:** 6,000. **Conventions/Meetings:** semiannual conference and trade show (exhibits).

3984 ■ Warehousing Education and Research Council (WERC)
1100 Jorie Blvd., Ste.170
Oak Brook, IL 60523-4423
Ph: (630)990-0001
Fax: (630)990-0256
E-mail: wercoffice@werc.org
URL: http://www.werc.org
Contact: Robert L. Shaunnessey, Exec. Dir.
Founded: 1977. **Members:** 4,000. **Membership Dues:** regular, $265 (annual) ● educator, $80 (annual) ● student, $40 (annual). **Staff:** 9. **Budget:** $1,800,000. **Regional Groups:** 14. **Description:** Represents distribution and warehousing professionals who lead, direct, and manage the efficient flow of information, materials, and finished goods throughout the supply chain. Provides practical ways that can be apply to improve service and reduce costs. **Libraries: Type:** reference. **Holdings:** 25; books, reports. **Subjects:** warehousing, distribution. **Publications:** *WERCsheet*, 11/year. Newsletter. Focuses on association and industry issues, news, and trends. Includes calendar of events. **Price:** $80.00 /year for members. **Circulation:** 4,000 ● Membership Directory, annual ● Reports. **Conventions/Meetings:** annual conference ● seminar, management - 8-10/year.

3985 ■ World Food Logistics Organization (WFLO)
1500 King St., Ste.201
Alexandria, VA 22314
Ph: (703)373-4300
Fax: (703)373-4301
E-mail: email@wflo.org
URL: http://www.wflo.org
Contact: J. William Hudson, Pres./CEO
Founded: 1943. **Members:** 1,000. **Membership Dues:** individual, $400 (annual) ● sustaining, $1,000 (annual) ● sponsoring, $2,000 (annual). **Staff:** 17. **Description:** Firms engaged in refrigerated warehousing; associate members are firms interested in refrigeration but not engaged in warehousing. Sponsors graduate-level scientific research on the refrigeration of perishable commodities. Sponsors annual training institute for public refrigerated warehouse personnel. **Libraries: Type:** reference. **Formerly:** The Refrigeration Research Foundation; (1999) Refrigeration Research and Education Foundation. **Publications:** *Cold Connection*, weekly. Reprint. Contains timely news, announcements and publications. ● *Cold Facts*, bimonthly. Newsletter. **Advertising:** accepted. Alternate Formats: online ● *Commodity Storage Manual*, periodic. Contains manual specifics of temperatures and humidities appropriate for storage. ● *Information Bulletin*, monthly ● Also publishes research papers. **Conventions/Meetings:** annual trade show and convention, held in conjunction with International Association of Refrigerated Warehouses (exhibits) - 2009 Apr. 18-23, San Antonio, TX.

Waste

3986 ■ American Coal Ash Association (ACAA)
15200 E Girard Ave., Ste.3050
Aurora, CO 80014
Ph: (720)870-7897
Fax: (720)870-7889
E-mail: info@acaa-usa.org
URL: http://www.acaa-usa.org
Contact: David C. Goss, Exec. Dir.
Founded: 1968. **Members:** 80. **Membership Dues:** electric utility producer (category U), $1,650-$15,000 (annual) ● voting: non-utility producer, organization, individual, academia, and specialty marketer, $3,300 (annual) ● non-voting: non-utility producer (category N), organization (category O), specialty marketer, and associate, $1,650 (annual) ● marketer (category M), $6,000-$13,500 (annual) ● non-voting: individual (category I) and academia (category A), $300 (annual). **Staff:** 2. **Budget:** $500,000. **Description:** Represents Electric utility companies and systems, coal and transportation companies, engineering, research, and development organizations, and ash marketing companies. Purposes are to provide technical assistance and information to coal ash producers, transporters, marketers, consumers, and other groups; to stimulate research and employment of ash uses, transport, and disposal; to promote utilization of ash through advertising and public relations programs, dissemination of information on ash production, transport, storage, utilization, and research. Compiles statistics. **Libraries: Type:** reference. **Holdings:** 1,000; books, papers. **Awards:** Achievement Award. **Type:** recognition ● Honorary Membership. **Type:** recognition. **Committees:** Communications and Marketing; Government Relations; Technical. **Task Forces:** Alkali-Silica-Reactivity; Ammonia Test; Foam Index. **Formerly:** (1985) National Ash Association. **Publications:** *Ash at Work*, semiannual. Magazine. Provides information on the utilization of ash in manufacturing and engineering, including specifications and other technical data. **Circulation:** 300. Alternate Formats: online ● *Fly Ash Facts for Highway Engineers*, periodic. **Price:** $5.00 for members; $10.00 for nonmembers ● *Process and Technical Data*, periodic ● *Publications List*, periodic ● Annual Report, annual. **Conventions/Meetings:** meeting and workshop - 3/year ● seminar ● biennial symposium ● workshop.

3987 ■ Asphalt Recycling and Reclaiming Association (ARRA)
PMB 250
3 Church Cir.
Annapolis, MD 21401

Ph: (410)267-0023
Fax: (410)267-7546
E-mail: krissoff@arra.org
URL: http://www.arra.org
Contact: Michael R. Krissoff, Exec. Dir.
Founded: 1976. **Members:** 200. **Membership Dues:** contractor, supplier, $2,500 (annual) ● affiliate, $250 (annual). **Staff:** 3. **Budget:** $300,000. **Description:** Represents contractors and engineers engaged in the reworking of asphalt; contractors employed in connection with the services of regular members and suppliers of material or equipment to members; governmental representatives, architects, and interested persons dealing with asphalt recycling; honorary members. Promotes asphalt recycling. Maintains speakers' bureau. **Awards:** Excellence in Recycling. **Frequency:** annual. **Type:** recognition. **Recipient:** for public officials and consulting engineers. **Committees:** Cold In-Place Recycling; Cold Planning; Full Depth Reclamation; Hot In-Place Recycling; Hot Recycling; Recycling Education. **Publications:** *Basic Asphalt Recycling Manual*, 7/year. **Price:** $27.50 each (for 1 to 9 copies); $25.00 each (for 10 to 24 copies); $22.50 each (for 25 to 49 copies); $20.00 each (for 50 to 99 copies) ● Membership Directory, annual. Lists companies and their employees. **Price:** included in membership dues. **Circulation:** 2,000. **Advertising:** accepted ● Newsletter, quarterly. Covers membership activities; includes membership directory update. **Price:** available to members only. **Circulation:** 2,000. **Advertising:** accepted ● Also publishes specifications and guidelines. **Conventions/Meetings:** annual convention ● annual meeting ● semiannual seminar.

3988 ■ Automotive Recyclers Association (ARA)
3975 Fair Ridge Dr., Ste.20 N
Fairfax, VA 22033
Ph: (703)385-1001
Free: (888)385-1005
Fax: (703)385-1494
E-mail: george@a-r-a.org
URL: http://www.a-r-a.org
Contact: George K. Eliades CAE, CEO
Founded: 1943. **Members:** 1,000. **Membership Dues:** branch, $375 (annual) ● associate/affiliate chapter, $625 (annual) ● central office, $2,500 (annual) ● direct corporation/firm (depends on the numbers of employees), $375-$1,000 (annual) ● all Canadian-based company, $375 (annual). **Staff:** 3. **Budget:** $2,500,000. **State Groups:** 38. **Description:** Firms selling recycled auto, truck, motorcycle, bus, and farm and construction equipment parts, retail and wholesale; operators of long line (telephone) circuits; firms selling equipment and services to the industry. Seeks to improve business practices and operating techniques through exchange of information via publications and meetings. Cooperates with public and private agencies in beautification efforts and developing solutions to the abandoned car and auto theft problems. Offers seminars and various training classes during annual convention and exposition. Maintains scholarship foundation, and educational foundation. Supports a certification program for members. **Awards:** ARA Scholarship Foundation. **Frequency:** annual. **Type:** scholarship. **Recipient:** for children of employees of direct member companies. **Committees:** Budget; Government Affairs; Insurance; Salvage Acquisition and Procurement. **Formerly:** (1955) National Auto Wreckers Association; (1972) National Auto and Truck Wreckers Association; (1977) Association of Auto and Truck Recyclers; (1982) Automotive Dismantlers and Recyclers of America; (1993) Automotive Dismantlers and Recyclers Association. **Publications:** *ARA E-Newsletter*, monthly. Contains pertinent/timely industry and association-related news and information. **Price:** free for members. **Circulation:** 1,000 ● *Automotive Recycling*, bimonthly. Magazine ● *Employee Safety Handbook*. Contains guidelines on how to lessen unsafe operations and accidents. **Price:** $2.50 for members; $7.00 for nonmembers ● *Safety and Loss Control Manual*. Provides information on recommended safe operating procedures and guidelines. **Price:** $25.00 for members; $45.00 for nonmembers ● *Storm Water Guidance Manual*. Provides detailed instructions on how to create a Storm Water Pollution Prevention Plan. **Price:** $100.00 for members; $250.00 for nonmembers ● Membership Directory, annual. Contains list of contacts and member company information. **Price:** $100.00 for nonmembers, plus shipping and handling; $20.00 for members. **Advertising:** accepted. **Conventions/Meetings:** annual meeting, for association and industry leaders (exhibits) ● annual trade show (exhibits).

3989 ■ Center for Waste Reduction Technologies (CWRT/AICHE)
c/o American Institute of Chemical Engineers
3 Park Ave.
New York, NY 10016-5991
Free: (800)242-4363
Fax: (212)591-8888
E-mail: cwrt@aiche.org
URL: http://www.aiche.org/cwrt
Contact: Dana Ponciroli, Mgr.
Founded: 1991. **Members:** 26. **Staff:** 3. **Description:** Businesses and corporations, government agencies, academicians, and interested others. Promotes public awareness of sustainable development and environmental stewardship. Identifies areas for research; conducts educational programs. Facilitates exchange of information. **Awards: Frequency:** periodic. **Type:** grant. **Additional Websites:** http://198.6.4.175/cwrt. **Affiliated With:** American Institute of Chemical Engineers. **Publications:** *Current and Potential Future Industrial Practices for Reducing and Controlling Volatile Organic Compounds* ● *Environmental Considerations in Process Design and Simulation* ● *Pollution Prevention: Homework and Design Problems for Engineering Curriculum* ● *Waste Reduction Priorities in Manufacturing: A DOE/CWRT Workshop*. **Price:** $25.00 ● Newsletter, bimonthly ● Brochures. **Conventions/Meetings:** conference - 2-3/year.

3990 ■ Coalition for Responsible Waste Incineration (CRWI)
1615 L St. NW, Ste.1350
Washington, DC 20036
Ph: (202)452-1241
Fax: (202)887-8044
E-mail: mel@crwi.org
URL: http://www.crwi.org
Contact: Mr. Melvin Keener, Exec. Dir.
Founded: 1987. **Members:** 10. **Budget:** $270,000. **Description:** Manufacturing companies; academic institutions; interested individuals and organizations. Promotes responsible incineration of industrial wastes as part of an overall waste management strategy. Serves as a forum for exchange of information among members and supplies members with technical, safety, health, and environmental information concerning waste incineration. Provides information on industrial incineration systems to the public, the media, and government officials at the local, state, and federal levels. Monitors and reports on the formulation of legislative and regulatory guidelines for industrial waste incineration. Encourages research in incineration. **Publications:** *CRWI Update*, monthly. Newsletter. Alternate Formats: online ● Proceedings, annual. **Conventions/Meetings:** biennial International Congress on Toxic Combustion By-Products: Formation and Control ● annual seminar and workshop.

3991 ■ Council for Textile Recycling (CTR)
c/o Secondary Materials and Recycled Textiles Association
131 E Broad St., Ste.206
Falls Church, VA 22046
Ph: (703)538-1000
Fax: (703)538-6305
E-mail: smartasn@erols.com
URL: http://www.smartasn.org
Contact: Bob Travis, Contact
Founded: 1990. **Members:** 50. **Membership Dues:** for profit entity, $200 (annual) ● nonprofit organization, $35 (annual). **Staff:** 3. **Description:** Textile and clothing manufacturers; national, state, and local recycling organizations; trade associations; state and local government agencies; interested individuals. Works to create greater awareness of the benefits of textile recycling; seeks to develop new markets and uses for recycled textiles. **Additional Websites:** http://www.textilerecycle.org. **Conventions/Meetings:** semiannual meeting, held in conjunction with International Association of Wiping Cloth Manufacturers.

3992 ■ Environmental Industry Associations (EIA)
4301 Connecticut Ave. NW, Ste.300
Washington, DC 20008-2304
Ph: (202)244-4700
Free: (800)424-2869
Fax: (202)966-4818
E-mail: membership@envasns.org
URL: http://www.envasns.org
Contact: Bruce Parker, Pres.
Founded: 1968. **Members:** 2,000. **Membership Dues:** affiliate, $150 (annual) ● international, $645 (annual). **Staff:** 35. **Budget:** $13,000,000. **State Groups:** 22. **Description:** Compiles statistics; conducts research and educational programs. **Telecommunication Services:** electronic mail, bparker@envasns.org. **Publications:** *Be Safe, Be Proud*. Videos ● *Legal Bulletin*, monthly. Newsletter ● *Waste Industry News*, monthly. Newsletter. Features articles on topical industry news and developments. **Price:** included in membership dues; $50.00 for nonmembers ● Manuals. Includes topics on safety and training. **Price:** $60.00 for members; $175.00 for nonmembers. **Conventions/Meetings:** convention ● annual Waste Expo - meeting (exhibits).

3993 ■ Environmental Technology Council (ETC)
734 15th St. NW, Ste.720
Washington, DC 20005-1013
Ph: (202)783-0870
E-mail: comments@etc.org
URL: http://www.etc.org
Contact: Scott Slesinger, VP
Founded: 1982. **Members:** 14. **Staff:** 3. **Budget:** $1,000,000. **National Groups:** 14. **Description:** Firms dedicated to the use of high technology treatment in the management of hazardous wastes and to the restricted use of land disposal facilities in the interests of protecting human health and the environment. Advocates minimization of hazardous wastes and the use of alternative technologies in their treatment, including chemical and biological treatments, fixation, neutralization, reclamation, recycling, and thermal treatments such as incineration. Encourages land disposal prohibitions. Promotes reductions in the volume of hazardous waste generated annually and expansion of EPA hazardous waste list. Advocates use of treatment technology as a more cost-effective approach to Superfund site cleanups. Works with state, national, and international officials and firms to assist in development of programs that utilize treatment and minimize land disposal. Provides technical and placement assistance to members; sponsors special studies, technical seminars, and workshops; participates in federal legislation, litigation, and regulatory development. Maintains library of materials on new technologies; operates speakers' bureau; compiles statistics and mailing list. **Telecommunication Services:** electronic mail, rcra-docket@epamail.epa.gov. **Formerly:** (1998) Hazardous Waste Treatment Council. **Publications:** *Membership Capability Profiles*, annual ● Proceedings, annual. **Conventions/Meetings:** annual conference (exhibits).

3994 ■ Ground Water Protection Council (GWPC)
13308 N MacArthur Blvd.
Oklahoma City, OK 73142
Ph: (405)516-4972
Fax: (405)516-4973
E-mail: mpaque@gwpc.org
URL: http://www.gwpc.org
Contact: Mike Paque, Exec. Dir.
Founded: 1983. **Members:** 2,000. **Membership Dues:** corporate, $3,000-$10,000 (annual). **Staff:** 7.

Description: Professionals and corporations involved in groundwater protection and underground injection control (the underground disposal of drilling by-products and other hazardous materials). Works to protect the groundwater supply of the U.S. Conducts research in groundwater and underground injection and hazardous materials problems. Provides training for wellhead protection and mechanical integrity testing involved with underground injection. Serves as a liaison between industry and state and federal environmental groups. Represents states at congressional hearings. Maintains speakers' bureau. **Libraries: Type:** reference. **Holdings:** 1,379; maps, papers. **Subjects:** ground water, underground injection. **Formerly:** (1993) Underground Injection Practices Council. **Publications:** *The Communique*, bimonthly. Newsletter ● *Journal of Applied Ground Water Protection*, semiannual ● Books. **Conventions/Meetings:** semiannual National Policy Meeting (exhibits) ● periodic symposium.

3995 ■ Institute of Scrap Recycling Industries (ISRI)
1615 L St. NW, Ste.600
Washington, DC 20036-5610
Ph: (202)662-8500
Fax: (202)626-0900
E-mail: isri@isri.org
URL: http://www.isri.org
Contact: Robin Wiener, Pres.
Founded: 1987. **Members:** 1,250. **Membership Dues:** active (based on annual gross sales), $511-$16,714 (annual) ● associate (domestic and paper mill), $925 (annual) ● international associate, $957 (annual) ● consumer (based on annual gross sales), $511-$2,724 (annual). **Staff:** 36. **Budget:** $6,500,000. **Local Groups:** 21. **Multinational. Description:** Represents processors, brokers, and consumers engaged in the recycling of ferrous, nonferrous, paper, plastics, glass, textiles, rubber and electronics scrap. Conducts specialized education and research programs. **Formed by Merger of:** (1987) Institute of Scrap Iron and Steel; (1987) National Association Recycling Industries. **Publications:** *Institute of Scrap Recycling Industries Directory of Members*, annual ● *ISRI Digest*, bimonthly ● *ISRI Focus*. Newsletter. **Price:** free for members ● *Scrap Magazine*, bimonthly. **Price:** free for members. Alternate Formats: online ● Also publishes scrap specifications. **Conventions/Meetings:** annual convention (exhibits) - usually March/April.

3996 ■ International Cartridge Recycling Association (ICRA)
Address Unknown since 2007
Founded: 1991. **Members:** 310. **Membership Dues:** active, $150 (annual) ● associate, $150 (annual). **Staff:** 2. **Budget:** $300,000. **Description:** Small and large printer cartridge remanufacturers, rechargers and recyclers; office supply dealers; and parts and service suppliers to the cartridge recycling industry. Promotes recycling and remanufacturing of laser printer cartridges and other computer products and services. Develops regulations and standards for recycling and remanufacuturing of laser printer cartridges and services. Promotes the recycling and remanufacturing industry. Disseminates information. Serves as network. **Formerly:** (1990) International Computer Products Remanufacturing Association. **Publications:** *ICRA Membership Directory*, annual. **Advertising:** accepted ● *ICRA ReNews*, bimonthly. Newsletter. Provides current information on industry and association news. **Price:** free for members. **Advertising:** accepted. **Conventions/Meetings:** semiannual trade show (exhibits); **Avg. Attendance:** 250.

3997 ■ National Association for PET Container Resources (NAPCOR)
PO Box 1327
Sonoma, CA 95476
Ph: (707)996-4207
Fax: (707)935-1998
E-mail: information@napcor.com
URL: http://www.napcor.com
Contact: Mr. Dennis Sabourin, Exec. Dir.
Founded: 1987. **Members:** 13. **Description:** Members are Polyethylene Terephthalate (PET) bottle and resin producers, and suppliers to the PET industry. Seeks to facilitate the economic recovery of PET plastic containers through collection, reclamation, and development of end-use markets. Provides technical, marketing, and promotional support for plastics recycling programs. **Committees:** Communications; Legislative; Strategic Planning; Technical. **Formerly:** (2001) National Association for Plastic Container Recovery. **Publications:** *PET Container Recycling Rate Report*, annual ● *PET Recycling: No. 1 Success Story*. Video. **Price:** free in U.S. and Canada. Alternate Formats: CD-ROM.

3998 ■ National Association of Wastewater Transporters (NAWT)
336 Chestnut Ln.
Ambler, PA 19002-1001
Ph: (215)643-6798
Free: (800)236-NAWT
Fax: (267)200-0279
E-mail: info@nawt.org
URL: http://www.nawt.org
Contact: A. Thomas Ferrero Jr., Exec. Dir.
Founded: 1983. **Members:** 3,000. **Membership Dues:** individual, $150 (annual) ● associate, $300 (annual) ● company, $300 (annual). **Staff:** 3. **Budget:** $100,000. **Regional Groups:** 2. **State Groups:** 22. **Description:** Septic contractors. Strives to raise the level of professionalism in the liquid waste industry. Conducts educational, charitable, and research programs. **Libraries: Type:** not open to the public. **Holdings:** books, periodicals. **Awards:** Person of the Year. **Frequency:** annual. **Type:** recognition. **Computer Services:** database ● mailing lists. **Publications:** *NAWT News*, monthly. Newsletter. **Advertising:** accepted. **Conventions/Meetings:** annual convention (exhibits).

3999 ■ National Office Paper Recycling Project
c/o United States Conference of Mayors
1620 Eye St. NW
Washington, DC 20006
Ph: (202)293-7330
Fax: (202)293-2352
E-mail: jwelfley@usmayors.org
URL: http://www.usmayors.org/uscm/uscm_projects_services/environment
Contact: J. Thomas Cochran, Exec. Dir.
Founded: 1990. **Members:** 1,300. **Membership Dues:** principal benefactor, $25,000 (annual). **Description:** Corporations committed to increasing their recycling of office paper and use of recycled products. Seeks to triple the amount of paper recycled by corporations. Disseminates information. **Awards:** Recycling At Work Awards. **Frequency:** periodic. **Type:** recognition. **Recipient:** for outstanding recycling programs. **Publications:** *Office Paper Recycling Guide*. Booklet. **Price:** free. Alternate Formats: online ● *Recycling At Work*, quarterly. Newsletter. Alternate Formats: online ● *Toner Cartridge Recycling*. Brochure. Alternate Formats: online. **Conventions/Meetings:** periodic meeting ● periodic seminar.

4000 ■ National Recycling Coalition (NRC)
805 15th St. NW, Ste.425
Washington, DC 20005
Ph: (202)789-1430
Fax: (202)789-1431
E-mail: info@nrc-recycle.org
URL: http://www.nrc-recycle.org
Contact: Kate Krebs, Exec. Dir.
Founded: 1978. **Members:** 3,600. **Membership Dues:** associate, $30 (annual) ● individual, $55 (annual) ● non-profit organization, $150 (annual) ● government agency, $275 (annual) ● small/local business, $500 (annual) ● trade association, $1,500 (annual) ● large business, $2,000 (annual). **Staff:** 11. **State Groups:** 28. **Description:** Individuals and environmental, labor, and business organizations united to encourage the recovery, reuse, and conservation of materials and energy, and to make the benefits of recycling more widely known. Seeks to help change national policies on energy, waste management, taxes, and transportation that hinder recycling efforts. Believes consumers should be informed that recycled products are not inherently inferior to products made with virgin materials. Encourages manufacturers to invest in the equipment required to make recycled products, and to make more of such products available at reasonable prices. Advocates recycling and resource conservation. Acts as information network for persons interested in recycling. Answers requests for information. **Libraries: Type:** reference. **Subjects:** recycling. **Awards:** Beth Brown Boettner Award for Outstanding Government Leadership. **Type:** recognition ● Fred Schmitt Award for Outstanding Corporate Leadership. **Type:** recognition ● Recycler of the Year. **Frequency:** annual. **Type:** recognition ● Recycling Works Recognition Awards. **Frequency:** annual. **Type:** recognition. **Recipient:** for organizations that have made significant commitments to recycling as national advocates and leaders ● Tim McClure Award for Outstanding Environmental and Community Leadership. **Type:** recognition. **Councils:** College and University Recycling; Minorities Recycling; Nonprofit Recyclers; Rural Recycling. **Absorbed:** (1981) Association for a National Recycling Policy. **Publications:** *Federal Legislation in 102nd Congress* ● *Measurement Standards and Reporting Guidelines* ● *Multifamily/Apartment Recycling* ● *National Policy on Recycling* ● *NRC Connection*, bimonthly. Newsletter ● *Rural and Small Town Recycling* ● Proceedings, annual. **Conventions/Meetings:** annual congress (exhibits).

4001 ■ National Waste Prevention Coalition (NWPC)
c/o King County Solid Waste Division
201 S Jackson St., No. 701
Seattle, WA 98104-3855
Ph: (206)296-4481
Fax: (206)296-4475
E-mail: tom.watson@kingcounty.gov
URL: http://www.metrokc.gov/dnrp/swd/nwpc
Contact: Tom Watson, Coor.
Founded: 1994. **Description:** Works to prevent waste from being created, and for reduction in the use of resources. Members are primarily in the solid waste management field.

4002 ■ Paper Stock Industries Chapter of ISRI (PSI)
3300 PGA Blvd., Ste.635
Palm Beach Gardens, FL 33410-2811
Ph: (561)627-9191
E-mail: nktraders@tradersintl.net
URL: http://paperstockindustries.org
Contact: Mr. Crawford Carpenter, Pres.
Founded: 1987. **Members:** 1,300. **Staff:** 35. **Local Groups:** 21. **Languages:** English, Spanish. **Description:** Promotes the recycling of scrap paper and paperboard. Hosts an annual conference/industry meeting each year. **Awards:** RRF/Paper Stock Industries Scholarship Program. **Frequency:** annual. **Type:** scholarship. **Recipient:** for company members, employees only. **Telecommunication Services:** electronic mail, ccarpenter@tngus.com. **Affiliated With:** Institute of Scrap Recycling Industries. **Formerly:** (1952) Paper Stock Institute of America; PSI Chapter. **Publications:** *Scrap Specifications Circular*. Booklet. Contains guidelines for buying scrap and selling scrap. ISSN: PS94-PS96. **Conventions/Meetings:** annual convention, paper recyclers convention (exhibits) - always October or November.

4003 ■ Portable Sanitation Association International (PSAI)
7800 Metro Pkwy., Ste.104
Bloomington, MN 55425
Ph: (952)854-8300
Free: (800)822-3020
Fax: (952)854-7560
E-mail: portsan@aol.com
URL: http://www.psai.org
Contact: Mr. William Carroll, Exec. Dir.
Founded: 1971. **Members:** 700. **Membership Dues:** regular in U.S. (based on the number of units), $180-$1,100 (annual) ● associate, $365 (annual) ● regular outside U.S. (based on the number of units), $170-$510 (annual). **Staff:** 3. **Budget:** $400,000. **Multina-**

tional. Description: Portable sanitation and construction site services contractors and manufacturers. Firms renting and servicing portable sanitation facilities (primarily portable chemical toilets). Offers specialized education programs, including certification program for portable sanitation workers. **Awards:** M.Z. "Andy" Gump Award. **Frequency:** annual. **Type:** recognition. **Recipient:** for achievements and contributions to the industry ● **Frequency:** annual. **Type:** scholarship. **Recipient:** to an incoming freshman ● **Frequency:** annual. **Type:** scholarship. **Recipient:** to a current undergraduate student. **Formerly:** (1987) Portable Sanitation Association. **Publications:** *Guide to Clean Portable Restrooms* ● *Guidelines Brochure* ● *Industry Catalog*, annual ● *Portable Sanitation Service Contract Manual*, annual ● *PSAI in Action*, bimonthly. Newsletter. Features informative articles and member press releases. **Conventions/Meetings:** annual conference (exhibits).

4004 ■ Steel Recycling Institute (SRI)
680 Andersen Dr.
Pittsburgh, PA 15220-2700
Ph: (412)922-2772
Free: (800)876-7274
Fax: (412)922-3213
E-mail: gcrawford@steel.org
URL: http://www.recycle-steel.org
Contact: Mr. Gregory L. Crawford, VP of Operations
Founded: 1988. **Staff:** 10. **Description:** Educates the solid waste management industry, government, business and the consumer about the economic and environmental benefits of recycling steel. **Computer Services:** database. **Affiliated With:** American Iron and Steel Institute. **Formerly:** Steel Can Recycling Institute. **Conventions/Meetings:** periodic meeting (exhibits).

4005 ■ Waste Equipment Technology Association (WASTEC)
c/o Gary T. Satterfield, Exec. VP
4301 Connecticut Ave. NW, Ste.300
Washington, DC 20008-2304
Ph: (202)244-4700
Fax: (202)966-4824
E-mail: wastecinfo@wastec.org
URL: http://www.wastec.org
Contact: Gary T. Satterfield, Exec. VP
Founded: 1972. **Members:** 190. **Membership Dues:** independent consultant, $250 (annual) ● consulting firm, financial service, distributor with limited manufacturing, $1,545 (annual) ● business service, distributor, equipment rental service, used/refurbished equipment supplier, $670 (annual) ● affiliate international firm (not selling in North America), $1,340 (annual) ● original equipment manufacturer (based on gross revenue from solid waste-related products), $1,590-$15,450 (annual) ● original equipment manufacturer component/material supplier (based on gross revenue from solid waste-related products), $1,060-$5,305 (annual) ● medical waste equipment manufacturer, $1,590 (annual). **Staff:** 6. **Budget:** $600,000. **Multinational. Description:** Manufacturers, designers, and distributors of waste collection, treatment, and storage equipment; waste handling consultants. Promotes effective processing of solid and hazardous wastes and more extensive use of recycling. Represents members' interests; conducts research and educational programs; maintains hall of fame; compiles statistics. **Awards:** Distinguished Service. **Frequency:** annual. **Type:** recognition. **Recipient:** for members who have rendered service in pursuit of WASTEC's mission ● Employee of the Year. **Frequency:** annual. **Type:** recognition. **Recipient:** for sales/marketing, engineering, production ● Environmental Industry Associations Hall of Fame Award. **Frequency:** annual. **Type:** recognition. **Recipient:** for manufacturers and technology providers ● Member of the Year. **Frequency:** annual. **Type:** recognition. **Recipient:** for members who exemplify extraordinary service to WASTEC. **Computer Services:** Electronic publishing ● mailing lists ● online services, Buyer's Guide. **Programs:** Education and Information; Executive; Market Enhancement; Technical. **Formerly:** (1992) Waste Equipment Manufacturers Institute. **Publications:** *Listing of Rated Stationary Compactors*, 3/year. Brochure ● *Products and Services Directory*, annual ● *WASTEC E-News*, 8/year. Newsletter. **Circulation:** 850. Alternate Formats: online ● *WASTEC's Equipment Technology News*, quarterly. Newsletter. **Circulation:** 250. **Conventions/Meetings:** annual conference ● annual roundtable, for executives.

Water

4006 ■ American Decentralized Wastewater Association (ADWA)
918 Cong. Ave., Ste.200
Austin, TX 78701
Free: (800)993-5002
Fax: (800)993-5010
E-mail: don@adwwa.org
URL: http://www.adwwa.org
Contact: Don Canada, Exec. Dir.
Description: Promotes rules, standards, training and related activities consistent with contemporary public health and environmental protection standards, engineering practices, technologies and an open and fair market. Promotes third-party certification of onsite wastewater treatment devices and components. Seeks to eliminate biases against third-party certification. **Awards:** Award of Excellence. **Frequency:** periodic. **Type:** recognition. **Recipient:** for outstanding wastewater treatment companies. **Publications:** Brochure. Outlines the goals of the organization. Alternate Formats: online.

4007 ■ American Ground Water Trust (AGWT)
16 Centre St.
Concord, NH 03301
Ph: (603)228-5444
Fax: (603)228-6557
E-mail: trustinfo@agwt.org
URL: http://www.agwt.org
Contact: Ed Breiner, Chm.
Founded: 1986. **Membership Dues:** individual, $30-$100 (annual) ● company, association/organization, $250-$5,000 (annual). **Staff:** 5. **Description:** Disseminates public education information about ground water to industry, government, educational institutions, and the public. Conducts educational forums, conferences and workshops. **Awards:** American Ground Water Trust Scholarship. **Frequency:** annual. **Type:** scholarship. **Recipient:** for undergraduate students. **Publications:** *The American Well Owner*, quarterly. Contains information about ground water. **Price:** $7.00/year. Alternate Formats: online ● *Water Well Basics*. Video. **Price:** $20.00 ● *Wetlands and Ground Water in the U.S.*. Book. **Price:** $15.00 ● Also publishes slide sets, transparencies, poster, fact sheets, flyers and stickers. **Conventions/Meetings:** conference and workshop - 20/year.

4008 ■ American Water Works Association (AWWA)
6666 W Quincy Ave.
Denver, CO 80235-3098
Ph: (303)794-7711
Free: (800)926-7337
Fax: (303)347-0804
E-mail: rrenner@awwa.org
URL: http://www.awwa.org
Contact: Jack W. Hoffbuhr, Exec. Dir.
Founded: 1881. **Members:** 56,000. **Membership Dues:** individual, $150 (annual) ● operation/administrative (in U.S., Canada, and Mexico), $62 (annual) ● student, $28 (annual) ● utility (maximum; based on number of customer service connections), $15,905 (annual) ● international utility (maximum; based on number of customer service connections), $12,120 (annual) ● manufacturer/associate (based on gross annual sales to water supply industry), $950-$5,080 (annual) ● consultant (based on number of employees engaged in services to water supply industry), $1,520-$5,050 (annual) ● technical service, $1,050 (annual) ● service provider (based on gross annual sales), $1,120-$5,645 (annual). **Staff:** 150. **Budget:** $26,000,000. **Regional Groups:** 7. **State Groups:** 42. **Description:** Water utility managers, superintendents, engineers, chemists, bacteriologists, and other individuals interested in public water supply; municipal- and investor-owned water departments; boards of health; manufacturers of waterworks equipment; government officials and consultants interested in water supply. Develops standards and supports research programs in waterworks design, construction, operation, and management. Conducts in-service training schools and prepares manuals for waterworks personnel. Maintains hall of fame. Offers placement service via member newsletter; compiles statistics. Offers training; children's services; and information center on the water utilities industry, potable water, and water reuse. **Libraries: Type:** reference. **Holdings:** archival material. **Awards:** Abel Wolman Fellowship. **Frequency:** annual. **Type:** scholarship. **Recipient:** for promising doctoral students pursuing advanced training and research in the field of water supply and treatment ● Academic Achievement Award. **Frequency:** annual. **Type:** recognition. **Recipient:** for contributions to the field of public water supply ● Holly Cornell Scholarship. **Frequency:** annual. **Type:** scholarship. **Recipient:** for outstanding female or minority students pursuing advanced training in the field of water supply and treatment ● Larson Aquatic Research Support. **Frequency:** annual. **Type:** scholarship. **Recipient:** to outstanding graduate students preparing for careers in the fields of science or engineering ● Thomas R. Camp Scholarship. **Frequency:** annual. **Type:** scholarship. **Recipient:** for outstanding students doing applied research in the drinking water field. **Computer Services:** database, Waternet (file 245), available on Dialog and CD-ROM ● mailing lists, for a fee ● online services, forums. **Councils:** Standards; Technical and Professional; Water Utility. **Affiliated With:** Water Environment Federation. **Publications:** *AWWA Journal* (in English and Spanish), monthly. Magazine. **Price:** included in membership dues. ISSN: 0003-150X. **Advertising:** accepted. Alternate Formats: online; CD-ROM ● *AWWA Publications Catalog*, periodic ● *MainStream*, quarterly. Newsletter. Contains news and feature items about events and issues of import to the water and wastewater professionals. **Price:** included in membership dues; $13.00 /year for nonmembers in U.S.; $18.50 /year for nonmembers outside U.S. ISSN: 0273-3218. Alternate Formats: online ● *Officers and Committee Directory*, annual. Alternate Formats: online ● *OpFlow*, monthly. Newsletter. **Price:** included in membership dues; $9.50 /year for nonmembers. ISSN: 0149-8029. Alternate Formats: online ● *Washington Report*, monthly ● *WaterWeek*, weekly. Newsletter. **Price:** $115.00 /year for members; $172.00 /year for nonmembers. Alternate Formats: online ● Books ● Manuals ● Also publishes standards. Conducts various conference and seminar proceedings. **Conventions/Meetings:** competition (exhibits) ● annual conference (exhibits) - 2009 June 14-18, San Diego, CA ● Distribution and Plant Operations Conference (exhibits) ● annual Water Quality Technology Conference (exhibits).

4009 ■ Association of Water Technologies (AWT)
15245 Shady Grove Rd., Ste.130
Rockville, MD 20850
Ph: (301)740-1421
Fax: (301)990-9771
E-mail: hzimmerman@awt.org
URL: http://www.awt.org
Contact: Ms. Heidi Zimmerman, Exec. Dir.
Founded: 1985. **Members:** 2,000. **Membership Dues:** associate, $740 (annual) ● full, $485 (annual) ● consultant, $485 (annual). **Staff:** 3. **Description:** Provides regional water treatment companies with technical education, industry communication, access to information, group purchasing discounts, legislative affairs, and sound management techniques. Also supplies certification of professional water technologists and regulatory monitoring. **Awards:** Ray Braum Memorial Award. **Frequency:** annual. **Type:** recognition. **Recipient:** for contributions to the field of water treatment. **Computer Services:** database. **Committees:** Bylaws; Communications; Convention; Educa-

tion and Certification; Legislative and Regulatory; Long Range Planning; Marketing; Technical. **Publications:** *The Analyst*, quarterly. Magazine. **Price:** included in membership dues; $100.00 for nonmembers in U.S.; $125.00 for nonmembers in Canada, Mexico; $200.00 for nonmembers in other countries. **Circulation:** 2,500. **Advertising:** accepted ● *Technical Reference and Training Manual*. **Price:** $100.00 for members; $250.00 for nonmembers ● Membership Directory. **Price:** included in membership dues. Alternate Formats: online ● Papers. Alternate Formats: online. **Conventions/Meetings:** annual convention (exhibits) - held in October and November. 2008 Nov. 5-6, Austin, TX; 2009 Aug. 26-29, Hollywood, FL; 2011 Sept. 14-17, Atlanta, GA.

4010 ■ National Association of Water Companies (NAWC)

1725 K St. NW, Ste.200
Washington, DC 20006
Ph: (202)833-8383
Fax: (202)331-7442
E-mail: peter@nawc.com
URL: http://www.nawc.org
Contact: Peter L. Cook, Exec. Dir.

Founded: 1895. **Members:** 340. **Staff:** 10. **Budget:** $2,500,000. **Regional Groups:** 12. **Description:** Investor-owned and operated water companies; associate members are individuals with an engineering, scientific, or other professional interest in the association. Conducts research and keeps members informed of economic, legal, and regulatory developments; encourages communication between investor-owned water companies and regulatory agencies; seeks to improve members' service to the public. Works with National Association of Regulatory Utility Commissioners (see separate entry). Compiles statistics. **Libraries: Type:** not open to the public. **Holdings:** books. **Committees:** Accounting; Customer Service; Finance; Government Relations; Membership; Past Presidents; Rates and Revenue; Regulatory Law; Regulatory Relations; Small Companies; Taxation. **Formerly:** (1971) National Water Company Conference. **Publications:** *Economic Primer*. Book. **Price:** $50.00 for members; $75.00 for nonmembers ● *Financial and Operating Data for Investor-Owned Water Utilities*, annual. Contains statistical report on member companies having gross revenues over $1 million. **Price:** included in membership dues; $50.00/copy for nonmembers. **Circulation:** 750 ● *Financial Summary for Investor-Owned Water Utilities*, annual. Report. Contains balance sheets, income statements, and selected data on sources of supply, plant expenditures, and water sales for seven revenue groups. **Price:** included in membership dues; $50.00/copy for nonmembers. **Circulation:** 750 ● *NAWC Privatization Study: A Survey of the Use of Public-Private Partnerships in the Drinking Water Sector*. **Price:** $50.00 plus shipping and handling ($5) ● *Newsflow*, bimonthly. Newsletter. Provides updates on government affairs and upcoming events. **Circulation:** 1,500 ● *Sourcebook of Regulatory Techniques*. **Price:** $200.00 for nonmembers ● *Sourcebook Supplement*. **Price:** $50.00 plus shipping and handling ($5); $25.00 for active member water company and PUC, plus shipping and handling ($5) ● *2000 Financial and Operating Data*. **Price:** $100.00 plus shipping and handling ($5) ● *2000 Financial and Operating Summary*. **Price:** $100.00 for year 2000, plus shipping and handling ($5); $50.00 each (previous years (1995-1999)); $25.00 each year for Electronic F&O Data ● *2005 Water Policy Forum*. Report. **Price:** $50.00 for nonmembers ● *Valuation Work Book: Valuing a Water Utility*. **Price:** $150.00 plus shipping and handling ($5) ● *Water Policy Forum - 1999 Regulatory Incentives for Consolidation*. **Price:** $50.00 plus shipping and handling ($5) ● *Water Policy Forum - 1997 Customer Focused Service*. **Price:** $50.00 plus shipping and handling ($5) ● *Water Policy Forum - 2000 The Changing Utility Environment*. **Price:** $50.00 plus shipping and handling ($5). **Conventions/Meetings:** annual conference.

4011 ■ National Ground Water Association (NGWA)

601 Dempsey Rd.
Westerville, OH 43081-8978
Ph: (614)898-7791
Free: (800)551-7379
Fax: (614)898-7786
E-mail: ngwa@ngwa.org
URL: http://www.ngwa.org
Contact: Kevin B. McCray CAE, Exec. Dir.

Founded: 1948. **Members:** 14,000. **Membership Dues:** contractor (based on category), $40-$305 (annual) ● scientist, engineer (based on category), $25-$305 (annual) ● manufacturer, manufacturer representative (based on sales volume), $315-$1,395 (annual) ● supplier (based on category), $40-$385 (annual) ● associate - individual, $105 (annual) ● associate - international, $120 (annual). **Staff:** 40. **Budget:** $6,000,000. **State Groups:** 47. **Multinational. Description:** Ground water drilling contractors; manufacturers and suppliers of drilling equipment; ground water scientists such as geologists, engineers, public health officials, and others interested in the problems of locating, developing, preserving, and using ground water supplies. Conducts seminars, and continuing education programs. Encourages scientific education, research, and the development of standards; offers placement services; compiles market statistics. Offers charitable program. Maintains speakers' bureau. **Libraries: Type:** reference. **Holdings:** 40,000; articles, books, periodicals. **Subjects:** ground water, hydrogeology, waterwell technology, environmental remediation. **Awards:** Equipment Design Award. **Frequency:** annual. **Type:** recognition. **Recipient:** to an individual or team, for excellence in the design of an equipment or a product that promotes safety as well as efficiency and ease of operation ● Individual Safety Advocate Award. **Frequency:** annual. **Type:** recognition. **Recipient:** to an individual who has made a contribution to promote, improve, maintain, and enhance safety in daily working operations ● Life Member Award. **Frequency:** annual. **Type:** recognition. **Recipient:** to retired members, or members of retirement age, who have contributed a special service in the furtherance of the ground water industry or to NGWA ● M. King Hubbert Award. **Frequency:** annual. **Type:** recognition. **Recipient:** to a person who has made a major science or engineering contribution to the ground water industry through research, technical papers, teaching, and practical applications ● Manufacturer Award. **Frequency:** annual. **Type:** recognition. **Recipient:** to a Manufacturers Division member ● Outstanding Project in Ground Water Protection Award. **Frequency:** annual. **Type:** recognition. **Recipient:** for outstanding science, engineering, or innovation in the area of protecting ground water ● Outstanding Project in Ground Water Remediation Award. **Frequency:** annual. **Type:** recognition. **Recipient:** for outstanding science, engineering, and/or innovation in the area of remediating ground water ● Outstanding Project in Ground Water Supply Award. **Frequency:** annual. **Type:** recognition. **Recipient:** for outstanding science, engineering, and/or contractor innovation in the area of supplying ground water ● Ross L. Oliver Award. **Frequency:** annual. **Type:** recognition. **Recipient:** to a member who has made outstanding contribution to the ground water industry ● Standard Bearer Award. **Frequency:** annual. **Type:** recognition. **Recipient:** to an outstanding volunteer involved in the legislative process on behalf of NGWA and its initiatives ● Supplier of the Year. **Frequency:** annual. **Type:** recognition. **Recipient:** to a supplier division member ● Technology Award. **Frequency:** annual. **Type:** recognition. **Recipient:** to a person who has made a major contribution to the ground water industry in the development of ideas, tools, and equipment. **Computer Services:** database, ground water. **Additional Websites:** http://www.wellowner.org. **Telecommunication Services:** electronic mail, kmccray@ngwa.org. **Committees:** Business Information; Education; Government Affairs; Policy and Bylaws; Public Affairs. **Divisions:** Association of Ground Water Scientists and Engineers; Contractors; Manufacturers; Suppliers. **Special Interest Groups:** Geothermal Energy; Ground Water Availability; Ground Water Modeling; Horizontal Well; Internet Ground Water Data; Microbial Ground Water Quality; Regulator. **Formerly:** (1991) National Water Well Association. **Publications:** *Ground Water*, bimonthly. Journal ● *Ground Water Monitoring and Remediation*, quarterly. Magazine ● *Newsletter of AGWSE*, bimonthly ● *Water Well Journal*, monthly ● *Well Log*, monthly. Newsletter ● Manuals ● Membership Directory, triennial ● Proceedings, annual. **Conventions/Meetings:** annual conference ● annual National Ground Water Convention and Exposition - trade show (exhibits).

4012 ■ Native American Water Association (NAWA)

1662 Hwy. 395, Ste.212
Minden, NV 89423
Ph: (775)782-6636
Free: (877)888-6292
Fax: (775)782-1021
E-mail: nawa@msn.com
URL: http://www.nawainc.org
Contact: Tom Crawford, Contact

Membership Dues: individual, $300 (triennial) ● tribal utility, $500 (triennial) ● organization, $1,000 (triennial) ● corporation, $1,500 (triennial). **Description:** Provides training and technical assistance to tribal water and wastewater operators, managers, utility commissions and tribal leadership. Works to strengthen tribal sovereignty and self-determination and to protect the environment and the overall health of Indian communities. Offers tribal water and wastewater operator certification programs, on-site training, utility ordinance development, operation and maintenance assessments. **Publications:** *The Source*, quarterly. Newsletter. **Price:** included in membership dues.

4013 ■ Water Quality Association (WQA)

4151 Naperville Rd.
Lisle, IL 60532-1088
Ph: (630)505-0160
Fax: (630)505-9637
E-mail: info@wqa.org
URL: http://www.wqa.org
Contact: Peter J. Censky, Exec. Dir.

Founded: 1974. **Members:** 2,500. **Membership Dues:** dealer in U.S. and Canada, consulting, $365 (annual) ● manufacturer's representative, $890 (annual) ● manufacturer/supplier in U.S. and Canada, $1,250 (annual). **Staff:** 27. **Budget:** $3,700,000. **Description:** Individuals or firms engaged in the manufacture and/or assembly and distribution and/or retail selling of water treatment equipment, supplies, and services. Promotes the acceptance and use of industry equipment, products, and services. Provides activities, programs, and services designed to improve economy and efficiency within the industry. Conducts expositions and certification and equipment validation programs. Compiles statistics. **Libraries: Type:** reference. **Holdings:** books. **Subjects:** water quality improvement. **Awards:** Hall of Fame Award. **Frequency:** annual. **Type:** recognition. **Recipient:** for lifetime dedication and service to the industry and the association. **Telecommunication Services:** electronic mail, pcensky@wqa.org. **Committees:** Technical; Technical Standards; Water Sciences. **Formed by Merger of:** Water Conditioning Association International; Water Conditioning Foundation. **Publications:** *Internews*, bimonthly. Alternate Formats: online ● *Water Treatment Fundamentals*. Book. Covers water quality, chemistry, water problems, treatment technologies, and installation procedure issues. **Price:** $154.00 ● *Water Treatment Fundamentals Seminar Audio Cassette Series*. Audiotape. Contains a must-know information - ideal for person wanting to take the Certified Water Specialist exam. **Price:** $200.00 ● *WQA NewsFax*, bimonthly. Newsletter. Alternate Formats: online ● Membership Directory, annual. **Price:** available to members only. **Conventions/Meetings:** annual Water Opportunity Show - convention and symposium (exhibits).

4014 ■ Water Systems Council (WSC)

1101 30th St. NW, Ste.500
Washington, DC 20007
Ph: (202)625-4387
Free: (888)395-1033
Fax: (202)625-4363

E-mail: wsc@watersystemcouncil.org
URL: http://www.watersystemscouncil.org
Contact: Dennis Coggins, Pres.

Founded: 1966. **Members:** 9. **Membership Dues:** individual, $100 (annual) ● allied interest organization, $500 (annual) ● distributor, $727 (annual) ● manufacturer (based on sales volume in water system industry), $3,280-$41,365 (annual). **Staff:** 2. **Description:** Manufacturers of pitless adapters and units for water wells. Promotes sound principles of pitless equipment construction and installation; maintains standards. Seeks to educate customers and users of pitless adapters. Conducts workshops for local health officials. Maintains speakers' bureau and library of state water well regulations. **Computer Services:** database, State Well Codes. **Committees:** Members Services and Recruitment; Pitless Adapter Standard; Programs Oversight; Water Systems Tank. **Formerly:** (1998) Pitless Adapter Division of Water Systems Council. **Publications:** *Large Submersible Water Pump - 4th Edition*. Manual. **Price:** $30.00 for nonmembers (with CD-ROM); $20.00 for nonmembers. Alternate Formats: CD-ROM ● *Water Systems Handbook - 12th Edition*. **Price:** $65.00 for nonmembers ● *Well Connected*, quarterly. Newsletter. **Price:** free for members. **Conventions/Meetings:** annual meeting - always spring ● annual meeting - always fall.

Weather

4015 ■ Weather Risk Management Association (WRMA)

1156 15th St. NW, Ste.900
Washington, DC 20005
Ph: (202)289-3800
Fax: (202)223-9741
E-mail: wrma@kellencompany.com
URL: http://www.wrma.org
Contact: Valerie Cooper CAE, Exec. Dir.

Founded: 1999. **Members:** 75. **Membership Dues:** regular, $5,000 (annual) ● associate, $2,000 (annual) ● end-user, $500 (annual). **Staff:** 4. **Budget:** $305,000. **Multinational. Description:** Seeks to educate companies on how to avoid the damaging financial effects of weather. Works to advocate in issues affecting weather risk management. Provides forums for discussion and interaction among members. Supplies information to end-users and facilitates the growth of industry. **Publications:** *WRMA Wire*, periodic. Newsletter. Alternate Formats: online. **Conventions/Meetings:** annual convention.

Weighing

4016 ■ International Society of Weighing and Measurement (ISWM)

15245 Shady Grove Rd., Ste.130
Rockville, MD 20850
Ph: (301)258-1115
Fax: (301)990-9771
E-mail: staff@iswm.org
URL: http://www.iswm.org
Contact: Richard Sharpe, Pres.

Founded: 1916. **Members:** 900. **Membership Dues:** independent, $130 (annual) ● manufacturer, $465 (annual) ● distributor, dealer, end user, $285 (annual) ● individual affiliate of a corporate, government, retired, $52 (annual). **Regional Groups:** 14. **Multinational. Description:** Persons engaged in the manufacture, construction, repair, installation, design, or sale of weighing and measuring equipment and peripherals; industry suppliers, consumers, and government and weights and measures officials. Committed to promoting the technical advancements created by and for the weighing and measuring industry. Compiles statistics. **Awards:** Mic Hendrick Memorial Award. **Frequency:** annual. **Type:** recognition. **Recipient:** for any person credited with a discovery principle or concept, which has benefited the weighing industry ● Rapp/Mantes Education Fund. **Frequency:** annual. **Type:** scholarship. **Recipient:** for members of the scale industry, their children, and grandchildren. **Committees:** Certification and Handbook 44; Mic Hendrick Memorial Award; Rapp/Mantes Education Fund; Website. **Formerly:** (1985) National Scale Men's Association. **Publications:** *Educational*. Yearbook ● *ISWM Membership Directory and Product Guide*, annual. Lists of members alphabetically and by ISWM division; also includes alphabetical product guide and listing product categories. **Price:** $25.00 for members; $50.00 for nonmembers. **Circulation:** 2,000. **Advertising:** accepted ● *ISWM News*, 3/year. Newsletter. Contains calendar of events, new product information, industry updates, technical articles, and association news. **Price:** available to members only. **Circulation:** 1,200. **Advertising:** accepted ● *Scaleman's Handbook of Metrology*. **Price:** $20.00 for members; $40.00 for nonmembers ● *Technical Publications Packet* ● Brochure. **Conventions/Meetings:** semiannual show.

4017 ■ Scale Manufacturers Association (SMA)

6724 Lone Oak Blvd.
Naples, FL 34109
Ph: (239)514-3441
Fax: (239)514-3470
E-mail: phil@scalemanufacturers.org
URL: http://www.scalemanufacturers.org
Contact: Robert A. Reinfried, Exec. Dir.

Founded: 1945. **Members:** 15. **Membership Dues:** company (0-16 million annual sales), $1,000-$12,000 (annual) ● company (16-50 million annual sales; maximum), $15,000 (annual) ● company (above 50 million annual sales), $20,000 (annual). **Staff:** 4. **Budget:** $200,000. **Description:** Manufacturers of commercial weighing equipment. **Telecommunication Services:** electronic mail, bob@scalemanufacturers.org. **Committees:** International Trade; Statistics; Strategy and Planning; Technical. **Programs:** Production Meets Type Conformity Assessment. **Formerly:** (1956) National Association of Scale Manufacturers. **Publications:** *Scale Manufacturers Association—Directory*, annual. Membership Directory. **Price:** available to members only ● *Weighlog*, semiannual. Newsletter. Covers association meetings and activities. **Price:** available to members only ● Also publishes technical literature. **Conventions/Meetings:** semiannual meeting.

Wholesale Distribution

4018 ■ Council of Supply Chain Management Professionals (CSCMP)

333 E Butterfield Rd., Ste.140
Lombard, IL 60148
Ph: (630)574-0985 (630)645-3458
Fax: (630)574-0989
E-mail: cscmpadmin@cscmp.org
URL: http://www.cscmp.org
Contact: Rick Blasgen, Pres./CEO

Founded: 1963. **Members:** 10,000. **Membership Dues:** individual, $295 (annual) ● student, $25 (annual) ● associate, $150 (annual). **Staff:** 30. **Budget:** $4,901,000. **Regional Groups:** 80. **Description:** Business executives with a professional interest in logistics and physical distribution management; includes members from industrial concerns as well as consultants and educators. Aims to advance and promote the management science of integrating transportation, warehousing, material handling, protective packaging, inventory size and location, and other areas of customer service, to reduce overall costs of selling and marketing while improving competitive status. Conducts research. Compiles bibliography available on web site regarding subjects related to logistics issues. Provides employment clearinghouse. **Awards:** Distinguished Service Award. **Frequency:** annual. **Type:** recognition. **Recipient:** for career-long contributions to the logistics profession ● Doctoral Dissertation Award. **Frequency:** annual. **Type:** recognition. **Recipient:** for a doctoral dissertation in logistics or a related field that demonstrates significant originality and technical competence while contributing to the logistics knowledge base ● George A. Gecowets Graduate Scholarship. **Frequency:** annual. **Type:** scholarship. **Recipient:** to students with academic achievement, work experience and leadership qualities. **Computer Services:** Mailing lists, of members. **Committees:** Education Program Development; Education Strategies; Professional Development; Research Strategies; Roundtable Advisory. **Formerly:** (1985) National Council of Physical Distribution Management; (2005) Council of Logistics Management. **Publications:** *Council of Logistics Management—Conference Proceedings*, annual. Contains a variety of papers on subjects presented at annual conference. **Price:** included in membership dues; $40.00 for nonmembers. **Circulation:** 15,000 ● *Creating Logistics Value: Themes for the Future*. Book. **Price:** $39.95 ● *Development and Implementation of Reverse Logistics Programs*. Book. **Price:** $74.95 ● *The Growth and Development of Logistics Personnel*. Book. **Price:** $39.95 ● *Improving Quality and Productivity in the Logistics Process*. **Price:** $40.00 for members; $75.00 for nonmembers ● *Journal of Business Logistics*, semiannual. Contains information on logistics operations and management. **Price:** $40.00 /year for members; $75.00 /year for nonmembers ● *Keeping Score: Measuring the Business Value of Logistics in the Supply Chain*. Book. **Price:** $74.95 ● *Logistics Comment*, 5/year. Newsletter. Reports on logistics. Includes book reviews and calendar of events. **Price:** included in membership dues. **Circulation:** 15,000 ● *Logistics Software*. **Price:** $75.00 for members; $100.00 for nonmembers. Alternate Formats: CD-ROM ● *21st Century Logistics: Making Supply Chain Integration A Reality*. Book. **Price:** $74.95 ● *World Class Logistics: The Challenge of Managing Continuous Change*. **Price:** $40.00 for members; $75.00 for nonmembers ● Membership Directory. **Price:** $49.95 for members ● Newsletters. Alternate Formats: online. **Conventions/Meetings:** annual conference - always mid September-October. 2008 Oct. 5-8, Denver, CO; 2009 Sept. 20-23, Chicago, IL ● periodic seminar and workshop, subjects include reverse logistics, quality and productivity, and logistics in service industries.

4019 ■ Distribution Business Management Association (DBMA)

2938 Columbia Ave., Ste.1102
Lancaster, PA 17603
Ph: (717)295-0033
Fax: (717)299-2154
E-mail: dbminfo@dbm-assoc.com
URL: http://www.dcenter.com
Contact: Amy Z. Thorn, Exec. Dir.

Founded: 1992. **Members:** 15,000. **Budget:** $1,500,000. **Description:** Management personnel in the wholesale distribution industries. Promotes education and continuing professional development in the materials handling, distribution, and supply chain industries. Conducts educational programs. **Awards:** Circle of Excellence Award. **Frequency:** annual. **Type:** recognition. **Recipient:** for an outstanding company. **Publications:** *Distribution Business Management Journal*, semiannual. Features academic studies to real-life implementations and industry case studies. **Price:** $25.00 in U.S.; $60.00 outside U.S. ISSN: 1535-1254. **Circulation:** 50,000. **Advertising:** accepted. Alternate Formats: online. **Conventions/Meetings:** annual conference, with speakers (exhibits).

4020 ■ Distribution Research and Education Foundation (DREF)

c/o Ron Schreibman, Exec. Dir.
1725 K St. NW, Ste.300
Washington, DC 20006
Ph: (202)872-0885
Fax: (202)785-0586
E-mail: rschreibman@nawd.org
URL: http://www.naw.org/Template.cfm?section=DREF
Contact: Ron Schreibman, Exec. Dir.

Founded: 1967. **Description:** Firms that are members of the National Association of Wholesaler-Distributors (see separate entry), wholesalers, and trade associations. Seeks to advance knowledge in the field of wholesale distribution by means of long-range research projects. **Publications:** *The Acquisitive Distributor.* Book. Focuses on distribution acquisitions. **Price:** $79.00 for NAW direct members; $89.00 for members of NAW member association; $99.00 for nonmembers ● *Connect with Your Suppliers: A Wholesaler-Distributor's Guide to Electronic Communications Systems.* Book. Focuses on the exchange of information among distributors, suppliers, third-party service providers, and customer companies. **Price:** $79.00 for NAW direct members; $89.00 for members of NAW member association; $99.00 for nonmembers ● *Facing the Forces of Change: The Road to Opportunity*, triennial. Report. Provides strategic insights into key issues impacting the wholesale distribution supply chain through 2008. **Price:** $249.00 for nonmembers; $175.00 for NAW direct members; $199.00 for members of NAW member association ● *Price for Success: A Practical Guide for Improving Margins in Wholesale Distribution.* Book. Contains strategies, tactics, and case studies to help executives, sales managers, and pricing managers build a pricing foundation. **Price:** $79.00 for NAW direct members; $89.00 for members of NAW member association; $99.00 for nonmembers. **Conventions/Meetings:** semiannual board meeting.

4021 ■ General Merchandise Distributors Council (GMDC)
1275 Lake Plaza Dr.
Colorado Springs, CO 80906
Ph: (719)576-4260
Fax: (719)576-2661
E-mail: info@gmdc.org
URL: http://gmdc.com
Contact: David T. McConnell Jr., Pres./CEO
Founded: 1970. **Members:** 650. **Membership Dues:** regular (wholesaler/retailer), $2,000 (annual) ● associate (manufacturer), $2,500 (annual). **Staff:** 12. **Description:** General merchandise (nonfood) units of wholesale grocers, cooperatives, and voluntaries (110); chain food stores, service merchandisers, drug chains, mass merchandisers, wholesale drug companies, and wholesale clubs; manufacturers or suppliers of general merchandise (540) and health and beauty care products. Works to improve management operations, marketing programs, sales techniques, merchandising, and distribution functions of members; furthers management education and employee training; and promotes understanding and cooperation among members, the public, and government. Conducts research and compiles statistics. **Publications:** *Conference Chronicles*, semiannual ● *Focus*, quarterly ● *Legislative Advisory*, monthly ● *Marketing Conference Transcripts*, semiannual ● *Off the Shelf*, quarterly. Newsletter. Alternate Formats: online ● *Seminar Educational Transcripts*, semiannual ● *White Paper.* Alternate Formats: online ● Membership Directory, annual. **Price:** $200.00 for nonmembers; included in membership dues. **Conventions/Meetings:** annual HBW Marketing - conference - 2008 Sept. 5-8, Scottsdale, AZ; 2009 Sept. 11-14, Orlando, FL; 2010 Sept. 10-13, Scottsdale, AZ ● annual GM Marketing - conference, discusses merchandise marketing - 2009 May 29-June 2, Fort Worth, TX; 2010 June 4-9, Orlando, FL; 2011 June 3-7, Orlando, FL.

4022 ■ Independent Sealing Distributors (ISD)
105 Eastern Ave., Ste.104
Annapolis, MD 21403
Ph: (410)263-1014
Fax: (410)263-1659
E-mail: isd@isd.org
URL: http://www.isd.org
Contact: Joseph M. Thompson Jr., Exec. Dir.
Founded: 1992. **Members:** 180. **Membership Dues:** distributor (with $200,000-$10 million and up annual sales), $205-$1,031 (annual) ● associate/manufacturer (with $250,000-$50 million and up annual sales), $205-$2,494 (annual) ● affiliate, $391-$781 (annual). **Staff:** 7. **Budget:** $200,000. **Description:** Distributors and manufacturers of hydraulic seals, gaskets, and fluid sealing products. Works to strengthen the positions of members in the distribution link between manufacturer and user. Provides information on technical, management and regulatory issues; offers educational programs and insurance programs. **Libraries: Type:** reference; lending. **Holdings:** 50; articles, audiovisuals, books, business records, periodicals. **Subjects:** business management, gasket and sealing industry. **Telecommunication Services:** electronic mail, jthompson@isd.org. **Committees:** Benefits and Resources; Communication/Technology; Program Development. **Publications:** *ISD Insider*, quarterly. Newsletter. **Advertising:** accepted ● Membership Directory, annual. **Conventions/Meetings:** annual meeting and convention (exhibits) ● University of Industrial Distribution - seminar, four-day educational and training program, offered in March and October.

4023 ■ National Association of Sign Supply Distributors (NASSD)
5024-R Campbell Blvd.
Baltimore, MD 21236-5975
Ph: (410)931-8100 (410)933-3453
Fax: (410)931-8111
E-mail: cal@clemonsmgmt.com
URL: http://www.nassd.org
Contact: Cal Clemons CAE, Exec. Dir.
Founded: 1991. **Members:** 51. **Membership Dues:** distributor, $1,500-$2,000 (annual) ● associate, $2,000 (annual). **Staff:** 3. **Description:** Sign distributors, product manufacturers and suppliers. Seeks to better serve the industry by improving communication between manufacturers, distributors and sign companies. Conducts educational programs. **Libraries: Type:** lending; not open to the public. **Holdings:** audiovisuals. **Computer Services:** database, membership directory. **Committees:** Education; Program; Public Relations. **Conventions/Meetings:** annual meeting and board meeting.

4024 ■ National Association of Wholesaler-Distributors (NAW)
1725 K St. NW, Ste.300
Washington, DC 20006-1419
Ph: (202)872-0885
Fax: (202)785-0586
E-mail: naw@nawd.org
URL: http://www.naw.org
Contact: Dirk Van Dongen, Pres.
Founded: 1946. **Members:** 45,000. **Membership Dues:** direct (based on annual sales volume), $720-$21,380 (annual) ● associate, $950 (annual). **Budget:** $6,600,000. **Description:** Federation of national, state, and regional associations, and individual wholesaler-distributor firms. Represents industry's views to the federal government. Analyzes current and proposed legislation and government regulations affecting the industry. Maintains public relations and media programs and a research foundation. Conducts wholesale executive management courses. **Telecommunication Services:** electronic mail, dvandongen@nawd.org. **Committees:** Wholesaler-Distributor Political Action. **Programs:** Benchmarking; Government Relations; Large Company Emphasis. **Affiliated With:** Distribution Research and Education Foundation. **Formerly:** (1970) National Association of Wholesalers. **Publications:** *NAW Report*, bimonthly. Provides information on government issues and actions affecting wholesaler distributors. **Price:** included in membership dues. **Circulation:** 15,000 ● *SmartBrief.* Newsletter. **Price:** free. Alternate Formats: online ● Books. Includes topics on wholesaling. ● Bulletin. Covers legislative issues. **Conventions/Meetings:** annual meeting.

4025 ■ Office Furniture Distribution Association (OFDA)
739 Daniel Shays Hwy., D-16
Athol, MA 01331
Ph: (978)249-0303
Fax: (978)249-5937
E-mail: kmiller@mass.rr.com
URL: http://www.theofda.org
Contact: Kenneth E. Miller, Managing Dir.
Founded: 1976. **Members:** 55. **Membership Dues:** full/associate, $250 (annual). **Staff:** 3. **Description:** Works to elevate office furniture distribution levels of service utilizing best practices to provide logistic solutions and create value for customers. **Publications:** *Freight Traffic Newsletter*, monthly. Alternate Formats: online. **Conventions/Meetings:** annual meeting and seminar.

4026 ■ U.S. Aquaculture Suppliers Association (USASA)
Address Unknown since 2008
URL: http://www.aquaculturesuppliers.com
Founded: 1989. **Members:** 200. **Membership Dues:** corporate, $125 (annual) ● individual, $75 (annual). **Staff:** 2. **Description:** Promotes interests of members. Supports aquaculture industry through the National Aquaculture Association and provides a unified voice for suppliers to the industry. **Computer Services:** database, tradeshow information. **Publications:** Directory, annual. **Conventions/Meetings:** annual Aquaculture America - meeting.

Wildlife

4027 ■ National Wildlife Control Operators Association (NWCOA)
PO Box 402
Neotsu, OR 97364
Ph: (541)994-8900
Fax: (866)576-3926
E-mail: eric.arnold@nwcoa.com
URL: http://www.nwcoa.com
Contact: Tim Julien, Pres.
Members: 650. **Membership Dues:** regular, $65 (annual) ● vendor, $250 (annual) ● associate, $25 (annual) ● professional, $100 (annual). **Staff:** 12. **Regional Groups:** 8. **State Groups:** 12. **Description:** Assists persons or organizations providing commercial wildlife damage management and control activities. **Libraries: Type:** reference; open to the public. **Programs:** National Certification. **Publications:** *NWCOA News*, bimonthly. Newsletter. Contains up-to-date information on events in U.S. and Canada. **Price:** included in membership dues. **Advertising:** accepted. **Conventions/Meetings:** annual conference and seminar.

4028 ■ North American Elk Breeders Association (NAEBA)
PO Box 1640
Platte City, MO 64079
Ph: (816)431-3605
Fax: (816)431-2705
E-mail: info@naelk.org
URL: http://www.naelk.org
Contact: Joel Espe, Pres.
Members: 1,800. **Membership Dues:** basic, $200 (annual) ● bronze, corporate, $300 (annual) ● silver, $600 (annual) ● gold, $1,000 (annual) ● diamond, $2,500 (annual) ● associate, $75 (annual) ● life, $2,000 ● junior, $25 (annual). **Staff:** 2. **Multinational. Description:** Promotes the North American elk farming and ranching industry; maintains registry of purebred elk; provides education in management and breeding practices. **Publications:** Journal, bimonthly. Includes important information to the elk industry. **Price:** included in membership dues ● Newsletters. Highlights information on issues affecting the elk industry. **Price:** included in membership dues. **Conventions/Meetings:** annual convention - held in late winter.

Window

4029 ■ Efficient Windows Collaborative (EWC)
c/o Nils Petermann, Research Assoc.
Alliance to Save Energy
1850 M St. NW, Ste.600
Washington, DC 20036
Ph: (202)530-2254
Fax: (202)331-9588

E-mail: ewc@ase.org
URL: http://www.efficientwindows.org
Contact: Nils Petermann, Research Assoc.
Description: A coalition of window, door, skylight and component manufacturers, research organizations, federal, state and local government agencies and others interested in promoting the benefits of energy-efficient windows. **Telecommunication Services:** electronic mail, npetermann@ase.org. **Conventions/Meetings:** workshop, held at major tradeshows and conferences.

4030 ■ Window Covering Safety Council (WCSC)
355 Lexington Ave., Ste.1500
New York, NY 10017
Ph: (212)297-2109
Free: (800)506-4636
Fax: (212)370-9047
URL: http://www.windowcoverings.org
Contact: Cara Clinton, Contact
Founded: 1994. **Description:** Major U.S. manufacturers, importers and retailers of window coverings. Strives to educate consumers about potential window-cord hazards to children; provides consumers with free cord-safety devices and information; promotes product quality and safety.

Wine

4031 ■ Specialty Wine Retailers Association (SWRA)
915 L St., Ste.1000
Sacramento, CA 95814
Ph: (916)446-4708
Fax: (916)442-0382
E-mail: info@specialtywineretailers.org
URL: http://www.specialtywineretailers.org
Contact: Dottie H. Johnson, Admin. Asst.
Founded: 2005. **Membership Dues:** retailer (based on annual gross wine volumes), $300-$2,500 (monthly) ● associate winery, $100 (annual) ● associate industry, $1,500 (annual). **Description:** Aims to create a national marketplace for direct-to-consumer wine sales. Seeks to replace laws that prevent consumers from gaining access to a diverse supply of local and imported wine. Serves its members in various legislative and regulatory arenas. **Publications:** Membership Directory. **Price:** included in membership dues.

4032 ■ WineAmerica National Association of American Wineries
1212 New York Ave., Ste.425
Washington, DC 20005
Ph: (202)783-2756
Fax: (202)347-6341
E-mail: info@wineamerica.org
URL: http://www.wineamerica.org
Contact: Bill Nelson, Pres.
Founded: 1978. **Members:** 800. **Membership Dues:** winery (minimum, based on gallons sold), $250 (annual) ● supplier, silver, $250 (annual) ● supplier, gold, $500 (annual) ● supplier, platinum, $1,000 (annual). **Regional Groups:** 5. **State Groups:** 4. **Description:** Encourages the dynamic growth and development of American wineries and wine growing through the advancement and advocacy of sound public policy. **Computer Services:** database ● information services ● online services. **Councils:** State Associations. **Publications:** Newsletter, monthly. Alternate Formats: online.

Women

4033 ■ African-American Female Entrepreneurs Alliance (AAFEA)
c/o Ms. Margo L. Davidson, Pres./Founder/CEO
333 Clearbrook Ave., Ste.200
Lansdowne, PA 19050
Ph: (215)747-9282
Fax: (610)394-0264
E-mail: aafea@prodigy.net
URL: http://www.aafea.net
Contact: Ms. Margo L. Davidson, Pres./Founder/CEO
Founded: 1998. **Membership Dues:** basic/active, $79 (annual) ● millionaire's club, $1,000 (annual) ● success track, $500 (annual). **Description:** Seeks to strengthen, expand and increase the visibility and profitability of African-American female businesses through education, mentoring and networking. Increases the awareness of political and government officials on the issues that affect the business climate as it relates to African-American female entrepreneurs. Works to change or eliminate systems that discriminate against businesses because of race or sex. Provides a vehicle of support and networking for African-American female entrepreneurs. **Publications:** Newsletter, quarterly. Highlights and markets businesses in the Alliance.

4034 ■ Association for Women in Aviation Maintenance (AWAM)
c/o Marcia Buckingham, Treas.
PO Box 1030
Edgewater, FL 32132-1030
Ph: (386)416-0248 (386)424-5780
Fax: (386)236-0517
E-mail: whq@awam.org
URL: http://www.awam.org
Contact: Denise Waters, Pres.
Founded: 1997. **Members:** 500. **Membership Dues:** individual, $25 (annual) ● student, $15 (annual) ● corporate, $300 (annual) ● educational institution, $150 (annual) ● life, $500. **Local Groups:** 4. **Multinational. Description:** Supports women's professional growth and enrichment in the aviation maintenance fields. Provides opportunities for sharing information and networking, education, fostering a sense of community and increasing public awareness of women in the industry. Offers scholarships, local chapters, networking, community outreach and maintenance training with career development seminars. **Libraries: Type:** reference. **Awards:** Beyond All Odds. **Frequency:** annual. **Type:** monetary. **Recipient:** for an individual who has become successful despite enormous challenges ● Student of the Year. **Frequency:** annual. **Type:** monetary. **Recipient:** for a hardworking student with a great attitude ● Teacher of the Year. **Frequency:** annual. **Type:** recognition. **Recipient:** for the teacher who has inspired others. **Computer Services:** Electronic publishing, E-Flashes (electronic news for members only); E-Briefs (AWAM electronic news distributed worldwide). **Publications:** *AWAM News*, quarterly. Newsletter. Contains update on current activities, scholarships, technical tips, bios of women in maintenance, historical information on aviation. **Price:** included in membership dues; $25.00 /year for nonmembers. **Circulation:** 1,200. **Advertising:** accepted ● *Women in Aviation Maintenance*. Brochure. Contains career education information for women thinking of a career in the field of aviation maintenance. Alternate Formats: online. **Conventions/Meetings:** annual Aviation Maintenance - seminar ● annual Professional Growth - seminar.

4035 ■ Association of Women in the Metal Industries (AWMI)
19 Mantua Rd.
Mount Royal, NJ 08061
Ph: (856)423-3201
Fax: (856)423-3420
E-mail: hbrust@talley.com
URL: http://www.awmi.com
Contact: Haley J. Brust, Exec. Dir.
Founded: 1981. **Members:** 2,000. **Membership Dues:** individual, $175 (annual) ● platinum corporate, $5,000 (annual) ● gold corporate, $3,500 (annual) ● silver corporate, $2,000 (annual) ● bronze corporate, $1,000 (annual). **Staff:** 4. **Budget:** $180,000. **Regional Groups:** 5. **State Groups:** 24. **Description:** Works to promote professionalism and advancement of women in the metal industries. Advocates on behalf of women in metal-related industries; conducts educational programs and activities; provides a forum for exchanging information and networking. **Awards:** Member of the Year. **Frequency:** annual. **Type:** recognition ● Service Awards. **Frequency:** annual. **Type:** recognition. **Computer Services:** database, mailings, conference registrations, and invoices. **Councils:** Region. **Publications:** *Coast to Coast*, quarterly. Newsletter. **Price:** free for members. **Circulation:** 2,000. **Advertising:** accepted ● Membership Directory, annual. **Price:** free for members. **Circulation:** 2,200. **Advertising:** accepted. **Conventions/Meetings:** biennial National All Member Conference ● biennial National Board Conference.

4036 ■ Business Women's Network (BWN)
1990 M St. NW, Ste.700
Washington, DC 20036
Ph: (202)466-8209
Free: (800)48W-OMEN
Fax: (202)833-1808
E-mail: inquire@tpag.com
URL: http://www.bwni.com
Contact: Edie Fraser, Pres./Founder
Founded: 1993. **Membership Dues:** individual, $59 (annual) ● student, $49 (annual). **Description:** Supports women in business; provides ongoing programs on mentoring, networking and managing skills. **Divisions:** Business Women's Education Fund. **Publications:** *Directory of Women's Association*. **Price:** $70.90 plus shipping and handling. Alternate Formats: online ● *Women and Diversity WOW! Facts 2002* ● Newsletter, monthly. **Price:** included in membership dues. Alternate Formats: online.

4037 ■ Center for Women's Business Research
1411 K St. NW, Ste.1350
Washington, DC 20005
Ph: (202)638-3060
Fax: (202)638-3064
E-mail: info@womensbusinessresearch.org
URL: http://www.cfwbr.org
Contact: Dr. Sharon G. Hadary, Exec. Dir.
Founded: 1989. **Membership Dues:** associate, $200 (annual) ● mentor, $500 (annual) ● friend, $100 (annual) ● advisor, $1,000 (annual) ● champion, $2,000 (annual). **Staff:** 10. **Description:** Women business owners. Supports the growth of women business owners and their enterprises by conducting research, sharing information and increasing knowledge. Offers marketing consulting and seminars. **Formerly:** (2002) National Foundation for Women Business Owners. **Publications:** *Key Facts about Women-Owned Businesses*. Brochure. **Price:** $70.00/bundle of 100. Alternate Formats: online ● *News*. Newsletter. **Price:** included in membership dues. Alternate Formats: online.

4038 ■ Executive Women's Council (EWC)
425 6th Ave., Ste.1860
Pittsburgh, PA 15219
Ph: (412)731-1500
E-mail: info@ewcpittsburgh.org
URL: http://www.ewcpittsburgh.org
Contact: Joan Ellenbogen, Pres.
Founded: 1975. **Members:** 100. **Membership Dues:** full, $125 (annual) ● associate, $85 (annual). **Staff:** 1. **Description:** Women who hold an executive position. Seeks to support and enrich members' careers through networking and education. **Publications:** Newsletter, monthly. **Circulation:** 100. **Advertising:** accepted. **Conventions/Meetings:** monthly board meeting.

4039 ■ German Professional Women's Association (GPWA)
PO Box 476
Lake Orion, MI 48361-0476
E-mail: info@gpwa-usa.com
URL: http://www.gpwa-usa.com
Contact: Christina Griesser, Pres.
Founded: 1997. **Membership Dues:** regular, $45 (annual). **Multinational. Description:** Serves the business and cultural interests of German-speaking women in the United States. Promotes business networking, the development of ideas and the exchange of information among German-speaking professional women. Provides professional support

for career, education and business development. **Publications:** Newsletter, monthly. Contains news and updates about the organization's activities. **Price:** included in membership dues.

4040 ■ Hard Hatted Women (HHW)
3043 Superior Ave.
Cleveland, OH 44114
Ph: (216)861-6500
Fax: (216)861-7204
E-mail: info@hardhattedwomen.org
URL: http://www.hardhattedwomen.org
Contact: Debbi Perkul, Exec. Dir.
Founded: 1979. **Members:** 300. **Membership Dues:** supporting/regular, $35 (annual). **Staff:** 6. **Budget:** $490,000. **Description:** Tradeswomen. Support group for women in the trades offering education, outreach and advocacy. **Telecommunication Services:** electronic mail, dperkul@hardhattedwomen.org. **Publications:** *Riveting News*, bimonthly. Newsletter. **Price:** included in membership dues. **Advertising:** accepted.

4041 ■ Hispanic Professional Women's Association (HPWA)
700 12th St., Ste.700
Washington, DC 20005
Ph: (202)250-0887
Fax: (703)880-4831
E-mail: info@hpwa.org
URL: http://www.hpwa.org
Contact: Laura Ramirez Drain, Founder
Founded: 2004. **Members:** 150. **Membership Dues:** professional, $50 (annual) ● corporate, $1,000 (annual) ● small business/non-pro lit, $150 (annual) ● student, $25 (annual). **Local Groups:** 8. **Description:** Raises awareness of the skills and talents of Hispanic women. Contributes to the growth and development of women in work and life. **Committees:** Events; Mentoring; Public Relations. **Programs:** Alcanzado Metas. **Publications:** Newsletter, quarterly.

4042 ■ Institute for Women in Trades, Technology and Science (IWITTS)
1150 Ballena Blvd., Ste.102
Alameda, CA 94501-3696
Ph: (510)749-0200
Fax: (510)749-0500
E-mail: info@iwitts.com
URL: http://www.iwitts.com
Contact: Donna Milgram, Exec. Dir.
Founded: 1994. **Members:** 17. **Description:** Works to integrate women into the full range of trades, technology and science careers. **Projects:** Cisco Learning Institute Gender Initiative; Law Enforcement Environmental Assessment Tools; National Institute of Justice; National Science Foundation; New Workplace for Women; Recruiting Women to Policing Workshops; School-To-Work; WomenTech; WomenTechWorld.Org. **Publications:** *Women in Policing*. Newsletter. Contains information on recruiting, retaining and promoting women officers. **Price:** free. Alternate Formats: online ● *WomenTech Educators*. Newsletter. Contains information in preparing women for technology careers. **Price:** free. Alternate Formats: online ● *WomenTechWorld*. Newsletter. Contains tips for women to succeed in tech education. **Price:** free. Alternate Formats: online.

4043 ■ International Women's Media Foundation (IWMF)
1625 K St. NW, Ste.1275
Washington, DC 20006
Ph: (202)496-1992
Fax: (202)496-1977
E-mail: info@iwmf.org
URL: http://www.iwmf.org
Contact: Jane Ransom, Exec. Dir.
Founded: 1990. **Membership Dues:** associate, $50 (annual). **Multinational. Description:** Women in the news media. Designed to help women fulfill their capacity as leaders within the international news media. Sponsors seminars and training sessions. **Awards:** Courage in Journalism Awards. **Frequency:** annual. **Type:** recognition. **Recipient:** for women journalists who demonstrated exceptional bravery in reporting. **Publications:** *IWMFwire*, quarterly. Newsletter. **Price:** included in membership dues. Alternate Formats: online. **Conventions/Meetings:** periodic seminar.

4044 ■ National Women's Business Council (NWBC)
409 3rd St. SW, Ste.210
Washington, DC 20024
Ph: (202)205-3850 (202)205-6828
Fax: (202)205-6825
E-mail: info@nwbc.gov
URL: http://www.nwbc.gov
Contact: Margaret Mankin Barton, Exec. Dir.
Founded: 1988. **Members:** 15. **Staff:** 4. **Description:** Women business owners. Strives to promote initiatives, policies, and programs designed to support women's business enterprises. **Publications:** *Engage*, bimonthly. Newsletter. Brings issues of interest and activities to the women's business and policy communities. Alternate Formats: online ● *2000 U.S. Case Study: Successful Public and Private Sector Initiatives Fostering the Growth of Women's Business Ownership*. Report.

4045 ■ Professional Women in Healthcare (PWH)
c/o Lyn Rawdon
310 Montgomery St.
Alexandria, VA 22314
Ph: (703)838-6138
E-mail: aeitingklamar@midmark.com
URL: http://www.hida.org
Contact: Anne Eiting Klamar MD, Chair
Founded: 2004. **Membership Dues:** individual, $200 (annual) ● distributor (NDC or IMCO member), $175 (annual) ● manufacturer (HIDA or HEF member), $125 (annual). **Description:** Facilitates growth and progressive leadership for women management professionals in the healthcare industry. Addresses the issues concerning women in the healthcare industry. Seeks to create an environment of professional and personal development by leveraging the intellectual capital of industry leaders through networking, education, and mentoring. **Affiliated With:** Health Industry Distributors Association. **Publications:** *Connections*, quarterly. Newsletter. **Price:** included in membership dues ● Membership Directory. **Price:** included in membership dues.

4046 ■ Springboard Enterprises
2100 Foxhall Rd. NW
Washington, DC 20007
Ph: (202)242-6282 (202)242-6280
Fax: (202)242-6284
E-mail: info@springboardenterprises.org
URL: http://www.springboardenterprises.org
Contact: Amy Millman, Pres.
Description: Aims to accelerate women's access to the equity markets. Promotes women's entrepreneurial development through alliances, partnerships and direct programming. Employs a community building approach to preparing and presenting new women-led technology companies to investors and business partners. Produces programs that educate, showcase and support entrepreneurs as they seek equity capital and grow their companies. **Telecommunication Services:** electronic mail, amy@springboardenterprises.org.

4047 ■ Women in Aviation International (WAI)
Morningstar Airport
3647 State Rte. 503 S
West Alexandria, OH 45381
Ph: (937)839-4647
Fax: (937)839-4645
E-mail: scoon@wai.org
URL: http://www.wai.org
Contact: Dr. Peggy Chabrian, Pres./Founder
Founded: 1994. **Members:** 6,000. **Membership Dues:** individual, $39 (annual) ● student, $29 (annual) ● corporate, $400 (annual) ● international, $49 (annual) ● family, $20 (annual) ● supersonic corporate, $500 (annual). **Staff:** 4. **Local Groups:** 18. **Description:** Promotes the advancement of women in aviation. Encourages women to seek opportunities in aviation; provides resources to assist women in aviation; conducts education outreach programs; compiles statistics; maintains Hall of Fame. **Libraries: Type:** reference. **Holdings:** 350; articles, audiovisuals, books, business records, clippings, periodicals. **Awards:** Pioneer Hall of Fame. **Type:** recognition. **Recipient:** for outstanding women in the society of aviation ● **Type:** scholarship. **Recipient:** for WAI members. **Computer Services:** database ● mailing lists ● online services. **Publications:** *Aviation for Women*, bimonthly. Magazine. **Circulation:** 4,500. **Advertising:** accepted. **Conventions/Meetings:** annual conference and trade show (exhibits).

4048 ■ Women Contractors Association (WCA)
PO Box 6757
Houston, TX 77265
Ph: (713)807-9977
Fax: (713)807-9917
E-mail: akalmin@womencontractors.org
URL: http://www.womencontractors.org
Contact: Amy Kalmin, Exec. Dir.
Founded: 1994. **Members:** 85. **Membership Dues:** associate, $250 (annual) ● contractor, $600 (annual). **Staff:** 1. **Description:** Women contractors. Promotes the growth of women owners and executives in the construction industry. **Awards:** Mary Gayle Brindley Award. **Frequency:** annual. **Type:** recognition. **Recipient:** to volunteers working for the association. **Publications:** Newsletter, monthly. **Conventions/Meetings:** monthly luncheon.

4049 ■ Women in Engineering ProActive Network (WEPAN)
c/o C. Diane Matt, CAE, Exec. Dir.
1901 E Asbury Ave.
Denver, CO 80208
Ph: (303)871-4643
Fax: (303)871-6833
E-mail: dmatt@wepan.org
URL: http://www.wepan.org
Contact: C. Diane Matt CAE, Exec. Dir.
Founded: 1990. **Members:** 600. **Membership Dues:** executive corporate, $5,000 (annual) ● senior corporate, $2,500 (annual) ● corporate, $1,000 (annual) ● institutional (includes 3 representatives), $225 (annual) ● individual, $80 (annual) ● student, $15 (annual) ● community college, retired, K-12, $40 (annual). **Description:** Women in engineering professions. Includes key strategies such as education and training, research, collaboration, leadership, diversity, advocacy, networking, sustainability, accountability, and volunteerism in order to be a catalyst for change that enhances the success of women in the engineering professions. **Awards:** The Betty Vetter Award for Research. **Frequency:** annual. **Type:** recognition. **Recipient:** for notable achievement in research related to women in engineering ● The Distinguished Service Award. **Frequency:** annual. **Type:** recognition. **Recipient:** for member whose individual service has made a significant impact for the organization ● The WEPAN Breakthrough Award. **Frequency:** periodic. **Type:** recognition. **Recipient:** to an employer for creating a work environment that enhances the career success of women engineers of all ethnicities ● Women in Engineering Initiative (WIEI) Award. **Frequency:** annual. **Type:** recognition. **Recipient:** for an outstanding program or project that serves as a model for other institutions. **Publications:** *Evaluation Resource*. Book. **Price:** $15.00 for members; $25.00 for nonmembers ● *Factors in the Underrepresentation of Women in Science & Engineering*. Paper. **Price:** $10.00 for members; $15.00 for nonmembers ● *Increasing Access for Women in Engineering*. Book. **Price:** $80.00 for members; $120.00 for nonmembers ● *Making the Connection*. Newsletter. **Price:** $35.00 for members; $50.00 for nonmembers ● *Training Curriculum for Mentors & Mentees*. **Price:** $100.00 for members; $150.00 for nonmembers ● *WEPAN National Conference Proceedings*. **Price:** $20.00 for members; $35.00 for nonmembers ● *WEPANEWS*, 3/year. Newsletter. **Price:** free. Alternate Formats: online ● *What Do Engineers Do?*. **Price:** $30.00 for members; $45.00 for nonmembers ● Membership Directory, semiannual. **Price:** included in membership dues; $20.00 for nonmembers. Alternate Formats: online. **Conventions/Meetings:** annual conference.

4050 ■ Women Entrepreneurs in Science and Technology (WEST)
155 Seaport Blvd., 11th Fl.
Boston, MA 02210
Ph: (617)988-6120
E-mail: info@westorg.org
URL: http://www.westorg.org
Contact: Janice Bourque, Chair
Membership Dues: individual, $85 (annual) ● student, $40 (annual). **Description:** Seeks to advance women in science and technology to achieve success and recognition as contributors and leaders. Develops and offers programs that cover issues that are relevant to the career and business issues in the diverse environments of life sciences, biotech, engineering, technology and research. Serves as a forum for men and women, educational institutions, service organizations and corporations. **Publications:** *WEST News*, monthly. Newsletter. Contains news and other updates on the organization's activities. Alternate Formats: online.

4051 ■ Women in Flavor and Fragrance Commerce (WFFC)
3301 Rte. 66, Ste.205, Bldg. C
Neptune, NJ 07753
Ph: (732)922-0500
Fax: (732)922-0560
E-mail: info@wffc.org
URL: http://www.wffc.org
Contact: Marie Cenno, Pres.
Founded: 1982. **Members:** 350. **Membership Dues:** regular in U.S. and Canada, $75 (annual) ● international, $90 (annual). **Description:** Women in the flavor and fragrance industry. Provides a center of education, camaraderie, support, and networking opportunities. **Publications:** Newsletter, quarterly. Alternate Formats: online. **Conventions/Meetings:** annual dinner ● annual meeting.

4052 ■ Women's Business Enterprise National Council (WBENC)
1120 Connecticut Ave. NW, Ste.1000
Washington, DC 20036
Ph: (202)872-5515 (972)359-0697
Fax: (202)872-5505
E-mail: ldenny@wbenc.org
URL: http://www.wbenc.org
Contact: Linda J. Denny, Pres.
Founded: 1997. **Staff:** 19. **Description:** Works as third-party certifier of women's business enterprises. Fosters diversity in the world of commerce with programs and policies designed to expand opportunities and eliminate barriers in the marketplace for women business owners. **Awards:** Applause Award. **Frequency:** annual. **Type:** recognition. **Recipient:** to barrier breakers who expand opportunities for women business owners with a significant first time contribution ● Dorothy B. Brothers Executive Scholarship. **Frequency:** annual. **Type:** scholarship. **Recipient:** to qualifying, certified women business owners who provide access to continuing executive management education. **Computer Services:** database. **Programs:** Tuck-WBENC Executive. **Publications:** Annual Report, annual. Alternate Formats: online.

4053 ■ Women's Regional Publications of America (WRPA)
c/o Jill Duval, VP/Membership Chair
PO Box 12955
Albuquerque, NM 87195
Ph: (505)247-9195 (904)992-7228
Free: (800)282-8749
E-mail: kgreen@womsdigest.net
URL: http://www.womensyellowpages.org
Contact: Karen Green, Pres.
Founded: 1986. **Members:** 22. **Membership Dues:** regular, $150 (annual). **Description:** Objectives are: to provide a forum where publishers of women's publications and business directories share information and resources; increase the visibility, authority, influence and status of women's business for the purpose of promoting growth and support of women; educate the general public about the need to support women-owned businesses, including equal opportunity employers and contractors. Directories published annually to reach out to the women's business community. **Formerly:** (2003) National Association of Women's Yellow Pages.

Wood

4054 ■ American Hardwood Information Center
c/o Hardwood Manufacturers Association
400 Penn Center Blvd., Ste.530
Pittsburgh, PA 15235
Ph: (412)829-0770
Free: (800)373-WOOD
Fax: (412)829-0844
URL: http://www.hardwood.org
Description: Works to provide information on hardwoods and hardwood products.

4055 ■ Composite Wood Council (CWC)
18922 Premiere Ct.
Gaithersburg, MD 20879-1574
Ph: (301)670-0604
Fax: (301)840-1252
E-mail: info@pbmdf.com
URL: http://www.pbmdf.com
Contact: Allyson S. O'Sullivan, Dir. of Member Services
Founded: 1989. **Membership Dues:** business (with gross annual sales of $5 million), $900 (annual) ● business (with gross annual sales of $5 million to $100 million), $1,300 (annual) ● business (with gross annual sales of more than $100 million), $1,800 (annual). **Description:** Promotes increased consumer preference for products made from composite wood and allied materials. **Affiliated With:** Composite Panel Association. **Publications:** Reports, annual. **Conventions/Meetings:** annual meeting, council meeting - fall.

4056 ■ Hardwood Council (HWC)
PO Box 525
Oakmont, PA 15139
URL: http://www.hardwoodcouncil.com
Founded: 1993. **Members:** 12. **Multinational. Description:** Promotes the increased use of North American hardwood flooring, paneling, furniture, cabinetry and decorative millwork to architects, designers and builders. **Publications:** *Finishing Touch*. **Price:** free. Alternate Formats: CD-ROM ● *Tips and Techniques*. Alternate Formats: online.

4057 ■ Southern Pine Council (SPC)
c/o SFPA
2900 Indiana Ave.
Kenner, LA 70065-4605
Ph: (504)443-4464
Fax: (504)443-6612
URL: http://www.southernpine.com
Contact: Steven Bean, VP of Marketing
Description: Joint promotional body of Southern Forest Products Association and Southeastern Lumber Manufacturers Association.

Wood Trades

4058 ■ Association of Woodworking and Furnishings Suppliers (AWFS)
500 Citadel Dr., Ste.200
Commerce, CA 90040
Ph: (323)838-9440
Free: (800)946-2937
Fax: (323)838-9443
E-mail: info@awfs.org
URL: http://www.awfs.org
Contact: Dale Silverman CAE, Exec. VP
Founded: 1979. **Members:** 450. **Membership Dues:** regular, associate, cooperating association, $285-$595 (annual) ● educational institution, $125-$175 (annual). **Staff:** 14. **Budget:** $3,000,000. **National Groups:** 2. **Description:** Provides programs and services that benefit members. Promotes a growing and financially sound woodworking and furnishings industry. **Computer Services:** Online services, product directory. **Committees:** West Coast Furniture Fabric Club; Young Furniture Associates. **Publications:** *Suppliers Edge*, monthly. Newsletter. Alternate Formats: online. **Conventions/Meetings:** semiannual Fabric Fair - conference - held spring and fall in Los Angeles, California ● annual Woodworking Industry Conference - meeting ● biennial Woodworking Machinery and Furniture Supply Fair - trade show (exhibits) - held in odd-numbered years.

Workmen's Compensation

4059 ■ American Cooperative Council on Compensation Technology (ACCCT)
7701 France Ave., Ste.450
Minneapolis, MN 55435
Ph: (952)897-1737
E-mail: linda.hanson@mwcia.org
URL: http://www.accct.org
Contact: Linda Hanson, Contact
Description: Operates as a joint venture of independent workers' compensation advisory and rating organizations. Fosters software development and technical cooperation on a project basis among its membership. Facilitates cooperation by providing a venue and support for legal services, billing, and bookkeeping.

Writers

4060 ■ American Screenwriters Association (ASA)
269 S Beverly Dr., Ste.2600
Beverly Hills, CA 90212-3807
Free: (866)265-9091
Fax: (866)265-9091
E-mail: asa@goasa.com
URL: http://www.asascreenwriters.com
Contact: John E. Johnson, Exec. Dir.
Members: 1,300. **Membership Dues:** professional, $60 (annual) ● platinum, $249 (annual) ● life, $1,500. **Multinational. Description:** Promotes the art and craft of screenwriting. Provides writers with practical resources and educational opportunities to enhance their skills. Assists writers who wish to sell their film and television scripts, or are currently working in film or television and are looking to advance their careers. **Awards:** ASA African American Screenwriters Scholarship. **Frequency:** annual. **Type:** scholarship. **Recipient:** for writers ● ASA Hispanic Screenwriters Scholarship. **Frequency:** annual. **Type:** scholarship. **Recipient:** for deserving writers ● The David Angell Humanitarian Award. **Frequency:** annual. **Type:** recognition. **Recipient:** for an individual in the entertainment industry who contributes to global well-being ● Discover Screenwriter Award. **Frequency:** annual. **Type:** recognition. **Recipient:** for writers who had screenplay made into a film ● The Epstein Award. **Frequency:** periodic. **Type:** recognition. **Recipient:** for individuals whose body or work, screenwriting experience or sharing of knowledge have advanced the art and craft of screenwriting ● Lew and Pamela Hunter Screenwriting Scholarship. **Frequency:** annual. **Type:** scholarship. **Recipient:** for full-time college students ● Mick Caswell Screenwriting Award. **Frequency:** annual. **Type:** recognition. **Recipient:** to the winner of the ASA International Screenplay Competition. **Additional Websites:** http://www.goasa.com. **Publications:** *Script Notes*. Newsletter. Contains information on screenwriting, programs and services. **Circulation:** 12,000. **Advertising:** accepted. Alternate Formats: online.

4061 ■ Asian American Writers' Workshop (AAWW)
16 W 32nd St., Ste.10A
New York, NY 10001
Ph: (212)494-0061
Fax: (212)494-0062
E-mail: desk@aaww.org
URL: http://www.aaww.org
Contact: Jeannie L. Wong, Admin. Dir.
Founded: 1991. **Membership Dues:** student, $25 (annual) ● friend, $45 (annual) ● organization, $55 (annual) ● bookworm, $100 (annual). **Description:** Dedicated to the creation, development, publication, and dissemination of Asian American literature. **Awards:** Asian American Literary Awards. **Fre-**

quency: annual. **Type:** recognition. **Recipient:** to writers. **Publications:** *Asian Pacific American Journal*, semiannual ● *Ten*. Magazine.

4062 ■ International Association of Obituarists
c/o Carolyn Milford Gilbert, Founder
8409 Pickwick Ln., No. 312
Dallas, TX 75225
Ph: (214)502-7801 (972)980-2868
Fax: (972)661-5825
E-mail: obituarist@sbcglobal.net
URL: http://www.obitpage.com
Contact: Carolyn Milford Gilbert, Founder
Membership Dues: regular, $50 (annual). **Multinational. Description:** Promotes the study and appreciation of the art of obituary. Serves as an advocate for obituary writers and their craft. Acts as a clearinghouse for inquiries and dissemination of information pertaining to obituaries. Maintains public awareness of the importance of the obituary. Provides direct contact with obituarists around the world. **Telecommunication Services:** electronic mail, carolyngilbert1@yahoo.com ● electronic mail, obitpage_tech@yahoo.com. **Publications:** Newsletter. **Price:** included in membership dues.

4063 ■ National Resume Writers' Association (NRWA)
PO Box 475
Tuckahoe, NY 10707
Ph: (631)930-6287
Free: (877)843-6792
Fax: (631)980-4355
E-mail: adminmanager@nrwaweb.com
URL: http://www.nrwaweb.com
Contact: Kathy Sweeney CPRW, Pres.
Founded: 1997. **Membership Dues:** regular, $150 (annual) ● associate, $95 (annual) ● additional fee, in U.S., $50 (annual). **Multinational. Description:** Promotes high standards of excellence in resume writing through mentoring, education and support services. Represents the interests of writers, recruiters, counselors and other employment and career-related professionals. **Computer Services:** database, list of consultants. **Programs:** Affiliate Partners; Certification; Mentoring. **Publications:** *Resume Writers' Digest*, bimonthly. Newsletter. Contains current topics on resume writing and other industry-specific issues.

4064 ■ National Verbatim Reporters Association (NVRA)
207 3rd Ave.
Hattiesburg, MS 39401
Ph: (601)582-4345
Fax: (601)582-3354
E-mail: nvra@nvra.com
URL: http://www.nvra.org
Contact: Jo Elizabeth M. Wheat CVR, Pres.
Founded: 1967. **Membership Dues:** general, $200 (annual) ● associate, $185 (annual) ● military, $150 (annual) ● student, retired, $100 (annual). **Description:** Voice writers. Strives to educate the public and legal community toward a better understanding of the voice writing system and to assist members to perform their duties more effectively. **Awards:** Horace Webb Scholarship. **Frequency:** annual. **Type:** monetary. **Recipient:** for voice writing student in NVRA endorsed school. **Publications:** *eVoice*, biweekly. Newsletter. Alternate Formats: online ● *The Verbatim Record*, quarterly. Newsletter. Alternate Formats: online. **Conventions/Meetings:** annual convention - 2008 July 30-Aug. 1, Savannah, GA.

4065 ■ North American Case Research Association (NACRA)
c/o Bob Crowner, Sec.-Treas.
466 Owen Bldg.
Ypsilanti, MI 48197
Ph: (734)487-2215
E-mail: rpcrowner@nacra.net
URL: http://www.nacra.net
Contact: Rebecca Morris, Pres.
Founded: 1958. **Members:** 500. **Membership Dues:** individual, $50 (annual). **Regional Groups:** 4. **Multinational. Description:** Promotes excellence in case research, writing, and teaching in business and other academic disciplines; advances the status of case research and pedagogy within academic institutions and professional associations; disseminates cases in multiple media globally. **Boards:** Eastern U.S.; Midwestern U.S.; Southeastern U.S.; Southwestern U.S.; Western U.S. **Councils:** Advisory. **Programs:** Conference; Grants; Latin America; Membership; Publisher Relations. **Affiliated With:** World Association for Case Method Research and Application. **Formerly:** (1982) Southern Case Writers; (1986) Case Research Association. **Publications:** *Case Research Journal*, quarterly. Features teaching cases grounded in research. **Price:** included in membership dues. **Advertising:** accepted. **Conventions/Meetings:** annual conference and roundtable ● seminar, offers professional development in case research, writing, and teaching.

4066 ■ North American Travel Journalist Association (NATJA)
531 Main St., No. 902
El Segundo, CA 90245
Ph: (310)836-8712
Fax: (310)836-8769
E-mail: info@natja.org
URL: http://www.natja.org
Contact: Elizabeth Beshear, Exec. Dir.
Founded: 1992. **Members:** 500. **Membership Dues:** media, $150 (annual) ● associate, $500 (annual). **Staff:** 5. **For-Profit. Multinational. Description:** Represents travel and hospitality industries. **Awards:** NATJA Awards. **Frequency:** annual. **Type:** recognition. **Recipient:** for journalists, publications and PR firms. **Computer Services:** database, membership, listserv. **Also Known As:** East West News Bureau. **Publications:** *Travelworld*, bimonthly. Magazine. Features stories and photos from members. **Circulation:** 75,000. **Advertising:** accepted. Alternate Formats: online ● *The Wayfarer*, bimonthly. Newsletter. Includes industry news and media relation contacts. Alternate Formats: online. **Conventions/Meetings:** annual conference - always May.

4067 ■ Novelists, Inc. (NINC)
PO Box 2037
Manhattan, KS 66505
Fax: (785)537-1877
E-mail: ninc@varney.com
URL: http://www.ninc.com
Contact: Ms. Laura Resnick, Pres.
Founded: 1989. **Members:** 600. **Membership Dues:** individual, $65 (annual) ● foreign, $75 (annual). **Multinational. Description:** Works to serve the needs of multi-published writers of popular fiction. **Telecommunication Services:** electronic mail, brendahb@aol.com. **Publications:** *NINK*, monthly. Newsletter. Offers advice and wisdom from other writers. **Price:** free, for members only. **Circulation:** 600. Alternate Formats: online. **Conventions/Meetings:** annual conference.

4068 ■ Public Safety Writers Association (PSWA)
2024 Falcon Ct.
Bellingham, WA 98229
Ph: (360)647-1785
E-mail: molsen@policewriter.com
URL: http://www.policewriter.com
Contact: Marilyn Olsen, Pres.
Founded: 1997. **Membership Dues:** writer, $55 (annual) ● corporate sponsor, $250 (annual). **Description:** Aims to provide resources and services to police writers aspiring to become published authors. Offers free manuscript review by experienced editors and publishers. **Computer Services:** database, cop tales ● information services, tips and ideas ● mailing lists. **Telecommunication Services:** electronic mail, tdees@policewriter.com. **Programs:** Manuscript Review. **Publications:** *The Public Safety Writer*, quarterly. Newsletter. Keeps members informed of news and opportunities in police writing. **Conventions/Meetings:** annual conference.

4069 ■ Sisters in Crime (SinC)
PO Box 442124
Lawrence, KS 66044
Ph: (785)842-1325
E-mail: sinc@sistersincrime.org
URL: http://www.sistersincrime.org
Contact: Roberta Isleib, Pres.
Founded: 1986. **Members:** 3,400. **Membership Dues:** regular in U.S. and Canada, $40 (annual) ● regular outside U.S. and Canada, $45 (annual). **Multinational. Description:** Writers, readers, booksellers, librarians, agents, editors, reviewers, and teachers promoting the work of women mystery writers; SinC archives are housed at the Mabel Smith Douglass Library of Douglass College, Rutgers University, New Brunswick, New Jersey. **Projects:** Bookstore; Monitoring. **Publications:** *Breaking and Entering in the New Millennium*. Book ● *InSinC*, quarterly. Newsletter. Covers upcoming events, member news, and publishing news. ● *Shameless Promotion for Brazen Hussies*. Book ● *So You're Doing an Author Signing*. Book ● Directory, annual.

4070 ■ Society of Midland Authors (SMA)
PO Box 10419
Chicago, IL 60610
E-mail: tomfrisbie@aol.com
URL: http://www.midlandauthors.com
Contact: James L. Merriner, Pres.
Founded: 1915. **Members:** 375. **Membership Dues:** individual, $35 (annual) ● patron, $500 (annual) ● sponsor, $250 (annual) ● fellow, $100 (annual). **Budget:** $35. **Description:** Works to create a closer association among writers of the Middle West. Stimulates creative literary effort and encourage an interest in reading and literature. **Awards:** Society of Midland Authors Awards. **Frequency:** annual. **Type:** monetary. **Publications:** *Literary License*, monthly. Newsletter. Contains reports. Alternate Formats: online ● Membership Directory. **Conventions/Meetings:** annual banquet ● monthly meeting, with programs - every second Tuesday.

4071 ■ Women Writing the West (WWW)
8547 E Arapahoe Rd.
Greenwood Village, CO 80112-1436
Ph: (303)773-8349
E-mail: wwwadmin@lohseworks.com
URL: http://www.womenwritingthewest.org
Contact: Jane Kirkpatrick, Pres.
Membership Dues: basic, $50 (annual) ● sustaining, $100 (annual). **Description:** Serves as a forum for writers and other professionals writing and promoting the Women's West founded by Sybil Downing and Jerrie Hurd. Promotes the legacy of earlier women writers who depicted the life during the hard and dangerous times of the Western American era. **Awards:** WILLA Literary Award. **Frequency:** annual. **Type:** recognition. **Recipient:** for books featuring women's stories set in the West. **Computer Services:** Information services, member news, links to member websites ● mailing lists, of members. **Publications:** Newsletter, quarterly. Alternate Formats: online ● Catalog, annual. Lists books written by members. **Advertising:** accepted. **Conventions/Meetings:** annual conference.

Youth

4072 ■ Youth Venture (YV)
1700 N Moore Ave., Ste.2000
Arlington, VA 22209
Ph: (703)527-4126
Fax: (703)527-8383
E-mail: info@youthventure.org
URL: http://www.youthventure.org
Contact: Roy Gamse, Acting Pres.
Founded: 1997. **Budget:** $1,073,414. **Description:** Works to empower young people to create and launch their own enterprises in order to take greater responsibility for their lives and communities. **Councils:** National Youth. **Publications:** *Venture Voice*. Newsletter. Alternate Formats: online. **Conventions/Meetings:** workshop.

Section 2: Environmental and Agricultural Organizations

Agribusiness

4073 ■ Agribusiness Council (ABC)
1312 18th St. NW, Ste.300
Washington, DC 20036
Ph: (202)296-4563 (202)887-0238
Fax: (202)887-9178
E-mail: info@agribusinesscouncil.org
URL: http://www.agribusinesscouncil.org
Contact: Nicholas E. Hollis, Pres./CEO

Founded: 1967. **Members:** 400. **Staff:** 3. **Local Groups:** 9. **Description:** Business organizations, universities and foundations, and individuals interested in stimulating and encouraging agribusiness in cooperation with the public sector, both domestic and international. Seeks to aid in relieving the problems of world food supply. Supports coordinated agribusiness in the developing nations by identifying opportunities for investment of U.S. private-sector technology management and financial resources. Advises agribusiness leaders about selected developing countries with good investment climates; brings potential investment opportunities to the attention of U.S. agribusiness firms; coordinates informal network of state agribusiness councils and grassroots organization; encourages companies to make investment feasibility studies in agribusiness; provides liaison and information exchange between agribusiness firms, governments, international organizations, universities, foundations, and other groups with the objective of identifying areas of cooperation and mutual interest; encourages projects geared to the conversion of subsistence farming to intensive, higher income agriculture in order to bring the world's rural populations, wherever feasible, into the market economy. **Libraries: Type:** reference. **Holdings:** biographical archives. **Subcommittees:** Ag Transport/Distribution; Agricultural Education/Media; Agricultural Environment/Natural Resource Management; Agro/Hi-Technology; Food Safety; Heritage Preservation; International Trade and Investment; Non-Traditional Ag Finance; Renewable Energy Technology. **Publications:** Reports, periodic. **Price:** free for members. **Conventions/Meetings:** annual meeting.

4074 ■ American Society of Agricultural Consultants (ASAC)
N78W14573 Appleton Ave., No. 287
Menomonee Falls, WI 53051
Ph: (262)253-6902 (785)336-1228
Fax: (262)253-6903
E-mail: cmerry@agconsultants.org
URL: http://www.agconsultants.org
Contact: Sam N. Bartee CAC, Pres.

Founded: 1963. **Members:** 200. **Membership Dues:** certified independent (ICACF) or certified allied (CAC), $350 (annual) ● sustaining, $500 (annual) ● student, retired, $50 (annual). **Staff:** 1. **Budget:** $120,000. **Description:** Members are independent, full-time consultants in many specialty areas serving agribusiness interests throughout the world. Strives to maintain high standards of ethics and competence in the consulting field. Provides referral service to agribusiness interests seeking consultants having specific knowledge, experience, and expertise. Maintains liaison with governmental agencies utilizing consultants and with legislative and administrative acts affecting consultants. **Computer Services:** database, qualified agricultural consultants. **Telecommunication Services:** electronic mail, cmerry@countryside-marketing.com. **Committees:** Awards; Bylaws; Certification; Education; Electronic Media and Systems; Ethics; Global Networking; Grievance; Legislative and Regulatory Matters; Marketing and Membership Development; Meetings; Membership Review. **Affiliated With:** American Society of Farm Managers and Rural Appraisers; National Alliance of Independent Crop Consultants. **Publications:** *ASAC Membership Directory*, annual. **Price:** included in membership dues. Alternate Formats: online ● *ASAC News*, quarterly. Newsletter. **Price:** included in membership dues. **Circulation:** 325. **Advertising:** accepted. **Conventions/Meetings:** annual meeting and conference.

4075 ■ Coalition for a Competitive Food and Agricultural System
Address Unknown since 2007

Members: 120. **Description:** Represents interested working for market-based policies designed to benefit people working in the U.S. food and agricultural system.

4076 ■ Communicating for America (CA)
PO Box 677
Fergus Falls, MN 56538-0677
Ph: (218)739-3241
Free: (800)432-3276
Fax: (218)739-3832
E-mail: lgodwin@cainc.org
URL: http://www.selfemployedcountry.org
Contact: Wayne Nelson, Pres.

Founded: 1972. **Members:** 80,000. **Budget:** $2,000,000. **Description:** Promotes the general health, well being and advancement of people in agriculture and agribusiness. Participates in federal and state issues that affect the quality of life in rural America and provides members with a variety of money-saving benefit programs. Conducts grants program, research on rural issues, and international exchange programs with an agricultural focus. **Libraries: Type:** reference. **Holdings:** archival material. **Formerly:** (1977) Creamery Association; (2000) Communicating for Agriculture; (2007) Communicating for Agriculture and the Self Employed. **Publications:** *CA Highlights*, monthly. Newspaper. Covers agricultural news and association activities. Includes legislative update from Washington. **Price:** free for members; $12.00 for nonmembers. **Circulation:** 90,000 ● *CAEP In Touch*, quarterly. Newspaper. Contains international exchange activities. **Price:** free to exchange participants. **Circulation:** 5,000 ● *Smart Choices*, quarterly. Magazine. **Conventions/Meetings:** annual meeting - always first Friday in April, Fergus Falls, MN.

4077 ■ Geode Resource, Conservation, and Development (GRCD)
308 N 3rd St.
Burlington, IA 52601
Ph: (319)752-6395
Fax: (319)752-0106
E-mail: geode@geodercd.org
URL: http://www.geodercd.org
Contact: Christa Perkins, Coor.

Founded: 1985. **Members:** 12. **Membership Dues:** $125 (annual). **Staff:** 7. **Budget:** $500,000. **For-Profit. Description:** Provides rural development services in natural resources in such areas as water quality, crop diversification, grant writing, community facilities or services, and planning resource economic development projects for an administration cost. **Telecommunication Services:** electronic mail, cperkins@geodercd.org. **Subgroups:** Geode Forestry; Regional Development.

4078 ■ National Alliance of Independent Crop Consultants (NAICC)
349 E Nolley Dr.
Collierville, TN 38017
Ph: (901)861-0511 (319)352-0919
Fax: (901)861-0512
E-mail: jonesnaicc@aol.com
URL: http://www.naicc.org
Contact: Allison Jones, Exec. VP

Founded: 1978. **Members:** 575. **Membership Dues:** voting, provisional, associate, $225 (annual) ● additional provisional, voting, associate from the same company, $175 (annual) ● student, $10 (annual) ● retired, $65 (annual) ● additional sustaining, $200 (annual). **Staff:** 1. **Budget:** $300,000. **Description:** Independent crop consultants and contract researchers united to promote agriculture and professionalism in the field. Seeks to: assist in the formation of state and national policies relating to agricultural production and of crop management philosophies; support agricultural crop producers by the most ecologically sound, environmentally safe, and economical means. Encourages members to expand their knowledge concerning crop management practices and techniques; participates in research in this area. Provides assistance in the formation of state and regional consultant organizations; offers referral system for members. Compiles statistics; sponsors educational programs. **Awards:** Consultant of the Year Award. **Frequency:** annual. **Type:** recognition ● Service to Agriculture Award. **Frequency:** annual. **Type:** recognition. **Publications:** Directory, annual ● Newsletter, monthly. **Circulation:** 800. **Advertising:** accepted. Alternate Formats: online. **Conventions/Meetings:** annual conference (exhibits).

4079 ■ National Council of Agricultural Employers (NCAE)
1112 16th St. NW, Ste.920
Washington, DC 20036
Ph: (202)728-0300
Fax: (202)728-0303

E-mail: info@ncaeonline.org
URL: http://www.ncaeonline.org
Contact: Sharon M. Hughes CAE, Exec. VP

Founded: 1964. **Members:** 270. **Membership Dues:** associate, $400. **Staff:** 2. **Budget:** $350,000. **Description:** Growers of agricultural commodities who employ hand labor for field crops; processors and handlers, farm and commodity organizations, and others whose business is related to labor - intensive farming in the U.S. Aims to improve the position and image of U.S. agriculture as an employer of labor and to facilitate and encourage the establishment and maintenance of an adequate force of agricultural employees. Serves as clearinghouse for exchange of information on labor supply, length of employment, and other conditions of work. Does not engage in recruitment, housing, supplying, or employment of agricultural workers, and does not represent its members or others in negotiating with labor unions or other organizations, or in agreeing to any contract relating to hours, wages, or working conditions. Keeps members abreast of national legislation affecting agricultural labor. **Libraries: Type:** reference. **Holdings:** papers. **Committees:** EPA/OSHA; Immigration/H2A; Labor Relations/Employee Benefits; MSPA/Labor Standards. **Publications:** Newsletter, monthly. **Price:** free for members; $75.00 for nonmembers. **Circulation:** 500. **Conventions/Meetings:** annual conference - late January or early February.

4080 ■ New Uses Council
c/o Dan Manternach, Exec. Dir.
91 W Galloway
Memphis, TN 38111
Ph: (901)309-1668
Fax: (901)452-5500
E-mail: dmanternach@newuses.org
URL: http://www.newuses.org
Contact: Dan Manternach, Exec. Dir.

Founded: 1990. **Members:** 1,000. **Membership Dues:** individual, $100 (annual) ● government agency/nonprofit, $250 (annual) ● company, corporation (based on annual sales), $250-$5,000 (annual). **Staff:** 1. **Budget:** $50,000. **Regional Groups:** 12. **State Groups:** 52. **Local Groups:** 250. **National Groups:** 7. **Multinational**. **Description:** Seeks to promote the development and commercialization of new uses for traditional and new agricultural and forestry crops and residues. Provides information on new industrial, energy and non-food uses of agricultural goods; promotes and educates consumers, the media and policy makers on renewable resource products; supports research and development to advance new crops; maintains speakers' bureau. **Computer Services:** database ● electronic publishing ● mailing lists ● online services. **Publications:** *Bioproducts Directory*, annual. Includes listings, descriptions, and addresses for organizations and individuals. **Price:** $80.00 for nonmembers; $40.00 for members. **Advertising:** accepted. Alternate Formats: online ● Reports. Alternate Formats: online.

4081 ■ Organization for Competitive Markets (OCM)
PO Box 6486
Lincoln, NE 68506
Ph: (402)817-4443
Fax: (208)441-5092
E-mail: ocm@competitivemarkets.com
URL: http://www.competitivemarkets.com
Contact: Keith Mudd, Pres.

Membership Dues: founding, $1,000 (annual) ● regular, $200 (annual) ● nonvoting, $50 (annual). **Description:** Works for increased competition and protection for the agricultural marketplace. Works against "abuse of corporate power and consolidation of the agricultural market". **Libraries: Type:** reference. **Holdings:** articles, reports. **Subjects:** agriculture. **Divisions:** Competitive Market Litigation Clearinghouse. **Subcommittees:** speakers' bureau. **Publications:** *A Food and Agricultural Policy for the 21st Century*. Papers ● *OCM Newsletter*. Alternate Formats: online.

4082 ■ Samuel Roberts Noble Foundation
2510 Sam Noble Pkwy.
Ardmore, OK 73401
Ph: (580)223-5810 (580)221-7400
Free: (866)223-5810
Fax: (580)224-6240
E-mail: srporter@noble.org
URL: http://www.noble.org
Contact: Michael A. Cawley, CEO/Pres.

Founded: 1945. **Description:** Strives to promote agriculture, the ranching industry, and plant biology. Hosts the "Junior Beef Excellence Program". **Awards: Type:** grant. **Publications:** *Noble Forum*, quarterly. Newsletter ● Annual Report, annual.

4083 ■ Southern U.S. Trade Association (SUSTA)
2 Canal St., Ste.2515
New Orleans, LA 70130
Ph: (504)568-5986
Fax: (504)568-6010
E-mail: susta@susta.org
URL: http://www.susta.org
Contact: Sharon Courtney, Office Mgr.

Founded: 1973. **Members:** 285. **Membership Dues:** associate, $400 (annual). **Staff:** 8. **Budget:** $8,000,000. **Regional Groups:** 4. **State Groups:** 16. **Local Groups:** 185. **Languages:** English, Spanish. **Description:** Departments of agriculture of the Southern states; food and agricultural manufacturers and exporters operating in the southern United States. Promotes the export of high-value food and agricultural products of the South, Participates in international trade exhibitions and conducts point of sale promotions in food chains and restaurants worldwide; organizes overseas trade missions and other promotional campaigns; "provides information and assistance with transportation and financing of export sales and works closely on an individual basis with its export company membership to develop and expand their share of agricultural export markets". Sponsors economics and marketing research and educational programs. **Awards:** E-Award. **Type:** recognition. **Telecommunication Services:** electronic mail, sharon@susta.org. **Programs:** Market Access. **Publications:** *Insight*, bimonthly. Newsletter. Alternate Formats: online.

4084 ■ United Agribusiness League (UAL)
54 Corporate Park
Irvine, CA 92606-5105
Ph: (949)975-1424
Free: (800)223-4590
Fax: (949)975-1671
E-mail: bgoodrich@ual.org
URL: http://www.ual.org
Contact: Bill Goodrich, Pres./CEO

Founded: 1980. **Members:** 1,400. **Staff:** 90. **Description:** Agricultural industries and businesses. Promotes "the development and common interest of the agricultural industry". Works to coordinate members' activities to advance agribusiness in general; provides services and benefits to enable members to realize greater productive efficiency. Serves as a clearinghouse on international agribusiness. Provides employee health care plans and other insurance to agribusinesses. **Awards:** UAL/UABI Annual Scholarship Program. **Frequency:** annual. **Type:** monetary. **Recipient:** for students studying for agriculture degrees. **Telecommunication Services:** electronic mail, ceinsmann@ual.org. **Publications:** *Ag Crime Prevention Brochures* ● *Ag News and Views*, monthly. Newsletter ● *Crime Prevention*, quarterly. Newsletter ● *Healthy Times*, monthly. Newsletter ● Membership Directory, annual. **Conventions/Meetings:** annual meeting.

4085 ■ Women in Agribusiness (WIA)
Address Unknown since 2007

Founded: 1985. **Members:** 400. **Description:** Women in agribusiness. Provides a forum for the discussion of ideas and information related to agribusiness. Offers placement, networking, and peer/mentor support services. **Awards:** CERES. **Frequency:** annual. **Type:** recognition. **Recipient:** bestowed to outstanding women in agribusiness. **Publications:** *Women in Agribusiness Bulletin*, quarterly. **Price:** $15.00/year in U.S.; $20.00/year outside U.S. **Advertising:** accepted.

Agricultural Development

4086 ■ Armenian Technology Group (ATG)
PO Box 5969
Fresno, CA 93755-5969
Ph: (559)224-1000
Fax: (559)224-1002
E-mail: info@atgusa.org
URL: http://www.atgusa.org
Contact: Varoujan Der Simonian MA, Exec. Dir.

Founded: 1989. **Languages:** Arabic, Armenian, English, Turkish. **Description:** Agronomists, office workers, engineers, veterinarians, and other individuals with an interest in Armenian agriculture. Seeks to increase agricultural production in Armenia through introduction of improved farming techniques and technologies. Identifies and distributes appropriate technologies; conducts training programs for farmers wishing to employ new methods; conducts projects in areas including weed control, fertilizers, production of animal feed, and testing of new seed varieties. **Awards: Type:** recognition. **Programs:** Civil Society and Humanitarian Aid; Diagnostic Lab; Restoring Reviving Karabagh's Grapes Industry; Reviving Karabagh's Honey Industry; Seed Multiplication. **Projects:** Wheat. **Publications:** Newsletter, semiannual. **Circulation:** 6,000. Alternate Formats: online ● Annual Report, annual. Alternate Formats: online. **Conventions/Meetings:** quarterly board meeting.

4087 ■ Compatible Technology International (CTI)
800 Transfer Rd., Ste.6
St. Paul, MN 55114
Ph: (651)632-3912
Fax: (651)204-9033
E-mail: cti@compatibletechnology.org
URL: http://www.compatibletechnology.org
Contact: Bruce L. Humphrys, Exec. Dir.

Founded: 1981. **Staff:** 4. **Budget:** $321,000. **Multinational**. **Description:** Seeks to increase the food production capabilities of small farms in the developing world through the introduction of more effective farming techniques and technologies. Develops, introduces, and trains indigenous people to make use of appropriate technologies and improved productive techniques. Encourages establishment of agricultural microenterprises to increase the economic viability of rural areas in the developing world. **Committees:** Africa; Americas; Asia; Technology. **Formerly:** (2001) Compatible Technology. **Publications:** *Harvest*, semiannual. Newsletter. **Price:** free. **Circulation:** 2,000. Alternate Formats: online.

4088 ■ Double Harvest (DH)
55 S Main St.
Oberlin, OH 44074
Ph: (440)714-1694
E-mail: vernon@doubleharvest.org
URL: http://www.doubleharvest.org
Contact: Jaclyn van Wingerden, Contact

Multinational. **Description:** Promotes increased agricultural production and reforestation in developing regions worldwide. Provides land, equipment, and technical assistance to farms and nurseries; conducts training in water resources management and soil conservation.

4089 ■ Future Harvest
Address Unknown since 2008

Multinational. **Description:** Educates the general public and decision makers on the importance of food production and the role of agricultural science in meeting human and environmental challenges. Provides financial support for scientific research and charitable projects that bring results to rural communities and farmers in developing countries. **Computer Services:** Mailing lists.

4090 ■ International Sprout Growers Association (ISGA)
2150 N 107th St., Ste.205
Seattle, WA 98133-9009
Ph: (206)367-8704
E-mail: office@isga-sprouts.org
URL: http://www.isga-sprouts.org
Contact: Frank Crikelair, Contact

Founded: 1989. **Members:** 150. **Membership Dues:** grower, $450 (annual) ● associate, $750 (annual) ● affiliate, $45 (annual). **Multinational. Description:** Professional association of sprout companies supplying products and services to the sprout industry. Promotes the exchange of information among industry members. **Publications:** Newsletter. **Price:** included in membership dues.

Agricultural Education

4091 ■ National Council for Agricultural Education
1410 King St., Ste.400
Alexandria, VA 22314
Ph: (703)838-5882 (703)838-5881
Free: (800)772-0939
Fax: (703)838-5888
E-mail: pholbert@ffa.org
URL: http://www.teamaged.org/councilindex.cfm
Contact: Mr. C. Coleman Harris, Exec. Sec.

Founded: 1983. **Description:** Strives to stimulate positive growth in agricultural education. **Formerly:** Agricultural Education National Headquarters. **Publications:** *Council Brochure*. Alternate Formats: online ● *Monday Morning Monitor*, weekly, every Monday. Newsletter. Alternate Formats: online ● *The National Strategic Plan and Action Agenda for Agricultural Education*. Brochure. Alternate Formats: online ● *State Staff Directory*. Alternate Formats: online.

Agricultural Equipment

4092 ■ Midwest Equipment Dealers Association (MEDA)
5330 Wall St., Ste.100
Madison, WI 53718
Ph: (608)240-4700
Fax: (608)240-2069
E-mail: meda@medaassn.com
URL: http://www.meda-online.com
Contact: Gary Manke CAE, Exec. VP

Founded: 1991. **Members:** 375. **Membership Dues:** Wisconsin agricultural equipment-main store, $425 (annual) ● Wisconsin agricultural equipment-branch store, Wisconsin dairy or farmstead, $240 (annual) ● Illinois agricultural equipment-main store, $450 (annual) ● Illinois agricultural equipment-branch store, Illinois dairy or farmstead mech, $255 (annual) ● associate, $200 (annual) ● associate (each additional), $75 (annual) ● Wisconsin outdoor power equipment, Wisconsin commercial/light industry, $240 (annual) ● Illinois outdoor power equipment, Illinois commercial/ light industry, Illinois construction equipment dealer, $255 (annual). **Staff:** 4. **Budget:** $1,000,000. **Regional Groups:** 1. **For-Profit. Description:** Promotes the farm, industrial, outdoor power equipment, dairy and farmstead mechanization industry. **Awards:** Ag Mechanical/Service Tech Awards. **Frequency:** annual. **Type:** scholarship. **Recipient:** to rural youth. **Telecommunication Services:** electronic mail, gmanke@medaassn.com. **Committees:** Insurance, Education and Training; Long Range Planning; Political Education, Legislation and Dealer-Manufacturer Relations. **Councils:** Outdoor Power Equipment Dealer. **Affiliated With:** Association of Bridal Consultants; Association for Wedding Professionals International; North American Equipment Dealers Association. **Publications:** *Guidelines to Profit*, monthly. Newsletter. **Advertising:** accepted. **Conventions/ Meetings:** annual conference ● annual Midwest Ag Expo - convention (exhibits).

Agricultural Science

4093 ■ Agriculture, Food and Human Values (AFHVS)
PO Box 118545
Gainesville, FL 32611
Ph: (352)392-0958
Fax: (352)392-5577
E-mail: rhaynes@phil.ufl.edu
URL: http://www.afhvs.org
Contact: Richard P. Haynes, Exec. Sec.

Founded: 1987. **Membership Dues:** student, $25 (annual) ● ordinary, $30 (annual). **Description:** Scholars working in the fields of agricultural and rural studies. Promotes interdisciplinary research and scholarship to encourage interaction between liberal arts and agricultural disciplines. Serves as a forum for "examining the values that underlie various visions of food and agricultural systems". Facilitates cooperation and exchange of information among members; provides technical assistance to organizations and agencies guiding the development of food and agricultural systems. **Publications:** *Agriculture and Human Values*, quarterly. Journal ● Newsletter, periodic. **Conventions/Meetings:** annual meeting - always early June.

4094 ■ Agriservices Foundation (AF)
Address Unknown since 2007

Founded: 1964. **Description:** Governed by a board of trustees and a board of advisors, whose purposes are to foster and support programs of education, research, and development that will contribute toward wider and more effective application of science and technology to the practice of agriculture. Programs include: alleviating world food hunger and malnutrition; sponsorship of travel-study groups abroad, which are in-depth studies of agriculture in other countries; short courses abroad. **Conventions/Meetings:** annual meeting.

4095 ■ American Farm Bureau Foundation for Agriculture (AFBFA)
600 Maryland Ave. SW, Ste.100W
Washington, DC 20024
Ph: (202)406-3662 (202)406-3631
Free: (800)443-8456
Fax: (202)406-3604
E-mail: foundation@fb.org
URL: http://www.agfoundation.org
Contact: Brad Eckart, Managing Dir.

Founded: 1967. **Staff:** 2. **Budget:** $600,000. **Description:** Initiates and finances agricultural research and education programs. **Additional Websites:** http://www.ageducate.org. **Formerly:** (1997) American Farm Bureau Research Foundation. **Supersedes:** American Farm Research Association. **Publications:** *Leading the Challenge*, quarterly. Newsletter. Alternate Formats: online ● Reports. Contains information on research project results. **Conventions/Meetings:** periodic symposium and meeting.

4096 ■ American Society of Agronomy (ASA)
677 S Segoe Rd.
Madison, WI 53711
Ph: (608)273-8080
Fax: (608)273-2021
E-mail: headquarters@agronomy.org
URL: http://www.agronomy.org
Contact: Ellen G.M. Bergfeld, CEO

Founded: 1907. **Members:** 11,500. **Membership Dues:** active, $82 (annual) ● graduate student, $27 (annual) ● sustaining, $510 (annual). **Staff:** 37. **Budget:** $2,500,000. **Regional Groups:** 4. **Description:** Professional society of agronomists, plant breeders, physiologists, soil scientists, chemists, educators, technicians, and others concerned with crop production and soil management, and conditions affecting them. Sponsors fellowship program and student essay and speech contests. Provides placement service. **Awards:** Agronomic Extension Education Award. **Type:** recognition. **Recipient:** for extension agronomists ● Agronomic Industry Award. **Type:** recognition. **Recipient:** for an outstanding private sector agronomist ● Agronomic Resident Education Award. **Type:** recognition. **Recipient:** for excellent resident teacher ● Carl Sprengel Agronomic Research Award. **Type:** recognition. **Recipient:** for major research accomplishments ● International Service in Agronomy Award. **Type:** recognition. **Recipient:** for outstanding contributions on research made outside of the U.S. ● Monsanto Professional Certification Service Award. **Type:** recognition. **Recipient:** for an outstanding registrant ● Syngenta Crop Protection Recognition Award. **Type:** recognition. **Recipient:** for outstanding performance in teaching and service in agronomy. **Committees:** Agronomic Industry; Information Retrieval; International Agronomy. **Divisions:** Agricultural Research Station Management; Agroclimatology and Agronomic Modeling; Environmental Quality; Extension Education; Military Land Use and Management; Resident Education; Soil and Plant Science Applications. **Subgroups:** Student Activities. **Publications:** *Agronomy Abstracts*, annual. **Price:** $15.00 ● *Agronomy Journal*, bimonthly. Alternate Formats: online ● *CSA News*, monthly. Newsletter. Contains information on agronomy, crop science, soil science, and related topics; also includes society news and calendar of events. **Price:** included in membership dues; $12.00 /year for nonmembers. **Circulation:** 12,500. **Advertising:** accepted. Alternate Formats: online ● *Journal of Environmental Quality*, quarterly ● *Journal of Natural Resources and Life Sciences Education*, semiannual ● Monographs. **Conventions/Meetings:** annual convention (exhibits).

4097 ■ American Society for Plasticulture (ASP)
526 Brittany Dr.
State College, PA 16803-1420
Ph: (814)238-7045
Fax: (814)238-7051
E-mail: info@plasticulture.org
URL: http://www.plasticulture.org
Contact: Patricia E. Heuser, Exec. Dir.

Founded: 1959. **Members:** 119. **Membership Dues:** grower in U.S., Canada, Mexico, $60 (annual) ● grower outside U.S., $80 (annual) ● academic in U.S., Canada, Mexico, $60 (annual) ● academic outside U.S., $80 (annual) ● commercial, $200 (annual) ● sponsor, $600 (annual). **Budget:** $50,000. **Description:** University departments of agriculture, horticulture, vegetable crops, and agricultural engineering conducting research, extension, and teaching; industrial sales and product development departments; professional growers of agricultural crops. Advances agriculture through the use of plastics. Conducts research and education programs. **Libraries: Type:** reference. **Subjects:** research reports. **Awards:** Best Paper Award. **Type:** scholarship ● Distinguished Service Award. **Type:** recognition. **Recipient:** for exceptional or special activity by an ASP member ● Pioneer Award. **Frequency:** annual. **Type:** recognition. **Recipient:** for contributions to plasticulture. **Computer Services:** Mailing lists, for members ● online services, membership list. **Committees:** Awards; Congress; Executive; Nominating. **Formerly:** (1990) National Agricultural Plastics Association. **Publications:** *Agri-Plastics Report*, semiannual. Newsletter. Provides information on research projects, new agri-business products, environmental issues and news about members. **Price:** included in membership dues. ISSN: 1073-1776. **Circulation:** 300. Alternate Formats: online. Also Cited As: *Agri-Plastic News* ● *Proceedings of National Congresses*, periodic, every 18 months, per Congress. Alternate Formats: online ● Membership Directory ● Bulletins. **Conventions/Meetings:** National Agricultural Plastics Congress - congress and tour, with research presentations and demonstrations (exhibits) - every 12 to 20 months.

4098 ■ Association for Communication Excellence in Agriculture, Natural Resources, and Life and Human Sciences (ACE)
PO Box 110811
Gainesville, FL 32611
Ph: (352)392-9588
Fax: (352)392-8583

E-mail: ace@ifas.ufl.edu
URL: http://www.aceweb.org
Contact: Bob Sams, Pres.

Founded: 1912. **Members:** 700. **Membership Dues:** active, $100 (annual) ● graduate, new, retired, $50 (annual) ● life, $250. **Staff:** 1. **Budget:** $80,000. **Regional Groups:** 4. **State Groups:** 50. **Description:** Develops professional skills of education, government, and research communicators and information technologists to extend knowledge about agriculture, natural resources and human sciences. **Awards:** Reuben Brigham Award. **Frequency:** annual. **Type:** recognition. **Recipient:** for private industry media firm supporting agriculture. **Programs:** Critique and Awards. **Formerly:** (1978) American Association of Agricultural College Editors; (2000) AG Communications in Education; (2004) Agricultural Communicators in Education. **Publications:** *ACE Archives Directory*. Provides a comprehensive documentation of ACE's history. ● *Journal of Applied Communications*, quarterly. Features abstracts of articles and full text of reviews. **Price:** $75.00 /year for libraries and nonmembers; $15.00/back issue for nonmembers; included in membership dues. ISSN: 1051-0834. Alternate Formats: online ● *Signals*, bimonthly. Newsletter. Features news of interest to members. Includes articles with a professional development focus. Alternate Formats: online. **Conventions/Meetings:** annual international conference.

4099 ■ Crop Science Society of America (CSSA)

677 S Segoe Rd.
Madison, WI 53711
Ph: (608)273-8080
Fax: (608)273-2021
E-mail: headquarters@crops.org
URL: http://www.crops.org
Contact: Henry L. Shands, Pres.

Founded: 1955. **Members:** 4,200. **Membership Dues:** active (base), $82 (annual) ● student (graduate/doctoral), $27 (annual) ● student (undergraduate), $10 (annual) ● sustaining, $510 (annual). **Staff:** 30. **Budget:** $2,500,000. **Multinational. Description:** Plant breeders, physiologists, ecologists, crop production specialists, seed technologists, turf grass specialists, and others interested in improvement, management, and use of field crops. Seeks to advance research, extension, and teaching of all basic and applied phases of the crop sciences and to cooperate with all other organizations and societies similarly interested in the improvement, production, management, and utilization of field crops. Maintains numerous committees including Coordination of Resident Education Activities, Crop Registration, Crop Science Teaching Improvement, Crop Terminology, Intersociety Committee on Plant Terminology, and Preservation of Genetic Stocks; also supports various intersociety collaboration committees. **Awards:** Crop Science Extension Education Award. **Frequency:** annual. **Type:** recognition. **Recipient:** to individuals who have demonstrated excellence in extension teaching activities in the area of crop science ● Crop Science Research Award. **Frequency:** annual. **Type:** recognition. **Recipient:** to recognize outstanding research contributions in crop science ● Crop Science Teaching Award. **Frequency:** annual. **Type:** recognition. **Recipient:** to recognize excellence in resident classroom teaching of crop science ● Frank N. Meyer Medal. **Frequency:** annual. **Type:** recognition. **Recipient:** for an individual who has made significant contributions in conserving the earth's genetic resources ● **Frequency:** annual. **Type:** scholarship. **Recipient:** for graduate and undergraduate students ● Young Crop Scientist Award. **Frequency:** annual. **Type:** recognition. **Recipient:** to young crop scientists who have made outstanding contributions in any area of crop science. **Divisions:** Crop Breeding, Genetics, and Cytology; Crop Ecology, Management and Quality; Crop Physiology and Metabolism; Forage and Grazing Lands; Genomics, Molecular Genetics, and Biotechnology; Plant Genetics and Resources; Seed Physiology, Production and Technology; Turfgrass Science. **Affiliated With:** American Society of Agronomy; Soil Science Society of America. **Formerly:** (1955) Crop Science Division of the American Society of Agronomy. **Publications:** *Crop Science*, bimonthly. Journal ● *CSA News*, monthly. Newsletter. **Price:** included in membership dues ● *Journal of Environmental Quality*, quarterly ● Annual Reports. **Conventions/Meetings:** annual convention, held in conjunction with the American Society of Agronomy and The Soil Science Society of America (exhibits) ● annual meeting - 2008 Oct. 26-30, Chicago, IL.

4100 ■ Ecological Farming Association (EFA)

406 Main St., Ste.313
Watsonville, CA 95076
Ph: (831)763-2111
Fax: (831)763-2112
E-mail: info@eco-farm.org
URL: http://www.eco-farm.org
Contact: Timothy J. Sullivan, Exec. Dir.

Founded: 1981. **Members:** 2,000. **Membership Dues:** seed sower, $50 (annual) ● barefoot gardener (student), $35 (annual) ● cultivator, $100 (annual) ● sustainer, $250 (annual) ● earth guardian, $500 (annual) ● eco legend, $1,000 (annual). **Staff:** 10. **Budget:** $250,000. **Description:** Organic farmers; wholesalers and retailers of natural foods; university level researchers and educators; consumers concerned with food safety, environmental, and land use issues. Seeks to promote agricultural practices that are "ecologically sound, economically viable, and socially just." Works to increase the number of growers using sustainable practices and consumers demanding organically-grown foods. Sponsors harvest fairs, farm tours, and ecological farming conference, and other educational events for sustainable agriculture. **Formerly:** (1989) Steering Committee for Sustainable Agriculture; (2001) Committee for Sustainable Agriculture. **Publications:** *Organic Matters*, annual. Newsletter. Alternate Formats: online. Also Cited As: *Food Organic Matters* ● *Participant Directory*, annual. **Conventions/Meetings:** annual conference ● annual Eco-Farm Conference (exhibits) - always in Asilomar, CA ● annual Heartland Conference and Country Fair - workshop and festival ● annual Hoes Down Harvest Festival ● periodic Sustainable AG Farming Series - workshop.

4101 ■ Farm Foundation (FF)

1301 W 22nd St., Ste.615
Oak Brook, IL 60523
Ph: (630)571-9393
Fax: (630)571-9580
E-mail: walt@farmfoundation.org
URL: http://www.farmfoundation.org
Contact: Walter J. Armbruster, Pres.

Founded: 1933. **Staff:** 3. **Nonmembership. Description:** Cooperates with existing agencies in stimulating research and educational activities to improve the economic, social, and cultural conditions of rural life. Sponsors regional and national committees, studies, publications, conferences, and training courses. **Awards: Type:** fellowship. **Recipient:** to agricultural extension workers for graduate training in the social sciences. **Publications:** *The Catalyst*, quarterly. Newsletter. Contains information on the work of Farm Foundation. Alternate Formats: online ● *Issue Report*. Alternate Formats: online ● *Public Issues Education: Increasing Competence, Enabling Communities*. Booklet. Contains materials and programs for training Extension professions in public issues education. **Price:** free. Alternate Formats: online ● Annual Report, annual. Provides a summary of yearly programs by priority area. Alternate Formats: online.

4102 ■ International Weed Science Society (IWSS)

c/o Dr. Albert Fischer, Sec.-Treas.
Univ. of California-Davis
Plant Sciences Dept., Mail Stop No. 4
1 Shields Ave.
Davis, CA 95616
Ph: (530)752-7386
Fax: (530)752-4604
E-mail: ajfischer@ucdavis.edu
URL: http://iws.ucdavis.edu
Contact: Dr. Albert Fischer, Sec.-Treas.

Founded: 1975. **Members:** 1,000. **Membership Dues:** individual, $15 (annual) ● associate, $50 (annual) ● life, $200. **Multinational. Description:** Individuals (1000) and organizations (30) interested in weed science research and training. Promotes weed control technology and education, training in weed science and technology, and communications among members. Sponsors workshops; stimulates research and regulatory programs. Encourages development of, and maintains liaison with, weed science and related organizations. Provides calendar of events. **Awards:** IWSS Outstanding Achievement in Weed Science. **Frequency:** quadrennial. **Type:** recognition. **Publications:** *Symposia Proceedings*, periodic. Alternate Formats: CD-ROM ● Brochure ● Newsletter, semiannual. **Conventions/Meetings:** quadrennial Weed Science Congress (exhibits).

4103 ■ IRI Research Institute (IRI)

PO Box 1276
169 Greenwich Ave.
Stamford, CT 06904-1276
Ph: (203)327-5985
Fax: (203)359-1595
E-mail: iriresrch@aol.com
URL: http://www.dizons.com/johnnyczar/IRI
Contact: Jerome F. Harrington, Pres.

Founded: 1950. **Staff:** 15. **Budget:** $1,000,000. **Description:** International technical specialists working in agricultural and agribusiness development. Provides projects such as: development and management of pasture seed industry in Venezuela; livestock improvement in Belize; nontraditional crop improvement program in the Dominican Republic; roadside vegetation and rice production in Brazil; food crops extension program in Indonesia; rice production and management in Guyana; a crop diversification program in Peru, including the Amazon region; coffee production, El Salvador feasibility and evaluation studies, most recently in Costa Rica, Ecuador, Egypt, Honduras, Kenya, Paraguay, Guyana, Saudi Arabia, and the Yemen Arab Republic. Incorporates a training program for academic credit or practical on-the-job training. **Convention/Meeting:** none. **Libraries: Type:** reference. **Holdings:** 2,500. **Subjects:** country profiles, crop production, sustainable agriculture practices, environment, forestry, coffee production. **Computer Services:** database ● online services. **Formerly:** (1963) IBEC Research Institute. **Publications:** Bulletin (in English, Portuguese, and Spanish), periodic ● Also publishes progress reports.

4104 ■ Josephine Porter Institute for Applied Bio-Dynamics (JPI)

PO Box 133
Woolwine, VA 24185
Ph: (276)930-2463
Fax: (276)930-2475
E-mail: info@jpibiodynamics.org
URL: http://www.jpibiodynamics.org

Founded: 1985. **Description:** Seeks to produce quality bio-dynamic agricultural preparations based on the scientific research of Rudolph Steiner (1861-1925). (Bio-dynamic farming stresses restoration of organic matter to the soil.) Offers educational programs on the making of bio-dynamic preparations. Conducts research; disseminates information. **Libraries: Type:** reference. **Publications:** *Applied Biodynamics*, quarterly. Newsletter. **Price:** $35.00/year ● Brochures. **Conventions/Meetings:** periodic workshop.

4105 ■ National Institute for Science, Law and Public Policy (NISLAPP)

1400 16th St. NW, Ste.101
Washington, DC 20036
Ph: (202)462-8800
Fax: (202)315-2501
E-mail: jim@swankin-turner.com
Contact: James S. Turner, Principal/Co-Founder

Founded: 1978. **Membership Dues:** general, $25 (annual). **Staff:** 3. **Description:** Seeks to influence public policies on food production topics, including sustainable agriculture, food safety, and nutrition by uniting individuals working to develop sustainable forms of agriculture and consumers concerned about health and quality food. Promotes agricultural techniques that do not involve the use of chemical fertilizers or pesticides. Monitors federal regulatory practices in the areas of milk pricing, the use of prescription drugs, and interpretation of food and drug law. Operates information clearinghouse on the food additive aspartame (Nutrasweet); maintains Takoma Urban Farm using sustainable agriculture methods. Makes available internships in law, food safety, and publishing; provides training in sustainable agriculture. Disseminates information; maintains speakers' bureau. **Libraries: Type:** not open to the public. **Subjects:** food safety regulation, aspartame. **Committees:** Enterprise; Legal. **Divisions:** Aspartame Consumer Safety Network; Healthy Harvest Society; Potomac Valley Press. **Publications:** *The Earth and You Eating for Two*. Book. Provides information for enviro-friendly households. **Price:** $9.00 plus shipping and handling. ISSN: 0938-4430.

4106 ■ North American Weed Management Association (NAWMA)
PO Box 687
Meade, KS 67864
Ph: (620)873-8730
Fax: (620)873-8733
E-mail: nawma@sbcglobal.net
URL: http://www.nawma.org
Contact: Jim Larson, Pres.
Membership Dues: sustaining, $100-$1,000 (annual). **Multinational. Description:** Provides education, regulatory direction, professional improvement and environmental awareness of the negative impacts of noxious weeds and exotic plants. Protects the natural resources from the degrading impacts of exotic and invasive noxious weeds. Empowers North American noxious weed managers by improving their image and professionalism. **Committees:** Audit; Awards; Conference and Trade Show; Mapping Standards; National Issues/Regulatory Direction; Personal Improvement/Education; Weed Free Forage. **Publications:** *NAWMAlogue*, periodic. Newsletter. Alternate Formats: online.

4107 ■ Potash and Phosphate Institute (PPI)
655 Engg. Dr., Ste.110
Norcross, GA 30092-2837
Ph: (770)447-0335
Fax: (770)448-0439
E-mail: ppi@ppi-ppic.org
URL: http://www.ppi-ppic.org
Contact: David W. Dibb, Pres.
Founded: 1935. **Members:** 9. **Staff:** 50. **Description:** Supports scientific research, particularly in the areas of soil fertility evaluation, soil testing, plant analysis, and tissue testing in state universities and experiment stations; participates in growers' meetings, dealer training courses, crops and soils workshops, and diagnostic clinics. Produces publications for educational use. **Formerly:** (1970) American Potash Institute; (1976) Potash Institute of North America; (1977) Potash Institute. **Publications:** *Better Crops with Plant Food*, quarterly. Magazine. **Circulation:** 16,000. Alternate Formats: online ● *2005 Catalog*. Alternate Formats: online ● Booklets ● Newsletter, periodic ● Reprints.

4108 ■ Rural Advancement Foundation International - USA (RAFI-USA)
PO Box 640
Pittsboro, NC 27312
Ph: (919)542-1396
Fax: (919)542-0069
E-mail: bbailey@rafiusa.org
URL: http://www.rafiusa.org
Contact: Betty T. Bailey, Exec. Dir.
Founded: 1990. **Staff:** 13. **Nonmembership. Description:** Promotes community, equity and diversity for family farmers and rural communities. **Telecommunication Services:** electronic mail, regina@rafiusa.org. **Programs:** Contract Agriculture Reform; Farm Preservation; On Farm Research; Tobacco Communities Initiatives. **Also Known As:** (1990) RAFI-USA. **Formerly:** (1986) International Genetic Resources Programme; (1990) Rural Advancement Fund International.

4109 ■ Weed Science Society of America (WSSA)
PO Box 7050
Lawrence, KS 66044-8897
Free: (800)627-0629
Fax: (785)843-1274
E-mail: jlancaster@allenpress.com
URL: http://www.wssa.net
Contact: Joyce Lancaster, Exec. Sec.
Founded: 1950. **Members:** 2,300. **Membership Dues:** regular, $155 (annual) ● student, $60 (annual). **Description:** Serves as a professional society of biological and chemical scientists and engineers involved in weed control research, extension, teaching, and regulatory activities; research and sales personnel from chemical and equipment industries. **Awards:** Honorary Member Award. **Frequency:** annual. **Type:** recognition. **Recipient:** for members who rendered meritorious service to the field of science. **Committees:** Education; Legislative; Terminology. **Absorbed:** (1956) Association of Regional Weed Control Conferences. **Formerly:** (1967) Weed Society of America. **Publications:** *Abstracts*, annual ● *Weed Science*, bimonthly. Journal. ISSN: 0043-1745. Alternate Formats: online ● *Weed Technology*, quarterly. Journal. ISSN: 0890-037X. Alternate Formats: online ● Newsletter, quarterly. **Price:** included in membership dues. Alternate Formats: online. **Conventions/Meetings:** annual meeting - always February.

Agriculture

4110 ■ Association for the Advancement of Industrial Crops (AAIC)
c/o USDA-ARS-ALARC
21881 Cardon Ln.
Maricopa, AZ 85239
Ph: (520)316-6426
E-mail: aaic@wiu.edu
URL: http://www.aaic.org
Contact: C. Gardner, Pres.-Elect
Founded: 1988. **Membership Dues:** regular, $30 (annual) ● regular (with journal subscription), $130 (annual). **Description:** Encourages and promotes the activities of those involved in the production, processing, development, and commercialization of industrial crops and by-products. Provides the public, industry, and government policy makers with expert scientific, engineering, and business information on developments in the utilization and commercialization of industrial products from agricultural crops. **Awards:** Anson Ellis Thompson Career Service Award. **Frequency:** annual. **Type:** recognition ● International Flora Technology Student Award for Outstanding Contributions to Jojoba Research. **Type:** recognition. **Recipient:** for a full time student who has early personal involvement in jojoba research and development ● Jojoba Growers and Processors Student Award. **Frequency:** annual. **Type:** recognition ● Outstanding Researcher Award. **Frequency:** annual. **Type:** recognition. **Recipient:** for research contribution in the development of industrial crops ● Special Recognition. **Frequency:** annual. **Type:** recognition. **Recipient:** for a person who has effectively promoted the study and/or development of industrial crops and products ● Student of the Year Award. **Frequency:** annual. **Type:** recognition. **Computer Services:** Information services, crop resources. **Committees:** Awards. **Divisions:** General Crops and Products; Meadowfoam; Medicinal and Nutriceutical Plants; Natural Rubber and Resins; Oilseeds. **Publications:** *Elsevier: Industrial Crops and Products*, bimonthly. Journal. Alternate Formats: online ● Newsletter, quarterly. Contains information on upcoming events. Alternate Formats: online. **Conventions/Meetings:** annual International Conference on Industrial Crops and Rural Development, plenary session, field trip, technical sessions and poster display (exhibits).

4111 ■ Black Farmers and Agriculturists Association (BFAA)
PO Box 61
Tillery, NC 27887
Ph: (252)826-2800 (252)826-3017
Fax: (252)826-3244
E-mail: info@bfaa-us.org
URL: http://bfaa-us.org
Contact: Gary R. Grant, Pres.
Founded: 1997. **Membership Dues:** adult, $40 (annual) ● college student, $25 (annual) ● youth, $12 (annual). **Description:** Grassroots organization united in direct response to the decline in African-American farmers and landowners. **Publications:** Newsletter ● Videos.

4112 ■ Consortium for International Crop Protection (CICP)
c/o Paul Jepson, Dir.
Oregon State Univ.
2040 Cordley Hall
Corvallis, OR 97331-2915
Ph: (541)737-3541 (541)737-9082
Fax: (541)737-3080
E-mail: jepsonp@science.oregonstate.edu
URL: http://www.ipmnet.org
Contact: Dr. Richard E. Ford, Exec. Dir.
Founded: 1978. **Members:** 14. **Membership Dues:** institution, $10,000. **National Groups:** 12. **Multinational. Description:** Advances economically efficient, and environmentally sound crop protection practices in developing countries to ensure health of rural and urban communities. **Libraries: Type:** reference. **Holdings:** 8,000; articles, books, periodicals. **Subjects:** international crop protection. **Computer Services:** database, IPM resources. **Publications:** *IPMnet News*, monthly. Newsletter. Contains a review of major information, summaries of research and success of IPM practices in various countries. **Price:** free. ISSN: 1523-7893. **Circulation:** 5,000. Alternate Formats: online. **Conventions/Meetings:** conference ● workshop.

4113 ■ National Urban Agriculture Council (NUAC)
1015 18th St. NW, No. 600
Washington, DC 20036
Ph: (202)429-4344
Fax: (202)429-4342
E-mail: rogerwaters@nuac.org
URL: http://www.nuac.org
Contact: Roger Waters, Pres.
Membership Dues: platinum, $10,000 (annual) ● gold, $5,000 (annual) ● silver, $1,500 (annual) ● bronze, $500 (annual). **Description:** Advocates for effective water management. Provide products, services and research on recycled water and water conservation. **Libraries: Type:** reference. **Holdings:** papers. **Publications:** *Pipeline*, quarterly. Newsletter. Alternate Formats: online.

4114 ■ North American Farm Show Council (NAFSC)
c/o R. Craig Fendrick, Exec. Coor.
11240 Beacom Rd.
Sunbury, OH 43074
Ph: (740)524-0658
Fax: (740)524-0658
E-mail: fendrick.1@osu.edu
URL: http://www.ag.ohio-state.edu/~farmshow
Contact: R. Craig Fendrick, Exec. Coor.
Founded: 1972. **Members:** 29. **Membership Dues:** associate, $100 (annual) ● regular, $700 (annual). **Description:** Annual farm shows. Represents members' and exhibitors' interests. **Publications:** *NAFSC Directory*, biennial. Brochure. Includes a membership directory and a calendar. Alternate Formats: online. **Conventions/Meetings:** annual conference - held in May.

4115 ■ Sustainable Harvest International (SHI)
779 N Bend Rd.
Surry, ME 04684
Ph: (207)669-8254
Free: (866)683-6594

Fax: (207)669-8255
URL: http://www.sustainableharvest.org
Contact: Florence Reed, Founder/Exec. Dir.
Founded: 1997. **Languages:** English, Spanish. **Multinational.** **Description:** Works for environmental, economic and social sustainability. Facilitates implementation of a program that allows poor farmers to take responsibility for reversing environmental degradation and achieving economic viability within their own countries. Addresses the tropical deforestation crisis in Central America by providing farmers with sustainable alternatives to slash-and-burn agriculture. **Computer Services:** Mailing lists. **Programs:** International; Small World. **Publications:** *La Cosecha*, semiannual. Newsletter. Alternate Formats: online ● Annual Reports.

4116 ■ USA Dry Pea and Lentil Council (USADPLC)
2780 W Pullman Rd.
Moscow, ID 83843-4024
Ph: (208)882-3023
Fax: (208)882-6406
E-mail: pulse@pea-lentil.com
URL: http://www.pea-lentil.com
Contact: Tim D. McGreevy, Exec. Dir.
Founded: 1965. **Membership Dues:** Western Pea and Lentil Growers Association, $50 (annual) ● associate, $150 (annual) ● SM/MD exporter, $375 (annual) ● LG exporter, associate international, $650 (annual) ● warehouse, broker, $325 (annual) ● retired, $25 (annual). **Staff:** 7. **Multinational.** **Description:** Growers, processors and exporters. Supports research, guarantees quality of chickpeas worldwide with a target audience of importers, manufacturers, food service and consumers. **Libraries: Type:** lending; open to the public; reference. **Holdings:** 100; archival material, articles, books, papers, periodicals, reports. **Subjects:** marketing, research, statistics, recipes, chemicals, history. **Awards:** USPLTA - Annual Golf Tournament. **Frequency:** annual. **Type:** trophy ● USPLTA - Carol Hahner Award. **Frequency:** annual. **Type:** recognition ● USPLTA - Honorary Life Membership Award. **Frequency:** annual. **Type:** recognition ● USPLTA - Special Recognition Award. **Frequency:** annual. **Type:** recognition ● WPLGA - John Carter Memorial Golf Tournament. **Frequency:** annual. **Type:** trophy ● WPLGA - Lentil Family of the Year. **Frequency:** annual. **Type:** recognition ● WPLGA - Special Recognition Award. **Frequency:** annual. **Type:** recognition. **Computer Services:** database ● electronic publishing ● mailing lists. **Boards:** U.S. Pea and Lentil Trade Association; Western Pea Lentil Growers Association. **Commissions:** Idaho Dry Pea and Lentil; Washington Dry Pea and Lentil. **Publications:** *Guidelines for the Manufacture of Canned and Frozen Peas*. Booklet ● *Pulse Pipeline*, biweekly. Newsletter. **Price:** $50.00 /year for members. **Circulation:** 800. **Advertising:** accepted. Alternate Formats: online ● *USA Dry Peas, Lentils and Chickpeas: Simple Foods for a Healthy Lifestyle* (in English and Spanish), annual. Brochures. **Price:** free for 1st 100. **Conventions/Meetings:** annual convention (exhibits).

4117 ■ Wallace Genetic Foundation
4910 Massachusetts Ave. NW, Ste.221
Washington, DC 20016
Ph: (202)966-2932
Fax: (202)966-3370
E-mail: wgfdn@aol.com
URL: http://www.wallacegenetic.org
Contact: Jean Douglas, Pres.
Founded: 1959. **Description:** Works to support agricultural research, preservation of farmland, ecology, conservation, and sustainable development. **Awards: Type:** grant.

4118 ■ Western United States Agricultural Trade Association (WUSATA)
4601 NE 77th Ave., Ste.120
Vancouver, WA 98662-4730
Ph: (360)693-3373
Fax: (360)693-3464
E-mail: andy@wusata.org
URL: http://www.wusata.org
Contact: Andy Anderson, Exec. Dir.
Founded: 1980. **Members:** 2,500. **Staff:** 9. **State Groups:** 13. **Description:** Provides integrated marketing services to help Western United States' agribusinesses develop and expand export sales, activities include trade missions, in-store promotions, market research, and menu promotions. Offers the Distributor Development Service, in-country, cost-effective marketing expertise in Japan, Singapore, Thailand, Malaysia, Indonesia, and Mexico. **Libraries: Type:** reference. **Subjects:** agriculture, international export. **Publications:** *Western Agri-Export Quarterly*. Newsletter. Contains current, informative information. **Price:** free. **Circulation:** 3,200.

Agroforestry

4119 ■ Association for Temperate Agroforestry (AFTA)
203 ABNR Bldg.
Univ. of Missouri
Columbia, MO 65211
Ph: (573)884-3216
Fax: (573)882-1977
E-mail: afta@aftaweb.org
URL: http://www.aftaweb.org
Contact: James P. Lassoie, Pres.
Founded: 1991. **Membership Dues:** regular, $20 (annual) ● student, $10 (annual) ● sustaining, $50 (annual) ● life, $300. **Description:** Promotes the wider adoption of agroforestry by landowners in temperate regions of North America. Conducts activities like networking, information exchange, public education and policy development. Serves as an information resource for natural resource educators, researchers, policy makers and land managers. Facilitates the exchange of scientific and practical information about temperate agroforestry. **Publications:** *Agroforestry Newsline*, monthly. Newsletter. Contains news of developments related to agroforestry. Alternate Formats: online ● *The Temperate Agroforester*, quarterly. Newsletter. Contains in-depth articles on agroforestry research, education and practice. **Price:** $40.00 /year for institutions, corporate; $20.00 /year for libraries, nonprofit organizations and public agencies. Alternate Formats: online ● Reports. Alternate Formats: online.

Animal Breeding

4120 ■ Alpaca Owners and Breeders Association
5000 Linbar Dr., Ste.297
Nashville, TN 37211
Ph: (615)834-4195
Free: (800)213-9522
Fax: (615)834-4196
E-mail: info@aobamail.com
URL: http://www.alpacainfo.com
Contact: Andrea Waugh, Event Mgr.
Membership Dues: associate, $75 (annual) ● farm, $125 (annual). **Description:** Promotes appreciation of the Alpaca breed and industry.

4121 ■ Alpines International (AI)
c/o Tina Antes, Sec.-Treas.
7195 City Rd. 315
Silt, CO 81652
Ph: (970)876-2738 (209)632-3764
E-mail: mammkey@sopris.net
URL: http://www.alpinesinternationalclub.com
Contact: Sheila Nixon, Pres.
Founded: 1958. **Members:** 175. **Membership Dues:** individual, $15 (annual). **Multinational.** **Description:** Owners and breeders of French Alpine and American Alpine Dairy goats, breeds noted for their vitality, stylishness, hardiness, heavy production, long lactation period, high butterfat, and good dairy conformation. Promotes the French Alpine and American Alpine breeds; fosters communication among club members. **Awards:** Steven Schack Memorial Youth Award. **Frequency:** annual. **Type:** recognition. **Recipient:** to the Premier Alpine Youth Exhibitor. **Programs:** All-American; Futurity; Performance; Specialty Shows. **Publications:** *Alpines International Newsletter*, quarterly. **Conventions/Meetings:** competition ● annual meeting.

4122 ■ American Angora Goat Breeder's Association (AAGBA)
PO Box 195
Rocksprings, TX 78880
Ph: (830)683-4483
URL: http://www.aagba.org
Contact: J.W. Adams, Contact
Founded: 1900. **Members:** 2,064. **Staff:** 1. **Description:** Owners and breeders of Angora goats. Maintains registry for purebred Angora goats showing ownership, transfers, and pedigrees. **Libraries: Type:** open to the public. **Holdings:** photographs. **Conventions/Meetings:** annual meeting - always October in Rocksprings, TX.

4123 ■ American Beefalo World Registry (ABWR)
10892 Yakima Valley Hwy.
Zillah, WA 98953
Free: (866)374-2297
Fax: (866)374-2297
E-mail: ideranch@embarqmail.com
URL: http://www.abwr.org
Contact: Buzz Ide, Sec.
Founded: 1983. **Members:** 150. **Membership Dues:** regular, $50 (annual) ● associate, $30 (annual) ● junior, $20 (annual). **Staff:** 1. **Regional Groups:** 6. **Description:** Breeders of beefalo (a cross between American bison and domestic cattle) in Europe and North, Central, and South America. Promotes the advantages of beefalo over domestic cattle. Disseminates information on bison genetic traits that result in lower maintenance costs for the breeder, including the beefalo's increased adaptability to climatic changes, greater foraging ability, calving ease, longer productive life span, and meat that is higher in protein and lower in fat and cholesterol. Assists in the analysis of beefalo meat in order to develop an accurate blood typing procedure for bison percentage cattle. Has developed full-blood and purebred strains of beefalo and maintains breed registry and herd books for 5 types of registration. Coordinates markets for beefalo meat. Conducts research and specialized education programs; compiles statistics. **Committees:** Bull and Sanctioned Sale Inspection; Promotion; Research. **Absorbed:** Bison Hybrid International Association. **Formed by Merger of:** International Beefalo Breeders Registry; American Beefalo Association; World Beefalo Association. **Publications:** *The ABWR Newsletter*, bimonthly. **Price:** $10.00/year; $18.00/year outside U.S. **Advertising:** accepted. **Conventions/Meetings:** semiannual show (exhibits).

4124 ■ American Cavy Breeders Association (ACBA)
c/o James D. Nielsen, Sec.-Treas.
1157 E San Angelo Ave.
Gilbert, AZ 85234
Ph: (480)545-1785 (765)453-9264
E-mail: acbasec-treas@nghs.net
URL: http://www.acbaonline.com
Contact: Jim Hupp, Pres.
Founded: 1943. **Members:** 1,200. **Membership Dues:** adult, $25 (annual) ● family, $30 (annual) ● youth, $20 (annual). **Regional Groups:** 25. **State Groups:** 50. **Description:** Promotes cavies (guinea pigs) and cavy breeding. Sponsors youth club. **Libraries: Type:** reference. **Holdings:** articles, photographs. **Awards:** Hall of Fame. **Frequency:** annual. **Type:** recognition ● Master Breeder. **Type:** recognition. **Computer Services:** Mailing lists. **Committees:** Advertising; Awards/Specials; Ballots; Constitution; Genetics Consultant; Guidebook; Hall of Fame; Master Breeder; Membership Services; Parliamentarian; Publicity; Specialty Show; Standards; Sweepstakes Records; Youth. **Affiliated With:** American Rabbit Breeders Association. **Publications:** *The Cavy Fancy*. Pamphlet ● *Guide Book*. **Advertising:**

accepted ● *Journal of the American Cavy Breeders Association*, quarterly. Newsletter. Contains informative articles, show listings, and reports. **Price:** included in membership dues. **Advertising:** accepted ● *Your Pet Cavy*. Pamphlet ● Articles. Alternate Formats: online. **Conventions/Meetings:** semiannual conference (exhibits) ● semiannual convention (exhibits).

4125 ■ American Council of Spotted Asses (ACOSA)
c/o Coreen Eaton, Sec.-Treas.
914 Riske Ln.
Wentzville, MO 63385
Ph: (636)828-5955 (563)735-5533
Fax: (636)828-5431
E-mail: acosa_main@spottedass.com
URL: http://www.spottedass.com
Contact: Bob Norton, Pres.

Founded: 1969. **Members:** 340. **Membership Dues:** life, $100 ● individual, $10 (annual). **Staff:** 2. **Description:** Owners of spotted asses (donkeys or burros) and interested individuals united to promote the breed. (Spotted asses are an endangered species of donkey; there are less than 1800 registered in the world.) Maintains registry and stud book. Conducts charitable programs. **Libraries: Type:** reference. **Holdings:** photographs. **Awards:** National Championships. **Frequency:** annual. **Type:** trophy. **Computer Services:** database, breeders listing. **Telecommunication Services:** electronic mail, acosa_president@spottedass.com. **Publications:** *Spotlight*, quarterly. Magazine. Contains up-to-date breeder listings, classified ads, educational and historical articles. **Price:** included in membership dues. **Circulation:** 350. **Advertising:** accepted. **Conventions/Meetings:** annual show - usually October.

4126 ■ American Dairy Goat Association (ADGA)
PO Box 865
209 W Main St.
Spindale, NC 28160
Ph: (828)286-3801 (740)969-4905
Fax: (828)287-0476
E-mail: info@adga.org
URL: http://www.adga.org
Contact: Shirley C. McKenzie, Mgr.

Founded: 1904. **Members:** 13,000. **Membership Dues:** junior, $10 (annual) ● regular, $35 (annual). **Staff:** 12. **Budget:** $1,000,000. **Description:** Breeders, owners, and dairymen interested in French Alpine, Nubian, Saanen, Toggenburg, LaMancha, and Oberhasli dairy goats. Maintains registry for purebred dairy goats, showing ownership, transfers, and pedigree records. Maintains open herdbooks for experimental animals. Sanctions official shows and conducts training conferences for judges. Offers herd improvement testing program for milk production and linear appraisal; sponsors one-day milking competitions. **Awards:** ADGA/Dean Family Scholarships. **Frequency:** annual. **Type:** scholarship. **Recipient:** for ADGA members ● Award of Merit. **Frequency:** annual. **Type:** recognition. **Recipient:** for ADGA members ● Friend of ADGA. **Frequency:** annual. **Type:** recognition. **Recipient:** for individuals or organization who rendered special service to ADGA ● Helen C. Hunt Distinguished Service Award. **Frequency:** annual. **Type:** recognition. **Recipient:** for ADGA members ● Mary L. Farley Award. **Type:** recognition. **Recipient:** for ADGA members. **Publications:** *ADGA News & Events*, quarterly. Newsletter. **Circulation:** 10,000 ● *Own A Dairy Goat*. Booklet ● Membership Directory, annual. **Price:** $2.00. **Conventions/Meetings:** annual meeting and convention (exhibits).

4127 ■ American Donkey and Mule Society (ADMS)
PO Box 1210
Lewisville, TX 75067
Ph: (972)219-0781
Fax: (972)420-9980
E-mail: lovelongears@hotmail.com
URL: http://www.lovelongears.com
Contact: Leah Patton, Office Mgr.

Founded: 1967. **Members:** 5,000. **Membership Dues:** individual, family in U.S., $23 (annual) ● individual, family in Canada, $30 (annual) ● overseas, $35 (annual). **Staff:** 4. **Budget:** $75,000. **Regional Groups:** 35. **Description:** Represents individuals and local organizations working to protect and promote the donkey and the mule and to provide services for their owners and clubs, disseminate information, and coordinate international activities. Maintains American Mule and Donkey Register (stud book) and national show standards; certifies inspector-judges and conducts teaching clinics for them. Operates museum, and Hee Haw Book Service (mail order book service). Maintains Miniature Donkey Registry of the United States and hall of fame. **Libraries: Type:** reference. **Holdings:** 1,000; articles, books, periodicals. **Subjects:** donkeys, mules, horses. **Awards:** Versatility Hall of Fame. **Type:** recognition. **Recipient:** for the accomplishments of donkeys and mules in open shows and events, and the achievements of offspring of outstanding sires and dams. **Computer Services:** database, breeders. **Telecommunication Services:** electronic mail, adms@juno.com. **Publications:** *Brayer*, bimonthly. Magazine. Contains articles on training, care, feeding, and human interest. **Price:** included in membership dues; $3.00 back issues as sample copies. **Circulation:** 5,000. **Advertising:** accepted. Alternate Formats: CD-ROM; online ● *Hee Haw Book Service Catalog*. Contains list of titles available through ADMS. **Price:** free. **Conventions/Meetings:** annual National Show - competition ● periodic show.

4128 ■ American Goat Society (AGS)
c/o Amy Kowalik, Office Mgr.
735 Oakridge Ln.
Pipe Creek, TX 78063
Ph: (830)535-4247 (817)270-4883
Fax: (830)535-4561
E-mail: agsoffice@earthlink.net
URL: http://www.americangoatsociety.com
Contact: Amy Kowalik, Office Mgr.

Founded: 1936. **Members:** 650. **Membership Dues:** life, $150 ● individual, $20 (annual) ● junior, $10 (annual) ● senior, $15 (annual) ● family, $30 (annual). **Staff:** 1. **Description:** Breeders, dairymen, owners, and exhibitors of dairy goats and their products, together with research and promotion field personnel. Maintains dairy goat registry. Sanctions show and fair exhibition program which leads to master championships of record. **Awards:** American Goat Society. **Frequency:** annual. **Type:** scholarship. **Recipient:** for AGS members who have an interest in agriculture ● Championship Certificate. **Type:** recognition. **Recipient:** for qualifying animals ● Milk Production Awards. **Frequency:** annual. **Type:** recognition. **Recipient:** for animals that completed the minimum production requirements ● Mrs. J.C. Lincoln Awards. **Frequency:** annual. **Type:** monetary. **Recipient:** for three goats that produce the highest amount of milk in 305 days or less during the year. **Telecommunication Services:** electronic mail, texasflatrock@earthlink.net. **Committees:** Conformation Classification; DHI; Exhibition Promotion and Judge Education; Official Milk and Butterfat Production Testing. **Publications:** *ABC's of Milk Testing*. Brochure. Alternate Formats: online ● *Beginners Guide to Dairy Goats*. Brochure. Alternate Formats: online ● *Introduction to the American Goat Society*. Brochure. **Advertising:** accepted. Alternate Formats: online ● *Judges Training Manual*. **Price:** $10.00 ● *Roster*, annual. Membership Directory ● *Showmanship Guide*. Brochure. Alternate Formats: online ● *2004 Members Handbook*. Alternate Formats: online ● *The Voice of AGS*, quarterly. Newsletter. Alternate Formats: online. Also Cited As: *News Dispatch—The Voice of AGS*. **Conventions/Meetings:** annual conference (exhibits).

4129 ■ American Legend (AL)
c/o Motorcycle Trailers Inc.
903 S Praireview Rd.
Mahomet, IL 61853
Ph: (217)586-2201
Free: (888)463-1917
Fax: (217)586-4830
E-mail: bob@legendaryinnovations.com
URL: http://www.american-legend.com
Contact: Anthony Parkhill, Owner

Founded: 1985. **Members:** 1,200. **Budget:** $1,200,000. **Description:** Breeders of ranch minks. Supervises sorting, matching, and grading of pelts; establishes color trademarks; promotes furs meeting its standards under the EMBA and BLACKGLAMA brands. **Libraries: Type:** open to the public. **Holdings:** photographs. **Formed by Merger of:** Great Lakes Mink Association; Emba Mink Breeders Association. **Publications:** Newsletter, monthly. **Conventions/Meetings:** annual meeting (exhibits) - always August.

4130 ■ American Mammoth Jackstock Registry (AMJR)
PO Box 1723
Johnson City, TX 78636
Ph: (830)868-2357
Fax: (830)868-2357
E-mail: register@amjr.us
URL: http://www.amjr.us
Contact: Linda Coffman, Owner

Founded: 1888. **Staff:** 4. **Description:** Maintains an office for registration and ownership transfer of jack (male) and jennet (female) Mammoth asses. Provides specific information on Mammoth Jack stock; conducts pedigree research; compiles statistics. **Libraries: Type:** open to the public. **Holdings:** archival material. **Telecommunication Services:** electronic mail, linda@jackstock.us. **Formerly:** (1989) Standard Jack and Jennet Registry of America; (1991) American Mammoth Jack Stock Registry. **Publications:** *Greatest Jack Stock Importations 1885 to 1889*, quarterly. Newsletter. **Price:** $25.00. **Advertising:** accepted. Alternate Formats: CD-ROM; online.

4131 ■ American Mule Association (AMA)
PO Box 1349
Yerington, NV 89447
Ph: (775)463-1922 (760)378-2222
E-mail: masmules@aol.com
URL: http://www.americanmuleassociation.com
Contact: Marsha Arthur, Sec.

Founded: 1976. **Members:** 450. **Membership Dues:** voting, $20 (annual) ● family, $35 (annual) ● junior, $12 (annual) ● life, $250. **Staff:** 16. **Description:** Individuals interested in breeding, racing, showing, and raising mules. Encourages the development of public interest in mules through the promotion and sponsorship of public mule contests. Maintains a registry of mules and issues certificates to individual mules, jacks, jennets, and hinnies; seeks to educate the public regarding the history, breeding, and raising of mules. Plans to: establish an association for the prevention of cruelty to mules and other animals; encourage the scientific development and scientific breeding of finer mules; provide for community recreation through the sponsorship of contests, races, and exhibitions of mules. Establishes rules for mule contests, races, and exhibitions, and standardizes election and equipment of judges, directors, and spokespersons for such functions. **Awards:** All Around Mule. **Frequency:** annual. **Type:** recognition. **Recipient:** to high point earner ● Division Champions. **Frequency:** annual. **Type:** recognition. **Recipient:** to high point for specific division ● Long Ears Versatility Award. **Frequency:** annual. **Type:** recognition. **Recipient:** for excellent donkey/mule and rider partnership ● Saddle Sore Award. **Frequency:** annual. **Type:** recognition. **Recipient:** to the donkey and rider with the longest miles ridden and driven. **Telecommunication Services:** electronic mail, buckaroomac@msn.com ● electronic mail, jporter@lightspeed.net. **Committees:** Packing and Driving; Performance; Racing. **Publications:** *Mules Newsletter*, monthly. Features shows results, association news and events. **Price:** included in membership dues; $13.50 /year for nonmembers. **Advertising:** accepted ● Handbook. **Conventions/Meetings:** semiannual board meeting.

4132 ■ American Ostrich Association (AOA)
PO Box 166
Ranger, TX 76470
E-mail: aoa@ostriches.org
URL: http://www.ostriches.org
Contact: Carole A. Price DVM, Pres.
Founded: 1987. **Members:** 100. **Membership Dues:** domestic, $150 (annual) ● international, $200 (annual). **Budget:** $25,000. **Description:** Supports the American Ostrich Industry through: government and legislative action; promotion of ostrich and ostrich products; information and referral services for breeders and allied businesses; and scientific research conducted in partnership with the American Ostrich Research Foundation. **Publications:** Newsletters, quarterly. Provides current information and events regarding the ostrich industry. **Price:** included in membership dues. Alternate Formats: online. **Conventions/Meetings:** annual Ostrichfest - convention (exhibits).

4133 ■ Cotswold Breeders Association (CBA)
PO Box 441
Manchester, MD 21102
E-mail: heritage.genetics@vallnet.com
URL: http://www.cotswoldbreedersassociation.org
Contact: Kim Caulfield, Pres.
Founded: 1996. **Members:** 90. **Membership Dues:** regular, $20 (annual) ● associate, $10 (annual) ● junior (under 18), $5 (annual). **Regional Groups:** 4. **Description:** Preserves and promotes the breed. Provides registration for all purebred Cotswolds, information, and support for mutual benefit of all members and breeders. Sponsors competitions and educational programs. **Libraries: Type:** not open to the public. **Subjects:** Cotswold sheep. **Awards:** Junior Breeder of the Year. **Frequency:** annual. **Type:** recognition. **Computer Services:** Mailing lists, sheep registration member list. **Publications:** *Cotswold Connection*, quarterly. Newsletter. **Circulation:** 100. **Advertising:** accepted. **Conventions/Meetings:** annual meeting.

4134 ■ Empress Chinchilla Breeders Cooperative (ECBC)
PO Box 318
Sixes, OR 97476
Ph: (541)332-3222 (479)754-5764
Fax: (541)332-4704
E-mail: empressc@harborside.com
URL: http://personal.kitusa.com/empressc
Contact: Dick Bradford, Pres.
Founded: 1965. **Members:** 200. **Membership Dues:** progressive, $45 (annual) ● associate, $15 (annual) ● 4H/FFA, $25 (annual). **Staff:** 1. **Regional Groups:** 3. **State Groups:** 13. **Description:** Breeders of chinchillas for fur. Conducts research; supervises live animal and pelt shows. **Telecommunication Services:** electronic mail, ladymj@centurytel.net. **Publications:** *Empress Chinchilla Breeder Magazine*, monthly. **Price:** $50.00. ISSN: 0094-3282. **Advertising:** accepted. **Conventions/Meetings:** annual meeting.

4135 ■ International Nubian Breeders Association (INBA)
c/o Caroline Lawson, Sec.-Treas.
5124 FM 1940
Franklin, TX 77856
Ph: (845)744-6089 (979)828-4158
E-mail: president@i-n-b-a.org
URL: http://www.i-n-b-a.org
Contact: Lynn Fleming, Pres.
Members: 500. **Membership Dues:** individual, $10 (annual) ● family, $20 (annual) ● youth, $5 (annual). **Multinational. Description:** Promotes, preserves and improves the Nubian dairy goat breed. **Libraries: Type:** reference. **Holdings:** archival material. **Subjects:** dairy goats. **Awards:** All-American Award. **Frequency:** annual. **Type:** recognition. **Recipient:** for excellence in production and type ● Breeder of Excellence Award. **Frequency:** annual. **Type:** recognition. **Recipient:** to a breeder who has made a significant contribution to the Nubian breed as a whole. **Computer Services:** Information services, Nubian breed resources ● mailing lists. **Telecommunication Services:** electronic mail, webmaster@i-n-b-a.org. **Committees:** All American; Breed Standards; Breeder of Excellence; Elections; Fundraising; Merit and Awards; Publicity/Membership; Specialty Shows. **Formerly:** National Nubian Club. **Publications:** *Nubian Newsletter*, quarterly. **Price:** included in membership dues. **Advertising:** accepted. **Conventions/Meetings:** annual conference ● specialty show.

4136 ■ Llama Association of North America (LANA)
1800 S Obenchain Rd.
Eagle Point, OR 97524
Ph: (541)830-5262 (541)826-6115
Fax: (541)830-5262
E-mail: llamainfo@aol.com
URL: http://www.llamainfo.org
Contact: Cathy Spalding, Pres.
Founded: 1981. **Members:** 560. **Membership Dues:** owner, $40 (annual) ● breeder, $60 (annual) ● youth, $15 (annual) ● youth club, $30 (annual). **Staff:** 1. **Description:** Llama and alpaca owners and breeders; interested others. Sponsors educational events, research and youth programs related to the care of llamas. **Libraries: Type:** not open to the public. **Holdings:** 36; articles, books, periodicals, video recordings. **Subjects:** young and alpaca care, training, showing. **Awards:** LANA Youth Project Award. **Frequency:** annual. **Type:** scholarship. **Recipient:** for project detailing llama related activities submitted by a youth. **Publications:** *Breeder's List*, annual. Directory. **Price:** free ● *LANA News*, quarterly. Newsletter. Helps the members keep in touch with what is going on in LANA and the Llama community. ● Membership Directory, annual. Provides a listing of referral services in addition to member information. ● Also publishes youth program material. **Conventions/Meetings:** annual conference, includes llama show (exhibits).

4137 ■ Miniature Donkey Registry (MDR)
c/o American Donkey and Mule Society
PO Box 1210
Lewisville, TX 75067
Ph: (972)219-0781
Fax: (972)420-9980
E-mail: adms@juno.com
URL: http://www.lovelongears.com
Contact: Leah Patton, ADMS Office Mgr.
Founded: 1958. **Members:** 5,000. **Membership Dues:** regular in U.S., $20 (annual) ● regular in Canada, $27 (annual) ● regular outside U.S. and Canada, $30 (annual). **Staff:** 4. **Description:** Maintained by the American Donkey and Mule Society. Studbook for owners of registered miniature donkeys. (Miniature donkeys measure no more than 36 inches high at the withers, range in color from mouse gray to reddish brown to black, and have a dark stripe that runs down the back and across the shoulders to form a cross.) Assists purchasers in locating breeders in their vicinity; provides information about the breed to the public. Compiles statistics; maintains miniature donkey registry (stud book); issues registration certificates. **Convention/Meeting:** none. **Libraries: Type:** reference. **Holdings:** 1,000; articles, books, periodicals, photographs. **Subjects:** donkeys, mules. **Computer Services:** Mailing lists, user services. **Additional Websites:** http://www.geocities.com/regminidonks/geninfo.html. **Affiliated With:** American Donkey and Mule Society. **Formerly:** Miniature Donkey Registry of the United States. **Publications:** *The Brayer*, bimonthly. Magazine. **Price:** included in membership dues. **Circulation:** 5,000. **Advertising:** accepted. Alternate Formats: CD-ROM; magnetic tape; online ● *The Hee-Haw Book Service*. Catalog. Alternate Formats: online ● *Membership Handbook*.

4138 ■ Mohair Council of America (MCA)
233 W Twohig Ave.
PO Box 5337
San Angelo, TX 76903
Ph: (325)655-3161
Free: (800)583-3161
E-mail: mohair@mohairusa.com
URL: http://www.mohairusa.com
Contact: Zane Willard, Exec. Dir.
Founded: 1966. **Staff:** 3. **Description:** Mohair growers throughout the U.S. Promotes the use of mohair. Conducts cooperative advertising and promotion with mills, manufacturers, and retailers. Sponsors competitions; compiles statistics. **Awards: Type:** recognition. **Affiliated With:** Texas Sheep and Goat Raisers Association. **Publications:** *Cape Sale Report*. Alternate Formats: online. **Conventions/Meetings:** semiannual board meeting ● annual meeting, for members.

4139 ■ National Bison Association (NBA)
8690 Wolff Ct., No. 200
Westminster, CO 80031
Ph: (303)292-2833
Fax: (303)659-3739
E-mail: david@bisoncentral.com
URL: http://www.bisoncentral.com
Contact: Dave Carter, Exec. Dir.
Founded: 1995. **Members:** 2,400. **Membership Dues:** active, $200 (annual) ● allied, $250 (annual) ● affiliate, $75 (annual) ● life, $3,000. **Staff:** 4. **Budget:** $600,000. **Regional Groups:** 15. **State Groups:** 20. **Description:** Buffalo ranchers and individuals interested in the preservation, production, and marketing of bison. Holds annual consignment auction; bison promotional projects; bison registration system based on blood analysis. Conducts Gold Trophy Show and Sale. **Libraries: Type:** open to the public. **Holdings:** 25; articles, books, periodicals. **Subjects:** bison history, management techniques, public herd information. **Awards:** Gold Trophy Awards. **Frequency:** annual. **Type:** recognition. **Recipient:** for best animals. **Committees:** Animal REG-NABR; Legislation; Marketing/Promotion; National Western Stock Show; Science, Research & Animal Health. **Subgroups:** Dr. Ken Throlson American Bison Foundation. **Formerly:** (1987) American Buffalo Association; (1994) National Buffalo Association; (1994) American Bison Association. **Publications:** *American Bison*. Booklet ● *Bison, Bison; Why Bison?*. Brochures ● *Bison Breeders Handbook* ● *Bison Connection*, weekly. Newsletter. Provides timely bison sale, auction data and classified ads from members. ● *Bison World*, quarterly. Magazine. **Price:** $75.00/year in U.S.; $80.00/year in Canada. **Advertising:** accepted. **Conventions/Meetings:** annual conference and seminar (exhibits) - always 3rd week in January and August.

4140 ■ National Committee on Pot Bellied Pigs (NCOPP)
Address Unknown since 2007
Membership Dues: household, $25 (annual) ● household, $45 (biennial) ● household life, $300. **Description:** Promotes the potbellied pig breed; provides a registry service for potbellied pigs. **Awards:** Diamond Trophy Awards. **Type:** recognition. **Recipient:** for earning four legs or having two Permanent Champion offspring ● High Point Herd Award. **Type:** recognition. **Recipient:** for highest amount of points from exhibition at NCOPP show for calendar year ● NCOPP Keith Connell Memorial Award. **Type:** recognition. **Recipient:** for outstanding service to the potbellied pig industry ● NCOPP Service Award. **Type:** recognition. **Recipient:** for outstanding service to NCOPP ● Storman Norman Perpetual Supreme Champion Award. **Frequency:** annual. **Type:** recognition. **Recipient:** to the two Supreme Champions ● Versatility Permanent Champion. **Type:** recognition. **Publications:** Newsletter, monthly. Contains network news. **Price:** included in membership dues; $15.00 for nonmembers. **Conventions/Meetings:** annual World Championship Show - specialty show, with awards.

4141 ■ National Pedigreed Livestock Council (NPLC)
c/o Zane Akins, Sec.-Treas.
177 Palermo Pl.
The Villages, FL 32159
Ph: (352)259-6005
Fax: (352)259-6005

E-mail: zane@thevillages.net
URL: http://www.nplc.net
Contact: Zane Akins, Sec.-Treas.
Founded: 1911. **Members:** 55. **Membership Dues:** voting, $175 (annual) ● associate, $100 (annual). **Staff:** 1. **Budget:** $25,000. **Description:** Federation of breeders of beef and dairy cattle, horses, swine, sheep, goats, and ponies. Registers pedigrees of animals, maintain records of ownership, foster breed improvement, and promote respective breeds. Conducts national advertising campaigns and programs of herd improvement; emphasizes youth involvement. **Awards:** Distinguished Service Award. **Frequency:** annual. **Type:** recognition. **Recipient:** for distinguished service. **Formerly:** (1985) National Society of Live Stock Record Associations. **Publications:** *National Pedigreed Livestock Council Annual Report, Directory and Career Opportunities*, annual. **Circulation:** 15,000. **Advertising:** accepted ● Membership Directory, annual. Contains information about NPLC, pedigreed livestock industry and career opportunities. **Price:** included in membership dues. **Conventions/Meetings:** annual conference - always the second week of May.

4142 ■ National Pygmy Goat Association (NPGA)

1932 149th Ave. SE
Snohomish, WA 98290
Ph: (425)334-6506 (530)878-8775
Fax: (425)334-5447
E-mail: npgaoffice@aol.com
URL: http://www.npga-pygmy.com
Contact: Ray Hoyt, Pres.
Founded: 1975. **Members:** 1,980. **Membership Dues:** youth, $20 (annual) ● active, $25 (annual) ● family, $35 (annual) ● contributing active, $55 (annual) ● senior, $25 (annual) ● business, $35 (annual) ● charter, $125 (annual) ● patron, $500-$1,000 (annual) ● benefactor, $1,000 (annual). **Staff:** 1. **Budget:** $129,000. **Description:** Pygmy goat breeders, veterinarians, hobbyists, small livestock farmers, and medical research groups. Encourages breeding and registration of pygmy goats; facilitates registration of purebred pygmy goats; promotes the breed; gathers and disseminates information about the breed. (The pygmy goat is noted for its hardiness and good nature, its ability to provide milk, its adaptability to climates, and its suitability as a research subject.) Sanctions shows; conducts judges' training school and workshops. Sponsors competitions; compiles statistics. **Committees:** Arbitration; Breed Standard; Certification; Judge's Training; Merchandising; Show; Youth. **Publications:** *Basic Owner Manual*. **Price:** $4.00 ● *Best of Memo '88-'96*. Book. **Price:** $11.00 ● *Best of Memo '81-'87*. Book. **Price:** $11.00 ● *Best of Memo '76-'81*. Book. **Price:** $11.00 ● *Judge's Training Manual* ● *Membership Roster*, annual. Membership Directory ● *The Memo*, quarterly. Magazine. **Price:** included in membership dues; $20.00 /year for nonmembers in U.S.; $30.00 /year for nonmembers outside U.S. Alternate Formats: online ● *Pygmy Goat Memo*, bimonthly ● *Showmanship Manual*. **Price:** $10.00 ● Brochure. **Price:** $4.75. **Conventions/Meetings:** annual meeting (exhibits).

4143 ■ National Saanen Breeders Association (NSBA)

c/o Lisa Shepard, Sec.-Treas.
PO Box 315
Santa Margarita, CA 93453
Ph: (805)461-5547 (804)529-6195
E-mail: secretary-treasurer@nationalsaanenbreeders.com
URL: http://nationalsaanenbreeders.com
Contact: Jolene K. Self, Pres.
Founded: 1954. **Members:** 300. **Membership Dues:** regular, $15 (annual). **Description:** Represents individuals, firms, associations, partnerships, or corporations interested in the breeding, sale, or promotion of the Saanen dairy goat. Circulates information and cooperates with other organizations in the development and promotion of the dairy goat. **Awards: Type:** recognition. **Recipient:** for show-winning and high-producing bucks and does. **Telecommunication Services:** electronic mail, shepard@thegrid.net. **Formerly:** (1980) National Saanen Club. **Publications:** *Saanen News*, quarterly. Newsletter. **Price:** included in membership dues. **Advertising:** accepted.

4144 ■ North American Gamebird Association (NAGA)

201 N Main
Eureka, KS 67045
Ph: (620)583-8779 (570)758-6284
E-mail: bill@pheasant.com
URL: http://www.naga.org
Contact: Bill MacFarlane, Pres.
Founded: 1931. **Members:** 1,600. **Membership Dues:** regular, $65 (annual) ● business, $125 (annual) ● sponsor, $300 (annual). **Staff:** 2. **Budget:** $100,000. **Description:** Commercial gamebird breeders and operators of shooting preserves for sportsmen; researchers, educators, and administrators connected with commercial gamebird management and propagation. Promotes the quality of shooting preserves; monitors local, state, and federal legislative matters. Cooperates in research affecting the quality and economic demands of the industry. Sponsors specialized education. **Awards:** NAGA College Scholarship. **Frequency:** annual. **Type:** scholarship. **Formerly:** (1980) North American Game Breeders and Shooting Preserve Association. **Publications:** *Wildlife Harvest Magazine*, monthly. **Price:** included in membership dues. **Circulation:** 2,500. **Advertising:** accepted ● Membership Directory, annual. **Conventions/Meetings:** annual conference and convention (exhibits) ● annual convention.

4145 ■ North American Potbellied Pig Association (NAPPA)

c/o Jamie Holley, Pres.
3850 Dacy Ln.
Kyle, TX 78640
Ph: (512)295-7897
E-mail: pigpatch@yahoo.com
URL: http://www.petpigs.com
Contact: Jamie Holley, Pres.
Founded: 1989. **Membership Dues:** individual, $30 (annual) ● commercial, certified breeder, outside U.S., $50 (annual). **Multinational. Description:** Educational organization committed to protecting and preserving the potbellied pig as a pet. **Funds:** Educational; Memorial; Shelter and Sanctuary. **Publications:** *NAPPA News*, monthly. Newsletter. Features topics such as health, nutrition and behavior of the potbellied pig. **Price:** included in membership dues. **Advertising:** accepted. Alternate Formats: online ● Brochures. Covers topics such as care, training, and medical information regarding the potbellied pig breed.

4146 ■ Oberhasli Breeders of America (OBA)

c/o Elise Shope Anderson, Sec.-Treas.
1035 Bardin Rd.
Palatka, FL 32177
E-mail: president@oberhasli.net
URL: http://www.oberhasli.net
Contact: Bob Taylor, Pres.
Founded: 1976. **Members:** 60. **Membership Dues:** association, $12 (annual). **State Groups:** 47. **Description:** Persons involved in breeding Oberhasli goats. Seeks to improve the breed without changing the Oberhasli's unique characteristics. **Libraries: Type:** open to the public. **Subjects:** all phases Oberhasli, Oberhasli history and pedigrees. **Awards:** All American. **Frequency:** annual. **Type:** recognition. **Recipient:** to show winners ● Premier Youth. **Frequency:** annual. **Type:** recognition. **Recipient:** for a young person with outstanding showmanship of an Oberhasli ● Swiss Belle. **Frequency:** annual. **Type:** recognition. **Recipient:** for milk production and composition. **Telecommunication Services:** electronic mail, webmaster@oberhasli.net. **Committees:** OBA Breed Standard. **Affiliated With:** American Dairy Goat Association. **Publications:** *Breeders Directory*, annual. **Circulation:** 60. **Advertising:** accepted. Alternate Formats: online ● *Oberhasli Swiss Newsletter*, 5/year. **Price:** included in membership dues. **Conventions/Meetings:** annual meeting (exhibits) - always October.

4147 ■ PIGS - A Sanctuary

1112 Persimmon Ln.
Shepherdstown, WV 25443
Ph: (304)262-0080
E-mail: farmmanager@pigs.org
URL: http://www.pigs.org
Contact: Melissa Susko, Exec. Dir.
Founded: 1992. **Description:** Seeks to improve the quality of life for farm and domestic animals and to provide adoption and rescue service. **Computer Services:** Mailing lists. **Publications:** *P.I.G.S.*, quarterly. Newsletter. **Conventions/Meetings:** tour, educational tours to the general public - by appointment only.

4148 ■ Rocky Mountain Llama and Alpaca Association (RMLA)

c/o Robert Hance, Membership Chm.
11818 W 52nd Ave.
Wheat Ridge, CO 80033
Ph: (303)422-4681
Fax: (303)422-3568
E-mail: hancelama@att.net
URL: http://www.rmla.com
Contact: Robert Hance, Membership Chm.
Founded: 1982. **Members:** 550. **Membership Dues:** adult, $40 (annual) ● youth/young adult, $10 (annual) ● life, $500. **Budget:** $20,000. **Regional Groups:** 1. **Description:** Owners and breeders of llamas, alpacas, or guanacos; interested individuals. Disseminates information on llama health care, reproduction, packing techniques, marketing and tax data, herd management, and training. Promotes llama research, education, and ethical business practices; provides a forum for exchanging ideas and methods. **Libraries: Type:** reference. **Holdings:** 300; books, clippings, video recordings. **Subjects:** health training, fiber use. **Publications:** *Breeders and Owners Directory*, annual. **Price:** free for members. **Circulation:** 500 ● *Caring for Llamas and Alpacas*. Book. Covers all of the routine health maintenance issues concerning llamas and alpacas in an easy to understand format. **Price:** $28.95 each, plus shipping and handling ● *4-H Youth Llama Manual*. Covers nearly all aspects of Llama; care, feeding, grooming, training and husbandry for use in 4H projects. **Price:** $3.00 each ● *RMLA Brochure and Service Directory*, annual. Includes categorized list of owners. **Circulation:** 2,000. **Advertising:** accepted ● Newsletter, bimonthly. Includes feature articles, news, announcements of upcoming events, and classified ads. **Price:** included in membership dues; $10.00 /year for nonmembers. **Circulation:** 500. **Advertising:** accepted. **Conventions/Meetings:** biennial meeting and seminar (exhibits) - always fall ● seminar.

Animal Science

4149 ■ American Embryo Transfer Association (AETA)

1111 N Dunlap Ave.
Savoy, IL 61874
Ph: (217)398-2217
Fax: (217)398-4119
E-mail: aeta@assochq.org
URL: http://www.aeta.org
Contact: Dr. Ron Kling, Pres.
Founded: 1982. **Members:** 320. **Membership Dues:** regular, $150 (annual) ● associate, $125 (annual) ● full-time student, $25 (annual). **Staff:** 2. **Description:** Commercial embryo transfer companies and interested individuals. (Embryo transfer involves removing fertilized ova from the uterus of one animal and implanting them in the uterus of another.) Promotes the use of embryo transfer for the improvement of livestock. Serves as information clearinghouse on matters involving embryo transfer of cattle and other species. Seeks to expand and create markets for members. Encourages cooperation among individuals and companies dealing with embryo transfer. Provides information to government regulatory agencies for the establishment of feasible regulations. Works to create a certification procedure to ensure the accuracy of parentage and offspring records.

Provides a patent alert system to inform members of patents issued, thus avoiding possible infringement. **Committees:** Audit; Certification; Convention Exhibit; Government Liaison and Animal Health; Industry Information; Newsletter; Nominating; Publicity and Promotion. **Publications:** *Closer Look*, quarterly. Newsletter. **Advertising:** accepted. Alternate Formats: online ● *Convention Proceedings*, annual ● Books ● Brochures ● Manuals ● Membership Directory, annual. **Conventions/Meetings:** annual meeting (exhibits) - always October. 2008 Oct. 14-19, Kansas City, MO.

4150 ■ American Society of Animal Science (ASAS)
1111 N Dunlap Ave.
Savoy, IL 61874
Ph: (217)356-9050
Fax: (217)398-4119
E-mail: asas@assochq.org
URL: http://www.asas.org
Contact: Meghan Wulster-Radcliffe PhD, Exec. Dir.

Founded: 1908. **Members:** 4,588. **Membership Dues:** student (graduate/undergraduate), $20 (annual) ● professional, $110 (annual) ● individual sustaining, $350 (annual) ● postdoctoral fellow, $55 (annual) ● corporate sustaining, $1,000 (annual). **Staff:** 4. **Budget:** $1,400,000. **Regional Groups:** 4. **Description:** Professional organization for animal scientist designed to help members provide effective leadership through research, extension, teaching, and service for the animal industries. **Awards:** American Feed Industry Association Award in Nonruminant Nutrition Research. **Frequency:** annual. **Type:** recognition. **Recipient:** for members of the society except officers, members of the Board of Directors and Awards committee ● American Feed Industry Association Award in Ruminant Nutrition Research. **Frequency:** annual. **Type:** recognition. **Recipient:** for members of the society except officers, members of the Board of Directors and Awards Committee ● Animal Growth and Development Award. **Frequency:** annual. **Type:** recognition. **Recipient:** for members of the society except officers, members of the Board of Directors and Awards committee ● Animal Industry Service Award. **Frequency:** annual. **Type:** recognition. **Recipient:** for members of the society except officers, members of the Board of Directors and Awards committee ● Animal Management Award. **Frequency:** annual. **Type:** recognition. **Recipient:** for members of the society except officers, members of the Board of Directors and Awards committee ● Animal Physiology and Endocrinology Award. **Frequency:** annual. **Type:** recognition. **Recipient:** for members of the society except officers, members of the Board of Directors and Awards committee ● Boutfault International Animal Agriculture Award. **Frequency:** annual. **Type:** recognition. **Recipient:** for members of the society except officers, members of the Board of Directors and Awards committee ● Corbin Companion Animal Biology Award. **Frequency:** annual. **Type:** recognition. **Recipient:** for members of the society except officers, members of the Board of Directors and Awards committee ● Distinguished Teacher Award. **Frequency:** annual. **Type:** recognition. **Recipient:** for members of the society except officers, members of the Board of Directors and Awards committee ● Extension Award. **Frequency:** annual. **Type:** recognition. **Recipient:** for members of the society except officers, members of the Board of Directors and Awards committee ● Fellow Award. **Frequency:** annual. **Type:** recognition. **Recipient:** for members of the society except officers, members of the Board of Directors and Awards committee ● L.E Casida Award. **Frequency:** annual. **Type:** recognition. **Recipient:** for members of the society except officers, members of the Board of Directors and Awards committee ● Meats Research Award. **Frequency:** annual. **Type:** recognition. **Recipient:** for members of the society except officers, members of the Board of Directors and Awards committee ● The Morrison Award. **Frequency:** annual. **Type:** recognition. **Recipient:** for members of the society except officers, members of the Board of Directors and Awards committee ● Omega Protein Innovative Research Award. **Frequency:** annual. **Type:** recognition. **Recipient:** for members of the society except officers, members of the Board of Directors and Awards committee ● The Rockefeller Prentice Memorial Award in Animal Breeding and Genetics. **Frequency:** annual. **Type:** recognition. **Recipient:** for members of the society except officers, members of the Board of Directors and Awards committee ● Special Board of Directors Award. **Frequency:** annual. **Type:** recognition. **Recipient:** for members of the society except officers, members of the Board of Directors and Awards committee. **Committees:** ASAS-ADSA Joint Program; Award; Program. **Publications:** *Animal and Dairy News*. Newsletter. **Advertising:** accepted. Alternate Formats: online ● *ASASynopsis*, semiannual. Newsletter. Alternate Formats: online ● *Combined Abstracts*, annual ● *Journal of Animal Science*, monthly. **Price:** included in membership dues. Alternate Formats: online ● Handbooks. Alternate Formats: online ● Reports. **Conventions/Meetings:** annual conference and meeting (exhibits) - 2008 July 7-11, Indianapolis, IN; 2009 July 12-16, Montreal, QC, Canada; 2010 July 11-15, Denver, CO.

4151 ■ Federation of Animal Science Societies (FASS)
1111 N Dunlap Ave.
Savoy, IL 61874
Ph: (217)356-3182
Fax: (217)398-4119
E-mail: fass@assochq.org
URL: http://www.fass.org
Contact: Mr. Anthony Pescatore, Pres.

Founded: 1998. **Members:** 10,000. **Description:** Represents animal science professionals. Strives to broaden the effective understanding and exchange of scientific information and to improve the impact of the animal sciences.

4152 ■ National Animal Supplement Council (NASC)
PO Box 2568
Valley Center, CA 92082
Ph: (760)751-3360
Fax: (760)751-5027
E-mail: b.bookout@nasc.cc
URL: http://www.nasc.cc
Contact: Bill Bookout, Pres.

Founded: 2001. **Description:** Aims to protect and enhance the health of companion animals and horses. **Committees:** Audit; Media; Political Action; Regulatory Affairs; Scientific Advisory; Website. **Funds:** Legislative Defense. **Programs:** Compliance PlusSM. **Publications:** Newsletter. **Price:** free ● Brochure. Alternate Formats: online.

Animal Welfare

4153 ■ Fur Free Alliance (FFA)
c/o Andrea Cimino
2100 L St. NW
Washington, DC 20037
Ph: (301)258-3109
E-mail: furfree@hsus.org
URL: http://infurmation.com
Contact: Nicki Brooks, Co-Chair

Multinational. Description: Works to "stop the killing and exploitation of animals for their fur. Raises public awareness of the cruelty and negative environmental impacts associated with the global fur trade. Advances legislative actions and in-depth investigations on animal killing and exploitation.". **Libraries: Type:** reference. **Holdings:** articles, papers, reports. **Subjects:** fur trade, fur industry. **Computer Services:** Information services, consumer information ● information services, fur trade resources.

4154 ■ Grassroots Endangered Species Coalition
PO Box 423
Battle Ground, WA 98604
Ph: (206)687-2505
Fax: (206)687-2973
Contact: Kathleen Benedetto, Contact

Members: 250. **Description:** Committed to reforming the old Endangered Species Act in a way that benefits both wildlife and people.

4155 ■ International Society for Cow Protection (ISCOWP)
RD 1, Box 322A
Moundsville, WV 26041
Ph: (304)843-1658
E-mail: iscowp@earthlink.net
URL: http://www.iscowp.org
Contact: William E. Dove, Pres.

Founded: 1990. **Membership Dues:** in U.S., $21 (annual) ● rest of the world, $25 (annual). **Multinational. Description:** Promotes cow protection. Aims to present alternatives to agricultural practices that support and depend upon the meat industry and industrialized, petroleum powered machinery. Offers cow protection classes and seminars, and training for teamsters and oxen. Facilitates cooperation and communication among members. **Publications:** Newsletter. Alternate Formats: online.

Animals

4156 ■ American Sanctuary Association (ASA)
2308 Chatfield
Las Vegas, NV 89128
Ph: (702)804-8562
Fax: (702)804-8561
E-mail: asarescue@aol.com
URL: http://www.asaanimalsanctuaries.org
Contact: Vernon Weir, Treas.

Description: Provides sanctuary for homeless, abandoned and abused domestic and wild animals. Certifies sanctuaries that provide high quality animal care and housing. Supports legislation that protects animals. Increases public awareness of humane and compassionate care for animals. **Computer Services:** Information services, lists of accredited sanctuaries ● online services, internet discussion lists. **Telecommunication Services:** electronic mail, tippilion@aol.com. **Publications:** Newsletter.

4157 ■ Animals as Intermediaries (AAI)
PO Box 155
Concord, MA 01742
Ph: (978)369-2585
Fax: (978)369-2815
E-mail: info@aai-nature.org
URL: http://www.aai-nature.org
Contact: Janey Tallarida, Exec. Dir.

Founded: 1983. **Description:** Represents the interests of individuals dedicated to supporting the human spirit by offering and building connections between people and the natural world. Provides educational and therapeutic nature-based programs to youth and elders and the staff who serve them at institutions where access to the natural world is limited. **Telecommunication Services:** electronic mail, janey@aai-nature.org.

4158 ■ Elephant Managers Association (EMA)
c/o Daryl Hoffman, Exec. Dir.
Buffalo Zoo
300 Parkside Ave.
Buffalo, NY 14214
Ph: (407)938-1988
E-mail: emaboard@elephant-managers.com
URL: http://www.elephant-managers.com
Contact: Daryl Hoffman, Exec. Dir.

Membership Dues: professional, contributing professional, supporting professional, $45 (annual) ● associate, $40 (annual) ● institutional, $75 (annual) ● gold, $250 (annual) ● ivory, $500 (annual). **Multinational. Description:** Works for the welfare of the world's elephants through conservation, husbandry, research, education and communication. **Computer Services:** Online services, message board. **Publications:** *Gray Matters*, bimonthly. Newsletter. Features breaking news, job announcements and EMA updates. ● Journal. Contains articles and photos of elephants around the world.

4159 ■ Fund for Horses
1918 Restridge Dr.
Houston, TX 77055
Ph: (713)650-1973
Free: (866)409-2312
Fax: (832)201-8847
E-mail: info@fund4horses.org
URL: http://www.fund4horses.org
Contact: Vivian Farrell, Chm./Pres.
Multinational. **Description:** Promotes and safeguards the health, safety and welfare of all equines. Works for the conservation of wild horses, asses, mules, donkeys, burros and zebras in their natural habitats. **Computer Services:** Online services, message board. **Boards:** Advisory. **Also Known As:** (2005) International Fund for Horses. **Publications:** Brochure. Alternate Formats: online.

4160 ■ National Opossum Society (NOS)
PO Box 21197
Catonsville, MD 21228
Ph: (410)233-1102
URL: http://www.opossum.org
Contact: Janice Hughlett, Contact
Founded: 1986. **Membership Dues:** general, $25 (annual). **Description:** Serves as a resource for current and correct diet, medical and general knowledge of opossums. Educates the public on the benefits of opossums in the environment. Works with agencies to improve management and handling of opossums in the environment. **Computer Services:** Information services, opossums resources. **Publications:** Newsletter, periodic.

4161 ■ Rabbits Unlimited Inc. (RUI)
Address Unknown since 2008
URL: http://www.rabbitsunlimited.org
Membership Dues: regular, $20 (annual) ● family, $30 (annual) ● charter, $40 (annual) ● club, $200 (annual) ● individual sponsor, $100 (annual) ● corporate sponsor, $500 (annual). **Description:** Represents the interests of individuals dedicated to the enhancement of the rabbit. Focuses on the conservation, preservation, education and the reestablishment of habitat that is needed to sustain a healthy population of rabbits and other game species.

Apiculture

4162 ■ American Association of Professional Apiculturists (AAPA)
c/o Eric Mussen, PhD
UC Davis, Dept. of Entomology
One Shields Ave.
Davis, CA 95616-8584
Ph: (530)752-0472
Fax: (530)754-7757
E-mail: ecmussen@ucdavis.edu
URL: http://entomology.ucdavis.edu/faculty/mussen.cfm
Contact: Eric Mussen PhD, Contact
Founded: 1980. **Members:** 150. **Membership Dues:** active, associate, student, $15 (annual). **Staff:** 3. **Budget:** $5,000. **Description:** Apiculturists and individuals engaged in extension, regulation, teaching, and research programs relating to honey bees. Promotes increased understanding of beekeeping, pollination, and the manufacture of honey. Serves as a clearinghouse on apiculture; conducts research and educational programs; sponsors competitions; maintains speakers' bureau. **Libraries: Type:** reference. **Subjects:** bee biology, bee management, pollination. **Awards:** Award for Apicultural Excellence. **Frequency:** annual. **Type:** recognition ● Student Paper Award. **Frequency:** annual. **Type:** recognition ● Student Scholarship. **Frequency:** annual. **Type:** scholarship. **Telecommunication Services:** electronic bulletin board. **Committees:** Member Awards; Nominations; Pesticide Efficacy and Registration; Regulations; Student Awards. **Special Interest Groups:** American Bee Research Conference. **Publications:** *Bee Pollinators in Your Garden*. Bulletin. **Price:** $2.50 each; for 1-9 copies; $2.00 each; for 10-99 copies; $1.50 each; for 100-999 copies; $1.00 each; for 1000 or more copies. **Conventions/Meetings:** annual conference, held in conjunction with American Bee Research Conference.

4163 ■ American Honey Producers Association (AHPA)
c/o Mark Brady, Pres.
3307 Sanger Creek Way
Waxahachie, TX 75165
Ph: (972)937-2022 (785)778-2002
Fax: (972)937-2022
E-mail: beeman52@sbcglobal.net
URL: http://www.americanhoneyproducers.org
Contact: Mark Brady, Pres.
Founded: 1969. **Members:** 800. **Membership Dues:** associate individual, $40 (annual) ● hobbyist, $50 (annual) ● associate firm/state, sideliner, $150 (annual) ● commercial, $300 (annual). **Staff:** 1. **Budget:** $250,000. **Description:** Commercial and avocational beekeepers. Represents the interests of beekeepers in agricultural research programs and before legislative bodies, and marketing. **Telecommunication Services:** electronic mail, webmaster@americanhoneyproducers.org. **Publications:** *American Honey Producers*, quarterly. Magazine. **Price:** included in membership dues; $20.00 for nonmembers. **Circulation:** 1,200. **Advertising:** accepted. Also Cited As: *AHPA Report*. **Conventions/Meetings:** annual convention, educational, technical, supply manufacturers (exhibits) - always January.

4164 ■ Apiary Inspectors of America (AIA)
c/o Minnesota Department of Agriculture
625 Robert St. N
St. Paul, MN 55155-2538
Ph: (651)201-6095 (320)239-4725
Free: (800)967-2474
E-mail: daniel.pasche@state.mn.us
URL: http://www.mda.state.mn.us/animals/animals/apiaryprogram.htm
Contact: Daniel Pasche, Inspector
Founded: 1926. **Members:** 85. **Membership Dues:** full, $100 (annual) ● associate, $35 (annual). **Description:** State and provincial apiarists; individuals interested in beekeeping and bee research are associate members. Seeks to promote and protect the beekeeping industry of North America. Participates in research meetings at United States Department of Agriculture-Science and Educational Administration laboratories. **Publications:** Newsletter, periodic ● Proceedings, annual. **Conventions/Meetings:** annual conference.

4165 ■ Eastern Apicultural Society of North America (EAS)
c/o Loretta Surprenant, Sec.
PO Box 300
Essex, NY 12936
Ph: (518)963-7593
E-mail: secretary@easternapiculture.org
URL: http://www.easternapiculture.org
Contact: Loretta Surprenant, Sec.
Founded: 1955. **Members:** 1,600. **Membership Dues:** individual, family, $25 (annual) ● life, $250. **Regional Groups:** 30. **Description:** Hobbyist beekeepers and producers of honey; supporting members are manufacturers of beekeeping equipment and packers of honey. Provides an educational program for hobbyist beekeepers and the public on the science of apiculture (beekeeping). **Awards:** DiVelbiss Award. **Frequency:** annual. **Type:** recognition. **Recipient:** to a beekeeper teaching the non-beekeeping public ● EAS Student Apiculture Award. **Frequency:** annual. **Type:** recognition. **Recipient:** for students studying apiculture ● James I. Hambleton Award. **Frequency:** annual. **Type:** recognition. **Recipient:** for research excellence in apiculture ● Roger A. Morse Outstanding Teaching/Extension Service/Regulatory Award. **Frequency:** annual. **Type:** recognition. **Recipient:** to an outstanding individual in the field of apiculture. **Computer Services:** database ● mailing lists. **Committees:** Annual Honey Show; Awards; Editorial; Nominations; Public Relations; Research; Short Course; Sites. **Affiliated With:** International Federation of Beekeepers' Associations. **Formerly:** (1967) Eastern Apicultural Society. **Publications:** *EAS Journal*, quarterly ● *Proceedings of Board of Directors*, 3/year ● Annual Report, annual. **Conventions/Meetings:** annual Beekeeping Short Course - seminar (exhibits) ● annual conference (exhibits) ● annual Cookery Contest - competition ● annual Gadget Show ● annual Honey Show ● annual Mead Making Show ● annual show and workshop (exhibits).

4166 ■ Mid-U.S. Honey Producers Marketing Association
3499 75th St. SW
Waverly, MN 55390
Ph: (763)658-4645 (763)658-4193
Fax: (763)658-4036
Contact: Darrel Rufer, Pres.
Founded: 1968. **Members:** 30. **Membership Dues:** $50 (annual). **Description:** Keepers of colonies of 500 or more bees who works with national beekeeping groups and the International Trade Commission to insure that the marketing of honey is maintained for the highest profitability. **Publications:** Newsletter. **Conventions/Meetings:** annual meeting - held every third Friday of August.

Aquaculture

4167 ■ Alternative Aquaculture Association
630 Independent Rd.
Breinigsville, PA 18031
Ph: (610)398-1062 (610)393-5918
Fax: (610)395-8202
E-mail: altaqua@ptd.net
URL: http://www.altaqua.com
Description: Promotes alternative aquaculture for small-scale businesses and recreation. **Publications:** *Network*. Newsletter ● *Small Scale Aquaculture*. Book. Contains aquaculture techniques, from bio filtration to spawning. **Price:** $20.00.

4168 ■ Aquaculture Certification Council (ACC)
12815 72nd Ave. NE
Kirkland, WA 98034
Ph: (425)825-7935
Fax: (425)650-3001
E-mail: info@aquaculturecertification.org
URL: http://www.aquaculturecertification.org
Contact: James Heerin, Pres.
Founded: 2002. **Nonmembership**. **Multinational**. **Description:** Certifies social, environmental and food safety standards at aquaculture facilities throughout the world. Helps educate the aquaculture public on the benefits of applying best management practices and the use of advanced scientific technology. **Computer Services:** Information services, technical, aquaculture, farm and plant resources. **Telecommunication Services:** electronic mail, jheerin@aquaculturecertification.org. **Committees:** Oversight. **Publications:** *Blue Standard*. Newsletter. Provides news and information relevant to the aquaculture industry. Alternate Formats: online.

4169 ■ Aquaculture International
c/o Charles W. Johnson, Founder/Pres.
PO Box 606
Andrews, NC 28901
URL: http://www.aquacultureinternational.org
Contact: Charles W. Johnson, Founder/Pres.
Multinational. **Description:** Promotes the development of the aquaculture industry through education and consultation. Establishes practical and innovative demonstration facilities that are economically feasible and can be replicated by farmers, missionaries and other interested individuals. **Computer Services:** Information services, aquaponics resources.

4170 ■ Catfish Farmers of America (CFA)
1100 Hwy. 82 E, Ste.202
Indianola, MS 38751
Ph: (662)887-2699
Fax: (662)887-6857
E-mail: hmccall1@jam.rr.com
URL: http://www.catfishfarmersamerica.org
Contact: Hugh Warren, Exec. VP
Founded: 1968. **Members:** 1,600. **Membership Dues:** regular, $40 (annual). **Staff:** 4. **Budget:** $500,000. **Description:** Represents farmers who raise catfish commercially; membership centered primarily in Alabama, Arkansas, Louisiana, and Mississippi. **Committees:** Legislative; Member Services; Processing; Research. **Publications:** *Catfish Journal*, monthly. Covers technical advances and management techniques. Contains listing of new products, calendar of events, and recipes. **Circulation:** 5,100. **Advertising:** accepted. **Conventions/Meetings:** annual conference.

4171 ■ The Catfish Institute (TCI)
5420 I-55 N, Ste.F
Jackson, MS 39211
Ph: (601)977-9559
E-mail: info@catfishinstitute.com
URL: http://www.catfishinstitute.com
Contact: Jason Stemm, Contact
Founded: 1986. **Description:** Seeks to increase public awareness and promote the qualities of Mississippi farm-raised catfish. Monitors the industry and acts as liaison among processors and farmers; serves as information and resource center.

4172 ■ Florida Tropical Fish Farms Association (FTFFA)
PO Box 1519
Winter Haven, FL 33882
Ph: (863)293-5710 (305)251-1398
Fax: (863)299-5154
E-mail: ftffa@yahoo.com
URL: http://www.ftffa.com
Contact: David Boozer, Exec. Dir.
Founded: 1964. **Members:** 330. **Membership Dues:** regular, associate, $75 (annual) ● firm outside U.S., $100 (annual) ● student, $20 (annual). **Staff:** 2. **Budget:** $900,000. **Description:** Growers of tropical fish and aquatic plants; associate members are manufacturers and suppliers of allied products in Florida and elsewhere in the U.S. Seeks to elevate trade standards and promote the industry. Sponsors quarterly meeting to hear speakers on the care of tropical fish, applicable laws, and other aspects of the trade. Resources include an organization-owned co-op. **Libraries: Type:** not open to the public; reference. **Holdings:** photographs. **Awards:** FTFFA Hall of Fame. **Frequency:** annual. **Type:** recognition. **Telecommunication Services:** electronic mail, webmaster@ftffa.com. **Affiliated With:** Pet Industry Joint Advisory Council. **Publications:** Newsletter, bimonthly ● Membership Directory, annual. Lists 350 members. **Price:** free. **Conventions/Meetings:** annual Fish Show (exhibits).

4173 ■ Global Aquaculture Alliance (GAA)
5661 Telegraph Rd., Ste.3A
St. Louis, MO 63129
Ph: (314)293-5500
Fax: (314)293-5525
E-mail: homeoffice@gaalliance.org
URL: http://www.gaalliance.org
Contact: George Chamberlain, Pres.
Founded: 1997. **Membership Dues:** individual, $60 (annual) ● sustaining, $1,000 (annual) ● governing, $1,500-$15,000 (annual) ● association, $500 (annual). **Multinational. Description:** Promotes management practices for sustainable aquaculture through the programs, conferences and other activities. Advocates aquaculture as an answer to global food needs. Develops and encourages the use of aquaculture system designs, installations and operations sensitive to and compatible with environmental and community needs. **Computer Services:** Information services, articles on aqua-issues ● online services, store. **Telecommunication Services:** electronic mail, georgec@gaalliance.org. **Programs:** Responsible Aquaculture. **Publications:** *Codes of Practice for Responsible Shrimp Farming*. Manual. Serves as a guide for establishing standards of good practice for responsible aquaculture. Alternate Formats: online ● *Global Aquaculture Alliance Update*. Newsletter. Contains articles and reports about the organization's international activities. Alternate Formats: online ● *Global Aquaculture Advocate*, bimonthly. Magazine. Presents practical information on current seafood issues, efficient and responsible aquaculture technology, and alliance activities. **Price:** $60.00/year; $96.00/2 years; $40.00/year for students. **Circulation:** 3,500. **Advertising:** accepted ● Articles. Contains anti-dumping articles. Alternate Formats: online.

4174 ■ Hydroponic Society of America (HSA)
c/o Bill Graham, VP
569 E Evelyn Ave.
Mountain View, CA 94041
Ph: (650)968-4070
Fax: (650)968-4051
E-mail: hsa@purefood.com
Contact: Bill Graham, VP
Founded: 1978. **Members:** 900. **Membership Dues:** student, $20 (annual) ● individual, $40 (annual) ● business/corporate, $250 (annual). **Staff:** 1. **Budget:** $80,000. **Regional Groups:** 2. **Description:** Commercial and hobby hydroponic growers, researchers, and equipment manufacturers. (Hydroponics is the growing of plants in nutrient solutions.) Promotes and encourages worldwide interest in scientific research and educational studies concerning hydroponics. Provides a forum for research reporting, lectures, and public discussion; disseminates information on hydroponic installations. **Libraries: Type:** reference. **Holdings:** archival material, books, periodicals. **Subjects:** hydroponics. **Publications:** *Directory of Suppliers of Nutrient, Seed, Systems, Equipment and Services for Hydroponic Growers, Commercial and Hobby*, periodic. Includes book list. **Advertising:** accepted ● *Soiless Grower: The Official Publication of the Hydroponic Society of America*, bimonthly. Newsletter. Includes book reviews and research reports. **Price:** free, for members only. **Circulation:** 1,000. **Advertising:** accepted ● *Symposium Proceedings*, annual. **Conventions/Meetings:** annual conference and symposium (exhibits) ● seminar.

4175 ■ Marine Aquarium Council (MAC)
923 Nu'uanu Ave.
Honolulu, HI 96817
Ph: (808)550-8217
Fax: (808)550-8317
E-mail: info@aquariumcouncil.org
URL: http://www.aquariumcouncil.org
Contact: David Mainenti, Exec. Dir.
Multinational. Description: Brings together marine aquarium animal collectors, exporters, importers, retailers, aquarium keepers, conservation organizations and government agencies. Conserves coral reefs and other marine ecosystems by creating standards and certification for those engaged in the collection and care of ornamental marine life from reef to aquarium. **Telecommunication Services:** electronic mail, paul.holthus@aquariumcouncil.org. **Publications:** *MAC News*. Newsletter. Alternate Formats: online.

4176 ■ Marine Aquarium Societies of North America (MASNA)
c/o Bob Lemcke, Treas.
937 Roper Rd.
Canton, GA 30115
Ph: (770)565-9841
Fax: (770)794-6909
E-mail: join@masna.org
URL: http://www.masna.org
Contact: Bob Lemcke, Treas.
Members: 1,200. **Membership Dues:** individual (prorated quarterly), $20 (annual) ● club (prorated quarterly), $50 (annual) ● corporate (prorated quarterly), $100 (annual). **Description:** Represents saltwater aquarium owners and other marine aquaculture hobbyists. Promotes effective care and breeding of marine plants and animals; encourages participation in the hobby of marine aquaculture. Conducts educational programs. **Awards:** Club Website Awards. **Frequency:** annual. **Type:** recognition ● MASNA Award. **Frequency:** annual. **Type:** recognition. **Recipient:** to an individual who has made an outstanding contribution to marine aquarium hobby. **Computer Services:** database, national clubs ● database, national speakers. **Publications:** *Marine Scene*, quarterly. Newsletter. **Advertising:** accepted. Alternate Formats: online.

4177 ■ Muskies Inc. (MI)
14257 Waters Edge Trail
New Berlin, WI 53151-9508
Ph: (262)789-1255
Free: (888)710-8286
E-mail: secretary@muskiesinc.org
URL: http://www.muskiesinc.org
Contact: David Cates, Pres.
Founded: 1966. **Members:** 6,500. **Membership Dues:** regular individual, $35 (annual) ● regular junior, $20 (annual) ● family, $47 (annual) ● active military, $30 (annual) ● life (age 0-29), $600 ● life (age 30-44), $550 ● life (age 45-49), $500 ● life (age 50-55), $450 ● life (age 56-60), $400 ● life (age 61-65), $350 ● life (age 66-up), $300 ● life (spouse, significant other, family-same household), $100. **Staff:** 3. **Budget:** $150,000. **Regional Groups:** 40. **Local Groups:** 41. **Description:** Fishermen united to promote and protect muskellunge sport fisheries. (The muskellunge is a large North American fish weighing up to 60 pounds.) Establishes muskellunge hatcheries; introduces muskellunge into suitable waters; supports selected conservation practices; seeks reduction in water pollution levels. Distributes information; promotes fellowship and sportsmanship among members. Conducts muskellunge research; provides youth services. Compiles statistics. **Libraries: Type:** reference. **Holdings:** archival material, video recordings. **Subjects:** muskellunge research and management. **Awards:** Angler Award. **Frequency:** annual. **Type:** recognition. **Recipient:** for the largest and longest fish caught and released. **Computer Services:** Mailing lists, labels. **Committees:** Educational Endowment; Research; Video Handbook. **Publications:** *Muskie*, monthly. Magazine. Contains statistical information. **Price:** $30.00. **Circulation:** 6,000. **Advertising:** accepted ● Brochures. **Conventions/Meetings:** semiannual board meeting (exhibits) ● competition ● seminar.

4178 ■ National Aquaculture Association (NAA)
111 W Washington St., Ste.1
Charles Town, WV 25414
Ph: (304)728-2167
Fax: (304)728-2196
E-mail: naa@frontiernet.net
URL: http://www.nationalaquaculture.org
Contact: Dr. Randy MacMillan, Pres.
Membership Dues: individual, voting, $250 (annual) ● affiliate, non-voting, $25 (annual) ● silver, $1,000-$2,499 (annual) ● gold, $2,500-$4,999 (annual) ● platinum, $5,000 (annual). **Description:** Represents all segments of the aquaculture industry in the U.S. **Committees:** Review. **Publications:** *Action Alerts*. Contains information on current issues of national importance and industry activities. ● *Industry Updates*. Contains information on current issues of national importance and industry activities. ● *NAA Close-Up*. Contains information on current issues of national importance and industry activities. ● *Who are the Stakeholders*. Contains information on current issues of national importance and industry activities. **Conventions/Meetings:** conference.

4179 ■ National Aquaculture Council (NAC)
Address Unknown since 2007
Description: Companies that grow, process, or distribute aquaculture products. Promotes the aquaculture industry in the U.S; acts as a regulatory body within the industry. Conducts lobbying activities; operates speakers' bureau. **Publications:** none. **Conventions/Meetings:** semiannual meeting - always April and October.

4180 ■ National Association of State Aquaculture Coordinators (NASAC)
c/o Florida Department of Agriculture and Consumer Services
Division of Aquaculture
1203 Governor's Square Blvd., Fifth Fl.
Tallahassee, FL 32301
Ph: (850)488-4033
E-mail: wilhels@doacs.state.fl.us
URL: http://www.ncagr.com/markets/aquaculture/nasac.html
Contact: Sherman Wilhelm, Pres.
Founded: 1991. **Description:** Enhances communication among state aquaculture coordinators and resolves conflicts within and among federal, state and international components of the aquaculture industry, while being a strong advocate of responsible development. **Computer Services:** database, directory of state aquaculture coordinators ● information services, aquaculture drug and effluent update. **Affiliated With:** National Association of State Departments of Agriculture. **Publications:** *Aquaculture in North Carolina - Inputs, Outputs and Economics*. Booklets. Contains general statistics and information on the species production cycle and estimates on investments costs and operating costs and returns. Alternate Formats: online ● *NASAC Ramblings*. Newsletter. Alternate Formats: online.

4181 ■ National Ornamental Goldfish Growers Association (NOGGA)
Address Unknown since 2008
Founded: 1981. **Members:** 6. **Description:** Commercial growers and breeders of ornamental goldfish. Conducts and sponsors research on diseases affecting ornamental goldfish. **Publications:** none. **Committees:** Research. **Conventions/Meetings:** annual meeting.

4182 ■ Pacific Shellfish Institute (PSI)
120 State Ave. NE, No. 142
Olympia, WA 98501
Ph: (360)754-2741
E-mail: psi@pacshell.org
URL: http://www.pacshell.org
Contact: Dr. Daniel Cheney, Exec. Dir.
Founded: 1995. **Staff:** 6. **Description:** Specializes in bivalve shellfish and environmental research and education. Addresses issues that affect all growers and harvesters of shellfish products by focusing largely on applied shellfish research and outreach activities. **Telecommunication Services:** electronic mail, cheney@pacshell.org. **Programs:** Hood Canal Dissolved Oxygen. **Projects:** Alternative Shellfish Culture; Burrowing Shrimp; Cadmium Health Risk Assessment; Oyster Mortality; Pet Waste Education Campaign; Research Regarding Toxic Phytoplankton Occurring in the Pacific Northwest; Scoopy Doo Pet Waste.

4183 ■ United States Aquaculture Society (USAS)
Louisiana State Univ.
143 J.M. Parker Coliseum
Baton Rouge, LA 70803
Ph: (225)578-3137
Fax: (225)578-3493
E-mail: wasmas@aol.com
URL: http://www.was.org/Usas/Default.htm
Contact: Dr. Jimmy Avery, Pres.
Membership Dues: regular, $5 (annual). **Description:** Represents individuals interested in the advancement of the aquaculture industry. Provides a national forum for the exchange of information among aquaculture researchers, students and industry members in the United States. Aims to secure, evaluate, promote and distribute educational, scientific, and technological advancement of aquaculture and mariculture. Addresses issues of importance to the U.S. Aquaculture Community. **Awards:** Distinguished Early Career Award. **Frequency:** annual. **Type:** recognition. **Recipient:** to an individual who has been involved in U.S. aquaculture for 10 years or less ● Distinguished Life-time Achievement Award. **Frequency:** annual. **Type:** recognition. **Recipient:** to an individual who has made contributions and broad impacts throughout his/her career to aquaculture in the United States ● Distinguished Service Award. **Frequency:** annual. **Type:** recognition. **Recipient:** to an individual who has made outstanding personal contributions to the U.S. WAS Chapter and/or the U.S. aquaculture industry. **Affiliated With:** World Aquaculture Society. **Publications:** Newsletter, semiannual. Alternate Formats: online.

4184 ■ U.S. Trout Farmers Association (USTFA)
111 W Washington St., Ste.1
Charles Town, WV 25414-1529
Ph: (304)728-2189
Fax: (304)728-2196
E-mail: ustfa@frontiernet.net
URL: http://www.ustfa.org
Contact: John Bechtel, Pres.
Founded: 1954. **Members:** 250. **Membership Dues:** student, $30 (annual) ● foreign, associate, library, $50 (annual) ● active, $50-$400 (annual) ● patron, $500-$1,500 (annual). **Description:** Trout farmers, suppliers, academics, students, and individuals interested in the trout farming industry. Promotes the trout farming industry and recreational trout fishing. Establishes Trout Farmers Quality Assurance Program; monitors legislation related to the aquaculture industry. **Awards:** Clark and Mimi White Distinguished Service Award. **Frequency:** annual. **Type:** recognition. **Affiliated With:** National Aquaculture Association; National Aquaculture Council. **Publications:** *Salmonid*. Journal ● *Trout Talk*, quarterly. Newsletter. **Conventions/Meetings:** annual meeting and trade show (exhibits).

4185 ■ World Aquaculture Society (WAS)
Louisiana State Univ.
143 J.M. Parker Coliseum
Baton Rouge, LA 70803
Ph: (225)578-3137
Fax: (225)578-3493
E-mail: carolm@was.org
URL: http://www.was.org
Contact: Dr. Carol Mendoza, Home Office Dir.
Founded: 1970. **Members:** 3,000. **Membership Dues:** individual, $60 (annual) ● life, $1,000 ● sustaining, $100 (annual) ● corporate, $250 (annual) ● student, $40 (annual). **Staff:** 3. **Budget:** $500,000. **National Groups:** 2. **Description:** Institutions, students and interested individuals. Aims to secure, evaluate, promote and distribute educational, scientific, and technological advancement of aquaculture and mariculture throughout the world. Promotes exchange and cooperation between persons interested in aquaculture (the cultivation of plants and animals in both freshwater and marine environments for domestic purposes, especially food.) Provides a forum for the exchange of information among scientists, fish farmers, business persons, bureaucrats and others; promotes and evaluates the educational, scientific and technological development of aquaculture throughout the world. Advocates the training of aquaculture workers in accredited colleges and universities. Encourages private industry and government agencies to support aquaculture research, development, and educational activities. Disseminates information on the status, potential and problems of aquaculture. Sponsors competitions and special interest workshops. **Formerly:** (1986) World Mariculture Society. **Publications:** *Advances in World Aquaculture*, periodic. Books. ISSN: 9624-529X ● *Journal of the WAS*, quarterly. Includes papers on all aspects of the production of aquatic animals and plants for food. Contains information for researchers and students. **Price:** $105.00/year in U.S.; $115.00/year in Canada, Mexico, and South America; $135.00/year all other countries. ISSN: 0893-8849. **Circulation:** 3,000 ● *World Aquaculture*, quarterly. Magazine. Includes aquaculture science and technology news and social, political, biological, and financial updates. **Price:** $50.00/year in U.S.; $65.00/year outside U.S. ISSN: 1041-5602. **Circulation:** 4,300. **Advertising:** accepted ● Membership Directory, periodic. **Price:** available to members only. Alternate Formats: online ● Also publishes proceedings and workshop series. **Conventions/Meetings:** annual symposium ● annual World Aquaculture - conference and trade show (exhibits).

Arts

4186 ■ River of Words (ROW)
2547 8th St., Studio 13B
Berkeley, CA 94710
Ph: (510)548-7636
Fax: (510)548-2095
E-mail: info@riverofwords.org
URL: http://www.riverofwords.org
Contact: Pamela Michael, Co-Founder/Exec. Dir.
Founded: 1995. **Description:** Educates children about the importance of water in their lives. Utilizes the avenue of creative expression. Conducts training workshops for teachers, park naturalists, grassroots groups, state resource agencies, librarians and individuals that help incorporate observation-based nature exploration and the arts into their work with young people. Provides traveling exhibitions and consulting services. **Awards:** River of Words Teacher of the Year. **Frequency:** annual. **Type:** recognition. **Recipient:** for a teacher whose creative implementation of River of Words has generated exemplary student work.

Aviation

4187 ■ International Association of Natural Resource Pilots (IANRP)
c/o Fred Kruger, Treas.
27102 County Rd. A
Spooner, WI 54801
Ph: (715)635-7788
E-mail: frkruger@juno.com
URL: http://ianrp.org
Contact: Fred Kruger, Treas.
Membership Dues: in U.S., $35 (annual) ● in Canada, C$45 (annual). **Multinational. Description:** Represents pilots who utilize aircraft in the field of renewable resources. Promotes the recognition of the importance of sound aviation practices in resource management. Encourages and develops the educational, social, and economic interests of aviation in resource management. **Libraries: Type:** reference. **Holdings:** archival material, articles, reports. **Subjects:** aircraft, aircraft installation. **Publications:** *Conservation Aeronautics*. Newsletter. Contains features on aeronautics and conservation, and other news articles. **Price:** free. Alternate Formats: online.

4188 ■ National Agricultural Aviation Association (NAAA)
1005 E St. SE
Washington, DC 20003-2847
Ph: (202)546-5722
Fax: (202)546-5726
E-mail: information@agaviation.org
URL: http://www.agaviation.org
Contact: Andrew D. Moore, Exec. Dir.
Founded: 1966. **Members:** 1,339. **Membership Dues:** operator, $400 (annual) ● affiliated operator, pilot, affiliated allied, $150 (annual) ● participating operator, $800 (annual) ● participating pilot, $300 (annual) ● allied, $400-$1,500 (annual) ● associate, $75 (annual) ● international, $200 (annual) ● state/regional association, organization, $600 (annual). **Staff:** 6. **Multinational. Description:** Represents owner/operators of agricultural aviation operations, pilots, airframe dealers, insurance companies, and propulsion, airframe, chemical, and system manufacturers. Carries out national legislative and educational activities; acts as liaison between state and national regulatory government agencies. **Libraries: Type:** reference. **Holdings:** books, periodicals, video recordings. **Subjects:** agricultural aviation. **Awards: Frequency:** annual. **Type:** recognition. **Recipient:** for members of NAAA ● WNAAA Scholarship Award. **Frequency:** annual. **Type:** scholarship. **Recipient:** for members of NAAA. **Computer Services:** database, Pilot/Operator Career ● information services, agricultural aviation security and safety information.

Telecommunication Services: electronic mail, lbarber@agaviation.org. **Affiliated With:** Women of the National Agricultural Aviation Association. **Formerly:** (1970) National Aerial Applicators Association. **Publications:** *Agricultural Aviation*, bimonthly. Magazine. **Price:** $30.00 for nonmembers in U.S.; $45.00 for nonmembers outside U.S. **Circulation:** 6,200. **Advertising:** accepted ● Membership Directory, annual. **Advertising:** accepted ● Newsletter, periodic. **Conventions/Meetings:** annual convention (exhibits) - always December.

4189 ■ Women of the National Agricultural Aviation Association (WNAAA)
1005 E St. SE
Washington, DC 20003-2847
Ph: (202)546-5722
Fax: (202)546-5726
E-mail: information@agaviation.org
URL: http://www.agaviation.org/wnaaamain.htm
Contact: Teresa Bair, Pres.

Founded: 1976. **Members:** 30. **Description:** Women of members of the National Agricultural Aviation Association (See Separate Entry.) Assists NAAA members with public relations and recreational activities. Sponsors educational programs. Provides scholarship program for children or grandchildren of agricultural aviators. **Publications:** none. **Awards:** WNAAA Scholarship. **Frequency:** annual. **Type:** scholarship. **Recipient:** for NAAA members only. **Conventions/Meetings:** annual convention - December.

Bird

4190 ■ American Game Fowl Society (AGFS)
PO Box 800
Belton, SC 29627
Ph: (864)237-5280
E-mail: gamefowls4all@yahoo.com
URL: http://americangamefowl.org
Contact: Anthony Saville, Pres.

Membership Dues: regular (with newsletter subscription), $40 (annual) ● regular (without newsletter subscription), $25 (annual). **Description:** Represents the rights of members to show American Game Fowls in the show pen at any venue throughout the United States. Ensures the rights of American Game Fowls and defends any mistreatment. Offers Game Fowl owners advice on the keeping and showing of American Game Fowl and bantams. **Publications:** *American Game Fowl Standard*, quarterly. Newsletter. Alternate Formats: online.

4191 ■ American Mookee Association (AMA)
Rte. 1, Box 4050
Clinton, OK 73601
Ph: (864)876-2543 (580)323-0824
E-mail: okie73601@sbcglobal.net
URL: http://aviangems.com/AMA
Contact: Larry Pridmore, Pres.

Founded: 1988. **Membership Dues:** adult, $10 (annual) ● family, $15 (annual) ● junior, $5 (annual). **Description:** Promotes the breeding, exhibition and improvement of the Mookee pigeon. **Computer Services:** Information services, Mookee resources. **Telecommunication Services:** electronic mail, lnjpridmore@backroads.net.

4192 ■ Asiatic Breeders Association (ABA)
c/o Joyce Baum, Pres.
PO Box 8265
Tucson, AZ 85738
Ph: (928)474-3322
E-mail: ringnecklady@msn.com
Contact: Joyce Baum, Pres.

Founded: 1996. **Multinational. Description:** Educates the people on the proper care, handling and maintenance of Asiatics. Encourages selective breeding of Asiatics. Promotes the use of close banding and record keeping of the Asiatic breed. Enhances the development of color mutations of Asiatics through the study of genetics.

4193 ■ Avian Welfare Coalition (AWC)
PO Box 40212
St. Paul, MN 55104
E-mail: monica@api4animals.org
URL: http://www.avianwelfare.org
Contact: Monica Engebretson, Contact

Founded: 2000. **Description:** Raises awareness of the plight of parrots and other captive birds. Serves as an educational resource for the humane community, lawmakers and the general public. **Telecommunication Services:** electronic mail, denise@avianwelfare.org. **Subgroups:** Education and Outreach; Public Outreach; Shelter Outreach.

4194 ■ Brotogeris Society International (BSI)
PO Box 14891
Shawnee Mission, KS 66285-4891
E-mail: emysemys@pacbell.net
URL: http://www.brotosociety.org
Contact: Yvonne Gomez, Pres.

Membership Dues: standard, $20 (annual) ● regular, outside U.S., $25 (annual) ● business, $40 (annual). **Multinational. Description:** Seeks to conserve and promote Brotogeris species. Encourages breeding and good husbandry practices of Brotogeris Parakeets. Promotes avian education to breeders, owners and the public. **Computer Services:** Online services, Yahoo groups.

4195 ■ Canary and Finch Society
c/o Ray Terrazas, Treas.
PO Box 79311
Houston, TX 77279
Ph: (409)744-3141
E-mail: mlshearn@houston.rr.com
URL: http://canaryfinchsociety.tripod.com
Contact: Helen Jones, Pres.

Membership Dues: single, $20 (annual) ● dual, $25 (annual). **Description:** Promotes all caged birds, particularly canaries and finches. Provides educational programs and group discussion on canaries and finches. **Publications:** Newsletter, monthly ● Catalog, in September. **Conventions/Meetings:** monthly meeting - every 2nd Sunday in Pasadena, TX.

4196 ■ Guinea Fowl Breeders Association (GFBA)
c/o Phyllis Bender, Sec.-Treas.
4 Coach Ln.
Westport, CT 06880
E-mail: phyllis@gfba.org
URL: http://www.gfba.org
Contact: Jeannette Ferguson, Pres.

Founded: 1999. **Membership Dues:** general, $10 (annual). **Description:** Represents individuals interested in raising guinea fowl. Encourages, supports and educates people about the benefits of raising guinea fowl. Provides information and support to those who own or plan to own guinea fowl. **Computer Services:** Information services, facts in raising guinea fowl ● online services, chat room ● online services, message board. **Telecommunication Services:** electronic mail, information@gfba.org. **Publications:** *GFBA Newsletter*. **Conventions/Meetings:** annual convention - spring.

4197 ■ Guinea Fowl International Association (GFIA)
PO Box 367
Paradise, TX 76073
E-mail: membership@guineafowlinternational.org
URL: http://www.guineafowlinternational.org
Contact: Cindy Gibson, Pres.

Membership Dues: single, $20 (annual) ● family, $28 (annual) ● junior (age 15 and under), $5 (annual). **Multinational. Description:** Supports the responsible keeping and breeding of Guinea Fowl. Educates on the care and habits of Guinea Fowl. Assists individuals interested in the incubation, hatching and keeping of Guinea Fowl. **Telecommunication Services:** electronic mail, brenscozysilkies@thecozynest.com.

4198 ■ Hummingbird Society
6560 Hwy. 179, Ste.204
Sedona, AZ 86351
Ph: (928)284-2251
Free: (800)529-3699
E-mail: info@hummingbird.org
URL: http://www.hummingbirdsociety.org
Contact: Dr. Ross Hawkins, Sec./Exec. Dir.

Founded: 1996. **Membership Dues:** individual, family in U.S., $30 (annual) ● individual, family outside U.S., $36 (annual) ● business, $100 (annual). **Description:** Promotes understanding and conservation of hummingbirds. **Publications:** *The Hummingbird Connection*, quarterly. Journal. Features articles about hummingbirds from various perspectives. **Price:** included in membership dues ● Brochure. Alternate Formats: online ● Catalog.

4199 ■ International Aviculturists Society (IAS)
PO Box 341852
Memphis, TN 38184
Fax: (901)371-0537
URL: http://funnyfarmexotics.com/IAS
Contact: Richard Porter MD, Contact

Multinational. Description: Aviculturists. Strives to protect, preserve, and enhance the keeping and breeding of exotic birds through educational programs, cooperative breeding programs, and avian research and conservation programs. Hosts conventions.

4200 ■ Quaker Parakeet Society (QPS)
PO Box 7241
Eugene, OR 97401
E-mail: qpsociety@hotmail.com
URL: http://qp-society.com

Founded: 1999. **Membership Dues:** single in U.S., $20 (annual) ● single in Canada, $22 (annual) ● student, $15 (annual). **Multinational. Description:** Supports the responsible keeping and breeding of Quaker Parakeets. Strives to provide factual, detailed information on Quakers. Encourages the legalization of Quakers in states where the birds are currently banned and strives to prevent further restrictions of ownership. Promotes protection and preservation of Quaker natural habitats. **Computer Services:** Information services, Quaker resources ● online services, discussion list. **Committees:** Fundraising. **Programs:** Quaker Parakeet Society Rescue And Placement. **Publications:** *The Sentinel*, quarterly. Journal. **Price:** included in membership dues.

4201 ■ Serama Council of North America (SCNA)
c/o Jerry Schexnayder, Treas.
PO Box 159
Vacherie, LA 70090
E-mail: serama4sale@jerschex.com
URL: http://www.seramacouncilofnorthamerica.com
Contact: Jerry Schexnayder, Treas.

Founded: 2003. **Membership Dues:** family, $20 (annual) ● individual, $15 (annual) ● junior, $10 (annual). **Multinational. Description:** Represents individuals dedicated to the introduction and promotion of the American Serama. Promotes the further breeding, development and improvement of the Serama in North America. Seeks to improve the beauty, quality, health and vigor of the American Serama. Offers educational and support programs for members, breeders and judges alike.

4202 ■ Tanygnathus Society
4510 Buckingham Rd.
Fort Myers, FL 33905
E-mail: jungalajune@earthlink.net
URL: http://thetanygnathussociety.org
Contact: June Dinger, Pres.

Founded: 2000. **Members:** 20. **Membership Dues:** single in U.S., $20 (annual) ● single in Canada, $26 (annual). **Multinational. Description:** Represents aviculturists interested in Tanygnathus Genus Parrots. Seeks to assist in the preservation and breeding of the Tanygnathus species. Takes census of genus population; disseminates information; promotes responsible aviculture. **Awards: Type:** recognition.

Recipient: for domestic breeding. **Publications:** *The Tanygnathus Society Bulletin*, 3/year. **Price:** free for members. **Advertising:** accepted.

Butterfly

4203 ■ International Butterfly Breeders Association (IBBA)
c/o Renee Cooke, Exec. Dir.
7917 Breeezy Point Rd.
Melrose, FL 32666
Ph: (352)258-0324
E-mail: executive_director.ibba@yahoo.com
URL: http://www.butterflybreeders.org
Contact: Renee Cooke, Exec. Dir.
Founded: 1998. **Membership Dues:** regular, $160 (annual) ● second/international/associate, $105 (annual) ● student, $55 (annual). **Multinational. Description:** Promotes high standards of ethics, competence and professionalism in the breeding of quality Lepidoptera through research, education, market development, and habitat conservation and restoration. **Computer Services:** Information services, butterfly resources ● mailing lists, of members. **Committees:** Business Relations and Business Development; Butterfly Breeders Formal Charities; Butterfly Gardening; Bylaws; Political Action and Strategic Planning; Scientific Research; State Agricultural Officials Contact. **Programs:** Wings of Hope. **Publications:** *Board Orientation Manual*. Provides information to new and prospective board members about the role and responsibilities of being a board member. Alternate Formats: online.

Cat

4204 ■ American Keuda Cat Association (AKCA)
PO Box 636
Palmer, TX 75152
Free: (866)841-2813
E-mail: keuda@yahoo.com
URL: http://www.hercurian.com/keuda
Contact: Jacque Brown, Pres.
Description: Seeks to promote and preserve the Keuda Cat breed. Develops breeding standards. Serves as a forum for the Keuda Cat owners and breeders. **Computer Services:** Information services, breed standard. **Telecommunication Services:** electronic mail, pattist@earthlink.net. **Publications:** Brochure. Alternate Formats: online.

4205 ■ The International Bengal Breeders' Association (TIBBA)
2336 Pleasant Grove
Westmoreland, TN 37186
Ph: (615)644-2992
E-mail: tibba@tibba.8k.com
URL: http://www.tibba.8k.com
Contact: Bonnie Clark, Sec.-Treas.
Founded: 2000. **Membership Dues:** general, $20 (annual) ● general (life), $200 ● breeder, $40 (annual) ● breeder (life), $400 ● family, $10 (annual) ● family (life), $100. **Multinational. Description:** Seeks to preserve and promote the future of domestic Bengal Cats. Provides education to the general public, pet owners and Bengal Cat breeders. **Computer Services:** database, breeders' lists ● information services, Bengal Cat resources ● mailing lists. **Committees:** Bengal Education; Bengal Rescue; E-mail List; Fundraising; Genetics; Historical; Legislative; Public Relations. **Publications:** *Bengal Tails*, quarterly. Newsletter. **Price:** $24.00 plus shipping and handling (for CD copy). Alternate Formats: online; CD-ROM.

4206 ■ The International Bengal Cat Society (TIBCS)
PO Box 50198
Long Beach, CA 90815
E-mail: president@tibcs.com
URL: http://www.bengalcat.com
Contact: Nancy Prince, Pres.
Membership Dues: general, junior, $30 (annual) ● breeder, $45 (annual) ● family in U.S. and international, $60 (annual). **Multinational. Description:** Seeks to promote and preserve the Bengal breed of domestic cats. Promotes high breeding standards. Disseminates information about the Bengal Cat. Serves as a forum for Bengal Cat owners and breeders. **Computer Services:** database, breeder directory ● information services, Bengal Cat resources. **Telecommunication Services:** electronic mail, msecretary@tibcs.com. **Publications:** *Bengal Bulletin*, quarterly. Newsletter. **Price:** included in membership dues.

4207 ■ International Desert Lynx Cat Association (IDLCA)
PO Box 511
Selma, OR 97538
E-mail: dlynxcat@earthlink.net
URL: http://www.idlca.com
Contact: Arlene Magrino, Pres.
Membership Dues: general, $20 (annual) ● breeder, $30 (annual) ● life, $200-$300. **Multinational. Description:** Seeks to preserve and improve the Desert Lynx Cat breed. Serves as a forum for Desert Lynx Cat owners and breeders. Develops Desert Lynx Cat breeding standards. **Computer Services:** database, owner/breeders lists ● information services, Desert Lynx Cat breed history and standards ● mailing lists ● online services, discussion. **Publications:** Newsletter, quarterly. Alternate Formats: online.

4208 ■ The International Savannah Breeders' Association (TISBA)
571 Millcross Rd.
Lancaster, PA 17601
E-mail: tisba@tisba.8k.com
URL: http://tisba.8k.com
Contact: Allison Navarro, Pres.
Founded: 2000. **Membership Dues:** general, $20 (annual) ● general (life), $200 ● breeder, $30 (annual) ● breeder (life), $300 ● family, $10 (annual) ● family (life), $100. **Multinational. Description:** Seeks to improve and preserve Savannah Cats. Provides education to the general public, pet owners and Savannah breeders. **Computer Services:** database, breeders list ● mailing lists ● online services, discussion forum. **Publications:** Newsletter, quarterly. Alternate Formats: online.

4209 ■ International Society for Endangered Cats (ISEC)
3070 Riverside Dr., Ste.160
Columbus, OH 43221
Ph: (614)487-8760
Fax: (614)487-8769
E-mail: felineinfo@isec.org
Founded: 1988. **Membership Dues:** student, $18 (annual) ● individual, $25 (annual) ● family, $50 (annual) ● supporting, $100 (annual) ● sustaining, $500 (annual) ● patron, $1,000 (annual). **Multinational. Description:** Raises public understanding and knowledge of wild cats. Supports research on ecology, captive breeding and reintroduction of cats to their native habitats. **Telecommunication Services:** electronic mail, membership@isec.org ● electronic mail, education@isec.org. **Programs:** Educational. **Publications:** Newsletter. Alternate Formats: online.

4210 ■ National Alliance of Burmese Breeders (NABB)
c/o Prudence Dorazio, Sec.
40 Morgan Point
Groton, CT 06340
E-mail: prudencedorazio@aol.com
URL: http://www.burmesecat.org
Contact: Prudence Dorazio, Sec.
Membership Dues: full, $25 (annual) ● associate, $20 (annual) ● family (2 or more members in the same household), $30 (annual). **Description:** Preserves the Burmese breed. Promotes the welfare of all cats. Encourages excellence in breeding practices. Provides information pertaining to health, genetic traits and other characteristics of the Burmese breed. Assists in the placement of homeless, displaced and abandoned Burmese cats. **Computer Services:** database, breeders directory ● database, pedigree ● information services, Burmese resources ● online services, Burmese Rescue Yahoo group. **Programs:** Burmese Rescue. **Affiliated With:** Cat Fanciers' Association. **Publications:** Newsletter, quarterly.

4211 ■ Savannah Cat Club (SVCC)
571 Millcross Rd.
Lancaster, PA 17601
E-mail: secretary@savannahcatclub.com
URL: http://www.savannahcatclub.com
Contact: Jennifer Miller, Pres.
Membership Dues: general, $25 (annual) ● breeder, $40 (annual). **Multinational. Description:** Promotes interest in and knowledge of Savannah Cats. Develops and promotes high breeding standards. Advances the Savannah breed. Serves as a forum for Savannah cat owners. **Publications:** *The Savannah Signal Newsletter*. **Price:** included in membership dues.

Cattle

4212 ■ American Angus Association (AAA)
3201 Frederick Ave.
St. Joseph, MO 64506
Ph: (816)383-5100 (816)383-5169
Fax: (816)233-9703
E-mail: angus@angus.org
URL: http://www.angus.org
Contact: John R. Crouch, Exec. VP
Founded: 1883. **Members:** 35,000. **Membership Dues:** regular, $80 (annual) ● junior, $20 (annual). **Staff:** 140. **Budget:** $16,000,000. **Regional Groups:** 30. **State Groups:** 40. **Local Groups:** 30. **Description:** Breeders and owners of purebred Angus cattle. Maintains registry for purebred Angus cattle. Collects, verifies, and publishes performance information, pedigrees, and transfers of ownership; offers premiums for the public exhibition of cattle. Promotes sale of Angus cattle in the U.S. through advertising, public information programs, and the Certified Angus Beef CAB Program. Sponsors educational programs; offers youth services. **Computer Services:** Information services, Angus facts and resources. **Telecommunication Services:** electronic mail, jcrouch@angus.org. **Formerly:** (1956) American Aberdeen-Angus Breeder's Association. **Publications:** *AAA 1,2,3*. Newsletter. Alternate Formats: online ● *Angus Journal*, monthly. Contains articles for breeders of registered Angus Cattle. **Price:** $50.00/year. **Circulation:** 21,500. **Advertising:** accepted. **Conventions/Meetings:** competition ● annual meeting, held in conjunction with the North American International Livestock Exposition - always Louisville, KY.

4213 ■ American Belgian Blue Breeders
PO Box 154
Hedrick, IA 52563
Ph: (641)661-2332
Fax: (641)661-2332
E-mail: info@belgianblue.org
URL: http://www.belgianblue.org
Contact: Connie Brooks, Pres.
Founded: 1988. **Members:** 85. **Membership Dues:** regular, $50 (annual). **Staff:** 1. **Budget:** $37,000. **Regional Groups:** 6. **State Groups:** 6. **Description:** Represents breeders of Belgian Blue cattle. Promotes the Belgian Blue breed of cattle; provides registry for cattle pedigrees. Maintains library; compiles statistics. Organizes shows. **Awards:** Junior Member Scholarships-College/University. **Frequency:** annual. **Type:** scholarship ● Premier Breeder and Premier Exhibitor Award. **Frequency:** annual. **Type:** recognition. **Telecommunication Services:** electronic mail, stevedollarhide@yahoo.com. **Formerly:** (1999) American Belgian Blue Association; (2003) American Belgian Blue Breeders Association. **Publications:** *Journal of the American Belgian Blue Breeders*, semiannual. Includes quarterly newsletter. **Conventions/Meetings:** annual meeting, national show, sales, and annual membership meeting.

4214 ■ American Black Hereford Association (ABHA)
25333 Wolcott Rd.
Leavenworth, KS 66048
Ph: (913)727-1266

Fax: (913)351-1515
E-mail: mail@blackhereford.com
URL: http://www.blackhereford.com
Contact: Joe Hoagland, Exec. Off.
Founded: 1994. **Membership Dues:** life, $500 ● individual, $100 (annual) ● associate, $50 (annual). **Description:** Collects, records and preserves the pedigrees of Black Hereford cattle. Stimulates and regulates any and all other matters that pertain to the history, breeding, exhibition, publicity, sale or preservation of the Black Hereford breed. **Computer Services:** database, breeders list.

4215 ■ American Blonde d'Aquitaine Association (ABAA)
7407 VZ County Rd. 1507
Grand Saline, TX 75140
Ph: (903)570-0568 (334)222-9631
E-mail: info@blondecattle.org
URL: http://www.blondecattle.org
Contact: Clayton Bryant, Pres.
Founded: 1973. **Members:** 65. **Membership Dues:** active, $50 (annual) ● associate, $25 (annual). **Staff:** 2. **Budget:** $25,000. **Regional Groups:** 4. **Description:** Registers and promotes the blonde d'Aquitaine breed of cattle in the U.S. **Computer Services:** Mailing lists ● online services, herd book. **Absorbed:** (1986) National Blonde D'Aquitaine Foundation. **Publications:** *Blonde Bulletin*, quarterly. Newsletter. **Circulation:** 1,200. **Advertising:** accepted ● Brochures ● Directory, periodic ● Membership Directory. Alternate Formats: online. **Conventions/Meetings:** annual meeting (exhibits).

4216 ■ American Brahman Breeders Association (ABBA)
3003 S Loop W, Ste.520
Houston, TX 77054
Ph: (713)349-0854
Fax: (713)349-9795
E-mail: abba@brahman.org
URL: http://www.brahman.org
Contact: Armelinda Ibarra, Office Mgr./Recording Sec.
Founded: 1924. **Members:** 1,700. **Membership Dues:** active, $100 (annual). **Staff:** 8. **Budget:** $550,000. **State Groups:** 11. **Description:** Breeders of purebred registered Brahman cattle and others interested in Brahmans or their use for crossbreeding. Works to: keep proper records of pedigree and transfer of ownership of Brahman cattle entered in the Herd Register; assist in the sponsorship of cattle exhibitions and shows; aid scientific education concerning the breeding of Brahman cattle. **Libraries: Type:** reference. **Holdings:** reports. **Telecommunication Services:** electronic mail, cshivers@brahman.org. **Committees:** Breed Improvement; Communications; Finance; International; Research; Show; Youth Activities. **Programs:** Carcass Evaluation. **Publications:** *ABBA Membership Handbook*. **Price:** $25.00 ● *The Brahman Journal* (in English, French, German, Portuguese, and Spanish), monthly. Alternate Formats: online ● *Membership List*, annual. Membership Directory. **Price:** available to members only. **Conventions/Meetings:** annual conference - always February, Houston, TX.

4217 ■ American Brahmousin Council (ABC)
PO Box 88
Whitesboro, TX 76273
Ph: (903)564-3995
E-mail: info@brahmousin.org
URL: http://www.brahmousin.org
Contact: Bob Cummins, Interim Dir.
Members: 95. **Description:** Breeders of Brahmousin cattle. **Publications:** *Brahmousin Connection*, quarterly.

4218 ■ American British White Park Association (ABWPA)
PO Box 957
Harrison, AR 72602
Free: (877)900-BEEF
Fax: (208)979-2008
E-mail: info@whitecattle.org
URL: http://www.whitecattle.org
Contact: Glenn Wenger, Pres.
Founded: 1975. **Members:** 528. **Membership Dues:** adult, associate, $100 (annual) ● junior (under 18 years old), $10 (annual) ● junior (over 18 years old), $90 (annual). **Staff:** 1. **State Groups:** 3. **Description:** Owners and others interested in White Park cattle. Collects, verifies, records, preserves, and publishes pedigrees of White Park cattle. Aims to maintain the purity of the breed and to seek identification of the breed as "genetically superior". **Telecommunication Services:** electronic mail, gwenger@wengers.com. **Formerly:** (2000) White Park Cattle Association of America. **Publications:** *White Cattle Journal*, quarterly. **Conventions/Meetings:** annual meeting.

4219 ■ American Chianina Association (ACA)
1708 N Prairie View Rd.
PO Box 890
Platte City, MO 64079
Ph: (816)431-2808 (706)693-4133
Fax: (816)431-5381
E-mail: amerchianina@earthlink.net
URL: http://www.chicattle.org
Contact: Glen Klippenstein, CEO
Founded: 1972. **Members:** 6,200. **Membership Dues:** adult, $100 (annual) ● junior, $25 (annual). **Staff:** 6. **Regional Groups:** 9. **Description:** Promotes and registers Chianina cattle. **Libraries: Type:** open to the public. **Holdings:** articles. **Telecommunication Services:** electronic mail, geuns@msu.edu. **Publications:** *American Chianina Journal*. **Price:** included in membership dues. **Advertising:** accepted. Alternate Formats: online. Also Cited As: *ACJ*. **Conventions/Meetings:** annual meeting.

4220 ■ American Devon Cattle Association (ADCA)
c/o Martha Trantham, Exec. Sec.
43 Lenoir Ln.
Canton, NC 28716
Ph: (828)235-8269
E-mail: tranthamsdevon@cbvnol.com
URL: http://www.americandevon.com
Contact: Martha Trantham, Exec. Sec.
Founded: 1918. **Members:** 125. **Membership Dues:** general, $50 (annual) ● junior, $5 (annual). **Staff:** 5. **Budget:** $10,000. **Description:** Breeders of purebred registered Devon cattle. Maintains registry, pedigree records, and hall of fame. Encourages a program of performance testing for the genetic improvement of the breed. Sponsors competitions; compiles statistics. **Committees:** Breed Improvement; Promotion; Publicity; Show and Sale. **Formerly:** (1971) American Devon Cattle Club. **Publications:** *Devon Cattle Quarterly*. Newsletter ● Brochures. **Advertising:** accepted. **Conventions/Meetings:** quadrennial World Devon Congress - meeting.

4221 ■ American Dexter Cattle Association (ADCA)
4150 Merino Ave.
Watertown, MN 55388
Ph: (952)215-2206 (970)858-1931
E-mail: adca@dextercattle.org
URL: http://dextercattle.org
Contact: David Jones, Pres.
Founded: 1912. **Members:** 650. **Membership Dues:** regular, $30 (annual). **Description:** Breeders of purebred Dexter cattle. Dexter cattle were brought to the U.S. from Ireland in 1912; the breed is America's smallest, weighing 650-1000 lbs. Seeks to ensure the quality of the breed. **Telecommunication Services:** electronic mail, djones2for2@yahoo.com. **Committees:** Five Year Goals for the ADCA. **Formerly:** (1957) American Kerry and Dexter Club. **Publications:** *Dexter Cattle*. Book. **Price:** $9.25 ● *Herd Book*, annual ● *2005 American Dexter Cattle Association Membership Directory* ● Bulletin, bimonthly. Contains information of interest and offerings of animals and semen for sale. **Conventions/Meetings:** annual meeting.

4222 ■ American Galloway Breeders' Association (AGBA)
310 W Spruce
Missoula, MT 59802
Ph: (406)728-5719 (262)377-7292
E-mail: doublejj@americangalloway.com
URL: http://www.americangalloway.com
Contact: Steven Castner, Pres.
Founded: 1888. **Members:** 125. **Membership Dues:** active, associate, $20 (annual) ● individual, $75 (annual) ● life, $250. **Staff:** 1. **Regional Groups:** 4. **Description:** Breeders of registered Galloway cattle. Promotes the breed and maintains a registry. Champions steers at major cattle shows. **Telecommunication Services:** electronic mail, slcastner@americangalloway.com. **Absorbed:** (1973) Galloway Performance International. **Publications:** *Breeder's Directory*, annual. Membership Directory. Lists members in U.S. and Canada. **Price:** free. **Advertising:** accepted ● *The Galloway Globe*, quarterly. Newsletter. **Price:** $20.00 included in membership dues; $20.00/year in U.S.; $25.00/year outside U.S. ● *Midwest Galloway News*, quarterly. Newsletter. **Price:** $10.00/year ● Brochure. **Conventions/Meetings:** annual Field Days - meeting (exhibits) - usually June ● annual meeting and show, held in conjunction with the Northern International Livestock Exposition, Billings, Montana (exhibits) - always October.

4223 ■ American Gelbvieh Association (AGA)
10900 Dover St.
Westminster, CO 80021
Ph: (303)465-2333
Fax: (303)465-2339
E-mail: info@gelbvieh.org
URL: http://www.gelbvieh.org
Contact: Wayne Vanderwert, Exec. Dir.
Founded: 1971. **Members:** 2,200. **Membership Dues:** active, $75 (annual) ● active in Canada and Mexico, $100 (annual) ● active in all other countries, $125 (annual) ● junior, $10 (annual). **Staff:** 15. **Budget:** $1,400,000. **Regional Groups:** 4. **State Groups:** 25. **Description:** Individuals who breed Gelbvieh cattle. Objectives are the registration of Gelbvieh cattle and the promotion of the breed. Maintains sire evaluation program. **Libraries: Type:** reference. **Holdings:** photographs. **Computer Services:** database, of members. **Telecommunication Services:** electronic mail, waynev@gelbvieh.org. **Programs:** Commercial Marketing; SmartBuy; SmartCross. **Publications:** *Gelbvieh World*, 11/year, 1 edition for June/July. Magazine. **Price:** $25.00/year. **Advertising:** accepted. Alternate Formats: diskette; CD-ROM ● Membership Directory, annual ● Also publishes sire summary. **Conventions/Meetings:** annual meeting - always January.

4224 ■ American Guernsey Association (AGA)
7614 Slate Ridge Blvd.
Reynoldsburg, OH 43068
Ph: (614)864-2409 (614)575-4620
Fax: (614)864-5614
E-mail: info@usguernsey.com
URL: http://www.usguernsey.com
Contact: Seth Johnson, Exec. Sec.-Treas.
Founded: 1877. **Members:** 1,500. **Membership Dues:** senior life, $150 ● junior, $5 ● junior converting to senior, $75. **Staff:** 6. **Budget:** $500,000. **State Groups:** 35. **Local Groups:** 10. **Description:** Breeders of registered Guernsey dairy cattle. Seeks to: conduct research to assist in the development of breeding a more profitable animal; improve marketing strategy for Guernsey milk; develop motivational programs for Guernsey breeders. **Awards:** Distinguished Service. **Frequency:** annual. **Type:** recognition ● Living Lifetime Production Award. **Frequency:** annual. **Type:** recognition. **Recipient:** to the cow with the top lifetime milk, fat and protein production ● Master Breeder. **Frequency:** annual. **Type:** recognition ● Max Dawdy Scholarship. **Frequency:** annual. **Type:** scholarship. **Recipient:** to one or more junior member ● National Outstanding Young Farmer. **Frequency:** annual. **Type:** recognition. **Recipient:** to an individual under age of 35 with notable contribution to the Guernsey breed ● Outstanding Youth. **Fre-**

quency: annual. **Type:** recognition ● Production Award. **Frequency:** annual. **Type:** recognition. **Recipient:** to a junior member who owns and breeds animals that excel in production ● Youth Scholarship. **Frequency:** annual. **Type:** scholarship. **Recipient:** to one junior member. **Computer Services:** Information services. **Telecommunication Services:** electronic mail, ialbert@usguernsey.com. **Divisions:** Extension; Information; Journal; Marketing; Records. **Programs:** Youth Lease. **Formerly:** (1987) American Guernsey Cattle Club. **Publications:** *Guernsey Breeders Journal*, 10/year. Includes information on shows and awards. **Price:** $15.00/year in U.S.; $18.00/year outside U.S. ISSN: 0017-5100. **Circulation:** 1,800. **Advertising:** accepted ● *National Guernsey Directory 2003-2004*. Alternate Formats: online. **Conventions/Meetings:** annual meeting (exhibits).

4225 ■ American Hereford Association (AHA)

PO Box 014059
Kansas City, MO 64101
Ph: (816)842-3757
Fax: (816)842-6931
E-mail: aha@hereford.org
URL: http://www.hereford.org
Contact: Craig Huffhines, Exec. VP

Founded: 1881. **Members:** 20,000. **Membership Dues:** life, $1,000 ● recording, $30 (annual). **Staff:** 50. **Budget:** $3,500,000. **State Groups:** 37. **Local Groups:** 75. **Description:** Breeders of purebred Hereford cattle. Maintains registry, pedigree, and performance records; provides fieldman assistance and guidance; conducts research programs; maintains hall of fame and museum; sponsors competitions; compiles statistics. **Libraries: Type:** reference. **Holdings:** 300. **Subjects:** Hereford history. **Awards: Type:** recognition. **Telecommunication Services:** electronic mail, chuffhin@hereford.org. **Committees:** Legislative; Research. **Absorbed:** (1999) American Polled Hereford Association. **Publications:** *Hereford World*, monthly. Journal. Contains Hereford news and information. **Price:** $25.00 /year for individuals. **Circulation:** 12,000. **Advertising:** accepted. **Conventions/Meetings:** annual meeting - always November, Kansas City, MO.

4226 ■ American Herens Association (AHA)

Address Unknown since 2008

Founded: 1983. **Members:** 25. **Description:** Individuals who own and raise Herens cattle. Seeks to introduce and establish Herens cattle in the U.S. The breed originated in Herens Valley in Switzerland and has only recently been imported to the U.S. **Publications:** none. **Convention/Meeting:** none. Only herd in North America located in Lewisburg, W. VA.

4227 ■ American Highland Cattle Association (AHCA)

200 Livestock Exchange Bldg.
4701 Marion St.
Denver, CO 80216
Ph: (303)292-9102
Fax: (303)292-9171
E-mail: info@highlandcattleusa.org
URL: http://www.highlandcattleusa.org
Contact: Eddie Mackay, Pres.

Founded: 1948. **Members:** 1,200. **Membership Dues:** individual in U.S., $60 (annual) ● life in U.S., $1,000 ● life outside U.S., $1,325 ● individual outside U.S., $80 (annual). **Staff:** 2. **Budget:** $200,000. **Regional Groups:** 9. **Description:** Represents highland cattle producers and enthusiasts. Maintains cattle registry, promotion, research, and education related to this breed. **Formerly:** American Scotch Highland Breeders Association. **Publications:** *The Bagpipe*, quarterly. Journal. Contains breed happenings, show and sale results, articles of general interest to cattle breeders, and member advertising. **Price:** included in membership dues; $16.00/year in U.S.; $28.00/year outside U.S. **Circulation:** 1,200. **Advertising:** accepted ● Brochures ● Pamphlets. **Conventions/Meetings:** annual meeting and trade show (exhibits) - usually held in the summer during June.

4228 ■ American-International Charolais Association (AICA)

11700 NW Plaza Cir.
Kansas City, MO 64153
Ph: (816)464-5977 (636)285-2554
Fax: (816)464-5759
E-mail: north@charolaisusa.com
URL: http://www.charolaisusa.com
Contact: J. Neil Orth, Exec. VP

Founded: 1957. **Members:** 4,200. **Membership Dues:** regular, active, $75 (annual) ● junior, $20 (annual). **Staff:** 23. **Budget:** $1,300,000. **Description:** Breeders of Charolais and Charolais crossbred cattle in Canada, Mexico, South Africa, United Kingdom, and United States. Maintains registry and pedigree records. Conducts cattlemen's seminars. Sponsors the International Junior Charolais Association. **Libraries: Type:** reference. **Holdings:** articles. **Telecommunication Services:** electronic mail, mwegner@charolaisusa.com. **Committees:** Advertising and Marketing; Affiliate; Breed Improvement; Charbray; Commercial; Junior; Long Range Planning; Rules and Ethics. **Absorbed:** (1967) American Charbray Breeders Association. **Formed by Merger of:** American Charolais Breeders Association; International Charollaise Association. **Publications:** *Charolais Journal*, monthly. **Price:** $50.00 in U.S.; $75.00 in Canada, foreign ● Membership Directory, annual. **Conventions/Meetings:** semiannual conference.

4229 ■ American International Marchigiana Society

PO Box 198
Walton, KS 67151-0198
Ph: (620)837-3303
Fax: (316)283-8379
E-mail: info@marchigiana.org
URL: http://www.marchigiana.org

Founded: 1973. **Description:** Marchigiana cattle breeders. Sponsors organized breeding-up program.

4230 ■ American Jersey Cattle Association (AJCA)

6486 E Main St.
Reynoldsburg, OH 43068-2362
Ph: (614)861-3636 (614)755-5857
Fax: (614)861-8040
E-mail: nsmith@usjersey.com
URL: http://www.usjersey.com
Contact: Neal Smith, Exec. Sec./CEO

Founded: 1868. **Members:** 2,400. **Membership Dues:** life, $100. **Staff:** 35. **Budget:** $1,800,000. **State Groups:** 46. **Description:** Owners and breeders of Jersey cattle. Promotes sale and use of Jersey milk through National All-Jersey, Inc., an affiliate. **Awards:** Cedarcrest Farms Scholarship. **Frequency:** annual. **Type:** scholarship. **Recipient:** for a student in a large veterinary practice ● Distinguished Service Award. **Frequency:** annual. **Type:** recognition. **Recipient:** for members who have rendered outstanding service ● Master Breeder Award. **Frequency:** annual. **Type:** recognition. **Recipient:** for members who have made notable contributions to the Jersey breed ● Reuben R. Cowles Jersey Youth Award. **Frequency:** annual. **Type:** scholarship. **Recipient:** for Jersey youth living in southeastern states ● Young Jersey Breeder Award. **Frequency:** annual. **Type:** recognition. **Recipient:** for members who have shown expertise in dairy farming and Jersey cattle breeding. **Additional Websites:** http://www.jerseydirectory.com. **Telecommunication Services:** electronic mail, pengland@usjersey.com. **Formerly:** American Jersey Cattle Club. **Publications:** *Jersey Directory*, every 18 months. Lists dairies by state. **Price:** $50.00/listing. **Circulation:** 5,000. **Advertising:** accepted. Alternate Formats: online ● *Jersey Journal*, monthly. **Price:** $25.00/year. **Circulation:** 3,000. **Advertising:** accepted. Alternate Formats: online ● Annual Report, annual. Alternate Formats: online. **Conventions/Meetings:** annual meeting and convention (exhibits) - usually June.

4231 ■ American Junior Brahman Association (AJBA)

c/o American Brahman Breeders Association
3003 S Loop W, Ste.520
Houston, TX 77054
Ph: (713)349-0854 (979)732-4175
Fax: (713)349-9795
E-mail: abba@brahman.org
URL: http://www.brahman.org/ajba.html
Contact: Janie Tipp, Pres.

Founded: 1980. **Members:** 1,322. **Membership Dues:** regular, $10 (annual). **Staff:** 1. **Regional Groups:** 12. **State Groups:** 12. **Description:** Individuals less than 21 years of age who are interested in Brahman cattle. **Awards: Type:** recognition ● **Type:** scholarship. **Telecommunication Services:** electronic mail, cshivers@brahman.org. **Committees:** Youth Activities. **Affiliated With:** American Brahman Breeders Association. **Publications:** *The Brahman Journal*, monthly. Magazine. **Price:** $15.00/year. **Advertising:** accepted. **Conventions/Meetings:** annual All-American Junior Brahman Show - always July.

4232 ■ American Junior Chianina Association (AJCA)

c/o American Chianina Association
1708 N Prairie View Rd.
PO Box 890
Platte City, MO 64079
Ph: (816)431-2808
Fax: (816)431-5381
E-mail: amerchianina@earthlink.net
URL: http://www.chicattle.org/ajca.html
Contact: Andy Higgins, Pres./Dir.

Founded: 1978. **Members:** 1,855. **Membership Dues:** individual, $25. **Staff:** 2. **Budget:** $30,000. **Regional Groups:** 9. **State Groups:** 14. **Description:** Individuals under age 21 who raise Chianina cattle. Registers and promotes Chianina cattle. **Awards: Type:** recognition. **Affiliated With:** American Chianina Association. **Publications:** *American Chianina Journal*, bimonthly. **Price:** $25.00/year. **Circulation:** 2,500. **Advertising:** accepted. Alternate Formats: online. **Conventions/Meetings:** annual National Junior Heifer Show - competition (exhibits) ● annual show.

4233 ■ American Junior Shorthorn Association (AJSA)

c/o American Shorthorn Association
8288 Hascall St.
Omaha, NE 68124
Ph: (402)393-7200
Fax: (402)393-7203
E-mail: info@shorthorn.org
URL: http://www.shorthorn.org
Contact: Greg Ruehle, Exec. Sec.

Founded: 1968. **Members:** 3,500. **Staff:** 2. **State Groups:** 30. **Description:** Young people involved in the U.S. beef industry. Aims to educate and interest young people in Shorthorn and Polled Shorthorn cattle. **Awards: Type:** recognition. **Telecommunication Services:** electronic mail, greg@shorthorn.org. **Programs:** Annual National Junior Shorthorn Show; Annual National Shorthorn Youth Conference. **Affiliated With:** American Shorthorn Association. **Publications:** *Shorthorn Country*, monthly. Magazine. **Advertising:** accepted. **Conventions/Meetings:** competition ● annual meeting.

4234 ■ American Maine-Anjou Association (AMAA)

204 Marshall Rd.
PO Box 1100
Platte City, MO 64079-1100
Ph: (816)431-9950
Fax: (816)431-9951
E-mail: maine@kc.rr.com
URL: http://www.maine-anjou.org
Contact: John Boddicker, Exec. VP

Founded: 1969. **Members:** 2,400. **Membership Dues:** adult, $50 (annual) ● junior, $15 (annual). **Staff:** 7. **Budget:** $1,100,000. **State Groups:** 18. **Description:** Works for the promotion and registration of the Maine-Anjou breed of beef cattle. Has registered 117,000 cattle. Compiles statistics. **Telecommunication Services:** electronic mail, amaajohn@kc.rr.com. **Formerly:** (1971) Maine-Anjou Society; (1975) International Maine-Anjou Association. **Publications:** *The Maine-Anjou Voice*, bimonthly. Magazine. **Price:** $20.00/year in U.S.; $25.00/year in Canada; $35.00/year for other foreign subscriptions. **Advertising:** accepted. Alternate Formats: online ● *The Maine Edition*, quarterly. Newsletter. Alternate Formats: online ● *Sale Reports*. Alternate Formats: online ● *Show Reports*. Alternate Formats: online. **Conventions/Meetings:** board meeting ● executive committee meeting ● annual meeting and convention.

4235 ■ American Milking Devon Cattle Association (AMDCA)
c/o Sue Randall, Registrar
135 Old Bay Rd.
New Durham, NH 03855
Ph: (603)859-6611
E-mail: mdevons@worldpath.net
URL: http://www.milkingdevons.org
Contact: Sue Randall, Registrar
Founded: 1978. **Members:** 85. **Membership Dues:** voting, associate, $20 (annual). **Description:** Breeders working to promote Devon cattle, a rare breed of red dairy cattle from England. Strives to promote historic breed as the premier breed of cattle for sustainable healthy agriculture to benefit both future farmers and the evolving health conscious consumer in the marketplace. **Computer Services:** database ● online services, breeder's list. **Conventions/Meetings:** annual meeting.

4236 ■ American Milking Shorthorn Junior Society (AMSJS)
800 Pleasant St.
Beloit, WI 53511-5456
Ph: (608)365-3332
Fax: (608)365-6644
E-mail: info@milkingshorthorn.com
URL: http://www.milkingshorthorn.com
Contact: Theresa Krause, Pres.
Founded: 1970. **Members:** 350. **Staff:** 2. **State Groups:** 30. **Description:** Individuals from birth to 20 years of age interested in the Milking Shorthorn breed of cattle. Sponsors competitions. **Awards: Type:** recognition. **Telecommunication Services:** electronic mail, cows_23@hotmail.com. **Publications:** *Milking Shorthorn Journal*, bimonthly. **Price:** $3.00/issue; $20.00/year foreign. **Conventions/Meetings:** meeting, held in conjunction with the American Milking Shorthorn Society.

4237 ■ American Milking Shorthorn Society (AMSS)
c/o David J. Kendall, Exec. Sec.
800 Pleasant St.
Beloit, WI 53511-5456
Ph: (608)365-3332
Fax: (608)365-6644
E-mail: info@milkingshorthorn.com
URL: http://www.milkingshorthorn.com
Contact: David J. Kendall, Exec. Sec.
Founded: 1920. **Members:** 400. **Membership Dues:** full, $45 (annual) ● associate, $30 (annual) ● junior, $25 (annual). **Staff:** 2. **Budget:** $150,000. **State Groups:** 30. **Description:** Breeders of registered Milking Shorthorn cattle producing both milk and beef. Maintains the official registration office for Milking Shorthorn cattle in the U.S. **Affiliated With:** American Milking Shorthorn Junior Society; Purebred Dairy Cattle Association. **Publications:** *Milking Shorthorn Journal*, bimonthly. Includes information on society's rules and regulations, calendar of events, national sales and shows, and breeder interest articles. **Price:** included in membership dues; $15.00 /year for nonmembers in U.S.; $20.00 /year for nonmembers outside U.S. ISSN: 1073-9394. **Circulation:** 700. **Advertising:** accepted. **Conventions/Meetings:** annual competition and convention (exhibits).

4238 ■ American Miniature Jersey Cattle Registry
Address Unknown since 2007
Description: Promotes the American Miniature Jersey Cattle breed; provides a breed registry.

4239 ■ American Murray Grey Association (AMGA)
PO Box 60748
Reno, NV 89506
Ph: (775)972-7526
Fax: (775)972-7526
E-mail: amgaoffice@murraygreybeefcattle.com
URL: http://www.murraygreybeefcattle.com
Contact: John E. Gerow, Exec. Dir.
Founded: 1970. **Members:** 200. **Membership Dues:** regular, $50 (annual) ● associate, $25 (annual) ● junior, $10 (annual). **Staff:** 2. **Regional Groups:** 3. **State Groups:** 1. **Description:** Livestock breeders. Promotes the Murray Grey breed of beef cattle. **Committees:** Exhibition; Performance; Promotion. **Programs:** Certified Murray Grey Beef. **Publications:** *American Murray Grey News*, quarterly. Newsletter. Includes new members list, calendar of events, and national show results. **Advertising:** accepted ● *The Herd Book*, biennial ● Yearbook. **Conventions/Meetings:** annual meeting ● seminar, educational.

4240 ■ American National CattleWomen (ANCW)
PO Box 3881
Englewood, CO 80155
Ph: (303)694-0313
Fax: (303)694-2390
E-mail: ancw@beef.org
URL: http://www.ancw.org
Contact: Marcie Hervey, Exec. Dir.
Founded: 1952. **Members:** 2,300. **Membership Dues:** basic, $50 (annual) ● sustaining, $75 (annual) ● collegiate, $30 (annual) ● state affiliate, $150 (annual) ● associate (business, corporation, private enterprise, individual), $100 (annual). **Staff:** 1. **Regional Groups:** 7. **State Groups:** 31. **Description:** Individuals who are employed or interested in the cattle industry. Promotes versatility and healthfulness of beef. Conducts promotional and educational programs including National Beef Cook-Off and Beef Ambassador Competition. **Committees:** Animal Care; Education; Legislative; National Beef Ambassador; National Beef Cook-Off; Promotion; Publicity. **Formerly:** (1986) American National CowBelles. **Publications:** *American CattleWoman*, quarterly. Newsletter. Provides timely information about organizational activities and beef industry issues. **Price:** $30.00. ISSN: 1042-5293. **Circulation:** 7,000. **Conventions/Meetings:** semiannual conference (exhibits) - always summer and spring ● annual convention and trade show - 2009 Jan. 28-31, Phoenix, AZ; 2010 Jan. 27-30, San Antonio, TX.

4241 ■ American Pinzgauer Association (APA)
PO Box 147
Bethany, MO 64424
Ph: (660)425-8617
Free: (800)914-9883
Fax: (660)425-8374
E-mail: info@pinzgauers.org
URL: http://www.pinzgauers.org
Contact: Glenn Erickson, Pres.
Founded: 1973. **Members:** 508. **Membership Dues:** junior, $5 (annual) ● adult, $50 (annual) ● life, $500 ● junior initial fee, $10 ● associate, $100 (annual). **Staff:** 1. **Budget:** $50,000. **Regional Groups:** 6. **Description:** Cattle breeders. Promotes and develops the Pinzgauer breed and works to ensure that it will make a significant contribution to the cattle industry. Operates systems for the registration, evaluation, and recording of Pinzgauer cattle. Maintains high breeding standards with emphasis on beef production. **Awards: Type:** recognition. **Recipient:** for breeders and directors. **Computer Services:** database, pedigree records and performance data for Pinzgauer cattle in U.S. ● mailing lists, membership, breed interest. **Publications:** *Pinzgauer Journal*, quarterly. Magazine. **Price:** $12.00 in U.S.; $24.00 outside U.S. **Advertising:** accepted ● Membership Directory. Alternate Formats: online. **Conventions/Meetings:** annual meeting and show, held in conjunction with national sale - always September or October.

4242 ■ American Red Brangus Association (ARBA)
3995 E Hwy. 290
Dripping Springs, TX 78620
Ph: (512)858-7285
Fax: (512)858-7084
E-mail: arba@texas.net
URL: http://www.americanredbrangus.org
Contact: Elaine Monaghan, Pres.
Founded: 1956. **Members:** 1,950. **Membership Dues:** active, associate, active junior, $75 (annual) ● junior, $30 (annual). **Staff:** 3. **Regional Groups:** 8. **Description:** Breeders of Red Brangus cattle; interested individuals. Provides for the registration, preservation of blood purity, and improvement of the Red Brangus breed, a crossbreed of purebred Brahman and Angus cattle. Sponsors field programs to aid in furthering the education of members in selecting profitable breeding stock; assists and cooperates with members who sponsor sales. Conducts annual contest in which heifers are judged and sold at auction. **Computer Services:** Mailing lists, registry. **Committees:** Breed Improvement; Journal Policy/Advertising; Junior; Public Relations. **Publications:** *Bull Pen*, monthly. Newsletter. Provides information on how to improve the breeding, feeding, and marketing of Red Brangus cattle. **Price:** included in membership dues. **Advertising:** accepted ● *Membership Mailings*, monthly ● *Red Brangus Bull-Pen*, monthly ● Membership Directory, annual ● Brochure. Alternate Formats: online. **Conventions/Meetings:** annual convention, with cattle, cattle producers, computer services (exhibits) - always November in Texas.

4243 ■ American Red Poll Association (ARPA)
PO Box 147
Bethany, MO 64424
Ph: (660)425-7318
Fax: (660)425-8374
E-mail: info@redpollusa.org
URL: http://www.redpollusa.org
Contact: Leo Young, Pres.
Founded: 1883. **Members:** 1,069. **Membership Dues:** regular, junior, $25 (annual). **Staff:** 1. **State Groups:** 11. **Description:** Represents breeders of purebred Red Poll cattle. Maintains registry showing ownership, transfers, and pedigree records of Red Poll cattle. **Absorbed:** Red Poll Beef Breeders International. **Formerly:** (1976) Red Poll Cattle Club of America. **Publications:** *Breeder Directory*, periodic ● *The Maternal Breed*. Brochure. Alternate Formats: online ● *Red Poll Beef Journal*, semiannual. **Conventions/Meetings:** annual meeting.

4244 ■ American Romagnola Association (ARA)
3815 Touzalin, Ste.104
Lincoln, NE 68507
Ph: (402)466-3334
Fax: (402)466-3338
E-mail: arabeef@aol.com
URL: http://www.americanromagnola.com
Contact: Stephanie Nelson, Sec./Office Mgr.
Founded: 1974. **Members:** 100. **Membership Dues:** active, $100 (annual). **Staff:** 1. **Description:** Represents cattle breeders. Maintains herd book and promotes Romagnola cattle, a breed noted for hardiness and foraging ability, low fat beef, and adaptability. Compiles statistics. **Awards: Type:** recognition. **Publications:** *Association Publication*. Brochures ● *Beefstock*, periodic. Newsletter ● *California Cattleman* ● *Cattle Today* ● *Dover's Journal*, periodic. **Advertising:** accepted ● *Livestock Digest* ● *Southwest Stockman* ● *Western Livestock Reporter*. **Conventions/Meetings:** competition ● annual meeting.

4245 ■ American Salers Association (ASA)
19590 E.Main St., No. 202
Parker, CO 80138
Ph: (303)770-9292
Fax: (303)770-9302

E-mail: sherry@salersusa.org
URL: http://www.salersusa.org
Contact: Ronnie Reece, Pres.
Founded: 1974. **Members:** 1,200. **Membership Dues:** regular, $50 (annual) ● life, $500 ● junior, $15 (annual). **Staff:** 5. **Description:** Breeders of Salers, a French breed of cattle introduced into the United States in 1975, and raised for meat products. Promotes interest in the breed throughout the cattle industry. Maintains registry; sanctions livestock shows; sponsors American Salers Junior Association (see separate entry). **Affiliated With:** American Salers Junior Association. **Publications:** *American Salers*, 9/year. Journal. **Price:** included in membership dues; $15.00 for associate members. **Circulation:** 5,000. **Advertising:** accepted. **Conventions/Meetings:** annual meeting, in conjunction with National Western Stock Show - always January in Denver, CO.

4246 ■ American Salers Junior Association (ASJA)
c/o American Salers Association
19590 E Main St., No. 202
Parker, CO 80138
Ph: (303)770-9292
Fax: (303)770-9302
E-mail: sherry@salersusa.org
URL: http://www.salersusa.org
Contact: Sherry Doubet, Exec. VP
Founded: 1983. **Members:** 600. **Membership Dues:** regular, $50 (annual) ● life, $500 ● junior, $15 (annual). **Description:** Represents cattlemen aged 21 or younger with an interest in Salers, a French breed of cattle. **Affiliated With:** American Salers Association. **Publications:** *Voice of Salers*. Magazine. Contains reports and important issues for the Salers cattle breeder and the beef industry. **Conventions/Meetings:** annual National Salers Junior Heifer Show and Seminar - meeting - usually summer.

4247 ■ American Shorthorn Association (ASA)
8288 Hascall St.
Omaha, NE 68124-3234
Ph: (402)393-7200 (402)393-7051
Fax: (402)393-7203
E-mail: info@shorthorn.org
URL: http://www.shorthorn.org
Contact: Greg Ruehle, Exec. Sec.
Founded: 1872. **Members:** 2,500. **Membership Dues:** junior (21 years of age), $20 ● senior, $35 (annual). **Staff:** 13. **Budget:** $750,000. **Regional Groups:** 5. **State Groups:** 40. **Local Groups:** 75. **Description:** Breeders of registered Shorthorn and Polled Shorthorn beef cattle. Seeks to record pedigrees and improve the breed. Sponsors Shorthorn Foundation. **Telecommunication Services:** electronic mail, greg@shorthorn.org. **Programs:** Durnham Natural Gold Beef; Whole Herd Reporting Gold. **Formerly:** (1975) American Shorthorn Breeders Association. **Publications:** *Shorthorn Country*, monthly. Magazine. **Price:** $24.00/year in U.S.; $30.00/year in Canada and outside U.S. **Circulation:** 5,000. **Advertising:** accepted. **Conventions/Meetings:** annual meeting - even-numbered years always November in Louisville, KY and odd-numbered years always January in Denver, CO.

4248 ■ American Simmental Association (ASA)
1 Simmental Way
Bozeman, MT 59715
Ph: (406)587-4531
Fax: (406)587-9301
E-mail: simmental@simmgene.com
URL: http://www.simmental.org
Contact: Jerry Lipsey PhD, Exec. VP
Founded: 1969. **Members:** 12,500. **Membership Dues:** adult, $100 (annual) ● junior, $50 (annual) ● household, $150 (annual). **Budget:** $2,350,000. **State Groups:** 36. **Description:** Promotes registration and improvement of the breeds of Simmental and Simbrah cattle in the U.S. **Computer Services:** database, animal. **Programs:** Commercial; Performance. **Absorbed:** (1979) American Junior Simmental Association. **Publications:** *The Register*, monthly. Magazine. Contains official breed publication. **Price:** $30.00/year. **Advertising:** accepted. Alternate Formats: online. **Conventions/Meetings:** annual meeting (exhibits).

4249 ■ American Tarentaise Association (ATA)
PO Box 594
Red Oak, IA 51566
Ph: (402)639-9808
E-mail: tarentaise@yahoo.com
Contact: Dan Braesch, Pres.
Founded: 1973. **Members:** 250. **Membership Dues:** associate, $30 (annual) ● junior, $25 ● life, $50. **Staff:** 4. **Budget:** $250,000. **State Groups:** 8. **Local Groups:** 2. **Description:** Cattlemen raising the Tarentaise breed of cattle (originally imported from France into the U.S.) and who are united for the promotion of the breed. Maintains the history, records, and pedigrees of individual animals. **Computer Services:** database, registry. **Publications:** *Discover Tarentaise*, monthly. Brochure. **Advertising:** accepted ● *Mamma's Boys*. Brochure ● *Tarentaise Journal*, bimonthly. **Circulation:** 1,500. **Advertising:** accepted ● *Today's Tarentaise*. Brochure. **Advertising:** accepted. Alternate Formats: online ● Membership Directory. Alternate Formats: online. **Conventions/Meetings:** semiannual meeting and board meeting ● annual meeting, with sale ● show.

4250 ■ American Wagyu Association (AWA)
c/o Ms. Jeanene de Avila
PO Box 547
Pullman, WA 99163
Ph: (509)397-1011
E-mail: deavila@colfax.com
URL: http://www.wagyu.org
Contact: Ms. Jeanene de Avila, Contact
Membership Dues: active, $100 (annual). **Multinational. Description:** Promotes and preserves the Wagyu breed. **Computer Services:** Information services, facts about the Wagyu breed.

4251 ■ Amerifax Cattle Association (ACA)
Address Unknown since 2008
Founded: 1977. **Members:** 150. **Staff:** 1. **State Groups:** 2. **Description:** Breeders of Amerifax cattle (derived from American Friesian-Angus cross). Maintains purebred herdbooks, promotes the breed, and disseminates information. **Publications:** *The Amerifax*, quarterly. Newsletter. **Price:** free. **Circulation:** 2,000. **Conventions/Meetings:** annual competition ● annual meeting.

4252 ■ Ankole Watusi International Registry (AWIR)
22484 W 239 St.
Spring Hill, KS 66083-9306
Ph: (913)592-4050
E-mail: watusi@aol.com
URL: http://www.awir.org
Contact: Dr. Elizabeth Lundgren, Exec. Sec.
Founded: 1983. **Members:** 144. **Membership Dues:** associate, $20 (annual) ● regular, $25 (annual) ● life, $250. **Staff:** 1. **Description:** Individuals, families, ranches, and corporations interested in promoting and preserving the Ankole-Watusi cattle breed. Works to protect the ancient and unique heritage of the breed, which originated in Africa; increase public awareness of Ankole-Watusi cattle as a distinct breed; preserve bloodline purity through proper breed practices; recognize present breeders and encourage new breeders; aid in the study and dissemination of knowledge of the past ancestry and future breeding of the cattle. Collects and disseminates information relative to the Ankole-Watusi breed; issues certificates of breeding; engages in collective advertising and other promotional and publicity campaigns to inform the public of the benefits and advantages of the Watusi breed. Sponsors full blood and cross breeding-up breeding programs. Compiles statistics. **Libraries: Type:** reference. **Holdings:** archival material, books, clippings, periodicals. **Subjects:** Ankole Watusi bloodlines and history. **Computer Services:** Information services, Ankole-Watusi breed facts. **Publications:** *Watusi*, quarterly, published in January, April, July, and October. Magazine. **Price:** included in membership dues. **Advertising:** accepted ● Plans to publish directory and prepare a videotape. **Conventions/Meetings:** annual banquet (exhibits) ● periodic competition, full blood and cross breeding-up competitions ● annual conference, in conjunction with Amarillo Tri-State Fair ● periodic seminar ● periodic show ● periodic tour.

4253 ■ Ayrshire Breeders' Association (ABA)
1224 Alton Creek Rd., Ste.B
Columbus, OH 43228
Ph: (614)335-0020
Fax: (614)335-0023
E-mail: info@usayrshire.com
URL: http://www.usayrshire.com
Contact: Becky Payne, Exec. Sec.
Founded: 1875. **Members:** 1,500. **Membership Dues:** adult, $25 (annual) ● junior, $10. **Staff:** 2. **State Groups:** 38. **Local Groups:** 60. **Description:** Breeders of Ayrshire cattle. Sponsors competitions and marketing service; compiles statistics; maintains registry of Ayrshire cattle. **Telecommunication Services:** electronic mail, bpayne@usayrshire.com. **Programs:** Classification; Genetic Recovery; Gold; Rewards. **Publications:** *Ayrshire Digest*, bimonthly. Magazine. **Price:** $20.00. ISSN: 0005-2450. **Circulation:** 1,500. **Advertising:** accepted. Alternate Formats: online ● Membership Directory. Alternate Formats: online ● Brochure. Alternate Formats: online. **Conventions/Meetings:** annual meeting - usually June.

4254 ■ Barzona Breeders Association of America (BBAA)
480 Jason Rd.
Fort Collins, CO 80524
Ph: (970)498-9306 (641)743-6610
Fax: (970)498-9940
E-mail: havens@mddc.com
URL: http://www.barzona.com
Contact: Karen Havens, Dir.
Founded: 1968. **Members:** 80. **Budget:** $60,000. **Description:** Purebred and commercial cattle breeders, colleges, and agribusiness organizations. Permits the "breeding up" of Barzona cattle by providing for registration of animals with purebred Barzona registry animals in the pedigree. Provides information of what Barzona breeders do with their cattle, and how they perform in various environments and operations. **Publications:** *Barzona Story*. Booklet. Provides information on the development of the Barzona, which may be the first composite breed of cattle developed in the US. ● *The Barzonian*, quarterly. Newsletter. Contains updates about the organization activities and highlights different breeders and operations across the US. **Price:** free. **Circulation:** 1,700. **Advertising:** accepted ● Video. Contains information on breed history. **Conventions/Meetings:** annual meeting.

4255 ■ Beefmaster Breeders United (BBU)
6800 Park 10 Blvd., Ste.290 W
San Antonio, TX 78213
Ph: (210)732-3132
Fax: (210)732-7711
E-mail: wschronk@beefmasters.org
URL: http://www.beefmasters.org
Contact: Wendell Schronk, Exec. VP
Founded: 1961. **Members:** 4,800. **Membership Dues:** life, $1,000 ● active, associate, $80 (annual) ● junior, $40 (annual). **Regional Groups:** 5. **Description:** Individuals and groups owning Beefmaster cattle. Improves the breed through performance and quality control programs and provides better marketing through promotion and BBU-approved sales. Conducts advertising and promotional activities. **Programs:** Breed Enhancement; Essential Commercial Female. **Formerly:** (2002) Beefmaster Breeders Universal. **Publications:** *The Beefmaster Cowman*, monthly. **Price:** $25.00/year in U.S.; $45.00/year outside U.S. ● *Membership List*, annual. Membership Directory ● Also publishes brochure. **Conventions/Meetings:** annual meeting and convention - always October.

4256 ■ Belted Galloway Society
c/o Laura Glassmann, Sec.
PO Box 316
Bendersville, PA 17306-0316
Ph: (717)677-9655
Fax: (717)677-9755
E-mail: beltiecows@aol.com
URL: http://www.beltie.org
Contact: Laura Glassmann, Sec.
Founded: 1951. **Members:** 900. **Membership Dues:** junior, $10 (annual) ● regular, $50 (annual) ● life, $550 ● associate, $25 (annual) ● junior (one time fee), $20. **Staff:** 2. **Budget:** $75,000. **Regional Groups:** 3. **State Groups:** 4. **Description:** Breeders of Belted Galloway cattle, a minor breed of beef type of Scotch origin. **Awards: Type:** recognition. **Committees:** Advertising/Promotion; Breed Standards; Fundraising; Grievance; Long Range Planning; Show; Society Sales. **Subgroups:** Belie Youth. **Formerly:** American Belted Galloway Cattle Breeders' Association. **Publications:** *Breeders Directory*. Alternate Formats: online ● *U.S. Beltie News*, monthly. Newsletter. Contains information on cattle health, feed, member activities, and regional news. **Circulation:** 525. **Advertising:** accepted. Alternate Formats: online. **Conventions/Meetings:** semiannual Breed Show ● annual meeting - always fall.

4257 ■ Braunvieh Association of America (BAA)
3815 Touzalin Ave., Ste.103
Lincoln, NE 68507-1600
Ph: (402)466-3292
Fax: (402)466-3293
E-mail: braunaa@attglobal.net
URL: http://www.braunvieh.org
Contact: Mark Nelson, Exec. VP
Founded: 1984. **Membership Dues:** individual/associate, $50 (annual) ● junior/sponsor, $25 (annual). **Description:** Provides current data and performance information about the Braunvieh breed of cattle, including efficiency of Braunvieh growth, maternal and feedlot profitability. **Telecommunication Services:** electronic mail, marknelson@inebraska.com.

4258 ■ Brown Swiss Cattle Breeders Association of the U.S.A. (BSCBA)
800 Pleasant St.
Beloit, WI 53511-5456
Ph: (608)365-4474
Fax: (608)365-5577
E-mail: info@brownswissusa.com
URL: http://www.brownswissusa.com
Contact: David J. Kendall, Exec. Sec.
Founded: 1880. **Members:** 1,100. **Membership Dues:** association/affiliate, $20 (annual) ● association/affiliate, $80 (quinquennial). **Staff:** 10. **Budget:** $520,000. **State Groups:** 31. **Description:** Breeders of registered Brown Swiss cattle. Sponsors Brown Swiss shows; participates in research programs; maintains records on Brown Swiss cattle. **Awards: Type:** recognition. **Telecommunication Services:** electronic mail, davetmb@tds.net. **Publications:** *Advertisers Directory*, biennial ● *Brown Swiss Bulletin*, monthly ● *Brown Swiss Performance Summary*, semiannual. **Conventions/Meetings:** annual conference (exhibits) - always July.

4259 ■ Buelingo Beef Cattle Society (BBCS)
15904 W Warren Rd.
Warren, IL 61087-9601
Ph: (815)745-2311
E-mail: bldaibue@aeroinc.net
URL: http://www.buelingo.com
Contact: Dean Monson, Pres.
Membership Dues: active, $35 (annual) ● associate, $12 (annual) ● junior, $5 (annual) ● life (active), $300. **Description:** Fosters the continued development of the finest breed of beef cattle in the industry. Registers and collects data on all BueLingo animals. Provides a means for breeders to network with other BueLingo producers. Introduces prospective breeders to the benefits of the breed. **Telecommunication Services:** electronic mail, elainef@leru.net.

4260 ■ Bukovina Society of the Americas
PO Box 81
Ellis, KS 67637
E-mail: info@bukovinasociety.org
URL: http://www.bukovinasociety.org
Contact: Ralph Honas, Pres.
Founded: 1988. **Members:** 350. **Membership Dues:** regular, $15 (annual) ● life, $150. **Staff:** 1. **Budget:** $5,000. **Multinational. Description:** Promotes a respect for and recognition of the history and accomplishments of the immigrants from Bukovina. **Libraries: Type:** open to the public. **Holdings:** 200; books, periodicals. **Subjects:** genealogy, history. **Computer Services:** Mailing lists, of members. **Publications:** *Bukovina Society*, quarterly. Newsletter. **Price:** included in membership dues. **Circulation:** 350. Alternate Formats: online. **Conventions/Meetings:** annual Bukovinafest - convention.

4261 ■ Cattlemen's Beef Promotion and Research Board (CBB)
9000 E Nichols Ave., Ste.303
Centennial, CO 80112-3450
Ph: (303)220-9890
Fax: (303)220-9280
E-mail: beefboard@beefboard.org
URL: http://www.beefboard.org
Contact: Tom Ramey, CEO
Founded: 1986. **Members:** 108. **Staff:** 9. **Budget:** $45,000,000. **Description:** Beef producers. Coordinates public relations, marketing, and dissemination of information through the Beef Checkoff Program. Conducts promotional, consumer information, and industry information campaigns; fosters communication among beef producers; sponsors research. Produces television and radio advertisements. **Committees:** Beef Promotion Operating; Joint Industry Audit; Joint Industry Budget; Joint Industry Evaluation; Joint Industry Program. **Programs:** Checkoff. **Formerly:** (2004) Beef Promotion and Research Board. **Publications:** *Update*, periodic. Newsletter ● Annual Report, annual. **Conventions/Meetings:** semiannual board meeting.

4262 ■ Gelbray International (GI)
Rte. 1, Box 273C
Madill, OK 73446
Ph: (580)223-5771
Fax: (580)226-5773
E-mail: yeager@brightok.net
Contact: Don M. Yeager, Sec.
Founded: 1981. **Members:** 50. **Membership Dues:** general, $25 (annual). **Description:** Breeders of Gelbray cattle. Promotes and perpetuates the registration and breeding of Gelbray cattle. The Gelbray breed is the result of crossbreeding between the Brahman, Gelbvieh and Angus. Registers Gelbray. **Formerly:** (1986) Gelbray Association. **Conventions/Meetings:** competition ● show.

4263 ■ Holstein Association USA (HAU)
1 Holstein Pl.
Brattleboro, VT 05302-0808
Ph: (802)254-4551
Free: (800)952-5200
Fax: (802)254-8251
E-mail: info@holstein.com
URL: http://www.holsteinusa.com
Contact: Randolph E. Gross, Pres.
Founded: 1885. **Members:** 35,000. **Membership Dues:** adult, associate, $25 (annual) ● junior, $15. **Staff:** 180. **State Groups:** 50. **Local Groups:** 450. **Description:** Breeders of Holstein cattle. Provides information to dairy producers for breeding, management, and marketing. **Libraries: Type:** reference; not open to the public. **Holdings:** 1,000; books, papers, periodicals, reports. **Subjects:** dairy, agriculture, management, finance. **Awards: Frequency:** annual. **Type:** recognition. **Recipient:** for a Registered Holstein producer or producer couple demonstrating the additional opportunities of Registered Holsteins ● Rumler Scholarship. **Frequency:** annual. **Type:** scholarship. **Recipient:** for MBA students with Bachelor's degree in animal or dairy science. **Computer Services:** database, maintenance and management of records on all registered Holsteins in U.S. ● information services, Holstein breed facts and resources ● online services, consulting service and genetic research ● online services, development of e-commerce website by subsidiary InSinc. **Formed by Merger of:** (1885) Dutch-Friesian Association of America; Association of Breeders of Thoroughbred Holstein Cattle. **Formerly:** Holstein-Friesian Association of America; Holstein Association of America. **Publications:** *Holstein Association News*, bimonthly. Newsletter. Features articles about the Holstein cattle industry, association members and association programs. **Price:** free to active members. **Circulation:** 15,400. Alternate Formats: online ● *The Holstein Pulse*, quarterly. Magazine. **Price:** free for members. **Conventions/Meetings:** annual National Holstein Convention - convention and general assembly (exhibits) - usually June.

4264 ■ Holstein Junior Program
c/o Holstein Association USA, Inc.
1 Holstein Pl.
Brattleboro, VT 05302-0808
Ph: (802)254-4551
Free: (800)952-5200
Fax: (802)254-8251
E-mail: kdunklee@holstein.com
URL: http://www.holsteinusa.com
Contact: Kelli F. Dunklee, Program Specialist
Founded: 1885. **Members:** 10,000. **Membership Dues:** individual, $15. **Staff:** 1. **Budget:** $50,000. **State Groups:** 40. **Description:** Represents young people interested in the dairy industry. Encourages interest in animals, especially Holstein cattle. Sponsors youth-operated and educational programs. Disseminates information. **Libraries: Type:** reference. **Awards:** Distinguished Junior Member. **Frequency:** annual. **Type:** recognition. **Recipient:** for 17 to 21 years old who has excelled in preparing for their life's work while contributing to their local, district and state activities. **Publications:** *Junior Holstein Bulletin*, annual. Newsletter. Alternate Formats: online. **Conventions/Meetings:** annual Junior Holstein Convention (exhibits) ● annual National Junior Holstein Convention - competition - always June.

4265 ■ International Brangus Breeders Association (IBBA)
PO Box 696020
San Antonio, TX 78269-6020
Ph: (210)696-4343
Fax: (210)696-8718
E-mail: joemassey@int-brangus.org
URL: http://www.int-brangus.org
Contact: Dr. Joseph M. Massey, Exec. VP
Founded: 1949. **Members:** 2,000. **Membership Dues:** senior, $125 (annual) ● junior, associate, $25 (annual). **Staff:** 8. **Budget:** $1,100,000. **Regional Groups:** 13. **State Groups:** 10. **Description:** Breeders of registered Brangus cattle (a combination of 3/8 Brahman and 5/8 Aberdeen-Angus cattle); currently register 33,300 head of cattle. **Computer Services:** database, cattle inventory. **Committees:** Breed Improvement; Commercial Marketing; Finance; Junior Programs; Promotions; Show Advisory. **Formed by Merger of:** (1958) American Brangus Breeders Association. **Publications:** *Brangus Journal*, monthly. **Price:** $25.00. **Advertising:** accepted ● *Commercial Brangus Edition*, semiannual. Newspaper ● Membership Directory, annual ● Brochures ● Catalogs. **Conventions/Meetings:** annual convention - always March in Houston, TX ● seminar.

4266 ■ International Junior Brangus Breeders Association (IJBBA)
5750 Epsilon Dr.
San Antonio, TX 78249
Ph: (210)696-4343
Fax: (210)696-8718
E-mail: ktbrangus@hotmail.com
URL: http://junior.int-brangus.org
Contact: Katy White, Pres.
Founded: 1977. **Members:** 750. **Membership Dues:** senior, $80 (annual) ● associate, junior, $25 (annual). **Description:** Individuals 22 years of age and under. Seeks to improve and develop the capabilities of youth in the breeding, raising, and exhibition of the

Brangus breed of cattle. Promotes quality in all beef animals, especially the Brangus breed. Sponsors breeding programs and youth activities that include National Junior Brangus Show, Junior Brangus Herd Improvement Program, Queen Contest, National Public Speaking Contest, National Showmanship Contest, and a National Board of Directors. **Awards: Frequency:** annual. **Type:** scholarship. **Publications:** *Junior Ear*, semiannual. Newsletter. **Price:** free. **Circulation:** 750. **Conventions/Meetings:** meeting and general assembly ● annual National Junior Brangus Show (exhibits) ● workshop.

4267 ■ International Miniature Cattle Breeders Society and Registry
25204 156th Ave. SE
Covington, WA 98042
Ph: (253)631-1911
Fax: (253)631-5774
E-mail: info@minicattle.com
URL: http://www.minicattle.com
Contact: Prof. Richard Gradwohl, Founding Dir.
Founded: 1966. **Members:** 10,000. **Membership Dues:** life, $200. **Staff:** 3. **Budget:** $100,000. **Regional Groups:** 18. **State Groups:** 14. **Local Groups:** 12. **National Groups:** 27. **For-Profit. Multinational. Description:** Promotes the 22 breeds of miniature cattle, 42 inches or less at maturity to be classified as full miniature, over 42 inches and up to 48 inches are classified as midsize miniature. These breeds include the Miniature American Beltie; Miniature Auburnshire; Australian Miniature Kyrhet; Miniature Angus, American and Lowline; Miniature Barbee Cattle; Miniature Belmont (Irish Jersey); Miniature Black Baldie; Miniature Burienshire; Miniature Covingtonshire; Miniature Dexter; Miniature Durham/Shorthorn; Miniature Grad-Wohl; Miniature Happy Mountain Cattle; Miniature Hereford; Miniature Highland; Miniature Jersey (lessor Jerseys); Miniature Kentshire; Miniature Kingshire; Miniature Panda Cattle; Miniature Zebu; Miniature Texas Longhorn; Open Breeds. **Libraries: Type:** not open to the public. **Holdings:** 800; articles, books, periodicals. **Subjects:** cattle. **Awards:** Honorary Degrees - Doctoral and Masters. **Frequency:** annual. **Type:** recognition. **Computer Services:** Mailing lists ● online services, sample breeders' directory. **Publications:** *Information Packet*, bimonthly. Newsletter. Includes a sample breeders list. **Price:** $28.00 includes postage and handling. **Circulation:** 15,000. **Advertising:** accepted ● *Miniature Cattle Breeds Newsletter*, quarterly. **Price:** $28.00/year. **Circulation:** 15,000. **Advertising:** accepted. Also Cited As: *MCBN*. **Conventions/Meetings:** annual conference.

4268 ■ International Miniature Zebu Association (IMZA)
c/o Maureen Neidhardt, Registrar
PO Box 66
Crawford, NE 69339
Ph: (308)665-3919 (309)756-0506
Fax: (308)665-3919
E-mail: rarebreed@bbc.net
URL: http://www.miniature-zebu-cattle.com
Contact: Maureen Neidhardt, Registrar
Founded: 1991. **Membership Dues:** in U.S., $35 (annual) ● outside U.S., $50 (annual). **Description:** Promotes the Miniature Zebu; provides a birth registry. **Publications:** Directory, annual. Contains a listing of Miniature Zebu owners. ● Newsletter. **Price:** included in membership dues.

4269 ■ International Texas Longhorn Association (ITLA)
PO Box 2610
Glen Rose, TX 76043
Ph: (254)898-0157
Fax: (254)898-0165
E-mail: staff@itla.com
URL: http://www.itla.com
Contact: Larry Smith II, Pres.
Membership Dues: active, $60 (annual) ● youth, $15 (annual) ● associate, $40 (annual) ● life, $700. **Multinational. Description:** Represents individuals dedicated to the development, registration and promotion of the Texas Longhorn breed of cattle. Works to assist, encourage and educate breeders engaged in the breeding and propagation of Texas Longhorn cattle. Provides public awareness of the benefits of Texas Longhorn cattle. **Computer Services:** Information services, Longhorn resources ● online services, message board. **Publications:** *Longhorn Drover*. Magazine. Provides news and information for Texas Longhorn owners, breeders and enthusiasts. **Advertising:** accepted.

4270 ■ Irish Blacks Association
25377 Weld County Rd. 17
Johnstown, CO 80534
Ph: (970)587-2252
Fax: (970)587-2252
E-mail: mmboney@webtv.net
URL: http://www.irishblacks.com
Contact: Maurice W. Boney, Pres.
Founded: 1972. **Members:** 100. **Staff:** 1. **Description:** Breeders of Irish Black cattle. (Irish Black cattle originated in Europe and differ from dairy/beef cattle in that they are raised solely for slaughter.) Seeks to promote the breed and improve its characteristics. **Formerly:** (2004) Beef Friesian Society. **Publications:** *Beef Friesian Society Newsletter*, periodic. **Conventions/Meetings:** annual board meeting.

4271 ■ Marky Cattle Association (MCA)
PO Box 198
Walton, KS 67151-0198
Ph: (620)837-3303
Fax: (316)283-8379
E-mail: info@marchigiana.org
URL: http://www.marchigiana.org
Contact: Martie TenEyck, Exec. Sec.
Founded: 1973. **Members:** 50. **Membership Dues:** regular, $25 (annual) ● regular (initial), $100 ● junior (initial; under 18), $10 ● junior, $5 (annual). **Staff:** 1. **Regional Groups:** 2. **Description:** Breeders or owners of Marchigiana cattle; cattle companies; investors. Seeks to improve the beef industry by encouraging the efficient production of high quality beef. Maintains records on numbers of Marchigiana cattle in the U.S. and their performance data. **Also Known As:** American International Marchigiana Society. **Publications:** Newsletter, periodic. **Price:** $10.00/year. **Advertising:** accepted ● Booklets. **Conventions/Meetings:** annual meeting.

4272 ■ Miniature Hereford Breeders Association (MHBA)
31270 Private Rd. 23
Elizabeth, CO 80107
E-mail: info@mhbaonline.org
URL: http://www.mhbaonline.org
Contact: Jami Mattson, Treas.
Founded: 1999. **Membership Dues:** in U.S., $50 (annual) ● in Canada and Mexico, $55 (annual) ● international, $60 (annual). **Multinational. Description:** Represents the interests of Miniature Hereford breeders across the country. Promotes the Miniature Hereford breed and encourages the success of each individual breeder. Sponsors events to raise public awareness of the Miniature Hereford cattle and the benefits of owning them. **Telecommunication Services:** electronic mail, jmatts4@hotmail.com.

4273 ■ National American Indian Cattlemen's Association (NAICA)
Address Unknown since 2008
Founded: 1974. **Staff:** 1. **Description:** Indian cattle producers. Carries on all activities necessary for the betterment of the Indian cattle industry and serves as clearinghouse for the accumulation and dissemination of information concerning the Indian cattle industry. Compiles statistics; conducts research. **Convention/Meeting:** none. Presently inactive.

4274 ■ National Dairy Herd Improvement Association (NDHIA)
PO Box 930399
Verona, WI 53593-0399
Ph: (608)848-6455
Fax: (608)848-7675
E-mail: dhia@dhia.org
URL: http://www.dhia.org
Contact: Jay Mattison, CEO/Admin.
Description: Owners and breeders of dairy cattle. Seeks to improve the bloodlines of dairy cattle of all breeds. Works to improve data collection concerning dairy cattle breeding and bloodlines. Serves as an information repository on dairy cattle breeding; maintains breed registries; formulates codes of ethics and uniform data collection practices; undertakes herd testing profiles. **Libraries: Type:** reference. **Subjects:** dairy cattle breed records. **Awards:** Martin A. Wilson Memorial Award. **Frequency:** annual. **Type:** recognition. **Recipient:** to person who has been employed in a DHIA management position for at least five years ● National DHIA H. Victor Joaquim Distinguished Leadership Award. **Frequency:** annual. **Type:** recognition. **Recipient:** to DHIA dairy producer and/or spouse who has been a leader in DHIA ● National DHIA Outstanding Service Award. **Frequency:** annual. **Type:** recognition. **Recipient:** to person who has been dedicated to the improvement of DHIA for many years ● **Frequency:** annual. **Type:** scholarship. **Recipient:** to outstanding incoming and continuing students at technical, two, and four-year institutions. **Telecommunication Services:** electronic mail, jmattison@requestltd.com. **Committees:** Audit Review; Quality Certification Services Advisory. **Programs:** National Dairy Herd Improvement.

4275 ■ National Junior Angus Association (NJAA)
3201 Frederick Ave.
St. Joseph, MO 64506
Ph: (816)383-5100
Fax: (816)233-9703
E-mail: info@njaa.info
URL: http://www.njaa.info
Contact: Alex Tolbert, Chm.
Founded: 1956. **Members:** 11,000. **Membership Dues:** individual, $20 (annual). **Staff:** 2. **Regional Groups:** 2. **State Groups:** 41. **Local Groups:** 29. **Description:** Individuals under 21 years of age with an interest in Angus cattle. Works to develop personal skills and leadership abilities among young people, and to improve and promote Angus cattle. Encourages young people to initiate ideas, programs, and projects at the national, regional, and local levels. Provides educational and leadership conferences and literature. **Awards:** Angus Foundation Scholarships. **Frequency:** annual. **Type:** scholarship. **Recipient:** to junior Angus members ● Bronze Award. **Type:** recognition. **Recipient:** for members based on participation and activities ● Gold Award. **Type:** recognition. **Recipient:** for members based on participation and activities ● Outstanding Leadership Award. **Frequency:** annual. **Type:** recognition. **Recipient:** to members 14 years old and above ● Silver Award. **Type:** recognition. **Recipient:** for members based on participation and activities. **Programs:** Leadership Development; Mentoring; National Junior Recognition; Photography Contest; Public Speaking Contest; Sales Contest. **Affiliated With:** American Angus Association. **Formerly:** (1980) Junior Activities Department of the American Angus Association. **Publications:** *Angus Journal*, semiannual. **Circulation:** 21,000. **Advertising:** accepted ● *Fitting, A behind the scenes look*. Brochure. Alternate Formats: online ● *NJAA Directions*, semiannual. Newsletter. Alternate Formats: online ● *The Road To Success*. Pamphlet. Alternate Formats: online ● *Your Angus Heifer*. Booklet. **Conventions/Meetings:** annual meeting (exhibits) ● National Junior Angus Showmanship Contest - competition.

4276 ■ National Junior Hereford Association (NJHA)
c/o American Hereford Association
PO Box 014059
Kansas City, MO 64101
Ph: (816)842-3757
Fax: (816)842-6931
E-mail: aha@hereford.org
URL: http://www.hereford.org/tailored.aspx?alias=NJHA&init
Contact: Catie Sims, Pres.
Founded: 1965. **Members:** 6,000. **Membership Dues:** ordinary, $30 (annual). **Staff:** 1. **State Groups:**

38. **Description:** Members of state junior Hereford associations under 22 years of age seeking to assist in the education and training of youth in leadership and the production and handling of beef cattle. Holds educational meetings, field days, and demonstrations to familiarize rural youth with the latest techniques. Sponsors competitions. **Awards: Type:** recognition. **Recipient:** for scholarship, achievement, public speaking, and beef cattle exhibitions. **Computer Services:** Online services, publication. **Telecommunication Services:** electronic mail, cstephens@hereford.org. **Affiliated With:** American Hereford Association. **Formerly:** (2000) American Junior Hereford Association. **Publications:** *Commercial Hereford*, semiannual. Newsletter ● *Hereford World*, 11/year. Journal. **Price:** $40.00/year. **Circulation:** 12,000. **Advertising:** accepted. Alternate Formats: online. **Conventions/Meetings:** annual convention and workshop, on leadership - always November in Kansas City, MO.

4277 ■ National Junior Santa Gertrudis Association (NJSGA)
PO Box 1257
Kingsville, TX 78364
Ph: (361)592-9357
Fax: (361)592-8572
E-mail: sgbi@sbcglobal.net
URL: http://www.santagertrudis.com
Contact: Ervin Kaatz, Exec. Dir.
Founded: 1977. **Members:** 1,000. **Membership Dues:** junior, $51 (annual) ● commercial, $30 (annual) ● active, $102 (annual). **Staff:** 3. **Regional Groups:** 6. **Local Groups:** 27. **Description:** Young people ages 9 to 21 who are admirers of Santa Gertrudis cattle. Conducts junior competitions and awards cash prizes to winning entries; sponsors educational and recreational activities; offers scholarship. Compiles statistics and conducts research. Maintains library of periodicals, audiovisual materials, and artwork. Contributes monthly article to the Santa Gertrudis Journal. Bestows scholarship, performance, and show animal awards. **Computer Services:** database, registered animals. **Affiliated With:** Santa Gertrudis Breeders International. **Publications:** *American Original Beef Breed Article*. Alternate Formats: online ● *Santa Gertrudis World*, monthly. Journal. **Price:** free with membership. **Circulation:** 4,000. **Conventions/Meetings:** annual meeting ● annual National Junior Heifer Show - meeting - always June.

4278 ■ North American Corriente Association (NACA)
c/o James Spawn, Sec.-Treas./Exec. Dir.
PO Box 12359
North Kansas City, MO 64116
Ph: (816)421-1992
Fax: (816)421-1991
E-mail: info@corrientecattle.org
URL: http://www.corrientecattle.org
Contact: James Spawn, Sec.-Treas./Exec. Dir.
Founded: 1982. **Members:** 700. **Membership Dues:** active, $35 (annual) ● associate, $20 (annual) ● life, $350. **Staff:** 4. **Budget:** $150,000. **Regional Groups:** 5. **Description:** Breeders of Corriente cattle, a breed developed in Mexico from Spanish cattle and used for team roping and bulldogging because of their endurance and small size. Promotes the use of Corriente cattle as a rodeo animal and to preserve the purity of the breed by instituting and monitoring a registered breeding program. Creates classification rules for full, half, three-quarter, and seven-eighths blood Corrientes in order to upgrade the status of the breed. Refers buyers to registered Corriente breeders. **Publications:** *Corriente Corresponder*, quarterly. Newsletter. Contains news and information about Corriente Cattle, events and producers. **Circulation:** 1,200. **Advertising:** accepted ● Membership Directory. Alternate Formats: online ● Handbook. **Conventions/Meetings:** annual conference - always spring.

4279 ■ North American Limousin Foundation (NALF)
7383 S Alton Way, Ste.100
Englewood, CO 80112
Ph: (303)220-1693
Fax: (303)220-1884
E-mail: limousin@nalf.org
URL: http://www.nalf.org
Contact: Kent Andersen PhD, Exec. VP
Founded: 1968. **Members:** 12,000. **Staff:** 14. **Description:** Represents individuals who own and raise Limousin cattle. Aims to promote the Limousin breed; record performance of the cattle; issue registrations and keep the herd book. **Telecommunication Services:** electronic mail, kent@nalf.org. **Publications:** *Limousin World*, monthly. Magazine. Provides information about one of the Limousin breed of beef cattle in the United States. **Advertising:** accepted. **Conventions/Meetings:** annual meeting - always January in Denver, CO.

4280 ■ North American Limousin Junior Association (NALJA)
c/o North American Limousin Foundation
7383 S Alton Way, Ste.100
Centennial, CO 80112
Ph: (303)220-1693
Fax: (303)220-1884
E-mail: r_wulf@hotmail.com
URL: http://www.nalf.org/programs/juniors.html
Contact: Rachel Wulf, Pres.
Members: 3,000. **Membership Dues:** junior, $50 (annual). **Budget:** $100,000. **Description:** People under the age of 21 who are involved in breeding Limousin cattle. Aims to teach members how to raise and show cattle. (Named for their native regions of Limousin and March in south-central France, the naturally red, horned Limousin were first imported to North America in November 1968 and are raised purely for their exceptionally lean beef, unlike most European breeds that are raised for both milk and meat.) Sponsors National Junior Heifer Show and contests including National Ambassador, showmanship, quiz bowl, sales talk, steer evaluation, and overall sweepstakes. Awards engraved silver Limousin belt buckles to exhibitors of county fair champion Limousin cattle. **Awards: Type:** grant. **Recipient:** for states wishing to organize Limousin field days ● Leonard and Vi Wulf NALJA Scholarship. **Frequency:** annual. **Type:** scholarship. **Recipient:** for young Limousin enthusiasts who possess outstanding character, perseverance, work ethic, ingenuity and demonstrated scholastic achievement ● NALJA Awards of Excellence. **Frequency:** annual. **Type:** recognition. **Recipient:** for active individuals in some segment of the beef industry or enrolled in an agricultural major in college. **Programs:** Awards of Excellence; Limouselle Scholarships; Limousin Sweepstakes. **Affiliated With:** North American Limousin Foundation.

4281 ■ North American Normande Association (NANA)
c/o Michael Mueller, Treas./Registry Sec.
748 Enloe Rd.
Rewey, WI 53580
Ph: (608)943-6091
Free: (800)573-6254
E-mail: mwbeef4u@mhtc.net
URL: http://www.normandeassociation.com
Contact: Michael Mueller, Treas./Registry Sec.
Founded: 1982. **Members:** 30. **Membership Dues:** active, $40 (annual) ● associate, $20 (annual). **Staff:** 1. **Budget:** $10,000. **Description:** Represents cattle breeders interested in importing purebred cattle and participating in a pedigree program for the development of the Normande breed in the U.S. and Canada. Seeks to promote registration of the Normande breed, and to ensure that the Normande breed will make a significant contribution to the improvement of the cattle industry. **Absorbed:** (1985) American Normande Association. **Publications:** *Normande Office News*, quarterly. Newsletter. **Price:** $10.00. **Advertising:** accepted. **Conventions/Meetings:** annual meeting, for members.

4282 ■ North American Piedmontese Association (NAPA)
PO Box 330
Valleyford, WA 99036-0330
Ph: (306)329-8600
E-mail: napa@yourlink.ca
URL: http://www.piedmontese-napa.com
Contact: Vicki Johnson, Exec. Dir.
Membership Dues: general, $70 (annual). **Multinational. Description:** Promotes and preserves the Fullblood Piedmontese cattle and the Naturalean cattle. Assists in the development and improvement of the Piedmontese breed. Establishes rules and policies for the registration of Piedmontese cattle. **Computer Services:** Information services, Piedmontese breed resources ● online services, message board. **Publications:** *Your Piedmontese Voice*, quarterly. Magazine. **Price:** $15.00 /year for nonmembers; included in membership dues. **Advertising:** accepted.

4283 ■ North American Romagnola and RomAngus Association (NARRA)
14305 W 379th St.
LaCygne, KS 66040-4077
Ph: (913)594-1080
Fax: (913)849-3794
E-mail: admin@romcattle.com
URL: http://www.romcattle.com
Contact: Tom Dixon, Pres.
Membership Dues: active (installation fee), $100 ● active, $45 (annual) ● associate (installation fee), change from junior to regular, $50 (annual) ● associate, $30 (annual) ● junior (installation fee), $25 ● junior, $20 (annual). **Description:** Promotes the Romagnola and RomAngus cattle breed. Works to actively pursue breed improvement and to be the registry of Romagnola and RomAngus cattle. **Publications:** *NARRA Newsletter*, quarterly.

4284 ■ North American South Devon Association (NASDA)
19590 E Main St., Ste.202
Parker, CO 80138
Ph: (303)770-3130
Fax: (303)770-9302
E-mail: nasouthdevon@aol.com
URL: http://www.southdevon.com
Contact: Sherry Doubet, Contact
Founded: 1974. **Members:** 185. **Membership Dues:** active, associate, $25 (annual) ● junior (initiation fee), $15. **Budget:** $100,000. **Description:** Owners and breeders interested in encouraging the development, registration, and promotion of South Devon cattle. Conducts junior educational and training programs; compiles performance data on breeders' cattle. **Awards:** Commercial Producer of the Year. **Frequency:** annual. **Type:** recognition ● Seedstock Producer of the Year. **Frequency:** annual. **Type:** recognition. **Publications:** *The North America South Devon*, quarterly. Newsletter. Provides information on promotions, upcoming events, and performance. **Price:** free for members. **Circulation:** 250. **Advertising:** accepted ● *Sire Summary*, annual. **Conventions/Meetings:** annual meeting and show, includes Junior Heifer Show; held in conjunction with the National Western Stock Show in Denver, CO (exhibits) - always in January.

4285 ■ North American Tuli Association (NATA)
c/o Ray E. Record, Exec. Sec.
10853 Forest Dr.
College Station, TX 77845
Ph: (979)774-9095
Fax: (979)774-0348
E-mail: rayerecord@msn.com
URL: http://www.tuliassociation.com
Contact: Ray E. Record, Exec. Sec.
Membership Dues: junior, $12 (annual) ● associate, $25 (annual) ● active, $100 (annual) ● life, $500 ● foundation, $1,000. **Description:** Serves to educate and promote the Tuli cattle breed. **Computer Services:** Information services, Tuli breed resources. **Publications:** *Tuli Times*, quarterly. Newsletter.

4286 ■ Parthenais Cattle Breeders Association
982 Hutchins Ln.
Chipley, FL 32428
Free: (800)762-0164

E-mail: parthenaiscattle@hotmail.com
URL: http://www.parthenaiscattle.org
Contact: Todd Smith, Pres.
Membership Dues: active, $100 (annual) ● associate, $50 (annual) ● junior, $25 (annual). **Description:** Parthenais cattle breeders. Promotes Parthenais cattle; maintains the herdbook and pedigree information on the Parthenais breed of cattle in the United States. Provides a current list of member breeders. **Conventions/Meetings:** annual meeting.

4287 ■ Piedmontese Association of the United States (PAUS)
343 Barrett Rd. 1
Elsberry, MO 63343-4137
Ph: (573)384-5685
Fax: (573)384-5567
E-mail: staff@pauscattle.org
URL: http://pauscattle.org
Contact: Dennis Hennerberg, Pres.
Founded: 1984. **Members:** 300. **Membership Dues:** individual, $100 (annual) ● associate, $50 (annual) ● junior, $25 (annual) ● life, $1,000. **Staff:** 1. **Regional Groups:** 3. **Description:** Breeders of Piedmontese cattle, which are raised for beef production and are renowned for the low fat content of their meat. Promotes use of Piedmontese cattle by the U.S. beef industry. Conducts research; compiles statistics. **Telecommunication Services:** electronic mail, d.hennerberg@pauscattle.org. **Absorbed:** (1986) American Piedmontese Association. **Publications:** *Piedmontese Profile*, quarterly. Magazine. **Price:** $35.00/year in U.S. **Circulation:** 450. **Advertising:** accepted. **Conventions/Meetings:** annual meeting and symposium.

4288 ■ Purebred Dairy Cattle Association (PDCA)
Address Unknown since 2008
Founded: 1940. **Members:** 7. **Staff:** 1. **State Groups:** 15. **Description:** Federation of seven dairy cattle breeders associations: Ayrshire, Brown Swiss, Guernsey, Holstein, Jersey, Milking Shorthorn, and Red and White. **Conventions/Meetings:** annual meeting - Madison, WI - **Avg. Attendance:** 15.

4289 ■ Purebred Dexter Cattle Association of North America (PDCA)
25979 Hwy. EE
Prairie Home, MO 65068
Ph: (660)841-9502
E-mail: pdca.dextercattle@gmail.com
URL: http://www.purebreddextercattle.org
Contact: Mark Muir, Pres.
Membership Dues: full/family/associate/provisional, $20 (annual) ● subscriber, $10 (annual) ● junior, $5 (annual) ● junior - new, $10. **Description:** Promotes and preserves the Dexter Cattle breed. Provides a classification system that reflects the multi-purpose nature of Dexter cattle. Develops a list of breeding bulls that have been tested negative for the chrondrodyplasia gene. Establishes an updated on-line pedigree registry that will provide accurate pedigree information to members. **Computer Services:** Information services, Dexter Cattle resources. **Publications:** *The Record*, quarterly. Newsletter. **Advertising:** accepted.

4290 ■ Ranchers-Cattlemen Action Legal Fund, United Stockgrowers of America (R-CALF USA)
PO Box 30715
Billings, MT 59107
Ph: (406)252-2516
Fax: (406)252-3176
E-mail: r-calfusa@r-calfusa.com
URL: http://www.r-calfusa.com
Contact: Bill Bullard, CEO
Founded: 1998. **Membership Dues:** general/voting, $50 (annual) ● affiliate, $200-$500 (annual) ● general, $140 (triennial). **Description:** Represents the U.S. cattle industry in trade and marketing issues to ensure the continued profitability and viability of independent U.S. cattle producers. **Publications:** *Cattlemen's Journal USA*, quarterly. Magazine ● *The Cattlemen's Newsletter*, monthly.

4291 ■ Red Angus Association of America (RAAA)
4201 N, Interstate 35
Denton, TX 76207
Ph: (940)387-3502
Fax: (940)383-4036
E-mail: info@redangus.org
URL: http://redangus.org
Contact: Dr. R.L. Hough, Exec. Sec.
Founded: 1954. **Members:** 1,800. **Membership Dues:** junior, $20 (annual) ● regular, $60 (annual). **Staff:** 15. **Budget:** $2,000,000. **Regional Groups:** 8. **State Groups:** 22. **Languages:** English, Spanish. **Description:** Breeders of purebred Red Angus cattle. Seeks to improve the breed through application of scientific methods of selection. Conducts performance testing program as prerequisite to registry of animals. Sponsors Red Angus divisions in livestock shows; compiles statistics. Issues registration papers for purebred Red Angus cattle. **Awards:** Merit Award Program. **Frequency:** annual. **Type:** recognition. **Recipient:** for individual merits, hard work and accomplishments. **Computer Services:** Online services, registration and ownership records. **Telecommunication Services:** electronic mail, bob@redangus.org. **Committees:** Alliance; Breed Improvement; Constitution; Junior Foundation; Promotion; Registration; Show and Sale; Strategic Planning. **Publications:** *American Red Angus*, 10/year. Magazine. **Price:** $25.00/year in U.S.; $40.00/year in Canada; $50.00/year outside U.S. and Canada. **Circulation:** 7,000. **Advertising:** accepted ● *Membership List*, annual. Directory ● Pamphlets. **Conventions/Meetings:** annual convention, with trade show booths (exhibits) - usually September.

4292 ■ Santa Gertrudis Breeders International (SGBI)
PO Box 1257
Kingsville, TX 78364
Ph: (361)592-9357
Fax: (361)592-8572
E-mail: sgbi@sbcglobal.net
URL: http://santagertrudis.com
Contact: Ervin Kaatz, Exec. Dir.
Founded: 1951. **Members:** 3,000. **Membership Dues:** active (plus $2.50 per head fair share and breed promotion), $100 (annual) ● junior (plus $1 per head breed promotion), $50 (annual) ● commercial, $20 (annual). **Staff:** 7. **Budget:** $650,000. **Local Groups:** 20. **Description:** Producers of Santa Gertrudis beef cattle. Seeks to continue and promote Santa Gertrudis cattle. Includes activities such as classification and registration of cattle. Sponsors approved livestock shows and youth endowment fund; maintains individual herd inventory and Total Performance Program. **Awards:** **Type:** scholarship. **Computer Services:** Information services, Santa Gertrudis breed facts. **Telecommunication Services:** electronic mail, ekaatz.sgbi@sbcglobal.net. **Committees:** Breed Promotion; Breed Standards; Finance and Auditing; Marketing and Promotion; Nominating; Research and Education; Shows and Exhibits. **Publications:** *Marketing Directory*, periodic ● *Santa Gertrudis USA*, monthly. Journal ● Membership Directory, annual ● Also publishes reference guide and testing handbook. **Conventions/Meetings:** annual meeting (exhibits).

4293 ■ Senepol Cattle Breeders Association (SCBA)
PO Box 429
O'Fallon, IL 62269
Ph: (910)617-6355
Free: (800)736-3765
Fax: (240)223-0200
E-mail: info@breedercare.com
URL: http://www.senepolcattle.com
Contact: Mr. Hans Lawaetz, Pres.
Membership Dues: active, $100 (annual) ● international, $50 (annual) ● junior, $20 (annual) ● new active, associate, $25. **Description:** Represents individuals interested in the Senepol Cattle breed. Promotes and preserves the Senepol breed. **Computer Services:** Information services, Senepol breed resources. **Programs:** SCBA Youth Loan. **Publications:** *Senepol World*. Newsletter ● Brochure.

4294 ■ Texas Longhorn Breeders Association of America (TLBAA)
2315 N Main St., Ste.402
PO Box 4430
Fort Worth, TX 76164
Ph: (817)625-6241
Fax: (817)625-1388
E-mail: tlbaa@tlbaa.org
URL: http://www.tlbaa.org
Contact: Ben Gravett, Chm.
Founded: 1964. **Members:** 5,000. **Membership Dues:** active, $100 (annual) ● life, $1,000 ● junior, $25 (annual). **Staff:** 8. **Budget:** $600,000. **Regional Groups:** 32. **Local Groups:** 33. **Description:** Individuals, firms, and organizations interested in the Texas Longhorn breed of cattle. Promotes public awareness of the Texas Longhorn, its link with history, and its role in modern beef production. Encourages practices to preserve purity of the breed and recognizes Texas Longhorn cattle breeders. Maintains registry for purebred Texas Longhorns. Provides speakers on limited basis; sponsors junior competitions; compiles breed and research statistics. Coordinates promotion and research to encourage the use of Longhorns by cattlemen. **Libraries:** **Type:** open to the public. **Holdings:** 12; periodicals. **Subjects:** Texas longhorn cattle. **Awards:** Breeder of the Year. **Frequency:** annual. **Type:** recognition ● Elmer Parker Award. **Frequency:** annual. **Type:** recognition. **Telecommunication Services:** electronic mail, gravett@erols.com. **Committees:** Advertising; Breed Research; Historical; Marketing and Education; Public Relations. **Programs:** Youth Scholarship. **Publications:** *Texas Longhorn Trails*, monthly. Magazine. **Price:** $60.00/year in U.S.; $70.00/year outside U.S. **Circulation:** 5,000. **Advertising:** accepted. Alternate Formats: CD-ROM; online. **Conventions/Meetings:** annual convention (exhibits) - always November ● annual show - always June.

4295 ■ United Braford Breeders (UBB)
422 E Main, No. 218
Nacogdoches, TX 75961
Ph: (936)569-8200
Fax: (936)569-9556
E-mail: ubb@brafords.org
URL: http://www.brafords.org
Contact: Rodney L. Roberson PhD, Exec. Dir.
Founded: 1969. **Members:** 500. **Membership Dues:** gift, $50 (annual) ● active, full, $75 (annual) ● junior, $50. **Staff:** 3. **Budget:** $125,000. **Regional Groups:** 3. **State Groups:** 2. **Description:** Producers of Braford cattle. Registers pedigrees and records production data. Encourages and assists with field days, auction sales, and promotional activities. **Telecommunication Services:** electronic mail, roberson@brafords.org. **Formerly:** International Braford Association. **Publications:** *Braford News*, quarterly. Magazine. **Circulation:** 3,000. **Advertising:** accepted. **Conventions/Meetings:** annual meeting.

4296 ■ Women in Livestock Development (WILD)
c/o Heifer Project International
PO Box 8058
Little Rock, AR 72203
Free: (800)422-0474
E-mail: info@heifer.org
URL: http://www.heifer.org
Contact: Jo Luck, Pres./CEO
Founded: 1990. **Description:** Seeks to address gender issues in development projects involving livestock. Group maintains that women gain respect in traditional societies if they acquire ownership of livestock, and that such ownership will not upset the existing social structure. Conducts research and educational programs. **Awards:** Wild Award. **Frequency:** annual. **Type:** monetary. **Recipient:** for outstanding achievement in livestock community development. **Publications:** *Focus on Women in*

Livestock Development, quarterly. Newsletter. **Conventions/Meetings:** periodic workshop (exhibits).

4297 ■ World Watusi Association (WWA)
PO Box 14
Crawford, NE 69339-0014
Ph: (308)665-3919
Fax: (308)665-1931
E-mail: mail@watusicattle.com
URL: http://www.watusicattle.com
Contact: Maureen Neidhardt, Exec. Sec.
Founded: 1985. **Members:** 300. **Membership Dues:** regular, $25 (annual) ● life, $250 ● associate, $15 (annual). **Staff:** 1. **Budget:** $25,000. **Description:** Membership in 3 countries includes: enthusiasts of animal novelty breeds; ranchers; members of the rodeo industry; investors; cow or bull owners. Promotes the Watusi breed of cattle and disseminates information on their uses and value. Conducts periodic cattle shows and sales. (The Watusi breed originated in Africa and is sometimes referred to as the African Longhorn because the cattle possess the largest and longest horns of any cattle in the world.) Registers cattle pedigrees. **Formerly:** (1985) Watusi International Association. **Publications:** Also publishes brochures and flyers. **Conventions/Meetings:** annual meeting.

Chimpanzee

4298 ■ Save the Chimps (STC)
PO Box 12220
Fort Pierce, FL 34979
Ph: (772)429-0403
Fax: (772)460-0720
E-mail: info@savethechimps.org
URL: http://www.savethechimps.org
Contact: Carole Noon PhD, Founder/Dir.
Founded: 1997. **Membership Dues:** regular, $25. **Description:** Works to save captive chimpanzees. Seeks to create a sanctuary where rescued chimpanzees can live out their lives without the threat of ever returning to a laboratory. Educates people about the chimpanzees and conservation issues. **Publications:** Newsletter. **Price:** included in membership dues.

Coal

4299 ■ Citizens Coal Council (CCC)
PO Box 964
Washington, PA 15301
Ph: (724)222-5602
Fax: (724)222-5609
E-mail: ccc@citizenscoalcouncil.org
URL: http://www.citizenscoalcouncil.org
Members: 54. **Membership Dues:** basic, $25-$250 (annual) ● low income student, $15 (annual). **Description:** Promotes social and environmental justice; works to protect communities and environment from damage caused by mining and burning coal; seeks to restore law and order through enforcement of federal Surface Mining Control and Reclamation Act.

Colleges and Universities

4300 ■ Campus Safety, Health and Environmental Management Association (CSHEMA)
c/o Rebecca Page
12100 Sunset Hills Rd., Ste.130
Reston, VA 20190-3221
Ph: (703)234-4141
Fax: (703)435-4390
E-mail: info@cshema.org
URL: http://www.cshema.org
Contact: Ms. Susan Lewis, Division Mgr.
Founded: 1953. **Members:** 936. **Membership Dues:** 3 or less EHS employees, $200 (annual) ● 4 to 10 EHS employees, $325 (annual) ● 11 to 25 EHS employees, $450 (annual) ● 26 to 40 EHS employees, $575 (annual) ● more than 40 EHS employees, $700 (annual) ● international institution, $200 (annual). **Budget:** $50,000. **Description:** Represents professionals responsible for environmental health and safety in the higher education sector. **Libraries: Type:** reference. **Holdings:** monographs, reports. **Subjects:** safety, compliance. **Awards:** Complete Safety Program Award. **Frequency:** annual. **Type:** recognition. **Recipient:** for health and safety programs ● Distinguished Service to Safety Award. **Frequency:** annual. **Type:** recognition. **Recipient:** for members who are actively involved in the Campus Society Division ● Homepage Award. **Frequency:** annual. **Type:** recognition. **Recipient:** for websites of member universities and colleges ● Honorary Life Membership Award. **Frequency:** annual. **Type:** recognition. **Recipient:** for individuals who have made significant, meaningful contributions to a division ● Newsletter Award of Excellence. **Frequency:** annual. **Type:** recognition. **Recipient:** for members and editors ● Perks for Peers Award. **Frequency:** annual. **Type:** recognition. **Recipient:** for project development programs ● Scholarship Award. **Frequency:** annual. **Type:** scholarship. **Recipient:** to undergraduate and graduate students in all majors/disciplines enrolled in 12 credit hours per semester, trimester or quarter ● Unique or Innovative Program Award. **Frequency:** annual. **Type:** recognition. **Recipient:** for schools or institutions. **Computer Services:** database. **Committees:** Awards and Recognition; Fire and Life Safety; Government Relations; Nominations; Professional Relations. **Programs:** Complete Environmental Health and Safety; Scholarship; Unique or Innovative. **Publications:** *Leadership Manual*. Expands the operating procedures or formal organizational by-laws of CSHEMA. Alternate Formats: online ● *Safety and Health*. Magazine. **Price:** included in membership dues ● Newsletter. **Price:** included in membership dues. Alternate Formats: online ● Membership Directory. **Price:** included in membership dues ● Survey. Alternate Formats: online. **Conventions/Meetings:** annual conference, with speakers.

Commodities

4301 ■ Amcot, Inc. (AI)
PO Box 259
Bakersfield, CA 93302
Ph: (661)327-5961
Fax: (661)861-9870
E-mail: atlamcot@aol.com
URL: http://www.amcot.org
Contact: T.W. Smith, Chm.
Membership Dues: active, associate, $25 (annual). **Description:** Serves as sales organization for raw cotton. **Formerly:** American Cotton Cooperative.

4302 ■ American Commodity Distribution Association (ACDA)
c/o W. Kenneth Shifflett, Exec. Sec.
11358 Barley Field Way
Marriottsville, MD 21104
Ph: (410)442-4612
Fax: (410)442-4613
E-mail: wkshifflett@verizon.net
URL: http://www.commodityfoods.org
Contact: W. Kenneth Shifflett, Exec. Sec.
Founded: 1975. **Members:** 350. **Membership Dues:** industry, $400 (annual) ● state/territory, associate, allied and agriculture, individual, $300 (annual) ● recipient agency, $150 (annual). **Staff:** 2. **Budget:** $75,000. **Regional Groups:** 7. **State Groups:** 50. **Description:** State agencies, companies, and agricultural organizations involved in food distribution, warehousing, transporting, or brokering; interested others. Acts as a clearinghouse for the exchange of information on commodity processing, distribution, and marketing and commodity regulations, changes, and purchases. Lobbies government on commodity issues. Coordinates members' activities to promote agriculture, nutrition, and the Federally Donated Food Program. Sponsors education, research, and charitable programs and children's services; compiles statistics. Maintains speakers' bureau. **Libraries: Type:** reference. **Holdings:** archival material, business records, clippings, periodicals. **Subjects:** USDA donated foods and processing of those foods. **Computer Services:** database ● mailing lists. **Publications:** *Calendar of Events*, periodic. Newsletter ● *Commodity Key*, bimonthly. **Price:** included in membership dues ● Membership Directory, annual. **Conventions/Meetings:** annual conference.

4303 ■ American Malting Barley Association (AMBA)
740 N Plankinton Ave., Ste.830
Milwaukee, WI 53203-2403
Ph: (414)272-4640
E-mail: info@ambainc.org
URL: http://www.ambainc.org
Contact: Michael P. Davis, Pres.
Founded: 1982. **Members:** 9. **Staff:** 3. **Description:** Malting and brewing companies. Works to improve malting barley through education and research. Maintains collection of scientific and other information on malting barley. **Libraries: Type:** reference. **Holdings:** reports. **Telecommunication Services:** electronic mail, mpdavis@execpc.com. **Supersedes:** Malting Barley Improvement Association. **Publications:** *Barley Newsletter*. Alternate Formats: online ● *Barley Variety Dictionary*. Alternate Formats: online ● *Know Your Malting Barley Varieties*. Alternate Formats: online ● *Proceedings of Barley Improvement Conference*, biennial. Alternate Formats: online ● *Red River Valley Barley Day*, biennial. Proceedings. Alternate Formats: online. **Conventions/Meetings:** biennial Red River Valley Barley Day - conference.

4304 ■ American Soybean Association (ASA)
12125 Woodcrest Executive Dr., Ste.100
St. Louis, MO 63141-5009
Ph: (314)576-1770
Free: (800)688-7692
Fax: (314)576-2786
E-mail: scensky@asaim.soy.org
URL: http://www.soygrowers.com
Contact: Stephen L. Censky, CEO
Founded: 1920. **Members:** 32,000. **Staff:** 45. **Description:** Develops and implements policies to increase the profitability of its members and the entire soybean industry. **Libraries: Type:** reference. **Holdings:** 5,000. **Subjects:** soybean industry. **Committees:** Commodity Classic; Conservation; Strategic Planning; Trade Policy and International Affairs. **Publications:** *ASA Today*, 10/year. Newsletter. **Price:** free for members. Alternate Formats: online ● *ASA Weekly News*. Newsletter. **Price:** free for members. Alternate Formats: online. **Conventions/Meetings:** annual Commodity Classic - conference (exhibits) - always February.

4305 ■ Hop Growers of America (HGA)
PO Box 9218
Yakima, WA 98909
Ph: (509)248-7043
Fax: (509)248-7044
E-mail: info@usahops.org
URL: http://www.usahops.org
Contact: Douglas MacKinnon, Exec. Dir.
Founded: 1956. **Members:** 140. **Staff:** 2. **Languages:** Chinese, English, German, Japanese, Spanish. **Description:** National association of hop growers in Washington, Oregon, and Idaho. **Committees:** Research. **Publications:** *HOPS USA*, monthly. Bulletin. **Conventions/Meetings:** annual meeting - always January.

4306 ■ International Cotton Advisory Committee (ICAC)
1629 K St. NW, Ste.702
Washington, DC 20006-1636
Ph: (202)463-6660
Fax: (202)463-6950
E-mail: secretariat@icac.org
URL: http://www.icac.org
Contact: Terry P. Townsend, Exec. Dir.
Founded: 1939. **Members:** 43. **Staff:** 10. **Budget:** $1,200,000. **Languages:** Arabic, English, French, Russian, Spanish. **Multinational. Description:** Observes developments affecting the cotton industry;

collects and disseminates statistics on cotton production, trade, consumption, stocks, and prices. Offers recommendations to members on measures leading to development of a sound cotton economy. Serves as a forum for international discussion of cotton matters. **Libraries: Type:** open to the public. **Holdings:** 15,000; books, periodicals. **Subjects:** cotton. **Computer Services:** database ● online services. **Committees:** Standing. **Publications:** *Cotton: Monthly Update of the World Situation* (in English, French, and Spanish). **Price:** $250.00/year; $225.00 internet/email. Alternate Formats: online; CD-ROM ● *COTTON: Review of the World Situation* (in English, French, and Spanish), bimonthly. **Price:** $190.00/year - hard copy; $160.00/year - internet. ISSN: 0010-9754. Alternate Formats: online ● *Cotton: World Statistics*, annual. Provides world cotton supply/demand statistics since 1980, by country on a crop year basis. **Price:** $200.00 hard copy; $160.00 internet. Alternate Formats: online ● *Current Research Projects in Cotton*, biennial. **Price:** $100.00 ● *ICAC documents on CD-ROM*. **Price:** $395.00 ● *The ICAC Recorder* (in English, French, and Spanish), quarterly. **Price:** $170.00/year - hard copy; $140.00/year - internet ● *Outlook for Cotton Supply*, annual. Provides an overview of factors affecting world cotton prices; provides statistics on aggregate world cotton supply and use, with price forecasts. **Price:** $100.00 internet; $125.00 hardcopy. Alternate Formats: online ● *Proceedings of Plenary Meetings* (in English, French, and Spanish), annual. **Price:** $50.00 hardcopy; $25.00 internet/email. Alternate Formats: online ● *Survey of Cotton Production Practices*. Provides information on how cotton is grown in 28 countries. **Price:** $150.00 hardcopy; $100.00 internet. Alternate Formats: online ● *Survey of the Cost of Production of Raw Cotton*. Compares the cost of production of cotton grown under a wide range of growing conditions. **Price:** $150.00 ● *Tis Report A Look Into the Future*. **Price:** $50.00 hard copy; $25.00 internet/email. Alternate Formats: online ● *World Cotton Trade*, annual. Discusses trade developments in raw cotton since 1980; analyzes world trade by region, and provides import/export projections by country. **Price:** $175.00 hard copy; $150.00 internet. Alternate Formats: online ● *World Textile Demand*, annual. Contains analyses and projections of world end-use consumption of textiles, mill use, and production of cotton and chemical yarn and fabric. **Price:** $300.00 hardcopy; $275.00 internet. Alternate Formats: online ● Catalog. Alternate Formats: online. **Conventions/Meetings:** annual Plenary Meeting, cotton producers and consumers forum.

4307 ■ International Wild Rice Exchange

PO Box 1247
Woodland, CA 95776-1247
Ph: (530)669-0150
Fax: (530)668-9317
E-mail: czambe9067@aol.com
Contact: Carlos Zambello, Pres.

Founded: 1969. **Members:** 65. **Membership Dues:** $150 (annual). **Staff:** 1. **Budget:** $12,000. **Regional Groups:** 5. **Description:** Growers, producers, processors, and marketers of wild rice. Disseminates information on research findings, weather conditions, planting methods, and diseases. Expands domestic and foreign markets for wild rice. Has held tours of processing and packaging plants and lakes and paddies where wild rice is grown. Conducts research. **Formerly:** (1982) Wild Rice Growers Association; (1999) International Wild Rice Association. **Publications:** *Manomin News*, quarterly. Newsletter. **Price:** included in membership dues. **Circulation:** 250. **Advertising:** accepted. **Conventions/Meetings:** annual conference (exhibits) - always January.

4308 ■ Kamut Association of North America (KANA)

333 Kamut Ln.
Big Sandy, MT 59520
Ph: (406)378-3105
Free: (800)644-6450
Fax: (406)378-3106
E-mail: debby@kamut.com
URL: http://www.kamut.com
Contact: Debby Quinn Blyth, Coor.

Founded: 1990. **Members:** 80. **Staff:** 2. **Regional Groups:** 1. **Description:** Growers, manufacturers, and distributors of kamut grain. Educates the public, consumers, retailers, and manufacturers on the nutritional and flavor benefits of kamut grain. Compiles statistics. Sponsors research and educational programs. **Libraries: Type:** reference. **Telecommunication Services:** electronic mail, bob.quinn@kamut.com. **Publications:** *The Goldern Kernel*, quarterly. **Conventions/Meetings:** annual conference.

4309 ■ National Association of Wheat Growers (NAWG)

415 2nd St. NE
Washington, DC 20002-4993
Ph: (202)547-7800
Fax: (202)546-2638
E-mail: wheatworld@wheatworld.org
URL: http://www.wheatworld.org
Contact: Daren Coppock, CEO

Founded: 1950. **Members:** 25,000. **Membership Dues:** regular, $100 (annual). **Staff:** 7. **Budget:** $1,300,000. **State Groups:** 19. **Description:** Federation of 19 state wheat growers associations. Represents wheat grower interest in educational, legislative, and regulatory projects and issues for wheat farmers in Washington, DC. Sponsors research and transportation, and leadership conferences; conducts seminars. Conducts charitable programs. **Libraries: Type:** reference. **Awards: Type:** recognition. **Committees:** Budget; Domestic Policy; Environmental Policy; International Policy; Operations and Planning; Research and Value Added. **Subcommittees:** Biotechnology; Joint Trade Policy. **Publications:** *Report From Washington*, weekly. Newsletter. Talks on legislative activities in Congress and federal government as it pertains to wheat growers and the industry. **Price:** included in membership dues; $50.00 /year for nonmembers (plus distribution charges). Alternate Formats: online. **Conventions/Meetings:** annual Commodity Classic - convention and trade show, with wheat, corn and soybeans growers (exhibits).

4310 ■ National Corn Growers Association (NCGA)

632 Cepi Dr.
Chesterfield, MO 63005-1221
Ph: (636)733-9004
Fax: (636)733-9005
E-mail: corninfo@ncga.com
URL: http://www.ncga.com
Contact: Rick Tolman, CEO

Founded: 1957. **Members:** 29,800. **Staff:** 30. **Budget:** $5,000,000. **State Groups:** 25. **Local Groups:** 100. **Description:** Growers of corn. Furthers the use, proper marketing, legislative position, and efficient production of corn. Conducts research and educational programs. Sponsors National Yield Contest; compiles statistics. **Telecommunication Services:** electronic mail, tolman@ncga.com. **Committees:** Communications and Education; Government Relations; Industry Relations; Marketing; Research and Commercialization; State Relations. **Publications:** *National Corn Grower*, quarterly. Newsletter. Includes calendar of annual state meetings. **Price:** included in membership dues. **Circulation:** 30,000 ● Directory, annual ● Report, annual ● Also publishes *World of Corn, Corn Commentary, Government Relations Bulletins*. **Conventions/Meetings:** annual Commodity Classic - convention and trade show, held in conjunction with NCGA and American Soybean Association (exhibits).

4311 ■ National Sorghum Producers (NSP)

4201 N Interstate 27
Lubbock, TX 79403-7507
Ph: (806)749-3478
Fax: (806)749-9002
E-mail: christi@sorghumgrowers.com
URL: http://www.sorghumgrowers.com
Contact: Tim Lust, CEO

Founded: 1955. **Members:** 2,000. **Membership Dues:** regular, $60 (annual) ● supporting, $100 (annual) ● contributing, $250 (annual) ● sustaining, $500 (annual). **Staff:** 9. **Budget:** $500,000. **State Groups:** 7. **Description:** Growers of grain sorghum and grain sorghum processing facilities. Promotes growth in the grain sorghum industry. Represents members' interests; conducts research and educational programs. **Formerly:** (2005) National Grain Sorghum Producers. **Publications:** *Grain Sorghum News*, monthly. Newsletter. **Conventions/Meetings:** annual conference.

4312 ■ National Sunflower Association (NSA)

4023 State St.
Bismarck, ND 58503-0690
Ph: (701)328-5100 (701)328-5103
Free: (888)718-7033
Fax: (701)328-5101
E-mail: klngrtnr@sunflowernsa.com
URL: http://www.sunflowernsa.com
Contact: Larry Kleingartner, Exec. Dir.

Founded: 1981. **Members:** 32,000. **Membership Dues:** associate, $325 (annual) ● regular, foreign, $500 (annual) ● farmer, $40 (annual) ● check-off elevator, $250 (annual). **Staff:** 3. **Budget:** $1,000,000. **Languages:** English, Spanish. **Description:** Growers, firms, and organizations associated with the sunflower and its products, including growers' councils, seed companies, processors, exporters, researchers, chemical firms, and merchandisers. Promotes the development of the sunflower industry. Seeks to improve sunflower production through research and education and to expand markets for sunflower products in the U.S. and abroad. Sponsors educational events; provides financial support for scientific research projects; disseminates information. **Committees:** Confectionery; Nusun Oil; Research. **Supersedes:** Sunflower Association of America. **Publications:** *The Sunflower*, bimonthly. Magazine. Provides information on production and marketing of sunflower products. **Price:** free for members and selected others; $9.00 /year for nonmembers. **Circulation:** 18,500. **Advertising:** accepted ● *Sunflower Species of the United States* ● *Sunflower Week in Review*, bimonthly. Newsletter. Provides sunflower information and updated prices. **Price:** free for members and selected others ● *U.S. Sunflower Crop Quality Report*, annual. Includes statistics on sunflower industry production, supply, geography, economics, research, seed, oil, exports, and grades and standards. **Price:** free. **Conventions/Meetings:** annual Sunflower Research Forum - workshop.

4313 ■ Organization for the Advancement of Knowledge (OAK)

c/o Richard Alan Miller, Dir.
1212 SW 5th St.
Grants Pass, OR 97526-6104
Ph: (541)476-5588
Fax: (541)476-1823
E-mail: drram@magick.net
URL: http://www.nwbotanicals.org/oak/oak.html
Contact: Richard Alan Miller, Dir.

Founded: 1974. **Staff:** 3. **For-Profit. Description:** Profit sharing cooperatives involved with rural economic development and production of herbs, spices, and medicinal plants for export. Compiles statistics; maintains speakers' bureau; offers educational programs. Conducts monthly workshops; sponsors seminars and research. **Computer Services:** Information services, alternative crops marketing services ● information services, farm plans ● information services, seed sources (price/cultivar comparisons). **Telecommunication Services:** information service, crop reports (AGRICOLA/CRIS). **Publications:** *Herb Market Report: For the Herb Farmer and Forager*, monthly. Newsletter. Features information on the marketing of herbs. **Price:** $18.00/year; $15.00/year in Canada ● *The Magical and Ritual Use of Aphrodisiacs*. Book ● *The Magical and Ritual Use of Herbs*. Book ● *Magical and Ritual Use of Perfumes*. Book ● *Native Plants of Commercial Importance*. Book.

Price: $16.50 ● *Potential of Herbs as a Cash Crop*. Book. **Price:** $15.00.

4314 ■ Pacific Northwest Grain and Feed Association (PNWGFA)
200 SW Market St., Ste.190
Portland, OR 97201
Ph: (503)227-0234
Fax: (503)227-0059
E-mail: pnwgfa@pnwgfa.org
URL: http://www.pnwgfa.org
Contact: Dave Gordon, Pres.
Founded: 1917. **Members:** 256. **Staff:** 3. **Budget:** $250,000. **Description:** Represents firms involved in the grain business; suppliers; retired grain executives. Conducts seminars and workshops. Offers honorary memberships. **Committees:** Grades; Scholarship; Transportation; Warehousemen's. **Affiliated With:** National Grain and Feed Association. **Formed by Merger of:** Pacific Northwest Grain Dealers; Washington Feed Association. **Formerly:** (1975) Pacific Northwest Pea Growers and Dealers. **Publications:** Directory, annual ● Newsletter, biweekly. **Conventions/Meetings:** annual convention (exhibits).

4315 ■ Plains Cotton Growers (PCG)
4517 W Loop 289
Lubbock, TX 79414
Ph: (806)792-4904
Fax: (806)792-4906
E-mail: mail@plainscotton.org
URL: http://www.plainscotton.org
Contact: Steve Verett, Exec. VP
Founded: 1956. **Members:** 25,000. **Staff:** 5. **Description:** Represents cotton producers, ginners, oil mills, warehouses, and allied businesses; membership concentrated in west Texas. Furthers the use of high plains cotton through research, promotion, advertising, legislative activities, and technical assistance to cotton mills. Provides statistics on cotton production, acreage, quality, varieties, and spinning performance. Conducts educational programs. **Libraries: Type:** reference. **Holdings:** archival material, audiovisuals. **Subjects:** cotton production, harvesting, manufacturing. **Committees:** Legislative; Marketing; Research. **Publications:** *Cotton News*, weekly. Newsletter. Contains a variety of interesting facts and statistics pertaining to legislation, regulatory affairs and current events. **Conventions/Meetings:** quarterly board meeting - always January, April, July, October ● annual meeting.

4316 ■ Soyfoods Association of North America (SANA)
1050 17th St. NW, Ste.600
Washington, DC 20036
Ph: (202)659-3520
E-mail: info@soyfoods.org
URL: http://www.soyfoods.org
Contact: Ted Nordquist, Pres.
Founded: 1978. **Members:** 60. **Membership Dues:** company (with less than 1000000 gross sales), $500 (annual) ● company (with 1000000 gross sales), $1,000 (annual) ● company (with 5000000 gross sales), $3,500 (annual) ● company (with 10000000 gross sales), $7,000 (annual) ● company (with 20000000 gross sales), $14,000 (annual) ● individual (professional), $250 (annual). **Staff:** 3. **Description:** Represents nutritionists, researchers, growers and brokers of soybeans and related products; trade associations and manufacturers of foods made from soybeans. Works to establish standards within the soyfoods industry and to represent the industry before government bodies. Responds to phone inquiries concerning soyfoods; compiles statistics; conducts research programs. Conventions/Meetings: annual Soy Symposium. **Libraries: Type:** reference. **Holdings:** 3,720; archival material, books, periodicals. **Subjects:** soyfoods, soybean utilization, soybeans, soybean history. **Computer Services:** Bibliographic search, SoyaScan: 66200 records. **Committees:** Standards. **Formerly:** (1981) Soycrafters Association of North America. **Publications:** *SANA Consumer Packet*. Brochures ● Newsletter, monthly ● Also publishes news releases.

4317 ■ Supima
4141 E Broadway Rd.
Phoenix, AZ 85040
Ph: (602)437-1364
Fax: (602)437-0143
E-mail: info@supima.com
URL: http://www.supima.com
Contact: Jesse W. Curlee, Pres.
Founded: 1954. **Members:** 2,400. **Membership Dues:** cotton grower, $3 (annual). **Staff:** 5. **Budget:** $2,300,000. **Description:** Southwestern producers of domestic, extra-long staple cotton. Compiles statistics; conducts promotional activities and research programs. **Committees:** Political Action. **Absorbed:** (1978) Arizona Cotton Planting Seed Distributors. **Formerly:** (2004) Supima Association of America. **Publications:** *Supima News*, monthly. Newsletter. Reports export and domestic consumption figures for Pima cotton; also includes association news and statistics. **Price:** included in membership dues. **Circulation:** 2,200. Alternate Formats: online. **Conventions/Meetings:** annual regional meeting - always September.

4318 ■ United States Durum Growers Association (USDGA)
2409 Jackson Ave.
Bismarck, ND 58501
Ph: (701)214-3203 (701)626-7378
Fax: (701)250-1730
E-mail: dawn@durumgrowers.com
URL: http://www.durumgrowers.com
Contact: Dawn Watson, Exec. Dir.
Founded: 1957. **Members:** 400. **Membership Dues:** grower, $75 (annual) ● associate, $100 (annual) ● life, $1,000. **Description:** Durum wheat growers. Cooperates with other organizations to promote favorable conditions for the production and marketing of durum wheat. **Committees:** Legislative; Marketing; Promotion; Research. **Publications:** *Durum Kernels*, monthly. **Conventions/Meetings:** annual International Durum Forum - meeting ● annual meeting - always November in Minot, ND.

4319 ■ U.S. Wheat Associates (USW)
1620 I St. NW, Ste.801
Washington, DC 20006-4005
Ph: (202)463-0999
Fax: (202)785-1052
E-mail: info@uswheat.org
URL: http://www.uswheat.org
Contact: Leonard Schock, Chm.
Founded: 1980. **Members:** 20. **Staff:** 82. **Budget:** $14,000,000. **Languages:** Chinese, English, French. **Multinational**. **Description:** Works as the industry export market development organization. **Computer Services:** Information services, wheat facts and resources. **Formed by Merger of:** Great Plains Wheat; Western Wheat Association. **Publications:** *Wheat Letter*, biweekly. Newsletter. Covers trade issues, markets, and organizational updates. **Price:** free. **Circulation:** 2,500. Alternate Formats: online ● Reports. Alternate Formats: online. **Conventions/Meetings:** board meeting - 3/year.

4320 ■ United Weighers Association (UWA)
Address Unknown since 2008
Description: Weighers and supervisors of raw commodities (sugar, coffee, cocoa, rubber, tin, and wool) imported to U.S. by ship.

4321 ■ U.S.A. Rice Council (USARC)
4301 N Fairfax Dr., Ste.425
Arlington, VA 22203
Ph: (703)236-2300
Fax: (703)236-2301
E-mail: riceinfo@usarice.com
URL: http://www.usarice.com
Contact: John King III, Chm.
Founded: 1956. **Members:** 45,000. **Staff:** 27. **Budget:** $5,000,000. **State Groups:** 6. **Description:** Rice producers, millers, dryers, packagers, and others in the rice industry in Arkansas, California, Louisiana, Mississippi, Missouri, and Texas. Provides worldwide advertising and promotion services to the rice industry. **Programs:** Rice Fits. **Absorbed:** U.S. Rice Export Development, Association. **Also Known As:** Rice Council of America. **Formerly:** (1960) The Rice Industry; (1991) Rice Council for Market Development. **Publications:** Newsletter, quarterly ● Also publishes recipe leaflets and educational material. **Conventions/Meetings:** annual meeting.

4322 ■ Wheat Quality Council (WQC)
c/o Ben Handcock, Exec. VP
106 W Capitol, Ste.2
PO Box 966
Pierre, SD 57501-0966
Ph: (605)224-5187
Fax: (605)224-0517
E-mail: bhwqc@aol.com
URL: http://www.wheatqualitycouncil.org
Contact: Ben Handcock, Exec. VP
Founded: 1938. **Members:** 150. **Membership Dues:** professional organization (based on production figures), $2,000-$6,000 (annual) ● allied company (minimum), $250 (annual) ● seed breeder/distributor, $100-$1,000 (annual) ● grain company, $250-$1,000 (annual) ● wheat food user, $500-$7,500 (annual) ● miller, $750-$12,750 (annual). **Staff:** 2. **Budget:** $250,000. **Description:** Members of the breadstuffs industry with an interest in wheat and wheat flour products. Works for charitable, educational, and research purposes in support of agricultural crop improvement, conservation, and protection. Involves in wheat quality studies and reporting. Compiles statistics; engages in educational activities for wheat quality evaluation for bread and other uses. **Libraries: Type:** reference. **Subjects:** wheat production, qualities of wheat of the U.S. **Committees:** Technical. **Formerly:** (1980) Kansas Wheat Improvement Association Hard Winter Wheat Quality Council. **Publications:** *Wheat Briefs*, 2-4/year. Newsletter. Provides information on the improvement of wheat for agribusiness and the baking industry. **Price:** included in membership dues. **Circulation:** 1,600 ● Annual Report, annual. Compares new wheat varieties to performance of old popular varieties. Includes data on milling and baking properties and wheat statistics. **Price:** included in membership dues. **Circulation:** 800. **Conventions/Meetings:** competition ● annual conference.

Commodity Exchanges

4323 ■ Board of Trade of the Wholesale Seafood Merchants (BTWSM)
Address Unknown since 2008
Founded: 1933. **Members:** 400. **Staff:** 4. **Description:** Credit and collection agencies for U.S. and Canadian wholesale seafood merchants.

4324 ■ CME Group
20 S Wacker Dr.
Chicago, IL 60606
Ph: (312)930-1000
Free: (800)331-3332
E-mail: info@cme.com
URL: http://www.cme.com
Contact: Craig S. Donohue, Dir./Pres.
Founded: 1898. **Members:** 2,724. **Staff:** 880. **Budget:** $90,000,000. **Multinational**. **Description:** Commodity futures exchange for live hogs, feeder cattle, live beef cattle, frozen pork bellies (bacon), lumber, gold, foreign currencies, government securities, bank debt, and equity financial instruments; deals with options on equity futures, interest rates, foreign currencies, and livestock. Maintains speakers' bureau; conducts research programs to help develop new contracts and update existing contracts; compiles statistics. **Libraries: Type:** reference. **Holdings:** 3,000; books. **Subjects:** aspects of futures trading. **Committees:** Audit; Compensation; Governance; Market Regulation Oversight; Marketing and Public Relations Advisory. **Divisions:** AG Marketing; Building Operations; Compliance; Financial Instruments Marketing; Government Relations; Legal and Regulatory; Main Frame Systems and Programs; Mainframe Software Support; Marketing; Price Quotations; Support Facilities Statistics. **Formed by Merger of:**

(2007) Chicago Mercantile Exchange and Chicago Board of Trade. **Formerly:** (1919) Chicago Butter and Egg Board. **Publications:** *Bibliography and Information Source Lists*, annual ● *Chicago Mercantile Exchange—Annual Report* ● *CME Magazine*. Features customer case histories, trend stories, editorials and news briefs. Alternate Formats: online ● *Open Outcry*, monthly ● *RCR Report*, quarterly ● Membership Directory, annual ● Newsletter, monthly ● Yearbook ● Also publishes contract specifications brochures and fundamental factor books. **Conventions/Meetings:** annual meeting - always November.

4325 ■ Fort Worth Grain Exchange (FWGE)
Address Unknown since 2008
Founded: 1907. **Members:** 36. **Staff:** 19. **Description:** Grain dealers, mills, and elevators. Maintains a protein laboratory, grain weighing department, and central facility for grain grading. **Formerly:** Fort Worth Grain and Cotton Exchange. **Conventions/Meetings:** annual meeting - always April or May. Ft. Worth, TX.

4326 ■ Greenwood Cotton Exchange (GCE)
Address Unknown since 2007
Founded: 1927. **Members:** 31. **Membership Dues:** $75. **Staff:** 2. **Description:** Commodity exchange - cotton. **Publications:** *Greenwood Cotton Exchange*, annual. **Conventions/Meetings:** annual meeting - always second Tuesday in July.

4327 ■ Kansas City Board of Trade (KCBT)
4800 Main St., Ste.303
Kansas City, MO 64112
Ph: (816)753-7500
Free: (800)821-5228
Fax: (816)753-3944
E-mail: kcbt@kcbt.com
URL: http://www.kcbt.com
Contact: Jeffrey C. Borchardt, Pres./CEO
Founded: 1856. **Members:** 260. **Staff:** 25. **For-Profit. Description:** Commodity exchange and clearing organization - cash grains, wheat futures, wheat options, Value Line stock index futures, and ISDEX Internet futures. **Telecommunication Services:** additional toll-free number, (800)821-4444. **Committees:** Appeals; Arbitration; Marketing; Stock Index; Wheat Contracts. **Departments:** Audits and Investigations; Marketing; Operations. **Formerly:** (2004) Board of Trade of Kansas City, Missouri. **Publications:** *Annual Statistical Report*, annual. Annual Report. Alternate Formats: diskette ● *Kansas City Grain Market Review*, daily ● *KCBT Market Watch*, periodic. Newsletter. Contains information for futures traders and brokerage firm executives covering Kansas City Board of Trade commodities and strategies. **Price:** included in membership dues. **Circulation:** 8,500 ● Membership Directory, annual ● Book ● Brochures.

4328 ■ Memphis Cotton Exchange (MCE)
c/o Cotton Museum
65 Union Ave.
Memphis, TN 38103
Ph: (901)531-7826
Fax: (901)531-7827
URL: http://www.memphiscottonmuseum.org
Contact: Mr. Calvin J. Turley, Pres.
Founded: 1873. **Members:** 94. **Membership Dues:** individual, $45 (annual) ● dual, $60 (annual) ● family, $75 (annual). **Staff:** 11. **Description:** Commodity exchange - cotton. Maintains the Cotton Museum. **Committees:** Arbitration; Futures; National Affairs; Trade. **Publications:** *Directory of the Cotton Trade*, annual. **Conventions/Meetings:** annual meeting - always first Wednesday of January in Memphis, TN.

4329 ■ Minneapolis Grain Exchange (MGEX)
400 S 4th St.
130 Grain Exchange Bldg.
Minneapolis, MN 55415
Ph: (612)321-7101
Free: (800)827-4746
Fax: (612)339-1155
E-mail: mgex@mgex.com
URL: http://www.mgex.com
Contact: Mark G. Bagan, Pres./CEO
Founded: 1881. **Members:** 402. **Description:** Commodity exchange. Trades spring wheat, durum wheat, cottonseed, Twin Cities electricity, white wheat, and white and black tiger shrimp futures and options; compiles grain and oil seed stock, movement, and price information. Conducts options and futures seminars. **Telecommunication Services:** electronic mail, mbagan@mgex.com ● hotline, marketing, (612)321-7131. **Committees:** Business Conduct; Futures Contract; Options. **Divisions:** Sampling; Weighing. **Publications:** *Annual Statistical Report*, annual. Annual Report ● *Trading Trends*. Newsletter ● Membership Directory, periodic. **Price:** available to members only.

4330 ■ New England Fish Exchange (NEFE)
Address Unknown since 2008
Founded: 1908. **Members:** 26. **Staff:** 4. **Description:** Commodity exchange for buyers and sellers of fish landed by fishing boats and fish trucked by auto and rail to Boston Fish Pier. Compiles statistics. **Publications:** *Boston Directory*, periodic.

4331 ■ New Orleans Board of Trade (NOBOT)
316 Bd. of Trade Pl.
New Orleans, LA 70130
Ph: (504)262-0412
E-mail: sas112274@aol.com
URL: http://www.neworleansbot.com
Contact: Brett Bourgeois, Exec. Dir.
Founded: 1880. **Members:** 250. **Membership Dues:** full/associate, $150. **Staff:** 5. **Description:** Members include representatives of commodity, transportation, export-import, utility, banking, insurance, warehouse, and other interests. Promotes trade and commerce in New Orleans, LA area and port. Operates Marine Exchange, which reports all ocean vessels entering and exiting the Mississippi River. Sponsors the Society of Maritime Arbitrators (see separate entry). Offers seminars on trade-related subjects. **Libraries: Type:** reference. **Holdings:** archival material, books, business records, periodicals. **Awards: Type:** recognition. **Computer Services:** database, ships. **Committees:** Coffee; Finance and Executive; Freight Forwarders and Freight Brokers; Insurance; Maritime; Supervisory. **Subgroups:** Society of Maritime Arbitrators. **Formerly:** (1889) New Orleans Produce Exchange. **Publications:** *Maritime Report*, daily. **Conventions/Meetings:** annual meeting, with election - always January.

4332 ■ New York Cotton Exchange (NYCE)
1 N End Ave.
New York, NY 10282-1101
Ph: (212)748-4094 (212)748-4000
Free: (800)HED-GEIT
E-mail: webmaster@nybot.com
Contact: Regina Rocker, VP, eCOPS Marketing and Administration
Founded: 1870. **Members:** 416. **Staff:** 85. **Description:** Commodity exchange - cotton and frozen concentrated orange juice. Develops new products; provides market information; compiles statistics. Collaborates with the Citrus Associates of the New York Cotton Exchange; operates Financial Instruments Exchange, in conjunction with the New York Stock Exchange. **Telecommunication Services:** hotline, emergency announcement line, (877)877-8890. **Departments:** Compliance; Floor Operations; Legal; Market Surveillance; Marketing; Research; Statistics. **Publications:** *Cotton Exchange Newsletter*, quarterly ● *Finex Report*, quarterly. Newsletter ● *Market Report*, daily ● *Weekly Trade Report* ● Annual Report, annual ● Brochures ● Membership Directory, annual ● Also publishes leaflets and rules and regulations.

4333 ■ New York Mercantile Exchange (NYMEX)
World Financial Ctr.
1 N End Ave.
New York, NY 10282-1101
Ph: (212)299-2000 (212)748-5265
Free: (800)438-8616
Fax: (212)301-4700
E-mail: exchangeinfo@nymex.com
URL: http://www.nymex.com
Contact: James E. Newsome, Pres./CEO
Founded: 1872. **Members:** 816. **Staff:** 227. **Description:** Brokerage houses, businesses with commercial interests in commodities, and professional traders. Provides a mechanism for trading futures and options. Compiles trading statistics for public distribution. Operates library of government and trade publications related to commodity futures contracts currently traded. Maintains numerous committees. **Divisions:** Compliance; Information Systems; Marketing; Research. **Formerly:** (1880) Butter, Cheese, and Egg Exchange of the City of New York. **Publications:** *Daily Futures Report* ● *Daily Options Report* ● *Energy in the News*, quarterly. Report ● *Exchange By-Laws and Rules*. Report ● *Metal in the News*, semiannual. Report ● *The Month at NYMEX*. Report ● *New York Mercantile Exchange Guide*. Report ● Newsletter, weekly ● Membership Directory, annual. **Conventions/Meetings:** annual meeting - always second Tuesday of March.

4334 ■ Salina Board of Trade (SBT)
Address Unknown since 2008
Founded: 1915. **Members:** 37. **Description:** Commodity exchange - grain.

Community Development

4335 ■ Green Empowerment
140 SW Yamhill St.
Portland, OR 97204
Ph: (503)284-5774
Fax: (503)460-0450
E-mail: info@greenempowerment.org
URL: http://www.greenempowerment.org
Contact: Michael Royce, Pres.
Founded: 1997. **Staff:** 12. **Multinational. Description:** Promotes community-based renewable energy, potable water delivery and watershed restoration projects. Facilitates environmental education, resource conservation, and protection activities. **Computer Services:** Information services, environmental quality resources ● online services, discussion/chatroom. **Councils:** Advisory; Technical Experts. **Projects:** The Alliance in Ecuador; Burma Solar Clinic; Nicaragua Solar Water Pump; Water for Drinking and Irrigation in the Philippines. **Publications:** Newsletter, quarterly. Alternate Formats: online.

4336 ■ Renew America
PO Box 77636
Washington, DC 20013
Fax: (972)436-5161
URL: http://www.renewamerica.us
Contact: Carla Michele, Contact
Founded: 1989. **Description:** Coordinates a network of community and environmental groups, businesses, government leaders and civic activists. Exchanges ideas and expertise for improving the environment. Finds and promotes programs that help inspire communities and businesses. **Awards:** The National Awards for Sustainability. **Frequency:** annual. **Type:** recognition. **Recipient:** for success stories and exemplary programs on environmental protection, social equity and economic progress.

Concrete

4337 ■ Cement Kiln Recycling Coalition (CKRC)
1001 Connecticut Ave. NW, Ste.615
Washington, DC 20036
Ph: (202)466-6802
Fax: (202)466-5009
E-mail: info@ckrc.org
URL: http://www.ckrc.org
Contact: Mike Benoit, Exec. Dir.
Members: 100. **Description:** Cement companies engaged in the use of fuel derived from hazardous waste; collectors, processors, managers, and market-

ers of cement kiln fuel derived from hazardous waste. Promotes environmentally responsible use of hazardous waste as fuel for cement kilns. Develops and enforces standards of conduct and practice for members; supports regulations and permit provisions for the use of fuel derived from hazardous waste that protect human and environmental health; works to create generally accepted environmental evaluation procedures for the cement kiln industry.

Conservation

4338 ■ Abundant Life Seed Foundation (ALSF)
PO Box 157
Saginaw, OR 97472-0157
Ph: (541)767-9606
Fax: (866)514-7333
E-mail: als@abundantlifeseeds.com
URL: http://www.abundantlifeseeds.com
Founded: 1975. **Members:** 1,200. **Membership Dues:** individual, $30 (annual). **Staff:** 6. **Budget:** $150,000. **Description:** Home gardeners, small farmers, students. Acquires, propagates, and preserves the plants and seeds of the Pacific Northwest, with particular emphasis on those species not commercially available, including rare and endangered species and heirlooms. Maintains permanent garden with seed saving as its primary purpose. **Publications:** *Seed Midden*, 3/year. Newsletter ● Catalog, annual. Alternate Formats: online.

4339 ■ Acres Land Trust
1802 Chapman Rd.
Huntertown, IN 46748
Ph: (260)637-2273
Fax: (260)637-2273
E-mail: acres@acreslandtrust.org
URL: http://acreslandtrust.org
Contact: Jason Kissel, Exec. Dir.
Founded: 1960. **Members:** 1,100. **Membership Dues:** individual, $20 (annual) ● family, $30 (annual) ● senior citizen, student, $15 (annual) ● life, $1,500 ● share-the-expense, club/organization, $50 (annual) ● patron, $100 (annual). **Staff:** 4. **Budget:** $100,000. **Description:** Promotes the preservation and acquisition of natural areas in northeastern Indiana. Seeks to acquire and administer natural areas as living museums for educational and scientific purposes and for public enjoyment. Maintains 53 nature preserves in 13 counties in Northeast Indiana. Works to protect other natural areas. Conducts guided field trips, concerts, canoe trips and special events. **Libraries: Type:** reference. **Formerly:** ACRES, Inc. **Publications:** *ACRES Quarterly*. Newsletter. **Price:** included in membership dues. **Circulation:** 2,500.

4340 ■ The Adirondack Council (TAC)
103 Hand Ave., Ste.3
PO Box D-2
Elizabethtown, NY 12932
Ph: (518)873-2240
Free: (877)873-2240
Fax: (518)873-6675
E-mail: info@adirondackcouncil.org
URL: http://www.adirondackcouncil.org
Contact: Brian Houseal, Exec. Dir.
Founded: 1975. **Members:** 18,000. **Membership Dues:** individual, $35 (annual). **Staff:** 14. **Budget:** $1,400,000. **Description:** Dedicated to ensuring the ecological integrity and wild character of New York's six-million-acre Adirondack Park through research, education, advocacy, and legal action. Aims to protect the NYS Constitution's Forever Wild clause, which bans logging and development of public lands; opposes development projects on private lands that threaten the park's natural resources; assists in and creates environmental education projects. Promotes interest in the problem of acid rain. Provides speakers. **Libraries: Type:** by appointment only. **Holdings:** archival material, audio recordings, books, clippings, reports, video recordings. **Awards:** Conservationist of the Year. **Frequency:** annual. **Type:** scholarship. **Recipient:** for person/organization whose actions had the most dramatic positive effect on the wild character and ecological integrity of the Adirondack Park ● Lifetime Achievement Award. **Frequency:** quinquennial. **Type:** recognition. **Recipient:** for person whose contributions to the health and beauty of the Adirondack Park over many years have inspired others to act on behalf of the park ● **Type:** recognition. **Telecommunication Services:** hotline, Albany office and acid rain information, (800)842-PARK. **Affiliated With:** National Audubon Society; National Parks Conservation Association; Natural Resources Defense Council; The Wilderness Society. **Publications:** *A Gift of Wildness*. Report ● *Acid Rain - A Continuing National Tragedy*. Report ● *Adirondack Poster Map* ● *Adirondack Wildguide*. Book ● *The Adirondacks, Wild Island of Hope*. Book. **Price:** $23.00 ● *After the Fact: The Truth About Environmental Enforcement in the Adirondack Park*. Report ● *Beside the Stilled Waters*. Report ● *Falling Farther Behind: Environmental Enforcement in the Adirondack Park*. Report ● *Lake Champlain: Mirror on the Mountains*. Report ● *Managing Growth and Development in Unique Natural Settings*. Proceedings ● *State of the Park Report*, annual, in October ● *2020 VISION*. Reports. Features research series with 3 volumes, on how to complete the Adirondack Forest Preserve and Safeguard Biological Diversity. ● Newsletter, 3/year, winter, spring, summer. **Conventions/Meetings:** quarterly Adirondack Executive Directors Group - executive committee meeting ● annual Adirondack Water Quality Conference - late summer ● annual Forever Wild Dinner - mid-July ● semiannual Oswegatchie Roundtable.

4341 ■ Africa Rainforest and River Conservation (ARRC)
PO Box 2594
Jackson, WY 83001
Ph: (307)734-0077
E-mail: info@africa-rainforest.org
URL: http://www.africa-rainforest.org
Contact: Brian Whitlock, Media Coor.
Founded: 1998. **Multinational. Description:** Aims to increase the awareness of endangered rainforest and river ecosystems in Africa. Gathers and disseminates information that will help the public understand the problems and will aid agencies and governments in developing programs to halt the destruction of those systems.

4342 ■ African Blackwood Conservation Project (ABCP)
c/o James E. Harris
PO Box 26
Red Rock, TX 78662
E-mail: info@blackwoodconservation.org
URL: http://www.blackwoodconservation.org
Contact: James E. Harris, Contact
Founded: 1996. **Multinational. Description:** Aims to help replenish the African Blackwood (Mpingo) in Tanzania. Educates Tanzanians about the ecological and commercial importance of Mpingo. Influences individual Tanzanian citizens to raise Mpingo on private and public lands. Assists in the founding of local environmental groups that establish micro-enterprises for the dual purposes of economic self-empowerment and environmental restoration. Helps community educational and reforestation efforts for the conservation of Mt. Kilimanjaro. **Publications:** *Kibosho East Environmental Handbook*. Contains environmental conservation information and advice. Alternate Formats: online ● Newsletter, annual. Alternate Formats: online ● Annual Report, annual. Alternate Formats: online.

4343 ■ Alaska Coalition (AC)
122 C St. NW, Ste.240
Washington, DC 20001
Ph: (202)544-5205
Fax: (202)544-5197
E-mail: info@alaskacoalition.org
URL: http://www.alaskacoalition.org
Contact: Dan Ritzman, Exec. Dir.
Founded: 1978. **Description:** National, state, and local environmental and conservation organizations. Promotes education, research, and legislative pressure in an effort to preserve Alaska's wild heritage and natural resources. Works to preserve the Arctic National Wildlife Refuge and prevent its exploration and development by oil and gas industries. Works for passage of the Alaska National Interest Lands Conservation Act, commonly known as the Alaska Lands Bill. Following passage of the bill in 1980, the coalition became inactive. The group reactivated in 1983 and succeeded in opposing proposed legislation that would have opened 12 million acres to sports hunting of the 24 million acres protected by the bill; this area is currently open only for subsistence hunting by rural Alaskans. **Publications:** *Alerts*, periodic ● *Bear Facts*, quarterly. Newsletter.

4344 ■ Alliance for International Reforestation (AIR)
421 N Woodland Blvd., Unit 8301
DeLand, FL 32723
Ph: (386)822-7575
E-mail: ahallum@stetson.edu
URL: http://www.stetson.edu/org/forest
Contact: Dr. Anne M. Hallum, Chair
Founded: 1992. **Multinational. Description:** Aims to assist local communities in Central America. Helps to conserve the environment through reforestation and sustainable farming. Establishes permanent tree nurseries and assists community groups to establish, manage and maintain tree nurseries. Educates the community about the impact of deforestation and the importance of conserving the environment. **Publications:** *AIRLines*. Newsletter. Alternate Formats: online.

4345 ■ American Cave Conservation Association (ACCA)
PO Box 409
119 E Main St.
Horse Cave, KY 42749
Ph: (270)786-1466 (270)786-1468
Fax: (270)786-1467
E-mail: acca@cavern.org
URL: http://www.cavern.org
Contact: David G. Foster, Exec. Dir.
Founded: 1977. **Members:** 600. **Membership Dues:** individual, $25 (annual) ● family, $35 (annual) ● supporter, $50 (annual) ● sustainer, $100 (annual) ● patron, $1,000 (annual) ● guarantor, $200 (annual). **Staff:** 10. **Budget:** $300,000. **Description:** Individuals and organizations interested in the conservation of caves, karstlands, and groundwater resources. Seeks to increase public awareness of the value of caves and the unique life-forms and resources associated with them. Serves as a support service offering: consulting on development and evaluation of cave management plans, land use activities, and educational programs; clearinghouse on cave management and conservation information; referral service for those involved in cave and karst management. Provides assistance to research programs and cave management projects including those that help better enforce state and federal environmental laws and policies. Sponsors educational development and training programs, primarily among elementary and secondary schoolchildren and professional land managers. Operates the American Cave and Karst Center and museum and Hidden River Cave. Offers training seminars and courses; conducts periodic National Cave Management Training Seminar; offers reward to those helping to deter vandalism of cave and karst resources. **Libraries: Type:** reference. **Holdings:** 2,000; books, periodicals. **Subjects:** caves, karst, groundwater, biology, geology. **Programs:** Caving Adventure Tour; Clues from the Past; Elementary Cavers; Fabulous Fossils; Karst Geology; Secret Sink; Troglotek; Water Works. **Also Known As:** American Cave and Karst Center; American Cave Museum. **Publications:** *American Cave Adventures*, semiannual. Newspaper. Features student newsletter. Focuses on groundwater/care issues. **Price:** free for teachers. **Circulation:** 45,000 ● *American Caves*, periodic. Magazine. Includes information on national and local cave issues and calendar of events. **Price:** included in membership dues; $5.00 for nonmembers. **Advertising:** accepted. **Conventions/Meetings:** board meeting - 3/year.

4346 ■ American Conservation Association (ACA)
Address Unknown since 2008
Founded: 1958. **Description:** Works to raise public awareness of environmental and conservation issues. Acts as clearinghouse for information on the environment. Sponsors programs to preserve and develop natural resources. Offers educational and research programs.

4347 ■ American Forests
PO Box 2000
Washington, DC 20013
Ph: (202)737-1944
Fax: (202)737-2457
E-mail: info@amfor.org
URL: http://www.americanforests.org
Contact: Deborah Gangloff, Exec. Dir.
Founded: 1875. **Members:** 117,000. **Membership Dues:** regular, $25 (annual) ● forest protector, $100 (annual) ● forest steward, $250 (annual) ● forest guardian, $500 (annual) ● forest legacy, $1,000 (annual). **Staff:** 25. **Budget:** $3,600,000. **Description:** Works to advance the intelligent management and use of forests, soil, water, wildlife, and all other natural resources. Promotes public appreciation of natural resources, helps plant trees to restore areas damaged by wildfire. **Libraries: Type:** reference. **Holdings:** 600. **Subjects:** forestry, conservation, wildlife. **Telecommunication Services:** electronic mail, gangloff@amfor.org. **Programs:** Forest Policy Center; Global ReLeaf; Urban Forest Center. **Formerly:** (1875) American Forestry Association. **Publications:** *ForestBytes*, monthly. Newsletter. Contains the latest news and events. Alternate Formats: online ● *National Register of Big Trees and Famous and Historic Trees*, semiannual ● Magazine, quarterly. Includes book reviews. **Price:** included in membership dues; $25.00 /year for nonmembers. ISSN: 0002-8541. **Circulation:** 25,000. **Advertising:** accepted. Alternate Formats: CD-ROM; online ● Books ● Reprints. **Conventions/Meetings:** biennial National Urban Forest Conference (exhibits).

4348 ■ American Land Conservancy (ALC)
250 Montgomery St., Ste.210
San Francisco, CA 94104
Ph: (415)912-3660
Fax: (415)912-3662
E-mail: info@alcnet.org
URL: http://www.alcnet.org
Contact: Mark Bergstrom, Pres.
Founded: 1990. **Description:** Protects land for the benefit of people and wildlife. Coordinates with communities, landowners and other parties to find effective conservation solutions for threatened natural resources. Develops long-term natural landscape preservation programs that focus on the preservation of certain natural landscapes.

4349 ■ American Medical Fly Fishing Association (AMFFA)
c/o Dr. Veryl F. Frye, Sec.-Treas.
PO Box 768
Lock Haven, PA 17745
Ph: (570)769-7375
E-mail: amffa@cub.kcnet.org
URL: http://www.amffa.org
Contact: Dr. Veryl F. Frye, Sec.-Treas.
Founded: 1969. **Members:** 220. **Membership Dues:** basic, $35 (annual) ● conservation, $50 (annual) ● sustaining, $100 (annual). **Staff:** 1. **Description:** Offers physicians interested in conservation and environmental and ecological problems an opportunity to work toward achieving a better environment. **Publications:** *American Medical Fly Fishing Association—Newsletter*, periodic. Covers membership activities. **Price:** included in membership dues. **Conventions/Meetings:** annual conference ● annual meeting - always in West Yellowstone, MT at Stage Coach Inn.

4350 ■ American Resources Group (ARG)
374 Maple Ave. E, Ste.310
Vienna, VA 22180-4751
Ph: (703)255-2700
Fax: (703)281-9200
E-mail: info@american-resources.org
URL: http://www.firetower.org
Contact: Dr. Keith A. Argow, Pres.
Founded: 1981. **Staff:** 5. **Budget:** $250,000. **Regional Groups:** 4. **State Groups:** 32. **Nonmembership. Description:** Conservation service organization providing land acquisition and forestry services for membership organizations. Engages in monitoring educational and research activities that promote a more sensible use of U.S. natural resources, especially small, private forestlands. Maintains speakers' bureau; compiles statistics; provides land acquisition services. Sponsors National Historic Lookout Register. **Libraries: Type:** reference. **Holdings:** 230. **Subjects:** watershed, land management, forestry. **Computer Services:** database, natural area. **Publications:** *The Forestry Advantage*, quarterly. Newsletter ● *National Woodlands Magazine*, quarterly. Covers current forestry and legislative issues. **Advertising:** accepted. **Conventions/Meetings:** seminar.

4351 ■ American Rivers (AR)
1101 14th St. NW, Ste.1400
Washington, DC 20005
Ph: (202)347-7550
Free: (877)347-7550
Fax: (202)347-9240
E-mail: amrivers@americanrivers.org
URL: http://www.americanrivers.org
Contact: Rebecca R. Wodder, Pres.
Founded: 1973. **Members:** 32,000. **Membership Dues:** individual, $20 ● family, $60 ● corporate, sustainer, $100 ● associate, $250 ● patron, $500 ● river guardian, $1,000. **Staff:** 50. **Budget:** $5,000,000. **Regional Groups:** 9. **Description:** A public interest group working to preserve and restore America's river systems; fosters a river stewardship ethic. Focuses on all types of river protection methods. **Absorbed:** (1984) River Conservation Fund. **Formerly:** (1986) American Rivers Conservation Council. **Publications:** *American Most Endangered Rivers*, annual. Report ● *American Rivers Guide to Wild and Scenic River Designation* ● *Grassroots River Protection*. Report ● *Mississippi Monitor/Missouri Monitor*, monthly. Report ● Newsletter, quarterly. **Price:** included in membership dues.

4352 ■ American Shore and Beach Preservation Association (ASBPA)
5460 Beaujolais Ln.
Fort Myers, FL 33919-2704
Ph: (239)489-2616
E-mail: exdir@asbpa.org
URL: http://www.asbpa.org
Contact: Harry Simmons, Pres.
Founded: 1926. **Members:** 1,000. **Membership Dues:** individual corporate/association, $250 (annual) ● individual regular, international individual, $100 (annual) ● library, $75 (annual) ● corporate, business, $1,000 (annual) ● college and university, $500 (annual) ● government (municipality and other district), $500-$1,000 (annual). **Staff:** 2. **Budget:** $300,000. **Regional Groups:** 2. **State Groups:** 2. **Description:** Federal, state, local, and foreign government agencies; private groups and individuals interested in conservation, development, and restoration of beaches and shorefronts of oceans, lakes, and rivers. **Awards:** Coastal Project Award. **Frequency:** annual. **Type:** recognition. **Recipient:** for a coastal project that has stood the test of time and has shown a positive environmental, social, or recreational benefit ● Congressional Awards. **Frequency:** annual. **Type:** recognition. **Recipient:** for members of congress who have worked on behalf of America's coast ● Educational Award. **Frequency:** annual. **Type:** trophy. **Recipient:** for an undergraduate or graduate student who, through his or her research, is furthering the state of science of coastal or river systems as it relates to the goals and mission of ASBPA ● Member of the Year. **Frequency:** annual. **Type:** recognition. **Recipient:** for an individual who has contributed time and talent to reach the goals and objectives of ASBPA during the previous year ● Morrough P. O'Brien Award. **Frequency:** annual. **Type:** recognition. **Recipient:** for coastal engineering ● Top Restored Beaches. **Frequency:** annual. **Type:** recognition. **Recipient:** for building awareness of and appreciation for the value and importance of America's restored beaches. **Publications:** *Coastal Voice*, monthly. Newsletter. Features articles on current coastal and ocean management issues. **Price:** included in membership dues. **Circulation:** 300. **Advertising:** accepted. Alternate Formats: online ● *Shore and Beach*, quarterly. Journal. Features articles by coastal zone management professionals. **Price:** included in membership dues. ISSN: 0037-4237. **Circulation:** 800. **Advertising:** accepted. **Conventions/Meetings:** annual conference, technical and policy conference addressing the coast - usually fall.

4353 ■ American Society for the Protection of Nature in Israel (ASPNI)
28 Arrandale Ave.
Great Neck, NY 11024-1804
Free: (800)411-0966
E-mail: robin@aspni.org
URL: http://www.aspni.org
Contact: Robin Gordon, Outreach Dir.
Founded: 1986. **Members:** 3,000. **Membership Dues:** environmental support, $36 (annual). **Staff:** 1. **Budget:** $500,000. **Description:** Persons interested in and concerned with conservation and environmental protection in Israel. Supports the work of the Society for the Protection of Nature in Israel. Educates the public about environmental issues in Israel, and provides information on SPNI guided hikes and field school activities. **Libraries: Type:** open to the public. **Holdings:** books, periodicals. **Subjects:** nature. **Computer Services:** Mailing lists. **Boards:** Professional Advisory. **Affiliated With:** Society for the Protection of Nature in Israel. **Publications:** *SPNI Newsletter*, 3-4/year. **Circulation:** 5,000 ● Bulletins.

4354 ■ American Wildlands (AWL)
PO Box 6669
Bozeman, MT 59771
Ph: (406)586-8175
Fax: (406)586-8242
E-mail: info@wildlands.org
URL: http://www.wildlands.org
Contact: Tom Skeele, Exec. Dir.
Founded: 1977. **Members:** 1,000. **Membership Dues:** individual, $25 (annual) ● family/business, $40 (annual) ● contributing, $100 (annual) ● Living Lightly, $15 (annual) ● Wildlands Protector, $250 (annual) ● Wildlands Vanguard, $500 (annual). **Staff:** 9. **Budget:** $350,000. **Regional Groups:** 1. **Description:** Aims to conserve the nation's wildland resources. Promotes the protection and responsible management of wildland resources, including wilderness, watersheds, wetlands, free-flowing rivers, fisheries, forests, rangelands, and wildlife; works to identify and investigate wilderness areas, wild and scenic rivers, and other natural areas needing protection; conducts scientific and economic research of wildland resources, making findings available to the public. Sponsors programs, forums, and institutes on proper land and water management on publicly owned lands. Conducts Timber Management Policy Reform and Sustainable Forestry Program which seeks reform on national forest policy and Corridors of Life, a scientific prospect to identify and protect habitat linkages in the Northern Rockies. Promotes proper use of earth, soil, water, plant, animal, and atmospheric resources; studies the interrelationship between man and wildland resources. Organizes citizen support to protect the wildlands resources, assists citizens through technical assistance programs. **Libraries: Type:** reference; open to the public. **Holdings:** articles. **Subjects:** timber reform, wildlife, endangered species, archives on Alaska. **Computer Services:** Mailing lists. **Projects:** Corridors of Life; GIS Mapping; Human Connections; Living Waters. **Formerly:** (1989) American Wilderness Alliance. **Publications:** *On the Wild Side*, quarterly. Journal. Contains articles, photos, profiles on issues and people/action alerts. **Price:** included in membership dues. **Circulation:** 2,000. **Advertising:** accepted. **Conventions/Meetings:** annual Corridors of Life Conference - convention ● Law Conference - meet-

ing ● annual Membership Meeting ● Native Fish Conference ● Range and Timber Clinics - meeting.

4355 ■ Americans for Our Heritage and Recreation (AHR)
c/o The Conservation Fund
1800 N Kent St., Ste.1120
Arlington, VA 22209-2156
Ph: (703)525-6300
E-mail: ahr@ahrinfo.org
URL: http://www.ahrinfo.org
Contact: Tom St. Hilaire, Exec. Dir.
Founded: 1997. **Staff:** 5. **Budget:** $500,000. **Description:** Represents recreational goods manufacturers, conservationists, park and recreation specialists, advocates for urban and wilderness areas, and preservationists of cultural and historic sites. Works to strengthen the nation's investment in places that conserve the American natural and cultural heritage, while providing recreational opportunities for all Americans, and protecting individual quality of life. Advocates revitalizing the Land and Water Conservation Fund.

4356 ■ Ancient Forest International (AFI)
PO Box 1850
Redway, CA 95560
Ph: (707)923-4475
Fax: (707)923-4475
E-mail: afi@ancientforests.org
URL: http://www.ancientforests.org
Contact: Rick Klein, Dir.
Founded: 1989. **Staff:** 5. **Budget:** $100,000. **Languages:** English, Spanish. **Nonmembership**. **Description:** Individuals interested in the conservation and wise use of natural resources, particularly native forests. Promotes public awareness of environmental issues; gathers and disseminates information on ecological problems and their solutions; upholds the human rights of indigenous peoples. Focuses on the acquisition of old-growth forests in rainforests of America, South and North. **Libraries: Type:** open to the public. **Holdings:** 50. **Publications:** *Chile's Native Forests*. Book. **Price:** $19.95.

4357 ■ Association of Conservation Engineers (ACE)
c/o Greg Mihalevich, Sec.
PO Box 180
Jefferson City, MO 65102
Ph: (573)522-4115
Fax: (573)522-2324
E-mail: greg.mihalevich@mdc.mo.gov
URL: http://conservationengineers.org
Contact: Greg Mihalevich, Sec.
Founded: 1961. **Members:** 300. **Membership Dues:** regular, $25 (annual). **Description:** Persons employed by or retired from any state, federal, or provincial agency or allied discipline working to develop fisheries, wildlife forestry, or recreational facilities, either in an administrative, professional engineering, engineer-in-training, or general construction superintendent capacity. Encourages the educational, social, and economic interests of engineering practices which further the cause of fish, wildlife, and recreational developments. **Awards:** Carl Anderson Conservation Project Engineering. **Frequency:** annual. **Type:** recognition. **Recipient:** for promising members ● Eugene Baker Conservation Engineering Award. **Frequency:** annual. **Type:** recognition. **Recipient:** for best conservation design project. **Affiliated With:** Association of Fish and Wildlife Agencies. **Publications:** *Conference Proceedings*, annual ● *Conservation Engineering Handbook*, periodic ● Membership Directory, annual ● Newsletter, semiannual. **Conventions/Meetings:** annual conference (exhibits).

4358 ■ Association for Conservation Information (ACI)
c/o Randall T. Cox, Esq., Legal Counsel
First Interstate Bldg., Ste.701
222 S Gillette Ave.
Gillette, WY 82716
Ph: (304)269-0463
E-mail: mburke@wlf.louisiana.gov
URL: http://www.aci-net.org
Contact: Marianne Burke, Pres.
Founded: 1938. **Members:** 800. **Membership Dues:** agency/organization, $200 (annual) ● individual, $25 (annual) ● sponsor, $500 (annual) ● associate, $50 (annual) ● supporting, $250 (annual) ● sustaining, $100 (annual). **Budget:** $20,000. **State Groups:** 45. **Description:** Professional society of information and education personnel of state, provincial, federal, and private conservation agencies. **Awards:** ACI Annual Awards Program. **Frequency:** annual. **Type:** recognition. **Recipient:** for conservation communication work. **Committees:** Awards; History; International Select Issues; Liaison; National Fishing Day; State-Federal Relationships. **Affiliated With:** Association of Fish and Wildlife Agencies. **Formerly:** American Association for Conservation Information. **Publications:** *The Balance Wheel*, quarterly. Newsletter. **Circulation:** 800. Alternate Formats: online ● Membership Directory, annual. **Conventions/Meetings:** annual conference - always July.

4359 ■ Association of Environmental and Resource Economists (AERE)
c/o Marilyn M. Voight, Exec. Dir.
1616 P St. NW, Rm. 600
Washington, DC 20036
Ph: (202)328-5125
Fax: (202)939-3460
E-mail: info@aere.org
URL: http://www.aere.org
Contact: Marilyn M. Voight, Exec. Dir.
Founded: 1981. **Members:** 900. **Membership Dues:** individual, $90 (annual) ● student, $55 (annual) ● editor, $40 (annual). **Staff:** 1. **Description:** Professionals, economists, and individuals from universities and governmental agencies interested in resource and environmental issues. Addresses the problems and concerns in resource management. Is concerned with issues such as water and land resources and air pollution. **Awards:** Publication of Enduring Quality Award. **Frequency:** annual. **Type:** recognition. **Telecommunication Services:** electronic mail, voigt@rff.org. **Publications:** *AERE Newsletter*, semiannual. Contains information about upcoming conferences and a variety of notices related to environmental research and policy. **Price:** free for members. **Advertising:** accepted ● *Journal of Environmental Economics and Management*, bimonthly. Includes articles by economists. ● Membership Directory. Alternate Formats: online ● Handbook. Alternate Formats: online. **Conventions/Meetings:** annual conference, held in conjunction with Allied Social Science Associations - always in January ● meeting ● annual workshop - June.

4360 ■ Association of Fish and Wildlife Agencies
444 N Capitol St. NW, Ste.725
Washington, DC 20001
Ph: (202)624-7890
Fax: (202)624-7891
E-mail: info@fishwildlife.org
URL: http://www.fishwildlife.org
Contact: Edward Parker, Pres.
Founded: 1902. **Members:** 450. **Staff:** 19. **Budget:** $1,000,000. **Description:** State and provincial fish and wildlife agencies (68) and officials (382). Educates the public about the economic importance of conserving natural resources and managing wildlife property as a source of recreation and a food supply; supports better conservation legislation, administration, and enforcement. **Awards:** Ernest Thompson Seton Award. **Frequency:** annual. **Type:** recognition. **Recipient:** to a state, provincial, or federal agency that best promoted a public awareness campaign of the need to support the science and practice of wildlife management ● Mark J. Reeff Memorial Award. **Frequency:** annual. **Type:** recognition. **Recipient:** to people under 35 for outstanding service in the conservation of fish and wildlife resources ● Seth Gordon Award. **Frequency:** annual. **Type:** recognition. **Recipient:** for distinguished service in wildlife conservation ● Special Recognition Awards. **Frequency:** annual. **Type:** recognition. **Recipient:** for distinguished record of accomplishment. **Telecommunication Services:** electronic mail, baughman@fishwildlife.org. **Committees:** Education/Outreach/Diversity; Fish and Wildlife Health; Fisheries/Water Resources Policy; International Relations; Law Enforcement; Threatened/Endangered Species Policy; Wildlife Resource Policy. **Formerly:** (1917) National Association of Game Commissioners and Wardens; (1976) International Association of Game, Fish, and Conservation Commissioners; (2006) International Association of Fish and Wildlife Agencies. **Publications:** *International Association Convention Proceedings*, annual. **Price:** $20.00 plus shipping and handling ● Newsletter, monthly. Alternate Formats: online. **Conventions/Meetings:** annual meeting - always September.

4361 ■ Association to Preserve Cape Cod (APCC)
PO Box 398
3010 Main St.
Barnstable, MA 02630-0398
Ph: (508)362-4226
Free: (877)955-4142
Fax: (508)362-4227
E-mail: info@apcc.org
URL: http://www.apcc.org
Contact: Margaret A. Geist, Exec. Dir.
Founded: 1968. **Members:** 5,500. **Membership Dues:** basic, $30 (annual) ● family, $50 (annual) ● supporter, $100 (annual) ● associate, $250 (annual) ● partner, $500 (annual) ● benefactor, $1,000 (annual). **Staff:** 6. **Budget:** $535,000. **Description:** Works to protect the natural resources of Cape Cod. Offers technical, advisory, and referral services. Conducts educational programs. **Libraries: Type:** reference; open to the public. **Subjects:** environmental protection and preservation. **Publications:** *Shore Lines*, quarterly. Newsletter. **Price:** included in membership dues. **Conventions/Meetings:** annual meeting.

4362 ■ Association of State Floodplain Managers (ASFPM)
2809 Fish Hatchery Rd., Ste.204
Madison, WI 53713
Ph: (608)274-0123
Fax: (608)274-0696
E-mail: asfpm@floods.org
URL: http://www.floods.org
Contact: Mr. Larry A. Larson CFM, Exec. Dir.
Founded: 1977. **Members:** 6,500. **Membership Dues:** individual, $100 (annual) ● agency, $250 (annual) ● student, $25 (annual). **Staff:** 10. **Budget:** $150,000. **Regional Groups:** 10. **State Groups:** 24. **Description:** Corporations, agencies, and individuals interested in and responsible for floodplain management including coastal policies, flood insurance, floodplain regulations, mapping and engineering standards, mitigation issues, stormwater management, and information and education. Supports environmental protection for floodplain areas. Represents state and local flood hazard programs to national agencies; provides information for federal flood hazard management policies and programs. Encourages cooperation and the exchange of information on developments in the field; supports continuing education in floodplain management. Sponsors research. Maintains speakers' bureau and biographical archives; compiles statistics; sponsors competitions and symposia; maintains a clearinghouse of information related to flood hazard management. **Libraries: Type:** open to the public. **Awards: Frequency:** annual. **Type:** monetary ● **Frequency:** annual. **Type:** scholarship. **Committees:** Arid Regions; Coastal Issues; Flood Insurance; Flood Mitigation; Floodplain Regulations; Floodproofing/Retrofitting; International Issues; Mapping and Engineering; Multi-Objective Management; Professional Development; Public Education; Urban Stormwater. **Affiliated With:** Council of State Governments; National Association of Conservation Districts. **Publications:** *Alluvial Fans, Mudflows, and Mud Floods* ● *Arid West Floodplain Management Issues* ● *Avoiding Liability in Floodplain Management* ● *Flood Planning Assistance to Small Towns* ● *Floodplain Management* ● *Insider*,

bimonthly. **Price:** available to members only ● *Model State Legislation* ● *News and Views/Insider*, monthly. Newsletter ● *Partnerships: Effective Flood Hazard Management* ● *Proceedings of Annual Conference*, annual ● *State and Local Programs* ● *Strengthening State Floodplain Management* ● Report, biennial ● Membership Directory, annual ● Also publishes surveys and brochures. **Conventions/Meetings:** annual National Floodplain Managers - conference (exhibits).

4363 ■ Association of State Wetland Managers (ASWM)
2 Basin Rd.
Windham, ME 04062
Ph: (207)892-3399
Fax: (207)892-3089
E-mail: jeanne.christie@aswm.org
URL: http://www.aswm.org
Contact: Jeanne Christie, Exec. Dir.
Founded: 1984. **Members:** 1,000. **Membership Dues:** individual, $60 (annual) ● corporate, $150-$300 (annual) ● student, $25 (annual) ● agency/NGO, $150 (annual). **Staff:** 5. **Description:** Professionals and other interested individuals who are involved in wetland management. Seeks to: promote and improve protection and management of U.S. wetlands; fosters cooperation among government agencies and integration of public, private, and academic protection programs. Encourages the exchange and dissemination of information and ideas between members; identifies, coordinates, and conducts research concerning wetland protection needs and techniques. Works to improve public knowledge and awareness of the field. Provides technical assistance in areas such as regulations, management, acquisition, assessment, mitigation, and land-use incentives. **Publications:** *Wetland Breaking News*, biweekly. Newsletter. Contains information on wetlands and other water resources. Alternate Formats: online ● *Wetland News*, quarterly. Newsletter. Contains news update, review of publications and calendar of wetland conferences and events of the association. ● *Wetland NewsLink*, monthly. Newsletter. Highlights international wetlands and migratory bird activities. ● Reports. **Conventions/Meetings:** annual lecture (exhibits) ● seminar ● annual symposium ● workshop.

4364 ■ Audubon Naturalist Society of the Central Atlantic States (ANS)
8940 Jones Mill Rd.
Chevy Chase, MD 20815
Ph: (301)652-9188
Fax: (301)951-7179
E-mail: contact@audobonnaturalist.org
URL: http://www.audubonnaturalist.org
Contact: Neal Fitzpatrick, Exec. Dir.
Founded: 1897. **Members:** 10,000. **Membership Dues:** individual, $40 (annual) ● family, $50 (annual) ● nature steward, $75 (annual). **Staff:** 30. **Budget:** $180,000. **Description:** Persons interested in environmental education and protection. Seeks to further sound conservation practices, and to protect birds and other wildlife and the environment on which they depend. Conducts special program of natural history field studies jointly with the graduate school of the U.S. Department of Agriculture, an ecology program for inner-city schools in Washington, DC, and environmental education programs for children and adults. Operates Woodend, a 40-acre urban environmental education center in Chevy Chase, MD; has nature sanctuaries in Loudoun and Fairfax Counties, VA. Sponsors series of illustrated lectures and field trips to varied habitats in the mid-Atlantic states; compiles statistics on local natural history; maintains museum. Operates speakers' bureau. Maintains Voice of Naturalist, a weekly recording of bird sightings. **Libraries: Type:** reference. **Holdings:** 2,500. **Awards:** Paul Bartsch Award. **Type:** recognition. **Recipient:** for distinguished contribution to natural history. **Committees:** Conservation; Education. **Formerly:** (1960) Audubon Society of the District of Columbia. **Publications:** *Audubon Naturalist News*, monthly. Newsletter. **Price:** included in membership dues. **Advertising:** accepted ● Report, annual ● Also publishes results of observations and studies.

4365 ■ Bamboo of The Americas (BOTA)
c/o Gib Cooper, Exec. Dir.
28446 Hunter Creek Loop
Gold Beach, OR 97444
Ph: (541)247-0835 (541)247-0160
Fax: (541)247-0835
E-mail: gib@bamboodirect.com
URL: http://www.bambooofthe americas.org
Contact: Gib Cooper, Exec. Dir.
Languages: English, Spanish. **Description:** Ensures the sustained viability of native bamboo species throughout the Americas. Establishes national collections of native bamboo species. Implements human resources and economic plans for the distribution and utilization of selected native bamboo species. Works together for the conservation of native bamboo resources. Enhances awareness of the benefits of bamboo through eco-tourism and other educational activities. **Publications:** Report, semiannual. Alternate Formats: online.

4366 ■ Big Island Rainforest Action Group (BIRAG)
PO Box 341
Kurtistown, HI 96760
Ph: (808)966-7622
E-mail: ja@interpac.net
Contact: Jim Albertini, Contact
Founded: 1989. **Description:** Organizes and administers efforts to preserve the rainforests of the Hawaiian Islands, particularly those directed at stopping geothermal development in the Wao Kele O Puna forest on the Island of Hawaii. Conducts programs such as: testimony at public hearings, letter-writing campaigns, demonstrations, and civil disobedience. Maintains speakers' bureau. **Libraries: Type:** reference. **Publications:** *BIRAG Rag*, periodic. Newsletter. Includes calendar of events. **Circulation:** 1,000. **Advertising:** accepted ● Also publishes leaflets; makes available slideshow and videotapes. **Conventions/Meetings:** weekly meeting - always Thursday.

4367 ■ Big Thicket Association (BTA)
PO Box 198
Saratoga, TX 77585
Ph: (409)382-5102 (936)262-8522
E-mail: ellen.buchanan@tpwd.state.tx.us
URL: http://www.btatx.org
Contact: Dr. Bruce Drury, Pres.
Founded: 1964. **Members:** 315. **Membership Dues:** active, $15 (annual) ● student, senior citizen, $10 (annual) ● life, $500 ● institutional, group, business, $25 (annual). **Budget:** $10,000. **Description:** Conservationists and others interested in preserving the wilderness area of Southeast Texas known as the "Big Thicket." Monitors welfare of the Preserve, supporting efforts to protect it; maintains interest in state parks, nature sanctuaries, environmental education, and local history. Operates field research Station for Big Thicket National Preserve. **Awards:** Lubbert Superior Achievement Award. **Frequency:** annual. **Type:** monetary. **Recipient:** for an outstanding employee of Big Thicket National Preserve with a minimum of 3 years of service ● R.E. Jackson Award. **Frequency:** periodic. **Type:** recognition. **Recipient:** for significant lifetime contributions. **Formerly:** (1957) East Texas Big Thicket Association. **Publications:** *Big Thicket Reporter*, bimonthly. Newsletter. **Price:** $15.00. **Circulation:** 365 ● *Re Jackson and Big Thicket Conservation: Setting the Stage*. **Price:** $2.50 ● *Temple Big Thicket Series, Nos. 1-4*. **Price:** $3.00 ● *Unlikely Critters of the Big Thicket*. **Price:** $3.00 ● Also publishes pamphlets, a bibliography, and educational materials. **Conventions/Meetings:** annual Big Thicket Day - meeting, with programs, business meeting hikes - always October.

4368 ■ Big Thicket Natural Heritage Trust (BTNHT)
PO Box 1049
Kountze, TX 77625
E-mail: bdrury@gt.rr.com
URL: http://www.btatx.org/BTNHT
Contact: Dr. Bruce Drury, Pres.
Membership Dues: student, $15 ● regular, $25 ● supporting, $50 ● family, $60 ● sustaining, $75 ● small business, $100 ● corporate, $250 ● benefactor, $1,000. **Description:** Seeks to reduce the negative effects of sub urbanization and resource extraction on plants, animals, and the quality of life in the Big Thicket region. Protects wildlife diversity and natural communities of the Big Thicket. Promotes respect for and enjoyment of the rural character and culture of the region through encouragement of land stewardship values that promote sustainable communities. Networks with citizens, corporations, business, developers, conservation groups and governmental organizations to seek out the most significant unprotected lands in the Big Thicket. **Affiliated With:** Big Thicket Association.

4369 ■ Camp Fire Club of America (CFCA)
230 Camp Fire Rd.
Chappaqua, NY 10514
Ph: (914)769-5508
Fax: (914)923-9977
E-mail: lvallen491@aol.com
URL: http://www.conservationforum.org/nwcp/partners/partner.asp?p_acronym=cfc
Contact: Michael Burkhart, Pres.
Founded: 1897. **Members:** 455. **Description:** Sportsmen dedicated to the preservation of wildlife habitat and wise use of natural resources. Sponsors Camp Fire Conservation Fund. Sponsors competitions. **Libraries: Type:** reference. **Holdings:** 2,500; books. **Subjects:** wildlife, hunting, fishing, conservation. **Awards: Type:** recognition. **Committees:** Campcraft; Campfire; Conservation; Fishing; Lake Management; Pistol; Rifle; Shotgun; Sports Activities; Wildlife. **Publications:** *Backlog*, annual ● *Green Sheet*, monthly. Newsletter. **Conventions/Meetings:** annual meeting - always March.

4370 ■ Camp Fire Conservation Fund (CFCF)
Address Unknown since 2008
Founded: 1977. **Members:** 300. **Membership Dues:** regular, $50 (annual) ● life membership, $1,500. **Description:** Individuals concerned with the conservation of forests and wildlife. Seeks to: inform the public and governmental agencies on the use of natural resources; restore and publicize the role of the sportsman in conservation; organize and fund educational and public information projects. Coordinates activities of sportsmen's and conservation organizations. Supports wildlife conservation research. **Publications:** *Camp Fire Conservation Fund*, quarterly. Newsletter. News on Fund projects. **Price:** free. **Conventions/Meetings:** annual meeting.

4371 ■ CEDAM International
1 Fox Rd.
Croton-on-Hudson, NY 10520
Ph: (914)271-5365
Fax: (914)271-4723
E-mail: cedam@bestweb.net
URL: http://www.cedam.org
Contact: Susan Sammon, Contact
Founded: 1967. **Members:** 1,000. **Membership Dues:** family, $35 (annual) ● single, $25 (annual) ● student, $12 (annual) ● life, $1,000. **Description:** Members actively pursuing underwater research, exploration and marine conservation. Purposes are to promote: conservation of marine environment; preservation of underwater maritime historical sites. Sponsors studies of coral reefs and other marine environments. Conducts scuba diving expeditions. **Awards:** Honorary Membership. **Frequency:** periodic. **Type:** recognition. **Recipient:** for outstanding and distinguished service to marine conservation ● Lloyd Bridges Scholarship. **Frequency:** annual. **Type:** scholarship. **Recipient:** for teacher or educator working in marine sciences. **Also Known As:** Conservation, Education, Diving, Awareness, Marine Research. **Publications:** *Reef Explorer*, quarterly. Newsletter ● Also publishes guide books. **Conventions/Meetings:** annual meeting.

4372 ■ Center for Plant Conservation (CPC)
PO Box 299
St. Louis, MO 63166-0299
Ph: (314)577-9450
Fax: (314)577-9465
E-mail: cpc@mobot.org
URL: http://www.centerforplantconservation.org
Contact: Kathryn L. Kennedy PhD, Pres./Exec. Dir.
Founded: 1984. **Members:** 500. **Membership Dues:** friend of CPC, $35 (annual) ● family, $75 (annual) ● benefactor, $250 (annual) ● preserving, $500 (annual) ● conserving, $1,000 (annual) ● president's circle, $5,000 (annual). **Staff:** 5. **Budget:** $400,000. **Regional Groups:** 30. **Description:** Individuals and organizations interested in rare plant conservation at botanical gardens and arboreta. Gathers and disseminates information regarding rare and endangered plants indigenous to the U.S. Saves seeds and cuttings of rare and endangered plants to preserve their genetic patterns. Presents educational slide shows. Compiles statistics. **Libraries: Type:** open to the public. **Holdings:** articles. **Subjects:** rare plant conservation. **Awards:** Catherine H. Beattie. **Frequency:** annual. **Type:** fellowship. **Computer Services:** database, rare plants. **Councils:** Corporate; National Volunteer; Science Advisory. **Programs:** Plant Sponsorship. **Publications:** *America's Vanishing Flora*. Features stories of endangered plants from the fifty states and efforts to save them. ● *Ex Situ Plant Conservation*. Book. **Price:** $40.00 paperback copy; $80.00 cloth (cover); $4.75 plus shipping and handling ● *Guidelines to the Management of Orthodox Seeds*. **Price:** $14.00 ● *Plant Conservation*, semiannual. Newsletter. Features reports on center activities and botanical garden network. **Price:** included in membership dues. **Circulation:** 11,000. Alternate Formats: online ● *Restoring Diversity*. Serves as a guide to educational resources on rare negative plant conservation. **Conventions/Meetings:** annual meeting (exhibits).

4373 ■ Center for Resource Management (CRM)
200 Intl. Dr., Ste.201
Portsmouth, NH 03801
Ph: (603)427-0206
Fax: (603)427-6983
E-mail: info@crminc.com
URL: http://www.crminc.com
Contact: Dr. Mary Ann Lachat EdD, Pres.
Founded: 1982. **Staff:** 5. **Budget:** $600,000. **Description:** Promotes a balance between the preservation and use of America's natural resources. Educates businesspersons, environmental leaders, and the government on solving resource management problems. Offers conflict resolution mediation; encourages cooperation in the use and preservation of natural resources. **Formerly:** (1997) Institute for Resource Management. **Publications:** *Symposium Proceedings*, 2-3/year. Contains environmental principles for golf courses in United States. **Price:** $5.00. **Conventions/Meetings:** biennial Golf and the Environment - conference ● symposium - 2-3/year.

4374 ■ Chihuahuan Desert Research Institute (CDRI)
PO Box 905
Fort Davis, TX 79734
Ph: (432)364-2499
Fax: (432)364-2686
E-mail: choyt@cdri.org
URL: http://www.cdri.org
Contact: Cathryn A. Hoyt PhD, Exec. Dir.
Founded: 1974. **Members:** 600. **Membership Dues:** individual, $35 (annual) ● student, senior, $25 (annual) ● family, $50 (annual) ● sustaining, $500 (annual) ● corporate/contributing, $100 (annual) ● friend, $250 (annual) ● life, $1,000. **Staff:** 7. **Budget:** $70,000. **Description:** Professionals and students of all disciplines. Seeks to promote an understanding and appreciation of the Chihuahuan Desert region of the U.S. and Mexico through scientific research and public education. (The region, which for the most part is sparsely populated, contains potentially valuable undeveloped resources.) Conducts research programs, expedites the research efforts of others, and serves as clearinghouse for information relating to the Chihuahuan Desert. Sponsors charitable programs and children's services. Maintains museum; compiles statistics. Provides consulting services, teaching materials, and teacher training workshops. **Libraries: Type:** reference. **Holdings:** 1,500; archival material. **Subjects:** natural sciences. **Awards: Type:** scholarship ● W. Frank Blair Award. **Frequency:** annual. **Type:** recognition. **Recipient:** for the best paper. **Telecommunication Services:** electronic mail, andy.price@tpwd.state.tx.us. **Departments:** Education; Media; Research. **Publications:** *The Chihuahuan Desert Discovery*, semiannual. Magazine. Includes calendar of events and research updates. **Price:** included in membership dues. **Circulation:** 1,000. Alternate Formats: online ● *Chihuahuan Newsbrief*, semiannual ● Papers. **Conventions/Meetings:** quadrennial meeting and symposium.

4375 ■ Coast Alliance
3331/2 Pennsylvania Ave. SE
Washington, DC 20003
Ph: (202)546-9554
E-mail: coast@coastalliance.org
Contact: Dery Bennett, Chair
Founded: 1979. **Staff:** 4. **Budget:** $300,000. **State Groups:** 500. **Description:** Concerned groups and individuals. Seeks to increase public awareness of coastal ecology, the value of coastal resources, and the need to protect coastal ecosystems through governmental programs and policies. Conducts educational programs. **Publications:** *Getting to the Bottom of It: Threats to Human Health and the Environment from Contaminated Underwater Sediments*. Report ● *Mission Possible: Controlling Runoff Under the Coastal Non-point Pollution Control Program*. Report ● *Muddy Waters: The Toxic Wasteland Below America's Oceans, Rivers & Lakes*. Report. **Price:** $25.00 ● *Pointless Pollution: Preventing Polluted Runoff & Protecting America's Coasts*. Report ● *State of the Coasts: A State-By State Analysis of the Vital Link Between Healthy Coasts and a Healthy Economy*. Report ● *Storm on the Horizon*. Report ● *Upstream Solutions to Downstream Pollutions*. Book ● *Using Common Sense to Protect the Coasts*. Report.

4376 ■ Coastal Conservation Association (CCA)
6919 Portwest Dr., Ste.100
Houston, TX 77024
Ph: (713)626-4234
Free: (800)201-FISH
Fax: (713)961-3801
E-mail: ccantl@joincca.org
URL: http://www.joincca.org
Contact: David G. Cummins, Pres.
Founded: 1977. **Members:** 90,000. **Membership Dues:** standard, $25 (annual) ● print, $100 (annual) ● associate, $15 (annual) ● sponsor, $200 (annual) ● patron, $500 (annual) ● life, $1,000 ● new tide, $10 (annual). **Staff:** 55. **Budget:** $9,000,000. **State Groups:** 15. **Local Groups:** 175. **Description:** Organizations, corporations, and individuals interested in conserving the natural resources of U.S. saltwater coastal areas. Seeks to advance the protection and conservation of marine life. Operates GCCA/John Wilson Hatchery near Corpus Christi, TX, and Sea Center Texas, in Lake Jackson, TX to bolster the redfish population in the Gulf of Mexico. Lobbies federal and state governments to enact legislation favorable to conservation and sport fishing. Conducts seminars regarding current topics in marine conservation; maintains New Tide youth program. **Formerly:** (1985) Gulf Coast Conservation Association. **Publications:** *Rising Tide*, quarterly. Newsletter ● *Tide*, bimonthly. Magazine. **Conventions/Meetings:** annual meeting.

4377 ■ Connecticut River Watershed Council (CRWC)
15 Bank Row
Greenfield, MA 01301
Ph: (413)772-2020
Fax: (413)772-2090
E-mail: cgwyther@ctriver.org
URL: http://www.ctriver.org
Contact: Chelsea Reiff Gwyther, Exec. Dir.
Founded: 1952. **Members:** 1,400. **Membership Dues:** individual/family, $35 (annual) ● business, $50 (annual). **Staff:** 7. **Budget:** $350,000. **State Groups:** 4. **Description:** Individuals, corporations, businesses, and conservation organizations. Works in partnership with people and communities to promote the conservation and wise use of natural resources in the Connecticut River Valley. Objectives include river restoration, habitat and water quality protection, environmental networking, and public education. **Libraries: Type:** reference. **Holdings:** 3,000; archival material, audiovisuals, books, business records, clippings, periodicals. **Subjects:** environment, water, natural resources. **Awards:** Conservation Education & Research PRG. **Frequency:** annual. **Type:** grant. **Recipient:** to college or high school students and nonprofit organizations. **Committees:** Land Conservancy. **Programs:** American Heritage River Initiatives; Conservation Education Research Grants; Environmental Awareness; Migratory Fish Restoration; River Steward; The River That Connects Us; Water Quality. **Publications:** *A Fishway for Your Stream*. Booklet. Features guide on how to provide fish passage around tributary dams. **Price:** included in membership dues ● *The Complete Boating Guide to the Connecticut River*. Book. Contains information about the Connecticut river. ● *Current & Eddies*, quarterly. Newsletter. Contains information about the organization and the Connecticut river. ● *The River That Connects Us*. **Price:** $10.00 ● *Tidewaters of the Connecticut River: An Explorer's Guide to Hidden Coves and Marshes*. Book. **Price:** $20.00 ● *The Watershed Curriculum*. Monographs. **Conventions/Meetings:** quarterly board meeting.

4378 ■ ConservAmerica
3200 Carlisle Blvd. NE, Ste.113
Albuquerque, NM 87110-1600
Ph: (505)889-4576
E-mail: administrator@conservamerica.org
URL: http://www.conservamerica.org
Contact: James A. Rowan Jr., Chm.
Description: Educates and builds a conservative constituency for environmental protection. Educates lawmakers and the general public about the need to support natural resource conservation and sound environmental protection. **Publications:** *Conservative Environmental Policy*, quarterly. Newsletter.

4379 ■ Conservation Breeding Specialist Group (CBSG)
12101 Johnny Cake Ridge Rd.
Apple Valley, MN 55124-8151
Ph: (952)997-9800
Fax: (952)997-9803
E-mail: office@cbsg.org
URL: http://www.cbsg.org
Contact: Dr. Robert C. Lacy, Chm.
Founded: 1979. **Members:** 966. **Staff:** 7. **Description:** A project of the International Union for the Conservation of Nature and Natural Resources. Individuals interested in maintaining global biodiversity. Promotes conservation and wise use of natural resources; works to protect endangered plant and animal species. Provides conservation assessment and management plans to areas threatened by human encroachment; conducts research and educational projects; makes available assistance to conservation programs worldwide. Consults with government agencies and nongovernmental organizations active in conservation and environmental protection activities. **Libraries: Type:** open to the public. **Holdings:** 210. **Subjects:** endangered species. **Publications:** *CBSG Donor News*. Newsletter. Alternate Formats: online ● *CBSG News*, semiannual. Newsletter. **Price:** $35.00/year. **Circulation:** 1,000. Alternate Formats: online ● Books ● Reports. Alternate Formats: online. **Conventions/Meetings:** annual meeting.

4380 ■ The Conservation Fund (TCF)
1655 N Ft. Myer Dr., Ste.1300
Arlington, VA 22209-3199
Ph: (703)525-6300

Fax: (703)525-4610
E-mail: postmaster@conservationfund.org
URL: http://www.conservationfund.org
Contact: Lawrence A. Selzer, Pres./CEO
Founded: 1985. **Staff:** 79. **Nonmembership. Description:** Established to work with public and private organizations and agencies to protect land, including parks, wildlife habitats, and historic sites. Aims to advance conservation through creative ideas and new resources. Projects include: American Greenways, helping establish public and private open space corridors to link natural, historic, and recreation areas; Civil War Battlefield Campaign, preserving historic battlefield lands; Conservation Leadership, increasing the effectiveness of nonprofit conservation organizations; Land Advisory Service, providing specialized skills in environmental land planning; Freshwater Institute, using new techniques to protect groundwater reserves. **Awards:** Alexander Calder Conservation Award. **Frequency:** annual. **Type:** recognition. **Recipient:** for demonstrating positive value of cooperative partnerships between business and conservation ● CF Industries National Watershed Awards. **Frequency:** annual. **Type:** recognition. **Recipient:** for corporate and community excellence in watershed protection ● Gene Cartledge Award for Excellence in Environmental Education. **Frequency:** annual. **Type:** recognition. **Recipient:** for excellence in environmental education. **Publications:** *Common Ground*, bimonthly. Newsletter. Includes current events, trends and ideas on conservation. **Circulation:** 16,000 ● Newsletter. Alternate Formats: online.

4381 ■ Conservation International - USA (CI)
2011 Crystal Dr., Ste.500
Arlington, VA 22202
Ph: (703)341-2400
Free: (800)429-5660
E-mail: inquiry@conservation.org
URL: http://www.conservation.org
Contact: Peter A. Seligmann, Chm./CEO
Founded: 1987. **Members:** 70,402. **Membership Dues:** individual, $35 (annual) ● advocate, $100 (annual) ● sponsor, $500 (annual). **Staff:** 1,250. **Budget:** $50,000,000. **Languages:** Arabic, English, French, German, Italian, Japanese, Portuguese, Russian, Spanish, Swahili. **Description:** Preserves and promotes awareness about the world's most endangered biodiversity, through scientific programs, local awareness campaigns and economic initiatives. Works with multinational institutions, provides economic analyses for political leaders, and promotes best practices that will allow for sustainable development. **Computer Services:** database, technical support. **Conventions/Meetings:** quarterly board meeting.

4382 ■ Conservation and Preservation Charities of America (CPCA)
1100 Larkspur Landing Cir., Ste.340
Larkspur, CA 94939
Free: (800)626-6685
Fax: (415)924-1379
E-mail: info@conservenow.org
URL: http://www.conservenow.org
Contact: Ms. Karen Piatak, Treas.
Description: Works to protect and restore the Earth's natural environment and historic treasures through workplace giving campaigns. **Publications:** Annual Report, annual. Alternate Formats: online,

4383 ■ Conservation and Research Foundation (CRF)
Dept. of Special Collections
Charles E. Shain Lib.
Connecticut Coll.
New London, CT 06320-4196
URL: http://www.conncoll.edu/is/info-resources/special-collections/crf/crfguide.html
Contact: Mary B. Goodwin, Founder
Founded: 1953. **Members:** 13. **Budget:** $28,000. **Multinational. Description:** Seeks to: encourage biological research; promote conservation of renewable natural resources; deepen the understanding of the relationship between humans and the environment; promoting methods of limiting human fertility. **Awards:** Environmental Grants. **Type:** grant. **Recipient:** for conservation and research ● Jeanette Siron Pelton Award. **Type:** recognition. **Recipient:** for outstanding published contributions in experimental plant morphology. **Publications:** *Five Year Report*, annual. Annual Report.

4384 ■ Conservation Technology Information Center (CTIC)
1220 Potter Dr. W, Ste.170
West Lafayette, IN 47906
Ph: (765)494-9555
Fax: (765)494-5969
E-mail: ctic@conservationinformation.org
URL: http://www.conservationinformation.org
Contact: Karen A. Scanlon, Exec. Dir.
Founded: 1982. **Members:** 200. **Membership Dues:** individual, $25 (annual) ● institutional, $250 (annual) ● corporate (less than $100 million gross income), $500 (annual) ● corporate (greater than $100 million and less than $500 million gross income), $2,000 (annual) ● corporate (greater than $500 million gross income), $6,500 (annual) ● individual outside U.S., $50 (annual). **Staff:** 4. **Budget:** $1,200,000. **Description:** Envisions agriculture using environmentally beneficial and economically viable natural resource systems; promotes development of public/private partnerships that promote the enhancement of soil and water quality by equipping agriculture with realistic, affordable and integrated solutions. **Libraries: Type:** reference; open to the public. **Holdings:** 35. **Subjects:** conservation, tillage, watershed, nutrient and pest management. **Awards: Frequency:** periodic. **Type:** recognition. **Formerly:** (2003) Conservation Tillage Information Center. **Publications:** *Conservation Impact*, 11/year. Magazine. **Price:** $25.00 /year for individuals; $35.00 outside U.S. ISSN: 1056-9707. **Advertising:** accepted. Alternate Formats: online ● *CTIC Partners*, quarterly. Magazine. **Price:** $25.00 /year for individuals; $50.00 outside U.S. ISSN: 1056-9707. **Circulation:** 25,000. **Advertising:** accepted. Alternate Formats: online ● *National Crop Residue Management Survey*, semiannual. Contains a survey of acres planted under various tillage methods by farmers nationwide. **Conventions/Meetings:** quarterly board meeting ● quarterly meeting.

4385 ■ Conservation Treaty Support Fund (CTSF)
3705 Cardiff Rd.
Chevy Chase, MD 20815
Ph: (301)654-3150
Free: (800)654-3150
Fax: (301)652-6390
E-mail: ctsf@conservationtreaty.org
URL: http://www.conservationtreaty.org
Contact: George A. Furness Jr., Pres./Operating Off.
Founded: 1986. **Staff:** 21. **Budget:** $100,000. **Description:** Supports international treaties on conservation of wild natural resources and habitat. Promotes public awareness and understanding of these treaties and their goals; works to enhance public support, compliance, and funding. Assists conservation treaties in obtaining funding from individuals, corporations, foundations, and government agencies. Maintains the Conservation Treaty Support Fund and the CITES Ambassadors Club, which provide financial assistance to international conservation efforts including the Convention on International Trade in Endangered Species, the Convention on Wetlands of International Importance (known as Ramsar, the city in Iran where it was negotiated) and the Convention on Migratory Species. **Awards:** Honorary Membership in Cites Ambassadors Club. **Type:** recognition. **Recipient:** for extraordinary service in support of conservation treaties. **Affiliated With:** Convention on International Trade in Endangered Species of Wild Fauna and Flora. **Publications:** *CITES Endangered Species Book*. **Price:** $5.00 each; $2.50/copy (order of 20 or more); $200.00/box of 90 copies ● *CITES Video*. **Price:** $10.00 each ● *Wetland World Video*. **Price:** $10.00 each ● Also publishes posters and prints. **Conventions/Meetings:** periodic meeting (exhibits).

4386 ■ Conservatree
100 Second Ave.
San Francisco, CA 94118
Ph: (415)561-6530
Fax: (509)756-6987
E-mail: paper@conservatree.org
URL: http://www.conservatree.org
Contact: Susan Kinsella, Exec. Dir.
Founded: 1976. **Nonmembership. Description:** Works to provide technical, strategic, and information tools, as well as implementation assistance to paper buyers wishing to convert to environmental papers.

4387 ■ The Cycad Society (TCS)
c/o Dr. Bart Schutzman
Univ. of Florida
Environmental Horticulture Dept.
1531 Fifield Hall
Gainesville, FL 32611-0670
E-mail: cycad@mail.ifas.ufl.edu
URL: http://www.cycad.org
Contact: Jody Haynes, Pres./Webmaster
Founded: 1977. **Members:** 400. **Membership Dues:** regular, in U.S., $25 (annual) ● foreign, $35 (annual). **Multinational. Description:** Represents individuals interested in conservation and propagation of endangered cycad species. Facilitates exchange of information about all phases of horticultural endeavor, ecology in habitat, and other scientific efforts. Conducts research on artificial propagation, pollen, and embryo culture; maintains seed bank. **Libraries: Type:** not open to the public. **Holdings:** articles. **Subjects:** cycad species. **Awards: Frequency:** annual. **Type:** grant. **Recipient:** to individuals, educational, and research institutions, and organizations that support cycad research, education, and conservation efforts and/or promote the legal propagation and horticultural interest of cycads. **Publications:** *CYCAD Newsletter*, quarterly. **Price:** included in membership dues. **Circulation:** 400. **Advertising:** accepted ● Also publishes annual membership roster. **Conventions/Meetings:** annual board meeting.

4388 ■ Desert Fishes Council (DFC)
PO Box 337
Bishop, CA 93515
Ph: (760)872-8751
Fax: (760)872-8751
E-mail: phil@desertfishes.org
URL: http://www.desertfishes.org
Contact: E. Phil Pister, Exec. Sec.
Founded: 1970. **Members:** 300. **Membership Dues:** regular, $25 (annual) ● student, $15 (annual) ● patron, $1,000 (annual) ● family, sustaining, $35 (annual) ● life, $625. **Staff:** 10. **Budget:** $15,000. **Regional Groups:** 12. **Languages:** English, Spanish. **Description:** Scientists, resource specialists, members of conservation organizations, and individuals concerned with long-term environmental values. Originally concerned with native fish of the Death Valley region, the group's interest has spread to habitat integrity throughout the American Southwest and Northern Mexico. Promotes proper management of this resource; encourages research relative to desert ecosystems. **Libraries: Type:** reference. **Awards:** Carl L. Hubbs. **Frequency:** annual. **Type:** recognition. **Recipient:** for best student paper ● Frances Hubbs Miller. **Frequency:** annual. **Type:** recognition. **Recipient:** for best paper presented by a Mexican student. **Telecommunication Services:** electronic mail, secretary@desertfishes.org. **Publications:** *Proceedings of The Desert Fishes Council* (in English and Spanish), annual. Journal. Contains resource status and research papers. **Price:** free for members. ISSN: 1068-0381. **Circulation:** 500. Alternate Formats: online. **Conventions/Meetings:** annual symposium - usually in November.

4389 ■ Desert Protective Council (DPC)
PO Box 3635
San Diego, CA 92163-1635
Ph: (619)342-5524

E-mail: information@dpcinc.org
URL: http://www.dpcinc.org
Contact: Nick Ervin, Pres.
Founded: 1954. **Members:** 400. **Membership Dues:** student, senior, associate, $15 (annual) ● single, $25 (annual) ● joint, $35 (annual) ● life, $300. **Description:** Persons interested in safeguarding desert areas of unique, scenic, scientific, historical, spiritual, and recreational value. Seeks to educate children and adults to promote a better understanding of the desert. Works to bring about establishment of wildlife sanctuaries for protection of indigenous plants and animals. The Desert Protective Council Foundation, formed in 1989, supports educational and non-legislative desert protection programs. **Awards:** Award of Merit. **Frequency:** annual. **Type:** recognition. **Recipient:** for outstanding contributions to desert protection. **Funds:** Imperial County. **Publications:** *Educational Bulletins*, quarterly. Features desert and wildlife articles. **Price:** included in membership dues; free on request. **Circulation:** 1,000. Alternate Formats: online ● *El Paisano*, quarterly. Newsletter. Focuses on the status of the ecology, archeology, natural history, biology, and geography of the desert. **Price:** included in membership dues. **Circulation:** 700 ● Annual Report, annual. Contains information on DPC's annual meetings. Alternate Formats: online ● Articles. Alternate Formats: online. **Conventions/Meetings:** annual meeting - always October.

4390 ■ Desert Tortoise Preserve Committee (DTPC)
4067 Mission Inn Ave.
Riverside, CA 92501
Ph: (951)683-3872
Fax: (951)683-6949
E-mail: dtpc@pacbell.net
URL: http://www.tortoise-tracks.org
Contact: Michael J. Connor PhD, Exec. Dir.
Founded: 1974. **Members:** 1,500. **Membership Dues:** individual, $15 (annual) ● family, $20 (annual) ● sponsor, $30 (annual) ● benefactor, $75 (annual) ● patron, $100 (annual) ● life, $500. **Description:** Individuals, conservation organizations, wildlife groups, and scientists interested in the protection and preservation of the Desert Tortoise Natural Area and other tortoise preserves in the West Mojave Desert. (The Desert Tortoise Natural Area encompasses 38 square miles in the Northwestern Mojave Desert and contains one of the finest remaining populations of the desert tortoise, Gopherus Agassizii, the official California State Reptile.) Works to assure the continued survival of viable populations of the desert tortoise. Aims to raise funds for purchasing privately owned parcels of land within the Desert Tortoise critical habitat. Cooperates with the Bureau of Land Management. Conducts conservation education programs and guided tours for schools, museums, and other groups. Maintains speakers' bureau. **Awards: Type:** recognition. **Programs:** Harper Lake Road Fencing Mitigation. **Projects:** Mojave Desert Discovery Centers. **Publications:** *Tortoise Tracks*, quarterly. Newsletter. **Price:** $15.00/year. Alternate Formats: online ● Reports. Alternate Formats: online. **Conventions/Meetings:** annual meeting - always January.

4391 ■ EarthEcho International
888 16th St. NW, Ste.800
Washington, DC 20006
Ph: (202)349-9828
Fax: (202)355-1399
E-mail: info@earthecho.org
URL: http://www.earthecho.org
Contact: Philippe Cousteau Jr., Co-Founder/Pres./CEO
Founded: 2000. **Multinational**. **Description:** Encourages individuals to become better stewards of water resources and enables them to adopt and maintain behaviors that are more consistent with sustainable living. Maintains strong relationships with scientists and researchers and employs them actively in educational and informational campaigns. Communicates with the public through online discussions.

4392 ■ Environmental Entrepreneurs (E2)
c/o Priscilla Bayley
Natural Resources Defense Coun.
40 W 20th St.
New York, NY 10011
Ph: (212)727-4422
Fax: (212)727-1773
E-mail: thanggi@nrdc.org
URL: http://www.e2.org
Contact: Teryn Hanggi, Program Mgr.
Founded: 2000. **Membership Dues:** steering committee, $25,000 ● principal, $24,999 ● partner, $2,500-$9,999 ● associate, $1,000-$2,499. **State Groups:** 22. **Description:** Represents business people who believe in protecting the environment while building economic prosperity. Serves as a champion on the economic side of good environmental policy by taking an economically sound approach to environmental issues. Focuses on environmental policies that drive economic growth in a healthy direction. **Telecommunication Services:** electronic mail, pbayley@nrdc.org. **Publications:** *Environmental Entrepreneurs Update*, monthly. Newsletter. Features articles on pressing environmental issues and includes updates on significant E2 and NRDC developments. **Price:** included in membership dues. Alternate Formats: online ● Reports. Presents an analysis of the financial benefits of environmental policy, and how it can affect the economy. Alternate Formats: online.

4393 ■ FishAmerica Foundation (FAF)
225 Reinekers Ln., Ste.420
Alexandria, VA 22314
Ph: (703)519-9691
Fax: (703)519-1872
E-mail: info@asafishing.org
URL: http://www.fishamerica.org
Contact: Johanna Laderman, Exec. Dir.
Founded: 1983. **Staff:** 3. **Budget:** $1,300,000. **Nonmembership**. **Description:** Provides funding for local projects aimed at enhancing fish populations, improving water quality and/or advancing applied fisheries research, thereby improving the opportunity for sportfishing success. Works to form public/private partnerships to address common water conservation problems and encourages anglers and other conservationists to demonstrate voluntary conservation measures. **Telecommunication Services:** electronic mail, fishamerica@asafishing.org ● electronic mail, jladerman@asafishing.org. **Committees:** Conservation Projects; Research Projects. **Publications:** *American Sportfishing*, monthly. Newsletter. **Price:** included in membership dues.

4394 ■ Forest Guild
PO Box 519
Santa Fe, NM 87504-0519
Ph: (505)983-8992
Fax: (505)986-0798
E-mail: info@forestguild.org
URL: http://www.forestguild.org
Contact: Howard Gross, Exec. Dir.
Founded: 1984. **Members:** 600. **Membership Dues:** sustaining, $100 (annual) ● supporting, $20-$99 (annual) ● student, $15 (annual). **Staff:** 15. **Budget:** $1,275,000. **Regional Groups:** 6. **Description:** Focuses on the protection of America's forests. Works to protect the integrity of the forest ecosystem and improve the lives of people in rural communities. Challenges traditional forest management philosophies and provides resource protection strategies to grassroots environmental organizations, rural communities, and public agencies. **Libraries: Type:** reference. **Holdings:** 4,000. **Subjects:** forestry, rural development, ecology. **Telecommunication Services:** electronic mail, howard@forestguild.org. **Subgroups:** Community Forestry; Land Stewardship; Land Trust; National Forest Planning and Policy; Sustainable Forestry. **Formerly:** (2004) Forest Trust. **Publications:** *Forest WISDOM*, 3/year. Newsletters. **Circulation:** 2,400. Alternate Formats: online ● Proceedings. **Conventions/Meetings:** annual Forest Stewards Guild Meeting - conference (exhibits).

4395 ■ Forestry Conservation Communications Association (FCCA)
PO Box 3217
Gettysburg, PA 17325
Ph: (717)388-1505
Fax: (717)334-5656
E-mail: nfc@fcca-usa.org
URL: http://www.fcca-usa.org
Contact: Ralph Haller, Exec. Dir.
Founded: 1944. **Members:** 273. **Staff:** 4. **Budget:** $200,000. **Regional Groups:** 4. **State Groups:** 50. **Description:** Communications engineers, directors, radio frequency coordinators, and advisers in state forestry and wildlife conservation work; state foresters and forest fire chiefs, state wildlife conservation administrators and park lands managers. Represents forestry and conservation agencies before the Federal Communications Commission; aids in development of communications equipment, systems, and procedures; promotes increased cooperation in the activities of state forestry and wildlife conservation agencies. **Telecommunication Services:** electronic mail, ed@fcca-usa.org. **Committees:** FCC Dockets; Legislation; Radio Frequency Coordinators; Radio Interference; Technical. **Affiliated With:** Association of Fish and Wildlife Agencies; National Association of State Foresters. **Publications:** Newsletter, quarterly. **Circulation:** 300. **Advertising:** accepted. **Conventions/Meetings:** annual conference, covers FCCA technical, FCC, and business issues (exhibits) - always third weekend in July.

4396 ■ Foundation for Research on Economics and the Environment (FREE)
662 Ferguson Rd.
Bozeman, MT 59718
Ph: (406)585-1776
Fax: (406)585-3000
E-mail: jbaden@free-eco.org
URL: http://www.free-eco.org
Contact: John A. Baden PhD, Chm./Founder
Founded: 1985. **Description:** Intellectual entrepreneurs. Works to advance conservation and environmental values by applying modern science and America's funding ideals to policy debates. Hosts Seminars for Federal Judges, Law Professors Program and Environmental Entrepreneurship's. **Publications:** *Judge Dave and the Rainbow People*. Book ● *Perspectives*. Newsletter. Alternate Formats: online.

4397 ■ Friends of the Earth (FOE)
1717 Massachusetts Ave. NW, Ste.600
Washington, DC 20036-2002
Ph: (202)783-7400
Free: (877)843-8687
Fax: (202)783-0444
E-mail: foe@foe.org
URL: http://www.foe.org
Contact: Brent Blackwelder PhD, Pres.
Founded: 1969. **Members:** 26,000. **Membership Dues:** regular, $35 (annual). **Staff:** 33. **Budget:** $4,000,000. **Regional Groups:** 1. **National Groups:** 70. **Description:** Dedicated to protecting the planet from environmental disaster; preserving biological and ethnic diversity; empowers citizens to have an effective voice in environmental decision; promotes use of tax dollars to protect the environment; other interests include groundwater and ozone protection, toxic waste cleanup, and reforming the World Bank and sustainable development which addressed the need to reduce over-consumption in the U.S. **Computer Services:** database ● mailing lists. **Committees:** Activist Members. **Programs:** Community, Health and Environment; Economics for the Earth; International; Legislative; Regional. **Affiliated With:** Oceanic Society. **Absorbed:** (1989) Environmental Policy Institute; (1989) Oceanic Society. **Publications:** *Arming NGO's With Knowledge: A Guide to the International Monetary Fund*. Handbook. Contains information on nature, structure and activities of the IMF. **Price:** $10.00. Alternate Formats: online ● *Crude Awakening, The Oil Mess in America: Wasting Energy, Jobs & the Environment*. Book. Reports on oil industries waste and inefficiency. **Price:** $35.00 ● *Earth Budget: Making Our Tax Dollars Work for the*

Environment. Book. Features an analysis of the Federal Budget. **Price:** $30.00 ● *Green Scissors*. Report. **Price:** $15.00. Alternate Formats: online ● *The Green Solution to Red Ink: Cutting Wasteful and Environmentally Harmful Spending*. Reports. Outlines environmentally harmful spending programs. **Price:** $5.00 ● *Into the Sunlight: Exposing Methyl Brodide's Threat to the Ozone Layer*. Reports. Dangers of the ozone-destroying pesticide methyl bromide. **Price:** $12.00 ● *Tax Reform for Sustainable Agriculture*. Report. **Price:** $10.00. Alternate Formats: online ● Magazine, quarterly. Discusses general environmental issues and organization. **Price:** $25.00 /year for individuals and nonprofit organizations; $25.00/year for corporations. ISSN: 0194-1062. Alternate Formats: online ● Annual Report, annual. Alternate Formats: online. **Conventions/Meetings:** annual meeting, with Board of Directors election - always summer.

4398 ■ Friends of the Everglades (FE)
7800 Red Rd., Ste.215K
Miami, FL 33143
Ph: (305)669-0858
Fax: (305)669-4108
E-mail: info@everglades.org
URL: http://www.everglades.org
Contact: David P. Reiner II, Pres.
Founded: 1969. **Members:** 4,000. **Membership Dues:** individual, $35 (annual) ● family, $50 (annual) ● supporting, $100 (annual) ● steward, corporate support, $500 (annual) ● everglades defender, corporate patron, $1,000 (annual) ● corporate defender, $5,000 (annual). **Staff:** 1. **Budget:** $100,000. **Description:** Concerned citizens working cooperatively with local, state and federal agencies as well as academics, scientists and other knowledgeable persons to represent the public interest. Seeks to educate public and political interests on the significance of the Everglades ecosystem and the best means to protect the resources therein. Works to develop and comment on local, state and federal environmental projects, regulations and permit applications, and when necessary, engage in administrative procedures to challenge permits and actions. Seeks restoration of the Kissimmee/Okeechobee/Everglades ecosystem and supports the Federal Ecosystem Restoration Task Force efforts to design and execute that proposal. Seeks strong environmental protection laws and enforcement, groundwater protection and drinking water quality, and works to increase public knowledge and participation in environmental issues. Provides environmental education in Dade County through the public school system and a "Young Friends of the Everglades" program. Maintains both an archival library and a library of current plans and studies. **Libraries: Type:** by appointment only. **Holdings:** archival material, periodicals, reports. **Subjects:** environmental topics, local, state and federal plans, Florida statutes and administrative code. **Programs:** Joan and Hy Rosner Environmental Education Fund; Young Friends of the Everglades. **Publications:** *An Evaluation of the Scientific Basis for Restoring Florida Bay by Increasing Freshwater Runoff from the Everglades*. Report. Alternate Formats: online ● *The Dade County Environmental Story*. Book. Serves as anthology and resource book. ● *Everglades Reporter*, quarterly. Newsletter. Lists updated issues and activities. **Price:** included in membership dues. **Circulation:** 4,000. Alternate Formats: online ● *Lake Okeechobee: A Lake in Peril* ● *The Nature of Dade County - A Hometown Handbook* (in English and Spanish) ● *Who Knows the Rain?* ● *Young Friends of the Everglades Newsletter*. Covers issues and activities of Young Friends of the Everglades; distributed to Miami-Dade County public schools. **Price:** included in membership dues. **Conventions/Meetings:** annual meeting - every spring, Miami, FL.

4399 ■ Friends of the River (FOR)
915 20th St.
Sacramento, CA 95811
Ph: (916)442-3155
Fax: (916)442-3396
E-mail: info@friendsoftheriver.org
URL: http://www.friendsoftheriver.org
Contact: Peter Ferenbach, Exec. Dir.
Founded: 1973. **Members:** 6,000. **Membership Dues:** friend, $35 (annual) ● River Guardian, $250 (annual) ● Watershed Warrior, $100 (annual) ● Stream Saver, $50 (annual) ● student, $15 (annual). **Staff:** 15. **Budget:** $1,270,000. **Local Groups:** 2. **Description:** California's statewide river conservation group, protects and restores rivers, streams and their watersheds through public education, citizen activist training and organizing and expert advocacy to influence public policy. Projects include: winning federal Wild and Scenic River status for Tuolumne, Kings, Kern, and Merced rivers; efforts to defeat construction of Auburn Dam on North Fork American River; campaign to win Wild and Scenic River protection for more than 100 rivers and streams on National Forest Land in California; campaign to reform legislation which provides unfair incentives to hydropower developers intent on damming rivers for economic profit; development of a new water agenda to help guide future water policy. Sponsors work-study and internship programs, research, political organizing, and fundraising projects. Projects funded through Friends of the River Foundation. **Libraries: Type:** reference. **Holdings:** 100. **Subjects:** water policy, water law, river preservation. **Awards:** Mark Dubois River Conservationist Award. **Frequency:** annual. **Type:** recognition. **Recipient:** for outstanding river conservation efforts in California. **Telecommunication Services:** electronic mail, sevans@friendsoftheriver.org. **Programs:** Rafting. **Publications:** *Headwaters*, quarterly. Newsletter. **Price:** included in membership dues. **Circulation:** 8,000. **Advertising:** accepted ● *Potential Wild and Scenic Rivers in California*. Report. Alternate Formats: online ● *Rivers of Power*. Report. Alternate Formats: online ● Brochures. **Conventions/Meetings:** annual Rivers Festival (exhibits) - 1st weekend of April.

4400 ■ Friends of the Trees Society (FTS)
PO Box 4469
Bellingham, WA 98227
Ph: (360)927-1274
E-mail: friendsofthetrees@yahoo.com
URL: http://www.friendsofthetrees.net
Contact: Michael Pilarski, Founder/Dir.
Founded: 1978. **Staff:** 3. **Description:** Promotes reforestation and sustainable agriculture. Conducts workshops on reforestation, permaculture, and related topics. **Libraries: Type:** reference. **Holdings:** audiovisuals, books, periodicals. **Computer Services:** Online services, TERN (Traveler's Earth Repair Network), linking ecoconscious travelers with host organizations worldwide for volunteer work. **Publications:** *International Green Front Report*, periodic. Newsletter. Reports on projects and events; contains book reviews. **Price:** $7.00 plus shipping and handling. **Circulation:** 8,000 ● *Kiwi Enthusiasts Journal*, annual. **Price:** $14.95 plus shipping and handling ● *Third World Resource Guide*, periodic. Contains names, addresses and brief descriptions of groups working in forestry, sustainable agriculture, and conservation. **Price:** $5.00. **Conventions/Meetings:** periodic conference.

4401 ■ Galapagos Conservancy (GC)
407 N Washington St., Ste.105
Falls Church, VA 22046-3436
Ph: (703)538-6833
Fax: (703)538-6835
E-mail: ambassadors@galapagos.org
URL: http://www.galapagos.org
Contact: Mr. William A. Nitze, Chm.
Founded: 1959. **Budget:** $650,000. **Description:** Supports, organizes, and administers research work at a station authorized by the government of Ecuador, with primary emphasis on science and conservation. Provides for the protection of the wildlife of the Galapagos Islands; disseminates research findings; encourages and aids scientific education, particularly in Ecuador. Maintains museum with collection of Galapagos biological specimens. Conducts research and specialized education programs. **Libraries: Type:** reference. **Subjects:** Galapagos. **Awards: Type:** scholarship. **Recipient:** for Ecuadorian science students to work at the Charles Darwin Research Station in the Galapagos. **Telecommunication Services:** electronic mail, comments@galapagos.org. **Formerly:** (2002) Charles Darwin Foundation for the Galapagos Isles; (2006) Charles Darwin Foundation. **Publications:** *Galapagos News*, semiannual. Newsletter. Alternate Formats: online ● *Noticias de Galapagos*, semiannual. Journal. Contains information on Science and Conservation in the Galapagos Islands. Alternate Formats: online ● Annual Report (in English and Spanish), annual. Alternate Formats: online. **Conventions/Meetings:** semiannual board meeting.

4402 ■ Garden Conservancy
PO Box 219
Cold Spring, NY 10516
Ph: (845)265-2029
Fax: (845)265-9620
E-mail: info@gardenconservancy.org
URL: http://www.gardenconservancy.org
Contact: Antonia F. Adezio, Pres.
Founded: 1989. **Membership Dues:** individual, $35 ● family/organization, $50 ● friend, $100 ● sponsor, $250 ● patron, $500 ● society of fellow, $1,500 ● President's Circle sustainer, $2,500 ● President's Circle benefactor, $5,000 ● Chairman's Circle, $10,000. **Description:** Preserves exceptional American gardens for the public's education and enjoyment. Works in partnership with individual garden owners, public and private organizations, and uses its legal, financial, and horticultural resources to secure each garden's future and to make it permanently accessible to the public. **Awards:** Marco Polo Stufano Garden Conservancy Fellowship. **Frequency:** annual. **Type:** fellowship. **Recipient:** to a gardener capable of making a significant contribution to American gardens. **Programs:** Open Days; Pacific Northwest Garden Conservancy Forum. **Projects:** Preservation. **Publications:** *Taking a Garden Public: Feasibility and Startup*. Handbook. **Price:** $25.00 plus shipping and handling ● *Taking a Garden Public: Fund Raising and Development*. Handbook. **Price:** $25.00 plus shipping and handling ● Newsletter, quarterly. Contains articles about Conservancy projects and garden restoration and preservation. **Price:** included in membership dues ● Annual Report, annual. **Price:** included in membership dues.

4403 ■ Global Coral Reef Alliance (GCRA)
c/o Dr. Thomas J. Goreau, Pres.
37 Pleasant St.
Cambridge, MA 02139
Ph: (617)864-4226 (617)864-0433
E-mail: goreau@bestweb.net
URL: http://www.globalcoral.org
Contact: Dr. Thomas J. Goreau, Pres.
Founded: 1990. **Description:** Conducts scientific research on coral reef ecosystems and the environmental factors that are affecting them. Disseminates information to the public and policy makers about the ecological, environmental, and economic importance of coral reefs. Develops policies to protect coral reefs and change the worldwide trend toward degradation. Supports conservation of reefs. Especially, does research on the significance and spread of mass coral reef "bleaching" which is caused by a rise in ocean temperature and threatens the existence of the reefs. Works to improve technology for the creation of artificial reefs, coastal protection, and building materials from seawater-derived minerals, using renewable energy.

4404 ■ Grassland Heritage Foundation (GHF)
PO Box 394
Shawnee Mission, KS 66201
Ph: (913)262-3506 (785)748-0955
E-mail: email@grasslandheritage.org
URL: http://www.grasslandheritage.org
Contact: Rex Powell, Contact
Founded: 1979. **Members:** 350. **Membership Dues:** individual, $20 ● family, $35 ● steward, benefactor, $50 ● sustaining, $100 ● conserver, $250 ● patron, $500 ● student/retired, $15. **Staff:** 1. **Budget:** $15,000. **Local Groups:** 1. **Description:** Aims to foster appreciation for, create interest in, and promote a better understanding of the value of America's native grassland prairies; to purchase, lease, or acquire, for the public benefit, native tallgrass prairies in the U.S. for scientific, educational, and recreational

purposes; to encourage the protection of natural prairie lands, including such lands now or at any subsequent time employed as grazing lands for domestic cattle, from forces alien to a natural prairie environment or a grazing economy. Owns and manages a 160 acre prairie site near Topeka, Kansas. Maintains speakers' bureau; sponsors student naturalist sessions. **Libraries: Type:** reference. **Holdings:** 100. **Subjects:** preservation, environment, aviary, ecology. **Committees:** Friends of the Prairie Center. **Formerly:** (1980) Tallgrass Prairie Foundation. **Publications:** *GHF News*, quarterly. Newsletter. Contains updates on group activities and events. **Price:** included in membership dues. **Conventions/Meetings:** annual board meeting - 4th Saturday in January ● bimonthly board meeting ● monthly meeting - every third Saturday.

4405 ■ Great Lakes United (GLU)
Buffalo State Coll.
Cassety Hall
1300 Elmwood Ave.
Buffalo, NY 14222
Ph: (716)886-0142
Fax: (716)204-9521
E-mail: glu@glu.org
URL: http://www.glu.org
Contact: Jim Mahon, Pres.
Founded: 1982. **Members:** 780. **Membership Dues:** basic/organization (with $15000 or less annual budget), $35 (annual) ● organization, $100 (annual) ● supporting/library, $50 (annual) ● student/unwaged, $20 (annual). **Staff:** 8. **Budget:** $370,000. **Regional Groups:** 150. **Languages:** English, French. **Description:** International conservation coalition formed by representatives of environmental, sports, union, community, and business groups that promote the protection and restoration of the Great Lakes ecosystem; interested individuals. Serves as an advisory organization and source of information exchange. Target issues include: hazardous and toxic substances; biodiversity and habitat protection; pollution protection in areas of concern; sustainable use of water resources. **Libraries: Type:** open to the public. **Holdings:** 1,000; articles, books, periodicals. **Subjects:** Great Lakes water quality, habitats, community health. **Telecommunication Services:** electronic mail, jmahon@glu.org. **Committees:** Clean Production; Habitat and Biodiversity; Healthy Communities in Areas of Concern; Sustainable Water Resources. **Divisions:** Lake Erie; Lake Huron; Lake Michigan; Lake Ontario; Lake Superior; St. Lawrence River. **Projects:** Binational Toxics Strategy; Lake Erie Dead Zone; Restoration; River to River-Africa: Niger; Source Water; Trade. **Publications:** *The Fate of the Great Lakes: Sustaining or Draining the Sweetwater Seas.* Report. **Price:** $7.00 for members; $10.00 for nonmembers ● *Taking Stock of Our Future: A Conference on the Impacts of Fish Stocking in the Great Lakes.* Reprint ● *The United Times*, quarterly. Newsletter. **Price:** $25.00 /year for individuals; $50.00 /year for libraries; $100.00/year for organizations. **Circulation:** 7,000. **Advertising:** accepted ● *Water Use and Ecosystem Restoration: An Agenda for the Great Lakes and St. Lawrence River.* Reprint ● Annual Report, annual. **Conventions/Meetings:** annual meeting (exhibits) - always May or June.

4406 ■ Greater Yellowstone Coalition (GYC)
PO Box 1874
Bozeman, MT 59771
Ph: (406)586-1593
Free: (800)775-1834
Fax: (406)556-2839
E-mail: gyc@greateryellowstone.org
URL: http://www.greateryellowstone.org
Contact: Michael Scott, Exec. Dir.
Founded: 1983. **Members:** 13,000. **Membership Dues:** badger, $35 (annual) ● lynx, $50 (annual) ● river otter, $150 (annual) ● wolverine, $250 (annual) ● mountain lion, $500 (annual) ● gray wolf, $1,000 (annual). **Staff:** 23. **Budget:** $2,400,000. **Regional Groups:** 110. **Description:** Brings together individuals and groups concerned with conservation, wildlife, and the environment. Seeks to conserve and protect the Greater Yellowstone Ecosystem, the 18 million acre area including and surrounding Yellowstone National Park, WY, and Grand Teton National Park, WY, and the full range of its life. Seeks to create a national awareness of issues and threats facing the GYE. Concerns include mining, drilling, logging, road construction, and destruction of wildlife habitat and human overuse of land in the region. **Councils:** Science. **Publications:** *Action Alert*, periodic ● *An Environmental Profile of the Greater Yellowstone Ecosystem* ● *Greater Yellowstone Report*, quarterly. Journal ● *Sustaining Greater Yellowstone: A Blueprint for the Future.* **Conventions/Meetings:** annual Journey Back to Nature - conference, scientific (exhibits).

4407 ■ Greensward Foundation (GF)
PO Box 610
New York, NY 10021
Ph: (212)625-8733
E-mail: info@greenswardparks.org
URL: http://www.greenswardparks.org
Contact: Ms. Celeste Holm, Sec.
Founded: 1964. **Members:** 2,300. **Description:** Works for the improvement of natural landscape urban parks, the proper understanding of these parks by the public, and the proper care of these parks by their custodians. Sponsors: Friends of Central Park, Friends of Prospect Park, and Friends of Fort Greene Park in New York; Friends of Branch Brook Park, in Newark, NJ; Friends of Cadwalader Park, in Trenton, NJ; Friends of Druid Hill Park, in Baltimore, MD. Encourages the maintenance of urban parks to be made labor intensive by hiring and properly supervising unskilled and unemployed workers. Sponsors year-round walking tours. Raises funds to save historic, century-old trees in city parks, and to restore the Vale of Cashmere in Prospect Park. Publishes books and maps on urban parks, including Bridges in Central Park, Tree Trails in Central Park, Rock Trails in Central Park, Central Park/Prospect Park, a New Perspective, and maps of Central Park, Prospect Park, Branch Brook Park, and Ft. Greene Park. **Publications:** *Bridges of Central Park.* Book. **Price:** $12.50. Alternate Formats: online ● *Central Park/Prospect Park - A New Perspective.* Book. **Price:** $12.50 ● *Little News*, quarterly. Bulletin ● *The Making of Prospect Park: Notes for a Projected Historical Study.* Pamphlet ● *Map: Branch Brook Park* ● *Map: Central Park* ● *Map: Fort Greene Park* ● *Map: Prospect Park/Brooklyn Botanic Garden* ● *The Men Who Made Central Park.* Pamphlet. **Price:** $1.75 ● *Prospect Park Handbook.* **Price:** $8.00. Alternate Formats: online ● *Requiem for an Elm.* Pamphlet. Alternate Formats: online ● *Rock Trails in Central Park.* Book. **Price:** $8.00. Alternate Formats: online ● *Rockefeller New York: A Tour by Henry Hope Reed.* Book. Alternate Formats: online ● *Tree Trails in Central Park.* Book. **Price:** $9.00 ● *Tree Trails in Prospect Park.* Pamphlet. Alternate Formats: online. **Conventions/Meetings:** annual meeting.

4408 ■ Holistic Management International
1010 Tijeras Ave. NW
Albuquerque, NM 87102
Ph: (505)842-5252
Fax: (505)843-7900
E-mail: hmi@holisticmanagement.org
URL: http://www.holisticmanagement.org
Contact: Shannon Horst, Exec. Dir.
Founded: 1984. **Members:** 1,500. **Membership Dues:** individual in U.S., $30 (annual) ● individual outside U.S., $35 (annual). **Staff:** 10. **Budget:** $2,500,000. **Regional Groups:** 4. **State Groups:** 7. **National Groups:** 7. **Languages:** English, French, Spanish. **Multinational. Description:** Ranchers, farmers, foresters, environmentalists, conservationists, educators, business leaders, politicians, and interested persons. Seeks to improve the human environment and quality of life through Holistic Resource Management. Objectives are to: produce stable environments with sound watersheds; restore profitability to agriculture; increase wildlife species and stability of populations; improve water resources of cities, industry, and agriculture; reestablish seriously damaged riparian (streamside) areas; prevent waste of financial resources by governments, international agencies, and private individuals due to poor resource management. Fosters citizen participation in sound resource management; works extensively on combatting the desertification process. Conducts training programs for educators in Holistic Resource Management. Collects and disseminates information; maintains Speaker's Bureau. Provides scientific and educational presentations and interviews. Operates land management and advisory services. **Formerly:** (2001) Center for Holistic Management; (2006) Allan Savory Center for Holistic Management. **Publications:** *Holistic Management In Practice*, bimonthly. Newsletter. Includes advice for practitioners, upcoming events, and information on new ideas and innovations. **Price:** $27.00/year. ISSN: 1069-2789. **Circulation:** 2,000. **Advertising:** accepted. **Conventions/Meetings:** annual meeting.

4409 ■ Interfaith Council for the Protection of Animals and Nature (ICPAN)
3691 Tuxedo Rd. NW
Atlanta, GA 30305
Ph: (404)814-1371
E-mail: regenstein@mindspring.com
Contact: Lewis G. Regenstein, Dir.
Founded: 1980. **Members:** 3,000. **Membership Dues:** $10 (annual). **Description:** Individuals of all religious faiths who share an interest in conservation of natural resources and environmental protection. Works to make religious leaders, institutions, and the public aware of humanity's "moral and spiritual obligation," as emphasized in the Bible and many religious teachings, to protect animals and the natural environment. Conducts educational campaigns including lectures and slide shows. **Affiliated With:** Humane Society of the United States. **Publications:** *Cleaning Up America The Poisoned: How to Survive our Polluted Society.* Book ● *Replenish the Earth: The Bible's message of Conservation and Kindness to Animals.* Booklet ● *Replenish the Earth: The Teachings of the World's Religions on Protecting Animals and Nature.* Book ● Brochures.

4410 ■ International Association for the Study of Common Property (IASCP)
PO Box 2355
Gary, IN 46409
Ph: (219)980-1433
Fax: (219)980-2801
E-mail: iascp@indiana.edu
URL: http://www.iascp.org
Contact: Ms. Michelle Curtain, Exec. Dir.
Founded: 1989. **Members:** 1,000. **Membership Dues:** individual (with income of $50,000 and above), $100 (annual) ● individual (with income of $20,000-49,999), $50 (annual) ● individual (with income of $19,999 and below), $10 (annual). **Staff:** 1. **Budget:** $90,000. **Regional Groups:** 3. **Description:** Scholars, government officials, development consultants, resource managers, and other interested individuals. Devoted to understanding and improving the management of environmental resources that are held or used collectively by communities in developing or developed countries. Promotes an interdisciplinary approach to resource management. **Libraries: Type:** open to the public. **Holdings:** 52. **Subjects:** common property. **Computer Services:** Mailing lists ● online services. **Publications:** *Common Property Resource Digest*, quarterly. Newsletter. **Price:** included in membership dues. **Circulation:** 4,200. Alternate Formats: online. **Conventions/Meetings:** biennial conference (exhibits).

4411 ■ International Erosion Control Association (IECA)
3001 S Lincoln Ave., Ste.A
Steamboat Springs, CO 80487
Ph: (970)879-3010
Free: (800)455-4322
Fax: (970)879-8563
E-mail: ecinfo@ieca.org
URL: http://www.ieca.org
Contact: Ronald Faucher, Pres.
Founded: 1972. **Members:** 3,500. **Membership Dues:** student, emeritus, $55 (annual) ● professional, $170 (annual) ● corporate, $320 (annual) ● emerald,

$595 (annual) ● cornerstone, $2,500 (annual). **Staff:** 13. **Regional Groups:** 10. **Description:** Landscape contractors, government officials, landscape architects, engineers, manufacturers and suppliers, and others in 50 countries. Encourages the exchange of information and ideas concerning effective and economical methods of erosion control. Recognizes the need for an organized discipline in soil erosion and sediment control so that laws, specifications, procedures, and restrictions concerning land disturbances may be written by qualified professionals. Offers short courses and annual conference. **Libraries: Type:** reference. **Holdings:** periodicals. **Awards:** Contractor of the Year Award. **Frequency:** annual. **Type:** recognition. **Recipient:** for excellence in the execution and application of effective erosion and sediment control practices ● Environmental Achievement Award. **Frequency:** annual. **Type:** recognition. **Recipient:** for an outstanding program that demonstrates excellence in natural resources conservation ● Most Distinguished Technical Paper Award. **Frequency:** annual. **Type:** recognition. **Recipient:** for excellence in the advancement of erosion control knowledge and education ● Sustained Contributor Award. **Frequency:** annual. **Type:** recognition. **Recipient:** for significant and long term contribution to the erosion and sediment control industry. **Sections:** Slope Technology; Storm Water Management; Stream Restoration; Vegetative Establishment. **Publications:** *Erosion Control Journal*, 9/year. Magazine. **Price:** $43.00. **Advertising:** accepted ● *News to Use*, quarterly. Newsletter. **Advertising:** accepted ● *Proceedings of Conferences*, annual ● Membership Directory, annual. **Advertising:** accepted ● Also publishes material on erosion and sediment control technology, revegetation, and related subjects. **Conventions/Meetings:** annual Environmental Connection - conference and lecture, about the erosion and sediment control industry (exhibits) - 2009 Feb. 9-12, Reno, NV; 2010 Feb. 14-17, Dallas, TX.

4412 ■ International Union for the Conservation of Nature and Natural Resources U.S. (IUCN USA)

1630 Connecticut Ave. NW, 3rd Fl.
Washington, DC 20009
Ph: (202)387-4826
Fax: (202)387-4823
E-mail: postmaster@iucnus.org
URL: http://www.iucn.org
Contact: Scott A. Hajost, Exec. Dir.

Founded: 1948. **Members:** 78. **Staff:** 11. **Budget:** $100,000. **Description:** States, governmental agencies, political and/or economic integration organizations, and international and national non-governmental organizations. Seeks to influence, encourage, and assist societies throughout the world to conserve the integrity and diversity of nature and to ensure that any use of natural resources is equitable and ecologically sustainable. **Additional Websites:** http://www.iucn.org/places/usa. **Telecommunication Services:** electronic mail, mhansen@iucnus.org. **Affiliated With:** IUCN - The World Conservation Union. **Publications:** *IUCN Today* (in English, French, and Spanish), bimonthly. Newsletter ● Catalog. Alternate Formats: online. **Conventions/Meetings:** annual board meeting.

4413 ■ Izaak Walton League of America (IWLA)

707 Conservation Ln.
Gaithersburg, MD 20878
Ph: (301)548-0150
Free: (800)IKE-LINE
Fax: (301)548-0149
E-mail: general@iwla.org
URL: http://www.iwla.org
Contact: David W. Hoskins, Exec. Dir.

Founded: 1922. **Members:** 40,000. **Membership Dues:** student, $18 (annual) ● youth, $7 (annual) ● family, $54 (annual) ● master, $100 (annual) ● family life benefactor, $1,500 ● supporting, $75 (annual) ● life, $500 ● life family, $750 ● life benefactor, $1,000 ● regular at-large, $36 (annual). **Staff:** 35. **Budget:** $3,000,000. **State Groups:** 21. **Local Groups:** 350. **Description:** Works to educate the public about conserving, maintaining, protecting, and restoring the soil, forest, water, and other natural resources of the U.S; promotes the enjoyment and wholesome utilization of these resources. Sponsors environmental programs including Sustainability Education Project, Outdoor Ethics, Save Our Streams, Midwest Energy Efficiency Program, Sustainable Agriculture and Wetlands, and Hunter and Angler Issues Program. **Libraries: Type:** reference; by appointment only. **Holdings:** archival material, books, business records, clippings, periodicals. **Telecommunication Services:** electronic mail, executivedirector@iwla.org. **Programs:** Agricultural; Clean Air; Clean Water; Sustainability Education; Wilderness and Public Lands. **Projects:** Fish Kill Advisory Network; Mississippi River Program; Missouri River Initiative; Protect Our Wetlands; Save Our Streams. **Absorbed:** (1961) Friends of the Land. **Publications:** *Outdoor America*, quarterly. Magazine. Features stories about current conservation issues. **Advertising:** accepted. Alternate Formats: online ● Annual Report, annual. Alternate Formats: online ● Newsletters. Alternate Formats: online ● Reports. Alternate Formats: online. **Conventions/Meetings:** annual convention (exhibits) - always July ● workshop.

4414 ■ Izaak Walton League of America Endowment (IWLAE)

c/o Charles L. Eldridge, Pres.
523 14th St.
Des Moines, IA 50309
Ph: (515)244-0932 (515)276-0767
Fax: (515)244-0951
E-mail: eldwldmch@msn.com
URL: http://www.iwla-endowment.org
Contact: Charles L. Eldridge, Pres.

Founded: 1922. **Members:** 50,000. **Staff:** 28. **Budget:** $4,000,000. **Regional Groups:** 1. **State Groups:** 300. **Description:** Works for the conservation, protection, maintenance and restoration of America's natural resources, particularly its soil, water, woods, air and wildlife; most acquisitions are resold to the U.S. Forest Service and the National Park Service, at cost or less, to become part of the nation's parks, forests and public recreation areas, although some are donated to federal and state governments. Places increasing emphasis on youth and conservation education programs, providing funding for youth conferences and educational activities. Provides funding for the television show Make Peace With Nature. **Affiliated With:** Izaak Walton League of America. **Publications:** Brochure. **Conventions/Meetings:** annual conference - always July.

4415 ■ Land Improvement Contractors of America (LICA)

3080 Ogden Ave., Ste.No. 300
Lisle, IL 60532
Ph: (630)548-1984
Fax: (630)548-9189
E-mail: nlica@aol.com
URL: http://www.licanational.com
Contact: Eileen Levy, Natl. Office Mgr.

Founded: 1951. **Members:** 2,500. **Staff:** 2. **Regional Groups:** 8. **State Groups:** 28. **Description:** Federation of 28 state chapters of land improvement, excavation, and conservation contractors. Seeks to: protect the soil and foster efficient business principles on the basis of private and free enterprise in the field of soil saving and soil building; promote clean water. Conducts educational and research programs. **Awards: Type:** recognition ● **Type:** scholarship. **Computer Services:** database, government relations. **Committees:** By-Laws; Convention; Education; Legislative; On-Site Waste Management; Public Relations; Technology; Water Table Management. **Publications:** *Applications Handbook* ● *LICA Membership Directory and Buyer's Guide*, annual. Lists national contractors and associate members. **Circulation:** 3,000. **Advertising:** accepted ● *Official Handbook* ● Newsletter, monthly. Contains Washington Report, employment listing, and information on professionalism, projects, business, insurance, history, and equipment. **Circulation:** 3,000. **Advertising:** accepted. Alternate Formats: online ● Brochures. **Conventions/Meetings:** annual meeting (exhibits).

4416 ■ Land Trust Alliance (LTA)

1660 L St. NW, Ste.1100
Washington, DC 20036
Ph: (202)638-4725
Fax: (202)638-4730
E-mail: lta@lta.org
URL: http://www.lta.org
Contact: Peter Hausmann, Chm.

Founded: 1982. **Members:** 1,000. **Membership Dues:** steward, $1,000 (annual) ● trustee, $750 (annual) ● conservator, $500 (annual) ● caretaker, $250 (annual) ● protector, $100 (annual) ● partner, $35 (annual) ● land trust (based on previous year's operating expenses), $225-$2,500 (annual) ● nonprofit, government, professional partner (based on benefits), $250-$1,000 (annual). **Staff:** 45. **Budget:** $6,800,000. **Regional Groups:** 6. **Description:** Local, regional, and national land conservation organizations, organized as land trusts; interested individuals. Promotes voluntary land conservation and strengthens the land trust movement by providing the leadership, information, skills, and resources land trusts need to conserve land for the benefit of communities and natural systems. Works to advance the land trust movement; makes available resources and training services to land trusts. Fosters supportive public policies and seeks to increase public awareness of land trusts and their goals. Compiles statistics. Promotes voluntary land conservation and strengthens the land trust movement by providing the leadership, information, skills and resources that land trusts need to conserve land for the benefit of communities and natural systems. **Libraries: Type:** not open to the public. **Holdings:** books, periodicals. **Subjects:** conservation easements. **Computer Services:** database, directory of members ● mailing lists. **Formerly:** (1990) Land Trust Exchange. **Publications:** *Appraising Easements: Guidelines for the Valuation of Historic Preservation and Land Conservation Easements.* Contains a digest of revenue procedures and revenue rulings. **Price:** $26.00 for organizational members and partners; $32.00 for nonmembers ● *The Conservation Easement Handbook: Managing Land Conservation and Historic Preservation Easement Programs.* **Price:** $39.95 for members; $49.95 for nonmembers. Alternate Formats: CD-ROM ● *Conservation Easement Stewardship Guide: Designing, Monitoring, and Enforcing Easements.* Handbook. Covers baseline documentation, stewardship funds and easement enforcement. **Price:** $20.00 for organizational members and partners; $25.00 for nonmembers ● *Conservation Options: A Landowner's Guide.* Contains information on how to conserve open spaces. **Price:** $7.00 for organizational members and partners; $8.50 for nonmembers (1-49 copies); $6.50 for nonmembers (50 or more copies) ● *Conservation Options for Private Landowners.* Brochure. Covers various types of land donations and bargain sales. **Price:** $10.00 for members; $14.00 regular (bundle of 150); $45.00 for nonmembers; $55.00 regular ● *Doing Deals: A Guide to Buying Land for Conservation.* Book. Includes information on working with landowners. **Price:** $32.00 for nonmembers; $25.00 for organizational members and partners ● *Exchange*, quarterly. Journal. **Price:** $16.00/year (additional subscription). ISSN: 0885-4106. **Circulation:** 1,800. Alternate Formats: online. Also Cited As: *Land Trust Exchange* ● *Federal Tax Law of Conservation Easements.* Covers historic preservation easements. **Price:** $95.00 for nonmembers; $69.00 for members ● *For the Common Good-Preserving Private Lands with Conservation Easements.* Video. Features three case studies to explain the workings and public benefits of conservation easement. **Price:** $19.50 for members; $25.00 for nonmembers ● *How Strong Are Our Defenses: The Results of the Land Trust Alliance's Northern New England Conservation Easement Quality Research Project.* Book. Features an assessment of the stewardship practices of large, staffed land trust in New Hampshire, Maine and Vermont. **Price:** $15.00 for nonmembers; $12.00 for members ● *InfoPaks.* Includes collection of information on frequently requested topics. **Price:** $20.00 for nonmembers; $15.00 for members ● *Land Trusts in America: Guardians of the Future.* Video. **Price:** $14.50 for members; $21.00 for nonmembers ●

Model Conservation Easement and Historic Preservation Easement. Handbook. **Price:** $20.00 for nonmembers; $16.00 for members ● *National Directory of Conservation Land Trusts*, biennial. Also Cited As: *Directory of Local and Regional Land Conservation Organizations* ● *National Land Conservation Conference-Rally 2005: Conservation in the Heartland.* Brochure. Alternate Formats: online ● *Preserving Family Lands*, biennial. Directory. **Price:** $9.00. Also Cited As: *Directory of Local and Regional Land Conservation Organizations* ● *Preserving Family Lands: Book II.* Features examples of basic estate and gift tax rules. **Price:** $18.00 for members; $23.00 for nonmembers ● *Protecting Your Land with a Conservation Easement.* Brochure. Contains an explanation on how easements work. **Price:** $14.00 regular (pack of 25); $10.00 for members; $45.00 for nonmembers; $55.00 regular (pack of 150) ● *Second Supplement to the Federal Tax Law Conservation Easements.* Book. **Price:** $11.00 for nonmembers; $8.00 for members ● *Standards and Practices Guidebook: An Operating Manual for Land Trusts.* Handbook. Contains information on every aspect of land trusts operations. **Price:** $65.00 for nonmembers; $45.00 for members ● *Starting a Land Trust: A Guide to Forming a Land Conservation Organization.* Handbook. **Price:** $45.00 for nonmembers; $35.00 for members ● *Statement of Land Trusts Standards and Practices.* Booklet. **Price:** free first copy; $2.00 for nonmembers; more than one copy; $1.00 for members; more than one copy ● *Third Supplement to the Federal Tax Law of Conservation Easements.* Book. Contains an interpretation of the Tax Court cases. **Price:** $20.00 for members; $26.00 for nonmembers ● *Your Land is Your Legacy, A Guide to Planning for the Future of Your Farm.* Booklet. Includes newest tax laws. **Price:** $11.95 for members; $13.95 for nonmembers. **Conventions/Meetings:** annual National Land Conservation Conference-Rally - conference and rally, a gathering of land conservation leaders (exhibits).

4417 ■ League to Save Lake Tahoe (LTSLT)
955 Emerald Bay Rd.
South Lake Tahoe, CA 96150
Ph: (530)541-5388
Fax: (530)541-5454
E-mail: info@keeptahoeblue.org
URL: http://www.keeptahoeblue.org
Contact: Rochelle Nason, Exec. Dir.

Founded: 1957. **Members:** 5,000. **Membership Dues:** Rubicon, $5,000 (annual) ● Emerald Bay, $10,000 (annual) ● sustaining, $50 (annual) ● family, $75 (annual) ● Tahoe, $100 (annual) ● Echo, $250 (annual) ● Tallac, $500 (annual) ● Crystal Bay, $1,000 (annual) ● Mt. Rose, $2,500 (annual). **Staff:** 10. **Budget:** $700,000. **Regional Groups:** 1. **Local Groups:** 1. **Description:** Seeks to preserve the environmental balance, scenic beauty and recreational opportunities of the Tahoe Basin. **Awards:** Friends of the Lake Awards. **Frequency:** annual. **Type:** recognition. **Recipient:** for significant contributions and efforts to protect Lake Tahoe ● Star Volunteer Awards. **Frequency:** annual. **Type:** recognition. **Projects:** Cattle Grazing in Meiss Meadows; Forest; Jet Skis; Lake Tahoe Airport; Martis Valley; Scenic Ordinances. **Formerly:** (1957) Tahoe Improvement and Conservation Association. **Publications:** *Keep Tahoe Blue*, quarterly. Newsletter. **Price:** included in membership dues. Alternate Formats: online ● Annual Report, annual. Alternate Formats: online. **Conventions/Meetings:** annual meeting and dinner - usually 4th Saturday in August, Lake Tahoe, CA.

4418 ■ LightHawk (LH)
PO Box 653
Lander, WY 82520
Ph: (307)332-3242
Fax: (307)332-1641
E-mail: info@lighthawk.org
URL: http://www.lighthawk.org
Contact: C. Rudy Engholm, Exec. Dir.

Founded: 1979. **Members:** 600. **Membership Dues:** individual, $35 (annual) ● co-pilot, $50 (annual) ● aviator, $100 (annual) ● protector, $500 (annual) ● senior/volunteer/student, $20 (annual) ● founder, $250 (annual). **Staff:** 11. **Budget:** $1,412,941. **Regional Groups:** 4. **Description:** Champions environmental protection utilizing the unique perspective of flight. Supports key partner organizations through the provision of flights over areas of environmental concern in the US, Canada, and Meso-America. By flying activists, industry and media representatives, decision makers, park officials, and local citizens over threatened and protected areas alike, it gives passengers both intellectual and visceral understanding of what is at stake. More than 160 volunteer pilots throughout the program regions donate their time, expertise and the use of their aircraft. Addresses critical issues in forests, including: related watersheds, deserts, shrublands, and grasslands, ocean and coastal issues, and rivers and other inland waterways. Examines how practices like industrial-scale timber cutting, off-road vehicle use and road-building, mineral exploration and extraction, and urban sprawl affect the various biomes. **Formerly:** (1989) Project Lighthawk. **Publications:** *Lighthawk Newsletter*, quarterly. Contains information on programs and various flights. **Price:** included in membership dues. Alternate Formats: online ● Annual Report, annual. Alternate Formats: online.

4419 ■ Marine Fish Conservation Network
600 Pennsylvania Ave. SE, Ste.210
Washington, DC 20003
Ph: (202)543-5509
Free: (866)823-8552
Fax: (202)543-5774
E-mail: network@conservefish.org
URL: http://www.conservefish.org
Contact: Bruce Stedman, Exec. Dir.

Members: 190. **Staff:** 12. **Description:** Works to promote the long-term sustainability of marine fish populations. Protects, restores and conserves marine fish. Educates policymakers, the fishing industry and the public about the need for sound conservation and better management practices. **Computer Services:** Information services, fish issues and resources ● mailing lists. **Publications:** *Network News*, quarterly. Newsletter. Contains information on fisheries management and conservation issues. Alternate Formats: online ● Reports. Alternate Formats: online ● Brochure.

4420 ■ National Association of Conservation Districts (NACD)
c/o Krysta Harden, CEO
509 Capitol Ct. NE
Washington, DC 20002-4937
Ph: (202)547-6223
Fax: (202)547-6450
E-mail: krysta-harden@nacdnet.org
URL: http://www.nacdnet.org
Contact: Krysta Harden, CEO

Founded: 1947. **Members:** 3,000. **Membership Dues:** supporter, $35 (annual) ● advocate, $60 (annual) ● partner, $100 (annual). **Staff:** 45. **Budget:** $4,100,000. **Regional Groups:** 7. **State Groups:** 54. **Description:** Soil and water conservation districts organized by the citizens of watersheds, counties, or communities under provisions of state laws. Directs and coordinates, through local self-government efforts, the conservation and development of soil, water, and related natural resources. Includes districts over 90&percent; of the nation's privately owned land. Conducts educational programs and children's services. **Libraries: Type:** reference. **Holdings:** 1,500. **Awards:** Conservation Education Award. **Frequency:** annual. **Type:** recognition. **Recipient:** for districts and teachers ● Excellent in Communications Award. **Frequency:** annual. **Type:** recognition. **Recipient:** for outstanding communications effort ● NACD Distinguished Service Award. **Frequency:** annual. **Type:** recognition. **Recipient:** for individual with significant contributions to the conservation and proper management of natural resources ● NACD Friend of Conservation Awards. **Frequency:** annual. **Type:** recognition. **Recipient:** for individual, business and agency with outstanding contributions to the conservation and proper management of natural resources ● NACD President's Award. **Frequency:** annual. **Type:** recognition. **Recipient:** for individual or organization that has been helpful to the conservation during the president's term ● Partnership Diversity Award. **Frequency:** annual. **Type:** recognition. **Recipient:** for conservation district, RC&D councils and state conservation agencies that are addressing diversity needs. **Computer Services:** Mailing lists. **Committees:** Agriculture Resource Conservation; Business Alliance; District Operations; Environmental Policy; Forestry; Grazing Lands and Public Lands; Great Plains; Information and Education; Legislative; Urban, Community, and Coastal Resources; Water Resources. **Formerly:** National Association of Soil Conservation Districts; (1970) National Association of Soil and Water Conservation Districts. **Publications:** *Buffer Notes*, monthly. Newsletter. Alternate Formats: online ● *News & Views*, bimonthly. Newsletter. **Price:** included in membership dues ● *Proceedings of Annual Convention* ● Directory, annual ● Catalogs ● Videos ● Annual Report, annual ● Reports. Alternate Formats: online ● Also offers films and slide sets. **Conventions/Meetings:** competition ● annual convention (exhibits) ● annual meeting.

4421 ■ National Association of Resource Conservation and Development Councils (NARC&DC)
444 N Capitol St. NW, Ste.345
Washington, DC 20001
Ph: (202)434-4780 (202)434-4779
Fax: (202)434-4783
E-mail: dhunter@sso.org
URL: http://www.rcdnet.org
Contact: Sharon Ruggi, Pres.

Founded: 1988. **Regional Groups:** 5. **Description:** Assists local councils to identify, address and solve challenges to sustain and improve the quality of life in communities. Develops and implements solutions to widespread problems. Creates opportunities that will help sustain rural communities, local economies and natural resources. **Publications:** *The National Catalyst.* Newsletter. Alternate Formats: online.

4422 ■ National Audubon Society (NAS)
700 Broadway
New York, NY 10003
Ph: (212)979-3000
Fax: (212)979-3188
E-mail: boardservice@audubon.org
URL: http://www.audubon.org
Contact: Elizabeth Horsburgh, Contact

Founded: 1905. **Members:** 600,000. **Membership Dues:** individual in U.S., $20 (annual) ● individual in Canada, $45 (annual) ● individual outside U.S. and Canada, $50 (annual). **Staff:** 300. **Budget:** $44,000,000. **Regional Groups:** 9. **State Groups:** 40. **Local Groups:** 520. **Description:** Works to conserve and restore natural ecosystems, focusing on birds and other wildlife for the benefit of humanity and the earth's biological diversity. **Awards:** Audubon Medal. **Frequency:** annual. **Type:** medal. **Recipient:** for distinguished service to conservation ● Palladium Medal. **Frequency:** annual. **Type:** medal. **Recipient:** for best conservation efforts made by an engineer. **Computer Services:** Online services, CompuServe Forum. **Telecommunication Services:** electronic mail, wmones@audubon.org ● hotline, legislative issues, (202)547-9017. **Divisions:** Education and Communication; Field Offices; Operations; Public Policy; Science; Television. **Publications:** *Audubon*, bimonthly. Magazine. Features articles on wildlife topics. **Price:** included in membership dues; $20.00 /year for nonmembers. ISSN: 0097-7136. **Advertising:** accepted ● *Audubon Activist*, bimonthly. Magazine ● *Audubon Adventures*, bimonthly. Newspaper. For children. ● *Field Notes*, bimonthly. Journal.

4423 ■ National Coalition for Marine Conservation (NCMC)
4 Royal St. SE
Leesburg, VA 20175
Ph: (703)777-0037
Fax: (703)777-1107

E-mail: christine@savethefish.org
URL: http://www.savethefish.org
Contact: Ken Hinman, Pres.
Founded: 1973. **Membership Dues:** regular, $30-$100 (annual) ● student, $15 (annual) ● sponsor, $250 (annual) ● patron, $500 (annual) ● steward, $1,000 (annual) ● benefactor, $1,500 (annual) ● fellow, $2,500 (annual). **Staff:** 4. **Description:** Works for the conservation of ocean fish and their environment. Promotes awareness of the threats to marine fisheries. Strives to convince policy-makers to restore and protect publicly-owned fishery resources. **Publications:** *Marine Bulletin*, quarterly. Newsletter. Contains news and information regarding the association's projects. **Price:** included in membership dues.

4424 ■ National Forest Foundation (NFF)
Bldg. 27, Ste.3
Ft. Missoula Rd.
Missoula, MT 59804
Ph: (406)542-2805
Fax: (406)542-2810
E-mail: info@natlforests.org
URL: http://www.natlforests.org
Contact: William J. Possiel, Pres.
Founded: 1990. **Members:** 5,000. **Membership Dues:** small business associate, $250-$999 (annual) ● corporate, $1,000-$10,000 (annual). **Staff:** 12. **Description:** Chartered by Congress, engages America in community-based and national programs that promote the health and public enjoyment of the 192 million acre National Forest System, and administers private gifts of funds and land for the benefit of the National Forests. **Awards:** Community Assistance Program. **Frequency:** quarterly. **Type:** grant. **Recipient:** to newly forming organizations ● Matching Awards Program. **Frequency:** semiannual. **Type:** recognition. **Recipient:** to nonprofits. **Councils:** National Leadership. **Publications:** *Mosaic*, semiannual. Newsletter. Contains news of Foundation accomplishments, US Forest Service activities, upcoming events, and current issues involving the nation's forests. **Price:** free. Alternate Formats: online ● *Treemail*, monthly. Newsletter. Alternate Formats: online ● Annual Report, annual. Alternate Formats: online. **Conventions/Meetings:** triennial board meeting.

4425 ■ National Mitigation Banking Association (NMBA)
PO Box 547881
Orlando, FL 32854-7881
Free: (888)272-6622
E-mail: info@mitigationbanking.org
URL: http://www.mitigationbanking.org
Contact: Don Ewoldt, Pres.
Founded: 1998. **Membership Dues:** mitigation banker, $5,000 (annual) ● affiliate, $2,500 (annual) ● associate, $1,000 (annual). **Description:** Works to restore and conserve America's wetlands and other natural resources. Promotes federal legislation and regulatory policy that encourages mitigation banking and conservation banking as means of compensating for adverse impacts to the environment. Provides research, education, and outreach programs. **Publications:** *NMBA News*, quarterly. Newsletter. Contains news and updates on the organization and its activities. **Price:** free. Alternate Formats: online.

4426 ■ National Wildlife Federation (NWF)
11100 Wildlife Center Dr.
Reston, VA 20190-5362
Free: (800)822-9919
E-mail: info@nwf.org
URL: http://www.nwf.org
Contact: Larry J. Schweiger, Pres./CEO
Founded: 1936. **Members:** 4,400,000. **Membership Dues:** wild animal baby, $19 (annual) ● adult, Your Big Backyard, $15 (annual) ● Ranger Rick, $17 (annual). **Staff:** 400. **Budget:** $96,000,000. **Description:** Serves as a member-supported conservation group, with over four million members and supporters. Federation of state and territorial affiliates, associate members and individual conservationist-contributors. Seeks to educate, inspire and assist individuals and organizations of diverse cultures to conserve wildlife and other natural resources and to protect the earth's environment in order to achieve a peaceful, equitable and sustainable future. Encourages the intelligent management of the life-sustaining resources of the earth and promotes greater appreciation of wild places, wildlife and the natural resources shared by all. Publishes educational materials and conservation periodicals. **Libraries: Type:** reference. **Holdings:** 6,000; books, periodicals. **Subjects:** natural history, conservation, endangered species, water quality. **Awards:** Conservation Hall of Fame. **Frequency:** annual. **Type:** recognition. **Recipient:** for outstanding and lasting contributions to wildlife preservation ● National Conservation Achievement Awards. **Frequency:** annual. **Type:** recognition. **Recipient:** for outstanding contributions to natural resources conservation and environmental protection. **Departments:** Communications; Conservation Programs; Constituent Programs; Customer Services; Education; Internet and Cause Marketing; National Wildlife Productions. **Publications:** *Conservation Directory*, annual ● *EnviroAction*, monthly. Report. Keeps members and grassroots activists informed about pending legislation and other critical environmental issues. ● *International Wildlife*, bimonthly. Magazine. Contains feature articles on natural history and wildlife topics; also covers trends, issues, and news of conservation. **Price:** $16.00. ISSN: 0020-9112 ● *National Wildlife*, bimonthly. Magazine. Covers conservation issues, wildlife features and award-winning photos. **Price:** included in membership dues. ISSN: 0028-0402 ● *Ranger Rick's Nature*, monthly. Magazine. Features information for young children. ● *Wild Animal Baby*, 10/year. Magazine. Features information for babies and toddlers. ● *Your Big Backyard*, monthly. Magazine. Features information for pre-schoolers. ● Also publishes press releases and conservation materials, action alerts and newsletters, special reports on conservation topics. **Conventions/Meetings:** annual meeting (exhibits).

4427 ■ Native Forest Council (NFC)
PO Box 2190
Eugene, OR 97402
Ph: (541)688-2600
Fax: (541)461-2156
E-mail: info@forestcouncil.org
URL: http://www.forestcouncil.org
Contact: Timothy G. Hermach, Pres./Founder
Founded: 1988. **Members:** 3,500. **Membership Dues:** individual, $35 (annual) ● supporter, $50 ● contributor, $100 ● sponsor, $250 ● sustaining, $500 ● benefactor, $1,000 ● international, $60. **Staff:** 5. **Budget:** $300,000. **Description:** Business and professional people concerned about the destruction of the national forests. Seeks to provide leadership and ensure the integrity of native forest ecosystems; proposes an immediate stop on the cutting of old growth trees on public lands, cessation in clear cutting and road construction, and a halt to the export of unrefined and barely processed logs. Serves as a clearinghouse for articles, studies, and tapes. Maintains speakers' bureau; compiles statistics; conducts research and educational programs. **Convention/Meeting:** none. **Libraries: Type:** reference. **Holdings:** audio recordings, books, clippings, periodicals, video recordings. **Telecommunication Services:** electronic mail, tim@forestcouncil.org. **Publications:** *Forest Voice*, quarterly. Newspaper. **Price:** $35.00/year; free for members. ISSN: 1069-2002. **Circulation:** 15,000 ● *Stop the Chainsaw Massacre*. Booklet.

4428 ■ Native Forest Network (NFN)
PO Box 8251
Missoula, MT 59807
Ph: (406)542-7343
Fax: (406)542-7347
E-mail: nfn@wildrockies.org
URL: http://www.nativeforest.org
Contact: Matthew Koehler, Exec. Dir.
Founded: 1992. **Members:** 1,500. **Membership Dues:** subscriber, $20 (annual) ● living lightly, $15 (annual) ● individual, $25 (annual) ● donor, $50 (annual) ● sustainer, $100 (annual) ● life, $500. **Budget:** $150,000. **Regional Groups:** 21. **Local Groups:** 200. **Languages:** English, Spanish. **Description:** Works to protect and preserve forests. Confronts multinational corporations responsible for deforestation. Conducts educational programs. **Projects:** Public Lands. **Publications:** *Forest Advocate*. Newspaper. Contains information on the national campaign to protect and restore America's National Forests. Alternate Formats: online ● *Native Forest News*, quarterly. Newsletter ● *NFN Action Alerts*, bimonthly. Article. **Conventions/Meetings:** annual South American Forest Conference (exhibits).

4429 ■ Native Seeds/SEARCH (NS/S)
526 N 4th Ave.
Tucson, AZ 85705-8450
Ph: (520)622-5561
Free: (866)622-5561
Fax: (520)622-5591
E-mail: info@nativeseeds.org
URL: http://www.nativeseeds.org
Contact: Ms. Carolyn Owens, Grants and Development Assoc.
Founded: 1983. **Members:** 5,300. **Membership Dues:** squash, $25 (annual) ● gourd, $45 (annual) ● bean, $100 (annual) ● chili, $250 (annual) ● corn, $500 (annual) ● Sunflower Guild, $1,000 (annual) ● Native American (outside Greater Southwest area), $20 (annual). **Staff:** 18. **Description:** Works to conserve southwestern traditional crop seeds and related wild seeds. Coordinates networking and distribution of seeds; offers members discounts on seeds. Provides speakers; maintains demonstration and research garden. **Programs:** Arizona RegisTREE; Native American Outreach. **Projects:** Conservation Farm; Culture Memory Bank; Desert Foods for Diabetes; Seed Bank. **Also Known As:** Native Seeds/Southwestern Endangered Arid-Land Resource Clearing House. **Formerly:** (1983) Southwest Traditional Crop Conservancy Garden and Seed Bank. **Publications:** *Seed Listing*, annual. Directory. Contains annual listings of seeds, crafts, books on desert gardening, ethnobotany, cookbooks and more. **Circulation:** 25,000 ● *Seedhead News*, quarterly. Newsletter. **Price:** included in membership dues. **Conventions/Meetings:** workshop.

4430 ■ Natural Areas Association (NAA)
PO Box 1504
Bend, OR 97709
Ph: (541)317-0199
Fax: (541)317-0140
E-mail: mail@naturalarea.org
URL: http://www.naturalarea.org
Contact: Karen Smith, Sec.
Founded: 1980. **Members:** 2,200. **Membership Dues:** individual, $40 (annual) ● library, $100 (annual) ● agency/institution (non profit/agency), $150 (annual) ● corporate, $250 (annual) ● student, $20 (annual) ● retired, $25 (annual) ● life (individual), $500. **Staff:** 1. **Description:** Individuals promoting the preservation and effective management of natural areas and other elements of natural diversity. Aims to: provide a channel for the exchange of information on natural area preservation and management; promote preservation techniques consistent with sound biological and ecological principles to benefit society; increase public awareness of natural areas; support research. Formulates and adopts statements of policy. **Libraries: Type:** not open to the public. **Awards:** George Fell Award. **Frequency:** annual. **Type:** recognition. **Recipient:** for outstanding contribution to natural areas of identification, protection or management. **Committees:** Awards and Recognition; Communications; Education and Outreach; Future Conferences; Management and Technology Development; Marketing and Development; Program Assistance; Steering. **Publications:** *Natural Area News*, periodic. Newsletter. **Price:** included in membership dues; $20.00 for members, plus shipping and handling; $30.00 for nonmembers, plus shipping and handling. Alternate Formats: online ● *Natural Areas Journal*, quarterly. Covers landscape ecology, conservation biology, natural area management techniques, applied research, conservation forum, and stewardship issues. **Price:** included in

membership dues. ISSN: 0885-8608. **Circulation:** 2,200. Alternate Formats: online ● *Old-Growth Forest Compendium.* Book. **Conventions/Meetings:** annual conference (exhibits) ● annual workshop.

4431 ■ Natural Resources Council of America (NRCA)
1616 P St. NW, Ste.340
Washington, DC 20036
Ph: (202)232-6531
Fax: (240)465-0467
E-mail: bboteler@naturalresourcescouncil.org
URL: http://www.naturalresourcescouncil.org
Contact: Kathleen Rogers, Chair
Founded: 1946. **Members:** 75. **Membership Dues:** supporter, $100 (annual). **Staff:** 3. **Budget:** $160,000. **Description:** Federation of national and regional conservation organizations and scientific societies dedicated to the professional conservation, protection, and responsible management of the world's natural resources. Encourages communication and cooperation among member organizations and promotes the adoption of public policies that further natural resource conservation. Gathers and disseminates information on conservation issues to its constituent members and policy makers. Conducts studies and surveys. Sponsors occasional commemorative events. **Awards:** Award of Achievement. **Frequency:** annual. **Type:** recognition. **Recipient:** to member, organization and people that improve the state of natural resources ● Award of Honor. **Frequency:** annual. **Type:** recognition. **Recipient:** to individuals with lifetime dedication on service for conservation ● Leadership Award. **Frequency:** annual. **Type:** recognition. **Recipient:** for individuals, organizations or coalition that served in conservation community ● National Environment Quality Award. **Frequency:** annual. **Type:** recognition. **Recipient:** to individuals who have demonstrated a special long-term commitment for the National Environmental Policy Act ● Public Service Award. **Frequency:** annual. **Type:** recognition. **Recipient:** to individuals who have been exemplary champions of the nation's natural resources. **Programs:** Leadership Training; Networking; Services. **Publications:** *Conservation Voice*, bimonthly. Newsletter. Contains news and events on conservation movement. **Price:** included in membership dues ● *National Leaders of American Conservation* ● *NEPA News*, quarterly. Newsletter. Contains issues related to the National Environment Policy Act. **Price:** included in membership dues; $20.00 for nonmembers (e-mail); $25.00 for nonmembers (print) ● *NRCA News*, bimonthly. Newsletter ● Books. **Conventions/Meetings:** meeting - 3/year.

4432 ■ Natural Resources Defense Council (NRDC)
40 W 20th St.
New York, NY 10011
Ph: (212)727-2700
Fax: (212)727-1773
E-mail: nrdcinfo@nrdc.org
URL: http://www.nrdc.org
Contact: Frances G. Beinecke, Pres.
Founded: 1970. **Members:** 550,000. **Membership Dues:** general, $10. **Staff:** 215. **Budget:** $45,855,801. **Description:** Uses law, science, and support of more than 550,000 members nationwide to protect the planet's wildlife and wild places and to ensure a safe and healthy environment for all living things. **Awards:** John B. Oakes Award for Distinguished Environmental Journalism. **Frequency:** annual. **Type:** recognition. **Additional Websites:** http://www.savebiogems.org. **Projects:** Air/Energy; Health; International; Land; Nuclear; Urban; Water and Oceans. **Publications:** *Nature's Voice*, bimonthly. Journal ● *OnEarth*, quarterly. Magazine ● Also publishes pamphlets, brochures, books, and reports on the atmosphere, energy, costal waters, nuclear weapons, and preservation of the earth. **Conventions/Meetings:** annual board meeting.

4433 ■ Nature Conservancy (TNC)
4245 Fairfax Dr., Ste.100
Arlington, VA 22203-1606
Ph: (703)841-5300
Free: (800)628-6860
Fax: (703)841-1283
E-mail: comment@tnc.org
URL: http://www.nature.org
Contact: Steven J. McCormick, Pres./CEO
Founded: 1951. **Members:** 1,000,000. **Membership Dues:** individual/couple, $50 (annual). **Staff:** 2,600. **Budget:** $245,000,000. **Regional Groups:** 12. **State Groups:** 50. **Multinational. Description:** Strives to preserve biological diversity through land and water protection of natural areas. Identifies ecologically significant lands and protects them through gift, purchase, or cooperative management agreements with government or private agencies, voluntary arrangements with private landowners, and cost-saving methods of protection. Provides long-term stewardship for 1340 conservancy-owned preserves and makes most conservancy lands available for nondestructive use on request by educational and scientific organizations. Compiles statistics. **Awards: Type:** recognition. **Formerly:** (1946) Committee on Preservation of Natural Conditions Ecological Society of America; (1950) Ecologists Union. **Publications:** *Landmarks*, quarterly. Magazine ● *Nature Conservancy Magazine*, quarterly. Contains articles on ecosystems and preserving biodiversity and TNC lands. **Price:** available to members only ● Annual Report, annual. **Conventions/Meetings:** annual meeting.

4434 ■ New England Wild Flower Society (NEWFS)
180 Hemenway Rd.
Framingham, MA 01701
Ph: (508)877-7630 (508)877-9553
Fax: (508)877-3658
E-mail: newfs@newfs.org
URL: http://www.newfs.org
Contact: Ms. Gwen Stauffer, Exec. Dir.
Founded: 1900. **Members:** 6,000. **Membership Dues:** individual, $50 (annual) ● family, friend, $70 (annual) ● contributor, $100 (annual) ● supporter, $250 (annual) ● sustainer, $500 (annual) ● patron, $1,000 (annual) ● life, $5,000 ● associate, $40 (annual) ● group, $150 (annual) ● group plus, $225 (annual) ● student, $38 (annual) ● dual, $60 (annual) ● garden club/nonprofit, $48 (annual). **Staff:** 18. **Budget:** $2,000,000. **Description:** Individuals, families, and horticultural and botanical organizations. Promotes conservation of temperate North American flora through horticulture, education, research, habitat preservation, and advocacy. Acts as clearinghouse for plant projects (particularly research, education, and legislation) in New England. Conducts activities such as classes for adults and children; field trips; garden tours. Displays landscaped collection of wildflowers in the Garden in the Woods, a 45-acre botanic garden of native plants. Maintains 7 other sanctuaries. **Libraries: Type:** reference. **Holdings:** 4,500; books, photographs. **Subjects:** flora of native plants, native plant I.D., natural history, native plant garden design. **Awards:** Conservation Award. **Frequency:** annual. **Type:** recognition. **Recipient:** for outstanding achievement in conservation ● Education Award. **Frequency:** annual. **Type:** recognition ● State Award. **Frequency:** annual. **Type:** recognition. **Additional Websites:** http://www.newenglandwildflower.org. **Committees:** Education; Horticulture; Library; Natural Areas; Visual Resources. **Formerly:** (1971) New England Wild Flower Preservation Society. **Publications:** *Botanical Clubs and Native Plant Societies of the U.S.* ● *Conservation Notes*, annual. Magazine ● *Garden in the Woods Cultivation Guide* ● *New England Wild Flower*, semiannual. Magazine. **Price:** included in membership dues; $4.00 for nonmembers ● *Nursery Sources: Native Plants and Wild Flowers* ● *Propagation of Wildflowers* ● *Seed and Book Catalogue*, annual. **Conventions/Meetings:** annual meeting - always fall, Boston, MA.

4435 ■ Ocean Conservancy
2029 K St. NW
Washington, DC 20006
Ph: (202)429-5609
Free: (800)519-1541
Fax: (202)872-0619
E-mail: vspruill@oceanconservancy.org
URL: http://www.oceanconservancy.org
Contact: Vikki N. Spruill, Pres./CEO
Founded: 1972. **Members:** 150,000. **Membership Dues:** basic, $25-$45 ● advocate, $50-$95 ● protector, $100-$225 ● Guardian of the Sea, $250-$750 ● President's Circle, $1,000-$7,500. **Staff:** 60. **Budget:** $110,000. **Regional Groups:** 3. **Description:** Works for the conservation and protection of the marine wildlife and their habitats. Promotes public awareness and education. Advocates correct management of marine resources and promotes conservation of endangered species and their habitats. Seeks to insure that human activities will not lead to the extinction of these species. Includes activities such as beach cleanups resulting in new state programs to reduce marine debris in the Gulf of Mexico and the establishment of a sanctuary for critically endangered humpback whales in the Caribbean. Conducts programs in fisheries, conservation, species recovery, habitat conservation, and pollution prevention. Operates the Marine Debris Information Office. Works to prevent accidental entanglement and drowning of marine animals in debris and fishing gear and has repeatedly thwarted efforts to increase international trade in sea turtle products. **Telecommunication Services:** electronic mail, membership@oceanconservancy.org ● electronic mail, corporate@oceanconservancy.org. **Absorbed:** Sea Turtle Rescue Fund; (1988) Whale Protection Fund; (1988) Marine Mammal Conservation Fund. **Formerly:** (1974) Delta Organization; (1988) Center for Environmental Education; (2002) Center for Marine Conservation. **Publications:** *Blueplanet Quarterly*. Magazine. Alternate Formats: online ● *Coastal Connection*, quarterly. Newsletter ● *Marine Conservation News*, quarterly. Newsletter. Updates members on organizational activities. **Price:** included in membership dues ● *Sanctuary Currents*, quarterly. Article. Updates current issues regarding marine sanctuaries. ● Newsletter. Alternate Formats: online.

4436 ■ Ocean Research and Conservation Association (ORCA)
Duerr Lab. for Marine Conservation
1420 Seaway Dr., 2nd Fl.
Fort Pierce, FL 34949
Ph: (772)467-1600
Fax: (772)467-1602
E-mail: inquiries@oceanrecon.org
URL: http://www.oceanrecon.org
Contact: Keith J. Paglen, CEO/Co-Founder
Founded: 2005. **Description:** Aims to preserve and protect marine ecosystems and the species they sustain through the development of innovative technologies, science-based conservation action, and public education. Addresses environmental issues concerning the trend of oceanic and near-shore marine ecosystem degradation. Conducts research on the structure and function of marine ecosystems.

4437 ■ Oceana
2501 M St. NW, Ste.300
Washington, DC 20037-1311
Ph: (202)833-3900
Free: (877)7-OCEANA
Fax: (202)833-2070
E-mail: info@oceana.org
URL: http://www.oceana.org
Contact: Andrew Sharpless, CEO
Founded: 2001. **Membership Dues:** regular, $20 (annual). **National Groups:** 150. **Multinational. Description:** Dedicated to the restoration and protection of the world's oceans. **Awards:** Partners Award. **Frequency:** annual. **Type:** recognition. **Recipient:** to individuals who have made outstanding contributions through their personal commitment to the cause of protecting the world's oceans ● Ted Danson Ocean Hero Award. **Frequency:** annual. **Type:** recognition. **Recipient:** to individuals who embody Ted's vision as bold and staunch defenders of the world's oceans. **Computer Services:** Mailing lists. **Telecommunication Services:** additional toll-free number, (800)8-OCEAN0. **Programs:** E-Activist. **Projects:** Ocean Law. **Publications:** *Deep Sea Corals: Out of Sight, But No Longer Out of Mind.* Report. Alternate For-

mats: online ● *If We Take Everything Out Of The Oceans.*. Brochure. Alternate Formats: online ● *Oceana protege los oceanos del planeta* (in Spanish). Alternate Formats: online ● *Splash!*, quarterly. Newsletter. **Price:** included in membership dues ● *Wasted Catch and the Destruction of Ocean Life.* Report. Alternate Formats: online ● Newsletter. Contains news and information updates on environmental campaigns and issues concerning the world's oceans. **Price:** free. Alternate Formats: online ● Magazine. Alternate Formats: online ● Reports. Alternate Formats: online.

4438 ■ Ozark Society (OSI)
PO Box 2914
Little Rock, AR 72203
Ph: (501)847-3738 (501)219-4293
Fax: (501)537-6656
E-mail: alice209ok@yahoo.com
URL: http://www.ozarksociety.net
Contact: Alice Barrett Andrews, Pres.
Founded: 1962. **Members:** 1,600. **Membership Dues:** family, $15 (annual) ● contributing, $25 (annual) ● life, $200. **Local Groups:** 8. **Description:** Individuals united for conservation, education, and recreation. Aims to preserve the scenic rivers, unique natural areas, and wilderness areas, particularly in the Ozark-Ouachita mountain region. Sponsors hiking and boating trips, and clean-up campaigns. **Committees:** Conservation. **Publications:** *Pack and Paddle*, periodic. Newsletter. Alternate Formats: online ● Books. Covers outdoor topics in Ozark-Ouachita region. ● Also publishes canoeing guides. **Conventions/Meetings:** semiannual meeting - always spring and fall.

4439 ■ Partners in Parks
PO Box 130
Paonia, CO 81428-0130
Ph: (970)527-6675
E-mail: partpark@mindspring.com
URL: http://www.partnersinparks.org
Contact: Sarah G. Bishop, Chair
Founded: 1988. **Staff:** 2. **Budget:** $100,000. **Description:** Creates educational opportunities in national parks for volunteers and students. Recruits highly skilled individuals to conduct research and preservation projects in these special places. **Publications:** Annual Report.

4440 ■ Pele Defense Fund (PDF)
PO Box 404
Volcano, HI 96785
E-mail: info@peledefensefund.org
URL: http://www.peledefensefund.org
Contact: Ralph Palikapu Dedman, Pres.
Founded: 1985. **Staff:** 3. **Budget:** $35,000. **Nonmembership. Description:** Individuals following traditional Hawaiian religious practices, particularly worship of Pele, the volcano goddess. Seeks to: perpetuate Hawaiian religion and culture through revitalization of beliefs, traditions, and practices regarding nature and the earth; gather and disseminate funds for research grants and an ethnographic research project; disseminate research findings through publications and other media to educate Hawaiian communities and the general public. Lobbies local and federal governments; opposes geothermal development in Hawaii as desecration of the goddess Pele. Conducts public forums. Sponsors religious ceremonies and activities. **Libraries: Type:** reference.

4441 ■ Rainforest Action Network (RAN)
221 Pine St., 5th Fl.
San Francisco, CA 94104
Ph: (415)398-4404
Fax: (415)398-2732
E-mail: answers@ran.org
URL: http://www.ran.org
Contact: Michael Brune, Exec. Dir.
Founded: 1985. **Members:** 35,000. **Membership Dues:** regular, $35 (annual). **Staff:** 36. **Budget:** $2,100,000. **Regional Groups:** 150. **Description:** Seeks to protect the earth's rainforests and the rights of their inhabitants through education, grassroots organizing, and direct action. Current campaigns include the Old Growth Forest Campaign and the Campaign for a Sane Economy. **Libraries: Type:** reference. **Holdings:** 1,000; books. **Subjects:** rainforests, sustainable development, international conservation, globalization. **Awards:** World Rainforest Awards. **Frequency:** annual. **Type:** recognition. **Computer Services:** Mailing lists. **Absorbed:** (1988) People of the Earth. **Publications:** *Action Alert*, bimonthly. Bulletin. Reports on issues requiring immediate public action. Includes addresses of influential individuals and organizations for members. **Price:** included in membership dues. **Circulation:** 27,000. Alternate Formats: online ● *Amazonia: Voices From the Rainforest* (in English, Portuguese, and Spanish). Report. Contains an overview of Amazon rainforest issues. **Price:** $5.00 plus shipping and handling ● *Cut Waste, Not Trees.* Report. Contains information about reducing wood and paper consumption; includes resource information. **Price:** $5.00 plus shipping and handling ● Also publishes fact sheets and distributes teacher's packet and booklet. **Conventions/Meetings:** annual Rainforest Action Group Chautauqua - conference - always August.

4442 ■ Rainforest Alliance (RA)
665 Broadway, Ste.500
New York, NY 10012
Ph: (212)677-1900
Free: (888)MY-EARTH
Fax: (212)677-2187
E-mail: info@ra.org
URL: http://www.rainforest-alliance.org
Contact: Tensie Whelan, Exec. Dir.
Founded: 1987. **Members:** 19,000. **Membership Dues:** general (minimum), $25 (annual) ● general (maximum), $1,000 (annual). **Staff:** 70. **Budget:** $8,880,000. **Languages:** English, Spanish. **Description:** Works for the conservation of tropical forests for the benefit of the global community. Develops and promotes economically viable and socially desirable alternatives to the destruction of tropical forests, an endangered, biologically diverse natural resource. Educates and researches the social and natural sciences; develops cooperative partnerships with businesses, governments and local peoples. **Awards:** Catalyst Grants. **Frequency:** periodic. **Type:** grant. **Recipient:** for local initiatives in tropical forest conservation ● Kleinhans Fellowships. **Frequency:** biennial. **Type:** fellowship. **Recipient:** for graduate research, particularly in tropical agriculture. **Programs:** Conservation Agriculture Program/ECO-O.K.; Conservation Media Center; Smartwood. **Formerly:** (1988) New York Rainforest Alliance. **Publications:** *The Canopy*, quarterly. Newsletter. Covers RA special events and breaking news. **Price:** included in membership dues. Alternate Formats: online ● *Eco-Education Matters*, monthly. Newsletter. Includes topics on conservation. Alternate Formats: online ● *Eco-Exchange* (in English and Spanish), bimonthly. Bulletin. Covers breaking environmental news in the tropics. Alternate Formats: online ● *Rainforest Matters*, monthly. Newsletter. Includes articles on conservation, program developments, poetry, interviews and species profile. Alternate Formats: online ● Annual Report, annual. Alternate Formats: online. **Conventions/Meetings:** conference.

4443 ■ Renewable Natural Resources Foundation (RNRF)
5430 Grosvenor Ln.
Bethesda, MD 20814-2142
Ph: (301)493-9101
Fax: (301)493-6148
E-mail: info@rnrf.org
URL: http://www.rnrf.org
Contact: Robert D. Day, Exec. Dir.
Founded: 1972. **Members:** 16. **Membership Dues:** individual associate, $50-$99 (annual) ● sustaining associate, $100-$499 (annual) ● sponsor associate, $500-$999 (annual) ● patron, $1,000 (annual) ● institutional, $300 (annual). **Staff:** 5. **Budget:** $1,000,000. **Description:** Members are American Fisheries Society, American Geophysical Union, American Meteorological Society, American Society of Agronomy, American Society of Civil Engineers, Society of Landscape Architects, American Society for Photogrammetry and Remote Sensing, American Water Resources Association, Association of American Geographers, Humane Society of the United States, Society for Range Management, Society of Wood Science and Technology, Society of Environmental Toxicology and Chemistry, Soil and Water Conservation Society, Universities Council on Water Resources, and Wildlife Society. Concerned with renewable natural resources subjects and public policy alternatives. Develops 35-acre, forested Renewable Natural Resources Center, an office-park complex for natural resources and other nonprofit organizations. **Libraries: Type:** reference. **Awards:** Excellence in Journalism. **Frequency:** annual. **Type:** recognition. **Recipient:** for promotion of scientific-based, accurate reporting ● Outstanding Achievement Award. **Frequency:** annual. **Type:** recognition. **Recipient:** for program, legislation, publication or other concrete accomplishment ● Sustained Achievement Award. **Frequency:** annual. **Type:** recognition. **Recipient:** to an individual with long-term commitment to natural resource sciences. **Programs:** International Activities; Legislative/Public Policy Briefings; National Congress. **Publications:** *Renewable Resources Journal*, quarterly. Contains information on renewable natural resources and public policy. **Price:** $25.00 /year for individuals in U.S.; $44.00 /year for institutions in U.S.; $30.00 /year for individuals outside U.S.; $50.00 /year for institutions outside U.S. ISSN: 0738-6532. **Circulation:** 2,000. **Conventions/Meetings:** annual Congress on Emerging Contaminants, new topic selected each year; attendance by invitation ● annual meeting.

4444 ■ Republicans for Environmental Protection (REP)
3200 Carlisle Blvd., Ste.114
Albuquerque, NM 87110
Ph: (505)889-4544
E-mail: info@repamerica.org
URL: http://www.repamerica.org
Contact: Ruth Fish, Exec. Asst.
Founded: 1995. **Membership Dues:** individual, family, $40 (annual) ● contributing, $75-$250 (annual) ● full-time student, low-income, $25 (annual). **Description:** Aims to restore natural resource conservation and sound environmental protection as fundamental elements of the Republican Party's vision for America. Educates the public and elected officials about the need to protect the environment and conserve the wildlands and natural resources. Advocates legislation to accomplish those goals while adhering to the basic Republican principles of fiscal responsibility and smaller government. **Awards:** Environmental Legislator of the Year. **Frequency:** annual. **Type:** recognition. **Recipient:** for legislators who have made contributions/laws for environment protection ● Founder's Award. **Frequency:** annual. **Type:** recognition. **Recipient:** to recognize founding members on their contributions ● Green Elephant Award for Citizen Achievement. **Frequency:** annual. **Type:** recognition. **Recipient:** for citizens who have contributed to environmmental protection ● Pelican Island Award for Habitat Conservation. **Frequency:** annual. **Type:** recognition. **Recipient:** for habitat conservation. **Publications:** *Green Elephant*, QRT. Newsletter. **Price:** $25.00 for nonmembers (minimum donation); included in membership dues.

4445 ■ River Management Society (RMS)
PO Box 9048
Missoula, MT 59807-9048
Ph: (406)549-0514
Fax: (406)542-6208
E-mail: rms@river-management.org
URL: http://www.river-management.org
Contact: Caroline Tan, Program Dir.
Founded: 1996. **Members:** 400. **Membership Dues:** student, $20 (annual) ● professional, $40 (annual) ● organizational, $100 (annual) ● life, $350 ● associate, $25 (annual). **Staff:** 1. **Budget:** $40,000. **Description:** Individuals, organizations, and agencies with an interest in the conservation of riverine ecosystems. Seeks to advance the profession of river management. Serves as a clearinghouse on riverine

conservation; conducts continuing professional development courses for river managers; functions as a liaison linking river managers with environmental protection organizations and government agencies. **Awards:** Frank Church Wild and Scenic Rivers Award. **Frequency:** annual. **Type:** recognition. **Recipient:** to an individual who has demonstrated, developed or creatively adapted innovative WSR management techniques ● Outstanding Contribution to River Management Award. **Frequency:** annual. **Type:** recognition. **Recipient:** to an outstanding individual in the field of river management ● Outstanding Contribution to River Management Society Award. **Frequency:** annual. **Type:** recognition. **Recipient:** to a member who has provided an outstanding example of the RMS spirit, mission and goals ● River Manager of the Year Award. **Frequency:** annual. **Type:** recognition. **Recipient:** to a member who has provided leadership in promoting and protecting natural, cultural and recreational resources. **Committees:** Awards and Elections; Fundraising; Public Policy; Symposium. **Publications:** *Better Boater Bathrooms: A Sourcebook for River Managers*. Handbook ● *River Information Digest*, quarterly. Newsletter. Features one of seven regional chapters on a rotating schedule. Reports timely river news. **Price:** included in membership dues. Alternate Formats: online ● Membership Directory, periodic. **Conventions/Meetings:** biennial Collaborating in the Current - symposium ● periodic River Management and Planning - symposium.

4446 ■ River Network (RN)
520 SW 6th Ave., No. 1130
Portland, OR 97204
Ph: (503)241-3506
Fax: (503)241-9256
E-mail: info@rivernetwork.org
URL: http://www.rivernetwork.org
Contact: Don Elder, Pres.

Founded: 1988. **Staff:** 19. **Budget:** $3,000,000. **Nonmembership. Description:** Helps people organize to protect and restore rivers and watersheds. Supports river and watershed advocates at the local, state and regional levels. Helps build effective organizations, and promotes working together to build a nationwide movement for rivers and watersheds. Acquires and conserves riverlands that are critical to the services that rivers perform for human communities: drinking water supply, floodplain management, fish and wildlife habitat, recreation, and open space. **Awards:** Watershed Assistance Grant. **Frequency:** annual. **Type:** grant. **Recipient:** to partner organizations. **Computer Services:** Mailing lists, of members. **Telecommunication Services:** electronic mail, delder@rivernetwork.org. **Programs:** Health and Environmental Justice; River Heroes; River Protection and Restoration; River Rally; River Smart; River Watch; Watershed. **Publications:** *A Citizen's Guide to Conserving Riparian Forests* ● *Directory of Funding Sources for Grassroots River and Watershed Conservation Groups* ● *How to Save a River*. Handbook. Contains topics encouraging citizen action. **Price:** $14.00 plus shipping and handling ● *1998-1999 River and Watershed Conservation Directory* ● *River Fundraising Alert*, quarterly. Newsletter ● *River Voices*, quarterly. Newsletter ● *Starting Up: A Handbook for New River and Watershed Organizations* ● *The Watershed Innovators Workshop Proceedings* ● Annual Report, annual. Alternate Formats: online. **Conventions/Meetings:** annual National River Rally (exhibits).

4447 ■ Sailors for the Sea
56 Commercial Wharf E
Boston, MA 02110
E-mail: info@sailorsforthesea.org
URL: http://www.sailorsforthesea.org
Contact: David Rockefeller Jr., Pres./Co-Founder

Membership Dues: student, $20 (annual) ● basic, $40 (annual) ● contributor, $80 (annual) ● sponsor, $150 (annual) ● watch captain, $250 (annual) ● navigator, $500 (annual). **Description:** Promotes ocean awareness to the public. Aims to restore and protect the sea. Identifies and broadcasts local, regional and national opportunities for citizen participation in protecting the integrity of marine life in U.S. waters.

4448 ■ Save America's Forests
4 Lib. Ct. SE
Washington, DC 20003
Ph: (202)544-9219
URL: http://www.saveamericasforests.org
Contact: Carl Ross, Founder/Dir.

Founded: 1990. **Membership Dues:** individual, group or business, $25 (annual). **Description:** Coalition of groups, businesses, and individuals united to pass national laws protecting forest ecosystems.

4449 ■ Save Our Seas (SOS)
PO Box 813
Hanalei, HI 96714
Ph: (808)651-3452
E-mail: sos@saveourseas.org
URL: http://www.saveourseas.org
Contact: Capt. Paul Clark, Pres.

Founded: 1993. **Membership Dues:** charter, $500 (annual). **Multinational. Description:** Utilizes education and research to preserve, protect and restore the world's oceans for future generations. Strives to unite people, community organizations, sources of information and solutions to ensure the restoration of oceans. Cooperates with state and local units of government, and private landowners around the world. **Telecommunication Services:** electronic mail, paul@saveourseas.org. **Publications:** *The Coconut Wireless*, quarterly. Magazine. Includes news, art, photography and issues related to Global Oceanic conservation. **Price:** included in membership dues. **Advertising:** accepted. Alternate Formats: online.

4450 ■ Save the Redwoods League (SRL)
114 Sansome St., Rm. 1200
San Francisco, CA 94104-3823
Ph: (415)362-2352
Free: (888)836-0005
Fax: (415)362-7017
E-mail: info@savetheredwoods.org
URL: http://www.savetheredwoods.org
Contact: Ruskin Hartley, Sec./Exec. Dir.

Founded: 1918. **Members:** 60,000. **Membership Dues:** contributor, $25 (annual) ● sustainer, $100 (annual) ● steward, $500 (annual) ● benefactor, $250 (annual) ● redwood leadership society, $1,000 (annual) ● family, $50 (annual) ● steward, $500 (annual). **Staff:** 13. **Description:** Helps acquire 6 out of every 10 acres of redwoods now in protected ownership. Purchases ancient forestlands and their watershed regions at fair market value; provides education, research grants and reforestation programs to foster and encourage a better and more general understanding of the redwood forests. **Libraries: Type:** not open to the public. **Holdings:** 1,000. **Subjects:** redwoods, parks, forestry. **Awards:** Education Grant. **Frequency:** annual. **Type:** grant. **Recipient:** to schools, interpretative associations and other qualified non-profits engaged in quality redwood education ● Research Grant. **Frequency:** annual. **Type:** grant. **Recipient:** for scientists studying various aspects of the coast redwood, giant sequoia and their ecosystem. **Programs:** Education Grants; Land Acquisition; Research Grants. **Projects:** Corridor from the Redwoods to the Sea. **Task Forces:** Master Plan. **Publications:** *Coast Redwood Bibliography*. Alternate Formats: online ● *Guide to Redwood Parks*. Booklet ● *The Redwood Forest*. Book. **Price:** $35.00 includes tax, posting and packing ● *Redwoods of the Past*. Pamphlet. **Price:** $1.00 ● *Save-the-Redwoods League Bulletin*, semiannual. **Price:** free. **Circulation:** 50,000. Alternate Formats: online ● *Story Told by a Fallen Redwood*. Pamphlet. **Price:** $1.00 ● *Trees, Shrubs, and Flowers of the Redwood Forest*. Pamphlet. **Price:** $3.00 ● Brochure, annual ● Annual Report, annual. Alternate Formats: online.

4451 ■ Seacoast Anti-Pollution League (SAPL)
PO Box 1136
Portsmouth, NH 03802-1136
Ph: (603)431-5089
E-mail: info@sapl.org
URL: http://www.sapl.org
Contact: David E. Hills, Pres.

Founded: 1969. **Members:** 600. **Membership Dues:** sustaining, $250 (annual) ● individual, $35 (annual) ● family, $50 (annual) ● contributing, $100 (annual). **Staff:** 1. **Budget:** $60,000. **Description:** Serves as a citizen-based environmental organization concerned with health and safety issues affecting the regional seacoast environment and its population. Seeks to prevent ecological, economic and public health damage from the Seabrook nuclear reactor and monitors the clean-up effort at the Portsmouth Naval Shipyard. **Committees:** Fundraising; Nuclear Issues; Public Events; Shipyard. **Formerly:** The Seacoast Anti-Pollution League. **Publications:** *SAPL News*, *Action Alerts*. Newsletter. Includes topical articles on issues and activities of the organization. **Price:** included in membership dues. **Conventions/Meetings:** annual meeting.

4452 ■ Society of Wetland Scientists (SWS)
1313 Dolley Madison Blvd., Ste.402
McLean, VA 22101
Ph: (703)790-1745
Fax: (703)790-2672
E-mail: sws@burkinc.com
URL: http://www.sws.org
Contact: Ms. Mary Kentula, Pres.

Members: 4,300. **Membership Dues:** active, regular, $100 (annual) ● student, $35 (annual) ● institutional, corporate, $500 (annual) ● library, $200 (annual) ● family, $125 (annual) ● emeritus, $60 (annual) ● life, $1,000. **Description:** Seeks to foster wetland conservation and research. Educates the public on wetland resources; provides a forum for exchange of ideas; develops and supports student education; and encourages sound management of wetlands. **Awards:** Best Student Paper and Poster Awards. **Type:** recognition. **Recipient:** for students ● Fellow Award. **Type:** recognition. **Recipient:** for outstanding individuals ● International Fellow Award. **Type:** recognition. **Recipient:** for outstanding wetland scientists ● International Travel Awards. **Type:** recognition. **Recipient:** for wetland scientists ● Lifetime Achievement Award. **Type:** recognition. **Recipient:** for wetland scientists ● Merit Award. **Type:** recognition. **Recipient:** for outstanding individuals ● President's Service Award. **Type:** recognition. **Recipient:** for members of the society ● Sponsors and Endowment Award. **Type:** recognition. **Recipient:** for individuals, organizations and corporations ● Student Scholarships. **Type:** scholarship. **Recipient:** for graduate and undergraduate students. **Telecommunication Services:** electronic mail, clove3pp@msn.com. **Publications:** *SWS Bulletin*, quarterly. **Price:** included in membership dues. ISSN: 0277-5212 ● *Wetlands*, quarterly. Journal ● Membership Directory. **Conventions/Meetings:** annual conference.

4453 ■ Soil and Water Conservation Society (SWCS)
945 SW Ankeny Rd.
Ankeny, IA 50023-9723
Ph: (515)289-2331
Fax: (515)289-1227
E-mail: swcs@swcs.org
URL: http://www.swcs.org
Contact: Craig A. Cox, Exec. Dir.

Founded: 1943. **Members:** 11,000. **Membership Dues:** conservationist, $80 (annual) ● student, $25 (annual) ● leader, $130 (annual) ● President's Club, $200 (annual). **Staff:** 16. **Budget:** $1,800,000. **Local Groups:** 85. **Description:** Soil and water conservationists and others in fields related to the use, conservation, and management of natural resources. Aims to advance the science and art of good land and water use. Offers unpaid internships to qualified students. **Awards:** Commendation Award. **Frequency:** annual. **Type:** recognition. **Recipient:** to members who render services to their chapters ● Fellow Award. **Frequency:** annual. **Type:** recognition. **Recipient:** to members with exceptional service in advocating for the conservation of natural resources ● Harold and Kay School Excellence in

Conservation Award. **Frequency:** annual. **Type:** monetary. **Recipient:** to individuals who creatively and effectively provide technical assistance in conservation planning and plan application ● Honor Award. **Frequency:** annual. **Type:** recognition. **Recipient:** to members/nonmembers with outstanding accomplishments ● Hugh Hammond Bennett Award. **Frequency:** annual. **Type:** recognition. **Recipient:** to members and nonmembers ● Merit Award. **Frequency:** annual. **Type:** recognition. **Recipient:** to groups, business firms, corporations or organizations with outstanding products, activities or services ● Outstanding Service Award. **Frequency:** annual. **Type:** recognition. **Recipient:** to members with distinguished service in helping the society ● Research Scholarship. **Frequency:** annual. **Type:** scholarship. **Recipient:** for individuals/students ● Soil Conservation Scholarship. **Frequency:** annual. **Type:** scholarship. **Recipient:** for individuals/students ● Student Leader Conservation Scholarship. **Frequency:** annual. **Type:** scholarship. **Recipient:** for individuals/student leaders. **Formerly:** (1987) Soil Conservation Society of America. **Publications:** *Conservation Voices*, bimonthly. Magazine ● *Conservogram*, monthly. Newsletter. Contains information on the activities of the society and chapters. **Price:** included in membership dues. Alternate Formats: online ● *Journal of Soil and Water Conservation*, bimonthly. Promotes creative thinking and encourages investigation on conservation issues. **Price:** included in membership dues. **Advertising:** accepted ● *Technical Monographs*, periodic ● Booklets. Contains educational information for children. **Price:** $12.00 sample set (includes shipping and insurance); $40.00 teacher's pack (includes shipping and insurance) ● Books ● Also publishes software for erosion prediction modeling. **Conventions/Meetings:** annual meeting (exhibits) - always summer ● periodic workshop.

4454 ■ The Steamboaters (TS)
c/o Steamboat Inn
42705 N Umpqua Hwy.
Idleyld Park, OR 97447-9729
Ph: (541)498-2230
Free: (800)840-8825
Fax: (541)498-2411
E-mail: steamboatinn@hughes.net
URL: http://www.steamboaters.org
Contact: Peter Tronquet, Pres.
Founded: 1966. **Members:** 300. **Description:** Fly fishermen who support the conservation of fishing waters and game fish. **Additional Websites:** http://www.thesteamboatinn.com. **Affiliated With:** Federation of Fly Fishers. **Publications:** *Steamboat Whistle*, quarterly. Newsletter. Alternate Formats: online. **Conventions/Meetings:** annual meeting, with spring banquet - always first Saturday after Labor Day.

4455 ■ Student Conservation Association (SCA)
PO Box 550
Charlestown, NH 03603-0550
Ph: (603)543-1700
Fax: (603)543-1828
E-mail: ask-us@thesca.org
URL: http://www.thesca.org
Contact: Dale Penny, Pres.
Founded: 1957. **Members:** 38,000. **Staff:** 130. **Budget:** $20,000,000. **Regional Groups:** 5. **Description:** Works to build the next generation of conservation leaders and inspire lifelong stewardship of the environment and communities by engaging young people in hands-on service to the land. Provides conservation service opportunities, outdoor education and leadership development for young people. Offers college and graduate students, as well as older adults expense-paid conservation internships, these positions includes wildlife research, wilderness patrols and interpretive opportunities and provide participants with valuable hands-on career experience. Places 15-19 year old high school students in four-week volunteer conservation crews in national parks forests and refuges across the country each summer to accomplish a range of trail building and habitat conservation projects. Offers year-round diversity conservation programs for young women and young persons of color in leading metropolitan areas of U.S. **Computer Services:** Mailing lists. **Councils:** SCA National. **Programs:** Conservation Corps; Conservation Crews; Conservation Internships; International Conservation Leadership Initiative; Urban initiatives. **Projects:** California Wildfire Recovery; SCA Fire Education. **Publications:** *Lightly on the Land: The SCA Trail Building and Maintenance Manual*. Book. Provides valuable information on topics ranging from trail construction to camping safety. **Price:** $21.99 ● *The Volunteer*, quarterly. Newsletter. Alternate Formats: online ● Annual Report, annual. Alternate Formats: online ● Papers. Alternate Formats: online.

4456 ■ Tall Timbers Land Conservancy (TTLC)
c/o Tall Timbers Research Station
13093 Henry Beadel Dr.
Tallahassee, FL 32312
Ph: (850)893-4153
E-mail: kmcgorty@ttrs.org
URL: http://www.talltimbers.org/ttlc.htm
Contact: Kevin McGorty, Dir.
Founded: 1990. **Staff:** 4. **Description:** Individuals and organizations dedicated to conservation and preservation of the Red Hills, a semicircular 25-mile-wide region between Albany, GA and Tallahassee, FL. Promotes increased public awareness of the resources in the region; conducts inventories of natural areas and historical sites. Hopes to develop a program to preserve and interpret the area through educational programs. The Red Hills region encompasses historic archaeological and architectural structures, natural areas, and scenic landscapes; the region also harbors nearly 85 threatened species of plants and animals. **Affiliated With:** Nature Conservancy; Tall Timbers Research Station; Trust for Public Land. **Formerly:** (2007) Red Hills Conservation Program.

4457 ■ Tall Timbers Research Station (TTRS)
13093 Henry Beadel Dr.
Tallahassee, FL 32312-0918
Ph: (850)893-4153
E-mail: rose@ttrs.org
URL: http://www.talltimbers.org
Contact: Mr. Lane Green, Exec. Dir.
Founded: 1958. **Members:** 1,000. **Membership Dues:** Stoddard Society, $10,000 (annual) ● benefactor, $5,000 (annual) ● patron, $2,500 (annual) ● sponsor, $1,000 (annual) ● sustaining, $500 (annual) ● supporting, $250 (annual) ● contributing, $125 (annual) ● friend, $65 (annual). **Staff:** 39. **Budget:** $2,345,275. **Regional Groups:** 4. **State Groups:** 3. **Description:** Dedicated to protecting wildlands and preserving natural habitats. Promotes public education on the importance of natural disturbances to the environment and the subsequent need for wildlife and land management. Conducts fire ecology research and other biological research programs through the Tall Timbers Research Station. Operates museum. **Libraries: Type:** reference. **Holdings:** 13,000; books, papers, periodicals. **Subjects:** fire ecology, botany, conservation, forestry, plant ecology, ornithology, land and wildlife management. **Computer Services:** Bibliographic search, includes all Tall Timbers Fire Ecology Conferences; 12,000 records ● database, E.V. Komarek Fire Ecology. **Telecommunication Services:** electronic mail, lane@ttrs.org. **Divisions:** Conservation; Development; Education; Land Management; Research. **Formerly:** (1994) Tall Timbers; (1998) Tall Timbers Research. **Publications:** *Quail and Conservation Report to Donors*, annual ● *Quail Call*, annual. Newsletter ● *Tall Timber News*, annual. Newsletter ● Annual Report, annual. **Conventions/Meetings:** Fire Ecology Conference, topics relating to fire ecology (exhibits) - every 2-3 years in various locations ● annual Game Bird Management Field Day - meeting - always fall ● annual Game Bird Management Seminar - always spring ● annual Open House - meeting - fall.

4458 ■ Theodore Roosevelt Conservation Partnership (TRCP)
555 Eleventh St. NW, 6th Fl.
Washington, DC 20004
Ph: (202)654-4600
Free: (877)770-8722
E-mail: info@trcp.org
URL: http://www.trcp.org
Contact: George Cooper, Pres./CEO
Description: Preserves and protects hunting and fishing heritage and fish and wildlife habitat. Expands access to hunting and fishing places. Increases funding for conservation and management of fish and wildlife habitat. **Telecommunication Services:** electronic mail, gcooper@trcp.org.

4459 ■ Tree Musketeers
136 Main St., Ste.A
El Segundo, CA 90245
Ph: (310)322-0263
Free: (800)473-0263
Fax: (310)322-4482
E-mail: info@treemusketeers.org
URL: http://www.treemusketeers.org
Contact: Gail Church, Exec. Dir.
Founded: 1987. **Membership Dues:** family, $25 (annual) ● corporate/organization, $50 (annual) ● adult, $15 (annual) ● youth, $10 (annual). **Staff:** 6. **Budget:** $500,000. **Description:** Children interested in the environment. Promotes environmental improvement through the actions of children (the children themselves administer the organization); encourages other young people and businesses to join the youth environmental movement. Efforts include waste management, urban forestry, public education, and youth leadership. Supports young people and groups across the country in dealing with their own hometown environmental problems. Unites kids and adults through Partners for the Planet Network in a "by youth" movement with a hotline, resources exchange, National and Regional Youth Summits, and a speakers' bureau. **Publications:** *TrunkLine*, semiannual. Newsletter. Describes the organization's activities in the prior 6 months along with appropriate articles relating to urban forestry and the environment. **Price:** included in membership dues.

4460 ■ TreePeople (TP)
12601 Mulholland Dr.
Beverly Hills, CA 90210
Ph: (818)753-4600 (818)753-4631
Fax: (818)753-4635
E-mail: info@treepeople.org
URL: http://www.treepeople.org
Contact: Andy Lipkis, Pres.
Founded: 1973. **Members:** 21,000. **Membership Dues:** regular, $25 (annual) ● oak leaf, $250-$499 (annual). **Staff:** 50. **Budget:** $4,500,000. **Description:** Environmental problem solving organization, operating primarily in Southern California, promoting community action, global awareness, environmental education, and an active role in the planting and care of trees. Conducts education and training seminars. Volunteers plant trees throughout Los Angeles, CA and its surrounding mountain area. Operates Environmental Leadership Program for schoolchildren and Citizen's Forester Training Program for adults. Maintains 45-acre Wilderness Park with recycling education exhibits. **Formerly:** (1986) California Conservation Project. **Publications:** *Second Nature: Adapting LA's Landscape for Sustainable Living*. Book ● *Seedling News*, quarterly. Newsletter ● *The Simple Act of Planting a Tree*. Book.

4461 ■ Trust for Public Land (TPL)
116 New Montgomery St., 4th Fl.
San Francisco, CA 94105
Ph: (415)495-4014
Free: (800)714-LAND
Fax: (415)495-4103
E-mail: info@tpl.org
URL: http://www.tpl.org
Contact: Matthew Shaffer, Contact
Founded: 1972. **Staff:** 400. **Regional Groups:** 6. **Description:** Works on the acquisition and preservation of lands in urban and rural areas for public use. Provides urban and community groups with training and technical assistance in land acquisition. Acquires recreational, historic, and scenic lands for conveyance to local, state, and federal agencies and non-

profit organizations for open space protection and public use. **Convention/Meeting:** none. **Awards:** Conservation Awards. **Frequency:** 3/year. **Type:** recognition. **Recipient:** to officials elected or appointed from NACo member counties. **Programs:** Center for Land and People; Children's Gardening; Conservation Finance; Federal Affairs; Green Printing; Tribal Lands; Twin Cities Mississippi River; Water. **Publications:** *Healing America's Cities: How Urban Parks Can Make Cities Safe and Healthy*. Report ● *Land and People*, semiannual. Magazine. Contains feature articles, interviews and news briefs about land-for-people conservation. **Price:** free. **Circulation:** 45,000 ● Annual Report, annual. Alternate Formats: online ● Newsletters, semiannual. Alternate Formats: online ● Handbooks. Alternate Formats: online ● Reports. Alternate Formats: online ● Land Link; Public Finance publication.

4462 ■ United States Tourist Council (USTC)
Address Unknown since 2007
Founded: 1969. **Members:** 18,700. **Description:** Conservation-concerned individuals who travel; institutions and industries that supply goods and services to the traveler. Objectives are to achieve: historic and scenic preservation; wilderness and roadside development; ecology through sound planning and education; support of scientific studies of natural wilderness areas. **Libraries: Type:** reference. **Publications:** Bulletin, periodic.

4463 ■ Upper Mississippi River Conservation Committee (UMRCC)
555 Lester Ave.
Onalaska, WI 54650
Ph: (608)783-8432
E-mail: umrcc@mississippi-river.com
URL: http://www.mississippi-river.com/umrcc
Contact: Kevin Stauffer, Chm.
Founded: 1943. **Members:** 250. **Staff:** 1. **Budget:** $10,000. **Regional Groups:** 1. **Description:** Natural resources managers and biologists. Objectives are: to promote the preservation and wise use of the natural and recreational resources of the upper Mississippi River; to formulate policies, plans, and programs for conducting cooperative studies. Creates cooperative projects that include creel census, commercial fishing statistics, waterfowl and wildlife censuses, hunter surveys, fish tagging, and collection of boating and other recreational use data. Helps to define land management for public properties such as public hunting grounds, wildlife refuges, flood plain reserves, and recreational lands. Works as an advisory body on all technical aspects of fish, wildlife, and recreation. Makes recommendations on conservation laws, programs, and legislation to state and federal governments. Maintains a continuing evaluation of the effects of water control regulation and recreational resources. Sponsors research programs. **Libraries: Type:** reference. **Holdings:** 5,000. **Subjects:** Mississippi River resources management. **Awards:** UMRCC Conservation Award. **Frequency:** annual. **Type:** recognition. **Computer Services:** database, Upper Mississippi River issues ● mailing lists, members, tech sections. **Working Groups:** Fisheries; Law Enforcement; Recreation; Water Quality; Wildlife. **Publications:** *UMRCC Annual Proceedings*, annual. **Price:** $15.00 ● Newsletter, quarterly. **Price:** free. **Circulation:** 700. Alternate Formats: online ● Reports. Alternate Formats: online. **Conventions/Meetings:** annual meeting and conference (exhibits) - always March.

4464 ■ Walden Pond Advisory Committee (WPAC)
Address Unknown since 2007
Founded: 1974. **Members:** 7. **Description:** Representatives of communities and organizations interested in the preservation and restoration of Walden Pond. (Walden Pond is an area where author Henry David Thoreau spent two solitary years writing and communing with nature. The pond has been a Massachusetts public reservation since 1922.) The committee is concerned about destruction of the vegetation, damage to the woods, and littering which the group claims is caused by careless crowds (an estimated 5000 persons may visit the area on a given weekend). Reviews maintenance and management practices, long-term master plan objectives, and capital improvement programs at Walden Pond on an annual basis. **Formerly:** (1974) Walden Pond Restoration Committee.

4465 ■ Waterfowl U.S.A. (WUSA)
Box 50
Waterfowl Bldg.
Edgefield, SC 29824
Ph: (803)637-5767
Fax: (803)637-6983
E-mail: president@waterfowlusa.org
URL: http://www.waterfowlusa.org
Contact: Roger L. White, Pres./CEO
Founded: 1983. **Members:** 20,000. **Membership Dues:** regular, $25 (annual) ● charter, $30 (annual) ● sponsor, $200 (annual) ● life, $1,000 ● bronze sponsor, $2,500 ● silver sponsor, $5,000 ● gold sponsor, $7,500 ● life sponsor, $10,000 ● diamond life sponsor, $25,000. **Staff:** 9. **Budget:** $1,250,000. **State Groups:** 37. **Local Groups:** 100. **Description:** Hunters, conservationists, and others dedicated to raising money for developing, preserving, restoring, and maintaining waterfowl habitats in the U.S. Seeks to: publicize the needs of waterfowl; develop state and local wetland projects; improve waterfowl resting areas, wood duck nest boxes, and planting areas that feed migrating and resident waterfowl; establish public shooting areas. Conducts wood duck research. Cooperates with other waterfowl groups. **Libraries: Type:** reference. **Computer Services:** database. **Funds:** Waterfowl USA Endowment Fund. **Programs:** Youth Education. **Projects:** Sample Habitat. **Formerly:** (1990) National Waterfowl Alliance, Waterfowl United States of America. **Supersedes:** North American Waterfowlers. **Publications:** *Waterfowl Magazine*, bimonthly. Informs members on the accomplishments and achievements of the organization. **Price:** included in membership dues. **Circulation:** 20,000. **Advertising:** accepted. Alternate Formats: online ● Pamphlets. **Conventions/Meetings:** annual conference.

4466 ■ Western Gamebird Alliance (WGA)
PO Box 14152
Tucson, AZ 85732
Ph: (520)241-3534
E-mail: info@gamebird-alliance.org
Contact: Dave Lukens, Pres.
Multinational. Description: Addresses the issues affecting upland gamebirds. Protects and restores upland gamebird habitat throughout the West. Improves gamebird habitat and hunter access on public lands all over the West. **Telecommunication Services:** electronic mail, dlukens@gamebird-alliance.org. **Publications:** *The Western Uplander*. Newsletter. **Price:** free.

4467 ■ Wild Earth
PO Box 455
Richmond, VT 05477
Ph: (802)434-4077
Fax: (802)434-5980
E-mail: info@wildlandsproject.org
URL: http://www.wild-earth.org
Contact: Mary Granskou, Pres.
Founded: 1991. **Membership Dues:** regular, $25 (annual). **Staff:** 6. **Description:** Melding conservation biology with grassroots activism, publishes a quarterly journal of wilderness advocacy and publishing voice of the Wildlands Project. **Publications:** Journal, quarterly. **Price:** $25.00/year. **Circulation:** 7,000. **Advertising:** accepted.

4468 ■ The Wilderness Society (TWS)
1615 M St. NW
Washington, DC 20036
Ph: (202)833-2300
Free: (800)843-9453
E-mail: member@tws.org
URL: http://www.wilderness.org
Contact: Brenda Davis, Chair
Founded: 1935. **Members:** 255,000. **Membership Dues:** regular, $30 (annual) ● introductory, $15 (annual) ● student, senior, limited income renewal, $10 (annual). **Staff:** 130. **Budget:** $17,000,000. **Description:** Works for the establishment of the land ethic as a basic element of American culture and philosophy, and the education of a broader and more committed wilderness preservation and land protection constituency. Focuses on federal, legislative, and administrative actions affecting public lands, including national forests, parks, and wildlife refuges, and Bureau of Land Management lands. Encourages Congress to designate appropriate public lands as wilderness areas. Programs include grass roots organizing, economic analysis, lobbying, research, and public education. Compiles statistics. **Awards: Frequency:** annual. **Type:** recognition. **Publications:** *From Despair to Hope: A Chronicle of Federal Old-Growth Forest Policy in the Pacific Northwest*. Paper. Features values and aspirations that most people in Western Oregon have for their national forests. Alternate Formats: online ● *National Landscape Conservation System*. Booklet. Features nation's newest system of public lands. Alternate Formats: online ● *Wilderness*, annual. Magazine. **Price:** included in membership dues ● *Wilderness Act Handbook-40th Anniversary Edition (2004)*, periodic. Serves as reference for those working to protect what is left of wild America. ● *Wilderness Report*, biweekly. Newsletter. Alternate Formats: online ● *The Wilderness Society's Newsletter*, quarterly ● Annual Report. Alternate Formats: online ● Also publishes reports, brochures, fact sheets, and alerts on critical conservation issues. **Conventions/Meetings:** semiannual meeting.

4469 ■ Wildlife Conservation Society (WCS)
2300 Southern Blvd.
Bronx, NY 10460
Ph: (718)220-5100 (718)220-5111
E-mail: membership@wcs.org
URL: http://www.wcs.org
Contact: Dr. Steven E. Sanderson, Pres./CEO
Founded: 1895. **Members:** 105,000. **Membership Dues:** individual, $75 (annual) ● individual premium, $90 (annual) ● family, $120 (annual) ● family premium, $150 (annual) ● conservation supporter, $250 (annual) ● conservation fellow, $500 (annual) ● conservation partner, $750 (annual) ● patron, $1,500 (annual) ● associate, $25 (annual). **Staff:** 880. **Budget:** $95,000,000. **Multinational. Description:** Represents supporters of international species survival strategies and habitat/ecosystem conservation projects. Operates Bronx Zoo, Aquarium for Wildlife Conservation, and three other wildlife centers in New York. Publishes and disseminates environmental education curricula to nationwide school audience, including extensive teacher training programs. Conducts baseline, field studies, provides professional training of foreign field of biologists, and prepares recommendations for parks and protected area management. Maintains an office in Nairobi, Kenya. **Libraries: Type:** by appointment only. **Holdings:** 6,000. **Subjects:** conservation biology, zoo biology. **Telecommunication Services:** electronic mail, ssautner@wcs.org. **Affiliated With:** Association of Zoos and Aquariums. **Formerly:** New York Zoological Society; NYZS/The Wildlife Conservation Society; (1984) Animal Research and Conservation Center; (1984) Wildlife Conservation International. **Publications:** *Wildlife Conservation*, bimonthly. Magazine. **Price:** $19.95/year in U.S.; $26.95/year outside U.S. ISSN: 1048-4949. **Advertising:** accepted ● Bulletin ● Annual Report, annual. **Advertising:** accepted. Alternate Formats: online. **Conventions/Meetings:** annual meeting.

4470 ■ Wildlife Habitat Council (WHC)
8737 Colesville Rd., Ste.800
Silver Spring, MD 20910
Ph: (301)588-8994
Fax: (301)588-4629
E-mail: whc@wildlifehc.org
URL: http://www.wildlifehc.org
Contact: Mr. Robert Johnson, Pres.
Founded: 1988. **Members:** 140. **Membership Dues:** corporate, $850-$5,000 (annual) ● national conservation, $550 (annual) ● local conservation, $50 (an-

nual) ● national sponsor, $1,500 (annual) ● state/local sponsor, $250 (annual) ● contributor, $25-$500 (annual). **Staff:** 18. **Budget:** $1,500,000. **Regional Groups:** 4. **Description:** A joint effort between the conservation and corporate communities designed to help corporations develop their lands for wildlife. Provides technical assistance in establishing and maintaining responsible corporate wildlife management practices, habitat certification, information sharing, employee involvement, and community outreach. **Awards:** Corporate Wildlife Habitat Program Certification. **Frequency:** annual. **Type:** recognition. **Recipient:** for improvement to habitat, scope of projects. **Telecommunication Services:** electronic mail, publications@wildlifehc.org. **Programs:** Corporate Lands for Learning; Corporate Wildlife Certification; Waterways for Wildlife; Wildlife at Work. **Formerly:** (1994) Wildlife Habitat Enhancement Council. **Publications:** *Habitat Quarterly*. Bulletin. Contains articles addressing issues dealing with wildlife habitat management. **Price:** $29.00/year. ISSN: 1088-0917. **Circulation:** 600 ● *Registry of Certified Corporate Wildlife Habitat Programs*, annual. **Price:** $12.00 ● *Wildlife Habitat*, quarterly. Newsletter. **Price:** $25.00/year. **Conventions/Meetings:** annual symposium (exhibits) - always November, usually in Maryland or Washington DC.

4471 ■ Wildlife Management Institute (WMI)
1146 19th St. NW, Ste.700
Washington, DC 20036
Ph: (202)371-1808
Fax: (202)408-5059
E-mail: rmccabe@wildlifemgt.org
URL: http://www.wildlifemanagementinstitute.org
Contact: Richard E. McCabe, Exec. VP

Founded: 1911. **Membership Dues:** supporting, $35 (annual) ● professional, $100 (annual) ● retired, student, $15 (annual) ● agency, corporate, $1,500 (annual) ● NGO, $750 (annual) ● industry, $375 (annual). **Staff:** 15. **Description:** Promotes improved professional management and wise utilization of all renewable natural resources in the public interest. **Awards:** The Distinguished Service Award. **Frequency:** annual. **Type:** recognition. **Recipient:** for a person who has dedicated his or her career to the principles and practices of conservation and whose accomplishments have been significant ● The Presidents Award. **Frequency:** annual. **Type:** recognition. **Recipient:** for federal, state or provincial natural resource agency division, department, office or program ● The Touchstone Award. **Frequency:** annual. **Type:** recognition. **Recipient:** for the achievement of a natural resource management program, professional or group of professionals in the public or private sector. **Formerly:** (1946) American Wildlife Institute. **Publications:** *Outdoor News Bulletin*, monthly ● *Transactions of Annual North American Wildlife and Natural Resources Conference*, annual. Book. **Price:** $38.00 ● Books ● Monographs. **Conventions/Meetings:** annual North American Wildlife and Natural Resources Conference (exhibits).

4472 ■ Wolf Haven International
3111 Offut Lake Rd.
Tenino, WA 98589
Ph: (360)264-4695
Free: (800)448-9653
Fax: (360)264-4639
E-mail: director@wolfhaven.org
URL: http://www.wolfhaven.org
Contact: Mr. John Blankenship, Exec. Dir.

Founded: 1982. **Members:** 2,650. **Membership Dues:** lone wolf, $30 (annual) ● beta, $95 (annual) ● alpha, $250 (annual) ● pack leader, $500 ● life, $5,000 ● wolf adoption, $25 (annual) ● classroom adoption, $35 (annual) ● wolf sponsorship, $125 (annual). **Staff:** 14. **Budget:** $800,000. **Multinational. Description:** Individuals interested in the conservation and understanding of wolves and wolf populations. Seeks to educate the public and increase awareness of the need for conservation. Provides presentations to school, civic, and professional groups. Offers educational on-site and outreach programs. Encourages research. Operates a sanctuary for wolves that have been raised in captivity and cannot be released into the wild. Works to educate the public about the problems of taking wildlife as pets. Is one of three institutions in the nation to assist with breeding and releasing the critically endangered Mexican gray wolf. **Libraries: Type:** reference. **Holdings:** 50. **Subjects:** wolves and related animals, wildlife conservation. **Publications:** *WolfTracks - Newsletter*, quarterly. **Price:** $2.00/copy. **Circulation:** 25,000.

4473 ■ World Association of Soil and Water Conservation (WASWC)
c/o John M. Laflen, Treas.
5784 Hwy. 9
Buffalo Center, IA 50424
E-mail: laflen@wctatel.net
URL: http://waswc.ait.ac.th
Contact: Miodrag Zlatic, Pres.

Members: 500. **Membership Dues:** individual (in developed country/international organization), $10 (annual) ● individual (in developing country/gift), $5 (annual) ● life, $80-$160 ● organization (based on number of persons), $100-$200 (annual). **Multinational. Description:** Promotes the sustained use of the earth's soil and water resources. Enhances the policies, approaches and technologies to improve the care of soil and water resources. Encourages discussion about good soil and water conservation practices. **Computer Services:** database, conservation activities and technology. **Publications:** *Journal of WASWC*. Contains repository of well conducted scientific work, including review and synthesis. Also Cited As: *JWASWC* ● *Proceedings of WASWC*. Includes reports, unreplicated studies, preliminary results, and other works. Also Cited As: *PWASWC* ● Newsletter (in Chinese, English, French, Portuguese, Russian, Spanish, and Vietnamese), quarterly. Includes conservation meetings and international news on conservation. Alternate Formats: online.

4474 ■ World Environment Center (WEC)
1300 Pennsylvania Ave. NW, Ste.550
Mailbox 142
Washington, DC 20004
Ph: (202)312-1210 (202)312-1370
Fax: (202)682-1682
E-mail: tyosie@wec.org
URL: http://www.wec.org
Contact: Dr. Terry F. Yosie, Pres./CEO

Founded: 1974. **Staff:** 4. **Budget:** $900,000. **Description:** Works to strengthen industrial and urban environmental, health, and safety policies by establishing and promoting partnerships among industry, government, and nongovernmental organizations. Facilitates information and expertise. Encourages corporate environmental leadership and responsibility. Provides training and technical cooperation programs utilizing volunteer experts. **Awards:** WEC Gold Medal for International Corporate Achievement in Sustainable Development. **Frequency:** annual. **Type:** medal. **Recipient:** for a corporation that demonstrated preeminent industry leadership, worldwide environmental quality, and global sustainable development. **Computer Services:** Online services, WEC Infolink. **Telecommunication Services:** electronic mail, info@wec.org ● electronic mail, wecgoldmedal2008@wec.org. **Programs:** Capacity Building: Advancing Sustainable Solutions; Gold Medal: Honouring Industry Excellence; Membership Roundtables: Learning and Building Competency. **Formerly:** (1980) Center for International Environment Information. **Publications:** *Greening the Supply Chain Initiative*. Brochure. Alternate Formats: online. **Conventions/Meetings:** periodic seminar and workshop.

4475 ■ World Environmental Organization
2020 Pennsylvania Ave. NW, No. 2001
Washington, DC 20006
Free: (800)800-2SUN
Fax: (888)777-8090
URL: http://www.world.org/weo
Contact: Jeff Gold, Chm./Pres.

Multinational. Description: Aims to preserve the natural diversity of plant and animal species, and their habitats, through the prevention of environmental degradation and destruction. Develops and implements scientific strategies for decreasing fossil fuel use. Prevents climate change and preserves plant and animal species and their habitats. Educates the public about a wide variety of environmental topics. **Publications:** Newsletter, several times each year. Contains environmental news and helpful tips for the environment. **Price:** free. Alternate Formats: online.

4476 ■ World Preserve
782 S Grand Hwy.
Clermont, FL 34711
Ph: (352)406-7128
Fax: (352)243-9559
E-mail: worldpreserve@hotmail.com
URL: http://www.worldpreserve.com
Contact: Christine Dykstra, Exec. Dir.

Founded: 2005. **Membership Dues:** regular, $20 (annual). **Description:** Raises public awareness of environmental and conservation issues. Promotes preservation and restoration of the natural resources. Attempts to combat environmental damage through clean-up, recycling and pollution reduction.

4477 ■ World Resources Institute (WRI)
10 G St. NE, Ste.800
Washington, DC 20002
Ph: (202)729-7600 (202)729-7675
Fax: (202)729-7610
E-mail: jlash@wri.org
URL: http://www.wri.org
Contact: Jonathan Lash, Pres.

Founded: 1982. **Staff:** 120. **Budget:** $10,000,000. **Description:** Scientists and other academics with an interest in the environment and development. Promotes environmentally sustainable economic and community development globally; seeks to identify and introduce alternative and renewable energy sources. Assists government agencies, development organizations, and private sector organizations address the needs of human beings without causing environmental harm. Sponsors research; identifies emerging energy sources and appropriate technologies and conducts training courses in their use; conducts natural resources management assessments. Maintains Center for International Development and Environment. **Libraries: Type:** by appointment only. **Holdings:** books. **Subjects:** sustainable development, environment, agriculture and food, biodiversity and protected areas, climate and atmosphere, coastal and marine ecosystems, economics, business and the environment, energy and resource, governance and institutions, forests and grasslands, water resources, freshwater ecosystems. **Computer Services:** Mailing lists, of partners. **Projects:** The Access Initiative; Beyond Grey Pinstripes; Business-Environment Learning and Leadership; Capital Markets Research; Carbon Capture and Storage; Climate Analysis and Indicators; Global Forest Watch; Globalization, Environment and Communities. **Publications:** *Chile's Frontier Forests: Conserving a Global Treasure* ● *Power Politics: Equity and Environment in Electricity Reform* ● *Tomorrow's Markets: Global Trends and Their Implications for Business* ● *Understanding the Ancillary Effects of Climate Change Policies: A Research Agenda* ● Books ● Papers ● Reports. **Conventions/Meetings:** periodic conference ● periodic seminar.

4478 ■ World Wildlife Fund (WWF)
PO Box 97180
Washington, DC 20090-7180
Ph: (202)293-4800
Free: (800)225-5993
Fax: (202)293-9211
E-mail: plannedgiving@wwfus.org
URL: http://www.worldwildlife.org
Contact: Mr. Carter S. Roberts, Pres./CEO

Founded: 1961. **Members:** 1,200,000. **Membership Dues:** individual, $15 (annual). **Staff:** 275. **Budget:** $60,000,000. **Description:** Seeks to protect the biological resources upon which human well-being depends. Emphasizes preservation of endangered and threatened species of wildlife and plants as well as habitats and natural areas anywhere in the world. Produces immediate and long-term conservation benefits. Provides models for natural management techniques and policies. Supports public and private conservation agencies and governments in carrying out projects and services. **Convention/Meeting:** none. **Libraries: Type:** reference. **Holdings:** 10,000. **Awards:** J. Paul Getty Wildlife Conservation Prize. **Frequency:** annual. **Type:** recognition. **Recipient:** to individuals with outstanding contributions to international conservation. **Committees:** Corporate Advisory; Migratory Bird; Public Information Advisory; Scientific Advisory. **Absorbed:** Conservation Foundation. **Formerly:** (1986) World Wildlife Fund - U.S. **Publications:** *Focus*, bimonthly. Newsletter ● Annual Report, annual. **Price:** $15.00.

Containers

4479 ■ Container Recycling Alliance (CRA)
700 E Butterfield Rd., Ste.480
Lombard, IL 60148
Ph: (630)572-2480
Fax: (630)572-2428
URL: http://www.crarecycling.com
Contact: Tom Riek, CEO

Description: Recovers glass containers from the waste stream for reuse in the manufacture of new glass products. Produces and markets cullet, the crushed and cleaned post-consumer glass used primarily for reuse in new glass packaging. Utilizes state-of-the-art technology in glass container recycling process.

4480 ■ Container Recycling Institute (CRI)
1776 Massachusetts Ave. NW, Ste.800
Washington, DC 20036-1904
Ph: (202)263-0999
E-mail: info@container-recycling.org
URL: http://www.container-recycling.org
Contact: Betty McLaughlin, Exec. Dir.

Founded: 1991. **Description:** Seeks to move social and environmental costs associated with manufacturing, recycling and disposal of container and packaging waste from government and taxpayers to producers and consumers.

Cooperatives

4481 ■ ACDI/VOCA
50 F St. NW, Ste.1075
Washington, DC 20001
Ph: (202)638-4661
Fax: (202)626-8726
E-mail: webmaster@acdivoca.org
URL: http://www.acdivoca.org
Contact: Carl H. Leonard, Pres./CEO

Founded: 1963. **Members:** 34. **Membership Dues:** voting (farmer cooperatives and farm credit banks), $4,000 (annual) ● associate (non co-op business and agricultural organization), $500 (annual) ● individual, $100 (annual). **Staff:** 600. **Description:** Agricultural cooperatives, agribusinesses, farmers' organizations, and farm credit banks in the United States. Assists in organizing and providing technical assistance for cooperatives and agribusinesses in developing countries, usually under contract with the Agency for International Development. Advises governmental and other agencies in agricultural marketing, supply, and credit; carries out feasibility studies for specific agribusiness ventures; arranges formal and on-the-job training in cooperative practices for government officials, cooperative functionaries, and rural leaders; conducts short- and long-term technical assistance programs. Conducts extensive global volunteer programs that introduce American agricultural and financial know-how to developing economies, an exchange that furthers international cooperation and fellowship and promotes global business. Invites resumes of U.S. agriculture, business, and finance experts who are willing to serve overseas on short-term assignments. **Libraries: Type:** reference. **Subjects:** world agriculture, cooperative development. **Telecommunication Services:** electronic mail, cleonard@acdivoca.org. **Affiliated With:** Farm Credit Council; National Council of Farmer Cooperatives. **Formed by Merger of:** (1963) Farmers Union International Association Corporation; (1963) International Cooperative Development Association; Agricultural Cooperative Development International; Volunteers in Overseas Assistance. **Formerly:** (1998) Agricultural Cooperative Development International and Volunteers in Cooperative Assistance. **Publications:** *World Report*, quarterly. Newsletter. Contains editorials and profiles of agricultural entrepreneurs. **Price:** free. **Circulation:** 6,000 ● Annual Report, annual. Alternate Formats: online ● Brochure ● Reports. **Conventions/Meetings:** annual meeting, in conjunction with National Council of Farmer Cooperatives (exhibits).

4482 ■ Farmland Industries (FI)
Address Unknown since 2008

Founded: 1929. **Members:** 1,820. **Staff:** 7,400. **Description:** Regional federation of local cooperative organizations. Manufactures and sells petroleum products, fertilizer, feed, and other supplies to farmers. Processes and markets pork products through its subsidiary, Farmland Foods, Inc. **Committees:** Farmland Political Action. **Formerly:** (1935) Union Oil Company Cooperative; (1966) Consumers Cooperative Association. **Publications:** *Farmland News*, monthly. Newsletter. Tabloid; contains information on estate planning. **Price:** $3.60 /year for members; $7.00 /year for nonmembers. ISSN: 0093-5832. **Circulation:** 170,000. **Advertising:** accepted. Alternate Formats: microform; online. Also Cited As: *Cooperative Consumer, Farmland*. **Conventions/Meetings:** annual meeting - always Kansas City, MO.

4483 ■ National Council of Farmer Cooperatives (NCFC)
50 F St. NW, Ste.900
Washington, DC 20001
Ph: (202)626-8700
Fax: (202)626-8722
E-mail: jmpeltier@ncfc.org
URL: http://www.ncfc.org
Contact: Jean-Mari Peltier, Pres.

Founded: 1929. **Members:** 60. **Staff:** 14. **Description:** Serves as a federation of farmers' marketing, purchasing, and credit cooperatives serving total farm membership of nearly two million. Works to protect the right of farmers to organize and operate their own cooperative associations; assist the agricultural industry to obtain a share of the total national income commensurate with the share obtained for the same productive and marketing efficiency by other segments of the nation's economy. **Committees:** Agriculture, Trade, and Credit; Budget and Audit; Co-op/PAC Advisory; Cotton; Dairy; Education; Energy; Grain; Legal, Tax, and Accounting; Member and Public Relations; Specialty Crops; Yearbook. **Affiliated With:** ACDI/VOCA; Farm Credit Council. **Absorbed:** (1973) National Federation of Grain Cooperatives. **Publications:** *American Cooperation Yearbook*, annual ● Newsletter. **Conventions/Meetings:** annual meeting - always January.

4484 ■ Universal Cooperatives
1300 Corporate Center Curve
Eagan, MN 55121
Ph: (651)239-1000
Fax: (651)239-1080
E-mail: info@ucoop.com
URL: http://www.ucoop.com
Contact: Terrance J. Bohman, Pres./CEO

Founded: 1972. **Members:** 17. **Membership Dues:** regular, $10,000. **Staff:** 850. **Description:** Works as a federation of regional agricultural cooperative associations. Engages in buying, manufacturing, importing and distributing activities. Focuses on tires, batteries, and accessories; twine; farm supplies; lubricants; animal health products; agricultural chemicals. **Divisions:** Animal Health and Nutrition; Automotive; Farm Chemical; International. **Affiliated With:** National Cooperative Business Association; National Council of Farmer Cooperatives. **Formed by Merger of:** (1972) National Cooperatives; United Cooperatives. **Conventions/Meetings:** annual Shareholder Meeting (exhibits) - always October.

Dairies

4485 ■ American Dairy Science Association (ADSA)
c/o Peter Studney, Exec. Dir.
1111 N Dunlap Ave.
Savoy, IL 61874
Ph: (217)356-5146
Fax: (217)398-4119
E-mail: adsa@assochq.org
URL: http://www.adsa.org
Contact: Peter Studney, Exec. Dir.

Founded: 1906. **Members:** 3,200. **Membership Dues:** professional, $110 (annual) ● graduate, $10 (annual) ● undergraduate, $5 (annual) ● journal, domestic, $50 (annual) ● foreign, $75 (annual) ● corporate sustaining, $1,000 (annual) ● post doctorate, $55 (annual). **Staff:** 25. **Budget:** $900,000. **Regional Groups:** 3. **Description:** Represents dairy educators, scientists, researchers, and extension workers; dairy equipment manufacturers and suppliers; commercial dairy plants, breeding associations, farmers, and others. Promotes the dairy industry by stimulating scientific research, improving educational methods, and encouraging worthy intra and inter-industry cooperative endeavors. **Awards:** Agway Inc. Young Scientist Award. **Frequency:** annual. **Type:** recognition. **Recipient:** for young scientists ● Alfa Laval Agri Dairy Extension Award. **Frequency:** annual. **Type:** recognition ● American Feed Industry Association Award. **Frequency:** annual. **Type:** recognition. **Recipient:** for research in dairy cattle nutrition ● Award of Honor. **Frequency:** annual. **Type:** recognition. **Recipient:** for outstanding and consistent contributions to the welfare of the association ● Borden Award. **Frequency:** annual. **Type:** recognition ● Distinguished Service Award. **Frequency:** annual. **Type:** recognition. **Recipient:** for outstanding contributions to the welfare of the dairy industry ● Gist-Brocades Award. **Frequency:** annual. **Type:** recognition ● International Dairy Foods Association Research Award in Dairy Foods Processing. **Frequency:** annual. **Type:** recognition. **Recipient:** for research in dairy foods processors ● International Dairy Production Award. **Frequency:** annual. **Type:** recognition. **Recipient:** for research in dairy production ● J.L. Lush Award in Animal Breeding. **Frequency:** annual. **Type:** recognition ● Merck Agvet Dairy Management Research Award. **Frequency:** annual. **Type:** recognition ● Milk Industry Foundation and Kraft General Foods Teaching Award in Dairy Manufacturing. **Frequency:** annual. **Type:** recognition ● National Milk Producers Federation Richard M. Hoyt Award. **Frequency:** annual. **Type:** recognition. **Recipient:** for research in US dairy industry problems ● Nutrition Professionals, Inc. Applied Dairy Nutrition Award. **Frequency:** annual. **Type:** recognition. **Recipient:** for outstanding achievement in research, teaching, extension and/or industry in applied dairy nutrition ● Pharmacia & Upjohn Physiology Award. **Frequency:** annual. **Type:** recognition ● Pioneer Hi-Bred Forage Award. **Frequency:** annual. **Type:** recognition. **Recipient:** for research in the area of forage production, processing, storage, or utilization ● Purina Mills, Inc. Teaching Award in Dairy Production. **Frequency:** annual. **Type:** recognition ● West Agro, Inc. Award. **Frequency:** annual. **Type:** recognition. **Recipient:** for research on milk quality. **Committees:** Awards; Education; Public Health; Student Affiliate. **Sections:** Extension; Industry and Business; Manufacturing; Production. **Publications:** *Journal of Dairy Science*, monthly. **Price:** $40.00 for members; $100.00 for nonmembers. **Advertising:** accepted. Alternate Formats: CD-ROM; online ● *Scientific Reader Series: Current Research for Improved Calf and Heifer Raising*. **Price:** $25.00 for members; $40.00 for nonmembers. Alternate Formats: online ● *Scientific Reader Series: Mastitis Control and Milk Quality*. **Price:** $25.00 for members; $40.00 for nonmembers ● Newsletter, quarterly. **Price:** free ● Newsletter, semiannual. Alternate Formats: online. **Conventions/Meetings:** annual conference and meeting (exhibits) - 2008 July 7-11, Indianapolis, IN.

4486 ■ Dairylea Cooperative (DC)
PO Box 4844
Syracuse, NY 13221-4844

Ph: (315)433-0100
Free: (800)654-8838
Fax: (315)433-2345
E-mail: webmaster@dairylea.com
URL: http://www.dairylea.com
Contact: Clyde E. Rutherford, Pres.
Founded: 1907. **Members:** 2,500. **Staff:** 100. **Description:** Regional cooperative representing milk producers. **Formerly:** (1969) Dairymen's League Cooperative Association. **Conventions/Meetings:** annual meeting - always October.

4487 ■ International Milk Producers Association
c/o NMPF
2101 Wilson Blvd., Ste.400
Arlington, VA 22201
Ph: (703)243-6111
Fax: (703)841-9328
Founded: 1980. **Members:** 60. **Staff:** 3. **Budget:** $750,000. **Description:** National committee of the International Dairy Federation. Represents dairy and scientific associations, food manufacturers, universities, consultants, and individuals concerned about scientific, technical, and economic problems in the dairy industry. Advises and cooperates with dairy industry organizations. Conducts congresses and other meetings. **Libraries: Type:** open to the public. **Holdings:** 50; periodicals. **Subjects:** dairy industry. **Computer Services:** database ● mailing lists ● online services. **Formerly:** (1999) United States of America National Committee of the International Dairy Federation. **Publications:** *USNAC Annual Report* ● Catalog (in English and French), periodic. Lists publications available for purchase. **Price:** free. **Advertising:** accepted ● Newsletter ● Also publishes program of work. **Conventions/Meetings:** semiannual general assembly, held at the USA-IDF Annual ● seminar (exhibits) ● symposium ● workshop.

4488 ■ National Dairy Shrine (NDS)
c/o Mr. Maurice E. Core, Exec. Dir.
1224 Alton Darby Creek Rd.
Columbus, OH 43228-9792
Ph: (614)878-5333
Fax: (614)870-2622
E-mail: shrine@cobaselect.com
URL: http://www.dairyshrine.org
Contact: Mr. Maurice E. Core, Exec. Dir.
Founded: 1949. **Members:** 17,000. **Membership Dues:** life, $50. **Staff:** 1. **Description:** Represents persons interested in the dairy industry, including cattle breeders and educators. Maintains portrait gallery and museum in Ft. Atkinson, WI "to honor great dairymen of the past, recognize great dairymen of the present, and inspire dairy leaders of the future." Conducts specialized education programs. **Libraries: Type:** reference; open to the public. **Holdings:** 200; books, photographs. **Subjects:** history of dairy industry, collegiate and 4-H dairy judging contest winners. **Awards:** Distinguished Dairy Cattle Breeder. **Frequency:** annual. **Type:** recognition ● DMI/NDS Scholarships. **Frequency:** annual. **Type:** scholarship. **Recipient:** for undergraduate students ● Guest of Honor Award. **Frequency:** annual. **Type:** recognition. **Recipient:** for contemporary dairy leaders with outstanding contributions to the dairy industry ● M.E. McCullough Memorial Scholarships. **Frequency:** annual. **Type:** scholarship. **Recipient:** for high school senior planning to pursue a major in dairy/animal science ● NDS/lager Scholarship. **Frequency:** annual. **Type:** scholarship. **Recipient:** to a college student majoring in dairy or animal science ● NDS/Klussendorf Association Scholarship. **Frequency:** annual. **Type:** scholarship. **Recipient:** to a college student majoring in dairy science ● Pioneer Award. **Frequency:** annual. **Type:** recognition ● Student Recognition Program. **Frequency:** annual. **Type:** recognition. **Recipient:** for leadership skills, academic ability and interest in dairy cattle. **Committees:** Breeder Award; Permanent Home; Portrait; Scholarship; Student Recognition. **Formerly:** Dairy Shrine. **Publications:** *The Chronicle*, semiannual. Newsletter. Covers award winners and distinguished individuals in the industry. **Price:** included in membership dues. **Circulation:** 12,000 ● *National Dairy Shrine's First Fifty Years*. Book. **Conventions/Meetings:** annual banquet, awards presentations.

4489 ■ National Milk Producers Federation (NMPF)
2101 Wilson Blvd., Ste.400
Arlington, VA 22201
Ph: (703)243-6111
Fax: (703)841-9328
E-mail: info@nmpf.org
URL: http://www.nmpf.org
Contact: Jerry Kozak, Pres./CEO
Founded: 1916. **Members:** 30. **Staff:** 18. **Budget:** $3,000,000. **Description:** Works as a federation of 30 dairy cooperatives whose members produce the majority of the U.S. milk supply. Serves as "the voice of 60,000 daily producers" on Capitol Hill and with government agencies. **Awards: Type:** recognition. **Recipient:** for outstanding cheese, excellence in cooperative communications, and exemplary agricultural leadership. **Absorbed:** (1966) National Creameries Association. **Formerly:** National Cooperative Milk Producers Federation. **Publications:** *Dairy Producer Highlights*, annual ● *News for Dairy Co-ops*, biweekly. Newsletter. Contains the latest dairy policy information. Alternate Formats: online ● Brochure. Contains information about the organization and the dairy industry. Alternate Formats: online. **Conventions/Meetings:** annual meeting.

4490 ■ Pioneer Dairymen's Club of America (PDCA)
3097 145th St. NW
Monticello, MN 55362
Ph: (763)878-2636
Contact: Don Biske, Pres.
Founded: 1932. **Members:** 106. **Membership Dues:** $10 (annual). **Staff:** 1. **State Groups:** 17. **Description:** Retired and active dairymen who have worked in the industry for at least 25 years. Informs dairymen of current developments and changes in the industry. Facilitates communication and information exchange among members. Holds jamborees. **Awards: Type:** recognition. **Recipient:** to lifetime members ● **Type:** recognition. **Recipient:** for outstanding performance in the dairy industry. **Publications:** Membership Directory, annual. **Price:** free, for members only ● Newsletter, semiannual. **Conventions/Meetings:** annual meeting - 1st Wednesday of October.

4491 ■ United States Dairy Export Council (USDEC)
2101 Wilson Blvd., Ste.400
Arlington, VA 22201-3061
Ph: (703)528-3049
Fax: (703)528-3705
E-mail: info@usdec.org
URL: http://www.usdec.org
Contact: Dan Ingram, Contact
Description: Represents U.S. milk producers, dairy cooperatives, proprietary processors, export traders, industry suppliers. **Computer Services:** database, Biotech. **Telecommunication Services:** information service, U.S. Dairy Export Guide. **Publications:** *Dairy Market Outlook*, monthly. Manual. Details world dairy commodity, trade and DEIP activity. ● *Export Profile*, quarterly. Features news for the U.S. dairy industry. Alternate Formats: online ● *Facts on Dairy Exports*, weekly. Newsletter. Contains current information on trade policy issues. ● *USDEC Bakery Recipe Book for U.S. Dairy Ingredients*. Manual. Includes an introduction on how to use dairy ingredients in bakery applications and 26 recipes provided in part by USDEC members and industry experts. ● *World Dairy Markets and Outlook*, quarterly. Newsletter. Features analyses and perspectives on specific export market opportunities. **Price:** included in membership dues.

Dairy Products

4492 ■ Cheese of Choice Coalition (CCC)
c/o Oldways Preservation and Exchange Trust
266 Beacon St.
Boston, MA 02116
Ph: (617)421-5500
Fax: (617)421-5511
E-mail: oldways@oldwayspt.org
Multinational. Description: Organizes to oppose governmental agencies that want to ban production and sale of cheese made from unpasteurized milks.

4493 ■ National Conference on Interstate Milk Shipments (NCIMS)
c/o Leon Townsend, Exec. Sec.
123 Buena Vista Dr.
Frankfort, KY 40601
Ph: (502)695-0253
Fax: (502)695-0253
E-mail: ltownsend@ncims.org
URL: http://www.ncims.org
Contact: Leon Townsend, Exec. Sec.
Founded: 1950. **Members:** 350. **Membership Dues:** regular, $350 (biennial). **Staff:** 1. **Description:** Members are persons involved in the dairy industry: dairy farmers, processing plant personnel, persons involved in inspecting the dairy farmer's operation and/or the processing plant, persons who make laws concerning inspections, those who enforce the laws, academic researchers and advisers, consumers of dairy products. Aims to deliberate proposals submitted by various individuals from state or local regulatory agencies, FDA, USDA, producers, consumers etc. who have an interest in ensuring that the dairy products to consume are safe. **Conventions/Meetings:** biennial conference - 2009 Apr. 17-22, Orlando, FL.

4494 ■ National Dairy Council (NDC)
10255 W Higgins Rd., Ste.900
Rosemont, IL 60018
Ph: (312)240-2880
E-mail: ndc@dairyinformation.com
URL: http://www.nationaldairycouncil.org
Founded: 1915. **Description:** Promotes the health benefits of dairy products, including milk, cheese and yogurt. Provides nutrition information to the media, physicians, dietitians, nurses, educators, consumers and others concerned about fostering a healthier society. Sponsors educational programs for school children. **Publications:** Brochures. Contains information about food, nutrition, diet and health. ● Booklets. Contains information about food, nutrition, diet and health.

4495 ■ Wisconsin Dairy Products Association (WDPA)
8383 Greenway Blvd.
Middleton, WI 53562
Ph: (608)836-3336
Fax: (608)836-3334
E-mail: info@wdpa.net
URL: http://www.wdpa.net
Contact: Brad Legreid, Exec. Dir.
Founded: 1973. **Members:** 190. **Staff:** 2. **Description:** Represents dairy processors united to promote legislation favorable to the dairy industry of Wisconsin. **Formed by Merger of:** Wisconsin Creameries Association; Wisconsin Dairy Foods Association. **Publications:** Membership Directory, monthly. Includes newsletter covering legislative and regulatory issues affecting the industry. Contains calendar of events and research reports. **Conventions/Meetings:** annual meeting.

Dog

4496 ■ American Rare Breed Association (ARBA)
9921 Frank Tippett Rd.
Cheltenham, MD 20623
Ph: (301)868-5718
Fax: (301)868-6409
E-mail: info@arba.org
URL: http://www.arba.org
Founded: 1991. **Membership Dues:** basic, $30. **Description:** Serves and protects the "Rare Breed Dog" in the United States. Promotes and educates the public and dog fanciers about over 130 breeds from

around the world that are not currently recognized by the American Kennel Club. **Computer Services:** Information services, breed standards. **Telecommunication Services:** electronic mail, sales@arba.org ● electronic mail, drslack@verizon.net ● electronic mail, laurice@arba.org ● electronic mail, robert@arba.org.

Ecology

4497 ■ Arcosanti, A Project of the Cosanti Foundation
HC 74, Box 4136
Mayer, AZ 86333
Ph: (928)632-7135 (928)632-6217
Fax: (928)632-6229
E-mail: info@arcosanti.org
URL: http://www.arcosanti.org
Contact: Mr. Stefan Grace, Public Relations Coor.
Founded: 1965. **Membership Dues:** student, $15 ● individual, $25 ● family, $50 ● contributing, $100 ● donor, $500 ● sustaining, $1,000 ● patron, $5,000. **Staff:** 32. **Budget:** $800,000. **Languages:** English, French, German, Italian, Japanese. **Description:** Main concern of the foundation is the building of the energy-efficient town of Arcosanti, an arcology prototype. (The foundation defines arcology as a methodology that combines architecture with ecology, and recognizes the necessity for radical reorganization of the sprawling urban landscape into dense, integrated, three-dimensional towns and cities.) Maintains the Arcosanti Project which facilitates the construction of Arcosanti through the fabrication and sale of ceramic and bronze windbells, donations and tuition from educational programs. Conducts specialized group activities at Arcosanti including tours, seminars, workshops, and music events at the Colly Soleri Music Center at Arcosanti. **Libraries: Type:** reference. **Holdings:** 10,000; archival material, books, periodicals. **Awards: Type:** scholarship. **Divisions:** Bell Making; Colly Soleri Music Center; Education; Habitat (Construction); Landuse. **Programs:** Architecture and Ecology; Music; Philosophy. **Formerly:** (1993) Arcosanti. **Publications:** *Arcosanti: An Urban Laboratory*. Book ● *Arcosanti Workshops*. Brochures ● *Colly Soleri Music Center*. Brochures ● *Reinvent the American Dream*. Brochures. **Conventions/Meetings:** annual AZ State Poetry Festival and Slab City Slam, three days of poetry and performance, featuring poets, musicians, and performers from around the State (exhibits).

4498 ■ Association for Arid Lands Studies (AALS)
c/o International Center for Arid and Semiarid Land Studies
PO Box 41036
Lubbock, TX 79409-1036
Ph: (806)742-2218
Fax: (806)742-1954
E-mail: icasals@ttu.edu
URL: http://www.iaff.ttu.edu/home/icasals/aals.asp
Contact: A.C. Correa, Contact
Founded: 1977. **Members:** 250. **Membership Dues:** student, $10 (annual) ● individual, $20 (annual). **Description:** Scientists, social scientists, and humanists interested in the study of arid lands. Encourages an increased awareness of the problems and potentials of arid and semiarid lands and man's impact on them. Seeks to stimulate interdisciplinary research and teaching. Sponsors professional programs and meetings. **Affiliated With:** Western Social Science Association. **Publications:** *Forum of the Association for Arid Lands Studies*, annual. Includes selected papers from annual AALS meeting. **Price:** included in membership dues. **Conventions/Meetings:** annual conference, held in conjunction with the Western Social Sciences Association.

4499 ■ Association of Ecosystem Research Centers (AERC)
c/o Robin Graham, Sec.
Environmental Sciences Div.
Oak Ridge Natl. Lab.
PO Box 2008
Oak Ridge, TN 37831-2008
Ph: (865)576-7756
E-mail: grahamrl@ornl.gov
URL: http://www.ecosystemresearch.org
Contact: Lucinda Johnson, Pres.-Elect
Founded: 1985. **Members:** 41. **Membership Dues:** center (first two years), $200 (annual) ● center (after two years), $400 (annual). **Description:** Ecosystem research centers and laboratories representing 800 individuals. Promotes ecosystem science as a specific branch of the field of ecology. Provides information to Congress, other federal agencies, and the public about ecosystem science and its application to policy issues. Monitors government agencies regarding their use of ecosystem science in determining policy. Assists in the establishment of new research centers. **Telecommunication Services:** electronic mail, ljohnson@nrri.umn.edu. **Affiliated With:** American Institute of Biological Sciences. **Publications:** *AERC News*, semiannual. Newsletter ● *The Association of Ecosystem Research Centers*. Brochure ● *Directory of Member Centers*, periodic. **Conventions/Meetings:** annual meeting ● workshop.

4500 ■ Canyonlands Field Institute (CFI)
PO Box 68
Moab, UT 84532
Ph: (435)259-7750
Free: (800)860-5262
Fax: (435)259-2335
E-mail: info@canyonlandsfieldinst.org
URL: http://www.canyonlandsfieldinst.org
Contact: Karla VanderZanden, Exec. Dir.
Founded: 1984. **Members:** 1,000. **Membership Dues:** individual, $25 (annual) ● family, $40 (annual) ● business, supporting, $100 (annual) ● Plateau Society, $500 (annual) ● student, $15 (annual) ● corporate sponsor, $2,500 (annual) ● Westwater Society, $5,000 (annual). **Staff:** 5. **Budget:** $400,000. **Description:** Seeks to educate the public on the Canyonlands area (a section of the Colorado Plateau in southeast Utah) and the environmental effects of humans. Encourages environmental responsibility for the area. Maintains speakers'/instructors' bureau. Conducts research and educational programs; offers children's programs (K-12) and youth educational camps; land- and river-based "outdoor science school". **Libraries: Type:** reference. **Holdings:** 500. **Awards:** Educators Scholarship. **Frequency:** monthly. **Type:** scholarship ● Joy Ungricht Carbor Scholarship. **Frequency:** monthly. **Type:** scholarship. **Recipient:** for women pursuing outdoor education or guiding careers. **Boards:** Friends of CFI (Fundraising); Trustees. **Publications:** *Desert Winds*, annual. Newsletter. **Price:** included in membership dues. Alternate Formats: online. **Conventions/Meetings:** seminar ● workshop.

4501 ■ Center for Ecoliteracy (CEL)
2528 San Pablo Ave.
Berkeley, CA 94702
Ph: (510)845-4595
Fax: (510)845-1439
E-mail: info@ecoliteracy.org
URL: http://www.ecoliteracy.org
Contact: Zenobia Barlow, Exec. Dir./Co-Founder
Founded: 1995. **Staff:** 8. **Budget:** $1,500,000. **Description:** Works to foster children's experience and understanding of the natural world through educational activities and a grant-giving program. Believes that the greatest challenge of the time is to create sustainable communities and that there are lessons to be learned from ecosystems "which are sustainable communities of plants, animals, and microorganisms". Seeks to educate school children (particularly elementary and secondary students in the bay area bioregion) in ecoliteracy. **Libraries: Type:** reference. **Holdings:** books, periodicals. **Awards:** BBC Environment Award. **Type:** recognition. **Computer Services:** Mailing lists, of members. **Formerly:** (1995) Elmwood Institute. **Publications:** *Earth in Mind: On Education, Environment, and the Human Prospect*. Book. **Price:** $16.95 ● *Ecological Literacy: Education and the Transition to a Postmodern World*. Book. **Price:** $16.95 ● *Ecology and Community*. Reprint. Contains reprinted lecture by Fritjof Capra. **Price:** $2.00 ● *The Elmwood Quarterly*. Newsletter. Contains articles on systemic thinking; includes book summaries and members' forum. **Price:** $5.00/copy; $2.00 for 1991 issues; $35.00 for 1991-1995 anthology. **Circulation:** 1,500 ● *From the Parts to the Whole-Systems Thinking in Ecology and Education*. Article. **Price:** $2.00 ● *Getting Started: A Guide for Creating School Gardens as Outdoor Classrooms*. Handbook. **Price:** $7.95 ● *Guide to Ecoliteracy: A New Context for School Restructuring*. Book. **Price:** $15.00 ● *The Turning Point*. Book. **Price:** $14.95. **Conventions/Meetings:** periodic meeting.

4502 ■ Earth Charter USA Campaign
2100 L St. NW
Washington, DC 20037
Ph: (202)778-6133
Fax: (202)778-6138
E-mail: info@earthcharterusa.org
URL: http://www.earthcharterusa.org
Contact: Richard M. Clugston, Dir.
Founded: 1995. **Multinational. Description:** Citizen's organizations and grassroots groups, religious and spiritual groups of all faiths, professional associations, labor and workers groups, academic and educational community, business groups, politics and government, and media. Aims to build a society where people, animals and Earth can thrive together. Has developed a global people's treaty that promotes the awareness of and commitment to the values necessary to create a sustainable future. **Publications:** Newsletter.

4503 ■ Earth Ecology Foundation (EEF)
6120 W Tropicana, No. A16-303
Las Vegas, NV 89103
Ph: (702)340-3925
E-mail: erikwunstell@aol.com
URL: http://www.westvegas.com/earth_ecology_foundation.html
Contact: Erik Wunstell, Dir.
Founded: 1980. **Members:** 12. **Staff:** 1. **Description:** Individuals interested in earth science and human ecology. Purposes are: to study the interrelationship between mankind, technology, and nature; to provide modern solutions to ecological problems; to develop management plans pertaining to climate change and weather disasters. Promotes the scientific and humane use of earth's ecology through natural and technological means. Seeks the effective utilization of both natural and manmade systems. Works to produce more progressive and futuristic forms of civilization. Envisions the successful unification between meeting human needs and the preservation of earthly biosphere. Conducts research and gathers information. Provides educational materials to students, scholars, schools and libraries worldwide. Plans to open research laboratories, science museums, nature centers, video archives, botanical gardens, and disaster management stations throughout North America and Europe. **Convention/Meeting:** none. **Libraries: Type:** reference. **Holdings:** 4,000; audiovisuals, books, periodicals, reports. **Subjects:** nature, ecology, science, technology, geography, weather, population, civilization, urban planning, architecture, energy, transportation, pollution control, disaster management, space technology, education, cyberculture. **Also Known As:** The Earthology Foundation. **Publications:** *Citizen's Guide to Disaster Recovery*. Newsletter ● *Earth Echo*, semiannual. Newsletter ● *Earthology - The Physics of Solar Relativity*. Book ● *Earth's Unified Solar Field Pattern*. Book ● *Ecological Civilization 2020*. Book ● *The Geometric Progression of Space and Time*. Book ● *Our Planetary Future*. Book.

4504 ■ EarthSave International
PO Box 96
New York, NY 10108
Ph: (718)459-7503
Free: (800)362-3648
Fax: (718)228-2491
E-mail: information@earthsave.org
URL: http://www.earthsave.org
Contact: Caryn Hartglass, Exec. Dir.
Founded: 1988. **Members:** 2,569. **Membership Dues:** student, senior, $25 (annual) ● individual, $35

(annual) ● family, foreign, $50 (annual) ● patron, $100 (annual) ● sustainer, $500 (annual) ● life, $1,000. **Staff:** 2. **Budget:** $300,000. **Local Groups:** 37. **Description:** Promotes food choices that are healthy for the planet. Seeks to educate, inspire and empower people to take positive action for all life on Earth. **Formerly:** (1996) Earthsave Foundation. **Publications:** *EarthSave*, quarterly. Magazine. Features articles regarding food choices and effect on life; chapter information. Alternate Formats: online ● *EarthSave Educational Series*. **Price:** free. Alternate Formats: online ● Newsletter, quarterly. **Price:** free for members. **Conventions/Meetings:** annual EarthSave Summit - retreat and seminar - usually late October.

4505 ■ EcoLogic Development Fund

25 Mt. Auburn St., Ste.203, Harvard Sq.
Cambridge, MA 02138
Ph: (617)441-6300
Fax: (617)441-6307
E-mail: info@ecologic.org
URL: http://www.ecologic.org
Contact: Shaun Paul, Exec. Dir.

Founded: 1993. **Staff:** 7. **Multinational. Description:** Works to preserve the biodiversity of tropical ecosystems and promote the well-being of threatened local habitats through small-scale, community-based development. Supports the productive use of local resources to meet local needs. Encourages communities to identify and solve their ecological and economic problems in ways that respect both their cultural integrity and the natural limits of their ecosystem. Works with communities to design programs that allow the communities to retain or reclaim traditional knowledge while providing access to resources and information that will enable them to improve their living conditions. Conducts research. Maintains speakers' bureau. **Awards: Type:** grant. **Recipient:** to local and regional organizations in Latin America that share EcoLogic's commitment to integrate community development and conservation. **Computer Services:** Mailing lists. **Publications:** Newsletter, semiannual. **Price:** free. **Circulation:** 3,000. Alternate Formats: online.

4506 ■ Ecological Society of America (ESA)

1707 H St. NW, Ste.400
Washington, DC 20006
Ph: (202)833-8773
Fax: (202)833-8775
E-mail: esahq@esa.org
URL: http://www.esa.org
Contact: Katherine S. McCarter, Exec. Dir.

Founded: 1915. **Members:** 9,700. **Membership Dues:** regular (based on annual income), $50-$95 (annual) ● student, $25 (annual) ● contributing, $250 (annual). **Staff:** 24. **Budget:** $2,700,000. **Regional Groups:** 4. **National Groups:** 13. **Description:** Educators, professional ecologists, and scientists interested in the study of plants, animals, and man in relation to their environment. Seeks to develop better understanding of biological processes and their contribution to agriculture, forestry, wildlife and range management, fisheries, industry, public health, and conservation. **Awards:** Braun. **Frequency:** annual. **Type:** recognition. **Recipient:** for excellence in ecology ● Buell. **Frequency:** annual. **Type:** recognition. **Recipient:** for excellence in ecology ● Corporate. **Frequency:** annual. **Type:** recognition. **Recipient:** for a corporation, business, division, or an individual of a company ● Eminent Ecologist. **Frequency:** annual. **Type:** recognition. **Recipient:** to a senior ecologist ● George Mercer. **Frequency:** annual. **Type:** recognition. **Recipient:** for an outstanding ecological research paper ● Honorary Member. **Frequency:** annual. **Type:** recognition. **Recipient:** to a distinguished ecologist ● Robert H. MacArthur Award. **Frequency:** biennial. **Type:** recognition. **Recipient:** to a distinguished ecologist ● W.S. Cooper Award. **Frequency:** annual. **Type:** recognition. **Recipient:** for an outstanding contributor to the fields of geobotany and/or physiographic ecology. **Telecommunication Services:** electronic mail, ksm@esa.org. **Sections:** Applied Ecology; Aquatic Ecology; Asian Ecology; Education; International Affairs; Long-term Studies; Paleoecology; Physiological Ecology; Plant Population Ecology; Soil Ecology; Statistical Ecology; Theoretical Ecology; Vegetation. **Affiliated With:** American Association for the Advancement of Science; American Institute of Biological Sciences; ASPRS - The Imaging and Geospatial Information Society; Renewable Natural Resources Foundation. **Publications:** *Ecological Applications*, quarterly. Articles. Contains research articles. **Price:** $65.00 for members (regular); $55.00 for members (student); $265.00 /year for institutions. ISSN: 1051-0761. **Circulation:** 4,200. **Advertising:** accepted. Alternate Formats: online ● *Ecological Monographs*, quarterly. **Price:** $40.00 for members (regular); $35.00 for members (student); $148.00 /year for institutions. ISSN: 0012-9615. **Circulation:** 3,500. **Advertising:** accepted. Alternate Formats: online ● *Ecological Society of America Bulletin*, quarterly. **Price:** $35.00. ISSN: 0012-9623. **Circulation:** 6,900 ● *Ecological Society of America Bulletin, Supplement*, annual. Directory. **Price:** $10.00. ISSN: 0012-9623. **Circulation:** 6,900 ● *Ecology*, monthly. Articles. Contains research articles. **Price:** $85.00 for members (regular); $70.00 for members (student); $680.00 /year for institutions. ISSN: 0012-9658. **Circulation:** 6,400. **Advertising:** accepted. Alternate Formats: online. **Conventions/Meetings:** annual conference, scientific symposia, presented papers, posters, and business meetings (exhibits) - always August.

4507 ■ Environmental and Energy Study Institute (EESI)

122 C St. NW, Ste.630
Washington, DC 20001
Ph: (202)628-1400
Fax: (202)628-1825
E-mail: eesi@eesi.org
URL: http://www.eesi.org
Contact: Carol Werner, Exec. Dir.

Founded: 1984. **Staff:** 18. **Budget:** $1,600,000. **Description:** Promotes environmentally sustainable societies by working to educate policy makers and the general public on related issues including groundwater protection, water efficiency, and global climate change. Cooperates with NGOs governmental organizations and private sector. Conducts educational programs. **Awards:** Congressional Leadership Award. **Type:** recognition. **Telecommunication Services:** electronic mail, cwerner@eesi.org. **Projects:** Climate; Energy; International; Transportation; Water. **Working Groups:** Energy Efficiency; Renewable Energy; World Forest Agreement. **Publications:** *Briefing Book*, annual. **Price:** $75.00. Alternate Formats: online ● Bulletin, weekly. Tracks congressional action on energy, environment, and natural resources issues. **Price:** $395.00/year. **Conventions/Meetings:** annual Congressional Leadership Dinner.

4508 ■ Foundation for Deep Ecology

Bldg. 1062, Ft. Cronkhite
Sausalito, CA 94965
Ph: (415)229-9339
Fax: (415)229-9340
E-mail: info@deepecology.org
URL: http://www.deepecology.org
Contact: Douglas Tompkins, Pres.

Founded: 1990. **Staff:** 12. **Multinational. Description:** Environmental advocates. Strives to promote environmental ethics and issues. **Awards:** Ecological Agriculture Grant. **Frequency:** periodic. **Type:** grant. **Recipient:** to small or large groups working on alternative models of agriculture ● Globalization and Megatechnology Grant. **Frequency:** periodic. **Type:** grant. **Recipient:** to projects that attempt to educate the public about the impacts of globalization and the technological systems that serve it. **Publications:** *Clearcut: The Tragedy of Industrial Forestry*. Book. Contains information on industrial forestry. ● *Fatal Harvest: The Tragedy of Industrial Agriculture*. Book. Contains information on industrial farming. ● *Thrillcraft: The Environmental Consequences of Motorized Recreation*. Book ● *Welfare Ranching: The Subsidized Destruction of the American West*. Book. Contains information supporting the elimination of grazing cattle on public lands.

4509 ■ Gaia Institute

440 City Island Ave.
Bronx, NY 10464
Ph: (718)885-1906
E-mail: info@gaiainstituteny.org
URL: http://www.gaiainstituteny.org
Contact: Paul Mankiewicz PhD, Dir.

Founded: 1985. **Members:** 200. **Staff:** 20. **Budget:** $200,000. **Description:** Individuals and organizations working to enhance understanding of global problems created by industrial societies, including acid rain, ozone depletion, and worldwide distribution of toxics. Promotes the Gaia Hypothesis, stating that conditions on the earth's surface are maintained and affected by the interactions between ecological communities. Works to focus attention on ways that humans and other organisms are active participants in global and ecological change. Calls for positive restructuring of society to deepen understanding of the earth and its organisms. Current projects include: recycling organic wastes, waste water, and sewage treatment to revegetate the environment; establishing urban rooftop greenhouses to economically provide organic produce in cities; landfill detoxification and bioremediation; fostering positive adaptation of regulatory systems in biological systems; integration of architecture and ecology in the design of human communities. Conducts programs in conjunction with public schools, including ecological restoration of the South Bronx and Bronx River edge in New York City. **Libraries: Type:** not open to the public. **Holdings:** 3,000; articles, books, periodicals. **Subjects:** biology, ecology, engineering, physics, chemistry. **Publications:** *The Gaia Newsletter*, periodic. Includes book reviews and synopses of literature pertaining to the Gaia Hypothesis. **Price:** included in membership dues. **Circulation:** 1,000. **Conventions/Meetings:** monthly workshop and seminar (exhibits).

4510 ■ Institute for Sustainable Desert Occupancy (ISDO)

Address Unknown since 2007

Founded: 1989. **Description:** Conducts research and educational activities about the desert and semi-desert regions of the earth, and the sustainability of their use by humans, including habitation, resource development and conservation. **Publications:** *I.S. D.O Review and Outlook*, quarterly. Newsletter. **Price:** free.

4511 ■ International Association for the Advancement of Earth and Environmental Sciences (IAAEES)

Address Unknown since 2007

Founded: 1972. **Regional Groups:** 6. **Description:** Promotes the advancement of earth and environmental sciences for the betterment of mankind. Stresses interdisciplinary cooperation and the relationship between science and social studies. Seeks to improve and encourage the study of science at elementary, secondary, and university levels. Initiates educational and research programs; conducts scientific meetings and symposia; develops model studies in various countries. Encourages interaction among private industry, the academic community, and society. Disseminates information on the status of earth resources. **Publications:** none. **Convention/Meeting:** none. **Committees:** Energy Resources; Integration of Sciences; Mineral and Natural Resources; Research Projects; Water Resources.

4512 ■ International Council for Human Ecology and Ethnology (ICHEE)

PO Box 7024
New York, NY 10128-0010
Ph: (212)410-6560
Fax: (212)410-6560
E-mail: ichee@aol.com
URL: http://www.ichee.org
Contact: Dr. Robert John, Dir. Gen.

Founded: 1987. **Members:** 6,000. **Description:** Individuals and organizations interested in human ecology and ethnology. Seeks to protect the integrity of tribal, racial, and national ethnic groups, which the Council believes are the result of biological and cultural evolution. Opposes programs that distort ecological systems by foreign intervention or colonization or encouraging immigration. Promotes regional ethnic conflict resolution considering possible scenarios that offer new boundaries based on common history and culture. Maintains speakers' bureau. **Libraries: Type:** not open to the public. **Subjects:** ecology, ethnology, geopolitics and relevant history. **Formerly:** (1987) International Association for the Advancement of Ethnology and Eugenics; (1990) International Council on Human Ecology; (2001) International Commission for Human Ecology and Ethnology. **Publications:** *ICHEE Bulletin*, periodic. Newsletter. Contains news, ideas, and views on human ecology. Alternate Formats: online ● *The Sage of San Diego-A New Enlightenment from the Western Tradition*. Book. **Price:** $10.00 postpaid.

4513 ■ International Institute for Baubiologie and Ecology (IBE)

PO Box 387
Clearwater, FL 33757
Ph: (727)461-4371
Fax: (727)441-4373
E-mail: baubiologie@earthlink.net
URL: http://www.buildingbiology.net
Contact: Megan George, Exec. Dir.

Founded: 1987. **Membership Dues:** individual, gift, $45 (annual) ● student, senior, limited income, $25 (annual) ● BBEC member, $65 (annual) ● contributing, $100 (annual) ● life, $1,000. **Staff:** 5. **Local Groups:** 1. **Multinational. Description:** Seeks to advance public awareness of health hazards in homes and workplaces; offers correspondence courses and consulting services. **Libraries: Type:** reference. **Holdings:** articles, books, clippings, periodicals. **Subjects:** ecology, environment, home, workplace health hazards. **Computer Services:** database ● mailing lists ● online services, study and seminars. **Publications:** *EcoDwell Online*, 2-3/year. Newsletter. **Price:** included in membership dues. Alternate Formats: online. **Conventions/Meetings:** Indoor Air, Water and Materials - seminar, home environmental hazards: identification, testing, and remediation ● workshop and lecture.

4514 ■ International Society for Ecological Modelling (ISEM)

PMB 255
550 M Ritchie Hwy.
Severna Park, MD 21146
E-mail: bfath@towson.edu
URL: http://www.isemna.org
Contact: Brian D. Faith, Pres.

Founded: 1975. **Membership Dues:** student, $10 (annual) ● regular, $20 (annual) ● institutional, $100 (annual). **Multinational. Description:** Individuals and organizations with an interest in ecology and ecological modelling. Seeks to advance the study, teaching, and practice of ecological modelling. Conducts educational and continuing professional development courses for members; serves as a clearinghouse on ecological modelling; sponsors research programs. Plans to offer discounts on ecological modelling products and services to members. **Computer Services:** Online services, chat room. **Telecommunication Services:** electronic mail, dmauriello@isemna.org ● electronic mail, glarocque@isemna.org. **Publications:** *Ecological Modelling*, periodic. Journal. **Price:** $188.00 paper and electronic copy; $125.00 electronic copy only. Alternate Formats: online ● *ECOMOD*, quarterly. Newsletter. **Price:** included in membership dues. Alternate Formats: online.

4515 ■ International Society for Microbial Ecology (ISME)

c/o David A. Stahl
Univ. of Washington
Dept. of Civil and Env. Engg.
302 More Hall
Seattle, WA 98195-2700
Ph: (206)685-3464
Fax: (206)543-1543
E-mail: office@isme-microbes.org
URL: http://www.isme-microbes.org
Contact: Ms. Sarash de Wilde, Office and Editorial Asst.

Founded: 1998. **Membership Dues:** full, $120 (annual) ● student, $65 (annual). **Description:** Fosters the exchange of scientific information by organizing international symposia as well as specific workshops, sponsoring publications, and promoting education and research. Provides services to the scientific as well as to the wider community. **Awards:** Jim Tiedje Award. **Frequency:** biennial. **Type:** recognition. **Recipient:** for outstanding lifetime contribution to microbial ecology ● Young Investigator Award. **Frequency:** biennial. **Type:** recognition. **Recipient:** for scientist who has made a significant contribution to microbial ecology. **Publications:** *Microbial Ecology*, 8/year. Journal. ISSN: 0095-3628. **Circulation:** 1,500. **Advertising:** accepted. Alternate Formats: online. **Conventions/Meetings:** biennial symposium (exhibits) - 2008 Aug. 17-22, Cairns, QL, Australia - **Avg. Attendance:** 2000.

4516 ■ North American Benthological Society (NABS)

PO Box 1897
Lawrence, KS 66044-8897
Ph: (785)843-1235
Free: (800)627-0629
Fax: (785)843-1274
E-mail: poff@lamar.colostate.edu
URL: http://www.benthos.org
Contact: N. LeRoy Poff, Pres.

Founded: 1953. **Members:** 2,000. **Membership Dues:** regular, $70 (annual) ● student, $35 (annual). **Multinational. Description:** Researchers in aquatic ecology. Promotes better understanding of the benthic biological community and its role in freshwater aquatic ecosystems. (Benthic refers to the study of ecology relating to, or occurring at, the bottom of a body of water.) Conducts research into specific aquatic groups such as algae, vascular plants, zooplankton, phytoplankton, insects, crustaceans, mollusks, and fishes. Other areas of interest include: classification of aquatic biota; determination of pollution-tolerance ranges of aquatic species; the effect of water quality on distribution and abundance in the benthic community; hydrology; methods of sampling and measuring components of aquatic ecosystems. Disseminates information to the scientific community. **Awards:** Award of Excellence. **Frequency:** annual. **Type:** recognition. **Recipient:** to an aquatic scientist ● Distinguished Service Award. **Frequency:** annual. **Type:** recognition. **Recipient:** to members who have contributed a substantial amount of time and energy to the society over a number of years ● Environmental Stewardship Award. **Frequency:** annual. **Type:** recognition. **Recipient:** for an individual who has contributed substantially to environmental and ecological concerns through fostering a better understanding of scientific underpinnings and communication ● Hynes Award for New Investigators. **Frequency:** annual. **Type:** recognition. **Recipient:** to a new investigator who has recently published a monumental paper on aquatic ecology. **Committees:** Awards Selection; Conservation and Environmental Issues; Constitutional Revision; Education and Diversity; Elections and Place; Endowment; Graduate Resources; International Profiles; Public Information and Publicity; Science and Policy; Taxonomic Certification; Technical Issues. **Formerly:** Midwest Benthological Society. **Publications:** *Bulletin of the North American Benthological Society*, 3/year ● *Current and Selected Bibliography of Benthic Biology*, annual ● *Journal of the North American Benthological Society*, quarterly. Includes articles that promote understanding of Benthic communities. **Price:** $65.00 for members (print copy); $135.00 for libraries and institutions (print copy); $110.00 for libraries and institutions (online); $190.00 for libraries and institutions (online and print). ISSN: 0887-3593. Alternate Formats: online ● Membership Directory, periodic. **Conventions/Meetings:** annual conference and symposium (exhibits) ● annual meeting.

4517 ■ North American Coalition for Christianity and Ecology (NACCE)

866 Park Pl.
Brooklyn, NY 11216-4004
Ph: (718)496-5139
E-mail: nacce1@verizon.net
URL: http://www.nacce.org
Contact: Elizabeth Dyson, Dir./Ed.

Founded: 1986. **Members:** 200. **Membership Dues:** basic, $25 (annual) ● congregational, sustaining, $50 (annual). **Budget:** $15,000. **Description:** Promotes study of ecological issues in the context of Biblical theology and contemporary science. Invites people into a loving relationship with Earth through the formation of local Earthkeeping circles and regional conferences. **Projects:** Earthkeeping Circles. **Formerly:** (1998) North American Conference on Christianity and Ecology. **Publications:** *Earthkeeping News*. Newsletter. Alternate Formats: online. **Conventions/Meetings:** Bringing the Church Back Down to Earth - conference ● monthly Earthkeeping Circles - meeting, promotes formation of local ecumenical earthkeeping circles around the country.

4518 ■ People-Plant Council (PPC)

2021 Throckmorton Plant Sciences Ctr.
Manhattan, KS 66506-5501
Ph: (785)532-6170
E-mail: cshoemak@ksu.edu
Contact: Dr. Diane Relf, Contact

Founded: 1990. **Membership Dues:** trade affiliate, $2,000 (annual) ● professional/amateur affiliate, $1,000 (annual). **Budget:** $6,000. **Description:** Encourages researchers to document the effects plants and flowers have on human life. Conducts studies on psychological, sociological, physiological, economic, and environmental factors. Conducts educational programs. Disseminates information to public. **Libraries: Type:** reference. **Holdings:** audio recordings, books, clippings, periodicals, video recordings. **Subjects:** horticultural therapy, people-plant interaction. **Publications:** *The Healing Dimensions of People-Plant Relations: A Research Symposium*. Book. **Price:** $39.00 ● *People-Plant Council Newsletter*, quarterly. **Price:** free. ISSN: 1061-3460. **Circulation:** 1,500 ● *People-Plant Relationships: Setting Research Priorities*. Book. **Price:** $54.00 ● *The Role of Horticulture in Human Well-Being and Social Development*. Book. **Price:** $50.00. **Conventions/Meetings:** biennial symposium (exhibits).

4519 ■ Point Foundation (PF)

5757 Wilshire Blvd., Ste.370
Los Angeles, CA 90036
Free: (866)337-6468
Fax: (866)397-6468
E-mail: info@pointfoundation.org
URL: http://www.thepointfoundation.org
Contact: Bruce C. Lindstrom, Founder/Chm.

Staff: 8. **Budget:** $800,000. **Description:** Sponsors educational and ecological publications. **Awards:** Point Scholarship. **Frequency:** annual. **Type:** scholarship. **Recipient:** for students who are underprivileged ● Walter M. Decker Scholarship. **Frequency:** annual. **Type:** scholarship. **Recipient:** for outstanding students. **Computer Services:** Mailing lists. **Funds:** Carlos Enrique Cisneros Scholarship; Merle Aronson Scholarship. **Programs:** Point Foundation Mentoring. **Publications:** *Millennium Whole Earth Catalog*, quadrennial. Book. **Circulation:** 200,000 ● *Whole Earth: Access to Tools, Ideas and Practices*, quarterly. Magazine. Provides unorthodox coverage of contemporary social, cultural, political, environmental, and economic topics. Includes annual subject index. **Price:** $24.00/year; $12.00 for back issues. ISSN: 0749-5056. **Circulation:** 40,000. **Advertising:** accepted. Alternate Formats: microform.

4520 ■ Sierra Club (SC)

85 2nd St., 2nd Fl.
San Francisco, CA 94105
Ph: (415)977-5500 (202)547-1141
Fax: (415)977-5799

E-mail: information@sierraclub.org
URL: http://www.sierraclub.org
Contact: Carl Pope, Exec. Dir.
Founded: 1892. **Members:** 550,000. **Membership Dues:** regular, $39 (annual) ● supporting, $75 (annual) ● contributing, $150 (annual) ● life, $1,000 ● student, senior, limited income, $25 (annual). **Staff:** 294. **Budget:** $43,000,000. **State Groups:** 65. **Local Groups:** 398. **Description:** Individuals concerned with nature and its interrelationship to human beings. Promotes protection and conservation of the natural resources of the U.S. and the world; and educates others about the need to preserve and restore the quality of the environment and the integrity of those ecosystems. Works on urgent campaigns to save threatened areas; and is concerned with problems of wilderness, forestry, clean air, coastal protection, energy conservation, population, international development lending, and land use. Attempts to influence public policy at all governmental levels through legislative, administrative, legal, and electoral means. Schedules wilderness outings and chapters and committees schedule outings, talks, films, exhibits, and conferences. **Libraries: Type:** reference. **Holdings:** 11,000; biographical archives, books, maps, periodicals, photographs. **Subjects:** mountaineering and environmental topics. **Awards: Type:** recognition. **Computer Services:** Mailing lists, of members. **Telecommunication Services:** electronic mail, carl.pope@sierraclub.org. **Committees:** Agriculture; Air Quality; Binational Great Lakes; Canadian National; Clean Air; Coastal; Economics; Energy; Environmental Education; Hazardous Materials; International Environment; Labor Liaison; Military Impacts on the Environment; Native American Sites; Political Education; Population; Public Lands; Solid Waste; Urban Environment; Water Resources; Wetlands; Wildlife. **Departments:** Books; Conservation; Development; Outings; Public Affairs; Sierra; Volunteer Development. **Task Forces:** Alaska; Biodiversity; Biotechnology; Corporate Behavior; James Bay. **Affiliated With:** IUCN - The World Conservation Union. **Publications:** *Sierra*, bimonthly. Magazine. Provides essays on the wilderness, reports on environmental politics, conservation movement, and outdoor adventure; includes color photographs. **Price:** included in membership dues; $15.00 /year for nonmembers. ISSN: 0161-7362. **Circulation:** 408,000. **Advertising:** accepted. Alternate Formats: microform; online ● *Sierra Club National News Report*, semimonthly. Contains information on news concerning the environment and environmental legislation. **Price:** $18.00 for members; $20.00 for nonmembers ● Newsletters. Alternate Formats: online ● Also publishes books on environmental issues and outdoor activities.

4521 ■ Sierra Student Coalition (SSC)
408 C St. NE
Washington, DC 20002
Ph: (202)548-4592
Free: (888)JOIN-SSC
Fax: (202)547-6009
E-mail: sierra.student@sierraclub.org
URL: http://www.ssc.org
Contact: Katherine McEachern, Chair
Founded: 1991. **Members:** 20,000. **Membership Dues:** student/introductory (individual), $25 (annual) ● student (joint), $35 (annual) ● regular (individual), $39 (annual) ● regular (joint), $49 (annual) ● supporting (individual), $75 (annual) ● supporting (joint), $100 (annual) ● contributing (individual), $150 (annual) ● contributing (joint), $175 (annual) ● life (individual), $1,000 ● life (joint), $1,250. **Staff:** 3. **Budget:** $200,000. **Regional Groups:** 30. **Local Groups:** 250. **Description:** Students interested in ecology and environmental protection. Activist program of the Sierra Club. Serves as a network of student-run grass roots environmental organizations. Develops and implements strategies for grass roots environmental action, local issues campaigns, and social justice initiatives. Provides information, resources, and assistance to local organizations. Conducts leadership training programs; sponsors charitable activities; makes available children's services. **Libraries: Type:** reference. **Holdings:** clippings. **Subjects:** environmental protection, social activism. **Computer Services:** Mailing lists, of members. **Publications:** *Generation E*, bimonthly. Newsletter ● Brochure ● Bulletin ● Directory, periodic. **Conventions/Meetings:** semiannual board meeting.

4522 ■ Society for Ecological Restoration International (SER)
285 W 18th St., Ste.1
Tucson, AZ 85701
Ph: (520)622-5485
Fax: (520)626-5485
E-mail: info@ser.org
URL: http://www.ser.org
Contact: Mary Kay C. LeFevour, Exec. Dir.
Founded: 1987. **Members:** 2,500. **Membership Dues:** associate, $5 (annual) ● basic, $25 (annual) ● full, $45 (annual) ● student/basic (developing country), $10 (annual) ● full (developing country), $20 (annual) ● professional, $125 (annual) ● professional (developing country), $75 (annual) ● organizational, $250 (annual) ● organizational (developing country), $175 (annual). **Staff:** 3. **Regional Groups:** 5. **Description:** Scientists, researchers, educators, academics, environmental consultants, and other interested individuals; government agencies. Promotes ecological restoration as a scientific and technical discipline that provides a strategy for environmental conservation, a technique for ecological research, and a means of developing a "mutually beneficial relationship" between humans and nature. **Telecommunication Services:** electronic mail, krod17@msn.com. **Formerly:** Society for Ecological Restoration and Management; (2005) Society for Ecological Restoration. **Publications:** *Restoration and Management Notes*, semiannual. Journal ● *Restoration Ecology*, quarterly. Journal ● *The Role of Restoration in Ecosystem Management*. Proceedings. From the 1996 Conference. **Price:** $35.00 in U.S.; $40.00 outside U.S. ● *SER News*, quarterly. Newsletter. **Conventions/Meetings:** annual conference (exhibits).

4523 ■ Thorne Ecological Institute (TEI)
PO Box 19107
Boulder, CO 80308-2107
Ph: (303)499-3647 (720)981-5035
Fax: (720)565-3873
E-mail: info@thorne-eco.org
URL: http://www.thorne-eco.org
Contact: Kelly Keena, Interim Exec. Dir.
Founded: 1954. **Staff:** 3. **Budget:** $210,000. **Description:** Works for the application of ecological principles, stewardship of natural resources, and improvement of the human environment. Offers children's programs in the natural sciences, arts and crafts, outdoor skills, and ecology. Offers hands-on environmental education to young people along the Front Range of Colorado. Envisions a thriving, healthy environment that supports all life. **Libraries: Type:** by appointment only. **Holdings:** 100; articles, books, films, papers, photographs, reports. **Awards:** Thorne Environmental Award. **Frequency:** annual. **Type:** recognition. **Recipient:** to individuals who have demonstrated a deep devotion and outstanding leadership for the earth through education, business ethics, stewardship, or community organizing. **Formerly:** (1971) Thorne Ecological Foundation. **Publications:** *Dragonfly News*. Newsletter. Alternate Formats: online ● *Issues and Technology in the Management of Impacted Wildlife*, biennial. Proceedings. Contains symposium proceedings of technical papers on management, mitigation, and research of impacted wildlife for biologists. **Price:** $35.00/copy.

Economics

4524 ■ Council on Food, Agricultural and Resource Economics (C-FARE)
c/o Tamara Wagester, Exec. Dir.
900 Second St. NE, Ste.205
Washington, DC 20002
Ph: (202)408-8522
Fax: (202)408-5385
E-mail: tamarawagester@cfare.org
URL: http://www.cfare.org
Contact: Tamara Wagester, Exec. Dir.
Description: Seeks to strengthen the national presence of the agricultural economics profession. Helps agricultural economists contribute to public and private sector decisions. Fosters support for agricultural research. Raises awareness of agricultural economics contributions in solving societal issues. **Publications:** *The Council Caller*. Newsletter. Alternate Formats: online ● Annual Reports. Alternate Formats: online.

Education

4525 ■ Project Food, Land and People (FLP)
c/o John H. Davis
65 Poinsetta Rd. SE
Scio, OH 43988
E-mail: info@foodlandpeople.org
URL: http://www.foodlandpeople.org
Contact: Christopher Williams, Steering Committee Chm.
Founded: 1988. **Description:** Addresses critical needs of agriculture, education and the environment. Promotes approaches to learning to help people better understand the interrelationships among agriculture, the environment and people of the world. Works to enhance sustainable agricultural practices and informed consumer choices. **Publications:** Newsletter, semiannual. Alternate Formats: online.

Energy

4526 ■ Center for Energy Efficiency and Renewable Technologies (CEERT)
1100 11th St., Ste.311
Sacramento, CA 95814
Ph: (916)442-7785
Free: (877)758-4462
Fax: (916)447-2940
E-mail: info@ceert.org
URL: http://www.ceert.org
Contact: V. John White, Exec. Dir.
Founded: 1990. **Description:** Environmental organizations, public interest groups, technology companies. Strives to work with its members to develop America's clean, renewable energy resources. Campaigns for sustainable electrical generation policies. **Publications:** *Clean Power Journal*, quarterly. Newsletter ● *Crude Reckoning: The Impact of Petroleum on California's Public Health and Environment*. Report.

4527 ■ Energy Communities Alliance (ECA)
1101 Connecticut Ave. NW, Ste.1000
Washington, DC 20036-4374
Ph: (202)828-2317
Fax: (202)828-2488
E-mail: sethk@energyca.org
URL: http://www.energyca.org
Contact: Seth Kirshenberg, Exec. Dir.
Founded: 1992. **Description:** Dedicated to meeting the broad ranging needs of energy communities. Develops customized research on specific problems facing energy communities. **Telecommunication Services:** electronic mail, paulk@energyca.org. **Publications:** *ECA Bulletin*, monthly. Updates members on issues impacting ECA member communities including legislative and regulatory updates and Federal Register monitoring. **Price:** included in membership dues.

4528 ■ Northwest Energy Efficiency Alliance (NEEA)
529 SW 3rd Ave., Ste.600
Portland, OR 97204
Ph: (503)827-8416
Free: (800)411-0834
Fax: (503)827-8437

E-mail: info@nwalliance.org
URL: http://www.nwalliance.org
Contact: Margie Gardner, Exec. Dir.
Founded: 1996. **Description:** Committed to supporting regional programs that make affordable, energy efficient products and services available in the marketplace. **Computer Services:** Mailing lists, listserv for members. **Projects:** Architecture and Energy: Building Excellence in the Northwest; BacGen; BetterBricks; Building Commissioning Association; Building Operator Certification; Building Performance Services; Commercial Windows Initiative; Compressed Air Challenge.

Environment

4529 ■ African American Environmentalist Association (AAEA)
9903 Caltor Ln.
Fort Washington, MD 20744
Ph: (301)265-8185
Fax: (301)265-2952
E-mail: africanamericanenvironmentalist@msn.com
URL: http://groups.msn.com/AAEA
Contact: Norris McDonald, Pres.
Founded: 1985. **Description:** Aims to increase African-American participation in the environmental movement. Seeks to protect the environment and enhance human, animal and plant ecologies. Promotes the efficient use of natural resources. **Computer Services:** Information services, environmental legislation ● information services, environmental resources ● online services, chat room ● online services, message board. **Telecommunication Services:** electronic mail, norrismcdonald@msn.com. **Publications:** *The African American Environmentalist.* Newsletter. Alternate Formats: online.

4530 ■ African Environmental Research and Consulting Group (AERCG)
14912 Walmer St.
Overland Park, KS 66223
Ph: (913)897-6132
Fax: (913)897-6132
E-mail: aercgc31@juno.com
URL: http://www.africaenviro.org
Contact: Dr. Peter A. Sam, Chm.
Founded: 1990. **Members:** 1,300. **Staff:** 6. **Regional Groups:** 7. **State Groups:** 2. **Local Groups:** 1. **National Groups:** 2. **For-Profit. Multinational. Description:** African and African-American professionals. Promotes mitigation of environmental hazards in Africa. Provides voluntary technical assistance and financial support to environmental protection and mitigation programs; promotes collaboration between African and American scientists working in pollution control and related fields; seeks to raise public awareness in the United States regarding environmental problems in Africa. Conducts preliminary assessments to identify environmental hazards; facilitates technology transfers. **Libraries: Type:** reference. **Subjects:** environmental management. **Awards:** Environmental Personality of the Year in Africa. **Frequency:** annual. **Type:** recognition. **Recipient:** for achievements in environmental management and community education. **Computer Services:** database ● mailing lists. **Publications:** *International Environmental Consulting Practice.* **Price:** $60.00/copy.

4531 ■ Amazon Alliance
1367 Connecticut Ave. NW, Ste.400
Washington, DC 20036-1860
Ph: (202)785-3334
Fax: (202)785-3335
E-mail: amazon@amazonalliance.org
URL: http://www.amazonalliance.org
Contact: Johnson Cerda, Co-Dir.
Founded: 1990. **Members:** 80. **Membership Dues:** individual, $40 (annual). **Staff:** 3. **Description:** Indigenous People of Amazon and U.S. Environmental groups nominated for membership. Works to strengthen and broaden the alliance between indigenous peoples of the Amazon and those who share their concerns for the Amazon's future. **Committees:** Alliance; Evaluation/Management; Fundraising. **Councils:** Steering. **Working Groups:** Brazil, the Guyanas, and the Andean-Amazon Countries. **Publications:** *Amazon Update*, monthly. Newsletter. Alternate Formats: online. **Conventions/Meetings:** biennial assembly, evaluate and plan work to be done in defense of the Amazonian peoples.

4532 ■ America the Beautiful Fund (ABF)
725 15th St. NW, Ste.605
Washington, DC 20005
Ph: (202)638-1649
Free: (800)522-3557
Fax: (202)638-2175
E-mail: info@america-the-beautiful.org
URL: http://www.america-the-beautiful.org
Contact: Nanine Bilski, Pres./CEO
Founded: 1965. **Membership Dues:** general, $10 (annual). **Staff:** 5. **Budget:** $5,000,000. **Local Groups:** 20,000. **Description:** Provides grants of vegetable, flower and herb seed to groups growing food for the needy, to beautify public spaces and promote environmental stewardship. **Awards:** National Recognition Award. **Frequency:** annual. **Type:** recognition. **Recipient:** for superior projects in U.S. **Publications:** *Better Times*, periodic. Newsletter. Covers projects and events in community improvement, environmental education, growing food for the needy, and ABF Awards. **Price:** $10.00 suggested annual donation for individual. **Circulation:** 10,000.

4533 ■ American Lands Alliance
726 7th St. SE
Washington, DC 20003
Ph: (202)547-9400
Fax: (202)547-9213
E-mail: info@americanlands.org
URL: http://www.americanlands.org
Contact: Taylor McKinnon, Pres.
Founded: 1991. **Staff:** 7. **Regional Groups:** 8. **State Groups:** 2. **Description:** Works to protect wildlife and wild places. Educates and advocates for sound forests and wildlands protection. **Computer Services:** Online services, listserv. **Publications:** Reports.

4534 ■ Association for Gnotobiotics Research and Technology
c/o Dr. Philip B. Carter, Interim Exec. Sec.-Treas.
North Carolina State Univ.
Coll. of Veterinary Medicine
4700 Hillsborough St.
Raleigh, NC 27606
Ph: (919)513-6278
Fax: (919)848-2192
E-mail: philipcarter@earthlink.net
URL: http://www.gnotobiotics.org
Contact: Leda Vieira, Pres.
Founded: 1961. **Membership Dues:** regular, $25 (annual) ● student, $5 (annual) ● institutional, $250 (annual). **Description:** Any person engaged or interested in the field of gnotobiotics. Goals are to stimulate research in the field of basic and applied gnotobiotics; expedite the dissemination of information relative to gnotobiotics and gnotobiotic technology; stimulate production, maintenance, distribution and use of gnotobiotes; establish standards; and establish an acceptable nomenclature in the field of gnotobiotics. **Committees:** Archives; History of the Association; Student Travel Fellowship; Technical Education. **Publications:** Newsletter ● Membership Directory. Alternate Formats: online. **Conventions/Meetings:** annual meeting.

4535 ■ Beldon Fund
99 Madison Ave., 8th Fl.
New York, NY 10016
Ph: (212)616-5600
Free: (800)591-9595
Fax: (212)616-5656
E-mail: info@beldon.org
URL: http://www.beldon.org
Contact: Bill Roberts, Exec. Dir./Pres.
Staff: 9. **Description:** Strives to promote environment issues. **Funds:** Beldon Discretionary. **Programs:** Human Health and the Environment; Key States. **Publications:** Annual Report, annual.

4536 ■ Center for Alternative Mining Development Policy (CAMDP)
210 Avon St., Ste.4
La Crosse, WI 54603
Ph: (608)784-4399
Fax: (608)785-8486
E-mail: gedicks.al@uwlax.edu
Contact: Al Gedicks, Exec. Dir.
Founded: 1977. **Members:** 600. **Description:** Native Americans, farmers, and those living in urban areas concerned about threats to the environment of the Lake Superior region. Seeks to provide information and technical assistance to Indian tribes and rural communities affected by plans for mining development. Focuses on issues such as mining taxation, groundwater quality, hazards of uranium exploration, and the environmental impact of metallic sulfide mining. Operates speakers' bureau. Consults with similar international and national groups. **Libraries: Type:** reference. **Holdings:** 1,000. **Subjects:** mining, radioactive waste. **Publications:** *Anishinaabe Niijii (Friends of the Chippewa).* Video ● *Keepers of the Water.* Video ● *LAND GRAB: The Corporate Theft of Wisconsin's Mineral Resources* ● *The New Resource Wars.* Video ● *The New Resource Wars: Native and Environmental Struggles Against Multinational Corporations.* Book. **Price:** $18.00 ● *Questions and Answers about BHP Billiton's Proposed Crandon Mine in Wisconsin.* Brochures ● *Resource Rebels: Native Challenges to Mining and Oil Corporations.* Book. **Price:** $18.00 ● Brochures. **Conventions/Meetings:** periodic Tri State Anti Uranium Organizers Training Conference ● periodic workshop, informs citizens on how to involve them in the environmental decision-making process.

4537 ■ Center for Environmental Information (CEI)
55 St. Paul St.
Rochester, NY 14604
Ph: (585)262-2870
Fax: (585)262-4156
E-mail: cei@ceinfo.org
URL: http://www.ceinfo.org
Contact: Lee M. Loomis, Dir.
Founded: 1974. **Members:** 400. **Membership Dues:** basic, $25 (annual) ● student, $10 (annual) ● family, sustaining, $50 (annual) ● Maple Society, $100 (annual) ● Oak Society, $200 (annual). **Staff:** 4. **Budget:** $250,000. **Description:** Disseminates information on environmental issues. Conducts annual climate issues conference. **Libraries: Type:** reference. **Holdings:** 10,000; books, clippings, periodicals. **Subjects:** environmental topics. **Awards:** Environmental Stewardship Award. **Frequency:** annual. **Type:** recognition ● Hartwell Volunteer Award. **Frequency:** annual. **Type:** recognition ● Hugh Cumming Environmental Quality Award. **Frequency:** annual. **Type:** recognition. **Telecommunication Services:** electronic mail, lloomis@ceinfo.org. **Publications:** *CEI Sphere*, quarterly. Newsletter. Alternate Formats: online ● *Directory of Environmental Organizations in the Rochester Area*, annual. Alternate Formats: online. **Conventions/Meetings:** annual conference, on climate issues.

4538 ■ Center for Environmental Study (CES)
Address Unknown since 2008
Founded: 1969. **Members:** 120. **Membership Dues:** general, $25 (annual) ● life, $10,000. **Staff:** 3. **Budget:** $250,000. **Description:** Seeks to increase public awareness of environmental processes and issues by the development and implementation of educational and informational programs and materials. Focus is regional but does provide research materials nationwide. **Libraries: Type:** reference; lending; open to the public. **Holdings:** 100; archival material, audiovisuals, books, clippings, periodicals. **Subjects:** environment, tropical forests, Great Lakes, biodiversity. **Computer Services:** Online services, awareness information. **Publications:** *Birds of Michigan*, annual. Book. Describes birds, habitats, feeding and other aspects of Michigan birds. **Price:** $8.00 ● *Car-*

ing for Planet Earth: The Great Lakes an Interactive, Multimedia Educational Program. **Price:** $19.00. Alternate Formats: CD-ROM ● *Research Bibliography of Mahogany.* **Price:** free. Alternate Formats: diskette.

4539 ■ Charles A. and Anne Morrow Lindbergh Foundation
2150 3rd Ave. N, Ste.310
Anoka, MN 55303-2200
Ph: (763)576-1596
Fax: (763)576-1664
E-mail: info@lindberghfoundation.org
URL: http://www.lindberghfoundation.org
Contact: Kelley Welf, Communications Mgr.
Founded: 1977. **Members:** 1,400. **Membership Dues:** individual grant sponsor, $15,000 (annual) ● life, associate, $5,000 ● patron associate, $2,500 (annual) ● associate, $1,000 (annual) ● sponsoring associate, $500 (annual) ● partnering associate, $250 (annual) ● sustaining associate, $100 (annual) ● family associate, $55 (annual) ● individual associate, $35 (annual) ● corporate grant sponsor, $25,000. **Staff:** 3. **Budget:** $360,000. **Description:** Perpetuates the partnership of aviator Charles A. Lindbergh (1902-1974) and Anne Morrow Lindbergh (1906-2001) and promotes their vision of balance between technological advancement and environmental preservation. Conducts educational programs. Awards research grants. **Awards:** Anne Spencer Lindbergh Prize. **Frequency:** biennial. **Type:** monetary. **Recipient:** to the author of a fantasy novel ● Lindbergh Award. **Frequency:** annual. **Type:** recognition. **Recipient:** to an individual for his or her significant contributions toward the foundation ● Lindbergh Grants. **Frequency:** annual. **Type:** grant. **Recipient:** by application. **Formerly:** Lindbergh Memorial Fund; Charles A. Lindbergh Fund. **Publications:** Newsletter, 3/year. Includes historical items on Lindbergh and aviation; reports on upcoming events and programs. **Price:** free for members. **Circulation:** 2,500 ● Annual Report, annual. **Conventions/Meetings:** annual Lindbergh Award Lecture - usually May, in New York City ● periodic symposium.

4540 ■ Clean Beaches Council (CBC)
1225 New York Ave. NW, Ste.450
Washington, DC 20005
Ph: (202)682-9507
Fax: (202)682-9506
E-mail: info@cleanbeaches.org
URL: http://www.cleanbeaches.org
Contact: Mr. Robert F. Van Voorhees Esq., Gen. Counsel
Founded: 1998. **Description:** Increases public awareness and volunteer participation in beach sustainability. Protects the earth's pristine coastal regions. Promotes sustainable habitation between humans and the environment.

4541 ■ Clean Islands International (CII)
8219 Elvaton Dr.
Pasadena, MD 21122-3903
Ph: (410)647-2500
Fax: (410)647-4554
E-mail: linkages@verizon.net
URL: http://www.islands.org/cii/ciipage.htm
Contact: Allan Hunt, Pres.
Founded: 1992. **Description:** Provides educational and technical assistance to island communities seeking to implement sustainable economic development programs while maintaining environmental quality. Conducts educational programs. **Telecommunication Services:** electronic mail, ahunt.gov@ibl.bm. **Conventions/Meetings:** periodic conference ● periodic workshop.

4542 ■ Climate Institute
1785 Massachusetts Ave. NW
Washington, DC 20036
Ph: (202)547-0104
Fax: (202)547-0111
E-mail: info@climate.org
URL: http://www.climate.org
Contact: John C. Topping, Pres.
Founded: 1986. **Members:** 1,500. **Membership Dues:** regular, $95 (annual) ● supporting, $150 (annual) ● contributing, $250 (annual) ● life, $1,000 ● student, $50 (annual). **Staff:** 8. **Budget:** $600,000. **Description:** Scientists, policy makers, and interested individuals. Acts as an international liaison between the scientific community and policy makers. Conducts seminars on environmental issues. Devoted to helping maintain the balance between climate and life on earth. **Libraries: Type:** reference. **Holdings:** 1,500. **Subjects:** climate change, related issues, energy. **Awards:** Global Environmental Leadership Award. **Frequency:** annual. **Type:** recognition. **Recipient:** for distinguished ability in global environmental leadership. **Telecommunication Services:** electronic mail, jtopping@climate.org. **Publications:** *Climate Alert*, quarterly. Newsletter. Covers global climate change issues. **Price:** $95.00. ISSN: 1071-3271. **Circulation:** 1,500. **Conventions/Meetings:** Seattle Summit on Protecting the World's Climate - meeting.

4543 ■ Coalition to End Childhood Lead Poisoning
2714 Hudson St.
Baltimore, MD 21224
Ph: (410)534-6447
Free: (800)370-5323
Fax: (410)534-6475
E-mail: info@leadsafe.org
URL: http://www.leadsafe.org
Contact: Ruth Ann Norton, Exec. Dir.
Founded: 1991. **Members:** 250. **Membership Dues:** general support, $100. **Staff:** 10. **Budget:** $900,000. **State Groups:** 1. **Local Groups:** 1. **Languages:** English, French, Spanish. **Description:** Works to prevent lead poisoning in children. Promotes a lead-free environment. Maintains speakers' bureau. **Libraries: Type:** reference. **Holdings:** artwork, audiovisuals, books, business records, clippings, periodicals. **Subjects:** lead poisoning. **Computer Services:** database ● online services. **Also Known As:** Coalition Against Childhood Lead Poisoning and Parents Against Lead. **Publications:** *Get the Lead Out!*. Newsletter. **Conventions/Meetings:** annual roundtable ● monthly Statewide Partnerships - meeting.

4544 ■ Coalition for Environmentally Responsible Economies (CERES)
99 Chauncy St., 6th Fl.
Boston, MA 02111
Ph: (617)247-0700
Fax: (617)267-5400
E-mail: lubber@ceres.org
URL: http://www.ceres.org
Contact: Mindy S. Lubber, Pres.
Founded: 1989. **Staff:** 20. **Budget:** $1,500,000. **Description:** Represents environmental groups, religious groups, labor and public interest groups. Encourages ethical environmental practices through negotiation, public education, and shareholder activism. Disseminates and promotes adherence to its principles, a ten-point code of environmental performance for businesses. **Awards:** Ceres-ACCA Sustainability Reporting Award. **Frequency:** annual. **Type:** recognition. **Recipient:** for the best sustainability report. **Computer Services:** Online services. **Telecommunication Services:** electronic mail, massie@ceres.org. **Projects:** Corporate Disclosure; Electronic Power Dialogue; Green Hotel Initiative; Insurance; Investors Network and Climate Risk; North East and Canada Climate Program; Research; Shareholder Action. **Publications:** *CERES Report* ● Newsletter. Alternate Formats: online ● Reports. **Conventions/Meetings:** annual conference.

4545 ■ Concern
1794 Columbia Rd. NW
Washington, DC 20009
Ph: (202)328-8160
Fax: (202)387-3378
E-mail: concern@concern.org
URL: http://www.sustainable.org
Contact: Susan Boyd, Dir.
Founded: 1970. **Staff:** 7. **Budget:** $100,000. **Description:** Provides environmental information to individuals and groups and encourages them to act in their communities. Funded by contributions from individuals, foundation grants, and proceeds from the sale of its publications. **Convention/Meeting:** none. **Computer Services:** database, community sustainability. **Publications:** *Drinking Water: A Community Action Guide.* Booklet. **Price:** $4.00 plus shipping and handling ($1.50) for first copy ● *Farmland: A Community Issue.* **Price:** $4.00 plus shipping and handling ● *Global Warming and Energy Choices.* **Price:** $4.00 plus shipping and handling ● *Household Wastes: Issues and Opportunities.* **Price:** $4.00 plus shipping and handling ● *Pesticides in Our Communities: Choice for Change.* **Price:** $4.00 plus shipping and handling ● *Waste: Choices for Communities.* **Price:** $4.00 plus shipping and handling.

4546 ■ Conservation Northwest
1208 Bay St., No. 201
Bellingham, WA 98225-4301
Ph: (360)671-9950
Free: (800)878-9950
Fax: (360)671-8429
E-mail: roliver@conservationnw.org
URL: http://www.conservationnw.org
Contact: Rose Oliver, Office Mgr./Events Coor.
Founded: 1989. **Members:** 8,000. **Membership Dues:** individual, $30 (annual) ● family, $35 (annual) ● living lightly, $15 (annual) ● supporter, $50 (annual) ● sustainer, $100 (annual) ● sponsor, $250 (annual) ● hero, $500 (annual). **Staff:** 26. **Budget:** $750,000. **Description:** Protects and connects old-growth forests and other wild areas from the Washington Coast to the BC Rockies: vital to a healthy future for you, the children, and wildlife. **Formerly:** (1995) Greater Ecosystem Alliance; (2005) Northwest Ecosystem Alliance. **Publications:** *Cascadia Wild: Protecting an International Ecosystem.* Book. **Price:** $12.95 ● *Conservation Northwest Quarterly.* Newsletter. **Price:** included in membership dues; $30.00 /year for nonmembers. **Circulation:** 8,000.

4547 ■ Earth Communications Office (ECO)
16815 Victory Blvd., No. 226
Van Nuys, CA 91406-5550
Ph: (818)787-9550 (213)321-2104
E-mail: lancecoach@aol.com
URL: http://www.oneearth.org
Contact: Lance Coach, Admin. Dir.
Founded: 1989. **Members:** 150. **Membership Dues:** individual, $40 (annual) ● sponsor, $75 (annual) ● contributing, $100 (annual). **Staff:** 4. **Budget:** $350,000. **Description:** Uses the power of communication to improve the global environment. Works within the Hollywood community to produce annual public service campaigns for movie theatres, television, radio, and the Internet that reach more than one billion people worldwide. **Libraries: Type:** not open to the public. **Holdings:** books, business records, clippings. **Subjects:** environment. **Publications:** *Earth Communique*, quarterly. Newsletter. **Price:** $40.00/year. **Circulation:** 2,000. **Advertising:** accepted. Alternate Formats: online.

4548 ■ Earth Day Network (EDN)
1616 P St. NW, Ste.340
Washington, DC 20036
Ph: (202)518-0044
Fax: (202)518-8794
E-mail: earthday@earthday.net
URL: http://www.earthday.net
Contact: Kathleen Rogers, Pres.
Founded: 1970. **Members:** 5,000. **Membership Dues:** individual, $15 (annual). **Staff:** 2. **Budget:** $50,000. **Languages:** Albanian, Arabic, Bulgarian, English, French, Hebrew, Japanese, Macedonian, Russian, Serbian, Spanish, Ukrainian. **Description:** Individuals interested in the environment. Coordinates annual Earth Day Events and activities in the United States; Earth Day is observed internationally on April 22 and is intended to increase global awareness of environmental issues. Campaigns for truth on environmental claims on labeling and in advertising. Reports on products and services that are good for the environment. Conducts research and educational programs. **Computer Services:** database, Earth Day events. **Councils:** International; U.S. **Formerly:** (2001) Earth Day 2000. **Publications:** *Countdown*

2000 Report, annual, published each Earth Day. Contains updates about the progress being made in meeting the global goals set out at Earth Day 1991. ● *Don't Be Fooled Report: Top Ten Greenwashers of the Year*, annual. Reprint. Features companies who make misleading claims about environmental benefits of the company or their products. ● *Earth Day 2000 Newsletter*, bimonthly. Reports on products and services that are environmentally friendly. **Price:** $15. 00/year. **Circulation:** 5,000 ● *Worldwide Network Directory*. Contains a listing of organizations involved in Earth Day Network campaigns.

4549 ■ Earth Force
2120 W 33rd Ave.
Denver, CO 80211
Ph: (703)299-9400
Fax: (703)299-9485
E-mail: earthforce@earthforce.org
URL: http://www.earthforce.org
Contact: Vince Meldrom, Pres.
Founded: 1994. **Nonmembership. Description:** Assists youth in discovering and implementing solutions to environmental issues in the community. **Telecommunication Services:** electronic mail, vmeldrum@ earthforce.org. **Boards:** Youth Advisory. **Programs:** Community Action and Problem Solving; Earth Force After School; Global Rivers Environmental Education Network. **Publications:** *Cross Cultural Watershed Partners Activities Manual*. **Price:** $9.99 ● *Field Manual for Water Quality Monitoring*. **Price:** $25.95.

4550 ■ Earth Island Institute (EII)
300 Broadway, Ste.28
San Francisco, CA 94133
Ph: (415)788-3666
Fax: (415)788-7324
E-mail: kgosling@earthisland.org
URL: http://www.earthisland.org
Contact: Karen L. Gosling, Membership Dir.
Founded: 1982. **Members:** 10,000. **Membership Dues:** regular, $25 (annual) ● student/low-income, $15 (annual). **Staff:** 15. **Budget:** $1,500,000. **Languages:** English, Russian, Spanish. **Multinational. Description:** "Believes that the most promising, creative solutions to urgent environmental problems spring from inspired and informed individuals." Works to develop environmental leadership by promoting citizen action and incubating a diverse network of projects. **Libraries: Type:** open to the public. **Subjects:** environmental issues. **Awards:** Brower Youth Awards. **Frequency:** annual. **Type:** monetary. **Recipient:** for young people aged 13 to 22. **Publications:** *Earth Island Journal*, quarterly. Magazine. **Price:** included in membership dues. ISSN: 1041-0406. **Circulation:** 20,000. **Advertising:** accepted. Alternate Formats: online. Also Cited As: *EIJ*.

4551 ■ Earth Liberation Front (ELF)
Address Unknown since 2004
Founded: 1997. **Description:** "Works to inflict economic damage on those profiting from destruction and exploitation of the natural environment".

4552 ■ Earth Regeneration Society (ERS)
c/o Alden Bryant, Pres.
1442A Walnut St., No. 57
Berkeley, CA 94709
Ph: (510)527-9716
Fax: (510)559-8410
E-mail: alden@earthregenerationsociety.org
URL: http://www.imaja.com/change/environment/ers/ ERSHomePage.html
Contact: Alden Bryant, Pres.
Founded: 1983. **Members:** 500. **Membership Dues:** subscriber, $25 (annual) ● sponsor, $100 (annual). **Description:** Represents scientists and other individuals organized to study and develop practical and scientific solutions to environmental issues. Concerns include climate stabilization, reduction of atmospheric carbon dioxide through soil remineralization, reforestation, conservation, and the development of alternative energy technology to abate the glaciation process. Maintains Speaker's Bureau; conducts research and educational programs. **Libraries: Type:** reference. **Holdings:** audiovisuals, books, clippings, monographs, periodicals. **Subjects:** climate change, soil, forests, energy, pollution, ozone conditions. **Additional Websites:** http://www.earthregenerationsociety.org. **Publications:** periodic *Whose World to Lose?*. Book ● Newsletter, periodic ● Papers ● Also publishes materials for the public and legislators, and list of recommended documents related to climate change and stabilization. **Conventions/Meetings:** periodic conference ● periodic international conference.

4553 ■ Earth Society Foundation (ESF)
238 E 58th St., Ste.2400
New York, NY 10022
E-mail: tomcdowd2@aol.com
URL: http://www.earthsocietyfoundation.org
Contact: Thomas C. Dowd, Pres.
Founded: 1976. **Members:** 115. **Membership Dues:** individual, $35 (annual). **Staff:** 10. **Budget:** $1,000,000. **Regional Groups:** 3. **State Groups:** 7. **National Groups:** 2. **Languages:** English, French, German. **Description:** Represents individuals interested in peace on earth and peace with earth; members are "involved citizens who care about peace, justice and care of the earth". Acts as an information clearinghouse, with support groups and persons concerned with individual rights, peace and environmental care and protection of the earth. Fosters worldwide participation in Earth Day (March 20) celebrations. Sponsors research programs; maintains archives. Operates speakers' bureau and charitable programs, such as symposia, workshops, panel discussions, and town meetings. **Libraries: Type:** reference. **Holdings:** 2,000; archival material, artwork, books, clippings. **Subjects:** environment, human rights, United Nations. **Awards:** Earth Day Award. **Frequency:** annual. **Type:** recognition. **Recipient:** for individuals who have served in the interest of harmony between man and nature ● **Type:** recognition. **Committees:** Earth Day; Earth Trustee. **Affiliated With:** The American Chestnut Foundation. **Publications:** *Earth Day Brochure*, annual. Contains history of Earth Day, details of annual ceremonies at United Nations in New York and Vienna. **Price:** $5. 00. **Circulation:** 2,000. **Advertising:** accepted. Alternate Formats: online ● *Earth Journal*, quarterly ● *History of the Earth Society and Earth Day* ● *John McConnell: The Man, who founded Earth Day* ● Monographs ● Also publishes educational literature. **Conventions/Meetings:** board meeting, to determine policies, discuss fund-raising, adopt progress reports, and discuss Earth Day - 10/year ● annual Margaret Mead Lecture Series - conference ● annual meeting, for members.

4554 ■ EarthAction International (EI)
30 Cottage St.
Amherst, MA 01002
Ph: (413)549-8118
Fax: (413)549-0544
E-mail: contact@earthaction.org
URL: http://www.earthaction.org
Contact: Lois Barber, Exec. Dir.
Founded: 1988. **Members:** 2,000. **Membership Dues:** individual, $25 (annual). **Staff:** 6. **Budget:** $800,000. **Languages:** English, French, Spanish. **Description:** Individuals and organizations in 161 countries. Seeks to mobilize international public pressure on key decision makers when important global decisions are being made. **Computer Services:** database, of 10,000 non-governmental organizations; 6,000 parliamentarians; 6,000 media. **Formerly:** (1990) Earthvote Network; (1991) Earthvote International. **Publications:** *EarthAction Alert* (in English, French, and Spanish), monthly. Each Action Kit focuses on one global environment, development, peace or human rights issue. **Price:** $25.00/year. Alternate Formats: online ● *Editorial Advisories* ● *Parliamentary Alerts*.

4555 ■ EarthVoice
2100 L St. NW
Washington, DC 20037
Ph: (202)778-6146
Fax: (202)778-6134
E-mail: earthvoice@earthvoice.org
Contact: Jan Hartke, Exec. Dir.
Founded: 1991. **Description:** Creates a humane society by protecting animals and ecosystems. Promotes environmental and humane educational programs. Increases awareness of the consequences of unsustainable activities. **Computer Services:** Information services, environmental sustainability resources.

4556 ■ EarthWave Society (EWS)
16151 Hwy., 377 S
Fort Worth, TX 76126
Ph: (817)443-3780
Free: (800)668-9283
Fax: (817)443-3858
URL: http://www.earthwave.org
Contact: Betty Wills, Exec. Dir.
Description: Educates the people on biodiversity, conservation and prudent utilization of the world's natural resources. Preserves wetlands and riverine habitats.

4557 ■ EcoVillage at Ithaca (EVI)
100 Rachel Carson Way
Ithaca, NY 14850
Ph: (607)272-5149
E-mail: ecovillage@cornell.edu
Contact: Liz Walker, Dir.
Founded: 1991. **Members:** 700. **Membership Dues:** student, low income, $15 (annual) ● individual, $30 (annual) ● family, $40 (annual) ● sustaining, $100 (annual). **Staff:** 1. **Budget:** $30,000. **Local Groups:** 1. **Description:** Promotes a whole-systems approach to ecological living that strives for the "harmonious integration of landscape and people providing their food, energy, shelter, and other material and non-material needs in a sustainable way." Currently consists of two co-housing neighborhoods, an organic farm, on a 175-acre site, of which 90 percent is conserved as open space. Conducts educational programs on: sustainable living, community tours for student and other visitors. Holds lectures and works with professors and college students on research projects. Maintains speakers' bureau. **Affiliated With:** Center for Religion, Ethics and Social Policy. **Publications:** *EcoVillage at Ithaca Newsletter*, semiannual. **Circulation:** 500. **Conventions/Meetings:** periodic conference.

4558 ■ Environmental Action Foundation (EAF)
2300 Wilson Blvd., Ste.400
Arlington, VA 22201
Ph: (703)837-5335
Fax: (703)837-5401
E-mail: kennedym@agc.org
URL: http://www.agc.org
Contact: Michael Kennedy, Contact
Founded: 1970. **Members:** 10,000. **Membership Dues:** individual, $25 (annual). **Staff:** 12. **Budget:** $1,000,000. **Description:** Environmental research and educational organization that serves as a resource for concerned citizens and organizations in the areas of energy policy, toxic substances, and solid waste reduction. Is currently concentrating on energy efficiency, utility deregulation, solid waste management, and toxic substances. Promotes solar energy as a safe, economical alternative to nuclear power. Works for changes in utility pricing structures to promote energy efficiency and protect persons on low and fixed incomes. Advocates recycling, source reduction and control of hazardous waste, energy efficiency measures, and renewable energy sources. **Computer Services:** database, electronic data transfers and index searches. **Projects:** Utility Reform. **Absorbed:** Environmental Action; (1987) Environmental Task Force. **Formerly:** (1972) Environmental Resource. **Publications:** *Environmental Action*, quarterly. Magazine. Covers the environmental movement and its goals and policies. Includes book reviews. **Price:** included in membership dues; $2.50/ issue for nonmembers. ISSN: 0013-992X. **Advertising:** accepted ● *Wastelines*, quarterly. Newsletter. Features waste reduction efforts. **Price:** $10.00/year.

Circulation: 800. **Advertising:** accepted ● Books ● Brochures ● Manuals ● Pamphlets ● Also publishes fact packets.

4559 ■ Environmental Assessment Association (EAA)

1224 N Nokomis NE
Alexandria, MN 56308
Ph: (320)763-4320
Fax: (320)763-9290
E-mail: eaa@iami.org
URL: http://www.iami.org/EAA/home.cfm
Contact: Robert G. Johnson, Exec. Dir.

Founded: 1982. **Members:** 8,200. **Membership Dues:** regular, $195 (annual). **Staff:** 23. **Budget:** $4,000,000. **Description:** Environmental professionals. Dedicated to providing members with information and education in the environmental industry concerning environmental inspections, testing and hazardous material removal. Works with government and environmental agencies; monitors legislation; conducts educational programs. **Awards:** Presidents Club. **Frequency:** monthly. **Type:** recognition. **Computer Services:** Mailing lists ● online services. **Publications:** *Environmental Guidebooks*. Reports ● *Environmental Times*, bimonthly. Newsletter. **Price:** $5. 50/copy. **Advertising:** accepted. Alternate Formats: online ● Membership Directory. Alternate Formats: online ● Booklets. **Conventions/Meetings:** annual conference (exhibits).

4560 ■ Environmental Business Council of New England (EBC-NE)

18 Tremont St., Ste.402
Boston, MA 02108
Ph: (617)725-0207
Fax: (617)227-5532
E-mail: ebc@ebcne.org
URL: http://www.ebcne.org
Contact: Daniel K. Moon, Pres.

Founded: 1990. **Members:** 200. **Membership Dues:** business (based on number of employees), $206-$1,725 (annual) ● non-profit (based on number of employees), $112-$900 (annual) ● government (based on number of employees), $318-$1,275 (annual). **Staff:** 3. **Description:** Firms that manufacture environmental and/or energy products and provide environmental and/or energy services. Fosters the development of an effective and competitive envirotech industry for the purpose of enhancing and maintaining a clean and productive environment. Provides a forum for environmental and energy company executives to network with each other and to meet leading members of the academic, nonprofit, and government communities to discuss issues of concern to the environmental industry. Provides business development and educational services. **Awards:** EBEE Award. **Frequency:** annual. **Type:** recognition. **Recipient:** to outstanding individuals, companies, or organizations from the New England area who helps promote environmental business. **Computer Services:** Mailing lists, of members. **Telecommunication Services:** electronic mail, dkmoon@ebcne.org. **Publications:** Newsletter, monthly. Contains information about the members and the association. Alternate Formats: online.

4561 ■ Environmental Conservation Organization (ECO)

PO Box 191
Hollow Rock, TN 38342
Ph: (731)986-0099
E-mail: karen@freedom.org
URL: http://www.eco.freedom.org
Contact: Henry Lamb, Exec. VP

Founded: 1988. **Membership Dues:** Paul Revere, $35 ● Patrick Henry, $50 ● Thomas Jefferson, $100. **Description:** Strives to share the belief that the environment includes human beings who prosper or perish as the result of their stewardship of natural resources. Rejects the notion that the environment is "fragile" and must be protected from human use by massive federal and international regulations. **Publications:** *Eco-logic Journal*, bimonthly.

4562 ■ Environmental Defense

257 Park Ave. S
New York, NY 10010
Ph: (212)505-2100
Free: (877)677-7397
Fax: (212)505-2375
E-mail: members@environmentaldefense.org
URL: http://www.environmentaldefense.org
Contact: Fred D. Krupp, Pres.

Founded: 1967. **Members:** 500,000. **Membership Dues:** individual, $25 (annual) ● family, $35 (annual) ● individual outside U.S., $35 (annual). **Staff:** 260. **Budget:** $45,000,000. **Regional Groups:** 6. **Description:** Links science, law, economics, and engineering to create innovative and economically viable solutions to environmental problems. Focuses on four areas such as: protecting and restoring biodiversity (with an emphasis on rivers and watersheds); stabilizing climate by developing policies to reduce dependence on fossil fuels; reducing risks to human health from exposure to toxic chemicals; and protecting oceans from pollution and overfishing. **Libraries: Type:** not open to the public. **Computer Services:** Online services, environmental Information Exchange, which provides state environmental organizations access to scientific, economic, legal and regulatory information. **Programs:** Climate and Air; Ecosystem Restoration; Living Cities; Oceans. **Formerly:** (2001) Environmental Defense Fund. **Publications:** *Solutions*, bimonthly. Newsletter. Reports on environmental protection activities. Includes staff and trustee profiles. **Price:** included in membership dues; free for nonmembers; single copy only. ISSN: 0163-2566. **Circulation:** 200,000. Alternate Formats: online ● Annual Report, annual. Alternate Formats: online. **Conventions/Meetings:** annual symposium.

4563 ■ Environmental Risk Resources Association (ERRA)

4901 Pine Cone Cir.
Middleton, WI 53562
Free: (877)735-0800
Fax: (608)798-1013
E-mail: webmaster@erraonline.org
URL: http://www.erraonline.org
Contact: Anne Simmons, Dir.

Membership Dues: individual, $225 (annual) ● office, $1,000 (annual). **Description:** Expands the use of environmental insurance as a risk management tool through education, technology, resources, innovation and networking. **Computer Services:** database, environmental insurance professionals directory ● information services, environmental insurance resources ● online services, education courses ● online services, message board. **Committees:** Expert Witness; Financial Responsibility. **Programs:** Environmental Insurance. **Publications:** Newsletter, quarterly. Alternate Formats: online.

4564 ■ Environmental Working Group (EWG)

1436 U St. NW, Ste.100
Washington, DC 20009
Ph: (202)667-6982
Fax: (202)232-2592
E-mail: info@ewg.org
URL: http://www.ewg.org
Contact: Kenneth A. Cook, Pres./Founder

Founded: 1993. **Description:** Seeks to improve public health and to protect the environment by reducing pollution in water and food. **Telecommunication Services:** electronic mail, ken@ewg.org. **Publications:** *EWG Bulletin*, monthly. Newsletter ● Reports. Alternate Formats: online.

4565 ■ George Wright Society (GWS)

PO Box 65
Hancock, MI 49930-0065
Ph: (906)487-9722
Fax: (906)487-9405
E-mail: info@georgewright.org
URL: http://www.georgewright.org
Contact: David Harmon, Exec. Dir.

Founded: 1980. **Members:** 700. **Membership Dues:** individual, library, $55 (annual) ● student, $25 (annual) ● life, $1,000 ● patron, $1,000 (annual) ● supporting, $150 (annual) ● institutional, $110 (annual). **Staff:** 3. **Budget:** $100,000. **Multinational. Description:** Represents protected area professionals. Uses research and education to preserve and protect parks, protected natural areas, and cultural sites. **Awards:** G.M. Wright Award. **Frequency:** biennial. **Type:** recognition. **Recipient:** for excellence in the field ● GWS Communication Award. **Frequency:** annual. **Type:** recognition. **Recipient:** for outstanding efforts in communicating highly technical or controversial park-related subjects to the public ● GWS Cultural Resource Management Award. **Frequency:** annual. **Type:** recognition. **Recipient:** for excellent management of cultural resources ● GWS Natural Resource Management Award. **Frequency:** annual. **Type:** recognition. **Recipient:** for excellent management of natural resources. **Publications:** *The George Wright Forum*, quarterly. Journal. **Price:** included in membership dues. ISSN: 0732-4715. Alternate Formats: CD-ROM; online. **Conventions/Meetings:** biennial Research and Resource Management in Parks, Protected Areas, and Cultural Sites - conference, park research and resource management.

4566 ■ Global Green USA (GGUSA)

2218 Main St., 2nd Fl.
Santa Monica, CA 90405
Ph: (310)581-2700
Fax: (310)581-2702
E-mail: ggusa@globalgreen.org
URL: http://www.globalgreen.org
Contact: Matt Petersen, Pres./CEO

Founded: 1993. **Staff:** 11. **Description:** Fosters "global value shift toward a sustainable and secure world through programs focused on safe elimination of weapons of mass destruction". **Awards:** Designing a Sustainable and Secure World Awards. **Frequency:** annual. **Type:** recognition. **Recipient:** for industry, media, organization, and individual ● Green Cross Millennium Awards. **Frequency:** annual. **Type:** recognition. **Recipient:** for individuals and organizations. **Computer Services:** Mailing lists, of members. **Telecommunication Services:** electronic mail, mpetersen@globalgreen.org. **Programs:** Legacy. **Projects:** CHEMTRUST. **Publications:** *A Blueprint for Greening Affordable Housing: Developer Guidelines for Resource Efficiency and Sustainable Communities*. Book. **Price:** $25.00 for non-profit; $35.00 for profit ● Newsletter. Contains information about projects and environmental issues. Alternate Formats: online. **Conventions/Meetings:** annual Global Green Legacy Forum - meeting.

4567 ■ Global Response

PO Box 7490
Boulder, CO 80306-7490
Ph: (303)444-0306
Fax: (303)449-9794
E-mail: info@globalresponse.org
URL: http://www.globalresponse.org
Contact: Paula Palmer, Exec. Dir.

Founded: 1990. **Members:** 6,000. **Membership Dues:** student, low income, $20 (annual) ● general, $50 (annual) ● sustaining, $200 (annual) ● major, $1,000 (annual) ● educator/classroom, $30 (annual). **Staff:** 3. **Budget:** $100,000. **Multinational. Description:** Seeks to prevent environmental destruction. Writes letters to government and corporate decision makers. Participates in global citizen cooperation and earth stewardship. **Telecommunication Services:** electronic mail, paula@globalresponse.org ● electronic mail, erin@globalresponse.org. **Publications:** *Eco-Club Action*, 8-10/year. Bulletin. Written for high school students, teachers, and environmental clubs. **Price:** included in membership dues. Alternate Formats: online ● *Global Response Action*, 8-10/year. Bulletin. Covers toxic waste, hazardous waste, resource exploitation, rainforest destruction, nuclear disarmament, ocean dumping, air pollution, and extinction. **Price:** included in membership dues. Alternate Formats: online ● *YEA Teachers' Packet* ● *Young Environmentalist's Action*, 8-10/year. Bulletin. Written for elementary and junior high school students, teachers, and environmental clubs. **Price:** included in membership dues.

4568 ■ Global Warming International Center (GWIC)
PO Box 50303
Palo Alto, CA 94303-0303
Ph: (630)910-1551
Fax: (630)910-1561
E-mail: gw17@globalwarming.net
URL: http://www.globalwarming.net
Contact: Dr. Sinyan Shen, Dir.
Founded: 1986. **Members:** 12,381. **Membership Dues:** student, $50 (annual) ● associate, $72 (annual) ● institution, $143 (annual). **Staff:** 17. **Budget:** $75,000,000. **Regional Groups:** 5. **Description:** Ministerial agencies and industrial corporations. Concerns with impacts and effects of global warming. Provides a focus for governments, the private sector, and academia to share information on global warming internationally. Coordinates training for personnel dealing with environmental issues, energy planning, and natural resource management through the Institute for World Resource Research. Establishes the Global Warming Index (GWI) and the Extreme Event Index (EEI) for international standardization. Maintains speaker's bureau; compiles statistics; operates placement service; conducts research and educational programs. **Libraries: Type:** reference. **Holdings:** 50,000; archival material, books, monographs, periodicals. **Subjects:** global warming, natural resource management. **Awards:** The GWIC Award. **Type:** recognition. **Recipient:** for contributions to global warming science and policy worldwide in his or her area of specialty ● **Type:** monetary ● **Type:** recognition ● **Type:** scholarship. **Committees:** Agriculture; Energy; Global Warming Index; Public Health; Reforestation; Telecommunication; World Resource Review. **Publications:** *World Resource Review*, quarterly. Journal. **Price:** $167.00. ISSN: 1042-8011. **Circulation:** 9,000. **Advertising:** accepted. **Conventions/Meetings:** annual meeting, provides review of Kyoto conference by 150 countries, reports on impacts of climate change on the global environment, natural resource management, and the world economy (exhibits).

4569 ■ The Green Life (TGL)
29 Temple Pl.
Boston, MA 02111
Ph: (617)426-2502
Free: (877)EARTH46
E-mail: info@thegreenlife.org
URL: http://www.thegreenlife.org
Contact: Ms. Jemilah Magnusson, Program Coor.
Founded: 1991. **Membership Dues:** basic, $25 (annual). **Staff:** 1. **Description:** Works to help keep the grassroots spirit of Earth Day alive and provide environmentally friendly alternatives to big box consumption. Serves as an anti-greenwashing watchdog. Provides materials and services to community organizers, educators, college activists, or simply concerned citizens. Senda out featured greenwasher alerts and eco-events calendars to members. Provides background information on companies and issues, along with options for making a difference. **Awards:** Earth Day Spring Clean Grant. **Frequency:** annual. **Type:** grant. **Computer Services:** database, Earth Day events and organizers. **Formerly:** (2004) Earth Day Resources. **Publications:** *Earth Day Curriculum*. Book. **Price:** $10.00 ● *50 Simple Things to Protect the Water*. Book. **Price:** $5.00 ● *Guide to Recycling*. Book. **Price:** $12.00 ● *Guide to Ridesharing*. Book. **Price:** $12.00. **Conventions/Meetings:** annual Earth Day Spring Clean - meeting.

4570 ■ Greening Earth Society
Address Unknown since 2008
Description: Strives to promote the benign effects of carbon dioxide (CO2) on the earth's biosphere and humankind. **Publications:** *The Greening of Planet Earth*, annual. Video ● *The Greening of Planet Earth Continues*, annual. Video.

4571 ■ Greenpeace U.S.A. (GPUSA)
702 H St. NW
Washington, DC 20001
Ph: (202)462-1177
Free: (800)326-0959
E-mail: info@wdc.greenpeace.org
Contact: John Passacantando, Exec. Dir.
Founded: 1971. **Members:** 250,000. **Membership Dues:** regular, $30 (annual). **Staff:** 70. **Description:** Independent campaigning organization that uses non-violent creative confrontation to expose global environmental problems, and to force solutions that are essential to a green and peaceful future. Works to save ancient forests, stop global warming, protect the oceans, stop toxic pollution, end nuclear threats, and end threats posed by genetic engineering. Conducts research and lobbying efforts and media campaigns. **Affiliated With:** Greenpeace Netherlands. **Publications:** *Greenpeace*, quarterly. Newsletter. **Price:** included in membership dues ● Also publishes campaign fact sheets and reports. **Conventions/Meetings:** board meeting - 3/year.

4572 ■ Hikers Against Doo Doo (HADD)
c/o Trionics International, Inc.
66 Upper Oak Point Rd.
Winterport, ME 04496
Fax: (207)848-5649
E-mail: haddusa@aol.com
Contact: Dr. A. Bern Hoff, Pres.
Founded: 1990. **Members:** 11,843. **Membership Dues:** regular, $15 (annual). **Staff:** 4. **Budget:** $59,500. **Languages:** English, Spanish. **For-Profit. Description:** Works to gather and spread information on the proper handling and disposal of human and pet droppings on hiking trails and in parks. Maintains clearinghouse for written policies and ordinances concerning feces removal from hiking trails; seeks new environmentally safe disposal techniques; promotes facilities improvements on hiking trails. **Libraries: Type:** not open to the public. **Holdings:** 276. **Computer Services:** Electronic publishing. **Subgroups:** Facilities Improvements; Information Database; Legal/Ordinances; New Disposal Techniques. **Publications:** *HADD News*, annual. Newsletter. **Price:** included in membership dues. **Advertising:** accepted. Alternate Formats: online. **Conventions/Meetings:** annual board meeting ● International Congress.

4573 ■ Institute for Conservation Leadership (ICL)
6930 Carroll Ave., Ste.420
Takoma Park, MD 20912
Ph: (301)270-2900
Fax: (301)270-0610
E-mail: icl@icl.org
URL: http://www.icl.org
Contact: Dianne Russell, Exec. Dir.
Founded: 1990. **Staff:** 9. **Nonmembership. Description:** Provides leadership development and organizational development training, technical assistance, and facilitation for organizations and leaders working toward the protection and conservation of the environment. Provides networking opportunities. Conducts educational programs for a fee. **Convention/Meeting:** none. **Telecommunication Services:** electronic mail, dianne@icl.org. **Programs:** Complete Fundraiser; Cultivating Leadership for a Changing Agriculture; Executive Director Leadership; Freshwater Leadership Initiative; Organizational Leadership and Effectiveness for the Environment; Strengthening Organizations and Leaders for the Environment; Sustainable Campaigns; Sustainable Organizations. **Publications:** *The Network*, periodic. Newsletter. Presents a diverse collection of pertinent news and information for people working in the environmental arena. Alternate Formats: online ● Articles. Alternate Formats: online ● Bibliographies.

4574 ■ Institute of Global Environment and Society (IGES)
4041 Powder Mill Rd., Ste.302
Beltsville, MD 20705-3106
Ph: (301)595-7000
Fax: (301)595-9793
E-mail: www@cola.iges.org
URL: http://grads.iges.org
Contact: Jagadish Shukla, Pres.
Staff: 5. **Multinational. Description:** Works to improve understanding and prediction of the variations of the Earth's climate. **Telecommunication Services:** electronic mail, nichole@cola.iges.org.

4575 ■ Institute for the Human Environment (IHE)
Address Unknown since 2008
Founded: 1972. **Staff:** 3. **Nonmembership. Description:** International group whose objective is to improve the quality of land use and policy decisions involving sustainability and the man-made environment. Facilitates problem-solving in a variety of human environment issues internationally. **Councils:** Action for Sustainable Communities. **Publications:** Also publishes reports. **Conventions/Meetings:** periodic meeting.

4576 ■ Institute of Professional Environmental Practice (IPEP)
333 Fisher Hall
600 Forbes Ave.
Pittsburgh, PA 15282
Ph: (412)396-1703 (412)396-1581
Fax: (412)396-1704
E-mail: ipep@duq.edu
URL: http://www.ipep.org
Contact: Amy Paff, Rep.
Founded: 1993. **Members:** 1,300. **Membership Dues:** qualified environmental professional, $150 (annual) ● environmental professional intern, $75 (annual). **Staff:** 2. **Multinational. Description:** Strives to improve the practice and educational standards of environmental professionals through administering the Qualified Environmental Professional (QEP) and Environmental Professional Intern (EPI) certifications. **Computer Services:** Mailing lists. **Committees:** Admissions; Environmental Professional Intern; Ethics; Exam Advisory; Examination Administration; Government Agency Support; International Development; Marketing.

4577 ■ International Arid Lands Consortium (IALC)
c/o Dr. Jim P.M. Chamie, Managing Dir.
1955 E 6th St.
Tucson, AZ 85719-5224
Ph: (520)621-3024
Fax: (520)621-3816
E-mail: ialc@ag.arizona.edu
URL: http://ag.arizona.edu/OALS/IALC/Home.html
Contact: Dr. Jim P.M. Chamie, Managing Dir.
Founded: 1990. **Multinational. Description:** Promotes development, management, restoration, reclamation of arid and semiarid lands in the U.S., Middle East, and elsewhere in the world. **Awards:** Peace Fellowship Award. **Type:** monetary. **Recipient:** for outstanding undergraduate and graduate students. **Computer Services:** database, IALC researchers. **Committees:** Program Priorities; Research and Demonstration Advisory. **Programs:** Peace Fellowship. **Publications:** *Peace Fellowship Final Report*. Reports. Alternate Formats: online ● *Peace Fellowship Program Brochure*. Alternate Formats: online ● Videos. Alternate Formats: online. **Conventions/Meetings:** conference and workshop.

4578 ■ International Center for the Solution of Environmental Problems (ICSEP)
5120 Woodway, Ste.8009
Houston, TX 77056-1788
Ph: (713)527-8711
Fax: (713)961-5157
E-mail: icsep@airmail.net
URL: http://www.icsep.com
Contact: Joseph L. Goldman PhD, Technical Dir.
Founded: 1975. **Staff:** 1. **Multinational. Description:** Institutes, corporations, and individuals engaged in scientific, engineering, management, economic, and offshore environmental activities. Uses a multidisciplinary approach to anticipate upcoming environmental problems and provide solutions for avoiding or reducing them. Is involved in numerous civic activities related to the environment. Conducts research projects on: anticipating the effects of storms and reducing their causes and occurrences off- and onshore; effects of storms related to city design; changes in surface vegetation caused by spreading

urbanization; flood control; reduction of land erosion; remote sensing applications; land subsidence and flooding by over-pumping; decline in land value resulting from these changes; the effect of weather on soil and agriculture; the effect of herbicide sprays on users and groundwater. **Libraries: Type:** reference. **Holdings:** 3,000; books, monographs, periodicals. **Subjects:** meteorology, oceanography, physical science, psychology, environmental science, literature, art. **Publications:** Brochure ● Newsletter, annual. **Conventions/Meetings:** annual Earthday - general assembly, art and science exhibits related to the environment (exhibits).

4579 ■ International Society for Environmental Ethics (ISEE)
c/o Dr. Lisa Newton, Treas.
Fairfield Univ.
Prog. in Environmental Stud.
Fairfield, CT 06824
Ph: (203)254-4128
E-mail: lhnewton@fair1.fairfield.edu
URL: http://www.cep.unt.edu/ISEE.html
Contact: Dr. Lisa Newton, Treas.
Founded: 1990. **Members:** 350. **Membership Dues:** regular, $25 (annual) ● student, $15 (annual). **National Groups:** 20. **Description:** Focuses on environmental ethics. **Computer Services:** Bibliographic search, contains over 7,000 entries on environmental ethics. **Telecommunication Services:** electronic mail, mwoods@sandiego.edu. **Projects:** Environmental Ethics Syllabus. **Publications:** *ISE Master Bibliography 2004*. Alternate Formats: online ● *ISEE Newsletter*, quarterly, April, July, October, January. **Price:** included in membership dues. Alternate Formats: online.

4580 ■ International Society for Industrial Ecology (ISIE)
c/o Yale School of Forestry and Environmental Studies
Yale Univ.
205 Prospect St.
New Haven, CT 06511-2189
Ph: (203)436-4835
Fax: (203)432-5912
E-mail: is4ie@yale.edu
URL: http://www.is4ie.org
Contact: John Ehrenfeld, Exec. Dir.
Founded: 2001. **Membership Dues:** individual, $125 (annual) ● student, $45 (annual) ● individual (developing country), $55 (annual). **Staff:** 2. **Multinational. Description:** Promotes industrial ecology as a way of finding solutions to complicated environmental problems. Encourages the use of industrial ecology in research, education, policy, community development and industrial practices. **Committees:** Awards; Education and Human Resources; Meetings; Topical Groups. **Publications:** Newsletter, quarterly. Includes news and information about industrial ecology. Alternate Formats: online.

4581 ■ International Society for Reef Studies (ISRS)
c/o Richard Aronson, Pres.
Dauphin Island Sea Lab
101 Bienville Blvd.
Dauphin Island, AL 36528
E-mail: raronson@disl.org
URL: http://www.fit.edu/isrs
Contact: Richard Aronson, Pres.
Founded: 1980. **Members:** 1,000. **Membership Dues:** individual, $80 (annual) ● family, $90 (annual) ● student, $25 (annual) ● sustaining, $200 (annual). **Multinational. Description:** Promotes for the benefit of the public, the production and dissemination of scientific knowledge and understanding of living and fossil coral reefs. **Awards:** Darwin Medal. **Frequency:** quadrennial. **Type:** medal. **Recipient:** to a senior member. **Telecommunication Services:** electronic mail, n.polunin@ncl.ac.uk. **Publications:** *Coral Reefs*. Journal. ISSN: 0722-4028. Alternate Formats: online ● *Reef Encounter*. Newsletter. Alternate Formats: online ● Papers. Alternate Formats: online. **Conventions/Meetings:** annual meeting.

4582 ■ International Sonoran Desert Alliance (ISDA)
PO Box 687
Ajo, AZ 85321
Ph: (520)387-6823
Fax: (520)387-5626
E-mail: tracy@isdanet.org
URL: http://www.isdanet.org
Contact: Jim Reiman, Pres.
Founded: 1992. **Staff:** 3. **Multinational. Description:** Protects the unique biological and cultural diversity of the Sonoran Desert through international dialogue, education, sustainable development and community action. **Computer Services:** Mailing lists. **Programs:** Community Projects and Plans; Youth Activities. **Projects:** Curley School. **Publications:** *Vista*. Newsletter. Alternate Formats: online.

4583 ■ Jessie Smith Noyes Foundation
6 E 39th St., 12th Fl.
New York, NY 10016-0112
Ph: (212)684-6577
Fax: (212)689-6549
E-mail: noyes@noyes.org
URL: http://www.noyes.org
Contact: Victor De Luca, Pres.
Founded: 1947. **Description:** Works to protect and restore the earth's natural systems. Promotes a sustainable society; funds environmental, reproductive rights initiatives. **Awards: Type:** grant. **Publications:** *The Challenge of Diversity*. Brochure. Alternate Formats: online.

4584 ■ Keep America Beautiful (KAB)
1010 Washington Blvd.
Stamford, CT 06901
Ph: (203)323-8987
Fax: (203)325-9199
E-mail: info@kab.org
URL: http://www.kab.org
Contact: G. Raymond Empson, Pres.
Founded: 1953. **Members:** 300. **Staff:** 16. **State Groups:** 21. **Local Groups:** 495. **Description:** Promotes litter prevention and ways to reduce, reuse, recycle, and waste management. **Awards:** Vision for America. **Frequency:** annual. **Type:** recognition. **Recipient:** for responsible corporations. **Departments:** Administration; Communications; Development Government; Training and Affiliate Services; Training and Program Development. **Programs:** Great American Cleanup; Litter Index; National Awards. **Publications:** *Affiliate Times*, bimonthly. Newsletter. Offers information about new programs, tools, resources, grant opportunities, important dates and recognition among their peers. Alternate Formats: online ● *Community Matters*. Newsletter. **Price:** free. Alternate Formats: online ● *Keep America Beautiful—Annual Review*. Annual Report. Includes listing of certified and pre-certified communities arranged by state; lists members and contributors. **Price:** free ● *Keep America Beautiful-Network News*, 3/year. Newspaper. Covers the litter prevention, voluntary recycling, and community improvement programs and activities of KAB. **Circulation:** 6,000 ● Also publishes guides, curricula, and instructional materials. **Conventions/Meetings:** annual conference ● annual Mid-Year Affiliates Forum - meeting.

4585 ■ Kids for a Clean Environment (Kids FACE)
PO Box 158254
Nashville, TN 37215
Ph: (615)331-7381
Free: (800)952-3223
E-mail: kidsface@mindspring.com
URL: http://www.kidsface.org
Contact: Melissa Poe, Founder
Founded: 1989. **Members:** 300,000. **Membership Dues:** general, $25 (annual). **Description:** Children, parents, teachers, and others working to improve the environment. Focuses on children organizing and implementing ideas and programs on their own, supported and assisted by parents and teachers Provides children's services and educational programs. Operates Environmental Resource Center. **Publications:** *Kids FACE Illustrated*, quarterly. Newsletter. **Price:** $25.00. **Circulation:** 2,000,000. **Advertising:** accepted ● *Our World, Our Future*. Book.

4586 ■ Legal Environmental Assistance Foundation (LEAF)
1114 Thomasville Rd., Ste.E
Tallahassee, FL 32303-6290
Ph: (850)681-2591
Fax: (850)224-1275
E-mail: leaf@leaflaw.org
URL: http://www.leaflaw.org
Contact: Cynthia Valencic, Contact
Founded: 1979. **Members:** 500. **Membership Dues:** basic, $25 (annual) ● supporter, $50 ● sponsor, $100 ● silver LEAF club, $250 ● gold LEAF club, $500 ● student/senior, $15. **Staff:** 3. **Budget:** $450,000. **Description:** Promotes the protection of the environment and health of the community by enforcing environmental regulations, discouraging harmful toxic and hazardous waste dumping, and encouraging energy efficiency. Works to enforce facilities and companies to comply with environmental laws and regulations. Participates in federal and state policy making. Sues governmental agency and industry personnel who violate environmental laws. Conducts education and legal workshops for professionals and interested individuals. **Awards:** Environmental Advocacy and LEAF Honor Roll. **Frequency:** annual. **Type:** recognition. **Recipient:** for environmental protection services. **Programs:** Air; Community Health; Land; Water. **Publications:** *LEAF Briefs*, quarterly. Newsletter. **Price:** free for members. **Circulation:** 1,000. **Conventions/Meetings:** annual meeting - January or February.

4587 ■ Merck Family Fund
303 Adams St.
Milton, MA 02186
Ph: (617)696-3580
Fax: (617)696-7262
E-mail: merck@merckff.org
URL: http://www.merckff.org
Contact: Jenny D. Russell, Exec. Dir.
Founded: 1954. **Description:** Works to restore and protect the natural environment and ensure a healthy planet for generations to come. **Awards: Type:** grant.

4588 ■ NAEM - National Association for Environmental Management (NAEM)
1612 K St. NW, Ste.1102
Washington, DC 20006-2830
Ph: (202)986-6616
Free: (800)391-NAEM
Fax: (202)530-4408
E-mail: programs@naem.org
URL: http://www.naem.org
Contact: Carol Singer Neuvelt, Exec. Dir.
Founded: 1990. **Members:** 1,300. **Membership Dues:** individual, $195 (annual) ● corporate (based on gross revenues), $900-$5,000 (annual) ● non-profit, government, $750 (annual) ● affiliate (based on annual revenues), $1,000-$3,000 (annual). **Staff:** 5. **Budget:** $650,000. **Regional Groups:** 8. **Description:** Works for the advancement of professional environment, health and safety management. **Awards:** Environmental Excellence Awards. **Frequency:** annual. **Type:** recognition. **Recipient:** for corporate and environmental manager. **Computer Services:** database ● mailing lists ● online services. **Programs:** Carnegie Mellon Business. **Formerly:** (2001) National Association for Environmental Management. **Publications:** *BNA's Environment, Health and Safety Benchmarks 2004*. Report. **Price:** $695.00 ● *Network News*, bimonthly. Newsletter. **Conventions/Meetings:** annual conference (exhibits) ● monthly meeting ● bimonthly Strategic Environmental Management Course - meeting.

4589 ■ National Association of Environmental Professionals (NAEP)
389 Main St., Ste.202
Malden, MA 02148
Ph: (781)397-8870
Free: (888)251-9902
Fax: (781)397-8887

E-mail: naep@guildassoc.com
URL: http://www.naep.org
Contact: Jim Melton, Pres.
Founded: 1975. **Members:** 2,000. **Membership Dues:** associate, $125 (annual) ● general, $150 (annual) ● student, $40 (annual) ● spouse, $65 (annual) ● corporate (primary office), $750 (annual) ● corporate (branch office), $375 (annual). **Budget:** $330,000. **State Groups:** 10. **Description:** Promotes ethical practice, technical competency, and professional standards in the environment field. Provides access to the latest trends in environmental research, technology, law, and policy. **Libraries: Type:** reference. **Holdings:** articles. **Awards:** National Environmental Excellence Award. **Frequency:** annual. **Type:** recognition ● Student Award. **Frequency:** annual. **Type:** recognition. **Recipient:** for outstanding student research project. **Computer Services:** Online services. **Telecommunication Services:** electronic mail, jmelton@bresnan.net. **Working Groups:** Professional Interest. **Publications:** *Environmental Practice*, quarterly. Journal. Provides stimulating research and commentary on significant environmental issues. **Price:** included in membership dues. ISSN: 0191-5398. **Circulation:** 2,000. **Advertising:** accepted. Alternate Formats: online ● *NAEP National E-News*, bimonthly. Newsletter. **Price:** included in membership dues. Alternate Formats: online. **Conventions/Meetings:** annual conference (exhibits).

4590 ■ National Environmental Satellite, Data, and Information Service (NESDIS)
1335 East-West Hwy., SSMC1, 8th Fl.
Silver Spring, MD 20910
Ph: (301)713-3578
Fax: (301)713-1249
E-mail: answers@noaa.gov
URL: http://www.nesdis.noaa.gov
Contact: Mary Ellen Kicza, Asst. Admin.
Founded: 1965. **Staff:** 824. **Description:** A major line component of the National Oceanic and Atmospheric Administration, U.S. Department of Commerce. Is responsible for acquiring, processing, archiving, recalling, and disseminating worldwide environmental data and environmental science information concerning the atmosphere, oceans, solid earth, and near space. Provides information on products for use by governmental agencies, the national and international scientific and engineering community, industry, commerce, agriculture, and the public. These products include assessments of the impact of environmental fluctuations on the national economy, national defense, energy development, global food supplies, natural resources, natural hazards, and human health. Maintains and services an archive of all data and information acquired by NOAA's operational geostationary and polar-orbiting satellites. Operates the National Climatic Data Center in Asheville, NC; the National Oceanographic Data Center in Washington, DC; and the National Geophysical Data Center in Boulder, CO. **Formerly:** (1980) Environmental Data Service; (1982) Environmental Data and Information Service. **Publications:** *Climatic Data for the World*, monthly ● *Local Climatological Data*, monthly ● *Mariners Weather Log*, bimonthly ● *Solar Geophysical Data*, monthly ● *Storm Data*, monthly ● Report, annual. **Conventions/Meetings:** periodic conference and workshop (exhibits).

4591 ■ National Environmental Trust (NET)
1200 18th St. NW, 5th Fl.
Washington, DC 20036
Ph: (202)887-8800
Fax: (202)887-8877
E-mail: cdelany@net.org
URL: http://www.net.org
Contact: Phil Clapp, Pres.
Founded: 1994. **Description:** Promotes citizen awareness on environmental issues and ways they affect public health and quality of life. **Publications:** Reports. Alternate Formats: online.

4592 ■ National Forest Protection Alliance (NFPA)
423 W 1st Ave., Ste.240
Spokane, WA 99201
Ph: (509)838-4912
Fax: (509)838-5155
E-mail: nfpa@landscouncil.org
URL: http://www.forestadvocate.org
Contact: Mike Petersen, Pres.
Founded: 1999. **Members:** 130. **Membership Dues:** individual, $35-$250 (annual). **Staff:** 4. **Description:** Promotes social change and environmental protection. Works to end industrial exploitation of federal public lands, starting with commercial logging. **Computer Services:** database, network directory. **Boards:** Advisory. **Programs:** Grassroots Development.

4593 ■ National Registry of Environmental Professionals (NREP)
PO Box 2099
Glenview, IL 60025
Ph: (847)724-6631
Fax: (847)724-4223
E-mail: nrep@nrep.org
URL: http://www.nrep.org
Contact: Richard A. Young PhD, Exec. Dir.
Founded: 1983. **Members:** 15,000. **Membership Dues:** re-certification, $90 (annual). **Staff:** 5. **Regional Groups:** 30. **Multinational. Description:** Certifies auditors, property assessors, lending analysts, indoor air quality specialists, hazardous and chemical material managers, ISO program administrators, environmental managers, engineers, technologists, scientists, and technicians. Promotes legal and professional recognition through professional registration credentialing. Offers accreditation. Provides lists of qualified environmental professionals to governmental agencies. Sponsors workshops through 30 official test center universities and online certification workshops through ESS. **Libraries: Type:** not open to the public. **Holdings:** 200. **Subjects:** environmental management, auditing and assessment. **Boards:** Certification Exam Development; Environmental Educators; Government Liaison; Governmental Regulators; Industrial Environmental Managers; Professional Practice and Ethics. **Divisions:** Office of Infrastructure Preparedness. **Affiliated With:** Environmental Information Association; International Association Emergency Managers; National Safety Management Society. **Absorbed:** (1994) International Academy of Toxicological Risk Assessment. **Conventions/Meetings:** annual meeting (exhibits).

4594 ■ National Tree Society
PO Box 10808
Bakersfield, CA 93389
Ph: (805)589-6912
URL: http://www.natural-connection.com/institutes/national_tree.html
Contact: Gregory W. Davis, Pres.
Founded: 1989. **Members:** 1,000. **Membership Dues:** regular, $36 (annual). **Staff:** 7. **Budget:** $350,000. **Regional Groups:** 3. **State Groups:** 7. **Local Groups:** 9. **Description:** Interested individuals organized to preserve the earth's biosphere by planting and caring for trees. Seeks to raise public understanding of the need for trees and the role they play in maintaining a healthy environment; works to acquire forest and other lands to ensure the continued growth of trees on such lands; establishes nurseries to supply the trees needed to "replace the millions destroyed annually and to offset Man's ever increasing use of combustion." Offers training in the planting and caring of trees; fosters research; is developing a specialized library focusing on the biosphere. Maintains and promotes the National Tree Fund, which provides financial support to plant and care for trees. Compiles statistics; maintains speakers' bureau. **Publications:** Brochures. Explains mission of National Tree Society. **Price:** free ● Newsletter, periodic ● Also issues press releases.

4595 ■ Native American Fish and Wildlife Society (NAFWS)
8333 Greenwood Blvd., Ste.260
Denver, CO 80221
Ph: (303)466-1725
Fax: (303)466-5414
URL: http://www.nafws.org
Contact: Ronald D. Rodgers, Deputy Dir.
Founded: 1983. **Members:** 224. **Membership Dues:** tribal individual, $20 (annual) ● affiliate organization, $120 (annual) ● student, $12 (annual). **Staff:** 14. **Regional Groups:** 7. **Description:** Works for the protection, conservation and enhancement of Native American fish and wildlife resources. Educates Native Americans about fish and wildlife management practices. **Publications:** *From the Eagle's Nest*, quarterly. Newsletter. Alternate Formats: online.

4596 ■ Native Habitat Organization (NHO)
c/o Nol Ward, Pres.
PO Box 101071
Fort Worth, TX 76185
Ph: (817)396-4370
E-mail: nol@consolidated.net
URL: http://www.nativehabitat.org
Contact: Nol Ward, Pres.
Description: Committed to understanding the responsibilities towards the natural world; aims to develop a code of land ethics; and promotes land use practices to meet human needs present and future.

4597 ■ New Environment Association (NEA)
821 Euclid Ave.
Syracuse, NY 13210
Ph: (315)446-8009
E-mail: hs38@mailbox.syr.edu
URL: http://www.newenvironment.org
Contact: Harry Schwarzlander, Contact
Founded: 1974. **Members:** 45. **Membership Dues:** individual, $25 (annual). **Description:** Exploration of new approaches to a sustainable future through participatory projects and educational programs. **Libraries: Type:** by appointment only; reference. **Holdings:** 950; articles, books, periodicals. **Subjects:** personal growth, social change, sustainable communities, environment. **Publications:** *New Environment Bulletin*, monthly. Newsletter. Contains articles, book reviews, commentaries, reports of recent activities, schedule of upcoming events, letters, etc. **Price:** $12.00/year; $22.00/2 years. **Circulation:** 160 ● *The New Environment Process*. Pamphlet ● Annual Report, annual. **Price:** free for members; $1.50 per back reports. **Conventions/Meetings:** monthly meeting.

4598 ■ North American Coalition on Religion and Ecology (NACRE)
Address Unknown since 2007
Founded: 1989. **Members:** 500. **Staff:** 3. **Budget:** $300,000. **Local Groups:** 1. **Description:** Encourages North American religious communities to involve and educate themselves in the environmental movement. Works to educate society on the moral and ethical implications of environmental action. Seeks to unite religion, science, and society in a discussion of global ethical principles. Conducts educational programs; maintains speakers' bureau. Sponsors discussion groups. **Publications:** *Getting Involved in the Earth Summit* ● *Race to Save the Planet Eco-Action: A Facilitator's Guide* ● *Race to Save the Planet Eco-Action: A Viewers Guide*. **Conventions/Meetings:** conference.

4599 ■ Open Space Institute (OSI)
1350 Broadway, Ste.201
New York, NY 10018-7799
Ph: (212)290-8200
Fax: (212)244-3441
E-mail: tblumberg@osiny.org
URL: http://www.osiny.org
Contact: Joseph J. Martens, Pres.
Founded: 1973. **Staff:** 10. **Budget:** $1,000,000. **State Groups:** 1. **Description:** Protects open space and promotes environmental values through public education and land conservation. Provides administrative and bookkeeping services to citizen environmental projects. **Formerly:** Open Space Action Committee. **Publications:** Annual Report, annual. **Price:** free. **Conventions/Meetings:** annual meeting.

4600 ■ Political Economy Research Center - The Center for Free Market Environmentalism (PERC)
2048 Anal. Dr., Ste.A
Bozeman, MT 59718
Ph: (406)587-9591
E-mail: perc@perc.org
URL: http://www.perc.org
Contact: Terry L. Anderson, Exec. Dir.
Description: Focuses on original research that brings market principles to resolving environmental problems. **Libraries: Type:** reference. **Holdings:** archival material, books, reports. **Subjects:** environment. **Awards:** Graduate and Law Student Fellowships. **Type:** scholarship ● Julian Simon Fellowship. **Type:** scholarship. **Telecommunication Services:** electronic mail, tla@perc.org. **Programs:** Environmental Education; Kinship Conservation Institute for Early Career Professionals; Roe Legal Fellowship and Outreach. **Publications:** *Agriculture and the Environment, Searching for Greener Pastures.* Book ● *Breaking the Environmental Policy Gridlock.* Book ● *Eco-Sanity: A Common Sense Guide to Environmentalism.* Book ● *Facts, Not Fear: Teaching Children About the Environment.* Book ● *Free Market Environmentalism - Revised Edition.* Book ● *Greening of U.S. Foreign Policy.* Book ● *Guide to Smart Growth: Shattering Myths, Providing Solutions.* Book ● *Multiple Conflicts Over Multiple Uses.* Book ● *Political Environmentalism.* Book ● Articles ● Reports. **Conventions/Meetings:** conference.

4601 ■ Quebec-Labrador Foundation/Atlantic Center for the Environment (QLF)
55 S Main St.
Ipswich, MA 01938
Ph: (978)356-0038
Fax: (978)356-7322
E-mail: atlantic@qlf.org
URL: http://www.qlf.org
Contact: Robert A. Bryan, Chm.
Founded: 1961. **Staff:** 18. **Budget:** $2,000,000. **Languages:** English, French. **Description:** Environmental education professionals, students, and others interested in conservation and improving the environment. Promotes education and involvement of the public in resource management and other environmental issues. Conducts research and educational programs. Provides technical assistance resource services such as assessments, conservation planning, and policy analysis; cooperates with other organizations in North America, Latin America, the Caribbean, Central Eastern Europe, and the Middle East. **Convention/Meeting:** none. **Awards:** Caring for the Earth. **Frequency:** annual. **Type:** recognition. **Recipient:** for persons who exemplify the principles of sustainability ● The Sounds Conservancy Grants Program. **Frequency:** annual. **Type:** grant. **Recipient:** for projects in marine conservation. **Formerly:** (1998) Atlantic Center for the Environment. **Publications:** *Compass*, annual. Magazine ● Handbooks ● Papers, periodic ● Also publishes educational materials.

4602 ■ Rene Dubos Center for Human Environments (RDCHE)
The Rene Dubos Ctr., Ste.387
Bronxville, NY 10708
Ph: (914)337-1636
Fax: (914)771-5206
E-mail: dubos@mindspring.com
URL: http://www.dubos.org
Contact: Ruth A. Eblen, Pres./Co-Founder
Founded: 1969. **Description:** Education and research organization focusing on the social and humanistic aspects of environmental problems. Seeks to help the general public and decision makers develop creative policies for the resolution of environmental conflicts and formulate new environmental values. Organizes and conducts forums on environmental issues and related activities. **Awards:** Rene Dubos Environmental Award. **Frequency:** annual. **Type:** recognition. **Recipient:** for individuals who exemplify leadership in keeping the organization's mission. **Formerly:** (1968) Total Education in the Total Environment; (1975) Rene Dubos Forum. **Publications:** *The Encyclopedia of the Environment.* Book. **Price:** $49.95 ● *Forum Proceedings*, annual. Includes directory of participants. ● *The World of Rene Dubos: A Collection of His Writings.* **Conventions/Meetings:** annual meeting, trustees ● annual roundtable, by invitation only - usually in May.

4603 ■ Resource Policy Institute (RPI)
Address Unknown since 2007
Founded: 1975. **Languages:** English, French, Spanish. **Description:** Research, education, and consulting group concerned with environmental and resource policy issues dealing with water and minerals, resource conservation, energy and technology policy, and national waste issues. Specializes in sustainability planning and pollution prevention. Resource Auditing Program; provides information on alternative energy, toxic substances, and the impact of federal legislation. **Convention/Meeting:** none. **Publications:** *Reports*, periodic.

4604 ■ Rock the Earth
1536 Wynkoop St., Ste.B200
Denver, CO 80202
Ph: (303)454-3304
Fax: (303)454-3306
E-mail: info@rocktheearth.org
URL: http://www.rocktheearth.net
Contact: Marc Ross, Pres./Exec. Dir.
Founded: 2003. **Membership Dues:** fan, $25 ● roadie, $50 ● crew, $100 ● sound engineer, $150 ● band manager, $250 ● tour manager, $500 ● rock star, $1,000 ● rock legend, $5,000. **Description:** Seeks to protect and defend America's natural resources through partnerships with the music industry and the world-wide environmental community. Advocates for a sustainable and healthy environment. Represents individuals and communities whose environment or natural surroundings are directly and adversely affected by others. **Projects:** Environmental Asset Monopolies; High Impact Polluters; The Mattaponi River; Preserving National Forests; Protecting Endangered Species from Pesticides; Protecting Public Lands from Livestock Grazing; Protecting Wilderness from Drilling; Raw Sewage Discharges. **Publications:** Newsletter.

4605 ■ Sacred Earth Network (SEN)
93A Glasheen Rd.
Petersham, MA 01366
Ph: (978)724-0120
E-mail: bill@sacredearthnetwork.org
URL: http://www.sacredearthnetwork.org
Contact: Bill Pfeiffer, Pres./Founder
Founded: 1985. **Members:** 500. **Membership Dues:** general, $35 (annual). **Staff:** 3. **Budget:** $200,000. **Languages:** English, Russian. **Description:** Environmentalists. Works to empower people to set up inexpensive and decentralized communications systems for the purpose of providing information and professional exchanges to strengthen ecological awareness. Encourages worldwide communication through electronic systems. Focuses on biodiversity issues in the former Soviet Union. Conducts workshops and retreats for environmental activists in the US. **Libraries: Type:** reference. **Holdings:** business records, clippings, periodicals. **Subjects:** environmental problems in the former Soviet Union. **Publications:** *Sacred Earth Network Newsletter.* Provides cutting edge ideas and solutions to environmental problems. **Price:** included in membership dues.

4606 ■ Scenic America (SA)
1634 I St. NW, Ste.510
Washington, DC 20006
Ph: (202)638-0550
Fax: (202)638-3171
E-mail: scenic@scenic.org
URL: http://www.scenic.org
Contact: Kevin Fry, Pres.
Founded: 1982. **Members:** 7,500. **Membership Dues:** individual, $35 (annual) ● regular, $35 ● contributor, regional organization, $50 (annual) ● sponsor, national organization, $100 (annual) ● donor, $250 (annual) ● landscape guardian, $500 (annual). **Staff:** 3. **Budget:** $410,000. **State Groups:** 7. **Description:** Safeguards natural beauty and community character through billboard and sign control, appropriate siting of cellular towers and other utilities, promotion of scenic byways, context-sensitive highway design, and protection of scenic landscapes and cityscapes. Advocates for the preservation of scenic beauty, open space, and quality of life. Fights billboard proliferation and other forms of visual pollution; works for the conservation of scenic byways and for context-sensitive highway design. **Libraries: Type:** reference. **Awards:** Stafford Award. **Frequency:** biennial. **Type:** recognition. **Telecommunication Services:** electronic mail, fry@scenic.org. **Formerly:** (1984) National Coalition to Preserve Scenic Beauty; (1989) Coalition for Scenic Beauty. **Publications:** *Aesthetics, Community Character, and the Law.* Book. Features design review, view protection, tree protection, sign protection, and updates based on developments in the law and in planning practice. **Price:** $34.00 ● *Fighting Billboard Blight: An Action for Citizens and Public Officials.* Handbook. Features a step-by-step guide in developing a campaign to fight against the proliferation of billboards. **Price:** $20.00 ● *Getting It Right In the Right-of-Way: Citizen Participation in Context-Sensitive Highway Design.* Includes information on community involvement in transportation planning. **Price:** $8.00 ● *Gift of the Journey: America's Scenic Roadways.* Video. **Price:** $8.00 ● *The Highway Beautification Act: A Broken Law.* **Price:** $10.00 ● *Looking at Change Before it Occurs.* Video. **Price:** $20.00 ● *Power to the People: Strategies for Reducing the Visual Impact of Overhead Utilities.* Contains information on preparing a comprehensive utility relocation plan. **Price:** $8.00 ● *Signs, Signs: The Economic and Environment Benefits of Community Sign Control.* Video. **Price:** $20.00 each ● *Taming Wireless Telecommunications Towers.* Provides citizens with background and advice on dealing with wireless telecommunications facilities through the planning and legislative process. **Price:** $8.00 ● *Tree Conservation Ordinances: Land Use Regulations Go Green.* Discusses valuation of trees, how to write an effective ordinance and common enforcement mistakes. **Price:** $32.00 ● *Trees Are Treasure: Sustaining the Community Forest.* Video. **Price:** $20.00 ● *Viewpoints*, quarterly. Newsletter. Contains information that pertains to sign control. **Price:** $25.00/year. **Circulation:** 5,000. Alternate Formats: online. **Conventions/Meetings:** biennial conference ● seminar.

4607 ■ Student Environmental Action Coalition (SEAC)
PO Box 31909
Philadelphia, PA 19104-0609
Ph: (215)222-4711
E-mail: seac@seac.org
URL: http://www.seac.org
Contact: Matt Reitmann, Natl. Council Coor.
Founded: 1988. **Members:** 1,500. **Membership Dues:** student, youth, $25 (annual) ● alumnus, $35 (annual) ● friend, $36-$100 (annual) ● sponsor, $101-$500 (annual). **Staff:** 3. **Budget:** $48,000. **Regional Groups:** 17. **State Groups:** 50. **Local Groups:** 1,500. **Description:** Students and student organizations; interested others. Seeks to empower students working for environmental justice. Serves as a clearinghouse on student environmental and social justice issues. Coordinates national and regional activities. Sponsors speakers' bureau and educational programs. **Libraries: Type:** reference. **Holdings:** articles, books, video recordings. **Subjects:** environmental justice, globalization, student power. **Computer Services:** Mailing lists ● online services, discussion forum. **Committees:** Kyoto Now Campaign; Militarism and the Environment Campaign; People of Color Caucus; Queer Caucus; Regional and State Networks; Tampaction Campaign; Women's Caucus; Working Class Caucus. **Publications:** *Threshold*, quarterly. Magazine. **Price:** free for members. **Circulation:** 1,000. **Advertising:** accepted. Alternate Formats: online; CD-ROM. **Conventions/Meetings:** annual Activist Training Camp - meeting, teaches skills on developing campaigns and building strong groups ● semiannual meeting.

4608 ■ Thornton W. Burgess Society
6 Discovery Hill Rd.
East Sandwich, MA 02537
Ph: (508)888-6870
Fax: (508)888-1919
E-mail: tburgess@capecod.net
URL: http://www.thorntonburgess.org
Contact: Jeanne Johnson, Exec. Dir.

Founded: 1976. **Members:** 2,000. **Membership Dues:** individual, $25 (annual) ● family, grandparent, $35 (annual) ● friend, $100 (annual) ● supporting, $40 (annual) ● sponsor, $50 (annual) ● patron, $500 (annual) ● benefactor, $1,000 (annual) ● business, $250 (annual). **Staff:** 27. **Budget:** $600,000. **Description:** Individuals interested in promoting and continuing the work of children's author and naturalist Thornton W. Burgess (1874-1965). Seeks to "inspire reverence for wildlife and concern for the natural environment". Operates the Thornton W. Burgess Museum and the Green Briar Nature Center. Offers educational programs. **Libraries: Type:** open to the public. **Holdings:** 1,600. **Subjects:** natural history of the Northeastern United States. **Awards: Type:** scholarship. **Recipient:** for studying environmental science. **Publications:** *Briar Patch Observer*, semiannual. Newsletter. Includes activities updates, natural history items, and membership information. **Price:** free for members. **Circulation:** 2,000 ● *Burgess Book Collector's Bulletin*, 3/year. Newsletter ● *Thornton W. Burgess: A Descriptive Book Bibliography*. **Price:** $25.00. **Conventions/Meetings:** annual meeting - always February.

4609 ■ Threshold
c/o Sacred Passage and The Way of Nature
PO Box 3388
Tucson, AZ 85722-3388
Free: (877)818-1881
E-mail: info@sacredpassage.com
URL: http://www.sacredpassage.com
Contact: John P. Milton, Founder/Pres.

Founded: 1971. **Regional Groups:** 12. **Languages:** English, Spanish. **Description:** Conducts wilderness retreats, vision quests, and awareness training programs in nature. Fosters training in meditation, T'ai Chi, Qi Gong, Taoist Yoga, shamanism, and spiritual cultivation in wilderness. Promotes environmental conservation and protection of endangered ecosystems such as the tropical rain forests. Encourages global awareness of environmental destruction. Facilitates coalition-building among environmental organizations in an effort to resolve issues. Conducts and supports projects through the Environmental Crisis Fund; has worked for resolution of environmental issues in the Amazon Basin, the Pacific region, Latin America, Europe, Asia, Africa, and North America. Conducts research and educational programs; provides technical assistance and planning information. **Libraries: Type:** reference. **Holdings:** 20,000. **Awards: Type:** recognition. **Publications:** *Passages*. Newsletter.

4610 ■ Trees, Water and People (TWP)
633 Remington St.
Fort Collins, CO 80524
Ph: (970)484-3678
Free: (877)606-4TWP
Fax: (970)224-1726
E-mail: twp@treeswaterpeople.org
URL: http://www.treeswaterpeople.org
Contact: Stuart Conway, Co-Founder/Intl. Dir.

Founded: 1998. **Multinational. Description:** Improves people's lives through protection, conservation and management of natural resources. Protects the sustainability of the world's forests and watersheds. **Programs:** Tribal Lands; Watershed Protection.

4611 ■ Turner Foundation
133 Luckie St. NW, 2nd Fl.
Atlanta, GA 30303
Ph: (404)681-9900
Fax: (404)681-0172
URL: http://www.turnerfoundation.org
Contact: Michael Finley, Pres.

Founded: 1990. **Description:** Environmental advocates. Works to prevent damage to the natural systems including water, air, and land. **Awards: Type:** grant. **Programs:** Air Quality, Energy and Transportation; Habitat; Population; Water and Toxics.

4612 ■ United States-Asia Environmental Partnership (US-AEP)
709 Potomac St.
Alexandria, VA 22314-3859
Ph: (202)835-0333
Fax: (202)835-0366
E-mail: dcallihan@usaep.org
URL: http://www.usaep.org

Founded: 1992. **National Groups:** 11. **Description:** Promotes environmentally sustainable development in Asia. **Programs:** Technology Cooperation; Urban. **Subgroups:** Policy.

4613 ■ United States Committee for the United Nations Environment Program (US UNEP)
47914 252nd St.
Sioux Falls, SD 57198-0002
Ph: (605)594-6117
Fax: (605)594-6119
E-mail: singh@usgs.gov
URL: http://grid2.cr.usgs.gov
Contact: Dr. Ashbindu Singh, Regional Coor.

Founded: 1984. **Members:** 1,000. **Description:** Individuals interested in raising public awareness of the importance of a global environmental effort. Encourages activism in support of the United Nations Environment Program. Acts as a liaison between the UNEP and the public. Sponsors educational programs and children's services. Offers placement services to job seekers in international environmental work. Maintains speakers' bureau. **Awards: Type:** recognition. **Formerly:** (1990) Friends of the United Nations Environment Program. **Publications:** *Update*, monthly ● *US/UNEP News*, quarterly. Newsletter. Reports on UNEP and international environmental issues and events. **Price:** included in membership dues ● *US/UNEP Topics*, quarterly ● Brochures. **Price:** free. **Circulation:** 3,000. **Conventions/Meetings:** competition ● periodic meeting.

4614 ■ Wildlands Project
PO Box 5284
Titusville, FL 32783
Free: (877)554-5234
Fax: (877)554-5234
E-mail: info@wildlandsproject.org
URL: http://www.twp.org
Contact: Mary Granskou, Pres.

Founded: 1991. **Staff:** 8. **Budget:** $1,000,000. **Regional Groups:** 25. **Description:** Individuals and organizations with an interest in the natural heritage of North America. Seeks to protect and restore North American wildlife and habitats. Works to establish a connected system of wildlands, landscape connections, and wildland buffer zones throughout North America, which the group believes will enable the reintroduction of large predators and the restoration of healthy ecosystems. Coordinates the activities of conservation organizations; conducts fundraising and educational programs. **Programs:** Conservation; Network; Partnership. **Publications:** *Wild Earth*, quarterly. Journal. Contains conservation biology focus. **Price:** $6.95. **Circulation:** 10,000 ● Newsletter. Alternate Formats: online.

4615 ■ Windstar Foundation (WF)
PO Box 656
Snowmass, CO 81654-0656
Ph: (970)927-5430
Free: (866)927-5430
Fax: (970)927-9342
E-mail: windstarco@wstar.org
URL: http://www.wstar.org
Contact: John Denver, Founder

Founded: 1976. **Members:** 2,000. **Membership Dues:** youth (age 14 and under), $10 ● senior/student, $25 ● individual, $35 ● household, $75 ● guardian, $100 ● supporter, $250 ● patron, $500 ● sponsor, $1,000 ● sustainer, $2,500 ● benefactor, $5,000 ● corporate, $10,000. **Staff:** 2. **State Groups:** 2. **Local Groups:** 1. **National Groups:** 12. **Description:** Seeks to create opportunities for individuals to acquire the knowledge, skills, experiences, and commitment necessary to build a healthy and sustainable future for humanity; publicizes steps that individuals can take to improve environmental quality. Conducts a variety of educational programs for children through adults. Assists individuals and communities worldwide in creating effective environmental education programs through Windstar Connection Groups. **Telecommunication Services:** electronic mail, president@wstar.org. **Publications:** *Windstar Vision*, quarterly. Newsletter. **Price:** $35.00/year ● Videos. **Conventions/Meetings:** annual New Choices for Your Future - symposium, with presentations from a wide variety of renowned environmental speakers accompanied by an on-line classroom curriculum for middle and high school teachers.

4616 ■ Women's Voices for the Earth (WVE)
PO Box 1067
Bozeman, MT 59771
Ph: (406)585-5549 (406)585-9009
Fax: (406)585-5549
E-mail: wve@womenandenvironment.org
URL: http://www.womenandenvironment.org
Contact: Lisa Woll, Pres.

Founded: 1995. **Membership Dues:** general, $35 (annual). **Staff:** 8. **Description:** Increases women's leadership and effectiveness in environmental decision-making. Reduces environmental toxins that negatively impact women's health. Builds alliances with, and provides support to, other groups also disproportionately impacted by environmental contamination. **Computer Services:** Information services, toxics campaign ● mailing lists. **Telecommunication Services:** electronic mail, lwoll@erols.com. **Boards:** Advisory. **Programs:** Environmental Alliance; Girls Using Their Strengths; Smart Growth Leadership Skills. **Publications:** *Weavings*, quarterly. Newsletter. Alternate Formats: online.

4617 ■ World Parks
2806 P St. NW
Washington, DC 20007
Ph: (202)333-1044
E-mail: worldparks@worldparks.org
URL: http://www.worldparks.org
Contact: Byron Swift, Pres.

Multinational, Description: Preserves the Earth's threatened species and ecosystem. Purchases and protects lands that are critical for preventing immediate species extinctions. Provides local conservation organizations with financial resources needed to purchase and protect critical lands for biodiversity conservation. **Programs:** Alliance for Zero Extinction. **Projects:** Landscape. **Publications:** Annual Report, annual.

4618 ■ WorldWIDE Network, Women in Development and Environment
Address Unknown since 2007

Founded: 1982. **Members:** 7,500. **Staff:** 3. **Description:** Women and men interested in environmental protection and sustainable development. Promotes strengthening the role of women in the development and implementation of environmental and natural resource policies. Educates and promotes communication among members concerning the consequences of decisions affecting the environment, especially the contamination and destruction of ecological systems. Encourages members to include environmental and natural resource management activities in their lives; seeks to educate policymakers about problems of women and the environment and to foster increased inclusion of women and their perspectives in the development and implementation of policies and programs. Keeps members informed of environmental projects and women's activities in related areas. Believes that women can serve as agents of change on environmental issues. Conducts educational programs; maintains speakers' bureau.

Libraries: Type: reference. **Holdings:** books, periodicals. **Councils:** International Advisory. **Also Known As:** WorldWIDE. **Formerly:** (1988) World Women Dedicated to the Environment; (1991) World Women in the Environment; (1993) Worldwide Network. **Publications:** *Proceedings of the Global Assembly* ● *Women and Environment: An Analytical Review* ● *WorldWIDE Directory of Women in Environment*, annual ● *WorldWIDE News, 1982-1995*, quarterly. Bulletin ● Pamphlet. **Conventions/Meetings:** periodic Global Assembly of Women on Environment - Partners in Life - meeting ● periodic regional meeting.

Environmental Education

4619 ■ Association of Women in Environmental Professions (AWEP)
PO Box 748
Seattle, WA 98111-0748
E-mail: awep@awep.org
URL: http://www.awep.org
Contact: Katherine Chesick, Pres.
Membership Dues: individual, $25 (annual) ● student, $15 (annual) ● corporate, $250 (annual). **Staff:** 6. **Description:** Advocates for environmental education and the advancement of women interested in the environment. Educates the public about environmental issues. Provides networking opportunities for environmental professionals and those interested in becoming one. **Publications:** Directory ● Newsletter, quarterly. Features articles on technical and professional issues, a calendar of upcoming events, and profiles of active members. **Advertising:** accepted.

4620 ■ Center for Respect of Life and Environment (CRLE)
2100 L St. NW
Washington, DC 20037
Ph: (202)778-6133
Fax: (202)778-6138
E-mail: info@crle.org
URL: http://www.crle.org
Contact: Richard M. Clugston, Exec. Dir.
Founded: 1986. **Description:** Recognizes a growing environmental crisis. Works to awaken community's ecological sensibilities, to transform lifestyles, institutional practices, and social policies to support the community of life. Programs identify approaches to economic and social development that recognize links between ecology, spirituality, and sustainability. **Publications:** *Earth Ethics*. Journal. Promotes alternative models for sustainable communities and lifestyles, based on ecospiritual practice and principle.

4621 ■ Children of the Earth United
PO Box 816
Columbia, MD 21044
Ph: (443)321-4617
E-mail: info@childrenoftheearth.org
URL: http://www.childrenoftheearth.org
Contact: Jennifer Reinfeld, Founder/Exec. Dir.
Founded: 1998. **Multinational. Description:** Aims to help foster a greater understanding and respect for the environment. Educates the general public on environmental issues and ecological concepts. Provides a forum for children and adults to share knowledge and ideas, and learn about animals, plants and the environment. Offers educational programs for children and educational information system accessible through the internet. **Telecommunication Services:** electronic mail, entry@childrenoftheearth.org ● electronic mail, comments@childrenoftheearth.org.

4622 ■ Eco-Spirit
PO Box 239
Clarksburg, MD 20871
Free: (866)709-0131
E-mail: info@eco-spirit.org
URL: http://www.eco-spirit.org
Contact: David E. Reeves, Pres./Chm.
Membership Dues: basic, $15 (annual). **Multinational. Description:** Advocates for the advancement of environmental education, spirituality, and activism. Strives to protect the Earth's land, water, air, animals, and plants by fostering a desire among all people to live in harmony with the Earth, its ecosystems, and other living organisms in an environmentally sustainable and ethical manner. Educates members and the general public on how to practice environmental sensitivity and voluntary simplicity to reduce pollution, cut energy use and limit the consumption of the Earth's natural resources. Seeks to build an international community of like-minded people dedicated to living environmentally sustainable and eco-spiritual lives. **Publications:** *Environmental Living and Eco-Spirituality*, bimonthly. Newsletter. Alternate Formats: online.

4623 ■ EcoVentures International (EVI)
1519 Connecticut Ave. NW, Ste.301
Washington, DC 20036
Ph: (202)667-0802
Fax: (202)667-0803
E-mail: info@eco-ventures.org
URL: http://www.eco-ventures.org
Contact: Margie Brand, Exec. Dir.
Founded: 2002. **Multinational. Description:** Trains and supports the youth to become environmental entrepreneurs. Seeks to integrate environmental education movements with the small businesses, entrepreneurship education and micro-enterprise training sectors to foster sustainable economic, social, and environmental growth and development. Assists individuals and communities to find the linkages between environment, economy, and society. **Telecommunication Services:** electronic mail, margie@eco-ventures.org. **Programs:** Advocacy Initiatives; EcoPreneurs Network; Environmental Enterprise Training; Training-of-Trainers and Capability Building. **Publications:** Newsletter. Alternate Formats: online.

4624 ■ Indigenous Environmental Network (IEN)
PO Box 485
Bemidji, MN 56619
Ph: (218)751-4967
Fax: (218)751-0561
E-mail: ien@igc.org
Contact: Tom Goldtooth, Exec.Dir.
Founded: 1990. **Description:** People interested in protecting the Earth. Strives to protect the Earth from contamination and exploitation. Holds conferences, meetings and publishes books. **Programs:** Globalization, Trade and Environment; Water is Life; Youth Program and Youth Leadership Training Project. **Publications:** Books. **Conventions/Meetings:** conference.

4625 ■ Youth for Environmental Sanity (YES)
420 Bronco Rd.
Soquel, CA 95073-9510
Ph: (831)465-1091
Fax: (831)462-6970
E-mail: info@yesworld.org
URL: http://www.yesworld.org
Contact: Ocean Robbins, Co-Founder/Dir.
Founded: 1990. **Staff:** 4. **Budget:** $400,000. **Description:** Educates, inspires and empowers young people to join forces for social justice and environmental sanity. Addresses school assemblies and college venues, holds day-long workshops and week-long youth training events. **Libraries: Type:** not open to the public. **Holdings:** books, video recordings. **Subjects:** environment, social change. **Awards:** Scholarships. **Type:** scholarship. **Publications:** *Choices for Our Future*. Video. **Price:** $10.00 ● *Connect* ● *Green Schools Manual*. Also available on VHS tape. **Price:** $10.00 ● Manuals. **Conventions/Meetings:** Youth Jams - conference - several per year.

Environmental Health

4626 ■ Alliance of Veterinarians for the Environment (AVE)
c/o Gwen Griffith, DVM
836 W Hillwood Dr.
Nashville, TN 37205
Ph: (615)353-0272
Fax: (615)353-8904
E-mail: avegwen@aol.com
URL: http://www.aveweb.org
Contact: Gwen Griffith DVM, Contact
Founded: 1995. **Membership Dues:** full, $25 (annual) ● associate/student, $15 (annual) ● institution/library, $20 (annual). **Description:** Seeks to promote environmental health and the conservation of nature through education and research within the veterinary profession. Advances the participation of veterinary medicine in environmental problem-solving. Produces national and international environmental education programs. Provides a national forum on veterinary environmental issues for educators, natural resource managers and policy decision-makers.

4627 ■ American Association of Pesticide Safety Educators (AAPSE)
c/o Carol Ramsay
Washington State Univ.
PO Box 646382
Pullman, WA 99164-6382
Ph: (509)335-9222
Fax: (509)335-1009
E-mail: ramsay@wsu.edu
URL: http://www.aapse.org
Contact: Carol Ramsay, Contact
Membership Dues: basic, $50 (annual) ● supporting, $100 (annual). **Description:** Provides science-based pesticide safety education programs; seeks to protect human health and environment through education. **Committees:** Issues and Evaluation; Nominations/Elections; Public Relations; Recognitions and Resolutions. **Publications:** *Journal of Pesticide Safety Education*. Alternate Formats: online ● *Position Papers*. Alternate Formats: online.

4628 ■ Global Environmental Management Initiative (GEMI)
1155 15th St. NW, Ste.500
Washington, DC 20005
Ph: (202)296-7449
Fax: (202)296-7442
E-mail: info@gemi.org
URL: http://www.gemi.org
Contact: Steve Hellem, Exec. Dir.
Founded: 1990. **Members:** 40. **Membership Dues:** company, $20,000 (annual). **Multinational. Description:** Helps businesses improve environmental, healthy and safety performance. Provides a forum for corporate environmental leaders to work together and share experiences and ideas. Shares tools and information to help businesses achieve environmental, health and safety excellence. **Publications:** *GEMI News*, monthly. Newsletter. **Price:** included in membership dues ● Reports. Alternate Formats: online.

4629 ■ Healthy Building Network (HBN)
927 15th St. NW, 4th Fl.
Washington, DC 20005
Ph: (202)898-1610
Fax: (202)898-1612
E-mail: info@healthybuilding.net
URL: http://www.healthybuilding.net
Contact: Bill Walsh, National Coor.
Description: Promotes healthier building materials as a means of improving public health and preserving the global environment. Focuses on green building strategies that are closely linked to the goals of the environmental health movement. Brings the perspectives of people directly impacted by the source, production, use and disposal of building materials to green building professionals.

4630 ■ Interamerican Association for Environmental Defense (AIDA)
c/o Earthjustice
426 17th St., 6th Fl.
Oakland, CA 94612
Ph: (510)550-6753
Fax: (510)550-6740

E-mail: aida@aida-americas.org
URL: http://www.aida-americas.org
Contact: Martin Wagner, Contact
Founded: 1996. **Languages:** English, Spanish. **Multinational. Description:** Promotes the ability of citizens to protect their health and environment through the development and enforcement of national and international environmental laws. Provides a forum for environmental law organizations to jointly design and apply solutions to shared environmental problems. Works with technical experts and transfers needed information to NGOs, communities and governments throughout the hemisphere.

Environmental Quality

4631 ■ Clean Production Action (CPA)
PO Box 153
Spring Brook, NY 14140
Ph: (716)805-1056
E-mail: alexandra@cleanproduction.org
URL: http://www.cleanproduction.org
Contact: Alexandra McPherson, Proj. Dir.
Staff: 3. **Multinational. Description:** Promotes the use of products that are safer and cleaner across their life cycle for consumers, workers and communities. Promotes societal realization of Clean Production and Sustainable Consumption. Analyzes research, policy and market developments to identify and promote technical, academic and industry expertise on Clean Production. Works with environmental and public health advocates, trade unions, progressive companies, and governments around the world.

4632 ■ Environmental Council of the States (ECOS)
444 N Capitol St. NW, Ste.445
Washington, DC 20001
Ph: (202)624-3660
Fax: (202)624-3666
E-mail: ecos@sso.org
URL: http://www.ecos.org
Contact: R. Steven Brown, Exec. Dir.
Founded: 1993. **Description:** Represents state and territorial environmental commissioners. Works to improve the environment. **Committees:** Air; Compliance; Cross-Media; Planning; Waste; Water. **Publications:** *ECOStates*, quarterly. Journal. **Price:** $80.00/year. Alternate Formats: online ● *State Environmental Agency Contributions to Enforcement and Compliance*. Report. Alternate Formats: online ● Annual Report. Alternate Formats: online ● Reports. Alternate Formats: online.

4633 ■ Environmental Research and Education Foundation (EREF)
901 N Pitt St., Ste.270
Alexandria, VA 22314
Ph: (703)299-5139
Fax: (703)299-5145
E-mail: mcagney@erefdn.org
URL: http://www.erefdn.org
Contact: Michael J. Cagney, Pres./CEO
Founded: 1992. **Description:** Dedicated to developing environmental solutions for waste management for the future. **Awards:** Francois Fiessinger Memorial Scholarship Fund. **Frequency:** annual. **Type:** scholarship. **Recipient:** for excellence in PhD or postdoctoral environmental research and education ● Research Grant. **Frequency:** annual. **Type:** grant. **Recipient:** to person who conducts research and education related to solid waste management. **Publications:** *EREF NEWS*. Newsletter. Alternate Formats: online ● *Research Bulletin*, quarterly. Alternate Formats: online ● Annual Reports, annual. Alternate Formats: online.

4634 ■ Filipino American Coalition for Environmental Solidarity (FACES)
1808 Fifth St.
Berkeley, CA 94710
Ph: (510)549-1808
Fax: (510)644-1808
E-mail: info@facessolidarity.org
URL: http://www.facessolidarity.org
Contact: Lea Patricia L. Francisco, Admin.
Founded: 2000. **Multinational. Description:** Represents environmental, peace and justice groups, students, scientists, professionals, and other concerned citizens who are committed to seeking environmental justice for the communities affected by toxic contamination at former U.S. military bases in the Philippines. Protects and preserves the resources of the environment and sustains all living creatures for present and future generations. Works for environmental justice within communities in the United States and in the Philippines, and builds partnerships through advocacy, education, service, and organizing. **Publications:** *Facing Justice*, quarterly. Newsletter. Alternate Formats: online.

4635 ■ Healthy Schools Network
110 Maryland Ave. NE, Ste.505
Washington, DC 20002
Ph: (202)543-7555
E-mail: info@healthyschools.org
URL: http://www.healthyschools.org
Contact: John Shaw, Pres.
Founded: 1995. **Description:** Seeks to ensure that every child has a healthy learning environment that is clean and in good repair. Documents and publicizes school environmental problems. Fosters research, education, coalition-building, and advocacy.

4636 ■ International Coalition for Children and the Environment (ICCE)
161 Water St.
Norwich, CT 06360
Ph: (860)885-1000
Fax: (860)885-0320
E-mail: rlharris@internationalcoalition.org
URL: http://www.internationalcoalition.org
Contact: Mr. Michael Van Leesten, Chm./Pres.
Founded: 2000. **Multinational. Description:** Aims to build a stronger community and raise awareness about indigenous people and the environment. Promotes and supports worldwide efforts of creating more environmentally friendly activities. Encourages self-respect, a sense of responsibility and confidence in the youth to become advocates for a sustainable environmental future. Provides youth with the skills and knowledge to respect, support, share and celebrate diversity of peoples and cultures. Facilitates discussions on innovative, adaptable, efficiently utilized and replicable uses of renewable resources. **Telecommunication Services:** electronic mail, info@internationalcoalition.org.

4637 ■ SkyTruth
PO Box 3283
Shepherdstown, WV 25443-3283
Ph: (304)876-9113
Fax: (304)876-0646
E-mail: into@skytruth.org
URL: http://www.skytruth.org
Contact: John F. Amos, Founding Dir./Exec. Dir.
Founded: 2001. **Staff:** 4. **Description:** Promotes environmental awareness and protection with remote sensing and digital mapping technology. Works with environmental NGOs and government management agencies to conduct projects that address critical environmental issues. Seeks to motivate people to take action for environmental protection and human sustainability. Uses pictures taken from orbiting satellites and aircraft to show people the impacts of human activities on the planet.

Farm Management

4638 ■ Agricultural Personnel Management Association (APMA)
Address Unknown since 2008
Membership Dues: individual/non-resident, $95 (annual) ● company, $195 (annual) ● student, $25 (annual). **Description:** Encourages leadership and effective personnel management in the agribusiness community. Works for the advancement of human resources and safety management through education, information and interaction. **Publications:** *Harvester*, bimonthly. Newsletter. Features articles on agricultural issues, safety and management matters. ● Membership Directory. Includes individuals and companies, addresses and types of businesses.

4639 ■ National Farm and Ranch Business Management Education Association (NFRBMEA)
6540 65th St. NE
Rochester, MN 55906-1911
Ph: (507)252-6928
Fax: (507)252-6928
E-mail: paul.gorman@southcentral.edu
URL: http://www.nfrbmea.org
Contact: Paul Gorman, Pres.-Elect
Founded: 1973. **Membership Dues:** active, $30 (annual) ● affiliate, $10 (annual). **Multinational. Description:** Works to bring ideas and techniques in farm and ranch business management education to its members. **Publications:** *NUTS & BOLTS*, 3/year. Newsletter. Features current ideas in farm and ranch management education. ● Annual Report, annual. Alternate Formats: online. **Conventions/Meetings:** annual conference.

4640 ■ Northwest Farm Managers Association (NWFM)
c/o Institute for Regional Studies and University Archives
PO Box 5599
Fargo, ND 58105-5599
Ph: (701)231-8914
Fax: (701)231-5632
E-mail: daakre@ndsuext.nodak.edu
URL: http://www.lib.ndsu.nodak.edu/ndirs/index.html
Contact: Dwight C. Aakre, Exec. Sec.
Founded: 1909. **Members:** 300. **Description:** Represents manager-operators of commercial farms and agriculturists interested in research in farm management, marketing, and agribusiness. **Awards:** H.W. Herbison Memorial Scholarship. **Frequency:** annual. **Type:** scholarship ● Pioneer of the Year Award. **Frequency:** annual. **Type:** recognition. **Recipient:** for a farmer or agri-businessperson who has a history of service and leadership in farming innovation and service to the community. **Publications:** *Northwest Farm Managers Association Membership Directory*, annual. **Price:** included in membership dues. **Circulation:** 300 ● *Plowshares to Printouts*. Book. **Conventions/Meetings:** annual meeting, with educational program - always first Tuesday and Wednesday of February, Fargo, ND.

Farming

4641 ■ Alliance for Sustainability
c/o Hillel Center
Univ. of Minnesota
1521 Univ. Ave. SE
Minneapolis, MN 55414
Ph: (612)331-1099
Fax: (612)379-1527
E-mail: iasa@mtn.org
URL: http://www.allianceforsustainability.net
Contact: Sean Gosiewski, Exec. Dir.
Founded: 1983. **Members:** 3,500. **Membership Dues:** basic, $40 ● four elements-earth, $500 ● four elements-wind, $250 ● four elements-fire, $100 ● four elements-water, $50 ● planetary partner, $5,000 ● green future, $2,500 ● tree of life, $1,000. **Staff:** 4. **Budget:** $50,000. **Description:** Development specialists, farmers, researchers, and other individuals; cooperatives and agricultural, consumer, and environmental groups. Aims to promote and contribute to the establishment of projects that are economically viable, ecologically sound, and socially just and humane. Sponsors programs in education, information dissemination, organizational support, network building, and policy. Promotes information sharing and cooperation through conferences, work exchanges, and organized tours. Furnishes technical expertise in farm practices, market development, and

financial planning. Operates speakers' bureau; conducts workshops. Maintains resource center providing information on biological pest control, pesticides, and sustainable agriculture, sustainability and more. Conducts projects stressing the theme of sustainability: The Natural Step Framework Training Seminars, Junk Mail Tree Project, and Skiers Ending Hunger. **Libraries: Type:** open to the public. **Holdings:** 1,200; periodicals. **Subjects:** pesticides, agriculture, sustainable agriculture. **Awards:** Sustainability Awards. **Frequency:** annual. **Type:** recognition. **Recipient:** for individuals, groups, and institutions that made significant contributions to sustainability. **Projects:** Alliance Retail; Junk Mail Tree. **Formerly:** (1997) International Alliance for Sustainable Agriculture. **Publications:** *Benefits of Diversity: An Incentive Towards Sustainable Agriculture.* Book. Discusses important concepts in sustainable agriculture and 21 case studies from around the Third World. **Price:** $10.00 plus $3 shipping ● *Breaking the Pesticide Habit: Alternatives to 12 Hazardous Pesticides.* Book. Provides background on the pesticide problem, case studies, safer alternatives to the twelve most menacing pesticides. **Price:** $19.95 plus $3 surface shipping in U.S. ● *Manna Newsletter*, monthly. Covers worldwide agricultural topics. Includes book reviews, calendar of events, conference reports, and information on new members. **Price:** free for members; $15.00 /year for nonmembers. Alternate Formats: online. **Conventions/Meetings:** periodic The Natural Step to Sustainable Business & Community - seminar.

4642 ■ American Farm Bureau Federation (AFBF)
600 Maryland Ave. SW, Ste.1000W
Washington, DC 20024
Ph: (202)406-3600
Free: (800)572-1090
Fax: (202)406-3602
E-mail: bstallman@fb.org
URL: http://www.fb.org
Contact: Bob Stallman, Pres.

Founded: 1919. **Members:** 5,000,000. **Staff:** 82. **State Groups:** 50. **Description:** Federation of 50 state farm bureaus and Puerto Rico, with membership on a family basis. Analyzes problems of members and formulates action to achieve educational improvement, economic opportunity, and social advancement. Maintains speakers' bureau; sponsors specialized education program. **Libraries: Type:** reference. **Holdings:** 9,175; books, periodicals. **Subjects:** agricultural economics and finance, trade. **Divisions:** Economic Analysis; Organization; Public Policy; Telecommunications. **Affiliated With:** American Farm Bureau Foundation for Agriculture. **Also Known As:** Farm Bureau. **Publications:** *Farm Bureau News*, weekly. Newsletter ● *Farm Bureau Working for You*, annual. Brochure. Outlines the many ways Farm Bureau works for America's farmers and ranchers. **Price:** $38.00/bundle of 200 ● *Farm Facts.* Booklet. Contains information on the business of farming and agriculture. **Price:** $4.00 single copy. **Conventions/Meetings:** annual convention (exhibits) - always January.

4643 ■ Biodynamic Farming and Gardening Association (BDA)
25844 Butler Rd.
Junction City, OR 97448
Ph: (541)998-0105 (916)961-8727
Free: (888)516-7797
Fax: (541)998-0106
E-mail: info@biodynamics.com
URL: http://www.biodynamics.com
Contact: Neil Austin, Contact

Founded: 1938. **Members:** 1,500. **Membership Dues:** regular, $45 (annual) ● contributing, $75 (annual) ● supporting, $100 (annual). **Staff:** 4. **Budget:** $400,000. **Regional Groups:** 31. **Description:** Farmers, gardeners, consumers, physicians, and scientists interested in improving nutrition and health through the production of high quality food using bio-dynamic farming. (Bio-dynamic farming stresses restoration of organic matter to the soil, use of special preparations to stimulate biological activity of soil and plant growth, crop rotation, proper cultivation to avoid structural damage to soil, and establishment of beneficial environmental conditions such as forests, wind protection, and water regulation). **Libraries: Type:** reference. **Holdings:** articles, periodicals. **Committees:** Land Trust; Research; Training. **Departments:** Bio-Dynamic Extension Service. **Publications:** *BIO-DYNAMICS*, quarterly. Journal. Includes calendar of events. **Advertising:** accepted ● Also publishes books on bio-dynamic agriculture and community supported agriculture. **Conventions/Meetings:** annual board meeting and conference (exhibits).

4644 ■ Demeter Association
PO Box 1390
Philomath, OR 97370
Ph: (541)929-7148
Fax: (541)929-4387
E-mail: demeter@peak.org
URL: http://www.demeter-usa.org
Contact: Jim Fullmer, Dir.

Founded: 1982. **Staff:** 1. **Budget:** $90,000. **Description:** Certifies Biodynamic farms. (Biodynamic farming predates organic farming and is based on lectures by Austrian philosopher Rudolf Steiner.). **Affiliated With:** Biodynamic Farming and Gardening Association. **Publications:** *The Voice of Demeter*, semiannual. Newsletter. Updates activities, policies, issues, and listing of certified farms. **Price:** free ● Magazine ● Articles. Alternate Formats: online ● Also publishes certification standards and P.O.P materials.

4645 ■ Family Farm Defenders (FFD)
PO Box 1772
Madison, WI 53701
Ph: (608)260-0900
Fax: (608)260-0900
E-mail: familyfarmdefenders@yahoo.com
URL: http://www.familyfarmdefenders.org
Contact: John E. Peck, Exec. Dir.

Founded: 1994. **Members:** 1,500. **Membership Dues:** general, $25 (annual). **Staff:** 1. **Budget:** $75,000. **Description:** Represents individuals and organizations dedicated to principles of sustainable agriculture, family farm livelihood, food safety, animal welfare, consumer right to know, workers' rights, fair trade, rural justice, and democratic sovereignty. **Libraries: Type:** open to the public. **Subjects:** agriculture, food, politics, globalization, workers rights, biotech, rural justice. **Projects:** Family Farmer Fair Trade Cheese; Yahara Food Farm Coalition. **Affiliated With:** 50 Years is Enough: U.S. Network for Global Economic Justice; National Family Farm Coalition; Rural Coalition. **Publications:** *The Defender*, quarterly. Newsletter. **Price:** included in membership dues. **Circulation:** 1,500. **Conventions/Meetings:** annual meeting - usually March/April.

4646 ■ International Flying Farmers (IFF)
PO Box 9124
Wichita, KS 67277-0124
Ph: (316)943-4234 (785)528-3197
Free: (800)266-5415
Fax: (800)266-5415
E-mail: support@flyingfarmers.org
URL: http://www.flyingfarmers.org
Contact: Jamie Sossaman, Pres.

Founded: 1944. **Members:** 2,000. **Membership Dues:** family, $60 (annual). **Staff:** 1. **Budget:** $300,000. **State Groups:** 33. **Multinational. Description:** Families in the U.S. and Canada interested in aviation or agriculture. Promotes the practical use of the airplane in agriculture; encourages soil and water conservation through education derived from aerial conservation flights; promotes safe flying through continued education and upgrading. Members collectively own 2000 planes, most of which are flown from their privately owned landing strips. Compiles information on private landing strips for planes. Offers insurance. Voluntary annual proficiency test enables members to keep check on their piloting proficiency and improve in specific areas. Organizes International Flying Farmer Teens to afford youth the opportunity to participate in worthwhile projects and to stimulate social activities under adult guidance. Conducts children's services and tours. **Awards:** The Gift of Flight - A Flight Incentive Scholarship. **Frequency:** annual. **Type:** scholarship. **Recipient:** to unmarried girls who have no previous flight instruction ● Memorial Fund Award for College Completion. **Frequency:** annual. **Type:** scholarship. **Recipient:** to a well-rounded individual whose education would be hindered without financial assistance. **Computer Services:** Online services, bulletin board. **Committees:** Insurance; Medical Advisory; Tours; Upgrading. **Programs:** APT. **Formerly:** (1961) National Flying Farmers Association. **Publications:** *The National Flying Farmer*, bimonthly. Magazine. Includes obituaries, internal committee reports, member profiles, and calendar of events. **Price:** included in membership dues; $25.00 for nonmembers in U.S.; $30.00 for nonmembers in Canada; $35.00 for nonmembers outside U.S. and Canada. ISSN: 0020-675X. **Circulation:** 2,000. **Advertising:** accepted ● Membership Directory, biennial. **Conventions/Meetings:** competition ● annual conference (exhibits) ● seminar.

4647 ■ The Land Institute (TLI)
2440 E Water Well Rd.
Salina, KS 67401-9051
Ph: (785)823-5376
Fax: (785)823-8728
E-mail: theland@landinstitute.org
URL: http://www.landinstitute.org
Contact: Mr. Wes Jackson, Pres.

Founded: 1976. **Members:** 2,200. **Staff:** 22. **Budget:** $1,250,000. **Description:** Natural Systems Agriculture (NSA) Program of long-term research to develop grains using perennials grown in mixtures mimicking native prairie; the Prairie Writers Circle disseminates op-ed articles to newspapers on sustainability topics. **Libraries: Type:** not open to the public. **Holdings:** articles, books, periodicals. **Subjects:** environment, sustainability, science, agriculture, community. **Awards:** Natural Systems Agriculture Graduate Research Fellowship. **Frequency:** annual. **Type:** grant. **Publications:** *The Land Report*, 3/year. Describes Land Institute activities, including Natural Systems Agriculture and subjects of ecological sustainability. **Price:** $25.00. ISSN: 1093-1171. **Circulation:** 3,500. **Conventions/Meetings:** annual Prairie Festival - festival and lecture, music, food - September.

4648 ■ National Association of Farmers' Market Nutrition Programs (NAFMNP)
PO Box 9080
Alexandria, VA 22304
Ph: (703)837-0451
Fax: (703)837-9304
E-mail: phil@triangleassociatesinc.com
URL: http://www.nafmnp.org
Contact: Phil Blalock, Exec. Dir.

Founded: 1992. **Membership Dues:** growing partner - supporting, $10 (annual) ● growing partner - sustaining, $20 (annual) ● growing partner - leadership, $30 (annual) ● growing partner - national, $50 (annual) ● sustaining - donor level, $500 (annual) ● sustaining - patron level, $1,000 (annual) ● sustaining - benefactor level, $3,000 (annual) ● sustaining - founder level, $5,000 (annual) ● sustaining - partnership level, $10,000 (annual). **Regional Groups:** 7. **Description:** Aims to cultivate opportunities for consumers to buy fresh produce from local growers. Provides networking and educational opportunities for its members as well as representation on key legislative and regulatory issues. **Telecommunication Services:** electronic mail, strattonka@michigan.gov. **Publications:** *Fresh from the Farmers' Market*, monthly. Newsletter. Features news and articles about the association and its activities. Alternate Formats: online ● *Program Impact Report for the WIC Farmers' Market Nutrition Program*, annual. Alternate Formats: online ● Annual Report. Alternate Formats: online.

4649 ■ National Farm-City Council (NFCC)
600 Maryland Ave. SW, Ste.1000W
Washington, DC 20024
Ph: (202)406-3706
Fax: (202)406-3756

E-mail: marshap@fb.org
URL: http://www.farmcity.org
Contact: Marsha Purcell, Sec.-Treas.
Founded: 1955. **Budget:** $35,000. **State Groups:** 48. **Local Groups:** 12,000. **Description:** Individual and corporate members, including businesses, industries, associations, publications, government agencies, and youth and service groups. Works to bring about better understanding between the rural and urban segments of American and Canadian society and thus strengthen the nations and their free economic society. Sponsors Farm-City Week in November. Distributes educational and consumer-oriented materials. Works through all communications media to "tell the agricultural story to city people and the city business story to farmers.". **Awards: Frequency:** annual. **Type:** recognition. **Recipient:** for outstanding events/activities in the state ● **Type:** recognition. **Recipient:** to organizations, businesses, groups or individuals for exemplary work on Farm City programs. **Committees:** Awards; Participation Development; Publicity and Public Relations; Special Events. **Formerly:** (1970) National Farm-City Committee. **Publications:** *Farm-City Connection*, 3/year. Newsletter. Alternate Formats: online ● Booklets ● Brochures ● Also publishes Farm-City Week kits and produces audio public service announcements. **Conventions/Meetings:** annual conference.

4650 ■ National Farmers Organization (NFO)
528 Billy Sunday Rd., Ste.100
Ames, IA 50010-2000
Free: (800)247-2110
E-mail: nfo@nfo.org
URL: http://www.nfo.org
Contact: Perry Garner, Communications Dir.
Founded: 1955. **Membership Dues:** individual, $75 (annual) ● life, $1,000. **State Groups:** 22. **Description:** Nonpartisan organization of farmers who bargain collectively to obtain contracts with buyers, processors, and exporters for the sale of farm commodities. Works to continuously improve such contracts. Conducts educational programs; maintains speakers' bureau. **Libraries: Type:** not open to the public. **Awards:** NFO Scholarship. **Frequency:** annual. **Type:** scholarship. **Divisions:** Cattle (Slaughter and Feeder); Dairy; Grain (Corn, Beans, Wheat); Hog; Organic Grains; Specialty Crop. **Publications:** *NFO Reporter*, quarterly. Newspaper. Alternate Formats: online. **Conventions/Meetings:** annual convention (exhibits).

4651 ■ National Farmers Union (NFU)
5619 DTC Pkwy., Ste.300
Greenwood Village, CO 80111-3136
Ph: (303)337-5500
Free: (800)347-1961
Fax: (303)771-1770
E-mail: tbuis@nfudc.org
URL: http://www.nfu.org
Contact: Tom Buis, Pres.
Founded: 1902. **Members:** 293,000. **Staff:** 20. **State Groups:** 20. **Local Groups:** 3,000. **Description:** Farm families interested in agricultural welfare. Carries on educational, cooperative and legislative activities. Represents members' interests especially in acquiring a more equitable share of the food dollar. Assists farm families in developing self-help institutions such as cooperatives. **Computer Services:** database, cooperatives. **Committees:** Political Action. **Formerly:** (1991) Farmers' Educational and Cooperative Union of America. **Publications:** *National Farmers Union News*, monthly. Newsletter. Reports on legislation and federal government activities and other issues concerning agriculture and rural America. **Price:** $10.00/year. ISSN: 0027-9226. **Circulation:** 30,000. **Conventions/Meetings:** annual convention (exhibits).

4652 ■ National Grange (NG)
1616 H St. NW
Washington, DC 20006
Ph: (202)628-3507
Free: (888)4GRANGE
Fax: (202)347-1091
E-mail: info@nationalgrange.org
URL: http://www.nationalgrange.org
Contact: William Steel, Pres.
Founded: 1867. **Members:** 300,000. **Membership Dues:** national associate, $25 (annual). **Staff:** 20. **Budget:** $1,200,000. **State Groups:** 37. **Local Groups:** 4,300. **Description:** Rural family service organization with a special interest in agriculture. Promotes mission and goals through legislative, social, educational, community service, youth and member services programs. Sponsors needlework and stuffed toy contests. **Awards: Type:** recognition. **Recipient:** for community service. **Telecommunication Services:** electronic mail, bsteel@nationalgrange.org. **Committees:** Membership Development; Membership Services. **Divisions:** Junior Granges; Legislative Activities; Women's Activities; Youth. **Programs:** Community Service; Grange Action. **Publications:** *Grange Today*, bimonthly. Newsletter. **Price:** available to members only ● *National Grange-Journal of Proceedings*, annual. Covers annual convention proceedings. ● *National Grange-Official Roster*, annual. Membership Directory ● *View from the Hill*, monthly. Newsletter. **Conventions/Meetings:** annual convention - always November. 2008 Nov. 11-15, Cromwell, CT; 2009 Nov. 17-21, Grand Rapids, MI.

4653 ■ National Young Farmer Educational Association (NYFEA)
PO Box 20326
Montgomery, AL 36120
Ph: (334)213-3276
Fax: (334)213-3276
E-mail: natloffice@nyfea.org
URL: http://www.nyfea.org
Contact: Gordon Stone, Exec. VP
Founded: 1982. **Members:** 14,000. **Membership Dues:** regular, $15 (annual) ● plus, $35 (annual) ● leader for agriculture, $100 (annual) ● life, $300. **Staff:** 3. **Budget:** $185,000. **State Groups:** 25. **Local Groups:** 1,000. **Description:** Farmers and ranchers involved in agricultural production. Seeks to encourage young farmers and to educate members on the latest production, management, and marketing techniques in farming. Promotes good urban-rural relations and provides information on agricultural issues affecting urban consumers. Assists young farmers in developing leadership skills and works with similar organizations to help improve the economic, educational, and social conditions of rural life. Conducts educational programs. Operates speakers' bureau and charitable program. **Awards: Type:** recognition. **Computer Services:** Online services, membership list. **Telecommunication Services:** electronic mail, gstone@nyfea.org. **Programs:** National Agricultural Advisor Subscription. **Publications:** *Agricultural Leaders Update*, 3/year. Newsletter. Covers NYFEA activities; serves to educate young farmers in the latest production and marketing management techniques. **Price:** included in membership dues. Also Cited As: *NYFEA Update* ● *The Leader for Agriculture*, semiannual. Magazine. **Price:** included in membership dues ● *National Young Farmer*, 3/year. Newsletter. **Price:** included in membership dues. **Circulation:** 26,000 ● *National Young Farmer Directory*, semiannual. Contains listing of officers and state associations. **Price:** free. **Conventions/Meetings:** annual National Agricultural Leadership Conference - convention ● annual National Young Farmer Educational Institute - competition and convention (exhibits).

4654 ■ North American Deer Farmers Association (NADeFA)
1215 N 7th St., Ste.104
Lake City, MN 55041
Ph: (651)345-5600
Fax: (651)345-5603
E-mail: info@nadefa.org
URL: http://www.nadefa.org
Contact: Phyllis Menden, Exec. Dir.
Founded: 1983. **Members:** 2,500. **Membership Dues:** active, associate, $100 (annual) ● patron, $500 (annual) ● practitioner/student, $35 (annual) ● additional active, $50 (annual). **Staff:** 3. **Budget:** $257,000. **State Groups:** 6. **Description:** Small farmers, farming suppliers, and individuals interested in environmentally-friendly farming alternatives. Promotes the production of venison and other agricultural products. Offers educational programs and research through its Cervid Livestock foundation. **Libraries: Type:** reference; not open to the public. **Holdings:** articles, books, clippings. **Subjects:** deer farming and ranching. **Awards:** Distinguished Service. **Frequency:** periodic. **Type:** recognition. **Councils:** Fallow Deer; Red Deer; Whitetail Deer. **Publications:** *Conference Proceedings*, annual. **Price:** $25.00. **Circulation:** 400. **Advertising:** accepted ● *News RoundUp*, quarterly. Newsletter. **Price:** included in membership dues. **Circulation:** 800 ● *North American Deer Farmer*, quarterly. Journal. **Price:** included in membership dues. ISSN: 1084-0583. **Circulation:** 1,200. **Conventions/Meetings:** annual conference (exhibits) - always end of February or early March ● periodic workshop.

4655 ■ Organic Crop Improvement Association (OCIA)
1340 N Cotner
Lincoln, NE 68505
Ph: (402)477-2323
Fax: (402)477-4325
E-mail: info@ocia.org
URL: http://www.ocia.org
Contact: Jeff Dewald, Pres.
Founded: 1985. **Members:** 30,000. **Membership Dues:** regular, $100 (annual) ● chapter, $150 (annual) ● corporation, $250 (annual) ● supporting, $50 (annual) ● general, $95 (annual). **Description:** Certification organization representing growers, processors, and manufacturers worldwide. Seeks to improve credibility of certified products through audit trail and crop improvement. **Publications:** *Communicator*, bimonthly. Newsletter. Alternate Formats: online. **Conventions/Meetings:** annual meeting.

4656 ■ People Food and Land Foundation (PFLF)
35751 Oak Springs Dr.
Tollhouse, CA 93667-9611
Ph: (559)855-3710
Free: (888)303-0103
E-mail: sunmt@sunmt.org
URL: http://www.sunmt.org
Contact: George Elfie Ballis, Coor.
Founded: 1974. **Members:** 500. **Staff:** 4. **Budget:** $40,000. **Description:** Small farmers, consumers, and individuals concerned with low-water use, arid land crops, organic methods for small farmers and gardeners, and low-tech passive solar models for farm, food processing, and home use. Sponsors Sun Mountain Research Center. Activities include: a "Seminar in Reality"; herbal food preparation; floral; medicinal, and culinary uses of native plants; shamanism; self-healing. Operates speakers' bureau. Sponsors intern program. **Libraries: Type:** reference. **Holdings:** 2,500. **Subjects:** agriculture, gardening, land, irrigation control. **Telecommunication Services:** electronic mail, mail@sunmt.org. **Formerly:** (1983) National Land for People. **Publications:** Bulletin, monthly.

4657 ■ Professional Farmers of America (PFA)
PO Box 36
Cedar Falls, IA 50613
Ph: (319)277-1278
Free: (800)772-0023
E-mail: editors@profarmer.com
URL: http://www.agweb.com/profarmer.asp
Contact: Chip Flory, Ed.
Founded: 1973. **Members:** 20,000. **For-Profit. Description:** Provides farmers with marketing strategies, data on market trends, and analyses of market-impacting developments worldwide. Offers seminars and home study courses. Sponsors commercial exhibits. **Publications:** *LandOwner*, semimonthly. Newsletter. **Price:** $99.00 /year for individuals ● *Pro Farmer*, weekly. Newsletter. **Price:** $149.00 /year for individuals.

4658 ■ Rural Restoration Adopt
PO Box B
Sikeston, MO 63801
Ph: (573)471-7966 (573)472-9673
Free: (800)472-4674
Fax: (573)471-3700
E-mail: webmaster@farmersruralrestoration.com
URL: http://www.farmersruralrestoration.com
Contact: Mary W. Myers, Pres.
Founded: 1988. **Members:** 1,000. **Membership Dues:** donor, $10 (monthly). **Staff:** 3. **Budget:** $65,000. **Regional Groups:** 10. **Description:** Seeks to restore and revitalize rural America to ensure the food supply for future generations. Works to raise public awareness as to the value and dignity of farm and ranch families. Offers personal assistance to farm families. Fosters communication and exchange between members of rural and urban communities. Organizes prayer groups and promotes Christian values. **Computer Services:** Mailing lists, of members. **Formerly:** (1998) Adopt-A-Farm-Family of America. **Publications:** *The Sower*, bimonthly. Magazine. **Price:** free to contributors of ministry. **Circulation:** 12,000. **Advertising:** accepted. Alternate Formats: online. **Conventions/Meetings:** annual Rural Restoration Conference - conference and lecture, with speakers from across the nation (exhibits).

4659 ■ Universal Proutist Farmers Federation (UPFF)
6810 Tilden Ln.
Rockville, MD 20852
Ph: (301)231-0110
E-mail: nysector@prout.org
URL: http://www.prout.org
Contact: Dada Shubhacetanananda, Contact
Founded: 1982. **Members:** 1,000. **Staff:** 4. **Regional Groups:** 1. **State Groups:** 1. **Local Groups:** 1. **Description:** Farmers involved with small scale organic farming. Advocates the Prout philosophy that resources should be shared in order to guarantee basic human needs, such as food, water, shelter, and education. (Prout is an acronym for Progressive Utilization Theory, a social, economic, and political theory based on the writings of the philosopher P.R. Sarkar.) Seeks government recognition of small farmers' needs, which include proper financing and management training. Provides information on large scale organic farming. Sponsors food distribution slide shows. Offers children's services. Compiles statistics. Plans to form producer cooperatives, seed distribution centers, farmworkers' and credit unions, information resource center on organic and traditional farming, legal information center, and "future farmers" cooperatives made up of urban dwellers. **Telecommunication Services:** electronic mail, csny@prout.org. **Publications:** *Farming the Future*, monthly. Newsletter ● *Prout Farming Information*, semiannual. **Conventions/Meetings:** semiannual meeting and seminar (exhibits) - always January and August.

4660 ■ U.S.A. Plowing Organization (USAPO)
c/o Roger Neate, Sec.-Treas.
14837 Greenville Rd.
Van Wert, OH 45891
Ph: (419)965-2284
Fax: (419)965-2281
E-mail: maestrolaw@msn.com
URL: http://usapo.org
Contact: Roger Neate, Sec.-Treas.
Founded: 1963. **Members:** 225. **Membership Dues:** regular, $20 (annual). **State Groups:** 9. **Description:** Current and former plowing competitors; individuals interested in plowing contests. Aims to promote interest in and understanding of land tillage. Sponsors annual national contest wherein winners may qualify to compete in annual World Ploughing Contest. Conducts seminars and training meetings. **Affiliated With:** World Ploughing Organisation. **Publications:** Newsletter, quarterly. Alternate Formats: online ● Also publishes rule book. **Conventions/Meetings:** annual National Contest and Farm Progress Show - competition, farm machinery and national plowing contests (exhibits).

4661 ■ Wild Farm Alliance (WFA)
PO Box 2570
Watsonville, CA 95077
Ph: (831)761-8408
Fax: (831)761-8103
E-mail: info@wildfarmalliance.org
URL: http://wildfarmalliance.org
Contact: Jo Ann Baumgartner, Dir.
Description: Represents group of wildlands proponents and ecological farming advocates who share a concern for the land and its wild and human inhabitants. Promotes a healthy, viable agriculture that helps protect and restore wild nature. Supports farming practices that accommodate wild habitat and native species. Fosters agricultural practices that strive to eliminate the use of environmentally toxic chemicals and contamination of soil and water resources. **Publications:** *Biodiversity: What it is and how to increase it on your farm.* Brochure. Alternate Formats: online.

Feed

4662 ■ Feed Microscopy Division
c/o American Oil Chemists' Society
2710 S Boulder
Urbana, IL 61802-6996
Ph: (217)359-2344
Fax: (217)351-8091
E-mail: general@aocs.org
URL: http://www.aocs.org/member/division/feed
Contact: Marj McCutcheon, Chair
Founded: 1953. **Members:** 210. **Membership Dues:** full, $12 (annual). **Description:** Professional society of microscopic analysts for state feed control departments, feed manufacturing companies, and universities. **Awards:** Fellow Award. **Frequency:** annual. **Type:** recognition. **Recipient:** for outstanding contribution to the field of microscopy. **Telecommunication Services:** electronic mail, mmccutcheon@ag.state.wv.us. **Committees:** Collaborative Check Sample; Methods; Problem Sample; Training. **Formerly:** (2005) American Association of Feed Microscopists Division. **Publications:** *Manual of Microscopic Analysis of Feedstuff*. **Price:** $65.00 for members; $75.00 for nonmembers, plus $15 shipping outside North America ● *Proceedings of Annual Meeting*, annual ● Newsletter, 3/year. Contains information relevant to the Feed Microscopy audience. Alternate Formats: online ● Also offers slide collection of feed ingredients and weed seeds. **Conventions/Meetings:** annual meeting, with course in feed microscopy (exhibits).

4663 ■ National Barley Growers Association (NBGA)
c/o Dale Thorenson
600 Pennsylvania Ave.
Washington, DC 20003
Ph: (202)969-8900
E-mail: dthorenson@gordley.com
URL: http://www.nationalbarley.org
Contact: Dale Thorenson, Contact
Founded: 1987. **State Groups:** 7. **Local Groups:** 3. **Description:** Seeks to enhance and maintain the profitability of the US barley industry through reduced costs, effective risk management tools, competitive market prices and an adequate federal safety net. **Computer Services:** Information services, industry links and resources. **Affiliated With:** American Malting Barley Association; U.S. Grains Council. **Publications:** *June 2004 NBGA Policy Paper*. Alternate Formats: online.

4664 ■ U.S. Grains Council (USGC)
1400 K St. NW, Ste.1200
Washington, DC 20005
Ph: (202)789-0789
Fax: (202)898-0522
E-mail: grains@grains.org
URL: http://www.grains.org
Contact: Kenneth Hobbie, Pres./CEO
Founded: 1960. **Members:** 94. **Staff:** 50. **Budget:** $4,000,000. **Multinational**. **Description:** Federation of feed grain producer organizations, seed trade associations, and organizations of grain processors, exporters, dealers and related agribusiness manufacturers. Maintains 10 international offices for development of foreign markets in over 80 countries for barley, corn, grain sorghum and related products. **Computer Services:** database, iMIS - maintains membership records, generates reports and events ● information services, barley, corn and sorghum resources ● information services, buying US grains. **Telecommunication Services:** electronic mail, khobbie@grains.org. **Committees:** Asia; Biotechnology Education; Membership and Communications; Rest of the World. **Departments:** Trade Policy; Value-Added. **Formerly:** (1998) U.S. Feed Grains Council. **Publications:** *Global Update*, biweekly. Newsletter ● *World Feed Grains Demand Forecast*, semiannual. Report ● Annual Report, annual. Alternate Formats: online. **Conventions/Meetings:** annual board meeting - always July. 2008 July 19-23, Anchorage, AK ● annual meeting - always February.

Fertilizer

4665 ■ IFDC - An International Center for Soil Fertility and Agricultural Development (IFDC)
PO Box 2040
Muscle Shoals, AL 35662
Ph: (256)381-6600
Fax: (256)381-7408
E-mail: general@ifdc.org
URL: http://www.ifdc.org
Contact: Dr. Amit H. Roy, Pres./CEO
Founded: 1974. **Staff:** 180. **Budget:** $20,000,000. **Languages:** English, French, Spanish. **Multinational**. **Description:** Participants include scientists, engineers, economists and specialists in market research and development, communications and personnel development. Seeks to alleviate world hunger by increasing agricultural production in the tropics and subtropics through development of improved fertilizer and fertilizer use. Studies ways of processing indigenous resources of phosphate rock into efficient fertilizers; conducts nitrogen efficiency research; examines the agronomic efficiency of sulfur sources such as gypsum, anhydrite and pyrites; sponsors studies of potassium, magnesium and calcium use. Conducts in-depth studies of fertilizer markets in order to design plans for the implementation of appropriate working systems. Sponsors human resource development programs in the areas of fertilizer marketing, evaluation and use and production. Offers production courses on fluid fertilizers, granulation, ammonia/urea plant operations, sustainable crop production, environmental issues and manufacturing process economics. Compiles and analyzes data in areas including plant investment, worldwide production capacity, price trends, raw materials deposits and distribution costs. Advises countries on agribusiness policies and technologies with the goal of economic development and increased production. Maintains laboratories and greenhouses, pilot-scale fertilizer manufacturing plants and training centers. **Libraries:** **Type:** reference. **Holdings:** 20,000; audiovisuals, books, periodicals. **Subjects:** fertilizer, agribusiness, marketing, chemistry, developing countries. **Computer Services:** database, fertilizer topics, agriculture, agribusiness. **Divisions:** Africa in Lome Togo; Asia-Dhaka Bangladesh; Market Development-Alabama, US; Resource Development-Alabama, US. **Programs:** Agribusiness; Market and Trade Policy; Natural Resource Management; Soil Fertility and Nutrient Dynamics. **Formerly:** (2003) International Fertilizer Development Center - USA. **Publications:** *IFDC Corporate Report*, annual. Annual Report. ISSN: 1536-0660. **Circulation:** 3,000 ● *IFDC Report*, semiannual. Bulletin ● Brochures ● Manuals ● Report, quarterly. **Conventions/Meetings:** annual board meeting.

Fishing Industries

4666 ■ American Tilapia Association (ATA)
111 W Washington St., Ste.1
Charles Town, WV 25414-1529

Ph: (304)728-2167
Fax: (304)728-2196
E-mail: ata1@frontiernet.net
URL: http://ag.arizona.edu/azaqua/ata.html
Contact: Mark Willows, Pres.

Membership Dues: supporter, $100 (annual) ● active, $50 (annual) ● sustaining, $25 (annual). **Description:** Supports and facilitates the growth of Tilapia production and consumption within the United States. Provides education, member information and networking, government interactions and support for research and promotion of the Tilapia industry. **Computer Services:** Information services, tilapia production and industry related resources ● online services, tilapia farming software. **Telecommunication Services:** electronic mail, naffc@mlgc.com. **Publications:** *Introduction to Tilapia Reproduction.* Paper. Alternate Formats: online ● Proceedings. Includes 72 papers regarding topics relevant to tilapia raising. **Price:** $48.00.

4667 ■ Association for Professional Observers (APO)
PO Box 30167
Seattle, WA 98103
E-mail: apo@apo-observers.org
URL: http://www.apo-observers.org
Contact: Dave Wagenheim, Contact

Membership Dues: observer, $15 (annual) ● supporting, $10 (annual). **Description:** Aims to strengthen fisheries observer programs through advocacy and education. Provides information for observers on issues related to their career and work environment. Facilitates the exchange of information for observers regarding fisheries in the United States territorial waters. Encourages the conservation and sustainability of marine and other aquatic resources. **Publications:** *Mail Buoy.* Newsletter. **Price:** included in membership dues. Alternate Formats: online.

4668 ■ Gulf and Caribbean Fisheries Institute (GCFI)
c/o Florida Fish and Wildlife Conservation Commission
Marine Res. Inst.
2796 Overseas Hwy., Ste.119
Marathon, FL 33050
Ph: (305)289-2330 (561)462-1660
Fax: (305)289-2334
E-mail: creswell@gcfi.org
URL: http://www.gcfi.org
Contact: LeRoy Creswell, Exec. Sec.

Founded: 1947. **Members:** 950. **Membership Dues:** regular, $50 (annual). **Staff:** 1. **Description:** Fishermen, fishery scientists, and administrators. Provides a forum for the exchange of ideas and information on fishery research, management, policy issues, conservation, aquaculture, and waste treatment. Suggests future business strategies and economic development. Provides technical training for fishermen and technicians. Selects papers for presentation at meetings and for publication. Furnishes advisory services (including library research, consultation, and referral) on fisheries and coastal zone problems. **Awards:** GCFI Travel Awards. **Frequency:** annual. **Type:** recognition. **Recipient:** for students in the U.S. and Caribbean Region ● Outstanding Student Awards for Academic Achievement. **Frequency:** annual. **Type:** recognition. **Recipient:** for the best student's oral or poster presentation ● Ron Schmied Scholarship. **Frequency:** annual. **Type:** scholarship. **Recipient:** for students with management perspective on recreational fisheries. **Publications:** *MPA Reports.* Alternate Formats: online ● *SPAG Reports.* Alternate Formats: online ● *Strombus gigas.* Book ● Proceedings (in English, French, and Spanish), annual. Includes English abstracts that have Spanish translation; Spanish and French are also translated into English. **Price:** included in membership dues; $30.00 /year for libraries in U.S.; $35.00 /year for libraries outside U.S., includes postage. **Circulation:** 300. **Conventions/Meetings:** annual conference (exhibits) - always November.

4669 ■ Pacific Coast Federation of Fishermen's Associations (PCFFA)
PO Box 29370
San Francisco, CA 94129-0370
Ph: (415)561-5080
Fax: (415)561-5464
E-mail: fish1ifr@aol.com
URL: http://www.pcffa.org
Contact: Zeke Grader, Exec. Dir.

Founded: 1976. **Members:** 22. **Membership Dues:** patron, highliner fishery steward, $1,000 (annual) ● benefactor, $500 (annual) ● sponsor, $250 (annual) ● supporter, $50 (annual) ● fishery steward, $350 (annual) ● fishery steward emeritus, $100 (annual) ● associate fishery steward, $35 (annual). **Staff:** 4. **Description:** Commercial fishermen's organizations in California and Alaska. Works to: preserve and improve the resources of the commercial fishing industry; protect rivers from herbicide and pesticide applications that may threaten salmon populations; maintain activity within the industry; regain local control over fisheries management. Assisted the California Coastal Commission in establishing new port facilities. Strongly opposes oil drilling in fishing grounds. Has worked to reduce high insurance rates of fish processors and boatyards, as well as to improve shoreside processing facilities; has initiated work in the development of new types of fisheries. Represents members' interests in legislative activities. **Projects:** California Hydropower Dam Environmental Review. **Publications:** *PCFFA FRIDAY*, biweekly. Newsletter. Covers developments in offshore oil drilling, logging, water quality, and other matters impacting on fisheries. **Price:** $30.00/year. **Circulation:** 1,300.

4670 ■ Striped Bass Growers Association (SBGA)
111 W Washington St., Ste.1
Charles Town, WV 25414
Ph: (304)728-2167
Fax: (304)728-2196
E-mail: sbga@frontiernet.net
URL: http://www.aquanic.org/sbga
Contact: Dr. Ron Hodson, Pres.

Membership Dues: active, $75 (annual) ● associate, $20 (annual) ● student, $10 (annual) ● sustaining, $300 (annual). **Description:** Promotes the advancement of the commercial cultivation of striped bass and its hybrids. Aims to enhance profitability in production and marketing of striped bass and hybrid bass culture. Provides opportunities for a collective representation of the striped bass industry. **Awards:** Walter Landry Memorial Award. **Frequency:** annual. **Type:** recognition. **Recipient:** for a student's outstanding achievements in research on any of the species in the Morone genus and/or hybrids. **Telecommunication Services:** electronic mail, ronald_hodson@ncsu.edu. **Publications:** *The Striper.* Newsletter. Alternate Formats: online.

4671 ■ Women's Fisheries Network (WFN)
2442 NW Market St., No. 199
Seattle, WA 98107
Ph: (206)789-1987
Fax: (206)789-1987
E-mail: wfn-nw@home.com
URL: http://www.fis.com/wfn
Contact: Karen A. Hauger, Admin.

Founded: 1993. **Members:** 250. **Membership Dues:** associate, $100 (annual) ● individual, $40 (annual) ● student, $25 (annual). **Staff:** 1. **Budget:** $5,000. **Regional Groups:** 3. **Description:** Men and women dedicated to education of issues confronting the fishing and seafood industry. Conducts educational programs. **Publications:** *WFN Roster*, annual. Directory. Contains membership directory, categorized by business type and areas of expertise. **Conventions/Meetings:** annual meeting, with annual report.

Flowers

4672 ■ American Clematis Society (ACS)
c/o Edith Malek, Pres.
PO Box 17085
Irvine, CA 92623-7085
E-mail: info@clematis.org
URL: http://clematis.org
Contact: Edith Malek, Pres.

Founded: 1996. **Members:** 301. **Membership Dues:** individual, $20 (annual) ● international, $22 (annual) ● household/family (two persons), $22 (annual) ● corporate, $100 (annual) ● friend, $50 (annual) ● life, $250. **Description:** Seeks to improve and promote the understanding and the knowledge of Clematis. Offers educational programs. **Libraries: Type:** not open to the public. **Holdings:** archival material, books, clippings, periodicals. **Subjects:** clematis. **Publications:** *The Clematis Chronicle*, quarterly. Journal. Features American Clematis Society's Guide to Growing Clematis in the United States. **Price:** $19.99. **Circulation:** 270. **Advertising:** accepted. **Conventions/Meetings:** bimonthly board meeting.

4673 ■ Passiflora Society International (PSI)
c/o Butterfly World
3600 W Sample Rd.
Coconut Creek, FL 33073
E-mail: info@passiflora.org
URL: http://www.passiflora.org
Contact: Ron Boender, Founder

Founded: 1990. **Members:** 300. **Membership Dues:** regular, $30 (annual). **Multinational. Description:** Represents the interests of hobbyists, commercial growers, leading experts and other Passiflora enthusiasts. Promotes the cultivation of various Passiflora species and hybrids. Maintains a plant collection database, and local and international seed banks. **Publications:** Newsletter, quarterly. **Price:** included in membership dues.

Food

4674 ■ Alliance for Better Foods
Address Unknown since 2007

Description: Supports biotechnology as a safe way to provide for an abundant, nutritious and high quality food supply.

4675 ■ Center for Food Safety (CFS)
Natl. HQ
660 Pennsylvania Ave. SE, Ste.302
Washington, DC 20003
Ph: (202)547-9359
Free: (800)600-6664
Fax: (202)547-9429
E-mail: office@centerforfoodsafety.org
URL: http://www.centerforfoodsafety.org
Contact: Andrew Kimbrell, Exec. Dir.

Founded: 1997. **Membership Dues:** student, low income, $15 ● regular, $35 (annual) ● business, $100. **Description:** Promotes sustainable agriculture and food safety. **Publications:** *Corporate Lies: Busting the Myths of Industrial Agriculture* ● *Fatal Harvest: The Tragedy of Industrial Agriculture.* Book. Contains over 30 essays on sustainable agriculture. **Price:** $75.00 hardcover; $45.00 paperback ● *Food Safety Now!*, quarterly. Newsletter ● *Food Safety Review* (in English and Spanish) ● *Genetically Modified (GM) Crops and Foods: Worldwide Regulation, Prohibition and Production.*

4676 ■ Food Alliance (FA)
1829 NE Alberta, Ste.5
Portland, OR 97211
Ph: (503)493-1066
Fax: (503)493-1069
E-mail: info@foodalliance.org
URL: http://www.foodalliance.org
Contact: Scott Exo, Exec. Dir.

Founded: 1997. **Membership Dues:** basic, $25 (annual) ● supporter, $50 (annual) ● associate, $100 (annual) ● advocate, $250 (annual) ● sustainer, $500 (annual) ● benefactor, $1,000 (annual). **Description:** Promotes sustainable agriculture by recognizing and rewarding farmers who produces food in environmentally and socially responsible ways. Creates market incentives for adoption of sustainable agricultural practices. Educates business leaders and other food system stakeholders on the benefits of sustainable agriculture. Develops formal "market partnerships" to increase demand for and facilitate sales of certified products. **Telecommunication Services:** electronic mail, scott@foodalliance.org. **Councils:** Stewardship. **Programs:** Certification; Eco-labeling.

4677 ■ True Food Network
2601 Mission St., Ste.803
San Francisco, CA 94110
Ph: (415)826-2770
E-mail: office@centerforfoodsafety.org
URL: http://www.truefoodnow.org
Contact: Andrew Kimbrell, Exec. Dir.
Founded: 2000. **Members:** 40,000. **Description:** Aims to stop genetic engineering of food and farms. Engages farmers in the struggle against genetically engineered crops. Creates a socially just, democratic and sustainable food system.

Forestry

4678 ■ Alliance for Community Trees (ACT)
4603 Calvert Rd.
College Park, MD 20740-3421
Ph: (301)277-0040 (301)220-2251
Fax: (301)277-0042
E-mail: info@actrees.org
URL: http://www.actrees.org
Contact: Alice Ewen Walker, Exec. Dir.
Founded: 1993. **Membership Dues:** non-profit (based on annual budget), $100-$500 (annual) ● friend (maximum), $50 (annual) ● associate, $50-$99 (annual) ● forestry leader, $100-$499 (annual) ● Caliper Circle, $500-$4,999 (annual) ● government agency (minimum; based on annual budget), $500 (annual). **Description:** Supports grassroots, citizen-based nonprofit organizations dedicated to urban and community tree planting, care, conservation and education. Pulls together the pioneering work of citizen foresters across the country through information sharing, training, technical assistance, policy and program development and advocacy.

4679 ■ American Forest and Paper Association (AF&PA)
1111 19th St. NW, Ste.800
Washington, DC 20036
Ph: (202)463-2700
Free: (800)878-8878
E-mail: info@afandpa.org
URL: http://www.afandpa.org
Contact: Celena NuQuay, Dir.
Founded: 1932. **Members:** 250. **Membership Dues:** association, $2,000-$4,000 (annual) ● associate (maximum; forestry and/or wood products group), $25,000 (annual) ● converter associate, $2,500 (annual) ● student, $50 (annual) ● design professional in U.S. and Canada, $100 (annual) ● design professional outside U.S. and Canada, $150 (annual). **Staff:** 154. **Budget:** $38,000,000. **Regional Groups:** 3. **Description:** National trade association of the forest, pulp, paper, paperboard and wood products industry. Represents approximately 400 member companies and related trade associations that grow, harvest, and process wood and wood fiber, manufacture pulp, paper and paperboard from both virgin and recycled fiber, and produce solid wood products. **Libraries: Type:** not open to the public. **Subjects:** forest, paper pulp, paperboard, wood products. **Awards:** American Wood Council Wood Design Award. **Frequency:** annual. **Type:** recognition. **Recipient:** for outstanding examples of wood construction exemplifying the practical environmental benefits of wood as well as wood's versatility ● Environmental and Energy Achievement Award. **Frequency:** annual. **Type:** recognition. **Recipient:** for companies displaying significant innovations and accomplishments in five major environmental and energy areas: air pollution control, water pollution control, solid waste management, energy management and innovation, and forest management ● Forest Management Award. **Frequency:** annual. **Type:** recognition. **Recipient:** for advancement in forest management and land use ● George Olmsted Award. **Frequency:** annual. **Type:** monetary. **Recipient:** for original and outstanding paper industry-related research by young scientists and engineers ● Safety Excellence Awards. **Frequency:** annual. **Type:** recognition. **Recipient:** to member companies with an exemplary record in the health and safety area ● Wildlife Stewardship Awards. **Frequency:** annual. **Type:** recognition. **Recipient:** for significant achievements by wildlife and fisheries biologists and managers. **Formed by Merger of:** (1992) American Paper Institute; National Forest Products Association; American Forest Council. **Publications:** *American Tree Farmer: The Official Magazine of the American Tree Farm System*, bimonthly. Provides information for and about forest landowners. Includes book reviews, product reviews, tax column, and annual equipment issue. **Price:** free to certified tree farmers; $15.00/year for others. **Circulation:** 85,000. **Advertising:** accepted ● *The Branch: The Official Magazine of Project Learning Tree*. **Price:** free. **Circulation:** 80,000 ● *Paper, Paperboard and Wood Pulp Capacity and Fiber Consumption*, annual. Contains capacity estimates for major grades of paper, paperboard and wood pulp from a comprehensive annual survey of each mill in the U.S. **Price:** $375.00 in U.S.; $395.00 outside U.S. ● *Statistical Summary of Recovered Paper Utilization*, annual. Provides historical consumption of recovered paper by major grade, by U.S. region, state and end use. **Price:** $60.00 ● *Statistics of Paper, Paperboard and Wood Pulp*, annual. Provides an overall, long-run view of the paper industry. **Price:** $365.00 ● Booklets. Contains technical data on uses of wood for architects, builders, and homeowners. ● Brochures. Alternate Formats: online ● Catalogs ● Annual Report, annual. Alternate Formats: online ● Papers. Alternate Formats: online ● Also publishes design specifications for wood construction, wood structural design data, and materials on timber supply and forest management issues. **Conventions/Meetings:** Forest Resources Legislative Conference - meeting ● annual Paper Week - conference.

4680 ■ Association of Consulting Foresters of America (ACF)
312 Montgomery St., Ste.208
Alexandria, VA 22314
Ph: (703)548-0990
Fax: (703)548-6395
E-mail: director@acf-foresters.org
URL: http://www.acf-foresters.org
Contact: Lynn C. Wilson, Exec. Dir.
Founded: 1948. **Members:** 650. **Membership Dues:** individual, $50. **Staff:** 2. **Budget:** $200,000. **Regional Groups:** 4. **State Groups:** 26. **Description:** Professional foresters in the field of applied forestry and forest utilization who work for private landowners or industry on a contract or contingency basis. Members must be graduates of an association-approved forestry school and have five years experience in forest administration and management. Provides client referral service. Compiles statistics. **Libraries: Type:** reference. **Awards:** Distinguished Forester. **Frequency:** annual. **Type:** recognition ● Public Service Award. **Frequency:** annual. **Type:** recognition. **Committees:** Continuing Education; Ethics; Industry Relations; Legislative; Publicity. **Formerly:** (1990) Association of Consulting Foresters. **Publications:** *The Consultant*, quarterly. Journal. **Price:** included in membership dues; $25.00 /year for nonmembers. **Circulation:** 1,000. **Advertising:** accepted ● *Membership Specialization Directory*, biennial. **Price:** included in membership dues; $9.95 for nonmembers ● Newsletter, bimonthly. **Price:** included in membership dues. Alternate Formats: online. **Conventions/Meetings:** annual meeting (exhibits) - always last week of June or first week of July.

4681 ■ Council on Forest Engineering (COFE)
620 SW 4th St.
Corvallis, OR 97333
Ph: (541)754-7558
Fax: (541)754-7559
E-mail: office@cofe.org
URL: http://cofe.org
Contact: Daniel Guimier, Chm.
Founded: 1978. **Members:** 400. **Membership Dues:** individual, $15 (annual) ● student, $5 (annual). **Regional Groups:** 3. **Description:** Individuals actively engaged in forest engineering or forest-based industry; retired forest engineers and students. Works to promote the most effective methods of managing and operating public and private forests through the development of forest engineering in industry, government, and the private sector. Formulates policies and industry standards. Sponsors research and educational programs; compiles statistics. **Libraries: Type:** reference. **Publications:** *Annual Meeting Proceedings* ● Newsletter, semiannual. **Conventions/Meetings:** annual meeting.

4682 ■ Elm Research Institute (ERI)
11 Kit St.
Keene, NH 03431
Ph: (603)358-6198
Free: (800)FOR-ELMS
Fax: (603)358-6305
E-mail: info@elmresearch.org
URL: http://www.libertyelm.com
Contact: John P. Hansel, Founder
Founded: 1967. **Members:** 2,000. **Membership Dues:** single, $25 (annual) ● family, $35 (annual) ● organization, $100 (annual). **Staff:** 5. **Budget:** $450,000. **National Groups:** 750. **Description:** Individuals; landscape architects; municipalities; local, state, and national organizations (including corporations, garden clubs, conservation groups, golf courses, cemeteries, and universities) interested in restoration and preservation of the American elm. Develops support from the private sector for independent research on Dutch elm disease; funds university research on Dutch elm disease controls and the development of disease-resistant varieties of American elms. Distributes the only disease-resistant, street-proven American elm, with a lifetime warranty against Dutch elm disease, called the American Liberty Elm. **Libraries: Type:** reference. **Holdings:** papers. **Subjects:** Dutch elm disease. **Computer Services:** database, elms in the national test pilot and on historic elms. **Programs:** Johnny Elmseed; Matching Tree Grant. **Supersedes:** Elms Unlimited. **Publications:** *Conscientious Injectors Handbook*. Features a guide for organizing a volunteer corps for preventive treatment of American Elms in control of Dutch Elm Disease. ● *Elm Leaves*, semiannual. Newsletter. Includes information on treatment of DED and on distribution of disease resistant American Liberty Elms. ● *Press Release*, quarterly ● *Progress Report*, annual ● *Re-Elming America*. Video. Features a twelve-minute video. **Conventions/Meetings:** annual meeting.

4683 ■ Forest Landowners Association (FLA)
900 Circle Pkwy., Ste.205
Atlanta, GA 30339
Ph: (404)325-2954
Free: (800)325-2954
Fax: (404)325-2955
E-mail: info@forestlandowners.com
Contact: Mr. Otis Ingram, Pres.
Founded: 1941. **Members:** 10,000. **Membership Dues:** individual, $55 (annual) ● consulting forester, $100 (annual) ● student, sponsor, $25 (annual). **Staff:** 7. **Budget:** $500,000. **Description:** Private owners and managers of 47,200,000 acres of timberland who grow and process timber in 17 southern states. Works to: expand the timber industry and bring commercial forest areas of the South to maximum production; reduce waste caused by fire, insects, disease, and inefficient harvesting and processing; ensure a favorable tax base and encourage government and private forest and forest products research. **Libraries: Type:** not open to the public. **Holdings:** periodicals. **Subjects:** forestry. **Awards:** Extension Forester of the Year. **Frequency:** annual. **Type:** recognition. **Recipient:** for exceptional contributions to forest landowner education, issues, and services ● Forest Landowner of the Year Award. **Frequency:** annual. **Type:** recognition. **Recipient:**

for outstanding service to southern forestry. **Computer Services:** Mailing lists. **Committees:** Forest Landowners Foundation; Forest Landowners Government Affairs; Forest Landowners Political Action. **Formerly:** (1996) Forest Farmers Association. **Publications:** *FLA Fast Facts*, weekly. Newsletter. Contains up-to-date forest industry and association information. Alternate Formats: online ● *Forest Landowner Magazine*, bimonthly. Contains articles on growing trees and managing tree farms. **Price:** $50.00. ISSN: 0015-7406. **Circulation:** 10,000. **Advertising:** accepted ● *Forest Landowner Manual*, biennial. **Price:** $35.00 ● *Hunt Club Digest*, 3/year. Magazine. Contains information on hunt club management, habitat management, and hunting gear. ● *Washington Update Newsletter*, quarterly. Contains information on federal legislation. Alternate Formats: online ● Annual Report, annual. Alternate Formats: online. **Conventions/Meetings:** annual National Forestry Conference (exhibits).

4684 ■ Forest Stewardship Council - United States (FSC-US)
1155 30th St. NW, Ste.300
Washington, DC 20007
Ph: (202)342-0413
Fax: (202)342-6589
E-mail: info@fscus.org
URL: http://www.fscus.org
Contact: Ned Daly, VP of Operations
Founded: 1995. **Membership Dues:** individual, $100 (annual) ● non-profit organization (based on number of employees), $150-$5,000 (annual) ● for-profit organization (based on number of employees), $200-$10,000 (annual). **Description:** Promotes and enhances well-managed forests through credible certification. Encourages the efficient use of the forest's resources and services to ensure economic viability, and environmental and social benefits. Maintains and enhances the long-term social and economic well being of forest workers and local communities. **Telecommunication Services:** electronic mail, ndaly@fscus.org. **Publications:** Brochure. Alternate Formats: online ● Papers. Alternate Formats: online.

4685 ■ ForestEthics
One Haight St., Ste.B
San Francisco, CA 94102
Ph: (415)863-4563
Free: (800)725-0087
E-mail: info@forestethics.org
URL: http://www.forestethics.org
Contact: Allison DeLauer, Acting Development Dir.
Founded: 1994. **Multinational. Description:** Protects endangered forests, wildlife, and human well-being. Encourages corporations across the United States, Canada and Chile to participate in its Corporate Action Program. Provides assistance to corporations who are willing to contribute for the preservation of wildlife. Encourages corporations to initiate environmental reforms. **Telecommunication Services:** electronic mail, allison@forestethics.org. **Publications:** Reports. Alternate Formats: online.

4686 ■ International Association of Wildland Fire (IAWF)
PO Box 261
Hot Springs, SD 57747-0261
Ph: (605)890-2348
Free: (888)440-IAWF
Fax: (206)600-5113
E-mail: iawf@iawfonline.org
URL: http://www.iawfonline.org
Contact: Chuck Bushey, Pres.
Founded: 1983. **Members:** 1,000. **Membership Dues:** individual, $60 (annual) ● student, $25 (annual) ● corporate/library, $75 (annual) ● corporate (with 5 subscriptions to Wildfire Magazine), $250 (annual) ● corporate (with 25 subscriptions to Wildfire Magazine), $1,100 (annual). **Staff:** 1. **Budget:** $400,000. **Description:** Fire scientists, managers, and individuals concerned with wildland fires. Acts as a forum for the exchange of information on wildland fires and fire prevention. **Libraries: Type:** reference. **Holdings:** 50,000. **Subjects:** forest fire. **Awards:** Wildland Fire Safety Award. **Frequency:** annual. **Type:** recognition. **Computer Services:** database, 55K bibliography of fire ● database, 100,000 names and addresses in forest fire. **Formerly:** Fire Research Institute. **Publications:** *Current Titles in Wildland Fire*, monthly. Bulletin ● *International Journal of Wildland Fire*. **Price:** $115.00 /year for individuals. Alternate Formats: online ● *Wildfire*, quarterly. Magazine. **Advertising:** accepted. Alternate Formats: online ● Proceedings. Alternate Formats: online ● Also distributes books and other materials on forest fire. **Conventions/Meetings:** annual Safety Summit - conference.

4687 ■ International Society of Tropical Foresters (ISTF)
5400 Grosvenor Ln.
Bethesda, MD 20814
Ph: (301)897-8720
Fax: (301)897-3690
E-mail: webmaster@istf-bethesda.org
URL: http://www.istf-bethesda.org
Contact: J.L. Whitmore, Pres.
Founded: 1950. **Members:** 1,500. **Membership Dues:** individual in developing country, $10 (annual) ● individual in developed country, $25 (annual) ● student in developed country, $10 (annual) ● student in developing country, $5 (annual) ● sustaining in developed country, $100 (annual) ● sustaining in developing country, $50 (annual). **Staff:** 7. **Budget:** $60,000. **Regional Groups:** 5. **Languages:** English, Spanish. **Description:** Aims for the transfer of technology and science to those concerned with the management, protection and rational use of tropical forests; all individuals and organizations interested in tropical forests and natural resources are eligible for membership. **Libraries: Type:** by appointment only. **Holdings:** archival material, articles, books, papers, periodicals. **Subjects:** tropical forestry. **Publications:** *ISTF News* (in English and Spanish), quarterly. Newsletter. Provides members with latest knowledge needed to better conserve tropical forests. Includes membership directory published yearly. **Price:** $10.00 for individuals in a developing country; $25.00 for individuals in a developed country; $30.00 for libraries in a developing country; $40.00 for libraries in a developed country. ISSN: 0276-2056. **Circulation:** 1,500. **Advertising:** accepted ● *ISTF Noticias* (in English and Spanish), quarterly. Newsletters. **Price:** $10.00 for individuals in developing countries; $25.00 for individuals in developed countries; $30.00 for libraries/organizations in developing country; $40.00 for libraries/organizations in developed country. ISSN: 0743-5991. **Circulation:** 350. **Advertising:** accepted. Alternate Formats: online. **Conventions/Meetings:** meeting - first Monday of February, in Washington, DC.

4688 ■ Live Oak Society (LOS)
3609 Purdue Dr.
Metairie, LA 70003
Ph: (504)887-1800
E-mail: cpl70600@aol.com
URL: http://www.louisianagardenclubs.org
Contact: Coleen Perilloux Landry, Chm.
Founded: 1934. **Members:** 5,666. **Staff:** 1. **Budget:** $250. **Description:** Officers (except for the chairperson) are live oak trees (species Quercus Virginiana) and are found in the states of Alabama, California, the Carolinas, Florida, Georgia, Kentucky, Louisiana, Mississippi, Tennessee, Texas, and Virginia. Qualifies those trees that have girth of at least 8 feet measured four feet above the ground for the Junior League Status, while any live oak measuring 16 feet or greater is qualified as centenarian. Promotes the culture, distribution, preservation and appreciation of the live oak tree, scientifically known as Quercus Virginiana. **Libraries: Type:** by appointment only. **Holdings:** archival material, articles, biographical archives, business records, clippings.

4689 ■ National Association of State Foresters (NASF)
444 N Capitol St. NW, Ste.540
Washington, DC 20001
Ph: (202)624-5415
Fax: (202)624-5407
E-mail: nasf@stateforesters.org
URL: http://www.stateforesters.org/index.html
Contact: C.T. Howlett Jr., Exec. Dir.
Founded: 1920. **Members:** 53. **Regional Groups:** 3. **State Groups:** 53. **Local Groups:** 1. **Description:** Chief officials of state forestry agencies. Promotes cooperation in forestry matters among states and between states and the federal government. Acts on national legislation relating to forestry issues. Maintains history of state forestry agencies; conducts educational programs on forestry issues; compiles statistics. **Awards:** Golden Smokey Award. **Type:** recognition. **Recipient:** for outstanding work in forest fire protection. **Committees:** Cooperative Forest Fire Prevention and Control; Environmental Regulations; Forest Inventory; Forest Pests; Forest Resource Planning; Forestry Assistance; Legislative; Resources Planning Act; Urban Forestry Assistance; Water Resources; Wood Energy. **Affiliated With:** Natural Resources Council of America. **Supersedes:** Association of Eastern Foresters. **Publications:** *Directory of State Foresters*, annual ● *NASF State Forestry Statistics*, annual ● *NASF Washington Update*, periodic. Newsletter. Contains reports on issues and events in the forestry community. Alternate Formats: online ● Reports, periodic. Contains issues of concern for the State Foresters. Alternate Formats: online. **Conventions/Meetings:** annual meeting (exhibits).

4690 ■ National Council for Air and Stream Improvement (NCASI)
PO Box 13318
Research Triangle Park, NC 27709-3318
Ph: (919)941-6400 (352)331-1745
Fax: (919)941-6401
E-mail: ryeske@ncasi.org
URL: http://www.ncasi.org
Contact: Carol Williams, Contact
Founded: 1943. **Members:** 100. **Staff:** 100. **Budget:** $10,000,000. **Regional Groups:** 4. **Description:** Conducts research on environmental problems related to industrial forestry and the manufacture of pulp, paper, and wood products. **Libraries: Type:** not open to the public. **Holdings:** 1,500; books. **Subjects:** chemistry, biochem, environmental issues, toxicology, forestry. **Publications:** *National Council of the Paper Industry for Air and Stream Improvement—Bulletin Board*, biweekly. Newsletter. **Price:** free for members. **Circulation:** 1,500 ● *National Council of the Paper Industry for Air and Stream Improvement—Technical Bulletin*, 40/year. Reports. Contains information on the forest product industries' environmental quality management interests. **Price:** $1,058.00/year. **Circulation:** 1,500 ● Reports. **Conventions/Meetings:** annual meeting - always March, New York City.

4691 ■ National Council on Private Forests (NCPF)
c/o Ian MacFarlane, Chm.
444 N Capitol St. NW
Washington, DC 20001
Ph: (202)624-5977
Fax: (202)624-5407
E-mail: info@ncpf.org
URL: http://www.ncpf.org
Contact: Ian MacFarlane, Chm.
Founded: 1985. **Members:** 13. **Description:** Landowner associations, forestry associations, and federal agencies and associations involved in the management of non-industrial private forest lands. Informs decision-makers in the private and public sectors of the effects of their policies on forest management. **Publications:** none.

4692 ■ National Network of Forest Practitioners (NNFP)
8 N Court St., Ste.411
Athens, OH 45701
Ph: (740)593-8733

E-mail: info@nnfp.org
URL: http://www.nnfp.org
Contact: Colin Donohue, Exec. Dir.
Founded: 1990. **Membership Dues:** regular, $35 (annual) ● small organization/business (5 or less employees), $60 (annual) ● organization, business, $100 (annual) ● institutional, agency, university, $250 (annual) ● partner, $500 (annual) ● supporting individual, $120 (annual). **Description:** Promotes the mutual well-being of workers, rural communities and forests. Supports individuals and groups that build sustainable relationships between forests and people. **Publications:** *Practitioner*. Newsletter. **Price:** included in membership dues. Alternate Formats: online ● Membership Directory. **Price:** included in membership dues.

4693 ■ National Woodland Owners Association (NWOA)
374 Maple Ave. E, Ste.310
Vienna, VA 22180
Ph: (703)255-2700
Free: (800)476-8733
Fax: (703)281-9200
E-mail: info@woodlandowners.org
URL: http://www.woodlandowners.org
Contact: Dr. Keith A. Argow, Pres.
Founded: 1983. **Members:** 42,000. **Membership Dues:** individual, $25 (annual). **Staff:** 4. **Regional Groups:** 4. **State Groups:** 32. **Description:** A member of the Natural Resources Council of America and the National Council on Private Forests. Woodland owners united to promote wise management of nonindustrial private forest lands. Works with cooperating and affiliated state woodland owners' associations and serves as voice for private landowners on forestry, wildlife, and resource conservation issues. Conducts management seminars in conjunction with state associations. Maintains speakers' bureau; compiles statistics. **Convention/Meeting:** none. **Libraries: Type:** reference. **Holdings:** 1,500. **Subjects:** non-industrial private forestry. **Awards:** Forest Stewardship State of the Year. **Frequency:** annual. **Type:** recognition ● Outstanding Forestry Legislation Award. **Frequency:** annual. **Type:** recognition. **Computer Services:** database, forestry incentives and forest management plan ● database, membership. **Affiliated With:** National Council on Private Forests; Natural Resources Council of America. **Publications:** *National Woodlands Magazine*, quarterly. Includes conservation news digest. **Price:** included in membership dues. ISSN: 0279-9812. **Circulation:** 2,400. **Advertising:** accepted. Alternate Formats: online ● *Woodland Report*. Newsletter. Reports legislative and association news; for private landowners on forestry, wildlife, and resource conservation issues. **Price:** included in membership dues. **Circulation:** 2,400.

4694 ■ Redwood Region Logging Conference (RRLC)
5601 S Broadway
Eureka, CA 95502-7127
Ph: (707)443-4091
Fax: (707)443-0926
E-mail: rrlc@humboldt1.com
URL: http://www.rrlc.net
Contact: Katherine Ziemer, Exec. Dir.
Founded: 1936. **Members:** 500. **Membership Dues:** firm (required for vendor), $75 (annual) ● individual, $15 (annual). **Budget:** $287,325. **Description:** Designs to "educate industry workers, students, and community members about forest ecosystems and timber harvest methods used throughout the North Coast.". **Awards:** Emmanuel Fritz Memorial Scholarship. **Frequency:** annual. **Type:** scholarship. **Recipient:** for freshmen, juniors or returning sophomores ● Kent L. Holmgren Memorial Scholarship. **Frequency:** annual. **Type:** scholarship. **Recipient:** for freshmen or sophomores. **Committees:** Education. **Programs:** Natural Resource Education Funding. **Conventions/Meetings:** annual conference and banquet, with art show and sale, entertainment, auction (exhibits).

4695 ■ Society of American Foresters (SAF)
5400 Grosvenor Ln.
Bethesda, MD 20814-2198
Ph: (301)897-8720
Free: (866)897-8720
Fax: (301)897-3690
E-mail: safweb@safnet.org
URL: http://www.safnet.org
Contact: Michael T. Goergen Jr., Exec. VP/CEO
Founded: 1900. **Members:** 17,000. **Membership Dues:** international, corresponding, conditional/technician/associate (0-5 years), professional (0-5 years), $79 (annual) ● professional (6 years), $99 (annual) ● professional (retired), conditional/technician/associate (6-49 years), $105 (annual) ● professional (7 years), $118 (annual) ● professional (8-49 years), $133 (annual) ● student, $35 (annual). **Staff:** 27. **Budget:** $4,500,000. **Regional Groups:** 33. **Local Groups:** 210. **Description:** National scientific and educational organization representing forestry in the United States. Aims to advance the science, education, technology, and practice of forestry. Supports 28 subject-oriented working groups. **Awards:** Carl Alwin Schenck Award. **Frequency:** annual. **Type:** recognition. **Recipient:** for outstanding performance in the field of forestry education ● Gifford Pinchot Medal. **Frequency:** biennial. **Type:** medal. **Recipient:** for outstanding contributions by a forestry professional ● Outstanding Communicator Award. **Frequency:** annual. **Type:** recognition. **Recipient:** for SAF member who displays the ability, talent, and skill to lead ● Sir William Schlich Memorial Award. **Frequency:** biennial. **Type:** medal. **Recipient:** for contributions to the field of forestry. **Affiliated With:** International Society of Tropical Foresters. **Publications:** *Forest Science*, quarterly. Journal. Includes topics such as silviculture, soils, biome disease, recreation, tree physiology. **Price:** $90.00 for members in U.S. and Canada; $120.00 foreign; $60.00 student members in U.S. and Canada; $130.00 for nonmembers in U.S. and Canada. ISSN: 0015-749X. **Advertising:** accepted. Alternate Formats: online ● *The Forestry Source*, monthly. Newspaper. Offers timely news for forest resource professionals. **Price:** free for members; $30.00 for nonmembers in U.S. and Canada; $55.00 for nonmembers outside U.S. and Canada; $60.00 for institutions in U.S. and Canada. Alternate Formats: online ● *Journal of Forestry*, 8/year. Contains information on significant developments and ideas in forest science, natural resources management, and forest policy. **Price:** free for members; $85.00 for nonmembers in U.S. and Canada; $115.00 for nonmembers outside U.S. and Canada; $185.00 for institutions in U.S. and Canada. **Advertising:** accepted. Alternate Formats: online ● *Northern Journal of Applied Forestry*, quarterly. **Price:** $52.00 for members in U.S. and Canada; $26.00 for student members in U.S. and Canada; $75.00 for nonmembers in U.S. and Canada; $170.00 for institutions in U.S. and Canada. Alternate Formats: online ● *Southern Journal of Applied Forestry*, quarterly. **Price:** $52.00 for members in U.S. and Canada; $26.00 for student members in U.S. and Canada; $75.00 for nonmembers in U.S. and Canada; $170.00 for institutions in U.S. and Canada. Alternate Formats: online ● *Western Journal of Applied Forestry*, quarterly. **Price:** $52.00 for members in U.S. and Canada; $26.00 for student members in U.S. and Canada; $75.00 for nonmembers in U.S. and Canada; $170.00 for institutions in U.S. and Canada. Alternate Formats: online ● Annual Report, annual. Alternate Formats: online. **Conventions/Meetings:** meeting, national, regional, and local technical and scientific gatherings ● annual meeting and convention (exhibits) - 2008 Nov. 5-9, Reno, NV.

4696 ■ Thoreau Institute
PO Box 1590
Bandon, OR 97411
Ph: (541)347-1517
E-mail: rot@ti.org
URL: http://www.ti.org
Contact: Randal O'Toole, Sr. Economist
Founded: 1975. **Staff:** 5. **Budget:** $100,000. **Description:** Serves as a consulting firm supported by individuals, foundations, and corporations. Aids citizens in influencing public forest management, and natural resource agencies. Proposes reforms of public forest and natural resource management and policy that would save taxpayers money and resolve environmental controversies. Conducts research and educational programs. **Libraries: Type:** by appointment only. **Holdings:** 4,000. **Subjects:** natural resources planning and management. **Formerly:** (1995) Cascade Holistic Economic Consultants. **Publications:** *Electronic Drummer*. Reports.

4697 ■ Trees for Tomorrow (TFT)
PO Box 609
519 Sheridan St.
Eagle River, WI 54521
Ph: (715)479-6456
Free: (800)838-9472
Fax: (715)479-2318
E-mail: learning@treesfortomorrow.com
URL: http://www.treesfortomorrow.com
Contact: Maggie Bishop, Exec. Dir.
Founded: 1944. **Members:** 300. **Membership Dues:** friend, $25 ● supporting, $50 ● patron, $100 ● sustaining, $500 ● champion/executive, $1,000 ● associate, $500. **Staff:** 24. **Budget:** $900,000. **Description:** Serves as an accredited natural resources specialty school sponsored by corporations, service organizations, and individuals. Features multi-day workshops for elementary, middle and high school students from Wisconsin, Michigan and Illinois. Aims to familiarize students with renewable resources of the northern forest ecosystem, urge conservation, and demonstrate good resource stewardship. Comprises of five thousand students and teachers that are served annually. Provides programs for other groups on request. **Libraries: Type:** reference. **Awards: Type:** recognition ● **Type:** scholarship. **Committees:** Business Management; Planning and Development; Promotion. **Publications:** *Northbound*, quarterly. Newsletter. Contains information on a variety of natural resources topics. **Price:** included in membership dues. **Circulation:** 3,000. Alternate Formats: online ● Brochures. Describes various educational programs. **Conventions/Meetings:** periodic conference ● periodic Student and Teacher Workshops.

4698 ■ Tropical Forest Foundation (TFF)
c/o Keister Evans, Exec. Dir.
2121 Eisenhower Ave., Ste.200
Alexandria, VA 22314
Ph: (703)518-8834
Fax: (703)518-8974
E-mail: tff@igc.org
URL: http://www.tropicalforestfoundation.org
Contact: Keister Evans, Exec. Dir.
Founded: 1990. **Members:** 100. **Staff:** 4. **Budget:** $800,000. **Description:** Individuals united to preserve the global ecosystem through the wise use and conservation of tropical forests. Sponsors educational programs; disseminates information on tropical forest products and maintenance. **Libraries: Type:** reference. **Holdings:** 100. **Subjects:** tropical forestry. **Awards:** TFF Award for Exemplary Forestry. **Frequency:** annual. **Type:** recognition. **Recipient:** for nomination and documented demonstration of exemplary forest management practices. **Publications:** *Ecology, Conservation and Management of Southeast Asian Rainforests*. Book. Consists of 304 pages with tables, figures and photos. **Price:** $35.00 ● *TFF Newsletter*, quarterly ● *Tropical Forests*, quarterly. Newsletter ● Bulletins, periodic ● Sustainable Forest Management Project in Brazil, publication number 1 model specifications for architects and designers. **Conventions/Meetings:** semiannual board meeting ● periodic conference ● annual symposium.

4699 ■ United States Department of Agriculture - Forest Service Volunteers Program (USDA-SYVP)
1400 Independence Ave. SW
Washington, DC 20250-0003
Ph: (703)605-4851 (202)205-8333
E-mail: webmaster@fs.fed.us
URL: http://www.usda.gov
Contact: Donald A. Hansen, Program Mgr.
Founded: 1972. **Regional Groups:** 9. **Description:** Volunteers interested in providing their services to maintain national forests and natural resources

values. Recruits individuals and organizations on forest-related tasks. Maintains contacts in 156 national forests, 9 forest experiment stations, a forest products laboratory, and 19 national grasslands. **Additional Websites:** http://www.fs.fed.us/fsjobs/forest-service/contact.html.

4700 ■ Western Forestry and Conservation Association (WFCA)
4033 SW Canyon Rd.
Portland, OR 97221
Ph: (503)226-4562
Fax: (503)226-2515
E-mail: richard@westernforestry.org
URL: http://www.westernforestry.org
Contact: Richard A. Zabel, Exec. Dir.
Founded: 1909. **Members:** 300. **Staff:** 2. **Budget:** $140,000. **Description:** Forest landowners, forestry associations, and individual foresters in private, federal, and state agencies from eight western states and Canada. Fosters cooperative effort among all forestry agencies in Western North America; promotes forest stewardship in western North America. **Awards: Type:** recognition. **Recipient:** for lifetime and current achievement. **Computer Services:** Mailing lists, of members. **Committees:** Fire; Forest Health; Land Use; Reforestation; Stand Management. **Publications:** Publishes tree seed zone map. **Conventions/Meetings:** annual Western Forestry Conference (exhibits) - always first week of December.

4701 ■ World Forestry Center (WFC)
4033 SW Canyon Rd.
Portland, OR 97221
Ph: (503)228-1367 (503)488-2111
Fax: (503)228-4608
E-mail: mail@worldforestry.org
URL: http://www.worldforestry.org
Contact: Gary Hartshorn PhD, Pres./CEO
Founded: 1964. **Members:** 1,000. **Membership Dues:** individual, $35 (annual) ● family, $45 (annual) ● individual plus, $40 (annual) ● family plus, $50 (annual). **Staff:** 24. **Description:** Professional foresters; individuals concerned with forests and forest management. Educational organization promoting public awareness of world forests and forest resources. Serves as an information clearinghouse. Provides education on subjects such as woodland management, forest products, and forest environments. Maintains museum. Sponsors exhibits. **Formerly:** (1986) Western Forestry Center. **Publications:** *Branching Out*, quarterly. Newsletter. **Price:** free for members. **Circulation:** 1,000.

Fruits and Vegetables

4702 ■ American Cranberry Growers Association (ACGA)
Address Unknown since 2008
Founded: 1869. **Members:** 75. **Description:** Cranberry farmers; interested others. Promotes propagation, interest, and development of cranberries. Provides information on the status of cranberry crops in New Jersey. Conducts educational programs. **Awards:** Outstanding Contributions to Cranberries. **Frequency:** annual. **Type:** recognition. **Publications:** Proceedings, semiannual. **Conventions/Meetings:** semiannual meeting - always winter and summer. Chatsworth, NJ - **Avg. Attendance:** 60.

4703 ■ American Mushroom Institute (AMI)
Washington, D.C. Off.
1 Massachusetts Ave. NW, Ste.800
Washington, DC 20001
Ph: (202)842-4344
Fax: (202)408-7763
E-mail: ami@mwmlaw.com
URL: http://www.americanmushroom.org
Contact: Laura L. Phelps, Pres.
Founded: 1955. **Members:** 450. **Membership Dues:** associate, grower (under 1.4 million lbs./year), $350 (annual). **Staff:** 3. **Description:** Mushroom growers, processors, suppliers, and researchers united to promote the growing and marketing of cultivated mushrooms. Aims to: increase cultivated mushroom consumption; develop better and more economical methods of growing and marketing mushrooms; collect and disseminate the latest statistics and other information; foster research programs beneficial to the industry; aid members with any problems. Supports a short course on mushroom science at Penn State University and an international congress on mushroom science. **Libraries: Type:** reference. **Holdings:** 250; books, periodicals. **Subjects:** mushrooms, cultivation of mushrooms. **Awards:** James W. Sinden Scholarship Award. **Frequency:** annual. **Type:** scholarship. **Recipient:** for students pursuing degrees beyond the bachelors level at an accredited college or university within the U.S. in a field of study involving the technical and scientific aspects of commercially cultivated edible fungi. **Committees:** Community Awareness; Food Science; Government Relations; Research. **Task Forces:** Environmental. **Publications:** *American Mushroom Institute—Membership Directory*, annual. **Price:** available to members only. **Circulation:** 450. **Advertising:** accepted ● *Mushroom Lover's Cookbook*. Contains collection of recipes. **Price:** $10.00 ● *Mushroom News*, monthly. Magazine. Contains advertisers' index, calendar of events, articles on marketing, production, and research in the mushroom industry. **Price:** $275.00. ISSN: 0541-3869. **Circulation:** 1,000. **Advertising:** accepted ● Brochures. **Conventions/Meetings:** triennial North American Mushroom Conference (exhibits).

4704 ■ American Pomological Society (APS)
c/o R.M. Crassweller, Treas.
103 Tyson Bldg.
University Park, PA 16802-4200
Ph: (814)863-6163
Fax: (814)237-3407
E-mail: aps@psu.edu
URL: http://www.americanpomological.org
Contact: Ed Stover, Pres.
Founded: 1848. **Members:** 1,000. **Membership Dues:** individual in U.S., $40 (annual) ● individual, $110 (triennial) ● library/institution, individual in Canada and Mexico, $50 (annual) ● library/institution, $150 (triennial) ● individual outside U.S., Canada, and Mexico, $60 (annual). **Staff:** 1. **Description:** Represents professional horticulturists, fruit growers, amateur fruit breeders, testers, and individuals in the nursery business devoted to fruit variety improvement. **Awards:** Shepard Award. **Frequency:** annual. **Type:** recognition. **Recipient:** for the best article published in the journal ● U.P. Hedrick Award. **Type:** recognition. **Recipient:** for best papers by undergraduate or graduate students ● Wilder Medal. **Frequency:** annual. **Type:** recognition. **Recipient:** for service in the field of horticulture. **Committees:** Editorial; Registration of New Fruit and Nut Varieties; Shepard Award; U.P. Hedrick Award; Wilder Medal Award. **Publications:** *History of Fruit Growing and Handling in U.S.A. and Canada, 1860-1972*. Book ● *Journal American Pomological Society*, quarterly. Covers fruit improvement. **Price:** included in membership dues. **Circulation:** 1,250. **Advertising:** accepted. Also Cited As: *Fruit Varieties and Horticultural Digest* ● *North American Apples: Varieties, Rootstocks, and Outlook*. Book. **Conventions/Meetings:** annual meeting, held in conjunction with the American Society for Horticultural Science.

4705 ■ Apple Products Research and Education Council
5775 Peachtree-Dunwoody Rd., Bldg. G, Ste.500
Atlanta, GA 30342
Ph: (404)252-3663
E-mail: info@appleproducts.org
URL: http://www.appleproducts.org
Contact: Andrew G. Ebert PhD, Pres.
Founded: 1951. **Members:** 80. **Staff:** 5. **Description:** Represents processors of apple products and suppliers to the industry. Conducts program to improve business conditions in the apple products industry and to enable the industry to serve the interests of consumers. Conducts research programs on the health benefits of apple products. **Committees:** Technical. **Formerly:** (2005) Processed Apples Institute. **Publications:** *Reference Manual for the Processed Apples Industry*, periodic. **Price:** $250.00 for nonmembers ● Membership Directory, annual. **Price:** free for members ● Newsletter, quarterly. **Conventions/Meetings:** annual convention ● annual Scientific/Technical Seminar.

4706 ■ Apricot Producers of California (APC)
PO Box 974
Turlock, CA 95381
Ph: (209)632-9777
Fax: (209)632-9779
E-mail: apricots@apricotproducers.com
URL: http://www.apricotproducers.com
Contact: William C. Ferriera, Pres.
Founded: 1961. **Members:** 90. **Budget:** $200,000. **Description:** Represents members (apricot growers) in negotiations with processors (canners, driers, and freezers) over prices, contracts of sale, and harvest conditions. Maintains the highest quality of production and to foster meaningful communication. Represents growers' viewpoints before state and federal bodies. **Committees:** Governmental Relations; Marketing. **Publications:** *Annual Calendar*, annual ● Newsletters. Alternate Formats: online. **Conventions/Meetings:** annual conference.

4707 ■ California Avocado Commission (CAC)
38 Discovery, Ste.150
Irvine, CA 92618
Ph: (949)341-1955
Fax: (949)341-1970
E-mail: tbellamore@avocado.org
URL: http://www.avocado.org
Contact: Mark Affleck, Pres./CEO
Founded: 1978. **Members:** 5,500. **Staff:** 14. **Budget:** $14,000,000. **Description:** Marketing organization for growers and packers of California avocados. Administers promotion program, directs marketing research, and creates and implements national advertising programs for California avocados. **Libraries: Type:** reference. **Holdings:** papers, reports. **Subjects:** avocado research. **Divisions:** Industry Affairs; Marketing and Production Research. **Formerly:** (1961) California Avocado Advisory Board.

4708 ■ California Avocado Society (CAS)
PO Box 1317
Carpinteria, CA 93014
Ph: (805)684-2804
Fax: (805)684-5352
E-mail: administration@californiaavocadosociety.org
URL: http://www.californiaavocadosociety.org
Contact: Trish Shade, Exec. Admin.
Founded: 1915. **Members:** 1,100. **Membership Dues:** regular, $40 (annual) ● sustaining, $200 (annual) ● patron, $350 (annual) ● life, $5,000. **Staff:** 1. **Description:** Seeks to improve the culture and production of avocados; promotes the general welfare of the avocado industry. Supports research. **Awards:** Award of Honor. **Frequency:** annual. **Type:** recognition. **Recipient:** for meritorious contribution to the avocado industry. **Affiliated With:** California Avocado Commission. **Formerly:** (1941) California Avocado Association. **Publications:** Yearbook, annual. Contains avocado grower information. **Price:** $35.00. ISSN: 0096-5960. **Circulation:** 1,100. **Advertising:** accepted. **Conventions/Meetings:** annual conference (exhibits).

4709 ■ California Canning Peach Association (CCPA)
2300 River Plaza Dr., Ste.110
Sacramento, CA 95833
Ph: (916)925-9131
Fax: (916)925-9030
E-mail: tmelchiori@calpeach.com
URL: http://www.calpeach.com
Contact: Rich Hudgins, Pres./CEO
Founded: 1922. **Members:** 625. **Staff:** 13. **Description:** California cling peach growers. Works to market members' production and obtain a reasonable return for cling peach growers' raw product. Conducts research on breeding new varieties of cling peaches. Compiles statistics on the cling peach industry.

Awards: Quality Award. **Frequency:** annual. **Type:** recognition. **Recipient:** for the lowest off grade. **Committees:** PeachPac. **Publications:** *Cling Peach Almanac*, periodic ● *Cling Peach Review*, semiannual. Magazine ● *Peach Fuzz*, monthly. Newsletter. Alternate Formats: online. **Conventions/Meetings:** annual meeting (exhibits) - always first week in February.

4710 ■ California Cling Peach Board (CCPAB)
c/o Jim Melban
531-D N Alta Ave.
Dinuba, CA 93618-3203
Ph: (559)595-1425
Fax: (559)591-5744
E-mail: jim@tabcomp.com
URL: http://www.calclingpeach.com
Contact: Jim Melban, Contact
Founded: 1946. **Members:** 800. **Staff:** 2. **Budget:** $2,000,000. **Description:** Represents growers and canners of cling peaches in California. Promotes the sale of canned cling peaches and fruit cocktail and conducts quality control programs and research on cling peaches. **Committees:** Advertising and Promotion; Research and Statistics. **Formerly:** (1996) Cling Peach Advisory Board; (2003) California Cling Peach Advisory Board. **Publications:** *Peach Press*. Newsletter. Alternate Formats: online.

4711 ■ California Date Administrative Committee (CDAC)
PO Box 1736
Indio, CA 92202-1736
Ph: (760)347-4510
Free: (800)223-8748
Fax: (760)347-6374
E-mail: dates2000@earthlink.net
URL: http://www.datesaregreat.com
Contact: Lorrie Cooper, Mgr.
Founded: 1996. **Members:** 18. **Staff:** 4. **Budget:** $650,000. **Description:** Serves as a marketing organization for growers and handlers of 4 varieties of California dates, under a federal marketing order. Represents various producers and packers within the industry. Administers quality regulations. Sponsors generic market promotion programs. Compiles statistics. **Libraries: Type:** reference; by appointment only. **Holdings:** archival material, business records, photographs, reports. **Computer Services:** database ● mailing lists ● online services. **Formerly:** (1970) Date Administrative Committee; (2001) California Date Administrative Committee; (2005) California Date Commission. **Conventions/Meetings:** annual meeting - always October.

4712 ■ California Dried Plum Board (CDPB)
3840 Rosin Ct., Ste.170
Sacramento, CA 95834
Ph: (916)565-6232
Fax: (916)565-6237
URL: http://www.californiadriedplums.org
Contact: Richard L. Peterson, Exec. Dir.
Founded: 1952. **Members:** 1,250. **Staff:** 5. **Budget:** $4,000,000. **Description:** California prune producers, prune packers, and one public sector member. Operates the California Dried Prune Marketing Order, as amended, under the authority of the Secretary of the California Department of Food and Agriculture, and collects assessments on packers and producers. Uses funds for non-brand advertising and promotion of prunes and prune products. Handles requests for recipes and resource material. **Formerly:** (1980) California Prune Advisory Board; (2003) California Prune Board. **Publications:** *California Dried Plum News*, quarterly. Newsletter ● *California Prune Buyer's Guide* ● *The New Mom's Survival Guide*. Brochure ● *Statistical Report*, periodic.

4713 ■ California Dry Bean Advisory Board (CDBAB)
531-D N Alta Ave.
Dinuba, CA 93618-3203
Ph: (559)591-4866
Fax: (559)591-5744
E-mail: jim@tabcomp.com
URL: http://www.calbeans.com
Contact: Jerry Munson, Board Mgr.
Founded: 1970. **Members:** 20. **Staff:** 2. **Budget:** $1,100,000. **Description:** Growers and handlers of all varieties of dry beans produced in California. Conducts research to improve quality and marketability; carries on limited promotion; seeks to establish quality standards for California dry beans. **Committees:** Product and Market Development; Reports and Collections; Research Promotion. **Councils:** Baby Lima; Blackeye; Garbanzo; Large Lima; Miscellaneous; Red Kidney. **Publications:** *California Bean Marketer: Newsletter for Growers and Handlers of California Dry Beans*, quarterly. Covers the dry bean industry, with emphasis on advertising and promotion. Includes statistics on California dry beans. **Price:** free for members. **Conventions/Meetings:** semiannual board meeting.

4714 ■ California Fig Advisory Board (CFAB)
7395 N Palm Bluffs Ave., Ste.106
Fresno, CA 93711-5767
Ph: (559)440-5400
Free: (800)588-2344
Fax: (559)438-5405
E-mail: info@californiafigs.com
URL: http://www.californiafigs.com
Contact: Richard Matoian, Mgr.
Founded: 1953. **Members:** 125. **Staff:** 5. **Budget:** $900,000. **Description:** Commercial fig growers in California. Operates under the State Department of Agriculture for the advertising and merchandising of figs and fig products. **Affiliated With:** California Fig Institute. **Formerly:** (1986) California Dried Fig Advisory Board. **Publications:** *Statistical Review of the California Dried Fig Industry*, annual.

4715 ■ California Fig Institute (CFI)
7395 N Palm Bluffs Ave., Ste.106
Fresno, CA 93711-5767
Ph: (559)440-5400
Free: (800)588-2344
Fax: (559)438-5405
E-mail: info@californiafigs.com
URL: http://www.californiafigs.com
Contact: Richard Matoian, Managing Dir.
Founded: 1937. **Members:** 200. **Staff:** 4. **Budget:** $100,000. **Description:** Commercial fig growers in California. Conducts research program. **Publications:** *Statistical Review*, annual. **Conventions/Meetings:** annual meeting - always Fresno, CA.

4716 ■ California Grape and Tree Fruit League (CG&TFL)
978 W Alluvial, Ste.107
Fresno, CA 93711-5700
Ph: (559)226-6330
Fax: (559)222-8326
E-mail: cgtfl@cgtfl.com
URL: http://www.cgtfl.com
Contact: Jerry DiBuduo, Chm.
Founded: 1936. **Members:** 350. **Membership Dues:** grower, $125 (annual) ● shipper, marketer, $250 (annual) ● associate, $425 (annual). **Staff:** 7. **Description:** Growers and shippers of fresh deciduous tree fruits and table grapes in California. Offers group insurance programs. **Committees:** Environmental Resources; Government Relations; Insurance & Financial Benefits; Labor; Marketing; Political Action; Standardization and Packaging; Traffic. **Formed by Merger of:** California Grape and Tree Fruit Association; California Growers and Shippers Protective League. **Publications:** *CG&TFL Membership Roster*, annual. Membership Directory. **Price:** included in membership dues. **Circulation:** 500 ● *On Target*, biweekly. Newsletter. Contains brief news items on association and industry activities. Contains legislative update. **Price:** included in membership dues. **Circulation:** 600. **Conventions/Meetings:** annual meeting - always March ● workshop and seminar, on operations.

4717 ■ California Kiwifruit Commission (CKC)
770 E Shaw, Ste.220
Fresno, CA 93710
E-mail: kiwifruit@kiwifruit.org
Contact: Linda LaFrancis, Pres.
Founded: 1979. **Members:** 350. **Staff:** 3. **Budget:** $500,000. **Description:** California kiwifruit growers. Conducts cultural and market research; promotes use of kiwifruit internationally and in the U.S. Compiles statistics. **Committees:** Advertising/Promotion; Cultural Research. **Conventions/Meetings:** semiannual board meeting.

4718 ■ California Melon Research Board (CMRB)
531-D N Alta Ave.
Dinuba, CA 93618
Ph: (559)591-0435
E-mail: contact@cmrb.org
URL: http://www.cmrb.org
Contact: J.D. Allen, Mgr.
Founded: 1972. **Members:** 20. **Staff:** 3. **Budget:** $240,000. **Description:** Participants are California melon growers. Conducts research on new varieties, pest control management, and disease control for melons grown in California. (California is the leading melon-growing state in the U.S., producing approximately 80-85&percent; of the annual U.S. melon crop.) Provides funding to universities for research programs. **Committees:** Research. **Publications:** *California Melon Research Board-Annual Report*. Provides technical research reports on disease control and new varieties of melons. **Price:** free. **Conventions/Meetings:** annual meeting (exhibits).

4719 ■ California Rare Fruit Growers (CRFG)
The Fullerton Arboretum-CSUF
PO Box 6850
Fullerton, CA 92834-6850
Ph: (415)839-0102 (415)469-0966
Free: (866)510-0737
Fax: (415)294-5369
E-mail: admin@crfg.org
URL: http://www.crfg.org
Contact: Bill Grimes, Pres.
Founded: 1968. **Members:** 4,300. **Membership Dues:** regular, in U.S., $30 (annual) ● regular, in Canada and Mexico, $40 (annual) ● regular, outside U.S., Canada, and Mexico, $53 (annual). **Staff:** 2. **Budget:** $40,000. **State Groups:** 3. **Local Groups:** 15. **National Groups:** 16. **Description:** Horticulturists united to transmit information regarding introduction and growing of rare fruit, to upgrade familiar fruits, and to increase the use of less common fruit. Maintains program to discover, register, and propagate superior fruit trees. Develops rare fruit areas at Quail Garden Arboretum in North San Diego County, CA, and Fullerton Arboretum in Orange County, CA. Conducts research program. Maintains seed, plant, and scion wood exchange. Teaches grafting at high schools, colleges and local garden clubs. **Publications:** *Fruit Facts*, periodic. Provides information on a single fruit including botanical identification, culture notes, and characteristics of cultivars. ● *The Fruit Gardener*, bimonthly. Magazine. Contains articles on pest control, tips for beginners, fruit recipes, book reviews, and do-it-yourself instructions for garden devices. **Price:** included in membership dues; $10.00/issue for nonmembers. ISSN: 1049-4545. **Advertising:** accepted. **Conventions/Meetings:** annual meeting (exhibits) - usually third Saturday of March.

4720 ■ California Strawberry Commission (CSC)
PO Box 269
Watsonville, CA 95077
Ph: (831)724-1301
Fax: (831)724-5973
E-mail: info@calstrawberry.com
URL: http://www.calstrawberry.com
Contact: Mark Murai, Pres.
Founded: 1955. **Members:** 58. **Staff:** 17. **Description:** Provides information about strawberries and the people who grow them. Answers questions, offers new recipes containing strawberries, and an-

nounces the latest news about strawberries. **Formerly:** California Strawberry Advisory Board.

4721 ■ California Table Grape Commission (CTGC)
392 W Fallbrook, Ste.101
Fresno, CA 93711-6150
Ph: (559)447-8350
Fax: (559)447-9184
E-mail: info@freshcaliforniagrapes.com
URL: http://www.tablegrape.com
Contact: Kathleen Nave, Pres.
Founded: 1968. **Members:** 1,100. **Staff:** 18. **Description:** Grape growers united to promote California table grapes. Conducts research on grape production. **Committees:** Issue Management; Research; Trade Management. **Programs:** Education and Outreach. **Publications:** *Grower Report*, quarterly ● *Natural News*, periodic. Newsletter.

4722 ■ Cherry Central Cooperative (CCC)
PO Box 988
Traverse City, MI 49685-0988
Ph: (231)946-1860
Fax: (231)941-4167
E-mail: info@cherrycentral.com
URL: http://www.cherrycentral.com
Contact: Richard L. Bogard, Pres./Gen. Mgr.
Founded: 1973. **Members:** 13. **Staff:** 47. **Regional Groups:** 3. **Description:** Represents fruit and vegetable growers, processors, and marketers.

4723 ■ Cherry Marketing Institute (CMI)
PO Box 30285
Lansing, MI 48909-7785
Ph: (517)669-4264
Fax: (517)669-3354
E-mail: info@usacherries.com
URL: http://www.usacherries.com
Contact: Philip J. Korson II, Pres./Managing Dir.
Founded: 1988. **Description:** Represents growers of tart cherries. Promotes and encourages the consumption of cherries. Conducts research. **Absorbed:** (1988) National Red Cherry Institute.

4724 ■ Concord Grape Association (CGA)
1100 Johnson Ferry Rd., Ste.300
Atlanta, GA 30342
Ph: (404)252-3663
Fax: (404)252-0774
E-mail: info@concordgrape.org
URL: http://www.concordgrape.org
Contact: Ms. Pamela A. Chumley, Pres.
Founded: 1966. **Members:** 11. **Description:** Processors of Concord grape products. Promotes the interests of members, and the welfare of the industry. **Formerly:** (1972) Concord Grape Council; (1974) American Concord Grape Association. **Publications:** Membership Directory. **Price:** free, for members only. **Conventions/Meetings:** annual meeting.

4725 ■ Cranberry Institute (CI)
3203-B Cranberry Hwy.
East Wareham, MA 02538
Free: (800)295-4132
Fax: (508)759-6294
E-mail: cinews@earthlink.net
URL: http://www.cranberryinstitute.org
Contact: Mr. Bill Cutts, Board Member
Founded: 1951. **Members:** 1,000. **Staff:** 2. **Description:** Cranberry growers and handlers in the United States and Canada. Gathers and disseminates information and helps members resolve horticultural and environmental issues related to growing cranberries. **Publications:** *Cranberry Health News*, quarterly. Newsletter. Contains the latest cranberry-related health research, news and information. Alternate Formats: online. **Conventions/Meetings:** periodic board meeting - 3/year.

4726 ■ DFA of California
710 Striker Ave.
Sacramento, CA 95834
Ph: (916)561-5900
Fax: (916)561-5906
E-mail: richn@dfaofca.com
URL: http://dfaofca.com
Contact: Richard W. Novy, Pres./CEO
Founded: 1908. **Members:** 42. **Membership Dues:** associate, $300 (annual). **Staff:** 30. **Description:** Represents processors, packers, grower packers, and wholesalers of prunes, raisins, and other dried fruits, and almonds, pistachios, and walnuts. Performs inspection and certification, research and development, and traffic and sanitation services. **Formerly:** Dried Fruit Association of California. **Conventions/Meetings:** annual meeting.

4727 ■ Florida Citrus Mutual (FCM)
PO Box 89
Lakeland, FL 33802
Ph: (863)682-1111
Fax: (863)682-1074
E-mail: mikes@flcitrusmutual.com
URL: http://www.flcitrusmutual.com/content
Contact: Mike Sparks, Exec. VP/CEO
Founded: 1948. **Members:** 12,000. **Staff:** 23. **Budget:** $2,000,000. **Description:** Supplies market and price information to members; marketing of fruit is handled by affiliated shippers and processors. **Divisions:** Economics and Statistics; Grower and Contracts; Marketing Information; Public Information. **Publications:** *Market News Bulletin*, semiweekly, mid-October through mid-June. Provides information on current citrus prices. **Price:** included in membership dues. **Circulation:** 900 ● *Triangle*, weekly, except July. Newsletter. Reports on the Florida citrus industry and developments affecting Florida citrus growers. **Price:** included in membership dues. **Circulation:** 12,300. **Conventions/Meetings:** annual conference - always second Wednesday of June.

4728 ■ Florida Citrus Nurserymen's Association (FCNA)
PO Box 12852
Fort Pierce, FL 34979-2852
Ph: (941)658-3400
Fax: (941)658-3469
E-mail: rrouse@ufl.edu
URL: http://www.floridacitrusnursery.com
Contact: Bob Rouse, Sec.
Founded: 1957. **Members:** 77. **Membership Dues:** active, $100 (annual) ● associate, allied, $60 (annual). **Description:** Florida citrus nurserymen seeking to promote and support research, education, and self-regulation concerning quality citrus nursery stock. Develops greenhouse techniques for containerized nursery plants. **Committees:** Executive. **Publications:** *Florida Citrus*, quarterly. Newsletter. Contains industry and society news. **Price:** free. **Circulation:** 400 ● *Membership List*, quarterly. Membership Directory. **Conventions/Meetings:** quarterly meeting (exhibits) ● annual meeting (exhibits) - always April.

4729 ■ Florida Department of Citrus (FDOC)
PO Box 148
Lakeland, FL 33802-0148
Ph: (863)499-2500
Fax: (863)284-4300
E-mail: info@citrus.state.fl.us
URL: http://www.floridajuice.com
Contact: Ken Keck, Exec. Dir.
Founded: 1935. **Staff:** 72. **Budget:** $64,000,000. **Description:** Established by an act of the Florida legislature and governed by the Florida Citrus Commission, a body of 12 citrus industry members appointed by the governor to staggered 3-year terms. Administers the citrus laws of the state; has regulatory authority over the packing, processing, labeling, and handling of citrus fruits and products. Conducts advertising and merchandising activities, and product marketing, scientific, and economic research. Investigates areas of flavor control, juice yield, mechanical harvesting, shipping, and production. Compiles statistics. Develops processes used by the industry for producing frozen concentrated orange juice. Operates through the finances provided by an excise tax in Florida on each box of fruit moved in commercial channels. **Also Known As:** Florida Citrus Commission. **Publications:** Annual Report, annual ● Booklets ● Brochures ● Reports ● Also publishes recipe booklets and menu cards.

4730 ■ Florida Fruit and Vegetable Association (FFVA)
PO Box 948153
Maitland, FL 32794-8153
Ph: (321)214-5200
Fax: (321)214-0210
E-mail: information@ffva.com
URL: http://www.ffva.com
Contact: Mike Stuart, Pres.
Founded: 1943. **Members:** 4,500. **Membership Dues:** producer, $250 (annual). **Staff:** 45. **Description:** Growers and shippers of Florida vegetables, sugar cane, citrus, and tropical fruits. **Libraries:** **Type:** open to the public; reference. **Committees:** Political Action. **Divisions:** Communications and Education; Environmental and Pest Management; Labor Relations. **Publications:** *Harvester*, monthly. Magazine ● *Rap-Up*, weekly. Newsletter ● Directory, annual ● Bulletin, periodic. **Conventions/Meetings:** annual conference - usually September.

4731 ■ Florida Gift Fruit Shippers Association (FGFSA)
5500 W Concord Ave.
Orlando, FL 32808
Ph: (407)295-1491
Free: (800)741-1491
Fax: (407)290-0918
E-mail: donnag@fgfsa.com
URL: http://www.fgfsa.com
Contact: Ms. Donna Garren, Exec. VP
Founded: 1946. **Members:** 65. **Staff:** 7. **Languages:** English, Spanish. **For-Profit. Description:** Firms packing and shipping gift fruit packages. **Committees:** Citrus Liaison; Marketing; Transportation. **Formerly:** Florida Express Fruit Shippers Association. **Publications:** *Orange Peel*, periodic. Bulletin. Features information used to direct association shipping program. **Conventions/Meetings:** annual trade show (exhibits) - always August or September.

4732 ■ Florida Lychee Growers Association (FLGA)
Address Unknown since 2007
Founded: 1952. **Members:** 10. **Membership Dues:** growers, $25 (annual). **Staff:** 1. **For-Profit. Description:** Marketing organization of growers of lychee fruit, including longans, mangos, avocadoes, and carambola. **Publications:** none. **Committees:** Research. **Conventions/Meetings:** annual meeting - spring; **Avg. Attendance:** 10.

4733 ■ Florida Tomato Committee
800 Trafalgar Ct., Ste.300
Maitland, FL 32751-7135
Ph: (407)660-1949
Fax: (407)660-1656
E-mail: info@floridatomatoes.org
URL: http://www.floridatomatoes.org
Contact: Samantha Winters, Dir.
Founded: 1974. **Members:** 35. **Staff:** 6. **Description:** Shippers and packagers of fresh Florida tomatoes. Seeks to promote the efficient production, packaging, distribution, and sale of Florida tomatoes. Co-sponsors research projects. **Telecommunication Services:** electronic mail, samantha@floridatomatoes.org. **Formerly:** (2002) Florida Tomato Exchange. **Publications:** News releases. **Conventions/Meetings:** annual meeting.

4734 ■ Home Orchard Society (HOS)
PO Box 230192
Tigard, OR 97281-0192
Ph: (503)293-1468 (503)266-6745
E-mail: membership@homeorchardsociety.org
URL: http://www.homeorchardsociety.org
Contact: Karen Tillou, Contact
Founded: 1975. **Members:** 900. **Membership Dues:** student, senior, $20 (annual) ● family, $25 (annual) ● friend, supporter, $40 (annual) ● life, $375. **Local Groups:** 4. **Description:** Professional and amateur home orchardists and others interested in the grow-

ing of small orchards at home. Promotes the science, culture, and enjoyment of growing fruit-bearing trees, shrubs, vines, and plants in the home landscape. Conducts educational programs on topics such as fruit propagation and disease, identification of fruit, cultural practices, and maintenance procedures. Holds winter care programs, spring scion events, and fall fruit show. Maintains arboretum which assists in the development and maintenance of public arboreta; develops a breeding program for science, perpetuation of historic trees, and preservation of pioneer varieties; collects existing varieties of trees with emphasis on the quality of flavor, texture, aroma, and succession of harvest. Conducts workshop on pruning, grafting, and budding. Plans include: holding public demonstrations, shows, and competitions to encourage amateur pomologists; developing and maintaining a library. **Awards: Type:** scholarship. **Recipient:** to students from Oregon who are interested in the study of horticulture or pomology. **Telecommunication Services:** electronic mail, arboretum@homeorchardsociety.org. **Publications:** *POME News*, quarterly. Journal. **Price:** included in membership dues; $3.00 for nonmembers. **Advertising:** accepted ● *Rootstocks, Basics and More.* **Conventions/Meetings:** annual All About Fruit Show, member grown fruit displays, extensive tasting display (exhibits).

4735 ■ Idaho Potato Commission (IPC)

661 S Rivershore Ln.
Eagle, ID 83616-5396
Ph: (208)334-2350
Fax: (208)334-2274
E-mail: ipc@potato.idaho.gov
URL: http://www.famouspotatoes.org
Contact: Frank W. Muir, Pres./CEO

Founded: 1937. **Staff:** 16. **Budget:** $10,000,000. **Description:** Encompasses a department of the State of Idaho in which commissioners are appointed by the governor. Administers by five commissioners that are active potato growers who represent five growers' organizations; two commissioners are shippers or handlers of Idaho potatoes; and two represent the Idaho potato processors and their associations. Works with the advertising, public relations, and field merchandising of Idaho-grown potatoes. Selects and directs an active research and educational program in cooperation with the University of Idaho extension service and others. Holds the copyrighted "Idaho" and "Grown in Idaho" seal; manages, licenses, and contracts for its use and reproduction in promoting Idaho potato products. **Committees:** Certification, Containers and Identification; Research and Education. **Programs:** Idaho Potato Harvest Festival; Idaho Potato Spud Festival. **Formerly:** Idaho Potato and Onion Commission. **Publications:** *A Way to Fuel Up.* Pamphlet ● *Fresh Shippers and Processors.* Directory ● *Idaho Potato Microwave Cookbook.* **Price:** $1.50 ● *Marketing Edge*, bimonthly. Report.

4736 ■ International Banana Association (IBA)

1901 Pennsylvania Ave. NW, Ste.1100
Washington, DC 20006
Ph: (540)314-3214
E-mail: info@eatmorebananas.com
URL: http://www.eatmorebananas.com
Contact: Tim Debus, VP

Founded: 1982. **Members:** 7. **Staff:** 3. **Description:** Promotes the banana industry throughout North America. **Computer Services:** database, recipes ● information services, banana facts. **Committees:** Finance and Audit; Marketing; Production; Science and Research. **Conventions/Meetings:** quarterly conference.

4737 ■ International Society of Citriculture (ISC)

c/o Dr. Carol Lovatt, Sec.-Treas.
Univ. of California
Dept. of Botany and Plant Sciences
Riverside, CA 92521-0124
Ph: (909)787-4663
Fax: (909)787-4437
E-mail: iscucr@ucr.edu
URL: http://www.lal.ufl.edu/societies/ISC/index.htm
Contact: Dr. Carol Lovatt, Sec.-Treas.

Founded: 1970. **Members:** 1,400. **Membership Dues:** individual, $30 (quadrennial). **Multinational. Description:** Scientists, professors, corporations and citrus growers and processors. Promotes and encourages research and the exchange of scientific information and education in the production, handling and distribution of fresh citrus fruits and products. **Awards:** Honorary Fellow. **Frequency:** periodic. **Type:** recognition ● Honorary Membership. **Frequency:** periodic. **Type:** recognition. **Computer Services:** Mailing lists, of members. **Affiliated With:** Food and Agriculture Organization of the United Nations - Regional Office for Europe. **Publications:** *Conference Proceedings*, periodic. Contains comprehensive collection of research papers on all aspects of citrus production, handling and processing. **Price:** $85.00/set ● Newsletter, annual. Alternate Formats: online ● Also publishes industry-related materials. **Conventions/Meetings:** quadrennial congress (exhibits) - 2008 Oct. 26-31, Wuhan, HU, People's Republic of China.

4738 ■ Leafy Greens Council (LGC)

c/o Ray L. Clark, Exec. Dir.
33 Pheasant Ln.
St. Paul, MN 55127
Ph: (651)484-3321
Fax: (651)484-1098
URL: http://www.leafy-greens.org
Contact: Ray L. Clark, Exec. Dir.

Founded: 1976. **Members:** 100. **Membership Dues:** affiliate, $100 (annual) ● regular (based on annual sales volume), $250-$600 (annual) ● supplier, $600 (annual). **Budget:** $40,000. **Description:** Growers, shippers, packers, and terminal agents. Promotes greater consumption of cabbage, celery, escarole, kale, leaf lettuce, parsley, romaine, spinach, Swiss chard, and greens. Provides a forum for discussion of common industry problems. Compiles marketing and serving suggestions for products. **Affiliated With:** United Fresh Produce Association. **Formerly:** (1976) National Spinach Association. **Conventions/Meetings:** annual meeting, held in conjunction with United Fresh Fruit and Vegetable Association - always February.

4739 ■ Michigan Apple Committee (MAC)

13105 Schavey Rd., Ste.2
DeWitt, MI 48820
Ph: (517)669-8353
Free: (800)456-2753
Fax: (517)669-9506
E-mail: staff@michiganapples.com
URL: http://www.michiganapples.com
Contact: Denise Yockey, Exec. Dir.

Founded: 1965. **Members:** 1,500. **Staff:** 6. **Description:** Marketing commodity association for Michigan apples and apple products. Offers seminars; sponsors competitions; compiles statistics. Conducts research programs. **Publications:** *Directory of Apple Fresh and Processed*, periodic ● *Michigan Apple News*, bimonthly. Newsletter. Includes marketing updates, public relations activities, and research updates. **Circulation:** 1,900 ● Also publishes point-of-sale materials and recipes.

4740 ■ Michigan Association of Cherry Producers (MACP)

c/o Cherry Marketing Institute
PO Box 30285
Lansing, MI 48909-7785
Ph: (517)669-4264
Fax: (517)669-3354
E-mail: info@usacherries.com
Contact: Philip J. Korson II, Pres./Managing Dir./Exec. Dir.

Founded: 1938. **Members:** 2,000. **Staff:** 5. **Description:** Carries out educational and promotional work for Michigan tart and sweet cherry growers. **Conventions/Meetings:** annual meeting - always late December.

4741 ■ National Cherry Growers and Industries Foundation (NCGIF)

2667 Reed Rd.
Hood River, OR 97031
Ph: (541)386-5761
Fax: (541)386-3191
URL: http://www.nationalcherries.com
Contact: Dana Branson, Admin.

Founded: 1954. **Staff:** 2. **Description:** Represents growers and processors of brine, canned and frozen cherries. Promotes the cherry industry through research, advertising, and recipes, marketing and product development. Provides recipes, point-of-sale materials, and special promotional assistance. **Formerly:** Cherry Growers and Industries Foundation. **Publications:** *Annual Statistical Summary*, annual. **Price:** free. **Conventions/Meetings:** annual meeting - always November.

4742 ■ National Mushroom Growers' Association (MGA)

c/o Mushroom Information Center
35 E 21st St.
New York, NY 10010
E-mail: l-n@mushroominfo.com

Founded: 1934. **Members:** 14. **Languages:** English, Spanish. **For-Profit. Description:** Represents wholesalers of fresh fruits and vegetables. Address mail c/o *Encyclopedia of Associations.* **Formerly:** (2003) Mushroom Growers Association.

4743 ■ National Onion Association (NOA)

822 7th St., Ste.510
Greeley, CO 80631-3941
Ph: (970)353-5895
Fax: (970)353-5897
URL: http://www.onions-usa.org
Contact: Darrell Duda, Pres.

Founded: 1913. **Members:** 675. **Membership Dues:** allied, $360 (annual) ● commercial, $630 (annual) ● associate, $150 (annual). **Staff:** 3. **Budget:** $400,000. **Description:** Growers, brokers, grower-shippers, shippers, suppliers, and support professionals engaged in the onion industry. Promotes the onion industry. Compiles monthly statistical report of stocks-on-hand, acreage, yield, and production of onions in the U.S. Lobbies issues of importance to national onion industry. **Computer Services:** database ● mailing lists. **Committees:** Environmental; Industry/Export; Legislative; Meetings; Promotion. **Programs:** Consumer education; Foodservice education; Nutrition. **Formerly:** National Statistical Onion Association. **Publications:** *Legislative Onion Outlook*, annual. Bulletin. Covers current industry-related legislation. **Circulation:** 625 ● *National Onion Association—Newsletter*, monthly. Provides information on the onion industry. **Price:** free for members. **Circulation:** 625. **Advertising:** accepted ● *National Onion Association—Statistical Report*, 8/year. Reports on onion stocks on hand and crop conditions in the U.S., Canada, and Mexico. **Circulation:** 625 ● Membership Directory, annual. **Price:** included in membership dues. **Advertising:** accepted. **Conventions/Meetings:** annual convention - usually first week of December ● annual convention and regional meeting - usually summer.

4744 ■ National Peach Council (NPC)

12 Nicklaus Ln., Ste.101
Columbia, SC 29229
Ph: (803)788-7101
Fax: (803)865-8090
E-mail: peachcouncil@att.net
URL: http://www.nationalpeach.org
Contact: Charles Walker, Managing Dir.

Founded: 1941. **Members:** 400. **Staff:** 1. **Budget:** $27,000. **Description:** Represents peach growers, allied industries, and research and extension personnel. Lobbies the U.S. Congress on behalf of fresh market peach growers, compiles and publishes statistics on the peach industry and prepares annual preseason crop estimates. **Awards:** Achievement Award. **Frequency:** annual. **Type:** recognition ● Carroll R. Miller Award. **Type:** recognition. **Committees:** Awards; Marketing; Promotions; Research. **Publications:** *Peach Statistical Yearbook*, annual ● *Peach*

Times, quarterly. Newsletter. **Price:** $40.00/year. **Circulation:** 2,175. **Advertising:** accepted. Alternate Formats: CD-ROM; online. **Conventions/Meetings:** annual meeting (exhibits) - usually January.

4745 ■ National Peach Partners (NPP)
c/o Maple Lawn Farms
251 E Maple Lawn Rd.
New Park, PA 17352
Ph: (717)382-4878
Fax: (717)382-4879
E-mail: gailmc@maplelawnfarms.com
URL: http://www.maplelawnfarms.com
Contact: Gail S. McPherson, Ed.
Founded: 1977. **Members:** 50. **Membership Dues:** active, $20 (annual). **Staff:** 1. **Description:** Women who work, or whose spouses work, in the peach industry; women who wish to promote the industry. Raises funds for the National Peach Council (see separate entry) through the sale of peach-related items and products. **Publications:** *Peach Connection*, semiannual. Newsletter. **Conventions/Meetings:** annual conference (exhibits).

4746 ■ National Potato Council (NPC)
1300 L St. NW, No. 910
Washington, DC 20005-4107
Ph: (202)682-9456
Fax: (202)682-0333
E-mail: spudinfo@nationalpotatocouncil.org
URL: http://www.nationalpotatocouncil.org
Contact: Don Sklarczyk, Pres.
Founded: 1948. **Members:** 10,500. **Membership Dues:** silver (grower, local business), $50 (annual) ● gold, platinum (producer, local business), $100-$200 (annual) ● sustaining (regional, national business), $2,500 (annual). **Staff:** 4. **Budget:** $600,000. **Description:** Commercial potato growers. Takes action on national potato legislative, regulatory, and environmental issues. **Committees:** Environmental Affairs; Grower/Public Relations; Legislative/Government Affairs; Trade Affairs. **Publications:** *NPC Insider Report*, weekly. Newsletter. Provides updates on legislative and regulatory industry issues and related topics, including a schedule of industry events and activities. **Price:** included in membership dues. Alternate Formats: online ● *Potato Statistical Yearbook*, annual. Contains data on potato production, marketing, consumption, trade, prices and margins, average prices, and consumer and shipping point prices. **Price:** free for members; $25.00 for nonmembers. **Circulation:** 11,000. **Advertising:** accepted ● *Spudletter*, bimonthly. Newsletter. Provides information on current legislative, regulatory, and environmental issues affecting the potato grower. Also includes membership news. **Price:** free for members. **Circulation:** 11,000. Also Cited As: *National Potato Council—Action Report*. **Conventions/Meetings:** annual convention (exhibits) ● annual meeting.

4747 ■ National Watermelon Association (NWA)
c/o Bob Morrissey, Exec. Dir.
1305 W Martin Luther King, Jr. Blvd., Ste.1
Plant City, FL 33563
Ph: (813)754-7575
Fax: (813)754-1118
E-mail: bmorrissey@tampabay.rr.com
URL: http://www.nationalwatermelonassociation.com
Contact: Bradley O'Neal, Pres.
Founded: 1914. **Members:** 700. **Membership Dues:** individual, $100 (annual). **Staff:** 3. **Budget:** $500,000. **State Groups:** 11. **Description:** Individuals involved in the production, marketing, and sales of watermelon. Maintains files of clippings and business records. Maintains speakers' bureau and conducts educational programs. **Awards:** National Watermelon Queen. **Frequency:** annual. **Type:** scholarship. **Recipient:** for member of chapter ● **Frequency:** annual. **Type:** recognition. **Recipient:** for marketing and service excellence. **Telecommunication Services:** electronic mail, eleanor@websign.net. **Committees:** Grades and Standards; Public Affairs; Research, Marketing and Promotion; Transportation; Young Spokesperson. **Publications:** *Annual Convention Proceedings*, annual ● *The Vineline*, bimonthly. Bulletin. **Price:** included in membership dues. **Advertising:** accepted. **Conventions/Meetings:** annual National Watermelon Convention - meeting, with tabletop exhibits (exhibits) - always February.

4748 ■ New Jersey Asparagus Industry Council (NJAIC)
PO Box 330
Trenton, NJ 08625-0330
Ph: (609)292-8853 (609)292-3976
Fax: (609)292-3978
E-mail: charles.kuperus@ag.state.nj.us
Contact: Charles M. Kuperus, Sec.
Founded: 1959. **Members:** 10. **Staff:** 1. **Description:** Persons concerned with the growing and marketing of asparagus in the state of New Jersey, appointed by the New Jersey State Board of Agriculture. Seeks to foster and promote better methods of producing, merchandising, and advertising New Jersey asparagus (financed by an excise tax on the sale of asparagus produced in New Jersey).

4749 ■ North American Blueberry Council (NABC)
PO Box 1036
Folsom, CA 95763
Ph: (916)983-2279
Fax: (916)983-9370
E-mail: info@nabcblues.org
URL: http://www.nabcblues.org
Contact: Mark Villata, Exec. Dir.
Founded: 1965. **Members:** 45. **Staff:** 2. **Description:** Represents blueberry growers and marketers in the U.S. and Canada. Acts as clearinghouse for research and development activities in blueberry production and aims to provide a central publicity and promotion agency for all production areas. Provides information; compiles statistics. **Publications:** *The Calyx*, annual. Newsletter. Promotes the blueberry industry. **Price:** available to members only ● Directory, annual. **Price:** available to members only. **Conventions/Meetings:** annual general assembly.

4750 ■ North American Strawberry Growers Association (NASGA)
c/o Steve Polter, Pres.
Polter Berry Farm Inc.
2275 CR 239
Fremont, OH 43420
Ph: (419)332-5890 (419)332-8217
Fax: (419)332-8217
E-mail: steve@poltersberryfarm.com
URL: http://www.nasga.org
Contact: Steve Polter, Pres.
Founded: 1978. **Members:** 400. **Membership Dues:** business in U.S., Canada, and Mexico, $85 (annual) ● business outside U.S. and Canada, $95 (annual) ● individual in U.S., Canada, and Mexico, $55 (annual) ● individual outside U.S. and Canada, $65 (annual). **Staff:** 2. **Description:** Strawberry growers, nurserymen, and professional researchers. Works to develop strawberry production and marketing; collects and disseminates information to members. Conducts research in the industry on areas such as: alternate markets for strawberries; breeding disease and insect resistant varieties; improved renovation methods; integrated pest management techniques. Organizes joint action on behalf of members on important legislative issues. **Committees:** Legislative; Marketing; Research. **Publications:** *Advances in Strawberry Production*, annual. Journal. Contains research programs report. **Price:** included in membership dues. **Circulation:** 350 ● Newsletter, periodic. Provides current industry news. **Price:** included in membership dues; $55.00 /year for nonmembers. **Advertising:** accepted ● Proceedings, annual. Includes transcripts of annual meeting speeches, announcements, and reports. **Price:** included in membership dues. **Conventions/Meetings:** annual conference (exhibits) - always early February ● annual convention and meeting, 4-day educational meeting (exhibits) ● workshop.

4751 ■ Northwest Cherry Growers (NWCG)
105 S 18th St., Ste.205
Yakima, WA 98901-2149
Ph: (509)453-4837
URL: http://www.nwcherries.com
Contact: B.J. Thurlby, Pres.
Founded: 1947. **Staff:** 10. **Description:** Works to promote fresh sweet cherries from Washington, Oregon, Idaho and Utah. **Libraries: Type:** reference. **Holdings:** archival material. **Subjects:** fresh cherry production and promotion. **Conventions/Meetings:** annual Cherry Institute - regional meeting and workshop - always January.

4752 ■ Northwest Fruit Exporters (NFE)
105 S 18th St., Ste.227
Yakima, WA 98901
Ph: (509)576-8004
Fax: (509)576-3646
E-mail: nfe@goodfruit.com
Contact: James Archer, Mgr.
Founded: 1976. **Members:** 98. **Membership Dues:** cherry exporter, $1,500 (annual) ● apple exporter, $1,000 (annual). **Staff:** 5. **Budget:** $1,000,000. **Description:** Growers and exporters of fresh sweet cherries and apples in the Pacific Northwest. Seeks to overcome Japanese trade barriers that block the importation of foreign agricultural products. Conducts promotional activities. **Publications:** none. **Committees:** Apple Commodity; Cherry Commodity. **Conventions/Meetings:** semiannual board meeting - January and August.

4753 ■ Northwest Horticultural Council (NHC)
105 S 18th St., Ste.105
Yakima, WA 98901
Ph: (509)453-3193
Fax: (509)457-7615
E-mail: general@nwhort.org
URL: http://www.nwhort.org
Contact: Christian Schlect, Pres.
Founded: 1947. **Members:** 8. **Staff:** 6. **Description:** Coordinates federal and international policies of Washington, Oregon, and Idaho tree fruit industries. **Publications:** *NHC News*, monthly. Bulletin.

4754 ■ Paw Paw Foundation (PPF)
c/o Paw Paw Research
129 Atwood Res. Fac.
Kentucky State Univ.
Frankfort, KY 40601-2355
Ph: (502)597-6174 (502)597-5942
Fax: (502)597-6381
E-mail: kpomper@dcr.net
URL: http://www.pawpaw.kysu.edu
Contact: Kirk W. Pomper PhD, Pres.
Founded: 1988. **Members:** 350. **Membership Dues:** general, $20 (annual). **Budget:** $7,000. **Description:** Horticulturists with an interest in the paw paw, the largest fruit indigenous to North America. Promotes commercial farming and sale of paw paws; seeks to improve paw paw strains. Conducts research in areas including paw paw breeding, horticulture, harvesting, and commercial use. Collects and evaluates paw paw germplasm; provides technical assistance to horticulturists working with paw paws; disseminates quality paw paw samples for use by chefs and scientists and in consumer trials and market research. **Publications:** *From the Pawpaw Patch*, semiannual. Newsletter. Provides citation and summary of professional journal articles as well as observations and experimental results contributed by readers. **Price:** free for members ● Membership Directory, periodic. Contains a list of PawPaw Foundation members. **Price:** available to members only; $5.00 for additional copies ● Brochure. Contains a brief history and description of pawpaws, purpose and activities of the PawPaw Foundation, mailing address and membership form.

4755 ■ Pear Bureau Northwest
4382 SE Intl. Way, Ste.A
Milwaukie, OR 97222-4635
Ph: (503)652-9720
Fax: (503)652-9721

E-mail: info@usapears.com
URL: http://www.usapears.com
Contact: Cristie Mather, Communications Mgr.
Founded: 1931. **Description:** Promotes pears grown in the Northwest; provides materials for uses and recipes for pears; provides information to consumers, educators, health professionals and food industry members. **Telecommunication Services:** electronic mail, lwieking@usapears.com. **Publications:** Newsletter, periodic. Features recipes, special offers, and seasonal tips. Alternate Formats: online ● Reports.

4756 ■ Pineapple Growers Association of Hawaii (PGAH)
Address Unknown since 2007
Founded: 1943. **Members:** 3. **Staff:** 1. **Description:** Growers and canners of pineapple in Hawaii. Promotes sale of fresh and canned pineapple products. **Convention/Meeting:** none. **Supersedes:** Pineapple Producers Cooperative Association.

4757 ■ Potato Association of America (PAA)
Univ. of Maine
5715 Coburn Hall, Rm. 6
Orono, ME 04469-5715
Ph: (207)581-3042
Fax: (207)581-3015
E-mail: umpotato@maine.edu
URL: http://www.umaine.edu/paa
Contact: Sam Thornton, Pres.
Founded: 1913. **Members:** 1,000. **Membership Dues:** graduate student, $20 (annual) ● individual, organization, $100 (annual) ● sustaining, $500 (annual). **Staff:** 5. **Budget:** $87,000. **Description:** Represents breeders, entomologists, horticulturists, plant pathologists, soil and fertilizer specialists, food technologists, producers, and handlers. **Awards:** Honorary Life Membership. **Frequency:** annual. **Type:** recognition. **Recipient:** for individuals who have made outstanding contributions to the potato industry. **Committees:** Editorial; Graduate Student Awards; Honorary Life Member; International Relations; Local Arrangements. **Sections:** Breeding and Genetics; Extension; Pathology and Entomology; Physiology; Production and Management; Seed Certification; Utilization. **Publications:** *American Journal of Potato Research*, bimonthly. **Price:** included in membership dues. ISSN: 1099-209X ● *PAA Insider*, quarterly. Newsletter. **Price:** included in membership dues; $5.00 for nonmembers, plus shipping and handling ● Directory. **Price:** included in membership dues; $5.00 for nonmembers, plus shipping and handling. **Conventions/Meetings:** annual conference - usually July.

4758 ■ Raisin Administrative Committee (RAC)
PO Box 5217
Fresno, CA 93755
Ph: (559)225-0520
Fax: (559)225-0652
E-mail: info@raisins.org
URL: http://www.raisins.org
Contact: Ron Worthley, Pres./Gen. Mgr.
Founded: 1949. **Members:** 47. **Staff:** 16. **Description:** Represents producers of grapes that are processed as raisins and processors of raisins. Establishes minimum quality standards; develops and releases industry statistics; works to improve market discipline. **Publications:** Brochures. Alternate Formats: online.

4759 ■ Raisin Bargaining Association (RBA)
1300 E Shaw Ave., Ste.175
Fresno, CA 93710-7911
Ph: (559)221-1925
Fax: (559)221-0725
E-mail: raisinbargaining@sbcglobal.net
URL: http://www.raisinbargaining.com
Contact: Glen S. Goto, CEO
Founded: 1966. **Members:** 2,000. **Staff:** 4. **Description:** Represents raisin growers. Acts as bargaining agency between members and raisin packers and processors. **Publications:** *RBA Newsletter*, monthly. **Circulation:** 2,000. Alternate Formats: online. **Conventions/Meetings:** annual luncheon (exhibits).

4760 ■ Rare Fruit Council International (RFCI)
PO Box 660506
Miami Springs, FL 33266
Ph: (305)554-1333
E-mail: imaguire@ufl.edu
URL: http://www.tropicalfruitnews.org
Contact: Maurice Kong, Contact
Founded: 1955. **Members:** 1,000. **Membership Dues:** domestic, $40 (annual) ● supporting, $100 (annual) ● family, overseas, $50 (annual). **Staff:** 5. **Budget:** $35,000. **State Groups:** 7. **Description:** Individuals in 34 countries interested in propagating and raising tropical fruit plants. Promotes tropical pomology in suitable areas of the world and informs the public of the merits of tropical fruit. Introduces and distributes new species, improved varieties, mutations, and clones of fruit plants. Conducts research and educational programs. **Libraries: Type:** reference. **Holdings:** 200; books, periodicals. **Subjects:** tropical plants, fruit. **Committees:** Fruit Display; Fruit Recipes; Horticultural Education; Plant Exchange; Plant Importation; Plant Names; Plant Sale; Research; Seed Exchange. **Formerly:** (1980) Rare Fruit Council. **Publications:** *Tropical Fruit News*, bimonthly. Magazine. Provides information on fruit enthusiast organizations, current topics of interest to tropical fruit growers, and articles about fruit. **Price:** included in membership dues. ISSN: 1075-6108. **Circulation:** 1,000. **Advertising:** accepted. **Conventions/Meetings:** monthly general assembly and lecture, includes slides and discussion panels (exhibits) - always second Wednesday, Miami, FL.

4761 ■ Specialty Crop Trade Council (SCTC)
710 Striker Ave.
Sacramento, CA 95834
Ph: (916)561-5900
Fax: (916)561-5906
E-mail: richn@dfaofca.com
URL: http://www.cdfea.org
Contact: Richard W. Novy, Pres./CEO
Founded: 1925. **Members:** 37. **Description:** Represents firms that are engaged in the export of California dried fruit and tree nuts. **Formerly:** (2006) California Dried Fruit Export Association. **Conventions/Meetings:** annual meeting.

4762 ■ Sun-Maid Growers of California (SMGC)
13525 S Bethel Ave.
Kingsburg, CA 93631
Ph: (559)896-8000
Fax: (559)897-6348
E-mail: info@sunmaid.com
URL: http://www.sun-maid.com
Contact: Barry Kriebel, Pres.
Founded: 1912. **Members:** 1,100. **Staff:** 200. **Description:** Agricultural processing and marketing cooperative. Processes and markets all types and varieties of raisins in bulk and consumer packages, raisin bread, dried fruits, (apples, apricots, cranberries, dates, figs, peaches, pears, prunes, and mixtures of dried fruits), and beverage alcohol. **Conventions/Meetings:** annual meeting - always December in Fresno, CA.

4763 ■ Sunkist Growers (SG)
PO Box 7888
Van Nuys, CA 91409-7888
Ph: (818)986-4800
E-mail: info@sunkistgrowers.com
URL: http://www.sunkist.com
Contact: T.J. Lindgren, Pres.
Founded: 1893. **Members:** 6,500. **Staff:** 1,500. **Description:** Serves as a citrus fruit marketing cooperative. **Awards:** A.W. Bodine-Sunkist Memorial Scholarship. **Frequency:** annual. **Type:** monetary. **Recipient:** for undergraduate students with agricultural backgrounds who are in need of financial assistance. **Formerly:** California Fruit Growers Exchange. **Conventions/Meetings:** annual meeting - always January or February.

4764 ■ Sunsweet Growers (SG)
901 N Walton Ave.
Yuba City, CA 95993
Ph: (530)674-5010
Free: (800)417-2253
Fax: (530)751-5395
E-mail: sunsweet@casupport.com
URL: http://www.sunsweet.com
Contact: Gary Thiara, Chm.
Founded: 1917. **Members:** 400. **Description:** Works as handler of dried tree fruits including cranberries, apricots and prunes. Is a grower-owned marketing cooperative representing more than two-thirds of the prune market worldwide, processes more than 50,000 tons of prunes a year. Produces and markets the dried fruit production of more than 400 grower-members with orchard holdings primarily in California's Sacramento and San Joaquin valleys. Boasts an enviable brand recognition of 85 percent in American households, placing it in the very top rank of long-standing successful American products. **Additional Websites:** http://www.plumsmart.net. **Conventions/Meetings:** annual meeting.

4765 ■ Tomato Genetics Cooperative (TGC)
c/o J.W. Scott, PhD, Managing Ed.
Univ. of Florida
Gulf Coast Res. and Educ. Center
14625 County Rd. 672
Wimauma, FL 33598-6101
Ph: (813)634-0000
Fax: (813)634-0001
E-mail: jwsc@ifas.ufl.edu
URL: http://tgc.ifas.ufl.edu
Contact: J.W. Scott PhD, Managing Ed.
Founded: 1950. **Members:** 250. **Membership Dues:** regular in U.S., $20 (annual) ● regular outside U.S., $25 (annual). **Multinational. Description:** Represents research geneticists, plant breeders, and individuals interested in tomato genetics and the exchange of research information and stocks. **Libraries: Type:** open to the public. **Holdings:** 55. **Computer Services:** Mailing lists. **Publications:** *Report of the Tomato Genetics Cooperative*, annual. Journal. **Conventions/Meetings:** annual meeting.

4766 ■ United Fresh Produce Association
1901 Pennsylvania Ave. NW, Ste.1100
Washington, DC 20006
Ph: (202)303-3400 (202)303-3404
Fax: (202)303-3433
E-mail: united@unitedfresh.org
URL: http://www.unitedfresh.org
Contact: Thomas E. Stenzel, Pres./CEO
Founded: 1904. **Members:** 1,000. **Membership Dues:** regular (minimum), $755 (annual) ● regular (maximum), $20,915 (annual) ● customer (based on the number of stores/units), $695-$1,295 (annual) ● associate, $1,295-$2,375 (annual) ● allied (based on annual budget), $475-$6,995 (annual) ● university, government, $250 (annual). **Staff:** 19. **Budget:** $4,600,000. **Regional Groups:** 9. **Languages:** English, Spanish. **Description:** Promotes the growth and success of produce companies and their partners. Represents interests of growers, shippers, processors, brokers, wholesalers and distributors of produce, working together with their customers at retail and food service, suppliers at every step in the distribution chain, and international partners. Provides leadership to shape business, trade and public policies that drive the industry. Works with thousands of industry members, provides fair and balanced forum to promote business solutions; helps build strong partnerships among all segments of the industry, promotes increased produce consumption; provides scientific and technical expertise essential to competing effectively in today's marketplace. **Telecommunication Services:** electronic mail, joberman@unitedfresh.org. **Committees:** Fresh PAC; Political Action; Produce Microbiology; Science and Technology. **Divisions:** Brokers; Distribution; Food Service; Grower/Shipper; International Trade; Processing; Retail; Wholesale. **Absorbed:** (1952) National League of Wholesale Fresh Fruit and Vegetable Distributors. **Formed by Merger of:** (1937) Western Fruit Jobbers Association; (2006) United Fresh Fruit

and Vegetable Association and International Fresh-Cut Produce Association; American Fruit and Vegetable Shippers Association. **Publications:** *A User's Guide to the New PACA*. Booklet. Provides a complete overview and clear explanation of how to operate legally under the Perishable Agricultural Commodities Act. **Price:** $175.00 for members; $350.00 for nonmembers ● Also publishes guides for food safety and other quality measures associated with fresh produce production. **Conventions/Meetings:** annual United Produce Expo and Conference (exhibits) ● annual Washington Public Policy Conference - meeting.

4767 ■ United Soybean Board (USB)
16640 Chesterfield Grove Rd., Ste.130
Chesterfield, MO 63005
Ph: (636)530-1777
Free: (800)989-8721
Fax: (636)530-1560
E-mail: ydock@unitedsoybean.com
URL: http://www.unitedsoybean.org
Contact: Yvonne Dock, Exec. Dir.
Founded: 1990. **Members:** 61. **Description:** Volunteer soybean farmers. Supports growers and processors of soybeans; seeks to advance soybean marketing and research. Conducts educational programs to raise awareness of the nutritional value of soybeans among health care and foodservice providers, food manufacturers, and the public. Sponsors research; addresses scientific issues affecting soybean growers and processors. **Committees:** Audit and Evaluation; Competitiveness; Domestic Marketing; International Marketing; New Uses; Production. **Publications:** *Biobased Solutions*, monthly. Newsletter. Discusses new soybean uses, from products to research, for industry stakeholders. Also Cited As: *Feedstocks* ● *Checkoff Chronicles*, annual. Newsletter. Alternate Formats: online. Also Cited As: *Soysource Newsletter* ● *Production Quarterly*. Newsletter. Examines progress being made to keep U.S. soybean farmers competitive and U.S. soybean production efficient through checkoff-funded research. ● *SoyLine*, monthly. Newsletter. Focuses on soybean checkoff accomplishments and activities. Alternate Formats: online ● Annual Report, annual ● Brochure. Alternate Formats: online.

4768 ■ U.S. Apple Association
8233 Old Courthouse Rd., Ste.200
Vienna, VA 22182
Ph: (703)442-8850
Fax: (703)790-0845
E-mail: shaaga@usapple.org
URL: http://www.usapple.org
Contact: Stacie Haaga, Membership/Communications Mgr.
Founded: 1970. **Members:** 400. **Membership Dues:** regular in U.S. (based on volume of apples sold annually), $100-$2,000 (annual) ● regular outside U.S., $1,000 (annual) ● professional, local associate, $100 (annual) ● national associate, allied industry association, $500 (annual). **Staff:** 8. **Description:** Represents all segments of the apple industry; over 400 individual firms involved in the apple business, as well as 40 state and regional apple associations representing over 9000 apple growers throughout the country. Seeks to provide the means for all segments of the apple industry to join in appropriate collective efforts to profitably produce and market apples and apple products. Unifies a diverse industry to achieve three primary goals: to represent the entire industry on national issues; to increase demand for apples and apple products; and to provide information on matters pertaining to the apple industry. **Computer Services:** Information services, consumer resources. **Committees:** Industry Information; Membership Services; National Apple Month; Public Affairs; Public Relations. **Councils:** U.S. Apple Export. **Formed by Merger of:** International Apple Association; National Apple Institute. **Formerly:** (1996) International Apple Institute. **Publications:** *An Apple A Day*, quarterly. Newsletter. Alternate Formats: online ● *Apple News*, monthly. Newsletter. Reports national and international events; includes statistics and article title index in each issue. **Price:** free for members. **Circulation:** 2,000. Alternate Formats: online ● *Market News*, 10/year. Reports. Alternate Formats: online. **Conventions/Meetings:** annual U.S. Apple Crop Outlook and Marketing - conference - mid-August.

4769 ■ United States Dry Bean Council (USDBC)
PO Box 550
Grapeview, WA 98546
Ph: (360)277-0112
Fax: (360)233-0621
E-mail: info@usdrybeans.com
URL: http://www.usdrybeans.com
Contact: Randy Duckworth, Exec. Dir.
Founded: 1950. **Members:** 13. **Staff:** 5. **Regional Groups:** 13. **Description:** Promotes the interests of dry bean producers and workers. **Formerly:** (2005) National Dry Bean Council. **Conventions/Meetings:** semiannual board meeting - always in Washington, DC.

4770 ■ United States Potato Board (USPB)
7555 E Hampden Ave., Ste.412
Denver, CO 80231-4835
Ph: (303)369-7783 (303)873-2320
Fax: (303)369-7718
E-mail: info@uspotatoes.com
URL: http://www.healthypotato.com
Contact: Tim O'Connor, Pres./CEO
Founded: 1971. **Members:** 6,200. **Staff:** 17. **Budget:** $8,500,000. **Description:** Growers of five or more acres of potatoes. Provides a way to organize and finance a national promotion program for potatoes, to increase consumption, expand markets, and make the growing and marketing of potatoes a better business for all; carries out effective and continuous coordinated marketing research, retail marketing, consumer advertising, public relations, and export programs. **Computer Services:** database ● mailing lists. **Additional Websites:** http://www.uspotatoes.com. **Telecommunication Services:** electronic mail, toconnor@uspotatoes.com. **Committees:** Domestic Marketing; Finance; Grower Relations; International Marketing; Policy and Management; Research and Evaluation. **Also Known As:** The Potato Board. **Formerly:** The National Potato Board; (2002) National Potato Promotion Board. **Publications:** *Tuber News*, bimonthly. Newsletter. Contains industry reports on program activities. **Price:** free. **Circulation:** 17,000 ● Brochures. **Conventions/Meetings:** annual board meeting - always in Denver, CO.

4771 ■ United States Sweet Potato Council
12 Nicklaus Ln., Ste.101
Columbia, SC 29229-3363
Ph: (803)788-7101
Fax: (803)865-8090
E-mail: sweetpotatousa@att.net
URL: http://www.sweetpotatousa.org
Contact: Mr. Charles Walker, Exec. Sec.
Founded: 1962. **Members:** 1,000. **Staff:** 1. **Budget:** $22,500. **State Groups:** 6. **Description:** Sweet potato producers, packers, processors, equipment manufacturers and suppliers; research and educational personnel. Conducts educational programs, promotes the industry, represents the industry on national issues affecting it, provides information and statistics. **Awards:** Distinguished Service Awards. **Type:** recognition. **Publications:** *Cooking with Sweet Potatoes*. Booklet. Contains recipes. ● *National Sweet Potato Newsletter*, semiannual. Alternate Formats: online ● *Sweet Potatoes Statistical*, annual. Yearbook. **Price:** $25.00 in U.S.; $30.00 outside U.S. **Conventions/Meetings:** annual meeting (exhibits) - always the last weekend in January.

4772 ■ Valley Fig Growers (VFG)
2028 S 3rd St.
Fresno, CA 93702
Ph: (559)237-3893
Fax: (559)237-3898
E-mail: info@valleyfig.com
URL: http://www.valleyfig.com
Contact: James Gargiulo, Sec.-Treas./VP of Finance
Founded: 1959. **Members:** 30. **Staff:** 90. **Description:** Growers of dried fruit. Processes and packages dried fruit; jointly markets and distributes commodities with Sun-Diamond Growers of California, Sun-Maid Growers of California, Sunsweet Growers, and Diamond Walnut Growers.

4773 ■ Washington State Apple Commission (WSAC)
PO Box 18
Wenatchee, WA 98807-0018
Ph: (509)663-9600
Fax: (509)662-5824
E-mail: info@waapple.org
URL: http://www.bestapples.com
Contact: Don Zones, Operations Mgr.
Founded: 1937. **Members:** 4,500. **Staff:** 48. **Description:** Represents apple growers in the state of Washington united for advertising, promotion, and publicity of Washington apples. **Libraries: Type:** reference. **Conventions/Meetings:** annual meeting - always third Wednesday of March in Yakima or Wenatchee, WA.

4774 ■ Western Growers Association (WGA)
PO Box 2130
Newport Beach, CA 92658
Ph: (949)863-1000 (949)885-2257
Free: (800)333-4942
Fax: (949)863-9028
E-mail: info@wga.com
URL: http://www.wga.com
Contact: Thomas A. Nassif, Pres./CEO
Founded: 1926. **Members:** 3,500. **Membership Dues:** regular, associate, $400 (annual). **Staff:** 283. **Regional Groups:** 12. **Description:** California and Arizona growers, shippers, and packers of fresh produce; brokers, distributors, jobbers, and members of allied industries. Represents members' concerns in areas including transportation; legislation; standardization; labor relations; marketing services; public relations; legal services; insurance compensation. **Telecommunication Services:** additional toll-free number, (800)777-7898. **Committees:** International Trade; Labor; Legislative; Marketing and Transportation; Public Relations; Water, Energy, and Topics. **Formerly:** (1942) Western Growers Protective Association. **Publications:** *Export Directory*, annual. Lists grower-shippers who are engaged in export business. ● *Update*, semimonthly. Newsletter ● *Western Grower and Shipper*, monthly. Magazine. **Price:** $18.00 in U.S.; $36.00 outside U.S. **Advertising:** accepted ● Directory, annual. **Conventions/Meetings:** annual meeting and workshop.

4775 ■ Wild Blueberry Association of North America (WBANA)
PO Box 100
Old Town, ME 04468
Ph: (207)570-3535
Fax: (207)581-3499
E-mail: wildblueberries@gwi.net
URL: http://www.wildblueberries.com
Founded: 1981. **Members:** 50. **Budget:** $800,000. **Description:** Companies and individuals involved in growing and processing wild blueberries. Seeks to promote the use of wild blueberries throughout North America and overseas. **Committees:** Canadian Promotion; Communications; Food Safety; Fresh Pack; Overseas Promotion; Research and Development; Strategic Planning; U.S. Promotion. **Publications:** *Wild Blueberry Newsletter*, quarterly. Includes association, industry, and activities information. **Circulation:** 3,000 ● Brochures. **Conventions/Meetings:** annual meeting.

Fuel

4776 ■ National Ethanol Vehicle Coalition (NEVC)
3216 Emerald Ln., Ste.C
Jefferson City, MO 65109
Ph: (573)635-8445
Free: (877)485-8595
Fax: (573)635-5466

E-mail: info@e85fuel.com
URL: http://www.e85fuel.com
Contact: Phillip J. Lampert, Exec. Dir.
Founded: 2000. **Membership Dues:** individual, $50 (annual) ● Clean Cities Coalition, $50 (annual). **Description:** Promotes the use of 85 percent ethanol as a renewable form of alternative transportation fuel. Aims to enhance agricultural profitability, to advance environmental stewardship and to promote national energy independence. **Telecommunication Services:** electronic mail, plampert@e85fuel.com. **Publications:** *FYI*, bimonthly. Newsletter. **Price:** free. Alternate Formats: online.

Gardening

4777 ■ Aquatic Gardeners Association (AGA)
c/o Cheryl Rogers, Membership Coor.
PO Box 51536
Denton, TX 76206-1536
E-mail: membership@aquatic-gardeners.org
URL: http://www.aquatic-gardeners.org
Contact: Larry Lampert, Pres.
Membership Dues: in U.S., Canada, Mexico, $20 (annual) ● in U.S., Canada, Mexico, $38 (biennial) ● in U.S., Canada, Mexico, $54 (triennial) ● other country, airmail, $33 (annual) ● other country, airmail, $63 (biennial) ● other country, airmail, $90 (triennial). **Multinational. Description:** Promotes aquatic plants and planted aquaria, for the beginner to the experienced hobbyist. **Publications:** *The Aquatic Gardener*, bimonthly. Journal. Focuses primarily on the aquatic aquarium plants. **Conventions/Meetings:** Aquascaping Contest - competition, online contest ● annual convention, with speakers, vendors, and field trips (exhibits).

4778 ■ The Gardeners of America/Men's Garden Clubs of America (TGOA/MGCA)
PO Box 241
Johnston, IA 50131-6245
Ph: (515)278-0295
Fax: (515)278-6245
E-mail: tgoasecy@dwx.com
URL: http://www.tgoa-mgca.org
Contact: Steven H. Bush, Treas.
Membership Dues: local, national, $25-$35 (annual). **Staff:** 2. **Budget:** $128,000. **State Groups:** 26. **Local Groups:** 70. **Description:** Promotes gardening education and related environmental issues through charitable, educational and scientific means. **Libraries: Type:** lending. **Holdings:** audio recordings, video recordings. **Subjects:** gardening, horticulture. **Awards: Frequency:** annual. **Type:** scholarship. **Recipient:** to students enrolled in an accredited community college or university. **Telecommunication Services:** electronic mail, bushfinancial@mchsi.com. **Publications:** *American Gardener*, bimonthly. Newsletter. **Price:** included in membership dues ● Newsletter, bimonthly. **Price:** included in membership dues. **Conventions/Meetings:** annual convention.

Genetics

4779 ■ State Public Interest Research Groups' Campaign on Genetically Engineered Foods
c/o U.S. PIRG Education Fund
218 D St. SE
Washington, DC 20003-1900
Ph: (202)546-9707
Fax: (202)546-2461
E-mail: webmaster@pirg.org
URL: http://pirg.org/ge
Contact: Ms. Alison Cassady, Research Dir., US PIRG
Description: Acts to call on government and corporate leaders to ensure genetically engineered food ingredients or crops not be allowed on the market unless they meet specific standards. **Additional Websites:** http://www.uspirg.org/issues/food-safety. **Publications:** *Fact Sheets.* Alternate Formats: online ● *Kraft Foods and Genetically Engineered Foods: The Experiment on You.* Video. Alternate Formats: online ● Reports. Alternate Formats: online.

Goats

4780 ■ American Kiko Goat Association (AKGA)
c/o Jean Thomure, Sec.
295 Cardinal Ln.
Trenton, GA 30752
Ph: (706)657-8649
E-mail: 2meracre@tvn.net
URL: http://www.kikogoats.com
Contact: Robert B. Mayer II, Pres.
Membership Dues: breeder, $55 (annual) ● associate, $25 (annual) ● life, $500. **Description:** Promotes the Kiko goat in North America. Assists members in breeding, raising and registering Kiko goats. Educates the public on the advantages of the Kiko goat as a premier meat breed. **Publications:** *The AKGA Update.* Magazine. Contains topics of interest to members. **Price:** $25.00 for associate members.

4781 ■ American Tennessee Fainting Goat Association (ATFGA)
Address Unknown since 2007
Founded: 1985. **Members:** 2,800. **Membership Dues:** $15 (annual). **Description:** Seeks to preserve, protect and promote the American Tennessee fainting goat breed. **Publications:** Newsletter, quarterly. **Conventions/Meetings:** Sanctioned shows.

4782 ■ Colored Angora Goat Breeders Association (CAGBA)
c/o Laurie Lee, Treas.
5390 Piney Woods Rd.
Riner, VA 24149
Ph: (540)797-8601
E-mail: gretadise@yahoo.com
URL: http://www.cagba.org
Contact: Greta Dise, Pres.
Founded: 1998. **Membership Dues:** youth, $5 (annual) ● single, $15 (annual) ● couple, $20 (annual). **Regional Groups:** 7. **Description:** Serves as a registry for Colored Angora Goats. Provides education to breeders about the proper caring of livestock. Encourages closer fellowship among the members through meetings, correspondence, circulation of useful information, news and ideas. Seeks cooperation with other organizations in the development of the Colored Angora Goat. **Computer Services:** Information services, color genetics ● online services, breeder locator. **Publications:** *An Introduction to Colored Angora Goat Breeders Association.* Brochure. Alternate Formats: online ● Newsletter, quarterly.

4783 ■ International Boer Goat Association
PO Box 1045
Whitewright, TX 75491
Ph: (903)364-5735
Free: (877)402-4242
Fax: (903)364-5741
E-mail: intlboer@intlboergoat.org
URL: http://www.intlboergoat.org
Contact: Derrie Minyard, Pres.
Founded: 1997. **Members:** 3,700. **Membership Dues:** individual, $40 (annual) ● ranch, family, $60 (annual). **Staff:** 5. **Multinational. Description:** Promotes the Boer goat meat industry and the Boer goat breed; provides genetic testing. **Awards: Type:** scholarship. **Computer Services:** database ● mailing lists ● online services. **Committees:** Ethics; Judges; Marketing/Merchandising; Newsletter; Show. **Programs:** Herdsman; Registry; Youth. **Publications:** *Boer Breeder*, bimonthly. Magazine. Contains educational articles about new medication, nutrition, genetics and current sanctioned show results. **Price:** included in membership dues. **Advertising:** accepted ● Videos. **Conventions/Meetings:** Field Days - meeting ● Goat Evaluation Clinics - regional meeting ● seminar ● show.

4784 ■ International Fainting Goat Association (IFGA)
c/o Lottie Long, Registrar
2455 Deanburg Rd.
Pinson, TN 38366
Ph: (402)782-2089 (402)564-7097
E-mail: barngodd@barngoddessfainters.com
URL: http://www.faintinggoat.com
Contact: Stephanie Dicke, Sec.
Founded: 1989. **Membership Dues:** regular, $25 (annual) ● youth, $10 (annual). **Description:** Represents goat breeders who wish to preserve the Fainting Goat as a pure breed. Assists in pedigree documentation. Educates the public about the uniqueness of the breed. **Computer Services:** database, membership directory ● information services, breed information and buyers guide. **Publications:** *Myotonic Messenger*, quarterly. Newsletter. Provides a variety of information and ideas to members.

4785 ■ International Goat Association (IGA)
c/o Christian DeVries, Operations Dir.
1 World Ave.
Little Rock, AR 72202
Ph: (501)454-1641
Fax: (501)907-2805
E-mail: goats@heifer.org
URL: http://www.iga-goatworld.org
Contact: Chris Lu, Pres.
Founded: 1982. **Multinational. Description:** Represents educators, scientists, veterinarians, technologists, producers, extensionists, project leaders and development experts that advance goat management and sale of goat products to improve human condition, social welfare and sustainable development. Encourages goat research and development to increase their productivity and usefulness throughout the world. **Projects:** Goat Products. **Publications:** *Atlas of Goat Products.* Handbook. Describes 210 goat products around the world. Alternate Formats: online ● *Small Ruminant Research.* Journal ● Newsletter. Alternate Formats: online.

4786 ■ Kinder Goat Breeders Association (KGBA)
PO Box 1575
Snohomish, WA 98291-1575
Ph: (360)668-4559
Fax: (360)668-4559
E-mail: kgbassn@aol.com
URL: http://www.kindergoats.com
Contact: Pat Showalter, Pres.
Founded: 1988. **Membership Dues:** youth, $10 (annual) ● active, $15 (annual) ● family, $25 (annual). **Description:** Promotes the Kinder goat breed; maintains the herdbook and breed registry of the Kinder goat. **Publications:** Newsletter. **Price:** included in membership dues. **Advertising:** accepted. **Conventions/Meetings:** specialty show.

4787 ■ National Toggenburg Club (NTC)
c/o Tracey Jones, Specialty Show Chair
2754 Crooked Finger Rd.
Scotts Mills, OR 97375-9640
Ph: (503)873-8512
E-mail: mossridge@netzero.net
URL: http://www.nationaltoggclub.org
Contact: Tracey Jones, Specialty Show Chair
Membership Dues: individual in U.S., $15 (annual) ● individual outside U.S., $21 (annual). **Description:** Represents breeders and fanciers devoted to the promotion of Toggenburg dairy goats. **Programs:** All-American. **Publications:** *TOGG News*, quarterly. Newsletter ● Reports. **Conventions/Meetings:** specialty show.

4788 ■ Nigerian Dwarf Goat Association (NDGA)
c/o Jim Mannos, Pres.
1414 Wilson Rd.
Lancaster, TX 75146
Ph: (972)227-7311 (928)445-3423
Fax: (972)227-7075

E-mail: info@ndga.org
URL: http://www.ndga.org
Contact: Jim Mannos, Pres.

Founded: 1996. **Membership Dues:** individual, $25 (annual) ● family, business, club, $35 (annual). **Regional Groups:** 3. **Description:** Preserves and promotes the small functional, dairy-type Nigerian Dwarf goats. Supports breeders and owners of dwarf goats through promotional efforts and assistance programs. **Computer Services:** database, membership directory ● information services, news bulletin ● mailing lists, of members. **Committees:** Judges Training; Merchandise; Milk Production; National Show Chair; Show. **Programs:** Milk Testing. **Publications:** *Dwarf Digest*. Journal.

4789 ■ United States Boer Goat Association (USBGA)
PO Box 663
Spicewood, TX 78669
Free: (866)668-7242
Fax: (877)640-4060
E-mail: office@usbga.org
URL: http://usbga.org
Contact: Ron McGill, CEO

Founded: 1997. **Membership Dues:** junior, $15 (annual) ● individual, $40 (annual) ● ranch/family, $60 (annual) ● life, $300. **Description:** Promotes and improves the Boer goat breed through pedigree tracking and maintenance by registration. Educates members on the benefits of Boer goat breeding. Advances the Boer goat industry through education, promotion and marketing. **Telecommunication Services:** electronic mail, usbgaoffice@aol.com. **Publications:** *The US Boer Goat*, bimonthly. Magazine. **Advertising:** accepted. Alternate Formats: online.

Grain

4790 ■ United States Rice Producers Association (USRPA)
2825 Wilcrest Dr., Ste.505
Houston, TX 77042-6041
Ph: (713)974-7423
Fax: (713)974-7696
E-mail: dwight@usriceproducers.com
URL: http://www.usriceproducers.com
Contact: Dwight Roberts, Pres./CEO

Membership Dues: affiliate, $500 (annual). **Description:** Represents rice producers located in the United States. **Conventions/Meetings:** annual Conservation Systems Cotton and Rice Conference.

4791 ■ Wheat Export Trade Education Committee (WETEC)
415 2nd St. NE, Ste.300
Washington, DC 20002
Ph: (202)547-2004
Fax: (202)546-2638
E-mail: wetec@wetec.org
Contact: Lynn Blair, Chair

Founded: 1999. **Staff:** 4. **Description:** Represents industry on matters affecting U.S. wheat exports and trade policy. **Conventions/Meetings:** annual board meeting, held in conjunction with the Wheat Industry Conference & Exposition - winter ● annual board meeting, held in conjunction with the U.S. Wheat Associates meeting - summer.

Grass

4792 ■ Chewings Fescue and Creeping Red Fescue Commission (CFCRFC)
c/o Oregon Seed Council
1193 Royvonne Ave. S, Ste.11
Salem, OR 97302
Ph: (503)585-1157
Fax: (503)585-1292
E-mail: dlnassoc@aol.com
URL: http://forages.oregonstate.edu/organizations/seed/offc
Contact: David S. Nelson, Exec. Sec.

Founded: 1956. **Staff:** 1. **Budget:** $225,000. **Description:** Serves an agency of the state of Oregon. Conducts educational and promotional activities for Oregon-grown fine leaf fescues. (Fescues are tufted, perennial grasses having small flowered spikes.) Establishes and finances the growers of chewings fescue and creeping red fescue. **Conventions/Meetings:** quarterly board meeting.

4793 ■ International Turf Producers Foundation (ITPF)
c/o Turfgrass Producers International
2 E Main St.
East Dundee, IL 60118
Ph: (847)649-5555
Free: (800)405-8873
Fax: (847)649-5678
E-mail: info@turfgrasssod.org
URL: http://www.turfgrasssod.org
Contact: Mr. Kirk Hunter, Exec. Dir.

Founded: 1993. **Staff:** 7. **Budget:** $200,000. **Nonmembership. Description:** Supports research and educational activities related to the planting, growing, and marketing of turfgrass sod. **Publications:** none. **Convention/Meeting:** none. **Awards:** ITPF Fellowship/Scholarship. **Frequency:** annual. **Type:** scholarship. **Recipient:** for a winning proposal ● ITPF Research Grant. **Frequency:** annual. **Type:** grant. **Recipient:** to persons studying the field.

4794 ■ Lawn Institute (LI)
2 E Main St.
East Dundee, IL 60118
Ph: (847)649-5555
Free: (800)405-8873
Fax: (847)649-5678
E-mail: info@thelawninstitue.org
URL: http://www.lawninstitute.com
Contact: James Novak, Media Relations Coor.

Founded: 1955. **Members:** 1,100. **Staff:** 6. **Budget:** $1,500,000. **Multinational. Description:** Producers of lawn seed and lawn products. "Seeks to help bridge the gap between professional research and an increasingly sophisticated consumer." Promotes better lawns through use of quality materials, research, and education. **Libraries: Type:** reference. **Awards:** Distinguished Service. **Frequency:** annual. **Type:** recognition. **Recipient:** nominated by industry peers ● Honorary Member. **Frequency:** annual. **Type:** recognition. **Recipient:** nominated by industry peers ● Innovation Award. **Frequency:** annual. **Type:** recognition. **Recipient:** nominated by industry peers. **Computer Services:** database. **Additional Websites:** http://www.turfgrasssod.org. **Formerly:** (1952) Better Lawn and Turf Institute/American Sod Producers Association. **Publications:** *Turf News*, annual. Magazine. Provides the latest information on lawn and sports turf establishment, maintenance, and renovation. **Price:** free. **Circulation:** 1,500. **Advertising:** accepted. Alternate Formats: CD-ROM. **Conventions/Meetings:** annual Mid-Winter Conference (exhibits) - every mid-winter ● annual Summer Convention and Field Days (exhibits) - every summer.

4795 ■ Manhattan Ryegrass Growers Association (MRGA)
Address Unknown since 2008

Founded: 1973. **Members:** 20. **Description:** Growers of Manhattan ryegrass. Works to promote, market, research, and develop Manhattan ryegrass, which is grown only in Oregon, and to ensure the purity of the grass. Compiles statistics. **Awards: Type:** grant. **Recipient:** for universities for research in improving the strain. **Publications:** Newsletter, semiannual. **Conventions/Meetings:** periodic meeting (exhibits).

4796 ■ O.J. Noer Research Foundation (OJNRF)
PO Box 94
Juneau, WI 53039-0094
Ph: (863)619-9822
Fax: (863)619-7441
E-mail: administrator@noerfoundation.org
URL: http://www.ojnoerfoundation.org
Contact: J.I. Wiley, Pres.

Founded: 1959. **Members:** 68. **Membership Dues:** supporting, $50 (annual). **Description:** Individuals and corporations involved in the turfgrass industry, including manufacturers and distributors of turf, golf course superintendents, and trade magazine editors. Promotes scientific research in turfgrass and related fields by providing funds to students and research projects; disseminates information about research findings to members. (Organization is named for turfgrass agronomist O.J. Noer). **Conventions/Meetings:** annual meeting, held in conjunction with Golf Course Superintendents Association of America.

4797 ■ Oregon Highland Bentgrass Commission (OHBC)
PO Box 3366
Salem, OR 97302-0366
Ph: (503)364-2944 (503)769-2205
Fax: (503)581-6819
E-mail: bryan@ostlund.com
URL: http://forages.oregonstate.edu/organizations/seed/ohbc/default.cfm
Contact: Ken Doerfler, Chm.

Founded: 1959. **Budget:** $29,000. **Description:** Seed growers and handlers. Provides funds for promotional activities and supports research projects. **Convention/Meeting:** none. **Libraries: Type:** reference. **Holdings:** reports. **Telecommunication Services:** electronic mail, forages@oregonstate.edu.

4798 ■ Oregon Ryegrass Growers Seed Commission (ORGSC)
PO Box 3366
Salem, OR 97302-0366
Ph: (503)364-2944
Fax: (503)581-6819
URL: http://www.ryegrass.com
Contact: Bryan Ostlund, Admin.

Founded: 1966. **Budget:** $500,000. **Description:** Promotes and distributes information on the Oregon ryegrass seed industry. Disseminates literature; sponsors advertisements; conducts research. **Convention/Meeting:** none.

4799 ■ Turfgrass Producers International (TPI)
2 E Main St.
East Dundee, IL 60118
Ph: (847)649-5555
Free: (800)405-8873
Fax: (847)649-5678
E-mail: info@turfgrasssod.org
URL: http://www.turfgrasssod.org
Contact: Kirk Hunter, Exec. Dir.

Founded: 1967. **Members:** 1,100. **Staff:** 6. **Budget:** $1,000,000. **Multinational. Description:** Turfgrass sod producers, equipment manufacturers, suppliers, and other interested professionals or business people; educators and research and extension personnel. Encourages efficient and economical production of turfgrass sod; develops standards in the industry; promotes the superiority of turfgrass sod; increases public awareness of the industry; services members in related programs. Conducts educational programs and field days; sponsors research. **Libraries: Type:** reference. **Holdings:** 27. **Subjects:** turfgrass sod production. **Computer Services:** Mailing lists, of members ● online services, member bulletin board. **Formerly:** (1994) American Sod Producers Association. **Publications:** *Business Management Newsletter*, bimonthly. **Price:** available to members only. **Circulation:** 1,100 ● *Turf News*, bimonthly. Magazine. **Price:** available to members only. **Advertising:** accepted ● *Turfgrass Producers International—Membership Directory*, annual. **Price:** available to members only ● Booklets ● Brochures ● Manuals ● Also produces slide-cassette presentation. **Conventions/Meetings:** semiannual meeting (exhibits) - always January/February and July. 2008 July 28-Aug. 1, Calgary, AB, Canada.

Greyhound

4800 ■ GREY2K USA
PO Box 442117
Somerville, MA 02144
Free: (866)247-3925
Fax: (617)666-3568
E-mail: info@grey2kusa.org
URL: http://www.grey2kusa.org
Contact: Carey M. Theil, Pres.
Founded: 2001. **Description:** Works for the welfare of greyhounds in the United States. Serves as a network of humane-minded citizens who work to pass stronger dog protection laws and close down existing greyhound racetracks. Works with animal-friendly lawmakers, greyhound adoption advocates, and local and national animal protection organizations.

Grounds Management

4801 ■ National Institute on Park and Grounds Management (NIPGM)
Address Unknown since 2008
Founded: 1975. **Members:** 350. **Membership Dues:** individual, $145 (annual). **Staff:** 2. **Description:** Managers in charge of large outdoor areas such as parks, campuses, and industrial areas. Goals are to inform, educate, and exchange information to improve grounds management. **Awards:** Excellence in Maintenance. **Frequency:** annual. **Type:** recognition. **Recipient:** for members only. **Sections:** Campus; Parks. **Publications:** *Park and Grounds Messenger*, monthly. Newsletter. Articles on grounds maintenance and management. **Price:** available to members only. **Circulation:** 350. **Advertising:** accepted ● Membership Directory, annual. Contains a list of current members by category and state. **Price:** available to members only. **Advertising:** accepted ● Also publishes management guides. **Conventions/Meetings:** annual conference and tour, with educational sessions, on-site tours, and networking opportunities (exhibits) ● annual meeting, open to all grounds management professionals (exhibits).

4802 ■ National Roadside Vegetation Management Association (NRVMA)
c/o John Reynolds, Exec. Dir.
5616 Lynchburg Cir.
Hueytown, AL 35023
Ph: (205)491-7574
Fax: (205)491-2725
E-mail: jreynoldsnrvma@charter.net
URL: http://www.nrvma.org
Contact: John Reynolds, Exec. Dir.
Founded: 1984. **Members:** 900. **Membership Dues:** individual, $25 (annual). **Budget:** $50,000. **Description:** Individuals involved in roadside vegetation management through employment, research, education, regulation, contracting, manufacturing, or merchandising. Promotes vegetation management activities regarding safety, functional and operational characteristics, economy, roadside beautification and aesthetics, and ecological soundness. Seeks to establish and administer standards of recognition and implementation of the practices of roadside vegetation management and its component skills. Offers manufacturers of materials and equipment an opportunity to introduce and demonstrate their products. Sponsors lectures on topics such as: landscaping and beautification; growing wildflowers and native plants; herbicides and their use; the art of managing roadsides; roadside parks; wetlands protection. **Awards:** National Roadside Excellence Award. **Frequency:** annual. **Type:** recognition. **Recipient:** for beauty, safety, usefulness, and innovation. **Publications:** Newsletter, quarterly. **Price:** free for members ● Proceedings. **Conventions/Meetings:** annual conference and trade show (exhibits) - usually September or October.

4803 ■ Professional Grounds Management Society (PGMS)
720 Light St.
Baltimore, MD 21230-3816
Free: (800)609-7467
Fax: (410)752-8295
E-mail: pgms@assnhqtrs.com
URL: http://www.pgms.org
Contact: Thomas C. Shaner CAE, Exec. Dir.
Founded: 1911. **Members:** 1,500. **Membership Dues:** active (prorated over the year), $175-$225 (annual) ● affiliate, $125 (annual) ● supplier, $400 (annual) ● student, educator, researcher, $35 (annual). **Staff:** 3. **Budget:** $400,000. **Regional Groups:** 8. **Local Groups:** 8. **Description:** Professional society of grounds managers of large institutions of all sorts and independent landscape contractors. Establishes grounds management as a profession; secures opportunities for professional advancement of well-qualified grounds managers; acquaints the public with "the distinction between competent ground managers, equipped through practical experience and systematic study, and self-styled 'maintenance' personnel, lacking these essentials." Sponsors contests. Conducts research and surveys; sponsors certification program for professional grounds managers and grounds keepers. Takes action with the legislative and executive branches of government on issues affecting grounds managers; keeps members informed on matters affecting the profession. **Awards:** Professional Grounds Management Award. **Frequency:** annual. **Type:** recognition. **Recipient:** for best-maintained sites, in each of 13 categories. **Computer Services:** database ● mailing lists. **Committees:** Certification; Education; Scholarship. **Divisions:** National Awards. **Formerly:** National Association of Gardeners. **Publications:** *Grounds Maintenance Estimating Guidelines*, periodic. Manual. **Price:** included in membership dues; $30.00 for nonmembers ● *Grounds Maintenance Management Guidelines*. Manual. **Price:** free for members; $25.00 for nonmembers ● *Grounds Management Forms and Job Descriptions Guide*. Booklet. **Price:** free for members; $25.00 for nonmembers ● *Grounds Management Forum*, bimonthly. Newsletter. Provides information on grounds management and association activities. Also includes information on new members, and upcoming events. **Circulation:** 1,500 ● *Grounds Management Guide*. Manual ● *Grounds Manager Certification Program*. Brochure ● *Landscape Management Supervisory Training Manual*. **Price:** $40.00 for members; $69.95 for nonmembers ● *Professional Grounds Management Society Membership Directory*, annual. **Price:** included in membership dues; $400.00 for nonmembers ● *The Professional Grounds Manager*. Brochure. **Conventions/Meetings:** annual Conference and GIE Expo - conference and meeting (exhibits) - always October. 2008 Oct. 22-25, Louisville, KY; 2009 Oct. 28-31, Louisville, KY.

Hazardous Material

4804 ■ Academy of Certified Hazardous Materials Managers (ACHMM)
9650 Rockville Pike
Bethesda, MD 20814
Ph: (301)634-7430
Free: (800)437-0137
Fax: (301)634-7431
E-mail: academy@achmm.org
URL: http://www.netforumachmm.org/eweb/StartPage.aspx?site=061128ACHM
Contact: Ms. Laureen A. McMurray Boyle, Pres.
Members: 6,000. **Membership Dues:** certified/affiliate, $85 (annual) ● student, $20 (annual) ● retired, $10 (annual). **Description:** Professionals in the field of hazardous materials. Envisions a world where the natural environment is unburdened by pollution, workers are not exposed to unhealthy conditions, and hazardous materials are used and transported safely and efficiently. Conducts educational programs, provides technical information, helps define industry standards. **Awards:** Champions of Excellence. **Type:** recognition. **Recipient:** for introducing the philosophy of CHMM ● Chapter of the Year. **Frequency:** annual. **Type:** recognition. **Recipient:** to the most accomplished chapter ● Chapter Website Award. **Frequency:** annual. **Type:** recognition. **Recipient:** to the most updated chapter website ● Friend of the Academy Award. **Frequency:** periodic. **Type:** recognition. **Recipient:** for non-CHMM member ● Hazardous Materials Manager of the Year. **Frequency:** annual. **Type:** recognition. **Recipient:** for an outstanding accomplishment in the environmental, health and safety field ● Honor Roll of Champions. **Frequency:** annual. **Type:** recognition. **Recipient:** for a chapter that sponsors a CHMM Overview course and subsequent examination ● Pete Cook Founders Award. **Frequency:** periodic. **Type:** recognition. **Recipient:** to the most outstanding member ● Special Achievements for the ACHMM. **Frequency:** periodic. **Type:** recognition. **Recipient:** to the most outstanding senior member ● Sponsor Appreciation Award. **Frequency:** annual. **Type:** recognition. **Recipient:** for a private corporation, public agency, nonprofit organization and/or educational institution ● Unsung Hero Award. **Frequency:** periodic. **Type:** recognition. **Recipient:** for CHMM or non-CHMM who contributed skills, time, and effort ● Young CHMM of the Year. **Frequency:** annual. **Type:** recognition. **Recipient:** to the most outstanding young member. **Telecommunication Services:** electronic mail, laureen.mcmurray@shawgrp.com.

4805 ■ Institute of Hazardous Materials Management (IHMM)
11900 Parklawn Dr., Ste.450
Rockville, MD 20852-2624
Ph: (301)984-8969
Fax: (301)984-1516
E-mail: ihmminfo@ihmm.org
URL: http://www.ihmm.org
Contact: John Frick PhD, Exec. Dir.
Founded: 1984. **Members:** 9,000. **Membership Dues:** certificant, $70 (annual). **Staff:** 10. **Budget:** $750,000. **Description:** Provides credentialed recognition to professionals engaged in the management and control of hazardous materials who have attained the required level of education, experience, and competence. **Awards:** Scholarships. **Frequency:** annual. **Type:** scholarship. **Recipient:** to students studying in the field of hazardous materials management. **Telecommunication Services:** electronic mail, jfrick@ihmm.org.

4806 ■ North American Hazardous Materials Management Association (NAHMMA)
3030 W 81st Ave.
Westminster, CO 80031-4111
Ph: (303)433-4446
Free: (877)292-1403
Fax: (303)458-0002
E-mail: nahmma@imigroup.org
URL: http://www.nahmma.org
Contact: Kolin Anglin, Pres.
Founded: 1993. **Membership Dues:** business, $150-$350 (annual) ● government, $150-$300 (annual) ● trade, $500 (annual) ● individual (sole proprietor, student, professor, retiree), $50 (annual) ● non-profit, $100 (annual). **Description:** Aims to prevent pollution and reduce the hazardous constituents entering municipal waste streams from households, small businesses and other entities that may be exempted from local, regional or national regulations. Encourages the development and use of non-hazardous products, constituents, processes and methods. Promotes the collection of products and materials that contain hazardous components for reuse and recycling. **Computer Services:** Online services, discussion board. **Committees:** Affiliations; Awards; Conference; Operations; Policy; Publicity; Strategic; Training. **Publications:** Newsletter. Alternate Formats: online.

Historic Preservation

4807 ■ Death Valley '49ers
PO Box 338
Death Valley, CA 92328
E-mail: deathvalley49ers@starband.net
URL: http://www.deathvalley49ers.org
Contact: Marvin Jensen, Pres.
Membership Dues: regular, $20 (annual) ● contributing, $50 (annual) ● corporation, $200 (annual) ●

life, $300. **Description:** Seeks to expand public awareness of Death Valley, a highly valued national resource and recreational area that is protected and preserved by the National Park Service and others for use and enjoyment of present and future generations. Special recognition is given to the California bound pioneer wagon parties of 1849-50. **Awards:** Death Valley '49ers Scholarship. **Frequency:** annual. **Type:** scholarship. **Recipient:** for Death Valley area high school graduating senior. **Publications:** *Keepsake.* Booklet ● Booklets. **Conventions/Meetings:** Death Valley History - conference ● annual Encampment - rally ● Invitational Art Show.

Horses

4808 ■ Akhal-Teke Association of America (ATAA)
PO Box 1635
Rolla, MO 65402
Ph: (573)426-5207
E-mail: info@akhal-teke.org
URL: http://www.akhal-teke.org
Contact: Martha Bowles, Sec.
Founded: 1983. **Members:** 80. **Membership Dues:** individual, $48 (annual) ● friend, junior, $25 (annual) ● family, $80 (annual). **Staff:** 7. **Description:** Owners of Akhal-Teke horses united to promote the breed in the United States. (Now used in competitive equine sports, the Akhal-Teke is a descendant of the wild steppe horse and is noted especially for its stamina and the golden color of its shiny coat.) Oversees Akhal-Teke Registry of America for purebreds and Akhal-Teke Sporthorse Registry of America for crosses of one half or better Akhal-Teke blood. **Libraries: Type:** reference. **Holdings:** 10; books. **Subjects:** U.S., Russian, German studbooks. **Awards:** Accomplishment Awards. **Frequency:** annual. **Type:** recognition ● Extraordinary Volunteer. **Frequency:** annual. **Type:** recognition. **Computer Services:** Mailing lists, of breeders. **Formerly:** (1998) Akhal-Teke Association of America; (1999) Akhal-Teke Association of America - Inc. in Missouri. **Publications:** *Akhal-Teke News*, quarterly. Newsletter. Covers news, information, and articles from around the world. **Price:** $12.00/year in U.S. **Advertising:** accepted. **Conventions/Meetings:** annual North American Akhal-Teke Conference (exhibits).

4809 ■ American Appaloosa Association Worldwide (AApA)
PO Box 429
Republic, MO 65738-0429
Ph: (417)466-2046
Fax: (417)466-3633
E-mail: heidi@amappaloosa.com
URL: http://www.amappaloosa.com
Founded: 1983. **Members:** 2,000. **Membership Dues:** single, $22 (annual) ● family (husband, wife and children under 18), $32 (annual) ● single (foreign), $30 (annual) ● family (foreign), $40 (annual). **Multinational. Description:** Provides a proper atmosphere and opportunity for the enjoyment of the Appaloosa horse. Seeks to provide permanent recognition of the characteristic Appaloosa horse. Recognizes the efforts of the breeders and owners of such horses. **Computer Services:** database, horses for sale ● information services, Appaloosa resources. **Telecommunication Services:** electronic mail, amappaloosaassn@sofnet.com. **Programs:** Open Show Points; Saddle and/or Driving Log.

4810 ■ American Association of Owners and Breeders of Peruvian Paso Horses (AAOBPPH)
Address Unknown since 2008
URL: http://www.aaobpph.org
Founded: 1962. **Members:** 500. **Membership Dues:** owner/breeder, $50 (annual) ● aficionado, $25 (annual) ● junior, $15 (annual) ● life, $600. **Staff:** 1. **Budget:** $150,000. **Regional Groups:** 14. **Description:** Owners and breeders of purebred registered Peruvian Paso Horses. Maintains hall of fame. Compiles statistics. Bestows awards. **Awards:** Harry Bennett Award. **Frequency:** annual. **Type:** recognition. **Recipient:** for high point horses in 10 different areas ● Lifetime Hall of Fame Awards. **Frequency:** annual. **Type:** recognition. **Computer Services:** database, pedigree information. **Telecommunication Services:** electronic mail, office@aaobpph.org. **Committees:** Budget; Ethics and Grievance; Membership; Promotion; Stud Book. **Publications:** *Official AAOBPPH Newsletter*, 3/year. **Price:** included in membership dues. **Circulation:** 600. **Advertising:** accepted. **Conventions/Meetings:** annual show and meeting (exhibits).

4811 ■ American Azteca Horse International Association (AAHIA)
PO Box 1577
Rapid City, SD 57709
Ph: (605)342-2322
E-mail: office@americanazteca.com
URL: http://americanazteca.com
Contact: Rita Greslin, Pres.
Founded: 2000. **Membership Dues:** full, $40 (annual) ● associate, $25 (annual). **Regional Groups:** 7. **Multinational. Description:** Serves as a venue for registering and promoting the American Azteca horses. Works to emphasize the qualities of American Azteca horses. **Computer Services:** Information services, breed resources ● online services, classified ads. **Publications:** *American Azteca News.* Newsletter. **Advertising:** accepted. Alternate Formats: online.

4812 ■ American Bashkir Curly Registry (ABCR)
PO Box 151029
Ely, NV 89315
Ph: (775)289-4999 (775)852-2223
Fax: (775)289-8579
E-mail: secretary@abcregistry.org
URL: http://www.abcregistry.org
Contact: Donna Bronson, Sec.
Founded: 1971. **Members:** 510. **Membership Dues:** adult, $35 (annual) ● youth, $20 (annual) ● family (2 adults and 2 or more children), $90 (annual). **Staff:** 3. **For-Profit. Description:** Individuals united for the registration and promotion of American Bashkir Curly horses. Compiles statistics; conducts research; maintains museum. **Libraries: Type:** reference. **Holdings:** photographs. **Subjects:** curly-coated horses. **Awards:** National Breed Promotion Award. **Frequency:** annual. **Type:** recognition ● **Frequency:** annual. **Type:** trophy. **Recipient:** for the top show and endurance performances by Bashkir Curly horses ● Youth Award. **Frequency:** annual. **Type:** recognition. **Computer Services:** database, horse registration. **Committees:** Breeders; Grievance; Horse Show; I.D.; Rose Parade. **Publications:** *American Bashkir Curly Registry Listings*, periodic. Book ● *Curly Cues*, quarterly. Newsletter. Lists horses registered and member activities. **Price:** included in membership dues; $2.00/issue for nonmembers; $20.00 /year for nonmembers. ISSN: 0887-2406. **Circulation:** 700. **Advertising:** accepted. **Conventions/Meetings:** annual Fifteen-Class All-Curly Horse Show (exhibits).

4813 ■ American Buckskin Registry Association (ABRA)
PO Box 493850
Redding, CA 96049
Ph: (530)223-1420
Fax: (530)223-1420
E-mail: georgijones@aol.com
URL: http://www.americanbuckskin.org
Contact: Ken Pickering, Pres.
Founded: 1963. **Members:** 5,500. **Membership Dues:** youth, $10 (annual) ● single, $15 (annual) ● joint, business, $20 (annual) ● life, $200. **Description:** Persons seeking to promote and increase the value of the Buckskin horse. Maintains stud book, registry, and pedigree records. **Awards:** Register of Merit/Champion Award. **Type:** recognition. **Recipient:** for horses earning a specific number of points in approved shows. **Telecommunication Services:** electronic mail, kdpick2902@sbcglobal.net. **Formerly:** (1965) Buckskin Registry Association. **Publications:** *Buckskin Journal*, monthly. **Price:** $15.00/year ● *Stud Book*, triennial ● Handbook, annual. **Conventions/Meetings:** annual meeting.

4814 ■ American Collegiate Horsemen's Association (ACHA)
PO Box 1322
Findlay, OH 45840
Ph: (740)361-9411
E-mail: danielsj@findlay.edu
URL: http://www.acha-horsemen.org
Contact: Jessica Daniels, Pres.
Founded: 2003. **Membership Dues:** club, $50 (annual) ● individual, $5 (annual). **Description:** Seeks to unite collegiate horsemen of all levels and disciplines from across the nation through the promotion of leadership, education, and service. Promotes the equine industry and disseminates knowledge of all its aspects to collegiate members. Brings about a cordial relationship between members and leaders of the equine industry through affiliations. **Publications:** Newsletter, monthly. **Price:** included in membership dues. **Conventions/Meetings:** annual convention.

4815 ■ American Connemara Pony Society (ACPS)
c/o Marynell Eyles, Sec.
PO Box 100
Middlebrook, VA 24459
E-mail: marynelleyles@hughes.net
URL: http://www.acps.org
Contact: Marynell Eyles, Sec.
Founded: 1956. **Members:** 800. **Membership Dues:** senior, $40 (annual) ● junior, $20 (annual) ● associate, $25 (annual) ● joint, $60 (annual) ● life, $600. **Staff:** 2. **Regional Groups:** 12. **Description:** Assists and promotes the breeding, registration, training, exhibition, equestrian competition and general use of the Connemara. Preserves the unique qualities of the breed and keep members informed in all matters concerning Connemara. **Libraries: Type:** reference. **Holdings:** books. **Subjects:** Connemara ponies. **Awards:** Achievement Awards. **Frequency:** annual. **Type:** scholarship. **Recipient:** for excellence in a variety of competitive and noncompetitive disciplines ● Hall of Fame Trophies. **Frequency:** annual. **Type:** trophy. **Recipient:** for outstanding ponies for their lifetime achievements ● USAE Award. **Frequency:** annual. **Type:** recognition ● USDF Award. **Frequency:** annual. **Type:** recognition. **Computer Services:** Online services, stud book computerized, Connemara page. **Boards:** Governors. **Committees:** Standing. **Publications:** *American Connemara*, bimonthly. Magazine. Features news, stories, and information on the Connemara. **Price:** $3.00/issue; $15.00/year. **Circulation:** 800. **Advertising:** accepted ● *Connemara Guide.* Handbook ● *Connemara Stud Book*, annual ● *Directory of Breeders*, periodic. **Conventions/Meetings:** annual meeting (exhibits) - always September.

4816 ■ American Cream Draft Horse Association (ACDHA)
193 Crossover Rd.
Bennington, VT 05201
Ph: (802)447-7612
Fax: (802)447-0711
E-mail: info@acdha.org
URL: http://www.acdha.org
Contact: Nancy H. Lively, Sec.-Treas.
Founded: 1944. **Members:** 89. **Membership Dues:** associate, full, $30 (annual) ● regular, $25 (annual). **Description:** Owners and livestock breeders of American Cream Draft horses, the only breed of draft horses originating in the United States. Seeks to preserve and upgrade the American Cream Draft horse. (The ideal American Cream is a medium cream color with white mane and tail, pink skin, and amber-colored eyes). **Affiliated With:** American Livestock Breeds Conservancy. **Formerly:** (1992) American Cream Draft Horse Association of America. **Publications:** *American Cream News*, semiannual. Newsletter. **Price:** available to members only. **Circulation:** 150 ● *The Cream of Draft Horses.* Brochure ● Pamphlets. **Conventions/Meetings:** annual meet-

ing, includes updates on by-laws, election of directors, and financial reports - always second Saturday of July.

4817 ■ American Dartmoor Pony Association (ADPA)
203 Kendall Oaks Dr.
Boerne, TX 78006
E-mail: adpasec@aol.com
URL: http://members.aol.com/_ht_a/adpasec/myhomepage
Contact: Joyce Pedrotti, Sec./Registrar
Founded: 1992. **Members:** 25. **Membership Dues:** single, business sponsorship, $20 (annual) ● family, farm, $25 (annual). **Staff:** 6. **Description:** Breeders and owners of Dartmoor ponies; interested others. (The Dartmoor pony, originally from the Dartmoor moorlands of southwestern England, is a riding and driving pony.) Promotes and preserves the breed in America. **Awards:** High Point Award for Rider & Pony. **Frequency:** annual. **Type:** trophy. **Publications:** *ADPA Diary*, annual. Magazine. Includes report of meeting, sales lists, letters from members etc. **Price:** included in membership dues. **Advertising:** accepted ● *ADPA Newsletter*, periodic ● *Stud Book*, periodic. **Conventions/Meetings:** annual meeting.

4818 ■ American Equestrian Trade Association (AETA)
591 North Ave., Ste.3-2
Wakefield, MA 01880-1617
Ph: (781)246-0486
Fax: (781)245-6487
E-mail: equestriantrade@verizon.net
URL: http://www.aetanews.com
Contact: Tom MacGuinness, Pres.
Founded: 2006. **Membership Dues:** retailer, $125-$225 (annual) ● manufacturer/distributor, $250-$450 (annual) ● supplier, $150 (annual) ● industry partner, sales agent/sales representative, $100 (annual) ● affiliate, $50 (annual). **Description:** Advances and safeguards the business interests of those who provide products and services to the equestrian community. Acts as an industry resource and provides a strong voice representing all sectors of the industry. Encourages and nurtures interest in equestrian activities in the United States. **Publications:** *AETA News*. Newsletter. Alternate Formats: online.

4819 ■ American Equine Association (AEA)
Address Unknown since 2007
Members: 56,000. **For-Profit. Description:** Individuals interested in maintaining a place for the horse in American society. Seeks to unite horsepeople. Makes available credit cards and horse-related products to members. Provides public relations assistance to organizations promoting heightened public awareness of equine issues and preservation of pastureland. **Publications:** *American Equine Association Newsletter*, monthly.

4820 ■ American Hackney Horse Society (AHHS)
4059 Iron Works Pkwy., A-3
Lexington, KY 40511-8462
Ph: (859)255-8694
Fax: (859)255-0177
E-mail: info@hackneysociety.com
URL: http://www.hackneysociety.com
Contact: Frances E. Bjalobok MS, Exec. Sec.
Founded: 1891. **Members:** 850. **Membership Dues:** individual, $35 (annual) ● family, $50 (annual) ● junior, $15 (annual) ● life, $500. **Staff:** 2. **Budget:** $150,000. **Regional Groups:** 11. **Languages:** English, Italian, Spanish. **Description:** Registers Hackney horses and ponies; promotes the breeding and showing of Hackney horses and ponies. Sponsors competitions; maintains registry; provides educational programs and children's services. **Libraries: Type:** open to the public. **Holdings:** 30; audiovisuals, books. **Subjects:** English, Canadian, American Hackney. **Awards:** AHHS National Futurity. **Frequency:** annual. **Type:** recognition ● AHHS Sweepstakes. **Frequency:** annual. **Type:** recognition ● AHHS Youth Medallion. **Frequency:** annual. **Type:** medal ● Youth Medallion National Championship. **Frequency:** annual. **Type:** medal. **Computer Services:** database ● mailing lists. **Boards:** Directors. **Committees:** Annual Awards; By-Laws; Convention Coordinator; Driving Competition; Executive; Finance; Foundation Liaison; Horse Liaison; Limited Breeders Weanling Stakes; Membership; National Breeders Futurity; Nominating; Regional Associations; Registry; Stud Book; Trophies; UPHA Classics Liaison; Web Page/Internet; Youth Medallion Program. **Publications:** *American Hackney Stud Book*, biennial. Lists transfers and registrations. ● *The Hackney*. Brochure ● Newsletter, quarterly. **Price:** included in membership dues. **Circulation:** 850. **Advertising:** accepted. **Conventions/Meetings:** annual convention (exhibits) - always January ● semiannual dinner.

4821 ■ American Haflinger Registry (AHR)
1686 E Waterloo Rd.
Akron, OH 44306
Ph: (330)784-0000
Fax: (330)784-9843
E-mail: ahaflinger@sbcglobal.net
URL: http://www.haflingerhorse.com
Founded: 1998. **Members:** 2,400. **Membership Dues:** full, $65 (annual). **Staff:** 4. **Regional Groups:** 11. **State Groups:** 1. **Description:** Owners, breeders, and other individuals interested in promoting Haflinger horses. (Haflingers are small horses renowned for their versatility and friendly temperament.) Maintains registry of pure bred Haflingers in North America. Keeps members abreast of breed improvements; licenses Haflinger breeding stallions and provides certificates of registry; disseminates information on pedigrees, licenses, stallion services, and sale and show dates. Facilitates participation by members in livestock shows. **Committees:** Futurity; National Show; Sales. **Absorbed:** (2000) Haflinger Association of America. **Formerly:** (1999) Haflinger Registry North America. **Publications:** *Haflinger Horse*, bimonthly. Magazine. **Advertising:** accepted ● Also publishes name lists and reports; makes available promotional materials. **Conventions/Meetings:** annual National Show - meeting ● semiannual Sale - meeting.

4822 ■ American Half-Quarter Horse Registry (AHQHR)
PO Box 1198
Apache Junction, AZ 85217-1198
Ph: (480)982-1551
E-mail: lzmqhorses@earthlink.net
URL: http://www.halfquarterhorseregistry.com
Founded: 1963. **Staff:** 1. **Description:** Quarter horse breeders and enthusiasts. Promotes the identification and registration of half-bred quarter horses. Encourages owners of grade mares to breed them with quarter horses, since foals with half-quarter horses must have one parent registered with the American Quarter Horse Association (see separate entry). Supports research and educational programs, including Morris Animal Foundation (see separate entry), 4-H Horse Program, and horse research at University of California, Davis and California State Polytechnic University. **Affiliated With:** American Quarter Horse Association; Morris Animal Foundation.

4823 ■ American Hanoverian Society (AHS)
4067 Iron Works Pkwy., Ste.1
Lexington, KY 40511-8483
Ph: (859)255-4141
Fax: (859)255-8467
E-mail: ahsoffice@aol.com
URL: http://www.hanoverian.org
Contact: Hush Bellis-Jones, Exec. Dir.
Founded: 1971. **Members:** 2,000. **Membership Dues:** active, $80 (annual) ● associate, $55 (annual) ● junior, $25 (annual) ● life, $800. **Staff:** 4. **Description:** Seeks for the development of a superior horse for jumping, and dressage. Serves as registry and maintains a studbook for Hanoverian horses. Selects and approves breeding stallions and mares. Offers breeding and advertising services; disseminates information to interested parties. Conducts stallion and mare inspections. **Awards: Frequency:** annual. **Type:** recognition. **Recipient:** for best Hanoverian hunter, jumper, dressage, and three-day event horse. **Computer Services:** database, horses ● online services, breeder profiles. **Committees:** Approval and Registration; Education; Grievances; Mare and Stallion Approval; Public Relations, Education, and Publicity. **Affiliated With:** United States Dressage Federation; Verband Hannoverscher Warmblutzuechter. **Publications:** *The American Hanoverian*, quarterly. Magazine. **Price:** included in membership dues; $8.00 for nonmembers, includes shipping. **Advertising:** accepted ● *Stallion Directory*. Yearbook. **Conventions/Meetings:** annual meeting.

4824 ■ American Holsteiner Horse Association (AHHA)
222 E Main St., Ste.1
Georgetown, KY 40324-1712
Ph: (502)863-4239
Fax: (502)868-0722
E-mail: ahhambr@bellsouth.net
URL: http://www.holsteiner.com
Contact: Bruce Cottew, Exec. Dir.
Founded: 1978. **Members:** 700. **Membership Dues:** full, $85 (annual) ● associate, $50 (annual) ● junior (18 years old or younger), $35 (annual) ● life, $850. **Staff:** 3. **Budget:** $220,000. **Description:** Promotes breeding standards for the Holsteiner horse, noted for its endurance, jumping ability, friendliness, and willingness to perform. **Awards:** Performance Records for Awards Programs. **Frequency:** annual. **Type:** recognition. **Computer Services:** database. **Committees:** Advertising. **Absorbed:** (1987) American Association of Breeders of Holsteiner Horses. **Formerly:** (1987) American Holstein Horse Association. **Publications:** *Impulsion*, quarterly. Newsletter. **Price:** included in membership dues. **Circulation:** 750. **Advertising:** accepted. Alternate Formats: online ● *Stallion Roster*, annual. Handbook. Includes listing of activated stallions and pedigree and breeding statistics. **Price:** free. **Advertising:** accepted. Alternate Formats: online. **Conventions/Meetings:** semiannual board meeting ● annual Breeding Stock Approvals - meeting - always September.

4825 ■ American Horse Council (AHC)
1616 H St. NW, 7th Fl.
Washington, DC 20006
Ph: (202)296-4031
Fax: (202)296-1970
E-mail: ahc@horsecouncil.org
URL: http://www.horsecouncil.org
Contact: James J. Hickey Jr., Pres.
Founded: 1969. **Members:** 2,000. **Staff:** 5. **Description:** Equine breed registries, horse-related organizations, and commercial businesses; individuals with commercial interest in the equine industry; those who have a recreational and pleasure interest in the horse industry. Represents the horse industry before congress and federal agencies. Promotes equitable taxation and legislation; maintains liaison with government agencies and advises members of current national developments affecting the equine industry. Provides advisory, consulting, and referral services; offers tax and information service. Sponsors public affairs program on the contributions of the horse industry to the American economy and quality of life. Compiles statistics. **Committees:** Animal Welfare Advisory; Health and Regulatory Advisory; Horse Shows Advisory; Racing Advisory; Recreation Advisory; State Horse Council Advisory. **Publications:** *AHC News*, quarterly. Newsletter. **Price:** available to members only ● *AHC Tax Bulletin*, bimonthly. **Price:** available to members only ● *Horse Industry Directory*, annual. Lists more than 1,500 equine organizations and publications in the U.S., Canada, South America, and Europe. **Price:** $25.00/copy. ISSN: 0890-233X. **Circulation:** 3,000 ● *Horse Owners and Breeders Tax Handbook*, periodic. Manual. Contains comprehensive, up-to-date explanation of how federal tax laws and regulations apply to a horse business. **Price:** $85.00/copy, includes shipping ● Also publishes news releases and position papers. **Conventions/Meetings:** annual meeting (exhibits).

4826 ■ American Horse Defense Fund (AHDF)
1718 M St. NW, Unit 191
Washington, DC 20036-4505

Ph: (202)609-8198
E-mail: president@ahdf.org
URL: http://www.ahdf.org
Contact: Shelley Sawhook, Pres.

Founded: 2000. **Membership Dues:** individual, $25 (annual) ● junior (16 and under), $15 (annual) ● supporter, $100 (annual) ● corporate, $500 (annual) ● educational and non-profit institution, protector, $250 (annual) ● advocate, $50 (annual). **State Groups:** 51. **Description:** Facilitates the protection, conservation and humane treatment of members of all Equid species. Works to address the inhumane treatment of horses, ponies, donkeys, mules and burros, both wild and domesticated. Provides education, advocacy and litigation in the state, federal and international arenas. **Computer Services:** Online services, message board. **Boards:** Advisory.

4827 ■ American Indian Horse Registry (AIHR)
Rancho San Francisco
9028 State Park Rd.
Lockhart, TX 78644
Ph: (512)398-6642
E-mail: nanci@indianhorse.com
URL: http://www.indianhorse.com
Contact: Nanci Falley, Pres.

Founded: 1961. **Members:** 1,208. **Membership Dues:** individual, $20 (annual). **Staff:** 3. **Regional Groups:** 6. **Local Groups:** 2. **National Groups:** 2. **For-Profit. Description:** Persons who own or desire to own American Indian Horses (those that come directly from Indian reservations or are direct descendants of reservation horses). Registers and aims to preserve the pedigrees of American Indian horses. Maintains Indian Horse Hall of Fame and museum of saddles, bridles, and art representing 19th century southwestern America. **Libraries: Type:** open to the public. **Holdings:** 500; films. **Subjects:** Western America, Indians, horses. **Awards:** Horseback Awards and Indian Horse Hall of Fame. **Type:** recognition. **Publications:** *American Indian Horse Catalog*, annual. **Price:** free. **Advertising:** accepted. Alternate Formats: online ● *American Indian Horse News*, quarterly. Newsletter. Features breed news and member articles. **Price:** $20.00/year. **Circulation:** 300. **Advertising:** accepted ● *American Indian Horse Studbook*, annual. **Price:** $30.00. **Conventions/Meetings:** annual National American Indian Horse Show - meeting - always 3rd weekend of September.

4828 ■ American Junior Paint Horse Association (AJPHA)
PO Box 961023
Fort Worth, TX 76161-0023
Ph: (817)834-2742
Fax: (817)834-3152
E-mail: coordinator@ajpha.com
URL: http://www.ajpha.com
Contact: Laura Akerlund, Pres.

Founded: 1974. **Members:** 6,500. **Membership Dues:** individual, $15 (annual). **Regional Groups:** 30. **Description:** Represents young men and women 18 years of age or younger. Seeks to improve and promote the American Paint Horse, a breed characterized by markings of irregular patterns of white on the horse's body. Aims to enhance the capabilities of members in the breeding, raising, and exhibition of horses. Develops members' academic and leadership skills. Conducts horse shows and judging contest. **Awards:** Club of the Year. **Frequency:** annual. **Type:** recognition. **Recipient:** for AJPHA regional clubs ● Youth Member of the Year. **Frequency:** annual. **Type:** recognition. **Recipient:** for exemplifying the spirit of community involvement and leadership. **Formerly:** American Paint Horse Association. **Publications:** *Generation J*, quarterly. Newsletter. **Price:** included in membership dues. Alternate Formats: online. **Conventions/Meetings:** annual Judging Contest - competition ● annual Youth Leadership Conference - convention ● annual Youth World Championship - meeting (exhibits).

4829 ■ American Kerry Bog Pony Society (AKBPS)
c/o Linda C. Ashar, Pres.
13010 W Darrow Rd.
Vermilion, OH 44089
Ph: (440)967-2680
Fax: (440)967-2696
E-mail: inquiry@kerrybogpony.org
URL: http://www.kerrybogpony.org
Contact: Linda C. Ashar, Pres.

Founded: 2004. **Membership Dues:** junior, $20 (annual) ● associate, $25 (annual) ● senior, $40 (annual) ● joint, $75 (annual) ● life, $500 ● family (additional fee per child), $10 (annual). **Multinational. Description:** Educates the public about the Kerry Bog Pony. Assists in and promotes the breeding, registration, training, exhibition and general use of the Kerry Bog Pony. Promotes equestrian competition. **Computer Services:** Information services, Kerry Bog resources. **Telecommunication Services:** electronic mail, akbps@yahoo.com. **Publications:** *The Kerry Ring*. Newsletter.

4830 ■ American Miniature Horse Association (AMHA)
5601 S Interstate 35 W
Alvarado, TX 76009
Ph: (817)783-5600
Fax: (817)783-6403
E-mail: information@amha.org
URL: http://www.amha.org
Contact: Pam Pruitt, Registration Supervisor

Founded: 1978. **Members:** 8,000. **Membership Dues:** regular in U.S., associate in Canada, $75 ● associate in U.S., $55 ● regular in Canada, $95 ● regular outside U.S. and Canada, $120 ● associate outside U.S. and Canada, $100. **Staff:** 14. **Budget:** $1,000,000. **Description:** Represents individuals interested in the American Miniature horse breed. Promotes the breed; maintains a permanent registry. Sponsors competitions. Compiles statistics. **Absorbed:** (1985) International Miniature Horse Registry. **Publications:** *Miniature Horse World*, bimonthly. Magazine. Provides articles by breeders and experts in the field. Includes show calendar. **Price:** $30.00/year in U.S.; $42.00/year in Canada and Mexico; $70.00/year elsewhere. **Circulation:** 3,800. **Advertising:** accepted ● Also publishes brochure and breeders list. **Conventions/Meetings:** annual meeting.

4831 ■ American Morgan Horse Association (AMHA)
122 Bostwick Rd.
Shelburne, VT 05482-4417
Ph: (802)985-4944
Fax: (802)985-8897
E-mail: info@morganhorse.com
URL: http://www.morganhorse.com
Contact: Julie Broadway, Exec. Dir.

Founded: 1909. **Members:** 13,000. **Membership Dues:** general, $50 (annual) ● youth, $15 (annual) ● life, $800 ● life (youth), $100. **Staff:** 20. **Budget:** $2,700,000. **Regional Groups:** 10. **State Groups:** 50. **Local Groups:** 96. **For-Profit. Description:** Breeders and owners of purebred Morgan horses. Maintains registry showing ownership, transfers, and pedigree records. Promotes and sponsors youth programs. Maintains speakers' bureau, museum, and hall of fame. Compiles statistics. Sponsors Morgan horse sales program. Conducts educational programs; offers children's services. **Libraries: Type:** reference. **Holdings:** 100. **Subjects:** Morgan horses. **Awards: Frequency:** annual. **Type:** recognition. **Committees:** AHSA Rules; Archives; Breed Promotion; Driving and Dressage Education; Hunter/Jumper; International Relations; Judging Seminars; Judging Standards; Magazine Steering; Open Competition; Point Reyes Advisory; Register; Trail Riding; Youth Steering. **Subgroups:** Advertising; Art and Production; Communication; Editorial; Promotional Sales; Youth and Education. **Formerly:** (1971) Morgan Horse Club. **Publications:** *AMHA News and Morgan Sales Network*, monthly. Newsletter. Includes news, membership information, and sales tips. **Price:** included in membership dues. **Circulation:** 15,000. **Advertising:** accepted ● *Morgan Horse Magazine*, monthly. Contains directories of accredited clubs, board members, and breeders and owners. **Price:** $31.50/year. **Circulation:** 10,000. **Advertising:** accepted ● Brochures ● Catalog ● Newsletter, monthly. **Conventions/Meetings:** competition ● Grand National Show ● annual meeting and convention (exhibits) - always February ● regional meeting and show.

4832 ■ American Mustang Association (AMA)
Address Unknown since 2007

Founded: 1962. **Members:** 1,000. **Description:** Owners and breeders of the American Mustang. Works to preserve the Mustang and give the breed an honored place in the horseman's world; to increase their value by controlled registration and by providing them with classes in recognized horse shows. **Awards: Frequency:** annual. **Type:** recognition. **Recipient:** for horse/rider accomplishments. **Computer Services:** Mailing lists. **Departments:** Public Relations; Registration. **Publications:** *American Mustang World*, quarterly. Newsletter. **Price:** included in membership dues. **Advertising:** accepted ● *Breeders' Listing*, annual ● *Show Program*, annual ● Also publishes general information and registration materials. **Conventions/Meetings:** annual National Horseshow.

4833 ■ American Mustang and Burro Association (AMBA)
PO Box 1013
Grass Valley, CA 95945-1013
E-mail: ambainc@bardalisa.com
URL: http://www.ambainc.net
Contact: George W. Berrier Jr., CEO

Founded: 1981. **Members:** 2,000. **Membership Dues:** individual, $20 (annual) ● family, $25 (annual) ● junior, $15 (annual) ● business, patron, $50 (annual) ● silver, $75 (annual) ● life (gold), $200 ● life (diamond family), $400. **State Groups:** 40. **Description:** Owners of adopted wild horses and burros; interested individuals. Seeks to promote the cause of wild horses and burros. Conducts educational programs concerning America's wild equine, such as the Adopt-A-Horse Program (see separate entry); also sponsors its own horse and burro adoption program and rescues and relocates previously wild horses and burros. Promotes social and competitive events. Maintains speakers' bureau, archive, and wild equine registry. Operates hall of fame; sponsors competitions. Establishes American Mustang and Burro Museum and Library, a collection of books and videos on wild horses, burros, training, feeding, and care. **Awards:** U.S. Dressage Federation. **Frequency:** annual. **Type:** recognition. **Recipient:** for members having registered AMBA horse/horses. **Committees:** Adoption Compliance; Assistance; Protection and Preservation; Speakers' Bureau. **Publications:** *American Mustang and Burro Association Journal*, quarterly ● *American Mustang and Burro Association Studbook*, annual. **Conventions/Meetings:** annual meeting - always third Saturday of January, Lincoln, CA.

4834 ■ American Paint Horse Association (APHA)
PO Box 961023
Fort Worth, TX 76161-0023
Ph: (817)834-2742 (817)222-6438
Fax: (817)834-3152
E-mail: askapha@apha.com
URL: http://www.apha.com
Contact: Jerry Circelli, Dir. of Public Relations/Marketing

Founded: 1962. **Members:** 108,000. **Membership Dues:** general, $35 (annual) ● junior, $15 (annual) ● life, $400. **Staff:** 150. **Budget:** $15,000,000. **Regional Groups:** 112. **Multinational. Description:** Owners and admirers of Paint Horses, a breed characterized by color patterns on the horse's body. Collects, records and preserves the pedigrees of Paint horses; conducts research; stimulates and regulates matters pertaining to the history, breeding, exhibition, publicity, sale, racing, or improvement of the breed. Holds annual World Championship Show, Youth World Show, and Paint Horse Sale. Has established Youth Development Foundation, which provides a comprehensive recognition and scholarship program to educate and reward young horsemen. **Computer Services:** database, breed registration, horse racing, horse showing, general information ● information services, American Painthorse resources. **Committees:** Amateur; Breed Improvement; General Show and Contest Rules; Judges; Promotion; Racing; Registration; Rules; Ways and Means; Youth. **Departments:** Accounting; Administration; Data Processing; Facilities Management; Field Services; Human Resources; Journal; Marketing; Member Services; Performance and Racing; Registration; Youth Activities. **Formed by Merger of:** (1965) American Paint Stock Horse Association; American Paint Quarter Horse Association. **Publications:** *APHA Connection*, quarterly. Newsletter. **Price:** included in membership dues. **Circulation:** 108,000 ● *Paint Horse Journal*, monthly. Magazine. Includes breed promotion information. **Price:** $30.00 for members; $35.00 for nonmembers. **Circulation:** 28,000. **Advertising:** accepted ● *Paint Perspective*, 3/year. Newsletter ● *Stud Book and Registry*, annual. **Conventions/Meetings:** annual convention and workshop.

4835 ■ American Part-Blooded Horse Registry (APB)
12294 SE 104th Ct.
Portland, OR 97086
Ph: (503)698-9615
E-mail: information@apbhorseregistry.com
URL: http://www.apbhorseregistry.com
Contact: Betty Seymour, Registrar
Founded: 1939. **Staff:** 2. **Description:** A facility for registration of horses that are not purebred, but whose breeding lines are important. Registers half-bloods (one purebred parent), grade (more than 50&percent; purebred), and cross-bred (registered purebred parents of different breeds) horses. Keeps records for Morgans, American Saddlebred, Standardbred, quarter horse, Tennessee Walking horse, Hackney and Welsh horses, and other less widely known breeds. **Convention/Meeting:** none. **Also Known As:** APB Registry.

4836 ■ American Paso Fino Horse Association (APFHA)
PO Box 2363
Pittsburgh, PA 15230
Ph: (724)437-5170
Fax: (724)438-4471
Contact: Warren R. Hull, Pres.
Founded: 1964. **Members:** 500. **Description:** Persons united to promote the breed of Paso Fino horses. Maintains stud book and breed records. **Affiliated With:** United States Equestrian Federation. **Publications:** *American Paso Fino World*, quarterly ● Also publishes handbook and stud book. **Conventions/Meetings:** annual Horse Show - meeting - always fall.

4837 ■ American Pinto Arabian Registry (APAR)
608 Pecan
Ferris, TX 75125
Ph: (972)544-2717
E-mail: texasapar@wmconnect.com
URL: http://ampintoarabs.topcities.com/index.html
Membership Dues: regular, $25 (annual) ● life, $200. **Description:** Promotes Pinto and Arabian horses, colored and non-colored.

4838 ■ American Quarter Horse Association (AQHA)
PO Box 200
Amarillo, TX 79168
Ph: (806)376-4811
E-mail: aqhamail@aqha.org
URL: http://www.aqha.com
Contact: Bill Brewer, Exec. VP
Founded: 1940. **Members:** 348,000. **Membership Dues:** youth, $15 (annual) ● regular, $35 (annual) ● amateur, $40 (annual) ● life, $400 ● youth life, $50. **Staff:** 300. **Budget:** $42,000,000. **Regional Groups:** 83. **State Groups:** 50. **Languages:** English, Spanish. **Description:** Breeders, owners, trainers, and others interested in the American Quarter Horse. Registers pedigrees and maintains records. Hosts shows, contests, recreational rides, and races. **Publications:** *American Quarter Horse Journal*, monthly. **Price:** $25.00/year. ISSN: 0164-6656. **Circulation:** 77,000. **Advertising:** accepted. Alternate Formats: online ● *American Quarter Racing Journal*, monthly. Covers topics in the sport of quarter horse racing; includes race schedules. **Price:** $25.00/year. ISSN: 0899-3130. **Circulation:** 9,300. **Advertising:** accepted. Alternate Formats: online ● *America's Horse*, bimonthly. Magazine. Provides general interest topics covering equine lifestyle. **Price:** free for members ● Books ● Brochures. **Conventions/Meetings:** annual convention - usually in March ● annual show (exhibits).

4839 ■ American Quarter Horse Youth Association (AQHYA)
c/o American Quarter Horse Association
1600 Quarter Horse Dr.
PO Box 200
Amarillo, TX 79104
Ph: (806)376-4811
Fax: (806)349-6409
E-mail: youth@aqha.org
URL: http://www.aqha.com
Contact: Jackie Rapp, VP
Founded: 1970. **Members:** 31,000. **Membership Dues:** youth, $15 (annual) ● amateur, $40. **Staff:** 240. **Budget:** $420,000. **Regional Groups:** 6. **State Groups:** 70. **Languages:** English, Spanish. **Description:** Youth division of the American Quarter Horse Association (see separate entry). Quarter horse enthusiasts 18 years old and younger. Promotes expanded involvement between young people and the quarter horse. Conducts programs on improving and developing skills of young horse owners and on breeding, raising, and showing quarter horses. Sponsors Horse Sense Clinics throughout the U.S. Maintains museum and hall of fame. **Libraries: Type:** reference. **Awards:** AQHF Scholarship. **Frequency:** annual. **Type:** scholarship. **Recipient:** for college students ● **Type:** recognition. **Committees:** Youth Activities. **Formerly:** (1995) American Junior Quarter Horse Association. **Publications:** *The American Quarter Horse Journal*, monthly. Alternate Formats: online ● *America's Horse*, bimonthly. Magazine. Contains informative, educational, and entertaining articles that promote the benefits of owning an American Quarter Horse and belonging to AQHA. **Price:** free for members. **Conventions/Meetings:** annual World Championship Quarter Horse Show - competition, for the National Champion title and awards in various classes (exhibits) - always August in Fort Worth, TX.

4840 ■ American Quarter Pony Association (AQPA)
PO Box 30
New Sharon, IA 50207
Ph: (641)675-3669
Fax: (641)675-3969
E-mail: jarrod@netins.net
URL: http://www.aqpa.com
Contact: Linda Grim, Sec.
Founded: 1964. **Members:** 5,000. **Membership Dues:** regular, $10 (annual). **Description:** Breeding stables and private owners, breeders, trainers, and other individuals interested in quarter ponies and quarter-type ponies and horses noted for their suitability for riders of all ages. Develops and maintains a registry on Quarter ponies and other small horses of unknown parentage. Compiles statistics; conducts regional classes. **Awards:** Certificate of Excellence. **Type:** recognition ● Plaque of Supreme Excellence. **Type:** recognition ● Superior Pony. **Type:** recognition. **Publications:** *Quarter Pony News*, quarterly. Newsletter. **Advertising:** accepted. **Conventions/Meetings:** periodic competition ● periodic show.

4841 ■ American Ranch Horse Association (ARHA)
PO Box 186
Nancy, KY 42544
Ph: (606)872-2742 (606)271-2963
Fax: (606)636-4212
E-mail: arhainfo@aim.com
URL: http://www.americanranchhorse.net
Membership Dues: individual, $25 (annual) ● family, farm, amateur, $35 (annual) ● life, $250. **Description:** Encourages, promotes, advertises and develops the ranch type horse as a unique and excellent athlete. Promotes the abilities of the all around versatile working horse, regardless of breed, through shows, clinics and sales in a positive atmosphere where honesty, personal growth and politeness towards fellow horsemen exists. **Awards:** ARHA High Point Horse. **Frequency:** annual. **Type:** recognition. **Recipient:** to the horse earning the most points during a year than any other horse has earned in all events ● Honor Roll Titles. **Frequency:** annual. **Type:** recognition. **Recipient:** to the horse earning the most points in each event during the year ● Rookie Of The Year. **Frequency:** annual. **Type:** recognition. **Recipient:** to the amateur and youth horse/rider combination that accumulates the greatest number of points during the year. **Publications:** *ARHA News*. Newsletter. **Advertising:** accepted. Alternate Formats: online.

4842 ■ American Saddlebred Horse Association (ASHA)
4083 Iron Works Pkwy.
Lexington, KY 40511
Ph: (859)259-2742
Fax: (859)259-1628
E-mail: saddlebred@asha.net
URL: http://www.saddlebred.com
Contact: Alan F. Balch, Exec. Sec.
Founded: 1891. **Members:** 7,300. **Membership Dues:** senior, $60 (annual) ● contributing, $100 (annual) ● charter club affiliate, special junior, $50 (annual) ● junior (includes special junior), $25 (annual) ● life, $1,500 ● youth club affiliate, $40 (annual). **Staff:** 15. **Budget:** $1,200,000. **Regional Groups:** 6. **State Groups:** 51. **Description:** Maintains registry and pedigree records of American Saddlebred horses throughout the world, associated with museum and hall of fame. Compiles statistics. Provides free promotional literature; offers videotape rental and sales. Administers youth programs and horse show prize program. **Libraries: Type:** reference. **Holdings:** 1,000; archival material, books. **Subjects:** horses. **Awards:** Frank Ogletree Award. **Frequency:** annual. **Type:** recognition. **Recipient:** for breeders, sportsmanship, youths. **Computer Services:** database, progency and pedigree ● mailing lists, membership. **Committees:** ASHA Foundation; Pleasure Horses; Promotion; Youth Events. **Absorbed:** (1983) American Saddlebred Pleasure Horse Association; (1983) International American Saddlebred Pleasure Horse Association. **Formerly:** (1980) American Saddle Horse Breeders Association. **Publications:** *American Saddle Horse Registry*, annual. Contains pedigree info on all registered horses. ● *American Saddlebred*, bimonthly. Magazine. Contains calendar of events, member profiles, feature articles, and statistics. **Price:** $40.00/year. ISSN: 0746-6153. **Circulation:** 7,000. **Advertising:** accepted ● *Horse America Made* ● Membership Directory, annual. **Conventions/Meetings:** competition ● annual convention (exhibits).

4843 ■ American Saddlebred Sporthorse Association (ASBSA)
520 Byers Rd.
Chester Springs, PA 19425
Ph: (610)458-8652
E-mail: info@americansaddlebredsporthorse.com
URL: http://www.americansaddlebredsporthorse.com
Membership Dues: junior (9-17), $15 (annual) ● individual, $25 (annual) ● family, $30 (annual) ● patron, $100 (annual) ● life, $500. **Description:** Promotes the American Saddlebred horses. Offers education, resources, opportunities, support and encouragement to owners, breeders and trainers who seek to explore the viability of the American Saddlebred as a premier sport horse. **Awards:** ASBSA Ambassador Awards. **Frequency:** annual. **Type:** recognition. **Recipient:** to members who have attended 3 to 9 events in a year ● Year-End Awards.

Frequency: annual. **Type:** recognition. **Recipient:** to members who have promoted American Saddlebreds in dressage, eventing, hunting, expos, breed demos and parades. **Computer Services:** Information services, facts about American Saddlebreds ● online services, chat ● online services, discussion forum. **Publications:** Newsletter, quarterly.

4844 ■ American Shagya Arabian Verband (ASAV)
15918 Porter Rd.
Verona, KY 41092
E-mail: contact@shagya-arabian-horses-asav.org
URL: http://www.shagya-arabian-horses-asav.org
Contact: Kilian Dill, Pres.
Membership Dues: full, $35 (annual) ● associate, $15 (annual) ● junior, $10 (annual) ● life, $200. **Description:** Promotes the general interests of the Shagya Arabian breed of horse. Educates owners about the history and evolution of the breed. Promotes and coordinates with Shagya breeders in the USA and throughout the world. **Awards:** Shagya Journal Awards. **Frequency:** annual. **Type:** recognition. **Recipient:** to the outstanding journal for the year. **Programs:** Just Ride Competitive Trail and Endurance; Just Ride Horse Show; Ride With Me Trail; Ride With Me Youth. **Publications:** Newsletter. **Price:** included in membership dues.

4845 ■ American Shetland Pony Club/American Miniature Horse Registry (ASPC/AMHR)
81-B Queenwood Rd.
Morton, IL 61550
Ph: (309)263-4044 (641)454-2050
Fax: (309)263-5113
E-mail: info@shetlandminiature.com
URL: http://www.shetlandminiature.com
Contact: Dennis O'Keefe, Pres.
Founded: 1888. **Members:** 6,500. **Membership Dues:** individual, $45 (annual) ● secondary, $15 (annual). **Staff:** 12. **Budget:** $900,000. **Description:** Breeders and owners of registered Shetland ponies. Maintains registry and pedigree records, All-Star Awards System, and hall of fame. **Committees:** Breed Promotion; National Shetland Futurity; Show Rules. **Publications:** *The Journal*, bimonthly. Magazine. Covers all aspects of breeding, selling, and showing Shetland and Miniature horses. **Price:** $30.00 /year for nonmembers; $56.00/year outside U.S. **Circulation:** 6,500. **Advertising:** accepted. **Conventions/Meetings:** annual competition (exhibits) - always November ● annual convention, open to membership (exhibits) - always 1st Wednesday through Saturday of November.

4846 ■ American Shire Horse Association (ASHA)
c/o Pamela Correll, Admin. Sec.
1211 Hill Harrell Rd.
Effingham, SC 29541
Ph: (843)629-0072
E-mail: secretary@shirehorse.org
URL: http://www.shirehorse.org
Contact: Pamela Correll, Admin. Sec.
Founded: 1885. **Members:** 650. **Membership Dues:** individual in U.S., $50 (annual) ● life, in U.S., $600 ● life, outside U.S., $700 ● individual outside U.S., $60 (annual) ● corporate, $275 (annual). **Staff:** 1. **Budget:** $40,000. **Description:** Breeders of Shire draft horses. Maintains breed registry. Compiles statistics on animals registered and transferred annually. **Libraries: Type:** reference. **Awards: Frequency:** annual. **Type:** recognition. **Publications:** Newsletter, quarterly. Includes lists of new registrations and transfers. **Price:** included in membership dues. **Circulation:** 550. **Advertising:** accepted ● Membership Directory, annual ● Also publishes studbooks and breed brochure. **Conventions/Meetings:** annual National Shire Show ● annual Regional Shire Show.

4847 ■ American Suffolk Horse Association (ASHA)
c/o Mary Margaret M. Read, Sec.
4240 Goehring Rd.
Ledbetter, TX 78946-5004
E-mail: suffolks@cvtv.net
URL: http://www.suffolkpunch.com
Contact: Mary Margaret M. Read, Sec.
Members: 200. **Membership Dues:** initial, $35 ● renewal, $30 (annual). **Staff:** 1. **Description:** Owners and breeders of the Suffolk-Punch horse. Compiles statistics annually on animals registered and transferred. **Libraries: Type:** reference. **Holdings:** 100; books. **Subjects:** English and American Suffolk studs. **Publications:** *History of Suffolk*, periodic. Pamphlet. **Price:** free ● Newsletter, 3/year. **Price:** free for members. **Conventions/Meetings:** annual meeting, includes field day demonstrations.

4848 ■ American Trakehner Association (ATA)
1536 W Church St.
Newark, OH 43055
Ph: (740)344-1111
Fax: (740)344-3225
E-mail: atahorses@alltel.net
URL: http://www.americantrakehner.com
Contact: Brad Kerbs, Pres.
Founded: 1974. **Members:** 1,300. **Membership Dues:** active, $75 (annual) ● junior (age 21 and under), $35 (annual) ● life, $750. **Staff:** 3. **Budget:** $250,000. **Regional Groups:** 1. **Languages:** English, German. **Multinational. Description:** Owners, breeders, riders and trainers of Trakehner horses. Encourages the development of the Trakehner horse for the equestrian sports exemplifying beauty, endurance, balance and intelligence. Objectives are: to maintain a public registry of horses of Trakehner and East Prussian origin; to disseminate information on the breeding and raising of these horses; to promote their performance in dressage, hunting, jumping and special events; to mark or brand approved stallions, mares, and foals. Sponsors visits to breeding operations that focus on proper breeding, safety and selection procedures. Conducts equine clinics that feature movies and slides, professional judges, breeders and stud directors. Compiles statistics. **Awards:** Gerda Friedrichs Memorial Award. **Frequency:** annual. **Type:** recognition. **Recipient:** for breeding success of an ATA studbook registered Trakehner broodmare and her foals ● Horse of the Year. **Frequency:** annual. **Type:** recognition. **Recipient:** for breeding and performance ● James Shover Memorial Trophy. **Frequency:** annual. **Type:** trophy. **Recipient:** to junior riders competing on Trakehner horses ● Karl-Heinz Barton Trophy. **Frequency:** annual. **Type:** trophy. **Recipient:** for exemplary service to the organization. **Computer Services:** Information services, Trakehner Horse resources. **Telecommunication Services:** electronic mail, bjkerbs@worldnet.att.net. **Committees:** Advertising; Awards; Branding; Corporate regulations; Education; Futurity; Inspection; Public Relations; Publications; Registration; Trakehner Auction. **Formerly:** (2000) North American Trakehner Association. **Publications:** *The American Trakehner*, quarterly. Magazine. Includes international news. **Price:** included in membership dues; $5.00/issue for nonmembers. ISSN: 0730-2975. **Circulation:** 3,500. **Advertising:** accepted ● *The Trakehner Horse* ● *Trakehner Mares in America, Vol. I, II and III* ● *Trakehner Stallions in America*. Book. Provides stud information. ● *Trakehner Times*, bimonthly. Newsletter ● Handbook, annual ● Membership Directory, annual. **Conventions/Meetings:** annual convention and banquet - 2008 Nov. 20-22, Burbank, CA ● annual meeting and competition, with auction (exhibits).

4849 ■ American Trote and Trocha Association (ATTA)
17050 SW 20th Avenue Rd.
Ocala, FL 34473-8808
Ph: (352)347-7761
Fax: (352)347-7752
E-mail: info@usatta.org
URL: http://www.usatta.org
Contact: Lori Perez, Pres.
Founded: 2001. **Membership Dues:** individual, $30 (annual) ● junior, $10 (annual) ● business/corporate, family, $50 (annual) ● life, $500. **Description:** Aims to protect the integrity, Spanish heritage, and promotion of all Paso horses. Maintains the registry of diagonal Paso horses. Sponsors horse festivals. **Publications:** Newsletter. Alternate Formats: online.

4850 ■ American Walking Pony Association (AWPA)
PO Box 5282
Macon, GA 31208
Ph: (478)743-2321 (478)742-1001
Fax: (478)738-0310
E-mail: awpony@bellsouth.net
Contact: Joan Hudson Brown, Exec. Sec.
Founded: 1968. **Members:** 90. **Membership Dues:** individual, $10 (annual). **Staff:** 1. **Description:** Equine enthusiasts and American Walking Pony breeders. Maintains registry and promotes the breed of the American Walking Pony. Has established standards for the breed. **Convention/Meeting:** none. **Publications:** *A Dream Walking*. Brochure. **Price:** free.

4851 ■ American Warmblood Registry (AWR)
PO Box 197
Carter, MT 59420
Ph: (406)734-5499
Fax: (775)667-0516
E-mail: amerwarmblood@aol.com
URL: http://www.americansportpony.com
Founded: 1981. **Members:** 783. **Membership Dues:** individual, $75 (annual). **Staff:** 6. **Regional Groups:** 7. **For-Profit. Description:** Breeders and owners of the American Warmblood, a fullbred or crossbred sport horse that excels in dressage, combined training, hunting, and jumping. Helps insure quality by including all imported horses and their American offspring. Issues registration certificates. Compiles statistics; operates speaker's bureau and teaches seminars. **Awards:** Breed Award. **Frequency:** annual. **Type:** recognition. **Recipient:** for inspections and show records ● Dressage Award USDF. **Frequency:** annual. **Type:** recognition ● Futurity and National Performance Awards. **Frequency:** annual. **Type:** recognition. **Computer Services:** database, horses and ponies registered. **Additional Websites:** http://www.americanwarmblood.com. **Telecommunication Services:** electronic mail, amsportpony@aol.com. **Committees:** Breed; Competition; Sportpony. **Affiliated With:** American Quarter Horse Association; United States Dressage Federation. **Formerly:** (1998) American Sportpony Registry. **Publications:** *Selected Sires*, annual. Directory ● *Warmblood News*, bimonthly. Newsletter. **Price:** $24.00 in U.S.; $37.00 outside U.S. ISSN: 1079-4433. **Circulation:** 4,300. **Advertising:** accepted ● *Yearbook of American Warmblood Stallions*, annual. Includes listing of approved stallions. **Price:** free for members; $5.00 for nonmembers. **Advertising:** accepted. Alternate Formats: CD-ROM. **Conventions/Meetings:** annual board meeting.

4852 ■ American Warmblood Society (AWS)
2 Buffalo Run Rd.
Center Ridge, AR 72027-8347
Ph: (501)893-2777
Fax: (501)893-2779
E-mail: aws@americanwarmblood.org
URL: http://www.americanwarmblood.org
Contact: Jean Brooks, Natl. Dir.
Founded: 1983. **Members:** 5,200. **Membership Dues:** owner/rider, pony in U.S., $45 (annual) ● outside U.S., $60 (annual) ● life in U.S., $450 ● life outside U.S., $600. **Staff:** 6. **Budget:** $100,000. **Regional Groups:** 10. **State Groups:** 50. **Multinational. Description:** Promotes, represents, records and registers Horses for the Olympic Sports and Combined Driving worldwide and is actively involved with the issues of breeding selection, performance indexing, research and continuing education in the sport horse industry. **Libraries: Type:** reference; lending; not open to the public. **Holdings:** books, video recordings. **Subjects:** horses, riding, driving. **Awards:** Breeder of the Year. **Frequency:** annual. **Type:** recognition. **Recipient:** for a current member with the highest score of the year ● Director of the Year. **Frequency:** annual. **Type:** recognition. **Recipient:** for a well-respected and hard working member ● Horse of the Year Awards. **Frequency:** annual.

Type: medal. **Recipient:** for dressage, show jumping, combined training and driving, inspections and in hand at all levels ● Local Recognized Show Awards. **Type:** medal ● Regional Champion Awards. **Frequency:** annual. **Type:** medal. **Recipient:** to highest scoring at Regional Championships ● Volunteer/ Organizer of the Year. **Frequency:** annual. **Type:** recognition. **Recipient:** for a volunteer/organizer who exemplifies a well respected and hard working member. **Computer Services:** database, registry of information about warm-blooded horses breeders and trainers including pedigree, competition scores, and training specialties ● database, statistics on bloodlines in performance ● electronic publishing, quarterly newsletter for sporthorses ● mailing lists, of members. **Telecommunication Services:** information service, American warmblood horses. **Subgroups:** State Volunteer Staffs. **Affiliated With:** American Driving Society; United States Dressage Federation; United States Equestrian Federation; United States Eventing Association. **Absorbed:** (1992) North American Warmblood Association; (1996) Quarter Sport Horse Registry. **Publications:** *Sport Horse Guide*, annual. Journal. Recognizes all "Approved for Breeding" Stallions and Mares. **Price:** free. **Circulation:** 2,000. **Advertising:** accepted. Alternate Formats: online ● *Stallion Service Auction*, annual. Annual Report. Contains brochure of all donated stallions for the Annual Stallion Service Auction. **Price:** free. **Circulation:** 2,000. **Advertising:** accepted. Alternate Formats: online ● *Warmblood Whisper*, quarterly. Newsletter. Contains educational equine articles and member accomplishments. **Price:** free. **Circulation:** 2,500. **Advertising:** accepted. **Conventions/Meetings:** quarterly conference, covers dressage, combined training, show jumping, combined driving (exhibits) ● annual meeting, covers dressage, combined training, show jumping, combined driving (exhibits).

4853 ■ American Warmblood and Sport Horse Guild (AW&SHG)
Address Unknown since 2007
Founded: 1984. **Membership Dues:** registration fee per horse, for lifetime, $55. **For-Profit. Description:** Breeders and owners of registered warmbloods and sport-type performance horses. Promotes the breeding and use of these horses. Seeks to establish a breedable foundation for American cross breds of existing registered parentage and warmblood-type horses. **Convention/Meeting:** none. **Libraries: Type:** reference. **Holdings:** archival material, business records. **Publications:** *AW&SHG Rules and Regulations*. Brochure.

4854 ■ American Welara Pony Society (AWPS)
PO Box 401
Yucca Valley, CA 92286-0401
Fax: (760)364-2048
E-mail: awps@copper.net
URL: http://www.welararegistry.com
Contact: John H. Collins, Registrar
Founded: 1980. **Members:** 443. **Membership Dues:** junior, $14 (annual) ● senior, $16 (annual) ● farm/ breeder, $45 (triennial) ● life, farm breeder, $175 ● associate, $40 (annual) ● farm, $28 (annual). **Staff:** 13. **Budget:** $20,000. **For-Profit. Multinational. Description:** Horse breeders with an interest in the Welara pony (Welsh and Arabian). Collects, records, and preserves the pedigrees of Welara ponies. Promotes the breeding, improvement, exhibition, and sale of the breed internationally. Seeks to increase Welara foundation stock. Maintains registry of Welara, Welara Sports Ponies, Arabian, and Welsh horses. Maintains points program. **Libraries: Type:** reference. **Awards:** Hi-Point. **Type:** trophy. **Computer Services:** database, breeder's directory. **Telecommunication Services:** electronic bulletin board, public equine related bulletin board service ● electronic mail, info@welararegistry.com. **Publications:** *Showing the Welara*, annual. Book. Provides information on rules and showing. **Price:** $2.00 each, for nonmembers; free for members. **Circulation:** 1,500 ● *Stud Book*, annual. Contains information on all animals registered with AWPS. Includes photo. **Price:** $2.00 for nonmembers; free for members. **Circulation:** 800. **Advertising:** accepted. Alternate Formats: CD-ROM ● *Welara Journal*, semiannual. Features list of breeders and information about registry, shows, and related events. Includes research reports. **Price:** included in membership dues; $4.00 /year for nonmembers in U.S.; $5.00 /year for nonmembers outside U.S. **Conventions/Meetings:** annual meeting (exhibits) ● show.

4855 ■ American White Horse and American Creme Horse Registry (AWACHR)
90000 Edwards Rd.
Naper, NE 68755
Ph: (402)832-5560
E-mail: carleyd@juno.com
URL: http://www.whitehorseranchnebraska.com/registry.htm
Contact: Carley Daugherty, Sec.-Treas.
Founded: 1936. **Members:** 225. **Membership Dues:** individual in U.S., $15 (annual) ● family in U.S., $25 (annual) ● individual outside U.S., $20 (annual) ● family outside U.S., $30 (annual). **Staff:** 2. **Budget:** $6,000. **State Groups:** 2. **Description:** Official registry for pure white, or cream-colored and pink skinned white/cream horses and ponies. Encourages better breeding programs. Aids state club organizations; assists with competitive shows. Maintains museum. **Awards:** High Points Champion Stallion/ Mare. **Frequency:** annual. **Type:** recognition ● International Grand Champion. **Frequency:** annual. **Type:** recognition ● USA Grand National Champion. **Frequency:** annual. **Type:** recognition. **Formerly:** (1998) International American Albino Association. **Supersedes:** World-Wide White and Creme Horse Registry; American Albino Association; American Albino Horse Club. **Publications:** *Sending Your Horse to School*. Booklet ● *White Horse Ranch*. Booklet ● Newsletter, quarterly. Provides news and helpful tips for horse owners and members. **Price:** included in membership dues. **Advertising:** accepted. **Conventions/Meetings:** annual meeting - always Father's Day weekend in Naper, NE.

4856 ■ American Youth Horse Council (AYHC)
6660 No. D-451 Delmonico
Colorado Springs, CO 80919
Ph: (719)594-9778
Free: (800)TRY-AYHC
Fax: (775)256-0382
E-mail: info@ayhc.com
URL: http://www.ayhc.com
Contact: Cindy Schonholtz, Exec. Dir.
Founded: 1968. **Members:** 400. **Membership Dues:** adult leader, $25 (annual) ● association, education institution, $100 (annual) ● student leader, $15 (annual) ● local horse club, family, $40 (annual) ● corporation, $150 (annual). **Description:** Works as the umbrella organization providing resources and leadership to the youth horse industry. Promotes the youth horse industry and responsible equine management practices. Provides a forum for information exchange within the horse industry. Conducts educational forums for youth leaders. Establishes youth conference guidelines. **Libraries: Type:** reference. **Holdings:** books. **Subjects:** horse management. **Awards:** Distinguished Service Award. **Frequency:** annual. **Type:** recognition ● Leader of the Year Award. **Frequency:** annual. **Type:** recognition. **Recipient:** for adults offering outstanding leadership to young people within the horse industry ● National Youth Horse Leader of the Year. **Frequency:** annual. **Type:** recognition ● Regional Youth Leader Symposium Grant. **Frequency:** annual. **Type:** grant. **Computer Services:** database. **Programs:** Grants and Scholarship; Leader of the Year Award. **Affiliated With:** American Horse Council. **Publications:** *Horse Industry Handbook: A Guide to Equine Care and Management*. **Price:** $49.95 for members; $59.95 for nonmembers ● *News Network*, quarterly. Newsletter. **Price:** included in membership dues ● *Safety Manual*. **Price:** $8.00 for members; $10.00 for nonmembers ● *Youth Leaders Manual*. Book. Contains 60 lesson plans on three skills level to teach responsible horse care. **Price:** $34.95 for members; $43.95 for nonmembers ● Brochures. Alternate Formats: online. **Conventions/Meetings:** annual National Youth Horse Leaders Symposium - workshop and symposium, with educational seminars for adult leaders of youth involved with horses - always first quarter.

4857 ■ Appaloosa Horse Club (ApHC)
2720 W Pullman Rd.
Moscow, ID 83843
Ph: (208)882-5578
Fax: (208)882-8150
E-mail: ceo@appaloosa.com
URL: http://www.appaloosa.com
Contact: Steve Taylor, CEO
Founded: 1938. **Members:** 32,000. **Membership Dues:** individual, $55 (annual) ● couple, $80 (annual) ● family, $95 (annual) ● youth, $10 (annual) ● life - adult, $500 ● life - youth, $75. **Staff:** 57. **Budget:** $6,500,000. **Regional Groups:** 148. **Multinational. Description:** Works to promote and preserve the Appaloosa breed. Serves as a registry; sets official standards and establishes guidelines for acceptance and classification for the breed; issues and records certificates of registration. Sponsors four trail rides per year and two championship shows. Maintains breeding records. Offers extensive youth programs. Operates museum and hall of fame. **Awards: Type:** recognition. **Recipient:** for achievements in Show and Race ● **Frequency:** annual. **Type:** scholarship. **Recipient:** for seven to ten qualified individuals. **Programs:** ACCAP; Non-Pro; Trail and Distance; Youth. **Publications:** *Appaloosa Journal*, monthly. **Price:** $3.00/issue. **Circulation:** 32,000. **Advertising:** accepted. **Conventions/Meetings:** annual National Appaloosa Horse Show - competition, with professional, amateur and youth competition (exhibits) - always July ● annual World Championship Appaloosa Horse Show - competition, with professional and amateur competition (exhibits) - always November.

4858 ■ Arabian Horse Association (AHA)
10805 E Bethany Dr.
Aurora, CO 80014
Ph: (303)696-4500
Fax: (303)696-4599
E-mail: info@arabianhorses.org
URL: http://www.arabianhorses.org
Contact: Myron Krause, Pres.
Founded: 1908. **Members:** 40,000. **Membership Dues:** adult, $25 (annual) ● adult, $70 (triennial) ● youth, $20 (annual) ● business, $55 (annual) ● life, $650. **Staff:** 26. **Description:** Maintains purebred Arabian registry. **Formed by Merger of:** (2003) Arabian Horse Registry of America and International Arabian Horse Association. **Formerly:** (1969) Arabian Horse Club Registry of America. **Publications:** *Arabian Horse Bookshelf*, annual. Contains data on purebred Arabian Horses. **Price:** $75.00. Alternate Formats: CD-ROM ● *Registry News*, quarterly. Newsletter. **Conventions/Meetings:** board meeting - always January, May, and September.

4859 ■ Arabian Horse Breeders Alliance (AHBA)
28150 N Alma School Pkwy., Ste.103-474
Scottsdale, AZ 85262
Ph: (480)415-8921
Fax: (480)907-2253
E-mail: info@arabianbreedersworldcup.com
URL: http://www.arabians.com
Contact: Scott Bailey, Contact
Membership Dues: individual, $25 (annual) ● family, $50 (annual) ● life, $500 ● contributing, $1,000-$5,000. **Multinational. Description:** Seeks to unite breeders to enhance their experience with Arabian horses. Encourages Arabian horse ownership among others. Promotes appreciation of the Arabian breed through education, competition, and selective promotion and publicity. **Telecommunication Services:** electronic mail, info@arabhorse.com. **Publications:** Newsletter. Alternate Formats: online.

4860 ■ Arabian Horse Owners Foundation (AHOF)
PO Box 30924
Tucson, AZ 85751
Ph: (520)760-0682
Free: (800)892-0682

Fax: (520)749-2572
E-mail: info@ahof.org
URL: http://www.arabianhorseowners.org
Contact: Howard F. Shenk, Exec. Dir.
Founded: 1957. **Members:** 40. **Membership Dues:** individual, $25 (annual). **Staff:** 2. **Budget:** $150,000. **Description:** Aims to promote Arabian horses, preserve related historical information, memorabilia, and artifacts, and educate owners regarding management and understanding of horses. Conducts seminars and workshops in horse training, showing, judging, and management. Operates mail order gift shop. Maintains museum and Speaker's Bureau. Operates hall of fame. **Libraries: Type:** reference. **Holdings:** 1,500; archival material, books. **Subjects:** historical map, horse breeding, horse training. **Awards: Type:** recognition. **Committees:** Research; Show. **Publications:** Brochures ● Catalog. **Conventions/Meetings:** competition.

4861 ■ Arabian Horse Trust (AHT)
Address Unknown since 2007
Founded: 1974. **Membership Dues:** $35 (annual). **Staff:** 6. **Description:** Dedicated to the preservation of the Arabian breed through the world's largest Arabian museum, library, art gallery and theatre. All proceeds are directed in the areas of heritage, breed research, public education, youth programs/scholarships and the preservation of rare books, art and photographs. **Libraries: Type:** reference. **Holdings:** 2,600; artwork, audiovisuals, books, clippings, periodicals. **Subjects:** Arabian horses, Middle Eastern history related to horses, horse training, and special collections. **Awards:** Gladys Brown Edwards Scholarship. **Frequency:** annual. **Type:** scholarship. **Recipient:** for a college junior or senior student with skills in communications and an interest in Arabian horses ● William Zekan Memorial Scholarship. **Frequency:** annual. **Type:** scholarship. **Recipient:** for a senior high school student or college undergraduate needing financial support. **Affiliated With:** Arabian Horse Association; International Arabian Horse Association. **Publications:** *Update*, quarterly. Newsletter. Features Arabian Horse Trust news and events. **Price:** included in membership dues. **Circulation:** 6,000. **Advertising:** not accepted.

4862 ■ Arabian Professional and Amateur Horseman's Association (APAHA)
14900 N Pennsylvania Ave., No. 421
Oklahoma City, OK 73134
E-mail: chtrncntr@aol.com
URL: http://www.apaha.com
Contact: Chris Culbreth, Pres.
Founded: 1986. **Membership Dues:** voting, $75 (annual) ● affiliate, $30 (annual). **Description:** Represents the collective voice of the active exhibitors of Arabian and Half-Arabian horses. Promotes and upholds a fair and level playing field in the horse show arena. Promotes a kind and ethical treatment of horses. **Awards:** Breeder of the Year. **Frequency:** annual. **Type:** recognition. **Recipient:** to outstanding breeder of the year ● Horseman of the Year. **Frequency:** annual. **Type:** recognition. **Recipient:** to outstanding horseman of the year ● Horsewoman of the Year. **Frequency:** annual. **Type:** recognition. **Recipient:** to outstanding horsewoman of the year. **Computer Services:** Online services, forums.

4863 ■ Azteca Horse Registry of America
PO Box 998
Ridgefield, WA 98642-0998
Ph: (360)887-3259
Fax: (360)887-3259
E-mail: azteca@pacifier.com
URL: http://www.azteca-horse.com
Contact: Dolores Dougherty, Pres.
Description: Promotes the Azteca horse breed. **Awards:** Awards. **Type:** recognition. **Programs:** Awards; Patches. **Publications:** *The Azteca Horse*. Newsletter. Alternate Formats: online.

4864 ■ Back in the Saddle Horse Adoption (BITS)
c/o Joni Fink, Exec. Dir.
1313 Youngs Rd.
Linden, PA 17744
Ph: (570)974-1087
Fax: (866)869-6861
E-mail: bitsinfo@comcast.net
URL: http://www.bitshorseadopt.org
Contact: Joni Fink, Exec. Dir.
Description: Represents the interests of individuals dedicated to finding new homes and careers for horses. Provides rehabilitation and training to prepare horses for their new homes. **Programs:** Foster. **Publications:** *BITS of News*. Newsletter.

4865 ■ Belgian Draft Horse Corporation of America (BDHCA)
PO Box 335
Wabash, IN 46992
Ph: (260)563-3205
Fax: (260)563-3205
E-mail: belgian@belgiancorp.com
URL: http://www.belgiancorp.com
Contact: Vicki Knott, Sec.-Treas.
Founded: 1887. **Members:** 5,500. **Membership Dues:** regular, $39 (annual) ● youth, $25 (annual). **Staff:** 6. **Budget:** $500,000. **Description:** Owners, breeders, and importers of purebred Belgian draft horses. Issues certificates of registry and transfer. Compiles statistics. **Awards: Type:** recognition. **Formerly:** (1937) American Association of Importers and Breeders of Belgian Draft Horses. **Publications:** *Belgian Review*, annual. **Price:** $10.00/back issue (plus $2 shipping and handling). **Conventions/Meetings:** annual meeting.

4866 ■ Blazer Horse Association (BHA)
820 N Can-Ada Rd.
Star, ID 83669
Ph: (208)286-7267
E-mail: lorenzo@integrity.com
URL: http://www.integrity.com/homes/lorenzo/bha.htm
Contact: Neil Hinck, Pres.
Founded: 1967. **Members:** 100. **Membership Dues:** family, $15 (annual). **Staff:** 4. **Description:** Blazer horses are a well-rounded and muscled, short-backed breed known for its gentle and willing disposition. Promotes the breeding, raising, care, and training of Blazer horses. Conducts tests of horse stamina, speed, and training; maintains hall of fame records. Encourages competitions and horse shows. Compiles statistics. **Awards:** All Around Man/Woman Award. **Frequency:** annual. **Type:** recognition. **Recipient:** for paid members ● Blazer Hall of Fame. **Frequency:** annual. **Type:** recognition. **Recipient:** for paid members ● Brood Mares Award. **Frequency:** annual. **Type:** recognition. **Recipient:** for paid members ● Brood Stallions Award. **Frequency:** annual. **Type:** recognition. **Recipient:** for paid members ● Endurance Riders Award. **Frequency:** annual. **Type:** recognition. **Recipient:** for paid members ● High Point Honors. **Frequency:** annual. **Type:** recognition. **Recipient:** for winners of timed events ● Judged Show Person Award. **Frequency:** annual. **Type:** recognition. **Recipient:** for paid members ● Performance Gelding Award. **Frequency:** annual. **Type:** recognition. **Recipient:** for paid members ● Performance Mares Award. **Frequency:** annual. **Type:** recognition. **Recipient:** for paid members ● Performance Stallion Award. **Frequency:** annual. **Type:** recognition. **Recipient:** for paid members ● Provisional Horse Award. **Frequency:** annual. **Type:** recognition. **Recipient:** for paid members ● Speed Event Riders Award. **Frequency:** annual. **Type:** recognition. **Recipient:** for paid members. **Publications:** Brochures. Records the history of the breed and qualifications for registration. **Price:** $2.00. **Conventions/Meetings:** annual banquet, includes awards - always last Saturday of February ● annual meeting and symposium.

4867 ■ Bright Futures Farm
44793 Harrison Rd.
Spartansburg, PA 16434-1809
Ph: (814)827-8270
Fax: (814)827-8278
E-mail: info@brightfuturesfarm.org
URL: http://www.brightfuturesfarm.org
Contact: Beverlee Dee, Executor
Description: Aims to provide homes and/or sponsorship for unwanted horses, including injured or retired Thoroughbreds and "Premarin Foals"; trains adoptable horses; those that cannot be adopted retire at the Bright Futures Farm. Conducts a 50-50 raffle. **Publications:** *Progress Report*, semiannual. Contains information about adopted horses. ● Newsletter. Contains information about adopted horses.

4868 ■ Bureau of Land Management National Wild Horse and Burro Program
c/o US Bureau of Land Management
Off. of Public Affairs
1849 C St., Rm. 406-LS
Washington, DC 20240
Ph: (202)452-5125
Free: (866)4MUSTANGS
Fax: (202)452-5124
E-mail: woinfo@blm.gov
URL: http://www.wildhorseandburro.blm.gov
Contact: Lili Thomas, Program Chief
Founded: 1973. **Staff:** 5. **Description:** Operates by the Bureau of Land Management of the United States Department of the Interior. Functions as the primary means of placing into private care excess wild horses and burros removed from public lands in the western U.S. The animals are removed in an effort to maintain an ecological balance on public lands. Qualifiers may adopt, for a fee, up to four such animals per year. Coordinates with the U.S. government that retains ownership of the animals for one year, after which time the adopters are allowed to claim title if the animals have been treated humanely. Sponsors competitions; conducts educational programs. **Formerly:** Adopt-A-Horse Program. **Publications:** *National Wild Horse & Burro News*, quarterly. Contains news on BLM wild horses and burros. ● *So You'd Like to Adopt a Wild Horse or Burro*, periodic. **Price:** free.

4869 ■ Caspian Horse Society of the Americas (CHSA)
PO Box 1589
Brenham, TX 77834-1589
Ph: (979)251-7305 (979)830-9046
Fax: (979)830-1566
E-mail: mccfarmsbr@aol.com
URL: http://www.caspian.org
Contact: Joyce Covington, Treas.
Founded: 1994. **Description:** Strives to preserve and promote the Caspian horse breed. Maintains a purebred and partbred permanent registry devoted to the interests of the Caspian horse in the Western Hemisphere. Provides pertinent information on Caspian horses.

4870 ■ Champagne Horse Breeders' and Owners' Association (CHBOA)
2033 Meander Run Rd.
Locust Dale, VA 22948
Ph: (910)892-2332
E-mail: stephanie@chboa.com
URL: http://www.chboa.com
Contact: Stephanie Pennell, Pres.
Founded: 2005. **Membership Dues:** regular, $20 (annual) ● life, $200. **Description:** Works to document and register equines carrying the Champagne gene. Raises public knowledge of the gene, and creates a cooperative of Champagne breeders and enthusiasts who work together to promote the Champagne horse. Aims to provide a supportive environment for members to interact, share information and develop camaraderie.

4871 ■ Cleveland Bay Horse Society of North America (CBHSNA)
PO Box 483
Goshen, NH 03752
Ph: (352)489-2768 (603)863-5193

E-mail: info@clevelandbay.org
URL: http://www.clevelandbay.org
Contact: Faye M. Mulvey, Sec.
Founded: 1885. **Membership Dues:** individual, $45 (annual) ● family, $60 (annual) ● junior, $15 (annual) ● life, $450. **Description:** Breeders and owners of purebred and partbred Cleveland Bay horses, breed originated in the vale of Cleveland, Yorkshire, England. Aims to promote and educate people about this critically rare breed. **Awards:** Performances. **Frequency:** annual. **Type:** recognition. **Recipient:** for top, enrolled, pure/part bred horse in multiple disciplines of riding. **Publications:** *Baywatch*, bimonthly. Newsletter. **Price:** included in membership dues; $20.00 for nonmembers. **Advertising:** accepted. **Conventions/Meetings:** annual meeting.

4872 ■ Clydesdale Breeders of the U.S.A. (CBUS)
17346 Kelley Rd.
Pecatonica, IL 61063
Ph: (815)247-8780
Fax: (815)247-8337
E-mail: secretary@clydesusa.com
URL: http://www.clydesusa.com
Contact: Betty J. Groves, Sec.
Founded: 1879. **Members:** 900. **Staff:** 2. **Description:** Owners and breeders of registered Clydesdale horses. Maintains registry and pedigree records. **Formerly:** American Clydesdale Association; (1977) Clydesdale Breeders Association of the United States. **Publications:** *Clydesdale News*, annual. Magazine. **Price:** $15.00/each. **Advertising:** accepted. **Conventions/Meetings:** annual general assembly - always April.

4873 ■ Colorado Ranger Horse Association (CRHA)
c/o Laurel Kosior, Newsletter Ed./Exec. Sec.
1510 Greenhouse Rd.
Wampum, PA 16157
Ph: (724)535-4841
Fax: (724)535-4841
E-mail: kozyk_farm@hotmail.com
URL: http://www.coloradoranger.com
Contact: Barbara Summerson, Floating Dir.
Founded: 1938. **Members:** 3,000. **Membership Dues:** individual in U.S., $20 (annual) ● individual outside U.S., $25 (annual) ● youth, $15 (annual). **Staff:** 1. **Regional Groups:** 4. **Description:** Owners, breeders, and trainers of Colorado Ranger horses; interested individuals. Records and registers horses that can trace unbroken and direct descent from one of two foundation sires, Patches 1 and Max 2. Maintains registry and stud book library. Conducts youth and adult shows and an endurance riding program. Conducts research programs; maintains hall of fame. Sponsors national advertising program. **Libraries: Type:** open to the public. **Holdings:** 27; books, periodicals. **Subjects:** Colorado Ranger horses. **Awards:** John Morris Most Versatile Horse Award. **Frequency:** annual. **Type:** recognition ● Mike Ruby Honorarium. **Frequency:** annual. **Type:** recognition. **Recipient:** for members who support the association. **Telecommunication Services:** electronic mail, ridearangerhorse@yahoo.com. **Publications:** *Rangerbred News*, periodic. Newsletter. Contains member profiles and information on current events. **Price:** included in membership dues. **Advertising:** accepted ● Also publishes reference and studbooks. **Conventions/Meetings:** annual show, with an auction (exhibits) - always 3rd weekend of September.

4874 ■ Curly Sporthorse International (CSI)
PO Box 129
Cross Anchor, SC 29331
Ph: (864)316-4672
E-mail: csi@curlysporthorse.org
URL: http://www.curlysporthorse.org
Contact: Elaine Elmer, Pres./Founder
Founded: 2003. **Membership Dues:** individual, $25 (annual) ● family, $40 (annual) ● life - individual, $200 ● life - family, $300. **Multinational. Description:** Helps promote, market and selectively breed Curly Sporthorses. Improves the quality of the Curly Sporthorse. Educates and guides Curly Sporthorse owners and breeders. **Awards:** CSI Horse of the Year Awards. **Frequency:** annual. **Type:** recognition. **Recipient:** for qualified CSI registered horse, the owner must be a member in good standing.

4875 ■ Dales Pony Association of North America (DPANA)
PO Box 585
New Portland, ME 04954
Ph: (207)628-6061
E-mail: info@dalesponyassoc.com
URL: http://www.dalesponyassoc.com
Contact: Nan Berry, Sec.
Founded: 1998. **Membership Dues:** pony owner, $20 (annual) ● associate/non-pony owner, $12 (annual) ● family, $24 (annual) ● junior, $12 (annual) ● corporate, $80 (annual). **Multinational. Description:** Works for the humane and ethical treatment of Dale ponies. Educates the general public about Dale ponies.

4876 ■ Dales Pony Society of America (DPSA)
c/o Heather Loeber, Registrar/Treas.
32 Welsh Rd.
Lebanon, NJ 08833
Ph: (908)236-6087
Fax: (419)818-9048
E-mail: dpregistrar@yahoo.com
URL: http://www.dalesponies.com
Contact: Heather Loeber, Registrar/Treas.
Membership Dues: general, $25 (annual). **Description:** Works to preserve, promote and protect the Dales pony in the United States.

4877 ■ Egyptian Arabian Horse Alliance (EAHA)
PO Box 262
Cleburne, TX 76033-0262
E-mail: eahatx@aol.com
URL: http://www.eahatx.org
Contact: Diane Malone, Pres.
Description: Preserves Egyptian Arabian bloodlines and characteristics. Increases awareness of the value and availability of the Egyptian Arabian horse. Strives to educate horse enthusiasts about the benefits of owning Egyptian Arabians. **Computer Services:** database, membership directory. **Telecommunication Services:** electronic mail, tfranch@aol.com.

4878 ■ Fell Pony Society and Conservancy of the Americas
c/o Victoria Tollman, Sec.-Treas.
10844 Hwy. 172
West Liberty, KY 41472
E-mail: fellinfo@yahoo.com
URL: http://www.fellpony.org
Contact: Victoria Tollman, Sec.-Treas.
Founded: 1999. **Membership Dues:** individual, in North America, $25 (annual) ● family, in North America, $35 (annual) ● junior, in North America, $10 (annual) ● individual, outside North America, $35 (annual) ● family, outside North America, $45 (annual) ● junior, outside North America, $20 (annual). **Multinational. Description:** Conserves and promotes the Fell Pony breed. Protects the genetic diversity of the Fell pony through collective conservation efforts, educational promotion and by supporting the network of like-minded breeders, enthusiasts and breed associations around the globe, with special emphasis on the breed in the Americas. **Committees:** Educational Development; Show. **Publications:** *The Bulletin*. Newsletter. **Price:** included in membership dues.

4879 ■ Fell Pony Society of North America (FPSNA)
c/o Lisa Lindholm, Gen. Sec.
2626 Diane Ln.
Hibbing, MN 55746
Ph: (218)263-5217
E-mail: info@fpsna.org
URL: http://www.fpsna.org
Contact: Lisa Lindholm, Gen. Sec.
Founded: 2001. **Membership Dues:** basic, $30 (annual) ● overseas patron, $30 (annual). **Multinational. Description:** Promotes and preserves the Fell Pony breed in North America. Represents the interests of owners and breeders in North America. **Publications:** *Fell Pony Express*, semiannual. Newsletter.

4880 ■ Friesian Horse Association of North America (FHANA)
4037 Iron Works Pkwy., Ste.160
Lexington, KY 40511-8483
Ph: (859)455-7430
Fax: (859)455-7457
E-mail: fhana@fhana.com
URL: http://www.fhana.com
Contact: Rick Simonetti, Exec. Dir.
Membership Dues: associate, non-owner or non-resident of North America, $30 (annual) ● individual, $110 (annual) ● family, $130 (annual) ● business, $150 (annual) ● life, $1,000 ● associate, $60 (annual). **Multinational. Description:** Promotes the Friesian horse. **Awards:** President's Trophies for Driving. **Frequency:** annual. **Type:** trophy. **Recipient:** for highest placing driver ● **Type:** recognition. **Publications:** *The Friesian*, quarterly. Magazine. **Advertising:** accepted.

4881 ■ Front Range Equine Rescue
PO Box 307
Larkspur, CO 80118
E-mail: info@frontrangeequinerescue.org
URL: http://www.frontrangeequinerescue.org
Contact: J.J. Kane, Contact
Founded: 1997. **Description:** Works to stop the abuse and neglect of horses. Educates new, potential and existing horse owners on basic horse care topics. Provides direct care and rehabilitation for horses. **Programs:** Adoption; Education; Fire Evacuation; Foster; Rescue; Sponsor-a-Horse; Stop the Backyard Breeder.

4882 ■ Gaited Horse International Association
c/o Whispering Pine Press, Inc.
PO Box 1469
Spokane Valley, WA 99037-1469
Ph: (509)927-0404
Fax: (509)927-1550
E-mail: info@gaitedhorse.com
URL: http://www.gaitedhorse.com
Multinational. Description: Promotes care, training, well being of all gaited horse breeds on an international level. **Publications:** *Gaited Horse International*, annual. Book. **Price:** $25.95 comb-bound; $15.95 electronic download; $17.95 compact disc ● *The Gaited Horse International Magazine*, quarterly. **Price:** $25.00/year in U.S.; $35.00/year in Canada; $45.00/year outside U.S. and Canada; $45.00/2 years in U.S. ● *Gaited Newsletter*, quarterly. **Price:** free for members.

4883 ■ Galiceno Horse Breeders Association (GHBA)
Address Unknown since 2008
Founded: 1959. **Members:** 400. **Staff:** 1. **Regional Groups:** 3. **State Groups:** 6. **Description:** Breed enthusiasts united to: collect, record, and preserve the pedigree of Galiceno horses; publish a stud book and registry; regulate all matters pertaining to the history, breeding, exhibition, publicity, sale, racing, or improvement of the breed. Sponsors shows and showing and training clinics. **Publications:** Newsletter, monthly ● Also publishes rules and regulations handbook.

4884 ■ Gliding Horse and Pony Registry (GHPR)
Address Unknown since 2007
Founded: 1973. **Description:** Registers lateral gaited horses and ponies. Compiles statistics. **Conventions/Meetings:** competition.

4885 ■ Gotland-Russ Association of North America (GRANA)
811 Carpenter Hill Rd.
Medford, OR 97501
Ph: (541)535-6756
E-mail: jams811@mac.com
URL: http://gotlandponies.org
Contact: Joyce Moreno, Chair/Registrar
Founded: 1997. **Members:** 25. **Membership Dues:** regular, $25 (annual). **Description:** Owners and admirers of Gotland ponies. Promotes breeding of Gotland ponies; encourages responsible horse ownership. Facilitates communication among members; maintains breed registry, newsletters and website. **Computer Services:** database, registry available to all. **Publications:** *Gotland Glimpses*, periodic. Newsletter. **Price:** free for members. **Advertising:** accepted. **Conventions/Meetings:** annual meeting.

4886 ■ Grayson-Jockey Club Research Foundation (GJC)
821 Corporate Dr.
Lexington, KY 40503
Ph: (859)224-2850
Fax: (859)224-2853
E-mail: contactus@grayson-jockeyclub.org
URL: http://www.grayson-jockeyclub.org
Contact: Edward L. Bowen, Pres.
Founded: 1940. **Members:** 511. **Staff:** 5. **Budget:** $800,000. **Description:** Represents organizations and individuals interested in horses and in supporting equine medical research. Funds research projects on horse health and care. **Awards: Type:** grant. **Recipient:** for equine research. **Computer Services:** database, equine research. **Absorbed:** (1984) Jockey Club Research Foundation. **Formerly:** (1940) Grayson Foundation. **Publications:** *Research Today*, bimonthly. Newsletter. Reports on equine research. Alternate Formats: online ● Annual Report, annual. **Conventions/Meetings:** annual meeting - always second week of August, Saratoga Springs, NY.

4887 ■ Gypsy Vanner Horse Society (GVHS)
PO Box 507
Willington, CT 06279
Ph: (352)250-8908
Fax: (860)631-1035
E-mail: registrar@vanners.org
URL: http://www.vanners.org
Contact: William Ricci, Pres.
Membership Dues: regular, $25 (annual). **Description:** Promotes understanding and recognition of the Gypsy Vanner horse breed. **Computer Services:** Online services, breeders' list. **Telecommunication Services:** electronic mail, gypsyhorses@wildcreekfarm.com.

4888 ■ Haflinger Breeders Organization (HBO)
PO Box 205
Conesville, OH 43811-0205
Ph: (740)622-3091 (740)622-0081
Fax: (740)622-0063
E-mail: hbo@coshocton.com
URL: http://www.haflingerbreedersorganization.com
Contact: Dean Woodward, Sec.
Founded: 1993. **Members:** 300. **Membership Dues:** individual, $25 (annual). **Staff:** 2. **Description:** Owners and breeders of Haflinger horses. Seeks to advance the Haflinger breed; promotes responsible horse ownership. Inspects, approves, and registers Haflinger horses; maintains breed registry. **Publications:** *HBO Cable*, bimonthly. Newsletter.

4889 ■ Half Saddlebred Registry of America (HSRA)
4083 Iron Works Pkwy.
Lexington, KY 40511-8462
Ph: (859)259-2742
Fax: (859)259-1628
E-mail: saddlebred@asha.net
URL: http://www.saddlebred.com
Contact: Charlotte Tevis, Admin. Mgr.
Founded: 1971. **Membership Dues:** youth club affiliate, $40 (annual) ● special junior, charter affiliate, $50 (annual) ● junior, $25 (annual) ● senior, $60 (annual) ● contributing, $100 (annual) ● life, $1,500. **Description:** Serves as registry in the equine trade. **Telecommunication Services:** electronic mail, c.tevis@asha.net. **Publications:** Pamphlets. **Conventions/Meetings:** annual meeting.

4890 ■ Horse Protection League (HPL)
PO Box 741089
Arvada, CO 80006
Ph: (303)216-0141
E-mail: info@cohpl.org
URL: http://www.cohpl.org
Contact: Pat Lamprey, Sec.
Founded: 1994. **Members:** 400. **Membership Dues:** basic, $25 (annual) ● family, $50 (annual) ● yearling, $100 (annual) ● mare, $250 (annual) ● stallion, $500 (annual) ● life, $5,000. **State Groups:** 5. **Description:** Seeks to rescue horses living in undesirable circumstances and place them for adoption, and also provide a lifetime commitment to each horse rescued. Sponsors the Angel Program for sponsoring a special horse and the Emergency Horse Fund for a one-time contribution. **Publications:** Newsletter, quarterly. **Conventions/Meetings:** monthly meeting.

4891 ■ Hungarian Horse Association of America (HHAA)
c/o George Cooksley, Treas.
HC 71 Box 108
Anselmo, NE 68813
Ph: (308)749-2411 (308)749-2413
E-mail: info@hungarianhorses.org
URL: http://hungarianhorses.org
Contact: George Cooksley, Treas.
Founded: 1966. **Members:** 125. **Membership Dues:** individual, $25 (annual). **Description:** Records and preserves the bloodlines of horses imported from Hungary after World War II; promotes the breed. Maintains registry. **Awards:** USDF All Breeds Award. **Frequency:** annual. **Type:** recognition. **Affiliated With:** United States Dressage Federation. **Formerly:** (1997) Hungarian Horse Association. **Publications:** Newsletter, 3/year. **Circulation:** 150. Alternate Formats: online. **Conventions/Meetings:** annual meeting.

4892 ■ Iberian Sport Horse and Warmblood Registry
c/o Dolores Dougherty, Pres.
PO Box 998
Ridgefield, WA 98642
Ph: (360)887-3259
Fax: (360)887-3259
URL: http://www.iberiansporthorse.com
Contact: Dolores Dougherty, Pres.
Founded: 1998. **Description:** Works as Iberian sport horse and warmblood registry.

4893 ■ Icelandic Horse Trekkers (IHT)
Address Unknown since 2007
Founded: 1982. **Members:** 300. **Description:** Breeders, enthusiasts, and distance and trail riders of the Icelandic horse. Seeks to encourage the development of the Icelandic breed and the sport of pony trekking. Works to promote the stamina, smooth gait, and excellent disposition of the Icelandic horse and fosters the preservation of the breed. Provides forum for information exchange among members and attempts to locate additional Icelandic horses and their owners. Maintains clearinghouse for physiological research on horses and their riders. Provides marketing service for buyers and sellers of Icelandic horses. **Awards: Type:** recognition. **Formerly:** (1989) Icelandic Pony Trekkers. **Publications:** *Icelandic Horse Trekkers Newsletter*, quarterly. **Price:** $7.50/year in U.S.; $10.00/year outside U.S. **Advertising:** accepted.

4894 ■ International Andalusian and Lusitano Horse Association (IALHA)
101 Carnoustie N, Box 200
Birmingham, AL 35242
Ph: (205)995-8900
Fax: (205)995-8966
E-mail: office@ialha.org
URL: http://www.ialha.com
Contact: Martina Philpott, Exec. Dir.
Founded: 1963. **Members:** 1,700. **Membership Dues:** associate/business, $50 (annual) ● full, $150 (annual). **Staff:** 4. **Budget:** $350,000. **Regional Groups:** 7. **Languages:** English, Spanish. **Multinational. Description:** Conducts research on Andalusian and Lusitano equine bloodlines. Owns set of Spanish and Portuguese stud books. Sponsors regional and national shows for purebred and half-bred Andalusians and Lusitanos. Conducts educational programs. Maintains U.S. registry for Andalusians and Half-Andalusians. **Computer Services:** database, breeders ● information services, Andalusian breed resources. **Additional Websites:** http://www.ialha.org. **Telecommunication Services:** electronic mail, martina@ialha.org. **Formerly:** (1995) American Andalusian Association. **Publications:** *The Andalusian*, quarterly. Magazine. **Price:** $30.00 in U.S. for nonmembers; included in membership dues. **Advertising:** accepted ● *International Andalusian and Lusitano Horse Association Handbook*, annual. **Conventions/Meetings:** annual meeting and show - usually October ● annual National Show - competition.

4895 ■ International Arabian Horse Association (IAHA)
Address Unknown since 2008
Founded: 1950. **Members:** 28,000. **Membership Dues:** youth affiliate; direct - youth, $14-$20 (annual) ● adult affiliate, $39-$45 (annual) ● associate, $20 (annual) ● direct, $79-$85 (annual) ● business, $54 (annual) ● life, $1,000. **Staff:** 65. **Budget:** $5,000,000. **Regional Groups:** 18. **Description:** Registers half-Arabian and Anglo-Arabian horses, administers more than $4 million in prize money annually, produces national events and provides activities and programs that enhance Arabian horse ownership. **Awards:** Dressage, Achievement, Distance Ride, and National Show Awards, Recreational Ride. **Frequency:** annual. **Type:** recognition. **Computer Services:** Mailing lists. **Committees:** Amateur; Combined Training; Dressage; Equine Stress; Equitation; Ethical Practice Review Board; International Arabian Horse Cover Review; Judges and Stewards Selection; National Championship and Regional Classes; Professional Horsemen; Sport Horse; Youth Activities. **Publications:** *IAHA Handbook*, annual. Alternate Formats: online ● *International Arabian Horse Magazine*, bimonthly. **Price:** $24.00/year. **Circulation:** 28,000. **Advertising:** accepted. **Conventions/Meetings:** annual Canadian National Arabian and Half-Arabian Championship Horse Show (exhibits) ● annual convention ● annual National Championship Arabian and Half-Arabian/Anglo-Arabian Competitive Trail Ride - competition ● annual National Championship Arabian and Half-Arabian/Anglo-Arabian Endurance Ride - competition ● annual U.S. National Arabian and Half-Arabian Championship Horse Show (exhibits) ● annual Youth National Arabian and Half-Arabian Championship Horse Show (exhibits).

4896 ■ International Buckskin Horse Association (IBHA)
PO Box 268
Shelby, IN 46377
Ph: (219)552-1013
E-mail: ibhainc@sbcglobal.net
URL: http://www.ibha.net
Contact: Richard Kurzeja, Exec. Sec.
Founded: 1971. **Members:** 3,500. **Membership Dues:** amateur, youth, $10 (annual) ● individual, $25 (annual) ● life, $200. **Staff:** 4. **Budget:** $200,000. **State Groups:** 21. **For-Profit. Description:** Represents owners of Buckskin, Dun or Grulla horses united to promote the breeding of such horses and preserve records of accomplishments and pedigrees. Sponsors research; offers children's services. **Libraries: Type:** reference. **Awards:** High Point Award. **Frequency:** annual. **Type:** recognition ● Lifetime Award. **Frequency:** annual. **Type:** recognition ● World Champion. **Frequency:** annual. **Type:** monetary ● Youth Activity Annual Accomplishment Award.

Frequency: annual. **Type:** recognition ● Youth Scholarships. **Frequency:** annual. **Type:** scholarship. **Recipient:** to members for 2 years. **Computer Services:** database, charter clubs ● database, Gateway Circuit winners. **Committees:** Amateur; Color Data; Convention; Drug Abuse and Illegals; Dun Factor and Color; Judges and Ethics; National Queen; Registration; Show Rules; World Show; World Show Sale; Youth Activity; Youth Scholarship. **Formerly:** (1971) International Buckskin Horse Registry. **Publications:** *Horse Circuit News*, monthly. Newspaper. **Price:** included in membership dues. **Circulation:** 3,500. **Advertising:** accepted ● *International Buckskin Horse Association Information Booklet*. **Conventions/Meetings:** annual convention ● periodic seminar.

4897 ■ International Colored Appaloosa Association (ICAA)
PO Box 99
Shipshewana, IN 46565
Ph: (574)825-3331
E-mail: icaa@aol.com
URL: http://www.icaainc.com
Contact: Penny Kowalski, Pres.

Members: 1,500. **Membership Dues:** individual adult, $15 (annual) ● family (head of household, spouse, children under 18 years old), $22 (annual) ● youth (18 years old and under), $5 (annual). **Multinational. Description:** Represents the interests of Appaloosa enthusiasts dedicated to the development and preservation of the Appaloosa as a purebred blood-breed. Works to develop, preserve, protect and promote a purebred blood-breed Appaloosa. **Publications:** *ICAA Newsletter*, monthly. **Price:** for members. Alternate Formats: online ● Annual Report. **Price:** for members.

4898 ■ International Curly Horse Organization (ICHO)
c/o Tina Estridge, Office Mgr.
2690 Carpenter Rd.
Jamestown, OH 45335
Ph: (515)204-6211
Fax: (563)405-7979
E-mail: office@curlyhorses.org
URL: http://www.curlyhorses.org
Contact: Tina Estridge, Office Mgr.

Founded: 2000. **Membership Dues:** regular, $25 (annual) ● junior, $20 (annual) ● family, $45 (annual) ● life, $300. **Staff:** 6. **Multinational. Description:** Protects and preserves curly horses. Registers and tracks pedigrees of North American curly horses. Funds and supports research on curly horses. Provides continuing education to breeders and members for maximum understanding of curly horse genetics. **Computer Services:** Mailing lists. **Committees:** Convention; Fundraising; Genesis; Promotions; Show. **Departments:** Member Support; Research. **Publications:** *ICHO Gazette*, quarterly. Newsletter.

4899 ■ International Generic Horse Association (IGHA)
PO Box 6778, Eastview
San Pedro, CA 90734-6778
E-mail: volunteer@equinerescue.net
URL: http://www.igha.org

Founded: 1975. **Description:** Owners and breeders of horses. Promotes "a better understanding, appreciation, and development of all equine types and breeds without prejudice or fault due to any known or unknown origin, lineage or breeding." Maintains registry of horses of unknown or crossbreeding; collects data relevant to the well-being of crossbred horses. **Publications:** *IGHA/HA Catalog*, periodic ● *IHG/HA Informational Brochure*, periodic.

4900 ■ International Morab Breeders' Association (IMBA)
24 Bauneg Rd.
Sanford, ME 04073
Free: (866)667-2246
E-mail: imba@morab-imba.com
URL: http://www.morab.com
Contact: Karen Smith, Exec. Dir.

Founded: 1986. **Members:** 576. **Membership Dues:** associate, $25 (annual) ● individual owner/breeder, $30 (annual) ● family, $40 (annual) ● individual - life, $200 ● individual youth/youth family, $10 (annual). **Staff:** 3. **Regional Groups:** 10. **State Groups:** 2. **Local Groups:** 7. **National Groups:** 3. **Multinational. Description:** Persons owning or breeding Morab horses and owners of Arabian, or Morgan horses capable of producing Morab foals; interested others. (The Morab horse, established as a breed in 1973, is produced by the cross-breeding of Arabian and Morgan horses. The Morab is characterized by powerful lungs and great endurance, a short back, and an intelligent and affectionate nature.) Promotes the Morab horse worldwide. Sponsors trail rides, shows, futurities, and riding events. Conducts educational programs. International Morab Registry Computerized Registry established - 1993. **Libraries: Type:** reference. **Holdings:** artwork, audiovisuals, clippings, photographs. **Awards:** Breeder of the Year. **Frequency:** annual. **Type:** recognition. **Recipient:** for Morab breeder ● Meritorious Service. **Frequency:** periodic. **Type:** recognition. **Recipient:** to IMBA member ● Morab Horse of the Year. **Frequency:** annual. **Type:** recognition. **Computer Services:** database, registry and awards systems, sale horses. **Funds:** Morab Breeders Trust. **Programs:** Lifetime Achievement Award; Youth. **Subgroups:** Partners and Performance. **Also Known As:** Morab Community Network. **Publications:** *Breeders Guide*, annual. Membership Directory. **Price:** free for members. **Circulation:** 500. **Advertising:** accepted ● *Morab Moments*. Book. **Price:** $40.00. ISSN: 0966-3113 ● *Morab Perspective*, quarterly. Newsletter. Includes articles, breeders' tips, and announcements of new foals. **Price:** free for members. **Advertising:** accepted ● Brochure ● Also publishes breed history. **Conventions/Meetings:** annual banquet and convention - every first Saturday in November ● annual Region Morab Championship Show, with horse fair.

4901 ■ International Morab Registry (IMR)
c/o International Morab Breeders Association
24 Bauneg Beg Rd.
Sanford, ME 04073
Free: (866)667-2246
E-mail: imba@morab-imbaa.com
URL: http://www.morab.com
Contact: Jackie Briscoe, Registrar

Founded: 1992. **Members:** 500. **Membership Dues:** associate, $25 (annual) ● individual owner/breeder, $30 (annual) ● family, $40 (annual) ● life, $200 ● youth individual/family, $10 (annual). **Staff:** 2. **Regional Groups:** 10. **State Groups:** 2. **Local Groups:** 7. **National Groups:** 3. **Multinational. Description:** Breeders, owners, and admirers of Morab horses. Promotes advancement of the Morab breed. Serves as the breed registry of International Morab Breeders Association. Conducts promotional and marketing activities. Engages in computerized research. **Awards:** Breeder of the Year. **Frequency:** annual. **Type:** recognition. **Recipient:** to Morab breeder for foal production, stallion service, IMBA sponsored Morab Futurity placement and other contributions ● Breeders Crop. **Frequency:** annual. **Type:** recognition ● Hearst Memorial Performance Award. **Frequency:** annual. **Type:** recognition ● Lifetime Achievement Award Program. **Frequency:** periodic. **Type:** recognition ● Meritorious Service Award. **Frequency:** annual. **Type:** recognition. **Recipient:** to a member for services in promotion of the Morab ● Morab Horse of the Year. **Frequency:** annual. **Type:** recognition. **Recipient:** to Morabs that are out being ambassadors of the Morab breed ● Partnership with AERC-Morab. **Frequency:** annual. **Type:** recognition ● Partnership with USDF All Breed-Morab. **Frequency:** annual. **Type:** recognition. **Also Known As:** The Morab Registry. **Publications:** *History of the Morab*. Brochure ● *The Morab Perspective*, quarterly. Newsletter. **Price:** included in membership dues. **Advertising:** accepted. **Conventions/Meetings:** periodic show.

4902 ■ International Pedigree Assignment and Bloodline Research Association (IPABRA)
c/o Chris Wallbruch, Pres./Treas.
321 N Martha St.
Lombard, IL 60148
E-mail: wombats@earthlink.net
URL: http://www.ipabra.org
Contact: Chris Wallbruch, Pres./Treas.

Members: 100. **Membership Dues:** in U.S., $10 (annual) ● outside U.S., $15 (annual). **Multinational. Description:** Promotes the practice of pedigree assignment in the model horse hobby. Provides useful information to people who share a common interest in pedigree assignment. Maintains a registry for purposes of compiling stud books and assisting members with sire and dam searches. **Awards:** Cumulative Awards. **Frequency:** annual. **Type:** recognition. **Recipient:** to breeders and their horses with the most accumulated points in a lifetime ● Year End Awards. **Frequency:** annual. **Type:** recognition. **Recipient:** to breeders and their horses with the most points accumulated in a given show year. **Telecommunication Services:** electronic mail, anniemare@neb.rr.com. **Publications:** *Bloodlines*, bimonthly. Newsletter. **Price:** included in membership dues. **Advertising:** accepted ● *IPABRA Stud Book*, periodic. Contains a comprehensive listing of members and their registered breeding stock. **Price:** $15.00/copy ● *Pedigree Assignment 101!*. Booklet. Features advertising, organizing and research tips. **Price:** $3.00/copy ● Membership Directory. Alternate Formats: online.

4903 ■ International Quarab Horse Association (IQHA)
PO Box 263
Hopkins, MI 49328-0263
Ph: (269)672-9175
Fax: (269)793-7984
E-mail: quarabregistry@aol.com
URL: http://www.quarabs.org
Contact: Corrina Wilbur, Contact

Membership Dues: youth, $5 (annual) ● individual, $10 (annual) ● family, $15 (annual) ● individual (initial), $15 ● family (initial), $20 ● life, $100. **Multinational. Description:** Maintains the registry for the Quarab breed. Promotes the responsible breeding of Quarabs by specific pedigree, conformation type and performance. Encourages good horsemanship and sportsmanship. **Computer Services:** Mailing lists, of members. **Programs:** Outside Show Activities.

4904 ■ International Quarter Pony Association (IQPA)
PO Box 125
Sheridan, CA 95681
Ph: (916)645-9313
E-mail: iqpaqp@pacbell.net
URL: http://netpets.org/~iqpa
Contact: LaDonna Foster, Exec. Sec.

Founded: 1994. **Membership Dues:** regular, $15 (annual). **Multinational. Description:** Works to record and preserve pedigrees of International Quarter Ponies. **Publications:** *International Quarter Pony Journal*. **Price:** $15.00/year. **Advertising:** accepted ● *Registry*. Book ● *Stud Book* ● Articles. Alternate Formats: online.

4905 ■ International Sport Horses of Color (SHOC)
PO Box 1710
Cottage Grove, OR 97424
Ph: (541)836-3000
E-mail: info@shoc.org
URL: http://www.shoc.org

Founded: 1998. **Membership Dues:** individual, $45 (annual) ● family, $65 (annual) ● life, $500. **Multinational. Description:** Provides the worldwide, color-oriented, sport horse and pony registry to unite sport horse breeders. **Awards:** Horse of the Year. **Frequency:** annual. **Type:** recognition.

4906 ■ International Sporthorse Registry (ISR)
517 DeKalb Ave.
Sycamore, IL 60178
Ph: (815)899-7803
Fax: (815)899-7823
E-mail: isreg@aol.com
URL: http://www.isroldenburg.org
Contact: Ekkehard L. Brysch, CEO
Founded: 1983. **Members:** 1,998. **Membership Dues:** ordinary, $80 (annual). **Staff:** 9. **Description:** Owners and breeders of sport horses. Seeks to improve sport horse bloodlines. Formulates and enforces standards of breed conformance; maintains breed registry. **Libraries: Type:** reference. **Subjects:** copies of Breeders Guide. **Awards:** Champion Foal Award. **Frequency:** annual. **Type:** trophy. **Recipient:** for the highest scoring foal at each inspection ● Champion Mare Award. **Frequency:** annual. **Type:** trophy ● USDF All Breed Award. **Frequency:** annual. **Type:** trophy. **Affiliated With:** United States Dressage Federation. **Publications:** *Breeders Guide*, annual. Book. Includes breeding statistics and information about the stallions. ● Newsletter, quarterly. Includes actual information about events, inspections, seminars, and show results. **Conventions/Meetings:** annual board meeting.

4907 ■ International Spotted Horse Registry Association (ISHR)
PO Box 412
Anderson, MO 64831-0412
Ph: (417)475-6273
Free: (866)201-3098
E-mail: ishrppa@aol.com
URL: http://members.tripod.com/~spottedhorses/index.html
Contact: Rebecca Rogers, Founder/Pres.
Founded: 1990. **Members:** 400. **Membership Dues:** individual/family, $10 (annual) ● life, $85. **Staff:** 19. **Multinational. Description:** Color registry for any/all types of spotted horses. Drafts to miniatures, grade to purebred, champion to family pet. Spots from Paints to Pintaloosas; each horse gets a permanent registration number. Conducts several programs for members and horses for year-end awards and rewards. **Libraries: Type:** reference. **Holdings:** articles, books, business records, periodicals. **Subjects:** spotted horses. **Awards:** ROM Year End High Point Trophies. **Frequency:** annual. **Type:** trophy. **Recipient:** for barrels, jumping showmanship, horsemanship, halter, dressage, driving, walk/trot, open contest and gymkhana, champion, supreme champion ● Special Year End Awards. **Frequency:** annual. **Type:** recognition. **Committees:** Judge; Show. **Publications:** *Foundation Stallions, Foundation Broodmares*, annual. Books ● *Rainbow Connection*, bimonthly. Newsletter. **Conventions/Meetings:** annual Open Horse Show (exhibits).

4908 ■ International Warlander Society and Registry
PO Box 110545
Palm Bay, FL 32911-0545
Ph: (321)953-1410
E-mail: warlandersr@cs.com
Contact: Meaza Ridley, Registrar
Multinational. Description: Promotes the Warlander horse, the rare Friesian and Andalusian breeds. **Publications:** *Horse of Kings*, annual. Magazine. Contains reports on the historical significance of royal Baroque horses. **Price:** $30.00 in U.S.; $42.00 outside U.S.

4909 ■ Irish Draught Horse Society of North America (IDHS (NA))
c/o Rachel Cox, Information Off.
HC65 Box 45
Pleasant Mount, PA 18453-9605
Free: (866)434-7621
E-mail: rachael@nep.net
URL: http://www.irishdraught.com
Contact: Gina Kirby, Pres.
Founded: 1993. **Membership Dues:** single (voting), $50 (annual) ● single (non-voting), $40 (annual) ● family (voting), $75 (annual) ● junior, business (non-voting), $25 (annual) ● life, (voting), $550. **Multinational. Description:** Promotes and preserves the Irish Draught Horse breed. Promotes and raises awareness of its successful crossbreed, the Irish Draught Sport Horse. **Awards:** Performance Awards. **Frequency:** annual. **Type:** recognition. **Recipient:** to members with an outstanding performance during shows and events. **Computer Services:** Information services, Irish Draught Horse resources. **Telecommunication Services:** electronic mail, gina@irishjumpersandhunters.com. **Committees:** Credentials; Marketing Team. **Publications:** *The Blarney*, quarterly. Newsletter. Contains timely, educational and entertaining articles on breeding and bloodlines. **Advertising:** accepted.

4910 ■ Kiger Mesteno Association (KMA)
11124 NE Halsey, Ste.591
Portland, OR 97220
E-mail: info@kigermustangs.org
URL: http://www.kigermustangs.org
Contact: Kevin Sink, Pres.
Founded: 1988. **Members:** 500. **Membership Dues:** individual, $30 (annual). **Description:** Protects, preserves, promotes and enhances the wild herd of mustangs. Establishes the use of the Kiger Mustang in all applicable areas of recreation, competition and work. Promotes activities and fellowship among the owners, breeders and individuals interested in the Kiger Mustang. **Awards:** Member of the Year. **Frequency:** annual. **Type:** recognition. **Recipient:** to the outstanding member ● Ron Harding Annual High Point Perpetual Trophy Award. **Frequency:** annual. **Type:** trophy. **Recipient:** to the horse with the highest annual grand total points from all fields of competition. **Computer Services:** Online services, message board. **Committees:** Medallion Awards Program. **Publications:** *Kiger Focus Newsletter*. **Advertising:** accepted.

4911 ■ Lipizzan Association of North America (LANA)
PO Box 1133
Anderson, IN 46015-1133
Fax: (765)641-1208
E-mail: sandy@lipizzan.org
URL: http://www.lipizzan.org
Contact: Sandy Heaberlin, Dir./Trustee
Founded: 1968. **Members:** 200. **Membership Dues:** individual/corporation, $45 (annual) ● friend, $15 (annual). **Staff:** 9. **Description:** Owners of Lipizzan horses; individuals interested in Lipizzans. (Lipizzans are smooth-gaited show and pleasure horses.) Promotes the Lipizzan as a competition, show, and pleasure horse. Maintains placement service and Speaker's Bureau. Conducts educational programs. **Awards:** United States Dressage Federation All Breed Award. **Frequency:** annual. **Type:** recognition. **Formed by Merger of:** (1992) Lipizzan Association of American; Lipizzan Society of North America. **Formerly:** (1980) Royal International Lipizzan Club; (1992) Lipizzan Association of America. **Publications:** *American Lipizzan: A Pictorial History*, annual. Book. Provides a comprehensive history of the breed in North America. **Price:** $40.00 ● *The Haute Ecole*, quarterly. Newsletter. **Advertising:** accepted. Alternate Formats: online ● *The Lipizzan Association of North America Studbook*. Contains information on imported and American breed horses. **Price:** $125.00 ● *Lipizzan Association of North America, V.2*, annual. Book ● Brochure. **Price:** $75.00. **Conventions/Meetings:** annual congress.

4912 ■ Lippitt Morgan Breeders Association (LMBA)
c/o Brenda Vincent
6395W US Hwy. 2
Manistique, MI 49854
Ph: (906)341-6372
E-mail: president@lippittmorganbreedersassociation.com
URL: http://www.lippittmorganbreedersassociation.com
Contact: Denise Erway, Pres.
Founded: 1995. **Membership Dues:** voting, $30 (annual) ● farm voting, $45 (annual) ● associate and non-voting, $30 (annual). **Description:** Preserves and promotes the Lippitt Morgan horse. Improves the condition of individuals engaged in the breeding of the Lippitt Morgan horse. **Computer Services:** Information services, Lippitt resources ● online services, message board. **Telecommunication Services:** electronic mail, bvincent@atsup.net. **Publications:** *Lippitt Morgan Breeders' Guide and Bulletin*, bimonthly. **Advertising:** accepted.

4913 ■ Missouri Fox Trotting Horse Breed Association (MFTHBA)
PO Box 1027
Ava, MO 65608-1027
Ph: (417)683-2468
E-mail: donnawatson@mfthba.com
URL: http://www.MFTHBA.com
Contact: Donna Watson, Asst. Sec.-Treas.
Founded: 1948. **Members:** 8,500. **Membership Dues:** individual, youth, associate, $15 (annual) ● life, $150 ● corporate, $25 (annual). **Staff:** 6. **Regional Groups:** 40. **Description:** Promoters, breeders, trainers, and owners of Missouri Fox Trotting horses. Seeks to gain acceptance of the Missouri Fox Trotting horse as a family horse. Sponsors sales, trail rides, and promotional activities. Maintains hall of fame and show arena. Conducts training programs. **Libraries: Type:** not open to the public. **Holdings:** periodicals. **Awards:** Fox Trot America Award. **Frequency:** annual. **Type:** recognition. **Recipient:** for MFTHBA's horses' participation in organized trail or distance rides ● National Trail Ride. **Frequency:** annual. **Type:** recognition. **Recipient:** for MFTHBA members. **Computer Services:** Online services. **Telecommunication Services:** electronic mail, mfthbawebmaster@mfthba.com. **Committees:** Budget; Ethics; Hall of Fame; Judges; Promotion; Show; Trail; Versatility. **Publications:** *Annual Show & Celebration Catalog*, annual. **Circulation:** 8,000 ● *The Journal*, monthly. Newspaper. **Price:** $25.00 /year for nonmembers; included in membership dues. **Circulation:** 6,500. **Advertising:** accepted ● *Official Rule Book* ● *Show and Celebration Catalog*, annual ● Videos. **Price:** $25.00. **Conventions/Meetings:** competition ● annual Futurity Show ● seminar, for judges and youth.

4914 ■ Morab Breeders Consortium
c/o Donna Lassanske
PO Box 203
Hodgenville, KY 42748-0203
Ph: (270)358-8727
Fax: (270)358-8727
E-mail: info@morabnet.com
URL: http://www.morabnet.com
Contact: Donna Lassanske, Contact
Membership Dues: $20 (annual) ● in addition to regular membership, to have promotional farm site, be listed as MBC breeder, place horses on PMHA Breeders Registry, $100 (annual). **Description:** Morab breeders dedicated to breeding and promoting Morabs of documented bloodlines consisting of Arabian and Morgan heritage. **Computer Services:** Mailing lists. **Affiliated With:** Purebred Morab Horse Association/Registry.

4915 ■ Morgan Single-Footing Horse Foundation (MSFHA)
c/o Ken Thomas, Pres.
650 E 1070 N
Richfield, UT 84701
Ph: (435)896-6824
E-mail: msfha@msfha.com
URL: http://www.msfha.com
Contact: Ken Thomas, Pres.
Membership Dues: regular, $20 (annual). **Description:** Promotes all Morgan horse types and disciplines, particularly the inherent four beat gaits within present registry. **Computer Services:** Mailing lists, of members. **Telecommunication Services:** electronic mail, kenthomas@msfha.com.

4916 ■ Mountain Pleasure Horse Association (MPHA)
PO Box 112
Mount Olivet, KY 41064
Ph: (606)724-2961 (606)932-4945

E-mail: mike@spradlinrealestate.com
URL: http://www.mtn-pleasure-horse.org
Contact: Mike Spradlin, Contact
Membership Dues: individual, $25 (annual) ● life, $500. **Description:** Promotes, breeds, and develops the Mountain Pleasure Horse throughout the United States. **Publications:** Newsletter. Contains news and information about horse care. **Conventions/Meetings:** periodic meeting.

4917 ■ National Chincoteague Pony Association (NCPA)
2595 Jensen Rd.
Bellingham, WA 98226
Ph: (360)671-8338
Fax: (360)671-7603
E-mail: gfreder426@aol.com
URL: http://www.pony-chincoteague.com
Contact: Gale Park Frederick, Contact
Founded: 1985. **Membership Dues:** individual, $10 (annual) ● pony registry, $75 (annual) ● life, $100. **Languages:** English, Spanish. **Description:** Admirers of Chincoteague ponies, a rare breed of horse which developed on Chincoteague Island off the coast of Virginia. Promotes responsible horse ownership; seeks to improve the Chincoteague pony. Facilitates communication and cooperation among members; maintains breed registry; establishes standards required for breed conformation; arranges Chincoteague pony sales. **Libraries: Type:** by appointment only; reference. **Holdings:** archival material, audio recordings, books, business records, periodicals, video recordings. **Subjects:** Chincoteague ponies and their history. **Additional Websites:** http://www.pony-chincoteague.org.

4918 ■ National Cutting Horse Association (NCHA)
260 Bailey Ave.
Fort Worth, TX 76107-1862
Ph: (817)244-6188 (903)873-2000
Fax: (817)244-2015
E-mail: lmayfield2@hotmail.com
URL: http://www.nchacutting.com
Contact: Bob Mayfield, Pres.
Founded: 1946. **Members:** 12,300. **Membership Dues:** individual, $60 (annual) ● life, $750 ● youth, $15 (annual) ● life (youth), $100. **Staff:** 29. **Budget:** $12,400,000. **State Groups:** 108. **Description:** Persons interested in the Cutting Horse (a saddle horse used to separate cattle from a herd). Promotes exhibition and breeding activities. Draws up rules and regulations for showing. Sponsors Cutting Horse Hall of Fame, NCHA Cutting Horse Futurity and other competitions. **Libraries: Type:** reference; not open to the public. **Holdings:** 48; periodicals. **Subjects:** cutting horses. **Awards: Type:** scholarship. **Recipient:** for youth cutting ● **Type:** trophy. **Recipient:** for winners and finalists. **Computer Services:** database, standings. **Publications:** *The Cutting Horse Chatter*, monthly. Magazine. Contains articles, ads, and schedules concerning cutting activities. **Price:** included in membership dues. ISSN: 1061-3986. **Circulation:** 11,767. **Advertising:** accepted ● *Judging Casebook*, annual ● *NCHA Yearbook*, annual ● *Rule Book*, annual. Handbook. Alternate Formats: online. **Conventions/Meetings:** annual convention - always June.

4919 ■ National Horse Show Commission (NHSC)
PO Box 167
1021 Colloredo Rd.
Shelbyville, TN 37162
Ph: (931)684-9506
Fax: (931)684-9538
URL: http://www.nationalhorseshowcommission.org
Contact: Lonnie Messick, Exec. VP
Founded: 1990. **Members:** 11. **Staff:** 4. **Description:** Seeks to standardize show rules for trainers, owners, and exhibitors of horses. Provides judge licensing; awards designated qualified person licensing certification. **Affiliated With:** Racking Horse Breeders' Association of America; Tennessee Walking Horse Breeders' and Exhibitors' Association; Walking Horse Owners' Association; Walking Horse Trainers Association.

4920 ■ National Morgan Reining Horse Association (NMRHA)
7701 Olivas Ln.
Vacaville, CA 95688
Ph: (608)835-7442
Fax: (608)835-7442
E-mail: travisnrha@aol.com
URL: http://www.nmrha.com
Contact: Travis Filipek, Pres.
Founded: 1996. **Members:** 80. **Membership Dues:** junior (under age 18), $5 (annual) ● individual, $20 (annual) ● family, $30 (annual) ● life, $300 ● associate, $10 (annual). **Staff:** 5. **Description:** Owners, breeders, and admirers of Morgan Reining horses. Promotes responsible horse ownership; seeks to improve the Morgan horse breed. Develops standards for breed conformance; maintains breed registry; conducts educational programs and competitions. **Libraries: Type:** lending; not open to the public. **Holdings:** audio recordings, video recordings. **Subjects:** Morgan horses. **Awards:** NMRHA Derby. **Frequency:** annual. **Type:** recognition ● NMRHA Non Pro Championship. **Type:** recognition ● NMRHA Novice. **Type:** recognition ● NMRHA Youth Reining Challenge. **Type:** recognition ● NRHA Competition Awards. **Type:** recognition. **Publications:** *NMRHA Reiner*, bimonthly. Newsletter. **Conventions/Meetings:** annual meeting, in conjunction with the Grand National Horse Show.

4921 ■ National Mustang Association (NMA)
PO Box 1367
Cedar City, UT 84721
Free: (888)867-8662
E-mail: mustangs@infowest.com
URL: http://www.nmautah.org
Contact: June Sewing, Exec. Sec.
Founded: 1964. **Members:** 2,500. **Membership Dues:** adult, $12 (annual) ● junior, $6 (annual) ● senior, $6 (annual). **Staff:** 1. **Description:** Aims to preserve the wild and free roaming horses. Provides better utilization of public land by improving grazing conditions and water development. Maintains a ranch as a sanctuary for horses removed from public lands. **Publications:** *The Mustang*, bimonthly. Newsletter. **Conventions/Meetings:** annual meeting - usually fall.

4922 ■ National Quarter Horse Registry (NQHR)
PO Box 716
New Harmony, UT 84757-0716
Ph: (435)251-7224
Fax: (320)205-0285
E-mail: questions@nqhr.org
URL: http://www.nqhr.com
Contact: Tamara Holdaway, Exec. Dir.
Founded: 1956. **Members:** 1,000. **Membership Dues:** silver, $200 (annual) ● gold, $300 (annual) ● regular, $25 (annual). **Regional Groups:** 6. **For-Profit. Description:** Records and maintains the ownership and breeding records of all eligible equine. Offers four sections: Quarter Horse, for horses resulting from the breeding of two verifiably registered Quarter Horses; Quarter Type, for horses with one Quarter Horse registered parent or deemed to be obvious Quarter breeding and type by a director; Paint Type, for horses of obvious or known Paint breeding or meeting the markings guideline; and Registration of Ownership, which is an open section for registration of ownership of any known history/pedigree. Seeks to remain current on the latest genetic color research in an effort to also correctly preserve and record equine color breeding history. **Libraries: Type:** reference. **Holdings:** 100; archival material, business records, papers, photographs, reports. **Subjects:** pedigrees, ownership records of all registered horses. **Awards:** Supreme Stallion Award. **Frequency:** annual. **Type:** recognition. **Computer Services:** Online services, forms. **Absorbed:** (1961) Race Horse Club; (1984) International Quarter Horse Registry; (1985) Capital Quarter Horse Registry. **Publications:** Newsletter, quarterly. Contains updates for members. **Price:** included in membership dues. **Advertising:** accepted. Alternate Formats: online. **Conventions/Meetings:** periodic board meeting.

4923 ■ National Quarter Pony Association (NQPA)
3232 U.S. 42 S
Delaware, OH 43015
E-mail: info@nqpa.com
URL: http://www.nqpa.com
Contact: Wendy Stephey, Sec.
Founded: 1975. **Members:** 400. **Membership Dues:** individual (19 years old and over), $15 (annual) ● family, $25 (annual) ● youth (18 years old and under), $10 (annual). **State Groups:** 4. **Description:** Owners and others interested in quarter ponies (Registered Quarter Horses 58 inches and under or Quarter/type ponies 58 inches and under). Records and preserves pedigrees of quarter ponies; provides information on matters pertaining to shows, contests, and projects designed to improve the breed. **Telecommunication Services:** electronic mail, stephey@bright.net. **Publications:** *The NQPA News Journal*, quarterly. **Price:** included in membership dues. **Advertising:** accepted ● Brochure. **Price:** free for members. **Circulation:** 250. **Advertising:** accepted. **Conventions/Meetings:** annual convention.

4924 ■ National Reining Horse Association (NRHA)
3000 NW 10th St.
Oklahoma City, OK 73107-5302
Ph: (405)946-7400 (209)274-0142
Fax: (405)946-8425
E-mail: media@nrha.com
URL: http://www.nrha.com
Contact: Mike Boyle, Pres.
Founded: 1966. **Members:** 12,400. **Membership Dues:** general/non-pro in U.S., $60 (annual) ● general/non-pro in U.S., $165 (triennial) ● life/life non-pro, $600 ● youth/youth non-pro, $30 (annual). **Staff:** 20. **Budget:** $75,000. **Regional Groups:** 4. **Multinational. Description:** Promotes and encourages the showing of reining horses. Develops standards of performance and judging; develops and disseminates informational material designed to provide contestants and spectators with an understanding of performance standards for this all-breed Western sport. Maintains videotape collection. Sanctions over 405 events each year internationally. **Awards:** Vaquero Media Awards. **Frequency:** annual. **Type:** recognition. **Computer Services:** Online services, horse earnings. **Publications:** *NRHA Reiner*, monthly. Magazine. **Price:** $25.00 for members; $50.00 in Canada; $75.00 international. ISSN: 0199-6762. **Circulation:** 9,000. **Advertising:** accepted. Alternate Formats: online. **Conventions/Meetings:** Derby - competition - always May ● annual Futurity and Championship Show - meeting.

4925 ■ National Show Horse Registry (NSHR)
10368 Bluegrass Pkwy.
Louisville, KY 40299
Ph: (502)266-5100
Fax: (502)266-5806
E-mail: nshowhorse@aol.com
URL: http://www.nshregistry.org
Contact: Gayle Garrett, Exec. Dir.
Founded: 1982. **Members:** 5,500. **Membership Dues:** adult, farm, corporate, $60 (annual) ● youth, $25 (annual) ● associate, $30 (annual) ● life, $1,000. **Staff:** 3. **Budget:** $860,000. **Regional Groups:** 8. **Description:** Owners of registered national show horses. Promotes amateur equestrian and open competitions for national show horses. Compiles statistics. **Awards:** National Championship. **Frequency:** annual. **Type:** monetary ● **Frequency:** annual. **Type:** recognition ● **Frequency:** annual. **Type:** scholarship. **Computer Services:** Online services, association's forms ● online services, show horse registry. **Affiliated With:** American Horse Council; United States Equestrian Federation. **Publications:** *National Show Horse*, bimonthly. Magazine. Covers industry information; includes briefs column, horsemanship column, editorials, and shows results. **Price:**

included in membership dues; $25.00 for nonmembers. **Circulation:** 5,000. **Advertising:** accepted ● *Nominated Stallion Directory*, annual. **Conventions/Meetings:** annual National Show Horse Finals Competition, for judges, owners, and exhibitors (exhibits) ● seminar ● annual show (exhibits).

4926 ■ National Snaffle Bit Association (NSBA)
4845 S Sheridan, Ste.515
Tulsa, OK 74145
Ph: (918)270-1469
Fax: (918)270-1471
E-mail: reichert@netins.net
URL: http://www.nsba.com
Contact: J.R. Reichert, Pres.
Founded: 1983. **Members:** 4,900. **Membership Dues:** regular, $45 (annual) ● youth, $25 (annual) ● life, $250. **Staff:** 3. **Budget:** $360,000. **State Groups:** 3. **Description:** Persons with an interest in showing and training pleasure horses. Aims to promote and improve the use of the snaffle bit and to train and develop all horses in a humane manner. Seeks to establish a greater market for pleasure horses. Conducts events for eligible horses registered with a recognized breed association. Maintains hall of fame and speakers' bureau. Compiles statistics. Sanctions events, awards to year-end high point winners in 28 categories or divisions. **Libraries: Type:** reference. **Holdings:** 2; video recordings. **Subjects:** western pleasure, longer line. **Awards:** Hall of Fame. **Frequency:** annual. **Type:** recognition ● Jack Benson Award. **Frequency:** periodic. **Type:** recognition. **Publications:** *The Way to Go*, monthly. Magazine. **Price:** included in membership dues; $30.00 /year for nonmembers. **Circulation:** 5,000. **Advertising:** accepted ● Brochures ● Videos ● Also publishes a list of recommended judges. **Conventions/Meetings:** annual banquet and meeting, for members - always June or July ● symposium.

4927 ■ National Spotted Saddle Horse Association (NSSHA)
PO Box 898
Murfreesboro, TN 37133-0898
Ph: (615)890-2864
Fax: (615)890-2864
E-mail: nssha898@aol.com
URL: http://www.nssha.com
Contact: Donna West Fletcher, Mgr.
Founded: 1979. **Members:** 2,200. **Membership Dues:** family, $45 (annual). **Staff:** 2. **Budget:** $100,000. **For-Profit. Description:** Owners, breeders, and trainers of Spotted Saddle horses; farmers and other interested individuals. (The Spotted Saddle horse is a relatively new breed native to middle Tennessee that has a smooth, easy gait, which can be traced to its ancestors, the Tennessee Walking horse and the standardbred.) Registers Spotted Saddle horses. Offers children's services. Conducts charitable activities; maintains hall of fame. **Computer Services:** Information services. **Publications:** Journal, quarterly. **Conventions/Meetings:** competition ● annual meeting - always January.

4928 ■ National Walking Horse Association (NWHA)
4059 Iron Works Pkwy., Ste.4
Lexington, KY 40511
Ph: (859)252-6942
Fax: (859)252-0640
E-mail: president@nwha.com
URL: http://www.nwha.com
Contact: Juana Grover, Pres.
Membership Dues: youth, $10 (annual) ● individual, $50 (annual) ● family, $100 (annual) ● life, $500 ● supporting, $25 (annual). **Description:** Represents individuals committed to preserving and fostering the natural abilities and welfare of the Walking Horse. Increases public awareness of the natural abilities of the Walking Horse. Improves the lives of horses and people by encouraging responsibility and sportsmanship. Promotes educational and recreational activities. Serves as an advocate for the Walking Horse against abusive and inhumane treatment. **Awards:** Neil Clark Memorial Youth Achievement Award. **Type:** recognition. **Recipient:** to the youth member who has an outstanding performance in NWHA events ● Order of the Equinus. **Type:** recognition. **Recipient:** to the youth horse rider who has earned the Versatility, Pleasure and Model Championship Awards. **Committees:** Futurity; Horse Show Development; Trail; Trainers; Versatility; Youth. **Programs:** Lifetime Superior Achievement; Trail Rider. **Publications:** *NWHA National News*. Newspaper. **Advertising:** accepted. Alternate Formats: online.

4929 ■ New Forest Pony Association and Registry (NFPA)
c/o Lucille Guilbault, VP
PO Box 206
Pascoag, RI 02859-0206
Ph: (401)568-8238
Fax: (401)567-0311
E-mail: lugilbo@cox.net
URL: http://www.newforestpony.net
Contact: Lucille Guilbault, VP
Founded: 1989. **Members:** 50. **Membership Dues:** general, $30 (annual) ● farm/family, $50 (annual). **Staff:** 2. **Budget:** $2,000. **Regional Groups:** 2. **Description:** Owners, breeders, and admirers of New Forest ponies. Seeks to advance the breed. Maintains New Forest pony registry; conducts educational clinics and demonstrations on horse ownership and breeding. **Libraries: Type:** reference. **Holdings:** archival material, articles, business records. **Subjects:** New Forest ponies. **Awards:** Year End Awards - USDF Breed Awards. **Frequency:** annual. **Type:** recognition. **Recipient:** to outstanding riders and breeders of New Forest ponies. **Computer Services:** Mailing lists, for all affiliated show information. **Affiliated With:** United States Dressage Federation. **Formerly:** (2001) New Forest Pony Association. **Publications:** *The New Forester*, quarterly. Newsletter. Contains what's new and old in The New Forest Pony World. Updates regarding registry and breed information. **Price:** included in membership dues. **Circulation:** 200. **Advertising:** accepted. **Conventions/Meetings:** annual board meeting.

4930 ■ North American Danish Warmblood Association (NADWA)
c/o Karin Dilou, Pres.
PO Box 536
Nicasio, CA 94946
Ph: (415)662-9555
Fax: (415)662-9550
E-mail: karin@danishwarmblood.net
URL: http://www.danishwarmblood.org
Contact: Karin Dilou, Pres.
Founded: 2001. **Membership Dues:** youth, $25 (annual) ● associate, $40 (annual) ● active, $55 (annual) ● family, $85 (annual) ● corporate, $125 (annual) ● gold, $150 (annual) ● life, $1,000. **Multinational. Description:** Helps strengthen the Danish breed in North America. Promotes the Danish Warmblood in North America by adhering to the European guidelines made by Danish Warmblood in Denmark. Represents owners, trainers, riders and competitors dedicated to bettering Danish Warmbloods in North America. **Awards:** Sport Horse Award. **Frequency:** annual. **Type:** recognition. **Recipient:** for high level of achievement of Danish Warmbloods. **Publications:** *Sport and Breeding*. Magazine. **Price:** free ● Newsletter, monthly. Alternate Formats: online.

4931 ■ North American Department of the Royal Warmblood Studbook of the Netherlands (NA/WPN)
PO Box 0
Sutherlin, OR 97479
Ph: (541)459-3232
Fax: (541)459-2967
E-mail: office@kwpn-na.org
URL: http://www.nawpn.org
Contact: Allison Hagen, Treas.
Founded: 1983. **Members:** 1,275. **Membership Dues:** participating, $85 (annual) ● associate, $50 (annual) ● life, $850 ● youth, $35 (annual). **Staff:** 4. **Budget:** $75,000. **Languages:** Dutch, English. **Description:** Represents owners and breeders of Dutch warmbloods, sport horses bred especially for Olympic and international equestrian competitions. Conducts educational programs for members on breeding and management of Dutch warmbloods. **Awards:** FEI Horse of the Year. **Frequency:** annual. **Type:** recognition. **Recipient:** for a horse owned by a NA/WPN subscriber ● Member of the Year. **Frequency:** annual. **Type:** recognition. **Recipient:** for NA/WPN subscriber ● North American Breeder of the Year. **Frequency:** annual. **Type:** recognition. **Recipient:** for NA/WPN subscriber. **Also Known As:** (2001) Dutch Warmblood Studbook in North America. **Publications:** *Breeder's Directory*, annual ● *Stallion Directory*, annual ● Newsletter, bimonthly. **Conventions/Meetings:** annual meeting, with horse inspections - held in September or October ● annual Members' Meeting - usually held in March.

4932 ■ North American Horsemen's Association (NAHA)
PO Box 223
Paynesville, MN 56362
Ph: (320)243-7250
Free: (800)328-8894
Fax: (320)243-7224
E-mail: insurance@arkagency.com
URL: http://www.arkagency-naha.com
Contact: Linda L. Liestman, Pres.
Founded: 1987. **Members:** 1,100. **Membership Dues:** associate, $50 (annual) ● full, $100 (annual) ● life, $600. **Staff:** 11. **Budget:** $101,000. **For-Profit. Description:** Represents individual horse owners and clubs. Promotes interests of members. Encourages equine safety. Maintains a reference library of books, periodicals, and clippings on equine law and safety in business issues. Bestows annual certificate of commendation for safety. Gathers statistics, conducts research, maintains hall of fame, and provides educational programs. **Libraries: Type:** not open to the public. **Holdings:** 350. **Subjects:** equine-related. **Awards:** Artist of Distinction. **Frequency:** annual. **Type:** recognition ● Horseman of Distinction. **Frequency:** annual. **Type:** recognition ● Horsewoman of Distinction. **Frequency:** annual. **Type:** recognition ● Safety Award Program. **Frequency:** annual. **Type:** recognition. **Publications:** *Risk Reduction Program Catalog*, semiannual. **Price:** $20.00. **Circulation:** 2,500 ● *Yearbook of News*, annual. Magazine. **Price:** $4.00/issue. **Circulation:** 15,000 ● Also publishes "Welcome to the Wonderful World of Horses: What a Beginner Needs to Know".

4933 ■ North American Mustang Association and Registry (NAMAR)
Address Unknown since 2008
Founded: 1986. **Members:** 100. **Membership Dues:** $20 (annual). **Staff:** 1. **For-Profit. Description:** Mustang owners and other interested individuals. Promotes friendly competition among members through horse shows. Compiles statistics. Registers horses; conducts training clinics. Operates charitable program; offers placement and children's services; maintains hall of fame. **Awards:** All-Around Mustang Award. **Frequency:** annual. **Type:** recognition. **Recipient:** for the horse earning the most show points. **Computer Services:** Horse-net, NAMAR1. **Publications:** *NAMAR Newsletter*, bimonthly. Includes information on shows of related organizations. **Price:** included in membership dues. **Advertising:** accepted. **Conventions/Meetings:** annual competition, photo contest ● annual Points and Awards Show - always first Saturday in November. Sunnyvale, TX.

4934 ■ North American Peruvian Horse Association (NAPHA)
3095 Burleson Retta Rd., Ste.B
Burleson, TX 76028
Ph: (817)447-7574
Fax: (817)447-2450
E-mail: info@napha.net
URL: http://www.napha.net
Contact: Linda Virgin, Pres.
Founded: 1970. **Members:** 1,100. **Membership Dues:** junior, $25 (annual) ● aficionado, $50 (annual) ● regular, $70 (annual). **Staff:** 3. **Regional Groups:** 32. **Multinational. Description:** Breeders and own-

ers of Peruvian Paso horses; others interested in the breed. Seeks to: aid and encourage traditional breeding, training, and showing of the Peruvian Paso; maintain an authentic registry for purebred Peruvian Pasos; institute and standardize rules for judging; promote the uniqueness of the Peruvian Paso. Sponsors clinics on topics such as training and artificial insemination. Provides computerized services. **Awards: Type:** recognition. **Computer Services:** database, directory of trainers ● database, listing of horses for sale ● database, listing of stallion at stud. **Committees:** Horse Improvement Program; Judges Accreditation; Rules; Show. **Absorbed:** American Peruvian Paso Horse Registry; (1982) International Peruvian Paso Horse Association; (1989) Peruvian Paso Part-Blood Registry. **Formerly:** (2005) Peruvian Paso Horse Registry of North America. **Publications:** *Nuestro Caballo*, periodic. Newsletter. Covers association activities. Includes information about shows, coming events, clinics, rule changes, registrations, and articles of interest. **Price:** free for members. **Circulation:** 1,200 ● Membership Directory, annual. Lists members geographically and alphabetically. ● Also publishes studbook. **Conventions/Meetings:** annual Governing and Rotating Governing Members Meeting - congress ● U.S. National Peruvian Paso Horse Show - competition.

4935 ■ North American Selle Francais Association (NASFA)

PO Box 579
Waynesboro, VA 22980
Ph: (540)932-9160
Fax: (540)932-9163
E-mail: sellefrancais@starpower.net
URL: http://www.sellefrancais.org

Membership Dues: life, $750 ● active, $80 (annual) ● junior, $25 (annual). **Multinational. Description:** Promotes the Selle Francais horse, a breed of equine athletes. **Publications:** Newsletter.

4936 ■ North American Shagya-Arabian Society (NASS)

c/o Gwyn Davis, VP/Information Off.
9797 S Rangeline Rd.
Clinton, IN 47842
Ph: (765)665-3851
E-mail: gwyn@starband.net
URL: http://www.shagya.net
Contact: Gwyn Davis, VP/Information Off.

Founded: 1986. **Members:** 120. **Membership Dues:** life, $500 ● active, associate, $45 (annual) ● junior, $25 (annual). **Budget:** $11,900. **Description:** Owners, breeders, and admirers of Shagya Arabian horses, a rare breed of horse originally bred in the military stables of the Austro-Hungarian monarchy. Seeks to promote and improve the breed. Gathers and disseminates information about the breed; approves pedigree of breeding stock; maintains registry of approved Shagya Arabians in the U.S. Works with other Shagya Arabian organizations. **Awards: Frequency:** annual. **Type:** recognition. **Recipient:** for registered Shagya horse. **Committees:** Breeding. **Publications:** *NASS News*, annual. Magazine. **Advertising:** accepted ● Newsletter, quarterly. Alternate Formats: online. **Conventions/Meetings:** periodic competition.

4937 ■ North American Single-footing Horse Association (NASHA)

PO Box 3170
Carefree, AZ 85377
Ph: (480)488-7169
E-mail: contact@singlefootinghorse.com
URL: http://www.singlefootinghorse.com
Contact: Patty L. McNutt, Dir.

Founded: 1978. **Members:** 1,000. **Membership Dues:** stable, family, $40 (annual). **State Groups:** 50. **Description:** Owners and admirers of trail, field, and pleasure horses. Promotes responsible horse care and safe and enjoyable horseback riding. Provides advice and assistance to horse owners and riders; conducts research and educational programs; maintains speakers' bureau. **Libraries: Type:** reference. **Holdings:** 125; audio recordings, periodicals, video recordings. **Subjects:** horse care, horseback riding, horse training. **Formerly:** (1998) North American Single-Footed Horse Association; (1999) North American Singlefooting Horse Association. **Publications:** *History*. Brochure ● *Horse and Handler Safety*. Book ● Newsletter, periodic. **Conventions/Meetings:** periodic regional meeting (exhibits).

4938 ■ North American Spotted Draft Horse Association (NASDHA)

c/o Sherry Shank, Sec.-Treas./Registrar
17420 US Hwy. 20
Goshen, IN 46528
Ph: (574)825-1924
E-mail: naspotteddrafts@yahoo.com
URL: http://www.nasdha.net
Contact: Tom Bihn, Pres.

Founded: 1995. **Members:** 300. **Membership Dues:** youth, $25 (annual) ● adult, $35 (annual) ● couple, $40 (annual) ● family, farm/ranch, $45 (annual). **Multinational. Description:** Preserves and promotes spotted draft horses. Increases public awareness of draft horses with pinto spotting. Strives to improve the quality of these horses. **Publications:** *The Spot Light*, quarterly. Newsletter. Contains news, stallion advertisements, spotted drafts for sale, official reports and articles of interest. **Price:** included in membership dues ● Handbook, annual.

4939 ■ Norwegian Fjord Horse Registry (NFHR)

1203 Appian Dr.
Webster, NY 14580
Ph: (585)872-4114
Fax: (585)787-0497
E-mail: registrar@nfhr.com
URL: http://www.nfhr.com
Contact: Mike May, Exec. Dir./Registrar

Founded: 1981. **Members:** 1,000. **Membership Dues:** single adult, $40 (annual) ● family, $50 (annual) ● individual (life), $400 ● family (life), $600. **Staff:** 1. **Multinational. Description:** Promotes the Norwegian Fjord horse. **Awards:** Hours of Fun with Fjord/s Award. **Type:** recognition ● Register of Excellence Award. **Type:** trophy ● Steppin Out with Your Fjord/s Award. **Type:** recognition ● Trail Riding/Driving Award. **Type:** recognition ● Versatility Award. **Type:** trophy. **Computer Services:** Online services, Fjord Herald farm directory. **Publications:** *Fjord Herald*, quarterly. Magazine. **Price:** included in membership dues; $30.00 for nonmembers. **Circulation:** 1,000. **Advertising:** accepted ● *NFHR Evaluation Handbook*. Alternate Formats: online.

4940 ■ Oldenburg Registry N.A. (OLD NA)

517 DeKalb Ave.
Sycamore, IL 60178
Ph: (815)899-7803
Fax: (815)899-7823
E-mail: isreg@aol.com
URL: http://www.isroldenburg.org
Contact: Ekkehard L. Brysch, CEO

Founded: 1983. **Members:** 1,998. **Staff:** 9. **Description:** Owners and breeders of modern sport horses used as dressage, hunter/jumpers, and performance horses. Seeks to improve sport horse bloodlines. Maintains breed registry; formulates and enforces standards of breed conformance. **Libraries: Type:** reference. **Subjects:** copies of Breeders Guide. **Awards:** Champion Foal Award. **Frequency:** annual. **Type:** trophy. **Recipient:** for the highest scoring foal at each inspection ● Champion Mare Award. **Frequency:** annual. **Type:** trophy ● USDF All Breed Award. **Frequency:** annual. **Type:** trophy. **Affiliated With:** United States Dressage Federation. **Publications:** Newsletter, bimonthly. **Price:** included in membership dues. **Advertising:** accepted. **Conventions/Meetings:** annual board meeting.

4941 ■ Palomino Horse Association (PHA)

Rte. 1, Box 125
Nelson, MO 65347
Ph: (660)859-2064 (660)859-2058
E-mail: palominorebuck@yahoo.com
URL: http://www.palominohorseassoc.com
Contact: Patricia Rebuck, Contact

Founded: 1936. **Members:** 317. **Membership Dues:** regular, in U.S., $25 (annual) ● regular, outside U.S., $30 (annual) ● life, $250. **Staff:** 5. **Description:** Maintains registry of pedigrees, transfers, and record ownerships. **Awards:** Register of Merit Award. **Frequency:** periodic. **Type:** recognition. **Recipient:** for a horse receiving 25 points in any performance or halter event. **Publications:** *Palomino Parade*, bimonthly. Newsletter. **Price:** included in membership dues. **Advertising:** accepted. **Conventions/Meetings:** annual meeting.

4942 ■ Palomino Horse Breeders of America (PHBA)

15253 E Skelly Dr.
Tulsa, OK 74116-2637
Ph: (918)438-1234
Fax: (918)438-1232
E-mail: yellahorses@palominohba.com
URL: http://www.palominohba.com
Contact: Alda Buresh, Pres.

Founded: 1941. **Members:** 12,134. **Membership Dues:** individual, $30 (annual) ● joint, $60 (annual) ● amateur, novice amateur, $40 (annual) ● youth, novice youth, $10 (annual) ● life, $400. **Staff:** 7. **State Groups:** 45. **Description:** Owners, breeders, and exhibitors of purebred Palomino horses. Maintains registry of pedigrees. Maintains hall of fame; compiles statistics. Offers children's services; conducts charitable program. **Libraries: Type:** reference. **Holdings:** archival material. **Awards:** Hall of Fame Awards. **Type:** recognition ● Youth, Amateur, and Open Awards. **Type:** recognition. **Computer Services:** database, AS400-200. **Telecommunication Services:** electronic mail, assist@palominohba.com. **Committees:** Affiliate Palomino Associations and Membership; Amateur; Animal Welfare Awards; Breeders; Bylaws and Legal; Cattle Events; Financial Management; Hall of Fame; Judges; Public Relations; Racing; Registration; Show Rules; World Championship Horse Show; World Championship Sale; Youth. **Publications:** *Palomino Horses Magazine*, monthly. **Price:** $30.00 for members; $40.00 for nonmembers. ISSN: 0031-045X. **Circulation:** 6,658. **Advertising:** accepted. **Conventions/Meetings:** annual convention and conference - usually in March ● annual World Championship Palomino Horse Show - competition (exhibits) - every July in Tulsa, OK.

4943 ■ Paso Fino Horse Association (PFHA)

101 N Collins St.
Plant City, FL 33563-3311
Ph: (813)719-7777
Fax: (813)719-7872
E-mail: execdir@pfha.org
URL: http://www.pfha.org
Contact: C.J. Marcello Jr., Exec. Dir.

Founded: 1972. **Members:** 8,700. **Membership Dues:** junior, $35 (annual) ● individual, $55 (annual) ● family, business/corporate, $75 (annual) ● life, $2,000. **Staff:** 11. **Budget:** $1,600,000. **Regional Groups:** 24. **Description:** Owners and breeders of Paso Fino horses; interested individuals. Promotes the Paso Fino in the U.S., Canada, Europe and South America. Maintains registry. Conducts judges' and showmanship clinics. Supervises annual show circuit of All-Paso Fino shows. **Libraries: Type:** reference. **Holdings:** video recordings. **Awards:** PFHA Youth Scholarship. **Type:** scholarship. **Recipient:** for members. **Formerly:** (1986) Paso Fino Owners and Breeders Association. **Publications:** *Farm Directory*, biennial. Contains history of Association, paso fino, and list of farms. **Price:** free. **Advertising:** accepted ● *Paso Fino Horse World*, monthly. Magazine. Contains information about paso fino horse breeders, show schedules, current point standings, activities, regional events, and association activities. **Price:** $22.00 /year for members; $30.00 /year for nonmembers; $45.00 in Canada; $95.00 outside U.S. and Canada. **Circulation:** 4,200. **Advertising:** accepted ● *Rule*, periodic. Book. **Price:** $10.00 ● *The Smoothest Ride*. Video. **Price:** $14.95/year ● Membership Directory, periodic. **Price:** $30.00 for members;

$75.00 for nonmembers. **Conventions/Meetings:** annual Grand National Championship Show - always September ● annual meeting, for membership - always January.

4944 ■ Pinto Horse Association of America (PtHA)
7330 NW 23rd St.
Bethany, OK 73008
Ph: (405)491-0111
Fax: (405)787-0773
E-mail: membership@pinto.org
URL: http://www.pinto.org
Contact: Darrell L. Bilke, Exec. VP/Chief Operating Off.
Founded: 1956. **Members:** 13,000. **Membership Dues:** youth, $15 (annual) ● individual, joint, corporation, $30 (annual) ● amateur, novice amateur, $10 (annual) ● life (youth), $100 ● life (individual), $300. **Staff:** 13. **Budget:** $1,300,000. **Regional Groups:** 43. **Description:** Persons interested in the promotion and improvement of the Pinto breed of horses. Maintains registry. Offers Register of Merit Programs including: ROM; Certificate of Achievement; Certificate of Ability; Championship; Supreme Champion. **Awards:** Horse of the Year Awards. **Frequency:** annual. **Type:** recognition. **Recipient:** for 44 categories. **Committees:** Education; Futurity; Judges; National Show Advisory; Publicity; Queen; Racing; ROM and Championship; Show Rules; Youth Activities. **Publications:** *Pinto Horse*, bimonthly. Magazine. Includes charter news information concerning rule changes, show results, show schedule, award winners, and news features. **Price:** $20.00 for members; $25.00 for nonmembers. ISSN: 8750-7269. **Circulation:** 3,000. **Advertising:** accepted ● Also publishes registry and rule book. **Conventions/Meetings:** annual Pinto Convention - conference and meeting.

4945 ■ Pony of the Americas Club (POAC)
3828 S Emerson Ave.
Indianapolis, IN 46203
Ph: (317)788-0107
Fax: (317)788-8974
E-mail: poac@poac.org
URL: http://www.poac.org
Contact: Sid Hutchcraft, Exec. Sec.
Founded: 1954. **Members:** 3,000. **Membership Dues:** junior, $25 (annual) ● active outside U.S., regular, $62 (annual). **Staff:** 4. **Budget:** $1,100,000. **Regional Groups:** 14. **State Groups:** 42. **National Groups:** 3. **Description:** Persons interested in the Pony of the Americas breed, a large Western and English type pony 46 to 56 inches in height with Appaloosa coloring. The breed is popular among children and is also used for pleasure, work stock, or show in Western and English classes. Maintains registry of over 40000 horses. Sponsors breed promotion sale of registered stock. Holds classes in shows for age groups 8 and under, 9 to 12, and 13 to 18. Compiles and disseminates free educational data for agricultural colleges, 4-H clubs, and other groups. Local, state, and national groups hold judging and riding clinics, shows, sales, and trail rides. **Awards: Type:** recognition ● Youth Scholarships. **Frequency:** annual. **Type:** scholarship. **Computer Services:** Online services, information and forms. **Committees:** Breeders; Futurity; International Show; Judges; Long Range Planning; Promotion and Marketing; Rules; Sale; Show Rules. **Absorbed:** (1991) National Appaloosa Pony. **Publications:** *POA Magazine*, monthly. **Price:** $27.00 in U.S.; $39.00 outside U.S. **Advertising:** accepted ● *POAC Official Handbook*, biennial ● *Stud Book*, biennial. **Conventions/Meetings:** annual trade show, with equine related products and services (exhibits) - always February.

4946 ■ Pure Puerto Rican Paso Fino Federation of America (PPRPFFA)
PO Box 280444
Columbia, SC 29228
Ph: (203)799-9792
E-mail: prpasofinos@aol.com
URL: http://www.puertoricanpasofino.org
Contact: Gail Brown, Pres.
Membership Dues: family, $35 ● individual, $25 ● youth, $20 ● contributing, $75 ● life, $300. **Description:** Educates individuals about the Puerto Rican Paso Fino breed. Trains, improves, protects and promotes the breed. Preserves the true four-beat laterally-gaited Puerto Rican Paso Fino. **Telecommunication Services:** electronic mail, gailbrown45@hotmail.com. **Publications:** Newsletters. **Price:** free, for members.

4947 ■ Purebred Morab Horse Association/Registry (PMHA)
PO Box 280
Sherwood, WI 54169
Ph: (920)358-8727
Fax: (920)687-0189
E-mail: registry@tds.net
URL: http://www.puremorab.com
Contact: Patricia Fochs, Exec. Dir.
Founded: 1984. **Members:** 200. **Membership Dues:** individual, $20 (annual) ● club, $50 (annual) ● family, $35 (annual) ● corporate, $100 (annual) ● registered prefix, $25 (annual). **Regional Groups:** 4. **State Groups:** 15. **Multinational. Description:** Registers and promotes the Morab horse (a fusion of Morgan and Arabian breeds) and preserves Morab bloodlines. Compiles statistics. **Awards:** Morab Horseman of the Year Award. **Frequency:** annual. **Type:** recognition. **Recipient:** for a horseman who has made outstanding contribution to the preservation of the Morab breed during the last five years ● National Award Morab Program. **Frequency:** annual. **Type:** recognition. **Recipient:** for any purebred Morab horse registered with PMHA ● Youth Coordinator Award. **Frequency:** annual. **Type:** recognition. **Recipient:** for an adult who has made outstanding contributions to Morab Youth Program. **Absorbed:** (1986) Hearst Memorial Morab Registry. **Formerly:** (1998) North American Morab Horse Association/Registry. **Publications:** *Morab Visions*, quarterly. Newsletter ● Brochures. **Price:** free for members. **Circulation:** 300. **Advertising:** accepted. **Conventions/Meetings:** annual meeting.

4948 ■ Racking Horse Breeders' Association of America (RHBAA)
67 Horse Center Rd.
Decatur, AL 35603
Ph: (256)353-7225
Fax: (256)353-7266
E-mail: rhbaa67horse@aol.com
URL: http://www.rackinghorse.com
Contact: Judy Jones, Pres.
Founded: 1971. **Members:** 3,500. **Membership Dues:** regular, $35 (annual) ● family, $45 (annual). **Staff:** 10. **Budget:** $1,000,000. **State Groups:** 50. **Local Groups:** 28. **Description:** Persons directly connected with Racking horses and the Racking horse industry. Aims to improve and promote the breed and maintain a studbook and registry. Sanctions events; sets rules and standards; qualifies official commissioners and judges; furnishes judges for official shows. **Committees:** Delegate; Judges; Rules Enforcement. **Publications:** *Racking Horse Directory*, annual ● *Racking Review*, monthly. Newsletter. **Conventions/Meetings:** annual competition.

4949 ■ Rocky Mountain Horse Association (RMHA)
PO Box 129
Mount Olivet, KY 41064-0129
Ph: (606)724-2354
Fax: (606)724-2153
E-mail: information@rmhorse.com
URL: http://www.rmhorse.com
Contact: Pat Brandenburg, Pres.
Founded: 1986. **Members:** 2,000. **Membership Dues:** single, junior, $25 (annual) ● family, legal entity, $50 (annual) ● life - single, $350 ● life - family, $675. **Staff:** 18. **Budget:** $100,000. **Regional Groups:** 5. **State Groups:** 6. **Description:** Owners and breeders of Rocky Mountain horses. (Rocky Mountain horses are medium-sized and of gentle temperament, with an ambling four-beat gait.) Preserves the breed, increases the number of horses of the breed, and expand knowledge of the breed. Compiles statistics. Sponsors research projects. **Awards:** Sam Tuttle Memorial Award. **Frequency:** annual. **Type:** recognition. **Computer Services:** Online services, horse registry. **Telecommunication Services:** electronic mail, footloosefarms@aol.com. **Publications:** *Natural Gait News*, monthly. Newspaper. Contains information about the Rocky Mountain Horse, horses for sale, breeders and more. **Price:** included in membership dues; $18.00 /year for nonmembers. **Circulation:** 3,000. **Advertising:** accepted ● *Rocky Mountain Horse*. Brochure. **Conventions/Meetings:** annual International Horse Show (exhibits) - always 3rd week of September ● annual meeting ● annual picnic - always June.

4950 ■ Show Horse Alliance (SHA)
c/o National Show Horse Registry
10368 Bluegrass Pkwy.
Louisville, KY 40299
Ph: (502)266-5100
Fax: (502)266-5806
URL: http://www.nshregistry.org/SHAall.asp?ID=90
Membership Dues: cross bred horse (not eligible for registration), $250 ● National Show Horse registered horse, $150. **Description:** Encourages breeders to create an extreme Saddle Seat type horse, relatively free of blood content restrictions. Only restriction required is that one parent in the first generation must be one of the following: National Show Horse, Arabian or Saddlebred.

4951 ■ Southwest Spanish Mustang Association (SSMA)
PO Box 948
Antlers, OK 74523
Ph: (580)326-6005 (580)326-8069
E-mail: sistymonroe@aol.com
URL: http://www.southwestspanishmustangassociation.com
Contact: Bryant Rickman, Chm.
Founded: 1978. **Members:** 350. **Membership Dues:** regular, $5 (annual). **Staff:** 6. **Description:** Owners of Spanish mustangs; interested individuals. Seeks to preserve the purest bloodlines of the Spanish mustang through strict registration and record-keeping. (The Spanish mustang evolved from horses brought to the New World by the Spanish Conquistadors in the 16th and 17th centuries; by 1890 the pure breed had nearly been eliminated because of slaughter, cross-breeding, and castration.) Promotes the mustang and publicizes its stamina and endurance; holds semiannual trail rides and playdays. **Libraries: Type:** reference; open to the public. **Subjects:** mustangs, Spanish mules, Western Americana. **Awards: Frequency:** semiannual. **Type:** trophy. **Publications:** *SSMA Breeder's List*. Directory ● Newsletter, semiannual. **Price:** free for members. **Circulation:** 350. **Advertising:** accepted. **Conventions/Meetings:** semiannual meeting - always May 23-25 and third weekend of October, in Finley, OK.

4952 ■ Spanish-Barb Breeders Association (SBBA)
PO Box 1628
Silver City, NM 88062
E-mail: info@spanishbarb.com
URL: http://www.spanishbarb.com
Contact: Jane Dobrott, Contact
Founded: 1972. **Members:** 125. **Membership Dues:** owner/breeder, $25 (annual) ● individual, $15 (annual) ● family, $20 (annual). **Description:** Individuals interested in the Spanish-barb horse. Collects, records, and preserves pedigrees and publishes a studbook and registry; stimulates, promotes, and regulates matters pertaining to the history, breeding, exhibition, publicity, or sale of this breed. **Publications:** *The Spanish-Barb: An American Legacy*. Booklet ● *Spanish-Barb Journal*, annual. **Price:** included in membership dues. **Advertising:** accepted ● *Spanish-Barb Update*, semiannual. Newsletter ● Papers. **Conventions/Meetings:** annual meeting ● annual show.

4953 ■ Spanish Mustang Registry (SMR)
c/o Carol Dildine, Sec.
323 County Rd. 419
Chilton, TX 76632
Ph: (254)546-2177 (512)966-6065

E-mail: dildine@hotl.net
URL: http://www.spanishmustang.org
Contact: Carol Dildine, Sec.

Founded: 1957. **Members:** 384. **Membership Dues:** junior, $15 (annual) ● single, $20 (annual) ● family, $25 (annual). **Staff:** 6. **Description:** Persons interested in registering and preserving the Spanish mustang. Conducts historical research and maintains slide collection. **Libraries: Type:** not open to the public. **Holdings:** articles, books. **Awards: Frequency:** annual. **Type:** recognition. **Computer Services:** database ● mailing lists. **Committees:** Historical; Horse Shows; Studbook. **Publications:** *Rule Book* ● *Studbook*, annual. Magazine ● Newsletter, quarterly. **Conventions/Meetings:** annual meeting - 3rd weekend of June.

4954 ■ Spanish-Norman Horse Registry

c/o Linda Osterman-Hamid, Registrar
PO Box 985
Woodbury, CT 06798
Ph: (203)266-4048
Fax: (203)263-3306
E-mail: info@spanish-norman.com
URL: http://www.spanish-norman.com
Contact: Linda Osterman-Hamid, Registrar

Founded: 1991. **Description:** Promotes the Spanish-Norman horse. **Publications:** Newsletter. Alternate Formats: online.

4955 ■ Spotted Saddle Horse Breeders' and Exhibitors' Association (SSHBEA)

PO Box 1046
Shelbyville, TN 37162
Ph: (931)684-7496
Fax: (931)684-7215
E-mail: jprince@sshbea.org
URL: http://www.sshbea.org
Contact: Janice Prince, Exec. Sec.

Founded: 1985. **Members:** 4,000. **Membership Dues:** adult, $35 (annual) ● life, $600. **Description:** Promotes and preserves the pedigree of the Spotted Saddle Horse. Facilitates the public exhibition of the Spotted Saddle Horse. Establishes official rules for registering and showing of the Spotted Saddle Horse. Develops and implements educational programs and clinics. **Computer Services:** Information services, Spotted Saddle Horse facts and resources. **Committees:** Amateur; Financial; Fund Raiser; Halter; Hearing; Performance; Political Action; Promotional and Class Sheet. **Publications:** *Spotted Saddle Horse News*, bimonthly. Magazine. **Price:** included in membership dues. **Advertising:** accepted ● Newsletter, periodic. **Price:** included in membership dues. Alternate Formats: online.

4956 ■ Standardbred Retirement Foundation (SRF)

108F Old York Rd.
Hamilton, NJ 08620
Ph: (609)324-1500
Fax: (609)324-1526
E-mail: srfmail1@verizon.net
URL: http://www.adoptahorse.org
Contact: George S. Brodey, Exec. Dir.

Founded: 1989. **Members:** 750. **Membership Dues:** starting gate, $25 (annual) ● quarter pole, $50 (annual) ● turning for home, $100 (annual) ● finish line, $250 (annual) ● winner's circle, $500 (annual) ● triple crown, $1,000 (annual) ● club house, $2,500 (annual) ● benefactor (minimum), $5,000 (annual). **Staff:** 6. **Budget:** $350,000. **Description:** Places noncompetitive racehorses in adoptive homes for use as pleasure horses and follows up to ensure their good care. Runs therapeutic equine programs for misguided youth and youth court ordered to serve community service hours, using race horse retirees. Conducts charitable and educational programs/humane services for horses. **Awards:** International Animal Welfare Award. **Type:** recognition. **Recipient:** for outstanding humane service to animals. **Programs:** Youth In Focus. **Publications:** Newsletter, quarterly.

4957 ■ Swedish Gotland Breeders' Society (SGBS)

3240 Hinton-Webber Rd.
Corinth, KY 41010-8952
Ph: (859)234-5707
E-mail: kokovoko@kih.net
URL: http://www.gotlands.net
Contact: Leslie Bebensee, Founder

Founded: 1990. **Members:** 200. **Description:** Owners and breeders of Swedish Gotland ponies. Promotes the Swedish Gotland pony as an ideal horse for riding, driving, racing, and work, for children and smaller adults. Serves as a clearinghouse on Swedish Gotland ponies. **Libraries: Type:** by appointment only; reference. **Holdings:** archival material. **Subjects:** history of Swedish Gotland ponies, studbooks. **Formerly:** (1999) Swedish Gotland Breeder's Association.

4958 ■ Swedish Warmblood Association of North America (SWANA)

PO Box 788
Socorro, NM 87801
Ph: (505)835-1318
Fax: (505)835-1321
E-mail: office@swanaoffice.org
URL: http://www.swedishwarmblood.org
Contact: Carol Reid, Exec. Dir.

Founded: 1992. **Members:** 500. **Membership Dues:** active, $75 (annual) ● junior and inactive, $60 (annual). **Staff:** 2. **Regional Groups:** 3. **Description:** Breeders, owners, and riders of Swedish warmblood horses. Inspects, licenses, and brands horses of Swedish descent. Arranges tours; holds auctions; sponsors genetics clinics. **Awards:** Eventing Award. **Frequency:** annual. **Type:** recognition ● Hunter Award. **Frequency:** annual. **Type:** recognition. **Recipient:** to the top horse nationally in children's-adult/amateur, junior-amateur/owner, and open hunters ● USA-E Jumping Award. **Frequency:** annual. **Type:** recognition ● USDF All-Breed Awards. **Frequency:** annual. **Type:** recognition. **Recipient:** for an active member of SWANA riding Swedish Warmblood Horse. **Computer Services:** database, for members of horses they own ● electronic publishing, email newsletter ● mailing lists, available for members ● online services, stallion directory; rules and regulations. **Telecommunication Services:** electronic mail, swana@sdc.org. **Committees:** Award; Inspection; Marketing. **Affiliated With:** United States Dressage Federation. **Formerly:** (1993) Swedish Warm Blood Association of North America. **Publications:** *Awards Book*, annual ● *Breeders Guide*, annual ● *SWANA News*, quarterly. Newsletter. **Price:** included in membership dues. **Advertising:** accepted. **Conventions/Meetings:** annual meeting, membership.

4959 ■ Tennessee Walking Horse Breeders' and Exhibitors' Association (TWHBEA)

PO Box 286
Lewisburg, TN 37091
Ph: (931)359-1574
Free: (800)359-1574
Fax: (931)359-7530
E-mail: mcook@twhbea.com
URL: http://www.twhbea.com
Contact: Charles R. Cadle, Exec. Dir./CEO

Founded: 1935. **Members:** 20,000. **Membership Dues:** adult/young adult, $60 (annual) ● junior, $10 (annual) ● life, $1,000. **Staff:** 27. **Budget:** $4,800,000. **State Groups:** 44. **Multinational. Description:** Owners, breeders, trainers, exhibitors, and others interested in the Tennessee Walking horse. Maintains registry of pedigrees and ownership. Operates speakers' bureau. **Affiliated With:** American Horse Council. **Formerly:** (1974) Tennessee Walking Horse Breeders' Association of America. **Publications:** *The Voice of the Tennessee Walking Horse*, monthly. Journal. **Price:** $30.00/year. **Circulation:** 20,000. **Advertising:** accepted. **Conventions/Meetings:** annual convention ● semiannual meeting - always fourth Saturday of May and first Saturday of December, Lewisburg, TN.

4960 ■ Tiger Horse Association (THA)

1604 Fescue Cir.
Huddleston, VA 24104
Ph: (540)297-2276
Fax: (540)297-7134
E-mail: information@tigerhorses.org
URL: http://www.tigerhorses.org

Membership Dues: junior (18 and under), $15 (annual) ● individual, $25 (annual) ● family, $40 (annual) ● life - individual, $500. **Description:** Promotes and protects the Tiger Horse breed. Acts as an information source for members and the general public about the breed. Increases public awareness and understanding of the Tiger Horse breed. **Awards:** Annual High Point Awards. **Frequency:** annual. **Type:** recognition. **Recipient:** to one gelding, one mare and one stallion who accumulates the most points during the year. **Computer Services:** Information services, Tiger Horse resources. **Programs:** Saddle Time; Tiger Youth. **Publications:** *Eye Of The Tiger*. Newsletter.

4961 ■ United Professional Horsemen's Association (UPHA)

4059 Iron Works Pkwy., Ste.2
Lexington, KY 40511
Ph: (859)231-5070
Fax: (859)255-2774
E-mail: uphakgr@aol.com
URL: http://www.uphaonline.com
Contact: Karen G. Richardson, Exec. Sec.

Founded: 1968. **Members:** 1,200. **Membership Dues:** active, associate, $50 (annual) ● junior (17 years old and below), $25 (annual). **Staff:** 1. **Regional Groups:** 18. **Description:** Professional horse trainers involved in the show horse industry; horse owners and breeders. Seeks to educate the public about show horses and improve the industry. Sponsors classics for Three-and Four-Year Olds. Maintains hall of fame. **Awards:** Horse of the Year Award. **Frequency:** annual. **Type:** recognition ● Horse Show Awards. **Type:** recognition. **Computer Services:** database. **Committees:** Classics; Equitation; Hackney-Harness-Roadster; Morgan; Saddlebred; Stable Management. **Publications:** Membership Directory, semiannual. **Conventions/Meetings:** annual meeting (exhibits) - always January ● seminar, for judges.

4962 ■ United States Icelandic Horse Congress (USIHC)

6800 E 99th Ave.
Anchorage, AK 99507
Ph: (907)346-2223
Fax: (907)346-2223
E-mail: info@icelandics.org
URL: http://www.icelandics.org
Contact: Bernie Willis, Pres.

Founded: 1987. **Members:** 750. **Membership Dues:** individual, $40 (annual) ● family, $60 (annual) ● individual (international), $55 (annual) ● family (international), $75 (annual). **Staff:** 1. **Budget:** $20,000. **Regional Groups:** 11. **Description:** Owners and admirers of Icelandic horses. Promotes public awareness of the Icelandic horse and Icelandic history and culture. Collects and disseminates information regarding Icelandic horses; facilitates communication among horse owners. Sponsors shows; conducts educational programs; plans to develop youth, family, senior citizen, and therapeutic programs. Compiles statistics. **Libraries: Type:** reference. **Holdings:** audiovisuals, books, clippings, periodicals. **Computer Services:** Mailing lists, of members. **Telecommunication Services:** electronic mail, president@icelandics.org. **Publications:** *The Icelandic Horse Quarterly*. Article. Alternate Formats: CD-ROM ● *Keilir*, monthly. Newsletter. Covers Iceland, Icelandic horses, and association activities. **Price:** $15.00. **Circulation:** 1,200. **Advertising:** accepted ● Plans to issue a study book. **Conventions/Meetings:** annual competition ● seminar, covers breeding, training, and horse care.

4963 ■ United States Lipizzan Registry (USLR)

707 13th St. SE, Ste.275
Salem, OR 97301
Ph: (503)589-3172

Fax: (503)362-6393
E-mail: uslroffice@aol.com
URL: http://www.uslr.org
Contact: Tim Foley, Pres.
Founded: 1980. **Members:** 250. **Membership Dues:** participating, $55 (annual) ● family, $80 (annual) ● associate, $35 (annual) ● corporation/partnership, $95 (annual) ● junior/civic organization, $25 (annual). **Staff:** 1. **Budget:** $25,000. **Regional Groups:** 4. **Description:** Individuals connected with the Lipizzan horse industry. Preserves and promotes the breed. Maintains a studbook and registry. **Awards:** All Breed Awards. **Frequency:** annual. **Type:** trophy. **Telecommunication Services:** electronic mail, tfoley@sbcoe.k12.ca.us. **Publications:** *USLR News*, quarterly. Newsletter. **Circulation:** 300. **Advertising:** accepted. Alternate Formats: online ● Membership Directory, annual ● Reports. **Conventions/Meetings:** annual convention, horse show (exhibits).

4964 ■ United States Peruvian Horse Association (USPHA)
PO Box 9074
Pahrump, NV 89060
Ph: (775)727-1099
E-mail: uspha.office@verizon.net
URL: http://www.uspha.net
Contact: Raul Del Solar, Pres.
Membership Dues: owner/breeder, $50 (annual) ● aficionado, $25 (annual) ● junior, $15 (annual). **Description:** Encourages the breeding of Peruvian horses. Promotes, encourages, and recognizes the versatility and achievements of the Peruvian horse. Protects the integrity and accuracy of breed records and the registration process. Educates and informs the public regarding the history and unique attributes of the Peruvian horse. Provides services to meet the needs of the owner/ breeder member. Promotes the legacy and future of the Peruvian horse. **Telecommunication Services:** electronic mail, grnorman@windrockranch.com.

4965 ■ Walkaloosa Horse Association (WHA)
PO Box 3170
Carefree, AZ 85377
Ph: (480)488-7169
E-mail: contact@walkaloosaregistry.com
URL: http://walkaloosaregistry.com
Contact: Lee Waddle, Registrar
Founded: 1983. **Members:** 365. **Staff:** 2. **For-Profit. Multinational. Description:** Members are owners of registered Walkaloosa horses. (Walkaloosa horses are four-beat intermediate gaited Appaloosa colored horses.) Maintains registry for Indian shuttling ApHC horses and for crossbreed of Tennessee Walking and Appaloosa horses or the Missouri Fox Trotter and Paso Fino horses. Works to promote and market the Walkaloosa horse. Compiles statistics. **Libraries: Type:** reference. **Holdings:** books, clippings, periodicals. **Subjects:** gaited horses, Appaloosas, Walkaloosas. **Publications:** *Walkaloosa News*, quarterly. Newsletter. **Price:** free. **Circulation:** 365. **Advertising:** accepted.

4966 ■ Walking Horse Owners' Association (WHOA)
PO Box 4007
Murfreesboro, TN 37129
Ph: (615)494-8822
Fax: (615)494-8825
E-mail: whoa@walkinghorseowners.com
URL: http://walkinghorseowners.com
Contact: Tommy Hall, Exec. Dir.
Founded: 1976. **Members:** 5,200. **Membership Dues:** regular, $60 (annual) ● family, $100 (annual) ● youth, $20 (annual) ● life (based on age), $200-$1,000. **Staff:** 6. **Budget:** $500,000. **State Groups:** 50. **Description:** Promotes the exhibition of the Tennessee Walking Horse as a sport and as a family activity; works to ensure fair play and equality at such exhibitions. Works to develop a positive identification program; seeks enactment and enforcement of uniform rules used in horse shows. Sponsors International Grand Championship Walking Horse Show. Compiles statistics; offers children's services. **Awards:** High Point Award. **Type:** recognition ● National High Point Award. **Frequency:** annual. **Type:** recognition. **Recipient:** for walking horses and their owners ● Register of Merit Award. **Frequency:** annual. **Type:** recognition ● Versatility High Point Award. **Frequency:** annual. **Type:** recognition. **Recipient:** for horses and their owners. **Committees:** Appeals; Convention; Horse Show; International Show; Licensing and Enforcement; Nominating; Pleasure; Rules. **Publications:** *The Directory*, annual. Newsletter. Contains listing of owners. **Price:** free for members. **Circulation:** 5,000. **Advertising:** accepted ● *WHOA News and Events*, monthly. Newsletter. Includes calendar of horse shows. **Price:** free for members. **Advertising:** accepted ● Membership Directory. **Conventions/Meetings:** annual convention (exhibits).

4967 ■ Walking Horse Trainers Association (WHTA)
PO Box 61
Shelbyville, TN 37162
Ph: (931)684-5866
Fax: (931)684-5895
E-mail: whta@walkinghorsetrainers.com
URL: http://www.walkinghorsetrainers.com
Contact: Wink Groover, Pres.
Founded: 1968. **Members:** 850. **Membership Dues:** license AAA, AA and A, associate, $250 (annual). **Staff:** 1. **Budget:** $75,000. **Description:** Trainers of Tennessee Walking horses. Works for unity in the horse industry. Sponsors continuing research. **Libraries: Type:** reference. **Awards:** Assistant Trainer of the Year. **Frequency:** annual. **Type:** recognition. **Recipient:** for assistant trainers ● Horse of the Year Award. **Frequency:** annual. **Type:** recognition. **Recipient:** for outstanding service ● Trainer of the Year Award. **Frequency:** annual. **Type:** recognition. **Recipient:** for horses and trainers. **Committees:** Budget; Building; Ethics; Horse Show; NHSC; Pleasure Horse; Scholarship. **Councils:** Youth. **Formerly:** Walking Horse Trainers Association. **Publications:** *From the Horses Mouth*, quarterly. Newsletter. **Price:** available to members only. **Circulation:** 800 ● *The Updater*. Newsletter. **Price:** included in membership dues ● Directory. **Conventions/Meetings:** annual banquet (exhibits) - always December ● annual National Walking Horse Trainers Show (exhibits) - always March.

4968 ■ Warmblood Breeders of North America (WBNA)
PO Box 2221
Vashon, WA 98070
Ph: (206)567-4346
Fax: (206)567-4346
E-mail: questions@warmbloodbreedersna.com
URL: http://www.warmbloodbreedersna.com
Contact: Dayna Gant, Pres.
Membership Dues: general, $25 (annual). **Description:** Promotes warmblood breeding in North America. Provides marketing and communication networks, breeder support forums and educational and advisory opportunities. **Computer Services:** Online services, forum. **Telecommunication Services:** electronic mail, dayna@warmbloodbreedersna.com. **Committees:** Growth; Marketing; Nomination.

4969 ■ Welsh Pony and Cob Society of America (WPCSA)
720 Green St.
Stephens City, VA 22655
Ph: (540)868-7669
Fax: (540)667-3766
E-mail: info@welshpony.org
URL: http://www.welshpony.org
Contact: Lisa L. Landis, Exec. Sec.-Treas.
Founded: 1906. **Members:** 1,800. **Membership Dues:** individual, $45 (annual) ● individual/junior, life, $1,000 ● associate, $30 (annual) ● family/firm, $55 (annual) ● junior, $25 (annual). **Staff:** 5. **Budget:** $120,000. **Description:** Registry of purebred Welsh ponies, Welsh cobs, and Half-Welsh ponies. Maintains library of complete set of *English Stud Book Indexes* and *American Stud Books*. **Awards:** All Around High Point Youth Award. **Frequency:** annual. **Type:** trophy. **Recipient:** for a junior exhibitor who accumulates the most points ● High Point. **Frequency:** annual. **Type:** recognition. **Recipient:** for ponies accumulating the highest total number of points in various show divisions. **Committees:** Administrative; By-Laws; Ethics/Hearing; High Score; Public Relations; Qualifications; Stud Book; Youth. **Formerly:** (1946) Welsh Pony and Cob Society of America; (1986) Welsh Pony Society of America. **Publications:** *Member-Breeder List*, annual. Directory. **Price:** free for members ● *2005 WPCSA Stallion Directory*. Alternate Formats: online ● *WPCSA Rule Book*. **Price:** free for members. Alternate Formats: online ● Newsletter, quarterly. **Price:** included in membership dues ● Yearbook, annual. **Conventions/Meetings:** annual meeting.

4970 ■ Western International Walking Horse Association (WIWHA)
c/o Kim Swingley, Sec.
PO Box 872228
Vancouver, WA 98687-2228
Ph: (503)570-0108
Contact: Kim Swingley, Sec.
Founded: 1980. **Members:** 8. **Multinational. Description:** Tennessee Walking Horse clubs. Goals are to assist in the promotion of the walking horse as a breed and as an industry. Is certified by the U.S. Department of Agriculture to train and license qualified persons to inspect walking horses. Sponsors breeders futurity. **Awards: Type:** recognition. **Committees:** Futurity; Rules and Enforcement. **Publications:** *WIWHA Rulebook*, annual. **Price:** $10.00 each. Alternate Formats: online. **Conventions/Meetings:** annual meeting - always first Saturday of March ● annual show - always third weekend of September.

4971 ■ Western Saddle Clubs Association (WSCA)
c/o Teri Spence, Sec.
47009 Company Rd. 13
St. Peter, MN 56082
Ph: (507)345-5856
E-mail: secretary@wsca.org
URL: http://www.wsca.org
Contact: Ben Sparks, Pres.
Founded: 1955. **Members:** 17,250. **Membership Dues:** individual ($65 for the first year), $60 (annual). **Description:** Promotes Western-type horses and trail riding. **Awards: Type:** scholarship. **Committees:** Alternate Facilities; Champshow; Drills and Squares; Futurity; Queens; Rule Book; Trails. **Publications:** *Rulebook* ● *Spotlight*, monthly. Newsletter. **Price:** $24.00/year. **Advertising:** accepted. **Conventions/Meetings:** Championship Horse Show - competition.

Horticulture

4972 ■ All-America Rose Selections (AARS)
c/o Erin Walsh
Ruder Finn/San Francisco
388 Market St., Ste.1400
San Francisco, CA 94111
Ph: (415)348-2731
E-mail: walshe@ruderfinn.com
URL: http://www.rose.org
Contact: Steve Hutton, Pres.
Founded: 1938. **Members:** 16. **Membership Dues:** individual, $3,000 (annual). **Staff:** 4. **Description:** Works to develop and introduce exceptional roses. Encourages the rose industry to improve the vitality, strength and beauty of roses for the American Home gardener. **Awards:** AARS Citation. **Frequency:** annual. **Type:** recognition. **Recipient:** for hybrid roses that are considered to be of superior quality ● President's Award. **Frequency:** annual. **Type:** recognition. **Recipient:** to best maintained public rose gardens ● Winning Roses. **Frequency:** annual. **Type:** recognition. **Recipient:** for roses that embody the consumers' desires in a garden plant. **Computer Services:** database, public gardens ● mailing lists. **Publications:** Brochure, annual ● Newsletter, quarterly. Alternate Formats: online. **Conventions/Meetings:** annual meeting, held in conjunction with American Association of Nurserymen.

4973 ■ American Public Gardens Association (APGA)
100 W 10th St., Ste.614
Wilmington, DE 19801-6604
Ph: (302)655-7100
Fax: (302)655-8100
E-mail: dstark@publicgardens.org
URL: http://www.publicgardens.org
Contact: Daniel J. Stark, Exec. Dir.
Founded: 1940. **Members:** 3,000. **Membership Dues:** individual (affiliated), retired, volunteer, $65 (annual) ● individual (non-affiliated), $80 (annual) ● student, $35 (annual) ● institution (international), $320 (annual) ● institution (based on budget category), $160-$2,500 (annual). **Staff:** 8. **Budget:** $630,000. **Regional Groups:** 8. **Description:** Directors and staffs of botanical gardens, arboreta, institutions maintaining or conducting horticultural courses, and others. Seeks to serve North American public gardens and horticultural organizations by promoting professional development through its publications and meetings, advocating the interests of public gardens in political, corporate, foundation, and community arenas, and encouraging gardens to adhere to professional standards in their programs and operations. **Libraries: Type:** open to the public. **Holdings:** 1,000. **Awards: Frequency:** annual. **Type:** recognition. **Recipient:** to individuals and organizations for outstanding contributions to horticulture. **Computer Services:** database ● mailing lists. **Committees:** College and University Gardens; Computer Information; Conservatory; Development; Grounds Management; Historic Landscapes; Human Issues in Horticulture; Municipal Gardens; Plant Collections; Plant Conservation; Plant Nomenclature and Registration; Public Garden Administration; Public Garden Education; Student Education; Volunteerism. **Working Groups:** Urban Forestry. **Formerly:** American Association of Botanical Gardens and Arboretums; (2005) American Association of Botanical Gardens and Arboreta. **Publications:** *Internship Directory*. Provides information on internships. **Price:** $10.00 ● *Public Garden*, quarterly. Journal. Covers subjects of concern to public gardens and their professional staffs. Includes case studies, book reviews, and research reviews. **Price:** included in membership dues; $40.00 /year for nonmembers in U.S., Canada, and Mexico; $50.00 /year for nonmembers outside North America. ISSN: 0885-3894. **Circulation:** 3,000. **Advertising:** accepted ● Newsletter, monthly. Includes funding sources, meeting calendar, and garden news. **Price:** included in membership dues; $65.00 /year for libraries in U.S., Canada, and Mexico; $90.00 /year for libraries outside North America. ISSN: 0569-2423. **Circulation:** 3,000. **Advertising:** accepted ● Papers ● Surveys. **Conventions/Meetings:** annual conference (exhibits).

4974 ■ Association of Zoological Horticulture (AZH)
PO Box 135776
Clermont, FL 34713
Ph: (407)939-1609
E-mail: wendy.andrew@disney.com
URL: http://www.azh.org
Contact: Wendy Andrew, Pres.
Membership Dues: professional, associate, $40 (annual) ● student, $15 (annual) ● organizational, commercial, $150 (annual). **Description:** Aids, fosters, and engages in the exchange of horticultural specimens and propagules for exhibition, conservation, and research. Fosters and cultivates the social, educational, and business relations of its members. **Awards:** AZH Conservation Award. **Frequency:** periodic. **Type:** grant. **Recipient:** for plant conservation projects. **Publications:** Newsletter, bimonthly. **Price:** included in membership dues; $25.00 for nonmembers ● Membership Directory, annual. **Price:** included in membership dues.

4975 ■ Bonsai and Orchid Association (BOA)
26 Pine St.
Dover, DE 19901
Ph: (302)736-6781
Free: (800)801-3791
Fax: (302)736-6763
E-mail: leroyrench@comcast.net
Founded: 1980. **Members:** 2,200. **Membership Dues:** regular, $50 (annual). **Staff:** 5. **Budget:** $50,000. **Description:** Growers, florists, pot manufacturers, greenhouse operators, importers, exporters, distributors, and individuals involved in the bonsai and orchid industry. Promotes international trade; assists in adding new items to the bonsai and orchid market. Maintains speakers' bureau; conducts charitable programs. **Libraries: Type:** reference. **Awards: Type:** recognition. **Formerly:** (1980) International Garden Horticultural Industry Association. **Publications:** *Bonsai and Orchid Buyers Guide*, annual. Directory. Lists members and products. **Price:** free for members; $10.00 for nonmembers in U.S.; $12.00 for nonmembers outside U.S. **Circulation:** 5,000. **Advertising:** accepted. Alternate Formats: CD-ROM ● *Green World News*, monthly. Newsletter. Includes calendar of events, information on new products, and research updates. **Price:** included in membership dues; $20.00 /year for nonmembers. **Circulation:** 2,300. **Conventions/Meetings:** annual Bonsai and Orchid Expo - convention and trade show (exhibits) ● competition.

4976 ■ Crape Myrtle Society of America (CMSOA)
PO Box 2758
McKinney, TX 75070-2758
E-mail: info@cmsoa.org
URL: http://www.crapemyrtlesocietyofamerica.com
Contact: Dr. Gary Knox, Natl. Pres.
Founded: 1999. **Members:** 325. **Membership Dues:** general, $20 (annual) ● life, $200. **Staff:** 3. **Budget:** $3,000. **Description:** Growers and admirers of crape myrtle, a ground-covering plant. Seeks to improve crape myrtle strains; promotes study and appreciation of crape myrtle. Serves as a clearinghouse on crape myrtle; facilitates exchange of information among members. **Libraries: Type:** not open to the public; by appointment only. **Holdings:** 200; books. **Subjects:** Crape myrtle. **Awards:** Photography Awards. **Frequency:** annual. **Type:** monetary. **Recipient:** for best 35mm transparencies depicting crape myrtle. **Formerly:** (2002) American Crape Myrtle Society.

4977 ■ Hardy Fern Foundation (HFF)
PO Box 3797
Federal Way, WA 98063-3797
E-mail: hff@hardyferns.org
URL: http://www.hardyferns.org
Founded: 1989. **Members:** 250. **Membership Dues:** active, $25 (annual) ● student, $10 (annual) ● family, $30 (annual) ● contributing, $100 (annual) ● supporting, $500 (annual) ● patron, $1,000 (annual). **Staff:** 2. **Budget:** $10,000. **Regional Groups:** 13. **Description:** Individuals and organizations with an interest in hardy ferns. Seeks to establish "a comprehensive collection of the world's hardy ferns for display, testing, public education and introduction to the gardening and horticultural community". Collaborates with gardeners, scientists, and arboreta to establish and develop hardy fern collections; maintains spore exchange network; sponsors research and educational programs. Tests rare fern varieties to determine their hardiness and suitability for garden use in various North American climates. **Publications:** *Directory of Fern Gardens And Nurseries*. **Price:** $10.00 ● *The Fern Propagation Handbook*. Booklet. **Price:** $10.00 in U.S.; $11.00 for Canadian orders (postage included); $12.00 for other countries (postage included) ● Newsletter, quarterly.

4978 ■ Heliconia Society International (HSI)
c/o Raymond F. Baker
3860 Manoa Rd.
Honolulu, HI 96822-1180
Ph: (808)988-0455
Fax: (808)988-0462
URL: http://www.heliconia.org
Contact: Raymond F. Baker, Contact
Founded: 1985. **Members:** 500. **Membership Dues:** corporate, $100 (annual) ● family, $40 (annual) ● individual, $35 (annual) ● library, $25 (annual) ● student, $10 (annual) ● contributing, $50 (annual). **Regional Groups:** 4. **Multinational. Description:** Promotes understanding and appreciation of the genus Heliconia and all relatives of the plant order Zingiberales—Gingers, Birds of Paradise, Bananas, Cannas, Costus, and Prayer plants. Provides access to information and contact from around the globe. **Publications:** Bulletin, quarterly. **Price:** free for members ● Membership Directory. **Price:** free for members. **Conventions/Meetings:** biennial conference.

4979 ■ InterAmerican Society for Tropical Horticulture (ISTH)
c/o Dr. Richard Campbell, Exec. Sec.-Treas.
Fairchild Tropical Garden
11935 SW Old Cutler Rd.
Miami, FL 33156
Ph: (305)667-1651
Fax: (305)665-8032
E-mail: rcampbell@fairchildgarden.org
URL: http://www.ashs.org/isth/index.html
Contact: Dr. Richard Campbell, Exec. Sec.-Treas.
Founded: 1951. **Membership Dues:** regular, $45 (annual) ● sustaining, $60 (annual) ● patron, $125 (annual) ● student, $15 (annual). **Description:** Promotes the study, appreciation and economic viability of horticultural crops in the tropics. **Publications:** Proceedings, annual ● Newsletter, semiannual. Alternate Formats: online.

4980 ■ International Cut Flower Growers Association (ICFG)
PO Box 99
Haslett, MI 48840
Ph: (517)655-3726
Fax: (517)655-3727
E-mail: icfg@voyager.net
URL: http://www.rosesinc.org
Contact: Jay Stawarz, Exec. Dir.
Founded: 1937. **Members:** 500. **Membership Dues:** grower, supplier, $500 (annual) ● associate, $300 (annual). **Staff:** 4. **Regional Groups:** 2. **Description:** Commercial rose growers, rose plant producers, and representatives of segments of floriculture industry. **Committees:** Marketing and Trade Relations; Packaging; Quality Control; Research. **Formerly:** (2002) Roses Incorporated. **Publications:** Bulletin, monthly. **Advertising:** accepted. Alternate Formats: online. **Conventions/Meetings:** semiannual meeting, with special events, production schools, and study tours - always spring and fall.

4981 ■ International Plant Propagators Society (IPPS)
615 Williams Grove Rd.
Mechanicsburg, PA 17055-7512
Ph: (717)691-8898
Fax: (717)691-5440
E-mail: secretary@ipps.org
URL: http://www.ipps.org
Contact: Ms. Patricia Heuser, Sec.-Treas.
Founded: 1951. **Members:** 2,500. **Membership Dues:** international, $46 (annual). **Budget:** $150,000. **Regional Groups:** 9. **Multinational. Description:** Individuals dedicated to the art and science of plant propagation. Disseminates information on all practical aspects of plant propagation and plant growth. **Libraries: Type:** not open to the public. **Holdings:** 52. **Subjects:** agriculture, plant science. **Computer Services:** Online services. **Programs:** Exchange. **Publications:** *Combined Proceedings, International Plant Society*, annual. **Price:** available to members only. ISSN: 0538-9143. **Circulation:** 2,700. Alternate Formats: CD-ROM ● Membership Directory. **Price:** $5.00 for members. **Conventions/Meetings:** annual regional meeting.

4982 ■ National Garden Bureau (NGB)
1311 Butterfield Rd., Ste.310
Downers Grove, IL 60515
Ph: (630)963-0770
Fax: (630)963-8864
URL: http://www.ngb.org
Contact: Nona Wolfram-Koivula, Exec. Dir.
Founded: 1920. **Members:** 48. **Description:** Serves as an educational service of the home garden seed

industry. Provides pictures and information to garden writers, food editors, newspapers, magazines, and radio and television stations on flower and vegetable gardening from seed.

4983 ■ North American Flowerbulb Wholesalers Association (NAFWA)
c/o Marlboro Bulb Company
2424 Hwy. 72/221 E
Greenwood, SC 29649
Ph: (864)229-1618
Fax: (864)229-5719
E-mail: nafwa1@aol.com
Contact: Jack C. De Vroomen, Sec.-Treas.
Founded: 1983. **Members:** 50. **Membership Dues:** regular, $550 (annual). **Languages:** Dutch, English. **Description:** Wholesalers and dealers of flower bulbs and related floricultural commodities. **Awards:** Bulb Booster Award. **Type:** recognition. **Supersedes:** Horticultural Dealers Association. **Publications:** *NAFWA News*, quarterly. Newsletter. **Circulation:** 350. **Conventions/Meetings:** annual conference.

4984 ■ North American Horticultural Supply Association (NAHSA)
100 N 20th St., 4th Fl.
Philadelphia, PA 19103-1443
Ph: (215)564-3484
Fax: (215)963-9784
E-mail: nahsa@fernley.com
URL: http://www.nahsa.org
Contact: Sarah Hagy, Exec. Dir.
Founded: 1988. **Members:** 110. **Membership Dues:** distributor, manufacturer, $745 (annual) ● affiliate, $695 (annual). **Staff:** 3. **Budget:** $100,000. **Description:** Horticultural hard goods distributors and manufacturers. (Horticultural hard goods include such items as greenhouse building materials and supplies, pesticides, and fertilizer.) Seeks to strengthen and enhance the relationship between horticultural hard goods manufacturers and distributors; promotes distribution in the market. Serves as a forum for exchange of information among members. **Committees:** Communication; Management Information; Membership. **Publications:** *Industry Calendar*, annual. Contains calendar of events throughout the green industry. ● *The Landscape*, monthly. Newsletters. Features updates on membership and association events. **Conventions/Meetings:** annual meeting (exhibits).

4985 ■ Perennial Plant Association (PPA)
3383 Schirtzinger Rd.
Hilliard, OH 43026
Ph: (614)771-8431
Fax: (614)876-5238
E-mail: ppa@perennialplant.org
URL: http://www.perennialplant.org
Contact: Dr. Steven M. Still, Exec. Dir.
Founded: 1983. **Members:** 2,000. **Membership Dues:** researcher, librarian, educator, education personnel, allied trade, amateur gardener, additional member of a voting firm, $80 (annual) ● broker, wholesaler (based on total volume of business in perennials), $80-$500 (annual) ● student (full time or undergraduate), $20 (annual) ● international (except Canada), $125 (annual). **Staff:** 4. **Description:** Growers, merchandisers, landscapers, and educators; those who sell products related to perennials; individuals interested in perennials. Aims are to: exchange information; educate the public on the care of perennials; promote the ornamental or economic use of perennials; advance and support research. Encourages the development of perennial-oriented curricula; evaluates standards in the industry. **Awards: Type:** grant. **Recipient:** to non-profit entity in the United States or Canada with the best research proposal relating to the herbaceous perennial industry ● **Type:** scholarship. **Recipient:** to college students studying horticulture or a related subject area. **Committees:** Education and Research; Promotion; Public Relations; Standards. **Publications:** *Guide to Herbaceous Perennial Gardens in the United States and Canada*. Booklet. Features a list of excellent public and private perennial gardens found in United States and Canada. ● *Perennial Plants Journal*, quarterly. Contains useful articles about research and growing tips. **Advertising:** accepted ● *Plant of the Year*. Brochure ● *Symposium Proceedings*, annual. Contains compilation of the speakers' presentations at the annual symposium. ● Membership Directory, annual. Provides listing of name and addresses with affiliations to facilitate communication. ● Newsletter, bimonthly. Contains information on the current events of the association. ● Catalog ● Manual. **Conventions/Meetings:** annual Perennial Plant Symposium - meeting and symposium (exhibits).

4986 ■ Tropical Flowering Tree Society (TFTS)
c/o Fairchild Tropical Botanical Garden
10901 Old Cutler Rd.
Coral Gables, FL 33156
E-mail: zurs2580@aol.com
URL: http://www.tfts.org
Membership Dues: regular, $30 (annual) ● international, $35 (annual) ● regular, $50 (biennial) ● patron, $150 (annual) ● regular, $120 (quinquennial) ● sponsor, $500 (annual). **Multinational. Description:** Represents the interests of individuals dedicated to the propagation and dissemination of information about tropical flowering trees and plants. Promotes, propagates and preserves the tropical flowering trees. Provides members with the opportunity to participate in plant sale and plant auction, field trips, picnics and conferences. **Publications:** Newsletter, quarterly. **Conventions/Meetings:** monthly meeting - held every 2nd Monday at Fairchild Tropical Botanical Garden, Miami, Florida.

Ichthyology

4987 ■ Bonefish and Tarpon Unlimited (BTU)
c/o Aaron Adams, PhD, Dir. of Operations and Research
PO Box 2197
Pineland, FL 33945
Ph: (239)283-1622
Fax: (239)283-2466
E-mail: aadams@mote.org
URL: http://www.tarbone.org
Contact: Aaron Adams PhD, Dir. of Operations and Research
Membership Dues: associate, $50 (annual) ● regular, $100 (annual) ● executive, $100 (annual) ● flats partner, $250 (annual) ● conservation partner, $500 (annual) ● gray ghost, $1,000 ● silver king, $2,500 ● life sponsor, $10,000. **Description:** Protects and enhances Bonefish and Tarpon species by gaining a better understanding of their habits. Supports projects and research to help understand, nurture and enhance a healthy Bonefish and Tarpon population. Gathers information related to the condition of these fishes and their behavior and life cycles. Provides educational material to the public and to fishermen. **Programs:** Tagging. **Publications:** Newsletter. **Conventions/Meetings:** annual symposium.

Interdisciplinary Education

4988 ■ Interdisciplinary Environmental Association (IEA)
c/o Dr. Michael A. Reiter, Chm.
Delaware State Univ.
Dept. of Agriculture and Natural Resources
1200 N DuPont Hwy.
Dover, DE 19901
Ph: (302)857-6412
Fax: (302)857-6455
E-mail: mreiter@desu.edu
URL: http://ieaonline.org
Contact: Dr. Michael A. Reiter, Chm.
Founded: 1990. **Membership Dues:** individual, $80 (annual) ● student, $40 (annual) ● institution (based on participants), $600-$2,400 (annual). **Multinational. Description:** Strives to bring together all disciplines so that environmental knowledge is enhanced through interdisciplinary communications. Educates the public about current concerns, research, plans and the prospects of a cleaner future. Encourages scholars to educate each other in an interdisciplinary format, and to present disciplinary perspectives of environmental problems to people outside of those disciplines. **Telecommunication Services:** electronic mail, dkantar@assumption.edu ● electronic mail, khickey@assumption.edu. **Publications:** *Interdisciplinary Environmental Review*. Journal. Contains interdisciplinary research and survey papers. **Price:** included in membership dues. ISSN: 0023-6234. **Conventions/Meetings:** annual conference.

Landscaping

4989 ■ Ecological Landscaping Association (ELA)
60 Thoreau St., No. 252
Concord, MA 01742-2456
Ph: (617)436-5838
URL: http://ecolandscaping.org
Contact: Chris O'Brien, Pres.
Founded: 1992. **Membership Dues:** associate, $50 (annual) ● professional, $75 (annual) ● supporting, $125 (annual) ● sustaining, $250 (annual). **Multinational. Description:** Advocates for environmentally responsible stewardship of land and natural resources in the landscaping and horticultural practices of professionals and the public. Promotes the design, installation and maintenance of landscapes through education and collaboration. Provides networking opportunities for people to exchange information concerning the environmental issues associated with ecological landscaping. **Publications:** *Discover Ecological Landscaping*. Brochure ● *The Ecological Landscaper*, quarterly. Newsletter. **Price:** included in membership dues. **Advertising:** accepted ● *Guide to Healthy Landscapes*, quarterly. Handbook. Provides information about soil management for long-term health of landscapes. **Price:** $25.00 for members; $30.00 for nonmembers, plus shipping and handling. **Advertising:** accepted.

4990 ■ Northeastern Weed Science Society (NEWSS)
c/o Jerry J. Baron, Pres.-Elect
IR-4, Rutgers Univ.
681 US Hwy. 1 S
North Brunswick, NJ 08902-3390
Ph: (732)932-4605
Fax: (732)932-8481
E-mail: jbaron@aesop.rutgers.edu
URL: http://www.newss.org
Contact: Jerry J. Baron, Pres.-Elect
Description: Individuals and organizations interested in weed science, and manufacturers or distributors of herbicides, equipment manufacturers or related industries that contribute to the support of the society. Serves the Northeastern states by promoting a better understanding of the common issues and progress among those concerned with research and education in weeds and weed control; cooperates with other weed control societies and the Weed Science Society of America. **Committees:** Archives; Audit; Awards; Collegiate Weed Contest; Nomination; Program; Resolutions; Site Selection. **Publications:** *Manual of Operating Procedures*. Alternate Formats: online ● *NEWSS News*. Newsletter. Alternate Formats: online ● Proceedings. **Price:** $25.00. **Conventions/Meetings:** annual meeting.

4991 ■ Project EverGreen
c/o Den Gardner, Exec. Dir.
PO Box 156
New Prague, MN 56071
Ph: (952)758-9135
Free: (877)758-4835
E-mail: dengardner@projectevergreen.com
URL: http://www.projectevergreen.com
Contact: Den Gardner, Exec. Dir.
Description: Raises the awareness of the environmental, economic and lifestyle benefits of landscapes. Promotes the significance of those who preserve and enhance green spaces at home, work and play. Promotes healthy landscapes and green spaces us-

ing public relations, public affairs and other tactics. **Telecommunication Services:** electronic mail, barbulschmid@projectevergreen.com. **Publications:** Brochure. Alternate Formats: online.

Livestock

4992 ■ Alpaca Breeders of the Rockies (ABR)

c/o Ron Hinds, Dir.
5704 Canyon Trail
Elizabeth, CO 80107
Ph: (303)646-1320
E-mail: pacaron@estreet.com
URL: http://www.alpacabreeders.org
Contact: Ron Hinds, Dir.

Founded: 1994. **Members:** 100. **Membership Dues:** associate, $36 (annual) ● farm, $120 (annual) ● business, $60 (annual). **Budget:** $9,000. **Description:** Breeders of Alpacas (an Alpaca is a close relative of the Llama); processors and distributors of Alpaca products. Promotes public awareness of Alpacas; seeks to advance the Alpaca industries. Facilitates communication and cooperation among members; conducts marketing campaigns. Participates in agricultural fairs; sponsors parades and other social activities. **Libraries: Type:** reference. **Holdings:** archival material, artwork, audio recordings, business records, video recordings. **Subjects:** Alpaca breeding, Alpaca wool and its uses, fiber marketing. **Awards:** Hummdinger. **Frequency:** annual. **Type:** recognition. **Telecommunication Services:** electronic mail, anniesalpacaranch@msn.com. **Committees:** Breed Standards; Education; Fiber Arts; Great Western Stock Show; National Western Stock Show; Nominating; Shows and Events; Veterinary Scholarship. **Publications:** *'Paca Parade*. Newsletter. **Advertising:** accepted. Alternate Formats: online. **Conventions/Meetings:** annual Fall Festival - meeting - always September/October.

4993 ■ American Emu Association (AEA)

PO Box 2502
San Angelo, TX 76902-2502
Ph: (541)332-0675
E-mail: info@aea-emu.net
URL: http://www.aea-emu.org
Contact: Charles Ramey, Pres.

Founded: 1989. **Members:** 1,000. **Membership Dues:** regular first time, $300 ● regular renewal, $100 (annual) ● certified business, international, $350 (annual) ● renewing international, $150 (annual) ● junior, $10 (annual). **Staff:** 1. **Budget:** $250,000. **Regional Groups:** 6. **State Groups:** 35. **Description:** Works to develop a world market for emu products. Promotes production, marketing, sales and commercial use of emu goods. Conducts educational and research programs. Compiles statistics. **Libraries: Type:** reference; open to the public. **Holdings:** audiovisuals, books, clippings, periodicals. **Computer Services:** Mailing lists, of members ● online services, breeder directory. **Publications:** *AEA EMUpdate*, bimonthly. Newsletter. **Advertising:** accepted. Alternate Formats: CD-ROM. **Conventions/Meetings:** annual convention and board meeting (exhibits) - always July.

4994 ■ American Livestock Breeds Conservancy (ALBC)

PO Box 477
Pittsboro, NC 27312
Ph: (919)542-5704
Fax: (919)545-0022
E-mail: albc@albc-usa.org
URL: http://www.albc-usa.org
Contact: Charles R. Bassett, Exec. Dir.

Founded: 1977. **Members:** 4,000. **Membership Dues:** individual, $30 (annual) ● contributor, $50 (annual) ● husbandry giving club, $100-$249 (annual) ● heritage giving club, $250-$499 (annual) ● legacy giving club (minimum), $500 (annual). **Staff:** 7. **Budget:** $500,000. **Regional Groups:** 6. **Description:** Works to promote and conserve endangered breeds of livestock and poultry in America. Encourages the use of rare breeds in appropriate commercial operations, diversified farms, living history museums, and zoos. Conducts research on breed status and characteristics. Operates semen bank for rare breeds. **Libraries: Type:** reference. **Holdings:** 800; artwork, books, periodicals. **Subjects:** livestock and poultry. **Awards:** Breed Conservation Award. **Frequency:** annual. **Type:** recognition. **Recipient:** for significant contribution to the conservancy of a breed or species. **Computer Services:** Information services, livestock registry. **Formerly:** American Minor Breeds Conservancy. **Publications:** *A Conservation Breeding Handbook*. **Price:** $12.95 plus shipping and handling. **Advertising:** accepted ● *A Rare Breeds Album of American Livestock*. **Price:** $29.95 plus shipping and handling ● *ALBC News*, bimonthly. Newsletter. **Price:** included in membership dues. ISSN: 1064-1599. **Circulation:** 4,000. **Advertising:** accepted ● *The Art of American Livestock Breeding*. Catalog. **Price:** $12.00 plus shipping and handling ● *Birds of a Feather: Saving Rare Turkeys from Extinction*. Documents the history of the domestic turkey; discusses strategies for conserving the genetics of rare birds. **Price:** $21.95 ● *Breeders Directory*, annual. **Price:** included in membership dues ● *The Sheep Book, A Hand book for the Modern Shepherd*. Handbook. Discusses new medications and progress in reproductive technology. **Price:** $24.95 ● *Taking Stock: The North American Livestock Census*. Survey. Includes data from comprehensive livestock census. Discusses the value and importance of genetic conservation. **Price:** $8.50 ● *Waterfowl Census*. Survey. Alternate Formats: online ● Books. **Conventions/Meetings:** annual conference (exhibits).

4995 ■ American Royal Association (ARA)

1701 Amer. Royal Ct.
Kansas City, MO 64102
Ph: (816)221-9800
Fax: (816)221-8189
E-mail: info@americanroyal.com
URL: http://www.americanroyal.com
Contact: Jim McNair, Pres./CEO

Founded: 1899. **Members:** 1,050. **Staff:** 8. **Budget:** $2,400,000. **Description:** Business firms and individuals are sponsors. Seeks to further livestock breeds and the agricultural industry through the annual American Royal Livestock, Horse Show and Rodeo. **Awards:** Royal Six. **Frequency:** annual. **Type:** scholarship. **Recipient:** for college sophomores and juniors pursuing a 4-year degree in agricultural related field. **Programs:** Adult; Collegiate; Elementary; KALF; Royal Six Leadership. **Conventions/Meetings:** annual meeting (exhibits) - always November, Kansas City, MO.

4996 ■ American Water Buffalo Association (AWBA)

c/o Dr. Hugh Popenoe, Pres.
PO Box 13533
Gainesville, FL 32604
Ph: (352)392-2643
Fax: (352)846-0816
E-mail: hlp@ufl.edu
URL: http://www.americanwaterbuffalo.org
Contact: Dr. Hugh Popenoe, Pres.

Founded: 1986. **Members:** 200. **Membership Dues:** student, $15 (annual) ● individual, $25 (annual) ● corporate, $50 (annual). **Staff:** 1. **Budget:** $5,000. **Multinational. Description:** Owners, breeders, and marketers of water buffalo. Promotes advancement of water buffalo breeds and care; seeks to expand demand for water buffalo products. Conducts educational and marketing programs; serves as a clearinghouse on water buffalo breeding and husbandry. **Libraries: Type:** open to the public; by appointment only; reference. **Holdings:** archival material, books, clippings, periodicals. **Subjects:** water buffalo. **Computer Services:** Information services ● online services, herd registration. **Publications:** *Water Buffalo Newsletter*, quarterly. **Price:** included in membership dues. **Conventions/Meetings:** annual meeting.

4997 ■ Food Animal Concerns Trust (FACT)

PO Box 14599
Chicago, IL 60614
Ph: (773)525-4952
Fax: (773)525-5226
E-mail: info@fact.cc
URL: http://204.200.206.238
Contact: Richard Wood, Exec. Dir.

Founded: 1982. **Budget:** $400,000. **Description:** Foundations and individuals opposed to the industrialization of livestock and poultry production. Examines the adverse impact of "factory farming" on farm income, public health, and animal welfare, and promotes new methods of livestock and poultry production. Maintains speakers' bureau. **Programs:** Food Safety; Humane Farming. **Projects:** Control of Salmonella in Egg Production; Nest Eggs. **Also Known As:** Fact, Inc. **Formerly:** (1982) Farm Animal Care Trust. **Publications:** *Fact Acts*, 3-4/year. Newsletter ● Report ● Also issues papers and handouts on food animal safety concerns.

4998 ■ International Livestock Identification Association (ILIA)

c/o Rick Wahlert, Sec.-Treas.
4701 Marion St., Ste.201
Denver, CO 80216
Ph: (303)294-0895
Free: (800)242-7820
Fax: (303)294-0918
E-mail: rick.wahlert@ag.state.co.us
URL: http://4ilia.com
Contact: Rick Wahlert, Sec.-Treas.

Founded: 1946. **Members:** 33. **Membership Dues:** regular, $75 (annual). **State Groups:** 30. **Description:** State and provincial employees engaged in regulatory work; officials of livestock associations. Conducts research, educational, and discussion programs dealing with use of livestock brands, recording and inspection of brands, cattle theft law, and prosecutions. Maintains speakers' bureau. **Libraries: Type:** reference. **Holdings:** biographical archives. **Awards: Type:** recognition. **Computer Services:** database, stolen livestock. **Committees:** Audit; Board Members; Brand Recorders; Electronic Data; Identification; Investigators; Nominating; Site Selection. **Formerly:** International Livestock Identification and Theft Investigators Association; (1969) National Livestock Brand Conference; (1982) International Livestock Brand Conference; (1988) International Livestock Brand and Theft Conference. **Publications:** *Fact Acts*, 3-4/year. Newsletter ● *Livestock Laws of Participating States* ● Proceedings, annual ● Newsletter, quarterly ● Also publishes papers, and information handouts on safety concerns. **Conventions/Meetings:** annual conference and meeting - always July.

4999 ■ International Livestock Investigators Association (ILIA)

c/o Rick Wahlert, Sec.-Treas.
Capitol Sta.
PO Box 202001
Helena, MT 59620-2001
Ph: (406)444-2043 (406)444-7323
Free: (800)523-3162
E-mail: livemail@mt.gov
URL: http://www.mt.gov/liv
Contact: Rick Wahlert, Sec.-Treas.

Founded: 1978. **Description:** Law enforcement officers specializing in livestock investigation. Seeks to reduce crimes associated with livestock, such as theft. **Conventions/Meetings:** annual conference.

5000 ■ International Miniature Donkey Registry

1338 Hughes Shop Rd.
Westminster, MD 21158
Ph: (410)875-0118
Fax: (410)857-9145
E-mail: donks@flash.net
URL: http://www.qis.net/~minidonk/imdr.htm
Contact: Edward M. Gross, Pres.

Founded: 1992. **Members:** 1,100. **Membership Dues:** ordinary, $18 (annual) ● life, $180. **Staff:** 4. **Description:** Owners and enthusiasts of miniature donkeys. Seeks to improve the bloodlines of miniature donkeys; promotes responsible donkey ownership. Serves as a clearinghouse on miniature donkeys; maintains breed registry. **Libraries: Type:** reference.

Holdings: archival material, books. **Subjects:** miniature donkeys. **Additional Websites:** http://www.miniaturedonkeyinfo.com. **Formerly:** IMDR. **Publications:** *Miniature Donkey Talk*, quarterly. Magazine. **Price:** $25.00/year. **Circulation:** 5,800. **Advertising:** accepted. Also Cited As: *MDT*.

5001 ■ International Yak Association (IYAK)
c/o Cynthia Huber, Sec.-Treas./Registrar
PO Box 27
Hillside, CO 81232
Ph: (719)942-4181
E-mail: ckhdcr@aol.com
URL: http://www.iyak.org
Contact: Cynthia Huber, Sec.-Treas./Registrar
Founded: 1992. **Membership Dues:** regular, $60 (annual) ● life, $400. **Multinational. Description:** Aims to collect, record and preserve the pedigrees of Yak. Seeks to advance Yak breeding. Raises awareness of Yak fiber and meat production and processing, halter training and hook trimming.

5002 ■ National Association of Animal Breeders (NAAB)
PO Box 1033
Columbia, MO 65205
Ph: (573)445-4406
Fax: (573)446-2279
E-mail: naab-css@naab-css.org
URL: http://www.naab-css.org
Contact: Dr. Gordon A. Doak, Pres.
Founded: 1947. **Members:** 22. **Membership Dues:** regular, $100 (annual) ● associate, $125 (annual). **Staff:** 5. **Description:** Farmer cooperatives and private businesses interested in the improvement of farm livestock in the U.S., Canada, Mexico, and other countries. Represents 60&percent; of farmer cooperatives and 40&percent; of private businesses in the US. **Awards:** Distinguished Service Award. **Frequency:** annual. **Type:** recognition. **Recipient:** for long term distinguished service to the industry ● Member Director Award. **Frequency:** annual. **Type:** recognition. **Recipient:** for long term service as a member of a NAAB Board of Directors ● Pioneer Award. **Frequency:** annual. **Type:** recognition. **Recipient:** for long term distinguished service to the AI industry ● Research Award. **Frequency:** annual. **Type:** recognition. **Recipient:** for stimulating and encouraging research in artificial insemination and reproduction. **Computer Services:** database, active AI sire list ● database, AI sire controller numbers ● database, AI sire (cross reference) ● database, expected net revenue ● database, international sire evaluation ● database, international sire list ● database, sire evaluation ● database, uniform breed codes. **Committees:** Beef Development; Custom Freezing; Directors; Managers; Marketing; Research; Sire Evaluation; Sire Health; Technical. **Programs:** Awards; Coordinated Research; Marketing and Promotion. **Formerly:** National Association of Artificial Breeders. **Publications:** *Illustrated Anatomy of the Bovine Male and Female Reproductive Tracts*. Book. Alternate Formats: online ● Pamphlets ● Proceedings, annual. **Conventions/Meetings:** annual convention (exhibits).

5003 ■ National Institute for Animal Agriculture (NIAA)
1910 Lyda Ave.
Bowling Green, KY 42104-3326
Ph: (270)782-9798
Fax: (270)782-0188
E-mail: niaa@animalagriculture.org
URL: http://www.animalagriculture.org
Contact: Michele Vise-Brown, CEO
Founded: 1916. **Membership Dues:** national association, commercial organization, $1,000 (annual) ● state-level association, publicly supported institution/agency, $500 (annual) ● self-employed individual, $250 (annual) ● affiliate, $100 (annual). **Budget:** $250,000. **Description:** Producers, industry professionals, state and federal regulators, and researchers interested in discussing common issues, building consensus, and offering solutions to the challenges facing meat animal production in North America. Produces educational materials. Addresses industry issues including animal health, livestock care and handling, food safety, and uniform livestock identification. **Awards:** Chairman's Award. **Frequency:** annual. **Type:** recognition. **Recipient:** for volunteers possessing the true spirit of voluntarism ● Meritorious Service Award. **Frequency:** annual. **Type:** recognition. **Recipient:** for membership ● President's Award. **Frequency:** annual. **Type:** recognition. **Recipient:** for chairperson/leaders. **Committees:** Animal Care; Brucellosis; Cattle Health Management; Emergency Diseases; Equine Health; Food Safety Assurance; Livestock Care; Livestock Identification; Poultry Health; Pseudorabies; Sheep Health Management; Swine Health Management. **Formed by Merger of:** (1980) National Livestock Sanitary Committee; National Livestock Loss Prevention Board. **Formerly:** (1976) Livestock Conservation, Inc.; (2001) Livestock Conservation Institute. **Publications:** *Animal Agriculture Quarterly*. Newsletter. Provides communications link between producers, veterinarians, researchers, academicians, government veterinarians and regulatory personnel. Alternate Formats: online ● *The Final Countdown: Brucellosis Progress Report*, quarterly. Newsletter ● *Food Safety Digest*, bimonthly. Newsletter ● *LCI News*, bimonthly. Newsletter ● *Official Annual Meeting Proceedings*, annual ● *PRV Progress Report*, bimonthly. Newsletter ● *Scrapie Progress Report*, quarterly. Newsletter ● Videos. Covers livestock diseases and handling. **Price:** $75.00 ● Pamphlets. Covers livestock diseases and handling. ● Reports, quarterly. Alternate Formats: online ● Also publishes material on food safety, livestock diseases and handling. **Conventions/Meetings:** annual conference and meeting (exhibits).

5004 ■ National Miniature Donkey Association (NMDA)
c/o Lynn Gattari, Gen. Mgr.
6450 Dewey Rd.
Rome, NY 13440
Ph: (315)336-0154
Fax: (315)339-4414
E-mail: nmdaasset@aol.com
URL: http://www.nmdaasset.com
Contact: Lynn Gattari, Gen. Mgr.
Founded: 1990. **Members:** 900. **Membership Dues:** in U.S., $35 (annual) ● outside U.S., $45 (annual) ● contributing in U.S., $50 (annual). **Staff:** 1. **Description:** Owners and admirers of Miniature Donkeys (which are indigenous to the islands of Sicily and Sardinia and reach a maximum height of 36 inches). Promotes the Miniature Donkey as an ideal pet. Gathers and disseminates information on Miniature Donkeys and their care and management. **Programs:** Ambassadors for the Breed; Gelding Incentive. **Publications:** *Asset*, quarterly. Magazine. **Advertising:** accepted ● *Miniature Donkeys*. Brochures. **Price:** $15.00 for 50 copies; $25.00 for 100 copies ● *Training Mules and Donkeys: A Logical Approach to Longears*. Videos. Includes workbooks and fieldcards. **Price:** $39.95/tape (series of 3).

5005 ■ North American Rhea Association
Address Unknown since 2007
Description: Promotes the production of the Rhea in the livestock industry. Rhea are part of the bird family which includes ostriches and emus.

Marine

5006 ■ Alliance of Marine Mammal Parks and Aquariums (AMMPA)
c/o Dave DeNardo
WCS/New York Aquarium
W 8th and Surf Ave.
Coney Island
Brooklyn, NY 11224
E-mail: ammpa@aol.com
URL: http://www.ammpa.org
Contact: Jay Sweeney, Pres.
Founded: 1987. **Membership Dues:** regular, in U.S., $6,000-$9,000 (annual) ● regular, outside U.S., $3,000 (annual) ● pinniped, $4,500 (annual) ● research facility, $1,250 (annual). **Multinational. Description:** Maintains the highest standards of care for marine mammals. Promotes conservation in the wild through public education, scientific study and wildlife presentations. Fosters research that benefits the health and well-being of marine mammals living in public display facilities and in the wild. Aims to rescue, rehabilitate and release stranded marine mammals. **Computer Services:** Information services, dolphin resources. **Programs:** Education.

5007 ■ American Marinelife Dealers Association (AMDA)
c/o Liz Harris, Sec.
Creatures Featured
PO Box 1052
Madison, FL 32341
Ph: (850)973-3488
E-mail: president@amdareef.com
URL: http://www.amdareef.com
Contact: Burton Patrick, Pres.
Founded: 1995. **Membership Dues:** standard, $50 (annual) ● contributor, $250 (annual) ● sponsor, $500 (annual) ● donor, $1,500 (annual) ● benefactor, $5,000 (annual). **Description:** Promotes marine aquariums-keeping as an entertaining, educational and worthwhile leisure time activity. Raises public awareness of the industry's role in marine conservation. Encourages responsible husbandry through education and training. **Computer Services:** database, directory of Captive Bred Livestock ● database, Ecolist ● information services, marine life resources ● online services, message board. **Telecommunication Services:** electronic mail, treasurer@amdareef.com. **Publications:** Newsletter, quarterly.

5008 ■ Blue Dolphin Alliance (BDA)
PO Box 2481
Harmony, CA 93435
Free: (877)257-6265
E-mail: bluedolphin.org@thegrid.net
URL: http://www.bluedolphin.org
Contact: Alan Godley, Dir.
Founded: 1989. **Membership Dues:** student, $15 (annual) ● senior, $20 (annual) ● individual and family, $25 (annual). **Description:** Raises awareness of whales, dolphins and all marine life. Supports the rehabilitation and release of marine mammals and other wildlife. **Affiliated With:** Earth Island Institute.

5009 ■ International Marine Minerals Society (IMMS)
Univ. of Hawaii
1000 Pope Rd., MSB 303
Honolulu, HI 96822
Ph: (808)956-6036
Fax: (808)956-9772
E-mail: karynnem@hawaii.edu
URL: http://www.immsoc.org
Contact: Cornel de Ronde, Pres.-Elect
Founded: 1987. **Membership Dues:** individual, $15 (annual). **Multinational. Description:** Promotes interest in the diverse aspects of marine minerals. **Awards:** The Moore Medal. **Frequency:** periodic. **Type:** medal. **Recipient:** to an individual who has made a distinction on the development of marine minerals. **Additional Websites:** http://www.underwatermining.org. **Telecommunication Services:** electronic mail, imms@soest.hawaii.edu. **Publications:** *The Code for Environmental Management of Marine Mining*. Alternate Formats: online ● *Soundings*, semiannual. Newsletter. Features the latest developments in the field of marine minerals. ● Papers ● Reports. **Conventions/Meetings:** annual meeting, held in conjunction with Underwater Mining Institute.

5010 ■ International SeaKeepers Society
4101 Ravenswood Rd., Ste.128
Fort Lauderdale, FL 33312
Ph: (954)766-7100 (561)392-3648
Fax: (954)252-4595
E-mail: info@seakeepers.org
URL: http://www.seakeepers.org
Contact: John Englander, CEO
Founded: 1998. **Multinational. Description:** Protects the oceans by equipping luxury yachts, other

vessels, and platforms around the world with sophisticated ocean and atmospheric monitoring sensors. Gathers and transmits compact and high-tech monitors via satellite to the international scientific community critically-needed data on the health of the oceans, changing weather and climate patterns, sources of pollution and other threats to human life and marine resources. **Computer Services:** Online services, data services/access. **Telecommunication Services:** electronic mail, englander@seakeepers.org. **Publications:** Newsletter.

5011 ■ PACON International
2525 Correa Rd., HIG 407A
Honolulu, HI 96822
Ph: (808)956-6163
Fax: (808)956-2580
E-mail: pacon@hawaii.edu
URL: http://www.hawaii.edu/pacon
Contact: Dr. Narenda Saxena, Founding Pres.
Membership Dues: individual, $50 (annual) ● life, $1,000 ● student, $15 (annual) ● corporate (full), $850 (annual) ● corporate (associate), $350 (annual) ● corporate (introductory), $350 (annual). **Multinational. Description:** Shares scientific and technical information to individuals interested in the future of the world's oceans. Promotes utilization and sustainable development of the ocean's resources. Seeks to emphasize the need for sound ocean policies through education and public programs. Advances the various disciplines involved in marine science and technology. **Awards:** Distinguished Member Award. **Frequency:** annual. **Type:** recognition. **Recipient:** for extraordinary work and support in promoting PACON International ● International Award. **Frequency:** biennial. **Type:** recognition. **Recipient:** for significant contribution to the advancement of ocean science or technology ● Ocean Service Award. **Frequency:** annual. **Type:** recognition. **Recipient:** for significant contribution to marine science and technology in general ● Service Award. **Frequency:** annual. **Type:** recognition. **Recipient:** for significant contribution to the organization or to one of the conferences of the organization. **Publications:** Newsletter, quarterly.

5012 ■ Reef Check
PO Box 1057
Pacific Palisades, CA 90272-1057
Ph: (310)230-2371 (310)230-2360
Fax: (310)230-2376
E-mail: rcinfo@reefcheck.org
URL: http://www.reefcheck.org
Contact: Gregor Hodgson PhD, Founder/Exec. Dir.
Founded: 1996. **Membership Dues:** general (donation), $25. **Multinational. Description:** Educates the public about the coral reef crisis. Creates a network of volunteer teams that monitor and report on reef health. Facilitates collaboration that produces sustainable solutions for the coral reef crisis. Stimulates local community action to protect remaining pristine reefs. Rehabilitates damaged reefs worldwide. **Computer Services:** Information services, coral reef resources ● mailing lists, of members. **Publications:** *The Global Coral Reef Crisis*, quinquennial. Report ● *The Transect Line*, quarterly. Newsletter. Alternate Formats: online.

5013 ■ Reef Relief
PO Box 430
Key West, FL 33041
Ph: (305)294-3100
Fax: (305)294-9515
E-mail: info@reefrelief.org
URL: http://www.reefrelief.org
Contact: DeeVon Quirolo, Exec. Dir.
Membership Dues: general, $50 (annual). **Multinational. Description:** Protects and preserves coral reef ecosystems. Increases public awareness of the importance and value of living coral reef ecosystems. Enhances scientific understanding and knowledge of living coral reef ecosystems. **Computer Services:** Information services, coral reef resources ● mailing lists. **Programs:** Coral Reef Conservation. **Projects:** Coral Photo Monitoring Survey; Key West Marine Park. **Publications:** *Reef Line*, quarterly. Newsletter. Alternate Formats: online.

5014 ■ ReefGuardian International (RGI)
2829 Bird Ave., Ste.5
PMB 162
Miami, FL 33133-4668
Ph: (305)358-4600
Fax: (301)371-6188
E-mail: info@reefguardian.org
URL: http://www.reefguardian.org
Membership Dues: regular, $25 (annual) ● friend, $100 (annual) ● sponsor, $250 (annual) ● guardian, $500 (annual) ● champion, $1,000 (annual). **Multinational. Description:** Represents the interests of individuals dedicated to the protection of coral reefs and their marine life. Creates coral reef marine protected areas. Stops dredging and burial of reefs. Prevents ship traffic threats to reefs. Safeguards reefs from pollution and offshore oil.

5015 ■ SeaWeb
8401 Colesville Rd., Ste.500
Silver Spring, MD 20910
Ph: (301)495-9570
Fax: (301)495-4846
E-mail: contactus@seaweb.org
URL: http://www.seaweb.org
Contact: Dawn M. Martin, Pres.
Multinational. Description: Promotes ocean conservation by raising public awareness, advancing science-based solutions and mobilizing decision-makers. Combines science, communications and policy work to "amplify leading voices" for ocean conservation. Uses communications expertise to translate science into understandable, actionable initiatives and to push for sound policies in ocean protection. **Programs:** Asia-Pacific; Marine Photo Bank. **Projects:** The LegaSea. **Publications:** *Ocean Update*, monthly. Newsletter. Summarizes recent news, views and events concerning marine and coastal environments. Alternate Formats: online.

5016 ■ Sirenian International
200 Stonewall Dr.
Fredericksburg, VA 22401-2110
E-mail: caryn@sirenian.org
URL: http://www.sirenian.org
Contact: Caryn Self Sullivan, Contact
Membership Dues: neonate (student), $10 (annual) ● mother/calf pair (family/classroom), $40 (annual) ● mermaid (individual), $25 (annual) ● mating herd (patron), $100 (annual) ● population, $500 (annual) ● specie, $1,000 (annual). **Multinational. Description:** Promotes the long term conservation of Manatee and Dugong populations through research, education and inter-cultural collaboration. Encourages sound and professional scientific research related to sirenian populations by providing feedback, support and funding. Enhances awareness, knowledge and use of collaborative problem-solving approaches to management of conflicts related to conservation of sirenians and their aquatic habitats. **Computer Services:** Information services, Sirenians resources ● mailing lists ● online services, slide shows ● online services, Yahoo groups. **Councils:** Scientific Advisory. **Publications:** *Manatee News*, quarterly. Report.

5017 ■ Society for Marine Mammalogy (SMM)
c/o Heather Koopman, Sec.
Univ. of North Carolina at Wilmington
601 S Coll. Rd.
Wilmington, NC 28403
Ph: (910)962-7199
Fax: (910)962-4066
E-mail: koopmanh@uncw.edu
URL: http://www.marinemammalogy.org
Contact: Heather Koopman, Sec.
Founded: 1981. **Membership Dues:** life, $1,200 ● institution, $100 (annual) ● associate, $70 (annual) ● emeritus, student, $50 (annual) ● full, $75 (annual). **Multinational. Description:** Promotes the educational, scientific and managerial advancement of marine mammal science. Provides scientific information on conservation and management of marine mammal resources. **Committees:** Awards and Scholarships; Conference; Education; International Relations; Investment; Nominations/Elections; Scientific Advisors; Scientific Program. **Publications:** *Marine Mammal Science*, quarterly. Journal. Alternate Formats: online ● Newsletter, quarterly. Alternate Formats: online ● Membership Directory, biennial.

5018 ■ Water Planet USA
203 Greenwood Dr.
Panama City Beach, FL 32407
Ph: (850)230-6030
Free: (866)449-5591
E-mail: info@waterplanetusa.com
URL: http://www.waterplanetusa.com
Contact: Denis Richard, Pres.
For-Profit. Multinational. Description: Works for the development of ecotourism. Designs a program that allows families with disabled children to have the adventure of being in the water and in the presence of wild dolphins. Promotes exchanges between ecosystems and organizations involved in the protection of nature and people interested in rediscovering their link to animals, plants and minerals. **Computer Services:** Information services, dolphin resources. **Programs:** Special Needs Children; Swim With the Dolphins; Therapeutic.

Marine Biology

5019 ■ Shark Research Institute (SRI)
PO Box 40
Princeton, NJ 08540
Ph: (609)921-3522
Fax: (609)921-1505
E-mail: media@sharks.org
URL: http://www.sharks.org
Contact: L.J.V. Compagno PhD, Dir.
Founded: 1991. **Membership Dues:** individual, $35 (annual) ● individual sponsor, $45 (annual) ● family sponsor, $60 (annual) ● contributing sponsor, $100 (annual) ● individual patron, $250 (annual) ● corporate, $500 (annual) ● corporate patron, $1,500 (annual) ● corporate sponsor, $2,500 (annual). **Multinational. Description:** Promotes public awareness of sharks and their vital role in the marine ecosystem. Establishes marine sanctuaries for sharks. Maintains a global database of shark attacks and develops resources to aid shark attack victims. Conducts and sponsors behavioral studies of sharks and supports research into their biology, distribution and global movements. Works to correct misperceptions about sharks and stop the slaughter of 100 million sharks annually. **Computer Services:** database, educational materials ● information services, shark resources. **Telecommunication Services:** electronic mail, development@sharks.org. **Publications:** Newsletter, quarterly. Alternate Formats: online.

Marketing

5020 ■ German Agricultural Marketing Board - CMA (CMA)
1800 Diagonal Rd., Ste.210
Alexandria, VA 22314
Ph: (703)739-8900
Fax: (703)739-8910
E-mail: feedback@germanfoods.org
URL: http://www.germanfoods.org
Contact: Arnim von Friedeburg, Managing Dir.
Founded: 1969. **Staff:** 4. **Languages:** English, German. **Description:** Promotes imported German foods, beverages, and agricultural products in the U.S. and Canada through advertising, public relations programs, and promotional campaigns with supermarket chains and individual retailers. Acts as a liaison between U.S. and Canadian importers and German manufacturers and exporters. Provides assistance to German manufacturers and their importers and distributors in complying with U.S. regulations. **Computer Services:** database, imported German foods and beverages, manufacturers, and exporters. **Publications:** *Buyers Guide to Imported German Foods and Beverages*, biennial. Directory. Lists importers and distributors of German products according to product group and alphabetically by

company name. **Price:** free ● *GermanFoods.org*, monthly. Newsletter. Alternate Formats: online ● *Lucull Export Catalog*, biennial. Directory. Lists German manufacturers and exporters of food and beverages according to product group. **Price:** free ● *Shelf Talk*, quarterly. Newsletter. **Price:** free ● Brochures. Covers various German food and beverage product categories such as beer, pickles, sauerkraut and cheese. **Price:** free.

5021 ■ Livestock Marketing Association (LMA)
10510 NW Ambassador Dr.
Kansas City, MO 64153
Ph: (816)891-0502
Free: (800)821-2048
Fax: (816)891-7926
E-mail: lmainfo@lmaweb.com
URL: http://www.lmaweb.com
Contact: Mark Mackey, CEO
Founded: 1976. **Staff:** 38. **Budget:** $4,000,000. **Description:** Livestock marketing businesses and livestock dealers. Sponsors annual World Livestock Auctioneer Championships. Offers management and promotional services. **Awards: Type:** recognition. **Divisions:** Livestock Board of Trade. **Programs:** LMA-Vaccinated and Certified Calf. **Subgroups:** Livestock Marketing Insurance Agency. **Formed by Merger of:** Competitive Livestock Marketing Association; National Livestock Dealers Association. **Publications:** *The Risk Manager*, monthly. Newsletter. Contains industry-related articles, legislative information, and risk management tips. **Price:** included in membership dues ● Membership Directory, annual ● Annual Report, annual ● Reports. Alternate Formats: online. **Conventions/Meetings:** annual meeting.

5022 ■ National Association of Produce Market Managers (NAPMM)
PO Box 291284
Columbia, SC 29229
Ph: (410)379-5760
Fax: (410)379-5773
E-mail: sbrannan@mfca.state.md.us
URL: http://www.napmm.com
Contact: Ronnie Best, Pres.
Founded: 1947. **Members:** 110. **Membership Dues:** executive, associate, $50 (annual) ● commercial partner, $300 (annual) ● retired executive, $5 (annual). **Regional Groups:** 5. **State Groups:** 28. **Description:** Produce market managers and industrial produce dealers; associate members are county agents and state employees in agriculture. Seeks to improve market conditions. **Awards:** Market Manager of the Year Award. **Frequency:** annual. **Type:** recognition. **Committees:** Constitution/History; Convention; International; Market Manager of the Year; NAPMM Handbook; Nominations; Site Selection. **Publications:** *Convention Proceedings*, annual ● *The Green Book Produce Market Information Directory* ● *Green Sheet*, quarterly. Newsletter. Alternate Formats: online ● Membership Directory. Alternate Formats: online ● Handbook. **Conventions/Meetings:** annual conference.

5023 ■ National Cattlemen's Beef Association (NCBA)
9110 E Nichols Ave., Ste.300
Centennial, CO 80112
Ph: (303)694-0305
Free: (866)233-3872
Fax: (303)694-2851
E-mail: membership@beef.org
URL: http://www.beefusa.org
Contact: Michael E. John, Pres.
Founded: 1922. **Staff:** 72. **Description:** Represents 149 organizations of livestock marketers, growers, meat packers, food retailers, and food service firms. Conducts extensive program of promotion, education and information about beef, veal, and associated meat products. Conducts projects such as recipe testing and development, food demonstrations, food photography, educational service to colleges, experimental meat cutting methods, merchandising programs, and preparation of materials for newspapers, magazines, radio, and television. **Libraries: Type:** reference. **Holdings:** 4,000; artwork, audiovisuals, books, clippings, monographs, periodicals. **Subjects:** food, human nutrition, meat science, promotion. **Awards:** Distinguished Service Award. **Frequency:** annual. **Type:** recognition. **Recipient:** for a meat science professional ● **Type:** grant. **Recipient:** for research on red meat in the diet and its relation to health. **Computer Services:** Online services, data times ● online services, dialog ● online services, Dow Jones ● online services, orbit ● online services, wilsonline. **Committees:** Lamb (see separate entry); Processed Meats (see separate entry). **Councils:** Beef Industry (see separate entry). **Departments:** Creative Services; Education; Foodservice; Home Economics; Meat Industry Information Center; Merchandising; News Service; Nutrition Research; Pork Industry; Revenue Development. **Affiliated With:** American Meat Science Association. **Absorbed:** (1962) National Beef Council. **Formerly:** (1997) National Live Stock and Meat Board. **Publications:** *Beef Promotion Bullhorn*, semimonthly ● *Food and Nutrition News*, 5/year. Newsletter ● *Meat Board Reports*, monthly ● *Pork Industry Group Letter*, semimonthly ● *Proceedings of Reciprocal Meat Conference*, annual ● Annual Report, annual ● Brochures ● Catalog ● Films ● Manuals ● Pamphlets. **Conventions/Meetings:** competition, intercollegiate meat judging contest ● annual conference and trade show, for discussion of market development issues (exhibits).

5024 ■ National Livestock Producers Association (NLSPA)
660 Southpointe Ct., Ste.314
Colorado Springs, CO 80906
Ph: (719)538-8843
Free: (800)237-7193
Fax: (719)538-8847
E-mail: nlpa@nlpa.org
URL: http://www.nlpa.org
Contact: R. Scott Stuart, Pres./CEO
Founded: 1921. **Members:** 11. **Staff:** 2. **Regional Groups:** 18. **Description:** Federation of cooperative livestock marketing agencies and regional credit corporations, with a combined membership of 200,000 individual livestock farmers and producers. Conducts marketing research; maintains government liaison. **Formerly:** (1943) National Live Stock Marketing Association. **Publications:** *Producer News*, quarterly ● Yearbook, annual. **Conventions/Meetings:** semiannual conference - always March and November.

5025 ■ North American Agricultural Marketing Officials (NAAMO)
c/o Mary Jordan, Sec.-Treas.
251 Causeway St., Ste.500
Boston, MA 02114-2151
Ph: (617)626-1750
Fax: (617)626-1850
E-mail: mary.jordan@state.ma.us
URL: http://www.naamo.org
Contact: Tom Slade, Pres.
Founded: 1920. **Members:** 50. **Membership Dues:** executive, $300 (annual) ● associate, $25 (annual). **Budget:** $30,000. **Regional Groups:** 4. **Description:** State and Canadian provincial marketing officials responsible for administration of state and provincial agricultural marketing programs. Seeks to improve the marketing, handling, storage, processing, transportation, and distribution of agricultural products. **Awards:** NAAMO Pride Award. **Frequency:** annual. **Type:** trophy. **Recipient:** to the region with the greatest attendance and participation ● **Type:** recognition. **Recipient:** for marketing activities. **Telecommunication Services:** electronic mail, tom.slade@ncmail.net ● electronic mail, kkrug@cdfa.ca.gov. **Committees:** Agricultural; Economic Development; International Trade; Market Development; Regulatory Services and Governmental Relations; Transportation, Distribution, and Packaging; Workshop. **Task Forces:** NAMO/USDA Industry. **Affiliated With:** National Association of Produce Market Managers; National Association of State Departments of Agriculture. **Formerly:** (1975) National Association of Marketing Officials; (1992) National Agricultural Marketing Officials. **Publications:** *National Agricultural Marketing Officials—Directory and Report of Annual Convention*, annual. **Price:** $25.00 ● *National Agricultural Marketing Officials—Newsletter*, periodic ● Annual Report, annual. **Price:** included in membership dues. **Conventions/Meetings:** annual conference (exhibits) ● regional meeting.

5026 ■ North American Farmers' Direct Marketing Association (NAFDMA)
62 White Loaf Rd.
Southampton, MA 01073
Ph: (413)529-0386
Free: (888)884-9270
Fax: (413)529-2471
E-mail: nafdma@map.com
URL: http://www.nafdma.com
Contact: Charlie Touchette, Exec. Dir.
Membership Dues: individual, $150 (annual). **Description:** Represents family farmers, extension agents, and farm market managers. Promotes networking with members on the profitability of direct marketing; develops ideas to attract guests to earn more farm income. **Awards:** Farm Direct Marketer of the Year. **Frequency:** annual. **Type:** recognition. **Recipient:** for outstanding marketer members ● Farmers' Market Manager of the Year. **Frequency:** annual. **Type:** recognition. **Recipient:** for outstanding market manager. **Telecommunication Services:** electronic mail, charlie@whiteloafridge.com. **Publications:** *Market Connection*, quarterly. Newsletter ● *Membership Handbook and Conference Digest*, annual. Yearbook. Provides contact list of the Board of Directors and current members. **Conventions/Meetings:** annual conference and tour, marketing (exhibits) ● annual show, media event.

5027 ■ Organic Trade Association (OTA)
PO Box 547
Greenfield, MA 01302
Ph: (413)774-7511
Fax: (413)774-6432
E-mail: info@ota.com
URL: http://www.ota.com
Contact: Linda Lutz, Membership Mgr.
Founded: 1985. **Members:** 1,500. **Membership Dues:** business associate (based on annual revenue), $500-$3,000 (annual) ● government, nonprofit, provisional, $300 (annual) ● trade (based on annual revenue), $300-$1,200 (annual). **Staff:** 15. **Budget:** $1,800,000. **Regional Groups:** 1. **Description:** Producers, processors, distributors, retailers, individuals and others involved in the organic products industry. Promotes the industry; heightens production and marketing standards. Provides certification guidelines. **Libraries: Type:** not open to the public. **Holdings:** reports. **Awards:** Organic Leadership Award. **Frequency:** annual. **Type:** recognition. **Recipient:** for outstanding contribution to further the organic industry. **Computer Services:** Online services, directory of products and services offered by members ● online services, organic export directory. **Additional Websites:** http://www.theorganicreport.org. **Committees:** Ethics; Government Relations; International Relations; Marketing; Quality Assurance. **Councils:** Canadian; Organic Coffee; Organic Fiber; Organic Suppliers Advisory. **Programs:** Organic Export. **Absorbed:** Legislative Council; Organic Certifiers Caucus; (1991) Organic Food Alliance. **Publications:** *The American Organic Standards* ● *Good Organic Retailing Practices Manual*, annual ● *Guide to the U.S. Organic Foods Production Act of 1990*. Paper ● *How to Harvest the Profits of Organic Produce*. Booklet ● *The Organic Report*, quarterly. Newsletter. **Advertising:** accepted ● *What's News in Organic*, 3-4/year. Newsletter. Alternate Formats: online ● Directory ● Booklet. **Conventions/Meetings:** annual All Things Organic - conference and workshop, with educational sessions (exhibits) ● seminar, covering marketing and labeling.

5028 ■ Produce Marketing Association (PMA)
1500 Casho Mill Rd.
Newark, DE 19714-6036
Ph: (302)738-7100

Fax: (302)731-2409
E-mail: bsilbermann@pma.com
URL: http://www.pma.com
Contact: Bryan Silbermann CAE, Pres.
Founded: 1949. **Members:** 2,400. **Membership Dues:** corporate in U.S. and Canada, $955-$2,120 (annual) ● commodity board/association, food service operator in U.S. and Canada, $955 (annual) ● corporate outside U.S. and Canada, $750-$1,990 (annual) ● commodity board/association, food service outside U.S. and Canada, $750 (annual) ● floral industry, $580 (annual) ● student, $25 (annual). **Staff:** 75. **Budget:** $12,000,000. **Languages:** English, Spanish. **Multinational. Description:** Represents marketers of fresh fruits, vegetables, and related products worldwide. Members are involved in the production, distribution, retail, and foodservice sectors of the industry. Works to create a favorable, responsible environment that advances the marketing of produce and floral products and services for North American buyers and sellers and their international partners. **Libraries: Type:** not open to the public. **Holdings:** 5,000; books, reports. **Subjects:** post-harvest marketing of fruits, vegetables, floral products. **Computer Services:** database ● mailing lists ● online services. **Formerly:** (1956) Produce Prepackaging Association; (1967) Produce Packaging Association; (1971) Produce Packaging and Marketing Association. **Publications:** *Freshline*, weekly. Newsletter. Covers events in the association and the produce industry. **Price:** free for members. Alternate Formats: online ● *FreshTrack*, biennial. Survey. Provides industry performance benchmarks and articles on topical issues. **Price:** $150.00 for members; $600.00 for nonmembers. **Conventions/Meetings:** annual Foodservice Conference, Tours and Expo, with tours (exhibits) - always in Monterey, CA. 2008 July 25-27, Monterey, CA ● annual Fresh Summit International Convention and Exposition - conference and convention (exhibits) - always October. 2008 Oct. 24-27, Orlando, FL; 2009 Oct. 2-5, Anaheim, CA ● annual Retail Produce Solutions - conference, with tours.

5029 ■ Producers Livestock Marketing Association
c/o Rick Lovell, Gen. Mgr.
PO Box 540477
North Salt Lake, UT 84054-0477
Ph: (801)936-2424
E-mail: homeoffice@producerslivestock.com
URL: http://www.producerslivestock.com
Contact: Rick Lovell, Gen. Mgr.
Members: 7,000. **Staff:** 50. **Description:** Represents livestock producers. Conducts cooperative livestock marketing program. **Programs:** Feeding and Grazing. **Affiliated With:** National Livestock Producers Association. **Formerly:** (1998) Producers Commission Association. **Publications:** *Producers News*, bimonthly. Newsletter ● Reports. Alternate Formats: online. **Conventions/Meetings:** annual meeting - always first Saturday of February, Sioux City, IA.

5030 ■ United Producers
PO Box 29800
Columbus, OH 43229
Ph: (614)890-6666
Free: (800)456-3276
Fax: (614)890-4776
E-mail: sgardner@uproducers.com
URL: http://www.uproducers.com
Contact: Dennis Bolling, Pres./CEO
Members: 23,519. **Membership Dues:** individual, $20 (annual). **Staff:** 225. **Description:** Cooperative marketing organization for livestock producers in the Midwest. Conducts livestock marketing program. Owns Illinois Livestock Marketing Company. Works with Illinois, Iowa, and Missouri farm bureaus. **Departments:** Auction Markets; Contract Feed Lot Selling; Contract Feeder Cattle; Contract Slaughter Hogs; Country Marketing; Feeder Cattle; Feeder Pigs; Forward Pricing; Terminal Market Operations. **Formerly:** (2001) Interstate Producers Livestock Association. **Conventions/Meetings:** annual meeting - always December, Chicago, IL.

Meat

5031 ■ Food Safety Consortium (FSC)
Univ. of Arkansas
110 Agriculture Bldg.
Fayetteville, AR 72701
Ph: (479)575-5647
Fax: (479)575-7531
E-mail: dedmark@uark.edu
URL: http://www.uark.edu/depts/fsc
Contact: Dave Edmark, Communications Dir.
Founded: 1988. **Description:** Consortium of researchers from the University of Arkansas, Iowa State University, and Kansas State University, established by Congress through a special Cooperative State Research Service grant. Conducts investigation into all areas of poultry, beef and pork meat production, from the farm to the consumer. Each member of the consortium performs research associated with specific animal species: University of Arkansas, poultry; Iowa State University, pork; and Kansas State University, beef. Research projects are coordinated with scientists at the University of Arkansas for Medical Sciences and Arkansas Children's Hospital. **Committees:** Steering. **Publications:** *The Food Safety Consortium Newsletter*, quarterly. Covers research activities. **Price:** free. **Circulation:** 750. Alternate Formats: online ● *FSC Personnel Directory*. Alternate Formats: online ● Annual Report, annual. Alternate Formats: online. **Conventions/Meetings:** annual meeting.

Media

5032 ■ EMS/Science Communication Network (EMS/SCN)
1320 18th St. NW, Ste.500
Washington, DC 20036
Ph: (202)463-6670
E-mail: amy@ems.org
URL: http://www.ems.org
Contact: Amy Kostant, Exec. Dir.
Founded: 1994. **Description:** Promotes media expansion coverage of critical environmental and public health issues. Establishes relationships with top scientists, physicians and other experts to bring journalists the latest and most credible information. **Computer Services:** Online services, library. **Telecommunication Services:** electronic mail, gabriela@ems.org. **Formerly:** (2006) Environmental Media Services.

Military

5033 ■ Military Toxics Project (MTP)
PO Box 558
Lewiston, ME 04243
Ph: (207)783-5091
Fax: (207)783-5096
E-mail: mtp@miltoxproj.org
URL: http://www.miltoxproj.org
Contact: Tara Thornton, Exec. Dir.
Description: Promotes clean up of military pollution, safeguards transportation of hazardous materials, advances development of preventative solutions to toxic, radioactive pollution from military activities. **Libraries: Type:** reference. **Holdings:** reports. **Additional Websites:** http://www.stopmilitarytoxics.org. **Telecommunication Services:** electronic mail, tara@miltoxproj.org. **Publications:** *MTP Newsletter*, monthly.

Mollusks

5034 ■ Freshwater Mollusk Conservation Society (FMCS)
c/o Steve Ahlstedt, Pres.
US Geological Survey
1820 Midpark Dr.
Knoxville, TN 37921
E-mail: ahlstedt@usgs.gov
URL: http://ellipse.inhs.uiuc.edu/FMCS
Contact: Steve Ahlstedt, Pres.
Founded: 1998. **Description:** Advocates the conservation of freshwater molluscan resources of North America. Serves as a source of information and facilitates public awareness about freshwater mollusks. Promotes science-based management of freshwater mollusks. **Awards:** Best Student Presentation Award. **Frequency:** biennial. **Type:** recognition. **Recipient:** for the best individual oral and poster presentation in the symposium ● Lifetime Achievement Award. **Frequency:** biennial. **Type:** recognition. **Recipient:** to an individual for singular accomplishment in the conservation and science of freshwater mollusks at a national or international level ● Meritorious Service Award. **Frequency:** biennial. **Type:** recognition. **Recipient:** for past or present FMCS member with singular accomplishments or long-term contribution to the society ● Student Travel Award Program. **Frequency:** biennial. **Type:** monetary. **Recipient:** for undergraduate and graduate student members of the society ● William J. Clench Memorial Award. **Frequency:** biennial. **Type:** recognition. **Recipient:** to an individual for singular accomplishment in the advancement of the natural history of freshwater mollusks at an academic or non-academic setting. **Telecommunication Services:** electronic mail, gzimmerman@enviroscienceinc.com. **Publications:** *Ellipsaria*, April, August and December. Newsletter. Includes news, general announcements and articles. ● Report, triennial. Alternate Formats: online.

Mushrooms

5035 ■ Mushroom Council
2880 Zanker Rd., Ste.203
San Jose, CA 95134
Ph: (408)432-7210
Fax: (408)432-7213
E-mail: info@mushroomcouncil.org
URL: http://www.mushroomcouncil.org
Contact: Robert Crouch, Sec.
Description: Promotes mushrooms; provides information about mushrooms and recipes. **Publications:** Reports. Alternate Formats: online.

Native American

5036 ■ Intertribal Bison Cooperative (ITBC)
2497 W Chicago St.
Rapid City, SD 57702
Ph: (605)394-9730
Fax: (605)394-7742
E-mail: itbc@enetis.net
URL: http://itbcbison.com
Contact: Ervin Carlson, Pres.
Founded: 1990. **Members:** 51. **Membership Dues:** calf, $10 (annual) ● yearling, $25 (annual) ● herd, $35 (annual) ● buffalo benefactor, $50 (annual) ● herd bull/lead cow, $100 (annual) ● buffalo dancer, $1,000 (annual) ● buffalo national patron (life), $10,000. **State Groups:** 16. **Description:** Committed to restoring the American bison to its "rightful range". **Publications:** *Buffalo Tracks*, quarterly. Newsletter. **Price:** included in membership dues ● Annual Report, annual. **Conventions/Meetings:** conference.

5037 ■ National Environmental Coalition of Native Americans (NECONA)
c/o Claremore Veterans Center
PO Box 988
Claremore, OK 74018
Ph: (918)342-3041
E-mail: noteno_84@hotmail.com
Contact: Grace Thorpe, Pres.
Description: Educates Indians and Non-Indians on health dangers of radioactivity and transportation of nuclear waste on rails and roads. Networks with Indian and Non-Indian environmentalists. Declares tribal nuclear free zone across the nation.

Natural Disasters

5038 ■ Floodplain Management Association (FMA)
PO Box 712080
Santee, CA 92072-2080
Ph: (619)204-4380
E-mail: admin@floodplain.org
URL: http://www.floodplain.org
Contact: Iovanka Todt, Exec. Dir.
Founded: 1990. **Membership Dues:** individual, $45 (annual) ● organizational, $125 (annual) ● student, $25 (annual). **Description:** Promotes flood reduction losses; encourages protection and enhancement of natural floodplain values. **Conventions/Meetings:** annual conference.

Natural Resources

5039 ■ International Association for Society and Natural Resources (IASNR)
c/o Richard S. Krannich, Exec. Dir.
Inst. for Social Sci. Res. on Natural Resources
Utah State Univ.
0730 Old Main Hill
Logan, UT 84322-0730
Ph: (435)797-1241
Fax: (435)797-1240
E-mail: rkranich@hass.usu.edu
Contact: Richard S. Krannich, Exec. Dir.
Founded: 2001. **Membership Dues:** professional, $90 (annual) ● student, $60 (annual). **Multinational. Description:** Fosters interdisciplinary social scientific understanding of the relationships between humans and natural resources. Seeks to advance the application of social science information in natural resources decision-making. Provides a mechanism for dialogue and information exchange among social scientists, resource managers, practitioners, agency personnel and decision makers. **Publications:** *Keeping in Touch*. Newsletter. Alternate Formats: online ● *Society and Natural Resources*. Journal. Includes research articles and policy analyses pertaining to relationships between social and biophysical systems. **Price:** included in membership dues. **Conventions/Meetings:** annual symposium.

5040 ■ International Joint Commission (IJC)
1250 23rd St. NW, Ste.100
Washington, DC 20440
Ph: (202)736-9024
Fax: (202)467-0746
E-mail: bevacquaf@washington.ijc.org
URL: http://www.ijc.org
Contact: Frank Bevacqua, Public Information Off.
Founded: 1911. **Members:** 6. **Staff:** 22. **Budget:** $7,500,000. **Languages:** English, French. **Description:** Joint U.S.-Canada quasi-judicial and advisory tribunal on boundary and transboundary water problems. Established from Boundary Waters Treaty of 1909 to prevent disputes on the use of boundary and transboundary waters and investigate questions arising from transboundary issues. Approves and disapproves applications from governments, companies, and individuals for obstructions, uses, and diversions of water that affect the natural level and flow of water on the other side of the international boundary; investigates particular questions, reports findings to the U.S. and Canadian governments, and offers recommendations; monitors compliance with IJC orders of approval. Maintains advisory boards of scientists, engineers, and other experts to supply IJC with technical studies and field work; answers student inquiries regarding the environmental quality of the Great Lakes. Conducts public hearings. **Boards:** Air Quality Advisory; Council of Great Lakes Research Managers; Great Lakes Science Advisory; Great Lakes Water Quality; Rainy River Pollution; Red River; St. Croix River; Souris River. **Publications:** *Biennial Report on Great Lakes Water Quality*. Contains information on water quality in the Great Lakes system. Alternate Formats: online ● *Focus*, 3/year. Newsletter. Contains information on current activities. ISSN: 1024-5219. **Circulation:** 6,000. Alternate Formats: online ● Reports. Contains information on governmental efforts to reduce pollution in the Great Lakes. **Conventions/Meetings:** seminar and workshop.

5041 ■ World Bamboo Organization (WBO)
c/o Ms. Susanne Lucas, Chair
9 Bloody Pond Rd.
Plymouth, MA 02360
E-mail: info@world-bamboo.org
URL: http://www.world-bamboo.org
Contact: Ms. Susanne Lucas, Chair
Founded: 1992. **Membership Dues:** corporate, $500 (annual) ● corporate, $1,350 (triennial). **Multinational. Description:** Promotes and supports the use of bamboo as a sustainable and alternative natural resource. Works to develop partnerships and alliances and create mechanisms for global communication, information exchange and technology transfer. **Telecommunication Services:** electronic mail, membership@worldbamboo.org ● electronic mail, susannelucas@worldbamboo.org. **Publications:** *World Bamboo News*. Newsletter. Alternate Formats: online ● Proceedings. Alternate Formats: online ● Journal. Alternate Formats: online.

Nurseries

5042 ■ American Nursery and Landscape Association (ANLA)
1000 Vermont Ave. NW, Ste.300
Washington, DC 20005-4914
Ph: (202)789-2900
Fax: (202)789-1893
E-mail: jbardzik@anla.org
URL: http://www.anla.org
Contact: Robert J. Dolibois CAE, Exec. VP
Founded: 1876. **Members:** 2,200. **Membership Dues:** introductory (first year), $200 ● active (minimum), $295 (annual) ● supplier/allied associate, $315 (annual) ● Canadian associate, $250 (annual) ● professional associate, $130 (annual) ● international associate, $325 (annual). **Staff:** 15. **Budget:** $3,600,000. **Description:** Vertical organization of wholesale growers; landscape firms; garden centers; mail order nurseries; suppliers. Promotes the industry and its products. Offers management and consulting services and public relations programs. Provides government representation and bank card plan for members. Maintains hall of fame. **Awards: Type:** recognition. **Computer Services:** database ● mailing lists, of members. **Committees:** Allied Associate; Botanical Gardens and Arboreta; Horticultural Distribution; Horticultural Standards; Information Management; Legislation; Nursery Industry Political Action; Pest Management; Quarantine; Water Management; Wholesale Plant Sales Professionals. **Councils:** Tree and Landscape Appraisers; Young Executive Forum. **Divisions:** Garden Centers of America; Horticultural Research Institute; National Associate of Plant Patent Owners; National Landscape Association; Wholesale Nursery Growers of America. **Formerly:** (1921) American Association of Nurserymen, Florists and Seedsmen; (1998) American Association of Nurserymen. **Publications:** *AAN Today*, bimonthly. Newsletter. **Advertising:** accepted ● *UPDATE*, every 3 weeks. Newsletter ● *Who's Who in the Nursery Industry*, annual. Membership Directory. **Price:** $250.00 ● Also publishes special research project reports. **Conventions/Meetings:** annual conference - always first weekend of February, Louisville, KY ● annual convention, includes learning retreat - always July.

5043 ■ Garden Centers of America (GCA)
PO Box 2945
LaGrange, GA 30241
Ph: (706)298-0287
Free: (888)648-6463
Fax: (706)883-8215
E-mail: info@gardencentersofamerica.org
URL: http://www.gardencentersofamerica.org
Contact: John Trax Jr., Pres.
Founded: 1973. **Members:** 525. **Staff:** 2. **Description:** Garden center operators. Aims to meet the daily needs of efficient garden center management. Conducts marketing surveys; offers specialized education programs. **Awards: Type:** recognition. **Computer Services:** database ● mailing lists. **Publications:** *Garden Center Newsletter*, bimonthly ● *Who's Who in the Nursery Industry*, annual. Directory ● Booklets. Provides information on business management. ● Also publishes sales/advertising aids. Produces publications in conjunction with American Association of Nurserymen. **Conventions/Meetings:** annual Management Clinic - meeting, in conjunction with National Landscape Association and Wholesale Nursery Growers of America - first weekend of February.

5044 ■ Horticultural Research Institute (HRI)
1000 Vermont Ave. NW, Ste.300
Washington, DC 20005-4914
Ph: (202)789-2900
Fax: (202)789-1893
E-mail: tjodon@amla.org
URL: http://www.anla.org/research
Contact: Teresa Jodon, Endowment Program Admin.
Founded: 1962. **Members:** 250. **Membership Dues:** individual, association, educator, $200 (annual). **Staff:** 2. **Description:** Nursery firms; nursery supply companies; state and regional nurserymen's associations. Conducts nursery industry research in areas of management, marketing, production, integrated pest management, water use, and a continuing study of the industry scope. Administered by the staff of the American Nursery and Landscape Association. **Awards: Frequency:** annual. **Type:** scholarship. **Recipient:** for research. **Computer Services:** database, horticultural research scientists. **Funds:** Horticultural Research Institute Endowment. **Publications:** *Horticultural Research Institute—New Horizons*, periodic. Newsletter. Reports research on the art and science of landscape and nursery plant production, marketing, and care. **Price:** included in membership dues ● *Journal of Environmental Horticulture*, quarterly. **Price:** $65.00 for members; $120.00 international. ISSN: 0738-2898. **Circulation:** 700 ● Manuals ● Also publishes information releases on current research and glossaries. **Conventions/Meetings:** annual convention (exhibits) - always summer.

5045 ■ Landscape Nursery Council (LANCO)
1611 Creekview Dr.
Florence, KY 41042
Ph: (859)525-1809 (859)525-7884
Fax: (859)525-9114
E-mail: swills1809@aol.com
Contact: Steve Wills, Exec.Dir.
Founded: 1952. **Members:** 11. **Staff:** 2. **Budget:** $5,000,000. **Description:** Serves as nursery and agricultural association. Encourages the exchange of information. Sponsors research and educational programs. Compiles statistics. **Awards: Type:** recognition. **Publications:** Directory, annual. **Conventions/Meetings:** annual conference.

5046 ■ National Association of Plant Patent Owners (NAPPO)
c/o American Nursery and Landscape Association
1000 Vermont Ave. NW, Ste.300
Washington, DC 20005
Ph: (202)789-2900
Fax: (202)789-1893
URL: http://www.anla.org/industry/patents
Contact: Robert J. Dolibois, Pres.
Founded: 1940. **Members:** 60. **Membership Dues:** associate, $100 (annual). **Staff:** 2. **Description:** Owners of patents on newly propagated trees, shrubs, fruits, and other plants. Seeks to keep members informed of plant patents issued, provisions of patent laws, changes in practice, and new legislation. **Affiliated With:** American Nursery and Landscape Association. **Publications:** *Roster*, annual. Membership Directory ● Bulletin, periodic. **Conventions/Meetings:** annual meeting - always July.

5047 ■ Nursery and Landscape Association Executives of North America (NLAE)
c/o Beverly Gelvin, Exec. Dir.
968 Trinity Rd.
Raleigh, NC 27607

Ph: (919)816-9120
Fax: (919)816-9118
E-mail: bgelvin@mail.nlae.org
URL: http://www.nlae.org
Contact: Beverly Gelvin, Exec. Dir.
Founded: 1947. **Members:** 65. **Description:** Professional society of executives of state, national, regional, and provincial nursery trade associations. **Computer Services:** Mailing lists. **Formerly:** Nursery Association Secretaries; (1987) Nursery Association Executives; (2004) Nursery Association Executives of North America. **Publications:** *Nursery Association Executives—Newsletter*, quarterly. **Conventions/Meetings:** semiannual conference - always February and July.

Nuts

5048 ■ Almond Board of California (ABC)
1150 9th St., Ste.1500
Modesto, CA 95354
Ph: (209)549-8262
Fax: (209)549-8267
E-mail: staff@almondboard.com
URL: http://www.almondsarein.com
Contact: Scott Hunter, Chm.
Founded: 1950. **Members:** 104. **Staff:** 15. **Budget:** $4,900,000. **Languages:** Chinese, English, French, German, Japanese, Korean, Russian. **Description:** Participants are almond packers and growers. Aims to administer the federal marketing order for almonds regarding the production research, quality control, and supply allocation of almonds. **Computer Services:** database, almond trade and handler list. **Additional Websites:** http://www.almondboard.com. **Committees:** Food Quality and Safety; International; Production Research; Public Relations and Advertising; Reserve. **Formerly:** (1976) Almond Control Board. **Publications:** *Almond Almanac*, annual. Report. Contains statistical report and board activities. Alternate Formats: online ● *California Almond News*, quarterly. Newsletter ● *Food Quality and Safety Manual*. Alternate Formats: online ● *Position Report*, monthly. Contains recent almond trade statistics. Alternate Formats: online. **Conventions/Meetings:** annual Almond Industry Conference (exhibits) - always December.

5049 ■ American Peanut Council (APC)
1500 King St., Ste.301
Alexandria, VA 22314
Ph: (703)838-9500
Fax: (703)838-9508
E-mail: info@peanutsusa.com
URL: http://www.peanutsusa.com
Contact: Patrick Archer, Pres.
Founded: 1997. **Members:** 250. **Staff:** 7. **Budget:** $1,000,000. **Languages:** English, German, Spanish. **Description:** Growers, shellers, brokers, processors, and manufacturers; allied businesses providing goods and services to the peanut industry. Encourages research to improve quality of peanuts. **Awards:** Peanut Hall of Fame. **Type:** recognition. **Recipient:** for lifetime achievement. **Committees:** Communications and Consumer Affairs; Domestic Marketing; International Marketing; Science and Technology. **Formerly:** (1998) National Peanut Council. **Publications:** *American Peanut News*, monthly. Newsletter. Includes membership activities. **Price:** free for members ● *Fast Facts*. Brochure. Contains facts and nutritional information. ● *Peanut Industry Directory*, annual. Arranged by type of activity. Includes alphabetical index. **Price:** $25.00 for nonmembers ● Also publishes educational materials. **Conventions/Meetings:** annual conference (exhibits) - always June/July.

5050 ■ American Peanut Research and Education Society (APRES)
c/o Dr. J. Ronald Sholar, Exec. Off.
Oklahoma State Univ.
376 AG Hall
Stillwater, OK 74078
Ph: (405)372-3052
Fax: (405)624-6718
E-mail: nickeli@provalue.net
URL: http://www.apres.okstate.edu
Contact: Dr. J. Ronald Sholar, Exec. Off.
Founded: 1969. **Members:** 550. **Membership Dues:** individual, institutional, $80 (annual) ● organizational, $100 (annual) ● student, $20 (annual) ● sustaining, $300 (annual). **Staff:** 2. **Budget:** $75,000. **Description:** Federal, state, and private company employees involved in the peanut industry. Works to improve the welfare of all segments of the peanut industry. Provides for exchange of information, cooperative planning, and review of all phases of peanut research and extension being carried on by government agencies and private industry. **Awards:** APRES Fellow Award. **Frequency:** annual. **Type:** recognition. **Recipient:** for outstanding contributions in an area of specialization ● Bailey Award. **Type:** recognition. **Recipient:** for outstanding research paper at annual conference. **Committees:** Bailey Award; Fellows; Peanut Quality; Public Relations. **Formerly:** (1979) American Peanut Research and Education Association. **Supersedes:** Peanut Improvement Working Group. **Publications:** *Advances in Peanut Sciences*. Book. Features updates on the latest advances in peanut science. **Price:** $45.00/copy ● *Peanut Research*, quarterly. Newsletter. Contains information on the current events of the association. **Price:** $2.00/issue ● *Peanut Science*, semiannual. Journal. Features updates on latest research results. **Price:** $9.00 volumes 1-13, domestic; $11.00 volumes 1-13, overseas; $17.00 volumes 14-current, domestic; $19.00 volumes 14-current, overseas ● *Peanut Science and Technology*. Book. **Price:** $15.00/copy. Alternate Formats: online ● Proceedings, annual. Contains directory. **Price:** $8.00 volumes 1-19, domestic; $11.00 volumes 1-19, overseas; $13.00 volumes 20-current, domestic; $16.00 volumes 20-current, overseas. Alternate Formats: online. **Conventions/Meetings:** annual meeting (exhibits).

5051 ■ American Peanut Shellers Association (APSA)
2336 Lake Park Dr.
Albany, GA 31707
Ph: (229)888-2508
Fax: (229)888-5150
E-mail: info@peanut-shellers.org
URL: http://www.peanut-shellers.org
Contact: Jack Chastain, Chm.
Founded: 1919. **Members:** 200. **Membership Dues:** associate, $400 (annual). **Staff:** 5. **Description:** Commercial peanut shellers and crushers in Alabama, Florida, Georgia, Texas, Virginia; associate members are brokers, equipment manufacturers, producers and warehousers, and other allied or supporting businesses. **Committees:** American Peanut Political Action; American Sheller Rules; Engineering and Research; Legislative; Market Development; Safety and Sanitation; Trade Rules; Warehousing and Handling. **Formerly:** Southeastern Peanut Association. **Publications:** *American Peanut Association Membership Directory*, annual. **Price:** $25.00 for nonmembers. Alternate Formats: online ● *APSA Newsletter*, monthly. **Price:** included in membership dues ● *Regulation*. Newsletters. **Conventions/Meetings:** annual USA Peanut Congress - conference, held in conjunction with American Peanut Council (exhibits).

5052 ■ Blue Diamond Growers (BDG)
PO Box 1768
Sacramento, CA 95814
Ph: (916)442-0771
Fax: (916)446-8489
E-mail: feedback@bdgrowers.com
URL: http://www.bluediamond.com
Contact: Douglas D. Youngdahl, Pres./CEO
Founded: 1910. **Members:** 4,000. **Staff:** 1,200. **Description:** California almond growers. Processes and markets Blue Diamond almonds, hazelnuts, macadamias for members on a cooperative basis. **Committees:** Liaison; Political Action. **Programs:** Issues Action; Leadership. **Formerly:** (1988) California Almond Growers Exchange. **Publications:** *Almond Facts*, bimonthly. Magazine. Covers cultural practices, Blue Diamond marketing efforts, and new products. **Price:** free for members; $25.00 /year for nonmembers in U.S.; $45.00 /year for nonmembers outside U.S. **Circulation:** 8,000. **Advertising:** accepted ● *California Almond Growers Exchange—Annual Report*. Contains report reviewing the production, sales, and exports of almonds in the previous year; provides consolidated balance sheets. **Price:** free. **Circulation:** 8,000 ● Brochure. Alternate Formats: online. **Conventions/Meetings:** annual meeting - always November in California.

5053 ■ California Macadamia Society (CMS)
PO Box 1298
Fallbrook, CA 92088-1298
Ph: (760)728-8081
Fax: (760)728-8081
E-mail: calmacsociety@aol.com
URL: http://members.aol.com/CalMacSociety
Contact: Jim Russell, Pres.
Founded: 1955. **Members:** 650. **Membership Dues:** individual, $17 (annual) ● family, $20 (annual) ● individual life, $150 ● family life, $175. **Staff:** 1. **Description:** Nut growers, researchers, and nurserymen. Aims to: furnish authoritative and timely information on macadamia culture; assist growers with harvesting and marketing data; advise nurserymen on varieties and propagation; encourage the University of California to assist the industry with research; formulate policies, where indicated, for presentation to the state legislature. **Committees:** County Education Fair Exhibits; Field Trips; Marketing; Publicity; Research; Variety. **Publications:** *California Macadamia Society—Newsletter*, quarterly ● *California Macadamia Society—Yearbook*, annual ● Booklets. **Conventions/Meetings:** annual meeting - always March.

5054 ■ California Pistachio Commission (CPC)
1318 E Shaw Ave., Ste.420
Fresno, CA 93710
Ph: (559)221-8294
Fax: (559)221-8044
E-mail: info@pistachios.org
URL: http://www.pistachios.org
Contact: Karen Reinecke, Pres.
Founded: 1981. **Members:** 500. **Staff:** 7. **Budget:** $6,500,000. **Description:** Eight commission members and eight alternate members elected by the 520 pistachio producers in California. Aims to develop domestic and international markets for California pistachios through promotion and public relations; conduct production and marketing research; and improve communication among growers. **Committees:** Administrative; Marketing; Research. **Publications:** *California Pistachio Industry Annual Report*, annual. Provides synopses of promotional and marketing activities of the commission. Includes research articles for the reported crop year. **Price:** free for California growers; $150.00 out of state, non-growers. **Advertising:** accepted ● *Pistachio Perspectives*, quarterly. Newsletter. Covers industry and commission activities. **Price:** free for California Growers. **Conventions/Meetings:** annual conference (exhibits) - always March.

5055 ■ Diamond Walnut Growers
c/o Diamond Foods, Inc.
1050 S Diamond St.
Stockton, CA 95205
Ph: (209)467-6000
URL: http://www.diamondnuts.com
Contact: Michael Mendes, Pres./CEO
Founded: 1912. **Members:** 2,350. **Description:** Walnut processing and marketing organization. **Affiliated With:** Sun-Maid Growers of California; Sunsweet Growers; Valley Fig Growers. **Formerly:** (1956) California Walnut Growers Association. **Publications:** *Diamond Walnut News & Review*, semiannual. Magazine.

5056 ■ Georgia Peanut Commission (GPC)
PO Box 967
110 E 4th St.
Tifton, GA 31794

Ph: (229)386-3470
Free: (800)346-4993
Fax: (229)386-3501
E-mail: info@gapeanuts.com
URL: http://www.gapeanuts.com
Contact: Armond Morris, Chm.
Founded: 1961. **Members:** 5,800. **Staff:** 7. **Budget:** $2,000,000. **Description:** Peanut farmers whose goals are to research, disseminate information on, and promote Georgia's peanut crop. Conducts specialized education programs; sponsors events. Compiles statistics. **Libraries: Type:** reference. **Holdings:** archival material. **Awards: Type:** recognition. **Affiliated With:** American Peanut Council; American Peanut Shellers Association; National Agri-Marketing Association; Peanut Advisory Board. **Publications:** *News Release*, periodic ● *The Source*, monthly. Newsletter. **Price:** free. **Circulation:** 10,000 ● *Southeastern Peanut Farmer*, 10/year. Tabloid reporting on the production, marketing, and consumption of peanuts; includes legislative and export reports, and calendar of events. **Price:** free to qualified peanut farmers; $5.00 /year for nonmembers. ISSN: 0038-3694. **Circulation:** 18,000. **Advertising:** accepted. Alternate Formats: microform ● Reports. Alternate Formats: online ● Also publishes promotional material. **Conventions/Meetings:** competition ● annual Farm Show (exhibits) ● seminar.

5057 ■ National Peanut Buying Points Association
PO Box 314
115 W 2nd St.
Tifton, GA 31793
Ph: (229)386-1716
Fax: (229)386-8757
E-mail: spearmanagency@friendlycity.net
Contact: Tyron Spearman, Exec. Sec.
Founded: 1957. **Members:** 150. **Membership Dues:** regular, $400 (annual) ● elite, $500 (annual). **Staff:** 2. **Budget:** $55,000. **Description:** Comprised of peanut warehousers. **Awards:** Distinguished Service. **Frequency:** annual. **Type:** recognition. **Computer Services:** Mailing lists. **Formerly:** (1998) Southern Peanut Warehousemen's Association. **Publications:** *Peanut Farm Market News*, weekly. Newsletter. **Price:** $480.00/year. **Circulation:** 400. **Conventions/Meetings:** annual USA Peanut Congress - conference (exhibits).

5058 ■ National Peanut Festival Association (NPFA)
5622 Hwy. 231 S
Dothan, AL 36301
Ph: (334)793-4323
Free: (866)277-3962
Fax: (334)793-3247
E-mail: nationalpeanut@aol.com
URL: http://www.nationalpeanutfestival.com
Contact: Pat Holland, Pres.
Founded: 1938. **Staff:** 2. **Description:** Conducts annual festival to promote peanuts and all agribusiness in the Wiregrass area. Sponsors educational programs. **Awards: Type:** recognition. **Publications:** *National Peanut Festival Association—Tabloid*, annual. Newspaper. Promotes peanut festival. Includes calendar of events and biographies of festival honorees. **Price:** free. **Circulation:** 85,000 ● Brochures ● Pamphlets. **Conventions/Meetings:** annual festival (exhibits) - always Dothan, AL.

5059 ■ National Pecan Shellers Association (NPSA)
1100 Johnson Ferry Rd., Ste.300
Atlanta, GA 30342
Ph: (404)252-3663
Fax: (404)252-0774
E-mail: info@ilovepecans.org
URL: http://www.ilovepecans.org
Contact: Russ Lemieux, Exec. Dir.
Founded: 1943. **Members:** 60. **Staff:** 1. **Description:** Shellers and processors of pecans. Promotes the welfare and interests of the pecan shelling and processing industry. **Publications:** *I'm Nuts For Pecans*. Newsletter ● *Perfect Performance with Pecans*. **Price:** free. Alternate Formats: online ● Membership Directory, periodic ● Brochure. Alternate Formats: online. **Conventions/Meetings:** semiannual convention (exhibits) - always February and September.

5060 ■ Peanut Advisory Board (PAB)
1025 Sugar Pike Way
Canton, GA 30115
Ph: (770)998-7311
Fax: (770)998-5962
E-mail: lpwagner@comcast.net
URL: http://www.peanutbutterlovers.com
Contact: Leslie Wagner, Exec. Dir.
Founded: 1980. **Members:** 10,000. **Staff:** 2. **Description:** Represents 10,000 peanut farmers in Georgia, Alabama, and Florida. Promotes the sale of U.S.-grown peanuts and educates the public on the peanut and peanut products. **Conventions/Meetings:** annual conference (exhibits).

5061 ■ Peanut Institute
PO Box 70157
Albany, GA 31708-0157
Ph: (229)888-0216
Free: (888)8PE-ANUT
Fax: (229)888-5150
E-mail: info@peanut-institute.org
URL: http://www.peanut-institute.org
Description: Promotes the peanut as a nutritionally healthy food; provides information on nutrition, diets, and educational materials. Conducts peanut recipe contests.

5062 ■ Southwestern Peanut Growers Association (SWPGA)
PO Box 338
304 SE Lubbock
Gorman, TX 76454
Ph: (254)734-2222
Fax: (254)734-2288
E-mail: info@swpga.com
URL: http://www.swpga.com
Contact: Dan Hunter, Mgr.
Founded: 1937. **Members:** 6,500. **Staff:** 30. **Description:** Represents peanut growers in the southwestern United States. Administers peanut price support program in the Southwest. **Publications:** *Southwestern Peanut Growers' News*, quarterly. Newspaper. **Price:** $3.00 in U.S.; $10.00 outside U.S. **Circulation:** 11,000. **Advertising:** accepted. Alternate Formats: online. **Conventions/Meetings:** annual symposium and meeting - in July.

5063 ■ Virginia-Carolina Peanut Association (VCPA)
PO Box 8
Nashville, NC 27856-0088
Ph: (252)459-9977
Fax: (252)459-7396
E-mail: info@aboutpeanuts.com
URL: http://www.aboutpeanuts.com
Contact: Betsy H. Owens, Exec. Dir.
Founded: 1933. **Members:** 10. **Description:** Peanut millers and shellers and manufacturers of peanut products. **Convention/Meeting:** none.

5064 ■ Virginia-Carolina Peanut Promotions (VCPP)
103 Triangle Ct.
Nashville, NC 27856-0008
Ph: (252)459-9977
Fax: (252)459-7396
E-mail: info@aboutpeanuts.com
URL: http://www.aboutpeanuts.com
Contact: Betsy H. Owens, Exec. Dir.
Founded: 1967. **Staff:** 2. **Budget:** $195,000. **Description:** Promotes the increased use and consumption of peanuts and peanut products. **Publications:** *The Gold Peanut*. Book. **Circulation:** 20,000. **Advertising:** accepted ● *Having Fun with Peanuts* ● *Peanut Fun Under the Big Top* ● *Presenting the Peanut* ● *Virginia Carolina Peanut News*, 3/year. Provides information on planning for planting, growing, and harvesting peanuts. **Price:** $10.00/year. Alternate Formats: online.

5065 ■ Walnut Council (WC)
c/o Wright Forestry Center
1011 N 725 W
West Lafayette, IN 47906-9431
Ph: (765)583-3501
Fax: (765)583-3512
E-mail: jackson@purdue.edu
URL: http://www.walnutcouncil.org
Contact: Liz Jackson, Exec. Dir.
Founded: 1970. **Members:** 1,000. **Membership Dues:** regular, in U.S., $25 (annual) ● life, $500 ● regular, in Canada, $30 ● regular, outside U.S. and Canada, $40 ● supporting, $60 ● student, $10. **Staff:** 1. **Budget:** $48,000. **State Groups:** 12. **Description:** Walnut growers, foresters, landowners, wood industry employees, and university representatives. Seeks to further the science, technology, and practice of walnut culture. Promotes new plantings, good management of walnut stands, and the use of all walnut products. Encourages the exchange of research data, propagational material, and nursery stock. Serves as forum for the discussion of developments concerning walnut culture. Maintains placement service. **Awards:** Black Walnut Achievement Award. **Frequency:** annual. **Type:** recognition. **Telecommunication Services:** hotline, (217)442-1691. **Committees:** Economics; Education; Immediate Past President Awards and Nominations; Legislative; Nut Culture; Protection; Silviculture; State Chapters. **Publications:** Bulletin, quarterly. **Price:** free for members. **Advertising:** accepted. Alternate Formats: online. **Conventions/Meetings:** annual meeting (exhibits).

5066 ■ Walnut Marketing Board (WMB)
101 Parkshore Dr., Ste.250
Folsom, CA 95630
Ph: (916)932-7070
Fax: (916)932-7071
E-mail: wmbcwc@walnuts.org
URL: http://www.walnut.org
Contact: Dennis A. Balint, Exec. Dir.
Founded: 1948. **Members:** 65. **Staff:** 7. **Budget:** $1,200,000. **Description:** Handlers, shellers, and processors of California English walnuts. Administers marketing order program providing quality control, production research, and promotion and market development of domestic markets. **Publications:** *Walnuts: Essential Food for Health*. Brochure. Features the latest walnut health information. **Price:** free. Alternate Formats: online ● Report, monthly. Alternate Formats: online. **Conventions/Meetings:** semiannual meeting - second week in February and September.

Organic Farming

5067 ■ Independent Organic Inspectors Association (IOIA)
PO Box 6
Broadus, MT 59317-0006
Ph: (406)436-2031
E-mail: ioia@ioia.net
URL: http://www.ioia.net
Contact: Luis Brenes, Chm.
Founded: 1991. **Members:** 325. **Membership Dues:** inspector, $75 (annual) ● business, organization, $100 (annual) ● certification agency, $250 (annual) ● patron, $500 (annual) ● sustainer, $1,000 (annual) ● student, senior citizen, $25 (annual). **National Groups:** 20. **Multinational. Description:** Addresses issues and concerns relevant to organic inspectors. Provides inspector training. Promotes integrity and consistency in the organic certification process. **Telecommunication Services:** electronic mail, ioiassistant@rangeweb.net. **Publications:** *Inspector's Report*, quarterly. Newsletter. **Price:** free for members ● *Training Coordinator Manual* ● Brochure ● Membership Directory, annual ● Manuals. **Conventions/Meetings:** annual meeting.

5068 ■ Mountain State Organic Growers and Buyers Association (MSOGBA)
c/o Scott Snyder, Pres.
Healing Hills Herb Farm
HC 83, Box 79
Ellenboro, WV 26346

Ph: (304)684-5585 (304)477-3299
E-mail: healinghillsherbs@yahoo.com
Contact: Scott Snyder, Pres.
Membership Dues: regular, $25 (annual). **Description:** Promotes organic food production. Represents home gardeners, livestock producers, university professors, market gardeners, herbalists, food processors, retailers and consumers. **Publications:** *The Organic Harvester*, quarterly. Newsletter. Features important organic issues. Alternate Formats: online ● Membership Directory. **Conventions/Meetings:** conference ● workshop.

5069 ■ Organic Consumers Association (OCA)
6771 S Silver Hill Dr.
Finland, MN 55603
Ph: (218)226-4164
Free: (888)403-1007
Fax: (218)353-7652
E-mail: information@organicconsumers.org
URL: http://www.organicconsumers.org
Contact: Ronnie Cummins, Natl. Dir.
Founded: 1998. **Members:** 850,000. **Description:** Concerned with food safety, organic farming, sustainable agriculture, fair trade and genetic engineering (biotechnology, transgenic). **Computer Services:** database, 500,000 people in network. **Telecommunication Services:** electronic mail, ronnie@organicconsumers.org. **Boards:** Policy Advisory. **Programs:** Appetite for a Change; Campaign Against GE Corn; Campaign to Stop GM Wheat; Clothes for a Change Campaign; Coming Clean/Bodycare Campaign; Protest Stardocks; Supermarket Campaign. **Publications:** *Organic Bytes*, biweekly. Newsletter. **Price:** free online. **Circulation:** 300,000. **Advertising:** accepted. Alternate Formats: online ● *Organic View*, biennial, fall/winter and spring/summer. Newsletter. **Circulation:** 30,000.

5070 ■ Organic Growers and Buyers Association (OGBA)
Address Unknown since 2008
Founded: 1977. **Description:** Organic food and fiber industry, including producers (farmers), processors/ manufacturers, warehouses, food handlers, brokers, traders and retailers. Provides organic certification services in food and fiber, including soybeans, grains, seeds, vegetables, fruits, livestock, dairy products, eggs, greenhouses, flowers, tofu, miso, seaweed, kuzu, rice, koji, umeboshi, tamari, assorted teas, coffee, maple syrup, sugar, juices, wild harvested products, herbs, frozen products, canned products, wholesale, etc; promotes education; assists in marketing efforts.

Parks and Recreation

5071 ■ National Park Trust (NPT)
51 Monroe St., Ste.110
Rockville, MD 20850
Ph: (301)279-PARK
Fax: (301)279-7211
E-mail: npt@parktrust.org
URL: http://www.parktrust.org
Contact: Mr. Davinder Khanna, Sr. VP
Founded: 1983. **Staff:** 6. **Languages:** English, Spanish. **Description:** Seeks to preserve the integrity of America's natural, historic and cultural resources. Secures privately held property in or adjacent to parks for sale or donation to the Park Service. Acquires land to create new national parks. **Awards:** Bruce F. Vento Public Service Award. **Frequency:** annual. **Type:** recognition. **Recipient:** to individual who has demonstrated a lifetime of skill and innovation. **Additional Websites:** http://www.parklandpreservation.org. **Telecommunication Services:** electronic mail, davinder@parktrust.org. **Programs:** National Park Travel. **Publications:** *Alaska: The Greatest Trip of Our Lives*. Report. Alternate Formats: online ● *National Park Trust News*, 3/year. Newsletter. **Circulation:** 8,000 ● *Parkland News*, weekly, on Mondays. Newsletter. Covers issues concerning parklands, wildlife habitats and open spaces. Alternate Formats: online ● *Saving the Legacy of the National System of Parks*, annual. Annual Report. Alternate Formats: online ● Brochure. **Conventions/Meetings:** board meeting.

Pest Control

5072 ■ American Mosquito Control Association (AMCA)
15000 Commerce Pkwy., Ste.C
Mount Laurel, NJ 08054
Ph: (856)439-9222
Fax: (856)439-0525
E-mail: amca@mosquito.org
URL: http://www.mosquito.org
Contact: Joe Conlon, Technical Advisor
Founded: 1935. **Members:** 2,000. **Membership Dues:** regular, $120 (annual) ● associate, $50 (annual) ● student, $30 (annual) ● government sustaining, $500 (annual) ● corporate sustaining, $1,000 (annual). **Staff:** 5. **Budget:** $535,000. **Regional Groups:** 9. **State Groups:** 41. **Local Groups:** 485. **National Groups:** 4. **Multinational. Description:** Entomologists, biologists, medical personnel, engineers, public health officials, military personnel, and others interested in mosquito control and related work. **Libraries: Type:** not open to the public. **Holdings:** 10,000. **Subjects:** mosquito and vector control. **Awards:** Industry Award. **Frequency:** annual. **Type:** recognition. **Recipient:** to a representative of mosquito/vector related industry who advanced the work of mosquito and/or vector control or research ● John N. Belkin Award. **Frequency:** annual. **Type:** recognition. **Recipient:** for meritorious contributions to the field of mosquito systematic and/or biology ● Medal of Honor. **Frequency:** annual. **Type:** medal. **Recipient:** for outstanding member with exceptional contributions to mosquito control ● Memorial Lecture Honoree and Memorial Lecture Award. **Frequency:** annual. **Type:** recognition. **Recipient:** for an individual who has made exceptional contributions to the broad field of mosquito control during his lifetime ● Meritorious Service Award. **Frequency:** annual. **Type:** recognition. **Recipient:** for outstanding service of an individual ● Presidential Citation. **Frequency:** annual. **Type:** recognition. **Recipient:** for outstanding individuals ● Student Paper Competition Awards. **Frequency:** annual. **Type:** recognition. **Recipient:** to student. **Computer Services:** Mailing lists, of members ● online services, member's area. **Committees:** International Exchange; Research. **Formed by Merger of:** (1944) Eastern Association of Mosquito Control Workers. **Publications:** *AMCA Newsletter*, bimonthly. Covers association activities and news affecting mosquito control. Includes employment listings and meetings calendar. **Price:** included in membership dues. ISSN: 0195-4180. **Circulation:** 2,000 ● *WingBeats*, quarterly. Includes interesting technical or field-related articles about mosquitoes, mosquito control, and related topics. Alternate Formats: online ● Journal, quarterly. Contains research articles on mosquitoes and closely related Diptera, and their control. Advertisers' index each issue; subject and author indexes. **Price:** included in membership dues; $85.00 /year for institutions. ISSN: 8756-971X. **Circulation:** 2,000. **Advertising:** accepted ● Bibliographies ● Books ● Bulletins. **Conventions/Meetings:** annual meeting (exhibits).

5073 ■ Association of Applied IPM Ecologists (AAIE)
PO Box 12181
Fresno, CA 93776
Ph: (559)907-4897
E-mail: director@aaie.net
Contact: Bill Rothfus, Exec. Dir.
Founded: 1967. **Members:** 300. **Membership Dues:** professional, corporate, sponsor, $100 (annual) ● general, $50 (annual) ● associate, $35 (annual) ● student, $15 (annual). **Staff:** 1. **Budget:** $50,000. **State Groups:** 1. **Description:** Professional agricultural pest management consultants, entomologists, and field personnel. Promotes the implementation of integrated pest management in agricultural and urban environments. Provides a forum for the exchange of technical information on pest control. Offers placement service. **Awards:** Member of the Year. **Frequency:** annual. **Type:** recognition ● Outstanding Achievement. **Frequency:** annual. **Type:** recognition. **Committees:** Research. **Formerly:** (2002) Association of Applied Insect Ecologists. **Publications:** *AAIE Conference Program*, annual. Proceedings. **Advertising:** accepted. Alternate Formats: online ● *Handling Beneficial Organisms on the Farm*. Video ● *Professional Members Directory*. Membership Directory ● Bulletin, quarterly. **Price:** $15.00/year. **Circulation:** 400. **Advertising:** accepted. **Conventions/Meetings:** annual conference.

5074 ■ Association of Natural Biocontrol Producers (ANBP)
c/o Maclay Burt, Exec. Dir.
2230 Martin Dr.
Tustin, CA 92782
Ph: (714)544-8295
Fax: (714)544-8295
E-mail: execdir@anbp.org
URL: http://www.anbp.org
Contact: Richard Ward, Pres.
Founded: 1990. **Membership Dues:** associate, $25 (annual) ● distributor, $250 (annual) ● producer, $550 (annual) ● practitioner, $125 (annual). **Description:** Represents the biological pest management industry. Promotes and encourages augmentative biological control, which utilizes beneficial insects, mites and nematodes to manage agricultural, horticultural and plant pest. Addresses key issues of the augmentative biological control industry through advocacy, education and quality assurance. **Computer Services:** Information services, biocontrol and biotechnology resources ● online services, member products. **Telecommunication Services:** electronic mail, rward@biobest.ca. **Publications:** *Bio-control Matters*, quarterly. Newsletter. Provides members with information, thought and opinion on biological control affairs. Alternate Formats: online ● *Biocontrol News*. Newsletter. Alternate Formats: online. **Conventions/Meetings:** annual Making Connections - conference, with thousands of entemologists and professionals from related disciplines.

5075 ■ Bio-Integral Resource Center (BIRC)
PO Box 7414
Berkeley, CA 94707
Ph: (510)524-2567
Fax: (510)524-1758
E-mail: birc@igc.org
URL: http://www.birc.org
Contact: William Quarles, Managing Ed.
Founded: 1978. **Members:** 5,000. **Membership Dues:** professional - individual, $35 (annual) ● professional - business/institution, $60 (annual) ● associate - individual, $30 (annual) ● associate - business/institution, $50 (annual) ● dual - individual, $55 (annual) ● dual - business/institution, $85 (annual). **Staff:** 7. **Budget:** $500,000. **Description:** Provides publications and consultations for pest management professionals, farmers, foresters, park service resource managers, environmentalists, and interested individuals. Provides practical information on methods of managing pests and land resource problems. Evaluates and disseminates information on the least toxic method of managing weed, vertebrate, insect, and microbe pests in urban, agricultural, forestall, and veterinary environments. Develops integrated pest management programs for community groups, public agencies, and private institutions. (IPM involves integrating biological, horticultural, mechanical, and chemical strategies to suppress pest populations below levels causing economic, medical, or aesthetic damage.) Areas of technical assistance include: consultation of community pest problems; identification of pests and their natural enemies; pest control program evaluation; development of contract specifications; landscape design and design plan review; integration of IPM methods and sustainable agriculture. Reports on educational opportunities; sponsors workshops and lectures. **Libraries: Type:** reference. **Holdings:** 15,000. **Computer Services:** database, least toxic pest control methods. **Pro-**

grams: International Information Exchange. **Publications:** *Common Sense Pest Control.* Book ● *Common Sense Pest Control Quarterly.* Journal. Features least-toxic solutions to pest problems. **Price:** $30.00/year. **Circulation:** 2,000. **Advertising:** accepted ● *IPM for Schools: A How To Manual.* **Price:** $45.00 ● *IPM Practitioner*, 10/year. Magazine. Features management alternatives for pests. **Price:** $35.00/year; $60.00/year for businesses and institutions. **Circulation:** 4,000. **Advertising:** accepted ● *2005 Directory of Least-Toxic Pest Control Products.* **Price:** $15.00.

5076 ■ National Animal Damage Control Association (NADCA)
c/o Art Smith, Pres.
Dept. of Game, Fish and Parks
523 E Capitol Ave.
Pierre, SD 57501
Ph: (402)472-8961
Fax: (402)472-8390
E-mail: svantassel2@unl.edu
URL: http://nadca.unl.edu
Contact: Art Smith, Pres.
Founded: 1979. **Members:** 600. **Membership Dues:** student, $10 (annual) ● active, $20 (annual) ● sponsor, $40 (annual) ● patron, $100 (annual). **State Groups:** 2. **Description:** Vertebrate pest controllers; nuisance wildlife control operators; trappers; federal, state, and local directors, managers, and employees concerned with wildlife management; individuals concerned with creating a more favorable attitude toward vertebrate pest management. Strives to increase public awareness and understanding of the purposes and principles of animal damage control. Supports the use of vertebrate pest management programs as a wildlife management tool. Promotes the animal damage control profession as it relates to the agribusiness community, wildlife resource management, and various government and private entities. Conducts educational and informational programs designed to aid in public and private decision-making concerning animal damage control. Maintains information center on animal damage control problems; sponsors seminars and workshops on vertebrate pest management. **Awards:** Best Student Presentation Award. **Frequency:** annual. **Type:** recognition. **Committees:** College Curricula for Animal Damage Control. **Publications:** *The Probe*, monthly. Newsletter. **Price:** included in membership dues. **Circulation:** 650. **Conventions/Meetings:** annual conference (exhibits).

5077 ■ National Association of Exotic Pest Plant Councils (NAEPPC)
c/o Tony Pernas, Chm.
Natl. Park Ser.
Florida/Caribbean EPMT
18001 Old Cuttler Rd., Ste.419
Palmetto Bay, FL 33157
Ph: (305)252-0347
Fax: (305)253-0463
E-mail: tony_pernas@nps.gov
URL: http://www.naeppc.org
Contact: Tony Pernas, Chm.
Founded: 1995. **Description:** Focuses on issues of exotic pest plants in natural areas and other wildlands. Seeks to improve the methods of prevention of new infestations of exotic pest plants from importation into the USA and through interstate movement. Aims to increase biological control funding.

5078 ■ National Gypsy Moth Management Board
Address Unknown since 2008
Founded: 1987. **Members:** 350. **Description:** State, local, and federal governmental officials, industry representatives, and private organizations with interest in European and Asian strains of gypsy moth. Gypsy moth is the most economically important forest and urban pest and it feeds on over 500 species of trees and plants. Serves as a coordinating body to dispense information about the gypsy moth and responds to requests for information from the public. **Awards:** Distinguished Service Award. **Frequency:** annual. **Type:** recognition. **Committees:** Audit; Awards; Executive; Nominating; Program. **Formerly:** (1968) National Gypsy Moth Council. **Publications:** *Yearly Proceedings of Annual Review Meeting*, annual. **Price:** $5.00. **Conventions/Meetings:** annual Gypsy Moth Review - convention, exhibit space paid for by Exhibitor if commercial, free to non-profits (exhibits) - usually October or November.

5079 ■ Society for Vector Ecology (SOVE)
1966 Compton Ave.
Corona, CA 92881-3318
Ph: (951)340-9792
Fax: (951)340-2515
E-mail: sove@sove.org
URL: http://www.sove.org
Contact: Major S. Dhillon PhD, Sec.-Treas.
Founded: 1968. **Members:** 820. **Membership Dues:** regular, $70 (annual) ● student, $35 (annual) ● sustaining/institutional, $100 (annual). **Budget:** $60,000. **Regional Groups:** 7. **Description:** Persons with a bachelor's or master's degree from an accredited college or university, plus two or more years experience in vector ecology or related fields of education and research; persons with at least seven years of technical or administrative service in the field. Objectives are: to provide educational meetings and otherwise facilitate the exchange of information among members; to examine the full spectrum of problems caused by vector and nuisance species (especially insects and rodents) and define areas needing additional research and technological development; to encourage the study and suppression of disease vectors and nuisance organisms through environmental management and the conservation of water, land, and reusable waste products; to encourage public recognition of vector ecology as a professional activity. Wishes to develop high ethical and professional standards in an effort to provide the greatest possible service to the public. Sponsors seminars, field trips, and regional conferences. **Libraries: Type:** open to the public. **Holdings:** 22. **Subjects:** disease and vector research. **Awards:** Distinguished Achievement. **Frequency:** annual. **Type:** recognition ● Distinguished Service. **Frequency:** annual. **Type:** recognition. **Telecommunication Services:** electronic mail, mdhillon@northwest-mvcd.org. **Committees:** Public Education. **Formerly:** (1988) Society of Vector Ecologists. **Publications:** *Journal of Vector Ecology*, semiannual. **Price:** included in membership dues. ISSN: 1081-1710. **Circulation:** 800. **Advertising:** accepted. Alternate Formats: online ● *Vector Ecology Newsletter*, quarterly. Alternate Formats: online. **Conventions/Meetings:** annual international conference ● quadrennial International Congress of Vector Ecology.

Photography

5080 ■ International League of Conservation Photographers (ILCP)
432 Walker Rd.
Great Falls, VA 22066
Ph: (703)304-1440
Fax: (703)759-5370
E-mail: info@conservationphotography.net
URL: http://www.ilcp.com
Contact: Cristina G. Mittermeier, Dir.
Founded: 2005. **Staff:** 3. **Multinational. Description:** Furthers environmental and cultural conservation through photography. Seeks to help educate the world community and to further conservation goals. Creates compelling and informed images and develops visually based campaigns to promote conservation issues. Facilitates the connection of photography with environmental, scientific and cultural media, and with governmental, religious and educational resources. **Publications:** *Conservation of Island Biodiversity: Importance, Challenges, and Opportunities.* Brochure. Alternate Formats: online ● *Transboundary Conservation: A New Vision for Protected Areas.* Book. Reviews the history of the transboundary conservation concept and application. Alternate Formats: online ● *The Wealth of Islands: A Global Call for Conservation.* Brochure. Alternate Formats: online ● Newsletter, quarterly. Features news about ILCP's projects and initiatives. Alternate Formats: online ● Annual Report, annual. Alternate Formats: online.

Pollution Control

5081 ■ Air and Waste Management Association (A&WMA)
1 Gateway Ctr., 3rd Fl.
420 Ft. Duquesne Blvd.
Pittsburgh, PA 15222-1435
Ph: (412)232-3444
Free: (800)270-3444
Fax: (412)232-3450
E-mail: info@awma.org
URL: http://www.awma.org
Contact: Adrianne Carolla, Exec. Dir./Sec.
Founded: 1907. **Members:** 17,000. **Membership Dues:** individual, $180 (annual) ● student, $35 (annual) ● affiliate, $93 (annual) ● organization, $435 (annual) ● individual, $310 (biennial) ● deluxe individual, $214 (annual) ● deluxe affiliate, $132 (annual). **Staff:** 50. **Budget:** $8,000,000. **Regional Groups:** 29. **Local Groups:** 76. **Description:** Serves as environmental, educational, and technical organization. Seeks to provide a neutral forum for the exchange of technical information on a wide variety of environmental topics. **Libraries: Type:** reference; open to the public. **Holdings:** archival material, books, monographs, periodicals. **Subjects:** air pollution, solid and hazardous waste, water pollution, environmental management. **Awards:** Frank A. Chambers Award. **Frequency:** annual. **Type:** recognition. **Recipient:** for outstanding achievement in the science and art of air pollution control ● Honorary A&WMA Membership Award. **Frequency:** annual. **Type:** recognition. **Recipient:** to person with eminent attainment in some field related to the mission and objective of the association ● J. Deane Sensenbaugh Award. **Frequency:** annual. **Type:** recognition. **Recipient:** for outstanding organizational achievement in waste management ● Lyman A. Ripperton Award. **Frequency:** annual. **Type:** recognition. **Recipient:** for inspiring students to achieve excellence ● Richard Beatty Mellon Award. **Frequency:** annual. **Type:** recognition. **Recipient:** for civic contributions to the association's objectives ● S. Smith Griswold Award. **Frequency:** annual. **Type:** recognition. **Recipient:** for accomplishment in prevention and control of air pollution ● Waste Management Award. **Frequency:** annual. **Type:** recognition. **Recipient:** for outstanding achievement in waste management, waste prevention, or as an educator in waste management. **Committees:** Communications and Marketing; Education; Sections and Chapters; Technical Council. **Divisions:** Air; Environmental Management; Waste. **Formerly:** Smoke Prevention Association of American; (1987) Air Pollution Control Association; (1989) APCA. **Publications:** *Air Pollution Engineering Manual* ● *APCA: The International Journal of the Air and Waste Management*, monthly. Includes peer-reviewed technical papers. **Price:** included in membership dues; $200.00 /year for nonmembers. ISSN: 1047-3289. **Circulation:** 18,000. **Advertising:** accepted. Alternate Formats: microform ● *Environmental Manager*, monthly. Magazine. Includes calendar of events, association news, business news, new product information, and legislative reports. **Price:** $200.00 for nonmembers. **Circulation:** 18,000. **Advertising:** accepted ● *Five-Year Cumulative Index* ● *Proceedings Digests*, annual ● *Resource Book and Membership Directory*, annual. **Price:** available to members only. **Circulation:** 17,000 ● Manuals ● Proceedings ● Videos ● Membership Directory. Alternate Formats: online ● Also publishes summary guides and educational materials. **Conventions/Meetings:** annual meeting and conference (exhibits) - always June ● periodic symposium and conference (exhibits).

5082 ■ American Indoor Air Quality Council (AmIAQ)
PO Box 11599
Glendale, AZ 85318-1599

Ph: (623)582-0832
Free: (800)942-0832
Fax: (623)581-6270
E-mail: info@iaqcouncil.org
URL: http://www.iaqcouncil.org
Contact: Mr. Charlie Wiles, Exec. Dir.
Founded: 1993. **Staff:** 7. **State Groups:** 50. **Nonmembership. Description:** Establishes credible certifications that provides lasting value to professionals, clients, and the public. Serves the public interest with integrity as an independent certifying body. **Telecommunication Services:** electronic mail, charlie@iaqcouncil.org.

5083 ■ Center for Clean Air Policy (CCAP)
750 First St. NE, Ste.940
Washington, DC 20002
Ph: (202)408-9260
Fax: (202)408-8896
E-mail: communications@ccap.org
URL: http://www.ccap.org
Contact: Ned Helme, Pres.
Founded: 1985. **Staff:** 13. **Budget:** $1,500,000. **Description:** Participants are U.S. state governors and corporate, academic, and public interest leaders. Develops and analyzes approaches to resolving environmental and energy issues. Seeks to inform decision makers and the public of the underlying environmental and economic implications of air pollution controls. Organizes and mediates discussions between all parties with an interest in the environment and economic impacts of air pollution control legislation. Conducts study projects to measure the impact of acid rain control strategies and policies, energy conservation efforts, and economic, environmental, and waste management control options; is currently engaged in environmental exchange programs with Germany and the Czech Republic. **Telecommunication Services:** electronic mail, skallan@ccap.org. **Formerly:** Center for Acid Rain and Clean Air Policy Analyses. **Publications:** *A Natural Approach: Forestry and Global Climate Changes* ● *Acid Rain: Road to a Middleground Solution* ● *Air Quality and Electricity Restructuring* ● *An Efficient Approach to Reducing Acid Rain: The Environment Benefits of Energy Conservation* ● *Cooling the Greenhouse Effect: Options and Costs for Reducing CO2 Emissions from the American Electric Power Company* ● *Strengthening Demand Side Management In Ohio.* Report. Includes information of the progress of Ohio's investor-owned utilities to implement DSM programs. **Price:** $30.00 ● *The Untold Story: The Silver Lining for West Virginia in Acid Rain Control* ● *Wisconsin's Strategy: Cleaning the Air, Protecting the Climate, Sustaining the Economy.* **Conventions/Meetings:** annual board meeting.

5084 ■ Citizens for Alternatives to Chemical Contamination (CACC)
8735 Maple Grove Rd.
Lake, MI 48632-9511
Ph: (989)544-3318
Fax: (989)544-3318
E-mail: jwitucki@peoplepc.com
URL: http://www.caccmi.org
Contact: John Witucki, Dir.
Founded: 1978. **Members:** 500. **Membership Dues:** individual, $15 (annual) ● family, $20 (annual) ● organization, $25 (annual). **Staff:** 1. **Budget:** $75,000. **Local Groups:** 4. **Description:** Grassroots environmental education and advocacy organization dedicated to the principles of social justice, pollution prevention, empowerment, and the protection of the Great Lakes human and natural ecosystem. Works to increase public awareness of toxic chemical threats to the environment. Conducts research and educational programs; offers children's services. **Libraries: Type:** lending; reference; not open to the public. **Holdings:** 500. **Subjects:** environment. **Awards: Frequency:** annual. **Type:** recognition. **Recipient:** for outstanding work for environmental equity and social justice, especially from grassroots. **Publications:** *CACC Clearinghouse*, monthly. Newsletter. **Price:** included in membership dues. **Circulation:** 750. **Advertising:** accepted. **Conventions/Meetings:** annual Backyard Eco Conference (exhibits) - always May/June in Central Michigan.

5085 ■ Clean Air Trust (CAT)
1625 K St. NW, Ste.790
Washington, DC 20006
Ph: (301)941-1987
E-mail: frank@cleanairtrust.org
URL: http://www.cleanairtrust.org
Founded: 1995. **Description:** Aims to educate the public and policymakers about the value of the Clean Air Act; promotes effective enforcement of the Act. **Publications:** Bulletins.

5086 ■ Clean Fuels Development Coalition (CFDC)
c/o Douglas A. Durante, Exec. Dir.
4641 Montgomery Ave., Ste.350
Bethesda, MD 20814
Ph: (301)718-0077
Fax: (301)718-0606
E-mail: cfdcinc@aol.com
URL: http://www.cleanfuelsdc.org
Contact: Douglas A. Durante, Exec. Dir.
Founded: 1988. **Description:** Advocates the development of a national energy policy that addresses environmental concerns and provides for increased production and use of non-petroleum motor fuels. Has identified an environmentally safe energy mix that includes the use of ethanol, methanol, natural gas, ethers, electricity, and other natural resources. Provides support in areas such as education, promotion, and research; represents members' interests before Congress and federal agencies. Analyzes pertinent legislation and regulatory action; disseminates environmental, production, and usage information. **Publications:** *Clean Fuels: Paving the Way for Americas Future.* Brochures ● Magazines.

5087 ■ Clean Water Action (CWA)
4455 Connecticut Ave. NW, Ste.A300
Washington, DC 20008-2328
Ph: (202)895-0420
Free: (866)928-7363
Fax: (202)895-0438
E-mail: cwa@cleanwater.org
URL: http://www.cleanwateraction.org
Contact: David Zwick, Pres.
Founded: 1972. **Members:** 700,000. **Membership Dues:** family, $25 (annual) ● newsletter, $36 (annual) ● sustainer, $60 (annual). **Staff:** 450. **Budget:** $9,000,000. **Description:** Works locally, statewide, and nationally for clean, safe, and affordable water. Seeks to: prevent health-threatening pollution; create environmentally safe jobs and businesses; empower people to make democracy work. Organizes grassroots groups, coalitions, and campaigns to protect the environment, economic well-being, and quality of life. **Formerly:** (1975) Fisherman's Clean Water Action Project; (1988) Clean Water Action Project. **Publications:** *Clean Water Action News*, quarterly. Newsletter. Reports on efforts to preserve clean and safe water, control toxic chemicals, and protect the nation's natural resources. **Price:** $25.00/year. **Circulation:** 300,000. **Advertising:** accepted. Alternate Formats: online ● Reports. **Conventions/Meetings:** semiannual board meeting.

5088 ■ Clean Water Fund (CWF)
4455 Connecticut Ave. NW, Ste.A300-16
Washington, DC 20008-2328
Ph: (202)895-0432
Free: (866)928-7363
Fax: (202)895-0438
E-mail: cwf@cleanwater.org
URL: http://www.cleanwaterfund.org
Contact: Peter Lockwood, Pres.
Founded: 1974. **Members:** 700,000. **Staff:** 70. **Budget:** $2,500,000. **State Groups:** 17. **Description:** Research and educational organization promoting public interest and involvement in issues related to water, toxic materials, and natural resources. Participants include scientific and policy experts, writers of environmental legislation, politicians, and grassroots organizers. Works to improve the effectiveness of local environmental groups. Seeks to: protect marine habitats; secure safe water supplies for the future through groundwater conservation and restricted use of pesticides; stop environmental crime and prevent pollution; devise practical solutions to the U.S. solid waste disposal crisis. Encourages cooperation between business, labor, sportsmen, and conservationists in devising solutions to environmental problems. Provides research, scientific, and technical assistance to local environmental organizations whose programs emphasize: development of long-term solutions to environmental problems; close public scrutiny of government agencies, public officials, and corporations to ensure their compliance with environmental protection laws and regulations; coalition building and networking to strengthen the environmental movement nationwide. Compiles statistics. **Programs:** Clean and Safe Water; Environment - Economy Initiatives; Pollution Prevention: Persistent Poisons; Research, Training, Outreach Education; Sustainable Energy. **Publications:** Reports. Alternate Formats: online.

5089 ■ ETAD North America - Ecological and Toxicological Association of Dyes and Organic Pigments Manufacturers
1850 M St. NW, Ste.700
Washington, DC 20036
Ph: (202)721-4154
Fax: (202)296-8120
E-mail: helmest@socma.com
URL: http://www.etad.com
Contact: C. Tucker Helmes PhD, Exec. Dir.
Founded: 1981. **Members:** 10. **Staff:** 3. **Budget:** $500,000. **Description:** U.S. member companies of the Ecological and Toxicological Association of the Dyestuffs Manufacturing Industry. Works with government agencies in identifying and controlling potential health or environmental hazards from dyes. **Programs:** DyeCare; Environment; Exposure Reduction; Pollution Prevention; Toxicology. **Affiliated With:** Ecological and Toxicological Association of Dyes and Organic Pigments Manufacturers; Synthetic Organic Chemical Manufacturers Association. **Formerly:** (1992) United States Operating Committee of ETAD; (2002) United States Dye Manufacturers Operating Committee of ETAD. **Publications:** *Guidelines for Safe Handling of Dyes.* Brochure. Contains guidelines for safe work practices. **Price:** $5.00 ● *Pollution Prevention Guidance Manual for the Dye Manufacturing Industry.* **Conventions/Meetings:** annual general assembly - always May.

5090 ■ Federation of Environmental Technologists (FET)
9451 N 107th St.
Milwaukee, WI 53224
Ph: (414)354-0070
Fax: (414)354-0073
E-mail: info@fetinc.org
URL: http://www.fetinc.org
Contact: Barbara Hurula, Exec. Dir.
Founded: 1983. **Members:** 700. **Membership Dues:** individual, $115 (annual) ● patron company, $250 (annual) ● government employee, $75 (annual) ● student, unemployed, $30 (annual). **Staff:** 2. **State Groups:** 5. **Local Groups:** 5. **Description:** Industries, educational groups, governmental agencies, and consultants professionally involved in pollution prevention and regulation. Seeks to prevent pollution and support economic growth. Conducts professional training courses. **Awards:** Wisconsin Governor's Award for Excellence in Environmental Performance. **Frequency:** annual. **Type:** recognition. **Recipient:** for reduction or prevention of hazardous waste. **Computer Services:** Mailing lists. **Committees:** Air; EMS; Hazardous Solid Waste; Health and Safety; Municipal; Water. **Publications:** *ENVIRONOTES*, monthly. Newsletter. Contains meeting and seminar minutes, employment opportunities, and calendar of events. **Price:** included in membership dues. **Circulation:** 800 ● Membership Directory, annual. **Conventions/Meetings:** annual Environment - conference (exhibits) ● seminar.

5091 ■ Freshwater Society
2500 Shadywood Rd.
Excelsior, MN 55331

Ph: (952)471-9773
Fax: (952)471-7685
E-mail: freshwater@freshwater.org
URL: http://www.freshwater.org
Contact: James J. Heintzman, Exec. Dir.

Founded: 1968. **Members:** 1,200. **Staff:** 8. **Budget:** $1,000,000. **Description:** Protects freshwater resources by promoting rational freshwater management, by providing publications and sponsoring educational programs. **Publications:** *Aquatic Nuisance Species Digest*, quarterly. Newsletter ● *Citizens Guide to Lake Protection*. Booklet ● *Facets of Freshwater*, monthly. Newsletter ● *Groundwater: Understanding Our Hidden Resource*. Pamphlet ● *Hazardous Waste In Our Water*. Pamphlet ● *National Water Quality News*, quarterly. Newsletter ● *Understanding Your Septic System*. Pamphlet ● *Understanding Your Shoreline*. Pamphlet ● *Waste Is a Water Problem*. Pamphlet ● *Water Filters*. Pamphlet.

5092 ■ Get Oil Out! (GOO!)

c/o Environmental Defense Center
Santa Barbara Off.
906 Garden St.
Santa Barbara, CA 93101
Ph: (805)963-1622
Fax: (805)962-3152
E-mail: japowell@getoilout.org
URL: http://www.getoilout.org
Contact: John Abraham Powell, Pres.

Founded: 1969. **Description:** Monitors and seeks to limit offshore oil and gas operations in the Santa Barbara Channel. Supports state and national legislation related to its objectives. Maintains the Get Oil Out Education and Legal Fund. Has become a national center for information and research on oil pollution and oil development, supplying universities, schools, organizations, and individuals with information, slides, and other visual aids. Maintains library. **Convention/Meeting:** none.

5093 ■ Indoor Air Quality Association (IAQA)

12339 Carroll Ave.
Rockville, MD 20852
Ph: (301)231-8388
Fax: (301)231-8321
E-mail: iaqglenn@aol.com
URL: http://www.iaqa.org
Contact: Glenn Fellman, Exec. Dir.

Founded: 1995. **Membership Dues:** corporate, $250 (annual) ● individual, $125 (annual) ● student, $45 (annual) ● individual government, $65 (annual) ● corporate franchisor, $750 (annual) ● corporate affiliate, corporate franchisee, $200 (annual) ● individual affiliate, $75 (annual). **Description:** Promotes the exchange of indoor environmental information. Provides education and research for the safety and well-being of the general public. Advances standards, procedures and protocols in the Indoor Air Quality industry. **Telecommunication Services:** electronic mail, iaqa@aol.com. **Committees:** Annual Meeting; Certification; Education; Guidelines; Legal and Legislative Affairs; Research and Technical. **Publications:** *In the Air*, quarterly. Newsletter. Features industry news, field studies, technical articles and IAQA activities. **Conventions/Meetings:** annual convention, with symposiums.

5094 ■ International Commission on Atmospheric Chemistry and Global Pollution (ICACGP)

c/o Dr. Anne M. Thompson, Pres.
NASA/Goddard Flight Ctr., Code 916
Bldg. 33, Rm. E417
Greenbelt, MD 20771
Ph: (301)614-5731
Fax: (301)614-5903
E-mail: thompson@gator1.gsfc.nasa.gov
URL: http://croc.gsfc.nasa.gov/cacgp
Contact: Dr. Anne M. Thompson, Pres.

Founded: 1957. **Multinational. Description:** Studies atmospheric science and global pollution. **Affiliated With:** International Association of Meteorology and Atmospheric Sciences.

5095 ■ Midwest Center for Environmental Science and Public Policy (MCESPP)

1845 N Farewell Ave., Ste.100
Milwaukee, WI 53202
Ph: (414)271-7280
Fax: (414)273-7293
E-mail: mcespp@mcespp.org
Contact: Jeffery A. Foran PhD, Pres.

Founded: 1971. **Members:** 30,000. **Membership Dues:** subscribing, $30 (annual). **Staff:** 8. **Budget:** $200,000. **Regional Groups:** 1. **Description:** Works to reduce exposure to toxic substances in air, water, and land. Focuses on research, public information, and advocacy, including formal and informal interaction with policy-making bodies on a state, regional, and national level. **Libraries: Type:** reference. **Holdings:** articles, books, reports. **Subjects:** environmental pollution. **Formerly:** (2005) Citizens for a Better Environment. **Publications:** *CBE Review*, semiannual, plus 2 updates/year. Newsletter ● Also publishes research reports, comments, and fact sheets.

5096 ■ National Biosolids Partnership (NBP)

601 Wythe St.
Alexandria, VA 22314
Ph: (703)684-2400
Fax: (703)684-2492
E-mail: shadeed@wef.org
URL: http://www.biosolids.org
Contact: Sam Hadeed, Communications Dir.

Founded: 1997. **Description:** Advances environmentally sound and accepted biosolids management practices. Develops a comprehensive environmental management system (EMS) for biosolids that will serve as a model for the wastewater profession. Develops and administers a centralized clearinghouse for biosolids information. **Libraries: Type:** open to the public; reference. **Holdings:** archival material, articles, papers, reports. **Subjects:** biosolids, environment management system. **Affiliated With:** Water Environment Federation. **Publications:** *NewsRoom*, weekly. Newsletter. Contains news about the organization and its EMS Program, and other updates. Alternate Formats: online ● Annual Report, annual. Contains reviews on the activities of the organization during the past year. **Price:** free. Alternate Formats: online ● Brochures. Contains news and information about the environmental management system. **Price:** free. Alternate Formats: online.

5097 ■ National Environmental, Safety and Health Training Association (NESHTA)

PO Box 10321
Phoenix, AZ 85064-0321
Ph: (602)956-6099 (602)956-6998
Fax: (602)956-6399
E-mail: info@neshta.org
URL: http://www.neshta.org
Contact: Charles L. Richardson, Exec. Dir.

Founded: 1977. **Members:** 1,400. **Membership Dues:** individual, $90 (annual) ● organization (mail), $460 (annual) ● organization (online), $360 (annual). **Staff:** 4. **Budget:** $500,000. **Multinational. Description:** Professional society for environmental training professionals organized to promote competency and standards. Purposes are: to encourage communication among individual trainers, training institutions, and governmental agencies; to promote environmental personnel training and education; to set minimum standards for training and education programs. Sponsors research programs. Conducts a national certification program for environmental trainers. **Awards:** Environmental Education Award. **Frequency:** annual. **Type:** recognition. **Recipient:** for distinction in regional, national or international training accomplishments ● Trainer-of-the-Year Award. **Frequency:** annual. **Type:** recognition. **Recipient:** for distinction in local or regional training development and/or delivery of training programs. **Computer Services:** Information services, referrals to training specialists ● mailing lists. **Telecommunication Services:** electronic mail, rick@neshta.org. **Boards:** Certified Environmental, Safety and Health Trainer Board of Certification. **Formerly:** (2004) National Environmental Training Association. **Publications:** *CET Exam Guide*. **Price:** $35.00 for members; $45.00 for nonmembers ● *Creative Environment Safety & Health Training*. Manual. **Price:** $45.00 for members; $55.00 for nonmembers ● *Designing and Delivering Effective Training*. Book. **Price:** $35.00 for members; $45.00 for nonmembers ● *Lead-Based Paint Maintenance Training Program*. **Price:** $129.00 ● *Lead-Based Paint Planning Tool*. **Price:** $10.00 ● *NESHTA eNews*, periodic. Newsletter. Covers association activities. Includes calendar of events. **Price:** $12.00. **Circulation:** 900. Alternate Formats: online. **Conventions/Meetings:** annual conference (exhibits) - always June ● seminar.

5098 ■ National Pollution Prevention Roundtable (NPPR)

11 Dupont Cir. NW, Ste.201
Washington, DC 20036
Ph: (202)299-9701
Fax: (202)299-9704
E-mail: staff@p2.org
URL: http://www.p2.org
Contact: Jeffrey Burke, Exec. Dir.

Founded: 1985. **Members:** 200. **Membership Dues:** individual, $150 (annual) ● organizational, $400 (annual) ● student, $30 (annual). **Staff:** 4. **Budget:** $900,000. **Regional Groups:** 10. **State Groups:** 40. **Description:** Works to promote pollution prevention at its source. Conducts educational and research programs; provides a forum for dialogue regarding pollution. **Libraries: Type:** open to the public. **Holdings:** books. **Subjects:** pollution prevention. **Computer Services:** Mailing lists, of members. **Telecommunication Services:** electronic mail, jeff@p2.org. **Working Groups:** Education, Training and Learning; Facility Planning; Info and Tech Transfer; International; Local Government; Regulatory Integration; Research and Technology Transfer; Small Business. **Formerly:** (1994) National Roundtable of State P2 Programs. **Publications:** *Journal of Cleaner Production*. **Price:** $95.00. ISSN: 0959-6526 ● *P2ost*, bimonthly. Newsletter. Contains highlights around the P2 community. **Conventions/Meetings:** annual National Environmental Partnership Summit - conference (exhibits) - usually spring.

5099 ■ Occupational Knowledge International (OK International)

220 Montgomery St., Ste.1027
San Francisco, CA 94104
Ph: (415)362-9898
Fax: (415)362-9410
E-mail: info@okinternational.org
URL: http://www.okinternational.org
Contact: Mr. Perry Gottesfeld, Exec. Dir./Pres.

Multinational. Description: Seeks to address inequities in environmental standards between developed and developing countries. Works to build capacity in developing countries to identify, monitor and mitigate environmental and occupational exposures to hazardous materials in order to protect public health and the environment. Provides technical assistance through partnerships, training, and environmental audit and certification programs, with a commitment to public health tenets, scientific principles, and corporate responsibility. **Programs:** Environmental Education; Lead Battery Environmental Audit and Certification; Plant/Product Certification; Site Inventors; Technical Assistance/Grantmaking. **Projects:** Heavy Metal Contamination from a U.S. Owned Smelter in Peru; Reducing Health Hazards Among Stone Crusher Mill Workers; Reducing Mercury Contamination from Small Scale Gold Refining Operations.

5100 ■ Solar Cookers International (SCI)

1919 21st St., Ste.101
Sacramento, CA 95814
Ph: (916)455-4499
Fax: (916)455-4498
E-mail: info@solarcookers.org
URL: http://solarcookers.org
Contact: Patrick Widner, Exec. Dir.

Founded: 1987. **Members:** 3,400. **Membership Dues:** basic, $50 (annual) ● sustainer, $120 (annual) ● gold benefactor, $1,000 (annual). **Staff:** 11. **Budget:** $699,000. **Multinational. Description:** Promotes the spread of solar cooking to help people and environments worldwide. Solar cooking consists of using a variety of devices that use sunlight to cook meals and to pasteurize drinking water. Provides information exchange. Helps other organizations adapt solar cooking to diverse needs. Develops educational materials and training programs. Focuses on communities in Eastern Africa. **Affiliated With:** Interaction/American Council for Voluntary International Action. **Formerly:** Solar Box Cookers International. **Publications:** *Advances in Solar Cooking: Proceedings of International Conferences on Solar Cookers Use and Technology*, biennial. **Price:** $15.00 ● *Letters From Kenya*. Video. Describes solar cooking in a refugee camp in Kenya. **Price:** $15.00 ● *Solar Cooker Review*, 3/year. Newsletter. **Price:** $10.00/year. **Conventions/Meetings:** biennial international conference (exhibits).

5101 ■ Water Environment Federation (WEF)
601 Wythe St.
Alexandria, VA 22314-1994
Ph: (703)684-2400 (703)684-2452
Free: (800)666-0206
Fax: (703)684-2492
E-mail: csc@wef.org
URL: http://www.wef.org
Contact: William Bertera, Exec. Dir.
Founded: 1928. **Members:** 37,080. **Staff:** 87. **Budget:** $18,000,000. **Regional Groups:** 79. **National Groups:** 30. **Multinational. Description:** Technical societies representing chemists, biologists, ecologists, geologists, operators, educational and research personnel, industrial wastewater engineers, consultant engineers, municipal officials, equipment manufacturers, and university professors and students dedicated to the enhancement and preservation of water quality and resources. Seeks to advance fundamental and practical knowledge concerning the nature, collection, treatment, and disposal of domestic and industrial wastewaters, and the design, construction, operation, and management of facilities for these purposes. Disseminates technical information; and promotes good public relations and regulations that improve water quality and the status of individuals working in this field. Conducts educational and research programs. **Libraries: Type:** reference. **Holdings:** 150; archival material, books, business records, clippings, monographs, periodicals. **Subjects:** water quality and related topics. **Awards:** Charles Alvin Emerson Medal for Outstanding Service to the Wastewater Collection and Treatment Industry. **Frequency:** annual. **Type:** medal. **Recipient:** for contributions to the wastewater collection and treatment industry ● Harry E. Schlenz Medal for Achievement in Public Education. **Frequency:** annual. **Type:** recognition. **Recipient:** to an individual who takes up the banner of water environment public education and presents it to the public in a productive process ● High School Science Fair National Award. **Frequency:** annual. **Type:** recognition ● Honorary Membership. **Frequency:** annual. **Type:** recognition. **Recipient:** to persons who have proven their preeminence in the fields of activity encompassed by Federation objectives. **Additional Websites:** http://www.weftec.org. **Telecommunication Services:** electronic mail, wbertera@wef.org. **Committees:** Agricultural and Industrial Residuals; Air Quality and Odor Control; Bioenergy Technology; Disinfection; Ecology Aquatic Resources; Environmental Management Systems; Government Affairs; Groundwater; Industrial Wastes; International Coordination; Literature Review; Plant Operations and Maintenance; Public Education; Residuals and Biosolids; Safety and Occupational Health; Small Community; Students and Young Professionals; Sunset Review; Technical Practice; Water Environment Research; Water Reuse; Watershed Management. **Formerly:** (1949) Federation of Sewage Works Associations; (1959) Federation of Sewage and Industrial Wastes Associations; (1991) Water Pollution Control Federation. **Publications:** *Highlights*, monthly. Newsletter. **Price:** $19.00/year for nonmembers; $19.00 /year for institutions; $1.50/issue. **Circulation:** 42,000. Alternate Formats: online ● *Industrial Wastewater*, bimonthly. Bulletin. **Price:** $129.00 /year for nonmembers; $116.00 /year for institutions; $18.00/issue for members; $22.00/issue for nonmembers ● *Literature Review*, annual ● *Manuals of Practice* ● *Water, Environment, and Technology*, monthly. Magazine. **Price:** $178.00 /year for nonmembers; $178.00 /year for institutions; $14.00/issue for members; $16.00/issue for nonmembers. **Advertising:** accepted ● *Water Environment Laboratory Solutions*, 9/year. Bulletin. **Price:** $99.00 /year for nonmembers; $99.00 /year for institutions; $18.00/issue for members; $22.00/issue for nonmembers ● *Water Environment Regulation Watch*, monthly. Bulletin. **Price:** $129.00 /year for nonmembers; $129.00 /year for institutions; $18.00/issue for members; $22.00/issue for nonmembers ● *Water Environment Research*, bimonthly. Journal ● Also publishes a water quality curriculum for school children. **Conventions/Meetings:** biennial Odors and Air Emissions - conference, designed to foster informed decision-making and encourage the use of effective innovative technologies (exhibits) ● annual Residuals and Biosolids Management Conference - conference and meeting (exhibits).

Poultry

5102 ■ American Bantam Association (ABA)
PO Box 127
Augusta, NJ 07822
Ph: (973)383-8633 (209)296-8084
E-mail: aba@bantamclub.com
URL: http://www.bantamclub.com
Contact: Jim Sallee, Pres.
Founded: 1914. **Members:** 2,500. **Membership Dues:** regular, $20 (annual) ● life, $250 ● associate, $25 (annual). **Description:** Breeders, exhibitors, judges, and others interested in bantams (miniature domestic breeds of poultry). **Libraries: Type:** open to the public. **Committees:** Breed Standard; Constitution and By-Laws; Grievance; Judges Licensing; Publicity; Ways and Means. **Publications:** *Bantam Chicken* ● *Bantam Duck Standard* ● *Bantam Standard* ● *Black East Indie* ● *Book of Bantams*. **Price:** $8.50 ● *Breed Book of Old English and Modern Game Bantams* ● *Cochin Bantams*. **Price:** $6.00 ● *Crested Bantams* ● *Modern Game Bantams* ● *Modern Waterfront Management* ● Yearbook, annual. **Price:** free for members. **Advertising:** accepted. **Conventions/Meetings:** semiannual meeting.

5103 ■ American Dutch Bantam Society (ADBS)
c/o Kristi van Greunen, Pres.
1910 Union St.
Alameda, CA 94501
E-mail: kristi@fynbosfarmpoultry.com
URL: http://www.dutchbantamsocietyamerica.com
Contact: Kristi van Greunen, Pres.
Founded: 1986. **Membership Dues:** general, $15 (annual) ● junior, $5 (annual). **Multinational. Description:** Promotes the Dutch Bantam breed in the United States and Canada through education and communication. Aims to improve the breeding of Dutch Bantams. **Computer Services:** Information services, Dutch Bantam resources ● online services, discussion board. **Publications:** Newsletter. Alternate Formats: online.

5104 ■ American Egg Board (AEB)
1460 Renaissance Dr., Ste.301
Park Ridge, IL 60068
Ph: (847)296-7043
Fax: (847)296-7007
E-mail: aeb@aeb.org
URL: http://www.aeb.org
Contact: Wayne Mooney, Chair
Founded: 1976. **Members:** 350. **Staff:** 20. **Budget:** $20,000,000. **Description:** Board of American egg producers appointed by the Secretary of Agriculture. Offers advertising, educational, research, and promotional programs designed to increase consumption of eggs and egg products. Conducts consumer educators and food-service seminars, and food safety education programs. **Departments:** Advertising; Communications; Consumer Education; Foodservice; Materials Distribution; Nutrition; Product and Market Development; State Support. **Formerly:** (1973) Poultry and Egg National Board. **Publications:** Annual Report, annual. Alternate Formats: online ● Newsletter, biweekly ● Also publishes a variety of cookbooks and recipes.

5105 ■ American Langshan Club (ALC)
c/o Forrest Beauford, Sec.-Treas.
18077 S Hwy. 88
Claremore, OK 74017
Ph: (918)341-2238
E-mail: langshan_99@yahoo.com
URL: http://groups.yahoo.com/group/Langshans
Contact: Forrest Beauford, Sec.-Treas.
Founded: 1945. **Members:** 80. **Membership Dues:** regular, $10 (annual) ● family, $15 (annual) ● life, $100. **Staff:** 10. **For-Profit. Description:** Breeders of Langshan poultry. Promotes improvement of the breed. Sponsors national, regional, and state meets. **Awards: Frequency:** annual. **Type:** recognition. **Additional Websites:** http://www.geocities.com/langshan_99/AMERICAN_LANGSHAN_CLUB.html. **Formerly:** National Black Langshan Club. **Publications:** *The Langshan News*, quarterly. Newsletter. **Conventions/Meetings:** periodic conference (exhibits).

5106 ■ American Pastured Poultry Producers Association (APPPA)
36475 Norton Creek Rd.
Blodgett, OR 97326
Ph: (541)453-4557
E-mail: grit@apppa.org
URL: http://www.apppa.org
Contact: Karen Black, Exec. Dir.
Founded: 1997. **Membership Dues:** basic, $30 (annual) ● producer plus, $50 (annual) ● business, $200 (annual). **Description:** Encourages and promotes the production, processing and marketing of poultry raised on pasture. Serves as a clearinghouse for innovations and refinements to the pastured poultry model. Provides opportunities for people to learn and exchange information about raising poultry on pasture. **Publications:** *APPPA Grit!*, bimonthly. Newsletter. Contains information on current happenings in the pastured poultry industry. **Price:** included in membership dues. Alternate Formats: online ● *Raising Poultry on Pasture: Ten Years of Success*. Book. **Price:** $39.95 for nonmembers, plus shipping and handling; $34.95 for members, plus shipping and handling; $29.95 renewal, plus shipping and handling.

5107 ■ American Poultry Association (APA)
c/o Dave Anderson, Pres.
947 Grand Ave.
Fillmore, CA 93015
Ph: (805)524-4046 (805)524-5588
E-mail: danderson@keygroupinc.com
URL: http://www.amerpoultryassn.com
Contact: Dave Anderson, Pres.
Founded: 1873. **Members:** 3,200. **Membership Dues:** individual in U.S., $15 (annual) ● associate, individual outside U.S. and Canada, $25 (annual) ● junior (18 years old and below), $10 (annual) ● endowment trust in U.S. and Canada (life), $220 ● endowment trust outside U.S. and Canada (life), $440 ● individual in U.S., $40 (triennial). **Description:** Poultry industry. Strives to protect and promote the standard-bred poultry industry in all of its phases. **Publications:** Yearbook, annual ● Newsletter, quarterly.

5108 ■ American Poultry International (API)
PO Box 16805
Jackson, MS 39236
Ph: (601)956-1715
Fax: (601)956-1755
E-mail: apiltd@apipoultry.com
URL: http://www.apipoultry.com
Contact: Gerry Holaday, Pres./CEO
Founded: 1978. **Members:** 6. **Budget:** $50,000. **Description:** Exporters of frozen chicken, turkey, ham, beef and pork products. **Formerly:** (1998) Management Company for American Poultry U.S.A. **Conventions/Meetings:** annual meeting, for stockholders.

5109 ■ American Silkie Bantam Club (ASBC)
c/o Sheila Gordon, Sec.-Treas.
41429 Butler Ct.
Indio, CA 92203
Ph: (760)342-1649
E-mail: sgordonwindsor@earthlink.net
URL: http://www.americansilkiebantamclub.org
Contact: Sheila Gordon, Sec.-Treas.
Founded: 1923. **Members:** 230. **Membership Dues:** individual, $15 (annual) ● junior, $10 (annual) ● family, foreign, $20 (annual). **Description:** People who breed Silkie Bantam chickens as a hobby. Promotes the breeding and exhibiting of Silkie Bantams. **Awards: Type:** recognition. **Affiliated With:** American Bantam Association. **Publications:** *Membership List*, annual. Membership Directory ● Newsletter, bimonthly ● Articles. Alternate Formats: online. **Conventions/Meetings:** annual meet.

5110 ■ Egg Clearing House, Inc. (ECI)
PO Box 817
Dover, NH 03821
Free: (800)872-3324
Fax: (800)736-7286
E-mail: webmaster@eggs.org
URL: http://www.eggs.org
Contact: Tom Hertzfeld II, Chm.
Founded: 1971. **Membership Dues:** individual, $1,000. **Description:** Buyers and sellers of eggs. Provides buyers and sellers a daily trading forum to satisfy their procurement or marketing needs.

5111 ■ National Chicken Council
1015 15th St. NW, Ste.930
Washington, DC 20005-2622
Ph: (202)296-2622
Fax: (202)293-4005
E-mail: ncc@chickenusa.org
URL: http://www.eatchicken.com
Contact: Richard L. Lobb, Dir. of Communications
Founded: 1954. **Members:** 225. **Staff:** 12. **Budget:** $3,000,000. **Description:** Membership includes producers/processors of broiler chickens; distributors and allied industry. Sponsors National Chicken Cooking Contest and National Chicken Month. Compiles statistics; conducts generic promotion program for chicken; provides government relations services for member companies and the broiler industry. **Awards:** Broiler Research Award. **Frequency:** annual. **Type:** monetary. **Recipient:** for outstanding research that made a positive contribution to the commercial poultry industry. **Additional Websites:** http://www.nationalchickencouncil.com. **Committees:** Communications; Marketing; Poultry Health; Safety and Health; Technical and Regulatory. **Absorbed:** National Broiler Association. **Formerly:** (1998) National Broiler Council. **Publications:** *Washington Report*, weekly. Newsletter. **Price:** included in membership dues. **Circulation:** 2,000. Alternate Formats: online ● Also publishes special summary reports. **Conventions/Meetings:** annual conference, government affairs conference and membership meeting - October ● annual Marketing Seminar - always mid-July.

5112 ■ National Poultry Improvement Plan (NPIP)
1498 Klondike Rd., Ste.101
Conyers, GA 30094-5169
Ph: (770)922-3496
Fax: (770)922-3498
E-mail: andrew.r.rhorer@aphis.usda.gov
Contact: Andrew R. Rhorer, Dir.
Founded: 1935. **Members:** 4,000. **Staff:** 4. **Budget:** $800,000. **State Groups:** 48. **Description:** Hatcheries, dealers, and independent poultry breeding flock owners. Tests and classifies poultry breeding flocks and hatcheries. Monitors and seeks to prevent egg-transmitted/hatchery-disseminated diseases. Provides a cooperative state-federal program through which new technology can be effectively applied to the improvement of poultry and poultry products. **Publications:** *National Poultry Improvement Plan and Auxiliary Provisions*, annual. Alternate Formats: online ● *Participant Directories*, annual ● Also publishes tables on testing and participation. **Conventions/Meetings:** biennial conference.

5113 ■ National Turkey Federation (NTF)
1225 New York Ave., Ste., 400
Washington, DC 20005
Ph: (202)898-0100
Fax: (202)898-0203
E-mail: info@turkeyfed.org
URL: http://www.eatturkey.com
Contact: Joel Brandenberger, Pres.
Founded: 1939. **Members:** 4,000. **Membership Dues:** associate, $625 (annual) ● primary packaging, $625-$9,375 (annual) ● box supplier, pharmaceutical, $1,250 (annual) ● local, $150 (annual). **Staff:** 9. **State Groups:** 48. **Description:** Serves as the national advocate for all segments of the turkey industry. Provides services and conducts activities that increase demand for its members' products by protecting and enhancing their ability to profitably provide wholesome, high-quality, and nutritious products. **Publications:** *Turkey Today and Tomorrow*, monthly. Newsletter. **Circulation:** 4,000. **Advertising:** accepted ● Brochure, annual. **Conventions/Meetings:** annual convention - always February ● annual meeting - always June or July.

5114 ■ Plymouth Rock Fanciers Club (PRFC)
c/o Pat Horstman, Sec.-Treas.
5 S Kings Creek Rd.
Burgettstown, PA 15021
Ph: (856)825-2484 (724)729-3701
E-mail: horstcon@yahoo.com
URL: http://www.crohio.com/rockclub
Contact: Richard Hickman, Pres.
Founded: 1973. **Members:** 150. **Membership Dues:** individual, $15 (annual) ● junior, $5 (annual) ● life, $100. **Regional Groups:** 8. **Description:** Breeders and exhibitors. Aims to promote the breeding of exhibition Plymouth Rock poultry and to improve the varieties of the breed. Awards trophies, rosettes, and ribbons at exhibitions. Maintains hall of fame. Compiles statistics. **Libraries: Type:** reference. **Holdings:** photographs, reports. **Awards: Type:** recognition. **Affiliated With:** American Bantam Association. **Absorbed:** (1978) American Barred Plymouth Rock Club. **Publications:** *Breeding Buff Color*. Article. Alternate Formats: online ● Newsletter, quarterly ● Yearbook, annual. **Conventions/Meetings:** annual meet and competition.

5115 ■ Poultry Breeders of America
1530 Cooledge Rd.
Tucker, GA 30084-7303
Ph: (770)493-9401
Fax: (770)493-9257
E-mail: ddalton@poultryegg.org
URL: http://www.poultryegg.org
Contact: Don Dalton, Pres.
Founded: 1959. **Members:** 15. **Membership Dues:** regular, associate, allied, international, $300 (annual). **Description:** Represents breeders of poultry. **Publications:** *Poultry Breeders' Roundtable Proceedings*, annual. **Price:** $25.00. **Conventions/Meetings:** annual National Breeders Roundtable - conference and seminar.

5116 ■ Poultry Science Association (PSA)
1111 N Dunlap Ave.
Savoy, IL 61874
Ph: (217)356-5285
Fax: (217)398-4119
E-mail: drew.giesen@novusint.com
URL: http://www.poultryscience.org
Contact: John B. Carey, Pres.
Founded: 1908. **Members:** 2,000. **Membership Dues:** active, $120 (annual) ● graduate, undergraduate student, $30 (annual) ● corporate, $1,000 (annual). **Staff:** 4. **Budget:** $500,000. **Description:** Members are from academia, industry, and government, with many involved in the research, teaching, or extension of poultry science and related fields. **Awards: Frequency:** annual. **Type:** recognition. **Publications:** *First International Symposium on the Artificial Insemination of Poultry*. Book. Contains male breeder management, semen handling, female breeder management, fertility evaluation and poultry germplasm preservation. **Price:** $35.00 ● *Poultry Science*, monthly. Journal. **Price:** $400.00. ISSN: 0032-5791. **Circulation:** 3,200. **Advertising:** accepted. Alternate Formats: online ● *Practical Poultry Research Collection*. Journal. **Price:** $40.00 for members; $100.00 for nonmembers ● Newsletter, semiannual. Alternate Formats: online. **Conventions/Meetings:** annual meeting (exhibits).

5117 ■ Sebright Club of America (SCA)
Address Unknown since 2008
Founded: 1930. **Members:** 250. **Description:** Persons who breed Sebright bantam fowl as a hobby. **Awards: Type:** recognition. **Publications:** *Sebright Manual* ● *Sebright Newsletter*, quarterly. **Conventions/Meetings:** annual meeting.

5118 ■ Silver Wyandotte Club of America (SWCA)
Address Unknown since 2008
Founded: 1901. **Members:** 100. **Description:** Breeders of standard-bred and Bantam Silver Laced Wyandotte poultry. Promotes the exchange of information among members. **Awards: Type:** monetary. **Recipient:** to winners of meets. **Publications:** Membership Directory, periodic ● Newsletter, quarterly. **Conventions/Meetings:** annual meet.

5119 ■ Society for the Preservation of Poultry Antiquities (SPPA)
c/o Dr. Charles Everett, Sec.-Treas.
1057 Nick Watts Rd.
Lugoff, SC 29078
Ph: (803)408-9846
E-mail: crheverett@bellsouth.net
URL: http://www.feathersite.com/Poultry/SPPA/SPPA.html
Contact: Dr. Charles Everett, Sec.-Treas.
Founded: 1971. **Members:** 800. **Membership Dues:** regular, $12 (annual) ● regular, $21 (biennial) ● regular, $27 (triennial) ● life, $200. **Staff:** 2. **Budget:** $5,000. **Description:** Individuals united to preserve poultry antiquities. Sponsors competitions. **Awards: Type:** recognition. **Publications:** *Breeders Directory*, biennial. Lists breeders and location of breeds facing extinction. **Price:** included in membership dues. **Advertising:** accepted ● Newsletter, quarterly. Alternate Formats: online. **Conventions/Meetings:** annual meeting and show.

5120 ■ United Egg Association Further Processors (UEA)
1720 Windwind Concourse, Ste.230
Alpharetta, GA 30005
Ph: (770)360-9220
Fax: (770)360-7058
E-mail: hmagwire@mwmlaw.com
URL: http://www.unitedegg.org
Contact: Howard Magwire, Staff Coor.
Founded: 1984. **Members:** 45. **Staff:** 2. **Budget:** $250,000. **Description:** Represents manufacturers of liquid, dried and frozen egg products. **Affiliated With:** Animal Agriculture Alliance; International Egg Commission. **Publications:** *United Voices*, bimonthly. Newsletter. **Circulation:** 250.

5121 ■ United Egg Producers (UEP)
1720 Windward Concourse, Ste.230
Alpharetta, GA 30005
Ph: (770)360-9220
Fax: (770)360-7058
E-mail: info@unitedegg.org
URL: http://www.unitedegg.org
Contact: Gene Gregory, Pres./CEO
Founded: 1968. **Members:** 500. **Staff:** 19. **Budget:** $1,900,000. **Description:** Represents regional egg marketing cooperatives whose members are independent egg producers. Aids members in improving efficiency in production, distribution, and marketing of eggs. Maintains legislative office in Washington, DC, which serves as congressional liaison. Compiles statistics; provides specialized education programs. **Awards:** Egg Producer of the Year Award. **Frequency:** annual. **Type:** recognition ● Maurice M. Stein Scholarships. **Frequency:** annual. **Type:** scholarship. **Recipient:** for two graduate students in poultry science. **Committees:** Marketing; United Egg

Political Action. **Divisions:** Government Relations; Nutrition and Consumer Affairs. **Formerly:** (2000) United Egg Association. **Publications:** *The New Yolk Times*, quarterly ● Newsletter, biweekly. **Conventions/Meetings:** quarterly board meeting ● annual conference.

5122 ■ U.S. Poultry and Egg Association
1530 Cooledge Rd.
Tucker, GA 30084-7303
Ph: (770)493-9401
Fax: (770)493-9257
E-mail: ddalton@poultryegg.org
URL: http://www.poultryegg.org
Contact: Don Dalton, Pres.

Founded: 1947. **Members:** 600. **Membership Dues:** regular, $300 (annual) ● associate, $300 (annual) ● allied, $300 (annual) ● international, $300 (annual). **Staff:** 21. **State Groups:** 26. **Description:** Producers, hatcherymen, feed millers, processors, packagers, manufacturers and suppliers of products and services used in the production cycle of poultry products. Identifies problem areas and needs of the membership and concentrates industry efforts toward solutions. Represents the industry in its relationships with government agencies, members of Congress, and other related industry groups. Coordinates research needs and funding. Conducts research in the areas of vaccine development, improved diagnostic methodologies, innovative carcass disposal methods, manure utilization, microbiological quality of finished product, further processing, processing, product development, poultry housing and husbandry. Sponsors ongoing research programs on production and animal health. **Libraries: Type:** reference. **Holdings:** films, video recordings. **Awards:** Work Horse of the Year Award. **Frequency:** annual. **Type:** recognition. **Recipient:** for contribution to poultry industry. **Committees:** Air Cargo; Animal Welfare; Awards and Recognition; Environmental Impact; Exhibitor; Exposition Program; Grower Relations; Long Range; Nominating; Personnel; Poultry Health; Research Technical Advisory. **Councils:** Fowl Processor; Poultry Breeders of America; Poultry Protein and Fat; U.S. Poultry Science Club. **Formerly:** (1998) Southeastern Poultry and Egg Association. **Publications:** *Member Report*, annual ● *News and Views*, monthly. Newsletter. **Circulation:** 1,200. **Conventions/Meetings:** annual International Poultry Exposition - conference (exhibits) - always January, Atlanta, GA ● seminar, management development.

5123 ■ U.S.A. Poultry and Egg Export Council (USAPEEC)
2300 W Park Pl. Blvd., Ste.100
Stone Mountain, GA 30087
Ph: (770)413-0006
Fax: (770)413-0007
E-mail: usapeec@usapeec.org
URL: http://www.usapeec.org
Contact: James H. Sumner, Pres.

Founded: 1984. **Members:** 230. **Staff:** 11. **Budget:** $10,000,000. **Description:** Poultry and egg producers, processors, and traders. Promotes increased exportation of United States poultry products. Represents members' interests; conducts promotional campaigns; facilitates establishment of international business contacts by members. **Telecommunication Services:** electronic mail, jsumner@usapeec.org. **Conventions/Meetings:** semiannual meeting - always spring and fall.

5124 ■ Virginia Poultry Breeders Association (VPBA)
c/o Judy Sanderlin, Sec.
3816 Wayside Rd.
Charles City, VA 23030
E-mail: vpba1963@aol.com
URL: http://www.vpba.net
Contact: Judy Sanderlin, Sec.

Founded: 1963. **Members:** 272. **Membership Dues:** single, $10 (annual) ● family, $15 (annual). **State Groups:** 5. **Description:** Individuals interested in the preservation and betterment of purebred poultry. Encourages youth to raise traditional breeds of poultry. Sponsors annual picnic and competitions. **Affiliated With:** American Bantam Association. **Formerly:** (1985) Virginia Poultry Breeders Club. **Publications:** *The Peep*, quarterly. Newsletter. Includes membership directory as well as letters from members, show data, and research and editor's reports. **Price:** included in membership dues. **Advertising:** accepted ● *Show Catalog*, annual. **Conventions/Meetings:** annual meeting (exhibits).

5125 ■ World's Poultry Science Association, U.S.A. Branch (WPSA)
c/o Dr. Paul Aho, Sec.
Poultry Perspective
20 Eastwood Rd.
Storrs, CT 06268
Ph: (860)429-3053
Fax: (860)487-0572
E-mail: paulaho@paulaho.com
URL: http://www.wpsa.com
Contact: Dr. Paul Aho, Sec.

Founded: 1965. **Members:** 400. **Membership Dues:** individual, $35 (annual). **Description:** Americans with financial interest, through ownership, employment, or avocation, in the poultry industry or allied industries and who are members of the World's Poultry Science Association. Provides for the participation of the U.S. in the quadrennial World's Poultry Congress. Promotes member and industry participation in the meetings. Cooperates with trade associations in promoting better understanding between the poultry industry in the U.S. and in other parts of the world. Works together with the Poultry Science Association in promoting participation of poultry scientists in all international affairs related to poultry science and industry and in providing grants to assist scientists in the participation in World's Poultry Congress. Supports youth poultry training programs. **Awards:** Student Award. **Frequency:** annual. **Type:** grant. **Publications:** *World's Poultry Science Journal*, 3/year. Contains directory. Also Cited As: *WPSJ*. **Conventions/Meetings:** quadrennial World's Poultry Congress (exhibits).

Public Lands

5126 ■ Forest Service Employees for Environmental Ethics
PO Box 11615
Eugene, OR 97440-3815
Ph: (541)484-2692
Fax: (541)484-3004
E-mail: fseee@fseee.org
URL: http://www.fseee.org
Contact: Andy Stahl, Exec. Dir.

Founded: 1989. **Members:** 12,000. **Membership Dues:** regular, $35 (annual) ● sustaining, $50 (annual) ● advocate, $100 (annual) ● patron, $500 (annual) ● outside U.S., $40 (annual). **Staff:** 9. **Budget:** $900,000. **For-Profit. Description:** Present, former, and retired U.S. Forest Service employees, workers from other land management agencies, and concerned citizens. Works to create a responsible value system for the Forest Service based on a land ethic that ensures ecologically and economically sustainable resource management. Seeks to revise and replace the Forest Service's present practice of encouraging overuse of public land by timber companies, mining firms, and cattle owners with a more ecological system of resource management. Acts as a support system for Forest Service employees who do not agree with the Service's present land management ethics. Provides a forum for exchange of information and ideas. Disseminates information on conservation and the misuse of the resources in national forests. Sponsors educational programs. **Convention/Meeting:** none. **Libraries: Type:** reference. **Holdings:** books, periodicals. **Subjects:** forests, public lands, ecosystem management, biodiversity, grazing. **Telecommunication Services:** electronic mail, andys@fseee.org. **Publications:** *Forest Magazine*, quarterly. Includes articles on the use and abuse of public lands. **Price:** $3.50. **Circulation:** 12,000. **Advertising:** accepted ● Brochures.

5127 ■ Public Lands Council (PLC)
1301 Pennsylvania Ave. NW, Ste.300
Washington, DC 20004-1701
Ph: (202)347-0228
Fax: (202)638-0607
E-mail: jeisenberg@beef.org
URL: http://67.100.156.138/plc2/default.asp
Contact: Jeff Eisenberg, Exec. Dir.

Founded: 1968. **Members:** 26,000. **Staff:** 4. **Description:** Ranchers who hold permits and leases for grazing livestock (cattle and sheep) on public lands in 14 western states. Represents the interests of public land ranchers before the U.S. Congress and the Executive Branch. Conducts specialized education and research programs. **Libraries: Type:** reference. **Holdings:** 500. **Telecommunication Services:** electronic mail, mbeal@beef.org. **Affiliated With:** American Sheep Industry Association. **Conventions/Meetings:** annual meeting.

5128 ■ Public Lands Foundation (PLF)
PO Box 7226
Arlington, VA 22207
Ph: (703)790-1988
Fax: (703)821-3490
E-mail: leaplf@erols.com
URL: http://www.publicland.org
Contact: George Lea, Pres.

Founded: 1985. **Membership Dues:** regular, $25 (annual). **State Groups:** 12. **Local Groups:** 6. **Description:** Retired members of the Bureau of Land Management (BLM); associate members are current employees and supporters of the BLM. Works to: keep public lands public; to increase public understanding of public lands and related issues by providing a "more balanced, non-political presentation of issues." Fosters effective management of public lands and natural resources under BLM management by supporting the use of professional, career employees. Promotes optimum implementation of the Federal Land Policy and Management Act of 1976. Conducts and sponsors research; maintains speakers' bureau. **Awards:** Outstanding Public Lands Professional Award. **Frequency:** annual. **Type:** recognition. **Publications:** *The Public Lands Monitor*, quarterly. Newsletter. **Price:** free for members ● Also publishes position statements and analytical papers. **Conventions/Meetings:** annual conference.

5129 ■ Sustainable Obtainable Solutions (SOS)
PO Box 1424
Helena, MT 59624
Ph: (406)495-0738
Fax: (406)495-9703
E-mail: ask_us@s-o-solutions.org
URL: http://www.s-o-solutions.org
Contact: Gloria Flora, Dir.

Founded: 2001. **Description:** Works to increase understanding of sustainability and the interrelationships of people and nature, especially on public lands. Seeks to ensure that current uses of public lands do not deny future generations the same benefits that people enjoy now. Helps concerned communities and organizations understand and apply systems thinking and sustainability criteria to their deliberations on the use of public lands. **Publications:** *Collaborative Spunk: The Feisty Guide for Reviving People and Our Planet*. Book. **Price:** $18. 00/copy.

Public Policy

5130 ■ Equestrian Land Conservation Resource (ELCR)
4037 Iron Works Pike, Ste.120
Lexington, KY 40511
Ph: (859)455-8383
Fax: (859)455-8381
E-mail: corr@elcr.org
URL: http://www.elcr.org
Contact: Carolyn L. Orr PhD, Acting Dir.

Founded: 1997. **Membership Dues:** basic, $25 ● field steward, $26-$49 ● meadow defender, $50-$99

● valley preserver, $100-$499 ● trails keeper, $500-$999 ● plains champion, $1,000-$2,499 ● foothills guardian, $2,500-$9,999 ● mountain conservator (minimum), $10,000. **Description:** Preserves access to open land for equestrian use across America. Acts as a clearinghouse for information concerning land protection, land use policy and equestrian land stewardship. Educates equestrians on the techniques of acquiring the permanent or long-term right to use land for equestrian activities. **Libraries: Type:** reference. **Publications:** Newsletter, quarterly. Includes issues on land access and protection.

Rabbits

5131 ■ American Belgian Hare Club (ABHC)

c/o Linda Telega
6456 Spencer Clark Rd.
Fowler, OH 44418
Ph: (330)722-2817
E-mail: ltelegat@aol.com
Contact: Linda Telega, Contact

Members: 60. **Membership Dues:** individual, $5 (annual). **Description:** Breeders promoting the exhibition and raising of Belgian hares. **Awards:** Sweepstakes. **Frequency:** annual. **Type:** trophy ● Top Five. **Frequency:** annual. **Type:** trophy. **Affiliated With:** American Rabbit Breeders Association. **Publications:** *The Spotlight*, quarterly. Newsletter. Lists show winners, sweepstakes standings, and letters from officers. **Advertising:** accepted. **Conventions/Meetings:** annual convention, held in conjunction with ARBA Convention (exhibits) - October or November.

5132 ■ American Checkered Giant Rabbit Club (ACGRC)

542 Aspen St. NW
Toledo, OR 97391
E-mail: cedwards@harborside.com
URL: http://www.acgrc.com
Contact: Danny Long, Pres.

Founded: 1919. **Members:** 300. **Membership Dues:** single, $15 (annual). **State Groups:** 15. **Description:** Works as a specialty club chartered by the American Rabbit Breeders Association (see separate entry). Breeders and exhibitors of checkered giant rabbits. **Libraries: Type:** open to the public. **Holdings:** articles. **Awards: Type:** recognition. **Computer Services:** database, membership history file ● database, membership list ● mailing lists, labels. **Telecommunication Services:** electronic mail, webmaster@acgrc.com. **Affiliated With:** American Rabbit Breeders Association. **Formerly:** (1959) American Checkered Giant Club. **Publications:** *Guide Book and Standard*, bimonthly. Newsletter ● *News Bulletin*, bimonthly. **Conventions/Meetings:** annual meeting, held in conjunction with ARBA ● show.

5133 ■ American Dutch Rabbit Club (ADRC)

c/o Barb Kline, Sec.-Treas.
4664 S C Rd. 591
New Riegel, OH 44853
Ph: (419)595-2050
E-mail: adrcsecretary@aol.com
URL: http://www.dutchrabbit.com
Contact: Barb Kline, Sec.-Treas.

Founded: 1939. **Members:** 900. **Membership Dues:** youth, $8 (annual) ● single adult, $10 (annual) ● husband/wife, $14 (annual) ● family, $20 (annual). **Description:** A specialty club chartered by the American Rabbit Breeders Association (see separate entry). Rabbit breeders interested in promoting the Dutch rabbit for show or commercially, for meat. Conducts annual sweepstakes to honor those with the highest number of points from year-round competitions. **Awards:** Hall of Fame. **Frequency:** annual. **Type:** recognition. **Recipient:** for service to Dutch rabbit and club. **Telecommunication Services:** electronic mail, mstremkowski@attwb.net. **Publications:** *Dutch Reporter*, quarterly. Newsletter. Features upcoming events, Dutch news and breeders. **Advertising:** accepted. Alternate Formats: online ● Also publishes guidebook. **Conventions/Meetings:** annual meeting, held in conjunction with the ARBA (exhibits) ● annual National Dutch Show.

5134 ■ American English Spot Rabbit Club (AESRC)

c/o Rosalie Berry, Sec.-Treas.
513 E Kent Rd.
Lubbock, TX 79403
Ph: (806)762-1918 (502)535-7051
E-mail: rosalie@berrypatch.net
URL: http://englishspots.8m.com
Contact: Rosalie Berry, Sec.-Treas.

Founded: 1924. **Members:** 180. **Membership Dues:** single adult, $10 (annual) ● youth, $7 (annual) ● rabbitry, $13 (annual). **Regional Groups:** 1. **State Groups:** 4. **Description:** Individuals interested in the progress and promotion of the English spot rabbit. Promotes the English Spot Sweepstakes (open and youth) and the National All-English Show Membership Contest. Conducts judging seminars in conjunction with the American Rabbit Breeders Association (see separate entry) convention. Offers children's services. Maintains hall of fame. **Libraries: Type:** open to the public. **Holdings:** articles. **Telecommunication Services:** electronic mail, onthespotrabbitry@hotmail.com. **Committees:** Hall of Fame; Standards. **Affiliated With:** American Rabbit Breeders Association. **Publications:** *Spot News*, quarterly. Newsletter. Contains group and general club information and question and answer section. **Price:** included in membership dues; $10.00/year for adults; $7.00/year for youth; $13.00/year for rabbitry or husband/wife. **Conventions/Meetings:** competition ● annual convention (exhibits) - October or November ● annual National All English Show - meeting - always Memorial Day weekend.

5135 ■ American Federation of New Zealand Rabbit Breeders (AFNZRB)

c/o John Neff
1351 Holder Ln.
Geneva, FL 32732
Ph: (407)349-0450
E-mail: newzealand1121@aol.com
URL: http://www.arba.net/nationalclub.htm
Contact: John Neff, Contact

Founded: 1918. **Members:** 2,000. **Membership Dues:** adult (new), husband/wife (renewal), Canadian (renewal), $14 (annual) ● husband/wife (new), Canadian (new), $16 (annual) ● family (new), $27 (annual) ● youth (new), adult (renewal), $12 (annual) ● foreign (new), $40 (annual) ● life, $240. **Staff:** 1. **State Groups:** 8. **Description:** Breeders and others united to promote the breeding and exhibition of New Zealand rabbits. Sponsors shows on local, state, and national levels annually. Compiles statistics; sponsors competitions. **Awards: Frequency:** annual. **Type:** scholarship. **Recipient:** to active showing member. **Affiliated With:** American Rabbit Breeders Association. **Publications:** *New Zealand Guidebook*, quinquennial. **Advertising:** accepted ● *New Zealand Times*, bimonthly. Newsletter. **Advertising:** accepted. Alternate Formats: online ● Also publishes articles. **Conventions/Meetings:** annual meeting (exhibits) - always fall ● annual trade show - always spring.

5136 ■ American Harlequin Rabbit Club (AHRC)

c/o Judy Bustle, Sec.-Treas.
132 Farmers Ln.
State Road, NC 28676
Ph: (336)874-7438 (812)843-5460
E-mail: rogrrabbit@webtv.net
URL: http://www.geocities.com/~harlies
Contact: Pam Granderson, Pres.

Founded: 1973. **Members:** 150. **Membership Dues:** regular, $5 (annual). **Staff:** 1. **Description:** Represents individuals interested in breeding and showing Harlequin rabbits. Promotes interest in Harlequin rabbits. **Libraries: Type:** reference. **Holdings:** archival material. **Awards: Type:** recognition. **Telecommunication Services:** electronic mail, carrollc@nb-net.nb.ca. **Committees:** Standards. **Affiliated With:** American Rabbit Breeders Association. **Publications:** *American Harlequin Rabbit Club 2001-2005 Official Guidebook*, quinquennial. **Price:** included in membership dues, available to members only ● *Harlequin Happenings*, bimonthly. Newsletter. **Price:** included in membership dues. **Conventions/Meetings:** annual show and meeting (exhibits).

5137 ■ American Himalayan Rabbit Association (AHRA)

c/o Errean Kratochvil, Sec.-Treas.
7715 Callan Ct.
New Port Richey, FL 34654
Ph: (727)847-1001
E-mail: himi1@yahoo.com
URL: http://ahra.himmie.net
Contact: Errean Kratochvil, Sec.-Treas.

Founded: 1931. **Members:** 250. **Membership Dues:** youth, $8 (annual) ● H&W, $12 (annual) ● adult, $10 (annual) ● family, $12 (annual). **Regional Groups:** 1. **State Groups:** 5. **Multinational. Description:** A specialty club of the American Rabbit Breeders Association. Individuals or families interested in raising the Himalayan rabbit as a pet or for show. Promotes the Himalayan rabbit. **Awards: Type:** recognition. **Affiliated With:** American Rabbit Breeders Association. **Publications:** *The Himmie News*, bimonthly. Newsletter. **Price:** free to members. **Advertising:** accepted. **Conventions/Meetings:** periodic competition ● semiannual meeting, held in conjunction with ARBA/with AHRA national show.

5138 ■ American Netherland Dwarf Rabbit Club (ANDRC)

c/o Sue Travis-Shutter, Sec.-Treas.
326 Travis Ln.
Rockwall, TX 75032
Ph: (925)687-7656
E-mail: webmaster@andrc.com
URL: http://www.andrc.com
Contact: Sue Travis-Shutter, Sec.-Treas.

Founded: 1970. **Members:** 1,600. **Membership Dues:** adult new, $15 ● adult renewal, $13 (annual) ● adult new, $40 ● adult renewal, $35 (triennial) ● youth (up to 18 years of age) new, $10 ● youth (up to 18 years of age) renewal, $8 (annual) ● youth (up to 18 years of age) new, $25 ● youth (up to 18 years of age) renewal, $20 (triennial) ● family (2 individuals) new, $20 ● family (2 individuals) renewal, $15 (annual) ● family (2 individuals) new, $45 ● family (2 individuals) renewal, $37 (triennial) ● family (3 plus individuals) new, $25 ● family (3 plus individuals) renewal, $20 (annual) ● family (3 plus individuals) new, $50 ● family (3 plus individuals) renewal, $42 (triennial). **Staff:** 3. **Budget:** $80,000. **Regional Groups:** 30. **Description:** Promotes breeding of American Netherland Dwarf rabbits. **Awards:** Best in Show. **Frequency:** annual. **Type:** recognition. **Recipient:** to the member who is the owner of the winning rabbit ● Darrell Bramhall Youth Scholarship. **Frequency:** annual. **Type:** scholarship. **Recipient:** to the member who has been in the club for three years and a graduating high school student. **Publications:** *Dwarf Digest*, quarterly. Magazine. **Price:** $3.00/issue for nonmembers; included in membership dues. **Circulation:** 1,500. **Advertising:** accepted. **Conventions/Meetings:** annual convention.

5139 ■ American Rabbit Breeders Association (ARBA)

PO Box 5667
Bloomington, IL 61702
Ph: (309)664-7500 (913)585-1434
Fax: (309)664-0941
E-mail: arbapost@aol.com
URL: http://www.arba.net
Contact: Brad Boyce, Exec. Dir.

Founded: 1910. **Members:** 32,000. **Membership Dues:** adult, $20 (annual) ● youth, $12 (annual) ● family, $20 (annual). **Staff:** 5. **State Groups:** 30. **Local Groups:** 900. **Description:** Promotes, encourages, and development of the domestic rabbit industry and fancy which includes registration, showing, pets, and commercial purposes. **Libraries: Type:** open to the public. **Subjects:** breeds of rabbits, cavies. **Awards:** Youth Scholarship. **Frequency:** annual. **Type:** scholarship. **Recipient:** for youth member. **Telecommunication Services:** electronic mail, arbainformation@aol.com. **Committees:** Advertising and Publicity; Commercial; Credentials; Research and Development; Resolutions; Show Rules; Standards; Youth. **Formerly:** (1923) National Breeders and Fanciers Association; (1928) American Pet Stock Association; (1934) American Rabbit and Cavy Breeders Association. **Publications:** *Domestic Rabbits*, bimonthly. Magazine. Features upcoming events, reports about rabbit and cavy news. **Price:** included in membership dues. **Circulation:** 20,000. **Advertising:** accepted ● *Official Guide to Raising Better Rabbits & Caview Rev. 2000*. Yearbook. Contains articles written by experienced breeders covering matters such as husbandry, rabbits and cavies. **Price:** $10.00 included in initial membership package ● *Standards of Perfection*. Book. Contains the standards of each recognized breed of rabbit and cavy, and photographs of rabbits. **Price:** $15.00 ● Yearbook. Contains lists of names and addresses of entire membership. **Price:** included in initial membership package ● Also publishes cookbook. **Conventions/Meetings:** annual convention (exhibits) - always October/November.

5140 ■ American Satin Rabbit Breeders' Association (ASRBA)

c/o Clarence Linsey, Sec.-Treas.
316 S Mahaffie
Olathe, KS 66061-4756
Ph: (913)764-1531
E-mail: clinsey@mnu.edu
URL: http://www.asrba.com
Contact: Clarence Linsey, Sec.-Treas.

Founded: 1946. **Members:** 1,000. **Membership Dues:** individual, $15 (annual) ● couple, $17 (annual) ● youth, $13 (annual) ● family, $19 (annual). **State Groups:** 20. **Description:** Represents breeders of satin rabbits. Works to promote and improve satin rabbits. Sponsors competitions; compiles statistics. Conducts specialized education and research programs. **Awards:** **Type:** recognition. **Committees:** Standards. **Publications:** *Satin News*, bimonthly. Newsletter ● *Satin Standards and Guide Book*, quinquennial. **Conventions/Meetings:** annual National All Satin Show - always April or May.

5141 ■ American Standard Chinchilla Rabbit Breeders Association (ASCRBA)

c/o Patricia Gest, Sec.-Treas.
1607 9th St. W
Palmetto, FL 34221
Ph: (941)729-1184
E-mail: cgest@aol.com
URL: http://www.arba.net
Contact: Patricia Gest, Sec.-Treas.

Founded: 1949. **Members:** 80. **Membership Dues:** adult, $8 (annual) ● youth, $5 (annual) ● husband/wife, $12 (annual) ● life, $100. **Staff:** 1. **Regional Groups:** 3. **Description:** A specialty club chartered by the American Rabbit Breeders Association (see separate entry). Breeders of standard chinchilla rabbits. Presents Youth Sweepstake Points trophies and Adult Sweepstakes Points trophies. **Additional Websites:** http://www.freewebs.com/ascrba/index.htm. **Affiliated With:** American Rabbit Breeders Association. **Formerly:** (1959) American Standard Chinchilla Association; (2007) American Standard Chinchilla Rabbit Association. **Publications:** Newsletter, quarterly. **Advertising:** accepted. **Conventions/Meetings:** annual meeting, in conjunction with the ARBA.

5142 ■ Californian Rabbit Specialty Club (CRSC)

c/o Donald Mersiovsky, Sec.-Treas.
1156 Elm Grove Spur
Belton, TX 76513
Ph: (254)939-0345 (517)851-7337
E-mail: secretary@nationalcalclub.com
URL: http://www.nationalcalclub.com
Contact: Darrell Howe, Pres.

Founded: 1946. **Members:** 900. **Membership Dues:** adult, $10 (annual) ● husband, wife, $15 (annual) ● youth, $5 (annual). **State Groups:** 15. **Description:** Serves as a specialty club chartered by the American Rabbit Breeders Association (see separate entry). Represents individuals interested in the Californian rabbit. Promotes the Californian rabbit for show, hobby, and meat production. Conducts educational programs and children's services. **Libraries:** **Type:** reference. **Holdings:** archival material. **Awards:** **Type:** recognition. **Telecommunication Services:** electronic mail, ddhowe@fnwusers.com. **Publications:** *Californian Rabbit Guide Book* ● *Californian Rabbit News*, quarterly. Newsletter. Includes show reports. **Price:** included in membership dues. **Circulation:** 1,500. **Advertising:** accepted. **Conventions/Meetings:** competition ● annual conference (exhibits).

5143 ■ Champagne d'Argent Rabbit Federation (CDRF)

Address Unknown since 2008

Founded: 1921. **Members:** 300. **Description:** Breeders of Champagne D'Argent rabbits. Encourages the breeding of the Champagne D'Argent rabbit and the improvement of the breed. Conducts research. Encourages and educates prospective breeders. **Awards:** **Type:** recognition. **Affiliated With:** American Rabbit Breeders Association. **Formerly:** Champagne d'Argent Federation. **Publications:** *Champagne News*, monthly. Newsletter ● Directory, annual. **Conventions/Meetings:** competition ● annual meeting - always fall.

5144 ■ Cinnamon Rabbit Breeders Association (CRBA)

c/o Nancy Searle
550 Amherst Rd.
Belchertown, MA 01007
Ph: (413)253-7721
E-mail: nsearle@umext.umass.edu
URL: http://www.arba.net/nationalclub.htm
Contact: Nancy Searle, Contact

Founded: 1977. **Members:** 20. **Membership Dues:** adult ($4 for youth), $8 (annual) ● family (plus $2 for each youth), $12 (annual). **Description:** A specialty club of the American Rabbit Breeders Association (see separate entry). Breeders of Cinnamon rabbits, which are cinnamon-colored commercial rabbits with smoke grey tickings on the back and midsection and circles of dark color around the eyes. Promotes the breed; disseminates information about the breed to members. Sponsors competitions; bestows awards; compiles statistics. **Publications:** *Cinnamon News*, quarterly. Newsletter. **Price:** $4.00/year. **Conventions/Meetings:** annual meeting, held in conjunction with ARBA - always fall.

5145 ■ Havana Rabbit Breeders Association (HRBA)

c/o Julia Rittenour, Sec.-Treas.
5554 Old State Rd.
Whittemore, MI 48770
Ph: (989)387-5095
E-mail: jrpalace@hotmail.com
URL: http://www.arba.net/nationalclub.htm
Contact: Julia Rittenour, Sec.-Treas.

Founded: 1925. **Members:** 225. **Membership Dues:** youth, $6 (annual) ● adult, $8 (annual) ● family (plus $3.50 per youth at the same address), $11 (annual). **Description:** A specialty club chartered by the American Rabbit Breeders Association (see separate entry). Breeders of the Havana rabbit united to advance the breed and promote cooperation among breeders. Sanctions over 500 shows annually; presents trophies. **Affiliated With:** American Rabbit Breeders Association. **Publications:** Newsletter, bimonthly. **Price:** for members. **Advertising:** accepted ● Also publishes reports and notices. **Conventions/Meetings:** annual All-Havana Rabbit Show - meeting (exhibits).

5146 ■ Holland Lop Rabbit Specialty Club (HLRSC)

2633 Seven Eleven Rd.
Chesapeake, VA 23322
Ph: (757)421-9607
E-mail: hlrscsec@aol.com
URL: http://www.hlrsc.com
Contact: Pandora Allen, Sec.

Founded: 1980. **Members:** 1,200. **Membership Dues:** adult, $15 (annual) ● youth, $12 (annual) ● combination, $19 (annual) ● family, $22 (annual). **Description:** Owners and breeders of Holland lop rabbits. Promotes the Holland lop rabbit and seeks to educate members concerning the animal's care and breeding. Sponsors competitions. **Awards:** **Type:** recognition. **Affiliated With:** American Rabbit Breeders Association. **Publications:** *Holland Lop Guide Book*, quarterly. Breed and club information included. **Price:** free for members. **Advertising:** accepted ● *Hollander*, quarterly. **Conventions/Meetings:** annual meeting.

5147 ■ Hotot Rabbit Breeders International (HRBI)

c/o Laurie Staley-Jones, Sec.-Treas.
51 S Olive Church Rd.
Paragon, IN 46166
E-mail: lazyslops@yahoo.com
URL: http://www.geocities.com/blancdehototclub
Contact: Michelle Sauerwein, Pres.

Founded: 1979. **Members:** 60. **Membership Dues:** individual, $10 (annual) ● husband-wife, $14 (annual) ● youth (18 and under), $5 (annual). **Description:** A specialty club chartered by the American Rabbit Breeders Association (see separate entry). Rabbit breeders and others interested in promoting and developing the hotot rabbit breed. (The Hotot originated in France in the early 1900s and was first imported into the U.S. in 1978. Raised primarily for breeding purposes, the hotot is white with black bands encircling brown eyes.) Compiles statistics. **Awards:** **Type:** recognition. **Affiliated With:** American Rabbit Breeders Association. **Publications:** *Hotot International News*, quarterly. Newsletter. **Conventions/Meetings:** competition ● annual meeting, held in conjunction with ARBA (exhibits).

5148 ■ Lop Rabbit Club of America (LRCA)

c/o Jeanne Welch, Sec.-Treas.
PO Box 236
Hornbrook, CA 96044
Ph: (530)475-3371
E-mail: lrcasecretary@aol.com
URL: http://www.lrca.net
Contact: Jeanne Welch, Sec.-Treas.

Founded: 1971. **Members:** 1,000. **Membership Dues:** adult (new), $11 ● husband/wife (new), $15 ● youth (new), $10 ● adult (renewal), $8 (annual) ● husband/wife (renewal), $12 (annual) ● youth (renewal), $7 (annual). **Staff:** 1. **Description:** A specialty club chartered by the American Rabbit Breeders Association (see separate entry). Breeders, exhibitors, and fanciers of French and English lops. **Awards:** Sweepstakes. **Frequency:** annual. **Type:** recognition. **Affiliated With:** American Rabbit Breeders Association. **Publications:** *Guidebook*, quinquennial. Journal. **Price:** included in membership dues. **Circulation:** 600. **Advertising:** accepted ● *Lop Digest*, quarterly. Newsletter. **Price:** included in membership dues. **Conventions/Meetings:** semiannual competition and meeting, club business (exhibits) - spring and fall.

5149 ■ Mini Lop Rabbit Club of America (MLRCA)

c/o Pennie Grotheer, Sec.-Treas.
PO Box 17
Pittsburg, KS 66762
Ph: (417)842-3317
Fax: (417)842-3217
E-mail: minilop@tiadon.com
URL: http://www.minilop.org
Contact: Pennie Grotheer, Sec.-Treas.

Founded: 1979. **Members:** 900. **Membership Dues:** youth, $10 (annual) ● adult, $15 (annual) ● husband, wife, $18 (annual) ● family, $20 (annual). **Staff:** 1. **Regional Groups:** 9. **Description:** Owners of mini lop rabbits. Promotes the breed, which has long, horseshoe-shaped ears that hang down the sides of the head instead of standing upright. Encourages fellowship among those interested in the breed as pets and show animals. **Awards:** District Breeder of the Year. **Frequency:** annual. **Type:** recognition ● Sweepstakes. **Frequency:** annual. **Type:** recognition ● Top Lop. **Frequency:** annual. **Type:** recognition. **Publications:** *The Advocate*, quarterly. Newsletter. **Advertising:** accepted ● *Membership List*, periodic. **Conventions/Meetings:** annual Rabbit Show -

competition and show, held in conjunction with American Rabbit Breeders Association - fall and spring.

5150 ■ National Angora Rabbit Breeders Club (NARBC)
c/o Margaret Bartold, VP
909 Hwy. E
Silex, MO 63377
Ph: (573)384-5866
E-mail: fantasylandangoras@yahoo.com
URL: http://www.nationalangorarabbitbreeders.com
Contact: Beverly DeVone, Sec.

Founded: 1965. **Members:** 800. **Membership Dues:** single youth, $5 (annual) ● single adult, $10 (annual) ● one rabbitry, $15 (annual) ● family, $20 (annual). **Regional Groups:** 9. **State Groups:** 11. **Description:** Breeders and fanciers of Angora rabbits. Plans to: serve as a forum for exchange of ideas among members; help young people interested in breeding Angora rabbits; show Angoras at all rabbit shows; sponsor annual all-Angora show. Assists cottage industry promotion of wool. Compiles statistics. **Awards:** President's Award. **Frequency:** annual. **Type:** recognition. **Computer Services:** Mailing lists. **Committees:** Commercial; Show Rules; Standards; Sweepstakes. **Publications:** *Angora News*, quarterly. Newsletter. **Price:** included in membership dues. **Circulation:** 1,000. **Advertising:** accepted ● *NARBC Fiber Guide*. Book. **Price:** $11.50 plus shipping and handling ● *NARBC Guidebook on Angoras*. **Conventions/Meetings:** competition ● annual convention (exhibits).

5151 ■ National Federation of Flemish Giant Rabbit Breeders (NFFGRB)
c/o Judith Welch, Sec.-Treas.
1460 McGill Hollow Rd.
Linden, PA 17744-7722
Ph: (570)321-1013
E-mail: flemishsec@aol.com
URL: http://www.nffgrb.com
Contact: Judith Welch, Sec.-Treas.

Founded: 1915. **Members:** 500. **Membership Dues:** single, $10 (annual) ● husband/wife, $15 (annual) ● family (plus $2/child), $20 (annual). **Staff:** 1. **Regional Groups:** 4. **State Groups:** 5. **Description:** Breeders of purebred Flemish giant rabbits. Promotes and works to improve Flemish giant rabbits; disseminates information to members; encourages the exhibition of all varieties of Flemish giant rabbits. **Awards: Type:** recognition. **Affiliated With:** American Rabbit Breeders Association. **Formerly:** (1959) National Federation of Flemish Giant Breeders. **Publications:** *Breeders Directory*. **Price:** free for members. Alternate Formats: online ● *Membership List*, annual. Membership Directory ● Newsletter, quarterly. **Price:** included in membership dues. Alternate Formats: online ● Also publishes guidebook. **Conventions/Meetings:** competition (exhibits) ● annual meeting, held in conjunction with the ARBA.

5152 ■ National Jersey Wooly Rabbit Club (NJWRC)
c/o Amanda Pitsch, Sec.
PO Box 264
Marne, MI 49435
Ph: (616)498-2330
E-mail: amanda@pitschfork.com
URL: http://www.njwrc.net
Contact: Lisa Smith, Pres.

Founded: 1986. **Members:** 700. **Membership Dues:** adult, $14 (annual) ● youth, $9 (annual). **Regional Groups:** 9. **Multinational. Description:** Promotes the Jersey Wooly rabbit breed. **Committees:** Constitution and By-Laws; Guidebook; Newsletter; Promotions/Sales and Advertisements; Standard; Sweepstakes; Youth. **Publications:** *Breeders' Color Registry* ● *Guidebook*. Features information on rabbit management, breeding, grooming, and showing. **Price:** included in membership dues ● Newsletter, quarterly. Contains informative articles, photos, club activities, district directors' articles, and results. **Price:** included in membership dues. **Conventions/Meetings:** annual Membership Contest - competition ● annual National Show and Convention - specialty show - held in spring ● annual Sweepstakes Contest - competition.

5153 ■ National Lilac Rabbit Club of America (NLRCA)
c/o Chris Schmidt, Sec.-Treas.
771 E-1000S
Warren, IN 46792
Ph: (260)375-2892
E-mail: clddsch@hotmail.com
URL: http://www.geocities.com/nlrca2002
Contact: Chris Schmidt, Sec.-Treas.

Founded: 1960. **Members:** 75. **Membership Dues:** youth, $4 (annual) ● family, $8 (annual). **Description:** A specialty club of the American Rabbit Breeders Association (see separate entry). Represents owners of lilac rabbits. Promotes the lilac rabbit breed. Compiles statistics. **Awards: Type:** recognition. **Telecommunication Services:** electronic mail, bobkoch@execpc.com. **Affiliated With:** American Rabbit Breeders Association. **Publications:** *Lilac Club Newsletter*, quarterly ● *The National Lilac Club Report*, quarterly. **Conventions/Meetings:** competition ● annual meeting and show, held in conjunction with ARBA (exhibits).

5154 ■ National Mini Rex Rabbit Club (NMRRC)
c/o Doug King, Sec.-Treas.
2719 Terrace Ave.
Sanger, CA 93657
Ph: (559)787-2588
E-mail: kingsminirex@msn.com
URL: http://www.nmrrc.com
Contact: Joey Shults, Pres.

Founded: 1985. **Members:** 1,500. **Membership Dues:** individual, youth, $15 (annual) ● husband/wife, $20 (annual) ● family, individual/youth outside U.S., $30 (annual) ● husband/wife outside U.S., $40 (annual) ● family outside U.S., $60 (annual) ● individual, youth, $40 (triennial) ● husband/wife, $50 (triennial) ● family, $75 (triennial) ● individual, youth outside U.S., $80 (triennial) ● husband/wife outside U.S., $100 (triennial) ● family outside U.S., $150 (triennial). **Multinational. Description:** Promotes and represents the Mini Rex rabbit. **Awards:** Youth Scholarship. **Frequency:** annual. **Type:** scholarship. **Recipient:** for a graduating/first year college youth member of the club. **Publications:** *Dwarfism in Mini Rex Rabbits*. Article ● *Guidebook*. **Price:** included in membership dues ● Newsletter. **Price:** included in membership dues. **Conventions/Meetings:** convention ● annual specialty show.

5155 ■ National Rex Rabbit Club (NRRC)
c/o Arlyse DeLoyola, Sec.-Treas.
117 Allegheny Ct.
San Marcos, TX 78666
Ph: (512)392-6033
E-mail: deloyola@centurytel.net
URL: http://www.nationalrexrc.com
Contact: Arlyse DeLoyola, Sec.-Treas.

Founded: 1958. **Members:** 600. **Membership Dues:** individual (in U.S.), $15 (annual) ● individual (outside U.S.), $25 (annual) ● individual (renewal in U.S.), $10 (annual) ● individual (renewal outside U.S.), $20 (annual). **Description:** Breeders of rex rabbits. Promotes the rex rabbit breed, whose fur is used for commercial purposes. Holds rabbit shows; sponsors competitions. **Awards:** Youth Scholarship Award. **Frequency:** annual. **Type:** scholarship. **Recipient:** for the outstanding member of the National Rex Rabbit Club. **Affiliated With:** American Rabbit Breeders Association. **Publications:** *Rex World*, quarterly. Magazine ● *World of Rex Booklet* ● Yearbook, annual. **Conventions/Meetings:** semiannual meeting.

5156 ■ National Silver Rabbit Club (NSRC)
c/o Laura Atkins, Sec.-Treas.
1030 SW KK Hwy.
Holden, MO 64040
Ph: (816)732-6208
E-mail: silverabt@yahoo.com
URL: http://natlsilverrabbitclub.tripod.com
Contact: Laura Atkins, Sec.-Treas.

Founded: 1972. **Members:** 75. **Membership Dues:** open, $7 (annual) ● youth, $5 (annual) ● family, $12 (annual). **Description:** A specialty club of the American Rabbit Breeders Association (see separate entry). Owners of silver rabbits. Promotes and improves the silver rabbit breed. Sponsors national and local rabbit shows; maintains speakers' bureau; compiles statistics. **Libraries: Type:** reference. **Holdings:** archival material, audiovisuals. **Subjects:** silver rabbits, club records. **Awards:** Sweepstakes. **Frequency:** annual. **Type:** recognition. **Telecommunication Services:** electronic mail, tnthavanas@mcmays.com. **Affiliated With:** American Rabbit Breeders Association. **Publications:** *Membership List*, periodic. Membership Directory ● *Silver Bullet*, quarterly. Newsletter. Covers communication between breeders, show reports, sweepstakes rankings, upcoming shows, and ARBA and association news. **Price:** included in membership dues; one free copy upon request from nonmembers. **Circulation:** 75. **Advertising:** accepted. **Conventions/Meetings:** competition ● annual show, held in conjunction with ARBA - always spring.

5157 ■ North American Lionhead Rabbit Club (NALRC)
c/o Arden Wetzel, Sec.
23657 140th Ave.
Milaca, MN 56353
Ph: (320)983-5715
E-mail: awwetzel03@frontiernet.net
URL: http://www.lionhead.us
Contact: Arden Wetzel, Sec.

Founded: 2001. **Members:** 150. **Membership Dues:** single adult, $15 (annual) ● single adult, $35 (triennial) ● single youth, $10 (annual) ● single youth, $25 (triennial) ● group, $20 (annual) ● group, $50 (triennial). **Multinational. Description:** Promotes the breeding, showing, advancement and development of the Lionhead rabbit. Works to advance the Lionhead rabbit to breed status with the American Rabbit Breeders Association. Cooperates with the American Rabbit Breeders Association in all matters of national policy. **Publications:** *The Mane Musing*, quarterly. Newsletter. **Price:** included in membership dues. **Advertising:** accepted ● *Official Guide Book*. **Price:** included in membership dues ● Newspaper. Alternate Formats: online.

5158 ■ Palomino Rabbit Co-Breeders Association (PRCBA)
c/o Deb Morrison, Sec.
396202 W 4000 Rd.
Skiatook, OK 74070
Ph: (918)396-3587
E-mail: morepals@aol.com
URL: http://www.geocities.com/petsburgh/park/4198
Contact: Deb Morrison, Sec.

Founded: 1953. **Members:** 166. **Membership Dues:** adult, $8 (annual) ● youth, $5 (annual) ● husband/wife or 2 adults at same address, $12 (annual) ● family of 2 adults (plus 2.50/youth at same address), $12 (annual) ● family of 1 adult (plus 2.50/youth at same address), $8 (annual) ● foreign (extra/person), $2 (annual). **Description:** Breeders, exhibitors, and owners of Golden and Lynx Palomino rabbits. Promotes the development of Palomino rabbits, a breed used for meat and show. **Awards: Frequency:** annual. **Type:** recognition. **Affiliated With:** American Rabbit Breeders Association. **Publications:** *PAL News*, quarterly. Newsletter. **Price:** included in membership dues. **Circulation:** 110. **Advertising:** accepted. **Conventions/Meetings:** annual meeting, held in conjunction with American Rabbit Breeders Association (exhibits) ● annual National All Pal Show.

5159 ■ Rhinelander Rabbit Club of America (RRCA)
c/o Linda Carter, Sec.-Treas.
1560 Vine St.
El Centro, CA 92243
Ph: (530)432-3964

E-mail: cartersdesert1@juno.com
URL: http://www.hop.to/rhinelanders
Contact: Linda Carter, Sec.-Treas.
Members: 70. **Membership Dues:** adult, $10 (annual) ● husband and wife, $15 (annual) ● youth, $6 (annual). **Description:** Represents persons who are interested in and who breed Rhinelander rabbits. **Publications:** *The Calico Chronicle*, quarterly. Newsletter. Alternate Formats: online.

5160 ■ Silver Marten Rabbit Club (SMRC)
c/o Leslie Tucker, Sec.-Treas.
2113 Sommer St.
Napa, CA 94559
Ph: (707)255-2821
E-mail: ltucker@silvermarten.com
URL: http://www.silvermarten.com
Contact: Larry Peralta, Pres.
Members: 200. **Membership Dues:** single adult, $12 (annual) ● husband and wife (plus $3/youth), $16 (annual) ● single youth (under 19), $9 (annual). **Staff:** 1. **Description:** Breeders of Silver Marten rabbits. Promotes the rabbit breeding industry; strives to improve the Silver Marten rabbit. Works with youth and 4-H clubs and state Silver Marten clubs. Conducts seminars. **Conventions/Meetings:** annual meeting, held in conjunction with American Rabbit Breeders Association.

Radiation

5161 ■ International Commission on Radiation Units and Measurements (ICRU)
7910 Woodmont Ave., Ste.400
Bethesda, MD 20814-3076
Ph: (301)657-2652
Fax: (301)907-8768
E-mail: icru@icru.org
URL: http://www.icru.org
Contact: Patricia Russell, Exec. Sec.
Founded: 1925. **Members:** 15. **Staff:** 2. **Description:** Commission members, senior advisors, consultants, and representatives of report committees in 12 countries. Develops internationally acceptable recommendations regarding: quantities and units of radiation and radionuclides; procedures suitable for the measurement and application of these quantities in clinical radiology and radiobiology; physical data needed in the application of these procedures, the use of which tends to assure uniformity in reporting. The commission has divided its field of interest into 15 technical areas. **Libraries: Type:** open to the public. **Holdings:** 8,000. **Subjects:** selected topics in radiation protection. **Awards:** ICRU Gray Medal. **Type:** recognition. **Recipient:** for outstanding contributions in scientific fields of interest to ICRU. **Programs:** Diagnostic Radiology and Nuclear Medicine; Radiation in Science; Radiation Protection; Radiation Therapy. **Affiliated With:** International Society of Radiology. **Formerly:** (1931) International X-Ray Unit Committee; (1950) International Committee for Radiological Units; (1956) International Commission on Radiological Units; (1965) International Commission on Radiological Units and Measurements. **Publications:** *ICRU News*, periodic. Newsletter. Contains scientific papers and information of interest. ISSN: 1473-6691. Alternate Formats: online ● *ICRU Reports*, periodic ● *Journal of the ICRU*, semiannual. **Conventions/Meetings:** annual conference, attendance by invitation only, reviews scientific program.

Rain Forests

5162 ■ International Society for Preservation of the Tropical Rainforest (ISPTR)
c/o Roxanne Kremer, Exec. Dir./Founder
3302 N Burton Ave.
Rosemead, CA 91770
Ph: (626)572-0233
Fax: (626)572-9521
E-mail: pard_expeditions@yahoo.com
URL: http://www.isptr-pard.org
Contact: Roxanne Kremer, Exec. Dir./Founder
Founded: 1986. **Members:** 100. **Membership Dues:** regular, $35 (annual). **Regional Groups:** 2. **Languages:** English, Spanish. **Multinational. Description:** Pilots projects and sustainable development in the Amazon rainforest. Combats illegal activity by commercial interests overfishing rivers, poaching, and logging. Provides free medical clinic to 20 from "Dolphin Corners" communities in Upper Amazon Lodge, Peru. **Libraries: Type:** not open to the public. **Publications:** *Amazon Frontline*. Newsletter.

5163 ■ Pachamama Alliance
PO Box 29191
San Francisco, CA 94129-9191
Ph: (415)561-4522
Fax: (415)561-4521
E-mail: info@pachamama.org
URL: http://www.pachamama.org
Contact: Bill Twist, Pres.
Multinational. Description: Aims to address the issues concerning efforts to conserve and maintain the tropical rainforests in the Amazon region of Ecuador. Provides access to technical expertise and funding in supporting the Achuar, an indigenous group living in the Amazon basin in southeastern Ecuador. Collaborates with the leaders of remote indigenous groups in the Amazon region of Ecuador. **Publications:** *New Moon Update*, monthly. Newsletter. Alternate Formats: online ● Annual Report, annual. Alternate Formats: online.

5164 ■ Rainforest Relief
PO Box 298
New York, NY 10008-0298
Ph: (917)543-4064
E-mail: info@rainforestrelief.org
URL: http://www.rainforestrelief.org
Contact: Tim Keating, Exec. Dir.
Founded: 1989. **Description:** Works to end the loss of the world's tropical and temperate rainforests. Protects the human and non-human inhabitants by reducing the demand for the products of rainforest logging, mining and agricultural conversion. **Computer Services:** Information services, rainforests resources ● mailing lists. **Telecommunication Services:** electronic mail, relief@rainforestrelief.org. **Projects:** Forest Banana. **Publications:** *Raindrops*, 3/year. Newsletter. Alternate Formats: online ● *Stealing Home*. Report. Alternate Formats: online.

Rangeland

5165 ■ American Forage and Grassland Council (AFGC)
350 Poplar Ave.
Elmhurst, IL 60126
Ph: (630)941-3240
Free: (800)944-AFGC
Fax: (630)359-4274
E-mail: info@afgc.org
URL: http://www.afgc.org
Contact: Michael J. Brandy, Assoc. Dir.
Founded: 1944. **Members:** 6,000. **Membership Dues:** individual, $30 (annual) ● student, $5 (annual) ● affiliate council (per member), $10 (annual) ● corporate copper, $250 (annual) ● corporate bronze, $500 (annual) ● corporate silver, $750 (annual) ● corporate gold, $1,000 (annual) ● corporate platinum, $2,500 (annual). **Budget:** $90,000. **State Groups:** 33. **Description:** Federation of agricultural associations and individuals interested in grassland farming and dedicated to the production and utilization of quality forage. Coordinates and distributes new information on grassland farming. Maintains speakers' bureau. **Awards: Frequency:** annual. **Type:** recognition. **Committees:** Awards; Corporate Liaison; Forage Leader; Forage Progress; International Organizational Liaison; Publicity/Promotion; Research; Ways and Means. **Affiliated With:** American Dairy Science Association; American Seed Trade Association; American Society of Agricultural and Biological Engineers; National Hay Association; Potash and Phosphate Institute; Society for Range Management; The Sulphur Institute. **Formerly:** (1958) Joint Committee on Grassland Farming; (1966) American Grassland Council. **Publications:** *Forage and Grassland Conference Proceedings*, annual. **Price:** $25.00 plus shipping and handling ● *The Forage Leader*, quarterly. Magazine. Contains articles and information of general interest to producers. **Price:** free for members ● Books. Provides information on good grassland farming practices. ● Membership Directory, annual ● Newsletter, quarterly. **Conventions/Meetings:** annual competition (exhibits) ● annual conference (exhibits).

5166 ■ Society for Range Management (SRM)
10030 W 27th Ave.
Wheat Ridge, CO 80215-6601
Ph: (303)986-3309 (406)677-0247
Fax: (303)986-3892
E-mail: info@rangelands.org
URL: http://www.rangelands.org
Contact: Jason Campbell, Exec. VP
Founded: 1948. **Members:** 3,500. **Membership Dues:** regular, $85 ● student, $35 ● institutional, $205 ● commercial, $525 ● life, $1,500 ● life family, $1,750. **Staff:** 7. **Budget:** $1,000,000. **Regional Groups:** 21. **State Groups:** 21. **Local Groups:** 22. **Description:** Professional international society of scientists, technicians, ranchers, administrators, teachers, and students interested in the study, use, and management of rangeland resources for livestock, wildlife, watershed, and recreation. **Libraries: Type:** reference. **Subjects:** range management. **Awards:** Masonic-Range Science Scholarship. **Frequency:** annual. **Type:** scholarship. **Telecommunication Services:** electronic mail, lradtke@rangelands.org. **Committees:** Coordinated Resource Management; Employment Affairs; Excellence in Range Management; History, Archives, and Library; Honor Awards; Information and Education; International Affairs; Leadership Development; Professional Affairs; Public Affairs; Rangeland Assessment and Monitoring; Remote Sensing/GIS; Research Affairs; Student Affairs; Technology Transfer; Wildlife Habitat. **Programs:** Conservation Research. **Task Forces:** Endangered Species. **Formerly:** International Society for Range Management; (1971) American Society of Range Management. **Publications:** *Rangeland Ecology and Management*, bimonthly. Journal. Includes information on topics such as range plant physiology, range improvement and revegetation, range livestock, and wildlife nutrition. **Price:** $40.00 for members; price varies for non-members. ISSN: 1551-5028. **Circulation:** 4,000. **Advertising:** accepted. Alternate Formats: microform; online. Also Cited As: *Journal of Range Management* ● *Rangeland News*, monthly. Newsletters. **Advertising:** accepted. Alternate Formats: online ● *Rangelands*, bimonthly. Magazine. Contains annual index, legislative updates, nontechnical articles, and lists of current literature and employment opportunities. **Price:** free for members; price varies for nonmembers. ISSN: 1551-501X. **Circulation:** 4,000. **Advertising:** accepted. Alternate Formats: online ● Also publishes papers. **Conventions/Meetings:** annual meeting (exhibits).

Recreation

5167 ■ Tread Lightly!
298 24th St., Ste.325
Ogden, UT 84401
Ph: (801)627-0077
Free: (800)966-9900
Fax: (801)621-8633
E-mail: treadlightly@treadlightly.org
URL: http://www.treadlightly.org
Contact: Lori Davis, Exec. Dir.
Membership Dues: individual, $25 (annual) ● retailer/outfitter, $50 (annual) ● dealer, $150 (annual) ● club, $100 (annual) ● official partner club, $250 (annual). **Description:** Aims to construct and restore recreational sites across the country. Empowers generations to enjoy the outdoors responsibly through

education and restoration. Furthers the goals of responsible and ethical recreation. Offers educational materials, training courses and restoration opportunities. **Publications:** *Trails*, semiannual. Newsletter. Alternate Formats: online.

Recycling

5168 ■ Association of Lighting and Mercury Recyclers (ALMR)
c/o Paul Abernathy, Exec. Dir.
2436 Foothill Blvd., Ste.B
Calistoga, CA 94515
Ph: (707)942-2197
Fax: (707)942-2198
E-mail: mail@almr.org
URL: http://www.almr.org
Contact: Paul Abernathy, Exec. Dir.
Description: Represents the majority of the commercial processors of mercury-bearing wastes in the US. Assists in collecting, processing, recycling and recovery of spent mercury lamps, ballast, batteries, electronic products and other wastes with hazardous levels of mercury throughout North America. Identifies, develops and expands market opportunities for recycling products that contain mercury. **Computer Services:** Information services, mercury recycling resources. **Projects:** Lamp Recycling Outreach. **Publications:** Newsletter. Alternate Formats: online.

Reptiles

5169 ■ Global Gecko Association (GGA)
c/o Leann Christenson, Membership Sec.
1155 Cameron Cove Cir.
Leeds, AL 35094
E-mail: membership@gekkota.com
URL: http://www.gekkota.com
Contact: Leann Christenson, Membership Sec.
Membership Dues: individual/family (in U.S.), $32 (annual) ● individual/family (in Canada and Mexico), $34 (annual) ● individual/family (overseas), $36 (annual) ● student, $15 (annual) ● institutional, $45 (annual) ● contributing, $50 (annual) ● patron, $250 (annual) ● life, $1,000. **Multinational. Description:** Promotes general interest, education, and conservation of Gekkota globally. Acts for the protection of habitats related to Gekkonids. Encourages responsible academic research regarding Gekkonids. Provides a vehicle for the exchange and sharing of resources, information, and ideas relating to all aspects of Gekkota. Facilitates closer cooperation between those interested in Gekkonids at both the amateur and professional level. **Publications:** *Chit-Chat*, quarterly. Newsletter. Contains GGA information, reviews of current gecko literature, veterinary advice, and Gecko News from around the world. **Price:** included in membership dues. **Advertising:** accepted ● *Gekko*, semiannual. Journal. Contains articles and papers, book reviews and interviews. **Advertising:** accepted.

Restaurant

5170 ■ Green Restaurant Association
89 South St., Ste.LL02
Boston, MA 02111
Ph: (858)452-7378
E-mail: gra@dinegreen.com
URL: http://www.dinegreen.com
Founded: 1990. **Description:** Strives to help restaurants become more environmentally sustainable in ways that are convenient and cost effective. Focuses on research, environmental consulting, education, public relations and marketing, and community organizing and consumer activism.

Seafood

5171 ■ Marine Stewardship Council (MSC)
2110 N Pacific St., Ste.102
Seattle, WA 98103
Ph: (206)691-0188
Fax: (206)691-0190
E-mail: jim.humphreys@msc.org
URL: http://www.msc.org
Contact: Jim Humphreys, Regional Dir.
Founded: 1997. **Languages:** English, French, Spanish. **Description:** Works to enhance responsible management of seafood resources, ensure sustainability of global fish stocks and health of marine ecosystems.

5172 ■ Shrimp Council
7918 Jones Br. Dr., Ste.700
McLean, VA 22102
Ph: (703)524-8880
E-mail: info@eatshrimp.com
URL: http://www.eatshrimp.com/about/contact_us.cfm
Staff: 18. **Budget:** $3,000,000. **Description:** Those involved in the shrimp industry. **Awards:** Finesse Awards. **Frequency:** annual. **Type:** recognition.

Seed

5173 ■ American Seed Research Foundation (ASRF)
225 Reinekers Ln., Ste.650
Alexandria, VA 22314-2875
Ph: (703)837-8140
Fax: (703)837-9365
URL: http://www.amseed.com/asrf
Contact: Suzanne R. Nicoles, Sec.-Treas.
Founded: 1959. **Members:** 100. **Membership Dues:** business (based on annual gross sales), $200-$8,500 (annual) ● equipment company, $500 (annual) ● state/regional seed association, $300 (annual). **Budget:** $45,000. **Description:** Breeders, producers, and distributors of seeds. Seeks to advance seed technology by supporting research on seeds. **Libraries: Type:** reference. **Holdings:** 47; periodicals, reports. **Subjects:** seed research. **Publications:** *Search*, annual. Journal. Describes research projects funded by grants. **Price:** free. **Conventions/Meetings:** annual general assembly and meeting - usually June.

5174 ■ American Seed Trade Association (ASTA)
225 Reinekers Ln., Ste.650
Alexandria, VA 22314-2875
Ph: (703)837-8140
Free: (888)890-SEED
Fax: (703)837-9365
E-mail: alozanom@sakata.com.mx
URL: http://www.amseed.com
Contact: Paul Bennett, Chm.
Founded: 1883. **Members:** 850. **Membership Dues:** Canadian and Mexican, $550 (annual) ● active (based on services performed), $750-$1,250 (annual) ● corresponding, $1,000 (annual) ● affiliate, $100 (annual). **Staff:** 10. **Budget:** $2,000,000. **State Groups:** 53. **Description:** Breeders, growers, assemblers, conditioners, wholesalers, and retailers of grain, grass, vegetable, flower, and other seed for planting purposes. **Committees:** ASTA International. **Divisions:** Associates; Brokers; Corn and Sorghum; Farm Seed; Lawn Seed; Soybean; Vegetable and Flower. **Publications:** *ASTA's Membership Directory*. Alternate Formats: online ● *Corn and Sorghum Proceedings*, annual. **Price:** $30.00 for members; $100.00 for nonmembers. Alternate Formats: CD-ROM ● *Inside ASTA*, monthly. Newsletter ● *Soybean Seed Proceedings*, annual ● Yearbook. **Conventions/Meetings:** annual convention - usually June.

5175 ■ National Council of Commercial Plant Breeders (NCCPB)
225 Reinekers Ln., Ste.650
Alexandria, VA 22314
Ph: (703)837-8140
Fax: (703)837-9365
E-mail: ajorss@amseed.org
URL: http://www.nccpb.org
Contact: Ann Jorss, Sec.-Treas.
Founded: 1954. **Members:** 65. **Budget:** $30,000. **Description:** Commercial seed firms. Engages in plant research and breeding programs in order to develop and market new and improved seeds and plants. Promotes and seeks to protect the interests of private industry in seed development, processing, and marketing. Monitors legislative matters pertaining to the seed industry and public agency programs as they affect private firms engaged in plant breeding. **Awards:** NCCPB Genetics and Plant Breeding Award. **Frequency:** annual. **Type:** recognition. **Recipient:** for scientists chosen for contributions to the field of genetics and plant breeding; one from academic and another from industry. **Computer Services:** Mailing lists ● online services. **Publications:** *Membership List*, annual. Membership Directory. **Conventions/Meetings:** annual meeting - always June.

5176 ■ Society of Commercial Seed Technologists (SCST)
101 E State St., No. 214
Ithaca, NY 14850
Ph: (607)256-3313
Fax: (607)256-3313
E-mail: scst@twcny.rr.com
URL: http://www.seedtechnology.net
Contact: Anita Hall, Exec. Dir.
Founded: 1922. **Members:** 253. **Membership Dues:** individual, $200 (annual) ● researcher, $150 (annual) ● associate, $75 (annual). **Staff:** 7. **Description:** Registered Seed Technologists. Maintains proficiency and professional standards among members. Promotes interests of the seed industry. Registers seed technologists. Tests and ensures seed quality; issues internationally recognized Reports of Analyses used to market seed. **Libraries: Type:** reference; open to the public. **Holdings:** articles, books, periodicals. **Awards:** Merit Award and Honorary Member Award. **Frequency:** annual. **Type:** recognition. **Recipient:** for persons who have rendered signal service ● **Frequency:** annual. **Type:** recognition. **Affiliated With:** Association of Official Seed Analysts. **Publications:** *SCST Newsletter*, 3/year ● *The Seed Technologist Newsletter*, 3/year. Contains information about training opportunities, upcoming events, employment, regional news, and technical issues. **Price:** $35.00. Alternate Formats: CD-ROM. **Conventions/Meetings:** annual meeting, held in conjunction with the Association of Official Seed Analysts (exhibits).

Sheep

5177 ■ American Border Leicester Association (ABLA)
c/o Polly Hopkins, Treas.
494 Evans Rd.
Chepachet, RI 02814
Ph: (401)949-4619
E-mail: khop4811@aol.com
URL: http://www.ablasheep.org
Contact: Polly Hopkins, Treas.
Founded: 1973. **Members:** 175. **Membership Dues:** active, $20 (annual) ● junior (under 18), $15 (annual). **Staff:** 10. **Budget:** $10,000. **Description:** Owners and admirers of Border Leicester sheep. Promotes Border Leicesters as a source of wool and meat. Sets breed standards and confers certification; maintains breed registry. Sponsors competitions; conducts educational programs. **Awards:** Junior Shepherd Award. **Frequency:** annual. **Type:** recognition. **Computer Services:** database ● mailing lists ● online services ● record retrieval services. **Publications:** *American Border Leicester Association Quarterly News*. Newsletter. **Circulation:** 200. **Advertising:** accepted. Alternate Formats: online ● *Border Leicester*. Brochure ● Directory, annual. **Conventions/Meetings:** annual Maryland Sheep and Wool Festival - convention and board meeting (exhibits) - always first weekend in May.

5178 ■ American Cheviot Sheep Society (ACSS)
c/o Jo Bernard, Sec.-Treas.
PO Box 367
New Richland, MN 56072
Ph: (507)465-8474
Fax: (507)465-8474
E-mail: jo@cheviots.org
URL: http://www.cheviots.org
Contact: Jo Bernard, Sec.-Treas.
Founded: 1924. **Members:** 700. **Membership Dues:** regular, $10 (annual). **Staff:** 1. **Description:** Breeders of Cheviot (border) sheep. Maintains registry; issues certificates of registration and transfer; compiles statistics. **Committees:** Youth. **Publications:** *Banner*, monthly. Magazine ● *Breeders Directory*, annual. **Circulation:** 1,500. **Advertising:** accepted ● *Cheviot Journal*, annual ● *It's Cheviot You Need*. Brochure. **Conventions/Meetings:** annual meeting - always November, Louisville, KY.

5179 ■ American Cormo Sheep Association (ACSA)
HC 59, Box 25
Broadus, MT 59317
Ph: (406)427-5449
E-mail: info@cormosheep.com
URL: http://www.cormosheep.com
Contact: Charlotte Carlat, Sec.-Treas.
Founded: 1976. **Members:** 30. **Membership Dues:** regular, $15 (annual). **Staff:** 1. **Description:** Purebred sheep breeders who seek to promote and sustain the Cormo sheep, which were introduced into the U.S. in 1976 and are noted for their high yield of fine wool and productivity on western rangelands. **Computer Services:** Mailing lists. **Telecommunication Services:** electronic mail, carlat@midrivers.com ● electronic mail, amcormosheepassoc@egroup.com. **Affiliated With:** American Sheep Industry Association. **Publications:** Newsletter, quarterly. **Price:** free for members.

5180 ■ American Corriedale Association (ACA)
c/o Marcia E. Craig, Exec. Sec.
PO Box 391
Clay City, IL 62824
Ph: (618)676-1046
Fax: (618)676-1133
E-mail: info@americancorriedale.com
URL: http://www.americancorriedale.com
Contact: Marcia E. Craig, Exec. Sec.
Founded: 1916. **Members:** 1,000. **Membership Dues:** full, $25 (annual) ● junior (ages 8-21), $7 (annual). **Staff:** 1. **Budget:** $35,000. **Regional Groups:** 2. **State Groups:** 10. **Description:** Breeders of purebred Corriedale sheep. Maintains registry showing ownership, transfers, and pedigree records. **Telecommunication Services:** electronic mail, sbarssheep@compuserve.com. **Publications:** *Corriedale Courier*, semiannual. Newsletters. **Circulation:** 1,000. **Advertising:** accepted ● *Corriedale Extra*, semiannual. Magazine. **Price:** free. **Circulation:** 1,000. **Advertising:** accepted. **Conventions/Meetings:** annual National Corriedale Show and Sale - general assembly - always June.

5181 ■ American Cotswold Record Association (ACRA)
PO Box 59
Plympton, MA 02367
Ph: (781)585-2026
Fax: (781)585-2026
E-mail: acrasheep@aol.com
Contact: Vicki Rigel, Sec.-Treas.
Founded: 1878. **Members:** 70. **Membership Dues:** regular, $10 (annual). **Staff:** 1. **For-Profit. Description:** Breeders and exhibitors of purebred white Cotswold sheep. Promotes the breed through involvement in fleece and sheep shows exhibits and advertising throughout the U.S. Maintains registry showing ownership, transfers, and pedigrees. Compiles statistics. **Formerly:** (1904) American Cotswold Sheep Association. **Publications:** *Cotswold News*, semiannual, every winter and summer. Newsletter. Provides membership activities news; includes reports on genetics and diseases of sheep. ● Booklet ● Brochures ● Directory, annual. **Conventions/Meetings:** competition ● annual conference (exhibits) - usually November ● annual meeting - in November.

5182 ■ American Delaine and Merino Record Association (ADMRA)
c/o Connie M. King, Sec.
59419 Walters Rd.
Jacobsburg, OH 43933-9731
Ph: (740)686-2172
E-mail: kingmerino@alltel.net
URL: http://www.admra.org
Contact: Connie M. King, Sec.
Founded: 1890. **Members:** 200. **Membership Dues:** life, $15 ● individual, $20 (annual). **Staff:** 1. **Description:** Breeders of registered American and Delaine Merino sheep. Seeks to propagate and improve fine wool sheep. **Publications:** *Consider Merinos*. Booklet. **Price:** free. **Conventions/Meetings:** annual meeting and show.

5183 ■ American Dorper Sheep Breeders' Society (ADSBS)
PO Box 796
Columbia, MO 65201
Ph: (573)442-8257
Fax: (573)874-8843
E-mail: adsbsoffice@centurytel.net
URL: http://www.dorperamerica.org
Contact: Ronda Sparks, Registrar
Founded: 1995. **Membership Dues:** general, $50 (annual). **Multinational. Description:** Supports the establishment of the Dorper breed on the North American Continent. Organizes and promotes educational and commercial events about the breed. Encourages and supports university research projects involving Dorper genetics. **Publications:** Magazine, quarterly. Alternate Formats: online.

5184 ■ American Finnsheep Breeders Association (FBA)
c/o Cynthia Smith, Sec.
HC 65, Box 517
Hominy, OK 74035
Ph: (918)519-4140 (540)463-4594
Free: (800)628-5262
E-mail: cindyusmith@yahoo.com
URL: http://www.finnsheep.org
Contact: Dr. Paul Hunter, Pres.
Founded: 1971. **Members:** 585. **Membership Dues:** new, $60 ● continuing, $25 (annual). **Description:** Breeders of Finnsheep and their crosses; research universities, agricultural schools, and private owners. (Finnsheep are native to Finland and are highly adaptable to most climates and varied feeds.) Promotes the Finnsheep breed and seeks to increase public awareness of its attributes. Advocates the role of Finnsheep in the U.S. sheep industry as that of a crossbred mother because of the ewe's ability to multiply and produce. Registers purebred and crossbred animals; processes transfers of ownership; issues pedigrees. Sponsors annual national sale. **Libraries: Type:** reference. **Holdings:** archival material. **Publications:** *Breeders' Directory*, annual. Alternate Formats: online ● *Finnsheep Short Tales*, semiannual. Newsletter. Alternate Formats: online ● Brochure ● Also issues breed standard guidelines. **Conventions/Meetings:** annual meeting (exhibits).

5185 ■ American Hampshire Sheep Association (AHSA)
15603 173rd Ave.
Milo, IA 50166-8940
Ph: (641)942-6402
Fax: (641)942-6502
E-mail: info@hampshires.com
URL: http://www.countrylovin.com/ahsa/index.html
Contact: Karey Claghorn, Sec.-Treas.
Founded: 1889. **Members:** 3,000. **Membership Dues:** senior, $25 (annual) ● active senior, $15 (annual) ● active junior, $10 (annual). **Staff:** 3. **Budget:** $115,000. **Description:** Promoters of purebred Hampshire sheep. Maintains registry and pedigree records. **Telecommunication Services:** electronic mail, rkdrealt@triwest.net. **Committees:** Advertising; Centennial; Junior Activities. **Publications:** Membership Directory, biennial. **Conventions/Meetings:** annual meeting.

5186 ■ American Karakul Sheep Registry (AKSR)
11500 Hwy. 5
Boonville, MO 65233
Ph: (660)838-6340
Fax: (660)838-6322
E-mail: aksr@iland.net
URL: http://www.karakulsheep.com
Contact: Rey Perera, Sec.
Founded: 1929. **Members:** 50. **Membership Dues:** adult, $15 (annual) ● junior, $5 (annual). **Staff:** 1. **Description:** Owners of Karakul sheep. **Convention/Meeting:** none. **Libraries: Type:** reference. **Holdings:** books, business records. **Subjects:** breeding and raising of Karakul sheep. **Formerly:** Karakul Fur Sheep Registry; (1980) Empire Karakul Registry; (1984) American Karakul Fur Sheep Registry. **Publications:** *Breeders List*, periodic. Directory ● *Karakul Friends Newsletter*, periodic. **Price:** included in membership dues ● Also distributes Karakul note cards.

5187 ■ American Lamb Council (ALC)
c/o American Sheep Industry Association
9785 Maroon Cir., Ste.360
Englewood, CO 80112
Ph: (303)771-3500
Fax: (303)771-8200
E-mail: info@sheepusa.org
URL: http://www.sheepusa.org
Contact: Angelo Theos, Co-Chm.
Founded: 1954. **Members:** 68,000. **Membership Dues:** individual (minimum, based on number of sheep), $25 (annual). **Staff:** 8. **Description:** A division of the American Sheep Industry Association (see separate entry). Promotes lamb meat and wool for the producer. **Publications:** *Sheep Industry News*, monthly. Newspapers. **Conventions/Meetings:** annual board meeting.

5188 ■ American Miniature Cheviot Sheep Breeders Association (AMCSBA)
403 Cheryl Way
Silver Springs, NV 89429
Ph: (775)629-1211
E-mail: eddieannmiller@hotmail.com
URL: http://www.minicheviot.com
Contact: Eddie Miller, Registrar
Founded: 2005. **Membership Dues:** general, $24 (annual). **Description:** Develops, promotes, and protects the miniature Cheviot sheep breed. Maintains the purity and standards of miniature Cheviot sheep through record-keeping. Facilitates exchange of information among association members and the public. Cooperates with all other organizations promoting sheep.

5189 ■ American North Country Cheviot Sheep Association (ANCCSA)
c/o Sandy Thomas, Sec.-Treas.
10506 S 875 E
Walkerton, IN 46574
Ph: (574)586-3778 (503)792-3448
E-mail: thomasfarms@localnet.com
URL: http://northcountrycheviot.com
Contact: Bonnie Henny, Pres.
Founded: 1962. **Members:** 250. **Membership Dues:** senior, $10 (annual). **Staff:** 1. **Regional Groups:** 3. **Description:** Breeders of purebred North Country Cheviot sheep. Records registration and transfer of ownership of purebred sheep; compiles statistics; maintains collection of registration certificates. **Awards:** American North Country Cheviot Hall of Fame. **Frequency:** biennial. **Type:** recognition. **Recipient:** for service to breed and sheep industry. **Computer Services:** database ● mailing lists ● online services. **Publications:** *North Country Cheviot*, biennial. Membership Directory ● *North Country News*. Newsletter. **Price:** free. **Circulation:** 500. **Advertising:** accepted. **Conventions/Meetings:** biennial International North Country Cheviot Show & Sale, includes sale ● show and regional meeting.

5190 ■ American Oxford Sheep Association (AOSA)
1960 E 2100 North Rd.
Stonington, IL 62567
Ph: (217)325-3515 (563)785-6608
Fax: (217)325-3515
E-mail: doaoxfords@hotmail.com
URL: http://www.americanoxfords.org
Contact: Justin O'Brien, Pres.
Founded: 1882. **Members:** 585. **Membership Dues:** junior, $5 (annual) ● senior, $10 (annual). **Regional Groups:** 2. **State Groups:** 4. **Description:** Breeders of purebred Oxford Down sheep. Purposes are: to encourage new and old breeders to use modern feeding and management methods to take full advantage of the excellent production potential of Oxfords; to improve standards of excellence; to provide for increased advertising, stepped up premiums in carcass shows, and a workable ram certification program. Provides extra premiums and trophies for established junior shows at state fairs and regional shows. Maintains registry showing ownership, transfers, and pedigree records. Sponsors projects throughout boys' homes in Minnesota, South Dakota, and Ohio. **Formerly:** American Oxford Down Record Association. **Publications:** *Membership Newsletter*, semiannual. **Price:** included in membership dues ● Brochure, annual. Contains membership lists. **Price:** included in membership dues. **Advertising:** accepted. **Conventions/Meetings:** annual meeting.

5191 ■ American Polypay Sheep Association (APSA)
c/o Karey Claghorn, Sec.
15603 173rd Ave.
Milo, IA 50166
Ph: (641)942-6402 (641)765-4595
Fax: (641)942-6502
E-mail: info@polypay.org
URL: http://www.countrylovin.com/polypay
Contact: Brad Dunne, Pres.
Founded: 1980. **Members:** 235. **Membership Dues:** adult, $50 (annual) ● junior, $5 (annual). **Description:** Promotes the polypay sheep breed. (Developed by the U.S. Sheep Experiment Station, the breed consists of 25&percent; Rambouillet, 25&percent; Targhee, 25&percent; Dorset, and 25&percent; Finnish-Landrace.) Records the ancestry of the sheep; maintains stud books, registry, and performance records on animal weight gain, offspring, and wool production; monitors improvement of the breed. Maintains research programs. **Awards: Type:** recognition. **Computer Services:** database. **Telecommunication Services:** electronic mail, sammons@theinter.com. **Committees:** Advertising; Sales. **Publications:** *American Polypay Sheep Association Breeder's Directory*, periodic. Alternate Formats: online ● *The American Polypay Sheep News*, monthly. Newsletter. **Advertising:** accepted. Alternate Formats: online ● Brochure ● Membership Directory. **Conventions/Meetings:** annual meeting.

5192 ■ American Rambouillet Sheep Breeders' Association (ARSBA)
1610 S State Rd. 3261
Levelland, TX 79336-9230
Ph: (806)894-3081
E-mail: contact@rambouilletsheep.org
URL: http://www.rambouilletsheep.org
Contact: Ron Sutherland, Pres.
Founded: 1889. **Members:** 500. **Membership Dues:** junior, $15 (annual) ● regular, $25 (annual). **Description:** Owners and breeders of registered Rambouillet sheep. Maintains registry and pedigree records. **Committees:** Register of Merits. **Publications:** *Bouilletin*, quarterly. Newsletter. Contains association news and activities. **Price:** included in membership dues. **Advertising:** accepted. Alternate Formats: online ● *Rambouillet Newsletter*, quarterly ● Also publishes a description of the operations of the association. **Conventions/Meetings:** annual meeting, breeder participation show and sale.

5193 ■ American Romney Breeders' Association (ARBA)
744 Riverbanks Rd.
Grants Pass, OR 97527-9607
Ph: (541)476-6428
E-mail: secretary@americanromney.org
URL: http://www.americanromney.org
Contact: Jean Kamenicky, Sec.-Treas.
Founded: 1912. **Members:** 500. **Membership Dues:** breeder, $15 (annual) ● junior, $5 (annual). **Staff:** 12. **Budget:** $25,000. **Regional Groups:** 6. **Description:** Breeders of purebred Romney sheep. Conducts lamb and wool shows and purebred exhibits to demonstrate the excellence of purebred Romney sheep. Records registrations and .transfers of the breed in the U.S. and Canada and those imported into the U.S. **Publications:** *American Romney*. Pamphlet. Covers the history of Romney sheep in America. ● *Romney Ramblings*, 3/year. Newsletter. **Advertising:** accepted ● Membership Directory, annual. **Price:** free. **Conventions/Meetings:** annual meeting, with banquet.

5194 ■ American Sheep Industry Association (ASI)
9785 Maroon Cir., Ste.360
Centennial, CO 80112
Ph: (303)771-3500
Fax: (303)771-8200
E-mail: info@sheepusa.org
URL: http://www.sheepusa.org
Contact: Burdell Johnson, Pres.
Founded: 1989. **Members:** 19,500. **Staff:** 9. **Budget:** $9,000,000. **Regional Groups:** 7. **State Groups:** 50. **Description:** Producers of sheep and wool. Goal is to advance the standards and profitability of the sheep industry. Conducts lobbying activities to promote legislation beneficial to the industry. **Libraries: Type:** not open to the public. **Awards:** Camptender Award. **Frequency:** annual. **Type:** recognition. **Recipient:** for a professional position related to sheep production ● Environmental Stewardship Award. **Frequency:** annual. **Type:** recognition. **Recipient:** for individuals actively involved in sheep production ● Flock Guardian Award. **Frequency:** annual. **Type:** recognition. **Recipient:** for an outstanding producer or industry professional ● McClure Silver Ram Award. **Frequency:** annual. **Type:** recognition. **Recipient:** for sheep producer ● Sheep Heritage Foundation. **Frequency:** annual. **Type:** scholarship. **Recipient:** for graduate students involved in sheep research ● Shepherd's Voice Award. **Frequency:** annual. **Type:** recognition. **Recipient:** for outstanding year-long print coverage of sheep industry ● Shepherd's Voice Award for Broadcast Media. **Frequency:** annual. **Type:** recognition. **Recipient:** for outstanding year-long broadcast coverage of sheep industry. **Telecommunication Services:** electronic mail, djlbek@bektel.com. **Councils:** Lamb; Legislative; Producer Education and Research; Resource Management; Wool. **Formed by Merger of:** (1989) American Sheep Producers' Council; National Wool Growers Association. **Publications:** *ASI Lamb and Wool Market News*, weekly. Newsletter. Provides prices of lamb, wool markets; includes industry briefs. **Price:** $35.00/year; $150.00/year by fax. **Circulation:** 1,000 ● *National Lamb and Wool Grower*, monthly. Magazine. **Circulation:** 21,000 ● *Sheep Industry News*, monthly. Newspaper ● Brochures. **Conventions/Meetings:** annual convention and trade show (exhibits) - always January or February.

5195 ■ American Shropshire Registry Association (ASRA)
c/o Mark McCabe, Youth Page Coor.
5154 Nickelson Rd.
Prospect, OH 43342
Ph: (740)494-2969
E-mail: mamccabe51@hotmail.com
URL: http://www.shropshires.org
Contact: Mark McCabe, Youth Page Coor.
Founded: 1884. **Members:** 650. **Membership Dues:** life, $20 ● adult, $20 (annual) ● junior, $10 (annual). **Staff:** 1. **Budget:** $27,000. **Regional Groups:** 4. **State Groups:** 10. **Description:** Breeders and owners of purebred Shropshire sheep. Maintains records of breeders, registrations, transfers, and pedigrees; issues performance registry certificates for lambs of outstanding quality. Promotes the qualities of the Shropshire breed. **Awards:** Shropshire Master Shepherd Award. **Frequency:** periodic. **Type:** recognition. **Recipient:** for contributions to the sheep industry and the Shropshire breed ● Shropshire Scholarships. **Frequency:** annual. **Type:** monetary. **Recipient:** for scholastic record, leadership, extracurricular activities and involvement with the sheep industry in general and the Shropshire breed in particular. **Committees:** Advertising; Breed Promotion and Awards; Direction and Planning; Junior Activities. **Publications:** *Breeder Directory*, triennial. **Price:** free for members. **Advertising:** accepted ● *Shropshire Voice*, 3/year. Journal. Features show and sale results and educational information. **Price:** free. **Circulation:** 600. **Advertising:** accepted. **Conventions/Meetings:** annual meeting and banquet (exhibits).

5196 ■ American Southdown Breeders' Association (ASBA)
100 Cornerstone Rd.
Fredonia, TX 76842
Ph: (325)429-6226 (909)877-1028
Fax: (325)429-6225
E-mail: gary@southdownsheep.org
URL: http://www.southdownsheep.org
Contact: Lee Pettey, Pres.
Founded: 1882. **Members:** 758. **Membership Dues:** individual, $10 (annual). **Staff:** 1. **Regional Groups:** 16. **Description:** Adult (654) and junior (104) breeders of purebred Southdown sheep. Maintains registry and pedigree records. Sponsors competitions. **Libraries: Type:** reference. **Holdings:** archival material. **Awards: Type:** recognition. **Telecommunication Services:** electronic mail, southdown@ctesc.net. **Publications:** *The American Southdown*, 3/year. Journal. **Price:** $10.00 for nonmembers. **Advertising:** accepted. Alternate Formats: online ● *Southdown Handbook*, biennial. Membership Directory. **Conventions/Meetings:** annual meeting.

5197 ■ ARCA: American Romeldale/CVM Association
c/o Barbara Kloese, Registrar
429 W US Hwy. 30
Valparaiso, IN 46385
Ph: (219)759-9665
URL: http://www.arcainc.org
Contact: Barbara Kloese, Registrar
Membership Dues: adult, $20 (annual) ● junior, associate, $10 (annual). **Description:** Promotes and protects the Romeldale/CVM sheep breed. Encourages the registration of all prime breeding stock to conserve this critically endangered breed. Facilitates collaboration and exchange of information among members.

5198 ■ Barbados Blackbelly Sheep Association International (BBSAI)
815 Bell Hill Rd.
Cobden, IL 62920
Ph: (618)893-4568
E-mail: secretary@blackbellysheep.org
URL: http://www.blackbellysheep.org
Contact: Mary Swindell, Sec.-Treas.
Membership Dues: junior, $15 (annual) ● associate, $25 (annual) ● regular, $30 (annual) ● family, $45 (annual) ● life, $200. **Multinational. Description:** Aims to raise, preserve, improve, promote and publish facts pertaining to American Blackbelly and Barbados Blackbelly sheep. Works to register and keep on file all records of registrations and transfers of American Blackbelly and Barbados Blackbelly sheep in the United States. Supports and promotes the interests of American Blackbelly and Barbados Blackbelly sheep breeders. **Publications:** Newsletter, quarterly. **Price:** included in membership dues.

5199 ■ Black Top and National Delaine Merino Sheep Association (BTNDMSA)
Address Unknown since 2007
Founded: 1938. **Members:** 8. **Membership Dues:** individual, $5. **Staff:** 1. **Description:** Breeders of purebred black top and delaine merino sheep.

Maintains registry showing ownership, transfers, and pedigree records. **Conventions/Meetings:** annual meeting.

5200 ■ Bluefaced Leicester Union of North America (BLU)

c/o Kelly Ward, Sec.-Treas.
760 W VW Ave.
Schoolcraft, MI 49087
Ph: (269)679-5497
Fax: (269)679-2153
E-mail: wardfarm@net-link.net
URL: http://www.bflsheep.com
Contact: Kelly Ward, Sec.-Treas.

Membership Dues: full/active, $15 (annual) ● associate, $10 (annual). **Multinational. Description:** Represents the interests of owners, enthusiasts, and breeders of Bluefaced Leicester sheep. Educates the general public regarding the advantages of the Bluefaced Leicester sheep. Seeks to expand the numbers of purebred Bluefaced Leicesters in North America.

5201 ■ Columbia Sheep Breeders Association of America (CSBA)

15603 173rd Ave.
Milo, IA 50166
Ph: (641)942-6402 (573)886-9419
E-mail: shull@netzero.com
URL: http://www.columbiasheep.org
Contact: Steve Hull, Pres.

Founded: 1942. **Members:** 1,000. **Membership Dues:** junior, $15 (annual) ● senior, $50 (annual). **Staff:** 2. **State Groups:** 12. **Description:** Breeders of Columbia sheep. Sponsors competitions. **Awards: Type:** recognition ● **Type:** recognition. **Telecommunication Services:** electronic mail, columbias@centurytel.net. **Publications:** *Speaking of Columbias*, monthly. Magazine. Features all the latest happenings in the Columbia world. **Conventions/Meetings:** competition ● annual meeting.

5202 ■ Continental Dorset Club (CDC)

PO Box 506
North Scituate, RI 02857-0506
Ph: (401)647-4676 (405)666-1088
Fax: (401)647-4679
E-mail: cdcdorset@cox.net
URL: http://www.dorsets.homestead.com
Contact: Debra Hopkins, Exec. Sec.-Treas.

Founded: 1898. **Members:** 2,500. **Membership Dues:** life, $20 ● adult, $7 ● junior, $3. **Staff:** 2. **State Groups:** 10. **Description:** Owners and breeders of registered Dorset sheep. Issues certificates of registration. Conducts advertising and promotional work. **Telecommunication Services:** electronic mail, kgstamps@hotmail.com. **Publications:** *Dorset Connection*, 3/year. Newsletter. **Price:** free for members. **Circulation:** 2,500. **Advertising:** accepted. **Conventions/Meetings:** annual meeting.

5203 ■ Jacob Sheep Breeders Association (JSBA)

c/o Lane Harris, Membership Sec.
PO Box 10427
Bozeman, MT 59719
Ph: (406)580-6832
E-mail: spottedsheep@yahoo.com
URL: http://www.jsba.org
Contact: Lane Harris, Membership Sec.

Founded: 1988. **Members:** 250. **Membership Dues:** junior, $10 (annual) ● ordinary, $30 (annual). **Regional Groups:** 5. **Description:** Owners and breeders of Jacob sheep. Promotes preservation of the Jacob breed. Maintains breed registry; facilitates exchange of information among members; serves as a clearinghouse on Jacob sheep and other minor breeds. **Telecommunication Services:** electronic mail, information@jsba.org. **Publications:** *Jacob Sheep Breeders Association Newsletter*, quarterly. **Price:** $10.00 /year for nonmembers; included in membership dues. **Conventions/Meetings:** annual meeting - every 3rd or 4th weekend of June.

5204 ■ Miniature and Novelty Sheep Breeders Association and Registry (MNSBAR)

113 Blake Rd.
Toledo, WA 98591
Ph: (360)864-6116
Fax: (360)864-6214
URL: http://www.toledotel.com/~smokeyvly/Reg.htm
Contact: Michelle Shannon, Contact

Membership Dues: regular, $20 (annual). **Description:** Aims to preserve miniature and novelty sheep. Promotes and protects true and rare breeds of small sheep. Ensures the conservation and survival of these unique sheep breeds through inspection, registration and education. Encourages breeding and exhibition of quality registered small, miniature, toy and novelty sheep. Seeks to develop and promote good fellowship among breeders of miniature and novelty sheep.

5205 ■ Montadale Sheep Breeders Association (MSBA)

2514 Willow Rd. NE
Fargo, ND 58102
Ph: (701)297-9199 (605)329-2478
Fax: (701)297-9199
E-mail: info@montadales.com
URL: http://www.countrylovin.com/msba/index.html
Contact: Mildred E. Moore, Exec. Sec.

Founded: 1945. **Members:** 800. **Membership Dues:** senior, $10 (annual) ● junior, $15 (annual). **Staff:** 1. **State Groups:** 9. **Description:** Breeders of purebred Montadale sheep. Maintains registry showing ownership, transfers, and pedigree records. **Publications:** *Montadale Breeders Directory*, annual ● *Montadale Mover Express*, quarterly. Magazine. **Advertising:** accepted. Alternate Formats: online. **Conventions/Meetings:** annual show - every June held in Springfield, Illinois.

5206 ■ National Lamb Feeders Association (NLFA)

1270 Chemeketa St. NE
Salem, OR 97301-4145
Ph: (503)370-7024 (503)364-5462
Free: (866)327-LAMB
Fax: (503)585-1921
E-mail: info@nlfa-sheep.org
URL: http://www.nlfa-sheep.org
Contact: Don Beerwinkle, Pres.

Founded: 1951. **Members:** 300. **Membership Dues:** feeder, plus 10 cents/head, $100 (annual) ● associate (packer, breaker, etc.), $500 ● non-voting (academia, press, etc.), $25. **Staff:** 1. **Budget:** $40,000. **Description:** Lamb feeders and representatives of associated industries, including feed manufacturers, drug manufacturers, and meat processors. Promotes lamb feeding through legislative representation and support for reasonable industry regulations, plus research, education and promotional efforts to benefit the lamb industry. Sponsors annual Howard Wyman Sheep Industry Leadership School. **Publications:** *Feeder News*, bimonthly. Newsletter. Contains industry and association news. **Price:** included in membership dues. **Circulation:** 425. **Advertising:** accepted. **Conventions/Meetings:** annual convention and board meeting, held in conjunction with American Sheep Industry Association Convention.

5207 ■ National Lincoln Sheep Breeders' Association (NLSBA)

15603 173rd Ave.
Milo, IA 50166
Ph: (608)437-5086 (269)623-2549
E-mail: kclaghorn@earthlink.net
URL: http://www.lincolnsheep.org
Contact: Brian Larson, Pres.

Founded: 1889. **Members:** 120. **Membership Dues:** regular, $10 (annual). **Staff:** 1. **Description:** Owners and breeders of purebred Lincoln sheep. Maintains registry showing ownership, transfers, and pedigree records. **Telecommunication Services:** electronic mail, watkins@mhtc.net. **Publications:** *The Lincoln Letter*. Newsletter. Alternate Formats: online ● Membership Directory. Alternate Formats: online. **Conventions/Meetings:** biennial Business Management Meeting.

5208 ■ National Tunis Sheep Registry, Inc. (NTSRI)

c/o Barbara Cassell, Sec.
15603 173rd Ave.
Milo, IA 50166
Ph: (641)942-6402
Fax: (641)942-6502
E-mail: barbaracassell@hotmail.com
URL: http://www.tunissheep.org
Contact: Barbara Cassell, Sec.

Founded: 1896. **Members:** 120. **Membership Dues:** regular, $10 (annual). **Staff:** 2. **Description:** Represents breeders of registered Tunis sheep. **Telecommunication Services:** electronic mail, djbrown@unicornerfarm.com. **Formerly:** (1929) American Tunis Sheep Breeders' Association. **Publications:** *Tun-US-IN*, quarterly. Newsletter. **Conventions/Meetings:** annual meeting - always Syracuse, NY.

5209 ■ Natural Colored Wool Growers Association (NCWGA)

429 W US30
Valparaiso, IN 46385
Ph: (219)759-9665 (503)632-3354
Fax: (219)759-9665
E-mail: kloese@gte.net
URL: http://www.ncwga.org
Contact: Barbara Kloese, Registrar

Founded: 1977. **Members:** 850. **Membership Dues:** regular, $20 (annual) ● junior, $5 (annual) ● associate, $15 (annual). **Staff:** 2. **Regional Groups:** 11. **Multinational. Description:** Breeders or owners of colored sheep and others interested in colored wool; spinners and weavers. Assists members in the development of colored wool; promotes the usefulness of colored wool products. Natural colored sheep wool ranges in color from black, silver, and gray, to brown, blond, beige, and red. Conducts training programs on the production and sale of colored sheep and woolen products. Sponsors sheep contests, fleece shows, and spinning and weaving competitions. Maintains a sheep registration program concentrating on flock, certified, and breeding line registries. **Committees:** Animal Registration. **Publications:** *The Marker*, quarterly. Newsletter ● *News and Membership Directory*, annual. **Conventions/Meetings:** annual meeting (exhibits).

5210 ■ Navajo-Churro Sheep Association (NCSA)

PO Box 94
Ojo Caliente, NM 87549
Ph: (505)737-0488
E-mail: churro@newmex.com
URL: http://www.navajo-churrosheep.com
Contact: Connie Taylor, Registrar

Founded: 1986. **Members:** 160. **Membership Dues:** active breeder/associate, $25 (annual) ● introductory, $15 (annual). **Budget:** $2,000. **Regional Groups:** 4. **Description:** Owners and breeders of Navajo-Churro sheep; fiber artists and collectors of textiles. Promotes preservation the Navajo-Churro breed of sheep. Facilitates breeding of Navajo-Churro sheep and maintains breed registry. **Libraries: Type:** reference. **Holdings:** archival material, audio recordings, books, business records, clippings, video recordings. **Subjects:** Navajo-Churro sheep. **Computer Services:** Online services, breeder listing. **Formerly:** (1998) Churro; Navajosa. **Publications:** *Catch Pen*, quarterly. Newsletter ● *Flockbook*, annual. Contains membership list, sheep registered, photos. **Conventions/Meetings:** annual meeting and workshop.

5211 ■ North American Babydoll Southdown Sheep Association and Registry (NABSSAR)

PO Box 146
Wellsville, KS 66092
Ph: (785)883-4774
Fax: (785)883-4778

E-mail: president@babydollsheep.org
URL: http://www.babydollsheep.org
Contact: Jeff Jager, Pres.
Founded: 2001. **Membership Dues:** senior/adult (single), $20 (annual) ● senior/adult (dual/family), $30 (annual) ● junior (single), $25 (annual) ● associate (single), $10 (annual) ● associate (dual/family), $15 (annual) ● life (single), $300 ● life (dual/family), $450 ● corporate (10 year fee), $500. **Multinational. Description:** Protects and promotes the breed of Babydoll Southdown Sheep. Provides its members the opportunity to meet and exchange information for the purpose of making better breeding choices. Preserves the standards of the breed. **Publications:** Newsletter, quarterly. **Price:** included in membership dues.

5212 ■ North American Clun Forest Association (NACFA)
c/o Bets Reedy, Sec.-Treas.
Bramble Hill
21727 Randall Dr.
Houston, MN 55943
Ph: (507)864-7585 (540)937-6124
E-mail: bramble@acegroup.cc
URL: http://www.clunforestsheep.org
Contact: Bets Reedy, Sec.-Treas.
Founded: 1973. **Members:** 60. **Membership Dues:** non-voting, $10 (annual) ● voting, $25 (annual) ● life, $100. **Staff:** 1. **Description:** Owners and breeders of registered Clun Forest sheep. Promotes the breed in North America. Prohibits adult show competition in efforts to emphasize performance and productivity rather than cosmetic qualities. Seeks to maintain the breed's natural characteristics by guarding against reduction in the genetic bank. Permits young members' participation in shows sponsored by Future Farmers of America and 4-H Program and Youth Development (see separate entries). Compiles statistics. **Computer Services:** database. **Telecommunication Services:** electronic mail, alan@touchstonefarm.org. **Publications:** Articles ● Brochures. **Conventions/Meetings:** annual meeting - usually September.

5213 ■ North American Shetland Sheepbreeders Association (NASSA)
c/o Karey Claghorn
NASSA Registry
15603 173rd Ave.
Milo, IA 50166
Ph: (641)942-6402
E-mail: registrar@shetland-sheep.org
URL: http://www.shetland-sheep.org
Contact: Gail Former, Pres.
Founded: 1991. **Members:** 680. **Membership Dues:** regular, $25 (annual) ● junior, $10 (annual). **Staff:** 9. **Budget:** $27,000. **Description:** Breeders of Shetland Sheep in North America. Assists breeders in maintaining the quality of the breeder and provides accurate registration and pedigree records for informed breeding decisions. **Publications:** *NASSA Flock Book*, annual ● *NASSA News*, quarterly. Newsletter. Contains news and information about Shetlands, a forum for breeder exchange, and breeder profiles. **Price:** $4.00. **Circulation:** 680. **Advertising:** accepted. **Conventions/Meetings:** annual meeting.

5214 ■ North American Wensleydale Sheep Association (NAWSA)
4589 Fruitland Rd.
Loma Rica, CA 95901
Ph: (530)743-5262
E-mail: info@wensleydalesheep.org
URL: http://www.wensleydalesheep.org
Contact: Barbara Burrows, Pres.
Founded: 1999. **Membership Dues:** active, $25 (annual) ● associate, $15 (annual). **Multinational. Description:** Establishes and supports the Wensleydale breed of sheep in North America. Engages in the education and promotion of Wensleydale sheep. Registers and keeps pedigree records of all animals that qualify as percentage blood and purebred Wensleydale sheep according to the guidelines of the association. Provides information about Wensleydale sheep and their products. **Publications:** Brochure. Alternate Formats: online.

5215 ■ Painted Desert Sheep Society (PDSS)
c/o Anita Garza, Founder/Registrar
11819 Puska Rd.
Needville, TX 77461
Ph: (979)793-4207
E-mail: cascabel@consolidated.net
URL: http://www.elcascabel.com/PDSSmain.htm
Contact: Anita Garza, Founder/Registrar
Membership Dues: family, $25 (annual). **Description:** Seeks to promote and preserve the Painted Desert sheep. Educates the public and members about the breed. Works to register and keep pedigree records of all animals that qualify as purebred Painted Desert sheep. Facilitates communication and collaboration among members.

5216 ■ Scottish Blackface Sheep Breeder's Association (SBSBA)
1699 HH Hwy.
Willow Springs, MO 65793
Ph: (417)962-5499
E-mail: sbsba@pcis.net
URL: http://www.geocities.com/blackies_sbsba/sbsba.html
Contact: Richard J. Harward, Sec.
Founded: 1982. **Members:** 150. **Membership Dues:** regular, $10. **Staff:** 1. **Description:** Represents breeders of Scottish Blackface sheep and others interested in the breed. Promotes the breed and works to establish its pedigree. **Publications:** *Breeders List*. **Price:** free ● Booklet ● Brochure. Contains information on the Scottish Blackface Sheep.

5217 ■ Sheep Industry Development Program (SID)
c/o American Sheep Industry Association
9785 Maroon Cir., Ste.360
Englewood, CO 80112
Ph: (303)771-3500
Fax: (303)771-8200
E-mail: info@sheepusa.org
URL: http://www.sheepusa.org
Contact: Peter Orwick, Exec. Dir.
Founded: 1967. **Members:** 68,000. **Staff:** 10. **Description:** A program of the American Sheep Industry Association. Develops production and management systems to make lamb and wool production consistently profitable and to encourage research that will benefit the sheep industry. Gathers, evaluates, and disseminates research information on sheep production and management; determines the need for research projects. Conducts field tests of industry innovations. **Computer Services:** database ● mailing lists. **Affiliated With:** American Sheep Industry Association. **Publications:** *SID/Sheep Production Handbook*, periodic. **Conventions/Meetings:** annual meeting (exhibits) - January.

5218 ■ Soays of America (SOA)
PO Box 551
Gig Harbor, WA 98335
E-mail: acornhillfarms@att.net
URL: http://www.soaysofamerica.org
Contact: Holly Aichem, Pres.
Founded: 2001. **Membership Dues:** active, farm manager, $20 (annual) ● associate, $15 (annual) ● junior, $12 (annual). **Multinational. Description:** Represents breeders, enthusiasts and other individuals committed to the promotion and protection of the viability of Soay Sheep in North America. Seeks to conserve and preserve the American Soay Sheep. Promotes interest in the Soay breed of sheep to attract new breeders for the conservation and well being of the breed. Maintains a conservancy, and fosters a sense of community for its members. **Telecommunication Services:** electronic mail, membership@soaysofamerica.org. **Publications:** Newsletter. **Price:** $3.50 per back issue.

5219 ■ United Suffolk Sheep Association (USSA)
PO Box 256
Newton, UT 84327-0256
Ph: (435)563-6105 (734)586-8444
Fax: (435)563-9356
E-mail: unitedsuffolk@comcast.net
URL: http://www.u-s-s-a.org
Contact: Jim Heggemeier, Pres.
Founded: 1999. **Members:** 3,000. **Membership Dues:** Suffolk breeder, $25 (annual) ● junior, $12 (annual). **Staff:** 7. **Description:** Breeders of purebred Suffolk sheep. Maintains flock book and registry showing pedigree, ownership, and transfer records. Sponsors competitions; offers special awards at national and regional sheep shows. Provides educational materials on the breed for 4-H Program and Youth Development and Future Farmers of America members. **Telecommunication Services:** electronic mail, heggemeier@hotmail.com. **Committees:** Advertising; National Suffolk Show and Sale; Office Management; Research and Development; Youth. **Affiliated With:** Families, 4-H, and Nutrition. **Formed by Merger of:** (1999) American Suffolk Sheep Society; (1999) National Suffolk Sheep Association. **Formerly:** (2003) United Suffolk Sheep Society. **Publications:** *Suffolk News*, bimonthly. Magazine. Contains Suffolk business news, junior news and industry updates. **Price:** $6.00. **Advertising:** accepted ● *The Suffolk News*, periodic. Membership Directory ● *Suffolk Success Story*, periodic ● *USSA Breeders Directory*. **Conventions/Meetings:** annual meeting.

5220 ■ Western Range Association (WRA)
Address Unknown since 2007
Founded: 1950. **Members:** 300. **Description:** Wool growers in 11 western states. Supplies sheepherder labor to members through domestic sources and importations from foreign countries. **Conventions/Meetings:** annual conference - always third Tuesday in June.

Soil

5221 ■ Association for the Environmental Health of Soils (AEHS)
150 Fearing St.
Amherst, MA 01002
Ph: (413)549-5170
Free: (888)540-2347
Fax: (413)549-0579
E-mail: paul@aehs.com
URL: http://www.aehs.com
Contact: Paul Kostecki PhD, Exec. Dir./Exec. Ed.
Founded: 1989. **Members:** 600. **Membership Dues:** student (with proof of status), $75 (annual) ● regular, $125 (annual). **Description:** Individuals interested in soil contamination and the analysis, assessment, remediation, and regulation of soils. Seeks to facilitate communication and foster cooperation among members. Serves as a network linking members; serves as a clearinghouse on soil contamination and remediation; sponsors educational programs. Makes available discounts on books to members. **Publications:** *International Journal of Phytoremediation*, periodic. **Price:** $65.00 /year for members ● *Journal of Soil Contamination*, periodic. **Price:** $65.00 /year for members ● *Soil and Groundwater Cleanup Magazine*, 9/year. **Conventions/Meetings:** annual conference ● periodic seminar ● periodic workshop.

5222 ■ National Society of Consulting Soil Scientists (NSCSS)
PO Box 1724
Sandpoint, ID 83864
Free: (800)535-7148
Fax: (208)263-7013
E-mail: info2007@nscss.org
URL: http://www.nscss.org
Contact: Lari Baldwin, Pres.-Elect
Founded: 1921. **Membership Dues:** regular, $100 (annual) ● student, $15 (annual) ● affiliate, $50 (annual). **Staff:** 850. **Description:** Aims to advance the

discipline and practice of soil science by professionals. Promotes quality interaction between professional soil scientists and their communities. Represents the diverse consulting, service, and business experiences within the society. Fosters professional and ethical conduct in the soil science discipline. **Computer Services:** database, listings of soil teaching resources ● information services, links to related sites ● mailing lists, e-mail discussion group. **Programs:** Liability Insurance. **Affiliated With:** Soil Science Society of America. **Publications:** *Soil Profiles*, quarterly. Newsletter. Provides information about conditions, research, and treatments for its readership. Alternate Formats: online.

5223 ■ United States Consortium of Soil Science Associations (USCSSA)
c/o Mr. Jim Culver, Coor.
611 Jeffrey Dr.
Lincoln, NE 68505
Ph: (402)483-0604
E-mail: j4culver@aol.com
URL: http://soilsassociation.org
Contact: Mr. Jim Culver, Coor.
Regional Groups: 3. **State Groups:** 44. **National Groups:** 3. **Description:** Aims to provide a communication and coordination resource for individual state soil scientist societies and associations. Supports the activities of field soil scientists, researchers, and educators in providing quality soil survey information. **Computer Services:** database, congress contacts, SCSSA societies and associations, consultants ● information services, state soils, state certification, registration of soil scientists ● online services, feedback form. **Subgroups:** Advisory. **Publications:** *A New Framework for Communications and Marketing*. Brochure. Alternate Formats: online.

Soil Conservation

5224 ■ Erosion Control Technology Council (ECTC)
PO Box 18012
St. Paul, MN 55118
Ph: (651)554-1895
Fax: (651)450-6167
E-mail: laurie@ectc.org
URL: http://www.ectc.org
Contact: Laurie L. Honnigford, Exec. Dir.
Founded: 1992. **Members:** 35. **Membership Dues:** directing, $6,000 (annual) ● corporate associate, $400 (annual) ● individual associate, $100 (annual). **Staff:** 2. **Budget:** $85,000. **Multinational. Description:** Seeks to advance the use of rolled erosion control materials. **Committees:** Market Data Reporting; Marketing; Testing and Standards. **Publications:** *Technical Guidance Manual*.

Sugar

5225 ■ American Sugar Cane League of the U.S.A. (ASCL)
PO Drawer 938
Thibodaux, LA 70301
Ph: (985)448-3707
Fax: (985)448-3722
E-mail: lasugar@amscl.org
URL: http://www.amscl.org
Contact: John P. Constant, Business Mgr.
Founded: 1922. **Members:** 650. **Staff:** 5. **Description:** Comprises of Louisiana sugar cane growers and processors. **Committees:** American Sugar Cane League Political Action. **Formed by Merger of:** (1922) Louisiana Sugar Planters Association, American Cane Growers Association and; Producers and Manufacturers Association. **Publications:** *The Sugar Bulletin*, monthly. Serves as a communication tool to keep League members up to date on the ongoings of the industry. **Price:** included in membership dues; $15.00 /year for nonmembers; $50.00/year for foreign. **Circulation:** 1,950. **Advertising:** accepted. **Conventions/Meetings:** annual meeting - always February.

5226 ■ American Sugarbeet Growers Association (ASGA)
1156 15th St. NW, Ste.1101
Washington, DC 20005
Ph: (202)833-2398
Fax: (202)833-2962
E-mail: info@americansugarbeet.org
URL: http://www.americansugarbeet.org
Contact: Luther Markwart, Exec. VP
Founded: 1975. **Members:** 23. **Staff:** 3. **Budget:** $500,000. **Regional Groups:** 12. **Description:** Represents state and regional sugar beet growers associations engaged in lobbying for the sugarbeet industry. **Committees:** Bylaws; Finance; International Affairs; Legislative; Meeting/Awards; Political Action; Public Relations. **Publications:** *ASGA Directory*, annual. Lists board of directors of ASA and regional associations. **Conventions/Meetings:** annual meeting, review of policy provisions passed by Congress that affect sugar growers.

5227 ■ Beet Sugar Development Foundation (BSDF)
800 Grant St., Ste.300
Denver, CO 80203
Ph: (303)832-4460
E-mail: tom@bsdf-assbt.org
URL: http://www.bsdf-assbt.org
Contact: Thomas K. Schwartz, Exec. VP
Founded: 1945. **Members:** 15. **Staff:** 30. **State Groups:** 7. **Description:** Represents sugar beet processing companies in the U.S. and Canada and major beet seed producing firms. Aims to conduct and promote research in beet sugar processing and sugar beet improvement. **Conventions/Meetings:** meeting - 3/year ● meeting, for members' representatives and USDA and state research personnel.

5228 ■ Hawaii Agriculture Research Center (HARC)
99-193 Aiea Heights Dr., Ste.300
Aiea, HI 96701-3911
Ph: (808)487-5561 (808)486-5310
Fax: (808)486-5020
E-mail: swhalen@harc-hspa.com
URL: http://www.hawaiiag.org/harc
Contact: Stephanie A. Whalen MS, Pres./Dir.
Founded: 1882. **Members:** 150. **Staff:** 65. **Budget:** $4,500,000. **Description:** Sugar companies raising sugarcane and manufacturing sugar; individuals connected with these firms. Seeks to improve and protect the sugar industry of Hawaii; supports experiment station. Conducts training sessions for members of the sugar industry; compiles statistics. Encompasses research in forestry, coffee, forage, vegetable crops, and tropical fruits. **Libraries: Type:** reference. **Holdings:** 90,000. **Subjects:** agriculture. **Committees:** Accounting; Energy; Environmental Standards; Experiment Station Advisory; Human Resources; Land and Water; Legal Advisory; Legislative; Raw Sugar Technical; Tax. **Departments:** Crop Science; Environmental Science; Genetics and Pathology; Sugar Technology. **Formerly:** Planters' Labor and Supply Company; (1998) Hawaiian Sugar Planters' Association. **Publications:** *Hawaii's Sugar*. Booklet ● Annual Report. Provides report regarding research undertaken during the previous year. **Price:** free for members. **Conventions/Meetings:** annual meeting - always November/December in Honolulu, HI ● seminar.

5229 ■ Red River Valley Sugarbeet Growers Association (RRVSGA)
1401 32nd St. SW
Fargo, ND 58103-3428
Ph: (701)239-4151
Fax: (701)239-4276
E-mail: rrvsga@corpcomm.net
URL: http://www.sbreb.org/brochures/RRVSGA/rrvsga.htm
Founded: 1926. **Members:** 2,500. **Staff:** 2. **Budget:** $500,000. **Description:** Sugar beet growers in North Dakota and Minnesota. Promotes the realization of a strong and stable sugar industry, and the well-being of its members. Concerns include: migrant seasonal farm workers, unemployment and workers' compensation, transportation, and highway use laws including truck weight, truck taxes, railroad service, and labor union issues. Favors U.S. participation in an International Sugar Agreement to better stabilize world sugar production, and investigates restrictions and regulations on products containing sugar. Conducts public relations campaign on the "value of sugar as a good food." Lobbies state and national legislators. Sponsors research and education board to aid extension services in Minnesota and North Dakota in developing research; conducts research program on the use of herbicides and fungicides. **Committees:** Sugarbeet Institute; Sugarbeet Research and Education Board of Minnesota and North Dakota. **Publications:** Newsletter, monthly. **Price:** free for members. **Circulation:** 2,500 ● Pamphlets. **Conventions/Meetings:** annual convention and conference - always December, Fargo, ND ● annual Sugarbeet Institute - meeting - always March.

Swine

5230 ■ American Berkshire Association (ABA)
PO Box 2436
West Lafayette, IN 47996
Ph: (765)497-3618
Fax: (765)497-2959
E-mail: berkshire@nationalswine.com
URL: http://www.americanberkshire.com
Contact: Amy Smith, Contact
Founded: 1875. **Members:** 400. **Membership Dues:** senior, $10 (annual) ● active, $20 (annual). **Staff:** 3. **Description:** Breeders and sellers of Berkshire hogs. Collects, records, and preserves the pedigrees and histories of purebred Berkshire swine. Studies the general improvement in swine type and practice; promotes use of the Berkshire breed and Berkshire Gold Program. **Telecommunication Services:** electronic mail, berkshire@americanberkshire.com. **Publications:** *The Berkshire News*, bimonthly. Magazine. **Price:** $10.00/year; $25.00/3 years; $25.00/year outside U.S. **Circulation:** 2,000. **Advertising:** accepted ● *Membership Handbook*. Alternate Formats: online ● Also publishes pedigrees and histories of purebred Berkshires. **Conventions/Meetings:** annual conference - always July ● annual meeting - always July.

5231 ■ American Guinea Hog Association (AGHA)
PO Box 719
New Boston, NH 03070
E-mail: agha@sullbarfarm.com
URL: http://www.americanguineahogassociation.org
Contact: Jim Barnett, Pres.
Founded: 2005. **Membership Dues:** active, $20 (annual) ● life, $200. **Description:** Promotes interest in and educates about the American Guinea Hog to attract new breeders for the conservation and well-being of the breed. Protects the genetic diversity of American Guinea Hogs. Works to register and keep pedigree records of all animals that qualify as American Guinea Hogs according to the guidelines of AGHA. Provides technical support to a network of breeders to further their work in conserving the American Guinea Hog. **Publications:** Newsletter. Alternate Formats: online.

5232 ■ American Landrace Association (ALA)
c/o National Swine Registry
PO Box 2417
West Lafayette, IN 47996
Ph: (765)463-3594
Fax: (765)497-2959
E-mail: nsr@nationalswine.com
URL: http://www.nationalswine.com/industryreference/indrefswinebrLand.html
Contact: Darrell D. Anderson, CEO
Founded: 1950. **Members:** 350. **Staff:** 3. **State Groups:** 20. **Description:** Breeders of registered Landrace hogs. Maintains hall of fame, registry, and pedigree records. Compiles statistics; sponsors competitions. **Awards: Type:** recognition. **Computer**

Services: Mailing lists. **Affiliated With:** National Association of Swine Records. **Publications:** *For the Record*, quarterly. Newsletter. Features association news and information. Alternate Formats: online ● *Seedstock Edge*, 9/year. Magazine. **Price:** $25.00/year; $60.00/year (first class); $60.00/3 years; $50.00 outside U.S. **Advertising:** accepted. Alternate Formats: online ● *Standards of Performance*. Report ● Directory, periodic. **Conventions/Meetings:** annual meeting.

5233 ■ American Yorkshire Club (AYC)
c/o National Swine Registry
PO Box 2417
West Lafayette, IN 47996
Ph: (765)463-3594
Fax: (765)497-2959
E-mail: nsr@nationalswine.com
URL: http://www.nationalswine.com
Contact: Darrell D. Anderson, CEO
Founded: 1935. **Members:** 1,000. **Staff:** 10. **State Groups:** 25. **Description:** Maintains registry for purebred Yorkshire swine showing ownership, transfers, and pedigree records. **Publications:** *Purebred Yorkshire Directory*, annual ● Journal, 9/year. **Conventions/Meetings:** semiannual conference.

5234 ■ Chester White Swine Record Association (CWSRA)
PO Box 9758
Peoria, IL 61612-9758
Ph: (309)691-0151 (765)653-0710
Fax: (309)691-0168
E-mail: cpspeoria@mindspring.com
URL: http://www.cpsswine.com
Contact: Paul Beaver, Pres.
Founded: 1930. **Members:** 3,872. **Membership Dues:** senior, junior, $10 (annual). **Staff:** 3. **Budget:** $300,000. **State Groups:** 14. **Description:** Owners and breeders of purebred Chester white swine. Maintains registry showing ownership, transfers, and pedigree records. Sponsors specialized education programs. **Awards: Type:** recognition. **Publications:** *Chester White Journal*, semiannual. **Circulation:** 1,645. **Advertising:** accepted. **Conventions/Meetings:** annual meeting ● show, national - 3/year.

5235 ■ National Association of Swine Records (NASR)
c/o National Swine Registry
PO Box 2417
West Lafayette, IN 47996
Ph: (765)463-3594
Fax: (765)497-2959
E-mail: nsr@nationalswine.com
URL: http://www.nationalswine.com
Contact: Mike Paul, Pres.
Founded: 1994. **Members:** 8. **Description:** Secretaries of swine record associations that register purebred hogs, representing a total of 10,000 members. Develops health and management guidelines for members. Conducts research to identify potential export markets for purebred hogs. Sponsors competitions; compiles statistics. **Awards: Type:** recognition ● **Type:** scholarship. **Computer Services:** database. **Telecommunication Services:** electronic mail, mike@nationalswine.com. **Committees:** Health; Product Evaluation. **Publications:** *Buyer's Guide*, biennial. Directory. **Conventions/Meetings:** annual meeting ● semiannual show.

5236 ■ National Hereford Hog Record Association (NHHRA)
Address Unknown since 2008
Founded: 1934. **Members:** 4,000. **Membership Dues:** life, $10. **Staff:** 1. **Budget:** $10,000. **State Groups:** 2. **Description:** Breeders of purebred Hereford hogs. Maintains registry showing ownership, transfers, and pedigree records. **Awards: Frequency:** annual. **Type:** recognition. **Publications:** *Hereford Hog Advertiser*, quarterly. Newsletter. **Advertising:** accepted ● Bulletin, annual. News from breeders. **Advertising:** accepted. **Conventions/Meetings:** annual National Hereford Hog Show and Sale, with hog sales (exhibits) - 3rd weekend in August.

5237 ■ National Junior Swine Association (NJSA)
PO Box 2417
West Lafayette, IN 47996-2417
Ph: (765)463-3594
Fax: (765)497-2959
E-mail: nsr@nationalswine.com
URL: http://www.nationalswine.com/njsa/njsa.html
Contact: Jennifer Shike, Dir. of Junior Activities
Founded: 2000. **Members:** 9,525. **Description:** Provides a network for purebred swine enthusiasts through a youth organization. Sponsors conferences, scholarships programs, national and regional junior shows featuring numerous educational contests. **Awards:** Outstanding Member of the Year Scholarships. **Type:** scholarship. **Recipient:** to student members. **Telecommunication Services:** electronic mail, jennifer@nationalswine.com. **Publications:** *The Pinnacle*, quarterly. Newsletter. Features activities and events, show tips, feeding advice, fun facts, puzzles, and feature stories. Alternate Formats: online. **Conventions/Meetings:** annual Eastern Regional - regional meeting - always in Harrisburg, PA ● annual National Junior Summer Spectacular - meeting, held in conjunction with the Summer Type Conference, with gilt show, showmanship contest, skillathon, photography contest - always in Louisville, KY ● annual Southwest Regional - meeting - always in Lawton, OK ● annual Western Regional - regional meeting - always in Bakersfield, CA.

5238 ■ National Pork Producers Council (NPPC)
122 C St. NW, Ste.875
Washington, DC 20001
Ph: (202)347-3600 (515)278-8012
Fax: (202)347-5265
E-mail: webmaster@nppc.org
URL: http://www.nppc.org
Contact: Neil Dierks, CEO
Founded: 1954. **Members:** 85,000. **Staff:** 8. **Budget:** $25,000,000. **State Groups:** 44. **Description:** Federation of state pork producer associations. Promotes the pork industry through research programs, consumer education, and lobbying activities. Compiles statistics; maintains speakers' bureau and hall of fame. **Libraries: Type:** reference. **Holdings:** books, periodicals. **Subjects:** swine, pork, food, agriculture. **Awards:** National Pork Fellowship. **Frequency:** annual. **Type:** scholarship ● Research Grant. **Frequency:** annual. **Type:** grant. **Telecommunication Services:** electronic mail, dierksn@nppc.org. **Committees:** Demand Enhancement; Environmental Issues; Government Relations; Market Technology; Pork Political Action; Production Technology; Quality Assurance; Resource Management; Revenue Development; State and Associate Relations; Swine Health and Pork Safety. **Absorbed:** (1992) National Pork Council Women. **Formerly:** National Swine Growers Council. **Publications:** *Annual Research Review*, *Seminar Proceedings* ● *Pork Leader*, biweekly. Newsletter ● *Pork Report*, bimonthly. Magazine. **Conventions/Meetings:** annual Pork Industry Forum - meeting - always March ● annual World Pork Expo - meeting - always June.

5239 ■ National Spotted Swine Record (NSSR)
PO Box 9758
Peoria, IL 61612-9758
Ph: (309)693-1804 (937)548-7909
Fax: (309)691-0168
E-mail: cpspeoria@mindspring.com
URL: http://www.cpsswine.com
Contact: Ron Pierce, Pres.
Founded: 1914. **Members:** 643. **Membership Dues:** senior, junior, $10 (annual). **Staff:** 3. **Budget:** $250,000. **State Groups:** 18. **Description:** Breeders of purebred spotted hogs, formerly known as Spotted Poland China hogs. **Libraries: Type:** reference. **Holdings:** 6; periodicals. **Subjects:** information on shows. **Affiliated With:** National Association of Swine Records. **Formerly:** (1916) American Spotted Poland China Record; (1960) National Spotted Poland China Record; (1965) Spotted Swine Record. **Publications:** *Spotted News*, bimonthly. Journal. **Price:** included in membership dues; $10.00 /year for nonmembers. ISSN: 0038-8432. **Circulation:** 1,675. **Advertising:** accepted. **Conventions/Meetings:** annual conference ● biennial meeting - always summer.

5240 ■ National Swine Improvement Federation (NSIF)
c/o Kenneth J. Stalder, PhD, Sec.-Treas.
Iowa State Univ.
Dept. of Animal Sci.
109 Kildee Hall
Ames, IA 50011-3150
Ph: (515)294-4683
Fax: (515)294-5698
E-mail: stalder@iastate.edu
URL: http://www.nsif.com
Contact: Kenneth J. Stalder PhD, Sec.-Treas.
Founded: 1975. **Members:** 60. **Membership Dues:** regular, associate, $100 (annual). **Description:** Central testing stations, on-the-farm testing programs, and industry and purebred breed associations actively involved in swine performance testing and genetic improvement programs concerned with the collection, evaluation, and use of performance data. Establishes uniform procedures for performance testing and facilitates cooperation among member organizations and all segments of the pork industry in developing and utilizing performance testing. Identifies areas for genetic research and supports research projects. **Awards:** Distinguished Service. **Frequency:** annual. **Type:** recognition. **Recipient:** for distinguished service toward genetic improvement in swine ● Graduate Student. **Frequency:** annual. **Type:** recognition. **Recipient:** for outstanding research in swine genetics. **Committees:** Audit; Awards; Central Test Station; Certification; Fact Sheet Review; Membership; Performance Testing; Program; Representation; Technical. **Publications:** *Guidelines for Uniform Swine Improvement Programs*, periodic. Booklet. **Price:** free ● *Proceedings of the Annual Conference*, annual. Contains information on the annual conference. Alternate Formats: online ● *Report Proceedings*, annual. Includes membership directory, officer and directors, and committees. ● *Swine Genetics*. Handbook. Contains fact sheets that explain the concept in swine improvement. Alternate Formats: online. **Conventions/Meetings:** annual conference and meeting (exhibits).

5241 ■ National Swine Registry (NSR)
PO Box 2417
West Lafayette, IN 47996
Ph: (765)463-3594
Fax: (765)497-2959
E-mail: nsr@nationalswine.com
URL: http://www.nationalswine.com
Contact: Darrell D. Anderson, CEO
Founded: 1994. **Members:** 2,000. **Membership Dues:** regular, $75 (annual). **Staff:** 15. **Budget:** $2,000,000. **Description:** Maintains registry for purebred Duroc, Yorkshire, Hampshire, and Landrace swine showing ownership, transfers, and pedigree records. **Computer Services:** database, directory of staffs and breeders. **Telecommunication Services:** electronic mail, darrell@nationalswine.com. **Departments:** Commercial Services; Communications; Junior Activities; Pedigree. **Formed by Merger of:** (1998) United Duroc Swine Registry; (1998) Hampshire Swine Registry. **Formerly:** (1957) United Duroc Record Association. **Publications:** *For the Record*, quarterly. Newsletter. Features association news and information. Alternate Formats: online ● *Seedstock Edge*, 9/year. Magazine. Features the latest information about shows and sales in the purebred swine registry, as well as production tips and trends. **Price:** $25.00/year in U.S.; $60.00/year (first class); $60.00/three years in U.S.; $50.00/year outside U.S. **Circulation:** 5,000. **Advertising:** accepted. Alternate Formats: online. **Conventions/Meetings:** annual meeting.

5242 ■ Poland China Record Association (PCRA)
PO Box 9758
Peoria, IL 61612-9758
Ph: (309)691-6301

Fax: (309)691-0168
E-mail: cpspeoria@mindspring.com
Contact: J.R. Reid, Pres.
Founded: 1876. **Members:** 323. **Membership Dues:** individual, $75 (annual). **Staff:** 3. **Budget:** $100,000. **Description:** Breeders of purebred Poland China hogs. Maintains registry showing ownership, transfers, and pedigree records. Sponsors prolificacy, meat type evaluation, and rate of gain and feeding efficiency measuring programs. **Publications:** *Poland China Advantage*, bimonthly. Directory. **Price:** $10.00/year; $25.00/3 years. ISSN: 1082-6920. **Circulation:** 2,500. **Advertising:** accepted. Alternate Formats: online; CD-ROM. **Conventions/Meetings:** annual conference.

5243 ■ United Duroc Swine Registry
PO Box 2417
West Lafayette, IN 47996-2417
Ph: (765)463-3594
Fax: (765)497-2959
E-mail: nsr@nationalswine.com
URL: http://www.nationalswine.com/industryreference/indrefswinebrDuroc.html
Contact: Jessica Goyette, Sec.
Founded: 1934. **Description:** Promotes the Duroc swine breed in the U.S. **Telecommunication Services:** electronic mail, jessica@nationalswine.com. **Publications:** *Seedstock Edge*, 9/year. Magazine. **Price:** included in membership dues.

Tea

5244 ■ International Compost Tea Council (ICTC)
14150 NE 20th St., Ste.293
Bellevue, WA 98007
Ph: (425)614-4282
Free: (866)558-0990
E-mail: ctinfo@intlctc.org
URL: http://www.intlctc.org
Contact: Seaneen Hummel, Pres.
Membership Dues: small business, $50 (annual) ● non-profit, academic, government, $75 (annual) ● large business, $100 (annual) ● individual, $25 (annual). **Description:** Promotes awareness of compost tea. Provides a forum to discuss the history, philosophy, science and actual practice of using compost tea. Provides opportunities and information that promote integrity, professionalism and education in the compost tea industry and all related industries, including agriculture, landscape, forestry, soil science and geotechnical engineering. **Boards:** Advisory.

Tobacco

5245 ■ Burley Stabilization Corporation (BSC)
PO Box 6447
Knoxville, TN 37914
Ph: (865)525-9381
Fax: (865)525-8383
E-mail: burleytobacco@aol.com
URL: http://www.burleystabilization.com
Contact: Mr. George Marks, Pres.
Founded: 1953. **Members:** 140,000. **Staff:** 3. **Description:** Burley tobacco growers' cooperative marketing organization. Coordinates the price support program for burley tobacco in Tennessee, North Carolina, and Virginia under contract with Commodity Credit Corporation. **Conventions/Meetings:** monthly board meeting.

5246 ■ Burley Tobacco Growers Cooperative Association (BTGCA)
620 S Broadway
Lexington, KY 40508
Ph: (859)252-3561
Fax: (859)231-9804
E-mail: stephanie@burleytobacco.com
URL: http://www.burleytobacco.com
Contact: Roger Quarles, Pres.
Founded: 1921. **Members:** 150,000. **Staff:** 14. **Description:** Represents producers of burley tobacco in Kentucky, Indiana, Ohio, West Virginia, and Missouri. Administers government price supports on tobacco for the Commodity Credit Corporation in this area. **Convention/Meeting:** none. **Publications:** Articles. Alternate Formats: online.

5247 ■ Eastern Dark-Fired Tobacco Growers Association (ED-FTGA)
Address Unknown since 2008
Founded: 1932. **Members:** 18,000. **Staff:** 4. **Description:** Dark tobacco growers. Membership concentrated in Kentucky and Tennessee. **Conventions/Meetings:** annual meeting - always third Wednesday in November; **Avg. Attendance:** 100.

5248 ■ Flue-Cured Tobacco Cooperative Stabilization Corporation (FCTCSC)
1304 Annapolis Dr.
Raleigh, NC 27608
Ph: (919)821-4560 (919)645-6006
Fax: (919)821-4564
E-mail: arnoldh3151@ipass.net
URL: http://www.fctcsc.com
Contact: L. Arnold Hamm, CEO/Gen. Mgr.
Founded: 1946. **Members:** 750,000. **Staff:** 47. **Description:** Represents flue-cured tobacco producers' marketing cooperative for six southern states. **Publications:** *Scoop*, monthly. Newsletter. Provides news and information about the Cooperative, world markets, and world tobacco sales. Alternate Formats: online ● Annual Report, annual. Alternate Formats: online. **Conventions/Meetings:** annual meeting (exhibits) - always last Friday in May, Raleigh, NC.

5249 ■ Society for Research on Nicotine and Tobacco (SRNT)
2810 Crossroads Dr., Ste.3800
Madison, WI 53718
Ph: (608)443-2462
Fax: (608)443-2474
E-mail: info@srnt.org
URL: http://www.srnt.org
Contact: Dr. Bruce Wheeler, Exec. Dir.
Founded: 1994. **Members:** 530. **Membership Dues:** full, affiliate, $120 (annual) ● student, $35 (annual) ● retired, $60 (annual). **Staff:** 10. **National Groups:** 3. **Languages:** English, French. **Description:** Seeks to foster the exchange of information on the entire spectrum of research concerning nicotine use and tobacco dependence and to stimulate the generation of new knowledge concerning nicotine in all its manifestations. **Awards:** Doll/Wynder Award. **Frequency:** biennial. **Type:** monetary ● Ferno Award. **Frequency:** triennial. **Type:** monetary ● Young Investigator Award. **Type:** monetary. **Computer Services:** database, available in English and French ● mailing lists, of members ● online services, listserv for members. **Telecommunication Services:** electronic mail, bwheeler@reesgroupinc.com. **Publications:** *Nicotine and Tobacco Research*, quarterly. Journal. **Circulation:** 575. Alternate Formats: online ● *SRNT Newsletter*, quarterly. **Circulation:** 530. Alternate Formats: online. **Conventions/Meetings:** annual conference ● annual convention (exhibits) ● biennial meeting, special interest ● annual meeting (exhibits).

Trapping

5250 ■ Fur Takers of America (FTA)
c/o Ramona Plueger, Membership Coor.
17453 130th Ave.
Monticello, IA 52310
E-mail: secretary@furtakersofamerica.com
URL: http://www.furtakersofamerica.com
Contact: Carol Krumwiede, Sec.
Founded: 1968. **Members:** 20,000. **Membership Dues:** regular, $25 (annual) ● junior (below 18 years old), $12 (annual) ● life (below 64 years old), $500 ● life (65 years old and above), $200 ● sustaining, $20 (annual). **Staff:** 2. **Budget:** $70,000. **Regional Groups:** 8. **State Groups:** 38. **Local Groups:** 92. **Description:** Fur trappers, fur buyers, trapping supply people, hunters, fur dressers, conservationists, and other interested individuals. Seeks to educate trappers in humane methods of trapping and conservation ethics. Has established a professional trapping school. Offers public information programs emphasizing the historic significance of the fur trade. Promotes trapping through education. Sponsors world trap setting contest. Maintains hall of fame; compiles statistics. **Awards:** National Charlie Dobbins. **Frequency:** annual. **Type:** scholarship. **Recipient:** for Fur takers of American member. **Telecommunication Services:** electronic mail, ckrum2003@yahoo.com ● electronic mail, ftamembership@yahoo.com. **Committees:** Conservation; Education; Trap Improvement. **Affiliated With:** U.S. Sportsmen's Alliance. **Publications:** *The Fur Taker*, monthly. Magazine. **Price:** included in membership dues. ISSN: 0016-2965. **Circulation:** 2,500. **Advertising:** accepted ● *Introduction to FTA*. Brochure. **Price:** free ● *Is Mother Nature Humane?*. Brochure. Alternate Formats: online. **Conventions/Meetings:** annual The Fur Taker of America National Rendezvous - convention ● annual North American Fur Taker Rendezvous - congress, trapping (exhibits) - always June.

5251 ■ National Trappers Association (NTA)
2815 Washington Ave.
Bedford, IN 47421
Ph: (812)277-9670
Fax: (812)277-9672
E-mail: ntaheadquarters@nationaltrappers.com
URL: http://www.nationaltrappers.com
Contact: Jim Buell, Pres.
Founded: 1959. **Members:** 12,000. **Membership Dues:** regular in U.S., $25 (annual) ● household, $10 (annual) ● junior, $15 (annual) ● regular outside U.S., $35 (annual) ● life (age 70 and older), $200 ● life (under age 70), $750 ● life (outside U.S.), $300. **Staff:** 7. **Budget:** $750,000. **State Groups:** 55. **Description:** Harvesters of furbearers (muskrat, fox, coyote, mink, beaver, raccoon, bobcat, and others) for the purpose of wildlife management, animal damage control, and outdoor recreation. Promotes sound environmental education programs and conservation of natural resources. Compiles statistics. **Awards:** Charles Dobbins Memorial Scholarship. **Frequency:** annual. **Type:** scholarship. **Recipient:** for wildlife management students ● Conservationist of the Year. **Frequency:** annual. **Type:** recognition ● President's Award. **Frequency:** annual. **Type:** recognition ● Trapper of the Year. **Frequency:** annual. **Type:** recognition. **Telecommunication Services:** electronic mail, info@nationaltrappers.com ● electronic mail, buell@nationaltrappers.com. **Committees:** Conservation. **Funds:** Charles Dobbins Memorial. **Publications:** *American Trapper*, bimonthly. Magazine. Contains reports, tips, editorials, and legislative news. **Price:** $3.00/past issues; $10.00 /year for libraries; $3.00/copy. **Advertising:** accepted ● *Balancing Nature*. Video. **Price:** $19.95 for 1 copy; $10.00 for 2-49 copies; $6.00 for 50 or more copies (regular rate); $6.00 for 25 or more copies (educational rate) ● *Facts About Fur*. **Price:** $1.00 ● *Furbearer Management - Myths and Facts* ● *Master Trappers*. Video. Features 10 trappers sharing their expertise. **Price:** $40.00/volume; $75.00 volumes 1/2 ● *NTA Trapping Handbook*. **Price:** $8.00 softbound; $12.00 hardbound; $3.00 educational rate ● *Teacher's Guide and Lesson Plan*. Booklet. **Price:** $2.00 ● *Traps Today - Myths and Facts* ● . **Price:** Also publishes other educational materials. **Conventions/Meetings:** annual convention (exhibits) - usually first week in August.

Travel

5252 ■ Sustainable Travel International (STI)
PO Box 1313
Boulder, CO 80306
Ph: (720)273-2975

E-mail: info@sustainabletravel.com
URL: http://www.sustainabletravelinternational.org
Contact: Brian Thomas Mullis, Pres.
Founded: 2002. **Membership Dues:** premium partner, $500 (annual) ● supporting business (based on annual gross revenue), $100-$300 (annual) ● contributing individual, $25 (annual). **Multinational. Description:** Promotes ecotourism and sustainable development. Seeks to educate travelers and travel-related companies to protect the environment and cultures they visit. Develops, adopts and markets sustainable tourism standards and practices through the Sustainable Tourism Eco-Certification Program. **Publications:** *Responsible Travel Report*, monthly. Newsletter. **Price:** included in membership dues. Alternate Formats: online.

Trees and Shrubs

5253 ■ American Conifer Society (ACS)

c/o John Martin, Office Mgr.
175 Charisma Ln.
Lewisville, NC 27023-9611
Ph: (336)945-0483
Fax: (336)945-0484
E-mail: nationaloffice@conifersociety.org
URL: http://www.conifersociety.org
Contact: John Martin, Office Mgr.
Founded: 1983. **Members:** 2,000. **Membership Dues:** basic, in U.S. and Canada, $30 (annual) ● institutional, $30 (annual) ● corporate, business, $100 (annual) ● basic, outside U.S. and Canada, $40 (annual) ● life, $1,000 ● sustaining, $50 ● patron, $130 (annual) ● joint in U.S. and Canada, $35 (annual) ● joint outside U.S. and Canada, $45 (annual). **Budget:** $100,000. **Regional Groups:** 4. **Description:** Arboretums, libraries, and landscapers, botanists, gardeners, and other interested individuals. Seeks to increase public interest in the development, preservation, and propagation of conifers, particularly those that are dwarf or unusual. Works to standardize nomenclature and education on conifers. Offers educational programs in taxonomy. Provides public speakers. **Libraries: Type:** reference. **Holdings:** archival material. **Awards:** ACS Scholarship. **Frequency:** annual. **Type:** scholarship. **Recipient:** for members of the society ● Jean Iseli Memorial Fund. **Frequency:** annual. **Type:** monetary. **Recipient:** for arboreta and horticultural related colleges. **Computer Services:** database, conifer. **Committees:** Conifer Quarterly Advisory; The Website Advisory. **Also Known As:** The Conifer Society. **Publications:** *Conifer Quarterly*. Magazine. **Price:** included in membership dues. ISSN: 8755-0490. **Circulation:** 1,700. **Advertising:** accepted. **Conventions/Meetings:** annual seminar (exhibits).

5254 ■ American Society of Consulting Arborists (ASCA)

15245 Shady Grove Rd., Ste.130
Rockville, MD 20850
Ph: (301)947-0483
Fax: (301)990-9771
E-mail: asca@mgmtsol.com
URL: http://www.asca-consultants.org
Contact: Beth Palys CAE, Exec. Dir.
Founded: 1967. **Members:** 525. **Membership Dues:** individual, $365 (annual). **Staff:** 5. **Budget:** $500,000. **Description:** Arboriculture professionals who possess extensive technical knowledge and experience including skills in the areas of written and oral communications, consulting ethics, expert witness activities, and practice management. Allows members to provide independent diagnoses, opinions, appraisal of value, and condition evaluation on trees for clients in the legal, insurance, and development communities as well as the general public. **Libraries: Type:** reference. **Awards:** Chadwick Scholarship Fund. **Frequency:** annual. **Type:** scholarship. **Programs:** Plant Health Care; Tree Planting. **Projects:** Tree Protection for Construction. **Also Known As:** ASCA (acronym). **Publications:** *A Consultant's Guide to Writing Effective Reports*. Book. **Price:** $60.00 for members, plus shipping and handling; $90.00 for nonmembers, plus shipping and handling ● *Arboricultural Consultant*, quarterly. Newsletter. **Price:** free for members. **Circulation:** 500. **Advertising:** accepted ● *Arboriculture and the Law*. Manual. **Price:** $35.00 for members, plus shipping and handling; $50.00 for nonmembers, plus shipping and handling ● *The Arborthority*. Newsletter ● *Example Report Book*. **Price:** $45.00 for members, plus shipping and handling; $70.00 for nonmembers, plus shipping and handling. **Conventions/Meetings:** annual conference (exhibits) - always December ● annual Consulting Academy - workshop - late February, early March.

5255 ■ American Willow Growers Network

c/o English Basketry Willows
412 County Rd. 31
Norwich, NY 13815-3149
Ph: (607)336-9031
Fax: (607)336-9031
E-mail: bonwillow@frontiernet.net
URL: http://www.msu.edu/user/shermanh/galeb
Contact: Bonnie Gale, Proprietor
Founded: 1988. **Members:** 400. **Membership Dues:** in U.S., $10 (annual) ● in Canada, C$13 (annual) ● outside U.S. and Canada, $15 (annual). **Staff:** 1. **Description:** Individuals interested in willows. Serves as a clearinghouse for the exchange of information on willow growth and usage including basketry, furniture making, timber production and biomass, windbreaks, and soil stabilization and amelioration. Provides for the exchange and sale of willow cuttings. **Convention/Meeting:** none. **Libraries: Type:** reference. **Publications:** *Newsletter of the American Willow Growers Network*, annual. Includes articles on growing, harvesting, and processing of willow; covers all aspects of the use of willow. **Price:** included in membership dues.

5256 ■ Holly Society of America (HSA)

c/o Rondalyn Reeser, Sec.
PO Box 803
309 Buck St.
Millville, NJ 08332-0803
Ph: (856)825-4300
E-mail: secretary@hollysocam.org
URL: http://www.hollysocam.org
Contact: Rondalyn Reeser, Sec.
Founded: 1947. **Members:** 550. **Membership Dues:** standard (individual/joint), $30 (annual) ● life, $600 ● sustaining, standard (commercial/institutional), $60 (annual) ● sponsoring, sustaining (commercial/institutional), $120 (annual). **Staff:** 3. **Regional Groups:** 7. **Description:** Nurserymen, landscape architects, florists, wreath and spray holly dealers, and individuals interested in holly culture. Aims to: promote research on growing holly and on controlling insect pests and diseases of holly; study methods of conservatively cutting market holly for Christmas decoratives; locate and preserve holly stands of great natural beauty; encourage the establishment of "Living Memorials" of native holly stands as memorials to servicemen. Maintains speakers' bureau; conducts research programs; compiles statistics. **Libraries: Type:** open to the public. **Holdings:** 20. **Awards:** Best in Show in the Amateur Division. **Frequency:** annual. **Type:** recognition. **Recipient:** for shows in the amateur division ● Stewart McLean Award. **Frequency:** annual. **Type:** recognition. **Recipient:** for the best show for the professional division ● Wilson T. Mott Award. **Frequency:** annual. **Type:** recognition. **Recipient:** for the best evergreen sprig in the amateur division ● Wolf-Fenton Award. **Frequency:** periodic. **Type:** recognition. **Recipient:** to an individual with outstanding contributions and dedicated service in the field of holly. **Committees:** Advertising; Arboretum; Auction; Awards; Disease and Pest Control; Investment; Registration; Research and Development. **Publications:** *Holly Society Journal*, quarterly. Contains informative articles and photographs, technical data, and research results. **Price:** included in membership dues; $3.50/copy for nonmembers. ISSN: 0738-2421. **Circulation:** 800. **Advertising:** accepted ● Brochure ● Books. **Conventions/Meetings:** annual meeting and dinner, also holds Holly auction and cutting exchange - always October or November.

5257 ■ International Fruit Tree Association (IFTA)

c/o Susan M. Pheasant, PhD, Exec. Dir.
PO Box 5006
Wenatchee, WA 98807-5006
Ph: (509)884-5651
Fax: (509)884-1858
E-mail: pheasant@ifruittree.org
URL: http://www.ifruittree.org
Contact: Susan M. Pheasant PhD, Exec. Dir.
Founded: 1958. **Membership Dues:** individual, $85 (annual). **Multinational. Description:** Individuals in 30 countries. Promotes research and disseminates information concerning the growing of dwarf fruit trees. **Awards: Type:** recognition. **Recipient:** for honorary memberships. **Committees:** Awards; Rootstock Research. **Formerly:** (1975) Dwarf Fruit Tree Association; (2005) International Dwarf Fruit Tree Association. **Publications:** *Compact Fruit Tree*, annual. **Conventions/Meetings:** annual conference - always February ● annual Orchard Tour - always June or July.

5258 ■ International Oak Society

c/o Richard Jensen, Membership Chm.
Dept. of Biology
St. Mary's Coll.
Notre Dame, IN 46556
Ph: (574)284-4674
Fax: (574)284-4716
E-mail: rjensen@saintmarys.edu
URL: http://www.saintmarys.edu/~rjensen/ios.html
Contact: Richard Jensen, Membership Chm.
Founded: 1985. **Members:** 500. **Membership Dues:** family, $30 (annual) ● individual, $25 (annual) ● life, $400. **Staff:** 15. **Description:** Those interested in advancing the state of scientific knowledge regarding oaks and Oakland ecology. Works to further the study, sustainable management, preservation, appreciation, and dissemination of knowledge to the public about oaks (genus Quercus) and their ecosystems. Encourages, recognizes, and honors outstanding achievements by individuals and organizations advancing the goals of the society. **Awards:** Special Service Awards. **Frequency:** 3/year. **Type:** recognition. **Recipient:** for outstanding service to the society in enhancing the knowledge about oaks and oak ecosystems. **Publications:** *International Oaks*, annual. Journal. **Price:** included in membership dues. **Circulation:** 500. Also Cited As: *Journal of the International Oak Society* ● *Oak News and Notes*, semiannual. Newsletter. **Price:** included in membership dues. **Circulation:** 500. **Advertising:** accepted. Also Cited As: *Intoaks*. **Conventions/Meetings:** triennial International Oak Conference - conference and workshop, with formal paper sessions.

5259 ■ International Society of Arboriculture (ISA)

PO Box 3129
Champaign, IL 61826-3129
Ph: (217)355-9411
Free: (888)472-8733
Fax: (217)355-9516
E-mail: isa@isa-arbor.com
URL: http://www.isa-arbor.com
Contact: Jim Skiera, Exec. Dir.
Founded: 1924. **Members:** 14,500. **Membership Dues:** library, $75 (annual) ● professional, $105 (annual) ● sustaining, $500 (annual) ● life, $1,050 ● student, senior, $25 (annual). **Staff:** 20. **Budget:** $4,500,000. **Regional Groups:** 32. **Description:** Individuals engaged in commercial, municipal, and utility arboriculture; city, state, and national government employees; municipal and commercial arborists; others interested in shade tree welfare. Disseminates information on the care and preservation of shade and ornamental trees. Supports research projects at educational institutions. **Awards:** John Z. Duling Grants. **Frequency:** annual. **Type:** grant ● Research Trust Funds. **Frequency:** annual. **Type:** monetary. **Committees:** Arbor Day; Awards; Certifications Liaisons; Diversity; Educational Goods and Services; Safety Standards/Performance Standards; Shade Tree Evaluation; Urban Forestry. **Formerly:** (1924) National Shade Tree Evaluation; (1974) International

Shade Tree Conference. **Publications:** *Arborist News*, bimonthly. **Circulation:** 11,000. **Advertising:** accepted. Alternate Formats: online ● *Journal of Arboriculture*, bimonthly ● Brochures ● Videos ● Yearbook. **Conventions/Meetings:** annual meeting, educational meeting (exhibits).

5260 ■ Metropolitan Tree Improvement Alliance (METRIA)
c/o Dr. Bert Cregg, Sec.-Treas.
Michigan State Univ.
Dept. of Horticulture
East Lansing, MI 48824-1325
E-mail: cregg@msu.edu
URL: http://www.ces.ncsu.edu/fletcher/programs/nursery/metria
Contact: Dr. Bert Cregg, Sec.-Treas.
Founded: 1976. **Members:** 350. **Description:** Arborists, tree nurserymen, city foresters, and research scientists. Attempts to provide, through education and research, opportunities for collaboration in developing better trees for metropolitan landscapes. Is concerned with the management and selection of urban trees, the breeding and use of improved cultivars, and better cultural techniques. **Publications:** *Metrian*, quarterly ● Also publishes proceedings of technical conferences. **Conventions/Meetings:** biennial conference.

5261 ■ National Christmas Tree Association (NCTA)
16020 Swingley Ridge Rd., Ste.300
Chesterfield, MO 63017
Ph: (636)449-5070
Fax: (636)449-5051
E-mail: info@realchristmastrees.org
URL: http://www.realchristmastrees.org
Contact: Rick Dungey, Contact
Founded: 1955. **Members:** 1,650. **Membership Dues:** associate, $65 ● general, $164 ● premier (major grower), $364 ● premier (wholesale, commercial retail), $264 ● premier (choose and cut), $214 ● related industry, $165-$765. **Staff:** 6. **Budget:** $450,000. **State Groups:** 36. **Description:** Exists to promote the use of real Christmas trees and support the industry that provides them. Includes grower-wholesalers, grower-retailers, and all other retailers that sell real Christmas trees and related green products. Sponsors National Christmas Tree Contest. Maintains information and referral service and provides the option of liability insurance for retailers, and choose and cut growers. **Computer Services:** Mailing lists. **Committees:** Communications; Educational Conferences; Environmental Concerns; Holiday Safety; Legislative/Regulatory Affairs; Member Development; Public Relations; Real Tree Development; Youth and Schools. **Sections:** Choose and Cut Growers; Commercial Retailers; Major Growers; Wholesale. **Formerly:** (1974) National Christmas Tree Growers Association. **Publications:** *American Christmas Tree Journal*, 5/year, January, March, July, October and May. Features marketing information. **Price:** included in membership dues; $45.00 /year for libraries. ISSN: 0569-3845. **Circulation:** 1,850. **Advertising:** accepted ● Bulletins. **Conventions/Meetings:** annual Christmas Trees PLUS - A Premier Event - conference, for marketing - usually February ● biennial convention and trade show (exhibits) - usually August.

5262 ■ Tree Care Industry Association
3 Perimeter Rd., Unit 1
Manchester, NH 03103
Ph: (603)314-5380
Free: (800)733-2622
Fax: (603)314-5386
E-mail: tcia@treecareindustry.org
URL: http://www.treecareindustry.org
Contact: Cynthia Mills CAE, Pres./CEO
Founded: 1938. **Members:** 2,300. **Membership Dues:** associate-dealer, distributor, industry support, $384 (annual) ● associate-manufacturer, $537 (annual) ● business (with annual gross volume of $0-$100,000), $359-$574 (annual) ● business (with annual gross volume of $500,001-$1,000,000), $790-$1,004 (annual) ● business (with annual gross volume of $1,000,001-$20,000,000), $1,436-$2,010 (annual) ● business (with annual gross volume of $20,000,001 and above), $3,444 (annual). **Staff:** 20. **Budget:** $4,000,000. **Languages:** English, Spanish. **Multinational. Description:** Represents commercial tree service companies. Works to improve arboricultural practices and inform the public of the need for preservation and proper care of shade trees. Runs Certified Treecare Specialist Program for practitioners and Accreditation program for companies. Conducts specialized education programs. **Awards:** Award of Merit. **Frequency:** annual. **Type:** recognition. **Recipient:** for a living person whose legacy has positively influenced the practice of arboriculture ● Legislator of the Year. **Frequency:** annual. **Type:** recognition. **Recipient:** to a member of congress who extols the virtues and is supportive of legislative and regulatory measures that facilitate and advance the commercial tree care industry ● Professional Communications Awards. **Frequency:** annual. **Type:** recognition. **Recipient:** for marketing and communication ● Safety Award. **Frequency:** annual. **Type:** recognition. **Recipient:** for exemplary safety programs. **Additional Websites:** http://www.tcia.org. **Formerly:** (2004) National Arborist Association. **Publications:** *The Reporter*, monthly. Newsletter. Includes industry surveys. **Price:** available to members only. **Circulation:** 2,350 ● *Tree Care Industry Magazine*, monthly. **Price:** $30.00. **Circulation:** 27,500. **Advertising:** accepted ● *The Treeworker*, monthly. Newsletter. Contains general safety-oriented and educational articles on arboricultural topics for arborists and field employees. **Price:** $14.50/year. **Circulation:** 3,000 ● Also issues several guides, pamphlets, and videocassette programs on various aspects of arboriculture. **Conventions/Meetings:** annual Tree Care Industry Expo - trade show - always November ● annual Winter Management Conference - always February.

5263 ■ Trees for the Future (TFTF)
PO Box 7027
Silver Spring, MD 20907
Free: (800)643-0001
Fax: (301)565-5012
E-mail: info@treesftf.org
URL: http://www.treesftf.org
Contact: Mr. David Deppner, Pres.
Founded: 1988. **Members:** 6,000. **Membership Dues:** standard, $40 (annual) ● grove, $100 (annual) ● whole village, $480 (annual). **Staff:** 4. **Budget:** $310,000. **Languages:** Amharic, English, Filipino, French, Indonesian, Spanish, Swahili. **Description:** Supports grassroots reforestation efforts, working with developing communities and university research teams in 64 tropical countries. Dedicated to helping people of developing communities to begin environmentally sustainable and regenerative projects. Since 1989 the association has supervised the planting of 20 million trees. **Convention/Meeting:** none. **Libraries: Type:** by appointment only. **Subjects:** collection of materials published by USAID and other agencies, nitrogen fixing trees and crops. **Computer Services:** database, tree planting programs around the world ● mailing lists, of members. **Publications:** *Global Cooling Handbook*. Contains introduction to carbon storage. ● *Johnny Ipil-Seed News*, quarterly. Newsletter. **Price:** included in membership dues. Alternate Formats: online ● Newsletter, monthly. Alternate Formats: online.

Virgin Islands

5264 ■ Friends of Virgin Islands National Park
PO Box 811
St. John, VI 00831
Ph: (340)779-4940
Fax: (340)693-9973
E-mail: info@friendsvinp.org
URL: http://www.friendsvinp.org
Contact: Joe Kessler, Pres.
Members: 3,000. **Membership Dues:** individual, $30 (annual) ● family, $50 (annual) ● sustaining, $100 (annual) ● patron, $500 (annual) ● gold, $1,000 (annual) ● platinum, $5,000 (annual) ● business (based on number of employees), $50-$5,000 (annual). **Staff:** 4. **Budget:** $400,000. **State Groups:** 50. **National Groups:** 10. **Description:** Promotes programs of Virgin Islands National Park, including historical, environmental, and cultural activities; encourages environmental conservation, supports research. **Telecommunication Services:** electronic mail, jkessler@friendsvinp.org. **Councils:** Advisory. **Programs:** Affinity Partners; Annaberg Docent; Archeology. **Projects:** Canon Coral Restoration; Cultural Preservation; Environmental Education; Natural Resource Protection. **Publications:** *Friends Tidings*, quarterly. Newsletter. Presents news and articles about Virgin Islands National Park and the Friends. Alternate Formats: online ● *Living Art*. Book. Features the natural beauty of St. John in 182 photographs. **Price:** $60.00 for 1-3 copies; $57.00 for 4-11 copies; $54.00 for 12 copies ● Report. Alternate Formats: online. **Conventions/Meetings:** periodic seminar.

Waste

5265 ■ Alliance of Foam Packaging Recyclers (AFPR)
1298 Cronson Blvd., Ste.201
Crofton, MD 21114
Ph: (410)451-8340
Fax: (410)451-8343
E-mail: info@epspackaging.org
URL: http://www.epspackaging.org
Founded: 1991. **Members:** 45. **Staff:** 3. **Budget:** $250,000. **Description:** Promotes public and industry understanding of the benefits of EPS foam packaging as an environmentally safe and efficient packaging material. **Publications:** *Molding the Future*, quarterly. Newsletter. Updates readers on latest technical and recycling trends in EPS industry. **Price:** free.

5266 ■ Center For Health, Environment and Justice (CHEJ)
PO Box 6806
Falls Church, VA 22040-6806
Ph: (703)237-2249
Fax: (703)237-8389
E-mail: chej@chej.org
URL: http://www.chej.org
Contact: Lois Marie Gibbs, Exec. Dir.
Founded: 1981. **Members:** 27,599. **Membership Dues:** individual, $35 (annual) ● group, $100 (annual). **Staff:** 13. **Budget:** $1,300,000. **Regional Groups:** 50. **State Groups:** 250. **Local Groups:** 8,000. **Description:** Promotes environmental justice and empowerment through community organization. **Libraries: Type:** open to the public. **Holdings:** 3,000; archival material, books, periodicals. **Subjects:** environmental waste management, waste, environmental justice. **Computer Services:** database, corporations, chemicals, health effects. **Telecommunication Services:** electronic mail, info@chej.org. **Committees:** Research; Superfund. **Programs:** Roundtable Series on Dioxin and Public Policy Issues; State and Regional Leadership Development Training and CEO Training. **Projects:** Health Care Without Harm; Protecting Our Children; Stop Dioxin Exposure Campaign. **Formerly:** (1997) Citizens Clearinghouse for Hazardous Waste. **Publications:** *Everyone's Backyard*, quarterly. Magazine. Includes science and legal articles and coverage of local grassroots groups. **Price:** $35.00/year; $5.00/copy. ISSN: 0749-3940. **Circulation:** 15,000. **Advertising:** accepted. Alternate Formats: online ● *Journal of the Grassroots Movement*. Alternate Formats: online ● Books ● Manuals ● Handbooks ● Catalog. Alternate Formats: online ● Also publishes over 123 additional publications and fact packs. **Conventions/Meetings:** quinquennial conference (exhibits).

5267 ■ Community Environmental Council (CEC)
26 W Anapamu St., 2nd Fl.
Santa Barbara, CA 93101
Ph: (805)884-0459 (805)963-0583
Fax: (805)962-9080

E-mail: cecadmin@cecmail.org
URL: http://www.communityenvironmentalcouncil.org
Contact: Mr. David D. Davis, Exec. Dir.
Founded: 1970. **Members:** 900. **Membership Dues:** individual, $50 (annual) ● corporate, $500 (annual). **Staff:** 45. **Budget:** $5,000,000. **Languages:** English, Spanish. **Description:** Individuals and environmental organizations whose prime objective is environmental education, research, and technical assistance. Current focus is on alternative energy policy and technology, and land-use policy. Runs the South Coast Watershed Resource Center. Conducts educational programs. **Libraries: Type:** not open to the public. **Holdings:** 800. **Awards:** Award for Environmental Stewardship. **Type:** recognition. **Publications:** *Alternatives to Household Chemicals*. Reports. **Price:** free ● *Garden Detectives*. Books. **Price:** $16.95 ● *Gildea Review*, semiannual. Newsletter. Covers environmental issues, with emphasis on waste management, land use, recycling, water conservation, and public decision making; includes reviews. **Price:** included in membership dues; $5.00/issue for nonmembers. **Circulation:** 900. Alternate Formats: online ● *What To Do When Your Garden Has Bugs*. Papers. **Price:** free ● Videos.

5268 ■ Global Alliance for Incinerator Alternatives (GAIA)
1442A Walnut St., No. 20
Berkeley, CA 94709
Ph: (510)883-9490
Fax: (510)883-9493
E-mail: gaia@no-burn.org
URL: http://www.no-burn.org
Contact: Ann Leonard, Intl. Coor.
Founded: 2000. **Multinational. Description:** Works to end the incineration of all forms of waste. Encourages sustainable waste prevention and discard management practices. Promotes the implementation of clean production and the reused, repaired and recycled back of products into the marketplace. **Also Known As:** Global Anti-Incinerator Alliance. **Publications:** *GAIA Campaigner*, quarterly. Newsletter. Alternate Formats: online.

5269 ■ Household Hazardous Waste Project (HHWP)
c/o Office of Waste Management
Univ. of Missouri Extension
Columbia, MO 65211
Ph: (573)882-5011
E-mail: owm@missouri.edu
URL: http://outreach.missouri.edu/owm/hhw.htm
Contact: Marie Steinwachs, Dir.
Founded: 1987. **Staff:** 2. **Budget:** $45,000. **Description:** An education program of the University of Missouri Extension. Aids the public in making informed decisions about the use, storage, and disposal of hazardous household products. Assists communities in developing management plans. Provides education to other unregulated generators of hazardous wastes including small businesses, home businesses, schools, farms, artists, and crafts persons. Emphasizes source reduction, waste minimization, and preventive practices in an attempt to change consumers' behavior toward hazardous products. Develops educational tools and materials. Operates an information request and referral service. **Publications:** *Guide to Hazardous Products Around the Home*. Manual. Alternate Formats: online ● *Home Hazardous Product Survey*. Alternate Formats: online ● *Household Hazardous Waste: Consumer Information*. Alternate Formats: online ● *Lessons in Household Hazardous Waste Management*. For grades K-3 or 4-8. Alternate Formats: online ● *Material Safety Data Sheets: Identifying Product Hazards*. Alternate Formats: online ● *Safe Use, Storage and Disposal of Paint*. Alternate Formats: online ● *Safe Use, Storage and Disposal of Pesticides*. Alternate Formats: online ● *Selecting Household Safety Equipment*. Alternate Formats: online ● *Setting Up Collection Sites for Antifreeze*. Bulletin. Alternate Formats: online ● *Setting Up Collection Sites for Used Oil*. Bulletin. Alternate Formats: online ● *Stored Waste Abatement Program*. Alternate Formats: online ● *What Your Home Haz*. Alternate Formats: online ● Brochures.

5270 ■ Integrated Waste Services Association (IWSA)
1331 H St. NW, Ste.801
Washington, DC 20005
Ph: (202)467-6240
Fax: (202)467-6225
E-mail: tmichaels@wte.org
URL: http://www.wte.org
Contact: Ted Michaels, Pres.
Founded: 1991. **Members:** 50. **Membership Dues:** municipal associate, $750 (annual) ● small business associate, $1,000 (annual) ● business associate, $3,000 (annual). **Staff:** 3. **Description:** Promotes integrated solutions to municipal solid waste management issues. Interacts with government agencies, public policy organizations, the media and public to encourage program implementation. **Computer Services:** database, waste to energy facilities. **Publications:** *Update*, quarterly. Newsletter. **Circulation:** 2,600 ● Bulletin, weekly ● Directory. Alternate Formats: online. **Conventions/Meetings:** annual meeting and board meeting.

5271 ■ National Onsite Wastewater Recycling Association (NOWRA)
PO Box 1270
Edgewater, MD 21037
Ph: (410)798-1697
Free: (800)966-2942
Fax: (410)798-5741
E-mail: lhbonner@hanifin.com
URL: http://www.nowra.org
Contact: Jerry Stonebridge PhD, Pres.
Founded: 1991. **Membership Dues:** regular, $140 (annual) ● regulator, $60 (annual) ● student, $35 (annual). **Description:** Onsite wastewater treatment providers including manufacturers, installers, field practitioners, suppliers, engineers, designers, researchers and academicians, and government regulatory personnel. Seeks to advance and promote the onsite wastewater treatment industry. Gathers and disseminates information on wastewater treatment; conducts educational programs to increase public awareness on the value of wastewater treatment; formulates and enforces standards of ethics and practice for the wastewater treatment industry. Assists in the development of sound ecological practices in wastewater treatment; compiles industry statistics. **Committees:** Communications/Promotion; Conference; Ethics and Licensing; Fundraising; Government Relations; Model Performance Code; State Association Presidents; Technical Practices. **Programs:** Business Benefits. **Publications:** *Onsite Journal*. **Advertising:** accepted. **Conventions/Meetings:** annual Installer Academy - conference, consists of technical sessions needed to succeed in business (exhibits) - always December in Las Vegas, NV.

5272 ■ Zero Waste Alliance (ZWA)
One World Trade Ctr.
121 SW Salmon St., Ste.210
Portland, OR 97204
Ph: (503)279-9383
Fax: (503)279-9381
E-mail: info@zerowaste.org
URL: http://zerowaste.org
Contact: Larry Chalfan, Exec. Dir.
Multinational. Description: Promotes the use of zero waste strategies. Provides improved profitability, competitiveness and environmental performance through the development and implementation of practices that lead to the reduction and elimination of waste and toxics. **Computer Services:** Information services, zero waste resources.

Water

5273 ■ Keepers of the Waters
1415 SE Tacoma St.
Portland, OR 97202
E-mail: bdamon7367@aol.com
URL: http://www.keepersofthewaters.org
Contact: Betsy Damon, Founder/Dir.
Founded: 1991. **Multinational. Description:** Brings together artists, scientists, and other community members to address water quality in ways that can initiate changes in the environment. Inspires and promotes projects that combine art, science, and community involvement to restore, preserve, and remediate water sources. Serves as an international communications network for people actively engaged in projects that transform human relationship to water. **Telecommunication Services:** electronic mail, lfeather@lonniefeather.com. **Publications:** Newsletter. **Price:** included in membership dues. Alternate Formats: online.

5274 ■ Society of Environmental Understanding and Sustainability (SEUS)
c/o Mr. Kenneth Davis, Pres.
716 Kent Rd.
Kenilworth, IL 60043
Ph: (847)251-2079
E-mail: kendavis@voyager.net
URL: http://www.kjd.com/Society.html
Contact: Mr. Kenneth Davis, Pres.
Description: Seeks to provide clean water for children who do not have access to it. Provides education for the public on how to deliver clean water for children. Strives to bring together leaders/perspectives from the government, the corporate world and the academe in a non-confrontational manner in order for them to learn from each other and from those who have special insights into the environmental issues of today. Supports the efforts and projects of organizations with similar goals. **Telecommunication Services:** electronic mail, topgunmsu@hotmail.com.

Water Conservation

5275 ■ Groundwater Foundation
PO Box 22558
Lincoln, NE 68542-2558
Ph: (402)434-2740
Free: (800)858-4844
Fax: (402)434-2742
E-mail: info@groundwater.org
URL: http://www.groundwater.org
Contact: Susan Seacrest, Pres.
Founded: 1985. **Members:** 1,200. **Membership Dues:** individual in U.S., $35 (annual) ● organizational in U.S., $85 (annual) ● family in U.S., $60 (annual). **Staff:** 10. **Description:** Environmental educators. Strives to inform the public about groundwater and concerns related to groundwater. **Awards:** E. Benjamin Nelson Government Service Award. **Frequency:** annual. **Type:** recognition. **Recipient:** for an elected or appointed public official who has significantly advanced environmental and groundwater stewardship ● Edith Stevens Groundwater Educator Award. **Frequency:** annual. **Type:** recognition. **Recipient:** for groundwater educators who understand the importance of groundwater, motivate others to protect groundwater, and lead by personal example ● Vern Haverstick Groundwater Hero Award. **Frequency:** annual. **Type:** recognition. **Recipient:** for groundwater protection activities by the unsung, yet heroic, efforts of community residents ● Youth Award for Excellence and Leadership in Groundwater. **Frequency:** annual. **Type:** recognition. **Recipient:** to students ages 12-17 in the U.S. who give time, energy, and knowledge to promote the protection of groundwater in their community. **Programs:** Awesome Aquifers for Science Olympiad; Fee for Services; Festival Expedition; Groundwater Guardian; H20 on the Go; Youth Groundwater Congress. **Publications:** *The Aquifer*, quarterly. Newsletter. Contains groundwater information. **Price:** included in membership dues. **Conventions/Meetings:** annual conference, focuses on current groundwater-related issues held in various cities throughout the United States (exhibits).

5276 ■ Groundwater Management Districts Association (GMDA)
c/o Wayne Bossert, Sec.-Treas.
PO Box 905
Colby, KS 67701-0905

Ph: (913)462-3915
Fax: (913)462-2693
E-mail: wab@gmd4.org
URL: http://www.gmdausa.org/Organization.htm
Contact: Wayne Bossert, Sec.-Treas.
Membership Dues: district, $300 (annual) ● organizational, $200 (annual) ● affiliate, $100 (annual) ● individual, $25 (annual). **Description:** Provides programs for the management, development, utilization, conservation, protection, and control of groundwater. **Awards: Type:** recognition. **Recipient:** for individuals or organizations. **Committees:** Awards; Clean Water Act; Endangered Species Act; Groundwater; Safe Drinking Water Act. **Publications:** Newsletter, semiannual. Alternate Formats: online.

5277 ■ National Organization for Water Awareness
Address Unknown since 2008
Founded: 1998. **Staff:** 5. **Nonmembership. Description:** Works to find practical solutions for safer drinking water. Validates scientific proof that many health problems are attributable to poor drinking water. Offers public health forums and workshops.

5278 ■ Restore America's Estuaries (RAE)
3801 N Fairfax Dr., Ste.53
Arlington, VA 22203
Ph: (703)524-0248
Fax: (703)524-0287
E-mail: jbenoit@estuaries.org
URL: http://www.estuaries.org
Contact: Jeff Benoit, Pres.
Founded: 1995. **Members:** 250,000. **Staff:** 5. **Regional Groups:** 11. **Description:** Committed to preserving America's estuaries by protecting and restoring the lands and waters essential to richness and diversity of coastal life. **Publications:** Annual Report. Alternate Formats: online.

5279 ■ WateReuse Association
1199 N Fairfax St., Ste.410
Alexandria, VA 22314
Ph: (703)548-0880
Fax: (703)548-5085
E-mail: information@watereuse.org
URL: http://www.watereuse.org
Contact: G. Wade Miller, Exec. Dir.
Founded: 1990. **Members:** 300. **Membership Dues:** individual, $150 (annual) ● associate, $250 (annual). **Staff:** 8. **Budget:** $935,000. **State Groups:** 4. **Local Groups:** 3. **Description:** Aims to advance the beneficial and efficient use of water resources through education, sound science, and technology using reclamation, recycling, reuse, and desalination for the benefit of members, the public, and the environment; membership includes water and wastewater agencies, federal and state agencies, public health officials, equipment suppliers, consultants, and prominent researchers from the academic community. **Publications:** *WateReuse Update*, quarterly. Newsletter. **Price:** included in membership dues. **Circulation:** 300. **Conventions/Meetings:** annual WateReuse Symposium - conference.

Water Pollution

5280 ■ Ocean Futures Society (OFS)
325 Chapala St.
Santa Barbara, CA 93101
Ph: (805)899-8899
E-mail: contact@oceanfutures.org
URL: http://www.oceanfutures.org
Contact: Jean-Michel Cousteau, Pres./Chm.
Description: Provides the global community with a forum for exploring issues affecting the ocean, its inhabitants, and its habitats. **Telecommunication Services:** electronic mail, leda.bozaciyan@jmcbrasil.org.br. **Formerly:** (2005) Ocean Futures. **Publications:** *Jean-Michel Cousteau Dispatch*, monthly. Newsletter. Contains latest conservation news, research, exploration and education activities of the society, and other issues affecting the ocean. **Price:** free. Alternate Formats: online.

Water Resources

5281 ■ Clean Water Council (CWC)
c/o National Utility Contractors Association
4301 N Fairfax Dr., Ste.360
Arlington, VA 22203-1627
Ph: (703)358-9300
Fax: (703)358-9307
E-mail: eben@nuca.com
URL: http://www.nuca.com
Contact: Eben Wyman, VP, Government Relations
Founded: 1990. **Description:** Construction, engineering, manufacturing, distribution, labor, and general business associations. Promotes increased federal funding for water quality infrastructure. Conducts educational programs to raise public awareness of water quality issues; conducts lobbying activities.

5282 ■ Puerto Rico Water and Environment Association (PRW&EA)
PO Box 13702
San Juan, PR 00908-3702
E-mail: membresias@prwea.org
URL: http://www.prwea.org
Contact: Ing. Juan R. Rodriguez, Pres.-Elect
Founded: 1974. **Languages:** English, Spanish. **Nonmembership. Description:** Environmental professionals.

5283 ■ Southeast Desalting Association (SEDA)
2409 SE Dixie Hwy.
Stuart, FL 34996
Ph: (772)781-7698
Fax: (772)463-0860
E-mail: administrator@southeastdesalting.com
URL: http://www.southeastdesalting.com
Contact: Jill Manning-Hudkins PE, Pres.
Founded: 1994. **Membership Dues:** public agency, industrial user, water supplier, small firm (with fewer than 5 employees), $195 (annual) ● certified operation individual, $25 (annual) ● manufacturer, supplier, consulting firm, $375 (annual) ● library, well-wisher, student, $50 (annual). **Description:** Commits to improve the quality of water supplies through membrane desalting and filtration, water reuse, and other water sciences. **Telecommunication Services:** electronic mail, jill.hudkins@tetratech.com. **Committees:** Legislative; Membership; Operator; Program; Public Relations; Technology Transfer. **Affiliated With:** American Membrane Technology Association. **Publications:** Report, quarterly ● Newsletter, quarterly. Alternate Formats: online. **Conventions/Meetings:** biennial National Technical Conference.

Wetlands

5284 ■ National Wetlands Coalition (NWC)
1050 Thomas Jefferson St. NW, Ste.700
Washington, DC 20007
Ph: (202)298-1800
Fax: (202)338-2416
Contact: Russell Riggs, Contact
Description: Local governments, ports, water agencies, the development community, agriculture groups, electric utilities, oil and gas pipelines and producers, the mining industry, banks, environmental and engineering consulting firms and Native American groups. Working with Congress and the Administration for legislative reform of and regulatory improvements to the federal wetlands permitting program.

Whales

5285 ■ World Whale Police (WWP)
PO Box 814
Olympia, WA 98506
Ph: (360)561-7492
E-mail: info@worldwhalepolice.org
URL: http://www.worldwhalepolice.org
Contact: Bill Moss, Contact
Multinational. Description: Educates the public about the necessity for marine mammal protection. Raises public awareness of safety through lectures, literature and on-site response to incidents of threats to marine mammals. **Computer Services:** Mailing lists ● online services, onsite reports. **Telecommunication Services:** electronic mail, worldwhalepolice@hotmail.com.

Wildlife

5286 ■ Watchable Wildlife
PO Box 319
Marine on St. Croix, MN 55047
Ph: (651)433-4100
Fax: (651)433-4101
E-mail: info@watchablewildlife.org
URL: http://www.watchablewildlife.org
Description: Seeks to advance wildlife viewing as a viable economic and conservation enterprise for communities throughout the United States, Canada, and Mexico. **Conventions/Meetings:** annual conference.

Wildlife Conservation

5287 ■ Abundant Wildlife Society of North America (AWS)
PO Box 2
Beresford, SD 57004
Ph: (605)751-0979
E-mail: research@bmtc.net
URL: http://www.aws.vcn.com
Contact: Troy Mader, Research Dir.
Founded: 1991. **Nonmembership. Description:** Interested individuals. Supports multiple use of public lands for grazing, logging, mining, hunting, fishing, trapping, and recreational use. Promotes management and use of wildlife "for good and useful purposes and the benefit of mankind". Encourages predator control; does not endorse exploitation of wildlife or needless destruction of habitat. Keeps members apprised of environmental and animal rights agenda. **Publications:** *Abundant Wildlife - Newsletter*, bimonthly. **Price:** included in membership dues ● *Conservation-vs-Environmentalism: A Look at Two Roads*. Brochures ● *Fact Sheet: Wolf Reintroduction in the United States*. Reports ● *Seven Popular Myths about Livestock Grazing on Public Lands*. Book ● *Trashing the Planet*. Book ● *Unnatural Wolf Transplant Yellowstone National Park*. Book ● *Wolf Hunter*. Book ● *Wolf Reintroduction in Yellowstone National Park: A Historical Perspective*. Book.

5288 ■ African Wild Dog Conservancy
PO Box 30692
Tucson, AZ 85751
E-mail: lycaonpictus@earthlink.net
URL: http://awdconservancy.org
Contact: Dr. Robert Robbins, Co-Founder
Founded: 2001. **Multinational. Description:** Strives to conserve African Wild Dogs through scientific research and education. Supports long-term conservation programs involving local communities. Implements programs integrating applied field and captive conservation research. **Computer Services:** Information services, African Wild Dogs resources. **Projects:** Community; Zoo.

5289 ■ African Wildlife Foundation (AWF)
1400 16th St. NW, Ste.120
Washington, DC 20036
Ph: (202)939-3333
Free: (888)494-5354
Fax: (202)939-3332
E-mail: africanwildlife@awf.org
URL: http://www.awf.org
Contact: Patrick J. Bergin PhD, Pres./CEO
Founded: 1961. **Members:** 65,000. **Membership Dues:** individual, $35 (annual). **Staff:** 21. **Budget:** $8,000,000. **Description:** Works with people to craft

and deliver creative solutions for the long-term well being of Africa's remarkable species, their habitats and the people who depend upon them. **Libraries: Type:** by appointment only. **Holdings:** 180; books. **Subjects:** Africa, general history, natural history, ecology, African fiction. **Programs:** African Heartlands; Conservation Enterprise; Critical Species Research and Conservation; Education and African Leadership. **Formerly:** (1982) African Wildlife Leadership Foundation. **Publications:** *African Wildlife News*, quarterly. Newsletter. Features stories on AWF projects, developments in wildlife conservation and opinion pieces. **Price:** $35.00/year. **Circulation:** 20,000. Alternate Formats: online ● Annual Report, annual. Alternate Formats: online ● Also publishes wildlife handbooks and park guides. **Conventions/Meetings:** semiannual board meeting.

5290 ■ American Bird Conservancy (ABC)

PO Box 249
The Plains, VA 20198-0249
Ph: (540)253-5780
Free: (888)BIRD-MAG
Fax: (540)253-5782
E-mail: abc@abcbirds.org
URL: http://www.abcbirds.org
Contact: Dr. George H. Fenwick, Pres.

Founded: 1922. **Members:** 2,200. **Membership Dues:** Vireo, $40 (annual) ● Meadowlark, $100 (annual) ● Tanager, $250 (annual) ● Curlew, $500 (annual) ● Falcon Club, $1,000 (annual) ● outside U.S., $55 (annual). **Staff:** 9. **Budget:** $80,000. **Description:** Aims for the conservation of wild birds and their habitats in the Americas. Seeks to build coalitions of conservation groups, scientists, and members of the public, to tackle key bird priorities using the best resources available. **Awards: Type:** grant. **Recipient:** for foreign ornithologists and conservationists to come to the U.S. and investigate conservation problems and methods. **Telecommunication Services:** electronic mail, gfenwick@abcbirds.org. **Programs:** Birds and Public Policy; Cats Indoors; Climate Change; Conservation Alliances; Important Bird Areas; International; NABCI; Partners in Flight. **Formerly:** International Council for Bird Preservation. **Publications:** *All the Backyard Birds: East*. Book. **Price:** $7.95 ● *All the Backyard Birds: East and West*. Book. **Price:** $10.95 ● *All the Backyard Birds: West*. Book. **Price:** $7.95 ● *All the Birds of North America*. Book. **Price:** $19.95 ● *All the Song Birds: Eastern Trailside*. Book. **Price:** $8.50 ● *The American Bird Conservancy Guide to the 500 Most Important Bird Areas in the United States*. Book. **Price:** $25.95 ● *Bird Calls*, 3/year. Newsletter. Contains information on ABC's achievements in conserving birds. Alternate Formats: online ● *Bird Conservation*, quarterly. Magazine. Features issues affecting wild birds in the U.S., Canada, Latin America and the Caribbean. ● Annual Report, annual. Alternate Formats: online ● Reports. Contains information on the impact of long line fishing to seabirds. Alternate Formats: online. **Conventions/Meetings:** semiannual Partner's in Flight Pan American Roundtable - meeting ● Policy Council Meeting - 3/year.

5291 ■ American Horse Protection Association (AHPA)

Address Unknown since 2008
URL: http://www.equineprotectionnetwork.com

Founded: 1966. **Members:** 15,000. **Membership Dues:** individual, $20 (annual) ● organization, $25 (annual). **Staff:** 4. **Budget:** $298,000. **Description:** Individuals interested in the protection and welfare of horses, both wild and domestic. Gained passage of the Horse Protection Act of 1970, which makes illegal the showing of "sored" horses in interstate commerce, and the Wild Horse and Burro Protection Act of 1971 and the Commercial Transportation of Equines for Slaughter Act of 1996. **Publications:** *AHPA Newsletter*, quarterly. Contains news of association efforts to end abuse of horses and burros. Includes schedule of activities. **Price:** included in membership dues. **Circulation:** 15,000.

5292 ■ American Pheasant and Waterfowl Society (APWS)

c/o E.T. Trader, Treas.
6220 Bullbeggar Rd.
Withams, VA 23488
E-mail: alpat@apexotics.com
URL: http://www.apws.org
Contact: Al Novosad, Pres.

Founded: 1936. **Members:** 2,000. **Membership Dues:** regular, in U.S., $25 (annual) ● regular, outside U.S., $35 (annual) ● life, $500. **Description:** Hobbyists, aviculturists, and zoos. Works to perpetuate all varieties of upland game, ornamental birds, and waterfowl. Maintains speakers' bureau; compiles statistics. **Libraries: Type:** reference. **Holdings:** audiovisuals. **Awards:** Breeders Award. **Frequency:** annual. **Type:** recognition. **Recipient:** for success in breeding birds ● Service Award. **Frequency:** annual. **Type:** recognition. **Recipient:** for service to aviculture. **Committees:** Awards; Education-Information; Legislation. **Formerly:** (1962) American Pheasant Society. **Publications:** Magazine, 10/year. Includes breeders' directory. **Price:** $25.00 in U.S.; $35.00 outside U.S. ISSN: 0892-6387. **Circulation:** 1,800. **Advertising:** accepted ● Membership Directory. **Conventions/Meetings:** annual convention (exhibits) ● Photo Contest - competition ● Youth Art Contest - competition ● Youth Photo Contest - competition.

5293 ■ Appalachian Bear Rescue (ABR)

PO Box 364
Townsend, TN 37882
Ph: (865)448-0143 (865)525-5134
Fax: (865)448-0141
E-mail: jcburgin@kramer-rayson.com
URL: http://www.appalachianbearrescue.org
Contact: Jack Burgin, Pres.

Founded: 1991. **Members:** 1,500. **Membership Dues:** regular, $30 (annual). **Budget:** $80,000. **Description:** Strives to educate the public about black bears, rehabilitate orphaned and injured bears for release to the wild, and carry out research on bears. Sponsors an Adopt-a-Bear program. **Formerly:** (2006) Appalachian Bear Center.

5294 ■ Association Promoting Education and Conservation in Amazonia (APECA)

21338 Dumetz Rd.
Woodland Hills, CA 91364
Ph: (818)348-6614
E-mail: apecausa@apecaperu.org
URL: http://www.apecaperu.org
Contact: Ruth Abel, Chair

Founded: 1993. **Languages:** English, Spanish. **Multinational. Description:** Promotes education and conservation of the Peruvian Amazon rain forest. Aims to develop sustainable methods of health care, education, and conservation for Peruvian communities. Offers research internships. **Telecommunication Services:** electronic mail, rabel@apecaperu.org. **Publications:** *APECA News*. Newsletter. Alternate Formats: online.

5295 ■ Atlantic Flyway Council (AFC)

Virginia Dept. of Game & Inland Fisheries
PO Box 11104
Richmond, VA 23230
Ph: (804)367-1000
Fax: (804)367-9147
E-mail: dgifweb@dgif.virginia.gov
URL: http://www.dgif.state.va.us
Contact: David Cob, Chm.

Founded: 1952. **Members:** 23. **Description:** Fish and game directors or fish and wildlife organizations of each of 17 Atlantic coastal states and six Canadian provinces. Coordinates waterfowl research and management in the Atlantic Flyway. **Committees:** Banding; Black Duck; Canada Goose; Diving Duck; Environmental Pollution; Habitat Management; Harvest Management; Land Acquisition; Marine Resources; Snow Goose, Brant and Swan; Wood Duck. **Sections:** Technical. **Formed by Merger of:** Northeast Waterfowl Committee; Southeast Waterfowl Committee. **Formerly:** Atlantic Waterfowl Council. **Publications:** *Techniques of Waterfowl Habitat Development and Management*. **Conventions/Meetings:** semiannual conference - always March and July.

5296 ■ Bat Conservation International (BCI)

PO Box 162603
Austin, TX 78716
Ph: (512)327-9721
Free: (800)538-2287
Fax: (512)327-9724
E-mail: batinfo@batcon.org
URL: http://www.batcon.org
Contact: Dr. Merlin D. Tuttle, Pres./Founder

Founded: 1982. **Members:** 14,000. **Membership Dues:** basic, $35 (annual) ● senior, student, educator, $30 (annual) ● friend, $45 (annual) ● supporting, $60 (annual) ● contributing, $100 (annual) ● patron, $250 (annual) ● sustaining, $500 (annual) ● Founder's Circle, $1,000 (annual). **Staff:** 30. **Budget:** $3,000,000. **Languages:** English, French, Spanish. **Description:** Members in 76 countries. Documents the value and conservation needs of bats. Seeks to increase public awareness of the ecological importance of bats and promote bat conservation and management efforts. Publicizes conservation needs of bats worldwide. **Libraries: Type:** reference. **Holdings:** 22; articles, books. **Subjects:** bats, conservation. **Awards:** Student Research Scholarship. **Frequency:** annual. **Type:** scholarship. **Recipient:** for bat conservation students. **Computer Services:** Bibliographic search. **Publications:** *The Bat House Builder's Handbook*. **Price:** $8.95 ● *Bats*, quarterly. Magazine. Covers latest news in field of bat conservation. **Conventions/Meetings:** annual workshop, hands-on field activities involving bats - usually summer.

5297 ■ Bear Trust International

PO Box 4006
Missoula, MT 59806-4006
Ph: (406)523-7779
E-mail: info@beartrust.org
URL: http://www.beartrust.org
Contact: A.C. Smid, Pres.

Founded: 1999. **Multinational. Description:** Promotes the conservation and sound management of wild bears, other wildlife and their natural habitat. Fosters cooperation among governments, federal and state agencies, public and private organizations, and individuals in wildlife management and habitat conservation. Promotes international research and program funding for wild bear and habitat projects. **Programs:** Adopt-a-Dumpster; Wild Bear Conservation. **Publications:** *The Bear Book*, periodic. Covers a series of real-life field stories about bears. **Price:** $25.00.

5298 ■ The Billfish Foundation (TBF)

2161 E Commercial Blvd., 2nd Fl.
Fort Lauderdale, FL 33308
Ph: (954)938-0150
Free: (800)438-8247
Fax: (954)938-5311
E-mail: tbf@billfish.org
URL: http://www.billfish.org
Contact: Ellen M. Peel JD, Pres.

Founded: 1986. **Members:** 5,000. **Membership Dues:** spearfish (junior, under 13), $15 (annual) ● sailfish, $25 (annual) ● striped marlin, $75 (annual) ● white marlin, $125 (annual) ● swordfish, $250 (annual) ● blue marlin, $500 (annual) ● black marlin, $1,000 (annual) ● grand slam, $2,500 (annual) ● super slam, $5,000 (annual) ● bronze patron, $10,000 (annual). **Description:** Promotes the conservation of billfish through scientific research and education. Works to develop an international management plan to ensure the survival of billfish. Lobbies Congress and regulators to provide greater protection for the billfish. Disseminates research and other information to commercial fishermen and the general public. Sponsors educational and research programs. Acts as a clearinghouse for information on billfish conservation. **Awards:** Conservation Awards. **Frequency:** annual. **Type:** recognition. **Recipient:** for groups and individuals who have made significant contributions to worldwide billfish conservation ● Release Certificate Awards. **Frequency:** annual. **Type:** recognition. **Programs:** Circle Hook; Release Certificate. **Projects:** Ace, Growth and Migration Studies; Genetic Analysis and Protein Sampling; Longline Bycatch Data Assessment; Research and Development of Cutting Edge Tagging Technology; Socio Economic Studies; Stock Assessment Workshops. **Publications:** *The Billfish*, quarterly. Newsletter. **Price:** included in membership dues ● *TBF Newsletter*, quarterly. Alternate Formats: online. **Conventions/Meetings:** annual banquet, includes awards presentation.

5299 ■ Bird Strike Committee USA (BSC-USA)
6100 Columbus Ave.
Sandusky, OH 44870
Ph: (419)625-0242
Fax: (419)625-8465
E-mail: richard.a.dolbeer@aphis.usda.gov
URL: http://www.birdstrike.org
Contact: Richard A. Dolbeer, Chm.
Founded: 1991. **Description:** Facilitates information exchange regarding bird and other wildlife strikes to aircraft; promotes technologies to reduce wildlife hazards. **Conventions/Meetings:** annual meeting.

5300 ■ Birds of Prey Foundation (BPF)
2290 S 104th St.
Broomfield, CO 80020
Ph: (303)460-0674
E-mail: raptor@birds-of-prey.org
URL: http://www.birds-of-prey.org
Contact: Sigrid N. Ueblacker, Pres./Founder
Founded: 1984. **Members:** 200. **Membership Dues:** falcon, $20 (annual) ● hawk, $30 (annual) ● owl, $45 (annual) ● eagle, $75 (annual). **Description:** Concerned with the preservation and rehabilitation of birds of prey. Conducts educational programs focusing on raptors and their relation to the environment. **Libraries: Type:** reference. **Publications:** *The Windwalker*, annual. Newsletter. Alternate Formats: online ● Brochures ● Pamphlets. **Conventions/Meetings:** annual meeting ● monthly meeting.

5301 ■ Boone and Crockett Club (B&C)
250 Sta. Dr.
Missoula, MT 59801
Ph: (406)542-1888
Free: (888)840-4868
Fax: (406)542-0784
E-mail: bcclub@boone-crockett.org
URL: http://www.boone-crockett.org
Contact: George Bettas, Exec. Dir.
Founded: 1887. **Members:** 200. **Membership Dues:** associate, non-associate, $25 (annual) ● associate, non-associate, $45 (biennial) ● associate, non-associate, $100 (quinquennial). **Staff:** 12. **Description:** Dedicated to the preservation of North American wildlife. Sponsors record keeping program on native North American big game trophies, and graduate-level research and workshops on wildlife species. Members were founders of the American Committee for International Conservation (see separate entry). Conducts competitions; sponsors educational programs. Compiles statistics. **Libraries: Type:** reference. **Holdings:** archival material, books. **Awards:** Special Sagamore Hill Award. **Frequency:** annual. **Type:** medal. **Recipient:** for distinguished devotion. **Committees:** Conservation; Editorial and Historical; National Collection of Heads and Horns; Records of North American Big Game. **Publications:** *The Black Bear in Modern North America*. Book ● *Boone and Crockett Club's 25th Big Game Awards*. Book. **Price:** $35.95/copy for associate member; $44.95/copy for non-associate member ● *Fair Chase*, quarterly. Magazine. **Price:** $25.00/year; $45.00/2 years; $100.00/5 years; $1,000.00 lifetime subscription. ISSN: 1077-3274 ● *Measuring and Scoring North American Big Game Trophies*. Book ● *Records of North American Big Game*. Book. **Price:** $39.95/copy for associate member; $49.95/copy for non-associate member ● *Records of North American Elk and Mule Deer*. Book ● *Records of North American Whitetail Deer*. Book ● *The Wild Sheep in Modern North America*. Book ● Also publishes From the Peace to the Fraser, African Game-Lands. **Conventions/Meetings:** annual meeting.

5302 ■ Boreal Songbird Initiative (BSI)
1904 Third Ave., Ste.305
Seattle, WA 98101
Ph: (206)956-9040
Fax: (206)728-0552
E-mail: info@borealbirds.org
URL: http://www.borealbirds.org
Contact: Marilyn Heiman, Dir.
Multinational. Description: Works to educate Americans about the importance of the Boreal Forest to migratory birds. Raises awareness of the Boreal Forest and assists efforts in Canada and Alaska to conserve. Educates the public about major conservation issues.

5303 ■ Bounty Wildlife Information Service (BIS)
Address Unknown since 2008
Founded: 1965. **Members:** 2,000. **Staff:** 350. **Description:** Individuals interested in the removal of wildlife bounties in the U.S. and Canada. Organizes bounty removal programs; publishes literature on the bounty system and methods for removal; compiles annual summary of bounties in North America; executes individual studies of areas. **Formerly:** (1995) Bounty Information Service. **Publications:** *A Decade of Bounties* ● *Guide for the Removal of Bounties* ● *News*, 1-3/year. **Conventions/Meetings:** biennial conference - always fall.

5304 ■ Brooks Bird Club (BBC)
PO Box 4077
Wheeling, WV 26003
E-mail: gusind@juno.com
URL: http://www.brooksbirdclub.org
Contact: Carl Slater, Admin.
Founded: 1932. **Members:** 2,500. **Membership Dues:** individual, $25 (annual) ● student, $10 (annual) ● family, $30 (annual). **Staff:** 7. **Regional Groups:** 5. **State Groups:** 2. **Local Groups:** 2. **Description:** Conducts bird population studies and surveys, winter bird and hawk counts, and field trips. Compiles migration records; sponsors backyard sanctuaries program and 2-week biotic study. **Libraries: Type:** reference. **Holdings:** 900; archival material, artwork, books, clippings, periodicals. **Subjects:** natural history, wildlife, conservation. **Awards:** Bartley Award. **Frequency:** annual. **Type:** recognition. **Recipient:** for best article of study published in Redstart ● **Type:** scholarship. **Committees:** Environmental; Land Acquisition; Research. **Publications:** *Mail Bag*, quarterly. Newsletter. Includes correspondence and news of members and their activities. **Price:** included in membership dues. **Circulation:** 600 ● *Redstart*, quarterly. Includes field and banding notes. **Price:** included in membership dues; $25.00/year. ISSN: 0034-2165. **Conventions/Meetings:** annual meeting - always October ● annual Mid-Winter Meeting - always February.

5305 ■ Caribbean Conservation Corporation and Sea Turtle Survival League (CCC)
4424 NW 13th St., Ste.B-11
Gainesville, FL 32609
Ph: (352)373-6441
Free: (800)678-7853
Fax: (352)375-2449
E-mail: ccc@cccturtle.org
URL: http://www.cccturtle.org
Contact: David Godfrey, Exec. Dir.
Founded: 1959. **Members:** 6,500. **Membership Dues:** individual, $25-$45 (annual) ● green sea turtle, $50 (annual) ● leatherback sea turtle, $100 (annual) ● loggerhead sea turtle, $250 (annual). **Staff:** 15. **Budget:** $1,000,000. **Multinational. Description:** Works to study, preservation, and rehabilitation of marine turtles in the Caribbean and Atlantic. Sponsors the Joshua B. Powers Fellowship, which brings biology and fishery specialists to the Green Turtle Research Station at Tortuguero, Costa Rica. Coordinates Adopt-A-Turtle program, which supports research and conservation efforts. Conducts educational and charitable programs. **Programs:** Florida Sea Turtle Grants; Sea Turtle Migration-Tracking Education; Sea Turtle Survival League. **Projects:** Bermuda Turtle; Chiriqui Beach Hawksbill and Leatherback Research and Conservation Program; Tortuguero Sea Turtle Monitoring and Conservation Program. **Also Known As:** Sea Turtle Survival League. **Publications:** *Turtle Tides* ● *Velador*, quarterly. Newsletter. **Price:** $25.00 for nonmembers; included in membership dues. **Circulation:** 6,500.

5306 ■ Cetacean Society International (CSI)
PO Box 953
Georgetown, CT 06829
Ph: (203)770-8615
Fax: (860)561-0187
E-mail: rossiter@csiwhalesalive.org
URL: http://www.csiwhalesalive.org
Contact: William W. Rossiter, Pres.
Founded: 1974. **Members:** 400. **Membership Dues:** regular, $20 (annual) ● student, senior, $15 (annual) ● contributing/family, $30 (annual) ● supporting, $50 (annual) ● sustaining, $100 (annual) ● patron, $500 (annual). **Budget:** $30,000. **Languages:** English, Portuguese, Spanish. **Description:** Serves as an all-volunteer, conservation, educational and research Organization to benefit whales, dolphins, porpoises and the marine environment. Promotes education and conservation programs, including whale and dolphin watching, and non-invasive, benign research. Advocates for laws and treaties to prevent commercial whaling, habitat destruction and other harmful or destructive human interactions. World goal is to minimize cetacean killing and captures, to maximize human activities that neither harm nor harass, and to enhance public awareness of and concern for cetaceans and the marine environment. Based in the USA, with volunteer representation in 25 countries. **Libraries: Type:** open to the public; by appointment only. **Holdings:** 200. **Subjects:** marine science and conservation. **Awards:** Cetacean Citation. **Type:** recognition. **Recipient:** for the exceptional work. **Formerly:** (1986) Connecticut Cetacean Society. **Publications:** *Meet the Great Ones* (in English and Spanish). Book. Contains entry-level book on whales. **Price:** $12.00 in U.S. ● *Whales Alive*, quarterly. Newsletter. **Price:** included in membership dues. **Circulation:** 800. Alternate Formats: online. **Conventions/Meetings:** quarterly meeting (exhibits).

5307 ■ Defenders of Wildlife
1130 17th St. NW
Washington, DC 20036
Free: (800)385-9712
E-mail: defenders@mail.defenders.org
URL: http://www.defenders.org
Contact: Rodger Schlickeisen, Pres./CEO
Founded: 1947. **Members:** 180,000. **Membership Dues:** regular, $25 (annual). **Staff:** 60. **Budget:** $7,000,000. **Regional Groups:** 7. **Description:** Persons interested in wildlife and conservation. Promotes the preservation and protection of wildlife and wildlife habitat through education, litigation, research, and advocacy. Programs focus on habitat preservation for biological diversity, endangered species recovery, international wildlife trade, and wildlife on public lands such as wildlife refuges and national forests. Provides wildlife education and information. Publishes reports and Defenders magazine. **Committees:** Green (Activist Network). **Programs:** California; Canadian; Defenders of Wildlife Habitat Conservation; Defenders of Wildlife Policy Leadership; Defenders of Wildlife Species Conservation; Internal. **Formerly:** Defenders of Furbearers. **Publications:** *Action Alert*, periodic ● *Defenders Magazine*, quarterly. Features articles on important conservation issues. **Price:** $20.00 /year for libraries; $3.00/copy (back issues). Alternate Formats: online ● *Endangered Species Report*, periodic ● *Wolf Action Newsletter*, periodic ● Annual Report, annual. Alternate Formats: online.

5308 ■ Delta Waterfowl Foundation
PO Box 3128
Bismarck, ND 58502
Free: (888)987-3695
E-mail: media@deltawaterfowl.org
URL: http://www.deltawaterfowl.org
Contact: Rob Olson, Pres.
Founded: 1911. **Members:** 35,000. **Membership Dues:** friend, $25 (annual) ● under 17 years old, $15

(annual) ● supporter, $50 (annual) ● sponsor, $100 (annual) ● canvasback sponsor, $250 (annual) ● President's Circle, $1,000 (annual) ● life, $10,000 ● patron, $500 (annual). **Staff:** 25. **Budget:** $1,700,000. **Description:** Focuses on research, education and advocacy in support of the continent's diverse waterfowl and their habitats. Supports hunting and recognizes waterfowl hunters as essential contributors to waterfowl conservation. Assists in graduate education, and plays key role in the evaluation of agricultural, habitat and hunting related policy. Recognizes that private land is the vast majority of waterfowl and wildlife abound and has a strong advocacy for conservation and agricultural policy that benefits private landowners. **Programs:** Student Research. **Formerly:** North American Wildlife Foundation; (1935) American Game Protective Association; (1946) American Wildlife Institute; (1951) American Wildlife Foundation. **Publications:** *Delta Waterfowl*, quarterly. Magazine. **Price:** included in membership dues. **Circulation:** 40,000. Alternate Formats: online ● Newsletter. Alternate Formats: online. **Conventions/Meetings:** annual meeting.

5309 ■ Desert Tortoise Council (DTC)

PO Box 3273
Beaumont, CA 92223
E-mail: mojotort@yahoo.com
URL: http://www.deserttortoise.org
Contact: Pat von Helf, Corresponding Sec.

Founded: 1975. **Members:** 175. **Membership Dues:** regular, $15 (annual) ● organization, $55 (annual) ● student, $10 (annual) ● contributing, $50 (annual) ● life, $300. **Staff:** 15. **Description:** State and federal biologists, herpetologists, universities, museums, zoos, turtle and tortoise clubs, other conservation-oriented groups, and concerned individuals. Seeks to ensure the survival of viable populations of the desert tortoise (tiopherus agassizii) throughout its existing range. Serves in a professional advisory capacity on matters involving management, conservation, and protection of desert tortoises. Stimulates and encourages studies on the status and phases of Life history, biology, physiology, management, and protection of desert tortoises. Acts as information clearinghouse for agencies, organizations, and individuals engaged in work on desert tortoises. **Libraries: Type:** open to the public. **Holdings:** 18; archival material. **Subjects:** tortoise biology, disease, conservation. **Awards:** Annual Award. **Frequency:** annual. **Type:** recognition. **Recipient:** for outstanding service to the DTC ● Best Student Paper Award. **Frequency:** annual. **Type:** recognition. **Recipient:** for the best student paper ● Certificates of Recognition. **Frequency:** annual. **Type:** recognition ● Special Award. **Frequency:** annual. **Type:** recognition. **Committees:** Awards; Public Information and Education; Research Advisory. **Publications:** *Annotated Bibliography of the Desert Tortoise*. Journal. Includes proceedings of annual symposium. **Price:** $10.00 for members; $15.00 for nonmembers. ISSN: 0191-3875 ● *Answering Questions About Desert Tortoises: A Guide For People Who Work With the Public*. Booklet. Alternate Formats: online ● Newsletter. Alternate Formats: online ● Proceedings. Contains information on DTC's annual symposiums. **Price:** $13.00 for members in U.S.; $16.00 for members outside U.S.; $18.00 for nonmembers in U.S.; $21.00 for nonmembers outside U.S. **Conventions/Meetings:** annual meeting and symposium (exhibits).

5310 ■ Dian Fossey Gorilla Fund International

800 Cherokee Ave. SE
Atlanta, GA 30315-1440
Ph: (404)624-5881
Free: (800)851-0203
Fax: (404)624-5999
E-mail: 2help@gorillafund.org
URL: http://www.gorillafund.org
Contact: Clare Richardson, Pres./CEO

Founded: 1978. **Members:** 5,000. **Membership Dues:** regular, $30 (annual) ● supporter, $50 (annual) ● sponsor, $100 (annual) ● gorilla, $250 (annual) ● silverback, $500 (annual). **Staff:** 3. **Budget:** $1,100,000. **Local Groups:** 1. **Languages:** English, French. **Multinational. Description:** Dedicated to studying and protecting the endangered mountain gorillas of central Africa; as of 2001 there were less than 350 gorillas living in Rwanda, Uganda, and the Democratic Republic of the Congo (ex-Zaire). Promotes preservation and conservation of the gorillas' rain forest habitat; is the sole operator of the Karisoke Research Center for the study of gorilla behavior and the environment. Operates Rwandan anti-poaching patrols to guard the gorillas and monitor their well-being; gorillas are often caught in traps and snares set for other animals. Makes available curriculum for elementary and middle schools. Organization was founded by primatologist Dian Fossey (1932-1985) in memory of the gorilla she named Digit, who was killed by poachers. **Libraries: Type:** reference. **Holdings:** biographical archives. **Subjects:** primates and habitat. **Computer Services:** database, contains donor records and demographic data on gorillas and habitat. **Committees:** Scientific Advisory. **Formerly:** Digit Fund; (1998) Dian Fossey Fund. **Publications:** *Digit News*, quarterly. Newsletter. Includes updates on current research, status of gorillas, current affairs in Rwanda and Democratic Republic of Congo and fundraising. **Price:** free for members. **Circulation:** 10,000. **Conventions/Meetings:** annual meeting.

5311 ■ Ducks Unlimited (DU)

1 Waterfowl Way
Memphis, TN 38120
Ph: (901)758-3825
Free: (800)45-DUCKS
Fax: (901)758-3850
URL: http://www.ducks.org
Contact: W. Bruce Lewis, Pres.

Founded: 1937. **Members:** 733,000. **Membership Dues:** adult, $25-$249 (annual) ● bronze and silver sponsor, $250-$999 (annual) ● gold sponsor, $1,000 (annual). **Staff:** 450. **Budget:** $128,000,000. **Regional Groups:** 3,500. **State Groups:** 50. **Description:** Conservationists in the U.S., Canada, Mexico, New Zealand, and Australia interested in migratory waterfowl and wildlife habitat conservation. Works to restore or enhance natural wetland areas for migratory waterfowl in the prairie provinces of Canada, which provide 70 percent of North America's wild geese and ducks, in prime nesting, staging, and wintering areas of the U.S., and in Mexico where millions of waterfowl spend winter. Raises funds for construction and rehabilitation work carried on by the field operating organizations. **Libraries: Type:** reference. **Holdings:** films, photographs. **Subjects:** waterfowl. **Absorbed:** (1936) More Game Birds in America. **Publications:** *The Ducks Unlimited Story*. Brochure. **Price:** included in membership dues ● *International Waterfowl Symposium Transactions*, periodic ● *Puddler Magazine*, quarterly. For children. ● Magazine, bimonthly. **Advertising:** accepted ● Annual Report, annual. Alternate Formats: online. **Conventions/Meetings:** annual meeting.

5312 ■ Earthtrust

c/o Windward Environmental Center
1118 Maunawili Rd.
Kailua, HI 96734
Ph: (808)261-5339
Fax: (206)202-3893
E-mail: info@earthtrust.us
URL: http://www.earthtrust.org
Contact: Don White, Pres.

Founded: 1976. **Description:** Works to preserve wildlife and the environment. Investigates threats to wildlife, documents illegal wildlife products in marketplaces, illegal driftnetting; specializes in marine mammal and sustainable fisheries issues; advocates for increasing protection of all wildlife. Active in CITES and IWC issues. Works in cooperation with donors, governments, fisheries, and corporations to formulate and enforce legislation to protect the earth and its species. **Projects:** Anti-whaling; Delphis Dolphin Cognition Research Lab; Flipper Seal of Approval Campaign; International Dolphin Campaigns; Save the Whales International; Saving Whales Through DNA Analysis. **Affiliated With:** United Nations. **Publications:** *President's Letter*, 3/year. Newsletter. Features the activities of the association. ● Pamphlets.

5313 ■ Elephant Care International

166 Limo View Ln.
Hohenwald, TN 38462
Ph: (931)796-7102
E-mail: hh@elephantcare.org
URL: http://www.elephantcare.org
Contact: Hank Hammatt, Co-Founder/Exec. Dir.

Membership Dues: student associate, $10 (annual) ● basic associate, $20 (annual) ● e-leader associate, $50 (annual) ● conservation partner, $500 (annual) ● patron, $1,000 (annual) ● life - patron, $10,000. **Multinational. Description:** Aims to improve elephant healthcare. Promotes harmony and well-being of humans and elephants where they share natural environments. Provides direct care and information resources for caregivers. Supports community-based initiatives to reduce deaths and injuries caused by human-elephant conflict. Aims to advance research studies pertinent to diseases of captive and wild elephants. **Publications:** Newsletter, quarterly.

5314 ■ Elephant Research Foundation (ERF)

Address Unknown since 2008

Founded: 1977. **Members:** 400. **Membership Dues:** $30 (annual). **Budget:** $5,000. **Description:** University faculty and students, farmers, zoo keepers, circus animal trainers, and others interested in the study of elephants. Promotes interest in and strives to increase public knowledge of elephants; work to protect elephant species; collects and disseminates information needed for education, and research on, and conservation of elephants. Works in cooperation with the East African Wildlife Society, International Union for Conservation of Nature and Natural Resources, and World Wildlife Fund. **Libraries: Type:** reference. **Holdings:** 1,000; articles, books, periodicals. **Subjects:** elephants, related species. **Committees:** Bibliography. **Absorbed:** (1992) Elephant Interest Group. **Publications:** *Elephant*, Irregular. Journal. Covers scientific articles, census, bibliography, members' activities. **Price:** $30.00. ISSN: 0737-108X. **Circulation:** 500.

5315 ■ Endangered Species Coalition (ESC)

PO Box 65195
Washington, DC 20035
Ph: (202)244-7138 (202)955-5609
Fax: (202)955-5789
E-mail: lgodfrey@stopextinction.org
URL: http://www.stopextinction.org
Contact: Brock Evans, Pres.

Founded: 1982. **Members:** 430. **Membership Dues:** national organization, $50-$3,500 ● regional/state/local organization, $35-$800. **Staff:** 10. **Budget:** $450,000. **Description:** Speaks on endangered species issues for over 430 environmental, religious, scientific, and business groups around the country. Seeks to secure a strong legal base for the effective conservation and recovery of plants and animals that are now, or may become, in danger of extinction and to ensure that the Endangered Species Act furthers the purposes and policies that it now specifies. Encourages public participation through petitions for the listing of particular species and the initiation of citizens' lawsuits and promotes state development of effective complementary conservation programs. Conducts educational, grass roots, and some lobbying activities, organizes meetings and letter-writing and telephone campaigns. **Telecommunication Services:** electronic mail, bevans_esc2004@yahoo.com. **Publications:** *ESA Today*, quarterly. Magazine. Alternate Formats: online ● *For All Things Wild*. Report. Contains information on the Federal Register. Alternate Formats: online ● Articles. Concerns with endangered species and the Endangered Species Act Reauthorization Bills. Includes fact sheets, position papers, and bill summaries. ● Also issues press releases, action alerts, and information fact sheets.

5316 ■ Exotic Wildlife Association (EWA)
105 Henderson Br. Rd. W
Ingram, TX 78025
Ph: (830)367-7761
Fax: (830)367-7762
E-mail: info@exoticwildlifeassociation.com
URL: http://www.exoticwildlifeassociation.com
Contact: Charly Seale, Exec. Dir.
Founded: 1967. **Members:** 1,000. **Membership Dues:** active, $150 (annual) ● patron, active corporate, $500 (annual) ● associate corporate, $200 (annual) ● associate, sportsman, $75 (annual) ● student, $25 (annual) ● life, $1,500. **Staff:** 4. **Description:** Encourages conservation of indigenous and non-indigenous hoofstock animals, and helps members develop and strengthen the markets for their animals. Educates policy-makers, the media and the public through research and advocacy. **Libraries: Type:** reference. **Subjects:** exotic wildlife, wildlife management. **Publications:** *Exotic Wildlife*, bimonthly. Magazine. **Price:** included in membership dues; $4.50 for nonmembers. **Advertising:** accepted ● *Game Ranch Directory*. **Advertising:** accepted. **Conventions/Meetings:** annual Fund Raiser/Awards Banquet - dinner, includes Trophy Game Records of the World ● annual meeting, for members (exhibits).

5317 ■ Florida Keys Wild Bird Rehabilitation Center (FKWBC)
93600 Overseas Hwy.
Tavernier, FL 33070
Ph: (305)852-4486
Fax: (305)852-3186
E-mail: info@fkwbc.org
URL: http://www.fkwbc.org
Contact: Laura B. Quinn, Chief Exec.
Founded: 1984. **Membership Dues:** individual, $25 (annual) ● family, $50 (annual) ● corporate, $250 (annual) ● patron, $1,000 (annual). **Staff:** 8. **Description:** Offers emergency therapy, rehabilitation, medical, and convalescent services to sick and injured wild birds in the Florida Keys. Collects data in order to aid in the detection of potential environmental concerns in the Florida Keys. Plans to develop captive breeding program using permanently injured wading birds of special concern. Educates the public on how man impacts the environment of the various local birds by touring the facility. **Computer Services:** database, statistics on wild birds. **Affiliated With:** National Wildlife Rehabilitators Association. **Publications:** *Footprints*, quarterly. Newsletter. Alternate Formats: online.

5318 ■ Foundation for North American Wild Sheep (FNAWS)
720 Allen Ave.
Cody, WY 82414-3402
Ph: (307)527-6261
Fax: (307)527-7117
E-mail: fnaws@fnaws.org
URL: http://www.fnaws.org
Contact: Ray Lee, Pres./CEO
Founded: 1977. **Members:** 6,000. **Membership Dues:** regular, $45 (annual) ● family, $80 (annual) ● junior, $10 (annual) ● international, $100 (annual) ● company, $200 (annual) ● life, $1,000 ● life (ages 59-64), $750 ● life (ages 65 & over), $500. **Staff:** 7. **State Groups:** 9. **Description:** Works to promote the management of and to safeguard against the extinction of all species of wild sheep native to the continent of North America. Provides funds for projects in areas including biological studies, buffer land acquisition, wild sheep transplants, re-establishment of wild sheep populations in historic habitats, wildlife habitat enhancement, prevention of poaching, and advancement of sportsmen's rights. **Awards:** Distinguished Service. **Frequency:** annual. **Type:** recognition. **Recipient:** for members with outstanding support to FNAWS mission from the ground up ● Federal Statesman. **Frequency:** annual. **Type:** recognition. **Recipient:** for members with outstanding support to resource management through the Healthy Forest Initiative ● Frank Golata Award. **Frequency:** annual. **Type:** trophy. **Recipient:** to outfitters who have exemplified the honor and dignity of the outfitting profession ● G.C.F. Dalziel Outstanding Guide Award. **Frequency:** annual. **Type:** trophy. **Recipient:** for members ● Grass Roots. **Frequency:** annual. **Type:** recognition. **Recipient:** for members with outstanding efforts on behalf of the many chapters and affiliates of FNAWS ● International Service. **Frequency:** annual. **Type:** recognition. **Recipient:** for members with outstanding efforts on behalf of wild sheep internationally ● Outstanding Achievement. **Frequency:** annual. **Type:** recognition. **Recipient:** for members with outstanding support on behalf of the wild sheep of Nevada ● Outstanding Conservationist. **Frequency:** annual. **Type:** recognition. **Recipient:** for members with outstanding contributions to wild sheep throughout North America ● Special Achievement and Recognition. **Frequency:** annual. **Type:** recognition. **Recipient:** for members with perseverance, patience, hard work and attention to detail ● State Statesman. **Frequency:** annual. **Type:** recognition. **Recipient:** for members with outstanding support on behalf of the wild sheep of Texas. **Telecommunication Services:** electronic mail, rlee@fnaws.org. **Funds:** Endowment; Life Membership. **Programs:** Grant-in-Aid. **Projects:** Hells Canyon. **Publications:** *Wild Sheep*, periodic. **Advertising:** accepted ● Books ● Videos. **Conventions/Meetings:** annual meeting and convention, fundraiser and membership meeting (exhibits).

5319 ■ Friends of the Australian Koala Foundation
c/o Nolan Lehr Group
224 W 29th St., 15th Fl.
New York, NY 10001
Ph: (212)967-8200
Free: (800)695-6252
Fax: (212)967-7292
E-mail: akf@savethekoala.com
URL: http://www.savethekoala.com
Contact: Deborah Tabart, CEO
Founded: 1989. **Membership Dues:** individual, $25 (annual). **Description:** Interested individuals. Raises private sector funds for research projects and educational programs to help preserve the koala and its habitat. Encourages biological research and disease control. Supports the studies of habitat usage and preservation, and town planning to minimize habitat destruction koala population dynamics. Sponsors public service announcements and special events. **Publications:** *Australian Koala Foundation Newsletter*, quarterly. **Price:** included in membership dues.

5320 ■ Friends of the Sea Otter (FSO)
93 Via Ventura
Monterey, CA 93940
Ph: (831)373-2747
Fax: (831)373-2749
E-mail: info@seaotters.org
URL: http://www.seaotters.org
Contact: D'Anne Albers, Exec. Dir.
Founded: 1968. **Members:** 5,000. **Membership Dues:** individual, classroom, $30 (annual) ● student, senior, $15 (annual) ● family, classroom plus, international, $50 (annual) ● steward, $100 (annual) ● advocate, $250 (annual) ● activist, $500 (annual). **Staff:** 5. **Description:** Citizens organized to aid in the protection and maintenance of a healthy population of sea otters and their marine habitat along the California coast and throughout their North Pacific range. Works to educate the public. Monitors and alerts members to actions affecting the otter's welfare. **Publications:** *Beneath the Surface*. Video. **Price:** $19.95 ● *The Otter Raft*, semiannual. Newsletter. Contains scientific and educational information. Alternate Formats: online ● *The Otter's Trove*, annual. Catalog. **Conventions/Meetings:** annual meeting, for members only - always third weekend in October, Monterey, CA.

5321 ■ Golden Lion Tamarin Management Committee (GLTMC)
Address Unknown since 2007
Founded: 1980. **Members:** 90. **Description:** Representatives from research and zoological institutions who participate in the Golden Lion Tamarin Conservation Program. Fosters conservation of the Golden Lion tamarin, a small marmoset indigenous to South America. Compiles statistics. **Computer Services:** database. **Publications:** *International Golden Lion Tamarin Studbook*, annual. **Price:** available to members only. **Circulation:** 300. **Advertising:** not accepted. **Conventions/Meetings:** annual conference.

5322 ■ Great Bear Foundation (GBF)
PO Box 9383
Missoula, MT 59807-9383
Ph: (406)829-9378
Fax: (406)829-9379
E-mail: gbf@greatbear.org
URL: http://www.greatbear.org
Contact: Dr. Charles Jonkel, Pres.
Founded: 1982. **Members:** 2,500. **Membership Dues:** individual, $30 (annual) ● family, $40 (annual) ● student, senior, $20 ● bear cub, $50 ● black bear, $100 ● brown bear, $250 ● polar bear, $500 ● life, $1,000. **Staff:** 3. **Budget:** $175,000. **Description:** Individuals interested in the conservation of the eight species of wild bears in the world. Operates conservation, education, research, and information services related to bears. **Awards: Type:** grant. **Recipient:** for individuals and organizations whose educational work and research benefit bears. **Projects:** Babine River Grizzly; Bear Hunting: Baiting, Hound, Spring and Den Hunts; Grizzly Bear Recovery; Malayan Sun Bears; Poaching and Illegal Trade of Bear Body Parts; Polar Bears, Arctic Ecosystems, and Global Climate Change; Spirit Bear. **Subgroups:** ASUM Student Chapter. **Publications:** *Bear News*, quarterly. Newsletter. Covers bears. **Price:** included in membership dues. ISSN: 0885-615X. **Advertising:** accepted. **Conventions/Meetings:** annual conference and meeting (exhibits).

5323 ■ Great Lakes Indian Fish and Wildlife Commission (GLIFWC)
PO Box 9
Odanah, WI 54861
Ph: (715)682-6619
Fax: (715)682-9294
E-mail: sue@glifwc.org
URL: http://www.glifwc.org
Contact: James Zorn, Exec. Admin.
Founded: 1983. **Members:** 11. **Staff:** 61. **Regional Groups:** 11. **Description:** Chippewa tribes concerned with wildlife conservation in the Great Lakes region. Assists member tribes in the conservation and management of fish, wildlife, and natural resources. Promotes tribal self-government; encourages ecosystem protection. Sponsors educational and research programs. **Publications:** *A Guide to Understanding Ojibwe Treaty Rights*. Booklet. **Price:** $3.00. Alternate Formats: online ● *BIZHIBAYASH: Circle of Flight*. Booklet. **Price:** free ● *Chippewa Treaties Understanding and Impact*. Booklet. **Price:** $2.00 ● *Chippewa Treaty Rights* ● *Fishery Status Update*. Booklet. **Price:** free ● *MAZINA'IGAN*, quarterly. Newspaper. **Price:** free ● *Ojibwe Treaty Rights and Resource Management*. Brochure ● *Poisoning the Circle: Mercury In Our Ecosystem*. Video. **Price:** $5.00 ● *Seasons of the Ojibwe*. Booklet. **Price:** $3.00 ● *Spearfishing Coverage Compilation*. Video. **Price:** $5.00 ● *Sulfide Mining: The Process and The Price*. Booklet. **Price:** free ● *With an Eagle's Eyes: Protecting Ojibwe Off-Reservation Treaty Rights and Resources*. Video. **Price:** $8.00 ● Annual Report, annual ● Manuals ● Reports.

5324 ■ Hawk Mountain Sanctuary (HMSA)
1700 Hawk Mountain Rd.
Kempton, PA 19529
Ph: (610)756-6961 (610)756-6000
Fax: (610)756-4468
E-mail: info@hawkmountain.org
URL: http://www.hawkmountain.org
Contact: Wendy McLean, Sec.
Founded: 1934. **Members:** 10,000. **Membership Dues:** individual, $35 ● family, $40 ● sustaining, $75 ● family plus, $50 ● Business Broad Wing Club, $100 ● Business Merlin, $250 ● Business Golden Eagle Club, $500 ● Business Gyrfalcon, $1,000 ● Business Millennium Club, $25,000. **Staff:** 15. **Budget:**

$1,000,000. **Description:** Conserves and protects wildlife, especially birds of prey such as eagles, hawks, and falcons. Maintains 2,400-acre wildlife sanctuary through which more than 20,000 birds of prey migrate each fall. Sponsors annual lecture series and research programs; conducts international internship program. Provides specialized education programs. Monitors public policy issues related to raptor conservation. Maintains visitors' center and hiking trails. **Convention/Meeting:** none. **Libraries: Type:** reference. **Holdings:** 2,000; books, clippings, monographs, periodicals. **Subjects:** raptors, birds. **Awards:** Hawk Mt. Research Grant. **Frequency:** annual. **Type:** grant. **Recipient:** for graduate student research related to raptor conservation. **Publications:** *Breeding Bird Census*. Report. Alternate Formats: online ● *Hawk Mountain News*, semiannual. Magazine. Includes migration reports. **Price:** included in membership dues ● *Hawk Mountain Sanctuary Conservation Status Report*. Alternate Formats: online ● *Kestrel Video*. Includes tips on building and setting up a nest box. **Price:** $15.00 ● *KJB-211*. Newsletter. Alternate Formats: online ● *Raptor Watch: A Global Directory of Raptor Migration Sites*. Book. Contains information on the numbers and kinds of raptors. ● Annual Report, annual.

5325 ■ International Association for Bear Research and Management (IBA)

c/o Joseph Clark, Sec.
Southern Appalachian Field Lab.
Univ. of Tennessee
274 Ellington Hall
Knoxville, TN 37996
Ph: (865)974-4790
Fax: (865)974-3555
E-mail: jclark1@utk.edu
URL: http://www.bearbiology.com
Contact: Joseph Clark, Sec.

Founded: 1968. **Members:** 700. **Membership Dues:** standard, $50 (annual) ● institutional, $100 (annual) ● low-cost, $25 (annual). **Description:** Research biologists, animal and land managers, professionals, and laypersons in 46 countries. Fosters communication and cooperation in research, care, and management of bears and their habitat. Conducts international conferences every 3 years and regional bear workshops. **Awards:** John Sheldon Bevins Memorial Foundation. **Frequency:** annual. **Type:** grant. **Recipient:** for research projects; travel grants for conference participants. **Formerly:** (1977) Bear Biology Association; (1999) International Association for Bear Research and Management; (2002) International Bear Association. **Publications:** *International Bear News*, quarterly. Newsletter. Alternate Formats: online ● *URSUS*, annual. Journal. Contains proceedings from Annual Conferences. Includes a variety of articles on all aspects of bear management and research worldwide. **Price:** $40.00 ● Also publishes a series of monographs. **Conventions/Meetings:** international conference (exhibits) - every 18 months ● periodic workshop.

5326 ■ International Bird Rescue Research Center (IBRRC)

4369 Cordelia Rd.
Fairfield, CA 94534
Ph: (707)207-0380
Fax: (707)207-0395
E-mail: jay@ibrrc.org
URL: http://www.ibrrc.org
Contact: Jay Holcomb, Exec. Dir.

Founded: 1971. **Members:** 400. **Description:** Represents individuals, researchers, and associations wishing to contribute and receive information regarding the deleterious effects of man-made and natural phenomena on birds and on methods of bird rehabilitation. Develops methods for the rehabilitation of oiled water birds because of the great losses in bird population caused by oil slicks. Coordinates research in this field. Provides consulting services for governmental and industrial contingency planning; also offers consulting assistance in the event of an oil spill emergency. Conventions/Meetings: none. **Publications:** *Cleaning Oiled Birds*. Video ● *Rehabilitating Oiled Sea Birds*. Manual ● *Saving Oiled Seabirds*. Manual.

5327 ■ International Crane Foundation (ICF)

PO Box 447
E-11376 Shady Lane Rd.
Baraboo, WI 53913-0447
Ph: (608)356-9462
Fax: (608)356-9465
E-mail: dana@savingcranes.org
URL: http://www.savingcranes.org
Contact: James Hook, Pres.

Founded: 1973. **Members:** 6,000. **Membership Dues:** individual, $35 (annual) ● family, $50 (annual) ● associate, $100 (annual) ● student, senior, $25 (annual) ● sustaining, $250 (annual) ● sponsor, $500 (annual) ● patron, $1,000 (annual) ● benefactor, $2,000 (annual). **Staff:** 25. **Budget:** $1,000,000. **Description:** Scientists and interested individuals in 20 countries committed to the preservation of the crane. Seeks to preserve and restock the crane population in its natural habitat and to increase captive propagation. Cooperates with universities in student research projects; provides tours of facilities. Operates speakers' bureau. Maintains aviculture facilities and an educational complex. **Libraries: Type:** reference. **Holdings:** 13,200; articles, books, periodicals. **Subjects:** bird conservation, ornithology, cranes, ecology, zoology, botany. **Departments:** Crane Conservation; Field Ecology; Site Administration; Veterinary Services. **Publications:** *The ICF Bugle*, quarterly. Newsletter ● *Proceedings of the 1983 International Crane Workshop* ● *Reflections - A Study of Cranes*. Newsletter. **Conventions/Meetings:** annual meeting - always September in Baraboo, WI.

5328 ■ The International Osprey Foundation (TIOF)

PO Box 250
Sanibel, FL 33957-0250
Fax: (720)223-2051
E-mail: tiof@ospreys.com
URL: http://www.ospreys.com
Contact: Timothy A. Gardner, Pres.

Founded: 1981. **Members:** 300. **Membership Dues:** individual, $20 (annual) ● family, $25 (annual) ● sustaining, $30 (annual) ● supporting, corporate, $50 (annual) ● contributing, $100 (annual) ● donor, $250 (annual) ● life, $500 ● student, $8 (annual). **Regional Groups:** 1. **Languages:** English, German. **Multinational. Description:** Professional and amateur ornithologists and other interested individuals who promotes the study and preservation of the osprey (a large fish-eating hawk) and other birds of prey. Mediates the exchange of information; compiles statistics; maintains speakers' bureau and a program of public education on the ecology and status of ospreys. Monitors ospreys on Sanibel Island, FL. **Awards:** Endowment Honor Roll. **Frequency:** annual. **Type:** grant. **Recipient:** for graduate studies pertaining to osprey (or other raptors). **Publications:** *International Newsletter*, annual. Features osprey-related topics. ● *Osprey Observer*, annual. Newsletter. **Conventions/Meetings:** annual meeting - always February or March, Sanibel, FL.

5329 ■ International Snow Leopard Trust (ISLT)

4649 Sunnyside Ave. N, Ste.325
Seattle, WA 98103
Ph: (206)632-2421
Fax: (206)632-3967
E-mail: info@snowleopard.org
URL: http://www.snowleopard.org
Contact: Brad Rutherford, Exec. Dir.

Founded: 1981. **Members:** 1,700. **Membership Dues:** associate, $35 (annual) ● patron, $50 (annual) ● advocate, $100 (annual) ● sponsor, $250 (annual) ● colleague, $500 (annual) ● student, $15 (annual). **Staff:** 6. **Budget:** $500,000. **Multinational. Description:** Works to conserve the endangered snow leopard and its fragile mountain habitat through a balanced approach that considers the needs of the local people and the environment. **Computer Services:** database, publications ● database, snow leopards. **Publications:** *Annotated Bibliography of Literature of the Snow Leopard* ● *Eighth International Snow Leopard Symposium*. Proceedings ● *Review of the Studies and Ecology of the Snow Leopard* ● *Snow Leopard Survey and Conservation*. Handbook ● *Snow Line*, periodic. Newsletter ● Bibliography ● Proceedings ● Journal. **Price:** free ● Also publishes status review. **Conventions/Meetings:** periodic symposium ● workshop.

5330 ■ International Society for the Protection of Mustangs and Burros (ISPMB)

PO Box 55
Lantry, SD 57636-0055
Ph: (605)964-6866 (605)365-6991
E-mail: ispmb@lakotanetwork.com
URL: http://www.ispmb.org
Contact: Karen A. Sussman, Pres.

Founded: 1960. **Members:** 19,000. **Membership Dues:** junior/senior, $15 (annual) ● individual, $35 (annual) ● association/contributing, $50 (annual) ● sponsor, $100 (annual) ● corporate, $5,000 (annual) ● sustaining, $500 (annual) ● benevolent, $1,000 (annual) ● senior, $25 (annual). **Description:** Persons interested in the protection and preservation of wild horses and burros. Goals are to recognize wild horses and burros as a valuable resource contributing to the biological diversity of the land and enriching the lives of human beings; acknowledge that wild horses and burros are one of the last living symbols of the heritage of many cultures; maintain organizational trust, credibility, and leadership; ensure the enforcement and prevent erosion of existing laws and assist in the development of new laws for the protection and preservation of wild horses and burros and their habitat; encourage and implement research and educational programs that increase appreciation, understanding, and preservation of wild horses, burros, and their habitat; promote humane treatment of wild horses and burros worldwide; and foster cooperative efforts with government agencies and other organizations in attaining quality programs relating to wild horses and burros and their habitat. Develops an ecotourism center on Cheyenne River Reservation Indian reservation; gives tours of two wild horse ranges. Center combines preservation of wild horses, conservation of the land and celebration of traditional Lakota heritage. **Absorbed:** Wild Horses of America Registry. **Formerly:** (1965) International Mustang Club. **Publications:** *Wild Horse and Burro Diary*, quarterly. Newsletter. **Conventions/Meetings:** annual meeting.

5331 ■ International Wild Waterfowl Association (IWWA)

c/o John Nuccitelli, Treas.
438 Quaker Meeting House Rd.
Honeoye Falls, NY 14472
Ph: (585)624-4608
Fax: (585)624-5175
E-mail: jnooch@aol.com
URL: http://www.wildwaterfowl.org
Contact: Walter Sturgeon Jr., Pres.

Founded: 1958. **Members:** 500. **Membership Dues:** regular, $30 (annual) ● life, $500 ● organization, $50 (annual). **Description:** Individuals in 15 countries concerned with conservation and the preservation of wild waterfowl. Works toward protection, conservation, and reproduction of any species considered in danger of eventual extinction; encourages the breeding of well-known and rare species in captivity so that more people may learn about them by observation and enjoy them in the natural habitats created for this purpose. Maintains speakers' bureau. Has established Avicultural Hall of Fame. **Libraries: Type:** reference. **Holdings:** 600; books. **Subjects:** birds. **Awards:** Conservation Award. **Frequency:** periodic. **Type:** recognition. **Recipient:** for outstanding contributions to wildlife conservation ● First Breeding Award. **Frequency:** periodic. **Type:** recognition. **Recipient:** for the first breeding of species in North America ● Hancock Memorial Award. **Frequency:** periodic. **Type:** recognition. **Recipient:** for outstanding contribution to the collective knowledge of waterfowl through field research, captive research, or photography ● Jean Delacour Avicultural Award. **Fre-**

quency: periodic. **Type:** recognition. **Recipient:** to an individual member or organization for outstanding contribution to the betterment of aviculture and the association in particular ● McQuade Memorial Award. **Frequency:** periodic. **Type:** recognition. **Recipient:** for outstanding breeding success by a novice member ● Southwick Memorial Award. **Frequency:** periodic. **Type:** recognition. **Recipient:** to a member for illustrious avicultural effort with waterfowl, particularly those directed toward establishing new species in captivity or for their conservation in the wild. **Projects:** Friends of the white-fronted goose; Nene O Molak'i; Orinoco Goose Nest Box; Torrent Duck. **Publications:** *First Breedings of Wild Waterfowl*, periodic. Newsletter ● *IWWA Membership Roster*, annual. Membership Directory ● *IWWA Newsletter*, quarterly. Alternate Formats: online ● *Surplus Lists of Waterfowl*, semiannual. **Conventions/Meetings:** annual conference (exhibits).

5332 ■ International Wildlife Coalition - USA (IWC)
70 E Falmouth Hwy.
East Falmouth, MA 02536
Ph: (508)457-1898
Free: (800)548-8704
Fax: (508)457-1898
E-mail: iwchq@iwc.org
URL: http://www.iwc.org
Contact: Heather Rockwell, Asst. Dir.

Founded: 1984. **Members:** 150,000. **Membership Dues:** regular, $25 (annual). **Staff:** 12. **Budget:** $3,000,000. **Multinational. Description:** Works to preserve wildlife and wildlife habitats in United States, Sri Lanka, Brazil, Australia, United Kingdom, and Canada. Publicizes the coalition's cause and activities; conducts research. Maintains Speaker's Bureau; conducts educational programs. **Convention/Meeting:** none. **Affiliated With:** Whale Adoption Project. **Formerly:** (1986) I KARE - Individuals Against Killing Animals for Recreational Enjoyment. **Publications:** *Information Packets*, monthly ● *Whales of the World Teacher's Kit* ● *Whalewatch*, quarterly. Newsletter ● *Wildlife and You*. Pamphlet ● *Wildlife Watch*, quarterly. Newsletter.

5333 ■ International Wildlife Rehabilitation Council (IWRC)
PO Box 8187
San Jose, CA 95155
Ph: (408)271-2685
Fax: (408)271-9285
E-mail: office@iwrc-online.org
URL: http://www.iwrc-online.org
Contact: Susan Heckly, Sec.

Founded: 1972. **Members:** 2,000. **Membership Dues:** individual in U.S., library outside U.S., $40 (annual) ● individual outside U.S., family in U.S., $50 (annual) ● library in U.S., $30 (annual) ● family outside U.S., $60 (annual) ● organizational in U.S., $52 (annual) ● organizational outside U.S., $62 (annual). **Staff:** 3. **Budget:** $276,000. **Description:** Individuals interested in the rehabilitation of wildlife; organizations that handle sick and injured wild animals. Aims to offer the most current information in the field. Maintains wildlife rehabilitation standards program. Conducts seminars and specialized education programs; compiles statistics. **Computer Services:** database, membership list. **Committees:** Conference/Skills Seminars; Literature; Species Paper. **Formerly:** (1985) Wildlife Rehabilitation Council. **Publications:** *Basic Wildlife Rehabilitation* (in English and Spanish). Manual. **Price:** $30.00 plus shipping and handling. **Circulation:** 8,000. Also Cited As: *IAB Manual* ● *Conference Proceedings*, annual ● *Journal of Wildlife Rehabilitation*, quarterly. Includes news of rehabilitation efforts nationwide and book reviews. Articles on species rehab and related topics peer reviewed. **Price:** $40.00 for individuals; $50.00 for families; $52.00 for organizations. ISSN: 1071-2232. **Circulation:** 2,000. **Advertising:** accepted ● *Raccoon Rehabilitation*. Manual ● Membership Directory, annual. **Price:** included in membership dues ● Also publishes works dealing with rehabilitation of wild animals. Literature catalog available. **Conventions/Meetings:** annual conference, with paper and workshop presentations (exhibits) - usually October or November.

5334 ■ Jane Goodall Institute for Wildlife Research, Education, and Conservation (JGI)
4245 N Fairfax Dr., Ste.600
Arlington, VA 22203
Ph: (703)682-9220
Free: (800)592-5263
Fax: (703)682-9312
E-mail: info@janegoodall.org
URL: http://www.janegoodall.org
Contact: William Johnston, Pres.

Founded: 1977. **Members:** 13,000. **Membership Dues:** contributing, $35-$499 (annual) ● conservator, $500-$999 (annual). **Staff:** 9. **Budget:** $2,000,000. **Regional Groups:** 1. **Description:** Commits to wildlife research, environmental education and the conservation and welfare of animals, particularly chimpanzees. Operates a number of projects, including Roots and Shoots, an environmental and humanitarian education program for young people; TACARE, a reforestation project in Western Tanzania; ChimpanZoo, an international research program dedicated to the study of captive chimpanzees; sanctuaries for orphaned chimpanzees; and the Gombe Stream Research Center for ongoing field research on wild chimpanzees. **Telecommunication Services:** electronic mail, cirwin@janegoodall.org. **Programs:** Chimp Guardian; ChimpanZoo; Employer's Matching Gift; Leadership Giving; Roots and Shoots. **Projects:** Central African World Heritage Forest Initiative; Chimpanzee Reintroduction; Community-Centered Conservation Initiatives. **Publications:** *ChimpanZoo Proceedings* ● *The Jane Goodall Institute Today*. Newsletter. Alternate Formats: online ● *JGI World Report*. Newsletter. **Price:** included in membership dues. **Circulation:** 30,000. **Advertising:** accepted ● *Roots and Shoots Network*. Newsletter. **Advertising:** accepted ● Brochure ● Annual Report, annual. **Conventions/Meetings:** annual ChimpanZoo Conference - meeting, highlights behavioral primatology research (exhibits) - always fall ● annual Roots and Shoots North American Youth Summit - meeting, environmental education - usually fall.

5335 ■ Keeping Track
PO Box 444
Huntington, VT 05462
Ph: (802)434-7000
Fax: (802)434-5383
URL: http://www.keepingtrack.org
Contact: Susan C. Morse, Founder/Dir.

Membership Dues: individual, $25 (annual) ● supporting, $50 (annual) ● life, $500. **Description:** Inspires community participation in the long-term stewardship of wildlife habitat. Teaches adults and children to observe, interpret, record and monitor evidence of wildlife habitat in their communities. Supports the use of monitoring data in local and regional conservation planning. **Publications:** Newsletter, quarterly.

5336 ■ Last Chance Forever (LCF)
PO Box 460993
San Antonio, TX 78246-0993
Ph: (210)499-4080
Fax: (210)499-4305
E-mail: raptor@ddc.net
URL: http://www.lastchanceforever.org
Contact: John A. Karger, Exec. Dir.

Founded: 1978. **Staff:** 5. **Description:** Aims to: shelter and rehabilitate birds of prey; conduct research and compile data; educate the public concerning birds of prey and their relation to the environment. Sponsors speaker and slide show exhibitions featuring birds for civic organizations and schools. Offers tours at summer festivals and environmental exhibits. **Convention/Meeting:** none. **Computer Services:** Online services, Friends of the Last Chance Forever, a listing of contributors and supporters. **Publications:** *A Feather in the Wind*, semiannual. Newsletter. Alternate Formats: online.

5337 ■ Lewa Wildlife Conservancy (USA)
c/o Paula Morris, Admin.
PO Box 7943
Woodbridge, VA 22195
Ph: (703)680-3182 (650)851-7738
E-mail: lewausa@verizon.net
URL: http://www.lewa.org/lewa_USA.php
Contact: Linda Millard, Exec. Dir.

Founded: 1997. **Membership Dues:** Rhino, $1,000 (annual) ● Grevy, $500 (annual) ● Impala, $100 (annual). **Description:** Works as a catalyst for the conservation of wildlife and its habitat. Provides financial, in-kind, and administrative back-up support for the Lewa Wildlife Conservancy and other wildlife conservation oriented entities in Kenya. Addresses the issues of sustainable wildlife conservation, educational programming, and community development in Kenya. **Telecommunication Services:** electronic mail, linda.millard@gmail.com. **Publications:** Newsletter.

5338 ■ Marine Mammal Stranding Center (MMSC)
PO Box 773
3625 Brigantine Blvd.
Brigantine, NJ 08203
Ph: (609)266-0538
Fax: (609)266-6300
E-mail: mmsc@verizon.net
URL: http://www.marinemammalstrandingcenter.org
Contact: Robert C. Schoelkopf, Dir./Founder

Founded: 1978. **Members:** 3,000. **Membership Dues:** child, senior, $15 (annual) ● regular, $25 (annual) ● benefactor, $50 (annual) ● donor, $100 (annual) ● sponsor, $500 (annual) ● corporate, $1,000 (annual). **Staff:** 5. **Budget:** $300,000. **State Groups:** 1. **Description:** Rescues, rehabilitates, and releases when possible stranded marine mammals that come ashore from the Atlantic Ocean; rescue activities are centered in New Jersey, but assistance is provided for rescues in other states. Operates seal census, college internships, animal first aid courses, museum, and gift shop. **Libraries: Type:** reference. **Programs:** Adopt A Seal. **Publications:** *The Blowhole*, quarterly. Newsletter. Includes updated list of strandings and rescue attempts, and reports on upcoming projects and activities. **Price:** included in membership dues. Alternate Formats: online ● Brochures. **Conventions/Meetings:** annual meeting, year-end summary of activities for members only (exhibits).

5339 ■ Midwest Association of Fish and Wildlife Agencies (MAFWA)
c/o Ollie Torgerson, Coor.
Wisconsin Dept. of Natural Resources
107 Sutliff Ave.
Rhinelander, WI 54501
Ph: (715)365-8924
Fax: (715)365-8932
E-mail: ollie.torgerson@dnr.state.wi.us
URL: http://mafwa.iafwa.org
Contact: Ollie Torgerson, Coor.

Founded: 1934. **Members:** 17. **Membership Dues:** state, $300 (annual) ● province, $100 (annual). **Staff:** 1. **State Groups:** 14. **Description:** Fish and game commissioners and directors of 14 Midwestern states and three Canadian provinces. Promotes conservation of wildlife and outdoor recreation. **Libraries: Type:** open to the public. **Holdings:** 64. **Awards:** Resource Contribution Awards. **Frequency:** annual. **Type:** recognition. **Committees:** Auditing; By-Laws; Legal; National Conservation Needs; Nominating/Awards; Public Land Management; Resolutions; Wildlife and Fish Health. **Working Groups:** Private Lands. **Affiliated With:** Association of Fish and Wildlife Agencies; Western Association of Fish and Wildlife Agencies. **Formerly:** (1975) Association of Midwest Fish and Game Commissioners; (1977) Association of Midwest Fish and Wildlife Commissioners; (2002) Association of Midwest Fish and Wildlife Agencies. **Publications:** Proceedings, annual. **Conventions/Meetings:** annual Director's Meeting - conference (exhibits).

5340 ■ Mission: Wolf
PO Box 1211
Westcliffe, CO 81252
Ph: (719)859-2157
E-mail: kent@missionwolf.com
URL: http://www.missionwolf.com
Contact: Kent Weber, Contact
Founded: 1988. **Members:** 4,500. **Membership Dues:** student, senior, $25 (annual) ● individual, $40 (annual) ● group, family, $100 (annual). **Staff:** 7. **Budget:** $110,000. **Description:** Serves as nature center and captive wolf sanctuary. Works to educate the public about wild wolves, the downfalls of wolf and wolf-dog cross pet ownership, and how to live sustainably. Travels with live wolves throughout the country each year through the Ambassador Wolf Program. Maintains sanctuary located in the remote mountains of Southern Colorado and provides a home for unwanted and cast-off captive-born pet wolves and wolf-dog crosses; the sanctuary is staffed only by volunteers and is open to visitors year round. **Libraries: Type:** open to the public. **Holdings:** audiovisuals, books, business records, clippings, monographs, periodicals. **Subjects:** wolves, habitats, predators, wolf recovery, environmental issues. **Awards:** Col. Smart Growth Award. **Frequency:** annual. **Type:** recognition. **Computer Services:** Online services, giftshop. **Publications:** *Wolf Visions*, semiannual. Newsletter. Contains current events of the refuge and the traveling education program and Wild Wolf recovery. **Price:** free. **Circulation:** 10,000. **Advertising:** accepted.

5341 ■ Mountain Lion Foundation
PO Box 1896
Sacramento, CA 95812
Ph: (916)442-2666
Fax: (916)442-2871
E-mail: lynnsadler@mountainlion.org
URL: http://www.mountainlion.org
Contact: Lynn Sadler, Pres./CEO
Founded: 1986. **Members:** 35,000. **Membership Dues:** individual, $35 (annual). **Staff:** 6. **Description:** Strives for the preservation and long-term survival of the mountain lion, other wildlife, and their habitat. Conducts educational and research programs. **Libraries: Type:** not open to the public. **Holdings:** articles, books, video recordings. **Subjects:** mountain lions, other large predators, such as bobcats, tigers, grizzlies; endangered species. **Awards:** Wildlife Protection Award. **Type:** recognition. **Telecommunication Services:** electronic mail, tdunbar@mountainlion.org. **Formerly:** (1992) Mountain Lion Preservation Foundation. **Publications:** *Cougar: The American Lion*. Book. **Price:** $19.95 ● *Crimes Against the Wild: Poaching in California* ● *Habitat Preservation* ● *Mountain Lion Foundation Review*, biennial. Newsletter. **Price:** free. **Circulation:** 35,000 ● *Preserving Cougar Country*.

5342 ■ National Military Fish and Wildlife Association (NMFWA)
c/o Terry Bashore, Pres.
2220 Somerset Pl.
Newport News, VA 23602
Ph: (757)225-4965
Fax: (757)764-6009
E-mail: terry.bashore@nmfwa.org
URL: http://68.178.187.196/index.cfm
Contact: Terry Bashore, Pres.
Founded: 1983. **Members:** 600. **Description:** Fish and wildlife managers and professionals in related fields. Provides professional resource management for the Department of Defense's fish and wildlife resources. Serves as a communication network. **Awards:** Presidential Award. **Frequency:** annual. **Type:** recognition. **Recipient:** for past or present DOD employees ● Professional Award. **Frequency:** annual. **Type:** recognition. **Recipient:** for management, law enforcement, and technical persons ● Support Award. **Frequency:** annual. **Type:** recognition. **Recipient:** for military and civilians ● Volunteer Award. **Frequency:** annual. **Type:** recognition. **Recipient:** for education and management. **Computer Services:** Mailing lists. **Publications:** *FAWN - Fish and Wildlife News*, 3/year. Newsletter. Pertains to natural resource management on Department of Defense lands. **Price:** free. **Circulation:** 600. Alternate Formats: online. **Conventions/Meetings:** annual Law Enforcement Refresher Course - meeting, for Department of Defense ● annual workshop, technical presentations on natural resource management of military lands (exhibits) - usually March.

5343 ■ National Wild Turkey Federation (NWTF)
PO Box 530
Edgefield, SC 29824-0530
Ph: (803)637-3106
Free: (800)THE-NWTF
Fax: (803)637-9170
E-mail: mgalloway@nwtf.net
URL: http://www.nwtf.org
Contact: Rob Keck, CEO
Founded: 1973. **Members:** 584,000. **Membership Dues:** regular, $30 (annual) ● sponsor, $225 (annual) ● JAKES/Hunting Heritage Club/extreme JAKES, $5 (annual) ● Women in the Outdoors/ Wheelin' Sportsmen, $25 (annual) ● Women in the Outdoors Sponsor/Wheelin' Sportsmen Sponsor, $200 (annual) ● senior sponsor, $1,000 ● bronze sponsor, $2,000 ● silver life sponsor, $5,000 ● gold life sponsor, $7,500 ● diamond life sponsor, $10,000 ● patron life sponsor, $25,000 ● guardian life sponsor, $50,000 ● centurion life sponsor, $100,000 ● military, student, $10 (annual) ● regular, $50 (biennial). **Staff:** 225. **Budget:** $58,000,000. **State Groups:** 50. **Local Groups:** 2,050. **National Groups:** 14. **Description:** Wild turkey enthusiasts and hunters. Promotes wise conservation and management of the American wild turkey as a valuable natural resource. Assists state wildlife agencies, universities, and other state or local organizations in conducting research, management, and restoration programs. Maintains Wild Turkey Center and financial assistance programs for agencies, organizations, and individuals. Sponsors annual wild turkey stamp and print art program, turkey calling competition, and banquets. **Libraries: Type:** open to the public. **Holdings:** 600; articles, books, periodicals. **Subjects:** wild turkeys. **Awards:** Research Grants. **Frequency:** annual. **Type:** monetary. **Recipient:** for turkey research. **Committees:** Awards; Building; Conservation; Convention; Membership Services; Technical. **Publications:** *The Caller*, quarterly. Newspaper. **Price:** included in membership dues. **Circulation:** 155,000. **Advertising:** accepted ● *Turkey Call*, bimonthly. Magazine. **Circulation:** 150,000 ● *Wildlife Bulletins*. **Conventions/Meetings:** annual convention, with sports show and auction dinners (exhibits) - always February or March.

5344 ■ National Wilderness Institute (NWI)
PO Box 25766
Washington, DC 20007
Ph: (703)836-7404
Fax: (703)836-7405
E-mail: nwi@nwi.org
URL: http://www.nwi.org
Contact: Robert Gordon, Exec.Dir.
Description: Promotes the wise management of natural resources using science, recognizing wildlife, fish, wetlands, wilderness, forest, range, air, water and soil respond positively to wise management. **Publications:** *Fresh Tracks*. Newsletter. Environmental bulletin. ● *NWI Resource*. Magazine. Features information on wildlife biology, technology, energy, agriculture, environmental regulation. ● Reports. Alternate Formats: online.

5345 ■ National Wildlife Refuge Association (NWRA)
1901 Pennsylvania Ave. NW, Ste.407
Washington, DC 20006
Ph: (202)333-9075
Free: (877)396-NWRA
Fax: (202)333-9077
E-mail: nwra@refugenet.org
URL: http://www.refugenet.org
Contact: Jeffrey Smith, Chm.
Founded: 1975. **Members:** 2,000. **Membership Dues:** individual, $25 (annual). **Staff:** 5. **Budget:** $700,000. **Description:** Works exclusively to protect, enhance and expand the National Wildlife Refuge System. By combining policy, grassroots development and public education objectives, it seeks to ensure that the country continues to support a diverse spectrum of plants and wildlife well into the future. Works with local refuge "friends" groups to promote America's diverse wildlife heritage. **Awards:** Friends Group of the Year. **Frequency:** annual. **Type:** recognition ● National Wildlife Refuge System Employee of the Year. **Frequency:** annual. **Type:** recognition ● Outstanding Refuge Manager of the Year. **Frequency:** annual. **Type:** recognition ● Outstanding Refuge System Volunteer of the Year. **Frequency:** annual. **Type:** recognition. **Publications:** *Wildlife Refuge*, semiannual. Magazine. Showcases the National Wildlife Refuge System. **Price:** included in membership dues. **Advertising:** accepted. **Conventions/ Meetings:** annual board meeting.

5346 ■ National Wildlife Rehabilitators Association (NWRA)
2625 Clearwater Rd., Ste.110
St. Cloud, MN 56301
Ph: (320)230-9920
Fax: (320)230-3077
E-mail: nwra@nwrawildlife.org
URL: http://www.nwrawildlife.org
Contact: Lessie Davis, Pres.
Founded: 1982. **Members:** 1,900. **Membership Dues:** active, $40 (annual) ● student, $20 (annual) ● family, $70 (annual) ● life, $1,500. **Staff:** 3. **Description:** Wildlife rehabilitators and other interested individuals including state and federal agency personnel, conservationists, educators, naturalists, researchers, veterinarians, and zoo and humane society staff. Supports the science and profession of wildlife rehabilitation and its practitioners. (Wildlife rehabilitation is the practice of assisting injured, orphaned, diseased, or displaced animals, with the goal of enabling such wildlife to be returned to its natural habitat.) Works to improve the profession through the development of high standards of practice, ethics, and conduct. Disseminates and stimulate the growth of knowledge in the field. Fosters cooperation of professional and governmental agencies and other similar groups with the wildlife rehabilitation community. Develops the Minimum Standards for Wildlife Rehabilitation, in conjunction with the International Wildlife Rehabilitation Council, to encourage the development of outstanding rehabilitation programs. Provides research grants; conducts networking; offers consulting referrals. **Awards:** Lifetime Achievement Award. **Frequency:** annual. **Type:** recognition. **Recipient:** to a person whose primary identification is with the field of wildlife rehabilitation and who has made significant contributions for many years ● Marlys J. Bulander: Working Together for Wildlife Award. **Frequency:** annual. **Type:** recognition. **Recipient:** to a person or group who has brought together individuals, organizations, rehabilitation facilities, agencies, industries, businesses, and/or academia in a cooperative effort to make a difference for wildlife ● Significant Achievement. **Frequency:** annual. **Type:** recognition. **Recipient:** to a person who has made a major contribution to the field of wildlife rehabilitation within the last two years. **Committees:** Education; Honors, Awards, Grants; Membership; Public Relations and Information; Publications; Standards; Veterinary. **Publications:** *Wildlife Rehabilitation*, annual. Proceedings ● *Wildlife Rehabilitation Bulletin*, semiannual. Journal. **Price:** included in membership dues. **Advertising:** accepted ● *The Wildlife Rehabilitator*, semiannual. Newsletters. Contains information on NWRA accomplishments and activities. **Price:** $7.00. **Advertising:** accepted ● Membership Directory, annual. **Price:** included in membership dues. **Conventions/Meetings:** annual meeting (exhibits) - always March.

5347 ■ Native Fish Society (NFS)
PO Box 19570
Portland, OR 97280
Ph: (503)977-3133
Fax: (503)977-0026

E-mail: info@nativefishsociety.org
URL: http://204.203.92.17
Contact: Bill Bakke, Exec. Dir.
Founded: 1995. **Members:** 700. **Membership Dues:** regular, $50 (annual) ● student, $25 (annual) ● contributor, $100 (annual) ● charter, $150 (annual) ● organizational, $200 (annual) ● benefactor, $500 (annual) ● corporate, $1,000 (annual). **Staff:** 3. **Description:** Individuals interested in the protection of fish species native to the Northwestern Continental United States. Advocates sound fishery and conservation programs to insure preservation of native fish stocks and habitats. Promotes public debate on fishery-related conservation issues. Gathers and disseminates information to improve public awareness of fishery and related conservation issues. Develops and implements fishery management policies and programs designed to maintain genetic diversity in native fish stocks. Conducts watershed analyses, conservation audits, and research to determine spawning requirements for native fish species and subspecies; establishes measurable biological objectives for fishery and conservation programs. **Libraries: Type:** reference. **Holdings:** 2,050. **Subjects:** native fish conservation with emphasis on salmonids. **Study Groups:** Fish Cons. **Publications:** *Program Report*. Alternate Formats: online ● *Strong Runs*, quarterly. Newsletter. Contains conservation reports, action alerts and invitations to special events. **Price:** included in membership dues. **Conventions/Meetings:** annual meeting, membership meeting.

5348 ■ New York Turtle and Tortoise Society (NYTTS)
PO Box 878
Orange, NJ 07051-0878
E-mail: qanda@nytts.org
URL: http://nytts.org
Contact: Lori Cramer, Contact
Founded: 1970. **Members:** 1,500. **Membership Dues:** individual, $25 (annual). **Description:** Veterinarians, zookeepers, biologists, and pet owners nationwide. Works to conserve, preserve, and propagate turtles and tortoises. Advocates protective legislation for endangered species; encourages enforcement of humane laws. Disseminates information on the care and breeding of turtles and tortoises. Maintains the Turtle Rehab Program, dedicated to the care and rehabilitation of injured turtles found in the wild. Conducts annual seminar. Maintains speakers' bureau. Provides adoption program for unwanted animals; Sponsors field trips. **Committees:** Adoption; Education; Rehabilitation. **Publications:** *NYTTS NewsNotes*, periodic. Newsletter ● *NYTTS Vet List*, periodic. Directory ● *Plastron Papers*, semiannual. Journal. Includes information on turtle behavior, husbandry, diet, medical care, habitat, conservation, legislation, and turtle lore. ● *Turtle Help Network*, periodic. Directory. Lists volunteers and their areas of interest and expertise. **Conventions/Meetings:** monthly meeting - always New York City ● annual show - always June, in New York City.

5349 ■ Norcross Wildlife Foundation
250 W 88th St., No. 806
New York, NY 10024
Ph: (212)362-4831
E-mail: john@norcrossws.org
URL: http://www.norcrossws.org
Contact: John G. McMurray, Program Off.
Founded: 1966. **Description:** Strives to protect, enhance, and expand habitat for wildlife, primarily at the Norcross Wildlife Sanctuary. Hosts educational programs.

5350 ■ North American Bear Center (NABC)
1926 Hwy. 169
Ely, MN 55731
Ph: (218)365-7879
E-mail: info@bear.org
URL: http://www.bear.org
Contact: Dr. Lynn Rogers, Chair
Founded: 1994. **Description:** Enhances the understanding of the general public of the habits, needs, and environment of bears in North America. **Publications:** *Bear Facts*, quarterly. Newsletter. **Conventions/Meetings:** monthly board meeting.

5351 ■ North American Bear Society (NABS)
Address Unknown since 2008
Founded: 1986. **Members:** 8,000. **Membership Dues:** student (under 21), $15 ● supporting, $25 ● family, $40 ● supporting, $50 (biennial) ● supporting, $100 (quinquennial) ● life, $1,000. **Staff:** 21. **Budget:** $100,000. **Regional Groups:** 3. **State Groups:** 6. **Local Groups:** 3. **Description:** Promotes the conservation and management of bears and other North American wildlife. Works to increase public awareness of wildlife conservation issues. Encourages hunter education in areas of "ethical sportsmanship," safety, and environmental concerns. Conducts educational and research programs; maintains speakers' bureau. **Libraries: Type:** reference. **Holdings:** 680; archival material, audiovisuals, books, business records, clippings, periodicals. **Subjects:** black, grizzly, and polar bears. **Awards:** Silver Tip Award. **Frequency:** annual. **Type:** monetary. **Computer Services:** database ● mailing lists. **Programs:** The Adaptable Arizona Black Bear; Bears of North America. **Publications:** *Bear Tracker*, quarterly. Newsletter. **Price:** included in membership dues. **Circulation:** 8,000. **Advertising:** accepted. Alternate Formats: online ● *NABS Membership Brochure* ● *URSUS*, annual. Magazine. **Price:** included in membership dues; $25.00/year for nonmembers. **Circulation:** 10,000. **Advertising:** accepted. Alternate Formats: online. **Conventions/Meetings:** competition ● annual conference (exhibits) - always March, Scottsdale, AZ.

5352 ■ North American Bluebird Society (NABS)
PO Box 43
Miamiville, OH 45147
Ph: (812)988-1876 (512)268-5678
E-mail: info@nabluebirdsociety.org
URL: http://www.nabluebirdsociety.org
Contact: Jonathan Ridgeway, Pres.
Founded: 1978. **Members:** 3,500. **Membership Dues:** subscribing, $20 (annual) ● supporting, $40 (annual) ● contributing, $75 (annual) ● guardian, $100 (annual) ● small business, $50 (annual) ● corporation, $125 (annual) ● life, $500. **Staff:** 4. **Budget:** $100,000. **Description:** Conservationists and other individuals and groups interested in bluebirds and other native cavity nesting birds of North America. Works to alert the public to the slow but definite disappearance of the bluebird due to lack of suitable nesting cavities and severe weather; to encourage establishment of bluebird trails of nesting boxes or individual nesting boxes; to keep scientific records of the bluebird's nesting habits and act as information clearinghouse. Presents slide shows; provides lecture demonstrations to schools and interested youth groups. Conducts research; compiles statistics; and maintains speakers' bureau. **Awards:** The North American Bluebird Society Award. **Frequency:** annual. **Type:** grant. **Recipient:** for outstanding contribution to the field of bluebird conservation ● **Type:** recognition. **Committees:** Catalog; Education; Education Advisory; Research. **Publications:** *Bluebird*, quarterly. Journal. Includes research reports, bibliography, and statistics. **Price:** available to members only. **Advertising:** accepted ● *Bluebird Bibliography*. **Price:** $1.00. **Conventions/Meetings:** annual Bluebird Convention, nest box displays, trail monitoring workshops, bluebird ecology programs (exhibits).

5353 ■ North American Crane Working Group
PO Box 566
Gambier, OH 43022
Ph: (206)286-8607
E-mail: thoffmann@hoffmanns.com
URL: http://www.nacwg.org
Contact: Tom Hoffmann, Treas.
Founded: 1988. **Members:** 160. **Membership Dues:** active, $10 (annual) ● sustaining, $20 (annual) ● contributing, $50 (annual). **Description:** Professional biologists, aviculturists, land managers, and interested individuals. Works to: promote the conservation of cranes and their habitats in North America; encourage research on crane conservation; increase public awareness and appreciation of cranes and their habitats. Provides educational programs. Disseminates information. **Publications:** *Proceedings of the North American Crane Workshop*, periodic ● *Unison Call*, semiannual. Newsletter. **Price:** included in membership dues. **Conventions/Meetings:** periodic workshop (exhibits).

5354 ■ North American Grouse Partnership (NAGP)
c/o C. Sealing
1670 N 1/2 Rd.
Fruita, CO 81521
Ph: (970)858-9659
Fax: (970)858-3704
E-mail: nagp@grousepartners.org
URL: http://www.grousepartners.org
Contact: James A. Mosher PhD, Exec. Dir.
Founded: 1999. **Membership Dues:** regular, $35 (annual) ● contributing, $50 (annual) ● sustaining, $100 (annual) ● steward, $250 (annual) ● patron, $500 (annual) ● benefactor, $1,000 (annual). **Multinational. Description:** Promotes the conservation of grouse and the habitats necessary for their survival and reproduction. Seeks to implement solutions to the problems that cause the decline in grouse population. Encourages public policies and management decisions that will enhance important habitats and grouse populations. **Publications:** *Grouse Partnership News*, annual. Magazine.

5355 ■ North American Loon Fund (NALF)
Address Unknown since 2007
Founded: 1979. **Members:** 1,800. **Membership Dues:** $30 (annual). **Staff:** 1. **Budget:** $125,000. **State Groups:** 18. **Description:** Individuals, institutions, and other organizations interested in preservation of the loon. Seeks to protect loons and their habitat by constructing artificial nesting sites, educating the public. Provides educational programs in areas where loons and humans coexist. Conducts research on: loon biology and behavior; the impact of human activity and water pollution on loon reproduction; loon population levels in various regions. **Awards:** North American Loon Fund Grants. **Frequency:** annual. **Type:** grant. **Recipient:** for research and management efforts. **Computer Services:** database. **Publications:** *The Loon Call*, 3/year. Newsletter. Contains reports on research and management projects, photographs, and publication notices. **Price:** included in membership dues. **Advertising:** accepted ● *Loon Resource Directory*. Provides resources for teaching about loons. **Price:** $2.00. **Advertising:** not accepted ● *Voices of the Loon* ● Also publishes conference papers, a bibliography on Loons, and produces records, cassettes, and compact disks. **Conventions/Meetings:** semiannual conference (exhibits); **Avg. Attendance:** 50.

5356 ■ North American Plant Preservation Council (NAPPC)
c/o Barry Glick, Exec. Dir.
HC 67 Box 539B
Renick, WV 24966
Ph: (304)497-2208
Fax: (304)497-2698
E-mail: barry@sunfarm.com
Contact: Barry Glick, Exec. Dir.
Founded: 1990. **Members:** 7,866. **Membership Dues:** regular, $25 (annual). **Staff:** 23. **Budget:** $103,000. **State Groups:** 50. **Local Groups:** 404. **Description:** Individuals interested in protecting and preserving endangered North American plant species. Promotes formation of local and regional collections of endangered indigenous plants; facilitates botanical and horticultural study. Gathers and disseminates information on the care of endangered plants. Conducts research, educational, and charitable programs; makes available children's services; maintains speakers' bureau; compiles statistics. **Libraries: Type:** reference; open to the public. **Holdings:** 1,850; archival material, articles, monographs. **Subjects:** endangered plants, botany, horticulture. **Computer Services:** database ● mailing lists ● on-

line services. **Publications:** *Directory of Collections*, annual. **Conventions/Meetings:** annual board meeting.

5357 ■ North American Wildlife Enforcement Officers Association (NAWEOA)
c/o Steve Kleiner, Sec.-Treas.
PO Box 22
Hollidaysburg, PA 16648
Ph: (801)942-9432
Fax: (206)201-6953
E-mail: naweoa@ureach.com
URL: http://www.naweoa.org
Contact: Marion Hoffman, Pres.
Founded: 1980. **Members:** 8,000. **Membership Dues:** individual regular/individual student, $10 (annual) ● individual associate, $20 (annual) ● affiliated organization, $200 (annual) ● student affiliated organization, $100 (annual) ● life (regular), $150 ● life (associate), $200. **Description:** Represents the interests of wildlife law enforcement professionals committed to wildlife protection and public service. Supports the activities of many major conservation organizations through membership and active participation. **Awards:** Certificate of Award. **Frequency:** annual. **Type:** recognition. **Recipient:** for outstanding achievement or service in the field of wildlife law enforcement ● Certificate of Valor. **Frequency:** annual. **Type:** recognition. **Recipient:** to the officer who performs a heroic act in an attempt to protect himself or a member from a dangerous situation ● Lifesaving Award. **Frequency:** annual. **Type:** recognition. **Recipient:** to an officer whose actions save the life of another person ● Officer Of the Year. **Frequency:** annual. **Type:** recognition. **Recipient:** to officer who is competent and promotes wildlife law enforcement ● Torch Award. **Frequency:** annual. **Type:** recognition. **Recipient:** to an officer from each region. **Telecommunication Services:** electronic mail, president@naweoa.org. **Publications:** Newsletter, biennial.

5358 ■ North American Wildlife Park Foundation (NAWPF)
Wolf Park
4012 E 800 N
Battle Ground, IN 47920
Ph: (765)567-2265
Fax: (765)567-4299
E-mail: wolfpark@wolfpark.org
URL: http://www.wolfpark.org
Founded: 1972. **Members:** 1,500. **Membership Dues:** individual, $25 (annual) ● sponsor, $145 (annual) ● family, $40 (annual) ● group, $50 (annual). **Staff:** 8. **Budget:** $350,000. **Description:** Conservationists and others interested in wolves and wildlife. Operates Wolf Park in Battle Ground, IN; conducts ongoing research into animal behavior; provides research opportunities to scientists and students; sponsors quarterly wolf behavior seminar, as well as lectures, college internships, and teaching programs. Monitors legislation affecting predatory animals. **Publications:** *Wolf Park News*, periodic ● *Wolf!*, quarterly. **Price:** $22.50/year. ISSN: 1042-6426. **Circulation:** 800. **Advertising:** accepted.

5359 ■ North American Wolf Association (NAWA)
23214 Tree Bright
Spring, TX 77373
Ph: (281)821-4439
E-mail: nawa@nawa.org
URL: http://www.nawa.org
Contact: Rae Evening Earth Ott, Dir.
Founded: 1994. **Staff:** 2. **Nonmembership. Multinational. Description:** Professional biologists/zoologists, libraries, lay conservationists, state and federal agencies, and related organizations. Encourages a rational approach to the conservation of the wolf and other wild canids of North America. Seeks to provide accurate insight into the realities of wildlife and the wilderness today. Has conducted research of Potential of Wolf Transplant or Reintroduction Programs via State Wildlife Divisions; Survey of U.S. Zoos Regarding Number and Subspecies of Wolves in Captivity. Conducts survey of private ownership of wolves and wolf hybrids. **Publications:** *A List of Coyote Literature*. Bibliography ● *A List of Wolf Literature*. Bibliography ● *A Natural History of Coyotes*. Includes bibliography. ● *A Natural History of Wolves*. Includes bibliography, distribution map, and population estimates. ● *Activities for Educators* ● *Endangered Species Act*. History of the Act and an account of its application. Includes bibliography. ● *Predator Controls and Coyotes* ● *Red Wolves* ● *Wolf Recovery*, annual. Summary of wolf recovery efforts. Includes bibliography and world wide population efforts. ● *Wolfdogs* ● *Wolves as Pets* ● *Wolves in Alaska*. Describes wolf management activities in Alaska.

5360 ■ Organization of Wildlife Planners (OWP)
c/o Andrea Crews, Treas.
PO Box 53465
Oklahoma City, OK 73152
Ph: (405)522-0769 (907)267-2366
E-mail: acrews@odwc.state.ok.us
URL: http://www.owpweb.org
Contact: Andrea Crews, Treas.
Founded: 1978. **Members:** 56. **Membership Dues:** associate individual, $25 (annual) ● associate organization, $50 (annual) ● governmental, $250 (annual). **Regional Groups:** 6. **State Groups:** 23. **Description:** Professional state and federal fish and wildlife planners, natural resource educators, professional conservationists and associated interests dedicated to improving, through education and training, the quality of wildlife management and planning. Seeks to develop the necessary tools and skills to conduct effective planned management systems. **Awards:** Paul C. Weikel Memorial Award. **Frequency:** annual. **Type:** recognition. **Recipient:** for individuals with outstanding contributions to improved agency management. **Subgroups:** Management Training; Marketing and Human Resources; Merit Awards; Technical Assistance. **Affiliated With:** Association of Fish and Wildlife Agencies. **Publications:** *A Handbook for Members and Customers*, annual. Includes organizational services, membership lists, and by-laws. **Price:** free ● *Developing Comprehensive Management Systems for Wildlife Agencies*, annual. Manual. Covers training course. **Price:** included in course registration fee ● *Management Tracks*, semiannual. Newsletter. **Price:** free. Alternate Formats: online. Also Cited As: *Tomorrow's Management* ● *Proceedings of the OWP Conference*, annual. Includes session papers. **Price:** free. **Conventions/Meetings:** annual conference (exhibits) ● annual meeting.

5361 ■ Pacific Marine Mammal Center (PMMC)
20612 Laguna Canyon Rd.
Laguna Beach, CA 92651
Ph: (949)494-3050
Fax: (949)494-2802
E-mail: info@pacificmmc.org
URL: http://www.pacificmmc.org
Contact: Michele Hunter, Dir. of Operations
Founded: 1971. **Members:** 5,000. **Membership Dues:** elephant seal, $25 (annual) ● harbor seal, $50 (annual) ● sea lion, $100 (annual) ● Pacific pinniped, $300 (annual). **Staff:** 6. **Budget:** $385,000. **Description:** Seeks to rescue, medically treat and rehabilitate seals, sea lions, dolphins and whales stranded in Orange County due to injury or illness. Releases healthy animals back to their natural habitat. Works to increase public awareness of the marine environment through education and research. **Libraries: Type:** reference. **Holdings:** 100; books. **Subjects:** marine mammals, marine environment and conservation. **Formerly:** Friends of the Sea Lion Marine Mammal Center. **Publications:** Newsletter, quarterly. **Price:** included in membership dues. **Circulation:** 800. Alternate Formats: online ● Brochures. Alternate Formats: online.

5362 ■ Pacific Seabird Group (PSG)
c/o Ron LeValley, Treas.
920 Samoa Blvd., Ste.210
Arcata, CA 95521
Ph: (707)826-0300 (907)786-3584
Fax: (707)826-0540
E-mail: info@pacificseabirdgroup.org
URL: http://www.pacificseabirdgroup.org
Contact: Ron LeValley, Treas.
Founded: 1972. **Members:** 450. **Membership Dues:** individual, family, $30 (annual) ● student, $24 (annual) ● life, $900. **Description:** Persons interested in the study and conservation of Pacific seabirds which includes over 275 species of birds all related by their dependence on the ocean environment. Aims to increase the flow of information among seabird researchers, and to inform members and the public of conservation issues relating to seabirds and the marine environment. **Committees:** Conservation; Japan Seabird Conservation; Marbled Murrelet Technical; Publications; Restoration; Seabird/Fisheries Interaction; Seabird Monitoring; Xantus's Murrelet Technical. **Affiliated With:** American Bird Conservancy. **Publications:** *Marine Ornithology*. Journal. Alternate Formats: online ● *Pacific Seabird*, semiannual. Bulletin. **Price:** available to members only. **Circulation:** 450. Alternate Formats: online; CD-ROM ● Membership Directory, periodic ● Papers. Alternate Formats: online. **Conventions/Meetings:** annual conference ● annual meeting.

5363 ■ Pacific Whale Foundation (PWF)
300 Maalaea Rd., Ste.211
Wailuku, HI 96793
Ph: (808)249-8811
Free: (800)942-5311
Fax: (808)243-9021
E-mail: info@pacificwhale.org
URL: http://www.pacificwhale.org
Contact: Gregory D. Kaufman, Pres./Founder
Founded: 1980. **Membership Dues:** senior, student, $35 (annual) ● individual, $40 (annual) ● family, international, $55 (annual) ● institution, $100 (annual) ● supporting, $250 (annual) ● contributing, $500 (annual) ● patron, $1,000 (annual). **Budget:** $270,000. **Description:** Scientists, conservationists, and volunteers united to prevent biological extinction of marine mammals. Aims to scientifically identify adverse factors affecting the recovery of endangered marine mammals and work to eradicate those factors. Provides research, conservation, and educational programs involving whales, dolphins, porpoises, and other marine mammals. Believes that aside from philosophical, ethical, and emotional issues, whales, dolphins, and porpoises are biologically essential to the earth's ecosystem. Establishes primary and long-term contact with marine mammals in their natural environment allowing scientists to observe and analyze animal behavior and thus create and modify conservation programs to meet their needs. Conducts research programs throughout the Pacific, with recent whale studies in Hawaii, American and Western Samoa, Tonga, Fiji, Australia, and Alaska. Sponsors lectures for schools, community groups, and universities. Solicits funds through the Adopt-A-Whale Program, merchandise sales, whalewatching cruises, expeditions, and internships. Maintains speakers' bureau. Compiles statistics. Is currently studying the effects of increased human activity in the humpback whale's Hawaiian breeding grounds as a possible contributor to the whale's reduced biological fitness. **Libraries: Type:** reference. **Holdings:** books. **Subjects:** marine mammals and their habitat. **Programs:** Adopt-a-Dolphin; Adopt-a-Whale; Marine Education; Marine Mammal Project; Ocean Outreach; Ocean Science Discovery Center. **Publications:** *Fin and Fluke Report*, annual. Journal ● *Maui Outdoor Adventure*, semiannual. Newsletter ● *Soundings*, semiannual. Newsletter ● *Whalewatching Guide* ● Books ● Monographs ● Videos.

5364 ■ Pelican Man's Bird Sanctuary (PMBS)
1708 Ken Thompson Pkwy.
Sarasota, FL 34236-1000
Ph: (941)388-4444
Fax: (941)388-3258
E-mail: mail@pelicanman.org
Contact: Roger Hammond, Contact
Founded: 1985. **Members:** 12,000. **Membership Dues:** individual, $35 (annual) ● family, $50 (annual)

● supporter, $100 (annual) ● sustaining, $150 (annual) ● patron, $250 (annual) ● sponsor, $500 (annual) ● benefactor, $1,000 (annual). **Staff:** 25. **Budget:** $1,000,000. **Description:** Wildlife rescue and rehabilitation center. Rescues birds, deer, raccoons, opossums, bats, fox, bobcat, turtles, iguanas, and other birds, including pelicans, owls, woodpeckers, egrets, blue herons, redbirds, bluebirds, doves and more. Seeks to rescue wildlife animals, rehabilitate them back to health and wellness and release them into their natural habitats. **Awards:** Volunteer Service Award. **Frequency:** periodic. **Type:** recognition. **Recipient:** for outstanding service. **Computer Services:** Mailing lists, of members. **Committees:** Education; Environmental Boat Tours; Rescue and Rehabilitation; Winter Feeding Program. **Formerly:** (1988) Protect Our Pelicans Society. **Publications:** *The Peligram*, semiannual. Newsletter. **Price:** included in membership dues; free to sanctuary supporters. **Circulation:** 25,000 ● Brochures. **Conventions/Meetings:** annual meeting.

5365 ■ The Peregrine Fund (TPF)
5668 W Flying Hawk Ln.
Boise, ID 83709
Ph: (208)362-3716 (208)362-8687
Fax: (208)362-2376
E-mail: tpf@peregrinefund.org
URL: http://www.peregrinefund.org
Contact: J. Peter Jenny, Pres./CEO
Founded: 1970. **Members:** 5,000. **Membership Dues:** individual, $25 (annual) ● contributor, $50 (annual) ● sponsor, $100 (annual) ● conservator, $250 (annual) ● benefactor, $500 (annual) ● Chairman's Circle, $1,000 (annual) ● Founding Chairman's Circle, $2,500 (annual) ● Premiere Chairman's Circle, $5,000 (annual). **Staff:** 49. **Budget:** $5,500,000. **Multinational. Description:** Serves as a science-based organization focusing on birds for the conservation of nature. Seeks to re-establish natural populations of endangered and threatened birds, conserve habitat and biological diversity, and develop infrastructures for in-country conservation. Informs the public of the value and the need for conservation. Operates World Center for Birds of Prey to serve as a research and education facility and to maintain and propagate rare birds of prey. **Libraries: Type:** reference. **Holdings:** 7,200; books, monographs, periodicals. **Subjects:** birds, conservation biology. **Publications:** *Falcon Propagation: A Manual on Captive Breeding* ● *Guide to Management of Peregrine Falcons at the Eyrie*. Book ● *Hacking: A Method for Releasing Peregrine Falcons and Other Birds of Prey*. Manual ● *Peregrine Falcon Populations: Their Management and Recovery*. Book ● *Return of the Peregrine, A North American Saga of Tenacity and Teamwork*. Book ● Annual Report, annual. **Price:** included in membership dues. **Circulation:** 9,000 ● Books ● Newsletter, semiannual. **Conventions/Meetings:** semiannual board meeting.

5366 ■ Pheasants Forever (PF)
1783 Buerkle Cir.
St. Paul, MN 55110
Ph: (651)773-2000
Free: (877)773-2070
Fax: (651)773-5500
E-mail: contact@pheasantsforever.org
URL: http://www.pheasantsforever.org
Contact: Howard K. Vincent, Pres./CEO
Founded: 1982. **Members:** 100,000. **Membership Dues:** associate, $30 (annual) ● rooster booster, $50 (annual) ● magnum, $100 (annual) ● sponsor, $250 (annual) ● life, $1,000 ● patron, $10,000. **Staff:** 50. **Budget:** $20,000,000. **State Groups:** 28. **Local Groups:** 600. **Description:** Dedicated to the protection and enhancement of pheasants and other upland wildlife through habitat improvement, public awareness and education, and land management policy changes. **Awards: Type:** scholarship. **Publications:** *Journal of Upland Conservation* ● *Pheasants Forever Journal*, 5/year. **Price:** included in membership dues. **Circulation:** 90,000. **Advertising:** accepted ● *Ringnecks*, periodic. Newsletter. **Price:** $15.00. **Circulation:** 10,000 ● *Ringnecks*, quarterly. Magazine ● *Ringnecks*. Manual. Contains outlines for successful youth mentoring programs. **Price:** $20.00 ● *Strides*, quarterly. Newsletter. Contains information about Aldo Leopold, his teaching techniques and the latest program developments.

5367 ■ Polar Bears International (PBI)
PO Box 66142
Baton Rouge, LA 70896
Ph: (225)923-3114
Fax: (225)923-3114
E-mail: website@polarbearsalive.org
URL: http://www.polarbearsinternational.org
Contact: Robert Buchanan, Pres.
Founded: 1992. **Membership Dues:** friend, $25-$99 (annual) ● mother and club, $100-$249 (annual) ● arctic circle, $250-$499 (annual) ● Lord of the Arctic, $500-$999 (annual) ● ursus maritimus, $2,500 (annual) ● Northern Light, $1,000-$2,499 (annual). **Multinational. Description:** Conserves polar bears through research and education. Promotes teamwork and encourages constructive dialogue on polar bear conservation. Serves as the central educational resource on polar bears worldwide. **Libraries: Type:** reference. **Computer Services:** Bibliographic search, scientific papers to popular articles and children's books ● information services, bear resources. **Committees:** Captive Bear Advisory; Wild Bear Advisory. **Councils:** Advisory. **Publications:** Newsletter.

5368 ■ Predator Conservation Alliance (PCA)
PO Box 6733
Bozeman, MT 59771
Ph: (406)587-3389
Fax: (406)587-3178
E-mail: pca@predatorconservation.org
URL: http://www.predatorconservation.org
Contact: Janelle Holden, Exec. Dir.
Founded: 1991. **Members:** 1,600. **Membership Dues:** individual, $35 (annual) ● supporting, $50 (annual) ● sustaining, $100 (annual) ● patron, $250 (annual). **Staff:** 11. **Budget:** $600,000. **Description:** Wildlife supporters dedicated to protecting imperiled and other predatory species and their habitats across North America. Believes that wild creatures have an inherent right to exist and that they are necessary to maintain the natural balance of native fauna and ecosystems as a whole. Challenges and calls for reform of USDA Wildlife Services (formerly known as Animal Damage Control). Works for the recovery and conservation of prairie grassland predators and prey and forest furbearers. Protects black bears and mountain lions from excessive exploitation. Conducts public outreach through public speaking and slide show presentations. **Computer Services:** Mailing lists, of members. **Formerly:** (1999) Predator Project. **Publications:** *Home Range*, quarterly. Newsletter. **Circulation:** 3,000. Alternate Formats: online ● *The Inside Scoop*, quarterly. Report ● *Wild Guardian*, quarterly. Journal. Alternate Formats: online ● Annual Report, annual. Alternate Formats: online. **Conventions/Meetings:** annual Predators, People and Places - meeting and lecture, features films, panel discussions, and wildlife viewing - every 1st weekend.

5369 ■ Purple Martin Conservation Association (PMCA)
301 Peninsula Dr., Ste.6
Erie, PA 16505
Ph: (814)833-7656
Fax: (814)833-2451
E-mail: generalinfo@purplemartin.org
URL: http://www.purplemartin.org
Contact: John Tautin, Exec. Dir.
Founded: 1987. **Members:** 6,500. **Membership Dues:** student/senior/educator, $20 (annual) ● basic/Canadian, $25 (annual) ● family, $30 (annual) ● donor, $50 (annual) ● benefactor, $100 (annual). **Staff:** 10. **Description:** Individuals interested in the Purple Martin (a small bird, whose range includes North, South, and Central America, that is dependent upon humans for its survival due to its almost exclusive use of human-supplied nesting sites). Gathers and disseminates information on techniques of attracting martins and managing nesting sites; conducts research on martin biology and breeding and migratory habits; cooperates with other organizations and government agencies to promote martin conservation. Operates Purple Martin Colony Registry Program, which seeks to locate and register every martin breeding site in North America. Conducts annual martin nesting survey; makes available martin husbandry supplies including bird houses, audiotaped martin calls for use in attracting birds, and house sparrow and starling traps. Maintains speakers' bureau; compiles statistics. **Convention/Meeting:** none. **Awards:** PMCA's Annual Research and Conservation Grant. **Frequency:** annual. **Type:** grant. **Recipient:** for individuals engage in Purple Martin research. **Computer Services:** Bibliographic search, materials on the Purple Martin ● database. **Telecommunication Services:** electronic mail, martininfo@purplemartin.org. **Publications:** *Purple Martin Update*, quarterly. Magazine. Includes reports from Brazil, the wintering ground of the Purple Martin. **Price:** included in membership dues. **Circulation:** 6,500 ● Brochure.

5370 ■ Quail Unlimited (QU)
PO Box 610
Edgefield, SC 29824
Ph: (803)637-5731
Fax: (803)637-0037
E-mail: national@qu.org
URL: http://www.qu.org
Contact: Joseph R. Evans, Pres.
Founded: 1981. **Members:** 55,000. **Membership Dues:** regular, $30 (annual) ● mentor, $50 (annual) ● sponsor, $250 (annual) ● life, $1,500 ● sentry, $100 (annual). **Staff:** 31. **Budget:** $44,000,000. **Regional Groups:** 10. **State Groups:** 21. **Local Groups:** 400. **Description:** Works for quail and upland bird conservation through its habitat management program and research. Conducts regional seminars; sponsors university research and scholarship programs. Operates Project Yield (Youth Involvement in Educational Land Development). **Awards: Type:** recognition. **Computer Services:** database ● mailing lists ● online services, publishing information. **Telecommunication Services:** electronic mail, getinvolved@qu.org ● electronic mail, revans@qu.org. **Committees:** Chapter Development; Fund Raising; Research; Youth Involvement. **Publications:** *JR's Covey*, quarterly. Magazine. **Price:** included in membership dues; $30.00 for nonmembers. **Circulation:** 5,000. **Advertising:** accepted. Also Cited As: *Junior Covey*. **Conventions/Meetings:** annual meeting (exhibits) ● annual support group meeting, with representatives and members to present awards, participate in workshops, view new merchandise, and learn about new research, studies and techniques (exhibits).

5371 ■ Raptor Education Foundation (REF)
PO Box 200400
Denver, CO 80220
Ph: (303)680-8500
Fax: (303)680-8502
E-mail: raptor2@usaref.org
URL: http://www.usaref.org
Contact: Mr. Peter Reshetniak, Sec.
Founded: 1980. **Members:** 4,000. **Membership Dues:** active, $25 (annual) ● student, $15 (annual) ● nest (family), $50 (annual) ● buteo, $30-$99 (annual) ● accipiter, $100-$2,499 (annual) ● falcon, $2,500-$4,999 (quinquennial) ● eagle (life), $5,000 ● special, $65 (semiannual). **Staff:** 3. **Languages:** English, French, Russian. **Multinational. Description:** Promotes environmental literacy by using its live nonreleasable collection of eagles, hawks, falcons, and owls to advance environmental concepts and issues. Provides lectures with live raptors for classrooms, youth and senior groups, civic clubs, professional organizations, and public/private events. Publishes books focused on raptors and science for children and adults. Provides consulting services for entities requiring a variety of creative and scientific services dealing with natural history concerns. Its membership program includes an extensive volunteer training course, and has an international membership base. Has created and manages the only environmental license plate program in Colorado, which benefits REF members exclusively. The Foundation is in-

volved in supporting West Nile Virus research using its captive raptor collection as a database for several research organizations. Has also developed a unique technological response to deal with over populations of pests of avian and mammalian species. **Libraries: Type:** not open to the public; reference. **Holdings:** 5,000; archival material, articles, artwork, books, photographs, reports. **Subjects:** raptors, ecology, environment, biology, zoology. **Awards:** Volunteer Awards. **Frequency:** annual. **Type:** recognition ● Volunteer of the Year. **Frequency:** annual. **Type:** recognition. **Recipient:** for individual(s) who has contributed in a wide variety of areas supporting the foundation's activities and mission. **Additional Websites:** http://www.raptoreducationfoundation.org. **Programs:** Eagle Summit; Face to Face; Falcon Summit; General Workshops; Owl Summit; Programs and Workshops; Raptor Summit; Raptors and the Environment; Teacher's Workshops. **Publications:** *Fidget's Freedom*. Book. Introduces the scientific concept of "hacking" which was used to re-establish peregrine falcon populations worldwide. **Price:** $17.95 for nonmembers; $12.95 for members ● *Raptors*. Book. Provides an easy and accurate introduction to the world of North American raptors. **Price:** $7.95 for nonmembers; included in membership dues. **Conventions/Meetings:** annual Awards Banquet.

5372 ■ Raptor Research Foundation (RRF)

c/o Leonard Young, Pres.
1640 Oriole Ln. NW
Olympia, WA 98502-4342
Ph: (360)943-7394 (360)561-8125
Fax: (360)943-7394
E-mail: leonardyoung1@comcast.net
URL: http://raptorresearchfoundation.org
Contact: Leonard Young, Pres.

Founded: 1966. **Members:** 1,200. **Membership Dues:** regular, $43 (annual) ● sustaining, $100 (annual) ● contributing, $50 (annual) ● life, $1,000 ● student, $30 (annual) ● contributing, $50 (annual). **Budget:** $60,000. **Description:** Individuals interested in birds of prey. Provides a forum for exchanging information concerning research in the biology and management of birds of prey. Promotes a better understanding and appreciation of the value of these birds. Conducts research and disseminates information. **Awards:** Dean Amadon Grant. **Frequency:** annual. **Type:** grant. **Recipient:** for persons working in the area of distribution and systematic (taxonomy) of raptors ● Fran and Frederick Hamerstrom Award. **Frequency:** annual. **Type:** recognition. **Recipient:** for individuals with significant contributions to the understanding of raptor technology and natural history ● James R. Koplin Travel Award. **Frequency:** annual. **Type:** recognition. **Recipient:** to a student who is the senior author and presenter of a paper or poster to be presented at the RRF meeting ● Leslie Brown Memorial Grant. **Frequency:** annual. **Type:** grant. **Recipient:** for the research on African birds of prey ● Morley Nelson Fellowship. **Frequency:** annual. **Type:** recognition. **Recipient:** for applicants pursuing projects on raptors ● Stephen R. Tully Memorial Grant. **Frequency:** annual. **Type:** grant. **Recipient:** for students and amateurs ● Tom Cade Award. **Frequency:** annual. **Type:** recognition. **Recipient:** for individuals who have made significant advances in the area of captive propagation and reintroduction of raptors ● William C. Andersen Memorial Award. **Frequency:** annual. **Type:** recognition. **Recipient:** to the best oral and poster presentation. **Committees:** Awards; Conferences; Conservation; Education; Eurasian; Nominations; Resolutions; Scientific Program. **Publications:** *Journal of Raptor Research*, quarterly. **Price:** $20.00/year; $7.50 back issues. ISSN: 0892-1016 ● *The Kettle*, biennial. Membership Directory. **Price:** available to members only. **Circulation:** 1,200 ● *The Wingspan*, semiannual. Newsletter. **Price:** free for members; $10.00 for nonmembers ● Reports, periodic. **Conventions/Meetings:** annual conference and meeting (exhibits).

5373 ■ RARE

1840 Wilson Blvd., Ste.204
Arlington, VA 22201
Ph: (703)522-5070
Fax: (703)522-5027
E-mail: rare@rareconservation.org
URL: http://www.rareconservation.org
Contact: Brett Jenks, Pres./CEO

Founded: 1973. **Members:** 2,400. **Membership Dues:** individual (donation), $30-$1,000 (annual). **Staff:** 30. **Budget:** $4,200,000. **Description:** Seeks the protection of wild lands of globally significant biological diversity by enabling local people to benefit from their preservation. **Computer Services:** Mailing lists. **Programs:** Rare Enterprises; Rare Pride; Rare Radio. **Also Known As:** RARE Center. **Formerly:** (1987) Rare Animal Relief Effort; (1992) Rare Center for Tropical Bird Conservation; (2004) RARE Center for Tropical Conservation. **Publications:** *Field Notes*, semiannual. Newsletter ● Annual Report, annual. Alternate Formats: online. **Conventions/Meetings:** board meeting - 3/year.

5374 ■ Rocky Mountain Elk Foundation (RMEF)

5705 Grant Creek Rd.
Missoula, MT 59808
Ph: (406)523-4500
Free: (800)225-5355
Fax: (406)523-4550
E-mail: info@rmef.org
URL: http://www.rmef.org
Contact: Andrew Hoxsey, Chm.

Founded: 1984. **Members:** 140,000. **Membership Dues:** supporting in U.S., $35 (annual) ● sponsor, $300 (annual) ● life, $1,500 ● supporting outside U.S., $45 (annual) ● family, $75 (annual) ● sustaining, $100 (annual). **Staff:** 150. **Local Groups:** 500. **Description:** Seeks to ensure the future of elk and other wildlife and their habitat. **Libraries: Type:** reference. **Holdings:** archival material, audio recordings, books, clippings, periodicals, video recordings. **Subjects:** current historical conservation activities, hunting issues, fictional and non-fictional accounts, biological studies of elk. **Awards:** Wallace Fennell Pate Wildlife Conservation Award. **Frequency:** annual. **Type:** recognition. **Recipient:** for an individual or group who has made outstanding contributions in the field of wildlife conservation ● Wildlife Leadership Award. **Frequency:** annual. **Type:** recognition. **Recipient:** for junior and senior college undergraduates in recognized wildlife programs. **Publications:** *BUGLE Magazine*, bimonthly. **Price:** included in membership dues. ISSN: 0889-6445. **Circulation:** 140,000. **Advertising:** accepted. Alternate Formats: online ● *WAPITI Newsletter*, bimonthly. **Price:** available to volunteers only. ISSN: 1041-3359. Alternate Formats: online. **Conventions/Meetings:** annual Elk Camp and Exposition - convention (exhibits).

5375 ■ Roo Rat Society (RRS)

Address Unknown since 2007

Founded: 1963. **Members:** 330. **State Groups:** 4. **Description:** Persons dedicated to the study and conservation of wildlife and natural resources on local, national, and international levels. Supports conservation projects by encouraging members to write to political leaders.

5376 ■ Ruffed Grouse Society (RGS)

451 McCormick Rd.
Coraopolis, PA 15108
Ph: (412)262-4044
Free: (888)564-6747
Fax: (412)262-9207
E-mail: rgs@ruffedgrousesociety.org
URL: http://www.ruffedgrousesociety.org
Contact: Michael D. Zagata, Exec. Dir./CEO

Founded: 1961. **Members:** 23,000. **Membership Dues:** junior, $10 (annual) ● regular, $25 (annual) ● conservation, $50 (annual) ● sustaining, $100 (annual) ● centurion, $1,000 (annual) ● sponsor-habitat, $250 (annual) ● sponsor-conservation, $500 (annual) ● sponsor-sustaining, $1,000 (annual) ● sponsor-strutter, $5,000 (annual) ● sponsor-life, $10,000. **Staff:** 23. **Budget:** $3,000,000. **Local Groups:** 140. **Description:** Conservationists dedicated to improving the environment for ruffed grouse, woodcock, and other forest wildlife. Encourages private, industrial, state, county, and federal landowners to manage their woodlands to benefit forest wildlife. Assists landholders by: publishing and distributing guides for habitat improvement; sponsoring training sessions and on- and off-site consultations; directing and sponsoring habitat improvement demonstration areas. Provides funds to governmental agencies to assist in management of forest lands. Supports projects designed to obtain additional information on improving woodland habitat for wildlife. Conducts specialized education for adults. **Awards:** Gordon W. Gullion Award for Excellence in Forest Wildlife Research. **Type:** recognition. **Committees:** Projects. **Programs:** Coverts; Management Area; Research and General Education. **Formerly:** (1971) Ruffed Grouse Society of America; (1977) Ruffed Grouse Society of North America. **Publications:** *A Guide to Capturing and Banding American Woodcock Using Pointing Dogs*. Booklet. **Price:** $3.00 ● *Managing Northern Forests for Wildlife*. Booklet. **Price:** free to forest landowners; $4.00 for nonmembers ● *Managing Woodlots for Fuel and Wildlife*. Booklet. **Price:** free to forest landowners; $2.00 for nonmembers ● *Managing Your Oak Forests for Ruffed Grouse*. Booklet. **Price:** free to forest landowners; $1.00 for nonmembers ● *RGS: The Ruffed Grouse Society Magazine*, quarterly. **Price:** included in membership dues. **Advertising:** accepted ● *Surface Mine Reclamation: A Wildlife Habitat Opportunity*. Booklet. **Price:** free to forest landowners; $2.00 for nonmembers.

5377 ■ Safari Club International (SCI)

4800 W Gates Pass Rd.
Tucson, AZ 85745-9490
Ph: (520)620-1220
Free: (888)HUNT-SCI
Fax: (520)622-1205
E-mail: showsci@safariclub.org
URL: http://www.scifirstforhunters.org
Contact: Dennis Anderson, Pres.

Founded: 1971. **Members:** 20,000. **Membership Dues:** regular life (in U.S., Canada and Mexico), $1,000 ● regular life (other countries), $1,500 ● senior life (in U.S., Canada and Mexico), $750 ● senior life (other countries), $1,250 ● regular (in U.S., Canada and Mexico), $55 (annual) ● regular (other countries), $80 (annual) ● regular (in U.S., Canada and Mexico), $150 (triennial) ● regular (other countries), $225 (triennial) ● youth (in U.S., Canada and Mexico), $15 (annual) ● youth (other countries), $30 (annual). **Regional Groups:** 90. **Description:** Represents sportsmen united to encourage conservation of wildlife. Promotes hunting as a wildlife management tool; aims to preserve public hunting and protect hunters' rights. Fosters public education concerning conservation; sponsors research. Supports communication and good fellowship among members. Operates hall of fame. **Awards: Type:** recognition. **Publications:** *African Special* ● *Deer Special* ● *North of the 48* ● *Record Book of Trophy Animals* ● *Safari Magazine*, bimonthly ● *Safari Times*, monthly. Newsletter ● *Sheep Special*. **Conventions/Meetings:** annual convention (exhibits) ● seminar.

5378 ■ Save the Manatee Club (SMC)

500 N Maitland Ave.
Maitland, FL 32751
Ph: (407)539-0990
Free: (800)432-5646
Fax: (407)539-0871
E-mail: membership@savethemanatee.org
URL: http://www.savethemanatee.org
Contact: Patrick M. Rose, Exec. Dir.

Founded: 1981. **Members:** 39,000. **Membership Dues:** associate, $25 (annual) ● friend, $35 (annual) ● sponsor, $50 (annual) ● guardian, $100 (annual) ● steward, $500 (annual) ● school class, group adoption, $20 (annual). **Staff:** 17. **Budget:** $1,400,000. **Languages:** English, Spanish. **Description:** Naturalists, students, businessmen, and other individuals. Works to help save and protect the West Indian manatee, an endangered marine mammal, and its habitat. Seeks to heighten public awareness and education regarding sanctuary areas, boating speed signs, and laws pertaining to protection of the manatees. Conducts the Adopt-a-Manatee program. Sponsors public service announcements that are distributed to media throughout the country, educational outreach programs for school classes and clubs, and manatee awareness workshops. Raises funds for research programs on manatee mortality reduction, population trends, and life history, and for the purchase of manatee warning signs to be posted in inland waterways. Conducts lobbying activities. Maintains speakers' bureau; conducts educational programs. **Convention/Meeting:** none. **Libraries: Type:** reference. **Holdings:** audiovisuals, video recordings. **Subjects:** West Indian manatees. **Telecommunication Services:** electronic mail, education@savethemanatee.org. **Programs:** Adopt A Manatee; Communications; Conservation; Manatee Gift Items; Research. **Publications:** *Adopt-A-Manatee Brochure*, quarterly ● *Feeding Manatees-Don't Do It* ● *Guidelines for Protecting Manatees* ● *Manatee Messages*. Video. **Price:** free ● *The Manatee Zone*, quarterly. Newsletter. **Price:** included in membership dues ● *Manatees: An Educator's Guide* ● *Save the Manatee Club Brochure* ● *West Indian Manatee Booklet* ● Handbook. **Price:** included in membership dues.

5379 ■ Save the Whales

1192 Waring St.
Seaside, CA 93955
Ph: (831)899-9957
Fax: (831)394-5555
E-mail: maris@savethewhales.org
URL: http://www.savethewhales.org
Contact: Maris Sidenstecker, Exec. Dir.

Founded: 1977. **Members:** 10,000. **Membership Dues:** child, $15 (annual) ● student, $20 (annual) ● regular, $25 (annual) ● t-shirt, $40 (annual) ● adopt a whale, $50 (annual). **Staff:** 2. **Budget:** $80,000. **State Groups:** 1. **Description:** Aims to educate children and adults about marine mammals, their environment and their preservation. Educates over 250,000 students about marine mammals and the fragile ocean environment through STW hands-on educational outreach program, Whales On Wheels (WOW). Disseminates educational information via mail, email, website, Adopt A Whale kits, newsletters, events, books, media and radio appearances. Prevents the Navy from detonating 269 explosives over a period of 5 years in a marine sanctuary inhabited by endangered whales. Provides and supports grants, donations, memberships, and bequests. **Libraries: Type:** reference. **Holdings:** articles, audio recordings, books, photographs, video recordings. **Programs:** Adopt A Whale; Whales on Wheels. **Publications:** *Adopt A Whale kit*. Newsletter. Includes orca photo and personalized adopt a whale certificate. **Price:** $15.00. Alternate Formats: online ● Newsletter, quarterly. **Price:** $25.00 ● Also distributes brochures, flyers, whale cd's, t-shirts and educational products through website.

5380 ■ Sea Shepherd Conservation Society (SSCS)

PO Box 2616
Friday Harbor, WA 98250
Ph: (360)370-5650
Fax: (360)370-5651
E-mail: info@seashepherd.org
URL: http://www.seashepherd.org
Contact: Capt. Paul Watson, Founding Dir.

Founded: 1977. **Members:** 35,000. **Membership Dues:** regular, in U.S. and Canada, $25 (annual) ● international, $35 (annual). **Staff:** 5. **Budget:** $500,000. **Multinational. Description:** International activist conservation society concerned with the protection and conservation of marine mammals. Operates research ships with volunteer crew. Opposes exploitation of all marine life and fights the problem through education, confrontation, and enforcement, although primary involvement is in enforcement of international laws, treaties, and regulations against driftnetting, illegal whaling, and sealing activities. Conducts research on issues of conservation, national and international law, and environmental pollution. **Convention/Meeting:** none. **Publications:** *Sea Shepherd Log*, quarterly. Newsletter. Provides information on the society's actions, involvement opportunities, marine issues. **Price:** free for members. ISSN: 1075-4660. **Circulation:** 35,000.

5381 ■ Society for the Conservation of Bighorn Sheep (SCBS)

PO Box 94182
Pasadena, CA 91109-4182
Ph: (310)679-2102
E-mail: info@scbs-desertbighorn.com
URL: http://mysite.verizon.net/res8q66y/bighorn/bighorn.htm
Contact: Steve Marschke, Pres.

Founded: 1964. **Members:** 250. **Membership Dues:** regular, $35 (annual) ● student, $20 (annual) ● life, $300 ● corporate, $1,000 (annual). **Staff:** 1. **Budget:** $100,000. **Regional Groups:** 2. **State Groups:** 2. **Description:** Conservation group organized to study, research, and monitor the status of bighorn sheep. Conducts wildlife census operations; coordinates activities with state and federal agencies; works to plan, develop, and maintain water resources for desert wildlife. **Affiliated With:** Foundation for North American Wild Sheep. **Publications:** *Sheep Sheet*, quarterly. Newsletter.

5382 ■ Society for the Preservation of Birds of Prey (SPBP)

12335 Santa Monica Blvd.
PMB 345
West Los Angeles, CA 90025
Ph: (310)840-2322
Contact: J. Richard Hilton, Pres.

Founded: 1966. **Staff:** 1. **Description:** Advocates the strictest possible protection for birds of prey. Seeks to educate the public about the role of raptors in the ecosystem; opposes unnecessary harvesting practices and supports captive raptor breeding for conservation. Maintains archives at The American Heritage Center library at The University of Wyoming/Laramie. **Libraries: Type:** reference. **Holdings:** 210; articles, books, papers. **Subjects:** raptors, birds of prey. **Computer Services:** Mailing lists. **Also Known As:** The Birds of Prey Society. **Publications:** *Leaflets Series*, periodic. Pamphlets. Covers selected topics. **Price:** free. **Circulation:** 700 ● *The Raptor Report*, periodic. Newsletter. Examines the coexisting relationship between humans and raptors. ISSN: 1048-8030.

5383 ■ Society of Tympanuchus Cupido Pinnatus (STCP)

Address Unknown since 2008

Founded: 1960. **Members:** 600. **Membership Dues:** $35 (annual). **Description:** Seeks to preserve the prairie chicken and other watched, threatened, and endangered species native to the state of Wisconsin. (The Society calls itself by the Latin name of the prairie chicken). **Publications:** *Boom*, quarterly. Newsletter. Review of charitable grants and articles dealing with the purpose of the society. ● *Prairie Grouse* ● *Prairie Grouse! A History of the Society of Tympanuchus Cupido Pinnatus, Ltd.*. **Conventions/Meetings:** annual meeting - always December. Milwaukee, WI.

5384 ■ Sumatran Orangutan Society USA (SOS USA)

7017 Highview Terr., Apt. No. 102
Hyattsville, MD 20782
Ph: (301)648-3855
E-mail: bali@orangutans-sos.org
URL: http://www.orangutans-sos.org
Contact: Avanti Mallapur, Coor.

Founded: 1997. **Membership Dues:** regular, $45 (annual) ● student, $25 (annual) ● life, $300. **Multinational. Description:** Seeks to conserve the endemic Sumatran orangutan (pongo abelii) and its native habitat. Promotes public awareness of, and participation in, conservation strategies for the Sumatran orangutan through campaigns, community education and global communication. Collaborates with Indonesian conservationists in the establishment and running of the Orangutan Information Center. **Telecommunication Services:** electronic mail, sumatran_orangutan_society@yahoo.com.

5385 ■ TortoiseAid International

PO Box 260
Apple Valley, CA 92307-0005
E-mail: tortoiseaid@tortoise-aid.org
URL: http://tortoise-aid.org
Contact: Annie Lancaster, Dir.

Multinational. Description: Strives to protect and preserve tortoises, turtles, terrapins, and their habitats by providing assistance in the care and management of captive species. Seeks to achieve measurable and long-term success through research and conservation programs. Educates individuals and organizations concerning issues of habitat destruction, trade, and other forms of exploitation which face chelonia and other wildlife. **Telecommunication Services:** electronic mail, tortoiseaid@yahoo.com.

5386 ■ TRAFFIC North America

1250 24th St. NW
Washington, DC 20037
Ph: (202)293-4800
Fax: (202)775-8287
E-mail: tna@wwfus.org
URL: http://www.traffic.org
Contact: Simon Habel, Dir.

Founded: 1972. **Staff:** 5. **Description:** Represents conservation, government, university, press, foreign, and private groups. Provides scientific and statistical information-gathering program, monitoring use and trade in wild plants and animals in North America and internationally. Maintains branches in the U.K. **Projects:** Protect Seashores; TRAFFIC Study. **Affiliated With:** World Wildlife Fund. **Formerly:** (1989) TRAFFIC - U.S.A. **Publications:** *A Tale of Two Cities: A Comparative Study of Traditional Chinese Medicine Markets in San Francisco and New York City*. Survey. Alternate Formats: online ● *Ancient Traditions. New Alternatives*. Brochure. Alternate Formats: online ● *Buyer Beware - Caribbean*. Brochure. Alternate Formats: online ● *TRAFFIC Report* (in English and Spanish), semiannual. Newsletter. Features international trade in wildlife and wildlife products. **Price:** free. ISSN: 0740-199X. **Circulation:** 3,500. Alternate Formats: online ● Reports. Alternate Formats: online.

5387 ■ Trout Unlimited (TU)

1300 N 17th St., Ste.500
Arlington, VA 22209
Ph: (703)522-0200 (703)284-9401
Free: (800)834-2419
Fax: (703)284-9400
E-mail: trout@tu.org
URL: http://www.tu.org
Contact: Charles Gauvin, Pres./CEO

Founded: 1959. **Members:** 130,000. **Membership Dues:** youth/student, senior, $20 (annual) ● regular, $35 (annual) ● family/contributor, $50 (annual) ● sponsor, $100 (annual) ● business, $200 (annual) ● conservator, $250 (annual) ● life, $1,000 ● family life, $1,100. **Staff:** 43. **Budget:** $10,000,000. **Regional Groups:** 10. **State Groups:** 32. **Local Groups:** 465. **National Groups:** 2. **Description:** Works to conserve, protect, and restore the cold-water habitat of trout, salmon, and steelhead by influencing the activities and programs of governmental agencies, by keeping the public informed on water management problems, and by restoring and maintaining streams and rivers through local volunteer efforts. **Libraries: Type:** not open to the public. **Holdings:** papers, reports. **Awards:** Trout Conservation Award. **Frequency:** annual. **Type:** recognition. **Programs:** Bring Back the Natives; Embrace A Stream; National Park Service Restoration; Strategies for Restoring Native Trout. **Projects:** Jefferson River; Kettle Creek; South Fork Snake River; Western Water. **Publications:** *Lines to Leaders*, monthly. Newsletter ● *Trout*, quarterly. Magazine. Contains information on trout and salmon fishing and trout unlimited activities around the country. **Price:** included in membership dues. ISSN: 0041-3364. **Circulation:** 125,000. **Advertising:** accepted. Alternate Formats: online ● Annual Report, annual. Alternate Formats: online ● Manual. Alternate Formats: online. **Conventions/Meetings:** annual convention (exhibits).

5388 ■ The Trumpeter Swan Society (TTSS)
12615 County Rd. 9, Ste.No. 100
Plymouth, MN 55441-1248
Ph: (763)694-7851
Fax: (763)557-4943
E-mail: ttss@threeriversparkdistrict.org
URL: http://www.trumpeterswansociety.org
Contact: Madeleine Linck, Admin. Asst.
Founded: 1968. **Members:** 500. **Membership Dues:** regular, $25 (annual) ● student/retired, $15 (annual) ● family, $30 (annual) ● organization, $50 (annual) ● supporting, $100 (annual) ● life, $500. **Budget:** $50,000. **Description:** Private waterfowl propagators; federal, state, and provincial waterfowl and nongame biologists; public zoos and park systems; federal, state, and county agencies; libraries; interested individuals. Promotes research in ecology and management of the trumpeter swan throughout North America; advances the science and art of trumpeter swan management, both in captivity and in the wild; assembles data and exchange information. Advocates restoration of trumpeter swans in their original range and makes funds available for research. **Funds:** North American Swan. **Programs:** Adopt A Swan. **Projects:** Trumpeter Swan Migration. **Publications:** *North American Swans*, annual. Bulletin. **Price:** included in membership dues ● *Swan and Goose Identification*. Brochure. Alternate Formats: online ● *Trumpetings*, quarterly. Newsletter. **Price:** included in membership dues. Alternate Formats: online ● Newsletter, semiannual ● Proceedings, biennial ● Papers. **Conventions/Meetings:** biennial conference.

5389 ■ Turkey Vulture Society
6622 Wise Ave.
St. Louis, MO 63139
E-mail: vulturesociety@gmail.com
URL: http://vulturesociety.homestead.com
Contact: Bill Lynch, Pres.
Founded: 1994. **Membership Dues:** regular, $25-$49 (annual) ● supporter, $50-$99 (annual) ● scientific sponsor, $100-$499 (annual) ● friend, $500-$999 (annual) ● benefactor (minimum), $1,000 (annual). **Description:** Promotes the scientific study of the life habits and needs of the Turkey Vulture. Protects the vulture and its habitat. Informs the public of the services vultures provide to humans and to the environment. **Libraries: Type:** reference. **Holdings:** books, clippings, papers, periodicals, reports, software. **Subjects:** turkey vulture, new world vultures. **Telecommunication Services:** electronic mail, turkeyvultur@ntelos.net. **Publications:** *News from the Blue Skies Above*, bimonthly. Newsletter. **Price:** included in membership dues.

5390 ■ Whale Adoption Project (WAP)
7 Nelson St.
Plymouth, MA 02360
Ph: (508)746-2522
Free: (888)699-4253
Fax: (508)746-2522
E-mail: contact@whales.org
URL: http://whales.org
Contact: Ms. Regina Asmutis-Silvia, Sr. Biologist
Membership Dues: standard whale adoption, $30 (annual) ● deluxe whale adoption, $55 (annual). **Description:** Serves as a voice for the protection of whales, dolphins and their environment. Offers whale adoptions and raise funds for programs such as: See a Spout, SAVE Whales, Project WET, SPAW, Driven by Demand, Classroom Education, Dolphin SMART, Anti Whaling. **Awards:** Profiles in Conservation. **Frequency:** annual. **Type:** recognition. **Recipient:** for efforts to conserve aquatic mammals and or their environment. **Publications:** *Whalewatch*, quarterly. Newsletter ● Also publishes brochures; produces bumper stickers, photographs, and adoption certificates.

5391 ■ Whitetails Unlimited (WTU)
PO Box 720
Sturgeon Bay, WI 54235
Ph: (920)743-6777
Free: (800)274-5471
Fax: (920)743-4658
E-mail: nh@whitetailsunlimited.com
URL: http://www.whitetailsunlimited.com
Contact: Peter J. Gerl, Exec. Dir.
Founded: 1982. **Members:** 75,000. **Membership Dues:** associate, $25 (annual) ● junior, $10 (annual) ● double buck, $50 (biennial) ● sponsor, $250 (annual) ● life, $400. **Staff:** 23. **Budget:** $6,000,000. **Local Groups:** 360. **Description:** Promotes sound deer management. Supports research on the white-tailed deer. Sponsors fundraising events and educational programs. Maintains Hall of Fame. **Libraries: Type:** reference. **Holdings:** video recordings. **Subjects:** white-tailed deer. **Awards: Type:** recognition. **Computer Services:** Mailing lists. **Programs:** DEER; Educational Booklets; HOPE for Wildlife; Hunting Tradition; Whitetail Watch. **Projects:** POLITE. **Publications:** *Deer Stand*, quarterly. Newsletter. Includes letter to volunteers. **Price:** free. **Circulation:** 1,500 ● Magazine, quarterly. **Price:** included in membership dues. **Circulation:** 65,000. **Advertising:** accepted. Alternate Formats: online. **Conventions/Meetings:** competition ● seminar and workshop, to educate the public about deer management.

5392 ■ Whooping Crane Conservation Association (WCCA)
c/o Keith Durham, Web Admin.
715 Earl Dr.
Lawrenceburg, TN 38464
E-mail: webadmin@whoopingcrane.com
Contact: Judith Buhrman, Sec.
Founded: 1961. **Members:** 700. **Membership Dues:** individual, $7 (annual) ● sustaining, $30 (annual) ● life, $150. **Description:** Naturalists, ornithologists, and aviculturists. Works to prevent the extinction of the whooping crane; ensures that a proper management program is carried out for captive propagation to serve as a backup for the wild population; supports the establishment of a second wild population to reinforce survival against disaster; promotes harmony and unity among all organizations, institutions, and agencies involved in the preservation of endangered wildlife; collects and disseminates information to advocate and encourage public appreciation and understanding of the whooping crane's educational, scientific, aesthetic, and economic values. Conducts captive management studies for perpetuation of the species; distributes information and statistics on species to the press and interested individuals. **Awards:** Honor Award. **Frequency:** annual. **Type:** recognition. **Recipient:** for contributions to North American wildlife conservation. **Formerly:** (1982) Whooping Crane Conservation Group. **Publications:** *Grus Americana*, quarterly. Newsletter. **Price:** included in membership dues. **Circulation:** 700. Alternate Formats: online ● *Today's Whooper Report*. Alternate Formats: online ● Membership Directory, annual. **Conventions/Meetings:** annual meeting.

5393 ■ Wild Canid Survival and Research Center (WCSRC)
PO Box 760
Eureka, MO 63025
Ph: (636)938-5900
Fax: (636)938-6490
E-mail: wildcanidcenter@onemain.com
URL: http://www.wolfsanctuary.org
Contact: Susan Lyndaker Lindsey PhD, Exec. Dir.
Founded: 1971. **Members:** 1,500. **Membership Dues:** individual, $30 (annual) ● family pack, $50 (annual) ● contributor, $100 (annual) ● sponsor, $250 (annual) ● benefactor, $500 (annual) ● alpha wolf, $1,000 (annual) ● adopt-a-wolf, $125 (annual). **Staff:** 10. **Description:** Works for the preservation of endangered canids and their habitat through captive breeding and educational programs. Maintains captive breeding programs for red and Mexican gray wolves; houses South American maned wolves, swift foxes, and African wild dogs. Provides tours and programs both on and off site. **Libraries: Type:** by appointment only. **Holdings:** archival material, books, films, periodicals, video recordings. **Subjects:** endangered species. **Publications:** *The Wild Canid Center Review*, quarterly. Bulletin. Provides updates on endangered wolves and conservation efforts. **Price:** free for members ● *Wolf Pack Press*, monthly. Newsletter. **Price:** free ● Annual Report, annual. Alternate Formats: online ● Also publishes special alerts. **Conventions/Meetings:** periodic conference ● annual meeting, open house - always first Sunday of October.

5394 ■ Wild Horse Organized Assistance (WHOA)
PO Box 555
Reno, NV 89504
URL: http://www.wildhorseorganizedassistance.org
Contact: Dawn Y. Lappin, Co-Founder/Chair
Founded: 1971. **Members:** 12,000. **Description:** Unites for the welfare and perpetuation of wild free-roaming horses and burros. Seeks to provide surveillance patrols to assure the well-being of these animals; assist in the development and expansion of programs to provide for their care and protection; conduct research and field studies on wild horse and burro behavior patterns on the range; provide scholarships to encourage student research studies; maintain a national research center, library, and museum; maintain visitors' information centers at wild horse and burro ranges which may be designated and created by federal or state governments, or contributed by individuals. **Conventions/Meetings:** biennial board meeting.

5395 ■ Wild Horses of America Registry (WHAR)
c/o Karen A. Sussman, Registrar
PO Box 55
Lantry, SD 57636-0055
Ph: (605)964-6866
E-mail: ispmb@lakotanetwork.com
URL: http://www.ispmb.org/registry.shtml
Contact: Karen A. Sussman, Registrar
Founded: 1975. **Members:** 1,051. **Membership Dues:** junior, $15 (annual) ● senior, $25 (annual) ● individual, $35 (annual) ● family, $45 (annual) ● contributing, $50 (annual) ● sponsor, $100 (annual) ● sustaining, $500 (annual) ● benevolent, $1,000 (annual) ● family, $50 (annual) ● corporate, $5,000 (annual). **Description:** A program of the International Society for the Protection of Mustangs and Burros; wild horse and burro registries organized to give recognition to America's wild horses removed from public lands. Aims to establish a uniform program of management, protection, and control of wild horses and burros as called for under the Wild Horse and Burro Act of 1971. Unlike other equine registries, eligibility is not based on bloodlines or conformation to specific standards. Seeks to educate the public on the traits of wild horses and their suitability for show, for trail and endurance riding, and for use as children's horses. Conducts educational programs for schools and interested groups; supports research on wild horses and burros. Plans include annual horse show and trail rides. **Affiliated With:** International Society for the Protection of Mustangs and Burros. **Conventions/Meetings:** annual board meeting.

5396 ■ WildAid
450 Pacific Ave., Ste.201
San Francisco, CA 94133
Ph: (415)834-3174
Fax: (415)834-1759
E-mail: info@wildaid.org
URL: http://www.wildaid.org
Contact: Peter Knights, Exec. Dir.
Multinational. Description: Aims to decimate the illegal wildlife trade. Disrupts wildlife trade by reducing poaching, targeting illegal traders and smugglers, and drastically lowering consumer demand for endangered species parts and products. Strives to bring wildlife conservation to the top of the international agenda. **Computer Services:** Information services, wildlife resources. **Boards:** International Advisory. **Programs:** Active Conservation Awareness; Activist Training; Cambodia Conservation; Campaigns (Shrimp and Shark); Galapagos Forever; Marine Reserves; Surviving Together Thailand. **Publications:** Newsletter. Alternate Formats: online.

5397 ■ Wildfowl Trust of North America (WTNA)
600 Discovery Ln.
PO Box 519
Grasonville, MD 21638
Ph: (410)827-6694
Fax: (410)827-6713
E-mail: info@bayrestoration.org
URL: http://www.bayrestoration.org
Contact: Judy Wink, Exec. Dir.
Founded: 1979. **Members:** 900. **Membership Dues:** individual, $35 (annual) ● family, $50 (annual) ● contributor, $150 (annual) ● Underwater Grass Steward, $500 (annual) ● Oyster Steward, $1,000 (annual) ● student, teacher, $15 (annual) ● Blue Crab Steward, $2,500 (annual) ● Partner in Restoration, $5,000 (annual). **Staff:** 6. **Budget:** $500,000. **Description:** Strives to preserve wetlands and wildfowl through education, conservation and research. Creates and maintains wildfowl and wetlands centers where the best examples of conservation, education and research resources would be available. Participates in the development of international wetland and waterfowl education projects. Operates the Chesapeake Bay Environmental Center, a 510-acre public visitation site hosting more than 10000 students and visitors annually. Conducts educational and research programs to cultivate respect for the environment and the need to preserve it. Offers internships. **Libraries: Type:** reference. **Holdings:** archival material, artwork, books, clippings, periodicals. **Subjects:** wildlife, wetlands, waterfowl, environment, education. **Publications:** Brochures ● Newsletter, quarterly. Includes calendar of events, children's page, and waterfowl and conservationist profiles. **Price:** free for members. **Circulation:** 1,000 ● Offers maps.

5398 ■ Wildlife Disease Association (WDA)
PO Box 1897
Lawrence, KS 66044-8897
Ph: (785)843-1221
Free: (800)627-0629
Fax: (785)843-1274
E-mail: sstarr@allenpress.com
URL: http://www.wildlifedisease.org
Contact: Scott Wright, Pres.
Founded: 1951. **Members:** 1,017. **Membership Dues:** regular, $95 (annual) ● student, $40 (annual) ● associate, $22 (annual). **Multinational. Description:** Professional workers in wildlife disease research, wildlife management, and public and veterinary health; others interested in the study of the factors that promote or prevent the successful propagation of wild animals as free living populations or as captives. Is concerned with diseases, nutritional requirements, physiological responses to population density, and relationship of population to environment. Maintains collection of audiovisual aids. **Computer Services:** database, membership list. **Committees:** Awards; Promotions; Public Awareness; Student Activities. **Publications:** *Journal of Wildlife Diseases*, quarterly. **Price:** $85.00. ISSN: 0090-3558. **Circulation:** 1,425 ● Papers ● Also publishes abstracts. **Conventions/Meetings:** annual meeting - always in August.

5399 ■ Wildlife Forever
2700 Freeway Blvd., No. 1000
Brooklyn Center, MN 55430
Ph: (763)253-0222
Fax: (763)560-9961
E-mail: info@wildlifeforever.org
URL: http://www.wildlifeforever.org
Contact: Douglas H. Grann, Pres./CEO
Founded: 1987. **Members:** 65,000. **Membership Dues:** supporter, $30 (annual) ● associate, $60 (annual) ● Eagle, $125 (annual) ● Golden Eagle, $250 (annual) ● Bald Eagle, $500 (annual) ● life, $1,000 ● contributor, $20 (annual). **Staff:** 14. **Budget:** $3,857,800. **Description:** Individuals united to preserve America's wildlife heritage through the conservation and management of habitats, plant life, and wildlife. Offers research and education grants. **Affiliated With:** North American Fishing Club; North American Hunting Club. **Publications:** *Cry of the Wild!*, quarterly. Newsletter. **Circulation:** 60,000.

5400 ■ Wildlife Information Center (WIC)
PO Box 198
Slatington, PA 18080-0198
Ph: (610)760-8889
Fax: (610)760-8889
E-mail: wiclgap@ptd.net
Contact: Dan R. Kunkle, Exec.Dir.
Founded: 1986. **Members:** 200. **Membership Dues:** friend of Lehigh Gap Wildlife Refuge, $20 (annual) ● family, $50 (annual) ● individual, $35 (annual) ● student, $25 ● sustaining, $100 ● contributing, $250 ● Golden Eagle, $10,000. **Budget:** $30,000. **Description:** Individuals preserving wildlife and habitat through education, research and conservation for the benefit of the earth and all its inhabitants. research programs. Produces slide shows and videotapes about wildlife, land preservation, ecotourism. Owns 750 acre wildlife refuge and community nature center, operates educational programs for children through adults. **Libraries: Type:** reference. **Holdings:** 2,300; archival material, periodicals. **Subjects:** wildlife, conservation, environment, natural history. **Awards:** Student Ecologist Awards. **Frequency:** annual. **Type:** recognition. **Recipient:** for extraordinary work on behalf of wildlife in Lehigh Valley. **Projects:** Kittatinny Raptor Corridor; Lehigh Gap Restoration. **Publications:** *American Hawkwatcher*, annual. Journal. Contains information on original Raptor research. **Price:** $12.00/issue. ISSN: 0748-8319. **Advertising:** accepted ● *Bake Oven Knob Hawk Count Protocol Guide*. Brochure. Describes in detail the techniques and methods used for Bake Oven Knob Hawk Count. ● *Kittatinny Raptor Corridor Handbook*. Bulletins. Contains short bulletins arranged in loose-leaf format. Alternate Formats: online ● *Lehigh Gap Update*, semiannual. Newsletter. Contains information on the progress of the Lehigh Gap Restoration Project. ISSN: 0891-2734. Alternate Formats: online ● *Wildlife Activist*, 3/year. Newsletter. Includes news from the Kittatinny Raptor Corridor Project, Wildlife Notes, and an extensive section called Wildlife Book Reviews. ISSN: 0894-4660. Alternate Formats: online ● *Wildlife Conservation Report*, periodic. ISSN: 0891-2734 ● Books ● Also publishes articles in wildlife magazines and newspapers; issues news releases and public service announcements. **Conventions/Meetings:** conference ● seminar ● workshop.

5401 ■ The Wildlife Society (TWS)
5410 Grosvenor Ln., Ste.200
Bethesda, MD 20814-2144
Ph: (301)897-9770
Fax: (301)530-2471
E-mail: tws@wildlife.org
URL: http://www.wildlife.org
Contact: Michael Hutchins, Exec. Dir.
Founded: 1937. **Members:** 9,200. **Membership Dues:** regular, $64 (annual) ● student, retired, $32 (annual) ● family, $103 (annual) ● international regular, $44 (annual) ● international student, retired, $22 (annual). **Staff:** 13. **Budget:** $1,850,000. **Regional Groups:** 7. **State Groups:** 54. **Local Groups:** 63. **National Groups:** 13. **Description:** Scientific and educational society of wildlife biologists, research scientists, conservation law enforcement officers, resource managers, and others interested in resource conservation and wildlife management on a sound biological basis. Takes an active role in preventing human-induced environmental degradation; works to increase awareness and appreciation of wildlife values; seeks the highest standards in all activities of the wildlife profession. Believes that wildlife, in its myriad forms, is a basic component of a high quality human culture. **Awards:** Aldo Leopold Award. **Frequency:** annual. **Type:** recognition. **Recipient:** to an outstanding wildlife professional ● **Frequency:** annual. **Type:** recognition. **Recipient:** for publications, group achievement, conservation education, and special recognition in the wildlife field. **Formerly:** (1936) Society of Wildlife Specialists. **Publications:** *Human Dimensions of Wildlife Management in North America*. Book ● *Journal of Wildlife Management*, quarterly. Covers research in all aspects of wildlife science and management. Contains book reviews. **Price:** $87.00 /year for members; $140.00 /year for nonmembers. ISSN: 0022-541X. **Circulation:** 7,000 ● *Research and Management Techniques for Wildlife and Habitats*. Book ● *Wildlife Monographs*, periodic. Covers administration, contemporary problems, economics, education, law enforcement, management, and philosophy related to wildlife. **Price:** $87.00 /year for members; $140.00 /year for nonmembers. ISSN: 0091-7648 ● *The Wildlife Professional*, quarterly. Magazine. **Advertising:** accepted. Alternate Formats: online ● *Wildlife Society Bulletin*, quarterly. Covers administration, contemporary problems, economics, education, law enforcement, management, and philosophy related to wildlife. **Price:** $83.00 /year for members; $110.00 /year for nonmembers. ISSN: 0091-7648. **Advertising:** accepted. **Conventions/Meetings:** semiannual board meeting, in conjunction with North American Wildlife and Natural Resources Conference ● annual conference (exhibits).

5402 ■ Wildlife Trust
460 W 34th St., 17th Fl.
New York, NY 10001
Ph: (212)380-4460
Fax: (212)380-4465
E-mail: homeoffice@wildlifetrust.org
URL: http://www.wildlifetrust.org
Contact: Mary C. Pearl PhD, Pres.
Founded: 1971. **Members:** 3,000. **Membership Dues:** individual, $25 (annual) ● family, $35 (annual) ● student/senior citizen, $15 (annual) ● sustaining, $50 (annual) ● sponsor, $100 (annual) ● preserver, $250 (annual) ● protector, $500 (annual) ● guardian, $1,000 (annual) ● conservator, $2,500 (annual) ● benefactor, $5,000 (annual) ● patron, $10,000 (annual). **Staff:** 35. **Budget:** $2,600,000. **Description:** Conserves threatened wild species and their habitats in partnership with local scientists and educators around the world. **Awards: Type:** grant. **Recipient:** for conservation and education projects including those involving tamarins in South America, thick-billed parrots and black-footed ferrets in the U.S., and birds and lemurs in Madagascar. **Committees:** Conservation; Development; Executive; Finance; Nominating and Governance. **Councils:** Scientific Advisory. **Projects:** California: Marbled Murrelet Ecology and Health; Evaluation of Jet-boat Technology to Reduce Manatee Injury and Deaths; Manatee Biology and Carrying Capacity at Warm Water; New York Bioscape Initiative; Northern Right Whale Survey Analysis; Post Release Monitoring of Rehabilitated Manatees. **Formerly:** (2001) Wildlife Preservation Trust International. **Publications:** *Conservation Medicine: Ecological Health in Practice*. Book. Examines ecological health issues from various standpoints. ● *The Dodo*, annual. Journal ● *Manatees: Natural History and Conservation*. Book. Offers scientific insights and information about the manatee and its cousin, the dugong. **Price:** $16.95 plus shipping and handling ● *On the Edge*, 3/year. Newsletter. Contains association and industry news, plus Annual Report issue. ● Annual Report, annual. Alternate Formats: online ● Monographs ● Also publishes posters, maps, and informational sheets.

5403 ■ World Bird Sanctuary (WBS)
125 Bald Eagle Ridge Rd.
Valley Park, MO 63088
Ph: (636)861-3225 (636)225-4390
Fax: (636)861-3240
E-mail: developmentwbs@aol.com
URL: http://www.worldbirdsanctuary.org
Contact: Walter C. Crawford Jr., Exec. Dir.
Founded: 1977. **Members:** 2,000. **Membership Dues:** individual, $25 (annual) ● family, $50 (annual). **Staff:** 35. **Description:** Seeks to preserve the earth's biological diversity and to secure the future of threatened bird species in their natural environments. Coordinates a hands-on internship program. Conducts educational, propagation, and rehabilitation programs. **Formerly:** (1992) Raptor Rehabilitation and Propagation Project. **Publications:** *Methods of Feather Replacement in Birds of Prey*. Paper. Paper presented as a workshop for NWRA. **Price:** $2.00 ●

Mews News, quarterly. Newsletter. **Price:** included in membership dues ● *Techniques for Artificial Incubation and Hand-Rearing of Raptors*. Book.

5404 ■ World Wildlife Preservation Society (WWPS)

19400 Santa Rita St.
Tarzana, CA 91356-3021
Ph: (818)345-5140
Fax: (818)881-7459
E-mail: cheetahtu@aol.com
Contact: Jan Giacinto, Pres.

Founded: 1958. **Members:** 200. **Membership Dues:** associate, $15 (annual) ● ordinary, $20 (annual). **Staff:** 4. **Regional Groups:** 2. **Local Groups:** 1. **Description:** Individuals with exotic pets. Promotes responsible exotic pet ownership. Provides support and services to individuals wishing to keep exotic pets. Provides educational speakers for schools and club groups and will bring exotic animals to show to discuss laws required for owning these animals and why some people should not own them. **Libraries: Type:** not open to the public. **Holdings:** articles, books, periodicals. **Subjects:** exotic pets, wild cats - ownership and care. **Awards:** Membership Award. **Type:** recognition. **Formerly:** (2000) World Pets Society. **Publications:** *Fur, Fin and Feather*, bimonthly. Newsletter. Includes all types of animal news, mostly exotic. **Price:** included in membership dues; $20.00 /year for nonmembers. **Circulation:** 200. **Advertising:** accepted. **Conventions/Meetings:** bimonthly general assembly and workshop - January, March, May, July, September, November; in Tarzana, California.

5405 ■ Xerces Society (XS)

4828 SE Hawthorne Blvd.
Portland, OR 97215
Ph: (503)232-6639
Fax: (503)233-6794
E-mail: info@xerces.org
URL: http://www.xerces.org
Contact: Scott Hoffman Black, Exec. Dir.

Founded: 1975. **Members:** 5,000. **Membership Dues:** individual, $25 (annual) ● supporter, institution, library, school, organization, $50 (annual) ● benefactor, $500 (annual) ● friend, $100 (annual) ● patron, $250 (annual) ● sustainer, $1,000 (annual) ● limited income, $15 (annual). **Staff:** 5. **Budget:** $230,000. **Description:** Scientists working in conservation-related fields; interested individuals. Named for an extinct San Francisco butterfly, the Xerces Blue; devoted to the preservation of invertebrates. Identifies and seeks to protect critical invertebrate habitats and their endangered ecosystems. Conducts pollinator conservation program. **Awards:** Joan Mosenthal DeWind Award. **Frequency:** annual. **Type:** scholarship. **Recipient:** to students who are engaged in research related to Lepidoptera conservation. **Telecommunication Services:** electronic mail, sblack@xerces.org. **Programs:** Aquatic Invertebrate Conservation; California Monarch Butterfly Conservation Campaign; Endangered Invertebrate Conservation; Pollinator Conservation. **Publications:** *Butterfly Gardening: Creating Summer Magic In Your Garden*. Book. Includes photographs of butterflies and plants. **Price:** $21.00 for members; $25.95 for nonmembers ● *Farming for Bees: Guidelines for Providing Native Bee Habitat on Farms*. Booklet. Contains information on protecting and enhancing native pollinator habitat in the farm landscape. **Price:** $7.50 for members; $10.00 for nonmembers ● *Pollinator Conservation Handbook*. **Price:** $18.45 for members; $22.45 for nonmembers ● *Wings: Essays on Invertebrate Conservation*, semiannual. Magazine. Includes essays by scientists and conservationists. **Price:** included in membership dues; $3.50/back issue for nonmembers. Alternate Formats: online.

5406 ■ Yellowstone Grizzly Foundation

Address Unknown since 2007

Description: Conducts behavioral research and educational programs on grizzly bears.

Wine

5407 ■ American Society for Enology and Viticulture (ASEV)

PO Box 1855
Davis, CA 95617-1855
Ph: (530)753-3142
Fax: (530)753-3318
E-mail: society@asev.org
URL: http://www.asev.org
Contact: Lyndie M. Boulton, Exec. Dir.

Founded: 1950. **Members:** 2,400. **Membership Dues:** regular, $170 (annual) ● international, $175 (annual) ● student in U.S., $35 (annual) ● student outside U.S., $40 (annual) ● industrial affiliate (with AJEV online), $600 (annual) ● industrial affiliate (with AJEV print and online), $650 (annual). **Staff:** 6. **Budget:** $700,000. **Regional Groups:** 3. **Description:** Persons concerned with the management and technical aspects of the wine and grape industry including owners, technicians, academic personnel, and farm advisors. Promotes technical advancement in enology and viticulture through integrated research by science and industry; provides a medium for the free exchange of technical information and information on problems of interest to the wine and grape industries. **Awards:** Merit Award. **Frequency:** annual. **Type:** recognition ● **Frequency:** annual. **Type:** scholarship. **Recipient:** to students pursuing a degree in enology and viticulture. **Committees:** Awards; Chapter Liaison; Policy; Public Relations; Technical Projects. **Formerly:** (1983) American Society of Enologists. **Publications:** *American Journal of Enology and Viticulture*, quarterly. Includes abstracts, technical briefs, and reviews. **Price:** $205.00 in U.S.; $225.00 outside U.S. ISSN: 0002-9254. **Circulation:** 3,300. **Advertising:** accepted. Alternate Formats: magnetic tape ● *Technical Abstracts*. Booklet. **Price:** $10.00 for members; $20.00 for nonmembers ● Directory, annual. **Price:** $150.00 for members; $300.00 for nonmembers ● Newsletter, quarterly. **Conventions/Meetings:** annual meeting, with technical sessions; preceded by an international symposium (exhibits) - 2008 June 18-20, Portland, OR.

5408 ■ American Vineyard Foundation (AVF)

PO Box 5779
Napa, CA 94581
Ph: (707)252-6911 (530)752-1902
Fax: (707)252-7672
URL: http://www.avf.org
Contact: Hal Huffsmith, Chm.

Founded: 1978. **Staff:** 1. **Budget:** $1,000,000. **Description:** Collects funds for research on grape growing and wine making. **Libraries: Type:** reference. **Holdings:** reports. **Publications:** *American Vineyard Foundation Annual Research Report*, annual.

5409 ■ American Wine Alliance for Research and Education (AWARE)

PO Box 765
Washington, DC 20004-0765
Free: (800)700-4050
E-mail: phjuerg@olemiss.edu
URL: http://www.olemiss.edu/orgs/AWARE
Contact: Dr. John P. Juergens, Chm.

Founded: 1989. **Members:** 1,200. **Staff:** 5. **Description:** Individuals interested in wine industry. Monitors research and conducts educational programs aimed at presenting the role of wine in society. Focuses on health issues. Seeks to provide an international resource center. **Libraries: Type:** reference. **Subjects:** alcohol, health. **Publications:** *AWARE Newsletter*, periodic. Features health and social issues articles. **Circulation:** 3,500.

5410 ■ American Wine Society (AWS)

c/o Mary Ann Coskery, Exec. Dir.
113 S Perry St.
Lawrenceville, GA 30045
Ph: (678)377-7070
Fax: (678)377-7005
E-mail: coskery@americanwinesociety.org
URL: http://www.americanwinesociety.org
Contact: Mary Ann Coskery, Exec. Dir.

Founded: 1967. **Members:** 5,900. **Membership Dues:** individual/couple, $57 (annual) ● professional, $80 (annual) ● senior citizen - life, $600. **Staff:** 3. **Regional Groups:** 30. **Local Groups:** 100. **National Groups:** 100. **Description:** Amateur and professional winegrowers, winemakers, wine connoisseurs, wine merchants, and other interested persons. Seeks to further the knowledge, appreciation and enjoyment of wines produced on the American continent without bias toward European or other wines. Encourages legislation requiring honest labeling of both American and imported wines; fosters production of home winemakers; seeks to further the use of American terms for American wines. Sponsors educational programs at national and local levels. Conducts wine tastings and trips to vineyards and wineries; arranges gourmet wine dinners; provides speakers on grape growing, wine-making, and wine appreciation. **Libraries: Type:** reference. **Holdings:** 200; books. **Subjects:** wine. **Awards:** Award of Merit. **Frequency:** annual. **Type:** recognition. **Recipient:** for significant contribution to the advancement of American wines. **Computer Services:** database ● mailing lists. **Committees:** Enology; Viticulture; Wine Appreciation Instructors; Wine Cookery; Wine Education; Wine Legislation and Practices. **Programs:** Wine Judge Training. **Publications:** *American Wine Society—Journal*, quarterly. Includes directory and book reviews. **Price:** $4.00. ISSN: 0364-698X. **Circulation:** 5,900. **Advertising:** accepted ● *AWS News*, quarterly. Newsletter. Contains society news. **Price:** included in membership dues. **Circulation:** 5,900. **Advertising:** accepted. Alternate Formats: online ● *Bulletins and Essays*, periodic ● *Cumulative Index to the American Wine Society Journal 1974-89* ● *Guide to Wine Grape Growing* ● Manual, quarterly ● Also publishes other instructional manuals covering aspects of wine making and grape growing. **Conventions/Meetings:** annual competition and conference, for amateur and commercial wine (exhibits).

5411 ■ Brotherhood of the Knights of the Vine (KOV)

3343 Indus. Dr., Ste.2
Santa Rosa, CA 95403
Ph: (707)579-3781
Fax: (707)579-3996
E-mail: info@kov.org
URL: http://www.kov.org
Contact: Carol Bade, Exec. Dir.

Founded: 1964. **Members:** 1,200. **Staff:** 2. **State Groups:** 7. **Local Groups:** 1. **National Groups:** 21. **Description:** Vintners, grape growers, wine wholesalers and retailers, professors of enology (the study of wine and wine-making), wine lovers with an interest in American grapes and wine. Seeks to promote wine as a healthy, hygienic beverage. Bestows titles of Supreme Knight, Master Knight, Knight or Gentle Lady, and Supreme Lady for services rendered to the cause of vines and wines of America. Sponsors Knights of the Vine Scholarship Fund at the University of California-Davis, Washington State University, Fresno State University, and Texas A&M University. National chapters conduct educational programs on wine. **Awards:** Supreme Knight and Supreme Lady. **Frequency:** periodic. **Type:** recognition. **Recipient:** for major contribution to wine industry. **Committees:** Gold Vine Award; Knight Vine Scholarship Fund. **Publications:** *The Arbor*, semiannual. Magazine. Includes articles about wine and the history of wine. Contains book reviews, membership directory, recipes, calendar of events, and chapter news. **Price:** free for members; $15.00 /year for nonmembers. **Advertising:** accepted. **Conventions/Meetings:** annual World Congress - FICB, gathering of wine brotherhood from around the world.

5412 ■ California Association of Winegrape Growers (CAWG)

601 Univ. Ave., Ste.135
Sacramento, CA 95825
Ph: (916)924-5370
Free: (800)241-1800

Fax: (916)924-5374
E-mail: info@cawg.org
URL: http://www.cawg.org
Contact: Karen Ross, Pres.
Founded: 1974. **Membership Dues:** grower (minimum; based on land acre), $150 (annual) ● major associate, $2,000 (annual) ● corporate associate, $1,500 (annual) ● benefactor associate, $1,000 (annual) ● patron associate, $750 (annual) ● friend associate, $500 (annual) ● supporter associate, $250 (annual). **Staff:** 3. **Budget:** $600,000. **Description:** Corporations, associations, and individuals who grow grapes in California for wine and related products. Serves as a unified voice to address issues aimed at improving the domestic and foreign market for California wines and wine grapes. Lobbies state and federal legislatures and regulatory agencies. Holds annual reception for the California Legislature and annual Wines of America Reception for Congress; co-sponsors the annual Unified Wine and Grape Symposium. **Telecommunication Services:** electronic mail, karen@cawg.org. **Projects:** California Code of Sustainable Winegrowing Practices; Good Neighbor and Community Relations; Pest Management Alliance; Private Lands Partnership; Vineyards and Wildlife Habitat. **Publications:** *The Crush*, monthly. Newsletter ● Annual Report, annual. Alternate Formats: online. **Conventions/Meetings:** annual Unified Wine and Grape Symposium, with seminars (exhibits) - always in Sacramento, CA. 2009 Jan. 27-29, Sacramento, CA; 2010 Jan. 26-28, Sacramento, CA.

5413 ■ Finger Lakes Wine Growers Association (FLWGA)
PO Box 222
Hammondsport, NY 14840
Ph: (607)569-6133
Fax: (607)569-6135
E-mail: mike@pleasantvalleywine.com
Contact: Michael J. Doyle, Pres.
Description: Wineries in the New York State Finger Lakes wine-producing region. Promotes the wine industry. **Conventions/Meetings:** periodic meeting.

5414 ■ Monterey County Vintners and Growers Association (MCVGA)
PO Box 1793
Monterey, CA 93942-1793
Ph: (831)375-9400
Fax: (831)375-1116
E-mail: info@montereywines.org
URL: http://www.montereywines.org
Contact: Rhonda Motil, Exec. Dir.
Founded: 1975. **Members:** 65. **Staff:** 4. **Description:** Represents grape growers and wine producers of Monterey County, CA. Seeks to develop awareness and promote the image of Monterey wines. **Formerly:** (2003) Monterey Wine Country Association. **Conventions/Meetings:** monthly board meeting.

5415 ■ Napa Valley Grapegrowers (NVG)
811 Jefferson St.
Napa, CA 94559
Ph: (707)944-8311
Fax: (707)224-7836
E-mail: info@napagrowers.org
URL: http://www.napagrowers.org
Contact: Jennifer Kopp, Exec. Dir.
Founded: 1975. **Members:** 325. **Membership Dues:** friend, $50 (annual) ● associate, $250 (annual) ● vineyard manager, $350 (annual) ● grower, $250-$3,000 (annual). **Staff:** 3. **Budget:** $59,000. **Local Groups:** 1. **Description:** Grape growers, wineries, businesses that work with growers, and others interested in the wine grape growing industry with particular emphasis on the Napa Valley. Provides marketing assistance to growers; promotes legislation at the local and state levels that will benefit growers. Has established a Napa Valley viticultural area designation, and is involved in the technical aspects of grape growing. Cosponsors marketing and promotional programs. Compiles statistical data on Napa Valley grapes and local markets. **Libraries: Type:** open to the public. **Holdings:** articles, books, periodicals. **Subjects:** wine grape growing. **Formerly:** (2006) Napa Valley Grape Growers Association. **Publications:** *Premium Grower*, quarterly. Newsletter. Covers Napa Valley grape and wine industry trends, prices, and events; provides some technical information on viticultural practices. **Price:** free for members; $100.00 /year for nonmembers. **Circulation:** 1,400. **Advertising:** accepted. **Conventions/Meetings:** semiannual Napa Valley Viticultural Fair - trade show and seminar, wine grape industry (exhibits).

5416 ■ Napa Valley Vintners Association (NVV)
PO Box 141
St. Helena, CA 94574
Ph: (707)963-3388
Free: (800)982-1371
Fax: (707)963-3488
E-mail: reception2@napavintners.com
URL: http://www.napavintners.com
Contact: Linda Reiff, Exec. Dir.
Founded: 1943. **Members:** 150. **Staff:** 15. **Budget:** $3,000,000. **Description:** Promotes Napa Valley, CA, wines and wineries; disseminates information about Napa Valley wines to the public. **Telecommunication Services:** electronic mail, pmcgaughy@napavintners.com. **Conventions/Meetings:** monthly meeting - always in St. Helena, CA ● annual Napa Valley Wine Auction - meeting (exhibits) - always June in St. Helena, CA.

5417 ■ New York Wine/Grape Foundation (NYWGF)
800 S Main St., Ste.200
Canandaigua, NY 14424
Ph: (585)394-3620
Fax: (585)394-3649
E-mail: info@newyorkwines.org
URL: http://www.newyorkwines.org
Contact: James Trezise, Pres.
Founded: 1985. **Members:** 335. **Staff:** 4. **Description:** Grape growers from New York State; wineries and juice processors, suppliers, financiers, insurance representatives, consultants to growers, restaurateurs, and consumers. Promotes the demand for and sale of grapes and grape products through advertising and promotional work; assist members by performing services relative to the production, harvesting, and marketing of wine grapes, and any related research; provide members with production and marketing information; promote mutual understanding and goodwill between growers and processors of grapes. Seeks to educate consumers on the variety and quality of grapes grown and grape products made in New York State. Sponsors Women for New York State Wines, consisting of women supporting the New York State wine industry; WNYSW promotes wine sales and holds wine tasting to teach people how to read wine labels and distinguish between wines made from various types of wine grapes. **Committees:** Research; Women's Promotion. **Formed by Merger of:** New York Association of Wine Producers; New York State Wine Grape Growers. **Formerly:** (1985) New York Wine Council. **Publications:** *Uncork New York*. Brochure ● *Wine Country Calendar*, annual ● *Wine Press*, weekly. Bulletin ● Reports. **Conventions/Meetings:** annual meeting and banquet ● annual New York Wine and Food Classic - competition.

5418 ■ Organic Grapes Into Wine Alliance (OGWA)
Address Unknown since 2008
URL: http://www.organicwine.com
Founded: 1989. **Membership Dues:** wine producer/winegrower/wholesaler/retailer/importer/associate, $100 (annual) ● supporting, $30 (annual). **Description:** Represents the interests of wine makers, grape growers and wine trades people. Supports the production of wines made from organically grown grapes by establishing production standards, education, cooperation and leadership.

5419 ■ San Joaquin Valley Wine Growers Association (SJVWGA)
Address Unknown since 2007
Founded: 1933. **Members:** 33. **Description:** Wineries (18); banks and suppliers to the industry (15). Promotes wines produced in the San Joaquin Valley region of California; cooperates with other regional groups to promote American wines in general. Aids in lobbying efforts to curb "unfair competition" of foreign wines in the U.S. market. Offers scholarships for outstanding students in fields related to wine production. **Committees:** Scholarship. **Affiliated With:** Wine Institute. **Formerly:** (1946) Sweet Wine Producers Association. **Conventions/Meetings:** annual meeting.

5420 ■ Santa Cruz Mountains Winegrowers Association (SCMWA)
7605-A Old Dominion Ct.
Aptos, CA 95003
Ph: (831)685-8463
Fax: (831)688-6961
E-mail: info@scmwa.com
URL: http://www.scmwa.com
Founded: 1976. **Members:** 48. **Membership Dues:** regular, $200 (annual) ● associate, $150 (annual). **Staff:** 4. **Budget:** $300,000. **Local Groups:** 1. **Description:** Wineries in the Santa Cruz Mountains area. Facilitates exchange of information among members. Promotes wines of the Santa Cruz Mountains appellation. Holds grape growing and winemaking seminars. **Awards:** Commercial Wine Competition. **Frequency:** annual. **Type:** recognition. **Formerly:** Santa Cruz Mountain Vintners.

5421 ■ Sonoma County Grape Growers Association (SCGGA)
PO Box 1959
Sebastopol, CA 95473
Ph: (707)829-3963
E-mail: info@scgga.org
URL: http://www.scgga.org
Contact: Dennis Black, Pres.
Founded: 1983. **Membership Dues:** bearing acre, $12 (annual) ● non-bearing acre, $5 (annual) ● associate, $250 ● sponsor, $500-$10,000. **Staff:** 4. **Description:** Growers of wine grapes for commercial sale to wineries. Promotes the wines of Sonoma County, CA; addresses agricultural issues that affect grape growers. Provides information on Sonoma County food and wine. Maintains speakers' bureau. **Awards:** Viticultural Award of Excellence. **Frequency:** annual. **Type:** recognition. **Recipient:** for contributions to Sonoma County viticulture. **Additional Websites:** http://www.sonomagrapevine.org. **Publications:** *SCGGA News*, bimonthly. Newsletter. Provides wine community news with emphasis on news and events with local impact. **Price:** included in membership dues; $250.00 for associates; $500.00 for sponsors. **Circulation:** 1,000. Alternate Formats: online. **Conventions/Meetings:** annual Buyers & Sellers BBQ & Trade Show - meeting, with networking opportunity (exhibits) ● seminar, on integrated pest management.

5422 ■ Sonoma County Vintners (SCV)
420 Aviation Blvd., Ste.106
Santa Rosa, CA 95403
Ph: (707)522-5840 (707)522-5842
Free: (800)939-7666
Fax: (707)573-3942
E-mail: info@sonomawine.com
URL: http://www.sonomawine.com
Contact: Honore Comfort, Exec. Dir.
Founded: 1946. **Members:** 140. **Membership Dues:** regular, $350 (annual). **Staff:** 3. **Budget:** $800,000. **Languages:** English, French, German, Japanese. **Description:** Wineries that produce and label at least one wine made in Sonoma County. Promotes the wines of Sonoma County. Conducts events designed to educate the public about wine, wine tasting, and wine-producing regions. Sponsors annual national wine tasting tour in March and April, and Canadian tour in October and November. **Affiliated With:** Sonoma County Grape Growers Association. **Formerly:** (1986) Sonoma County Wine Growers As-

sociation; (2006) Sonoma County Wineries Association. **Publications:** *Tasting Book*, annual. Directory. **Circulation:** 50,000. **Advertising:** accepted ● Also publishes educational brochures and menu book; produces poster and map of wine producing regions; makes available videotape. **Conventions/Meetings:** quarterly meeting ● annual Showcase of Food and Wine - dinner, includes Barrel Auction - always second weekend of July.

5423 ■ Vinifera Wine Growers Association (VWGA)
PO Box 10045
Alexandria, VA 22310
Ph: (703)922-7049
Fax: (703)922-0617
E-mail: thewinexchange@aol.com
Contact: Gordon W. Murchie, Pres.

Founded: 1973. **Members:** 300. **Membership Dues:** general, $45 (annual). **Description:** Promotes public appreciation and understanding of wine and its production. Supports state and national wine educational forums and research. Provides technical, cultural, and historical wine information. Promotes wine enjoyment and responsible consumption as part of a healthy lifestyle. Supports quality production and sales of all grape wines. Lobbies on behalf of state and federal legislation favorable to the growth and economic viability of the U.S. wine industry. Strengthens cooperation with other wine organizations in addressing wine issues of common concern. **Awards:** Best of Show Jefferson Loving Cup. **Frequency:** annual. **Type:** recognition. **Recipient:** for the best show in the annual VWGA-sponsored estate wine competition ● Monteith Trophy. **Frequency:** annual. **Type:** trophy. **Recipient:** for major contributors to the growth of the U.S. wine industry ● Wine Grape Productivity Tray. **Frequency:** annual. **Type:** recognition. **Recipient:** for major contributors to the growth of the U.S. wine industry. **Publications:** Special reports on wine production in China, South Africa, and Australia. **Conventions/Meetings:** periodic seminar, on wine education and appreciation ● annual Virginia Wine Festival - meeting and competition, arts and crafts (exhibits) - always last weekend of August in Historic Long Branch, Millwood, VA.

5424 ■ Wine Appreciation Guild (WAG)
360 Swift Ave., Unit 30-40
South San Francisco, CA 94080
Ph: (650)866-3020
Free: (800)231-9463
Fax: (650)866-3513
E-mail: info@wineappreciation.com
URL: http://www.wineappreciation.com
Contact: Bryan Imelli, Contact

Founded: 1973. **Members:** 1,476. **Membership Dues:** industry, $400 (annual). **Staff:** 31. **Budget:** $1,000,000. **Regional Groups:** 2. **Description:** Represents winery owners and distributors. Disseminates information on wine, with emphasis on American wines. Conducts wine evaluations and research programs on wine and health, cooking with wine, and consumer wine. Offers wine study courses and compiles statistics. Sponsors competitions. **Libraries: Type:** not open to the public; reference. **Holdings:** 3,200; audio recordings, audiovisuals, biographical archives, books, video recordings. **Subjects:** wine, food. **Awards:** Wine Literary Award. **Frequency:** annual. **Type:** recognition. **Recipient:** to an author for his/her substantial contribution to the literature of American wine. **Committees:** Consumer; Culinary and Recipes; Health and Social Issues; Trade. **Affiliated With:** Wine Institute. **Supersedes:** Wine Advisory Board. **Publications:** *American Wine Directory*, annual ● *Benefits of Moderate Drinking* ● *Consumers Guide to Jug Wine*, annual ● *Consumers Guide to Varietal Wines*, annual ● *Drinking and Health* ● *Encyclopedia of American Wine*, biennial ● *Pocket Encyclopedia of California Wines*, annual ● *Vindex* ● *Wine Cookbook Series*, biennial ● *Winery Technology and Operations* ● Also publishes material on wine study courses for consumers and professionals. **Conventions/Meetings:** annual conference (exhibits) - always April ● annual Wine Literary Award Banquet - meeting - always February in San Francisco, CA.

5425 ■ Wine Institute (WI)
425 Market St., Ste.1000
San Francisco, CA 94105
Ph: (415)512-0151
Fax: (415)442-0742
E-mail: horiuchi@wineinstitute.org
URL: http://www.wineinstitute.org
Contact: Robert P. Koch, Pres./CEO

Founded: 1934. **Members:** 400. **Membership Dues:** regular, $180 (annual) ● associate, $1,500 (annual). **Staff:** 45. **Budget:** $5,000,000. **Description:** Initiates and advocates state, federal, and international public policy to enhance the environment for the responsible consumption and enjoyment of wine. **Libraries: Type:** reference. **Holdings:** 3,500; archival material, books. **Committees:** Communications; International; Public Policy; Research and Education. **Publications:** *News Briefs*, monthly ● *Wine Institute News*, monthly. Newsletter. **Price:** available to members only ● *Wine Issues Monitor* ● Reports. **Conventions/Meetings:** annual meeting - always June in San Francisco, CA.

Accounting

5426 ■ Association of Government Accountants (AGA)
2208 Mt. Vernon Ave.
Alexandria, VA 22301-1314
Ph: (703)684-6931
Free: (800)AGA-7211
Fax: (703)548-9367
E-mail: rvandaniker@agacgfm.org
URL: http://www.agacgfm.org
Contact: Relmond Van Daniker Jr., Exec. Dir.
Founded: 1950. **Members:** 18,500. **Membership Dues:** full, government, $90 (annual) ● early career, $45 (annual) ● student, $30 (annual) ● private sector, $150 (annual). **Staff:** 19. **Budget:** $3,500,000. **Regional Groups:** 16. **State Groups:** 99. **Description:** Professional society of financial managers employed by federal, state, county, and city governments in financial management and administrative positions. Conducts research; offers education and professional development programs. **Awards:** Federal Leadership Award. **Frequency:** annual. **Type:** recognition. **Recipient:** for outstanding financial leaders in the federal government ● Robert W. King Memorial Award. **Frequency:** annual. **Type:** recognition. **Recipient:** for achievements or service that enhanced the prestige of AGA. **Computer Services:** Mailing lists, of members. **Committees:** Early Careers; Education; Emerging Issues; Ethics; Financial Management and Standards; International Development; Public Service; Research. **Formerly:** Federal Government Accountants Association. **Publications:** *Government Financial Management Topics*, monthly ● *The Journal of Government Financial Management*, quarterly. **Price:** $95.00/year in U.S.; $115.00/year outside U.S. ISSN: 1533-1385. **Circulation:** 14,500. **Advertising:** accepted. **Conventions/Meetings:** annual Federal Leadership Conference (exhibits) - usually January ● annual Professional Development Conference, attracts top government financial managers (exhibits) - 2008 July 27-30, Atlanta, GA; 2009 June 21-24, New Orleans, LA.

5427 ■ Governmental Accounting Standards Board (GASB)
PO Box 5116
Norwalk, CT 06856-5116
Ph: (203)847-0700
Fax: (203)849-9714
E-mail: rhattmore@gasb.org
URL: http://www.gasb.org
Contact: Robert H. Attmore, Chm.
Founded: 1984. **Members:** 7. **Staff:** 16. **Description:** Establishes standards for local and state governments. Holds public hearings. Maintains speakers' bureau; conducts research programs. **Libraries: Type:** not open to the public. **Holdings:** books, periodicals, reports. **Computer Services:** database, governmental accounting research system. **Councils:** Governmental Accounting Standards Advisory. **Formerly:** Financial Accounting Foundation. **Supersedes:** (1984) National Council on Governmental Accounting. **Publications:** *The GASB Report*, monthly. Newsletter ● Also publishes statements and interpretations of accounting standards. **Conventions/Meetings:** board meeting - always Norwalk, CT; every 6 weeks.

5428 ■ National Association of State Boards of Accountancy (NASBA)
150 4th Ave. N, Ste.700
Nashville, TN 37219
Ph: (615)880-4200
Fax: (615)880-4290
E-mail: communications@nasba.org
URL: http://www.nasba.org
Contact: David A. Costello CPA, Pres./CEO
Founded: 1908. **Members:** 55. **Staff:** 125. **Budget:** $19,771,891. **Regional Groups:** 8. **Description:** Comprises 54 state boards of accountancy. Serves as a forum for the boards, which administer the Uniform CPA Examination, license certified public accountants, and regulate the practice of public accountancy in the United States. Sponsors committee meetings, conferences, programs and services designed to enhance the effectiveness of its member boards. **Awards:** Distinguished Service Award. **Frequency:** annual. **Type:** recognition. **Recipient:** for outstanding service ● William H. Van Rensselaer Public Service Award. **Frequency:** annual. **Type:** recognition. **Recipient:** for outstanding leadership. **Computer Services:** Information services, statistical. **Boards:** CPA Examination Review; International Qualifications Appraisal. **Committees:** Awards; Bylaws; CPE Advisory; Education; Ethics; Examinations; Legal Counsel; Professional and Regulatory Response; Regulatory Structures; Relations With Member Boards; Strategic Initiatives; Uniform Accountancy Act. **Programs:** CPA Examination Services; CPEMARKET.COM; CredentialNet; Licensure and Practice; National Registry of CPE Sponsors; Quality Assurance Service. **Formerly:** (1969) Association of Certified Public Accountant Examiners. **Publications:** *Annual Meeting Presentations*, annual. Audiotapes. Alternate Formats: magnetic tape ● *Complaint Referral Handbook: A Guide for Federal Agencies*, periodic ● *CPA Candidate Performance on the Uniform CPA Examination*, annual. Book. Contains charts and statistics analyzing the performance of CPA candidates. **Price:** $115.00. **Circulation:** 500 ● *Digest of State Accountancy Laws and State Board Regulations*, biennial. **Price:** $32.00 for NASBA or AICPA member; $40.00 for nonmembers, plus shipping and handling. **Circulation:** 1,500 ● *NASBA Annual Report*, annual. Alternate Formats: online ● *State Board Report*, monthly. Newsletter. Contains current developments affecting state accountancy boards. **Price:** $65.00. **Circulation:** 1,400 ● *State Boards of Accountancy of the United States*, periodic. Directory. **Price:** $150.00 ● *Uniform Accountancy Act and Rules*, periodic. **Conventions/Meetings:** periodic conference ● annual meeting ● annual regional meeting.

Administrative Services

5429 ■ Association of Local Government Auditors (ALGA)
449 Lewis Hargett Cir., Ste.290
Lexington, KY 40503-3669
Ph: (859)276-0686
E-mail: jim.williamson@okc.gov
URL: http://www.governmentauditors.org
Contact: Jim Williamson, Pres.
Founded: 1989. **Members:** 2,300. **Membership Dues:** individual/associate, $250 (annual) ● audit organization, $150-$500 (annual). **Description:** Audit professionals. Dedicated to providing a forum for issues that concern local auditors and voice their interests. Conducts educational programs. **Computer Services:** database ● mailing lists. **Committees:** Advocacy; Awards; Benchmarking/Best Practices; Bylaws; Conference; Education; Professional Issues; Website. **Formerly:** (2006) National Association of Local Government Auditors. **Publications:** *Local Government Auditors Newsletter*, quarterly ● Directory. **Conventions/Meetings:** board meeting ● annual convention.

African-American

5430 ■ National Black State Troopers Coalition (NBSTC)
c/o Kim Hoffman-Davis, Treas.
PO Box 2661
Joliet, IL 60434-2661
Free: (866)363-0467
E-mail: nbstc1@nbstc.org
URL: http://www.nbstc.org
Contact: Robert Guilbeaux, Pres.
Founded: 1985. **Description:** Promotes communication among minority state troopers; encourages members to participate in self-improvement programs; prepares and competes for promotions; and requests assignments to specialized units to advance careers and better serve communities. **Conventions/Meetings:** meeting.

Agricultural Law

5431 ■ American Agricultural Law Association (AALA)
PO Box 2025
Eugene, OR 97402-0009
Ph: (541)485-1090
Fax: (541)302-1958
E-mail: roberta@aglaw-assn.org
URL: http://www.aglaw-assn.org
Contact: Robert P. Achenbach Jr., Exec. Dir.
Founded: 1980. **Members:** 700. **Membership Dues:** regular, $90 (annual) ● student, $30 (annual) ●

foreign, outside North America, $125 (annual) ● institutional, $250 (annual) ● sustaining, $175 (annual). **Staff:** 2. **Budget:** $100,000. **Description:** Law professors, agricultural law teachers from agricultural economics departments, government agency representatives, practicing attorneys, and other professionals and students working in agricultural law. Seeks to advance understanding and awareness of agricultural law by facilitating research, instruction, information, extension, practice, and other activities, and to share ideas and information on new developments in agricultural law. **Publications:** *Agricultural Law Review*, annual. Journal. **Price:** included in membership dues ● *Agricultural Law Update*, monthly. Newsletter. **Price:** included in membership dues ● *American Agricultural Law Association Membership Directory*, annual. **Conventions/Meetings:** annual Agricultural Law Symposium - conference (exhibits) - usually October ● seminar, on agricultural law topics.

Agriculture

5432 ■ Association of American Feed Control Officials (AAFCO)

c/o Dr. Rodney J. Noel, Sec.-Treas.
Purdue Univ.
Off. of Indiana State Chemist
175 S Univ. St.
West Lafayette, IN 47907-2063
Ph: (765)494-1561
Fax: (765)496-6349
E-mail: noelr@purdue.edu
URL: http://www.aafco.org
Contact: Dr. Rodney J. Noel, Sec.-Treas.

Founded: 1909. **Members:** 200. **Staff:** 1. **Description:** Represents officials of federal, state, and provincial government agencies regulating the manufacture, sale, and distribution of animal feeds and remedies. Promotes uniformity in legislation, definitions, and rulings and the enforcement of laws. **Committees:** Collaborative Check Sample; E-Commerce; Enforcement Issues; Environmental Issues; Feed Labeling; Feed Manufacturing; Ingredient Definitions; Inspection and Sampling. **Publications:** *Official Publication, AAFCO*, annual. Contains definitions of feed ingredients, model regulations, and addresses. **Price:** $50.00 in U.S. and Canada; $65.00 outside U.S. and Canada. **Conventions/Meetings:** annual conference - always first week of August.

5433 ■ Association of American Plant Food Control Officials (AAPFCO)

Fertilizer/Ag Lime Control Ser.
Univ. of Missouri-Columbia
Columbia, MO 65211-8080
Ph: (573)882-0007
Fax: (573)882-4543
E-mail: slaterj@missouri.edu
URL: http://www.aapfco.org
Contact: Joe Slater, Sec.

Founded: 1946. **Members:** 200. **Membership Dues:** organization, $100 (annual). **Description:** Represents officials of state agencies concerned with enforcement of laws relating to control of sale and distribution of mixed fertilizer and fertilizer materials. **Libraries:** **Type:** reference. **Holdings:** reports. **Awards:** Certificate of Appreciation. **Frequency:** periodic. **Type:** recognition. **Recipient:** for members who have completed a minimum of 10 years of active service and performed meritorious service to the association, principles of plant food control and promoting harmonious and cooperative relationship between the association and the industry ● D.S. Coltrane Award. **Frequency:** periodic. **Type:** recognition ● Life Membership. **Frequency:** periodic. **Type:** recognition. **Recipient:** for members who have completed a minimum of 8 years active committee service or 15 years in a member agency. **Computer Services:** database, National Fertilizer Tonnage. **Committees:** Education and Information; Environmental Affairs; Good Manufacturing Practices; Industry-Regulatory; Labeling; Magruder Check Sample; Official Terms and Definitions; Seminars, Uniform Reports, Uniform Bills; Slow Release Fertilizers. **Formerly:** (1969) Association of American Fertilizer Control Officials. **Publications:** *Association of American Plant Food Control Officials-Official Publication*, annual. Proceedings. Provides information on annual meeting and directory of members. Contains list of official fertilizer terms and definitions. **Price:** $25.00. **Circulation:** 400 ● *Commercial Fertilizers*, annual. Booklet. Features summary of fertilizer used in the U.S. **Price:** $30.00 ● *Inspector's Manual*, periodic. **Price:** $20.00. **Conventions/Meetings:** semiannual conference and meeting - always first week of August and sometimes in February.

5434 ■ Association of American Seed Control Officials (AASCO)

c/o Anita Hall
101 E State St., No. 214
Ithaca, NY 14850
Ph: (607)256-3313
Fax: (607)256-3313
E-mail: scst@twcny.rr.com
URL: http://www.seedcontrol.org
Contact: Joe Garvey, Pres.

Founded: 1956. **Members:** 53. **Membership Dues:** state, federal, province, $150 (annual). **Regional Groups:** 4. **Description:** Officials who administer U.S. federal and state, and Dominion of Canada seed laws. Promotes uniformity in seed laws, rules and regulations, and in the administration of laws relative to the sale and distribution of seeds; furthers the exchange of constructive ideas among administrators of seed laws; seeks to study and suggest improvements in proposed seed legislation; cooperates with administrators of state, federal, and Canadian seed laws; promotes a general appreciation of the benefits of seed control to farmers, seedsmen, and the public by encouraging the marketing and use of correctly labeled seed of high quality. **Committees:** Administration and Enforcement; Information and Education; Labeling and Legislative Review; Official Definitions; RUSSL Review; Seed Inspector Qualification and Training. **Publications:** *Handbook on Seed Sampling*. Presents methods, guidelines and equipment for both regulatory and industry applications. **Price:** $40.00 1-9 copies; $35.00 10 or more copies; $30.00 for educational institution; $5.00 for bulk and international order ● *Manual for Seed Inspectors* ● *Official Publication and Proceedings of the Annual Meeting*, annual. Directory. **Price:** $20.00 ● *Uniform State Seed Law, Policies Labeling Info*, annual ● Newsletter, quarterly. **Conventions/Meetings:** annual meeting.

5435 ■ Association of Official Seed Analysts (AOSA)

Mail Boxes Etc., No. 285
601 S Washington
Stillwater, OK 74074-4539
Ph: (405)780-7372 (541)737-5094
Fax: (405)780-7372
E-mail: aosaoffice@sbcglobal.net
URL: http://www.aosaseed.com
Contact: Janice Osburn, Exec. Asst.

Founded: 1908. **Members:** 60. **Membership Dues:** official, $600 (annual) ● associate, allied, $175 (annual). **Staff:** 1. **Budget:** $100,000. **Description:** Officials of 60 federal, state, and provincial seed testing and research laboratories. Seeks to: develop uniform rules for testing field, vegetable, flower, and tree seeds; encourage the use of high quality seed; promote research; foster the training of seed analysts. **Awards:** Merit Award. **Frequency:** annual. **Type:** recognition. **Computer Services:** database, membership, book, and subscription listings. **Telecommunication Services:** electronic mail, daniel.curry@oregonstate.edu. **Committees:** Certification of Analysts; Referee; Research; Research Funding; Rules; Seed Pathology; Testing Uniformity. **Affiliated With:** American Seed Trade Association; Association of American Seed Control Officials; Association of Official Seed Certifying Agencies; Society of Commercial Seed Technologists. **Publications:** *Cultivar Purity Testing Handbook*, periodic. **Price:** $25.00. Alternate Formats: CD-ROM ● *Rules for Testing Seed*, annual. Handbook. **Price:** $55.00 ● *Seed Technologist Newsletter*, 3/year. Reports on research on seed technology; offers information on purity and germination testing of seeds. **Price:** $35.00/year. **Circulation:** 450 ● *Seedling Evaluation Handbook*, annual. **Price:** $40.00 ● *Uniform Classification Handbook*, annual. **Price:** $40.00 ● *Uniform Classification of Weed and Crop Seeds, No. 25*, annual. Handbook. **Conventions/Meetings:** annual conference and meeting (exhibits).

5436 ■ Association of Official Seed Certifying Agencies (AOSCA)

1601 52nd Ave., Ste.1
Moline, IL 61265
Ph: (309)736-0120
Fax: (309)736-0115
E-mail: cboruff@aosca.org
URL: http://www.aosca.org
Contact: Chet Boruff, Sec.-Treas./CEO

Founded: 1919. **Members:** 396. **Membership Dues:** associate, affiliate, $50 (annual). **Languages:** English, Spanish. **Description:** State seed certifying agencies. Promotes breeding, production, and distribution of foundation, registered, and certified seed stocks. Establishes and adopts minimum standards for certification of field and vegetable crops. **Committees:** Corn; Cotton; Forage; Grains; Grasses and Legumes; Peanuts; Rice; Soybeans; Tobacco; Tree Seed; Vegetables. **Formerly:** (1968) International Crop Improvement Association. **Publications:** *Acres Approved for Certification*, annual ● Also publishes certification handbook. **Conventions/Meetings:** annual meeting.

5437 ■ National Association of Agriculture Employees (NAAE)

c/o Mike Randall, Pres.
PO Box 31143
Honolulu, HI 96820-1143
Ph: (808)861-8449 (734)942-9005
Free: (888)631-3249
E-mail: sarahclore@yahoo.com
URL: http://www.aginspectors.org
Contact: Sarah Clore, Sec.

Founded: 1954. **Members:** 500. **Local Groups:** 44. **Description:** Federal plant protection and quarantine employees, including entomologists, plant pathologists, and agricultural and biological scientists. Protects the agricultural interests and economy of the U.S. by the enforcement of the Federal Plant Pest and Plant Quarantine Acts, and animal health laws; is recognized as exclusive bargaining agent of federal plant protection and quarantine employees. **Committees:** Government Relations; Safety; Welfare. **Formerly:** (1981) Federal Plant Quarantine Inspectors National Association. **Publications:** *NAAE Yellow Book*. Manual. Alternate Formats: online ● Newsletter, bimonthly. **Price:** free for members. **Conventions/Meetings:** biennial meeting.

5438 ■ National Association of County Agricultural Agents (NACAA)

252 N Park St.
Decatur, IL 62523
Ph: (217)424-5144 (806)373-7946
Fax: (217)424-5115
E-mail: exec-dir@nacaa.com
URL: http://www.nacaa.com
Contact: Fred Miller, Pres.

Founded: 1915. **Members:** 7,000. **Budget:** $400,000. **State Groups:** 49. **Description:** County agricultural agents and extension workers. Serves the county agents of 50 state associations. **Awards:** Distinguished Service Award. **Frequency:** annual. **Type:** recognition. **Recipient:** for top educators ● **Type:** scholarship. **Recipient:** for agents. **Computer Services:** Mailing lists, of members. **Committees:** Association Policy; Communications; Extension Programs; 4-H Youth; Professional Training; Program Development; Public Relations; Recognitions and Awards; Scholarships; State Relations. **Publications:** *County Agents*, periodic ● Videos. **Conventions/Meetings:** annual meeting (exhibits) - 2008 July 13-17, Greensboro, NC.

5439 ■ National Association of State Departments of Agriculture (NASDA)
1156 15th St. NW, Ste.1020
Washington, DC 20005
Ph: (202)296-9680
Fax: (202)296-9686
E-mail: nasda@nasda.org
URL: http://www.nasda.org
Contact: Richard W. Kirchhoff, Exec. VP/CEO
Founded: 1916. **Members:** 54. **Membership Dues:** Tier I, $20 (annual) ● Tier II, $18 (annual) ● Tier III, $16 (annual) ● Tier IV, $14 (annual) ● Tier V, $11 (annual) ● Tier VI, $8 (annual) ● Tier VII, $5 (annual) ● Tier VIII, $3 (annual). **Staff:** 9. **Budget:** $20,000,000. **Regional Groups:** 4. **Description:** Directors of state and territorial departments of agriculture. Coordinates policies, procedures, laws, and activities between the states and federal agencies and Congress. Conducts research. **Awards:** Honor Award. **Frequency:** annual. **Type:** recognition. **Recipient:** for employees of the state departments of agriculture. **Committees:** Animal and Plant Industries; Food Regulation and Nutrition; International Marketing and Trade; Natural Resources and Pesticide Stewardship; Rural Development and Financial Security. **Task Forces:** Biotechnology; Farm Labor; Specialty Crop. **Formerly:** (1957) National Association of Commissioners, Secretaries and Directors of Agriculture. **Publications:** *NASDA Directory*, annual. Alternate Formats: online ● *NASDA News*, weekly. Newsletter ● Annual Report, annual. Alternate Formats: online ● Brochure. **Conventions/Meetings:** annual American FoodFair - trade show, for U.S. producers, retailers, and wholesalers (exhibits) - always May in Chicago, IL ● annual conference - usually September ● annual Mid-Winter Conference - usually February in Washington, DC ● annual United States Food Export Showcase - trade show, for U.S. producers, retailers, and wholesalers (exhibits) - always May in Chicago, IL.

5440 ■ National Plant Board (NPB)
c/o Aurelio Posadas
PO Box 847
Elk Grove, CA 95759
Ph: (916)709-3484
Fax: (916)689-2385
E-mail: aureliop@elkgrove.net
URL: http://www.nationalplantboard.org
Contact: Kenneth J. Rauscher, Pres.
Founded: 1925. **Members:** 51. **Staff:** 1. **Budget:** $8,000. **Regional Groups:** 4. **Description:** Members represent the states of the U.S. and Puerto Rico in plant inspection, quarantine, and regulatory matters. Seeks to advance and protect agriculture, horticulture, and forestry on state, national, and international levels. **Awards:** Carl Carlson Memorial Award. **Frequency:** annual. **Type:** monetary. **Recipient:** for individuals who have distinguished themselves in the field of regulatory plant protection. **Committees:** Interstate Pest Control Compact Technical Advisory; Legislative Analysis; Quarantine and Nursery Standards and Certification. **Councils:** National Plant Board. **Affiliated With:** National Association of State Departments of Agriculture. **Publications:** *Minutes*, annual ● *Proceedings of the Annual Meeting*. **Conventions/Meetings:** annual meeting (exhibits) - always August.

5441 ■ Organization of Professional Employees of the United States Department of Agriculture (OPEDA)
c/o U.S. Department of Agriculture
PO Box 381
Washington, DC 20044
Ph: (202)720-4898
Fax: (202)720-2799
E-mail: opeda@usda.gov
URL: http://www.usda.gov/opeda
Contact: Mr. Farook Sait, Natl. Pres.
Founded: 1929. **Members:** 3,500. **Membership Dues:** employed, $52 (annual) ● retiree, $25 (annual). **Staff:** 1. **Budget:** $100,000. **Regional Groups:** 28. **Description:** Professional, scientific, technical, and administrative personnel of U.S. Department of Agriculture and in government classified grades. Seeks to provide enlightened guidance and representation before Congress, the administration and the public on matters that promote efficient and effective operation of USDA agencies. **Awards:** JW Peterson Scholarship Award. **Frequency:** annual. **Type:** scholarship. **Recipient:** for USDA employee or child/spouse of an employee ● Unsung Hero Award. **Frequency:** annual. **Type:** recognition. **Recipient:** for extraordinary service to fellow employees and/or the community and acts of bravery. **Committees:** Economic; Member Services; Professional; Public Service. **Publications:** *OPEDA News*, monthly. Newsletter. Covers industry, association and chapter news, and legislative issues. ISSN: 0277-1993. **Conventions/Meetings:** annual conference - always October.

Air Force

5442 ■ 80th Fighter Squadron Headhunters' Association
c/o Tom Reichert
5263 Winchester Ln.
Ogden, UT 84403-4329
Ph: (706)324-7360
Fax: (706)324-7360
E-mail: jaybird@80fsheadhunters.org
URL: http://80fsheadhunters.org
Contact: Col. Jay E. Riedel, Pres.
Founded: 1998. **Members:** 1,000. **Membership Dues:** individual, $10 (annual). **Multinational. Description:** Brings together the members, former members and families of the 80th Fighter Squadron of the US Air Force. Holds reunions every 18 months. **Libraries: Type:** not open to the public. **Holdings:** archival material, audio recordings, books, papers, photographs, video recordings. **Computer Services:** database, master e-mail list of 650 people ● database, master roster of 1,900 people ● mailing lists, for quarterly newsletter. **Also Known As:** The Headhunters. **Publications:** *Headhunter Headlines*, quarterly. Newsletter. Includes quarterly roster and email updates. **Price:** included in membership dues. **Circulation:** 900. **Conventions/Meetings:** Headhunter Reunion - every 18 months, spring and fall. 2008 Oct. 2-5, Destin, FL.

5443 ■ 511th Aircraft Control and Warning Group
c/o Don Simmons, Sec.
704 S Grove Rd.
Richardson, TX 75081
Ph: (972)231-6518
E-mail: japan511@aol.com
URL: http://hometown.aol.com/reunion511
Contact: Don Simmons, Sec.
Members: 1,700. **Membership Dues:** $20 (annual). **Description:** Reunion association of U.S. Air Force personnel and civilian technicians assigned to the Air Defense of Northern Japan from 1947 through 1960. Organizes members meet once a year to renew old friendships and welcome new members. **Publications:** Newsletter, quarterly. **Conventions/Meetings:** annual reunion.

Alcoholic Beverages

5444 ■ Alcohol Beverage Legislative Council (ABLC)
5101 River Rd., Ste.108
Bethesda, MD 20816-1560
Ph: (301)656-1494
Fax: (301)656-7539
E-mail: wiles@ablusa.org
URL: http://www.ablusa.org
Contact: Harry G. Wiles, Exec. Dir.
Founded: 1985. **Members:** 100. **Membership Dues:** diamond, $25,000 ● platinum, $15,000 ● gold, $10,000 ● silver, $5,000 ● bronze, $2,500 ● national associate affiliate, $1,000. **Staff:** 5. **Description:** Represents alcohol beverage retailers and retail companies. Aims to build a network of politically active retailers and a legal and legislative department to advise and assist the network on national issues affecting alcohol beverage retailers nationwide. Encourages members to communicate on behalf of the industry; provides timely information on federal issues such as national tax increases and efforts to limit the availability of alcoholic beverages. **Publications:** *ABL Leader*, monthly. Newsletter. Alternate Formats: online ● *Alcohol Beverage Legislative Council Bulletin*, periodic. Report. **Conventions/Meetings:** annual convention ● annual meeting, held in conjunction with the National Association of Beverage Retailers.

5445 ■ Joint Committee of the States (JCS)
c/o National Alcohol Beverage Control Association
4401 Ford Ave., Ste.700
Alexandria, VA 22302-1473
Ph: (703)578-4200
Fax: (703)820-3551
E-mail: info@nabca.org
URL: http://www.nabca.org
Contact: James M. Sgueo, Pres./CEO
Membership Dues: supplier, associate (national), $1,500 (annual) ● broker/allied, associate (state), $750 (annual) ● government, $500 (annual). **Description:** A committee of the National Alcohol Beverage Control Association and the national Conference of State Liquor Administrators. Undertakes studies in areas of mutual interest and concern to state liquor control agencies. **Formed by Merger of:** National Alcohol Beverage Control Association; National Conference of State Liquor Administrators. **Formerly:** (2003) Joint Committee of the States to Study Alcohol Beverage Laws. **Publications:** *NABCA Contacts Directory*. Compiles names and addresses of every member organization and its top officials. **Price:** included in membership dues; $295.00 for nonmembers ● *NABCA Survey Book*, annual. Covers operational and regulatory information from the 19 control jurisdictions. **Price:** included in membership dues; $295.00 for nonmembers. **Conventions/Meetings:** annual conference.

5446 ■ National Alcohol Beverage Control Association (NABCA)
4401 Ford Ave., Ste.700
Alexandria, VA 22302-1473
Ph: (703)578-4200
Fax: (703)820-3551
E-mail: info@nabca.org
URL: http://www.nabca.org
Contact: James M. Sgueo, Pres./CEO
Founded: 1938. **Members:** 143. **Membership Dues:** supplier (base due), national association, $1,500 (annual) ● broker, allied, state association, $750 (annual) ● governmental, $500 (annual). **Staff:** 22. **Budget:** $2,000,000. **Description:** State agencies controlling the purchase, distribution, and sale of alcoholic beverages under the control system; distillery firms and trade associations are associate members. **Publications:** *The Effects of Privatization of Alcohol Control Systems*. Report. Analyzes some of the dimensions of alcohol control and privatization. ● *NABCA Contacts Directory*, annual. Features a compilation of the names and addresses of every member organization and its top officials. **Price:** free for members; $295.00 for nonmembers, plus shipping and handling ● *NABCA Survey Book*. Includes over 35 surveys on an annual basis covering operational and regulatory information from the 19 control jurisdictions. **Price:** free for members; $295.00 for nonmembers, plus shipping and handling ● *Statistical Reports*, monthly. Includes quarterly and annual cumulation. ● Also publishes public service announcements on moderate drinking, surveys, and other materials. **Conventions/Meetings:** annual conference.

5447 ■ National Conference of State Liquor Administrators (NCSLA)
c/o Ms. Pamela D. Salario, Exec. Dir.
6183 Beau Douglas Ave.
Gonzales, LA 70737
Ph: (225)473-7209
Fax: (225)257-4498

E-mail: pamsalario@cox.net
URL: http://www.ncsla.org
Contact: Ms. Pamela D. Salario, Exec. Dir.
Founded: 1934. **Members:** 117. **Membership Dues:** regular-state agency, $225 (annual). **Budget:** $200,000. **Regional Groups:** 4. **Description:** State agencies administering liquor control laws and collecting beverage taxes under a license system rather than a state-controlled monopoly stores system. **Publications:** *NCSLA Official Directory*, annual. Membership Directory. Lists state liquor control administrators; arranged geographically. **Price:** included in membership dues. Alternate Formats: online. **Conventions/Meetings:** annual conference.

Arbitration and Mediation

5448 ■ American Arbitration Association (AAA)

1633 Broadway, 10th Fl.
New York, NY 10019
Ph: (212)716-5800
Free: (800)778-7879
Fax: (212)716-5905
E-mail: websitemail@adr.org
URL: http://www.adr.org
Contact: William K. Slate II, Pres./CEO
Founded: 1926. **Staff:** 650. **Regional Groups:** 30. **Nonmembership. Multinational. Description:** Works to achieve the resolution of disputes through the use of mediation, arbitration, democratic elections, and other voluntary methods. Provides administrative services for arbitrating, mediating, or negotiating disputes and impartial administration of elections. Maintains National Roster of Arbitrators and Mediators for referrals to parties involved in disputes. Conducts skill-building sessions to promote a more complete understanding of conflict resolution processes. **Divisions:** International Centre for Dispute Resolution. **Formed by Merger of:** Arbitration Foundation; Arbitration Society of America. **Publications:** *Dispute Resolution Journal*, quarterly. **Price:** included in membership dues; $55.00 /year for nonmembers ● Books ● Films ● Manuals ● Newsletter, monthly. Includes reports on labor arbitration in private industry, schools, and government. Contains semiannual index and summaries of cases. **Price:** $90.00/year. **Circulation:** 3,500. **Conventions/Meetings:** seminar ● workshop.

5449 ■ American Bar Association Section of Dispute Resolution (ABASODR)

740 15th St. NW
Washington, DC 20005-1019
Ph: (202)662-1680
Fax: (202)662-1683
E-mail: dispute@abanet.org
URL: http://www.abanet.org/dispute
Contact: Lela Love, Chair-Elect
Founded: 1987. **Members:** 9,000. **Membership Dues:** attorney, $45 ● associate, $35. **Staff:** 10. **Description:** A section of the American Bar Association (see separate entry). Lawyers, judges, law professors, and other legal professionals and laypersons. Serves as an information clearinghouse on dispute resolution; provides technical services; coordinates actions of dispute resolution programs worldwide. Conducts workshops at legal conferences; aids law schools in establishing sound dispute resolution curricula. Encourages the participation of state and local bar associations in dispute resolution activities. **Libraries: Type:** reference. **Holdings:** 500; books, periodicals. **Subjects:** dispute resolution mechanisms. **Formerly:** (1981) American Bar Association Committee on the Resolution of Minor Disputes; (1987) American Bar Association Special Committee on Dispute Resolution; (1993) American Bar Association Standing Committee on Dispute Resolution. **Publications:** *Confidentiality in Mediation*. Monographs ● *Dispute Resolution Magazine*, quarterly. **Price:** included in membership dues; $30.00 /year for nonmembers. ISSN: 0271-2709 ● *Dispute Resolution Program Directory 1993*, annual. **Price:** $60.00. **Circulation:** 3,000. **Advertising:** accepted. Alternate Formats: online ● *Law School Directory*, periodic ● *Legislative Updates*, periodic ● *Mediation: The Coming of Age* ● *1989 Federal and State DR Legislative Monograph*, periodic. **Price:** $30.00. **Circulation:** 2,000. **Conventions/Meetings:** annual conference ● annual meeting, held in conjunction with ABA ● semiannual meeting - always spring and fall.

5450 ■ Association for Conflict Resolution (ACR)

1015 18th St. NW, Ste.1150
Washington, DC 20036
Ph: (202)667-9700 (301)365-9307
Fax: (202)464-9720
E-mail: acr@acrnet.org
URL: http://www.acrnet.org
Contact: Linda Baron, Interim Exec. Dir.
Founded: 2001. **Members:** 6,500. **Membership Dues:** individual, $195 (annual) ● advanced practitioner, $230 (annual) ● youth (grades K-12), $35 (annual) ● affiliate associate, $95 (annual) ● practitioner, educator, researcher, $205 (annual) ● student, $80 (annual) ● retiree, $50 (annual) ● organization (based on size and status), $325-$1,400 (annual). **Staff:** 11. **Regional Groups:** 21. **Multinational. Description:** Professional organization dedicated to enhance the practice and public understanding of conflict resolution. **Telecommunication Services:** electronic mail, hlanier@wmata.com. **Sections:** Commercial; Community; Consumer; Court; Criminal Justice; Crisis Negotiation; Education; Environmental/Public Policy; Family; Health Care; International; Ombudsman; Online Dispute Resolution; Organizational Conflict Management; Spirituality; Training; Workplace. **Formed by Merger of:** (2001) Society of Professionals in Dispute Resolution; (2001) Conflict Resolution Education Network; (2001) Academy of Family Mediators. **Publications:** *ACResolution*, quarterly. Journal ● *Conflict Resolution Quarterly*. Journal. **Conventions/Meetings:** annual conference and seminar.

5451 ■ Center for Dispute Settlement (CDS)

1666 Connecticut Ave. NW
Washington, DC 20009-1039
Ph: (202)265-9572
Fax: (202)332-3951
E-mail: cconnelly@cdsusa.org
URL: http://www.cdsusa.org
Contact: Linda R. Singer, Pres.
Founded: 1971. **Staff:** 14. **Description:** Seeks to design, implement, and evaluate programs that apply mediation and other dispute resolution techniques to government, interpersonal, community, business, and institutional problems. Manages complaint center and operates service for the mediation of disputes. Offers consulting and training services. **Formerly:** (1976) Center for Correctional Justice; (1987) Center for Community Justice. **Conventions/Meetings:** annual Mediation for the Professional Advanced Mediation Techniques - meeting.

5452 ■ Center for Medical Ethics and Mediation

PO Box 86110
San Diego, CA 92138-6110
Ph: (619)296-7268
Free: (888)614-3832
Fax: (619)296-7268
E-mail: cmem@flash.net
URL: http://www.cmem.org
Contact: Robert J. Wagener, Pres.
Founded: 1993. **Members:** 9. **Membership Dues:** individual, $45 (annual) ● group, $65 (annual) ● student, senior, $25 (annual). **Budget:** $90,000. **Description:** Provides training, education, and consultation services to health and legal professionals, health care consumers, and the general public in matters related to health, health care, law, alternative dispute resolution, and ethics. Trains institutional ethics committees to employ alternative forms of dispute resolution in ethics consultations, including mediation and other collaborative facilitation models. Conducts research and educational programs. **Libraries: Type:** reference; by appointment only. **Holdings:** 1,000; audiovisuals, books, clippings, periodicals. **Subjects:** medical ethics, alternative dispute resolution (mediation). **Computer Services:** Mailing lists. **Publications:** *Pontis*, quarterly. Bulletin. Contains conference announcements, editorials, and articles on medical issues. **Advertising:** accepted ● Brochure. Describes the center's mission, training programs, and faculty. **Conventions/Meetings:** conference and board meeting.

5453 ■ General Arbitration Council of the Textile and Apparel Industries (GAC)

c/o American Arbitration Association
335 Madison Ave., 10th Fl.
New York, NY 10017-4605
Ph: (212)716-5800
Free: (800)778-7879
Fax: (212)716-5905
E-mail: websitemail@adr.org
URL: http://www.adr.org
Contact: L'Tanya Keith-Robinson, Dir.
Founded: 1930. **Members:** 15. **Staff:** 7. **Description:** Serves the needs of the workers of the textile and apparel industries. **Committees:** Rules and Qualifications of Arbitrators. **Formerly:** (1983) General Arbitration Council of the Textile Industry. **Conventions/Meetings:** annual meeting - usually February, New York City.

5454 ■ Institute for International Mediation and Conflict Resolution (IIMCR)

1424 K St. NW, Ste.650
Washington, DC 20005
Ph: (202)347-2042
Fax: (202)347-2440
E-mail: info@iimcr.org
Contact: Sergio Sanchez, Pres.
Founded: 1995. **Staff:** 6. **Budget:** $500,000. **Languages:** Dutch, English, French, German, Spanish. **Description:** Aims to put dedicated students and young professionals from all parts of the world in direct contact with international leaders, policy makers, and experts in negotiation and conflict resolution through seminars and symposia. **Libraries: Type:** not open to the public. **Holdings:** 1,000. **Subjects:** international politics, conflict resolution. **Computer Services:** database, listserver. **Conventions/Meetings:** annual symposium - July/August.

5455 ■ Institute for Mediation and Conflict Resolution (IMCR)

384 E 149th St., Ste.330
Bronx, NY 10455
Ph: (718)585-1190
E-mail: info@imcr.org
URL: http://www.imcr.org
Contact: Stephen E. Slate, Exec. Dir.
Founded: 1969. **Languages:** English, Spanish. **Description:** Agency, supported by foundation grants and contracts, to which community disputants can turn for assistance in resolving differences on a voluntary basis. Seeks to: mediate community conflicts; train people in mediation techniques and conflict resolution skills; design dispute settlement systems. Facilitates discussion on current trends in dispute resolution. **Telecommunication Services:** electronic mail, seslate19@imcr.org. **Also Known As:** IMCR Dispute Resolution Center. **Publications:** *F.Y.I.*, quarterly. Newsletter. **Conventions/Meetings:** quarterly Dispute Resolution Forum - meeting.

5456 ■ Inter-American Commercial Arbitration Commission (IACAC)

c/o American Arbitration Association
140 W 51st St.
New York, NY 10020-1201
Ph: (212)484-4000
Fax: (212)765-4874
URL: http://www.adr.org
Contact: William K. Slate III, Dir.
Founded: 1934. **Staff:** 3. **National Groups:** 17. **Languages:** English, Spanish. **Description:** Companies, businessmen, bankers, lawyers, investors, and interested others in 34 North and South American countries. Arbitrates or negotiates adjustment of international trade controversies. Promotes effective

national arbitration laws in member countries of the Organization of American States. Conducts promotional and educational programs. **Additional Websites:** http://www.sice.oas.org/dispute/comarb/iacac/iacac1e.asp. **Conventions/Meetings:** biennial Inter-American Conference on International Commercial Arbitration - international conference.

5457 ■ International Centre for Settlement of Investment Disputes (ICSID)
1818 H St. NW
Washington, DC 20433
Ph: (202)458-1534
Fax: (202)522-2615
URL: http://www.worldbank.org/icsid
Contact: Ana Palacio, Sec. Gen.
Founded: 1966. **Members:** 140. **Description:** Countries that are members of the International Bank for Reconstruction and Development, or, by invitation, parties to the Statute of the International Court of Justice. Provides facilities for the conciliation and arbitration of investment disputes between members and nationals of other members in accordance with the provisions of the Convention on the Settlement of Investment Disputes between States and Nationals of Other States. Collects and disseminates information relating to legislation, international agreements, and other investment matters. **Publications:** *Contracting States and Measures Taken by Them for the Purpose of the Convention*, periodic. Report. **Price:** free ● *ICSID Review: Foreign Investment Law Journal*, semiannual. Contains information on laws and practices relating to foreign investment. **Price:** $70.00/year for those in OECD country; $35.00/year for others. **Advertising:** accepted ● *International Centre for Settlement of Investment Disputes—Annual Report* (in English, French, and Spanish). **Price:** free ● *Investment Laws of the World*, periodic. Books. Contains texts of basic investment laws of over 90 countries. **Price:** $995.00/set ● *Investment Treaties*, annual. Books. Provides texts of selected bilateral promotion and protection treaties entered into since 1960 by developed and developing countries. **Price:** $695.00/set ● *News From ICSID*, semiannual. Newsletter. Covers disputes before the centre and centre activities. **Price:** free ● *Rules and Regulations* (in English, French, and Spanish). Handbook. **Price:** free. **Conventions/Meetings:** annual meeting, held in conjunction with American Arbitration Association and International Chamber of Commerce.

5458 ■ Mediators Without Borders (MWB)
1807 Jancey St.
Pittsburgh, PA 15206-1065
Ph: (412)441-1151
Fax: (412)441-1152
E-mail: mediatorswithoutborders@gmail.com
URL: http://www.mediatorswithoutborders.org
Contact: Kenneth Cloke, Founder/Pres.
Founded: 2006. **Membership Dues:** mediator, $360 (annual) ● citizen supporter, $36 (annual) ● student supporter, $18 (annual). **Description:** Brings together mediators to collaborate and participate in mitigating violent conflict and organizing alternative approaches to expressing, negotiating, and resolving political, economic, social, ethnic, and religious differences. Fosters collaborative initiatives in partnership with local indigenous efforts. Assists in building and sustaining local capacity and training in ways that encourage forgiveness and reconciliation and integrate peace with justice. **Publications:** Newsletter, biweekly. Alternate Formats: online.

5459 ■ National Academy of Arbitrators (NAA)
1 N Main St., Ste.412
Cortland, NY 13045
Ph: (607)756-8363 (516)621-6960
Fax: (607)756-8365
E-mail: naa@naarb.org
URL: http://www.naarb.org
Contact: Barbara Zausner, Pres.
Founded: 1947. **Members:** 700. **Staff:** 3. **Regional Groups:** 17. **National Groups:** 17. **Description:** Labor-management arbitrators. Works to improve general understanding of the nature and use of arbitration as a means of settling labor disputes. Conducts research and educational programs. **Committees:** Ethics and Grievances; International Studies; Law and Legislation; Legal Affairs; Legal Representation; Professional Responsibility and Grievances; Public Employment Disputes Settlement; Research and Education. **Publications:** Proceedings, annual ● Newsletter, quarterly. **Conventions/Meetings:** Fall Education Conference (exhibits) - 2008 Oct. 3-5, Seattle, WA ● annual meeting (exhibits).

5460 ■ National Association for Community Mediation (NAFCM)
PO Box 3263
Washington, DC 20010
Ph: (202)545-8866
Fax: (202)545-8873
E-mail: jordway@nafcm.org
URL: http://www.nafcm.org
Contact: Irvin Foster, Exec. Dir.
Founded: 1993. **Members:** 650. **Membership Dues:** individual, $30 (annual) ● program (based on annual budget), $25-$300 (annual). **Staff:** 4. **Description:** Supports the maintenance and growth of community-based mediation programs and processes. Presents a voice in appropriate policy making, legislative, professional, and other arenas. Encourages the development and sharing of resources for these efforts. **Libraries: Type:** reference. **Holdings:** articles, books. **Subjects:** mediation, conflict resolution. **Awards:** Mini-grants. **Frequency:** semiannual. **Type:** grant ● Volunteer Mediator of the Year. **Frequency:** biennial. **Type:** recognition. **Recipient:** for an outstanding volunteer mediator. **Computer Services:** Online services, listserv. **Programs:** Mini-Grant; National AmeriCorps. **Projects:** National Research. **Publications:** *Community Dispute Resolution, Empowerment, and Social Justice: The Origin, History and Future of a Movement*. Book. **Price:** $16.95 for members; $19.95 for nonmembers ● *Community Mediation*, annual. Directory. Describes over 250 community mediation programs across the country. **Price:** free for members; $20.00 for nonmembers ● *Community Mediation Center Self-Assessment Manual*. **Price:** $25.00/copy ● *The Community Mediator*, quarterly. Newsletter. **Price:** included in membership dues. **Advertising:** accepted. Alternate Formats: online ● *Practice Notes*. Articles. Contains tips, insights and directions for further reading on topics ranging from learning styles to preventing volunteer burnout. **Price:** $5.00/copy.

5461 ■ National Center for Mediation Education (NCME)
1160 Spa Rd., No. 1B
Annapolis, MD 21403-1022
Ph: (410)280-8888
Free: (800)781-7500
Fax: (410)295-9190
E-mail: makranitz@aol.com
Contact: Martin Kranitz, Dir.
Founded: 1984. **Members:** 1,500. **Staff:** 4. **Budget:** $35,000. **Description:** Serves as a center that trains mediators for their role in separation and divorce cases. Provides instruction to various professionals, including lawyers and mental health and social workers; acts as a clearinghouse for information and referrals. Maintains speakers' bureau. Offers basic and advanced professional training in structured mediation for separation and divorce cases. **Divisions:** Referral; Standards; Training. **Publications:** *Starting Your Own Mediation Practice: A Workbook*. **Price:** $39.95 plus shipping and handling ● Distributes a disk of forms for mediation practice from workbook. **Conventions/Meetings:** annual Advanced Mediation Training - workshop ● quarterly Basic Mediation Training - workshop.

5462 ■ Professional Mediation Association (PMA)
1645 Martha Leeville Rd.
Lebanon, TN 37090
E-mail: contact@promediation.com
URL: http://www.promediation.com
Membership Dues: general (professional, institutional or corporate), $75 (annual). **Description:** Facilitates coordination for the development of alternative dispute resolution and mediation. Enhances the standards and training in all areas of alternative dispute resolution. Provides referrals to industry, agencies and individuals. **Computer Services:** database, listing of mediators ● information services, mediation resources ● mailing lists, of members.

5463 ■ Society of Maritime Arbitrators (SMA)
30 Broad St., 7th Fl.
New York, NY 10004-2304
Ph: (212)344-2400
Fax: (212)344-2402
E-mail: info@smany.org
URL: http://www.smany.org
Contact: Klaus C.J. Mordhorst, Pres.
Founded: 1963. **Members:** 130. **Description:** Helps settle disputes arising from contracts for any and all movements by water or involving shipbuilding and repair; maintains uniformity in U.S. maritime arbitration proceedings. Holds arbitration workshop. **Publications:** *Arbitration Award Service*, bimonthly. **Price:** $495.00/year ● *The Arbitrator*, quarterly. Alternate Formats: online ● *Maritime Arbitration Rules*. **Conventions/Meetings:** annual International Congress of Maritime Arbitrators.

Architecture

5464 ■ Environmental Design Research Association (EDRA)
PO Box 7146
Edmond, OK 73083-7146
Ph: (405)330-4863
Fax: (405)330-4150
E-mail: edra@edra.org
URL: http://edra.org
Contact: Janet Singer, Exec. Dir.
Founded: 1968. **Members:** 600. **Membership Dues:** regular, $125 (annual) ● student (full-time), retiree, $65 (annual) ● sustaining (wayfinder), $200 (annual) ● sustaining (placemaker), $400 (annual). **Staff:** 3. **Budget:** $150,000. **Description:** Represents design professionals, social scientists, students, educators, and environmental managers. Advances the art and science of environmental design research. Improves understanding of the relationships between people and their surroundings. Works to create environments responsive to human needs. Promotes design and building processes that incorporate more information about user requirements. Examines the effects of designed environments on family organization, worker productivity, and the recovery rate of hospital patients. Encourages the education of designers, clients, and users about the behavioral consequences of designed environments. **Libraries: Type:** open to the public. **Holdings:** 231. **Subjects:** environmental. **Awards:** EDRA Career Award. **Frequency:** annual. **Type:** recognition. **Recipient:** for sustained contribution to the field. **Computer Services:** Mailing lists, for a fee. **Committees:** Education; Information; Interdisciplinary Relations; Professional Practice. **Publications:** *Design Research News*, quarterly. Newsletter. **Price:** $24.00/year in U.S.; $28.00/year outside U.S. **Advertising:** accepted ● *Proceedings of Annual Meeting* ● Monograph, annual. **Conventions/Meetings:** annual Linking Differences/Defining Actions - conference (exhibits).

5465 ■ International Institute of Site Planning (IISP)
715 G St. SE
Washington, DC 20003
Ph: (202)546-2322
Fax: (202)546-2722
E-mail: iisitep@aol.com
Contact: Beatriz de Winthuysen Coffin, Dir.
Founded: 1976. **Languages:** English, Spanish. **Nonmembership. Multinational. Description:** Acts as a liaison among professionals by promoting stimulating and creative correspondence concerning development and design of sites. Directs research and provides information on site planning; conducts study/travel programs in the U.S. and abroad. **Libraries:**

Type: reference. **Holdings:** 175. **Subjects:** site planning, landscape architecture, civil engineering. **Publications:** *Gardens of Spain*. Catalog ● *In Situ*, quarterly. Bulletin. **Price:** $20.00/year. **Conventions/Meetings:** periodic lecture and seminar (exhibits).

5466 ■ National Council of Architectural Registration Boards (NCARB)
1801 K St. NW, Ste.1100-K
Washington, DC 20006-1310
Ph: (202)783-6500
Fax: (202)783-0290
E-mail: customerservice@ncarb.org
URL: http://www.ncarb.org
Contact: Douglas K. Engebretson, Pres.
Founded: 1919. **Members:** 55. **Membership Dues:** intern/ARE applicant, $50 (annual) ● registered architect, $150 (annual). **Staff:** 65. **Budget:** $11,500,000. **Regional Groups:** 6. **State Groups:** 55. **Description:** Federation of state boards for the registration of architects in the United States, District of Columbia, Puerto Rico, Virgin Islands, Guam, and the Northern Mariana Islands. **Libraries: Type:** reference. **Holdings:** archival material, books, business records. **Awards:** NCARB Prize for Creative Integration of Practice and Education in the Academy. **Frequency:** annual. **Type:** monetary. **Committees:** Architect Registration Examination; Education; Intern Development; International Relations; Member Board Executives; Procedures and Documents; Professional Conduct; Professional Development. **Publications:** *Architect Overseas Practice Standard*. Alternate Formats: online ● *ARE Study Guide: Graphic Divisions*. **Price:** $50.00 plus shipping and handling ● *ARE Study Guide: Multiple Choice Divisions*. **Price:** $50.00 plus shipping and handling ● *Cracking the Codes*. Newsletter. **Price:** $270.00 for members; $200.00 for current NCARB certificate holders ● *Direct Connection*, semiannual. Newsletter ● *Energy-Conscious Architecture*. **Price:** $195.00 for members; $125.00 for current NCARB certificate holders ● *Fire Safety in Buildings*. **Price:** $195.00 for members; $125.00 for current NCARB certificate holders ● *Indoor Environment*. **Price:** $195.00 for members; $125.00 for current NCARB certificate holders ● *Low-Slope Roofing I*. **Price:** $195.00 for members; $125.00 for current NCARB certificate holders ● *Low-Slope Roofing II*. **Price:** $245.00 for members; $175.00 for current NCARB certificate holders ● *Member Board Requirements Chart*, annual. **Price:** free. Alternate Formats: online ● *Member Board Roster*, annual. Membership Directory ● *Professional Conduct*. **Price:** $195.00 for members; $125.00 for current NCARB certificate holders ● *Seismic Mitigation*. **Price:** $195.00 for members; $125.00 for current NCARB certificate holders ● *Subsurface Conditions*. **Price:** $195.00 for members; $125.00 for current NCARB certificate holders ● *Sustainable Design*. **Price:** $195.00 for members; $125.00 for current NCARB certificate holders ● *Why Buildings Fail*. **Price:** $195.00 for members; $125.00 for current NCARB certificate holders ● *Wind Forces*. **Price:** $245.00 for members; $175.00 for current NCARB certificate holders ● Annual Report, annual. **Conventions/Meetings:** annual conference and meeting.

Armed Forces

5467 ■ 107th Engineer Association
900 Palms Ave.
Ishpeming, MI 49849-1064
Ph: (906)486-8741
Fax: (906)486-4946
E-mail: secretary@107engineers.org
URL: http://www.107thEngineers.org
Contact: Thomas Perry, Sec.
Founded: 1960. **Members:** 800. **Membership Dues:** 107th Engr. (c) Bn, Regt; 254th Engr. (c) Bn; 522nd Engr. (c) Co., 112th Engr. Reg., $5 (annual). **Staff:** 4. **Local Groups:** 1. **Description:** Promotes the military interest of and pursues patriotic obligation to the USA. Encourages social relations between all members, past and present. Compiles lists of names and addresses of men eligible to the association membership. Holds conventions for the purpose of renewing old military friendships and promoting new. **Libraries: Type:** reference. **Holdings:** archival material, articles, books, periodicals. **Subjects:** military history of the 107th Engineer Battalion since 1881, World War II for 254th Engineers, 522nd Engineers, 112th Engineers. **Publications:** *Bull Sheet*, annual. Newsletter. Features 18-20 pages with information about next reunion, military history, stories, battles, and pictures. **Circulation:** 1,000. Alternate Formats: online. **Conventions/Meetings:** annual reunion - 2008 Aug. 15-17, Baraga, MI.

5468 ■ USS Nitro (AE-2/AE-23) Association
c/o Robert F. Eberlein, VP/Founder
12215 Ashland St.
Granger, IN 46530-9654
Ph: (574)277-3128
E-mail: ebb23@aol.com
URL: http://www.ussnitro.org
Contact: Robert F. Eberlein, VP/Founder
Membership Dues: crew, $24 (annual) ● associate, $14 (annual). **Description:** Committed to uniting former crewmembers who served aboard the U.S. Navy ships named NITRO. **Publications:** Membership Directory. **Price:** included in membership dues ● Newsletter, quarterly. **Price:** included in membership dues. **Conventions/Meetings:** annual reunion - 2008 June 19-22, Branson, MO.

Army

5469 ■ Army Engineer Association (AEA)
PO Box 30260
Alexandria, VA 22310-8260
Ph: (703)428-7084 (703)428-6049
Fax: (703)428-6043
E-mail: xd@armyengineer.com
URL: http://www.armyengineer.com
Contact: Ret. Col. Jack O'Neill, Exec. Dir.
Membership Dues: regular, $25 (annual) ● junior rank (15 months), $15 ● life, $300 ● large firm (with more than 250 employees), $500 (annual) ● small firm (with less than 250 employees), $250 (annual). **Description:** Promotes the history and traditions of Army engineering. Recognizes the service dedication of Army engineers. Provides programs in support of the Army and the Army Engineer Regiment. **Awards:** ACES Award. **Frequency:** annual. **Type:** recognition. **Recipient:** for best Combat Engineer Squad Leader in every Combat Engineer Battalion ● Best Platoon Leader. **Frequency:** annual. **Type:** recognition. **Recipient:** for outstanding Engineer Lieutenant Platoon Leader ● Caterpillar Silver Star deFleury. **Frequency:** annual. **Type:** medal. **Recipient:** for officially retired members of the Regiment who retired from service between 1945 and 1975 ● SUPER SAPPER Award. **Frequency:** annual. **Type:** recognition. **Recipient:** for best Engineer Soldier in every Engineer Battalion. **Computer Services:** database, listings of military units ● information services, veteran's resources. **Publications:** *The Army Engineer*, biennial. Magazine. Contains articles about functions, activities and units. **Advertising:** accepted.

Asian

5470 ■ Asian American Justice Center (AAJC)
1140 Connecticut Ave. NW, Ste.1200
Washington, DC 20036
Ph: (202)296-2300
Fax: (202)296-2300
E-mail: veng@advancingequality.org
URL: http://www.advancingequality.org
Contact: Mr. Vincent Eng Esq., Deputy Dir.
Founded: 1991. **Staff:** 20. **Budget:** $3,000,000. **Regional Groups:** 3. **Local Groups:** 100. **Nonmembership. Description:** Works to advance the human and civil rights of Asian Americans through advocacy, public policy, public education, and litigation. Focuses its work to promote civic engagement, to forge strong and safe communities, and to create an inclusive society in communities on a local, regional, and national level. Focuses on the issues about the Asian American community such as: affirmative action, anti-Asian violence prevention/race relations, census, immigrant rights, immigration, language access, and voting rights. **Awards:** American Courage Award. **Frequency:** annual. **Type:** recognition. **Recipient:** to an individual, company, or organization that has shown extraordinary courage or commitment to the cause of civil rights ● Bridge Builder Award. **Frequency:** annual. **Type:** recognition. **Recipient:** to an individual or community based organization that has developed an innovative approach to successful community empowerment. **Formerly:** (2006) National Asian Pacific American Legal Consortium.

Attorneys

5471 ■ American Academy of Adoption Attorneys (AAAA)
PO Box 33053
Washington, DC 20033
Ph: (202)832-2222
E-mail: info@adoptionattorneys.org
URL: http://www.adoptionattorneys.org
Contact: Herbert A. Brail, Pres.
Founded: 1990. **Members:** 330. **Description:** Attorneys who practice or have otherwise distinguished themselves in the field of adoption law. Promotes the reform of adoption laws and disseminating information on ethical adoption practices. Offers educational and charitable programs and a speakers' bureau. **Computer Services:** Mailing lists, of members. **Publications:** *Agency Directory*. Alternate Formats: online ● Membership Directory. Alternate Formats: online ● Newsletter. **Conventions/Meetings:** annual convention and board meeting.

5472 ■ American Academy of Appellate Lawyers (AAAL)
15245 Shady Grove Rd., Ste.130
Rockville, MD 20850
Ph: (301)258-9210
Fax: (301)990-9771
E-mail: info@appellateacademy.org
URL: http://www.appellateacademy.org
Contact: Ms. Beth Palys CAE, Exec. Dir.
Founded: 1990. **Members:** 288. **Membership Dues:** individual, $350 (annual). **Staff:** 4. **Description:** Promotes the improvement of appellate advocacy and the administration of the appellate courts. **Awards:** Eisenberg Prize. **Frequency:** annual. **Type:** monetary. **Recipient:** for best article on appellate practice and procedure. **Publications:** *The Appellate Advocate*, quarterly. Newsletter ● Reports. **Conventions/Meetings:** semiannual meeting - always fall and spring.

5473 ■ American Academy of Estate Planning Attorneys (AAEPA)
6050 Santo Rd., Ste.240
San Diego, CA 92124
Ph: (858)453-2128
Free: (800)846-1555
Fax: (858)874-5804
E-mail: information@aaepa.com
URL: http://www.aaepa.com
Contact: Robert Armstrong, Pres.
Description: Attorneys providing estate planning services. Fosters excellence in estate planning; promotes successful practice of estate planning. Provides products, services, and technical support to members; serves as a clearinghouse on estate planning; conducts continuing education courses. **Programs:** Deed Processing Assistance. **Publications:** *Conference Call*. Audiotapes. Alternate Formats: online.

5474 ■ American Association of Visually Impaired Attorneys (AAVIA)
c/o American Council of the Blind
1155 15th St. NW, Ste.1004
Washington, DC 20005

Ph: (202)467-5081
Free: (800)424-8666
Fax: (202)467-5085
E-mail: austingl@bellsouth.net
URL: http://www.visuallyimpairedattorneys.org
Contact: Ellen Telker, Pres.
Founded: 1969. **Members:** 250. **Description:** Blind lawyers and blind law students. Seeks to: provide a forum for discussion of the special problems encountered by blind persons licensed to practice law and by blind students training for the legal profession; protect the interests of blind members of the legal profession; acquire, preserve, and maintain law libraries and periodicals of special interest to blind lawyers and blind law students; promote the production of and disseminate information concerning legal materials in Braille or recorded form; advance the legal profession. Conducts educational research, and professional training programs. Operates speakers' bureau. Maintains index of legal material in Braille and on cassette; reproduces items from the *American Bar Journal* and related publications on cassettes. **Committees:** Employment; Law Student Activities; Library. **Affiliated With:** American Council of the Blind. **Formerly:** (2004) American Blind Lawyers Association. **Publications:** Newsletter, bimonthly. Alternate Formats: magnetic tape. **Conventions/Meetings:** annual meeting (exhibits) - always July.

5475 ■ American Bar Association (ABA)
321 N Clark St.
Chicago, IL 60610
Ph: (312)988-5000 (312)988-5522
Free: (800)285-2221
E-mail: askaba@abanet.org
URL: http://www.abanet.org
Contact: Karen J. Mathis, Pres.
Founded: 1878. **Members:** 400,000. **Membership Dues:** lawyer, $125 (annual) ● law student, $25 (annual) ● associate, $175 (annual). **Staff:** 800. **Budget:** $65,000,000. **Description:** Attorneys in good standing of the bar of any state. Conducts research and educational projects and activities to: encourage professional improvement; provide public services; improve the administration of civil and criminal justice; increase the availability of legal services to the public. Sponsors Law Day USA. Administers numerous standing and special committees such as Committee on Soviet and East European Law, providing seminars and newsletters. Operates 25 sections, including Criminal Justice, Economics of Law Practice, and Family Law. Sponsors essay competitions. Maintains library. **Awards: Type:** recognition. **Computer Services:** database, AMBAR. **Commissions:** Mentally Disabled; National Institute of Justice; Public Understanding of Law; Reduce Court Costs and Delays. **Publications:** *ABA Journal*, monthly. Includes association activities and developments in law and the profession. **Price:** included in membership dues; $48.00/year for non-lawyers. ISSN: 0747-0088 ● *Administrative Law Review*, quarterly. Journal. Covers developments in the field of administrative law. **Price:** included in membership dues; $35.00/year for non-lawyers. ISSN: 0001-8368 ● *American Bar Association—Washington Letter*, monthly. Newsletter. Reports on congressional activity affecting legislation of interest to lawyers and the Bar. **Price:** $21.00 /year for members; $26.00 /year for nonmembers. ISSN: 0516-9968 ● *Antitrust*, 3/year. Magazine. Covers developments in antitrust law; contains Antitrust Law Section calendar and list of upcoming publications. **Price:** included in membership dues; $22.00/year for non-lawyers ● *Antitrust Law Journal*, quarterly. Includes proceedings of Antitrust Law Section meetings, section reports, and positions on legislation, as well as content of national institutes. **Price:** $30.00/ year for non-lawyers ● *Barrister*, quarterly. Magazine. Contains general articles on the legal profession, the law, and society. **Price:** included in membership dues; $19.95/year for non-lawyers. ISSN: 0094-5277. **Advertising:** accepted ● *The Brief*, quarterly. Magazine. Contains news and feature articles on current events in the fields of tort and insurance law. **Price:** included in membership dues; $18.00/year for non-lawyers. ISSN: 0273-0995 ● *Business Lawyer*, quarterly. Journal. Covers current legal topics and section programs relating to business and financial law. **Price:** included in membership dues; $28.00/ year for non-lawyers. ISSN: 0007-6899 ● *China Law Reporter*, quarterly. Journal. Covers issues of interest to lawyers and scholars concerned with business and law in the People's Republic of China. **Price:** $43.00/ year ● *Communications Law*, quarterly. Newsletter. Includes reports on activities of the ABA Forum on Communication Law. **Price:** included in membership dues; $15.00/year for non-lawyers. ISSN: 0737-7622 ● *The Compleat Lawyer*, quarterly. Magazine. Provides articles on substantive areas of law, news of the ABA General Practice Section council and committees, and updates on legislative actions. **Price:** included in membership dues; $23.00/year for non-lawyers. ISSN: 0741-9066 ● *Criminal Justice*, quarterly. Magazine. Covers various aspects of criminal law and reporting on legislative, policymaking, and educational activities of the section. **Price:** included in membership dues; $33.00/year for non-lawyers. ISSN: 0887-7785 ● *The Entertainment and Sports Lawyer*, quarterly. Newsletter. Reports on the activities of the ABA Forum on Entertainment and Sports Industries and recent developments in the field. **Price:** included in membership dues; $30.00/year for non-lawyers. ISSN: 0732-1880 ● *Family Advocate*, quarterly. Journal. Provides practical information on divorce, mental health, juveniles, custody, support, and problems of the aging; covers current trends. **Price:** included in membership dues; $37.00/year for non-lawyers. ISSN: 0163-710X ● *Family Law Quarterly*. Journal. Covers judicial decisions, legislation, and taxation in regard to divorce, custody, support, aging, and other issues. **Price:** included in membership dues; $34.00/year for non-lawyers. ISSN: 0014-729X ● *Franchise Law Journal*, quarterly. Provides information on current legal trends in franchising and reports on the activities of the ABA Forum on Franchising. **Price:** included in membership dues; $31.00/ year for non-lawyers. ISSN: 8756-7962 ● *Human Rights*, 3/year. Magazine. Covers human rights, and individual rights and responsibilities. **Price:** included in membership dues; $18.00/year for non-lawyers. ISSN: 0046-8185 ● *International Lawyer*, quarterly. Journal. Covers the fields of international business transactions, public international law, and comparative law. **Price:** included in membership dues; $31. 00/year for non-lawyers. ISSN: 0020-7810 ● *The Judges' Journal*, quarterly. Guides judges and lawyers on successful court innovations and major jurisprudential issues. **Price:** included in membership dues; $23.00/year for non-lawyers. ISSN: 0047-2972 ● *Jurimetrics: Journal of Law, Science and Technology*, quarterly. Covers legal issues in science and technology. **Price:** included in membership dues; $29.00/year for non-lawyers. ISSN: 0022-6793. **Conventions/Meetings:** annual meeting ● annual meeting - always midyear.

5476 ■ American Bar Association Center for Professional Responsibility (ABACPR)
321 N Clark St., 15th Fl.
Chicago, IL 60610-4714
Ph: (312)988-5325
Free: (800)285-2221
Fax: (312)988-5491
E-mail: cpr@abanet.org
URL: http://www.abanet.org/cpr
Founded: 1978. **Membership Dues:** lawyer, associate, $100 (annual) ● law student, $20 (annual). **Staff:** 26. **Description:** Supports the work of committees of the American Bar Association involved in the design and implementation of policy in the fields of legal ethics, professional discipline and regulation, professionalism, unauthorized practice of law, and client security funds. Maintains liaison with courts, disciplinary agencies, and advisory committees in each state. Operates reference library on lawyer discipline. **Computer Services:** database, national discipline data bank. **Publications:** *The Professional Lawyer*, quarterly. Magazine. Features updates and analysis on professional responsibility law and programs. **Price:** included in membership dues; $40.00 for nonmembers. **Conventions/Meetings:** annual National Conference of Professional Responsibility - 2009 May 27-30, Chicago, IL.

5477 ■ American Bar Association Young Lawyers Division (ABAYLD)
321 N Clark
Chicago, IL 60610
Ph: (312)988-5614
Fax: (312)988-6231
E-mail: mccallj@staff.abanet.org
URL: http://www.abanet.org/yld
Contact: Jill Eckert McCall, Staff Dir.
Founded: 1934. **Members:** 140,000. **Staff:** 8. **Budget:** $1,600,000. **Description:** Members of the American Bar Association who are under the age of 36 or have been accepted to the bar for 5 years or less. Provides information to lawyers who are beginning their legal careers; assists state bar associations to facilitate public service initiatives. **Publications:** *The Affiliate*, bimonthly. Newsletters. **Circulation:** 2,000 ● *Committee Newsletter*, periodic. Covers specific legal topics. ● *The Young Lawyer*, monthly. Newsletter. **Price:** free for members; $29.95 for nonmembers. ISSN: 1090-6878. Alternate Formats: online ● Membership Directory. Contains listing of all officers, constitutional representatives, directors, coordinators, boards, teams and liaisons. Alternate Formats: online. **Conventions/Meetings:** semiannual Affiliate Outreach National Public Service Conferences, in conjunction with ABA ● semiannual meeting and conference, held in conjunction with ABA Annual and mid-Winter Meetings.

5478 ■ American Board of Certification (ABC)
101 2nd St. SE, Ste.904
Cedar Rapids, IA 52401
Ph: (319)365-2222
Fax: (319)363-0127
E-mail: certification@abcworld.org
URL: http://www.abcworld.org
Contact: Dian Gilmore, Exec. Dir.
Founded: 1998. **Members:** 1,000. **Staff:** 2. **Description:** Attorneys engaged in the practice of bankruptcy and creditors' rights law. Seeks to improve the quality of bankruptcy and creditors' rights law bars. Develops standards of training, ethics, and practice for members; certifies qualifying attorneys in the fields of business bankruptcy, consumer bankruptcy, and creditors' rights law. **Publications:** Annual Report, annual. Alternate Formats: online.

5479 ■ American College of Real Estate Lawyers (ACREL)
1 Central Plz.
11300 Rockville Pike, Ste.903
Rockville, MD 20852
Ph: (301)816-9811
Fax: (301)816-9786
E-mail: webmaster@acrel.org
URL: http://www.acrel.org
Contact: Ms. Jill Pace, Exec. Dir.
Description: Attorneys practicing real estate law. Promotes adherence to high standards of ethics and practice by members; seeks to advance the real estate law profession. Serves as a clearinghouse on real estate law; facilitates exchange of information among members; addresses legislative and legal reform issues impacting on the practice of real estate law; consults and cooperates with bar associations and government agencies with an interest in real estate law. Produces and distributes educational materials. **Publications:** *ACREL News*. Newsletter. Alternate Formats: online.

5480 ■ American Lawyers Auxiliary (ALA)
2010 E 46th St.
Tulsa, OK 74105
E-mail: barneya@staff.abanet.org
Contact: Linda Jarvis, Pres.
Founded: 1958. **Members:** 50,000. **Membership Dues:** individual, $25 (annual) ● life, $300 ● state auxiliary, $50 (annual) ● local auxiliary, $30 (annual) ● law school auxiliary/spouse, $15 (annual). **State Groups:** 15. **Local Groups:** 90. **Description:** Acts as a clearinghouse for state and local groups throughout the country, promoting educational programs pertaining to the law. Encourages members to volunteer their services to legal services programs

and to juvenile courts. Cooperates with the organized bar in public service activities and programs such as Law Day and courthouse tours; promotes public service programs such as advocacy for people with disabilities. Compiles statistics. Maintains 15 committees. **Awards:** Alice Carr Memorial. **Frequency:** annual. **Type:** monetary. **Recipient:** to 3 elementary, middle, high school LRE teachers ● Auxiliary Excellence Award. **Type:** monetary. **Recipient:** to affiliated auxiliaries with outstanding service to their community ● Citizen Awareness of the Law. **Frequency:** annual. **Type:** recognition ● Law Day U.S.A. **Frequency:** annual. **Type:** recognition ● Law Related Education Resource Award. **Type:** monetary. **Recipient:** to students and teachers who have made excellent use of Third Grade LRE Teaching Unit ● Law Related Education Teacher of the Year. **Frequency:** annual. **Type:** monetary. **Recipient:** to elementary, middle and high school teachers who have made outstanding contributions to law related education ● Outstanding Individual Volunteer Award. **Type:** recognition. **Recipient:** to individual member who most effectively increases member and public understanding of law and the American legal system. **Formerly:** (1983) National Lawyers Wines. **Publications:** *ALA News*, quarterly. Newsletter. **Conventions/Meetings:** annual meeting.

5481 ■ American Prosecutors Research Institute (APRI)

99 Canal Center Plz., Ste.510
Alexandria, VA 22314
Ph: (703)549-9222
Fax: (703)836-3195
E-mail: mediacontact@ndaa-apri.org
URL: http://www.ndaa-apri.org/apri
Contact: Paul A. Logli, Pres.

Founded: 1984. **Staff:** 35. **Languages:** English, German, Greek, Spanish. **Nonmembership. Description:** Acts as a clearinghouse, providing information and referrals to interested individuals in regard to all areas of criminal justice and on topics such as child abuse, environmental crime prosecution, and narcotics prosecution. Provides research and training in child abuse, environmental crime, drug, and impaired driving prosecution. **Programs:** Child Abuse and Exploitation; Child Protection; Community Prosecution; DNA Forensics; Drug Prosecution and Prevention; Gun Violence Prosecution; Juvenile Justice; Research; Traffic Law; Violence Against Women; White Collar Crime. **Affiliated With:** National District Attorneys Association. **Publications:** *Between the Lines*, quarterly. Newsletter. Covers the prosecution of vehicular offenses. Alternate Formats: online ● *In-Re*, quarterly. Newsletter. Contains information on juvenile justice issues. Alternate Formats: online ● *Investigation and Prosecution of Child Abuse*. Manual. Contains the latest in case law and research on nearly every facet of child sexual abuse, physical abuse and neglect. **Price:** $64.95 ● *The Silent Witness*, quarterly. Newsletter. Features issues related to DNA in courts. Alternate Formats: online ● *Update*, monthly. Newsletter. Covers prosecution of child abuse. Alternate Formats: online ● Also publishes summaries of relevant state legislation. **Conventions/Meetings:** annual conference - every summer. 2008 July 13-16, Tucson, AZ.

5482 ■ Armenian Bar Association

c/o Lisa Boyadjian, Admin. Asst.
PO Box 29111
Los Angeles, CA 90029
Ph: (323)666-6288
E-mail: info@armenianbar.org
URL: http://www.armenianbar.org
Contact: Betty A. Jamgotchian, Exec. Dir.

Founded: 1989. **Members:** 300. **Membership Dues:** attorney, $100 (annual) ● attorney (in practice less than 2 years), law clerk, $50 (annual) ● law student, $25 (annual) ● sponsor, $1,000 (annual). **Languages:** Armenian, English. **For-Profit. Description:** Armenian attorneys; interested others. Works to enable attorneys of Armenian heritage to better serve the legal profession and the Armenian community. Provides pro bono services; offers legal education in Armenian communities. Sponsors programs and exchanges to promote democracy and rule of law in the Republic of Armenia. **Publications:** Newsletter, quarterly. **Circulation:** 2,800. **Advertising:** accepted. Alternate Formats: online. **Conventions/Meetings:** semiannual meeting - always spring and fall.

5483 ■ Association of Attorney-Mediators (AAM)

PO Box 741955
Dallas, TX 75374-1955
Ph: (972)669-8101 (713)977-1717
Free: (800)280-1368
Fax: (972)669-8180
E-mail: aam@attorney-mediators.org
URL: http://www.attorney-mediators.org
Contact: Brenda Rachuig, Exec. Dir.

Founded: 1989. **Members:** 300. **Staff:** 10. **Description:** Qualified, independent attorney-mediators. Strives to promote the use of mediation and protects the mediation process. Conducts seminars for attorneys, assists the Judiciary in drafting and implementing local rules and procedures for mediation: submits amicus briefs to the Courts on selected issues involving mediation and monitors legislation concerning the mediation process. **Publications:** *Association of Attorney-Mediators Newsletter*. Alternate Formats: online.

5484 ■ Association of Black Women Attorneys (ABWA)

255 W 36th St., Ste.800
New York, NY 10018
Ph: (212)300-2193
E-mail: abwagroup@yahoo.com
URL: http://www.geocities.com/abwagroup
Contact: Margo Brodie, Pres.

Founded: 1976. **Members:** 90. **Membership Dues:** regular, $50 (annual) ● associate, $35 (annual) ● student, $20 (annual). **Description:** Organization for black women lawyers. Aims to encourage and enhance the professional development of women of color. Provides information, networking opportunities, mentoring opportunities, and CLE programs. **Awards:** Ruth Whitehead Whaley. **Frequency:** annual. **Type:** recognition. **Additional Websites:** http://www.abwanewyork.org.

5485 ■ Association of Commercial Finance Attorneys (ACFA)

c/o Richard K. Brown, Sec.
Kennedy Covington Lobdell & Hickman, LLP
214 N Tryon St., Hearst Tower, 43rd Fl.
Charlotte, NC 28202
Ph: (704)331-7403
E-mail: info@acfa.cc
URL: http://www.acfa.cc
Contact: Richard K. Brown, Sec.

Members: 350. **Membership Dues:** regular, $225 (annual). **Description:** Attorneys practicing in the area of commercial finance. Conducts seminars and other educational programs. **Telecommunication Services:** electronic mail, rbrown@kennedycovington.com. **Publications:** Directory, annual. **Price:** free for members. **Conventions/Meetings:** annual meeting.

5486 ■ Association for Honest Attorneys (A.H.A!)

PO Box 558
Derby, KS 67037
Ph: (316)788-0901
Fax: (316)788-7990
E-mail: support@assocforhonestattys.com
URL: http://assocforhonestattys.com
Contact: Joan Heffington, Founder/CEO

Founded: 2003. **Membership Dues:** general, $12 (annual). **Description:** Seeks to improve the legal system in America and "gain respect for the legal profession by striving to keep attorneys honest." Offers assistance with attorney difficulties, education regarding the legal system, and a quick resolution of legal matters.

5487 ■ Association of Professional Responsibility Lawyers (APRL)

134 N LaSalle St., Ste.1600
Chicago, IL 60602
Ph: (312)782-4396
Fax: (312)782-4725
E-mail: admin@aprl.net
URL: http://www.aprl.net
Contact: Steven L. Lee, Pres.

Membership Dues: full, $150 (annual). **Description:** Promotes professional responsibility and legal ethics for all professionals involved in law. **Publications:** Articles ● Newsletter. Alternate Formats: online. **Conventions/Meetings:** annual meeting ● seminar.

5488 ■ The Attorney's Group (TAG)

Hillsboro Executive Center North
350 Fairway Dr., Ste.200
Deerfield Beach, FL 33441-1834
Ph: (954)571-1877
Free: (800)221-2168
Fax: (954)571-8582
E-mail: membership@assnservices.com
URL: http://www.tag-assn.com
Contact: Jack Furnari, Exec. Dir.

Founded: 1976. **Members:** 4,000. **Membership Dues:** regular, $35 (annual) ● regular, $85 (triennial). **Staff:** 15. **Description:** Represents practicing attorneys. Provides economic benefits and services, unsecured loan plans, mortgage loans, group insurance discounts, accounts receivable collections, office supplies, wealth protection and a vision and dental plan. **Publications:** *Quarterly Forum*, semiannual. Newsletter. **Advertising:** accepted.

5489 ■ Croatian American Bar Association (CABA)

1850 Whittier Ave., Unit E201
Costa Mesa, CA 92627
E-mail: marko@croatianamericanbar.com
URL: http://www.croatianamericanbar.com
Contact: Marko Zoretic, Pres.

Founded: 2005. **Membership Dues:** regular, $40 (annual) ● student, $10 (annual) ● international association, $20 (annual). **Multinational. Description:** Promotes the advancement of lawyers and law students of Croatian heritage in the legal profession. Provides a forum for professional networking, support, and exchange of ideas among its members. Supports the provision of legal services to the Croatian-American community. Fosters camaraderie among its members. **Libraries: Type:** reference. **Holdings:** articles, books. **Publications:** Membership Directory. Alternate Formats: online.

5490 ■ Decalogue Society of Lawyers (DSL)

39 S LaSalle St., Ste.410
Chicago, IL 60603
Ph: (312)263-6493
Fax: (312)263-6512
E-mail: decaloguesociety@aol.com
URL: http://decaloguesociety.com
Contact: James A. Shapiro, Pres.

Founded: 1934. **Members:** 1,500. **Membership Dues:** attorney in Illinois, $110 (annual) ● attorney outside Illinois (fully retired or less than 4 years since admitted to Bar), $60 (annual). **Staff:** 1. **Budget:** $50,000. **Languages:** English, Hebrew. **Description:** Represents lawyers of the Jewish faith. Seeks to promote and cultivate social and professional relations among members of the legal profession. Conducts a forum on topics of general and Jewish interest. Maintains placement service to help members find employment and office facilities. **Awards:** Merit Award. **Frequency:** annual. **Type:** recognition. **Recipient:** for distinguished service to humanity ● **Type:** scholarship. **Committees:** Civil Rights; Good and Welfare; Insurance; Job Placement; Legislation; Long Range Planning; Programs; Public Relations; speakers' bureau. **Divisions:** Law Student. **Publications:** *The Decalogue Tablets*, quarterly. Newsletter. **Price:** free. **Circulation:** 1,800. **Advertising:** accepted. Alternate Formats: online ● Membership Directory, periodic. **Conventions/Meetings:** lecture and seminar, covers recent decisions, legislation, and developments in the law - 30/year ● annual meeting - always June in Chicago, IL.

5491 ■ Fair Elections Legal Network (FELN)
1730 Rhode Island Ave. NW, Ste.712
Washington, DC 20036
Ph: (202)331-0114
Fax: (202)331-1663
E-mail: admin@fairelectionsnetwork.com
URL: http://www.fairelectionsnetwork.com
Contact: Robert M. Brandon, Pres./Co-Founder
Founded: 2006. **Description:** Represents experienced election lawyers who are involved in removing impediments to increased voter participation. Seeks to help bring about increased voter participation by traditionally under-represented constituencies. Serves as a legal clearinghouse for attorney referrals and contacts. Promotes communication among election lawyers. **Telecommunication Services:** electronic mail, rbrandon@fairelectionsnetwork.com.

5492 ■ Federal Bar Association (FBA)
2011 Crystal Dr., Ste.400
Arlington, VA 22202
Ph: (703)682-7000
Fax: (703)682-7001
E-mail: fba@fedbar.org
URL: http://www.fedbar.org
Contact: David L. Guerry, Pres.
Founded: 1920. **Members:** 15,000. **Membership Dues:** active (private sector), $75-$150 (annual) ● active (public sector), $60-$115 (annual) ● sustaining (public and private sector), $60 (annual) ● foreign associate (public and private sector), $150 (annual) ● law student associate (public and private sector), $25 (annual). **Staff:** 15. **Budget:** $2,000,000. **Local Groups:** 74. **Description:** Attorneys employed by the federal government as legislators, judges, lawyers, or members of quasi-judicial boards and commissions; those with previous government legal experience; and those with a substantive interest in federal law and who practice before a federal court or agency. Over 100 specialized committees, operating through 24 Sections and Divisions, provide various programs such as continuing legal education and professional and community service. **Computer Services:** Mailing lists, of members. **Telecommunication Services:** electronic mail, membership@fedbar.org. **Affiliated With:** Foundation of the Federal Bar Association. **Publications:** *The Federal Lawyer*, 10/year. Magazine. **Price:** $35.00 /year for nonmembers in U.S.; $45.00 /year for nonmembers outside U.S. **Advertising:** accepted ● Membership Directory, quinquennial ● Newsletter, quarterly. **Conventions/Meetings:** annual conference, for Indian Law (exhibits) ● annual conference, about Tax Law ● annual meeting and convention (exhibits) ● annual seminar, about Insurance Tax.

5493 ■ Federal Circuit Bar Association (FCBA)
1620 I St. NW, Ste.900
Washington, DC 20006
Ph: (202)466-3923
Fax: (202)833-1061
E-mail: brookshire@fedcirbar.org
URL: http://www.fedcirbar.org
Contact: James E. Brookshire Esq., Exec. Dir.
Membership Dues: regular, associate, $225 (annual) ● government, educator, $85 (annual) ● retired, $65 (annual). **Description:** Represents all areas of the legal community of the Federal Circuit. Seeks to unite different groups who practice within the legal community of the Federal Circuit. Offers a forum for common concerns and dialogue between bar and court, government counsel and private practitioner, litigator, and corporate counsel. **Awards:** Giles Sutherland Rich Memorial Scholarship. **Frequency:** annual. **Type:** scholarship. **Recipient:** to a law student (either in undergraduate studies or in law school) showing financial need and demonstrated academic promise ● Howard T. Markey Scholarship. **Frequency:** annual. **Type:** scholarship. **Recipient:** to a law student (either in undergraduate studies or in law school) showing financial need, demonstrated academic promise, and service. **Publications:** *Federal Circuit Bar Association Newsletter*. **Price:** included in membership dues ● *Federal Circuit Bar Journal*, quarterly. Provides scholarly articles in the substantive and procedural law areas. **Price:** included in membership dues.

5494 ■ Fellows of the American Bar Foundation (FABF)
750 N Lake Shore Dr.
Chicago, IL 60611-4403
Ph: (312)988-6596
Free: (800)292-5065
Fax: (312)988-6579
E-mail: eschexnayder@abfn.org
URL: http://fellows.abfn.org
Contact: Mr. Edward Schexnayder, Contact
Founded: 1955. **Members:** 8,000. **Staff:** 5. **Multinational. Description:** Membership is elected and limited to one third of one percent of the lawyers in each U.S. jurisdiction, with a minimum quota of eight per jurisdiction, no more than 50 members-at-large and about 2500 life members. Membership is considered "evidence of professional distinction", and asserts that members "are among the major contributors" of the American Bar Foundation. **Awards:** Outstanding Scholar Award. **Frequency:** annual. **Type:** recognition. **Recipient:** for outstanding research in law and government ● Outstanding Service Award. **Frequency:** annual. **Type:** recognition. **Recipient:** for 50 years of distinguished service to the legal profession. **Committees:** Fellows Research Advisory. **Publications:** *Fellows Handbook*. Alternate Formats: online ● *Fellows News*, quarterly. Newsletter. **Circulation:** 7,000. **Advertising:** accepted. Alternate Formats: online ● *Roster of the Fellows*, annual. Membership Directory. **Conventions/Meetings:** annual convention, held in conjunction with the ABF and ABA.

5495 ■ Foundation of the American Board of Trial Advocates
Bryan Tower, Ste.3000
2001 Bryan St.
Dallas, TX 75201
Ph: (214)871-7523
Free: (800)932-2682
Fax: (214)871-6025
E-mail: national@abota.org
URL: http://www.abota.org/foundation
Contact: Brian Tyson, Exec. Dir.
Founded: 1958. **Members:** 5,000. **State Groups:** 88. **Description:** Attorneys. Strives to improve the "ethical and technical standards of practice in the field of advocacy to the end that individual litigants may receive more effective representation and the general public benefit by more efficient administration of justice consistent with time-tested and traditional principles". **Publications:** *Voi Dire*, quarterly. Magazine. Alternate Formats: online.

5496 ■ Hispanic National Bar Association (HNBA)
1101 Connecticut Ave. NW, Ste.1000
Washington, DC 20036
Ph: (202)223-4777
Fax: (202)223-2324
E-mail: jreyna@williamsmullen.com
URL: http://www.hnba.com
Contact: Jimmie V. Reyna, Pres.
Founded: 1972. **Members:** 25,000. **Membership Dues:** attorney/foreign attorney, $75 (annual) ● attorney affiliate, legal assistant, or legal administrator, $20 (annual) ● Benjamin Aranda, life, $1,250. **Staff:** 2. **Budget:** $300,000. **Regional Groups:** 13. **Languages:** English, Spanish. **Description:** Works to cultivate the science of jurisprudence; promote reform in the law; facilitate the administration of justice; advance the standing of the legal profession; promote high standards of integrity, honor, and professional courtesy among Hispanic lawyers. Counsels Hispanics interested in law careers; offers placement service; provides financial assistance; compiles statistics. Conducts professional training seminars. **Awards:** Law Student Scholarship. **Frequency:** annual. **Type:** scholarship. **Recipient:** for Hispanic law students. **Committees:** Amicus Curiae; Annual Convention; Business Development; D.C. Office Implementation; Immigration; International Law; Judicial Appointments. **Programs:** New Lawyers. **Formerly:** (1978) La Raza National Lawyers Association; (1980) La Raza National Bar Association. **Publications:** *National Directory*, semiannual. **Price:** $100.00. **Advertising:** accepted ● *Noticias*, quarterly. Newsletter. Alternate Formats: online. **Conventions/Meetings:** semiannual conference ● annual convention (exhibits) - always October.

5497 ■ International Academy of Trial Lawyers (IATL)
5841 Cedar Lake Rd., Ste.204
Minneapolis, MN 55416-5657
Ph: (952)546-2364
Free: (866)823-2443
Fax: (952)545-6073
E-mail: iatl@llmsi.com
URL: http://www.iatl.net
Contact: Robert T. Hall, Pres.
Founded: 1954. **Members:** 554. **Staff:** 2. **Budget:** $250,000. **Multinational. Description:** Represents the interests of attorneys who have been practicing for a minimum of 12 years and who are principally engaged in trial and appellate practice. Maintains museum-type Lincoln Library, including old and rare books. Operates charitable program. **Libraries:** **Type:** reference. **Holdings:** 500. **Awards:** Student Advocacy Award. **Frequency:** annual. **Type:** recognition. **Committees:** Admissions; International Democracy; International Relations; Lee S. Kreindler Memorial Lectureship; Long Range Planning; Media; National Judicial College. **Programs:** China. **Publications:** *Dean's Address*, annual. Alternate Formats: online ● *24 Dramatic Cases of Trial Lawyers* ● Membership Directory, biennial ● Journal, semiannual. **Conventions/Meetings:** semiannual meeting.

5498 ■ International Alliance of Holistic Lawyers (IAHL)
PO Box 371
Milton, DE 19968
Fax: (302)684-5644
E-mail: info@iahl.org
URL: http://iahl.org
Contact: Felicity Lavelle, Dir.
Membership Dues: general public, $75 (annual) ● law student, $25 (annual) ● lawyer, $100 (annual). **Multinational. Description:** Represents and promotes the interests of holistic lawyers. Seeks to transform the practice of law through education and support of holistic practices. Provides a forum for networking, progress and new vision in the legal profession. **Telecommunication Services:** electronic mail, director@iahl.org. **Publications:** *The Whole Lawyer*. Newsletter. **Price:** included in membership dues. Alternate Formats: online.

5499 ■ International Association of Defense Counsel (IADC)
1 N Franklin St., Ste.1205
Chicago, IL 60606
Ph: (312)368-1494
Fax: (312)368-1854
E-mail: info@iadclaw.org
URL: http://www.iadclaw.org
Contact: L. Gino Marchetti Jr., Pres.
Founded: 1920. **Members:** 2,500. **Staff:** 9. **Budget:** $2,500,000. **Description:** Attorneys practicing defense trial law in 13 countries. Organizes research projects; offers continuing legal education programs including the Defense Counsel Trial Academy for young trial lawyers. Conducts annual legal writing contest. Maintains 26 substantive law committees in addition to 20 standing committees. **Awards:** Yancey Memorial Award. **Frequency:** annual. **Type:** recognition. **Recipient:** for best journal article. **Boards:** Continuing Legal Education. **Committees:** Corporate Counsel; Insurance Executive; Multi-National; Open Forum; Professional Responsibility; Senior Advisory; Technology. **Affiliated With:** Defense Research Institute. **Formerly:** (1927) General Counsels' Association of Accident and Health Counsels; (1986) International Association of Insurance Counsel. **Publications:** *Committee Newsletter*, monthly ● *Defense*

Counsel Journal, quarterly. **Price:** $50.00/year. **Circulation:** 5,000 ● *IADC Docket*, quarterly. Newsletter. **Price:** $5.00/year. **Circulation:** 5,000 ● *The Joan Fullam Irick Privacy Project Phase I and II*. Book. Provides critical insights into the latest privacy issues affecting the corporate and defense bar. **Price:** $30.00 each; $50.00 for two volumes ● Membership Directory, annual ● Also publishes monographs. **Conventions/Meetings:** semiannual meeting ● annual meeting.

5500 ■ International Municipal Lawyers Association (IMLA)
1110 Vermont Ave. NW, Ste.200
Washington, DC 20005
Ph: (202)466-5424
Fax: (202)785-1052
E-mail: info@imla.org
Contact: Henry W. Underhill Jr., Exec. Dir.
Founded: 1935. **Members:** 1,500. **Staff:** 11. **Budget:** $1,200,000. **Description:** Seeks to promote and advance the development of local government law and. Serves as a clearinghouse of local law materials; collects and disseminates information; assists government agencies to prepare for litigation and develop new local laws; provides legal research and writing services; offers continuing legal education opportunities; conducts research programs. **Libraries: Type:** reference; not open to the public. **Holdings:** articles, books, clippings, periodicals. **Computer Services:** database ● online services. **Programs:** Legal Advocacy. **Sections:** Economic Development, Taxation and Finance; Ethics; Health and Environment; Litigation and Risk Management; Municipal Operations. **Absorbed:** (1998) National IST of Municipal Law Officers. **Publications:** *Municipal Lawyer*, bimonthly. Magazine. **Circulation:** 2,500. **Advertising:** accepted. **Conventions/Meetings:** semiannual conference.

5501 ■ International Network of Boutique Law Firms (INBLF)
c/o Gallion and Spielvogel
1225 Franklin Ave., Ste.325
Garden City, NY 11530
Ph: (516)512-8899
Fax: (516)512-8980
E-mail: info@inblf.com
URL: http://www.inblf.com
Contact: Steven Spielvogel Esq., Pres.
Members: 250. **Multinational. Description:** Ensures that each firm's clients will receive quality legal representation. Provides a healthy referral network among the high performing, single focus law firms. Promotes a network that connects small law firms around the country and the world giving the small law firms a way to compete with the larger national and global firms. **Publications:** Newsletter, monthly.

5502 ■ International Senior Lawyers Project (ISLP)
c/o Ms. Jean C. Berman, Esq., Exec. Dir.
31 W 52nd St., 3rd Fl.
New York, NY 10019
Ph: (212)880-5836
Fax: (212)878-8375
E-mail: jberman@islp.org
URL: http://www.islp.org
Contact: Ms. Jean C. Berman Esq., Exec. Dir.
Founded: 2000. **Multinational. Description:** Provides volunteer legal services by highly skilled and experienced attorneys to advance democracy and the rule of law, protect human rights and promote equitable economic development worldwide. Helps governments and citizens develop and implement legal reforms. Assists programs that advance the social and economic well-being of people in developing countries. Builds the capacity of local organizations and professionals to meet the needs of their communities. **Programs:** Access to Justice; Economic Development and Participation in the Global Economy; Human Rights and Social Justice. **Publications:** *The ISLP News*, biennial. Newsletter. Includes articles about ISLP projects, interviews with volunteers and updates on organizational developments. Alternate Formats: online.

5503 ■ International Society of Primerus Law Firms
171 Monroe Ave. NW, Ste.750
Grand Rapids, MI 49503
Ph: (616)454-9939
Free: (800)968-2211
Fax: (616)458-7099
E-mail: jbuchanan@primerus.com
URL: http://www.primerus.com
Contact: John C. Buchanan Esq., Pres.
Founded: 1992. **Multinational. Description:** Represents independent law firms. Helps restore honor and dignity to the legal profession. Strives to rebuild the public's trust in lawyers and the judicial system. Facilitates communication and cooperation among members.

5504 ■ Iranian American Bar Association (IABA)
1025 Connecticut Ave. NW, Ste.1012
Washington, DC 20036
E-mail: iaba@iaba.us
URL: http://www.iaba.us
Contact: John Radsan, Pres.
Founded: 2000. **Membership Dues:** private sector attorney (with 2 or more years of experience), $125 (annual) ● private sector attorney (with less than 2 years of experience), $60 (annual) ● public sector attorney (with 2 or more years of experience), $60 (annual) ● public sector attorney (with less than 2 years of experience), $30 (annual) ● law student, $20 (annual). **Description:** Works to educate and inform the Iranian American community about legal issues of interest. Seeks to ensure that the American public at large, Iranian American representatives and other government officials are fully and accurately informed on legal matters of interest and concern to the Iranian American community. Promotes the social, economic, professional and educational advancement of the Iranian American community. Strives to publicize and promote the achievements of Iranian American lawyers and other legal professionals. **Publications:** *IABA Newsletter*. Alternate Formats: online ● *The IABA Review*. Report. Alternate Formats: online.

5505 ■ Lawyers Associated Worldwide (LAW)
15424 Holdridge Dr. E
Wayzata, MN 55391
Ph: (952)404-1546
Fax: (952)404-1796
E-mail: admin@lawyersworldwide.com
URL: http://www.lawyersworldwide.com
Contact: Hallie J. Mann, Exec. Dir.
Multinational. Description: Represents members who specialize in alternative dispute resolution. Works with other organizations to provide quality, cost effective alternative dispute resolution firms. Allows member firms to service the legal needs of clients that are expanding their operations and relationships into new domestic and foreign markets because of the increasing globalization of the business world. Assists clients with legal and business issues in the areas of corporate and financial transactions, real estate, intellectual property and information technology, litigation, and private client practice. **Telecommunication Services:** electronic mail, halliemann@lawyersworldwide.com. **Publications:** Newsletter. Alternate Formats: online.

5506 ■ Lex Mundi
2100 W Loop S, Ste.1000
Houston, TX 77027
Ph: (713)626-9393 (925)962-0115
Fax: (713)626-9933
E-mail: lexmundi@lexmundi.com
URL: http://www.lexmundi.com
Contact: Carl E. Anduri Jr., Pres.
Founded: 1989. **Members:** 167. **Staff:** 7. **Budget:** $1,400,000. **Multinational. Description:** Independent law firms. Provides an exchange of professional information about local and global practice and development of law, facilitates and disseminates communications among members, and improves members' abilities to serve their clients. **Computer Services:** Mailing lists, of members. **Subgroups:** Agribusiness; Business Crimes and Compliance; E-Commerce; Environmental; Health Care; Immigration; State and Local Tax; Trusts and Estates. **Publications:** *eWorld Reports*. Newsletter. Contains articles on law from around the world. Alternate Formats: online. **Conventions/Meetings:** conference - 5/year.

5507 ■ Lithuanian-American Bar Association (LABAS)
c/o Patricia A. Streeter, Pres.
221 N Main St., Ste.300
Ann Arbor, MI 48104
Ph: (734)222-0088
Fax: (734)769-2196
E-mail: pas@patstreeter.com
URL: http://javadvokatai.org
Contact: Patricia A. Streeter, Pres.
Founded: 1991. **Membership Dues:** attorney, $60 (annual) ● law student, $30 (annual). **Multinational. Description:** Organizes, sponsors, and supports educational programs promoting the highest standards in legal scholarship and its application. Advances an understanding of the legal system of the United States of America in the Republic of Lithuania, and of the legal system of the Republic of Lithuania in the United States of America. Promotes a harmonious and productive relationship between the United States of America and the Republic of Lithuania. **Publications:** Membership Directory. Alternate Formats: online.

5508 ■ National Association of Assistant United States Attorneys (NAAUSA)
12427 Hedges Run Dr., Ste.104
Lake Ridge, VA 22192-1715
Ph: (703)426-4266
Free: (800)455-5661
Fax: (800)528-3492
E-mail: info@naausa.org
URL: http://www.naausa.org
Contact: Richard L. Delonis, Pres.
Founded: 1992. **Members:** 1,700. **Membership Dues:** regular, $130 (annual) ● associate, $25 (annual). **Staff:** 2. **Budget:** $190,000. **Regional Groups:** 15. **Description:** Assistant U.S. attorneys. Promotes professional advancement among members. Conducts continuing professional development programs. **Publications:** *NAAUSA Quarterly*. Newsletter. **Advertising:** accepted. **Conventions/Meetings:** annual Lobby Day - convention - February-April, Washington, DC.

5509 ■ National Association of Bench and Bar Spouses (NABBS)
c/o Lyla R. Coleman, Pres.
6837 Lakeshore Dr.
Raytown, MO 64133
Ph: (816)353-4899
Free: (866)353-0008
Fax: (816)353-4899
E-mail: lylacoleman@aol.com
URL: http://www.nabbsinc.org
Contact: Lyla R. Coleman, Pres.
Founded: 1951. **Members:** 400. **Regional Groups:** 4. **Description:** Spouses of attorneys united to conduct civic, cultural, and social activities in order "to enhance the prestige of the legal profession" and to encourage fellowship among attorneys' spouses. Sponsors conferences on the family and child advocacy programs; maintains Dorothy Atkinson Legal Scholarship Fund for worthy law students and college students interested in careers in law. **Affiliated With:** National Bar Association. **Formerly:** (1987) National Barristers' Wives. **Publications:** Membership Directory, annual ● Newsletter, semiannual ● Also publishes historical brochure and program aids. **Conventions/Meetings:** annual meeting, held in conjunction with NBA.

5510 ■ National Association of Consumer Bankruptcy Attorneys (NACBA)
2300 M St., Ste.800
Washington, DC 20037
Ph: (202)331-8005
Fax: (202)331-8535

E-mail: maureent@nacba.org
URL: http://www.nacba.org
Contact: Henry J. Sommer, Pres.

Founded: 1992. **Members:** 1,300. **Membership Dues:** regular, $150-$450 (annual) ● non-profit/educational institution, $75 (annual) ● clerk, judge, trustee, $150 (annual). **State Groups:** 16. **Multinational. Description:** Provides educational programs, support and services to debtors, members, policy makers and the general community. Serves the needs of consumer bankruptcy attorneys. Protects the rights of consumer debtors and their attorneys in bankruptcy. **Awards:** Champion of Consumer Rights. **Frequency:** annual. **Type:** recognition. **Recipient:** for extraordinary service in protecting American consumers. **Computer Services:** Information services, bankruptcy practice resources.

5511 ■ National Association of Muslim Lawyers (NAML)

c/o Sadia Ali, Treas.
3225 Woodland Park Dr., Apt. 1562
Houston, TX 77082
Ph: (202)448-9978
Fax: (202)448-2871
URL: http://www.namlnet.org
Contact: Farhana Khera, Pres./Exec. Dir.

Founded: 1996. **Membership Dues:** private practice/corporate counsel, $50-$100 (annual) ● government/public interest/military, $25-$75 (annual) ● academia/judge, $75 (annual) ● law student, $15 (annual) ● non-lawyer associate, $100 (annual) ● corporate/sustaining, $500 (annual). **Description:** Represents the Muslim legal profession. Promotes justice and improvements in the American legal system. Fosters meaningful access to legal representation for Muslims. Promotes full, fair and equal participation by Muslims in American society. **Publications:** Membership Directory. **Price:** included in membership dues.

5512 ■ National Association of Republican Attorneys (NARA)

PO Box 656513
Fresh Meadows, NY 11365-6513
Ph: (718)357-7075
E-mail: drtomstevens@aol.com
Contact: Dr. Thomas Robert Stevens, Pres.

Description: Encourages the organization of Republican Law Student associations nationwide. Promotes reform of the judicial system. Acts as a forum for networking.

5513 ■ National Association of Retail Collection Attorneys (NARCA)

1620 I St. NW, Ste.615
Washington, DC 20006
Ph: (202)861-0706
Free: (800)633-6069
Fax: (202)463-8498
E-mail: narca@narca.org
URL: http://www.narca.org
Contact: Ms. Cynthia R. White JD, Exec. Dir.

Founded: 1993. **Members:** 700. **Membership Dues:** law firm, $500 (annual). **Staff:** 5. **Budget:** $1,300,000. **Description:** Collection law firms. Assists consumer collection law firms and creditors. Establishes performance standards; lobbies for creditors' rights legislation; provides collection support; conducts educational programs. **Awards:** Community Service Award. **Frequency:** annual. **Type:** recognition. **Recipient:** for the law firm that has made an impact through community service ● Don Kramer Award. **Frequency:** annual. **Type:** recognition. **Recipient:** for outstanding contributions to the legal collection industry. **Committees:** Don Kramer Award; Education; Grievance; Laws and Legislation; Member Services; Outreach. **Publications:** *NARCA Newsletter*, quarterly. **Circulation:** 6,000. **Advertising:** accepted ● Membership Directory, annual. **Circulation:** 5,000. **Advertising:** accepted. Alternate Formats: online. **Conventions/Meetings:** semiannual convention, educational program for law firms and clients (exhibits).

5514 ■ National Association of Women Lawyers (NAWL)

Amer. Bar Center 15.2
321 N Clark St.
Chicago, IL 60610
Ph: (312)988-6186
Fax: (312)988-5491
E-mail: nawl@nawl.org
URL: http://www.abanet.org/nawl
Contact: Dr. Rickie Jacobs, Exec. Dir.

Founded: 1899. **Members:** 1,044. **Membership Dues:** sustaining, $120 (annual) ● regular, international, $80 (annual) ● associate or partner, $55 (annual) ● young lawyer, $45 (annual) ● life, $1,500. **Staff:** 1. **Description:** Membership is open to any person who is a member in good standing of the bar of any state or U.S. territory, any non-U.S. legal professional (attorney or judge), any prospective attorney currently attending law school, and any state or local bar or law school association with compatible objectives. Men are welcome and encouraged to join. **Awards:** Arabella Babb Mansfield Award. **Frequency:** annual. **Type:** recognition. **Recipient:** to an outstanding individual for professional success, positive influence and valuable contribution to women in the law and in society; named after the first American woman admitted to a state bar in the United States ● Outstanding Law Student Program. **Frequency:** annual. **Type:** recognition ● Outstanding Member. **Frequency:** annual. **Type:** recognition ● Service Award. **Frequency:** annual. **Type:** recognition ● Toch Award. **Frequency:** annual. **Type:** recognition. **Affiliated With:** American Bar Association; International Bar Association. **Absorbed:** Women Lawyers' Club. **Publications:** *Presidents' Newsletter*, quarterly. Provides information to members. ● *Women Lawyer's Journal*, quarterly. Magazine. Publishes articles addressing current issues in domestic and foreign law. **Price:** $16.00/year. ISSN: 0473-7468. **Advertising:** accepted. **Conventions/Meetings:** annual conference ● annual regional meeting.

5515 ■ National Bar Association (NBA)

1225 11th St. NW
Washington, DC 20001
Ph: (202)842-3900
Fax: (202)289-6170
E-mail: lf@williegary.com
URL: http://www.nationalbar.org
Contact: Linnes Finney Jr., Pres.

Founded: 1925. **Members:** 18,000. **Membership Dues:** regular (admitted to practice of less than 5 years), $100-$300 (annual) ● associate, $75 (annual) ● life (subscribing and regular), $3,000-$3,500. **Staff:** 10. **Budget:** $1,500,000. **Regional Groups:** 12. **State Groups:** 79. **Local Groups:** 76. **Description:** Professional association of minority (predominantly African-American) attorneys, members of the judiciary, law students, and law faculty. Represents the interests of members and the communities they serve. Offers continuing legal education programs. Maintains hall of fame. **Awards:** C. Francis Stradford Award. **Frequency:** annual. **Type:** recognition ● Equal Justice Award. **Type:** recognition ● Gertrude E. Rush Award. **Frequency:** annual. **Type:** recognition ● Ronald Harmon Brown Award of International Distinction. **Frequency:** annual. **Type:** recognition ● Wiley A. Branton Award. **Frequency:** annual. **Type:** recognition. **Telecommunication Services:** electronic mail, rturner@clarkhill.com. **Councils:** Judicial. **Divisions:** Government Lawyers; Law Professors; Law Students; Legislative Lawyers; Partners in Majority Firms; Small Firms/Solo Practitioners; Women Lawyers; Young Lawyers. **Publications:** Magazine, bimonthly. Legal information for minority legal professionals. Includes legal briefs and industry outlook. **Price:** included in membership dues; $60.00 /year for nonmembers. ISSN: 0741-0115. **Circulation:** 17,000. **Advertising:** accepted. **Conventions/Meetings:** annual convention (exhibits) ● annual Midyear Conference and Gertrude E. Rush Award Dinner - conference and dinner.

5516 ■ National Conference of Bar Presidents (NCBP)

c/o Pamela Robinson, Assoc. Dir.
Div. for Bar Services
321 N Clark St., 20th Fl.
Chicago, IL 60610
Ph: (312)988-5345 (312)988-5353
Fax: (312)988-5492
E-mail: robinsonp@staff.abanet.org
URL: http://www.ncbp.org
Contact: Pamela Robinson, Assoc. Dir.

Founded: 1950. **Members:** 300. **Membership Dues:** individual, $35 (annual) ● bar association (based on number of members), $130-$230 (annual) ● life, fellow, $1,000 ● sustaining, life (fellow), $100. **Staff:** 3. **Budget:** $300,000. **Description:** Presidents, presidents-elect, and past presidents of state, local, and specialty bar associations. Provides a forum for exchange of ideas; seeks to stimulate work in bar associations, and encourages closer coordination of bar activities with the American Bar Association (see separate entry). Conducts educational programs. **Telecommunication Services:** electronic mail, bware@staff.abanet.org. **Caucuses:** Metropolitan Bar. **Committees:** Communication; Finance/Sponsorship; Program. **Task Forces:** Diversity. **Publications:** *The Conference Call*, semiannual. Newsletter. **Circulation:** 1,200 ● *NCBP Best Projects*, annual ● Also publishes membership brochure. **Conventions/Meetings:** semiannual conference, held in conjunction with the ABA (exhibits) - always February and August.

5517 ■ National Conference of Black Lawyers (NCBL)

PO Box 80043
Lansing, MI 48908-0043
Free: (866)266-5091
URL: http://www.ncbl.org
Contact: Kamau Karl Franklin, Co-Chair

Founded: 1968. **Membership Dues:** life, $1,000 ● sustaining, $500 (annual) ● law student, $10 (annual) ● legal worker, $25 (annual) ● supporter/activist, $20 (annual) ● lawyer (based on salary), $100-$175 (annual). **Description:** "Committed in working with other organizations to end the oppression of people of color and the poor in this country and to support similar liberation movements throughout the world". **Computer Services:** database, membership directory.

5518 ■ National Conference of Women's Bar Associations (NCWBA)

PO Box 82366
Portland, OR 97282-0366
Ph: (503)657-3813
Fax: (503)657-3932
E-mail: info@ncwba.org
URL: http://www.ncwba.org
Contact: Lynn T. Albert, Pres.

Founded: 1981. **Members:** 110. **Membership Dues:** organizational (based on number of members), $75-$350 (annual). **Staff:** 1. **Description:** Umbrella organization for state and local women's bar associations. Promotes the interests of women lawyers. Serves as a forum for information exchange among women's bar associations. **Awards:** NCWBA Public Service Award. **Frequency:** annual. **Type:** recognition. **Recipient:** to women's bar; for community service. **Publications:** *NCWBA Newsletter*, quarterly. **Conventions/Meetings:** semiannual meeting and workshop, held in conjunction with American Bar Association - always February and August.

5519 ■ National Counsel of Black Lawyers (NCBL)

Address Unknown since 2008

Founded: 1968. **Members:** 1,000. **Staff:** 6. **Local Groups:** 15. **Description:** Attorneys throughout the U.S. and Canada united to use legal skills in the service of black and poor communities. Maintains projects in legal services to community organizations, voting rights, and international affairs; provides public education on legal issues affecting blacks and poor people. Researches racism in law schools and bar admissions. Conducts programs of continuing legal education for member attorneys. Maintains general law library. Compiles statistics; maintains lawyer referral and placement services. Provides speakers' bureau on criminal justice issues, international human rights law, and civil rights practice. **Awards:** **Type:** recognition. **Sections:** Bar Development;

Criminal Justice; Delivery of Legal Services; Economic and Social Rights; International Affairs and World Peace; Political Rights; Racially Targeted Violence; Rights of Women. **Formerly:** (1998) National Conference of Black Lawyers. **Publications:** *Notes*, quarterly. **Conventions/Meetings:** annual meeting - always late summer or early fall.

5520 ■ National Employment Lawyers Association (NELA)
44 Montgomery St., Ste.2080
San Francisco, CA 94104
Ph: (415)296-7629
Fax: (415)677-9445
E-mail: nelahq@nelahq.org
URL: http://www.nela.org
Contact: Terisa E. Chaw, Exec. Dir.
Founded: 1985. **Members:** 3,000. **Membership Dues:** lawyer in practice (less than 5 years), legal services/public interest organization lawyer, $235 (annual) ● lawyer in practice (5 to 9 years), associate, $310 (annual) ● lawyer in practice (over 10 years), $335 (annual) ● champion, $5,000 (annual) ● contributing, $450 (annual) ● sustaining, $550 (annual) ● advocate, $1,000 (annual) ● defender, $2,500 (annual) ● paraprofessional, $160 (annual) ● law student, $20 (annual). **Staff:** 7. **Budget:** $1,000,000. **Regional Groups:** 67. **Description:** Attorneys who represent individual employees in cases involving employment discrimination, wrongful termination, benefits, and other employment-related matters. Promotes the professional development of members through networking, publications, technical assistance, and education. Supports the workplace rights of individual employees via lobbying and other activities. Maintains informational bank of pleadings and briefs; does not operate a lawyer referral service. Conducts regional seminars; conducts educational programs. **Libraries: Type:** reference. **Telecommunication Services:** electronic bulletin board, NELANET, restricted to members only. **Committees:** Age Discrimination; Alternative Dispute Resolution; Disability Rights; ERISA; Ethics and Sanctions; Federal Employee Rights; International Employment Law; Privacy Law; Sexual Harassment Law; Sexual Orientation Discrimination; Title VII; Trial Practice; Wage and Hour Law; Whistleblower Law. **Formerly:** (1992) Plaintiff Employment Lawyers Association. **Publications:** *The Employee Advocate*, quarterly. Magazine. Contains activities, latest developments in employment law, best practice tips, briefs, and articles of interest to the members. **Price:** included in membership dues. **Circulation:** 3,000. **Advertising:** accepted ● *Employee Rights Litigation: Pleading and Practice.* Covers all aspects of employment law, including statutory and common law claims. Includes practitioners' tips. ● *Member Service Guide*, annual. Membership Directory. **Advertising:** accepted ● *NELA Directory* ● Annual Report, annual. Alternate Formats: online. **Conventions/Meetings:** annual convention and conference, for professional vendors, primarily publishers and software (exhibits) - late June ● semiannual seminar, specific fields of plaintiff employment law.

5521 ■ National Lawyers Association (NLA)
17201 E 40 Hwy., Ste.207
Independence, MO 64055
Free: (800)471-2994
Fax: (816)229-8425
E-mail: nla@nla.org
URL: http://www.nla.org
Contact: Mario Mandina, CEO
Membership Dues: attorney, $200 (annual) ● law student, $25 (annual). **Description:** Seeks to improve the image of the legal profession. Aims to advance legal institutions and respect for the law, and to educate the public on such matters. Provide services, benefits, technology, education, guidance and professional assistance to its members. **Telecommunication Services:** electronic mail, ceo@nla.org. **Publications:** *NLA Brief.* Newsletter. Alternate Formats: online.

5522 ■ National Lawyers Guild (NLG)
132 Nassau St., Rm. 922
New York, NY 10038
Ph: (212)679-5100
Fax: (212)679-2811
E-mail: nlgno@nlg.org
URL: http://www.nlg.org
Contact: Heidi Boghosian, Exec. Dir.
Founded: 1937. **Members:** 7,000. **Membership Dues:** attorney/legal worker, $50 (annual) ● law student, $15 (annual). **Staff:** 4. **Budget:** $300,000. **Regional Groups:** 9. **Local Groups:** 200. **Description:** Lawyers, law students, legal workers, and jailhouse lawyers dedicated to seek economic justice, social equality, and the right to political dissent. Serves as national center for progressive legal work providing training programs to both members and nonmembers. Sponsors skills seminars in different areas of law. Maintains speakers' bureau and offers legal referrals. **Libraries: Type:** by appointment only. **Subjects:** history of the guild. **Awards:** Haywood Burns Memorial Fellowship. **Frequency:** annual. **Type:** fellowship. **Recipient:** for outstanding law students. **Telecommunication Services:** electronic mail, director@nlg.org. **Committees:** Affirmative Action/Anti-Discrimination; Anti-Racism; Anti-Sexism; Civil Liberties; Criminal Law; International; Labor; Lesbian, Gay Rights; Summer Projects. **Projects:** National Immigration; National Police Accountability; Sugar Law Center. **Subcommittees:** AIDS Network; Cuba; Disinformation and Information Restriction; Faculty Network; IADL Representative; Middle East; Peace and Disarmament; Philippines; Puerto Rico; Southern Africa. **Task Forces:** Anti-Repression; Central America; Chile; Corporations, the Constitution and Human Rights; Disability Rights; Economic Rights; Ireland; Military Law. **Publications:** *National Lawyers Guild—Guild Notes*, quarterly. Newsletter. **Price:** $75.00 /year for institutions; $35.00 /year for individuals. **Circulation:** 10,000. **Advertising:** accepted ● *National Lawyers Guild—Guild Practitioner*, quarterly. **Price:** $40.00 /year for libraries and institutions; $25.00/year for lawyers; $10.00/year for students and legal workers ● *National Lawyers Guild—Referral Directory*, annual. Features geographically arranged directory of guild lawyers and their legal services. **Price:** $75.00 /year for institutions; $35.00 /year for individuals. **Advertising:** accepted ● *Rights on Trial.* **Conventions/Meetings:** annual convention (exhibits) - always October.

5523 ■ National Lesbian and Gay Law Association (NLGLA)
601 Thirteenth St. NW, Ste.1170 S
Washington, DC 20005-3823
Ph: (202)607-6384
E-mail: info@nlgla.org
URL: http://www.nlgla.org
Contact: D'Arcy A. Kemnitz, Exec. Dir.
Founded: 1988. **Members:** 400. **Membership Dues:** law student, $40 (annual) ● individual (income under $40,000), $60 (annual) ● individual (income $40,000-$79,999), $95 (annual) ● individual (income $80,000-$119,999), $125 (annual) ● individual (income $120,000 and above), $175 (annual). **Regional Groups:** 11. **Description:** Gay and lesbian lawyers and law students. Promotes public acceptance of difference in sexual preference; encourages professional advancement of members. Serves as a national voice representing members' interests; works to change the law and the legal profession in areas of concern to the homosexual community; functions as a forum for the discussion of legal and social matters of interest to members. Provides assistance to gay and lesbian law students; seeks to establish networks and coalitions pursuing the association's goals. Conducts educational programs; sponsors competitions; maintains speakers' bureau. **Awards:** Don Bradley Award. **Frequency:** annual. **Type:** recognition. **Computer Services:** Mailing lists, of members. **Formerly:** (2001) National Lesbian and Gay Lawyers Association. **Publications:** Newsletter, monthly. Alternate Formats: online ● Directory, annual. Alternate Formats: online. **Conventions/Meetings:** annual conference - 2008 Sept. 4-6, San Francisco, CA ● annual meeting - 2008 Aug. 7-12, New York, NY; 2009 July 30-Aug. 4, Chicago, IL; 2010 Aug. 5-10, San Francisco, CA.

5524 ■ National Network of Estate Planning Attorneys
3500 DePauw Blvd., Ste.2090
Indianapolis, IN 46268
Free: (800)638-8681
E-mail: info@nnepa.com
URL: http://the.nnepa.com/public
Contact: Daniel P. Stuenzi, CEO
Description: Estate attorneys. Promotes the understanding of estate planning to consumers.

5525 ■ Network of Trial Law Firms
303 S Broadway, Ste.222
Tarrytown, NY 10591
Ph: (914)332-4400
Fax: (914)332-1671
E-mail: emirsky@trial.com
URL: http://www.trial.com
Contact: Ellis R. Mirsky, Exec. Dir/Gen. Counsel
Founded: 1993. **Multinational. Description:** Provides clients with trial and litigation representation. Advances the education, technology, business and science of law profession. Fosters research and study of advances in the state-of-the-art of legal representation. Offers continuing legal education to counsel and insurance professionals.

5526 ■ Nigerian Lawyers Association (NLA)
321 Broadway, 3rd Fl.
New York, NY 10007
Ph: (212)566-9926
Fax: (212)571-4309
E-mail: feedback@nigerianlawyers.org
URL: http://www.nigerianlawyers.org
Contact: Placid Aguwa Esq., Pres.
Founded: 1999. **Membership Dues:** general (based on number of years admitted), $50-$100 (annual) ● provisional, $40 (annual). **Description:** Promotes the interests and advances the professional needs of its members. Strives to achieve fair and equitable administration of justice. Provides leadership and advocacy for the legal needs of the Nigerian community. **Publications:** Newsletter, monthly. **Price:** included in membership dues.

5527 ■ North American South Asian Bar Association (NASABA)
c/o Bharati Sharma, VP-Individual Membership
Schiffrin amd Barroway, LLP
280 King of Prussia Rd.
Radnor, PA 19087
Ph: (484)270-1456
Fax: (610)667-7056
E-mail: bsharma@sbclasslaw.com
URL: http://www.na-saba.org
Contact: Paul S. Grewal, Pres.
Membership Dues: individual, $25 (annual) ● organizational, $50 (annual). **Multinational. Description:** Promotes professional development for South Asians, attorneys and law students. Coordinates activities with other national bar associations. Provides a nationwide networking forum for all South Asian attorneys. Offers a referral network/service to the South Asian community. Seeks to educate and disseminate information to the South Asian community about the law, legal access, and relevant legal issues. **Telecommunication Services:** electronic mail, pgrewal@daycasebeer.com.

5528 ■ People Before Lawyers (PBL)
c/o Marc Perkel
309 N Jefferson, No. 220
Springfield, MO 65802
Ph: (417)866-1222
E-mail: marc@perkel.com
URL: http://www.perkel.com/pbl
Contact: Marc Perkel, Contact
Description: Provides information to people who want to represent themselves in court. Aims to restore integrity and honesty to the judicial system. Makes sure that judges and lawyers are required to follow their own rules.

5529 ■ Renaissance Lawyer Society (RLS)
4905 Glendarion Dr.
Durham, NC 27713
E-mail: mtholland@aol.com
URL: http://www.renaissancelawyer.org
Contact: Maureen Holland, Pres.
Founded: 2001. **Membership Dues:** general, $100 (annual) ● student, $25 (annual). **Description:** Seeks to address various issues concerning the legal system. Supports innovation and transformation in the legal profession. Provides a platform for exchange of ideas promoting understanding, collaboration, and cooperation in the legal community. Serves as a clearinghouse for legal information and resources. **Telecommunication Services:** electronic mail, kevinginsberg@renaissancelawyer.com.

5530 ■ Scandinavian American Lawyers Association
4177 Garrick
Warren, MI 48091
Ph: (586)757-4177
Fax: (313)557-6367
E-mail: anton_the_lord_hartforth@msn.com
Contact: Anton Anderssen, Contact
Founded: 1993. **Membership Dues:** $20 (annual). **Staff:** 1. **Languages:** English, Swedish. **Description:** Professional association of Scandinavian-American attorneys. Provides a forum to discuss and address issues of interest to members. Maintains a placement service. **Libraries: Type:** reference. **Holdings:** archival material.

5531 ■ Serbian Bar Association of America (SBAA)
c/o Kelly Pavich, Exec. Dir.
260 Maple St.
Beecher, IL 60401
E-mail: kellypavich@yahoo.com
URL: http://www.serbbar.org
Contact: Kelly Pavich, Exec. Dir.
Membership Dues: lawyer (served the law for 10 years or more), paralegal, $50 (annual) ● lawyer (served the law for less than 10 years), $100 (annual). **Multinational. Description:** Provides resource assistance to, and promotes the best interests of, the Serbian American community. Acts as a vehicle for making unified public pronouncements to represent and advocate the vital interests of the Serbian American community as a whole with respect to current social, political, economic, legal and other matters of vital concern. Serves as a national network of communication among members of the Serbian American legal community for purposes of networking, exchange of ideas, client referrals and career placement opportunities. **Awards:** Czar Dushan Award. **Frequency:** annual. **Type:** recognition. **Recipient:** to Serbian American lawyers who have excelled in their legal work and who have, through their legal careers, demonstrated leadership in the community ● Merit Award. **Frequency:** annual. **Type:** recognition. **Recipient:** to those individuals, both Serbs and non-Serbs, who through their work and life demonstrate support for the Serbian American community ● SBAA Scholarships. **Frequency:** annual. **Type:** scholarship. **Recipient:** to Serbians who are enrolled in an accredited law school in the USA.

5532 ■ Swedish-American Bar Association (SABA)
c/o Mikael Koltai, Esq., Founder
5020 Campus Dr.
Newport Beach, CA 92660
Ph: (949)706-9111
Free: (888)656-5824
Fax: (949)706-9155
E-mail: mikael@koltailaw.com
URL: http://www.saba-advokat.com
Contact: Mikael Koltai Esq., Founder
Founded: 1993. **Description:** Represents Swedish speaking attorneys in the United States. Provides sources of Swedish speaking professional legal services for Swedish-American businesses. Facilitates communication and collaboration among members.

5533 ■ Taiwanese American Lawyers Association (TALA)
c/o June J. Hsieh, Pres.
17800 Castleton St., Ste.383
City of Industry, CA 91748
Ph: (626)810-0685
Fax: (626)810-7300
E-mail: info@junehsiehlaw.com
URL: http://www.tala-la.org
Contact: June J. Hsieh, Pres.
Founded: 1994. **Membership Dues:** general, $100 (annual). **Multinational. Description:** Represents Taiwanese attorneys practicing law in the United States. Works to provide a forum for professional exchange and to serve the Taiwanese community in the United States. Raises the awareness and knowledge of U.S. laws, legal system and individual rights.

5534 ■ United States Law Firm Group (USLFG)
c/o John F. McClatchey , Exec. Dir.
3900 Key Ctr.
127 Public Sq.
Cleveland, OH 44114-1216
Ph: (216)566-5500 (216)566-5704
Fax: (216)566-5800
E-mail: john.mcclatchey@thompsonhine.com
URL: http://www.uslfg.com
Contact: John F. McClatchey, Exec. Dir.
Multinational. Description: Seeks to exchange ideas and experiences relating to law firm management, issues affecting law firms and legal developments in a variety of practice areas. Provides assistance in selecting competent counsel.

Automobile

5535 ■ American Association of Motor Vehicle Administrators (AAMVA)
4301 Wilson Blvd., Ste.400
Arlington, VA 22203
Ph: (703)522-4200
Fax: (703)522-1905
E-mail: info@aamva.org
URL: http://www.aamva.org
Contact: Mike Calvin, Interim Pres./CEO
Founded: 1933. **Members:** 1,500. **Membership Dues:** category 1, $2,200 (annual) ● local government, $750 (annual) ● category 2, $1,000 (annual). **Staff:** 75. **Regional Groups:** 4. **State Groups:** 50. **Languages:** English, French. **Description:** Officials representing 68 states, provinces, and territories who administer motor vehicle laws and regulations. Promotes reasonable and uniform laws and regulations governing registration, certification of ownership, equipment and operation of motor vehicles, and issuance of motor vehicle driver's licenses. **Awards:** AAMVA/NHTSA Safety Award. **Frequency:** annual. **Type:** recognition. **Recipient:** for jurisdictional information technology team that successfully implemented a new or innovative project to enhance highway/public safety ● AAMVA/NHTSA Security Award. **Frequency:** annual. **Type:** recognition. **Recipient:** for jurisdictional information technology team that successfully implemented a new or innovative project to enhance security ● Customer Service Excellence Award. **Frequency:** annual. **Type:** recognition. **Recipient:** for individuals, teams, and agencies who display exemplary service and either support, promote or provide a true quality service driven culture or experience ● Distinguished Service Award. **Frequency:** annual. **Type:** recognition. **Recipient:** for outstanding service in motor vehicle administration and law enforcement ● Harvard Fellowship. **Frequency:** annual. **Type:** fellowship ● Martha Irwin Distinguished Service Award for Safety. **Frequency:** annual. **Type:** recognition. **Recipient:** to a member of law enforcement jurisdiction, or an individual or organization whose primary function is directly associated with highway and traffic safety efforts ● Public Affairs and Consumer Education Awards. **Frequency:** annual. **Type:** recognition. **Recipient:** for public relations, public affairs, and consumer education excellence among the motor vehicle, law enforcement, and traffic safety agencies. **Committees:** Customer Service Delivery; Driver Licensing and Control; Financial Responsibility; Legal Services; Motor Carrier Services; Motor Vehicle Information Systems; Police Traffic Services; Public Affairs and Consumer Education; Vehicle Registration and Title; Vehicle Safety and Inspection. **Publications:** *MOVE Magazine*, 3/year. **Price:** included in membership dues; $26.00 for nonmembers. **Circulation:** 4,000. **Advertising:** accepted. Alternate Formats: online ● Membership Directory. Alternate Formats: online. **Conventions/Meetings:** annual international conference (exhibits).

5536 ■ International Association of Lemon Law Administrators (IALLA)
c/o Ms. Carol Roberts, Exec. Dir.
89 Annabessacook Dr.
Winthrop, ME 04364
Ph: (207)377-8752
Fax: (207)377-8752
E-mail: coroberts@adelphia.net
URL: http://www.ialla.net
Contact: Ms. Carol Roberts, Exec. Dir.
Membership Dues: full, $100 (annual) ● individual associate, student associate, $10 (annual) ● educational associate, $25 (annual). **Multinational. Description:** Promotes and supports effective lemon law legislation. Fosters and initiates intergovernmental activities that enhance marketplace fairness, harmonize consumer standards, increase the efficiency and effectiveness of member agencies, and reduce barriers to cross-jurisdictional enforcement of lemon laws. Represents the interests of its members on emerging public policy and legislative developments with emphasis on issues affecting consumers in the marketplace. **Publications:** Newsletter.

Aviation

5537 ■ Center for Aviation Research and Education (CARE)
1010 Wayne Ave., Ste.930
Silver Spring, MD 20910
Ph: (301)495-2848
Fax: (301)585-1803
URL: http://www.nasao.org/center/Center_Home_Page.htm
Contact: Henry M. Ogrodvinski, Pres./CEO
Founded: 1986. **Staff:** 4. **Description:** Research and educational arm of the National Association of State Aviation Officials. Supports and coordinates activities conducted by state and federal aviation agencies. Manages national airport safety data collection program; gathers and disseminates information on aerospace and aviation education programs offered by state governments. Conducts training courses in airport master planning, aviation system planning, airport management, airfield pavement evaluation, maintenance, and management. Compiles statistics. **Libraries: Type:** not open to the public. **Awards:** Aviation Education Award. **Frequency:** annual. **Type:** recognition. **Recipient:** for state programs. **Computer Services:** database, state aviation. **Affiliated With:** National Association of State Aviation Officials. **Formerly:** (1993) National Association of State Aviation Officials Center for Aviation Research and Education. **Conventions/Meetings:** annual Inspection Training - workshop.

5538 ■ Civil Air Patrol (CAP)
105 S Hansell St., Bldg. 714
Maxwell AFB, AL 36112-6332
Ph: (334)953-5463
Free: (877)227-9142
Fax: (334)953-1255
E-mail: webmaster@cap.gov
URL: http://www.cap.gov
Contact: Maj. Gen. Antonio J. Pineda CAP, Natl. Commander
Founded: 1941. **Members:** 60,000. **Membership Dues:** individual, $35 (annual) ● cadet, $25 (annual). **Staff:** 100. **Budget:** $30,000,000. **Regional Groups:** 8. **State Groups:** 52. **Local Groups:** 1,700. **Descrip-**

tion: Civilian volunteer auxiliary of the United States Air Force, with membership divided between senior members and business members and cadets ranging from 6th grade through age 21. Approximately 8,000 members are FAA licensed pilots, flying four out of every five hours on search and rescue missions directed by the Air Force Rescue Coordination Center. Members participate in rescue work during national disasters and cooperate with state and federal authorities in civil defense planning. They operate a network of approximately 20,000 fixed, mobile, and airborne emergency communications radio stations. Cadets study the social, cultural, economic, political, international, and vocational aspects of aerospace education. Courses are supplemented by practical experience in aviation, radio communications, and weather observation, and by training in leadership skills, physical fitness, and character building. Selected cadets participate in the International Air Cadet Exchange with cadets from an average of 15 foreign countries. Offers: regional and state encampments; flying training encampments; orientation courses in Federal Aviation Administration procedures and in jet, advanced jet, and space age familiarization; spiritual life conferences and counseling seminars. Cooperates with colleges and universities in conducting professional aerospace education workshops, in-service programs, and seminars for teachers and school administrators. Holds National Cadet Competition. Provides aerospace education materials upon request. Maintains Hall of Honor. Operates speakers' bureau. **Awards: Type:** recognition. **Recipient:** for individual and collective contributions to CAP ● **Type:** scholarship. **Recipient:** to cadets and senior members for academic and vocational purposes. **Publications:** *Annual Report to Congress*, annual. Alternate Formats: online ● *Civil Air Patrol News*, monthly. Newsletter ● Also publishes several aerospace education manuals with accompanying student workbooks, and instructor guides; also provides audiovisual training aids. **Conventions/Meetings:** annual National Congress on Aviation and Space Education (exhibits) - always mid-April.

5539 ■ Lawyer-Pilots Bar Association (LPBA)
PO Box 1510
Edgewater, MD 21037
Ph: (410)571-1750
Fax: (410)571-1780
E-mail: lpba@lan2wan.com
URL: http://www.lpba.org
Contact: Karen Griggs, Exec. Dir.
Founded: 1959. **Members:** 1,500. **Membership Dues:** individual, $99 (annual) ● law student, $49 (annual). **Description:** Lawyers who are licensed pilots and engaged in the practice of aviation law or interested in aviation. Is concerned with law, safety, and general aviation. **Libraries: Type:** reference. **Holdings:** photographs, reports. **Also Known As:** Legal Eagles. **Formerly:** (1965) Lawyer-Pilots Association. **Publications:** *LPBA Journal*, quarterly. **Price:** included in membership dues. Alternate Formats: online ● *Roster*, annual. Membership Directory. **Conventions/Meetings:** semiannual meeting - always summer and winter. 2008 July 30-Aug. 4, Oshkosh, WI.

5540 ■ National Association of State Aviation Officials (NASAO)
1010 Wayne Ave., Ste.930
Silver Spring, MD 20910
Ph: (301)588-0587
Fax: (301)585-1803
E-mail: henryo@nasao.org
URL: http://www.nasao.org
Contact: Henry M. Ogrodzinski, Pres./CEO
Founded: 1931. **Members:** 52. **Staff:** 4. **Budget:** $400,000. **Regional Groups:** 8. **Description:** Represents state aeronautics commissions or departments (including those in Guam and Puerto Rico) that promote, administer, and regulate aviation, and seek uniform aviation laws. Sponsors National Association of State Aviation Officials Center for Aviation Research and Education. **Libraries: Type:** not open to the public; reference. **Holdings:** reports. **Awards:** Distinguished Service. **Frequency:** annual. **Type:** recognition ● Most Innovative State Program. **Frequency:** annual. **Type:** recognition ● National Journalism. **Frequency:** annual. **Type:** recognition. **Telecommunication Services:** electronic mail, rjackson@nasao.org. **Committees:** Airports; Aviation Safety; Navigational Aids and Airspace. **Publications:** *NASAO Funding and Organizational Data Report*, annual. **Price:** $75.00 ● *NASAO Member Directory*, annual. Membership Directory. **Conventions/Meetings:** annual conference (exhibits) ● annual convention and trade show - 2008 Sept., Anchorage, AK; 2009 Sept., Phoenix, AZ.

5541 ■ National Black Coalition of Federal Aviation Employees (NBCFAE)
77 Southgate Rd.
Valley Stream, NY 11581
Ph: (516)245-3104
E-mail: hilary.king@nbcfae.org
URL: http://www.nbcfae.org
Contact: Shaun Sanders, Natl. Pres.
Founded: 1976. **Members:** 1,000. **Membership Dues:** retired, $50 (annual) ● corporate, $1,000 (annual) ● associate corporate, $500 (annual) ● associate, $50 (annual). **Regional Groups:** 8. **Description:** Federal Aviation Administration employees. Purposes are to: promote professionalism and equal opportunity in the workplace; locate and train qualified minorities for FAA positions; help the FAA meet its affirmative action goals; monitor black, female, and minority trainees; educate members and the public about their rights and FAA personnel and promotion qualifications; develop a voice for black, female, and minority FAA employees. Recruits minorities from community and schools who qualify for employment; sponsors seminars for members and for those who wish to be employed by the FAA. Maintains speaker's bureau; sponsors competitions. **Awards:** NBCFAE Scholarship. **Frequency:** annual. **Type:** scholarship. **Affiliated With:** National Association for the Advancement of Colored People; Organization of Black Airline Pilots. **Publications:** Also publish brochures. **Conventions/Meetings:** annual Training Conference - always October.

Bail

5542 ■ Professional Bail Agents of the United States (PBUS)
1301 Pennsylvania Ave. NW, Ste.925
Washington, DC 20004
Ph: (202)783-4120
Free: (800)883-PBUS
Fax: (202)783-4125
E-mail: info@pbus.com
URL: http://www.pbus.com
Contact: Stephen H. Kreimer, Exec. Dir.
Founded: 1981. **Members:** 2,000. **Membership Dues:** individual voting, $300 (annual) ● agency, $675 (annual) ● individual, $120 (annual) ● insurance company, $1,500 (annual). **Staff:** 4. **Budget:** $500,000. **State Groups:** 15. **Description:** Represents bail agents nationwide. Advances the profession through legislative advocacy, professional networking, continuing education, support of bail insurance, and development of a code of ethics. Sponsors the Certified Bail Agent Program, the only certification program designed especially for professional bail agents. Maintains a hall of fame. **Awards:** Bail Agent of the Year. **Frequency:** annual. **Type:** recognition ● Bail Individual of the Year. **Frequency:** annual. **Type:** recognition. **Computer Services:** database ● mailing lists. **Publications:** *Bail Agents Perspective*, quarterly. Magazine. **Advertising:** accepted. **Conventions/Meetings:** annual convention and meeting - always in February.

Banking

5543 ■ Banking Law Institute (BLI)
c/o Arkansas Bar Association
2224 Cottondale Ln.
Little Rock, AR 72202
Ph: (501)375-4606
Free: (800)609-5668
Fax: (501)375-4901
E-mail: mglasgow@arkbar.com
URL: http://www.arkbar.com
Founded: 1983. **Staff:** 15. **Budget:** $200,000. **Description:** Bank attorneys, bank external counsels, and bank officers interested in banking regulations. Acts as clearinghouse for information regarding laws and regulations that affect the financial services industry. **Conventions/Meetings:** seminar - 5-6/year.

5544 ■ Conference of State Bank Supervisors (CSBS)
1155 Connecticut Ave. NW, 5th Fl.
Washington, DC 20036-4306
Ph: (202)296-2840 (202)728-5718
Free: (800)886-2727
Fax: (202)296-1928
E-mail: nmilner@csbs.org
URL: http://www.csbs.org
Contact: Neil Milner CAE, Pres./CEO
Founded: 1902. **Members:** 54. **Membership Dues:** associate (sliding scale based on assets), $249-$8,510 (annual). **Staff:** 28. **Budget:** $4,000,000. **Regional Groups:** 5. **Description:** State officials responsible for chartering, regulating and supervising the nation's 6,220 state-chartered financial institutions and nearly 300 state-licensed branches and agencies of foreign banks; primary advocates for the state banking system nationwide. Advances the dual system of bank regulation. Represents the state banking system on Capitol Hill, among federal regulatory agencies and in the courts. **Libraries: Type:** reference. **Subjects:** state banking codes, regulations, and rulings, with supporting material. **Awards:** Graduate Banking Scholarships for Examiners. **Type:** fellowship. **Boards:** Bankers Advisory; International Bankers Advisory. **Committees:** Legislative; Performance Standards; Regulatory; Technology. **Formerly:** National Association of Supervisors of State Banks. **Publications:** *A Profile of State Chartered Banking*, biennial, even-numbered years. Contains statistical compendium of information on the state banking system. **Price:** $795.00 for nonmembers; $495.00 for members ● *Directory of State Bank Supervisors*, semiannual. **Price:** $50.00 for members; $115.00 for nonmembers ● *The Examiner*, weekly. Newsletter. **Conventions/Meetings:** annual meeting and conference.

Boating

5545 ■ National Association of State Boating Law Administrators (NASBLA)
1500 Leestown Rd., Ste.330
Lexington, KY 40511
Ph: (859)225-9487 (907)269-8705
Fax: (859)231-6403
E-mail: info@nasbla.org
URL: http://www.nasbla.org
Contact: Jeff Johnson, Pres.
Founded: 1959. **Members:** 125. **Membership Dues:** associate - non-profit organization, $300 (annual) ● associate - all other organization, $1,000 (annual). **Staff:** 7. **Budget:** $1,200,000. **Regional Groups:** 3. **Description:** State boating law administrators; associate members are persons from boating related businesses and organizations. Promotes boating safety by providing a medium for the exchange of views and experiences; fostering interstate and federal-state cooperation and coordination in boating problems; promoting greater uniformity in laws and regulations; increasing efficiency in administration and enforcement of boating laws. Conducts education programs; compiles statistics. **Libraries: Type:** reference. **Holdings:** books. **Committees:** Boat Accident Investigation, Reporting and Analysis; Boats and Associated Equipment; Education; Homeland Security; Law Enforcement; Numbering and Titling; Paddlesports; Waterways Management. **Publications:** *A Guide for Multiple Use Waterway Management, 2nd Edition*. Book. **Price:** $75.00 plus shipping and handling ● *National Boating Accident Investiga-*

tion Field Guide. Manual. **Price:** $49.00 plus shipping and handling ● *Small Craft Advisory*, bimonthly. Magazine. Contains authoritative articles featuring practices, procedures, research in recreation. **Price:** $12.00/year. ISSN: 1066-2383. **Circulation:** 12,000. Alternate Formats: online. **Conventions/Meetings:** annual conference and seminar, with awards and business session (exhibits) - always fall. 2008 Sept. 6-10, Burlington, VT; 2009 Sept. 26-30, Corpus Christi, TX.

5546 ■ National Boating Safety Advisory Council (NBSAC)
c/o Jeffrey N. Hoedt, Exec. Dir.
U.S. Coast Guard G-0PB-1
Washington, DC 20593-0001
Ph: (202)267-0950 (202)267-1077
Fax: (202)267-4285
E-mail: jhoedt@comdt.uscg.mil
URL: http://www.uscgboating.org/nbsac/nbsac.htm
Contact: Jeffrey N. Hoedt, Exec. Dir.
Founded: 1971. **Members:** 21. **Description:** Funded by the U.S. Coast Guard. State boating officials, boat and associated equipment manufacturers, national recreational boating organizations and the boating public. Advises the Secretary of Homeland Security and Commandant of the U.S. Coast Guard on boating safety and reviews proposed boating regulations. **Publications:** *Press Release*, periodic.

Building Codes

5547 ■ Association of Major City/County Building Officials (AMCBO)
505 Huntmar Park Dr., Ste.210
Herndon, VA 20170
Ph: (703)481-2038 (804)646-6624
Free: (800)DOC-CODE
Fax: (703)481-3596
E-mail: rwible@ncsbcs.org
URL: http://www.ncsbcs.org/newsite/AMCBO/amcbo_main_page.htm
Contact: Claude Cooper, Chm.
Founded: 1972. **Members:** 36. **Membership Dues:** jurisdiction, $300. **Staff:** 2. **Description:** Represents city and county building officials united to discuss mutual interests and problems. Focuses on issues of public safety in the buildings, administrative techniques, and building codes. Encourages the development of comprehensive training and educational programs for building code enforcement personnel. Provides scientific and technical resources for the improvement of building codes and for innovative building technology and products to reduce the cost of construction and maintain safety levels. **Telecommunication Services:** electronic mail, coopercg@ci.richmond.va.us. **Affiliated With:** National Conference of States on Building Codes and Standards. **Formerly:** (2001) Association of Major City Building Officials. **Conventions/Meetings:** annual meeting.

5548 ■ Building Officials and Code Administrators International (BOCA)
c/o International Code Council
Chicago District Off.
4051 W Flossmoor Rd.
Country Club Hills, IL 60478
Free: (888)422-7233
E-mail: webmaster@iccsafe.org
URL: http://www.iccsafe.org
Contact: Rick Weiland, CEO
Founded: 1915. **Members:** 14,500. **Membership Dues:** individual, $150 (annual). **Staff:** 100. **Budget:** $10,000,000. **Description:** Governmental officials and agencies and other interests concerned with administering or formulating building, fire, mechanical, plumbing, zoning, housing regulations. Promulgates the BOCA National Codes and the ICC International Codes suitable for adoption by reference by governmental entities. Provides services for maintaining the codes up-to-date. Maintains services for all members in connection with codes and their administration; provides consulting, training and education, plan review, and other advisory services; conducts correspondence courses; prepares in-service training programs and assists local organizations in such activities. Maintains placement services. **Libraries: Type:** not open to the public. **Awards:** Albert H. Baum. **Frequency:** annual. **Type:** recognition ● Walter S. Lee. **Frequency:** annual. **Type:** recognition. **Committees:** Building Code; Certification; Education; Fire Prevention Code; Housing Code; Interpretations; Mechanical Code; National Code; One- and Two-Family Dwelling Code; Plumbing Code; Property Maintenance; Research and Evaluation. **Formerly:** (1970) Building Officials Conference of America. **Publications:** *Annual Supplements to International Codes*, annual. Journal ● *BOCA Bulletin*, bimonthly ● *BOCA ES and NES Research Report*, quarterly ● *BOCA National Codes*, triennial ● *Building Code Manual and Property Maintenance Manual* ● *Code Commentaries*. Handbooks ● *The Code Official*, bimonthly. Magazine. **Price:** included in membership dues; $18.00 /year for nonmembers. **Advertising:** accepted ● *International Building Code*, triennial ● *International Energy Conservation Code*, triennial ● *International Fire Code*, triennial ● *International Fuel Gas code*, triennial ● *International Mechanical Code*, triennial ● *International One-and Two-Family Dwelling Code*, triennial ● *International Plumbing Code*, triennial ● *International Property Maintenance Code*, triennial ● Membership Directory, annual ● Also publishes code interpretations, department forms and permits, and textbooks. **Conventions/Meetings:** annual Code Development and Educational Conference (exhibits) ● annual meeting - always spring ● seminar.

5549 ■ International Association of Plumbing and Mechanical Officials (IAPMO)
5001 E Philadelphia St.
Ontario, CA 91761
Ph: (909)472-4100 (909)472-4203
Free: (800)854-2766
Fax: (909)472-4150
E-mail: iapmo@iapmo.org
URL: http://www.iapmo.org
Contact: G.P. Russ Chaney, Exec. Dir.
Founded: 1926. **Members:** 3,500. **Membership Dues:** government agency, $150-$300 (annual) ● individual, $75 (annual) ● senior, $15 (annual) ● organization, $425 (annual) ● student, apprentice, $25 (annual). **Staff:** 42. **Budget:** $7,000,000. **State Groups:** 35. **Description:** Government agencies, administrative officials, sales representatives, manufacturers, associations, and members of associations related to the plumbing field. Sponsors and writes Uniform Plumbing Codes; also sponsors Uniform Mechanical Code. Sponsors Speaker's Bureau. National Air Conditioning, Heating, Ventilating and Refrigeration Officials became a mechanical division of the Association in 1977. **Telecommunication Services:** electronic mail, russ.chaney@iapmo.org. **Committees:** Manufactured Housing and Recreational Vehicle Research; Manufactured Housing and Recreational Vehicle Standards; Plumbing Research; Plumbing Standards; Solar Energy Code; Swimming Pool; Uniform Mechanical Code; Uniform Plumbing Code. **Formerly:** (1966) Western Plumbing Officials Association. **Publications:** *Directory of Listed Plumbing Products*, monthly. Contains list of products found to conform to the Uniform Plumbing Code and applicable standards. **Price:** free to selected members; $94.75 /year for nonmembers. Alternate Formats: online ● *Directory of Listed Plumbing Products for Mobile Homes and Recreational Vehicles*, bimonthly. Lists plumbing parts found acceptable for installation in mobile homes and recreational vehicles. **Price:** $75.80/year ● *Interpretation Manual* ● *Official*, bimonthly. Magazine. **Price:** free for members; $29.00 /year for nonmembers. ISSN: 0192-5784. **Circulation:** 4,000. **Advertising:** accepted ● *Uniform Mechanical Code* ● *Uniform Plumbing Code Illustrated Training Manual* ● *Uniform Plumbing Code Study Guide* ● *Uniform Solar Energy Code* ● *Uniform Swimming Pool Code*. **Conventions/Meetings:** annual conference (exhibits) ● annual seminar, education and business conference (exhibits).

5550 ■ International Code Council (ICC)
500 New Jersey Ave. NW, 6th Fl.
Washington, DC 20001-2070
Ph: (562)699-0541
Free: (888)422-7233
Fax: (202)783-2348
E-mail: webmaster@iccsafe.org
URL: http://www.iccsafe.org
Contact: Walley Bailey CBO, Pres./CEO
Founded: 1972. **Members:** 50,000. **Membership Dues:** professional/cooperating, $150 (annual) ● student, $25 (annual) ● retired, $20 (annual) ● government, $100-$280 (annual) ● associate, $35 (annual) ● educational institution, $100 (annual) ● corporate/federal agency, $300 (annual) ● certified, $75 (annual). **Staff:** 300. **Budget:** $45,000,000. **State Groups:** 50. **Local Groups:** 300. **Description:** Represents three model code organizations with a membership of about 12,000 cities, states, counties, and towns. Represents building officials at all levels of government. Develops, recommends, and promotes new product acceptance, uniform regulations, and adoption of model codes. Maintains Board for the Coordination of the Model Codes and National Evaluation Service. Administers nationally recognized Certified Building Official Program. **Libraries: Type:** reference. **Holdings:** 500. **Subjects:** engineering, architecture. **Computer Services:** Mailing lists, administrative software ● online services, bulletin board, e-mail discussions. **Telecommunication Services:** electronic mail, members@iccsafe.org. **Committees:** Architectural and Engineering Services; Code and Standards Development Consensus; Code Revision; Exam Development. **Publications:** *International Building Code*, monthly. Magazine. **Circulation:** 50,000. **Advertising:** accepted ● *International Fire Code*, triennial ● *International Gas Code*, triennial ● *International Mechanical Code*, triennial ● *International Plumbing Code*, triennial ● *International Residential Code*. Manuals. **Conventions/Meetings:** annual conference - 2008 Sept. 14-20, Minneapolis, MN.

5551 ■ International Conference of Building Officials (ICBO)
c/o International Code Council
Los Angeles District Off.
5360 Workman Mill Rd.
Whittier, CA 90601
Free: (888)422-7233
Fax: (562)908-5524
E-mail: webmaster@iccsafe.org
URL: http://www.iccsafe.org
Contact: Rick Weiland, CEO
Founded: 1922. **Members:** 16,000. **Membership Dues:** governmental, $195 (annual). **Staff:** 135. **Budget:** $15,000,000. **Regional Groups:** 5. **State Groups:** 88. **Local Groups:** 3. **Description:** Representatives of local, regional, and state governments. Seeks to publish, maintain, and promote the Uniform Building Code and related documents; investigate and research principles underlying safety to life and property in the construction, use, and location of buildings and related structures; develop and promulgate uniformity in regulations pertaining to building construction; educate the building official; formulate guidelines for the administration of building inspection departments. Conducts training programs, courses, and certification programs for code enforcement inspectors. Maintains speakers' bureau. **Libraries: Type:** reference. **Holdings:** 250; archival material. **Subjects:** building codes. **Awards:** A.J. Lund Award. **Frequency:** annual. **Type:** recognition. **Recipient:** to an individual who made an outstanding contribution on promoting the group's objectives ● John Fies Award. **Type:** recognition. **Recipient:** to an outstanding representative of the building industry ● Phil Roberts Award. **Frequency:** annual. **Type:** recognition. **Recipient:** to an outstanding building official. **Computer Services:** Mailing lists ● record retrieval services, product information. **Departments:** Code Development; Education; Plan Check; Product Evaluation; Publishing. **Formerly:** (1956) Pacific Coast Building Officials Conference. **Publications:** *Building Standards Magazine*, bimonthly. Provides information for building construction and inspection techniques. **Price:** $24.00/year. **Circulation:** 18,000. **Advertising:** accepted ● *Building Standards Newsletter*, monthly ● *ICBO Certification Roster*, annual ●

The Uniform Building Code, triennial ● Membership Directory, annual ● Also publishes material on dwelling house construction and building inspection, a training manual for building inspectors, and other codes, manuals, and textbooks; makes available videos on building code enforcement and administration. **Conventions/Meetings:** annual conference, education and code development (exhibits) - always September ● seminar.

5552 ■ National Conference of States on Building Codes and Standards (NCSBCS)
505 Huntmar Park Dr., Ste.210
Herndon, VA 20170
Ph: (703)437-0100 (703)481-2024
Fax: (703)481-3596
E-mail: dbecker@ncsbcs.org
URL: http://www.ncsbcs.org
Contact: Debbie Becker, Admin. Asst.

Founded: 1967. **Members:** 320. **Membership Dues:** affiliate - private sector, $400 (annual) ● government, $100 (annual) ● academic, $75 (annual). **Staff:** 6. **Budget:** $1,000,000. **Regional Groups:** 4. **Description:** Assists in the development of programs leading to the adoption and administration of uniform comprehensive building codes and standards where such uniformity is deemed necessary for interstate purposes. Encourages acceptance of modular and industrialized building and pre-assembled building components. Develops standards and code practices that will encourage the introduction and uniform recognition of innovations in building materials. Establishes standards for building accessibility by disabled individuals. Supports the evolution of comprehensive training and educational programs at recognized educational institutions for personnel connected with the enforcement of building regulations. Fosters cooperation among government officials concerned with building regulations, and between these officials and the design, manufacturing, business, and consumer interests affected by their activities. Co-sponsors International Building Safety Week every April. **Libraries: Type:** reference. **Holdings:** 600. **Subjects:** state building codes, codes administration. **Awards:** Charles Mahaffy Award. **Frequency:** annual. **Type:** recognition ● Gene Rowland Award. **Frequency:** annual. **Type:** recognition ● President's Award. **Frequency:** annual. **Type:** recognition. **Computer Services:** database, state and major city code information. **Telecommunication Services:** electronic mail, atcfitch@ncsbcs.org. **Committees:** Factory-Built Structures; Regulatory Affairs. **Divisions:** Administrative Services; Association Services; Contract Services. **Subcommittees:** Information Technology Industry Advisory. **Task Forces:** Accessibility; Housing. **Affiliated With:** American Institute of Architects; American National Standards Institute; American Society of Heating, Refrigerating and Air-Conditioning Engineers; Association of Major City/County Building Officials; Council of State Community Development Agencies; Council of State Governments; International Code Council; National Association of Home Builders; National Conference of State Legislatures; National Fire Protection Association; National Governors Association. **Publications:** *Directory of Building Codes and Regulations*, annual ● *Introduction to Building Codes and Guide to Effective and Efficient Codes Administration*, annual. **Price:** $15.00. **Circulation:** 20,000 ● *Model One-Stop Permit Process for One- and Two-Family Dwellings* ● *NCSBCS News*. Newsletter ● *Reducing the Regulatory Portion of Housing Costs: Models of Effective and Efficient State Building Code Administration for Residential Structures* ● Reports. **Conventions/Meetings:** annual conference.

5553 ■ National Standard Plumbing Code Committee (NSPC)
180 S Washington St.
PO Box 6808
Falls Church, VA 22046
Ph: (703)237-8100
Free: (800)533-7694
Fax: (703)237-7442
E-mail: naphcc@naphcc.org
URL: http://www.phccweb.org
Contact: Dick Wagner, Chm.

Founded: 1970. **Members:** 12. **Staff:** 2. **Description:** Sponsored by National Association of Plumbing-Heating-Cooling Contractors. Has developed and updates a model plumbing code. Serves as a secretariat and publisher of the code. **Publications:** *National Standard Plumbing Code*, 3/year. Book. **Conventions/Meetings:** annual meeting - always August.

5554 ■ New Buildings Institute (NBI)
PO Box 2349
White Salmon, WA 98672
Ph: (509)493-4468
Fax: (509)493-4078
E-mail: info@newbuildings.org
URL: http://www.newbuildings.org
Contact: Dave Hewitt, Exec. Dir.

Founded: 1997. **Description:** Promotes energy efficiency in buildings through policy development, research, guidelines and codes. **Programs:** Public Interest Energy Research. **Projects:** Hot Dry Air Conditioner; Nonresidential Quality Assurance; Northeast Regional Building Energy Codes. **Publications:** Newsletter ● Annual Report, annual. Alternate Formats: online.

5555 ■ Southern Building Code Congress International (SBCCI)
c/o International Code Council
500 New Jersey Ave. NW, 6th Fl.
Washington, DC 20001-2070
Free: (888)422-7233
Fax: (703)379-2348
E-mail: webmaster@iccsafe.org
URL: http://www.iccsafe.org
Contact: Adolf A. Zubia, Contact

Founded: 1940. **Members:** 16,000. **Membership Dues:** professional, $250 (annual) ● student, $25 (annual). **Staff:** 95. **Budget:** $14,500,000. **State Groups:** 14. **Local Groups:** 95. **Description:** Active members are state, county, municipal, or other government subdivisions; associate members are trade associations, architects, engineers, contractors, and related groups or persons. Seeks to develop, maintain, and promote the adoption of the International Building, Residential Gas, Plumbing, Mechanical, Fire, and property maintenance Codes. Encourages uniformity in building regulations through the International Codes and their application and enforcement. Provides technical and educational services to members and others; participates in the development of nationally recognized consensus standards. Provides research on new materials and methods of construction; conducts seminars on code enforcement, inspection, and special topics. **Libraries: Type:** reference. **Holdings:** 500. **Subjects:** engineering, architecture. **Telecommunication Services:** TDD, (205)599-9742. **Committees:** Code Revision. **Publications:** *International Building Code*, triennial ● *International Fire Code*, triennial ● *International Gas Code*, triennial ● *International Mechanical Code*, triennial ● *International Plumbing Code*, triennial ● *International Residential Code*. Manuals ● *Southern Building Magazine*, bimonthly. **Circulation:** 16,000. **Advertising:** accepted ● Manuals, triennial ● Membership Directory, annual ● Pamphlets. **Conventions/Meetings:** annual meeting and conference (exhibits) - always October.

Cable Television

5556 ■ Association of Cable Communicators (ACC)
PO Box 75007
Washington, DC 20013-0007
Ph: (202)222-2370 (202)222-2373
Free: (800)210-3396
Fax: (202)222-2371
E-mail: services@cablecommunicators.org
URL: http://www.cablecommunicators.org
Contact: Steven R. Jones, Exec. Dir.

Founded: 1985. **Members:** 650. **Membership Dues:** individual, $200 (annual). **Staff:** 3. **Budget:** $750,000. **Description:** Supports the educational needs of professionals involved in public affairs, media, government and community relations, and communications within the cable telecommunications industry. Advocates public affairs professional's participation in all aspects of corporate decision-making process. Works to enhance each member's status and influence through skill building and educational development. **Awards:** Beacon. **Frequency:** annual. **Type:** monetary. **Computer Services:** Mailing lists. **Formerly:** (2006) Cable Television Public Affairs Association. **Publications:** *CPR Facts*, 26/year. Newsletter. **Price:** free for members ● *Public Affairs Issues*, quarterly. **Price:** included in membership dues ● Membership Directory, annual. **Price:** included in membership dues. **Conventions/Meetings:** annual conference, includes awards ceremony.

Caribbean

5557 ■ Association of Caribbean Electoral Organizations (ACEO)
c/o IFES
1101 15th St. NW, 3rd Fl.
Washington, DC 20005
Ph: (202)350-6700
Fax: (202)350-6701
E-mail: info@ifes.org
URL: http://www.ifes.org
Contact: Richard W. Soudriette, Pres./CEO

Founded: 1998. **Description:** Election officials. Promotes cooperation and mutual assistance among electoral authorities in the Caribbean, and the use of election processes that ensure free, fair and peaceful elections.

Catholic

5558 ■ American Catholic Lawyers Association (ACLA)
PO Box 10092
Fairfield, NJ 07004
Ph: (973)244-9895
Fax: (973)244-9897
E-mail: info@acla-inc.org
URL: http://www.americancatholiclawyers.org
Contact: Christopher A. Ferrara Esq., Pres./Chief Counsel

Founded: 1990. **Description:** Represents individuals dedicated to the free legal defense of and the rights of Catholics in America. Seeks to establish the "Social Kingship of Christ", and uphold the Divine prerogatives and moral law. Provides free legal services on behalf of Catholics needing legal defense in matters of faith and conscience. **Publications:** Newsletter. Alternate Formats: online.

Civil Defense

5559 ■ The American Civil Defense Association (TACDA)
11576 S State St., Ste.502
Draper, UT 84020
Free: (800)425-5397
Fax: (888)425-5339
E-mail: info@tacda.org
URL: http://www.tacda.org
Contact: Ms. Sharon Packer, Exec. Dir.

Founded: 1962. **Members:** 500. **Membership Dues:** contributing, $36 (annual). **Staff:** 3. **Budget:** $90,000. **Description:** Represents individuals and families from all walks of life, all sharing the common goal of preparing themselves, their families, and their communities against natural and manmade disasters. Aims to provide information, tools and resources that empower American Citizens with a comprehensive understanding of reasonable preparedness strategies and techniques; promoting a self-reliant, pro-active approach to protecting themselves, their families and their communities in the event of Nuclear, Biological,

Chemical or other manmade and natural disasters. Maintains Speakers' Bureau that organizes speaking opportunities by experts in their fields. **Libraries: Type:** reference. **Awards:** American Preparedness Award. **Frequency:** annual. **Type:** recognition. **Formerly:** (1977) Association for Community-Wide Protection from Nuclear Attack. **Publications:** *Journal of Civil Defense*, quarterly. Magazine. Includes book reviews, calendar of events, shelter articles, legislative news, survival news, and a listing of civil defense emergency services. **Price:** included in membership dues; $18.00 /year for nonmembers. ISSN: 0740-5537. **Circulation:** 2,000. **Advertising:** accepted. Alternate Formats: online ● Also publishes proclamations. **Conventions/Meetings:** annual seminar and conference (exhibits).

5560 ■ Disaster Emergency Response Association (DERA)

PO Box 797
Longmont, CO 80502
Ph: (970)532-3362
Fax: (970)532-2979
E-mail: dera@disasters.org
URL: http://www.disasters.org
Contact: Bascombe J. Wilson, Exec. Dir.

Founded: 1962. **Members:** 1,100. **Membership Dues:** professional, technical, academic, $50 (annual) ● executive management, nonprofit organization, $75 (annual) ● unpaid volunteer, student, retired, $25 (annual) ● government agency, $95 (annual) ● corporate sponsor, $500 (annual) ● life, $450. **Staff:** 4. **Budget:** $25,000. **Languages:** English, French, Italian, Portuguese, Spanish. **Description:** Individuals working in the field of disaster preparedness, including professional disaster researchers, response and recovery specialists, trainers, and project managers. Assists communities, businesses, and industries in preparing for emergencies. Conducts risk assessments, mitigation efforts, and information management and decision-making training programs. Provides disaster relief by mitigating hazards, improving emergency communications networks, and sponsoring emergency response teams. **Awards:** DERA Disaster Studies Award. **Frequency:** annual. **Type:** recognition. **Recipient:** for high school students who enter an excellent disaster related project in regional or state level science fairs. **Committees:** Disaster Mitigation; International Service Commission. **Sections:** Amateur Radio; Disaster Medicine; Disaster Mortuary; Search and Rescue. **Publications:** *Disaster Resource Center Update*, periodic. **Price:** $50.00/ year. **Circulation:** 7,500. **Advertising:** accepted. Alternate Formats: online ● *DisasterCom*, quarterly. Newsletter. **Price:** $45.00/year. ISSN: 1521-1592. Alternate Formats: online. **Conventions/Meetings:** annual Community Preparedness: Making a Safer Tomorrow - workshop (exhibits) - usually in February.

5561 ■ Disaster Preparedness and Emergency Response Association (DERA)

PO Box 797
Longmont, CO 80502
E-mail: dera@disasters.org
URL: http://www.disasters.org
Contact: Steven Keene, Chm.

Founded: 1962. **Members:** 750. **Membership Dues:** professional, technical, academic, $50 (annual) ● volunteer, student, retired, $25 (annual) ● executive, management, $75 (annual) ● nonprofit, $75 (annual) ● life, $450 ● small business, $125 (annual) ● governmental agency, $95 (annual) ● corporate, $500 (annual). **Staff:** 2. **Budget:** $24,000. **Regional Groups:** 10. **State Groups:** 54. **National Groups:** 8. **Languages:** Dutch, English, French, Italian, Portuguese, Spanish. **Multinational. Description:** Government agencies, nonprofit associations, educational institutions, corporations, emergency management professionals, volunteers, and other individuals and organizations with an interest in civil defense and disaster preparedness. Seeks to assist communities worldwide in disaster preparedness, response, and recovery. Serves as a network linking members; acts as a clearinghouse on civil defense and disaster preparedness. **Awards:** Student Achievement. **Frequency:** annual. **Type:** medal. **Recipient:** for noteworthy studies related to disaster preparedness. **Also Known As:** DERA International. **Publications:** *Disastercom*, quarterly. Newsletter. **Price:** free. ISSN: 1521-1592. **Advertising:** accepted. Alternate Formats: online. **Conventions/Meetings:** annual International Preparedness Workshop, membership meeting, preparedness symposium and strategic planning workshop (exhibits) - every February.

5562 ■ DRI International (DRII)

1400 Eye St. NW, Ste.1050
Washington, DC 20005
Ph: (202)962-3979
Fax: (202)962-3990
E-mail: driinfo@drii.org
URL: http://drii.org
Contact: Brent Woodworth, Chm.

Founded: 1988. **Members:** 2,700. **Membership Dues:** individual, $75 (annual). **Staff:** 5. **Budget:** $2,000,000. **Multinational. Description:** Serves as a certifying organization for professionals in the field of Business Continuity Management. Promotes advancement in the study, teaching, and practice of disaster recovery and business continuity. Seeks to ensure the existence of workable business recovery plans worldwide. Devises public and private infrastructure continuity plans and studies; sponsors professional development and other educational programs; conducts examinations and certifies business continuity professionals. **Boards:** Certification. **Formerly:** Disaster Recovery Institute International. **Publications:** Newsletter, quarterly. Alternate Formats: online. **Conventions/Meetings:** annual meeting and conference, in conjunction with Disaster Recovery Journal spring meeting.

5563 ■ International Association Emergency Managers (IAEM)

c/o Elizabeth B. Armstrong, CAE, Exec. Dir
201 Park Washington Ct.
Falls Church, VA 22046-4527
Ph: (703)538-1795 (502)852-2948
Fax: (703)241-5603
E-mail: info@iaem.com
URL: http://www.iaem.com
Contact: Elizabeth B. Armstrong CAE, Exec. Dir.

Founded: 1952. **Members:** 5,000. **Membership Dues:** individual, $170 (annual) ● affiliate, $500 (annual) ● student, $25 (annual). **Staff:** 6. **Budget:** $350,000. **Regional Groups:** 10. **State Groups:** 30. **Multinational. Description:** Individuals responsible for disaster preparedness, response, and recovery, including homeland security on the city and country levels. Serves as liaison among local units of government and state and federal emergency and civil defense agencies. Seeks to develop a comprehensive, workable, and effective all-hazard emergency and civil defense program through coordinated action. Conducts educational programs. Provides a professional certification program. **Awards:** Executive Citations. **Type:** recognition. **Recipient:** to the member of the association whose professional image and achievements enhance the field of emergency management ● Honorary Citations. **Frequency:** annual. **Type:** recognition. **Recipient:** to the individual who has visibly and actively supported the association in its efforts to improve the level of international preparedness ● Interagency Disaster Preparedness Awards. **Type:** recognition. **Recipient:** for cosponsorship with Homeland Protection Professional Magazine ● Media Awards. **Frequency:** annual. **Type:** recognition. **Recipient:** for local emergency managers. **Committees:** Awards and Recognition; Business and Industry; International Development; Training and Education. **Formerly:** (1983) United States Civil Defense Council; (1998) National Coordinating Council on Emergency Management. **Publications:** Bulletin, monthly. Includes updates on resources and policies affecting EM management, research, and technology to protect lives and property from disaster. **Price:** included in membership dues. **Circulation:** 3,000. **Advertising:** accepted ● Membership Directory, annual. **Price:** available to members only. **Conventions/Meetings:** annual meeting and conference (exhibits) - 2008 Nov. 15-20, Overland Park, KS; 2009 Oct. 31-Nov. 5, Orlando, FL.

5564 ■ International Resources Group (IRG)

1211 Connecticut Ave. NW, Ste.700
Washington, DC 20036
Ph: (202)289-0100
Fax: (202)289-7601
E-mail: info@irgltd.com
URL: http://www.irgltd.com
Contact: Philip Palmedo, Chm./CEO

Founded: 1978. **Staff:** 170. **Budget:** $25,000,000. **Languages:** English, French, German, Greek, Japanese, Mandarin, Portuguese, Russian, Spanish, Thai. **Multinational. Description:** Promotes disaster preparedness and mitigation and effective emergency management worldwide. Undertakes and administers housing, flood preparedness, emergency construction, community self-help, monitoring and evaluating transition from emergency to environmental disaster programs. **Libraries: Type:** not open to the public. **Holdings:** 2,000. **Subjects:** disaster, emergency management. **Formerly:** (2001) INTERTECT; (2005) IRG Ltd.

5565 ■ National Emergency Management Association (NEMA)

PO Box 11910
Lexington, KY 40578-1910
Ph: (859)244-8000 (859)244-8162
Fax: (859)244-8239
E-mail: nemaadmin@csg.org
URL: http://www.nemaweb.org/index.cfm
Contact: Trina R. Sheets, Exec. Dir.

Founded: 1950. **Members:** 380. **Membership Dues:** individual, $200 (annual) ● corporate, $500-$1,200 (annual) ● organizational, key state staff, and homeland security, $300 (annual) ● state, $3,200 (annual). **Staff:** 5. **Regional Groups:** 11. **State Groups:** 60. **Description:** State emergency management directors, individuals, associations, organizations, and corporations with an interest in emergency management. Seeks to improve relations within the emergency management community to provide a cohesive infrastructure for the protection of the public against natural and man-made hazards. Promotes state emergency management programs. Represents the state emergency management community before the federal government. Facilitates coordination of efforts between the government and the private sector. Produces position papers and resolutions on emergency management issues. Conducts specialized education programs; maintains speakers' bureau. **Awards:** Lacy E. Suiter Distinguished Service in Emergency Management. **Frequency:** annual. **Type:** recognition. **Recipient:** for individual who has made outstanding contributions throughout his career to any or all facets of emergency management. **Committees:** CSEPP; Emac; Information Infrastructure; Legal Counsel; Legislative; Mitigation; Preparedness; Private Sector; Public Affairs; Response and Recovery. **Projects:** Incident Command System; National Homeland Security. **Formerly:** (1974) National Association of State Civil Defense Directors; (1980) National Association of State Directors for Disaster Preparedness. **Conventions/Meetings:** semiannual conference (exhibits).

Civil Service

5566 ■ Association of Former International Civil Servants - New York (AFICS (NY))

One United Nations Plz., Rm. DC1-580
New York, NY 10017
Ph: (212)963-2943
Fax: (212)963-5702
E-mail: afics@un.org
URL: http://www.un.org/other/afics
Contact: Andres Castellanos, Pres.

Founded: 1970. **Members:** 3,141. **Membership Dues:** life, $250 ● individual, $25 (annual) ● associate, $12 (annual) ● life-associate, $125. **Staff:** 3. **Multinational. Description:** Association for former international civil servants of the United Nation's family of organizations. Aims to advise and assist former international civil servants and those about to separate from service on questions of pensions, residence, health care, taxation, social security and other important concerns. **Committees:** Aging and Assistance; Insurance; Legal; Pension. **Publications:** Bulletin, quarterly. Alternate Formats: online.

5567 ■ Council of Jewish Organizations in Civil Service (CJOCS)
Address Unknown since 2008
Founded: 1946. **Members:** 120,000. **Description:** Jewish civil servants employed at city, state, or federal levels. Seeks to prevent discrimination and to actively promote a merit system based on individual ability regardless of race, color, creed, or national origin. Activities include Hebrew and Yiddish cultural programs. **Awards: Type:** recognition ● **Type:** scholarship. **Publications:** *Council News*, biweekly. **Conventions/Meetings:** annual conference ● annual seminar.

5568 ■ National Association of Civil Service Employees (NACSE)
Address Unknown since 2008
Founded: 1973. **Members:** 40,000. **Staff:** 28. **State Groups:** 42. **Description:** Federal, state, county, and city civil service employees; association employees and counselors. Assists nonprofit charitable, educational, and scientific organizations in promoting social welfare. Conducts service and product consumer research and educational programs and symposia; sponsors competitions; maintains placement service. **Awards: Type:** grant. **Recipient:** for research reports or studies on educational subjects ● Legion of Honor Award. **Type:** recognition. **Recipient:** for outstanding members supporting association programs ● Recognition Awards. **Type:** recognition. **Recipient:** for individuals who have made outstanding contributions to the social welfare of the community. **Publications:** *Register*, monthly. **Conventions/Meetings:** annual meeting.

5569 ■ National Association of State Retirement Administrators (NASRA)
PO Box 14117
Baton Rouge, LA 70898
Ph: (225)757-9558 (512)868-2774
Fax: (225)757-9765
E-mail: glendac@nasra.org
URL: http://www.nasra.org
Contact: Glenda Chambers, Exec. Dir.
Founded: 1956. **Members:** 200. **Membership Dues:** regular, $2,400 (annual) ● associate, $2,700 (annual). **Staff:** 4. **Description:** Administrators of statewide public employee retirement systems. Encourages nationwide review of pension and retirement programs; sponsors conferences; provides technical and information services to members. **Libraries: Type:** reference. **Holdings:** reports. **Committees:** Audit and Budget; Code of Conduct; Constitution and Bylaws; Education; Legislative and Resolutions; Nominations; Program; Special Programs. **Publications:** *Membership List*, periodic. Membership Directory ● *Minutes of Conference*, annual ● *Public Fund*. Survey ● *Survey of State Retirement Systems*, biennial ● Newsletter, semiannual. Alternate Formats: online. **Conventions/Meetings:** annual conference - usually August. 2008 Aug. 1-6, Salt Lake City, UT; 2009 July 31-Aug. 5, Savannah, GA.

5570 ■ National Conference on Public Employee Retirement Systems (NCPERS)
444 N Capitol St. NW, Ste.221
Washington, DC 20001-1512
Free: (877)202-5706
Fax: (202)624-1439
E-mail: info@ncpers.org
URL: http://www.ncpers.org
Contact: Kim H. Hank Esq., Exec. Dir./Counsel
Founded: 1941. **Members:** 425. **Membership Dues:** retirement fund/associated organization (with 1-16501 organization members), $150-$600 (annual) ● corporate sponsor, $6,000 (annual). **Description:** National, state, and local organizations whose purpose is to promote and safeguard the rights and benefits of public employees in retirement systems. Serves as congressional liaison. **Libraries: Type:** reference. **Holdings:** archival material, reports. **Programs:** Life Insurance. **Task Forces:** Health Care. **Publications:** *First Report: NCPERS Task Force on Health Care Benefits of Public Employees and Retirees* ● *The Monitor*, monthly. Newsletter. Contains information on federal legislation and regulatory issues affecting public retirement plans. **Price:** included in membership dues. Alternate Formats: online ● *Persist*, quarterly. Journal. Includes investment and benefit reports, legal issues, and trustee continuing education. **Price:** included in membership dues. Alternate Formats: online ● *Word From Washington*, monthly ● Proceedings, annual ● Annual Report. **Conventions/Meetings:** annual conference (exhibits) - always April or May. 2009 Apr. 26-30, San Diego, CA ● annual workshop and conference, legislative ● annual workshop.

5571 ■ National Organization of Blacks in Government (BIG)
3005 Georgia Ave. NW
Washington, DC 20001-3807
Ph: (202)667-3280
E-mail: big@bignet.org
URL: http://www.bignet.org
Contact: Darlene H. Young, Pres.
Founded: 1975. **Members:** 25,000. **Membership Dues:** life, $300 ● regular, $35 (annual) ● associate, $25 (annual) ● gold plus, $175. **Staff:** 8. **Local Groups:** 100. **Description:** Federal, state, or local government employees or retirees concerned with the present and future status of Blacks in government. Develops training and other programs to enhance the liberty and sense of well-being of Blacks in government. Offers seminars and workshops for professional and nonprofessional government employees. **Telecommunication Services:** electronic mail, natbigpresident@aol.com. **Committees:** Agency Watch; Education; Legal; Legislative Review; Personnel Action Liaison; Public Relations. **Programs:** Attorney Assistance; Big National Health; Complaint Advisors and Assistance; Discrimination Awareness; Memorial Wall; Monetary Assistance. **Affiliated With:** National Conference of Black Mayors. **Publications:** *BIG Bulletin*, monthly. Newsletter ● *BIG Reporter*, quarterly. Newsletter ● *Blacks in Government—News*, quarterly. Newsletter. **Price:** included in membership dues. **Conventions/Meetings:** annual conference ● annual conference (exhibits) - always August.

5572 ■ Public Employees Roundtable (PER)
c/o Council for Excellence in Government
1301 K St. NW, Ste.450 W
Washington, DC 20005
Ph: (202)728-0418
Fax: (202)728-0422
E-mail: per@excelgov.org
URL: http://www.excelgov.org/index.php?keyword=a43bda2ade1cbd
Contact: Carl Fillichio, Exec. Dir.
Founded: 1982. **Members:** 34. **Membership Dues:** associate council, $1,000 (annual). **Staff:** 21. **Budget:** $400,000. **Regional Groups:** 5. **Description:** Promotes awareness of the contributions made by public employees to the quality of life of Americans. Encourages excellence, enthusiasm, and devotion in government, and promotes public service careers. Sponsors Public Service Recognition Week on the first week of May and the National Forensic League extemporaneous speech finals. Produces videos and public service announcements. **Awards:** Elliot Richardson Prize for Excellence in Public Service. **Frequency:** annual. **Type:** recognition. **Recipient:** for extraordinary, sustained accomplishment and integrity in government service ● Public Service Excellence Awards. **Frequency:** annual. **Type:** scholarship. **Recipient:** for students with 3.5 GPA; for public service aspirations. **Computer Services:** Mailing lists. **Telecommunication Services:** electronic mail, cfillichio@excelgov.org. **Publications:** *How to Celebrate*. Handbook ● *The Unsung Heroes*, quarterly. Newsletter. Includes facts and figures about public service contributions. **Price:** included in membership dues. **Circulation:** 8,000. **Conventions/Meetings:** annual Associate Council Members' Meeting - always December or January.

Colleges and Universities

5573 ■ AAUW Legal Advocacy Fund (LAF)
1111 16th St. NW
Washington, DC 20036
Ph: (202)785-7700
Free: (800)326-AAUW
Fax: (202)872-1425
E-mail: helpline@aauw.org
URL: http://www.aauw.org/laf/index.cfm
Contact: Leslie Annexstein, Dir.
Founded: 1981. **Members:** 100,000. **Membership Dues:** individual, member-at-large, $49 (annual) ● student, affiliate-at-large, $17 (annual). **Description:** Promotes equity for women in higher education; supports discrimination lawsuits against colleges and universities; provides financial support for sex discrimination lawsuits; works to educate the university community about sex discrimination, aims to improve conditions through campus outreach; provides consulting with women on legal strategies, resources and potential lawsuits. **Awards:** Progress in Equity Award. **Frequency:** annual. **Type:** recognition. **Recipient:** for a college or university program ● Speaking Out for Justice Award. **Frequency:** biennial. **Type:** recognition. **Recipient:** for a nationally prominent individual. **Telecommunication Services:** TDD, (202)785-7777. **Publications:** *AAUW Outlook*. Magazine. Includes articles, interviews, book reviews and excerpts, community action projects, and legislative updates. Alternate Formats: online ● *Legal Advocacy Fund Update*. Newsletter. Alternate Formats: online ● *Mission in Action*, periodic. Newsletter. Contains updates on the work of AAUW. Alternate Formats: online ● Annual Report, annual. Alternate Formats: online.

Commercial Law

5574 ■ American Bankruptcy Institute (ABI)
44 Canal Center Plz., Ste.404
Alexandria, VA 22314
Ph: (703)739-0800
Fax: (703)739-1060
E-mail: sgerdano@abiworld.org
URL: http://www.abiworld.org
Contact: Samuel J. Gerdano, Exec. Dir.
Founded: 1982. **Members:** 10,600. **Membership Dues:** individual, $250 (annual) ● government/professor/auctioneer/non-profit/international, $95 (annual). **Staff:** 25. **Budget:** $7,000,000. **Description:** Attorneys, accountants, and other providers of financial services, lending institutions, credit organizations, consumer groups, federal and state governments, and other interested individuals. Provides a multidisciplinary forum for the exchange of information on bankruptcy and insolvency issues. Fosters dialogue among lawyers, businesspersons, and legislators on current and potential bankruptcy problems. Reviews existing and proposed legislation as it affects bankruptcy and insolvency. Conducts nationally televised panel discussions and research projects; provides information to the public and legislators. Maintains speakers bureau; compiles statistics. Conducts research and educational programs. **Libraries: Type:** reference. **Awards:** Medal of Excellence. **Frequency:** annual. **Type:** medal. **Computer Services:** Mailing lists. **Telecommunication Services:** electronic mail, mkleppinger@abiworld.org. **Committees:** Asset Sales; Bankruptcy Administration; Bankruptcy Reorganization; Bankruptcy Taxation; Commercial Fraud Task Force; Consumer Bankruptcy; Ethics; Finance and Banking; Health Care; International; Law School; Legislation; Membership; Professional Compensation; Public Companies; Real Estate; Uniform Commercial Code; Unsecured Trade Creditors; Young Members. **Publications:** *ABI Annual Membership Directory*, annual. Contains listing of member's addresses and telephone numbers. **Price:** included in membership dues.

Advertising: accepted. Alternate Formats: CD-ROM ● *ABI Journal*, 10/year. Covers the entire range of insolvency issues, featuring timely articles written by some of the most knowledgeable professionals in the field. **Advertising:** accepted. Alternate Formats: online ● *ABI Law Review*, semiannual. Journal. **Price:** included in membership dues ● *ABI Update Newsletter*. Alternate Formats: online ● *Legislative Updates*. Reports ● Also publishes manuals. **Conventions/ Meetings:** annual Moot Court - competition, opportunity for law schools to compete on bankruptcy issues ● annual Winter Leadership Conference - convention (exhibits) - always December, in West Coast.

5575 ■ American College of Bankruptcy
11350 Random Hills Rd., Ste.800
Fairfax, VA 22030-6044
Ph: (703)934-6154
Fax: (703)802-0207
E-mail: college@amercol.org
URL: http://www.amercol.org
Contact: David T. Sykes, Chm.
Founded: 1989. **Members:** 650. **Membership Dues:** fellow, $250 (annual). **Staff:** 1. **Budget:** $50,000. **Description:** Bankruptcy attorneys, judges, and professors united to recognize and honor distinguished bankruptcy professionals in an effort to set standards of achievement in the field. Funds and assists projects that promote quality bankruptcy practice including undergraduate and graduate programs. Conducts research. **Libraries: Type:** reference. **Holdings:** archival material. **Subjects:** bankruptcy. **Awards:** Distinguished Service Award. **Frequency:** annual. **Type:** recognition. **Recipient:** for improving the administration of justice in the field of bankruptcy. **Committees:** Communications; Educational Programs; Future of the College; History of the College; Liaisons; Meetings and Events; Nominating; Pro Bono. **Publications:** *American College of Bankruptcy Directory*, annual ● *College Columns Newsletter*, quarterly. **Conventions/Meetings:** annual meeting.

5576 ■ Commercial Law League of America (CLLA)
70 E Lake St., Ste.630
Chicago, IL 60601
Ph: (312)781-2000 (516)677-8200
Fax: (312)781-2010
E-mail: info@clla.org
URL: http://www.clla.org
Contact: Wanda Borges Esq., Pres.
Founded: 1895. **Members:** 4,000. **Membership Dues:** regular US, Canadian and international applicant, $295 (annual) ● law professor/teacher, law clerk, editor, legal periodical, $50 (annual) ● law student, $10 (annual) ● special/short term rate, $130 ● optional and contribution: bankruptcy, creditor's right section, $80 (annual) ● sustaining, young member and fund for public education, $25-$35 (annual). **Staff:** 3. **Budget:** $2,000,000. **Regional Groups:** 5. **National Groups:** 4. **Multinational. Description:** Represents lawyers and other professionals engaged in bankruptcy and other commercial law areas; commercial collection agencies; law list publishers. Elevates the standards and improve the practice of commercial law. Promotes uniformity of legislation in matters affecting commercial law. Conducts educational programs on legal topics and issues of public interest at regional and national meetings. Maintains speakers' bureau and over 40 special and standing committees covering areas of commercial law including Bankruptcy and Uniform Commercial Code. **Libraries: Type:** reference. **Holdings:** papers, reports. **Awards:** President's Cup. **Frequency:** annual. **Type:** recognition. **Telecommunication Services:** electronic mail, dwatson@clla.org. **Committees:** Political Action. **Funds:** Patron; Public Education. **Sections:** Bankruptcy; Commercial Collection Agency; Creditors' Rights; Young Members. **Publications:** *Bankruptcy Reform Act Manual*. **Price:** $40.00 plus shipping and handling ● *Commercial Law Bulletin*, bimonthly. Magazine. Contains popular legal articles and CLLA news. Includes advertisers' index, calendar of events and practice tips. **Price:** $18.00 included in membership dues; $45.00 /year for nonmembers. **Circulation:** 6,000. **Advertising:** accepted. Alternate Formats: CD-ROM; microform ● *DePaul Business & Commercial Law Journal*, quarterly. Includes information on commercial and bankruptcy law. **Price:** $12.00 included in membership dues; $85.00 /year for nonmembers; $20.00/issue for nonmembers. ISSN: 0010-3055. **Circulation:** 6,000. **Advertising:** accepted ● *Member Roster*, annual. Membership Directory. **Advertising:** accepted ● Pamphlets ● Also publishes educational materials. **Conventions/Meetings:** annual convention - always July ● periodic regional meeting.

5577 ■ Forfeiture Endangers American Rights
20 Sunnyside Ave., Ste.A-419
Mill Valley, CA 94941
Ph: (415)389-8551
Free: (888)FEAR-001
Fax: (415)381-6105
E-mail: brenda@fear.org
URL: http://www.fear.org
Contact: Brenda Grantland Esq., Pres.
Founded: 1992. **Members:** 200. **Membership Dues:** general, $35 (annual). **Budget:** $5,000. **State Groups:** 10. **Description:** Represents victims of asset forfeiture laws, attorneys with an interest in forfeiture statutes, and other individuals advocating reform of forfeiture laws as a defense of the right of due process. Group believes that current forfeiture statutes (forfeiture is the loss of property due to a breach of legal obligation) place undo burdens on the defendant, who is often deprived of the means to finance legal defense by the act of forfeiture. Plans to operate state groups in all U.S. states. Maintains speakers' bureau. **Libraries: Type:** reference. **Also Known As:** FEAR. **Publications:** *FEAR Chronicles*, periodic. Newsletter. Covers current cases of forfeiture law abuse and reform. **Price:** $35.00/year. **Circulation:** 400. **Conventions/Meetings:** annual meeting.

5578 ■ National Association of Bankruptcy Trustees (NABT)
1 Windsor Cove, Ste.305
Columbia, SC 29223
Ph: (803)252-5646
Free: (800)445-8629
Fax: (803)765-0860
E-mail: info@nabt.com
URL: http://www.nabt.com
Contact: Samuel K. Crocker, Pres.
Founded: 1982. **Membership Dues:** trustee, $325 (annual) ● trustee assistant, $50 (annual) ● associate, $150 (annual) ● supplier, $300 (annual) ● Presidential Circle, $350 (annual). **Description:** Attorneys, court-appointed trustees, bankers, auctioneers, clerks, and others involved in bankruptcy proceedings. Seeks to help members manage their bankruptcy practices more efficiently and profitably. Provides continuing education on bankruptcy issues and office management procedures and systems. Seeks to obtain malpractice insurance for members. Lobbies the government and monitors legislation on bankruptcy issues. **Formerly:** National Association of Chapter 13 Trustees. **Publications:** *NABTalk*, quarterly. Newsletter. **Price:** included in membership dues. **Conventions/Meetings:** annual conference ● annual Full Speed Ahead - convention - 2008 Aug. 20-24, Anchorage, AK ● semiannual meeting (exhibits).

5579 ■ National Association of Shareholder and Consumer Attorneys (NASCAT)
c/o Barry A. Weprin, Treas.
One Pennsylvania Plz., 49th Fl.
New York, NY 10119
Ph: (212)946-9312
Fax: (212)273-4379
E-mail: bweprin@milbergweiss.com
URL: http://www.nascat.org
Contact: Carol Gilden, Pres.
Founded: 1988. **Members:** 100. **Description:** Lawyers and law firms that support strong federal and state securities and commercial laws. Promotes a free and fair market for investors and other consumers. **Telecommunication Services:** electronic mail, kroddy@wilentz.com. **Formerly:** (2004) National Association of Securities and Commercial Law Attorneys.

Communications

5580 ■ Federal Communications Bar Association (FCBA)
1020 19th St. NW, Ste.325
Washington, DC 20036-6101
Ph: (202)293-4000
Fax: (202)293-4317
E-mail: fcba@fcba.org
URL: http://www.fcba.org
Contact: Stanley D. Zenor, Exec. Dir.
Founded: 1936. **Members:** 3,500. **Membership Dues:** private sector attorney/private sector non-attorney, $125 (annual) ● government/academic attorney, $40 (annual) ● retired, $40 (annual) ● law student, $35 (annual) ● paralegal/legal assistant, $65 (annual) ● foreign attorney/foreign non-attorney, $130 (annual). **Staff:** 4. **Budget:** $1,000,000. **Regional Groups:** 8. **Description:** Attorneys and other professionals specializing in communications law and policy. Sponsors continuing legal education programs and seminars. **Computer Services:** database ● mailing lists, lists rentals to qualified organizations. **Telecommunication Services:** electronic mail, stan@fcba.org. **Committees:** FCC Enforcement Practice; National Telecommunications Moot Court; Professional Responsibility; Relations with Other Bar Associations; State and Local Practice; Transactional Practice; Wireless Telecommunications Practice; Young Lawyers. **Publications:** *CLE Seminars*. Audiotapes ● *FCBA News*, monthly. Newsletter. Alternate Formats: online ● *Federal Communications Law Journal*, 3/year. **Price:** $30.00/year in U.S.; $40.00/year in Canada and Mexico; $50.00/year, international. Alternate Formats: online ● *International Practice Handbook* ● Membership Directory, annual. **Price:** $55.00 for members; $30.00 for law student members; $110.00 for nonmembers. **Advertising:** accepted. **Conventions/Meetings:** annual conference (exhibits) ● annual dinner ● monthly luncheon ● monthly seminar.

5581 ■ Federal Publishers Committee (FPC)
Address Unknown since 2007
Founded: 1979. **Members:** 600. **Staff:** 4. **National Groups:** 1. **Description:** Representatives from executive branch agencies, the Joint Committee on Printing of the Congress, the Government Printing Office, the Library of Congress, and other organizations involved in federal publishing. Promotes cost-effective publications management in the federal government in the areas of planning, marketing, writing, graphic design, printing, promotion, and other aspects of publishing. Studies creation, production, marketing, distribution, and storage problems. **Publications:** *Reports of Meeting*, monthly ● *Special Reports—Roundtables*, periodic ● Handbook. **Conventions/Meetings:** monthly conference ● periodic symposium.

5582 ■ International Technology Law Association (ITechLaw)
401 Edgewater Pl., Ste.600
Wakefield, MA 01880
Ph: (781)876-8877 (508)487-1599
Fax: (781)224-1239
E-mail: office@itechlaw.org
URL: http://www.itechlaw.org
Contact: Susan L. Donegan Esq., Exec. Dir.
Founded: 1971. **Members:** 1,600. **Membership Dues:** attorney, $230-$280 (annual) ● regular 2, corporate counsel, $230 (annual) ● student, $45 (annual) ● government, law professor, $200 (annual) ● associate (non-lawyer), $500 (annual). **Staff:** 1. **Budget:** $75,000. **Description:** Lawyers, law students, and others interested in legal problems related to computer-communications technology. Aids in: contracting for computer-communications goods and services; perfecting and protecting proprietary rights

chiefly in software; and taxing computer-communications goods, services, and transactions, and liability for acquisition and use of computer-communications goods and services. Provides specialized educational programs; and offers limited placement service. Holds Annual Computer Law Update. **Telecommunication Services:** electronic mail, memberservices@itechlaw.org. **Committees:** Ethics and Professional Responsibility; International Associate Exchange Program. **Formerly:** (2006) Computer Law Association. **Publications:** *A Guide to European Data Protection and Privacy Laws for U.S. Companies*. Book. **Price:** $45.00 for members; $55.00 for nonmembers ● *Computer Law Association Newsletter*, quarterly ● Bulletin. Alternate Formats: online ● Membership Directory, annual ● Also publishes conference programs. **Conventions/Meetings:** periodic conference ● seminar.

5583 ■ National Association of Government Communicators (NAGC)
201 Park Washington Ct.
Falls Church, VA 22046-4527
Ph: (703)538-1787
Fax: (703)241-5603
E-mail: info@nagconline.org
URL: http://www.nagc.com
Contact: Gene Rose, Pres.
Founded: 1976. **Members:** 650. **Membership Dues:** active, $85 (annual) ● organization, agency, $340 (annual) ● affiliate individual, $125 (annual) ● retired, $45 (annual) ● student, $35 (annual) ● affiliate group, $500 (annual). **Staff:** 3. **Budget:** $300. **State Groups:** 10. **Local Groups:** 2. **Description:** Government employees, retired persons, non-government affiliates, and students. Seeks to advance communications as an essential professional resource at every level of national, state, and local government by: disseminating information; encouraging professional development, public awareness, and exchange of ideas and experience; improving internal communications. Maintains placement service. **Awards:** International Blue Pencil. **Frequency:** annual. **Type:** recognition. **Recipient:** for print media ● International Gold Screen. **Frequency:** annual. **Type:** recognition. **Recipient:** for audiovisual media. **Telecommunication Services:** electronic mail, gene.rose@ncsl.org. **Sections:** Audiovisual; Print Media; Public Affairs Directors. **Formed by Merger of:** (1925) Armed Forces Writers League; Federal Editors Association. **Formerly:** (1925) Government Information Organization. **Publications:** *GC Magazine*, bimonthly. **Price:** included in membership dues; $40.00 for nonmembers. ISSN: 1067-1722. **Advertising:** accepted. **Conventions/Meetings:** annual conference (exhibits).

5584 ■ Scribes - The American Society of Legal Writers
c/o Prof. Joseph Kimble, Exec. Dir.
PO Box 13038
Lansing, MI 48901
Ph: (517)371-5140
Fax: (517)334-5781
E-mail: kimblej@cooley.edu
URL: http://www.scribes.org
Contact: Prof. Joseph Kimble, Exec. Dir.
Founded: 1952. **Members:** 2,200. **Membership Dues:** individual, $65 (annual) ● institutional, $650 (annual). **Staff:** 2. **Budget:** $35,000. **Description:** Honors legal writers and improves legal writing. Members include authors of books or articles on law or subjects related to law; editors of journals on legal topics; judges; faculty at law schools. Offers professional training. **Awards:** Scribes Book Award. **Frequency:** annual. **Type:** recognition. **Recipient:** for law writers and editors ● Scribes Briefwriting Competition. **Frequency:** annual. **Type:** recognition ● Scribes Notes and Comments Competition. **Frequency:** annual. **Type:** recognition. **Committees:** Awards; Institutes; Membership Publications. **Also Known As:** American Society of Writers on Legal Subjects. **Formerly:** (2006) Scribes Administrative Office. **Publications:** *The Scribes Journal of Legal Writing*, annual. Contains articles about legal writing. **Price:** free for members. **Circulation:** 7,000 ● *The Scrivener*, quarterly. Newsletter. **Price:** free for members. **Circulation:** 1,100. **Conventions/Meetings:** annual meeting ● periodic meeting, held in conjunction with the American Bar Association ● periodic seminar.

Community Development

5585 ■ American Institute of Certified Planners (AICP)
1776 Massachusetts Ave. NW
Washington, DC 20036-1904
Ph: (202)872-0611
Free: (800)954-1669
Fax: (202)872-0643
E-mail: aicp@planning.org
URL: http://www.planning.org/aicp
Contact: Rudayna Abdo, Dir.
Founded: 1978. **Members:** 11,000. **Staff:** 6. **Budget:** $2,000,000. **Description:** Serves as the professional institute of the American Planning Association (see separate entry). Consists of members of the APA who have met the requirements of education, practice, and examination established for the professional practice of public planning. Provides continuing education and a written professional examination. Maintains code of ethics; conducts research. **Libraries: Type:** open to the public. **Holdings:** 4,200; articles, periodicals. **Subjects:** planning practice. **Awards:** AICP National Historic Planning Landmarks and Pioneers. **Frequency:** annual. **Type:** recognition. **Recipient:** for national planning historical landmarks, planning pioneers ● AICP Outstanding Student Awards. **Frequency:** annual. **Type:** recognition. **Recipient:** for outstanding planning students ● AICP Student Project Awards. **Frequency:** annual. **Type:** recognition. **Recipient:** for student project. **Affiliated With:** American Planning Association. **Formerly:** (1917) American Institute of Planners. **Publications:** *American Institute of Certified Planners—Membership Directory*. Includes list of universities granting accredited planning degrees. Alternate Formats: online ● *Practicing Planner*, quarterly. Newsletter. Explores new ideas and concepts of planning practice and methods. **Price:** free for members. Alternate Formats: online ● Also publishes training packages.

5586 ■ American Planning Association (APA)
122 S Michigan Ave., Ste.1600
Chicago, IL 60603-6107
Ph: (312)431-9100
Fax: (312)431-9985
E-mail: customerservice@planning.org
URL: http://www.planning.org
Contact: Paul Farmer, Exec. Dir./CEO
Founded: 1909. **Members:** 32,139. **Membership Dues:** planning board, $60 (annual) ● student, $40 (annual) ● regular, $120-$260 (annual). **Staff:** 68. **Budget:** $12,300,000. **Regional Groups:** 46. **Description:** Public and private planning agency officials, professional planners, planning educators, elected and appointed officials, and other persons involved in urban and rural development. Works to foster the best techniques and decisions for the planned development of communities and regions. Provides extensive professional services and publications to professionals and laypeople in planning and related fields; serves as a clearinghouse for information. Through Planning Advisory Service, a research and inquiry-answering service, provides, on an annual subscription basis, advice on specific inquiries and a series of research reports on planning, zoning, and environmental regulations. Supplies information on job openings and makes definitive studies on salaries and recruitment of professional planners. Conducts research; collaborates in joint projects with local, national, and international organizations. **Libraries: Type:** reference. **Holdings:** books. **Subjects:** urban planning. **Awards:** Charles Abrams Scholarship. **Type:** scholarship ● **Type:** fellowship ● **Type:** recognition. **Recipient:** for newspapers for public service ● **Type:** recognition. **Recipient:** for individuals involved with planning-related projects. **Computer Services:** Mailing lists, of members. **Committees:** National and State Planning Policy. **Departments:** Continuing Professional Development; Government Affairs; Public Information; Publications and Advertising; Research; Student Affairs. **Divisions:** City Planning and Management; Economic Development; Environment, Natural Resources and Energy; Federal Installation Planning; Housing and Human Services; Information Technology; Intergovernmental Affairs; International; Planning and Law; Planning and the Black Community; Planning and Women; Private Practice; Resorts and Tourism; Small Town and Rural Planning; Transportation Planning; Urban Design and Preservation. **Formed by Merger of:** (1978) American Institute of Planners; (1978) American Society of Planning Officials; (1994) National Conference on City Planning. **Publications:** *Journal of the American Planning Association*, quarterly. Provides information on planning, environmental, and urban affairs. Includes index, symposium proceedings, reports, research notes, and book reviews. **Price:** $37.00 /year for members in U.S.; $58.00 /year for members outside U.S.; $75.00 /year for nonmembers in U.S.; $102.00 /year for nonmembers outside U.S. ISSN: 0194-4363. **Circulation:** 12,800. **Advertising:** accepted. Alternate Formats: microform. Also Cited As: *APA Journal* ● *PAS Memo*, monthly. Newsletter. Covers city planning news. **Circulation:** 2,000 ● *Planning Advisory Service Reports*, 8/year. Monograph. Covers the technical aspects of city planning. **Price:** $1.00. **Circulation:** 2,000 ● *Planning & Environmental Law*, monthly. Journal. Contains information for professional city planners and lawyers covering judicial decisions and state laws in the area of zoning. **Price:** $285.00/year in U.S.; $315.00/year outside U.S. ISSN: 0094-7598. **Circulation:** 2,000 ● *Planning Magazine*, monthly. Covers news and analysis of city and regional planning issues. Includes book reviews and annual index. **Price:** $65.00/year in U.S.; $90.00/year outside U.S. ISSN: 0001-2610. **Circulation:** 30,000. **Advertising:** accepted ● *Zoning Practice*, monthly. Journal. Contains information for city officials and the general public covering zoning in local communities throughout the United States. **Price:** $60.00/year in U.S.; $65.00/year outside U.S. **Circulation:** 3,800 ● Bibliographies ● Books ● Reports. **Conventions/Meetings:** annual conference, planning consultants, computer mapping vendors (exhibits) - 2009 Apr. 25-29, Minneapolis, MN; 2010 Apr. 10-14, New Orleans, LA.

5587 ■ American Society of Consulting Planners (ASCP)
1776 Massachusetts Ave. NW
Washington, DC 20036-1904
Ph: (202)872-0611
Fax: (202)872-0643
E-mail: webmaster@planning.org
URL: http://www.planning.org
Founded: 1966. **Members:** 37. **Staff:** 1. **Budget:** $8,000. **Description:** Private firms engaged in city, regional, and other planning activities. Seeks to increase public awareness of the private practice of planning and to establish and enforce standards of technical and ethical performance. Compiles statistics; conducts research and specialized education programs. **Committees:** Education; Legislative; Marketing; Professional Development. **Publications:** *Administrative Manual for Consulting Planners* ● *ASCP Directory*, annual ● *Code of Professional Conduct* ● Booklets ● Brochures. **Conventions/Meetings:** semiannual conference, held in conjunction with American Planning Association and American Institute of Certified Planners ● semiannual workshop.

5588 ■ Center for Design Planning (CDP)
4224 Spanish Trail Pl.
Pensacola, FL 32504
Ph: (850)484-4100
Fax: (850)484-4100
E-mail: profhlm@msn.com
Contact: Prof. Harold Lewis Malt, Dir.
Founded: 1973. **Staff:** 4. **Nonmembership. Description:** Urban planners, researchers, designers. Investigates the public outdoor urban environment and seeks to improve it for users. Conducts feasibil-

ity studies and research on streetscape, commercial revitalization, pedestrianization, and cultural facilities. Participates in Transfer of Development Rights. Prepares comprehensive plans. **Convention/Meeting:** none. **Libraries: Type:** reference. **Holdings:** 8,000; audiovisuals, monographs. **Subjects:** urban environment.

5589 ■ National Association of County Planners (NACP)
c/o National Association of Counties
440 1st St. NW, 8th Fl.
Washington, DC 20001
Ph: (202)661-8807
Fax: (202)737-0480
E-mail: jdavenpo@naco.org
URL: http://www.countyplanning.org
Contact: James Davenport, Staff Liaison
Founded: 1965. **Members:** 150. **Membership Dues:** $35 (annual). **Staff:** 2. **Description:** Persons who serve in a planning capacity for a county or for a city-county, multi-county, or regional agency and those who have an interest in planning at the county level. Works to stimulate and contribute to improvement of county planning in the U.S; study the problems of county planning and disseminate information to members. Serves as a vehicle for the exchange of information among county planning directors, local elected officials, and the federal government. Provides exposure to local planning programs. **Formerly:** (1989) National Association of County Planning Directors. **Publications:** *Capital Improvement Project Guidebook* ● *NACP Directory*, annual. Contains member organization listings. ● *NACP News*, quarterly. Newsletter. **Price:** available to members only. **Circulation:** 500. **Advertising:** accepted ● *Roster*, biennial. Membership Directory. **Price:** available to members only. **Conventions/Meetings:** annual meeting.

5590 ■ National Association of Development Organizations (NADO)
400 N Capitol St. NW, Ste.390
Washington, DC 20001
Ph: (202)624-7806 (202)624-5947
Fax: (202)624-8813
E-mail: info@nado.org
URL: http://www.nado.org
Contact: Matthew Chase, Exec. Dir.
Founded: 1967. **Membership Dues:** platinum, $4,000 (annual) ● sustaining associate, $1,000 (annual) ● general, $2,000 (annual) ● sustaining, $3,000 (annual) ● associate, $500 (annual). **Staff:** 10. **Budget:** $2,000,000. **Description:** Represents multi-county planning and development organizations; educational institutions; businesses; individuals; city, county, and state agencies concerned with economic, community, and business development. Promotes economic development, primarily in rural areas and small towns; serves as a forum for communication and education. Aims to develop a balanced national growth policy. Testifies at congressional hearings. Provides technical assistance for members. **Awards:** Innovation Award. **Frequency:** annual. **Type:** recognition. **Recipient:** for devising creative programs of development districts ● President's Award. **Frequency:** annual. **Type:** recognition. **Recipient:** to an outstanding individual or organization ● **Frequency:** annual. **Type:** recognition. **Affiliated With:** National Association of Development Organizations Research Foundation. **Publications:** *Development Finance Reporter*, monthly. **Advertising:** accepted ● *NADO News*, weekly. Newsletter. **Price:** included in membership dues ● *Regional Development Digest*, periodic. Newspaper. Promotes innovative programs and practices of regional development organizations. **Circulation:** 8,000. Alternate Formats: online ● *Special Report*, 3-4/year ● Also publishes congressional alerts. **Conventions/Meetings:** annual Training Conference - always fall ● annual Washington Policy Conference - always spring.

5591 ■ National Association for Olmsted Parks (NAOP)
1111 16th St. NW, Ste.310
Washington, DC 20036
Ph: (202)223-9113
Free: (866)666-6905
Fax: (202)223-9112
E-mail: info@naop.org
URL: http://www.olmsted.org
Contact: Ms. Catherine Nagel, Exec. Dir.
Founded: 1980. **Members:** 1,000. **Membership Dues:** individual, $35 (annual). **Staff:** 1. **Budget:** $50,000. **State Groups:** 2. **Local Groups:** 8. **Description:** Represents design and preservation professionals, historic property and park managers, scholars, municipal officials, citizen activists and representatives of numerous Olmsted organizations around the United States. Promotes the philosophy of Frederick Law Olmsted Sr. and the firm founded by his sons, Olmsted Brothers Landscape Architects, about land use planning, quality design, democracy and land conservation. **Publications:** *An Ecosystem Approach to Woodland Management*. Book. **Price:** $7.50/year. **Circulation:** 1,000. **Advertising:** accepted ● *Field Notes*, 3/year. Newsletter. Includes summer update. **Price:** $12.00/year ● *Frederick Law Olmsted's First and Last Suburb: Riverside and Druid Hills and The Olmsteds at Biltmore*. Book. **Price:** $7.50 ● *Held in Trust: Charles Eliot's Vision for the New England Landscape*. Book. **Price:** $7.50 ● *Landscape Composition Preservation Treatments*. Book. **Price:** $7.50 ● *Workbook Series*. **Price:** $7.50 ● Makes available *The Olmsted Papers* and *The Master List of Design Projects of the Olmsted Firm, 1857-1950* (books) and Frederick Law Olmsted - Designing the American Landscape by Charles Beveridge and Paul Rocheleau. **Conventions/Meetings:** semiannual Partnerships in Parks - conference ● workshop.

5592 ■ National Association of State Development Agencies (NASDA)
10900 Univ. Blvd. MSN 1J2
Bull Run Hall Rm.
Manassas, VA 20110-2201
Ph: (703)993-9411
E-mail: mfriedman@nasda.com
Contact: Miles Friedman, Pres./CEO
Founded: 1946. **Members:** 250. **Membership Dues:** full, $9,500 (annual) ● affiliate, $2,500 (annual). **Budget:** $750,000. **Description:** Provides consultation and field services in the area of state economic development. Sponsors International Trade Specialist Training Program in conjunction with American Graduate School of International Management, Glendale, AZ. Monitors hearings and legislation in Congress and interprets national events for members. Serves as clearinghouse for all member agencies. **Computer Services:** database, State Export Program. **Divisions:** Business and Economic Development Financing; Economic Development Research and Data; Employment and Training; International Business Development; International Trade and Investment; Investment Attraction and Marketing; Local/Substate and Enterprise Zone; Travel and Tourism Development. **Formerly:** National Association of State Economic Development Agencies; (1969) Association of State Planning and Development Agencies. **Publications:** *Analysis of Innovative State Economic Development Financing Programs*. Report ● *Coordination of Employment and Training and Economic Development: A Resource Book* ● *Directory of Incentives for Business Investment in the U.S.: A State by State Guide*. Features major export development programs. **Price:** free for members; $300.00 for nonmembers. Alternate Formats: CD-ROM ● *NASDA Letter*, every 6-8 weeks ● *NASDA State Economic Development Expenditure Survey*, semiannual. Includes budgeted expenditures and salaries for all managers. **Price:** $250.00 for nonmembers; free for members. Alternate Formats: CD-ROM ● *Report on State Responses to the State Volume Limit on Private Activity Bonds* ● *State Ed Agency*. Directory. Contains a listing of directors and managers. **Price:** $150.00 /year for nonmembers; free for members ● *State Enterprise Zone Roundup*, annual ● *Trade Development Catalog*. **Conventions/Meetings:** annual conference.

5593 ■ National Policy Association (NPA)
Address Unknown since 2007
Founded: 1934. **Members:** 250. **Membership Dues:** friend, $100 (annual) ● sponsor, $1,000 (annual) ● supporter, $250 (annual) ● President's Circle, $2,000 (annual). **National Groups:** 1. **Languages:** English, Spanish. **Description:** Research institution that helps private and public sector leaders from agriculture, business, labor, and academia to better understand national economic and social issues. Conducts research and analysis on national and international economic and social issues. **Awards:** Gold Medal Award. **Frequency:** annual. **Type:** recognition. **Committees:** New American Realities; North American Committee. **Formerly:** (1941) National Economic and Social Planning Association; (1997) National Planning Association. **Publications:** *Looking Ahead*, quarterly. Journal. **Price:** $40.00. **Advertising:** not accepted ● Reports ● Also publishes policy statements and research reports. **Conventions/Meetings:** semiannual conference and seminar.

5594 ■ Partners for Livable Communities (PLC)
1429 21st St. NW
Washington, DC 20036
Ph: (202)887-5990
Fax: (202)466-4845
E-mail: livability@livable.com
URL: http://www.livable.com
Contact: Robert H. McNulty, Pres./CEO
Founded: 1977. **Members:** 1,200. **Staff:** 10. **Description:** Represents organizations and individuals dedicated to the improvement of community environments through cooperative efforts of the public and private sectors. Serves as a resource and information center offering civic improvements through special initiatives and technical assistance programs. Offers leadership training forums, workshops, and study tours. Sponsors Shaping Growth in American Communities, a program designed to help cities, states, and counties handle local level developments and to identify national trends in managing rapid physical, social, and economic changes. Maintains National Resource Center. Operates speakers' bureau; conducts research. **Libraries: Type:** open to the public. **Holdings:** 5,000. **Subjects:** aging in places from Urban Parks to Downtown. **Computer Services:** database, members, consultants, speakers, best practices, and publications. **Formerly:** (1997) Partners for Livable Places. **Publications:** *The Economics of Amenity* ● *Issues in Supporting the Arts* ● *Livability*, semiannual. Newsletter ● *Partners' Resources, 1975-2002*. Directory. Contains listing of available publications with corresponding descriptions. **Price:** $20.00 ● *The Return of the Livable City: Learning from America's Best*. **Conventions/Meetings:** annual meeting.

5595 ■ Public Works and Economic Development Association (PWEDA)
Address Unknown since 2007
Founded: 1981. **Members:** 300. **Membership Dues:** general, $495 (annual) ● associate, $190 (annual). **Staff:** 4. **Description:** Members consist of Economic Development Districts, state and local economic development agencies, University centers, trade adjustment assistant centers and interested parties in economic development. Objectives are to: support the economic development programs of the EDA (organized in 1965 to provide assistance to small industries); promote private sector activity that results in job creation; monitor tax policies and legislation that affect economic development; focus special attention on rural economic development programs. **Publications:** *Economic Development Monthly*. Newsletter. Contains information covering legislative activity and advances, trends and new technologies in economic development. **Price:** free. **Advertising:** not accepted ● *PWEDA Newsletter*, biweekly. Contains information covering legislative activity and advances, trends and new technologies in economic development. ● Also publishes brochures. **Conventions/Meetings:** annual meeting - always December, Washington, DC.

5596 ■ Regional Science Association International (RSAI)
c/o David Boyce, Archivist
2149 Grey Ave.
Evanston, IL 60201

E-mail: rsai@uiuc.edu
URL: http://www.regionalscience.org
Contact: David Boyce, Archivist
Founded: 1954. **Members:** 2,500. **Membership Dues:** regular, $60 (annual) ● student, $40 (annual). **Staff:** 1. **Regional Groups:** 78. **Multinational. Description:** Represents academic and professional individuals concerned with the practice and advancement of urban and regional analysis and related studies. **Formerly:** (1991) Regional Science Association. **Publications:** *Papers in Regional Science: Journal of the Regional Science Association International*, quarterly. ISSN: 1056-8190 ● *RSAI News*, 3/year. Newsletter. Alternate Formats: online ● Report. Alternate Formats: online. **Conventions/Meetings:** semiannual conference (exhibits) ● periodic meeting.

5597 ■ Urban Land Institute (ULI)
1025 Thomas Jefferson St. NW, Ste.500 W
Washington, DC 20007-5230
Ph: (202)624-7000
Free: (800)321-5011
Fax: (202)624-7140
E-mail: customerservice@uli.org
URL: http://www.uli.org
Contact: Todd Mansfield, Chm.
Founded: 1936. **Members:** 37,000. **Membership Dues:** private sector individual in U.S., $350 (annual) ● public sector individual in U.S., $200 (annual) ● young leader in U.S., $175 (annual) ● student in U.S., $75 (annual) ● private sector individual in U.S. (full), $1,090 (annual) ● public sector individual in U.S. (full), $385 (annual) ● private sector individual outside U.S., $165 (annual) ● young leader outside U.S., $115 (annual) ● student outside U.S., $50 (annual) ● public sector individual outside U.S., $120 (annual) ● private sector individual (full) outside U.S., $400 (annual) ● public sector individual (full) outside U.S., $205 (annual). **Staff:** 100. **Multinational. Description:** Real estate developers, planners, architects, engineers, academicians, government officials and financiers. Encourages effective urban planning and development through research and education. Twenty-five councils conduct studies of industrial potentials, downtown problems, and new area development. **Libraries: Type:** reference. **Holdings:** 12,000; articles, books, periodicals. **Subjects:** land use, real estate, shopping centers, environment. **Awards:** ULI Award for Excellence. **Frequency:** annual. **Type:** recognition. **Recipient:** for development projects that represent superior land planning and development, resourceful use of land, relevance to contemporary issues, and sensitivity to the environment. **Publications:** *Land Use Digest*, monthly. Newsletters. Summarizes reports on land use issues from trade, professional, and academic journals as well as from the institute's own research. **Price:** included in membership dues. **Circulation:** 13,000 ● *Urban Land*, monthly. Magazine. Covers urban development policies and regulations as well as topical issues such as zoning, infrastructure financing, and impact fees. **Price:** included in membership dues. **Circulation:** 13,000. **Advertising:** accepted. Alternate Formats: microform ● *The Urban Land Institute—Project Reference File*, quarterly. Monograph. Provides a "complete look at successful development in action". Includes developer comments and project data. **Price:** $70.00 /year for members; $85.00 /year for nonmembers. **Circulation:** 1,200. **Advertising:** accepted ● Books ● Manuals ● Reports. Alternate Formats: online. **Conventions/Meetings:** semiannual conference (exhibits) - always spring and fall.

Congress

5598 ■ Congressional Border Caucus (CBC)
1527 Lonworth Bldg.
Washington, DC 20515
Ph: (202)225-4831
Fax: (202)225-2016
URL: http://www.house.gov/reyes
Contact: Perry Finney, Chief of Staff
Founded: 1986. **Members:** 40. **Description:** Members of Congress who represent states bordering Mexico. Develops and promotes legislation and public policy relevant to the U.S.-Mexico border region. Conducts research programs; maintains speakers' bureau. **Conventions/Meetings:** quarterly meeting.

5599 ■ Congressional Management Foundation (CMF)
513 Capitol Ct. NE, Ste.300
Washington, DC 20002
Ph: (202)546-0100
Fax: (202)547-0936
E-mail: cmf@cmfweb.org
URL: http://www.cmfweb.org
Contact: Ms. Beverly Bell, Exec. Dir.
Founded: 1977. **Staff:** 7. **Budget:** $500,000. **Nonmembership. Description:** Works with academicians, individuals, and corporate representatives to provide management assistance to members of Congress and their staffs. Seeks to improve the quality of U.S. representative government. Provides consulting services, management training programs, and guidebooks to House and Senate offices. **Libraries: Type:** reference. **Holdings:** reports. **Projects:** Communicating with Congress. **Publications:** *Congress Online*. Newsletter. Alternate Formats: online ● *Congressional Intern Handbook*. Contains information in compliance with the Fair Labor Standards Act in the House and Senate. **Price:** $15.00 for Congressional offices; $17.50 for non-Congressional offices ● *Frontline Management: A Guide for Congressional District/State Offices*. Book. **Price:** $15.00 for Congressional offices; $20.00 for non-Congressional offices ● *House and Senate Salary Surveys* ● *Setting Course: A Congressional Management Guide*. Book. **Price:** $15.00 for Congressional offices; $20.00 for non-Congressional offices ● *Working in Congress: The Staff Perspective*. Book. **Price:** $10.00 for Congressional offices; $15.00 for non-Congressional offices ● Reports. Alternate Formats: online. **Conventions/Meetings:** seminar.

5600 ■ VoterWatch
695 Arkansas St.
San Francisco, CA 94107
E-mail: info@voterwatch.org
URL: http://www.voterwatch.org
Contact: Perla Ni, Co-Founder
Description: Encourages the community to find out more about important matters discussed in Congress. Provides an easy and convenient way to search videos of Congress to find out what is going on with the issues that matter most to the community. Maintains a site where users can search and easily write about or email just those parts that they need.

Conservative

5601 ■ American Society of Contrarian Speakers and Writers
Address Unknown since 2008
Founded: 1998. **Members:** 100. **Staff:** 2. **Description:** Conservative speakers and writers who address "insufficiency and ridiculous practices" in public policy, education, business and industry, the judicial system, the media and academia. Maintains speakers' bureau. **Libraries: Type:** reference. **Holdings:** 3,000; archival material, articles, books, periodicals. **Subjects:** public policy, history, education, sociology, psychology science. **Awards:** Finger in the Eye Award. **Frequency:** annual. **Type:** recognition. **Recipient:** for those who persistently annoy and pester bureaucracies, unions, the media and other unnecessary evils ● Old Coot Award. **Frequency:** annual. **Type:** recognition. **Recipient:** for the person who stubbornly prevails, despite resistance. **Publications:** *The Curmudgeon*, quarterly. Journal. **Conventions/Meetings:** periodic meeting.

5602 ■ Frontiers of Freedom (FF)
PO Box 69
Oakton, VA 22124
Ph: (703)246-0110
Fax: (703)246-0129
E-mail: info@ff.org
URL: http://www.ff.org
Contact: George C. Landrith, Pres.
Founded: 1995. **Membership Dues:** Leadership's Circle, $25-$500 (annual) ● John Adams' Circle, $1,000 (annual) ● Alexander Hamilton's Circle, George Washington's Circle, $10,000 (annual) ● James Madison's Circle, $25,000 (annual) ● Thomas Jefferson's Circle, $50,000 (annual). **Description:** Works to maintain and restore the American system of limited government and individual rights. **Publications:** *Freedom Report*, bimonthly. Newsletter. Alternate Formats: online ● Newsletters, weekly. **Price:** free.

Constitution

5603 ■ American Constitution Society for Law and Policy (ACS)
1333 H St. NW, 11th Fl.
Washington, DC 20005
Ph: (202)393-6181
Fax: (202)393-6189
E-mail: info@acslaw.org
URL: http://www.acslaw.org
Contact: Lisa Brown, Exec. Dir.
Founded: 2001. **Membership Dues:** private sector, $50 (annual) ● government/public interest/academia, $25 (annual) ● student, $10 (annual) ● friend, $125 (annual) ● patron, $250 (annual) ● sponsor, $500 (annual) ● Advocate's Circle, $1,200 (annual). **Description:** Ensures that the fundamental principles of human dignity, individual rights and liberties, genuine equality and access to justice are in their rightful place in American law. Fosters a progressive vision of the law. Works to strengthen the underpinnings for progressive law and policy in the United States. **Publications:** Bulletin, weekly. Alternate Formats: online ● Newsletter. **Price:** included in membership dues.

5604 ■ Constitution Society
7793 Burnet Rd., No. 37
Austin, TX 78757
Ph: (512)374-9585
E-mail: jon.roland@constitution.org
URL: http://www.constitution.org
Contact: Jon Roland, Contact
Founded: 1994. **Description:** Dedicated to research and public education on the principles of constitutional republican government. Publishes documentation, engages in litigation and organizes local citizens groups to work for reform.

Constitutional Law

5605 ■ First Amendment Lawyers Association (FALA)
c/o Wayne Giampietro, Gen. Counselor
121 S Wilke Rd., No. 500
Arlington Heights, IL 60005
Ph: (847)590-8700
Fax: (847)590-9825
E-mail: wgiampietro@skdaglaw.com
URL: http://firstamendmentlawyers.org
Contact: Wayne Giampietro, Gen. Counselor
Founded: 1970. **Members:** 180. **Membership Dues:** individual, $140 (annual). **Staff:** 1. **Description:** Lawyers who support and defend cases involving the First Amendment to the U.S. Constitution (i.e., freedom of religion, freedom of speech and the press, freedom to peaceably assemble, and freedom to petition the government for a redress of grievances). **Publications:** Bulletin, semiannual ● Directory, semiannual. **Conventions/Meetings:** semiannual seminar.

Construction

5606 ■ National Construction Investigators Association (NCIA)
Address Unknown since 2008
Membership Dues: general, $25 (annual). **Description:** Promotes interaction, communication and train-

ing between investigators and prosecutors. Protects the health, safety and welfare of the general public. Provides education and enforces laws that regulate the construction industry.

Consulting

5607 ■ Logistics Management Institute (LMI)
2000 Corporate Ridge
McLean, VA 22102-7805
Ph: (703)917-9800
Free: (800)213-4817
Fax: (703)917-7597
E-mail: pweiss@lmi.org
URL: http://www.lmi.org
Contact: Donald L. Pilling, Pres./CEO

Founded: 1961. **Staff:** 670. **Nonmembership. Description:** Provides consultations to government organizations in the areas of infrastructure, logistics, and resource management. Draws policies and procedures that assist government to effectively and efficiently acquire goods and services. Helps federal managers in civil and defense agencies make decisions to improve government performance. **Libraries: Type:** not open to the public. **Holdings:** 7,000; books, monographs, periodicals, reports. **Subjects:** logistics, operations research, management. **Computer Services:** database, reports. **Programs:** Resident Research Fellows; Young Professionals. **Publications:** *LMI Annual Report*, annual. Alternate Formats: online ● *The Public Manager*, quarterly. Journal. Alternate Formats: online.

Consumers

5608 ■ Conference on Consumer Finance Law (CCFL)
c/o Prof. Alvin C. Harrell, Exec. Dir.
Oklahoma City Univ. School of Law
2501 N Blackwelder
Oklahoma City, OK 73106
Ph: (405)521-5363
Fax: (405)521-5089
URL: http://www.theccfl.com
Contact: Prof. Alvin C. Harrell, Exec. Dir.

Founded: 1927. **Members:** 850. **Membership Dues:** individual, $95 (annual). **Staff:** 2. **Description:** Lawyers interested in the field of consumer finance law. Seeks to: encourage study and research in the field of financial services law; make available information on the history and current status of the laws and regulations relating to banking, consumer finance, and financial services; promote, through education, the sound development of consumer finance; stimulate, by discussion and publication, the improvement of legal procedures affecting consumer finance; provide a forum for the exchange of opinions. Presents a formal paper, program, or seminar speech on financial services law in conjunction with the American Bar Association. **Libraries: Type:** reference. **Holdings:** articles. **Affiliated With:** American Bar Association. **Formerly:** (1984) Conference on Personal Finance Law. **Publications:** *Consumer Finance Law Quarterly Report*. Journal. Contains analysis of current trends in financial services, banking, secured transactions, and consumer finance. **Price:** included in membership dues; $50.00 for nonmembers. **Circulation:** 1,200. **Advertising:** accepted. **Conventions/Meetings:** semiannual conference, held in conjunction with the ABA - always March/April and August.

5609 ■ National Association of Consumer Agency Administrators (NACAA)
2 Brentwood Commons, Ste.150
750 Old Hickory Blvd.
Brentwood, TN 37027
Ph: (615)371-6125 (608)224-4965
Free: (866)SAY-NACAA
Fax: (615)369-6225
E-mail: eowen@nacaa.net
URL: http://www.nacaa.net
Contact: Elizabeth Owen, Exec. Dir.

Founded: 1976. **Members:** 162. **Staff:** 2. **Budget:** $245,000. **Description:** Administrators of state, county, provincial, and local governmental consumer protection agencies; federal agencies and universities in the U.S. and several other countries. Seeks to enhance consumer services available to the public. Sponsors public policy forums. Acts as a clearinghouse for consumer education and legislation information. Works jointly with corporations, trade groups, non-profit organizations, and others to produce consumer education materials. **Awards:** Achievement Consumer Education Award. **Frequency:** annual. **Type:** recognition. **Recipient:** for outstanding educational publications and media presentations ● Consumer Agency Achievement Award. **Frequency:** annual. **Type:** recognition. **Recipient:** for outstanding performance by a NACAA member agency ● NACAA Advocate of the Year Award. **Frequency:** annual. **Type:** recognition. **Recipient:** for a person who exemplifies the best in enhancing and promoting consumer interests and fairness in the marketplace. **Telecommunication Services:** electronic mail, jim.rabbitt@wi.gov. **Publications:** *NACAA Forum*. Newsletter. Alternate Formats: online ● *NACAA News*, bimonthly. Newsletter. Includes reports from members and others about enforcement, administrative, educational, and legislative activities. **Price:** free for members; $75.00/year for consumer agencies and organizations; $95.00/year for businesses, media, and others. ISSN: 0739-392X. **Conventions/Meetings:** annual conference and workshop (exhibits) - always May or June ● regional meeting ● seminar.

5610 ■ National Association of Consumer Credit Administrators (NACCA)
PO Box 20871
Columbus, OH 43220-0871
Ph: (614)326-1165
Fax: (614)326-1162
E-mail: nacca2001@aol.com
URL: http://www.naccaonline.org
Contact: Theresa L. Brady, Pres.

Founded: 1935. **Members:** 46. **Membership Dues:** active, $500 (annual). **Staff:** 1. **Description:** Represents state government officials who administer consumer finance laws in the U.S., Guam, Puerto Rico, and Canada. Holds roundtable discussions to exchange views on consumer credit and administration of applicable laws. **Committees:** Amendment; Consumer Education; Nomination; Remembrance. **Formerly:** Association of Small Loan Administrators; National Association of Small Loan Supervisors. **Publications:** *Minutes of Annual Meeting*, annual. **Conventions/Meetings:** annual conference - usually fall ● Continuing Education School - meeting, for examiners of state credit regulators ● annual meeting - 2008 Sept. 30-Oct. 3, Beverly Hills, CA; 2009 Sept. 22-25, Miami Beach, FL.

5611 ■ National Consumer Law Center (NCLC)
77 Summer St., 10th Fl.
Boston, MA 02110-1006
Ph: (617)542-8010
Fax: (202)463-9462
E-mail: consumerlaw@nclc.org
URL: http://www.consumerlaw.org
Contact: Willard P. Ogburn, Exec. Dir.

Founded: 1969. **Staff:** 35. **Budget:** $3,500,000. **Description:** Serves as a specialized resource in consumer and energy law funded by federal, state, and foundation grants and donations. Lawyers provide research, technical consulting, and in-depth assistance to legal services, private lawyers, and state agencies throughout the nation. Defines recurring patterns in the problems of low-income consumers and develops a series of alternative solutions utilizing litigation, legislation, lawyer training, and development of new service delivery systems. Seeks consultants for an interdisciplinary approach to problems. Conducts analyses of weatherization and energy assistance programs for low-income homeowners, renters, and state and federal agencies. **Libraries: Type:** not open to the public; reference. **Holdings:** reports. **Publications:** *Learning Financial Literacy in Bankruptcy*. Report. Alternate Formats: online ● *NCLC Energy and Utility Update*, quarterly. Newsletter. Covers developments in state and federal low-income home energy and weatherization programs; and also monitors customer services and utilities issues. **Price:** $95.00/year for private-sector/industry; $45.00/year for government/nonprofit. **Circulation:** 1,000. Alternate Formats: online ● *NCLC Reports*, bimonthly. Newsletter. Covers new developments and ideas for the practice of consumer law for attorneys representing low-income clients. **Price:** free to legal services offices; $60.00 /year for nonmembers. **Circulation:** 2,500. Alternate Formats: online ● *Surviving Debt: A Guide for Consumers*. Handbook. **Price:** $15.00 ● *Utility Law Series*. Books. Covers tenants rights to utility service and the regulation of rural electric cooperatives. ● Manuals ● Brochures. Alternate Formats: online ● Also publishes 14-volume consumer credit and sales legal practice series on subjects such as consumer bankruptcy law and practice, sales of goods and services, unfair and deceptive acts and practices, debt collection harassment, repossessions, odometer law, truth in lending in transition, consumer usury and credit overcharges, and the Equal Credit Opportunity and Fair Credit Reporting Acts. **Conventions/Meetings:** annual Consumer Rights Litigation Conference.

Cooperative Extension

5612 ■ National Extension Association of Family and Consumer Sciences (NEAFCS)
14070 Proton Rd., Ste.100
Dallas, TX 75244-3601
Free: (800)808-9133
Fax: (972)490-4219
E-mail: dave@neafcs.org
URL: http://www.neafcs.org
Contact: Mr. David Beebe, Exec. Dir.

Founded: 1931. **Members:** 3,100. **Membership Dues:** individual (active), $60 (annual) ● life, $210. **Budget:** $450,000. **State Groups:** 50. **Description:** Represents extension educators in the area of Family and Consumer Sciences. Provides research-based educational programs in the areas of nutrition, food safety, health, parenting, child development, 4-H, youth development, housing, home care, aging, financial management, community development, and textiles. Sponsors conferences and trains volunteer leaders to work with individuals and groups. Conducts a public policy forum. **Awards: Frequency:** annual. **Type:** recognition. **Computer Services:** Mailing lists, of members. **Committees:** Awards and Recognition; Member Resources; Professional Development; Public Affairs. **Formerly:** National Home Demonstration Agents' Association; (1997) National Association of Extension Home Economists; (2004) National Extension Association of Family and Consumer Services. **Publications:** *The Communique*, annual. Newsletter. Includes up-to-date information for members. **Price:** $20.00 for nonmembers; free for members. **Circulation:** 3,200. **Advertising:** accepted ● *eNEAFCS*, monthly. Newsletter. Includes up-to-date information for members. **Price:** $20.00 for nonmembers; free for members. **Circulation:** 3,200. **Advertising:** accepted. Alternate Formats: online ● *The Journal of NEAFCS*, annual. **Price:** $20.00 for nonmembers; free for members. **Circulation:** 4,000. **Conventions/Meetings:** annual conference, includes concurrent sessions, special events and keynote speakers (exhibits) - 2009 Sept. 15-18, Birmingham, AL.

Copyright

5613 ■ Creative Commons (CC)
Corporate HQ
171 2nd St., Ste.300
San Francisco, CA 94105-3808
Ph: (415)369-8481
Fax: (415)278-9419

E-mail: info@creativecommons.org
URL: http://creativecommons.org
Contact: James Boyle, Founder
Founded: 2001. **Multinational. Description:** Founded on the notion that "some people may not want to exercise all of the intellectual property rights the law affords them." Aims to offer the public a set of copyright licenses free of charge, to help artists communicate that their copyrighted works are free for sharing, but only on certain conditions.

Corporate Law

5614 ■ Association of Corporate Counsel (ACC)

1025 Connecticut Ave. NW, Ste.200
Washington, DC 20036-5425
Ph: (202)293-4103
Fax: (202)293-4701
E-mail: krebs@acc.com
URL: http://www.acc.com
Contact: Frederick J. Krebs, Pres.
Founded: 1982. **Members:** 12,250. **Membership Dues:** individual, $225 (annual). **Staff:** 30. **Budget:** $4,500,000. **Local Groups:** 42. **National Groups:** 12. **Multinational. Description:** Attorneys who practice in the legal departments of corporations and other private sector organizations. Promotes the common interests of its members, contributes to their continuing education, seeks to improve understanding of the role of in-house attorneys, and encourages advancements in the standards of corporate legal practice. **Telecommunication Services:** electronic mail, chair@acc.com. **Committees:** Commercial Law; Corporate and Securities Law; Employment and Labor Law; Environmental Health and Safety; Information Technology Law and eCommerce; Insurance Staff Counsel; Intellectual Property; International Legal Affairs; Law Department Management; Litigation; New to In-house; Small Law Departments. **Formerly:** (2007) American Corporate Counsel Association. **Publications:** *ACCA Docket*, 10/year. Journal. Includes articles about substantive law and managerial matters of interest to in-house legal practitioners, and news of the association. **Price:** included in membership dues; $175.00 for nonmembers in U.S. **Circulation:** 33,000. **Advertising:** accepted. Alternate Formats: online ● Surveys. Alternate Formats: online. **Conventions/Meetings:** annual meeting, with networking events exclusively for in-house counsel (exhibits) - always October or November. 2008 Oct. 20-22, Seattle, WA; 2009 Oct. 19-21, Boston, MA; 2010 Oct. 25-27, San Antonio, TX.

5615 ■ Minority Corporate Counsel Association (MCCA)

1111 Pennsylvania Ave. NW
Washington, DC 20004
Ph: (202)739-5901 (202)739-5910
Fax: (202)739-5999
E-mail: info@mcca.com
URL: http://www.mcca.com
Contact: Veta T. Richardson, Exec. Dir.
Founded: 1997. **Membership Dues:** law department - per lawyer (1-10 attorneys), $250 (annual) ● law department (based on number of attorneys), $3,500-$7,500 (annual) ● sustaining, $15,000 (annual). **Description:** Advocates for the expanded hiring, retention, and promotion of minority attorneys in corporate law departments and the law firms that serve them. Collects and disseminates information about diversity in the legal profession. Creates effective professional skills development programs for minority attorneys. **Awards:** Employers of Choice Award. **Frequency:** annual. **Type:** recognition. **Recipient:** to industry leaders who have committed themselves to creating and maintaining an inclusive corporate legal department ● Lloyd M. Johnson, Jr. Scholarship Program. **Frequency:** annual. **Type:** scholarship. **Recipient:** to students from disadvantaged backgrounds who have been accepted into law school ● Rainbowmaker Award. **Frequency:** periodic. **Type:** recognition. **Recipient:** to an exceptional leader whose advocacy in support of a more diverse legal profession has created "rainbows" of opportunity for future generations of diverse lawyers ● Thomas . Sager Award. **Frequency:** annual. **Type:** recognition. **Recipient:** to law firms that have demonstrated sustained commitment to improve the hiring, retention, and promotion of minority attorneys ● Trailblazer Award. **Frequency:** periodic. **Type:** recognition. **Recipient:** to outstanding corporate minority lawyers who have made significant efforts to advance diversity in their corporations. **Telecommunication Services:** electronic mail, vetarichardson@mcca.com. **Publications:** *Diversity & The Bar*, quarterly. Magazine. **Price:** $35.00/issue. **Circulation:** 30,000 ● *Live Vine*. Newsletter. Features industry news, announcements, career development advice, and diversity research. Alternate Formats: online ● Articles. Alternate Formats: online.

Cosmetology

5616 ■ National - Interstate Council of State Boards of Cosmetology (NIC)

7622 Briarwood Cir.
Little Rock, AR 72205
Ph: (501)227-8262 (605)737-0095
Fax: (501)227-8212
E-mail: dnorton@nictesting.org
URL: http://www.nictesting.org
Contact: Rosanne Kinley, Pres.
Founded: 1956. **Members:** 250. **Membership Dues:** cosmetology licensing board, $200 (annual). **Staff:** 2. **Regional Groups:** 5. **Description:** Persons commissioned by 50 state governments as administrators of cosmetology laws and examiners of applicants for licenses to practice cosmetology. **Committees:** Education; Legislative; National Endorsement; NIC/Skin Care Liaison. **Formed by Merger of:** (1969) National Council of Boards of Beauty Culture; (1969) Interstate Council of State Boards of Cosmetology. **Publications:** *NIC Bulletin*, bimonthly. Alternate Formats: online ● Directory, annual ● Reports. Alternate Formats: online. **Conventions/Meetings:** annual conference ● annual seminar, on administration, examinations, law enforcement, legislation, and policy-making.

County Government

5617 ■ National Association of Black County Officials (NABCO)

440 1st St. NW, Ste.410
Washington, DC 20001
Ph: (202)347-6953
Fax: (202)393-6596
E-mail: nobco@naco.org
Founded: 1975. **Members:** 2,000. **Membership Dues:** individual, $100 (annual). **Staff:** 1. **Budget:** $500,000. **Regional Groups:** 4. **State Groups:** 5. **Description:** Black county officials organized to provide program planning and management assistance to counties in the U.S. Acts as a clearinghouse of technical information exchange to develop resolutions to problems on the local and national levels. Promotes the sharing of knowledge and methods of improving resource utilization and government operations. Conducts seminars and training sessions. Plans to maintain resource file on the achievements and history of black county officials. **Awards:** Chairman's Award. **Frequency:** annual. **Type:** recognition. **Recipient:** for a county or local official who has shown outstanding leadership ● Chairman's Award. **Frequency:** annual. **Type:** scholarship. **Recipient:** for high school graduates ● President's Award. **Type:** recognition. **Recipient:** for outstanding achievements. **Computer Services:** Mailing lists. **Boards:** Directors. **Formerly:** National Organization of Black County Officials. **Publications:** *County Compass*, quarterly. Newsletter. Includes calendar of events, member profiles, member news, programmatic and legislative updates. **Price:** free. **Circulation:** 3,500. **Advertising:** accepted ● *County to County*, bimonthly. Bulletin. Provides health education specifically AIDS prevention. **Circulation:** 2,500. **Conventions/Meetings:** periodic board meeting, in conjunction with the National Association of Counties (exhibits) ● annual Economic Development Conference - meeting (exhibits).

5618 ■ National Association of Counties (NACo)

25 Massachusetts Ave. NW
Washington, DC 20001
Ph: (202)393-6226 (202)942-4233
Fax: (202)393-2630
E-mail: rlipscom@naco.org
URL: http://www.naco.org
Contact: Larry E. Naake, Exec. Dir.
Founded: 1935. **Members:** 2,210. **Membership Dues:** corporate, $1,500 (annual). **Staff:** 80. **Budget:** $10,000,000. **State Groups:** 48. **Description:** Represents county governments in the United States. Provides essential services to the nation's 3,066 counties. Advances issues with a unified voice before the federal government, improves the public's understanding of county government, assists counties in finding and sharing innovative solutions through education and research, and provides value-added services to save counties and taxpayers money. **Awards:** County Leadership in the Arts Award. **Frequency:** annual. **Type:** recognition. **Recipient:** for an outstanding local official who supports the arts ● Distinguished Service Award for County Elected Officials. **Frequency:** annual. **Type:** recognition. **Recipient:** for a county elected official who has demonstrated exemplary performance in the promotion and continuous improvement of county workforce development programs ● Joe Cooney Award: Excellence in Workforce Development. **Frequency:** annual. **Type:** recognition. **Recipient:** for substantial contribution to employment and training ● NACO Achievement Award. **Frequency:** annual. **Type:** recognition. **Recipient:** for unique and innovative county programs ● Workforce Development Awards for Excellence. **Frequency:** annual. **Type:** recognition. **Recipient:** for exemplary programs that are developing the nation's workforce. **Computer Services:** database ● online services, InfoRamp. **Committees:** Agriculture & Rural Affairs; Community and Economic Development; Environment, Energy and Land Use; Finance and Intergovernmental Affairs; Health; Human Services and Education; Indoor Air Advisory; Intergovernmental Relations; Joint Center Advisory; Justice and Public Safety; Labor and Employment; Public Lands; Sustainability Leadership; Transportation; Watershed Management. **Task Forces:** Homeland Security. **Affiliated With:** National Animal Control Association; National Association of Black County Officials; National Association of County Civil Attorneys; National Association for County Community and Economic Development; National Association of County Engineers; National Association of County Health Facility Administrators; National Association of County Information Officers; National Association of County Park and Recreation Officials; National Association of County Planners; National Association of County Recorders, Election Officials, and Clerks; National Association of County Relations Officials; National Association of County Treasurers and Finance Officers; National Council of County Association Executives. **Formerly:** National Association of County Officials; (1981) National Association of County Welfare Directors; (1984) National Association of County of Employment and Training Administrators; (2000) National Association of County Training and Employment Professionals; (2000) National Association of County Human Services Administrators. **Publications:** *County News*, bimonthly. Newsletter. **Price:** $75.00/year. ISSN: 0744-9798. **Circulation:** 29,000. **Advertising:** accepted. Alternate Formats: online ● *JTPA Directory of Service Delivery Areas*, annual ● *Legislative Bulletin*. Alternate Formats: online ● *NACO Update on Job Training*, biweekly ● Annual Report, annual. Alternate Formats: online ● Report, annual. Alternate Formats: online ● Surveys. Alternate Formats: online. **Conventions/Meetings:** annual Employment and Human Services - conference (exhibits) - 2008 July 11-15, Kansas City, MO; 2009 July 24-29, Nashville, TN ● annual Legislative - conference - always March. 2009 Mar. 7-11, Washington, DC.

5619 ■ National Association of County Civil Attorneys (NACCA)
c/o Robert Spence, Pres.
2501 7th St., Ste.300
Tuscaloosa, AL 35401-1801
Ph: (205)349-3870 (202)942-4285
Fax: (205)345-9580
E-mail: rspence@hsmbb.com
URL: http://www.naco.org
Contact: Robert Spence, Pres.
Founded: 1963. **Members:** 100. **Description:** County civil attorneys. Aims to respond to growing organizational needs of the office of county civil attorney. Seeks to educate members in areas including environment, labor-management relations, consumer protection, land use, utilization of energy sources, traditional statutory and case law, national legislation, and Supreme Court decisions. Offers educational programs; and compiles statistics. **Telecommunication Services:** electronic mail, jbyers@naco.org. **Affiliated With:** National Association of Counties. **Conventions/Meetings:** semiannual conference, held in conjunction with National Association of Counties - always winter and summer ● periodic conference, primarily on liability issues ● periodic workshop.

5620 ■ National Association of County Information Officers (NACIO)
c/o Tom Goodman, Public Affairs Dir.
440 1st St. NW
Washington, DC 20001
Ph: (913)715-8572 (913)681-3200
Fax: (202)393-2630
E-mail: tucker@jcw.org
URL: http://www.nacio.org
Contact: Robert Tucker, Pres.
Founded: 1965. **Members:** 470. **Membership Dues:** county staff, $75 ● state association staff, $100 ● non-county government, $75 ● corporate, $250. **Regional Groups:** 5. **Description:** Information officers and others who perform public information functions for county governments in the U.S. Seeks to improve the performance and understanding of public information functions in county governments. **Computer Services:** Mailing lists, listserv. **Publications:** *The Art of Communication*, semiannual. Newsletter. **Advertising:** accepted. Alternate Formats: online ● Also publishes membership list. **Conventions/Meetings:** annual competition, recognizes outstanding public information programs ● annual Legislative Conference - always March in Washington, DC ● annual meeting, in conjunction with the National Association of Counties - always summer. 2008 July 11-15, Kansas City, MO; 2009 July 24-29, Nashville, TN.

5621 ■ National Association of County Recorders, Election Officials, and Clerks (NACRC)
2501 Aerial Center Pkwy., Ste.103
Morrisville, NC 27560
Ph: (919)459-2080 (407)836-5982
Fax: (919)459-2075
E-mail: info@nacrc.org
URL: http://www.nacrc.org
Contact: Sue Baldwin, Pres.
Founded: 1949. **Members:** 1,000. **Membership Dues:** public official, county population of 25,000 or less, $55 (annual) ● corporate/business, national association, $500 (annual) ● state association, $350 (annual) ● population of 25,001 to 75,000, $135 (annual) ● population of 75,001 to 200,000, $175 (annual) ● population of 200,000 to 500,000, $200 (annual) ● associate, $35 (annual) ● population over 500,001, $250 (annual) ● deputy/director of association, $50 (annual). **Staff:** 1. **Budget:** $130,000. **Description:** Represents elected and appointed county recorders, election officials, clerks and court clerks. Promotes efficient business methods in the conduct of the public's business, especially in the offices of county recorder, clerk, or elections official. Administers Certified Public Official Program and conducts seminars. **Libraries: Type:** reference. **Awards:** Linda S. Carter Award. **Frequency:** annual. **Type:** recognition. **Recipient:** for individuals who have exemplified leadership, ingenuity and excellence in their offices ● NACRC Public Official of the Year Award. **Frequency:** annual. **Type:** recognition. **Recipient:** for outstanding public service. **Computer Services:** database ● mailing lists. **Committees:** Clerks to Boards and Commissions; Election Administration; JEOLC; Land Records; Official Records Administration and Management. **Task Forces:** Property Records Industry Joint. **Affiliated With:** National Association of Counties. **Formerly:** National Association of County Recorders and Clerks. **Publications:** *For The Record*, semimonthly. Newsletter. Contains updates on technology and processes affecting the property records industry. ● *NACRC Bulletin*, quarterly. Newsletter. Features legislative updates and conference notes; and reports on pertinent activities and programs implemented around the U.S. **Price:** available to members only. **Advertising:** accepted ● Membership Directory, annual. **Conventions/Meetings:** annual conference, held in conjunction with the National Association of Counties (exhibits) - always July. 2008 July 10-13, Kansas City, MO ● annual Legislative Conferences (exhibits) - always Washington, DC ● annual Western Interstate Regional Conference (exhibits).

5622 ■ National Association of County Relations Officials
c/o Diane Hutchins, Pres.
141 Pryor St. SW
Atlanta, GA 30303-3444
Ph: (404)730-7375
Fax: (404)730-7500
E-mail: diane.hutchins@co.fulton.ga.us
URL: http://www.naco.org
Contact: Diane Hutchins, Pres.
Founded: 1966. **Members:** 300. **Staff:** 1. **Description:** Represents intergovernmental and grants coordinators. Advances the concept of county intergovernmental coordination as a valuable tool for local governments. Promotes greater exchange of ideas and information concerning federal and state aid programs. Improves techniques for securing and administering federal and state funds. Fosters better relations among federal, state, and local officials. Conducts grant training workshops. **Formerly:** (1973) National Conference of County Development Coordinators; (1989) Council of Intergovernmental Relations Officials; (1997) National Association of Intergovernmental Relations Officials. **Publications:** *A Guide to Grants-In-Aid in County Government*. Handbook ● Directory, biennial ● Also publishes topical manuals and handbook. **Conventions/Meetings:** semiannual meeting, in conjunction with the National Association of Counties.

5623 ■ National Association of County Surveyors (NACS)
c/o R. Charles Pearson, Sec.-Treas.
County Surveyor, Clackamas County
9101 SE Sunnybrook Blvd., Ste.428
Clackamas, OR 97015-6612
Ph: (503)353-4499
Fax: (503)353-4481
E-mail: chuckpear@co.clackamas.or.us
URL: http://www.naco.org/nacs/index.htm
Contact: R. Charles Pearson, Sec.-Treas.
Membership Dues: full, $50 (annual) ● associate, $25 (annual) ● affiliate organization, $100 (annual) ● corporate, $250 (annual). **Description:** County surveyors; state associations of counties. Seeks to raise the efficiency of county surveying programs; promotes professional advancement of members. Facilitates communication and cooperation among members; lobbies on behalf of legislation beneficial to county governments and surveyors. **Affiliated With:** National Association of Counties. **Publications:** Newsletter, quarterly. **Conventions/Meetings:** annual conference.

5624 ■ National Council of County Association Executives (NCCAE)
c/o Kaye Braaten
503 4th Ave. N
Wahpeton, ND 58075-4405
Ph: (701)642-2237 (609)394-3467
Fax: (701)642-2329
E-mail: kbraaten@naco.org
URL: http://www.naco.org
Contact: Celeste Carpiano, Pres.
Founded: 1967. **Description:** Represents full-time staff members of state county associations. Aims to strengthen and improve county government organizations. **Formerly:** (1973) Conference of Executives of State Associations of Counties. **Conventions/Meetings:** annual meeting - always October.

Court Employees

5625 ■ Conference of State Court Administrators (COSCA)
c/o National Center for State Courts
300 Newport Ave.
Williamsburg, VA 23185
Ph: (757)259-1841
Free: (800)877-1233
URL: http://cosca.ncsc.dni.us
Contact: Shelley Rockwell, Contact
Founded: 1953. **Members:** 56. **Description:** Administrators of state courts, courts of the District of Columbia, Guam, Virgin Islands, the Northern Mariana Islands, and Puerto Rico. Provides association management services. **Committees:** Alternative Dispute Resolution; Education; Equality in the Courts. **Affiliated With:** National Center for State Courts. **Formerly:** (1972) National Conference of Court Administrative Officers; (1975) National Conference of State Court Administrators. **Conventions/Meetings:** annual meeting - every summer.

5626 ■ Federal Court Clerks Association (FCCA)
c/o Sheryl L. Loesch, Pres.
U.S. District Ct. - Middle District of Florida
80 N Hughey Ave., Rm. 300
Orlando, FL 32801
Ph: (407)835-4222 (904)549-1901
Fax: (407)835-4228
E-mail: sheryl_loesch@flmd.uscourts.gov
URL: http://www.fcca.ws
Contact: Sheryl L. Loesch, Pres.
Founded: 1922. **Members:** 2,050. **Membership Dues:** clerk, $75 ● chief deputy, $50 ● deputy clerk, retiree, $20 ● corporate, $150. **Description:** Clerks and deputy clerks of U.S. Courts of Appeal, U.S. District Courts, and 6 independent courts. Seeks to: assist members in rendering the best services in the administration of justice; foster cooperation between the offices of Clerks of the U.S. Courts and the Clerks and Administrative Office of the U.S. Courts regarding any problem of any clerk's office; establish uniformity of practice and procedure in the courts of the several circuits and districts; encourage the adoption of standard and simplified systems of accounting and office methods; improve individual expertise and the efficient, prompt, and economical operation of offices; and maintain a high standard of integrity, honor, and courtesy in all relations. **Awards:** Carol C. Fitzgerald Scholarship. **Frequency:** annual. **Type:** scholarship. **Recipient:** for members. **Publications:** *Federal Court Clerks' News*, bimonthly. Newsletter ● Journal. **Advertising:** accepted. Alternate Formats: online. **Conventions/Meetings:** annual conference.

5627 ■ National Association for Court Management (NACM)
c/o Association of Management
300 Newport Ave.
Natl. Center for State Courts
Williamsburg, VA 23185-4147
Ph: (757)259-1841 (318)965-3739
Free: (800)616-6165
Fax: (757)259-1520
E-mail: nacm@ncsc.dni.us
URL: http://www.nacmnet.org
Contact: Howard Chesshire, Pres.
Founded: 1985. **Members:** 2,500. **Membership Dues:** associate, regular, $100 (annual) ● full-time student, retired, $70 (annual) ● sustaining, $325 (annual). **Multinational. Description:** Court management professionals. Aims to foster communication

among members. Conducts educational programs. **Libraries: Type:** reference. **Holdings:** articles. **Awards:** Award of Merit. **Type:** recognition ● Justice Achievement Award. **Type:** recognition. **Committees:** Planning; Professional Development; Publication/ Communications. **Formed by Merger of:** (1985) National Association for Court Administration; National Association of Trial Court Administrators. **Publications:** *Court Communique*, quarterly. Newsletter. Contains information on court projects, while keeping members informed of changes in the profession. **Price:** included in membership dues ● *The Court Manager*, quarterly. Journal. Provides members with useful articles and research specifically covering issues relevant to court managers. **Price:** included in membership dues; $45.00 /year for nonmembers. **Advertising:** accepted ● *Trial Court Management Guides*. Handbooks ● Reports. Alternate Formats: online. **Conventions/Meetings:** annual conference (exhibits) - 2008 July 13-17, Anaheim, CA; 2009 July 7-11, Boston, MA ● annual Midyear Conference (exhibits).

5628 ■ National Association of Judiciary Interpreters and Translators (NAJIT)
603 Stewart St., Ste.610
Seattle, WA 98101
Ph: (206)267-2300
Fax: (206)626-0392
E-mail: headquarters@najit.org
URL: http://www.najit.org
Contact: Andy Ozols, Exec. Dir.
Founded: 1978. **Members:** 1,054. **Membership Dues:** associate, $85 (annual) ● active, $105 (annual) ● organizational (nonprofit), $115 (annual) ● corporate, $160 (annual) ● student, $40 (annual). **Staff:** 3. **Description:** Interpreters working on a staff or per diem basis in municipal, state, or federal courts; translators specializing in legal translations. Establishes professional standards and provides forum for the exchange of information among members. **Awards:** NAJIT Scholars. **Frequency:** annual. **Type:** grant. **Telecommunication Services:** electronic mail, executivedirector@najit.org ● information service, replies to questions from the public about the profession. **Committees:** Advocacy; Bylaws and Governance; Conference; Education; Proteus; Publications; Website. **Formerly:** (1988) Court Interpreters and Translators Association. **Publications:** *Proteus*, quarterly. Newsletters. **Price:** included in membership dues; $16.00 for nonmembers. **Advertising:** accepted. Alternate Formats: online. **Conventions/Meetings:** annual conference, multi-track classes and workshops (exhibits) - always the third weekend of May.

5629 ■ National Conference of Appellate Court Clerks (NCACC)
c/o Sandra L. Skinner, Pres.
Missouri Court of Appeals, Southern Dist.
300 Hammons Pkwy.
Springfield, MO 65806
Ph: (417)895-6811
Fax: (417)895-6817
E-mail: sandra.skinner@courts.mo.gov
URL: http://www.appellatecourtclerks.org
Contact: Sandra L. Skinner, Pres.
Founded: 1973. **Members:** 220. **Membership Dues:** regular, sustaining, $100 (annual) ● retired, $25 (annual). **Description:** Works to improve judicial administration at the appellate level through education. The National Center for State Courts serves as the secretariat. **Telecommunication Services:** electronic mail, address@appellatecourtclerks.org. **Affiliated With:** National Center for State Courts. **Publications:** *The Docket*, quarterly. Newsletter. Alternate Formats: online. **Conventions/Meetings:** annual conference.

5630 ■ National Court Reporters Association (NCRA)
8224 Old Courthouse Rd.
Vienna, VA 22182-3808
Ph: (703)556-6272
Free: (800)272-6272
Fax: (703)556-6291
E-mail: msic@ncrahq.org
URL: http://www.ncraonline.org
Contact: Mark J. Golden CAE, Exec. Dir./CEO
Founded: 1899. **Members:** 27,000. **Membership Dues:** participating, $240 ● participating (international), $125 ● associate, $145 ● associate (international), $100 ● student, $60. **Staff:** 60. **Budget:** $7,800,000. **Description:** Represents independent state, regional, and local associations. Verbatim court reporters who work as official reporters for courts and government agencies, as freelance reporters for independent contractors, and as captioners for television programming; retired reporters, teachers of court reporting, and school officials; student court reporters. Conducts research; compiles statistics; offers several certification programs; and publishes journal. **Libraries: Type:** reference. **Holdings:** 3,000; books, monographs, periodicals. **Subjects:** shorthand reporting and reporters. **Awards:** Distinguish Service Award. **Frequency:** annual. **Type:** recognition. **Recipient:** for services to the profession and the association ● Endorsers of the Year. **Frequency:** annual. **Type:** recognition. **Recipient:** for contribution to the growth of NCRA. **Computer Services:** Mailing lists. **Telecommunication Services:** TDD, (703)556-6289. **Absorbed:** (1970) Associated Stenotypists of America. **Formerly:** (1991) National Shorthand Reporters Association. **Publications:** *Journal of Court Reporting*, 10/year. Serves court and freelance shorthand reporters who specialize in hearings, depositions, statements, conferences, captioning, and other fields. **Price:** included in membership dues; $5.00/copy, for nonmembers. ISSN: 0274-5860. **Circulation:** 35,000. **Advertising:** accepted. Also Cited As: *National Shorthand Reporter* ● *National Court Reporters Association—The Court Reporters Sourcebook*, annual. Membership Directory. Lists international shorthand reporters; geographically and alphabetically arranged. **Price:** $24.95 for members; $49.95 for nonmembers. **Circulation:** 3,500. **Advertising:** accepted ● Also publishes other guides. **Conventions/Meetings:** annual convention (exhibits) ● annual seminar.

5631 ■ Society for the Technological Advancement of Reporting (STAR)
222 S Westmonte Dr., Ste.101
Altamonte Springs, FL 32714
Ph: (407)774-7880
Free: (800)565-6054
Fax: (407)774-6440
E-mail: star@staronline.org
URL: http://www.staronline.org
Contact: Michael Miller, Pres.
Members: 700. **Membership Dues:** reporting, agency, $150 (annual) ● associate, $75 (annual) ● student, $40 (annual). **Description:** Promotes the profession of court reporting and court reporting technology. Provides forum for information exchange, product evaluations, and united voice to manufacturers of CAT technology and related products. **Publications:** *STAR-STAR*, quarterly. Newsletter. Contains information of interest to members. **Advertising:** accepted ● Membership Directory. **Conventions/Meetings:** annual conference and seminar - held in spring ● annual convention (exhibits).

5632 ■ United States Court Reporters Association (USCRA)
4731 N Western Ave.
Chicago, IL 60625-2012
Ph: (816)512-5608
Free: (800)628-2730
Fax: (816)512-5688
E-mail: uscra@uscra.org
URL: http://www.uscra.org
Contact: Kathleen M. Wirt, Pres.-Elect
Founded: 1945. **Membership Dues:** student, $35 (annual) ● regular - full time, $150 (annual) ● regular - job share, $75 (annual) ● associate, supporting, $50 (annual). **Description:** Federal court reporters. Promotes high standards of performance and professional ethics in the verbatim transcription of court proceedings. Establishes professional standards of practice; conducts continuing professional development programs. **Committees:** Auditing; Circuit Representative; Constitution and Bylaws; Convention; Ethics; Federal Legislation and Regulations; Nominating; President's Advisory. **Publications:** *Circuit Rider*, quarterly. Magazine. **Circulation:** 600. **Advertising:** accepted. **Conventions/Meetings:** annual board meeting and seminar - always March or April ● annual convention (exhibits) - always Columbus Day weekend. 2008 Oct. 9-13, Denver, CO.

Credit Unions

5633 ■ National Association of State Credit Union Supervisors (NASCUS)
1655 N Ft. Myer Dr., Ste.300
Arlington, VA 22209
Ph: (703)528-8351
Fax: (703)528-3248
E-mail: offices@nascus.org
URL: http://www.nascus.org
Contact: Mary Martha Fortney, Pres./CEO
Founded: 1965. **Members:** 850. **Membership Dues:** credit union advisory council ($10-$20 million worth of assets), $50 (annual) ● credit union advisory council (maximum; $20-$1 billion worth of assets), $7,500 (annual) ● credit union advisory council ($1 billion or more worth of assets), $12,000 (annual). **Staff:** 7. **Budget:** $1,000,000. **Regional Groups:** 12. **State Groups:** 48. **Description:** Represents credit union regulators and the credit union industry. Improves the competitive, financial, and service position of credit unions. Advances the quality of credit union examinations. Broadens and updates the skills of examiners and supervisory examination procedures to address the changes and advancements in credit union financial activity and products. Provides forum for the discussion and analysis of current and anticipated problems in the financial and operating structure of credit unions. Operates the National School for State Credit Union Examiners, which offers continuing education coordinating classroom lectures, pre-work, discussion groups, and case studies on issues confronting credit union examiners. **Awards:** John B. Rucker, Jr. **Frequency:** annual. **Type:** scholarship. **Committees:** Audit; Education; NISCUE; Performance Standards; Regulatory Development. **Task Forces:** Alternative Capital; NASCUS & NCUA Corporate Credit Union; NASCUS & NCUA HR 1151 Rules Working. **Formerly:** (2000) National Institute for State Credit Union Examination. **Publications:** *Facts From Washington*, bimonthly. Newsletter. Alternate Formats: online ● *NASCUS Stateline*, monthly. Newsletter. Includes legislative developments affecting credit unions. **Price:** free for members. **Circulation:** 1,000. Alternate Formats: online ● *President's Report*, annual. Annual Report. **Conventions/Meetings:** annual symposium and conference.

Crime

5634 ■ Association for Crime Scene Reconstruction (ACSR)
PO Box 51376
Phoenix, AZ 85076-1376
Ph: (602)534-9280
E-mail: brucemwiley@yahoo.com
URL: http://www.acsr.org
Contact: Bruce Wiley, Pres.
Founded: 1991. **Members:** 525. **Membership Dues:** regular, provisional, $30 (annual) ● supporting, $90 (annual). **Description:** Encourages the exchange of information and procedures useful in the reconstruction of crime scenes. Stimulates research on improved methods of crime scene reconstruction. Improves the professional expertise of individuals in the field of crime scene reconstruction through education and training seminars. **Publications:** Newsletter. Includes information on crime scene reconstruction. **Conventions/Meetings:** annual conference, with training.

5635 ■ Crime Prevention Coalition of America (CPCA)
1000 Connecticut Ave. NW, 13th Fl.
Washington, DC 20036

Ph: (202)466-6272
Fax: (202)296-1356
E-mail: membership@ncpc.org
URL: http://www.ncpc.org
Founded: 1980. **Members:** 350. **Membership Dues:** state/national organization, federal agency, $100 (annual) ● affiliate, $50 (annual) ● for profit organization, $2,500 (annual). **Description:** Aims to reduce crime in the United States. Commits to lead collective efforts of individuals, communities and government to improve the quality of life by preventing crime. **Affiliated With:** Advertising Council; National Crime Prevention Council. **Publications:** *Mobilizing the Nation*, annual. Annual Report. Illustrates preventive approaches to reduce crime, violence, and substance abuse in the U.S. Alternate Formats: online.

5636 ■ International Association of Asian Crime Investigators (IAACI)
PO Box 1327
Marina, CA 93933
Ph: (831)901-4595
Fax: (831)384-5321
E-mail: referee0090@hotmail.com
URL: http://www.iaaci.com
Contact: Bruce C. Martin, Pres.
Founded: 1987. **Membership Dues:** general, $35 (annual) ● associate, $25 (annual). **Multinational. Description:** Promotes awareness of combating Asian criminality worldwide. Serves as a conduit of information and criminal intelligence. Facilitates educational opportunities for members of the criminal justice community. Assists in the identification and apprehension of Asian criminals. **Publications:** *IACCI News*, quarterly. Newsletter. Contains information on criminal trends and investigative techniques. ● Membership Directory.

5637 ■ International Association of Bloodstain Pattern Analysts (IABPA)
12139 E Makohoh Trail
Tucson, AZ 85749-8179
Ph: (520)760-6620
Fax: (520)760-5590
E-mail: norman@bloody1.com
URL: http://www.iabpa.org
Contact: Mr. Norman Reeves, Sec.-Treas.
Founded: 1983. **Members:** 600. **Membership Dues:** general, $40 (annual). **Multinational. Description:** Enhances standardization and encourages research on bloodstain pattern analysis. **Libraries: Type:** reference. **Holdings:** 4; archival material, business records, photographs. **Awards:** Dan Rahn Grant. **Frequency:** annual. **Type:** grant. **Recipient:** for research in the field of bloodstain pattern analysis ● Distinguished Member. **Frequency:** periodic. **Type:** recognition. **Recipient:** for member who has made outstanding contributions in the field of bloodstain pattern analysis. **Computer Services:** Information services, bloodstain pattern analysis resources ● online services, bulletin board. **Committees:** Daubert; Educational; Ethics. **Publications:** Newsletter, quarterly. **Advertising:** accepted. Alternate Formats: online. **Conventions/Meetings:** annual conference, with training (exhibits).

5638 ■ National Alliance of Gang Investigators Associations (NAGIA)
c/o Rusty Keeble, Pres.
PO Box 608628
Orlando, FL 32860-8628
Ph: (321)388-8694
Fax: (407)836-3103
E-mail: rustykeeble@fgia.com
URL: http://www.nagia.org
Contact: Rusty Keeble, Pres.
Founded: 1998. **Members:** 15,000. **Regional Groups:** 16. **Description:** Promotes and coordinates national anti-gang strategies. Advocates the standardization of anti-gang training, establishment of uniform gang definitions, assistance for communities with emerging gang problems, and input to policymakers and program administrators. Facilitates and supports regional gang investigators associations; the Regional Information Sharing Systems; as well as federal, state, and local anti-gang initiatives. **Libraries: Type:** reference. **Holdings:** articles. **Subjects:** gangs, crime, law enforcement, violence, graffiti. **Computer Services:** Information services, gang-related articles. **Publications:** *National Gang Threat Assessment 2000*, quadrennial. Report. Provides an accurate and comprehensive picture of the threat posed by gangs in the US. Alternate Formats: online ● Articles. Alternate Formats: online.

5639 ■ Victims' Assistance Legal Organization (VALOR)
8180 Greensboro Dr., Ste.1070
McLean, VA 22102-3823
Ph: (703)748-0811
Fax: (703)356-5085
E-mail: info@valor-national.org
URL: http://www.valor-national.org
Contact: Eric Smith JD, Pres.
Founded: 1979. **Description:** Seeks to advance the rights and improve the treatment of crime victims in the criminal, juvenile and civil justice systems. Develops and administers national scope programs to address issues of concern to crime victims.

Criminal Justice

5640 ■ Center on Juvenile and Criminal Justice (CJCJ)
54 Dore St.
San Francisco, CA 94103
Ph: (415)621-5661
Fax: (415)621-5466
E-mail: dmacallair@cjcj.org
URL: http://www.cjcj.org
Contact: Daniel Macallair MPA, Exec. Dir.
Founded: 1985. **Staff:** 8. **Description:** Seeks to reduce society's reliance on the use of incarceration as a solution to social problems. **Publications:** *A Preliminary Analysis of Detention Expansion In Alameda County* ● *A Tale of Two Jurisdictions: Youth Crime and Detention Rates in Maryland and the District of Columbia* ● *An Analysis of San Francisco Juvenile Justice Reforms During The Brown Administration* ● *Barriers and Promising Approaches to Workforce and Youth Development for Young Offenders* ● *Drugs and Disparity: The Racial Impact of Illinois' Practice of Transferring Young Drug Offenders to Adult Court* ● *The History of the Presentence Investigation Report* ● *OFF BALANCE: Youth, Race and Crime in the News* ● *Prison Expansion in a Time of Austerity: An Analysis of the Governor's Proposed New Prison in Delano* ● *Reducing Disproportionate Minority Confinement: The Multnomah County Oregon Success Story and its Implications* ● *Restructuring Juvenile Corrections in California*. Report ● *Widening the Net in Juvenile Justice and the Dangers of Prevention and Early Intervention.*

5641 ■ Citizens United for Alternatives to the Death Penalty (CUADP)
PMB 335
2603 Dr. Martin Luther King Jr. Hwy.
Gainesville, FL 32609
Free: (800)973-6548
E-mail: cuadp@cuadp.org
URL: http://www.cuadp.org
Contact: Abraham J. Bonowitz, Dir./Co-Founder
Founded: 1997. **Members:** 100,000,000. **Budget:** $60,000. **For-Profit. Description:** Aims to abolish the death penalty in the U.S. through aggressive campaigns of public education and the promotion of tactical grassroots activism. **Computer Services:** Mailing lists, open to nonmembers. **Telecommunication Services:** electronic mail, abe@cuadp.org. **Committees:** Abolitionist Action; Floridians for Alternatives to the Death Penalty. **Affiliated With:** National Coalition to Abolish the Death Penalty. **Conventions/Meetings:** International Death Penalty Abolition Day - meeting - always May 1st.

5642 ■ Criminal Justice Legal Foundation (CJLF)
PO Box 1199
Sacramento, CA 95812
Ph: (916)446-0345
Fax: (916)446-1194
URL: http://www.cjlf.org
Contact: Michael Rushford, Pres./CEO
Founded: 1982. **Membership Dues:** basic support, $25 (annual). **Staff:** 8. **Budget:** $720,028. **Nonmembership. Description:** Strives to assure that people who are guilty of committing crimes receive swift and certain punishment in an orderly and thoroughly constitutional manner. **Libraries: Type:** not open to the public; reference. **Holdings:** 500; archival material, articles, papers, reports. **Subjects:** criminal law, criminal procedure, sentencing, prison administration, constitutional law, criminal justice policy, evidence, death penalty, victim's right, USA Patriot Act, Anti-Terrorism and Effective Death Penalty Act, Megan's Law, Three Strikes and You're Out. **Boards:** Texas. **Committees:** Legal Advisory. **Publications:** *Advisory*, quarterly. Newsletter. Reports on the Foundation's current activities.

5643 ■ Innocence Project
100 5th Ave., 3rd Fl.
New York, NY 10011
Ph: (212)364-5340
E-mail: info@innocenceproject.org
URL: http://www.innocenceproject.org
Contact: Barry C. Scheck, Co-Founder/Co-Dir.
Founded: 1992. **Description:** Serves as legal clinic handling cases where post-conviction DNA testing of evidence can yield conclusive proof of innocence to inmates who have exhausted their appeals and their means.

5644 ■ International Association of Law Enforcement Planners (IALEP)
PO Box 11437
Torrance, CA 90510-1437
Ph: (310)225-5148
E-mail: ialep@ialep.org
URL: http://www.ialep.org
Contact: Mr. Sanjena V. Clay, Pres.
Founded: 1991. **Members:** 1,000. **Membership Dues:** active/associate, $75 (annual). **Multinational. Description:** Represents law enforcement planning and research personnel. Strives to provide its members with information concerning innovations, problems, and solutions in the law enforcement industry. Holds weeklong Planner's course. **Awards:** Planner of the Year. **Frequency:** annual. **Type:** recognition. **Recipient:** to persons who have made significant contributions to the field of law enforcement planning ● Project of the Year. **Frequency:** annual. **Type:** recognition. **Recipient:** to projects that have made significant contributions to the field of law enforcement planning. **Computer Services:** database, project ● information services, listserver ● mailing lists, of members. **Publications:** *The Exchange*, 2-3/year. Newsletter. Contains information on IALEP. **Price:** free for members. Alternate Formats: online. **Conventions/Meetings:** annual conference.

5645 ■ National Alliance of Sentencing Advocates and Mitigation Specialists (NASAMS)
c/o Maureen B. James
1140 Connecticut Ave. NW, Ste.900
Washington, DC 20036
Ph: (202)452-0620
E-mail: m.james@nlada.org
URL: http://www.nlada.org/Defender/Defender_NASAMS
Contact: Lori James-Monroe, Chair
Founded: 1992. **Membership Dues:** professional, $65 (annual) ● student, $40 (annual). **Description:** Promotes fair, humane, and equitable sentencing and confinement decisions for all people in America. Advances the field of sentencing advocacy by fostering the professional development of its members and upholding the ethical standards of practice of the organization. Is a section of National Legal Aid and Defender Association. **Awards:** John Augustus Award. **Frequency:** annual. **Type:** recognition. **Recipient:** for outstanding contribution to the profession of sentencing advocacy ● Mim George Award. **Frequency:** annual. **Type:** recognition. **Recipient:** for outstanding contribution by an organization ● Presi-

dent's Award. **Frequency:** annual. **Type:** recognition. **Recipient:** for extraordinary dedication to the work of the governing board and association ● Sentencing Project Award. **Frequency:** annual. **Type:** recognition. **Recipient:** for exemplary performance in serving clients, courts and community. **Computer Services:** database, mitigation directory ● information services, mitigation resource ● mailing lists, listserv hosted by Yahoo Groups. **Formerly:** (2005) National Association of Sentencing Advocates. **Publications:** *NASA Notes*, 3/year. Newsletter. Contains information about philosophy and practice of sentencing advocacy. Alternate Formats: online ● Annual Reports. Highlights the activities and accomplishments of the association. Alternate Formats: online.

5646 ■ National Association of Federal Defenders (NAFD)
PO Box 22223
Nashville, TN 37202
E-mail: tim_crooks@fd.org
URL: http://www.federaldefenders.org
Contact: Tim Crooks, Pres.
Description: Aims to improve the quality of justice for those persons who are unable to afford counsel in federal criminal or habeas corpus cases. Strives to protect and insure by rule of law those individual rights guaranteed by the Federal Constitution. Preserves and protects the ability of federal defender organizations to attract and retain qualified persons for service in their organizations. **Publications:** *The Liberty Legend*, quarterly. Newsletter. Alternate Formats: online.

5647 ■ National Association of Forensic Counselors (NAFC)
PO Box 8827
Fort Wayne, IN 46898-8827
Ph: (260)426-7234
Fax: (260)426-7431
E-mail: nafc@locl.net
URL: http://www.nationalafc.com
Contact: Francis J. Deisler PhD, Pres./CEO
Founded: 1994. **Members:** 34,000. **State Groups:** 16. **Description:** Promotes competency and training among persons working with criminal offenders. Seeks to uphold postgraduate standards and professional responsibility in the specialized area of criminal justice counseling and evaluation. Administers credentialing certification and recertification for qualified forensic counseling practitioners. **Publications:** *The Forensic Therapist*. Journal ● Annual Report, annual. Alternate Formats: online.

5648 ■ National Association for Justice Information Systems (NAJIS)
c/o Jim Parsons, Pres.
PO Box 410
Vancouver, WA 98666
Ph: (360)397-2113
Fax: (360)759-5912
E-mail: jim.parsons@clark.wa.gov
URL: http://www.najis.org
Contact: Jim Parsons, Pres.
Description: Represents individuals who are responsible for the acquisition, operation and management of local, state and federal criminal justice information systems. Shares information to managers for the courts and allied agencies who are involved with automated information system. Assists individuals who are investigating, evaluating and purchasing software or hardware that facilitates case tracking and management. **Telecommunication Services:** electronic mail, mperbix@yahoo.com. **Publications:** *InfoSys*. Newsletter. Alternate Formats: online.

5649 ■ National Association of Probation Executives (NAPE)
c/o Ms. Christine Davidson, Exec. Dir.
Sam Houston State Univ.
Correctional Mgt. Inst. of Texas
George J. Beto Criminal Justice Center
Huntsville, TX 77341-2296
Ph: (936)294-3757
Fax: (936)294-1671
E-mail: davidson@shsu.edu
URL: http://www.napehome.org
Contact: Ms. Christine Davidson, Exec. Dir.
Founded: 1981. **Members:** 240. **Membership Dues:** regular, $50 (annual) ● regular, $95 (biennial) ● regular, $140 (triennial) ● organizational, $250 (annual) ● corporate, $500 (annual). **Description:** Probation executives. Focuses on enhancing the professionalism in the field of probation. Offers networking, management, program development, training, and research. **Awards:** Executive of the Year. **Frequency:** annual. **Type:** recognition. **Recipient:** for excellence in the field of community corrections ● William Faches Award for Exceptional Community Service. **Frequency:** annual. **Type:** recognition. **Recipient:** to an individual who has significantly impacted community corrections through community service. **Affiliated With:** American Correctional Association; American Probation and Parole Association. **Publications:** *Executive Exchange*, quarterly. Journal. Alternate Formats: online ● *Probation Safety Survey*. Alternate Formats: online. **Conventions/Meetings:** annual conference and meeting.

5650 ■ National Association of State Sentencing Commissions (NASC)
c/o Lynda Flynt
300 Dexter Ave.
Montgomery, AL 36104-3741
Ph: (334)353-4830
Fax: (334)353-5785
E-mail: lynda.flynt@alacourt.gov
URL: http://www.ussc.gov/states.htm
Contact: Lynda Flynt, Contact
Founded: 1995. **Description:** Facilitates the exchange and sharing of information ideas, data, expertise, and experiences. Educates on issues related to sentencing policies, sentencing guidelines and sentencing commissions. **Publications:** *The Sentencing Guideline*. Newsletter. Alternate Formats: online.

5651 ■ National Major Gang Task Force (NMGTF)
338 S Arlington Ave., Ste.112
Indianapolis, IN 46219
Ph: (317)322-0537
Fax: (317)322-0549
E-mail: nmgtf@earthlink.net
URL: http://www.nmgtf.org
Contact: Lina Presley, Treas./Membership Chair
Membership Dues: regular, $35 (annual) ● regular, $125 (quinquennial) ● regular (10 years), $250. **Description:** Provides leadership and information within the criminal justice system and other stakeholders to minimize the effects of security threat groups, gangs and terrorists in jails, prisons and communities. Offers technical assistance in the development of statewide gang/security threat group programs in numerous jurisdictions. Seeks to establish information-sharing standards with regard to gangs and security threat group management. **Publications:** Bulletin, semiannual. **Price:** included in membership dues.

Criminal Law

5652 ■ Americans for Effective Law Enforcement (AELE)
841 W Touhy Ave.
Park Ridge, IL 60068-3351
Ph: (847)685-0700
Fax: (847)685-9700
E-mail: info@aele.org
URL: http://www.aele.org
Contact: Wayne W. Schmidt, Exec. Dir.
Founded: 1966. **Staff:** 5. **Budget:** $850,000. **Nonmembership. Description:** Seeks to explore the need for effective enforcement of criminal law. Helps police, prosecutors, and the courts promote fairer, more effective administration of criminal law. Serves as a friend of the court, representing the law-abiding public, in cases before the United States Supreme Court or other courts where cases with a bearing on effective criminal law enforcement is being heard. Drafts model legislation and constitutional amendments to aid in effective law enforcement and public protection. States that it is concerned with equal justice for all and will reject support from "advocates of racial bias or other unconstitutional concepts." Maintains Law Enforcement Legal Defense Center that assists police administrators in defense of civil suits alleging police misconduct. **Libraries: Type:** reference. **Holdings:** 1,000; articles, books. **Subjects:** law. **Computer Services:** Electronic publishing, monthly publications and digests. **Telecommunication Services:** electronic mail, aele@aol.com. **Publications:** *Fire and Police Personnel Reporter*, monthly. Articles. Contains articles on litigation arising out of employee disciplinary action or labor laws; articles cover more than 200 topics. ISSN: 0164-6397. Alternate Formats: online ● *Jail and Prison Law Bulletin*, monthly. Contains articles on civil liability of officers and jails, detention centers and prisons, issues arising out of custody, detention or confinement. ISSN: 0739-0998 ● *Law Enforcement Legal Liability Reporter*, monthly. Articles. Contains articles on the civil liability of law enforcement officers and agencies. ISSN: 0271-5481. Alternate Formats: online ● Also publishes amicus curiae briefs. **Conventions/Meetings:** workshop.

5653 ■ Federal Criminal Investigators Association (FCIA)
PO Box 23400
Washington, DC 20026
Ph: (630)969-8537
Free: (800)403-3374
Fax: (800)528-3492
E-mail: fcianat@aol.com
URL: http://www.fedcia.org
Contact: Richard Zehme, Pres.
Founded: 1957. **Members:** 2,000. **Membership Dues:** associate, $45 (annual) ● retired, student, $25 (annual) ● regular, $50 (annual). **Staff:** 2. **Budget:** $50,000. **Regional Groups:** 10. **Local Groups:** 35. **Description:** Serves as professional fraternal organization dedicated to the advancement of federal law enforcement officers and the citizens they serve. Aims to ensure law enforcement professionals have the tools and support network to meet the challenges of future criminal investigations while becoming more community oriented. Intends to pursue mission by promoting professionalism, enhancing the image of federal officers, fostering cooperation among all law enforcement professionals, providing a fraternal environment for the advancement of the membership and community. Helps charitable programs and organizations. **Awards:** FIA Endowment Fund Scholarship. **Frequency:** annual. **Type:** scholarship. **Recipient:** for college students studying criminal investigation or law enforcement ● **Frequency:** annual. **Type:** recognition. **Computer Services:** database, membership. **Committees:** Communications; Legislation; National Meetings/Seminars; Recreation; Recruitment/Membership; Retiree/Disability; Scholarship. **Affiliated With:** National Center for Missing and Exploited Children; National Law Enforcement Council; National Law Enforcement Officers Memorial Fund. **Formerly:** (1969) U.S. Treasury Agents Association; (1991) Federal Criminal Investigators Association; (1992) Association of Federal Investigators; (1998) Federal Investigators Association. **Publications:** *Investigative and Related Positions in the Federal Government* ● Newsletter, quarterly. Covers legislative issues and other current information affecting federal law enforcement. Includes chapter news and employment opportunities. **Price:** included in membership dues. **Circulation:** 2,000. **Advertising:** accepted. **Conventions/Meetings:** annual meeting ● Training Conference and Awards Banquet - banquet and meeting (exhibits) - in Washington, DC.

5654 ■ International Criminal Court Alliance
11835 W Olympic Blvd., Ste.1090
Los Angeles, CA 90064
Ph: (310)473-0777 (310)379-8843
Free: (866)379-8843

E-mail: info@icc-alliance.org
URL: http://www.icc-alliance.org
Contact: Sean Butler, Pres./Sec.
Multinational. Description: Supports research and education regarding the participation of the United States in a permanent International Criminal Court. Promotes peace through International Law. Supports the International Criminal Court in promoting a just and equitable international legal system that will address crimes of genocide, crimes against humanity and war crimes, when there are no other courts willing or able to prosecute.

5655 ■ Justice Research Association (JRA)
PO Drawer 23557
Hilton Head Island, SC 29925
Ph: (843)689-6298
Fax: (202)478-0271
E-mail: admin@cjcentral.com
URL: http://www.cjcentral.com
Contact: Frank Schmalleger PhD, Dir.
Founded: 1994. **Members:** 16. **Staff:** 2. **Description:** Serves the needs of the nation's criminal justice planners, criminal justice agency administrators, attorneys practicing criminal law, and management personnel within the private security community. Provides consulting services, as well as research and data-gathering services. Offers educational and research programs. **Libraries: Type:** not open to the public. **Holdings:** 500; articles, books. **Subjects:** criminal justice. **Formerly:** (1991) Southern Planning Consultants. **Publications:** *The Definitive Guide to Criminal Justice and Criminology on the World Wide Web*. Book. **Price:** $21.40/copy ● *Your Criminal Justice Career: The Definitive Guide to Criminology and Criminal Justice on the World Wide Web*, every 2-3 years. Book. **Conventions/Meetings:** annual board meeting.

5656 ■ National Association of Criminal Defense Lawyers (NACDL)
1150 18th St. NW, Ste.950
Washington, DC 20036
Ph: (202)872-8600
Fax: (202)872-8690
E-mail: assist@nacdl.org
URL: http://www.criminaljustice.org
Contact: Norman L. Reimer, Exec. Dir.
Founded: 1958. **Members:** 11,000. **Membership Dues:** regular, $265 (annual) ● new lawyer, $140 (annual) ● public defender, professor/military, $125 (annual) ● judge, associate, $150 (annual) ● student, $30 (annual) ● sustaining, $400 (annual) ● life, $5,000. **Staff:** 18. **Budget:** $3,000,000. **Description:** Advances the mission of the nation's criminal defense lawyers to ensure justice and due process for persons accused of crime or other misconduct. A professional bar association that includes private criminal defense lawyers, public defenders, law professors, active military defense counsel and judges committed to preserving fairness within America's criminal justice system. **Libraries: Type:** reference. **Holdings:** archival material, video recordings. **Awards:** Champion of Justice Awards. **Frequency:** annual. **Type:** recognition. **Recipient:** for individuals who have staunchly preserved or defended the constitutional rights of American citizens ● Lifetime Achievement. **Frequency:** annual. **Type:** recognition. **Recipient:** for exceptional accomplishments over a lifetime of distinguished leadership and service on behalf of the law ● Marshall Stern Legislative Achievement Award. **Frequency:** annual. **Type:** recognition. **Recipient:** to a member who best demonstrates commitment to the legislative arena ● Robert C. Heeney Memorial Award. **Frequency:** annual. **Type:** recognition. **Recipient:** to a criminal defense attorney who best exemplifies the goals and values of NACDL, and the legal profession. **Computer Services:** Mailing lists ● online services, brief bank index. **Telecommunication Services:** electronic mail, norman@nacdl.org. **Committees:** Affiliates; Amicus Curiae; Death Penalty; Ethics Advisory; Hotline Panel of Legal Experts; Indigent Defense; Lawyers Assistance Strike Force; Legislative; Public Affairs; White Collar Crime. **Task Forces:** DNA; Forfeiture Abuse. **Formerly:** (1973) National Association of Defense Lawyers in Criminal Cases. **Publications:** *The Champion*, 10/year. Magazine. Discusses criminal justice issues and developments, as well as trial practice strategies and techniques. **Price:** $90.00 /year for nonmembers in U.S.; $105.00 /year for nonmembers outside U.S.; included in membership dues. ISSN: 0744-9488. **Circulation:** 12,500. **Advertising:** accepted. Alternate Formats: online ● *Membership Handbook*, annual. Membership Directory. Includes directory of members, arranged alphabetically and geographically. **Conventions/Meetings:** annual Law Student Trial Competition ● quarterly seminar and meeting, with continuing legal education programs (exhibits) - always February, May, August, and November.

5657 ■ National Criminal Defense College (NCDC)
c/o Mercer Law School
343 Orange St.
Macon, GA 31207
Ph: (478)746-4151
Fax: (478)743-0160
E-mail: deryld@ncdc.net
URL: http://www.ncdc.net
Contact: Deryl D. Dantzler, Dean
Founded: 1985. **Staff:** 3. **Budget:** $225,000. **Description:** Continuing legal education institution for criminal defense lawyers. Sponsors trial institute in two-week sessions in Macon, GA, twice each summer, and various shorter programs in other locations; holds seminars. **Telecommunication Services:** electronic mail, rosie@ncdc.net. **Affiliated With:** National Association of Criminal Defense Lawyers. **Supersedes:** National College for Criminal Defense. **Conventions/Meetings:** quarterly Board of Regents' Meeting - board meeting.

Criminology

5658 ■ International Association of Crime Analysts (IACA)
9218 Metcalf Ave., No. 364
Overland Park, KS 66212
Free: (800)609-3419
E-mail: iaca@iaca.net
URL: http://www.iaca.net
Contact: Christopher W. Bruce, Pres.
Founded: 1990. **Members:** 1,500. **Membership Dues:** individual, $25. **Multinational. Description:** Crime analysts. Strives to enhance the effectiveness and consistency in the fields of crime and intelligence analysis. **Committees:** Bylaw Revision. **Publications:** *Exploring Crime Analysis*. Book. Covers essential crime analysis skills. **Price:** $29.99 single copy ● *The Forecaster*. Newsletter. **Conventions/Meetings:** annual conference, for crime analysts.

Customs

5659 ■ Customs and International Trade Bar Association (CITBA)
c/o Allison M. Baron, Esq., Membership Chair
75 Broad St., 26th Fl.
New York, NY 10004
Ph: (212)425-0055
Fax: (212)425-1797
E-mail: abaron@spcblaw.com
URL: http://www.citba.org
Contact: Allison M. Baron Esq., Membership Chair
Founded: 1917. **Members:** 500. **Membership Dues:** active/associate, $75 (annual) ● retired/student, $25 (annual). **Description:** Represents attorneys admitted to practice before the U.S. Court of International Trade and U.S. Court of Appeals for the Federal Circuit, and who practice in the fields of customs and international trade law. Conducts special events. **Libraries: Type:** open to the public. **Holdings:** photographs. **Committees:** Continuing Legal Education and Professional Responsibility; Customs and Tariffs; International Trade; Judicial Selection; Liaison With Other Bar Associations; Meetings and Special Events; Membership; Publications; Trial and Appellate Practice. **Affiliated With:** International Bar Association. **Formerly:** (1981) Association of the Customs Bar. **Publications:** *CITBA Newsletter*, bimonthly. Alternate Formats: online. **Conventions/Meetings:** monthly dinner and seminar.

Democracy

5660 ■ Americans for Informed Democracy (AID)
45 Court St.
New Haven, CT 06511
Ph: (203)773-1202
E-mail: info@aidemocracy.org
URL: http://www.aidemocracy.org
Contact: Seth Green, Pres.
Description: Seeks to build a new generation of globally conscious leaders who can shape an American foreign policy appropriate for an increasingly interdependent world. Works to raise global awareness in U.S. university campuses. Coordinates town hall meetings on America's role in the world and holds leadership retreats.

5661 ■ Council for a Community of Democracies (CCD)
1801 F St. NW, Ste.308
Washington, DC 20006
Ph: (202)789-9771
Fax: (202)789-9764
E-mail: info@ccd21.org
URL: http://www.ccd21.org
Contact: Robert R. LaGamma, Exec. Dir.
Founded: 2000. **Multinational. Description:** Promotes democracy across the globe by fostering closer ties among democratic nations and institutions. Works closely with the United Nations to ensure that all democratic states work together to strengthen democracy across a wide spectrum of cultural and religious traditions. Promotes transparency of governmental processes, sound electoral systems, respect for human rights and the rule of law, active civic education, prevention of official corruption and related core values basic to democratic governance. **Libraries: Type:** open to the public. **Holdings:** articles, books, periodicals. **Subjects:** democracy, freedom, peace, foreign policy. **Caucuses:** UN Democracy.

5662 ■ Declaration Foundation (DF)
PO Box 1310
Herndon, VA 20191
E-mail: df@declarationfoundation.com
URL: http://www.declaration.net
Contact: Ms. Mary Parker Lewis, Exec. Dir.
Description: Strives to proclaim the ideas, principles, beliefs and convictions, which formed the foundation of America, found in the Declaration of Independence. Fosters an America reawakening to the power and potential of the ideas in the Declaration of Independence. Promotes truth to America as found in the Declaration of Independence and educates all generations. Reestablishes Declaration Principles as the unifying force for American citizenship. **Publications:** *America's Declaration Principles in Thought and Action*. Book. **Price:** $30.00 hardcopy; $15.00 softcopy. Alternate Formats: online.

5663 ■ Demos
220 Fifth Ave., 5th Fl.
New York, NY 10001
Ph: (212)633-1405 (212)389-1407
Fax: (212)633-2015
E-mail: info@demos.org
URL: http://www.demos.org
Contact: Miles Rapoport, Pres./CEO
Founded: 1999. **Description:** Democracy reform. **Publications:** *Around the Kitchen Table*, monthly. Journal. Alternate Formats: online ● *Democracy Dispatches*, biweekly. Journal. Tracks and analyzes legislative and political developments on democracy issues in the states. Alternate Formats: online ● *Engaging Democracy's Moment: The Report on a National Strategy Discussion*. Alternate Formats: online.

5664 ■ Preamble Center
2040 S St. NW
Washington, DC 20009
Ph: (202)265-3263
E-mail: preamble@preamble.org
URL: http://www.nypn.org/htm/Members/preamble/index.html
Description: Promotes vigorous public dialogue about the economic problems confronting America's working families and encourage the development of serious, workable solutions through research, analysis, and the dissemination of information to the public. **Publications:** Papers.

Democratic Party

5665 ■ 21st Century Democrats
1731 Connecticut Ave. NW, 2nd Fl.
Washington, DC 20009
Ph: (202)626-5620
Fax: (202)347-0956
E-mail: info@21stdems.org
URL: http://www.21stcenturydems.org
Contact: Kelly Young, Exec. Dir.
Description: Promotes the traditions of the Democratic Party through election of economically progressive, populist officials. Conducts a youth leadership development speaker series. **Programs:** Campaign Trainings; Field Organizer; Oregon Neighbor-to-Neighbor. **Projects:** Young Voter. **Conventions/Meetings:** conference, training ● annual dinner.

Democratic Socialism

5666 ■ Committees of Correspondence for Democracy and Socialism (CCDS)
545 8th Ave., 14th Fl. NE
New York, NY 10018
Ph: (212)868-3733
Fax: (212)868-3334
E-mail: national@cc-ds.org
URL: http://www.cc-ds.org
Contact: Leslie Cagan, Co-Chair
Membership Dues: individual, $31 (annual) ● household, $41 (annual) ● low income, student, unemployed, $16 (annual). **Description:** Activists in all social movements committed to democracy and socialism. **Publications:** *Dialogue and Initiative*, quarterly. Journal. **Price:** $5.00 /year for members; $10.00 /year for nonmembers. Alternate Formats: online ● *Mobilizer*, quarterly. Newsletter. **Price:** $10.00 /year for nonmembers; $25.00 /year for nonmembers outside U.S. Alternate Formats: online ● Articles. Alternate Formats: online.

District Attorneys

5667 ■ National College of District Attorneys (NCDA)
Univ. of South Carolina Law School
1600 Hampton St., Ste.414
Columbia, SC 29208
Ph: (803)705-5005
Fax: (803)705-5301
E-mail: registrar@ndaa.org
URL: http://www.ndaa-apri.org/ncda/ncda_home.php
Contact: Mary Galvin, Dean
Founded: 1970. **Staff:** 15. **Budget:** $1,000,000. **Description:** Represents students, state, local, federal, and municipal prosecutors, assistant attorneys general and military lawyers. Aims to provide high quality postgraduate education and training for lawyers engaged in public prosecution. Provides intensive two-week course for career prosecutors, one-week course for executive prosecutors, and continuing program of short courses across the country on topics of interest to prosecutors. Aids state training programs by assisting state training coordinators in presenting educational programs. Sponsors programs for administrative and investigative personnel of prosecutors' offices. Offers continuing legal education credit certification. **Awards:** Distinguished Faculty Award. **Frequency:** annual. **Type:** recognition. **Telecommunication Services:** electronic bulletin board, course information. **Subcommittees:** American Bar Association; American College of Trial Lawyers; National District Attorneys Association 1. **Affiliated With:** American Bar Association; American College of Trial Lawyers; National District Attorneys Association. **Publications:** *Menu*, semiannual. Catalog ● *NCDA Journal*. Newsletter ● *Office Administration Manual*. **Price:** $50.00 ● *The Practical Prosecutor*, annual. Magazine ● Books.

5668 ■ National District Attorneys Association (NDAA)
99 Canal CN Plz., Ste.510
Alexandria, VA 22314
Ph: (703)549-9222
Fax: (703)836-3195
E-mail: velva.walter@ndaa.org
URL: http://www.ndaa.org
Contact: Velva Walter, Media Relations Dir.
Founded: 1950. **Members:** 7,000. **Staff:** 24. **Description:** Elected/appointed prosecuting attorneys; associate members are assistant prosecuting attorneys, investigators, paralegals, and other prosecution office staff. Dedicated in providing information and a national forum for prosecuting attorneys. Seeks to serve prosecuting attorneys and to improve and facilitate the administration of justice in the U.S. Provides educational and informational services, technical assistance and research in areas such as vehicular crimes, juvenile justice, guns prosecution, community prosecution, DNA forensics, white collar crime, drug prosecution and child abuse prosecution through the American Prosecutors Research Institute. Prepares amicus curiae briefs. **Formerly:** National District Attorneys Association Foundation; (1959) National Association of County and Prosecuting Attorneys. **Publications:** *Directory of Prosecuting Attorneys*, semiannual ● *The Prosecutor*, bimonthly. Magazine. **Conventions/Meetings:** annual conference - usually July ● annual conference - usually summer ● annual Legislative Conference (exhibits) - usually May in Washington area.

Draft

5669 ■ Committee Opposed to Militarism and the Draft (COMD)
PO Box 15195
San Diego, CA 92175
Ph: (619)265-1369 (760)753-7518
E-mail: comd@comdsd.org
URL: http://www.comdsd.org
Membership Dues: individual, $16 (annual) ● student, low income, $8 (annual). **Description:** People opposed to militarism and the draft. Challenges the institution of the military, its effect on society, its budget and its role abroad and at home. Community education, direct action and youth outreach. **Publications:** *Draft Notices*.

Drug Abuse

5670 ■ National Institute on Drug Abuse (NIDA)
c/o National Institutes of Health
6001 Executive Blvd., Rm. 5213
Bethesda, MD 20892
Ph: (301)443-1124
E-mail: information@nida.nih.gov
URL: http://www.nida.nih.gov
Contact: Dr. Nora D. Volkow MD, Dir.
Languages: English, Spanish. **Description:** Promotes research into the prevention and treatment of drug abuse. **Divisions:** Basic Neurosciences and Behavioral Research; Epidemiology, Services and Prevention; Intramural Research; Treatment Research and Development. **Working Groups:** Genetics; Neuroscience; Translational Prevention/Development; Women and Gender Research. **Publications:** *Science and Practice Perspective*. Journal. Promotes a practical creative dialogue between scientists and drug abuse service providers. Alternate Formats: online ● Reports.

Drug Policy

5671 ■ National Alliance for Model State Drug Laws (NAMSDL)
700 N Fairfax St., Ste.550
Alexandria, VA 22314
Ph: (703)836-6100
Fax: (703)836-7495
E-mail: info@natlalliance.org
URL: http://www.natlalliance.org
Contact: Sherry Green, Exec. Dir.
Description: Acts as a resource for governors, state legislators, drug and alcohol professionals, community leaders, the recovering community, and others striving for comprehensive and effective state drug and alcohol laws and policies. Drafts, researches and analyzes model drug and alcohol laws and related state statutes. Provides access to the national network of drug and alcohol experts and facilitates working relationships among state and community leaders and drug and alcohol professionals.

5672 ■ National Association of State Controlled Substances Authorities (NASCSA)
c/o Katherine Keough, Exec. Dir.
72 Brook St.
Quincy, MA 02170
Ph: (617)472-0520
Fax: (617)472-0521
E-mail: kathykeough@nascsa.org
URL: http://www.nascsa.org
Contact: Katherine Keough, Exec. Dir.
Founded: 1984. **Members:** 52. **Membership Dues:** active, associate, $200 (annual). **Staff:** 1. **Budget:** $20,000. **State Groups:** 52. **Description:** Provides a forum for communication and exchange among state substance authorities. Disseminates information. **Libraries: Type:** reference; not open to the public. **Holdings:** archival material, books, clippings, periodicals. **Subjects:** drugs, controlled substances. **Conventions/Meetings:** annual conference - 2008 Oct. 21-25, Fort Lauderdale, FL.

Economics

5673 ■ Committee on the Status of Women in the Economics Profession (CSWEP)
c/o Lisa M. Lynch, Chair
Economic Affairs
Fletcher School of Law and Diplomacy
Tufts Univ.
160 Packard Ave.
Medford, MA 02155
E-mail: cswep@tufts.edu
Contact: Lisa M. Lynch, Chair
Founded: 1972. **Members:** 4,000. **Membership Dues:** professional, $25 (annual). **Staff:** 1. **Regional Groups:** 4. **Description:** A standing committee of American Economic Association (see separate entry). Women economists in the U.S. Aims to support and facilitate equality of opportunity for women economists. Disseminates information about job opportunities, research funding, and research related to the status of women in economics. Sponsors technical sessions. **Awards:** Carolyn Shaw Bell Award. **Frequency:** annual. **Type:** recognition. **Recipient:** for contribution to furthering women economists ● Elaine Bennet Award. **Frequency:** biennial. **Type:** recognition. **Recipient:** for research contribution by a female economist. **Affiliated With:** American Economic Association. **Publications:** *AEA-CSWEP Newsletter*, 3/year. **Price:** included in membership dues. **Circulation:** 4,000. **Conventions/Meetings:** annual Allied Social Science Meeting - conference, held in conjunction with AEA (exhibits) - always January.

5674 ■ Society of Government Economists (SGE)
PO Box 77082
Washington, DC 20013
Ph: (410)963-0134
E-mail: sge@sge-econ.org
URL: http://www.sge-econ.org
Contact: Jonathan Schwabish, Pres.
Founded: 1970. **Members:** 500. **Membership Dues:** regular, $25 (annual) ● institutional, $150 (annual). **Description:** Represents economists who are employed by governments or international organizations, or who are interested in economic policy issues. Objectives are to promote interaction between economists working for units of government and to further the application of economic principles and theory within the government. Seeks to improve economic indicators and aid economists by taking action on government standards. Conducts policy discussions. Maintains placement services. **Awards: Type:** recognition. **Additional Websites:** http://sge-econ.tripod.com. **Telecommunication Services:** electronic mail, jonathan.schwabisch@cbo.gov. **Publications:** *SGE Bulletin*, monthly. Newsletter. Alternate Formats: online ● Bulletin, monthly ● Membership Directory, semiannual. **Conventions/Meetings:** biennial conference ● monthly luncheon ● seminar and workshop.

Education Law

5675 ■ Center for Law and Education (CLE)
1875 Connecticut Ave. NW, Ste.510
Washington, DC 20009
Ph: (202)986-3000
Fax: (202)986-6648
E-mail: cle@cleweb.org
URL: http://www.cleweb.org
Contact: Kathleen Boundy, Co-Dir.
Founded: 1969. **Membership Dues:** professional, $50 (annual) ● individual, $35 (annual) ● student, $20 (annual) ● low-income, $5 (annual) ● sponsoring, $150 (annual). **Staff:** 14. **Description:** Provides support services on education issues to advocates working on behalf of low-income students and parents. **Computer Services:** Mailing lists. **Telecommunication Services:** electronic mail, pweckstein@cleweb.org. **Publications:** *CAPS Newsletter* ● *School Improvement Catalogs*, 3/year. **Price:** free. **Circulation:** 9,000. **Conventions/Meetings:** periodic workshop, held in conjunction with local legal services programs, school districts, or other organizations.

5676 ■ Education Law Association (ELA)
Mail Drop 0528
300 Coll. Park
Dayton, OH 45469
Ph: (937)229-3589
Fax: (937)229-3845
E-mail: ela@educationlaw.org
URL: http://www.educationlaw.org
Contact: Mandy Schrank, Exec. Dir.
Founded: 1954. **Members:** 1,400. **Membership Dues:** individual, $145 (annual) ● retired, $100 (annual) ● full-time student, $50 (annual). **Staff:** 4. **Budget:** $500,000. **Multinational. Description:** School attorneys, law professors, professors of education, school administrators, teachers, and school board members. Works for exchange of information on law school; seeks to stimulate research and publication in the field. **Libraries: Type:** reference. **Holdings:** books. **Subjects:** education law. **Awards:** Dissertation Award. **Frequency:** annual. **Type:** recognition ● McGhehey Award. **Frequency:** annual. **Type:** recognition ● Membership Award. **Frequency:** annual. **Type:** recognition ● Service Award. **Frequency:** annual. **Type:** recognition. **Computer Services:** Mailing lists, for a fee. **Committees:** Promotion of School Law and Research. **Formerly:** (1997) National Organization on Legal Problems of Education. **Publications:** *Annual Conference Papers*, annual. Proceedings. Includes compilation of all paper presentations given at annual conference. **Price:** $95.00 included in registration fee for attendees. **Advertising:** accepted. Alternate Formats: CD-ROM ● *Case Citation Series*, 2-3/year. Booklet. **Price:** $30.00 ● *ELA Notes*, quarterly. Newsletter. ISSN: 0047-8997. **Circulation:** 1,400. **Advertising:** accepted ● *School Law Reporter*, monthly. Journal. ISSN: 1059-4094. **Circulation:** 1,400 ● *Yearbook of Education Law*, annual. Includes subject index and table of cases. **Price:** $44.00 for members; $55.00 for nonmembers. **Circulation:** 1,500 ● Monographs. **Conventions/Meetings:** annual conference (exhibits).

5677 ■ National Association of College and University Attorneys (NACUA)
1 Dupont Cir., Ste.620
Washington, DC 20036
Ph: (202)833-8390
Fax: (202)296-8379
E-mail: nacua@nacua.org
URL: http://www.nacua.org
Contact: Kathleen Curry Santora, CEO
Founded: 1960. **Members:** 2,700. **Membership Dues:** associate institution, $1,150 (annual) ● institution ($175 per attorney), $560 (annual) ● associate individual, $580 (annual). **Staff:** 11. **Budget:** $1,000,000. **Multinational. Description:** Represents attorneys from U.S. and Canadian campuses, colleges and universities. Compiles and distributes legal decisions, opinions, and other writings and information on legal problems affecting colleges and universities. **Awards:** Distinguished Service Award. **Frequency:** annual. **Type:** recognition. **Recipient:** for extraordinary service both to NACUA and to institutions of higher learning over an extended period of time ● Fellows of the Association. **Frequency:** annual. **Type:** recognition. **Recipient:** to recognize exemplary service over an extended time ● Honorary Membership. **Frequency:** periodic. **Type:** recognition. **Recipient:** for substantial contributions to the understanding of legal issues affecting colleges and universities ● Life Membership. **Frequency:** annual. **Type:** recognition. **Recipient:** for outstanding service and substantial contributions. **Sections:** Affirmative Action and Non-Discrimination; Athletics; Employment Law; Environmental Law; Governance and Accountability; Health Sciences; Intellectual Property; Liability, Risk Management and Insurance; Litigation and Alternative Dispute Resolution; Student Affairs; Taxation. **Affiliated With:** American Bar Association. **Publications:** *Aids on Campus*. Pamphlet ● *College Law Digest*, monthly. Report. Includes reports on legal issues in higher education. **Price:** included in membership dues ● *Journal of College and University Law*, 3/year. Includes articles of current interest to college and university counsel, commentaries, annual conferences and workshops. **Price:** free online subscription for members; $64.00 for nonmembers; $23.00/copy in U.S.; $24.00/copy outside U.S. Alternate Formats: online ● *Legal Issues in Athletics*. Pamphlet ● *Racial Harassment on Campus*. Pamphlet ● *Sexual Harassment on Campus*. Pamphlet ● *Understanding Attorney-Client Privileges Issues in the College and University Setting*. Pamphlet ● Directory, annual. **Price:** included in membership dues. **Conventions/Meetings:** annual conference - 2008 June 22-25, New York, NY; 2009 June 24-27, Toronto, ON, Canada; 2010 June 27-30, Washington, DC; 2011 June 29-July 2, San Francisco, CA.

Employment

5678 ■ International Association of Industrial Accident Boards and Commissions (IAIABC)
5610 Medical Cir., Ste.24
Madison, WI 53719-1295
Ph: (608)663-6355
Fax: (608)663-1546
E-mail: fhowe@iaiabc.org
URL: http://www.iaiabc.org
Contact: Gregory Krohm, Exec. Dir.
Founded: 1914. **Members:** 450. **Membership Dues:** corporate, $1,000 (annual) ● individual/city/country, $500 (annual) ● jurisdictional, $950 (annual). **Staff:** 5. **Multinational. Description:** States and provinces having a workers' compensation law; organizations, including insurers, medical and rehabilitation providers and unions; self-insurers, lawyers, and others interested in workers' compensation. Works to develop standards for improving workers' compensation laws and their administration. Sponsors annual International Workers' Compensation College. Operates educational programs. **Libraries: Type:** reference. **Holdings:** audiovisuals, books, clippings, periodicals. **Subjects:** workers' compensation. **Committees:** Adjudication; Administration and Procedures; Legislation; Medical; Rehabilitation; Safety; Self Insurance; Statistics. **Publications:** Journal, semiannual. **Price:** $20.00 single issue, for members; $40.00 single issue, for nonmembers; $30.00 /year for members; $70.00 /year for nonmembers. **Advertising:** accepted. Alternate Formats: online ● Newsletter, periodic. **Conventions/Meetings:** annual convention (exhibits) - 2008 Oct. 25-31, Vancouver, BC, Canada.

5679 ■ International Association of Workforce Professionals (IAWP)
1801 Louisville Rd.
Frankfort, KY 40601
Ph: (502)223-4459
Free: (888)898-9960
Fax: (502)223-4127
E-mail: iapes@iapes.org
URL: http://www.iawponline.org
Contact: Mary Riddell, Mgr.
Founded: 1913. **Members:** 20,000. **Membership Dues:** full, $42 (annual) ● retired, $21 (annual). **Staff:** 4. **Budget:** $600,000. **Regional Groups:** 20. **State Groups:** 53. **Local Groups:** 55. **Description:** Officials and others engaged in job placement, unemployment compensation, and labor market information administration through municipal, state, provincial, and federal government employment agencies and unemployment compensation agencies. Conducts workshops and research. Offers professional development program of study guides and tests. **Libraries: Type:** reference. **Awards:** Award of Merit. **Frequency:** annual. **Type:** recognition ● Chapter Award. **Frequency:** annual. **Type:** recognition ● Citations of Merit. **Type:** recognition ● Veteran Award. **Type:** recognition. **Telecommunication Services:** electronic mail, maryr@iapes.org. **Committees:** Award of Merit; Education; International Development; Legislative; Services to People With Disabilities; Veteran Services. **Formerly:** (1952) International Association of Public Employment Services; (2005) International Association of Personnel in Employment Security. **Publications:** *Workforce Professional*, 8/year. Newsletter. **Price:** $25.00 for nonmembers ● Also publishes guide books. **Conventions/Meetings:** annual convention and conference (exhibits).

5680 ■ National Association of State Workforce Agencies (NASWA)
444 N Capitol St. NW, Ste.142
Washington, DC 20001
Ph: (202)434-8020
Fax: (202)434-8033
E-mail: ceser@naswa.org
URL: http://www.icesa.org
Contact: Richard A. Hobbie, Exec. Dir.
Founded: 1936. **Members:** 53. **Membership Dues:** regular, $18,000 (annual). **Staff:** 9. **Budget:** $1,200,000. **Description:** State agencies responsible for administering unemployment insurance, employment and training programs, labor market information and workforce development. Strives to improve the public employment service, unemployment insurance programs, and employment and training programs; to encourage effective state action in training and placing unemployed workers, paying unemployment benefits, stabilizing the labor market and developing labor market information; to engage in public policy research and education in order to secure enactment of sound legislation; to identify the positions of member agencies and act as their collective voice in communicating those positions to federal officials, to national groups, and to the public. **Awards:** Chavrid Award. **Frequency:** annual. **Type:** recognition ● Eagle Award. **Frequency:** annual. **Type:** recognition.

Recipient: for outstanding individuals ● Harris Award. **Frequency:** annual. **Type:** recognition ● Heartwell Award. **Frequency:** annual. **Type:** recognition. **Recipient:** for an individual outside the state workforce agency system ● James F. Walls Award. **Frequency:** annual. **Type:** recognition. **Recipient:** for a local employee or a one-stop center employee ● Mark Sanders Award. **Frequency:** annual. **Type:** recognition. **Recipient:** for a local office or one-stop center ● Merrill Baumgardner Award. **Frequency:** annual. **Type:** recognition. **Recipient:** for an individual in the field of automation in a state workforce agency ● Veterans Award. **Frequency:** annual. **Type:** recognition. **Additional Websites:** http://www.naswa.org. **Telecommunication Services:** electronic mail, rhobbie@naswa.org. **Committees:** Administrative and Finance; Communications and Legislative Relations; Employment and Training; Equal Opportunity Employment; Information Technology; Interstate Benefits; Labor Market Information; Unemployment Insurance; Veterans Affairs. **Formerly:** (1939) Interstate Conference of Unemployment Compensation Agencies; (2002) Interstate Conference of Employment Security Agencies. **Publications:** *Workforce Bulletin*, weekly. **Price:** $1,500.00. Alternate Formats: online ● Brochures ● Monographs ● Pamphlets. **Conventions/Meetings:** annual conference ● semiannual meeting (exhibits) - always March and September.

5681 ■ National Foundation for Unemployment Compensation and Workers Compensation (NFUCWC)
910 17th St., Ste.315
Washington, DC 20006
Ph: (202)223-8902
Fax: (202)783-1616
E-mail: info@uwcstrategy.org
URL: http://www.uwcstrategy.org
Contact: Douglas Holmes, Pres.

Founded: 1984. **Nonmembership. Description:** Conducts research on issues of unemployment and workers' compensation, with the objective of providing basic data to the public policy decision-makers so that unemployment and workers' compensation programs may be improved from an employer perspective. Provides training for business professionals concerned with unemployment and workers' compensation. **Awards:** Father Becker Award. **Frequency:** monthly. **Type:** recognition. **Recipient:** to an individual who has made major contributions to unemployment insurance research ● J. Eldred Hill Jr. Award. **Frequency:** annual. **Type:** recognition. **Recipient:** to an individual for excellence in the public policy arena and in service to the employer community ● UI Integrity Award. **Frequency:** annual. **Type:** recognition. **Recipient:** to an individual who has demonstrated courageous commitment to preserving the integrity of the unemployment system ● UWC Outstanding Contribution Award. **Frequency:** annual. **Type:** recognition. **Recipient:** for outstanding contributions to UWC or the national foundation for unemployment compensation and workers' compensation. **Affiliated With:** UWC - Strategic Services on Unemployment and Workers' Compensation. **Publications:** *Fiscal Data for State Unemployment Insurance Systems*, annual. Bulletin. **Price:** $25.00 for nonmembers; $20.00 for members ● *Fiscal Data for State Worker's Compensation Systems*, annual. Bulletin. **Price:** $25.00 for nonmembers; $20.00 for members ● *Highlights of State Unemployment Compensation Laws*, annual. Book. **Price:** $45.00 for members ● *State Unemployment Insurance Legislation and Related Changes*, annual. Bulletin. **Price:** $35.00 ● *State Workers' Compensation Legislation and Related Changes*, annual. Bulletin. **Price:** $30.00. **Conventions/Meetings:** annual Current Issues in Unemployment Insurance - conference (exhibits) - spring.

5682 ■ U.S. Equal Employment Opportunity Commission (EEOC)
1801 L St. NW, Ste.100
Washington, DC 20507
Ph: (202)663-4900 (202)419-0700
Free: (800)669-4000
Fax: (703)997-4890
E-mail: info@ask.eeoc.gov
URL: http://www.eeoc.gov
Contact: Naomi C. Earp, Chair

Founded: 1965. **Staff:** 2,400. **Budget:** $267,000,000. **Description:** Strives to promote equal opportunity in employment through administrative and judicial enforcement of the federal civil rights laws and through education and technical assistance. **Awards:** Freedom to Compete Award. **Frequency:** annual. **Type:** recognition. **Recipient:** for excellence in the implementation of specific equal employment opportunity practices. **Publications:** *Compliance Manual* ● *10 Reasons to Mediate*. Video. **Price:** free.

Energy

5683 ■ Energy Bar Association (EBA)
1020-19th St. NW, Ste.525
Washington, DC 20036
Ph: (202)223-5625
Fax: (202)833-5596
E-mail: admin@eba-net.org
URL: http://www.eba-net.org
Contact: Lorna Wilson, Admin.

Founded: 1946. **Members:** 2,300. **Membership Dues:** private sector, $120 (annual) ● government, academic, $40 (annual) ● student, $20 (annual). **Budget:** $400,000. **State Groups:** 3. **Multinational. Description:** Attorneys practicing in the U.S. and its territories, districts, and possessions. Seeks to promote the proper administration of laws relating to production, development, conservation, transmission, and economic regulation of energy. Conducts educational programs. **Computer Services:** database, job bank ● mailing lists, of members ● online services, Lexis/Nexus, UMI, Westlaw. **Committees:** Administrative Practice and Administrative Law Judges; Alternative Dispute Resolution; Antitrust; E-Commerce; Electric Utility Regulation; Environment and Public Lands; Ethics; FERC Administration; Finance and Transactions; Generation and Power Marketing; Hydroelectric Regulation; International Energy Transactions; Judicial Review; Legislation and Regulatory Reform; Natural Gas Regulation; Oil Pipeline Regulation; Programs and Meetings; Website; Young Lawyers. **Affiliated With:** American Bar Association. **Formerly:** (1977) Federal Power Bar Association; (2000) Federal Energy Bar Association. **Publications:** *Committee Reports*, annual. Journal. **Price:** $30.00 in U.S.; $36.00 in Canada; $42.00 outside U.S. and Canada. ISSN: 0270-9163. **Circulation:** 2,500. **Advertising:** accepted. Also Cited As: *Energy Law Journal* ● *EBA Update*, quarterly. Newsletter. Alternate Formats: online ● Membership Directory, annual ● Also publishes judicial and legislative materials. **Conventions/Meetings:** semiannual meeting ● annual meeting.

5684 ■ Interstate Oil and Gas Compact Commission (IOGCC)
PO Box 53127
Oklahoma City, OK 73152-3127
Ph: (405)525-3556
Free: (800)822-4015
Fax: (405)525-3592
E-mail: iogcc@iogcc.state.ok.us
URL: http://www.iogcc.state.ok.us
Contact: Christine Hansen, Exec. Dir.

Founded: 1935. **Members:** 864. **Staff:** 12. **Budget:** $1,300,000. **Description:** Promotes conservation and efficient recovery of domestic oil and natural gas resources. Works to protect health, safety, and the environment. **Libraries: Type:** reference. **Holdings:** 2,000. **Computer Services:** Mailing lists, of members. **Committees:** Energy Resources, Research and Technology; Environmental and Safety; Legal and Regulatory Affairs; Public Lands; Public Outreach; State Review. **Formerly:** (1991) Interstate Oil Compact Commission. **Publications:** *Marginal Oil & Gas Report*, annual. Survey. **Price:** $8.00 ● *Member Directory of the IOGCC and Oil and Gas Agencies*, annual. Membership Directory. **Price:** $11.00. **Conventions/Meetings:** annual Global Energy and the Environment - meeting.

5685 ■ National Association of State Energy Officials (NASEO)
1414 Prince St., Ste.200
Alexandria, VA 22314
Ph: (703)299-8800
Fax: (703)299-6208
E-mail: mnew@naseo.org
URL: http://www.naseo.org
Contact: Michelle New, Acting Exec. Dir.

Description: State energy officials. Promotes establishment and enforcement of effective state laws and regulations regulating the energy industries. Facilitates communication and cooperation among members; works to coordinate state and federal laws and regulations affecting the energy industries. **Committees:** Buildings; Energy Data and Security; Energy, Environment and Transportation; Energy Production; Government Affairs; Industrial. **Publications:** *NASEO News*, bimonthly. Newsletter. Alternate Formats: online. **Conventions/Meetings:** annual Energy Outlook Conference.

5686 ■ National Petroleum Council (NPC)
1625 K St. NW, Ste.600
Washington, DC 20006
Ph: (202)393-6100
Fax: (202)331-8539
E-mail: info@npc.org
URL: http://www.npc.org
Contact: Marshall W. Nichols, Exec. Dir.

Founded: 1946. **Members:** 150. **Staff:** 17. **Description:** Advisory council to the Secretary of Energy on matters relating to oil and gas. **Publications:** Reports. Contains advice on domestic refining capacity, product imports and inventories. **Conventions/Meetings:** semiannual meeting.

Entertainment Law

5687 ■ Black Entertainment and Sports Lawyers Association (BESLA)
PO Box 441485
Fort Washington, MD 20749-1485
Ph: (301)248-1818
Fax: (301)248-0700
E-mail: beslamailbox@aol.com
URL: http://www.besla.org
Contact: Ms. Phyllicia M. Hatton, Conference Mgr./Consultant

Founded: 1979. **Members:** 450. **Membership Dues:** general, $130 (annual) ● associate/affiliate, $105 (annual) ● student, $40 (annual) ● life, general, $1,500 ● life, associate, $1,000 ● recent law practitioner, $75 (annual). **Budget:** $1,150,000. **Description:** Represents black attorneys specializing in entertainment and sports law. Aims to provide more efficient and effective legal representation to entertainers and athletes. Offers referral system for legal representation and a resource bank for providing information to students, groups, and non-profit and civic organizations involved in the entertainment industry; and serves as an industry watchdog in protecting the rights of individuals within the entertainment community. Maintains hall of fame; conducts research programs. **Awards:** BESLA Award. **Frequency:** annual. **Type:** recognition. **Recipient:** for contribution to the organization and to the community ● BESLA/Budweiser Urban Scholarship Fund. **Type:** scholarship ● BESLA General Scholarship Fund. **Type:** scholarship ● Corporate Award. **Frequency:** annual. **Type:** recognition. **Recipient:** for contribution to the organization and to the community ● Founding Directors Scholarship Fund. **Type:** scholarship ● Jack and Sadye Gibson Scholarship Fund. **Type:** scholarship ● Legends Award. **Frequency:** annual. **Type:** recognition. **Recipient:** for contribution to the organization and to the community ● Malena Rance Scholarship Fund. **Type:** scholarship. **Committees:** Communications; Conference; Executive; Fund Raising; Program. **Formerly:** (1986) Black Entertainment Lawyers Association. **Publications:** *Annual Conference Pro-*

ceedings, annual. **Advertising:** accepted ● *BESLA Bulletin*, quarterly. **Price:** available to members only. **Conventions/Meetings:** annual conference, for members, students, and executives in the industry ● annual international conference.

Environmental Law

5688 ■ Association of State and Interstate Water Pollution Control Administrators (ASIWPCA)
1221 Connecticut Ave. NW, 2nd Fl.
Washington, DC 20036
Ph: (202)756-0600
Fax: (202)756-0605
E-mail: admin1@aswipca.org
URL: http://www.asiwpca.org
Contact: Linda Eichmiller, Sec.
Founded: 1960. **Members:** 57. **Staff:** 5. **Budget:** $1,000,000. **State Groups:** 50. **Description:** Represents administrators of state and interstate governmental agencies legally responsible for prevention, abatement, and control of water pollution. Promotes coordination among state agency programs and those of the Environmental Protection Agency, Congress, and other federal agencies. Conducts research; maintains speakers' bureau. **Task Forces:** Groundwater Protection; Information Management; Program and Policy Issues; Standards and Monitoring; State Revolving Loan Fund; Strategic Planning; Watershed Protection. **Publications:** *Association of State and Interstate Water Pollution Control Administrators—Position Statements*, annual ● *State's Evaluation of Progress*. Report. **Price:** $5.00 ● Annual Report, annual ● Brochures ● Membership Directory, annual. **Price:** $5.00 ● Proceedings. **Conventions/Meetings:** annual meeting - always August ● annual meeting - always February in Washington, DC.

5689 ■ Center for International Environmental Law (CIEL)
1350 Connecticut Ave. NW, Ste.1100
Washington, DC 20036
Ph: (202)785-8700
Fax: (202)785-8701
E-mail: info@ciel.org
URL: http://www.ciel.org
Contact: Jeffrey Wanha, Dir. of Finance and Admin.
Founded: 1989. **Staff:** 20. **Budget:** $2,000,000. **Languages:** English, Spanish. **Multinational. Description:** Environmental attorneys. Seeks to strengthen national, international, and comparative environmental law and public policy worldwide. Conducts environmental and legal research and provides recommendations to policy makers. **Libraries: Type:** open to the public. **Subjects:** environmental law (national and international), biodiversity, wildlife, climate change, air, trade, oceans, local resource management, capacity-building, international financial institutions, human rights, community rights. **Programs:** Biodiversity and Wildlife; Chemical Health and Safety; Climate Change; Environmental Law Education; Human Rights; Intellectual Property; International Financial Institutes; Law and Communities; NGO Development; Ozone Depletion; State of Environmental Law; Trade and Sustainable Development.

5690 ■ Earthjustice
426 17th St., 6th Fl.
Oakland, CA 94612-2820
Ph: (510)550-6700
Free: (800)584-6460
Fax: (510)550-6740
E-mail: info@earthjustice.org
URL: http://www.earthjustice.org
Contact: Mr. Buck Parker, Exec. Dir.
Founded: 1971. **Members:** 140,000. **Staff:** 140. **Budget:** $22,442,062. **Multinational. Description:** Public interest law firm committed to safeguarding public lands, national forests, parks, wilderness areas; reduce air and water pollution, prevent toxic contamination, preserve endangered species and wildlife habitat, achieve environmental justice. Represents clients without charge. **Libraries: Type:** reference. **Holdings:** video recordings. **Formerly:** (1997) Sierra Club Legal Defense Fund. **Publications:** *E-Brief*, monthly. Newsletter. Electronic newsletter. Alternate Formats: online ● *In Brief: Earthjustice*, quarterly. Newsletter ● *Salmon Recovery Under Attack*. Report. Alternate Formats: online ● *Victory Report*, annual. Brochure. Documents the year's victories. ● Annual Report, annual. **Circulation:** 3,500. Alternate Formats: online.

5691 ■ Environmental Law Alliance Worldwide - U.S. (E-LAW US)
1877 Garden Ave.
Eugene, OR 97403
Ph: (541)687-8454
Fax: (541)687-0535
E-mail: elawus@elaw.org
URL: http://www.elaw.org
Contact: Mr. Bern Johnson, Exec. Dir.
Founded: 1989. **Staff:** 9. **Budget:** $622,000. **Languages:** English, French, Russian, Spanish. **Description:** Global alliance of public interest attorneys and scientists in 50 countries who defend the environment through law. Gives advocates around the world access to the lessons and resources of U.S. efforts to protect the environment including regulatory models, case precedents from U.S. courts, U.S. legal scholarship and jurisprudence, and information about multinational corporations. **Publications:** *E-LAW Advocate*, quarterly. Newsletter. **Price:** free. Alternate Formats: online.

5692 ■ Environmental Law Institute (ELI)
2000 L St. NW, Ste.620
Washington, DC 20036
Ph: (202)939-3800
Free: (800)433-5120
Fax: (202)939-3868
E-mail: law@eli.org
URL: http://www.eli.org
Contact: Leslie Carothers, Pres.
Founded: 1969. **Members:** 4,000. **Membership Dues:** standard/individual outside U.S. (with soft copy of The Environmental Forum), $95 (annual) ● individual in U.S. (government, academic and public interest), $60 (annual) ● individual outside U.S. (with printed copy of The Environmental Forum), $115 (annual). **Staff:** 55. **Budget:** $6,000,000. **Multinational. Description:** Provides information services, training courses and seminars, and research programs. Works to develops effective solutions to pressing environmental problems. Governed by a board of directors who represent a "balanced mix of leaders within the environmental profession" and supported by individuals, foundations, government, corporations, law firms and other sources. Co-sponsors environmental law conferences with the American Bar Association, American Law Institute, and the Smithsonian Institution. Conducts summer and annual internship programs for law students. Research division includes projects on air and water pollution; wetlands; economics; state environmental law; toxic substances and hazardous waste; land use; biodiversity; smart growth/sprawl. **Awards:** Environmental Law Institute Award. **Frequency:** annual. **Type:** recognition. **Computer Services:** Online services, document source, downloadable collections, legal reporting service. **Additional Websites:** http://www.elr.info, http://www.endangeredlaws.org, http://www.elistore.org. **Telecommunication Services:** electronic mail, rose@eli.org. **Divisions:** Development; Education and Training; Publications; Research. **Affiliated With:** ALI-ABA Committee on Continuing Professional Education; American Bar Association; American Law Institute; International Union for the Conservation of Nature and Natural Resources U.S. **Absorbed:** (2003) Center for Native Lands. **Publications:** *Environmental Forum*, bimonthly. Journal. Contains information regarding environmental policy. **Price:** $95.00/year. **Circulation:** 4,000. **Advertising:** accepted ● *Environmental Law Reporter*, daily, weekly, monthly updates. Journal. **Price:** $1,255.00/year; $520.00 each. Alternate Formats: online ● *National Wetlands Newsletter*, bimonthly. **Price:** $48.00/year in U.S.; $55.00/year outside U.S. ● Books ● Brochures ● Reports. Covers air and water pollution, energy, land use, resource conservation and recycling, and toxic substances. ● ELR Deskbook Series. **Conventions/Meetings:** annual conference, held in conjunction with American Law Institute and American Bar Association - always February, Bethesda, MD ● Course on Environmental Law - seminar ● annual seminar and dinner.

5693 ■ Environmental Policy Center (EPC)
c/o Department of Environmental Health, University of Cincinnati
PO Box 670056
Cincinnati, OH 45267-0056
Ph: (513)558-5439
Fax: (513)558-4397
E-mail: jim.flessa@uc.edu
URL: http://www.eh.uc.edu/epc
Contact: Joyce Martin, Dir.
Founded: 1979. **Staff:** 10. **Description:** Operates the Global Cities Project which provides environmental information services to cities and communities to assist in building sustainable futures. Studies public policy issues with respect to local environmental concerns. **Formerly:** (1993) Center for the Study of Law and Politics. **Publications:** *Building Sustainable Communities: An Environmental Guide for Local Government*, periodic. Monographs. Provides information on air quality, solid waste, toxics, energy, transportation, water efficiency and quality, land use and urban forestry. **Price:** $40.00/copy; $20.00 for nonprofit, government, students ● *Case Studies*. Reports. Presents community profiles of local environmental management programs, including policy options, financial considerations and program effectiveness. **Conventions/Meetings:** periodic conference, on environmental policy.

5694 ■ Environmental Safety (ES)
1700 N Moore St., Ste.2000
Arlington, VA 22209
Ph: (703)527-8300
Fax: (703)527-8383
E-mail: info@ashoka.org
URL: http://www.ashoka.org
Contact: William Drayton, Pres./Founder
Founded: 1984. **Staff:** 5. **Budget:** $300,000. **Description:** Advisory committee of former officials of the Environmental Protection Agency; lawyers, public health officials, and environmental specialists. Ensures that the EPA and other federal agencies take active steps towards implementing their environmental protection responsibilities, particularly with respect to the dangers of toxic chemicals in the air, water, food, workplace, and waste streams. Collects and disseminates information on the EPA budget, budget trends, and funding of programs regarding specific environmental issues. Works to develop and test, with states, alternative approaches to implementing environmental laws. Supports "Get America Working" program that seeks to increase the demand for labor structurally while simultaneously reducing the economy's use of natural resources. **Convention/Meeting:** none. **Libraries: Type:** reference; not open to the public. **Holdings:** 1,000; archival material, books. **Subjects:** environment. **Awards:** International Environment Fellows. **Frequency:** periodic. **Type:** recognition. **Recipient:** for important environmental innovations. **Supersedes:** American Environmental Safety Council. **Publications:** *EPA's Real Needs*. Papers. Contains position papers and informational material on specific environmental issues.

5695 ■ Harvard Environmental Law Society (HELS)
1563 Massachusetts Ave.
Harvard Law School
Pound Hall
Cambridge, MA 02138
E-mail: els@law.harvard.edu
URL: http://www.law.harvard.edu/students/orgs/els
Contact: Kim Smaczniak, Pres.
Founded: 1945. **Members:** 250. **Description:** Represents Harvard law students united to protect the environment through legal research and educational programs. Conducts research projects on nuclear power, toxic wastes, land-use planning, and wilder-

ness preservation. Activities include advice, research, assistance to organizations with litigation and the drafting of legislation, promoting placement in environmental law, sponsoring speakers, symposia, lobbying, outings, and paper recycling. Operates placement services. **Libraries: Type:** reference. **Holdings:** 300. **Subjects:** environmental law. **Conventions/Meetings:** annual convention.

5696 ■ National Association of Clean Air Agencies (NACAA)
444 N Capitol St. NW, Ste.307
Washington, DC 20001
Ph: (202)624-7864
Fax: (202)624-7863
E-mail: 4clnair@4cleanair.org
URL: http://www.cleanairworld.org
Contact: S. William Becker, Exec. Dir.

Founded: 1968. **Members:** 54. **Staff:** 7. **Budget:** $1,100,000. **For-Profit. Description:** State and territorial air pollution program administrators and members of their staffs. Provides an opportunity for state officials who are responsible for implementing air pollution control programs established under the Clean Air Act to share air quality-related experiences and to discuss problems. Encourages communication and cooperation among federal, state, and local regulatory agencies. **Formed by Merger of:** (2006) State and Territorial Air Pollution Program Administrators and Association of Local Air Pollution Control Officials. **Publications:** *Washington Update*, weekly. Newsletter. Alternate Formats: online. **Conventions/Meetings:** semiannual conference.

5697 ■ National Association of Environmental Law Societies (NAELS)
c/o Dan Worth, Exec. Dir.
1227 Olivia Ave.
Ann Arbor, MI 48104
Ph: (734)709-8794
E-mail: dworth_99@yahoo.com
URL: http://www.naels.org
Contact: Dan Worth, Exec. Dir.

Founded: 1988. **Members:** 60. **Membership Dues:** ordinary, $40 (annual). **Description:** Student-run environmental law societies. Promotes awareness of environmental issues among law schools, the legal profession, and the public. Works to advance environmental law through development of improved curricula and materials. Encourages formation of environmental law societies. **Telecommunication Services:** electronic mail, sjanasie@kentlaw.edu. **Publications:** *NAELS Newsletter*, annual. Contains environmental news and annual conference updates. **Price:** free. **Advertising:** accepted. Alternate Formats: online. **Conventions/Meetings:** annual conference and workshop (exhibits) - always March.

Family Law

5698 ■ American Academy of Matrimonial Lawyers (AAML)
150 N Michigan Ave., Ste.2040
Chicago, IL 60601
Ph: (312)263-6477
Fax: (312)263-7682
E-mail: gferro@marvinandferro.com
URL: http://www.aaml.org
Contact: Gaetano Ferro, Pres.

Founded: 1962. **Members:** 1,600. **State Groups:** 25. **Description:** Represents board certified attorneys specializing in the field of matrimonial and family law. Seeks to encourage the study, improve the practice, elevate the standards, and advance the cause of matrimonial law in an effort to preserve the welfare of the family and society. Conducts legal institutes. Sponsors advanced mandatory continuing legal education program. **Telecommunication Services:** electronic mail, office@aaml.org. **Publications:** *Journal of the American Academy of Matrimonial Lawyers*, annual ● *List of Certified Fellows*, annual ● Newsletter, periodic ● Proceedings, semiannual. **Conventions/Meetings:** annual meeting.

5699 ■ Association of Family and Conciliation Courts (AFCC)
6525 Grand Teton Plz.
Madison, WI 53719-1083
Ph: (608)664-3750
Fax: (608)664-3751
E-mail: afcc@afccnet.org
URL: http://www.afccnet.org
Contact: Hon. William C. Fee, Pres.

Founded: 1963. **Members:** 1,916. **Membership Dues:** individual, $150 (annual) ● institutional, $360 (annual) ● student, $60 (annual) ● gift, $130 (annual). **Staff:** 5. **Budget:** $750,000. **Regional Groups:** 6. **State Groups:** 5. **Description:** Judges, counselors, family court personnel, attorneys, mediators, researchers, and teachers concerned with the resolution of family disputes as they affect children. Proposes to develop and improve the practice of dispute resolution procedure as a complement to judicial procedures. Aims to strengthen the family unit and minimize family strife by improving the process of marriage, family, and divorce counseling; and to provide an interdisciplinary forum for the exchange of ideas, for the creation of new approaches to child custody matters and solutions to problems of family discord. Collaborates with the National Council of Juvenile and Family Court Judges, National Judicial College, the National Center for State Courts, the American Bar Association and several universities, law schools, and state organizations responsible for providing ongoing training for attorneys, judges, and family therapists. Conducts research and offers technical assistance and training to courts, legal associations, judicial organizations, and behavioral science professionals. **Awards:** Distinguished Research Award. **Frequency:** annual. **Type:** monetary ● Distinguished Service Award. **Frequency:** annual. **Type:** monetary ● International Conference Attendance Scholarship. **Frequency:** annual. **Type:** monetary ● Law School Essay Contest. **Frequency:** annual. **Type:** monetary ● Meyer Elkin Essay Contest. **Type:** recognition. **Telecommunication Services:** electronic mail, wfee@co.steuben.in.us. **Affiliated With:** American Bar Association; National Center for State Courts; National Council of Juvenile and Family Court Judges; National Judicial College. **Publications:** *AFCC Newsletter*, quarterly. Contains new articles on the association and laws. **Price:** included in membership dues. **Advertising:** accepted ● *Family Court Review*, quarterly. Journal ● Membership Directory, annual ● Articles ● Manuals ● Pamphlets ● Papers ● Videos. **Conventions/Meetings:** annual conference, includes 15-20 exhibits (exhibits) - 2009 May 27-30, New Orleans, LA ● periodic regional meeting.

5700 ■ National Center for Youth Law (NCYL)
405 14th St., 15th Fl.
Oakland, CA 94612-2701
Ph: (510)835-8098
Fax: (510)835-8099
E-mail: info@youthlaw.org
URL: http://www.youthlaw.org
Contact: John F. O'Toole, Dir.

Founded: 1970. **Staff:** 15. **Budget:** $1,500,000. **Languages:** English, Spanish. **Description:** Employs eight attorneys on a full-time basis to provide assistance to legal services programs and private attorneys representing poor children and youth across the U.S. Provides assistance such as: consultation, training, legal research, drafting of pleadings and motions, aid in writing trial and appellate briefs, and participation in litigation in selected cases. Maintains collection of pleadings, memoranda, motions, briefs, and other specialized materials. Provides expertise in such areas as: abuse and neglect proceedings, termination of parental rights, foster care, children in institutions, public benefits for children, child and adolescent health, and housing discrimination against families with children and child support issues. **Telecommunication Services:** electronic mail, otoole@youthlaw.org. **Publications:** *Youth Law News*, quarterly. Journal. Reports and analyzes recent developments in youth law as they affect poor children and their families. **Price:** $60.00 /year for individuals; $125.00 /year for institutions. ISSN: 0882-8520. **Circulation:** 4,500.

5701 ■ National Child Support Enforcement Association (NCSEA)
444 N Capitol St., Ste.414
Washington, DC 20001-1512
Ph: (202)624-8180
Fax: (202)624-8828
E-mail: ncsea@ncsea.org
URL: http://www.ncsea.org
Contact: Colleen Delaney Eubanks CAE, Exec. Dir.

Founded: 1952. **Membership Dues:** individual, $95 (annual) ● state, tribal, or international IV-D agency, $1,200-$2,750 (annual) ● local or international IV-D agency, $300-$1,000 (annual) ● state, national, or international IV-D agency, $1,200-$2,750 (annual) ● local agency/non-profit, $300 (annual) ● corporate associate, $1,000-$5,000 (annual). **Staff:** 6. **Budget:** $1,500,000. **Description:** Promotes the well-being of children through professional development of its membership, advocacy and public awareness. Membership includes: Judges, court masters, hearing officers, district attorneys, government attorneys, private attorneys, social workers, child support enforcement caseworkers, state and county child support offices, probation departments, and child support advocates. Conducts monthly Tele-Talks, annual Policy Forum & Training Conference, Annual Training Conference & Expo. **Awards:** NCSEA Excellence Awards. **Frequency:** annual. **Type:** recognition. **Recipient:** for program and personal excellence in the child support community. **Telecommunication Services:** electronic mail, colleeneubanks@ncsea.org. **Committees:** Communications; Legislation; Research; Training Policy. **Formerly:** (1974) National Conference on Uniform Reciprocal Enforcement of Support; (1984) National Reciprocal and Family Support Enforcement Association. **Publications:** *Child Support Quarterly*. Magazine. **Advertising:** accepted ● *Rapid Read*, monthly. Newsletter ● Membership Directory, annual ● Annual Report, annual. Alternate Formats: online. **Conventions/Meetings:** annual conference (exhibits).

5702 ■ National Juvenile Court Services Association (NJCSA)
c/o Ian Curley, Staff Liaison
Univ. of Nevada
PO Box 8970
Reno, NV 89507
Ph: (775)784-6895
Fax: (775)784-6628
E-mail: icurley@ncjfcj.org
URL: http://www.njcsa.org
Contact: Ian Curley, Staff Liaison

Founded: 1972. **Members:** 350. **Membership Dues:** regular, $45 (annual) ● joint, $115 (annual). **Description:** Judges, probation officers, educators, lawyers, and other individuals interested in juvenile justice. Seeks to: educate juvenile and family court personnel; plan and coordinate educational programs in conjunction with the National Council of Juvenile and Family Court Judges. Develops rapport between juvenile court personnel and judges; raises professional competency; promotes community understanding; seeks greater support of treatment programs for juveniles; offers technical assistance. Sponsors professional courses and seminars. **Awards:** Juvenile Court Administrator Award. **Frequency:** periodic. **Type:** recognition. **Recipient:** to an administrator of juvenile court for outstanding leadership and significant skills in the development of the service delivery system in his or her community ● M. James Toner NJCSA Fellows Award. **Frequency:** annual. **Type:** recognition. **Recipient:** to individuals who have devoted a lifetime of service to the juvenile justice community, juveniles, and their families and for outstanding work related to juvenile justice in the communities they serve ● Outstanding Achievement Award. **Frequency:** periodic. **Type:** recognition. **Recipient:** to an individual or organization for outstanding contributions to the juvenile justice system for a lifetime of work. **Computer Services:** Mailing lists, of members. **Telecommunication Services:** electronic mail, colgov@core.com. **Committees:** Certification;

Legislation; Public Relations; Special Services; Training. **Publications:** *Juvenile and Family Court Journal*, quarterly. Contains articles of interest to the field of juvenile justice and related areas. **Price:** included in membership dues ● *Juvenile and Family Justice TODAY*, quarterly. Magazine. Contains organizational news and events in the field of juvenile and family law. **Price:** included in membership dues ● *Juvenile and Family Law Digest*. Booklet. Contains report and provides commentary on recent state court decisions. **Price:** included in membership dues ● *Rapport*, quarterly. Newsletter. Contains news and information concerning juvenile justice administration, local and regional activities, member activities. **Price:** $10.00 /year for nonmembers; $2.00/copy for nonmembers; included in membership dues. **Circulation:** 350. Alternate Formats: online ● Directory. Contains a listing of all members' names, addresses and telephone numbers. **Price:** included in membership dues. **Conventions/Meetings:** annual Juvenile Probation and Juvenile Justice Management Conference, features special training programs for juvenile justice personnel (exhibits).

5703 ■ National Law Center for Children and Families (NLC)
225 N Fairfax St.
Alexandria, VA 22314
Ph: (703)548-5522
Fax: (703)548-5544
E-mail: info@nationallawcenter.org
URL: http://www.nationallawcenter.org
Contact: Richard R. Whidden Jr., Exec. Dir.
Founded: 1991. **Staff:** 4. **Description:** Seeks to protect children and families from illegal pornography; strives to be a specialized resource of state and federal obscenity and child exploitation laws; aims to counsel federal, state and local legislators on existing criminal and civil codes; and provides training on specialized issues involved in illegal pornography and First Amendment related cases. Acts as a clearinghouse. **Libraries: Type:** reference. **Subjects:** child exploitation, pornography. **Publications:** *NLC Reporter*. Newsletter. Alternate Formats: online ● Manuals. Provides guidance for professionals. **Conventions/Meetings:** seminar, training for law enforcement.

Federal Government

5704 ■ Asian American Government Executives Network (AAGEN)
1001 Connecticut Ave. NW, Ste.530
Washington, DC 20036
Ph: (202)423-6801
Fax: (202)296-0540
E-mail: aagen@aagen.org
URL: http://www.aagen.org
Contact: Sharon Wong, Chair
Founded: 1994. **Membership Dues:** regular, $60 (annual) ● regular, $110 (biennial) ● regular, $150 (triennial) ● associate, $40 (annual) ● associate, $75 (biennial) ● associate, $105 (triennial). **Multinational. Description:** Represents Asian Americans in federal service. Promotes, expands and supports Asian Pacific American leadership in the federal, state and local governments. Promotes excellence in public service.

5705 ■ Council for Excellence in Government (CEG)
1301 K St. NW, Ste.450 W
Washington, DC 20005
Ph: (202)728-0418
Fax: (202)728-0422
E-mail: ceg@excelgov.org
URL: http://www.excelgov.org
Contact: Patricia McGinnis, Pres./CEO
Founded: 1983. **Members:** 750. **Membership Dues:** regular, $500 (annual). **Staff:** 25. **Budget:** $2,600,000. **Description:** Business leaders with executive-level government experience who wish to promote and support excellence in government. Seeks to strengthen the public service and improve the effectiveness of the U.S. government. Believes that good management in government, as in business, is essential to good performance, and that the nation needs high-performance government institutions to improve society and thrive in a global economy. Sponsors programs for mid-level career managers, senior executives, and congressional staff to interact with Council Principals in order to acquaint themselves with the best ideas and practices in management in the private and public sectors. Forms partnerships with executive teams to help them develop the leadership strategies and policies for their agencies. Works in strategic partnerships with other organizations to reach all levels of government. Sponsors lectures, workshops, and seminars. **Awards:** Good Housekeeping Award for Women in Government. **Frequency:** annual. **Type:** recognition. **Recipient:** for women who have made important contributions in public service. **Computer Services:** database ● mailing lists ● online services. **Formerly:** (1989) Center for Excellence in Government. **Publications:** *A Survivor's Guide for Government Executives*. Book ● *E-News*, bimonthly. Newsletter. Alternate Formats: online ● *The 1992 Prune Book: 50 Jobs That Can Change America* ● *The Prune Book: How to Succeed in Washington's Top Jobs* ● *The Prune Book: The 45 Toughest Financial Management Jobs in Washington* ● *The Prune Book: The 60 Toughest Science and Technology Jobs in Washington* ● *The Prune Book: Top Management Challenges for Presidential Appointees*.

5706 ■ Executive Women in Government (EWG)
PO Box 1046
Laurel, MD 20725-1046
Ph: (301)725-3500
Fax: (301)725-5323
E-mail: info@execwomeningov.org
URL: http://www.execwomeningov.org
Contact: Ms. Lynn Scarlet, Pres.
Founded: 1974. **Members:** 300. **Membership Dues:** individual, $65 (annual). **Staff:** 1. **Description:** Represents executive women in government. Advances women in senior leadership positions in federal government; advocates on issues related to the purposes and goals of the organization; provides mutual support to members in their professional pursuits and information exchange. **Publications:** Newsletter, periodic. Alternate Formats: online ● Membership Directory. **Conventions/Meetings:** annual conference, includes topics of benefit to senior level professionals ● annual conference, training conference to promote networking and professional development ● monthly meeting and lecture.

5707 ■ Federal Facilities Council (FFC)
c/o National Research Council
500 5th St. NW
Washington, DC 20001
Ph: (202)334-3374
Fax: (202)334-3370
E-mail: lstanley@nas.edu
URL: http://www7.nationalacademies.org/ffc
Contact: Lynda Stanley, Dir.
Founded: 1952. **Members:** 18. **Staff:** 2. **Budget:** $500,000. **Description:** Federal agencies responsible for design and construction and operation of government facilities or construction-related research. Fosters continuing cooperation among federal construction agencies in connection with the design, construction, and operation of federal facilities. Conducts studies and surveys, primarily for federal agency personnel through seven standing committees and ad hoc task groups. **Committees:** Design and Construction; Environmental Engineering; Operations and Maintenance; Organization and Administration; Procurement and Contracting; Project Management; Research. **Affiliated With:** National Academy of Sciences; National Research Council. **Formerly:** (1994) Federation Construction Council. **Publications:** *Investments in Federal Facilities: Asset Management Strategies for the 21st Century*. Report. Identifies 10 principles/policies used by best-practice organizations for facilities investment and management. **Price:** $31.28 for paperback. Alternate Formats: online ● *Starting Smart: Key Practices for Developing Scopes of Work for Facility Projects*. Report. Identifies key practices for developing scopes of work for design. **Price:** $16.20 for paperback. Alternate Formats: online ● Proceedings ● Reports. **Conventions/Meetings:** conference and seminar (exhibits).

5708 ■ Federal Managers Association (FMA)
1641 Prince St.
Alexandria, VA 22314-2818
Ph: (703)683-8700
Fax: (703)683-8707
E-mail: info@fedmanagers.org
URL: http://www.fedmanagers.org
Contact: Didier-Kim Q. Trinh, Exec. Dir.
Founded: 1913. **Membership Dues:** federal manager and supervisor, $18 (quarterly) ● member-at-large, $72 (annual). **Regional Groups:** 8. **Local Groups:** 170. **Description:** Represents managers and supervisors in all federal agencies. Promotes excellence in public service through effective management. Promotes and supports legislation beneficial to members, including workforce reshaping through mission analysis; compensation reform; and health and retirement benefits. Sponsors professional development program for managers as well as training seminars. **Awards:** Gil Guidry Award. **Frequency:** annual. **Type:** recognition ● Manager of the Year. **Frequency:** annual. **Type:** recognition. **Telecommunication Services:** electronic mail, darrylfma@aol.com. **Committees:** Federal Management Institute; Political Action. **Affiliated With:** Federal Employee Education and Assistance Fund; Public Employees Roundtable. **Formerly:** (1950) National Association of Supervisors; (1968) National Association of Supervisors, Department of Defense; (1979) National Association of Supervisors, Federal Government. **Publications:** *The Federal Manager*, quarterly. Magazine. Covers management and legislative issues in the government that affect federal managers. **Price:** $7.50/issue; $24.00/year. ISSN: 0893-8415. **Circulation:** 21,000. **Advertising:** accepted. Alternate Formats: online ● *The Washington Report*, bimonthly. Newsletter. **Conventions/Meetings:** annual Mid-Year Conference and Training Seminar - conference and seminar (exhibits) ● annual National Convention and Management Training Seminar - convention and seminar (exhibits) - always March.

5709 ■ Fund for Assuring an Independent Retirement (FAIR)
c/o National Association of Letter Carriers
100 Indiana Ave. NW, Ste.813
Washington, DC 20001-2144
Ph: (202)393-4695 (202)662-2836
Fax: (202)756-7400
E-mail: nalcinf@nalc.org
URL: http://www.nalc.org
Contact: William H. Young, Pres.
Founded: 1979. **Members:** 300,000. **Description:** Coalition of 32 organizations whose 13 million members are employed by or retired from the federal government. Seeks to protect the wages and benefits of such members. Conducts research and political education programs and analyzes legislative proposals for the benefit of member organizations and Congress. **Committees:** Communications; Legislation; Research. **Publications:** Report, monthly.

5710 ■ National Active and Retired Federal Employees Association (NARFE)
606 N Washington St.
Alexandria, VA 22314-1914
Ph: (703)838-7760
Free: (800)627-3394
Fax: (703)838-7785
E-mail: hq@narfe.org
URL: http://www.narfe.org
Contact: Charles L. Fallis, Pres.
Founded: 1921. **Members:** 430,000. **Membership Dues:** individual, $33 (annual). **Staff:** 65. **Budget:** $7,000,000. **State Groups:** 53. **Local Groups:** 1,740. **Description:** Retired U.S. Government civilian and District of Columbia employees, their spouses, persons drawing annuities as survivors of retired U.S.

government employees, present employees eligible for optional retirement, and federal employees with at least 5 years' service. Seeks to: serve annuitants and potential annuitants and their survivors under the retirement laws; sponsor and support beneficial legislation; promote the general welfare of civil service annuitants and their families. Also interested in pre-retirement programs, especially in federal and district government agencies. **Telecommunication Services:** electronic mail, natpres@narfe.org. **Committees:** National Association of Retired Federal Employees Political Action. **Formerly:** (1947) National Association of Retired Civil Employees; (2005) National Association of Retired Federal Employees. **Publications:** Magazine, monthly. Focuses on legislation and issues affecting federal civilian retirees and their dependents. **Price:** $1.00 for nonmembers; free for members. **Circulation:** 400,000. **Advertising:** accepted. Alternate Formats: online. **Conventions/Meetings:** biennial convention (exhibits) - even-numbered years.

5711 ■ National Association of Hispanic Federal Executives (NAHFE)

PO Box 23270
Washington, DC 20026-3270
Ph: (202)315-3942
Fax: (202)478-0806
E-mail: president@nahfe.org
URL: http://www.nahfe.org
Contact: Mr. Jose Osegueda, Pres./CEO

Founded: 1984. **Members:** 20,000. **Membership Dues:** individual, $36 (annual) ● corporate, $1,000 (annual). **Staff:** 3. **Budget:** $300,000. **Regional Groups:** 7. **Languages:** English, Spanish. **Description:** Hispanic and other federal employees ranked GS-12 and above; individuals in the private sector whose positions are equivalent to rank GS-12. Promotes the federal government as a model employer by encouraging qualified individuals to apply for federal government positions. Offers increased productivity training to federal employees. Maintains speakers' bureau and placement service. Offers educational programs; compiles statistics; conducts research. **Awards:** President's Award. **Frequency:** annual. **Type:** recognition. **Formerly:** Association of Hispanic Federation Executives. **Publications:** *The Hispanic Executive*, quarterly. Newsletter. **Price:** free for members. **Circulation:** 3,000. **Advertising:** accepted. **Conventions/Meetings:** annual Executive Leadership Training - conference (exhibits) - always November.

5712 ■ Professional Managers Association (PMA)

PO Box 77235
Washington, DC 20013
Ph: (202)874-1508
Fax: (202)874-1739
E-mail: info@promanager.org
URL: http://www.promanager.org
Contact: Mr. Thomas Burger, Pres.

Founded: 1981. **Members:** 3,000. **Membership Dues:** individual, $65 (annual) ● retired, $75 (5/year) ● individual, $2 (periodic). **Staff:** 2. **Budget:** $150,000. **Local Groups:** 30. **Description:** Federal civil service employees in management positions. Seeks to: improve the management, compensation, and public image of the federal work force; provide a vehicle for the advancement of interests and views of professional managers. Concentrates on issues affecting the interests of professional managers and their ability to efficiently conduct their duties. Includes issues such as: insuring fairness of pay and appraisal systems; reversing the erosion of federal benefits; encouraging innovation in management practices. Conducts research on management issues. **Libraries: Type:** not open to the public. **Holdings:** 300; articles, books, periodicals. **Subjects:** federal management issues. **Telecommunication Services:** electronic mail, burger@promanager.org. **Committees:** Communication; Legislative Issues; Management Improvement. **Publications:** Also publishes action memos and white papers. **Conventions/Meetings:** periodic meeting ● symposium.

5713 ■ Senior Executives Association

PO Box 44808
Washington, DC 20026-4808
Ph: (202)927-7000
E-mail: action@seniorexecs.org
URL: http://www.seniorexecs.org
Contact: Carol A. Bonosaro, Pres.

Founded: 1980. **Members:** 2,800. **Membership Dues:** active, $281 (annual) ● retiree, $100 (annual) ● life (active), $1,500 ● life (retired), $750. **Staff:** 8. **Budget:** $600,000. **Regional Groups:** 8. **Description:** Members of the Senior Executive Service, Senior Level and other Federal Career executives, and qualified GS-15s in the federal government. Seeks to: improve the efficiency, effectiveness, and productivity of the federal government; foster the professionalism of career federal executives; and enhance public recognition of the contributions of federal career executives. Presents the concerns of career executives to congress, executive branch political leaders, the press, and the public. Testifies before congressional committees; issues fact statements and news releases. Initiates legal action to protect the interests of members. Addresses issues including: compensation for government executives; management improvement initiatives; regional, state, local, and agency chapters. Compiles statistics. Holds professional development seminars through the Professional Development League. **Libraries: Type:** reference. **Holdings:** periodicals. **Awards: Type:** recognition. **Computer Services:** database, nonmember career federal executives ● mailing lists. **Publications:** *Action*, monthly. Newsletter. Covers association's activities and news affecting senior federal executives. Includes calendar of events and legislative updates. **Price:** free for members. **Circulation:** 3,200. **Advertising:** accepted. **Conventions/Meetings:** annual Career Executive Leadership - conference (exhibits) - always in Washington, DC.

5714 ■ Senior Executives Association Professional Development League (SEA PDL)

c/o SEA
PO Box 44808
Washington, DC 20026
Ph: (202)927-7000
Fax: (202)927-5192
E-mail: action@seniorexecs.org
URL: http://www.seniorexecs.org
Contact: Carol A. Bonosaro, Pres.

Founded: 1981. **Membership Dues:** active, $281 (annual) ● retiree, $100 (annual) ● life, $750-$1,500. **Staff:** 7. **Budget:** $225,000. **Description:** Participants are senior career executives of the federal government. Seeks to advance the professionalism of career federal executives through training and communications activities and research. Sponsors conferences and seminars designed to enhance executive abilities of the federal government career administrator, and research and recognition programs. **Libraries: Type:** reference. **Holdings:** monographs. **Also Known As:** Professional Development League. **Publications:** *Professional Development League*. Brochure. **Price:** free. **Conventions/Meetings:** annual Career Executive Leadership Conference (exhibits) - always in Washington, DC.

Fire Fighting

5715 ■ Fellowship of Christian Firefighters, International (FCF)

PO Box 901
Fort Collins, CO 80522-0901
Free: (800)322-9848
Fax: (970)416-9076
E-mail: fcfihq@aol.com
URL: http://www.fellowshipofchristianfirefighters.com
Contact: Gaius Reynolds, Pres.

Founded: 1978. **Members:** 1,950. **Membership Dues:** general, $25 (annual) ● life, $700. **Staff:** 2. **Budget:** $40,000. **Local Groups:** 70. **Description:** Christian fire fighters from Australia, Mexico, Philippines, Canada, and the United States. Provides support to members. Activities conducted at the chapter level include Bible studies and family camps. Maintains booth at fire service conferences. Supplies firehouses with Bibles at Chief's request. **Publications:** *The Encourager*, bimonthly. Newsletter. **Price:** included in membership dues. Alternate Formats: online ● Directory, biennial. **Conventions/Meetings:** annual International Family Conference - always June.

5716 ■ International Association of Arson Investigators (IAAI)

2151 Priest Bridge Dr., Ste.25
Crofton, MD 21114
Ph: (410)451-FIRE
Fax: (410)451-3049
E-mail: wlemire@foleymansfield.com
URL: http://www.firearson.com
Contact: Thomas J. Fee, Pres.

Founded: 1949. **Members:** 7,400. **Membership Dues:** individual, $75 (annual). **Staff:** 3. **Budget:** $500,000. **Description:** Arson investigators employed by fire and police departments, other law enforcement agencies, and fire underwriters agencies in 44 countries. Purposes are to: unite public officials and private persons engaged in the control of arson and kindred crimes; cooperate with law enforcement agencies and associations to further fire prevention and the suppression of crime; encourage high professional standards of conduct among arson investigators; continually strive to eliminate all factors that interfere with administration of crime suppression. Conducts specialized education and regional seminars. Maintains speakers' bureau. **Libraries: Type:** not open to the public. **Awards: Type:** recognition ● **Type:** scholarship. **Computer Services:** database, membership. **Telecommunication Services:** electronic mail, feeinvest@aol.com. **Committees:** Appellate Review; Chapter Liaison; Fire Investigation Standards; Fire Investigator Safety; Forensic Science; Strategic Planning; Training and Education; Wildland Arson. **Publications:** *Fire and Arson Investigator*, quarterly. Magazine. Contains articles on the problems of arson. Includes index, law reviews, research reports, and statistics. **Price:** included in membership dues. **Circulation:** 8,000. **Advertising:** accepted ● Membership Directory, annual. **Conventions/Meetings:** annual meeting, with training seminar (exhibits) - always April or May ● annual School Division Meeting - meeting and conference.

5717 ■ International Association of Black Professional Fire Fighters (IABPFF)

1020 N Taylor Ave.
St. Louis, MO 63113
Ph: (786)229-6914
Fax: (305)249-5230
E-mail: execdir411@hotmail.com
URL: http://www.iabpff.org
Contact: Johnny J. Brewington, Pres.

Founded: 1970. **Members:** 8,500. **Staff:** 2. **Budget:** $160,000. **Regional Groups:** 6. **Local Groups:** 125. **Description:** Fire fighters, dispatchers, and individuals in related professions. Strives to promote interracial communication and understanding, recruit blacks for the fire services, improve working conditions for blacks in the fire services, assist blacks in career advancement, promote professionalism, and represent black fire fighters before the community. **Computer Services:** Mailing lists. **Committees:** Political/Community Action. **Affiliated With:** National Association for the Advancement of Colored People; Southern Christian Leadership Conference. **Publications:** *National Express*, monthly. Bulletin ● *Smoke*, semiannual. Newsletter. **Conventions/Meetings:** biennial convention (exhibits) - always in even-numbered years. 2008 Aug. 3-8, Detroit, MI.

5718 ■ International Association of Fire Chiefs (IAFC)

4025 Fair Ridge Dr., Ste.300
Fairfax, VA 22033-2868
Ph: (703)273-0911
Free: (800)661-3336
Fax: (703)273-9363

E-mail: membership@iafc.org
URL: http://www.iafc.org
Contact: Garry L. Briese, Exec. Dir.
Founded: 1873. **Members:** 12,600. **Membership Dues:** individual (based on location in US region), $215-$260 (annual). **Staff:** 33. **Budget:** $5,200,000. **Regional Groups:** 8. **Description:** Fire Department chief officers, emergency services administrators and emergency medical services directors/managers and supervisors, career, volunteer, municipal and private, who are interested in improving fire, rescue, and EMS coverage to the general public. Provides leadership to career and volunteer chiefs, chief fire officers and managers of emergency service organizations throughout the international community through vision, information, education, services and representation to enhance their professionalism and capabilities. **Libraries: Type:** reference. **Holdings:** 5,000; articles, books, periodicals. **Subjects:** safety, municipal and administrative topics, fire protection, hazardous materials, labor relations. **Awards:** International Benjamin Franklin Award of Valor. **Frequency:** annual. **Type:** recognition. **Recipient:** to a deserving fire fighter. **Computer Services:** database. **Committees:** Accreditation; Arson; Codes Coordination; Communications; Emergency Management; Emergency Vehicle Certification; Fire Prevention; Hazardous Materials; Health and Safety; Nominations and Elections; Professional Development; Risk Management and Liability; Transportation Emergency Rescue; Urban Rescue/Structural Collapse; Volunteer Fire Service; Youth Activities. **Publications:** *On Scene*, bimonthly. Newsletter. Covers current news of interest to fire and emergency services managers. **Price:** included in membership dues; $74.00 /year for nonmembers. ISSN: 0893-3936. **Circulation:** 12,000. **Advertising:** accepted. Alternate Formats: online ● Books ● Manuals ● Reports. **Conventions/Meetings:** annual Fire Rescue International - conference (exhibits) - 2008 Aug. 14-16, Denver, CO.

5719 ■ International Fire Marshals Association (IFMA)

c/o Steven Sawyer, Exec. Sec.
1 Batterymarch Park
Quincy, MA 02169-7471
Fax: (617)984-7056
E-mail: ifma@nfpa.org
Contact: Steven Sawyer, Exec. Sec.
Founded: 1906. **Members:** 2,462. **Membership Dues:** associate, affiliate, $145 (annual). **Staff:** 2. **Regional Groups:** 23. **Description:** Municipal, county, state, and provincial fire marshals and fire prevention bureau officials. Works for professional improvement through information exchange, meetings, and conferences. Seeks to minimize the loss of life and property by fire through fire prevention education, enforcement of fire laws, investigation of fire causes, and fire hazard regulation. **Formerly:** (1999) Fire Marshals Association of North America. **Publications:** *IFMA Code of Ethics*. Paper. Contains code of ethics for members. **Price:** $1.00. Alternate Formats: online ● *International Fire Marshals Association—Membership Directory*, annual. **Price:** included in membership dues ● *Model Fireworks Law*. Manual. Features model law that prohibits the sale and possession of fireworks. **Price:** $1.00. Alternate Formats: online. **Conventions/Meetings:** annual meeting, held in conjunction with NFPA - June.

5720 ■ International Society for Fire Service Instructors (ISFSI)

2425 Hwy. 49 E
Pleasant View, TN 37146
Free: (800)435-0005
Fax: (615)746-1170
E-mail: info@isfsi.org
URL: http://www.isfsi.org
Contact: Timothy E. Sendelbach, Pres.
Founded: 1960. **Members:** 7,500. **Membership Dues:** regular, $75 (annual). **Staff:** 30. **Budget:** $3,000,000. **Description:** Umbrella organization for emergency management membership groups. Seeks to provide information, training, and education to fire officers, fire fighters, rescue, and emergency personnel. **Libraries: Type:** not open to the public. **Holdings:** 1,000; books, video recordings. **Subjects:** fire education. **Awards:** Innovator of the Year Award. **Frequency:** annual. **Type:** recognition. **Recipient:** to the most innovative technology applications ● Instructor of the Year Award. **Frequency:** annual. **Type:** recognition. **Recipient:** to the most innovative idea for fire safety implemented. **Formerly:** (1998) Alliance for Fire and Emergency Management. **Publications:** *Class A Foams*. Book. **Price:** $44.95/video; $535.00/instructional program ● *Fire Department Loss Control* ● *Hazmat Awareness Training Program* ● *Hazmat Operations Training Program* ● *Instruct-O-Gram*, monthly. **Price:** $24.00/year ● *Managing People, Books I, II and III* ● *Pre-Emergency Planning* ● *Rural Firefighting Operations Books I, II and III* ● *Voice*, monthly. **Price:** $72.00/year. **Advertising:** accepted. **Conventions/Meetings:** annual Fall Training - conference (exhibits) - locations vary ● periodic seminar.

5721 ■ National Association of Hispanic Firefighters (NAHF)

2821 McKinney Ave., Ste.7
Dallas, TX 75204
Ph: (972)223-5033
Free: (866)370-6243
E-mail: nahf@nahf.org
URL: http://www.nahf.org
Contact: Alberto N. Olmos, Pres.
Founded: 1995. **Members:** 2,500. **Membership Dues:** association, $24 (annual). **Staff:** 10. **Budget:** $100,000. **Regional Groups:** 3. **National Groups:** 10. **Description:** Aims to secure the rights of Hispanic firefighters. Fosters quality training and education. **Libraries: Type:** open to the public. **Holdings:** 100. **Awards:** FEMA Fire Prevention. **Frequency:** annual. **Type:** grant. **Recipient:** to Hispanic community. **Publications:** Newsletter, quarterly. **Price:** free. **Circulation:** 2,000. **Advertising:** accepted. Alternate Formats: online. **Conventions/Meetings:** annual conference (exhibits).

5722 ■ National Association of State Fire Marshals (NASFM)

1319 F St. NW, Ste.301
Washington, DC 20004
Ph: (202)737-1226
Free: (877)996-2736
Fax: (202)393-1296
E-mail: info@firemarshals.org
URL: http://www.firemarshals.org
Contact: James Narva, Exec. Dir.
Founded: 1989. **Members:** 51. **Membership Dues:** advocate, $1,600 (annual) ● association, $5,000 (annual) ● public service, $200 (annual). **Staff:** 11. **Budget:** $3,000,000. **Description:** State fire marshals. Promotes fire safety; seeks to increase the effectiveness of public fire fighting services. Serves as a forum for the exchange of information among members; sponsors educational and training programs. **Conventions/Meetings:** annual meeting.

5723 ■ National Volunteer Fire Council (NVFC)

1050 17th St. NW, Ste.490
Washington, DC 20036
Ph: (202)887-5700
Free: (888)ASK-NVFC
Fax: (202)887-5291
E-mail: nvfcoffice@nvfc.org
URL: http://www.nvfc.org
Contact: Heather Schafer, Exec. Dir.
Founded: 1976. **Members:** 2,500. **Membership Dues:** personal, $30 (annual) ● department, $50 (annual) ● state association, $500 (annual) ● corporate, $1,000-$10,000 (annual). **Staff:** 10. **Budget:** $450,000. **State Groups:** 49. **Local Groups:** 2,000. **Description:** State organizations representing volunteer fire departments; local fire departments and companies; commercial organizations that support volunteer firefighters. Provides a unified, national voice for volunteer firefighters. Promotes professional training of volunteer firefighters; seeks to enhance the public image of volunteer fire services. Conducts educational programs on fire prevention and self-protection for children, the elderly, and the handicapped. Gathers and disseminates information. Examines recruitment and retention techniques for volunteer firefighters. Represents the U.S. as a member of the Federation of Volunteer Firefighters' Associations. Organizes charitable program and maintains speakers' bureau. **Libraries: Type:** reference. **Awards:** Firefighter of the Year Award. **Frequency:** annual. **Type:** recognition. **Recipient:** for an exemplary performance in the fire service and community ● Marc Mueller Fire Prevention Award. **Frequency:** annual. **Type:** recognition. **Telecommunication Services:** electronic mail, hschafer@nvfc.org. **Publications:** *Dispatch*, quarterly. Newsletter. **Price:** included in membership dues; $50.00 for nonmembers. **Circulation:** 3,000. **Advertising:** accepted. Alternate Formats: CD-ROM ● *New Tools for Volunteer Firefighters* ● Fire Service Resource Guide and Final Report on Retention and Recruitment. **Conventions/Meetings:** semiannual meeting - always spring and fall.

5724 ■ Women in the Fire Service (WFS)

PO Box 5446
Madison, WI 53705
Ph: (608)233-4768
Fax: (608)233-4879
E-mail: info@wfsi.org
URL: http://www.wfsi.org
Contact: Terese M. Floren, Dir./Co-Founder
Founded: 1982. **Members:** 6,200. **Membership Dues:** individual in U.S., $40 (annual) ● institution in U.S., $50 (annual) ● individual outside U.S., $45 (annual) ● institution outside U.S., $55 (annual) ● supporting, $75 (annual) ● sustaining, $125 (annual). **Staff:** 3. **Budget:** $85,000. **Description:** Women working in the fire service, including career and volunteer firefighters, emergency medical technicians and paramedics, inspectors and arson investigators, fire safety educators, and administrators; women interested in careers in fire service; interested men. Provides support and advocacy for women in fire service; promotes professional development of members in an effort to make women more effective firefighters. Collects and disseminates information on issues affecting women in fire service; maintains resource bank on issues such as recruitment, physical agility testing, promotional testing, fitness training, firefighting techniques, and maternity leave. Offers guidance in decisions concerning sexual harassment, sexual discrimination, and other issues. Supports and facilitates the development of local groups. Maintains speakers' bureau; compiles statistics; conducts charitable and educational programs. **Libraries: Type:** reference; not open to the public. **Awards:** Molly Matthews Fund. **Type:** scholarship. **Formerly:** (1989) Women in Fire Suppression. **Publications:** *Firework*, 8/year. Newsletter. **Price:** $40.00 for nonmembers in U.S.; $45.00 for nonmembers outside U.S.; included in membership dues. **Circulation:** 800. Alternate Formats: online ● *Information Packets*. Includes topics of recruitment, sexual harassment, reproductive safety, and the history of women in firefighting; also physical abilities testing. ● *WFS Quarterly*. Journal. Focuses on gender integration of fire service. **Price:** $50.00 for nonmembers in U.S.; $55.00 for nonmembers outside U.S.; included in membership dues. ISSN: 1071-1767. **Circulation:** 250 ● Video. Features the recruitment of women firefighters. ● Also publishes flyers and a videotape for recruitment of women firefighters. **Conventions/Meetings:** biennial Fire Service Women's Leadership Training Seminar (exhibits) - always spring ● biennial International Conference of Fire Service Women (exhibits).

Firearms

5725 ■ Gun Owners of America (GOA)

8001 Forbes Pl., Ste.102
Springfield, VA 22151
Ph: (703)321-8585
Fax: (703)321-8408
E-mail: goamail@gunowners.org
URL: http://www.gunowners.org
Contact: Larry Pratt, Exec. Dir.
Founded: 1975. **Members:** 300,000. **Membership Dues:** full, $20-$250 (annual) ● life, $500. **Descrip-**

tion: Works to educate the public about the Second Amendment. **Publications:** *The Gun Owners*, QRT. Newsletter. Alternate Formats: online.

5726 ■ Gun Owners Foundation (GOF)
8001 Forbes Pl., Ste.102
Springfield, VA 22151
Ph: (703)321-8585
Fax: (703)321-8408
E-mail: gofmail@gunowners.org
URL: http://www.gunowners.com
Contact: Frank McGlynn, Exec. VP
Description: Works to educate the public about the importance of the Second Amendment and to provide legal, expert and support assistance for individuals involved in firearms-related cases.

5727 ■ Second Amendment Committee
PO Box 1776
Hanford, CA 93232
Ph: (559)584-5209 (559)582-8534
Fax: (559)584-4084
E-mail: liberty89@libertygunrights.com
URL: http://www.libertygunrights.com
Contact: Bernadine Smith, Founder
Founded: 1984. **Description:** Provides information for seeking a peaceful resolution to the gun crises in America. **Computer Services:** Mailing lists, updates.

Fishing

5728 ■ Atlantic Offshore Lobstermen's Association (AOLA)
c/o Bonnie Spinazzola, Exec. Dir./Sec.
54 Chatham Dr.
Bedford, NH 03110
Ph: (603)206-5468
Fax: (603)666-5601
E-mail: bonnie@offshorelobster.org
URL: http://www.offshorelobster.org
Contact: Bonnie Spinazzola, Exec. Dir./Sec.
Founded: 1971. **Members:** 75. **Membership Dues:** individual, $1,000 (annual). **Staff:** 1. **Description:** Offshore lobster boat owners, crewmen on fishing vessels, and businesses associated with fishing. Represents the interests of East Coast offshore lobstermen concerning foreign fishing control and domestic fishery regulations. Protects fishermen's interests in formulating fisheries management policy in the Fisheries Conservation Zone. Has participated in the development of fishery management plans for American lobster. It is concerned with issues including: resolution of conflicts between U.S. fixed and mobile gear fishermen; protection of the fishing industry from detrimental offshore petroleum development practices; economic development of the fishing industry through the New England Fishery Development Foundation; ocean dumping. Conducts research programs and seminars. Maintains speakers' bureau. **Libraries: Type:** reference. **Holdings:** 100. **Awards: Type:** recognition. **Formerly:** (1982) Atlantic Offshore Fish and Lobster Association; (1995) Atlantic Offshore Fishermen's Association. **Publications:** *Atlantic Fishermen Expo*, annual. **Circulation:** 3,000. **Advertising:** accepted ● *Matching Capital to Resources in the Fish Harvesting Industry* ● Newsletter, quarterly. **Conventions/Meetings:** annual Atlantic Fishermen's Expo - meeting - always February in Newport, RI.

5729 ■ Atlantic States Marine Fisheries Commission (ASMFC)
1444 Eye St. NW, 6th Fl.
Washington, DC 20005
Ph: (202)289-6400
Fax: (202)289-6051
E-mail: info@asmfc.org
URL: http://www.asmfc.org
Contact: John V. O'Shea, Exec. Dir.
Founded: 1942. **Members:** 45. **Staff:** 31. **Budget:** $5,000,000. **Regional Groups:** 5. **Description:** State administrators, governor's appointees, and state legislators from the 15 Atlantic coast states. Aims to promote better utilization of the fisheries (marine, shell, and anadromous) of the Atlantic seaboard by developing a joint program for the promotion and protection of such fisheries, and by preventing the physical waste of the fisheries from any cause. **Libraries: Type:** reference. **Awards:** Awards of Excellence. **Frequency:** annual. **Type:** recognition. **Recipient:** for important contributions of individuals to the success of the organization ● Captain David H. Hart Award. **Frequency:** annual. **Type:** recognition. **Recipient:** for individuals who have made outstanding contributions to the betterment of marine fisheries on the Atlantic Coast. **Telecommunication Services:** electronic mail, comments@asmfc.org. **Boards:** Species Management. **Committees:** Species Technical. **Programs:** Interstate Fisheries Management and Science. **Subcommittees:** Stock Assessment. **Publications:** *Annual Meeting Report*, annual ● *ASMFC Fisheries Focus*, monthly. Newsletter ● *Habitat Hotline Atlantic*, quarterly. Newsletter ● *Interstate Fisheries of the Atlantic Coast*. Book ● *Understanding Fisheries Management*. Manual ● Brochures ● Also publishes fisheries management plans and special reports. **Conventions/Meetings:** annual meeting.

5730 ■ Inter-American Tropical Tuna Commission (IATTC)
8604 La Jolla Shores Dr.
La Jolla, CA 92037-1508
Ph: (858)546-7100
Fax: (858)546-7133
E-mail: webmaster@iattc.org
URL: http://www.iattc.org
Contact: Dr. Robin Allen, Dir.
Founded: 1950. **Members:** 13. **Staff:** 68. **Budget:** $4,817,997. **Languages:** English, Spanish. **Multinational. Description:** Appointed commissioners representing Japan, France, Nicaragua, Guatemala, Peru, Mexico, Ecuador, El Salvador, Costa Rica, Panama, Vanuatu, Venezuela and the United States. Conducts studies on Pacific Ocean tunas and dolphins associated with tunas. Recommends conservation measures to member governments in order to maintain optimum levels of tuna stock and maximum level of dolphin stock. (Dolphins are frequently caught and inadvertently killed in tuna nets.) Monitors population and mortality levels; conducts research. Provides the secretariat for the International Dolphin Conservation Program. Responsibility are met with its two programs, the Tuna-Billfish Program and the Tuna-Dolphin program. The principal responsibilities of the Tuna-Billfish program are: to study the biology of tunas and related species of the eastern Pacific Ocean to estimate the effects that fishing and natural factors have on their abundance; to recommend appropriate conservation measures so that the stocks of fish can be maintained at levels which will afford maximum sustainable catches; to collect information on compliance with Commission resolutions. The principal responsibilities of the Tuna-Dolphin program are: to monitor the abundance of dolphins and their mortality incidental to purse-seine fishing in the eastern Pacific Ocean; to study the causes of mortality of dolphins during fishing operations and promote the use of fishing techniques and equipment that minimize these mortalities; to study the effects of different modes of fishing on the various fish and other animals of the pelagic ecosystem; and to provide a secretariat for the International Dolphin Conservation Program. **Libraries: Type:** reference. **Holdings:** 2,000; periodicals. **Computer Services:** database, tuna fishery statistics of the eastern Pacific Ocean. **Telecommunication Services:** teletext, 691115 TUNACOM. **Publications:** *Data Report*, periodic ● *Special Reports* (in English and Spanish), periodic. ISSN: 0749-8187. **Circulation:** 800 ● *Stock Assessment Report*, annual ● Annual Report (in English and Spanish), annual. **Price:** $5.00. ISSN: 0074-1000. **Circulation:** 1,000 ● Bulletin (in English and Spanish), periodic. ISSN: 0074-0993. **Circulation:** 800. **Conventions/Meetings:** annual conference ● periodic meeting.

5731 ■ International Pacific Halibut Commission (IPHC)
PO Box 95009
Seattle, WA 98145-2009
Ph: (206)634-1838
Fax: (206)632-2983
E-mail: info@iphc.washington.edu
URL: http://www.iphc.washington.edu
Contact: Dr. Bruce M. Leaman, Exec. Dir.
Founded: 1923. **Members:** 6. **Staff:** 25. **Budget:** $1,500,000. **Multinational. Description:** Intergovernmental organization of commissioners appointed by the United States (3) and Canada (3) to be responsible for management of the halibut fishery in the North Pacific and Bering Sea. Seeks to develop stocks of Pacific halibut to levels that will permit optimum sustained yield and to maintain stocks at those levels. Applies specific types of regulation and scientific investigations. Compiles catch statistics. **Telecommunication Services:** electronic mail, bruce@iphc.washington.edu. **Publications:** *Bluebook*, annual. Report ● Reports, annual. Contains technical data. ● Report, annual. **Conventions/Meetings:** annual meeting.

5732 ■ Pacific Fishery Management Council (PFMC)
7700 NE Ambassador Pl., Ste.200
Portland, OR 97220-1384
Ph: (503)820-2280
Free: (866)806-7204
Fax: (503)820-2299
E-mail: pfmc.comments@noaa.gov
URL: http://www.pcouncil.org
Contact: Dr. Don McIsaac, Exec. Dir.
Founded: 1976. **Members:** 18. **Staff:** 10. **Budget:** $1,907,750. **Description:** Established by the Magnuson-Stevens Fishery Conservation and Management Act of 1976 to compile and disseminate information for consideration by the Secretary of Commerce in adopting measures for West Coast fisheries management. **Telecommunication Services:** electronic mail, donald.mcisaac@noaa.gov. **Committees:** Coastal Pelagic Species; Groundfish Team; Habitat; Halibut; Highly Migratory Species; Salmon Team; Scientific and Statistical. **Publications:** *Fishery Management Plans*, annual ● *PFMC Newsletter*, bimonthly ● *Review of Ocean Salmon Fisheries*, annual. Contains research documents reviewing the salmon season for the preceding year. Includes statistics. **Price:** free ● *Roster*, periodic. Membership Directory ● *Status of the Pacific Coast Groundfish Fishery and Recommended Acceptable Biological Catches*, annual. Documents reviewing past year's fishery performance and Council management actions. **Price:** free. **Conventions/Meetings:** meeting - 5/year.

5733 ■ Pacific States Marine Fisheries Commission (PSMFC)
205 SE Spokane St., Ste.100
Portland, OR 97202
Ph: (503)595-3100
Fax: (503)595-3232
E-mail: info@psmfc.org
URL: http://www.psmfc.org
Contact: Mr. Randy Fisher, Exec. Dir.
Founded: 1947. **Staff:** 6. **State Groups:** 5. **Description:** State employees and appointees from Alaska, Idaho, Washington, Oregon, and California; advised by a scientific and industry advisory committee. Promotes and supports policies and activities directed at the conservation, development, and management of fishery resources of mutual concern to member states; coordinates a regional approach to research, monitoring, and utilization of resources. Compiles statistics. **Awards:** Outstanding Contribution to Pacific Coast Fisheries. **Frequency:** annual. **Type:** recognition. **Computer Services:** database, commercial fishery, landings Pacific Coast salmon coded wire tag release and recovery. **Committees:** Coastwide Data; Groundfish; Recreational Fisheries; Salmon-Steelhead; Salmon Tag Coordinators; Shellfish. **Formerly:** (1989) Pacific Marine Fisheries Commission. **Publications:** Annual Report, annual. **Conventions/Meetings:** annual meeting - always October/November.

5734 ■ Southeastern Association of Fish and Wildlife Agencies (SEAFWA)
c/o Robert M. Brantly, Exec. Sec.
8005 Freshwater Farms Rd.
Tallahassee, FL 32308

Ph: (850)893-1204
Fax: (850)893-6204
E-mail: seafwa@aol.com
URL: http://www.seafwa.org
Contact: Robert M. Brantly, Exec. Sec.
Founded: 1947. **Members:** 18. **Staff:** 1. **State Groups:** 18. **Description:** Directors of state game and fish commissions in 16 southern states, and the Commonwealth of Puerto Rico, and the Virgin Islands. Aims to: protect the right of jurisdiction of southeastern states over their wildlife resources on public and private lands; study state and federal wildlife legislation and regulations as they affect the area; consult with and make recommendations to federal wildlife and public land agencies on federal management programs and programs involving federal aid to southeastern states; serve as a clearinghouse for exchange of ideas on wildlife management and research techniques. Sponsors: Cooperative Fish Disease Study at Auburn University in Alabama; Cooperative Wildlife Disease Study at the University of Georgia in Athens. **Committees:** Constituent Outreach and Marketing; Cooperative Fish Disease Study; Cooperative Genetics and Fish Breeding; Fur Resources. **Affiliated With:** Association of Fish and Wildlife Agencies. **Formerly:** (1977) Southeastern Association of Game and Fish Commissioners. **Publications:** *Southeastern Association of Fish and Wildlife Agencies Proceedings*, annual. Contains information on fish and wildlife management and wild life law enforcement. **Price:** $22.00/ year. **Circulation:** 2,500 ● *Transactions*, annual ● Also publishes research papers. **Conventions/Meetings:** annual conference, forum for wildlife professionals from all disciplines to present information regarding management of wildlife and fishery resources (exhibits) - always fall.

5735 ■ Western Association of Fish and Wildlife Agencies (WAFWA)
c/o Larry L. Kruckenberg, Sec.
Wyoming Game and Fish Dept.
5400 Bishop Blvd.
Cheyenne, WY 82009
Ph: (307)777-4569
Fax: (307)777-4699
E-mail: larry.kruckenberg@state.wy.us
URL: http://www.wafwa.org
Contact: Larry L. Kruckenberg, Sec.
Founded: 1922. **Members:** 23. **Membership Dues:** regular, $500 (annual). **Description:** Represents officials of state and provincial wildlife and fish agencies of western states and provinces. Promotes fish and wildlife conservation in the West. **Formerly:** (1978) Western Association of State Game and Fish Commissioners. **Publications:** *Western Proceedings*, annual. **Price:** $20.00. **Circulation:** 500. **Conventions/Meetings:** annual conference (exhibits).

Food and Drugs

5736 ■ Association of Food and Drug Officials (AFDO)
2550 Kingston Rd., Ste.311
York, PA 17402
Ph: (717)757-2888
Fax: (717)755-8089
E-mail: afdo@afdo.org
URL: http://www.afdo.org
Contact: Steve Steinhoff, Chm.
Founded: 1896. **Members:** 700. **Membership Dues:** alumni/student, regulatory, consumer/educational, $50 (annual) ● small business/consultant, $225 (annual) ● associate industry, $325 (annual). **Staff:** 4. **Budget:** $250,000. **Regional Groups:** 6. **Description:** Officials who enforce federal, state, district, county, and municipal laws and regulations relating to food, drugs, cosmetics, consumer product safety, and similar areas. Prevents fraud in production, manufacturing, distribution, and sale of these items. Promotes uniform laws and administrative procedures; disseminates information concerning law enforcement. **Awards:** Harvey W. Wiley Awards. **Frequency:** annual. **Type:** recognition. **Committees:** Drugs, Devices and Cosmetics; Education and Training; Field; Food; International and Government Relations; Laws and Regulations; Media and Public Affairs; Product Safety; Resolutions; Retail Food; Science and Technology. **Formerly:** (1974) Association of Food and Drug Officials of the United States. **Publications:** *E-News*, quarterly. Newsletter ● Directory, semiannual. **Conventions/Meetings:** annual conference, provides information on current and emerging food and drug issues (exhibits) - usually second week of June.

5737 ■ Association of Technical and Supervisory Professionals (ATSP)
c/o Pete Bridgeman, Natl. Sec.
436 Park St. NE
Vienna, VA 22180
E-mail: petebridgeman@hotmail.com
URL: http://www.atsp.net
Contact: Pete Bridgeman, Natl. Sec.
Founded: 1974. **Members:** 402. **Description:** Technical and supervisory personnel involved in U.S. Department of Agriculture poultry and meat inspection programs. Consults with management of meat processing companies on matters of concern to members. Monitors legislation affecting the meat processing industry and informs members of pending regulatory agency policy revisions; conducts limited lobbying activities and organizes letter-writing campaigns to influence legislation. **Affiliated With:** Public Employees Roundtable. **Publications:** Newsletter, periodic. Alternate Formats: online. **Conventions/Meetings:** quarterly meeting, held in conjunction with USDA.

5738 ■ Food and Drug Law Institute (FDLI)
1155 15 St. NW, Ste.800
Washington, DC 20005-4903
Ph: (202)371-1420
Free: (800)956-6293
Fax: (202)371-0649
E-mail: comments@fdli.org
URL: http://www.fdli.org
Contact: James J. Kelly, Pres./CEO
Founded: 1949. **Members:** 548. **Membership Dues:** manufacturer, $2,000-$10,000 (annual) ● start-up manufacturer, $1,000 (annual) ● supplier, $2,000-$4,000 (annual) ● law firm, $3,000-$5,000 (annual) ● sole practitioner, $500 (annual) ● service organization, $1,800 (annual) ● international/nonprofit organization, $650 (annual) ● academic, $100 (annual) ● government staff, $40 (annual) ● student, $25 (annual). **Staff:** 16. **Budget:** $3,500,000. **Description:** Provides forum regarding laws, regulations and policies related to drugs, medical devices, and other health care technologies. **Libraries: Type:** reference. **Awards:** Internships. **Frequency:** annual. **Type:** scholarship. **Recipient:** for law students interested in the food, drug and medical device arena ● Writing Award. **Frequency:** annual. **Type:** recognition. **Recipient:** for papers on topics in the area of food and drug law and regulations. **Telecommunication Services:** electronic mail, jjk@fdli.org. **Boards:** Journal Editorial Advisory; Update Editorial Advisory. **Committees:** Academic Programs; Drugs and Biologics; Food and Dietary Supplement; Governance; Medical Device; Strategic Planning. **Formerly:** (1965) Food Law Institute. **Publications:** *FDLI Update*, bimonthly. Magazine. Includes listings of new members, member services, employment opportunities, and short substantive articles. **Price:** free for members; $50.00 for nonmembers. ISSN: 1075-7635. **Circulation:** 8,000. **Advertising:** accepted ● *Food and Drug Law Journal*, quarterly. Contains book reviews, article citations, and reports. **Price:** $299.00 for members; $379.00 for nonmembers. ISSN: 0015-6361. **Circulation:** 1,100. Also Cited As: *Food Drug Cosmetic Law Quarterly and Food Drug Cosmetic Law Journal* ● Audiotapes ● Videos ● Books. Alternate Formats: online; CD-ROM. **Conventions/Meetings:** annual conference ● annual meeting and conference, held in cooperation with the Food and Drug Administration (exhibits) - always in Washington, DC.

5739 ■ International Association for Food Protection (IAFP)
6200 Aurora Ave., Ste.200W
Des Moines, IA 50322-2864
Ph: (515)276-3344
Free: (800)369-6337
Fax: (515)276-8655
E-mail: info@foodprotection.org
URL: http://www.foodprotection.org
Contact: David W. Tharp CAE, Exec. Dir.
Founded: 1911. **Members:** 3,000. **Membership Dues:** student/retired, in U.S., $25 (annual) ● student/retired, in Canada and Mexico, $25 (annual) ● student/retired, international, $25 (annual) ● individual, in U.S., $50 (annual) ● individual, in Canada and Mexico, $50 (annual) ● individual, international, $265 (annual) ● sustaining, $750-$5,000 (annual). **Staff:** 12. **Budget:** $2,000,000. **Regional Groups:** 8. **State Groups:** 29. **Multinational. Description:** Food safety professionals. Provides educational programs and services to members. Functions as a clearinghouse on food safety; serves as a forum for the exchange of information among members. **Libraries: Type:** not open to the public. **Holdings:** 160; video recordings. **Subjects:** food safety, food science, food microbiology, sanitation. **Awards:** Educator Award. **Frequency:** annual. **Type:** recognition. **Recipient:** to members for contribution to food safety education ● Harold Barnum Industry Award. **Frequency:** annual. **Type:** recognition. **Recipient:** to members for contribution to industry of food safety ● Harry Haverland Citation Award. **Frequency:** annual. **Type:** recognition. **Recipient:** to members for service to the association ● Honorary Life Membership. **Frequency:** annual. **Type:** recognition. **Recipient:** to members for lifetime service to the association ● International Leadership Award. **Frequency:** annual. **Type:** recognition. **Recipient:** for a long history of outstanding contribution ● Sanitarian Award. **Frequency:** annual. **Type:** recognition. **Recipient:** to members for contribution to the sanitarian profession. **Computer Services:** Mailing lists. **Committees:** Applied Laboratory Methods; Communicable Diseases Affecting Man; Dairy Quality and Safety; Education; Food Safety Network; Food Sanitation; Foundation Fund; Fruit and Vegetable Safety and Quality; Meat and Poultry Safety and Quality; Microbial Food Safety Risk Assessment; Retail Food Safety and Quality; Sanitary Procedures; Seafood Safety and Quality; Student; Viral and Parasitic Foodborne Disease; Water Safety and Quality. **Formerly:** (1938) International Association of Dairy and Milk Inspectors; (1950) International Association of Milk Sanitarians; (1966) International Association of Milk and Food Sanitarians; (2000) International Association of Milk, Food and Environmental Sanitarians. **Publications:** *Food Protection Trends*, monthly. Journal. Contains refereed articles on applied research, applications of current technology and general interest subjects for food safety professionals. **Price:** included in membership dues; $248.00 /year for nonmembers in U.S.; $263.00 /year for nonmembers in Canada and Mexico; $278.00 /year for nonmembers outside North America. ISSN: 1541-9576. **Circulation:** 9,000. **Advertising:** accepted. Alternate Formats: online ● *Journal of Food Protection*, monthly. Contains scientific Research and authoritative review articles on food safety and quality. **Price:** included in membership dues; $504.00 /year for nonmembers in U.S.; $539.00 /year for nonmembers in Canada and Mexico; $584.00 /year for nonmembers outside North America. ISSN: 0362-028X. **Circulation:** 12,000. **Advertising:** accepted. Alternate Formats: microform; online. **Conventions/Meetings:** annual meeting, more than 500 presentations on the latest food science and food safety information (exhibits) - 2008 Aug. 3-6, Columbus, OH; 2009 July 12-15, Grapevine, TX; 2010 Aug. 1-4, Anaheim, CA.

5740 ■ International Association of Milk Control Agencies (IAMCA)
c/o Charles Huff, Sec.-Treas.
New York Dept. of Agriculture and Markets
10 B Airline Dr.
Albany, NY 12235

Ph: (518)457-5731
Fax: (518)485-8730
E-mail: charlie.huff@agmkt.state.ny.us
URL: http://www.maine.gov/agriculture/mmc/iamca
Contact: Charles Huff, Sec.-Treas.
Founded: 1935. **Members:** 26. **Membership Dues:** regular, $150 (annual) ● associate, $50 (annual). **Description:** State and provincial agencies administering regulations dealing with milk pricing. Compiles statistics. **Affiliated With:** National Association of State Departments of Agriculture. **Formerly:** National Association of Milk Control Boards of America. **Publications:** Proceedings, annual ● Membership Directory, annual. **Conventions/Meetings:** annual meeting.

5741 ■ International Narcotic Enforcement Officers Association (INEOA)
112 State St., Ste.1200
Albany, NY 12207-2023
Ph: (518)463-6232
Fax: (518)432-3378
E-mail: info@ineoa.org
URL: http://www.ineoa.org
Contact: John J. Bellizzi Jr., Exec. Dir.
Founded: 1975. **Members:** 15,000. **Membership Dues:** active, regular, associate, $40 (annual). **Staff:** 6. **Budget:** $500,000. **Description:** Narcotic enforcement officers, government employees, and others from 60 countries concerned with narcotics control. Seeks ways to improve: laws relative to narcotics, depressants, stimulants, and hallucinogens and enforcement of such laws; police methods; administration of justice. Provides and disseminates educational materials relating to control of drugs and prevention of narcotic addiction and drug abuse. Provides a forum for exchange of ideas; conducts study groups and seminars. Maintains speakers' bureau. **Libraries:** **Type:** reference. **Holdings:** 1,200; books, papers. **Subjects:** narcotic enforcement. **Awards:** Medal/Valor. **Frequency:** annual. **Type:** medal. **Recipient:** based on performance of duty. **Boards:** Directors. **Formerly:** (1962) National Narcotic Enforcement Officers Association. **Publications:** *International Drug Report*, quarterly. Newsletter. Covers current reports on drug issues, especially those affecting drug control. Includes legal decisions and listing of new members. **Price:** included in membership dues. ISSN: 0148-4648. **Circulation:** 10,000 ● *International Narcotic Enforcement Officers Association—Directory*, annual. **Price:** included in membership dues. **Circulation:** 10,000 ● *Narc Officer*, bimonthly. Journal. Provides information on drug abuse and various means of drug control for narcotics enforcement officers, government officials, and others. **Price:** included in membership dues; $35.00 /year for nonmembers. ISSN: 0889-7794. **Circulation:** 10,000. **Advertising:** accepted. **Conventions/Meetings:** annual International Drug Conference - meeting (exhibits).

5742 ■ International Narcotics Interdiction Association (INIA)
2523 Sand Shore Dr.
Conroe, TX 77304
Ph: (936)447-6759
Free: (888)842-8432
Fax: (936)588-6463
E-mail: info@inia.org
URL: http://www.inia.org
Contact: Dick Kempshall, Exec. Dir.
Members: 1,000. **Membership Dues:** individual, $30 (annual). **Multinational. Description:** Aims to improve the operation of targeting narcotics traffickers. Seeks to uphold the professional standards of drug interdiction. Provides specialized interdiction training for narcotics professionals. **Awards:** INIA Scholarship. **Frequency:** annual. **Type:** scholarship. **Recipient:** for children of INIA members ● Interdiction Group of the Year. **Frequency:** annual. **Type:** recognition. **Recipient:** to an interdiction unit that has made a significant contribution to the field of narcotics interdiction ● Narcotics Interdiction Officer of the Year. **Frequency:** annual. **Type:** recognition. **Recipient:** to a distinguished member of the international law enforcement community who has shown dedicated service and personal achievement in drug interdiction duties. **Publications:** Newsletter. **Price:** free. **Conventions/Meetings:** annual conference, with training classes.

Foreign Policy

5743 ■ Foreign Policy Research Institute (FPRI)
1528 Walnut St., Ste.610
Philadelphia, PA 19102
Ph: (215)732-3774
Fax: (215)732-4401
E-mail: fpri@fpri.org
URL: http://www.fpri.org
Contact: Robert L. Freedman, Chm.
Founded: 1955. **Membership Dues:** subscribing, $35 (annual) ● friend, $75 (annual) ● student, $30 (annual) ● associate, $125 (annual) ● sponsor, $250 (annual) ● patron, $500 (annual) ● fellow, $1,000 (annual). **Multinational. Description:** Seeks to bring insights that serve as factors on the development of US policies on other nations. Conducts research and consultations on global issues that may have implications on US standing in the international community. **Funds:** Marvin Wachman Fund for International Education. **Subgroups:** History Academy. **Publications:** *America the Vulnerable*. Book. Contains essays by respected thinkers in the United States. **Price:** $20.00 for nonmembers; free to members ● *BackChannel*. Newsletter. Alternate Formats: online ● *ORBIS*, quarterly. Journal. Offers informative and insightful disclosure on the full range of topics relating to American foreign policy and national security. Alternate Formats: online ● Bulletins, 50/year. Contains findings of research staff and associated scholars. Alternate Formats: online.

Foreign Service

5744 ■ American Academy of Diplomacy (AAD)
1800 K St. NW, Ste.1014
Washington, DC 20006
Ph: (202)331-3721
Fax: (202)833-4555
E-mail: academy@academyofdiplomacy.org
URL: http://www.academyofdiplomacy.org
Contact: Ambassador Bruce Laingen, Pres.
Founded: 1983. **Members:** 100. **Membership Dues:** general, $250 (annual). **Staff:** 2. **Budget:** $150,000. **Description:** Individuals who have served in positions of major foreign affairs responsibility. Promotes high standards in American diplomacy. Works to: improve American diplomatic representation abroad; increase public appreciation of the contributions of diplomacy to U.S. national interest; study the conduct and content of American foreign policy. Conducts seminars and research programs; makes available material on the qualifications of prospective diplomats to the U.S. Senate. **Libraries:** **Type:** open to the public. **Awards:** Douglas Dillon Award. **Frequency:** annual. **Type:** recognition. **Recipient:** for distinguished writing on American diplomacy ● Philip Merrill Fellowship. **Frequency:** annual. **Type:** fellowship. **Recipient:** for the best essay on the practice of American diplomacy ● Walter and Leonore Annenberg Award for Excellence in Diplomacy. **Frequency:** annual. **Type:** grant. **Recipient:** for individual who made exemplary contributions to the field of American diplomacy. **Programs:** Ansary. **Publications:** *First Line of Defense: Ambassadors, Embassies and American Interests Abroad*. Book. Contains an assessment of Sec. Powell's first year in office. **Price:** $9.95 plus shipping and handling ● Newsletter, quarterly. **Circulation:** 200. Alternate Formats: online.

5745 ■ Diplomatic and Consular Officers, Retired (DACOR)
1801 F St. NW
Washington, DC 20006
Ph: (202)682-0500
Free: (800)344-9127
Fax: (202)842-3295
E-mail: dacor@dacorbacon.org
URL: http://www.dacorbacon.org
Contact: Richard McKee, Exec. Dir.
Founded: 1952. **Members:** 3,000. **Membership Dues:** retired or former officer, $85-$258 (annual) ● active duty officer, former spouse, $64-$129 (annual) ● widow and widower, $32-$48 (annual) ● life, $3,285. **Staff:** 5. **Budget:** $500,000. **Description:** Retired and active members of the Foreign Service and other federal government agencies who have served in officer positions principally concerned with international relations. Operates Bacon House for members, and DACOR Bacon House Foundation for educational and charitable purposes. **Libraries:** **Type:** reference. **Holdings:** 2,000. **Subjects:** international relations. **Awards:** Foreign Service Cup. **Frequency:** annual. **Type:** recognition. **Recipient:** for post-retirement activities to strengthen the Foreign Service. **Computer Services:** database ● mailing lists. **Committees:** Departmental Liaison; Education; Legislative; Library; Memorial; Program; Welfare. **Formerly:** (1952) Retired Foreign Service Officers Association. **Publications:** Bulletin, monthly ● Annual Report, annual.

Forensic Sciences

5746 ■ American Academy of Forensic Psychology (AAFP)
c/o Alan M. Goldstein, PhD
13 Arden Dr.
Hartsdale, NY 10530
Ph: (914)693-7760
Fax: (914)674-6312
E-mail: alanmg@optonline.net
URL: http://www.aafp.ws
Contact: Alan M. Goldstein PhD, Contact
Founded: 1980. **Members:** 160. **Membership Dues:** fellow, $35 (annual). **Staff:** 3. **Description:** Individuals who have passed the Diplomate Examination in Forensic Psychology of the American Board of Professional Psychology. (Forensic psychology is the application of scientific principles to aid the adjudication of legal matters.) Seeks to promote forensic psychology as a viable area of psychological study. Conducts continuing education programs and research into primary education and training needs. Facilitates communication and cooperation with other groups on issues of common concern. Provides standards for the provision of forensic psychological services. Maintains speakers' bureau. Sponsors presentations at annual convention of American Psychological Association. **Awards:** Distinguished Contributions Award. **Frequency:** annual. **Type:** recognition. **Committees:** Continuing Education; Professional Standards. **Affiliated With:** American Board of Professional Psychology; American Psychological Association. **Publications:** *Bulletin of the American Academy of Forensic Psychology*, annual. Alternate Formats: online ● *Directory of Diplomates*, annual. **Conventions/Meetings:** conference and workshop - 5/year.

5747 ■ American Academy of Forensic Sciences (AAFS)
410 N 21st St.
Colorado Springs, CO 80904-2712
Ph: (719)636-1100
Fax: (719)636-1993
E-mail: awarren@aafs.org
URL: http://www.aafs.org
Contact: Anne Warren, Exec. Dir.
Founded: 1948. **Members:** 6,000. **Membership Dues:** associate, regular, fellow, and trainee affiliate, $145 (annual) ● student affiliate, $55 (annual). **Staff:** 11. **Budget:** $2,300,000. **Description:** Represents criminalists, scientists, members of the bench and bar, pathologists, biologists, psychiatrists, examiners of questioned documents, toxicologists, odontologists, anthropologists, and engineers. Works to: encourage the study, improve the practice, elevate the standards, and advance the cause of the forensic sciences; improve the quality of scientific techniques,

tests, and criteria; plan, organize, and administer meetings, reports, and other projects for the stimulation and advancement of these and related purposes. Maintains Forensic Sciences Job Listing; conducts selected research for the government; offers forensic expert referral service. **Libraries: Type:** reference. **Awards:** Distinguished Fellows Award. **Frequency:** annual. **Type:** recognition ● Gradwohl Award. **Frequency:** annual. **Type:** recognition ● Regional Award. **Type:** recognition ● Section Award. **Type:** recognition. **Sections:** Criminalistics; Engineering Sciences; General; Jurisprudence; Odontology; Pathology and Biology; Physical Anthropology; Psychiatry and Behavioral Science; Questioned Documents; Toxicology. **Affiliated With:** Forensic Sciences Foundation. **Publications:** *Academy News*, bimonthly. Newsletter. **Advertising:** accepted. Alternate Formats: online ● *Journal of Forensic Sciences*, bimonthly. Features professional and scientific articles on forensics. **Price:** $410.00 /year for institutions; $265.00 /year for individuals. **Circulation:** 7,000. Alternate Formats: online ● Membership Directory, annual. **Advertising:** accepted. **Conventions/Meetings:** annual meeting (exhibits) - 2009 Feb. 16-21, Denver, CO; 2010 Feb. 22-27, Seattle, WA ● seminar and workshop.

5748 ■ American Association of Police Polygraphists (AAPP)

PO Box 657
Waynesville, OH 45068-0657
Free: (888)743-5479
Fax: (937)488-1046
E-mail: nom@policepolygraph.org
URL: http://www.policepolygraph.org
Contact: Julie Gerspacher, Office Mgr.

Founded: 1977. **Members:** 700. **Membership Dues:** in U.S., $100 (annual) ● outside U.S., $125 (annual). **Budget:** $45,000. **Regional Groups:** 5. **Description:** Represents individuals currently affiliated with a public criminal justice agency or military service in the profession of polygraphy (operation of the polygraph or "lie detector") and former law enforcement polygraphists who remain active in the field. Encourages cooperation among members. Increases polygraph proficiency. Promotes and maintains the highest standards of ethics. Aims to upgrade the profession. Provides a forum for the exchange of information. Conducts specialized education and research; sponsors seminars; compiles statistics. Operates quality control program for members on a case-by-case basis. Maintains speakers' bureau. **Awards: Type:** recognition. **Recipient:** for outstanding contributions to polygraphy ● William Buddy Sentner Scholarship Award. **Frequency:** annual. **Type:** scholarship. **Recipient:** for qualified graduating high school or currently attending college. **Publications:** *American Association of Police Polygraphists—Journal*, semiannual. Contains updates on using the polygraph for police investigation. Includes information on legislation and techniques, and employment opportunities. **Price:** included in membership dues. **Advertising:** accepted ● Membership Directory, annual. **Conventions/Meetings:** annual seminar.

5749 ■ American Board of Criminalistics (ABC)

PO Box 1123
Wausau, WI 54402-1123
Ph: (715)845-3684
Fax: (715)845-4156
E-mail: abcreg@dwave.net
URL: http://www.criminalistics.com
Contact: Michael Healy, Pres.

Founded: 1989. **Members:** 600. **Regional Groups:** 5. **National Groups:** 3. **Description:** Regional and national organizations of forensic scientists and criminalists. Offers certificates of Professional Competency in Criminalistics as well as in specialty disciplines of forensic biology, drug chemistry, fire debris analysis, and various areas of trace evidence examination. Works to establish professional standards and promote growth within the industry. Answers questions regarding the certification process. **Committees:** Accreditation; Appeals; By-Laws; Certificate; Credentials; Ethics; Examination; FAQ; Proficiency Review; Recertification; Training and Education. **Conventions/Meetings:** semiannual board meeting.

5750 ■ American Board of Forensic Document Examiners (ABFDE)

7887 San Felipe, Ste.122
Houston, TX 77063
Ph: (713)784-9537
E-mail: joyce.lauterbach@ci.irs.gov
URL: http://www.abfde.org
Contact: Joyce Lauterbach, Pres.

Founded: 1977. **Description:** Represents and supports qualified forensic scientists; provides program of certification in forensic document examination. **Committees:** Professional Review. **Publications:** *ASQDE Journal*. **Conventions/Meetings:** annual meeting - 2009 Feb. 16-21, Denver, CO; 2010 Feb. 22-27, Seattle, WA; 2011 Feb. 21-26, Chicago, IL.

5751 ■ American College of Forensic Examiners International (ACFEI)

2750 E Sunshine
Springfield, MO 65804
Ph: (417)881-3818
Free: (800)423-9737
Fax: (417)881-4702
E-mail: cao@acfei.com
URL: http://www.acfei.com
Contact: Robert L. O'Block PhD, Exec. Dir.

Founded: 1992. **Members:** 14,000. **Membership Dues:** standard, $145 (annual) ● international, $170 (annual) ● student, $45 (annual) ● international student, $70 (annual) ● life, $2,500. **Staff:** 20. **Budget:** $2,000,000. **Description:** Professionals in the field of forensic examination, including the following disciplines: accounting, accident reconstruction, criminology, crisis intervention, counselors, social work, nursing and law enforcement hypnosis, all medical fields, physics, psychiatry, psychology, and toxicology. Works to advance the profession of forensic examination through education, training, and certification. **Libraries: Type:** not open to the public; lending. **Holdings:** 1,000. **Subjects:** forensic examination. **Awards:** Eagle Award. **Frequency:** annual. **Type:** recognition. **Telecommunication Services:** electronic bulletin board, ForensicNet. **Boards:** Certification in Homeland Security; Examiners in Crisis Intervention; Forensic Accounting; Forensic Counselors; Forensic Dentistry; Forensic Engineering and Technology; Psychological Specialties; Recorded Evidence. **Formerly:** American Board of Forensic Examiners; American College of Forensic Examiners. **Publications:** *The Forensic Examiner*, quarterly. Journal. Includes scientific articles, case studies, and new research in various areas of forensic examination. **Price:** included in membership dues; $130.00 /year for nonmembers. **Circulation:** 20,000. **Advertising:** accepted. **Conventions/Meetings:** annual conference (exhibits).

5752 ■ American College of Forensic Psychiatry (ACFP)

PO Box 130458
Carlsbad, CA 92013-0458
Ph: (760)929-9777
Fax: (760)929-9803
E-mail: psychlaw@sover.net
URL: http://www.forensicpsychiatry.cc
Contact: Debra Miller, Dir.

Founded: 1981. **Members:** 200. **Membership Dues:** psychiatrist (resident), $100 (annual) ● psychiatrist (non-resident), $220 (annual). **Multinational. Description:** Represents psychiatrists who testify in civil and criminal cases. Serves as a professional association and educational providers. **Additional Websites:** http://www.forensicpsychonline.com. **Publications:** *American Journal of Forensic Psychiatry*, quarterly. Contains interfacing issues in psychiatry and law. **Price:** $75.00 /year for individuals; $95.00 /year for institutions; $26.00/copy. ISSN: 0163-1942. **Circulation:** 800. **Advertising:** accepted ● *Civil and Criminal Mental Health Case Law*. Book. **Price:** $80.00 ● *Psychology of Murder: Readings in Forensic Science*. Book. **Price:** $55.00. **Conventions/Meetings:** annual conference and symposium, continuing medical education.

5753 ■ American Polygraph Association (APA)

PO Box 8037
Chattanooga, TN 37414-0037
Ph: (423)892-3992
Free: (800)272-8037
Fax: (423)894-5435
E-mail: manager@polygraph.org
URL: http://www.polygraph.org
Contact: Robbie S. Bennett, Natl. Office Mgr.

Founded: 1966. **Members:** 2,300. **Membership Dues:** $150 (annual). **Staff:** 1. **State Groups:** 55. **Local Groups:** 1. **Description:** Sets qualifications for polygraph examiners. Establishes polygraph instrument standards. Provides consultation to federal, foreign, and academic institutions. Examines individuals deemed wrongly accused. **Libraries: Type:** reference. **Holdings:** archival material. **Awards:** Al and Dorothea Clinchard Award. **Frequency:** annual. **Type:** recognition. **Recipient:** for outstanding service in APA ● David L. Motsinger Award. **Frequency:** annual. **Type:** recognition. **Recipient:** for outstanding contribution and loyalty to APA ● J.J. Heger Award. **Frequency:** annual. **Type:** recognition. **Recipient:** for promoting advanced ideas and goals ● John E. Reid Award. **Frequency:** annual. **Type:** recognition. **Recipient:** for distinguished achievements in relation with the polygraph field ● Leonarde Keeler Award. **Frequency:** annual. **Type:** recognition. **Recipient:** for long and distinguished service in the polygraph field ● William L. Bennett Memorial Award. **Frequency:** annual. **Type:** recognition. **Recipient:** for excellent display of ability on behalf of APA interest. **Committees:** Awards; Continuing Education/Certification; Educational Accreditation; Ethics and Grievance; International Membership Liaison; Legislation; Public Relations and Information; Research and Development. **Formed by Merger of:** (1994) American Academy of Polygraph Examiners; Academy of Scientific Interrogation. **Publications:** *American Polygraph Association—Membership Roster*, annual. Directory. Lists members arranged geographically. **Price:** $40.00/year. **Circulation:** 3,000. **Advertising:** accepted ● *American Polygraph Association—Newsletter*, bimonthly. Provides information on the detection of deception featuring articles on current court cases, technical interest cases, law changes, and seminars. **Price:** included in membership dues; $100.00 for members; $125.00 for nonmembers. **Circulation:** 3,600. **Advertising:** accepted ● *Lie Detector Test-Marston*. **Price:** $20.00 for nonmembers; $12.00 for members ● *Polygraph*, quarterly. Journal. Features articles on polygraph operations, research, history, psychology, physiology, instrumentation, law, and training. Includes abstracts. **Price:** included in membership dues; $100.00 /year for members; $125.00 /year for nonmembers. **Circulation:** 3,600. **Advertising:** accepted. Alternate Formats: microform ● *Polygraph: Issues and Answers*. **Price:** $10.00 for members; $15.00 for nonmembers ● *Quick Reference Guide to Polygraph Admissibility*. **Conventions/Meetings:** annual seminar and workshop (exhibits) - usually July/August ● seminar ● workshop.

5754 ■ American Society of Crime Laboratory Directors (ASCLD)

139K Tech. Dr.
Garner, NC 27529
Ph: (919)773-2044
Fax: (919)773-2602
E-mail: office@ascld.org
URL: http://www.ascld.org
Contact: Susan Scholl, Membership Chair

Founded: 1974. **Members:** 350. **Membership Dues:** retired, $50 (annual) ● regular, $100 (annual) ● affiliate, $75 (annual). **Budget:** $30,000. **Description:** Directors of crime laboratories or crime laboratory systems. Purposes are: to promote the common professional interest of its members; to promote and foster the development of crime laboratory management principles and techniques; to acquire, preserve and disseminate information related to the utilization of crime laboratories; to maintain and improve communications among crime laboratory directors; and to promote, encourage and maintain the highest standards of practice in the field of crime laboratory services. Monitors legislation affecting forensic science (forensic science refers to the application of science to problems at law) at the state and federal levels. Issues policy statements on areas of interest to forensic scientists. **Awards: Type:** scholarship. **Recipient:** for forensic science students. **Computer Services:** Mailing lists, of members. **Committees:** ABC Liaison; Bylaws; Criminal Justice; Education and Training; Ethical Practices; Health and Safety; Historical; International Liaison; Laboratory Facilities; Management Survey; Membership; Newsletter; Nominating; Proficiency Advisory Program; Publications; Strategic Planning. **Publications:** *ASCLD Newsletter*, quarterly. **Circulation:** 350. **Advertising:** accepted. Alternate Formats: online ● *Crime Laboratory Digest*, quarterly ● Manual ● Membership Directory, annual. **Price:** free for members ● Report, annual. Describes workload survey of forensic labs. **Conventions/Meetings:** annual symposium - usually September.

5755 ■ American Society of Questioned Document Examiners (ASQDE)
PO Box 18298
Long Beach, CA 90807
Ph: (562)901-3376
Fax: (562)901-3378
E-mail: webeditor@asqde.org
URL: http://www.asqde.org
Contact: Howard C. Rile, Pres.

Founded: 1942. **Members:** 131. **Membership Dues:** professional, $100 (annual). **Staff:** 6. **Multinational. Description:** Professional examiners of questioned documents in private practice and public service. Promotes justice through discovery and proof of facts relating to handwriting, typewriting, ink, paper, and other problems concerning documents. Fosters scientific research, development of scientific instruments and processes, and improvement of methods and procedures. Promotes ethical, technical, and educational standards in document examination and court testimony. **Libraries: Type:** reference. **Holdings:** 1,000; archival material, books, business records, periodicals. **Subjects:** forensic document examination. **Awards:** Albert S. Osborn Award of Excellence. **Frequency:** annual. **Type:** recognition. **Recipient:** for distinction in activities such as professional research or literary accomplishments which advance the field of questioned document examination and for service to the ASQDE over a long period of time. **Committees:** Annual General Meeting; Ethics; Evaluations and Examinations; Finance; Journal; Library; Membership and Credentials; Nominating; Society Communications; Strategic Planning. **Affiliated With:** American Board of Forensic Document Examiners. **Publications:** *Journal of the American Society of Questioned Document Examiners*, semiannual. Includes research in forensic document examination. **Price:** $40.00 individual; $110.00 agency/distribution; $85.00 individual international; $125.00 agency/distribution international. ISSN: 1524-7287. **Circulation:** 200. Alternate Formats: online. Also Cited As: *JASQDE*. **Conventions/Meetings:** annual meeting, for forensic document examiners, by invitation only (exhibits).

5756 ■ Association of Forensic DNA Analysts and Administrators (AFDAA)
Univ. of North Texas Hea. Sci. Center
3500 Camp Bowie Blvd.
Fort Worth, TX 76107
Ph: (817)735-5107
Fax: (817)735-5016
E-mail: jwarren@hsc.unt.edu
URL: http://www.afdaa.org
Contact: Joseph Warren, Chm.

Membership Dues: general, $20 (annual). **Description:** Represents professionals engaged in the forensic aspects of DNA analysis for the judicial system. Provides a forum for the exchange of ideas and information among forensic DNA scientists. **Conventions/Meetings:** semiannual meeting - usually January and July.

5757 ■ Association of Forensic Document Examiners (AFDE)
PO Box 31402
Cleveland, OH 44131
E-mail: expert@afde.org
URL: http://www.afde.org
Contact: Bonnie Schwid, Pres.

Founded: 1986. **Members:** 45. **Membership Dues:** general, $175 (annual) ● certified, $175 (annual) ● associate, $175 (annual) ● international, $75 (annual) ● affiliate, $75 (annual). **Multinational. Description:** Represents forensic document examiners and students of document examination. Sponsors annual continuing education conferences and offers a certification program. **Libraries: Type:** not open to the public. **Subjects:** forensic analysis, handwriting identification, question documents. **Publications:** *Journal of Forensic Document Examination*, annual. Includes case histories and technical papers and research. **Price:** $33.00 in U.S. and Canada; $36.00 outside U.S. and Canada. ISSN: 0895-0849. **Conventions/Meetings:** annual Continuing Education - symposium.

5758 ■ Association of Forensic Quality Assurance Managers (AFQAM)
c/o Suzanne Smith, Sec./Membership Chair
Fed. Bur. of Investigation
2501 Investigation Pkwy., Rm. 1115
Quantico, VA 22135
Ph: (703)632-8294
Fax: (703)632-8285
E-mail: membership@afqam.org
URL: http://www.afqam.org
Contact: Deborah Friedman, Pres.

Members: 142. **Membership Dues:** general, $50 (annual). **Multinational. Description:** Promotes and provides quality assurance support to the forensic science community. Promotes standardized practices and professionalism in quality assurance management for the forensic community. Supports and enhances quality assurance practices to provide the criminal justice system with the highest quality of laboratory results and service. **Telecommunication Services:** electronic mail, president@afqam.org.

5759 ■ Evidence Photographers International Council (EPIC)
229 Peachtree St. NE, No. 2200
Atlanta, GA 30303
Ph: (404)614-6406
Free: (866)868-EPIC
E-mail: cwerner@evidencephotographers.com
URL: http://www.epic-photo.org
Contact: Claire Werner, Mgr.

Founded: 1968. **Members:** 2,500. **Membership Dues:** active, $45-$100 (annual) ● sustaining, $100-$175 (annual). **Staff:** 3. **Budget:** $100,000. **Description:** Law enforcement and civil evidence photographers; others in related fields. Objectives are to: aid in the worldwide advancement of forensic photography; assist in research and development of new techniques; enhance professional education; inform members of new procedures. Maintains speakers' bureau. Offers certification upon satisfactory completion of an oral or written examination by a three-member panel, receipt of a minimum of 30 prints for review, and a $150 application fee. Provides an honors program to recognize those who have shown expertise in the field of forensic photography, and service to the Council. Sponsors the EPIC Witness Referral Service. **Libraries: Type:** reference. **Subjects:** evidence photography. **Awards:** R.C. Hakanson Annual Award. **Frequency:** annual. **Type:** fellowship. **Recipient:** for an outstanding photographer. **Committees:** Certification; Education; National Promotions. **Publications:** *Evidence Photographers International Council—Directory of Members*, semiannual. Membership Directory. **Circulation:** 2,500 ● *Evidence Photographers International Council—Newsletter*, semiannual. Alternate Formats: online ● *Journal of Evidence Photography*, semiannual. Contains articles, photographs, and techniques relating to the practice of forensic photography. **Price:** free for members; $5.00 /year for nonmembers. **Circulation:** 2,500. **Advertising:** accepted ● *Outline for Standard Crime Scene Photography* ● *Standards for Evidence Photography Criminal and Civil*. Booklet. **Price:** $7.95/copy. **Conventions/Meetings:** semiannual School of Evidence Photography - seminar (exhibits) ● periodic workshop.

5760 ■ Forensic Expert Witness Association (FEWA)
2549 Eastbluff Dr., No. 497
Newport Beach, CA 92660
Ph: (949)640-9903
Free: (888)322-3231
Fax: (949)640-9911
E-mail: info@forensic.org
URL: http://forensic.org
Contact: Mark McDonald, Pres.

Founded: 1996. **Membership Dues:** regular, $245 (annual) ● associate, $195 (annual) ● affiliate, $345 (annual). **Local Groups:** 4. **Description:** Encourages professional development among forensic consultants in all fields of forensic science. Provides an effective referral system that brings together the client and the appropriate member-consultant. Develops a system of standards and ethics, policies and procedures, and other tools needed in the course of forensic work. **Computer Services:** Information services, forensic resources. **Committees:** Education; Public Relations. **Publications:** *Expert Witness*, annual. Directory ● Newsletter, quarterly. Alternate Formats: online.

5761 ■ Forensic Sciences Foundation (FSF)
410 N 21st St.
Colorado Springs, CO 80904
Ph: (719)636-1100
Fax: (719)636-1993
E-mail: awarren@aafs.org
URL: http://www.aafs.org
Contact: Anne H. Warren BS, Exec. Dir.

Founded: 1969. **Staff:** 10. **Budget:** $75,000. **Nonmembership. Description:** Purposes are to: conduct research in the procedures and standards utilized in the practice of forensic sciences; develop and implement useful educational and training programs and methods of benefit to forensic sciences; conduct programs of public education concerning issues of importance to the forensic sciences; engage in activities which will promote, encourage, and assist the development of the forensic sciences. Provides referral service for forensic scientists. Compiles statistics. Operates the Forensic Sciences Foundation Press. **Libraries: Type:** reference. **Holdings:** biographical archives. **Awards:** Acorn Grants. **Frequency:** annual. **Type:** grant. **Recipient:** for AAFS members and affiliates ● Emerging Forensic Scientist Award. **Frequency:** annual. **Type:** recognition. **Recipient:** for paper presentation at the annual meeting of the American Academy of Forensic Sciences, judged by a panel of experts ● FSF Student Travel Grant Award. **Frequency:** annual. **Type:** grant. **Recipient:** for a student in FS; based on essay submission ● Jan Bashinski Criminalistics Graduate Thesis Assistance Grant. **Frequency:** annual. **Type:** grant. **Recipient:** for graduate students in order to complete his/her thesis or independent research project required for a graduate degree in criminalistic forensic sciences ● Lucas Grants. **Frequency:** annual. **Type:** grant. **Recipient:** for AAFS members and affiliates. **Affiliated With:** American Academy of Forensic Sciences. **Conventions/Meetings:** annual meeting (exhibits).

5762 ■ Independent Association of Questioned Document Examiners (IAQDE)
c/o Julie C. Edison
PO Box 1231
McLean, VA 22101-1231
Ph: (703)437-9801
E-mail: jjberrie@comcast.net
URL: http://www.iaqde.org
Contact: Jean Joanne Berrie-Perrino, Pres.

Founded: 1969. **Members:** 175. **Description:** Persons who are qualified in document examination, script-writing, and type-writing with photographic evidence. Aims to promote justice through the discovery and proof of the facts relating to questioned documents. Objectives are to: maintain the ethical, educational, and scientific standards of this profession; pursue scientific research, development and adaptation of scientific instruments and processes, and the advancement of skills and knowledge in the field of questioned document examination; continue comprehensive and thorough study as a basis for advancement of scientific skills; create confidence in the profession of questioned document examination through professional competency, integrity, good moral character, and strict ethical standards; promote through lectures, papers, and other appropriate means a better understanding of document examiners by the public, bar, and judiciary. Conducts national and regional workshops. Provides qualified members to assist in court cases involving questioned documents. Conducts examination for certification upon qualified members. Offers annual advancement examinations. Maintains library. **Committees:** Certification; Education; Ethics; Evidence Photography; Legal Procedures; Research. **Publications:** *IAQDE Membership Directory and By-Laws*, annual ● Journal, quarterly ● Newsletter, monthly. **Conventions/ Meetings:** annual conference and seminar (exhibits).

5763 ■ International Association for Identification (IAI)
2535 Pilot Knob Rd., Ste.117
Mendota Heights, MN 55120-1120
Ph: (651)681-8566
Fax: (651)681-8443
E-mail: iaisecty@theiai.org
URL: http://www.theiai.org
Contact: Joseph P. Polski, COO

Founded: 1915. **Members:** 5,000. **Membership Dues:** individual in U.S., $60 (annual) ● individual outside U.S., $50 (annual) ● sustaining in U.S., $600 (annual) ● sustaining outside U.S., $500 (annual). **Staff:** 12. **Budget:** $750,000. **Regional Groups:** 34. **State Groups:** 35. **Description:** Individuals engaged in forensic identification, investigation, and scientific crime detection. Strives to improve methods of scientific identification techniques used in criminal investigations. **Libraries: Type:** reference. **Holdings:** 500. **Awards:** Dondero Award. **Frequency:** annual. **Type:** recognition ● Good of Association Award. **Type:** recognition. **Boards:** Forensic Art Certification; Latent Print Certification; Voice Print and Acoustic Analysis Certification, Crime Scene Certification. **Subcommittees:** Bloodstain Pattern Analysis; Crime Scene Investigation; Fingerprint Identification; Firearms and Toolmark Identification; Footwork/Tiretrack; Forensic Art; Forensic Laboratory Analysis; Forensic Photography and Electronic Imaging; Innovative Techniques; Polygraph Examination; Questioned Documents. **Absorbed:** (1980) International Association of Voice Identification. **Formerly:** (1920) International Association for Criminal Identification. **Publications:** *ANSI-1 Fingerprint Identification Benchmark Standards*. Manual. **Price:** $48.00 ● *ANSI-2 Fingerprint Identification on Glossary of Terms and Acronyms*. **Price:** $48.00 ● *Composite Art Manual*. **Price:** $38.00 ● *Forensic Art Manual* ● *Inked Fingerprint Training Outline* ● *Journal of Forensic Identification*, bimonthly. **Price:** free for members; $140.00 /year for individuals; $170.00 /year for institutions and libraries in North America. ISSN: 0895-173X. **Circulation:** 4,600 ● *Latent Fingerprint Training Outline*. **Price:** $28.00 ● Membership Directory, annual. **Price:** included in membership dues. **Circulation:** 4,600. **Advertising:** accepted. **Conventions/Meetings:** annual seminar, for training purposes (exhibits) - 2008 Aug. 17-23, Louisville, KY.

5764 ■ International Society of Stress Analysts (ISSA)
Address Unknown since 2008

Founded: 1973. **Members:** 50. **Membership Dues:** $49 (annual). **Staff:** 2. **Budget:** $2,000. **Regional Groups:** 2. **Languages:** Arabic, English, French, Spanish. **Multinational. Description:** Jurists, attorneys, physicians, private detectives, law enforcement personnel, security personnel, scholar/ researchers, and individuals interested in stress analysis for lie detection/truth verification. Purposes are to: promote the science of psychological stress evaluation and the efficient administration of justice; aid indigent persons, without cost, who may be wrongfully accused; develop and maintain high educational standards; observe and evaluate training programs for the purpose of accreditation and endorsement. Sponsors and certifies schools; offers workshops and research and educational programs; conducts forums. Offers expertise, consultation, and advice; invites inquiries. **Libraries: Type:** reference. **Holdings:** 35; periodicals. **Subjects:** criminal justice. **Awards: Type:** recognition. **Computer Services:** Mailing lists. **Committees:** Research and Validation. **Formerly:** National Society of Stress Analysts. **Publications:** *Stressing Comments*, monthly. Journal. Covers information on current legislation, research, and professional activities of members. **Price:** included in membership dues. **Advertising:** accepted ● Membership Directory, annual. **Conventions/ Meetings:** competition ● annual conference ● semiannual seminar.

5765 ■ National Association of Document Examiners (NADE)
c/o Barbara Downer, CDE, Pres.
1734 E 30th Ave. N
Oxford, KS 67119
Ph: (620)455-9910
Free: (877)288-9410
Fax: (620)455-9910
E-mail: documentexam@earthlink.net
URL: http://www.documentexaminers.org
Contact: Barbara Downer CDE, Pres.

Founded: 1980. **Members:** 140. **Membership Dues:** professional, $100 (annual). **Description:** Handwriting experts who examine signatures and documents to determine authenticity or identify the originator. Conducts educational and research programs. Maintains speakers' bureau and referral service; compiles statistics. Certifies Document Examiners. Awards diplomatic status to deserving members. **Libraries: Type:** reference. **Holdings:** 200; archival material, books. **Subjects:** document examination. **Awards:** Certified Document Examiner, Diplomate. **Frequency:** 3/year. **Type:** recognition. **Recipient:** for service and experience. **Committees:** Diplomate; Education; Ethics; Professional-Certification. **Publications:** *Communique*, bimonthly. Newsletter. **Price:** free for members. **Circulation:** 200. **Advertising:** accepted. Alternate Formats: online ● *The NADE Journal*, quarterly. **Price:** free for members; $50.00 /year for nonmembers. **Circulation:** 200. **Conventions/Meetings:** annual conference (exhibits) - always spring.

5766 ■ National Forensic Center (NFC)
PO Box 270529
San Diego, CA 92198-2529
Free: (800)735-6660
Fax: (858)487-7747
E-mail: info@national-experts.com
URL: http://www.national-experts.com
Contact: Mark Haslam, Publication Dir.

Founded: 1979. **Members:** 5,000. **Staff:** 4. **For-Profit. Description:** Expert witnesses and litigation consultants who serve attorneys, insurance companies, and government agencies. Trains consultants to work with attorneys and to testify in court; trains individuals to serve as expert witnesses and litigation consultants. Makes speakers available upon request. Compiles statistics on experts' fees. **Computer Services:** Online services, access to Lexis-Nexis, and Westlaw. **Publications:** *The Expert and the Law*, bimonthly. Newsletter ● *Forensic Services Directory*, annual. Alternate Formats: CD-ROM ● *Guide to Fees*, annual ● *Marketing Your Expert Witness Practice* ● *National Directory of Expert Witnesses*, annual. Includes more than 1,500 expert listings nationwide in over 400 categories of technical, scientific and medical expertise. **Price:** $45.00 each. Alternate Formats: online ● Also publishes a catalogue of Forensic books. **Conventions/Meetings:** annual National Conference of Expert Witnesses, Litigation Consultants and Attorneys (exhibits) - always 1st weekend of November ● periodic seminar.

5767 ■ Society of Forensic Toxicologists (SOFT)
One MacDonald Center
1 N MacDonald St., Ste.15
Mesa, AZ 85201
Ph: (480)839-9106
Free: (888)866-7638
Fax: (480)839-9106
E-mail: trohrig@sedgwick.gov
URL: http://www.soft-tox.org
Contact: Timothy Rohrig PhD, Pres.

Founded: 1970. **Members:** 425. **Membership Dues:** full, associate, $50 (annual) ● student affiliate, $15 (annual). **Description:** Scientists who analyze tissue and body fluids for drugs and poisons and interpret the information for judicial purposes. Objectives are to establish uniform qualifications and requirements for certification of forensic toxicologists and promote support mechanisms for continued certification; to stimulate research and development; to provide review board for cases involving differences of professional opinion; to act on administrative and career problems affecting forensic toxicologists. Serves as clearinghouse; conducts proficiency testing programs; provides information on case histories and job opportunities. Sponsors American Board of Forensic Toxicology. **Awards:** Forensic Toxicology Educational Research Award. **Frequency:** annual. **Type:** recognition. **Committees:** Awards; Bylaws; Continuing Education and Training; Drugs and Driving; Ethics; Laboratory Guidelines; Nominating; Policy and Procedures. **Publications:** *Society of Forensic Toxicologists Directory*, triennial ● *Special Issue of Journal of Analytical Toxicology*, annual. **Price:** $120. 00/copy. **Advertising:** accepted ● *Tox Talk Newsletter*, quarterly. **Price:** $15.00 /year for nonmembers. **Conventions/Meetings:** annual meeting (exhibits) - always September/October ● workshop.

Freedom

5768 ■ Free Nation Foundation - Critical Institutions (FNF-CI)
111 W Corbin St.
Hillsborough, NC 27278
E-mail: richard.o.hammer@gmail.com
URL: http://freenation.org
Contact: Richard O. Hammer, Pres.

Founded: 2001. **Description:** Dedicated to the plan outlined in the book Toward a Free Nation, by Richard O. Hammer. Supports a small scholarship program. **Formerly:** (2001) Free Nation Foundation.

Fundraising

5769 ■ National Association of State Charity Officials (NASCO)
c/o Jody Wahl, Pres.
Off. of the Attorney Gen.
Bremer Tower
445 Minnesota St., 12th Fl.
St. Paul, MN 55101-2131
Ph: (651)297-4607
E-mail: jody.wahl@state.mn.us
URL: http://www.nasconet.org
Contact: Jody Wahl, Pres.

Founded: 1978. **Description:** Represents state officials who regulate charities under state statutes. Organized to facilitate administration of state laws regarding charitable solicitations and to facilitate regulation by developing recommended uniform formats for reporting charitable solicitations. **Conventions/Meetings:** annual seminar, in conjunction with the National Association of Attorney Generals.

5770 ■ WISH List
333 N Fairfax St., Ste.302
Alexandria, VA 22314
Ph: (703)778-5550
Free: (800)756-WISH
Fax: (703)778-5554

E-mail: wish@thewishlist.org
URL: http://www.thewishlist.org
Contact: Pat Giardina Carpenter, Pres.
Founded: 1992. **Membership Dues:** basic, $100 (annual) ● advocate, $250 (annual) ● champion, $500 (annual) ● under age of 30, $50 (annual) ● student, $20 (annual) ● cyber, $5 (annual) ● team, $1,000 (annual) ● trustee, $2,500 (annual) ● benefactor, $5,000 (annual) ● contributor, $10,000 (annual). **Description:** Fundraising network for pro-choice Republican women candidates in America. **Also Known As:** WISH.

Gambling

5771 ■ National Indian Gaming Association (NIGA)
224 Second St. SE
Washington, DC 20003
Ph: (202)546-7711
Fax: (202)546-1755
E-mail: estevens@indiangaming.org
URL: http://www.indiangaming.org
Contact: Ernest L. Stevens Jr., Chm.
Founded: 1985. **Members:** 205. **Membership Dues:** tribe not engaged in gaming, $800 (annual) ● gaming tribe (with gross annual revenue of less than 10 million), $1,500 (annual) ● gaming tribe (with gross annual revenue of 10-25 million), $3,500 (annual) ● gaming tribe (with gross annual revenue of 25-50 million), $7,500 (annual) ● gaming tribe (with gross annual revenue of 50-100 million), $15,000 (annual) ● gaming tribe (with gross annual revenue over 100 million), $25,000 (annual). **Staff:** 15. **Budget:** $2,000,000. **Description:** Indian nations operating gambling establishments are members; tribes, organizations, and businesses supporting Indian gaming establishments are associate members. Works to protect and preserve the welfare of tribes seeking to achieve economic self-sufficiency through the operation of gaming establishments. Seeks to expand political self-determination of Indian nations. Cooperates with government agencies in the formulation and application of laws and regulations applicable to Indian gaming. Provides technical assistance and other support to tribal gaming establishments. Conducts educational programs. **Publications:** *Handbook for Tribal Leaders*. **Price:** $20.00 for members; $40.00 for nonmembers ● *Indian Gaming Integrity*. Video. **Price:** $35.00 ● *2005 Indian Gaming Resource Directory*. Includes listing of regional gaming associations, Indian gaming facilities etc. **Price:** $30.00 for members; $55.00 for nonmembers ● Annual Report, annual. **Price:** $20.00 for members; $40.00 for nonmembers. **Conventions/Meetings:** annual Election Meeting - conference, includes annual election, membership meeting, regional caucuses and informative workshops (exhibits) ● periodic executive committee meeting ● periodic Legislative Meetings ● periodic seminar ● annual trade show and convention.

5772 ■ North American Gaming Regulators Association (NAGRA)
1000 Westgate Dr., Ste.252
St. Paul, MN 55114
Ph: (651)203-7244
Fax: (651)290-2266
E-mail: don.dutton@state.nm.us
URL: http://www.nagra.org
Contact: Don Dutton, Pres.
Founded: 1984. **Members:** 120. **Membership Dues:** regular, $425 (annual) ● trades affiliate, $650 (annual). **Staff:** 2. **Regional Groups:** 4. **Description:** Domestic and foreign governmental agencies, bureaus, commissions, and Native American tribes and First Nations charged with the regulation and enforcement of any type of gambling. Works for the mutual exchange of regulatory techniques for training enforcement personnel; provides a medium for communication of common problems; offers resources to states enacting legislation; speaks on matters concerning non-profit and related gambling. **Committees:** Casino and Electronic Gaming; Charitable Gaming; Indian Gaming; Internet Gaming; Investigators; Policy. **Formerly:** National Association of Gambling Regulatory Agencies. **Publications:** *Coin Operator Standards*. Report. Alternate Formats: online ● *NAGRA News*, 2-4/year. Newsletter. Contains news on upcoming conferences and training courses and association events. **Circulation:** 1,600. Alternate Formats: online ● *Standards on Bingo*. Report. Alternate Formats: online ● *Standards on Pull-Tabs*. Report. Alternate Formats: online. **Conventions/Meetings:** semiannual conference and seminar, includes training courses ● annual conference.

Gay/Lesbian

5773 ■ FireFlag/EMS
208 W 13th St.
New York, NY 10011
Ph: (917)885-0127
E-mail: firefitz289@hotmail.com
URL: http://www.fireflag.net
Contact: Mike Vissichelli, Pres.
Membership Dues: regular, $25 (annual). **Description:** Aims at uniting, empowering and protecting the interests and the general well being of gay, lesbian, bisexual and transgender firefighters, fire officers, emergency medical technicians, officers and paramedics who are active members and retired members of recognized fire and rescue services. **Computer Services:** Information services, news and events ● mailing lists, information distribution ● online services, message board.

Government

5774 ■ Association of Pacific Island Legislatures (APIL)
181 E Marine Corps Dr.
Carl Rose Bldg., Ste.207
Hagatna, GU 96910
Ph: (671)472-2719
Fax: (671)473-3004
E-mail: apil@guam.net
URL: http://www.pacificlegislatures.com
Founded: 1981. **Members:** 12. **Membership Dues:** legislative, $10,000 (annual). **Staff:** 1. **Budget:** $120,000. **Regional Groups:** 12. **Multinational. Description:** Works to organize a permanent associate of mutual assistance by representatives of the people of the Pacific Islands. **Conventions/Meetings:** annual board meeting.

5775 ■ International Association of Clerks, Recorders, Election Officials and Treasurers (IACREOT)
2400 Augusta Dr., Ste.250
Houston, TX 77057
Ph: (630)407-5600 (970)328-8868
Free: (800)890-7368
Fax: (713)789-1897
E-mail: tjsthree@msn.com
URL: http://www.iacreot.com
Contact: Mr. Tony J. Sirvello III, Exec. Dir.
Founded: 1971. **Members:** 1,700. **Membership Dues:** full, $145 (annual) ● associate, $95 (annual) ● corporate, $500 (annual). **Staff:** 1. **Budget:** $400,000. **Description:** Clerks, recorders, election officials, treasurers, and other officials performing similar duties as elected or appointed officials performing similar duties, including federal, state, county and city government officials. Provides a forum for the exchange of ideas among officials and a unified voice for members before state legislatures, county and city boards, and U.S. Congress in formulating laws and policies. Sponsors Chancellors Certificate in Public Administration Program in cooperation with the University of Missouri and offers Continuing Education Credits through seminars and workshops. Offers tradeshow for government organizations. **Awards:** Anita Rodeheaver Scholarship. **Frequency:** annual. **Type:** monetary. **Recipient:** to a child or grandchild of an IACREOT member. **Publications:** *The IACREOT News*, quarterly. Magazine. **Conventions/Meetings:** annual conference and trade show - 2008 July 19-23, Phoenix, AZ; 2009 July 7-11, Spokane, WA.

5776 ■ Worldwide Assurance for Employees of Public Agencies (WAEPA)
7651 Leesburg Pike
Falls Church, VA 22043
Ph: (703)790-8010
Free: (800)368-3484
Fax: (703)790-4606
E-mail: info@waepa.org
URL: http://www.waepa.org
Contact: John Seal, Pres.
Founded: 1943. **Members:** 30,000. **Staff:** 10. **Budget:** $1,700,000. **Description:** Represents federal civilian employees. Provides group life, accidental death and dismemberment, dependent group life insurance coverage and long-term care insurance to federal civilian employees at reasonable cost. **Formerly:** War Agencies Employee Protection Agency. **Publications:** *WAEPA News*, quarterly. Newsletter. **Conventions/Meetings:** annual board meeting, board of directors meets off-site - usually July.

Government Accountability

5777 ■ Association of Inspectors General
Historic Carpenters' Hall
320 Chestnut St.
Philadelphia, PA 19106
Ph: (360)265-7785
Fax: (360)638-2686
E-mail: roland@sandpiperconsulting.com
URL: http://www.inspectorsgeneral.org
Contact: Roland M. Malan, Exec. Dir.
Founded: 1996. **Membership Dues:** regular, $50 (annual) ● agency (up to 6 people), $250 (annual) ● student, $15 (annual). **Description:** Fosters public accountability and integrity in the general areas of prevention, examination, investigation, audit, detection, elimination, and prosecution of fraud, waste, and abuse through policy research and analysis. Seeks to standardize practices, policies, conduct, and ethics. Encourages professional development by providing and sponsoring educational programs and establishing professional qualifications, certifications, and licensing of officials. **Publications:** Newsletter, quarterly. Alternate Formats: online.

Government Employees

5778 ■ American Association of Port Authorities (AAPA)
1010 Duke St.
Alexandria, VA 22314-3589
Ph: (703)684-5700
Fax: (703)684-6321
E-mail: info@aapa-ports.org
URL: http://www.aapa-ports.org
Contact: Kurt J. Nagle, Pres.
Founded: 1912. **Members:** 500. **Membership Dues:** sustaining, $1,295 (annual). **Staff:** 16. **Budget:** $2,000,000. **Languages:** Spanish. **Multinational. Description:** Port administrative organizations of the U.S., Canada, the Caribbean, and Latin America; sustaining and associate members are private firms with an interest in port development, water transportation, or accessorial services. Holds status as a cooperating organization with the Organization of American States, particularly the Economic and Social Council, in relation to hemispheric port development from an economic standpoint. Conducts education and training seminars; sponsors environmental improvement and communications competitions; compiles statistics. **Libraries: Type:** reference. **Awards: Type:** recognition. **Telecommunication Services:** electronic mail, cosullivan@aapa-ports.org. **Committees:** Cruise; Facilities Engineering; Harbors, Navigation and Environment; Information Technology; Latin American Coordinating; Law Review; Maritime Economic Development; Operations; Port Finance; Port Planning and Research;

Projects and Publications; Public Relations; Safety; Security. **Publications:** *Committee Reports*, annual ● *Finance Survey* ● *Graphics Manual* ● *Mitigation Handbook*. Directory ● *Seaports Magazine*, semiannual ● *Seaports of the Americas*, annual. Directory. **Conventions/Meetings:** annual convention (exhibits).

5779 ■ National Association of Farm Service Agency County Office Employees (NASCOE)
c/o Jeanne Monday, Membership Chair
PO Box 336
Charleston, MS 38921
Ph: (662)647-8857
Fax: (662)647-5673
E-mail: jjmonday@bellsouth.net
URL: http://www.nascoe.org
Contact: Bonnie Heinzman, Pres.
Founded: 1959. **Members:** 9,000. **Membership Dues:** full, $40 (annual) ● associate, $20 (annual). **State Groups:** 50. **Description:** County office employees. Promotes effective operation of county agencies; facilitates cooperation between county, state, municipal, and federal authorities. Represents members in negotiations with federal government agencies; seeks to secure optimal conditions of employment for county employees. Provides group benefits to members including insurance and travel discounts, vision care programs, and legal and credit union services. **Awards:** Distinguished Service Awards. **Type:** recognition. **Recipient:** for members who have made outstanding contributions to the progress and advancement of the association ● Professional Improvement Awards. **Type:** recognition. **Recipient:** for members who take sufficient advantage of educational opportunities available to them ● **Frequency:** periodic. **Type:** scholarship. **Recipient:** for member's spouse, member's child, or member's legal dependent. **Committees:** Awards; Benefits; Emblems; Legislative; Membership; Publicity. **Formerly:** (2004) National Association of County Office Employees. **Publications:** Newsletter, bimonthly. **Price:** included in membership dues. **Circulation:** 11,000. **Conventions/Meetings:** convention.

Health Law

5780 ■ American Academy of Psychiatry and the Law (AAPL)
One Regency Dr.
PO Box 30
Bloomfield, CT 06002-0030
Ph: (860)242-5450
Free: (800)331-1389
Fax: (860)286-0787
E-mail: execoff@aapl.org
URL: http://www.aapl.org
Contact: Jacquelyn T. Coleman CAE, Exec. Dir.
Founded: 1969. **Members:** 1,500. **Membership Dues:** general, $250 (annual) ● resident, $55 ● corresponding, $50. **Staff:** 6. **Budget:** $500,000. **Regional Groups:** 11. **Description:** Psychiatrists who are members in good standing of the American Psychiatric Association or the American Academy of Child and Adolescent Psychiatry. Seeks to exchange ideas and experience in those areas where psychiatry and the law overlap; develop standards of practice in the relationship of psychiatry to the law and encourage the development of training programs for psychiatrists seeking skill and knowledge in this area; stimulate and encourage research in the field; improve relationships between psychiatrists and other professionals in the field; inform the public of problems in the area of psychiatry and the law and the potential contributions from psychiatry. **Awards:** Golden Apple Award. **Frequency:** annual. **Type:** recognition. **Recipient:** for outstanding contributions in the field ● Red Apple. **Frequency:** annual. **Type:** recognition ● Seymour Pollack Award. **Frequency:** annual. **Type:** recognition. **Recipient:** for distinguished contributions to the field of forensic psychiatry. **Committees:** Accreditation of Fellowship; Education; Ethics; International Relations. **Publications:** *Journal of the American Academy of Psychiatry and Law*, quarterly. **Price:** $25.00 ● *Newsletter of the American Academy of Psychiatry and Law*, 3/year. Contains scholarly articles on forensics psychiatry. **Price:** $140.00 /year for libraries and institutions; $90.00 /year for individuals; $15.00 each, plus shipping and handling (for non-US mailings). **Circulation:** 2,500 ● Membership Directory, annual. **Conventions/Meetings:** annual convention and meeting - usually October. 2008 Oct. 23-26, Seattle, WA; 2009 Oct. 29-Nov. 1, Baltimore, MD ● semiannual meeting - 2009 May 16-17, San Francisco, CA.

5781 ■ American Bar Association - Commission on Mental and Physical Disability Law (CMPDL)
740 15th St. NW, 9th Fl.
Washington, DC 20005
Ph: (202)662-1571
Fax: (202)662-1032
E-mail: cmpdl@abanet.org
URL: http://www.abanet.org/disability
Contact: John Parry, Dir.
Founded: 1976. **Staff:** 5. **Nonmembership. Description:** Gathers and disseminates information, via publications, on court decisions, legislation, and administrative developments affecting people with mental and physical disabilities. Covers topics such as: the ADA, court access, civil commitment, civil/criminal incompetence, diminished culpability, sex offenders, institutional rights, rights in the community, employment, housing/zoning, public accommodations, education of children with disabilities, discrimination against people with disabilities, guardianship, confidentiality, federal/state entitlement programs, and liability/professional issues. **Awards:** Paul G. Hearne Award for Disability Rights. **Frequency:** annual. **Type:** recognition. **Recipient:** for outstanding public service. **Programs:** Mentor. **Formerly:** (1988) Mental Disability Legal Resource Center; (1989) Mental and Physical Disability Legal Research Services and Databases; (1991) Commission on the Mentally Disabled. **Publications:** *Civil Law Handbook on Psychiatric and Psychological Evidence and Testimony (2001)* ● *Criminal Law Handbook on Psychiatric and Psychological Evidence and Testimony (2000)*. **Price:** $40.00 ● *Handbook on Disability Discrimination Law (2003)*. **Price:** $40.00 ● *Handbook on Mental Disability Law (2002)*. **Price:** $45.00 ● *Mental and Physical Disability Law Reporter*, bimonthly. Journal. **Price:** $384.00 for organization; $324.00 for individual. ISSN: 0883-7902. **Circulation:** 520. Alternate Formats: online ● *Monograph on State Disability Discrimination Laws—With State Charts or Employment, Public Services, Public Accommodations, Housing, and Education*. **Price:** $40.00.

5782 ■ American Health Lawyers Association (AHLA)
1025 Connecticut Ave. NW, Ste.600
Washington, DC 20036-5405
Ph: (202)833-1100
Fax: (202)833-1105
E-mail: pleibold@healthlawyers.org
URL: http://www.healthlawyers.org
Contact: Peter M. Leibold, Exec. VP/CEO
Founded: 1968. **Members:** 9,800. **Membership Dues:** attorney (admitted to the Bar for more than 8 years), health professional (graduate for more than 8 years), $335 (annual) ● attorney (admitted to the Bar from 4-8 years), health professional (graduate for 4-8 years), $295 (annual). **Staff:** 35. **Budget:** $1,500,000. **Description:** Focuses on the legal issues in the healthcare field. Provides resources to address the issues facing its active members who practice in law firms, government, in-house settings, and academia and who represent the entire spectrum of the health industry: physicians, hospitals and health systems, health maintenance organizations, health insurers, managed care companies, nursing facilities, home care providers, and consumers. **Special Interest Groups:** Antitrust; Fraud and Abuse, Self-Referrals, and False Claims; Health Information and Technology; Healthcare Liability and Litigation; HMOs and Health Plans; Hospitals and Health Systems; In-House Counsel; Labor and Employment; Life Sciences; Long Term Care; Medical Staff, Credentialing, and Peer Review; Physician Organizations; Regulation, Accreditation, and Payment; Tax and Finance; Teaching Hospitals and Academic Medical Centers. **Formerly:** (1971) Society of Hospital Attorneys; (1984) American Society of Hospital Attorneys; (1995) American Academy of Hospital Attorneys; (1998) American Academy of Healthcare Attorneys. **Conventions/Meetings:** annual In-House Counsel - meeting and conference (exhibits).

5783 ■ Health Law Section - American Bar Association
c/o American Bar Association
321 N Clark St.
Chicago, IL 60610
Ph: (312)988-5548
Fax: (312)988-6797
E-mail: jillpena@staff.abanet.org
URL: http://www.abanet.org/health/home.html
Contact: Jill C. Pena, Dir.
Founded: 1996. **Members:** 9,939. **Membership Dues:** attorney/associate, $50 (annual) ● law student, $10 (annual). **Description:** Seeks to enhance the practice of health lawyers and improve understanding and development of health laws. **Telecommunication Services:** electronic mail, healthlaw@abanet.org. **Committees:** Coordinating Committee on Diversity. **Special Interest Groups:** E-Health Privacy and Security; Employee Benefits and Executive Compensation; Healthcare Facility Operations; Healthcare Fraud and Compliance; Healthcare Litigation and Risk Management; Managed Care and Insurance; Medical Research, Biotechnology and Clinical Ethical Issues; Payment and Reimbursement; Public Health and Policy; Tax and Accounting; Transactional and Business Healthcare. **Publications:** *E-Health Business and Transactional Law*. Book ● *Health Care Fraud and Abuse: Practical Perspectives*. Book. **Price:** $175.00 ● *The Health Lawyer*, bimonthly. Newsletter. Provides current information on health law. **Price:** included in membership dues; $60.00 /year for nonmembers. Alternate Formats: online ● Monographs. **Conventions/Meetings:** Satellite Seminars ● seminar ● Teleconferences.

5784 ■ National Health Law Program (NHeLP)
2639 S La Cienega Blvd.
Los Angeles, CA 90034-2675
Ph: (310)204-6010
Fax: (310)204-0891
E-mail: nhelp@healthlaw.org
URL: http://www.healthlaw.org
Contact: Laurence Lavin, Dir.
Founded: 1969. **Staff:** 10. **Budget:** $900,000. **Languages:** English, Spanish. **Description:** Attorneys, health specialists, and other interested persons. Provides assistance to legal services program attorneys and their clients in matters involving health problems of the poor. Offers information, referral, and consultation on litigation strategy. Prepares materials for and conducts training sessions for and with field program attorneys and paralegals. Coordinates testimony for particular hearings. **Libraries: Type:** reference. **Subjects:** health law and policy. **Publications:** *Health Advocate*, quarterly. Newsletter. Updates on issues affecting low-income/disabled health care consumers. **Price:** $85.00/year. **Circulation:** 2,500 ● Also publishes law review articles and health advocates guides on issues such as Medicaid access to emergency health care.

Historic Preservation

5785 ■ Historic Hawaii Foundation
680 Iwilei Rd., Ste.No. 690
Honolulu, HI 96817
Ph: (808)523-2900
Fax: (808)523-0800
E-mail: member@historichawaii.org
URL: http://www.historichawaii.org
Contact: Kiersten Faulkner, Exec. Dir.
Founded: 1974. **Members:** 3,200. **Membership Dues:** individual, $35 (annual) ● student/senior, $25

(annual) ● family, $50 (annual) ● preservation partner, $100 (annual) ● preservation supporter, $250 (annual) ● preservation sponsor, $500 (annual) ● heritage associate, $1,000 (annual) ● heritage benefactor, $2,500 (annual) ● heritage patron, $5,000 (annual) ● heritage leader, $10,000 (annual). **Staff:** 3. **Budget:** $250,000. **Description:** State historic preservation organization. Promotes the importance of historic preservation. Provides a framework for interaction among members and other similar associations. Fosters exchange of information; sponsors professional development programs. Operates speakers' bureau. **Awards:** Historic Preservation Award. **Frequency:** annual. **Type:** recognition. **Affiliated With:** National Alliance of Preservation Commissions; National Conference of State Historic Preservation Officers; National Trust for Historic Preservation. **Formerly:** (1987) Statewide Steering Committee; (1998) National Alliance of Statewide Preservation Organizations. **Publications:** Newsletter, quarterly. **Circulation:** 3,500 ● Also contributes to *Preservation Forum*, a publication of the NTHP. **Conventions/Meetings:** annual conference and meeting - usually spring.

5786 ■ National Alliance of Preservation Commissions (NAPC)
Founders Garden House
325 S Lumpkin St.
Athens, GA 30602
Ph: (706)542-4731 (706)542-0169
Fax: (706)583-0320
E-mail: napc@uga.edu
URL: http://www.sed.uga.edu/pso/programs/napc/napc.htm
Contact: Drane Wilkinson, Program Coor.

Founded: 1983. **Members:** 1,200. **Membership Dues:** individual, $35 (annual) ● commission, community (based on budget), $80-$130 (annual). **Staff:** 2. **Budget:** $150,000. **Description:** Local historic preservation commissions and organizations, historic district architectural review boards, local and state governments, and businesses. Serves as a network for information exchange and education on local legislation affecting the preservation of historic districts and landmarks. Represents members before the National Trust for Historic Preservation, National Conference of State Historic Preservation Officers, and federal agencies. Makes available educational materials, forms, guidelines, and ordinances. **Publications:** *Alliance Review*, bimonthly. Newsletter. **Price:** included in membership dues ● *Editor and Designer*. Newsletter. **Conventions/Meetings:** annual meeting and workshop ● biennial National Commission Forum - conference, national training workshop for certified local governments and their historic preservation commissions and staff ● seminar.

5787 ■ National Conference of State Historic Preservation Officers (NCSHPO)
444 N Capitol St. NW
Hall of States, Ste.342
Washington, DC 20001-1512
Ph: (202)624-5465
Fax: (202)624-5419
E-mail: schamu@sso.org
URL: http://www.ncshpo.org
Contact: Nancy Miller Schamu, Exec. Dir.

Founded: 1969. **Members:** 57. **Staff:** 3. **Budget:** $250,000. **Description:** Officers and deputy officers appointed by the governor in each of the states and territories. Provides an exchange of information about state and federal preservation programs and legislative proposals, and maintains liaison with non-profit organizations and federal and state agencies administering historic preservation programs. Publicizes and elicits citizen support for historic preservation. Offers periodic training sessions for SHPO staff on responsibilities. Conducts periodic status surveys of state historic preservation programs. Conducts research; compiles statistics. **Awards: Type:** recognition. **Committees:** Critical Issues; National Park Service; State Programs. **Councils:** Advisory. **Publications:** *NCSHPO/Alert*, periodic ● *Preservation Tax Incentives for Historic Buildings*. Published in conjunction with the National Park Service. ● *SHPO Directory*, semiannual. **Conventions/Meetings:** annual meeting.

Housing

5788 ■ Council of Large Public Housing Authorities (CLPHA)
1250 Eye St. NW, Ste.901
Washington, DC 20005
Ph: (202)638-1300
Fax: (202)638-2364
E-mail: tmainor@clpha.org
URL: http://www.clpha.org
Contact: Sunia Zaterman, Exec. Dir.

Founded: 1981. **Members:** 64. **Staff:** 7. **Budget:** $975,000. **Description:** Authorities of large public housing facilities. Purpose is to support public housing by securing adequate federal funding for the operation, development, and improvement of housing of low-income persons. Collects information on housing developments and development of budget proposals of housing authorities; analyzes congressional and Department of Housing and Urban Development proposals on housing issues. Maintains legislative liaison in Washington, DC. **Libraries: Type:** reference; not open to the public. **Holdings:** archival material, books, periodicals. **Subjects:** public housing. **Telecommunication Services:** electronic mail, szaterman@clpha.org. **Publications:** *Applicant Screening and Nondiscrimination: Complying with HUD's Tenant Selection, 504 and Fair Housing Rules* ● *Basic Facts About Public Housing* ● *CLPHA Newsletter*, biweekly ● *Dealing with the HUD Inspector General: A Guide for Public Housing Authorities* ● *Demographic Characteristics of Public and Indian Housing Residents* ● *Lease and Grievance Procedure Workbook* ● *Public Housing: A Resource We Can't Afford to Lose* ● *Security, Crime and Drugs in Public Housing: A Review of Programs and Expenditures* ● *Trends in Public Housing Budgets and Finances, 1975-1990* ● Reports. **Conventions/Meetings:** quarterly meeting - always February, June, and September ● annual meeting - always fall.

5789 ■ Housing Statistics Users Group (HSUG)
c/o National Association of Home Builders
1201 15th St. NW
Washington, DC 20005
Ph: (202)266-2398 (202)266-8200
Free: (800)368-5242
Fax: (202)266-8400
URL: http://www.nahb.org
Contact: Elliot F. Eisenberg PhD, Housing Policy Economist

Founded: 1986. **Members:** 100. **Membership Dues:** regular, $125 (semiannual). **Staff:** 3. **Budget:** $5,000. **Regional Groups:** 1. **Description:** Represents organizations in the housing industry interested in the discussion of federal statistical programs related to the field. **Conventions/Meetings:** meeting - 3/year.

5790 ■ Institute for Responsible Housing Preservation (IRHP)
401 9th St. NW, Ste.900
Washington, DC 20004
Ph: (202)585-8739
Fax: (202)585-8080
E-mail: info@housingpreservation.org
URL: http://www.housingpreservation.org
Contact: Brian Poulin, Pres.

Founded: 1989. **Members:** 60. **Membership Dues:** executive circle, $7,500 (annual) ● sustaining, $2,000 (annual) ● non-profit/public agency, $500 (annual). **Budget:** $200,000. **Description:** Owners and managers of low-income housing; attorneys, accountants, appraisers, and consultants working in the field of low-income housing; mortgage lenders. Promotes continued funding for non-profit housing sales under the Low Income Housing Preservation and Resident Homeownership Act of 1990 (LIHPRHA). Represents the interests of low-income housing owners; keeps members abreast of legislative developments pertinent to the industry; conducts lobbying activities to insure funding for preservation vouchers and to secure further protection for the prepayment rights of housing owners. Provides legal services to members suing government agencies; assists members in securing public appropriations. **Publications:** *Responsible Owner*, periodic. Newsletter. **Price:** free, for members only. **Conventions/Meetings:** annual board meeting.

5791 ■ National American Indian Housing Council (NAIHC)
50 F St. NW, Ste.3300
Washington, DC 20001
Ph: (202)789-1754
Free: (800)284-9165
Fax: (202)789-1758
E-mail: housing@naihc.net
URL: http://www.naihc.net
Contact: Paul Lumley, Exec. Dir.

Founded: 1974. **Members:** 250. **Membership Dues:** individual, $150 (annual) ● associate, $500 (annual) ● voting (based on NAHASDA allocation for all tribes represented), $100-$5,000 (annual). **Staff:** 20. **Regional Groups:** 7. **Description:** Provides technical assistance, training, research, and advocacy services to tribes and tribal housing agencies. **Libraries: Type:** reference. **Holdings:** 350. **Subjects:** Indian housing and related issues. **Computer Services:** database, Native American Funding Resources. **Programs:** Custom Training; Technical Assistance. **Publications:** *Native American Housing News*, 9/year. Newspaper. **Circulation:** 1,000. Alternate Formats: online ● *Quick Facts*, biweekly. Newsletter. Alternate Formats: online ● Brochures. Alternate Formats: online ● Reports. Alternate Formats: online. **Conventions/Meetings:** annual conference - always February ● annual conference and convention, with trade show (exhibits) - June or July.

5792 ■ National Association of Housing Information Managers (NAHIM)
134 S 13th St., Ste.701
Lincoln, NE 68508
Ph: (402)476-9424
Free: (800)379-3807
E-mail: nahimexec@aol.com
URL: http://www.nahim.org
Contact: John E. Mooring, Exec. Dir.

Founded: 1992. **Members:** 200. **Membership Dues:** regular, $50-$125 (annual). **Staff:** 1. **Budget:** $25,000. **Description:** Public housing authority computer specialists are members; software vendors are associate members. Seeks to advance the computerized information systems maintained by public housing authorities. Promotes improvement in the maintenance, expansion, and availability of public housing data processing systems. Promotes cooperation and exchange of information among members; serves as a clearinghouse on public housing information systems. **Publications:** *NAHIM News*, monthly. Newsletter. **Price:** included in membership dues. Alternate Formats: online.

5793 ■ National Association of Housing and Redevelopment Officials (NAHRO)
630 Eye St. NW
Washington, DC 20001
Ph: (202)289-3500
Free: (877)866-2476
Fax: (202)289-8181
E-mail: nahro@nahro.org
URL: http://www.nahro.org
Contact: Saul N. Ramirez Jr., Exec. Dir.

Founded: 1933. **Members:** 9,000. **Membership Dues:** housing authority, $100-$15,000 (annual) ● allied individual, $25 (annual) ● manufacturer, supplier, $500 (annual) ● profit company, $415 (annual) ● nonprofit company, $250 (annual) ● public agency, $200-$600 (annual). **Staff:** 40. **Budget:** $4,000,000. **Regional Groups:** 8. **Local Groups:** 43. **Description:** Individuals and public agencies engaged in community rebuilding by community development, public housing, large-scale private or cooperative housing rehabilitation, and conservation of existing neighborhoods through housing code enforcement, voluntary citizen action, and government action. Develops new techniques in administrative practices, finance, design, construction, management, and community relations. Consults with federal government agencies and other policy-making bodies on questions of national and local policy. Aids in drafting legislation. Sponsors workshops and seminars on housing and community development. Offers training and certification programs. **Awards:** Awards of Excellence in Housing and Community Development. **Type:** recognition ● Awards of Merit in Housing and Community Development. **Type:** recognition ● C.F. "Buzz" Meadows Memorial Award. **Type:** recognition ● Elizabeth B. Wells Memorial Award. **Type:** recognition ● Frederic M. Vogelsang Memorial Award. **Type:** recognition ● John D. Lange International Award. **Type:** recognition ● M. Justin Herman Memorial Award. **Type:** recognition. **Computer Services:** Mailing lists, of members. **Boards:** Credentialing Trustees. **Committees:** Commissioners; Community Revitalization and Development; Housing; International; Professional Development. **Formerly:** (1963) National Association of Housing Officials. **Publications:** *Journal of Housing and Community Development*, bimonthly. **Price:** $33.00 /year for nonmembers; free with agency membership. **Circulation:** 13,000. **Advertising:** accepted ● *NAHRO Directory of Local Agencies* ● *NAHRO Monitor*, bimonthly. **Price:** $20.00/year for associates and allied members. Alternate Formats: online ● Monographs. **Conventions/Meetings:** annual conference (exhibits) - 3/year ● annual conference - 2009 Mar. 16-18, Washington, DC.

5794 ■ National Association of Local Housing Finance Agencies (NALHFA)
2025 M St. NW, Ste.800
Washington, DC 20036-3309
Ph: (202)367-1197
Fax: (202)367-2197
E-mail: info@nalhfa.org
URL: http://www.nalhfa.org
Contact: Mr. John C. Murphy, Exec. Dir.
Founded: 1982. **Members:** 250. **Membership Dues:** regular, $700-$1,690 (annual) ● non-profit, $471 (annual). **Staff:** 7. **Budget:** $750,000. **State Groups:** 30. **Local Groups:** 180. **National Groups:** 40. **Description:** City and county agencies that finance affordable, tax-exempt housing; affiliate members are organizations and firms, including underwriters, housing counsel, financial advisors, syndicators, and consulting firms, that work with local agencies to provide affordable housing opportunities. Provides advocacy on legislative and regulatory issues affecting affordable housing. Makes available information exchange and communication with others in the field. **Libraries: Type:** by appointment only. **Holdings:** 4; books, software. **Subjects:** bonds for beginners, housing bonds, tax credits for low-income housing. **Awards:** Meritorious Achievement. **Frequency:** semiannual. **Type:** recognition. **Telecommunication Services:** electronic mail, jmurphy@nalhfa.org. **Committees:** Awards; Legislation; Member Services; Nominating. **Formerly:** (2001) Association of Local Housing Finance Agencies. **Publications:** *Bonds for Beginners, ABCs of Housing Bonds, Tax Credit, Cash Flow* ● *Housing Finance Report*, bimonthly ● Annual Report, annual. **Price:** included in membership dues. **Conventions/Meetings:** semiannual conference, educational - always spring and fall ● Financing Affordable Housing I and II - seminar, issues include development, subsidy layering and bond issuance - 3/year.

5795 ■ National Council of State Housing Agencies (NCSHA)
444 N Capitol St., Ste.438
Washington, DC 20001
Ph: (202)624-7710
Fax: (202)624-5899
E-mail: bthompson@ncsha.org
URL: http://www.ncsha.org
Contact: Barbara J. Thompson, Exec. Dir.
Founded: 1974. **Staff:** 18. **Budget:** $3,000,000. **Nonmembership. Description:** State Housing Finance Agencies from 50 states, Puerto Rico, and the Virgin Islands; affiliate members include investment bankers, housing development firms, and other public and private agencies involved with low and moderate income single and multi-family housing finance, development, and management. Administers technical workshops and other educational activities. Serves as Washington, DC liaison for member agencies in dealing with the U.S. Department of Housing and Urban Development and other federal offices. Keeps members informed of congressional and administrative actions that could affect member agencies. Maintains files on all member agencies, including bond issue and program administration information, annual reports, and bylaws. Conducts specialized education and research programs; compiles statistics. **Libraries: Type:** not open to the public. **Awards:** Awards for Program Excellence. **Frequency:** annual. **Type:** recognition. **Recipient:** for homeownership, rental, special needs, legislative advocacy, and communications ● Leadership Award. **Frequency:** annual. **Type:** recognition. **Recipient:** for individuals who have given above and beyond the call of duty for the betterment of NCSHA. **Committees:** HomeOwnership; Rental Housing. **Formerly:** (1987) Council of State Housing Agencies. **Publications:** *Developer's Guide to the Low Income Housing Tax Credit*, annual. **Price:** $85.00 for housing finance agency members; $125.00 for affiliate members; $175.00 for nonmembers ● *HFA Fact Book: A National Survey of Program Activity Levels*, annual. **Price:** $25.00 for members; $35.00 for affiliate member; $50.00 for nonmembers ● *State Equity Funds: The New Capital Source for Low Income Rental Housing* ● *State HFA Program Catalog* ● *State Housing Finance*, quarterly. Newsletter ● *2005 Credit Opportunities Workshop Manual*. **Price:** $50.00 ● Membership Directory. **Price:** $10.00 for housing finance agency members; $20.00 for affiliate members; $150.00 for nonmembers. **Conventions/Meetings:** annual conference (exhibits) - usually fall ● annual conference and trade show ● annual Legislative Conference - usually March ● annual Tax Credit Conference - usually June ● annual workshop - usually May.

5796 ■ National Housing Law Project (NHLP)
614 Grand Ave., Ste.320
Oakland, CA 94610
Ph: (510)251-9400
Fax: (510)451-2300
E-mail: nhlp@nhlp.org
URL: http://www.nhlp.org
Contact: Gideon Anders, Exec. Dir.
Founded: 1968. **Staff:** 10. **Budget:** $1,000,000. **Description:** Provides back-up assistance, including research and litigation, to local legal services programs in areas of housing law such as: landlord-tenant law, the Federal Community Development Block Grant program, displacement, public housing and Section 8, HUD subsidized multi-family housing, rural housing, single-family housing and state housing finance agencies. Maintains Washington, DC, office. **Telecommunication Services:** electronic mail, ganders@nhlp.org. **Publications:** *Farmers Home Administration Housing: Tenants' and Homeowners' Rights*. Manual. **Price:** $350.00 ● *Housing Law Bulletin*, 10-12/year. Contains information about important developments in housing policy and law. **Price:** $150.00 for individuals outside California; $100.00 for individuals in California ● *HUD Housing Programs: Tenants' Rights*. Manual. **Price:** $350.00 ● *RHCDS (FmHA) Housing Programs: Tenants' and Purchaser's Rights*. Manual. **Price:** $55.00. **Conventions/Meetings:** seminar ● workshop.

5797 ■ Professional Housing Management Association (PHMA)
154 Ft. Evans Rd. NE
Leesburg, VA 20176
Ph: (703)771-1888
Fax: (703)771-0299
E-mail: jonmoore@earthlink.net
URL: http://www.phma.com
Contact: Jon R. Moore DHD, Exec. Dir.
Membership Dues: individual, $50 (biennial) ● life, $300 ● corporate gold, $1,000 (annual) ● corporate platinum, $3,500 (annual). **Description:** Promotes professionalism in all phases of housing and lodging management within the military departments. **Awards:** PHMA Scholarships. **Type:** scholarship. **Recipient:** for members in good standing or their immediate dependent family. **Conventions/Meetings:** annual competition, golf tournament to raise money for scholarship fund ● seminar, for multi-chapter training.

5798 ■ Public Housing Authorities Directors Association (PHADA)
511 Capitol Ct. NE
Washington, DC 20002-4937
Ph: (202)546-5445 (202)543-4381
Fax: (202)546-2280
E-mail: tkaiser@phada.org
URL: http://www.phada.org
Contact: Timothy G. Kaiser, Exec. Dir.
Founded: 1979. **Members:** 1,500. **Membership Dues:** housing authority (1-1400 units), $100-$1,230 ● housing authority (1401-3250 units), $1,350-$2,985 ● housing authority (over 3251 units), $3,050-$4,575. **Staff:** 9. **Budget:** $1,200,000. **Description:** Directors of public housing authorities in the U.S. or their designees. Aims to provide information on Department of Housing and Urban Development and congressional actions and activities related to public housing agencies. Focuses on individual services for members. **Awards: Type:** scholarship. **Recipient:** for low-income housing residents. **Committees:** Housing; Legislation; Professional Development. **Programs:** PHADA/Rutgers Executive Director Education. **Publications:** *Public Housing Authorities Directors Association—Advocate*, bimonthly. Newsletter. Covers legislation and regulatory actions affecting the housing industry. **Price:** included in membership dues. **Circulation:** 2,200. **Advertising:** accepted. **Conventions/Meetings:** annual convention (exhibits) ● quarterly Professional Development Conference ● workshop.

Human Resources

5799 ■ Marine Corps Recruiters Association (MCRA)
c/o Sgt. James Simmons, Sec.-Treas.
1705 N Main St.
Nevada, MO 64772
E-mail: jimandsally@sofnet.com
URL: http://www.marinerecruitersassoc.com
Contact: Sgt. James Simmons, Sec.-Treas.
Membership Dues: regular, $25 (annual). **Description:** Provides assistance to the U.S. Marine Corps Recruiting Service. Aims to preserve and strengthen camaraderie among members, regardless of race, color, national origin, age, gender, religion, or disabilities. Facilitates exchange of ideas and information concerning recruitment duties. **Publications:** Newsletter.

Human Rights

5800 ■ Citizens Equal Rights Alliance (CERA)
PO Box 93
Ronan, MT 59864
Ph: (605)374-5836
E-mail: feedback@citizensalliance.org
URL: http://www.citizensalliance.org
Contact: Elaine Willman, Chair
Membership Dues: individual, $35 (annual). **Description:** Protects and supports the constitutional rights of people, both Indian and non-Indian. Provides education and training concerning constitutional rights. Participates in legal actions that impact the constitutional rights of citizens. **Telecommunication Services:** electronic mail, toppin@aol.com. **Publications:** *CERA News*. Newsletter. Alternate Formats: online.

5801 ■ Human Rights Advocates (HRA)
PO Box 5675
Berkeley, CA 94705

E-mail: info@humanrightsadvocates.org
URL: http://www.humanrightsadvocates.org
Contact: Anne Wagley, Human Rights Attorney

Founded: 1978. **Members:** 100. **Membership Dues:** regular, $35 (annual) ● student or low-income, $20 (annual). **Languages:** English, French, Spanish. **Description:** International human rights lawyers and professionals. Objectives are to provide education about the application of human rights law and to promote this body of law domestically and internationally. Organizes public conferences, lectures, and seminars; submits amicus curiae briefs. Maintains library of current United Nations documents and materials on human rights organizations; has consultative status with ECOSOC. **Committees:** Amicus; Education; United Nations. **Programs:** Frank C. Newman Internship. **Projects:** California Corporate Accountability. **Publications:** *Accommodation: A Legal Analysis at the Accommodation Agreement Risky Between the US Government, the Hopi Tribe and the Navaho Nation* ● *Human Rights Advocates—Newsletter*, semiannual. Covers HRA's efforts to promote and protect fundamental human rights in the United States and worldwide. **Price:** included in membership dues. Alternate Formats: online ● *International Human Rights Law: What It Is and How It Can Be Used in State and Federal Courts.* **Conventions/Meetings:** annual Report on UN Sub-Commission: Report on Commission on Human Rights - meeting, with updates on developments at UN bodies.

5802 ■ International Association of Official Human Rights Agencies (IAOHRA)

444 N Capitol St. NW, Ste.536
Washington, DC 20001
Ph: (202)624-5410
Fax: (202)624-8185
E-mail: iaohra@sso.org
URL: http://www.iaohra.org
Contact: Jim Stowe, Pres.

Founded: 1949. **Members:** 187. **Staff:** 2. **Budget:** $100,000. **Regional Groups:** 5. **Description:** Governmental human rights agencies with legal enforcement powers. Objectives are to foster better human relations and to enhance human rights procedures under the law. Conducts training services that include: administration and management training; technical assistance in civil rights compliance and curriculum development for colleges and universities, business, industry, and other organizations; training for administrators and commissioners to promote awareness and capability in current literature, theory, and philosophy relative to equal opportunity. Maintains ongoing liaison with federal agencies involved with civil rights enforcement in order to coordinate development of state legislation. Develops and conducts training and technical assistance workshops for regional planning units and state planning agencies. Plans to establish a human rights training institute. Sponsors workshops; compiles statistics. **Computer Services:** Mailing lists, of members. **Telecommunication Services:** electronic mail, jlstowe@columbus.gov. **Publications:** *IAOHRA Newsletter*, quarterly. **Price:** included in membership dues ● Membership Directory, annual. **Price:** available to members only ● Also publishes technical notes. **Conventions/Meetings:** annual conference (exhibits).

5803 ■ International Justice Mission (IJM)

PO Box 58147
Washington, DC 20037-8147
Ph: (703)465-5495
Fax: (703)465-5499
E-mail: contact@ijm.org
URL: http://www.ijm.org
Contact: Gary A. Haugen, Pres./CEO

Founded: 1997. **Multinational. Description:** Aims to help people suffering injustice and oppression who cannot rely on local authorities for relief through the casework approach. (The approach consists of investigation and intervention between enforcement and legal professionals on behalf of victims in cases of abuse, oppression and injustice). **Departments:** Education. **Publications:** Reports, quarterly.

5804 ■ Meiklejohn Civil Liberties Institute (MCLI)

PO Box 673
Berkeley, CA 94701-0673
Ph: (510)848-0599
Fax: (510)848-6008
E-mail: 2007@mcli.org
URL: http://www.mcli.org
Contact: Ann Fagan Ginger, Exec. Dir.

Founded: 1965. **Staff:** 3. **Budget:** $90,000. **Description:** Works to collect attorney work papers and unreported rulings filed in courts in cases involving civil rights, due process, and civil liberties, in order to assist attorneys and legal workers confronted with similar issues. Concentrates effort on a peace law and education project, with a brief-bank of legal case files and in-depth findings and reports relating to current issues about U.S. military policies, conventional and nuclear war, and use of international treaties ratified by the U.S. Operates speakers' bureau. **Libraries: Type:** reference. **Holdings:** archival material. **Subjects:** case files, cold war period, civil rights movements, free speech movement, Vietnam War era, UN human rights treaties. **Computer Services:** Information services ● mailing lists. **Projects:** Archival; Human Rights; Right to Education. **Publications:** *Alexander Meiklejohn: Teacher of Freedom.* Book. **Price:** $13.95 cloth cover; $7.95 paperback ● *Challenging US Human Rights Violations Since 9/11.* Book ● *The Cold War Against Labor.* Booklets. **Price:** $22.95 cloth cover ● *Event Journal*, annual ● *The Ford Hunger March.* **Price:** $5.00 ● *Human Rights and Peace Law Docket: 1945-1993, 1995 Edition*, biennial. **Price:** $66.00 /year for libraries and institutions; $55.00 /year for individuals ● *Human Rights Docket* ● *Human Rights Organizations and Periodicals Directory, 1996 - 8th Edition*, biennial. **Price:** $125.00 for libraries and institutions; $45.00 for individuals ● *News from MCLI*, periodic ● *Peace Law Almanac*, periodic. Includes U.S. Constitution, UN Charter, Nuremberg Principles, Neutrality Act, UN & U.S. on Gulf War, International Covenant on Civil & Political Rights. **Price:** $40.00 ● *Peace Law Basics.* Contains excerpts from Peace Law Almanac. **Price:** $15.00 ● *PL Law School Reader* ● *PL Undergrad College Reader* ● Has also published materials for the public, and specialized materials for attorneys and social scientists. **Conventions/Meetings:** annual conference (exhibits).

Humanities

5805 ■ National Endowment for the Humanities (NEH)

1100 Pennsylvania Ave. NW
Washington, DC 20506
Ph: (202)606-8400
Free: (800)NEH-1121
E-mail: info@neh.gov
URL: http://www.neh.gov
Contact: Bruce Cole, Chm.

Founded: 1965. **Staff:** 160. **Description:** Grant-making agency of the U.S. government dedicated to supporting research, education, preservation and public programs in the humanities. **Awards:** Charles Frankel Prize. **Type:** recognition. **Recipient:** to recognize persons for outstanding contributions to the public's understanding of humanities ● The Jefferson Lecture Award. **Frequency:** annual. **Type:** recognition. **Recipient:** to an individual who has made significant scholarly contributions to the humanities ● National Humanities Medals. **Frequency:** annual. **Type:** recognition. **Recipient:** to individuals or groups whose work has deepened the nation's understanding of the humanities. **Telecommunication Services:** TDD, (866)372-2930. **Programs:** U.S. Newspaper. **Projects:** National Digital Newspaper. **Publications:** *Equal Employment Opportunity Data.* Report. Alternate Formats: online ● *Freedom of Information Act*, annual. Report. Alternate Formats: online ● *Humanities*, bimonthly. Magazine. **Price:** $24.00/year. Alternate Formats: online ● *NEH Connect!.* Newsletter. Alternate Formats: online.

Immigration

5806 ■ American Immigration Law Foundation (AILF)

918 F St. NW, 6th Fl.
Washington, DC 20004
Ph: (202)742-5600
Fax: (202)742-5619
E-mail: info@ailf.org
URL: http://www.ailf.org
Contact: Benjamin E. Johnson, Exec. Dir.

Founded: 1987. **Description:** Promotes public understanding of immigration law and policy through education, policy analysis, and support to litigators. **Awards:** AILF Torchlight Awards. **Frequency:** annual. **Type:** recognition. **Recipient:** for individuals or organizations that have made significant contributions in promoting the benefits of immigration ● American Heritage Awards. **Frequency:** annual. **Type:** recognition. **Recipient:** for outstanding immigrant group ● Dubroff Memorial Writing Contest. **Frequency:** annual. **Type:** scholarship. **Recipient:** for immigration law experts ● Immigrant Achievement Award. **Frequency:** annual. **Type:** recognition. **Recipient:** for outstanding newcomers.

5807 ■ American Immigration Lawyers Association (AILA)

918 F St. NW
Washington, DC 20004-1400
Ph: (202)216-2400
Fax: (202)783-7853
E-mail: executive@aila.org
URL: http://www.aila.org
Contact: Jeanne A. Butterfield Esq., Exec. Dir.

Founded: 1946. **Members:** 4,100. **Membership Dues:** student, $50 (annual) ● attorney (admitted to practice for less than 3 years), $295 (annual) ● attorney (admitted to practice for 3 years or more), $395 (annual) ● nonprofit attorney, $100 (annual). **Staff:** 19. **Budget:** $2,700,000. **Local Groups:** 34. **Languages:** English, Spanish. **Description:** Lawyers specializing in the field of immigration and nationality law. Fosters and promotes the administration of justice with particular reference to the immigration and nationality laws of the United States. **Libraries: Type:** reference. **Holdings:** archival material, books, periodicals. **Subjects:** immigration law. **Computer Services:** Mailing lists, of members. **Committees:** American Citizenship; Amicus Curiae; Asylum and Refugees; Ethics; Government Liaison; Immigration Legislation; Unlawful Practice of the Law; Visa Practice. **Special Interest Groups:** African-American; Asian; Gay and Lesbian; Hispanic/Latino; In-House Counsel; Indian Subcontinent; Law Professors; Middle Eastern. **Affiliated With:** American Bar Association. **Formerly:** (1981) Association of Immigration and Nationality Lawyers. **Publications:** *AILA Membership Directory*, annual ● *AILA Monthly Mailing.* Newsletter. Includes subject index. **Price:** included in membership dues; $295.00 /year for nonmembers. ISSN: 0898-1663. **Circulation:** 3,800. **Advertising:** accepted ● *Connect!.* Newsletter. Includes information useful to employers. Alternate Formats: online ● *Immigrants Action Alert* (in English and Spanish). Newsletter ● *Immigration and Nationality Law Handbook*, annual ● *Washington Update*, biweekly. Newsletter. Alternate Formats: online. **Conventions/Meetings:** annual conference (exhibits) - usually June. 2008 June 25-28, Vancouver, BC, Canada ● regional meeting and conference - 6-10/year ● seminar ● workshop, on immigration litigation.

5808 ■ Legal Immigrant Association (LIA)

PO Box 2082
Santa Clara, CA 95055
E-mail: pauldonelly@medialever.com
URL: http://legalimmigrant.org
Contact: Paul Donnelly, Contact

Founded: 2007. **Description:** Represents legal immigrant professionals. Promotes the social well-being of law-abiding skilled workers. Works to reduce the green card processing delays that have troubled the employment-based immigrant community.

5809 ■ Liberty's Promise
1010 Pendleton St.
Alexandria, VA 22314-1837
Ph: (703)549-9950
Fax: (703)549-9953
E-mail: lp-info@libertyspromise.org
URL: http://www.libertyspromise.org
Contact: Dr. Robert M. Ponichtera, Exec. Dir.
Founded: 2003. **Description:** Works to sustain and support young immigrants. Encourages immigrants to be active and conscientious American citizens. **Programs:** Best Practices; Civics and Citizenship; Lending a Hand; Opportunities Plus.

5810 ■ National Immigration Project of the National Lawyers Guild (NIP/NLG)
14 Beacon St., Ste.602
Boston, MA 02108
Ph: (617)227-9727
Fax: (617)227-5495
E-mail: dan@nationalimmigrationproject.org
URL: http://www.nationalimmigrationproject.org
Contact: Dan Kesselbrenner, Dir.
Founded: 1974. **Members:** 500. **Membership Dues:** general, $150 (annual) ● nonprofit attorney or public defender, $125 (annual) ● non-attorney, $50 (annual) ● law student, $25 (annual). **Staff:** 3. **State Groups:** 6. **Description:** Lawyers, law students, and legal workers. Educates and organizes for progressive immigration law. Works in defense of civil liberties of the foreign born. Holds immigration law skills seminars. Collects texts, manuals, and pamphlets on immigration law and problems of the foreign born in the U.S. Maintains Brief Bank, a library of memoranda, briefs, and immigration law decisions. **Computer Services:** Mailing lists, of members. **Publications:** *The Immigration Act of 1990 Handbook* ● *Immigration Law and Crime*. Book ● *Immigration Law and Defense*. Book ● *Immigration Law and the Family* ● *National Immigration Project Newsletter*, quarterly ● *U.S. Citizenship and Naturalization Handbook*. **Conventions/Meetings:** annual conference.

Industrial Development

5811 ■ Association of Defense Communities (ADC)
734 15th St. NW, Ste.900
Washington, DC 20005
Ph: (202)822-5256 (202)223-7800
Fax: (202)822-8819
E-mail: mail@defensecommunities.org
URL: http://www.naid.org
Contact: Jeffrey A. Finkle, CEO
Founded: 1978. **Members:** 70. **Membership Dues:** private company (based on the number of employees), $500-$1,200 (annual) ● closed base community (based on annual budget), $150-$350 (annual) ● active base community (based on population), $150-$450 (annual) ● affiliated organization (based on annual budget), $150-$350 (annual) ● all state or federal agency, emeritus (ADC member for 5 or more years), $150 (annual) ● sole practitioner, $250 (annual). **Staff:** 1. **Description:** Represents professionals involved in the conversion, reuse, and community development of former federal military installations. Provides a medium for exchanging ideas on the principles, practices, and experiences in the field. Assists in converting former government lands and buildings for public and private uses that generate employment. Provides a unified voice regarding the property conversion process. Monitors legislation and federal developments. **Formerly:** (2006) National Association of Installation Developers. **Publications:** *Defense Communities 360*, weekly. Newsletter. Features snapshots of issues facing defense communities. **Price:** free for members ● Membership Directory, annual. **Conventions/Meetings:** annual conference.

5812 ■ International Economic Development Council (IEDC)
734 15th St. NW, Ste.900
Washington, DC 20005
Ph: (202)223-7800
Fax: (202)223-4745
E-mail: cziegler@iedconline.org
URL: http://www.iedconline.org
Contact: Jeffrey A. Finkle, Pres./CEO
Founded: 1926. **Members:** 4,000. **Staff:** 25. **Budget:** $4,000,000. **Description:** Works to help economic development professionals improve the quality of life in their communities. Represents all levels of government, academia, and private industry; provides a broad range of member services including research, advisory services, conferences, professional certification, professional development, publications, legislative tracking and more. **Awards: Type:** recognition. **Boards:** Certification. **Committees:** Communications; Education; Educational Foundation; Fellow Review; Legislative. **Absorbed:** (2002) Council for Urban Economic Development. **Formerly:** (1980) American Industrial Development Council; (2002) American Economic Development Council. **Publications:** *Annual Federal Review and Budget Overview*, annual. Report ● *Economic Development Journal*, quarterly ● *Economic Development Now*, bimonthly. Newsletter. Contains articles and reports of interest to economic developers. **Price:** $50.00/year. ISSN: 0742-3713. **Circulation:** 3,000 ● *Federal Review*, annual. Report. **Circulation:** 3,000. **Advertising:** accepted. **Conventions/Meetings:** biennial Tech-Led Conference.

Information Management

5813 ■ American Council for Technology (ACT)
11350 Random Hills Rd., Ste.120
Fairfax, VA 22030
Ph: (703)218-1955
Fax: (703)218-1960
E-mail: act-iac@actgov.org
Contact: Ken Allen, Exec. Dir.
Founded: 1978. **Members:** 12,000. **Budget:** $25,000. **Regional Groups:** 26. **Description:** Federal, state, and local government information resource managers; government information processing line and staff managers. Reviews and comments on proposed legislation such as the Paperwork Reduction Act, Federal Procurement Regulations, and Federal Information Resources Management Regulations. Disseminates information to operating personnel in field installation on information policy and regulations. Provides a forum for information technology managers to discuss issues and solve mutual problems. Sponsors Information Resource Management Seminars and governmental training courses. Conducts studies and provides analysis of government ADP activities; maintains speakers' bureau. **Awards:** Intergovernmental Solutions Awards. **Frequency:** annual. **Type:** recognition. **Recipient:** for government programs and solutions that demonstrate proven results of transformation through integration of information technology ● Janice K. Mendenhall Award. **Frequency:** annual. **Type:** recognition. **Recipient:** for outstanding individual who embodies qualities and professional aspirations ● John J. Franke Award. **Frequency:** annual. **Type:** recognition. **Recipient:** to an individual who makes extraordinary long-term contributions to federal service. **Committees:** Education; Industry; Legislation. **Special Interest Groups:** eGovernment; Emerging Technology; Enterprise; Homeland Protection; Human Capital. **Formerly:** (2003) Federation of Government Information Processing Councils. **Publications:** *FedFacts*, quarterly. Newsletter. ISSN: 0896-579X ● *iACTion*. Newsletter. Alternate Formats: online ● Articles ● Directory, annual ● Proceedings. **Conventions/Meetings:** annual conference (exhibits).

5814 ■ American Society of Access Professionals (ASAP)
1444 I St. NW, Ste.700
Washington, DC 20005-6542
Ph: (202)712-9054
Fax: (202)216-9646
E-mail: asap@bostrom.com
URL: http://www.accesspro.org
Contact: Claire Shanley, Exec. Dir.
Founded: 1980. **Members:** 300. **Membership Dues:** individual, $35 (annual). **Budget:** $120,000. **Description:** Federal employees, attorneys, journalists, educators, and others working with, or having an interest in, advancing effective techniques and procedures for administering access statutes such as the Freedom of Information Act, the Federal Privacy Act, and other access and data protection laws. Seeks to: enhance responsible and cost effective administration of access laws; promote protection of personal privacy and fair information practices; offer training opportunities; provide a national and international forum for discussion of issues surrounding these laws; work for definition of job standards and recognition of access professionals. Offers job bank to assist members in locating new positions. Holds 5 or 6 training sessions a year. **Committees:** Awards; Legislative; Outreach; Professional Standards; Training. **Publications:** *American Society of Access Professionals—Membership Directory*, annual. **Price:** included in membership dues. **Circulation:** 300 ● *ASAP News*, bimonthly. Newsletter. Covers privacy, government policy, and other freedom of information issues. Includes book reviews, calendar of events, and personnel changes. **Price:** included in membership dues. **Conventions/Meetings:** bimonthly luncheon and meeting, with speakers ● annual symposium - always in Washington, DC ● annual Training Series - meeting - always September, in Washington, DC ● annual Western Regional Training Conference - symposium - usually March or April.

5815 ■ Association for Federal Information Resources Management (AFFIRM)
PO Box 2848
Alexandria, VA 22301
Ph: (703)549-1160
Fax: (703)995-4890
E-mail: info@affirm.org
URL: http://www.affirm.org
Contact: Chris Niedermayer, Pres.
Founded: 1979. **Members:** 275. **Membership Dues:** individual, $25 (annual) ● individual (with Academia subscription), $175 (annual) ● individual industry, $125 (annual) ● individual industry (with subscription), $650 (annual) ● corporate (with subscription), $450 (annual). **Description:** Professionals in disciplines related to Information Resources Management (IRM) including: automatic data processing; library and technical information; paperwork management; privacy and freedom of information; information security; records and statistical data collection; telecommunications. Aims to promote the concept and practice of IRM within the U.S. government. Acts as independent clearinghouse; arranges to hear speakers from government and private industry; researches new concepts and techniques to improve the quality and use of federal information systems and resources management personnel; provides representation before conferences, symposia, and seminars on federal government management. **Awards:** Executive Leadership Awards. **Frequency:** annual. **Type:** recognition. **Recipient:** for outstanding accomplishments of leaders in the IT community ● **Type:** scholarship. **Recipient:** for high school students. **Committees:** Communications; Programs; Scholarship. **Working Groups:** Emerging Technologies/Issues. **Publications:** *The Affirmation*, monthly. Newsletter ● Membership Directory, annual.

5816 ■ Council of Professional Associations on Federal Statistics (COPAFS)
2121 Eisenhower Ave., Ste.200
Alexandria, VA 22314
Ph: (703)836-0404
E-mail: copafs@aol.com
URL: http://members.aol.com/copafs
Contact: Edward J. Spar, Exec. Dir.
Founded: 1981. **Members:** 57. **Staff:** 2. **Budget:** $130,000. **Description:** Professional associations representing individuals united to: increase participation of professional associations in the development and improvement of federal statistics programs;

establish communication with federal agency personnel, congressional committees, and others involved in federal statistical policy and programs; make information on federal statistics available to members; encourage the discussion of issues of public concern. Works with representatives of statistical agencies, the presidential administration, and Congress to identify emerging issues and promote opportunities for improvement; and advises decision-makers of members' views. Is concerned with various aspects of statistical policy and programs including priorities and the scope, economy, and compatibility of data collection methods. Member associations include: American Agricultural Economics Association; American Association for Public Opinion Research; American College of Epidemiology; American Economic Association; American Marketing Association; American Political Science Association; American Psychological Association; American Public Health Association; American Sociological Association; American Statistical Association; Association of Public Data Users; Association for University Business and Economic Research; Association for Vital Records and Health Statistics; Gerontological Society of America; Industrial Relations Research Association; Population Association of America; Society of Actuaries. **Affiliated With:** American Agricultural Economics Association; American Association for Public Opinion Research; American College of Epidemiology; American Economic Association; American Marketing Association; American Political Science Association; American Psychological Association; American Public Health Association; American Sociological Association; American Statistical Association; Association of Public Data Users; Labor and Employment Relations Association; National Association for Public Health Statistics and Information Systems; Population Association of America; Rural Sociological Society. **Publications:** *News from COPAFS*, periodic. Newsletter. Covers developments in federal statistics policy and programs, including data collection efforts, quality of data, and access to information. **Price:** $30.00/year. **Circulation:** 700 ● Annual Report, annual ● Articles ● Brochures. **Conventions/Meetings;** quarterly meeting - always Washington, DC.

5817 ■ Federal Consumer Information Center Program (FCIC)

1800 F St. NW, Rm. G-142
Washington, DC 20405
Ph: (202)501-1794
Free: (800)FED-INFO
E-mail: catalog.pueblo@gsa.gov
URL: http://www.pueblo.gsa.gov

Founded: 1966. **Staff:** 24. **Description:** Serves as a nationwide federal consumer information service providing printed publications. Topics covered include: getting Federal benefits; dealing with consumer complaints; buying cars and houses; making investments and handling credit problems; researching health questions; and finding the best sources of Federal information and assistance. **Telecommunication Services:** additional toll-free number, (888)-878-3256 ● additional toll-free number, (800)688-9889. **Formerly:** (2001) Federal Information Center Program. **Publications:** *Consumer Information Catalog*, quarterly. **Price:** free ● Brochures, periodic.

5818 ■ Government Management Information Sciences (GMIS)

PO Box 365
Bayville, NJ 08721
Ph: (973)632-0470
Free: (800)460-7454
Fax: (732)606-9026
E-mail: headquarters@gmis.org
URL: http://www.gmis.org
Contact: Bruce Miller, Pres.

Founded: 1971. **Members:** 500. **Membership Dues:** regular, $75-$400 (annual) ● vendor/associate, $500 (annual). **Staff:** 1. **Budget:** $95,000. **State Groups:** 18. **Description:** Represents state and local government agencies involved in Information Technology; while member agencies differ in many aspects, it is a homogenous group with similar interests dedicated to sharing with each other. Provides organizational support to eighteen state chapters. State chapters enable member agencies within a geographical area to develop close relationships and to foster the spirit and intent through cooperation, assistance and mutual support. Affiliated with five international sister organizations of local governments: KommITS in Sweden, SOCITM in United Kingdom, VIAG in the Netherlands, MISA in Canada, and ALGIM in New Zealand. **Libraries: Type:** reference. **Holdings:** papers, reports. **Subjects:** technical. **Awards:** Ambassador of the Year. **Frequency:** annual. **Type:** recognition. **Recipient:** for a member who recruits the most number of new members in a year ● Government Management Information Sciences Award. **Frequency:** annual. **Type:** recognition ● Management Information Systems Annual Professional of the Year Award. **Frequency:** annual. **Type:** recognition ● Professional of the Year. **Frequency:** annual. **Type:** recognition. **Recipient:** for an individual whose performance has favorably reflected the information processing profession. **Computer Services:** Mailing lists, of members. **Telecommunication Services:** electronic mail, lcurley@monroecounty.gov. **Publications:** *General Educational Material*, bimonthly. Newsletter. Contains general educational material. **Advertising:** accepted. Alternate Formats: online. Also Cited As: *GEM* ● Survey, annual. Alternate Formats: online. **Conventions/Meetings:** annual international conference and trade show (exhibits) - always June.

5819 ■ IACP Law Enforcement Information Management Section (LEIM)

c/o International Association of Chiefs of Police
515 N Washington St.
Alexandria, VA 22314-2357
Ph: (703)836-6767
Free: (800)THE-IACP
Fax: (703)836-4543
E-mail: snyderm@theiacp.org
URL: http://www.theiacp.org
Contact: G. Matthew Snyder, Staff Liaison

Founded: 1989. **Members:** 300. **Staff:** 1. **Budget:** $30,000. **Description:** A section of the International Association of Chiefs of Police. Monitors trends and progress in law enforcement information systems management. Provides a forum for discussion of related issues including law enforcement data processing, telecommunications, and technical and automated information management systems. Conducts training programs. **Committees:** Special Projects; Training. **Affiliated With:** International Association of Chiefs of Police. **Formerly:** Law Enforcement Information Management Section. **Publications:** *LEIM Update*, quarterly. Contains information on trends in the industry and software and hardware system management updates. **Price:** included in membership dues. **Circulation:** 300. **Conventions/Meetings:** semiannual conference and symposium (exhibits) ● annual meeting.

5820 ■ National Association of Government Archives and Records Administrators (NAGARA)

90 State St., Ste.1009
Albany, NY 12207
Ph: (518)463-8644
Fax: (518)463-8656
E-mail: nagara@caphill.com
URL: http://www.nagara.org
Contact: Mary Beth Herkert, Pres.

Founded: 1974. **Members:** 190. **Membership Dues:** institutional (federal), $1,200 (annual) ● institutional (state/combined program), $600 (annual) ● institutional (state/separate program), $300 (annual) ● institutional (local government program), $150 (annual) ● individual, associate (federal, state, local), $75 (annual). **Budget:** $100,000. **Description:** Aims to improve the administration of government records and archives and to raise public awareness and increase understanding of government archives and records management programs. Works to: act as forum for members and foster exchange among government archives and records management agencies in order to improve their programs and services; promote research, development, and use of archival management methods; encourage research and examination of problems in the administration and preservation of government records; create and implement professional standards of administration of archival and government records. Develops and disseminates publications and program guidelines for state and local programs; reports on issues concerning federal records programs; works with local government associations and other organizations towards solving the special problems of county, municipal, and government records. Represents the government records community in national issues affecting records management and archival programs. **Committees:** Information Technology; Local Government Records; Preservation Issues; Terminology and Program Reporting Standards. **Projects:** Archival Clearinghouse Study; State Program Reporting Standards. **Formerly:** (1984) National Association of State Archives and Records Administrators. **Publications:** *Crossroads*, quarterly. Bulletin. Alternate Formats: online ● *NAGARA Clearinghouse*, quarterly. Newsletter. **Conventions/Meetings:** annual meeting (exhibits) - 2008 July 23-26, Atlanta, GA.

5821 ■ National Association of State Chief Information Officers (NASCIO)

c/o AMR Management Services
201 E Main St., Ste.1405
Lexington, KY 40507
Ph: (859)514-9212
Fax: (859)514-9166
E-mail: drobinson@amrms.com
URL: http://www.nascio.org
Contact: Mr. Doug Robinson, Exec. Dir.

Founded: 1969. **Members:** 1,300. **Membership Dues:** state, $7,800 (annual) ● corporate, $7,500 (annual) ● federal, local, international associate, non-profit organization, $500 (annual) ● territory, $1,500 (annual). **Staff:** 10. **Budget:** $4,000,000. **Description:** Represents the chief information officers of the fifty states, U.S. territories and the District of Columbia. Fosters government excellence through quality business practices, information management, and technology policy. Helps shape national IT policy through collaborative partnerships, information sharing and knowledge transfer across jurisdictional and functional boundaries. **Awards:** Meritorious Service Award. **Frequency:** annual. **Type:** recognition ● National Technology Champion Award. **Frequency:** annual. **Type:** recognition ● Recognition Awards for Outstanding Achievement in the Field of Information Technology. **Frequency:** annual. **Type:** recognition. **Recipient:** for innovative statewide systems. **Computer Services:** database, membership directory ● mailing lists, of members ● online services, document library. **Formerly:** (1969) Committee on Information Systems; (1989) National Association for State Information Systems; (1998) NASIRE; (2002) National Association of State Information Resource Executives. **Publications:** *Compendium of Digital Government*, annual. Report ● *Enterprise Architecture Development Tool-Kit*, periodic. Manual. Alternate Formats: CD-ROM; online ● *Fast Facts*, monthly. Newsletter. **Price:** free for members. **Conventions/Meetings:** annual conference ● annual Mid-Year Conference.

5822 ■ National Freedom of Information Coalition (NFOIC)

c/o Missouri School of Journalism
133 Neff Annex
Univ. of Missouri-Columbia
Columbia, MO 65211
Ph: (573)882-5736
Fax: (573)884-6204
E-mail: cdavis@nfoic.org
URL: http://www.nfoic.org
Contact: Charles Davis, Exec. Dir.

Founded: 1989. **Membership Dues:** state FOI organization, academic center, first amendment organization, $250 (annual) ● sustaining (underwriting), $5,000 (annual) ● media association, trade association, law firm, $1,000 (annual) ● individual, $25 (annual) ● government agency, newspaper, lawfirm, electronic media outlet, $100 (annual) ● non-profit organization, $50 (annual). **Description:** Seeks to protect the public's right to know. **Computer Services:** Mailing lists, of members. **Telecommunication Services:** electronic mail, daviscn@missouri.edu. **Projects:** Education for Freedom. **Conventions/Meetings:** conference ● Freedom Workshop - meeting ● workshop.

Inspectors

5823 ■ International Association of Bedding and Furniture Law Officials (IABFLO)
c/o Joan C. Jordan, Pres.
Dept. of Consumer Protection
165 Capitol Ave.
Hartford, CT 06106
Ph: (860)713-6123 (614)644-3964
E-mail: margaret.davis@vdh.virginia.gov
URL: http://abflo.info
Contact: Joan C. Jordan, Pres.
Founded: 1936. **Members:** 30. **Membership Dues:** regular, $50 (annual) ● associate, $150 (annual). **Description:** State and local officials supervising the inspection and labeling of mattresses, pillows, upholstered furniture, and similar items. Encourages and promotes the adoption of uniform bedding and upholstered furniture laws, rules, regulations, nomenclature, labeling requirements, and enforcement procedures. Secures, devises, tests, and adopts standard methods of inspection and sampling of bedding, quilted clothing, and upholstered furniture, and the analyses of filling material used. Secures uniformity in the statement of analytical results. Promotes, conducts, and encourages research in chemistry and allied fields. **Libraries: Type:** not open to the public. **Committees:** Laboratory; Nomenclature. **Publications:** *Official Methods of Analysis*. Book. **Price:** $150.00. **Conventions/Meetings:** annual conference - always in March or April.

5824 ■ National Board of Boiler and Pressure Vessel Inspectors (NBBI)
1055 Crupper Ave.
Columbus, OH 43229-1183
Ph: (614)888-8320 (614)431-3216
Fax: (614)888-0750
E-mail: getinfo@nationalboard.org
URL: http://www.nationalboard.org
Contact: Donald E. Tanner, Exec. Dir.
Founded: 1919. **Members:** 57. **Staff:** 60. **Budget:** $8,000,000. **Description:** Represents North American government agencies empowered to assure adherence to code construction and repair of boilers and pressure vessels. Promotes greater safety through maintaining uniformity in the construction, installation, repair, maintenance and inspection of boilers and pressure vessels. **Libraries: Type:** reference. **Holdings:** archival material, articles. **Awards:** D.J. McDonald Memorial Scholarships. **Frequency:** annual. **Type:** monetary ● Safety Medal Award. **Frequency:** annual. **Type:** medal. **Publications:** *National Board Bulletin*, quarterly. Magazine ● *National Board Inspection Code, 1998 Edition*. Alternate Formats: CD-ROM ● Proceedings, annual. **Price:** $25.00. **Conventions/Meetings:** annual meeting, includes technical presentation (exhibits) - always April or May. 2009 May 11-15, La Jolla, CA; 2010 May 3-7, San Antonio, TX; 2011 May 9-13, Las Vegas, NV.

Insurance

5825 ■ Association of Defense Trial Attorneys (ADTA)
c/o Glenn S. Morgan, Membership Chm.
PO Box 310
Rutland, VT 05702-0310
Ph: (802)786-1045
Fax: (802)786-1100
E-mail: gsm@rsclaw.com
URL: http://www.adtalaw.com
Contact: Glenn S. Morgan, Membership Chm.
Founded: 1941. **Members:** 700. **Membership Dues:** prime, $275 (annual) ● associate, $200 (annual). **Budget:** $50,000. **Description:** Trial lawyers who have over five years' experience in the preparation and trial of insurance cases and the handling of insurance matters, and who possess the knowledge, skill, and facilities to provide insurance companies and self-insurers a legal service of the highest standard. Maintains current biographical data on each member. **Libraries: Type:** not open to the public. **Subjects:** business addresses for members. **Committees:** Finance; Membership; Program; Publication. **Formerly:** (1988) Association of Insurance Attorneys. **Publications:** *The Association*. Newsletter. Alternate Formats: online ● *Membership Roster*, annual. Membership Directory. **Price:** free for members. **Conventions/Meetings:** annual conference ● annual meeting.

5826 ■ Association of Life Insurance Counsel (ALIC)
135 N Pennsylvania St., Ste.1600
Indianapolis, IN 46204
Ph: (317)684-5485
Fax: (317)223-0485
E-mail: bjeffery@bosepublicaffairs.com
URL: http://alic.cc
Contact: Phillip E. Stano, Sec.-Treas.
Founded: 1913. **Members:** 900. **Membership Dues:** individual, $150 (annual). **Description:** General legal counsel for life insurance companies. Seeks to further the education of members in areas of the law that affect life insurance; to promote efficiency in legal service to life insurance companies; to encourage cordial relations among legal representatives of life insurance companies. **Libraries: Type:** reference. **Awards:** Buist M. Anderson Distinguished Service Award. **Frequency:** annual. **Type:** recognition. **Recipient:** for longstanding members who provided outstanding service to the association, and to the life insurance community. **Sections:** Corporate; Insurance; Investment; Securities; Tax. **Publications:** Membership Directory, annual ● Proceedings, annual. **Conventions/Meetings:** annual meeting - always May.

5827 ■ Federation of Defense and Corporate Counsel (FDCC)
11812 N 56th St.
Tampa, FL 33617
Ph: (813)983-0022
Fax: (813)988-5837
E-mail: mstreeper@thefederation.org
URL: http://www.thefederation.org
Contact: Martha J. Streeper, Exec. Dir.
Founded: 1936. **Members:** 1,400. **Membership Dues:** individual, $250 (annual). **Budget:** $500,000. **Description:** Professional society of attorneys actively engaged in the legal aspects of the insurance industry; insurance company executives; corporate counsel involved in the defense of claims. Conducts research through Federation of Defense and Corporate Counsel Foundation. Sponsors annual essay competition for students at accredited law colleges. Maintains 36 law sections and committees. Conducts seminars and educational sessions. **Awards: Type:** recognition. **Formerly:** (1996) Federation of Insurance Counsel; (2003) Federation of Insurance and Corporate Counsel. **Publications:** *Biographical Roster*, annual. Membership Directory. **Price:** available to members only. **Circulation:** 1,400 ● *FDCC Quarterly*. Journal. Covers legal issues relevant to the insurance industry and corporate executives. **Price:** $34.00/year for university law libraries; $40.00/year all others. **Circulation:** 2,100. Alternate Formats: microform; online ● *FDCC Update: Annual Survey of Decision Law*, annual ● *Federation Flyer*, semiannual. Newsletter. Contains updates on activities of the organization. **Conventions/Meetings:** annual meeting (exhibits) - always winter. 2009 Feb. 22-Mar. 1, Kauai, HI ● annual meeting - 2008 July 27-Aug. 3, Banff, AB, Canada.

5828 ■ International Association of Insurance Fraud Agencies (IAIFA)
PO Box 10018
Kansas City, MO 64171
Ph: (816)756-5285
Fax: (816)756-5287
E-mail: moodym@sbcglobal.net
URL: http://www.iaifa.org
Contact: Maximiliane Moody, Exec. Dir.
Founded: 1986. **Members:** 250. **Membership Dues:** associate/regular, $200 (annual) ● corporate, $500 (annual). **Multinational. Description:** Seeks to prevent and fight insurance fraud worldwide through cooperation, training and education of the insurance industry, law enforcement agencies and governments. Works to break down jurisdictional barriers and cut red tape in order to track crime. **Publications:** Newsletter, periodic. **Conventions/Meetings:** annual meeting ● periodic seminar.

5829 ■ International Association for Insurance Law in the United States (AIDA-US)
PO Box 9001
Mount Vernon, NY 10552
Ph: (914)966-3180
Fax: (914)966-3264
E-mail: sa@cinn.com
URL: http://www.aidaus.org
Contact: Steve Acunto, Managing Dir.
Founded: 1963. **Members:** 79. **Description:** Attorneys, insurance company executives, state insurance regulators, professors, and others interested in international and comparative aspects of insurance law. Aims to further the development of international collaboration in insurance law. Promotes education; provides contacts among individuals in the field. **Also Known As:** International Association for Insurance Law, United States Chapter; United States of America Chapter of AIDA. **Publications:** *AIDA-US Newsletter*, quarterly ● *International Newsletter*, quarterly ● Directory, annual ● Also publishes monographs and treatises. **Conventions/Meetings:** annual Colloquium - meeting ● quadrennial World Congress.

5830 ■ National Association of Insurance Commissioners (NAIC)
2301 McGee St., Ste.800
Kansas City, MO 64108-2662
Ph: (816)842-3600
Fax: (816)783-8175
E-mail: news@naic.org
URL: http://www.naic.org
Contact: Walter Bell, Pres.
Founded: 1871. **Members:** 55. **Staff:** 404. **Budget:** $49,000,000. **Description:** State officials supervising insurance. Promotes uniformity of legislation and regulation affecting insurance to protect interests of policyholders. Conducts educational programs for insurance regulators. Compiles statistics from annual statement of solvency and profit data on all U.S. insurers of life, health, property, and casualty. **Libraries: Type:** reference; by appointment only. **Holdings:** 12,000; archival material, articles, books, monographs, periodicals. **Subjects:** insurance regulation. **Awards:** Journal of Insurance Regulation. **Type:** grant ● Robert Dineen Award. **Frequency:** annual. **Type:** recognition. **Recipient:** for state insurance department regulator ● Spencer Kimball Writing Award. **Type:** recognition. **Recipient:** for best example of regulatory research published in the Journal of Insurance Regulation. **Computer Services:** database, insurance regulatory information. **Committees:** Executive; Financial Condition; Financial Regulation Standards and Accreditation; Health Insurance and Managed Care; Life Insurance and Annuities; Market Conduct and Consumer Affairs; Property and Casualty Insurance; Special Insurance Issues. **Formerly:** (1936) National Convention of Insurance Commissioners. **Publications:** *Annual Statement Instructions*, annual. Manuals. Serves property/casualty, life, fraternal, and title insurers and health maintenance organizations; and other insurers and organizations. **Price:** $225.00/year ● *Database Sales Brochure* ● *Insurance Regulatory Information System Ratio Results*, annual. Includes explanations of ratio formulas and result benchmarks. Updates issued 3 times/year. **Price:** $125.00. **Circulation:** 425 ● *International Insurance Relations*, annual. Manual. Includes statutory accounting for property/casualty or life insurers or health maintenance organizations. **Price:** $200.00 ● *Issues*. Booklet. Contains compilation of NAIC's

current position on wide range of insurance regulatory issues. **Price:** $35.00 ● *Journal of Insurance Regulation*, quarterly. Provides current information, research, and regulatory reviews on the insurance industry. **Price:** $70.00/year in U.S.; $85.00/year outside U.S. ● *NAIC Model Laws, Regulations and Guidelines*, quarterly. Manual. Includes updating service containing all model insurance regulations and a history of which states have adopted the models. **Price:** $25.00/individual copy; $395.00/year; $395.00/year for updating service ● *NAIC News*, monthly. Newsletter. Summarizes current insurance topics, specifically insurance regulation. **Price:** $200.00/year ● *National Association of Insurance Commissioners—Proceedings*, quarterly. Contains four-volume set covering the four national meetings. **Price:** $325.00/year ● *Publications Catalog* ● *Retaliation: A Guide to State Retaliatory Taxes, Fees, Deposits and Other Requirements.* Manual. Lists each state's retaliatory tax rates resulting from companies selling insurance products across state lines. **Price:** $250.00/year. **Conventions/Meetings:** quarterly Legislative Meeting.

5831 ■ National Association of Unemployment Insurance Appellate Boards (NAUIAB)
c/o Alice S. Mitchell, Treas.
UI Appeals Tribunal
Georgia Dept. of Labor
1630 Phoenix Blvd., Ste.201
College Park, GA 30349
Ph: (770)994-2220
Fax: (770)996-6871
E-mail: alice.mitchell@dol.state.ga.us
URL: http://www.nauiab.org
Contact: Alice S. Mitchell, Treas.
Membership Dues: regular, $50 (annual). **Description:** Promotes opportunities for people who care about the Unemployment Insurance (UI) appellate process. Participates in actively seeking attainment of professional standards. Provides a forum for the exchange of ideas and opinions. Studies and advocates improved operating procedures and techniques in the administration on unemployment insurance appeals. Provides information and study material for continuing education of members. **Publications:** *Navigator*, 3/year. Newsletter. Alternate Formats: online.

5832 ■ National Conference of Insurance Legislators (NCOIL)
385 Jordan Rd.
Troy, NY 12180
Ph: (518)687-0178
Fax: (518)687-0401
E-mail: info@ncoil.org
URL: http://www.ncoil.org
Contact: Susan F. Nolan, Exec. Dir.
Founded: 1969. **State Groups:** 35. **Description:** Serves as an organization of state legislators whose main area of public policy concern is insurance legislation and regulation. Many legislators active in the Association are either chairs or members of the committees responsible for insurance legislation in their respective state houses across the country. **Committees:** Health Insurance; Life Insurance; Property/Casualty; State-Federal Relations; Workers Compensation. **Task Forces:** Availability and Market Capacity; Insurer Solvency. **Publications:** *NCOIL Insurance Legislative Fact Book and Almanac*, annual ● *NCOILetter*, monthly. Newsletter. Alternate Formats: online. **Conventions/Meetings:** annual meeting - always spring. 2009 Mar. 5-8, Washington, DC ● annual meeting - 2008 Nov. 20-23, Duck Key, FL; 2009 Nov. 19-22, New Orleans, LA.

5833 ■ Public Agency Risk Managers Association (PARMA)
PO Box 6810
San Jose, CA 95150
Free: (888)412-5913
E-mail: brenda.reisinger@parma.com
URL: http://www.parma.com
Contact: David Clovis ARM, Pres.
Founded: 1974. **Members:** 850. **Membership Dues:** regular, $100 (annual) ● associate, $275 (annual). **Staff:** 4. **Budget:** $500,000. **Regional Groups:** 4. **State Groups:** 1. **Description:** Public agencies (such as cities, counties, universities, school districts, special districts); interested private agencies; professionals. Purposes are to consider, discuss, and exchange ideas for the improvement and functioning of risk management in government agencies; to assist agencies and their governing bodies in fostering education, communication, and mutual cooperation. Provides input on bills pending before state legislatures affecting risk management in public agencies. **Awards:** Ben C. Frances Risk Management Education Fund. **Frequency:** annual. **Type:** scholarship. **Recipient:** for employees of a member public agency working towards an ARM designation. **Publications:** *Parmafacts*, bimonthly. Newsletter ● Membership Directory, annual. **Conventions/Meetings:** annual conference (exhibits) ● seminar.

5834 ■ Public Risk Management Association (PRIMA)
500 Montgomery St., Ste.750
Alexandria, VA 22314
Ph: (703)528-7701
Fax: (703)739-0200
E-mail: info@primacentral.org
URL: http://www.primacentral.org
Contact: Lisa Lopinsky, Exec. Dir.
Founded: 1978. **Members:** 2,300. **Membership Dues:** government, corporate associate, organizational affiliate, $310 (annual) ● corporate affiliate, $625 (annual) ● associate, $175 (annual) ● individual affiliate, $185 (annual). **Staff:** 11. **Budget:** $2,000,000. **State Groups:** 37. **Description:** Public agency risk, insurance, human resources, attorneys, and/or safety managers from cities, counties, villages, towns, school boards, and other related areas. Provides an information clearinghouse and communications network for public risk managers to share resources, ideas, and experiences. Offers information on risk, insurance, and safety management. Monitors state and federal legislative actions and court decisions that deal with immunity, tort liability, and intergovernmental risk pools. Maintains library containing current reports from governmental units on their insurance procedures, self-insurance plans, and loss control and safety programs; and copies of policy statements, job descriptions, contractual arrangements, and indemnification clauses. **Libraries: Type:** reference. **Holdings:** 3,000; business records, papers, reports, video recordings. **Subjects:** risk management, public health and safety, varied RFPs, job descriptions. **Awards:** Public Sector Risk Manager of the Year. **Frequency:** annual. **Type:** recognition. **Recipient:** for risk management achievements that overcame non-routine challenges. **Telecommunication Services:** electronic mail, llopinsky@primacentral.org. **Publications:** *Public Risk*, monthly, except June and December. Magazine. Contains feature articles on a wide range of risk management topics; also includes book reviews, and legislative news. **Price:** $130.00/year. ISSN: 0891-7183. **Circulation:** 3,000. **Advertising:** accepted. **Conventions/Meetings:** annual Conference for Public Agencies, includes education sessions (exhibits) - always May or June. 2009 May 31-June 3, Dallas, TX ● annual Government Risk Management Seminar.

Intellectual Property

5835 ■ American Intellectual Property Law Association (AIPLA)
241 18th St. S, Ste.700
Arlington, VA 22202
Ph: (703)415-0780
Fax: (703)415-0786
E-mail: aipla@aipla.org
URL: http://www.aipla.org
Contact: Judith M. Saffer, Pres.
Founded: 1897. **Members:** 14,500. **Membership Dues:** student/graduate affiliate, $45 (annual) ● regular, agent affiliate, $285 (annual) ● government, $80 (annual) ● junior, $120 (annual) ● affiliate outside U.S., $310 (annual). **Staff:** 15. **Description:** Voluntary bar association of lawyers practicing in the fields of patents, trademarks, copyrights, and trade secrets. Aids in the operation and improvement of U.S. patent, trademark, and copyright systems, including the laws by which they are governed and rules and regulations under which federal agencies administer those laws. Sponsors moot court and legal writing competitions. **Libraries: Type:** not open to the public. **Subjects:** intellectual property law. **Awards:** Jan Jancin Award. **Frequency:** annual. **Type:** recognition ● National Science Fair Award. **Frequency:** annual. **Type:** recognition. **Recipient:** for high school science fair ● Watson Award. **Frequency:** annual. **Type:** recognition. **Computer Services:** Mailing lists, of members. **Committees:** Alternate Dispute Resolution; Amicus; Antitrust; Biotechnology; Chemical Practice; Copyrights; Corporate Practice; Diversity in IP Law; Education; Electronic and Computer Law; Electronic Business, Automation and Harmonization of Standards; Emerging Technologies/Internet; Industrial Designs; Interference; International and Foreign Law; International Education; Inventor Issues; IP Law Associations; IP Practice in Europe; IP Practice in Japan; IP Practice in Latin America; IP Practice in the Far East; Law Practice Management; Licensing; Management of IP Assets; Mentoring; Patent Cooperation Treaty Issues; Patent Law; Patent Litigation; Patent-Relations with the USPTO; Professional Programs; Professionalism and Ethics; Public Appointments; Trade Secrets; Trademark; Trademark Internet/Cyberspace; Trademark Legislation; Trademark Litigation; Trademark-Relations w/the USPTO; Trademark Treaties and International Law; Women in IP Law; Young Lawyers. **Formerly:** (1914) Patent Law Association of Washington; (1984) American Patent Law Association. **Publications:** *AIPLA Bulletin*, 3/year. Contains compilation of papers presented at continuing legal education conferences and updates on legislation affecting intellectual property law. **Price:** free for members; $60.00 /year for nonmembers in U.S.; $70.00 /year for nonmembers outside U.S. **Circulation:** 14,000. **Advertising:** accepted ● *AIPLA Quarterly Journal.* Contains professional papers on intellectual property. **Price:** free for members; $70.00 /year for nonmembers in U.S.; $80.00 /year for nonmembers outside U.S. ● Membership Directory, biennial. Alternate Formats: online ● Also publishes a series of monographs. **Conventions/Meetings:** annual meeting, offers continuing legal education in the field of intellectual property (exhibits) - every October in Washington, DC. 2008 Oct. 23-25, Washington, DC ● annual meeting - April or May ● annual MidWinter Institute - meeting - January or February.

5836 ■ American Society of Composers, Authors and Publishers (ASCAP)
1 Lincoln Plz.
New York, NY 10023
Ph: (212)621-6000
Free: (800)95-ASCAP
Fax: (212)724-9064
E-mail: info@ascap.com
URL: http://www.ascap.com
Contact: Marilyn Bergman, Pres.
Founded: 1914. **Members:** 200,000. **Membership Dues:** music writer, $10 (annual) ● music publisher, $50 (annual). **Staff:** 300. **Budget:** $500,000,000. **Description:** Composers, lyricists, and publishers. Serves as clearinghouse in the field of music performing rights. Grants licenses and distributes royalties for the public performance of the copyrighted musical works of its members by broadcasters, symphony orchestras, and other users. **Awards: Frequency:** annual. **Type:** recognition. **Publications:** *The ASCAP Advantage* ● *ASCAP List of Members*, periodic. Membership Directory ● *Biographical Dictionary* ● *Playback*, quarterly. Magazine. Contains profiles of members, music event coverage and legislative updates. **Price:** $12.00/year. **Circulation:** 90,000. **Advertising:** accepted. **Conventions/Meetings:** meeting - 3/year in New York, NY, Los Angeles, CA, and Nashville, TN.

5837 ■ Americans for the Enforcement of Intellectual Property Rights (AEIPR)
PO Box 35215
Chicago, IL 60707-0215

Ph: (773)453-0080
Fax: (708)453-0083
E-mail: aeipr@rentamark.com
Contact: L. Stollen, Contact
Founded: 1975. **Members:** 80,032. **Membership Dues:** individual, $25 (annual) ● business, $100 (annual) ● corporate sponsor, $250 (annual). **Staff:** 10. **Description:** Individuals and organizations with an interest in intellectual property law. Promotes strict enforcement of laws protecting the rights of ownership of individuals to their own intellectual creations. Sponsors legal research and lobbying activities; works to strengthen statutory intellectual property protection. Serves as a platform to network lawyers to clients and lawyers nationwide on the net. **Libraries: Type:** not open to the public. **Holdings:** 15,000. **Subjects:** intellectual property law. **Awards:** Trademark Attorney of the Year. **Frequency:** annual. **Type:** recognition. **Computer Services:** Mailing lists ● online services, ad banner (468x60 pixel) advertising. **Also Known As:** (2000) American Intellectual Property Association. **Publications:** Journal, quarterly. Contains articles submitted by authors via email. **Price:** included in membership dues. **Circulation:** 125,000. **Advertising:** accepted. Alternate Formats: online. **Conventions/Meetings:** convention.

5838 ■ Association of University Technology Managers (AUTM)
60 Revere Dr., Ste.500
Northbrook, IL 60062
Ph: (847)559-0846
Fax: (847)480-9282
E-mail: info@autm.net
URL: http://www.autm.net
Contact: Vicki Loise CAE, Exec. Dir.
Founded: 1974. **Members:** 3,600. **Membership Dues:** individual, affiliate, $175 (annual) ● student, $87 (annual). **Staff:** 12. **Budget:** $1,000,000. **Regional Groups:** 5. **Description:** Technology Transfer managers from institutions of higher learning and affiliated hospitals; attorneys; foundations. Assists administrators in the licensing of technology and reporting of inventions. Recommends more effective technology transfer procedures. Sponsors national workshops, regional information sessions, and a basic and advanced licensing course. **Computer Services:** database, membership list. **Formerly:** (1989) Society of University Patent Administrators. **Publications:** *AUTM Journal*, annual. **Price:** included in membership dues ● *AUTM Membership Directory*, annual ● Newsletter, bimonthly. Contains information on university technology transfer and association activities. ● Also publishes AUTM Technology Transfer Practice Manual, Vol. I, II, III. **Conventions/Meetings:** annual Central Region Summer Meeting - conference - always June/July ● Eastern Region Summer Meeting - conference - always June/July ● annual meeting - always February or March. 2009 Feb. 12-14, Orlando, FL ● Western Region Summer Meeting - conference - always June/July.

5839 ■ Brand Names Education Foundation (BNEF)
1133 Ave. of the Americas
New York, NY 10036-6710
Ph: (212)768-9885
Fax: (212)768-7796
E-mail: info@bnef.org
URL: http://www.bnef.org
Contact: Alan C. Drewsen, Exec. Dir.
Founded: 1987. **Membership Dues:** regular, $850 (annual) ● supplementary, regular reduced member, $575 (annual) ● associate, $700 (annual) ● professor, $75 (annual) ● student, $25 (annual). **Staff:** 2. **Budget:** $1,000,000. **Description:** Promotes education in the trademark field; advances the brand name concept. Conducts annual Saul Lefkowitz Moot Court Competition. Promotes consumer education about the value and importance of brand names. **Awards:** Ladas Memorial Award. **Frequency:** annual. **Type:** recognition. **Recipient:** for the best paper on the subject of trademark law or a matter that directly relates to or affects trademarks ● Pattishall Medal for Teaching Excellence. **Frequency:** triennial. **Type:** recognition. **Recipient:** to educators in the business and legal fields for outstanding instruction in the trademark and trade identity field. **Additional Websites:** http://www.inta.org. **Telecommunication Services:** electronic mail, bnef@inta.org. **Committees:** Anti-Counterfeiting and Enforcement; Dilution and Well-Known Marks; Emerging Issues; Enforcement; Geographical Indications; International Amicus; Internet; Legislation and Regulation; Non-Traditional Marks; Parallel Imports; Trademark Office Practices; Treaty Analysis. **Publications:** Produces and distributes television public service announcements.

5840 ■ Business Software Alliance (BSA)
c/o BSA United States
1150 18th St. NW, Ste.700
Washington, DC 20036
Ph: (202)872-5500
Fax: (202)872-5501
E-mail: webmaster@bsa.org
URL: http://www.bsa.org
Contact: Robert Holleyman, Pres./CEO
Founded: 1988. **Members:** 8. **Staff:** 25. **Regional Groups:** 4. **Description:** Computer software publishers. Promotes the free world trade of business software by combating international software piracy, advancing intellectual property protection, and increasing market access. **Formerly:** (1990) Business Software Association. **Publications:** *Guide to Software Management*, annual. Assists organizations in software management. Available in 8 languages. Alternate Formats: online ● *Software Review*, quarterly. Newsletter.

5841 ■ Center for Social and Legal Research (CSLR)
2 Univ. Plz., Ste.414
Hackensack, NJ 07601
Ph: (201)996-1154
Fax: (201)996-1883
E-mail: ctrslr@aol.com
URL: http://www.privacyexchange.org
Contact: Ms. Lorrie Sherwood, Exec. Dir./Ed.
Founded: 1987. **Staff:** 12. **Multinational. Description:** Works to assist businesses in developing balanced consumer and employee privacy and data protection policies domestically and globally. Conducts privacy conferences and manages educational projects aimed at businesses that use personal information in their operations. Maintains free online privacy reference resource. **Libraries: Type:** reference. **Holdings:** clippings. **Subjects:** data protection, privacy, public policy, e-commerce, ID theft. **Awards:** Distinguished Privacy Leadership Award. **Frequency:** annual. **Type:** recognition. **Telecommunication Services:** electronic mail, admin@privacyexchange.org. **Formerly:** (1999) CSLR. **Publications:** *P&AB Privacy Litigation Report*, quarterly. Contains review and analysis of privacy-centered lawsuits. ● *Privacy and American Business*, monthly. Report. Contains information concerning current privacy issues. **Price:** $195.00. ISSN: 1070-0536. Alternate Formats: online ● *Privacy Newsflash*. Newsletter. Alternate Formats: online. **Conventions/Meetings:** annual conference - always spring ● Project Meetings.

5842 ■ Copyright Clearance Center (CCC)
222 Rosewood Dr.
Danvers, MA 01923
Ph: (978)750-8400
Fax: (978)646-8600
E-mail: info@copyright.com
URL: http://www.copyright.com
Contact: Joseph S. Alen, Pres./CEO
Founded: 1978. **Members:** 14,000. **Staff:** 160. **Description:** Facilitates compliance with U.S. copyright law. Provides licensing systems for the reproduction and distribution of copyrighted materials in print and electronic formats throughout the world. Manages rights relating to over 1.75 million works and represents more than 9600 publishers and hundreds of thousands of authors and other creators, directly or through their representatives. **Publications:** Annual Report, annual. Alternate Formats: online.

5843 ■ Copyright Society of the U.S.A. (CSUSA)
352 7th Ave., Ste.739
New York, NY 10001
Ph: (212)354-6401
Fax: (212)354-2847
E-mail: amy@csusa.org
URL: http://www.csusa.org
Contact: Helene Blue, Pres.
Founded: 1953. **Members:** 925. **Membership Dues:** individual, $125 (annual) ● sustaining, $750 (annual) ● patron, $500 (annual) ● contributing, $175 (annual) ● senior/junior, $50 (annual) ● full time student, $12 (annual). **Staff:** 1. **Regional Groups:** 8. **Description:** Lawyers and laymen; libraries, universities, publishers, and firms interested in the protection and study of rights in music, literature, art, motion pictures, and other forms of intellectual property. Promotes research in the field of copyright; encourages study of economic and technological aspects of copyright by those who deal with problems of communication, book publishing, motion picture production, and television and radio broadcasting. Seeks better understanding among students and scholars of copyright in foreign countries, to lay a foundation for development of international copyright. Co-sponsors (with New York University School of Law) the Walter J. Derenberg Copyright and Trademark Library, which includes foreign periodicals dealing with literary and artistic property and related fields. Sponsors symposia and lectures on copyright. Encourages study of copyright in U.S. law schools. **Libraries: Type:** reference. **Awards:** Seton Award. **Frequency:** annual. **Type:** grant. **Recipient:** for young lawyer. **Computer Services:** Online services, Westlaw journal. **Publications:** *Journal of the Copyright Society*, quarterly. **Price:** $25.00 /year for libraries. **Circulation:** 1,400. Alternate Formats: online. **Conventions/Meetings:** annual meeting - always June ● annual meeting - usually February.

5844 ■ Home Recording Rights Coalition (HRRC)
PO Box 14267
Washington, DC 20044-4267
Ph: (202)628-9212
Free: (800)282-8273
Fax: (202)628-9227
E-mail: info@hrrc.org
URL: http://www.hrrc.org
Contact: Gary Shapiro, Pres./CEO
Founded: 1981. **Description:** Consumers, retailers, and manufacturers of audio and video electronics products. Advocates the consumer's right to use consumer electronics equipment for private, noncommercial purposes; current issues range from new audio and video technologies to the digital information superhighway and multimedia. **Publications:** *The Case for Home Recording Rights*. Book ● *Compendium of Arguments* ● *HRRC Insider*, periodic. Newsletter. Details legislative and regulatory developments. **Price:** free, for members only. Alternate Formats: online.

5845 ■ Imaging Supplies Coalition (ISC)
1435 E Venice Ave., No. 104
MBN 249
Venice, FL 34292
Ph: (941)961-7897
E-mail: info@isc-inc.org
URL: http://www.isc-inc.org
Contact: Allen D. Westerfield, Contact
Founded: 1994. **Members:** 10. **Membership Dues:** regular, $20,000 (annual) ● associate, $1,000-$10,000 (annual). **Staff:** 1. **Description:** Equipment manufacturers of supplies and their licensees. Seeks to protect members and their customers from product and service counterfeiting by promoting intellectual property protection worldwide. Provides educational programs on telemarketing fraud and counterfeit products; conducts training seminars for law enforcement officials; conducts investigations and litigations; offers product authentication services. **Computer Services:** database. **Publications:** Newsletter, periodic. **Conventions/Meetings:** annual board meeting and conference (exhibits).

5846 ■ Intellectual Property Owners Association (IPO)
1255 23rd St. NW, Ste.200
Washington, DC 20037
Ph: (202)466-2396
Fax: (202)466-2893
E-mail: info@ipo.org
URL: http://www.ipo.org
Contact: Herbert C. Wamsley, Exec. Dir.
Founded: 1972. **Members:** 7,800. **Staff:** 10. **Budget:** $3,383,735. **Description:** Corporations, lawyers, and individuals interested in intellectual property (patents, trademarks, copyrights, and trade secrets). Seeks to support and strengthen the patent, trademark, copyright, and trade secret laws. Monitors related legislative activities. **Formerly:** (2000) Intellectual Property Owners. **Publications:** *IPO Daily News*. Newsletter. **Price:** available to members only, via email. **Conventions/Meetings:** periodic conference and meeting, includes exposition - always fall ● annual meeting - always spring.

5847 ■ International Intellectual Property Alliance (IIPA)
c/o Eric H. Smith, Pres./Co-Founder
800 Connecticut Ave. NW, Ste.500
Washington, DC 20006
Ph: (202)833-4198
Fax: (202)331-3101
E-mail: info@iipa.com
URL: http://www.iipa.com
Contact: Eric H. Smith, Pres./Co-Founder
Founded: 1984. **Members:** 6. **Multinational. Description:** Comprised of six trade associations, each representing a significant segment of the U.S. copyright community. Represents over 1,300 U.S. companies producing and distributing materials protected by copyright laws globally: computer software which includes business applications software and entertainment software (such as videogame CDs and cartridges, personal computer CD-ROMs and multimedia products); theatrical films, television programs, home videos and digital representations of audiovisual works, music, records, CDs, and audiocassettes; and textbooks, tradebooks, reference and professional publications and journals (in both electronic and print media). **Publications:** *Copyright Industries in the U.S. Economy: The 2004 Report*, semiannual. Book. **Price:** free. Alternate Formats: online.

5848 ■ International Intellectual Property Association (IIPA)
1255 23rd St. NW, Ste.200
Washington, DC 20037
Ph: (202)466-2396
Fax: (202)466-2893
E-mail: herb@ipo.org
URL: http://www.ipo.org
Founded: 1930. **Members:** 650. **Membership Dues:** individual, $150 (annual) ● corporate, $275 (annual). **Description:** Lawyers who have professional qualifications and interest in the international protection of patents, designs, trademarks, copyrights, and other intellectual property rights. American group of the International Association for the Protection of Industrial Property. Monitors international developments that may affect industrial property and related rights. Studies, discusses, and reports on proposed national and foreign legislation treaties and conventions that are likely to affect national and international intellectual property interests. **Committees:** Anti-Counterfeiting; Effect of Laws and Policies of Foreign Governments Respecting Use, Registration, Maintenance and Renewal of Trademarks; Employed Inventor's Laws in Foreign Countries; Industrial Designs; International Conventions and Treaties Involving Patent Rights and Technology; International Copyright Conventions and Treaties; Multinational Patents; Patent Cooperation Treaty, its Development and Administration; Relations with Foreign Patent and Trademark Offices; Software Protection; Trademark Registration Treaty. **Formerly:** (1989) International Patent and Trademark Association. **Publications:** Membership Directory, annual ● Also publishes minutes of committee and executive meetings. **Conventions/Meetings:** triennial international conference and congress.

5849 ■ International Licensing Industry Merchandisers' Association (LIMA)
350 5th Ave., Ste.1408
New York, NY 10118
Ph: (212)244-1944
Fax: (212)563-6552
E-mail: info@licensing.org
URL: http://www.licensing.org
Contact: Charles M. Riotto, Pres.
Founded: 1985. **Members:** 1,000. **Membership Dues:** licensee, licensor/licensing agent (based on licensing activity), $500-$2,500 (annual). **Staff:** 5. **Budget:** $1,800,000. **Regional Groups:** 5. **Languages:** Chinese, English, German, Japanese. **Multinational. Description:** Companies and individuals engaged in the marketing and servicing of licensed properties, both as agents and as property owners; manufacturers and retailers in the licensing business; supporters of the licensing industry. Professional association for the licensing industry worldwide. Objectives are to establish a standard reflecting a professional and ethical management approach to the marketing of licensed properties; to become the leading source of information in the industry; to communicate this information to members and others in the industry through publishing, public speaking, seminars, and an open line; to represent the industry in trade and consumer media and in relationships with the government, retailers, manufacturers, other trade associations, and the public. Conducts research programs. Compiles statistics; maintains hall of fame and placement service. **Libraries: Type:** reference. **Awards:** LIMA International Licensing Award. **Frequency:** annual. **Type:** recognition. **Computer Services:** database, licensing. **Formed by Merger of:** (1985) Licensed Merchandisers' Association; Licensing Industry Association. **Publications:** *BottomLine*, quarterly. Newsletter. Contains topical licensing issues. **Circulation:** 1,200. Alternate Formats: online ● *Worldwide Licensing Resource Directory*, annual. **Conventions/Meetings:** annual Licensing International and Licensing University - trade show and seminar, licensor properties (exhibits).

5850 ■ International Trademark Association (INTA)
655 3rd Ave., 10th Fl.
New York, NY 10017-5617
Ph: (212)642-1700
Fax: (212)768-7796
E-mail: info@inta.org
URL: http://www.inta.org
Contact: Alan C. Drewsen, Exec. Dir.
Founded: 1878. **Members:** 5,000. **Membership Dues:** regular, $850 (annual) ● supplementary, regular reduced, $575 (annual) ● student, $25 (annual) ● associate, $700 (annual) ● professor, $75 (annual). **Staff:** 44. **Budget:** $8,000,000. **Description:** Trademark owners; associate members are lawyers, law firms, advertising agencies, designers, market researchers, and others in the trademark industries. Seeks to: protect the interests of the public in the use of trademarks and trade names; promote the interests of members and of trademark owners generally in the use of their trademarks and trade names; disseminate information concerning the use, registration, and protection of trademarks in the United States, its territories, and in foreign countries. Maintains job bank and speakers' bureau. **Libraries: Type:** reference. **Holdings:** 3,000; books, periodicals. **Subjects:** trademarks. **Computer Services:** database, membership list. **Committees:** Education and Information Services; Governance; Participation; Policy Development and Advocacy. **Formerly:** (1993) U.S. Trademark Association. **Publications:** *INTA Bulletin*, biweekly. Newsletter ● *Trademark Checklist* ● *The Trademark Reporter*, bimonthly. Journal. Covers trademark and unfair competition law. Topics includes international developments and U.S. Patent and Trademark Office practice. **Price:** included in membership dues; $50.00 /year for libraries, school and government agency. ISSN: 0041-056X. **Circulation:** 3,900 ● Books ● Brochures ● Membership Directory, annual. **Conventions/Meetings:** annual meeting and convention (exhibits) - always May. 2009 May 16-20, Seattle, WA; 2010 May 22-26, Boston, MA.

5851 ■ Inventors Workshop International Education Foundation/Entrepreneurs Workshop (IWIEF)
PO Box 285
Santa Barbara, CA 93102-0285
Ph: (805)969-9250
Fax: (805)899-4927
E-mail: alan@inventorsworkshop.org
Contact: Alan A. Tratner, Pres.
Founded: 1971. **Members:** 32,000. **Membership Dues:** student, $35 (annual) ● college, $75 (annual) ● adult, $139 (annual). **Staff:** 3. **Budget:** $250,000. **State Groups:** 20. **Local Groups:** 9. **Languages:** English, Spanish. **Description:** Amateur and professional inventors in the U.S. Provides instruction, assistance, and guidance in areas including: patent protection; patent searches for inventions; offering inventions for sale; getting inventions and products designed, produced, and manufactured; choosing experts when required; performing as many of these vital actions as capabilities and resources provide. Organizes seminars and semiannual programs on invention promotion and "Reduction to Practice." Conducts research. Works in cooperation with Entrepreneurs Workshop International, which was formed to help inventor/members sell, market, or license their products. Offers children's services. Operates Green2Gold Incubator and workshops for energy and environmental technologies. **Libraries: Type:** reference. **Holdings:** 600. **Subjects:** invention, new product development, creativity. **Awards:** Great Idea Contest and Imagination Fairs. **Frequency:** annual. **Type:** recognition. **Subgroups:** Eco Inventing; Inventech Catalog; Medical; Preferrals; Seminars/Product Searches; Toys and Games; Vehicles. **Formerly:** (1984) Inventors Workshop International. **Publications:** *Complete Guide to Making Money With Your Inventions* ● *Eco Expo Resources Guide* ● *Invent!: The Magazine of Creativity, Invention and Entrepreneurship and The Lightbulb Journal*, bimonthly. Provides information on the business of inventing to inventors, innovators, entrepreneurs, designers, and engineers. Includes patent information. **Price:** free for members; $24.95 /year for nonmembers. **Circulation:** 14,000. **Advertising:** accepted ● *Inventors Bookshop*. Catalog. Contains information on publications and A.V.S. ● *Inventor's Guidebook* ● *Inventor's Journal* ● *The Lightbulb/Pathfinder Newsletter*, periodic ● *Little Inventions That Made Big Money* ● *Membership Resources Directory*. **Conventions/Meetings:** periodic Creativity in America: Inventech and Eco Expo - conference (exhibits) ● periodic Imagination Fair/Great Idea Contest - competition ● International Young Inventors and Entrepreneurs Conference ● periodic InvenTech Tradeshow - trade show (exhibits).

5852 ■ IP Justice (IPJ)
1192 Haight St.
San Francisco, CA 94117
Ph: (415)553-6261
Fax: (415)462-6451
E-mail: robin@ipjustice.org
URL: http://ipjustice.org
Contact: Atty. Robin D. Gross, Exec. Dir.
Membership Dues: basic, $50 (annual) ● supporter, $75 (annual) ● corporate, $500 (annual) ● patron, $1,000 (annual) ● visionary, $5,000 (annual) ● student/budget, $25 (annual). **Description:** Promotes balanced intellectual property law. Focuses on international treaties, directives and other trade agreements that address intellectual property rights. Advises policy makers on the impact of intellectual property rules. Raises global awareness of the threat to individual freedoms posed by expanding legal rights and technological restrictions. **Publications:** Reports. Alternate Formats: online.

5853 ■ Licensing Executives Society (LES)
1800 Diagonal Rd., Ste.280
Alexandria, VA 22314
Ph: (703)836-3106

Fax: (703)836-3107
E-mail: info@les.org
URL: http://www.usa-canada.les.org
Contact: Ken Schoppmann, Exec. Dir.
Founded: 1966. **Members:** 6,800. **Membership Dues:** active, $225 (annual) ● student, $35 (annual) ● associate, $112 (annual). **Budget:** $2,500,000. **Regional Groups:** 4. **Description:** U.S. and foreign businessmen, scientists, engineers, and lawyers having direct responsibility for the transfer of technology. Maintains placement service. **Libraries: Type:** reference. **Holdings:** audiovisuals, books, periodicals. **Committees:** Awards; Education; Ethics; International; Laws; Legislative; Publicity; Research; Transition in Licensing. **Publications:** *International Technology Transfer Directory*, biennial ● *Law and Business of Licensing*, periodic ● *Les Nouvelles*, quarterly. Journal ● *Licensing Executives Society—Membership Directory*, periodic ● *Viewpoints*, bimonthly. Newsletter. Contains information about association's activities. **Conventions/Meetings:** semiannual meeting - every winter and spring ● annual meeting - 2008 Oct. 19-23, Orlando, FL; 2009 Oct. 18-22, San Francisco, CA ● periodic regional meeting ● quarterly seminar.

5854 ■ Los Angeles Copyright Society (LACS)

c/o Greg P. Goeckner, Treas.
15503 Ventura Blvd.
Encino, CA 91436
E-mail: marie.varricchio-diaz@fox.com
URL: http://www.copr.org
Contact: Mark E. Meyerson, Pres.
Founded: 1952. **Members:** 300. **Membership Dues:** individual, $45 (annual). **Description:** Attorneys specializing in copyright, privacy, defamation, and other aspects of entertainment law in the motion picture, television, recording, and related entertainment industries. Sponsors lectures and discussions on all phases of entertainment law, both domestic and international. **Awards:** Peter D. Knecht Memorial Award. **Frequency:** periodic. **Type:** recognition. **Recipient:** for a deserving student who has displayed excellence in the field of contract and entertainment law. **Conventions/Meetings:** monthly meeting - September through May.

5855 ■ National Council of Intellectual Property Law Associations (NCIPLA)

Address Unknown since 2007
Founded: 1934. **Members:** 53. **Description:** State and local patent law associations, each represented by a councilman. Informs member associations of matters of interest in patent, trademark, and copyright fields and facilitates exchange of information among member associations. Cosponsors, with the Patent and Trademark Office, the National Inventors Hall of Fame Foundation. Maintains speakers' bureau; compiles statistics. **Awards: Type:** recognition. **Formerly:** (1988) National Council of Patent Law Associations. **Publications:** *National Council of Patent Law Associations—Chairman's Letter*, monthly ● *National Council of Patent Law Associations—Legislative Letter*, monthly ● *NCPLA Newsletter*, quarterly. Provides legal information concerning the patent, trademark, and copyright fields and news of the member state and local associations. **Price:** $50.00/year. **Circulation:** 400.

5856 ■ Patent Office Professional Association (POPA)

PO Box 2745
Arlington, VA 22202
Ph: (571)272-0897 (571)272-6930
URL: http://www.popa.org
Contact: Robert D. Budens, Pres.
Founded: 1964. **Members:** 3,300. **Membership Dues:** individual, $5 (biweekly). **Budget:** $200,000. **Description:** Professional, nontrademark, and nonmanagement employees of the U.S. Patent and Trademark Office. Works to establish better working conditions and professionalism. **Libraries: Type:** reference. **Holdings:** archival material, books, reports. **Subjects:** labor, legal issues. **Awards:** Outstanding Service Award. **Frequency:** annual. **Type:** recognition. **Affiliated With:** Fund for Assuring an Independent Retirement; Public Employees Roundtable. **Publications:** *POPA News*, monthly. Newsletter. Discusses congressional testimony regarding USPTO operations and a report on the increasingly unhealthy USPTO culture. **Price:** free. **Circulation:** 4,000. Alternate Formats: online. **Conventions/Meetings:** annual meeting - always first Thursday of December in Arlington, VA.

5857 ■ Patent and Trademark Office Society (PTOS)

PO Box 2089
Arlington, VA 22202
Ph: (571)272-4190 (571)272-4170
URL: http://www.ptos.org
Contact: Tonia Meonske, Pres.
Founded: 1917. **Members:** 2,000. **Membership Dues:** active, $52 (annual) ● active, $2 (biweekly) ● associate, $50 (annual). **Staff:** 50. **Budget:** $300,000. **Description:** Current and former employees of the U.S. Patent and Trademark Office; patent and trademark practitioners outside the patent office. Purposes are educational, social, and legislative; legislative program concerns federal patent and trademark legislation; social program is for members and their families; educational programs, including lectures, films, and classes, are designed for the public and for continuing professional education. Supplies judges for annual International Science Fair Competition and local fairs. **Libraries: Type:** reference. **Holdings:** archival material, photographs. **Awards:** Pasquale J. Federico Award. **Frequency:** annual. **Type:** recognition. **Recipient:** for outstanding public service in the field of intellectual property ● Rossman Award. **Frequency:** annual. **Type:** recognition. **Recipient:** for the best article in the Journal of the Patent and Trademark Office Society. **Formerly:** (1985) Patent Office Society. **Publications:** *Journal of the Patent and Trademark Office Society (JPTOS)*, monthly. Includes legal reviews. **Price:** included in membership dues. ISSN: 0882-9098. **Circulation:** 4,000. **Advertising:** accepted. Alternate Formats: online ● *Unofficial Gazette*, monthly. Newsletter. Alternate Formats: online ● Monographs. **Conventions/Meetings:** annual meeting.

5858 ■ Software and Information Industry Association (SIIA)

1090 Vermont Ave. NW, 6th Fl.
Washington, DC 20005-4930
Ph: (202)289-7442
Free: (800)388-7478
Fax: (202)289-7097
E-mail: industrydaily@siia.net
URL: http://www.siia.net
Contact: Ken Wasch, Pres.
Founded: 1984. **Members:** 750. **Staff:** 35. **Budget:** $4,000,000. **Description:** Seeks to promote the interest of the software and information industries. Protects intellectual property and advocate a legal and regulatory environment that benefits the industry. Serves as a resource to members. **Awards:** Codie Awards. **Frequency:** annual. **Type:** recognition. **Recipient:** for excellence in software and information services. **Committees:** Government Affairs. **Divisions:** Content; Education; Financial Information Services; Software. **Formed by Merger of:** (1999) Software Publishers Association and Information Industry Association. **Publications:** *Upgrade*, bimonthly. Magazine. **Price:** $79.00/6 issues. **Circulation:** 3,500. **Advertising:** accepted. **Conventions/Meetings:** annual conference.

5859 ■ Songwriters Guild of America (SGA)

209 Tenth Ave. S, Ste.321
Nashville, TN 37203
Ph: (615)742-9945
Fax: (615)742-9948
E-mail: nash@songwritersguild.com
URL: http://www.songwritersguild.com
Contact: Ms. Kitty Wright, Membership Services Mgr.
Founded: 1931. **Members:** 4,500. **Membership Dues:** gold, $60 (annual) ● platinum, $84 (annual) ● diamond, $108 (annual). **Staff:** 8. **State Groups:** 3. **Description:** Voluntary songwriters association run by songwriters for songwriters. Seeks to strengthen songwriters' rights and increase royalties through appropriate action directed at publishers, industry groups, and the courts of congress. Provides members with a wide range of services that are beneficial to songwriters. Maintains efforts to advance, promote, and benefit the profession of songwriting. **Awards:** Abe Olman Award. **Type:** scholarship. **Recipient:** for music students. **Telecommunication Services:** electronic mail, membership@songwritersguild.com ● electronic mail, royalties@songwritersguild.com ● electronic mail, copyright@songwritersguild.com ● electronic mail, licensing@songwritersguild.com. **Departments:** Catalog Administration; Copyright; Royalty. **Subgroups:** Songwriters Guild Foundation. **Absorbed:** (2003) National Academy of Songwriters. **Formerly:** (1958) Songwriters Protective Association; (1982) American Guild of Authors and Composers; (1986) Songwriters Guild. **Publications:** *Songwriters Guild of America—News*, monthly. Newsletter. Covers SGA and SGF activities and membership news. Includes obituaries, classified ads, and interviews with songwriters. **Price:** free. **Circulation:** 6,000. **Advertising:** accepted. **Conventions/Meetings:** annual meeting.

5860 ■ Trademark Society (TMS)

Gen. Info. Services
Patent and Trademark Off.
Crystal Plz., Rm. 2002
Washington, DC 20231
Ph: (703)308-4357
Free: (800)786-9199
E-mail: usptoinfo@uspto.gov
URL: http://www.uspto.gov
Contact: Jon W. Dudas, Dir.
Members: 100. **Description:** Represents labor union of trademark attorneys in the U.S. Department of Commerce. **Convention/Meeting:** none.

5861 ■ Visual Artists and Galleries Association (VAGA)

Address Unknown since 2008
Founded: 1975. **Members:** 5,000. **Membership Dues:** $50 (annual). **Staff:** 4. **Description:** Represents American (500) and European (4,500) artists, photographers, and art galleries. Allows members to control the reproduction of their works by arranging royalty agreements with the periodical, book, poster, and specialty publishing industries. Takes action on members' behalf against unauthorized reproductions of their works short of litigation; acts as a clearinghouse for licensing reproduction rights. Disseminates information about members and their works supplied by members themselves to users of art reproduction. Works to establish uniform art reproduction rights procedures throughout the industry. Offers protection against pirated art reproductions not only in the United States, but also throughout Europe and Japan its affiliation with other societies dealing with foreign artists' rights. Compiles statistics. **Libraries: Type:** reference. **Publications:** Newsletter, periodic. **Conventions/Meetings:** biennial conference.

Intelligence

5862 ■ Military Intelligence Corps Association (MICA)

PO Box 13020
Fort Huachuca, AZ 85670-3020
Ph: (520)456-6232
E-mail: info@micorps.org
URL: http://www.micorps.org
Contact: Les Siemens, Exec. Dir.
Membership Dues: individual (based on grade/status), $18-$40 (annual) ● corporate (based on number of employees), $150-$500 (annual) ● life (based on age), $250-$600. **Description:** Represents the active duty, reserve component and retired Army, and defense contractors and others who support the military intelligence mission. Seeks to enhance the military intelligence profession. Promotes military intelligence through a variety of programs. Fosters fraternal relations among members and throughout

the rest of the military intelligence community. **Awards:** Golden Rose Award. **Type:** recognition. **Recipient:** for a military spouse whose volunteer service contributes to the mission accomplishment of the military intelligence unit, activity, command or staff agency ● Knowlton Award. **Type:** recognition. **Recipient:** for individuals who have contributed significantly to the promotion of Army Intelligence ● **Frequency:** annual. **Type:** scholarship. **Recipient:** for undergraduate family members of active duty, reserve, national guard, and retired military intelligence soldiers. **Publications:** *The Vanguard*, quarterly. Journal.

International Law

5863 ■ American Bar Association Section of International Law

740 15th St. NW
Washington, DC 20005
Ph: (202)662-1661 (202)662-1000
Fax: (202)662-1669
E-mail: intlaw@abanet.org
URL: http://www.abanet.org/intlaw
Contact: Leanne Pfautz, Section Dir.

Founded: 1933. **Members:** 13,000. **Staff:** 10. **State Groups:** 60. **Description:** Attorneys licensed to practice law in the U.S; attorneys admitted to the bar in foreign countries; law students. Seeks to advance the rule of law worldwide; assists attorneys in practice involving international issues. Conducts continuing education programs; maintains over 60 committees including International Trade, International Litigation, Corporate Law, Human Rights, and Environmental Law. **Computer Services:** Mailing lists. **Divisions:** Business Regulation; Business Transactions and Disputes; Comparative Law; Constituent; Industries; Legal Practice; Public International Law; Taxes, Estates and Individuals. **Publications:** *International Law News*, quarterly. Newsletter. Contains articles on breaking issues for practitioners in the international arena. **Price:** free for members ● *International Lawyer*, quarterly. Journal. Contains articles on current issues and developments in international law and practice. ISSN: 0020-7810. Alternate Formats: online ● *Section Update E-newsletter*, monthly. Contains the latest on section's activities. Alternate Formats: online ● Booklets, 3-4/year ● Several books each year on various international law topics. **Conventions/Meetings:** meeting (exhibits) - 3/year, usually spring, August, and fall.

5864 ■ American Foreign Law Association (AFLA)

c/o Michael D. Patrick, Treas.
Fragomen, Del Rey, Bernsen and Loewy, LLP
515 Madison Ave.
New York, NY 10022
E-mail: mpatrick@fragomen.com
URL: http://www.afla-law.org
Contact: Andrew L. Odell, Pres.

Founded: 1925. **Members:** 650. **Membership Dues:** resident, $125 (annual) ● non-resident, law student, $75 (annual) ● sustaining, $150 (annual) ● patron, $250 (annual) ● firm, $300 (annual). **Description:** Represents attorneys, jurists, and law professors concerned with issues in international, comparative, and foreign law. Maintains non-governmental organization status with the United Nations. Conducts research. Sponsors educational programs, monthly luncheon programs, and International Law Weekend. **Awards: Type:** recognition. **Publications:** *American Foreign Law Association Newsletter*, 3/year ● *American Journal of Comparative Law*, quarterly. Includes annual directory. **Circulation:** 2,000. **Conventions/Meetings:** annual luncheon - always April/May, New York City.

5865 ■ American Society of Comparative Law (ASCL)

c/o Symeon C. Symeonides, Pres.
Willamette Univ. Coll. of Law
245 Winter St. SE
Salem, OR 97301
Ph: (503)370-6402
Fax: (503)370-6828
E-mail: symeon@willamette.edu
URL: http://www.comparativelaw.org
Contact: Symeon C. Symeonides, Pres.

Founded: 1951. **Members:** 100. **Membership Dues:** sponsor, $700 (annual) ● associate, $90 (annual) ● sustaining, $500 (annual). **Budget:** $60,000. **Description:** Members are law schools and law-related institutes. Promotes the comparative study of law and the understanding of foreign legal systems and private international law. Supports the American Journal of Comparative Law and other publications concerning comparative, foreign, and private international law; also co-sponsors conferences in these fields. **Libraries: Type:** not open to the public. **Holdings:** books, periodicals. **Awards:** Yntema Prize for Young Comparatists. **Frequency:** annual. **Type:** monetary. **Recipient:** for best writing in the American Journal of Comparative Law. **Computer Services:** database, Index to the American Journal of Comparative Law. **Formerly:** (1992) American Association for the Comparative Study of Law. **Publications:** *The American Journal of Comparative Law*, quarterly. Features topics on the field of comparative foreign, and private international law. **Price:** $30.00/year in U.S.; $32.00/year outside U.S. ISSN: 0002-919X. **Circulation:** 2,000. **Advertising:** accepted. Alternate Formats: online ● *United States Reports to the International Congress of Comparative Law*, quadrennial. **Price:** $30.00. **Conventions/Meetings:** annual conference and congress.

5866 ■ American Society of International Law (ASIL)

2223 Massachusetts Ave. NW
Washington, DC 20008
Ph: (202)939-6000
Fax: (202)797-7133
E-mail: services@asil.org
URL: http://www.asil.org
Contact: Elizabeth Andersen, Exec. Dir./Exec. VP

Founded: 1906. **Members:** 4,000. **Membership Dues:** regular, $180 (annual) ● professional, $95 (annual) ● student, $35 (annual) ● contributing, $300 (annual) ● special/retired, $120 (annual) ● patron, $10,000 (annual). **Staff:** 20. **Budget:** $1,500,000. **Description:** Scholars, practitioners, government officials, political scientists, and specialists in subjects. Such as human rights, law of the sea, disarmament and more. Provides access to insight and information on the world of international law. **Libraries: Type:** reference; open to the public. **Holdings:** 25,000; archival material, books, monographs, periodicals, video recordings. **Subjects:** international legal affairs. **Awards:** Certificate of Merit of ASIL. **Frequency:** annual. **Type:** recognition. **Recipient:** to authors of works that convey creative scholarship in the field of international law and high technical craftsmanship and utility to practicing lawyers and scholars. **Computer Services:** Mailing lists, of members. **Special Interest Groups:** Africa; Dispute Resolution; Human Rights; Intellectual Property; International Criminal Law; International Economic Law; International Health Law; International Law in Domestic Courts. **Publications:** *American Journal of International Law*, quarterly. **Price:** $140.00. ISSN: 0002-9300. **Circulation:** 6,600. **Advertising:** accepted. Alternate Formats: online. Also Cited As: *AJIL* ● *ASIL Newsletter*, 5/year. **Price:** $60.00 for nonmembers in U.S.; $80.00 for nonmembers outside U.S.; included in membership dues. Alternate Formats: online ● *Basic Documents of International Economic Law*. Alternate Formats: online ● *Careers in International Law*. **Price:** $30.00 ● *International Legal Materials*, bimonthly. Alternate Formats: microform; online ● *Studies in Transnational Legal Policy*. Monograph ● Membership Directory ● Proceedings, annual. **Conventions/Meetings:** annual meeting, international law publications and services (exhibits) - always late March or early April in Washington, DC.

5867 ■ International Law Institute (ILI)

The Foundry Bldg.
1055 Thomas Jefferson St. NW
Washington, DC 20007
Ph: (202)247-6006
Fax: (202)247-6010
E-mail: training@ili.org
URL: http://www.ili.org
Contact: Prof. Don Wallace Jr., Chm.

Founded: 1955. **Staff:** 24. **Budget:** $2,000,000. **Languages:** English, French, Russian, Spanish. **Description:** Offers a combination of research and training programs that focus on the legal aspect of international business transactions. Sponsors international conferences and service programs for foreign students and lawyers. **Libraries: Type:** not open to the public. **Divisions:** Development Negotiation Program; Foreign and Domestic Student Programs; Orientation in U.S. Legal System; Research and Publications. **Formerly:** (1979) Institute for International and Foreign Trade Law. **Publications:** *ILI News Quarterly*. Newsletter. Alternate Formats: online ● Books. Features topics on transnational litigation, international trade, international dispute resolution and foreign legal systems. ● Catalog ● Titles on topics in private international law and trade. **Conventions/Meetings:** monthly seminar, training programs.

5868 ■ International Law Students Association (ILSA)

25 E Jackson Blvd., Ste.518
Chicago, IL 60604
Ph: (312)362-5025
Fax: (312)362-5073
E-mail: ilsa@ilsa.org
URL: http://www.ilsa.org
Contact: Amity R. Boye, Exec. Dir.

Founded: 1961. **Members:** 10,000. **Membership Dues:** corporate, $225 (annual) ● student, $35 (annual) ● non-student, $60 (annual). **Staff:** 2. **Regional Groups:** 17. **Local Groups:** 200. **National Groups:** 3. **Languages:** English, French, Spanish. **Description:** International law societies at law schools worldwide; interns and associate members. Promotes the study and understanding of international law through cooperative development of programs. Provides support to local groups for on-campus programming and coordinates regional, national, and international events. Conducts annual Philip C. Jessup International Law Moot Court Competition (see separate entry), open to all international law societies. Administers the U.S. portion of the Student Trainee Exchange Program, a student administered internship exchange between U.S. and European law firms and legal organizations, and the Transamerica Student Exchange Program between the U.S. and Mexico. Provides research opportunities to undergraduate, graduate, and law students in the field of international law. Maintains speakers list; coordinates a book donation program. **Awards:** Dean Rusk Award. **Type:** recognition. **Recipient:** for students writing in student law journals ● Francis Deak Award. **Type:** recognition. **Computer Services:** Mailing lists, of members. **Formerly:** (1987) Association of Student International Law Societies. **Publications:** *Ad Rem: The Quarterly Magazine of The International Law Students Association*. Newsletter. **Price:** $15.00 in U.S.; $20.00 outside U.S. **Advertising:** accepted. Alternate Formats: online ● *ILSA Guide to Education and Career Development in International Law*. Books ● *ILSA Journal of International and Comparative Law*, 3/year. **Price:** $10.00/year. Also Cited As: *ASILS International Law Journal* ● *Jessup Competition Compendium, 1987-2000*. Catalog ● Videos. Alternate Formats: online. **Conventions/Meetings:** semiannual conference - always fall and spring ● annual The Philip C. Jessup International Law Moot Court Competition.

5869 ■ International Legal Defense Counsel (ILDC)

405 Lexington Ave., 26th Fl.
New York, NY 10174
Ph: (212)907-6442
URL: http://ildc-law.com
Contact: Michael J. Griffith, Contact

Founded: 1977. **Members:** 4. **Staff:** 4. **Languages:** English, Spanish. **Multinational. Description:** United States attorneys concerned with the plight of individuals encountering legal problems in countries other than their own. Provides legal assistance to Americans incarcerated abroad. Acts as liaison between the family, the foreign attorney, and the client in both civil and criminal cases; and assists in hiring legal counsel abroad. Provides continued legal representation in the U.S. for prisoners returned under prisoner transfer treaties. Increases public awareness of legal problems encountered while living and traveling abroad. Company services include: employee seminar aimed at avoiding legal troubles abroad; legal orientation to foreign laws and customs; legal counseling for employees living or traveling abroad; legal opinions on matters involving civil or criminal laws of foreign countries. Maintains speakers' bureau. **Libraries: Type:** reference. **Holdings:** 125. **Subjects:** international law. **Supersedes:** Committee of Concerned Parents. **Publications:** *Coming Home: A Handbook for Americans Imprisoned in Mexico* ● *The Hassle of Your Life: A Handbook for Families of Americans Jailed Abroad* ● *Prisoner Transfer Treaties, A Practical Guide.* Handbook ● *Repatriation: A Handbook for Americans Imprisoned in Europe.*

5870 ■ World Association of Judges (WAJ)
c/o World Jurist Association
1000 Connecticut Ave. NW, Ste.202
Washington, DC 20036
Ph: (202)466-5428
Fax: (202)452-8540
E-mail: wja@worldjurist.org
URL: http://www.worldjurist.org
Contact: Bola A. Ajibola, Pres.
Founded: 1966. **Membership Dues:** individual, judge, $150 (annual). **Staff:** 6. **Languages:** English, French, German, Spanish. **Description:** Members of courts in countries throughout the world. Promotes the expansion of the rule of law in the world community and the advancement and improvement of the administration of justice for all people. **Awards: Type:** recognition. **Affiliated With:** World Association of Law Professors; World Association of Lawyers; World Business Associates; World Jurist Association. **Conventions/Meetings:** biennial conference, held in conjunction with the WJA.

5871 ■ World Association of Law Professors (WALP)
c/o World Jurist Association
1000 Connecticut Ave. NW, Ste.202
Washington, DC 20036
Ph: (202)466-5428
Fax: (202)452-8540
E-mail: wja@worldjurist.org
URL: http://www.worldjurist.org
Contact: Salvador B. Lao, Pres.
Founded: 1975. **Membership Dues:** practitioner/student/law professor/professional, $100 (annual) ● business associate, $200 (annual) ● judge/lawyer, $250 (annual). **Staff:** 6. **Languages:** English, French, German, Spanish. **Description:** Law professors united to further international cooperation through the development of international law. Promotes the objectives and programs of World Jurist Association. **Affiliated With:** World Association of Judges; World Association of Lawyers; World Business Associates; World Jurist Association. **Conventions/Meetings:** biennial conference, held in conjunction with WJA.

5872 ■ World Association of Law Students and Young Jurists
1000 Connecticut Ave. NW, Ste.202
Washington, DC 20036
Ph: (202)466-5428
Fax: (202)452-8540
E-mail: wja@worldjurist.org
URL: http://www.worldjurist.org
Contact: Charles S. Rhyne Esq., Pres./Founder
Founded: 1977. **Membership Dues:** student, lawyer (under 36), $50 (annual). **Staff:** 6. **Languages:** English, French, German, Spanish. **Description:** Law students and young jurists in 40 countries who assist and support the World Jurist Association in its objective to develop law and legal institutions throughout the world. **Affiliated With:** World Association of Judges; World Association of Law Professors; World Association of Lawyers; World Jurist Association. **Conventions/Meetings:** biennial conference, held in conjunction with the World Jurist Association.

5873 ■ World Association of Lawyers (WAL)
1000 Connecticut Ave. NW, Ste.202
Washington, DC 20036
Ph: (202)466-5428
Fax: (202)452-8540
E-mail: wja@worldjurist.org
URL: http://www.worldjurist.org
Contact: Margaret M. Henneberry, Exec. VP
Founded: 1975. **Membership Dues:** law professor, legal professional, young lawyer, law student, $100 (annual) ● lawyer, judge, $250 (annual) ● business associate, $200 (annual). **Staff:** 6. **Languages:** English, French, Spanish. **Description:** Seeks the development of international law as a basis for the peaceful resolution of conflict. Promotes the goals and activities of World Jurist Association. **Affiliated With:** World Association of Judges; World Association of Law Professors; World Business Associates; World Jurist Association. **Publications:** *Law and Judicial Systems of Nations*. Handbook. Includes guide to the legal systems. **Price:** $100.00/copy; $100.00 for CD-ROM; $175.00/copy (with CD-ROM). Alternate Formats: CD-ROM ● *Law/Technology*, quarterly. Journal. Reports on the relation of technology to law. **Price:** $80.00 for members; $90.00 /year for nonmembers. ISSN: 0278-3916 ● *World Jurist*, bimonthly. Newsletter. Provides scholarly articles, information regarding WJA activities, and news of interest to members. **Price:** included in membership dues; $80.00 /year for nonmembers ● Paper, annual. Includes papers presented in conference and seminars. **Price:** $8.00 each. **Conventions/Meetings:** biennial international conference, held in conjunction with WJA.

5874 ■ World Business Associates
1000 Connecticut Ave. NW, Ste.202
Washington, DC 20036
Ph: (202)466-5428
Fax: (202)452-8540
E-mail: wja@worldjurist.org
URL: http://www.worldjurist.org
Contact: Rick A. Baltzersen, Pres.
Founded: 2000. **Membership Dues:** individual, nonlegal professional, $75 (annual). **Staff:** 6. **Languages:** English, French, German, Spanish. **Description:** Individuals not involved in the legal profession who support the goals and activities of the World Jurist Association. **Awards: Type:** recognition. **Affiliated With:** World Association of Judges; World Association of Law Professors; World Association of Lawyers; World Jurist Association. **Formerly:** (2000) World Association of Center Associates. **Conventions/Meetings:** biennial conference, held in conjunction with WJA (exhibits).

5875 ■ World Jurist Association (WJA)
7910 Woodmont Ave., Ste.1440
Bethesda, MD 20814
Ph: (202)466-5428
Fax: (202)452-8540
E-mail: wja@worldjurist.org
URL: http://www.worldjurist.org
Contact: Charles S. Rhyne Esq., Founder
Founded: 1963. **Members:** 8,000. **Membership Dues:** lawyer, judge, $250 (annual) ● law professor, legal professor, young lawyer, law student, $100 (annual) ● business associate, $200 (annual). **Staff:** 4. **Languages:** English, French, German, Spanish. **Description:** Lawyers, judges, law professors, jurists, law students, and nonlegal professionals in 140 countries and territories. Seeks to build laws and legal institutions for international cooperation. Conducts Global Work Program to recommend research and voluntary action for development of international law as a basis for promoting the rule of law and the resolution of disputes by peaceful means. Sponsors biennial World Law Day. Maintains biographical archives. Contains 21 Sections, including Constitutional Law, Foreign Trade and Investment, Human Rights, and Litigation. **Awards: Type:** recognition. **Affiliated With:** World Association of Judges; World Association of Law Professors; World Association of Lawyers; World Business Associates. **Formerly:** (1990) World Peace Through Law Center. **Publications:** *Law and Judicial Systems of Nations*, periodic. Book. Offers descriptions of different legal systems around the world. **Price:** $100.00 plus shipping and handling. Alternate Formats: CD-ROM ● *Law/Technology*, quarterly. Journal. Contains articles about the relation of technology to law. Includes bibliography of computers and law and book reviews. **Price:** $80.00 /year for members; $90.00 /year for nonmembers. ISSN: 0278-3916 ● *The World Jurist*, bimonthly. Newsletter. For those seeking to promote the rule of law and improvement of administration of justice in the world community. **Price:** included in membership dues; $80.00 /year for nonmembers ● Pamphlets. **Conventions/Meetings:** biennial Conference on the Law of the World - seminar and conference.

Investigation

5876 ■ Association of Christian Investigators (ACI)
c/o Kelly Riddle, Pres.
2553 Jackson Keller, Ste.200
San Antonio, TX 78230
Ph: (210)342-0509
Fax: (210)342-0731
E-mail: kelmar@stic.net
URL: http://www.a-c-i.org
Contact: Kelly Riddle, Pres.
Members: 500. **Membership Dues:** general, $25 (annual). **Description:** Integrates the investigative profession with Christian beliefs, standards and principles. Provides an environment in which investigators can create a meaningful and long-term relationship with other investigators. Provides referrals to Christians in need of an investigator. **Computer Services:** database, member directory ● mailing lists ● online services, chat board. **Publications:** Newsletter, monthly. Alternate Formats: online.

5877 ■ Association of Former Agents of the U.S. Secret Service (AFAUSSS)
525 SW 5th St., Ste.A
Des Moines, IA 50309-4501
Ph: (515)282-8192
Fax: (515)282-9117
E-mail: afausss@assoc-mgmt.com
URL: http://www.oldstar.org
Contact: Kathy Rickenberger, Exec. Dir.
Founded: 1971. **Members:** 1,600. **Membership Dues:** regular (retired or former agent), $50 (annual) ● associate (active agent) and affiliate (active/retired/former employee), $25 (annual). **Staff:** 3. **Description:** Former agents of the U.S. Secret Service united to assist members and promote good law enforcement. **Awards:** Explorer Award. **Frequency:** annual. **Type:** recognition. **Recipient:** to Boy Scouts of America ● Law Enforcement Award. **Type:** recognition ● Law Enforcement Scholarship Award. **Frequency:** annual. **Type:** scholarship. **Recipient:** for law enforcement only. **Publications:** *Pipeline*, quarterly. Newsletter. **Price:** free for members ● Directory, annual. **Conventions/Meetings:** annual conference (exhibits).

5878 ■ Association of Former Intelligence Officers (AFIO)
6723 Whittier Ave., Ste.303 A
McLean, VA 22101
Ph: (703)790-0320 (703)790-0321
Fax: (703)991-1278
E-mail: afio@afio.com
URL: http://www.afio.com
Contact: Elizabeth Bancroft, Exec. Dir./Sec.-Treas.
Founded: 1975. **Members:** 4,500. **Membership Dues:** in U.S., $50 (annual) ● outside U.S., $95 (annual). **Staff:** 4. **Budget:** $350,000. **Regional Groups:** 27. **Description:** Represents educational association of current and former intelligence professionals, security and counterterrorism practitioners and some U.S. citizens. Enhances public understanding of the role and importance of intelligence for national

security, counterterrorism and to deal with threats in the contemporary world. Engages in career guidance for young people who are interested in intelligence or homeland security careers. **Libraries: Type:** reference. **Holdings:** books. **Subjects:** intelligence and intel-related. **Awards:** Colby-Guth Intelligence Paper Award. **Frequency:** annual. **Type:** monetary. **Recipient:** for outstanding essays focusing on China, the Middle East and South Asia ● Lifetime Intelligence Achievement Award. **Frequency:** annual. **Type:** recognition. **Computer Services:** Bibliographic search, suggestions of the best intelligence books to read on specific topics. **Telecommunication Services:** electronic bulletin board, career listings sent to all members weekly. **Programs:** Academic Exchange. **Also Known As:** (2006) Association for Intelligence Officers. **Formerly:** (1976) Association of Retired Intelligence Officers. **Publications:** *The Intelligencer - Journal of US Intelligence Studies*, semiannual. Includes essays, professional insights, and book reviews on intelligence and intelligence-related issues. **Price:** $15.00/issue. **Circulation:** 5,500. **Advertising:** accepted ● *Periscope*, semiannual. Newsletter. Includes organization news and summaries of speeches and comments on current developments of intelligence interest. **Price:** $50.00/year; $10.00/issue for nonmembers. **Circulation:** 4,500. **Advertising:** accepted. Alternate Formats: online ● *Weekly Intelligence Notes (WINs)*. Contains summaries of intelligence events via email. **Price:** $50.00/year. **Circulation:** 4,500. Alternate Formats: online. **Conventions/Meetings:** annual National Convention and Awards Banquet - conference and banquet, with speakers ● annual National Intelligence Symposium - conference, intelligence, counterintelligence and security education ● quarterly Speaker Luncheon - conference and luncheon, discusses about intelligence education; with author signings on new books in this field (exhibits).

5879 ■ Federal Law Enforcement Officers Association (FLEOA)
PO Box 326
Lewisberry, PA 17339
Ph: (717)938-2300
Fax: (717)932-2262
E-mail: fleoa@fleoa.org
URL: http://www.fleoa.org
Contact: Art Gordon, Natl. Pres.
Founded: 1977. **Members:** 20,000. **Membership Dues:** regular, $105 (annual) ● retiree/resignee, $40 (annual) ● associate, $45 (annual) ● student, $55 (annual). **Local Groups:** 80. **Description:** Represents federal criminal investigators. Provides legal representation for members. Monitors related legislative and judiciary activities; keeps members informed on related tax, insurance, pension, and other financial matters. **Awards:** FLEOA Foundation Scholarship Program. **Frequency:** annual. **Type:** scholarship. **Recipient:** for high school graduates who are children of current, retired or deceased federal law enforcement officers. **Telecommunication Services:** electronic mail, president@fleoa.org. **Committees:** Legal; Legislative. **Publications:** *1811*, bimonthly. Newsletter. **Advertising:** accepted. **Conventions/Meetings:** biennial meeting.

5880 ■ High Technology Crime Investigation Association International (HTCIA)
c/o Carol Hutchings, Exec. Sec.
4021 Woodcreek Oaks Blvd., Ste.156
PMB 209
Roseville, CA 95747
Ph: (916)408-1751
Fax: (916)408-7543
E-mail: exec_secty@htcia.org
URL: http://www.htcia.org
Contact: Anthony Reyes, Pres.
Founded: 1980. **Members:** 100. **Membership Dues:** chapter, $25 (annual). **Staff:** 5. **Description:** Law enforcement personnel and other individuals making use of technology to aid in civil and criminal investigations. Promotes expanded application of technology to investigative work. Gathers and disseminates information; facilitates communication and cooperation among members. **Libraries: Type:** not open to the public. **Holdings:** 20. **Committees:** Annual Conference; Executive Secretary Selection; Internet; Legal Advisory. **Formerly:** (2001) High Technology Crime Investigation Association. **Conventions/Meetings:** annual meeting (exhibits).

5881 ■ International Association of Financial Crimes Investigators (IAFCI)
1020 Suncast Ln., Ste.102
El Dorado Hills, CA 95762
Ph: (916)939-5000
Fax: (916)939-0395
E-mail: admin@iafci.org
URL: http://www.iafci.org
Contact: Jan Moffett, Contact
Founded: 1968. **Members:** 3,500. **Membership Dues:** regular/associate in U.S., $115 (annual) ● regular/associate outside U.S., $77 (annual) ● law enforcement, $65 (annual). **Staff:** 4. **Budget:** $100,000. **Local Groups:** 42. **Description:** Special agents, investigators, and investigation supervisors who investigate criminal violations of credit card laws and prosecute offenders; law enforcement officers, prosecutors, or related officials who investigate, apprehend, and prosecute credit card offenders; employees of card issuing institutions who are responsible for credit card security and investigations; management personnel of companies performing services for the credit card industry. Aids in the establishment of effective credit card security programs; suppresses fraudulent use of credit cards; and detects and proceeds with the apprehension of credit card thieves. Emphasizes a professional approach to the investigative function, a free exchange of criminal intelligence, and a vigorous prosecution policy. Encourages members to use existing federal and local criminal statutes and to seek more effective legislation in areas where it is lacking. Provides workshops and training conferences to acquaint law enforcement bodies and the membership with technological advances in the industry. **Committees:** Legislative; Mailing Problems; Public Relations. **Formerly:** Association of Credit Card Investigators; (1996) International Association of Credit Cards; (2001) International Association of Financial Crimes. **Publications:** *IAFCI News*, quarterly. Newsletter ● Newsletter, quarterly. **Conventions/Meetings:** annual conference, with speakers and training sessions (exhibits) - 2008 Aug. 25-29, Hollywood, CA ● annual seminar.

5882 ■ International Association of Law Enforcement Intelligence Analysts (IALEIA)
PO Box 13857
Richmond, VA 23225
Ph: (520)547-8760
Fax: (804)565-2059
E-mail: lisa.palmieri@pol.state.ma.us
URL: http://www.ialeia.org
Contact: Lisa Palmieri, Pres.
Founded: 1980. **Members:** 1,700. **Membership Dues:** regular, associate, $50 (annual) ● developing country analyst, $10 (annual) ● corporate, $1,000 (annual) ● student, $25 (annual) ● academic, $150 (annual). **Staff:** 1. **Budget:** $50,000. **Regional Groups:** 10. **State Groups:** 14. **Local Groups:** 1. **National Groups:** 3. **Multinational. Description:** Civilian and sworn law enforcement intelligence analysts and officers. Works to promote standards of excellence in the field of law enforcement intelligence and to provide a forum for the exchange of ideas, methods of analysis, career development programs, and concepts in intelligence information management. **Awards: Frequency:** annual. **Type:** recognition. **Recipient:** for professional service. **Publications:** *IALEIA Journal*, semiannual. **Price:** $25.00/year. **Circulation:** 1,400. Also Cited As: *Law Enforcement Intelligence Analysis Digest* ● *Intelscope*, 3/year. Magazine. **Circulation:** 1,600. **Advertising:** accepted. Alternate Formats: online ● Membership Directory, annual. **Advertising:** accepted ● Booklets; annual; sponsorships accepted. **Conventions/Meetings:** annual meeting and conference, training (exhibits) ● semiannual meeting and conference, training.

5883 ■ International Homicide Investigators Association (IHIA)
10711 Spotsylvania Ave.
Fredericksburg, VA 22408
Free: (877)843-4442
Fax: (540)898-5594
E-mail: ihia@adelphia.net
URL: http://www.ihia.org
Contact: William Hagmaier, Exec. Dir.
Founded: 1988. **Membership Dues:** general, $50 (annual) ● international, $35 (annual). **National Groups:** 3. **Multinational. Description:** Supports law enforcement agencies and death investigation professionals. Provides leadership, training, resources and expertise that will enhance the ability to solve cases. **Awards:** Terece J. Green Distinguished Homicide Professional. **Frequency:** annual. **Type:** recognition. **Recipient:** for significant contributions to the profession of homicide. **Computer Services:** Online services, discussion board. **Boards:** Advisory. **Programs:** National Homicide Standards of Training; National Registry of Unidentified Dead. **Conventions/Meetings:** annual conference, with training.

5884 ■ International Latino Gang Investigator's Association (ILGIA)
4057 Hwy. 9
PMB 108
Howell, NJ 07731-3307
E-mail: gcmorales2002@yahoo.com
URL: http://www.ilgia.org
Contact: Gabe Morales, Pres.
Founded: 2002. **Membership Dues:** general, $20 (annual). **Regional Groups:** 11. **Multinational. Description:** Responds to the proliferation of gangs in the society. Seeks information on gang activities and international drug trade associated with Latino gangs. Increases awareness of gangs in the society. Assists law enforcement and related agencies to combat gang activities. **Boards:** Advisory. **Publications:** Newsletter.

5885 ■ National Association of Legal Investigators (NALI)
c/o Alan E. Goodman, Natl. Dir.
PO Box 8479
Portland, ME 04104
Free: (888)244-5685
Fax: (207)893-1457
E-mail: info@nalionline.org
URL: http://www.nalionline.org
Contact: Alan E. Goodman, Natl. Dir.
Founded: 1967. **Members:** 700. **Membership Dues:** active, retired, associate, and professional affiliate, $150 (annual). **Regional Groups:** 7. **State Groups:** 25. **Description:** Legal investigators, both independent and law firm staff, who specialize in investigation of personal injury matters for the plaintiff and criminal defense. Promotes professionalization of the legal investigator, accomplished by seminars and a professional certification program. Provides nationwide network of contact among members. Compiles statistics. **Awards:** Editor/Publisher Award. **Frequency:** annual. **Type:** recognition. **Telecommunication Services:** electronic mail, aeglis@aol.com. **Committees:** Certification; Constitutional Revision and Review; Continuing Education; Research. **Publications:** *Legal Investigator*, quarterly. Magazine. **Price:** $45.00 for nonmembers. **Circulation:** 1,500. **Advertising:** accepted ● Membership Directory, semiannual. **Conventions/Meetings:** annual conference and seminar (exhibits) - always January/June.

5886 ■ National Association of Property Recovery Investigators (NAPRI)
5715 Will Clayton, No. 1503
Humble, TX 77338
Ph: (386)479-5329
Fax: (309)422-2112
E-mail: info@napri.org
URL: http://www.napri.org
Contact: Alexander Rubino, Pres.
Founded: 1999. **Members:** 4,000. **Multinational. Description:** Increases the recovery and return of stolen property to victims of theft and identification and apprehension of criminals. Encourages legisla-

tion that will benefit law enforcement agencies in the investigation of property crimes. **Awards:** National Property Crime of the Year. **Frequency:** annual. **Type:** recognition. **Recipient:** for significant contribution to property crime investigation techniques ● National Superior Service and Devotion to Duty Award. **Frequency:** annual. **Type:** recognition. **Recipient:** for significant contribution to property crime investigation field. **Committees:** Computer and Technology; Legislative; Organized Retail Crime; Property Crime Investigator's Certification.

5887 ■ National Association of Traffic Accident Reconstructionists and Investigators (NATARI)
PO Box 2588
West Chester, PA 19382
Ph: (610)696-1919
E-mail: natari@natari.org
URL: http://www.natari.org
Contact: William C. Camlin, Pres.
Founded: 1984. **Members:** 200. **Membership Dues:** reconstructionist, investigator, associate, $60 (annual). **Budget:** $20,000. **Description:** Represents engineers, attorneys, police officers, private investigators, medical examiners, and other individuals involved in the analysis of motor vehicle traffic accidents. Gathers and disseminates information on techniques and equipment of potential use to members; reviews literature in the field. Participating Organization of the Accreditation Commission for Traffic Accident Reconstruction. **Awards:** Distinguished Service Award. **Frequency:** annual. **Type:** recognition ● Literary Award. **Frequency:** annual. **Type:** recognition ● Performance Award. **Frequency:** annual. **Type:** recognition. **Affiliated With:** National Association of Traffic Accident Reconstructionists and Investigators. **Publications:** *Accident Investigation Formula Book*, annual. Contains a list of formula's used in accident investigation and reconstruction. **Price:** $10.00 ● Newsletter, quarterly. **Price:** included in membership dues. **Circulation:** 200. **Advertising:** accepted. **Conventions/Meetings:** annual conference (exhibits) - usually first week of October.

5888 ■ National Defender Investigator Association (NDIA)
460 Smith St., Ste.K
Middletown, CT 06457
Ph: (860)635-5533
Fax: (860)613-1650
E-mail: ndia@cox.net
URL: http://www.ndia.net
Contact: Matthew W. Whalen, Pres.
Founded: 1969. **Members:** 750. **Membership Dues:** regular, $40 (annual). **Multinational. Description:** Defender investigators. Promotes the study of investigation of murder cases, robbery, sex crimes, child molestation, serial crimes, property crimes, forensics sciences, and investigative techniques, new procedures, and other considerations. **Conventions/Meetings:** annual conference and dinner.

5889 ■ National Military Intelligence Association (NMIA)
PO Box 479
Hamilton, VA 20159
Ph: (540)338-1143
Fax: (703)738-7487
E-mail: nmiassoc@comcast.net
URL: http://www.nmia.org
Contact: Debra Davis, Corporate Liaison
Founded: 1974. **Members:** 3,000. **Membership Dues:** regular, associate, $50 (annual) ● life (over 40 years of age), $700 ● life (under 40 years of age), $900 ● corporate small business, $750 (annual) ● corporate, $1,500 (annual). **Description:** Active duty, reserve, retired, and former military and civil service intelligence professionals and interested U.S. citizens. Enhances the military intelligence profession through educational means. Informs members of relevant legislation and actions; acts as a medium for the exchange of ideas and knowledge among the intelligence professionals of the Armed Services; interacts with other intelligence organizations on matters of importance to the profession; conducts local chapter meetings where members of the intelligence profession of all Services may meet professionally and socially; acts as unofficial spokesman of military intelligence to the public. Conducts research. Honors military scholars. **Awards:** Merit/Scholarship Program. **Frequency:** annual. **Type:** scholarship. **Recipient:** for members' children who are entering college ● **Type:** recognition. **Recipient:** to outstanding intelligence professionals of the Army, Navy, Air Force, Marine Corps, Coast Guard, and civilian agencies. **Publications:** *American Intelligence Journal*, semiannual. Provides readers the views of the intelligence leaders and thinkers. **Price:** $75.00 in U.S.; $135.00 outside U.S. ISSN: 0883-072X. **Circulation:** 3,000. **Advertising:** accepted ● *NMIA Newsletter*, bimonthly ● Also publishes supplements to the journal as needed. **Conventions/Meetings:** annual Counterintelligence Update - meeting - usually November, Bolling Air Force Base ● annual Information Warfare Update - meeting - usually May, Washington, DC ● annual National Intelligence Status - meeting - usually November ● annual symposium - usually February/March.

5890 ■ Society of Professional Investigators (SPI)
PO Box 1128
Bellmore, NY 11710
Ph: (516)781-5100
Fax: (516)783-0000
E-mail: info@spionline.org
URL: http://www.spionline.org
Contact: David E. Zeldin CFE, Pres.
Founded: 1955. **Members:** 350. **Membership Dues:** full, associate, student, affiliate, $50 (annual). **Description:** Persons with at least 5 years' investigative experience for an official federal, state, or local government agency or for a quasi-official agency formed for law enforcement or related activities. Seeks to advance knowledge of the science and technology of professional investigation, law enforcement, and police science; maintains high standards and ethics; promotes efficiency of investigators in the services they perform. **Libraries: Type:** reference. **Holdings:** books. **Subjects:** law enforcement. **Awards:** Irwin R. Rutman Award. **Frequency:** annual. **Type:** recognition. **Recipient:** for outstanding law enforcement achievement. **Committees:** Awards; Legislature; Press Relations and Public Affairs; Welfare. **Publications:** *Roster*, triennial. Membership Directory ● *SPI Newsletter*, 8/year. **Price:** free. **Circulation:** 500. **Advertising:** accepted. **Conventions/Meetings:** annual dinner ● monthly seminar.

Investments

5891 ■ Public Investors Arbitration Bar Association (PIABA)
2415 A Wilcox Dr.
Norman, OK 73069
Ph: (405)360-8776
Free: (888)621-7484
Fax: (405)360-2063
E-mail: piaba@piaba.org
URL: http://secure.piaba.org/piabaweb/html/index.php
Contact: Robin S. Ringo, Exec. Dir.
Founded: 1990. **Membership Dues:** regular, $495 (annual). **Description:** Promotes interests of the public investor in securities and commodities arbitration. **Computer Services:** database, directory of expert and consultant to assist PIABA members with their cases ● database, PDF files of the award submitted by various arbitration forums ● database, research ● mailing lists. **Telecommunication Services:** electronic bulletin board ● electronic mail, rsringo@piaba.org. **Committees:** Communications and Technology; Legislation; Program; Self-Regulated Organizations. **Publications:** *PIABA Bar Journal*, quarterly. **Price:** included in membership dues; $175.00 /year for libraries (law school libraries only); $250.00 /year for nonmembers. **Conventions/Meetings:** annual meeting - 2008 Oct. 23-25, Colorado Springs, CO.

Judiciary

5892 ■ American Judges Association (AJA)
300 Newport Ave.
Williamsburg, VA 23185-4147
Ph: (757)259-1841
Fax: (757)259-1520
E-mail: aja@ncsc.dni.us
URL: http://aja.ncsc.dni.us
Contact: Judge Steve Leben, Pres.
Founded: 1959. **Members:** 3,500. **Membership Dues:** individual, $125 (annual) ● retired judge, $50 (annual). **Budget:** $100,000. **Description:** Seeks to improve the administration of justice at all levels of the courts. **Awards:** Award of Merit. **Frequency:** annual. **Type:** recognition. **Committees:** Court Administration and Organization; Highway Safety; Judicial and Citizenry Education; Judicial Concerns and Standards; Legislation. **Formerly:** (1965) National Association of Municipal Judges; (1972) North American Judges Association. **Publications:** *AJA Benchmark*, quarterly. Newsletter ● *Court Review*, quarterly. Journal ● *Domestic Violence*. Booklet. Provides a judge with critical information about victims of domestic violence. **Conventions/Meetings:** conference, held in conjunction with American Judges Foundation (exhibits) - every fall ● annual meeting - mid-year.

5893 ■ American Judicature Society (AJS)
Drake Univ.
The Opperman Ctr.
2700 Univ. Ave.
Des Moines, IA 50311
Ph: (515)271-2281
Fax: (515)279-3090
E-mail: dperrault@ajs.org
URL: http://www.ajs.org
Contact: Neal Sonnett, Pres.
Founded: 1913. **Members:** 11,000. **Membership Dues:** regular, $100 (annual) ● judge, full-time professor, public/nonprofit sector, $75 (annual) ● retiree, $40 (annual) ● student, $35 (annual) ● sustaining, $250 (annual) ● leadership, $500 (annual) ● president, $1,000 (annual) ● founder, $1,500 (annual) ● life, $5,000. **Staff:** 12. **Budget:** $2,000,000. **Description:** Lawyers, judges, law teachers, government officials, and citizens interested in the effective administration of justice. Conducts research; presents educational programs; offers a consultation service; sponsors and organizes citizens' conferences on judicial improvement. Coordinates the work of states in judicial discipline and removal through its Center for Judicial Conduct Organizations. **Libraries: Type:** reference. **Holdings:** 5,000. **Subjects:** judicial administration. **Awards:** Edward J. Devitt. **Frequency:** annual. **Type:** recognition. **Recipient:** for a judge who has achieved an exemplary career and has made significant contributions to the administration of justice, the advancement of the role of law, and the improvement of society as a whole ● Elmo B. Hunter Award. **Type:** recognition. **Recipient:** for significant achievement in improving judicial selection ● Herbert Harley Award. **Type:** recognition. **Recipient:** for contributions to state justice system improvement ● Justice Award. **Frequency:** annual. **Type:** recognition. **Recipient:** for outstanding national contribution ● Opperman Award. **Frequency:** annual. **Type:** recognition. **Recipient:** for a state judge ● Toni House Journalism Award. **Frequency:** annual. **Type:** recognition. **Recipient:** for a reporting that has enhanced public understanding of the courts and/or significantly improved the administration of justice. **Publications:** *Judicature*, bimonthly. Journal. **Price:** included in membership dues; $9.00/issue. ISSN: 0022-5800. **Circulation:** 11,000. **Advertising:** accepted. Alternate Formats: online ● *Judicial Conduct Reporter*, quarterly. Newsletter. **Price:** $9.00/issue. **Advertising:** accepted. Alternate Formats: online ● Reports ● Videos ● Also publishes books, studies, pamphlets, and brochures. **Conventions/Meetings:** semiannual meeting.

5894 ■ Association of Administrative Law Judges (AALJ)
c/o Judge Thomas Snook, Co-Chm.
1454 Mendavia Ave.
Coral Gables, FL 33146

Ph: (414)297-3141 (305)536-5761
E-mail: info@aalj.org
URL: http://www.aalj.org
Contact: Ronald Bernoski, Pres.
Founded: 1966. **Members:** 675. **Description:** Represents administrative law judges in the Department of Health and Human Services. (Administrative law judges preside over Social Security disability cases and cases involving disputes over health benefits, hospital accreditation, and other health sanction issues.) Promotes efficiency of administrative justice. **Awards:** Vickery Award. **Frequency:** annual. **Type:** recognition. **Recipient:** for outstanding contributions to administrative justice system. **Formerly:** Association of Administrative Law Judges, Department of Health and Human Services. **Publications:** *Director's Update*, periodic. Newsletter ● Newsletter, bimonthly. **Conventions/Meetings:** semiannual Judicial Conference for Continuing Legal Education - board meeting.

5895 ■ Association of Reporters of Judicial Decisions
5711 Nevada St.
College Park, MD 20740
Ph: (202)479-3194
Fax: (202)479-3240
E-mail: bcauley@appellate.state.al.us
URL: http://arjd.washlaw.edu
Contact: Wilma Grant, Pres.
Founded: 1982. **Members:** 77. **Membership Dues:** reporter of decisions, $50 (annual) ● assistant or staff, $30 (annual). **Description:** Judicial reporters and professional staff. Works to advance the interests of judicial reporters, improve the accuracy and efficiency of reporting decisions of state and federal appellate courts, and provides a forum for communication and cooperation of members. Conducts educational and research programs. **Awards:** Henry C. Lind Award. **Frequency:** periodic. **Type:** recognition. **Recipient:** for individuals who have made significant contributions for improving the reporting of decisions or preserving historic court records. **Subgroups:** Education; Electronic Publishing; Honors. **Also Known As:** ARJD. **Publications:** *Catchline*, 3/year. Newsletter. **Advertising:** accepted. Alternate Formats: online ● Directory, annual. **Conventions/Meetings:** annual meeting - every August.

5896 ■ Conference of Chief Justices (CCJ)
c/o Association Management
300 Newport Ave.
Williamsburg, VA 23185-4147
Ph: (757)259-1841
Fax: (757)259-1520
E-mail: ccj@ncsc.dni.us
URL: http://ccj.ncsc.dni.us
Contact: Hon. Randall T. Shepard, Pres.
Founded: 1949. **Members:** 58. **For-Profit. Description:** Chief justices of supreme courts of the United States, District of Columbia, American Samoa, Guam, Puerto Rico, the Mariana Islands, and the Virgin Islands. **Boards:** Best Practices Institute. **Committees:** Access to and Fairness in the Courts; Courts and Children; International Agreements; Mass Torts; Public Trust and Confidence in the Judiciary. **Subcommittees:** Judicial Family Institute. **Conventions/Meetings:** annual conference - midyear.

5897 ■ Council for Court Excellence (CCE)
1111 14th St. NW, Ste.500
Washington, DC 20005
Ph: (202)785-5917
Fax: (202)785-5922
E-mail: office@courtexcellence.org
URL: http://www.courtexcellence.org
Contact: June B. Kress, Exec. Dir.
Founded: 1982. **Members:** 140. **Membership Dues:** law firm director on the board, $250-$7,500 (annual) ● business director on the board, $125-$5,000 (annual) ● civic, judicial, individual voting director on the board, $125 (annual). **Staff:** 6. **Budget:** $600,000. **Description:** Lawyers, business leaders, and civic and judicial branch members. Aims to develop and advocate methods of improving the administration of justice in local and federal courts. Stimulates understanding and communication between citizens and the courts. Conducts educational workshops. **Libraries: Type:** not open to the public. **Holdings:** 1,500. **Subjects:** legal reform, court management sentencing, court budgeting, jury management. **Awards:** Justice Potter Stewart Award. **Frequency:** annual. **Type:** recognition. **Recipient:** for distinguished service to improve court systems. **Committees:** Children in the Courts; Court Improvements; Criminal Justice; Public Service. **Publications:** *A Citizen's Guide to the Courts*. Brochure. **Price:** $5.00 ● *A Victim's Guide to the DC Criminal Justice System*. Brochure ● *Bankruptcy: Things to Consider Before You File*. Brochure ● *Child Neglect Practice Manual for District of Columbia* ● *Collecting the Money*. Brochure ● *Council for Court Excellence—Annual Report*. **Price:** free. **Circulation:** 3,500. Alternate Formats: online ● *Court Excellence*, periodic. Newsletter. For those interested in the administration of justice. **Price:** included in membership dues; $50.00 for nonmembers. **Circulation:** 3,500. Alternate Formats: online ● *Getting Help for the Mentally Ill*. Brochure ● *Juries for the Year 2000 and Beyond: Proposals to Improve the Jury Systems in Washington, DC*. Report ● *Recovering Your Stolen Property*. Brochure ● *When Someone Dies*. Brochure ● *Your Case on Appeal*. Brochure ● Reports. **Conventions/Meetings:** semiannual board meeting.

5898 ■ Equal Justice Works
c/o David Stern, CEO
2120 L St. NW, Ste.450
Washington, DC 20037-1541
Ph: (202)466-3686
Fax: (202)429-9766
E-mail: mail@equaljusticeworks.org
URL: http://www.equaljusticeworks.org
Contact: David Stern, CEO
Founded: 1986. **Staff:** 28. **Local Groups:** 131. **Description:** Works to surmount barriers to equal justice that affect millions of low-income individuals and families. Engaged in organizing, training, and supporting public service-minded law students and creates summer and postgraduate public interest jobs. **Awards: Type:** grant. **Recipient:** for students and recent graduates engaged in public interest employment. **Formerly:** (2002) National Association for Public Interest Law. **Publications:** *An Action Manual for Loan Repayment Assistance*. Contains step-by-step guide to starting loan repayment assistance programs at law schools. **Price:** $5.00 for students; $10.00 for others. Alternate Formats: online ● *Campaigning for Law School Pro Bono Requirements* ● *Choosing Wisely: NAPIL's Guide to Law Schools*. **Price:** $10.00 ● *Law Firms and Pro Bono*, annual. Details pro bono activities of national law firms. **Price:** $20.00 ● *Loan Repayment Assistance Plan Report*. Offers information on loan repayment programs for public interest attorneys. **Price:** $20.00 for students; $25.00 for others ● *NAPIL Connection*, quarterly. Newsletter. Contains information on fundraising tips and campus programs. Includes profiles of public interest organizations and a calendar of events. **Price:** $25.00 ● *NAPIL Directory of Public Interest Legal Internships*, annual. Lists summer and semester public interest employment programs. Includes student evaluations and information on summer funding programs. **Price:** $20.00 for students; $25.00 for others ● *The NAPIL Guide to Public Interest Career Resources*, annual. Bibliography. **Price:** $10.00 for students; $15.00 for others ● *NAPIL Member Group Directory*. Membership Directory. **Price:** $10.00 ● *The NAPIL Post-Graduate Fellowships Guide*. **Price:** $20.00 for students; $25.00 for others ● *Pro Bono in Law Schools*. **Price:** $5.00 for students; $10.00 for others. **Conventions/Meetings:** annual National Public Interest Law Conference and Career Fair.

5899 ■ Federal Administrative Law Judges Conference (FALJC)
2020 Pennsylvania Ave. NW
PMB 260
Washington, DC 20006
Ph: (202)675-3065
E-mail: plang@flra.gov
URL: http://www.faljc.org
Contact: Judge Paul Lang, Pres.
Founded: 1947. **Members:** 270. **Membership Dues:** new judge, $135 (annual) ● retired judge/voluntary sustaining, $25 (annual). **Staff:** 1. **Description:** Administrative law judges employed by federal agencies and departments who perform judicial functions in the federal service, presiding at administrative hearings, ruling on admissibility of evidence, making findings of fact and conclusions of law, and issuing decisions. **Awards: Type:** recognition. **Committees:** Legislation; Litigation; Pay and Compensation; Social. **Formerly:** Federal Trial Examiners Conference. **Publications:** *Directory of FALJC Members*. Membership Directory. Alternate Formats: online ● *Directory of FALJC Officers*. Alternate Formats: online ● *FALJC Newsletter*, periodic. Alternate Formats: online. **Conventions/Meetings:** monthly luncheon ● annual seminar - always September.

5900 ■ Federalist Society for Law and Public Policy Studies
1015 18th St. NW, Ste.425
Washington, DC 20036
Ph: (202)822-8138
Fax: (202)296-8061
E-mail: info@fed.org
URL: http://www.fed-soc.org
Contact: Eugene B. Meyer, Pres.
Founded: 1982. **Members:** 25,000. **Membership Dues:** general, lawyer, $50 (annual) ● faculty, public sector, non-profit, $25 (annual) ● student, $5 (annual). **Staff:** 14. **Budget:** $3,100,000. **Local Groups:** 200. **Description:** Conservative and libertarian lawyers, law students, law school faculty, and individuals interested in the current state of the legal order. Seeks to: bring about a reordering of priorities within the U.S. legal system that will emphasize individual liberty, traditional values, and the rule of law; restore recognition of these priorities among lawyers, judges, law students, and professors. Believes that the state exists to preserve freedom, and that the separation of powers is central to the Constitution. **Awards:** Bator Award. **Type:** recognition. **Publications:** *ABA Watch*, semiannual. Alternate Formats: online ● *Bar Watch Bulletin* ● *The Federalist Paper*, quarterly. Newsletter ● *Harvard Journal of Law and Public Policy*, 3/year. **Conventions/Meetings:** annual National Lawyers Convention ● periodic regional meeting ● annual symposium.

5901 ■ Fund for Modern Courts (FMC)
351 W 54th St.
New York, NY 10019
Ph: (212)541-6741
Fax: (212)541-7301
E-mail: justice@moderncourts.org
URL: http://www.moderncourts.org
Contact: Mr. Dennis R. Hawkins, Exec. Dir.
Founded: 1955. **Staff:** 7. **Budget:** $270,000. **Local Groups:** 3. **Languages:** English, Spanish. **Description:** Business and labor leaders, lawyers, civic groups, and others who seek public support for the improvement of the judicial system. Issues addressed include: reform of New York State Court System; judicial selection; judicial discipline; court administration; court structure; court financing; alternatives to traditional court procedures. Sponsors citizens court monitoring projects in 17 counties of New York State. Holds forums to educate the public on the judicial system; sponsors lectures. Operates speakers' bureau; compiles statistics. **Libraries: Type:** reference. **Holdings:** 2,000. **Subjects:** court reform. **Awards:** John J. McCloy Memorial Award. **Frequency:** annual. **Type:** recognition. **Recipient:** for lawyers who have made outstanding contributions to improving the administration of justice in New York ● Samuel J. Puboff Memorial Award. **Frequency:** annual. **Type:** recognition. **Recipient:** for non-lawyers who have made extraordinary contributions to improving the quality of justice in New York. **Committees:** Appellate Justice; Court Facilities; Criminal Justice; Judicial Conduct; Modern Courts. **Programs:** Citizen Court Monitoring; Education and Outreach. **Projects:** Citizens Jury. **Also Known As:** Committee for

Modern Courts Fund. **Publications:** *Modern Courts*, quarterly. Newsletter. **Price:** free. **Circulation:** 8,000 ● Annual Report, annual. Alternate Formats: online ● Surveys. Alternate Formats: online ● Also publishes reports on court monitoring pamphlets, guides, and studies on judicial reform. **Conventions/Meetings:** semiannual board meeting - always May and December ● seminar, educational and research public forums.

5902 ■ Institute of Judicial Administration (IJA)
c/o Prof. Oscar G. Chase, Exec. Co-Dir.
New York Univ. School of Law
Vanderbilt Hall
40 Washington Square Park, Rm. 413
New York, NY 10012
Ph: (212)998-6217 (212)998-6149
Fax: (212)995-4881
E-mail: alison.kinney@nyu.edu
URL: http://www.law.nyu.edu/institutes/judicial
Contact: Prof. Oscar G. Chase, Exec. Co-Dir.
Founded: 1952. **Members:** 100. **Membership Dues:** judicial, academic, court administrator, $75 (annual) ● regular, $150 (annual) ● contributing, $200 (annual) ● sustaining, $300 (annual) ● sponsoring, $500 (annual) ● individual fund gift, $1,000 (annual). **Staff:** 2. **Description:** Lawyers, judges, and laypersons with an interest in judicial administration. Promotes judicial, procedural, and administrative improvements in the courts; encourages dialogue among the bench, bar, and academy. Furthers empirical research on improving the understanding of the justice system. Offers educational programs for appellate and trial judges. **Publications:** *IJA Report*. Newsletter. Alternate Formats: online. **Conventions/Meetings:** annual New Judges Seminar, for appellate judges - always summer.

5903 ■ International Association of Lesbian and Gay Judges (IALGJ)
c/o Hon. D. Zeke Zeidler, Treas.
137 N Larchmont Blvd., No. 206
Los Angeles, CA 90004
E-mail: gcohen@provincialcourt.bc.ca
URL: http://home.att.net/~ialgj
Contact: Hon. J. Gary Cohen, Pres.
Founded: 1993. **Members:** 60. **Membership Dues:** individual, $50 (annual). **Multinational. Description:** Gay and lesbian judges. Promotes communication and mutual support among members. Encourages high standards of conduct. Represents members' interests.

5904 ■ National Alliance for Family Court Justice (NAFCJ)
c/o Elisabeth Richards, Natl. Dir.
4309 Greenberry Ln.
Annandale, VA 22003
Ph: (703)658-2308
E-mail: lizgoal@aol.com
URL: http://nafcj.org
Contact: Elisabeth Richards, Natl. Dir.
Founded: 1993. **Multinational. Description:** Seeks to represent "the interests of individuals dedicated to addressing system failure in the courts and social services resulting in retaliation against non-offending parents who complain of family abuse.". **Computer Services:** Online services, discussion. **Publications:** Articles. Alternate Formats: online.

5905 ■ National American Indian Court Judges Association (NAICJA)
4410 Arapahoe Ave., Ste.135
Boulder, CO 80303
Ph: (303)245-0786
Fax: (303)245-0785
E-mail: mail@naicja.org
URL: http://www.naicja.org
Contact: Judge Elbridge Coochise, Dir.
Founded: 1969. **Members:** 256. **Membership Dues:** active, associate, honorary, supporting, $75 (annual). **Regional Groups:** 8. **Description:** Seeks to strengthen and enhance tribal justice systems. **Projects:** National Tribal Justice Resource Center; Violence Against Women's Act. **Publications:** *NAICJA News*, periodic. Newsletter. **Price:** included in membership dues ● Annual Report, annual. Alternate Formats: online. **Conventions/Meetings:** annual National Tribal Judicial Conference.

5906 ■ National Association of Hearing Officials (NAHO)
PO Box 4999
Midlothian, VA 23112
Ph: (360)664-7268
E-mail: ellena@drs.wa.gov
URL: http://www.naho.org
Contact: Ellen G. Anderson, Pres.
Founded: 1986. **Membership Dues:** individual, $35 (annual) ● group (10 or more), $30 (annual) ● individual, $90 (triennial). **Regional Groups:** 6. **Description:** Dedicated to improving the administrative hearing process, promotes professionalism, provides training, continuing education, certification program, and a national forum for discussion of issues, and leadership concerning administrative hearings. **Libraries: Type:** reference; lending; not open to the public. **Holdings:** video recordings. **Subjects:** conference courses. **Publications:** *NAHO News*, quarterly. Newsletter. Alternate Formats: online. **Conventions/Meetings:** annual National Training Conference.

5907 ■ National Association of Women Judges (NAWJ)
1341 Connecticut Ave. NW, Ste.4.2
Washington, DC 20036
Ph: (202)393-0222
Fax: (202)393-0125
E-mail: nawj@nawj.org
URL: http://www.nawj.org
Contact: Drucilla Stender Ramey, Exec. Dir.
Founded: 1980. **Members:** 1,300. **Membership Dues:** associate/retired/amicus judicii, $175 (annual) ● life, $3,000. **Staff:** 4. **Budget:** $600,000. **Regional Groups:** 14. **Description:** Participants are women judges committed to strengthening the role of women in the American judicial system. Primary goals are to increase the number of women judges at all levels of the federal and state judiciary; minimize gender bias in the judicial system through support of special task forces, development of educational materials, and provision of training for male and female judges; increase the effectiveness of women judges through provision of education and other support programs. Has developed a curriculum on the judicial selection process and candidate skills. Provides assistance in developing and funding education programs of the National Association of Women Judges. Sponsors institutes. **Telecommunication Services:** electronic mail, dstender77@aol.com. **Committees:** Administrative Law; Amicus; By-Laws; Conference Planning; Conference Policy; Federal Judges; Gender Fairness; International Outreach. **Formerly:** Foundation for Women Judges; (1995) Women Judges' Fund for Justice. **Publications:** *Child Custody and Visitation: Facilitator's Manual*. **Price:** $20.00 ● *Family Violence: Effective Judicial Intervention*. **Price:** $20.00 ● *Learning From the New Jersey Supreme Court Task Force on Women in the Courts* ● *Medicine, Ethics and the Law: Pre-conception to Birth*. **Price:** free ● *National Conference on Bioethics, Family and the Law*. Proceedings. **Price:** $5.00 ● *Operating a Task Force on Gender Bias in the Courts: A Manual for Action*. **Price:** $35.00 ● *Planning for Evaluation: Guidelines for Task Forces on Gender Bias in the Courts*. **Price:** $10.00 ● *Promoting Gender Fairness Through Judicial Education: A Guide to the Issues and Resources*. **Price:** $20.00 ● *Spousal Support*. **Price:** $20.00 ● *What's A Judge to Do? Pregnant Substance Users and the Role of the Court*. **Price:** free ● *Women, Families and Reproduction: Judicial Decision Making*. Proceedings. **Price:** $10.00. **Conventions/Meetings:** annual conference.

5908 ■ National Center for State Courts (NCSC)
300 Newport Ave.
Williamsburg, VA 23185-4147
Ph: (757)259-1857
Free: (800)616-6164
Fax: (757)564-2022
E-mail: knowledge@ncsc.dni.us
URL: http://www.ncsconline.org
Contact: Ms. Mary Campbell McQueen, Pres.
Founded: 1971. **Staff:** 130. **Description:** Provides assistance to state and local trial and appellate courts in improving their structure and administration. Furnishes consultant services; conducts national studies and projects; acts as a clearinghouse for exchange of information on court problems; coordinates activities of other organizations involved in judicial improvement, providing secretariat services for several. Conducts conferences and training courses. Compiles statistics on state court caseload and administrative operations. Research includes: appellate procedures, pretrial services, court delay, alternatives to incarceration, juvenile justice, rural court services, alternative dispute resolution, jury management, and sentencing and judicial information systems. Offers placement service. **Libraries: Type:** by appointment only; lending; reference. **Holdings:** 30,000; books, monographs, periodicals, reports, video recordings. **Subjects:** judicial administration. **Awards: Type:** recognition. **Computer Services:** Information services, index of resources available from the NCSC. **Telecommunication Services:** electronic bulletin board, court technology. **Committees:** Access to and Fairness in the Courts; Court Management; Courts and Children; Mass Torts; Professionalism and Competence of the Bar; Public Trust and Confidence in the Judiciary; Security and Emergency Preparedness; Tribal Relations. **Divisions:** Institute for Court Management; Washington Office. **Publications:** *Judicial Salary Survey*, semiannual ● *Report*, monthly. Newsletter ● *State Court Journal*, quarterly ● Annual Report, annual ● Books ● Pamphlets ● Papers ● Reports. **Conventions/Meetings:** annual board meeting.

5909 ■ National Conference of Bankruptcy Judges (NCBJ)
c/o Ms. Christine J. Molick, Exec. Dir.
241 Aristides Dr.
Irmo, SC 29063
Ph: (803)749-4115
Fax: (803)749-4116
E-mail: cjmolick@sc.rr.com
URL: http://www.ncbj.org
Contact: Ms. Christine J. Molick, Exec. Dir.
Founded: 1926. **Members:** 320. **Description:** Represents active and former bankruptcy judges. Promotes improvements in law practice and administration of justice in U.S. bankruptcy courts; encourages uniformity in the administration of estates in bankruptcy. **Committees:** Automation and Technology; Ethics; Legislation. **Publications:** *American Bankruptcy Law Journal*, quarterly. **Price:** $65.00/year; $20.00 single issue. ISSN: 0027-9048 ● Newsletter, quarterly. **Conventions/Meetings:** annual conference (exhibits) - 2008 Sept. 24-27, Scottsdale, AZ; 2009 Oct. 18-21, Las Vegas, NV.

5910 ■ National Conference of Federal Trial Judges (NCFTJ)
c/o American Bar Association
321 N Clark St., 19th Fl.
Chicago, IL 60610
Ph: (312)988-5689
Free: (800)238-2667
Fax: (312)988-5709
E-mail: abajd@abanet.org
URL: http://www.abanet.org/jd/ncftj/home.html
Contact: Barbara M.G. Lynn, Chair
Founded: 1972. **Members:** 400. **Description:** Judges of the U.S. District Court, U.S. Tax Court, U.S. Court of International Trade, and U.S. Claims Court. Provides a forum for federal trial judges in order to improve the administration of justice in federal trial court. Sponsors seminars and educational programs; compiles and disseminates information. **Conventions/Meetings:** annual meeting - 2008 Aug. 7-12, New York, NY.

5911 ■ National Conference of Specialized Court Judges (NCSCJ)
c/o ABA Judicial Division
321 N Clark St., 19th Fl.
Chicago, IL 60610

Ph: (312)988-5705
Free: (800)238-2667
Fax: (312)988-5709
E-mail: abajd@abanet.org
URL: http://www.abanet.org/jd/ncscj
Contact: James M. Riehl, Chm.
Founded: 1969. **Members:** 487. **Staff:** 1. **Description:** A conference of the American Bar Association; city, state, municipal, county, and federal judges of limited jurisdiction courts. Offers professional training; holds seminars. Maintains over 30 committees including Bio-Ethics, Court Delay Reduction, Judicial Ethics, and Native American Tribal Courts. **Awards:** Education Award. **Type:** recognition. **Recipient:** for best state judicial education organization ● Flashner Board Award. **Type:** recognition. **Recipient:** for an outstanding limited jurisdiction judge in the U.S. **Formerly:** (2004) National Conference of Special Court Judges. **Publications:** *Special Court News*, quarterly. Newsletter. **Price:** included in membership dues. **Conventions/Meetings:** annual conference - midyear ● annual meeting.

5912 ■ National Council of Juvenile and Family Court Judges (NCJFCJ)
PO Box 8970
Reno, NV 89507
Ph: (775)784-6012
Fax: (775)784-6628
E-mail: staff@ncjfcj.org
URL: http://www.ncjfcj.org
Contact: Ms. Mary Mentaberry, Exec. Dir.
Founded: 1937. **Members:** 1,800. **Membership Dues:** regular, $195 (annual) ● associate, $145 (annual) ● student, $85 (annual). **Staff:** 112. **Budget:** $20,000,000. **State Groups:** 15. **Description:** Judges with juvenile and family court jurisdiction and others with a professional interest in the nation's juvenile justice system. Works to further more effective administration of justice for young people through the improvement of juvenile and family court standards and practices. Sponsors continuing education program. Compiles and disseminates research data. **Awards:** President's Award. **Frequency:** annual. **Type:** recognition. **Recipient:** to judges, individuals, states, and organizations for meritorious service to the children of America. **Formerly:** (1977) National Council of Juvenile Court Judges. **Publications:** *Juvenile and Family Court Journal*, quarterly. Contains articles on juvenile justice and family law. Includes statistics. **Price:** included in membership dues; $60.00 /year for nonmembers in U.S. and Canada; $68.00 /year for nonmembers outside U.S. and Canada. ISSN: 0161-7109. **Circulation:** 2,500. Alternate Formats: microform ● *Juvenile and Family Justice Today*, quarterly. Magazine. Includes calendar of events; legislative updates; articles on juvenile and family law. **Price:** included in membership dues; $40.00 /year for nonmembers. **Circulation:** 2,500. **Advertising:** accepted ● *Juvenile and Family Law Digest*, monthly. Journal. Provides current court decisions affecting the juvenile and family law fields. Includes index, cumulated annually. **Price:** included in membership dues; $160.00 /year for nonmembers. ISSN: 0279-2257. Alternate Formats: microform ● Monograph ● Also publishes textbook series. **Conventions/Meetings:** annual conference (exhibits).

5913 ■ National Judges Association (NJA)
c/o Ralph J. Zeller, Exec. Dir.
PO Box 160
Maud, OK 74854-0160
Ph: (405)374-2896
Free: (888)FON-ENJA
Fax: (405)374-2316
E-mail: rjzjd@sbcglobal.net
URL: http://www.nationaljudgesassociation.org
Contact: Ralph J. Zeller, Exec. Dir.
Founded: 1979. **Members:** 400. **Membership Dues:** retired, $25 (annual) ● regular (based on judicial salary), $25-$100 (annual) ● associate, $50 (annual) ● life, $300. **Staff:** 1. **Budget:** $23,000. **Description:** Incumbent nonlawyer judges and individuals working to publicize the contributions of nonlawyer judges to the court system. Opposes legislation limiting judicial positions to individuals with a law degree. Fosters exchange of ideas, methods, and experiences among members. Seeks to enhance members' judicial performance through further education. Maintains National Judges Education and Research Foundation, which seeks to improve the judicial image and performance through continuing education and training and information exchange. Offers educational courses. **Awards:** MacEachern Award. **Frequency:** annual. **Type:** recognition. **Recipient:** to an outstanding non-attorney judge. **Computer Services:** Mailing lists, of members. **Committees:** Credentials; Education; Legislative; Publicity/Liaison. **Publications:** *The Gavel*, quarterly. Newspaper. **Circulation:** 750. **Advertising:** accepted. **Conventions/Meetings:** annual Educational Conference (exhibits) - 2008 June 14-20, Savannah, GA ● annual meeting - mid-year ● seminar.

5914 ■ National Judicial College (NJC)
Univ. of Nevada
Judicial Coll. Bldg., MS 358
Reno, NV 89557
Ph: (775)784-6747
Free: (800)255-8343
Fax: (775)784-1253
E-mail: info@judges.org
URL: http://www.judges.org
Contact: William F. Dressel, Pres.
Founded: 1963. **Description:** Provides education and training for the nation's judges and other decision-makers. Seeks to improve the administration of justice. Conducts both resident courses and regional extension programs to improve judicial proficiency, performance, and productivity. Provides programs as an assistance to state judicial education offices; organizes special and innovative programs such as victims' rights, family violence, jail and prison crowding, equal justice citizens in the courts, and bioethics. Maintains speakers' bureau. **Libraries: Type:** open to the public. **Holdings:** 60,000. **Subjects:** law, judicial administration. **Awards: Type:** scholarship. **Computer Services:** Mailing lists. **Boards:** Visitors. **Councils:** Legacy. **Programs:** Comparative Law. **Formerly:** (1971) National College of State Trial Judges; (1978) National College of the State Judiciary. **Publications:** *Administrative Law Judge's Desk Book: Evidence* ● *Americans with Disabilities Act-An Instructional Guide for Judges and Court Administrators* ● *Capital Cases Benchbook* ● *Case in Point*, periodic. Magazine ● *Criminal Law Outline*, annual. Alternate Formats: diskette ● *Ethics for Judges* ● *Goldberg's Deskbook on Evidence for ALJs* ● *Inherent Powers of the Courts* ● *Judicial Discretion* ● *Managing Trails Effectively*. Contains planning/conducting course. ● *NJC Newsletter*, quarterly ● *Planning/Conducting a Faculty Development Workshop on Gender Fairness in the Courts* ● Videos ● Books. **Conventions/Meetings:** periodic meeting.

Juvenile Delinquency

5915 ■ Coalition for Juvenile Justice (CJJ)
1710 Rhode Island Ave. NW, 10th Fl.
Washington, DC 20036
Ph: (202)467-0864
Fax: (202)887-0738
E-mail: info@juvjustice.org
URL: http://www.juvjustice.org
Contact: Paul Lawrence, Natl. Chm.
Founded: 1984. **Members:** 1,500. **Staff:** 7. **Description:** Representatives from state and local government agencies and citizens interested in the juvenile justice system; promotes prevention services and treatment programs for delinquent and at-risk youth; provides forum for programs, practices, and procedures; assists in development of national policies and legislation; acts as national voice for members. **Awards:** National Board Leadership. **Type:** recognition ● National Executive Leadership. **Type:** recognition ● National Public Education. **Type:** recognition ● National Public Leadership. **Type:** recognition. **Subgroups:** Management Leadership; National Collaboration for Youth; Public Policy. **Task Forces:** Child Sex Abuse; Diversity; Inter-city Transportation Assistance. **Publications:** *AssemblyLine*. Newsletter. **Price:** included in membership dues ● *Some Assembly Required Calendar*, bimonthly. Presents a calendar of events. **Price:** included in membership dues. **Conventions/Meetings:** annual conference and retreat ● annual dinner, with presentation of the Excellence in National Leadership Awards.

Labor

5916 ■ International Labor History Association (ILHA)
706 Bruce Ct.
Madison, WI 53705
Ph: (608)231-1886
Contact: Ronald C. Kent, Ed.
Founded: 1988. **Description:** Trade unionists, writers, scholars, and other interested individuals. Seeks to advance the study and teaching of working-class history in each country of the world. Supports progressive labor movements and the cause of world peace. Works to improve critical labor histories in schools, universities, adult education institutions, and trade unions. Opposes racism, antisemitism, fascism, sexism, apartheid, and imperialism. Conducts research and educational programs. Operates speakers' bureau. **Libraries: Type:** reference. **Subjects:** educational teaching and reference materials on labor history. **Awards:** ILHA Book of the Year. **Frequency:** annual. **Type:** recognition. **Recipient:** to the author of an outstanding book in labor history. **Publications:** *ILHA Newsletter*, periodic. Contains teaching outlines on labor history. **Conventions/Meetings:** periodic board meeting.

5917 ■ National Association of Governmental Labor Officials (NAGLO)
PO Box 11910
Lexington, KY 40578-1910
Ph: (859)244-8221
Fax: (859)244-8001
E-mail: pplummer@csg.org
URL: http://www.naglo.org
Contact: Piper Plummer, Mgr.
Founded: 1914. **Members:** 51. **Membership Dues:** state government, $750 (annual). **Regional Groups:** 10. **Description:** Elected and appointed heads of state labor departments. Seeks to assist labor officials in performing their duties and to improve employment conditions for American workers and employers. **Formed by Merger of:** (1893) Association of Chiefs and Officials of Bureaus of Labor; International Association of Factory Inspectors. **Formerly:** (1928) Association of Governmental Labor Officials; (1933) Association of Government Officials in Industry of the United States and Canada; (1979) International Association of Governmental Labor Officials. **Publications:** *NAGLO Congressional Directory*. **Price:** $10.00 ● *NAGLO Membership Directory*, biennial. **Price:** $60.00 ● *NAGLO News*, periodic. Contains updates concerning developments in labor and employment laws. **Conventions/Meetings:** annual conference (exhibits) - always summer.

5918 ■ National Public Employer Labor Relations Association (NPELRA)
1012 S Coast Hwy., Ste.M
Oceanside, CA 92054
Ph: (760)433-1686
Free: (877)673-5721
Fax: (760)433-1687
E-mail: info@npelra.org
URL: http://www.npelra.org
Contact: Michael T. Kolb, Exec. Dir.
Founded: 1971. **Members:** 2,300. **Membership Dues:** associate, $150 (annual) ● active/affiliate, $175 (annual). **Staff:** 7. **Regional Groups:** 1. **State Groups:** 15. **Description:** Labor relations professionals working for special districts and federal, state, county, and city governments. Seeks to improve the quality of labor relations and employment relations in the public sector. **Libraries: Type:** reference. **Subjects:** labor relations, public sector. **Awards:** Pacesetter. **Frequency:** annual. **Type:** recognition. **Recipi-**

ent: for innovative approaches to human resources/ personnel labor management problem solving. **Committees:** Academy; Awards; Conference; Legislative; Mentoring/Coaching; Nominating; Sponsorship/Advertising; Training. **Publications:** *Developing A Supervisor's Labor Relations Guide.* Book. Covers training guidelines, labor relation concepts, grievances, and discipline. **Price:** $25.00 ● *Documenting Discipline.* Book. **Price:** $12.00 for members; $15.00 for nonmembers ● *Family Medical Leave Guide.* Provides full text of the 1993 federal law. **Price:** $50.00 for members; $57.50 for nonmembers ● *FLSA Public Sector Compliance Guide.* Covers all aspects of the law. **Price:** $95.00 for members; $130.00 for nonmembers ● *Handling Diversity in the Workplace: Communication is the Key.* **Price:** $12.00 for members; $15.00 for nonmembers ● *The Human Touch Performance Appraisal.* **Price:** $12.00 for members; $15.00 for nonmembers ● *I Have To Fire Someone!.* **Price:** $12.00 for members; $15.00 for nonmembers ● *In Defense of the Public Employer: Case Law and Litigation Strategies for Discrimination Claims.* Book ● *Interviewing: More Than a Gut Feeling.* Book. **Price:** $12.00 for members; $15.00 for nonmembers ● *Legal Issues for Managers: Essential Skills for Avoiding Your Day In Court.* **Price:** $12.00 for members; $15.00 for nonmembers ● *Maintaining Public Services: The NPELRA Strike Manual.* **Price:** $55.00 for members; $90.00 for nonmembers ● *National Public Employer Labor Relations Association—Newsletter,* monthly. Provides current information on labor relations developments affecting the public sector. Offers news, counsel, and new ideas. **Price:** available to members only. Also Cited As: *NPELRA Newsletter* ● *Negotiate with Confidence.* Book ● *The Sexual Harassment Prevention Training Game.* Features a board game that will train 4-5 people at a time. ● *Smarter Bargaining and Smarter Bargaining II.* Features contract language for the public sector. ● *Smarter Bargaining: Guide to Contract Language for Today's Public Sector Negotiator (Book I).* **Price:** $65.00 for members; $75.00 for nonmembers ● *Smarter Bargaining: Guide to Contract Language for Today's Public Sector Negotiator (Book II).* **Price:** $40.00 for members; $60.00 for nonmembers ● *Stopping Sexual Harassment Before It Starts: A Business and Legal Perspective.* Book. **Price:** $12.00 for members; $15.00 for nonmembers ● *Winning Arbitration.* **Price:** $55.00 for members; $90.00 for nonmembers ● *Working Together.* Video. **Conventions/Meetings:** annual conference (exhibits) - always March or April ● seminar.

5919 ■ Society of Federal Labor and Employee Relations Professionals (SFLERP)
PO Box 25112
Arlington, VA 22202
Ph: (703)685-4130
Fax: (703)685-1144
E-mail: info@sflerp.org
URL: http://www.sflerp.org
Contact: Paco Martinez Alvarez, Exec. Dir./Treas.
Founded: 1973. **Members:** 550. **Membership Dues:** sponsored, $15 (annual) ● general, $50 (annual) ● organization, $100 (annual) ● retiree, $35 (annual) ● student, $10 (annual) ● general, $90 (biennial) ● general, $135 (triennial). **Staff:** 1. **Local Groups:** 3. **Description:** Seeks to enhance the stature of the federal labor-management and employee relations profession, to increase understanding among federal labor parties, and to provide a forum for discussion of relevant issues. Society members are federal agency management officials, representatives of unions of federal employees, and neutrals who handle labor disputes in the federal sector. **Awards:** Labor-Management Cooperation Award. **Frequency:** annual. **Type:** recognition. **Recipient:** to the best Federal agency and union that best exemplify the Board's goal. **Formerly:** (2003) Society of Federal Labor Relations Professionals. **Publications:** *SFLRP Reporter,* quarterly. Newsletter. **Advertising:** accepted. **Conventions/Meetings:** annual symposium (exhibits).

Land Control

5920 ■ Lincoln Institute of Land Policy
113 Brattle St.
Cambridge, MA 02138
Ph: (617)661-3016
Free: (800)LAND-USE
Fax: (617)661-7235
E-mail: help@lincolninst.edu
URL: http://www.lincolninst.edu
Contact: Gregory K. Ingram, Pres./CEO
Founded: 1974. **Description:** Aims to study and teach about land policy, including land economics and land taxation. Sponsors programs on taxation of land and buildings, land markets and land as common property. **Publications:** *Land Lines,* quarterly. Magazine. Reports on the Institute's current research and educational programs. **Circulation:** 8,000. Alternate Formats: online.

Latin American

5921 ■ National Latino Officers Association (NLOA)
PO Box 02-0120
Brooklyn, NY 11201
Free: (866)579-5809
Fax: (646)772-3728
URL: http://www.nloaus.org
Contact: Anthony Miranda, Exec. Chm.
Membership Dues: regular, $30 (annual) ● associate, $25 (annual). **Description:** Aims to create a coordinated network of support without limitations or boundaries. Promotes tolerance toward and understanding of the Latino culture in all public and private agencies, especially in the law enforcement communities. Creates strong bonds between the Latino community and other law enforcement agencies. Ensures equal representation in hiring and promotional practices.

Law

5922 ■ American Bar Association Criminal Justice Section (CJS)
740 15th St. NW, 10th Fl.
Washington, DC 20005-1019
Ph: (202)662-1510 (202)662-1500
Fax: (202)662-1501
E-mail: crimjustice@abanet.org
URL: http://www.abanet.org/crimjust/home.html
Contact: Jack Hanna, Dir.
Founded: 1920. **Members:** 9,500. **Membership Dues:** individual, $35 (annual) ● law student, $7 (annual). **Staff:** 12. **Description:** A section of the American Bar Association. Attorneys and law students; judges, law professors, law enforcement and court personnel, and other interested individuals. Seeks to ensure quick, fair, and effective administration of criminal justice; monitors law enforcement procedures and developments in substantive and procedural criminal law. Assists lawyers and prosecutors in developing trial and appellate skills and in solving practice-related problems. Studies legal issues and recommends procedural and statutory improvements in areas such as the definition of crimes, arrest, pretrial release, postconviction procedures, rights of victims and witnesses, juvenile justice, and correction and rehabilitation of offenders. Lobbies federal government on issues of criminal justice on behalf of the ABA; cooperates with government bodies in the drafting of procedural guidelines and standards. Develops briefing materials for the ABA in the area of criminal justice; conducts continuing professional education programs for attorneys. Submits amicus curiae briefs to federal courts on contemporary criminal justice issues. **Libraries: Type:** open to the public. **Holdings:** 1,000; books, monographs, periodicals. **Awards:** Charles R. English Award. **Frequency:** annual. **Type:** recognition. **Recipient:** for CJS members ● Livingston Hall Juvenile Justice Award. **Frequency:** annual. **Type:** recognition. **Recipient:** for lawyers making exemplary contribution to juvenile justice ● Livy Hall Award. **Frequency:** annual. **Type:** recognition. **Recipient:** for a lawyer practicing in juvenile justice ● William Greenhalgh Student Essay Competition. **Frequency:** annual. **Type:** recognition. **Recipient:** for law students. **Telecommunication Services:** electronic mail, hannaj@staff.abanet.org. **Formerly:** Section of Criminal Law. **Publications:** *Criminal Justice,* quarterly. Magazine. Includes feature articles, as well as regular columns. **Price:** included in membership dues; $33.00 /year for nonmembers. ISSN: 0887-7785. **Circulation:** 9,000. **Advertising:** accepted. Alternate Formats: microform ● *Criminal Law Outline.* Book. Serves as a guide to U.S. Supreme Court decisions on the 4th, 5th, 6th, and 8th Amendments, and on miscellaneous federal/state due process problems. ● *Ethical Problems Facing The Criminal Defense Lawyer.* Book. **Price:** $59.95/copy; $49.95 section member discount ● *The Fourth Amendment Handbook.* Features a chronological survey of Supreme Court decisions. Examines 344 cases pertaining to the Fourth Amendment through 1991. ● *Practice Under the New Federal Sentencing Guidelines* ● *Protecting Yourself and Your Fee-A Defense Lawyer's Practice Guide in a New Age of Federal Law.* Explains the many new federal laws that hold potential personal liability for lawyers. Forms and Department of Justice Guidelines are included. **Price:** $25.00 for nonmembers; $20.00 for members ● Also publishes course materials. reports, pamphlets, monographs, and newsletters. Publishes ABA Standards for Criminal Justice and IJA/ABA Juvenile Justice Standards as well as a video tape covering cross-examination skills. **Conventions/Meetings:** Council Meeting - 3/year.

5923 ■ American Bar Foundation (ABF)
750 N Lake Shore Dr.
Chicago, IL 60611
Ph: (312)988-6500 (312)988-6511
Free: (800)292-5056
Fax: (312)988-6579
E-mail: rnelson@abfn.org
URL: http://www.abf-sociolegal.org
Contact: Robert L. Nelson, Dir.
Founded: 1952. **Staff:** 60. **Budget:** $4,100,000. **Description:** Research and educational organization. Studies the administration of justice; promotes the study of law and sociolegal research; conducts research on such topics as the work of lawyers, professionalism, alternative dispute resolution, tort reform, medical malpractice, the courts and judicial administration, and legal education. **Awards:** Post-doctoral Fellowship. **Frequency:** annual. **Type:** fellowship. **Recipient:** for writers of outstanding doctoral dissertations. **Publications:** *Fellows News.* Newsletter. Alternate Formats: online ● *Law and Social Inquiry,* quarterly. Journal. Contains articles on the legal profession, the provision of legal services, the operation of legal institutions, trends and policy developments. **Price:** $36.00 /year for individuals; $59.00 /year for institutions; $29.00/year for faculty and students. ISSN: 0361-9486. **Circulation:** 5,100 ● *Researching Law: An ABF Update,* quarterly. Newsletter. **Advertising:** accepted. Alternate Formats: online ● Annual Report, annual. Alternate Formats: online ● Also publishes working papers. **Conventions/Meetings:** annual meeting, in conjunction with the American Bar Association - always February.

5924 ■ American College of Tax Counsel (ACTC)
1156 15th St. NW, Ste.900
Washington, DC 20005-1704
Ph: (202)637-3243
Fax: (202)331-2714
E-mail: info@actconline.org
URL: http://www.actconline.org
Contact: Frederic L. Ballard Jr., Chm.
Founded: 1980. **Members:** 645. **Membership Dues:** regular, $225 (annual) ● retired/academic, $100 (annual). **Staff:** 5. **Budget:** $250,000. **Description:** Dedicated to the study of tax policy and seeks methods for improving the operation and administration of the tax system, especially those aspects that relate to voluntary compliance, professionalism, and ethics in the practice of tax law.

5925 ■ American Law Institute (ALI)
4025 Chestnut St.
Philadelphia, PA 19104-3099

Ph: (215)243-1600
Free: (800)253-6397
Fax: (215)243-1636
E-mail: ali@ali.org
URL: http://www.ali.org
Contact: Lance Liebman, Dir.
Founded: 1923. **Members:** 3,800. **Membership Dues:** invitational, $250 (annual). **Staff:** 15. **Budget:** $5,000,000. **Description:** Judges, law teachers, and lawyers. Promotes the clarification and simplification of the law and its better adaptation to social needs by continuing work on the Restatement of the Law, model and uniform codes, and model statutes. Conducts a program of continuing legal education jointly with the American Bar Association called "ALI-ABA" (see separate entry). **Libraries: Type:** reference. **Holdings:** 6,000; books, periodicals. **Subjects:** law, continuing legal education. **Awards:** Henry J. Friendly Medal. **Frequency:** annual. **Type:** medal. **Recipient:** for contributions to the Law in the Tradition of Judge Friendly and the Institute. **Computer Services:** Online services, Westlaw and Lexis-Nexis. **Committees:** Audit; Conflicts of Interest; Federal Judicial Code Revision; Institute Program; Institute Size; Investment; Nominating; Tax Program. **Affiliated With:** American Bar Association. **Publications:** *ALI Proceedings of Annual Meetings*, annual. Contains transcript of ALI Annual Meeting proceedings. ● *ALI Reporter*, quarterly. Newsletter. Reports on the activities of ALI. **Price:** included in membership dues. **Circulation:** 3,500. Alternate Formats: online ● *Capturing the Voice of The American Law Institute: A Handbook for ALI Reporters and Those Who Review Their Work*. Alternate Formats: online ● Annual Report, annual. Alternate Formats: online ● Also publishes tentative drafts and official versions of its work. **Conventions/Meetings:** annual general assembly ● annual meeting - always May.

5926 ■ American Tort Reform Association (ATRA)

1101 Connecticut Ave. NW, Ste.400
Washington, DC 20036
Ph: (202)682-1163
Fax: (202)682-1022
E-mail: sjoyce@atra.org
URL: http://www.atra.org
Contact: Sherman Joyce, Pres.
Founded: 1986. **Members:** 350. **Staff:** 8. **Budget:** $2,000,000. **State Groups:** 40. **Description:** Membership includes professional groups and businesses, nonprofit and trade associations. Advocates changes in the current tort system, returning fairness, efficiency, and predictability to the civil justice system. Offers advocacy information and public education on legal issues. Maintains speakers' bureau. **Libraries: Type:** reference. **Holdings:** archival material, books. **Computer Services:** database. **Committees:** Medical Liability Advisory; Products Liability Advisory; Professional Liability Advisory; Public Information; Punitives. **Publications:** *Legislative Watch*, weekly. Contains legislative updates on tort issues at the state and federal level. ● *The Reformer*, quarterly. Newsletter. Alternate Formats: online ● *Tort Reform Outlook*, annual. Features legislative forecast. ● *Tort Reform Record*, semiannual. Lists enactments from 1986 to present. **Conventions/Meetings:** annual conference - always in Washington, DC ● annual Legislative Conference for State Coalition Leaders and Lobbyists - conference and regional meeting, civil justice reform education, held in Chicago.

5927 ■ American Veterinary Medical Law Association (AVMLA)

c/o Karen M. Wernette, DVM, Exec. Dir.
511 N Country Ridge Ct.
Lake Zurich, IL 60047-2824
Ph: (847)719-1810
Fax: (847)719-1810
E-mail: info@avmla.org
URL: http://www.avmla.org
Contact: Karen M. Wernette DVM, Exec. Dir.
Founded: 1994. **Membership Dues:** active, associate, $100 (annual) ● student, $40 (annual). **Description:** Provides information to members regarding pertinent issues in the field of veterinary medical law. Increases public awareness and understanding of the impact of law on all aspects of veterinary medicine. Facilitates interactions among organizations, regulatory agencies and the courts for the benefit of society. **Publications:** *AVMLA Newsletter*, quarterly. Keeps members informed on legal issues in veterinary medicine and AVMLA activities. **Advertising:** accepted. Alternate Formats: online ● Proceedings, annual.

5928 ■ Asian Law Caucus (ALC)

939 Market St., Ste.201
San Francisco, CA 94103
Ph: (415)896-1701
Fax: (415)896-1702
E-mail: genf@asianlawcaucus.org
URL: http://www.asianlawcaucus.org
Contact: Gen Fujioka, Program Dir.
Founded: 1972. **Staff:** 10. **Languages:** Chinese, English, Vietnamese. **Description:** People interested in the legal and civil rights of the Asian Pacific American. Strives to promote, advance and represent the legal and civil rights of the Asian and Pacific Islander communities. Litigates cases, provides free legal representation to low-income clients. **Awards:** ALC Community Award. **Type:** recognition. **Publications:** *ALC Newsletter*. **Conventions/Meetings:** annual Caucus Golf Classic - competition.

5929 ■ Association of Legal Administrators (ALA)

75 Tri State Intl., Ste.222
Lincolnshire, IL 60069-4435
Ph: (847)267-1252
Fax: (847)267-1329
E-mail: jmichalik@alanet.org
URL: http://www.alanet.org
Contact: John J. Michalik, Exec. Dir.
Founded: 1971. **Members:** 10,000. **Membership Dues:** first time introductory, $250 ● regular, associate, student, $350 (annual) ● public interest, nonprofit, $200 (annual). **Staff:** 36. **Budget:** $6,500,000. **Regional Groups:** 6. **Multinational. Description:** Administrators of private law firms and corporate and governmental law departments. Promotes the exchange of information regarding administration and management problems particular to legal organizations; provides information on the value and availability of professional administrators; improves standards and qualifications; develops continuing education programs; participates in the advancement of legal administration. Offers classified advertising service. **Libraries: Type:** reference. **Holdings:** books, monographs, periodicals. **Subjects:** legal management. **Awards: Frequency:** annual. **Type:** recognition. **Committees:** Certification; Conference; Corporate/Government Planning; Intellectual Property; Large Firm Administrators Caucus Steering; Multicultural; Personal Injury Plaintiff; Principal Administrators; Vendor Relations. **Task Forces:** Diversity. **Publications:** *ALA News*, bimonthly. Magazine. Contains association news, advertisers, articles, calendar of events, chapter news, and course calendar. **Price:** included in membership dues; $36.00 /year for nonmembers. **Circulation:** 8,000. **Advertising:** accepted ● *ALA News International*, quarterly. Magazine. Covers association news and articles featuring law office management trends around the world. ● *Association of Legal Administrators—Directory*, annual. **Price:** included in membership dues. **Circulation:** 8,000. **Advertising:** accepted ● *Compensation Survey*, annual ● *Legal Management: The Journal of the Association of Legal Administrators*, bimonthly. Contains articles on legal administration. Includes advertisers' index, book reviews, and new products listing. **Price:** included in membership dues. **Circulation:** 25,000. **Advertising:** accepted. Alternate Formats: microform. **Conventions/Meetings:** annual conference (exhibits) - always April or May.

5930 ■ Atlantic Legal Foundation (ALF)

330 Madison Ave., 6th Fl.
New York, NY 10017
Ph: (212)867-3322
Fax: (212)867-1022
E-mail: atlanticlegal@atlanticlegal.org
URL: http://www.atlanticlegal.org
Contact: William H. Slattery, Pres.
Founded: 1976. **Description:** Works to promote and protect good science in the courtroom and to challenge governmental regulations. Advocates for the principles of free enterprise, the rights of individuals and limited government. **Telecommunication Services:** electronic mail, whslattery@atlanticlegal.org. **Publications:** *Atlantic Legal Annual Report*, annual. Alternate Formats: online ● *Atlantic Legal Bulletin*. Alternate Formats: online ● Reports. Alternate Formats: online.

5931 ■ Center for American and International Law

5201 Democracy Dr.
Plano, TX 75024-3561
Ph: (972)244-3400
Free: (800)409-1090
Fax: (972)244-3401
E-mail: cail@cailaw.org
URL: http://www.cailaw.org
Contact: Michael J. Marchand, Pres.
Founded: 1947. **Members:** 813. **Membership Dues:** individual, $500 (annual) ● business, $850 (annual). **Staff:** 20. **Description:** Provides continuing legal and law enforcement education, focusing primarily on continuing education programs for lawyers and management training programs for law enforcement officials. **Awards:** John Rogers Award. **Frequency:** annual. **Type:** recognition. **Recipient:** for a person associated with the petroleum industry ● Storey Award. **Frequency:** annual. **Type:** recognition. **Recipient:** for leadership in international law. **Telecommunication Services:** electronic mail, mikemarchand@cailaw.org. **Divisions:** Institute for Energy Law; Institute for International and Comparative Law; Institute for Law and Technology; Institute for Law Enforcement Administration; Institute for Litigation Studies; Institute for Local Government Studies; Institute for Transnational Arbitration. **Formerly:** (2002) Southwestern Legal Foundation. **Publications:** *Labor Law Developments*, annual ● *Oil and Gas Law*, monthly ● *Oil and Gas Reporter*, monthly ● *Planning, Zoning, and Eminent Domain*, annual ● *Private Investments Abroad*, annual ● *Proceedings of the Institute on Planning, Zoning, and Eminent Domain*, annual ● Annual Report, annual ● Brochures ● Also publishes programs for educational and special events.

5932 ■ Center for Democracy (CFD)

Address Unknown since 2007
Languages: English, Russian. **Description:** Attorneys and environmental professionals. Promotes judicial development and independence and environmental conservation in the former Soviet Union "undertakes programs and studies on major issues that confront democratic societies." Advocates an independent judiciary in central and eastern Europe and the former Soviet Union. Sponsors research and educational programs; conducts international exchanges; advises international development and environmental organizations and government agencies regarding legal issues. **Conventions/Meetings:** periodic conference ● periodic seminar.

5933 ■ Chinese Law Society of America (CLSA)

c/o Dr. C. Stephen Hsu, Chm.
1285 Ave. of the Americas
New York, NY 10019-6064
Ph: (212)373-3128
Fax: (212)373-2308
E-mail: info@chineselawsociety.org
URL: http://www.chineselawsociety.org
Contact: Dr. C. Stephen Hsu, Chm.
Founded: 1993. **Multinational. Description:** Represents Chinese legal scholars, practitioners and law students who have worked/studied or are currently working/studying in the US. Aims to promote the study, research, and understanding of Chinese and American law. Organizes academic and professional activities among its members. Assists in China's legal development and reform.

5934 ■ Coalition for International Justice
Address Unknown since 2008
Description: Supports and monitors for the international criminal tribunals for the former Yugoslavia and Rwanda. Works with concerned groups and individuals to help these tribunals function effectively. Strives to strengthen relations between them and people for whom they were established to provide justice. Uses its experience with these tribunals to further justice efforts for other conflict-stricken areas around the world. **Publications:** Reports. Alternate Formats: online ● Articles. Alternate Formats: online.

5935 ■ Commission on Law and Aging
c/o American Bar Association
740 15th St. NW
Washington, DC 20005-1022
Ph: (202)662-8690
Fax: (202)662-8698
E-mail: abaaging@abanet.org
URL: http://www.abanet.org/aging
Contact: Erica F. Wood, Asst. Dir.
Founded: 1978. **Members:** 15. **Description:** Works to examine law and policy issues affecting older persons. **Formerly:** (2004) Commission on Legal Problems of the Elderly. **Publications:** *Termination and Closure of Poor Quality Nursing Homes: What Are the Options?*. **Conventions/Meetings:** annual conference.

5936 ■ Commission on Women in the Profession
c/o American Bar Association
321 N Clark St., 18th Fl.
Chicago, IL 60610
Ph: (312)988-5715
Free: (800)285-2221
Fax: (312)988-5790
E-mail: abacwp1@abanet.org
URL: http://www.abanet.org/women
Contact: Pamela J. Roberts, Chair
Founded: 1987. **Staff:** 13. **Description:** Assesses the status of women in the legal profession. Strives to identify barriers to the advancement of women. Promotes the full and equal participation of women in the ABA, the legal profession, and the justice system. **Publications:** *Directory of Associations for Women Lawyers*, annual. Contains listings for national, state, and local women's bar associations and multicultural women's bar associations. ● *Perspective*, quarterly. Magazine. Contains in-depth articles for and about women lawyers. **Price:** $35.00/year.

5937 ■ Foundation of the Federal Bar Association (FFBA)
2011 Crystal Dr., Ste.400
Arlington, VA 22202
Ph: (703)682-7000
Fax: (703)682-7001
E-mail: foundation@fedbar.org
URL: http://www.fedbar.org
Contact: William LaForge, Pres.
Founded: 1954. **Members:** 250. **Budget:** $300,000. **Description:** Membership comprises 20 of the original incorporators of the foundation and 150 members of the national council of the Federal Bar Association (see separate entry). Acquires and administers funds for activities that promote and improve the administration of justice, including the study of means for the improved handling of the legal business of federal departments and establishments. Conducts research on such subjects as delays in justice. Co-sponsors five briefing conferences annually. Operates Law Observance program. **Telecommunication Services:** electronic mail, fba@fedbar.org. **Committees:** Fund Raising; Research Projects. **Affiliated With:** Federal Bar Association. **Conventions/Meetings:** competition ● quarterly meeting, in conjunction with FBA.

5938 ■ Global Advertising Lawyers Alliance (GALA)
599 Lexington Ave., 28th Fl.
New York, NY 10022
Ph: (212)549-0343
Fax: (212)521-5450
E-mail: sbess@gala-marketlaw.com
URL: http://www.gala-marketlaw.com
Contact: Stacy D. Bess, Exec. Dir.
Founded: 1998. **Members:** 53. **Membership Dues:** associate, $1,000 (annual). **Staff:** 1. **Regional Groups:** 3. **Multinational. Description:** Attorneys worldwide advising clients involved in cross-border commercial communication. **Additional Websites:** http://www.galagazette.com.

5939 ■ Incorporated Society of Irish/American Lawyers (ISIAL)
c/o Stacey Harb
15140 Farmington Rd.
Livonia, MI 48154
E-mail: michael.riordan@usdoj.gov
URL: http://home.earthlink.net/~isial/index.html
Contact: Michael Riordan, Pres.
Founded: 1978. **Members:** 600. **Membership Dues:** general, $40 (annual). **Description:** U.S. lawyers and judges of Irish ancestry. Promotes the doctrine of universal liberty, equal rights, and justice for all individuals; opposes anything that tends to impair the efficiency and permanency of free institutions. Facilitates exchange of ideas and information among members and with solicitors and barristers from other countries. Works to improve relations between legal professionals and the public. Preserves the memories and historical record of the Irish people. Maintains speakers' bureau; contributes to charities. **Awards:** Hon. Thomas P. Thornton Scholarship. **Frequency:** annual. **Type:** scholarship. **Recipient:** to a second year law school student of Irish ancestry. **Affiliated With:** Irish American Cultural Institute; Irish National Caucus. **Publications:** *A History of the Incorporated Society of Irish/American Lawyers*, monthly. Newsletter. Contains a history of the first 24 years of the society. **Price:** $15.00 ● Membership Directory, triennial ● Newsletter, monthly. **Conventions/Meetings:** monthly meeting.

5940 ■ Institute for Justice (IJ)
901 N Glebe Rd., Ste.900
Arlington, VA 22203
Ph: (703)682-9320
Fax: (703)682-9321
E-mail: general@ij.org
URL: http://www.ij.org
Contact: William H. Mellor, Pres./Gen. Counsel
Founded: 1991. **Staff:** 42. **State Groups:** 3. **Local Groups:** 1. **Description:** Works as libertarian public interest law firm; promotes civil rights activism. **Publications:** *Carry the Torch*. Alternate Formats: online ● *City Studies*. Alternate Formats: online ● *Liberty and Law*, bimonthly. Newsletter. Updates activities nationwide. Alternate Formats: online ● *Public Power; Private Gain*. Report. Alternate Formats: online ● Reports. Alternate Formats: online ● Brochure. Alternate Formats: online.

5941 ■ Inter-American Bar Association (IABA)
1211 Connecticut Ave. NW, Ste.202
Washington, DC 20036
Ph: (202)466-5944
Fax: (202)466-5946
E-mail: iaba@iaba.org
URL: http://www.iaba.org
Contact: Renaldy J. Gutierrez, Pres.
Founded: 1940. **Members:** 3,000. **Membership Dues:** student (last 2 years of law school), $50 (annual) ● junior (first 5 years after Bar admission), $160 (annual) ● senior (after 5th year of Bar admission), $200 (annual) ● contributing, $290 (annual) ● life, $3,500. **Staff:** 4. **Languages:** English, French, Portuguese, Spanish. **Description:** National, regional, and special associations of attorneys; individual lawyers. Purposes are to: advance the science of jurisprudence, and in particular, the study of comparative law; promote uniformity in commercial legislation; further the knowledge of laws of Western Hemisphere countries; propagate justificative administration through the creation and maintenance of independent judicial systems; protect and defend civil, human, and political rights of individuals; uphold the honor of the legal profession; encourage geniality and brotherhood among members. **Libraries: Type:** not open to the public. **Subjects:** law. **Awards:** Best Book. **Type:** recognition ● Best Paper. **Type:** recognition ● Honor Diploma. **Frequency:** annual. **Type:** recognition ● Inter-American Accents Justice Award. **Type:** recognition ● Inter-American Jurisprudence Award. **Type:** recognition ● Law Student Paper. **Type:** recognition. **Committees:** Administrative Law; Business, Banking and Securities Law; Civil Law and Procedure; Constitutional Law; Corporate and Institutional Counsel; Criminal Law and Procedure; Development and Integration Law; Fiscal Law; Human Rights Law; Intellectual and Industrial Property Law; International Arbitration Law; Labor Law and Social Security; Legal Education; Military Law; Natural Resources and Environmental Protection; Practice of Law; Public and Private International Law; Telecommunications, Science and Technology Law; Women's Rights. **Sections:** Administration of Justice; Law School Faculty; Law Students; Young Lawyers. **Publications:** *Campaign Brochure*. Alternate Formats: online ● *Inter-American Bar Association—Conference Proceedings* (in English and Spanish). Features a collection of papers presented at IABA conferences. **Advertising:** accepted. Alternate Formats: CD-ROM ● *Inter-American Bar Association—Membership Directory*, annual. **Price:** available to members only ● *Inter-American Bar Association Newsletter*, quarterly. Includes awards and calendar of events. Alternate Formats: online. **Conventions/Meetings:** annual conference (exhibits).

5942 ■ International Center for Law in Development (ICLD)
Address Unknown since 2008
Founded: 1978. **Staff:** 5. **Budget:** $220,000. **Description:** Nongovernmental agency that aims to: give systematic and continuing attention to the role of law in the development of modern nations; provide an international vehicle for collaborative projects to strengthen legal education, institutions, and services in Latin America, Asia, and Africa; help in the creation and mobilization of greater competence in the field of law and development. Sponsors research programs. **Supersedes:** (1978) International Legal Center. **Conventions/Meetings:** workshop and seminar.

5943 ■ International Center for Not-for-Profit Law (ICNL)
1126 16th St. NW, Ste.400
Washington, DC 20036
Ph: (202)452-8600
Fax: (202)452-8555
E-mail: infoicnl@icnl.org
URL: http://www.icnl.org
Contact: Sylvia Staggs, Office Mgr.
Founded: 1992. **Staff:** 16. **Budget:** $3,142,275. **Languages:** English, French, Mandarin Dialects, Polish, Russian, Spanish. **Multinational. Description:** Seeks to assist in the formation of laws and regulatory systems that stimulate activities of non-profit organizations worldwide. Provides technical assistance in the writing of laws and regulations governing non-profit organizations; assists in the privatization of social, educational, and cultural assets and programs internationally. **Libraries: Type:** by appointment only. **Subjects:** law. **Computer Services:** database ● online services. **Publications:** *The International Journal for Not-For-Profit Law*, quarterly. Also Cited As: *IJNL* ● Annual Report, annual. Alternate Formats: online.

5944 ■ International Paralegal Management Association (IPMA)
PO Box 659
Avondale Estates, GA 30002-0659
Ph: (404)292-4762
Fax: (404)292-2931
E-mail: info@paralegalmanagement.org
URL: http://www.paralegalmanagement.org
Contact: Michael J. Mazur Jr., Exec. Dir.
Founded: 1984. **Members:** 750. **Membership Dues:** regular, $175 (annual) ● associate, academic, $150 (annual) ● emeritus, $50 (annual) ● sustaining individual, $275 (annual) ● sustaining corporate, $1,100 (annual) ● government/not-for-profit organiza-

tion, $100 (annual). **Staff:** 4. **Budget:** $500,000. **Local Groups:** 20. **Multinational. Description:** Individuals who manage paralegals. Promotes the field of paralegal management; conducts continuing education program for members; provides for information exchange among members and those planning to enter the field. Maintains 20 chapters and speakers' bureau. **Awards:** Community Spirit. **Frequency:** annual. **Type:** recognition. **Recipient:** for excellence in individual service to a member's community ● President's Award. **Frequency:** annual. **Type:** recognition ● Pro Bono Award. **Frequency:** annual. **Type:** recognition. **Recipient:** for excellence in individual pro bono activities ● Therese Cannon Scholarship. **Frequency:** annual. **Type:** scholarship. **Recipient:** for continuing education or IPMA annual conference attendance. **Telecommunication Services:** electronic mail, mike@paralegalmanagement.org. **Formerly:** (2005) Legal Assistant Management Association. **Publications:** *Paralegal Management*, bimonthly. Magazine. Contains articles on current trends and issues in the field of paralegal management. **Price:** included in membership dues; $50.00 /year for nonmembers. **Circulation:** 600. **Advertising:** accepted. **Conventions/Meetings:** annual international conference (exhibits) - always fall. 2008 Oct. 15-18, New Orleans, LA - **Avg. Attendance:** 375; 2009 Oct. 14-17, Orlando, FL - **Avg. Attendance:** 425.

5945 ■ International Society for Law and Technology (ISLAT)

1811 W Katella Ave., No. 101
Anaheim, CA 92804
Ph: (714)778-3230
Fax: (714)778-5463
E-mail: secretariat@islat.org
URL: http://www.islat.org
Contact: Stephen Lesavich PhD, Pres.

Founded: 2001. **Multinational. Description:** Improves the understanding of the complex interrelationships between the law and technology. Promotes the regular exchange of new issues, ideas, and information related to the intersection of law and technology. Encourages collaboration between practicing lawyers, technologists, legal and technical academics, and the judiciary with respect to emerging areas related to new technologies and the law. Serves as facilitator and coordinator of new legal and technical information interchange worldwide. **Telecommunication Services:** electronic mail, lesavich@lesavich.net.

5946 ■ Law and Society Association (LSA)

217 Draper Hall
Univ. of Massachusetts
40 Campus Center Way
Amherst, MA 01003-9244
Ph: (413)545-4617
Fax: (413)577-3194
E-mail: pipkin@legal.umass.edu
URL: http://www.lawandsociety.org
Contact: Ronald M. Pipkin, Exec. Off.

Founded: 1964. **Members:** 1,600. **Membership Dues:** regular (annual income of $15,000 to over $125,000), $35-$180 (annual) ● student, $35 (annual) ● international (based on ISA country list), $20 (annual). **Staff:** 4. **Multinational. Description:** Social scientists, law professors, lawyers, and administrators for government and other agencies. Explores the relationships between law and society in order to contribute to the understanding of law as a social and political phenomenon and to expedite the use of law as an instrument of public policy. Promotes interdisciplinary ventures in the area of law and the social sciences. Sponsors activities that may stimulate criticism and new ideas among scholars and practitioners concerned with the interaction of society and law. Conducts joint panels and symposia with other professional associations; sponsors training institutes for socio-legal research and teaching. **Awards:** Hurst Prize, Kalven Prize, and Herbert Jacob Prize. **Frequency:** annual. **Type:** recognition. **Recipient:** to commemorate the work of J. Willard Hurst, Harry Kalven, and Herbert Jacob. **Committees:** Conditions of Work; Development; Diversity; Graduate Student Workshop; International Activities; Minority Fellowship; Nominations; Summer Institute. **Publications:** *Law and Society Newsletter*, 3/year. Alternate Formats: online ● *Law and Society Review*, quarterly. Journal. Contains research and educational information on the cultural, economic, political, psychological, and social aspects of law and the legal system. **Price:** included in membership dues. ISSN: 0023-9216. **Circulation:** 2,400. **Advertising:** accepted. Alternate Formats: online. **Conventions/Meetings:** annual conference (exhibits) ● annual meeting.

5947 ■ National Asian Pacific American Bar Association (NAPABA)

910 17th St. NW, Ste.315
Washington, DC 20006
Ph: (202)775-9555
Fax: (202)775-9333
E-mail: info@napaba.org
URL: http://www.napaba.org
Contact: Les Jin, Exec. Dir.

Founded: 1987. **Membership Dues:** bronze, $50 (annual) ● silver, $100 (annual) ● gold, $250 (annual) ● platinum, $500 (annual) ● law student, $25 (annual). **Description:** Promotes the interests of Asian Pacific American attorneys and their communities. **Awards: Frequency:** annual. **Type:** scholarship. **Recipient:** for law students. **Computer Services:** Mailing lists. **Telecommunication Services:** electronic mail, ed@napaba.org. **Publications:** *NAPABA Lawyer*. Newsletter. Contains updates on current events and programs. ● Reports. **Conventions/Meetings:** annual convention.

5948 ■ National Association of Bar Executives (NABE)

c/o Allan Head, Pres.
PO Box 3688
Cary, NC 27519
Ph: (919)677-0561
Fax: (919)677-0761
E-mail: ahead@ncbar.org
URL: http://www.abanet.org/nabe
Contact: Jill Werner, Staff Dir.

Founded: 1941. **Members:** 630. **Membership Dues:** regular, $100-$775 (annual). **Staff:** 2. **Budget:** $288,000. **Description:** Executive directors of national, state, county, or city bar associations; public information officers; legislative directors; continuing legal education directors; counsels and other professional bar staff. Aims to coordinate and exchange ideas on administration of organized bar activities on both state and local levels. Compiles statistics; conducts surveys of bar activities, bar association staff members, and salaries. Sponsors specialized education programs including bar association budgeting, tax consequences, and bar public relations workshop. Maintains numerous committees. **Awards:** Fred Bolton Award for Professional Excellence. **Frequency:** annual. **Type:** recognition. **Recipient:** for professional excellence, to an outstanding bar executive. **Telecommunication Services:** electronic mail, wernerj@staff.abanet.org ● electronic mail, johnsonmaria@staff.abanet.org. **Sections:** Administration and Finance; Communications and Public Relations; Continuing Legal Education; Government Relations. **Formerly:** (1962) National Conference of Bar Secretaries; (1965) National Conference of Bar Executives. **Publications:** *The Bar Executive*, quarterly. Newsletter ● *NABE Membership Directory and Bylaws*, annual. ● Also publishes handbook. **Conventions/Meetings:** semiannual conference, held in conjunction with American Bar Association (exhibits) - always August and February.

5949 ■ National Client Protection Organization (NCPO)

c/o A. Root Edmonson, Pres.
North Carolina Client Security Fund
PO Box 25908
Raleigh, NC 27611
Ph: (919)828-4620
Fax: (919)821-9168
E-mail: redmonson@ncbar.com
URL: http://www.ncpo.org
Contact: A. Root Edmonson, Pres.

Founded: 1998. **Members:** 110. **Membership Dues:** organization, $200 (annual) ● individual, $25 (annual). **Multinational. Description:** Promotes law client protection funds and programs to protect consumers from dishonest conduct in the practice of law. **Awards:** Isaac Hecht Award. **Frequency:** annual. **Type:** recognition. **Publications:** *The Client Protection Webb*, quarterly. Newsletter. Alternate Formats: online. **Conventions/Meetings:** annual seminar ● annual workshop.

5950 ■ National Conference of Bar Examiners (NCBE)

402 W Wilson St.
Madison, WI 53703-3614
Ph: (608)280-8550
Fax: (608)280-8552
E-mail: contact@ncbex.org
URL: http://www.ncbex.org
Contact: Dr. Michael T. Kane, Dir. of Research

Founded: 1931. **Staff:** 40. **Description:** Bar examiners and members of character committees designated by each state supreme court; lawyers appointed to handle applications for admission to practice law. Works to: increase efficiency of state boards of law examiners and character committees; formulate and distribute bar examination materials and data to members; aid in character investigations incident to admission to the practice of law; further studies and cooperate with other branches of the legal profession in relation to the problems of legal education and admissions to the bar. **Telecommunication Services:** TDD, (608)661-1275. **Publications:** *The Bar Examiner*, quarterly. Magazine. **Conventions/Meetings:** annual meeting - always August.

5951 ■ National Conference of Bar Foundations (NCBF)

c/o American Bar Association
Div. for Bar Services
321 N Clark St., Ste.2000
Chicago, IL 60610
Ph: (312)988-6008
Fax: (312)988-5492
E-mail: info@ncbf.org
URL: http://www.ncbf.org
Contact: Jill Werner, Staff Dir.

Founded: 1977. **Members:** 85. **Membership Dues:** individual, $25 (annual) ● organization, $150 (annual). **Staff:** 1. **Budget:** $25,000. **State Groups:** 1. **Description:** Bar and law foundations affiliated with state, local, national, and Canadian bar associations. Works to help bar foundations develop programs and achieve public interest objectives by providing a medium for the exchange of information. Compiles statistics. Conducts educational programs. Coordinates with the American Bar Association in developing public interest publications. **Libraries: Type:** reference. **Holdings:** audiovisuals, clippings, periodicals. **Subjects:** bar foundation issues, fund raising, grant making, board development. **Affiliated With:** American Bar Association. **Publications:** *Bar Foundation Activities Survey*, biennial. Contains results from bar associations. ● *NCBF Foundation Forum*, quarterly. Newsletter. Includes articles and meeting updates. **Price:** available to members only ● *NCBF Membership Roster and Bylaws*, annual. Membership Directory ● Brochures. **Conventions/Meetings:** semiannual conference, held in conjunction with the ABA (exhibits) - always February and August.

5952 ■ National Italian American Bar Association (NIABA)

PMB 932
2020 Pennsylvania Ave. NW
Washington, DC 20006-1846
Ph: (212)269-1400
Fax: (212)809-5449
E-mail: niaba@niaba.org
URL: http://www.niaba.org
Contact: Dominic H. Frinzi, Pres.

Founded: 1983. **Members:** 5,000. **Membership Dues:** regular, $50 (annual) ● sponsor, $100 (annual) ● patron, $250 (annual). **Staff:** 1. **State Groups:** 15. **Languages:** English, Italian. **Description:** Works to advance interests of the Italian-American legal community to improve the administration of justice. **Awards:** Distinguished Achievement. **Frequency:** annual. **Type:** scholarship. **Recipient:** to law students ● Distinguished Public Service. **Type:** recognition ● Pro Bono Award. **Type:** recognition. **Publications:** *The Digest*, annual. Journal ● *NIABA Newsletter*, quarterly. Contains items of interest and legal developments. Alternate Formats: online.

5953 ■ National Organization of Bar Counsel (NOBC)
c/o Nancy L. Cohen, Pres.
1560 Broadway, Ste.1800
Denver, CO 80210
Ph: (303)866-6577
Fax: (303)893-5302
E-mail: admin@nobc.org
URL: http://www.nobc.org
Contact: Nancy L. Cohen, Pres.
Founded: 1965. **Members:** 500. **Budget:** $20,000. **Description:** Attorneys for bar associations and disciplinary agencies in the U.S. and Canada who are professionally involved in representing their associations in all legal matters, with emphasis on matters of professional misconduct by lawyers. Participates in interpreting and prosecuting professional ethics, investigating unauthorized practice of law, and initiating improved legislation. **Telecommunication Services:** electronic mail, nancy.cohen@arc.state.co.us. **Publications:** *Current Developments*, biennial. Contains digest of recent disciplinary cases. Alternate Formats: online. **Conventions/Meetings:** semiannual conference, held in conjunction with American Bar Association - always February and August.

5954 ■ Southeastern Legal Foundation (SLF)
6100 Lake Forrest Dr. NW, Ste.520
Atlanta, GA 30328
Ph: (404)257-9667
Free: (800)474-8313
Fax: (404)257-0049
E-mail: info@southeasternlegal.org
URL: http://www.southeasternlegal.org
Contact: Shannon L. Goessling, Exec. Dir.
Founded: 1976. **Description:** Advocates limited government, individual economic freedom, and the free enterprise system in the courts of law and public opinion.

5955 ■ TechLaw Group
c/o Robert Cathey
Ackermann Pr.
1111 Northshore Dr., Ste.N-400
Knoxville, TN 37919
Ph: (865)588-7456
E-mail: lskinner@techlaw.org
URL: http://www.techlaw.org
Contact: Lisa Skinner, Exec. Dir.
Founded: 1986. **Members:** 17. **Staff:** 2. **Budget:** $125,000. **Description:** Technology law firms. Seeks to advance the practice of technology law. Represents the legal interests of corporations engaged in fields including aeronautics, computers, medicine and pharmaceuticals, plastics, and robotics. Conducts research and educational programs; maintains speakers' bureau. **Publications:** *Techlaw Update*, periodic. Newsletter ● Brochure. **Conventions/Meetings:** semiannual board meeting ● semiannual conference.

5956 ■ Tribal Court Clearinghouse
The Tribal Law & Policy Inst.
8235 Santa Monica Blvd., Ste.211
West Hollywood, CA 90046
Ph: (323)650-5467
Fax: (323)650-8149
E-mail: jerry@tlpi.org
URL: http://www.tribal-institute.org
Contact: Jerry Gardner, Exec. Dir.
Description: Works as a resource for tribal justice systems to enhance justice in Indian country and health, well-being, and culture of Native peoples.

5957 ■ World Society of Mixed Jurisdiction Jurists (WSMJJ)
c/o Prof. Vernon Palmer, Pres.
Tulane Law School
6329 Freret St.
New Orleans, LA 70118
Ph: (504)865-5978 (504)862-8859
E-mail: vpalmer@law.tulane.edu
URL: http://www.mixedjurisdiction.org
Contact: Prof. Vernon Palmer, Pres.
Founded: 2002. **Membership Dues:** individual in North America, Europe and other developed regions, $50 (annual) ● institution in North America, Europe and other developed regions, $150 (annual) ● individual in Africa, South America and other developed regions, $20 (annual) ● institution in Africa, South America and other developed regions, $60 (annual). **Multinational. Description:** Unites jurists and comparatists around the globe. Studies and advances the mixed jurisdictions. Stimulates comparative law research, and keeps its members abreast of interesting developments and new research in the field. **Publications:** Newsletter. Alternate Formats: online.

Law Enforcement

5958 ■ Airborne Law Enforcement Association (ALEA)
411 Aviation Way, Ste.200
Frederick, MD 21701
Ph: (301)631-2406
Fax: (301)631-2466
E-mail: singley@alea.org
URL: http://www.alea.org
Contact: Mr. Stephen Ingley, Exec. Dir.
Founded: 1968. **Members:** 3,500. **Membership Dues:** professional/technical specialist/associate (in U.S.), $35 (annual) ● professional/technical specialist/associate (outside U.S.), $60 (annual) ● affiliate, $360 (annual). **Staff:** 16. **Budget:** $750,000. **Description:** Law enforcement officers and personnel using aircraft. Works to encourage communication and liaison between law enforcement agencies interested in using aircraft for the suppression and prevention of crime. Offers educational programs; promotes public awareness; provides information to law enforcement agencies; compiles statistics. **Awards:** ALEA Safety Award. **Frequency:** annual. **Type:** recognition ● Capt. Gus Crawford Memorial Air Crew of the Year. **Frequency:** annual. **Type:** recognition ● Robert L. Cormier Memorial Award. **Frequency:** annual. **Type:** recognition ● **Frequency:** annual. **Type:** scholarship. **Recipient:** for high school seniors ● Technical Specialist of the Year. **Frequency:** annual. **Type:** recognition. **Computer Services:** database, law enforcement aviation unit information ● database, membership ● electronic publishing, electronic newsletter ● online services, membership, event registration, discussion area. **Committees:** Air Beat; ALEA Manuals; Awards and Scholarships; Conference and Seminars; Education and Training; Research and Surveys; Safety. **Councils:** Affiliate. **Publications:** *Air Beat Magazine*, bimonthly. **Circulation:** 7,000. **Advertising:** accepted ● *ALEA E-Newsletter*, monthly. Alternate Formats: online. **Conventions/Meetings:** annual conference and trade show (exhibits) - 2008 July 16-19, Houston, TX; 2009 July 22-25, Savannah, GA; 2010 July 14-17, Tucson, AZ.

5959 ■ American Association of Code Enforcement (AACE)
5310 E Main St., Ste.104
Columbus, OH 43213
Ph: (614)552-2633
Fax: (614)868-1177
E-mail: info@aace1.com
URL: http://www.aace1.com
Contact: Kathy Davis, Pres.
Founded: 1988. **Members:** 1,500. **Membership Dues:** active, associate, $75 (annual). **Staff:** 2. **Budget:** $135,000. **State Groups:** 15. **Description:** Works to advance the profession of federal, state, county, and city employees involved with enforcement of housing and land use codes. Conducts certification and training programs; disseminates information to the public. **Awards:** Code Enforcement Officer of the Year. **Frequency:** annual. **Type:** recognition. **Recipient:** nomination by peers. **Publications:** *AACE Perspective*, bimonthly. Journal. **Price:** included in membership dues. **Circulation:** 1,200. **Advertising:** accepted. **Conventions/Meetings:** annual conference (exhibits).

5960 ■ American Association of State Troopers (AAST)
1949 Raymond Diehl Rd.
Tallahassee, FL 32308
Ph: (850)385-7904
Free: (800)765-5456
Fax: (850)385-8697
E-mail: alpasini@statetroopers.org
URL: http://www.statetroopers.org
Contact: Al Pasini, Exec. Dir.
Founded: 1989. **Members:** 5,200. **Membership Dues:** active trooper, retired trooper, honorable service, $24 (annual) ● associate law enforcement, $35 (annual) ● VIP, $500 (annual) ● partner, $250 (annual) ● sponsor, $100 (annual). **Staff:** 5. **Budget:** $1,500,000. **State Groups:** 6. **Description:** Provides benefits and services to active and retired troop members. **Awards:** AAST Scholarship Foundation. **Frequency:** annual. **Type:** scholarship. **Recipient:** for dependents of trooper members, based on grade point average. **Publications:** *Trooper Connection*, quarterly. Newsletter.

5961 ■ American Deputy Sheriffs' Association (ADSA)
3001 Armand St., Ste.B
Monroe, LA 71201
Free: (800)937-7940
Fax: (318)398-9980
E-mail: adsa@deputysheriff.org
URL: http://www.deputysheriff.org
Contact: Sgt. Ashley Isaac, Pres.
Founded: 1996. **Members:** 30,000. **Description:** Dedicated to issues and needs of county law enforcement departments in the U.S. **Awards:** Academic Scholarship Program. **Frequency:** semiannual. **Type:** scholarship. **Recipient:** to dependents of members. **Departments:** Membership. **Publications:** *Informant*. Newsletter. Provides law enforcement information and new ideas and techniques. Alternate Formats: online.

5962 ■ American Federation of Police and Concerned Citizens (AFP&CC)
6350 Horizon Dr.
Titusville, FL 32780
Ph: (305)573-0070 (321)264-0911
Fax: (305)573-9819
E-mail: info@aphf.org
URL: http://www.aphf.org
Contact: Donna M. Shepherd, Exec. Dir.
Founded: 1961. **Members:** 104,000. **Membership Dues:** active, $36 (annual) ● associate, $20 (annual) ● active, $90 (triennial). **Staff:** 20. **Budget:** $4,000,000. **Description:** Governmental and private law enforcement officers (paid, part-time, or volunteer) united for the prevention of crime and the apprehension of criminals. Offers death benefits and training programs to members and police survivors. Sponsors American Police Academy. Maintains hall of fame. Conducts workshops. **Libraries: Type:** not open to the public. **Holdings:** 2,500. **Subjects:** law enforcement, security. **Awards: Frequency:** weekly. **Type:** recognition. **Recipient:** for service, valor or for community service. **Absorbed:** National Police and Fire Fighters Association; American Law Enforcement Officers Association; CB Radio Patrol of American Federation of Police. **Also Known As:** American Police Hall of Fame and Museum. **Formerly:** (1966) United States Federation of Police; (1997) American Federation of Police. **Publications:** *Police Times*, quarterly. Magazine. **Price:** included in membership dues. **Circulation:** 104,000. **Advertising:** accepted. **Conventions/Meetings:** annual conference.

5963 ■ American Society of Law Enforcement Training (ASLET)
Address Unknown since 2008
URL: http://aslet.org
Founded: 1987. **Members:** 7,000. **Membership Dues:** individual in U.S. and Canada and Mexico, $50 (annual) ● individual (international), $65 (annual) ● group, $40 (annual). **Staff:** 5. **Budget:** $1,000,000. **Regional Groups:** 10. **State Groups:** 50. **Description:** Association for those who teach and those who want to learn and improve law enforcement training. ASLET is dedicated to enhancing and promoting excellence in law enforcement training while increasing the effectiveness of its members to better serve their communities and society. **Awards: Frequency:** annual. **Type:** recognition. **Recipient:** for training. **Computer Services:** database, trainer specialization. **Committees:** Ethics; Health Advisory; Legal Liaison; Professional Development; Public Relations; Seminar Curriculum. **Formerly:** (2004) American Society of Law Enforcement Trainers. **Publications:** *Law Enforcement Trainer*, bimonthly. Journal. **Price:** available to members only. **Advertising:** accepted ● Brochures. **Conventions/Meetings:** competition ● annual Training Seminar - seminar and conference (exhibits) - always January.

5964 ■ Association for Explosive Detection K-9s, International (AEDK9)
c/o Nancy Bidwell, Pres.
PO Box 176
Aquilla, TX 76622
Ph: (386)788-4083 (254)722-9310
E-mail: info@explk9.org
URL: http://www.explk9.org
Contact: Nancy Bidwell, Pres.
Membership Dues: active/active associate, $30 (annual) ● corporate/associate sponsor, $50 (annual). **Multinational. Description:** Fosters continued professionalism of explosive detection dog handlers and their K-9 partners. Seeks to improve communication, coordination, and accreditation of professional private explosive detection teams. Provides certification to determine the proficiency and reliability of canine teams in the detection of explosives.

5965 ■ Black Cops Against Police Brutality (B-CAP)
PO Box 4256
East Orange, NJ 07019
Ph: (973)926-5717
E-mail: info@b-cap.org
URL: http://www.b-cap.org
Contact: Sgt. DeLacy Davis Ret., Contact
Founded: 1991. **Description:** Works to ensure that people of color are afforded their rights under the Constitution by police, especially in urban areas. Specializes in gang violence-prevention, youth violence reduction/intervention, police violence issues, and community empowerment and motivation. **Programs:** Auto Theft Prevention. **Conventions/Meetings:** annual Kwanzaa Cultural Celebration - meeting, with workshops.

5966 ■ Blacks in Law Enforcement (BLE)
591 Vanderbilt Ave., Ste.133
Brooklyn, NY 11238
Ph: (718)455-9059
E-mail: blacksnlaw@aol.com
URL: http://members.tripod.com/blacksnlaw
Contact: Ron Daniels, Exec. Dir.
Founded: 1986. **Members:** 900. **Membership Dues:** individual, $60 (triennial). **Staff:** 2. **Budget:** $65,000. **Description:** Blacks employed by law enforcement agencies in the U.S; others interested in the history of blacks in U.S. law enforcement. Seeks to educate the public concerning the contributions made by blacks in the field of law enforcement. Documents the lives and achievements of the first blacks to participate in law enforcement in the U.S. Develops programs to improve the public image of law enforcement officers; Has established a short-term training program for law enforcement officers. Provides children's services, including the operation of an animal farm. Operates hall of fame. Sponsors competitions; compiles statistics; Law Enforcement Children's Animal Ranch; maintains speakers' bureau. **Libraries: Type:** reference. **Awards:** Distinguished Officer of the Year Award. **Frequency:** annual. **Type:** recognition. **Recipient:** for community and department service. **Committees:** Animal Farm; Banquet; College Student. **Formerly:** (1988) Blacks in Law Enforcement. **Publications:** *NULEOA Student Chapter News*, quarterly. Newsletter. Distributes to all students in colleges and universities majoring in criminal justice. **Circulation:** 3,000. **Advertising:** accepted ● Magazine, annual. **Price:** $4.50. **Circulation:** 25,000. **Advertising:** accepted. **Conventions/Meetings:** annual Recruitment, Key to Building a Successful Agency - conference and banquet, with products, programs and support materials (exhibits).

5967 ■ Commission on Accreditation for Law Enforcement Agencies (CALEA)
10302 Eaton Pl., Ste.100
Fairfax, VA 22030-2215
Ph: (703)352-4225
Free: (800)368-3757
Fax: (703)591-2206
E-mail: calea@calea.org
URL: http://www.calea.org
Contact: Sylvester Daughtry Jr., Exec. Dir.
Founded: 1979. **Staff:** 16. **Budget:** $5,000,000. **Multinational. Description:** Aims to administer an accreditation program by which law enforcement agencies at local, county, state, national, and international levels can voluntarily demonstrate their compliance with professional criteria; has established a body of over 400 standards of evaluation. Seeks to improve the delivery of law enforcement services. Recruits, selects, and trains assessors who conduct on-site assessments of agency compliance with standards. Maintains speakers' bureau. **Publications:** *Accreditation Program Overview*, periodic. Brochure. Provides basic information about the cost, process, benefits, and history of law enforcement accreditation. **Price:** $20.00/item ● *Calea Update*, 3/year. Magazine. Contains current events and technical information about accreditation; includes list of accredited agencies. **Price:** free. **Circulation:** 6,000 ● *Standards for Law Enforcement Agencies*, periodic. Contains 436 standards, with commentary on all aspects of law enforcement operations and management. **Price:** $27.00. **Conventions/Meetings:** conference and workshop (exhibits) - 3/year.

5968 ■ Federal Bureau of Investigation Agents Association (FBIAA)
PO Box 250
New Rochelle, NY 10801
Ph: (914)235-7580
Fax: (914)235-8235
E-mail: fbiaa@fbiaa.org
URL: http://www.fbiaa.org
Contact: Glenn F. Kelly, Exec. Dir.
Founded: 1981. **Members:** 10,150. **Membership Dues:** active, $78 (annual) ● associate, $26 (annual). **Staff:** 4. **Regional Groups:** 4. **Description:** Active duty special agents in the Federal Bureau of Investigation. Promotes professional advancement of members. Facilitates communication and cooperation among members; sponsors research and educational programs. **Telecommunication Services:** electronic mail, gkelly@fbiaa.org. **Publications:** *FBI Agent*, quarterly. Newsletter.

5969 ■ Federal Hispanic Law Enforcement Officers Association (FHLEOA)
c/o Tom Allison, VP/Legal Advisor
4445 Summer Oak Dr.
Tampa, FL 33618
Ph: (813)390-7532
E-mail: edirector@fhleoa.org
URL: http://www.fhleoa.org
Contact: Jose L. Rivera, Exec. Dir.
Membership Dues: regular, $35 (annual). **Multinational. Description:** Supports equal treatment for all people in the law enforcement workplace. Acts as a collective voice and representation to address law enforcement concerns before legislative bodies, regulatory agencies, and the courts. Provides networking opportunities for its members. **Telecommunication Services:** electronic mail, legaladvisor@fhleoa.org. **Publications:** Newsletter, periodic. **Price:** included in membership dues. Alternate Formats: online.

5970 ■ Hispanic American Police Command Officers Association (HAPCOA)
6450 NW Loop 410, PMB 1546
San Antonio, TX 78238-1986
Ph: (210)431-7349
Fax: (210)434-8744
E-mail: info@hapcoa.org
URL: http://www.hapcoa.org
Contact: Frank Hernandez, Pres.
Founded: 1973. **Membership Dues:** regular, $100 (annual) ● associate, $75 (annual) ● supporting, $55 (annual) ● student, $25 (annual) ● life, $1,500 ● organizational/corporate, $2,500 (annual). **Description:** Assists law enforcement, criminal justice and community organizations nationwide in their efforts to recruit, train and promote qualified Hispanic American men and women. Collaborates with other non-profit organizations with the same interests. **Awards:** HAPCOA Aguila Awards. **Frequency:** annual. **Type:** recognition. **Recipient:** for exceptional contribution to the organization's mission and goals. **Projects:** Closing the Gap; Madrina-Padrino Public Safety.

5971 ■ International Association Auto Theft Investigators (IAATI)
c/o John V. Abounader, Exec. Dir.
PO Box 223
Clinton, NY 13323-0223
Ph: (315)853-1913
Fax: (315)793-0048
E-mail: jvabounader@iaati.org
URL: http://www.iaati.org
Contact: John V. Abounader, Exec. Dir.
Founded: 1952. **Members:** 4,300. **Membership Dues:** active/affiliate, $30 (annual). **Staff:** 25. **Regional Groups:** 8. **Multinational. Description:** Law enforcement officers in 36 countries responsible for investigating vehicle thefts; vehicle manufacturers, insurance investigators, claims handlers, U.S. and Canadian auto theft bureau agents, members of motor vehicle and rental vehicle agencies. Aims to encourage high professional standards among auto theft investigators; promote exchange of information and cooperation between law enforcement agencies; facilitate dissemination of technical information among members. **Awards:** A.T. Phillips Award. **Type:** recognition. **Recipient:** for an individual or unit of any insurance carrier for outstanding efforts resulting in the apprehension and/or detection of those individuals responsible for auto related criminal acts against the insurance industry ● AGC/IAATI Award. **Type:** recognition. **Recipient:** for field investigators or first-line supervisors who have distinguished themselves in the field of off-road (farm construction) equipment investigation/recovery ● IAATI Award of Merit. **Frequency:** annual. **Type:** recognition. **Recipient:** for a person, group, department or company for outstanding contribution in the area of vehicle theft investigation or prevention ● IAATI Lo-Jack Award. **Frequency:** annual. **Type:** recognition. **Recipient:** for law enforcement officers whose efforts, in conjunction with the use of an electronic tracking device, make the most significant impact on the recovery of stolen vehicles ● Raymond H. Dreher Memorial Award. **Type:** recognition. **Recipient:** for members who have distinguished themselves by service to the association or for other outstanding acts in the vehicle theft field ● 3M Vehicle Theft Investigators Award. **Frequency:** annual. **Type:** recognition. **Recipient:** for any person who has distinguished himself or herself in the vehicle theft investigations where a VIN label played a significant part in the success of the investigation. **Publications:** *The APB*, quarterly. Newsletter. **Advertising:** accepted ● Membership Directory, annual. **Conventions/Meetings:** annual meeting and seminar (exhibits) - always August.

5972 ■ International Association of Chiefs of Police (IACP)
515 N Washington St.
Alexandria, VA 22314-2344

Ph: (703)836-6767
Free: (800)THE-IACP
Fax: (703)836-4543
E-mail: information@theiacp.org
URL: http://www.theiacp.org
Contact: Joseph C. Carter, Pres.

Founded: 1893. **Members:** 19,000. **Membership Dues:** individual, $100 (annual). **Staff:** 100. **Budget:** $12,000,000. **Multinational. Description:** Represents police executives who are commissioners, superintendents, chiefs, and directors of national, state, provincial, and municipal departments; assistant and deputy chiefs; division or district heads. Provides consultation and research services in all phases of police activity. Conducts educational programs. **Awards:** PARADE/IACP Police Officer of the Year Award. **Frequency:** annual. **Type:** recognition. **Recipient:** for exceptional achievement in any police endeavor, including but not limited to, extraordinary valor, crime prevention, drug control and prevention, investigative work, community relations and traffic safety ● Webber Seavey Award for Quality in Law Enforcement. **Frequency:** annual. **Type:** recognition. **Recipient:** to agencies and departments worldwide for promoting a standard of excellence that exemplifies law enforcement's contribution and dedication to the quality of life in local communities. **Computer Services:** Information services, web-based dissemination of police-related matters ● online services, IACP Net. **Committees:** Arson and Explosives; Aviation; Chaplain; Civil Law Enforcement/Military; Communications and Technology. **Divisions:** International Policing; State and Provincial Police; State Associations of Chiefs of Police. **Formerly:** (1895) National Chiefs of Police Union; (1898) National Association of Chiefs of Police; (1902) Chiefs of Police of the U.S. and Canada. **Publications:** *Directory of IACP Members*, annual. Membership Directory. **Price:** $77.50. Alternate Formats: online ● *Model Policies*, periodic ● *Police Buyers' Guide*, annual ● *Police Chief: The Professional Voice of Law Enforcement*, monthly. Magazine. Covers all aspects of law enforcement duties, from improved administrative techniques to operational practices, legislative issues, and technology. **Price:** included in membership dues; $25.00 /year for nonmembers. ISSN: 0915-2571. **Circulation:** 17,000. **Advertising:** accepted ● *Training Keys*, periodic. **Price:** $11.50/volume, for members; $14.00/volume, for nonmembers; $3.00/item. **Conventions/Meetings:** annual conference (exhibits) - 2008 Nov. 8-12, San Diego, CA; 2009 Oct. 3-7, Denver, CO; 2010 Oct. 23-27, Orlando, FL.

5973 ■ International Association of Directors of Law Enforcement Standards and Training (IADLEST)

c/o Patrick J. Judge, Exec. Dir.
2521 Country Club Way
Albion, MI 49224
Ph: (517)857-3828
Fax: (517)857-3826
E-mail: pjudge@iadlest.org
URL: http://www.iadlest.org
Contact: Patrick J. Judge, Exec. Dir.

Membership Dues: director, $400 (annual) ● general, $100 (annual) ● sustaining, $200 (annual). **Multinational. Description:** Dedicated to the improvement of public safety personnel; works to establish standards for employment and training of peace officers. **Computer Services:** database, National Decertification ● online services, membership intranet ● online services, POST-Net. **Projects:** Model Minimum State Standards. **Publications:** *Driver Training Reference Guide* ● *IADLEST Sourcebook*. Handbook ● *Reciprocity Handbook*. **Price:** $22.00/copy.

5974 ■ International Association of Law Enforcement Firearms Instructors (IALEFI)

25 Country Club Rd., Ste.707
Gilford, NH 03249-6977
Ph: (603)524-8787
Fax: (603)524-8856
E-mail: info@ialefi.com
URL: http://www.ialefi.com
Contact: Robert D. Bossey, Exec. Dir./Treas.

Founded: 1981. **Members:** 5,000. **Membership Dues:** active, associate, $55 (annual) ● business, $550 (annual). **Budget:** $500,000. **Multinational. Description:** Law enforcement training officials from Australia, Canada, Europe, the South Pacific, and the United States. Promotes the best possible firearms training for law enforcement and corrections officers. **Publications:** *Firearms Training Standards for Law Enforcement Personnel*. Manual. Contains guide reference in setting up and maintaining a firearms program. **Price:** $15.00 for members; $25.00 for nonmembers ● *IALEFI Guidelines for Simulation Training Safety*. Manual. **Price:** $15.00 for members; $25.00 for nonmembers ● *Law Enforcement Firearms Instructors*, quarterly. Manual. Contains information about firearms program. **Price:** $25.00 for members; $35.00 for nonmembers ● *The MP-5 Submachine Gun Story*. Book. **Price:** $30.00 for members; $49.95 for nonmembers. Alternate Formats: CD-ROM ● *Tactical Firearms Handbook*. Manual. Contains the know-how instructions in firearms qualification and training. **Price:** $25.00 for members; $35.00 for nonmembers. **Conventions/Meetings:** annual conference, for training.

5975 ■ International Association for Property and Evidence (IAPE)

903 N San Fernando Blvd., Ste.4
Burbank, CA 91504-4327
Ph: (818)846-2926
Free: (800)449-4273
Fax: (818)846-4543
E-mail: mail@iape.org
URL: http://www.iape.org
Contact: Robert F. Giles, Pres.

Founded: 1993. **Membership Dues:** general, $50 (annual). **Multinational. Description:** Enhances the professional growth of law enforcement property and evidence personnel. Provides education and training related to handling, storage, maintenance and disposal of law enforcement-held property and evidence. **Computer Services:** Information services, property and evidence resources. **Publications:** *Evidence Log*, quarterly. Magazine.

5976 ■ International Association of Undercover Officers (IAUO)

142 Banks Dr.
Brunswick, GA 31523
Free: (800)876-5943
Fax: (800)876-5912
E-mail: charlie@undercover.org
URL: http://www.undercover.org
Contact: Brian Sallee, Pres.

Membership Dues: regular, $35 (annual) ● founding, $100 (annual) ● life, $350 ● group (trial), $100. **Multinational. Description:** Promotes safety and professionalism among undercover officers. Fosters mutual cooperation, discussions and interests among its members. Provides international network of intelligence gathering means for undercover officers. **Publications:** *The Brotherhood*, quarterly. Magazine. Contains articles and information on law enforcement and related topics.

5977 ■ International Footprint Association (IFA)

PO Box 1652
Walnut, CA 91788-1652
Free: (877)432-3668
E-mail: footprint@footprinter.org
URL: http://www.footprinter.org
Contact: Charles Zigler, Pres.

Founded: 1929. **Members:** 4,000. **Membership Dues:** individual (chapter), $30-$50 (annual). **Staff:** 1. **Budget:** $35,000. **Local Groups:** 40. **Description:** Represents law enforcement officers and citizens of all professions and businesses. Brings together, on a social basis, conscientious law enforcement personnel and others interested in improving knowledge of law enforcement problems. **Conventions/Meetings:** annual convention - always late June or early July.

5978 ■ International Law Enforcement Educators and Trainers Association (ILEETA)

PO Box 1003
Twin Lakes, WI 53181-1003
Ph: (262)279-7879
Fax: (262)279-5758
E-mail: info@ileeta.org
URL: http://www.ileeta.org
Contact: Ed Nowicki, Exec. Dir.

Membership Dues: regular, $50 (annual) ● foreign, $55 (annual). **Multinational. Description:** Reduces law enforcement risks. Enhances training of criminal justice practitioners. Promotes safety and security. **Awards: Frequency:** annual. **Type:** scholarship. **Boards:** Advisory. **Publications:** *ILEETA Digest*, quarterly. Journal. Contains articles for trainers and educators. Alternate Formats: online ● Bulletin, periodic. Alternate Formats: online.

5979 ■ International Police Work Dog Association (IPWDA)

PO Box 7455
Greenwood, IN 46143
E-mail: k9cop496@aol.com
URL: http://www.ipwda.org
Contact: Richard L. McQueary, Pres.

Membership Dues: regular/associate, $45 (annual). **Multinational. Description:** Aims to unite and assist all law enforcement agencies in the training and continued progress of all police work dogs. Seeks to establish a working standard for all police work dogs, handlers, and trainers through an accreditation program. Promotes the image of the police work dog. **Awards:** Award of Merit. **Frequency:** annual. **Type:** recognition. **Recipient:** for an outstanding job on a case or a long-term high level of performance in the field of police K-9 work ● Award of Valor. **Frequency:** annual. **Type:** recognition. **Recipient:** to a member, a member's K-9, or a team who took the risk in accomplishing their mission or saving someone threatened with severe injury or death ● Bill Faus, Jr. Lifetime Achievement Award. **Frequency:** annual. **Type:** recognition. **Recipient:** to an individual who has shown dedication for the betterment, education, training, and support of police K-9s ● Distinguished Service Award. **Frequency:** annual. **Type:** recognition. **Recipient:** to a member who has demonstrated a pattern of service for the improvement and betterment of the association. **Telecommunication Services:** electronic mail, ipwda1@yahoo.com.

5980 ■ Law Enforcement Alliance of America (LEAA)

7700 Leesburg Pike, Ste.421
Falls Church, VA 22043
Ph: (703)847-2677
Free: (800)766-8578
Fax: (703)556-6485
E-mail: membership@leaa.org
URL: http://www.leaa.org
Contact: James J. Fotis, Exec. Dir.

Founded: 1990. **Members:** 65,000. **Membership Dues:** individual, $26 (annual) ● family, $34 (annual) ● life, $200. **Staff:** 12. **Budget:** $1,500,000. **Description:** Works to improve the criminal justice system and keep citizens safe from violent crime. Provides representation in Washington, DC; introduces and passes legislative criminal justice reforms; promotes victims rights over criminal rights; supports an individual's right to choose to own a firearm. **Libraries: Type:** reference; not open to the public. **Holdings:** books, periodicals. **Awards: Type:** recognition. **Computer Services:** database ● mailing lists ● online services. **Telecommunication Services:** electronic bulletin board. **Task Forces:** Legislative. **Publications:** *LEAA Advisor*. Newsletter ● *The LEAA Advocate*, 3-4/year. Magazine. **Circulation:** 40,000. **Advertising:** accepted ● *LEAA Shield*. Magazine. **Advertising:** accepted. Alternate Formats: online. **Conventions/Meetings:** semiannual board meeting.

5981 ■ Law Enforcement Memorial Association (LEMA)

PO Box 72835
Roselle, IL 60172-0835
Ph: (312)623-1391

Fax: (847)524-1369
E-mail: forgottenheroes@comcast.net
URL: http://www.forgottenheroes-lema.org
Contact: Sgt. Ronald C. Van Raalte, Pres.

Founded: 1980. **Members:** 1,000. **Membership Dues:** individual, $25 (annual) ● supporter individual, organization, $100 (annual). **Staff:** 3. **Description:** Current and former law enforcement officers, lineal descendants of slain officers, and interested individuals working to compile a detailed, accurate, and documented list of police officers who died in the line of duty. Plans to establish a memorial museum and library and publish a memorial book. Conducts research. **Libraries: Type:** open to the public. **Holdings:** 400. **Subjects:** crime. **Awards:** Alan J. Vargo Memorial. **Type:** recognition. **Recipient:** for distinguished service. **Computer Services:** database. **Publications:** *Lema News*, 3/year. Newsletter.

5982 ■ Law Enforcement Thermographers' Association (LETA)
PO Box 6485
Edmond, OK 73083-6485
Ph: (405)330-6988
E-mail: information@leta.org
URL: http://www.leta.org
Contact: Doug Newman, Pres.

Founded: 1995. **Membership Dues:** active, $25 (annual) ● associate, $25 (annual) ● corporate, $1,000 (annual). **Multinational. Description:** Promotes legal and ethical use of thermal imaging on law enforcement operations. Provides training and certification to individuals in the field of law enforcement thermography. **Computer Services:** Information services, standards/protocols and law updates ● online services, feedback. **Publications:** *Hot Spot*. Newsletter. Alternate Formats: online. **Conventions/Meetings:** annual international conference, with training.

5983 ■ National Asian Peace Officers' Association (NAPOA)
PO Box 50973
Washington, DC 20091-0973
Ph: (202)431-2175
E-mail: info@napoaonline.org
URL: http://www.napoaonline.org
Contact: Rolland T. Ogawa, Pres.

Founded: 1980. **Description:** Promotes the interests of Asian American peace officers. Fosters the development of professional and fraternal relationships of Asian Pacific law enforcement communities in the United States. **Conventions/Meetings:** annual conference.

5984 ■ National Association of Asian American Law Enforcement Commanders (NAAALEC)
PO Box 131672
Houston, TX 77219
E-mail: tdmaru@comcast.net
URL: http://www.naaalec.org
Contact: Tom Maruyama, Pres.

Founded: 1994. **Membership Dues:** regular, sustaining, $150 (annual) ● associate/supporting, $50 (annual). **Description:** Represents the interests of Asian American law enforcement commanders. Improves the recruitment and selection of qualified Asian Americans in law enforcement careers. Encourages and assists members in attaining positions of higher responsibility. Aims to achieve greater understanding and network between the Asian American communities and their criminal justice agencies. Evaluates and recommends criminal legislation. **Publications:** Newsletter. Alternate Formats: online.

5985 ■ National Association for Civilian Oversight of Law Enforcement (NACOLE)
c/o Charles Reynolds, Sec.
PO Box 396
Dover, NH 03821
Free: (866)462-2653
E-mail: nacole@nacole.org
URL: http://www.nacole.org
Contact: Charles Reynolds, Sec.

Founded: 1995. **Membership Dues:** organization, $300 (annual) ● regular, $150 (annual) ● associate, $100 (annual). **Description:** Works to promote law enforcement through the practice of civilian oversight. Provides training, referrals, information sharing and technical assistance to the oversight community and to persons and jurisdictions attempting to establish oversight. Educates and encourages law enforcement agencies to respond on citizen's issues and complaints. **Publications:** *NACOLE Review*. Newsletter. Alternate Formats: online. **Conventions/Meetings:** annual conference.

5986 ■ National Association of Drug Diversion Investigators (NADDI)
PO Box 611
Manchester, MD 21102-0611
Ph: (443)398-6257
E-mail: ccichon@naddi.org
URL: http://www.naddi.org
Contact: Charlie Cichon, Exec. Dir.

Founded: 1987. **Members:** 2,000. **Membership Dues:** individual, $50 (annual). **State Groups:** 17. **Description:** Consists of members responsible for investigating and prosecuting pharmaceutical drug diversion. Supports pharmaceutical drug investigations. Provides education and training in pharmaceutical drug diversion. **Awards:** Investigator and Educator of the Year. **Frequency:** annual. **Type:** scholarship. **Telecommunication Services:** electronic mail, burke@naddi.org. **Publications:** *Abused Pharmaceutical Substance*. Brochure. Alternate Formats: online. **Conventions/Meetings:** annual Educational Training - conference (exhibits).

5987 ■ National Association of Field Training Officers (NAFTO)
PO Box 3236
Evansville, IN 47731
Ph: (812)436-7951
E-mail: director@nafto.org
URL: http://www.nafto.org
Contact: Chuck Knoll, Pres.

Founded: 1991. **Membership Dues:** regular, $40 (annual). **Description:** Promotes and fosters mutual cooperation between field training officers, other members of their agencies, private industry and the public. Provides a forum for the exchange of ideas and techniques. Conducts educational methodology research for the improvement in the areas of teaching and learning. Educates the public regarding apprenticeship training. **Awards:** National FTO of the Year Award. **Frequency:** annual. **Type:** recognition. **Recipient:** for field training officer who has excellence in the profession. **Telecommunication Services:** electronic mail, nafto@chorus.net. **Publications:** *The NAFTO News*. Newsletter. **Price:** included in membership dues.

5988 ■ National Association of Police Organizations (NAPO)
317 S Patrick St.
Alexandria, VA 22314
Ph: (703)549-0775
Free: (800)322-6276
Fax: (703)684-0515
E-mail: info@napo.org
URL: http://www.napo.org
Contact: William J. Johnson, Exec. Dir.

Founded: 1978. **Members:** 220,000. **Staff:** 12. **Local Groups:** 4,000. **Description:** Police officers united to promote the needs of members on a national level. Endorses candidates for national office. Conducts research on law enforcement related issues. Defends the rights of law enforcement officers in courts and conduct educational seminars. **Libraries: Type:** not open to the public. **Holdings:** 200; books. **Subjects:** labor law, criminal law. **Awards:** Top Cops Awards. **Frequency:** annual. **Type:** recognition. **Publications:** *Dinner Program, Convention Program*. Book. **Advertising:** accepted ● *Top Cops Awards*. Book. **Advertising:** accepted ● *Washington Report*, monthly. Newsletter. **Advertising:** accepted. **Conventions/Meetings:** annual convention and seminar (exhibits) - 2008 July 24-28, Rio Grande, PR.

5989 ■ National Association of Women Law Enforcement Executives (NAWLEE)
3 Dunham St.
Carver, MA 02330
Ph: (781)789-9500
Fax: (508)866-8707
E-mail: info@nawlee.com
URL: http://www.nawlee.com
Contact: Laura Forbes, Pres.

Membership Dues: executive, $100 (annual) ● associate, $75 (annual) ● supporting, $50 (annual). **Description:** Addresses the unique needs of women holding senior management positions in law enforcement. Provides a forum for the exchange of information concerning effective law enforcement. **Programs:** Mentor. **Publications:** Newsletter. Alternate Formats: online.

5990 ■ National Black Police Association (NBPA)
3251 Mt. Pleasant St. NW
Washington, DC 20010-2103
Ph: (202)986-2070
Fax: (202)986-0410
E-mail: nbpanatofc@worldnet.att.net
URL: http://www.blackpolice.org
Contact: Marcus G. Jones, Natl. Chm.

Founded: 1972. **Members:** 35,000. **Membership Dues:** individual, $100 (annual) ● chapter, $200 (annual). **Staff:** 2. **Budget:** $250,000. **Regional Groups:** 5. **State Groups:** 10. **Local Groups:** 140. **Description:** Male and female black police officers. Seeks to: improve relationships between police departments and the black community; recruit minority police officers on a national scale; eliminate police corruption, brutality, and racial discrimination. Maintains speakers' bureau. Operates charitable program. **Libraries: Type:** reference. **Holdings:** books. **Subjects:** blacks in law enforcement. **Awards: Type:** recognition ● **Type:** scholarship. **Publications:** *Black Police Membership Directory*, quinquennial. **Price:** included in membership dues ● *NBPA Advocate*, quarterly. Newsletter. Reports on legislation, court decisions, politics, and general police actions affecting black officers. **Price:** $20.00/issue. **Advertising:** accepted. **Conventions/Meetings:** annual National Educational and Training Conference (exhibits) - held in August.

5991 ■ National Center for Women and Policing (NCWP)
433 S Beverly Dr.
Beverly Hills, CA 90212
Ph: (310)556-2526
Fax: (310)556-2509
E-mail: womencops@feminist.org
URL: http://www.womenandpolicing.org
Contact: Margaret Moore, Dir.

Founded: 1995. **Members:** 300. **Membership Dues:** Lieutenant or above, policing consultant, $100 (annual) ● Sergeant or below, civilian in law enforcement, $50 (annual). **Staff:** 10. **Budget:** $500,000. **Regional Groups:** 56. **Description:** A division of the Feminist Majority Foundation. Persons in the criminal justice field, including educators. Seeks to increase the numbers of women in policing to improve police services to the community, especially in the area of violence against women. **Libraries: Type:** reference. **Holdings:** archival material, articles, books, periodicals, video recordings. **Subjects:** women and policing, crimes against women. **Awards:** Breaking the Glass Ceiling Award. **Frequency:** periodic. **Type:** recognition. **Recipient:** for women reaching a command position in a law enforcement organization ● Fighting for Equality Award. **Frequency:** annual. **Type:** recognition. **Recipient:** for women who have fought gender-based injustices ● Lifetime Achievement Award. **Frequency:** periodic. **Type:** recognition. **Recipient:** for women with distinguished careers in law enforcement. **Computer Services:** Mailing lists. **Affiliated With:** Feminist Majority Foundation. **Publications:** *Investigating Acquaintance Sexual Assault Training Manual*. **Price:** $10.00/CD; includes shipping and handling. Alternate Formats: CD-ROM ● *Recruiting and Retaining Women: A Self-Assessment Guide for Law Enforcement.* Book. Assists law enforcement agencies in identifying and removing obstacles to hiring more women. Alternate Formats: online ● *The Status of Women in Policing,* annual. Survey. Contains information for individual agencies and shows the number of women by rank and by race. **Conventions/Meetings:** annual Leadership Development Conference, highlights critical issues in policing.

5992 ■ National Constables Association (NCA)
16 Stonybrook Dr.
Levittown, PA 19055-2217
Ph: (215)547-6400 (318)256-0195
Free: (800)272-1775
Fax: (215)943-0979
E-mail: ntlconstable@lycos.com
URL: http://www.angelfire.com/la/nationalconstable
Contact: Bruce Speight, Natl. Dir. of Communications
Founded: 1973. **Members:** 7,200. **Membership Dues:** active (constable), $60 (annual) ● associate (non-constable), $30 (annual). **Staff:** 3. **Budget:** $50,000. **Regional Groups:** 6. **State Groups:** 34. **Local Groups:** 240. **National Groups:** 2. **Description:** Elected and appointed constables and individuals interested in preserving and upgrading the constable system. Seeks to re-establish and define the role of constables in the judicial and executive systems of local, county, state, and federal governments; train, educate, and upgrade the quality and performance of constables; encourage acceptance of constables within communities as trusted, responsible, elected, and appointed representatives of the people. Acts as a clearinghouse of information for constables. Compiles statistics. Maintains museum and hall of fame at American Police Hall of Fame, in Biscayne, FL. Operates speakers' bureau. **Libraries: Type:** reference. **Holdings:** archival material. **Subjects:** constable system. **Awards:** Community-Constable Partnership Award. **Frequency:** annual. **Type:** recognition. **Recipient:** for elected county officials ● Constable of the Year Award. **Type:** recognition ● Extraordinary Service Award. **Type:** recognition ● Fighter Against Drug Abuse Award. **Frequency:** annual. **Type:** recognition ● Hero Award. **Type:** recognition ● Outstanding Service to the Constable System by a Non-Constable Award. **Frequency:** annual. **Type:** recognition. **Computer Services:** database, membership list. **Committees:** Benefits; Training; Women's Activities. **Formerly:** (1981) National Police Constables Association. **Publications:** *All Points Bulletin,* quarterly. Newsletter. **Price:** free. **Advertising:** accepted. Alternate Formats: CD-ROM ● *Code of Ethics* ● *History of Constables* ● *National Constables Association News,* quarterly. Newsletter. Includes history, reports, and meeting summaries. **Price:** free. **Circulation:** 12,000. **Advertising:** accepted. **Conventions/Meetings:** annual board meeting and convention, minimal equipment and supplies (exhibits) - always first Thursday to Sunday of March.

5993 ■ National Drug Enforcement Officers Association (NDEOA)
Off. of Training/TRDS
FBI Acad.
PO Box 1475
Quantico, VA 22134-1475
Ph: (202)298-9653
E-mail: steven.r.peterson@usdoj.gov
URL: http://www.ndeoa.org
Contact: Steve Peterson, Pres.
Founded: 1970. **Membership Dues:** general, $45 (annual). **Description:** Law enforcement officers. Strives to promote the cooperation, education, and exchange of information among all law enforcement agencies involved in the enforcement of controlled substance laws. Hosts conferences and training seminars. **Awards:** NDEOA Educational Scholarship. **Type:** scholarship. **Committees:** Corporate Advisory.

5994 ■ National Law Enforcement Council (NLEC)
1620 Eye St. NW, Ste.210
Washington, DC 20006
Ph: (202)331-1275 (202)785-8940
Fax: (202)785-8949
Contact: Donald Baldwin, Exec. Dir.
Founded: 1978. **Members:** 35. **Staff:** 4. **Description:** Representatives of 15 principal law enforcement organizations with a total membership of over 485,000 law enforcement/criminal justice professionals. Sponsors luncheon meetings to discuss legislation of interest to the law enforcement/criminal justice community and to hear speakers who are national leaders in the law enforcement field. **Awards: Type:** recognition.

5995 ■ National Law Enforcement Officers Memorial Fund (NLEOMF)
400 7th St. NW, Ste.300
Washington, DC 20004
Ph: (202)737-3400
E-mail: info@nleomf.com
URL: http://www.nleomf.com
Contact: Craig W. Floyd, Chm./CEO
Founded: 1984. **Members:** 33. **Membership Dues:** friend, $1,000-$9,999 (annual) ● Rose and Shield Society (maximum), $25,000 (annual) ● Sterling Circle, $25,000 (annual). **Staff:** 33. **Description:** Professional law enforcement associations united to pay tribute to officers who have lost their lives in the line of duty through the National Law Enforcement Officers' Memorial in Washington, DC. Also seeks to educate the public regarding the risks associated with being a law enforcement officer and the need for a national museum through the news media, public speaking, and promotional activities. Member organizations include: Federal Law Enforcement Officers Association; Fraternal Order of Police, Grand Lodge; International Association of Chiefs of Police; International Brotherhood of Police Officers; International Union of Police Associations/AFL-CIO; National Association of Police Organizations; National Black Police Association; National Organization of Black Law Enforcement Executives; National Sheriffs Association; Police Executive Research Forum; Police Foundation; Concerns of Police Survivors; Fraternal Order of Police Auxiliary; National Troopers Coalition; United Federation of Police. **Awards:** Distinguished Service Award. **Frequency:** annual. **Type:** recognition. **Publications:** *Memorial News,* quarterly. Newsletter. Includes articles on contributions, memorial-related activities, and research updates. **Price:** free ● *Roll Call of Fallen Officers,* biweekly. Newsletter. Lists police officers killed in the line of duty. Alternate Formats: online. **Conventions/Meetings:** annual conference - 2008 Aug. 17-24, St. Louis, MO.

5996 ■ National Liquor Law Enforcement Association (NLLEA)
11710 Beltsville Dr., Ste.300
Beltsville, MD 20705-3102
Ph: (301)755-2795
E-mail: support@nllea.org
URL: http://www.nllea.org
Contact: Shawn Walker, Pres.
Membership Dues: individual, $20 (annual) ● associate, $50 (annual) ● agency, $200 (annual). **Description:** Represents the interests of law enforcement personnel dedicated to the enforcement of liquor laws and regulations. Seeks to improve the standards and practices of liquor law enforcement. Strives for public recognition of the role of liquor law enforcement in protecting and promoting public safety. Fosters a cooperative and mutually beneficial working relationship with alcohol research and public health organizations and responsible members of the liquor industry. **Awards:** John W. Britt Community Service Award. **Frequency:** annual. **Type:** recognition. **Recipient:** for a non-enforcement organization or agency that made a significant contribution to the efforts of liquor and/or tobacco law enforcement ● Liquor Enforcement Agency of the Year. **Frequency:** annual. **Type:** recognition. **Recipient:** for effectiveness and innovative programs by a liquor enforcement agency ● Liquor Enforcement Officer of the Year. **Frequency:** annual. **Type:** recognition. **Recipient:** for an act of heroism or bravery ● Most Innovative Liquor Law Enforcement Program. **Frequency:** annual. **Type:** recognition. **Recipient:** for an effective program which exhibited efficiency, fiscal savings or eye-catching campaigns. **Telecommunication Services:** electronic mail, shawn-walker@nllea.org. **Publications:** *NLLEAGRAM,* quarterly. Newsletter. Provides updates on NLLEA events, liquor laws and changes in Alcoholic Beverage Controls. Alternate Formats: online.

5997 ■ National Narcotic Detector Dog Association (NNDDA)
379 CR 105
Carthage, TX 75633
Free: (888)289-0070
E-mail: thenndda@yahoo.com
URL: http://www.nndda.org
Contact: Mark Treece, Pres.
Founded: 1978. **Membership Dues:** corporate, associate, $50 (annual) ● associate (non-law enforcement person), $30 (annual). **Description:** Works for the utilization and proficiency of scent detector dogs for the benefit of law enforcement and private industries. Provides training pertaining to the laws of search and seizure. **Libraries: Type:** reference. **Holdings:** articles. **Computer Services:** Information services, certification rules and standards. **Conventions/Meetings:** annual seminar, with training - usually March or April.

5998 ■ National Native American Law Enforcement Association (NNLEA)
PO Box 171
Washington, DC 20044
Free: (800)948-3863
E-mail: info@nnalea.org
URL: http://www.nnalea.org
Contact: Kim Baglio, Pres.
Founded: 1993. **Membership Dues:** general, $15 (annual). **State Groups:** 3. **Description:** Promotes mutual cooperation between American Indian Law Enforcement officers, agents, personnel, agencies, tribes and private industries. Provides media for the exchange of ideas and new techniques used by both criminals and investigators. Informs its members about judicial decisions as they relate to the law enforcement community. **Programs:** Academic Scholarship. **Publications:** Newsletter.

5999 ■ National Organization of Black Law Enforcement Executives (NOBLE)
4609-F Pinecrest Off. Park Dr.
Alexandria, VA 22312-1442
Ph: (703)658-1529
Fax: (703)658-9479
E-mail: jlee@noblenational.net
URL: http://www.noblenational.org
Contact: Jessie Lee, Exec. Dir.
Founded: 1976. **Members:** 3,500. **Membership Dues:** supporting, $55 (annual) ● associate, $100 (annual) ● regular, $150 (annual) ● sustaining, $525 (annual) ● life (regular), $1,525 ● life (associate, supporting), $1,095. **Staff:** 7. **Budget:** $1,500,000. **Regional Groups:** 6. **Local Groups:** 54. **Multinational. Description:** Represents law enforcement executives above the rank of lieutenant; police educators; academy directors; interested individuals and organizations. Provides a platform from which the concerns and opinions of minority law enforcement executives and command-level officers can be expressed. Facilitates the exchange of programmatic information among minority law enforcement executives. Aims to eliminate racism in the field of criminal justice and to increased cooperation from criminal justice agencies. Encourages coordination between law enforcement agencies and the community to prevent and abate crime and its causes. Conducts research and training and offers technical assistance in crime victim assistance, community oriented policing, domestic violence, use of deadly force, reduction of fear of crime, airport security assessment, and minority recruitment. Offers internships; operates Speaker's Bureau. **Libraries: Type:** reference. **Holdings:** 300. **Awards:** Irlet Anderson Scholarship

Award. **Frequency:** annual. **Type:** scholarship. **Recipient:** for criminal justice study ● NOBLE Fellowship Program. **Frequency:** annual. **Type:** fellowship ● **Type:** scholarship. **Recipient:** for students preparing for careers in law enforcement. **Computer Services:** database, domestic violence resources, community oriented policy training ● information services, virtual resource center. **Committees:** Civil Rights; Conference; Constitution and Bylaws; Education and Training; Legislative Affairs; Resolution; Strategic Planning; Ways and Means. **Publications:** *Hate Crimes: A Police Perspective*. Video ● *Minority Community Victim Assistance* ● *NOBLE Actions*, quarterly. Magazine. Reports on current law enforcement issues and activities. Contains employment opportunities, calendar of events, and legislative information. **Price:** included in membership dues; $25.00 /year for nonmembers. **Advertising:** accepted ● *Racial and Religious Violence: Final Report* ● Brochures ● Pamphlets. **Conventions/Meetings:** annual conference, with various products and services (exhibits) - always July.

6000 ■ National Police Bloodhound Association (NPBA)

Address Unknown since 2008

Founded: 1962. **Members:** 300. **Description:** Law enforcement officers at all levels; search and rescue personnel with law enforcement affiliations. Dedicated to the advancement and training of the man-trailing abilities of the purebred bloodhound in law enforcement and search and rescue. Conducts lectures on topics concerning working bloodhounds. Offers assistance from experts in mountain, desert, swamp, snow, city, and urban trailing. Makes available technical information on scent, the preservation of scent, and methods of developing cooperation from the departments. **Formerly:** (1966) Eastern Police Bloodhound Association. **Publications:** *Nose News*, quarterly ● Manual. Provides information to bloodhound handlers. ● Pamphlets.

6001 ■ National Police Officers Association of America (NPOAA)

c/o National Police and Security Officers Association of America
PO Box 663
South Plainfield, NJ 07080-0663
Ph: (908)226-8715
Fax: (908)226-8715
E-mail: npsoaa1@aol.com
URL: http://npoaa.tripod.com

Founded: 1955. **Members:** 6,000. **Membership Dues:** active, $35 (annual). **Staff:** 2. **Budget:** $25,000. **State Groups:** 4. **Description:** Professional and fraternal benefit organization of law enforcement, security, and military officers of federal, state, county, and local police departments, and civilians supporting law enforcement. Maintains Speaker's Bureau; conducts educational programs. **Awards:** Community Service Award. **Frequency:** periodic. **Type:** recognition. **Recipient:** for outstanding acts of community service ● Family Values Award. **Frequency:** periodic. **Type:** recognition. **Recipient:** for outstanding police work, including good arrests, bravery, merit, and valor ● Police and Security Training Scholarships. **Frequency:** periodic. **Type:** scholarship. **Recipient:** to NPOAA/NPSOAA members. **Additional Websites:** http://npsoaa.tripod.com, http://usccnii2000.tripod.com/deceptiondetection. **Publications:** *NPOAA/NPSOAA Review and Focus*, periodic. Newsletter. **Price:** included in membership dues; $25.00 /year for nonmembers in U.S.; $50.00 /year for nonmembers in Canada, Mexico, and outside North America. ISSN: 0042-2347. **Advertising:** accepted. Alternate Formats: online.

6002 ■ National Sheriffs' Association (NSA)

1450 Duke St.
Alexandria, VA 22314-3490
Ph: (703)836-7827 (703)838-5331
Free: (800)424-7827
Fax: (703)683-6541
E-mail: nsamail@sheriffs.org
URL: http://www.sheriffs.org
Contact: Aaron D. Kennard, Exec. Dir.

Founded: 1940. **Members:** 21,363. **Membership Dues:** corporate, $1,500 (annual) ● life retired paid-up-for-life (based on age bracket), $70-$308 ● paid-up-for-life (based on age bracket), $260-$517. **Staff:** 29. **Budget:** $4,000,000. **State Groups:** 50. **Description:** Works to enable sheriffs and other law enforcement to perform and serve jurisdictions. Promotes cooperative relationships with local, state, and federal governmental agencies across the nation to network and form partnerships beneficial to law enforcement, equating to training, equipment and personnel. Seeks grassroots guidance. Assists sheriffs' offices and state sheriffs' associations in locating and preparing applications for state and federal grant funding. Sponsors the National Sheriffs' Institute, the National Sheriff's Education Foundation, and the International Association of Court Officers and Services. **Awards:** Deputy Sheriff of the Year Award. **Frequency:** annual. **Type:** recognition. **Recipient:** for deputy sheriff with exemplary performance in all aspects of law enforcement, corrections, court service, and other related activities ● Ferris E. Lucas Award. **Frequency:** annual. **Type:** recognition. **Recipient:** to the Sheriff of the Year for his/her outstanding service to the Office of the Sheriff ● J. Stannard Baker Award. **Frequency:** annual. **Type:** recognition. **Recipient:** to individual law enforcement officers/deputies who have made significant contributions or outstanding achievements in highway safety enforcement and programs ● Law Enforcement Explorer Post Advisor Award. **Frequency:** annual. **Type:** recognition. **Recipient:** to an outstanding contribution by a Post Advisor to a Law Enforcement Explorer Post ● Medal of Merit. **Frequency:** annual. **Type:** medal. **Recipient:** for civil personnel of sheriff's department/office, members of sheriff's reserves and posses, and private citizens, who through acts of personal bravery assist a member of a sheriff's department/office in peril or to safety ● Medal of Valor. **Type:** medal. **Recipient:** to full-time sworn personnel of sheriff's department/office of sheriff for acts of outstanding personal bravery performed in the line of duty at imminent personal hazard of life ● Purple Heart. **Frequency:** annual. **Type:** recognition. **Recipient:** to full-time sworn personnel of sheriff's department/office who in the performance of duty, sustain personal injuries inflicted by an assailant with a dangerous or deadly weapon ● **Frequency:** annual. **Type:** scholarship. **Recipient:** for criminal justice students who are employees of a sheriff's office/sheriff's department or the sons or daughters of sheriffs' office/sheriff's department personnel ● Youth Service Medal. **Type:** medal. **Recipient:** for persons under the age of 19 with outstanding personal bravery performed in saving or attempting to save the life of a member of a sheriff's department/office. **Committees:** Accreditation/Detention and Corrections; Audit; Awards; Budget; Chaplains Advisory; Congressional Affairs; Constitution and By-Laws; Court Security/Prisoner Transportation and Service of Process; Crime Prevention; Criminal Justice Information Systems/Technology; Domestic Violence; Drug Enforcement; Educational Foundation; Exhibitor Advisory; Gift of Life; Indian Affairs; Insurance and Employee Benefits; Law Enforcement/Private Security; Major County Sheriffs Association; Marine; Membership; National Service Associates; National Sheriffs' Institute Advisory; Nominating; Resolutions; Standards and Ethics/Education and Training; State Executive Directors and Presidents; Traffic Safety; Youth Programs and Juvenile Justice. **Programs:** Chaplains; CNA Municipal Insurance; National Neighborhood Watch; Triad. **Sections:** Conference; Jail Operation; Publications; Research and Development. **Subcommittees:** Management. **Publications:** *Annual Directory of Sheriffs*, annual. Includes names, addresses of all 3,096 sheriffs from across the nation. **Price:** $50.00 for nonmembers; $35.00 for members. **Circulation:** 19,534. **Advertising:** accepted ● *First and Second Line Supervisors Program* ● *Jail Officers' Training Manual* ● *Jail Technician Program* ● *Sheriff*, bimonthly. Magazine. Covers association activities and topics of interest to the law enforcement community including legal updates and criminal justice strategies. **Price:** included in membership dues; $25.00 /year for nonmembers. ISSN: 1070-8170. **Advertising:** accepted. **Conventions/Meetings:** annual conference (exhibits) - 2008 June 27-July 2, Indianapolis, IN.

6003 ■ North American Police Work Dog Association (NAPWDA)

4222 Manchester Ave.
Perry, OH 44081-9611
Ph: (440)259-3169
Free: (888)4CANINE
Fax: (440)259-3170
E-mail: napwda@napwda.com
URL: http://www.napwda.com
Contact: Jim Watson, Natl. Sec.

Founded: 1977. **Members:** 3,600. **Membership Dues:** regular, associate, $35 (annual). **Staff:** 8. **Multinational. Description:** Active or retired law enforcement officers and military policemen who are or were canine handlers, trainers, or administrators; associate members are others involved with or interested in canine training or law enforcement. Seeks to unite all law enforcement agencies in the training and improvement of police work dogs. Has established a working standard for all police work dogs, handlers, and trainers; maintains accreditation program. Sponsors working seminars that allow handlers and their dogs to participate in specific training exercises. Conducts research on the legal ramifications of using police work dogs. Compiles statistics. **Awards:** Exceptional K9. **Frequency:** annual. **Type:** recognition. **Recipient:** for members who meet written requirements ● Outstanding K9. **Frequency:** annual. **Type:** recognition. **Recipient:** for members who meet written requirements ● Valor. **Frequency:** annual. **Type:** recognition. **Recipient:** for members who meet written requirements. **Computer Services:** database, K-9 certification tests and results. **Publications:** Newsletter, quarterly. **Advertising:** accepted ● Also publishes educational materials and training aids. **Conventions/Meetings:** annual workshop, covers all utility phases, including tactical techniques and scenarios, plus the specialty phases of narcotics, explosives, cadaver and accelerants (exhibits) - 2008 June 15-20, Indianapolis, IN.

6004 ■ Police Association for College Education (PACE)

63 Lake Forest Dr.
Mineral, VA 23117
Ph: (540)894-8781
Fax: (540)894-8782
E-mail: loumayo@police-association.org
URL: http://www.police-association.org
Contact: Dr. Louis A. Mayo PhD, Exec. Dir.

Description: Advances the quality of police agencies and services by recommending a minimum education level of a four-year college degree for officers. **Libraries: Type:** reference. **Holdings:** articles, biographical archives, papers, periodicals. **Subjects:** law, law enforcement, police. **Computer Services:** database, directory of member cities, NCRJ abstracts ● information services, open letters, speeches, resolutions ● online services, forum, photo gallery. **Programs:** Assessment and Planning; Job Placement; Special Events; Technical Assistance; Training. **Publications:** *Panel: Education, Discipline and Law Enforcement*. Proceedings. Alternate Formats: online ● Newsletter. Alternate Formats: online.

6005 ■ Police Executive Research Forum (PERF)

1120 Connecticut Ave. NW, Ste.930
Washington, DC 20036
Ph: (202)466-7820
Fax: (202)466-7826
E-mail: cwexler@policeforum.org
URL: http://www.policeforum.org
Contact: Chuck Wexler, Exec. Dir.

Founded: 1976. **Members:** 900. **Membership Dues:** general, $300 (annual) ● subscribing, $160 (annual). **Staff:** 38. **Budget:** $5,000,000. **Description:** Represents executive heads, department heads and executives of criminal justice agencies. Stresses cooperation with other professionals and organizations in the criminal justice system. Seeks to stimulate public understanding and discussion of important criminal justice issues. Encourages research and experimentation; disseminates research information. Sponsors annual Senior Management Institute for Police and Problem-Oriented Policing Conference. **Libraries:**

Type: reference. **Departments:** Center for Force and Accountability; Executive Search; Homeland Security and Development; Legislative Issues; Management Services; Publications and Information Services; Research; Training and Technical Assistance. **Publications:** *Deadly Force: What We Know*. Book. **Price:** $20.00 ● *Police Management: Issues and Perspectives*. Book. **Price:** $17.00 ● *Police Officer Training*. Manual ● *Problem Oriented Policing*. Books. **Price:** $75.00 ● *Problem Solving Quarterly*. Newsletter. **Price:** $35.00/year. ISSN: 1084-7316 ● *Solving Crimes: The Investigation of Burglary and Robbery*. Report. **Price:** $14.00 ● *Subject to Debate*, bimonthly. Newsletter ● *Using Research: A Primer for Law Enforcement Managers*. Book. **Price:** $19.00. **Conventions/Meetings:** annual meeting.

6006 ■ Police Foundation
1201 Connecticut Ave. NW
Washington, DC 20036
Ph: (202)833-1460
Fax: (202)659-9149
E-mail: pfinfo@policefoundation.org
URL: http://www.policefoundation.org
Contact: Ms. Mary Malina, Communications Dir.
Founded: 1970. **Staff:** 25. **Nonmembership. Description:** Aims to support innovation and improvement in policing through research and evaluation, technical assistance, training, technology, professional services and communication programs. Conducts research in police behavior, policy and procedure. Works closely with local agencies on important police operational and administrative concerns. Provides services to law enforcement agencies and state and local governments. Operates a Crime Mapping and Problem Analysis Laboratory that provides practical assistance and information to police departments and develops the physical and theoretical infrastructure needed for innovations of police and criminological theory. **Libraries: Type:** not open to the public. **Holdings:** 1,000; articles, books, periodicals. **Subjects:** policing, criminal justice. **Publications:** *Crime Mapping News*, quarterly. Newsletter. Provides information for crime mapping, GIS, problem analysis, and policing. **Price:** free. **Circulation:** 2,500. Alternate Formats: online ● *Ideas in American Policing*, semiannual. Newsletter. **Price:** single copies free, except international postage. ISSN: 1884-614X. **Circulation:** 5,000 ● Books ● Reports. **Conventions/Meetings:** quarterly board meeting.

6007 ■ Police Marksman Association (PMA)
200 Green St., Ste.200
San Francisco, CA 94111
Free: (888)765-4231
E-mail: pma@policemarksman.com
URL: http://www.policemarksman.com
Contact: Connie Bond, Ed.
Founded: 1976. **Members:** 18,000. **Membership Dues:** individual, $18 (annual). **Staff:** 5. **For-Profit. Description:** Represents law enforcement personnel. Provides firearms training and survival knowledge for effective performance in the line of duty. **Publications:** *The Police Marksman*, bimonthly. Magazine. **Price:** $18.95 in U.S.; $33.95 outside U.S. **Advertising:** accepted.

6008 ■ United States Police Canine Association (USPCA)
PO Box 80
Springboro, OH 45066-0080
Free: (800)531-1614
E-mail: uspcadir@aol.com
URL: http://www.uspcak9.com
Contact: Russell Hess, Natl. Exec. Dir.
Founded: 1971. **Members:** 5,000. **Membership Dues:** special, honorary, regular, associate, $40 (annual). **Staff:** 1. **Regional Groups:** 27. **Description:** Full-time paid law enforcement officers who are either military, federal, state, county, or municipal officers and who are canine handlers, trainers, or administrators. Purposes are to: unite in a common cause all law enforcement agencies utilizing the services of the canine; promote friendship and brotherhood among all those interested in the training and utilization of the canine in police work; coordinate and exchange advanced techniques of training of the police dog; improve the image of the working police dog to the populace in general through improved public service and the prevention and detection of crime. Sponsors regional mini-seminars. Conducts police service dog certification field trials in patrol, detector dog and tracking ability. Maintains police evaluators and certification process to provide qualified professional evaluations. Maintains a legal assistance fund to support proper use of police service dogs and departments in legal challenges. Maintains Speaker's Bureau. **Awards:** Eukanuba Awards. **Frequency:** quarterly. **Type:** recognition. **Recipient:** for outstanding patrol and detector cases ● Valor Award. **Frequency:** annual. **Type:** recognition. **Recipient:** to dogs killed in the line of duty. **Formed by Merger of:** Police K-9 Association; United States K-9 Association. **Publications:** *Canine Courier*, quarterly. Newspaper. Covers regional news about training, legal cases, and field work involving police dogs; includes veterinary articles. **Price:** included in membership dues; $20.00 /year for nonmembers. **Circulation:** 2,000. **Advertising:** accepted ● *Rules and Regulations of Police Service Dog Performance Standards and Evaluation Standards* ● Also publishes brochure. **Conventions/Meetings:** meeting - 3/year ● National Detector Dog Trials - competition and seminar, field trial ● National PDI Trials - meeting and seminar ● semiannual National Training Seminar, with hands-on training (exhibits).

6009 ■ United States Secret Service Uniformed Division Retirement Association (UDRA)
Address Unknown since 2008
Membership Dues: full, $30 (annual) ● associate, $15 (annual). **Description:** Retired persons from the U.S. Secret Service Uniformed Division, active personnel of the USSS Uniformed Division, and active and retired personnel of other law enforcement organization as associate members; surviving spouses of deceased USSS Uniformed Division retirees as honorary members. Promotes accomplishments of members; facilitates communication and continued camaraderie among members; monitors Congressional activity and informs members of relevant legislation. The U.S. Secret Service Uniformed Division is a permanent federal police force; its authority, powers, and duties are enumerated in the U.S. Code, Title 18, Section 3056A. **Publications:** Newsletter, 3-4/year.

6010 ■ Women in Federal Law Enforcement (WIFLE)
2200 Wilson Blvd., Ste.102, PMB-204
Arlington, VA 22201
Ph: (703)548-9211
Free: (866)399-4353
Fax: (410)451-7373
E-mail: wifle@comcast.net
URL: http://www.wifle.org
Contact: Margaret M. Moore, Exec. Dir.
Founded: 1999. **Membership Dues:** regular, $50 (annual) ● associate, $35 (annual) ● supporting, $250 (annual) ● student, $10 (annual) ● life, $500. **Description:** Aims to achieve gender equity in federal law enforcement. Seeks to enhance the image of law enforcement. Promotes the value of collaborative and cooperative leadership styles. Assists and monitors the progress of agencies in the recruitment, hiring, promotion, and retention of women in law enforcement. Conducts research on issues affecting women in law enforcement positions. **Awards:** Julie Y. Cross Award. **Frequency:** annual. **Type:** recognition. **Recipient:** for exceptional heroic achievement in law enforcement ● Outstanding Advocate for Women in Federal Law Enforcement. **Frequency:** annual. **Type:** recognition. **Recipient:** for substantial contribution in one or all areas of recruiting, retaining, or promoting women in law enforcement ● Outstanding Federal Law Enforcement Employee. **Frequency:** annual. **Type:** recognition. **Recipient:** for a sustained superior level of performance in law enforcement ● Top Prosecutor Award. **Frequency:** annual. **Type:** recognition. **Recipient:** for exceptional work resulting in the conviction of individual(s) for qualified federal violations ● WIFLE Scholarship. **Frequency:** annual. **Type:** scholarship. **Recipient:** to women who are interested in pursuing a career in law enforcement. **Telecommunication Services:** electronic mail, wifle@wifle.org. **Publications:** *WIFLE-Enews*, quarterly. Newsletter. **Price:** included in membership dues. Alternate Formats: online. **Conventions/Meetings:** annual conference, leadership training.

Legal

6011 ■ Clarity
c/o Prof. Joseph Kimble, Membership Sec.
Box 13038
Lansing, MI 48901-3038
Ph: (517)371-5140
Fax: (517)334-5748
E-mail: kimblej@cooley.edu
URL: http://www.clarity-international.net
Contact: Prof. Joseph Kimble, Membership Sec.
Membership Dues: general, $25 (annual). **Multinational. Description:** Promotes the use of good and clear language by the legal profession. Seeks to avoid archaic, obscure and overelaborate language in legal work. Drafts legal documents in language that is both certain in meaning and easily understandable. Facilitates exchange of ideas and precedents to produce good written and spoken legal language. **Publications:** Journal. Alternate Formats: online.

6012 ■ A Matter of Justice Coalition (AMOJ)
PO Box 1209
Dahlgren, VA 22448-1209
Ph: (540)663-0486
Fax: (540)644-1333
E-mail: justicematters@amatterofjustice.org
URL: http://www.amatterofjustice.org
Contact: Jacob Roginsky PhD, Pres.
Founded: 2000. **Description:** Educates the public about the issues and abuses of the United States legal system. Documents instances of abuse endured from lawyers, judges and other public servants. **Libraries: Type:** reference. **Computer Services:** Mailing lists.

6013 ■ NALS
314 E 3rd St., Ste.210
Tulsa, OK 74120
Ph: (918)582-5188
Fax: (918)582-5907
E-mail: info@nals.org
URL: http://www.nals.org
Contact: Tammy Hailey CAE, Exec. Dir.
Founded: 1929. **Members:** 6,000. **Membership Dues:** regular, $90 (annual). **Staff:** 6. **Regional Groups:** 8. **State Groups:** 23. **Local Groups:** 161. **Description:** Legal support professionals. Provides continuing legal education and resource materials, networking opportunities and professional certification programs and designations.

6014 ■ National Association of Litigation Support Managers (NALSM)
c/o Chad M. Papenfuss, Pres.
Fredrikson & Byron, P.A.
200 S 6th St., Ste.4000
Minneapolis, MN 55402
Ph: (612)492-7815
Fax: (612)492-7077
E-mail: cpapenfuss@fredlaw.com
URL: http://www.malsm.org
Contact: Chad M. Papenfuss, Pres.
Membership Dues: regular/vendor, $75 (annual) ● associate, $50 (annual) ● student, $35 (annual). **Description:** Promotes litigation support managers.

6015 ■ National Legal Sanctuary for Community Advancement (NLSCA)
444 DeHaro St., Ste.205
San Francisco, CA 94107
Ph: (415)553-7100

E-mail: akhlaghilaw@sbcglobal.net
URL: http://www.legalsanctuary.org
Contact: Banafsheh Akhlaghi Esq., Pres./CEO
Founded: 2001. **Description:** Protects the civil rights, human rights and dignity of Middle Eastern, Muslim and South Asian peoples in the United States through legal advocacy. Gives legal defense, policy advocacy and public education to advance social justice.

6016 ■ National Legal Video Association (NLVA)
80 Bloomfield Ave., Ste.104
Caldwell, NJ 07006
Ph: (973)228-8872
Fax: (973)228-6650
E-mail: support@nlva.com
URL: http://www.nlva.com
Membership Dues: corporate, $200 (annual) ● individual, $100 (annual). **Description:** Promotes professionalism, ethics, uniformity and specialized skills for individuals involved in legal videography. Creates awareness of the role of legal videographers. **Computer Services:** database, listing of legal professionals ● information services, federal rules ● online services, information survey. **Publications:** Newsletter, quarterly.

Legal Aid

6017 ■ Center for Law and Justice International (CLJI)
6375 New Hope Rd.
New Hope, KY 40052
Ph: (502)549-5454
Fax: (502)549-5252
E-mail: info@clji.org
URL: http://www.clji.org
Contact: Jane Adolphe, Pres.
Founded: 1984. **Description:** Attorneys interested in "fighting for human life and striving for a culture of life in which families may live in faith and freedom." Litigates at state and federal levels to protect all human rights; produces several newsletters. Have speakers available. **Affiliated With:** Catholics United for Life. **Publications:** Newsletter. **Price:** free. Alternate Formats: online.

Legal Education

6018 ■ National South Asian Bar Association (NASABA)
c/o Bharati Sharma, VP of Individual Membership
Schiffrin and Barroway, LLP
280 King of Prussia Rd.
Radnor, PA 19087
Ph: (484)270-1456
Fax: (610)667-7056
E-mail: bsharma@sbclasslaw.com
URL: http://www.na-saba.org
Contact: Bharati Sharma, VP of Individual Membership
Membership Dues: individual, $25 (annual) ● organization, $50 (annual). **Description:** Provides a link between South Asian lawyers and the South Asian community across North America. Promotes the South Asian bar and focuses on the legal needs of the South Asian community. Educates and disseminates information to the South Asian community about the law, legal access, and relevant legal issues. **Publications:** Newsletter.

Legal Services

6019 ■ American Guild of Court Videographers (AGCV)
1628 E Third St.
Casper, WY 82601
Ph: (307)472-9600
Free: (800)678-1990
Fax: (307)472-5048
E-mail: info@agcv.com
URL: http://www.agcv.com
Contact: Dr. Gayle Marquette PhD, Founder
Founded: 1995. **Description:** Represents legal videographers in America. Develops skills and acknowledges the qualifications of a properly trained legal video professional. Shares information for the advancement of the profession. Trains professional legal videographers in all aspects of video recording and visual evidence including the final preparation of the evidence. **Additional Websites:** http://www.legalvideographers.com. **Telecommunication Services:** additional toll-free number, membership, (866)688-8441. **Conventions/Meetings:** monthly seminar.

6020 ■ American Prepaid Legal Services Institute (API)
321 N Clark St.
Chicago, IL 60610
Ph: (312)988-5751
Fax: (312)988-5483
E-mail: info@aplsi.org
URL: http://www.aplsi.org
Contact: Alec M. Schwartz, Exec. Dir.
Founded: 1976. **Members:** 750. **Membership Dues:** regular, $325 (annual) ● provider, $120 (biennial) ● provider, $85 (annual) ● associate, $150 (annual). **Staff:** 4. **Budget:** $195,000. **Description:** Insurance companies, prepaid legal plan sponsors and administrators, lawyers and law firms, and others interested in prepaid/group legal services. The concept of prepaid legal services is similar to that of health insurance a consumer pays a fixed amount each year or month in exchange for certain (legal) service benefits to be used as and if needed. Acts as a national information and technical assistance resource. Provides information and assistance on regulation and tax status of prepaid and group legal plans. Reviews documents and makes suggestions. Arranges for speakers to participate in educational programs sponsored by other organizations. Conducts limited research for members and other groups. **Libraries: Type:** not open to the public. **Telecommunication Services:** electronic mail, tuckera@staff.abanet.org. **Committees:** Legislative; Public Education. **Publications:** *American Prepaid Legal Services Institute—Newsbriefs*, monthly. Newsletter. Provides general information on industry trends. **Price:** included in membership dues; $85.00 for nonmembers. **Circulation:** 800 ● *Membership Brochure*. Alternate Formats: online ● *Plan Newsletter*. **Price:** $22.00 ● *Prepaid Legal Service Plan Summaries*. Includes profiles of typical legal service paths with information on geographical areas served, enrollment mechanisms and benefits. **Price:** $21.50 ● *Regulation Reporter*, bimonthly. Book. Contains supplements on statues, ethics codes, resource data, federal law, model legislation/court decisions of 50 states, U.S. and Puerto Rico. **Price:** $325.00 initial 4 volumes; $175.00 annual supplements ● *Who's Who in Prepaid Legal Services: The API Membership Directory*, annual. **Price:** included in membership dues; $75.00 /year for nonmembers. **Advertising:** accepted. **Conventions/Meetings:** annual Chicago Connections - conference ● annual Educational Conference - meeting ● seminar.

6021 ■ American Pro Se Association (APSA)
1441 Prospect Ave.
Plainfield, NJ 07060
Ph: (908)753-4516
Fax: (908)753-2599
E-mail: support@legalhelp.org
URL: http://www.legalhelp.org
Contact: Roj Prasad, Pres.
Membership Dues: premium, $50 (annual). **Description:** Educates the public on the alternative and lower cost options of dispute resolutions. Aims to improve the orderly and fair administration of justice. Promotes the protection of citizen's liberties in keeping with the Bill of Rights of the United States. **Libraries: Type:** reference. **Holdings:** articles. **Subjects:** law. **Computer Services:** Information services, law resources. **Publications:** *Proceeding Pro Se*, quarterly. Newsletter. Alternate Formats: online.

6022 ■ Custom Legal Plans, LLC
139-30 Queens Blvd.
Briarwood, NY 11435-2926
Ph: (718)526-6100
URL: http://customlegalplans.com
Contact: Elliot Adler, Exec. Dir.
Founded: 1977. **Staff:** 6. **Budget:** $200,000. **Description:** Addresses legal programs in the U.S. and Canada (primarily group and prepaid legal plans); serves as a clearinghouse and advises individuals and groups seeking to establish or evaluate legal service plans or other legal services delivery innovations. Provides technical assistance and conducts research into new methods of legal practice. Operates national legal services plan for members of other non-profit organizations. **Libraries: Type:** reference. **Additional Websites:** http://www.unionplus.org. **Formed by Merger of:** (1975) National Consumer Center for Legal Services; Resource Center for Consumers of Legal Services. **Formerly:** (2004) National Resource Center for Consumers of Legal Services. **Publications:** Papers ● Survey ● Also publishes model plan documents and compendium.

6023 ■ Farmers' Legal Action Group (FLAG)
360 N Robert St., Ste.500
St. Paul, MN 55101-1589
Ph: (651)223-5400
Free: (877)860-4349
Fax: (651)223-5335
E-mail: lawyers@flaginc.org
URL: http://www.flaginc.org
Contact: Susan E. Stokes, Exec. Dir.
Founded: 1986. **Description:** Provides legal services to family farmers and rural communities. Works to protect and preserve the family farm system of agriculture in the U.S. Undertakes strategic litigation and class action lawsuits to change important areas of the law that will have an effect on a large number of family farmers. Submits formal comments on proposed agency regulations, testifies before federal and state legislative bodies and assists client organizations in their attempt to draft legislation. **Publications:** *Farmers' Legal Action Report*, quarterly. Newsletter. Provides information about agricultural law issues. **Price:** $30.00 regular; $20.00 special farmer.

6024 ■ Guam Bar Association (GBA)
120 West O'Brien Dr.
Guam Judicial Ctr., 2nd Fl.
Hagatna, GU 96910
Ph: (671)475-3396 (671)475-3397
Fax: (671)475-3400
E-mail: info@guambar.org
URL: http://www.guambar.org
Contact: Mr. Bruce Bradley, Exec. Dir.
Description: Legal professionals. Aims to improve the administration of justice and the standards of the legal profession; encourage higher and better education of its members; assist in the admission and discipline of its members and in the formulation and administration of measures to prevent the unauthorized practice of law; and assume such other responsibilities and duties as the Supreme Court of Guam may from time to time determine.

6025 ■ Justice Without Borders
PO Box 2400
Madison, WI 53701-2400
E-mail: ronwpor@hotmail.com
URL: http://www.justicewithoutborders.org
Contact: Nicholas L. Chiarkas, Contact
Founded: 1998. **Multinational. Description:** Promotes the exchange of information, ideas and expertise in providing legal representation to individuals that face deprivation of life or liberty. **Committees:** Management. **Subcommittees:** Communications; Core Values; Funding; Infrastructure; Mission/Summit.

6026 ■ Lawyers for Children America (LFCA)
c/o Swidler Berlin Shereff Friedman LLP
3000 K St. NW, Ste.125
Washington, DC 20007
Ph: (202)339-8943 (202)339-8941

Fax: (202)298-5558
E-mail: info@lawyersforchildrenamerica.org
URL: http://www.lawyersforchildrenamerica.org
Contact: Katherine McG. Sullivan, Chair
Founded: 1995. **Regional Groups:** 3. **Description:** Provides services that help children and youth who are victims of abuse and neglect. Provides training and ongoing support to attorneys who have committed them to providing pro bono representation to children. **Computer Services:** Online services, resources center. **Telecommunication Services:** hotline, report abuse and neglect, (800)422-4453. **Programs:** Internship. **Publications:** Newsletter. Alternate Formats: online.

6027 ■ Lawyers' Committee for Civil Rights Under Law (LCCRUL)
1401 New York Ave. NW, Ste.400
Washington, DC 20005
Ph: (202)662-8600 (202)662-8300
Fax: (202)783-0857
E-mail: barnwine@lawyerscommittee.org
URL: http://www.lawyerscomm.org
Contact: Barbara R. Arnwine, Exec. Dir.
Founded: 1963. **Members:** 218. **Staff:** 37. **Budget:** $3,500,000. **Local Groups:** 8. **Description:** Operates through local committees of private lawyers in eight major cities to provide legal assistance to poor and minority groups living in urban centers. National office undertakes reform efforts in such fields as employment, voting rights, housing discrimination and community development, education discrimination, and environmental justice. **Libraries: Type:** reference. **Additional Websites:** http://www.lawyerscommittee.org. **Telecommunication Services:** electronic mail, twierzbicki@lawyerscommittee.org. **Projects:** Education; Employment; Employment Testing; Environmental Justice; Fair Housing and Community Development; Voting Rights. **Publications:** *Call to Justice*, annual. Newsletter. Alternate Formats: online ● *Committee Report*, quarterly ● Annual Report, annual. **Conventions/Meetings:** bimonthly meeting.

6028 ■ Lawyers for One America (LFOA)
4136 Redwood Hwy., Ste.9
San Rafael, CA 94903
Ph: (415)479-3636
Fax: (415)479-3621
E-mail: lfoa@lfoa.org
URL: http://www.lfoa.org/default.htm
Contact: Teveia Rose Barnes, Pres./Exec. Dir.
Founded: 2000. **Membership Dues:** law student, $25 (annual) ● friend, $75 (annual) ● sponsor, $500 (annual) ● champion, $1,000 (annual) ● patron, $5,000 (annual) ● renaissance founder, $10,000 (annual). **Description:** Advocates and promotes greater racial and ethnic diversity in the legal profession. Advocates for law schools, lawyers and judicial systems that accurately reflect the communities that they serve. Provides civil pro bono legal services to underserved communities.

6029 ■ National Academy of Elder Law Attorneys (NAELA)
1604 N Country Club Rd.
Tucson, AZ 85716-3102
Ph: (520)881-4005
Fax: (520)325-7925
E-mail: info@naela.com
URL: http://www.naela.org
Contact: Susan McMahon, Exec. Dir.
Founded: 1987. **Members:** 4,300. **Membership Dues:** individual, $375 (annual). **Staff:** 18. **Budget:** $1,000,000. **Description:** Practicing attorneys, law professors, and others interested in the provision of legal services to the elderly. Promotes technical expertise and education for legal services addressing the needs of the elderly and their families. **Telecommunication Services:** TDD, (520)326-2467. **Publications:** *Conference Manuals* ● *Conference Tapes*, biennial. Audiotapes. Covers seminars. ● *NAELA News*, bimonthly. Newsletter. **Price:** included in membership dues; $95.00 /year for nonmembers. **Advertising:** accepted. Alternate Formats: diskette ● *NAELA Quarterly*. Journal. **Price:** included in membership dues; $95.00 /year for nonmembers. ISSN: 1070-3063. **Conventions/Meetings:** biennial symposium (exhibits).

6030 ■ National Center on Poverty Law (NCPL)
50 E Washington St., Ste.500
Chicago, IL 60602
Ph: (312)263-3830 (206)842-4764
Fax: (312)263-3846
E-mail: ritamclennon@povertylaw.org
URL: http://www.povertylaw.org
Contact: Rita A. McLennon, VP for External Affairs
Founded: 1967. **Staff:** 36. **Budget:** $3,000,000. **Description:** Legal services attorneys and programs; private attorneys; law universities and libraries; court judges and libraries; government organizations. Makes available information on case law with respect to issues relating to poor people. Operates extensive brief bank of cases and publications relating to poverty law and the consumer. Provides advocacy to the poor on welfare and housing issues. **Libraries: Type:** not open to the public. **Holdings:** 500,000; papers. **Computer Services:** database, abstracts of cases and other material relating to poverty law in private libraries on Lexis and Westlaw. **Telecommunication Services:** electronic mail, johnbouman@povertylaw.org. **Formerly:** (2001) National Clearinghouse for Legal Services. **Publications:** *Clearinghouse Review*, monthly. Journal. Includes bibliography. **Price:** $300.00/year ● Newsletter.

6031 ■ National Legal Aid and Defender Association (NLADA)
1140 Connecticut Ave. NW, Ste.900
Washington, DC 20036
Ph: (202)452-0620
Fax: (202)872-1031
E-mail: info@nlada.org
URL: http://www.nlada.org
Contact: Jo-Ann Wallace, Pres./CEO
Founded: 1911. **Members:** 2,800. **Membership Dues:** sustaining, $100 (annual) ● individual attorney, $90 (annual) ● non-attorney professional, $50 (annual) ● life, $1,000 ● individual client, $15 (annual) ● individual student/fellow, $25 (annual). **Staff:** 23. **Description:** Legal aid offices and public defender organizations representing the indigent and individual members. Provides technical and management assistance to local organizations offering legal services to poor persons in civil or criminal cases and to state and local units of government. Advocates for federally funded high quality legal services with the public, media, congress, and members of the Executive branch. Offers litigation support through amicus curiae capability to organizations providing legal services. Serves as clearinghouse for information on the provision of legal aid and defender services to persons without means to pay lawyers' fees. Sponsors training program covering substantive law, management issues and litigation skills. Matches private law firms with impact cases to facilitate increased pro bono participation. **Awards:** Harrison Tweed Award. **Frequency:** annual. **Type:** recognition. **Recipient:** for state and local bar associations that develop or significantly expand projects or programs to increase civil services ● Innovations in Technology Award. **Frequency:** annual. **Type:** recognition. **Recipient:** for individuals who have made outstanding career contributions to creativity and innovation in the delivery of legal service to poor people ● Kutak-Dodds Prize. **Frequency:** annual. **Type:** monetary. **Recipient:** for individuals who have contributed in a significant way to the enhancement of human dignity and quality of life ● National Exemplary Awards. **Frequency:** annual. **Type:** recognition. **Recipient:** for private bar that has demonstrated outstanding leadership in promoting and supporting equal justice. **Caucuses:** Rainbow. **Committees:** Civil; Defender. **Sections:** Appellate Defender; Assigned Counsel and Contract Defender; Death Penalty Litigation; Defender Trainers; Farmworker Law; Institutions and Alternative; Juvenile; Native American; Paralegal/Legal Assistants; Rural Advocacy; Social Services; Student Legal Services; Women's Issues. **Publications:** *Cornerstone*, quarterly. Newsletter. Contains technical information for public defenders, legal services attorneys, pro bono attorneys, and their clients. **Price:** included in membership dues. **Circulation:** 3,200 ● *Directory of Legal Aid and Defender Offices in the U.S.*, biennial. Lists civil and criminal legal assistance programs for the poor. **Price:** $15.00/copy for members; $60.00/copy for nonmembers ● Handbooks ● Reports. **Conventions/Meetings:** annual conference (exhibits).

6032 ■ National Legal Center for the Medically Dependent and Disabled (NLCMDD)
3 S 6th St.
Terre Haute, IN 47807
Ph: (812)232-2434
Fax: (812)235-3685
E-mail: bbostrom@bopplaw.com
Contact: Barry Bostrom, VP
Founded: 1984. **Staff:** 1. **Budget:** $160,000. **Nonmembership. Description:** Publishes Issues in Law & Medicine, a peer reviewed professional law journal. **Libraries: Type:** reference; not open to the public. **Subjects:** bioethical, medical, and legal information. **Publications:** *Issues in Law and Medicine*, 3/year. Journal. Contains articles examining the legal and medical issues related to the right of disabled persons to receive beneficial medical care, abortion, etc. **Price:** $69.00 /year for individuals; $89.00 /year for institutions. ISSN: 8756-8160. **Circulation:** 1,000. Alternate Formats: online.

6033 ■ National Structured Settlements Trade Association (NSSTA)
1800 K St. NW, Ste.718
Washington, DC 20006
Ph: (202)466-2714
Fax: (202)466-7414
URL: http://www.nssta.com
Contact: Henry Strong, Pres.
Founded: 1985. **Members:** 1,300. **Membership Dues:** producer company and professional, $7,820 (annual) ● provider company (based on premium volume), $55,000 (annual) ● user company, $920 (annual) ● associate, $690 (annual). **Staff:** 8. **Budget:** $1,000,000. **Description:** Structured settlement firms, life insurance companies, claims adjustors, attorneys, and other consultants involved in the tort process. Develops out-of-court settlements in personal injury accident suits and other tort actions. Conducts educational programs; maintains speakers' bureau. **Libraries: Type:** reference. **Holdings:** audiovisuals, books, clippings, periodicals. **Computer Services:** database, list of members. **Committees:** Asbestos; Education; Government Benefits; Legal; Legs and Regs; Long Range Planning; Marketing; Political Action; Public Relations; Technology. **Publications:** *Legislative Update*, bimonthly ● *NSSTA Newsletter*, bimonthly ● Brochure. **Conventions/Meetings:** annual conference ● regional meeting - 3/year.

6034 ■ Pretrial Justice Industry (PJI)
927 15th St. NW, 3rd Fl.
Washington, DC 20005
Ph: (202)638-3080
Fax: (202)347-0493
E-mail: pji@pretrial.org
URL: http://www.pretrial.org
Contact: Timothy J. Murray, Exec. Dir.
Founded: 1977. **Staff:** 12. **Description:** Provides criminal justice consulting services covering subjects such as data collection, jail overcrowding, and drug testing. Conducts seminars; maintains library. **Programs:** Pretrial Survey; State Court Processing Statistics. **Projects:** Building Blocks for Youth; Criminal Courts Technical Assistance; Criminal Justice/Mental Health Consensus; Juvenile Defendants in Criminal Courts; Juvenile Detention Alternatives Initiative; Processing of Domestic Violence Cases in State Courts. **Formerly:** (2007) Pretrial Services Resource Center. **Publications:** *Commercial Surety Bail: Assessing Its Role in the Pretrial Release and Detention Decision - 1997*. Monograph. Includes the analysis of state and federal case law and statutes on bail, media reports, and research on pretrial release. **Price:** $10.00. Alternate Formats:

online ● *Integrating Drug Testing Into a Pretrial Services System - 1999 Update.* Monograph. Contains an updated version of 1992 document. Alternate Formats: online ● *Pretrial Release and Supervision Program Training Supplement - 1997.* Manual. Includes a suggested bibliography for pretrial training. **Price:** $22.00 ● *Pretrial Reporter*, bimonthly. Newsletter. Contains the latest in case law and research related to the pretrial field. **Price:** $48.00/year; $80.00 for 2 years. **Conventions/Meetings:** semiannual meeting.

6035 ■ Street Law
1010 Wayne Ave., Ste.870
Silver Spring, MD 20910
Ph: (301)589-1130
Fax: (301)589-1131
E-mail: clearinghouse@streetlaw.org
URL: http://www.streetlaw.org
Contact: Ms. Allison Hawkins, Marketing and Communications Mgr.

Founded: 1975. **Staff:** 25. **Languages:** English, Spanish. **Description:** Works to bring practical, participatory education about law, democracy, and human rights to classroom teachers; health and social services professionals; juvenile justice professionals; law enforcement; the legal community; and NGO leaders. Provides the members with programs and publications to empower and transform democratic ideals into a citizen action. Conducts programs in 50 states and over 30 countries. **Telecommunication Services:** electronic mail, ahawkins@streetlaw.org ● TDD, (202)546-7591. **Committees:** National Advisory. **Formerly:** (1982) National Street Law Institute; (1998) National Institute for Citizen Education in the Law. **Publications:** *Street Law Annual Report*, annual. Annual Reports ● *Street Law Ink*, quarterly. Newsletters ● Also makes available textbooks and teachers guides; produces mock trial kits and filmstrips.

6036 ■ Volunteer Lawyers for the Arts (VLA)
1 E 53rd St., 6th Fl.
New York, NY 10022
Ph: (212)319-2787 (212)319-2910
Fax: (212)752-6575
E-mail: epaul@vlany.org
URL: http://www.vlany.com
Contact: Elena M. Paul Esq., Exec. Dir.

Founded: 1969. **Members:** 800. **Membership Dues:** arts professional, $100 (annual) ● student, $50 (annual) ● legal professional level 1 (1 to 5 years experience), $150 (annual) ● legal professional level 2 (5 or more years experience), arts organization (budget of $99,999 or less), $200 (annual) ● arts organization (budget of $100,000 to $999,999), $375 (annual) ● arts organization (budget of $1,000,000 or more), $1,500 (annual). **Staff:** 7. **Budget:** $500,000. **Regional Groups:** 41. **Description:** Volunteer lawyers who provide free legal services to artists and art organizations in art-related legal matters. Works to familiarize the legal profession and the arts community with legal problems confronting artists and provide them with available solutions. Conducts special initiatives, internship and educational programs, seminars, and workshops. Maintains speakers' bureau; offers translation services for Spanish-speaking clients. Funded by the New York State Council on the Arts, individual contributions, corporations, and private foundations. **Libraries: Type:** reference. **Telecommunication Services:** electronic mail, jtominar@vlany.org. **Divisions:** Legal Services. **Sections:** Education. **Publications:** *Artists' Guide to Small Claims Court* ● *VLA Copyright Guide for Visual Artists, Musicians, Composers, and Performing Artists* ● *VLA National Directory*, annual. Alternate Formats: online ● Monographs ● Pamphlets. **Conventions/Meetings:** annual conference.

6037 ■ Western Center on Law and Poverty (WCLP)
3701 Wilshire Blvd., Ste.208
Los Angeles, CA 90010-2809
Ph: (213)487-7211
E-mail: info@wclp.org
URL: http://www.wclp.org
Contact: Syd Whalley, Exec. Dir.

Founded: 1968. **Staff:** 23. **Budget:** $2,005,000. **Description:** Provides legal counsel and representation to individuals and groups whose actions may effect change in institutions affecting the poor. Specializes in poverty law in California, offering litigation assistance and services to all neighborhood legal services programs. Concentrates on substantive areas of law including housing, health, and welfare. Acts as co-counsel with local legal services programs. Provides technical and research assistance to all legal aid offices throughout California. **Libraries: Type:** reference. **Holdings:** 12,000. **Awards:** Community Advocacy Award. **Frequency:** annual. **Type:** recognition ● Community Service Award. **Frequency:** annual. **Type:** recognition ● Public Service Award. **Frequency:** annual. **Type:** recognition. **Publications:** *Directory, California and Nevada Legal Services Programs*, annual. **Price:** $1.00 ● Newsletter, periodic.

Legislative Reform

6038 ■ National Order of Women Legislators (NOWL)
910 16th St., Ste.100
Washington, DC 20006
Ph: (202)293-3040
Fax: (202)293-5430
E-mail: robin_read@womenlegislators.org
URL: http://www.womenlegislators.org
Contact: Rep. Robin Read, Pres./CEO

Founded: 1938. **Members:** 1,600. **Membership Dues:** regular, $50 (annual). **Staff:** 11. **Description:** Women legislators. Strives to educate members on critical issues; assists members to become more effective through networking, and honing political and communication skills. **Publications:** *Connection*. Newsletter.

Lending

6039 ■ National Association of Government Guaranteed Lenders (NAGGL)
215 E 9th Ave.
Stillwater, OK 74074
Ph: (405)377-4022
Fax: (405)377-3931
E-mail: info@naggl.com
URL: http://www.naggl.org
Contact: Anthony R. Wilkinson, Pres./CEO

Founded: 1984. **Membership Dues:** regular, $495-$2,095 (annual) ● associate, $700 (annual) ● indirect lender, $875 (annual) ● sustaining, $2,625 (annual). **Staff:** 8. **Description:** Aims to serve the needs and represents the interests of the small business lending community who utilize the Small Business Administrations and other government guaranteed loan programs.

Liability

6040 ■ American Board of Professional Disability Consultants (ABPDC)
Address Unknown since 2007

Founded: 1988. **Members:** 400. **Membership Dues:** certified specialist, $235 (annual) ● diplomate, $295 (annual). **Staff:** 9. **Budget:** $25,000. **For-Profit. Description:** Physicians, psychologists, counselors, attorneys, and ancillary heath professionals. Identifies and awards diplomate standing to specialists in disability and personal injury. Responds to inquiries on disability and personal injury. Maintains speakers' bureau. **Libraries: Type:** reference. **Holdings:** archival material. **Awards: Frequency:** annual. **Type:** scholarship. **Recipient:** for children of members to attend graduate school. **Computer Services:** Mailing lists. **Publications:** *National Register of Professional Disability Consultants*, periodic. Directory. **Price:** $6.95. **Advertising:** accepted ● *Newsbrief*, periodic. Newsletter ● *Questions and Answers on Disability and Personal Injury*. Pamphlet.

6041 ■ American Board of Professional Liability Attorneys (ABPLA)
170 Wright Ave.
Malverne, NY 11565
Ph: (516)599-7700
Fax: (516)599-7701
E-mail: info@abpla.org
URL: http://www.abpla.org
Contact: Thomas W. Malone, Pres.

Founded: 1972. **Members:** 200. **Membership Dues:** diplomate, associate, $350 (annual). **Staff:** 2. **Description:** Accredited by the American Bar Association to certify Attorneys in the areas of medical, legal or accounting professional. Liability litigation attorneys who have satisfied requirements of litigation experience and who have passed the written liability examination. Promotes and improves ethical and technical standards of advocacy and litigation practice in professional liability litigation; establishes basic standards for training, qualification, and recognition of specialists; fosters efficient administration of justice. Provides graduated training program for licensed attorneys desiring certification as specialists in the field. Offers placement service; compiles statistics. Maintains file of abstracts and program transcripts. **Publications:** *Directory of Diplomates*, annual ● Newsletter, 3/year ● Proceedings, annual. **Conventions/Meetings:** annual meeting and seminar.

6042 ■ Defense Research Institute (DRI)
150 N Michigan Ave., Ste.300
Chicago, IL 60601
Ph: (312)795-1101
Fax: (312)795-0747
E-mail: dri@dri.org
URL: http://www.dri.org
Contact: Patrick A. Long, Pres.

Founded: 1960. **Members:** 22,000. **Membership Dues:** individual (defense attorney, government attorney, or young lawyer), $130-$225 (annual) ● corporate, $500 (annual) ● law student, $20 (annual) ● senior, $50 (annual). **Staff:** 30. **Budget:** $6,000,000. **Description:** Lawyers, claims people, adjusters, insurance companies, trade associations, corporations, and "target" defendants in civil litigation, such as doctors, pharmacists, engineers, manufacturers, and other professional and skilled personnel. Seeks to increase the knowledge and improve the skills of defense lawyers and to improve the adversary system of justice. Maintains research facilities, including files of speeches, briefs, and names of expert witnesses in various fields. Maintains Expert Witness Index. **Awards:** DRI Community Service Award. **Frequency:** annual. **Type:** recognition. **Recipient:** for a current or past active contributing individual member of DRI ● DRI Law Firm Diversity Award. **Frequency:** annual. **Type:** recognition. **Recipient:** for a DRI member ● Fred H. Sievert Award. **Frequency:** annual. **Type:** recognition. **Recipient:** for the outstanding Defense Bar Leader ● Louis B. Potter Lifetime Professional Service Award. **Frequency:** annual. **Type:** recognition. **Recipient:** for a current or past active contributing attorney member of DRI ● Outstanding Committee Chair Award. **Frequency:** annual. **Type:** recognition. **Recipient:** for a current or immediate past DRI Substantive Law and Practice Area Committee Chair ● Outstanding State Representative Award. **Frequency:** annual. **Type:** recognition. **Recipient:** for a current or immediate past DRI State Representative ● Rich Krochock Award. **Frequency:** annual. **Type:** recognition. **Recipient:** for a DRI member who has provided exemplary leadership to the DRI Young Lawyers Committee ● Rudolf A. Janata Award. **Frequency:** annual. **Type:** recognition. **Recipient:** for the outstanding Defense Bar Association. **Computer Services:** database, Expert Witness. **Committees:** Aerospace Law; Alternative Dispute Resolution; Apellate Advocacy; Commercial Litigation; Employment Law; Insurance Law; International Law; Law Practice Management; Lawyers' Professionalism and Ethics; Life, Health and Disability; Medical Liability and

Health Care Law; Product Liability; Professional Liability; Trial Tactics; Workers' Compensation. **Divisions:** Arbitration Program; Individual Research Service. **Publications:** *Awards Brochure*, annual. Alternate Formats: online ● *Directory of Members*, biennial. Membership Directory ● *For the Defense*, monthly. Magazine. **Advertising:** accepted ● *Publications Catalog*, annual ● *The Voice*, weekly. Newsletter. Alternate Formats: online ● Also publishes reprints and other special reports, monographs and pamphlets. **Conventions/Meetings:** annual meeting (exhibits) ● quarterly meeting.

6043 ■ Inner Circle of Advocates (ICA)
c/o Dennis Donnelly, Pres.
1 Main St.
Chatham, NJ 07928
Ph: (973)635-5400
E-mail: inquiry@innercircle.org
URL: http://www.innercircle.org
Contact: Dennis Donnelly, Pres.
Founded: 1972. **Members:** 100. **Description:** Attorneys who have won jury damage awards for single personal injury or death claims of one million dollars or more (membership is by invitation only). Seeks to facilitate the exchange of views, information, and research. **Telecommunication Services:** electronic mail, ddonnell@njatty.com. **Conventions/Meetings:** annual conference.

6044 ■ National Association of Forensic Economics (NAFE)
PO Box 394
Mount Union, PA 17066
Ph: (814)542-3253
Free: (866)370-6233
Fax: (814)542-3253
E-mail: gskoog@umich.edu
URL: http://nafe.net
Contact: Gary R. Skoog, Pres.
Founded: 1986. **Members:** 800. **Membership Dues:** individual, institution, $165 (annual) ● student, $80 (annual). **Staff:** 3. **Regional Groups:** 4. **Description:** Economists, financial analysts, appraisers, attorneys, and libraries promoting research and professional development in forensic economics. (Forensic economics are applied when determining compensation in litigation involving economic liability, including personal injury and death, negligence, medical malpractice, discrimination, business valuation, contracts, anti-trust, and rehabilitation.) Sponsors professional seminars and workshops on economic testimony in litigation. Compiles statistics; maintains speakers' bureau. **Computer Services:** Electronic publishing, past issues of journal available on website. **Affiliated With:** Allied Social Science Associations. **Formerly:** (1992) National Association of Forensic Economists. **Publications:** *Journal of Forensic Economics*, 3/year. Contains articles of interest to economists, accountants, finance and business professionals, vocational counselors, lawyers, and actuaries. **Price:** included in membership dues. ISSN: 0898-5510. **Circulation:** 800. **Advertising:** accepted ● *Litigation Economics Review*, semiannual. Journal ● *NAFE News*, quarterly. Newsletter. Alternate Formats: online. **Conventions/Meetings:** annual luncheon, held in conjunction with ASSA - 1st week in January.

Libel

6045 ■ Media Law Resource Center (MLRC)
North Tower, 20th Fl.
520 Eight Ave.
New York, NY 10018
Ph: (212)337-0200
Fax: (212)337-9893
E-mail: medialaw@medialaw.org
URL: http://www.medialaw.org
Contact: Sandra S. Baron, Exec. Dir.
Founded: 1980. **Members:** 300. **Membership Dues:** associate, $500-$1,250 (annual) ● media company (minimum), $2,000 (annual). **Staff:** 7. **Description:** Provides support for media defendants in libel and privacy cases, including development of statistical and empirical data, assistance in locating expert witnesses or consultants, and help in coordinating amicus curiae briefs by supporting organizations. Maintains a brief, pleading, and information bank; collects and disseminates information on pending libel and privacy cases for use in legal defense against claims. Serves as a liaison with media organizations, attorneys, and other groups working to advance the defense of libel and privacy claims. Prepares bulletins and reports on current developments and cases, legal theories, privileges, and defenses. Compiles statistics on the incidence and cost of libel and privacy litigation. Provides employment for law student interns. Conducts educational and training workshops and programs; has established fellowship program in libel law. Operates MLRC Institute. **Libraries: Type:** reference. **Subjects:** libel, privacy, related law. **Awards:** William J. Brennan Jr. Defense of Freedom Award. **Frequency:** annual. **Type:** recognition. **Computer Services:** database, brief bank, brief digests, and case data bank. **Telecommunication Services:** electronic mail, sbaron@medialaw.org. **Sections:** Defense Counsel. **Formerly:** (2003) Libel Defense Resource Center. **Publications:** *Annual 50-State Survey of Media Privacy and Related Law; 50-State Survey-Employment Libel and Privacy Law; 50 State Survey Media Libel Law*, annual. **Price:** $175.00. **Circulation:** 500 ● *MediaLawLetter*, monthly. Newsletter. Contains articles and updates on court decisions and legislative initiatives of interest in the U.S. and abroad. ● Bulletin, quarterly. Reports on trends, developments, and news in First Amendment law and litigation. **Price:** $35.00/issue ● Also publishes special studies and reports. **Conventions/Meetings:** biennial Conference on Media Libel, Privacy and Related First Amendment Issues, held in conjunction with National Association of Broadcasters and Newspaper Association of America ● annual dinner.

Libertarianism

6046 ■ Libertarian Nation Foundation (LNF)
335 Mulberry St.
Raleigh, NC 27604
E-mail: info@libertariannation.org
URL: http://libertariannation.org
Contact: Bobby Yates Emory, Pres.
Founded: 2001. **Membership Dues:** regular, $30 (annual). **Description:** "The purpose of the Libertarian Nation Foundation is to advance the day when coercive institutions of government can be replaced by voluntary institutions of civil mutual consent, by developing clear and believable descriptions of those voluntary institutions, and by building a community of people who share confidence in these descriptions.". **Libraries: Type:** reference. **Telecommunication Services:** electronic mail, liberty1@deltaforce.net. **Affiliated With:** Free Nation Foundation - Critical Institutions. **Publications:** *Formulations*, quarterly. Journal. **Price:** $15.00/year; $4.00/issue ● Annual Report, annual ● Papers. **Conventions/Meetings:** board meeting.

Libraries

6047 ■ Office for Intellectual Freedom (OIF)
c/o Judith F. Krug, Dir.
Amer. Lib. Assn.
50 E Huron St.
Chicago, IL 60611
Free: (800)545-2433
Fax: (312)280-4227
E-mail: oif@ala.org
URL: http://www.ala.org/alaorg/oif
Contact: Judith F. Krug, Dir.
Description: Implements the intellectual freedom policies of the American Library Association; educates librarians and public on the Library Bill of Rights. **Publications:** *Intellectual Freedom Manual, 6th Edition*. Handbook ● *Newsletter on Intellectual Freedom*, bimonthly. Alternate Formats: online.

Lotteries

6048 ■ North American Association of State and Provincial Lotteries (NASPL)
6 N Broadway
Geneva, OH 44041
Ph: (440)466-5630
Fax: (440)466-5649
E-mail: info@nasplhq.org
Contact: Clint Harris, Pres.
Founded: 1973. **Members:** 50. **Membership Dues:** sanctioned state and provincial lottery, $12,000 (annual). **Staff:** 6. **Budget:** $1,000,000. **Regional Groups:** 4. **State Groups:** 38. **Description:** North American lottery organization directors. Conducts meetings to exchange information on security, sales, marketing, public relations, operations, and internal controls. Assists jurisdictions in establishing lotteries. **Libraries: Type:** not open to the public. **Holdings:** 100; articles, books, periodicals. **Subjects:** state and provincial lottery organizations. **Awards:** Batchy, Hickey, and Powers Award. **Frequency:** annual. **Type:** recognition. **Recipient:** for best TV, radio and print lottery ads. **Committees:** Awards; Education and Training; Legal; Research and Resources; Sales and Marketing; Security. **Formerly:** (1986) National Association of State Lotteries. **Publications:** *NASPL Lottery Insights*, monthly. Magazine. Contains lottery news. **Price:** $150.00/year. **Circulation:** 1,400. **Advertising:** accepted. **Conventions/Meetings:** annual conference and trade show (exhibits).

Maoism

6049 ■ Maoist Internationalist Movement (MIM)
c/o MIM Distributors
PO Box 29670
Los Angeles, CA 90029-0670
E-mail: mim@mim.org
URL: http://www.etext.org/Politics/MIM
Founded: 1983. **Multinational. Description:** Works to uphold communist ideology of Marxism-Leninism-Maoism; works to end oppression of all groups over other groups: classes, genders, nations. **Telecommunication Services:** electronic mail, mim3@mim.org. **Formerly:** (2003) Maoist International Movement. **Publications:** *Maoist Sojourner*, bimonthly. Newspaper. Focuses on societies where the labor aristocracy does not play a big role as it does in the imperialist countries. ● *MIM Notes* (in English and Spanish), bimonthly. Newsletter. Alternate Formats: online ● *MIM Theory*, 14/year. Journal. Includes collection of existing or emerging Maoist internationalist parties. **Price:** $59.00 ● *Notas Rojas* (in Spanish). Newspaper.

Marine

6050 ■ International Cargo Gear Bureau (ICGB)
321 W 44th St.
New York, NY 10036
Ph: (212)757-2011
Fax: (212)757-2650
E-mail: charles-visconti@icgb.com
URL: http://www.icgb.com
Contact: Charles G. Visconti, Pres./Chm.
Founded: 1954. **Description:** Provides recognized registration, inspection, certification, documentation, design evaluation and consultation services for materials handling equipment ashore and afloat. **Telecommunication Services:** electronic mail, roy-monturi@icgb.com. **Publications:** *ICGB-104 Guide* ● *Reference Manual* ● Directory, periodic. **Conventions/Meetings:** annual meeting.

6051 ■ United States Marine Safety Association (USMSA)
5050 Indus. Rd.
Farmingdale, NJ 07727
Ph: (732)751-0102

Fax: (732)751-0508
URL: http://www.usmsa.org
Contact: Tom Thompson, Exec. Dir.
Founded: 1987. **Members:** 150. **Membership Dues:** manufacturer, $1,235 (annual) ● secondary manufacturer, service organization, $5,775 (annual) ● associate, $375 (annual) ● subscriber, $195 (annual). **Staff:** 2. **Budget:** $90,000. **Description:** Represents service stations, manufacturers, manufacturers' representatives, distributors, trainers, and other individuals promoting safety at sea. **Committees:** Electronics; Immersion Suit; Life Raft Manufacturers; Pyrotechnics; Recreational; Service Station; Training/Medical. **Councils:** International Photoluminescent Safety Products. **Publications:** *Care and Inspection*. Booklet ● *Life Raft Servicing*. Pamphlet ● Newsletter, quarterly. **Price:** available to members only ● Membership Directory, annual. **Conventions/Meetings:** annual meeting.

Marine Corps

6052 ■ Marine Corps Aviation Reconnaissance Association (MCARA)
Address Unknown since 2008
URL: http://business.quadlink.net/adirondack/mcara
Founded: 1990. **Membership Dues:** officer, $15 (annual) ● enlisted, $25 (annual) ● life (for members over 62 years of age), $100. **Description:** Represents the interests of Marines who were attached to or served with units of the Marine Corps Aviation Reconnaissance Squadrons. Conducts aerial photographic reconnaissance and airborne electronic countermeasures in support of Fleet Marine Force Operations.

Maritime Law

6053 ■ Center for Seafarers' Rights (CSR)
c/o Seamen's Church Institute of New York/New Jersey
241 Water St.
New York, NY 10038
Ph: (212)349-9090
Fax: (212)349-8342
E-mail: csr@seamenschurch.org
URL: http://www.seamenschurch.org/CSR%20Website/center_for_seafarers.htm
Contact: Rev. Douglas B. Stevenson Esq., Dir.
Founded: 1982. **Staff:** 3. **Budget:** $300,000. **Local Groups:** 600. **Description:** A division of Seamen's Church Institute of New York/New Jersey. Aims to protect, empower, and support merchant seafarers through: researching maritime laws; advocating for national and international structures of legal protection for seafarers; advising individual seafarers and their advocates. Holds international seminars on seafarers' rights issues. **Libraries: Type:** reference. **Holdings:** 500. **Subjects:** maritime law and custom. **Publications:** *The Rights of Seafarers*, periodic.

6054 ■ Law of the Sea Institute (LOSI)
c/o Institute of Legal Research
381 Boalt Hall
Univ. of California, Berkeley
Berkeley, CA 94720-7200
Ph: (510)642-5125 (510)643-9788
Fax: (510)643-2698
E-mail: losi@law.berkeley.edu
URL: http://www.law.berkeley.edu/centers/ilr/lawofthesea.html
Contact: Prof. Harry N. Scheiber, Co-Dir.
Founded: 1965. **Members:** 200. **Staff:** 3. **Multinational. Description:** Works to stimulate and exchange information and ideas relating to international law, politics, economics, and technology of the sea. **Telecommunication Services:** electronic mail, scheiber@uclink.berkeley.edu. **Publications:** *Law of the Sea in the 1990s: A Framework for Further International Cooperation*. Book ● *The Law of the Sea: New Worlds, New Discoveries*. Book ● *The Marine Environment and Sustainable Development: Law, Policy, and Science*. Book ● *Moscow Symposium on the Law of the Sea*. Book ● *Proceedings of Annual Law of the Sea Institute Conference*, annual. **Price:** $58.00/copy. ISSN: 0557-8620 ● *The Role of the Oceans in the 21st Century*. Proceedings. **Price:** $58.00/copy ● *San Diego International Law Journal*, semiannual. Provides forum for legal scholarship with respect to the pertinent and pressing issues in international and comparative law. ● Papers. **Conventions/Meetings:** annual conference (exhibits) ● workshop.

6055 ■ Maritime Law Association of the U.S. (MLA)
80 Pine St.
New York, NY 10005-1759
Ph: (212)425-1900
Fax: (212)425-1901
E-mail: bonner@freehill.com
URL: http://www.mlaus.org
Contact: Patrick Bonner, Second VP
Founded: 1899. **Members:** 3,123. **Membership Dues:** individual, $125 (annual). **Description:** Lawyers and others interested in maritime law. Provides advisers to government and industry officials. Maintains microfiche collection. **Affiliated With:** American Bar Association. **Publications:** *Committee Reports*, periodic ● *MLA Report*, semiannual ● *President's Newsletter*, semiannual ● Membership Directory, annual ● Proceedings, semiannual. **Conventions/Meetings:** semiannual seminar - always first Friday in May and third Friday in October.

Merchant Marine

6056 ■ American Maritime Association (AMA)
Address Unknown since 2008
Founded: 1961. **Members:** 25. **Staff:** 1. **Description:** U.S. flag steamship companies, which operate vessels in foreign and domestic trades. Conducts collective bargaining with the various off-shore maritime unions and promotes a strong American Merchant Marine. **Publications:** none. **Convention/Meeting:** none.

6057 ■ American Maritime Congress (AMC)
400 N Capitol St. NW, Ste.G-50
Washington, DC 20001
Ph: (202)347-8020
Fax: (202)347-1550
E-mail: diannelauer@americanmaritime.org
URL: http://www.americanmaritime.org
Contact: Ron Davis, Chm.
Founded: 1977. **Staff:** 7. **Description:** Research and education organization representing major U.S.-flag ship operating companies that have contracts with the National Marine Engineers' Beneficial Association. Disseminates information for promotion of a strong U.S.-flag Merchant Marine. Maintains speakers' bureau; assists maritime researchers. **Libraries: Type:** reference. **Formerly:** (1989) Joint Maritime Congress. **Publications:** *American Maritime Congress Washington Letter*, weekly. Newsletter. **Price:** $295.00/year ● Directory, periodic.

6058 ■ American Maritime Officers Service (AMOS)
490 L'Enfant Plz. SW, Ste.7204
Washington, DC 20024
Ph: (202)479-1133
Fax: (202)479-1136
URL: http://www.amo.org
Contact: Gordon Spencer, Legislative Dir.
Founded: 1975. **Members:** 75. **Description:** Consists of U.S. shipping companies united to represent the interests of the U.S. Merchant Marine. Encourages development of a versatile maritime fleet; provides commercial vessels to support U.S. military operations during times of peace as well as conflict. **Publications:** *News Briefs*, quarterly. Magazine. **Conventions/Meetings:** semiannual meeting.

6059 ■ Chamber of Shipping of America (CSA)
1730 M St. NW, Ste.407
Washington, DC 20036-4517
Ph: (202)775-4399
Fax: (202)659-3795
URL: http://www.knowships.com
Contact: Joseph J. Cox, Pres./CEO
Founded: 1969. **Members:** 20. **Staff:** 3. **Budget:** $550,000. **Description:** U.S. based companies that own and operate tankers, dry bulk carriers, container ships, and other oceangoing vessels in U.S. foreign and domestic commerce. Serves as a spokesman for the U.S. shipping industry, with respect to maritime issues and establishment of a strong, well-balanced American flag fleet adequate to meet the national needs for both commerce and defense. Testifies before congressional committees in support of legislation to realize these goals. Keeps in touch with federal and state government agencies concerning maritime matters. Participates in numerous international forums such as International Maritime Organization, and International Labor Organization. U.S. member of International Chamber of Shipping and International Shipping Federation. **Awards:** Halert C. Shepheard Award. **Frequency:** periodic. **Type:** recognition. **Recipient:** to an individual in recognition of exceptional achievement toward merchant marine safety ● Jones F. Devlin Award. **Type:** recognition. **Recipient:** for achievement in merchant marine safety ● Ship Safety Achievement Award. **Type:** recognition. **Recipient:** to vessels that have outstanding feats of safety. **Formed by Merger of:** (1968) American Merchant Marine Institute; (1968) Pacific American Steamship Association; (1968) Committee of American Steamship Lines. **Formerly:** (1997) American Institute of Merchant Shipping; (1998) United States Chamber of Shipping. **Publications:** *Environmental Criminal Liability in the United States*. Handbook. **Price:** $50.00. Alternate Formats: online. **Conventions/Meetings:** annual meeting.

6060 ■ Maritime Institute for Research and Industrial Development (MIRAID)
Address Unknown since 2008
Founded: 1978. **Members:** 25. **Staff:** 6. **Description:** Inland and ocean-going maritime transportation companies. Purpose is to promote the U.S. merchant marine. Conducts research on legislation and federal agency regulations affecting the maritime industry. Acts as clearinghouse for members; compiles statistics. **Conventions/Meetings:** annual board meeting - always Washington, DC or Baltimore, MD.

Military

6061 ■ Adjutants General Association of the United States (AGAUS)
c/o Terri Kattes
Nebraska Military Dept.
1300 Military Rd.
Lincoln, NE 68508-1090
Ph: (402)309-7107
Fax: (402)309-7128
E-mail: terri.kattes@ne.ngb.army.mil
URL: http://www.ngaus.org
Contact: Major Gen. Roger P. Lempke, Pres.
Founded: 1909. **Members:** 54. **Membership Dues:** general, $250 (annual). **Budget:** $13,000. **State Groups:** 54. **Description:** Adjutants General (National Guard) of the states and territories. **Awards:** George Washington Freedom Award. **Frequency:** annual. **Type:** recognition. **Additional Websites:** http://www.agaus.org. **Conventions/Meetings:** annual conference (exhibits).

6062 ■ Air Force Association (AFA)
1501 Lee Hwy.
Arlington, VA 22209-1198
Ph: (703)247-5800
Free: (800)727-3337
Fax: (703)247-5853

E-mail: polcom@afa.org
URL: http://www.afa.org
Contact: Donald L. Peterson, Exec. Dir.
Founded: 1946. **Members:** 140,000. **Membership Dues:** individual, $36 (annual) ● life, $500 ● cadet/enlisted, $18 (annual) ● in Canada and Mexico, $46 (annual) ● foreign, $65 (annual). **Staff:** 76. **Budget:** $11,000,000. **State Groups:** 47. **Local Groups:** 330. **Description:** Promotes public understanding of aerospace power and the pivotal role it plays in the security of the nation. **Awards:** National Aerospace Award. **Frequency:** annual. **Type:** recognition. **Recipient:** for the most productive individual of the association ● Team of the Year Award. **Frequency:** annual. **Type:** recognition. **Recipient:** for professionals who display superior technical expertise and provide leadership and inspiration to their co-workers. **Telecommunication Services:** electronic mail, service@afa.org. **Councils:** Air National Guard; Civilian Personnel; Enlisted; Junior Officer Advisory; Reserve; Veterans/Retiree. **Affiliated With:** Arnold Air Society; Silver Wings. **Absorbed:** Air Reserve Association; (2006) Aerospace Education Foundation. **Publications:** Magazine, monthly. **Price:** $36.00/year; $4.00 each. **Advertising:** accepted. Alternate Formats: online. **Conventions/Meetings:** annual National Convention and Aerospace Technology Exposition - in Washington, DC ● annual symposium (exhibits) - in Los Angeles, California ● annual Tactical Air Warfare Symposium - in Orlando, Florida.

6063 ■ Air Force Sergeants Association (AFSA)
5211 Auth Rd.
Suitland, MD 20746
Ph: (301)899-3500
Free: (800)638-0594
Fax: (301)899-8136
E-mail: staff@afsahq.org
URL: http://www.afsahq.org
Founded: 1961. **Members:** 135,000. **Staff:** 28. **Budget:** $4,500,000. **Regional Groups:** 16. **Local Groups:** 302. **Description:** Any enlisted man or woman, active or retired, in the Air Force, Air National Guard, Air Force Reserve, Army Air Corps, or Army Air Forces; women auxiliaries. Works to: promote, preserve, and uphold fair and equitable legislation as it pertains to the welfare of the airmen who served and are serving in the U.S.A.F; maintain the highest professional standards and integrity among members; promote the interests of members, the U.S., and the rest of the "free world"; promote religious, educational, and recreational activities among members, in order to develop a better understanding and mutual respect. Sponsors educational seminars, Air Force training, JOBCAP - a job placement service, and programs for retired members. Provides congressional representation, insurance, and other services. **Awards:** Chapter of the Year. **Frequency:** annual. **Type:** recognition ● Member of the Year. **Frequency:** annual. **Type:** recognition ● **Type:** recognition. **Recipient:** for heroism and excellence ● **Type:** scholarship. **Recipient:** for dependent children. **Committees:** Field Operations; Government Relations; Marketing. **Publications:** *AFSA Newsletter*, weekly. Newsletters ● *Field Operations Management Manual* ● *Lobby Ledger*, periodic ● *Sergeants*, monthly. Magazine ● *Viewpoint*, quarterly ● *Worldwide Directory*, biennial. **Conventions/Meetings:** Professional Airmen's Conference and Annual Convention - meeting (exhibits) - always July/August.

6064 ■ American Logistics Association (ALA)
1133 15th St. NW, Ste.640
Washington, DC 20005
Ph: (202)466-2520
Fax: (202)296-4419
E-mail: membership@ala-national.org
URL: http://www.ala-national.org
Contact: John Molino, Pres.
Founded: 1920. **Members:** 2,000. **Membership Dues:** individual, $100 (annual). **Staff:** 12. **Budget:** $2,500,000. **Local Groups:** 24. **Description:** Promotes, protects and ensures the continued viability of the military resale (Commissary and Exchange Benefits) and Morale, Welfare and Recreations (MWR Benefits) industries. Acts as liaison between manufacturers and the Armed Forces' purchasing agencies. Promotes cooperation between the Congress, Defense Department and the industries which it conducts business. **Awards:** Distinguished Service Award. **Frequency:** annual. **Type:** recognition. **Telecommunication Services:** electronic mail, john@ala-national.org. **Committees:** Commissary; Exchange. **Formerly:** Defense Supply Association; Quartermaster Association. **Publications:** *Executive Briefing*, monthly. Newsletter. Alternate Formats: online ● *Worldwide Directory and FactBook*, annual. **Advertising:** accepted. **Conventions/Meetings:** annual All Services Exchange Roundtable ● annual convention ● annual Defense Commissary Agency (DeCA) Training Conference ● annual Government Relations Forum - trade show (exhibits) ● biennial MWR Expo (Morale, Welfare, and Recreation) - trade show (exhibits) ● annual Veterans Canteen Service (VCS) Show and Sell - trade show.

6065 ■ American Military Society (AMS)
PO Box 98186
Washington, DC 20090-8186
Free: (800)379-6128
Fax: (301)925-6920
URL: http://www.amsmilitary.org
Contact: Doug Russell, Pres.
Founded: 1982. **Members:** 30,000. **Membership Dues:** single, $20 (annual) ● joint, $30 (annual) ● joint life, $400 ● single life, $300. **Staff:** 3. **Budget:** $200,000. **Description:** Active or retired members of the armed services (Army, Navy, Air Force, Marine Corps, and Coast Guard), and civilians. Develops and supports activities which promote the general well-being of the members; upholds and defends the Constitution; supports national defense; and preserves the memories and traditions of the Armed Forces. **Computer Services:** database ● mailing lists ● online services. **Publications:** *Advocate*, bimonthly. Newsletter. Contains up-to-the-minute developments regarding military matters and legislative issues. **Advertising:** accepted. Alternate Formats: online. **Conventions/Meetings:** annual meeting.

6066 ■ American Society of Military Comptrollers (ASMC)
415 N Alfred St.
Alexandria, VA 22314
Ph: (703)549-0360
Free: (800)462-5637
Fax: (703)549-3181
E-mail: asmchq@asmconline.org
URL: http://www.asmconline.org
Contact: Hon. Robert F. Hale CDFM, Exec. Dir.
Founded: 1949. **Members:** 18,000. **Membership Dues:** active/associate, $26 (annual) ● corporate, $250 (annual). **Staff:** 3. **Budget:** $2,787,556. **Local Groups:** 145. **Description:** Civilians and military personnel who are now or who have been involved in the overall field of military comptrollership; other interested individuals. Conducts research programs. Compiles statistics; maintains speakers' bureau. Plans to establish library. **Publications:** *Armed Forces Comptroller*, quarterly. Journal. Covers financial management, resource management, and comptrollership in the Department of Defense and the Coast Guard. **Price:** included in membership dues; $15.00 for libraries and organizations in U.S.; $18.00 for libraries and organizations outside U.S. ISSN: 0004-2188. **Circulation:** 18,000. **Advertising:** accepted ● *Chapter Newsletter*. Booklet. Provides assistance to chapters already conducting newsletters by offering suggestions as to how these can be improved. ● Bulletin. Facilitates communication between chapters. ● Also plans to publish a directory. **Conventions/Meetings:** competition ● annual Professional Development Institute Conference - meeting (exhibits) - usually May ● seminar.

6067 ■ Armed Forces Communications and Electronics Association (AFCEA)
c/o Tobey Jackson, Promotions and PR Mgr.
4400 Fair Lakes Ct.
Fairfax, VA 22033-3899
Ph: (703)631-6100
Free: (800)336-4583
Fax: (703)631-6169
E-mail: promo@afcea.org
URL: http://www.afcea.org
Contact: Tobey Jackson, Promotions and PR Mgr.
Founded: 1946. **Members:** 30,000. **Membership Dues:** individual, corporate, $35 (annual). **Local Groups:** 134. **Multinational. Description:** Serves as a bridge between government requirements and industry capabilities. Represents top government, industry, and military professionals in the fields of communications, intelligence, information systems, imaging, and multi-media. Aims for the continuing education of its members and for peace through civil government effectiveness and military and industrial preparedness. Supports global security by providing an ethical environment encouraging a close cooperative relationship among civil government agencies, the military and industry. **Awards: Type:** recognition. **Telecommunication Services:** electronic mail, service@afcea.org. **Publications:** *SIGNAL*, monthly. Journal. Covers the international disciplines of communication, intelligence and information systems. **Price:** included in membership dues. ISSN: 0037-4938. **Circulation:** 32,000. **Advertising:** accepted. Alternate Formats: online. **Conventions/Meetings:** annual conference and trade show, conference and exposition focusing on current defense and IT issues (exhibits) ● annual Homeland Security IT Conference - conference and trade show, conference and exposition focusing on current defense and IT issues (exhibits) ● annual TechNet Asia-Pacific - conference and trade show, conference and exposition focusing on current defense and IT issues (exhibits) ● annual TechNet International - conference and trade show, conference and exposition focusing on current defense and IT issues (exhibits).

6068 ■ Armed Forces Hostess Association (AFHA)
The Pentagon, Rm. ID110
6604 Army Pentagon
Washington, DC 20310-6604
Ph: (703)697-3180 (703)697-6857
Fax: (703)693-9510
URL: http://www.army.mil/afha/main.html
Founded: 1949. **Description:** Information office operated by volunteer wives of the armed forces. Assists in welcoming service families to the Washington, DC area; provides information on living conditions at all U.S. installations in the U.S. and overseas. Maintains information files on topics ranging from animal care and camps to universities and local vacation areas. **Formerly:** (1949) Army Hostess Association.

6069 ■ Armed Forces Sports (AFS)
The Summit Center
4700 King St., 4th Fl.
Alexandria, VA 22302-4418
Ph: (703)681-7215
Free: (888)875-PLAY
Fax: (703)681-7245
E-mail: afs@cfs.army.mil
URL: http://www.armedforcessports.com
Contact: Suba Saty, Sec.
Founded: 1948. **Staff:** 2. **Description:** Persons serving as head of the morale and welfare activities of the U.S. Army, Navy, Marines, and Air Force. Encourages physical fitness in the armed forces through a policy of "sports for all"; has established uniform rules to govern all service sports within its jurisdiction. Conducts interservice sports championship competitions. Develops and encourages spectator interest sports for the individual services. Selects and sends military athletes and teams to national and international competitions; has representative on the Executive Board and House of Delegates of the U.S. Olympic Committee, various U.S. sports governing bodies, and the International Military Sports Council. Compiles statistics. **Formerly:** (1970) Interservice Sports Council; (1985) Interservice Sports Committee; (2001) Armed Forces Sports Committee. **Publications:** *U.S. Armed Forces Sports Yearbook*. **Con-**

ventions/Meetings: quarterly meeting - usually January, April, July, and October.

6070 ■ Army Aviation Association of America (AAAA)
755 Main St., Ste.4D
Monroe, CT 06468-2830
Ph: (203)268-2450
Fax: (203)268-5870
E-mail: aaaa@quad-a.org
URL: http://www.quad-a.org
Contact: William R. Harris Jr., Exec. Dir.

Founded: 1957. **Members:** 14,500. **Membership Dues:** individual, corporate, $26 (annual) ● student, $15 (annual) ● life, $480. **Staff:** 8. **Regional Groups:** 1. **State Groups:** 50. **Description:** Commissioned officers, warrant officers, and enlisted personnel serving in U.S. Army aviation assignments in the active U.S. Army, Army National Guard, and Army Reserve; Department of Army civilian personnel and industry representatives affiliated with army aviation. Fosters fellowship among military and civilian persons connected with army aviation, past or present; seeks to advance status, overall esprit, and general knowledge of professionals engaged in army aviation. Activities include locator and placement services, technical assistance, and biographical archives. Sponsors speakers' bureau; maintains hall of fame. **Awards:** Historical Award. **Frequency:** annual. **Type:** recognition. **Recipient:** for individuals who have made outstanding contributions or innovation in the employment of Army Aviation ● **Type:** scholarship. **Recipient:** to members and their siblings, children, and spouses. **Publications:** *Army Aviation*, 10/year. Magazine. Provides an essential public forum for the current and future leaders in the military community. **Price:** included in membership dues; $30.00 /year for nonmembers. ISSN: 0004-248X. **Circulation:** 14,000. **Advertising:** accepted. **Conventions/Meetings:** annual convention (exhibits).

6071 ■ Association of the United States Army (AUSA)
2425 Wilson Blvd.
Arlington, VA 22201
Ph: (703)841-4300
Free: (800)336-4570
Fax: (703)525-9039
E-mail: ausa-info@ausa.org
URL: http://www.ausa.org
Contact: Gen. Gordon R. Sullivan, Pres.

Founded: 1950. **Members:** 100,000. **Membership Dues:** individual, $12-$38 (annual) ● corporate (based on number of designees), $150-$585 (annual) ● life, $250-$525 ● sustaining, $5,000 (annual). **Staff:** 70. **Budget:** $12,000,000. **Regional Groups:** 10. **Local Groups:** 132. **Description:** Professional society of: active, retired, and reserve military personnel; West Point and Army ROTC cadets; civilians interested in national defense. Seeks to advance the security of the United States and consolidate the efforts of all who support the United States Army as an indispensable instrument of national security. Conducts industrial symposia for manufacturers of Army weapons and equipment, and those in the Department of the Army who plan, develop, test, and use weapons and equipment. Symposia subjects have included guided missiles, army aviation, electronics and communication, telemedicine, vehicles, and armor. Sponsors monthly PBS TV series America's Army. **Libraries: Type:** reference. **Holdings:** articles, books, periodicals. **Subjects:** military history, government. **Awards:** AUSA ROTC Medals. **Frequency:** annual. **Type:** medal. **Recipient:** for excellence in military studies, ROTC ● Certificate of Achievement. **Type:** recognition. **Recipient:** for outstanding accomplishments and service to the U.S. Army or AUSA ● Certificate of Appreciation. **Type:** recognition. **Recipient:** for outstanding contributions through service to AUSA or the U.S. Army ● Citation for Exceptional Service. **Type:** recognition. **Recipient:** for significant contributions to AUSA, U.S. Army, or national defense ● Gen. Creighton W. Abrams Medal. **Frequency:** annual. **Type:** medal. **Recipient:** for advancement of the U.S. Army ● George Catlett Marshall Medal. **Type:** medal. **Recipient:** for "selfless service to the United States of America" ● John W. Dixon Medal. **Frequency:** annual. **Type:** medal. **Recipient:** for member of industry, for outstanding contribution to national defense ● President's Medal. **Frequency:** annual. **Type:** medal. **Recipient:** for the advancement of the mission of AUSA ● **Type:** recognition. **Recipient:** for significant contributions to the advancement of the U.S. Army and the Association. **Computer Services:** database, only available to local chapters. **Telecommunication Services:** electronic mail, gsullivan@ausa.org. **Programs:** Book; Family. **Absorbed:** (1955) U.S. Antiaircraft Association. **Formerly:** U.S. Infantry Association; U.S. Field Artillery Association. **Publications:** *Army*, monthly. Journal. Includes letters from members and book reviews. **Price:** included in membership dues; $3.00/ issue; $33.00 /year for nonmembers; $90.00/3 years for nonmembers. ISSN: 0004-2455. **Circulation:** 90,000. **Advertising:** accepted. Alternate Formats: microform ● *AUSA News*, monthly. Covers association activities; includes legislative news and information regarding military reunions. **Price:** available to members only. ISSN: 1075-458X. **Advertising:** accepted ● *Defense Reports*, monthly ● *Land Warfare Essays*, 6-8/year ● *Land Warfare Papers*, 2-4/year ● *NCO Update*, bimonthly ● *Special Reports*, 4-5/year ● *Washington Update*, monthly. **Conventions/Meetings:** periodic symposium, focuses on army and industry information exchange (exhibits) - 5-6/year ● annual meeting, includes presentation by army leaders, scholarly presentation and association committee meetings and workshops (exhibits) - 2008 Oct. 6-8, Washington, DC; 2009 Oct. 5-7, Washington, DC; 2010 Oct. 8-10, Washington, DC.

6072 ■ Chief Warrant and Warrant Officers Association, United States Coast Guard (CWOA)
200 V St. SW
Washington, DC 20024
Ph: (202)554-7753
Fax: (202)484-0641
E-mail: cwoauscg@verizon.net
Contact: Mr. Ed Swift, Exec. Dir.

Founded: 1929. **Members:** 3,300. **Membership Dues:** individual, $36 (annual). **Staff:** 1. **Budget:** $180,000. **Local Groups:** 20. **Description:** Individuals who currently hold or once held the rank of Warrant Officer or Chief Warrant Officer on the active, retired, and reserve rolls of the U.S. Coast Guard. Works to aid members in advancing their professional abilities. Seeks to enhance their value, loyalty, and devotion to the service; promotes its unity and morale through social association. **Awards:** CWOA John A. Keller Scholarship Grant. **Frequency:** annual. **Type:** scholarship. **Recipient:** for members' children. **Committees:** Scholarship. **Publications:** *CWO News*, monthly. Newsletter. **Conventions/Meetings:** annual meeting - always April.

6073 ■ Citizen Soldier (CS)
267 5th Ave., Ste.901
New York, NY 10016
Ph: (212)679-2250
Fax: (212)679-2252
URL: http://www.citizen-soldier.org
Contact: Tod Ensign, Dir.

Founded: 1969. **Members:** 7,000. **Staff:** 2. **Budget:** $100,000. **Description:** Individuals concerned with military-civilian relationships within American society. Aims to help Vietnam War veterans who may have been harmed by highly toxic herbicides (including Agent Orange) that were used in Vietnam between 1962 and 1970. Works with veterans who were exposed to low-level radiation at Nevada and South Pacific A-bomb test sites and Persian Gulf War veterans suffering from unexplained chronic ailments. Represents GIs on active duty who are victims of military racism and/or sexism. Assists GIs who have been prosecuted or otherwise punished due to positive results on drug residue urine tests that CS believes to have been inaccurate because of defective laboratory work. Seeks to protect the rights of soldiers testing positive for the AIDS antibody. Advocates for veterans suffering from Persian Gulf Syndrome. Promotes a public service campaign to inform service members of their legal rights regarding the military's HIV testing program. Works with high school and college youths to address concerns on military recruiting practices. Maintains speakers' bureau. Advises GIs who wish alternatives to service in current Iraqi War. **Computer Services:** Mailing lists, donors. **Publications:** *America's Military Today*. Book. **Price:** $27.95 hard cover ● *Metal of Dishonor: Depleted Uranium Weapons*. Book. Deals with issues of chemical weapons exposure of US troops in Persian Gulf. **Price:** $12.00 postpaid.

6074 ■ Civil Affairs Association (CAA)
10130 Hyla Brook Rd.
Columbia, MD 21044-1705
Ph: (410)992-7724
Fax: (410)740-5046
E-mail: civilaffairs@earthlink.net
URL: http://www.civilaffairsassoc.org
Contact: Dennis C. Barlow, Pres.

Founded: 1947. **Members:** 2,500. **Membership Dues:** military officer, $25 (annual) ● military NCO/ enlisted, $15 (annual) ● international, civilian, $20 (annual) ● life (military officer/civilian), $175 ● life (military NCO/enlisted), $100. **Staff:** 1. **Budget:** $40,000. **Local Groups:** 43. **Multinational. Description:** U.S. Army active and reserve officers and enlisted personnel serving in Army or Marine Corps civil affairs units or in civil affairs staff positions in major military headquarters, and international members. Advocates and promotes a strong U.S. military civil affairs capability. **Awards:** Hilldring Award. **Frequency:** annual. **Type:** recognition ● Temple Award. **Frequency:** annual. **Type:** recognition. **Formerly:** Military Government Association. **Publications:** *Civil Affairs Journal and Newsletter*, quarterly. Includes articles on current civil affairs doctrine, issues, activities; news about civil affairs people, places, and things. **Price:** included in membership dues; $10.00 /year for nonmembers. ISSN: 0045-7035. **Circulation:** 2,000. Alternate Formats: online. Also Cited As: *Scroll and Sword*. **Conventions/Meetings:** annual conference, held in conjunction with the World Wide Civil Affairs Conference (exhibits) - usually in June.

6075 ■ Defense Advisory Committee on Women in the Services (DACOWITS)
4000 Defense Pentagon, Rm. 2C548A
Washington, DC 20301-4000
Ph: (703)697-2122
Fax: (703)614-6322
E-mail: dacowits@osd.mil
URL: http://www.dtic.mil/dacowits
Contact: Col. Denise Dailey, Military Dir.

Founded: 1951. **Members:** 13. **Description:** Civilians appointed by Secretary of Defense to provide recommendations to optimize utilization and quality of life for women in U.S. armed forces. Assists the Department of Defense by advising on specified matters relating to the recruitment and retention, treatment, employment, integration, and well-being of highly qualified professional women in the Services. Advises on family issues related to the recruitment and retention of a highly qualified professional military. **Subcommittees:** Equality Management; Forces Development and Utilization; Quality of Life. **Publications:** Books. Includes conference issue books. ● Reports, annual. Contains committee reports.

6076 ■ Enlisted Association of National Guard of the United States (EANGUS)
3133 Mt. Vernon Ave.
Alexandria, VA 22305
Ph: (703)519-3846
Free: (800)234-EANG
Fax: (703)519-3849
E-mail: eangus@eangus.org
URL: http://www.eangus.org
Contact: Msgt. Michael P. Cline, Exec. Dir./CEO

Founded: 1972. **Members:** 85,000. **Membership Dues:** individual, $9 (annual). **Staff:** 8. **Budget:** $3,000,000. **State Groups:** 54. **Description:** Active and retired members of the U.S. National Guard. Conducts educational, legislative and charitable programs. **Libraries: Type:** not open to the public.

Awards: CSM Virgil R. Williams. **Frequency:** annual. **Type:** scholarship ● We Care for America. **Frequency:** annual. **Type:** scholarship. **Computer Services:** database, membership ● mailing lists. **Telecommunication Services:** electronic bulletin board. **Publications:** *Legislative Updates*. Magazine. **Advertising:** accepted. Alternate Formats: CD-ROM; online ● *New Patriot*, quarterly. Magazine. **Advertising:** accepted. Alternate Formats: online. **Conventions/Meetings:** annual board meeting and convention (exhibits).

6077 ■ Inter-University Seminar on Armed Forces and Society (IUS)

Political Sci. Dept.
Loyola Univ. Chicago
6525 N Sheridan Rd.
Chicago, IL 60626
Ph: (773)508-2930
Fax: (773)508-2929
E-mail: asigart@luc.edu
URL: http://www.iusafs.org
Contact: Robert A. Vitas, Exec. Dir.

Founded: 1960. **Members:** 600. **Membership Dues:** fellow, scholar, $70 (annual). **Staff:** 2. **Budget:** $100,000. **Regional Groups:** 3. **Description:** Individuals from both public and private life in the academic, military, and government fields who are primarily researchers. Promotes the study of armed forces and society; provides a focal point for the exchange of information on the subject; stimulates research in the field on a cross-national basis. Compiles statistics; recommends a scholar to conduct seminars and give lectures. **Publications:** *Armed Forces and Society*, quarterly. Journal. Focuses on the multinational and interdisciplinary study of armed forces and society. **Price:** $48.00/year. ISSN: 0095-327X. **Circulation:** 5,000. **Advertising:** accepted ● *IUS Newsletter*, semiannual ● *IUS Special Edition on Armed Forces and Society*, periodic. Books. **Conventions/Meetings:** biennial international conference, for scholars and military professionals making presentations on issues related to civil/military and political/military relations.

6078 ■ Judge Advocates Association (JAA)

c/o Col. Amy Griese, USAFR
8109 Overlake Ct.
Fairfax Station, VA 22039
Ph: (703)474-7691
E-mail: jaa@jaa.org
URL: http://www.jaa.org
Contact: Brig. Gen. Edward F. Rodriguez Jr., Pres.

Founded: 1943. **Members:** 400. **Membership Dues:** junior (4 or less years of service), associate, $30 (annual) ● senior, $50 (annual) ● law student, $20 (annual) ● life (under 45 years of age), $500 ● life (over 45 years of age), $350. **Staff:** 1. **Budget:** $25,000. **Description:** Active, reserve, retired and former Judge Advocates of the Army, Navy, Air Force, Marine Corps, Coast Guard and practitioners of military and veterans law. Assists in the development of military law and an efficient military and veterans legal and judicial system. **Awards:** American Bar Association Award. **Frequency:** annual. **Type:** recognition. **Recipient:** to public lawyers with extraordinary achievements ● Chief Justice Marshall Lifetime Achievement Award. **Frequency:** annual. **Type:** recognition. **Recipient:** to a former judge advocate ● Outstanding Career Armed Services Attorney Award. **Frequency:** annual. **Type:** recognition. **Recipient:** for lawyers ● Robinson O. Everett Distinguished Life Service Award. **Frequency:** annual. **Type:** recognition. **Recipient:** to a very special individual. **Affiliated With:** American Bar Association. **Publications:** *The Military Advocate*, semiannual. Newsletter. Contains short articles on topics of interest to the military and veterans' bar, notices of activities, and upcoming events. **Price:** free for members. **Circulation:** 500. **Advertising:** accepted. Alternate Formats: online. **Conventions/Meetings:** annual The Military Administrative Law Conference (MALC) (exhibits) - every March ● annual The Military Appellate Advocacy Symposium (MAAS) - conference - every September.

6079 ■ Marine Corps Association (MCA)

715 Broadway St.
Quantico, VA 22134
Ph: (703)640-6161
Free: (800)336-0291
Fax: (703)640-0823
E-mail: mca@mca-marine.org
URL: http://www.mca-marines.org
Contact: Major Gen. Leslie M. Palm, Pres./CEO

Founded: 1913. **Members:** 87,000. **Membership Dues:** enlisted (with one magazine), $23 (annual) ● enlisted (with two magazines), $44 (annual) ● officer (with one magazine), $35 (annual) ● officer (with two magazines), $67 (annual). **Staff:** 50. **Description:** Represents active duty, reserve, retired, Fleet Reserve, honorably discharged Marines, and members of other services who have served with Marine Corps units. Disseminates information about the military arts and sciences to members; assists members' professional advancement; fosters the spirit and works to preserve the traditions of the United States Marine Corps. Maintains discount book service and group insurance plan for members. Association founded by members of the Second Provisional Marine Brigade at Guantanamo Bay, Cuba. **Awards: Type:** recognition. **Recipient:** to outstanding students in various Marine Corps Schools. **Computer Services:** Electronic publishing, MCA Today Newsletter. **Telecommunication Services:** electronic mail, customercare@mca-marines.org. **Absorbed:** (1976) Leatherneck Association. **Publications:** *Leatherneck*, monthly. Magazine. **Circulation:** 135,000. **Advertising:** accepted ● *Marine Corps Gazette*, monthly. Journal ● Books.

6080 ■ Marine Corps Aviation Association (MCAA)

715 Broadway St.
PO Box 296
Quantico, VA 22134
Ph: (703)630-1903
Free: (800)280-3001
Fax: (703)630-2713
E-mail: mcaa@flymcaa.org
URL: http://www.flymcaa.org
Contact: Lt. Col. R. Art Sifuentes USMC, Exec. Dir.

Founded: 1972. **Members:** 4,000. **Membership Dues:** individual, $35 (annual) ● individual, $95 (triennial). **Staff:** 3. **Budget:** $100,000. **Regional Groups:** 14. **Local Groups:** 25. **Description:** Members and former members of U.S. Marine aviation units and others with an interest in Marine Corps aviation; aerospace corporations. Aims to: perpetuate camaraderie in marine aviation; foster and encourage professional excellence and recognize important achievements in marine aviation. Conducts charitable programs. **Awards:** MCAA Aviation Awards. **Type:** recognition. **Recipient:** for 26 categories. **Absorbed:** First Marine Aviation Force Veterans Association. **Publications:** *Annual Symposium and Reunion Journal*, annual. **Price:** included in membership dues ● *Yellow Sheet*, 3/year. Magazine. **Price:** available to members only ● Membership Directory, periodic. Includes newsletter. **Price:** available to members only. **Conventions/Meetings:** annual reunion and symposium (exhibits).

6081 ■ Marine Corps League (MCL)

c/o Mr. Michael A. Blum, Exec. Dir.
PO Box 3070
Merrifield, VA 22116-3070
Ph: (703)207-9588
Free: (800)625-1775
Fax: (703)207-0047
E-mail: mclsarge@aol.com
URL: http://www.MCLeague.org
Contact: Mr. Michael A. Blum, Exec. Dir.

Founded: 1923. **Members:** 63,000. **Membership Dues:** $30 (annual). **Staff:** 14. **Budget:** $2,100,000. **Regional Groups:** 10. **State Groups:** 49. **Local Groups:** 1,014. **Description:** Represents men and women who are serving or who have served honorably in the United States Marine Corps, and U.S. Navy Corpsmen. Preserves the traditions and promotes the interests of the United States Marine Corps. Promotes the ideals of American freedom and democracy. Preserves the history and memory of the men who have given their lives to the nation. Maintains true allegiance to American institutions. Creates a bond of comradeship between those in the service and those who have returned to civilian life. Renders assistance to all Marines and former Marines as well as to their widows and orphans. **Awards:** Dickie Chapelle and Iron Mike Awards. **Frequency:** annual. **Type:** recognition. **Recipient:** for individuals who have supported the U.S. and the Marine Corps ● **Type:** recognition. **Recipient:** for outstanding enlistees in a variety of military occupational specialties ● **Frequency:** annual. **Type:** scholarship. **Recipient:** for a cadet at the Marine Military Academy. **Boards:** Trustees. **Committees:** Service; VA Volunteer Service; Veterans Day; Young Marines; Youth Physical Fitness. **Publications:** *SEMPER FI*, bimonthly. Magazine. Features articles and editorials of interest to marines and marine veterans. **Circulation:** 70,000. **Advertising:** accepted. **Conventions/Meetings:** annual meeting, military expositions (exhibits) - usually August for national or May/June for state.

6082 ■ Marine Corps Reserve Association (MCRA)

2020 Gen. Booth Blvd., Ste.200
Virginia Beach, VA 23454
Ph: (757)301-2032
Free: (800)927-6270
Fax: (757)301-6884
E-mail: kathleen@usmcra.org
URL: http://www.mcrassn.org
Contact: Colonel Richard H. Esau Jr., Exec. Dir.

Founded: 1926. **Members:** 6,000. **Membership Dues:** PLC/ROTC, PVT-Sgt., $15 (annual) ● SSgt.-MSgt./1st Sgt., $20 (annual) ● MGySgt./Sgt.Maj., WO/Lt./Capt., $25 (annual) ● Major, $35 (annual) ● Lt. Col., $40 (annual) ● Colonel, $50 (annual) ● General, $100 (annual) ● life (40 years and under to over 60 years), $300-$600. **Staff:** 3. **Budget:** $250,000. **Regional Groups:** 6. **Local Groups:** 103. **Description:** Marines who have served on active duty in peace or war. Seeks to: advance the professional skills of marines; represent and assist individual members; promote the interests of the U.S. Marine Corps in order to advance the welfare and preserve the security of the United States. Maintains speakers' bureau and placement service. **Awards:** MCJROTC Awards. **Frequency:** annual. **Type:** recognition. **Recipient:** to MCJROTC units nationally ● **Type:** recognition. **Recipient:** to outstanding units of the Selected Marine Corps Reserve ● **Type:** recognition. **Recipient:** to an outstanding individual who best supports the objectives of the association. **Telecommunication Services:** electronic mail, resau@mcrassn.org. **Formerly:** (2003) Marine Corps Reserve Officers' Association. **Publications:** *MCRA Membership Directory*, semiannual. **Price:** included in membership dues. **Circulation:** 7,500. **Advertising:** accepted ● *The Word*, bimonthly. Magazine. **Advertising:** accepted. **Conventions/Meetings:** annual conference (exhibits) - always April ● annual seminar (exhibits).

6083 ■ Military Law Task Force (MLTF)

318 Ortega St.
San Francisco, CA 94122
Ph: (619)233-1701 (415)566-3732
E-mail: kathleengilberd@aol.com
URL: http://www.nlgmltf.org
Contact: Kathleen Gilberd, Co-Chair

Founded: 1970. **Members:** 100. **Membership Dues:** regular, $25 (annual). **Description:** Counselors, attorneys, and law students concerned with military, selective service, and veterans' law. Purposes are to: assist active-duty personnel, veterans, and those affected by selective service; provide educational and political work focused on these areas of law; offer research assistance in military and veterans law; support networking among attorneys and counselors. Operates speakers' bureau; offers informal referral services and educational materials. **Affiliated With:** National Lawyers Guild. **Publications:** *On Watch*, quarterly. Newsletter. Features military and veterans law analysis. **Price:** $25.00 /year for nonmembers; $40.00 /year for institutions; free for members.

Alternate Formats: online ● Also publishes memos and counseling guides. **Conventions/Meetings:** annual seminar.

6084 ■ Montford Point Marine Association (MPMA)
27 Red Tail Ct.
Limerick, PA 19468
E-mail: cordobac@aol.com
URL: http://www.montfordpointmarines.com
Contact: Joseph Geeter, Natl. Pres.

Founded: 1965. **Members:** 4,000. **Membership Dues:** individual, $25 (annual) ● life (by age), $150-$300. **Staff:** 1. **Regional Groups:** 19. **Description:** Represents veterans and active members of all branches of the U.S. Armed Forces. Aims to support educational assistance programs, veterans programs and promotion of community services. Works to improve the social conditions of veterans, local families, youth and the growing population of senior citizens; named after Montford Point, New River, Camp Lejeune, NC, the only base in America used for the recruit or "Boot Camp" training of black Marines, 1942-49. **Conventions/Meetings:** annual convention.

6085 ■ National Association of Superintendents of U.S. Naval Shore Establishments (NASNSE)
c/o Mr. Larry Sands, Pres.
89 Pine Legde Dr.
Wells, ME 04090
Ph: (207)646-7316
E-mail: larry.sands@navy.mil
URL: http://nasnse.org
Contact: Mr. Larry Sands, Pres.

Founded: 1912. **Members:** 315. **Budget:** $30,000. **Local Groups:** 11. **Description:** Superintendents of production, maintenance, and public works branches of naval shore establishments. Promotes the general welfare of members professionally, intellectually, and socially; cultivates high standards of professional ethics. **Committees:** Credentials. **Formerly:** National Association of Master Workmen of Navy Yards and Naval Stations; (1969) National Association of Master Mechanics and Foreman of Naval Shore Establishments. **Conventions/Meetings:** annual congress - always in Washington, DC.

6086 ■ National Association for Uniformed Services (NAUS)
5535 Hempstead Way
Springfield, VA 22151-4094
Ph: (703)750-1342
Fax: (703)354-4380
E-mail: info@naus.org
URL: http://www.naus.org
Contact: Major Gen. William M. Matz Jr., Pres.

Founded: 1968. **Members:** 160,000. **Membership Dues:** single, $15 (annual) ● husband and wife, $25 (annual) ● widow(er), $12 (annual) ● life (single, by age), $130-$240 ● life (husband and wife, by age), $190-$360 ● life (widower, by age), $130-$220. **Staff:** 10. **Budget:** $4,000,000. **Description:** Members of the uniformed military services, active, retired or reserve, veteran, enlisted and officers, and their spouses or widows. Develops and supports legislation that upholds the security of the U.S., sustains the morale of the uniformed services, and provides fair and equitable consideration for all service people. Protects and improves compensation, entitlements, and benefits. Provides discount rates on travel, insurance, auto rentals, charge cards, prescription medicine, and legal services. **Computer Services:** database, membership. **Telecommunication Services:** electronic mail, wmatz@naus.org. **Committees:** Political Action. **Affiliated With:** Society of Military Widows. **Formerly:** National Association for Uniformed Services Retirees. **Publications:** *Uniformed Services Journal*, bimonthly. Magazine. **Conventions/Meetings:** annual meeting - always last week in October or first week of November in Washington, DC.

6087 ■ National Committee for Employer Support of the Guard and Reserve (NCESGR)
1555 Wilson Blvd., Ste.200
Arlington, VA 22209-2405
Ph: (703)696-1386
Free: (800)336-4590
Fax: (703)696-1411
E-mail: ncesgr-ombud@osd.mil
URL: http://www.esgr.org

Founded: 1972. **Members:** 4,000. **Staff:** 54. **Budget:** $20,000,000. **State Groups:** 56. **Description:** Provides free education, consultation, and if necessary, mediation for employers of guard and reserve members. Aims to ensure the national security. Promotes cooperation and understanding between reserve component members and their civilian employers and assists in the resolution of conflicts arising from an employee's military commitment. Operates with a network of almost 4,000 volunteers throughout 56 Committees located in each state, commonwealth, territory, and the District of Columbia. Operates an ombudsman program to assist in the informal resolution of employer-employee conflicts resulting from employee participation in the National Guard and Reserve. **Awards:** Above and Beyond Award. **Frequency:** annual. **Type:** recognition. **Recipient:** for employers of reserve component members who have gone above and beyond the requirements of the uniformed services employment and re-employment act ● Patriot Award. **Frequency:** annual. **Type:** recognition. **Recipient:** to managerial level individuals and the company by guard/reserve employees for their support to the reserve components ● Pro Patria Award. **Frequency:** annual. **Type:** recognition. **Recipient:** to two employers who are the most outstanding within the district, state, commonwealth, or territory for the calendar year ● Secretary of Defense Employer Support Freedom Award. **Frequency:** annual. **Type:** recognition. **Recipient:** to the top employers in the nation who have demonstrated exceptional support to guard and reserve employees. **Additional Websites:** http://www.esgr.mil. **Publications:** *E-ssentials*, monthly. Newsletter. Provides news, information and recognition. **Price:** free. **Circulation:** 6,000.

6088 ■ National Council of Industrial Naval Air Stations (NCINAS)
Address Unknown since 2008

Founded: 1957. **Members:** 20,000. **Regional Groups:** 6. **State Groups:** 4. **Local Groups:** 6. **Description:** Federation of local groups of government civilian employees at Industrial Naval Air Stations. **Formerly:** (1980) National Council of Naval Air Stations Employee Organizations. **Conventions/Meetings:** annual conference.

6089 ■ National Defense Industrial Association (NDIA)
2111 Wilson Blvd., Ste.400
Arlington, VA 22201-3061
Ph: (703)522-1820
Fax: (703)522-1885
E-mail: info@ndia.org
URL: http://www.adpa.org
Contact: Lt. Gen. Lawrence P. Farrell Jr., Pres./CEO

Founded: 1919. **Members:** 24,000. **Membership Dues:** individual, $30 (annual) ● individual - allied, $35 (annual) ● life, $400. **Staff:** 40. **Budget:** $8,000,000. **National Groups:** 58. **Description:** Concerned citizens, military and government personnel, and defense-related industry workers interested in industrial preparedness for the national defense of the United States. Operates Technology Services that provides a forum for discussion of defense industry programs and issues. Conducts 55 technical meetings per year. **Awards:** Defense Industry Award. **Frequency:** biennial. **Type:** recognition ● ROTC Award. **Type:** recognition. **Telecommunication Services:** electronic mail, jmattingly@ndia.org. **Divisions:** Advanced Information Systems; Air Armament; Ballistics; Combat Survivability; Environmental; Industrial Base Planning; Insensitive Munitions; International Affairs; Logistics; Munitions Technology; Night Operations; Robotics; Science and Engineering Technology; Security Technology; Small Arms System; Special Operations/Low Intensity Conflict; Statistical Process Control; Tank and Automotive; Technical Information; Test and Evaluation; Training Systems; Undersea Warfare Systems. **Absorbed:** (1965) Armed Forces Chemical Association; (1974) Armed Forces Management Association; (1992) National Training Systems Association. **Formerly:** (1948) Army Ordnance Association; (1973) American Ordnance Association; (1998) National Defense Preparedness Association; (2001) National Security Industrial Association. **Publications:** *National Defense*, monthly. Magazine. Covers Business and technology topics affecting the production and procurement of weapons systems; and their implications on the defense industrial base. **Price:** included in membership dues; $35.00 /year for nonmembers. ISSN: 0092-1491. **Circulation:** 28,000. **Advertising:** accepted ● *Washington Chapter Corporate Directory*, annual. **Conventions/Meetings:** annual meeting - always spring.

6090 ■ National Defense Transportation Association (NDTA)
50 S Pickett St., Ste.220
Alexandria, VA 22304-7296
Ph: (703)751-5011
Fax: (703)823-8761
E-mail: info@ndtahq.com
URL: http://www.ndtahq.com
Contact: Lt. Gen. Kenneth R. Wykle, Pres.

Founded: 1944. **Members:** 7,800. **Membership Dues:** individual, $35 (annual) ● life, $400 ● Chairman's Circle, $6,200 (annual) ● sustaining, $1,200 (annual) ● regional patron, $550 (annual) ● military - government rate, $20 (annual) ● student, $10 (annual). **Staff:** 8. **Budget:** $1,300,000. **Regional Groups:** 9. **State Groups:** 42. **Local Groups:** 61. **Languages:** Danish, English, German, Korean, Latin, Turkic Dialects. **Description:** Men and women in the field of transportation, travel logistics and related areas in the Armed Forces, federal government, private industry and the academic sector. Strives to foster a strong and efficient transportation system in support of national defense. Serves as link between government and industry on transportation matters. Operates a job placement service for members. **Awards:** National Transportation Award, Defense Distinguished Service and National Defense Leadership. **Frequency:** annual. **Type:** recognition. **Recipient:** for high level of achievements of national significance. **Telecommunication Services:** electronic mail, mark@ndtahq.com. **Committees:** Surface Transportation. **Divisions:** National Defense Transportation Foundation. **Formerly:** (1949) Army Transport Association. **Publications:** *Defense Transportation Journal*, bimonthly. **Price:** $35.00 in U.S.; included in membership dues; $45.00 overseas. **Circulation:** 10,000. **Advertising:** accepted ● *NDTA-Gram*, monthly. Newsletter. Includes news and information about the association. Alternate Formats: online. **Conventions/Meetings:** annual Transportation and Logistics Forum and Exposition - meeting and trade show (exhibits) - always September/October.

6091 ■ National Guard Association of the United States (NGAUS)
1 Massachusetts Ave. NW
Washington, DC 20001
Ph: (202)789-0031
Fax: (202)682-9358
E-mail: ngaus@ngaus.org
URL: http://www.ngaus.org
Contact: Ret. Brig. Gen. Stephen M. Koper, Pres.

Founded: 1878. **Members:** 56,000. **Membership Dues:** active (based on rank), $26-$153 (annual) ● active (life), $1,000 ● retired (life), $125 ● separated, associate, $45 (annual) ● associate (life), $500 ● gold corporate, $1,500 (annual) ● platinum corporate, $2,500 (annual) ● silver corporate, $1,000 (annual) ● bronze corporate, $500 (annual). **Staff:** 25. **Budget:** $3,500,000. **Regional Groups:** 6. **State Groups:** 54. **Description:** Active and Retired Officers and Warrant Officers of the Army National Guard and Air National Guard of the States, Commonwealth of Puerto Rico, the District of Columbia, Guam, and the

Virgin Islands. Goals include: adequate national security and a strong Army National Guard and Air National Guard of the United States as components of the armed forces. Sponsors public affairs competition for National Guard personnel. Maintains the Museum of the National Guard, containing rare art and artifacts relating to the militia and National Guard. **Libraries: Type:** reference. **Holdings:** 4,500; archival material, books. **Subjects:** military history. **Awards: Type:** recognition. **Recipient:** for achievement and heroism. **Computer Services:** Mailing lists, of members. **Telecommunication Services:** electronic mail, president@ngaus.org. **Publications:** *National Guard*, monthly. Magazine. **Advertising:** accepted. **Conventions/Meetings:** annual conference (exhibits) - always September/October.

6092 ■ National Guard Executive Directors Association (NGEDA)
3706 Crawford Ave.
Austin, TX 78731
Ph: (512)454-7300
Fax: (512)467-6803
E-mail: rlindner@ngat.org
URL: http://www.ngeda.org
Contact: Ray Linder, Sec.-Treas.
Description: Provides a forum for the exchange of information of common interest to members and the organizations they represent; encourages states to organize and maintain a National Guard association; participates in improving the operational readiness, training and image of the National Guard on both state and national levels. **Awards:** Col. James F. Gamble Award. **Frequency:** annual. **Type:** recognition. **Recipient:** for an individual with an exemplary performance and dedication in support of the member states and activities. **Affiliated With:** National Guard Association of the United States. **Conventions/Meetings:** semiannual conference and meeting, in conjunction with NGAUS general conference - always January ● annual meeting.

6093 ■ National Naval Officers Association (NNOA)
PO Box 10871
Alexandria, VA 22310-0871
Ph: (703)997-1068
E-mail: webmaster@nnoa.org
URL: http://www.nnoa.org
Contact: Capt. Bernard L. Jackson, Natl. Pres.
Founded: 1972. **Members:** 825. **Staff:** 15. **Budget:** $50,000. **Regional Groups:** 4. **Local Groups:** 39. **Description:** Active, reserve, and retired Navy, Marine, and Coast Guard officers and students in college and military sea service programs. Promotes and assists recruitment, retention, and career development of minority officers in the naval service. Conducts specialized education; maintains counseling, referral, and mentorship. Makes available non-ROTC grants-in-aid. Sponsors competitions; operates charitable program. **Awards: Type:** recognition. **Computer Services:** database, membership. **Telecommunication Services:** electronic bulletin board ● electronic mail, nnoa@nnoa.org. **Publications:** *NNOA Meridian*, quarterly. Newsletter. Covers sea service news and events; includes chapter news, news from other military services, statistics, and information about other organizations. **Price:** included in membership dues. **Circulation:** 900. **Advertising:** accepted. **Conventions/Meetings:** annual conference, professional seminars and networking conference (exhibits) - July or August.

6094 ■ Naval Civilian Managers Association (NCMA)
PO Box 215
Portsmouth, VA 23705
Ph: (757)396-2265
Fax: (757)396-7743
E-mail: clifford.elder@navy.mil
Contact: J. Clifford Elder, Natl.Pres.
Founded: 1947. **Members:** 800. **Budget:** $30,000. **Regional Groups:** 14. **Description:** Upper echelon civilian personnel in a naval organizational entity. Encourages improvement of administration and management of U.S. Navy. Compiles statistics. Maintains speakers' bureau, museum, and hall of fame. **Awards: Type:** recognition. **Committees:** Federal Employee; Legislative; Management Systems Improvement. **Formerly:** (1987) Naval Civilian Administrators Association. **Publications:** Membership Directory, annual ● Newsletter, quarterly ● Proceedings, annual. **Conventions/Meetings:** competition ● annual meeting - always May.

6095 ■ Naval Enlisted Reserve Association (NERA)
6703 Farragut Ave.
Falls Church, VA 22042-2189
Ph: (703)534-1329
Free: (800)776-9020
Fax: (703)534-3617
E-mail: members@nera.org
URL: http://www.nera.org
Contact: Capt. Stephen Sandy, Exec. Dir.
Founded: 1957. **Members:** 14,000. **Membership Dues:** active/associate, $25 (annual) ● life - active/associate, $250 ● active/associate, $47 (biennial) ● active/associate, $69 (triennial). **Staff:** 3. **Local Groups:** 108. **Description:** Enlisted personnel of the U.S. Naval Reserve, Marine Corps Reserve, and Coast Guard Reserve on active duty, inactive duty, or retired. Works to promote career enlisted service in the "sea-going" branches of the armed services; concerned with the readiness, training, morale, and well-being of all Reservists; obtains fair and proper recognition of the contributions made by Reservists to the national defense and to obtain protection and extension of benefits and entitlements for those Reservists who are currently serving and for those who have already served satisfactorily and have retired. Works with Congress and military leaders for legislation and proposals designed to improve and enhance the effectiveness of Reserve programs; also works to provide a communications link with the public. **Computer Services:** Online services, communications center for members. **Telecommunication Services:** electronic mail, neraexec@nera.org. **Publications:** *The Mariner*, bimonthly ● Manual. **Conventions/Meetings:** annual competition and meeting.

6096 ■ Naval Intelligence Professionals (NIP)
PO Box 11579
Burke, VA 22009-1579
Ph: (703)250-6765
E-mail: navintpro@aol.com
URL: http://www.navintpro.org
Contact: Radm. T.A. Brooks, Pres.
Founded: 1985. **Members:** 1,800. **Membership Dues:** general, $25 (annual). **Staff:** 1. **Budget:** $40,000. **Regional Groups:** 10. **Description:** Active duty and former naval intelligence officers; enlisted personnel; civilian professionals; corporations. Objectives are to: improve naval intelligence operations; act as a clearinghouse for information on scientific and technical advances in naval intelligence; provide a forum for the exchange of ideas. Encourages readiness for those who would be involved in a national crisis mobilization. **Publications:** *Naval Intelligence Professionals Quarterly*. Newsletter. Contains articles that describe historic events and people in naval intelligence community. Includes book reviews, obituaries, and promotions. **Price:** included in membership dues ● Membership Directory, annual. **Conventions/Meetings:** annual meeting.

6097 ■ Naval Reserve Association (NRA)
1619 King St.
Alexandria, VA 22314-2793
Ph: (703)548-5800
Free: (866)672-4968
Fax: (703)683-3647
E-mail: membership@navy-reserve.org
URL: http://www.navy-reserve.org
Contact: Casey Coane, Exec. Dir.
Founded: 1954. **Members:** 25,000. **Membership Dues:** regular, $40 (annual) ● regular, $105 (triennial). **Staff:** 8. **Budget:** $1,000,000. **Regional Groups:** 11. **Local Groups:** 187. **Description:** Naval officers on active or inactive duty or retired. Maintains involvement with legislation affecting U.S. Navy and Naval Reserve. Provides Naval Officer Promotion Record Reviews. Sponsors Naval Reserve Junior Officer of the Year Programs. Offers professional education; sponsors competitions; maintains speakers' bureau. **Libraries: Type:** reference. **Holdings:** 500. **Subjects:** naval history. **Awards:** Naval Awards. **Type:** recognition. **Telecommunication Services:** electronic mail, exec@navy-reserve.org. **Committees:** Health Affairs; Junior Officers; Legislation; Naval Air; Naval Surface/Subsurface; Policy; Public Relations; Retired Personnel. **Publications:** *NRA News*, monthly. Magazine. Provides legislative updates, member and chapter news, explanations of rights and benefits of reserve and retired officers, and descriptions. **Price:** included in membership dues; $8.00 /year for nonmembers. ISSN: 0162-2129. **Circulation:** 25,000. **Advertising:** accepted ● Also publishes Naval Reserve officer promotion statistics and other professional materials. **Conventions/Meetings:** semiannual conference and symposium (exhibits) ● semiannual meeting.

6098 ■ Naval Sea Cadet Corps (NSCC)
2300 Wilson Blvd.
Arlington, VA 22201-3308
Ph: (703)243-6910
Fax: (703)243-3985
E-mail: mford@navyleague.org
URL: http://www.seacadets.org
Contact: Capt. Michael D. Ford, Exec. Dir.
Founded: 1962. **Members:** 11,500. **Membership Dues:** for adult leader, $13 (annual) ● youth (ages 11-14), $46 (annual) ● youth (ages 13-17), $46 (annual). **Staff:** 16. **Budget:** $2,600,000. **Regional Groups:** 35. **Local Groups:** 320. **Description:** Youths aged 11-17 years interested in the Navy, Marine Corps, Coast Guard, and Merchant Marines. Works to instill good citizenship and patriotism in youth. Encourages qualities such as personal neatness, loyalty, obedience, dependability, and responsibility to others. Offers courses in physical fitness and military drill, first aid, water safety, basic seamanship, and naval history and traditions. **Awards: Type:** monetary. **Recipient:** to NSCC members ● **Frequency:** annual. **Type:** scholarship. **Recipient:** to sea cadets only. **Affiliated With:** Naval Sea Cadet Corps; Navy League of the United States. **Formerly:** Navy League Cadet Corps. **Publications:** *WASH - O - GRAM*, quarterly. Newsletter. Provides news on organization policy and personal news items. **Price:** included in membership dues. Alternate Formats: online. **Conventions/Meetings:** semiannual board meeting - usually June and November.

6099 ■ Navy Club of the United States of America (NCUSA)
6134 S 375 W
Lafayette, IN 47909
Free: (800)628-7265
E-mail: natloffice@navyclubusa.org
URL: http://www.navyclubusa.org
Contact: Edward L. Walter, Natl. Commandant
Founded: 1938. **Members:** 5,800. **Membership Dues:** individual, $20 (annual). **Staff:** 2. **State Groups:** 5. **Local Groups:** 31. **Description:** Persons who are, or have been, in the active service of the U.S. Navy, Naval Reserve, Marine Corps, Marine Corps Reserve, and Coast Guard. Promotes and encourages further public interest in the U.S. Navy and its history and to uphold the spirit and ideals of the U.S. Navy. Acts as public forum for members' views on national defense. Assists Navy Recruiting Command. Conducts charitable activities. **Awards:** Military Excellence Award. **Frequency:** weekly. **Type:** recognition. **Recipient:** for top boot camp graduate at Great Lakes naval training GR. **Telecommunication Services:** electronic mail, co166navy@aol.com. **Commissions:** Arizona Memorial. **Committees:** Anchor Day. **Publications:** *The Quarterdeck*, semiannual. Newsletter. **Price:** included in membership dues; $2.00 for nonmembers. **Circulation:** 5,850. **Advertising:** accepted. Alternate Formats: online. **Conventions/Meetings:** annual convention - usually June.

6100 ■ Navy Club of the United States of America Auxiliary (NCUSAA)
124 E Front St.
Delphi, IN 46923-1508
Ph: (765)564-6147
E-mail: ncauxshipswriter@hotmail.com
URL: http://www.navyclubusa.org
Contact: Judy Gainey, Natl. Auxiliary Shipswriter
Founded: 1941. **Members:** 700. **Regional Groups:** 5. **Local Groups:** 20. **Description:** Women relatives of men who have served in the United States Navy, Marine Corps, Coast Guard, and component reserve services; women who are eligible in their own right for membership in the Navy Club of the United States of America. Provides assistance to the Navy Club; promotes fraternal love and sociability; encourages interest in the U.S. Navy and its history. Activities include veterans' service, rehabilitation programs, child welfare assistance, handicapped services, and overseas relief, memorials, and community service. Supports U.S. Navy special services. Maintains museum. **Libraries: Type:** reference. **Subjects:** history. **Awards:** Activities Award. **Frequency:** annual. **Type:** recognition ● History Book Award. **Frequency:** annual. **Type:** recognition ● Membership Award. **Frequency:** annual. **Type:** recognition ● **Type:** recognition. **Recipient:** for outstanding accomplishments by individuals in the national security field ● Woman of the Year. **Frequency:** annual. **Type:** recognition. **Commissions:** Ebb-Tide. **Committees:** Americanism; Child Welfare; Legislation; Naval Relations; Parliamentarian; Rehabilitation; Shipswriter. **Affiliated With:** Freedoms Foundation at Valley Forge. **Publications:** *Ebb-Tide*, quarterly ● *Quarterdeck*, quarterly. Published in conjunction with NCUSA. Alternate Formats: online ● Proceedings, annual. **Conventions/Meetings:** convention ● annual reunion - always June.

6101 ■ Navy League of the United States (NLUS)
2300 Wilson Blvd., Ste.200
Arlington, VA 22201-3308
Ph: (703)528-1775
Free: (800)356-5760
Fax: (703)528-2333
E-mail: execdirector@navyleague.org
URL: http://www.navyleague.org
Contact: Stephen R. Pietropaoli, Natl. Exec. Dir.
Founded: 1902. **Members:** 74,000. **Membership Dues:** individual, $40 (annual) ● life - individual, $450 ● husband/wife, $70 (annual) ● life - husband/wife, $650 ● active duty spouse, $30 (annual) ● community affiliate, $400 (annual) ● corporate gold, $12,500 (annual) ● corporate, $4,000 (annual) ● business associate, $1,500 (annual). **Staff:** 38. **Budget:** $8,400,000. **Regional Groups:** 18. **State Groups:** 53. **Local Groups:** 345. **Multinational. Description:** Civilian organization that supports U.S. capability to keep the sea lanes open through a strong, viable Navy, Marine Corps, Coast Guard, and Merchant Marine. Seeks to awaken interest and cooperation of U.S. citizens in matters serving to aid, improve, and develop the efficiency of U.S. naval and maritime forces and equipment; acquires and disseminates information concerning the conditions of U.S. naval and maritime forces and equipment. **Libraries: Type:** reference. **Holdings:** 1,000. **Awards:** Navy League Endowed Scholarships. **Frequency:** annual. **Type:** scholarship. **Recipient:** for outstanding dependent or direct descendant of an individual who is currently serving the league. **Publications:** *Almanac of Sea Power*, annual. Contains basic information about ships, aircraft, personnel, and related topics as they pertain to military departments and merchant marines. ISSN: 0736-3559. **Circulation:** 75,000. **Advertising:** accepted. Alternate Formats: microform; online ● *Navy League of the U.S.—National Directory*, periodic ● *The Navy Leaguer*, periodic. Newsletter. **Circulation:** 65,000. **Advertising:** accepted ● *Sea Power*, monthly. Magazine. Addresses contemporary issues in the defense, foreign policy, and economic arenas. **Price:** included in membership dues; $40.00 /year for nonmembers. ISSN: 0199-1337. **Circulation:** 75,000. **Advertising:** accepted. Alternate Formats: microform. **Conventions/Meetings:** annual Sea-Air-Space Exposition and Technical Briefings - meeting (exhibits).

6102 ■ Non Commissioned Officers Association of the United States of America (NCOA)
10635 IH 35 N
San Antonio, TX 78233
Ph: (210)653-6161
Free: (800)662-2620
Fax: (210)637-3337
E-mail: natdir@ncoausa.org
URL: http://www.ncoausa.org
Contact: Gene Overstreet, Pres./CEO
Founded: 1960. **Members:** 65,000. **Membership Dues:** individual, $30 (annual). **Staff:** 10. **Budget:** $1,500,000. **Local Groups:** 100. **Description:** Noncommissioned and petty officers of the United States military serving in grades E1 through E9 from all five branches of the U.S. Armed Forces; includes active duty and retired personnel, members of the Reserve and National Guard components, and personnel who held the rank of NCO/PO at the time of separation from active duty under honorable conditions. Formed for patriotic, fraternal, social, and benevolent purposes. Offers veterans job assistance, legislative representation, and grants. Conducts charitable programs. **Awards:** NCOA Scholarships. **Frequency:** annual. **Type:** scholarship. **Recipient:** for members' dependents ● **Type:** recognition. **Also Known As:** NCO Association. **Publications:** *NCOA Journal*, quarterly. Magazine. **Price:** included in membership dues. **Advertising:** accepted. **Conventions/Meetings:** annual convention (exhibits).

6103 ■ Reserve Officers Association of the United States (ROA)
1 Constitution Ave. NE
Washington, DC 20002-5618
Ph: (202)479-2200
Free: (800)809-9448
Fax: (202)479-0416
E-mail: dmccarthy@roa.org
URL: http://www.roa.org
Contact: Lt. Gen. Dennis M. McCarthy USMC, Exec. Dir.
Founded: 1922. **Members:** 74,000. **Membership Dues:** regular, $40 (annual) ● spouse, $20 (annual) ● life (based on age), $280-$490 ● virtual, $100 (quinquennial) ● ROTC/officer, WO candidate, military academy student, $4 (annual). **Staff:** 28. **State Groups:** 55. **Local Groups:** 500. **Description:** Represents reserve members of the seven United States Uniformed Services-Army, Navy, Air Force, Marines, Coast Guard, Public Health Service, and National Oceanic and Atmospheric Administration Corps. Aims to "support and promote the development and execution of a military policy for the United States that will provide adequate National Security". **Libraries: Type:** reference. **Holdings:** 6,500. **Subjects:** military and national security. **Awards:** Henry J. Reilly Memorial Scholarship. **Frequency:** annual. **Type:** scholarship. **Recipient:** to members and members' dependents, college undergraduates and graduates. **Absorbed:** Reserve Officers of the Naval Services; (1948) Naval Reserve Officers Association. **Publications:** *The Officer*, 10/year. Magazine. **Circulation:** 80,000. **Advertising:** accepted. Alternate Formats: online ● *ROA National Security Report*, 10/year. **Conventions/Meetings:** annual conference and seminar, association business, leadership training, and awards banquet ● annual convention, election of officers, association business, educational and professional development seminars, and limited number of exhibits (exhibits) - June/July.

6104 ■ Retired Activities Branch
Navy Personnel Command, PERS-675
5720 Integrity Dr.
Millington, TN 38055-6220
Free: (866)827-5672
E-mail: mill_retiredactivities@navy.mil
URL: http://www.npc.navy.mil/CommandSupport/RetiredActivities
Contact: Mr. Dennis Mills Sr., Hd., Retired Operations Section
Founded: 1978. **Members:** 480,000. **Staff:** 2. **Regional Groups:** 65. **Description:** A program of the U.S. Department of the Navy. Assists Navy retirees and survivors with benefits and entitlement information. Maintains speakers' bureau. **Formerly:** (1987) Retired Affairs Officers; (1993) Retired Affairs Section. **Publications:** *All Hands*, monthly. Magazine. Looks at the lives of Navy service members. Alternate Formats: online ● *Shift Colors: The Newspaper for Navy Retirees*, triennial. Provides association news, contact information for agencies and organizations providing benefits to members, and other items of interest. Alternate Formats: online. **Conventions/Meetings:** annual Retiree Appreciation Day - seminar, for retirees and survivors (exhibits).

6105 ■ State Guard Association of the United States (SGAUS)
PO Box 1416
Fayetteville, GA 30214-1416
Ph: (770)460-1215
E-mail: director@sgaus.org
URL: http://www.sgaus.org
Contact: Col. Paul H. LaValle, Pres.
Founded: 1983. **Members:** 2,600. **Membership Dues:** enlisted personnel, $16 (annual) ● officer/civilian, $25 (annual) ● general officer, $30 (annual). **Staff:** 3. **State Groups:** 22. **Description:** Active and retired officers and enlisted personnel of State Defense Forces (SDF) including State Guard, State Military Reserve, National Reserve, Defense Force, Guard Reserve, and other militia. Promotes the SDF in states where they exist; lobbies on behalf of SDF before state and federal governments; fosters exchange among states to keep members abreast of changes in laws pertaining to the SDF. Seeks to educate the public and disseminates information on the history and mission of the militia and to advocate a viable state militia system. **Libraries: Type:** reference. **Holdings:** archival material, books, periodicals. **Subjects:** militia history. **Awards: Type:** recognition. **Formerly:** State Defense Force Association of the United States. **Publications:** *The SGAUS Journal*, quarterly. Covers state defense forces (militia units controlled by the states). **Price:** included in membership dues. **Circulation:** 3,200. **Conventions/Meetings:** conference.

6106 ■ Tailhook Association (TA)
9696 Businesspark Ave.
San Diego, CA 92131
Ph: (858)689-9223
Free: (800)322-HOOK
E-mail: thookassn@aol.com
URL: http://www.tailhook.org
Contact: Mr. J.R. Davis, Exec. Dir.
Founded: 1956. **Members:** 12,000. **Membership Dues:** individual, associate, in Canada, $40 (annual) ● domestic, $105 (triennial) ● foreign (air mail), $50 (annual) ● life, age 59 and under, $705 ● life, age 60-65, $705 ● life, age 66-70, $505 ● life, age 71 and over, $405. **Staff:** 5. **Budget:** $500,000. **Regional Groups:** 3. **Description:** Individuals who have been designated as Naval Aviators or Naval Flight Officers and have made carrier landings; other individuals who have made carrier landings or who have the background and interest to support the objectives of the association. Seeks to foster, develop, study, and support U.S. aircraft carriers and aircrews, and their role in the nation's defense system. **Libraries: Type:** not open to the public. **Holdings:** 700; books, photographs. **Subjects:** aviation, aircraft carriers. **Awards:** Tailhook Educational Foundation Scholarship Award. **Frequency:** annual. **Type:** scholarship. **Recipient:** for deserving individuals who have served or are the children of someone who has served on a U.S. aircraft carrier ● Tailhooker of the Year Award. **Frequency:** annual. **Type:** recognition. **Recipient:** for an individual's significant accomplishments in the advancement of carrier aviation. **Additional Websites:** http://www.tailhook.net. **Publications:** *The Hook*, quarterly. Journal. Covers the history of U.S. Navy carrier aviation. Includes book reviews. **Price:** included in membership dues. ISSN: 0736-9220. **Circulation:** 12,000. **Advertising:** accepted. **Conventions/Meetings:** annual convention (exhibits) - always September.

6107 ■ U.S. Armor Association (USAA)
PO Box 607
Fort Knox, KY 40121-0607
Ph: (502)942-8624
E-mail: brightcg@bbtel.com
URL: http://www.usarmor-assn.org
Contact: Connie Stiggers, Sec.-Treas.
Founded: 1885. **Members:** 6,500. **Membership Dues:** military, $20 (annual) ● non-military, $24 (annual). **Staff:** 3. **Description:** U.S. Army officers, noncommissioned officers, enlisted men, and veterans of all components. Disseminates professional knowledge of military art and science, especially mobile ground warfare. **Awards:** St. George, St. Joan, Noble Patron. **Type:** recognition. **Computer Services:** Mailing lists, of members. **Formerly:** United States Armored Cavalry Association; United States Cavalry Association. **Publications:** *Armor Magazine*, bimonthly. **Price:** $22.00 /year for members; $26.00 /year for nonmembers; $50.00 outside U.S. **Circulation:** 6,500. **Conventions/Meetings:** annual Armor Conference (exhibits) - always third weekend of May in Fort Knox, KY.

6108 ■ United States Army Warrant Officers Association (USAWOA)
462 Herndon Pkwy., Ste.207
Herndon, VA 20170-5235
Ph: (703)742-7727
Free: (800)587-2962
Fax: (703)742-7728
E-mail: usawoa@cavtel.net
URL: http://www.penfed.org/usawoa
Contact: Roy Valiant, Natl. Pres.
Founded: 1973. **Members:** 5,000. **Membership Dues:** regular/associate, $45 (annual) ● retired, $30 (annual) ● life (based on the age of the member), $260-$800 ● corporate, $1,200 (annual). **Staff:** 3. **Budget:** $220,000. **Regional Groups:** 6. **Local Groups:** 75. **Description:** Active duty, National Guard, Reserve, and retired U.S. Army warrant officers. Promotes the technical and social welfare of warrant officers. Recommends Army improvement programs. Circulates professional information among warrant officers. Stimulates patriotism, devotion to duty, and comradeship among members. **Awards: Frequency:** annual. **Type:** scholarship. **Recipient:** for family members of association members. **Telecommunication Services:** electronic mail, roy.valiant@apg.amedd.army.mil. **Publications:** *Newsliner*, 11/year. Magazine. **Price:** included in membership dues. **Advertising:** accepted. **Conventions/Meetings:** annual conference.

6109 ■ United States Marine Corps Drill Instructors Association (USMCDIA)
PO Box 5401
Parris Island, SC 29905
Ph: (912)632-4557
Fax: (912)632-4557
URL: http://www.usmcdiassn.com
Contact: Vic Ditchkoff, Natl. Pres.
Founded: 1986. **Members:** 3,500. **Membership Dues:** $25 (annual). **Staff:** 11. **Budget:** $15,000. **Regional Groups:** 2. **State Groups:** 4. **Description:** Present and former U.S. Marine Corps drill instructors. Fosters a spirit of comradery through social and recreational activities. Promotes the welfare of elderly, disabled, and needy veterans; sponsors patriotic, charitable, and educational programs. Maintains living memorial monument fund; conducts blood drives and active participants' toys 4 tots. **Libraries: Type:** reference. **Holdings:** books, periodicals. **Subjects:** military. **Awards:** L.D. Crow Crawford Scholarship Grant. **Frequency:** annual. **Type:** scholarship. **Recipient:** for a student who mantains B average. **Computer Services:** database, membership. **Publications:** *Field Hat*, quarterly. Newsletter. **Price:** free for members. **Circulation:** 3,600. **Advertising:** accepted. Alternate Formats: diskette. **Conventions/Meetings:** semiannual National Convention & Chapter Reunion (exhibits) - April or May.

6110 ■ United States Naval Institute (USNI)
291 Wood Rd.
Annapolis, MD 21402
Ph: (410)268-6110
Free: (800)233-8764
Fax: (410)269-7940
E-mail: twilkerson@usni.org
URL: http://www.navalinstitute.org
Contact: Thomas L. Wilkerson, CEO/Publisher
Founded: 1873. **Members:** 70,000. **Membership Dues:** regular, $39 (annual) ● life, $750-$1,500. **Staff:** 100. **Budget:** $12,000,000. **Description:** Regular, reserve, and retired professionals in the Navy, Marine Corps, and Coast Guard; civilians interested in the advancement of the knowledge of sea power and in advancing professional, literary, and scientific knowledge in the naval and maritime services. Conducts oral history and color print program. **Libraries: Type:** reference. **Holdings:** 5,000; photographs. **Subjects:** naval, maritime history, ships, submarine, aircraft. **Publications:** *Naval History*, bimonthly. Magazine. Includes eyewitness accounts, oral histories, book reviews, and essays; devoted to naval history. **Price:** $18.00 /year for members; $20.00 /year for nonmembers. ISSN: 1042-1920. **Circulation:** 35,000. **Advertising:** accepted ● *Naval Review*, annual ● Proceedings, monthly. Covers U.S. naval defense issues; includes book reviews and advertisers index. **Price:** included in membership dues; $35.00 /year for nonmembers. ISSN: 0041-798X. **Circulation:** 100,000. **Advertising:** accepted ● Books. Contains information on naval subjects, naval histories, biographies, and fiction. **Conventions/Meetings:** annual Essay and Photo Contests - meet and seminar (exhibits) ● quarterly seminar.

Military History

6111 ■ American Military Medical Impression (AMMI)
Address Unknown since 2008
Founded: 1997. **Members:** 502. **Membership Dues:** individual, $25 (annual). **Description:** Strives to educate people about the sacrifices and advances made by medical personnel during WWII. Operates a WWII field hospital and performs reenactments at airshows.

Military Law

6112 ■ Alliance Against the Uniformed Services Former Spouses Protection Act (USFSPA) Law (AAUL)
Address Unknown since 2008
URL: http://www.militarybetrayed.com
Description: "Seeks to make the USFSPA Law known to everyone it could affect; to reveal to the American public that the USFSPA situation hurts our society and our ability to maintain our national security; to show that the USFSPA Law is antiquated and out of date; and to make apparent (by example) the discrimination of the USFSPA.".

6113 ■ Servicemembers Legal Defense Network (SLDN)
PO Box 65301
Washington, DC 20035-5301
Ph: (202)328-3244
Fax: (202)797-1635
E-mail: sldn@sldn.org
URL: http://www.sldn.org
Contact: Aubrey Sarvis, Exec. Dir.
Founded: 1993. **Staff:** 14. **Budget:** $1,500,000. **Description:** Assists service members hurt by the "Don't Ask, Don't Tell, Don't Pursue, Don't Harass" policy. **Publications:** *Conduct Unbecoming: The Annual Report on 'Don't Ask, Don't Tell'*, annual. Contains policy report. Alternate Formats: online.

Mining

6114 ■ American Society of Mining and Reclamation (ASMR)
3134 Montavesta Rd.
Lexington, KY 40502-3548
Ph: (859)351-9032
Fax: (859)335-6529
E-mail: asmr2@insightbb.com
URL: http://ces.ca.uky.edu/asmr
Contact: Dr. Robert Darmody, Pres.
Founded: 1973. **Members:** 450. **Membership Dues:** full-time student, $10 (annual) ● regular, $50 (annual) ● sustaining, corporate, $100 (annual) ● part-time student, $25 (annual) ● life (regular), $500 ● life (sustaining, corporate), $1,000. **Staff:** 2. **Budget:** $25,000. **Description:** Mining companies and corporations; representatives from federal agencies and state governments; individuals from the academic community. Encourages efforts to protect and enhance land disturbed by mining. Promotes, supports, and assists in research and demonstrations; fosters communication among research scientists, regulatory agencies, landowners, and the surface mining industry; identifies experts for organizations needing assistance; promotes and supports educational programs; disseminates scientific information. Maintains the Register of Reclamation Research and Demonstration Plots on Lands Surface Mined for Coal to collect and preserve information on such areas and to promote better reclamation through wider use of research and demonstration areas. **Awards:** Memorial Scholarship Award. **Frequency:** annual. **Type:** recognition. **Recipient:** for one graduate student and one undergraduate student ● Reclamation Researcher of the Year. **Frequency:** annual. **Type:** recognition. **Recipient:** for research scientists ● Reclamationist of the Year Award. **Frequency:** annual. **Type:** recognition. **Recipient:** for outstanding accomplishments in the practical application or evaluation of reclamation technology ● William T. Plass Award. **Frequency:** annual. **Type:** recognition. **Recipient:** for outstanding contributions in the areas of mining, teaching, and research. **Divisions:** Ecology; Forestry and Wildlife; Geotechnical Engineering; International Tailing Reclamation; Land Use Planning and Design; Soils and Overburden; Water Management. **Formed by Merger of:** (1994) American Home Laundry Manufacturers Association and the Consumer Products Division of the National Electrical Manufacturers Association. **Formerly:** (1978) Council for Surface Mining and Reclamation Research in Appalachia; (1982) American Council for Reclamation Research; (2002) American Society for Surface Mining and Reclamation. **Publications:** *Meeting Proceedings*, annual. Alternate Formats: CD-ROM ● *Reclamation Matters*, semiannual. Magazine. Alternate Formats: online ● *Reclamation Newsletter*, 10/year. In conjunction with Canadian Land Reclamation Association. ISSN: 0826-7049 ● Brochures ● Membership Directory, annual. **Conventions/Meetings:** annual conference (exhibits) - 2008 June 13-19, Richmond, VA - **Avg. Attendance:** 250; 2009 May 30-June 5, Billings, MT - **Avg. Attendance:** 250.

6115 ■ Earthworks
1612 K St. NW, Ste.808
Washington, DC 20006
Ph: (202)887-1872
Fax: (202)887-1875
E-mail: info@earthworksaction.org
URL: http://www.mineralpolicy.org
Contact: Stephen D'Esposito, Pres.
Founded: 1988. **Members:** 2,600. **Membership Dues:** $25 (annual). **Staff:** 13. **Budget:** $900,000. **State Groups:** 2. **Description:** Seeks to prevent and clean up environmental problems caused by mining. Produces reports and factual material on the environmental and fiscal impacts of inadequate mining regulation and poor mining practices. Lobbies for the reform of the 1872 Mining Law, the Clean Water Act, CERCLA, and RCRA (as it applies to mining), and other laws and regulations for mineral development. **Additional Websites:** http://www.earthworksaction.org. **Formerly:** (2004) Mineral Policy Center. **Publications:** Journal, triennial. **Circulation:** 16,000.

6116 ■ Interstate Mining Compact Commission (IMCC)
445-A Carlisle Dr.
Herndon, VA 20170
Ph: (703)709-8654

Fax: (703)709-8655
E-mail: gconrad@imcc.isa.us
URL: http://www.imcc.isa.us
Contact: Gregory E. Conrad, Exec. Dir.
Founded: 1971. **Members:** 20. **Staff:** 4. **Budget:** $425,000. **Description:** States engaged in mining. Aims to: study and recommend techniques for the protection and restoration of land, water, and other resources affected by mining; assist in the reduction, elimination, or counteraction of pollution or deterioration of natural resources; encourage programs in member states that will achieve comparable results in protecting and improving the usefulness of natural resources; maintain an efficient and productive mining industry. Compiles statistics; disseminates studies and reports on surface mining, reclamation techniques, and legislative developments affecting member states. Maintains liaison between state and federal governments. **Libraries: Type:** by appointment only; open to the public. **Holdings:** archival material, articles, periodicals, reports. **Subjects:** mining and natural resources. **Awards:** Kenes C. Bowling National Reclamation Award. **Frequency:** annual. **Type:** recognition. **Recipient:** to states nominated through member state regulatory authorities ● National Mineral Education Awards. **Frequency:** annual. **Type:** recognition. **Recipient:** to states/persons/companies nominated through member state regulatory authorities. **Computer Services:** database. **Committees:** Abandoned Mine Lands; Education Work Group; Environmental Affairs; Mine Safety and Health. **Publications:** *The Compact*, quarterly. Newsletter. Features overview of current issues before the Compact and topics of interest to member states related to congressional and regulatory affairs. **Price:** free. Alternate Formats: online ● Annual Report, annual. Includes overview of activities of the Compact and its committees throughout the calendar year. **Price:** free ● Directory, semiannual. Contains list of member states and their Governors and Governors' official representatives; standing committee members; and state contact persons. **Price:** free. **Conventions/Meetings:** annual banquet and conference - always April/May ● executive committee meeting and luncheon - always September, October or November.

6117 ■ Mine Inspectors' Institute of America (MIIA)
319 Painterville Rd.
Hunker, PA 15639
Ph: (724)925-5150
Fax: (724)925-6190
URL: http://www.msha.gov
Members: 500. **Description:** Federal, state, and Canadian provincial mine inspectors; company safety officers. Disseminates information on mining. **Conventions/Meetings:** annual meeting - always June.

6118 ■ National Association of State Land Reclamationists (NASLR)
c/o Anna Harrington
Coal Res. Center
Southern Illinois Univ.
Carbondale, IL 62901-4623
Ph: (618)536-5521
Fax: (618)453-7346
E-mail: jsmoskie@gw.dec.ny.us
URL: http://www.crc.siu.edu/naslr/home.htm
Contact: Mr. Joseph S. Moskiewicz, Sec.-Treas.
Founded: 1973. **Members:** 140. **Membership Dues:** state, $200 (annual) ● individual, $10 (annual) ● corporate sponsorship, $100 (annual). **Staff:** 1. **State Groups:** 23. **Description:** Individuals involved in administering state-sponsored land reclamation programs. Seeks to bring together state officials for discussion of problems of national interest; to keep abreast of the art of land reclamation; to promote cooperation between states, private mining groups, and the federal government; to discuss, encourage, endorse, or sponsor activities, programs, and legislation that will advance mined land reclamation. **Awards:** Mined Land Reclamation Award. **Frequency:** annual. **Type:** recognition ● Reclamationist of the Year Award. **Frequency:** annual. **Type:** recognition. **Committees:** Cooperative Land Reclamation; Foreign Relations; Legislative; Public Relations and Education; Research for Improved Mining Methods. **Publications:** *NASLR Newsletter*, quarterly. **Price:** free for members. **Circulation:** 400. **Conventions/Meetings:** annual conference - usually fall.

Minorities

6119 ■ National Congress of Black Women (NCBW)
1224 W St. SE, Ste.200
Washington, DC 20020
Ph: (202)678-6788
E-mail: info@nationalcongressbw.org
URL: http://www.nationalcongressbw.org
Contact: Dr. E. Faye Williams, Chair
Founded: 1984. **Membership Dues:** life, $1,000 ● young adult (up to age 25), $25 ● general, $50 (annual) ● patron, $100 (annual) ● sponsor, $200 (annual) ● benefactor, $500 (annual) ● youth (up to 21 years of age), $10 (annual) ● young adult (up to 25 years of age), $25 (annual) ● life, $1,000. **Staff:** 7. **Description:** Works to encourage African American women to engage in political activities. Offers training in understanding and operating within the political process. Strives to develop, educate and encourage African American women to seek office. Encourages the appointment of these women at all levels of Government. **Formerly:** (2005) National Political Congress of Black Women.

Mortuary Science

6120 ■ International Conference of Funeral Service Examining Boards of the United States (ICFSEB)
1885 Shelby Ln.
Fayetteville, AR 72704
Ph: (479)442-7076
Fax: (479)442-7090
E-mail: info@theconferenceonline.org
URL: http://www.cfseb.org
Contact: Dalene Paull, Exec. Dir.
Founded: 1904. **Members:** 52. **Membership Dues:** regular, $250 (annual). **Staff:** 4. **Budget:** $650,000. **Description:** State licensing agencies (boards of health and departments of mortuary sciences) that govern the licensure of embalmers and funeral directors in the U.S. and in Ontario, Canada; membership includes executive secretaries and members of these boards. Accredited schools and colleges of mortuary science are associate members. Studies and recommends educational standards; examines and accredits embalming schools and colleges; cooperates in obtaining uniformity of rules and regulations governing state boards. Compiles and makes available to all member state boards and licensing agencies a standard examination to use in testing applicants. Participates in the American Board of Funeral Service Education (see separate entry) to create and maintain professional standards for schools and colleges. Maintains speakers' bureau and compiles statistics. **Libraries: Type:** reference. **Awards: Type:** recognition. **Telecommunication Services:** electronic mail, director@theconferenceonline.org. **Affiliated With:** American Board of Funeral Service Education. **Formerly:** (2003) Conference of Funeral Service Examining Boards of the United States. **Publications:** *The Conference Report*, 3/year. Newsletter ● *National Board Examination Brochure* ● Directory, annual. **Conventions/Meetings:** annual convention.

Municipal Employees

6121 ■ Society of Municipal Arborists (SMA)
PO Box 641
Watkinsville, GA 30677
Ph: (706)769-7412
Fax: (706)769-7307
E-mail: urbanforestry@prodigy.net
URL: http://www.urban-forestry.com
Contact: Jerri J. LaHaie CAE, Exec. Dir.
Founded: 1964. **Members:** 800. **Membership Dues:** senior, student, $25 (annual) ● professional, $60 (annual) ● corporate, $125 (annual). **Staff:** 1. **Description:** Arboriculture professionals, students of arboriculture, commercial companies in related fields, and interested individuals. Promotes the science of municipal arboriculture as a major ingredient of city planning. Provides accreditation to forestry departments that meet approved standards and application. Serves as a liaison between related groups; conducts research and publishes results. **Awards: Frequency:** annual. **Type:** recognition. **Committees:** Accreditation; Arbor Day; Awards; Editorial Advisory; Education Curriculum; Equipment; National Affairs; Public Relations; Tree Research and Selection. **Absorbed:** (1997) Municipal Arborists and Urban Foresters Society. **Publications:** *A Review of Planting Practices in Selected Cities* ● *City Trees*, bimonthly. Journal. Contains technical articles on species of trees, pest control, conservation, planning/design, and equipment. Includes research updates and statistics. **Price:** included in membership dues; $40.00 /year for nonmembers. **Circulation:** 800. **Advertising:** accepted. Alternate Formats: online ● *Meeting Proceedings*, annual ● Membership Directory, annual. **Conventions/Meetings:** annual conference (exhibits).

Municipal Government

6122 ■ Hispanic Elected Local Officials (HELO)
c/o National League of Cities
1301 Pennsylvania Ave. NW, Ste.550
Washington, DC 20004
Ph: (202)626-3000
Fax: (202)626-3043
E-mail: info@nlc.org
Contact: Carol Alvarado, Pres.
Founded: 1976. **Members:** 150. **Membership Dues:** elected official from NLC direct member city, $35 ● elected official from NLC non-member city, $45 ● supporting, $55 ● corporate, $150. **Staff:** 4. **Languages:** English, Spanish. **Description:** Hispanic elected officials at the local level. Seeks to allow members to share information and experiences concerning local government issues. **Formerly:** (1980) National League of Spanish Speaking Elected Officials; (1984) Elected Spanish Speaking Officials. **Publications:** *Constituency and Member Group Newsletter*, quarterly. Alternate Formats: online. **Conventions/Meetings:** annual Congressional City Conference - meeting, held in conjunction with the National League of Cities ● annual convention (exhibits).

6123 ■ International City/County Management Association (ICMA)
777 N Capitol St. NE, Ste.500
Washington, DC 20002-4201
Ph: (202)289-4262 (202)962-3680
Free: (800)745-8780
Fax: (202)962-3500
E-mail: roneill@icma.org
URL: http://icma.org
Contact: Robert O'Neill Jr., Exec. Dir.
Founded: 1914. **Members:** 8,400. **Membership Dues:** full/affiliate, $215 (annual) ● student, intern, $25 (annual). **Staff:** 125. **Budget:** $20,000,000. **Description:** International professional and educational organization for appointed administrators and assistant administrators serving cities, counties, districts, and regions. Provides publications, training, and management assistance to help local government professionals improve their skills and increase their knowledge. Collects data on local governments. **Libraries: Type:** reference. **Holdings:** audiovisuals, books, clippings, monographs, periodicals. **Subjects:** municipal management. **Awards: Frequency:** annual. **Type:** recognition. **Computer Services:** Online services, provides survey data for a fee. **Formerly:** (1969) International City Managers' Association;

(1990) International City Management Association. **Publications:** *ICMA Newsletter*, biweekly ● *IQ Report*, monthly ● *Job Opportunities Bulletin*, periodic. Lists employment opportunities of particular interest to women and minorities. ● *Municipal Management Series*, periodic ● *Municipal Year Book*, annual. Yearbook ● *Public Management*, monthly. Magazine. **Conventions/Meetings:** annual conference (exhibits) - 2008 Sept. 21-24, Richmond, VA; 2009 Sept. 13-16, Montreal, QC, Canada; 2010 Oct. 17-20, San Jose, CA.

6124 ■ International Institute of Municipal Clerks (IIMC)
8331 Utica Ave., Ste.200
Rancho Cucamonga, CA 91730
Ph: (909)944-4162
Free: (800)251-1639
Fax: (909)944-8545
E-mail: hq@iimc.com
URL: http://www.iimc.com
Contact: Marcella H. O'Connor MMC, Pres.
Founded: 1947. **Members:** 10,400. **Membership Dues:** full, $115-$200 (annual) ● additional, full, $75 (annual) ● retired, $25 (annual) ● corporate, $600 (annual) ● associate, $75 (annual). **Staff:** 12. **Budget:** $2,200,000. **Multinational. Description:** County, city, town, township, village, borough, regional, metropolitan, and district clerks, city secretaries, recorders, and clerks of council. Provides education at universities throughout the U.S. and Canada. Conducts surveys and research; provides information services annual conference. **Libraries: Type:** reference. **Holdings:** 600. **Subjects:** clerk field. **Awards:** Institute Directors Award of Excellence. **Frequency:** annual. **Type:** recognition. **Recipient:** for unique and exceptional contributions of current retired Institute Director in promoting quality education for municipal clerks ● President's Award of Merit. **Frequency:** annual. **Type:** recognition. **Recipient:** for members who have been instrumental in promoting the goals of the association ● Quill Award. **Frequency:** annual. **Type:** recognition. **Recipient:** for outstanding contribution to the association. **Computer Services:** database, salary information and salary profile (for members only). **Telecommunication Services:** electronic mail, moconnor@uralla.nsw.gov.au. **Committees:** Budget and Planning; Conference Policy; Education and Personal Growth; Election; International Relations; Program Review and Certification; Public Relations and Marketing; Research; Research and Information. **Publications:** *City Council Rules of Procedure*. Report. Contains sample guidelines. **Price:** $6.00 for members; $18.00 for nonmembers ● *Consent Agendas*. Bulletin. Contains procedures on handling matters on agenda expeditiously. **Price:** $6.00 for members; $18.00 for nonmembers ● *Election Management and Performance Indicators*. Bulletin. Features topics on managing elections. **Price:** $12.00 for members; $20.00 for nonmembers ● *How to Design a Disaster Recovery Program*. Bulletin. Outlines how to draft a disaster recovery plan for city. **Price:** $6.00 for members; $18.00 for nonmembers ● *News Digest*, monthly. **Advertising:** accepted ● *Short, Simple and Efficient Agendas*. Bulletin. Contains a system for agenda and minutes. **Price:** $6.00 for members; $18.00 for nonmembers ● *Technical Bulletin*, periodic. **Conventions/Meetings:** annual Educational Conference, equipment services for municipal government (exhibits) - 2009 May 19-23, Chicago, IL; 2010 May 16-20, Sydney, NW, Australia.

6125 ■ National Association of Local Government Environmental Professionals (NALGEP)
1333 New Hampshire Ave. NW, 2nd Fl.
Washington, DC 20036
Ph: (202)638-6254
Fax: (202)393-2866
E-mail: nalgep@spiegelmcd.com
URL: http://www.nalgep.org
Contact: Mr. Paul Connor, Exec. Dir.
Founded: 1993. **Membership Dues:** local government (based on number of people in the community), $175-$225 (annual) ● associate, $400 (annual). **Description:** Environmental officials responsible for municipal environmental compliance. Promotes effective administration of municipal environmental quality projects. Facilitates networking and exchange of information among members; promotes environmental education and training; conducts environmental policy projects; represents the collective views of local governments on environmental issues. **Projects:** Brownfields Showcase Community Network; Clean Air Transportation Communities; Community Revitalization Research Initiative; Smart Growth Business Partnership; Smart Growth for Clean Water. **Publications:** *NALGEP News Flash*, biweekly. Newsletters. **Price:** $1.00 for nonmembers; free for members. **Advertising:** accepted. Alternate Formats: online.

6126 ■ National Association of Towns and Townships (NATAT)
1130 Connecticut Ave. NW, Ste.300
Washington, DC 20036
Ph: (202)454-3954
Free: (866)830-0008
Fax: (202)331-1598
E-mail: info@natat.org
URL: http://www.natat.org
Contact: Mr. Keith Hite, Pres.
Founded: 1976. **Members:** 11,000. **Membership Dues:** associate, $100 (annual). **Staff:** 6. **Budget:** $750,000. **Regional Groups:** 11,000. **Local Groups:** 11. **National Groups:** 2. **Description:** Lobbying organization for towns and townships at the federal level. Conducts annual education and legislative conference. **Awards:** Grassroots Government Leadership Award. **Frequency:** annual. **Type:** recognition. **Telecommunication Services:** electronic mail, khite@psats.org. **Absorbed:** (1983) National Association of Smaller Communities. **Publications:** *The Americans with Disabilities Act—A Compliance Workbook for Small Communities* ● *Getting Online 2.0: A Small Town Guide to Creating 21st Century Communities* ● *Getting Out From Under—Underground Storage Tank Alternatives for Small Towns* ● *Growing Our Own Jobs—A Small Town Guide to Creating Jobs Through Agricultural Diversification* ● *Harvesting Hometown Jobs—A Small Town Guide to Economic Development* ● *Innovative Grassroots Financing-A Small Town Guide to Raising Funds and Cutting Costs* ● *Limiting Small Town Liability: A Risk Management Primer for Small Town Leaders* ● *Treat it Right—A local Official's Guide to Small Town Wastewater Treatment* ● *Washington Report*, monthly. Covers small town and rural government. **Price:** free for members. Alternate Formats: online ● *Why Waste A Second Chance? A Small Town Guide to Recycling*. **Conventions/Meetings:** annual America's Town Meeting - conference (exhibits) - September in Washington, DC ● periodic workshop, training.

6127 ■ National Black Caucus of Local Elected Officials (NBC-LEO)
c/o National League of Cities
1301 Pennsylvania Ave. NW
Washington, DC 20004-1763
Ph: (202)626-3169
Fax: (202)626-3043
E-mail: gordon@nlc.org
URL: http://www.nbc-leo.org
Contact: Mary France Gordon, Dir.
Founded: 1970. **Members:** 400. **Membership Dues:** regular, associate, $50 (annual). **Staff:** 4. **Regional Groups:** 18. **Description:** Elected black municipal and county officials united to recognize and deal with problems of members. Attempts to provide the organizational structure required to better present and respond to issues affecting constituents. Seeks to influence the National League of Cities in the development of policies affecting black Americans; promotes legislative and economic development initiatives directed toward the needs of the black community. **Awards:** City Cultural Diversity Award. **Frequency:** annual. **Type:** recognition. **Recipient:** for excellent achievements of cities ● Liberty Award. **Frequency:** annual. **Type:** recognition. **Affiliated With:** National League of Cities. **Publications:** *Consistency*, monthly. Journal. **Price:** free for members. **Circulation:** 500 ● *Member Group*, monthly. Newsletter. **Price:** free for members. **Circulation:** 500 ● *Newslines*, monthly. Newsletter. **Price:** free for members. **Circulation:** 500. Alternate Formats: online. **Conventions/Meetings:** annual Board of Directors Regional Conferences - meeting ● semiannual Congress of Cities - conference ● Congressional City Conference.

6128 ■ National Civic League (NCL)
1445 Market St., Ste.300
Denver, CO 80202
Ph: (303)571-4343
Free: (800)864-8622
Fax: (303)571-4404
E-mail: ncl@ncl.org
URL: http://www.ncl.org
Contact: Christopher T. Gates, Pres.
Founded: 1894. **Members:** 600. **Membership Dues:** individual, $75 (annual) ● nonprofit/public agency, $85 (annual) ● student/senior, $45 (annual) ● local government, $225-$425 (annual) ● corporate and sustaining, $1,000-$5,000 (annual). **Staff:** 14. **Budget:** $2,000,000. **Description:** Community leaders, civic leaders, educators, public officials, civic organizations, libraries, nonprofits and businesses interested in community building, transforming democratic institutions and developing techniques of citizen action and participation. Serves as a clearinghouse for information on healthy communities, community renewal, local campaign, finance reform, All-American cities, city and county charters, election systems and techniques of citizen participation. **Awards:** All-America City and Community Award. **Frequency:** annual. **Type:** recognition. **Recipient:** to 10 communities for extraordinary collaborative civic accomplishments. **Programs:** America's Future: Create It Together Research Program. **Projects:** Civic Assistance Program; Healthy Communities Initiative; National Civic League Press; Radon Action; Research Program. **Formerly:** (1981) National Municipal League; (1987) Citizens Forum on Self-Government/ National Municipal League. **Publications:** *Civic Action*, quarterly. Newsletter. **Price:** free for members. **Circulation:** 1,500. Alternate Formats: online ● *National Civic Review: Building Successful Communities*, quarterly. Journal. Covers community problem solving including information on technology transfer, government management and productivity, and performance measurement. **Price:** included in membership dues; $30.00 /year for nonmembers. ISSN: 0027-9013. Alternate Formats: microform ● Annual Report, annual ● Also publishes model charters, reports, pamphlets, and books on state and local government. **Conventions/Meetings:** annual National Conference on Governance - meeting.

6129 ■ National Conference of Black Mayors (NCBM)
1151 Cleveland Ave., Bldg. D
East Point, GA 30344
Ph: (404)765-6444
Fax: (404)765-6430
E-mail: info@ncbm.org
URL: http://www.ncbm.org
Contact: Mayor Robert L. Bowser, Pres.
Founded: 1974. **Members:** 462. **Staff:** 5. **Budget:** $400,000. **State Groups:** 17. **Description:** Nonpartisan organization dedicated to promoting the development of municipalities managed by black mayors. Objectives are to: improve the executive management capacity and efficiency of member municipalities in the delivery of municipal services; create viable communities within which normal government functions can be performed efficiently; provide the basis upon which new social overhead investments in the infrastructure of municipalities can utilize federal, state, local, and private resources to encourage new industry and increase employment; assist municipalities in stabilizing their population through improvements of the quality of life for residents and, concurrently, create alternatives to outward migration. Facilitates small town growth and development through energy conservation. Offers workshops; compiles demographic statistics. **Awards:** Fannie Lou Hamer Award. **Frequency:** annual. **Type:** recog-

nition ● Presidents' Award. **Frequency:** annual. **Type:** recognition ● Tribute to a Black American. **Frequency:** annual. **Type:** recognition. **Computer Services:** Mailing lists. **Programs:** Municipal Management Clinic; Youth Career Expos. **Task Forces:** Economic Development; Energy. **Formerly:** (1977) Southern Conference of Black Mayors. **Publications:** *Mayors Roster*, annual. Directory ● *Municipal Watch*, quarterly. **Conventions/Meetings:** annual conference (exhibits) - always April.

6130 ■ National League of Cities (NLC)
1301 Pennsylvania Ave. NW, Ste.550
Washington, DC 20004-1747
Ph: (202)626-3000
Fax: (202)626-3043
E-mail: info@nlc.org
URL: http://www.nlc.org
Contact: Donald J. Borut, Exec. Dir.
Founded: 1924. **Members:** 1,800. **Membership Dues:** associate, for-profit, $1,000 (annual) ● associate, nonprofit, $675 (annual). **Staff:** 97. **Budget:** $15,900,000. **State Groups:** 49. **Local Groups:** 1,700. **Description:** Federation of state leagues and cities. Develops and pursues a national municipal policy which can meet the future needs of cities and help cities solve critical problems they have in common. Represents municipalities before Congress and federal agencies. Offers training, technical assistance, and information to municipal officials to help them improve the quality of local government. Sponsors the National League of Cities Institute. Conducts research program and seminars. **Libraries: Type:** not open to the public. **Holdings:** 20,000; books, periodicals. **Subjects:** local government. **Awards:** Certificate of Achievement in Leadership Program. **Frequency:** annual. **Type:** recognition. **Recipient:** for local elected officials ● City Cultural Diversity. **Frequency:** annual. **Type:** recognition. **Recipient:** for cities that exhibit quality and innovation in promoting cultural diversity ● James C. Howland Award for Municipal Enrichment. **Frequency:** annual. **Type:** recognition. **Recipient:** for communities that have preserved and/or enriched a high quality of life in cities, towns, and villages. **Computer Services:** database, cities with population exceeding 10,000 ● mailing lists, names of 62,000 city officials. **Committees:** Community and Economic Development; Energy, Environmental and Natural Resources; Finance Administration and Intergovernmental Relations; Human Development; Information Technology and Communications; Public Safety and Crime Prevention; Transportation Infrastructure and Services. **Formerly:** American Municipal Association. **Publications:** *City Fiscal Conditions*, annual. Book. Contains survey of city financial conditions. **Price:** $15.00 ● *Directory of City Policy Officials*, annual. Lists names and city hall address and phone numbers for local elected officials in all cities with over 10,000 population. **Price:** $40.00. **Advertising:** accepted ● *Nation's Cities Weekly*. Newspaper. **Price:** $59.00 for members; $96.00 for nonmembers in U.S.; $128.00 for nonmembers in Canada and Mexico; $183.00 for nonmembers in other foreign countries. ISSN: 0164-5935. **Circulation:** 30,000. **Advertising:** accepted ● *The State of America's Cities*, annual. Book. Contains opinion survey of city leaders. **Price:** $10.00. Alternate Formats: online. **Conventions/Meetings:** annual Congress of Cities - convention (exhibits) - 2008 Nov. 11-15, Orlando, FL; 2009 Nov. 10-14, San Antonio, TX ● annual Congressional City Conference - always March in Washington, DC. 2009 Mar. 14-18, Washington, DC; 2010 Mar. 13-17, Washington, DC.

6131 ■ Reason Public Policy Institute
3415 S Sepulveda Blvd., Ste.400
Los Angeles, CA 90034
Ph: (310)391-2245
Fax: (310)391-4395
E-mail: david.nott@reason.org
Contact: David Nott, Pres.
Founded: 1976. **Staff:** 9. **Budget:** $1,500,000. **Description:** Aims to research and help implement public policy innovations; apply libertarian ideas to develop policy proposals that advance liberty and build the necessary coalitions based on shared goals to advance those ideas with motivated policymakers and overcome obstacles to change; stresses transparency and accountability for results in public policy; offers alternative institutional structures that incorporate flexibility, voluntarism, property rights, and competition. **Computer Services:** database, Directory of Private Service Providers, which lists companies that supply public services ● database, Privatization Bibliographic, which identifies cities and counties with privatized particular services ● database, Privatization, which lists state and local governments that have privatized services. **Formerly:** (1991) Local Government Center; (2003) Privatization Center. **Publications:** *Annual Privatization Report*. Annual Report. Describes developments in privatization at all levels of government and internationally, including activities of research institutes. **Price:** $35.00/year. **Circulation:** 10,000. **Advertising:** accepted ● *Policy Research Studies*, periodic. Papers ● *Privatization Watch*, monthly. Newsletter. Reports on the latest developments in privatization and market solutions to urban problems; includes corporate profiles. **Price:** $95.00/year. **Circulation:** 1,000. **Advertising:** accepted ● Books ● Brochure.

6132 ■ United States Conference of Mayors (USCM)
1620 Eye St. NW
Washington, DC 20006
Ph: (202)293-7330
Fax: (202)293-2352
E-mail: info@usmayors.org
URL: http://www.usmayors.org
Contact: J. Thomas Cochran, Exec. Dir.
Founded: 1932. **Members:** 1,050. **Staff:** 50. **Budget:** $11,000,000. **Description:** Cities with populations of over 30,000 represented by their mayors. Promotes improved municipal government by cooperation between cities and the federal government. Provides educational information, technical assistance, and legislative services to cities. Conducts research programs; compiles statistics. **Awards:** City Livability Award. **Frequency:** annual. **Type:** recognition. **Recipient:** for mayors of winning cities ● Excellence in Public/Private Partnership Award. **Frequency:** annual. **Type:** recognition. **Recipient:** for outstanding public/private partnership working together in improving the quality of life in American cities ● Municipal Water Conservation Achievement Award. **Frequency:** annual. **Type:** recognition. **Recipient:** for communities with excellent water conservation practices. **Computer Services:** Mailing lists, of members. **Committees:** Health; International Affairs; Jobs, Education and Family; Transportation and Communications; Urban Economic Policy. **Divisions:** Program Development and Issue Advocacy; Program Development and Technical Assistance. **Publications:** *The Mayors of America's Principal Cities*, semiannual ● *Resolutions Adopted*, annual ● *U.S. Mayor*, biweekly. Newspaper. **Price:** $35.00. **Advertising:** accepted. Alternate Formats: online. **Conventions/Meetings:** annual meeting (exhibits) - always June ● annual meeting - always January, Washington, DC.

6133 ■ Women in Government (WIG)
2600 Virginia Ave. NW, Ste.709
Washington, DC 20037-1925
Ph: (202)333-0825
Free: (888)333-0164
Fax: (202)333-0875
E-mail: abrady@womeningovernment.org
URL: http://www.womeningovernment.org
Contact: Susan Crosby, Exec. Dir./Pres.
Founded: 1988. **Members:** 1,200. **Membership Dues:** woman state legislator, $100 (annual) ● individual, $50 (annual) ● student, $20 (annual). **Staff:** 11. **Budget:** $1,500,000. **Description:** Coalition of elected women in state, national, and international governments. Promotes dialogue between the public and private sectors. Serves as an information clearinghouse. Conducts educational bipartisan seminars and discussions on issues affecting and affected by various legislative bodies. Conducts educational programs. **Telecommunication Services:** electronic mail, membership@womeningovernment.org. **Councils:** Business. **Programs:** Internship; State Directors. **Publications:** *The Legislative Voice*, quarterly. Newsletter. Alternate Formats: online ● Membership Directory, annual. **Conventions/Meetings:** monthly conference and roundtable, small group.

6134 ■ Women in Municipal Government (WIMG)
c/o National League of Cities
1301 Pennsylvania Ave. NW, Ste.550
Washington, DC 20004
Ph: (202)626-3000 (202)626-3169
Fax: (202)626-3043
E-mail: mitchell@nlc.org
Contact: Kay Senter, Pres.
Founded: 1974. **Members:** 200. **Membership Dues:** regular, $50 (annual) ● associate, $60 (annual) ● supporting, $75 (annual). **Staff:** 4. **Description:** Women who are elected and appointed city officials including mayors, council members, and commissioners. Seeks to: encourage active participation of women officials in the organizational and policy-making processes and programs of the National League of Cities and state municipal leagues; identify qualified women for service in the NLC and other national positions; promote issues of interest to women and the status of women in the nation's cities. **Publications:** *Constituency and Member Group Report*, quarterly. Newsletter. Offers news on all of NCC's constituency groups. **Price:** included in membership dues. **Circulation:** 1,400. **Conventions/Meetings:** annual conference and board meeting - always summer ● National League of Cities Congress of Cities ● National League of Cities Congressional City Conference ● seminar and workshop, includes plenary and governance sessions (exhibits) - always spring, summer, and fall.

Natural Resources

6135 ■ Association of Metropolitan Water Agencies (AMWA)
1620 I St. NW, Ste.500
Washington, DC 20006
Ph: (202)331-2820
Fax: (202)785-1845
E-mail: vandehei@amwa.net
URL: http://www.amwa.net
Contact: Diane VanDe Hei, Exec. Dir.
Founded: 1981. **Members:** 63. **Staff:** 6. **Description:** Represents municipal public water supply agencies. Represents members' interests before the Environmental Protection Agency and other federal bodies. **Awards:** Donald R. Boyd Award. **Frequency:** annual. **Type:** recognition. **Recipient:** for extraordinary personal service in drinking water quality field ● Gold Awards for Competitiveness Achievement. **Frequency:** annual. **Type:** recognition. **Recipient:** for public drinking water system ● Platinum Awards for Sustained Competitiveness Achievement. **Frequency:** annual. **Type:** recognition. **Recipient:** for previous Gold Award winners ● President's Award. **Frequency:** annual. **Type:** recognition. **Recipient:** for individuals who are currently or formerly representing AMWA member agencies. **Publications:** *Regulatory*, monthly. Report ● Also publishes proceedings and surveys. **Conventions/Meetings:** annual Legislative/Regulatory Meeting - always March or April, Washington, DC ● annual meeting - 2008 Oct. 19-22, New Orleans, LA.

6136 ■ Energy and Mineral Law Foundation (EMLF)
340 S Broadway, Ste.101
Lexington, KY 40508
Ph: (859)231-0271
Fax: (859)226-0485
E-mail: emlf@aol.com
URL; http://www.emlf.org
Contact: David G. Ries, Pres.
Founded: 1979. **Members:** 600. **Membership Dues:** contributing, $425 (annual) ● supporting, $1,100 (annual) ● sustaining, $2,200 (annual) ● associate, $100 (annual) ● law student, $20 (annual). **Staff:** 2. **Bud-**

get: $350,000. **Description:** Represents law firms, corporations, coal and gas producers, electric power companies, law schools, associations, consultants, and individuals interested in the development of natural resources and energy law. Established to stimulate research, discussion, and dissemination of information on the legal problems in the field. Sponsors institutes and educational programs. **Libraries: Type:** reference. **Holdings:** 19. **Subjects:** coal, oil, coalbed methane, mine safety, health, labor, gas transmission. **Awards: Type:** grant ● Law Student Scholarship. **Frequency:** annual. **Type:** scholarship. **Recipient:** for law student at member law school. **Formerly:** (1999) Eastern Mineral Law Foundation. **Publications:** *EMLF White Papers.* Contains chapters from the various proceedings of Annual Institutes of Energy and Mineral Law Foundation. **Price:** $10. 00. Alternate Formats: online ● *Institute Proceedings*, annual. Book. **Price:** $95.00. **Circulation:** 480. Alternate Formats: online ● *Special Institute Handbook Series*, periodic ● Membership Directory, annual. **Conventions/Meetings:** annual conference ● workshop and seminar - 3-5/year.

6137 ■ Great Lakes Commission (GLC)
Eisenhower Corporate Park
2805 S Indus. Hwy., Ste.100
Ann Arbor, MI 48104-6791
Ph: (734)971-9135
Fax: (734)971-9150
E-mail: teder@qlc.org
URL: http://www.glc.org
Contact: Tim A. Eder, Exec. Dir.
Founded: 1955. **Members:** 26. **Membership Dues:** $60,000 (annual). **Staff:** 32. **Budget:** $6,000,000. **Description:** Interstate Compact Commission. Designated or appointed officials (according to state statutes) in 8 states party to the Great Lakes Basin Compact. Serves as a research, coordinating, advisory, and advocacy agency on the development, use, and protection of the water and related land resources of the Great Lakes Basin. Compiles statistics and information on state, federal, and regional programs and projects. **Awards:** Carol A. Ratza Memorial Scholarship. **Frequency:** annual. **Type:** scholarship. **Recipient:** for outstanding achievement and vision in electronic communications technology ● Outstanding Service. **Frequency:** annual. **Type:** recognition. **Recipient:** for organizational leadership. **Computer Services:** database, Great Lakes Regional Water Use and Repository. **Boards:** Network Advisory. **Programs:** Administration; Communications and Internet Technology; Data and Information Management; Environmental Quality; Regional Coordination; Resource Management; Transportation and Sustainable Development. **Task Forces:** Air Toxics; Aquatic Nuisance Species; Coast Guard Funding; Ecosystem Charter; Emergency Preparedness; Great Lakes Circle Tour; Great Lakes Information; Soil Erosion and Sedimentation; Soo Locks Funding; Tourism and Outdoor Recreation; Water Resources Management. **Publications:** *Advisor*, bimonthly. Newsletter. **Price:** free. **Circulation:** 3,500. Alternate Formats: online ● *Great Lakes Research Checklist*, periodic ● *Membership List*, periodic. Membership Directory ● *Minutes of Regular Meeting*, semiannual ● *Special Publications*, periodic ● Annual Report, annual. **Price:** free. Alternate Formats: online. **Conventions/Meetings:** semiannual meeting ● annual meeting ● periodic meeting, for task forces ● seminar.

6138 ■ Interstate Council on Water Policy (ICWP)
51 Monroe St., Ste.PE-08A
Rockville, MD 20850
Ph: (301)984-1908 (703)622-6660
Fax: (301)984-5841
E-mail: icwp2005@yahoo.com
URL: http://www.icwp.org
Contact: Peter Evans, Exec. Dir.
Founded: 1959. **Members:** 60. **Membership Dues:** large state agency, $5,000 ● smaller state agency, interstate, regional, water resource organization, $3,500 ● affiliate, $1,500. **Budget:** $55,000. **Description:** State, interstate, and intrastate officials with responsibility for all water quantity- and quality-related matters. Affiliate members are individuals, businesses, universities, and governmental agencies with primary interest in water. Facilitates interstate cooperation and exchange of information. Presents views to Congress and federal agencies. Researches water management, water for energy, and water technology. **Telecommunication Services:** electronic mail, phe@riverswork.com. **Committees:** Drought; Groundwater; Legislative; Policy. **Formerly:** (1990) Interstate Conference on Water Policy. **Publications:** *Policy Statement*, annual ● Membership Directory, annual ● Papers ● Also publishes congressional testimony. **Conventions/Meetings:** annual conference ● annual roundtable - always in Washington, DC.

6139 ■ Mineral Economics and Management Society (MEMS)
c/o Lisa Morrison, Treas.
PO Box 656
Kennett Square, PA 19348
Ph: (610)925-1860
Fax: (610)925-1861
E-mail: lisa.morrison@crugroup.com
URL: http://www.minecon.org
Contact: Lisa Morrison, Treas.
Founded: 1990. **Members:** 120. **Membership Dues:** regular, $60 (annual) ● student, $30 (annual). **Budget:** $20,000. **Regional Groups:** 1. **Multinational. Description:** Represents natural resource economists, business and finance specialists, geologists, mineral and energy engineers, and others interested in the mineral industries. Seeks to further the application of management, economics, finance, and policy analysis to issues in the minerals and materials producing industries. **Awards:** Student Paper Awards. **Frequency:** annual. **Type:** recognition. **Recipient:** for quality of paper and presentation. **Computer Services:** Mailing lists. **Publications:** *Annual Conference Proceedings*, annual. Contains papers presented at the annual conference. **Price:** $20.00 for members in U.S. and Canada; $25.00 for members outside U.S. and Canada; $45.00 for nonmembers in U.S. and Canada; $50.00 for nonmembers outside U.S. and Canada. Alternate Formats: CD-ROM ● *MEMS Newsletter*, semiannual. Reports on society events and opportunities for professional activity. Alternate Formats: online. **Conventions/Meetings:** annual convention, displays publications of interest to members (exhibits) - always spring.

6140 ■ National Association of Flood and Storm Water Management Agencies (NAFSMA)
1301 K St. NW, Ste.800 E
Washington, DC 20005
Ph: (202)218-4122 (202)218-4133
Fax: (202)478-1734
E-mail: info@nafsma.org
URL: http://www.nafsma.org
Contact: Susan Gilson, Exec. Dir.
Founded: 1977. **Members:** 106. **Membership Dues:** regular (based on service population), $1,000-$9,000 (annual) ● subscribing (based on number of employees), $1,500-$2,500 (annual). **Staff:** 2. **Budget:** $200,000. **Description:** State, county, and local governments; special districts concerned with management of water resources. Objectives are to reduce or eliminate flooding and provide for improved storm water management and conservation of watersheds. **Telecommunication Services:** electronic mail, sgilson@carmengroup.com. **Committees:** Flood Management; Floodplain Management; Stormwater Management; Watershed Management. **Formerly:** (1988) National Association of Urban Flood Management Agencies. **Publications:** *Legislative Report*, periodic ● *NAFSMA Bulletin*, periodic ● *NAFSMA Newsletter*, monthly ● *Survey of Local Storm Water Utilities.* **Conventions/Meetings:** annual meeting and workshop.

6141 ■ Rocky Mountain Mineral Law Foundation (RMMLF)
9191 Sheridan Blvd., Ste.203
Westminster, CO 80031
Ph: (303)321-8100
Fax: (303)321-7657
E-mail: info@rmmlf.org
URL: http://www.rmmlf.org
Contact: David P. Phillips, Exec. Dir.
Founded: 1955. **Members:** 2,000. **Membership Dues:** individual, $450 (annual) ● university (faculty), $350 (annual) ● senior (fully retired), $120 (annual) ● firm, corporation, agency, organization, $915-$3,295 (annual). **Staff:** 9. **Multinational. Description:** Law schools; bar associations; mining, oil, and gas associations and companies; landmen; natural resource attorneys and law firms. Keeps abreast of the laws, regulations, decisions, and literature concerning mining, oil, gas, environmental, and water problems; disseminates this information and related research data to natural resource-oriented individuals, companies, and associations. Holds institutes on natural resource-related topics; conducts short courses. Sponsors Gower Federal Services, which provides monthly updates in each of several areas including royalty valuation and management, oil and gas, mining, and the outer continental shelf. **Committees:** Mining Joint Venture Agreement; Natural Resources Law Teaching; Site Selections; Special Institutes and Projects. **Publications:** *American Law of Mining*, annual ● *Annual Institute Proceedings* ● *Law of Federal Oil and Gas Leases* ● *Mineral Law Newsletter*, quarterly. **Price:** $72.00/year. Alternate Formats: online ● *Public Land and Resources Law Digest*, semiannual ● *Special Institute Manuals* ● *Water Law Newsletter*, 3/year. **Price:** $42.00/year. Alternate Formats: online ● Brochure. **Conventions/Meetings:** periodic conference ● workshop.

Naval Engineering

6142 ■ Marine Corps Engineer Association (MCEA)
PO Box 566
Jacksonville, NC 28541
Ph: (910)265-2701
E-mail: exdirmcea@yahoo.com
URL: http://www.marcorengasn.org
Contact: Sgt. Maj. Mike Cline USMC, Exec. Dir.
Membership Dues: individual, $15 (annual) ● individual, $40 (triennial) ● corporate, $400 (annual) ● life (individual), $500. **Description:** Promotes Marine Corps engineering in combat engineer, engineer equipment, utilities, bulk fuel, landing support (shore party), topographic and construction surveying/drafting. Fosters preservation of an accurate historical account of USMC engineering and the contributions of USMC engineers during combat operations. Recognizes and honors outstanding leadership and achievements of individual Marines and organizations within the engineer related fields. **Publications:** Newsletter. Alternate Formats: online.

Navy

6143 ■ AE Sailors Association (AESA)
c/o Nicholas Nicolai, Treas.
26355 Grace Dr.
Wind Lake, WI 53185
URL: http://www.aesailors.com
Contact: Nicholas Nicolai, Treas.
Members: 1,200. **Membership Dues:** $15 (annual). **Description:** Promotes shared experiences of AE sailors, regardless of ship. **Computer Services:** Online services, membership rosters. **Publications:** *Over the Waves.* Newsletter. **Conventions/Meetings:** reunion.

6144 ■ All Navy Women's National Alliance (ANWNA)
PO Box 147
Goldenrod, FL 32733-0147
E-mail: anwna@aol.com
URL: http://www.anwna.com
Description: Represents the interests of active duty, reserve, retired, and veteran Navy, Coast Guard, and Marine women. Honors the accomplishments and rich history of the women of the sea services.

Enhances the appreciation of the role of women in the naval service through educational programs and forums. **Computer Services:** Mailing lists.

6145 ■ Women of Naval Special Warfare (WNSW)
Address Unknown since 2007
Description: Works to meet the needs of female relatives, wives, widows, friends, special ex-wives, and the women attached to Navy SEAL, SWCC, SDV, SBT, and SEAL R. Teams, along with Naval Special Warfare Command.

Notaries Public

6146 ■ American Society of Notaries (ASN)
PO Box 5707
Tallahassee, FL 32314-5707
Ph: (850)671-5164
Free: (800)522-3392
Fax: (850)671-5165
E-mail: info@asnnotary.org
URL: http://www.asnnotary.org
Contact: Kathleen M. Butler, Exec. Dir.
Founded: 1965. **Members:** 20,000. **Membership Dues:** individual, $39 (annual). **Staff:** 5. **Budget:** $500,000. **Description:** Notaries Public. Provides members with educational services and technical support. Promotes high ethical standards for notaries. Seeks to increase public awareness of the valuable contribution of notaries. **Libraries: Type:** reference. **Holdings:** 500. **Subjects:** lawful notary procedures. **Committees:** Education; Government Relations; Membership; Public Relations. **Publications:** *American Notary*, bimonthly. Newsletter. Covers laws and state issues affecting notaries. **Price:** included in membership dues. ISSN: 0044-7773. **Circulation:** 22,000. **Advertising:** accepted. Alternate Formats: microform; online ● *Guidelines for Notaries*. Monograph ● Manuals. **Conventions/Meetings:** annual meeting.

6147 ■ National Notary Association (NNA)
9350 DeSoto Ave.
PO Box 2402
Chatsworth, CA 91313-2402
Free: (800)876-6827
Fax: (800)833-1211
URL: http://www.nationalnotary.org
Contact: Milton G. Valera, Pres./CEO
Founded: 1957. **Members:** 162,000. **Membership Dues:** individual, $49 (annual) ● attorney, $24 (annual) ● notary signing agent, $39 (annual) ● e-notarization, small business, immigration, $34 (annual). **Staff:** 115. **Description:** Notaries public (officers empowered to witness the signing of documents, identify the signers, take acknowledgments, and administer oaths). Works to teach notaries public in the U.S. their duties, powers, limitations, liabilities, and obligations. Keeps members informed of changes in notary law; offers various services, supplies, and insurance plans to members. Maintains speakers' bureau. **Libraries: Type:** reference. **Holdings:** articles, papers, reports. **Awards:** March Fong Eu Achievement Award. **Frequency:** annual. **Type:** recognition. **Recipient:** for the individual who has done the most to improve standards, image, and quality of the notary office ● Notary of the Year. **Frequency:** annual. **Type:** recognition. **Recipient:** for outstanding individual who sets a level of ethical and professional conduct as a notary public. **Commissions:** Notary Code of Professional Responsibility. **Committees:** Model Notary Act Drafting. **Publications:** *Arizona Notary Law Primer*. Book. Contains detailed information on state notary laws. ● *Home Business Made Easy*. Book ● *How to Get a Green Card*. Book ● *Independent Paralegal's Handbook* ● *Michigan Notary Law Primer*. Includes updated laws and regulations governing notaries in all 50 states as well as notary commission requirements. **Price:** included in membership dues ● *The National Notary*, bimonthly. Magazine. Contains general information on notarial subjects. **Price:** included in membership dues. **Advertising:** accepted ● *New Jersey Notary Law Primer*. **Price:** $29.65 for members; $39.95 for nonmembers ● *New York Notary Law Primer*. Book. **Price:** $49.65 for members; $65.00 for nonmembers ● *Notary Bulletin*, bimonthly. Newsletter. Features legislative updates. **Price:** included in membership dues. **Circulation:** 150,000 ● *Notary Law & Practice: Cases & Materials*. Book ● *Notary Seal and Certificate Verification Manual*. Provides preparation for the California Notary Public exam. ● *101 Law Forms for Personal Use*. Book ● *101 Useful Notary Tips*. Book ● *Preparing for the California Notary Public Exam*. Provides preparation for the California Notary Public exam. ● *The Quick and Legal Will Book* ● *Sorry, No Can Do*. Book ● *Start Your Business*. Book ● *12 Steps to a Flawless Notarization*. Book ● *2000 I.D. Checking Guide*. Book ● *U.S. Notary Reference Manual*. Book. Includes updated laws and regulations governing notaries in all 50 states as well as notary commission requirements. **Conventions/Meetings:** annual conference (exhibits).

Nuclear War and Weapons

6148 ■ Western States Legal Foundation (WSLF)
1204 Preservation Pkwy.
Oakland, CA 94612
Ph: (510)839-5877
Fax: (510)839-5397
E-mail: webmaster@wslfweb.org
URL: http://www.wslfweb.org
Contact: Jacqueline Cabasso, Exec. Dir.
Founded: 1982. **Description:** Strives to monitor and analyze U.S. nuclear weapons programs and policies. **Publications:** *The End of Disarmament and the Arms Races to Come*. Reprint. Alternate Formats: online ● *Western States Legal Foundation Information Bulletin*. Alternate Formats: online.

Paralegals

6149 ■ American Alliance of Paralegals, Inc. (AAPI)
16815 E Shea Blvd., Ste.110
PBM No. 101
Fountain Hills, AZ 85268
E-mail: info@aapipara.org
URL: http://www.aapipara.org
Contact: Deborah A. Repass RP, Pres.
Founded: 2003. **Membership Dues:** voting/associate, $20 (annual) ● sustaining, $50 (annual) ● sponsor/vendor, $200 (annual). **Description:** Strives to promote and improve the paralegal profession. Advances the educational and literary standard of the paralegal profession. Fosters, encourages and disseminates information concerning the profession. **Telecommunication Services:** electronic mail, president@aapipara.org. **Publications:** *The Alliance Echo*, quarterly. Newsletter. Contains news articles, legislation updates, and other information affecting the paralegal profession. **Price:** included in membership dues. Alternate Formats: online.

6150 ■ National Association of Legal Assistants (NALA)
1516 S Boston, Ste.200
Tulsa, OK 74119
Ph: (918)587-6828
Fax: (918)582-6772
E-mail: nalanet@nala.org
URL: http://www.nala.org
Contact: Marge Dover CAE, Exec. Dir.
Founded: 1975. **Members:** 9,000. **Membership Dues:** active, $99 (annual) ● student, $40 (annual) ● sustaining, $54 (annual) ● associate, $84 (annual). **Staff:** 8. **Budget:** $1,500,000. **State Groups:** 91. **Description:** Professional paralegals employed for over six months; graduates or students of legal assistant training programs; attorneys. Members subscribe to and are bound by the NALA Code of Ethics and Professional Responsibility. Cooperates with local, state, and national bar associations in setting standards and guidelines for legal assistants. Promotes the profession and attempts to broaden public understanding of the function of the legal assistant. Offers continuing education for legal assistants both nationwide and statewide, and professional certification on a national basis to members and nonmembers who meet certain criteria. **Awards:** Founders Award. **Frequency:** annual. **Type:** recognition. **Recipient:** for extraordinary contributions to the growth and future of the legal assistant profession. **Computer Services:** Online services, NALA NET. **Additional Websites:** http://www.nalacampus.com. **Publications:** *Alternative Dispute Resolution*. Book. Uncovers the distinguishing factors, advantages and disadvantages of the various processes in alternative dispute resolution. **Price:** $43.00 for members; $48.00 for nonmembers ● *Business Organizations Review*. Manual. Contains CLA Specialty Exam on business organizations. **Price:** $41.00 for members; $45.00 for nonmembers ● *CLA Mock Examination and Study Guide*. Book. Contains 100 pages of text and mock examination for the CLA exam. **Price:** $20.00 for members; $25.00 for nonmembers ● *CLA Review, 2nd Edition*. Manual. Contains extensive guidelines for effectively preparing for and taking the CLA examination. **Price:** $90.00 for members; $105.00 for nonmembers ● *NALA for Paralegals and Legal Assistants, 4th Edition*. Manual. Covers general skills including legal research, legal analysis, interviewing procedures, and communications. **Price:** $75.00 for members; $82.00 for nonmembers ● *National Association of Legal Assistants - Career Chronicle*, annual. Journal. Reviews significant developments within the career field. **Price:** included in membership dues. **Circulation:** 6,000. **Advertising:** accepted ● *National Association of Legal Assistants—Facts and Findings*, quarterly. Journal. Updates legal assistants on current federal and state legislation, and economic and ethical issues affecting the profession. Lists new members. **Price:** included in membership dues; $25.00 /year for nonmembers. **Circulation:** 6,000. **Advertising:** accepted ● *Occupational Survey Report*, biennial ● Manuals. **Conventions/Meetings:** annual convention and workshop (exhibits) - always July.

6151 ■ National Federation of Paralegal Associations (NFPA)
PO Box 2016
Edmonds, WA 98020
Ph: (425)967-0045
Fax: (425)771-9588
E-mail: info@paralegals.org
URL: http://www.paralegals.org
Contact: Anita G. Haworth RP, Pres.
Founded: 1974. **Members:** 15,000. **Membership Dues:** individual, $85 (annual) ● student, $50 (annual) ● organizational, $200 (annual). **Staff:** 8. **Budget:** $800,000. **Regional Groups:** 5. **State Groups:** 60. **Description:** State and local paralegal associations and other organizations supporting the goals of the federation; individual paralegals. Works to serve as a national voice of the paralegal profession; to advance, foster, and promote the paralegal concept; to monitor and participate in developments in the paralegal profession; to maintain a nationwide communications network among paralegal associations and other members of the legal community. Provides a resource center of books, publications, and literature of the field. Monitors activities of local, state, and national bar associations and legislative bodies; presents testimony on matters affecting the profession. Developed PACE exam for Registered Paralegal credentials. **Awards:** Local Outstanding Leader. **Type:** recognition ● Paralegal of the Year. **Frequency:** annual. **Type:** recognition ● Pro Bono Award. **Type:** recognition ● William R. Robie Award. **Frequency:** annual. **Type:** recognition. **Recipient:** for student or affiliate member who possesses outstanding leadership and dedication to the paralegal profession. **Telecommunication Services:** electronic mail, president@paralegals.org. **Committees:** Career Advancement; Education; Ethics and Professional Responsibility; Professional Development. **Publications:** *Bankruptcy and Collections: The Paralegal Perspective*. Book. **Price:** $35.00 ● *Directory of Paralegal Associations*, periodic ● *Directory of*

Paralegal Training Programs ● *Fee Recoverability*. Book ● *How to Choose a Paralegal Education Program*. Handbook ● *National Paralegal Reporter*, bimonthly. **Price:** $33.00/year. **Advertising:** accepted ● *The Reporter*, bimonthly. Magazine. Features topics on paralegal roles and choosing vendors. **Price:** $33.00/year; $59.00 for 2 years. **Circulation:** 17,000 ● *2001 Compensation and Benefits Report*, biennial. Book ● Booklets. **Conventions/Meetings:** annual convention and meeting (exhibits) - always spring.

6152 ■ National Paralegal Association (NPA)
Box 406
Solebury, PA 18963
Ph: (215)297-8333
Fax: (215)297-8358
E-mail: admin@nationalparalegal.org
URL: http://www.nationalparalegal.org
Contact: H. Jeffrey Valentine, Exec. Dir.
Founded: 1982. **Members:** 24,000. **Membership Dues:** student, $30 (annual) ● regular - initial, $70 ● regular, $45 (annual) ● paralegal school, $70 (annual). **Staff:** 9. **Description:** Paralegals, paralegal students, educators, supervisors, paralegal schools, administrators, law librarians, law clinics, and attorneys. Advances the paralegal profession by promoting recognition, economic benefits, and high standards. Registers paralegals; maintains speakers' bureau, job bank, and placement service; offers resume preparation assistance. Offers free job bank nationally. Sponsors commercial exhibits. Operates mail order bookstore and gift shop. Compiles statistics. Develops promotion and public relations, insurance, certification, and computer bank programs. Compiles and maintains for rental the largest list of paralegals nationwide. **Computer Services:** Mailing lists, of over 160000 paralegals. **Publications:** *Directory of Corporate Legal Departments*. Alternate Formats: diskette ● *Directory of Local Paralegal Clubs*, annual. Lists regional, state, and local paralegal groups. **Price:** $5.00. **Circulation:** 2,800. **Advertising:** accepted ● *Legal Book Publishers Directory* ● *Local Paralegal Club Directory* ● *National Paralegal Employment and Salary Survey*, periodic. Contains summary of salaries and benefits to paralegals on a national and nine regional areas. **Price:** $18.00 for members; $30.00 for nonmembers ● *The Paralegal Bookstore*, annual. Lists over 250 titles. ● *Paralegal Career Booklet*, periodic. Provides information on the paralegal profession as well as information for prospective students. **Price:** $8.00/copy. **Advertising:** accepted ● *The Paralegal Journal*, periodic. Covers paralegals in government, business, and finance. Includes information on the law, training, and education. **Price:** included in membership dues; $40.00 /year for nonmembers. ISSN: 0739-3601. **Circulation:** 35,000. **Advertising:** accepted ● *Paralegal School Directory*, semiannual. Lists colleges, universities, and schools offering paralegal programs; includes information for prospective students. **Price:** $10.00/copy; $2.50 for state editions. **Advertising:** accepted ● *Paralegal Schools-State Listings* ● Also publishes a paralegal information packet. **Conventions/Meetings:** competition ● workshop, teaching.

Parks and Recreation

6153 ■ American Park and Recreation Society (APRS)
c/o Mike Moran, CPRP, Pres.
220 S Gilbert St.
Iowa City, IA 52240
Ph: (319)356-5100
Fax: (319)356-5487
E-mail: aprs@nrpa.org
URL: http://www.nrpa.org/content/default.aspx?documentId=525
Contact: Mike Moran CPRP, Pres.
Founded: 1965. **Members:** 7,000. **Staff:** 2. **Budget:** $95,000. **Description:** A branch of the National Recreation and Park Association. Professional park and recreation directors who provide cultural, physical, and intellectual opportunities in recreational settings throughout the country. Seeks to provide a blend of professional enrichment and public advocacy in the parks and recreation field. Conducts educational sessions and research symposia at annual congressional meetings. Offers speakers' bureau. Maintains 24 committees. **Libraries: Type:** reference. **Awards: Type:** recognition. **Telecommunication Services:** electronic mail, mike-moran@iowa-city.org. **Formed by Merger of:** American Institute of Park Executives; American Recreation Society. **Conventions/Meetings:** annual congress and symposium (exhibits).

6154 ■ Association of National Park Rangers (ANPR)
PO Box 108
Larned, KS 67550-0108
Ph: (316)285-2107
E-mail: anprbusiness@anpr.org
URL: http://www.anpr.org
Contact: Lee Werst, Pres.
Founded: 1977. **Membership Dues:** active (individual), $25-$75 (annual) ● associate (student), $25-$40 (annual) ● life (individual, joint), $750-$1,000 ● active (joint), $40-$90 (annual) ● associate (regular), $45-$60 (annual) ● non-profit organization, $100 (annual) ● associate (other than NPS employees), $750-$1,000 (annual). **Description:** Supports the management and the perpetuation of the national park service and system. Provides education, training, advocacy and public information on national park protection. Enhances the park rangers' profession. Sets a forum for social enrichment. **Libraries: Type:** reference. **Publications:** *Live the Adventure: Join the National Park Service*. Booklet. Features the park ranger profession and issues. ● *Ranger*, quarterly. Magazine. **Price:** $100.00 /year for libraries. **Advertising:** accepted. Alternate Formats: online. **Conventions/Meetings:** annual Ranger Rendezvous - meeting.

6155 ■ National Association of County Park and Recreation Officials (NACPRO)
16 W 284-97th St.
Burr Ridge, IL 60527
Fax: (630)920-0333
E-mail: rdangooch@aol.com
URL: http://www.nacpro.org
Contact: Mr. R. Dan Gooch, Exec. Sec.
Founded: 1964. **Members:** 250. **Membership Dues:** county (with population of less than 100,000 up to 500,000 or more), $80-$100 (annual) ● corporate (include one web link category), $200 (annual). **Staff:** 1. **Description:** Members are elected or appointed county government officials with parks and/or recreation advisory, administrative, or policy-making authority. Stimulates interest in county park and recreation resources and works to obtain more effective use of public and privately owned land and water areas. **Awards: Type:** recognition. **Committees:** Federal, State and Local Issues; NACPRO/NRPA Liaison; Public Information. **Publications:** *NACPRO News*, quarterly. Newsletter. **Circulation:** 500. **Advertising:** accepted. Alternate Formats: online ● Brochures. **Conventions/Meetings:** semiannual meeting, in conjunction with National Association of Counties (exhibits).

6156 ■ National Association of Recreation Resource Planners (NARRP)
PO Box 221
Marienville, PA 16239
Ph: (814)927-8212
Fax: (814)927-6659
E-mail: info@narrp.org
URL: http://www.narrp.org
Contact: Glenn Haas, Pres.
Founded: 1980. **Members:** 200. **Membership Dues:** individual, $70 (annual) ● institutional, $195 (annual) ● student, $33 (annual). **Description:** Individuals working in state and federal recreation and resource agencies and private organizations who are responsible for recreation planning. Seeks to increase the professional expertise of membership and to coordinate positions with respect to federal planning requirements and policy and funding issues. **Awards:** Distinguished Service. **Frequency:** annual. **Type:** recognition. **Recipient:** for outstanding contributions to the profession of recreation resource planning ● National Recreation Resource Leadership. **Frequency:** annual. **Type:** recognition. **Recipient:** for leadership in park and recreation and natural resources management. **Formerly:** National Association of State Recreation Planners. **Publications:** *NARRP News*, quarterly. Newsletter. **Price:** free. **Circulation:** 300. **Advertising:** accepted ● Membership Directory, periodic. **Conventions/Meetings:** annual Recreation Resource Planning Conference - conference and workshop (exhibits) - usually in May.

6157 ■ National Association of State Outdoor Recreation Liaison Officers (NASORLO)
c/o Yvonne S. Ferrell, Exec. Dir.
3116 Woodbrook Pl.
Boise, ID 83706
Ph: (208)384-5421
Fax: (208)331-7757
E-mail: yferrell@earthlink.net
Contact: Yvonne S. Ferrell, Exec. Dir.
Founded: 1967. **Members:** 56. **Membership Dues:** state, $950 (annual). **Staff:** 1. **Budget:** $35,000. **Description:** Appointed state and territorial outdoor recreation liaison officers charged with administering the states' side of the Land and Water Conservation Fund Act. Seeks the improvement of practices, programs, and management of outdoor recreation in conjunction with the National Park Service. Under the Land and Water Conservation Fund Act, the National Park Service provides funds to states for planning, acquiring, and developing public outdoor recreational facilities; the states, in turn, make a portion of the grants available to local governments for their projects. **Affiliated With:** National Association of Recreation Resource Planners; National Association of State Park Directors. **Conventions/Meetings:** annual Healthy Landscapes, Healthy People - meeting.

6158 ■ National Association of State Park Directors (NASPD)
c/o Philip K. McKnelly, Exec. Dir.
8829 Woodyhill Rd.
Raleigh, NC 27613
Ph: (919)676-8365
Fax: (919)676-8365
E-mail: naspd@nc.rr.com
URL: http://www.naspd.org
Contact: Philip K. McKnelly, Exec. Dir.
Founded: 1962. **Members:** 50. **Membership Dues:** state, $1,400 (annual). **Staff:** 1. **Budget:** $75,000. **Regional Groups:** 6. **Description:** Directors of every state park system in the U.S. Purposes are to: provide a common forum for the exchange of information regarding state park programs; take collective positions on issues that affect state park programs; encourage the development of professional leadership in the administration of state park and recreational programs. Compiles statistics. **Awards:** Distinguished Professional. **Frequency:** annual. **Type:** recognition. **Recipient:** for total contribution as a state park director ● President's Award. **Frequency:** annual. **Type:** recognition. **Recipient:** for meritorious service to state parks ● Survivor. **Frequency:** annual. **Type:** recognition. **Recipient:** to individuals who have served five years as a state park director. **Computer Services:** database, of directors, information exchange. **Publications:** *National Association of State Park Directors—Annual Information Exchange*. Provides information about the nation's state park systems. **Price:** included in membership dues ● *National Association of State Park Directors—Directory*, semiannual. Lists state park directors. **Price:** included in membership dues. **Conventions/Meetings:** annual conference, with 250 participants from NASPD members and associates (exhibits).

6159 ■ National Park Foundation (NPF)
1201 Eye St. NW, Ste.550B
Washington, DC 20005
Ph: (202)354-6460
Fax: (202)371-2066

E-mail: ask-npf@nationalparks.org
URL: http://www.nationalparks.org
Contact: Vin Cipolla, Pres./CEO
Founded: 1967. **Staff:** 22. **Description:** Raises support from corporations, foundations, and individuals to preserve and enhance America's national parks. **Awards:** The Harry Yount National Park Ranger Award. **Frequency:** annual. **Type:** monetary. **Recipient:** for National Park Service Ranger who has demonstrated outstanding leadership and excellence in ranger's duties and skills. **Supersedes:** National Park Trust Fund Board. **Publications:** *Complete Guide to America's National Parks*, biennial. Directory. Provides visitor information on the 369 national park areas, as well as complete weather information on 40 areas. **Price:** $15.95/copy ● *National Park Forum*, quarterly. Newsletter ● Annual Report. Alternate Formats: online.

6160 ■ National Parks Conservation Association (NPCA)
1300 19th St. NW, Ste.300
Washington, DC 20036
Ph: (202)223-6722
Free: (800)628-7275
Fax: (202)659-0650
E-mail: npca@npca.org
URL: http://www.npca.org
Contact: Thomas C. Kiernan, Pres.
Founded: 1919. **Members:** 300,000. **Membership Dues:** individual, $15 (annual). **Staff:** 110. **Budget:** $17,000,000. **Regional Groups:** 10. **Description:** Dedicated solely to protecting, preserving, and enhancing the National Park System. **Computer Services:** Mailing lists, of members. **Formerly:** (1970) National Parks Association; (2000) National Parks and Conservation Association. **Publications:** *National Parks*, bimonthly. Magazine. **Price:** $15.00 for members. **Circulation:** 400,000. **Advertising:** accepted ● Annual Report. Alternate Formats: online. **Conventions/Meetings:** annual dinner, for fundraising.

6161 ■ National Recreation and Park Association (NRPA)
22377 Belmont Ridge Rd.
Ashburn, VA 20148-4501
Ph: (703)858-0784
Fax: (703)858-0794
E-mail: info@nrpa.org
URL: http://www.nrpa.org
Contact: John A. Thorner, Exec. Dir.
Founded: 1965. **Members:** 23,000. **Membership Dues:** professional, associate, $130 (annual) ● retired, $60 (annual) ● student, $40 (annual) ● citizen, $55 (annual) ● agency, $465 (annual) ● group, $285 (annual) ● corporate, $500 (annual). **Staff:** 50. **Regional Groups:** 8. **State Groups:** 52. **Description:** Park resource managers, planners, designers, rangers, and maintenance persons; nature interpreters and persons concerned with the preservation and use of natural, recreational, historic, and cultural resources. Cooperates with federal agencies, the states, and other groups to develop a national system of natural, historic, recreational, and cultural resources for public use; to assist professionals so they may provide adequate outdoor areas developed and managed to assure public enjoyment. Sponsors annual National Congress Recreation and Parks educational seminar; conducts annual training institute. **Libraries: Type:** reference. **Awards:** Recreation and Park Hall of Fame. **Frequency:** annual. **Type:** recognition. **Recipient:** for individuals ● William Penn Mott, Jr., Awards. **Frequency:** annual. **Type:** recognition. **Recipient:** for individuals and agencies. **Computer Services:** Mailing lists, available in label form or on disk. **Committees:** Accreditation; Awards; Congress Programs; Environmental Ethics; Legislative Action; Membership Development; Newsletter; Park Practice Advisory; Professional Development; Recreation and Parks Law Reporter; Regional Effectiveness; Tellers. **Formerly:** (1972) National Conference on State Parks. **Publications:** *Parks and Recreation*, monthly. Magazine. Informs, motivates and inspires professionals, civic leaders and citizens to elevate the value of parks and recreation as a public service. **Price:** $36.00 /year for nonmembers in U.S.; $48.00 /year for libraries in U.S.; $46.00 /year for nonmembers outside U.S.; $58.00 /year for libraries outside U.S. ISSN: 0031-2251. **Advertising:** accepted ● *Recreation and Parks Law Reporter*, quarterly. Journal. Provides background information for administrators, educators and attorneys. Examines recent court decisions affecting park and recreation facilities. **Price:** $50.00 /year for members; $75.00 /year for nonmembers. **Conventions/Meetings:** annual conference, training conference and exposition (exhibits).

6162 ■ Park Law Enforcement Association (PLEA)
c/o Steve Newsom, Pres.
Hamilton County Park District
10245 Winton Rd.
Cincinnati, OH 45231
Ph: (513)521-3980
E-mail: snewsom@greatparks.org
URL: http://www.parkranger.com
Contact: Steve Newsom, Pres.
Founded: 1984. **Membership Dues:** individual, $25 (annual) ● state affiliate, $75 (annual) ● agency (based on number of officers), $100-$200 (annual). **State Groups:** 4. **Description:** Represents park law enforcement professionals. Improves law enforcement and visitor protection services in park law enforcement and park recreation areas. Facilitates the exchange of information between park law enforcement personnel and other park and recreation professionals. Offers continuing education and technical assistance to persons working in park law enforcement. **Awards:** Lifetime Achievement Award. **Frequency:** annual. **Type:** recognition ● Park Law Enforcement Scholarship Award. **Frequency:** annual. **Type:** scholarship. **Recipient:** for high school students entering the park law enforcement field. **Computer Services:** Information services, ranger resources ● online services, discussion board. **Publications:** Newsletter, triennial. **Advertising:** accepted.

6163 ■ Society of Park and Recreation Educators (SPRE)
c/o Gallaudet University
22377 Belmont Ridge Rd.
U.S. Department of of Physical Educ. and Recreation
800 Florida Ave. NE
Washington, DC 20002
Ph: (202)651-5591
E-mail: carol.riddick@gallaudet.edu
URL: http://www.nrpa.org
Contact: Carol C. Riddick PhD, Pres.
Founded: 1966. **Members:** 700. **Description:** A branch of the National Recreation and Park Association (see separate entry). Professional society for park and recreation educators. Operates an information exchange, and sponsors educational programs. **Awards:** Distinguished Colleague Award. **Frequency:** annual. **Type:** recognition. **Recipient:** for outstanding park recreation educators ● Teaching Excellence. **Frequency:** annual. **Type:** recognition. **Recipient:** for outstanding park and recreation teaching. **Computer Services:** Online services, listserv: SPREnet. **Affiliated With:** National Recreation and Park Association. **Publications:** *Curriculum Catalog*, biennial. Contains a detailed listing of 100-125 parks and recreation programs. **Price:** $125.00 for members; $150.00 for nonmembers. **Circulation:** 500 ● *Journal of Leisure Research*, quarterly ● *Schole: A Journal of Leisure Studies and Recreation*, annual. **Conventions/Meetings:** annual congress, in conjunction with National Recreation and Park Association (exhibits).

Parole

6164 ■ American Probation and Parole Association (APPA)
2760 Res. Park Dr.
Lexington, KY 40511-8482
Ph: (859)244-8203 (859)244-8207
Fax: (859)244-8001
E-mail: appa@csg.org
URL: http://www.appa-net.org
Contact: Carl Wicklund, Exec. Dir.
Founded: 1975. **Members:** 3,500. **Membership Dues:** individual, $50 (annual) ● agency, $250-$650 (annual) ● affiliate, $250 (annual) ● corporate, $5,000 (annual) ● associate, $1,000 (annual) ● educational institution, $150 (annual) ● library, $60 (annual). **Staff:** 18. **Regional Groups:** 17. **Description:** Probation/parole executives, line officers, and other interested individuals. Seeks to: improve and advance progressive probation/parole practices through the development of knowledge, skills, resources, and legislation; encourage public awareness and support of probation/parole as an effective means of dealing with the prevention and correction of crime and delinquency; stimulate the development of services, research design, and program evaluation. Promotes legislative programs; sponsors research programs; conducts regional workshops. **Libraries: Type:** reference. **Holdings:** articles, books, periodicals. **Subjects:** community corrections. **Awards:** APPA Member of the Year Award. **Frequency:** annual. **Type:** recognition ● APPA Scholarship Community Awareness Through Media Award. **Frequency:** annual. **Type:** scholarship ● President's Award. **Frequency:** annual. **Type:** recognition ● Sam Houston State University. **Frequency:** annual. **Type:** recognition ● Scoha Knouff Line Officer of the Year Award. **Frequency:** annual. **Type:** recognition. **Recipient:** for an individual who has made significant contribution to probation and parole ● University of Cincinnati Award. **Frequency:** annual. **Type:** recognition ● Walter Dunbar Memorial Award. **Frequency:** annual. **Type:** recognition. **Computer Services:** Mailing lists, of members. **Telecommunication Services:** electronic mail, cwicklun@csg.org. **Committees:** Accreditation; Adult Education; Annual Institute Chair; Awards; Community Justice; Corporate Relations; Diversity; Investments; Juvenile Justice; Legislative; Nominations; Public Relations; Research and Development; Research and Technology; Statements/Positions; Training; Victims Issues. **Publications:** *Perspectives*, quarterly. Journal. Contains information on child abuse, drug abuse, probation and parole, AIDS, and innovative correctional programs. **Price:** included in membership dues. ISSN: 5611-5045. **Circulation:** 7,500. **Advertising:** accepted. Alternate Formats: CD-ROM; online. **Conventions/Meetings:** annual Training Institute/Winter Training Institute - conference and workshop (exhibits).

6165 ■ Association of Paroling Authorities International (APAI)
c/o Bea Leopold, Exec. Dir.
233 Canterbury Dr.
Wallingford, PA 19086
Ph: (610)872-4645
Fax: (610)872-1192
E-mail: bleopold@apaintl.org
URL: http://www.apaintl.org
Contact: Bea Leopold, Exec. Dir.
Founded: 1960. **Members:** 350. **Membership Dues:** individual, $50 (annual) ● organizational (with up to 8 members), $300 (annual) ● organizational (with 9 to 13 members), $400 (annual) ● corporate, $500 (annual). **Staff:** 2. **Budget:** $75,000. **Regional Groups:** 5. **Multinational. Description:** Chief administrators and members of paroling authorities in the U.S., Canada, U.S. territories, and countries outside North America. Seeks to develop and promote parole work and programs through conferences and cooperative programs and to secure effective legislation in this field. Maintains speakers' bureau. **Awards:** Vincent O'Leary Award. **Frequency:** annual. **Type:** recognition. **Recipient:** for outstanding contributions in parole administration. **Computer Services:** Mailing lists, of members. **Affiliated With:** American Correctional Association; American Probation and Parole Association. **Publications:** *A Resource Kit for New Parole Board Members*. Handbooks. Alternate Formats: online ● *Abolishing Parole: Why The Emperor Has No Clothes*, quarterly. Newsletter. **Price:** included in membership dues. **Circulation:** 350. **Advertising:** accepted ● *APAI News*, quarterly. Newsletter. **Price:**

included in membership dues. **Circulation:** 350. **Advertising:** accepted ● *Parole Work! Parole Board's Policies Programs, Procedures, Practices*, annual ● *The Practice of Parole Boards*, annual. **Conventions/Meetings:** annual Training Conference (exhibits).

6166 ■ Parole and Probation Compact Administrators' Association (PPCAA)
c/o Karen Tucker, Treas.
2601 Blair Stone Rd.
Tallahassee, FL 32399
Ph: (850)410-4324
E-mail: tucker.karen@mail.dc.state.fl.us
Contact: Karen Tucker, Treas.
Founded: 1946. **Members:** 25. **Membership Dues:** state, $2,000 (annual). **Description:** State administrators of the Interstate Compact for the Supervision of Parolees and Probationers as it concerns adults. (Originally passed in 1934 and revised in 1988, the compact allows parolees and probationers to cross state lines under the supervision of the receiving state.) Facilitates and promotes the exchange of information among members regarding the compact; seeks uniformity in the interpretation and practice of the compact; facilitates cooperation in the administration of the compact. **Committees:** Awards; Conference and Public Relations; Morrissey-Brewer Hearings; Nominations. **Formerly:** Association of Administrators of the Interstate Compact for the Supervision of Parolees and Probationers. **Publications:** *Interstate Compact for the Supervision of Parolees and Probationers Manual*. Handbook ● *Parole and Probation Compact Administrators Association Directory*, annual. Membership Directory. Arranged geographically. **Price:** included in membership dues ● *PPCAA Newsletter*, quarterly. Covers membership activities. **Price:** included in membership dues. **Circulation:** 150. **Conventions/Meetings:** annual meeting - midwinter.

Patent Law

6167 ■ National Association of Patent Practitioners (NAPP)
4680-18i Monticello Ave., PMB 101
Williamsburg, VA 23188
Free: (800)216-9588
Fax: (757)220-3928
E-mail: napp@napp.org
URL: http://www.napp.org
Contact: Ron Reardon, Pres.
Membership Dues: practitioner, $200 (annual) ● associate, $175 (annual) ● academic, $100 (annual). **Regional Groups:** 3. **Description:** Supports patent practitioners and those working in the field of patent law. Disseminates information related to patent prosecution practice and technology development. Creates a collective, nationwide voice to respond to proposed changes in the patent statutes, rules and PTO operations with a view to their relationship with their clients. **Computer Services:** database, job bank ● information services, all about patents ● mailing lists, general discussion. **Telecommunication Services:** phone referral service, national referral, (703)-308-5316. **Publications:** *The Disclosure*, monthly. Newsletter. Contains information about the affairs of the organization and issues and articles about patent. **Price:** $40.00 /year for members. **Advertising:** accepted. Alternate Formats: online. **Conventions/Meetings:** annual Patent Practice Update - meeting.

6168 ■ Patent and Trademark Depository Library Program (PTDL)
U.S. Patent & Trademark Off.
PO Box 1450
Alexandria, VA 22313-1450
Ph: (703)308-4357
Free: (800)786-9199
Fax: (571)273-9250
E-mail: trademarkassistancecenter@uspto.gov
URL: http://www.uspto.gov/go/ptdl/ptdlgen.htm
Contact: Amanda Putnam, Mgr.
Founded: 1871. **Members:** 86. **Staff:** 10. **Description:** Library designated by the U.S. Patent and Trademark Office to receive and house copies of U.S. patents and trademark materials, make them available to the public, and disseminate patent and trademark information. **Publications:** *Notes on Becoming a Patent and Trademark Depository Library*. Brochure. Alternate Formats: online ● Reports.

Pensions

6169 ■ American Benefits Council
1212 New York Ave. NW, Ste.1250
Washington, DC 20005-3987
Ph: (202)289-6700
Fax: (202)289-4582
E-mail: info@abcstaff.org
URL: http://www.americanbenefitscouncil.org
Contact: James A. Klein, Pres.
Founded: 1967. **Members:** 260. **Staff:** 12. **Budget:** $2,000,000. **Description:** Serves as national trade association for companies concerned about federal legislation and regulations affecting all aspects of the employee benefits system. Represents the entire spectrum of the private employee benefits community and sponsors or administers retirement and health plans covering more than one hundred million Americans. **Telecommunication Services:** electronic mail, jklein@abcstaff.org. **Committees:** Accounting and Investment Issues; ESOP; Health Care Issues; Political Action; Post-Employment Benefits; Retirement Savings/ERISA Tax; Social Security; Welfare Benefits. **Formerly:** (2000) Association of Private Pension and Welfare Plans. **Publications:** *Action Alert*, periodic ● *Benefits Byte*.

Pest Control

6170 ■ Association of American Pesticide Control Officials (AAPCO)
PO Box 466
Milford, DE 19963
Ph: (302)422-8152
Fax: (302)422-2435
E-mail: aapco-sfireg@comcast.net
URL: http://aapco.ceris.purdue.edu
Contact: Grier Stayton, Sec.
Founded: 1947. **Members:** 55. **Membership Dues:** individual, $100 (annual). **Staff:** 1. **Budget:** $10,000. **Description:** State agencies controlling the sale, use, and distribution of pesticides. Promotes uniform laws, regulations, and policies of enforcement. **Libraries: Type:** not open to the public. **Holdings:** reports. **Committees:** Information Technology; Laboratory; Legislation; Off-Target Movement of Pesticides; State Research and Evaluation; States-Industry Forum; Worker Protection. **Task Forces:** FIFRA Section 18. **Formerly:** Association of Economic Poisons Control Officials. **Publications:** Journal, annual. Lists names and addresses of state regulatory officials. **Price:** $30.00. Alternate Formats: online. **Conventions/Meetings:** annual board meeting and conference - always March in Washington, DC.

Police

6171 ■ Association of Retired Hispanic Police (ARHP)
PO Box 1735
Cathedral Sta.
New York, NY 10025
Ph: (718)246-4836
Fax: (718)246-4853
E-mail: arhp@excite.com
URL: http://www.arhpinc.org
Contact: Ralph Cabo, Pres.
Founded: 1996. **Description:** Retired Hispanic New York City police officers. Provides support, issues newsletters and plans events. **Publications:** *Hermandad* (in English and Spanish), quarterly. Newsletter. Contains information on the association and its members. Alternate Formats: online.

6172 ■ International Police Mountain Bike Association (IPMBA)
583 Frederick Rd., Ste.5B
Baltimore, MD 21228
Ph: (410)744-2400
Fax: (410)744-5504
E-mail: info@ipmba.org
URL: http://www.ipmba.org
Contact: Maureen Becker, Exec. Dir.
Founded: 1991. **Members:** 3,000. **Membership Dues:** regular, $50 (annual). **Staff:** 2. **Multinational. Description:** Provides resources, networking opportunities and training for public safety bicyclists, including police officers and EMS personnel. Conducts the IPMBA Police Cyclist Course and the EMS Cyclist Course. **Computer Services:** Mailing lists. **Telecommunication Services:** electronic mail, maureen@ipmba.org. **Publications:** *Complete Guide to Police Cycling*. Book. Contains information of interest to members. **Price:** $19.00 ● *IPMBA News*, quarterly. Newsletter. Features profiles of mountain bike patrols and EMS units, stories from the field, product reviews and discounts, etc. **Price:** free for members. **Advertising:** accepted. Alternate Formats: online. **Conventions/Meetings:** annual Police on Bikes - conference, public safety bicycle use (exhibits).

6173 ■ National Association of Chiefs of Police (NACOP)
6350 Horizon Dr.
Titusville, FL 32780
Ph: (321)264-0911
Fax: (321)264-0033
E-mail: policeinfo@aphf.org
URL: http://www.aphf.org
Contact: Donna Shepherd, Exec. Dir.
Members: 60,000. **Membership Dues:** active, $50 (annual) ● active, $125 (triennial). **Description:** Municipal, county, state, and federal law enforcement command officers and directors of security agencies. Acts as a liaison with congressional, White House and government agencies, provides training programs, death benefit insurance, and awards and honors. Supports and maintains the American Police Hall of Fame and Museum. **Libraries: Type:** reference. **Holdings:** films, video recordings. **Subjects:** municipal, county, state, federal law. **Publications:** *The Chief of Police*, bimonthly. Magazine. Covers legal issues and legislation. **Conventions/Meetings:** seminar ● workshop.

6174 ■ National Police Accountability Project (NPAP)
14 Beacon St., Ste.701
Boston, MA 02108
Ph: (617)227-6015
Fax: (617)227-6018
E-mail: npap@nlg.org
URL: http://www.nlg-npap.org
Contact: Brigitt Keller Esq., Exec. Dir.
Founded: 1999. **Membership Dues:** benefactor, $5,000 (annual) ● sustainer, $2,500 (annual) ● sponsor, $1,000 (annual) ● supporter, $500 (annual) ● non-NLG, $150 (annual) ● NLG, $125 (annual) ● student, $25 (annual) ● friend, $250 (annual). **Staff:** 1. **Description:** Aims to curtail police abuse of authority through coordinated legal action, public education and support for organizations that work with victims of police misconduct; a project of the National Lawyers Guild. Provides training and support for attorneys and legal workers, public education and information around issues relating to police misconduct, consulting services, support for legislative reform efforts aimed at raising the level of police accountability. **Libraries: Type:** reference. **Subjects:** police misconduct, civil rights. **Computer Services:** database ● mailing lists. **Affiliated With:** National Lawyers Guild. **Publications:** *Civil Rights Litigation and Attorney Fees*, annual. Handbook ● *Police Misconduct: Law and Litigation* ● Newsletters, periodic. **Conventions/Meetings:** periodic conference ● periodic meeting ● periodic workshop.

6175 ■ National Tactical Officers Association (NTOA)
PO Box 797
Doylestown, PA 18901
Free: (800)279-9127

Fax: (646)485-1182
E-mail: membership@ntoa.org
URL: http://www.ntoa.org
Contact: John Gnagey, Exec. Dir.
Founded: 1983. **Members:** 35,000. **Membership Dues:** individual, $40-$45 (annual) ● team, $150-$200 (annual). **Description:** Provides a communication link between SWAT/CNT and other tactical units in the United States. Serves as a clearinghouse for tactical information. Provides cost-effective tactical training. **Libraries: Type:** reference. **Computer Services:** database, national less lethal ● information services, tactical and intelligence report ● online services, forum. **Boards:** Advisory. **Departments:** Marketing and Publication; Training and Information. **Programs:** Special Assistance for Needed Tactical Officers Assets. **Publications:** *Crisis Negotiator*, quarterly. Newsletter ● *Tactical Edge*, quarterly. Journal. **Conventions/Meetings:** annual conference, tactical operations.

Political Reform

6176 ■ Brennan Center for Justice at NYU School of Law
c/o NYU School of Law
161 Ave. of the Americas, 12th Fl.
New York, NY 10013
Ph: (212)998-6730
Fax: (212)995-4550
E-mail: brennancenter@nyu.edu
URL: http://www.brennancenter.org
Contact: Michael Waldman, Exec. Dir.
Founded: 1995. **Staff:** 51. **Nonmembership. Description:** Unites thinkers and advocates in pursuit of inclusive and effective democracy. Aims to develop and implement a nonpartisan agenda of scholarship, public education, and legal action that promotes equality and human dignity, while safeguarding fundamental freedoms in the areas of democracy, poverty, and criminal justice. Strives for campaign finance reform to ensure that elected officials are not unduly influenced by donors, and that the elections embody the fundamental principle of political equality that underlies the Constitution. **Departments:** Criminal Justice; Democracy; Development; Poverty. **Publications:** *Judicial Independence Series, Campaign Finance Reform Series, and Raising Voices Series*, 3/year. Monographs. Alternate Formats: online ● *Policy*, 5/year. Reports. Alternate Formats: online ● Books ● Articles ● Journals ● Newsletters.

Politics

6177 ■ Political Research Associates (PRA)
1310 Broadway, Ste.201
Somerville, MA 02144
Ph: (617)666-5300
Fax: (617)666-6622
E-mail: pra@publiceye.org
URL: http://www.publiceye.org
Contact: Katherine Hancock Ragsdale, Exec. Dir.
Founded: 1981. **Staff:** 8. **Description:** Seeks to monitor and analyze organizations, leaders, ideas, and activities of the U.S. political right. **Libraries: Type:** reference. **Holdings:** archival material, audio recordings, books, clippings, video recordings. **Subjects:** antidemocratic, authoritarian, oppressive movements and trends in the United States. **Publications:** *Groups Building Democracy and Diversity*. Directory. Alternate Formats: online ● *PRA 20-Year Report*. Alternate Formats: online ● *PRAccess*. Newsletter. Alternate Formats: online ● *The Public Eye Magazine*. Alternate Formats: online ● Annual Report, annual. Alternate Formats: online.

Postal Service

6178 ■ National Association of Postmasters of the United States (NAPUS)
8 Herbert St.
Alexandria, VA 22305-2600
Ph: (703)683-9027
Fax: (703)683-6820
E-mail: napusinfo@napus.org
URL: http://www.napus.org
Contact: Ken Engstrom, Exec. Dir.
Founded: 1898. **Members:** 41,000. **Membership Dues:** active, $37-$355 (annual) ● associate, retired, $42 (annual). **Staff:** 10. **Budget:** $2,000,000. **State Groups:** 50. **Description:** Serves the professional interests of postmasters and promotes cooperation and interchange of ideas between members and officials of the U.S. Postal Service. **Telecommunication Services:** hotline, (703)683-9038. **Committees:** Diversity; Education and Development; Government Relations; PAC for Postmasters; Postmaster Representation; Services. **Publications:** *NAPUS Update*, monthly. Newsletter. **Price:** included in membership dues. ISSN: 0888-0182. **Circulation:** 28,000 ● *Postmasters Gazette*, monthly. Magazine. **Price:** $18.00 /year for nonmembers; included in membership dues. **Circulation:** 48,000. **Advertising:** accepted. Alternate Formats: online. **Conventions/Meetings:** annual convention (exhibits) - 2008 Aug. 23-28, St. Louis, MO ● annual Leadership Conference - meeting (exhibits) - always February.

6179 ■ National Postal Forum (NPF)
3998 Fair Ridge Dr., Ste.300
Fairfax, VA 22033
Ph: (703)218-5015 (703)293-2310
Fax: (703)218-5020
E-mail: info@npf.org
URL: http://www.npf.org
Contact: Michael J. Genick, Exec. Dir./COO
Founded: 1968. **Description:** Postal authorities and businesses making use of the postal service. Seeks to ensure the most efficient use of postal services by businesses. Serves as a clearinghouse on products and services offered by the U.S. Postal Service; conducts educational and training programs for business mailers. **Awards:** Mailing Excellence Awards. **Frequency:** annual. **Type:** recognition. **Telecommunication Services:** electronic mail, mgenick@npf.org. **Conventions/Meetings:** annual meeting.

6180 ■ Retired League Postmasters of the National League of Postmasters (RLP)
c/o National League of Postmasters
1 Beltway Ctr.
5904 Richmond Hwy., Ste.500
Alexandria, VA 22303-1864
Ph: (703)329-4550
Fax: (703)329-0466
E-mail: information@postmasters.org
URL: http://www.postmasters.org
Contact: Charles W. Mapa, Pres.
Founded: 1902. **Members:** 7,700. **Membership Dues:** individual, $72 (annual). **Budget:** $40,000. **State Groups:** 50. **Description:** Retired postmasters. Works to maintain an active participatory relationship with the National League of Postmasters of the United States. Conducts lobbying activities; disseminates information. Participates in a bi-partisan PAC. **Awards: Frequency:** periodic. **Type:** recognition. **Recipient:** for exceptional service to the organization. **Computer Services:** Mailing lists, desktop IBM. **Committees:** Code; Effective Service; Legislative; Membership; Resolution. **Affiliated With:** National League of Postmasters of the United States. **Publications:** *Advocate Express*, bimonthly. Newsletter. **Advertising:** accepted ● *Postmasters Advocate*, bimonthly. Newsletter. State branch newsletters mailed to other states. **Price:** included in membership dues. **Circulation:** 30,000. **Advertising:** accepted. **Conventions/Meetings:** annual convention - 2008 Aug. 3-7, Louisville, KY; 2009 Aug. 2-6, Buffalo, NY ● annual League of Postmasters Forum - meeting and workshop, legislative training (exhibits).

Press

6181 ■ Association of Capitol Reporters and Editors (ACRE)
c/o Charles Ashby, Treas.
2141 Eliot St.
Denver, CO 80211
Ph: (803)771-8658
E-mail: cashby@chieftain.com
URL: http://www.capitolbeat.org
Contact: Aaron Sheinin, Pres.
Founded: 1999. **Members:** 300. **Membership Dues:** professional, $50 (annual) ● student, $25 (annual). **Description:** Aims to revitalize journalism at the state and local levels. Seeks to advance public understanding of state government and the issues before state government. Educates and shares information with its members and the public on practices, tools, and techniques in state government reporting. **Awards:** Excellence in State House Reporting Awards. **Frequency:** annual. **Type:** recognition. **Recipient:** for the best state house reporting in print, broadcast and online media ● John Aubuchon Freedom of Information Award. **Frequency:** annual. **Type:** recognition. **Recipient:** for exemplary persistence by journalists in obtaining access to documents and meetings that are critical for public understanding of state government issues. **Telecommunication Services:** electronic mail, asheinin@thestate.com. **Publications:** Newsletter, quarterly. Alternate Formats: online.

6182 ■ Military Reporters and Editors (MRE)
c/o Medill School of Journalism
1325 G St. NW, Ste.730
Washington, DC 20005
Ph: (202)661-0141
E-mail: sigc@express-news.net
URL: http://www.militaryreporters.org
Contact: Sig Christenson, Pres.
Membership Dues: professional/academic/associate/retiree, $50 (annual) ● student, $25 (annual). **Description:** Seeks to advance public understanding of the military, national security and homeland defense. Educates members and the public on the best practices, tools and techniques for such coverage. Represents the interests of working journalists to the government and the military. Ensures that journalists have access to places where the US military and its allies operate.

Probate Law

6183 ■ American College of Trust and Estate Counsel (ACTEC)
3415 S Sepulveda Blvd., Ste.330
Los Angeles, CA 90034-6032
Ph: (310)398-1888
Fax: (310)572-7280
E-mail: info@actec.org
URL: http://www.actec.org
Contact: Gerry Vogt, Exec. Dir.
Founded: 1948. **Members:** 2,700. **Staff:** 9. **Budget:** $1,300,000. **Description:** Represents attorneys specializing in probate law. Sends delegates to American Bar Association's Real Property, Probate, and Trust Law Section; maintains liaison with other organizations involved in probate law. Operates ACTEC Foundation, which makes available grants. **Committees:** Computer; Elder Law; Employee Benefits in Estate Planning; Estate and Gift Tax; Expanded Practice and Personal Counseling; Fiduciary Income Tax; Fiduciary Litigation; Office Management; Professional Standards; State Laws; Transfer Tax Study. **Formerly:** (1990) American College of Probate Counsel. **Publications:** *Membership Roster*, annual. Membership Directory ● *Probate Lawyer*, annual. Journal. Covers topics in probate, trust, and estate law. **Price:** included in membership dues; $4.50 /year for nonmembers. **Circulation:** 2,800 ● Journal, quarterly. Provides information regarding changes in tax and non-tax estate planning law for probate attorneys; includes calendar of events and obituaries. **Price:** included in membership dues; $60.00 /year for nonmembers. **Circulation:** 2,800 ● Also publishes studies, charts, and other materials for members. **Conventions/Meetings:** annual conference and seminar ● annual workshop and meeting, members only - usually October, March, June.

Process Serving

6184 ■ National Association of Professional Process Servers (NAPPS)
PO Box 4547
Portland, OR 97208-4547

Ph: (503)222-4180
Free: (800)477-8211
Fax: (503)222-3950
E-mail: administrator@napps.org
URL: http://www.napps.org
Contact: Gary A. Crowe, Admin.
Founded: 1982. **Members:** 1,600. **Membership Dues:** individual, $150 (annual). **Budget:** $400,000. **State Groups:** 8. **Description:** Individuals and companies who serve summonses, complaints, subpoenas, and other legal documents. Goals are to: promote and upgrade the process-serving industry; establish high moral and ethical standards for the industry; monitor legislation at the state and federal level; assist in the formation and continuation of state associations representing the industry. Seeks to improve relations between process servers and members of the legal community such as attorneys, judges, clerks, and court officers. Assists with service of process in foreign countries through the Hague Service Convention; makes discount insurance programs available to members. **Libraries: Type:** not open to the public; reference. **Holdings:** archival material, articles, audio recordings, periodicals. **Subjects:** laws and procedures pertaining to service of process, general material on process serving, process serving. **Awards:** Donald C. MacDonald Award. **Frequency:** annual. **Type:** trophy. **Recipient:** for distinguished service to the process serving industry. **Computer Services:** Mailing lists, membership. **Telecommunication Services:** electronic mail, claire@napps.org. **Committees:** Education; eFiling/eService; International Relations; Legislative Affairs; Standards and Best Practices; State Associations. **Publications:** *Annual Seminar Conferences*. Audiotapes. Highlights the annual educational seminars. Alternate Formats: CD-ROM ● *The Docket Sheet*, bimonthly. Magazine. **Price:** included in membership dues; $35.00 /year for nonmembers. **Circulation:** 1,900. **Advertising:** accepted ● *Membership Directory and Civil Rules Guide*, semiannual. **Price:** available to members only. **Conventions/Meetings:** annual conference (exhibits) ● annual seminar.

Property

6185 ■ National Association State Agencies for Surplus Property (NASASP)

c/o Doug Coleman, Admin.
2301 C St.
Auburn, WA 98001-7401
E-mail: jim.smith@mail.state.ar.us
URL: http://www.nasasp.org/v3
Contact: James Smith, Pres.
Founded: 1947. **Members:** 66,000. **Membership Dues:** associate, $35 (annual). **Staff:** 2. **Budget:** $50,000. **Regional Groups:** 4. **State Groups:** 56. **Multinational. Description:** Represents surplus property agencies in the 50 states and the District of Columbia, Puerto Rico, Guam, Northern Marianas, and the Virgin Islands that distribute surplus federal property to public agencies and nonprofit educational and public health organizations; this property is distributed to eligible organizations at a fraction of the original acquisition cost. Sponsors competitions; operates charitable program. **Publications:** *NASASP Newsletter*, quarterly ● Directory, annual. **Conventions/Meetings:** annual conference.

6186 ■ National Association of Unclaimed Property Administrators (NAUPA)

c/o NAST
PO Box 11910
Lexington, KY 40578-1910
Ph: (859)244-8150
Fax: (859)244-8053
E-mail: naupa@csg.org
URL: http://www.unclaimed.org
Contact: Hon. John D. Perdue, Pres.
Founded: 1962. **Members:** 52. **Staff:** 1. **Description:** Represents state officials who administer unclaimed property laws. Promotes cooperation among the states and territories in administration of such laws; seeks to resolve jurisdictional conflicts without litigation and works to develop uniform legislation. Maintains speakers' bureau. **Formerly:** (1980) Association of Unclaimed Property Administrators. **Publications:** *NAUPA Newsletter*, quarterly. **Price:** $50.00/year. **Circulation:** 300. **Advertising:** accepted. Alternate Formats: online ● *Quick Reference Handbook*. Contains information in reporting unclaimed property. **Price:** $150.00 plus shipping and handling. Alternate Formats: online. **Conventions/Meetings:** annual conference, software companies, publishers, contract auditors (exhibits).

Property Rights

6187 ■ American Land Rights Association (ALRA)

PO Box 400
Battle Ground, WA 98604
Ph: (360)687-3087
Fax: (360)687-2973
E-mail: alra@pacifier.com
URL: http://www.landrights.org
Contact: Chuck Cushman, Exec. Dir.
Founded: 1978. **Members:** 19,400. **Membership Dues:** individual, $35 (annual). **Staff:** 8. **Budget:** $360,000. **State Groups:** 50. **Local Groups:** 1,800. **Description:** Individuals holding property, equity interest, grazing permits, leases, mining claims, or real estate in or adjacent to federally managed areas such as national parks, forests, and other federal lands. Also includes people affected by the Endangered Species Act and the Clean Water Act. Seeks to ensure that members are treated fairly and consistently. Works with federal agencies when conflicts arise to help find solutions; often travels to the site of conflicts and holds meetings with local land use organizations. Advises members on how to affect legislation. Conducts research programs. Sponsors internship and congressional placement programs. Maintains speakers' bureau; compiles statistics. **Awards:** Champion of Property Rights. **Frequency:** periodic. **Type:** recognition ● Golden Padlock. **Frequency:** annual. **Type:** recognition ● **Type:** grant ● **Type:** recognition. **Computer Services:** database, federal Land Users Data System, listing over 1 million persons owning land or holding permits, leases, or other equity on federally managed areas. **Telecommunication Services:** electronic mail, ccushman@pacifier.com. **Formerly:** (1980) National Parks Inholders Association; (1993) National Inholders Association; (1993) Land Rights; (2000) League of Private Property Owners. **Publications:** *American Land Rights Association Congressional Directory*, periodic. **Circulation:** 500,000 ● *Land Rights Advocate*, biennial. Newsletter. Contains how-to manual on dealing with congress and federal agencies. ● *Land Rights Alerts*, periodic. Directory. Provides issue-specific alerts in letter format. ● *Private Property Congressional Vote Index*, annual. Directory. **Price:** free. **Circulation:** 500,000 ● Directory. **Conventions/Meetings:** annual meeting (exhibits).

6188 ■ Defenders of Property Rights

1350 Connecticut Ave. NW, Ste.410
Washington, DC 20036
Ph: (202)822-6770
Fax: (202)822-6774
E-mail: mail@yourpropertyrights.org
Contact: Nancie G. Marzulla, Pres.
Founded: 1991. **Description:** Ensures that the property rights contained in the Constitution be given the full effect of the law. Works with victims of "overzealous" regulations and with elected representatives to pass legislation that will ease the danger property owners face from government regulation. Educates property owners about their rights and how best to protect them. **Publications:** Newsletter. Alternate Formats: online.

Public Administration

6189 ■ American Association of State Service Commissions (ASC)

1400 I St. NW, Ste.560
Washington, DC 20005-6526
Ph: (202)729-8263
Fax: (202)729-8265
E-mail: askus@asc-online.org
URL: http://www.asc-online.org
Contact: Kyle Caldwell, Chm.
Founded: 1997. **Description:** Represents the interests of state service commissions across the United States. Informs the state, national, public, private and nonprofit policy makers of the value of national and community service and volunteerism in the country's civil society. Supports the development of service commissions and volunteer organizations throughout the United States. **Libraries: Type:** reference. **Computer Services:** Information services, advocacy resources ● information services, service commissions. **Telecommunication Services:** electronic bulletin board ● electronic mail, kyle@connectmichiganalliance.org ● electronic mail, tbranen@asc-online.org. **Committees:** Steering. **Also Known As:** (2005) America's Service Commissions.

6190 ■ American Society for Public Administration (ASPA)

1301 Pennsylvania Ave. NW, Ste.840
Washington, DC 20004-1735
Ph: (202)393-7878 (202)585-4307
Fax: (202)638-4952
E-mail: info@aspanet.org
URL: http://www.aspanet.org
Contact: Antoinette Samuel CAE, Exec. Dir.
Founded: 1939. **Members:** 10,000. **Membership Dues:** individual, $100 (annual) ● supporting, $120 (annual) ● sustaining, $220 (annual) ● life, $2,000 ● electronic - outside U.S., Canada, Mexico, $30 (annual) ● family, $35 (annual) ● electronic - student, $40 (annual) ● full - student, $75 (annual) ● senior, $55 (annual). **Staff:** 13. **Budget:** $1,500,000. **Regional Groups:** 10. **Local Groups:** 128. **Multinational. Description:** Promotes excellence in public service, including government, non-profit and private sectors, and academic community. **Committees:** Ethics; Organizational Review and Evaluation; Policy Issues; Professional Development. **Publications:** *PA Times*, monthly. Newspaper. Includes book reviews. **Price:** $50.00 for first class mails; $75.00 for international air mails. **Circulation:** 11,500. **Advertising:** accepted. Alternate Formats: microform ● *Public Administration Review*, bimonthly. Journal. Serves governmental administrators, public officials, educators, research workers, and others interested in the public management profession. **Price:** $90.00/year. **Circulation:** 13,000. **Advertising:** accepted. Alternate Formats: microform ● National Conference Program book. **Conventions/Meetings:** annual conference (exhibits).

6191 ■ Conference of Minority Public Administrators (COMPA)

c/o American Society for Public Administration
1301 Pennsylvania Ave. NW, Ste.840
Washington, DC 20004
Ph: (202)393-7878
Fax: (202)638-4952
E-mail: info@aspanet.org
URL: http://www.natcompa.org
Contact: Mrs. Delores Strain, Pres.
Founded: 1971. **Members:** 460. **Membership Dues:** regular/international, $100 (annual) ● electronic student, $40 (annual) ● full, student, $75 (annual) ● senior, $55 (annual) ● international electronic, $30 (annual) ● family, $35 (annual) ● supporting individual, $120 (annual) ● sustaining individual, $220 (annual) ● life, $2,000. **Staff:** 11. **Description:** A section within the American Society for Public Administration. Members of ASPA who belong to a minority group or are interested in the promotion of minorities within public administration. Works to improve government and advance excellence in public service. **Awards:** COMPA Public Service Award. **Frequency:** annual. **Type:** recognition. **Recipient:** for a minority public administrator who has demonstrated overall outstanding achievement in the field of public service ● COMPA Travel Grant. **Frequency:** annual. **Type:** grant. **Recipient:** to an undergraduate or graduate student who is not employed full-time but aspires to attend the conference for the purpose of networking,

presenting theses or dissertations and/or participating as a panelist ● Ronald H. Brown Memorial Scholarship. **Frequency:** annual. **Type:** recognition. **Recipient:** for academic achievement and community involvement of talented minority students nationwide ● Sylvester Murray Distinguished Mentor Award. **Frequency:** annual. **Type:** recognition. **Recipient:** for a minority public administrator who has demonstrated overall outstanding mentorship capabilities in the field of public service. **Committees:** Resource Development. **Publications:** *COMPA Spectrum*, quarterly. Newsletter ● *Journal of Public Management and Social Policy*. Provides forum for scholarly research addressing diverse issues. Alternate Formats: online. **Conventions/Meetings:** annual meeting, in conjunction with ASAP.

6192 ■ Institute of Public Administration - USA (IPA)
Address Unknown since 2008
Founded: 1906. **Staff:** 21. **Budget:** $531,318. **Description:** Private research, educational, and consulting agency consisting of research staff, associates, and board of trustees. Conducts domestic and international research and education in public administration, public finance, citizenship and ethics, management, urban development and government organization and policy problems. Makes available consultation and technical services specializing in urban and metropolitan studies, governmental management, charter and code revision and reorganization, personnel and training for governmental service, public enterprise, financing and organization, urban transportation, contracting, ethics, and private-public sector cooperation in the United States and abroad. **Libraries: Type:** reference. **Holdings:** 50,000. **Telecommunication Services:** phone referral service, (212)730-5480. **Formerly:** (1921) Bureau of Municipal Research; (1931) National Institute of Public Administration. **Publications:** Reports, periodic.

6193 ■ National Academy of Public Administration (NAPA)
900 7th St. NW, Ste.600
Washington, DC 20001
Ph: (202)347-3190
Fax: (202)393-0993
E-mail: academy@napawash.org
URL: http://www.napawash.org
Contact: Mr. Howard Messner, Pres./CEO
Founded: 1967. **Members:** 550. **Membership Dues:** contribution, $300 (annual). **Staff:** 30. **Budget:** $8,000,000. **Multinational. Description:** Works to respond to specific requests from public agencies and non-governmental organizations. Promotes discourse on emerging trends in governance through standing panels and external funding. Assists federal agencies, congressional committees, state and local governments, civic organizations, and institutions overseas through problem solving, objective research, rigorous analysis, information sharing, development strategies for change, and connecting people and ideas. Promotes forward-looking ideas and of analyzing successes and failures of government reform. **Libraries: Type:** reference. **Holdings:** books, periodicals. **Awards:** Herbert Roback Scholarship. **Frequency:** annual. **Type:** scholarship ● Louis Brownlow Book Award. **Frequency:** annual. **Type:** recognition ● National Public Service Award. **Frequency:** annual. **Type:** recognition. **Subgroups:** Executive Program and Management; Federal Systems; International; Public Service; Social Equity. **Publications:** Annual Report, annual ● Papers, periodic ● Also publishes study results in panel reports. **Conventions/Meetings:** semiannual meeting - always spring and fall.

6194 ■ National Association of Schools of Public Affairs and Administration (NASPAA)
1029 Vermont Ave. NW, Ste.1100
Washington, DC 20005
Ph: (202)628-8965
Fax: (202)626-4978
E-mail: naspaa@naspaa.org
URL: http://www.naspaa.org
Contact: Laurel McFarland, Exec. Dir.
Founded: 1970. **Members:** 249. **Membership Dues:** associate, $610 (annual) ● international associate (OECD countries), $300 (annual) ● international associate (non-OECD countries), $150 (annual) ● institutional (based on the number of students), $728-$2,933 (annual). **Staff:** 7. **Budget:** $630,000. **Description:** Universities and government agencies dedicated to the advancement of education, research, and training in public affairs and public administration. Serves as a national center for information about programs and developments in this field. Fosters goals and standards of educational excellence and represents the concerns and interests of member institutions in the formulation and support of national policies for education in public affairs/public administration. Accredits master's degree program in public affairs and administration. Cooperates with governmental organizations, professional associations, and national public interest groups to improve the quality of public management. **Computer Services:** Mailing lists. **Commissions:** Peer Review and Accreditation. **Committees:** Annual Conference Program; Diversity; Doctoral Education; International Education; Marketing the MPA; Personnel; Policy Issues; Small Programs; Standards; Technology; Undergraduate; Urban Management and Education. **Sections:** Comprehensive Schools; Health Sector Management Education; Non-Profit Management Education; Political Science Based PA Programs; Undergraduate Programs. **Affiliated With:** Pi Alpha Alpha. **Formerly:** (1958) Council on Graduate Education for Public Administration. **Publications:** *Doctoral Policy Statement for Programs in Public Affairs/Public Administration* ● *Guidelines and Standards for Baccalaureate* ● *Journal of Public Affairs Education*, quarterly. Features pedagogical and curricula issues in public affairs education. **Price:** $45.00 /year for individuals; $35.00/year for students; $100.00 /year for institutions ● *Peer Review/Accreditation Policy* ● *Public Enterprise*, monthly. Newsletter. Contains articles of interest to deans, chairpersons, public administration faculty, and others interested in public service education. **Price:** included in membership dues ● *Roster of Accredited Programs*, annual ● *Standards for Masters*. **Conventions/Meetings:** annual conference.

6195 ■ National Association of State Facilities Administrators (NASFA)
PO Box 11910
Lexington, KY 40578-1910
Ph: (859)244-8181 (859)244-8121
Fax: (859)244-8001
E-mail: marcia@nasfa.net
URL: http://www.nasfa.net
Contact: Marcia Stone, Exec. Dir.
Founded: 1987. **Members:** 1,500. **Membership Dues:** state, corporate, $1,800 (annual) ● other governmental, $1,000 (annual). **Staff:** 2. **Budget:** $137,000. **Regional Groups:** 4. **Description:** State administrators involved in architecture, engineering, construction, maintenance, building operations, and real estate property management. Seeks to: provide a forum for the study of effective state facilities administration; develop cooperative mechanisms for the improvement of all aspects of state facilities administration and management. Conducts research on building issues; analyzes and disseminates information on topics such as state facilities policies and practices, legislation, and programs. **Libraries: Type:** reference. **Awards:** Innovations Award. **Frequency:** annual. **Type:** recognition. **Recipient:** for innovative facilities management programs. **Committees:** Annual Conference and Trade Show; Communications; Definitions; Executive; Innovation Award; Membership; Recognition; Special Projects. **Affiliated With:** Council of State Governments. **Publications:** *NASFA Representatives Directory*, periodic. Lists by state the key individuals responsible for specific facilities functions. **Price:** $30.00 ● *State Facilities Quarterly*. Newsletter. **Circulation:** 500. **Conventions/Meetings:** annual conference and trade show (exhibits) ● regional meeting ● seminar.

6196 ■ National Forum for Black Public Administrators (NFBPA)
777 N Capitol St. NE, Ste.807
Washington, DC 20002
Ph: (202)408-9300
Free: (888)766-9951
Fax: (202)408-8558
E-mail: jsaunders@nfbpa.org
URL: http://www.nfbpa.org
Contact: John E. Saunders III, Exec. Dir.
Founded: 1983. **Members:** 3,000. **Membership Dues:** individual, $175 (annual) ● student, $25 (annual) ● business (based on number of employees), $1,000-$5,000 (annual) ● associate sustaining, $2,000 (annual) ● associate primary, $1,000 (annual) ● associate gold, $5,000 (annual) ● provisional, $50 (annual) ● retired, $75 (annual) ● Board of Director, $3,000 (annual). **Staff:** 6. **Budget:** $1,200,000. **Local Groups:** 49. **Description:** Black city and county managers and assistant managers; chief administrative officers; agency directors; bureau and division heads; corporate executives; students. Works to promote, strengthen, and expand the role of blacks in public administration. Seeks to focus the influence of black administrators toward building and maintaining viable communities. Develops specialized training programs for managers and executives. Provides national public administrative leadership resource and skills bank. Works to further communication among black public, private, and academic institutions. Addresses issues that affect the administrative capacity of black managers. **Awards:** Marks of Excellence Award. **Frequency:** annual. **Type:** recognition. **Recipient:** to a black public administrator who has made outstanding contributions to public service. **Councils:** Academic Advisory; Corporate Advisory; Elected Officials Advisory. **Task Forces:** Black Homicide; Environmental Management Focus Group. **Publications:** *The Forum*, quarterly. Magazine. Includes articles on management and professional development; provides conference, chapter, and member information. **Advertising:** accepted. Alternate Formats: online ● *Resource Guide*, annual ● Membership Directory, semiannual. **Conventions/Meetings:** annual conference (exhibits) - always April.

6197 ■ Public Technology Institute (PTI)
1301 Pennsylvania Ave. NW, Ste.830
Washington, DC 20004
Ph: (202)626-2412 (202)626-2445
Free: (866)664-6368
Fax: (202)626-2498
E-mail: info@pti.org
URL: http://www.pti.org
Contact: Dr. Alan R. Shark, Exec. Dir.
Founded: 1971. **Members:** 160. **Membership Dues:** jurisdiction (city/county; minimum), $1,000 (annual) ● jurisdiction (city/county; maximum), $30,000 (annual). **Staff:** 25. **Budget:** $3,000,000. **Description:** Works as a Technical arm of International City/County Management Association, National League of Cities, and National Association of Counties. Conducts research and development activities for cities and counties. Serves as vehicle for transferring new technologies and solutions to local government problems; provides technical assistance and management training to local governments. Offers information online. Sponsors seminars and workshops. **Libraries: Type:** reference. **Holdings:** 350; books, papers, periodicals. **Awards:** Solutions Technology Achievement Award. **Frequency:** annual. **Type:** recognition ● Technology Leadership Award. **Frequency:** annual. **Type:** recognition. **Recipient:** for technology innovations and achievements by local governments. **Programs:** Urban Consortium for Technology Initiatives for Cities and Counties Over 250000. **Formerly:** (1971) Technology Applications Program, International City Management Association; (2005) Public Technology, Inc. **Publications:** *Prism Online*, monthly. Magazines. Alternate Formats: online ● *Publications Catalog*, annual. **Conventions/Meetings:** annual Congress of Public Technologists, showcases for best practice technology solutions in local government (exhibits).

6198 ■ Section for Women in Public Administration (SWPA)
1120 G St. NW, Ste.700
Washington, DC 20005-3885
Ph: (202)393-7878
Fax: (202)638-4952

E-mail: jhutch@vcu.edu
URL: http://www.swpanet.org
Contact: Janet Hutchinson, Contact
Founded: 1971. **Members:** 331. **Membership Dues:** regular, $17. **Staff:** 11. **Description:** Established by the American Society for Public Administration to initiate action programs appropriate to the needs and concerns of women in public administration. Promotes equal educational and employment opportunities for women in public service, and full participation and recognition of women in all areas of government. Develops strategies for implementation of ASPA policies of interest to women in public administration; recommends qualified women to elective and appointive ASPA governmental leadership positions; acts as forum for communication among professional and laypeople interested in the professional development of women in public administration. **Awards: Type:** grant. **Recipient:** to local ASPA chapters initiating programs encouraging career growth and professional development for women in public administration ● Joan Fiss Bishop Memorial Award. **Type:** recognition. **Committees:** Archivist and Constitution/By-Laws Revision; Awards; Conference; Contributions; Leadership; National; Nominations; Research. **Formerly:** (1973) Task Force for Women in Public Administration; (1982) National Committee for Women in Public Administration. **Publications:** *Bridging the Gap*, semiannual. Newsletter ● Membership Directory, periodic. **Conventions/Meetings:** annual conference, held in conjunction with ASPA (exhibits).

6199 ■ Southern Public Administration Education Foundation (SPAEF)
2103 Fairway Ln.
Harrisburg, PA 17112
Ph: (717)540-5477
Fax: (215)893-1763
E-mail: spaef@spaef.com
URL: http://spaef.com
Contact: Dr. T. Aaron Wachhaus, Contact
Founded: 1977. **Staff:** 5. **Local Groups:** 1. **Description:** Represents researchers and scholars. Produces publications to educate scholars and practitioners. Publishes electronic journals. **Publications:** *Journal of Health and Human Resources Administration*, quarterly. Features articles, symposia and book reviews on health, hospital and welfare administration. **Price:** $125.00 /year for individuals; $190.00 /year for libraries and institutions ● *Public Administration Quarterly*. Journal. Includes articles regarding public administration. **Price:** $111.00 /year for individuals; $185.00 /year for libraries and institutions.

Public Affairs

6200 ■ Air Force Public Affairs Alumni Association (AFPAAA)
PO Box 447
Locust Grove, VA 22508-0447
E-mail: membersvc@afpaaa.org
URL: http://www.afpaaa.org
Contact: Linda Arnold, Chm.
Founded: 1993. **Members:** 700. **Membership Dues:** life, $300 ● full, adjunct, affiliate, $25 (annual) ● associate, $10 (annual). **Description:** Preserves the heritage and professionalism of the public affairs, band and broadcasting career fields. Accumulates and preserves first-person historical accounts of national and international public affairs events and activities. Provides job transition resources for members. **Awards:** Best of the Best. **Frequency:** annual. **Type:** recognition. **Recipient:** for top performer in USAF public affairs. **Telecommunication Services:** electronic mail, arnold@afpaaa.org. **Programs:** Oral History. **Projects:** USAF Public Affairs Memorial. **Publications:** Newsletter, quarterly. Alternate Formats: online ● Membership Directory.

Public Finance

6201 ■ American Association for Budget and Program Analysis (AABPA)
PO Box 1157
Falls Church, VA 22041
Ph: (703)941-4300
Fax: (703)941-1535
E-mail: aabpa@aol.com
URL: http://www.aabpa.org
Contact: Teri Gullo, Pres.
Founded: 1976. **Members:** 600. **Membership Dues:** regular, $45 (annual) ● student, $15 (annual) ● corporate, $150 (annual). **Staff:** 1. **Budget:** $50,000. **Local Groups:** 1. **Description:** Professionals in budgeting, policy analysis, and program & management analysis evaluation who are employed by the federal government, state and local agencies, private companies, and academic institutions. Seeks to advance knowledge in budgeting management and program analysis. Promotes the exchange of ideas and information. Conducts monthly program with guest speakers from government agencies, congress, and institutions. **Libraries: Type:** reference. **Holdings:** archival material. **Awards:** Distinguished Service Award. **Frequency:** annual. **Type:** recognition. **Computer Services:** Mailing lists. **Telecommunication Services:** electronic mail, moravitz@us.ibm.com. **Absorbed:** American Public Policy Association. **Publications:** *The Bottom Line*, bimonthly. Newsletter ● *Journal of Public Budgeting and Finance*, quarterly. **Conventions/Meetings:** annual meeting (exhibits) - usually April and November ● symposium.

6202 ■ Association for Governmental Leasing and Finance (AGL&F)
19 Mantua Rd.
Mount Royal, NJ 08061
Ph: (856)423-3259
Fax: (856)423-3420
E-mail: aglfhq@talley.com
URL: http://www.aglf.org
Contact: Ken Cleveland, Exec. Dir.
Founded: 1981. **Members:** 290. **Membership Dues:** individual and governmental, not-for-profit organization, $350 (annual) ● limited, $750 (annual) ● basic, $1,250 (annual) ● industry leader, $2,500 (annual). **Staff:** 2. **Budget:** $350,000. **Description:** Aims to inform governmental issuers, investment bankers, institutional investors, and legislative bodies of the attributes of governmental leasing and other alternative finance methods available to state and local governments. Identifies and reports changes in legislation and case laws regarding leasing and finance. Researches tax-exempt municipal leases. Provides speakers' bureau. **Libraries: Type:** reference. **Holdings:** archival material. **Telecommunication Services:** electronic mail, leasing@aglf.org. **Publications:** *The Fifty State Survey: Federal Securities Law and of Legislation and Case Law in the Fifty States*, biennial. Journal. **Price:** $300.00 for nonmembers ● *Tell*, quarterly. Newsletter. **Price:** available to members only ● *Tell Flash*, periodic. Contains legislative updates. **Price:** available to members only. **Conventions/Meetings:** annual conference.

6203 ■ Association of Public Treasurers of the United States and Canada (APT US & C)
962 Wayne Ave., Ste.910
Silver Spring, MD 20910
Ph: (301)495-5560
Fax: (301)495-5561
E-mail: info@aptusc.org
URL: http://www.aptusc.org
Contact: Kelly Noone, Exec. Dir.
Founded: 1965. **Members:** 2,500. **Membership Dues:** associate, $409 ● sustaining, $57 ● active, $67 ● town, village, county, or state/province, $115-$345 ● special district/retirement system, $115-$344. **Staff:** 3. **Budget:** $350,000. **Regional Groups:** 17. **State Groups:** 17. **Description:** City, state, and town deputy treasurers, finance directors, controllers, and representatives of the public finance industry. Conducts regional education/training programs for municipal finance administrators. Offers seminars and workshops; provides speakers on municipal finance and personal and career development; offers publications on treasury issues. **Awards:** Certification of Excellence Award. **Type:** recognition. **Recipient:** for entities whose investment policies are approved and certified ● Certified Municipal Finance Administrator Award. **Type:** recognition ● Dr. Jackson R.E. Phillips Award. **Frequency:** annual. **Type:** recognition. **Recipient:** to a treasurer or finance officer for outstanding achievement in fiscal management ● **Frequency:** annual. **Type:** scholarship. **Recipient:** for an active member ● Service Award Program. **Frequency:** annual. **Type:** recognition. **Recipient:** for outstanding service. **Committees:** Accounting, Automation, and Internal Controls; Cash Management, Receipting and Banking Services; Debt Management; Education Certification; Investment Policies, Practices, and Certification. **Formerly:** (2003) Municipal Treasurers Association of the U.S. and Canada. **Publications:** *Technical Topics*, quarterly. Newsletter. **Price:** free for members. **Circulation:** 2,500 ● *Treasury Notes*, monthly. Newsletter. Provides information on all aspects of treasury management and news of Association activities. Includes calendar of events and legislative updates. **Price:** free for members. **Circulation:** 2,500 ● Brochures ● Membership Directory, annual. Alternate Formats: online. **Conventions/Meetings:** annual conference - always August. 2008 Aug. 19-13, Grand Rapids, MI.

6204 ■ Government Finance Officers Association of United States and Canada (GFOA)
203 N LaSalle St., Ste.2700
Chicago, IL 60601-1216
Ph: (312)977-9700
Fax: (312)977-4806
E-mail: inquiry@gfoa.org
URL: http://www.gfoa.org
Contact: Jeffrey L. Esser, Exec. Dir./CEO
Founded: 1906. **Members:** 14,000. **Membership Dues:** city and county, special district, retirement system (minimum), $145 (annual) ● city and county (maximum), $4,325 (annual) ● special district (maximum), $1,500 (annual) ● retirement system (maximum), $1,545 (annual) ● state and province, international, $145-$235 (annual) ● federal, $140 (annual) ● associate, $210 (annual) ● inactive, retired, $35 (annual) ● educational, $40 (annual). **Staff:** 65. **Description:** Finance officers from city, county, state, provincial, and federal governments, schools, and other special districts; retirement systems, colleges, universities, public accounting firms, financial institutions, and others in the United States and Canada interested in government finance. Maintains five centers: Finance and Operations; Federal Liaison; Research, Professional Development; and Technical Services. Supports the Governmental Accounting Standard Board. Maintains Washington, DC, office. **Libraries: Type:** not open to the public. **Holdings:** articles, books, periodicals, reports. **Subjects:** government finance topics. **Awards:** Award for Excellence in Government Finance. **Frequency:** annual. **Type:** recognition. **Recipient:** for outstanding financial management ● Certificate of Achievement for Excellence in Financial Reporting Award. **Frequency:** annual. **Type:** recognition. **Recipient:** for states and local government ● Distinguished Budget Presentation Award. **Frequency:** annual. **Type:** recognition. **Recipient:** for outstanding government ● Popular Reporting Awards. **Frequency:** annual. **Type:** recognition. **Recipient:** for outstanding government. **Computer Services:** Online services, software for debt issuance and governmental accounting. **Telecommunication Services:** electronic mail, membership@gfoa.org. **Committees:** Accounting, Auditing and Financial Reporting; Canadian; Cash Management; Governmental Budgeting and Management; Governmental Debt and Fiscal Policy; Retirement and Benefits Administration. **Formerly:** (1927) Association of Comptrollers and Accounting Officers; (1984) Municipal Finance Officers Association of U.S. and Canada. **Publications:** *GAAFR Review*, monthly. Newsletter. **Price:** $50.00 for active members; $60.00 for associate members; $85.00 for nonmembers ● *Government Finance Officers Association—Newsletter*, semimonthly. Provides updates on current events, innovations, and federal legislation affecting public finance management for state and local government. **Price:** free for members; $30.00 /year for nonmembers ● *Government Finance Review*, bimonthly. Magazine. **Price:** free for members; $30.00 /year for

nonmembers ● *Pension and Benefits Update*, bimonthly. Newsletter. **Price:** $40.00 for active members; $50.00 for associate members; $60.00 for nonmembers ● *Public Investor*, monthly. Newsletter. **Price:** $55.00 for active members; $70.00 for associate members; $85.00 for nonmembers ● Bulletin, periodic. Features a research on topics in government finance. **Price:** free for members ● Also publishes textbooks and reports focusing on various areas of public financial management. **Conventions/Meetings:** annual conference (exhibits) - usually May or June. 2008 June 15-18, Fort Lauderdale, FL; 2009 June 28-July 1, Seattle, WA ● National Training Seminar, beginning, intermediate, and advanced levels - 60/year.

6205 ■ National Association of County Treasurers and Finance Officers (NACTFO)
c/o Kim Reynolds, Treas.
PO Box 157
Osceola, IA 50213
Ph: (641)342-3311
Fax: (641)342-6260
E-mail: clarketr@cecnet.net
URL: http://www.nactfo.org
Contact: Barbara F. Coates, Pres.

Founded: 1954. **Members:** 2,985. **Membership Dues:** county (based on population), $60-$225 (annual) ● affiliate, $500 (annual). **Budget:** $65,000. **Description:** Elected and appointed county treasurers, tax collectors and finance officers. Promotes improved and efficient operating and financial procedures in the financial administration of county tax revenue collection. **Awards:** Public Service Award. **Frequency:** annual. **Type:** recognition. **Recipient:** for outstanding fiscal officer. **Affiliated With:** National Association of Counties. **Publications:** *County Treasury Marks*, semiannual. Newsletter. Alternate Formats: online. **Conventions/Meetings:** annual conference - usually February or March. 2009 Mar. 7-11, Washington, DC; 2010 Mar. 6-10, Washington, DC ● semiannual convention, general business (exhibits) - always July and February/March ● annual meeting, held in conjunction with the National Association of Counties - always July. 2008 July 11-15, Kansas City, MO; 2009 July 10-14, Nashville, TN; 2010 July 16-20, Reno, NV.

6206 ■ National Association of State Auditors, Comptrollers, and Treasurers (NASACT)
449 Lewis Hargett Cir., Ste.290
Lexington, KY 40503-3669
Ph: (859)276-1147
Fax: (859)278-0507
E-mail: kpoynter@nasact.org
URL: http://www.nasact.org
Contact: Kinney Poynter, Exec. Dir.

Founded: 1916. **Members:** 170. **Staff:** 14. **Budget:** $1,800,000. **Description:** Auditors, comptrollers, and treasurers of state fiscal agencies. Studies government, particularly finance, financial reporting, taxation, administration, office methods, procedures, and general administration of state government. Offers training program and peer review and technical services. **Awards:** President's Award. **Frequency:** annual. **Type:** recognition. **Recipient:** for an outstanding individual. **Computer Services:** Mailing lists, for a fee. **Telecommunication Services:** electronic mail, phackney@nasact.org. **Committees:** Intergovernmental Relations; State and Municipal Bonds. **Publications:** *NASACT News*, monthly. Newsletter. Alternate Formats: online ● Directory, annual ● Also publishes pamphlets on activities of auditors, comptrollers, and treasurers. **Conventions/Meetings:** annual conference - 2008 Aug. 9-13, Chicago, IL.

6207 ■ National Association of State Budget Officers (NASBO)
Hall of the States Bldg.
444 N Capitol St. NW, Ste.642
Washington, DC 20001-1511
Ph: (202)624-5382 (202)624-8804
Fax: (202)624-7745
E-mail: nasbo-direct@nasbo.org
URL: http://www.nasbo.org
Contact: Scott D. Pattison, Exec. Dir.

Founded: 1945. **Members:** 162. **Staff:** 7. **Description:** Budget directors, their deputies, and superior officers of the states and territories. Seeks to encourage study and research in state budgeting and promote cooperation and efficiency in budget programs. Conducts budget and legislative briefing every spring and four to five educational seminars each year. **Libraries: Type:** reference. **Holdings:** archival material, reports. **Awards:** George A. Bell Award. **Frequency:** annual. **Type:** recognition. **Recipient:** for outstanding contributions and services to public budgeting and management in state government ● Gloria Timmer Award. **Frequency:** annual. **Type:** recognition. **Recipient:** for significant achievements or a career of accomplishments that had significant impacts on the award recipient's state. **Telecommunication Services:** electronic mail, spattison@nasbo.org. **Committees:** Commerce, Physical Resources, and Transportation; Education and Human Resources; Financial Management, Systems, Data, and Reporting; Personnel Development. **Publications:** *Fiscal Survey of the States*, semiannual. **Price:** $25.00. ISSN: 0198-6562 ● Also publishes special reports. **Conventions/Meetings:** annual meeting, every spring ● annual meeting, every fall.

6208 ■ National Association of State Treasurers (NAST)
PO Box 11910
Lexington, KY 40578-1910
Ph: (859)244-8175
Fax: (859)244-8053
E-mail: nast@csg.org
URL: http://www.nast.net
Contact: Hon. Tate Reeves, Pres.

Founded: 1975. **Members:** 50. **Membership Dues:** subsidiary/associate, $1,000 (annual) ● principal, $3,000 (annual). **Staff:** 9. **Budget:** $1,000,000. **Regional Groups:** 4. **State Groups:** 50. **National Groups:** 3. **Description:** State, commonwealth, and territorial treasurers, deputies, and staff. Works to provide a forum for the exchange of information and to learn new techniques concerning investment and cash management. Receives assistance from Council of State Governments in planning conventions. **Libraries: Type:** not open to the public. **Subjects:** public finance. **Awards:** Jesse Unruh Treasurer Emeritus. **Frequency:** annual. **Type:** recognition. **Committees:** Intergovernmental Relations and Legislation. **Affiliated With:** Council of State Governments. **Publications:** *Corporate Affiliate Handbook*. **Price:** $40.00 ● *NAST Review*, quarterly. Newsletter ● *State Treasury Activities and Functions*, triennial. Directory ● *State Treasury Profiles*, semiannual. **Price:** $45.00 for nonmembers; $40.00 for members ● Directory, biennial. **Conventions/Meetings:** annual conference (exhibits) ● annual Issues Conference ● annual Legislative Conference.

6209 ■ Society of Financial Examiners (SOFE)
174 Grace Blvd.
Altamonte Springs, FL 32714
Ph: (407)682-4930
Free: (800)787-7633
Fax: (407)682-3175
E-mail: info@sofe.org
URL: http://www.sofe.org
Contact: Paula Keyes CPCU, Exec. Dir.

Founded: 1973. **Members:** 1,650. **Membership Dues:** general/regulatory, $65 (annual) ● associate, $250 (annual). **Staff:** 5. **Budget:** $400,000. **State Groups:** 50. **Description:** Current or former government examiners of banks, savings and loans, credit unions, and insurance companies in the U.S. and Canada and others interested in financial solvency. Aims to enhance the prestige of examiners by providing educational development programs and plateaus of recognizable achievement. Provides accreditation and certification through independently administered examinations. **Libraries: Type:** reference. **Holdings:** video recordings. **Awards:** Don Fritz Memorial Award. **Frequency:** annual. **Type:** recognition ● Editor's Choice Award. **Frequency:** annual. **Type:** recognition ● Founders Award. **Frequency:** annual. **Type:** recognition. **Telecommunication Services:** electronic mail, pkeyes@sofe.org. **Publications:** *Examiner*, quarterly. Magazine. Contains articles on issues affecting financial examiners. Includes directory, charts, and tables. **Price:** included in membership dues. ISSN: 0190-2733. **Circulation:** 2,500 ● *Insight*, monthly. Newsletter. Includes obituaries, member profiles, career development seminar proceedings, and classified advertisements; for financial examiners. **Price:** included in membership dues. **Advertising:** accepted. **Conventions/Meetings:** annual Career Development Seminar - meeting and seminar - usually July/August. 2008 Aug. 3-6, Nashville, TN; 2009 July 24-29, Sacramento, CA.

Public Health

6210 ■ Association of Health Facility Survey Agencies (AHFSA)
5105 Solemn Grove Rd.
Garner, NC 27529
Ph: (919)661-8774
E-mail: rgoodnow@bellsouth.net
URL: http://www.ahfsa.org
Contact: Mr. Robert Goodnow, Exec. Dir.

Founded: 1968. **Members:** 51. **Membership Dues:** regular, $500 (annual). **Staff:** 45. **Description:** Directors of state or territorial health facility licensure and certification programs; staff members of a state or territorial health facility licensure and certification agency; employees of the federal Health Care Financing Administration; interested individuals. Purposes are to exchange information among members and between members and the Association of State and Territorial Health Officials (see separate entry); constitute a "reservoir of expertise" to aid in the guidance of ASTHO; improve the quality of health facility licensure and certification programs; provide a forum for state and territorial issues at the national level. Has a representative on an ASTHO standing committee and liaises with the federal Department of Health and Human Services and the HCFA. Has developed new training programs with the HHS and testified before the U.S. Senate Special Committee on Aging on survey and certification procedures. **Awards:** Surveyor of the Year Award. **Frequency:** annual. **Type:** recognition. **Formerly:** (1991) Association of Health Facility Licensure and Certification Directors. **Publications:** *AHFSA Directory*, annual ● *Association of Health Facility Survey Agencies Newsletter*, semiannual. Reports on the quality of health facility licensure and certification programs and related issues. Includes calendar of events. **Price:** included in membership dues ● Papers. **Conventions/Meetings:** annual conference.

6211 ■ Association of State Drinking Water Administrators (ASDWA)
1025 Connecticut Ave. NW, Ste.903
Washington, DC 20036
Ph: (202)293-7655
Fax: (202)293-7656
E-mail: info@asdwa.org
URL: http://www.asdwa.org
Contact: Brad Addison, Pres.-Elect

Founded: 1984. **Members:** 56. **Membership Dues:** associate, $100 (annual). **Staff:** 5. **Budget:** $780,000. **Description:** Managers of state and territorial drinking water programs; state regulatory personnel. Works to meet communication and coordination needs of state drinking water program managers; facilitates the exchange of information and experience among state drinking water agents. Acts as a collective voice for the protection of public health through assurance of high quality drinking water; oversees the implementation of the Safe Drinking Water Act. Liaises with Congress and the Environmental Protection Agency. Holds training sessions. **Publications:** *ASDWA Update*, bimonthly. Newsletter. Contains latest issues related to drinking water. **Price:** included in membership dues; $40.00 /year for nonmembers. **Circulation:** 350 ● *Capacity Develop-*

ment Newsletter, quarterly. Contains articles that give insights into capacity development issues. Alternate Formats: online ● *Results and Analysis of the ASDWA Survey of Best Management Practices in Community Ground Water Systems.* Report. Highlights the results of a survey of 812 public water systems. **Price:** $25.00/copy ● *Source Water News*, bimonthly. Newsletter. Alternate Formats: online ● *State Sanitary Survey Resource Directory.* Includes a guidance document to assist states in reviewing their own sanitary survey programs. **Price:** $50.00/copy. **Conventions/Meetings:** annual conference (exhibits) ● seminar ● workshop.

6212 ■ Association of State and Territorial Health Officials (ASTHO)
2231 Crystal Dr., Ste.450
Arlington, VA 22202
Ph: (202)371-9090
Fax: (202)527-3189
E-mail: pjarris@astho.org
URL: http://www.astho.org
Contact: Paul E. Jarris MD, Exec. Dir.
Founded: 1942. **Members:** 57. **Staff:** 40. **Budget:** $7,500,000. **Description:** Represents the state and territorial public health agencies of the United States, the U.S. Territories, and the District of Columbia. Works to formulate and influence sound public health policy, and assure excellence in state-based public health practice. Seeks to assist state health departments in the development and implementation of programs and policies to promote health and prevent disease. Serves as an information resource to state health agencies, members and alumni on public policy. Addresses key public health issues and publishes newsletters, survey results, resource lists, and policy papers that assist states in the development of public policy. Promotes public health programs at the state level. **Libraries: Type:** not open to the public. **Holdings:** archival material, papers, periodicals, reports. **Awards:** Excellence in Public Health. **Frequency:** annual. **Type:** recognition. **Recipient:** for leaders at the national and local level, for their outstanding promotion of health and prevention of diseases ● The McCormack Award. **Frequency:** annual. **Type:** recognition. **Recipient:** for current or former public health official who has served for at least ten years and has made significant contribution to the knowledge and practice of the field ● The Nobel Swearingen Award. **Frequency:** annual. **Type:** recognition. **Recipient:** for an individual in public health administration with ten or more years of experience in a state health agency and five or more years of service to the management of a similar committee ● Vision Awards. **Frequency:** annual. **Type:** recognition. **Recipient:** for outstanding state health department programs and initiatives. **Computer Services:** Information services ● mailing lists. **Additional Websites:** http://www.statepublichealth.org. **Committees:** Environmental Health; Immunization Policy; Infectious Diseases; Informatics; Preparedness; Prevention and Chronic Disease; Primary Care. **Affiliated With:** Association of Health Facility Survey Agencies; Association of Maternal and Child Health Programs; Association of Public Health Laboratories; Association of State and Territorial Dental Directors; Council of State and Territorial Epidemiologists; Directors of Health Promotion and Education; National Alliance of State and Territorial AIDS Directors; State and Territorial Injury Prevention Directors Association. **Formerly:** (1975) Association of State and Territorial Health Officers. **Publications:** *ASTHO Report*, quarterly. Newsletter. **Circulation:** 2,000. **Conventions/Meetings:** annual conference (exhibits) ● quarterly meeting, on AIDS.

6213 ■ Association of State and Territorial Local Health Liaison Officials (ASTLHLO)
Empire State Plz.
Corning Tower Bldg., Rm. 821
Albany, NY 12237
Ph: (518)473-4223
Fax: (518)473-8714
URL: http://www.astlhlo.org
Contact: Sylvia Pirani, Pres.
Description: Represents and supports state health department officials in their roles of overseeing and providing support to local health agencies. Aims to improve overall local health infrastructure and performance. Advocates for a strong public health presence at both the state and local levels. **Publications:** Membership Directory. Alternate Formats: online.

6214 ■ Commissioned Officers Association of the United States Public Health Service (COA)
8201 Corporate Dr., Ste.200
Landover, MD 20785
Ph: (301)731-9080
Free: (866)366-9593
Fax: (301)731-9084
E-mail: gfarrell@coausphs.org
URL: http://www.coausphs.org
Contact: Jerry Farrell, Exec. Dir.
Founded: 1950. **Members:** 7,000. **Membership Dues:** retired, $105 (annual) ● inactive reserve officer, retired-associate, $50 (annual) ● active duty officer 03 and below, $60 (annual) ● active duty officer 04 and above, $105 (annual) ● co-step, life, $25 ● life (based on age), $440-$1,575. **Staff:** 6. **Budget:** $900,000. **Local Groups:** 52. **Description:** Commissioned officers of the U.S. Public Health Service; includes career active duty, retired, and inactive reserve officers who are physicians, dentists, scientists, engineers, pharmacists, nurses, and other types of professional personnel. Acts as an official spokesperson for the Commissioned Corps, as an information center for its members, and "as a sounding board where views and concerns of the Corps may be brought to the proper authorities for official action". **Absorbed:** (1976) United States Public Health Service Clinical Society. **Publications:** *Frontline*, 10/year. Bulletin. **Price:** included in membership dues. **Advertising:** accepted ● *Proceedings of Annual Meeting.* **Conventions/Meetings:** annual Scientific Meeting - conference (exhibits).

6215 ■ Directors of Health Promotion and Education (DHPE)
1101 5th St. NW, 3rd Fl.
Washington, DC 20005
Ph: (202)659-2230
Fax: (202)659-2339
E-mail: director@dhpe.org
URL: http://www.dhpe.org
Contact: Rose Marie Matulionis MSPH, Exec. Dir.
Founded: 1946. **Members:** 175. **Membership Dues:** voting, $200-$350 (annual) ● associate, $50 (annual). **Staff:** 8. **Description:** Directors of public health education in state and territorial departments of health and Indian health service areas. Seeks to improve the quality of public health education practice; promote information exchange and advocacy. Develops practice guidelines and supports collection and dissemination of data and information relevant to public health education. **Awards: Frequency:** annual. **Type:** recognition. **Committees:** Political Action. **Affiliated With:** Association of State and Territorial Health Officials. **Formerly:** (1989) Conference of State and Territorial Directors of Public Health Education; (2004) Association of State and Territorial Directors of Public Health Education; (2005) Association of State and Territorial Directors of Health Promotion and Public Health Education. **Publications:** *Conference Call*, quarterly. Newsletter ● *Roster of Members*, quarterly. Membership Directory ● *The Voice.* Bulletin. Alternate Formats: online ● Proceedings, annual. **Conventions/Meetings:** meeting (exhibits) ● annual National Conference on Health Education and Health Promotion (exhibits).

6216 ■ IUD Claims Information Source (ICIS)
PO Box 84151
Seattle, WA 98124
Ph: (206)329-1371
Fax: (206)329-0912
Contact: Constance Miller, Managing Dir.
Founded: 1989. **Staff:** 1. **Description:** Provides information and referrals to women filing lawsuits because of injuries sustained through use of an intrauterine contraceptive device (IUD). Offers professional seminars in claims filing and resolution. Maintains speakers' bureau. **Publications:** *Dalkon Shield Claims Guidebook* ● *Dalkon Shield Legal Guide.* **Conventions/Meetings:** annual board meeting.

6217 ■ National Association of County and City Health Officials (NACCHO)
1100 17th St. NW, 2nd Fl.
Washington, DC 20036
Ph: (202)783-5550
Fax: (202)783-1583
E-mail: info@naccho.org
URL: http://www.naccho.org
Contact: Patrick Libbey, Exec. Dir.
Founded: 1965. **Members:** 1,000. **Membership Dues:** student, $25 (annual) ● retiree, alumnus, $50 (annual) ● state public health department or government agency, non-profit or school of public health, $330 (annual) ● for-profit organization, $2,425 (annual). **Staff:** 43. **Budget:** $5,000,000. **Description:** County and city (local) health officials. Purposes are to stimulate and contribute to the improvement of local health programs and public health practices throughout the U.S; disseminate information on local health programs and practices; participate in the formulation of the policies of the National Association of Counties (see separate entry). Develops self-assessment instrument for use by local health officials. Operates Primary Care Project which helps to strengthen the link between local health departments and community health centers. Provides educational workshops for local health officials. **Awards: Type:** recognition. **Formerly:** National Association of County Health Officials; (1975) National Association of County Health Officers. **Publications:** *Achieving Healthier Communities through MAPP: A User's Handbook.* **Price:** $34.95 for members; $54.95 for nonmembers ● *Membership Monthly.* Brochure. Serves as an information guide for members. **Price:** included in membership dues ● *NACCHO Exchange*, quarterly. Newsletter. **Price:** included in membership dues; $10.00 for nonmembers ● *NACCHO News*, bimonthly. Newsletter. **Price:** included in membership dues. **Circulation:** 3,300. **Advertising:** accepted ● *Public Health Dispatch*, monthly. Newsletter. **Price:** included in membership dues ● Annual Report, annual. **Conventions/Meetings:** annual conference (exhibits) ● periodic meeting.

6218 ■ National Association for Public Health Statistics and Information Systems (NAPHSIS)
962 Wayne Ave., Ste.701
Silver Spring, MD 20910
Ph: (301)563-6001
Fax: (301)563-6012
E-mail: hq@naphsis.org
URL: http://www.naphsis.org
Contact: Garland Land, Exec. Dir.
Founded: 1933. **Members:** 300. **Budget:** $50,000. **Description:** Officials of state and local health agencies responsible for registration, tabulation, and analysis of births, deaths, fetal deaths, marriages, divorces, and other health statistics. **Telecommunication Services:** electronic mail, gland@naphsis.org. **Affiliated With:** Association of State and Territorial Health Officials. **Formerly:** (1958) American Association of Registration Executives; (1980) American Association for Vital Records and Public Health Statistics; (1997) Association for Vital Records and Health Statistics. **Publications:** Journal, bimonthly. **Conventions/Meetings:** annual conference (exhibits).

Public Interest Law

6219 ■ Alliance for Justice (AFJ)
11 Dupont Cir. NW, 2nd Fl.
Washington, DC 20036
Ph: (202)822-6070
Fax: (202)822-6068

E-mail: alliance@afj.org
URL: http://www.afj.org
Contact: Nan Aron, Pres.

Founded: 1979. **Members:** 50. **Membership Dues:** organization (initiation fee), $500 ● organization (based on budget), $500-$3,500 (annual). **Staff:** 35. **Budget:** $5,200,000. **Description:** Advocates for civil rights, social justice, consumer, and environmental protection. Works to strengthen the progressive community's role in public interest advocacy. Works with and on behalf of its members to safeguard the fairness of the public policy and federal judicial systems. Helps to ensure that the concerns of ordinary Americans, and the voice of the public interest, receive a fair hearing in the nation's legislatures and courts of law. Sponsors summer internship program for undergraduate students or law students interested in public interest law; compiles statistics. **Awards:** Ally of Justice Award. **Frequency:** annual. **Type:** recognition. **Recipient:** for the significant contribution to the cause of social justice. **Programs:** Student Action Campaign. **Affiliated With:** Citizens Communications Center Project of the Institute for Public Representation; Consumers Union of United States; Equal Rights Advocates. **Absorbed:** Judicial Selection Project. **Formerly:** (1980) Council for Public Interest Law. **Publications:** *Being a Player: A Guide to the IRS Lobbying Regulations for Advocacy Charities*. Book. Provides a plain language roadmap of IRS lobbying regulations. **Price:** $15.00 ● *The Co/Motion Guide to Youth-Led Social Change*. Manual. Engages young people in action by giving them the tools, skills, and strategies to solve problems. **Price:** $30.00 ● *The Connection: Strategies for Creating and Operating 501(c)(3)s, 501(c)(4)s, and PACs*. Book. Explains the advantages and issues to be considered in establishing each of the different types of organizations. **Price:** $25.00 ● *E-Advocacy for Nonprofits: The Law of Lobbying and Election-Related Activity on the Net*. Book. Addresses the law governing Internet advocacy. **Price:** $25.00 ● *First Monday Video: America Up In Arms*. Videos. Contains chronicle impact of gun violence on three families, their communities, and society as a whole. ● *First Monday Video: Bringing Justice Home*. Videos. Shows three vignettes dealing with the lack of affordable housing and housing discrimination. **Price:** $25.00 for colleges and non-profits; $50.00 for law firms, law schools, and graduate programs ● *First Monday Video: Justice for All*. Videos. Tells the story of a death row prisoner in Texas whose lawyer fell asleep during his trial and who has a strong claim of innocence. **Price:** $25.00 for non-profits; $50.00 for law firms ● *First Monday Video: Liberty and Justice for All*. Videos. Features two immigrants whose claims are jeopardized by laws that deprive the federal courts of the power to review INS policies. **Price:** $20.00 ● *Foundations and Ballot Measures: A Legal Guide*. Book. **Price:** $10.00 ● *Justice First*, quarterly. Newsletter. Contains articles describing recent developments in the public interest sector. Includes profiles of member organizations. **Price:** included in membership dues. **Circulation:** 10,000 ● *Justice for Sale: Shortchanging the Public Interest for Private Gain*. Analyzes efforts to elevate profits and private wealth over social justice and individual rights. **Price:** $15.00 ● *Liberty and Justice for All: Public Interest Law in the 1980s and Beyond* (in English and Spanish). Book. **Price:** $7.00 ● *Myth vs. Fact: Foundation Support of Advocacy*. Report. Dispels the myths associated with funding advocacy organizations. **Price:** $20.00 ● *No Free Lunch? The House and Senate Gift Rules and Nonprofit Organizations*. Paper. Assists non-profit organizations in deciphering the new House and Senate Gift Rules. **Price:** free ● *Regulation of Advocacy Activities of Nonprofits the Receive Federal Grants*. Paper. Summarizes the applicable federal regulations and Internal Revenue Code provisions. **Price:** free ● *The Rules of the Game: An Election Year Legal Guide for Nonprofit Organizations*. Book. Reviews federal tax and election law that govern nonprofits in an election year. **Price:** $20.00 ● *Seize the Initiative*. Book. Answers frequently asked questions by nonprofit organizations about work on ballot measures. **Price:** $20.00 ● *2000 Annual Report of the Judicial Selection Project*, annual. Analyzes the Clinton Administration's record on judicial appointments. **Price:** $5.00 reports from prior years available ● *What the "Intermediate Sanctions" Law Means for Nonprofit Organizations*. Paper. Reviews the major provisions of the new law, primarily new public disclosure requirements for IRS form 990 and what they mean for you. **Price:** free ● *Worry-Free Lobbying for Nonprofits: How to Use the 501(h) Election to Maximize Effectiveness*. Brochure. Describes how non-profits and the foundations that support them can take advantage of the clear and generous provisions in federal law. **Price:** free. **Conventions/Meetings:** annual Justice First - luncheon - always in Washington, DC.

6220 ■ Center for Law and Social Policy (CLASP)

1015 15th St. NW, Ste.400
Washington, DC 20005-2605
Ph: (202)906-8000
Fax: (202)842-2885
E-mail: ahouse@clasp.org
URL: http://www.clasp.org
Contact: Alan W. Houseman, Exec. Dir.

Founded: 1968. **Staff:** 32. **Budget:** $3,900,000. **Nonmembership. Description:** Works to improve the economic conditions of low-income families with children and to secure access for low-income households to the civil justice system. **Libraries: Type:** open to the public. **Holdings:** articles, books. **Subjects:** social welfare, child support, legal services, child care, workforce development and reproductive health, early education. **Additional Websites:** http://www.spdp.org. **Affiliated With:** National Legal Aid and Defender Association. **Publications:** *CLASP Update*, monthly. Newsletter. Features welfare and low-income family policy issues. **Price:** free. **Circulation:** 2,000 ● Manuals. Discusses child support enforcement, welfare reform, workforce development, reproductive health and teen parents, early education and child care, etc. ● Report, annual ● Periodic analytical reports on child support enforcement, welfare reform, child care, reproductive health and teen parents, workforce development, early education, legal aid for the poor, and disconnected youth.

6221 ■ Economic Justice Institute (EJI)

975 Bascom Mall
Madison, WI 53706-1399
Ph: (608)262-9143 (608)265-2058
E-mail: eji@law.wisc.edu
URL: http://www.law.wisc.edu/eji
Contact: Louise Trubek, Founder

Founded: 1974. **Description:** Provides advocate services for consumers and low-income families through education, research, training and representation. Aims to educate and empower consumers by providing services and information. **Libraries: Type:** reference. **Awards:** Public Interest. **Frequency:** annual. **Type:** recognition. **Recipient:** for Wisconsin citizens who have made outstanding contributions in public interest. **Divisions:** Advocacy; Citizen Information; Clinical Education; Research; Training. **Publications:** *The Public Eye*, semiannual. Newsletter ● Books ● Manuals ● Papers ● Brochure ● Handbook. **Conventions/Meetings:** periodic seminar, with training programs.

6222 ■ Equal Rights Advocates (ERA)

1663 Mission St., Ste.250
San Francisco, CA 94103-2488
Ph: (415)621-0672 (415)575-2383
Free: (800)839-4ERA
Fax: (415)621-6744
E-mail: info@equalrights.org
URL: http://www.equalrights.org
Contact: Irma D. Herrera, Exec. Dir.

Founded: 1974. **Members:** 5,300. **Staff:** 14. **Budget:** $1,300,000. **Languages:** English, Spanish. **Description:** Public interest law center specializing in sex discrimination. Focuses on discrimination issues in employment such as nontraditional work, sexual harassment, pregnancy-based discrimination, pay equity, and gender equity issues. Lectures to professional groups; advises local, state, and national attorneys, legislators, and other advocates. Provides legal advice and counsel to victims of race- and sex-based discrimination; conducts public education programs on discrimination issues. **Libraries: Type:** reference. **Subjects:** law. **Telecommunication Services:** electronic mail, iherrera@equalrights.org ● hotline, advice and counseling, (415)621-0505. **Publications:** *Affirmative Action Handbook: How to Start and Defend Affirmative Action Programs* ● *Equal Rights Advocates—Annual Report*. Includes summaries of significant legal decisions affecting women. **Circulation:** 1,000 ● *Keeping the Door Open-Women and Affirmative Action*. Booklet ● *Know Your Rights* (in English and Spanish). Brochures. **Price:** free. Alternate Formats: online ● *Pay Equity Sourcebook* ● Newsletter, quarterly. Reports on women's legal issues; provides analyses of cases and legislation of concern to women. Also includes organization news. **Price:** included in membership dues. **Circulation:** 5,000. **Conventions/Meetings:** monthly board meeting.

6223 ■ National Chamber Litigation Center (NCLC)

1615 H St. NW
Washington, DC 20062-2000
Ph: (202)463-5337 (202)659-6000
Free: (800)638-6582
E-mail: nclc@uschamber.com
URL: http://www.uschamber.com/nclc/default.htm
Contact: Thomas J. Donohue, Pres./CEO

Founded: 1977. **Members:** 400. **Membership Dues:** small business (with up to 50 employees, plus $100 per additional 5 employees), $365-$1,500 (annual). **Staff:** 8. **Budget:** $1,500,000. **Description:** Small and large businesses that view litigation as a means to curb the influence of government regulations on business. Represents business on national public policy issues before the courts and government agencies. Works to: overturn laws, regulations, and court rulings that violate businesses' constitutional rights and legal interests; contain the power of forces that disrupt sound labor-management relations, undermine businesses' potential strength, and bias government rulemaking activities; promote sensible rulemaking in national issues crucial to business such as consumer affairs, safety regulations, and environmental issues. **Libraries: Type:** not open to the public. **Committees:** Constitutional and Administrative Law Advisory; Environmental Law Advisory; Labor Law Advisory. **Affiliated With:** U.S. Chamber of Commerce. **Publications:** *National Chamber Litigation Center—Case List*, 8/year. Reports. Includes a summary of current NCLC legal cases. **Price:** included in membership dues; $15.00 /year for nonmembers and legal resource libraries. **Circulation:** 1,000 ● *100 Ways to Cut Legal Fees and Manage Your Lawyer*. Handbook ● Newsletter, weekly. Provides news on legislative and regulatory developments, economic forecasts and analysis, and higlights from small business toolkits. Alternate Formats: online. **Conventions/Meetings:** annual Supreme Court Press Briefing - meeting.

6224 ■ National Legal Center for the Public Interest (NLCPI)

1776 K St. NW, 8th Fl.
Washington, DC 20006-2844
Ph: (202)466-9360
Fax: (202)466-9366
E-mail: info@nlcpi.org
URL: http://www.nlcpi.org
Contact: Richard A. Hauser, Pres.

Founded: 1975. **Staff:** 5. **Budget:** $120,000. **Nonmembership. Description:** Law and education foundation. Seeks to foster knowledge about law and the administration of justice in a society committed to the rights of individuals, free enterprise, private ownership of property, balanced use of private and public resources, limited government, and a fair and efficient judiciary. Contributes to the development of public debate and policy by providing the public and private sectors with timely information and professional expertise on key legal, legislative, regulatory, and economic issues of national importance through educational publications and forums. **Libraries: Type:** reference. **Holdings:** books, periodicals. **Sub-**

jects: law, public rebury. **Publications:** *BRIEFLY. Perspectives on Legislation, Regulation and Litigation*, monthly. Book ● *The Judicial Legislative Watch Report*, monthly. Newsletter. Reports activities in Congress, the Executive Branch, and the Judiciary. Alternate Formats: online ● Newsletters ● Books. **Conventions/Meetings:** periodic conference ● annual General Counsel Briefing - conference, includes panel discussion ● periodic lecture ● annual Press Briefing - meeting ● Supreme Court Briefing - meeting ● annual Yauer Distinguished Lecture in Law and Public Policy.

6225 ■ National Legal Foundation (NLF)
PO Box 64427
Virginia Beach, VA 23467-4427
Ph: (757)463-6133
Fax: (757)463-6055
E-mail: nlf@nlf.net
URL: http://www.nlf.net
Contact: Steven W. Fitschen, Pres.
Founded: 1985. **Description:** Serves as public interest law firm dedicated to "the restoration and defense of constitutional freedoms in America". Litigates in defense of First Amendment liberties, with special focus on religious freedom. Prepares briefs, educational materials, and other publications on church-state issues for lawyers, teachers, and interested individuals. Holds seminars on First Amendment issues for attorneys. Maintains speakers' bureau. **Libraries: Type:** reference. **Holdings:** books, clippings, monographs, periodicals. **Subjects:** law. **Telecommunication Services:** electronic mail, swf@nlf.net. **Publications:** *Minuteman*, quarterly. Newsletter. Alternate Formats: online.

6226 ■ Pacific Legal Foundation (PLF)
3900 Lennane Dr., Ste.200
Sacramento, CA 95834-2918
Ph: (916)419-7111
Fax: (916)419-7747
E-mail: plf@pacificlegal.org
URL: http://www.pacificlegal.org
Contact: Robin L. Rivett, Pres.
Founded: 1973. **Staff:** 54. **Budget:** $5,000,000. **Description:** Litigates in state and federal courts challenging government actions, laws, and regulations that infringe on individual and economic freedoms. Defends and espouses the principles of private property rights, constitutionally limited government, free market enterprise, and individual responsibility. Opposes unfair tax assessment policies; challenges hiring and contracting quotas and preferences; supports education, tort, and welfare reforms. **Libraries: Type:** reference. **Holdings:** articles, biographical archives. **Sections:** Environmental; General Law; Property Rights. **Publications:** *At Issue*, 10/year. Report. Features news bulletins. ● *Guide Post*, quarterly. Newsletter ● *The PLF Sentry*. Newsletter. Alternate Formats: online ● Annual Report.

6227 ■ Public Justice
1825 K St. NW, Ste.200
Washington, DC 20006-1220
Ph: (202)797-8600 (202)701-3252
Fax: (202)232-7203
E-mail: tlpj@tlpj.org
URL: http://www.tlpj.org
Contact: Arthur H. Bryant, Exec. Dir.
Founded: 1982. **Members:** 2,500. **Membership Dues:** basic, $250 (annual) ● student, $25 (annual) ● supporting, $500 (annual) ● sustaining, $1,000 (annual) ● advocate, $2,500 (annual) ● benefactor, $5,000 (annual) ● patron, $10,000 (annual) ● champion, $25,000 (annual) ● associate, $100 (annual). **Staff:** 27. **Budget:** $3,000,000. **Description:** National public interest law firm specializing in precedent-setting and socially significant civil litigation requiring trial attorney skills. Fights for consumer and victims' rights, environmental protection and safety, civil rights and civil liberties, the preservation of the civil justice system, the elimination of secrecy in the court system, and the protection of the poor and powerless. Operates Speaker's Bureau; conducts educational programs. **Libraries: Type:** reference. **Awards:** Public Justice Achievement Award. **Frequency:** annual. **Type:** recognition. **Recipient:** for extraordinary work and achievement of trial lawyers ● Trial Lawyer of the Year. **Frequency:** annual. **Type:** recognition. **Recipient:** for trial lawyers who took great risk and overcame incredible odds to advance the common law, to make new law and to win justice for their clients. **Formerly:** (2007) Trial Lawyers for Public Justice. **Publications:** *TLPJ in the News*, annual ● *Trial Lawyers Doing Public Justice*, annual. Booklet ● Newsletter, quarterly ● Membership Directory, annual. **Conventions/Meetings:** quarterly board meeting ● semiannual convention ● quarterly meeting, for committee members.

6228 ■ United States Justice Foundation (USJF)
c/o Gary G. Kreep, Exec. Dir.
932 D St., Ste.2
Ramona, CA 92065-2355
Ph: (760)788-6624
Fax: (760)788-6414
E-mail: usjf@usjf.net
URL: http://www.usjf.net
Contact: Gary G. Kreep, Exec. Dir.
Founded: 1979. **Description:** Politically conservative attorneys dedicated to preserve the civil, property, and human rights of U.S. citizens. Provides free legal services to individuals, businesses, and other entities having problems with government agencies, government regulations, and government-supported organizations. Network of attorneys in 17 states who volunteer time to work on cases chosen by the board of directors. Provides analysis of legislation for federal, state, and local legislators on numerous subjects. Helps draft legislation and/or policies for state and local government entities. Provides legal assistance and support for parents rights groups across the United States. Active in the legal fight to uphold Proposition 13, the California tax relief initiative. Also active in the litigation to uphold Proposition 187, the ban on free public education, welfare, and non-emergency medical services for illegal aliens. Provides speaker services. **Libraries: Type:** reference. **Holdings:** archival material. **Publications:** *Justice Report*, quarterly. Newsletter. **Price:** $25.00. **Advertising:** accepted ● Brochures.

6229 ■ Washington Legal Foundation (WLF)
2009 Massachusetts Ave. NW
Washington, DC 20036-1004
Ph: (202)588-0302
Fax: (202)588-0386
E-mail: info@wlf.org
URL: http://www.wlf.org
Contact: Constance C. Larcher, Pres./CEO
Founded: 1976. **Staff:** 20. **Budget:** $4,500,000. **Nonmembership. Description:** Litigates in the courts and before government agencies; provides outreach program; publishes in seven educational formats. **Telecommunication Services:** electronic mail, administration@wlf.org ● electronic mail, clarcher@wlf.org. **Divisions:** Legal Studies. **Absorbed:** (1986) American Legal Foundation. **Publications:** *Contemporary Legal Notes* ● *Conversations With*, monthly ● *Counsel's Advisory*, monthly ● *Legal Backgrounders*, weekly ● *Legal Opinion Letters*. Monographs ● *WLF Monographs*, monthly ● *WLF Working Papers Studies*, monthly ● *Working Papers* ● Also publishes legal public policy monographs on regulatory and conservative judicial issues.

Public Policy

6230 ■ Evergreen Freedom Foundation (EFF)
PO Box 552
Olympia, WA 98507
Ph: (360)956-3482
Fax: (360)352-1874
E-mail: effwa@effwa.org
URL: http://www.effwa.org
Contact: Bob Williams, Pres.
Founded: 1991. **Members:** 4,500. **Membership Dues:** subscriber, $50 (annual) ● contributor, $100 (annual) ● sustainer, $250 (annual) ● patron, $500 (annual) ● sponsor, $1,000 (annual). **Staff:** 23. **Budget:** $1,850,000. **Description:** Works to advance individual liberty, free enterprise and limited, accountable government. **Publications:** *In-Brief*, 2-4/year. Alternate Formats: online ● *Living Liberty*, monthly. Newsletters. Alternate Formats: online ● *Policy Highlighter*, 15-20/year. Alternate Formats: online.

Public Relations

6231 ■ National Information Officers Association (NIOA)
PO Box 10125
Knoxville, TN 37939
Ph: (865)389-8736
E-mail: info@nioa.org
URL: http://www.nioa.org
Contact: Lisa McNeal, Exec. Dir.
Founded: 1989. **Members:** 600. **Membership Dues:** general, $75 (annual). **Description:** Represents the interests of emergency services and public safety information officers. Provides educational information, training opportunities and regional support to information officers. Promotes stronger media relations. **Publications:** *NIOA News*, bimonthly. Newsletter. Includes original articles and reprints of news items. **Advertising:** accepted. Alternate Formats: online. **Conventions/Meetings:** annual conference, training - 2008 Aug. 24-27, Reno, NV.

Public Welfare

6232 ■ National Center for Law and Economic Justice (NCLEJ)
275 7th Ave., Ste.1506
New York, NY 10001-6708
Ph: (212)633-6967
Fax: (212)633-6371
E-mail: info@nclej.org
URL: http://www.nclej.org
Contact: Henry A. Freedman, Exec. Dir.
Founded: 1965. **Staff:** 11. **Description:** Examines critical issues in welfare policy and law. Develops materials for policy makers, legal services lawyers and welfare recipient groups; provides information on welfare issues to a wide range of individuals and groups. **Libraries: Type:** reference. **Holdings:** reports. **Subjects:** poverty law. **Awards:** James Corman Award. **Frequency:** annual. **Type:** recognition. **Recipient:** for individuals in public service who have devoted their lives to the cause of economic justice. **Additional Websites:** http://www.lincproject.org. **Programs:** Current Economic Justice. **Projects:** Child-care Collaborative; Low-Income Networking and Communications. **Formerly:** (1998) Center on Social Welfare Policy and Law; (2006) Welfare Law Center. **Publications:** *Publications List*. **Price:** free ● *Welfare News and Welfare Bulletin*, periodic. Alternate Formats: online ● Annual Report. Alternate Formats: online.

Public Works

6233 ■ American Public Works Association (APWA)
2345 Grand Blvd., Ste.700
Kansas City, MO 64108-2625
Ph: (816)472-6100 (202)218-6700
Free: (800)848-APWA
Fax: (816)472-1610
E-mail: pking@apwa.net
URL: http://www.apwa.net
Contact: Peter King, Exec. Dir.
Founded: 1894. **Members:** 24,000. **Membership Dues:** individual, $129 (annual). **Staff:** 60. **Budget:** $7,500,000. **State Groups:** 64. **Description:** Chief administrators, commissioners, and directors of public works, city engineers, superintendents, and department heads of transportation, water, waste water, solid waste, equipment services, and buildings and grounds; federal, provincial, and state administrators

and engineers; consultants and educators; associate members are equipment manufacturers' representatives, utility company officials, and contractors; student members are engineering and public administration students interested in the theory and practice of the design, construction, maintenance, administration, and operation of public works facilities and services. Conducts historical research on public works subjects and demonstrates applicability of history to current public works problems and issues through Public Works Historical Society (see separate entry). Sponsors research and education foundations. **Libraries: Type:** reference. **Holdings:** audiovisuals, books, clippings, periodicals. **Subjects:** public works. **Awards:** Top Ten Public Works Leaders of the Year. **Frequency:** annual. **Type:** recognition. **Computer Services:** Online services, local government information network. **Telecommunication Services:** electronic mail, membership@apwa.net. **Committees:** Intergovernmental Relations. **Councils:** Administrative Management; Buildings and Grounds; Emergency Management; Equipment Services; Municipal Engineering; Program Coordination; Solid Wastes; Transportation; Utility Location and Coordination; Water Resources. **Affiliated With:** American Society of Civil Engineers; Associated General Contractors of America; National Association of Schools of Public Affairs and Administration; National Safety Council; Public Works Historical Society. **Formerly:** International Association of Public Works Officials; (1937) American Society of Municipal Engineers. **Publications:** *APWA Reporter*, monthly. Magazine. **Circulation:** 28,000. **Advertising:** accepted ● *Contracting Maintenance Services*. Book ● *Fight Winter and Win: A Service Guide for Public Officials*. Book ● *Financing Stormwater Facilities: A Utility Approach*. Book ● *Managing Public Equipment*. Book ● *One Call Systems Directory*, annual ● *Policy Statements*, annual ● *Public Works Management Practices*. Book. **Price:** $50.00. **Advertising:** accepted ● *Public Works Today: A Profile of Local Service Organizations and Managers*. Book ● Books ● Manuals ● Reports. Includes subjects such as solid waste collection and disposal, street and urban road maintenance, equipment management, urban drainage, etc. **Conventions/Meetings:** annual conference ● annual One Call Symposium ● annual congress (exhibits) - 2008 Aug. 17-20, New Orleans, LA; 2009 Sept. 13-16, Columbus, OH; 2010 Aug. 15-18, Boston, MA.

6234 ■ Council of Infrastructure Financing Authorities (CIFA)

1801 K St. NW, Ste.500
Washington, DC 20006
Ph: (202)973-3100
Fax: (202)973-3101
E-mail: cifa@navigantconsulting.com
URL: http://www.cifanet.org
Contact: Ms. Anna Miller, Pres.

Founded: 1988. **Members:** 100. **Membership Dues:** public (state with population exceeding 5 million), national affiliate, international, $5,000 (annual) ● public (state with population between 2-5 million), $3,000 (annual) ● public (state with population less than 2 million), associate, $1,000 (annual) ● regional affiliate, $2,500 (annual) ● academic/individual, $250 (annual). **Description:** Public agencies with a responsibility for financing infrastructure development and public works projects. Seeks to improve awareness and understanding of infrastructure financing issues. Serves as a clearinghouse on infrastructure financing; monitors business trends and legislation impacting the availability and terms of infrastructure financing. Lobbies for tax policies that encourage public investment; supports regulatory reform to discourage financing abuses; provides educational and training for infrastructure financing professionals; facilitates exchange of information among members. **Committees:** Education and Training; Municipal Market; SRF and Infrastructure Program. **Publications:** *Infrastructure Commentary*, semiannual. Newsletter ● *Washington Update*, semiannual. Newsletter. Alternate Formats: online ● Brochures ● Monographs. Alternate Formats: online ● Reports. Alternate Formats: online. **Conventions/Meetings:** annual Legislative Policy - conference - usually April-May ● annual State Revolving Fund - workshop (exhibits) - usually October-November. 2008 Oct. 19-21, Providence, RI.

6235 ■ Global Village Institute (GVI)

PO Box 90
Summertown, TN 38483-0090
Ph: (931)964-4474
Fax: (931)964-2200
E-mail: ecovillage@thefarm.org
URL: http://www.i4at.org
Contact: Albert K. Bates, Chm.

Founded: 1980. **Staff:** 5. **Budget:** $250,000. **Languages:** English, Spanish. **Description:** Engages in scientific research and education relating to small-scale, appropriate technologies which can provide basic human needs at a minimal economic and environmental cost. Conducts research in food sciences transportation and energy. **Libraries: Type:** reference. **Holdings:** 5,000. **Subjects:** environment, nuclear energy, chemicals, weapons, defense, sustainable development, agriculture. **Affiliated With:** Plenty International. **Formerly:** (1980) Shutdown Project; (1998) Natural Rights Center; (2000) Global Village Institute; (2001) Global Ecovillage Network. **Publications:** *Climate in Crisis*. Book ● *Ecovillages*, quarterly. Newsletter. **Conventions/Meetings:** bimonthly Courses in Ecological Design and Building - workshop.

6236 ■ International Association for Public Participation Practitioners (IAP2)

11166 Huron St., Ste.27
Denver, CO 80234-3339
Ph: (303)451-5945
Free: (800)644-4273
Fax: (303)458-0002
E-mail: iap2hq@iap2.org
URL: http://www.iap2.org
Contact: Scott Russell, Pres.

Founded: 1990. **Membership Dues:** full, $135 (annual) ● life, $1,350 ● small group, $650 (annual) ● corporate, $2,000 (annual) ● student, developing economy, $40 (annual) ● large group, $1,250 (annual). **National Groups:** 22. **Multinational. Description:** Public participation professionals, companies, and organizations; related individuals including policy makers, trainers, mediators, and citizen activists. Works to advance the study and practice of public participation worldwide. Advocates for and represents members' interests. Conducts research and educational programs; provides technical assistance to public participation projects. **Awards:** Organization of the Year Award. **Frequency:** annual. **Type:** recognition. **Recipient:** for the best organization ● Project of the Year Award. **Frequency:** annual. **Type:** recognition. **Recipient:** for projects that have achieved definable income. **Publications:** *Participation Quarterly*. Newsletter. Contains in-depth articles on public participation and related topics, case studies and announcements. ● Annual Report, annual. Alternate Formats: online. **Conventions/Meetings:** annual conference (exhibits).

6237 ■ National Association of Clean Water Agencies (NACWA)

1816 Jefferson Pl. NW
Washington, DC 20036-2505
Ph: (202)833-2672 (202)833-3743
Fax: (202)833-4657
E-mail: info@nacwa.org
URL: http://www.nacwa.org
Contact: Ken Kirk, Exec. Dir.

Founded: 1970. **Members:** 370. **Staff:** 20. **Budget:** $2,300,000. **Regional Groups:** 10. **Description:** Public waste water treatment facilities, consulting firms and other private and public organization. Seeks to advance knowledge in the management of metropolitan sewerage agencies and develop more effective public service by encouraging the establishment of sound sewage collection, treatment and disposal policies. **Libraries: Type:** reference. **Awards:** Excellence in Management Recognition Program. **Frequency:** annual. **Type:** recognition. **Recipient:** to member agencies who have implemented successful programs (over a continuous 3-year period) ● National Environmental Achievement Awards. **Frequency:** annual. **Type:** recognition. **Recipient:** to individuals and member agencies that have made outstanding contributions to environmental protection and wastewater management ● Peak Performance Awards. **Frequency:** annual. **Type:** recognition. **Recipient:** to individual NACWA member agency facilities for outstanding compliance with national pollutant discharge elimination system permit limits. **Telecommunication Services:** electronic mail, kkirk@nacwa.org. **Committees:** Air Quality; Biosolids; Comprehensive Watershed; Legal Affairs; Pretreatment and Pollution Prevention; Water Quality; Wet Weather Issues. **Formerly:** (2006) Association of Metropolitan Sewerage Agencies. **Publications:** *Clean Water Advocate*, 10/year. Newsletter. Includes reports of activities and projects. **Price:** free for members; $250.00 for nonmembers. Alternate Formats: online ● *Financial Survey*, triennial. Contains compilation of industry statistics based on a triennial survey. **Price:** $100.00 for nonmembers; $75.00 for members. Alternate Formats: CD-ROM ● *NACWA Index*, annual. Survey. Contains snapshot of industry statistics. **Circulation:** 2,000. Alternate Formats: online ● *Year in Review*, annual. Annual Reports. **Circulation:** 2,000. Alternate Formats: online. **Conventions/Meetings:** annual National Environmental Policy Forum - meeting - always in May ● semiannual Winter/Summer Technical Conference - meeting - always February and July. 2008 July 15-18, Anchorage, AK.

Purchasing

6238 ■ National Association of State Procurement Officials (NASPO)

201 E Main St., Ste.1405
Lexington, KY 40507-2004
Ph: (859)514-9159 (803)737-0600
Fax: (859)514-9188
E-mail: naspo@amrms.com
URL: http://www.naspo.org
Contact: Robert Voight Shealy, Pres.

Founded: 1947. **Members:** 125. **Membership Dues:** associate, $500 (annual) ● state, $1,200 (annual). **Staff:** 3. **Budget:** $150,000. **Regional Groups:** 4. **Description:** Purchasing officials of the states and territories. The Association Management Resources, Inc. serves as staff agency. Operates "Marketing to State Governments" seminar. Conducts research on special interest topics. Offers special training programs. **Libraries: Type:** reference. **Holdings:** papers. **Awards:** Cost Reduction Incentive Award. **Frequency:** annual. **Type:** recognition. **Recipient:** for cost reduction, transferability, and service ● Cronin Club Award. **Frequency:** annual. **Type:** recognition. **Recipient:** for clubs ● Guilio Mazzone Distinguished Service Award. **Frequency:** annual. **Type:** recognition. **Recipient:** to individuals, for a continuing exemplary service to the public purchasing profession. **Computer Services:** database, recycled commodities. **Telecommunication Services:** electronic mail, jgallt@amrms.com. **Committees:** Annual Meeting; Cooperative Purchasing; Emerging Issues; Federal/State Relations; Information Technology; Marketing Meeting; Member Services and Public Relations; Nominating; Research and Publications; Resolutions; States Helping States; Strategic Partnerships and Alliances; Time and Place. **Councils:** Universal Public Purchasing Certification. **Formerly:** (1998) National Association of State Purchasing Officials. **Publications:** *Contract Cookbook for Purchase of Services*. **Price:** $25.00 for nonmembers; $17.50 for members ● *Issues in Public Purchasing*. Book. **Price:** $29.95 ● *NASPO 2005 Vendor Guide: How to Do Business with the States*, annual. Directory. **Price:** $60.00. Alternate Formats: CD-ROM ● *State and Local Government Purchasing Principles and Practices*. **Price:** $75.00 for nonmembers; $60.00 for members ● *Survey of State Government Purchasing Practices*, biennial. Surveys. Alternate Formats: CD-ROM ● Brochure. Alternate Formats: online ● Papers. Alternate Formats: online ● Books. **Conventions/Meetings:** annual conference, closed meeting for NASPO members ● annual Vendor Seminar - meeting and seminar, educational conference for the vendor community - 2008 Sept. 8-11, St. Louis, MO.

6239 ■ National Institute of Governmental Purchasing (NIGP)
151 Spring St.
Herndon, VA 20170-5223
Ph: (703)736-8900 (845)364-3824
Free: (800)FOR-NIGP
Fax: (703)736-2818
E-mail: membershipinfo@nigp.org
URL: http://www.nigp.org
Contact: Rick Grimm, CEO

Founded: 1944. **Members:** 2,200. **Membership Dues:** agency, associate, $330-$5,400 (annual) ● individual, former public procurement professional, $175 (annual) ● retired, student, $35 (annual). **Staff:** 23. **Budget:** $4,000,000. **Regional Groups:** 8. **State Groups:** 67. **Description:** Federal, state, provincial, county, and local government buying agencies; hospital, school, prison, and public utility purchasing agencies in the U.S. and Canada. Also provides services to the International procurement community. Develops standards and specifications for governmental buying; promotes uniform purchasing laws and procedures; conducts specialized education and research programs. Administers certification program for the Universal Public Purchasing Certification Council (UPPCC) for Certified Professional Public Buyer (CPPB) and Certified Public Purchasing Officer (CPPO); offers audit consulting services and cost saving programs and tools for governmental agencies, including product commodity code to online specifications library. Maintains speakers' bureau; compiles statistics, web based products and services. **Libraries: Type:** open to the public. **Holdings:** 30,060; reports. **Subjects:** purchasing and materials management, survey and trends, position descriptions. **Awards:** Albert H. Hall Award. **Frequency:** annual. **Type:** recognition. **Recipient:** to a former or present member who has made outstanding contributions to NIGP over an extended period of time ● Best Practices Award. **Frequency:** annual. **Type:** recognition. **Recipient:** to a governmental entity that has achieved excellence and outstanding achievement ● Buyer of the Year. **Frequency:** annual. **Type:** recognition. **Recipient:** for individual purchasing professionals ● Chapter of the Year. **Frequency:** annual. **Type:** recognition. **Recipient:** for chapter members ● Distinguished Service Award. **Frequency:** annual. **Type:** recognition. **Recipient:** to individuals who have provided extraordinary service to their government entity, the community, the institute or the purchasing profession ● Innovative Practices Award. **Frequency:** annual. **Type:** recognition. **Recipient:** to leading public agencies that have developed cutting-edge, non-standard, forward thinking approaches for the procurement profession ● Manager of the Year. **Frequency:** annual. **Type:** recognition. **Recipient:** for individual purchasing professionals ● Outstanding Agency Accreditation Achievement. **Frequency:** annual. **Type:** recognition. **Recipient:** for agencies. **Telecommunication Services:** electronic mail, rgrimm@nigp.org. **Boards:** Editorial Advisory. **Committees:** Diversity; Education and Professional Development; Executive; Finance and Budget Review; Forum and Products Exposition; Honors and Awards; Lewis E. Spangler Professional Development Foundation; Marketing and Communications; Membership; Nominating; Research. **Councils:** Presidents; Supplier Partnership; Universal Public Purchasing Certification. **Publications:** *NIGP Buy-Weekly*, every other Wednesday. Bulletin. Alternate Formats: online ● *The NIGP Source*, quarterly. Magazine. Contains technical articles and manuscripts on contemporary procurement issues. Alternate Formats: online ● *The Procurement Professional*, bimonthly. Journal. **Price:** free for members; $50.00 for nonmembers. **Circulation:** 15,000 ● *The Public Purchaser*, bimonthly. Magazine. Contains general articles on purchasing and materials management. **Price:** free, upon request or with membership. **Circulation:** 24,000. **Advertising:** accepted. **Conventions/Meetings:** annual Forum and Products Exposition - seminar (exhibits) ● annual Professional Development Forum and Products Exposition - conference (exhibits).

Racing

6240 ■ Association of Racing Commissioners International (RCI)
2343 Alexandria Dr., Ste.200
Lexington, KY 40504-3283
Ph: (859)224-7070
Fax: (859)224-7071
E-mail: emartin@arci.com
URL: http://www.arci.com
Contact: Edward Martin, Pres./CEO

Founded: 1934. **Members:** 350. **Staff:** 5. **Budget:** $1,000,000. **Regional Groups:** 8. **State Groups:** 25. **National Groups:** 20. **Description:** Members of state racing commissions in the U.S. and racing commissions in Canada, Jamaica, Mexico, and Puerto Rico. Works for uniform procedures and reciprocity in enforcing rules, regulations, and penalties; promotes forceful and honest nationwide control of racing; provides bulletin service on rule changes and decisions of racetrack officials and state commissions; compiles statistical data. Sponsors research and educational programs. **Awards:** William May Award. **Frequency:** annual. **Type:** recognition. **Computer Services:** database, licensing and rulings information. **Committees:** Commission Secretaries and Supervisors of Racing; Constitution and Bylaws; Drug Testing Standards and Practices; Illegal Practices; Industry; Information and Public Relations; International Relations; Judiciary; Model Rules; Public Safety and Security; Uniform Rules and Practices; Winners Federation. **Programs:** Associate Membership; Information Data Base; Stewards and Judges Certification. **Projects:** Rule Codification and Standardization. **Formerly:** (1988) National Association of State Racing Commissioners. **Publications:** *Association of Racing Commissioners International—Bulletin*, bimonthly. Newsletter. Provides information for those interested in the pari-mutuel industry. **Price:** $125.00/year. **Circulation:** 700. Alternate Formats: online ● *Commissioners' Manual*, periodic. Alternate Formats: online ● *Racing Law and Racing Commissioners Manual* ● *Statistical Summary of Pari-Mutuel Wagering*, annual. Handbook. Contains news on pari-mutuel wagering; includes statistics and state revenue tax summaries for Jai-Alai, and horse and greyhound racing. **Price:** included in membership dues; $25.00/copy for nonmembers ● *Statistical Tables on Greyhound Racing*, annual ● *Statistical Tables on Horse Racing*, annual ● Brochure. Alternate Formats: online ● Paper. Alternate Formats: online. **Conventions/Meetings:** annual meeting (exhibits).

Radiation

6241 ■ Conference of Radiation Control Program Directors (CRCPD)
205 Capital Ave.
Frankfort, KY 40601-2832
Ph: (502)227-4543
Fax: (502)227-7862
E-mail: ssmith@crcpd.org
URL: http://www.crcpd.org
Contact: Sue Smith, Exec. Office Mgr.

Founded: 1968. **Members:** 947. **Membership Dues:** emeritus, $40 (annual) ● associate, $55 (annual) ● affiliate, $85 (annual) ● director, $130 (annual) ● international, $95 (annual). **Staff:** 11. **Budget:** $1,500,000. **Description:** State and local radiological program directors; individuals from related federal protection agencies. Serves as a forum for the interchange of experience, concerns, developments, and recommendations among radiation control programs and related agencies. Encourages cooperation between enforcement programs and agencies at state and federal levels. Promotes radiological health and uniform radiation control laws and regulations; supports radiation control programs; provides assistance with members' technical work and development. Researches and recommends radiation control regulations at state levels in an effort to implement uniform regulations nationwide. Collects and disseminates information, statistics, and data. Maintains speakers' bureau; conducts mammography training seminars. Maintains 30 committees. **Libraries: Type:** reference. **Awards: Type:** recognition. **Committees:** Decommissioning and Decontamination; Diagnostic X-ray; Emergency Response Planning; Low-Level Radio-Active Waste; Mammography; Radon. **Councils:** Environmental Nuclear; General; Healing Arts; Suggested State Regulations. **Publications:** *CRCPD Newsbrief*, monthly. Newsletter. Reviews federal and state legislation and regulation, conference membership, and executive board actions. **Price:** free for members; $35.00 /year for nonmembers. **Circulation:** 796. Alternate Formats: online ● *Directory of Personnel Responsible for Radiological Health Programs*, annual. Lists federal, state, and local agencies associated with CRCPD dealing directly or indirectly with radiation control. **Price:** $40.00/copy. **Advertising:** accepted ● *National Conference on Radiation Control—Proceedings*, annual. Includes papers presented at the National Conference on Radiation Control. **Price:** $50.00/copy. Alternate Formats: CD-ROM; online ● *Patient Exposure Guides for Diagnostic X-Ray*. **Conventions/Meetings:** annual National Conference on Radiation Control - meeting (exhibits) - always May.

6242 ■ National Council on Radiation Protection and Measurements (NCRP)
7910 Woodmont Ave., Ste.400
Bethesda, MD 20814-3076
Ph: (301)657-2652
Free: (800)229-2652
Fax: (301)907-8768
E-mail: schauer@ncrponline.org
URL: http://www.ncrponline.org
Contact: David A. Schauer, Exec. Dir.

Founded: 1929. **Members:** 94. **Staff:** 10. **Budget:** $1,400,000. **Description:** Represents scientists who share the belief that significant advances in radiation protection and measurement can be achieved through cooperative effort. Makes recommendations focused on safe occupational exposure levels and disseminates information. **Committees:** Basic Radiation Protection Criteria; Biological Aspects of Radiation Protection Criteria; Biological Effects and Exposure Criteria for Radiofrequency Electromagnetic Radiation; Biological Effects of Ultrasound; Control of Indoor Radon; Environmental Radiation; Operational Radiation Safety; Radon Measurements. **Formerly:** (1947) Advisory Committee on X-Ray and Radium Protection; (1957) National Committee on Radiation Protection; (1964) National Committee on Radiation Protection and Measurements. **Publications:** *NCRP Commentary*, periodic ● *NCRP Report*, periodic ● *NCRP Statement*, periodic ● *Symposium Proceedings*, periodic. **Conventions/Meetings:** annual Low Dose and Low Dose-Rate Radiation Effects and Models - meeting ● annual meeting, with guest speakers - always early spring in Washington, DC Area.

Real Estate

6243 ■ Association of Real Estate License Law Officials (ARELLO)
8361 Sangre de Cristo Rd., Ste.250
Littleton, CO 80127
Ph: (303)979-6190 (334)260-2928
Fax: (303)979-6187
E-mail: mailbox@arello.org
URL: http://www.arello.com
Contact: Mr. Fran Whitley, Pres.

Founded: 1930. **Members:** 900. **Membership Dues:** full (based on licensee/registrant), $195-$2,790 (annual) ● affiliate - single representative, $150 (annual) ● affiliate - institution, $750 (annual) ● associate, $75 (annual) ● allied, $175 (annual) ● individual, $20 (annual). **Staff:** 3. **Regional Groups:** 6. **State Groups:** 52. **National Groups:** 15. **Multinational. Description:** Represents government and other organization officials administering real estate licensing laws. Seeks to serve as the essential global resource for real estate regulatory information, to improve efficiency of license law administration and enforcement, and to elevate the standards of the real estate industry. Coordinates global conferences on regulatory issues. **Libraries: Type:** reference. **Subjects:** licensing statistics, educator requirements. **Computer Services:** database, of real estate licensees. **Additional Websites:** http://www.arello.org. **Formerly:** (1965) National Association of Real Estate License Law Officials. **Publications:** *ARELLOgram* (in English and Spanish), bimonthly. Newsletter. Covers association activities. Contains committee reports and calendar of events. **Price:** free for members. **Circulation:** 700. Alternate Formats: online ● *Boundaries*, bimonthly. Newsletter. **Price:** $75.00/year. **Circulation:** 500 ● *Digest of Real Estate License Laws*, annual. Includes information on legislation, reciprocity, and subdivided lands requirements. **Price:** $48.00/year. **Circulation:** 1,500 ● *International Directory of Real Estates Regulators and Organizations*, annual. **Price:** $20.00. **Conventions/Meetings:** annual conference, committee meetings, educational sessions and annual membership meeting - 2008 Oct. 17-20, Indianapolis, IN; 2009 Oct. 21-24, Miami, FL ● annual conference, midyear meetings - 2009 Apr. 27-29, Asheville, NC; 2010 Apr. 25-27, Colorado Springs, CO ● seminar, educational.

Regional Government

6244 ■ National Association of Regional Councils (NARC)

1666 Connecticut Ave. NW, Ste.300
Washington, DC 20009-1039
Ph: (202)986-1032
Fax: (202)986-1038
E-mail: cmoore@narc.org
URL: http://www.narc.org
Contact: Cameron Moore, Exec. Dir.

Founded: 1967. **Members:** 250. **Membership Dues:** regular, $1,000-$12,500 (annual) ● transportation, $1,250 (annual). **Staff:** 12. **Budget:** $1,800,000. **Description:** Active members are regional councils of local governments and governmental agencies; associate members are libraries, businesses, and other agencies and organizations interested in regionalism as an approach to meeting problems that cross local governmental boundaries, including economic development, transportation, environmental management, housing, services to the elderly, and rural development. Through this approach, local governments within a region pool resources to solve mutual problems on an area-wide basis instead of developing separate and duplicate or conflicting answers to problems. Councils vary from voluntary organizations to directly elected multi-jurisdictional entities. Provides legislative representation in Washington, DC, and technical assistance through workshops and training programs. **Libraries: Type:** not open to the public. **Holdings:** articles, books, periodicals. **Subjects:** regionalism. **Awards:** Achievement Awards. **Frequency:** annual. **Type:** recognition. **Recipient:** for regional councils and MPOs ● John Bosley Award. **Frequency:** annual. **Type:** recognition. **Recipient:** for individuals with outstanding service and contributions ● Ray Award. **Frequency:** annual. **Type:** recognition. **Recipient:** for state and multi-state associations of regional councils ● Tom Bradley Leadership Award. **Frequency:** annual. **Type:** recognition. **Recipient:** for NARC-member regional councils or MPO policy officials ● Walter Scheiber Leadership Award. **Frequency:** annual. **Type:** recognition. **Recipient:** for executive directors. **Telecommunication Services:** electronic mail, miko@narc.org. **Sections:** Major Metro; Medium Metro; Rural. **Formerly:** (1971) National Service to Regional Councils. **Publications:** *Directory of Regional Councils*, annual. **Price:** included in membership dues; $100.00 for nonmember businesses. **Advertising:** accepted. Alternate Formats: online ● *The Regionalist*, quarterly. Magazine ● *Regions*, bimonthly. Newspaper. **Price:** free for members; $30.00 for nonmembers ● *Special Reports*, periodic ● *State of the Regions*, annual. Report. **Conventions/Meetings:** annual conference and workshop (exhibits) ● annual Washington Policy Conference - always early February in Washington, DC.

Republican Party

6245 ■ Madison Project

PO Box 66128
Washington, DC 20035-6128
Ph: (202)747-1245
Fax: (202)318-1464
E-mail: info@madisonproject.com
URL: http://www.madisonproject.com
Contact: Bob Bobosky, Chm.

Founded: 1994. **Membership Dues:** regular, $25 (annual) ● supporter, $100 (annual) ● patron, $500 (annual) ● Madison Council, $1,000 (annual) ● National Advisory Board, $2,500 (annual). **Description:** Works to empower conservative candidates across the U.S. Values pro-life, pro-family, limited government, and religious freedom.

Rights of Way

6246 ■ International Right of Way Association (IRWA)

19750 S Vermont Ave., Ste.220
Torrance, CA 90502-1144
Ph: (310)538-0233
Fax: (310)538-1471
E-mail: info@irwaonline.org
URL: http://www.irwaonline.org
Contact: Dennis G. Stork, Exec. VP

Founded: 1934. **Members:** 8,300. **Membership Dues:** international, $205 (annual) ● Canadian international, $237 (annual). **Staff:** 17. **Budget:** $1,700,000. **Regional Groups:** 10. **State Groups:** 65. **Local Groups:** 10. **Description:** International professional society of appraisers, attorneys, engineers, negotiators, property managers, title examiners, and others whose principal interest is in the purchase of land and rights in land for the construction of transportation, utility, and other public service facilities. Sponsors educational institutes, seminars, and programs in the fields of right-of-way negotiation and valuation procedures, real estate appraisal, eminent domain law, property management, and administration. **Libraries: Type:** reference. **Holdings:** articles, photographs. **Awards:** Chapter Newsletter of the Year Award. **Frequency:** annual. **Type:** recognition. **Recipient:** for chapter newsletters that have exhibited exemplary qualities in their communication of chapter, regional, and international news ● Employer of the Year Awards. **Frequency:** annual. **Type:** recognition. **Recipient:** for associate companies ● Frank C. Balfour Professional of the Year Award. **Frequency:** annual. **Type:** recognition. **Recipient:** for professionals who have demonstrated exemplary support to the association during the past year ● Gene L. Land Award. **Frequency:** annual. **Type:** recognition. **Recipient:** to local IRWA chapters with the highest percentage gain and highest numerical gain in membership ● Louise L. and Y.T. Lum Award. **Frequency:** annual. **Type:** recognition. **Recipient:** for individuals who have made a distinguished contribution to education for the right-of-way profession ● Mark A. Green Award for Journalism Excellence. **Frequency:** annual. **Type:** recognition. **Recipient:** for articles published in the Right of Way magazine. **Telecommunication Services:** electronic mail, stork@irwaonline.org. **Committees:** Asset Management; Conference Host; Environmental; Ethics; Liaison; Local Public Agency; Nominations and Elections; Pipeline; Professional Development; Property Management; Public Relations; Relocation; Right-of-Way Environment; Right-of-Way Valuation; Survey; Transportation; Utilities; Valuation. **Programs:** Certification. **Formerly:** (1946) Southern California Right of Way Association; (1980) American Right of Way Association. **Publications:** *Right of Way*, bimonthly. Magazine. **Price:** included in membership dues; $30.00 /year for nonmembers. **Circulation:** 7,000. **Advertising:** accepted. Alternate Formats: online ● Catalog. Lists education programs. ● Newsletters, monthly. Alternate Formats: online. **Conventions/Meetings:** annual conference (exhibits) - always June. 2008 June 22-25, Austin, TX; 2009 June 28-July 1, Indianapolis, IN; 2010 June 27-30, Calgary, AB, Canada.

Rural Development

6247 ■ Rural Planning Organizations of America

c/o National Association of Development Organizations
400 N Capitol St. NW, Ste.390
Washington, DC 20001
Ph: (202)624-7806
Fax: (202)624-8813
E-mail: info@nado.org
URL: http://www.ruraltransportation.org
Contact: Jason Boehlert, Contact

Founded: 2006. **Description:** Enhances the professional and organizational development of rural transportation planners by providing information, peer networking and research initiatives. Serves as the national clearinghouse and forum for exchange among its rural transportation stakeholders. Develops and promotes research and information sharing of practices, activities, trends and issues involving rural transportation planning. Provides a forum for the exchange of information among individuals involved in the planning and development of the rural transportation. **Libraries: Type:** reference. **Holdings:** reports. **Subjects:** air quality, economic development, highways, safety, rail, planning, Geospatial Information Infrastructure (GIS), transit. **Affiliated With:** National Association of Development Organizations; National Association of Development Organizations Research Foundation. **Also Known As:** RPO America. **Publications:** *Rural Transportation*. Newsletter. Contains transportation news and notes from around the country. Alternate Formats: online.

Safety

6248 ■ Association of Public-Safety Communications Officials - International (APCO)

351 N Williamson Blvd.
Daytona Beach, FL 32114-1112
Ph: (386)322-2500 (202)833-9600
Free: (888)272-6911
Fax: (386)322-2501
E-mail: apco@apcointl.org
URL: http://www.apco911.org
Contact: Mr. George S. Rice Jr., Exec. Dir.

Founded: 1935. **Members:** 15,000. **Membership Dues:** regular, $64-$112 (annual) ● commercial, $144 (annual). **Staff:** 55. **Budget:** $6,900,000. **State Groups:** 43. **Description:** Employees of municipal, county, state, and federal public safety agencies such as 911 emergency phone line, fire, police, highway maintenance, forestry-conservation, civil defense, special emergency, and local government; individuals who sell public safety communication products. Objectives are to: foster the development and progress of the art of public safety communications; ensure greater cooperation in the correlation of the work and activities of the several town, county, state, and federal agencies; promote cooperation between these agencies and the Federal Communications Commission. Conducts surveys, management and training seminars, and grant-in-aid projects with federal funding agencies. Offers 40-hour and 80-hour training courses for telecommunications, public safety, and emergency medical dispatchers; provides information service. Compiles statistics. **Awards:** Communications Center Director of the Year. **Frequency:** annual. **Type:** recognition. **Recipient:** for a public safety communications center director who has demonstrated exemplary service ● Leadership in Advancing Communications Policy. **Frequency:** annual. **Type:** recognition. **Recipient:** to a FCC or executive branch member showing exemplary leadership in public safety communications policy ● Leadership in Advocacy Award. **Frequency:** annual. **Type:** recognition. **Recipient:** for leadership in public safety communications legislative and regulatory advocacy ● Leadership in Legislative Service. **Frequency:** annual. **Type:** recognition. **Recipient:** for legislative service on public safety communications issues ● Leadership in Regulatory Service. **Frequency:** annual. **Type:** recognition. **Recipient:** to a public servant who has demonstrated exemplary dedication on public safety communications issues ● Line Supervisor of the Year. **Frequency:** annual. **Type:** recognition. **Recipient:** to a public safety communications line supervisor who has demonstrated exemplary service ● Technician of the Year. **Frequency:** annual. **Type:** recognition. **Recipient:** to a public safety communications technician who has demonstrated exemplary service ● Telecommunicator of the Year. **Frequency:** annual. **Type:** recognition. **Recipient:** to a public safety communications telecommunicator who has demonstrated exemplary service. **Telecommunication Services:** electronic bulletin board, member ● electronic mail, membership@apco911.org. **Committees:** Commercial Advisory; Emergency Management; Emergency Medical Service; Emergency Number (911); Fire Service; Historical; Law Enforcement; Operating Procedure; Telecommunication Management. **Affiliated With:** Land Mobile Communications Council. **Formerly:** Associated Police Communications Officers; (1993) Associated Public-Safety Communications Officers. **Publications:** *APCO Membership Directory*, annual ● *Public Safety Communications*, monthly. Magazine. Focuses on public safety communications education, products, and technology. **Price:** $60.00. **Circulation:** 15,000. **Advertising:** accepted ● Manuals. Includes topics on operating procedure and coordinators. ● Also publishes police telecommunications systems text. **Conventions/Meetings:** annual conference, public safety communications products and service (exhibits) - 2008 Aug. 3-7, Kansas City, MO; 2009 Aug. 9-14, Las Vegas, NV; 2010 Aug. 1-5, Houston, TX.

6249 ■ Association of State Dam Safety Officials (ASDSO)

450 Old Vine St.
Lexington, KY 40507-1544
Ph: (859)257-5140
E-mail: info@damsafety.org
URL: http://www.damsafety.org
Contact: Lori C. Spragens, Exec. Dir.

Founded: 1984. **Members:** 2,000. **Membership Dues:** student, $20 (annual) ● senior, $35 (annual) ● associate, affiliate company employee, $45 (annual) ● affiliate company, $330 (annual) ● sustaining, $2,500 (annual) ● individual, $85 (annual). **Staff:** 4. **Budget:** $730,000. **Regional Groups:** 4. **Description:** State, local, and federal officials; Private sector engineers and contractors; other interested individuals; students. Aims to: provide a forum for the exchange of ideas and experiences on dam safety issues; provide information and assistance to state dam safety programs and foster interstate cooperation; provide representation of state interests before Congress and federal agencies; improve efficiency and effectiveness of state dam safety programs; act as an information clearinghouse. Compiles statistics. Provides research and educational programs. Maintains speakers' bureau. **Libraries: Type:** reference. **Holdings:** 2,000; audiovisuals, books, clippings, periodicals. **Subjects:** dam safety engineering. **Awards:** ASDSO Honorary Member. **Frequency:** periodic. **Type:** recognition. **Recipient:** for individuals who have contributed to the improvement of ASDSO and the advancement of dam safety over a lifetime of work ● ASDSO Presidents' Award. **Frequency:** annual. **Type:** recognition. **Recipient:** for contributions to the advancement of dam safety or for specific assistance to the president over his/her term of office ● ASDSO Undergraduate Scholarship. **Frequency:** annual. **Type:** scholarship. **Recipient:** for senior undergraduates in civil engineering, geology, hydrology or related programs who intend to pursue a career in dam safety ● Innovative Rehabilitation Design of the Year Award. **Frequency:** annual. **Type:** recognition. **Recipient:** to the designer of a unique remedial solution that advances the state-of-the-art in the field of dam safety and exemplifies high professional engineering standards ● National Award of Merit. **Frequency:** annual. **Type:** recognition. **Recipient:** for contributions to dam safety on a national level ● Regional Awards of Merit. **Type:** recognition. **Recipient:** to individuals, companies, organizations, municipalities, or other entities for outstanding contributions to dam safety on a regional level. **Computer Services:** Bibliographic search, covering journals, conference proceedings, books, videos, reports, and others ● information services ● mailing lists, of members ● online services, discussion forums, membership directory, state contact information, educational materials, downloads, calendar of events, student pages, links. **Telecommunication Services:** electronic bulletin board, selected information on request and job opportunities in dam safety. **Committees:** Annual Conference Planning; Dam Financing Solutions; Educational Outreach; Legal and Liability; Legislative Activities; National Dam Safety Program; Peer Review; Public Awareness; Resolutions; Scholarship; Technical. **Affiliated With:** Association of State Floodplain Managers; National Emergency Management Association; North American Lake Management Society; Rebuild America; United States Society on Dams. **Publications:** *Annual Conference Proceedings*, annual. Includes compilation of technical papers. **Price:** $30.00 for CD-ROM. ISSN: 1526-9191. Alternate Formats: CD-ROM ● *ASDSO E-News*, monthly. Newsletter. Includes technical reviews and calendar of events. **Price:** $15.00. ISSN: 1528-7351. **Circulation:** 2,000. **Advertising:** accepted. Alternate Formats: online ● *Journal of Dam Safety*, quarterly. Contains technical articles on dam safety issues, lessons learned, and new technology in the field of dam safety and dam engineering. **Price:** free for members ● Membership Directory, annual. **Conventions/Meetings:** annual conference (exhibits) ● State Technical Training Workshops.

6250 ■ Fire Department Safety Officers Association (FDSOA)

30 Main St., Ste.6
PO Box 149
Ashland, MA 01721-0149
Ph: (508)881-3114
Fax: (508)881-1128
E-mail: fdsoa@fdsoa.org
URL: http://www.fdsoa.org
Contact: Mary F. McCormack, Exec. Dir.

Founded: 1989. **Members:** 7,000. **Membership Dues:** individual, $85 (annual) ● department/agency, $385 (annual) ● sustaining, $500 (annual) ● student, $25 (annual). **Staff:** 3. **Budget:** $400,000. **Multinational. Description:** Works to provide educational and networking opportunities for safety officers. Represents officers nationally; provides members with information on safety for personnel and emergency vehicles as well as innovations and technology. **Committees:** Technical. **Publications:** *Health & Safety*, monthly. Newsletter. Accepts advertising from corporate sponsors only. **Price:** $36.00/year, libraries only ● *Safety Gram*, monthly. Bulletin. **Conventions/Meetings:** annual Apparatus Specification and Vehicle Maintenance Symposium - January or February ● annual conference.

6251 ■ International Municipal Signal Association (IMSA)

PO Box 539
Newark, NY 14513-0539
Ph: (315)331-2182
Free: (800)723-4672
Fax: (315)331-8205
E-mail: info@imsasafety.org
URL: http://www.imsasafety.org
Contact: Marilyn Lawrence, Exec. Dir.

Founded: 1896. **Members:** 10,000. **Membership Dues:** active, $60 (annual) ● sustaining, $350 (annual) ● public agency, $50 (annual) ● student, $35 (annual). **Staff:** 9. **Budget:** $1,000,000. **Regional Groups:** 23. **Description:** Professional organization of government officials responsible for municipal signaling, fire alarms, traffic signals, radio communication, street lighting, signs and marking, and other related services. **Libraries: Type:** reference. **Holdings:** audiovisuals, books, periodicals. **Subjects:** traffic signals, street signs and markings, roadway lighting, municipal fire alarm, interior fire alarm, electronic traffic signals, microprocessors in traffic signals, public safety dispatches, preventive maintenance of traffic signals. **Awards:** IMSA Scholarship. **Frequency:** annual. **Type:** scholarship. **Recipient:** for member pursuing a degree in public safety. **Computer Services:** database, information on certification, conferences, mailing labels and membership. **Telecommunication Services:** electronic mail, mel@imsasafety.org. **Committees:** Emergency Medical Services; Exhibits; Fire/Emergency Communications; Standardization; Street Lighting. **Divisions:** Sustaining Membership - Commercial Companies. **Programs:** Certification; Educational. **Affiliated With:** Institute of Transportation Engineers; International Association of Fire Chiefs; National Electrical Manufacturers Association; National Fire Protection Association. **Publications:** *Fire Alarm Manual* ● *IMSA Journal*, bimonthly. **Price:** $50.00/year; $5.00/copy for members; $6.00/copy for non-members ● *Microprocessor Manual for Traffic Signals* ● *Preventive Maintenance of Traffic Signals*. Manual ● *Wire and Cable Specifications*. **Conventions/Meetings:** annual conference, features products pertaining to traffic signals, street systems marking roadways, lighting, fire alarm, cable (exhibits) ● seminar.

6252 ■ National Association of Professional Accident Reconstructionists (NAPARS)

PO Box 65
Brandywine, MD 20613-0065
Ph: (301)843-0048
E-mail: president@napars.org
Contact: John H. Meserve, Pres.

Founded: 1984. **Members:** 1,100. **Membership Dues:** general, $60 (annual). **Multinational. Description:** Upgrades and professionalizes the accident reconstruction field. Conducts research, experimentation and exchange of ideas about technical accident reconstruction. Informs the public of accident investigation and reconstruction issues. Conducts seminars for members and others.

6253 ■ National Association of State Motorcycle Safety Administrators (SMSA)

c/o Ruth Wilson, Business Mgr.
7881 S Wellington St.
Centennial, CO 80122
Ph: (303)797-2318 (775)684-7480
Fax: (303)703-3569
E-mail: smsabusinessmgr@smsa.org
URL: http://www.smsa.org
Contact: Ruth Wilson, Business Mgr.

Founded: 1984. **Membership Dues:** voting, $500-$1,500 (annual) ● professional (non-profit corporation), $1,000 (annual) ● corporate (for-profit company), $1,500 (annual) ● supporting associate (unincorporated organization), $500 (annual) ● supporting, emeritus associate, $35 (annual). **Description:** Represents the interests of state motorcycle safety administrators. Fosters and promotes state-administered motorcycle safety programs. Represents state concerns relating to motorcycle safety by working cooperatively with those individuals and organizations having an interest in motorcycle safety. **Awards:** Chairpersons' Award. **Frequency:** annual. **Type:** recognition. **Recipient:** for outstanding contributions to motorcycle safety. **Publications:** *The Leading Edge*. Newsletter. **Price:** included in membership dues. Alternate Formats: online ● Annual Report.

6254 ■ REACT International (RI)

5210 Auth Rd., No. 403
Suitland, MD 20746-4393
Ph: (301)316-2900 (210)771-7075
Fax: (301)316-2903

E-mail: reacthq1@reactintl.org
URL: http://www.reactintl.org
Contact: Dora Wilbanks, Office Mgr.
Founded: 1962. **Members:** 4,000. **Membership Dues:** regular, $20 (annual) ● family, junior, $18 (annual) ● life, $300. **Staff:** 1. **Budget:** $120,000. **Regional Groups:** 9. **State Groups:** 36. **Local Groups:** 310. **National Groups:** 5. **Multinational. Description:** Independent, tax-exempt public service communications organization financially supported by commercial, governmental, and private and membership funds. Provides volunteer public service and emergency communications through citizens band two-way radio (CB radio has an average range of 15 miles, with 40 channels in the band), General Mobile Radio Service, UHF, amateur, and VHF radio equipment. Volunteer teams are organized and named on a local basis, operating independently of international headquarters. Each team maintains a station or system monitoring the official (by Federal Communications Commission regulation) CB Emergency and Motorists Assistance Channel (9) and GMRS (462.675 MHz) with 24-hour coverage, and agrees to assist in all local emergencies by furnishing instant radio communication in cooperation with proper authorities and agencies. Has cooperative understanding with American Red Cross, ARRL and Salvation Army. Supports charitable activities and community organizations. Consults with radio industry and government on safety communications matters. Maintains speakers' bureau; compiles statistics; operates museum. REACT stands for Radio Emergency Associated Communications Teams. **Awards:** K40/REACT International Achievement Award. **Frequency:** annual. **Type:** recognition. **Recipient:** for individuals, teams and councils. **Committees:** Convention and Site Selection; Emergency Response; Five Year Planning; Junior REACT; Public Relations; Retention; Training and Development; Ways and Means. **Affiliated With:** American Red Cross National Headquarters; Salvation Army. **Formerly:** REACT. **Publications:** *GMRS Basics-Training Manual*, annual. **Price:** $10.00 ● *Money Matters*. **Price:** $10.00 ● *Monitoring CB-Training Manual*. **Price:** $10.00 ● *REACT Team Directory*, annual ● *The REACTer*, bimonthly. Magazine. Contains news from headquarters and reports from various teams/councils around the world. **Price:** $2.50/issue. ISSN: 1055-9167. **Circulation:** 3,500. **Advertising:** accepted. Alternate Formats: online ● *RI Publication Guide and Style Manual*. Alternate Formats: online ● *Search and Rescue Manual*. **Price:** $10.00 ● Brochures ● Also publishes radio safety leaflets. **Conventions/Meetings:** annual competition (exhibits) ● annual conference (exhibits).

Securities

6255 ■ National Association of Bond Lawyers (NABL)
230 W Monroe St., Ste.320
Chicago, IL 60606-4715
Ph: (312)648-9590
Fax: (312)648-9588
E-mail: nabl@nabl.org
URL: http://www.nabl.org
Contact: Ken Luurs, Exec. Dir.
Founded: 1979. **Members:** 3,100. **Membership Dues:** individual, $195-$345 (annual) ● retired, $50 (annual). **Staff:** 8. **Budget:** $1,883,000. **Description:** Lawyers whose law practices deal with obligations issued by or on behalf of a state, territory, or possession of the United States; a political subdivision; the District of Columbia. Includes the rendering of legal opinions in connection with the delivery of such obligations. Aids in educating members and others in the law relating to state and municipal obligations. Provides advice and comments with regard to state and municipal obligations in proceedings before courts and administrative bodies through briefs and memoranda. Maintains ten committees and task forces. **Awards:** Bernard P. Friel Medal. **Frequency:** annual. **Type:** recognition ● Carlson Prize. **Frequency:** annual. **Type:** recognition ● Distinguished Service Award. **Frequency:** annual. **Type:** recognition ● **Type:** recognition. **Telecommunication Services:** electronic mail, kluurs@nabl.org. **Publications:** *Bond Attorneys' Workshop* ● *The Bond Lawyer*, quarterly. Newsletter. **Price:** available to members only ● *Fundamentals of Municipal Bond Law* ● Directory, annual. **Conventions/Meetings:** annual Bond Attorney's Workshop - conference.

Security

6256 ■ Institute for Defense Analyses (IDA)
4850 Mark Center Dr.
Alexandria, VA 22311-1882
Ph: (703)845-2000
Fax: (703)845-2588
E-mail: resumes@ida.org
URL: http://www.ida.org
Contact: Gen. Larry D. Welch USAF, Pres./CEO
Founded: 1956. **Staff:** 850. **Description:** Seeks to provide "an independent and objective source of analyses, evaluations and advice for the United States Government." Originally formed to meet the needs of the Department of Defense, works primarily for the Office of the Secretary of Defense and the Joint Chiefs of Staff; and also conducts research, systems evaluation and policy analysis for other Department of Defense offices as well as other agencies. Issues technical reports, which are announced and distributed by National Technical Information Service, U.S. Department of Commerce. Maintains 80,000 technical reports. **Convention/Meeting:** none. **Libraries: Type:** reference. **Holdings:** 12,000; archival material, books, reports. **Computer Services:** Information services. **Divisions:** Center for Communications Research-Princeton; Computer and Software Engineering; Cost Analysis and Research; Information Technology and Systems; Operational Evaluation; Science and Technology; Strategy, Forces, and Resources; Supercomputing Research Center; System Evaluation. **Publications:** Annual Report, annual.

6257 ■ Research Security Administrators (RSA)
c/o Audrey Holl, Sec.
99 Cleveland Rd., Apt. 24
Pleasant Hill, CA 94523
Ph: (925)935-4064
E-mail: acholl@cs.com
URL: http://www.researchsecurityadministrators.org
Contact: Audrey Holl, Sec.
Founded: 1956. **Description:** Concerned with all defense, technical, scientific, and social matters which have an impact on the security of the United States. Strives to advance technical knowledge and related topics of concern to the contemporary security professionals and their associates. **Awards:** Bob Donovan Scholastic Grant. **Frequency:** semiannual. **Type:** grant. **Recipient:** for students enrolled full time in an industrial security curriculum at an accredited college or university ● Ray Williams Scholastic Grant. **Frequency:** semiannual. **Type:** grant. **Recipient:** for students enrolled full time in an industrial security curriculum at an accredited college or university. **Computer Services:** Mailing lists. **Committees:** Grant. **Publications:** Articles. Alternate Formats: online. **Conventions/Meetings:** semiannual seminar - always in lower and upper California.

Social Justice

6258 ■ Equal Justice Society (EJS)
220 Sansome St., 14th Fl.
San Francisco, CA 94104
Ph: (415)288-8700 (415)288-8710
Fax: (415)288-8787
E-mail: info@equaljusticesociety.org
URL: http://www.equaljusticesociety.org
Contact: Eva Paterson, Pres.
Founded: 2000. **Membership Dues:** activist, $25 (annual) ● ally, $50 (annual) ● organizer, $100 (annual) ● scholar, $250 (annual) ● advocate, $500 (annual) ● visionary, $1,000 (annual). **Description:** Represents the interests of scholars, advocates and concerned individuals advancing legal strategies and public policy for enduring social change. Aims to reshape jurisprudence to ensure that the rights of all are expanded, rather than diminished, by the courts and policy makers. Develops and disseminates new legal theories to help ensure fairness and democracy. Forges connections between students and those who are already practicing law. **Telecommunication Services:** electronic mail, media@equaljusticesociety.net. **Publications:** Newsletter.

Social Security

6259 ■ National Conference of State Social Security Administrators (NCSSSA)
Social Security Div.
2 Northside 75, Ste.300
Atlanta, GA 30318-7778
Ph: (404)603-5608
Fax: (404)350-6309
E-mail: info@ncsssa.org
URL: http://www.ncsssa.org
Contact: Dean Conder, Pres./Co-Chair
Founded: 1951. **Members:** 52. **Membership Dues:** state government, $125 (annual). **Staff:** 50. **Budget:** $21,000,000. **Regional Groups:** 5. **Description:** State social security administrators and their subordinates. Encourages exchange of ideas on the administration of social security programs for public employees. **Committees:** Administrators Handbook; Arrangements; Auditing; Constitution and By-Laws; Government Affairs; Hospitality; Legislative; Program; Research and Information; Resolutions; Time and Place. **Formerly:** National Association of State Social Security Administrators; (1963) Conference of State Social Security Administrators. **Publications:** *History*, periodic ● *Manual of Operating Procedure for State Administrators*, periodic ● *NCSSSA-Today*. Newsletter. Alternate Formats: online ● *Roster of Administrators*, annual ● Directory, periodic ● Proceedings, annual. **Price:** available to members only. **Conventions/Meetings:** annual conference.

6260 ■ National Council of Social Security Management Associations (NCSSMA)
AJC Federal Bldg.
1240 E 9th St., Rm. 793
Cleveland, OH 44199
Ph: (216)522-3204 (202)547-8530
Fax: (603)925-1528
E-mail: dean.dal.ben@ssa.gov
URL: http://www.ncssma.org
Contact: Mr. Rick Warsinskey, Pres.
Founded: 1970. **Members:** 3,500. **Budget:** $150,000. **Regional Groups:** 10. **Description:** Managers and supervisors of the 1350 Social Security field offices and teleservice centers in the U.S. and Puerto Rico. Works to represent the interests of members before Congress, the media, and agency heads and to improve the image and professionalism of federal employees. Conducts research on federal employee pay and retirement benefits. Maintains speakers' bureau. **Libraries: Type:** not open to the public. **Holdings:** archival material. **Awards:** Community Service Award. **Frequency:** annual. **Type:** recognition. **Recipient:** to a member chosen for their involvement in their community. **Telecommunication Services:** electronic mail, ekildal@comcast.net. **Committees:** Automation; Communications; Disability; Grassroots; Management; Service Delivery; Staffing and Training; T16 Operations; T2 Operations. **Publications:** *Frontline*, monthly. Newsletter. **Price:** included in membership dues. **Circulation:** 4,000. Alternate Formats: online ● Papers. Alternate Formats: online ● Reports. **Conventions/Meetings:** competition ● annual conference - always October.

Social Welfare

6261 ■ American Association of Food Stamp Directors (AAFSD)
c/o Kathy Link, Pres.
Utah Dept. of Workforce Services
140 E 300 S, 5th Fl.
Salt Lake City, UT 84111-2305

Ph: (801)526-9230
Fax: (801)526-9239
E-mail: klink@utah.gov
URL: http://foodstamp.aphsa.org
Contact: Kathy Link, Pres.
Founded: 1975. **Members:** 200. **Staff:** 1. **Description:** State and local food stamp directors and others involved in food stamp program administration. Aims to strengthen the administration and management of the food stamp program. Assists state agencies and the National Council of State Human Service Administrators (see separate entry) in analyzing and responding to the laws and regulations affecting the program. Addresses program concerns; promotes professional development. **Affiliated With:** American Public Human Services Association. **Conventions/Meetings:** annual conference.

6262 ■ National WIC Association (NWA)
2001 S St. NW, Ste.580
Washington, DC 20009
Ph: (202)232-5492
Fax: (202)387-5281
E-mail: douglasg@nwica.org
URL: http://www.nwica.org
Contact: Rev. Douglas A. Greenaway, Exec. Dir.
Founded: 1983. **Members:** 666. **Membership Dues:** Business Partner Council, $25,000 (annual) ● founder, $20,000 (annual) ● benefactor, $10,000 (annual) ● patron, $5,000 (annual) ● donor, $2,500 (annual) ● local agency (1-7000 participants), $50 (annual) ● local agency (7001-42000 participants), $100-$300 (annual) ● local agency (over 42000 participants), $400 (annual) ● state association/nonprofit, $250 (annual). **Staff:** 4. **Budget:** $1,700,000. **Description:** Directors of state, territorial, and Native American Special Supplemental Nutrition Program for Women, Infants, and Children (WIC) programs; local WIC agencies; related organizations providing nutrition, breast-feeding, and health care education and services. Promotes availability and effectiveness of WIC programs; seeks to insure the healthy development of economically disadvantaged women and children. Lobbies for expansion of WIC and related programs at the federal and state levels; facilitates cooperation among members and between WIC and related agencies and organizations; provides "leadership in the WIC community". **Committees:** Breastfeeding; Bylaws; Calendar; Evaluation; Funding; Legislative; Membership Development; Nominating; Program Integrity; Technology. **Formerly:** (2004) National Association of WIC Directors. **Publications:** *Monday Morning Report*. Newsletter ● Books. **Conventions/Meetings:** annual conference.

6263 ■ United States Conference of City Human Services Officials (USCCHSO)
c/o United States Conference of Mayors
1620 Eye St. NW
Washington, DC 20006
Ph: (202)293-7330 (202)861-6707
Fax: (202)467-4276
E-mail: info@usmayors.org
URL: http://www.usmayors.org/humanservices
Contact: Crystal D. Swan, Contact
Founded: 1980. **Membership Dues:** regular (under 100000 population), $100 (annual) ● regular (100000-250000 population), $250 (annual) ● regular (250001-500000 population), $500 (annual) ● regular (500001-650000 population), $600 (annual) ● regular (650001-2000000 population), $1,000 (annual) ● regular (2000000 population and over), $1,500 (annual). **Staff:** 2. **Description:** Promotes improved coordination and management of human services in cities throughout the U.S. and provides useful information and assistance to city human services officials. Facilitates exchange of ideas and experiences among city human services officials; provides information on city human services activities to federal officials; promotes cooperation among federal, state, and local governments and between the public and private sectors in human services. Defines human services as assistance provided directly to the people such as social services, child day-care, income assistance, and employment and training and services to specific populations such as children and disabled persons. Offers technical assistance and referral services. **Affiliated With:** United States Conference of Mayors. **Publications:** *Impact of Unfunded Federal Mandates and Cost on U.S. Cities*. Report. Features the preliminary report on cost in 59 cities. ● Brochures ● Also publishes a National Directory of City Human Services Officials. **Conventions/Meetings:** annual meeting - always spring in Washington, DC.

Socialism

6264 ■ Freedom Road Socialist Organization (FRSO)
PO Box 1386
Stuyvesant Sta.
New York, NY 10009
E-mail: doneil@freedomroad.org
URL: http://www.freedomroad.org
Contact: Dennis O'Neil, Contact
Founded: 1985. **Description:** Represents organizations united to defend the rights and living standards of working people and other sections of the population.

6265 ■ Socialist Alternative
PO Box 45343
Seattle, WA 98145
Ph: (206)842-9487 (206)526-7185
E-mail: info@socialistalternative.org
URL: http://www.socialistalternative.org
Founded: 1986. **Multinational. Description:** Advocates for individuals in the workplace, communities and campuses against exploitation and injustice. **Publications:** *Socialism Today*, monthly. Magazine. Provides up-to-date analysis, from a socialist perspective, of events in Britain and internationally.

Sports Law

6266 ■ Sports Lawyers Association (SLA)
12100 Sunset Hills Rd., Ste.130
Reston, VA 20190
Ph: (703)437-4377
Fax: (703)435-4390
E-mail: info@sportslaw.org
URL: http://www.sportslaw.org
Contact: Richard A. Guggolz, Exec. Dir.
Founded: 1976. **Members:** 1,200. **Membership Dues:** law student, $75 (annual) ● law educator, $115 (annual) ● regular, $245 (annual) ● associate, $440 (annual). **Staff:** 2. **Budget:** $300,000. **Description:** Attorneys involved in sports law; students studying sports law. A law society for specialists in sports law; works for legislation regulating attorneys and agents who represent athletes. Offers sponsorship opportunities. Acts as a forum for discussion; provides educational materials. **Awards:** Award of Excellence. **Frequency:** annual. **Type:** recognition. **Recipient:** to an attorney noted for demonstrating distinguished characteristics and qualities within the legal profession. **Computer Services:** database. **Publications:** *The Sports Lawyer*, monthly. Newsletter. Includes issues affecting the practice of sports law. **Price:** included in membership dues. Alternate Formats: online ● *The Sports Lawyers Journal*, annual. Includes articles on the need for breadth and depth in today's sports law field. **Price:** included in membership dues. **Conventions/Meetings:** annual conference, three-day program for educational and networking opportunities - 2009 May 14-16, Chicago, IL; 2010 May 20-22, Phoenix, AZ.

Standards

6267 ■ American National Standards Institute (ANSI)
1819 L St. NW, 6th Fl.
Washington, DC 20036
Ph: (202)293-8020 (212)642-4900
Fax: (202)293-9287
E-mail: info@ansi.org
URL: http://www.ansi.org
Contact: Mr. S. Joe Bhatia, Pres./CEO
Founded: 1918. **Members:** 1,000. **Membership Dues:** company, government, educational, individual, $495 (annual) ● organizational, $2,995 (annual). **Staff:** 75. **Budget:** $25,000,000. **Description:** Industrial firms, trade associations, technical societies, labor organizations, consumer organizations, and government agencies. Serves as clearinghouse for nationally coordinated voluntary standards for fields ranging from information technology to building construction. Gives status as American National Standards to standards developed by agreement from all groups concerned, in such areas as: definitions, terminology, symbols, and abbreviations; materials, performance characteristics, procedure, and methods of rating; methods of testing and analysis; size, weight, volume, and rating; practice, safety, health, and building construction. Provides information on foreign standards and represents United States interests in international standardization work. **Awards:** ANSI Awards. **Frequency:** annual. **Type:** recognition. **Telecommunication Services:** electronic mail, membership@ansi.org. **Committees:** Certification. **Councils:** Board of Standards Review; Company Member; Consumer Interest; Executive Standards; Organizational Member. **Formerly:** (1918) American Engineering Standards Committee; (1928) American Standards Association; (1966) United States of America Standards Institute. **Publications:** *ANSI Reporter*, quarterly. Magazine. Covers issues that affect the voluntary standards system, including government standards-related proposals and actions. Includes calendar of events. **Price:** $100.00 for nonmembers; included in membership dues. ISSN: 0038-9676. **Circulation:** 2,000. **Advertising:** accepted. Alternate Formats: online ● *Catalog of American National Standards*, annual. Lists 11,500 current ANSI-approved standards by subject and by designation. **Price:** included in membership dues; $20.00 /year for nonmembers ● *Standards Action*, weekly. Newsletter. Lists all ISO, IEC, EN and ANSI standards in progress or newly published. Enables effective participation in the standards development process. **Price:** included in membership dues. ISSN: 0038-9633. Alternate Formats: online. **Conventions/Meetings:** annual meeting (exhibits) - September or October in Washington, DC.

6268 ■ International Association for the Properties of Water and Steam (IAPWS)
c/o Dr. R. Barry Dooley, Exec. Sec.
EPRI
1300 W W.T. Harris Blvd.
Charlotte, NC 28262
E-mail: bdooley@structint.com
URL: http://www.iapws.org
Contact: Dr. R. Barry Dooley, Exec. Sec.
Founded: 1971. **Members:** 11. **Description:** Countries represented by individuals united to discuss and provide representations of thermodynamic and some thermophysical properties of steam, water substance, and aqueous solutions. These representations are used throughout the world in the specification and design of power equipment. Develops new and improved representations. Conducts research. **Awards:** Gibbs Award. **Frequency:** quadrennial. **Type:** recognition. **Recipient:** to a senior researcher who has made outstanding technical achievements in areas of interest to IAPWS ● Helmholtz Award. **Frequency:** annual. **Type:** recognition. **Recipient:** for a junior researcher working in an area of interest to IAPWS. **Working Groups:** Industrial Requirements and Solutions; Physical Chemistry of Aqueous Solutions; Power Cycle Chemistry; Thermophysical Properties of Water and Steam. **Formerly:** (1990) International Association for the Properties of Steam. **Publications:** *Releases and Guidelines*, periodic ● Reports. **Conventions/Meetings:** International Conference on Properties of Steam - every 4-5 years.

6269 ■ National Conference on Weights and Measures (NCWM)
15245 Shady Grove Rd., Ste.130
Rockville, MD 20850-6240

Ph: (240)632-9454
Fax: (301)990-9771
E-mail: ncwm@mgmtsol.com
URL: http://www.ncwm.net
Contact: Beth W. Palys CAE, Exec. Dir.
Founded: 1905. **Members:** 3,000. **Membership Dues:** government, $75 (annual) ● industry, $90 (annual). **Staff:** 5. **Description:** State and local weights and measures officials; representatives of manufacturers of weighing and measuring devices, trade associations, industry (users of devices), and representatives of federal government. Promotes uniformity in weights and measures laws, regulations, specifications and tolerances. Sponsored by National Institute of Standards and Technology. **Committees:** Education, Administration and Consumer Affairs; Laws and Regulations; Professional Development; Specifications and Tolerances. **Publications:** *NIST Handbook 44, Specifications, Tolerances, and Other Technical Requirements for Weighing and Measuring Devices*, annual ● *NIST Handbook 130, Uniform Laws and Regulations*, annual ● *Printed Reports of National Conference on Weights and Measures*, annual. Includes conference proceedings. **Conventions/Meetings:** annual conference.

State Government

6270 ■ Council on Governmental Ethics Laws (COGEL)

PO Box 393
196 Alps Rd., Ste.2
Athens, GA 30606
Ph: (706)548-7758
Fax: (706)548-7079
E-mail: director@cogel.org
URL: http://www.cogel.org
Contact: Diane Gill, Exec. Dir.
Founded: 1978. **Members:** 212. **Membership Dues:** government agency, private organization, $445 (annual) ● individual, $150 (annual). **Staff:** 2. **Budget:** $100,000. **Description:** Governmental agencies and individuals with responsibilities in governmental ethics, elections, campaign finance, and lobby law regulation, including boards of ethics, electoral officers, electoral commissions, and state ethics commissions. Compiles and disseminates information regarding state elections, campaign finance, ethics, and lobbying registration and regulations. Promotes exchange of information among members. **Awards:** Council on Governmental Ethics Laws Award. **Frequency:** annual. **Type:** recognition. **Publications:** *COGEL Guardian*, quarterly. Newsletter. Includes a geographical arrangement summarizing news and cases in state and federal courts in the U.S. and Canada. **Price:** included in membership dues; $60.00 /year for nonmembers. ISSN: 1059-6224. **Conventions/Meetings:** annual conference.

6271 ■ Council on Licensure, Enforcement and Regulation (CLEAR)

403 Marquis Ave., Ste.200
Lexington, KY 40502
Ph: (859)269-1289
Fax: (859)231-1943
E-mail: rose.mccool@dora.state.co.us
URL: http://www.clearhq.org
Contact: Rosemary McCool, Pres.-Elect
Founded: 1980. **Members:** 400. **Membership Dues:** regular (individual licensing board), $230 ● regular (licensing agency based on the number of boards or professions), $165 ● regular (other government agency), associate (employee of government agency), $195 ● associate (national/state professional association), $455 ● agency (responsible for 10-19 regulated professions), $1,560 (annual) ● agency (responsible for 20 or more regulated professions), $2,600 (annual) ● regular association of agency, $455 (annual) ● associate - other organization, $780 (annual). **Staff:** 6. **Budget:** $730,000. **Languages:** Chinese, English, French, Japanese, Spanish. **Multinational. Description:** State and provincial officials and administrators involved with occupational licensing and regulation issues. Aims to improve the quality and understanding of professional and occupational regulation to enhance public protection. Conducts National Certified Investigator/Inspector Training Program and board member training. **Awards:** Investigator of the Year Award. **Frequency:** annual. **Type:** recognition. **Recipient:** for an excellent investigator ● Member Achievement Award. **Frequency:** annual. **Type:** recognition. **Recipient:** for an outstanding member ● Program Award. **Frequency:** annual. **Type:** recognition. **Recipient:** for a program or agency concerned with occupational and professional regulation that enhances regulatory process ● Recognition Award. **Frequency:** annual. **Type:** recognition. **Recipient:** for a nonmember who has made a broader public understanding on regulatory issues ● Service Award. **Frequency:** annual. **Type:** recognition. **Recipient:** for an individual who has made outstanding contribution and commitment to the organization. **Computer Services:** Mailing lists, free for members and nonmembers. **Affiliated With:** Council of State Governments. **Formerly:** (1991) National Clearinghouse on Licensure, Enforcement, and Regulation. **Publications:** *CLEAR Exam Review*, semiannual. Journal. **Price:** $30.00/year. **Advertising:** accepted ● *CLEAR News*, quarterly. Newsletter. Contains up-to-date news items. **Advertising:** accepted. Alternate Formats: online ● *Resource Briefs*, annual. Papers. Features current issues in occupational and professional regulations. **Price:** $10.00 plus shipping and handling. **Conventions/Meetings:** annual conference (exhibits) - always fall ● annual regional meeting - always winter.

6272 ■ Council of State Community Development Agencies (COSCDA)

1825 K St., Ste.515
Washington, DC 20006-1226
Ph: (202)293-5820 (919)733-2853
Fax: (202)293-2820
E-mail: dtaylor@coscda.org
URL: http://www.coscda.org
Contact: Dianne E. Taylor, Exec. Dir.
Founded: 1974. **Members:** 48. **Membership Dues:** associate, $1,000 (annual) ● corporate, $2,500 (annual). **Staff:** 6. **Budget:** $520,000. **State Groups:** 50. **Description:** Directors and staff of state community development agencies. Established by department of community affairs directors to create a forum for discussion of and action on national issues and to exchange information on their agencies' programs. Aims to promote the common interests and goals of the states, with major emphasis in the area of comprehensive community development. This includes planning, financial assistance, and direct action programs encompassing physical, human, and economic development. Assists local governments in strengthening their capabilities through improved intergovernmental relations and more effective utilization of local, state, and federal resources. Conducts workshops; disseminates information; offers technical assistance. **Awards:** COSCDA Sterling Achievement Awards. **Frequency:** annual. **Type:** recognition. **Recipient:** for state programs that have demonstrated, during a sustained period, positive results in improving the lives of lower income persons ● James Reeves Member Contribution Award. **Frequency:** annual. **Type:** recognition. **Recipient:** to individual member of COSCDA who has made the most significant and sustained contribution to the work and mission of the association during the last five years ● President's Award for Innovation. **Frequency:** annual. **Type:** recognition. **Recipient:** for innovative activities, policies or programs that have been implemented at the state level. **Committees:** Ad Hoc COSCDA Fundraising; Awards Selection; COSCDA Employee Policy and Procedures; Economic Development; Housing; Initiative and Innovations; Programs. **Subcommittees:** Community Development; Homeliness. **Formerly:** (1990) Council of State Community Affairs Agencies. **Publications:** *The National Line*, biweekly. Newsletter. Alternate Formats: online ● *Put Up or Give Way: States, Economic Competitiveness and Poverty* ● *The State Line*, quarterly. Newsletter ● Newsletter, bimonthly. Contains state legislative updates. **Price:** free for members ● Monographs ● Reports ● Annual Report, annual. Alternate Formats: online ● Brochure. Alternate Formats: online ● Survey. **Conventions/Meetings:** annual conference.

6273 ■ Council of State Governments (CSG)

2760 Res. Park Dr.
PO Box 11910
Lexington, KY 40511-8482
Ph: (859)244-8000 (859)244-8246
Free: (800)800-1910
Fax: (859)244-8001
E-mail: csg@csg.org
URL: http://www.csg.org
Contact: Daniel M. Sprague, Exec. Dir./CEO
Founded: 1933. **Members:** 1,700. **Staff:** 155. **Budget:** $12,000,000. **Regional Groups:** 4. **Description:** Serves all elected and appointed officials in all three branches of government in every state and territory. **Libraries: Type:** not open to the public. **Holdings:** 20,000; articles, books, periodicals. **Subjects:** state government. **Awards:** Corporate Associate of the Year. **Frequency:** annual. **Type:** recognition ● Innovation Awards. **Frequency:** annual. **Type:** recognition ● Toll Fellows Leadership Training. **Frequency:** annual. **Type:** recognition. **Computer Services:** database, library, states information center, and resource. **Committees:** Annual Meeting; CSG Associates Advisory; Intergovernmental Affairs; International; Strategic Planning; Suggested State Legislation. **Task Forces:** Agriculture and Rural Policy; Environmental; Health Capacity; Public Safety and Justice. **Affiliated With:** National Association of Governmental Labor Officials; National Association of Secretaries of State; National Association of State Facilities Administrators; National Association of State Personnel Executives; National Association of State Telecommunications Directors; National Association of State Treasurers; National Lieutenant Governors Association; Southern Governors' Association. **Supersedes:** American Legislators Association. **Publications:** *Book of the States*, annual. **Price:** $99.00 paperback; $125.00 hardcover; $63.20 paperback - state government officials and staff; $79.20 hardback - state government officials and staff. **Circulation:** 10,000. **Advertising:** accepted ● *Leaders Lens*, quarterly. Newsletter ● *State Leadership Directory I*, annual. Lists state members of all state legislatures. **Price:** $65.00 for state officials. Alternate Formats: CD-ROM ● *State Leadership Directory II*, annual. Lists state legislative committee leaders. **Price:** $45.00 for state officials ● *State Leadership Directory III*, annual. Lists of state administrative officials classified by function. **Price:** $65.00 for state officials ● *State News*, 10/year. Magazine. Covers topics of concern to state government officials. **Price:** $55.00/year; $90.00 for 2 years; $145.00 for 3 years. ISSN: 0039-0119. **Circulation:** 15,000. **Advertising:** accepted. Alternate Formats: online ● Newsletters. Alternate Formats: online. **Conventions/Meetings:** annual Midwestern Legislative - conference and meeting - 2008 July 13-16, Rapid City, SD; 2009 Aug. 9-12, Overland Park, KS ● annual Southern Legislative - conference and meeting - 2008 Aug. 16-20, Oklahoma City, OK; 2009 Aug. 15-19, Winston-Salem, NC ● annual Spring Committee and Task Force Meetings (exhibits) ● annual State Trends and Leadership Forum - meeting - 2008 Dec. 4-7, Omaha, NE.

6274 ■ Democratic Governors Association (DGA)

1401 K St. NW, Ste.200
Washington, DC 20005
Ph: (202)772-5600
Fax: (202)772-5602
E-mail: communications@democraticgovernors.org
URL: http://www.democraticgovernors.org
Contact: Nathan Daschlee, Exec. Dir.
Founded: 1983. **Members:** 28. **Staff:** 6. **Description:** Governors of the states and territories of the U.S. who are members of the Democratic Party. **Libraries: Type:** open to the public. **Formerly:** (1983) Democratic Governors Conference. **Publications:** *The Advance*. Magazine. Contains collection of videos, blog spots, news clips and editorials ranging from health care to energy. Alternate Formats: online

● *Update*, quarterly. Newsletter. **Conventions/Meetings:** semiannual meeting.

6275 ■ Fiscal Studies Program
Rockefeller Inst. of Govt.
411 State St.
Albany, NY 12203-1003
Ph: (518)443-5285
Fax: (518)443-5274
E-mail: fiscal@rockinst.org
Contact: Robert B. Ward, Deputy Dir.
Founded: 1990. **Nonmembership. Description:** Works to provide high-quality, practical and independent research on state and local programs and finances. Conducts research on trends affecting states; serves as a national information resource for public officials, the media and others; and compiles statistics. **Libraries: Type:** reference. **Holdings:** books, periodicals. **Computer Services:** Electronic publishing ● mailing lists ● online services. **Formerly:** (2001) Center for the Study of States. **Publications:** *State Fiscal Briefs*, quarterly. Bulletin ● *State Revenue Report*, quarterly. Newsletter. **Conventions/Meetings:** annual New York State Network for Economic Research - Economic Outlook Conference, includes presentation and discussion of papers - usually fall in Albany, NY.

6276 ■ National Association of Attorneys General (NAAG)
2030 M St. NW, 8th Fl.
Washington, DC 20036-3306
Ph: (202)326-6000 (202)326-6027
Fax: (202)331-1427
E-mail: pwarren@naag.org
URL: http://www.naag.org
Contact: Lynne Ross, Exec. Dir.
Founded: 1907. **Members:** 56. **Staff:** 33. **Budget:** $4,000,000. **Description:** Attorneys general of the 50 states, District of Columbia, American Samoa, Guam, Puerto Rico, Virgin Islands, and Northern Mariana Islands. Sponsors legal education seminars on consumer protection, environmental protection, antitrust, corrections, insurance, charitable trusts and solicitations, and Supreme Court practice. **Awards:** Wyman Award. **Frequency:** annual. **Type:** recognition. **Recipient:** to an attorney general who has done the most to advance the objectives of the association. **Committees:** Antitrust; Civil Rights; Consumer Protection; Criminal Law; Environment and Energy; Health Care Fraud; Supreme Court; Tobacco; Violence Against Women. **Task Forces:** Health Care. **Working Groups:** Federalism; Gaming. **Publications:** *A-G Bulletin*, monthly. Newsletter. Covers litigation that affects the powers and duties of state attorneys general, federal legislation, and association activities. **Price:** $75.00/year. **Circulation:** 300 ● *Antitrust Report*, 10/year. Newsletter. Contains reports on antitrust and commerce developments by state attorneys general. Includes subject index. **Price:** $145.00/year ● *Consumer Protection Report/ Telemarketing Fraud*, monthly. Newsletter. Contains reports on consumer protection enforcement activities by the state attorneys general. **Price:** $145.00/ year ● *Medicaid Fraud Report*, 10/year. Newsletter. Reports on state prosecution of Medicaid provider fraud; provides summaries of legal cases involving hospitals, nursing homes, and physicians. **Price:** $150.00/year ● *NAAG Handbook*, biennial. Lists state attorney generals, biographical information, photographs, key staff members, etc. **Price:** $35.00 ● *National Environmental Enforcement Journal*, 11/ year. Covers environmental enforcement issues on the federal, state, and local levels; covers civil proceedings, criminal prosecutions, and others. **Price:** $195.00/year; $95.00 /year for libraries, government and nonprofit organizations. **Circulation:** 850 ● *State Constitutional Law Bulletin*, 10/year. Summarizes major state constitutional law opinions and decisions. **Price:** $50.00/year. **Conventions/ Meetings:** periodic meeting - usually March, June, and December.

6277 ■ National Association of Secretaries of State (NASS)
c/o Hall of States
444 N Capitol St. NW, Ste.401
Washington, DC 20001-1557
Ph: (202)624-3525 (202)624-3528
Fax: (202)624-3527
E-mail: info@nass.org
URL: http://www.nass.org
Contact: Leslie Reynolds, Exec. Dir.
Founded: 1904. **Members:** 84. **Staff:** 3. **Budget:** $90,000. **Regional Groups:** 4. **Description:** Secretaries of state, lieutenant governors, and state officials acting as secretaries of state of the states and territories of the U.S. Aims to exchange suggestions for improvement among members, and information concerning the duties, responsibilities, and methods of operation of the secretary of state. Compiles statistics. **Libraries: Type:** reference. **Holdings:** archival material, periodicals. **Awards:** Exceptional Civic Journalism Award. **Frequency:** annual. **Type:** recognition. **Recipient:** for a journalist who has produced exemplary news coverage in educating the public about voting, helping to increase voter participation or clarifying some aspect of the voting process ● Margaret Chase Smith American Democracy Award. **Frequency:** annual. **Type:** recognition. **Recipient:** for public leaders ● NASS Freedom Award. **Frequency:** annual. **Type:** recognition. **Recipient:** for individuals who have made significant creative, procedural, and/or technological contributions to the free election process in the United States ● NASS Medallion Award. **Frequency:** annual. **Type:** medal. **Recipient:** for individuals, groups, or organizations with an established record of promoting the goals of NASS. **Committees:** Awards and Publications; Business Services; e-Government; Elections; International Relations; Nominations and Credentials; Securities; Voter Participation. **Programs:** NASS Medallion Awards. **Projects:** New Millennium. **Sections:** Administrative Codes and Registers. **Subcommittees:** Corporate Affiliate Advisory; Presidential Primaries. **Task Forces:** Bogus Filing. **Formerly:** (1921) Association of American Secretaries of State. **Publications:** *NASS New Millennium Best Practices*. Report. Alternate Formats: online ● *NASS News*, bimonthly. Newsletter. **Circulation:** 500 ● *The Office and Duties of the Secretary of State*, quadrennial ● Surveys. Alternate Formats: online. **Conventions/Meetings:** annual conference (exhibits) - every winter ● annual conference - every summer. 2008 July 24-28, Grand Rapids, MI.

6278 ■ National Association of State Chief Administrators (NASCA)
c/o Council of State Governments
PO Box 11910
Lexington, KY 40578-1910
Ph: (859)244-8181
Fax: (859)244-8001
E-mail: nasca@csg.org
URL: http://www.nasca.org
Contact: Ms. Marcia Stone, Exec. Dir.
Founded: 1976. **Members:** 40. **Membership Dues:** state, $2,000 (annual) ● corporate, $3,000 (annual). **Staff:** 2. **Budget:** $172,000. **Description:** Brings together chief officials from administration and general services to discuss and implement public policy and to improve government efficiency and effectiveness. Advances professional development and best management solutions for state government. Provides members with the opportunity to increase their knowledge of state government administration through education, networking and, information exchange on state government trends, innovations, standards and best practices. **Awards:** Outstanding Program Award. **Frequency:** annual. **Type:** recognition. **Recipient:** for state agencies, organizations, individuals, or state agency and private partnerships that have demonstrated outstanding leadership skills in innovation, originality, effectiveness, and applicability. **Computer Services:** database. **Formerly:** (1988) National Conference of State General Service Officers; (2000) National Association of State Directors of Administration and General Service Officers. **Conventions/Meetings:** annual conference - usually August.

6279 ■ National Association for State Community Services Programs (NASCSP)
400 N Capitol St. NW, Ste.395
Washington, DC 20001
Ph: (202)624-5866
Fax: (202)624-8472
E-mail: nascsp@sso.org
URL: http://www.nascsp.org
Contact: Timothy R. Warfield, Exec. Dir.
Founded: 1968. **Members:** 103. **Staff:** 8. **Budget:** $1,200,000. **Description:** Coalition of state administrators of Community Services Block Grant and Department of Energy's Low-Income Weatherization Assistance Program. Seeks to enhance state involvement in the formation, implementation, and coordination of antipoverty programs; assists states in identifying and overcoming social and economic constraints confronting their low-income citizens; protects and promotes the interests of poverty-level citizens by working for improvements in antipoverty programs. Gathers and disseminates ideas, information, and opinions to state community services program officers, state weatherization program directors, state and federal agencies, and interested national groups concerning program coordination, new proposals in antipoverty policy, CSBG, and weatherization legislation. Analyzes antipoverty benefits of public and private institutions and federal programs. **Libraries: Type:** reference. **Subjects:** weatherization, annual statistical report on the Community Services Block Grant. **Committees:** CSBG; Legislative; Weatherization. **Formerly:** National Association for State Economic Opportunity Office Directors. **Publications:** *Community Services Block Grant Statistics Report*, annual ● Newsletter, monthly. **Conventions/Meetings:** annual Legislative Conference ● annual seminar, training ● annual Training Conference.

6280 ■ National Association of State Personnel Executives (NASPE)
c/o Council of State Governments
PO Box 11910
Lexington, KY 40578-1910
Ph: (859)244-8182
Fax: (859)244-8001
E-mail: lscott@csg.org
URL: http://www.naspe.net
Contact: Jim Farrell, Pres.
Founded: 1977. **Members:** 125. **Membership Dues:** state, $2,500 (annual) ● corporate, $3,500 (annual). **Staff:** 3. **Budget:** $220,000. **Description:** Personnel directors for state and territorial governments. Develops equitable standards for personnel management and administration in government. **Libraries: Type:** reference. **Holdings:** archival material. **Awards:** Eugene H. Rooney, Jr. Awards. **Frequency:** annual. **Type:** recognition. **Recipient:** for innovative state human resource management programs and for leadership in state human resource management. **Computer Services:** database ● mailing lists, listserv for members. **Committees:** Executive. **Task Forces:** Workforce of the Future. **Publications:** *State Personnel Office: Roles and Functions, 4th Edition*, portions updated annually. Provides data on a variety of HRM functions in state government. **Price:** $75. 00. ISSN: C008-9600. Alternate Formats: CD-ROM ● *State Personnel Representatives Directory* ● *State Personnel View Newsletter*, quarterly. **Circulation:** 100. **Conventions/Meetings:** annual conference (exhibits).

6281 ■ National Black Caucus of State Legislators (NBCSL)
444 N Capitol St. NW, Ste.622
Washington, DC 20001
Ph: (202)624-5457
Fax: (202)508-3826
URL: http://www.dcwatch.com/issues/pbc010515b.htm
Contact: Rep. James L. Thomas, Pres.
Founded: 1977. **Members:** 600. **Membership Dues:** legislator, $100 (annual). **Staff:** 12. **Budget:** $800,000. **Regional Groups:** 12. **State Groups:** 44. **Description:** Black state legislators. Organized to provide more political networking to black legislators from the federal and state levels. Goals are to: provide a network through which state legislators can exchange information and ideas on state and national legislation; provide a unified front or platform; serve as a focal point for involvement of black legislators in

the "new federalism" and state based programs and funding. Activities include arranging meetings between all governmental groups and elected officials and analyzing and forming a position on the "new federalism" and block grants. Conducts seminars. Maintains speakers' bureau and biographical archives; compiles statistics. **Libraries: Type:** not open to the public. **Awards:** Legislator of the Year. **Frequency:** annual. **Type:** recognition. **Recipient:** for legislative and issue-based activities ● Nation Builders Award. **Frequency:** annual. **Type:** recognition. **Committees:** Agriculture; Business and Finance; Economic Development; Education; Elementary and Secondary Education; Energy; Environment; Ethics; Health; Housing; Human Services; Insurance; International Affairs; Labor and Management; Law and Justice; Military and Veterans' Affairs; Post-Secondary Education; Sports and Entertainment; Telecommunications; Transportation; Youth. **Roundtables:** Corporate; Labor. **Task Forces:** African American Males; Black Consumer and Corporate Responsibility; Election Reform; Healthcare Reform; Welfare Reform. **Publications:** *Directory of Black State Legislators*, biennial. **Price:** $25.00 each. **Circulation:** 3,000. Alternate Formats: diskette ● *The Legislator*, quarterly. Newsletter. Alternate Formats: online ● *NBCSL Resolution Policy Procedures Manual*. Alternate Formats: online. **Conventions/Meetings:** annual Legislative Conference (exhibits).

6282 ■ National Conference of Commissioners on Uniform State Laws (NCCUSL)
211 E Ontario St., Ste.1300
Chicago, IL 60611-3261
Ph: (312)915-0195 (312)915-0680
Fax: (312)915-0187
E-mail: nccusl@nccusl.org
URL: http://www.nccusl.org
Contact: Howard J. Swibel, Pres.

Founded: 1892. **Members:** 361. **Staff:** 9. **Description:** Judges, law school deans and professors, and practicing attorneys appointed by state governors. Promotes uniformity in state law on subjects where uniformity is deemed desirable and practicable. Also promotes uniformity of judicial decisions throughout the U.S. Drafts uniform and model acts on subjects suitable for interstate compact and subjects in which uniformity will make more effective the exercise of state powers and promote interstate cooperation. **Computer Services:** Mailing lists, of committee. **Telecommunication Services:** electronic mail, john.sebert@nccusl.org. **Committees:** Agricultural Cooperatives; American Indian Tribes and Nations; Anatomical Gift Act; Annual Meeting; Apportionment of Tort Responsibility Act; Arbitration; Assignment of Rents; Bank Deposits. **Also Known As:** Uniform Law Commissioners. **Publications:** *Handbook and Proceedings*, annual ● *NCCUSL Drafting Manual*. Alternate Formats: online ● *ULC Bulletin*. Newsletter. Alternate Formats: online ● Pamphlets. Discusses uniform laws and model acts adopted by the conference. ● Book ● Annual Report. Alternate Formats: online ● Reports. Alternate Formats: online ● Articles. **Conventions/Meetings:** annual meeting - 2008 July 18-25, Big Sky, MT; 2009 July 9-16, Santa Fe, MN.

6283 ■ National Conference of State Legislatures (NCSL)
7700 E First Pl.
Denver, CO 80230-7143
Ph: (303)364-7700
Fax: (303)364-7800
E-mail: ncslnet-admin@ncsl.org
URL: http://www.ncsl.org
Contact: William T. Pound, Exec. Dir.

Founded: 1975. **Staff:** 145. **Budget:** $11,500,000. **Description:** National organization of state legislators and legislative staff. Aims are: to improve the quality and effectiveness of state legislatures; to ensure states a strong, cohesive voice in the federal decision-making process; to foster interstate communication and cooperation. Compiles research data. Provides training and development, and service on current issues and concerns. Maintains Office of State-Federal Relations in Washington, DC, to monitor federal legislation and 22 committees. **Libraries: Type:** reference. **Holdings:** 4,500; archival material. **Computer Services:** database, LEGISNET (state legislative research). **Telecommunication Services:** electronic mail, deana.blackwood@ncsl.org. **Projects:** Education; Energy, Science, and Natural Resources; Fiscal Affairs; Human Services; Legislative Information Services; Legislative Management; State Issues and Policy Analysis. **Affiliated With:** Council of State Governments. **Formed by Merger of:** National Legislative Conference; National Conference of State Legislative Leaders; National Society of State Legislators. **Publications:** *Federal Update*, bimonthly ● *Fiscal Letter*, bimonthly ● *LegisBrief*, 48/year ● *Mandate Monitor*, 10-12/year ● *State Legislatures*, monthly. Magazine. **Price:** $49.00. **Advertising:** accepted ● Books ● Films ● Handbooks ● Reports ● Also publishes legislator guides and studies. **Conventions/Meetings:** annual Fall Forum - seminar ● annual meeting (exhibits) - 2008 July 20-27, New Orleans, LA.

6284 ■ National Governors Association (NGA)
Hall of States
444 N Capitol St., Ste.267
Washington, DC 20001-1512
Ph: (202)624-5300
Fax: (202)624-5313
E-mail: webmaster@nga.org
URL: http://www.nga.org
Contact: Raymond C. Scheppach, Exec. Dir.

Founded: 1908. **Members:** 55. **Staff:** 94. **Budget:** $26,211,600. **Description:** Governors of the 50 states, Guam, American Samoa, the Virgin Islands, the Northern Mariana Islands, and Puerto Rico. Serves as vehicle through which governors influence the development and implementation of national policy and apply creative leadership to state problems. Keeps the federal establishment informed of the needs and perceptions of states. Through its Center for Best Practices, it provides a vehicle for sharing information on innovative programs among the states and providing technical assistance to governors on a wide range of issues. **Libraries: Type:** reference. **Holdings:** archival material, articles. **Committees:** Economic Development and Commerce; Education, Early Childhood, Workforce; Executive; Health and Human Services; Natural Resources. **Affiliated With:** National Association of State Budget Officers. **Formerly:** Governors' Conference; (1977) National Governors' Conference. **Publications:** Monographs. **Conventions/Meetings:** semiannual conference - always winter and summer, Washington, DC.

6285 ■ National Lieutenant Governors Association (NLGA)
71 Cavalier Blvd., Ste.124
Florence, KY 41042-5168
Ph: (859)283-1400
Fax: (859)244-8001
E-mail: jhurst@csg.org
URL: http://www.nlga.us
Contact: Ms. Julia Hurst, Exec. Dir.

Founded: 1962. **Members:** 55. **Membership Dues:** conference associates partner, $5,000 (annual). **Staff:** 1. **Budget:** $200,000. **Regional Groups:** 4. **State Groups:** 55. **Description:** Lieutenant governors or their equivalents in states and territories. Develops policy work and research on non-partisan basis for officeholders first in line of gubernatorial succession. Compiles statistics and maintains information on the powers and duties of the office of lieutenant governors. Holds three meetings per year for members. Operates a private sector program for membership. Passes policy resolutions and statements. **Libraries: Type:** reference. **Holdings:** reports. **Affiliated With:** Council of State Governments. **Formerly:** (2002) National Conference of Lieutenant Governors. **Publications:** *NLGA Focus*, quarterly. Newsletter ● Newsletter, monthly. **Price:** $1.00. Alternate Formats: online. **Conventions/Meetings:** annual meeting (exhibits) - 2008 July 23-26, Buffalo, NY ● annual State Federal - meeting - every winter.

6286 ■ Republican Governors Association (RGA)
1747 Pennsylvania Ave. NW, Ste.250
Washington, DC 20006
Ph: (202)662-4140
Fax: (202)662-4924
E-mail: info@rga.org
URL: http://www.rga.org
Contact: Mr. Nick Ayers, Exec. Dir.

Founded: 1963. **Members:** 30. **Staff:** 16. **Budget:** $20,000,000. **Description:** Republican governors. Provides liaison with governors' offices; supports policy formulation. Works directly with Republican candidates for governorships. **Publications:** Newsletter. Contains latest events of the organization. Alternate Formats: online. **Conventions/Meetings:** annual conference - always November.

6287 ■ Southern Governors' Association (SGA)
444 N Capitol St. NW, Ste.200
Hall of the States
Washington, DC 20001
Ph: (202)624-5897
Fax: (202)624-7797
E-mail: sga@sso.org
URL: http://www.southerngovernors.org
Contact: Ms. Diane Duff, Exec. Dir.

Founded: 1934. **Members:** 17. **Staff:** 7. **Description:** Seeks to promote and coordinate regionally collaborative initiatives, to track and analyze federal legislation and regulations of interest to southern states, to advance and advocate before Congress and the executive branch the southern governors' policy agenda as expressed through approved policy resolutions, and to provide a forum for southern governors and their staffs to share ideas and experiences. The association's membership is composed of the governors of Alabama, Arkansas, Georgia, Kentucky, Louisiana, Maryland, Mississippi, Missouri, North Carolina, Oklahoma, Puerto Rico, South Carolina, Tennessee, Texas, the U.S. Virgin Islands, Virginia and West Virginia. Is a subsidiary organization of The Council of State Governments. **Formerly:** (1978) Southern Governors' Conference. **Publications:** *Best Practices in Southern Tourism and Destination Management*. Book ● *New Traditions: Options for Rural High School Excellence*. Report. Alternate Formats: online ● *Seeds for the New Economy: Research, Development and Technology*. Report. Alternate Formats: online ● *Southern Views*, bimonthly. Newsletter. Includes reports of SGA activities and issues. **Price:** free. Alternate Formats: online. **Conventions/Meetings:** annual conference and meeting - usually late August or September.

6288 ■ State Debt Management Network (SDMN)
c/o National Association of State Treasurers
2760 Res. Park Dr.
PO Box 11910
Lexington, KY 40578-1910
Ph: (859)244-8175
Fax: (859)244-8053
E-mail: nast@csg.org
URL: http://www.nast.net/debtnet/index.htm
Contact: Robert L. Watson, Chm.

Founded: 1991. **Membership Dues:** voting, professional, $250 (annual) ● associate, $50 (annual). **Description:** Managers, issuers of state bringing together public officials from branches of state government to share information on issuance, management, and oversight of public debt. **Awards:** Distinguished Service Award. **Type:** recognition. **Recipient:** to an individual for continued professionalism, support and commitment ● Tanya Gritz Award for Excellence in Public Finance. **Type:** recognition. **Recipient:** to an individual or group demonstrating excellence in authorization, planning, issuance and management of public debt. **Telecommunication Services:** electronic mail, rwatson@osc.state.ny.us. **Conventions/Meetings:** annual conference.

Substance Abuse

6289 ■ National Association of Drug Court Professionals (NADCP)
4900 Seminary Rd., Ste.320
Alexandria, VA 22311
Ph: (703)575-9400
Fax: (703)575-9402
E-mail: kfwilson@nadcp.org
URL: http://www.nadcp.org
Contact: Karen Freeman-Wilson, Exec. Dir.
Founded: 1994. **Membership Dues:** individual, $60 (annual) ● organization, $375 (annual) ● corporate, $25,000 (annual). **Staff:** 25. **Multinational. Description:** Represents professionals involved in the development, implementation and institutionalization of drug court programs. Reduces substance abuse, crime and recidivism. Advocates for the establishment and funding of drug courts. **Computer Services:** Information services, facts on drug courts. **Divisions:** National Drug Court Institute. **Publications:** *NADCP News*, quarterly. Newsletter. Alternate Formats: online.

Taxation

6290 ■ American Society of Tax Problem Solvers (ASTPS)
2250 Wehrle Dr., Ste.3
Williamsville, NY 14221
Ph: (716)630-1650
Fax: (716)630-1651
E-mail: ron@astps.org
URL: http://www.astps.org
Contact: Lawrence M. Lawler CPA, Natl. Dir.
Membership Dues: regular, $180 (annual). **Description:** Represents professionals who specialize in representing taxpayers before the IRS. Promotes education and professionalism in the area of Tax Problem Resolution. Advocates for taxpayer rights and responsiveness in taxing entities. Assists its members in maintaining a high level of skills, knowledge and professionalism in the area of tax representation. **Publications:** *The TAPeR Practitioner Times*, quarterly. Newsletter. Contains information on tax problem solving. **Price:** included in membership dues. Alternate Formats: online.

6291 ■ American Taxation Association (ATA)
c/o American Accounting Association
5717 Bessie Dr.
Sarasota, FL 34233-2399
Ph: (941)921-7747
Fax: (941)923-4093
E-mail: americantaxationassociation@aaahq.org
URL: http://aaahq.org/ata/index.htm
Contact: Terry Shevlin, Pres.
Founded: 1974. **Members:** 1,018. **Membership Dues:** accounting professor and practitioner, $20 (annual). **Budget:** $32,000. **Description:** Membership comprises primarily university professors teaching federal income tax, federal estate, and/or gift tax courses; other members are practitioners, including certified public accountants. Seeks to further taxation education. Researches the impact of the tax process, particularly tax code sections, on the social and economic structure of the U.S. Maintains speakers' bureau. **Libraries: Type:** reference. **Holdings:** reports. **Awards:** Dissertation Award. **Type:** recognition ● Tax Manuscript Award. **Type:** recognition. **Committees:** Computer Usage; International Taxation; Manuscript and Dissertation Awards; Practitioner Interests; Tax Policy; Tax Research. **Publications:** *Journal of the American Taxation Association*, semiannual. **Price:** $20.00/year. **Advertising:** accepted ● Newsletter, 3/year. **Conventions/Meetings:** annual meeting, held in conjunction with the AAA (exhibits) - February.

6292 ■ Federation of Tax Administrators (FTA)
444 N Capitol St. NW, Ste.348
Washington, DC 20001
Ph: (202)624-5890
Fax: (202)624-7888
URL: http://www.taxadmin.org
Contact: Harley T. Duncan, Exec. Dir.
Founded: 1937. **Members:** 53. **Staff:** 10. **Budget:** $1,000,000. **Description:** State revenue departments. Promotes advanced standards and improved methods of tax administration. Investigates administrative problems facing tax officials; prepares research reports on state tax issues. Maintains communications network. **Computer Services:** Mailing lists ● online services. **Committees:** Administrative Affairs; External Affairs; Internal Affairs; Nominations; Resolutions. **Projects:** Motor Fuel Uniformity. **Sections:** Motor Fuel Tax. **Absorbed:** (1988) National Association of Tax Administrators. **Publications:** *Tax Administrators News*, monthly. Newsletter. Covers developments in tax legislation, court decisions, compliance, and administrative practices. **Price:** $40.00/year. ISSN: 0039-9949. **Circulation:** 2,000. Alternate Formats: online ● *TaxExPRESS*, weekly. Newsletter. Provides information on current events. Alternate Formats: online ● Bulletins. Provides information on tax administration. ● Directories. **Price:** $15.00 for members; $20.00 for nonmembers (1-9 copies); $15.00 for nonmembers (10 or more copies) ● Proceedings, annual ● Reports. Alternate Formats: online. **Conventions/Meetings:** annual meeting, review of current trends in state taxes.

6293 ■ Forest Landowners Tax Council (FLTC)
PO Box 784
Alexandria, VA 22313-0784
Ph: (703)549-0747
E-mail: info@fltc.net
URL: http://www.fltc.net
Contact: Frank Stewart, Exec. Dir.
Membership Dues: benefactor, $1,000 (annual) ● patron, $500-$999 (annual) ● supporter, $250-$499 (annual) ● contributor, $100-$249 (annual). **Description:** Provides a unified voice for non-industrial, private forest landowners on federal tax issues. Seeks to provide technical research to identify opportunities for timber tax improvements. Serves as a source of education for those who wish to learn more about timber taxation. **Telecommunication Services:** electronic mail, director@fltc.net. **Publications:** *The FLTC Tax Report*. Alternate Formats: online ● *Timber Tax*. Newsletter. **Price:** included in membership dues.

6294 ■ Institute for Professionals in Taxation (IPT)
600 Northpark Town Center
1200 Abernathy Rd. NE, Ste.L-2
Atlanta, GA 30328
Ph: (404)240-2300
Fax: (404)240-2315
E-mail: ipt@ipt.org
URL: http://www.ipt.org
Contact: Billy D. Cook, Exec. Dir.
Founded: 1976. **Members:** 4,100. **Membership Dues:** associate, $225 (annual) ● regular, affiliate, $350 (annual). **Staff:** 13. **Budget:** $2,800,000. **Description:** Corporate property and sales tax representatives; attorneys, appraisers, consultants, and accountants who represent corporate taxpayers. Seeks to foster the education of members; promotes study in property and sales taxation; encourages the interchange of ideas and assistance among members; facilitates cooperation with governmental authorities in solving problems of ad valorem (imposed at a rate percent of value) and sales tax administration. Strives for high standards of competence and efficiency in corporate property and sales tax management. Offers professional certification for property and sales tax professionals. Presents views of members to other taxpayer organizations, governmental bodies, and interested persons. Analyzes existing and proposed legislation, regulations, administrative actions, and to her relevant matters; keeps members informed of findings. **Awards:** Distinguished Service Award. **Frequency:** annual. **Type:** recognition. **Recipient:** to individuals who have made outstanding contributions to the institute over an extended period of time ● Founders' Scholarship. **Type:** scholarship ● Literary Award. **Frequency:** annual. **Type:** recognition. **Recipient:** for papers by IPT members ● Special Award. **Frequency:** annual. **Type:** recognition. **Recipient:** for members who have contributed significantly to a special project, activity, or achievement of the institute. **Committees:** Admissions; Awards; By-Laws and Resolutions; Canadian Liaison; Certification/Licensing; Computer Usage; Information and Services; International Taxation; Legal; Legislative; Local Luncheon Liaison; Membership Promotions and Public Relations; Professional Ethics; Property Tax Education; Sales and Use Tax Education. **Councils:** Advisory. **Funds:** Education. **Formerly:** (1998) Institute of Property Taxation. **Publications:** *Property Tax Report*, monthly. Newsletter. Covers recent court cases and state developments. Includes listings of new publications and members, calendar of events, and employment opportunities. **Price:** included in membership dues. **Circulation:** 2,000 ● *Property Taxation*. Book. Provides coverage of all key issues and references local practice, assessors' manuals, statutes and case law. **Price:** $75.00 for members; $100.00 for staff of IPT member companies; $175.00 for nonmembers ● *Sales and Use Taxation*. Book. **Price:** $75.00 for members; $100.00 for staff of IPT member companies; $175.00 for nonmembers ● *Sales Tax Report*, monthly. Newsletter. Contains listings of publications of interest and new members and employment referral service. **Price:** free for members. **Circulation:** 1,800 ● *Third-Party Drop Shipment Survey*, semiannual. Book. **Price:** $175.00 ● Proceedings ● Brochures. Alternate Formats: online ● Papers. Alternate Formats: online. **Conventions/Meetings:** annual Basic and Intermediate Sales Tax - meeting ● annual Basic, Intermediate and Advanced Property Tax - meeting ● annual conference (exhibits) ● annual Property Tax - seminar ● annual Sales Tax - symposium (exhibits) ● annual Sales Tax Academy - seminar.

6295 ■ Institute of Tax Consultants (ITC)
7500 212th SW, Ste.205
Edmonds, WA 98026-7617
Ph: (425)774-3521
Fax: (425)672-0461
E-mail: kraemerc@juno.com
URL: http://www.taxprofessionals.homestead.com/welcome.html
Contact: Richard T. Hunt, Pres.
Founded: 1981. **Description:** Aims to provide tax practitioners with the opportunity to upgrade their professionalism through certification. Conducts educational programs and certification examinations. **Committees:** Certification; Education; Public Relations. **Publications:** *Don't Tax Yourself Out of the Tax Business*. Brochure ● Newsletter, periodic ● Also publishes a program/information guide. **Conventions/Meetings:** semiannual meeting.

6296 ■ International Association of Assessing Officers (IAAO)
314 W 10th St.
Kansas City, MO 64105-1616
Ph: (816)701-8100 (816)701-8120
Free: (800)616-4226
Fax: (816)701-8149
E-mail: daniels@iaao.org
URL: http://www.iaao.org
Contact: Lisa Daniels MPA, Exec. Dir.
Founded: 1934. **Members:** 7,600. **Membership Dues:** regular, $175 (annual) ● associate, $180 (annual) ● affiliate, $175 (annual). **Staff:** 20. **Budget:** $3,800,000. **Regional Groups:** 4. **State Groups:** 35. **Multinational. Description:** State and local officials concerned with valuation of property for ad valorem property tax purposes. Works to improve standards and conduct research on tax assessment. Offers educational programs and seminars; awards professional designations; makes available research and consulting services. Organizes task forces on special topics. **Libraries: Type:** reference; by appointment only. **Holdings:** 13,400; books, periodicals. **Subjects:** property tax and its administration, appraisal, land economics, land use, local government. **Commissions:** Nominating. **Committees:** Associate Members; Awards; Communications; Conference Content;

Ethics; Legal; Local Host; Planning and Rules; Professional Development; Research; Technical Standards. **Councils:** Metropolitan Jurisdiction. **Sections:** Computer Assisted Appraisal; Mapping; Personal Property; State/Provincial/Country Assessment Administration. **Formerly:** National Association of Assessing Officers. **Publications:** *Fair and Equitable*, monthly. Magazine. **Price:** $48.00 for nonmembers; free for members. **Circulation:** 8,000. **Advertising:** accepted ● *Journal of Property Tax Assessment and Administration*, quarterly. **Price:** $245.00 for nonmembers; free for members. ISSN: 1357-1419. **Advertising:** accepted. **Conventions/Meetings:** annual International Conference on Assessment Administration (exhibits).

6297 ■ Multistate Tax Commission (MTC)

444 N Capitol St. NW, Ste.425
Washington, DC 20001-1512
Ph: (202)624-8699
Fax: (202)624-8819
E-mail: mtc@mtc.gov
URL: http://www.mtc.gov
Contact: Joe Huddleston, Exec. Dir.

Founded: 1967. **Members:** 21. **Staff:** 40. **Budget:** $5,000,000. **Description:** States that have enacted the Multistate Tax Compact into law; states whose governors have requested associate membership or which have enacted the Compact legislation conditional upon congressional approval. Purposes are to: facilitate proper determination of state and local tax liability of multistate taxpayers, including the equitable apportionment of tax bases and settlement of apportionment disputes; promote uniformity or compatibility in significant components of tax systems; facilitate taxpayer convenience and compliance in the filing of tax returns and in other phases of tax administration; to avoid duplicative taxation. Performs corporate income tax audits, sales and use tax audits, and property tax audits in the form of a joint audit. (A joint audit is the audit of a corporate business on behalf of several states at one time.) Maintains National Nexus Program that encourages multistate businesses to comply with state tax laws. Represents states before Congress and the Executive Branch with respect to federal laws and policies having an impact on state tax authority. **Committees:** Litigation; Technology; Uniformity. **Programs:** Joint Audit; National Nexus. **Publications:** *MTC Review*, periodic. Newsletter. **Price:** free. **Circulation:** 3,500 ● *Multistate Tax Commission Review*. Journal. Alternate Formats: online ● Annual Report. Alternate Formats: online. **Conventions/Meetings:** annual conference and meeting.

6298 ■ National Association of Computerized Tax Processors (NACTP)

c/o Jamie Stiles, Pres.
235 E Palmer St.
Franklin, NC 28734
Ph: (828)524-8020
E-mail: president@nactp.org
URL: http://www.nactp.org
Contact: Jamie Stiles, Pres.

Founded: 1973. **Members:** 12. **Membership Dues:** regular, $500 (annual). **Staff:** 1. **Description:** Companies that process income tax returns via computer. Deals with common industry problems and concerns. Compiles statistics. **Committees:** Electronic Filing; IRS Testing; State Liaison. **Projects:** Piper. **Publications:** *Preparer's Guide to Electronic Filing Software and Services*, annual. Booklet ● *Supplement to Accounting Today*, annual. Book. **Price:** free ● Directory, annual. **Conventions/Meetings:** annual conference - always August, in conjunction with Internal Revenue Service.

6299 ■ National Association of Enrolled Agents (NAEA)

1120 Connecticut Ave. NW, Ste.460
Washington, DC 20036-3953
Ph: (202)822-6232
Fax: (202)822-6270
E-mail: info@naeahq.org
URL: http://www.naea.org
Contact: Susan Zuber CAE, Exec. VP

Founded: 1972. **Members:** 10,000. **Membership Dues:** regular, $165 (annual). **Staff:** 14. **Budget:** $1,000,000. **State Groups:** 39. **Local Groups:** 42. **Description:** Individuals who have gained Enrolled Agent status and are thus qualified to represent all classes of taxpayers at any administrative level of the Internal Revenue Service. Promotes ethical representation of the financial position of taxpayers before government agencies. Conducts seminars and conferences to keep members informed of legislation and regulations affecting the profession and taxpayers. Makes presentations to civic, community, educational, and employee groups to inform the public of its rights, privileges, and obligations under tax laws and regulations. Operates seminars in taxation and taxpayer representation including the National Tax Practice Institute, a 3-year, tri-level program in taxpayer representation and audit procedures. **Computer Services:** database, enrolled agents. **Telecommunication Services:** electronic mail, szuber@naeahq.org ● electronic mail, webmaster@naea.org ● 24-hour hotline, EA referral, (800)424-4339. **Committees:** Audit; Awards; Ethics and Professional Conduct; Government Relations; Nominating; NTPI Planning; Political Action; Public Information. **Formerly:** (1978) Association of Enrolled Agents. **Publications:** *E@lert*, weekly. Newsletter. Provides brief updates on the latest tax news. **Price:** included in membership dues. Alternate Formats: online ● *EA Journal*, bimonthly. Magazine. Provides current information on taxation and taxpayer representation issues. **Price:** included in membership dues; $48.00 /year for nonmembers. ISSN: 8750-7072. **Circulation:** 10,000. **Advertising:** accepted ● Membership Directory, annual. Includes membership listing, practitioner hotline and resource information. **Price:** free for members. **Circulation:** 9,500. **Conventions/Meetings:** annual convention and meeting (exhibits) - usually 3rd week of August.

6300 ■ National Association of Tax Consultants (NATC)

PO Box 90276
Portland, OR 97290-0276
Ph: (503)261-0878 (541)343-5336
Free: (800)745-6282
Fax: (503)261-0963
E-mail: natc2@juno.com
URL: http://www.natctax.org
Contact: Jayne T. Williams, Pres.

Founded: 1982. **Members:** 1,200. **Membership Dues:** Idaho/non-established state, $60 (annual) ● Oregon/Alaska/Washington, $90 (annual). **Staff:** 1. **State Groups:** 3. **Description:** Aims to provide a conduit of communication between its members and the Internal Revenue Service, to have a voice in the development of the national licensing of the tax preparer professional, to inspire preparers of individual income tax returns, business entity tax forms and fiduciary tax forms to expand their vision of professional service to the consumer, and to support state and local organizations in the development of a national professional standard. **Telecommunication Services:** electronic mail, office@natctax.org.

6301 ■ National Association of Tax Professionals (NATP)

PO Box 8002
Appleton, WI 54914-8002
Free: (800)558-3402
Fax: (800)747-0001
E-mail: natp@natptax.com
URL: http://www.natptax.com
Contact: Michael D. Whittle EA, Pres.

Founded: 1979. **Members:** 16,000. **Membership Dues:** individual, international, $148 (annual) ● individual discount, $106 (annual) ● academic, $53 (annual). **Staff:** 39. **Budget:** $5,000,000. **State Groups:** 35. **Description:** Serves professionals who work in all areas of tax practice, including individual practitioners, enrolled agents, certified public accountants, accountants, attorneys and certified financial planners. **Awards:** Tax Professional of the Year. **Frequency:** annual. **Type:** recognition. **Recipient:** for tax professionals who have outstanding achievements in service to their community and profession. **Computer Services:** Information services, federal tax facts and resources. **Telecommunication Services:** electronic mail, skath@natptax.com. **Committees:** Government Relations; Professional Development. **Programs:** Educational; Mentor. **Formerly:** (2003) National Association of Tax Practitioners. **Publications:** *TAXPRO Monthly*. Newsletter. Provides information on tax laws and procedures and developments in the field of federal taxation; association activities and practice management. **Price:** free for members. **Circulation:** 16,000 ● *TAXPRO Quarterly Journal*. **Price:** free for members. **Circulation:** 16,000. **Advertising:** accepted ● *TAXPRO Weekly E-Mail*. Newsletter. **Price:** free for members. **Circulation:** 10,000. Alternate Formats: online. **Conventions/Meetings:** annual conference (exhibits) - always July or August. 2008 July 7-10, Atlanta, GA; 2009 July 20-23, Reno, NV.

6302 ■ National Tax Association - Tax Institute of America (NTA)

725 15th St. NW, No. 600
Washington, DC 20005-2109
Ph: (202)737-3325
Fax: (202)737-7308
E-mail: natltax@aol.com
URL: http://www.ntanet.org
Contact: Ms. Charmaine J. Wright, Sec.

Founded: 1907. **Members:** 1,168. **Membership Dues:** government/academic individual, $100 (annual) ● retiree, $45 (annual) ● corporate individual/professional, $140 (annual) ● government agency, $370 (annual) ● corporation, $350 (annual) ● full-time student, $40 (annual) ● sustaining (minimum), $500 (annual). **Staff:** 3. **Budget:** $300,000. **Description:** Government and corporate tax officials, accountants, consultants, economists, attorneys, and others interested in the field of taxation. Promotes nonpartisan academics, study of taxation; encourages better understanding of the common interests of national, state, and local governments in matters of taxation and public finance; and disseminates higher quality research through publications and conferences. **Libraries: Type:** reference. **Holdings:** archival material, articles. **Awards:** Daniel M. Holland Medal. **Frequency:** annual. **Type:** medal. **Recipient:** for outstanding accomplishments in the field of public finance and distinguished contributions in the areas of research, teaching, practice or contributions to the National Tax Association ● Jeanne S. Mattersdorf Memorial Fund Award. **Frequency:** annual. **Type:** recognition. **Recipient:** for promising students to acquaint them with the objectives, activities, and programs of the association ● NTA-TIA Outstanding Doctoral Dissertation Honorable Mention Award. **Frequency:** annual. **Type:** monetary. **Recipient:** for two honorable mention dissertation entries ● Outstanding Doctoral Dissertation Award. **Frequency:** annual. **Type:** monetary. **Recipient:** for an outstanding dissertation dealing with taxation and finance. **Committees:** Education in Public Finance; Federal Taxation and Finance; Intergovernmental Fiscal Relations; International Public Finance; Local Non-Property Taxation; Property Taxation; State Income and Business Taxation; State Sales and Use Taxation; Taxation of Energy, Communications, and Transportation; Taxation of Financial Institutions, Products and Services. **Formed by Merger of:** (1973) National Tax Association; Tax Institute of America. **Publications:** *National Tax Journal*, quarterly. Covers topics of current interest in the field of taxation and public finance in the United States and foreign countries. **Price:** $60.00 /year for individuals in U.S.; $65.00 /year for individuals outside U.S.; $90.00 /year for libraries in U.S.; $95.00 /year for libraries outside U.S. ISSN: 0028-0283. **Circulation:** 3,500 ● *Proceedings of the Annual Conference on Taxation*, annual. Contains a compilation of papers presented at each annual conference on theory and practice of federal, state, and local taxation. **Price:** included in membership dues. **Circulation:** 3,200. **Conventions/Meetings:** Conference on Taxation, conference of tax professionals on important current public finance issues -

always fall ● annual Spring Symposium - conference - always May or June in Washington, DC.

6303 ■ Tax Council (TC)
1301 K St. NW, Ste.800W
Washington, DC 20005-3317
Ph: (202)822-8062
Fax: (202)414-1301
E-mail: general@thetaxcouncil.org
URL: http://www.thetaxcouncil.org
Contact: Roger J. LeMaster, Exec. Dir.

Founded: 1966. **Members:** 120. **Membership Dues:** general, $2,000 (annual). **Description:** Business organization concerned with sound federal tax and fiscal policies. Promotes a stable, capital-conscious federal tax policy. Presents testimony on tax issues and sponsors tax conferences. **Awards:** Tax Policy Achievement Award. **Frequency:** annual. **Type:** recognition. **Committees:** Communications; Foreign Tax; Programs; Tax Policy; Tax Reform. **Publications:** *Budget Analysis*, annual ● *Tax Council Informational Brochure* ● *Tax Policy Papers*, periodic. Provides analysis of various tax policy issues. **Conventions/Meetings:** annual conference and luncheon, discussion of current tax issues which impact major businesses ● annual Spring Legislative Conference, discussion of current tax issues which affect corporations and businesses - always spring.

6304 ■ Tax Executives Institute (TEI)
1200 G St. NW, Ste.300
Washington, DC 20005-3814
Ph: (202)638-5601
Fax: (202)638-5607
E-mail: administration@tei.org
URL: http://www.tei.org
Contact: David L. Bernard, Intl. Pres.

Founded: 1944. **Members:** 5,400. **Membership Dues:** general, $200 (annual) ● associate, $25 (annual). **Staff:** 13. **Budget:** $1,500,000. **Local Groups:** 52. **National Groups:** 52. **Multinational. Description:** Professional society of executives administering and directing tax affairs for corporations and businesses. Maintains TEI Education Fund. **Libraries: Type:** not open to the public. **Awards:** Distinguished Service Award. **Frequency:** annual. **Type:** recognition. **Recipient:** for outstanding contributions of public tax officials. **Telecommunication Services:** electronic mail, memberinfo@tei.org. **Committees:** Canadian Tax; Federal Tax; International Tax; IRS; Management; State and Local Tax; Tax Information. **Publications:** *The Structure and Size of the Corporate Tax Department: An Empirical Analysis*. Book. **Price:** $25.00 ● *The Tax Executive*, bimonthly. Journal. Includes book reviews and annual index. **Price:** included in membership dues; $22.00 individual issues, for nonmembers; $120.00 /year for nonmembers in U.S. and Canada; $145.00 /year for nonmembers outside U.S. and Canada. ISSN: 0040-0025. **Circulation:** 5,800. **Advertising:** accepted. Alternate Formats: microform ● *Value-Added Taxes - A Comparative Analysis*. Book. **Price:** $20.00. **Conventions/Meetings:** annual conference - usually mid-year ● annual conference.

6305 ■ Tax Foundation
2001 L St. NW, Ste.1050
Washington, DC 20036
Ph: (202)464-6200
Fax: (202)464-6201
E-mail: tf@taxfoundation.org
URL: http://www.taxfoundation.org
Contact: William Ahern, Communications Dir.

Founded: 1937. **Description:** Strives to educate the public about taxes. **Publications:** *Special Briefs*. Papers. Includes testimony and public speeches by Tax Foundation economists. ● *Tax Features*. Newsletter. **Price:** free for members. Alternate Formats: online ● *Tax Foundation Background Paper*. Alternate Formats: online ● *Tax Foundation Special Reports*. Alternate Formats: online ● *Tax Watch*, bimonthly. Newsletter. Alternate Formats: online ● Books ● Reports.

Telecommunications

6306 ■ National Association of State Telecommunications Directors (NASTD)
2760 Res. Park Dr.
Lexington, KY 40511-8482
Ph: (859)244-8187
Fax: (859)244-8001
E-mail: mmccord@csg.org
URL: http://www.nastd.org
Contact: Mark McCord, Exec. Dir.

Founded: 1978. **Members:** 130. **Membership Dues:** associate, $750 (annual) ● corporate, $3,500 (annual). **Staff:** 4. **Budget:** $400,000. **Regional Groups:** 4. **Description:** Represents directors of state telecommunications agencies. Aims to improve state telecommunications systems by allowing members to exchange information, ideas, concepts, and practices. Seeks to provide a unified voice on matters pertaining to national communications policies and regulatory issues. **Libraries: Type:** reference. **Subjects:** state telecommunications. **Committees:** Corporate Relations; Information Exchange and Education; Regulatory Action. **Affiliated With:** Council of State Governments. **Publications:** *NASTD Directory*, annual ● *NASTD Monitor*, monthly. Contains regulatory updates. ● *NASTD State Reports*, annual. **Conventions/Meetings:** annual conference and trade show (exhibits) - 2008 Aug. 23-27, Boston, MA.

6307 ■ National Association of Telecommunications Officers and Advisors (NATOA)
1800 Diagonal Rd., Ste.495
Alexandria, VA 22314
Ph: (703)519-8035
Fax: (703)519-8036
E-mail: info@natoa.org
URL: http://www.natoa.org
Contact: Elizabeth Beaty, Exec. Dir.

Founded: 1980. **Members:** 1,100. **Membership Dues:** individual, $395 (annual) ● associate (profit-making), $680 (annual) ● agency, $510-$750 (annual) ● student, $85 (annual) ● associate (non-profit), $310 (annual). **Budget:** $900,000. **Local Groups:** 17. **Description:** Elected and appointed government officials who represent cable television and telecommunications administrators; staff personnel from local governments and public interest groups. Seeks to: establish an information-sharing network among local telecommunications regulators and users in the public sector; provide education and training for local government officials to enhance their capacity to deal with cable and telecommunications issues; provide technical and policy development assistance to members. Maintains speakers' bureau. **Awards:** Government Programming Awards. **Frequency:** annual. **Type:** recognition. **Recipient:** for creativity in video programming including technical proficiency and diversity in programming. **Computer Services:** database ● online services, e-mail list serve. **Telecommunication Services:** electronic mail, lbeaty@natoa.org. **Committees:** Communications; Legal Affairs; Multimedia/Programming; Technology and Applications. **Publications:** *Journal of Municipal Telecommunications Policy*, quarterly ● *NATOA Update News*, monthly. Bulletin. Covers member activities and detailed updates on NATOA legislative and regulatory action. **Price:** included in membership dues. **Circulation:** 850 ● Membership Directory, annual. Includes monthly updates via web. **Conventions/Meetings:** annual conference (exhibits) ● Government Programming Awards - competition ● Litigation and Regulation - seminar ● regional meeting.

6308 ■ RTCA
1828 L St. NW, Ste.805
Washington, DC 20036
Ph: (202)833-9339
Fax: (202)833-9434
E-mail: info@rtca.org
URL: http://www.rtca.org
Contact: Mr. David S. Watrous, Pres.

Founded: 1935. **Members:** 305. **Membership Dues:** international government associate, $1,700 (annual) ● academic institution, $900 (annual) ● organization (with gross revenue of less than $1M), $475 (annual) ● organization (with gross revenue of $1M-$500M), $1,700-$3,300 (annual) ● organization (with gross revenue of over $500M), $7,500 (annual). **Staff:** 10. **Budget:** $1,600,000. **Description:** Addresses requirements, operational concepts, and industry standards for aviation. Advances the art and science of aviation and aviation electronic systems for the benefit of the public. Products are developed by volunteers from the entire aviation community and include consensus-based recommendations addressing the implementation of new operational capabilities, performance standards, transition and implementation strategies, as well as technical guidance documents and special topic reports. Recommendations are often used as the foundation for government policy and industry business decisions. Most activities function as Federal Advisory Committees. **Libraries: Type:** reference. **Awards:** William E. Jackson Award. **Frequency:** annual. **Type:** recognition. **Recipient:** to an outstanding graduate student in the field of aviation electronics and telecommunications. **Telecommunication Services:** electronic mail, membership@rtca.org. **Formerly:** (1992) Radio Technical Commission for Aeronautics. **Publications:** *RTCA Digest*, bimonthly. Newsletter. Includes association news and information about technical advances in aeronautical communications. **Price:** free for members. **Advertising:** accepted ● Proceedings, annual ● Also publishes performance standards, guidance documents and reports for communications, navigation, surveillance and air traffic management (CNS/ATM) system issues. **Conventions/Meetings:** annual symposium (exhibits).

Traffic

6309 ■ National Committee on Uniform Traffic Laws and Ordinances (NCUTLO)
107 S West St., No. 110
Alexandria, VA 22314-2824
Free: (800)807-5290
Fax: (540)465-5383
E-mail: twogen2@yahoo.com
URL: http://www.ncutlo.org
Contact: Lelia A. Osina, Exec. Dir.

Founded: 1926. **Members:** 150. **Membership Dues:** state, sponsor, nonprofit (over $1 million annual budget), $2,000 (annual) ● associate, nonprofit (under $1 million annual budget), $500 (annual) ● individual, $100 (annual). **Staff:** 2. **Budget:** $250,000. **Description:** Federal, state, and local highway, police, motor vehicle, and other officials; legislators; educational institutions; manufacturers of vehicles and equipment; insurance companies, motor clubs, and safety councils; other persons and organizations interested in uniform motor vehicle laws. Maintains small library on traffic law. Keeps the Uniform Vehicle Code, Collection of model laws. **Committees:** Operations and Drivers; Scope and Administration; Vehicle Regulations. **Formerly:** (1947) National Conference on Street and Highway Safety. **Publications:** *Uniform Vehicle Code*. **Price:** $100.00. Alternate Formats: online. **Conventions/Meetings:** periodic executive committee meeting ● annual meeting.

6310 ■ Traffic Court Program of the American Bar Association (ABA/TCP)
Address Unknown since 2008

Founded: 1942. **Staff:** 1. **Description:** Founded by the American Bar Association. Promotes observance of traffic laws; improve efficiency of traffic courts; promote respect for traffic laws; reduce traffic violations; increase dignity of and respect for traffic courts. Promotes acceptance of Standards for Traffic Justice as approved by the ABA. Conducts educational programs for traffic court personnel. Serves as contact point between the legal profession and private individuals and groups interested in traffic court and traffic law reform. **Affiliated With:** American Bar Association. **Publications:** *Traffic Court Procedure and Administration*. Book ● Pamphlets ● Videos ● Also publishes studies of various courts with traffic jurisdiction, and other materials. **Conventions/Meetings:** annual meeting (exhibits) ● annual seminar - always October.

Transportation

6311 ■ Alliance for a New Transportation Charter (ANTC)
c/o Surface Transportation Policy Project
1100 17th St. NW, 10th Fl.
Washington, DC 20036
Ph: (202)466-2636
Fax: (202)466-2247
E-mail: antc@transact.org
URL: http://www.transact.org/ANTC/about.asp
Founded: 2001. **Description:** Advocates for the development and the implementation of transportation policies that provide changes in transportation planning and investment. Promotes the use of transportation as a tool for achieving better outcomes in public health, affordable housing, job access, energy efficiency and social equity. **Computer Services:** Online services, discussion boards.

6312 ■ American Association of State Highway and Transportation Officials (AASHTO)
444 N Capitol St. NW, Ste.249
Washington, DC 20001-1539
Ph: (202)624-5800 (202)624-5811
Fax: (202)624-5806
E-mail: info@aashto.org
URL: http://www.transportation.org
Contact: John Horsley, Exec. Dir.
Founded: 1914. **Members:** 76. **Staff:** 34. **Description:** Represents highway and transportation departments of the 50 states, Puerto Rico, and the District of Columbia; U.S. Department of Transportation; affiliate members are national and territorial highway departments and state transportation agencies. Develops and improves methods of administration, design, construction, operation, and maintenance of a nationwide integrated transportation system; works to study all problems connected with such a system; counsels Congress on transportation legislation; develops technical administrative and highway operational standards and policies for all transportation modes; and cooperates with other agencies in the consideration and solution of transportation problems. Sponsors the National Cooperative Highway Research Program. **Awards:** Alfred E. Johnson Achievement Award. **Frequency:** annual. **Type:** recognition. **Recipient:** to individuals who have rendered the most outstanding service in the field of engineering or management ● President's Transportation Awards. **Frequency:** annual. **Type:** recognition. **Recipient:** to individuals who have performed exemplary service furthering the transportation activities of his/her member department or committee ● Thomas H. MacDonald Memorial Award. **Frequency:** annual. **Type:** recognition. **Recipient:** to individuals who have made exceptional contribution to the art and science of highway engineering ● 25-Year Award of Meritorious Service. **Frequency:** annual. **Type:** recognition. **Recipient:** to member department employees having the grade of district engineer or equivalent responsibility in the department. **Committees:** Administration; Aviation; Environment; Highway Traffic Safety; Highways; Planning; Policy; Public Transportation; Rail Transportation; Research Advisory; U.S. Route Numbering; Water Transportation. **Subcommittees:** Bridges and Structures; Construction; Design; Highway Transport; Maintenance; Materials; Public Affairs; Traffic Engineering. **Formerly:** (1973) American Association of State Highway Officials. **Publications:** *AASHTO Journal: Weekly Transportation News*. Newsletter. Gives a weekly overview of transportation issues. Alternate Formats: online ● *AASHTO Quarterly*. Magazine ● *The AASHTO Regulatory Monitor*, weekly. Report. Provides weekly updates on federal regulatory action related to transportation issues. Alternate Formats: online ● *Reference Book*, annual ● Books. Covers design, construction, and maintenance of transportation facilities. ● Proceedings, annual. **Conventions/Meetings:** annual meeting.

6313 ■ American Road and Transportation Builders Association (ARTBA)
The ARTBA Bldg.
1219 28th St. NW
Washington, DC 20007-3389
Ph: (202)289-4434
Fax: (202)289-4435
E-mail: pruane@artba.org
URL: http://www.artba.org
Contact: Peter Ruane, Pres./CEO
Founded: 1902. **Members:** 5,000. **Membership Dues:** primary (with less than $5000000 annual volumes), $600 (annual) ● public official, educational/research institution, $175 (annual) ● service membership, $200 (annual). **Staff:** 35. **Budget:** $6,400,000. **State Groups:** 33. **Languages:** Chinese, English, French, Russian, Spanish. **Description:** Highway, bridge, rail and airport contractors; federal, state, county, and municipal engineers and officials; engineers in private practice; manufacturers and distributors of construction equipment; producers and suppliers of materials and services; educators and students of highway engineering; representatives from the traffic safety industry; individuals engaged in other aspects of the design, manufacture, sale, fabrication, installation, and service of devices and materials relating to traffic control during the construction and operation of transportation facilities. Serves as liaison between the industry and government. Sponsors business insurance program, drug testing program, educational and technical workshops. Maintains committees including ARTBA-PAC. **Libraries:** **Type:** not open to the public. **Holdings:** 1,000; articles, books, periodicals. **Subjects:** transportation, construction. **Awards:** ARTBA Award. **Frequency:** annual. **Type:** recognition ● S.S. Steinberg Award. **Frequency:** annual. **Type:** recognition. **Recipient:** for outstanding contribution to transportation education. **Computer Services:** Online services, infostructure. **Telecommunication Services:** electronic mail, rbritton@artba.org. **Divisions:** Contractors; Education; Manufacturers; Materials and Services; Planning and Design; Public/Private Ventures; Traffic Safety Industry; Transportation Officials. **Absorbed:** (1969) Better Highway Information Foundation. **Formerly:** (1910) American Road Makers; (1977) American Road Builders Association. **Publications:** *Contractors Salary and Benefits Survey*, annual ● *Transportation Builder*. Magazine. **Advertising:** accepted ● *Transportation Officials and Engineers*, annual. Directory. **Price:** $195.00 for members; $249.00 for nonmembers ● Newsletter, monthly. **Conventions/Meetings:** annual convention ● annual Legislative Conference - convention (exhibits) - always spring in Washington, DC ● annual meeting - always fall ● Public Ventures - conference.

6314 ■ American Transit Service Council (ATSC)
Address Unknown since 2007
Description: Transportation companies, government agencies, and other organizations with an interest in public transit. Promotes development of market-responsive transit services through competitive contracting. Assists communities wishing to implement public transportation policies and services; serves as a clearinghouse on public transit and related issues.

6315 ■ Americans for Transportation Mobility (ATM)
U.S. Chamber of Commerce
Congressional and Public Affairs
Trans. and Infrastructure
1615 H St. NW
Washington, DC 20062
Ph: (202)463-5600
Fax: (202)887-3430
E-mail: mobility@uschamber.com
URL: http://www.a-t-m.org
Contact: Justin Lumadue, Contact
Founded: 2001. **Description:** Works to ensure that the nation's transportation infrastructure is improved to handle current and future demands. Educates the public, elected officials and other opinion leaders about the value of transportation to the economy and quality of life. **Publications:** *ATM Insider*, monthly. Newsletter. Alternate Formats: online.

6316 ■ Association of Transportation Law Professionals (ATLP)
c/o Lauren Michalski, Exec. Dir.
PO Box 5407
Annapolis, MD 21403-0702
Ph: (410)268-1311
Fax: (410)268-1322
E-mail: info@atlp.com
URL: http://www.atlp.org
Contact: Lauren Michalski, Exec. Dir.
Founded: 1929. **Members:** 750. **Membership Dues:** attorney, non-attorney, $195 (annual) ● university/college faculty, government employee, $100 (annual) ● retired, $75 (annual) ● student, $50 (annual). **Description:** Seeks to equip members with the necessary tools to be vital resources for their companies, firms, customers and clients who compete in a constantly changing and increasingly global transportation and logistics marketplace. Provides educational offerings that are designed, among other things, to eliminate surprises and afford opportunities for the exchange of information among professionals involved in logistics and all modes of transportation; encourages the highest standards of conduct among transportation and logistics professionals; promotes the proper administration of laws and policies affecting transportation and logistics. **Computer Services:** Online services, bulletin board. **Committees:** Membership and Diversity; Nominations; Practice and Procedure; Programs. **Formerly:** (1940) Association of Practitioners Before the Interstate Commerce Commission; (1984) Association of Interstate Commerce Commission Practitioners; (1994) Association of Transportation Practitioners; (2006) Association for Transportation Law, Logistics and Policy. **Publications:** *Annual Meeting Papers and Proceedings*, annual ● *Association Highlights*, bimonthly. Newsletter. **Price:** available to members only. **Advertising:** accepted ● *Comes Now the Interstate Commerce Practitioner*. Book ● *The Journal of Transportation Law, Logistics and Policy*, quarterly. **Price:** $100.00 in U.S.; $105.00 in Canada; $110.00 international. **Advertising:** accepted ● Membership Directory, biennial ● Books. **Conventions/Meetings:** annual meeting.

6317 ■ Governors Highway Safety Association (GHSA)
750 1st St. NE, Ste.720
Washington, DC 20002-8002
Ph: (202)789-0942
Fax: (202)789-0946
E-mail: headquarters@ghsa.org
URL: http://www.ghsa.org
Contact: Barbara L. Harsha, Exec. Dir.
Founded: 1969. **Members:** 105. **Membership Dues:** corporate, $750 (annual) ● non-profit, $500 (annual) ● small business, $250 (annual) ● emeritus, $100 (annual). **Staff:** 4. **Budget:** $277,000. **Regional Groups:** 10. **State Groups:** 55. **Local Groups:** 50. **National Groups:** 50. **Description:** Represents the interests of state and territorial officials who administer the Highway Safety Act of 1966. (The Highway Safety Act requires that states receiving highway safety grants under 23 U.S. Code 402 may not receive program approval unless the governor of each state or territory is responsible for administration of the program.) Works to reduce highway fatalities and automobile accidents; enforces the 55 mph speed limit; develops and maintains driver education and pedestrian and bicycle safety programs; manages alcohol safety and occupant protection programs. Conducts research through grant programs. Provides highway safety training in such areas as judicial training, engineering, traffic engineering, and traffic safety engineering. **Awards:** James J. Howard Trailblazer Award. **Frequency:** annual. **Type:** recognition ● Peter K. O'Rourke Special Achievement Award. **Frequency:** annual. **Type:** recognition. **Telecommunication Services:** electronic mail, jadkins@

ghsa.org. **Committees:** Member Services; National Policy; Organization and Finance; Public Relations; Research Evaluation and Assessments. **Subcommittees:** Enforcement and Engineering; Health and Injury Control; Impaired Driving; Occupant Protection. **Formerly:** (2003) National Association of Governors' Highway Safety Representatives. **Publications:** *Directions in Highway Safety*, quarterly. Newsletter. **Price:** included in membership dues; available to members only. **Circulation:** 1,200. Alternate Formats: online. Also Cited As: *GHSA News* ● *Highway Safety Policies and Priorities*. Book. Lists GHSA policy resolutions and all the positions and interests of the members adopted since 1974. Revised 1996-1997. **Conventions/Meetings:** periodic executive committee meeting, covers a variety of highway safety issues ● annual Lifesavers - conference, in conjunction with the National Highway Traffic Safety Administration and other highway safety organizations; for highway safety professionals only ● quarterly seminar, on program management ● periodic seminar, on program management ● workshop, covers a variety of highway safety issues ● annual convention and meeting, for establishing policy, sharing expertise, and networking (exhibits) - 2008 Sept. 7-10, Scottsdale, AZ; 2009 Aug. 29-Sept. 2, Savannah, GA.

6318 ■ International Bridge, Tunnel and Turnpike Association (IBTTA)
1146 19th St. NW, Ste.800
Washington, DC 20036-3725
Ph: (202)659-4620
Fax: (202)659-0500
E-mail: carnold@ibtta.org
URL: http://www.IBTTA.org
Contact: Patrick D. Jones, Exec. Dir.
Founded: 1932. **Members:** 280. **Staff:** 11. **Budget:** $2,000,000. **Multinational. Description:** Serves as the worldwide alliance of toll operators and associated industries that provides a forum for sharing knowledge and ideas to promote and enhance toll-financed transportation services. Helps members stay abreast of trends that will see the toll industry emerge as one of the most important forces in highway finance and operations around the world. Offers finance summits, meetings, exhibitions, and workshops throughout the year. Represents 280 members in 25 countries on six continents; members are leaders in technological innovation with expertise in the ways technology is reshaping road financing, organizational models and service delivery. **Libraries: Type:** reference. **Holdings:** papers, reports. **Subjects:** toll finance, operation, maintenance, technology. **Awards:** Toll Excellence Awards. **Type:** recognition. **Recipient:** to member toll agencies for furthering the aims of the industry through creative, innovative and positive programs. **Telecommunication Services:** electronic mail, info@ibtta.org. **Committees:** Administration; Concession, Marketing and Business Development; Engineering and Design; Finance; Law; Maintenance; Operations; Public Relations; Research; Risk Management; Security and Law Enforcement; Technology. **Formerly:** (1952) American Toll Bridge Association; (1964) American Bridge, Tunnel, and Turnpike Association. **Publications:** *ETTM System Survey*. Surveys ● *Tollways*, monthly. Newsletter. Focuses on trends, developments and news about the worldwide toll industry. **Circulation:** 2,000. **Conventions/Meetings:** annual conference (exhibits) - usually September. 2008 Sept. 20-24, Baltimore, MD; 2009 Sept. 12-16, Chicago, IL.

6319 ■ International Transportation Management Association (ITMA)
PO Box 924146
Houston, TX 77292-4146
Ph: (713)747-4909
Fax: (713)747-5330
E-mail: pvanetten@gwii.com
URL: http://itma-houston.org
Contact: Peter Van Etten, Pres.
Founded: 1975. **Membership Dues:** individual, $50 (annual) ● corporate, $150 (annual). **Multinational. Description:** Promotes the knowledge of international transportation issues. Educates members on the various aspects of international transportation. **Computer Services:** Mailing lists. **Publications:** Newsletter.

6320 ■ National Association for Pupil Transportation (NAPT)
1840 Western Ave.
Albany, NY 12203-4624
Ph: (518)452-3611
Free: (800)989-NAPT
Fax: (518)218-0867
E-mail: info@napt.org
URL: http://www.napt.org
Contact: Michael J. Martin, Exec. Dir.
Founded: 1974. **Members:** 2,300. **Membership Dues:** individual, $75 (annual) ● business partner, $1,350 (annual) ● state association, $2,500 (annual). **Staff:** 2. **Description:** Principals, transportation directors, bus drivers, bus mechanics, and interested individuals. Works for the improvement of safety, efficiency, and economy of pupil transportation in school districts that own and operate their own bus fleets. Promotes leadership for the advancement of the industry; collects and disseminates information. **Awards:** Schoolbus Fleet Director of the Year. **Type:** recognition ● Thomas Built Buses Continuing Education. **Type:** grant. **Recipient:** for private education ● Transportation Administrator of the Year. **Type:** recognition. **Computer Services:** Mailing lists, of members. **Telecommunication Services:** electronic mail, mike.martin@napt.org. **Publications:** *Human Resources Materials*, periodic ● *NAPT Member Handbook*, annual ● *NAPT News and Views*, 6/year. Newsletter. **Conventions/Meetings:** annual conference and workshop - first week of November.

6321 ■ National Association of Railroad Trial Counsel (NARTC)
1430 E Missouri, Ste.B200
Phoenix, AZ 85014
Ph: (602)265-2700
Fax: (602)265-2705
E-mail: info@nartc.org
URL: http://www.usnartc.org
Contact: Michelle Mills Thorpe, Exec. Dir.
Founded: 1955. **Members:** 1,200. **Membership Dues:** regular, $285 (annual). **Staff:** 4. **Budget:** $400,000. **Regional Groups:** 5. **Description:** Professional organization of defendant attorneys representing railroads. Sponsors educational programs. **Publications:** *NARTC Membership List*, periodic. Membership Directory ● Newsletter, monthly. **Conventions/Meetings:** quarterly conference ● conference and meeting.

6322 ■ National Conference of State Fleet Administrators (NCSFA)
1544 W 6785 S
West Jordan, UT 84084
Ph: (801)685-3040
Fax: (801)685-3040
E-mail: info@ncsfa.net
URL: http://www.ncsfa.net
Contact: Mr. Steven Saltzgiver, Exec. Dir.
Founded: 1987. **Members:** 100. **Membership Dues:** primary, $500 (annual) ● additional, $350 (annual) ● associate, $250 (annual). **Staff:** 1. **Budget:** $150,000. **Description:** State administrators and directors engaged in vehicle fleet management. Encourages effective exercise of fleet management functions in order to increase efficiency and economy in state fleet administration. Provides a forum enabling state vehicle fleet administrators to meet and exchange information. Promotes and encourages professional competence standards in state government fleet administration. Reports on matters relating to state fleet vehicles and transportation. Conducts educational programs; compiles statistics. **Awards:** Distinguished Member of the Year. **Frequency:** annual. **Type:** recognition. **Recipient:** to a member for exemplary service to NCSFA ● Honda Environmental Award. **Frequency:** annual. **Type:** recognition ● State Fleet of the Year Award. **Frequency:** annual. **Type:** recognition. **Computer Services:** Electronic publishing ● mailing lists ● online services. **Committees:** Awards; Manufacturers Liaison; Membership Retention; Website. **Publications:** *Fleet Administration News*, quarterly. Newsletter. **Price:** free for members and sponsors. **Circulation:** 250. Alternate Formats: online ● *NCSFA Roster*, periodic. Directory. **Conventions/Meetings:** annual conference and trade show (exhibits).

6323 ■ National Conference of State Transportation Specialists (NCSTS)
c/o Mr. Terry Willert, Pres.
Public Utilities Commn.
1560 Broadway, Ste.250
Denver, CO 80202
Ph: (303)894-2850
E-mail: terry.willert@dora.state.co.us
URL: http://www.naruc.org/NCSTS
Contact: Mr. Terry Willert, Pres.
Founded: 1958. **Members:** 250. **Description:** Comprised of state agencies and partners involved in transportation safety, insurance and consumer protection that promotes uniform, effective and fair laws in the public interest by providing representation and a forum for communication and education. **Affiliated With:** National Association of Regulatory Utility Commissioners. **Conventions/Meetings:** annual conference.

6324 ■ National Transit Benefit Association (NTBA)
PO Box 25
Clifton, VA 20124
Ph: (703)222-9373
Fax: (703)222-9374
E-mail: inquiries@ntba.info
URL: http://www.ntba.info
Contact: Larry Filler, Pres.
Description: Promotes transit and vanpooling through the use of federal, state and local tax programs. Reduces traffic congestion and improves air quality. Provides a network for organizations involved in commuter benefit issues.

6325 ■ Snow and Ice Management Association (SIMA)
2221-C Peninsula Dr.
Erie, PA 16510
Ph: (814)835-3577
Fax: (814)835-0527
E-mail: brian@sima.org
URL: http://www.sima.org
Contact: Brian Birch, Interim Exec. Dir.
Founded: 1996. **Members:** 1,100. **Membership Dues:** general, $170-$375 (annual) ● associate, $275-$375 (annual) ● affiliate, $240 (annual). **Staff:** 3. **Budget:** $500,000. **Description:** Provides a network of resources in the snow and ice industry. Promotes ethical, efficient, and environmentally sound risk management for members. Contractors, subcontractors, facility managers, educational and medical facilities, suppliers, manufacturers and government agencies. **Committees:** Communications; Conference; Education; Membership. **Publications:** *Snow Business*, quarterly. Magazine. **Price:** $3.00. **Circulation:** 40,000. **Advertising:** accepted. **Conventions/Meetings:** annual Snow and Ice Symposium (exhibits) - 2008 June 18, Buffalo, NY.

6326 ■ Transportation Lawyers Association (TLA)
PO Box 15122
Lenexa, KS 66285-5122
Ph: (913)895-4615
Fax: (913)895-4652
E-mail: tla-info@goamp.com
URL: http://www.translaw.org
Contact: Stephanie Newman, Exec. Dir.
Founded: 1937. **Members:** 900. **Membership Dues:** professional, $185 (annual) ● law professor, $75 (annual) ● government attorney, $125 (annual) ● student, $25 (annual). **Staff:** 3. **Budget:** $200,000. **Description:** Attorneys representing transportation interests throughout the U.S. and Canada. Assists members in the practice of transportation law through exchange of ideas, education, and participation in rule-making proceedings. Cosponsors annual Transportation Law Institute. **Awards:** Distinguished

Service Award. **Frequency:** annual. **Type:** recognition ● Lifetime Achievement Award. **Frequency:** annual. **Type:** recognition. **Recipient:** for service to the organization. **Committees:** Legislative; Practice and Procedure; Regulatory Reform. **Formerly:** (1983) Motor Carrier Lawyers Association. **Publications:** *The Transportation Lawyer*, 5/year. Journal ● Membership Directory, monthly. **Price:** included in membership dues. **Conventions/Meetings:** annual conference and meeting (exhibits).

Travel

6327 ■ Society of Government Travel Professionals (SGTP)
6935 Wisconsin Ave., No. 200
Bethesda, MD 20815
Ph: (301)654-8595
Fax: (301)654-6663
E-mail: govtvlmkt@aol.com
URL: http://www.government-travel.org
Contact: Duncan G. Farrell CMP, Gen. Mgr.

Founded: 1983. **Members:** 500. **Membership Dues:** supplier regular, $450 (annual) ● supplier supporting/associate/travel agent small business, $195 (annual) ● travel agent regular, $375 (annual). **Staff:** 2. **Budget:** $300,000. **Description:** Travel agencies, air/lodging/car rental suppliers, government travel managers and contractors. Promotes members' growth in professionalism in the $29 billion governmental travel market. Provides mentoring and networking opportunities; conducts workshops; provides information on key issues in the industry; offers professional development and educational programs. **Libraries: Type:** reference; not open to the public; by appointment only. **Holdings:** books, business records, monographs. **Subjects:** business and leisure travel marketing/management. **Awards:** Professional Development. **Frequency:** annual. **Type:** recognition. **Computer Services:** database ● mailing lists, rental at $100/use. **Formerly:** STAG; (2000) Society of Travel Agents in Government. **Publications:** *SGTP's Member Profiles Reference Manual*, semiannual. Alternate Formats: CD-ROM; online ● *STAG 101: Principals of Governmental Travel Management*. Manual. **Price:** $100.00 ● *Survival Guide for the $20 Billion Government Travel Market*. Newsletter. Contains list of frequently used acronyms and government terms. ● Newsletter. Alternate Formats: CD-ROM; online. **Conventions/Meetings:** semiannual Advanced Operations for Government Travel Managers - workshop (exhibits) - always September and February ● annual conference, educational ● semiannual Marketing for Suppliers - conference and workshop (exhibits) - always winter and fall.

Trial Advocacy

6328 ■ American Association for Justice (AAJ)
1050 31st St. NW
Washington, DC 20007-4405
Ph: (202)965-3500
Free: (800)424-2725
Fax: (202)298-6849
E-mail: membership@justice.org
URL: http://www.atla.org
Contact: Lewis S. Eidson Jr., Pres.

Founded: 1946. **Members:** 60,000. **Membership Dues:** regular/associate (based on number of years in practice), $50-$365 (annual) ● international, $125 (annual) ● government/paralegal affiliate, $75 (annual) ● law professor/military, $35 (annual) ● law student, $15 (annual). **Staff:** 165. **Budget:** $19,400,000. **State Groups:** 51. **Local Groups:** 5. **Description:** Represents lawyers, judges, law professors, paralegals, and students engaged in civil plaintiff or criminal defense advocacy. Advances jurisprudence and the law as a profession; encouraging mutual support and cooperation among members of the bar; advancing the cause of persons seeking redress for damages against person or property; training in advocacy; upholding and improving the adversary system and trial by jury. Holds year-round educational programs. Sponsors environmental law essay contest; student trial by jury program; public interest programs; and National Student Trial Advocacy Competition. Conducts research on insurance, product liability, premises liability, environmental torts, and medical malpractice. **Libraries: Type:** reference; not open to the public. **Holdings:** 20,000; articles, books, periodicals. **Subjects:** law. **Awards:** AAJ Paralegal of the Year Award. **Frequency:** annual. **Type:** recognition ● Alia Herrera Memorial Scholarship. **Type:** scholarship. **Recipient:** for law students who are entering their second or third year of law school, or having the equivalent of one year to complete ● Leesfield Scholarship. **Type:** scholarship. **Recipient:** for a law student for attendance at AAJ's annual convention ● Richard D. Hailey Scholarships. **Type:** scholarship. **Recipient:** for incoming first-, second-, and third-year African American, Hispanic, Asian American, Native American, and Bi-racial AAJ law student members ● Steven J. Sharp Award for Public Service. **Frequency:** annual. **Type:** recognition. **Recipient:** for attorneys and clients whose cases tell the story of American civil justice and help educate state and national policy makers and the public about the importance of consumers' rights ● Trial Advocacy Scholarship. **Type:** scholarship. **Recipient:** for second and third-year AAJ law student members. **Computer Services:** database, of products ● mailing lists ● online services, forums. **Committees:** Curriculum Development; Ethical Conduct; Exchange Advisory; International Relations; Lawyers Challenge for Children; Public Education; Section and Litigation Group Coordination; Speakers/Bureau People's Law School. **Affiliated With:** Pound Civil Justice Institute. **Formerly:** (1946) Association of American Trial Lawyers; (1960) National Association of Claimants Compensation Attorneys; (1964) NACCA Bar Association; (1972) American Trial Lawyers Association; (2006) Association of Trial Lawyers of America. **Publications:** *AAJmart*. Catalog. Features a list of products and services offered by advertising companies in the legal community. ● *Law News Digest*, weekly. Journal. Includes breaking news, timely features, and information important to the justice system and their practice. **Price:** free. Alternate Formats: online ● *Trial*, monthly. Magazine. Brings readers news of the latest legal trends and developments. **Advertising:** accepted. Alternate Formats: online ● Membership Directory, annual. Alternate Formats: online. **Conventions/Meetings:** semiannual convention (exhibits) - 2008 July 12-16, Philadelphia, PA; 2009 Feb. 7-11, New Orleans, LA; 2009 July 11-15, San Diego, CA; 2010 Jan. 30-Feb. 3, Maui, HI.

6329 ■ American Board of Trial Advocates (ABOTA)
2001 Bryan St., Bryan Tower, Ste.3000
Dallas, TX 75201-3078
Ph: (214)871-7523
Free: (800)932-2682
Fax: (214)871-6025
E-mail: national@abota.org
URL: http://www.abota.org
Contact: Mr. Brian Tyson, Exec. Dir.

Founded: 1958. **Members:** 5,805. **Membership Dues:** by invitation, $400 (annual). **Staff:** 6. **Budget:** $1,250,000. **Regional Groups:** 12. **State Groups:** 50. **Local Groups:** 90. **Description:** Civil trial plaintiff and defense attorneys. Seeks to preserve the jury system. Promotes the 7th Amendment. Fosters improvement in the ethical and technical standards of practice in the field of advocacy. Elevates the standards of integrity, honor and courtesy in the legal profession. Aids in further education and training of trial lawyers. Works for the preservation of the jury system. Improves the methods of procedure of the present trial court system. **Awards:** Chapter Activity. **Frequency:** annual. **Type:** recognition ● Masters In Trial. **Frequency:** annual. **Type:** recognition ● Media. **Frequency:** annual. **Type:** recognition ● Thomas Jefferson. **Frequency:** annual. **Type:** recognition. **Computer Services:** database. **Publications:** *President's Report*, quarterly. Newsletter. Contains local, state and national news and activities. **Price:** $30.00 for nonmembers; free for members. Alternate Formats: online ● *Voir Dire*, quarterly. Magazine. Provides members with chapter and national information. **Price:** included in membership dues; $35.00 /year for nonmembers ● Directory, annual. **Conventions/Meetings:** Masters in Trial - seminar.

6330 ■ American College of Trial Lawyers (ACTL)
19900 MacArthur Blvd., Ste.610
Irvine, CA 92612-8405
Ph: (949)752-1801
Fax: (949)752-1674
E-mail: nationaloffice@actl.com
URL: http://www.actl.com
Contact: David J. Beck, Pres.

Founded: 1950. **Members:** 5,300. **Multinational. Description:** Maintains and improves the standards of trial practice, the administration of justice and the ethics of the profession. Brings together members of the profession who are qualified and who, by reason of probity and ability, will contribute to the accomplishments and good fellowship of the College. **Awards:** Emil Gumpert Award. **Frequency:** annual. **Type:** recognition. **Recipient:** for programs with principal purpose of maintaining and improving the administration of justice ● George A. Spiegelberg Award. **Frequency:** annual. **Type:** recognition. **Recipient:** to the best advocate in the National Mock Trial Competition. **Publications:** *The Bulletin*. Newsletter. Alternate Formats: online. **Conventions/Meetings:** annual meeting - 2008 Sept. 25-28, Toronto, ON, Canada; 2010 Sept. 23-26, Washington, DC.

6331 ■ International Society of Barristers (ISOB)
802 Legal Res. Bldg.
Univ. of Michigan Law School
Ann Arbor, MI 48109-1215
Ph: (734)763-0165
Fax: (734)764-8309
E-mail: reedj@umich.edu
URL: http://www.internationalsocietyofbarristers.com
Contact: John W. Reed, Admin. Sec.

Founded: 1965. **Members:** 600. **Membership Dues:** regular, $500 (annual). **Budget:** $200,000. **Description:** Encourages the continuation of advocacy under the adversary system. Seeks young lawyers to enter advocacy and preserves the right of trial by jury. **Publications:** *International Society of Barristers Quarterly*. Journal. Contains articles, essays, and speeches covering trial lawyers and the litigation process. Includes illustrated membership roster. **Price:** included in membership dues; $10.00 /year for nonmembers. ISSN: 0020-8752. **Circulation:** 800. Alternate Formats: microform; online. **Conventions/Meetings:** annual board meeting and convention - 2009 Mar. 15-21, Scottsdale, AZ.

6332 ■ ITC Trial Lawyers Association (ITCTLA)
PO Box 6186
Benjamin Franklin Sta.
Washington, DC 20004
Ph: (202)429-3770
Fax: (202)857-7929
E-mail: admin@itctla.org
URL: http://www.itctla.org
Contact: Alice Kipel, Pres.

Founded: 1984. **Members:** 350. **Membership Dues:** non-government attorney, $75 (annual) ● U.S. government attorney, student, $25 (annual). **Budget:** $12,000. **Description:** Active members are lawyers in good standing with the bar of any state or the District of Columbia who have an interest in practice before the International Trade Commission; associate members are lawyers who are authorized to practice before a foreign court or agency in matters relating to the ITC or who otherwise have an interest in practice before the ITC. Disseminates information and facilitates communication among lawyers, the business community, and government bodies regarding Section 337 of the Omnibus Trade and Competitiveness Act of 1988. (Section 337 deals with cases brought before the ITC against imports that are alleged to be unfair because they violate U.S. intellectual property rights.). **Committees:** Amicus; International Affairs; ITC - Bar Liaison; Judicial Selection; Legislation; Professional Responsibility; Regulations. **Councils:** House. **Also Known As:** International Trade Commission Trial Lawyers Association. **Publications:** *337 Reporter*, 10/year. Newsletter. **Conventions/Meetings:** annual meeting - always fall ● periodic meeting - usually late spring.

6333 ■ National Board of Trial Advocacy (NBTA)
200 Stonewall Blvd., Ste.1
Wrentham, MA 02093-2210
Ph: (508)384-6565
Free: (866)384-6565
Fax: (508)384-8022
E-mail: rhugus@nbtanet.org
URL: http://www.nbtanet.org
Contact: Roberta Hugus, Exec. Dir.
Founded: 1977. **Members:** 2,100. **Membership Dues:** board certification, $725. **Staff:** 5. **Description:** Represents lawyers, judges, and educators. Improves the quality of trial advocacy and public access to trial advocates of demonstrated competence. Conducts National Certification of Family Law, Criminal and Civil Trial Advocates Program. Provides referral service for legal counsel. **Awards:** Theodore I. Koskoff Award. **Type:** recognition. **Recipient:** for commitment and proven enhancements to trial law and specialty certification. **Computer Services:** Mailing lists, for a fee with management approval. **Affiliated With:** American Academy of Matrimonial Lawyers; American Association for Justice; Federation of Defense and Corporate Counsel; Inner Circle of Advocates; International Academy of Trial Lawyers; International Association of Defense Counsel; International Society of Barristers; National Association of Criminal Defense Lawyers; National Association of Women Lawyers; National District Attorneys Association. **Publications:** *National Board of Trial Advocacy Membership Directory*, annual. **Price:** free. **Circulation:** 10,000. **Advertising:** accepted ● Brochures. **Conventions/Meetings:** semiannual board meeting.

6334 ■ National Institute for Trial Advocacy (NITA)
361 Centennial Pkwy., Ste.220
Louisville, CO 80027
Free: (800)225-6482
E-mail: lrose@nita.org
URL: http://www.nita.org
Contact: Lonny Rose, CEO
Founded: 1971. **Staff:** 60. **Description:** Represents the interests of lawyers and judges dedicated to improvement of the trial bar in the U.S. Trains lawyers in trial advocacy skills; develops methods for teaching and learning such skills in law schools and in continuing education programs. Sponsors regional training programs featuring student performance in a courtroom atmosphere augmented by team teaching, videotape review of the students' performances, demonstrations and lectures. Produces textbooks, audio and video tapes used by practitioners and law school students. **Publications:** *Law School Catalog*, annual. Contains complete listing of publications available to law school professors. ● *NITA Notes*, monthly. Newsletter. Contains information about NITA's new initiatives, programs, publications, and faculty. Alternate Formats: online ● Catalog, semiannual. Contains complete listing of seasonal CLE programming and publications.

6335 ■ Pound Civil Justice Institute
1054 31st St. NW, Ste.260
Washington, DC 20007-4453
Ph: (202)965-3500
Free: (800)424-2725
Fax: (202)342-0298
E-mail: pound@roscoepound.org
URL: http://www.roscoepound.org
Contact: Lajuan H. Campbell, Membership and Development Coor.
Founded: 1956. **Members:** 1,500. **Membership Dues:** associate fellow, $95 (annual) ● fellow, $145 (annual) ● sustaining fellow, $250 (annual) ● supporting fellow, $500 (annual) ● corporate fellow, $1,000 (annual). **Staff:** 4. **Budget:** $500,000. **Description:** Conducts research and educational activities. Supports the improvement and development of a more qualified trial bar, the better functioning of the adversary and jury system of trial and making the law more viable in meeting the needs of individual citizens in a modern, democratic society. Sponsors roundtables, forums and publications on civil law and social issues. **Awards:** Elaine Osborne Jacobson Scholarship. **Frequency:** annual. **Type:** scholarship. **Recipient:** to a woman law student who is committed to a career in health care law, working to support women, children, the elderly and the disabled ● Richard S. Jacobson Award. **Frequency:** annual. **Type:** grant. **Recipient:** to a full-time law professor for excellence in teaching trial advocacy ● Roscoe Hogan Environmental Law Essay Contest. **Frequency:** annual. **Type:** scholarship. **Recipient:** for an outstanding essay by a law student in the area of environmental law. **Formerly:** (1946) Roscoe Pound-NACCA Foundation; (1987) Roscoe Pound-American Trial Lawyers Foundation; (2000) Roscoe Pound Foundation; (2006) Roscoe Pound Institute. **Publications:** *Civil Justice Digest*, quarterly. Newsletter. Provides information for judges and academics. **Price:** free. Alternate Formats: online ● *Judges' Forum Reports*, annual. Contains papers presented at the respective Forum for State Appellate Court Judges and comments of judges who attended the Forum. ● *Papers of the Roscoe Pound Foundation*, periodic. **Conventions/Meetings:** annual Forum for State Court Judges - conference, forum for invited state court judges to discuss issues of legal and social importance to the U.S. judiciary ● annual meeting ● periodic roundtable, small group discussion among professionals.

Utilities

6336 ■ American Public Power Association (APPA)
2301 M St. NW
Washington, DC 20037-1427
Ph: (202)467-2900
Fax: (202)467-2910
E-mail: mrufe@appanet.org
URL: http://www.APPAnet.org
Contact: Terry J. Huval, Chair
Founded: 1940. **Members:** 2,000. **Membership Dues:** regular, $500 (annual) ● corporate associate, federal service contract, $3,000 (annual) ● private energy associate, $5,500 (annual) ● individual associate, $750 (annual) ● international associate, $1,500 (annual) ● government associate, $1,000 (annual). **Staff:** 60. **Description:** Municipally owned electric utilities, public utility districts, state and county-owned electric systems, and rural cooperatives. Conducts research programs; compiles statistics; offers utility education courses; sponsors competitions. **Libraries: Type:** reference. **Holdings:** 6,000. **Subjects:** the electric power industry, consumer affairs. **Committees:** Public Ownership of Electric Resources Political Action. **Sections:** Accounting Finance Rates and Information Systems; Energy/Customer Services and Communications; Engineering and Operations; Legal; Policy. **Publications:** *Annual Directory and Statistical Report*, annual. **Price:** $50.00 for members (first copy free for members); $125.00 for nonmembers ● *Public Power*, bimonthly. Magazine. Includes annual directory. **Advertising:** accepted. Alternate Formats: online ● *Public Power Weekly*. Newsletter. Alternate Formats: online ● Booklets ● Manuals ● Papers ● Surveys. **Conventions/Meetings:** annual meeting ● annual Engineering and Operations Technical Conference (exhibits) - 2008 June 21-25, New Orleans, LA; 2009 June 13-17, Salt Lake City, UT; 2010 June 20-23, Orlando, FL.

6337 ■ Association of Boards of Certification (ABC)
208 5th St.
Ames, IA 50010-6259
Ph: (515)232-3623
Fax: (515)232-3778
E-mail: abc@abccert.org
URL: http://www.abccert.org
Contact: Stephen W. Ballou, Exec. Dir.
Founded: 1972. **Members:** 87. **Membership Dues:** associate, $250 (annual) ● regular (1-500 persons certified), $300-$900 (annual) ● regular (501 to over 2001 persons certified), $1,200-$1,800 (annual). **Staff:** 9. **Description:** Governmental certification authorities for environmental control operating personnel and laboratory analysts. Seeks to strengthen state certification laws, their administration and effectiveness, and to establish uniform certification requirements among members. Promotes certification as a means to more efficient operation of public utilities; assists newly created boards in implementing certification programs. Conducts ABC Certification Program for certification of operators. **Computer Services:** database ● online services, testing. **Formerly:** (1982) Association of Boards of Certification for Operating Personnel in Water and Wastewater Utilities; (1986) Association of Boards of Certification for Operating Personnel. **Publications:** *ABC At A Glance*. Brochure. Contains information about membership and services offered by ABC. ● *The Certifier*, bimonthly. Newsletter. **Price:** included in membership dues; $30.00 for nonmembers ● *The Directory*, annual. Membership Directory. Lists state and provincial certification contacts in the fields of water, wastewater, and industrial waste treatment. **Price:** included in membership dues ● Also publishes certification tests, job analyses, and certification program standards. **Conventions/Meetings:** annual conference and workshop (exhibits) - usually late January ● semiannual meeting - always June and October.

6338 ■ International Utilities Revenue Protection Association (IUPRA)
c/o Jeff Cornelius, Chm.
PO Box 1310
Wauchula, FL 33873
Free: (800)282-3824
Fax: (863)773-3737
E-mail: jeff.cornelius@preco.coop
URL: http://iurpa.org
Contact: Jeff Cornelius, Chm.
Founded: 1990. **Membership Dues:** regular, $50 (annual). **Multinational. Description:** Represents revenue protection professionals dedicated to reducing revenue loss in the utility industry. Works to identify measures to protect companies from revenue losses associated with unauthorized use of service. Addresses the need for revenue protection, with primary focus on issues that deal with energy theft. Collects data from utilities around the world regarding their revenue protection programs. **Publications:** Newsletter.

6339 ■ National Association of Regulatory Utility Commissioners (NARUC)
1101 Vermont NW, Ste.200
Washington, DC 20005-3553
Ph: (202)898-2200 (202)898-2208
Fax: (202)898-2213
E-mail: admin@naruc.org
URL: http://www.naruc.org
Contact: Charles D. Gray, Exec. Dir.
Founded: 1889. **Members:** 409. **Staff:** 15. **Budget:** $2,200,000. **Regional Groups:** 5. **Description:** Represents public utility commissioners having jurisdiction over public utilities in the areas of gas, electricity, telecommunications and water. Aims to serve the consumer interest by working to improve the quality and effectiveness of regulation of public utilities. Works to: advance commission regulation through examination and discussion of subjects dealing with the operation and supervision of public utilities; promote uniformity of regulation of public utilities; foster coordinated action by regulatory commissions to protect the public interest. **Computer Services:** Online services, forum. **Committees:** Consumer Affairs; Electricity; Energy Resources and the Environment; Gas; International Relations; Telecommunications; Washington Action; Water. **Formerly:** (1918) National Association of Railway Commissioners;

(1923) National Association of Railway and Utilities Commissioners. **Publications:** *Bell Operating Companies Exchange Service Telephone Rates*, annual. Report. **Price:** $47.50 ● *Bell Operating Companies Long Distance Message Telephone Rates*, annual. Report. **Price:** $48.00/copy ● *Committee Reports*, annual ● *Directory of Communications Professionals*, annual. **Price:** $30.00 ● *Directory of Energy Professionals*, annual. **Price:** $40.00 ● *Executive Director Reports*, annual ● *NARUC Bulletin Service*, weekly. Newsletter. **Price:** $110.00 ● *NARUC Members and Governance*, quarterly. Report. **Price:** $20.00 ● *NARUC Members, Committees, Policy*, quarterly. Booklet. **Price:** $10.00 ● *National Association of Regulatory Utility Commissioners—Bulletin*, weekly. Reports on regulatory agency and court decisions, Congressional legislative matters, and other significant events. **Price:** $110.00/year ● *National Association of Regulatory Utility Commissioners—Proceedings*, annual. **Price:** $40.00/copy ● *Profiles of Regulatory Agencies of the U.S. and Canada*, annual. Yearbook. **Price:** $50.00 ● *Residential Electric Bills*, annual. Report. **Price:** $32.50 ● *Residential Gas Bills*, annual. Report. **Price:** $32.50 ● *Status of Competition in Intrastate Telecommunications*, annual. Report. **Price:** $40.00 ● Reports. **Conventions/Meetings:** annual convention (exhibits) - 2008 Nov. 16-19, New Orleans, LA; 2009 Nov. 15-18, Chicago, IL; 2010 Nov. 14-17, Atlanta, GA.

6340 ■ National Association of State Utility Consumer Advocates (NASUCA)
8380 Colesville Rd., Ste.101
Silver Spring, MD 20910-6267
Ph: (301)589-6313
Fax: (301)589-6380
E-mail: nasuca@nasuca.org
URL: http://www.nasuca.org
Contact: Charles A. Acquard, Exec. Dir.
Founded: 1979. **Members:** 44. **Staff:** 2. **Description:** Represents 44 state designated advocates in 42 states and the District of Columbia who represent consumers before state public service commissions. Represents the consuming public before regulatory agencies that establish rates for utility services. Testifies before Congress on national regulatory practices; intervenes in regulatory matters involving federal agencies. **Committees:** Consumer Protection; Economics and Finance; Electricity; Natural Gas; Public Relations; Tax and Accounting; Telecommunications; Water. **Publications:** *NASUCA Directory*, annual. **Price:** $100.00 ● *NASUCA News*, monthly. Newsletter. **Conventions/Meetings:** annual Capitol Hill Conference - convention and meeting - held in winter or spring in Washington, DC ● annual meeting.

6341 ■ Tennessee Regulatory Authority (TRA)
460 James Robertson Pkwy.
Nashville, TN 37243-0505
Ph: (615)741-4648 (615)741-3668
Free: (800)342-8359
Fax: (615)532-4698
E-mail: jessica.johnson@state.tn.us
URL: http://www.state.tn.us/tra
Contact: Eddie Roberson PhD, Chm.
Founded: 1996. **Members:** 150. **Description:** Staff members of state and federal regulatory commissions in the U.S. and Canada. Promotes fair and effective utility regulation in the public interest. Sponsored by National Association of Regulatory Utility Commissioners (see separate entry). **Telecommunication Services:** teletype, (888)276-0677. **Affiliated With:** National Association of Regulatory Utility Commissioners. **Formerly:** Conference of Utility Commission Engineers; (1973) Conference of State Utility Commission Engineers. **Publications:** Proceedings, annual. **Conventions/Meetings:** annual conference (exhibits).

Veterans

6342 ■ American Veterans Medical Airlift Service (AVMAS)
931 Flanders Rd.
PO Box 1065
La Canada Flintridge, CA 91011
Ph: (818)952-6212
E-mail: avmas98@aol.com
Contact: John M. Stratton, Chm./CEO
Founded: 1994. **Description:** Through volunteer civilian pilots and their privately owned aircraft the association provides the U.S. Department of Veteran Affairs the capability of transporting American Veteran Patients of the Veterans Administration from home to hospital and hospital to home for care when requested by a VA Medical Center. **Publications:** *The AMVAS Reporter*.

6343 ■ Federal Employees Veterans Association (FEVA)
PO Box 183
Merion Station, PA 19066
Contact: Lester Harris III, Exec. Off.
Founded: 1950. **Members:** 12,842. **Description:** Federal government employees who have veterans' preference in federal employment under the G. I. Bill. Works to maintain and increase veterans' preference in federal employment and prevent "the discrimination against the veteran that was rampant in federal agencies in the post-World War II era.". **Awards: Type:** recognition. **Conventions/Meetings:** annual meeting - always Washington, DC.

6344 ■ Korean War Project
PO Box 180190
Dallas, TX 75218-0190
Ph: (214)320-0342
E-mail: hbarker@kwp.org
URL: http://www.koreanwar.org
Contact: Hal Barker, Founder
Founded: 1979. **Members:** 4,195. **Membership Dues:** regular, $15 (annual). **Description:** Provides support to veterans of the Korean War and their families. **Libraries: Type:** reference. **Holdings:** books. **Telecommunication Services:** electronic bulletin board, Air Force ● electronic bulletin board, Army ● electronic bulletin board, Marine ● electronic bulletin board, Navy ● electronic bulletin board, DMZ ● electronic bulletin board, UN. **Projects:** Finding The Families. **Publications:** Newsletter, periodic. Alternate Formats: online.

6345 ■ National Association of State Approving Agencies (NASAA)
c/o Joan L. Ryan, Pres.
Dept. of Veterans' Affairs
PO Box 19432
Springfield, IL 62794-9432
Ph: (217)782-7838
E-mail: s-jlr@dva.state.il.us
URL: http://www.saavetrain.org
Contact: Joan L. Ryan, Pres.
Founded: 1947. **Members:** 65. **Regional Groups:** 4. **State Groups:** 50. **Description:** State agencies designated to administer federal law concerning approval and supervision of educational programs for military personnel, veterans, and dependents. Addresses issues of common concern to members and promotes professionalism among state approving agencies. **Awards: Type:** recognition. **Committees:** Apprenticeship and On-The-Job Training; Contract; Institutions of Higher Learning; Legislative; Military Education; Non-College Degree. **Publications:** Directory, annual ● Newsletter, quarterly. **Conventions/Meetings:** semiannual conference and workshop - always February and July.

6346 ■ National Association of State Directors of Veterans Affairs (NASDVA)
107 S West St., No. 570
Alexandria, VA 22314
Ph: (505)827-6312
Fax: (505)827-6372
E-mail: clayton.clark@state.vt.us
URL: http://www.nasdva.com
Contact: John M. Garcia, Pres.
Founded: 1946. **Members:** 55. **Membership Dues:** state director, $400 (annual). **Description:** Directors of veterans' affairs for state governments. Serves as medium for exchange of ideas among state veterans' officers. Maintains liaison with all congressionally chartered veterans' organizations. **Awards:** Melvin T. Dixon Memorial Plaque. **Type:** recognition. **Publications:** *Correspondence Guide*, periodic. Directory. **Conventions/Meetings:** annual conference.

6347 ■ National Association of Veterans' Research and Education Foundations (NAVREF)
5480 Wisconsin Ave., Ste.214
Chevy Chase, MD 20815
Ph: (301)656-5005
Fax: (301)656-5008
E-mail: navref@navref.org
URL: http://www.navref.org
Contact: Barbara F. West, Exec. Dir.
Founded: 1993. **Members:** 87. **Staff:** 3. **Budget:** $350,000. **Description:** Research foundations affiliated with VA medical centers. Works to provide educational activities for foundation directors. **Awards: Type:** recognition. **Computer Services:** database ● mailing lists ● online services. **Telecommunication Services:** electronic mail, bwest@navref.org. **Publications:** *NAVREF Up to Date*. Newsletter. **Conventions/Meetings:** annual conference - always March or April, Washington DC area ● annual convention.

6348 ■ National Organization of Veterans' Advocates (NOVA)
PO Box 65876
Washington, DC 20035-5876
Ph: (480)838-6566
E-mail: theodore.jarvi@azbar.org
URL: http://www.vetadvocates.com
Contact: Theodore C. Jarvi, Pres.
Founded: 1993. **Membership Dues:** sustaining, $400 (annual) ● associate/trial, $100 (annual) ● student, $25 (annual). **Description:** Provides representation to America's veterans and their dependents. Serves attorneys and non-attorney practitioners admitted to practice before the U.S. Court of Appeals for Veterans Claims (CAVC). Provides continuing legal education and support to individuals representing veterans.

Victims

6349 ■ National Crime Victim Bar Association (NCVBA)
2000 M St. NW, Ste.480
Washington, DC 20036
Ph: (202)467-8753
Free: (800)FYI-CALL
Fax: (202)467-8701
E-mail: victimbar@ncvc.org
URL: http://www.victimbar.org
Membership Dues: general, $245 (annual). **Description:** Provides technical support to attorneys representing crime victims in civil suits. Refers crime victims to lawyers in their local area. Increases general awareness on the availability of civil remedies for victims of crime. **Computer Services:** database, annotated summaries of civil cases ● information services, civil case resources. **Affiliated With:** National Center for Victims of Crime. **Publications:** *Civil Justice for Victims of Crime*. Brochure. Alternate Formats: online ● *Victim Advocate*, quarterly. Journal. Features articles about civil litigation involving crime victims. **Price:** $5.00.

Video

6350 ■ Law Enforcement and Emergency Services Video Association (LEVA)
PO Box 547
Midlothian, TX 76065
Ph: (972)291-5888
Fax: (972)291-5888
E-mail: president@leva.org
URL: http://www.leva.org
Contact: Susan Brinkley Krawczyk, Exec. Sec.
Members: 650. **Membership Dues:** public safety individual, $55 (annual) ● public safety organization, $150 (annual) ● associate, $70 (annual) ● corporate

sponsor, $275 (annual). **Multinational. Description:** Serves as a key resource to the global public safety community by focusing on the needs of video production and forensic imaging disciplines. Provides opportunities for professional development through quality training and informational exchange. Offers forensic video analysis training to law enforcement professionals. **Publications:** *Viewfinder*. Newsletter. Contains new product information and reviews. **Price:** included in membership dues ● Membership Directory, annual. **Price:** included in membership dues.

Vietnam Veterans

6351 ■ Private Agencies Collaborating Together (PACT)

1200 18th St. NW, Ste.350
Washington, DC 20036
Ph: (202)466-5666
Fax: (202)466-5669
E-mail: pact@pacthq.org
URL: http://www.pactworld.org
Contact: Sarah Newhall, Pres./CEO

Founded: 1971. **Description:** Represents nongovernmental organizations with an interest in political development. Promotes the establishment of a civil and just society. Provides support and assistance to local social justice initiatives; works to insure political freedom and respect for the rule of law. **Programs:** Capacity Building; Civil Society Strengthening; Community REACH HIV/AIDS; Omega Initiative. **Publications:** Annual Report, annual.

Voluntarism

6352 ■ National Association of Volunteer Programs in Local Government (NAVPLG)

c/o National Association of Counties
440 First St. NW
Washington, DC 20001
E-mail: info@navplg.org
URL: http://www.navplg.org

Membership Dues: local government individual, $20 (annual) ● local government group, $75 (annual) ● affiliate, $25 (annual). **Description:** Works to strengthen volunteer programs in local government. **Awards:** Excellence in Volunteer Management Award. **Frequency:** annual. **Type:** recognition. **Recipient:** to an administrator of a volunteer program in local government ● Innovative Program Award. **Frequency:** annual. **Type:** recognition. **Recipient:** to an outstanding local government program, for the creation and implementation of a program service. **Affiliated With:** National Association of Counties. **Publications:** *Plug into Your Peer Network*, quarterly. Newsletter. **Price:** included in membership dues. Alternate Formats: online. **Conventions/Meetings:** annual conference.

Waste

6353 ■ Association of State and Territorial Solid Waste Management Officials (ASTSWMO)

444 N Capitol St. NW, Ste.315
Washington, DC 20001
Ph: (202)624-5828 (202)624-5351
Fax: (202)624-7875
E-mail: swmtjk@sso.org
URL: http://www.astswmo.org
Contact: Thomas Kennedy, Exec. Dir.

Founded: 1974. **Members:** 56. **Staff:** 9. **Budget:** $2,400,000. **Description:** Represents state solid and hazardous waste directors. Works in close coordination with the Environmental Protection Agency to develop and advance positive programs in the management of all solid wastes by promoting uniform regulation and enforcement of pertinent laws and federal regulations at all levels of government. Disseminates information on technology and management techniques among and between states; conducts timely studies and analyses of critical issues; assists in the training of state employees in key areas of waste management. Compiles statistics. Membership and services limited to State program offices. **Telecommunication Services:** electronic mail, daniar@sso.org. **Committees:** CERCLA; Federal Facilities; Hazardous Waste; Training and Informational Exchange. **Subcommittees:** Tanks. **Publications:** Surveys. **Conventions/Meetings:** semiannual conference - October/April ● workshop, for training.

6354 ■ Municipal Waste Management Association (MWMA)

1620 Eye St. NW, Ste.600
Washington, DC 20006
Ph: (202)861-6775 (202)861-6760
Fax: (215)686-7812
E-mail: jsheahan@usmayors.org
URL: http://www.usmayors.org/uscm/mwma
Contact: Judy Sheahan, Asst. Exec. Dir.

Founded: 1982. **Members:** 285. **Membership Dues:** active - minimum (based on population), $510 (annual) ● active - maximum (based on population), $6,120 (annual) ● associate (based on number of employees), $310-$1,020 (annual). **Staff:** 3. **Budget:** $50,000. **Description:** City, county, and state governmental units, and other public authorities and agencies involved in resource recovery; associate members are interested individuals and private sector organizations including systems contractors, equipment suppliers, and consultants. Objectives are to promote the development and successful operation of resource recovery facilities and of district heating and cooling systems. Encourages development of recycling programs and urban waste energy systems whereby municipal solid waste is: processed and burned; converted into steam or electricity; sold to utilities, industry, and private users. Promotes development of thermal distribution systems utilizing urban waste energy. Acts as forum for exchange of information; offers professional and technical services; monitors related legislative activities. **Libraries: Type:** reference. **Holdings:** archival material. **Awards: Frequency:** annual. **Type:** fellowship. **Recipient:** for students selected by the Honorees to work on a specific solid waste management project ● **Frequency:** annual. **Type:** recognition. **Recipient:** for solid waste professionals (Honorees) who have made significant contributions to the development of the solid waste management field. **Telecommunication Services:** electronic mail, tfischer@usmayors.org. **Committees:** Operating Facilities; Recycling. **Affiliated With:** United States Conference of Mayors. **Publications:** *A Report to the Nation on Recycling in America's Cities: A Survey of 258 Municipal Recycling Programs* ● *America Recycles*. Video ● *Buy Recycled Paper Products Guide* ● *Changing Skylines: The Garbage Crisis*. Video ● *Directory of Associate Members*, annual ● *45 Questions and Answers About Composting* ● *Local Government Buy Recycled Technical Assistance Guide* ● *MWMA Membership Directory*, annual. Alternate Formats: online ● *MWMA Reporter*, periodic ● *National Composting Program Brochure* ● *The National "Recycling in Schools": Certification Program Application and Guidelines* ● *Office Paper Recycling Guide* ● *Public Place*, quarterly. Newsletters. **Advertising:** accepted. Alternate Formats: online ● *Recycling in America's Cities: A Summary of 163 City Recycling Programs* ● *Recycling in Schools: How to Develop Your Own Program* ● *Supply and Recycling Demand for Office Waste Paper 1990-1995* ● *U.S. Solid Waste Composting Facility Profiles Vol. I and II*. **Conventions/Meetings:** annual conference - always March, Washington, DC ● seminar.

6355 ■ Solid Waste Association of North America (SWANA)

1100 Wayne Ave., Ste.700
Silver Spring, MD 20910
Ph: (301)585-2898
Free: (800)467-9262
Fax: (301)589-7068
E-mail: info@swana.org
URL: http://www.swana.org
Contact: John H. Skinner PhD, Exec. Dir./CEO

Founded: 1961. **Members:** 7,000. **Membership Dues:** regular, $142 (annual) ● corporate, $270 (annual) ● small business, $227 (annual) ● student/retired, $59 (annual). **Staff:** 25. **Budget:** $4,000,000. **Regional Groups:** 5. **State Groups:** 46. **Local Groups:** 11. **National Groups:** 42. **Description:** Public agency officials and private corporate officials, including employees, managers of public solid waste management agencies and their manufacturers, suppliers, consultants, and contractors. Mission is to advance the practice of environmentally and economically sound municipal solid waste management in North America. Seeks to develop and promote policies to advance the mission of the Association, to provide training, continuing education and information for the practice of municipal solid waste management, and to further and encourage innovation in the field through research, development and demonstration. Sponsors programs for training. **Libraries: Type:** reference. **Holdings:** 8,000; archival material, audiovisuals, books, periodicals. **Subjects:** solid and hazardous waste management. **Awards:** Excellence Awards. **Frequency:** annual. **Type:** recognition. **Recipient:** for outstanding members and their programs that promote socially, environmentally and economically sound waste management ● Honorary Membership Award. **Frequency:** annual. **Type:** recognition. **Recipient:** for significant contributions to the field of environmental protection ● Life Member Award. **Frequency:** annual. **Type:** recognition. **Recipient:** for length of service, commitment to SWANA and its chapters, and superior commitment and service to his/her employer ● Professional Achievement Award. **Frequency:** annual. **Type:** recognition. **Recipient:** for distinguished contributions to SWANA, the individual's employing organization, and the general public ● Robert L. Lawrence Distinguished Service Award. **Frequency:** annual. **Type:** recognition. **Recipient:** to a member or nonmember who, by his or her service to the MSWM field, has demonstrated meritorious consideration ● Scholarship Awards. **Frequency:** annual. **Type:** scholarship. **Recipient:** to student members, children and grandchildren of members in good standing. **Computer Services:** Online services, information clearinghouse. **Divisions:** Collection and Transfer; Communication, Education, and Marketing; Landfill Gas Management; Landfill Management; Planning and Management; Special Waste Management; Waste Reduction, Recycling and Composting; Waste-to-Energy. **Programs:** Developing a MSW Business, Customer Service and Marketing Plan; Evaluating and Managing Privatization and MSW Management Services; Landfill Gas System Operation and Maintenance; Managing Landfill Operations; Managing MSW Collection Systems; Managing Recycling Systems; Managing Transfer Station Design and Operation; Operational Issues for Landfill Managers; Paying for Your MSW Management System; Principles of Managing Integrated MSW Collection Systems. **Formerly:** (1990) Governmental Refuse Collection and Disposal Association. **Publications:** *MSW Solutions and MSW Management*, monthly. Newsletter. Contains updates on all current news within the solid waste field. **Price:** free for members. **Advertising:** accepted. Alternate Formats: online ● Proceedings ● Brochures. Alternate Formats: online. **Conventions/Meetings:** annual International Waste-to-Energy Symposium ● annual Landfill Gas Symposium ● annual North American Waste to Energy Conference ● annual seminar ● annual WASTECON - symposium and show (exhibits) - October.

6356 ■ U.S. Composting Council (USCC)

4250 Veterans Memorial Hwy., Ste.275
Holbrook, NY 11741
Ph: (631)737-4931
Fax: (631)737-4939
E-mail: uscc@compostingcouncil.org
URL: http://www.compostingcouncil.org
Contact: Dr. Stuart Buckner, Exec. Dir.

Founded: 1990. **Members:** 275. **Membership Dues:** benefactor, $10,000 (annual) ● corporate sustaining, $5,000 (annual) ● corporate, $2,500 (annual) ● large business, $1,000 (annual) ● medium business, large government, $500 (annual) ● university, nonprofit, government, small business, $250 (annual) ● individual (non-voting), $100 (annual) ● student, $50 (annual). **Staff:** 4. **Budget:** $350,000. **State Groups:** 8. **Description:** Supports the recycling of all organic materials in the waste stream, including compostable materials from solid waste, wastewater, and agriculture that are not otherwise recycled. (Composting is a way of naturally recycling organic wastes and converting them into beneficial products that are safe to the public and the environment.) Works to improve public and market acceptance of composting processes and products; defines compost product standards; ensures that composting products are defined as "recycled" in federal, state, and local regulations and legislation; removes procedural and regulatory barriers; provides product classification and quality control for product liability and controlled use issues; and serves as an information clearinghouse. Maintains Speaker's Bureau; compiles statistics; and conducts research and educational programs. **Libraries: Type:** reference. **Holdings:** books, clippings, monographs, periodicals, video recordings. **Subjects:** composting issues. **Awards:** Hi Kellogg Award. **Frequency:** annual. **Type:** recognition. **Recipient:** for persons exhibiting excellence in the composting arena ● Outstanding Composter. **Type:** recognition ● Outstanding Researcher. **Type:** recognition ● Rufus Chaney Award. **Frequency:** annual. **Type:** recognition. **Recipient:** for excellence in the area of compost research. **Computer Services:** database, compost facility ● mailing lists. **Committees:** Information and Education; Legislative and Environmental Affairs; Marketing; Research; Standards and Practices. **Formerly:** Solid Waste Composting Council; (2000) Composting Council. **Publications:** *An Assessment of Health and Environmental Risks.* **Price:** $15.00 for members; $30.00 for nonmembers ● *Bioaerosols Associated with Composting Facilities.* **Price:** $10.00 for members; $15.00 for nonmembers ● *Biomass and Bioenergy.* **Price:** $10.00 for members; $20.00 for nonmembers ● *Compost Enhancement Guide.* **Price:** $15.00 for members; $20.00 for nonmembers ● *Compost Facility Financing Guide.* **Price:** $5.00 for members; $7.00 for nonmembers ● *Compost Facility Operating Guide.* **Price:** $75.00 for members; $125.00 for nonmembers ● *Compost Facility Planning Guide.* **Price:** $10.00 for members; $20.00 for nonmembers ● *Compost Facility RFQ/FRP Development Guide (U.S. Conference of Mayors).* **Price:** $10.00 for members; $15.00 for nonmembers ● *Compost Marketing: A Planning Guide for Local Governments (U.S. Conference of Mayors).* **Price:** $5.00 for members; $10.00 for nonmembers ● *Compost Marketing: National Composting Program.* **Price:** $5.00 for members; $7.00 for nonmembers ● *Compost Use on State Highway Applications (D.O.T.).* **Price:** $30.00 for members; $35.00 for nonmembers ● *Composting Council Cap.* **Price:** $10.00 for members; $15.00 for nonmembers ● *Composting Handbooks.* **Price:** $10.00 for members; $15.00 for nonmembers ● *Composting: "The Evolution of Recycling".* **Price:** $3.00 for members; $5.00 for nonmembers ● *Composting Thermometer.* **Price:** $3.00 for members; $5.00 for nonmembers ● *Farmer's Field Guide to Compost Production and Use.* **Price:** $6.00 for members; $10.00 for nonmembers ● *Field Guide to Compost Use.* Book. **Price:** $20.00 for members; $30.00 for nonmembers. Alternate Formats: CD-ROM ● *Landscape Architecture Specifications for Compost Utilization.* Book. **Price:** $25.00 for members; $30.00 for nonmembers. Alternate Formats: CD-ROM ● *National Backyard Composting Program.* **Price:** $150.00 for members; $200.00 for nonmembers ● *Watershed Manager's Guide to Organics: The Soil and Water Connection.* **Price:** $7.00 for members; $12.00 for nonmembers. **Conventions/Meetings:** annual conference (exhibits).

Weather Services

6357 ■ National Weather Service Employees Organization (NWSEO)
601 Pennsylvania Ave. NW, Ste.900
Washington, DC 20004
Ph: (703)293-9651
Fax: (703)293-9653
E-mail: director@nwseo.org
URL: http://www.nwseo.org
Contact: Dan Sobien, Pres.
Founded: 1976. **Members:** 1,400. **Membership Dues:** associate, $65 (annual) ● retiree, $45 (annual). **Staff:** 5. **Regional Groups:** 7. **Description:** Federal employees of the National Weather Service National Environment Satellite, Data Information Service, and the NOAA Office of General Counsel. Preserves and promotes the professionalism and excellence of weather services and support functions in the U.S. Represents members in transactions with the Department of Commerce, National Oceanic and Atmospheric Administration, National Weather Service, and other agencies concerning grievances, personnel policies and practices, and other matters. **Telecommunication Services:** electronic mail, wse.pres@nwseo.org. **Committees:** Reorganization; Weather Employees Political Action. **Publications:** *The Four Winds Flyer*, monthly. Newsletter. Alternate Formats: online ● *Four Winds Newsletter*, bimonthly. Reviews research and advances in the field and discusses government personnel policies and practices. Includes calendar of events. **Price:** included in membership dues. **Circulation:** 1,400. **Conventions/Meetings:** annual meeting.

Women

6358 ■ American Association of University Women Legal Advocacy Fund (AAUW/LAF)
1111 16th St. NW
Washington, DC 20036
Ph: (202)785-7750
Free: (800)326-AAUW
Fax: (202)463-7169
E-mail: laf@aauw.org
URL: http://www.aauw.org/laf/index.cfm
Contact: Ms. Joan C. Jupiter, Program Asst.
Founded: 1981. **Membership Dues:** member-at-large, $42 (annual) ● student affiliate-at-large, $17 (annual). **Description:** Promotes equity for women in higher education; supports discrimination lawsuits against colleges and universities; provides financial support for sex discrimination lawsuits; works to educate the university community about sex discrimination; aims to improve conditions through campus outreach; provides consulting with individuals on legal strategies, resources and potential lawsuits. **Awards:** Case Support. **Frequency:** 3/year. **Type:** monetary ● Progress in Equity Award. **Frequency:** annual. **Type:** monetary. **Recipient:** to college or university program making significant progress for women on campus. **Publications:** *LAF Update.* Newsletter. Alternate Formats: online.

6359 ■ National Foundation for Women Legislators (NFWL)
910 16th St., Ste.100
Washington, DC 20006
Ph: (202)293-3040
Fax: (202)293-5430
E-mail: nwfl@womenlegislators.org
URL: http://www.womenlegislators.org
Contact: Robin Read, Pres./CEO
Membership Dues: individual, $350 (annual) ● president (Corporate Leadership Circle), $50,000 (annual) ● senator (Corporate Leadership Circle), $35,000 (annual) ● representative (Corporate Leadership Circle), $25,000 (annual) ● governor (Corporate Leadership Circle), $15,000 (annual) ● mayor (Corporate Leadership Circle), $10,000 (annual) ● general (Corporate Leadership Circle), $5,000 (annual) ● platinum sponsor, $25,000 (annual) ● diamond sponsor, $20,000 (annual) ● gold sponsor, $15,000 (annual) ● silver sponsor, $10,000 (annual) ● elite sponsor, $5,000 (annual) ● friend of NFWL, $2,000 (annual) ● general sponsor, $1,000 (annual) ● women state legislator, $50 (annual). **Description:** Women legislators. Established to support the many programs and initiatives of the National Order of Women Legislators. **Publications:** *The Connection*, 3/year. Newsletter. **Price:** free for members. Alternate Formats: online.

6360 ■ Women in Military Service for America Memorial Foundation
Dept. 560
Washington, DC 20042-0560
Ph: (703)533-1155
Free: (800)222-2294
Fax: (703)931-4208
E-mail: hq@womensmemorial.org
URL: http://www.womensmemorial.org
Contact: Ann Marie Sharratt, Exec. Dir.
Description: Promotes the nation's first major national memorial dedicated to honoring women who have served in America's armed forces. **Libraries: Type:** reference. **Holdings:** 668; books, periodicals. **Subjects:** history of women in the military. **Awards:** LTC. Margaret L. Ellerman, USA, Ret., Scholarship. **Frequency:** annual. **Type:** scholarship ● Sarah Marjorie Kelley Scholarship. **Frequency:** annual. **Type:** scholarship. **Computer Services:** Mailing lists, ISO listing ● online services, gift shop. **Programs:** Women's Memorial's Education Outreach. **Publications:** *In Search Of.* Newsletter. **Price:** $1.50/issue. Alternate Formats: online.

6361 ■ Women's Bureau of the U.S. Department of Labor
200 Constitution Ave. NW, Rm. S-3002
Washington, DC 20210
Ph: (202)693-6710
Free: (800)827-5335
Fax: (202)693-6725
E-mail: wb-wwc@dol.gov
URL: http://www.dol.gov/wb/welcome.html
Contact: Shinae Chun, Dir.
Founded: 1920. **Staff:** 5. **Description:** Works to ensure the voices of working women are heard and their priorities represented in the public policy arena. Alerts women about their right in the workplace, proposes policies and legislation that benefit working women, researches and analyzes information about women and work and reports its findings to the President, Congress and the public.

Workers

6362 ■ Peggy Browning Fund
1818 Market St., Ste.2300
Philadelphia, PA 19103-3648
Ph: (215)665-6815
Fax: (215)564-2262
E-mail: mmoffa@peggybrowningfund.org
URL: http://www.peggybrowningfund.org
Contact: Joseph Lurie, Pres.
Description: Provides law students with work and educational experiences in the area of workers' rights. **Awards:** Summer Fellowships. **Type:** fellowship. **Recipient:** for law students. **Publications:** Newsletter. Alternate Formats: online.

Youth

6363 ■ Juvenile Justice Clearinghouse (JJC)
c/o Stephanie Bush-Baskette, Program Dir.
School of Criminology and Criminal Justice
Florida State Univ.
Bellamy Bldg., Rm. 155C
Tallahassee, FL 32306-2170
Ph: (850)644-4299
Fax: (850)644-9614
E-mail: sbushbas@garnet.acns.fsu.edu
URL: http://www.fsu.edu/~crimdo/jjclearinghouse/jjclearinghouse.html
Contact: Stephanie Bush-Baskette, Program Dir.
Founded: 1979. **Description:** Provides access to information and resources relating to juvenile justice topics. **Libraries: Type:** reference. **Computer Services:** database, abstracts ● information services, JUVJUST.

Acoustics

6364 ■ Acoustical Society of America (ASA)
2 Huntington Quadrangle, Ste.1N01
Melville, NY 11747-4505
Ph: (516)576-2360
Fax: (516)576-2377
E-mail: asa@aip.org
URL: http://asa.aip.org
Contact: Charles E. Schmid, Exec. Dir.

Founded: 1929. **Members:** 7,000. **Membership Dues:** full, $130 (annual) ● associate, $110 (annual) ● student, $45 (annual). **Staff:** 10. **Regional Groups:** 22. **Multinational. Description:** Represents physicists, engineers, psychologists, architects, neuroscientists and speech and hearing scientists covering fields of electroacoustics, ultrasonics, architectural acoustics, physiological and psychological acoustics, musical acoustics, noise, vibration control, underwater acoustics, biological response to vibration, animal bioacoustics, acoustical oceanography, speech communication, biomedical ultrasound, signal processing in acoustics and acoustical oceanography. Aims to increase and diffuse the knowledge of acoustics and to promote its practical applications. **Awards:** Distinguished Service Citation. **Frequency:** periodic. **Type:** recognition. **Recipient:** for outstanding service to the organization ● Gold Medal. **Frequency:** annual. **Type:** medal. **Recipient:** for contributions to acoustics ● Helmholtz-Rayleigh Interdisciplinary Silver Medal. **Frequency:** annual. **Type:** medal. **Recipient:** for contributions to the advancement of science, engineering or human welfare through the application of acoustic principles ● Pioneers of Underwater Acoustics Medal. **Frequency:** periodic. **Type:** medal. **Recipient:** for outstanding contributions to the science of underwater acoustics ● R. Bruce Lindsay Award. **Frequency:** annual. **Type:** recognition. **Recipient:** to an individual who is under 35 years of age and who has contributed substantially to the advancement of theoretical or applied acoustics or both ● Science Writing Award. **Frequency:** annual. **Type:** monetary. **Recipient:** for outstanding science writing in acoustics—one for a professional in acoustics and one for a journalist ● Silver Medal. **Frequency:** annual. **Type:** medal. **Recipient:** for contributions to the advancement of science, engineering or human welfare through the application of acoustic principles or through accomplishments in acoustics ● Trent-Crede Medal. **Frequency:** periodic. **Type:** medal. **Recipient:** for outstanding contributions to the science of mechanical vibration and shock ● Von Bekesy Medal. **Frequency:** periodic. **Type:** medal. **Recipient:** for outstanding contributions to the area of psychological or physiological acoustics ● Wallace Clement Sabine Medal. **Frequency:** periodic. **Type:** medal. **Recipient:** for furthering the knowledge of architectural acoustics. **Computer Services:** Electronic publishing, journal and research letters online. **Committees:** Acoustical Oceanography; Animal Bioacoustics; Architectural Acoustics; Biomedical Ultrasound/Biomedical Response to Vibration; Engineering Acoustics; Musical Acoustics; Noise; Physical Acoustics; Psychological and Physiological Acoustics; Signal Processing in Acoustics; Speech Communication; Structural Acoustics and Vibration; Underwater Acoustics. **Publications:** *JASA Express Letters*, article at a time. Papers ● *Journal of the Acoustical Society of America*, monthly. Covers basic research in all areas of acoustics. Includes subject and author indexes, book reviews, calendar of events, and chapter news. **Price:** included in membership dues; $1,425.00 /year for nonmembers. ISSN: 0001-4966. **Circulation:** 8,000. **Advertising:** accepted. Alternate Formats: microform; CD-ROM; online ● *Standards on Acoustics* ● Also publishes book reviews, references to contemporary papers in acoustics, and reviews of acoustical patents, and books on acoustics. **Conventions/Meetings:** semiannual Technical Conference (exhibits).

6365 ■ IEEE Signal Processing Society
445 Hoes Ln.
Piscataway, NJ 08854-4141
Ph: (732)562-3888
Free: (800)678-IEEE
Fax: (732)235-1627
E-mail: sp.info@ieee.org
URL: http://www.ieee.org/organizations/society/sp
Contact: Mercy Kowalczyk, Exec. Dir.

Founded: 1949. **Members:** 23,000. **Membership Dues:** regular, $27 (annual). **Staff:** 6. **Regional Groups:** 10. **Local Groups:** 71. **Description:** Promotes the theory and application of "filtering, coding, transmitting, estimating, detecting, analyzing, recognizing, synthesizing, recording, and reproducing signals by digital or analog devices or techniques". **Awards:** Best Paper Award. **Frequency:** annual. **Type:** recognition. **Recipient:** for the author of a paper of exceptional merit ● Young Author Best Paper Award. **Frequency:** annual. **Type:** recognition. **Recipient:** for the young author of a meritorious paper. **Formerly:** (1998) Signal Processing Society. **Publications:** *IEEE Signal Processing Magazine*, bimonthly. **Price:** included in membership dues. **Circulation:** 23,000. **Advertising:** accepted ● *IEEE Transactions*, monthly ● Journals ● Manuals. Alternate Formats: online. **Conventions/Meetings:** annual International Conference on Acoustics, Speech, and Signal Processing (exhibits) - always spring ● annual International Conference on Image Processing - meeting (exhibits) - fall.

6366 ■ IEEE Ultrasonics, Ferroelectrics, and Frequency Control Society
c/o IEEE Operations Center
445 Hoes Ln.
Piscataway, NJ 08854-4141
Ph: (732)981-0060
Free: (800)678-IEEE
Fax: (732)981-1721
E-mail: ieeeusa@ieee.org
URL: http://www.ieee-uffc.org
Contact: Arthur Ballato, Pres.

Members: 2,352. **Membership Dues:** regular, $20 (annual) ● student, $10 (annual). **Budget:** $400,000. **Local Groups:** 8. **Description:** A society of the Institute of Electrical and Electronics Engineers (see separate entry). Studies and disseminates information on subjects such as: acoustics, ferroelectrics, and frequency control; design of sonic and ultrasonic devices and their uses in biomedicine, signal processing, and industry; generation, transmission, and detection of bulk and surface mechanical waves. **Awards:** Achievement Award. **Frequency:** annual. **Type:** recognition. **Recipient:** to a member in special recognition of outstanding contributions ● Distinguished Lecturer Award. **Frequency:** annual. **Type:** recognition. **Recipient:** for lecturers ● Distinguished Service Award. **Frequency:** annual. **Type:** recognition. **Recipient:** to members for long term support to the society's activities ● Ferroelectrics Recognition Award. **Frequency:** annual. **Type:** recognition. **Recipient:** to members for outstanding achievements in their scientific work as well as in promoting the Ferroelectrics community ● Outstanding Paper Award. **Frequency:** annual. **Type:** recognition. **Recipient:** to the author of a paper published in the UFFC Society ● Rayleigh Award. **Frequency:** annual. **Type:** recognition. **Recipient:** to members for meritorious service to the UFFC Society in the field of Ultrasonics. **Committees:** Awards; Education; Ferroelectrics; Ultrasonics Web. **Affiliated With:** Institute of Electrical and Electronics Engineers. **Formerly:** IEEE Sonics and Ultrasonics Society. **Publications:** *Transactions on Ultrasonics, Ferroelectrics, and Frequency Control*, bimonthly. Journal. **Price:** included in membership dues. ISSN: 0885-3010. Alternate Formats: online ● Newsletter. **Price:** included in membership dues. Alternate Formats: online ● Papers ● Proceedings. Alternate Formats: online. **Conventions/Meetings:** annual conference (exhibits) ● annual Frequency Control Symposium ● biennial International Symposium on the Application of Ferroelectrics ● annual Ultrasonics Symposium.

Aerospace

6367 ■ Aerospace Electrical Society (AES)
18231 Fernando Cir.
Villa Park, CA 92861
Ph: (714)538-1002
Fax: (714)538-1002
Contact: Lloyd P. Appelman, Pres.

Founded: 1941. **Members:** 250. **Staff:** 9. **Regional Groups:** 3. **State Groups:** 2. **Description:** Technicians, engineers, and management personnel engaged in the development and use of electrical and electronic equipment and systems for air and space craft. **Committees:** Education; Youth Science. **Formerly:** (1960) Aircraft Electrical Society. **Publica-**

tions: *News & Views*, monthly. Newsletter. **Conventions/Meetings:** monthly board meeting (exhibits).

6368 ■ American Astronautical Society (AAS)

6352 Rolling Mill Pl., Ste.102
Springfield, VA 22152-2354
Ph: (703)866-0020
Fax: (703)866-3526
E-mail: aas@astronautical.org
URL: http://www.astronautical.org
Contact: James R. Kirkpatrick, Exec. Dir.

Founded: 1954. **Members:** 1,400. **Membership Dues:** individual, affiliate, $85 (annual) ● student, teacher, retired, $35 (annual) ● fellow, senior, $100 (annual). **Staff:** 2. **Budget:** $400,000. **Regional Groups:** 4. **Multinational. Description:** Network of space professionals, technical and non-technical. Researchers, scientists, executives, educators, and other professionals in the field of astronautics and related areas. Promotes and supports research related to the development of astronautical sciences. Offers scholarships. Participates in student science fairs. **Awards: Frequency:** annual. **Type:** recognition. **Recipient:** for space and flight achievements. **Committees:** Science; Technology; Utilization of Space. **Affiliated With:** American Association for the Advancement of Science; International Astronautical Federation. **Publications:** *AAS History Series: A Supplement to Advances in the Astronautical Sciences*, periodic. Proceedings. From symposia of the International Academy of Astronautics. ISSN: 0730-3564 ● *Advances in the Astronautical Sciences*, periodic. Proceedings. Contents derived from major society conferences. **Price:** $50.00. Alternate Formats: CD-ROM ● *American Astronautical Society—Science and Technology Series: A Supplement to Advances in the Astronautical Sciences*, periodic. Monograph. ISSN: 0278-4017 ● *Journal of the Astronautical Sciences*, quarterly. Covers the science and technology of astronautics. Includes annual index and book reviews. **Price:** included in membership dues; $155.00 /year for nonmembers in U.S.; $170.00 /year for nonmembers outside U.S. ISSN: 0021-9142. **Circulation:** 1,800. Alternate Formats: microform ● *Space Times*, bimonthly. Magazine. Features articles about developments in the commercial space arena, military defense issues, and problems and solutions for space exploration. **Price:** included in membership dues; $80.00 /year for nonmembers in U.S.; $90.00 /year for nonmembers outside U.S. **Circulation:** 1,700. **Advertising:** accepted. **Conventions/Meetings:** annual Goddard Memorial Symposium - always March ● annual National Conference - always November.

6369 ■ American Institute of Aeronautics and Astronautics (AIAA)

1801 Alexander Bell Dr., Ste.500
Reston, VA 20191-4344
Ph: (703)264-7500
Free: (800)NEW-AIAA
Fax: (703)264-7551
E-mail: custserv@aiaa.org
URL: http://www.aiaa.org
Contact: Dr. Paul D. Nielsen, Pres.

Founded: 1963. **Members:** 41,000. **Membership Dues:** student, $20 (annual) ● associate, professional, and senior, $85 (annual) ● life, $1,275 ● young professional, spouse, $42 (annual). **Staff:** 127. **Budget:** $15,000,000. **Regional Groups:** 6. **Local Groups:** 65. **Multinational. Description:** Represents scientists and engineers in the field of aeronautics and astronautics. Facilitates interchange of technological information through publications and technical meetings in order to foster overall technical progress in the field and increase the professional competence of members. Operates Public Policy program to provide federal decision-makers with the technical information and policy guidance needed to make effective policy on aerospace issues. Public Policy program activities include congressional testimony, position papers, section public policy activities, and workshops. Offers placement assistance; compiles statistics; offers educational programs. Provides abstracting services through its AIAA Access. **Libraries: Type:** reference. **Awards:** Certificate of Merit Award. **Frequency:** monthly. **Type:** recognition ● Distinguished Lectureship Award. **Type:** recognition ● Education Award. **Frequency:** annual. **Type:** recognition ● Goddard Astronautics Award. **Type:** recognition ● International Award. **Frequency:** annual. **Type:** recognition ● Publication Award. **Type:** recognition ● Reed Aeronautics Award. **Frequency:** annual. **Type:** recognition ● Section Award. **Type:** recognition ● Service Award. **Frequency:** annual. **Type:** recognition ● Technical Award. **Type:** recognition. **Formed by Merger of:** American Rocket Society; Institute of the Aerospace Sciences. **Publications:** *AAIA Bulletin*, monthly. Newsletter. Features calendar of events, employment listings, and new product information. **Price:** included in membership dues; free to qualified aerospace engineers; $75.00 /year for nonmembers. ISSN: 0740-722X. **Circulation:** 65,000 ● *Aerospace America*, monthly. Magazine. Covers aeronautics and space technology with special attention to aerospace defense, design, and electronics. **Price:** free for members; $163.00 for nonmembers in U.S.; $200.00 for nonmembers outside U.S. ISSN: 0740-722X. **Circulation:** 65,000. **Advertising:** accepted ● *AIAA Education Series* ● *AIAA Journal*, monthly. Covers new theoretical developments and experimental results on aeroacoustics, aerodynamics, combustion, and fundamentals of propulsion. **Price:** $75.00 /year for members in U.S.; $1,500.00 /year for nonmembers and institutions in U.S.; $135.00 /year for members outside U.S.; $1,640.00 /year for nonmembers and institutions outside U.S. ISSN: 0001-1452. **Circulation:** 5,000. Alternate Formats: microform ● *AIAA Student Journal*, quarterly. Magazine. Covers engineering trends, career development, placement opportunities, interviewing techniques, continuing education, and curricula. **Price:** free for members; $25.00 for nonmembers. ISSN: 0001-1460. **Circulation:** 8,000. **Advertising:** accepted ● *International Aerospace Abstracts*, monthly. Journal. Covers literature in aeronautics, astronautics, space science, and areas of related technologies and applied engineering. **Price:** $1,380.00/year. ISSN: 0020-5842. Alternate Formats: online ● *Journal of Aircraft*, bimonthly. Covers advances in and the use of aircraft. Topics include aircraft design, flight safety, air traffic control and computer application. **Price:** $65.00 /year for members in U.S.; $840.00 /year for nonmembers and institutions in U.S.; $95.00 /year for members outside U.S.; $910.00 /year for nonmembers and institutions outside U.S. ISSN: 0021-8669. **Circulation:** 3,400. Alternate Formats: microform ● *Journal of Guidance, Control, and Dynamics*, bimonthly. Covers dynamics, stability, guidance, control, navigation, optimization, electronics, avionics, and information processing related to marine systems. **Price:** $65.00 /year for members in U.S.; $840.00 /year for nonmembers and institutions in U.S.; $95.00 /year for members outside U.S.; $910.00 /year for nonmembers and institutions outside U.S. ISSN: 0731-5090. **Circulation:** 3,200. Alternate Formats: microform ● *Journal of Propulsion and Power*, bimonthly. Covers aerospace propulsion and power topics including airbreathing, electric, and exotic propulsion, and solid and liquid rockets. **Price:** $55.00 /year for members in U.S.; $910.00 /year for nonmembers and institutions in U.S.; $85.00 /year for members outside U.S.; $980.00 /year for nonmembers and institutions outside U.S. ISSN: 0748-4658. **Circulation:** 2,200. Alternate Formats: microform ● *Journal of Spacecraft and Rockets*, bimonthly. Covers the science and technology of spacecraft and missile systems and their associated missions and performance. **Price:** $55.00 /year for members in U.S.; $780.00 /year for nonmembers and institutions in U.S.; $85.00 /year for members outside U.S.; $850.00 /year for nonmembers and institutions outside U.S. ISSN: 0022-4650. **Circulation:** 3,400. Alternate Formats: microform ● *Journal of Thermophysics and Heat Transfer*, quarterly. Covers the properties and mechanisms of thermal energy transfer in gases, liquids, and solids including conductive, convective, and radiative models. **Price:** $50.00 /year for members in U.S.; $660.00 /year for nonmembers and institutions in U.S.; $70.00 /year for members outside U.S.; $710.00 /year for nonmembers and institutions outside U.S. ISSN: 0887-8722. **Circulation:** 1,400. Alternate Formats: microform ● *Progress in Astronautics and Aeronautics Series*. **Price:** $69.95 for members; $99.95 for nonmembers ● *Roster*, biennial. Membership Directory. **Price:** $39.95 for members; $79.95 for nonmembers ● Reports ● Also publishes career and educational information. **Conventions/Meetings:** annual Aerospace Sciences Meeting and Exhibit - meeting and conference (exhibits) ● annual Global Air and Space - conference, covers technical information (exhibits) ● annual Guidance, Navigation and Control - conference (exhibits) ● biennial International Communications Satellite Systems Conference (exhibits) ● annual Joint Propulsion Conference (exhibits) ● Life Sciences and Space Medicine Conference, covers technical information (exhibits) ● annual Space - conference (exhibits) ● annual Structures, Structural Dynamics, and Materials Conference (exhibits).

6370 ■ Association for Aviation Psychology (AAP)

c/o Lori McDonnell, Membership Service Coor.
NASA Ames Res. Center
Mail Stop 262-4
Moffett Field, CA 94035
Fax: (650)604-3729
E-mail: ahobbs@mail.arc.nasa.gov
URL: http://avpsych.org
Contact: Alan Hobbs, Pres.

Founded: 1960. **Members:** 350. **Membership Dues:** individual, $40 (annual). **Description:** Represents behavioral scientists who are employed or interested in the field of aviation psychology or related fields dealing with human factors in aviation; includes psychologists, engineers, physiologists, education specialists, sociologists, and statisticians employed by the federal government, universities, commercial airlines, industry, and the armed forces. Promotes aviation psychology and related aerospace and environmental disciplines through information exchange, meetings, stimulation of educational and research interest in the field, and application of psychological principles and research to problems in aviation. **Awards: Frequency:** annual. **Type:** grant. **Recipient:** to graduate students. **Publications:** *International Journal of Aviation Psychology*, quarterly. Includes papers and proceedings of the meeting. **Price:** included in membership dues ● Membership Directory, annual ● Newsletter, quarterly. Includes issues and events. Alternate Formats: online. **Conventions/Meetings:** biennial International Symposium on Aviation Psychology ● annual meeting.

6371 ■ Association of Space Explorers - U.S.A. (ASE-USA)

1150 Gemini Ave.
Houston, TX 77058
Ph: (281)280-8172
Fax: (281)280-8173
E-mail: andy@space-explorers.org
URL: http://www.space-explorers.org
Contact: Andy Turnage, Exec. Dir.

Founded: 1985. **Members:** 300. **Staff:** 1. **National Groups:** 2. **Languages:** English, Russian. **Multinational. Description:** Astronauts, cosmonauts, and other space travelers in 30 countries who have made at least 1 orbit around the earth performed in outer space. Promotes education in math, science and engineering; environmental stewardship; encourages international cooperation and space exploration for the benefit of all nations. **Awards:** Planetary Award/ Crystal Helmet. **Frequency:** annual. **Type:** recognition. **Recipient:** for significant contribution in the fields of manned space research, environmental awareness, or international cooperation. **Publications:** *Conference Proceedings*, annual. Alternate Formats: online ● *The Space Explorer*. Newsletter ● Annual Report, annual. **Price:** $5.00 ● Brochures. **Conventions/Meetings:** annual Planetary Congress.

6372 ■ Association of U.S. Members of the International Institute of Space Law (AUSMIISL)

Address Unknown since 2007

Members: 110. **Description:** National association to promote the participation of U.S. members in the International Institute of Space Law and to contribute to the solution of legal problems arising from the use and exploration of outer space. Membership is by invitation only. **Affiliated With:** International Institute of Space Law. **Conventions/Meetings:** annual meeting, held in conjunction with American Society of International Law - always spring, Washington, DC.

6373 ■ Experimental Aircraft Association (EAA)
EAA Aviation Center
PO Box 3086
Oshkosh, WI 54903-3086
Ph: (920)426-4800
Free: (800)843-3612
Fax: (920)426-4873
E-mail: webmaster@eaa.org
URL: http://www.eaa.org
Contact: Tom Poberezny, Pres.
Founded: 1953. **Members:** 170,000. **Membership Dues:** individual, $40-$60 (annual) ● family, $50 (annual) ● student, $23 (annual) ● school/library, $23 (annual) ● life, $975. **Staff:** 190. **Budget:** $11,000,000. **Local Groups:** 1,000. **Multinational. Description:** Represents individuals interested in sport and recreational flying. Seeks to make aviation accessible to all who wish to participate. Consists of members with a wide range of aviation interests and backgrounds. Offers the opportunity to make new aviation friends and form relationships while encouraging the sharing of information, stories and enthusiasm. **Libraries: Type:** reference. **Holdings:** 25,000; archival material, books, clippings, periodicals, photographs, video recordings. **Subjects:** aviation history and building. **Divisions:** International Aerobatic Club; Vintage Aircraft Association; Warbirds of America. **Affiliated With:** National Association of Flight Instructors. **Publications:** *Sport Aviation Magazine*, monthly. Monograph. Contains articles and features dealing with recreational aviation. **Circulation:** 150,000. **Advertising:** accepted ● *Sport Pilot and Light Sport Aircraft*, monthly. Magazine. Provides technical and how-to information on building light aircraft from kits or as homebuilts. Includes calendar of events. ISSN: 0894-1289. **Circulation:** 18,000. **Advertising:** accepted ● *Vintage Airplane*, monthly. Magazine. Concerned with the restoration, maintenance, and flying of antique and classic aircraft built from 1945-55. Includes calendar of events. **Price:** included in membership dues; $35.00 /year for nonmembers. ISSN: 0091-6943. **Circulation:** 8,000. **Advertising:** accepted ● *Warbirds*, 8/year. Magazine. Covers the restoration, maintenance, and flying of military aircraft built from World War II to the present; includes historical information. **Price:** included in membership dues. ISSN: 0744-6624. **Circulation:** 6,000. **Advertising:** accepted ● Manuals. Covers wood aircraft construction and aircraft welding. ● Also publishes historical series on museum aircraft. **Conventions/Meetings:** annual Air Venture Oshkosh - convention, world's largest sport aviation gathering with more than 750,000 people and 10,000 airplanes (exhibits).

6374 ■ High Frontier (HF)
500 N Washington St.
Alexandria, VA 22314-2314
Ph: (703)535-8774
Fax: (703)535-8776
E-mail: high.frontier@verizon.net
URL: http://www.highfrontier.org
Contact: Ambassador Henry F. Cooper, Chm.
Founded: 1982. **Staff:** 15. **Description:** Represents scientists, space engineers, strategists and economists. Advocates the use of outer space for non nuclear commercial and military purposes. Seeks to open space for both economic and defensive military uses by the U.S. and its allies. Aims to provide protection for Americans and their property. The group advocates use of equipment currently in development. Maintains Speaker's Bureau; sponsors educational programs. Has produced High Frontier: A New National Strategy (television documentary show). **Publications:** *A Defense That Defends*. Video ● *A Defense That Defends: Blocking Nuclear Attacks*. Book ● *High Frontier: A Strategy for National Survival*. Book ● *One Incoming*. Film ● *The Shield*, quarterly. Newsletter. Covers space development and exploration. **Price:** $25.00/year. **Circulation:** 25,000. **Advertising:** accepted ● Brochures ● Pamphlets ● Reports.

6375 ■ International Experimental Aerospace Society (IEAS)
14870 Granada Ave., No. 316
Apple Valley, MN 55124
Ph: (952)432-3918 (952)891-4319
E-mail: cab@ieas.org
URL: http://www.ieas.org
Contact: Carl A. Blood, Pres./Treas.
Membership Dues: participating, $20 (annual) ● student, $5 (annual). **Multinational. Description:** Represents education and research societies of rocketry and space technology experimenters from around the world. Promotes experimental aerospace. Provides opportunities for exchange of information and coordination of services that will enable private individuals to safely engage in experimental aerospace activities. Assists and encourages regulatory authorities to permit safe experimental activities.

6376 ■ International Space Exploration and Colonization Company (ISECCo)
PO Box 60885
Fairbanks, AK 99706-0885
Ph: (907)488-1001
E-mail: info@isecco.org
URL: http://isecco.org
Contact: Ray R. Collins, Pres.
Founded: 1988. **Members:** 250. **Membership Dues:** interested observer, $10 (quinquennial) ● contributor, $5 (monthly) ● general, $35 (monthly) ● supporter, $100 (monthly) ● colonist, $1,000 (monthly). **Staff:** 4. **Budget:** $2,000. **Multinational. Description:** Graduate students and other interested individuals. Supports research in areas that will promote space exploration and colonization. Conducts educational programs. **Libraries: Type:** not open to the public. **Holdings:** 50; books, periodicals. **Subjects:** space. **Computer Services:** Mailing lists, meeting notices, project updates. **Study Groups:** UAF Student Chapter. **Conventions/Meetings:** semimonthly meeting ● annual Workfest and Meeting of Members, with research and construction projects - last full week in May, Friday through Sunday.

6377 ■ National Space Club (NSC)
2025 M St. NW, Ste.800
Washington, DC 20036-2422
Ph: (202)973-8661
E-mail: info@spaceclub.org
URL: http://www.spaceclub.org
Contact: Rory M. Heydon, Exec. Dir.
Founded: 1957. **Members:** 1,000. **Membership Dues:** individual, $30 (annual). **Staff:** 1. **Description:** Nontechnical organization of individuals and companies affiliated with the missile and space fields in government, industry, the military and the press. Seeks to establish and maintain U.S. space leadership and stimulate the advancement of peaceful and military applications of space flight and related technologies. Sponsors Robert H. Goddard Historical Essay Competition. **Awards:** Dr. Robert H. Goddard Scholarship. **Frequency:** annual. **Type:** scholarship. **Recipient:** for students in the aerospace field ● **Frequency:** annual. **Type:** recognition. **Computer Services:** database, corporate members. **Telecommunication Services:** electronic mail, rory@spaceclub.org. **Programs:** National Space Club Scholars; NSC Youth Education Support Campaign. **Formerly:** National Rocket Club. **Publications:** Newsletter, monthly. **Conventions/Meetings:** annual dinner ● monthly luncheon ● annual National Space Outlook Conference.

6378 ■ National Space Society (NSS)
1620 I St. NW, Ste.615
Washington, DC 20006
Ph: (202)429-1600
Fax: (202)463-8497
E-mail: nsshq@nss.org
URL: http://www.nss.org
Contact: George T. Whitesides, Exec. Dir.
Founded: 1974. **Members:** 25,000. **Membership Dues:** individual, $20 (annual) ● student, $18 (annual) ● foreign, $35 (annual) ● contributor, $50 (annual) ● pathfinder, $100 (annual) ● explorer, $250 (annual) ● pioneer, $500 (annual) ● visionary, $1,000 (annual) ● Buzz Aldrin Council, $500 (annual). **Staff:** 4. **Budget:** $1,000,000. **Multinational. Description:** Individuals dedicated "to convincing the nation and its leadership of the critical need for a growing progressive American technology for which a strong space program provides the thrust and momentum." Seeks to: provide a forum for public participation to help insure that the space program is responsive to public priorities; inspire space enthusiasts to elicit their responses to key issues on the space program; promote and create self-sustaining communities, large-scale industrialization, and private enterprise in space; support scholarships, lectureships, libraries and museums, which encourage the study of space and related technologies. Activities include tours to launches and media program to communicate the benefits of the space program to the public. Maintains Speaker's Bureau. **Libraries: Type:** reference; not open to the public. **Holdings:** articles, books, periodicals. **Subjects:** science, technology, space exploration history, aerospace industry. **Formed by Merger of:** L5 Society; National Space Institute. **Publications:** *Ad Astra*, bimonthly. Magazine. Covers national and international space exploration and development. Includes book and computer software reviews and calendar of events. **Price:** included in membership dues; $3.50/copy, for nonmembers. **Circulation:** 30,000. **Advertising:** accepted. Alternate Formats: online ● Articles ● Bibliographies ● Books. **Conventions/Meetings:** annual International Space Development Conference (exhibits) - always Memorial Day weekend.

6379 ■ Naval Airship Association (NAA)
c/o Peter F. Brouwer, Treas.
1950 SW Cycle St.
Port St. Lucie, FL 34953-1778
Ph: (772)871-9379
Fax: (772)621-8769
E-mail: treasurer@naval-airships.org
URL: http://www.naval-airships.org
Contact: Peter F. Brouwer, Treas.
Founded: 1984. **Members:** 1,300. **Membership Dues:** individual, $25 (annual). **Staff:** 4. **Description:** Active or retired military personnel; interested others. Promotes knowledge of and interest in the U.S. Navy's involvement with lighter-than-air principles in military aviation. Supports the Naval Aviation Museum Foundation and the National Museum of Naval Aviation in their efforts to educate the public on naval employment of LTA principles. Assists governmental agencies in LTA development and applications. **Libraries: Type:** open to the public. **Computer Services:** database ● mailing lists. **Publications:** *Noon Balloon*, quarterly. Newsletter. **Price:** included in membership dues. **Circulation:** 1,300. **Conventions/Meetings:** annual reunion (exhibits).

6380 ■ Negro Airmen International (NAI)
PO Box 23911
Savannah, GA 31403
Ph: (912)964-6523 (912)232-1710
E-mail: jone973@comcast.net
URL: http://www.blackwings.com
Contact: Sam Louis Jones Jr., Pres.
Founded: 1967. **Members:** 1,000. **Membership Dues:** regular/associate, $35 (annual) ● student/family, $5 (annual). **Regional Groups:** 10. **Local Groups:** 25. **Multinational. Description:** Individuals holding at least a student pilot license who are active in some phase of aviation; members include both aviation professionals and others who are qualified pilots. Seeks greater participation by blacks in the field of aviation through the encouragement of broader job opportunities; promotes awareness by government and industry of the needs, attitudes, and interests of blacks concerning aviation. Encourages black youth to remain in school and to enter the field

of aviation. Operates speakers' bureau and placement service. **Libraries: Type:** reference. **Computer Services:** database, membership and demographics. **Committees:** Equal Opportunity; Government Liaison; Grants and Scholarships; Public Education; Public Relations; Social Programs; Training and Employment. **Formerly:** Black Wings in Aviation. **Publications:** Brochures, quarterly. **Price:** free for members. **Circulation:** 900 ● Newsletter, quarterly ● Also has produced a film on flight basics for youth. **Conventions/Meetings:** annual Fly-In - meeting - always Memorial Day weekend in Tuskegee, AL ● annual meeting ● annual Skyhook - competition ● annual Summer Flight Academy for Youth - meeting - always July in Tuskegee, AL.

6381 ■ Pacific Rocket Society (PRS)

PO Box 662
Mojave, CA 93502
Ph: (661)824-1662
E-mail: cyberplex@aol.com
URL: http://www.translunar.org/prs
Contact: Randa Milliron, Treas.

Founded: 1946. **Members:** 100. **Membership Dues:** student in U.S., $15 (annual) ● student outside U.S., resident in U.S., $25 (annual) ● resident outside U.S., $35 (annual) ● life, $350. **Description:** Represents individuals interested in experimental rocketry, especially advanced concepts, designs, and testing. Encourages education and participation in the design, construction, and testing of liquid and solid propellant rockets. Assists members in design and safety techniques. Maintains speakers' bureau. **Publications:** *Pacific Rockets Quarterly*. Newsletter. **Price:** $3.00/issue. **Advertising:** accepted ● *PRS/Translunar Research International Liquid Rocket*. Video ● *PRS/Translunar Research Rocket Tests*. Video. **Conventions/Meetings:** bimonthly meeting and seminar.

6382 ■ The Planetary Society (TPS)

65 N Catalina Ave.
Pasadena, CA 91106-2301
Ph: (626)793-5100
Fax: (626)793-5528
E-mail: tps@planetary.org
URL: http://www.planetary.org
Contact: Dr. Louis Friedman, Exec. Dir.

Founded: 1980. **Members:** 100,000. **Membership Dues:** student in Canada, $25 (annual) ● regular - in U.S. and Canada, $30 (annual) ● regular - other country, $45 (annual) ● student - other country, $35 (annual) ● student and senior in U.S., $20 (annual). **Staff:** 23. **Budget:** $4,000,000. **Description:** Represents individuals "devoted to a realistic continuing program of planetary exploration and the search for extraterrestrial life." Seeks to enhance public awareness and to stimulate fundamental research. Fosters communication among interested groups and individuals in the U.S. and 100 other countries; distributes information concerning the latest findings and discoveries in the field. Sponsors exhibits and research activities. Offers education programs. **Libraries: Type:** not open to the public. **Holdings:** 600; books, periodicals. **Subjects:** astronomy, planetary science. **Awards:** Thomas O. Paine Memorial Award. **Frequency:** annual. **Type:** monetary. **Recipient:** for individuals who have advanced the goal of the human exploration of Mars. **Projects:** Mars Exploration - the Mars Microphone; NEO Research and Missions; PlanetFest; Red Rover, Red Rover; Rover Technology; Search for Extraterrestrial. **Publications:** *Bioastronomy News*, quarterly. Newsletter. **Price:** $10.00. **Circulation:** 4,000 ● *Mars Underground News*, quarterly. **Price:** $10.00 ● *NEO News*, quarterly. **Price:** $10.00 ● *Planetary Report*, bimonthly. Journal. News about planetary missions, spacefaring nations, intrepid explorers, planetary science controversies, latest findings in human exploration. **Price:** included in membership dues. ISSN: 0736-3680. **Conventions/Meetings:** conference ● biennial meeting (exhibits).

6383 ■ SAFE Association

PO Box 130
Creswell, OR 97426-0130
Ph: (541)895-3012
Fax: (541)895-3014
E-mail: safe@peak.org
URL: http://www.safeassociation.com
Contact: Jeani Benton, Admin.

Founded: 1960. **Members:** 900. **Membership Dues:** individual, $60 (annual) ● corporate, $500 (annual) ● retired, $20 (annual) ● full-time student, $10 (annual). **Staff:** 1. **Regional Groups:** 10. **Multinational. Description:** Designers, engineers, manufacturers, and users of safety and survival equipment. Conducts research; encourages dissemination of information. **Awards: Frequency:** annual. **Type:** recognition. **Recipient:** for members only. **Affiliated With:** Aerospace Medical Association; Flight Safety Foundation. **Formerly:** Space and Flight Equipment Association; (1969) Survival and Flight Equipment Association. **Publications:** *SAFE Journal*, semiannual. Includes book reviews, chapter and membership news, and new member list. **Price:** included in membership dues; $25.00 /year for nonmembers in U.S.; $30.00 /year for nonmembers outside U.S. **Circulation:** 1,000. **Advertising:** accepted ● *SAFE—Symposium Proceedings*, annual. **Price:** $27.50/copy in U.S.; $30.00/copy outside U.S. Alternate Formats: CD-ROM. **Conventions/Meetings:** annual meeting - 2008 Oct. 27-29, Reno, NV ● annual symposium (exhibits) - usually from September through December.

6384 ■ Society of Experimental Test Pilots (SETP)

PO Box 986
Lancaster, CA 93584-0986
Ph: (661)942-9574
Fax: (661)940-0398
E-mail: setp@setp.org
URL: http://www.setp.org
Contact: Paula S. Smith, Exec. Dir.

Founded: 1955. **Members:** 2,000. **Membership Dues:** life (associate), $100 ● life (associate fellow, fellow), $110. **Staff:** 5. **Budget:** $400,000. **Regional Groups:** 1. **State Groups:** 3. **Local Groups:** 1. **National Groups:** 4. **Description:** Pilots engaged in experimental developmental flight testing of aircraft, engines or associated components. Seeks to promote that part of the aeronautical endeavor, which involves the moral obligation of the test pilot to the airplane passenger and the commercial, private or service pilot without affecting the competitive structure of the industry. Sponsors the SETP Scholarship Foundation. **Libraries: Type:** reference. **Holdings:** books, periodicals. **Awards:** Herman R. Salmon Award. **Frequency:** annual. **Type:** recognition. **Recipient:** for the best technical article printed in *Quarterly Cockpit* ● Iven C. Kincheloe Outstanding Test Pilot Award. **Frequency:** annual. **Type:** recognition. **Recipient:** for outstanding professional accomplishment in the conduct of flight testing ● James H. Doolittle Award. **Frequency:** annual. **Type:** recognition. **Recipient:** for outstanding accomplishment in technical management or engineering ● Tony LeVier Flight Test Safety Award. **Frequency:** annual. **Type:** recognition. **Recipient:** for significant achievement in flight test safety. **Publications:** *Quarterly Cockpit* ● *Symposium Proceedings*, annual. **Conventions/Meetings:** annual meeting and symposium (exhibits).

6385 ■ Society of Flight Test Engineers (SFTE)

44814 N Elm Ave.
Lancaster, CA 93534
Ph: (661)949-2095
Fax: (661)949-2096
E-mail: sfte@sfte.org
URL: http://www.sfte.org
Contact: Margaret Drury, Exec. Dir.

Founded: 1968. **Members:** 948. **Membership Dues:** individual, affiliate, associate, $55 (annual) ● senior, $30 (annual) ● student, $15 (annual) ● life (depends upon the age), $400-$1,400. **Staff:** 1. **Budget:** $80,000. **Regional Groups:** 10. **Local Groups:** 2. **National Groups:** 9. **Description:** Engineers and other professionals interested in the flight testing of aircraft. Works to advance flight test engineering throughout the aircraft industry by providing technical and fraternal communication on a domestic and international basis among individuals in the allied engineering fields of test operations, analysis, instrumentation, and data systems. **Libraries: Type:** open to the public. **Holdings:** 30. **Awards:** Flight Test Engineer of the Year Award. **Frequency:** annual. **Type:** recognition. **Publications:** *Flight Test News*, monthly. Newsletter. Covers the latest flight test developments. Includes new member list. **Price:** included in membership dues; $25.00 /year for nonmembers ● *Society of Flight Test Engineers—Membership Directory*, biennial. **Price:** available to members only ● Proceedings, annual. **Conventions/Meetings:** annual symposium (exhibits) ● workshop.

6386 ■ Space Energy Association (SEA)

PO Box 1136
Clearwater, FL 33757-1136
Ph: (954)749-6553
E-mail: spaceenergy@earthlink.net
URL: http://www.keelynet.com/sea.htm
Contact: Jim Kettner, Ed.

Founded: 1990. **Members:** 275. **Staff:** 2. **Budget:** $10,000. **Regional Groups:** 1. **State Groups:** 1. **For-Profit. Description:** Promotes the study and understanding of advanced energy systems. Conducts research programs. **Convention/Meeting:** none. **Libraries: Type:** reference. **Holdings:** 3; books, business records, periodicals. **Subjects:** advanced energy systems. **Publications:** *Space Energy Journal*, quarterly. Newsletter. Covers research and development in the advanced energy field. **Price:** $35.00 /year for members; $40.00/year in Canada and Mexico; $50.00/year in other countries. **Circulation:** 275.

6387 ■ Space Settlement Studies Program (SSSP)

Address Unknown since 2007

Founded: 1977. **Members:** 1,000. **Staff:** 2. **Description:** Individuals interested in the colonization of outer space. Functions as a clearinghouse on space habitation, focusing on the social and psychological needs of people living in space. Studies the process of colonizing space and transportation to and from earth. Also conducts attitudinal studies on space habitation. Maintains speakers' bureau; compiles statistics. **Libraries: Type:** open to the public. **Holdings:** 360. **Subjects:** space colonization. **Formerly:** (1980) Center for the Studies of Human Communities in Space. **Publications:** *Extraterrestrial Society*, semiannual. Newsletter ● *Space Journal*, periodic. **Conventions/Meetings:** periodic seminar.

6388 ■ Space Studies Institute (SSI)

PO Box 82
Princeton, NJ 08542
Ph: (609)921-0377
Fax: (609)921-0389
E-mail: info@ssi.org
URL: http://www.ssi.org
Contact: Ms. Bettie Gerber, Exec. Dir.

Founded: 1977. **Members:** 5,000. **Membership Dues:** senior associate, $100 (annual) ● regular, $25 (annual) ● senior citizen, student, $15 (annual). **Staff:** 4. **Budget:** $500,000. **Description:** Represents firms, organizations and individuals supporting space research. Promotes space manufacturing research and human exploration of space. Conducts educational programs; operates speakers' bureau. **Libraries: Type:** reference. **Holdings:** books, periodicals. **Publications:** *SSI Update*, bimonthly. Newsletter. Offers current news of SSI's research efforts in making the resources of space available for human benefit. **Price:** included in membership dues. **Circulation:** 5,000 ● Articles ● Brochures. **Conventions/Meetings:** biennial conference.

6389 ■ Space Transportation Association (STA)

c/o Richard Coleman, Pres.
4305 Underwood St.
University Park, MD 20782
Ph: (703)855-3917

E-mail: rich@spacetransportation.us
URL: http://www.spacetransportation.us
Contact: Richard Coleman, Pres.

Founded: 1989. **Members:** 20. **Staff:** 9. **Budget:** $120,000. **Description:** Consists of organizations who plan to develop and use space vehicles and systems for government and private use. Seeks to develop commercial space transportation as an economically feasible and profitable activity. Encourages the development of expendable and reusable launch vehicles. Works to amend government regulations and create new regulations to protect and encourage the development of space vehicles and space transportation. Educates the government, private industry, and public about the feasibility and technology of commercial space transportation. Sponsors research studies. **Computer Services:** database. **Affiliated With:** High Frontier. **Publications:** *Space, Energy and Transportation*, quarterly. Journal. **Price:** $30.00 for individuals; $200.00 for institutions. **Advertising:** accepted ● *SpaceTrans*, monthly. Newsletter. Includes articles on new developments in space transportation. **Conventions/Meetings:** semiannual board meeting ● monthly breakfast and meeting.

6390 ■ Student Experimental Payload Program (SEP)
Address Unknown since 2007

Description: Provides launch service for student designed and constructed payloads utilizing custom built Class B Tropospheric Sounding Rockets.

6391 ■ Trans Lunar Research (TLR)
c/o Randa Milliron, Co-Founder
PO Box 661
Mojave, CA 93502-0661
Ph: (661)824-1662 (661)965-0771
E-mail: tlr@translunar.org
URL: http://www.translunar.org
Contact: Randa Milliron, Co-Founder

Founded: 1996. **Members:** 50. **Membership Dues:** regular, $35 (annual) ● full-time student, $25 (annual). **Staff:** 2. **Description:** Individuals with an interest in manned planetary exploration and lunar colonization. Promotes exploration, commercial exploitation, and colonization of space. Advocates increase emphasis on manned interplanetary travel; supports private-sector space launch vehicle development, private space station construction, and lunar base research; maintains speakers' bureau. **Affiliated With:** Pacific Rocket Society. **Publications:** *Trans Lunar Research Journal*, annual. **Price:** $5.00/copy ● Papers. Alternate Formats: online.

6392 ■ Universities Space Research Association (USRA)
10211 Wincopin Cir., Ste.500
Columbia, MD 21044-3432
Ph: (410)730-2656
Fax: (410)730-3496
E-mail: info@hq.usra.edu
URL: http://www.usra.edu
Contact: Dr. Frederick A. Tarantino, Pres.

Founded: 1969. **Members:** 97. **Membership Dues:** university, $1,200. **Regional Groups:** 9. **Description:** Represents the International consortium of universities. Fosters cooperation among universities, research organizations and the U.S. government for the advancement of space research. Charter includes provision to acquire, plan, construct and operate laboratories and other facilities for research, development and education associated with space science and technology. Unites NASA engineers and engineering students on design projects for NASA through its educational programs. **Computer Services:** database, member institutions. **Publications:** *Lunar and Planetary Information Bulletin*, 3/year. Newsletter. Disseminates information and news of research in the lunar and planetary sciences. Includes calendar of events and news of personnel changes. **Price:** free. **Circulation:** 5,400 ● *USRA Quarterly*. **Conventions/Meetings:** annual meeting - always March in Washington, DC.

6393 ■ Women in Aerospace (WIA)
2200 Wilson Blvd., No. 102-248
Arlington, VA 22201
Ph: (703)522-7745
Fax: (703)522-4226
E-mail: info@womeninaerospace.org
URL: http://www.womeninaerospace.org
Contact: Dawn Sienicki, Pres.

Founded: 1985. **Members:** 250. **Membership Dues:** individual (in public sector, government, nonprofit), $45 (annual) ● individual (student, retiree), $20 (annual) ● corporate gold, $5,000 (annual) ● corporate silver, $2,500 (annual) ● corporate bronze, $1,000 (annual) ● nonprofit, $500 (annual) ● individual (private sector, corporate), $75 (annual) ● corporate platinum, $10,000 (annual). **Description:** Women and men working in aerospace and related fields; allied organizations and businesses. Seeks to increase women's visibility as aerospace professionals and to expand their opportunities for career advancement. Provides a forum for exchange of ideas and information among members and recognition of outstanding women in the field. Assists members in meeting and maintaining contact with peers and key players in the profession. Seeks to establish a positive public attitude toward the role of women as leaders in aerospace and related fields. Strives to influence the legislative process as it affects the industry. Educates the members about current issues in aerospace. Encourages students to develop interests and abilities in the field. Maintains speakers' bureau. **Awards:** Aerospace Awareness Award. **Frequency:** annual. **Type:** recognition. **Recipient:** to individuals with excellent outreach and building aerospace awareness ● Aerospace Educator Award. **Frequency:** annual. **Type:** recognition. **Recipient:** to an excellent full time aerospace educator ● International Achievement Award. **Frequency:** annual. **Type:** recognition. **Recipient:** to individuals with noteworthy contributions to aerospace ● Leadership Award. **Frequency:** annual. **Type:** recognition. **Recipient:** to individuals with exemplary leadership abilities ● Outstanding Achievement Award. **Frequency:** annual. **Type:** recognition. **Recipient:** to individuals with contributions to a single aerospace project. **Committees:** Communications; Professional Development; Programs. **Programs:** Annual Awards. **Publications:** Newsletter. **Conventions/Meetings:** annual Awards Reception - meeting - usually September ● monthly meeting.

African-American

6394 ■ African-American Women in Technology (AAWIT)
818-2 Twin Oaks Dr.
Decatur, GA 30030
E-mail: info@aawit.net
URL: http://www.aawit.net
Contact: Monique Boea, Pres.

Membership Dues: regular, $50 (annual). **Description:** Encourages, promotes and serves the interests of African-American women in Information Technology. Helps its members advance their careers and enhance their personal development through special resources and networking opportunities. **Computer Services:** Online services, big sister network, job postings for IT.

6395 ■ NIH Black Scientists Association (NIH BSA)
PO Box 2262
Kensington, MD 20891-2262
Ph: (301)435-4568
E-mail: smithj@nei.nih.gov
URL: http://bsa.od.nih.gov
Contact: Janine Smith MD, Pres.

Members: 100. **Membership Dues:** general, $25 (annual) ● student, $15 (annual). **Description:** Scientists, physicians, technologists and science administrators at the National Institute of Health (NIH). Provides communication and dissemination of information about issues of common interest, development of important personal and professional contacts, career support and enhancement, and group advocacy on issues of importance to under-represented minorities at NIH and beyond. Maintains membership database and speakers' bureau. **Committees:** Ad Hoc; Career Development; Communications and Membership. **Publications:** Brochure. **Conventions/Meetings:** monthly meeting ● seminar and workshop.

6396 ■ Program for Research on Black Americans (PRBA)
c/o 5062 Institute for Social Research
PO Box 1248
Ann Arbor, MI 48106-1248
Ph: (734)763-0045
Fax: (734)763-0044
E-mail: prba@isr.umich.edu
URL: http://rcgd.isr.umich.edu/prba
Contact: Harold W. Neighbors, Dir.

Founded: 1976. **Staff:** 35. **Description:** Collects, analyzes, and interprets empirical data, and disseminates findings based on national and international studies of people of African-American and African descent. Provides research and training opportunities for black social scientists and students. Fosters high quality research on factors related to mental health and mental disorders among Americans of African descent. **Convention/Meeting:** none. **Libraries: Type:** reference. **Subjects:** data tapes and reprints of published materials based on program data collections. **Awards:** Distinguished Faculty Service Award. **Type:** recognition. **Publications:** *African American Research Perspectives*, semiannual. Report. **Circulation:** 4,500. Alternate Formats: online ● *Program for Research on Black Americans Newsletter*, annual. **Circulation:** 4,500 ● *Research and Training Activities of the Program for Research on Black Americans*, quarterly. Report. **Circulation:** 2,000.

Agriculture

6397 ■ International Association for the Plant Protection Sciences (IAPPS)
c/o Dr. E.A. "Short" Heinrichs, Sec. Gen.
2270 Litton Reaves Hall
Virginia Tech
Blacksburg, VA 24061-0334
Ph: (540)231-3516
Fax: (540)231-3519
E-mail: ipm-dir@vt.edu
URL: http://www.plantprotection.org
Contact: Dr. E.A. "Short" Heinrichs, Sec. Gen.

Founded: 1999. **Membership Dues:** industrialized country scientist (new/renewal), $50 (annual) ● developing country scientist (new/renewal), $35 (annual) ● student, $30 (annual) ● additional for subscription to print version of journal Crop Protection, $50. **Multinational. Description:** Provides a global forum for the purpose of identifying, evaluating, integrating and promoting plant protection concepts, technologies and policies which are economically, environmentally and socially acceptable. Promotes the implementation of sustainable plant health management strategies. Ensures the production of sufficient quality of food/feed/fiber for a growing world population. **Publications:** *Crop Protection*. Journal. **Price:** included in membership dues. Alternate Formats: online ● *IAPPS Newsletter*, monthly. **Price:** included in membership dues. Alternate Formats: online. **Conventions/Meetings:** annual congress.

6398 ■ International Service for the Acquisition of Agri-biotech Applications (ISAAA)
c/o Ms. Patricia Meenen, Financial Mgr.
Cornell Univ.
417 Bradfield Hall
Ithaca, NY 14853
Ph: (607)255-1724
Fax: (607)255-1215
E-mail: americenter@isaaa.org
URL: http://www.isaaa.org
Contact: Ms. Patricia Meenen, Financial Mgr.

Founded: 1993. **Multinational. Description:** Delivers the benefits of new agricultural biotechnologies to the poor in developing countries. Increases crop productivity and income generation of poor farmers. Promotes safe environment and sustainable agricultural development. Builds partnerships between institutions in the South and the private sector in the North. Strengthens of South-South collaboration. **Additional Websites:** http://africenter.isaaa.org. **Programs:** Biosafety; Biotechnology Fellowships; Food Safety; Impact Assessment; Plant Genomics; Technology Transfer.

Alternative Technology

6399 ■ National Clean Cities (NCC)
1735 20th St. NW
Washington, DC 20009
E-mail: plampert@e85fuel.com
Contact: Phillip Lampert, Contact
Description: Works to promote and deploy alternative-fuel vehicles, alternative-fuel infrastructure and advanced transportation technologies. Provides national leadership to advance clean alternatives to petroleum use for transportation and increased vehicle efficiency.

Animal Research

6400 ■ Comparative Cognition Society (CCS)
c/o Jeff Katz, Sec./Conference Organizer
Dept. of Psychology
226 Thach Hall
Auburn University, AL 36849-5214
E-mail: michael.brown@villanova.edu
URL: http://www.comparativecognition.org
Contact: Michael Brown, Pres.
Founded: 1999. **Membership Dues:** faculty, $45 (annual) ● student, post-doctoral, retired faculty, $15 (annual). **Description:** Aims to advance the study of the mechanisms and evolution of cognition in animals. Promotes scientific understanding of perception, learning, memory, or other cognitive processes in animals. Encourages research on all aspects of animal cognition. **Awards:** Comparative Cognition Society Research Award. **Frequency:** annual. **Type:** recognition. **Recipient:** to individuals who have made outstanding contributions to the study of cognitive processes in animals. **Telecommunication Services:** electronic mail, ron@psyc.queensu.ca. **Publications:** *Comparative Cognition and Behavior Reviews*. Journal. Alternate Formats: online ● Proceedings. Alternate Formats: online.

Animal Science

6401 ■ International Marine Animal Trainers Association (IMATA)
1200 S Lake Shore Dr.
Chicago, IL 60605
Ph: (312)692-3193
Fax: (312)939-2216
E-mail: info@imata.org
URL: http://www.imata.org
Contact: Allan Kordowski, Pres.
Founded: 1972. **Members:** 1,000. **Membership Dues:** student, web affiliate, $40 (annual) ● professional, associate, $75 (annual) ● active, $60 (annual) ● organizational, $200 (annual). **Multinational. Description:** Individuals who "serve marine mammal science through training, public display, research, husbandry, conservation, and education". Promotes the continued existence of oceanaria, aquaria, and marine laboratories; seeks to advance the profession of marine animal training. Works to create a positive public image for members; serves as a forum for the exchange of information among marine animal trainers; serves as a clearinghouse on marine animal research and husbandry. **Publications:** *Soundings*, quarterly. Magazine. **Conventions/Meetings:** annual conference, with paper and poster presentations and discussion groups - 2008 Nov. 9-15, Cancun, QR, Mexico.

Anthropology

6402 ■ American Anthropological Association
2200 Wilson Blvd., Ste.600
Arlington, VA 22201-3357
Ph: (703)528-1902
Fax: (703)528-3546
E-mail: members@aaanet.org
URL: http://www.aaanet.org
Contact: Bill Davis, Exec. Dir.
Founded: 1902. **Members:** 11,000. **Membership Dues:** professional, retired (based on income level), $125-$290 (annual) ● student (based on income level), $65-$90 (annual) ● joint, $95 (annual) ● associate, $120 (annual) ● international, $142 (annual) ● life, $4,000. **Staff:** 23. **Description:** Aims to further the professional interests of anthropologists; to disseminate anthropological knowledge and its use to address human problems; to promote the entire field of anthropology in all its diversity; to represent the discipline nationally and internationally, in the public and private sectors; to bring together anthropologists from all subfields and specializations, providing networking opportunities across the broad range of the discipline. **Libraries: Type:** not open to the public. **Subjects:** anthropology. **Awards:** AAA/Mayfield Award in Excellence in Undergraduate Teaching in Anthropology. **Frequency:** annual. **Type:** recognition ● Anthropology in Media Award. **Frequency:** annual. **Type:** recognition ● Franz Boos Award for Exemplary Service to Anthropology. **Frequency:** annual. **Type:** recognition ● Textor and Family Prize for Excellence in Anticipatory Anthropology. **Frequency:** annual. **Type:** recognition. **Publications:** *American Anthropologist*, quarterly. **Price:** included in membership dues. **Circulation:** 11,000. Alternate Formats: online ● *Anthropology News*, 9/year. **Conventions/Meetings:** annual meeting (exhibits) - 2008 Nov. 19-23, San Francisco, CA; 2009 Dec. 2-6, Philadelphia, PA.

6403 ■ American Association of Physical Anthropologists (AAPA)
PO Box 7050
Lawrence, KS 66044
Free: (800)627-0326
Fax: (785)843-1234
E-mail: aapamember@allenpress.com
URL: http://www.physanth.org
Contact: Trudy R. Turner, Sec.-Treas.
Founded: 1930. **Members:** 1,800. **Membership Dues:** regular, special, $130 (annual) ● student, retired, $65 (annual) ● spouse, $15 (annual) ● life, $1,600. **Description:** Professional society of physical anthropologists and scientists in closely related fields interested in the advancement of the science of physical anthropology through research and teaching of human variation, paleoanthropology and primatology. **Awards:** Charles Darwin Lifetime Achievement Award. **Frequency:** annual. **Type:** recognition. **Recipient:** for contributions to the field of physical anthropology ● Student Prize Paper Award. **Frequency:** annual. **Type:** recognition. **Recipient:** for research papers prepared and presented by students. **Committees:** Education; History; Honors; Research; Training. **Publications:** *AAPA Newsletter*, quarterly. Alternate Formats: online ● *American Journal of Physical Anthropology*, monthly. Provides original scientific articles on skeletal anatomy and paleopathology; body composition, growth and adaptability; and dental morphology. **Price:** included in membership dues. **Circulation:** 2,000. **Advertising:** accepted ● *Career Information Bulletin*, periodic ● *Yearbook of Physical Anthropology*, annual. Journal. Contains review papers on nonhuman primate behavior and biology, genetics and demography, growth and aging and clinical medicine. **Price:** included in membership dues. **Conventions/Meetings:** annual meeting (exhibits).

6404 ■ American Ethnological Society (AES)
c/o Member Services - American Anthropological Association
4350 N Fairfax Dr., Ste.640
Arlington, VA 22203-1620
Ph: (703)528-1902
Fax: (703)528-3546
E-mail: aes@lists.princeton.edu
URL: http://www.aesonline.org
Contact: Ida Susser, Pres.
Founded: 1842. **Members:** 2,628. **Membership Dues:** regular, $45 (annual) ● student, $18 (annual) ● joint, $22 (annual). **Budget:** $140,000. **Description:** A division of the American Anthropological Association. Anthropologists and others interested in the field of ethnology and social anthropology. Conducts symposia. **Awards:** Senior Book Prize. **Frequency:** biennial. **Type:** recognition. **Recipient:** for a book by a senior scholar ● Sharon Stephens Prize. **Frequency:** biennial. **Type:** recognition. **Recipient:** for a junior scholar's first book. **Telecommunication Services:** electronic mail, frothstein@towson.edu. **Publications:** *American Ethnologist*, quarterly. Journal. Covers topics in ecology, economy, social organization, ethnicity, politics, ideology, personality, cognition, ritual, and symbolism. **Price:** included in membership dues; $113.00 /year for institutions; $75.00 /year for nonmembers. ISSN: 0094-0496. **Advertising:** accepted. Alternate Formats: online ● *Unit News in Anthropology Newsletter*, monthly ● Monographs, periodic. **Conventions/Meetings:** annual conference, held in conjunction with AAA (exhibits) - usually November or December ● annual meeting - always spring.

6405 ■ American Society of Primatologists (ASP)
c/o Karen L. Bales, Treas.
Univ. of California
Dept. of Psychology
1 Shields Ave.
Davis, CA 95616
Ph: (530)754-5890
Fax: (530)752-2087
E-mail: klbales@ucdavis.edu
URL: http://www.asp.org
Contact: Karen L. Bales, Treas.
Founded: 1976. **Members:** 600. **Membership Dues:** full, $90 (annual) ● student, $45 (annual) ● retired, $20 (annual). **Description:** Promotes the discovery and exchange of information regarding nonhuman primates, including all aspects of their anatomy, behavior, development, ecology, evolution, genetics, nutrition, physiology, reproduction, systematics, conservation, husbandry and use in biomedical research. **Awards:** Conservation Award. **Frequency:** annual. **Type:** recognition. **Recipient:** for students and young investigators from habitat countries who demonstrate potential for making significant contributions to primate conservation ● Distinguished Primatologist Award. **Frequency:** annual. **Type:** recognition. **Recipient:** for a primatologist who has had an outstanding career and has made significant contributions to the field ● Distinguished Service Award. **Frequency:** periodic. **Type:** recognition. **Recipient:** for deserving individuals who have contributed long-term service to the society ● Early Career Achievement Award. **Frequency:** annual. **Type:** recognition. **Recipient:** for exceptional work by a beginning scientist ● Senior Primatologist Award. **Frequency:** annual. **Type:** recognition ● Senior Research Award. **Frequency:** annual. **Type:** recognition. **Recipient:** for individuals who have made significant contributions to research activities supporting or enhancing knowledge relevant to primatology. **Committees:** Awards and Recognition; Conservation; Education; Program; Publication; Research and Development. **Publications:** *American Journal of Primatology*, monthly ● *ASP Bulletin*, quarterly. Newsletter ● Directory, annual. **Conventions/Meetings:** annual conference ● annual congress (exhibits).

6406 ■ Amerind Foundation (AF)
PO Box 400
2100 N Amerind Rd.
Dragoon, AZ 85609
Ph: (520)586-3666
Fax: (520)586-4679

E-mail: amerind@amerind.org
URL: http://www.amerind.org
Contact: John Ware PhD, Dir.

Founded: 1937. **Members:** 600. **Membership Dues:** individual, $30 (annual) ● family, $40 (annual) ● Cochise club, $100-$499 (annual) ● San Pedro club, $500-$999 (annual) ● Casas Grandes club, $1,000 (annual). **Staff:** 12. **Description:** Conducts research in anthropology and archaeology of the greater American southwest and northern Mexico and ethnology in the Western Hemisphere. Offers artist shows; volunteer opportunities, public programs, and visiting scholar program. Operates museum. **Libraries: Type:** not open to the public; by appointment only; reference. **Holdings:** 30,000; archival material, books, periodicals, photographs, reports. **Subjects:** anthropology, archaeology, ethnohistory of the Americas. **Publications:** *Amerind New World Studies Series*, periodic. Books ● *Amerind Publication Series*. **Conventions/Meetings:** semiannual board meeting.

6407 ■ Anthropology Film Center

HC70 Box 3209
Glorieta, NM 87535
Ph: (505)757-2219
E-mail: info@anthrofilm.org

Founded: 1965. **Members:** 6. **Staff:** 1. **Description:** General anthropologists, visual anthropologists, culture and communication specialists, applied anthropologists, musicologists, linguists, and educators. Seeks to further scholarship, research, and practice in visual anthropology by using consultation and research services, seminars, publications, teaching, equipment outfitting, and specialized facilities. Has Anthropology Film Center that develops, reviews, and administers research projects in the following areas: generation and analysis of anthropology film (design, collection, and investigation of naturally occurring human behavior in context through visual technologies and methodologies); film as visual communication; socio-vidistics (investigation of the social organization surrounding the production, use, and display of photographs and film materials in their cultural contexts); culture and human perception; visual/aural arts and media. Conducts other activities including: generation and publication of research films and reports; consultation with universities and institutions; resident fellow program. Offers Ethnographic and Documentary Film Program which provides introductory basics in photography, film making and ethnology, and hands on training with story boarding, camera, sound, editing and lighting exercises. **Libraries: Type:** reference. **Holdings:** 12,000; books, films, papers, periodicals. **Subjects:** visual anthropology, ethnographic film. **Awards: Frequency:** annual. **Type:** grant ● **Frequency:** annual. **Type:** scholarship. **Computer Services:** database, film budget programs. **Formerly:** (1978) Anthropology Film Institute; (2003) Anthropology Film Center Foundation. **Conventions/Meetings:** periodic seminar ● periodic workshop.

6408 ■ Association for Africanist Anthropology (AfAA)

c/o American Anthropological Association
2200 Wilson Blvd., Ste.600
Arlington, VA 22201-3357
Ph: (703)528-1902
Fax: (703)528-3546
E-mail: jrosborn@ucsd.edu
URL: http://www.ibiblio.org/afaa
Contact: J.R. Osborn, Contact

Membership Dues: general, $25 (annual). **Description:** Promotes the professional interests of Africanist anthropologists. Encourages stronger professional ethics in the anthropology of Africa. Encourages and promotes existing African Studies programs and fosters the development of such programs. Facilitates the discussion of Africanist scholarship. **Awards:** Distinguished Lecturers Award. **Frequency:** annual. **Type:** recognition. **Recipient:** for outstanding lecturer focusing on Africanist anthropology. **Affiliated With:** American Anthropological Association.

6409 ■ Association of Black Anthropologists (ABA)

c/o Dana-Ain Davis
Social Sciences Div.
735 Anderson Hill Rd.
Purchase, NY 10577-1402
Ph: (914)251-6624
E-mail: dana-ain.davis@purchase.edu
URL: http://www.aaanet.org/assembly.htm
Contact: Dana-Ain Davis, Contact

Founded: 1970. **Members:** 200. **Description:** A section of the American Anthropological Association. Anthropologists and others interested in the study of blacks and other people subjected to exploitation and oppression. Works to: formulate conceptual and methodological frameworks to advance understanding of all forms of human diversity and commonality; advance theoretical efforts to explain the conditions that produce social inequalities based on race, ethnicity, class, or gender; develop research methods that involve the people studied and local scholars in all stages of investigation and dissemination of findings. **Libraries: Type:** reference. **Holdings:** biographical archives. **Awards: Type:** recognition. **Computer Services:** Mailing lists, available for rental through the American Anthropological Association. **Boards:** Editorial. **Committees:** Anthropology Watch; Nominations; Public Relations; Recruitment and Retention. **Councils:** Advisory. **Formerly:** (1975) Caucus of Black Anthropologists. **Publications:** *Transforming Anthropology*, semiannual. Newsletter. Includes commentaries, essays, book reviews, and referred articles. **Price:** included in membership dues; $20.00 /year for nonmembers. **Advertising:** accepted ● Papers ● Also publishes collections of papers. **Conventions/Meetings:** annual meeting, held in conjunction with AAA.

6410 ■ Association of Latina and Latino Anthropologists (ALLA)

c/o American Anthropological Association
2200 Wilson Blvd., Ste.600
Arlington, VA 22201-3357
Ph: (703)528-1902
Fax: (703)528-3546
E-mail: president@aaalla.org
URL: http://www.aaalla.org
Contact: Paule Cruz Takash, Pres.

Membership Dues: individual, $20 (annual) ● student, $10 (annual). **Description:** Promotes research and distributes information on Latinos in the United States. Stimulates dialogue in academic and other circles about Latino community objectives and realities. Encourages respect for indigenous and insider views. Promotes alternative perspectives and paradigms in anthropology. **Awards:** ALLA Book Award. **Frequency:** biennial. **Type:** recognition. **Recipient:** for the best book on U.S. Latino/Latina culture ● ALLA Lifetime Achievement Award. **Type:** recognition. **Recipient:** for excellence in the practice of anthropology and/or service to the U.S. Latino and Latina population ● ALLA Student Paper Prize. **Frequency:** annual. **Type:** monetary. **Recipient:** for the best student paper on U.S. Latino/Latina culture. **Affiliated With:** American Anthropological Association.

6411 ■ Association for Political and Legal Anthropology (APLA)

c/o Bill Maurer, Pres.-Elect
Univ. of California - Irvine
Dept. of Anthropology
3272 Social Sciences Plz. B
Irvine, CA 92697-5100
Ph: (949)824-7602
Fax: (949)824-4717
E-mail: wmmaurer@uci.edu
URL: http://www.aaanet.org/apla
Contact: Bill Maurer, Pres.-Elect

Membership Dues: individual, $30 (annual) ● student, $20 (annual). **Description:** Represents individuals in the field of political and legal anthropology. Advances the study of political and legal processes. Encourages communication among academic community. **Awards:** Student Paper Prize. **Frequency:** annual. **Type:** monetary. **Recipient:** for outstanding analysis of political and legal institutions and processes. **Affiliated With:** American Anthropological Association. **Publications:** *PoLAR: The Political and Legal Anthropology Review*, semiannual. Journal. Contains articles and research material on the anthropology of law and politics. **Price:** included in membership dues; $49.00 /year for individuals and institutions.

6412 ■ Association of Senior Anthropologists (ASA)

c/o Paul Doughty, Chm.
1071 NW 21st Terr.
Gainesville, FL 32603-1034
Ph: (904)392-2031
Fax: (904)392-6929
URL: http://www.aaanet.org/asa
Contact: Paul Doughty, Chm.

Membership Dues: individual, $10 (annual). **Description:** Seeks to create a sense of community among senior anthropologists and to further their interests and concerns. Works to improve the professional relationships of senior anthropologists and the quality of anthropological study. Encourages camaraderie among senior anthropologists. **Affiliated With:** American Anthropological Association. **Publications:** *ASA Occasional Papers*. Contains anthropological articles, studies and research from senior anthropologists. **Price:** included in membership dues.

6413 ■ Association for Social Anthropology in Oceania (ASAO)

c/o Dr. Jocelyn Armstrong, Sec.
Dept. of Community Hea.
Univ. of Illinois MC-588
1206 S Fourth St.
Champaign, IL 61820
Ph: (217)244-1196
Fax: (217)333-2766
E-mail: jocelyn@uiuc.edu
URL: http://www.asao.org
Contact: Dr. Jocelyn Armstrong, Sec.

Founded: 1967. **Members:** 350. **Membership Dues:** general, $35 (annual) ● student/unemployed, $20 (annual). **Multinational. Description:** Represents individuals, university and college libraries, and professional associations. Works to advance the study of comparative social anthropology in Oceania through symposia, joint publication, and research coordination. **Formerly:** (1970) Association for Social Anthropology in Eastern Oceania. **Publications:** *ASAO Newsletter*, 3/year. ISSN: 1095-3000. Alternate Formats: online ● Monographs. **Conventions/Meetings:** annual conference.

6414 ■ Biological Anthropology Section (BAS)

c/o Jim Bindon
Univ. of Alabama
Dept. of Anthropology
PO Box 870210
Tuscaloosa, AL 35487
Ph: (205)348-1958
E-mail: jbindon@tenhoor.as.ua.edu
URL: http://www.as.ua.edu/bas
Contact: Trudy R. Turner PhD, Chair

Founded: 1984. **Members:** 512. **Description:** A unit of American Anthropological Association (see separate entry). International group of anthropologists concerned with the biological aspects of anthropology. Aims to maintain communication among biological anthropologists. Promotes scientific and public understanding of human origins and the interaction between biological and cultural dimensions that underlie the evolution of humans. **Publications:** Publishes periodic series on topics pertaining to biological anthropology. **Conventions/Meetings:** annual meeting, held in conjunction with AAA.

6415 ■ Council on Anthropology and Education (CAE)

c/o American Anthropological Association
2200 Wilson Blvd., Ste.600
Arlington, VA 22201-3357
Ph: (703)528-1902
Fax: (703)528-3546

E-mail: pgilmore@u.arizona.edu
URL: http://www.aaanet.org/cae/index.htm
Contact: Perry Gilmore, Pres.
Founded: 1968. **Members:** 720. **Membership Dues:** regular, $42 (annual) ● student, $11 (annual) ● associate, $22 (annual). **Multinational. Description:** Aims to advance and to stimulate interest and research in the coordination of anthropological perspectives, theories, methods and findings with educational problems, policies, practices, and institutions. **Awards:** Distinguished Scholarly Contributions Award. **Type:** recognition. **Recipient:** for individual who has published number of studies in the field of educational anthropology ● Distinguished Service Contributions Award. **Type:** recognition. **Recipient:** for individual with outstanding implementation of anthropological approaches to actual educational processes ● Ethnographic Evaluation Award. **Type:** recognition ● George and Louise Spindler Award. **Frequency:** annual. **Type:** recognition. **Recipient:** for scholars and practitioners ● Outstanding Dissertation Award. **Frequency:** annual. **Type:** recognition. **Recipient:** for individual with outstanding dissertation recently completed in the field of anthropology and education. **Committees:** Anthropological Studies of School and Culture; Anthropology of Post Secondary Education; Applied Work for Educational Futures; Blacks in Education; Culture, Ecology and Education; Ethnographic Approaches to Evaluation in Education; Gender and Schools and Society; Latinos and Education; Multicultural and Multilingual Education; Social and Cultural Contexts of Language, Literacy and Cognition; Study of Cultural Transmission / Acquisition; Transnational Issues in Education and Change. **Publications:** *Anthropology and Education Quarterly*. Journal. **Price:** $89.00 institution, for nonmembers. ISSN: 0161-7761. **Advertising:** accepted. Alternate Formats: online. **Conventions/Meetings:** annual meeting, held in conjunction with AAA - 2008 Nov. 19-23, San Francisco, CA; 2009 Dec. 2-6, Philadelphia, PA.

6416 ■ Evolutionary Anthropology Society (EAS)

c/o American Anthropological Association
2200 Wilson Blvd., Ste.600
Arlington, VA 22201-3357
Ph: (703)528-1902
Fax: (703)528-3546
E-mail: easmith@u.washington.edu
URL: http://www.anth.uconn.edu/eas
Contact: Eric Alden Smith, Pres.
Membership Dues: regular, $10 (annual) ● student, $5 (annual). **Description:** Promotes the development and application of modern evolutionary theory to the analysis of human behavior and culture. Fosters scholarly exchange between evolution-minded researchers in all subfields of anthropology. Supports the dissemination of evolutionary anthropology in teaching and research. Provides a forum for individuals who are concerned with the communication of anthropological research among the general public. **Awards:** Best New Investigator Award. **Frequency:** annual. **Type:** recognition. **Recipient:** for outstanding paper in evolutionary anthropology ● Best Student Investigator Award. **Frequency:** annual. **Type:** recognition. **Recipient:** for outstanding student paper in evolutionary anthropology. **Affiliated With:** American Anthropological Association.

6417 ■ General Anthropology Division of the American Anthropological Association (GAD)

c/o Karl G. Heider, Pres.
Univ. of South Carolina
Dept. of Anthropology
Columbia, SC 29208
Ph: (703)528-1902
Fax: (703)528-3546
E-mail: heiderk@gwm.sc.edu
URL: http://www.aaanet.org/gad
Contact: Karl G. Heider, Pres.
Founded: 1984. **Members:** 4,877. **Description:** A section of the American Anthropological Association (see separate entry), dedicated to the study of general anthropology (as opposed to specialized areas of anthropology such as medical, psychological, or biological anthropology). Promotes public awareness and understanding of practical, contemporary applications of anthropological studies. **Committees:** Anthropology of Jews and Judaism; Anthropology of Science, Technology and Computing; Teaching Anthropology. **Task Forces:** Famine in Africa. **Publications:** *American Anthropologist*, quarterly. Journal. Published in conjunction with AAA. **Price:** $50.00/year. ISSN: 0002-7294. **Circulation:** 8,500. **Advertising:** accepted ● *Anthropology Newsletter*, quarterly. Includes news on the activities of the organization. ● *General Anthropology*, periodic. Bulletin. Serves as the official bulletin of the section. **Conventions/Meetings:** annual meeting, held in conjunction with AAA.

6418 ■ Institute for the Study of Man (ISM)

1133 13th St. NW, Ste.C-2
Washington, DC 20005
Ph: (202)371-2700
Fax: (202)371-1523
E-mail: iejournal@aol.com
URL: http://www.jies.org
Contact: Roger Pearson PhD, Dir.
Founded: 1975. **Multinational. Description:** Aims to publish books and journals in areas related to anthropology, historical linguistics, and the human sciences. **Libraries: Type:** reference. **Holdings:** 12,000. **Publications:** *Journal of Indo-European Studies*, quarterly. **Advertising:** accepted ● Books. **Conventions/Meetings:** periodic convention and workshop, with anthropological topics.

6419 ■ International Primatological Society (IPS)

c/o Richard Wrangham, Pres.
Harvard Univ.
Peabody Museum
11 Divinity Ave.
Cambridge, MA 02138
Ph: (617)495-5948
Fax: (617)496-8041
E-mail: wrangham@fas.harvard.edu
URL: http://www.internationalprimatologicalsociety.org
Contact: Richard Wrangham, Pres.
Founded: 1966. **Members:** 1,500. **Membership Dues:** student, $20 (annual) ● regular, $40 (annual) ● life, $520. **Regional Groups:** 5. **Description:** Individuals interested in primate research. Facilitates cooperation among primatologists and fosters conservation and judicious use of primates in research. **Awards:** Galante. **Frequency:** annual. **Type:** grant. **Recipient:** for conservation research. **Committees:** Captive Care; Conservation. **Affiliated With:** American Society of Primatologists. **Publications:** *International Journal of Primatology*, quarterly. **Price:** $47.00/year. ISSN: 0164-0291 ● *IPS Bulletin*, biennial ● *Members' Handbook*, annual ● *Proceedings of the International Congress*, biennial. **Conventions/Meetings:** biennial congress (exhibits) - 2008 Aug. 3-8, Edinburgh, United Kingdom.

6420 ■ International Women's Anthropology Conference (IWAC)

Anthropology Dept.
25 Waverly Pl.
New York Univ.
New York, NY 10003
Ph: (212)998-8550
Fax: (212)995-4014
E-mail: constance.sutton@nyu.edu
URL: http://homepages.nyu.edu/~crs2/index.html
Contact: Prof. Connie Sutton, Pres.
Founded: 1978. **Description:** Women anthropologists and sociologists who are researching and teaching topics such as women's role in development, feminism, and the international women's movement. Encourages the exchange of information on research, projects, and funding; addresses policies concerning women from an anthropological perspective. Conducts periodic educational meetings with panel discussions. **Publications:** *IWAC Newsletter*, semiannual ● Bulletin, periodic. **Conventions/Meetings:** semiannual conference.

6421 ■ Kroeber Anthropological Society (KAS)

c/o University of California, Berkeley
Dept. of Anthropology
232 Kroeber Hall
Berkeley, CA 94720-3710
Ph: (510)642-3391
Fax: (510)643-8557
E-mail: kas@sscl.berkeley.edu
URL: http://anthropology.berkeley.edu/kas.html
Contact: Angela C. Jenks, Pres.
Founded: 1949. **Members:** 500. **Staff:** 7. **Description:** Represents anthropologists, students, interested laypersons and institutional members (300 major universities and anthropological institutions). **Publications:** *Kroeber Anthropological Society Papers*, 3/year. Journal. **Price:** $60.00/year in U.S.; $70.00/year outside U.S. ISSN: 0023-4869. **Circulation:** 500. **Conventions/Meetings:** annual conference - always spring in Berkeley, CA.

6422 ■ National Association for the Practice of Anthropology (NAPA)

c/o American Anthropological Association
2200 Wilson Blvd., Ste.600
Arlington, VA 22201
Ph: (703)528-1902
Fax: (703)528-3546
E-mail: wiedmand@fiu.edu
URL: http://www.practicinganthropology.org
Contact: Dennis Wiedman, Pres.
Founded: 1983. **Members:** 1,000. **Membership Dues:** regular, $175 (annual) ● student, $80 (annual) ● joint, $95 (annual) ● associate, $120 (annual) ● retired, $140 (annual) ● sustainer, $250 (annual). **Budget:** $33,661. **Description:** A section of the American Anthropological Association. Professional anthropologists serving social service organizations, government agencies, and business and industrial firms. Works to help anthropologists develop and market their expertise in areas such as social and political analysis, and program design, evaluation, and management. Compiles statistics. **Awards:** Student Achievement Award. **Frequency:** annual. **Type:** recognition. **Recipient:** for student's achievements in the area of practicing and applied technology. **Committees:** Business Anthropology; Local Practitioners Network. **Programs:** Councilor; Mentor. **Publications:** *Bulletin Series*, periodic ● Annual Report, annual. Alternate Formats: online ● Plans to publish *National Directory of Practicing Anthropologists* biennially. **Conventions/Meetings:** annual workshop and symposium, held in conjunction with AAA.

6423 ■ Society for the Anthropology of Europe (SAE)

c/o American Anthropological Association
2200 Wilson Blvd., Ste.600
Arlington, VA 22201
Ph: (703)528-1902
Fax: (703)528-3546
E-mail: akarakas@wellesley.edu
URL: http://www.h-net.org/~sae/sae/index.html
Contact: Anastasia Karakasidou, Pres.
Founded: 1986. **Members:** 525. **Membership Dues:** regular, $20 (annual) ● student, $10 (annual). **Budget:** $12,730. **Description:** Serves as section of the American Anthropological Association. Anthropologists. Works to promote the anthropological study of Europe and to facilitate communication among members in North America and Europe. **Publications:** *SAE Journal*, semiannual. **Price:** $20.00 for nonmembers in U.S.; $22.00 for nonmembers outside U.S.; included in membership dues ● *Society for the Anthropology of Europe Directory, 2nd Edition (1993)*. **Conventions/Meetings:** annual meeting, held in conjunction with AAA.

6424 ■ Society for the Anthropology of Food and Nutrition (SAFN)

c/o Craig Hadley, Sec.-Treas.
Univ. of Michigan
Center for Social Epidemiology and Population Hea.
1214 S Univ. Ave., 2nd Fl.
Ann Arbor, MI 48104-2592
Ph: (734)615-9215

E-mail: chadley@umich.edu
URL: http://www.aaanet.org/cna/index.htm
Contact: Andrea S. Wiley, Pres.
Founded: 1974. **Members:** 328. **Description:** A section of the American Anthropological Association. Represents anthropologists and nutritional scientists studying the interface between anthropology and nutrition. Facilitates communication among members and promotes research in areas including the social, cultural, and economic aspects of nutrition and food use. **Awards:** Christine Wilson Awards. **Frequency:** annual. **Type:** recognition. **Recipient:** for outstanding undergraduate and graduate research papers on a topic that combines perspectives in nutrition or food studies and anthropology. **Telecommunication Services:** electronic mail, wileyas@jmu.edu. **Committees:** Curriculum and Research; Meetings and Programs; Nominations; Policy and Liaison. **Formerly:** Council on Nutritional Anthropology. **Publications:** *Nutritional Anthropology*, semiannual. Journal. Includes book reviews, summaries of research projects, and profiles of researchers. **Price:** free through membership in AAA ● *Nutritional Anthropology Methods Handbook*. **Conventions/Meetings:** annual meeting, in conjunction with AAA (exhibits).

6425 ■ Society for the Anthropology of North America (SANA)

c/o American Anthropological Association
2200 Wilson Blvd., Ste.600
Arlington, VA 22201
Ph: (703)528-1902
Fax: (703)528-3546
E-mail: jeff_maskovsky@qc.edu
URL: http://sananet.org
Contact: Jeff Maskovsky, Pres.
Membership Dues: professor, professional, $25 (annual) ● student, $10 (annual). **Multinational. Description:** Promotes the anthropological study of North America. Addresses the need for a voice and institutional presence for the Anthropology of the United States, Canada and Mexico. Analyzes North American cultural life and promotes research in areas including ethnicity, race, class, gender and structured inequality. Facilitates communication among members. **Awards:** Delmos Jones and Jagna Sharff Memorial Book Prize for the Critical Study of North America. **Frequency:** annual. **Type:** recognition. **Recipient:** for outstanding book on North American cultural life ● SANA Prize for Distinguished Achievement in the Critical Study of North America. **Frequency:** annual. **Type:** recognition. **Recipient:** for contributions to research, teaching and service related to the development of critical studies of North America. **Affiliated With:** American Anthropological Association. **Publications:** *North American Dialogue*, semiannual. Journal. Contains features, research articles and news. **Price:** free. Alternate Formats: online.

6426 ■ Society for the Anthropology of Religion (SAR)

c/o Andrew Buckser
Purdue Univ.
Dept. of Sociology and Anthropology
700 W State St.
West Lafayette, IN 47907-1365
Fax: (765)496-1476
E-mail: bucksera@sri.soc.purdue.edu
URL: http://www.aaanet.org/sar
Contact: Ellen Badone, Pres.
Founded: 1997. **Membership Dues:** regular, $15 (annual) ● student, $10 (annual). **Description:** Facilitates teaching and research in the anthropological study of religion. Encourages and helps provide avenues for enhanced communication among scholars sharing the interests of anthropology and religion. Seeks to re-energize the study of the anthropology of religion. **Awards:** Clifford Geertz Prize in the Anthropology of Religion. **Frequency:** annual. **Type:** recognition. **Recipient:** for the most outstanding recent book in the anthropology of religion. **Publications:** Annual Report, annual. Contains notes on meetings, officers and other organization activities. **Price:** included in membership dues. Alternate Formats: online.

6427 ■ Society for Applied Anthropology (SfAA)

PO Box 2436
Oklahoma City, OK 73101-2436
Ph: (405)843-5113
Fax: (405)843-8553
E-mail: info@sfaa.net
URL: http://www.sfaa.net
Contact: Mr. J. Thomas May PhD, Exec. Dir.
Founded: 1941. **Members:** 2,300. **Membership Dues:** regular, $50 (annual) ● student, joint member, $30 (annual) ● sustaining fellow, $90 (annual) ● fellow, $62 (annual) ● joint fellow, $40 (annual) ● joint sustaining fellow, $75 (annual). **Staff:** 4. **Budget:** $200,000. **Description:** Professional society of anthropologists, sociologists, psychologists, health professionals, industrial researchers, and educators. Promotes scientific investigation of the principles controlling relations between human beings, and encourages wide application of these principles to practical problems. **Awards:** Bronislaw Malinowski Award. **Frequency:** annual. **Type:** recognition. **Recipient:** for career achievement ● Margaret Mead Award. **Frequency:** annual. **Type:** trophy ● Peter K. New Student Research Award. **Frequency:** annual. **Type:** trophy. **Recipient:** for quality of applied research ● Sol Tax. **Frequency:** annual. **Type:** trophy. **Publications:** *Human Organization*, quarterly. Journal. Contains information on social and behavioral sciences covering government and industry, health, medical care, and international affairs. **Price:** $75.00/year in U.S.; $85.00/year outside U.S. ISSN: 0018-7259. **Circulation:** 4,000. **Advertising:** accepted ● *Practicing Anthropology: A Career-Oriented Publication of the Society for Applied Anthropology*, quarterly. Journal. Provides professional information for anthropologists and other social scientists outside academia. **Price:** $35.00/year in U.S.; $40.00/year outside U.S. ● *SFAA Newsletter*, quarterly. **Price:** $10.00/year in U.S.; $15.00/year outside U.S. **Conventions/Meetings:** annual conference, with participation of professionals, including anthropologists, archaeologists, geographers, sociologists and folklorists (exhibits).

6428 ■ Society for Cultural Anthropology (SCA)

c/o Judith Farquhar, Pres.
Univ. of Chicago
Dept. of Anthropology
1126 E 59th St.
Chicago, IL 60637
E-mail: farquhar@uchicago.edu
URL: http://www.aaanet.org/sca
Contact: Judith Farquhar, Pres.
Founded: 1983. **Members:** 1,614. **Membership Dues:** individual, $38 (annual) ● institution, $83 (annual) ● student, $18 (annual). **Description:** A section of the American Anthropological Association (see separate entry), dedicated to the study of culture. Compiles statistics. **Computer Services:** database, membership roster. **Telecommunication Services:** electronic mail, blweis@wm.edu. **Publications:** *Cultural Anthropology*, quarterly. Journal. **Price:** $83.00 /year for institutions; $48.00 /year for nonmembers. ISSN: 1886-7356. **Circulation:** 1,400. Alternate Formats: online ● Also contributes to the AAA newsletter. **Conventions/Meetings:** annual meeting, held in conjunction with AAA ● symposium.

6429 ■ Society for East Asian Anthropology (SEAA)

c/o Prof. Lisa Hoffman, Sec.
Dept. of Urban Stud.
Univ. of Washington - Tacoma
1900 Commerce St.
Tacoma, WA 98402-3100
Ph: (253)692-5895
E-mail: hoffmanl@u.washington.edu
URL: http://www.aaanet.org/seaa
Contact: Yunxiang Yan, Pres.
Membership Dues: individual, $10 (annual) ● student, $5 (annual). **Description:** Advances the anthropological study of East Asian societies and cultures, of East Asia. Facilitates scholarly communications and collaborations among East Asianist anthropologists within and outside of East Asia. Encourages communication and utilization of the results obtained from anthropological studies of East Asia. **Awards:** David Plath Media Award. **Frequency:** annual. **Type:** monetary. **Recipient:** for the best media work on any aspect of East Asian anthropology ● Francis L.K. Hsu Book Prize. **Frequency:** annual. **Type:** monetary. **Recipient:** for English language book that has made the most significant contribution to East Asian anthropology ● Theodore C. Bestor Prize. **Frequency:** annual. **Type:** monetary. **Recipient:** for the best graduate student paper on any aspect of East Asian anthropology. **Affiliated With:** American Anthropological Association.

6430 ■ Society for Economic Anthropology (SEA)

c/o Judith E. Marti, Sec.-Treas.
Dept. of Anthropology
California State Univ. - Northridge
18111 Nordhoff St.
Northridge, CA 91330-8244
E-mail: judith.marti@csun.edu
URL: http://sea.org.ohio-state.edu
Contact: Jeff Cohen, Pres.
Founded: 1982. **Members:** 350. **Membership Dues:** basic student, $10 (annual) ● basic professional, $35 (annual) ● standard student, $30 (annual) ● standard professional, $50 (annual). **Description:** Anthropologists, archaeologists, economists, and other individuals with an interest in economic anthropology. Promotes study of diversity and change in the economic systems of the world. Gathers and disseminates information on economic anthropology; facilitates communication and exchange of information among members. **Awards:** Harold K. Schneider Student Paper Prize. **Frequency:** annual. **Type:** recognition. **Recipient:** for the best student paper on any aspect of economic anthropology or economic archaeology ● SEA Book Prize. **Frequency:** biennial. **Type:** recognition. **Recipient:** for the best-reviewed book on economic anthropology. **Publications:** *SEA Newsletter*, semiannual. **Price:** included in membership dues. Alternate Formats: online ● Monographs, annual. Includes monographs in economic anthropology series. **Price:** $25.00. **Conventions/Meetings:** semiannual board meeting ● annual meeting.

6431 ■ Society for Latin American Anthropology (SLAA)

c/o AAA Membership Services
4350 N Fairfax Dr., Ste.640
Arlington, VA 22203-1620
Ph: (703)528-1902
E-mail: mlavoie@indiana.edu
URL: http://www.indiana.edu/~wanthro/matt1.htm
Contact: Matthew Lavoie, Contact
Founded: 1969. **Members:** 773. **Membership Dues:** regular, $35 (annual) ● student, $20 (annual). **Budget:** $26,504. **Description:** Section of the American Anthropological Association. Represents anthropologists, graduate students in anthropology, academic and nonacademic institutions and individuals interested in Latin America. Encourages research in Latin American anthropology. **Formerly:** (1971) Ad Hoc Group on Latin American Anthropology; (1982) Latin American Anthropology Group. **Publications:** *Journal of Latin American Anthropology*, semiannual. **Conventions/Meetings:** annual symposium, held in conjunction with AAA.

6432 ■ Society of Lesbian and Gay Anthropologists (SOLGA)

4350 N Fairfax Dr., Ste.640
Arlington, VA 22203-1620
Ph: (703)528-1902
Fax: (703)528-3546
E-mail: ctw@usc.edu
URL: http://www.uvm.edu/~dlrh/solga/index.html
Contact: Marcia Ochoa, Interim Sec.
Founded: 1988. **Membership Dues:** student, $8 (annual) ● basic, $15 (annual). **Description:** Promotes communication, research, development of teaching materials. Serves the interests of gay and lesbian anthropologists. **Awards:** Kenneth W. Payne Student

Prize Award. **Frequency:** annual. **Type:** monetary. **Recipient:** for students and scholars of LGBT topics and issues in anthropology ● Ruth Benedict Prize Award. **Frequency:** annual. **Type:** scholarship. **Recipient:** for outstanding anthropological scholarship on lesbian, gay, bisexual, or transgendered topic. **Publications:** Newsletter, 3/year. **Conventions/Meetings:** meeting, with scientific panels.

6433 ■ Society for Linguistic Anthropology (SLA)
c/o Joel C. Kuipers, Pres.
George Washington Univ.
Dept. of Anthropology
2112 G St. NW, Rm. 201
Washington, DC 20052
Ph: (202)994-6545 (202)994-6075
E-mail: kuipers@gwu.edu
URL: http://www.aaanet.org/sla
Contact: Joel C. Kuipers, Pres.
Founded: 1983. **Members:** 512. **Membership Dues:** individual, $40 (annual) ● student, $20 (annual). **Description:** Serves as section of the American Anthropological Association (see separate entry). Represents University faculty; students. Promotes the anthropological study of language. **Awards:** Edward Sapir. **Frequency:** biennial. **Type:** recognition. **Recipient:** for a book that makes significant contribution to understanding of language in society ● Student Essay. **Frequency:** annual. **Type:** monetary. **Recipient:** for graduate and undergraduate. **Publications:** *Journal of Linguistic Anthropology*, semiannual, June and December. **Price:** $51.00 for nonmembers; included in membership dues. ISSN: 1055-1360. **Circulation:** 500. **Advertising:** accepted. **Conventions/Meetings:** annual meeting, held in conjunction with AAA ● semiannual meeting and symposium.

6434 ■ Society for Medical Anthropology (SMA)
c/o Marcia Inhorn, Pres.
Health Behavior and Health Education
School of Public Health
Univ. of Michigan
1420 Washington Heights
Ann Arbor, MI 48109-2029
E-mail: minhorn@umich.edu
URL: http://www.medanthro.net
Contact: Marcia Inhorn, Pres.
Founded: 1971. **Members:** 1,700. **Description:** Section of the American Anthropological Association (see separate entry). Promotes study of anthropological aspects of health, illness, health care and related topics. **Awards:** Career Achievement Award. **Frequency:** annual. **Type:** recognition. **Recipient:** for career-long contributions to establishing the practice of medical anthropology as a full partner in solving health problems ● Eileen Basker Memorial Prize. **Frequency:** annual. **Type:** monetary. **Recipient:** for large-scale work representing superior research in the area of gender and health ● Graduate Student Mentor Award. **Frequency:** annual. **Type:** recognition. **Recipient:** for excellence in graduate student mentorship ● Practicing Medical Anthropology Award. **Frequency:** annual. **Type:** recognition. **Recipient:** for scholars engaged in applying anthropological principles in particular health project settings. **Councils:** Anthropology and Reproduction; Nursing and Anthropology. **Special Interest Groups:** AIDS and Anthropology Research; Bioethics; Clinically Applied Medical Anthropology; Disability Research; Global Health and Emerging Diseases; Pharmaceutical Studies. **Publications:** *Medical Anthropology Quarterly*. Journal. Includes book reviews and research reports. **Price:** included in membership dues; $80.00 /year for nonmembers. ISSN: 0745-5194. **Circulation:** 2,000. **Advertising:** accepted. Also Cited As: *International Journal for the Cultural and Social Analysis of Health* ● *Special Publications*, periodic. **Conventions/Meetings:** annual meeting, held in conjunction with AAA (exhibits).

6435 ■ Society for Urban, National and Transnational/Global Anthropology (SUNTA)
c/o Deborah Pellow, Pres.-Elect
Syracuse Univ.
The Maxwell School
209 Maxwell Hall
Syracuse, NY 13244
E-mail: dpellow@maxwell.syr.edu
URL: http://www.sunta.org
Contact: Deborah Pellow, Pres.-Elect
Membership Dues: individual, $33 (annual) ● student, $15 (annual) ● joint, $10 (annual) ● associate, $20 (annual). **Description:** Seeks to advance the science and profession of urban, national and transnational/global anthropology. Promotes the advancement of research and the professional interests of urban national and transnational/global anthropologists. Encourages the distribution and application of knowledge acquired in the study of urban, national and transnational/global anthropology. **Awards:** Leeds Award. **Frequency:** annual. **Type:** recognition. **Recipient:** for relevant accomplishments and contributions in the field of urban studies in general. **Affiliated With:** American Anthropological Association. **Publications:** *City and Society*. Journal. Contains articles, research work, case studies, comparisons and syntheses. **Price:** included in membership dues.

6436 ■ Society for Visual Anthropology (SVA)
c/o Mary Strong, Sec.
1708 11th Ave.
Brooklyn, NY 11218
E-mail: rdomiurbi@aol.com
URL: http://www.societyforvisualanthropology.org
Contact: Anne Zeller, Pres.
Founded: 1968. **Members:** 525. **Membership Dues:** professional, $165 (annual) ● student, $75 (annual). **Description:** A section of the American Anthropological Association (AAA) (see separate entry). Represents individuals united to aid, support, and promote the anthropological study and use of visual forms. Sponsors training sessions. **Awards:** Film Festival at Annual AAA Meeting. **Type:** recognition. **Recipient:** for superior anthropological films and videotapes. **Formerly:** (1972) Program in Ethnographic Film; (1985) Society for the Anthropology of Visual Communication. **Publications:** *Directory of Visual Anthropology*, periodic ● *The Visual Anthropology Review*, semiannual. Journal. **Price:** included in membership dues; $25.00 for nonmembers. **Advertising:** accepted. **Conventions/Meetings:** annual conference, held in conjunction with AAA (exhibits) ● symposium.

Archaeology

6437 ■ American Committee to Advance the Study of Petroglyphs and Pictographs (ACASPP)
Address Unknown since 2008
Founded: 1979. **Members:** 302. **Membership Dues:** regular, $10 (annual). **Staff:** 2. **Languages:** English, French, Spanish, Vietnamese. **Description:** Professionals and students interested in the study of petroglyphs (from the Greek for "rock and carving") and pictographs (from the Greek for "picture and writing"), including interpretation, recording, documentation, analysis, conservation, and preservation. Objectives are to maintain: consistent standards of recording for petroglyphs and pictographs; permanent archives of data and reports; broad dissemination of results of study and analysis through publications, public meetings, conferences, and field schools. **Libraries: Type:** by appointment only. **Holdings:** 10,000; artwork, photographs. **Subjects:** archaeology, anthropology, language, linguistic, art, art history. **Publications:** *Rock Art*, semiannual. Newsletter ● Membership Directory, periodic ● Also publishes papers and educational materials. **Conventions/Meetings:** periodic meeting (exhibits).

6438 ■ American Rock Art Research Association (ARARA)
Arizona State Museum
Univ. of Arizona
Box 210026
Tucson, AZ 85721-0026
Free: (888)668-0052
E-mail: araraboard@gmail.com
URL: http://www.arara.org
Contact: Mavis Greer, Pres.
Founded: 1974. **Members:** 600. **Membership Dues:** individual, $45 (annual) ● family, $50 (annual) ● student, $35 (annual) ● institution/society, $60 (annual) ● donor (minimum), $120 (annual). **Staff:** 7. **Budget:** $59,550. **Description:** Archaeologists, artists, authors, social scientists, and interested individuals. Encourages and advances research in the field of rock art. (Rock art is petroglyphs and pictographs found painted on or etched into rock surfaces; rock art is thought to be a form of communication and a record of events used by prehistoric and historic people.) Promotes nondestructive utilization of rock art for scientific, educational, and artistic purposes. Works to protect and preserve rock art sites by encouraging cooperative action between private land owners and state and federal agencies. Rents rock art replicas and resource materials. **Libraries: Type:** open to the public. **Holdings:** articles, books, periodicals. **Subjects:** petroglyphs, pictographs. **Awards:** ARARA Conservation and Preservation Award. **Frequency:** annual. **Type:** recognition. **Recipient:** for significant contributions to the conservation or protection of rock art ● Castleton Award. **Frequency:** annual. **Type:** monetary. **Recipient:** for best essay on rock art ● Frank and A.J. Bock Award. **Frequency:** periodic. **Type:** recognition. **Recipient:** for extraordinary lifetime achievement in the rock art studies ● Klaus Wellmann Award. **Frequency:** annual. **Type:** recognition. **Recipient:** for distinguished service ● Oliver Rock Art Photography Award. **Frequency:** annual. **Type:** recognition. **Recipient:** for exceptional works that master the art and science of rock art photography. **Telecommunication Services:** electronic mail, mavis@greerservices.com. **Committees:** Conservation and Preservation; Education. **Publications:** *American Indian Rock Art*, annual. Journal ● *La Pintura*, quarterly. Newsletter. **Price:** included in membership dues. **Circulation:** 700 ● Films. Covers rock art. ● Also makes available slide presentations and other educational material. **Conventions/Meetings:** annual convention and symposium (exhibits) - usually Memorial Day weekend.

6439 ■ Archaeological Conservancy (AC)
5301 Central Ave. NE, Ste.902
Albuquerque, NM 87108-1517
Ph: (505)266-1540
Fax: (505)266-0311
E-mail: tacinfo@nm.net
URL: http://www.americanarchaeology.com
Contact: Mark Michel, Pres.
Founded: 1980. **Members:** 23,000. **Membership Dues:** individual, $25 (annual). **Budget:** $1,000,000. **Description:** People interested in preserving prehistoric and historic sites for interpretive or research purposes (most members are not professional archaeologists). Seeks to acquire for permanent preservation, through donation or purchase, the ruins of past American cultures, primarily those of American Indians. Works throughout the U.S. to preserve cultural resources presently on private lands and protect them from the destruction of looters, modern agricultural practices, and urban sprawl. Operates with government agencies, universities, and museums to permanently preserve acquired sites. **Convention/Meeting:** none. **Publications:** *American Archaeology*, quarterly. Magazine. Features news relating to archeology in the Americas. **Price:** included in membership dues. ISSN: 1093-8400. **Advertising:** accepted.

6440 ■ Archaeological Institute of America (AIA)
656 Beacon St., 6th Fl.
Boston, MA 02215-2006
Ph: (617)353-9361 (617)353-8706
Free: (877)524-5300
Fax: (617)353-6550
E-mail: aia@aia.bu.edu
URL: http://www.archaeological.org
Contact: Bonnie R. Clendenning, Exec. Dir.
Founded: 1879. **Members:** 8,500. **Membership Dues:** individual, $50 (annual) ● student, $26 (annual) ● dual, $95 (annual). **Staff:** 30. **Budget:** $5,000,000. **Local Groups:** 93. **Multinational. Description:** Educational and scientific society of archaeologists and others interested in archaeological study and research. Founded five schools of

archaeology: American School of Classical Studies (Athens, 1881); School of Classical Studies of the American Academy (Rome, 1895); American Schools of Oriental Research (Jerusalem, 1900 and Baghdad, 1921); School of American Research (1907, with headquarters at Santa Fe, NM). Is allied with three research institutes: American Research Institute in Turkey; American Institute of Iranian Studies; American Research Center in Egypt. Maintains annual lecture programs for all branch societies. Operates placement service for archeology educators. Sponsors educational programs for middle school children. **Libraries: Type:** reference. **Awards:** Gold Medal Award. **Frequency:** annual. **Type:** medal. **Recipient:** for distinguished archaeological achievement and scientific contributions to archaeology ● Olivia James Traveling Fellowship. **Frequency:** annual. **Type:** fellowship. **Recipient:** for travel and study in Rome and the Aegean area ● Science Medal Award. **Frequency:** annual. **Type:** recognition. **Recipient:** for distinguished archaeological achievement and scientific contributions to archaeology ● Wiseman Book Award. **Frequency:** annual. **Type:** recognition. **Recipient:** for distinguished archaeological achievement and scientific contributions to archaeology. **Computer Services:** Online services, forums. **Telecommunication Services:** electronic mail, bclendenning@aia.bu.edu. **Committees:** Annual Meeting Outreach; APA/AIA Placement; Archaeological Outreach Education; Archeology in American Higher Education; Archives; Awards; Conservation and Heritage Management; Corpus Vasorum Antiquorum; Development; Education; Fellowships; Gold Medal; Lecture Program; Nominating; Professional Responsibilities; Underwater Archaeology. **Affiliated With:** American Research Institute in Turkey; American Schools of Oriental Research. **Publications:** *AIA Newsletter*, quarterly. **Circulation:** 10,000 ● *American Journal of Archaeology*, quarterly. Covers archaeological subjects; illustrated with black-and-white photographs, drawings, and diagrams. Includes book reviews. **Price:** included in membership dues; $75.00 /year for individuals in U.S.; $95.00 /year for individuals outside U.S.; $250.00 /year for institutions in U.S. ISSN: 0002-9114. Alternate Formats: microform ● *Archaeological Fieldwork Opportunities Bulletin*, annual. Lists excavation sites and field schools for volunteers and employment opportunities. **Price:** $11.00 for members; $12.50 for nonmembers, plus shipping and handling. **Circulation:** 2,000. **Advertising:** accepted ● *Archaeology*, bimonthly. Magazine. **Price:** $21.95/year in U.S.; $36.95/year outside U.S., plus shipping and handling. ISSN: 0003-8113. **Circulation:** 175,000. **Advertising:** accepted ● Annual Report, annual ● Monographs. **Conventions/Meetings:** annual meeting (exhibits).

6441 ■ Archeology Division of the American Anthropological Association (AD)

c/o American Anthropological Association
2200 Wilson Blvd., Ste.600
Arlington, VA 22201
Ph: (703)528-1902
Fax: (703)528-3546
E-mail: sgillesp@ufl.edu
URL: http://www.aaanet.org/ad
Contact: Susan Gillespie RPA, Pres.

Founded: 1984. **Membership Dues:** regular, $45 (annual) ● student, $10 (annual) ● joint, foreign, retired, $15 (annual). **Description:** A unit of the American Anthropological Association (see separate entry). Represents University and college faculty and students of archaeology. Works to advance the study of archaeology as a branch of anthropology. Fosters the publication and dissemination of archaeological research to anthropologists, scholars, and the public. **Awards:** Alfred Vincent Kidder Award. **Frequency:** annual. **Type:** recognition. **Recipient:** for eminence in the field of American archaeology. **Formerly:** (2005) Archeology Section. **Conventions/Meetings:** annual meeting, held in conjunction with AAA.

6442 ■ Center for American Archeology (CAA)

PO Box 366
Kampsville, IL 62053
Ph: (618)653-4316
Fax: (618)653-4232
E-mail: caa@caa-archeology.org
URL: http://www.caa-archeology.org
Contact: Ms. Mary Pirkl, Dir. of Education

Founded: 1953. **Members:** 500. **Membership Dues:** regular, $50 (annual) ● supporting, $100 (annual) ● family, $75 (annual) ● senior, $45 (annual) ● contributing, $500 (annual) ● sustaining, $250 (annual). **Staff:** 20. **Budget:** $500,000. **Description:** Philanthropic organizations, foundations, corporations, professional and amateur archaeologists, students, and others interested in archaeology in the U.S. Conducts archaeological research and disseminates the results. Excavates, analyzes, and conserves archaeological sites and artifacts. Sponsors tours, lectures, and educational and outreach programs, including university, middle school and junior high, and high school field schools; offers professional training at levels of detail ranging from secondary to postgraduate. Maintains speakers' bureau. Operates Visitors Center. **Libraries: Type:** reference. **Holdings:** 15,000. **Programs:** Contract Archeology; Education; Public Outreach; Research. **Formerly:** (1981) Foundation for Illinois Archaeology. **Publications:** *Center for American Archeology Annual Report*, annual ● *Center for American Archeology Newsletter*, quarterly ● *Kampsville Archaeological Center Research Series*, periodic. Reports ● *Kampsville Archaeological Center Technical Report*, periodic ● *Kampsville Studies in Archeology and History*. Monographs. **Conventions/Meetings:** seminar ● workshop, for teachers.

6443 ■ Center for the Study of Beadwork (CSB)

PO Box 13719
Portland, OR 97213
Ph: (503)655-3078
E-mail: csb@europa.com
URL: http://www.europa.com/~alice
Contact: Alice Scherer, Dir.

Founded: 1986. **Budget:** $55,000. **Multinational. Description:** Individuals interested in beads and beadwork. Gathers and disseminates information on beadwork, which includes the working of seed and bugle beads. Studies and collects information on contemporary, older, ethnic, and Euro-American beadwork. Collects papers from beadwork artists, researchers, and collectors. Conducts research and educational programs; maintains speakers' bureau. Makes available books, resource lists, slide kits, postcards. Participates in larger bead conferences as a speaker. **Convention/Meeting:** none. **Libraries: Type:** reference. **Holdings:** 1,500; archival material, artwork, books, clippings, monographs, periodicals. **Subjects:** contemporary, Indian, African, European, Asian, and Japanese beadwork. **Also Known As:** CSB. **Publications:** *The New Beadwork*. Book. Covers contemporary beadwork as an art form. **Price:** $29.95 ● *Notes from a Beadworker's Journal*, periodic. Newsletter. Includes classified listings and news about bead-related organizations around the world; back issues only are available. **Price:** $2.50/back issue; $5.00/special issue. **Circulation:** 750. **Advertising:** accepted.

6444 ■ Early Sites Research Society (ESRS)

Address Unknown since 2007

Founded: 1973. **Members:** 225. **Description:** Individuals and organizations interested in the study of the nature, origin, and purpose of unidentified stone work or other unexplained antiquities in the United States. Research teams correlate activities and engage in field work. Has collection of material on stone work and related fields. Operates field school for children. **Libraries: Type:** reference. **Holdings:** 8,000; audiovisuals, books, films. **Awards: Type:** recognition. **Recipient:** for archaeological field work. **Committees:** Archaeology; Maritime Archaeology; Research. **Publications:** *ESRS Epigraphic Series*, periodic ● *Work Report*, periodic ● Books ● Bulletin, annual ● Newsletter, periodic ● Also publishes research materials. **Conventions/Meetings:** semiannual meeting - always spring and fall.

6445 ■ Epigraphic Society (ES)

c/o Mr. Donal B. Buchanan, Sec.-Treas./Ed.
97 Village Post Rd.
Danvers, MA 01923
Ph: (978)774-1275
E-mail: donalbb@epigraphy.org
URL: http://www.epigraphy.org
Contact: Mr. Donal B. Buchanan, Sec.-Treas./Ed.

Founded: 1974. **Members:** 800. **Budget:** $30,000. **Regional Groups:** 15. **Description:** Launches expeditions to North America and overseas. Reports discoveries and decipherments and assesses their historical implications. Participates in group lecture and teaching programs with other archaeological societies and university departments of archaeology and history. **Libraries: Type:** reference. **Holdings:** archival material. **Subjects:** archaeology, history. **Awards: Type:** recognition. **Publications:** *ESOP: Epigraphic Society Occasional Papers*, 1-2/year. Journal. Reports research on ancient inscriptions and linguistics. **Price:** included in membership dues; $32.50 /year for nonmembers. ISSN: 0192-5148. **Circulation:** 1,000. **Advertising:** accepted ● Also publishes dictionaries. **Conventions/Meetings:** biennial meeting.

6446 ■ Etruscan Foundation (EF)

PO Box 26
Fremont, MI 49412
Ph: (231)519-0675
Fax: (231)924-0777
E-mail: office@etruscanfoundation.org
URL: http://www.etruscanfoundation.org
Contact: Mr. Richard String, Exec. Dir.

Founded: 1958. **Members:** 301. **Membership Dues:** student, $25 (annual) ● active, $65 (annual) ● contributor, institutional, $100 (annual) ● sponsor, $250 (annual) ● friend, $500 (annual) ● patron, $1,000 (annual) ● benefactor, $2,500-$10,000 (annual). **Budget:** $100,000. **Multinational. Description:** Works for the study and understanding of the cultural and material history and heritage of the Etruscans, their neighbors and ancestors, by supporting research, education, conservation, and publication. **Publications:** *Etruscan Studies*, annual. Journal. Details activities in all areas of research and study related to the Etruscan civilization with articles contributed by scholars around the world. **Price:** $100.00 /year for libraries in U.S.; $50.00 /year for individuals in U.S.; $110.00 /year for libraries outside U.S.; $60.00 /year for individuals outside U.S.

6447 ■ Institute for American Indian Studies (IAIS)

38 Curtis Rd.
PO Box 1260
Washington, CT 06793-0260
Ph: (860)868-0518
Fax: (860)868-1649
E-mail: iais@charter.net
URL: http://www.birdstone.org
Contact: Elizabeth McCormick, Dir.

Founded: 1971. **Members:** 1,350. **Membership Dues:** student, $20 (annual) ● senior, $25 (annual) ● individual, $40 (annual) ● family, $55 (annual) ● contributor, $100 (annual) ● benefactor, $250 (annual) ● sponsor, $500 (annual) ● patron, $1,000 (annual). **Staff:** 10. **Budget:** $600,000. **Description:** Represents individuals, families, libraries and institutions. Discovers, preserves and interprets information about Native Americans of the northeastern woodlands area of the U.S., including their migration, survival patterns, cultural changes and beliefs; enhances appreciation for their cultures and achievements. Conducts archaeological field trips, research programs, surveys and excavations. Provides indoor and outdoor exhibits covering 12,000 years of North American prehistory, history and contemporary native themes. Maintains quarter-mile Quinnetukut Habitat Trail and Indian Encampment with three wigwams and a longhouse. Sponsors archaeological training sessions, teacher workshops, craft workshops, summer youth programs and film festivals. **Libraries: Type:** reference. **Holdings:** 2,000; audiovisuals, books, periodicals. **Telecommunication Services:** electronic mail, emccormick.iais@charter.net. **Com-**

mittees: Academic Advisory; Native American Advisory; Youth Advisory. **Departments:** Collections; Development; Education; Exhibits; Gift Shop; Research. **Formerly:** (1975) Shepaug Valley Archaeological Society; (1992) American Indian Archaeological Institute. **Publications:** *Calendars for Press*, 3/year ● *Netop*, bimonthly. Newsletter. **Price:** included in membership dues. **Circulation:** 1,350 ● Brochures ● Catalogs ● Pamphlets. **Conventions/Meetings:** lecture ● Native American Art and Literary Competitions, for 1st through 8th graders ● symposium.

6448 ■ Institute of Nautical Archaeology (INA)
PO Drawer HG
College Station, TX 77841-5137
Ph: (979)845-6694 (979)845-6355
Fax: (979)847-9260
E-mail: ina@tamu.edu
URL: http://ina.tamu.edu
Contact: Donny L. Hamilton PhD, Pres.
Founded: 1973. **Members:** 1,400. **Membership Dues:** seafarer, $75 (annual) ● student, retiree, $25 (annual) ● surveyor, $150 (annual) ● diver, $40 (annual) ● restorer, $500 (annual) ● curator, $1,000 (annual) ● excavator, $2,500 (annual) ● navigator, $5,000 (annual) ● institution, $100 (annual). **Staff:** 10. **Multinational. Description:** Individuals interested in nautical archaeology. Gathers information of man's past as left in the physical remains of his maritime activities and disseminates this information through scientific and popular publications, seminars, and lectures. Initially, work was concentrated in the Mediterranean and Aegean seas, but now encompasses five continents. Studies ship remains spanning 3400 years. Supports related research ranging from the treatment of waterlogged wood to the study of past sea-level changes. Sponsors master's and doctoral degree programs in nautical archaeology through Texas A&M University. **Libraries: Type:** reference. **Holdings:** 3,000; books. **Subjects:** nautical archaeology, history of seafaring. **Telecommunication Services:** electronic mail, dlhamilton@tamu.edu. **Formerly:** (1979) American Institute of Nautical Archeology. **Publications:** *The INA Quarterly*. Journal. Features articles about the underwater archaeological research being conducted or sponsored by INA. **Price:** $1.25 for members (from Volume 1 to 9); $2.50 for nonmembers; $1.75 for members (starting from Volume 10). Alternate Formats: online.

6449 ■ International Association for Obsidian Studies (IAOS)
c/o S. Colby Phillips, Sec.-Treas.
Univ. of Washington
Dept. of Anthropology
Box 353100
Seattle, WA 98195-3100
E-mail: colbyp@u.washington.edu
URL: http://www.peak.org/obsidian/obsidian.html
Contact: Anastasia Steffen, Pres.
Founded: 1989. **Members:** 110. **Membership Dues:** student, $10 (annual) ● regular, $20 (annual) ● institutional, $50 (annual) ● life, $200. **Budget:** $3,000. **Description:** Promotes use and application of obsidian chemical characterization data and dating methods and studies to archaeological problems. **Publications:** Newsletter, 3/year. **Price:** included in membership dues. **Circulation:** 110 ● Bulletin. **Price:** included in membership dues. Alternate Formats: online ● Articles. Alternate Formats: online ● Books. **Conventions/Meetings:** annual meeting, held in conjunction with SAA convention.

6450 ■ National Association of State Archaeologists (NASA)
c/o Arthur E. Spiess, Sec.-Treas.
Maine Historic Preservation Commn.
65 State House Sta.
Augusta, ME 04333-0065
Ph: (207)287-2132
Fax: (207)287-2335
E-mail: arthur.spiess@maine.gov
URL: http://www.uiowa.edu/~osa/nasa
Contact: Arthur E. Spiess, Sec.-Treas.
Founded: 1979. **Members:** 53. **Membership Dues:** individual, $25 (annual). **Description:** State archaeologists who oversee the archaeological functions of their state and participate in the management of the state's archaeological resources. Compiles statistics. **Publications:** Directory, annual ● Newsletter, quarterly. **Conventions/Meetings:** annual meeting and symposium, held in conjunction with the Society for American Archaeology.

6451 ■ Near East Archaeological Society (NEAS)
Horn Archaeological Museum
Andrews Univ.
Berrien Springs, MI 49104-0990
Ph: (269)471-3273
Fax: (269)471-3619
E-mail: publications@neasweb.org
URL: http://www.neasweb.org
Contact: Dr. Ronald Youngblood, Pres.
Founded: 1957. **Members:** 265. **Membership Dues:** regular, institution, associate in U.S., $30 (annual) ● student in U.S., $15 (annual) ● regular, institution, associate outside U.S., $35 (annual) ● student outside U.S., $20 (annual). **Staff:** 8. **Multinational. Description:** Evangelical institutions and individuals interested in archaeological research in the Mediterranean and its potential for enhancing biblical research. Promotes archaeological and biblical research in Palestine and the surrounding Near East region. Endorses and published preliminary reports of excavations. **Libraries: Type:** reference. **Holdings:** 48. **Telecommunication Services:** electronic mail, president@neasweb.org. **Publications:** *Artifax*, quarterly. Newsletter. Provides information about Near Eastern archaeology, archaeological research projects, and announcements of conferences and field work. **Price:** included in membership dues. **Circulation:** 400. **Advertising:** accepted ● *Near East Archaeological Society Bulletin*, annual. **Price:** included in membership dues ● *NEAS Bulletin*, annual. Journal. Contains articles about Near Eastern archaeology. Includes book reviews and conference reports. **Price:** included in membership dues; $25.00 /year for nonmembers; $25.00 /year for institutions; $15.00 for students. ISSN: 0739-0068. **Circulation:** 400. **Advertising:** accepted. **Conventions/Meetings:** annual meeting and board meeting, held in conjunction with the Evangelical Theological Society; presents scholarly papers and excavation reports - 2008 Nov. 19-21, Providence, RI; 2009 Nov. 18-20, New Orleans, LA; 2010 Nov. 17-19, Atlanta, GA.

6452 ■ New England Antiquities Research Association (NEARA)
94 Cross Point Rd.
Edgecomb, ME 04556
Ph: (207)882-9425
Fax: (207)882-8162
E-mail: krosspt@lincoln.midcoast.com
URL: http://www.neara.org
Contact: Roslyn Strong, Contact
Founded: 1964. **Members:** 500. **Membership Dues:** active, $35 (annual) ● patron, $50 (annual) ● sponsor, $75 (annual). **State Groups:** 10. **Description:** Works to study the nature, origin, history, and purpose of stoneworks and related structures in the northeastern U.S. Collects data on these sites and interprets it in relation to other disciplines, including archaeology, anthropology, geology, and astronomy. Provides current research projects including historical documentation research, involving recording and mapping of lithic sites; and professionally supervised limited excavation. Encourages other research. Compiles statistics; maintains file of site reports; provides slide show to interested organizations. **Libraries: Type:** reference. **Holdings:** 700. **Committees:** Research Assistance. **Publications:** *Nearo Transit*, semiannual. Newsletter. Includes chapter news and member activities. ● Journal, semiannual. Covers archaeology, anthropology, geology, archaeoastronomy, epigraphy, and earth mysteries. Includes chapter news and book reviews. **Price:** included in membership dues. ISSN: 0149-2551. **Circulation:** 500. **Advertising:** accepted ● Monographs. **Conventions/Meetings:** semiannual conference - always spring and fall.

6453 ■ Register of Professional Archaeologists (RPA)
5024-R Campbell Blvd.
Baltimore, MD 21236
Ph: (410)933-3486
Fax: (410)931-8111
E-mail: info@rpanet.org
URL: http://www.rpanet.org
Contact: Jeffrey H. Altschul, Pres.
Founded: 1976. **Members:** 1,531. **Membership Dues:** individual (member of sponsoring group/organization), $45 (annual) ● individual (without any affiliation), $125 (annual). **Description:** Represents archaeologists satisfying basic requirements in training and experience, including private consultants, individuals working with large firms, and academic personnel. Seeks to define professionalism in archaeology; provide a measure against which to evaluate archaeological actions and research; establish certification standards; provide for grievance procedures; demonstrate to other archaeologists and the public the nature of professional archaeology. Monitors related legislative activities; maintains register archives. Is developing educational programs and drafting standards and guidelines for field schools. **Awards:** Distinguished Service Award. **Frequency:** annual. **Type:** recognition. **Recipient:** for service in research, teaching, government, cultural resource management or public outreach ● Seiberling Award. **Frequency:** annual. **Type:** recognition. **Recipient:** for implementation of programs, policies, regulations, and guidance that benefited the conservation of archaeological resources ● Special Achievement Award. **Frequency:** annual. **Type:** recognition. **Recipient:** for action or program that merits national-level recognition. **Committees:** Certification; Ethics; Government Relations; Standards. **Formerly:** (1998) Society of Professional Archaeologists. **Publications:** *Directory of Professional Archaeologists*, annual. **Price:** included in membership dues ● Papers. **Conventions/Meetings:** annual meeting, held in conjunction with Society for American Archaeology.

6454 ■ SEARCH Foundation
PO Box 1729
Crestline, CA 92325
Ph: (909)338-2468
Fax: (909)338-2468
E-mail: jtmomega777@juno.com
Contact: John T. McIntosh, Pres.
Founded: 1969. **Description:** Seeks to locate and identify the remains of the Biblical Noah's Ark through research and field expeditions. (SEARCH is an acronym for Scientific Exploratory Archeological Research). **Libraries: Type:** not open to the public. **Holdings:** articles, photographs.

6455 ■ Society for American Archaeology (SAA)
900 2nd St. NE, No. 12
Washington, DC 20002-3560
Ph: (202)789-8200
Fax: (202)789-0284
E-mail: headquarters@saa.org
URL: http://www.saa.org
Contact: Tobi A. Brimsek CAE, Exec. Dir.
Founded: 1934. **Members:** 7,000. **Membership Dues:** regular, $125 (annual) ● student, $65 (annual) ● retired, $72 (annual) ● joint, $38 (annual) ● associate, $49 (annual) ● life, $5,200. **Staff:** 9. **Budget:** $1,100,000. **Description:** Professionals, vocationals, students, and others interested in American archaeology. Stimulates scientific research in the archaeology of the New World by: creating closer professional relations among archaeologists, and between them and others interested in American archaeology; advocating the conservation of archaeological data and furthering the control or elimination of commercialization of archaeological objects; promoting a more rational public appreciation of the aims and limitations of archaeological research. Maintains

placement service and educational programs. **Awards:** Book Award. **Frequency:** annual. **Type:** recognition. **Recipient:** for a recently published book that is expected to have a major impact on the direction and character of archaeological research ● The Crabtree Award. **Frequency:** annual. **Type:** recognition. **Recipient:** to individuals who made major contributions to American archaeology ● Fryxell Award for Interdisciplinary Research. **Frequency:** annual. **Type:** recognition. **Recipient:** for interdisciplinary excellence by a distinguished scientist whose research has contributed significantly to American archaeology ● Lifetime Achievement Award. **Frequency:** annual. **Type:** recognition. **Recipient:** for specific accomplishments in a wide range of areas relating to archaeology which are truly extraordinary, widely recognized as such and of a positive and lasting quality ● Poster Award. **Frequency:** annual. **Type:** recognition. **Recipient:** for the best accomplishments in this medium ● Presidential Recognition Award. **Frequency:** annual. **Type:** recognition. **Recipient:** to individuals who have provided extraordinary services to the society and the profession in the past year ● Public Service Award. **Frequency:** annual. **Type:** recognition. **Recipient:** to non-archaeologists who have made important contributions to the protection and preservation of cultural resources ● SAA Dissertation Award. **Frequency:** annual. **Type:** recognition. **Recipient:** to archaeologists just entering the profession whose doctoral dissertations are judged to be particularly outstanding. **Committees:** Ceremonial Resolutions; Consulting Archaeology; Curation; Ethics; Government Affairs; Government Archaeology; Latin American Relations; National Historic Landmarks; Native American Relations; Native American Scholarships; Public Education; Repatriation; Status of Women in Archaeology; Student Affairs; Survey Project Oversight. **Councils:** Affiliated Societies. **Publications:** *American Antiquity*, quarterly. Journal. Includes book reviews. **Price:** included in membership dues; $175.00 for nonmembers, institutional subscribers. ISSN: 0002-7316. **Circulation:** 6,200. **Advertising:** accepted. Alternate Formats: microform ● *Archaeology and Public Education*, 3/year. Newsletter. Aids educators, interpreters, and archaeologists who wish to teach the public about the value of archaeological research and resources. **Price:** free for members; $10.00 for nonmembers ● *Latin American Antiquity* (in English and Spanish), quarterly. Journal. Includes archaeology, prehistory, and ethnohistory of Mesoamerica, Central America, South America, and culturally related areas. **Price:** $50.00 for members; $115.00 for nonmembers, institutional subscribers. ISSN: 1045-6635. **Circulation:** 1,500. **Advertising:** accepted ● *SAA Archaeological Record*, 5/year. Magazine. Covers archaeological topics and society news. Includes book list and employment opportunities. **Price:** included in membership dues; $10.00 for back issues, plus shipping and handling. ISSN: 1741-5672. **Circulation:** 6,600. **Advertising:** accepted. Also Cited As: *SAA Bulletin* ● *Special Publications*, periodic. **Conventions/Meetings:** annual conference and meeting (exhibits) - usually March or April. 2009 Apr. 22-26, Atlanta, GA; 2010 Apr. 14-18, St. Louis, MO.

6456 ■ Society of Bead Researchers (SBR)

c/o Alice Scherer, Sec.-Treas.
PO Box 13719
Portland, OR 97213
E-mail: alice@europa.com
URL: http://sbrwebsite.home.comcast.net/index
Contact: Roderick Sprague, Pres.

Founded: 1981. **Members:** 130. **Membership Dues:** regular in North America, $20 (annual) ● regular outside North America, $30 (annual) ● sustaining, $45 (annual) ● patron, $75 (annual) ● benefactor, $150 (annual). **Budget:** $5,000. **Multinational. Description:** Represents the interests of amateur and professional archaeologists, ethnologists, museologists, and collectors in 11 countries. Aims to further research on beads of all periods. Disseminates results of research through publications. **Publications:** *Bead Forum*, semiannual. Newsletter. Includes short articles and new publications listing. **Price:** included in membership dues. ISSN: 0829-8726. **Circulation:** 300 ● *Beads*, annual. Journal. **Price:** C$17.50 in North America; C$22.50 outside North America. ISSN: 0843-5499. **Circulation:** 1,000.

6457 ■ Society for Historical Archaeology (SHA)

15245 Shady Grove Rd., Ste.130
Rockville, MD 20850
Ph: (301)990-2454
Fax: (301)990-9771
E-mail: hq@sha.org
URL: http://www.sha.org
Contact: Sara F. Mascia, Treas.

Founded: 1967. **Members:** 2,300. **Membership Dues:** student, $70 (annual) ● regular, $125 (annual) ● institution, $200 (annual) ● retired, $75 (annual) ● friend, $175 (annual) ● developer, $250 (annual) ● benefactor, $400 (annual) ● life, $3,600 ● adjunct, $40 (annual). **Description:** Represents archaeologists, historians, anthropologists, and ethnohistorians; other individuals and institutions with an interest in historical archaeology or allied fields. Aims to bring together persons interested in studying specific historic sites, manuscripts, and published sources, and to develop generalizations concerning historical periods and cultural dynamics as these emerge through the techniques of archaeological excavation and analysis. Main focus is the era beginning with the exploration of the non-European world by Europeans, and geographical areas in the Western Hemisphere, but also considers Oceanian, African, and Asian archaeology during the relatively late periods. **Awards:** Award of Merit. **Frequency:** annual. **Type:** recognition. **Recipient:** for specific achievements of individuals and organizations that have furthered the cause of historical archaeology ● Carol Ruppe Distinguished Service Award. **Frequency:** periodic. **Type:** recognition. **Recipient:** for individuals who have a record of sustained and truly outstanding service to the society ● Harrington Award. **Frequency:** periodic. **Type:** recognition ● John L. Cotter Award. **Frequency:** periodic. **Type:** recognition. **Recipient:** for single achievement of an individual that is truly outstanding in its respective category. **Telecommunication Services:** electronic mail, sasamascia@aol.com. **Publications:** *Guides to Historical Archaeological Literature*, periodic. Bibliography. Covers ethnic groups of the historic period. ISSN: 8868-1800. **Circulation:** 500. Also Cited As: *Guides to the Historical Archaeological Literature of the Immigrant Experience in America* ● *Historical Archaeology*, quarterly. Journal. Contains articles on theoretical perspectives, comparative studies, and artifact and site analyses. Includes book reviews. **Price:** included in membership dues. ISSN: 0440-9213. **Advertising:** accepted ● *Society for Historical Archaeology—Newsletter*, quarterly. Covers current archaeological research and cultural resource laws and regulations; includes information on society activities. **Price:** included in membership dues. Alternate Formats: online ● *Special Publications Series*, periodic. Monographs. Contains special thematic topics of interest to historical archaeology. ● *Underwater Archaeology*, annual. Brochure. Contains papers focusing on underwater archaeology. **Conventions/Meetings:** annual Conference on Historical and Underwater Archaeology (exhibits) - always January.

6458 ■ Society for Industrial Archeology (SIA)

c/o Don Durfee, Coor.
Social Sciences Dept.
Michigan Technological Univ.
1400 Townsend Dr.
Houghton, MI 49931-1295
Ph: (906)487-1889
E-mail: sia@mtu.edu
URL: http://www.sia-web.org
Contact: Don Durfee, Coor.

Founded: 1971. **Members:** 1,650. **Membership Dues:** individual, institutional, $50 (annual) ● joint, $55 (annual) ● student, $20 (annual) ● contributing, $100 (annual) ● sustaining, $150 (annual) ● corporate, $500 (annual). **Budget:** $60,000. **Regional Groups:** 8. **Description:** Historians, architects, architectural historians, teachers, museum technical staff, archaeologists, engineers, government staff, and other interested individuals. Promotes the identification, preservation, and use of historic industrial and engineering sites, structures, and equipment. Broadens public awareness of the social significance of America's industrial and technological heritage. Disseminates information; encourages research and field investigations of vanishing works and processes; conducts process tours; offers technical assistance. Members present technical papers. **Awards:** General Tools Award. **Frequency:** annual. **Type:** recognition. **Recipient:** for contribution to the field ● Robert M. Vogel Prize. **Frequency:** annual. **Type:** recognition. **Recipient:** for the best article in the journal. **Additional Websites:** http://www.siahq.org. **Publications:** *IA: The Journal of the Society for Industrial Archeology*, semiannual. Includes book reviews. **Price:** included in membership dues. ISSN: 0160-1040. **Circulation:** 1,650 ● *SIA Newsletter*, quarterly. **Price:** included in membership dues. ISSN: 0160-1067. Alternate Formats: online ● Bibliography, periodic ● Books ● Membership Directory, periodic ● Monographs ● Reports ● Also publishes data sheets; has produced slide film. **Conventions/Meetings:** annual conference, book sales (exhibits) - always spring ● annual tour - always fall.

6459 ■ Stonehenge Study Group (SSG)

Address Unknown since 2008

Founded: 1970. **Members:** 2,200. **Staff:** 2. **For-Profit. Description:** Participants are individuals interested in astronomy, geology, archaeology, anthropology, meteorology, epigraphy, rock art, and related arts and sciences. Activities include: expeditions to megalithic sites such as Stonehenge, Avebury, Newgrange, Callanish, and Carnac where stone circles are available for study; local lectures and study groups covering archaeoastronomy, druids, legends, biblical interpretations, pre-Columbian contacts, and Ogham epigraphy. **Libraries: Type:** reference. **Holdings:** 4,000; books, periodicals. **Subjects:** archaeology, astronomy, geology, meteorology, related arts and sciences. **Computer Services:** database, megalithic site survey information, epigraphic listings. **Affiliated With:** New England Antiquities Research Association. **Publications:** *A Search for Quetzalcoatl*. Book. **Price:** $8.00 ● *America's First Crop Circle*. Book ● *The Best of Stonehenge Viewpoint*. Book. Explores myth, ancient religions, earth mysteries, ancient legends, and prehistory through the disciplines of archaeology, epigraphy, and astronomy. **Price:** $10.00/year. ISSN: 0140-654X. **Circulation:** 2,200 ● *Cascading Comets*. Book ● *Celtic Secrets*. Book ● *The Colorado Ogam Album*. Book ● *Exploring Rock Art*. Book ● *King Arthur's Crystal Cave*. Book ● *Megalithic Adventures*. Book ● *Science of Ley Hunting*. Book ● *Seekers of the Linear Vision*. Book ● *Stonehenge Scrolls*. Book ● *Waters Above Firmament*. Book ● *The Whistler Serenade*. Book. **Conventions/Meetings:** annual conference - always in Santa Barbara, CA.

6460 ■ World Archaeological Society (WAS)

c/o Ron Miller, Dir.
120 Lakewood Dr.
Hollister, MO 65672
Ph: (417)334-2377
E-mail: ronwriterartist@aol.com
URL: http://www.worldarchaeologicalsociety.com
Contact: Ron Miller, Dir.

Founded: 1971. **Membership Dues:** regular in U.S., $16 (annual) ● regular outside U.S., $20 (annual). **Staff:** 2. **For-Profit. Description:** Professional and amateur archaeologists, anthropologists, and art historians in 32 countries. Promotes the scientific and constructive study of antiquity within the fields of archaeology, anthropology, and art history. Conducts research on biblical archaeology, democracy, and the anthropology of drug addiction. Projects include the "Living" Museum of Democracy and the restoration of old Bibles. Conducts special research projects upon request. Supplies tape lectures for special programs. Provides ink and color illustrations for researchers. **Libraries: Type:** reference. **Holdings:** 6,000; books, clippings. **Subjects:** archaeology, anthropology, art history, fine art, religion, literature, military history, general history. **Awards:** WAS Special Commendations. **Frequency:** periodic. **Type:** recognition. **Recipient:** for publishers and individual artists of publications, photographs, graphic art and film. **Publications:** *Special Publications*, periodic. Report. **Price:** included in membership dues. ISSN: 1060-2887. **Advertising:** accepted. Alternate Formats: online ● *WAS Fact Sheet* ● *WAS Newsletter*, occasional. Includes book reviews, articles, obituaries, and short articles. **Price:** free for members. ISSN: 0738-8063. **Advertising:** accepted. Alternate Formats: online.

Architecture

6461 ■ American Architectural Foundation (AAF)

1799 New York Ave. NW
Washington, DC 20006
Ph: (202)626-7318
Fax: (202)626-7420
E-mail: info@archfoundation.org
URL: http://www.archfoundation.org
Contact: Elizabeth Larouer, Exec. Asst. to the Pres./CEO

Founded: 1942. **Staff:** 13. **Budget:** $3,150,000. **Description:** Educates the public about the importance of architecture in daily life. **Libraries: Type:** reference. **Holdings:** artwork, photographs. **Awards:** Accent on Architecture. **Frequency:** annual. **Type:** grant. **Recipient:** for local non-profit design and civic organizations in producing innovative public education programs ● AIA/AAF Scholarships. **Frequency:** annual. **Type:** scholarship. **Recipient:** to high school seniors and college freshmen who plan to study architecture in an NAAB-accredited program ● Keystone Award. **Frequency:** annual. **Type:** recognition. **Recipient:** to an individual from outside the architecture and design field for exemplary leadership. **Affiliated With:** American Institute of Architects. **Formerly:** (1960) American Architectural Foundation; (1988) American Institute of Architects Foundation. **Publications:** Also publishes exhibition and competition catalogs, guides, indices, and other materials. **Conventions/Meetings:** semiannual meeting - usually April and November in Washington, DC.

6462 ■ American Indian Council of Architects and Engineers (AICAE)

c/o Jefferson Begay, Pres.
1707 E Highland Ave., Ste.200
Phoenix, AZ 85016
Ph: (602)222-5300
Fax: (602)789-5735
E-mail: jbegay@kitchell.com
URL: http://www.aicae.org
Contact: Jefferson Begay, Pres.

Founded: 1976. **Members:** 40. **Membership Dues:** individual, $50 (annual) ● voting ($50 times the index number), $150-$350 (annual) ● non-voting associate, $10-$100 (annual). **Description:** American Indian-owned architectural and engineering firms. Seeks to: enhance the role and improve the professional skills of American Indians in architecture and engineering; encourage American Indians to pursue careers in these fields. Represents interests of members at the national level. **Telecommunication Services:** electronic mail, sfricke@whiteshield.com. **Publications:** Directory, annual ● Newsletter, semiannual. **Conventions/Meetings:** semiannual conference.

6463 ■ American Institute of Architects (AIA)

1735 New York Ave. NW
Washington, DC 20006-5292
Ph: (202)626-7300
Free: (800)AIA-3837
Fax: (202)626-7547
E-mail: infocentral@aia.org
URL: http://www.aia.org
Contact: R.K. Stewart FAIA, Pres.

Founded: 1857. **Members:** 77,000. **Membership Dues:** architect, $136 (annual) ● associate in U.S., $54 (annual) ● international associate, $81 (annual) ● individual allied, $150 (annual) ● associate outside U.S., $48 (annual). **Staff:** 150. **Budget:** $32,000,000. **Regional Groups:** 19. **State Groups:** 50. **Local Groups:** 322. **Multinational. Description:** Represents architects, licensed architects, graduate architects, not yet licensed and retired architects. Fosters professionalism and accountability among members through continuing education and training. Promotes design excellence by influencing change in the industry. Sponsors educational programs with schools of architecture, graduate students, and elementary and secondary schools. Advises on professional competitions. Supplies construction documents. Established the American Architectural Foundation. Sponsors Octagon Museum; operates bookstore; stages exhibitions; compiles statistics. Provides monthly news service on design and construction. Conducts professional development programs, research programs, charitable activities, and children's services. **Libraries: Type:** reference; by appointment only. **Holdings:** 40,000; archival material, artwork, audiovisuals, books. **Subjects:** architecture, interior design, construction. **Awards:** Gold Medal Award. **Frequency:** annual. **Type:** medal. **Recipient:** for achievement in design ● National Honor Award. **Frequency:** periodic. **Type:** recognition. **Recipient:** for achievement in design. **Computer Services:** database, membership network ● online services, bibliographies. **Committees:** Architecture for Design; Architecture for Education; Architecture for Health; Corporate Architects; Historic Resources; Housing; Interiors; Justice; Urban Design and Planning. **Departments:** Communications; Component Relations; Contract Documents; Executive Office; Finance and Administration; Government Affairs; Human Resources; Knowledge Center; Meetings and Events; Membership Systems; Professional Practice; Publishing and Marketing; Stakeholder Relations; Technology. **Affiliated With:** American Architectural Foundation; Association of Collegiate Schools of Architecture; International Union of Architects; National Architectural Accrediting Board; National Council of Architectural Registration Boards. **Absorbed:** Western Association of Architects. **Publications:** *AIArchitect*, weekly. Newsletter. **Price:** included in membership dues. Alternate Formats: online ● *Architectural Record*. Magazine. **Price:** included in membership dues ● *ARCHITECTURE*, monthly. Journal. Covers architectural design, technology, and the profession. Includes new product information, book reviews, and calendar of events. **Price:** included in membership dues; $42.00 /year for nonmembers. ISSN: 0746-0554. **Circulation:** 79,000. **Advertising:** accepted ● *Profile*, annual. Membership Directory ● Newspaper, monthly. Provides members with information on products and services available from the institute. **Price:** included in membership dues; $50.00 /year for nonmembers. **Circulation:** 65,000. **Conventions/Meetings:** annual meeting and convention (exhibits).

6464 ■ American Institute of Building Design (AIBD)

7059 Blair Rd. NW, Ste.201
Washington, DC 20012
Free: (800)366-2423
Fax: (202)249-2473
E-mail: info@aibd.org
URL: http://www.aibd.org
Contact: Steven Mickley CPBD, Exec. Dir.

Founded: 1950. **Members:** 1,200. **Membership Dues:** general, $160 (annual) ● professional, $355 (annual) ● design student, $15 (annual) ● affiliate, $450 (annual) ● associate, $95 (annual) ● educator, $70 (annual). **Staff:** 3. **Budget:** $400,000. **Regional Groups:** 48. **State Groups:** 22. **Local Groups:** 55. **Description:** Represents professional building designers engaged in the professional practice of designing residential and light commercial buildings. Other membership categories include draftspersons, educators, and students. Corporate members are residential and light commercial building manufacturers. Keeps members informed of techniques and principles of building design; seeks to stimulate public interest in the aesthetic and practical efficiency of building design; engages in legislative activities and lobbying; provides consumer referral service. Aids in the development of better and continuing education. Local groups meet monthly. **Libraries: Type:** reference. **Subjects:** architecture. **Awards:** AIBD and Home Styles Annual Design Competition. **Frequency:** annual. **Type:** recognition. **Recipient:** for best examples of individual effort in building design and community betterment. **Computer Services:** database, building designer list. **Committees:** Education; Ethics; Examination; Legislative; Political Action. **Affiliated With:** International Conference of Building Officials; National Association of Home Builders. **Formerly:** (1950) United Designers Association. **Publications:** *AIBD Membership Directory*, annual. Contains national membership listing. ● *AIBD Update*, monthly ● *Copyright Manual*. Manuals ● *Design Line*, quarterly. Newsletter. Covers developments in building design products, economic and building trends, and association news. **Price:** included in membership dues. **Circulation:** 2,000. **Advertising:** accepted ● *History of Architecture Syllabus* ● *Home Design Journal*. Magazine ● Copyright Basics for Home Designers and Builders. **Conventions/Meetings:** annual convention (exhibits) - every July or August.

6465 ■ American Society of Golf Course Architects (ASGCA)

125 N Executive Dr., Ste.106
Brookfield, WI 53005
Ph: (262)786-5960
Fax: (262)786-5919
E-mail: info@asgca.org
URL: http://www.asgca.org
Contact: Chad Ritterbusch, Exec. Sec.

Founded: 1946. **Members:** 150. **Budget:** $250,000. **Description:** Represents architects and designers specializing in golf courses. **Awards:** Donald Ross Award. **Frequency:** annual. **Type:** recognition. **Recipient:** for individual who has impacted the profession of golf course design. **Formerly:** ASGCA. **Publications:** *American Society of Golf Course Architects—Membership Directory*, semiannual. **Price:** free ● *ASGCA Newsletter*, monthly. **Price:** available to members only. **Conventions/Meetings:** annual meeting.

6466 ■ American Society of Landscape Architects (ASLA)

636 Eye St. NW
Washington, DC 20001-3736
Ph: (202)898-2444
Free: (888)999-ASLA
Fax: (202)898-1185
E-mail: nsomerville@asla.org
URL: http://www.asla.org
Contact: Nancy C. Somerville, Exec. VP/CEO

Founded: 1899. **Members:** 17,000. **Membership Dues:** full, affiliate, international, $290 (annual) ● associate, $145 (annual) ● student/student affiliate, $43 (annual) ● corporate, $1,750 (annual). **Staff:** 44. **Budget:** $8,000,000. **Regional Groups:** 48. **Description:** Professional society of landscape architects. Promotes the advancement of education and skill in the art of landscape architecture as an instrument in service to the public welfare. Seeks to strengthen existing and proposed university programs in landscape architecture. Offers counsel to new and emerging programs; encourages state registration of landscape architects. Sponsors annual educational exhibit. Offers placement service; conducts specialized education and research. **Libraries: Type:** reference. **Holdings:** 1,500; books, periodicals, reports. **Subjects:** landscape architecture, planning, design, urban growth, historic preservation, horticulture. **Awards:** Alfred B. LaGasse Medal. **Frequency:** annual. **Type:** medal. **Recipient:** for notable contributions to the field of landscape architecture ● ASLA Medal. **Frequency:** annual. **Type:** medal. **Recipient:** for notable contributions to the field of landscape architecture ● Bradford Williams Medal. **Frequency:** annual. **Type:** medal. **Recipient:** for superior writing in Landscape Architecture magazine ● The Design Medal. **Frequency:** annual. **Type:** medal. **Recipient:** for an individual landscape architect who has produced a body of exceptional design work at a sustained level for a period of at least ten years ● Honorary Membership. **Frequency:** annual. **Type:** recognition. **Recipient:** for persons other than landscape architects whose achievements of national or international significance or influence have provided notable service to the profession of landscape architecture ● Jot D. Carpenter Teaching Medal. **Frequency:** annual. **Type:** medal. **Recipient:** for an individual who has made a sustained and significant contribution to landscape architecture education ● The Landscape Architecture Firm Award. **Frequency:** annual. **Type:** recognition. **Recipient:** for any firm or successor firms in which the continuing collaboration among individuals of the firm has been the principal force in consistently producing distinguished landscape architecture for a period of at least 10 years ● The Landscape Architecture Medal of Excellence. **Frequency:** annual. **Type:** medal. **Recipient:** for significant contributions to landscape architecture policy, research, education, project planning and design, or a combination of these items; for someone whose body of work has been maintained at a consistent level of excellence for 10 or more years ● Olmsted Medal. **Frequency:** annual. **Type:** medal. **Recipient:** for notable contribution to the field of landscape architecture by an individual or organization outside the field of landscape architecture ● President's Medal. **Frequency:** annual. **Type:** medal. **Recipient:** to a member for unselfish and devoted service to the ASLA at the national level over a period of not less than five years. **Computer Services:** Mailing lists, customized membership lists ● online services, job/resume listings, ASLA firms, supplier directory, bookstore catalog. **Committees:** Annual Meeting Steering; Archives and Collections; Campus Planning and Design; Context-Sensitive Design; Design/Build; Emerging Professionals; Historic Preservation; Housing and Community Design; International Practice; Landscape and Land Use Planning; Online; Parks and Recreation; Reclamation and Restoration; Residential Landscape Design; Rural Landscape Design; Therapeutic Garden Design; Urban Planning and Design; Water Conservation; Women in Landscape Architecture. **Councils:** Annual Meeting Expo Advisory; Chapter Presidents; Education; Fellows; Professional Interest Groups. **Affiliated With:** International Federation of Landscape Architects; Landscape Architecture Foundation. **Absorbed:** (1982) American Institute of Landscape Architects. **Publications:** *ASLA Members Handbook*, monthly. Membership Directory. Online version has a database searchable by name, geographical location, and employer. **Price:** included in membership dues. ISSN: 0192-5067. **Advertising:** accepted. Alternate Formats: online ● *Landscape Architecture*, monthly. Magazine. Covers landscape planning, design, and management. **Price:** included in membership dues; $49.00 /year for nonmembers; $32.00/year for students. ISSN: 0023-8031. **Circulation:** 25,000. **Advertising:** accepted ● *Landscape Architecture News Digest - LAND Online*, biweekly. Newsletter. Covers issues affecting the landscape architecture profession. Members receive electronic delivery. **Price:** included in membership dues. ISSN: 0023-754X. Alternate Formats: online. **Conventions/Meetings:** annual meeting, education sessions, professional awards presentation (exhibits) - 2008 Oct. 24-27, Philadelphia, PA; 2009 Oct. 1-4, Chicago, IL.

6467 ■ Arab American Association of Engineers and Architects (AAAEA)

PO Box 1536
Chicago, IL 60690-1536
Ph: (312)409-8560
E-mail: aaaea@aaaea.org
URL: http://www.aaaea.org
Contact: Jamal Grainawi SE, Pres.

Founded: 1996. **Membership Dues:** full/associate, $50 (annual) ● full, $100 (biennial) ● student, $10 (annual). **Description:** Represents the interests of architects, engineers and computer science professionals and students of Arab heritage residing in the USA. Seeks to help its members succeed and advance in their professions by networking and interacting among each others through technical, educational, and social activities and events. Promotes cooperation and mutual assistance among the members. **Awards:** AAAEA Scholarship Award. **Frequency:** annual. **Type:** scholarship. **Recipient:** to an undergraduate or graduate, engineer, architect or computer science student who is also a student member of AAAEA. **Publications:** *AAAEA Newsletter*. Alternate Formats: online.

6468 ■ Architectural Engineering Institute (AEI)

c/o American Society of Civil Engineers
1801 Alexander Bell Dr.
Reston, VA 20191-4400
Ph: (703)295-6393
Fax: (703)295-6371
E-mail: achaker@asce.org
URL: http://www.aeinstitute.org
Contact: Amar Chaker PhD, Dir.

Founded: 1998. **Members:** 4,500. **Multinational. Description:** Seeks to advance the state-of-the-art and state-of-the-practice of the building industry worldwide by facilitating effective and timely technology transfer. Provides a multidisciplinary forum for building industry professionals to examine technical, scientific and professional issues of common interest. **Absorbed:** (1998) National Society of Architectural Engineers. **Publications:** *Journal of Architectural Engineering*, quarterly. ISSN: 1076-0431. **Conventions/Meetings:** biennial conference.

6469 ■ Architectural Research Centers Consortium (ARCC)

c/o Prof. Stephen Weeks, Treas.
Univ. of Minnesota
Dept. of Architecture
Rapson Hall, Rm. 145
89 Church St.
Minneapolis, MN 55455
Ph: (612)624-2832
Fax: (612)624-5743
E-mail: weeks001@umn.edu
URL: http://www.arccweb.org
Contact: Prof. Michel Mounayar, Pres.

Founded: 1976. **Membership Dues:** small school/center, $250 (annual) ● medium school/center, $450 (annual) ● large school/center, $650 (annual) ● associate, $100 (annual). **Multinational. Description:** Architectural research centers and schools of architecture, industrial laboratories, government agencies, and architects in private practice. Promotes "the expansion of research culture" and the development of a supporting infrastructure in architecture and related design disciplines. Facilitates communication and cooperation among members; works to coordinate architectural research worldwide; conducts research and educational programs. **Libraries: Type:** reference. **Holdings:** periodicals. **Awards:** Haecker Award. **Frequency:** periodic. **Type:** recognition. **Conventions/Meetings:** annual conference, in conjunction with EAAE - 2008 June 25-28, Copenhagen, Denmark ● periodic workshop.

6470 ■ Asian American Architects and Engineers (AAAE)

c/o Samantha S. Low, Membership Chair
The Albert Gp.
114 Sansome St., Ste.710
San Francisco, CA 94104
Ph: (415)957-8788
E-mail: leschau@kennedyjenks.com
URL: http://www.aaaenc.org
Contact: Samantha S. Low, Membership Chair

Founded: 1978. **Members:** 120. **Membership Dues:** student, $25 (annual) ● regular/general/associate, $100 (annual) ● firm, $225 (annual) ● corporate sponsor, $500 (annual). **Description:** Minorities. Provides contracts and job opportunities for minorities in the architectural and engineering fields. Serves as a network for the promotion in professional fields. **Publications:** Directory, semiannual ● Newsletter, monthly. Alternate Formats: online. **Conventions/Meetings:** biweekly meeting.

6471 ■ Association for Bridge Construction and Design (ABCD)

PO Box 23264
Pittsburgh, PA 15222-6264
Ph: (412)257-8774 (412)824-4685
Fax: (412)257-8815
E-mail: podlipsky@abcdpittsburgh.org
URL: http://www.abcdpittsburgh.org
Contact: Gary B. O'Melia, Pres.

Founded: 1976. **Members:** 300. **Membership Dues:** individual, $20 (annual) ● sustaining, $150 (annual) ● student, $5 (annual). **Regional Groups:** 3. **State Groups:** 3. **Local Groups:** 1. **Description:** Represents persons and firms having a direct or indirect interest in the design and construction of bridges. **Awards: Frequency:** annual. **Type:** scholarship. **Publications:** *Information Publication About Bridge Crisis* ● Newsletter, monthly. Includes employment opportunities and obituaries. **Price:** included in membership dues. **Advertising:** accepted. **Conventions/Meetings:** annual meeting - usually June.

6472 ■ Association of University Architects (AUA)

1277 Univ. of Oregon
Eugene, OR 97403-1277
Ph: (541)346-3537
Free: (800)280-6218
Fax: (541)346-3545
E-mail: aua@auaweb.net
URL: http://www.auaweb.net
Contact: Jack Fenwick, Contact

Founded: 1955. **Members:** 130. **Description:** Licensed architects who are full-time employees of universities or four-year colleges, and who have as their primary duties professional responsibility for the physical development of their institutions. Seeks to achieve more effective planning of total physical environment in the field of higher education; to improve the design and construction standards of university buildings, recognizing the growing complexity of contemporary academic pursuits; to develop common bonds and establish standards that will ensure clarity of communications and enhance the interchange of information among members. Compiles and circulates statistics on costs and construction, and fosters exchange of information among members via questions and answers. **Awards:** AUA Honor Awards. **Frequency:** annual. **Type:** recognition. **Recipient:** for outstanding designs of campus facilities by AUA members ● Distinguished Service Award. **Type:** recognition. **Publications:** *Association of University Architects—Newsletter*, periodic. **Price:** available to members only ● *AUA Membership Roster*, annual. Membership Directory. Includes information about association activities and awards. **Price:** available to members only. **Conventions/Meetings:** annual conference.

6473 ■ Council of Landscape Architectural Registration Boards (CLARB)

3949 Pender Dr., Ste.120
Fairfax, VA 22030
Ph: (571)432-0332
Fax: (571)432-0442
E-mail: info@clarb.org
URL: http://www.clarb.org
Contact: Robert T. Van Hook, Interim Exec. Dir.

Founded: 1961. **Members:** 48. **Staff:** 10. **Budget:** $1,500,000. **Description:** State and provincial registration boards for landscape architects. Works for coordination of state and provincial registration; seeks to facilitate reciprocal registration between states and provinces. Prepares Annual Landscape Architect Registration. **Committees:** Continuing Education; Examination. **Publications:** *Environment and Design*, quarterly. Newsletter. **Circulation:** 1,500 ● *Understanding the L.A.R.E.*, annual. **Price:** $100.00. **Circulation:** 1,000. **Conventions/Meetings:** annual meeting.

6474 ■ Council on Tall Buildings and Urban Habitat (CTBUH)

Illinois Inst. of Tech.
S.R. Crown Hall
3360 S State St.
Chicago, IL 60616-3850

Ph: (312)909-0253 (610)694-0238
Fax: (610)419-0014
E-mail: info@ctbuh.org
URL: http://www.ctbuh.org
Contact: Antony Wood, Exec. Dir.
Founded: 1969. **Members:** 1,200. **Membership Dues:** individual, $150 (annual) ● retired, $75 (annual) ● student, $40 (annual) ● contributing participant, $750 (annual) ● contributor, $1,500 (annual) ● donor, $3,000 (annual) ● patron, $6,000 (annual) ● supporting contributor, $10,000 (annual). **Staff:** 4. **Regional Groups:** 8. **National Groups:** 7. **Multinational. Description:** Performs an "invaluable service in a world of exploding populations, urban sprawl and new security concerns". Creates and shares new knowledge about the urban habitat, tall buildings, and their growing impact on the urban environment. Disseminates findings at world congresses; international, regional and specialty conferences; technical forums; and through the publication of books, monographs, proceedings, reports and newsletters. Seeks to improve the urban habitat in order to provide adequate space for life and work by utilizing the latest innovations and by analyzing all other important social and cultural variables that influence both the natural and human built environments. **Libraries: Type:** reference. **Holdings:** 500; books, periodicals. **Subjects:** subject matter of council. **Awards:** Fazlur Rahman Khan Medal. **Frequency:** annual. **Type:** medal. **Recipient:** to an individual for his/her demonstrated excellence in design and/or research that has made a significant contribution to a discipline(s) for the design of tall buildings and the built urban environment ● Lynn S. Beedle Achievement Award. **Frequency:** annual. **Type:** recognition. **Recipient:** to individual who has contributed to the advancement of tall building technology or betterment of the built environment. **Subgroups:** Building Service Systems; Criteria and Loading; Development and Management; Planning and Environmental Criteria; Systems and Concepts; Tall Concrete and Masonry Buildings; Tall Steel Buildings; Urban Systems. **Affiliated With:** American Institute of Architects; American Planning Association; American Society of Civil Engineers; American Society of Interior Designers; Urban Land Institute. **Formerly:** (1976) Joint Committee on Tall Buildings. **Publications:** *CTBUH Review*, quarterly. Journal. Covers all aspects of tall buildings. Includes research, case studies and innovative building projects. **Price:** included in membership dues; $150.00 for nonmembers. **Circulation:** 1,500. **Advertising:** accepted. Alternate Formats: online ● *100 of the World's Tallest Buildings*. Book. **Price:** $59.95 ● *Tall Building Safety Assessment and Enhancement Guidebooks*. Booklets. **Price:** $15.00. **Conventions/Meetings:** Renewing the Urban Landscape - congress (exhibits) - every 4-5 years.

6475 ■ Institute for Urban Design
PO Box 835
New York, NY 10014
Ph: (212)741-2041
Fax: (212)633-0125
E-mail: info@instituteforurbandesign.org
URL: http://www.instituteforurbandesign.org
Contact: Ann Ferebee, Founding Dir.
Founded: 1979. **Members:** 500. **Membership Dues:** fellow, $300. **Description:** Architects, land architects, planners, and developers. Promotes professional awareness of the need for better urban design building construction. **Libraries: Type:** reference. **Holdings:** archival material, video recordings. **Publications:** *Urban Design Update*, bimonthly. Newsletter. Highlights urban design projects from the offices of the institute members. **Price:** $120.00/year in U.S.; $170.00/year in Canada; $210.00/year outside U.S. and Canada ● Directory, annual, every spring. Contains information on its members. ● Booklets, semiannual, after every symposium of fall and spring. Contains transcript of the discussion on the meeting. **Price:** free for members. **Conventions/Meetings:** semiannual symposium - every May and October.

6476 ■ Landscape Architecture Foundation (LAF)
818 18th St. NW, Ste.810
Washington, DC 20006
Ph: (202)331-7070
Fax: (202)331-7079
E-mail: rfigura@lafoundation.org
URL: http://www.lafoundation.org
Contact: L. Susan Everett, Exec. Dir.
Founded: 1966. **Staff:** 3. **Description:** Serves as an education and research vehicle for the landscape architecture profession in the U.S. Combines the capabilities of landscape architects, interests of environmentalists, and needs of agencies and resource foundations. Provides for the preparation and dissemination of educational and scientific information through publications, exhibits, lectures, and seminars. Solicits and expends gifts, legacies, and grants. Established an endowment fund for professorships at colleges and universities. Sponsors California Landscape Architectural Student Scholarship Fund. Conducts a study of the profession to establish goals in terms of education, research needs, practice, and formulation of public policy. **Awards:** ASLA Council of Fellows. **Frequency:** annual. **Type:** scholarship. **Recipient:** for promising students who would not otherwise have an opportunity to continue a professional program due to unmet financial need ● Dangermond Fellowship. **Frequency:** annual. **Type:** fellowship. **Recipient:** to graduate students of landscape architecture in the United States ● **Frequency:** annual. **Type:** scholarship. **Recipient:** for meritorious work. **Computer Services:** Information services, information and research clearinghouse containing over 50,000 bibliographic references and professional profiles of landscape architects. **Additional Websites:** http://www.laprofession.org. **Committees:** Recognition; Research. **Formerly:** American Society of Landscape Architects Foundation. **Publications:** *American Landscaper Report*, quarterly. Newsletter. Alternate Formats: online.

6477 ■ National Building Museum (NBM)
401 F St. NW
Washington, DC 20001
Ph: (202)272-2448
Fax: (202)272-2564
E-mail: crynd@nbm.org
URL: http://www.nbm.org
Contact: Chase Rynd, Exec. Dir.
Founded: 1980. **Members:** 5,000. **Membership Dues:** individual, $50 (annual) ● dual, $70 (annual) ● supporting, $250 (annual) ● student, $30 (annual) ● contributing, $125 (annual) ● sustaining, $500 (annual) ● senior, $40 (annual) ● family, $80 (annual). **Staff:** 60. **Budget:** $8,000,000. **Description:** Dedicated to exploring and celebrating architecture, design, engineering, construction, and urban planning. Offers rotating exhibitions and varied education programs for all audiences. Since it's founding in 1980, the Museum has become a vital forum for exchanging ideas and information about such topical issues as landmark preservation, urban revitalization, sustainable and affordable design, and suburban growth. **Libraries: Type:** reference. **Holdings:** archival material, artwork, maps, photographs. **Awards:** Honor Award. **Frequency:** annual. **Type:** recognition. **Recipient:** for individuals or organizations that contribute significantly to the built environment. **Telecommunication Services:** electronic mail, membership@nbm.org. **Affiliated With:** American Association of Museums. **Publications:** *Affordable Housing: Designing an American Asset*. Catalog ● *Blueprints: Journal of the National Building Museum*, quarterly. Contains articles which complement the museum's exhibition and programs schedule. **Price:** included in membership dues. Alternate Formats: online ● *Calendar of Events*, monthly. Provides information on exhibitions, events, and programs. ● *The Green House: New Directions in Sustainable Architecture*. Book ● *On the Job: Design and the American Office*. Catalog ● *World War II and the American Dream: How Wartime Building Changed a Nation*. Catalog ● Do It Yourself: Home Improvement in 20th Century.

6478 ■ National Organization of Minority Architects (NOMA)
Howard Univ.
Coll. of Engg., Architecture and Cmpt. Sciences
School of Architecture and Design
2366 Sixth St. NW, Rm. 100
Washington, DC 20059
Ph: (202)686-2780
E-mail: secretary@noma.net
URL: http://www.noma.net
Contact: Carlton Smith, Pres.
Founded: 1971. **Members:** 600. **Membership Dues:** student, $30 (annual) ● professional, allied professional, $200 (annual) ● architectural intern, associate, $100 (annual) ● supporting company representative, $500 (annual). **Staff:** 10. **Budget:** $250,000. **State Groups:** 10. **Local Groups:** 20. **Description:** Seeks to increase the number and influence of minority architects by encouraging minority youth and taking an active role in the education of new architects. Works in cooperation with other associations, professionals, and architectural firms to promote the professional advancement of members. Sponsors competitions; offers children's services, educational programs, and charitable programs; maintains Speaker's Bureau; compiles statistics. **Awards:** Design Excellence. **Frequency:** annual. **Type:** recognition. **Recipient:** for professionals and students ● **Type:** scholarship. **Formerly:** (1973) National Organization of Black Architects. **Publications:** *NOMA News*, quarterly. Newsletter. **Circulation:** 2,300. **Advertising:** accepted ● *Roster of Minority Firms*, periodic. Directory. **Conventions/Meetings:** annual convention (exhibits) - always October ● annual meeting and conference (exhibits).

6479 ■ Rice Design Alliance (RDA)
MS 51
PO Box 1892
Houston, TX 77251-1892
Ph: (713)348-5668 (713)348-4876
Fax: (713)348-5924
E-mail: rda@rice.edu
URL: http://www.rda.rice.edu
Contact: Ms. Linda Sylvan, Exec. Dir.
Founded: 1973. **Members:** 1,650. **Membership Dues:** sponsor, $150 (annual) ● patron, $250 (annual) ● sustaining, contributing firm, $500 (annual) ● corporation, $1,000 (annual) ● individual, $45 (annual) ● family, $75 (annual) ● corporate sponsor, $1,500 (annual) ● student, $15 (annual). **Staff:** 4. **Budget:** $700,000. **Description:** Works for the advancement of architecture, urban design, and the built environment in the Houston region. Conducts educational programs; sponsors lectures and seminars; and holds national design competitions. **Publications:** *CITE: The Architecture and Design Review of Houston*, quarterly. Magazine. Includes information on architectural issues that affects the environment both in Houston and the Southwest. **Price:** $5.00/issue; $25.00/year in U.S.; $50.00/year outside U.S. ISSN: 8755-0415. **Circulation:** 5,000. **Advertising:** accepted ● Offers supplemental publications and catalogues. **Conventions/Meetings:** annual meeting - always May or June ● annual tour.

6480 ■ Society of American Registered Architects (SARA)
14 E 38th St., 11th Fl.
New York, NY 10016
Ph: (218)724-5568
Free: (888)385-7272
Fax: (218)724-5589
E-mail: president@sara-national.org
URL: http://www.sara-national.org
Contact: Cathie Moscato, Exec. Dir.
Founded: 1956. **Members:** 800. **Membership Dues:** student, $18 (annual) ● associate, $78 (annual) ● professional, affiliate, $270 (annual) ● international, $295 (annual). **Staff:** 2. **Budget:** $150,000. **State Groups:** 7. **Local Groups:** 3. **Description:** Architects registered or licensed under the laws of states and territories of the U.S. Sponsors seminars and professional and student design competitions. Offers placement service. **Libraries: Type:** not open to the public. **Holdings:** biographical archives. **Awards:** Design Award. **Frequency:** annual. **Type:** recognition. **Recipient:** to members ● Honorary Award. **Type:** recognition. **Recipient:** to members ● Synergy Award. **Frequency:** annual. **Type:** recognition. **Recipient:** to outstanding members or nonmembers. **Computer Services:** database, only available to members. **Committees:** Awards and Certificates; By-

Laws Review; Continuing Education; Conventions; Education; Government Relations and Intra-Profession; Graphics; Insurance; International; Legal Activism; Liaison to Councils; Long Range Planning; Nominating; Past Presidents; Professional Design Competition; Public Relations; Publications; Services to Members; Student Design Competition; Student Fund. **Publications:** *SARA Membership Directory*, annual. **Advertising:** accepted ● *SARAScope Newsletter*, bimonthly. **Price:** available to members only ● Also publishes practice aid pamphlets. **Conventions/Meetings:** annual convention - always October.

6481 ■ Society for Design Administration (SDA)
5020 Clark Rd., No. 134
Sarasota, FL 34233-3231
Ph: (941)925-8402
Free: (800)711-8199
Fax: (941)921-3465
E-mail: admin@sdadmin.org
URL: http://www.sdadmin.org
Contact: Karenlee Oreo, Exec. Dir.
Founded: 1959. **Members:** 800. **Membership Dues:** regular/associate, $200 (annual) ● member-at-large, $250 (annual) ● student, $25 (annual) ● national emeritus, $50 (annual). **Description:** Aims to promote the exchange of ideas and to educate members in the related disciplines of design firm administration. **Computer Services:** Mailing lists. **Committees:** Awards; Certification; Education Services; Historical; Leadership; National Publication; Nominating; Public Relations. **Affiliated With:** American Institute of Architects.

6482 ■ Vernacular Architecture Forum (VAF)
c/o Gabrielle M. Lanier, Sec.
PO Box 1511
Harrisonburg, VA 22803-1511
E-mail: laniergm@jmu.edu
URL: http://www.vernaculararchitectureforum.org
Contact: Gabrielle M. Lanier, Sec.
Founded: 1980. **Members:** 894. **Membership Dues:** student, $25 ● active, $45 ● institution, contributing, $75 ● patron, $150 ● household, $65 ● life, $2,000. **Regional Groups:** 3. **Description:** Individuals interested in architecture, history, geography, material culture, and related subjects. Serves as a forum for professional interaction in vernacular architecture. (Vernacular architecture refers to traditional domestic and agricultural buildings, industrial and commercial structures, 20th century suburban houses, settlement patterns, and cultural landscapes.) Seeks to encourage the study and preservation of vernacular architecture. **Awards:** Abbott Lowell Cummings Award. **Frequency:** annual. **Type:** recognition. **Recipient:** for outstanding scholarly book about North American vernacular architecture ● Paul Buchanan Award. **Frequency:** annual. **Type:** recognition. **Recipient:** for outstanding non-published field-based work about North American vernacular architecture. **Publications:** *Perspectives in Vernacular Architecture*, annual. Journal. Contains an anthology of the best papers presented at VAF annual meeting. **Price:** free for members ● *Vernacular Architecture Newsletter*, quarterly. Includes book reviews, and features employment opportunities, current bibliographies, and membership directory every 2-3 years. **Price:** included in membership dues. **Conventions/Meetings:** annual conference (exhibits) - always May or June. 2009 June 11-13, Butte, MT.

Artificial Intelligence

6483 ■ American Association for Artificial Intelligence (AAAI)
445 Burgess Dr., Ste.100
Menlo Park, CA 94025
Ph: (650)328-3123
Fax: (650)321-4457
E-mail: info7contact@aaai.org
URL: http://www.aaai.org
Contact: Alan Mackworth, Pres.
Founded: 1979. **Members:** 6,200. **Membership Dues:** individual in U.S. and Canada, $95 (annual) ● student in U.S. and Canada, $35 (annual) ● individual outside U.S. and Canada, $135 (annual) ● individual life in U.S. and Canada, $1,350 ● individual life outside U.S. and Canada, $1,900 ● institution/library in U.S. and Canada, $190 (annual) ● institution/library outside U.S. and Canada, $230 (annual) ● student outside U.S. and Canada, $75 (annual). **Staff:** 6. **Description:** Artificial Intelligence researchers; students, libraries, corporations, and others interested in the subject. (Artificial Intelligence is a discipline in which an attempt is made to approximate the human thinking process through computers.) Seeks to unite researchers and developers of Artificial Intelligence in order to provide an element of cohesion in the field. Serves as focal point and organizer for conferences; areas of interest include interpretation of visual data, robotics, expert systems, natural language processing, knowledge representation, and Artificial Intelligence programming technologies. Holds tutorials. **Libraries: Type:** reference. **Holdings:** books, papers, periodicals, reports. **Subjects:** molecular biology, artificial intelligence research. **Awards:** AAAI Classic Paper Award. **Frequency:** annual. **Type:** recognition. **Recipient:** for authors of papers ● AAAI Distinguished Service Award. **Frequency:** annual. **Type:** recognition. **Recipient:** for individuals who have made extraordinary service to the AI community ● AAAI Effective Expository Writing Award. **Frequency:** annual. **Type:** recognition. **Recipient:** for the authors with effective piece of writing ● AAAI Fellows Program. **Frequency:** annual. **Type:** recognition. **Recipient:** for fellows who have made unusual distinction in the profession ● AAAI Intel Science and Engineering Awards. **Frequency:** annual. **Type:** recognition. **Recipient:** for outstanding achievement in the area of intelligent computation and robotics ● AAAI Outstanding Paper Award. **Frequency:** annual. **Type:** recognition. **Recipient:** for papers that exemplify high standards in technical contribution and exposition ● ACM/AAAI Allen Newell Award. **Frequency:** annual. **Type:** recognition. **Recipient:** for individuals who have breadth within computer science and other disciplines ● Innovative Applications of Artificial Intelligence Awards. **Frequency:** annual. **Type:** recognition. **Recipient:** for case-study papers that describe deployed applications with measurable benefits. **Computer Services:** Mailing lists, of members. **Publications:** *AAAI Press Catalog*. Contains brief listing of press books, technical reports, proceeding and AI magazine back issues. ● *AI Magazine*, quarterly. Informs members about new research and literature on the field of artificial intelligence. **Price:** included in membership dues. ISSN: 0738-4602. **Circulation:** 7,000. **Advertising:** accepted ● *Journal of Artificial Intelligence*, semiannual. Contains articles on all areas of artificial intelligence. **Price:** $85.00 for nonmembers; $68.00 for members. Alternate Formats: online ● *Proceeding of the National Conference on Artificial Intelligence*, annual. Proceedings. **Price:** $85.00 ● *Technical Report Series*. Provides members with speed access to state of the art research. ● Numerous proceedings, edited collections and technical reports published each year by AAAI Press. **Conventions/Meetings:** annual Fall Symposium Series ● annual Innovative Applications of Artificial Intelligence - conference - 2008 July 13-17, Chicago, IL ● annual National Conference on Artificial Intelligence - 2008 July 13-17, Chicago, IL ● annual Spring Symposium Series.

6484 ■ Cognitive Science Society (CSS)
c/o Deborah Gruber, Business Mgr.
Univ. of Texas
Dept. of Psychology
1 Univ. Sta. A8000
Austin, TX 78712-0187
Ph: (512)471-2030
Fax: (512)471-3053
E-mail: cogsci@psy.utexas.edu
URL: http://www.cognitivesciencesociety.org
Contact: Prof. Thomas B. Ward, Exec. Off.
Founded: 1979. **Members:** 1,200. **Membership Dues:** zone A, $75 (annual) ● student, $50 (annual) ● zone B, retiree, $30 (annual). **Staff:** 1. **Description:** Represents published PhD's (500); students and PhD's not actively publishing (300) in the fields of psychology, artificial intelligence, and cognitive science. Promotes the dissemination of research in cognitive science and allied sciences. (Cognitive science is a branch of artificial intelligence that seeks to simulate human reasoning and associative powers on a computer, using specialized software). **Computer Services:** Mailing lists. **Committees:** Events; Fellows; Publications; Software. **Publications:** *Cognitive Science*, bimonthly. Journal. **Price:** included in membership dues. Alternate Formats: online ● Membership Directory, biennial. **Conventions/Meetings:** annual conference.

6485 ■ International Association of Knowledge Engineers (IAKE)
973 Russell Ave., Ste.D
Gaithersburg, MD 20879
Ph: (301)948-5390
Fax: (301)926-4243
Contact: Julie Lowe, Exec. Dir.
Founded: 1987. **Staff:** 3. **Nonmembership. Multinational. Description:** Think tank for practitioners and professionals in the field of knowledge engineering. (Knowledge engineering is concerned with the design of reasoning machines and computer systems to receive, organize, and maintain human knowledge.) Seeks to establish standards in the field; promote documentation of knowledge engineering; develop technology for fields including mathematics and linguistics, engineering and physical science, philosophy and social science, and the arts. Maintains placement service. Provides for testing and certification. **Computer Services:** database, knowledge users and providers. **Telecommunication Services:** electronic bulletin board. **Publications:** *Artificial Intelligent Applications on Wall Street 1993, 1995.* Proceedings. **Price:** $65.00 ● *How to Start and Fund a High-Tech Company*. Manual. **Price:** $65.00 ● *Standards and Review in Knowledge Engineering*. Manual. **Price:** $65.00. **Conventions/Meetings:** conference (exhibits).

6486 ■ International Society of Applied Intelligence (ISAI)
Texas State Univ., San Marcos
Dept. of Cmpt. Sci.
601 Univ. Dr.
San Marcos, TX 78666-4616
Ph: (512)245-3409
Fax: (512)245-8750
E-mail: ma04@txstate.edu
URL: http://isai.cs.txstate.edu
Contact: Dr. Moonis Ali, Pres.
Founded: 1993. **Members:** 50. **Membership Dues:** student, associate, $50 (annual) ● full, $125 (annual) ● institutional, $500 (annual). **Staff:** 1. **Regional Groups:** 5. **Multinational. Description:** Researchers, academicians, computer scientists, industry professionals, and others with an interest in Intelligent systems' Technology. Promotes dissemination of Research in the area of intelligent systems' technology and improves scientific literacy. Sponsors an International conference on Industrial, Engineering, and other Applications of Applied Intelligent Systems. **Awards:** IAE/AIE Best Papers Award. **Frequency:** annual. **Type:** recognition. **Recipient:** for outstanding papers presented at ISAI conference. **Computer Services:** Online services. **Working Groups:** AI in Finance and Business; AI in Manufacturing Systems; Building and Architecture; Elements of Cooperation in AI; Verification and Validation. **Publications:** *Innovations in Applied Artificial Intelligence*, annual. Proceedings. Contains lecture notes in Artificial Intelligence by Springer-Verlag. ISSN: 0302-9743 ● *International Journal of Applied Intelligence*, bimonthly. Contains information on artificial intelligence, neural network, and its complex problem solving technologies. **Price:** $589.00 institutional; $276.00 individual. ISSN: 0924-669X. **Advertising:** accepted. Alternate Formats: online ● *ISAI Newsletter*, quarterly. **Price:** available for ISAI members only. Alternate Formats: online. **Conventions/Meetings:** annual International Conference on Industrial, Engineering and Other Applications of Applied Intelligent Systems (IEA/AIE), emphasizes the real world ap-

plications of Applied Intelligent Systems (exhibits) - 2008 June 24-27, Wroclaw, Poland - **Avg. Attendance:** 250.

6487 ■ Special Interest Group on Artificial Intelligence (SIGART)
c/o Irene Frawley
Assn. for Computing Machinery
2 Penn Plz., Ste.701
New York, NY 10121-0701
Ph: (212)869-7440 (212)626-0605
Free: (800)342-6626
Fax: (212)302-5826
E-mail: frawley@acm.org
URL: http://www.sigart.org
Contact: Irene Frawley, Contact
Members: 8,255. **Membership Dues:** individual, $25 (annual) ● student, $11 (annual). **Description:** A special interest group of the Association for Computing Machinery (see separate entry). Individuals interested in the application of computers to tasks normally requiring human intelligence. Enhances the capabilities of computers in this area. **Conventions/Meetings:** annual Agents and International Conference on Autonomous Agents - meeting (exhibits).

Astrology

6488 ■ American Federation of Astrologers (AFA)
6535 S Rural Rd.
Tempe, AZ 85283-3746
Ph: (480)838-1751
Free: (888)301-7630
Fax: (480)838-8293
E-mail: afa@msn.com
URL: http://www.astrologers.com
Contact: Robert W. Cooper, Exec. Sec.
Founded: 1938. **Members:** 3,100. **Membership Dues:** senior associate in U.S., $30 (annual) ● associate in U.S., senior associate outside U.S., $45 (annual) ● husband/wife outside U.S., $75 (annual) ● husband/wife in U.S., associate outside U.S., $60 (annual) ● group affiliate in U.S., $50 (annual) ● international group affiliate, $65 (annual) ● life - associate in U.S., $600 ● life - associate outside U.S., $1,000 ● associate researcher in U.S., $67 (annual) ● associate researcher outside U.S., $82 (annual) ● life - researcher outside U.S., $1,400. **Staff:** 6. **Description:** Local associations and individuals in 47 countries interested in the advancement of astrology through research and education. Administers certification examinations. **Libraries: Type:** reference. **Holdings:** 3,000. **Subjects:** astrology. **Absorbed:** (1969) National Astrological Library. **Publications:** *Today's Astrologer*, monthly. Journal. Provides astrological information and education and general membership news. **Price:** included in membership dues. ISSN: 0735-4797. **Circulation:** 3,000. Alternate Formats: diskette ● Approximately 3000 astrological titles, approximately publishing twelve (12) new titles per year. **Conventions/Meetings:** biennial conference and workshop, with more than 300 workshops (exhibits) - usually July or August of even-numbered years at Hotel Rio.

6489 ■ Association for Astrological Networking (AFAN)
8306 Wilshire Blvd., PMB 537
Beverly Hills, CA 90211
Ph: (212)726-1407
Free: (800)578-AFAN
E-mail: info@afan.org
URL: http://www.afan.org
Contact: Paula Dare, Membership Chair
Founded: 1982. **Members:** 500. **Membership Dues:** regular in North America, $30 (annual) ● regular outside North America, $40 (annual) ● regular in North America, $80 (triennial) ● regular outside North America, $110 (triennial) ● life, $350 ● senior (above 65 years old), student in North America, $25 (annual) ● student outside North America, $35 (annual) ● Astrological Association of Britain and Federation of Australian Astrologer member, $30 (annual). **Staff:** 12. **Budget:** $20,000. **Description:** Seeks to provide an accurate and professional image of astrology to the public and media. Serves as a link between astrologers and the community. Provides legal research resources and worldwide astrological contacts. Maintains speakers' bureau. **Libraries: Type:** reference. **Holdings:** archival material. **Awards:** Jim Lewis Community Service Award. **Frequency:** triennial. **Type:** recognition. **Telecommunication Services:** electronic mail, members@afan.org. **Committees:** Advisory; Community Activities; Correspondence; Democratic Procedures; Legal Information; Public Information and Education; Publications. **Publications:** *Astrology Now*. Brochure ● Newsletter, quarterly. **Price:** included in membership dues. **Circulation:** 2,500 ● Also produces lecture tapes. **Conventions/Meetings:** annual International Astrology Day - meeting - 3rd week of March, near Spring Equinox ● United Astrology Congress, held in conjunction with International Society for Astrological Research and National Council for Geocosmic Research (exhibits) - 3-5/year.

6490 ■ Association for Psychological Astrology (APA)
360 Quietwood Dr.
San Rafael, CA 94903
Ph: (415)479-5812
E-mail: glenn@aaperry.com
URL: http://www.aaperry.com
Contact: Glenn Perry PhD, Dir.
Founded: 1987. **Members:** 3,000. **Staff:** 3. **For-Profit. Description:** Psychologists, counselors, and astrologers. Works to enhance the credibility of astrology in the mental health professions by establishing general guidelines for the application of astrology to the fields of counseling and psychotherapy. Conducts educational programs, including lectures. **Libraries: Type:** reference. **Holdings:** 24; periodicals. **Subjects:** astrological psychology. **Computer Services:** Mailing lists. **Formerly:** (2004) Association for Astrological Psychology. **Publications:** *The AstroPsychology Newsletter*, monthly. Magazine. Alternate Formats: online. **Conventions/Meetings:** seminar ● workshop.

6491 ■ Astrologers' Guild of America (AGA)
Address Unknown since 2007
Founded: 1927. **Description:** Professionals, students, and others interested in astrology. Seeks to: promote astrological research and study; protect interests of qualified astrologers. Holds lectures and symposia. Presently inactive. **Publications:** *Astrological Review*, quarterly. **Conventions/Meetings:** annual meeting.

6492 ■ Astromusic
PO Box 3120
Ashland, OR 97520
Ph: (541)488-3344
Fax: (541)488-7870
E-mail: astromusic@wrightful.com
URL: http://www.astromusic.com
Contact: Gerald Jay Markoe, Contact
Founded: 1980. **Members:** 500. **For-Profit. Description:** Individuals interested in celestial music or "the music of the spheres", which is defined as a person's horoscope or actual birth chart translated into a musical composition. Integrating music and astronomy, the composition is a musical interpretation of planetary positions and angular separations at the time of an individual's birth, intended to enhance meditation, relaxation, and healing. Provides cassettes of compositions. **Formerly:** (1987) AstroMusical Research. **Conventions/Meetings:** annual Astro World Congress ● conference (exhibits) - 4-6/year.

6493 ■ Friends of Astrology (FOA)
208 Rosewood Ct.
Westmont, IL 60559-1577
E-mail: info@friendsofastrology.org
URL: http://friendsofastrology.org
Contact: Christine Arens, Pres.
Founded: 1938. **Members:** 500. **Membership Dues:** individual in U.S., $45 (annual) ● individual outside U.S., $60 (annual). **Local Groups:** 3. **Description:** Seeks to raise the standards of astrology through scientific research and educational programs. Operates speaker's bureau. Compiles statistics. **Libraries: Type:** reference; lending; not open to the public. **Holdings:** 1,500; archival material, artwork, books, periodicals. **Subjects:** astrology, ephemerides, astronomy, numerology, tarot, iching, palmistry, handwriting, kabbalah. **Awards: Type:** recognition. **Computer Services:** Online services, horoscope charts. **Affiliated With:** American Federation of Astrologers. **Publications:** *Friends of Astrology Bulletin*, monthly. Magazine. Contains astrological lessons, book reviews, and zodiac sign and monthly lunar forecasts. Includes personality analyses of newsworthy figures. **Price:** free for members; $25.00 /year for nonmembers. **Circulation:** 500. **Conventions/Meetings:** lecture - 3/month.

6494 ■ International Society for Astrological Research (ISAR)
PO Box 38613
Los Angeles, CA 90038
Ph: (805)525-0461
Free: (800)982-1788
Fax: (805)933-0301
E-mail: maitreya@csiway.com
URL: http://www.isarastrology.com
Contact: Raymond A. Merriman, Pres.
Founded: 1968. **Members:** 1,000. **Membership Dues:** regular in U.S. (surface mail), $39 (annual) ● regular outside U.S. (surface mail), $44 (annual) ● airmail, $45 (triennial) ● regular outside U.S., $115 (triennial) ● regular in U.S., $90 (triennial). **Staff:** 2. **Languages:** English, Japanese, Portuguese, Serbian, Spanish, Turkish. **Description:** Represents professional and nonprofessional astrologers. Provides research data and education for astrologers and interested individuals within the scientific community. **Libraries: Type:** reference. **Holdings:** 300; articles, books, periodicals. **Subjects:** astrological research. **Awards:** ISAR Research Grant. **Frequency:** periodic. **Type:** grant. **Recipient:** for research projects ● Regulus Awards. **Frequency:** triennial. **Type:** recognition. **Computer Services:** Online services, Microsoft Net. **Publications:** *Astrological Research Methods*. Book. **Price:** $35.00 ● *Frequency Analysis Tables* ● *International Astrologer*, quarterly. Journal. **Price:** included in membership dues. **Circulation:** 1,000. **Advertising:** accepted ● *Tables for Aspect Research*. **Price:** $12.00 ● Newsletter, weekly. Alternate Formats: online ● Newsletter, quarterly. **Conventions/Meetings:** annual conference and workshop, with booths (exhibits) ● annual congress (exhibits) ● monthly seminar.

6495 ■ Organization for Professional Astrology (OPA)
c/o Bob Mulligan, Pres.
PO Box 9237
Naples, FL 34101
Ph: (239)261-2840
Fax: (239)435-0967
E-mail: bobmulliga@aol.com
URL: http://www.professional-astrology.org
Contact: Bob Mulligan, Pres.
Membership Dues: regular, $60 (annual) ● life, $500. **Description:** Advances the cause of professional astrology. Assists astrologers to improve both personally and professionally. Aims to help astrologers get the information, tools, and experiences they need to improve their practices. Defines and maintains professional standards for the responsible use of astrology. **Publications:** *The Career Astrologer*, quarterly. Newsletter. **Price:** included in membership dues ● Newsletter, monthly. **Price:** included in membership dues. Alternate Formats: online.

Astronomy

6496 ■ Amateur Astronomers Association (AAA)
PO Box 383
Gracie Sta.
New York, NY 10028

Ph: (212)535-2922
E-mail: president@aaa.org
URL: http://www.aaa.org
Contact: Richard Rosenberg, Pres.

Founded: 1927. **Members:** 500. **Membership Dues:** regular, $25 (annual). **Local Groups:** 3. **Description:** Persons interested in astronomy, including amateur and career astronomers. Conducts educational program that includes lectures, classes, seminars, constellation study, outdoor observing, telescope assembly, and local field trips. Offers Amateur Astronomers Medal. Sponsors speakers' bureau; offers consulting and information services. **Libraries: Type:** reference. **Holdings:** 2,000. **Subgroups:** Observers. **Formerly:** (1988) Amateur Astronomers Association of New York City. **Publications:** *Enjoy the Stars*, annual. Brochure ● *Eyepiece*, monthly. Newspaper. Includes calendar of events. ISSN: 0146-7662. Alternate Formats: online ● *Sky and Telescope*, monthly. Magazine. **Conventions/Meetings:** annual meeting - always May in New York City, NY.

6497 ■ American Association of Variable Star Observers (AAVSO)

49 Bay State Rd.
Cambridge, MA 02138
Ph: (617)354-0484
Free: (888)802-7827
Fax: (617)354-0665
E-mail: aavso@aavso.org
URL: http://www.aavso.org
Contact: Dr. Arne Henden, Dir.

Founded: 1911. **Members:** 1,300. **Membership Dues:** regular (aged 21 and over), $70 (annual) ● associate, $35 (annual) ● sustaining, $140 (annual). **Staff:** 14. **Budget:** $230,000. **Description:** Professional and amateur astronomers who observe stars that vary in brightness. Compiles, processes, analyzes, and publishes variable star observations. Prepares and distributes finder charts of variable star fields and light curves of important variables; coordinates observations between professional and amateur astronomers. Solar Division has developed a radio technique for detecting solar flares. Their sunspot counts are the basis of the American Sunspot numbers published by the National Bureau of Standards. **Libraries: Type:** reference. **Holdings:** 2,000; books, periodicals. **Subjects:** astronomy and related subjects. **Awards:** Director's Award. **Frequency:** annual. **Type:** recognition. **Recipient:** to an outstanding observer who contributes to special observing projects ● Nova Award. **Frequency:** annual. **Type:** recognition. **Recipient:** to original discoverer of a nova by direct visual methods ● Observer Awards. **Frequency:** annual. **Type:** recognition. **Recipient:** to observers who have submitted to the AAVSO visual observations and photoelectric and CCD observations ● Solar Observer Awards. **Frequency:** annual. **Type:** recognition. **Recipient:** to solar observers who have reached milestones of 1000, 1500, and 2000 sunspot observations. **Committees:** Charged Coupled Device; Eclipsing Binaries; New Charts; Nova Search; Photoelectric Photometry; RR Lyrae Variables; Supernova Search; Telescope. **Divisions:** Solar. **Publications:** *AAVSO Circular*, monthly. Contains preliminary observations of eruptive and other information on variable stars. **Price:** $25.00 /year for nonmembers; $40.00 /year for institutions ● *AAVSO Monographs*, periodic. Provides computer-generated, long-term light curves of AAVSO observations. **Price:** $5.00 for members; $10.00 for nonmembers ● *AAVSO Newsletter*, semiannual. Contains updates as to the activities of the association. **Price:** free. Alternate Formats: online ● *American Association of Variable Star Observers—Bulletin*, annual. Publishes predicted dates of maxima and minima of 600 long period variable stars. **Price:** $25.00 /year for nonmembers; $40.00 /year for institutions. Alternate Formats: online ● *Journal of the AAVSO*, semiannual. Contains scientific research papers; also includes committee reports, annual report, book reviews, and table of AAVSO observers' totals. **Price:** $25.00 /year for nonmembers; $40.00 /year for institutions; free for members. Alternate Formats: online ● *Solar Bulletin*, monthly. Reports daily sunspot activity; also includes sudden ionospheric disturbance data. **Price:** $20.00 /year for members in U.S.; $24.00 /year for members outside U.S.; $40.00 /year for institutions in U.S.; $25.00 /year for nonmembers in U.S. **Conventions/Meetings:** semiannual conference - usually in late October and April or May.

6498 ■ American Astronomical Society (AAS)

2000 Florida Ave. NW, Ste.400
Washington, DC 20009-1231
Ph: (202)328-2010
Fax: (202)234-2560
E-mail: aas@aas.org
URL: http://www.aas.org
Contact: Kevin B. Marvel, Exec. Off.

Founded: 1899. **Members:** 6,500. **Membership Dues:** full, associate, $115 (annual) ● junior, $40 (annual) ● emeritus, $58 (annual). **Staff:** 13. **Budget:** $8,500,000. **Description:** Represents astronomers, physicists, and scientists in related fields. Conducts Visiting Professor in Astronomy Program. **Awards:** Beatrice M. Tinsley Prize. **Frequency:** biennial. **Type:** recognition. **Recipient:** to an outstanding research contribution to astronomy or astrophysics of an exceptionally creative or innovative character ● Chretien Award. **Frequency:** annual. **Type:** recognition ● Danny Heineman Prize for Astrophysics. **Frequency:** annual. **Type:** recognition. **Recipient:** for outstanding work in the field of astrophysics ● Education Prize. **Frequency:** annual. **Type:** recognition. **Recipient:** to an individual for outstanding contributions to the education of the public, students and/or the next generation of professional astronomers ● George Van Biesbroeck Prize. **Frequency:** biennial. **Type:** recognition. **Recipient:** to an individual for long-term extraordinary or unselfish service to astronomy ● Helen B. Warner Prize for Astronomy. **Frequency:** annual. **Type:** recognition. **Recipient:** to an astronomer for his/her significant contribution to observational or theoretical astronomy ● International Travel Grants. **Type:** grant. **Recipient:** for international travel to support U.S. attendance at selected foreign astronomical meetings ● Joseph Weber Award for Astronomical Instrumentation. **Frequency:** annual. **Type:** recognition. **Recipient:** to an individual for the design, invention or significant improvement of instrumentation leading to advances in astronomy ● Newton Lacy Pierce Prize in Astronomy. **Frequency:** annual. **Type:** recognition. **Recipient:** to an astronomer for outstanding achievement in observational astronomical research ● Small Research Grants. **Type:** grant. **Recipient:** for research. **Committees:** Annie Jump Cannon Award; Astronomy and Public Policy; Astronomy News; Beatrice M. Tinsley Prize; Dannie Heineman Prize; Education Advisory; Education Prize; Employment; George Van Biesbroeck Prize; Henri Chretien Grant; Joseph Weber Award for Astronomical Instrumentation; Light Pollution, Radio Interference and Space Debris; Status of Women in Astronomy; Working Group on Astronomical Imaging Technology; Working Group on Astronomical Software. **Divisions:** Dynamical Astronomy; High Energy Astrophysics; Historical Astronomy; Planetary Sciences; Solar Physics. **Affiliated With:** American Institute of Physics; International Astronomical Union. **Formerly:** (1914) Astronomical and Astrophysical Society of America. **Publications:** *AAS Job Register*, monthly. Lists employment opportunities nationally and internationally in astronomy. **Price:** free for members. **Circulation:** 2,100. **Advertising:** accepted. Alternate Formats: online ● *AAS Newsletter*, 5/year. **Price:** included in membership dues. Alternate Formats: online ● *American Astronomical Society—Membership Directory*, annual. **Price:** included in membership dues ● *Astronomical Journal*, monthly. **Price:** $550.00/year in U.S.; $628.50/year in Canada; $590.00/year in Mexico; $53.00/copy ● *Astrophysical Journal*, 3/month. **Price:** $300.00 in U.S., Canada and Mexico; $545.00 surface; $630.00 airfreight; $15.00/copy for members in U.S. Alternate Formats: online ● *Bulletin of the American Astronomical Society*. **Price:** $30.00 in U.S., Canada and Mexico; $45.00 all countries except U.S., Canada and Mexico; $55.00 all countries except Canada and Mexico - airfreight ● Also publishes a career brochure. **Conventions/Meetings:** semiannual conference and meeting (exhibits) - always winter and summer. 2009 Jan. 7-10, Long Beach, CA ● meeting, for discussion on scientific issues.

6499 ■ American Lunar Society (ALS)

c/o Eric Douglas, VP
10326 Tarleton Dr.
Mechanicsville, VA 23116
Ph: (804)550-1211
E-mail: ejdftd@mindspring.com
URL: http://www.amlunsoc.org
Contact: Eric Douglas, VP

Founded: 1982. **Members:** 120. **Membership Dues:** regular, in U.S., $15 (annual). **Staff:** 2. **Multinational. Description:** Scientists and interested individuals. Studies the astronomy of the moon and the history of its exploration; promotes lunar exploration. Exchanges ideas about moon exploration; studies the use of lunar resources; encourages the review of scientific works; promotes telescopic observation of the moon. **Committees:** Research. **Publications:** *Selenology*, quarterly. Newsletter. Reports on lunar science, history of moon exploration, and eclipses. Includes book reviews, calendar of events, and research updates. **Price:** included in membership dues; $15.00 /year for nonmembers. **Circulation:** 200.

6500 ■ American Meteor Society (AMS)

c/o Karl Simmons, Treas.
44017 Woodland Ct.
Callahan, FL 32011
E-mail: ksams32011@aol.com
URL: http://www.amsmeteors.org
Contact: Karl Simmons, Treas.

Founded: 1911. **Members:** 100. **Membership Dues:** associate, $8 (annual) ● student, observer, $6 (annual) ● group, $10 (annual). **Staff:** 3. **Budget:** $3,000. **Regional Groups:** 3. **Description:** Represents amateur and professional astronomers interested in observation of meteors and publication of research papers on fireball orbits and meteor radiant, catalog on the patterns of long-enduring trains of meteors, rate catalog, studies of radio and telescopic meteors, and descriptions of prominent meteor streams. **Convention/Meeting:** none. **Libraries: Type:** reference; not open to the public. **Holdings:** 200; archival material, articles, books. **Subjects:** meteoric astronomy. **Awards:** American Meteor Society Award. **Frequency:** annual. **Type:** monetary. **Recipient:** to a SUNY-Geneseo student who has contributed much to meteor research or the AMS ● AMS Research Grants. **Frequency:** annual. **Type:** monetary. **Recipient:** for annual proposal competition, selected by board of directors ● C.P. Olivier Award. **Frequency:** annual. **Type:** monetary. **Recipient:** to an individual who has contributed to meteor research or the AMS chosen by board of directors. **Publications:** *Meteor Trails: The Journal of American Meteor Society*, quarterly. Contains meteor observations and their scientific interpretation. **Price:** included in membership dues ● Annual Report, annual. Includes research reports. **Price:** included in membership dues. **Circulation:** 200 ● Monographs ● Reports ● Bulletins.

6501 ■ Association of Universities for Research in Astronomy (AURA)

1212 New York Ave. NW, Ste.450
Washington, DC 20005
Ph: (202)483-2101
Fax: (202)483-2106
E-mail: wsmith@aura-astronomy.org
URL: http://www.aura-astronomy.org
Contact: William S. Smith, Pres./CEO

Founded: 1957. **Members:** 40. **Membership Dues:** institution, $10,000 (annual) ● individual, $2,000 (annual). **Description:** A consortium of universities and related institutions formed to manage U.S. national astronomy observatories. Manages and operates the National Optical Astronomy Observatories (Kitt Peak National Observatory, near Tucson, AZ, the Cerro Tololo Inter-American Observatory, La Serena, Chile, and the National Solar Observatory at Sunspot, NM, and Tucson, AZ) under cooperative agreement with the National Science Foundation. NSF manages the international Gemini telescope project while NASA manages the Space Telescope Science Institute in Baltimore, MD. Conducts stellar, solar, planetary and space science research. **Publications:** Brochures ● Monographs. **Conventions/Meetings:** annual meeting.

6502 ■ Astronomical League
9201 Ward Pkwy., Ste.100
Kansas City, MO 64114
Ph: (816)333-7759 (937)678-5032
E-mail: aloffice@earthlink.net
URL: http://www.astroleague.org
Contact: Jackie Beucher, Exec. Sec.
Founded: 1946. **Members:** 18,000. **Membership Dues:** affiliate, $15 (annual) ● youth, $20 (annual) ● regular in U.S., $30 (annual) ● regular outside U.S., $40 (annual) ● supporting, $50 (annual) ● patron, $75 (annual) ● life, $400. **Regional Groups:** 10. **Local Groups:** 250. **Description:** Members of 250 astronomical societies and other interested individuals. Promotes the science of astronomy; encourages and coordinates activities of amateur astronomical societies; fosters observational and computational work and craftsmanship in various fields of astronomy; correlates amateur activities with professional research. Sponsors educational programs. **Awards:** Astronomical League Award. **Frequency:** annual. **Type:** recognition ● Horkheimer Award. **Frequency:** annual. **Type:** recognition. **Recipient:** for service to astronomy or club ● Leslie Peltier Award. **Frequency:** annual. **Type:** recognition. **Recipient:** for observational astronomy ● Mabel Sterns Award. **Frequency:** annual. **Type:** recognition. **Recipient:** for outstanding newsletter editor ● National Outstanding Young Astronomer Award. **Frequency:** annual. **Type:** recognition. **Recipient:** for outstanding achievements by high school astronomers. **Committees:** ARP-Peculiar Galaxy Club; Asteroid Club; Astronomy Day; Book Service; Deep Skies Binocular Club; Double Stars Club; Education; Galaxy Groups and Clusters Club; Herschel/Herschel II Club; Horkheimer Solar Imaging Award; Light Pollution; Lunar Club; Mabel Sterns Award; Messier Binocular Club; Messier Club; Meteor Club; NYA Award; Planetary Club; Southern Skies Binocular Club; Sunspotter Club; Urban Club. **Affiliated With:** American Association of Variable Star Observers; Astronomical Society of the Pacific; International Dark-Sky Association; International Planetarium Society. **Publications:** *Astronomy Teachers Handbook*. **Price:** $10.00 ● *The Herschel II Guide*. Book. **Price:** $15.00 ● *Math for Amateur Astronomers*. Book. **Price:** $7.00 ● *Observe and Understand the Sun*. Book. **Price:** $12.00 ● *Observe and Understand Variable Stars*. Book. **Price:** $15.00 ● *Observe Eclipses*. Book. **Price:** $15.00 ● *Observe Manuals*. **Price:** $8.00 ● *Reflector*, quarterly. Newsletter. Covers League functions; includes book reviews, calendar of events, and research updates. **Price:** included in membership dues; $8.00 for nonmembers in U.S.; $11.00 for nonmembers in Canada and Mexico; $16.00 for nonmembers in other countries. ISSN: 0034-2963. **Circulation:** 19,000. **Advertising:** accepted ● *The Universe Sampler*. Book. Contains observing guides to Messier and Herschel objects. **Price:** $7.00. **Conventions/Meetings:** annual meeting (exhibits).

6503 ■ Astronomical Society of the Pacific (ASP)
390 Ashton Ave.
San Francisco, CA 94112
Ph: (415)337-1100
Free: (800)335-2624
Fax: (415)337-5205
E-mail: jmanning@astrosociety.org
URL: http://www.astrosociety.org
Contact: James Manning, Exec. Dir.
Founded: 1889. **Members:** 7,000. **Membership Dues:** student, $35 (annual) ● individual, $48 (annual) ● family, $75 (annual). **Staff:** 22. **Budget:** $3,200,000. **Description:** Professional and amateur astronomers, educators, and laypeople. Aims to increase public understanding and appreciation of astronomy and to disseminate astronomical information. Sponsors lectures, conferences, and workshops for teachers and the public; acts as information resource service for teachers, librarians, and the media; maintains speakers' bureau. Produces and distributes audiovisual, computer, and observing materials on astronomy. **Libraries: Type:** reference. **Subjects:** astronomy. **Awards:** Amateur Achievement Award. **Frequency:** annual. **Type:** recognition. **Recipient:** for outstanding achievement ● Catherine Wolfe Bruce Medal. **Frequency:** annual. **Type:** recognition. **Recipient:** for lifetime accomplishment ● Klumpke-Roberts Award. **Frequency:** annual. **Type:** recognition. **Recipient:** for popularization of astronomy ● Maria and Eric Muhlman Award. **Frequency:** annual. **Type:** recognition. **Recipient:** for instrumentation development ● Robert J. Trumpler Award. **Frequency:** annual. **Type:** recognition. **Recipient:** for outstanding dissertation ● Thomas J. Brennan Award. **Frequency:** annual. **Type:** recognition. **Recipient:** for outstanding high school teaching. **Computer Services:** Mailing lists. **Telecommunication Services:** electronic mail, director@astrosociety.org. **Committees:** Awards; History of Astronomy. **Publications:** *ASP Conference Series*, periodic. Proceedings ● *Mercury*, bimonthly. Magazine. Features topics on astronomy intended for students, teachers, amateur astronomers, and astronomy buffs. ISSN: 0047-6773. **Circulation:** 7,000. **Advertising:** accepted ● *Publications of the ASP*, monthly. Journal. **Price:** $45.00 individual; $330.00 institutional. **Circulation:** 2,500 ● *Universe in the Classroom: An Online Newsletter on Teaching Astronomy*, quarterly. Provides information for grades 3-12. **Price:** free to teachers. **Circulation:** 12,000. **Conventions/Meetings:** annual meeting and lecture, for education and public outreach professionals (exhibits).

6504 ■ Central Bureau for Astronomical Telegrams (CBAT)
Mail Stop 18
Smithsonian Astrophysical Observatory
60 Garden St.
Cambridge, MA 02138
Ph: (617)495-7281
Fax: (617)495-7231
E-mail: iausubs@cfa.harvard.edu
URL: http://cfa-www.harvard.edu/iau/cbat.html
Contact: Dr. Daniel W.E. Green, Dir.
Founded: 1920. **Members:** 15. **Staff:** 3. **Description:** Astronomers. Receives, verifies, and disseminates reports on transient astronomical phenomena. Compiles statistics. **Awards:** The Edgar Wilson Award. **Frequency:** annual. **Type:** monetary. **Recipient:** for amateur comet discoverers. **Computer Services:** database, publishing information. **Affiliated With:** International Astronomical Union. **Publications:** *Catalogue of Cometary Orbits*. **Price:** $30.00 ● *Circulars*, 300/year. Brochure. Postcards that contain information on comets, novae, supernovae, and other astronomical phenomena. **Price:** $10.00/month. **Circulation:** 700. **Conventions/Meetings:** triennial meeting.

6505 ■ International Amateur-Professional Photoelectric Photometry (IAPPP)
4229 Franklin Rd.
Nashville, TN 37204
Ph: (615)383-4630
E-mail: douglas.s.hall@vanderbilt.edu
URL: http://www.iappp.org
Contact: Douglas S. Hall, Pres.
Founded: 1980. **Members:** 600. **Membership Dues:** individual, $25 (annual) ● life, $500. **Staff:** 3. **Regional Groups:** 23. **Multinational. Description:** Amateurs, students, and professionals interested in astronomy. Facilitates collaborative astronomical research between amateurs, students, and professional astronomers by providing a medium for the exchange of practical information not normally discussed at symposia or published in journals. Provides information on specialized aspects of photoelectric photometry. Solicits manuscripts relevant to astronomical research. Conducts educational and research programs. **Awards: Type:** grant ● Richard D. Lines Special Award in Astronomy. **Frequency:** annual. **Type:** monetary. **Recipient:** for a high school student entered in the International Science and Engineering Fair. **Publications:** *I.A.P.P.P. Communications*, quarterly. Journal. **Price:** included in membership dues. ISSN: 0886-6961. **Circulation:** 900. **Conventions/Meetings:** competition ● periodic convention and regional meeting ● periodic Techniques of Astronomical Photometry Summer School - workshop.

6506 ■ International Dark-Sky Association (IDA)
3225 N 1st Ave.
Tucson, AZ 85719-2103
Ph: (520)293-3198
Fax: (520)293-3192
E-mail: ida@darksky.org
URL: http://www.darksky.org
Contact: Christian Hanson CAE, Chief Admin. Off.
Founded: 1988. **Members:** 9,500. **Membership Dues:** in Canada, $40 (annual) ● small astronomy club, library, $50 (annual) ● governmental, $200 (annual) ● individual (sponsor, supporter, sustainer, patron), $50-$500 (annual) ● family (sponsor, supporter, sustainer, patron), $50-$650 (annual) ● organization (sponsor, supporter, sustainer, patron), $100-$2,000 (annual) ● life (individual, family, organization), $1,000-$3,000. **Staff:** 12. **Regional Groups:** 40. **Languages:** English, Spanish. **Multinational. Description:** Aims to preserve and protect the nighttime environment and our heritage of dark skies through quality outdoor lighting. Works to stop the adverse effects of light pollution on dark skies, including energy waste and air and water pollution caused by energy waste. Raises awareness about light pollution, its adverse effects, and its solutions. Educates everyone, everywhere, about the values of quality outdoor lighting. Helps stop other threats to our view of the universe, such as Radio Frequency Interference (RFI) and space debris. **Libraries: Type:** reference; by appointment only; open to the public. **Holdings:** 1,200; archival material, articles, biographical archives, books, clippings, periodicals. **Subjects:** astronomy, physics, weather, light pollution. **Awards:** Executive Director Special Awards. **Frequency:** annual. **Type:** recognition. **Recipient:** to individuals or organizations who have been helpful to IDA's mission ● George and Edythe Taylor Student Awards. **Frequency:** annual. **Type:** recognition ● Good Lighting Award. **Frequency:** periodic. **Type:** recognition ● Hoag/Robinson Award. **Frequency:** annual. **Type:** recognition. **Recipient:** to individuals who have been effective in educating about Outdoor Lighting Control Ordinances. **Working Groups:** Educational; Informational; Lighting Advisory; Lighting Research; Measuring Sky Brightness; Offices; Passenger; Photobiology and Pathology; Science Museums/Planetaria. **Publications:** *IDA Newsletter*, quarterly. Alternate Formats: online ● Also makes available slide presentation, and issues information sheets. **Conventions/Meetings:** annual Asia Pacific - conference, discusses the concept of dark sky lighting and deeper communications (exhibits).

6507 ■ International Occultation Timing Association (IOTA)
c/o Chad Ellington, Sec.-Treas.
PO Box 6356
Kent, WA 98064-6356
E-mail: business@occultations.org
URL: http://www.occultations.org
Contact: Chad Ellington, Sec.-Treas.
Founded: 1975. **Members:** 270. **Membership Dues:** individual, $30 (annual). **Description:** Amateur astronomers, professional astronomers affiliated with universities, amateur astronomical societies, university astronomy departments, and government institutions from 34 countries. Seeks to: predict and coordinate observations of grazing occultations (eclipses) of the stars by the moon, as well as occultations of stars by asteroids; observe occultations of planets by the moon, and solar eclipses; disseminate such data to national government institutions for analysis. Observation data of the moon and stars can be used to determine their precise positions, map the edge of the moon, and detect close double stars. Observation findings from stars and asteroids allow the diameter of the asteroid to be

calculated and possible satellites of the asteroid to be detected. Informs members of observations, discoveries, observational techniques, and equipment. Analyzes data for formal journal publication and occultation prediction improvement. Conducts seminars; maintains observation report file. **Publications:** *Occultation Newsletter*. **Price:** $20.00/year in U.S.; $25.00/year outside U.S. ISSN: 0737-6766. **Circulation:** 270 ● Membership Directory, periodic. **Conventions/Meetings:** annual meeting.

6508 ■ International Planetarium Society (IPS)
c/o Shawn Laatsch, Membership Chm./Treas.
Imiloa Astronomy Center of Hawaii
600 Imiloa Pl.
Hilo, HI 96720
Ph: (808)969-9735
Fax: (808)969-9748
E-mail: slaatsch@imiloahawaii.org
URL: http://www.ips-planetarium.org
Contact: Shawn Laatsch, Membership Chm./Treas.
Founded: 1970. **Members:** 650. **Membership Dues:** individual, $50 (annual) ● institutional, $100 (annual). **Regional Groups:** 21. **Description:** Planetarium staff members; planetarium equipment suppliers; students in planetarium education and astronomy. Encourages exchange of ideas relating to planetariums and the profession. Operates placement service. **Awards:** Service Award. **Frequency:** biennial. **Type:** recognition. **Computer Services:** Mailing lists, of members. **Formerly:** (1976) International Society of Planetarium Educators. **Publications:** *Directory of the World's Planetariums*, biennial. **Price:** $40.00. **Circulation:** 700. **Advertising:** accepted ● *Planetarian*, quarterly. Journal. **Price:** $36.00 /year for libraries. ISSN: 0090-3213. **Advertising:** accepted ● Reports. **Conventions/Meetings:** biennial conference (exhibits) - 2008 June 15-20, Chicago, IL.

6509 ■ Maria Mitchell Association (MMA)
4 Vestal St.
Nantucket, MA 02554
Ph: (508)228-9198 (508)228-2896
Fax: (508)228-1031
E-mail: info@mmo.org
URL: http://www.mmo.org
Contact: Janet E. Schulte PhD, Exec. Dir.
Founded: 1902. **Members:** 2,200. **Membership Dues:** individual/double star, $40 (annual) ● stargazer, $30 (annual) ● Centennial Circle, $2,500 (annual) ● Island Family, $50 (annual) ● Stellar Cluster, $75 (annual) ● Nebula, $100 (annual) ● Supernova, $250 (annual) ● Galaxy, $500 (annual) ● Maria Mitchell Circle, $1,000 (annual). **Staff:** 36. **Budget:** $440,000. **Description:** Professional researchers; scientists; interested others. Works to increase public knowledge of astronomy and awareness of Maria Mitchell (1818-1889), America's first recognized woman astronomer. Encourages study of the natural history of Nantucket, MA, where Mitchell lived. Operates the Maria Mitchell Science Center, which includes a library, aquarium, observatory, and natural science and historic house museums. Sponsors lectures, research, and educational programs. Conducts summer classes for children. **Libraries: Type:** reference; by appointment only; not open to the public. **Holdings:** 8,000; archival material, books, clippings, periodicals. **Subjects:** Maria Mitchell, astronomy, natural science, Nantucket history. **Awards:** Maria Mitchell Women in Science Award. **Frequency:** annual. **Type:** monetary. **Publications:** *E-Comet*, monthly. Newsletter. Provides up-to-date information on research, activities, programs and other happenings. Alternate Formats: online ● Annual Report, annual. **Price:** $5.00 for nonmembers; included in membership dues.

6510 ■ SETI League
PO Box 555
Little Ferry, NJ 07643
Ph: (201)641-1770
Free: (800)TAU-SETI
Fax: (201)641-1771
E-mail: info@setileague.org
URL: http://www.setileague.org
Contact: Dr. H. Paul Shuch, Exec. Dir.
Founded: 1994. **Members:** 1,470. **Membership Dues:** full, $50 (annual) ● supporting, $35 (annual) ● scholarship, $25 (annual) ● full - life, $1,000 ● additional household, $15 (annual) ● household - life, $300 ● patron - life, $10,000 ● director, $100,000 ● benefactor, $1,000,000. **Staff:** 1. **Budget:** $25,000. **Regional Groups:** 63. **Description:** Astronomers and other individuals with an interest in the search for extra-terrestrial intelligence (SETI). Seeks to continue the program of the original National Aeronautics and Space Administration SETI program, which was cancelled in 1993. Coordinates a global electromagnetic search for microwave signals generated by extra-terrestrial sources; serves as a forum for the exchange of information among SETI researchers. Assembles, operates, and maintains advanced optical and radio telescopes; disseminates instructions for the construction of amateur radio telescopes using discarded television satellite dishes. Operates EME moonbounce beacon for calibration and testing purposes. Sells SETI memorabilia. **Libraries: Type:** by appointment only; not open to the public; reference. **Holdings:** 400; archival material, articles, audio recordings, books, periodicals, video recordings. **Subjects:** astronomy, electronics, microwave communications, digital signal processing, aerospace technology, bioastronomy, SETI, search for extraterrestrial intelligence, EME, moonbounce. **Awards:** Giordano Bruno Memorial Award. **Frequency:** annual. **Type:** recognition. **Recipient:** to an individual making an outstanding contribution to the search for extra-terrestrial intelligence ● Orville N. Greene Service Award. **Frequency:** annual. **Type:** recognition. **Recipient:** to an individual making volunteer contributions or providing extraordinary service to the SETI League. **Computer Services:** Mailing lists, multiple email. **Also Known As:** Search for Extra-Terrestrial Intelligence League. **Publications:** *Project Cyclops*. Book. **Price:** $20.00 in U.S.; $25.00 outside U.S. ● *SearchLites*, quarterly. Newsletter. Contains news, reviews, papers, and articles. **Price:** included in membership dues. ISSN: 1096-5599. **Circulation:** 1,500. Alternate Formats: online ● *SETI League Technical Manual*. Handbook ● *Sing A Song of SETI*. Book. **Price:** $10.00 in U.S.; $13.00 outside U.S. ● *Sing More Songs of SETI*. Book. **Price:** $10.00 in U.S.; $13.00 outside U.S. **Conventions/Meetings:** annual meeting and seminar ● annual SETICon - convention and banquet, technical and theoretical papers, awards, demonstrations (exhibits).

6511 ■ Von Braun Astronomical Society (VBAS)
PO Box 1142
Huntsville, AL 35807
Ph: (256)539-0316
E-mail: executive.secretary@vbas.org
URL: http://www.vbas.org
Contact: Richard Norman, Exec. Sec.
Founded: 1954. **Members:** 170. **Membership Dues:** student, $12 (annual) ● regular, $24 (annual) ● family, $36 (annual). **Staff:** 13. **Budget:** $10,000. **Description:** Promotes interest in the descriptive and technical phases of astronomy. Encourages participation in observational, computational, and applied phases of this and related sciences. Membership concentrated in Huntsville, AL area (site of the U.S. Army Missile Command and NASA's G. C. Marshall Space Flight Center). Maintains 2 observatories and planetarium on Monte Sano Mountain; the observatories are equipped with a 53.34cm (21 in.) Cassegrainian reflector and a 40.6cm (16 in.) Celestron telescope; the planetarium seats 100 persons and utilizes a "GOTO Mercury Model" planetarium projector. Holds planetarium shows and star parties for the public on 3 Saturdays of each month, and schedules special shows and star parties upon request. Sponsors classes for members. **Libraries: Type:** not open to the public. **Holdings:** 600; books, video recordings. **Subjects:** astronomy, cosmology, optics. **Computer Services:** database, membership programs and mailing information. **Subgroups:** Activity; Junior Astronomers; Observers; Telescopes and Observing. **Affiliated With:** Astronomical League. **Formerly:** (1974) Rocket City Astronomical Association. **Publications:** *Via Stellaris*, monthly. Newsletter. Includes calendar of events, book reviews, members' articles, and astronomy club info. **Price:** included in membership dues. **Circulation:** 200. **Conventions/Meetings:** monthly general assembly.

6512 ■ Webb Society
c/o John Isles, North American Sec.-Treas.
10575 Darrel Dr.
Hanover, MI 49241
E-mail: jisles@hughes.net
URL: http://www.webbdeepsky.com
Contact: John Isles, North American Sec.-Treas.
Founded: 1967. **Members:** 400. **Membership Dues:** individual (in Europe - airmail), $30 (annual) ● individual (overseas - surface), $30 (annual) ● individual (overseas - air mail), $37 (annual) ● in UK, 16 (annual) ● (full) surface, $A 45 (annual) ● airmail, $A 50 (annual) ● student (in UK), 8 (annual) ● student (in Europe - airmail), $18 (annual) ● student (overseas - airmail), $32 (annual) ● student (surface), $29 (annual). **Multinational. Description:** Represents the interests of amateur and professional astronomers. Specializes in the observation of double stars and 'deep-sky' objects. **Awards:** Graphics Award. **Frequency:** annual. **Type:** monetary. **Recipient:** for best graphics contribution to the society's journal ● Webb Society Award. **Frequency:** annual. **Type:** monetary. **Recipient:** for best contribution to the society's journal. **Sections:** Double Stars; Galaxies; Nebulae and Clusters; Southern Sky. **Publications:** *Deep-Sky Observer*, quarterly. Journal. **Price:** included in membership dues. **Conventions/Meetings:** annual meeting.

Audiovisual Communications

6513 ■ HAVi
40994 Encyclopedia Cir.
Fremont, CA 94538
Ph: (510)979-1394
Fax: (510)979-1390
E-mail: a-shibata@itg.hitachi.co.jp
URL: http://www.havi.org
Contact: Akira Shibata, VP
Founded: 1999. **Membership Dues:** standard, $10,000 (annual) ● non-profit, $2,500 (annual). **Multinational. Description:** Promotes network architecture for home audio video interoperability. **Publications:** *HAVI Example by Example*. Book ● *HAVI, the A/V digital network revolution*. Papers. Alternate Formats: online ● Newsletter. **Price:** included in membership dues.

Automatic Control

6514 ■ IEEE Control Systems Society (IEEE/CSS)
445 Hoes Ln.
PO Box 1331
Piscataway, NJ 08855-1331
Ph: (732)981-0060 (908)562-5528
Free: (800)678-4333
Fax: (732)981-1721
E-mail: bushnell@ee.washington.edu
URL: http://www.ieeecss.org
Contact: Linda Bushnell, Admin./Sec.
Founded: 1954. **Members:** 12,200. **Membership Dues:** student, retiree (electronic access), $8 (annual) ● affiliate, $25 (annual) ● student, retiree, $13 (annual). **Budget:** $1,500,000. **Regional Groups:** 28. **Local Groups:** 39. **National Groups:** 30. **Description:** A society of the Institute of Electrical and Electronics Engineers. Disseminates information on automatic control systems and applications, covering subjects such as: real-time control; optimal control; adaptive and stochastic control; estimation and identification; linear systems; system modeling; applications of physical, economic, and social systems. Sponsors conference programs. **Awards:** CDC Best

Student-Paper. **Frequency:** annual. **Type:** recognition. **Recipient:** for excellent paper presented at the IEEE conference ● Control System Technology. **Frequency:** annual. **Type:** recognition. **Recipient:** for outstanding contributions in design ● Control Systems Magazine Outstanding Paper. **Frequency:** annual. **Type:** recognition. **Recipient:** for outstanding article published in the Control Systems Magazine ● George S. Axelby Outstanding Paper. **Frequency:** annual. **Type:** recognition. **Recipient:** for outstanding paper published in the Transaction on Automatic Control ● Outstanding Chapter. **Frequency:** annual. **Type:** recognition. **Recipient:** for outstanding CSS chapter ● Transactions On Control Systems Technology Outstanding Paper. **Frequency:** annual. **Type:** recognition. **Recipient:** for outstanding paper published in the Transaction on Automatic Control Technology. **Publications:** *Control Systems*, bimonthly. Magazine. **Price:** included in membership dues. ISSN: 0272-1708. **Circulation:** 15,000. **Advertising:** accepted ● *Transactions on Automatic Control*, monthly. Journal. **Price:** included in membership dues ● *Transactions on Control Systems Technology*, bimonthly. Journal. **Price:** included in membership dues. **Conventions/Meetings:** annual American Control Conference ● annual Conference on Control Applications - meeting ● annual Conference on Decision and Control.

Automation

6515 ■ Association for Laboratory Automation (ALA)
c/o Greg Dummer, CAE, Exec. Dir.
330 W State St.
Geneva, IL 60134
Ph: (630)208-6830
Free: (888)733-1252
Fax: (630)578-0172
E-mail: ala_office@labautomation.org
URL: http://labautomation.org
Contact: Greg Dummer CAE, Exec. Dir.

Founded: 1996. **Members:** 800. **Membership Dues:** individual, $120 (annual) ● sterling corporate, $1,500 (annual) ● bronze corporate, $750 (annual) ● student affiliate, $25 (annual). **Multinational. Description:** Works to support the advancement and education of automation technologies worldwide. Advances science and education related to laboratory automation by encouraging the study, advancing the science, and improving the practice of medical and laboratory automation. Seeks to improve the quality, efficiency and relevance of laboratory analysis. Provides a forum for the latest developments and ideas in the field of laboratory automation. **Awards:** Academic Travel Awards. **Frequency:** annual. **Type:** monetary. **Recipient:** for outstanding students, post-doctoral fellows and junior faculty ● ALA Innovation Award. **Frequency:** annual. **Type:** recognition. **Recipient:** for laboratory innovation and technology advancement. **Publications:** *Journal of the Association for Laboratory Automation*, bimonthly. Features articles about current developments in the field of laboratory robotics. **Price:** $194.00 /year for nonmembers in U.S.; $266.00 /year for institutions in U.S.; $219.00 /year for nonmembers outside U.S.; $292.00 /year for institutions outside U.S. Alternate Formats: online. Also Cited As: *JALA* ● *LabSnap*, monthly. Newsletter. **Price:** included in membership dues. Alternate Formats: online.

Automotive

6516 ■ Electric Auto Association (EAA)
323 Los Altos Dr.
Aptos, CA 95003-5248
Ph: (831)688-8669
E-mail: contact@eaaev.org
URL: http://eaaev.org
Contact: Ron Freund, Chm.

Founded: 1967. **Members:** 1,100. **Membership Dues:** regular in U.S., $39 (annual) ● regular in Canada, $42 (annual) ● regular in other country, $45 (annual) ● student, senior, $25 (annual) ● supporting, $120-$500 (annual). **Regional Groups:** 7. **State Groups:** 33. **Local Groups:** 7. **National Groups:** 33. **Multinational. Description:** Represents engineers, technicians, and hobbyists. Encourages development of electric vehicles for street use and sponsors public exhibitions of vehicles built by members. Conducts research on electric vehicles. **Libraries: Type:** reference. **Subjects:** electric vehicles. **Awards:** Technical Achievement Fellowship. **Frequency:** annual. **Type:** fellowship. **Recipient:** for outstanding members. **Telecommunication Services:** electronic mail, membership@eaaev.org. **Publications:** *Current Events*, monthly. Newsletter. Includes industry and EAA news, technical information, and helpful ideas. **Price:** included in membership dues. **Conventions/Meetings:** annual rally and symposium (exhibits).

6517 ■ Electric Drive Transportation Association (EDTA)
1101 Vermont Ave. NW, Ste.401
Washington, DC 20005
Ph: (202)408-0774
Fax: (202)408-7610
E-mail: info@electricdrive.org
URL: http://www.electricdrive.org
Contact: Brian P. Wynne, Pres.

Founded: 1990. **Members:** 86. **Membership Dues:** non-profit, $1,500 (annual) ● small business, $5,000 (annual) ● general, $8,000 (annual) ● board, $35,000 (annual). **Staff:** 6. **Description:** Represents corporations and government agencies developing electric- and hybrid-powered vehicles. Includes areas of interest such as: commercial development of batteries, fuel cells, propulsion systems, infrastructure, and complete vehicles. Encourages the introduction of electric and hybrid vehicles into the transportation sector. Functions as an information clearinghouse. **Libraries: Type:** reference. **Holdings:** archival material, audiovisuals, books, clippings, periodicals. **Subjects:** electric vehicles, supporting infrastructure. **Awards:** E-Visionary. **Type:** recognition ● Local EV Hero. **Type:** recognition. **Formerly:** (2003) Electric Vehicle Association of the Americas. **Publications:** *Electric Drive Update and Media Watch*, biweekly. Reports ● Also provides various members-only publications. **Conventions/Meetings:** annual Electric Transportation Industry Conference, focuses on EV technology and research; marketing and infrastructure development (exhibits) ● annual International Electric Vehicle Symposium (exhibits).

6518 ■ International Society for Terrain-Vehicle Systems (ISTVS)
c/o George L. Blaisdell, Gen. Sec.
Natl. Sci. Found.
4201 Wilson Blvd.
Arlington, VA 22230
Ph: (703)292-7447
E-mail: gblaisdell@nsf.gov
URL: http://istvs.com
Contact: George L. Blaisdell, Gen. Sec.

Founded: 1962. **Members:** 350. **Membership Dues:** engineer, scientist, $80 (annual). **Staff:** 4. **Regional Groups:** 3. **Multinational. Description:** Membership in 27 countries includes: professional automotive, civil, mechanical, and agricultural engineers; administrators; students; other scientific and technical personnel engaged in the area of off-road vehicles, terrain-vehicle systems or soil working machinery, and amphibians. Fosters research on the design and use of terramechanics including the scientific study of processes of vehicular movement, earth-moving, and agricultural implements. Maintains documentation center of technical journal reprints in Hanover, New Hampshire. **Awards:** Bekker-Reece-Radforth Award. **Frequency:** triennial. **Type:** monetary. **Recipient:** for outstanding young researcher ● Hata-Soehne-Juricka Award. **Frequency:** triennial. **Type:** monetary. **Recipient:** for outstanding young researcher. **Telecommunication Services:** electronic mail, rdwismer@aol.com. **Committees:** Laboratory-Field Test Procedures; Standardization. **Publications:** *Journal of Terramechanics*, quarterly ● *Proceedings of International Congress*, triennial ● *Regional Meetings Abstracts*, annual ● Membership Directory, annual. Contains information on members. ● Newsletter, quarterly. **Conventions/Meetings:** triennial conference ● periodic regional meeting.

6519 ■ Natural Gas Vehicle for America (NGVAmerica)
400 N Capitol St. NW
Washington, DC 20001
Ph: (202)824-7366
Fax: (202)824-7087
E-mail: rkolodziej@ngvamerica.org
URL: http://www.ngvc.org
Contact: Richard Kolodziej, Pres.

Founded: 1988. **Members:** 180. **Staff:** 7. **Budget:** $2,000,000. **Description:** Natural gas producers, engine, vehicle, and equipment manufacturers, environmental organizations, and service providers to the vehicular industries. Promotes development of commercially viable natural gas powered vehicles. Serves as the national voice of the natural gas vehicle industries; conducts promotional campaigns and lobbying activities; sponsors research and development programs; makes available support and services to members. **Formerly:** (2001) Natural Gas Vehicle Association; (2006) Natural Gas Vehicle Coalition. **Publications:** *Clean Bus Report*, quarterly. Alternate Formats: online ● *Technology Committee Bulletin* ● Newsletter, weekly.

6520 ■ SAE International - Society of Automotive Engineers (SAE)
400 Commonwealth Dr.
Warrendale, PA 15096-0001
Ph: (724)776-4841 (724)776-4970
Free: (877)606-7323
Fax: (724)776-0790
E-mail: customerservice@sae.org
URL: http://www.sae.org
Contact: Dr. Richard O. SchaumGreg, Pres.

Founded: 1905. **Members:** 80,000. **Membership Dues:** professional, $100 (annual) ● student, $10 (annual). **Staff:** 380. **Budget:** $452,000,000. **State Groups:** 66. **National Groups:** 9. **Description:** Collects and disseminates information on mobility technology. Fosters information exchange among the worldwide automotive and aerospace communities. Conducts educational programs. **Libraries: Type:** open to the public; reference. **Holdings:** 50,000. **Subjects:** automotive and aerospace engineering. **Computer Services:** database, Global Mobility containing technical papers and standards. **Committees:** Administrative; Technical. **Formed by Merger of:** (1917) American Society of Aeronautical Engineers; (1917) Society of Tractor Engineers. **Formerly:** Society of Automobile Engineers. **Publications:** *Aerospace Engineering*, monthly. Magazine. **Price:** $66.00/year in North America; $118.00/year outside North America. ISSN: 0736-2536. **Advertising:** accepted ● *Aerospace Standards* ● *Automotive Consultant's Directory*, annual ● *Automotive Engineering*, monthly. Magazine. **Price:** $96.00 in U.S.; $150.00 outside U.S. ISSN: 0098-2571. **Circulation:** 122,000. **Advertising:** accepted ● *Bosch Handbook*, annual. Contains book of ground vehicle standards. ● *Off Highway Engineering*, bimonthly. **Price:** $54.00/year in North America; $78.00/year outside North America. ISSN: 1074-6919. **Advertising:** accepted ● *Progress in Technology* ● *SAE Aerospace Material Specifications* ● *SAE Technical Papers* ● *SAE Transactions*, annual ● *SAE Update*, monthly. Newspaper. **Conventions/Meetings:** Automotive Manufacturing - meeting ● annual congress, showcases technical developments to the largest assembled audience of mobility engineers (exhibits) ● annual Fuels and Lubricants Meeting and Exposition - congress ● annual International Truck and Bus Meeting and Exposition - conference ● annual Offhighway and Powerplant Congress.

6521 ■ SFI Foundation (SFI)
15708 Pomerado Rd., Ste.N208
Poway, CA 92064
Ph: (858)451-8868
Fax: (858)451-9268

E-mail: sfi@sfifoundation.com
URL: http://www.sfifoundation.com
Contact: Arnold S. Kuhns, Pres.
Founded: 1978. **Staff:** 9. **Description:** Develops and administrates minimum performance specifications for the automobile industry, including consumer automotive, automotive aftermarket, and high performance racing products. Encourages suggestions on specifications as they are developed through committee meetings and public hearings. **Telecommunication Services:** electronic mail, specs@sfifoundation.com. **Committees:** Specification. **Programs:** Specs. **Formerly:** (1986) SEMA Foundation. **Publications:** Articles. Alternate Formats: online ● Specifications.

Behavioral Sciences

6522 ■ American Association of Behavioral and Social Sciences (AABSS)

c/o Diane Keffer
Dept. of SSME, Univ. of Tampa
401 W Kennedy Blvd.
Tampa, FL 33606-1490
E-mail: jdoyle@fullerton.edu
URL: http://www.aabss.org
Contact: John Doyle PhD, Ed.
Membership Dues: regular, $50 (annual). **Description:** Serves faculty and administrators at four-year colleges and universities. Provides a forum to share research, ideas for professional development, and academic concerns in all areas of the Behavioral and Social Sciences. Encourages students to participate in Behavioral and Social Sciences research. **Telecommunication Services:** electronic mail, crenold@fullerton.edu. **Publications:** *AABSS Journal*, annual. Alternate Formats: online ● *AABSS Perspectives*, annual. Journal. Alternate Formats: online. **Conventions/Meetings:** annual meeting.

6523 ■ American Institutes for Research in the Behavioral Sciences (AIR)

1000 Thomas Jefferson St. NW
Washington, DC 20007-3835
Ph: (202)342-5000
Fax: (202)403-5001
E-mail: inquiry@air.org
URL: http://www.air.org
Contact: Sol H. Pelavin, Pres./CEO
Founded: 1946. **Staff:** 1,100. **Nonmembership. Description:** Scientific and educational research organization. Conducts behavioral and social science research in fields of education, social program evaluation, healthcare, human performance in the workplace, usability engineering, human factors, problems of the specially challenged, education finance, employment equity, statistical methods and design. Supported by contracts and grants from industry, foundations, and government agencies. **Also Known As:** American Institutes for Research. **Publications:** *Air Newsletter*, annual. Describes research activities and key events. **Price:** free. **Circulation:** 4,000 ● Bibliography. Contains project reports.

6524 ■ American Society of Trial Consultants (ASTC)

1941 Greenspring Dr.
Timonium, MD 21093
Ph: (410)560-7949
Fax: (410)560-2563
E-mail: astcoffice@aol.com
URL: http://www.astcweb.org
Contact: Ronald J. Matlon PhD, Exec. Dir.
Founded: 1982. **Members:** 400. **Membership Dues:** individual, $185 (annual) ● student, $60 (annual). **Staff:** 3. **Description:** Consultants and researchers involved in the behavioral aspects of litigation. Provides opportunities for networking and dialogue among those who share similar professional interests in trial consulting, research, and teaching. Promotes effective utilization of social science knowledge by attorneys; promotes members' effective utilization of services offered by trial consultants. Fosters development of behavioral knowledge for current legal education and practice. Provides bar associations and law firms with lists of trial consultants. **Awards: Frequency:** annual. **Type:** monetary. **Telecommunication Services:** electronic mail, matlon1005@earthlink.net. **Committees:** Development; Membership and Membership Services; Pro-Bono Publico; Professional Standards; Professional Visibility; Research. **Formerly:** (1983) Association of Trial Behavior Consultants. **Publications:** *Court Call*, quarterly. Newsletter. **Advertising:** accepted ● Directory, annual. **Conventions/Meetings:** annual conference.

6525 ■ Armenian Behavioral Science Association (ABSA)

c/o Prof. Harold Takooshian, PhD, Exec. Off.
113 W 60th St., Rm. 916
New York, NY 10023
Ph: (212)636-6393
Fax: (201)262-7141
E-mail: takoosh@aol.com
Contact: Prof. Harold Takooshian PhD, Exec. Off.
Founded: 1987. **Members:** 600. **Description:** Works to advance the study of the behavioral science among Armenian-Americans through research, education, and practical application. Offers consulting services; advises students entering behavioral sciences fields; maintains Speaker's Bureau; conducts manpower surveys. Compiles statistics; sponsors educational programs. **Awards:** Outstanding Achievement Award. **Frequency:** semiannual. **Type:** recognition. **Recipient:** for outstanding contributions to behavioral sciences. **Computer Services:** database. **Divisions:** Economics; Political Science; Psychiatry; Psychology; Social Science; Sociology/Anthropology; Statistics. **Publications:** *ABSA Bulletin*, semiannual. **Circulation:** 540 ● *Directory of Armenian-American Behavioral Scientists*, biennial. **Conventions/Meetings:** semiannual meeting ● annual meeting.

6526 ■ Association for Behavior Analysis (ABA)

1219 S Park St.
Kalamazoo, MI 49001-5607
Ph: (269)492-9310 (269)492-9314
Fax: (269)492-9316
E-mail: mail@abainternational.org
URL: http://www.abainternational.org
Contact: Maria E. Malott PhD, Exec. Dir.
Founded: 1974. **Members:** 4,600. **Membership Dues:** chapter-adjunct, student, emeritus, $45 (annual) ● affiliate, full, $115 (annual) ● supporting, $152 (annual) ● sustaining, $280 (annual). **Staff:** 12. **Regional Groups:** 24. **State Groups:** 15. **Local Groups:** 1. **Multinational. Description:** Professionals, paraprofessionals, and students interested in the applied, experimental, and theoretical analysis of behavior. Promotes the development of behavior analysis as a profession and science. Provides a forum for the discussion of issues; disseminates information on behavior analysis. Conducts workshops and seminars in 16 specialty areas including: Behavioral Pharmacology and Toxicology; Developmental Disabilities; Organizational Behavior Analysis. Offers continuing education credits for psychologists. Maintains archives of the association's publications; offers placement service. **Computer Services:** Mailing lists, of members. **Committees:** Continuing Education; International Development. **Formerly:** (1980) Midwestern Association for Behavior Analysis. **Publications:** *ABA Newsletter*, 3/year. Includes employment opportunities and research updates. **Price:** included in membership dues; $30.00 /year for institutions and nonmembers. **Circulation:** 2,500. **Advertising:** accepted ● *The Analysis of Verbal Behavior*, annual. Journal ● *The Behavior Analyst*, semiannual. Journal ● *Concepts & Principles of Behavior Analysis* ● *Program Book*, annual. **Conventions/Meetings:** annual convention (exhibits) ● annual international conference.

6527 ■ Association for the Behavioral Sciences and Medical Education (ABSAME)

1460 N Center Rd.
Burton, MI 48509
Ph: (810)715-4365
Fax: (810)715-4371
E-mail: admin@absame.org
URL: http://www.absame.org
Contact: Mark Vogel PhD, Exec. Dir.
Founded: 1970. **Members:** 150. **Membership Dues:** regular, $125 (annual) ● student, $50 (annual) ● institutional, $550 (annual). **Description:** A member society of the Council of Academic Societies of the Association of American Medical Colleges. Physicians and behavioral scientists committed to developing and advancing the teaching of behavioral science. Seeks to improve the effectiveness, efficiency, and quality of health care through the application of social and behavioral science knowledge. Aids the continuing education of teachers, clinicians, researchers, and administrators in the behavioral sciences. Conducts educational programs. **Publications:** *ABSAME Newsletter*, semiannual. **Price:** included in membership dues. **Circulation:** 200. **Advertising:** accepted. Alternate Formats: online ● *Annals of Behavioral Science and Medical Education*, semiannual. Journal. ISSN: 1075-0930. **Circulation:** 250. **Advertising:** accepted ● *Membership List*, annual. Membership Directory. **Conventions/Meetings:** annual meeting and conference (exhibits).

6528 ■ Association of Management/International Association of Management

PO Box 64841
Virginia Beach, VA 23467-4841
Ph: (757)482-2273
Fax: (757)482-0325
E-mail: aomgt@inter-source.org
URL: http://www.aom-iaom.org
Contact: Dr. Willem Arthur Hamel, Co-Founder/Pres.
Founded: 1979. **Members:** 3,500. **Membership Dues:** academic, individual, $120 (annual). **Staff:** 6. **Budget:** $500,000. **Regional Groups:** 3. **National Groups:** 12. **Description:** Academics and practitioners of management. Seeks to align theory and practice in the study of human resource management, information and technology management, computer science, organizational studies, information systems, global health and ecology, transportation, travel and related technology, educational studies and research, management functions and applications, and multidisciplinary related issues. Encourages research in the fields. **Libraries: Type:** reference. **Holdings:** archival material, periodicals. **Awards:** Outstanding Professional Service Award. **Frequency:** annual. **Type:** recognition. **Recipient:** for professional service contributions to the association ● The Ram Award. **Frequency:** annual. **Type:** recognition. **Recipient:** for professional service contributions to the association. **Computer Services:** Mailing lists, of members. **Telecommunication Services:** electronic mail, aomgt@infi.net ● electronic mail, listproc@bilbo.isu.edu. **Formerly:** (1975) Training Research Assessment Consultants; (1983) Association of Human Resources Management and Organizational Behavior; (1996) Association of Management. **Publications:** *AoM Proceedings*, annual. Includes scholarly and practitioner papers. **Circulation:** 750. **Advertising:** accepted. Alternate Formats: CD-ROM; online ● *Global Information Systems*, quarterly. Journal. Includes academic and practitioner related research and scholarly information systems related articles bridging the academic/practitioner experience. ● *Journal of Information Technology Management*, quarterly. Includes case studies, management applications, information technology, and professional academic and practitioner related articles. **Price:** $65.00 for individuals; $165.00 for institutions. ISSN: 1042-1319 ● *Journal of Management Systems*, quarterly. Includes academic research and scholarly management systems related articles, case studies, and book reviews. **Price:** $65.00 /year for individuals; $165.00 /year for institutions. ISSN: 1041-2808 ● *Leadership and Leaders*, quarterly. Journal. **Conventions/Meetings:** annual conference (exhibits).

6529 ■ Association for the Treatment of Sexual Abusers (ATSA)

4900 SW Griffith Dr., Ste.274
Beaverton, OR 97005-4732
Ph: (503)643-1023

Fax: (503)643-5084
E-mail: atsa@atsa.com
URL: http://www.atsa.com
Contact: Maia Christopher, Exec. Dir.
Founded: 1984. **Members:** 2,200. **Membership Dues:** clinical, research, professional associate, $165 (annual) ● student, affiliate, $35 (annual). **Staff:** 3. **Budget:** $750,000. **State Groups:** 22. **Description:** Develops and disseminates professional standards and practices in the field of sex offender research, evaluation and treatment. Provides referrals for sex offender treatment providers. **Awards:** Best Graduate Research on Sexual Abuse Victims and Abusers. **Frequency:** annual. **Type:** grant. **Formerly:** (1986) Association for the Behavioral Treatment of Sexual Aggression; (1992) Association for the Behavioral Treatment of Sexual Abusers. **Supersedes:** Sexual Assault Research Association. **Publications:** *The Forum*, quarterly. Newsletter. **Price:** free for members ● *Sexual Abuse: A Journal of Research and Treatment*, quarterly. **Price:** $40.00 /year for nonmembers; free for members. **Advertising:** accepted. **Conventions/Meetings:** annual Research and Treatment Conference, offers opportunities for professional growth, networking, and the dissemination of the latest research findings in the area of sexual abuse and treatment (exhibits).

6530 ■ Federation of Behavioral, Psychological, and Cognitive Sciences (FBPCS)

750 1st St. NE, 9th Fl.
Washington, DC 20002
Ph: (202)336-5920
Fax: (202)336-5812
E-mail: federation@fbpcs.org
URL: http://www.thefederationonline.org
Contact: Barbara A. Wanchisen PhD, Exec. Dir.
Founded: 1980. **Members:** 10,000. **Membership Dues:** full rate (per relevant member of the society), $11-$13 (annual). **Staff:** 3. **Description:** Scientific societies representing 10,000 research scientists. Promotes research in behavioral, psychological, and cognitive sciences and their physiological bases and applications in health, education, and human development. Facilitates the exchange of information and interaction among governmental agencies and scientific organizations. Serves as a source of information and expertise on behavioral, psychological, and cognitive sciences. Works with other scientific societies in the fields of social science, psychology, education, and neurosciences. Encourages litigation and policies that provide training and research in these areas; represents interests of members before Congress. Conducts scientific seminars to demonstrate the utility of science in addressing public policy problems. Sponsors Forum on Research Management as a channel for increasing communication among university scientists and government officials. **Awards:** Richard T. Louttit Award. **Frequency:** biennial. **Type:** recognition. **Recipient:** for a person who had a distinguished career of service in government or other arena towards behavioral science. **Computer Services:** Electronic publishing. **Committees:** Animal Research; Forum on Research Management; Science Seminar. **Publications:** *Federation News*, monthly. Newsletter ● *Science and Public Policy Seminar Transcripts*, periodic ● Annual Report, annual. **Conventions/Meetings:** annual meeting.

6531 ■ Human Behavior and Evolution Society (HBES)

Univ. of Nebraska
Center for Great Plains Stud.
1155 Q St.
Lincoln, NE 68588-0214
Ph: (402)472-6240 (402)472-2865
Fax: (402)472-9642
E-mail: rhames@unl.edu
URL: http://www.hbes.com
Contact: Dr. Raymond Hames, Treas.
Founded: 1988. **Members:** 650. **Membership Dues:** student, $33 (annual) ● joint student, $38 (annual) ● regular, $66 (annual) ● joint regular, $76 (annual). **Staff:** 1. **Budget:** $49,000. **Description:** Scholars in the sciences, social sciences, and humanities who share a "perspective on human affairs that is rooted in modern evolutionary thought." Promotes advancement in the fields of ethnology and sociobiology. Gathers and disseminates information on human behavior and evolution. Makes available to members discounts on scholarly publications; provides job and scientific conference announcements. **Awards:** Best Poster Award. **Frequency:** annual. **Type:** monetary. **Recipient:** for the best poster presented at the annual meeting ● Distinguished Scientific Award for an Early Career Contribution to Evolution and Human Behavior. **Frequency:** annual. **Type:** monetary. **Recipient:** for research achievement within 8 years of receiving doctorate ● New Young Investigator. **Frequency:** annual. **Type:** monetary. **Recipient:** for significant research accomplishments within three years of receiving a doctorate. **Computer Services:** database ● mailing lists, rented to vendors of books and other products of interest to members. **Publications:** *Evolution and Human Behavior*, bimonthly. Journal. **Advertising:** accepted ● *HBES Membership Directory*, bimonthly. Lists members contact information and reserach interests. ● *HBES Newsletter*, quarterly. Features member news, conferences, personal profiles, teaching resources and journals. **Conventions/Meetings:** annual conference, with book displays (exhibits) ● annual meeting.

6532 ■ Human Resources Research Organization (HumRRO)

66 Canal Center Plz., Ste.400
Alexandria, VA 22314
Ph: (703)549-3611
Fax: (703)549-9025
E-mail: network@humrro.org
URL: http://www.humrro.org
Contact: Laurie Wise PhD, Pres.
Founded: 1951. **Staff:** 100. **Nonmembership. Description:** Behavioral and social science researchers seeking to improve human performance, particularly in organizational settings, through behavioral and social science research, development, consultation and instruction. Promotes research and development to solve specific problems in: training and education; development, refinement, and instruction in the technology of training and education; studies and development of techniques to improve the motivation of personnel in training and on the job; research of leadership and management, and development of leadership programs; criterion development, individual assessment, and program evaluation in training and operating systems; measurement and evaluation of human performance under varying circumstances; organizational development studies, including performance counseling, group decision-making, and factors that affect organizational competence; development of manpower information systems and the application of management science on personnel systems. Encourages use of high technology for instructional purposes by means of computer assisted instruction, interactive video, and computer literacy. Offers technical publication services including data analysis and editorial, word processing, production, and printing services. **Awards:** Meredith P. Crawford Fellowship in I/O Psychology. **Frequency:** annual. **Type:** fellowship. **Recipient:** to a graduate student demonstrating exceptional research skills in industrial/organization psychology or related field. **Divisions:** Employment Assessment and Development; Workforce Analysis and Training Systems. **Publications:** Bibliography, periodic ● Also publishes technical reports and professional papers.

6533 ■ International Society for Adaptive Behavior (ISAB)

c/o Prof. Herb Roitblat, VP
Dept. of Psychology
Univ. of Hawaii at Manoa
2430 Campus Rd.
Honolulu, HI 96822
Ph: (808)956-6727
Fax: (808)956-4700
E-mail: roitblat@hawaii.edu
URL: http://www.isab.org
Contact: Prof. Herb Roitblat, VP
Membership Dues: student, $49 ● full, $75. **Multinational. Description:** Represents individuals with background and interest in the field of adaptive behavior. Encourages education and furthers research on adaptive behavior in animals, software agents, and robots. Facilitates the exchange of information about events, job opportunities, and research results in adaptive behavior. **Publications:** *Adaptive Behavior*. Journal. Explores mechanisms, organizational principles, and architecture for generating action in environments. **Price:** included in membership dues. Alternate Formats: online ● Newsletter. **Price:** included in membership dues.

6534 ■ International Society for Human Ethology (ISHE)

c/o Dori LeCroy, Treas.
175 King St.
Charleston, SC 29401
Ph: (843)534-0526
Fax: (843)577-9645
E-mail: karl.grammer@univie.ac.at
URL: http://evolution.anthro.univie.ac.at/ishe
Contact: Glenn Weisfeld, Pres.
Founded: 1972. **Members:** 500. **Membership Dues:** regular/library, $20 (annual) ● retired/low income scholar, $10 (annual) ● regular/library, $50 (triennial) ● retired/low income scholar, $25 (triennial). **Staff:** 10. **Budget:** $50,000. **Multinational. Description:** Individuals active in psychology, psychiatry, anthropology, sociology, political science, zoology and others interested in promoting ethological perspectives in the study of human behavior. Encourages empirical research on questions of individual development and environmental, ecological, and social processes which elicit and support certain behavior patterns. Sponsors educational programs. Offers book reviews. **Awards:** Linda Mealey Award. **Frequency:** annual. **Type:** scholarship. **Recipient:** to outstanding researchers at the graduate school level ● Owen Aldis Scholarship Fund. **Frequency:** annual. **Type:** scholarship. **Recipient:** for doctoral students ● Young Investigator Award. **Frequency:** biennial. **Type:** monetary. **Recipient:** for research presentation excellence. **Telecommunication Services:** electronic bulletin board, 1.5 H.E., including graphics. **Publications:** *Human Ethology Bulletin*, quarterly. Includes essays, articles, book reviews, and announcements. **Price:** included in membership dues. ISSN: 0739-2036. **Circulation:** 500. Also Cited As: *Human Ethology Newsletter* ● Membership Directory, triennial. **Price:** $10.00/copy. **Circulation:** 500. **Conventions/Meetings:** biennial conference and congress, books, journals (exhibits).

6535 ■ International Society for Research on Aggression (ISRA)

c/o L. Rowell Huesmann, Ed.
426 Thompson St.
Ann Arbor, MI 48106-1248
E-mail: john-knutson@uiowa.edu
URL: http://www.israsociety.com
Contact: John Knutson, Exec. Sec.
Founded: 1970. **Members:** 200. **Membership Dues:** regular, $60 (annual). **Multinational. Description:** Represents scholars who have made substantial contributions to the research of problems of aggression as well as other professionals and students who support the society. Encourages the discovery and exchange of scientific information on causes and consequences of aggression with the goal of reducing harmful aggression. **Committees:** Ethics. **Publications:** *Aggressive Behavior*, bimonthly. Journal ● *ISRA Bulletin*, semiannual. **Conventions/Meetings:** symposium ● biennial World Meeting - 2008 July 8-13, Budapest, Hungary.

6536 ■ National Character Laboratory (NCL)

c/o Col. A.J. Stuart, Jr., Pres.
4635 Leeds Ave.
El Paso, TX 79903
Ph: (915)562-5046
Fax: (915)562-3110
E-mail: ajstuartjr@aol.com
URL: http://www.moralhealth.org
Contact: Col. A.J. Stuart Jr., Pres.
Founded: 1971. **Members:** 80. **Membership Dues:** regular, $5 (annual). **Staff:** 1. **Budget:** $10,000. **De-**

scription: Psychiatrists, psychologists, counselors, clergymen, teachers, and others with an interest in character research. Encourages, coordinates, and disseminates the results of character research at the national and state level. Works to reduce the incidence of crime and drug abuse by developing and promoting more effective methods of improving character and behavior. Seeks to influence the individual when and where his or her character is largely formed: by the parents, in the home, or while the person is young. Operates model city project in El Paso, TX. **Convention/Meeting:** none. **Libraries: Type:** open to the public. **Holdings:** 200; books, periodicals. **Subjects:** character. **Awards:** Honorary Life Membership. **Type:** recognition. **Recipient:** for major contribution via work. **Committees:** Crime Prevention. **Publications:** *Character Discipline*. Brochure. Contains information on suggested standardized terminology for character. **Circulation:** 100 ● *National Character Laboratory—Membership List*, annual. Directory. **Price:** free. **Circulation:** 100 ● *National Character Laboratory—Newsletter*, quarterly. **Price:** included in membership dues; $5.00 /year for nonmembers. **Circulation:** 200.

6537 ■ Organizational Behavior Teaching Society (OBTS)
c/o Dr. Cynthia Krom, Treas.
Mt. Saint Mary Coll.
330 Powell Ave.
Newburgh, NY 12550
E-mail: president@obts.org
URL: http://www.obts.org
Contact: Jeanie Forray, Pres.
Founded: 1973. **Members:** 400. **Membership Dues:** regular, $55 (annual) ● graduate student, $35 (annual). **Regional Groups:** 4. **Description:** Management consultants, trainers, professors, and other teaching professionals in management disciplines. Investigates the various theories and methods of teaching management in educational institutions, public administration, and publicly and privately sponsored training programs. **Awards:** David L. Bradford Distinguished Educator Award. **Frequency:** annual. **Type:** recognition. **Recipient:** to a person or a teaching team with demonstrated achievement over a lifetime ● Fritz Roethlisberger Award for the Best Paper in the Journal of Management Education. **Frequency:** annual. **Type:** monetary. **Recipient:** for a paper published in the current year ● Honor Roll. **Frequency:** annual. **Type:** recognition. **Recipient:** for individuals ● New Educator Award. **Frequency:** annual. **Type:** recognition. **Recipient:** for individuals ● Service Award. **Frequency:** annual. **Type:** recognition. **Recipient:** for voluntary contributions. **Publications:** *Journal of Management Education*, bimonthly. Contains articles that focus on teaching-learning in various settings. **Price:** included in membership dues; $77.00/copy for institutions; $21.00/copy for nonmembers; $419.00 /year for institutions. **Advertising:** accepted. Alternate Formats: online ● *Women and Men in Organizations: Teaching Strategies*. Manual ● Brochures. **Conventions/Meetings:** annual conference (exhibits).

6538 ■ Society for the Advancement of Behavior Analysis (SABA)
1219 S Park St.
Kalamazoo, MI 49001-5607
Ph: (269)492-9310
Fax: (269)492-9316
E-mail: mail@abainternational.org
URL: http://www.abainternational.org/saba
Contact: Maria E. Malott PhD, Sec.-Treas.
Founded: 1980. **Nonmembership. Multinational. Description:** Charitable foundation founded to disseminate information and support research and education in behavior analysis. Supports applications of behavior analysis in educational settings and the development and continuation of publications about behavior analysis. Conducts charitable, research, and educational programs, and sponsors competitions. **Computer Services:** database, contributors.

6539 ■ Society for Evolutionary Analysis in Law (SEAL)
c/o Janelle Steele, Admin. Asst.
Vanderbilt Univ. Law School
131 21st Ave. S
Nashville, TN 37203-1181
Ph: (615)343-2034
E-mail: seal@vanderbilt.edu
URL: http://law.vanderbilt.edu/seal
Contact: Janelle Steele, Admin. Asst.
Members: 350. **Membership Dues:** regular, $45 (annual) ● student, $22 (annual). **Multinational. Description:** Fosters interdisciplinary exploration of issues at the intersection of law, biology, and evolutionary theory. Strives to improve the models of human behavior relevant to law. Promotes the integration of life science and social science perspectives on law-relevant topics. Encourages scholarly interests in evolutionary processes and law, relevant disciplines including, among others, evolutionary and behavioral biology, cognitive science, neuroscience, complex adaptive systems, economics, evolutionary psychology, psychiatry, behavioral ecology, behavioral genetics, primatology, evolutionary anthropology, and gender relations. **Awards:** SEAL Scholarly Writing Prize. **Frequency:** annual. **Type:** recognition. **Recipient:** for exemplary scholarship on a topic related to organization's scope of interest.

6540 ■ Society for Human Performance in Extreme Environments (HPEE)
2652 Corbyton Ct.
Orlando, FL 32828
Ph: (407)381-7762
Fax: (386)226-7050
E-mail: society@hpee.org
URL: http://www.hpee.org
Contact: Jason P. Kring PhD, Pres.
Founded: 1997. **Membership Dues:** individual in U.S., $65 (annual) ● individual outside U.S., $75 (annual) ● student in U.S., $25 (annual) ● student outside U.S., $35 (annual). **Description:** Encourages and facilitates collaboration between researchers, practitioners and other professionals to improve human safety and performance in extremely risky and challenging settings. Promotes study and research in human behavior and performance with emphasis on complex human activities. Serves as a resource and means of information exchange for its members. **Publications:** *The Explorer*, quarterly. Newsletter. **Price:** included in membership dues ● *Journal of Human Performance in Extreme Environments*, semiannual. Features research and operational findings devoted to the study of human performance and behavior in high-stress environments. **Price:** included in membership dues. ISSN: 1529-5168. Also Cited As: *JHPEE*.

6541 ■ Society for Quantitative Analyses of Behavior (SQAB)
c/o Dr. Michael Lamport Commons, Co-Pres.
234 Huron Ave.
Cambridge, MA 02138-1328
Ph: (617)497-5270
Fax: (617)497-5270
E-mail: commons@tiac.net
URL: http://sqab.psychology.org
Contact: Dr. Michael Lamport Commons, Co-Pres.
Founded: 1978. **Members:** 650. **Membership Dues:** student, $35 (annual) ● regular, $65 (annual). **Budget:** $10,000. **Description:** Promotes the understanding of behavior using quantitative analyses; develops and uses mathematical formulations to characterize one or more dimensions of an obtained data set, derives predictions to be compared with data, and generates novel data analyses. **Libraries: Type:** reference. **Holdings:** 1,000; books. **Subjects:** quantitative analysis of behavior. **Computer Services:** Mailing lists. **Affiliated With:** Association for Behavior Analysis. **Publications:** *SQAB Proceedings*, annual. Informal videotapes of live ABA presentations at various levels for use in classroom or seminar setting, or for individual use. **Circulation:** 1,000 ● Videos, annual. Features informal videotapes of live ABA presentations at various levels for use in classroom or seminar setting, or for individual use. **Circulation:** 1,000 ● Papers. Contains abstracts of SQAB conference papers. ● Journal. **Conventions/Meetings:** annual Symposium on Quantitative Analyses of Behavior - meeting and symposium - May.

6542 ■ Special Interest Group on Computer and Human Interaction (SIGCHI)
1515 Broadway
New York, NY 10036
Ph: (212)626-0500
Free: (800)342-6626
Fax: (212)944-1318
E-mail: sigchi-president@acm.org
URL: http://sigchi.org
Contact: Julie Jacko, Pres.
Members: 4,700. **Membership Dues:** student, $42 (annual) ● professional, $99 (annual). **Description:** Computer professionals, systems designers, human factors scientists, and psychologists united to study the human-computer interaction process and user-centered system design. Conducts tutorials and conferences to enhance the design and evaluation of user interfaces. A special interest group of the Association for Computing Machinery. **Also Known As:** ACM SIGCHI. **Formerly:** (1982) Special Interest Group for Social and Behavioral Science Computing. **Publications:** *Interactions*, bimonthly. Magazine. Contains information for designers of interactive products. ● *SIGCHI Bulletin*, quarterly. Newsletter. Includes book reviews and conference, workshop, and research reports. **Price:** included in membership dues. **Circulation:** 5,000 ● *TOCHI*. Journal. Includes original research that spans the field of human-computer interaction. ● Proceedings, annual ● Membership Directory, periodic. **Conventions/Meetings:** annual conference (exhibits).

Beverages

6543 ■ International Society of Beverage Technologists (ISBT)
3340 Pilot Knob Rd.
St. Paul, MN 55121
Ph: (651)454-7250 (239)768-3480
Fax: (651)454-0766
E-mail: isbt@bevtech.org
URL: http://www.bevtech.org
Contact: Larry Hobbs, Exec. Dir.
Founded: 1953. **Members:** 1,000. **Membership Dues:** individual, $150 (annual) ● emeritus, $50 (annual). **Staff:** 2. **Budget:** $250,000. **Description:** Professional society of persons engaged in the scientific or technical phases of production, research, or quality control in the beverage industry. **Awards:** Best Paper-Best Committee. **Frequency:** annual. **Type:** recognition. **Recipient:** for best paper and committee ● Circle of Honor. **Type:** recognition. **Telecommunication Services:** electronic mail, larry_hobbs@comcast.net. **Committees:** Bottle and Closure; Can and End; Environmental Affairs; Global Issues and Technology; Manufacturing and Distribution Technology; Non-Traditional Beverages; Packaging Technology; Product and Ingredient Technology; Quality Control; Sanitation and Container Cleaning; Sweetener; Water Quality and Treatment. **Formerly:** (1995) Society of Soft Drink Technologists. **Publications:** *ISBT Update*, quarterly. Newsletter. Alternate Formats: online ● *Sanitation*. Manual. **Price:** $50.00 ● *Who's Who in Beverage Technology*, annual. Directory ● Manual. Alternate Formats: online ● Proceedings, annual. **Price:** $100.00. **Circulation:** 1,000. Alternate Formats: CD-ROM. **Conventions/Meetings:** annual Basic Course Beverage Production - seminar ● annual BevTech - meeting - always April or early May.

6544 ■ Master Brewers Association of the Americas (MBAA)
3340 Pilot Knob Rd.
St. Paul, MN 55121-2097
Ph: (651)454-7250
Fax: (651)454-0766
E-mail: mbaa@mbaa.com
URL: http://www.mbaa.com
Contact: Steve Nelson, Exec. VP
Founded: 1887. **Members:** 2,600. **Membership Dues:** professional, $123 (annual) ● student, $40 (annual). **Staff:** 3. **Description:** Provides opportunity for brewing professionals to interact with other

fermentation industry professionals and to learn practical solutions, resourceful safeguards, and innovative technologies. **Awards: Type:** recognition ● **Type:** scholarship. **Committees:** International Liaison; Technical. **Formerly:** (1976) Master Brewers Association of America. **Publications:** *MBAA Technical Quarterly*. Journal. Includes technical papers and association news. **Price:** included in membership dues; $60.00 for nonmembers in the brewing industry. **Advertising:** accepted ● Books. Contains information on brewer and beer packaging. **Conventions/Meetings:** annual convention (exhibits).

6545 ■ World Cocoa Foundation (WCF)

8320 Old Courthouse Rd., Ste.300
Vienna, VA 22182
Ph: (703)790-5012
Fax: (703)790-0168
E-mail: bill.guyton@worldcocoa.org
URL: http://www.worldcocoafoundation.org
Contact: William Guyton, Pres.

Founded: 1945. **Staff:** 7. **Description:** Supported by manufacturers of cocoa and chocolate products. Encourages educational and research projects in the cultivation of more cacao of better quality; strives to improve economic conditions of cacao farmers by increasing yields on farms and reducing the per unit production cost. Projects include: research on life history and control of insects attacking cacao; studies on principal cacao diseases; germ plasma assembly and testing; breeding for yield and disease resistance; and physiology. Sponsors exchanges of personnel and training fellowships. Disseminates information. **Libraries: Type:** reference. **Holdings:** articles, reports. **Subjects:** cocoa research. **Programs:** Cooperative Cocoa Research; Latin American Regional Farmer Support; Southeast Asia Regional Farmer Support; Sustainable Cocoa; West African Regional Farmer Support. **Formerly:** (1948) American Cocoa Research Committee; (2004) American Cocoa Research Institute. **Publications:** *WCF Newsletter*, bimonthly. Includes information about new members, events and updates. **Conventions/Meetings:** annual meeting.

Biochemistry

6546 ■ American Society for Biochemistry and Molecular Biology (ASBMB)

9650 Rockville Pike
Bethesda, MD 20814-3996
Ph: (301)634-7145
Fax: (301)634-7126
E-mail: asmb@asbmb.org
URL: http://www.asbmb.org
Contact: Barbara A. Gordon, Exec. Off.

Founded: 1906. **Members:** 11,900. **Membership Dues:** regular, $140 (annual) ● associate, $70 (annual) ● undergraduate, $20 (annual). **Staff:** 20. **Budget:** $16,000,000. **Description:** Biochemists and molecular biologists who have conducted and published original investigations in biological chemistry and/or molecular biology. Operates placement service. **Awards:** ASBMB-Amgen Scientific Achievement Award. **Frequency:** annual. **Type:** recognition. **Recipient:** to a new investigator for significant achievements ● ASBMB-Merck Award. **Frequency:** annual. **Type:** recognition. **Recipient:** for outstanding contributions to research ● ASBMB/Schering-Plough Institute Award. **Frequency:** annual. **Type:** recognition. **Recipient:** for outstanding contributions to biochemistry and molecular biology ● Avanti Award in Lipids. **Frequency:** annual. **Type:** recognition. **Recipient:** for outstanding research contributions in the area of lipids ● Herbert A. Sober Award. **Frequency:** semiannual. **Type:** recognition. **Recipient:** for outstanding biochemical and molecular biological research ● William C. Rose Award. **Frequency:** annual. **Type:** recognition. **Recipient:** for outstanding contributions to biochemical and molecular biology. **Formerly:** (1987) American Society of Biological Chemists. **Publications:** *ASBMB Today*, monthly. Magazine. **Advertising:** accepted. Alternate Formats: online ● *Biochemistry and Molecular Biology Education*, bimonthly. Journal. Features articles in related fields such as microbiology and cell biology. **Price:** $125.00 for members; $155.00 for nonmembers; $395.00 institutional ● *Journal of Biological Chemistry*, weekly. Covers research in the field. **Price:** $530.00 /year for members; $2,525.00 /year for nonmembers; $1,218.00 /year for members in Canada; $3,324.00 /year for nonmembers in Canada. ISSN: 0021-9258. **Circulation:** 7,000. **Advertising:** accepted. Alternate Formats: online ● *Journal of Lipid Research*, monthly. **Price:** $180.00 /year for nonmembers; $155.00 /year for members; $221.00 /year for members in Canada; $727.00 /year for nonmembers in Canada. Alternate Formats: online ● *Molecular and Cellular Proteomics*, monthly. Journal. Consists of original articles and short reviews that deal with the structural and functional properties of proteins and their expression. **Price:** $90.00 /year for members; $137.00 /year for members in Canada; $375.00 /year for nonmembers; $442.00 /year for nonmembers in Canada. Alternate Formats: online. **Conventions/Meetings:** annual meeting, in conjunction with Experimental Biology (exhibits).

6547 ■ American Society for Virology (ASV)

c/o Dorothea L. Sawicki, PhD, Sec.-Treas.
Dept. of Medical Microbiology and Immunology
Univ. of Toledo Coll. of Medicine
3000 Arlington Ave., Mail Stop 1021
Toledo, OH 43614
Ph: (419)383-5173
Fax: (419)383-2881
E-mail: asv@asv.org
URL: http://www.asv.org
Contact: Dorothea L. Sawicki PhD, Sec.-Treas.

Founded: 1981. **Membership Dues:** full, $100 (annual) ● associate, $30 (annual) ● associate (student), $15 (annual) ● life (full), $1,000. **Description:** Individuals possessing professional degrees who have published original investigations in virology, and are actively engaged in virological research. Serves as a forum for discussion and exchange of information among members. Makes available to members discount subscriptions to scholarly journals; represents members on national and international scientific councils. **Awards:** Travel Grant. **Frequency:** periodic. **Type:** grant. **Recipient:** for members wishing to attend national and international virology councils. **Committees:** Advisory; Education and Career Development; Graduate Student/Postdoctoral Fellow Travel Award; Nominating; Program Planning; Public Affairs. **Publications:** *President's Newsletter*, periodic ● *Secretary-Treasurer's Newsletter*, periodic. **Conventions/Meetings:** annual meeting - 2008 July 12-16, Ithaca, NY; 2009 July 11-15, Vancouver, BC, Canada; 2010 July 17-21, Bozeman, MT.

6548 ■ International Isotope Society (IIS)

c/o Dr. Brad D. Maxwell, Pres.
PO Box 4000
Princeton, NJ 08543
Ph: (609)252-5015
E-mail: brad.maxwell@bms.com
URL: http://www.intl-isotope-soc.org
Contact: Dr. Brad D. Maxwell, Pres.

Founded: 1986. **Members:** 500. **Membership Dues:** individual, $50 (annual) ● corporate, $350 (annual) ● individual, $100 (triennial). **Staff:** 1. **Regional Groups:** 9. **Local Groups:** 3. **National Groups:** 3. **Multinational. Description:** Represents individuals who conduct or have conducted research in the field of isotope synthesis or the applications of isotopes and isotopically-labelled compounds and corporations. Seeks to advance knowledge of the synthesis, measurement, and applications of isotopically labelled compounds. Serves as a forum for discussion among scientists working with isotopes; acts as liaison between members, other scientific organizations, and governments worldwide. Assists in maintaining links between academic and industrial organizations that use isotopes. Disseminates information to the public to promote awareness of the practical applications of isotopes. Plans to conduct educational programs. **Awards:** IIS Award. **Frequency:** triennial. **Type:** recognition. **Recipient:** for distinguished service ● Melvin Calvin Award. **Frequency:** triennial. **Type:** recognition. **Recipient:** for scientific achievement. **Computer Services:** Mailing lists, of members. **Committees:** Low Level Radioactive Waste; Nominations and Elections. **Publications:** *International Isotope Society Newsletter*, semiannual. Covers society activities. **Price:** included in membership dues. **Advertising:** accepted ● *Journal of Labelled Compounds and Radiopharmaceuticals*, monthly. **Price:** $3,160.00 plus shipping and handling. **Advertising:** accepted. Alternate Formats: online ● *Proceedings of the International Symposium*, triennial. **Conventions/Meetings:** triennial International Symposium on Synthesis and Applications of Isotopically Labelled Compounds and Isotopes - conference (exhibits).

6549 ■ International Proteolysis Society (IPS)

Wayne State Univ. School of Medicine
Scott Hall, Rm. 6304
540 E Canfield
Detroit, MI 48201
Ph: (313)577-0514
Fax: (313)577-6739
E-mail: ipssecretary@gmail.org
URL: http://www.protease.org
Contact: Rob Pike, Chm.

Founded: 1999. **Members:** 300. **Membership Dues:** active (full), $100 (biennial) ● in training, $40 (biennial). **Multinational. Description:** Aims to advance research studies on proteolysis. Encourages exchange of ideas and resources by supporting a member-driven society. Fosters links between academic and industrial organizations with common interests in proteolysis. **Telecommunication Services:** electronic mail, rob.pike@med.monash.edu.au.

6550 ■ International Society of Chemical Ecology (ISCE)

c/o Dr. Stephen Foster, Sec.
Dept. of Entomology
North Dakota State Univ.
Fargo, ND 58105
Ph: (701)231-6444
Fax: (701)231-8557
E-mail: stephen.foster@ndsu.edu
URL: http://www.chemecol.org
Contact: Dr. Stephen Foster, Sec.

Founded: 1983. **Members:** 750. **Membership Dues:** regular, $35 (annual) ● student, $15 (annual) ● life, $800 ● corporate associate, $1,000 (annual). **Staff:** 22. **Budget:** $75,000. **Description:** Chemists, ecologists, biologists, and others with an interest in chemical ecology. Promotes understanding of the origin, function, and importance of natural chemicals that mediate communication and interactions within and among organisms. Seeks to broaden the scope of chemical ecology and to stimulate cooperation and exchange of information among members of diverse scientific fields. Conducts educational programs designed to foster knowledge in the area of chemical ecology. **Awards:** ISCE Silver Medal. **Frequency:** annual. **Type:** recognition. **Recipient:** for merit ● Silverstein-Simeone Award Lecture. **Frequency:** annual. **Type:** recognition. **Recipient:** for merit ● Student Travel Awards. **Frequency:** annual. **Type:** recognition. **Recipient:** for merit and need. **Committees:** Executive. **Publications:** *ISCE Newsletter*, 3/year. Contains society news for members; annual meeting information. **Price:** free for members. **Circulation:** 600. **Advertising:** accepted ● *Journal of Chemical Ecology*, monthly ● *Proceedings of the Annual Meeting*. **Conventions/Meetings:** annual conference and meeting (exhibits) - usually summer ● annual convention (exhibits).

6551 ■ Pan-American Association for Biochemistry and Molecular Biology (PABMB)

c/o Dr. Jack Preiss
Michigan State Univ.
Dept. of Biochemistry and Molecular
East Lansing, MI 48824-1319
Ph: (517)353-3137
Fax: (517)353-9334

E-mail: preiss@pilot.msu.edu
URL: http://pabmb.fcien.edu.uy
Contact: Dr. Sergio T. Ferreira, Chm.
Founded: 1969. **Members:** 12. **National Groups:** 12. **Languages:** English, Portuguese, Spanish. **Description:** Societies of professional biochemists in the Americas and culturally related European countries. Promotes the science of biochemistry by disseminating information and encouraging contacts between its members. Cooperates with other organizations having similar objectives. Conducts workshops and symposia. **Committees:** Education; Scientific Exchanges. **Formerly:** Pan American Association of Biochemical Societies. **Publications:** *Symposium Proceedings*, periodic. **Advertising:** accepted. **Conventions/Meetings:** triennial conference and symposium, with scientific presentations (exhibits).

6552 ■ Protein Society
9650 Rockville Pike
Bethesda, MD 20814-3999
Ph: (301)634-7277
Free: (800)99A-MINO
Fax: (301)634-7271
E-mail: cyablonski@proteinsociety.org
URL: http://www.proteinsociety.org
Contact: Cindy A. Yablonski PhD, Exec. Off.
Founded: 1986. **Members:** 3,200. **Membership Dues:** full, $220 (annual) ● graduate student (online only), $60 (annual) ● post doctoral, $120 (annual) ● emeritus and undergraduate student (online only), undergraduate student, $25 (annual). **Staff:** 2. **Multinational. Description:** Furthers research and development in protein science; provides national and international forums to facilitate communication, cooperation and collaboration with respect to all aspects of the study of proteins. Publishes Protein Science journal; members have an opportunity to actively participate in the emerging fields of protein science including proteomics, bioinformatics, structural biology, and computational biology as they pertain to proteins at the molecular and cellular level. **Awards:** The Carl Branden Award. **Frequency:** annual. **Type:** recognition. **Recipient:** to an outstanding protein scientist who has made exceptional contributions in the areas of education and/or service to the science ● Christian B. Anfinsen Award. **Frequency:** annual. **Type:** recognition. **Recipient:** for significant technical achievements in the field of protein science ● The Dorothy Crowfoot Hodgkin Award. **Frequency:** annual. **Type:** recognition. **Recipient:** for exceptional contributions in protein science, which profoundly influence the understanding of biology ● Emil Thomas Kaiser Award. **Frequency:** annual. **Type:** recognition. **Recipient:** for a recent, highly significant contribution in applying chemistry to the study of proteins ● Hans Neurath Award. **Frequency:** annual. **Type:** recognition. **Recipient:** for a recent contribution of unusual merit to basic research in the field of protein science, including but not restricted to the chemistry, design, folding, structure, or biological function of proteins ● Irving Sigal Young Investigator Award. **Frequency:** annual. **Type:** recognition. **Recipient:** for an important contribution to the study of proteins by a scientist who is in the early stages of an independent career ● Stein and Moore Award. **Frequency:** annual. **Type:** recognition. **Recipient:** for the highest level of contribution to the study of proteins. **Computer Services:** database ● electronic publishing, journal access ● mailing lists. **Publications:** *Protein Science*, monthly. Journal. **Price:** included in membership dues. **Advertising:** accepted. Alternate Formats: online ● *The Protein Society News*, semiannual. Newsletters. Updates members on key activities. **Circulation:** 3,500 ● Membership Directory. **Conventions/Meetings:** biennial European Symposium (exhibits) ● annual US Symposium (exhibits) - 2008 July 19-23, San Diego, CA; 2009 July 25-29, Boston, MA; 2010 Aug. 1-5, San Diego, CA.

6553 ■ RNA Society (RNA)
9650 Rockville Pike
Bethesda, MD 20814-3998
Ph: (301)634-7120
Fax: (301)634-7420
E-mail: rna@faseb.org
URL: http://www.rnasociety.org
Contact: Evelyn Jabri, CEO
Founded: 1993. **Members:** 1,059. **Membership Dues:** full (print and electronic access), $155 (annual) ● full (electronic access only), $138 (annual) ● student (print and electronic access), $70 (annual) ● student (electronic access only), $30 (annual). **Staff:** 3. **Description:** Professionals working in molecular, evolutionary, and structural biology, biochemistry, biomedical sciences, chemistry, genetics, virology, and related disciplines with an interest in the structure and functions of Ribonucleic Acid (RNA). Serves as a multidisciplinary forum for exchange of information and research results among members. Promotes and supports RNA research; gathers and disseminates information. **Computer Services:** Mailing lists, of members. **Publications:** *RNA Journal*, monthly. **Price:** included in membership dues. **Circulation:** 40,000. **Advertising:** accepted. Alternate Formats: online ● Newsletter, semiannual. **Conventions/Meetings:** biennial meeting and symposium (exhibits) ● annual meeting - 2008 July, Berlin, Germany; 2009 May 26-31, Madison, WI.

Bioelectrics

6554 ■ Society for Physical Regulation in Biology and Medicine (SPRBM)
c/o Gloria L. Parsley, Exec. Dir.
2412 Cobblestone Way
Frederick, MD 21702-2626
Ph: (301)663-4556
Fax: (301)694-4948
E-mail: sprbmoffice@aol.com
URL: http://www.sprbm.org
Contact: Gloria L. Parsley, Exec. Dir.
Founded: 1980. **Members:** 100. **Membership Dues:** full, $75 (annual) ● associate, $20 (annual) ● sustaining, $1,000 (annual) ● retired, $30 (annual). **Staff:** 1. **Budget:** $40,000. **Multinational. Description:** Medical professionals, engineers, biological and physical scientists, and representatives of industry. Seeks to further international and interdisciplinary research, communication, cooperation, and education in the study and clinical applications of the effects of electricity and magnetism in growth, repair, and regeneration of human cells and tissues. **Libraries: Type:** reference. **Holdings:** archival material, periodicals. **Awards:** Kappa Delta. **Frequency:** annual. **Type:** recognition ● Yasuda Award. **Frequency:** annual. **Type:** recognition. **Formerly:** (1993) Bioelectrical Repair and Growth Society. **Publications:** *Transactions*, annual. Contains abstracts of works presented at the annual meeting. **Price:** $55.00/year. **Conventions/Meetings:** annual conference (exhibits).

Bioelectromagnetics

6555 ■ Bioelectromagnetics Society (BEMS)
2412 Cobblestone Way
Frederick, MD 21702-2626
Ph: (301)663-4252
Fax: (301)694-4948
E-mail: bemsoffice@aol.com
URL: http://www.bioelectromagnetics.org
Contact: Gloria L. Parsley, Exec. Dir.
Founded: 1978. **Members:** 800. **Membership Dues:** sustaining, $1,000 (annual) ● full, $85 (annual) ● associate, $70 (annual) ● student/emeritus, $30 (annual). **Staff:** 6. **Budget:** $300,000. **Multinational. Description:** Scientists, engineers, and others who conduct research in or are interested in the interaction of electromagnetic energy (at frequencies ranging from zero hertz through those of visible light) and acoustic energy with biological systems. Encourages clinical study in the field of bioelectromagnetics and disseminates information. Cooperates with other associations in sponsoring workshops and seminars. **Awards:** D'Arsonval Award. **Frequency:** biennial. **Type:** recognition. **Telecommunication Services:** electronic mail, ewa.czerska@fda.hhs.gov. **Publications:** *Bioelectromagnetics*, bimonthly. Journal. **Price:** $640.00 for nonmembers; $80.00 for members in U.S.; $100.00 for members outside U.S. Alternate Formats: online. **Conventions/Meetings:** annual conference and meeting, poster session (exhibits) ● quadrennial congress.

6556 ■ Bioelectromagnetics Special Interest Group (BEM SIG)
c/o American Mensa
1229 Corporate Dr. W
Arlington, TX 76006-6103
Ph: (817)607-0060
Free: (800)66-MENSA
Fax: (817)649-5232
E-mail: nationaloffice@americanmensa.org
URL: http://www.us.mensa.org
Contact: Heather Spillers, Natl. Groups Coor.
Founded: 1985. **Members:** 100. **Membership Dues:** individual, $20 (annual). **Staff:** 2. **Description:** A special interest group of Mensa. Reports on scientific literature concerning the interaction between electric and/or magnetic fields and living organisms. **Convention/Meeting:** none. **Libraries: Type:** reference. **Holdings:** audiovisuals, books, clippings, periodicals. **Subjects:** bioelectromagnetics. **Affiliated With:** American Mensa. **Publications:** *Resonance—Bioelectromagnetics Special Interest Group*, semiannual. Newsletter. **Price:** $10.00/year in U.S. (small size copy); $15.00/year outside U.S. (small size copy); $20.00/year in U.S. (large size copy); $25.00/year outside U.S. (large size copy). **Circulation:** 150. **Advertising:** accepted. Also Cited As: *BEM SIG Resonance*.

Bioethics

6557 ■ Center for Bioethics
Univ. of Minnesota
N504 Boynton Hea. Center
410 Church St. SE
Minneapolis, MN 55455-0346
Ph: (612)624-9440
Fax: (612)624-9108
E-mail: bioethx@umn.edu
URL: http://www.bioethics.umn.edu
Contact: Jeffrey P. Kahn PhD, Dir.
Founded: 1985. **Staff:** 25. **Budget:** $1,500,000. **Description:** Promotes ethical issues in health care and the life sciences; conducts original interdisciplinary research, public discussion and debate, and formulation of public policy. Offers educational programs and courses, and community outreach programs. **Boards:** Advisory. **Councils:** Dean's Policy. **Publications:** *Bioethics Examiner*, 3/year. Newsletter. **Circulation:** 8,500. Alternate Formats: online ● Annual Reports, annual. Overviews bioethics. **Conventions/Meetings:** conference and lecture.

6558 ■ Center for Bioethics
Univ. of Pennsylvania
3401 Market St., Ste.320
Philadelphia, PA 19104-3308
Ph: (215)898-7136
Fax: (215)573-3036
E-mail: caplan@mail.med.upenn.edu
URL: http://www.bioethics.upenn.edu
Contact: Arthur Caplan PhD, Dir.
Founded: 1994. **Staff:** 20. **Description:** Works as an interdisciplinary unit of the University of Pennsylvania Health System; seeks to advance scholarly and public understanding of ethical, legal, social and public policy issues in healthcare. Conducts research aimed at improving the practice and delivery of medical care. Offers degree programs. Maintains speakers' bureau. **Departments:** Faculty; Medical Ethics. **Projects:** Bioethics Internet. **Subgroups:** Penn Bioethics Society. **Publications:** *Penn Bioethics*. Journal. Contains articles from Penn and other schools. Alternate Formats: online ● *PennBioethics*, biennial. Newsletter. Contains short informative articles, opinion pieces, upcoming events, and activity updates. **Price:** free. **Conventions/Meetings:** annual

conference and seminar, for health care professionals and researchers in the University of Pennsylvania Health System ● lecture and symposium, on current ethical issues in health care.

Biology

6559 ■ American Academy of Microbiology (AAM)

1752 N St. NW
Washington, DC 20036
Ph: (202)737-3600
Fax: (202)942-9346
E-mail: academy@asmusa.org
URL: http://www.asm.org
Contact: R. John Collier, Chm.

Founded: 1955. **Members:** 2,000. **Membership Dues:** elected, $50 (annual). **Staff:** 6. **Multinational.** **Description:** Fosters and recognizes excellence in the microbiological sciences. Convenes critical issues colloquia and develops consensus-building position papers and expert scientific opinion and advice on current and emerging issues in microbiology. Encourages exchange of information among members. Sponsors American Board of Medical Laboratory Immunology, American Board of Medical Microbiology, National Registry of Microbiologists and Committee on Postgraduate Educational Programs. **Awards:** ASM Awards. **Frequency:** semiannual. **Type:** recognition. **Recipient:** for excellence in science. **Affiliated With:** American Society for Microbiology. **Publications:** *Academy News and Views*, quarterly. Newsletter. **Price:** free ● *Colloquia Reports*.

6560 ■ American Institute of Biological Sciences (AIBS)

1444 I St. NW, Ste.200
Washington, DC 20005
Ph: (202)628-1500
Free: (800)992-2427
Fax: (202)628-1509
E-mail: rogrady@aibs.org
URL: http://www.aibs.org
Contact: Dr. Richard T. O'Grady, Exec. Dir.

Founded: 1947. **Members:** 6,000. **Membership Dues:** regular, $125 (annual). **Staff:** 30. **Budget:** $4,250,000. **Description:** Professional member organization and federation of biological associations, laboratories, and museums whose members have an interest in the life sciences. Promotes unity and effectiveness of effort among persons engaged in biological research, education, and application of biological sciences, including agriculture, environment, and medicine. Seeks to further the relationships of biological sciences to other sciences and industries. Conducts roundtable series; provides names of prominent biologists who are willing to serve as speakers and curriculum consultants; provides advisory committees and other services to the Department of Energy, Environmental Protection Agency, National Science Foundation, Department of Defense, and National Aeronautics and Space Administration. Maintains educational consultant panel. **Awards:** Congressional Science Fellowship. **Frequency:** periodic. **Type:** fellowship ● Distinguished Service Award. **Frequency:** annual. **Type:** recognition ● Media Award. **Frequency:** annual. **Type:** recognition. **Computer Services:** Mailing lists, biologists, biology departments, biology laboratories. **Committees:** Awards; Education; Human Resources; Nominating; Public Policy Review; Publications. **Departments:** Communications Office; Conference and Meeting Services; Government Relations; Scientific Peer Advisory and Review Services. **Formerly:** (1969) American Society of Professional Biologists. **Publications:** *BioScience*, monthly. Journal. Covers institute news, peer reviewed scientific articles, feature articles, book reviews, calendar of events, and employment listings. **Price:** $90.00 family; $70.00 regular; $40.00 graduate student; $20.00 student (for K-12 or undergraduate). ISSN: 0006-3568. **Circulation:** 12,000. **Advertising:** accepted. Alternate Formats: microform; CD-ROM ● *What Will You Be Doing in 2020?*. Brochure ● Membership Directory, biennial. **Conventions/Meetings:** annual meeting (exhibits).

6561 ■ American Society of Biomechanics (ASB)

c/o Max Kurz , PhD, Membership Chm.
Univ. of Houston
Dept. of Hea. and Human Performance
104S Garrison
3855 Holman St.
Houston, TX 77004
Ph: (713)743-2274
E-mail: mkurz@mail.coe.uh.edu
URL: http://asbweb.org
Contact: Max Kurz PhD, Membership Chm.

Founded: 1977. **Members:** 640. **Membership Dues:** regular, $50 (annual) ● student, $15 (annual). **Description:** Consists of biomechanical researchers, students, and other individuals with an interest in biomechanics. Biomechanics refers to the study of the structure and function of biological systems using the methods of mechanics. Seeks to advance the study, teaching, and practice of biomechanics. Facilitates exchange of information between mechanical engineers, orthopedic surgeons, sports medical professionals, and others making use of biomechanical research. Sponsors research and educational programs. **Publications:** *American Society Biomechanics Newsletter*, semiannual. **Price:** included in membership dues. **Advertising:** accepted. Alternate Formats: online ● *Journal of Biomechanics*, periodic. **Conventions/Meetings:** annual meeting, in conjunction with the Canadian Society for Biomechanics - 2008 Aug. 5-9, Ann Arbor, MI.

6562 ■ American Society for Cell Biology (ASCB)

8120 Woodmont Ave., Ste.750
Bethesda, MD 20814-2762
Ph: (301)347-9300
Fax: (301)347-9310
E-mail: ascbinfo@ascb.org
URL: http://www.ascb.org
Contact: Ms. Cheryl Lehr, Exec. Asst./Office Mgr.

Founded: 1960. **Members:** 11,000. **Membership Dues:** individual, $125 (annual) ● student, $38 (annual) ● postdoc, $60 (annual) ● undergraduate, $20 (annual). **Staff:** 20. **Budget:** $4,500,000. **Description:** Represents scientists with educational or research experience in cell biology or an allied field. Offers placement service. **Awards:** Bruce Alberts Award for Excellence in Science Education. **Frequency:** annual. **Type:** recognition. **Recipient:** for innovative and sustained activities in science education with particular emphasis on the local, regional, and/or national impact of the nominee's activities ● E.B. Wilson Medal. **Frequency:** annual. **Type:** medal. **Recipient:** for an outstanding scientist in cell biology ● E.E. Just Lecture. **Frequency:** annual. **Type:** recognition. **Recipient:** for outstanding scientific achievement by a minority scientist ● Early Career Life Scientist Award. **Frequency:** annual. **Type:** monetary. **Recipient:** for outstanding scientist who earned his or her doctorate no more than 12 years earlier and who has served as an independent investigator for no more than seven years ● Keith Porter Lecture. **Frequency:** annual. **Type:** recognition. **Recipient:** to an eminent cell biologist ● MAC Poster Awards. **Frequency:** annual. **Type:** monetary. **Recipient:** for the best minorities' posters presented at the ASCB annual meeting ● MBC Paper of the Year. **Frequency:** annual. **Type:** recognition. **Recipient:** for the author of the paper judged to be the best for that year (from June to May) ● Merton Bernfield Memorial Award. **Frequency:** annual. **Type:** monetary ● Minorities Affairs Committee Travel Award. **Frequency:** annual. **Type:** monetary ● Predoctoral Student Travel Award. **Frequency:** annual. **Type:** monetary. **Recipient:** for minorities and students to attend the annual meeting ● Public Service Award. **Frequency:** annual. **Type:** medal. **Recipient:** for outstanding national leadership in support of biomedical research ● Women in Cell Biology Awards. **Frequency:** annual. **Type:** monetary. **Recipient:** for junior and senior women in cell biology. **Computer Services:** database ● online services, job board. **Boards:** Cell Biology Education Editorial; Molecular Biology of the Cell Editorial. **Committees:** Education; International Affairs; Minorities Affairs; Program (Scientific Meetings); Public Information; Public Policy; Women in Cell Biology. **Publications:** *ASCB Annual Meeting Abstracts*, annual. Proceedings ● *The ASCB Newsletter*, monthly ● *Cell Biology Education*, quarterly. Journal. **Price:** free. ISSN: 1536-7509. Alternate Formats: online ● *Molecular Biology of the Cell*, monthly. Journal. Contains peer-reviewed research articles. **Price:** free for members; $175.00 for nonmembers in U.S.; $225.00 for nonmembers outside U.S.; $375.00 for institutions in U.S. ISSN: 1059-1524. **Circulation:** 10,000. **Advertising:** accepted. **Conventions/Meetings:** international conference and symposium (exhibits).

6563 ■ American Society for Gravitational and Space Biology Student Association (ASGSB-SA)

Bone/Signal Lab.
NASA Ames Res. Center
Mail Stop 236-7
Moffett Field, CA 94035
Ph: (650)604-6014
Fax: (650)604-3159
E-mail: rocampo2359@hotmail.com
URL: http://www.asgsb-sa.org
Contact: Robbie Ocampo, Pres.

Founded: 1999. **Members:** 60. **Membership Dues:** student, $35 (annual). **Staff:** 5. **Budget:** $500. **Description:** Student affiliate of the national organization, American Society of Gravitational and Space Biology (ASGSB); fosters research, education, training, development in gravitational and space biology. **Conventions/Meetings:** annual conference.

6564 ■ American Society for Matrix Biology (ASMB)

c/o Delores M. Francis, Admin.
9650 Rockville Pike
Bethesda, MD 20814
Ph: (301)634-7120
Fax: (301)634-7420
E-mail: asmb@faseb.org
URL: http://www.asmb.net
Contact: Delores M. Francis, Admin.

Membership Dues: full, $90 (annual) ● postdoctoral fellow, $50 (annual) ● student, $15 (annual) ● corporate, $500 (annual) ● corporate sponsor, $1,000 (annual) ● corporate patron, $2,000 (annual). **Description:** Promotes matrix biology, focusing on the structure and function of components of the extracellular matrix, the interactions of these components with cells, the consequences of these interactions for intracellular signaling and gene expression, the orderly progression of processes utilizing these interactions during development, and the disruption of these processes in hereditary and acquired diseases of animals and humans. Matrix biology is also relevant to allied disciplines such as tumor biology, orthopedics, rheumatology, dermatology, and bioengineering. **Publications:** Newsletter. Alternate Formats: online. **Conventions/Meetings:** biennial meeting - 2008 Dec. 7-10, San Diego, CA.

6565 ■ American Society for Microbiology (ASM)

1752 N St. NW
Washington, DC 20036
Ph: (202)737-3600 (202)942-9207
Fax: (202)942-9333
E-mail: oed@asmusa.org
URL: http://www.asm.org
Contact: Michael I. Goldberg PhD, Exec. Dir.

Founded: 1899. **Members:** 42,000. **Membership Dues:** full, $53 (annual) ● transitional, postdoctoral, $33 (annual) ● student, $17 (annual). **Staff:** 115. **Local Groups:** 36. **Description:** Scientific society of microbiologists. Promotes the advancement of scientific knowledge in order to improve education in microbiology. Encourages the highest professional and ethical standards, and the adoption of sound legislative and regulatory policies affecting the discipline of microbiology at all levels. Communicates microbiological scientific achievements to the public.

Maintains numerous committees and 23 divisions, and placement services; compiles statistics. **Libraries: Type:** reference. **Holdings:** archival material. **Computer Services:** database, mailing information. **Programs:** International Professorship. **Affiliated With:** International Union of Microbiological Societies. **Formerly:** Society of American Bacteriologists. **Publications:** *Abstracts of Annual Meeting* ● *Antimicrobial Agents and Chemotherapy*, monthly. Journal. Covers all aspects of antimicrobial, antiparasitic, antiviral, and anticancer agents and chemotherapy. **Price:** $49.00 /year for members; $263.00 /year for nonmembers. ISSN: 0066-4804. **Circulation:** 7,823. **Advertising:** accepted. Alternate Formats: microform; CD-ROM ● *Applied and Environmental Microbiology*, monthly. Journal. Publishes research in the areas of industrial microbiology, biotechnology, food microbiology, and microbial ecology. **Price:** $50.00 /year for members; $265.00 /year for nonmembers. ISSN: 0099-2240. **Circulation:** 8,898. **Advertising:** accepted. Alternate Formats: microform; CD-ROM ● *ASM Directory of Members*, every 2-3 years. Membership Directory. **Price:** available to members only ● *ASM News*, monthly. Magazine. Provides information on a range of scientific and policy issues to the worldwide community of microbiologists. **Price:** included in membership dues; $25.00 /year for nonmembers. ISSN: 0044-7897. **Circulation:** 40,000. **Advertising:** accepted ● *Clinical Microbiology Reviews*, quarterly. Presents reviews of developments in clinical microbiology and immunology. Covers bacteriology, virology, mycology, and parasitology. **Price:** $20.00 /year for members; $121.00 /year for nonmembers. ISSN: 0893-8512. **Circulation:** 9,289. **Advertising:** accepted. Alternate Formats: microform; CD-ROM ● *Infection and Immunity*, monthly. Journal. Directed toward microbiologists, immunologists, epidemiologists, pathologists, and clinicians. Topics covered include ecology and epidemiology. **Price:** $51.00 /year for members; $368.00 /year for nonmembers. ISSN: 0019-9567. **Circulation:** 6,657. **Advertising:** accepted. Alternate Formats: microform; CD-ROM ● *International Journal of Systematic Bacteriology*, quarterly. Presents papers concerned with the systematics of bacteria, yeasts, and yeast-like organisms, including taxonomy, nomenclature and identification. **Price:** $35.00 /year for members; $158.00 /year for nonmembers. ISSN: 0020-7713. **Circulation:** 1,932. **Advertising:** accepted. Alternate Formats: microform; CD-ROM ● *Journal of Bacteriology*, semimonthly. Contains research articles on structure and function, cell surfaces, eucaryotic cells, genetics and molecular biology, and bacteriophages. **Price:** $79.00 /year for members; $378.00 /year for nonmembers. ISSN: 0021-9193. **Circulation:** 7,323. **Advertising:** accepted. Alternate Formats: microform; CD-ROM ● *Journal of Clinical Microbiology*, monthly. Covers current research on the microbiological aspects of human and animal infections and infestations. **Price:** $49.00 /year for members; $264.00 /year for nonmembers. ISSN: 0095-1137. **Circulation:** 13,644. **Advertising:** accepted. Alternate Formats: microform; CD-ROM ● *Journal of Virology*, monthly. Contains research reports on viruses, including the areas of biochemistry, biophysics, genetics, immunology, morphology, and physiology. **Price:** $81.00 /year for members; $380.00 /year for nonmembers. ISSN: 0022-538X. **Circulation:** 5,329. **Advertising:** accepted. Alternate Formats: microform; CD-ROM ● *Microbiological Reviews*, quarterly. Journal. Covers aspects of microbiology including bacteriology, virology, mycology, and parasitology. **Price:** $25.00 /year for members; $120.00 /year for nonmembers. ISSN: 0146-0749. **Circulation:** 11,944. Alternate Formats: microform; CD-ROM ● *Molecular and Cellular Biology*, monthly. Journal. Contains articles concerning all aspects of the molecular biology of eucaryotic cells, including regulation of gene expression, and transcription. **Price:** $80.00 /year for members; $379.00 /year for nonmembers. ISSN: 0270-7306. **Circulation:** 6,074. **Advertising:** accepted. Alternate Formats: microform; CD-ROM ● Books ● Manuals ● Reprints. **Conventions/Meetings:** competition ● annual Interscience Conference on Antimicrobial Agents and Chemotherapy - usually September/October ● annual meeting and conference (exhibits).

6566 ■ American Society for Photobiology (ASP)

PO Box 1897
Lawrence, KS 66044
Free: (800)627-0629
Fax: (785)843-1287
E-mail: phot@allenpress.com
URL: http://www.pol-us.net/ASP_Home/index.html
Contact: Linda Jones, Pres.

Founded: 1972. **Members:** 1,200. **Membership Dues:** full, $120 (annual) ● student, $45 (annual) ● emeritus, $60 (annual). **Staff:** 4. **Multinational. Description:** Persons who have educational, research, or practical experience in photobiology or an allied scientific field. Promotes original research in photobiology (includes all biological phenomena or responses due to chemical and/or physical changes induced by non-ionizing radiation). Facilitates the integration of different disciplines in the study of photobiology. Provides information on the photobiological aspects of national and international problems. **Awards:** ASP New Investigator Award. **Type:** recognition. **Recipient:** for promising quality research performed ● ASP Research Award. **Frequency:** annual. **Type:** monetary. **Recipient:** for individuals who have made major contributions to the field of photobiology, photochemistry, and photophysics ● Lifetime Achievement Award. **Type:** monetary. **Recipient:** for a senior researcher whose work has significantly advanced any of the research areas encompassed by the association ● Photon Award. **Frequency:** annual. **Type:** monetary. **Recipient:** for members who have made exceptional contributions and who have served the association above and beyond the call of duty. **Publications:** *American Society for Photobiology - Directory and Constitution*. **Circulation:** 2,200. **Advertising:** accepted. Alternate Formats: online ● *American Society for Photobiology - Newsletter*, quarterly. Alternate Formats: online ● *Photo Chemistry and Photobiology*, bimonthly. Journal. **Conventions/Meetings:** biennial conference.

6567 ■ American Type Culture Collection (ATCC)

PO Box 1549
Manassas, VA 20108
Ph: (703)365-2700
Free: (800)638-6597
Fax: (703)365-2701
E-mail: news@atcc.org
URL: http://www.atcc.org

Founded: 1925. **Staff:** 300. **Description:** Seeks to collect, propagate, preserve, and distribute authentic cultures of cells, microorganisms and genetic materials for reference purposes for use in educational, research, and other scientific and industrial activities. Conducts research in cryobiology, microbial systematics, and karyology. Maintains depository for cultures involved in patent applications and for confidential safekeeping of proprietary cultures. **Programs:** Accounting; Applied Sciences; Bacteriology; Bioinformatics; Cell Biology; Management Information Systems; Manufacturing; Marketing and Public Relations; Materials Management; Molecular Biology; Mycology and Botany; Patent Depository; Protistology; Sales; Virology. **Publications:** *ATCC Connection*, weekly. Newsletter ● Brochures ● Catalogs ● Manuals.

6568 ■ Anaerobe Society of the Americas (ASA)

PO Box 452058
Los Angeles, CA 90045
Ph: (310)216-9265
Fax: (310)216-9274
E-mail: asa@anaerobe.org
URL: http://www.anaerobe.org
Contact: Ronald Goldman PhD, Exec. Dir.

Founded: 1992. **Members:** 300. **Membership Dues:** student, retiree, $25 (annual) ● anaerobist (not holding a doctorate), $35 (annual) ● anaerobist (with a doctorate), $70 (annual). **Staff:** 1. **Multinational. Description:** Scientists, veterinary and medical health care professionals, and other individuals with an interest in anaerobic bacteria and related organisms. Promotes the advancement of the understanding of anaerobic organisms and their impact on human and animal health. Works to stimulate interest and facilitate interchange among anaerobists from all disciplines; sponsors research and educational programs. **Awards:** Lifetime Achievement Award. **Frequency:** biennial. **Type:** recognition. **Recipient:** for advancing the study and training in the field of anaerobes. **Publications:** *Anaerobe*, periodic. Journal ● *ASA News*, periodic. Newsletter ● Proceedings, biennial. **Conventions/Meetings:** biennial American Congress on Anaerobic Bacteria and Anaerobic Infections, international congress addressing research related to anaerobes (exhibits).

6569 ■ Association of Genetic Technologists (AGT)

PO Box 15945
Lenexa, KS 66285-5945
Ph: (913)541-0497 (913)895-4605
Fax: (913)895-4652
E-mail: agt-info@goamp.com
URL: http://www.agt-info.org
Contact: Stephanie Newman, Exec. Dir.

Founded: 1975. **Members:** 1,300. **Membership Dues:** regular (international), $110 (annual) ● regular, $85 (annual) ● student (international), $60 (annual) ● emeritus, collaborative, $40 (annual) ● student, $35 (annual). **Regional Groups:** 12. **Multinational. Description:** Promotes cooperation and exchange of information among those engaged in classical cytogenetics, molecular and biochemical genetics. Stimulates interest in genetics as a career. **Libraries: Type:** reference. **Holdings:** archival material. **Awards:** Outstanding Achievement Award. **Frequency:** annual. **Type:** recognition. **Recipient:** for individuals committed to furthering the field of genetics as demonstrated by their work, attitude and AGT activities. **Committees:** Education; Membership; Public Relations. **Formerly:** (1996) Association of Cytogenetic Technologists. **Publications:** *Journal of the Association of Genetic Technologists*, quarterly. Contains lists of new techniques for cytogeneticists. Includes book reviews, employment opportunities, and research reports. **Price:** included in membership dues; $105.00 for nonmembers. **Advertising:** accepted. **Conventions/Meetings:** annual conference and meeting (exhibits) - always June ● annual lecture and workshop.

6570 ■ Association for Tropical Biology and Conservation (ATBC)

c/o W. John Kress, Exec. Dir.
PO Box 37012
Washington, DC 20013-7012
Ph: (202)633-0920
Fax: (202)786-2563
E-mail: kressj@si.edu
URL: http://www.atbio.org
Contact: W. John Kress, Exec. Dir.

Founded: 1963. **Members:** 1,400. **Membership Dues:** individual, $65 (annual). **Languages:** English, Portuguese, Spanish. **Multinational. Description:** Promotes research and fosters the exchange of ideas among biologists working in tropical environments. Enhances the understanding of human-environment interactions in the tropics. **Awards:** Gentry Awards. **Frequency:** annual. **Type:** monetary. **Recipient:** for best student paper at annual meeting ● Honorary Fellow. **Frequency:** annual. **Type:** recognition. **Recipient:** for distinguished contributions to tropical biology. **Affiliated With:** American Institute of Biological Sciences; Organization for Tropical Studies. **Formerly:** (2005) Association for Tropical Biology. **Publications:** *Biotropica* (in English, French, Portuguese, and Spanish), quarterly. Journal. Contains original research in tropical biology. **Price:** included in membership dues. ISSN: 0006-3606. **Circulation:** 1,600 ● *Tropinet*, quarterly. Newsletter. **Conventions/Meetings:** annual conference (exhibits) ● periodic symposium.

6571 ■ Biological Stain Commission (BSC)

Univ. of Rochester, Medical Center
Pathology Dept.
575 Elmwood Ave.
Box 626
Rochester, NY 14642-0001
Ph: (585)275-2751 (585)275-6335
Fax: (585)442-8993

E-mail: mfranks@biostain.org
URL: http://www.biostains.org
Contact: David P. Penney PhD, Sec.-Treas.
Founded: 1922. **Members:** 75. **Membership Dues:** general, $40 (annual). **Staff:** 3. **Budget:** $200,000. **Description:** Professional scientists in biology, medicine, and related fields. Works for the establishment of standards for the identification, purity, performance, and labeling of the more important biological stains, in order that they may be relied upon as standard tools in biological research. In cooperation with manufacturers and distributors, conducts program of stain certification. Conducts and promotes research in the improvement and applications of biological stains. **Awards: Frequency:** annual. **Type:** grant. **Recipient:** for research on stains and staining. **Telecommunication Services:** electronic mail, dpenney@biostains.org. **Boards:** Trustees. **Formerly:** (1944) Commission on Standardization of Biological Stains. **Publications:** *Biotechnic and Histochemistry*, bimonthly. Journal. Covers all aspects of the preparation of biological specimens; contains articles on new dyes and staining methods. **Price:** included in membership dues; $64.00 /year for nonmembers; $109.00 /year for institutions; $36.00/ year for students. ISSN: 0038-9153. **Circulation:** 2,700. **Advertising:** accepted. Alternate Formats: microform; online. Also Cited As: *Stain Technology: A Journal for Microtechnic and Histochemistry* ● *Conn's Biological Stains*. Book ● *Staining Procedures*. Book. **Conventions/Meetings:** annual conference - always first weekend of June.

6572 ■ Biometric Application Programming Interface Consortium (BIOAPI)

c/o Steve Vinsik, Sec.
11491 Sunset Hills Rd.
Reston, VA 20190
Ph: (703)579-3064
Fax: (703)579-3217
E-mail: info@bioapi.org
URL: http://www.bioapi.org
Contact: Steve Vinsik, Sec.
Founded: 1998. **Members:** 133. **Description:** Works with industry biometric solution developers, software developers and system integrators to leverage existing standards and facilitate easy adoption and implementation. **Computer Services:** Information services, BioAPI references ● mailing lists, of members ● online services, discussion groups. **Working Groups:** Applications; Conformance Test; Device; External; Reference Implementation.

6573 ■ Cell Proliferation Society

c/o Yuriy Gusev
Johns Hopkins Univ. School of Medicine
720 Rutland Ave., Ross Bldg., Rm. 764
Baltimore, MD 21205
Ph: (410)502-6987
Fax: (410)955-1945
E-mail: jwj@po.cwru.edu
URL: http://odin.mdacc.tmc.edu/biomath/cellpro/cell3
Contact: James W. Jacobberger, Sec.
Founded: 1976. **Members:** 330. **Membership Dues:** regular, $55 (annual). **Description:** Clinical practitioners, experimentalists, and theoreticians interested in cell proliferation. (Cell kinetics is the study of the rates and mechanisms by which cells undergo a divisional cycle.) Goals are to: facilitate communication among those in the field; promote basic and clinical research; disseminate information on cell proliferation to all interested persons. **Awards:** Student Travel Award. **Type:** monetary. **Recipient:** for graduate students, first- and second- year post-doctorals, and medical residents whose work in the area of cell kinetics represents an outstanding scientific achievement. **Formerly:** (2002) Cell Kinetics Society. **Publications:** *Cell Proliferation*. Journal. **Conventions/ Meetings:** annual meeting and symposium - usually in North America, for 2-3 days in March or April.

6574 ■ Committee on the Status of Women in Microbiology (CSWM)

c/o Dr. Lorraine Findlay, PhD, Chair
Nassau County Coll. and Medical Center
Dept. of Allied Hea. Sciences
One Educ. Dr.
Garden City, NY 11530-6793
Ph: (516)572-7915
Fax: (516)572-7565
E-mail: lorraine.findlay@ncc.edu
URL: http://www.asm.org/Policy/index.asp-?bid=22282
Contact: Dr. Lorraine Findlay PhD, Chair
Founded: 1972. **Members:** 9. **Description:** A committee of the American Society for Microbiology (see separate entry). Microbiologists investigating the status of women in microbiology in relation to their male counterparts in the work place and within their professional society. Reports findings and conducts seminars at the annual meeting of the ASM. Works toward full and equal opportunity for educational, career, and personal development for male and female microbiologists. **Awards:** Alice Evans Award. **Frequency:** annual. **Type:** recognition. **Publications:** *The Communicator*, 3/year. Newsletter. **Price:** free. **Advertising:** accepted. **Conventions/Meetings:** annual meeting (exhibits).

6575 ■ Environmental Mutagen Society (EMS)

1821 Michael Faraday Dr., Ste.300
Reston, VA 20190
Ph: (703)438-8220
Fax: (703)438-3113
E-mail: emshq@ems-us.org
URL: http://www.ems-us.org
Contact: Martina Veigl PhD, Pres.
Founded: 1969. **Members:** 1,100. **Membership Dues:** regular (couple), $243 (annual) ● regular, $149 (annual) ● student, $26 (annual) ● postdoc, $81 (annual) ● postdoc (couple), $107 (annual) ● emeritus, $55 (annual). **Staff:** 2. **Description:** Bioscientists in universities, governmental agencies, and industry. Promotes basic and applied studies of mutagenesis (the area of genetics dealing with mutation and molecular biology); disseminates information relating to environmental mutagenesis. Offers placement service. **Awards:** Alexander Hollaender Award. **Frequency:** annual. **Type:** recognition ● EMS Award. **Frequency:** annual. **Type:** recognition. **Recipient:** for outstanding service in the field ● Student and New Investigator Travel Awards. **Type:** recognition. **Computer Services:** Mailing lists, of members. **Affiliated With:** International Association of Environmental Mutagen Societies. **Publications:** *EMS Newsletter*, semiannual. **Price:** included in membership dues; $15.00 /year for nonmembers. **Circulation:** 1,200. **Advertising:** accepted ● *Environmental and Molecular Mutagenesis*, 8/year. Journal. Includes book reviews. **Price:** included in membership dues; $504.00 /year for nonmembers in North America; $556.00 /year for nonmembers outside North America. ISSN: 0893-6692. **Advertising:** accepted ● Membership Directory, biennial. Contains updates on membership. **Price:** included in membership dues. **Circulation:** 1,200. **Advertising:** accepted. Alternate Formats: online. **Conventions/Meetings:** annual meeting (exhibits).

6576 ■ Federation of American Societies for Experimental Biology (FASEB)

9650 Rockville Pike
Bethesda, MD 20814
Ph: (301)634-7000
Fax: (301)634-7001
E-mail: membershipdirectoryinfo@faseb.org
URL: http://www.faseb.org
Contact: Robert E. Palazzo PhD, Pres.
Founded: 1912. **Members:** 10. **Staff:** 100. **Budget:** $12,700,000. **Description:** Federation of scientific societies with a total of 40,000 members: the American Physiological Society; American Society for Biochemistry and Molecular Biology; American Society for Pharmacology and Experimental Therapeutics; American Society for Investigative Pathology; American Society for Nutritional Sciences; the American Association of Immunologists; the American Society for Bone and Mineral Research; American Society for Clinical Investigation; the Indocrine Society; the American Society of Human Genetics; Society for Developmental Biology; Biophysical Society; American Association of Anatomists; and the Protein Society. Maintains placement service. **Libraries: Type:** not open to the public. **Holdings:** 2,000; periodicals. **Subjects:** biological and life sciences, health and health care, medicine, nutrition. **Awards:** Excellence in Science Award. **Frequency:** annual. **Type:** recognition. **Recipient:** for outstanding achievement by women in biological science ● Public Service Award. **Type:** recognition. **Recipient:** for supporting medical research. **Computer Services:** Mailing lists, of members. **Committees:** Public Affairs Advisory; Publications and Communications; Research and Education; Research Conferences Advisory. **Publications:** *The FASEB Journal*, monthly. Reports developments in the biological and biomedical sciences. Includes reviews, original communications, methodologies, and public affairs. **Price:** $49.00 /year for members; $118.00 /year for nonmembers; $335.00 /year for institutions; $25.00/year for students. ISSN: 0892-6638. **Circulation:** 9,000. **Advertising:** accepted. Alternate Formats: microform ● *Federation of American Societies for Experimental Biology—Directory of Members*, annual. Membership Directory. **Price:** included in membership dues; $60. 00/copy for nonmembers. **Circulation:** 31,000. **Advertising:** accepted ● *Federation of American Societies for Experimental Biology—Public Affairs Newsletter*, bimonthly. Summarizes FASEB and constituent societies' activities on legislation and developments affecting biomedical research. Includes "Guest Opinion" column. **Price:** included in membership dues; $60.00 /year for nonmembers. **Circulation:** 36,000. **Advertising:** accepted. Also Cited As: *FASEB Newsletter*. **Conventions/Meetings:** conference - 18/year ● annual meeting (exhibits).

6577 ■ Human Biology Association (HBA)

c/o Dr. Gillian Ice, Sec.-Treas.
Ohio Univ. Coll. of Osteopathic Medicine
Dept. of Social Medicine
309 Grosvenor Hall
Athens, OH 45701
Ph: (740)593-2128
Fax: (740)593-1730
E-mail: iceg@ohio.edu
URL: http://www.humbio.org
Contact: Dr. Gillian Ice, Sec.-Treas.
Founded: 1974. **Members:** 300. **Membership Dues:** fellow, regular, $90 (annual) ● student, emeritus, $50 (annual) ● benefactor, supporting, $110 (annual) ● spouse, $35 (annual). **Description:** Represents individuals who are involved in fields related to human biology, including physical anthropology, sports medicine, genetics, nutrition, physiology, epidemiology, growth and development and pediatrics. Promotes study of human biology and related topics; encourages communication and utilization of results from such studies; aids in education of persons involved in such studies. Seeks to stimulate discussions of common goals and problems among scientists in the field. Assists with scholarly research in human biological sciences. Sponsors courses. **Computer Services:** database, interest. **Affiliated With:** American Association for the Advancement of Science. **Publications:** *American Journal of Human Biology*, bimonthly. Contains information on human population biology; includes papers, articles, and book reviews. **Price:** $432.00 /year for nonmembers in U.S.; $525.00 /year for nonmembers outside U.S.; included in membership dues ● Directory, annual. **Conventions/Meetings:** annual meeting and seminar, held in conjunction with American Association of Physical Anthropologists ● seminar ● workshop.

6578 ■ International Association of Environmental Mutagen Societies (IAEMS)

c/o Leona Samson, VP
Massachusetts Inst. of Tech.
CEHS/Bio Engg., Rm. 56-235
77 Massachusetts Ave.
Cambridge, MA 02139
Ph: (617)258-7813
Fax: (617)253-8099
E-mail: lsamson@mit.edu
URL: http://www.iaems.org.nz
Contact: Leona Samson, VP
Founded: 1973. **Members:** 3,500. **Budget:** $5,000. **Regional Groups:** 6. **Multinational. Description:**

Chemical, biological, and medical scientists in 50 countries acting in research, teaching, or administration in the fields of environmental mutagens and carcinogens and their control. (Mutagens are substances that tend to increase the frequency or extent of mutation). Promotes international collaboration in related areas. Organizes training courses and workshops in test methods and interpretation of data. Sponsors the International Commission for Protection Against Environmental Mutagens and Carcinogens. **Computer Services:** database. **Affiliated With:** International Union of Biological Sciences. **Foreign language name:** Association Internationale de Societes s'Occupant des Agents Mutagenes Presents dans l'Environnement. **Conventions/Meetings:** quadrennial International Conference on Environmental Mutagens (exhibits).

6579 ■ International Canopy Network (ICAN)
2103 Harrison Ave. NW, PMB 612
Olympia, WA 98502-2607
Ph: (360)866-6788
Fax: (360)866-6788
E-mail: canopy@evergreen.edu
URL: http://www.evergreen.edu/ican
Contact: Nalini Nadkarni, Pres.
Founded: 1994. **Members:** 200. **Membership Dues:** regular, $30 (annual) ● student, $20 (annual) ● corporate, $50 (annual). **Staff:** 3. **Description:** Scientists, conservationists, educators, and environmental professionals with an interest in forest canopies. Facilitates interaction among canopy scientists worldwide. Seeks to increase public awareness of environmental issues affecting forests. Creates educational materials for school use. Gathers and disseminates information. **Libraries: Type:** open to the public. **Holdings:** articles. **Subjects:** forest canopy ecology. **Computer Services:** database, canopy science bibliography ● online services, publication. **Publications:** *What's Up*, quarterly. Newsletter. Highlights research and developments in the field of canopy ecology. **Price:** included in membership dues. **Circulation:** 200. Alternate Formats: online ● Membership Directory, periodic.

6580 ■ International Cytokine Society (ICS)
c/o Dr. Sherwood M. Reichard, Exec. Mgr.
119 Davis Rd., Ste.5A
Augusta, GA 30907-0219
Ph: (706)228-4655
Fax: (706)228-4685
E-mail: sherwoodreichard@earthlink.net
URL: http://www.weizmann.ac.il/cytokine
Contact: Dr. Sherwood M. Reichard, Exec. Mgr.
Founded: 1978. **Members:** 800. **Membership Dues:** student/affiliate, $25 (annual) ● full, $50 (annual) ● full outside U.S., $55 (annual) ● associate/affiliate outside U.S., $30 (annual). **Staff:** 5. **Multinational. Description:** Represents physicians and scientists associated with universities; private, industrial, and government institutes; hospital clinics; and the pharmaceutical industry. Promotes research into and awareness of the health importance of cytokines; fosters the dissemination and application of information in these fields; provides a forum for the multidisciplinary integration of current and basic clinical knowledge and concepts in the study of cytokines. **Awards:** Honorary Life Membership. **Frequency:** annual. **Type:** recognition. **Recipient:** for contributions to the field ● Outstanding Scholar Award. **Frequency:** annual. **Type:** monetary. **Recipient:** for full time graduate or medical student ● Postdoctoral Investigator Award. **Frequency:** annual. **Type:** monetary. **Recipient:** for members who completed their training and currently engaged in research ● Young Investigator Award. **Frequency:** annual. **Type:** monetary. **Recipient:** for outstanding papers presented by students in training. **Telecommunication Services:** electronic mail, trinchig@niaid.nih.gov. **Committees:** Honors and Awards; Organizing. **Affiliated With:** National Academy of Sciences. **Publications:** *Cytokine*, semimonthly. Journal. Provides comprehensive coverage of cytokines and their receptors. **Price:** $679.00 /year for individuals (except in Europe and Japan); $1,432.00 /year for institutions (except in Europe and Japan). ISSN: 1043-4666 ● *Directory and Constitution*, biennial ● Newsletter, quarterly. **Advertising:** accepted. **Conventions/Meetings:** annual Cytokines in Cancer and Infectious Diseases - conference (exhibits) - 2008 Oct. 12-16, Montreal, QC, Canada ● workshop.

6581 ■ International Federation of Cell Biology (IFCB)
c/o Dr. W. Elaine Hardman, Treas.
Marshall Univ. School of Medicine
1542 Spring Valley Dr.
Huntington, WV 25704-9388
Ph: (304)696-7339 (512)567-3817
E-mail: cameron@uthscsa.edu
URL: http://www.ifcbiol.org
Contact: Prof. Ivan L. Cameron, VP
Founded: 1972. **Members:** 21. **Languages:** English, French. **Description:** National and regional associations of cell biologists. Works to: promote international cooperation among scientists working in cell biology and related fields; contribute to the advancement of cell biology in all of its branches. Acts as coordinating body that initiates special studies and encourages research in subjects outside the normal scope of national societies, such as the problem of scientific communication. Conducts seminars. **Telecommunication Services:** electronic mail, hardmanw@marshall.edu. **Affiliated With:** International Union of Biological Sciences. **Supersedes:** International Society for Cell Biology; International Society for Experimental Cytology. **Publications:** *Cell Biology International Reports*, monthly ● *International Cell Biology - Review of International Congresses*. Proceedings. **Conventions/Meetings:** quadrennial international conference (exhibits).

6582 ■ International Organization for Mycoplasmology (IOM)
c/o Jacqueline Fletcher, Treas.
Oklahoma State Univ.
127 Noble Res. Ctr.
Stillwater, OK 74078
Ph: (405)744-9948
Fax: (405)744-6039
E-mail: jaf2394@okstate.edu
URL: http://mycoplasmas.vm.iastate.edu/IOM
Contact: Jacqueline Fletcher, Treas.
Founded: 1974. **Members:** 450. **Membership Dues:** sustaining, $1,000 (biennial) ● individual, $75 (biennial) ● student, retirement, $15-$20 (biennial). **Budget:** $30,000. **Multinational. Description:** Medical, veterinary, plant pathology, and molecular biology scientists who study mycoplasmas; commercial companies that produce diagnostic reagents; animal suppliers; pharmaceutical and chemical companies. Works to support and encourage mycoplasmal research and dissemination of information. (Mycoplasmas are microorganisms that cause disease in humans, animals, and a wide variety of plants. These include diseases characterized by yellowing, stunting and decline in plants; urogenital, respiratory, and joint diseases are found in poultry, swine, sheep, goats, and cows; pneumonia and genitourinary tract disease in humans.) Sponsors educational programs including a training program in methodology and a biennial techniques course. Offers placement service. Maintains speakers' bureau. **Libraries: Type:** reference. **Holdings:** archival material. **Awards:** Derrik Edward Award. **Type:** recognition. **Recipient:** for scientific achievement ● Emmy Klieneberger Award. **Type:** recognition. **Recipient:** for scientific achievement. **Committees:** Education; Publicity. **Publications:** *Congress Abstracts*, biennial ● *Congress Proceedings*, biennial ● *IOM Newsletter*, quarterly ● Membership Directory, periodic. **Conventions/Meetings:** biennial rally and symposium (exhibits).

6583 ■ International Society for Analytical Cytology (ISAC)
9650 Rockville Pike
Bethesda, MD 20814-3998
Ph: (301)634-7435
Fax: (301)634-7429
E-mail: isac@isac-net.org
URL: http://www.isac-net.org
Contact: J. Paul Robinson PhD, Pres.
Founded: 1978. **Members:** 1,500. **Membership Dues:** regular, $126 (annual) ● student, $71 (annual) ● student (without journal), $35 (annual) ● emeritus, $10 (annual) ● Clinical Cytometry Society, $95 (annual). **Staff:** 7. **Budget:** $1,300,000. **Description:** Researchers and academics from government and private sectors interested in the study of cytology using high power technical equipment. (Cytology is a branch of biology dealing with the study of the structure, function, multiplication, pathology, and life history of cells.) Works to improve the usage of this equipment and to discover new techniques. **Awards: Type:** recognition. **Telecommunication Services:** electronic mail, jpr@flowcyt.cyto.purdue.edu. **Formerly:** (1991) Society for Analytical Cytology. **Publications:** *Case Studies in Clinical Flow Cytometry*. Journal. Alternate Formats: online ● *Current Protocols in Cytometry*. Book. Represents the combined efforts of leading cytometry laboratories from around the world. ● *Cytometry*, monthly. Journal. **Price:** included in membership dues. ISSN: 1097-0320. **Conventions/Meetings:** biennial International Congress - conference and congress (exhibits).

6584 ■ International Society of Artificial Life (ISAL)
Reed Coll.
3203 SE Woodstock Blvd.
Portland, OR 97202-8199
Ph: (503)788-6697
Fax: (503)788-6643
E-mail: society@alife.org
URL: http://www.alife.org/index.html
Contact: Mark Bedau, Pres.
Founded: 2001. **Membership Dues:** individual, $65 (annual) ● student, $40 (annual). **Multinational. Description:** Promotes scientific research and education relating to artificial life. Raises awareness of ethical issues associated with artificial life.

6585 ■ International Society for Biological and Environmental Repositories (ISBER)
9650 Rockville Pike
Bethesda, MD 20814-3993
Ph: (301)634-7949
Fax: (301)634-7990
E-mail: isber@asip.org
URL: http://www.isber.org
Contact: Frank Simione MS, Pres.
Founded: 2000. **Membership Dues:** general, $140 (annual) ● official/organization, associate (based on number of employees), $325-$1,200 (annual). **Multinational. Description:** Provides information and guidance on the safe and effective management of specimen collections. Serves as an educational forum for the discussion of repository management. Disseminates information on repository management issues. **Computer Services:** Bibliographic search ● database, products and services directory ● information services, repository resources ● mailing lists. **Publications:** Newsletter, periodic.

6586 ■ International Society for Biosafety Research (ISBR)
c/o Alan McHughen, PhD, Treas.
Batchelor Hall 3110
Univ. of California
Riverside, CA 92521-0124
E-mail: alanmc@ucr.edu
URL: http://www.isbr.info
Contact: Alan McHughen PhD, Treas.
Membership Dues: regular, $20 (annual) ● sustaining (corporation and non-profit organization), $1,000 (annual). **Multinational. Description:** Aims to promote biosafety research by fostering communication and technical exchange among experts and scientists who study plants, animals, and microbes. Supports the science used in biosafety assessment processes. Addresses science-based biosafety issues associated with "genetically modified organisms" (GMOs). Aims to ensure the safety of GMO products through risk assessment that supports regulatory decision-making. **Publications:** *Environ-*

mental Biosafety Research, quarterly. Journal. Includes peer-reviewed original research papers and review articles. ISSN: 1635-7922. Alternate Formats: online. Also Cited As: *EBR* ● Newsletter. **Price:** included in membership dues ● Brochure. Alternate Formats: online ● Proceedings. Alternate Formats: online.

6587 ■ International Society for Chronobiology (ISC)
Univ. of Texas, Medical Br.
Dept. of Neuroscience and Cell Biology
Galveston, TX 77555-1069
Ph: (409)772-1294
Fax: (409)762-9382
E-mail: nhrubin@utmb.edu
URL: http://www.chronoint.org
Contact: Dr. Norma H. Rubin, Sec.-Treas.
Founded: 1937. **Members:** 680. **Budget:** $40,000. **Description:** Scientists, medical professionals, students, and other individuals; corporations and institutions interested in the study of chronobiology (basic and applied study of temporal parameters of biological rhythms in plants, animals and humans). Seeks to further contact among scientists and medical professionals in the field; encourage development and recognition of centers of research; establish chronobiology as an academic discipline in its own right. Sponsors technique training. **Libraries: Type:** reference. **Holdings:** periodicals. **Subjects:** chronobiology journals. **Awards:** Honorary Life Member. **Type:** recognition. **Recipient:** for distinguished career contributions to chronobiology. **Formerly:** (1971) Society for the Study of Biological Rhythms. **Publications:** *Agriculture* ● *Chronobiology Applications in General Medicine Biology* ● *Chronobiology International: A Journal for Biological Rhythm Research*, bimonthly. Contains research articles encompassing biological rhythm investigations of bio-periodicity in all life forms. **Price:** included in membership dues; $85.00 /year for institutions. ISSN: 0742-0528. **Circulation:** 1,000. **Advertising:** accepted. Alternate Formats: microform ● *Proceedings of 1989 XIX International Conference* ● Plans to publish directory. **Conventions/Meetings:** biennial conference (exhibits).

6588 ■ International Society of Differentiation (ISD)
PO Box 10854
St. Paul, MN 55110
Ph: (651)659-9493
Fax: (651)659-9493
E-mail: office@isdifferentiation.org
URL: http://www.isdifferentiation.org
Contact: H. Clevers, Pres.
Founded: 1971. **Members:** 300. **Membership Dues:** regular, $50 (annual) ● student, $30 (annual). **Multinational. Description:** Academic and industrial professionals. Promotes research and exchanges information concerning biological differentiation of normal and neoplastic cells at molecular, cellular, and tissue levels of organization. (Biological differentiation is the process leading to specializations of structure and function of cells, tissues, and intact organisms.) Offers professional training at conferences. **Publications:** *Conference Proceedings*, periodic ● *Differentiation*, bimonthly. Journal. **Price:** included in membership dues ● *ISD Newsletter*, periodic. **Conventions/Meetings:** biennial conference (exhibits).

6589 ■ International Society for Plant Molecular Biology (ISPMB)
Univ. of Georgia
Biochemistry and Molecular Biology Dept.
Athens, GA 30602
Ph: (706)542-3000
Fax: (706)542-2090
E-mail: lrl@uga.edu
URL: http://www.uga.edu/ispmb
Contact: Shannon Scott, Pres.
Founded: 1983. **Members:** 1,850. **Membership Dues:** regular, $50 (annual) ● student, $20 (annual) ● sustaining, $1,000 (annual). **Description:** Scientists whose research involves the molecular biology of plants. Coordinates exchange of information. **Libraries: Type:** not open to the public. **Holdings:** 15; periodicals. **Subjects:** plant molecular biology. **Computer Services:** Mailing lists, labels. **Formerly:** (1983) Plant Molecular Biology Association. **Publications:** *Plant Molecular Biology*, monthly. Journal ● *Plant Molecular Biology Reporter*, quarterly. Journal. Covers technical subjects, experimental protocols, and genetic resources. Includes calendar of events. **Price:** included in membership dues. ISSN: 0735-9640. **Circulation:** 2,200. **Advertising:** accepted. Alternate Formats: online ● Membership Directory, biennial. **Conventions/Meetings:** triennial International Congress of Plant Molecular Biology (exhibits).

6590 ■ Natural Science Collections Alliance (NSC Alliance)
1313 Dolley Madison Blvd., Ste.402
McLean, VA 22101
Ph: (703)790-1745
Fax: (703)790-2672
E-mail: nsca@burkinc.com
URL: http://www.nscalliance.org
Contact: Michael Mares, Pres.
Founded: 1972. **Members:** 225. **Staff:** 2. **Budget:** $200,000. **Description:** Represents educational institutions, museums, and government agencies (which maintain permanent collections in systematic biology). Aims to foster the care, management, preservation, and improvement of systematics collections and to facilitate their use in science and society by: providing representation for institutions housing systematics collections; encouraging direct interaction among those concerned with systematics collections and their use; providing a forum for consideration of mutual problems; promoting the role of systematics collections in research, education, and public service. **Libraries: Type:** not open to the public; reference. **Subjects:** systematics, collections, biodiversity, conservation. **Computer Services:** database. **Formerly:** (2001) Association of Systematics Collections. **Publications:** *The Washington Report*, biweekly. Newsletter. Covers political and public policy affecting natural science collections research. **Price:** included in membership dues. **Circulation:** 125. **Conventions/Meetings:** annual meeting.

6591 ■ Organization of Biological Field Stations (OBFS)
c/o Dr. Shorty Boucher
Univ. California - Davis
Environmental Sci. and Policy
1 Shields Ave.
Davis, CA 95616
Ph: (707)875-2020
Fax: (707)875-2009
E-mail: obfs@ucdavis.edu
URL: http://www.obfs.org
Contact: Dr. Claudia Luke, Sec.
Founded: 1968. **Members:** 205. **Membership Dues:** individual, $25 (annual) ● station, $100 (annual). **Description:** Representatives or directors of biological field stations and other interested individuals. Works toward the advancement of biological science by facilitating communication among biological field stations and by encouraging the use of field stations for education, training, and research. Promotes the funding of field station facilities, operations, programs, and research activities. Publicizes activities to user groups; does not provide funding or compile information on careers or employment opportunities. **Affiliated With:** American Institute of Biological Sciences. **Formerly:** (1975) Organization of Inland Biological Field Stations. **Publications:** *Annual Summer Course Announcement Poster*, annual. **Price:** free ● *Biological Field Station of North America*. Brochure ● *Biology on the Spot*. Brochure. **Price:** free ● *Data Management at Biological Field Stations and Coastal Marine Laboratories*. Report. **Price:** free ● *Guide to Biological Field Stations 1992*, semiannual. Newsletter. Includes list of new publications and new members. **Price:** included in membership dues. **Circulation:** 190 ● *OBFS Newsletter*, semiannual. Includes list of new publications and new members. **Price:** included in membership dues. **Circulation:** 190. Alternate Formats: online. **Conventions/Meetings:** annual meeting - always late September.

6592 ■ Pan-American Aerobiology Association (PAAA)
c/o Michael L. Muilenberg, Membership Sec.-Treas.
Harvard School of Public Hea., SPH-1, G-33
665 Huntington Ave.
Boston, MA 02115
Ph: (617)432-0642
Fax: (617)432-3349
E-mail: mmuil@hsph.harvard.edu
URL: http://www.geocities.com/paaaorg
Contact: Michael L. Muilenberg, Membership Sec.-Treas.
Founded: 1989. **Membership Dues:** individual, $40 (annual) ● student, $20 (annual). **Multinational. Description:** Scientists interested in the sources, dispersal, and deposition of airborne biological particles. **Awards:** Student Development Award. **Frequency:** annual. **Type:** scholarship. **Recipient:** for students of Aerobiology. **Computer Services:** database, aerobiological data. **Committees:** Latin American; Spore Counter Certification. **Working Groups:** Biological Sampling Strategies. **Publications:** *Allergy Pollen Key with Images*. Manual. **Price:** $10.00 ● *Cultural Heritage and Aerobiology*. Book ● *Flow of Life in the Atmosphere: An Airscape Approach to Understanding Invasive Organisms*. Book. **Price:** $38.95 ● *Methods in Aerobiology*. Book ● Newsletter, semiannual. Alternate Formats: online. **Conventions/Meetings:** annual conference ● quadrennial congress.

6593 ■ Society for Biological Engineering (SBE)
c/o American Institute of Chemical Engineers
3 Park Ave., 19th Fl.
New York, NY 10016
E-mail: bio@aiche.org
URL: http://www.aiche.org/SBE
Contact: June C. Wispelwey, Exec. Dir.
Membership Dues: professional, $75 (annual) ● undergraduate student, $5 (annual) ● graduate student, $25 (annual). **Multinational. Description:** Promotes the integration of biology with engineering and its benefits through bioprocessing, biomedical, and biomolecular applications. Raises interest, understanding, and recognition of engineers' and scientists' roles in biological engineering. Provides opportunities for the successful interaction of engineers and scientists. **Awards:** James E. Bailey Award. **Frequency:** annual. **Type:** recognition. **Recipient:** for outstanding contributions to the field of biological engineering. **Affiliated With:** American Institute of Chemical Engineers. **Publications:** *SBE Connections*, monthly. Newsletter. **Price:** included in membership dues. Alternate Formats: online. **Conventions/Meetings:** annual conference.

6594 ■ Society for Conservation Biology (SCB)
4245 N Fairfax Dr., Ste.400
Arlington, VA 22203-1651
Ph: (703)276-2384
Fax: (703)995-4633
E-mail: info@conbio.org
URL: http://www.conbio.org
Contact: Paul Beier, Sec.
Founded: 1985. **Members:** 6,000. **Membership Dues:** general, $10 (annual) ● life, $400. **Staff:** 10. **Local Groups:** 23. **Languages:** English, Spanish. **Multinational. Description:** Represents the interests of professional scientists and conservationists interested in the conservation of biological diversity. Promotes the scientific study of the phenomena that affect the maintenance, loss and restoration of biological diversity. Seeks to advance the science and practice of conserving the Earth's biological diversity. **Awards:** Distinguished Contributions to Conservation Biology Award. **Frequency:** annual. **Type:** recognition ● Student Awards. **Frequency:** annual. **Type:** recognition. **Recipient:** for outstanding students. **Publications:** *Conservation Biology*, bimonthly. Journal. Contains peer reviewed papers and book reviews. ISSN: 0888-8892. **Circulation:**

6,000. **Advertising:** accepted. Alternate Formats: online ● *Conservation In Practice*, quarterly. Magazine. Contains articles on innovative practices of Conservation biology aimed at managers, practitioners and policy makers. **Price:** $30.00 in U.S.; $35.00 in Canada and other developed countries; $30.00 developing countries ● *Society for Conservation Biology Newsletter*, quarterly. **Conventions/Meetings:** annual meeting (exhibits) - 2008 July 13-18, Chattanooga, TN.

6595 ■ Society for Developmental Biology (SDB)
9650 Rockville Pike
Bethesda, MD 20814-3998
Ph: (301)634-7815
Fax: (301)634-7825
E-mail: sdb@faseb.org
URL: http://www.sdbonline.org
Contact: Gail Martin PhD, Pres.
Founded: 1939. **Members:** 2,100. **Membership Dues:** student, $15 (annual) ● full, $60 (annual) ● postdoctoral, $35 (annual). **Staff:** 2. **Regional Groups:** 7. **Multinational. Description:** Professional society of biologists interested in problems of development and growth of organisms. **Awards:** Best Poster Awards. **Frequency:** annual. **Type:** recognition. **Recipient:** to students and postdocs at the annual meeting ● Developmental Biology - Society for Developmental Biology Lifetime Achievement Award. **Frequency:** annual. **Type:** recognition. **Recipient:** to a senior developmental biologist ● Edwin Conklin Award. **Frequency:** annual. **Type:** monetary. **Recipient:** for significant life-long contribution to the field of developmental biology. **Computer Services:** Mailing lists, of members. **Formerly:** Society for the Study of Development and Growth. **Publications:** *Developmental Biology*, biweekly. Journal. **Price:** $308.00. ISSN: 0012-1606. **Circulation:** 2,500. **Advertising:** accepted ● Newsletter. Alternate Formats: online. **Conventions/Meetings:** annual meeting, with platform presentations and poster sessions (exhibits).

6596 ■ Society of Ethnobiology (SE)
c/o Margaret Scarry, Sec.-Treas.
Univ. of North Carolina
Dept. of Anthropology
CB 3115, Alumni Bldg.
Chapel Hill, NC 27599-3155
Ph: (919)962-3841
Fax: (919)962-1613
E-mail: secretary@ethnobiology.org
URL: http://www.ethnobiology.org
Contact: Margaret Scarry, Sec.-Treas.
Founded: 1978. **Members:** 520. **Membership Dues:** individual (in U.S., Canada and Latin America), $50 (annual) ● individual (in Africa, Asia, Australia and Europe), $60 (annual) ● student (in U.S., Canada and Mexico), $35 (annual) ● student (elsewhere), $45 (annual) ● institution (in U.S., Canada and Mexico), $90 (annual) ● institution (outside U.S., Canada and Mexico), $100 (annual) ● resident of Mexico, $40 (annual). **Budget:** $30,000. **Languages:** English, Spanish. **Multinational. Description:** Represent individuals and institutions interested in ethnobiology. (Ethnobiology is the study of the relationship between plants and animals and specific peoples or regions, and can include the study of the medicinal uses of plant and animal products). **Libraries: Type:** open to the public. **Awards:** Barbara Lawrence Award. **Frequency:** annual. **Type:** monetary. **Recipient:** for best student paper. **Publications:** *Journal of Ethnobiology* (in English, French, and Spanish), semiannual. Includes scientific articles on ethnobiological subjects. **Price:** $35.00 /year for individuals in U.S. and Canada; $25.00 /year for individuals in Mexico; $80.00 /year for institutions in U.S., Canada and Mexico; $90.00 /year for institutions outside U.S., Canada and Mexico. ISSN: 0278-0771. **Circulation:** 520. **Advertising:** accepted. Alternate Formats: online. **Conventions/Meetings:** annual conference and meeting (exhibits).

6597 ■ Society for Experimental Biology and Medicine (SEBM)
197 W Spring Valley Ave.
Maywood, NJ 07607-1727
Ph: (201)291-9080
Fax: (201)291-2988
E-mail: sebm@inch.com
URL: http://www.sebm.org
Contact: Felice O'Grady, Exec. Dir.
Founded: 1903. **Members:** 1,500. **Membership Dues:** student, $20 (annual) ● regular, $70 (annual) ● associate, $50 (annual). **Staff:** 2. **Budget:** $400,000. **Regional Groups:** 2. **Description:** Society of scientists actively engaged in research in experimental biology and experimental medicine. Cultivates the experimental method of investigation in the sciences of biology and medicine. **Awards:** Best Paper Award. **Frequency:** annual. **Type:** monetary. **Recipient:** for outstanding research paper in the experimental biology area and in clinical, preclinical or translational research area ● Young Investigator Awards. **Frequency:** annual. **Type:** grant. **Recipient:** for members who are undergraduate, graduate students and/or individuals within 5 years of receiving doctoral degrees. **Additional Websites:** http://www.ebmonline.org. **Publications:** *Experimental Biology and Medicine*, monthly. Journal. Contains original research, mini reviews, brief articles and meeting symposia. 15 topic categories; 163 members of editorial board. **Price:** $545.00 for institutions in U.S. (print and online); $585.00 for institutions outside U.S. (print and online); $445.00 for institutions (online only). ISSN: 0037-9727. **Circulation:** 1,350. **Advertising:** accepted. Alternate Formats: online. **Conventions/Meetings:** annual meeting and symposium.

6598 ■ Society for In Vitro Biology (SIVB)
514 Daniels St., Ste.411
Raleigh, NC 27605
Ph: (919)420-7940 (662)325-7577
Free: (888)588-1923
Fax: (919)420-7939
E-mail: sivb@sivb.org
URL: http://www.sivb.org
Contact: Dr. Paul J. Price, Pres.
Founded: 1946. **Members:** 1,200. **Membership Dues:** individual, $160 (annual) ● student, $55 (annual) ● post-doctoral, $105 (annual) ● sustaining, $505 (annual). **Staff:** 3. **Budget:** $1,000,000. **Multinational. Description:** Professional society of individuals using mammalian, invertebrate, plant cell tissue, and organ cultures as research tools in chemistry, physics, radiation, medicine, physiology, nutrition, and cytogenetics. Aims are to foster collection and dissemination of information concerning the maintenance and experimental use of tissue cells in vitro and to establish evaluation and development procedures. Operates placement service. **Awards:** Earle Award. **Frequency:** annual. **Type:** recognition ● Fell Award. **Frequency:** annual. **Type:** recognition ● Hopps Award. **Frequency:** annual. **Type:** recognition ● Morgan Award. **Frequency:** annual. **Type:** recognition ● Song Award. **Frequency:** annual. **Type:** recognition ● Student Travel Awards. **Frequency:** annual. **Type:** recognition ● White Award. **Frequency:** annual. **Type:** recognition. **Computer Services:** Mailing lists, of members ● online services, journals. **Telecommunication Services:** electronic mail, president@sivb.org. **Committees:** Awards; Constitution and Bylaws; Development; Education; Laboratory and Biosafety Materials; Long-Range Planning; Nominating; Program; Public Policy; Publications; Records and Historical; Student Affairs; Terminology. **Sections:** In Vitro Animal Cell Sciences and Plant Biotechnology. **Formerly:** Tissue Culture Association; (1946) Tissue Culture Commission. **Publications:** *In Vitro Cellular and Developmental Biology - Animal*, 10/year, combined July/August and November/December issues. Journal. Covers in-vitro cultivation and characterization of cells, tissues and tumors. Provides an abstract issue in spring. **Price:** included in membership dues; $381.00 for nonmembers in U.S., Canada and Mexico; $421.00 for nonmembers outside U.S., Canada and Mexico. ISSN: 1071-2690. **Circulation:** 1,500. **Advertising:** accepted. Alternate Formats: microform; online ● *In Vitro Cellular and Developmental Biology - Plant*, bimonthly. Journal. Covers in-vitro cultivation of tissues, organs, or cells from plants. **Price:** included in membership dues; $273.00 for nonmembers in U.S., Canada and Mexico; $323.00 for nonmembers outside U.S., Canada and Mexico. ISSN: 1054-5476. **Circulation:** 3,600. **Advertising:** accepted ● *In Vitro Report*, quarterly. Newsletter. Includes national and international news relevant to the field. **Price:** included in membership dues; $55.00 for nonmembers in U.S., Canada and Mexico; $70.00 for nonmembers outside U.S., Canada and Mexico. ISSN: 1077-3975. **Circulation:** 1,800. **Advertising:** accepted. **Conventions/Meetings:** annual In Vitro Biology Meeting, international event, which focuses on issues pertinent to plant and animal research; participants receive a unique learning experience on cell culture and biotechnology (exhibits) - always May or June. 2008 June 14-18, Tucson, AZ - **Avg. Attendance:** 400.

6599 ■ Society for Industrial Microbiology (SIM)
3929 Old Lee Hwy., Ste.92A
Fairfax, VA 22030-2421
Ph: (703)691-3357
Fax: (703)691-7991
E-mail: simhq@simhq.org
URL: http://www.simhq.org
Contact: Christine Lowe, Exec. Dir.
Founded: 1949. **Members:** 1,300. **Membership Dues:** regular, in U.S., $100 (annual) ● regular, outside U.S., $115 (annual) ● student (SIM News and Journal), $60 (annual) ● student (SIM News only), $35 (annual) ● corporate bronze, $500 (annual) ● emeritus, $1 (annual) ● corporate silver, $750 (annual) ● corporate gold, $1,000 (annual) ● corporate diamond, $2,000 (annual). **Staff:** 6. **Local Groups:** 9. **Description:** Mycologists, bacteriologists, biologists, chemists, engineers, zoologists, and others interested in biological processes as applied to industrial materials and processes concerning microorganisms. Serves as liaison between the specialized fields of microbiology. Maintains placement service; conducts surveys and scientific workshops in industrial microbiology. **Awards:** Charles Porter Award. **Frequency:** annual. **Type:** recognition. **Recipient:** for members who have outstanding records of sustained service to the society ● Charles Thom Award. **Frequency:** annual. **Type:** recognition. **Recipient:** for contributions to research in industrial microbiology reflecting ideas and thoughts advancing basic and applied scientific knowledge ● Schering-Plough Young Investigators Award. **Type:** recognition. **Recipient:** for scientific contribution in biotechnology/industrial microbiology, must be 35 years old or younger or within 5 years of completing a PhD degree ● SIM Fellow Award. **Frequency:** annual. **Type:** recognition. **Recipient:** for demonstration of nominee's excellence in microbial research and contributions made in academic, government, industrial, military or public health positions ● Waksman Outstanding Educator Award. **Frequency:** annual. **Type:** recognition. **Recipient:** for professors working in a recognized institution of higher education for 10 years. **Computer Services:** Mailing lists, of members. **Telecommunication Services:** electronic mail, chris.lowe@simhq.org. **Committees:** Awards and Grants; Education. **Affiliated With:** American Institute of Biological Sciences. **Publications:** *Corporate Membership Brochure*. Alternate Formats: online ● *Journal of Industrial Microbiology and Biotechnology*, monthly. Provides reviews and reports of original research in specialized areas of microbiology. **Price:** included in membership dues. **Advertising:** accepted. Alternate Formats: online. Also Cited As: *JIM&B* ● *SIM News*, bimonthly. Magazine. **Price:** included in membership dues. **Advertising:** accepted ● Pamphlet. For use in high schools. **Conventions/Meetings:** annual Industrial Microbiology and Biotechnology Meeting - conference and symposium (exhibits).

6600 ■ Society for Mathematical Biology (SMB)
PO Box 11283
Boulder, CO 80301
Ph: (303)661-9942
Fax: (303)665-8264

E-mail: membership@smb.org
URL: http://www.smb.org
Contact: Dr. Mark Chaplain, Pres.
Membership Dues: student (group A), $25 (annual) ● full (group A), $50 (annual) ● student (group B), $20 (annual) ● full (group B), $35 (annual) ● joint, $40 (annual). **Description:** Biologists, mathematicians, and other individuals with an interest in the application of mathematics to biology. Serves as a forum for discussion and the exchange of information in the field of mathematical biology. Sponsors interdisciplinary research projects in areas including biophysics and computational biology. **Publications:** *Bulletin of Mathematical Biology*, periodic. Journal. **Price:** included in membership dues ● Newsletter, 3/year. **Conventions/Meetings:** annual meeting ● periodic workshop.

6601 ■ Society for Molecular Biology and Evolution (SMBE)
c/o Jianzhi George Zhang, Sec.
Univ. of Michigan
Dept. of Ecology and Evolutionary Biology
1075 Natural Sci. Bldg.
830 N Univ. Ave.
Ann Arbor, MI 48109-1048
Ph: (734)763-0527 (734)763-0514
Fax: (734)763-0544
E-mail: jianzhi@umich.edu
URL: http://www.smbe.org
Contact: Jianzhi George Zhang, Sec.
Founded: 1993. **Membership Dues:** regular, $112 (annual) ● student/post-doctoral researcher, $67 (annual). **Multinational. Description:** Seeks to further the goals of molecular evolutionary biology and its practitioners. Increases communication between the fields of evolution and molecular biology. Provides facilities for association and communication among molecular evolutionists. **Publications:** *Molecular Biology and Evolution*, monthly. Journal. **Conventions/Meetings:** annual meeting.

6602 ■ Teratology Society (TS)
1821 Michael Faraday Dr., Ste.300
Reston, VA 20190
Ph: (703)438-3104
Fax: (703)438-3113
E-mail: tshq@teratology.org
URL: http://www.teratology.org
Contact: Elaine M. Faustman PhD, Pres.
Founded: 1960. **Members:** 798. **Membership Dues:** student, emeritus (with subscription to journal), $65 (annual) ● regular, associate, $126 (annual). **Staff:** 2. **Budget:** $300,000. **Description:** Individuals from academia, government, private industry, and the professions. Stimulates scientific interest in, and promotes the exchange of ideas and information about, problems of abnormal biological development and malformations at the fundamental or clinical level. Sponsors annual education course, and presentations. Establishes archives of society documents and history. **Awards:** Eli Lilly Women and Minority Travel Award. **Frequency:** annual. **Type:** recognition. **Recipient:** for female minority graduate students and postdoctoral fellows ● F. Clarke Fraser New Investigator Award. **Frequency:** annual. **Type:** recognition. **Recipient:** for members with successful independent careers ● James C. Bradford Memorial Student Poster Award. **Frequency:** annual. **Type:** recognition. **Recipient:** for the best student ● James G. Wilson Publication Award. **Frequency:** annual. **Type:** recognition. **Recipient:** for the best paper published in Birth Defects Research Journal ● Josef Warkany Lecturer Award. **Frequency:** annual. **Type:** recognition. **Recipient:** for a scientist who has significantly contributed to the field of Teratology ● Marie Taubeneck Award. **Frequency:** annual. **Type:** recognition. **Recipient:** for graduate students and postdoctoral fellows ● Student Travel Awards. **Frequency:** annual. **Type:** monetary. **Recipient:** for a graduate student ● Wilson Presentation Award. **Frequency:** annual. **Type:** recognition. **Recipient:** for graduate students and postdoctoral fellows ● Young Investigator Travel Awards. **Frequency:** annual. **Type:** recognition. **Recipient:** for graduate students and postdoctoral fellows. **Committees:** Education; Public Affairs. **Publications:** *Teratology Society Newsletter*. Alternate Formats: online ● *Teratology: The International Journal of Abnormal Development*, monthly. Reports on studies in all areas of abnormal development and related fields. Includes abstracts of papers presented at annual meeting, book reviews. **Price:** included in membership dues. ISSN: 0040-3709. **Advertising:** accepted ● Membership Directory. Alternate Formats: online ● Articles. Alternate Formats: online. **Conventions/Meetings:** annual meeting and symposium (exhibits) - 2008 June 28-July 3, Monterey, CA; 2009 June 27-July 2, Rio Grande, PR.

6603 ■ U.S. Federation for Culture Collections (USFCC)
c/o Darrell Jay Grimes, Pres.
PO Box 7000
Ocean Springs, MS 39566-7000
Ph: (228)872-4211
E-mail: jay.grimes@usm.edu
URL: http://usfcc.us
Contact: Darrell Jay Grimes, Pres.
Founded: 1970. **Members:** 260. **Membership Dues:** individual, $25 ● affiliate, $45 ● sustaining, $200 ● student/emeritus, $12. **Description:** Persons interested in culture collections, particularly those involved in collecting, maintaining, and preserving microbial cultures. Works to maintain liaison among members, encourage research, find means of preserving collections of microorganisms, disseminate information, and encourage establishment of strain data services. Sponsors workshops on the preservation of microbial cultures and the operation of culture collections. **Libraries: Type:** reference. **Subjects:** catalogs of culture collections. **Awards:** J. Roger Porter Award. **Frequency:** annual. **Type:** recognition. **Recipient:** for an outstanding scientist who has made contributions to the federation's objectives. **Publications:** *Advances in Culture Collections*, periodic ● *United States Federation For Culture Collections Newsletter*, quarterly. **Advertising:** accepted. Alternate Formats: online ● Directory, semiannual. **Conventions/Meetings:** semiannual conference and symposium ● annual meeting, held in conjunction with American Society for Microbiology.

6604 ■ United States Human Proteome Organization (USHUPO)
2019 Galisteo St., Bldg. I-1
Santa Fe, NM 87505
Ph: (505)989-4876
E-mail: ushupo@ushupo.org
URL: http://www.ushupo.org
Contact: Catherine Fenselau, Pres.
Membership Dues: regular, $100 (annual) ● student, $50 (annual) ● corporate, $1,000 (annual). **Multinational. Description:** Engages in scientific and educational activities to encourage the spread of proteomics technologies. Disseminates knowledge pertaining to the human proteome. **Committees:** Open Source; Program. **Subgroups:** Outreach; Technology.

6605 ■ Waksman Foundation for Microbiology (WFM)
c/o Amy Cheng Vollmer, Pres.
Dept. of Biology
Swarthmore Coll.
500 Coll. Ave.
Swarthmore, PA 19081-1390
Ph: (610)328-8044
Fax: (610)328-8663
E-mail: avollme1@swarthmore.edu
URL: http://www.waksmanfoundation.org
Contact: Amy Cheng Vollmer, Pres.
Founded: 1951. **Members:** 11. **Staff:** 1. **Budget:** $80,000. **Description:** Encourages research in microbiology by: establishing lectureships; funding specialized courses in microbiology (must have international or national outreach); aiding in the publishing of scientific works concerning microbiology; supporting innovative educational programs dealing with microbiological topics; and making use of contemporary communication techniques, as well as programs concerned with enhancing public awareness of science, including K-12 teaching programs that make use of microorganisms. **Awards: Frequency:** quarterly. **Type:** recognition ● Selman A. Waksman Award in Microbiology. **Frequency:** biennial. **Type:** monetary. **Recipient:** for outstanding contributions to research in microbiology ● Selman A. Waksman Teaching Award. **Frequency:** annual. **Type:** monetary. **Recipient:** for excellence in teaching. **Boards:** Trustees. **Committees:** Electronic Techniques and Applications; K-12 Science Education; Planning. **Formerly:** (2000) Foundation for MicroBiology. **Publications:** *Foundation for Microbiology 1951-1995*, quinquennial. Report ● Report, annual. **Conventions/Meetings:** annual Trustees Meeting - board meeting.

Biomedical Engineering

6606 ■ Association for the Advancement of Medical Instrumentation (AAMI)
1110 N Glebe Rd., Ste.220
Arlington, VA 22201-4795
Ph: (703)525-4890
Free: (800)332-2264
Fax: (703)276-0793
E-mail: membership@aami.org
URL: http://www.aami.org
Contact: Michael J. Miller JD, Pres./CEO
Founded: 1965. **Members:** 6,000. **Membership Dues:** individual in U.S., $195 (annual) ● individual outside U.S., $255 (annual) ● student, $30 (annual) ● corporate (based on gross worldwide medical sales), $925-$41,000 (annual) ● professional, $55 (annual). **Staff:** 35. **Budget:** $5,000,000. **Multinational. Description:** Clinical engineers, biomedical equipment technicians, physicians, hospital administrators, consultants, engineers, manufacturers of medical devices, nurses, researchers and others interested in medical instrumentation. Works to improve the quality of medical care through the application, development, and management of technology. Maintains placement service. Offers certification programs for biomedical equipment technicians and clinical engineers. Produces numerous standards and recommended practices on medical devices and procedures. Offers educational programs. **Awards:** AAMI Foundation/Laufman-Greatbatch Award. **Frequency:** annual. **Type:** monetary. **Recipient:** for individuals or groups who have made a unique and significant contribution to the advancement of medical instrumentation ● Becton Dickinson Career Achievement Award. **Frequency:** annual. **Type:** monetary. **Recipient:** for outstanding achievement in the development or improvement of medical devices, instruments, or systems ● Clinical/Biomedical Engineering Achievement Award. **Frequency:** annual. **Type:** monetary. **Recipient:** for individual excellence and achievement in the field of clinical and biomedical engineering ● TISCOR/Herb Gardner Foundation Award. **Frequency:** annual. **Type:** monetary. **Computer Services:** database ● mailing lists. **Telecommunication Services:** electronic mail, careers@aami.org ● electronic mail, certifications@aami.org ● electronic mail, customerservice@aami.org ● electronic mail, webmaster@aami.org ● electronic mail, standards@aami.org. **Committees:** Clinical Engineering Management; International Standards; Standards. **Publications:** *AAMI News*, monthly. Newsletter. Informs members on legislative and regulatory proposals, proposed and final AAMI standards, and association policies and programs. **Price:** included in membership dues; $75.00 for nonmembers. ISSN: 0739-0270. **Circulation:** 6,000. **Advertising:** accepted ● *Biomedical Instrumentation and Technology*, bimonthly. Journal. Includes advertisers and annual subject indexes, book reviews, statistics, association news, information on medical instrumentation. **Price:** included in membership dues; $115.00 for nonmembers. ISSN: 0883-9093. **Circulation:** 6,000. **Advertising:** accepted ● Also publishes technology analyses and reviews and medical device standards and recommended practices. **Conventions/Meetings:** annual meeting and symposium (exhibits).

6607 ■ Biomedical Engineering Society (BMES)
8401 Corporate Dr., Ste.140
Landover, MD 20785-2224

Ph: (301)459-1999
Fax: (301)459-2444
E-mail: info@bmes.org
URL: http://www.bmes.org
Contact: Barbara Dunlavey CMP, Exec. Dir.
Founded: 1968. **Members:** 3,700. **Membership Dues:** full, associate, $175 (annual) ● student, $30 (annual) ● post graduate, $80 (annual) ● corresponding, $25 (annual). **Staff:** 6. **Budget:** $1,000,000. **Regional Groups:** 87. **Multinational. Description:** Biomedical, chemical, electrical, civil, agricultural and mechanical engineers, physicians, managers, and university professors representing all fields of biomedical engineering; students and corporations. Encourages the development, dissemination, integration, and utilization of knowledge in biomedical engineering. **Libraries: Type:** open to the public. **Holdings:** 100; articles, books. **Subjects:** biomedical engineering. **Awards:** BMES Distinguished Achievement Award. **Frequency:** annual. **Type:** recognition. **Recipient:** to a company, charitable foundation or non-academic institution ● BMES Distinguished Lecturer Award. **Frequency:** annual. **Type:** recognition. **Recipient:** to an outstanding individual in the field of science and biochemical engineering ● BMES Graduate Student Awards. **Frequency:** 5/year. **Type:** monetary. **Recipient:** for graduate students who have done an outstanding biomedical engineering research and/or design project ● BMES Undergraduate Student Awards. **Frequency:** 5/year. **Type:** monetary. **Recipient:** for undergraduate students who have done an outstanding biomedical engineering research and/or design project ● Rita Schaffer Young Investigator Award. **Frequency:** annual. **Type:** monetary. **Recipient:** for young investigators. **Computer Services:** Mailing lists, $300 per thousand names. **Telecommunication Services:** electronic mail, barb.dunlavey@bmes.org. **Affiliated With:** American Institute for Medical and Biological Engineering. **Publications:** *Annals of Biomedical Engineering*, monthly. Journal. **Price:** $50.00 for members. ISSN: 0090-6964. **Circulation:** 5,000. **Advertising:** accepted. Alternate Formats: online. Also Cited As: *ABME* ● *BMES Bulletin*, quarterly. Newsletter. **Advertising:** accepted. Alternate Formats: online ● *BMES Membership Directory*, annual. Alternate Formats: online ● *Planning a Career in Biomedical Engineering*. Brochure. **Conventions/Meetings:** annual conference and meeting, 13 tracks, over 1000 papers (exhibits) - always fall. 2008 Oct. 1-4, St. Louis, MO; 2009 Oct. 7-10, Pittsburgh, PA.

6608 ■ IEEE Engineering in Medicine and Biology Society (EMBS)
445 Hoes Ln.
Piscataway, NJ 08855-1331
Ph: (732)981-3433
Fax: (732)465-6435
E-mail: l.wolf@ieee.org
URL: http://www.embs.org
Contact: Laura J. Wolf, Exec. Dir.
Founded: 1952. **Members:** 8,200. **Staff:** 3. **Budget:** $2,500,000. **Regional Groups:** 10. **Multinational. Description:** A society of the Institute of Electrical and Electronics Engineers. Concerned with concepts and methods of the physical and engineering sciences applied in biology and medicine, including formalized mathematical theory, experimental science, technological development, and practical clinical application. Disseminates information on current methods and technologies used in biomedical and clinical engineering. **Awards:** Best Chapter Award. **Type:** recognition. **Recipient:** for outstanding activities and services ● Career Award. **Frequency:** annual. **Type:** recognition. **Recipient:** for body of work and service to the community ● Early Career Award. **Type:** recognition. **Recipient:** for body of work and service to the community ● Outstanding Performance Award for Student Club or Chapter. **Type:** recognition. **Recipient:** for the best performing Student Club or chapter ● Service Award. **Type:** recognition. **Recipient:** for body of work and service to the community. **Publications:** *Engineering in Medicine and Biology*, bimonthly. Magazine. **Price:** included in membership dues. **Circulation:** 10,000. **Advertising:** accepted. Alternate Formats: online. Also Cited As: *EMB Magazine* ● *Transaction on Biomedical Engineering*, monthly. Journal ● *Transactions on Computational Biology and Bioinformatics*. Journal ● *Transactions on Information and Technology in Biomedicine*, quarterly. Journal. Alternate Formats: online ● *Transactions on Medical Imaging*, quarterly. Journal ● *Transactions on NanoBioscience*, quarterly. Journal ● *Transactions on Neural Systems and Rehabilitation Engineering*, quarterly. Journal. **Conventions/Meetings:** annual international conference (exhibits) - always fall. 2008 Aug. 21-24, Vancouver, BC, Canada; 2009 Sept. 3-6, Minneapolis, MN ● International Conference on Biomedical Robotics and Biomechatronics ● International Symposium on Biomedical Imaging ● Special Topic Conference on Cellular, Molecular and Tissue Engineering ● Special Topic Conference on Information Technology in Biomedicine ● Special Topic Conference on Microtechnologies in Medicine and Biology ● Special Topic Conference on Neural Engineering.

6609 ■ Society For Biomaterials (SFB)
15000 Commerce Pkwy., Ste.C
Mount Laurel, NJ 08054
Ph: (856)439-0826
Fax: (856)439-0525
E-mail: info@biomaterials.org
URL: http://www.biomaterials.org
Contact: Dan Lemyre CAE, Exec. Dir.
Founded: 1974. **Members:** 2,100. **Membership Dues:** active, associate in U.S., $250 (annual) ● student in U.S. (with journal), $210 (annual) ● student in Canada and outside North America (without journal), $30 (annual) ● active, associate in Canada, $265 (annual) ● student in Canada (with journal), $225 (annual) ● active, associate outside North America, $338 (annual) ● student outside North America (with journal), $298 (annual) ● retired/senior (with journal), $200 (annual). **Staff:** 15. **Description:** Bioengineers and materials scientists; dental, orthopedic, cardiac, and other surgeons and scientists interested in developing biomaterials as tissue replacements in patients; corporations interested in the research manufacture of biomaterials. Provides an interdisciplinary forum for research in biomaterials. Promotes research, development, and education in the biomaterials sciences. **Libraries: Type:** reference. **Holdings:** 62. **Subjects:** biomedical materials research, applied biomaterials. **Awards:** Clemson Award. **Frequency:** annual. **Type:** recognition. **Recipient:** for outstanding contributions to biomaterials science ● Student Award. **Frequency:** semiannual. **Type:** recognition. **Recipient:** for best publication submitted for review. **Computer Services:** Mailing lists, of members. **Telecommunication Services:** electronic mail, dlemyre@ahint.com. **Committees:** Awards, Ceremonies, and Nominations; Devices and Materials; Education and Professional Development; Liaison; Local Arrangements. **Publications:** *A Bibliography of Monographic Works on Biomaterial and Biocompatibility*. Alternate Formats: online ● *Biomaterials Forum*, periodic. Newsletter. Reports on developments in the science of biomaterials; includes society news. **Price:** free for members. **Advertising:** accepted. Alternate Formats: online. Also Cited As: *The Torch* ● *Journal of Applied Biomaterials*, quarterly. **Price:** included in membership dues. **Advertising:** accepted ● *Journal of Biomaterials Science, Polymer Edition*. Alternate Formats: online ● *Journal of Biomedical Materials Research*, monthly. **Price:** included in membership dues. **Advertising:** accepted. **Conventions/Meetings:** annual symposium and meeting (exhibits) - always spring ● periodic symposium.

6610 ■ Tissue Engineering Society International (TESI)
Address Unknown since 2008
URL: http://www.tesinternational.org
Membership Dues: full, $135 (annual) ● young investigator, $100 (annual) ● student, $25 (annual) ● full (in developing region), $50 (annual) ● joint, $145 (annual). **Multinational. Description:** Represents individuals engaged or interested in the field of tissue engineering. Promotes education and research within the field of tissue engineering. Serves as an international forum to promote the informed discussion of the challenges and therapeutic benefits of the application of tissue engineering technologies. **Telecommunication Services:** electronic mail, dss@biocounsel.net. **Publications:** *interlink*, semiannual. Newsletter ● *Tissue Engineering*, bimonthly. Journal. **Price:** $77.00 in U.S. and Canada (print only); $115.00 international (print only); $90.00 in U.S. and Canada (print and online); $129.00 international (print and online). Alternate Formats: online. **Conventions/Meetings:** annual conference.

6611 ■ World Association for Chinese Biomedical Engineers (WACBE)
c/o Savio L-Y. Woo, PhD, Chm.
Univ. of Pittsburgh
Musculoskeletal Res. Ctr.
405 Center for Bioengineering
300 Tech. Dr.
Pittsburgh, PA 15219
Ph: (412)427-2000
Fax: (412)427-2001
E-mail: ddecenzo@pitt.edu
URL: http://www.pitt.edu/~zmli/wacbe
Contact: Savio L-Y. Woo PhD, Chm.
Founded: 2004. **Membership Dues:** student, $10 (annual) ● regular, $50 (annual) ● life, $500. **Multinational. Description:** Networks the worldwide Chinese professionals and students in the field of biomedical engineering. Promotes basic and translational research in the field. Encourages students to become biomedical engineers. Facilitates the professional and career development of members. Promotes cooperation among and between industrialists and academics. **Publications:** Journal. **Conventions/Meetings:** biennial congress.

Biophysics

6612 ■ Biophysical Society (BPS)
9650 Rockville Pike
Bethesda, MD 20814
Ph: (301)634-7114
Fax: (301)634-7133
E-mail: society@biophysics.org
URL: http://www.biophysics.org
Contact: Rosalba Kampman, Exec. Off.
Founded: 1957. **Members:** 7,000. **Membership Dues:** regular, $160 (annual) ● student, $25 (annual) ● early career, $55 (annual) ● regular (special international), $50 (annual) ● student (special international), $10 (annual) ● corporate platinum, $6,000 (annual) ● corporate gold, $4,000 (annual) ● corporate silver, $2,000 (annual). **Staff:** 13. **Budget:** $2,900,000. **Description:** Biophysicists, physical biochemists, and physical and biological scientists interested in the application of physical laws and techniques to the analysis of biological or living phenomena. Maintains placement service. **Awards:** Avanti Awards in Lipids. **Frequency:** annual. **Type:** recognition. **Recipient:** for an investigator who has made outstanding contributions in understanding Lipid Biophysics ● Distinguished Service Award. **Frequency:** annual. **Type:** recognition. **Recipient:** for contributions beyond achievements in research ● Emily M. Gray Award. **Frequency:** annual. **Type:** recognition. **Recipient:** for significant contributions to education in Biophysics ● Fellows of the Biophysical Society. **Frequency:** annual. **Type:** fellowship. **Recipient:** for members who have demonstrated excellence in science and to the expansion of Biophysics ● Founders Awards. **Frequency:** annual. **Type:** recognition. **Recipient:** for an outstanding achievement in any area of Biophysics ● Margaret Oakley Dayhoff Award. **Frequency:** annual. **Type:** recognition. **Recipient:** for the outstanding woman who has not yet reached a position of high recognition within the Academic society ● Michael and Kate Barany Award for Young Investigators. **Frequency:** annual. **Type:** recognition. **Recipient:** for an outstanding contribution to Biophysics ● U.S. Genomics Award. **Frequency:** annual. **Type:** recognition. **Recipient:** for an outstanding investigator in the field of Single Molecule Biology. **Computer Services:** Mailing lists,

of members. **Telecommunication Services:** electronic mail, rkampman@biophysics.org. **Committees:** Education; International Relations; Minority Affairs; Professional Opportunities for Women; Public Affairs; Publications. **Subgroups:** Bioenergetics; Biological Fluorescence; Exocytosis and Endocytosis; Membrane Biophysics; Membrane Structure and Assembly; Molecular Biophysics; Motility. **Absorbed:** (1958) National Biographysics Conference. **Publications:** *Annual Meeting Abstracts*, annual. Journal. **Price:** $70.00 print version. ISSN: 0006-3495. **Circulation:** 7,000. **Advertising:** accepted. Alternate Formats: CD-ROM. Also Cited As: *Biophysical Journal Supplement* ● *Biophysical Journal*, monthly. **Price:** $98.00 /year for members in U.S. (print version); $1,116.00 /year for institutions in U.S. (print version); free online; $178.00 in Canada (print version). ISSN: 0006-3495. **Circulation:** 7,000. **Advertising:** accepted. Alternate Formats: online ● *Biophysical Society—Directory*, annual. Includes geographic listing and buyer's guide. **Price:** available to members only. **Advertising:** accepted. Alternate Formats: online ● *Careers in Biophysics*. Brochure. Alternate Formats: online ● Newsletter, bimonthly. Includes society information and announcements, grant opportunities, and articles of interest. **Price:** included in membership dues. **Advertising:** accepted. Alternate Formats: online. **Conventions/Meetings:** annual meeting (exhibits) - 2009 Mar. 7-11, Fort Lauderdale, FL; 2010 Feb. 20-24, San Francisco, CA; 2011 Feb. 5-9, Baltimore, MD.

6613 ■ Society for Free Radical Biology and Medicine (SFRBM)
8365 Keystone Crossing, Ste.107
Indianapolis, IN 46240
Ph: (317)205-9482
Fax: (317)205-9481
E-mail: info@sfrbm.org
URL: http://www.sfrbm.org
Contact: Kent Lindeman CMP, Exec. Dir.

Founded: 1987. **Members:** 1,400. **Membership Dues:** active, $125 (annual) ● student, $20 (annual) ● postdoctoral fellow, $85 (annual). **Staff:** 5. **Budget:** $500,000. **Multinational. Description:** Scientists and physicians with an interest in the "chemistry, biology, and pathology of oxygen and its metabolites, related free radicals, and other activated or reactive species, and antioxidants." Works to advance understanding of oxygen and free radicals. Serves as a forum for exchange of information among members. Sponsors research programs. **Awards:** Young Investigator Award. **Frequency:** annual. **Type:** monetary. **Recipient:** for outstanding poster symposia display or oral presentation at annual meeting. **Affiliated With:** Society for Free Radical Biology and Medicine. **Formerly:** (2003) Oxygen Society. **Publications:** *Free Radical Biology and Medicine*, semimonthly. Journal. **Price:** $70.00 for members; $495.00 for nonmembers. **Advertising:** accepted. Alternate Formats: online. **Conventions/Meetings:** annual meeting and lecture, with oral abstract presentations, poster symposium (exhibits) - 2008 Nov. 19-23, Indianapolis, IN; 2009 Nov. 18-22, San Francisco, CA.

Biotechnology

6614 ■ Council for Biotechnology Information (CBI)
1225 Eye St. NW, Ste.400
Washington, DC 20005
Ph: (202)962-9200
E-mail: cbi@whybiotech.com
URL: http://www.whybiotech.com
Contact: Sean Darragh, Exec. Dir.

Founded: 2000. **Languages:** English, French, Spanish. **Multinational. Description:** Communicates science-based information about the benefits and safety of agricultural and food biotechnology. Raises consumer awareness on all aspects of plant biotechnology. Promotes the vital role of plant biotechnology in helping provide the world with more and better food while protecting the environment. **Publications:** *Good Ideas Are Growing*. Brochure. Addresses the benefits that biotechnology provides to consumers, farmers, and people in developing countries. Alternate Formats: online ● *Look Closer at Biotechnology*. Book. Contains short lessons, word puzzles, games and quizzes to help children learn more about biotechnology. Alternate Formats: online ● Papers. Provides science-based discussions on various issues related to biotech crops and foods. Alternate Formats: online.

6615 ■ Genetic Engineering Action Network (GEAN)
c/o Stephanie Weisenbach, Natl. Coor.
PO Box 194
Mechanicsville, IA 52306
Ph: (563)432-6735
E-mail: info@geaction.org
URL: http://www.geaction.org
Contact: Stephanie Weisenbach, Natl. Coor.

Description: Represents activists, non-governmental organizations, farmers and farm advocacy groups, academics and scientists who have come together to work on the many issues surrounding biotechnology. Seeks to support and further the work of those organizations and individuals working to address the risks to the environment, biodiversity, human health and the socioeconomic and ethical consequences of genetic engineering. **Telecommunication Services:** electronic mail, stephanie@geaction.org. **Affiliated With:** 20/20 Vision National Project; Campaign to Label Genetically Engineered Foods; Center for Food Safety; Citizens for Health; Clean Water Action; Council for Responsible Genetics; Farm Aid; Friends of the Earth; Greenpeace U.S.A.; Institute for Agriculture and Trade Policy; Institute for Food and Development Policy; International Society for Ecology and Culture; National Family Farm Coalition; Organic Consumers Association; Pesticide Action Network North America Regional Center; Rural Advancement Foundation International - USA; Sierra Club; Student Environmental Action Coalition.

6616 ■ International Society of Lyophilization - Freeze Drying (ISL-FD)
112A Bala Ave.
Bala Cynwyd, PA 19004
Ph: (610)660-9665 (610)660-9623
Fax: (610)660-9643
E-mail: jennings@phase-technologies.com
URL: http://www.islyophilization.org
Contact: Thomas A. Jennings PhD, Pres.

Founded: 2001. **Multinational. Description:** Promotes and advances the science and technology of lyophilization or freeze drying. Utilizes the Internet and other support programs that provide financial or material assistance to those who need it. Encourages fellowship and understanding throughout the International Community.

6617 ■ Surfaces in Biomaterials Foundation
1000 Westgate Dr., Ste.252
St. Paul, MN 55114
Ph: (651)290-6267 (651)290-6295
Fax: (651)290-2266
E-mail: surfacesinbiomaterials@ewald.com
URL: http://www.surfaces.org
Contact: Bill Monn, Exec. Dir.

Founded: 1990. **Members:** 100. **Membership Dues:** individual, $50 (annual) ● academic, $625 (annual) ● supporting, $2,500 (annual). **Description:** Strives to explore creative solutions to technical challenges at BioInterface by fostering education and multidisciplinary cooperation among industrial, academic, clinical, and regulatory communities. **Awards:** Excellence in Surface Award. **Frequency:** annual. **Type:** recognition. **Recipient:** for significant contributions to the field of surface science ● Student Excellence Award. **Frequency:** annual. **Type:** recognition. **Recipient:** for graduate/undergraduate student. **Publications:** *SurFacts*, 3/year. Newsletter. **Price:** included in membership dues. **Advertising:** accepted. Alternate Formats: online. **Conventions/Meetings:** annual Biointerface - workshop and symposium (exhibits) - 2008 Oct. 27-29, Minneapolis, MN.

6618 ■ Women in Bio (WIB)
PO Box 34043
Bethesda, MD 20827
Ph: (703)819-7647
E-mail: womeninbio@comcast.net
URL: http://www.womeninbio.org
Contact: Robbie Melton, Pres./Dir.

Founded: 2001. **Membership Dues:** individual, $35-$100 ● corporate, $250. **Description:** Aims to unite female entrepreneurs and executives in developing successful businesses in biotechnology and the life sciences. Serves the life sciences industry, with a shared interest in science and entrepreneurship. Fosters female participation in entrepreneurship and professional development in biotechnology and the life sciences.

Botany

6619 ■ American Bamboo Society (ABS)
315 S Coast Hwy. 101, Ste.U
PMB 212
Encinitas, CA 92024-3555
E-mail: membership@americanbamboo.org
URL: http://www.americanbamboo.org
Contact: David King, Sec.

Founded: 1979. **Members:** 1,450. **Membership Dues:** individual, $40 (annual) ● life, $600 ● patron, $120 (annual) ● supporting, $60 (annual). **Budget:** $45,000. **Regional Groups:** 12. **Multinational. Description:** Individuals interested in the bamboo plant. Aims to provide an information source on the culture, identification, propagation, use, and appreciation of bamboo; disseminate and store information; promote the use of desirable species; preserve and increase the number of bamboo species in the U.S; plant and maintain a bamboo garden for aesthetic purposes. Local chapters develop stocks of plants for distribution to botanical gardens and to the public, maintain bamboo quarantine greenhouses in California, Florida, Massachusetts, and Washington State in order to import selected species from foreign sources; hold plant sales. Provides plant material for research in taxonomy, propagation, and culture of as many species as possible. Services include: seed dispersal, and propagation trials. Compiles statistics. **Libraries: Type:** reference; not open to the public. **Awards: Frequency:** annual. **Type:** grant. **Recipient:** for research on bamboo and for bamboo art and crafts. **Telecommunication Services:** electronic mail, secretary@americanbamboo.org. **Publications:** *Bamboo Science and Culture: The Journal of the American Bamboo Society*, annual. Includes information on bamboo botany, culture, and uses. Also includes conference proceedings. **Price:** included in membership dues; $20.00 /year for nonmembers and institutions. ISSN: 0197-3789. **Circulation:** 1,400 ● *Bamboo Species Source List*, annual. Includes description of bamboo species currently available and their commercial suppliers. **Price:** included in membership dues; $3.00 each, for nonmembers. **Circulation:** 1,400. **Advertising:** accepted ● *Bamboo: The Magazine of the American Bamboo Society*, bimonthly, even numbered months. **Conventions/Meetings:** annual lecture and meeting, national; vendor displays and plants, with festival and auction (exhibits) - usually October ● periodic tour.

6620 ■ American Botanical Council (ABC)
PO Box 144345
Austin, TX 78714-4345
Ph: (512)926-4900
Free: (800)373-7105
Fax: (512)926-2345
E-mail: abc@herbalgram.org
URL: http://www.herbalgram.org
Contact: Neil Blomquist, Founder/Pres.

Founded: 1988. **Members:** 3,800. **Membership Dues:** individual in U.S., $50 (annual) ● individual outside U.S., $70 (annual) ● academic in U.S., $100 (annual) ● academic outside U.S., $120 (annual) ● professional in U.S., $150 (annual) ● professional outside U.S., $170 (annual) ● organization in U.S., $250 (annual) ● corporate, $500 (annual) ● basic sponsor, $1,200 (annual). **Staff:** 17. **Budget:** $1,500,000. **Description:** Seeks to gather and disseminate information on herbs, medicinal plants, and herbal research; increases public awareness and professional knowledge of the historical role and current potential of plants in medicine; promotes understanding regarding the importance of preserving native plant populations in temperate and tropical zones. Conducts educational and public outreach programs. Operates speakers' bureau. **Publications:** *The ABC Clinical Guide to Herbs*. Book. **Price:** $69.95/copy ● *The Complete German Commission E Monographs - Therapeutic Guide to Herbal Medicines*. **Price:** $89.00/copy ● *Herbal Medicine Expanded E Commission Monographs*. **Price:** $39.95/copy. Alternate Formats: CD-ROM; online ● *HerbalGram*, quarterly. Journal. Contains legal and media coverage updates. Includes book reviews, calendar of events, networking information, and conference and special report. **Price:** included in membership dues. ISSN: 0899-5648. **Circulation:** 28,000. **Advertising:** accepted.

6621 ■ American Bryological and Lichenological Society (ABLS)

Dept. of Biology
Univ. of Nebraska
Omaha, NE 68182-0040
Ph: (402)554-2491
Fax: (402)554-3532
E-mail: regan@mail.unomaha.edu
URL: http://mywebspace.wisc.edu/jpbennet/web/abls
Contact: Robert Egan, Sec.-Treas.

Founded: 1898. **Members:** 800. **Membership Dues:** regular, $20 (annual). **Multinational. Description:** Professional biologists, amateur biologists, biology teachers and hobbyists interested in the study of mosses, liverworts, and lichens. Maintains moss, lichen, and hepatic exchange clubs. **Affiliated With:** American Institute of Biological Sciences; Botanical Society of America. **Formerly:** (1949) Sullivant Moss Society; (1968) American Bryological Society. **Publications:** *Bryologist*, quarterly. Journal. Includes member news and current literature. **Price:** $70.00/year. ISSN: 0007-2745 ● *Evansia*, quarterly. Journal. **Price:** $15.00/year; $5.00 for members; $15.00 for libraries. **Conventions/Meetings:** annual meeting (exhibits).

6622 ■ The American Chestnut Foundation (TACF)

PO Box 4044
469 Main St., Ste.1
Bennington, VT 05201-4044
Ph: (802)447-0110
Fax: (802)442-6855
E-mail: chestnut@acf.org
URL: http://www.acf.org
Contact: Marshal T. Case, Pres./CEO

Founded: 1983. **Members:** 5,800. **Membership Dues:** regular, $40-$99 (annual) ● student, $15 (annual) ● chestnut leaf, $5,000 (annual) ● gold leaf, $1,000-$4,999 (annual) ● silver leaf, $500-$999 (annual) ● bronze leaf, $250-$499 (annual) ● green leaf, $100-$249 (annual). **Staff:** 10. **Budget:** $1,000,000. **State Groups:** 8. **Description:** Individuals involved in disciplines including genetics, plant breeding, plant pathology, forestry, and horticulture. Preserves and restores the American chestnut tree, a hardwood that was nearly destroyed during the early 1900s by a fungus blight in the U.S. which originated in the Orient. Funds a scientific breeding program and related research; organizes fundraising activities. Coordinates and seeks to stimulate related research and other efforts among members; provides scientific steering and review. Sponsors projects in areas such as in vitro propagation techniques, the collecting of American chestnut and resistant germ plasm, and the assembling of critical genetic stocks. Maintains research in Virginia where it is actively engaged in backcross breeding to produce blight resistant American chestnut trees. Cooperators include state chapters. **Awards: Type:** grant. **Recipient:** for scientists involved in other aspects of chestnut biology. **Programs:** Charlie Chestnut Environmental Education. **Projects:** American Chestnut Mined Land Reclamation. **Publications:** *Bark*, quarterly. Newsletter. Includes calendar of events. **Price:** included in membership dues. Alternate Formats: online ● *Growing Chestnut Trees - A Handbook* ● *Journal of The American Chestnut Foundation*, semiannual. Contains the latest information on chestnut research. **Price:** included in membership dues. Alternate Formats: online ● Annual Report. Alternate Formats: online. **Conventions/Meetings:** annual conference - in mid-October.

6623 ■ American Fern Society (AFS)

c/o Dr. George Yatskievych, Membership Sec.
PO Box 299
St. Louis, MO 63166-0299
Ph: (314)577-9522
E-mail: george.yatskievych@mobot.org
URL: http://amerfernsoc.org
Contact: Dr. George Yatskievych, Membership Sec.

Founded: 1893. **Members:** 1,000. **Membership Dues:** regular in North America, $12 (annual) ● journal in North America, $25 (annual) ● regular outside North America, $19 (annual) ● journal outside North America, $32 (annual). **Description:** Promotes the study of ferns and their allies by persons interested in the biology, taxonomy, and horticulture of ferns, club mosses, and horsetails. Sponsors spore exchange program. **Publications:** *American Fern Journal*, quarterly. **Price:** $35.00/year (USA/Canada/Mexico); $45.00/year foreign. ISSN: 0002-8444. **Circulation:** 1,000 ● *Fiddlehead Forum*, 5/year. Newsletter. Provides scientific and practical information on ferns, along with ephemeral material. Includes book reviews. **Price:** included with membership subscription to journal. **Circulation:** 1,150 ● *Pteridologia*, periodic. Monograph series. **Circulation:** 250. **Conventions/Meetings:** annual conference, held in conjunction with Botanical Society of America - early August.

6624 ■ American Herb Association (AHA)

PO Box 1673
Nevada City, CA 95959
Ph: (530)265-9552
URL: http://www.ahaherb.com
Contact: Kathi Keville, Dir./Ed.

Founded: 1981. **Members:** 1,000. **Membership Dues:** regular, $20 (annual) ● supporting, $35 (annual) ● foreign, $28 (annual) ● regular, in Canada and Mexico, $24 (annual). **Staff:** 5. **Description:** Enthusiasts and specialists of medicinal herbs and herbal products. Seeks to increase knowledge and provide up-to-date scientific and experiential information on herbs. Offers a network to exchange data and resources among members nationwide. Maintains herb garden. **Libraries: Type:** reference; not open to the public. **Holdings:** 1,000. **Subjects:** herb gardening, botany, botanical art, medicinal herbs. **Publications:** *Directory of Mail-Order Medicinal Herb Products*. **Price:** $4.00 for nonmembers; $3.50 for members ● *Herb Schools and Correspondence Courses*, semiannual. **Price:** $3.50 ● Newsletter, quarterly. Covers current information on botanical medicine including folklore, ethnobotany, scientific studies, and legal and political issues. **Price:** $4.00/sample copy. **Circulation:** 1,000. **Advertising:** accepted ● Also publishes list of recommended herb books.

6625 ■ American Orchid Society (AOS)

16700 AOS Ln.
Delray Beach, FL 33446-4351
Ph: (561)404-2000 (561)404-2010
Fax: (561)404-2100
E-mail: theaos@aos.org
URL: http://orchidweb.org/aos/orchids/page01.aspx
Contact: James Jordan, CEO

Founded: 1921. **Members:** 27,000. **Membership Dues:** single in U.S., $60 (annual) ● joint in U.S., $75 (annual) ● single outside U.S., $72 (annual) ● joint outside U.S., $87 (annual) ● student, $35 (annual). **Staff:** 20. **Budget:** $3,200,000. **National Groups:** 550. **Multinational. Description:** Represents hobbyists, professional growers, botanists, and others interested in extending the knowledge, production, perpetuation, use, and appreciation of orchids. Oversees competitions. Operates speakers' bureau. Sponsors charitable programs. Funds research and conservation grants. **Libraries: Type:** reference. **Holdings:** 3,000; biographical archives, books, periodicals. **Subjects:** orchids. **Computer Services:** Mailing lists. **Committees:** Affiliated Societies; Awards/Judging; Conservation; Education; Finance; Library/Archives; Publications; Research; Technology. **Publications:** *Awards Quarterly*. Journal. Includes photos and descriptions of orchids granted awards at shows. **Price:** $45.00 /year for members in U.S.; $65.00 /year for nonmembers in U.S.; $50.00 /year for members outside U.S.; $70.00 /year for nonmembers outside U.S. ISSN: 0747-3109. **Circulation:** 4,000 ● *Orchids - The Magazine of the American Orchid Society*, monthly. **Price:** $47.00 /year for members in U.S.; $56.00 /year for nonmembers in U.S.; $84.00 /year for members outside U.S.; $68.00 /year for nonmembers outside U.S. ● Publishes various handbooks. **Conventions/Meetings:** semiannual conference (exhibits) - always spring and fall ● triennial World Orchid Conference.

6626 ■ American Phytopathological Society (APS)

3340 Pilot Knob Rd.
St. Paul, MN 55121
Ph: (651)454-7250
Fax: (651)454-0766
E-mail: aps@scisoc.org
URL: http://www.apsnet.org
Contact: Steven C. Nelson, Exec. VP

Founded: 1908. **Members:** 5,000. **Membership Dues:** regular, $72 (annual) ● post-doctoral, $50 (annual) ● student, $26 (annual). **Staff:** 65. **Budget:** $2,250,000. **Regional Groups:** 6. **Description:** Represents the interests of professional educators, researchers, and individuals interested in the study and management of plant diseases. Maintains 46 committees. **Telecommunication Services:** electronic mail, snelson@scisoc.org. **Publications:** *Molecular Plant-Microbe Interactions*, monthly. Journal. Highlights the genetic, biochemical, and biophysical mechanisms of interactions of plants with viroids, viruses, procaryotes, and fungi. **Price:** $387.00 library in U.S.; $448.00 library outside U.S.; $79.00 for members in U.S.; $94.00 for members in Canada ($107 elsewhere, $57 online version). ISSN: 0894-0282. **Advertising:** accepted. Alternate Formats: online ● *Phytopathology*, monthly. Journal. Includes abstracts of annual meeting; international journal of plant pathology. **Price:** $88.00 for members in Canada; $95 elsewhere; $355.00 library in U.S.; $416.00 library outside U.S.; $73.00 for members in U.S. ISSN: 0031-949X ● *Phytopathology News*, monthly. Newsletter. Reports on current research in the field of plant diseases and their control; includes society news, book reviews, and calendar of events. **Price:** included in membership dues; $20.00 /year for nonmembers in U.S. ISSN: 0278-0267 ● *Plant Disease: An International Journal of Applied Plant Pathology*, monthly. Features articles that focus on the practical aspects of maintaining and improving plant health. Includes disease note and research articles. **Price:** $355.00 in U.S.; $416.00 outside U.S.; $73.00 member, in U.S.; $88.00 member, in Canada; $95 elsewhere. ISSN: 0191-2917. **Advertising:** accepted ● Films ● Also publishes series of disease compendia, slides, and illustrations. **Conventions/Meetings:** annual meeting (exhibits).

6627 ■ American Society for Horticultural Science (ASHS)

113 SW St., Ste.200
Alexandria, VA 22314-2851
Ph: (703)836-4606
Fax: (703)836-2024
E-mail: ashs@ashs.org
URL: http://www.ashs.org
Contact: Michael W. Neff, Exec. Dir.

Founded: 1903. **Members:** 4,000. **Membership Dues:** postdoctoral, $60 (annual) ● active, $105 (annual) ● emeritus, $55 (annual) ● graduate student, $40 (annual) ● undergraduate student, $25 (annual) ● corporate, $300 (annual) ● international college affiliate, $20 (annual). **Staff:** 12. **Budget:** $2,000,000.

Regional Groups: 3. **Description:** Promotes and encourages scientific research and education in horticulture throughout the world. Members represent all areas of horticulture science. **Awards:** Fellows Award. **Frequency:** annual. **Type:** fellowship. **Recipient:** for members ● Outstanding Extension Educator. **Frequency:** annual. **Type:** recognition. **Recipient:** for an educator who has made an outstanding contribution to horticultural science ● Outstanding Industry Scientist. **Frequency:** annual. **Type:** recognition. **Recipient:** for a horticultural crops scientist ● Outstanding International Horticulturist. **Frequency:** annual. **Type:** recognition. **Recipient:** for an international horticulturist who has made an outstanding contribution to international horticultural science ● Outstanding Researcher. **Frequency:** annual. **Type:** recognition. **Recipient:** for a horticultural crops scientist ● Outstanding Undergraduate Educator. **Frequency:** annual. **Type:** recognition. **Recipient:** for an educator who has had a distinguished undergraduate education teaching career in horticultural science. **Telecommunication Services:** electronic mail, mwneff@ashs.org. **Committees:** Career Award Selection; Nominations and Elections; Publication Award Screening. **Divisions:** Education; Extension; Industry; International; Research. **Publications:** *ASHS Newsletter*, monthly. Covers society activities, horticultural science, and news of people in the field. **Price:** included in membership dues. ISSN: 0882-8024. **Advertising:** accepted ● *Hort Technology*, quarterly. Journal. Provides science-based information to professional horticulturists, practitioners and educators. **Price:** $25.00 /year for members, paper only; $120.00 /year for institutions in U.S., Canada, and Mexico; $40.00 /year for members, full subscription; $30.00 /year for members, on-line access and CD archive. ISSN: 1063-0198. **Circulation:** 5,000. **Advertising:** accepted. Alternate Formats: online ● *HortScience*, bimonthly. Journal. Covers scientific and industry developments and significant research education and changes that affect the profession. **Price:** $55.00 /year for members, paper only; $70.00 /year for members, full subscription; $400.00 /year for institutions in U.S., Canada, and Mexico; $450.00 /year for institutions outside U.S., Canada, and Mexico. ISSN: 0018-5345. **Circulation:** 6,500. Alternate Formats: microform ● *Journal of the American Society for Horticultural Science*, bimonthly. Covers the results of original and completed basic or fundamental research. Includes annual and 5 year cumulative indexes. **Price:** $55.00 /year for members, paper only; $70.00 /year for members, full subscription; $400.00 /year for institutions in U.S., Canada, and Mexico; $450.00 /year for institutions outside U.S., Canada, and Mexico. ISSN: 0003-1062. **Circulation:** 5,500. Alternate Formats: microform ● Proceedings ● Membership Directory. **Price:** included in membership dues. Alternate Formats: online. **Conventions/Meetings:** annual meeting and conference (exhibits) - 2008 July 21-24, Orlando, FL; 2009 July 25-28, St. Louis, MO ● annual regional meeting (exhibits).

6628 ■ American Society of Plant Biologists (ASPB)

15501 Monona Dr.
Rockville, MD 20855-2768
Ph: (301)251-0560
Fax: (301)279-2996
E-mail: info@aspb.org
URL: http://www.aspb.org
Contact: Dr. Crispin Taylor, Exec. Dir.

Founded: 1924. **Members:** 6,000. **Membership Dues:** regular, $115 (annual) ● student, $45 (annual) ● post doctorate, $65 (annual). **Staff:** 22. **Budget:** $5,985,000. **Regional Groups:** 5. **Description:** Professional society of plant biologists, plant biochemists, and other plant scientists engaged in research and teaching. Offers placement service for members; conducts educational and public affairs programs. **Awards:** **Frequency:** annual. **Type:** recognition. **Recipient:** for outstanding research in plant physiology ● **Frequency:** biennial. **Type:** recognition. **Recipient:** for outstanding research in plant physiology. **Computer Services:** Mailing lists, of members. **Telecommunication Services:** electronic mail, ctaylor@aspb.org. **Committees:** Education; Education Foundation; International; Membership; Minority Affairs; Nominating; Program; Public Affairs; Publications; Women in Plant Biology. **Formerly:** (2001) American Society of Plant Physiologists. **Publications:** *ASPB Newsletter*, bimonthly. Covers current events of interest to plant physiologists and those in related disciplines. Includes calendar of events and regional section news. **Price:** included in membership dues; $30.00 /year for nonmembers. ISSN: 0279-9936. **Circulation:** 6,000. **Advertising:** accepted ● *Biochemistry and Molecular Biology of Plants*. Book ● *Final Program and Abstract Supplement*, annual. Contains abstracts of presentations to be made at the annual meeting. Includes author index. **Price:** included with meeting registration; $10.00/copy for nonsubscribers. ISSN: 0032-0889. **Circulation:** 2,000. **Advertising:** accepted ● *The Plant Cell*, monthly. Journal. Covers plant cellular, molecular, and developmental biology. Includes papers, reviews on important research areas, and commentary. **Price:** $160.00 for members; $110.00 for student/postdoctoral. **Circulation:** 4,500. **Advertising:** accepted ● *Plant Physiology*, monthly. Journal. Contains scientific papers, communications, and reviews on the physiology, molecular biology, environmental biology, biochemistry, and cell biology. **Price:** $185.00 for members; $135.00 for student/postdoctoral. ISSN: 0032-0889. **Circulation:** 5,300. **Advertising:** accepted. Alternate Formats: online ● Membership Directory, annual. **Advertising:** accepted ● Also publishes workshop summaries and vocational guidance bulletin. **Conventions/Meetings:** annual Plant Biology - meeting (exhibits) - 2008 June 27-July 2, Merida, YU, Mexico; 2009 July 18-22, Honolulu, HI.

6629 ■ American Society of Plant Taxonomists (ASPT)

Dept. of Botany 3165
Univ. of Wyoming
1000 E Univ. Ave.
Laramie, WY 82071
Ph: (307)766-2556 (307)766-2380
Fax: (307)766-2851
E-mail: aspt@uwyo.edu
Contact: Linda Brown, Business Office Mgr.

Founded: 1937. **Members:** 1,300. **Membership Dues:** regular, $53 (annual) ● student, $20 (annual). **Staff:** 1. **Budget:** $163,000. **Multinational. Description:** Promotes education and research in the field of plant taxonomy (classification of plants), including taxonomy and herbaria. **Awards:** Asa Gray Award. **Frequency:** annual. **Type:** recognition. **Recipient:** to outstanding scientists for their contributions to systematics research ● Cooley Award. **Frequency:** annual. **Type:** recognition. **Recipient:** for the best paper presented at the annual meeting by a person who is either a current graduate student or who has received a PhD within the previous 10 years ● Graduate Student Research Grants. **Frequency:** annual. **Type:** grant. **Recipient:** to students conducting fieldwork, herbarium travel, and/or laboratory research in any area of plant systematics ● Grady L. Webster Plant Systematics Publication Award. **Frequency:** annual. **Type:** recognition. **Recipient:** for the best published paper in systematic botany monographs ● Peter H. Raven Scientific Outreach Award. **Frequency:** annual. **Type:** recognition. **Recipient:** to a plant systematist for exceptional outreach activities that advance the public's understanding of plant systematic work and its value to society. **Computer Services:** Electronic publishing, beginning with Systematic Botany, volume 29 ● mailing lists, of members. **Affiliated With:** Botanical Society of America. **Publications:** *ASPT Newsletter*, semiannual. **Price:** for members only, by request. Alternate Formats: online ● *Systematic Botany*, quarterly. Journal. Covers research. **Circulation:** 1,800. Alternate Formats: online ● *Systematic Botany Monographs*, periodic. **Price:** available to nonmembers; price varies. **Circulation:** 250 ● Membership Directory, biennial. **Price:** included in membership dues. **Circulation:** 750. Alternate Formats: online. **Conventions/Meetings:** annual conference, held in conjunction with Botanical Society of America, with business meeting and papers presented (exhibits) - usually early August.

6630 ■ Aquatic Plant Management Society (APMS)

PO Box 821265
Vicksburg, MS 39182-1265
Ph: (601)634-2656
Fax: (601)634-2430
E-mail: linda.s.nelson@erdc.usace.army.mil
URL: http://www.apms.org
Contact: Dr. Linda Nelson, Sec.

Founded: 1961. **Members:** 330. **Membership Dues:** individual, $50 (annual) ● student, $20 (annual) ● sustaining, $500 (annual). **Regional Groups:** 7. **Description:** Scientists, engineers, water district managers, university and private industry personnel, and interested citizens dedicated to designing methods and operations for controlling the spread of aquatic plants that interrupt navigation and recreation in waterways. Conducts education and training to promote the management of aquatic plants including water hyacinth, hydrilla, Eurasian watermilfoil, and other nuisance, exotic aquatic plant species. Offers scholarships. **Affiliated With:** Council for Agricultural Science and Technology; Responsible Industry for a Sound Environment; Weed Science Society of America. **Formerly:** (1976) Hyacinth Control Society. **Publications:** *Aquatic Plant News*, 3/year. Newsletter. Includes calendar of events and book reviews. **Price:** included in membership dues. **Circulation:** 500 ● *Journal of Aquatic Plant Management*, semiannual. **Price:** included in membership dues. ISSN: 0146-6623. **Circulation:** 500. **Conventions/Meetings:** annual meeting (exhibits) - always July.

6631 ■ Arizona Cactus and Succulent Research (ACSR)

Address Unknown since 2008
URL: http://www.arizonacactus.com

Founded: 1981. **Members:** 590. **Membership Dues:** individual, $15 (annual) ● family, $25 (annual) ● outside U.S., $30 (annual) ● sustaining, $100 (annual) ● patron, $500 (annual) ● benefactor, $1,000 (annual). **Staff:** 3. **Budget:** $30,000. **Languages:** Spanish. **Multinational. Description:** Conducts research and disseminates information on the use of arid-land plants for landscaping. Operates and conducts tours of a botanical garden containing samples of over 800 varieties of high desert plant life; offers slide presentation, classes, and lectures; maintains speakers' bureau; sponsors seminars, field trips, exhibitions, and research and charitable programs. **Libraries: Type:** reference. **Holdings:** 2,200; archival material, books, clippings, monographs, photographs, reports. **Subjects:** cacti and succulents, deserts, ethnobotany, plants, animals. **Awards:** Arizona Clean and Beautiful Award. **Type:** recognition ● Governors Award for Recycling. **Type:** recognition. **Computer Services:** database ● mailing lists ● online services. **Also Known As:** Arizona Cactus. **Publications:** *Arizona Cactus News*, monthly. Newsletter. **Price:** $15.00/year. **Circulation:** 650 ● *Desert in Bloom* ● *Index of Cactus Illustrations*. Book ● *On the Desert*. Book. Includes essays of the American deserts. ● *On the Desert Vol. 2*. Book. Features Essays. **Conventions/Meetings:** annual Labor Day Fiesta - festival.

6632 ■ Botanical Society of America (BSA)

PO Box 299
St. Louis, MO 63166
Ph: (314)577-9566
Fax: (314)577-9515
E-mail: bsa-manager@botany.org
URL: http://www.botany.org
Contact: William Dahl, Exec. Dir.

Founded: 1906. **Members:** 2,800. **Membership Dues:** student, $30 (annual) ● professional, $50 (annual) ● life, $2,000 ● affiliated professional, $35 (annual) ● K-12 classroom teacher, associate, $10 (annual) ● amateur botanist, $20 (annual). **Budget:** $100,000. **Regional Groups:** 4. **Description:** Professional society of botanists and others interested in plant science. Conducts special research programs. **Awards:** Charles E. Bessey Award. **Frequency:** annual. **Type:** recognition. **Recipient:** for excellence in leadership in botanical education ● Darbaker Prize. **Frequency:** annual. **Type:** recognition. **Recipient:** for meritorious work in the study of microscopical algae ● Merit Award. **Frequency:** annual. **Type:** recognition. **Recipient:** for outstanding contributions to botanical science ● Samuel Noel Postlethwait Award. **Frequency:** annual. **Type:** recognition. **Recipient:** for exceptional teaching and service on behalf of the BSA. **Computer Services:** Mailing lists, of members. **Telecommunication Services:** electronic mail, wdahl@botany.org. **Committees:** Conservation; Education. **Sections:** Bryological and Lichenological; Developmental and Structural; Ecological; Economic Botany; Genetics; Historical; Mycological; Paleobotanical; Phycological; Physiological; Phytochemical; Pteridological; Systematics; Teaching; Tropical Biology. **Formed by Merger of:** Botanical Society; Society for Plant Morphology and Physiology; American Mycological Society. **Publications:** *American Journal of Botany*, monthly. Contains scientific articles on botany. **Price:** $510.00 /year for institutions (other countries); $470.00 /year for institutions (in U.S.); $485.00 /year for institutions (Canada/ Mexico). ISSN: 0002-9122. **Circulation:** 5,000. **Advertising:** accepted. Alternate Formats: online ● *Career Bulletin*, periodic ● *Careers in Botany*. Brochure. Outlines the nature of various career opportunities in the botanical disciplines. Alternate Formats: online ● *Plant Science Bulletin*, quarterly. Newsletter. Includes book reviews. ISSN: 0032-0919. **Circulation:** 6,000. Alternate Formats: online ● Membership Directory, biennial. **Price:** included in membership dues; $10.00/copy for nonmembers. **Circulation:** 3,000 ● Reports. Alternate Formats: online. **Conventions/Meetings:** annual conference and symposium, usually held in conjunction with American Institute of Biological Sciences (exhibits) - usually late July/August.

6633 ■ Desert Botanical Garden (DBG)

1201 N Galvin Pkwy.
Phoenix, AZ 85008
Ph: (480)941-1225 (480)481-8101
Fax: (480)481-8124
E-mail: administration@dbg.org
URL: http://www.dbg.org
Contact: John Sallot, Marketing Mgr.

Founded: 1937. **Members:** 8,300. **Membership Dues:** Aloe Vera Club, $55 (annual) ● Senita Club, $65 (annual) ● Cholla Club, $90 (annual) ● Agave Century Club, $150 (annual) ● Boojum Tree Club, $300 (annual) ● Ocotillo Club, $500 (annual) ● Golden Barrel Club, $700 (annual) ● Saguaro Society, $1,250 (annual). **Staff:** 86. **Budget:** $5,400,000. **Description:** Museum dedicated to the study, propagation, and display of the flora of arid lands. Holds public classes, tours, demonstrations, and workshops on desert flora, horticulture, and related subjects; offers children's programs. Maintains herbarium and living plant collections. **Libraries: Type:** reference. **Holdings:** 7,000; books, maps, periodicals. **Subjects:** desert botany, ecology, desert ethnobotany. **Computer Services:** database, living plant collections. **Departments:** Research. **Formerly:** (1979) Arizona Cactus and Native Flora Society. **Publications:** *Catalogue of the Flora of Arizona*. Book. **Price:** $4.95 ● *Desert Botanical Garden—Calendar*, quarterly. Brochure. Lists garden activities. **Price:** included in membership dues. **Circulation:** 15,000 ● *Sonoran Quarterly*. Journal. Concerned with desert plants, ethnobotany, ecology, and conservation; also includes information on desert landscaping. **Price:** included in membership dues; $2.00/copy for nonmembers. ISSN: 0735-8652. **Circulation:** 8,300 ● Brochures. **Conventions/Meetings:** annual meeting - usually held in May.

6634 ■ Friends of the National Arboretum (FONA)

3501 New York Ave. NE
Washington, DC 20002-1958
Ph: (202)544-8733
E-mail: khoran@fona.org
URL: http://www.fona.org
Contact: Kathy Horan, Exec. Dir.

Founded: 1983. **Members:** 2,000. **Membership Dues:** general, $35 (annual) ● family/joint, $50 (annual). **Staff:** 4. **Description:** Individuals and corporations. Maintains national and international tree and flower collections on 444 acres of land in the District of Columbia. Conducts educational and research activities. Operates charitable program. **Committees:** Ad Hoc Events; Annual Dinner; Development and Fundraising; Environment; Flowering Tree Walk; Garden Fair; Government Relations; Public Relations. **Formerly:** Friends of the U.S. National Arboretum. **Publications:** *Arbor Friends*, quarterly. Newsletter. Covers current developments in horticulture research and the Arboretum gardens/plant collection; also includes horticultural tips and calendar. **Price:** included in membership dues. **Circulation:** 4,000. **Conventions/Meetings:** lecture, on horticulture ● tour, garden.

6635 ■ Herb Research Foundation (HRF)

4140 15th St.
Boulder, CO 80304
Ph: (303)449-2265
Free: (800)748-2617
Fax: (303)449-7849
E-mail: info@herbs.org
URL: http://www.herbs.org
Contact: Robert S. McCaleb, Pres.

Founded: 1983. **Members:** 4,504. **Membership Dues:** regular, in U.S., $40-$500 (annual) ● regular, outside U.S., $95 (annual) ● professional, commercial (minimum), $260 (annual) ● professional, commercial (maximum), $6,000 (annual). **Staff:** 8. **Description:** Professionals in the health food industry, plant research scientists, herbal medicine practitioners and their patients, pharmacologists, herbal manufacturers and trade organizations, ethnobotanists, and interested consumers; scientists and students in the fields of pharmacognosy, botany, ethnobotany, and medicine. Encourages and supports research on the chemistry, pharmacology, and use of herbal folk medicines, teas, and other botanical products; provides a forum for discussion and cooperation among herbalists, physicians, health food advocates, and scientists. Works to form a liaison between the U.S. herbal movement and the worldwide scientific community. Disseminates research information on botanicals and serves as a source of information for the public and press on medicinal plants. Provides botanical literature research service. **Libraries: Type:** reference. **Holdings:** 250,000; papers, reports. **Subjects:** medical plants, pharmacognosy, pharmacology, botany, herbs, herbal medicine. **Computer Services:** Online services, research and ordering. **Publications:** *Herbal Research News*, quarterly. Newsletter ● *HerbalGram*, quarterly. Journal. Includes current research on botanicals, legal news, book reviews, and monographs. Published in conjunction with the American Botanical Council. **Price:** $35.00. **Circulation:** 20,000 ● *Herbs for Health*, bimonthly. Magazine. Contains information on how to use herbs and other supplements to maintain and improve health. ● Also issues abstracts and scientific literature.

6636 ■ Herb Society of America (HSA)

9019 Kirtland Chardon Rd.
Kirtland, OH 44094
Ph: (440)256-0514
Fax: (440)256-0541
E-mail: herbs@herbsociety.org
URL: http://www.herbsociety.org
Contact: Ms. Wendy Daugherty, Exec. Admin.

Founded: 1933. **Members:** 2,300. **Membership Dues:** individual, honorary, $50 (annual) ● joint, $75 (annual) ● student, $30 (annual) ● business, $85 (annual) ● international, $110 (annual) ● individual, life, $2,000 ● joint, life, $3,000 ● individual benefactor, $4,000 ● joint benefactor, $6,000. **Staff:** 8. **State Groups:** 43. **Local Groups:** 1. **Description:** Represents scientists, educators, and others interested in botanical and horticultural research on herbs and the culinary, economic, decorative, fragrant, and historic use of herbs. Maintains herb gardens in arboreta and other public sites. Establishes and maintains gardens for the blind. Planned and funded the National Herb Garden, which was donated to the National Arboretum in Washington, DC. Promotes the knowledge, use and delight of herbs through educational programs, research, and sharing the experience of its members with the community. **Libraries: Type:** reference. **Holdings:** 3,000; audiovisuals, books, periodicals. **Subjects:** botany, horticulture, herbs, folklore, gardening. **Awards:** The Helen de Conway Little Medal of Honor. **Frequency:** annual. **Type:** recognition. **Recipient:** for horticultural knowledge, research, or activity ● The Nancy Putnam Howard Award for Horticulture. **Frequency:** annual. **Type:** recognition. **Committees:** Botanical and Horticultural Research; Scholarship; Slide/Lecture. **Publications:** *The Beginners Herb Garden*, semiannual. Booklet. Discusses planting, propagation, and general care of herbs. **Price:** $6.95 for nonmembers, plus $2 postage; $5.50 for members ● *The Herb Society of America New Encyclopedia of Herbs and Their Uses*, published as necessary. Book. **Price:** $40.00 for nonmembers, plus $5 postage and handling ● *The Herb Society of America Newsletter*, quarterly ● *The Herbarist*, annual. Journal. **Price:** $12.00 for nonmembers; $8.00 for members (duplicates). ISSN: 0740-5979. **Circulation:** 3,000. **Advertising:** accepted ● Also publishes guides. **Conventions/Meetings:** annual Educational Conference - conference and meeting - 2008 June 26-28, Boston, MA.

6637 ■ International Bulb Society (IBS)

PO Box 336
Sanger, CA 93657-0336
Ph: (305)254-3635
E-mail: membership@bulbsociety.org
URL: http://www.bulbsociety.org
Contact: Alan Meerow PhD, Pres.

Founded: 1933. **Members:** 1,200. **Membership Dues:** regular in U.S., $40 (annual) ● regular in U.S., $75 (biennial) ● regular in U.S., $110 (triennial) ● regular outside U.S. (surface mail/airmail), $45-$50 (annual) ● regular outside U.S. (surface mail/airmail), $85-$95 (biennial) ● regular outside U.S. (surface mail/airmail), $125-$140 (triennial). **Staff:** 15. **Budget:** $75,000. **Regional Groups:** 3. **Description:** Studies the plant family Amaryllidaceae and all bulb families. Promotes the conservation of bulbs (both in habitat and in cultivation) and preservation of bulb habitats, and facilitates propagation and distribution of bulbs and their seeds to further bulb conservation and enjoyment. **Libraries: Type:** reference. **Holdings:** 4,000. **Subjects:** botanical, taxonomic, floristic topics. **Awards:** Herbert Medal. **Frequency:** periodic. **Type:** medal. **Recipient:** for an individual with meritorious achievements in advancing the knowledge of bulbous plants ● Traub Award. **Frequency:** periodic. **Type:** recognition. **Recipient:** for meritorious service to the society. **Absorbed:** (1985) Amaryllis Research Institute. **Also Known As:** American Amaryllis Society Group. **Formerly:** (1991) American Plant Life Society. **Publications:** *Bulbs*, semiannual. Magazine. Contains interviews with leading growers, breeders and researchers. **Advertising:** accepted ● *Herbertia*, annual. Journal. Covers bulbous monocot and dicot plants. **Price:** $30.00. ISSN: 8756-9418. **Circulation:** 750 ● *Review of Southern Africa Cyrtanthus*. **Conventions/Meetings:** annual Conference and Bulb Symposium - board meeting and symposium.

6638 ■ International Organization of Citrus Virologists (IOCV)

c/o Chester N. Roistacher, Sec.
Dept. of Plant Pathology
Univ. of California
Riverside, CA 92521
Ph: (951)787-1012
Fax: (951)787-4398
E-mail: chetroist@charter.net
URL: http://www.ivia.es/iocv
Contact: Chester N. Roistacher, Sec.

Founded: 1957. **Members:** 220. **Membership Dues:** individual, $30 (triennial). **Description:** Individuals engaged in research in citriculture, plant virus diseases, or plant protection; persons involved in nursery operations, fruit production, processing, and marketing related to citrus. Promotes cooperative study of citrus fruit disease and the exchange of information regarding their identity, relationships, effects, importance, means of spread, control, and/or prevention. Encourages personal contacts and the preparation and distribution of materials relevant to the study of citrus virus disease. Seeks to facilitate the development of mutual understanding among individuals, institutions, and agencies concerned with the production of citrus fruits. **Awards:** Wallace Award. **Frequency:** triennial. **Type:** recognition. **Publications:** *International Organization of Citrus Virologists—Proceedings*, triennial. Provides research reports on viral diseases affecting citrus trees. **Circulation:** 300. Alternate Formats: online ● Newsletter, every 2-3 months. Alternate Formats: online. **Conventions/Meetings:** triennial conference (exhibits).

6639 ■ International Organization of Plant Biosystematists (IOPB)
c/o Peter C. Hoch, PhD, Treas.
Missouri Botanical Garden
PO Box 299
St. Louis, MO 63166-0299
Ph: (314)577-5175
Fax: (314)577-0820
E-mail: nieto@ma-rjb.csic.es
URL: http://www.iopb.org
Contact: Gonzalo Nieto Feliner, Pres.
Founded: 1960. **Members:** 211. **Description:** Represents scientists in 35 countries interested in population biology, ecology, taxonomy, and evolution of plants. **Publications:** Newsletter, semiannual.

6640 ■ International Palm Society (IPS)
PO Box 1897
Lawrence, KS 66044-8897
Ph: (785)843-1274
Fax: (785)843-1274
E-mail: palms@allenpress.com
URL: http://www.palms.org
Contact: Paul Craft, Pres.
Founded: 1956. **Members:** 2,500. **Membership Dues:** individual in U.S., $35 (annual) ● family, commercial in U.S., $45 (annual) ● friend in U.S., $45-$99 (annual) ● supporting, $100-$499 (annual) ● life, $1,000 ● benefactor (one-time fee), $2,500 ● library in U.S., $40 (annual) ● outside U.S., $28 (annual). **Budget:** $100,000. **National Groups:** 30. **Multinational. Description:** Botanists, taxonomists, horticulturists, nurserymen, students, and amateurs interested in the study and cultivation of palms; institutions may become subscribers to the quarterly journal. Serves as clearinghouse for information about the palm family. **Awards:** Endowment Fund. **Frequency:** annual. **Type:** grant. **Computer Services:** Mailing lists, of members. **Formerly:** (1985) Palm Society. **Publications:** *Chamaedorea Palms*. Book. **Price:** $36.95 in U.S., surface delivery; $46.95 outside U.S., surface delivery; $59.95 outside U.S., airmail delivery ● *Genera Palmarum*. Book ● *Palms*, quarterly. Journal. Covers such topics as palm culture, research, and species identification. **Price:** included in membership dues. ISSN: 0032-8480. **Circulation:** 3,000. **Advertising:** accepted. Alternate Formats: online ● Membership Directory, annual ● Reprints. **Conventions/Meetings:** biennial conference ● seminar ● symposium.

6641 ■ International Society for Molecular Plant Microbe Interactions (IS-MPMI)
3340 Pilot Knob Rd.
St. Paul, MN 55121
Ph: (651)454-7250
Free: (800)481-2698
Fax: (651)454-0766
E-mail: ismpmi@scisoc.org
URL: http://www.ismpminet.org
Contact: Federico Sanchez, Pres.
Founded: 1990. **Members:** 500. **Membership Dues:** regular, $45 (annual) ● post-doctoral, $30 (annual) ● student, $15 (annual). **Staff:** 10. **Multinational. Description:** Studies and disseminates information on the molecular genetics of plant disease and problems of interaction between microbes and plants. **Publications:** *Molecular Plant-Microbe Interactions*, monthly. Journal. Features genetic, biochemical, and biophysical mechanisms of interactions of plants with uroids, viruses, procaryotes, and fungi. **Price:** $65.00/issue in U.S.; $70.00/issue outside U.S.; $312.00 online version in U.S.; $317.00 online version outside U.S. ISSN: 0894-0282. **Advertising:** accepted. Alternate Formats: online. **Conventions/Meetings:** biennial congress.

6642 ■ Lady Bird Johnson Wildflower Center
4801 La Crosse Ave.
Austin, TX 78739
Ph: (512)232-0100 (512)232-0200
Fax: (512)232-0156
E-mail: member@wildflower.org
URL: http://www.wildflower.org
Contact: Susan K. Rieff PhD, Exec. Dir.
Founded: 1982. **Members:** 20,000. **Membership Dues:** individual, $40 (annual) ● family, $65 (annual) ● supporter, $100 (annual) ● sustainer, $500 (annual) ● champion, $1,000 (annual) ● contributor, $250 (annual) ● dual, $50 (annual). **Staff:** 65. **Budget:** $5,200,000. **Description:** Aims to increase the sustainable use and conservation of native wildflowers, plants and landscapes. **Libraries: Type:** reference. **Holdings:** 1,500; articles, books, photographs. **Subjects:** native plants, wildflowers, landscape architecture, conservation, Lady Bird Johnson. **Computer Services:** database, native plant nurseries, seed companies, and related organizations in each state. **Publications:** *Wildflower Magazine*, quarterly. **Price:** included in membership dues. ISSN: 0898-8803. **Circulation:** 23,000. Alternate Formats: online ● *Wildflower Wire*, monthly. Newsletter. Contains advance notices of special events, classes, gift store specials, and other items of interest to native plant lovers. **Price:** free. Alternate Formats: online. **Conventions/Meetings:** semiannual board meeting.

6643 ■ Magnolia Society International (MSI)
c/o Elizabeth Edward, Sec.
3000 Henneberry Rd.
Jamesville, NY 13078
Ph: (315)677-7813
E-mail: beth.edward@gmail.com
URL: http://www.magnoliasociety.org
Contact: Elizabeth Edward, Sec.
Founded: 1961. **Members:** 700. **Membership Dues:** individual in U.S., $25 (annual) ● individual outside U.S., $30 (annual) ● life, $600. **Regional Groups:** 2. **Multinational. Description:** Represents botanists, horticulturists, commercial growers, and persons interested in study of all members of the magnolia family. Individual members are conducting research projects by hybridizing magnolias and testing for hardiness. Conducts international registration of magnolia clones and parentage of hybrids. **Awards:** Gresham Award. **Frequency:** annual. **Type:** recognition. **Committees:** Awards and Honors; Display and Test Gardens; Nominations/Endowment; Publicity; Round Robin; Scion/Pollen Exchange; Seed Counter; Slide Library. **Formerly:** (1986) American Magnolia Society; (2004) The Magnolia Society. **Publications:** *Check List of Cultivated Magnolias*. Journal. Published in cooperation with American Horticultural Society. **Price:** $18.50 for members in U.S.; $20.00 for members in Canada; $22.00 for members outside U.S. Alternate Formats: online ● *Magnolia: Journal of the Magnolia Society*, semiannual. Newsletter. Covers hybridization, seed collection, storing, mailing, genetics, the search for new species abroad, and society news. **Price:** included in membership dues. ISSN: 0738-3053. **Circulation:** 600. **Advertising:** accepted ● *Magnolia Magazine*, semiannual. Newsletter ● *Membership Roster*, triennial ● *Proceedings of International Symposium On the Family Magnoliaceae*. **Price:** $47.00 for members in U.S.; $52.00 for members in Canada; $57.00 for members outside U.S. ● Books. **Conventions/Meetings:** annual meeting and tour.

6644 ■ Musser International Turfgrass Foundation (MITF)
PO Box 124
Sharon Center, OH 44274
Ph: (330)239-2458 (330)239-2383
Fax: (330)239-1390
E-mail: fdobie@compuserve.com
Contact: D. Frank Dobie, Pres.
Founded: 1969. **Members:** 24. **Budget:** $5,000. **Description:** Turfgrass managers, research scientists, and executives of firms dealing in turf equipment and supplies. Named in honor of the late Prof. H. Burton Musser for his pioneer contributions to the turfgrass field. **Awards:** Award of Excellence. **Frequency:** annual. **Type:** scholarship. **Recipient:** for exceptional graduate students at turfgrass-oriented universities. **Committees:** Awards; Fund Raising; Publicity. **Divisions:** Golf Tournament. **Publications:** *List of Directors*, annual ● Also publishes information releases in trade magazines. **Conventions/Meetings:** annual board meeting.

6645 ■ Organization for Flora Neotropica (OFN)
New York Botanical Garden
Bronx, NY 10458-5126
Ph: (718)817-8625
Fax: (718)817-8648
E-mail: ofn@nybg.org
URL: http://www.nybg.org/botany/ofn
Contact: Dr. Wayt Thomas, Exec. Dir.
Founded: 1964. **Members:** 150. **Staff:** 1. **Languages:** English, French, Portuguese, Spanish. **Description:** Established by the United Nations Educational, Scientific and Cultural Organization. Representatives from countries (Mexico, Central America, the West Indies, South America, Europe, and the U.S.) and organizations actively concerned with the taxonomy of neotropical flora; interested individuals. Promotes research on plant systematics, particularly monographic research, of the American tropics and conservation of tropical American ecosystems exploration, strengthens herbaria that house important tropical collections, promotes the protection of natural tropical vegetation, and aids in the establishment and protection of biological reserves. Conducts research on plants of the New World. **Also Known As:** Flora Neotropica Organization. **Publications:** *Flora Neotropica Monographs* (in English, French, Portuguese, and Spanish), periodic. Provides information on morphology, taxonomy, nomenclature, geographical distribution, ecology, conservation and economic importance. ISSN: 0071-5794. **Circulation:** 1,000. **Conventions/Meetings:** annual board meeting.

6646 ■ Phycological Society of America (PSA)
c/o Blackwell Publishing, Inc.
350 Main St.
Malden, MA 02148
Ph: (781)388-8599
Free: (800)835-6770
Fax: (781)388-8232
E-mail: membershipservices@blackwellpublishing.com
URL: http://www.psaalgae.org
Contact: Robert A. Andersen, VP/Pres.-Elect
Founded: 1946. **Members:** 1,100. **Membership Dues:** regular, $95 (annual) ● student, $45 (annual) ● joint, $100 (annual) ● retired (with journal), $65 (annual) ● life, $2,000. **Budget:** $120,000. **Regional Groups:** 3. **Description:** Educators, researchers, and others interested in the pure, applied, or avocational study and utilization of algae. Maintains speakers' bureau. **Awards:** Croasdale. **Frequency:** annual. **Type:** monetary. **Recipient:** for fellowships to support student participation in field courses on algae ● Harold C. Bold Award. **Frequency:** annual. **Type:** monetary. **Recipient:** for best student oral presentation at the annual PSA meetings ● Hoshaw. **Frequency:** annual. **Type:** recognition. **Recipient:** for supporting student travel to annual PSA meetings ● Luigi Provasoli Award. **Frequency:** biennial. **Type:** monetary. **Recipient:** for best paper published in the Journal of Phycology during the previous year ● Prescott. **Frequency:** biennial. **Type:** recognition. **Recipient:** for best monograph or book about algae in preceding 1 to 2 years. **Computer Services:** Mailing lists, of members. **Committees:** Archives; Award of Excellence; Communications; Education; Election; Grants and Fellowship; Publication. **Funds:** Endow-

ment. **Affiliated With:** American Association for the Advancement of Science; American Institute of Biological Sciences. **Publications:** *Journal of Phycology*, bimonthly. Provides information on the study of seaweeds and algae. Includes book reviews and research reports. **Price:** included in membership dues; C$225.00 for nonmembers. ISSN: 0022-3646. **Circulation:** 2,000. **Advertising:** accepted ● *Phycological Newsletter*, 3/year. Includes book reviews, calendar of events, obituaries, and research updates. **Price:** included in membership dues. **Circulation:** 1,100. Alternate Formats: online ● *Phycological Society of America—Membership Directory*, biennial. **Price:** included in membership dues; C$35.00/copy for nonmembers. **Circulation:** 1,100. **Advertising:** accepted ● Books. **Conventions/Meetings:** annual conference and symposium, held in conjunction with American Institute of Biological Sciences (exhibits) - usually August ● annual meeting, scientific.

6647 ■ Plant Growth Regulation Society of America (PGRSA)

c/o Mr. Charles Hall, Exec. Sec.
PO Box 2945
LaGrange, GA 30241
Ph: (706)845-9085
Fax: (706)883-8215
E-mail: chall@asginfo.net
URL: http://www.pgrsa.org
Contact: Mr. Charles Hall, Exec. Sec.

Founded: 1973. **Members:** 160. **Membership Dues:** regular in U.S., Canada and Mexico, $40 (annual) ● international, $55 (annual) ● student, $15 (annual) ● sustaining, $500 (annual). **Staff:** 2. **Budget:** $45,000. **Description:** Represents scientists concerned with plant growth regulation. Seeks to foster a better understanding of the processes of plant growth and development. Promotes research; provides a forum for scientists from diverse disciplines to exchange information about the field of plant growth regulation. **Awards:** Bayer Crop Science Student Awards. **Frequency:** annual. **Type:** recognition. **Recipient:** for best graduate student oral and poster presentation at the annual meeting ● Valent Biosciences Best Paper Award. **Frequency:** annual. **Type:** recognition. **Recipient:** for best published manuscript in PGRSA Quarterly. **Formerly:** (1981) Plant Growth Regulator Working Group; (2001) Plant Growth Regulator Society of America. **Publications:** *Bioassays and Other Special Techniques for Plant Hormones and Plant Growth Regulators*. Book. **Price:** $20.00 ● *PGRSA Quarterly*. Journal. Contains technical reports, literature reviews, and dissertations and abstracts on the subject of plant growth. Includes association news. **Price:** included in membership dues; $72.00 for back issues. ISSN: 0163-6367. Alternate Formats: online. Also Cited As: *PGRSA Bulletin* ● *Plant Growth Regulator Society of America—Membership Directory*, annual. **Price:** included in membership dues; $16.00 for nonmembers ● *Plant Growth Regulator Society of America—Proceedings*, annual. **Price:** included in meeting registration; $40.00 in North America, current issues; $55.00 international, current issues; $30.00 back issues. **Conventions/Meetings:** annual meeting (exhibits).

6648 ■ Rhododendron Species Foundation (RSF)

PO Box 3798
Federal Way, WA 98063
Ph: (253)838-4646 (253)927-6960
Fax: (253)838-4686
E-mail: rsf@rhodygarden.org
URL: http://www.rhodygarden.org
Contact: Rick Peterson, Co-Exec. Dir./Garden Mgr.

Founded: 1964. **Members:** 750. **Membership Dues:** individual, $35 (annual) ● student, $15 (annual) ● family, $50 (annual) ● supporting, $100 (annual) ● sustaining, $250 (annual) ● patron, $500 (annual) ● garden society, $1,000 (annual) ● life, $5,000. **Staff:** 7. **Budget:** $400,000. **Description:** Dedicated to the conservation, research, acquisition, evaluation, cultivation, public display, and distribution of Rhododendron species; provides education relating to the Genus; and serves as an invaluable resource to scientific, horticultural, and educational communities worldwide. Maintains 22 acre garden, nursery, greenhouses, and related facilities. Visitor services include gift shop, guided tours by reservation, and plant sales area. Spring and fall plant sales are held annually. **Libraries: Type:** reference. **Holdings:** 1,900; books, monographs, periodicals. **Subjects:** rhododendrons, botanical reference, general horticulture. **Computer Services:** database, plant collection. **Committees:** Library; Photography; Research and Development. **Affiliated With:** American Rhododendron Society. **Also Known As:** Rhododendron Species Botanical Garden. **Publications:** *Rhododendron Species Foundation Newsletter*, quarterly. **Price:** free for members. **Circulation:** 1,000. **Advertising:** accepted ● Books. **Conventions/Meetings:** annual meeting - late April or early May ● seminar.

6649 ■ Society for Economic Botany (SEB)

PO Box 61788
Honolulu, HI 96839
E-mail: director@econbot.org
URL: http://www.econbot.org
Contact: Mr. Michael B. Thomas, Sec.

Founded: 1959. **Members:** 1,200. **Membership Dues:** student, emeritus/retired, $35 (annual) ● regular, $65 (annual) ● family, $75 (annual) ● sustaining, $100-$249 (annual) ● patron, $250-$499 (annual) ● benefactor, $500 (annual) ● life, $1,200 ● student/emeritus (online access only), $25 (annual) ● regular (online access only), $50 (annual) ● family (online access only), $60 ● life (online access only), $1,000 ● corporate/institution in U.S., $122 (annual) ● corporate/institution outside U.S., $134 (annual). **Multinational. Description:** Aims to foster and encourage scientific research, education, and related activities on the past, present, and future uses of plants, and the relationship between plants and people, and to make the results of such research available to the scientific community and general public through meetings and publications. With more than 1,000 members from all 50 U.S. states and more than 64 countries, serves as the world's largest professional society for individuals who are concerned with basic botanical, phytochemical and ethnological studies of plants known to be useful or those which may have potential uses so far undeveloped. It is recognized that the field of economic botany includes all or parts of many established disciplines such as: agronomy, anthropology, archaeology, chemistry, economics, ethnobotany, ethnology, forestry, genetic resources, geography, geology, horticulture, medicine, microbiology, nutrition, pharmacognosy, and pharmacology, in addition to the established botanical disciplines. **Awards:** Distinguished Economic Botanist Award. **Frequency:** annual. **Type:** recognition. **Recipient:** for an individual who has made outstanding accomplishments to the goals of the society ● Edmund Fulling Award. **Frequency:** annual. **Type:** monetary. **Recipient:** for an outstanding student paper presentation ● Julia Morton Award. **Frequency:** annual. **Type:** recognition. **Recipient:** for an outstanding student poster presentation ● Klinger Book Award. **Frequency:** annual. **Type:** recognition. **Recipient:** to an outstanding book at each annual meeting of the society for economic botany ● President's Award. **Frequency:** periodic. **Type:** recognition. **Recipient:** for outstanding service ● Richard E. Schultes Award. **Frequency:** annual. **Type:** grant. **Recipient:** to graduate students who are members of the society. **Boards:** Editorial. **Committees:** Archives; Auditing; Bylaws; Education and Outreach; Endowment; Ethics; Newsletter; Nominations and Awards; Program and Publicity; Student; Web Site. **Affiliated With:** American Association for the Advancement of Science; Botanical Society of America; Society of Ethnobiology. **Publications:** *Economic Botany*, quarterly. Journal. Contains book reviews and annotated bibliotheca and research articles. **Price:** included in membership dues. ISSN: 0013-0001. **Circulation:** 2,000. **Advertising:** accepted. Alternate Formats: online ● *SEB Brochure*. Alternate Formats: online ● *SEB Newsletter Plants and People*, semiannual. Contains original research articles on utilization of plants. Alternate Formats: online ● Membership Directory, biennial ● Also publishes occasional symposium volumes. **Conventions/Meetings:** annual symposium - 2009 June, Charleston, SC.

Building Industries

6650 ■ Alliance of Deep Foundation Testing Professionals (APTLY)

5 del Valle
Orinda, CA 94563
Ph: (925)254-0460
Fax: (925)254-0461
E-mail: aptly@insitutech.com
URL: http://www.insitutech.com/aptinfo.html
Contact: Mike Holloway, Contact

Founded: 1995. **Description:** Collaborates with the Deep Foundations Institute in testing and applying new methods available in the field. Provides networking and disseminates technical and commercial information to members. **Formerly:** (2004) Alliance of Pile Testing Laboratory Engineers.

6651 ■ American Society for Composites (ASC)

c/o Prof. James M. Whitney, Treas.
Dept. of Civil Engg.
422 Kettering Lab.
Univ. of Dayton
300 Coll. Park
Dayton, OH 45469-0243
Ph: (937)229-2979
Fax: (937)229-3491
E-mail: james.whitney@notes.udayton.edu
URL: http://www.asc-composites.org
Contact: Prof. James M. Whitney, Treas.

Founded: 1985. **Membership Dues:** student, $15 (annual) ● regular, $35 (annual) ● corporate, $500 (annual). **Description:** Provides a communication forum for the engineering and scientific communities in composite materials. Expedites the growth of knowledge in interdisciplinary engineering and scientific research in composite materials. Promotes the exploitation of the unique properties of composite materials in emerging applications. **Awards:** ASC Outstanding Research Award. **Frequency:** annual. **Type:** recognition. **Recipient:** for sustained research efforts and significant contributions to the composites community ● Best Paper Award. **Frequency:** annual. **Type:** recognition. **Recipient:** for the best paper within individual divisions at the Technical Conference ● PhD Research Scholarship Award. **Frequency:** annual. **Type:** recognition. **Recipient:** for outstanding composite materials research by PhD students ● Technomic Outstanding Service Award. **Frequency:** annual. **Type:** recognition. **Recipient:** for significant contributions to the composites community through applied research, practice, education, service, advocacy or leadership. **Publications:** Newsletter, semiannual. **Price:** included in membership dues. **Conventions/Meetings:** annual conference.

6652 ■ International Building Performance Simulation Association (IBPSA)

c/o Jeff Haberl
Energy Sys. Lab.
Dept. of Architecture
Texas A&M Univ.
College Station, TX 77843-3581
Ph: (979)845-1015
Fax: (979)862-1571
E-mail: jhaberl@esl.tamu.edu
URL: http://www.ibpsa.org
Contact: Jan Hensen, Pres.

Membership Dues: sustaining, $500 (annual) ● regular, $75 (annual) ● student, $25 (annual). **National Groups:** 10. **Multinational. Description:** Advances the science of building performance simulation. Improves the design, construction, operation and maintenance of new and existing buildings worldwide. **Awards:** IBPSA Distinguished Service Award. **Frequency:** annual. **Type:** recognition. **Recipient:** for distinguished record of contributions to the field of building simulation ● IBPSA Outstanding Practice Award. **Frequency:** annual. **Type:** recognition. **Recipient:** for significant contributions to the advancement of building simulation in practice ● IBPSA Outstanding Young Contributor Award. **Frequency:** annual. **Type:** recognition. **Recipient:** for significant contributions to the field of building simulation. **Computer Services:** Information services, building simulation resources ● mailing lists. **Publications:** *IBPSA News*, quarterly. Newsletter. Alternate Formats: online.

6653 ■ National Association of Tower Erectors (NATE)
8 2nd St. SE
Watertown, SD 57201-3624
Ph: (605)882-5865
Free: (888)882-5865
Fax: (605)886-5184
E-mail: nate@natehome.com
URL: http://www.natehome.com
Contact: Patrick Howey, Exec. Dir.

Founded: 1995. **Members:** 500. **Membership Dues:** voting, $1,000-$7,000 (annual) ● non-voting, $1,500-$3,500 (annual) ● support, $1,250-$2,500 (annual). **Staff:** 7. **Description:** Provides a unified voice to help shape the future of the tower industry. Formulates and adheres to uniform standards of safety to ensure the continued well-being of tower personnel. Educates the general public, applicable government agencies and clients on continued progress toward safer standards within the industry. Facilitates effective safety training for the industry. **Computer Services:** database, membership lists. **Committees:** OSHA Relations; Safety and Education; Trade Show. **Publications:** *Tower Times*, monthly. Magazine. **Advertising:** accepted. **Conventions/Meetings:** annual conference.

Cartography

6654 ■ Cartography and Geographic Information Society (CaGIS)
c/o Aileen R. Buckley, Pres.
ESRI, Inc.
380 New York St.
Redlands, CA 92373
Ph: (909)793-2853
Fax: (909)327-3067
E-mail: abuckley@esri.com
URL: http://www.cartogis.org
Contact: Aileen R. Buckley, Pres.

Founded: 1974. **Members:** 2,600. **Membership Dues:** full, associate, $140 (annual) ● student, $28 (annual). **Description:** Member organization of the American Congress on Surveying and Mapping (see separate entry). Fosters improvements in cartography and GIS; encourages professional growth, new techniques, the study of practical uses of maps, and the conservation and servicing of map collections. **Committees:** Automation; Awards; Certification; Facsimiles; History; Information Services; Large Scale Map Standards; Map Design Competition; Outreach; Research. **Formerly:** (1981) Cartography Division of the American Congress on Surveying and Mapping; (2002) American Cartographic Association. **Publications:** *ACSM Bulletin*, bimonthly. **Price:** $92.00 in U.S.; $110.00 outside U.S. ● *Careers in Cartography and GIS Brochure*. Alternate Formats: online ● *Cartography and Geographic Information Science*, quarterly. Journal. **Price:** $155.00 in U.S. (online); $175.00 outside U.S. (online); $195.00 in U.S. (paper and online); $175.00 in U.S. (paper and online). Alternate Formats: online. **Conventions/Meetings:** annual seminar.

6655 ■ International Map Trade Association (IMTA)
PMB 281
2629 Manhattan Ave.
Hermosa Beach, CA 90254-2411
Ph: (310)376-7731
Fax: (310)376-7287
E-mail: imta@maptrade.org
URL: http://www.maptrade.org
Contact: Mr. Sanford J. Hill, Exec. Dir.
Founded: 1981. **Members:** 700. **Membership Dues:** regular in North America (data provider/publisher/manufacturer/retailer/government organization/library/consultant), $150-$450 (annual) ● regular in Europe, Africa and Middle East, 150-455 (annual) ● regular in Australia, New Zealand, and Asia Pacific, $A 297 (annual) ● associate in north and south America, $100 (annual) ● associate in Europe, Asia, and Middle East, 89 (annual). **Staff:** 5. **Budget:** $200,000. **Multinational. Description:** Represents the international mapping, geospatial, and geographic information industry. Membership includes data and content providers, publishers/manufacturers/ distributors, and retailers. Members from over 50 countries and 6 continents, representing over 700 companies and organizations, join together to foster individual and industry growth. **Committees:** Americas Planning; Americas Web Site; EAME Retailer; EAME Technology; Marketing and Development; Web Site. **Formerly:** International Map Dealers Association. **Publications:** *Map Report*, monthly. Newsletter. Includes calendar of events, profiles of new members, and new product information. **Price:** included in membership dues; $75.00 for nonmembers. **Advertising:** accepted. Alternate Formats: online. **Conventions/Meetings:** annual conference and trade show, with approximately 50 exhibitors (exhibits).

6656 ■ North American Cartographic Information Society (NACIS)
c/o AGS Library
PO Box 399
Milwaukee, WI 53201-0399
Ph: (414)229-6282
Free: (800)558-8993
Fax: (414)229-3624
E-mail: business@nacis.org
URL: http://www.nacis.org
Contact: Jenny Marie Johnson, Pres.
Founded: 1980. **Members:** 400. **Membership Dues:** regular, $42 (annual) ● student, $20 (annual) ● affiliate, $72 (annual). **Description:** Cartographers, graphic artists, draftspersons, surveyors, commercial representatives, and photogrammetrists (those involved in the science of making reliable measurements by the use of aerial photographs); map librarians, archivists, collectors, geologists, and real property descriptors; geographers, planners, travelers, researchers, and historians; map distributors including government agencies and map retailers. Objectives are to: encourage communication, coordination, and cooperation among members; promote graphics and education in cartographic materials; coordinate the acquisition, preservation, and automatic retrieval of cartographic materials; influence related governmental policy. Sponsors map displays, business meetings, and field trips; disseminates industry news on new map publications, upcoming mapping conferences, new cartographic techniques, programs, and information systems. **Publications:** *Board Meeting Report*. Reports. Alternate Formats: online ● *Cartographic Perspectives*, 3/year. Journal. Reviews mapping software, cartographic literature, and new map publications. Contains cartographic perspectives on the news and lab activities. **Price:** included in membership dues; $72.00 for nonmembers. ISSN: 1048-9085. **Circulation:** 400. **Conventions/Meetings:** annual conference and meeting (exhibits) - usually October ● workshop.

Ceramics

6657 ■ American Ceramic Society (ACerS)
735 Ceramic Pl., Ste.100
Westerville, OH 43081-8728
Ph: (614)794-5855
Free: (866)721-3322
Fax: (301)206-9789
E-mail: customerservice@ceramics.org
URL: http://www.ceramics.org
Contact: Scott Steen, Exec. Dir.
Founded: 1898. **Members:** 10,600. **Membership Dues:** regular, $100 (annual) ● associate, senior (retired), $40 (annual) ● student, $25 (annual) ● corporate, $300-$950 (annual). **Staff:** 50. **Budget:** $8,000,000. **Regional Groups:** 32. **Local Groups:** 37. **Multinational. Description:** Professional society of scientists, engineers, educators, plant operators, and others interested in the glass, cements, refractories, nuclear ceramics, whitewares, electronics, engineering, and structural clay products industries. Disseminates scientific and technical information through its publications and technical meetings. Conducts continuing education courses and training such as the Precollege Education Program. Sponsors over 10 meetings yearly; encourages high school and college students' interest in ceramics. Maintains Ross C. Purdy Museum of Ceramics; offers placement service and speakers' bureau. **Libraries: Type:** reference. **Holdings:** 11,000; archival material, books, clippings, periodicals. **Subjects:** ceramic history, brick, cement, glass, and industrial and technical aspects of ceramics, porcelain, pottery. **Awards:** The John and Edith Wachtman Scholarship in Ceramics. **Frequency:** annual. **Type:** scholarship. **Recipient:** for high school senior planning to enter college and study ceramic science or ceramic engineering. **Computer Services:** database, Ceramic Abstracts ● database, Ceramic Futures - contains resumes. **Divisions:** Art; Basic Science; Cements; Electronics; Engineering Ceramics; Glass and Optical Materials; Materials and Equipment; Nuclear and Environmental Sciences; Refractory Ceramics; Structural Clay Products; Whitewares. **Affiliated With:** Ceramic Educational Council; National Institute of Ceramic Engineers. **Publications:** *American Ceramic Society Bulletin*, monthly. Includes monthly advertisers index, annual cumulative index, calendar of events, obituaries, new product information, program for meetings. **Price:** included in membership dues; $50.00 /year for nonmembers. ISSN: 0002-7812. **Circulation:** 14,400. **Advertising:** accepted ● *Ceramic Abstracts*, 5/year. Reports on significant literature in ceramics and related fields. Includes annual author and subject indexes. **Price:** $95.00 for members; $295.00 for nonmembers. ISSN: 0095-9960. **Circulation:** 2,400. Alternate Formats: online; CD-ROM ● *Ceramic Engineering and Science Proceedings*, 5/year. Contains technical papers presented at society's meetings. **Price:** $75.00 /year for members; $95.00 /year for nonmembers. ISSN: 0196-6219. **Circulation:** 1,200 ● *Ceramic Source*, annual. Directory. Lists organization and product information. Includes product and services services directory, organizational directory, and geographic index. **Price:** free for members; $45.00 /year for nonmembers. ISSN: 8756-8187. **Circulation:** 10,000. **Advertising:** accepted ● *Ceramics Monthly*. Magazine. **Price:** $24.00/year ● *Journal of the American Ceramic Society*, monthly. Presents the latest advances in ceramic science and engineering. **Price:** $85.00 /year for members; $355.00 /year for nonmembers. ISSN: 0002-7820. **Circulation:** 4,200. **Advertising:** accepted. Alternate Formats: online ● *Pottery Making Illustrated*, 5/year. Magazine. **Conventions/Meetings:** annual meeting (exhibits) - 2008 Oct. 5-9, Pittsburgh, PA; 2009 Oct. 25-30, Pittsburgh, PA ● annual meeting ● biennial Unified International Technical Conference on Refractories.

6658 ■ National Institute of Ceramic Engineers (NICE)
c/o Greg Geiger, Admin.
735 Ceramic Pl., Ste.100
Westerville, OH 43081-8728
Ph: (614)794-5858
Fax: (614)794-5882
E-mail: ggeiger@ceramics.org
URL: http://www.ceramics.org/membership/Sections_Classes/nice.aspx
Contact: Greg Geiger, Admin.
Founded: 1937. **Members:** 750. **Membership Dues:** full, associate, affiliate, fellow, distinguished sponsor, $40 (annual). **Staff:** 1. **Budget:** $40,000. **State Groups:** 1. **Description:** Promotes the profession of ceramic engineering, accreditation of educational programs in ceramic and glass engineering and science, and in materials science and engineering and high ethical engineering standards and practices.

Sponsors continuing education courses. Offers employment service and promotes professional engineer registration. Responsible for Professional Engineering exams in Ceramic Engineering. **Awards:** Arthur Friedberg Memorial Lecturer. **Frequency:** annual. **Type:** recognition. **Recipient:** for outstanding contributions to ceramics ● Best Student Chapter. **Frequency:** annual. **Type:** recognition. **Recipient:** for outstanding participation in student activities ● Graves-Walker Award. **Frequency:** annual. **Type:** recognition. **Recipient:** for outstanding service to ceramic profession ● Schwartzwalder-PACE Award. **Frequency:** annual. **Type:** recognition. **Recipient:** to a young scientist/engineer for contributions to the field. **Committees:** AAES; Accreditation; Awards; Chapters; Ethics; Professional Registration; Public Relations; Rules. **Affiliated With:** Ceramic Educational Council; Keramos. **Publications:** *NICE News*, monthly. Article. Appears in the bulletin of the American Ceramic Society. **Conventions/Meetings:** annual executive committee meeting ● annual meeting, held in conjunction with American Ceramic Society (exhibits) - usually April or May in the Midwest.

6659 ■ The Refractories Institute (TRI)
Centre City Tower
650 Smithfield St., Ste.1160
Pittsburgh, PA 15222-3907
Ph: (412)281-6787
Fax: (412)281-6881
E-mail: triassn@aol.com
URL: http://www.refractoriesinstitute.org
Founded: 1951. **Members:** 80. **Membership Dues:** active (minimum), $3,280 (annual) ● affiliate (minimum), $400 (annual) ● associate (minimum), $2,816 (annual) ● contractor, installer, $848 (annual). **Staff:** 1. **Budget:** $500,000. **Description:** Active members are producers of firebrick and other refractory materials; associate members are suppliers of refractory raw materials, production equipments, and services. **Awards:** Safety and President's Awards to Active Members. **Frequency:** annual. **Type:** recognition. **Committees:** Associates Advisory; Operations and Management; Regulatory. **Publications:** *Directory of the Refractories Industry*, quadrennial. Lists manufacturers, suppliers of raw materials and equipment, sales and plant locations, products and brand names. **Price:** $45.00 for members; $85.00 for nonmembers; $100.00 for foreign orders. **Advertising:** accepted ● *Refractories*. **Price:** $5.00 for members; $10.00 for nonmembers in U.S.; $12.00 for nonmembers outside U.S. ● *Refractory News*, monthly. Newsletter. **Price:** free for members; $24.00 /year for nonmembers. **Circulation:** 700. **Conventions/Meetings:** semiannual meeting.

Chemistry

6660 ■ AACC International
3340 Pilot Knob Rd.
St. Paul, MN 55121
Ph: (651)454-7250
Free: (800)328-7560
Fax: (651)454-0766
E-mail: aacc@scisoc.org
URL: http://www.aaccnet.org
Contact: Steven C. Nelson, Exec. VP
Founded: 1915. **Members:** 3,000. **Membership Dues:** student, $41 (annual) ● professional, $131 (annual) ● corporate (based on the number of employees), $425-$1,225 (annual) ● CDE, $39 (annual). **Staff:** 30. **Local Groups:** 15. **Multinational. Description:** Serves as professional society of scientists and other individuals in the grain processing industry (milling, baking, convenience foods, and feeds). Encourages research on cereal grains, oil seeds, pulses, and related materials, and studies their processing, utilization, and products. Seeks to develop and standardize analytical methods used in cereal and seed chemistry and to disseminate scientific and technical information through workshops and publications. Offers honors for outstanding research. Maintains over 20 technical subcommittees. Conducts short courses for continuing education and annual sanitation certification program. **Awards:** AACC Endowment Fund. **Type:** scholarship. **Recipient:** for students majoring in discipline related to cereal science. **Committees:** Approved Methods. **Divisions:** Biotechnology; Carbohydrate; Education; Engineering and Processing; Flavor and Food Ingredients; Milling and Baking; Nutrition; Protein; Rheology; Rice; Student. **Absorbed:** (1923) American Society of Milling and Baking Technology. **Formerly:** (2005) American Association of Cereal Chemists. **Publications:** *Cereal Chemistry*, bimonthly. Journal. Presents original research reports to scientists and students working in the areas of food chemistry and food processing. ISSN: 0009-0352. Alternate Formats: microform ● *Cereal Foods World*, bimonthly. Journal. Features research articles on developments in the industry. Includes updates on consumer trends, regulatory developments, and international news. ISSN: 0146-6283. **Advertising:** accepted. Alternate Formats: microform ● Books ● Monographs. **Conventions/Meetings:** annual congress (exhibits) - 2008 Sept. 21-24, Honolulu, HI.

6661 ■ Adhesion Society (AS)
2 Davidson Hall - 0201
Blacksburg, VA 24061
Ph: (540)231-7257
Fax: (540)231-3971
E-mail: adhesoc@vt.edu
URL: http://www.adhesionsociety.org
Contact: David Dillard, Pres.
Founded: 1978. **Members:** 500. **Membership Dues:** regular, $55 (annual) ● student/retiree, $20 (annual). **Staff:** 1. **Description:** Serves as professional association open to scientists and engineers whose work and interests include the broad field of adhesion and all of its aspects. **Libraries: Type:** reference. **Holdings:** archival material. **Awards:** Adhesion Society Award of Excellence. **Frequency:** annual. **Type:** recognition. **Recipient:** for research ● Alan Gent Best Student Paper Award. **Frequency:** annual. **Type:** scholarship. **Recipient:** for students ● Robert L. Patrick Fellowship. **Frequency:** annual. **Type:** fellowship. **Recipient:** for service/research. **Divisions:** Particle Adhesion; Pressure Sensitive Adhesives; Structural Adhesives. **Publications:** *Adhesion of Science and Technology*, annual. Journal. Provides forum for basic aspects, theories and mechanisms of adhesions. ● *Adhesion Society—Newsletter*, quarterly. Provides news of Society and Adhesion Community. **Price:** included in membership dues. **Circulation:** 500. Alternate Formats: online ● *Proceedings of the Annual Meeting*, annual. Contains papers presented at the meeting. **Price:** $80.00. **Conventions/Meetings:** annual meeting and symposium, presentation of papers on adhesion science (exhibits) ● annual symposium and meeting (exhibits).

6662 ■ American Association for Aerosol Research (AAAR)
15000 Commerce Pkwy., Ste.C
Mount Laurel, NJ 08054
Ph: (856)439-9080
Free: (877)777-6753
Fax: (856)439-0525
E-mail: info@aaar.org
URL: http://www.aaar.org
Contact: Amy Williams, Exec. Dir.
Founded: 1982. **Members:** 1,200. **Membership Dues:** student, retired, $33 (annual) ● full, $160 (annual) ● organizational, $1,944 (annual). **Staff:** 3. **Budget:** $140,000. **Description:** Represents scientists and engineers associated with universities, technical institutes and private firms; government representatives; interested firms and associations. Promotes aerosol research in areas including industrial processes, air pollution and industrial hygiene. **Awards:** Benjamin Y.H. Liu. **Frequency:** annual. **Type:** recognition. **Recipient:** for outstanding contributions to aerosol instrumentation and techniques ● David Sinclair Award. **Frequency:** annual. **Type:** recognition. **Recipient:** to senior scientist for excellence in aerosol research ● Kenneth T. Whitby Award. **Frequency:** annual. **Type:** recognition. **Recipient:** to a young scientist for outstanding technical contribution to aerosol science ● Sheldon K. Friedlander Award. **Frequency:** annual. **Type:** recognition. **Recipient:** for an outstanding dissertation by an individual who has earned a doctoral degree ● Thomas T. Mercer Joint Prize. **Frequency:** annual. **Type:** recognition. **Recipient:** for excellence in the areas of pharmaceutical aerosols and inhalable materials. **Telecommunication Services:** electronic mail, awilliams@ahint.com. **Publications:** *Aerosol Science and Technology*, monthly. Journal. **Price:** $1,127.00 for nonmembers. ISSN: 0278-6826. **Circulation:** 1,000. **Advertising:** accepted ● *American Association for Aerosol Research Directory: Officers and Membership*, annual ● *Annual Abstracts*, annual. Booklet. Lists abstracts of all papers presented at technical meeting. ● *Particulars*, 3/year. Newsletter. Contains up-to-date information about meetings, conferences, symposia, awards, job opportunities, and other official business. **Price:** included in membership dues. **Advertising:** accepted. **Conventions/Meetings:** annual conference (exhibits) - 2008 Oct. 20-24, Orlando, FL; 2009 Oct. 26-30, Minneapolis, MN.

6663 ■ American Carbon Society (ACS)
c/o Dr. Wesley Hoffman, Chm.
Air Force Research Laboratory, AFRL/PRSM
10 E Saturn Blvd.
Edwards, CA 93524-7680
Ph: (661)275-5768
Fax: (661)275-5007
E-mail: wesley.hoffman@edwards.af.mil
URL: http://www.americancarbonsociety.org
Contact: Nidia C. Gallego, Sec.-Treas.
Founded: 1957. **Members:** 500. **Membership Dues:** regular, $30 (annual). **Staff:** 1. **Description:** Physicists, chemists, technologists, and other scientific personnel worldwide who attend the biennial Carbon Conference organized by the society. Focuses on the physics, chemistry, and other scientific aspects of organic crystals, polymers, chars, carbons, and graphite materials. **Awards:** Charles Pettinos Award. **Frequency:** biennial. **Type:** recognition ● Graffin Lectureship Award. **Frequency:** annual. **Type:** recognition ● SGL Carbon Award. **Frequency:** biennial. **Type:** recognition. **Formerly:** (1973) American Carbon Committee. **Publications:** *American Carbon Society—Extended Abstracts of Conference Papers*, triennial. Book. **Price:** $62.50 ● *Carbon*, monthly. Journal. **Price:** included in membership dues. **Conventions/Meetings:** triennial International Carbon Conference - 2008 July 13-18, Nagano, Japan; 2009 June 14-19, Biarritz, France.

6664 ■ American Chemical Society (ACS)
1155 16th St. NW
Washington, DC 20036
Ph: (202)872-4600
Free: (800)227-5558
Fax: (202)872-4615
E-mail: help@acs.org
URL: http://portal.chemistry.org/portal/acs/corg/memberapp
Contact: Madeleine Jacobs, Exec. Dir./CEO
Founded: 1876. **Members:** 151,000. **Membership Dues:** regular/associate, $136 (annual) ● non-scientist/society affiliate, $102 (annual) ● student, $68 (annual). **Staff:** 1,950. **Budget:** $250,000,000. **Local Groups:** 187. **Description:** Scientific and educational society of chemists and chemical engineers. Conducts: studies and surveys; special programs for disadvantaged persons; legislation monitoring, analysis, and reporting; courses for graduate chemists and chemical engineers; radio and television programming. Offers career guidance counseling; administers the Petroleum Research Fund and other grants and fellowship programs. Operates Employment Clearing Houses. Compiles statistics. Maintains Speaker's Bureau and 33 divisions. **Libraries: Type:** reference. **Holdings:** 10,000. **Awards: Frequency:** annual. **Type:** recognition. **Recipient:** for scientific achievement in areas of chemical science. **Computer Services:** database, Chemical Journals of the ACS Online; contains full text of 23 ACS journals ● online services, CAS (Chemical Abstract Service), an interactive chemical information search service ● online services, STN International,

a scientific and technical information network. **Committees:** Chemistry and Public Affairs; Corporation Associates; Education; Grants and Awards; International Activities; Local Section Activities; Professional Relations; Women Chemists. **Publications:** *Accounts of Chemical Research*, monthly. Journal. **Price:** $29.00 /year for members; $204.00 /year for nonmembers. ISSN: 0009-2347. Alternate Formats: microform; online ● *Analytical Chemistry*, semimonthly. Journal. Covers developments in the field; includes author index, book reviews, and new products. **Price:** $40.00 /year for members; $85.00/year for individual nonmembers; $570.00/year for institution nonmembers. ISSN: 0003-2700. **Advertising:** accepted. Alternate Formats: microform ● *Biochemistry*, weekly. Journal. Covers biochemical research. **Price:** $115.00 /year for members; $1,517.00 /year for nonmembers. ISSN: 0006-2960. Alternate Formats: microform; online ● *Chemical and Engineering News*, weekly. Magazine. Describes policies and activities of the ACS. **Price:** included in membership dues; $120.00 /year for nonmembers. ISSN: 0009-2347. Alternate Formats: microform; online ● *Chemical Health and Safety*, bimonthly. Journal. **Price:** $25.00 /year for members; $50.00 /year for nonmembers; $250.00 /year for institutions. ISSN: 1074-9098. **Advertising:** accepted ● *Chemical Reviews*, 8/year. Journal. Contains critical evaluations of progress in particular fields. **Price:** $36.00 /year for members; $420.00 /year for nonmembers. ISSN: 0009-2665. Alternate Formats: microform; online ● *Chemistry of Materials*, monthly. Journal. Contains research, communications, and reviews of relevance to chemists, chemical engineers, and material scientists and technologists. **Price:** $50.00 /year for members; $435.00 /year for nonmembers. ISSN: 0897-4756. Alternate Formats: microform; online ● *Chemtech*, monthly. Magazine. Includes book and software reviews. **Price:** $42.00 /year for members; $85.00 /year for nonmembers; $395.00 /year for institutions. ISSN: 0009-2703. Alternate Formats: microform ● *Environmental Science and Technology*, monthly. Journal. Contains feature articles, regulatory news, and research papers. Includes advertisers index, book reviews, and consulting services. **Price:** $44.00 /year for members; $90.00 /year for nonmembers; $585.00 /year for institutions. ISSN: 0013-936X. **Advertising:** accepted. Alternate Formats: microform ● *Industrial and Engineering Chemistry Research*, monthly. Journal. Provides reports on original research in the field. **Price:** $65.00 /year for members; $695.00 /year for nonmembers. ISSN: 0888-5885. Alternate Formats: microform; online ● *Journal of Agricultural and Food Chemistry*, monthly. Reports on advances in the field; covers the applications of chemical disciplines in more efficient and economical production. **Price:** $35.00 /year for members; $420.00 /year for nonmembers. ISSN: 0021-8561. Alternate Formats: microform; online ● *Journal of Chemical and Engineering Data*, quarterly. **Price:** $37.00 /year for members; $395.00 /year for nonmembers. ISSN: 0021-9568. Alternate Formats: microform; online ● *Journal of Chemical Information and Computer Sciences*, bimonthly. Contains research papers. **Price:** $23.00 /year for members; $230.00 /year for nonmembers. ISSN: 0095-2338. Alternate Formats: microform; online ● *Journal of Medicinal Chemistry*, biweekly. Covers the relationship between chemistry and biological activity including advances in drug design and development. **Price:** $58.00 /year for members; $790.00 /year for nonmembers. ISSN: 0022-2623. Alternate Formats: microform; online ● *Journal of Organic Chemistry*, biweekly. Covers such areas as organic reactions, natural products, studies of mechanisms, bioorganic chemistry, and theoretical organic chemistry. **Price:** $76.00 /year for members; $920.00 /year for nonmembers. ISSN: 0022-3263. Alternate Formats: microform; online ● *Journal of Pharmaceutical Sciences*, monthly. **Price:** $30.00 /year for members; $85.00 /year for nonmembers; $310.00 /year for institutions. ISSN: 0022-3549. **Advertising:** accepted ● *Journal of Physical Chemistry*, weekly. Contains experimental and theoretical research dealing with fundamental aspects of physical chemistry and chemical physics. **Price:** $108.00 /year for members; $1,496.00 /year for nonmembers. ISSN: 0022-3654. Alternate Formats: microform; online ● *Journal of the American Chemical Society*, biweekly. Contains research articles. Includes author index and book reviews. **Price:** $107.00 /year for members; $1,396.00 /year for nonmembers. ISSN: 0002-7863. **Advertising:** accepted. Alternate Formats: microform; online ● *Langmuir*, monthly. Journal. Contains papers on ultra-high vacuum surface chemistry and spectroscopy, heterogeneous catalysis, interface chemistry involving fluids. **Price:** $69.00 /year for members; $874.00 /year for nonmembers. ISSN: 0743-7463. Alternate Formats: microform; online ● *Organometallics*, monthly. Journal. Contains articles and communications concerned with main group, transition, lanthanide, and actinide organometallic chemistry. **Price:** $80.00 /year for members; $1,025.00 /year for nonmembers. ISSN: 0276-7333. Alternate Formats: microform; online. **Conventions/Meetings:** semiannual meeting (exhibits) - 2008 Aug. 17-21, Philadelphia, PA; 2009 Mar. 22-26, Salt Lake City, UT; 2009 Aug. 16-20, Washington, DC.

6665 ■ American Institute of Chemical Engineers (AIChE)

3 Park Ave.
New York, NY 10016-5991
Ph: (212)591-8100
Free: (800)242-4363
Fax: (212)591-8888
E-mail: xpress@aiche.org
URL: http://www.aiche.org
Contact: Larry Evans, Pres.

Founded: 1908. **Members:** 59,000. **Membership Dues:** individual (without degree and with BS degree before 2005), $199 (annual) ● individual (with 2005-present BS degree), $100 (annual) ● current graduate student/unemployed, $50 (annual) ● student, $15 (annual). **Staff:** 103. **Local Groups:** 107. **Description:** Serves as professional society of chemical engineers. Establishes standards for chemical engineering curricula; offers employment services. Presents technical conferences, petrochemical and refining exposition, and continuing education programs. Sponsors competitions. Offers speakers' bureau; complies statistics. **Divisions:** Computing and Systems Technology; Engineering and Construction Contracting; Environmental; Food, Pharmaceutical and Bioengineering; Forest Products; Fuels and Petrochemical; Heat Transfer and Energy Conversion; Management; Marketing; Materials Engineering and Sciences; Nuclear Engineering; Safety and Health. **Affiliated With:** ABET. **Publications:** *AIChE Journal*, monthly. Covers fundamental research and developments in the field. Includes annual author, subject, and title index, book reviews, new book announcements. **Price:** $60.00 /year for members; $349.00 /year for nonmembers. ISSN: 0001-1541. **Circulation:** 3,900. **Advertising:** accepted. Alternate Formats: microform ● *AIChE Symposium Series*, bimonthly. Contains collected papers on specific subjects presented at symposia from AIChE meetings. Includes subject index. ISSN: 0065-8812 ● *AIChEMI Modular Instruction Series*, periodic. Monograph. Covers a specific area of process control. **Price:** $30.00/volume, for members; $60.00/volume, for nonmembers. ISSN: 0270-6229 ● *AIChExtra*, monthly. Newsletter. **Price:** free for members ● *Ammonia Plant Safety*, annual. Proceedings. Contains technical papers from the institute's annual ammonia symposium. **Price:** $50.00 for members; $100.00 for nonmembers. ISSN: 0149-3701. **Circulation:** 1,200 ● *Biotechnology Progress*, bimonthly. Journal. Reports recent research and developments affecting the food, pharmaceutical, bioengineering, and allied fields. **Price:** $30.00/year for AIChE and ACS members; $289.00/year for all others. ISSN: 8756-7938. **Circulation:** 3,400. Alternate Formats: microform ● *Chapter One*, quarterly. Magazine. Contains technical articles, advice on studying and future careers, reports from campuses, and book reviews. **Price:** included in membership dues (student members); $12.00 /year for nonmembers. ISSN: 0895-3384. **Circulation:** 7,500. **Advertising:** accepted ● *Chemical Engineering Faculties*, annual. Directory. Lists faculty members, department heads, and placement officers of approximately 151 U.S. and 281 foreign chemical engineering schools. **Circulation:** 1,200 ● *Chemical Engineering Progress*, monthly. Magazine. Presents technical articles on all core activities of the chemical process and related industries. **Price:** included in membership dues; $60.00 /year for nonmembers. ISSN: 0360-7275. **Circulation:** 47,500. **Advertising:** accepted. Alternate Formats: microform ● *Environmental Progress*, quarterly. Journal. For environmental engineers covering all aspects of pollution. **Price:** free for members of the Environmental Division; $33.00/year for other members. ISSN: 0278-4491. **Circulation:** 4,300. **Advertising:** accepted. Alternate Formats: microform ● *International Chemical Engineering*, quarterly. Journal. Provides English translations of papers originally published in foreign-language journals covering a broad range of clinical engineering topics. **Price:** $45.00 /year for members; $349.00 /year for nonmembers. ISSN: 0020-6318. **Circulation:** 1,100. Alternate Formats: microform ● *Plant/Operations Progress*, quarterly. Journal. Concerned with the design, operation, and maintenance of safe installations; technical papers report new techniques and advances. **Price:** free for members of the Safety and Health Division; $30.00/year for other members. ISSN: 0278-4513. **Circulation:** 2,100. **Advertising:** accepted. Alternate Formats: microform ● Directory, periodic. **Price:** available to members only ● Also publishes pamphlets, letter symbols for chemical engineering, directory of consultants, and standard testing procedures. **Conventions/Meetings:** conference - 3/year ● annual meeting - usually held in spring.

6666 ■ American Institute of Chemists (AIC)

315 Chestnut St.
Philadelphia, PA 19106-2702
Ph: (215)873-8224
Fax: (215)629-5224
E-mail: info@theaic.org
URL: http://www.theaic.org

Founded: 1923. **Members:** 3,000. **Membership Dues:** regular, $110 (annual) ● fellow, $150 (annual) ● corporate, $2,500 (annual) ● charter corporate, $3,500 (annual) ● student, $35 (annual) ● retired, $70 (annual) ● retired fellow, $75 (annual) ● life fellow, $1,200. **Staff:** 2. **Budget:** $200,000. **Regional Groups:** 12. **State Groups:** 12. **Local Groups:** 2. **Description:** Represents chemists and chemical engineers. Promotes advancement of chemical professions in the U.S; protects public welfare by establishing and enforcing high practice standards; represents professional interests of chemists and chemical engineers. Sponsors National Certification Commission in Chemistry and Chemical Engineering and AIC Foundation. **Libraries:** **Type:** reference. **Holdings:** 4; periodicals. **Subjects:** chemistry. **Awards:** Chemical Pioneers Award. **Frequency:** annual. **Type:** recognition. **Recipient:** to chemists and chemical engineers for outstanding contributions ● Gold Medal Award. **Frequency:** annual. **Type:** medal. **Recipient:** to an individual who has stimulated activities of service ● Joseph Hyman Ethics Award. **Frequency:** annual. **Type:** recognition. **Recipient:** for individuals who perform their duties for the public good ● Student Award. **Frequency:** annual. **Type:** recognition. **Recipient:** for outstanding seniors, post-baccalaureate, and postdoctoral students. **Computer Services:** Mailing lists, of 5,000 chemists, chemical engineers and biochemists. **Committees:** Awards; Bylaws; Education; Ethics; International; Local Institutes; National Meetings; Nominations and Elections; Publications; Younger Chemists. **Affiliated With:** American Association for the Advancement of Science; American Chemical Society; Chemical Heritage Foundation. **Publications:** *American Institute of Chemists—Professional Directory*, biennial. Includes professional biographical information. **Price:** $20.00 for members; $75.00/copy for nonmembers. **Circulation:** 5,500. **Advertising:** accepted ● *The Chemist*, quarterly. Magazine. Includes articles and reports of professional and personal interest to chemists. Also includes book reviews, and employment opportunities. **Price:** included in membership dues; $65.00 /year for nonmembers. ISSN: 0009-3025. **Circulation:** 5,000. **Advertising:** accepted. **Conventions/Meetings:** annual The Professional Chemist—Past, Present, Future - conference.

6667 ■ American Leather Chemists Association (ALCA)
1314 50th St., Ste.103
Lubbock, TX 79412-2940
Ph: (806)744-1798
Fax: (806)744-1785
E-mail: alca@leatherchemists.org
URL: http://www.leatherchemists.org
Contact: Carol Adcock, Exec. Sec.
Founded: 1903. **Members:** 500. **Membership Dues:** individual, $112 (annual) ● mutual, $201 (annual) ● student, $56 (annual). **Staff:** 3. **Budget:** $150,000. **Description:** Chemists, leather technologists, and educators concerned with the tanning and leather industry. Works to devise and perfect methods for the analysis and testing of leathers and materials used in leather manufacture. Promotes advancement of chemistry and other sciences, especially their application to problems confronting the leather industry. **Libraries: Type:** reference. **Holdings:** 98. **Subjects:** leather chemistry. **Committees:** Collagen Uses and Its Coproducts; Education; Environmental Affairs; Methods and Specification Review; Raw Stock; Research Liaison. **Publications:** *Directory of the American Leather Chemists Association*, annual. **Price:** included in membership dues; $20.00/copy for nonmembers. **Circulation:** 1,000. **Advertising:** accepted ● *Journal of the American Leather Chemists Association*, monthly. Contains research reports; covers patents and foreign research articles in abstract form. Includes book reviews, employment listings, and obituaries. **Price:** $115.00 /year for members; $115.00 /year for nonmembers in U.S. (plus $28 postages, $75 by air); $115.00 /year for nonmembers outside U.S. (plus $31 postages, $75 by air). ISSN: 0002-9726. **Conventions/Meetings:** annual conference, authors present research reports (exhibits) - always June.

6668 ■ American Microchemical Society (AMS)
c/o Herk Felder, Treas.
2 June Way
Middlesex, NJ 08846
E-mail: ella_osnovikova@permacel.com
URL: http://www.microchem.org
Contact: Ella Osnovikova, Chair
Founded: 1935. **Members:** 150. **Membership Dues:** individual, $10 (annual). **Description:** Promotes interest in the practice and teaching of microchemistry. Participates in exhibits and symposia. Maintains placement service. **Awards:** Benedetti-Pichler Award. **Frequency:** annual. **Type:** recognition. **Recipient:** for an outstanding research in the field of microchemistry ● **Type:** scholarship. **Recipient:** to chemistry students. **Funds:** Educational. **Formerly:** (1938) New York-New Jersey Section of the Microchemical Society; (1963) Metropolitan Microchemical Society. **Publications:** *Microchemical Journal*, bimonthly. **Conventions/Meetings:** meeting - 8-9/year ● annual symposium.

6669 ■ American Oil Chemists' Society (AOCS)
PO Box 17190
Urbana, IL 61803-7190
Ph: (217)359-2344
Fax: (217)351-8091
E-mail: general@aocs.org
URL: http://www.aocs.org
Contact: Jean Wills, Exec. VP
Founded: 1909. **Members:** 4,700. **Membership Dues:** active in U.S., $145 (annual) ● active outside U.S. (via air mail), $220 (annual) ● corporate (bronze level), $750 (annual) ● corporate (silver level), $2,500 (annual) ● corporate (gold level), $5,000 (annual) ● corporate (platinum level), $10,000 (annual). **Staff:** 6. **Budget:** $5,000,000. **Local Groups:** 9. **Multinational. Description:** Chemists, biochemists, chemical engineers, research directors, plant personnel, and others in laboratories and chemical process industries concerned with animal, marine, and vegetable oils and fats, and their extraction, refining, safety, packaging, quality control, and use in consumer and industrial products such as foods, drugs, paints, waxes, lubricants, soaps, and cosmetics. Sponsors short courses; certifies referee chemists; distributes cooperative check samples; sells official reagents. Maintains 100 committees. Operates job placement service for members only. **Libraries: Type:** reference. **Holdings:** books, monographs, periodicals. **Awards:** Honored Student Award. **Frequency:** annual. **Type:** monetary. **Recipient:** for graduate students who are doing research toward an advance degree ● Schroepfer Medal. **Frequency:** annual. **Type:** medal. **Recipient:** for scientists who have made major advances in the steroid field ● Stephen S. Chang Award. **Frequency:** annual. **Type:** recognition. **Recipient:** for a scientist or technologist ● Supelco/Nicholas Pelick-AOCS Research Award. **Frequency:** annual. **Type:** recognition. **Recipient:** for outstanding original research ● Thomas H. Smouse Memorial Fellowship. **Frequency:** annual. **Type:** monetary. **Recipient:** for outstanding graduate research in a field of study. **Divisions:** Topical. **Sections:** Geographical. **Formerly:** (1922) Society of Cotton Products Analysts. **Publications:** *INFORM*, monthly. Magazine. Contains information on new products and publications, Washington reports, and calendar of events. **Price:** $155.00 /year for individuals; $155.00 /year for institutions; $30.00 for members; $145.00 for student. ISSN: 0897-8026. **Circulation:** 6,100. **Advertising:** accepted. Alternate Formats: online ● *Journal of Surfactants and Detergents*, quarterly. Contains research articles, short communications, and methods papers related to surfactants and detergents field. **Price:** $120.00 for members in U.S.; $128.00 for members outside U.S.; $160.00 for nonmembers in U.S.; $168.00 for nonmembers outside U.S. ● *Lipids*, monthly. Journal. **Price:** $95.00 /year for members in U.S.; $115.00 /year for members outside U.S.; $293.00 /year for libraries and institutions in U.S.; $315.00 /year for libraries and institutions outside U.S. ISSN: 0024-4201. **Circulation:** 1,600 ● Journal, monthly. Contains papers covering research developments and processing of fats and oils and their derivative products. **Price:** $88.00 /year for members in U.S.; $108.00 /year for members outside U.S.; $295.00 /year for libraries and institutions; $315.00 /year for nonmembers outside U.S. ISSN: 0003-021X. **Circulation:** 3,500 ● Membership Directory, annual. **Price:** $280.00 /year for libraries and institutions in U.S.; $288.00 /year for libraries and institutions outside U.S. ● Monographs ● Proceedings. **Conventions/Meetings:** annual congress and meeting, for fats, oils, lipids, surfactants, detergents, and related materials research and processing (exhibits) ● annual meeting (exhibits) - 2009 May 3-6, Orlando, FL.

6670 ■ American Society of Brewing Chemists (ASBC)
3340 Pilot Knob Rd.
St. Paul, MN 55121-2097
Ph: (651)454-7250
Fax: (651)454-0766
E-mail: asbc@scisoc.org
URL: http://www.asbcnet.org
Contact: Steven C. Nelson, Exec. Off.
Founded: 1934. **Members:** 850. **Membership Dues:** individual in U.S., $115 (annual) ● student in U.S., $22 (annual) ● corporate in U.S., $243 (annual) ● corporate outside U.S., $260 (annual). **Staff:** 10. **Budget:** $280,000. **Multinational. Description:** Serves as professional organization of chemists in brewing and malting industries. Develops standard methods of analysis for raw materials, supplies, and products of brewing, malting, and related industries. Provides professional development resources to members through publications, continuing education courses. **Awards:** ASBC Foundation. **Frequency:** annual. **Type:** scholarship. **Recipient:** to graduate students ● ASBC Student Travel Grant. **Frequency:** annual. **Type:** grant. **Telecommunication Services:** electronic mail, snelson@scisoc.org. **Committees:** Technical. **Formerly:** Malt Analysis Standardization Committee. **Publications:** *ASBC Newsletter*, quarterly. Provides news items and technical reports on brewing and related matters, abstracts of technical papers, book reviews, and membership listings. **Price:** included in membership dues; $26.00 /year for nonmembers outside U.S., plus shipping and handling ($6). **Circulation:** 1,000. **Advertising:** accepted ● *Directory of Members, ASBC*, annual. Membership Directory ● *Journal of the American Society of Brewing Chemists*, quarterly. Presents scientific papers, review articles, and technical reports dealing with brewing chemistry, microbiology, technology, and techniques. **Price:** included in membership dues; $216.00 /year for nonmembers in U.S.; $231.00 /year for nonmembers outside U.S. ISSN: 0361-0470 ● *Methods to Analysis of the ASBC*. **Conventions/Meetings:** annual convention, with presentation of technical papers/posters, submission of reports, and society business (exhibits).

6671 ■ AOAC International
481 N Frederick Ave., Ste.500
Gaithersburg, MD 20877-2417
Ph: (301)924-7077
Free: (800)379-2622
Fax: (301)924-7089
E-mail: aoac@aoac.org
URL: http://www.aoac.org
Contact: E. James Bradford, Exec. Dir.
Founded: 1884. **Members:** 3,100. **Staff:** 30. **Budget:** $6,600,000. **Regional Groups:** 17. **Description:** Government, academic, and industry analytical scientists who develop, test, and collaboratively study methods for analyzing fertilizers, foods, feeds, pesticides, drugs, cosmetics, and other products related to agriculture and public health. Offers short courses for analytical laboratory personnel in chemical and microbiological quality assurance, lab waste management, statistics, giving expert testimony, and technical writing. **Computer Services:** Mailing lists, of members. **Formerly:** Association of Official Agricultural Chemists; (1991) Association of Official Analytical Chemists. **Publications:** *Journal of AOAC International*, bimonthly. Includes papers on original research and new techniques and applications, new product information, collaborative studies, and meeting symposia. **Price:** $144.00 for members; $208.00 for nonmembers. ISSN: 0004-5756. **Circulation:** 4,200. **Advertising:** accepted ● *Official Methods of Analysis of the AOAC*, quinquennial. Includes annual supplements. ● *Referee*, monthly. Newsletter ● Manuals ● Membership Directory, annual ● Monographs ● Proceedings. **Conventions/Meetings:** annual meeting (exhibits) - 2008 Sept. 21-25, Dallas, TX; 2009 Sept. 13-17, Philadelphia, PA; 2010 Sept. 26-30, Orlando, FL.

6672 ■ Association of Consulting Chemists and Chemical Engineers (ACC&CE)
PO Box 297
Sparta, NJ 07871-0297
Ph: (973)729-6671
Fax: (973)729-7088
E-mail: info@chemconsult.org
URL: http://www.chemconsult.org
Contact: Linda B. Townsend, Exec. Sec.
Founded: 1928. **Members:** 150. **Membership Dues:** full, $210 (annual). **Staff:** 2. **Budget:** $45,000. **Description:** Serves the chemical and related industries through its expertise on a wide variety of technical and business knowledge. Provides experienced counseling for new members. **Computer Services:** database, contains scope sheets and classifier identifying members in more than 1,500 specialized areas. **Telecommunication Services:** electronic mail, accce@chemconsult.org. **Publications:** *Online Directory of Consulting Services*. Alternate Formats: online ● Newsletter, bimonthly. Alternate Formats: online ● Also issues press releases. **Conventions/Meetings:** monthly Chem Show - show and conference (exhibits) - always last Tuesday in New York or New Jersey ● biennial symposium, "diversity in consulting" presented by member consultants (exhibits).

6673 ■ Association of Fertilizer and Phosphate Chemists (AFPC)
PO Box 1645
Bartow, FL 33831

E-mail: marlene.parrish@mosaicco.com
URL: http://www.afpc.net
Contact: Marlene Parrish, Pres.
Membership Dues: regular, $200 (annual). **Description:** Represents organizations engaged in analytical chemistry associated with mining and processing of phosphates in the United States. Promotes uniformity of analytical methods and procedures for the phosphate industry. Reviews and conducts research on new sampling methods for the fertilizer and phosphate industry. **Awards:** Hero of the Industry Award - Chemist of the Year. **Frequency:** annual. **Type:** recognition. **Recipient:** for outstanding contribution to the chemical industry. **Publications:** Pamphlet. Alternate Formats: online.

6674 ■ Association of Formulation Chemists (AFC)
Address Unknown since 2007
Description: Disseminates technical information on formulation technology pertaining to adhesives, drugs, cosmetics, pigments, foods, pesticides, in addition to other applications.

6675 ■ Center for Process Analytical Chemistry (CPAC)
Univ. of Washington
160 Chemistry Lib. Bldg.
Box 351700
Seattle, WA 98195-1700
Ph: (206)685-2326
Fax: (206)543-6506
E-mail: cpac@cpac.washington.edu
URL: http://www.cpac.washington.edu
Contact: Dr. Melvin Koch, Dir.
Founded: 1984. **Members:** 38. **Membership Dues:** sponsorship, $35,000 (annual). **Staff:** 3. **Budget:** $2,000,000. **Description:** Conducts research on novel sensors, data analysis methods, and instrumentation for real-time process monitoring and control. **Libraries: Type:** reference. **Awards:** CPAC Projects. **Frequency:** annual. **Type:** grant. **Recipient:** for research compatible with sponsor needs. **Committees:** IAB Steering. **Subgroups:** Sponsor Focus. **Publications:** *CPAC InterLink*, monthly. Newsletter. Provides information about the activities of CPAC. Alternate Formats: online. **Conventions/Meetings:** semiannual Sponsor Meeting (exhibits) - always 1st week of November and May.

6676 ■ Chlorine Chemistry Council (CCC)
1300 Wilson Blvd.
Arlington, VA 22209
Ph: (703)741-5000
Fax: (703)741-6084
E-mail: info@c3.org
URL: http://c3.org
Contact: C.T. Howlett Jr., Exec. Dir.
Founded: 1993. **Description:** Business council comprises of chlorine and chlorinated product manufacturers. Works toward achieving policies that promote the continuing responsible uses of chlorine-based products. Develops and implements programs to this end. Promotes the use of sound scientific practices. Sponsors and conducts research concerning the potential health and environmental effects of chlorine.

6677 ■ Commercial Development and Marketing Association (CDMA)
3 Park Ave., 19th Fl.
New York, NY 10016-5991
Ph: (203)702-7667
Free: (866)511-2362
Fax: (203)775-5177
E-mail: info@cdmaonline.org
URL: http://www.cdmaonline.org
Contact: Bruce E. Banyai, Pres.
Founded: 1999. **Members:** 605. **Membership Dues:** regular, $225 (annual) ● initiation, $125 ● emeritus, $95 (annual) ● regular, $595 (triennial). **Staff:** 2. **Budget:** $175,000. **Regional Groups:** 7. **Description:** Aims to foster, promote, and share business practices for long-term growth and value creation in the chemical and allied industries. **Awards:** Award for Executive Excellence. **Frequency:** annual. **Type:** recognition. **Recipient:** for outstanding contributions of an executive of a chemical or allied industry company. **Committees:** Planning and Policy. **Formed by Merger of:** (1999) Commercial Development Association; (1999) Chemical Management and Resources Association. **Formerly:** (1941) Technical Service Association; (1970) Commercial Chemical Development Association. **Publications:** Directory, annual. Alternate Formats: online. **Conventions/Meetings:** annual meeting (exhibits) - always March or April and September or October.

6678 ■ Controlled Release Society (CRS)
3340 Pilot Knob Rd.
St. Paul, MN 55121
Ph: (651)454-7250
Fax: (651)454-0766
E-mail: crs@scisoc.org
URL: http://www.controlledreleasesociety.org
Contact: Prof. Randall Mrsny, Pres.
Founded: 1973. **Members:** 3,000. **Membership Dues:** corporate, $300 (annual) ● individual, $120 (annual) ● student, $32 (annual). **Staff:** 6. **Description:** Individuals interested in controlled release delivery systems used in agriculture and veterinary pharmaceuticals. Controlled release delivery systems involve the use of time-release systems (such as time capsules and membranes used for medication) in the areas of agriculture and veterinary pharmaceuticals. Provides a forum for the dissemination of basic and applied research. **Awards:** *Journal of Controlled Release* Outstanding Paper Award. **Frequency:** annual. **Type:** recognition ● CRS-Cygnus Graduate Student Award. **Frequency:** annual. **Type:** recognition. **Recipient:** for outstanding work in drug delivery ● CRS Distinguished Service Award. **Type:** recognition ● CRS-Dow Corning Graduate Student Outstanding Research Award. **Type:** recognition ● CRS Founders Award. **Type:** recognition ● CRS/Prographarm Outstanding Pharmaceutical Paper Award. **Type:** recognition ● CRS-3M Pharmaceuticals Graduate Student Outstanding Research in Drug Delivery. **Type:** recognition ● Graduate Student/Postdoc Registration Lottery Awards. **Type:** recognition ● Graduate Student/Postdoc Travel Grant Lottery Awards. **Type:** recognition ● Outstanding Paper in Veterinary Field. **Type:** recognition. **Recipient:** for contributions of exceptional quality and originality in the field of veterinary science ● Young Investigator Research Achievement Award. **Frequency:** annual. **Type:** recognition. **Computer Services:** Mailing lists. **Publications:** *Biomaterials*. Journal. **Price:** $340.00. ISSN: 0142-9612 ● *Controlled Release Newsletter*, 3/year. Includes information, new publications, and calendar of events. **Price:** included in membership dues. **Advertising:** accepted. Alternate Formats: online ● *European Journal of Pharmaceutics and Biopharmaceutics (APV)*. **Price:** $80.00. ISSN: 0939-6411 ● *International Symposium on Controlled Release of Bioactive Materials*, annual. Contains abstracts of papers presented at the society's meeting covering controlled release oral delivery systems and related topics. **Price:** included in membership dues. **Circulation:** 3,000. **Advertising:** accepted ● *Journal of Controlled Release*, bimonthly. Covers the science and technology of the controlled release of active chemical agents. Includes job postings, book reviews, and new patents. **Price:** $105.00 /year for members. ISSN: 0168-3659. **Advertising:** accepted. **Conventions/Meetings:** annual International Symposium on Controlled Release of Bioactive Materials (exhibits) - early summer ● annual meeting (exhibits) - 2008 July 12-16, New York, NY.

6679 ■ Council for Chemical Research (CCR)
1730 Rhode Island Ave. NW, Ste.302
Washington, DC 20036
Ph: (202)429-3971
Fax: (202)429-3976
E-mail: danthony@ccrhq.org
URL: http://www.ccrhq.org
Contact: Dr. Donald Anthony ScD, Pres./Exec. Dir.
Founded: 1980. **Members:** 206. **Staff:** 3. **Budget:** $850,000. **Description:** Represents universities that grant advanced degrees in chemistry or chemical engineering; chemical companies, government laboratories, and independent research laboratories that employ chemists and chemical engineers in research and development. Aims to promote more effective interactions between university chemistry and chemical engineering departments and the research function of industry and government and to support basic research in chemistry and chemical engineering. Strives for continued vitality of chemical science, engineering, and technology in the U.S., and the greater recognition of the global nature of the chemical research enterprise. Sponsors charitable programs; produces educational materials; compiles statistics. Maintains speakers' bureau. **Awards:** Collaboration Success Award. **Frequency:** annual. **Type:** recognition ● Diversity Award. **Frequency:** annual. **Type:** recognition ● Malcom E. Pruitt Award. **Frequency:** annual. **Type:** recognition. **Recipient:** for excellence in promoting industry/academic/government research cooperation. **Committees:** Administration; Awards; Communications and Publicity; Government Relations; International; Program; Science Education and Human Resources; Strategic Advisory; University/Industry/Government Laboratory Interaction. **Publications:** *CCR's Year in Review*, annual. Annual Report. Alternate Formats: online ● *Measure for Measure: Chemical R&D Powers the U.S. Innovation Engine*. Report. **Price:** $25.00 for members; $75.00 for nonmembers. **Conventions/Meetings:** annual conference - usually spring.

6680 ■ Electrochemical Society (ECS)
65 S Main St., Bldg. D
Pennington, NJ 08534-2839
Ph: (609)737-1902
Fax: (609)737-2743
E-mail: ecs@electrochem.org
URL: http://www.electrochem.org
Contact: Roque J. Calvo, Exec. Dir.
Founded: 1902. **Members:** 7,000. **Membership Dues:** individual, $98 (annual) ● student, $18 (annual) ● benefactor, $5,000 (annual) ● patron, $2,500 (annual) ● sponsoring, $1,500 (annual) ● sustaining, $1,000 (annual). **Staff:** 20. **Local Groups:** 22. **Description:** Serves as technical society of electrochemists, chemists, chemical and electrochemical engineers, metallurgists and metallurgical engineers, physical chemists, physicists, electrical engineers, research engineers, teachers, technical sales representatives, and patent attorneys. Seeks to advance the science and technology of electrochemistry, electronics, electrothermics, electrometallurgy, and applied subjects. **Awards:** Summer Fellowship. **Frequency:** annual. **Type:** fellowship. **Telecommunication Services:** electronic mail, roque.calvo@electrochem.org. **Divisions:** Battery; Corrosion; Dielectrics Science and Technology; Electrodeposition; Electronics; Energy Technology; Fullerenes Group; High Temperature Materials; Industrial Electrolysis and Electrochemical Engineering; Luminescence and Display Materials; Organic and Biological Electrochemistry; Physical Electrochemistry. **Formerly:** (1930) American Electrochemical Society. **Publications:** *Extended Abstracts* ● *Interface*, quarterly. Magazine. Contains technical articles about the latest developments in the field, and presents news and information about and for members of ECS. **Advertising:** accepted ● *Monograph Volumes* ● *Proceedings Volumes*. Provides up-to-date views of specialized topics and frequently offer comprehensive treatment of rapidly developing areas. ● Journals, monthly. Alternate Formats: online ● Membership Directory, annual. **Price:** available to members only. **Conventions/Meetings:** biennial international conference (exhibits) ● semiannual symposium - 2008 Oct. 12-17, Honolulu, HI; 2009 May 24-29, San Francisco, CA; 2009 Oct. 4-9, Vienna, Austria.

6681 ■ Emulsion Polymers Institute (EPI)
Lehigh Univ.
Iacocca Hall, Rm. D-325
111 Res. Dr.
Bethlehem, PA 18015
Ph: (610)758-3590 (610)758-3602
Fax: (610)758-5880

E-mail: eric.daniels@lehigh.edu
URL: http://fp1.cc.lehigh.edu/inemuls/epi/epi_home_page.htm
Contact: Dr. Eric S. Daniels, Exec. Dir.
Founded: 1975. **Membership Dues:** industrial liaison, $13,000 (annual). **Staff:** 20. **Description:** Sponsored by Lehigh University and 25 member companies of the Emulsion Polymers Liaison Program. Aims are: to conduct scientific research on the production, characterization, and application of polymer colloids; to provide consultations, contract research, and other services to member companies. Conducts 2 annual short courses on emulsion polymerization and latex technology. **Publications:** *Graduate Research Progress Reports*, semiannual. Alternate Formats: CD-ROM ● Bulletin, semiannual. **Conventions/Meetings:** annual Advances in Emulsion Polymerization and Latex Technology - conference, advances in emulsion polymerization and latex technology.

6682 ■ Federation of Analytical Chemistry and Spectroscopy Societies (FACSS)
PO Box 24379
Santa Fe, NM 87502
Ph: (505)820-1648
Fax: (505)989-1073
E-mail: facss@facss.org
URL: http://www.facss.org
Contact: Cindi Lilly, Exec. Asst.
Founded: 1972. **Members:** 7. **Staff:** 5. **Budget:** $750,000. **Description:** Professional societies representing 9,000 analytical chemists and spectroscopists. Members are: Analysis Instrumentation Division of the Instrument Society of America; Association of Analytical Chemists; Coblentz Society; Division of Analytical Chemistry of the American Chemical Society; Division of Analytical Chemistry of the Royal Society of Chemistry; Society for Applied Spectroscopy. Aims to provide a forum to address the challenges of analytical chemistry, chromatography, and spectroscopy. Reviews technical papers; maintains placement service. **Awards:** Hirshfeld Award. **Frequency:** annual. **Type:** grant. **Recipient:** for an outstanding graduate student ● Professional Awards. **Frequency:** annual. **Type:** recognition. **Recipient:** for outstanding scientists ● Student Poster Award. **Frequency:** annual. **Type:** recognition. **Recipient:** for students who present the best papers. **Computer Services:** Mailing lists, registration and exhibitor. **Committees:** Awards. **Conventions/Meetings:** annual meeting and workshop (exhibits).

6683 ■ International Maillard Reaction Society (IMARS)
Wolstein Bldg.
2103 Cornell Rd., Rm. 5127
Cleveland, OH 44106
Ph: (216)368-2930
Fax: (216)368-1357
E-mail: imars@case.edu
URL: http://imars.case.edu
Contact: Vincent M. Monnier MD, Pres.
Founded: 2005. **Membership Dues:** student, $35 (annual) ● postdoctoral fellow, emeritus, $50 (annual) ● active, associate, $75 (annual) ● corporate, $3,000 (annual). **Multinational. Description:** Fosters a balanced approach to understanding both the advantageous and deleterious properties of carbonyl compounds and their end products in food science, technology and medicine. Supports and encourages the transfer of basic and applied knowledge about Maillard Reaction to the health professionals in academia and the industry. Interacts with public, private and industrial funding organizations. **Telecommunication Services:** electronic mail, vincent.monnier@case.edu. **Publications:** *The Maillard Reaction: Chemistry, Biochemistry and Implications*. Book. Provides treatise on the Maillard reaction. **Price:** 84.95 for nonmembers; $59.50 for members ● *Maillard Reaction Newsletter*, monthly. **Price:** included in membership dues. Alternate Formats: online.

6684 ■ International Organization for Chemical Sciences in Development (IOCD)
PO Box 8156
Falls Church, VA 22041
Ph: (703)845-9078
Fax: (703)845-9078
E-mail: iocd@igc.org
URL: http://www.iocd.org
Contact: Dr. Robert H. Maybury, Exec. Dir.
Founded: 1981. **Languages:** English, French. **Nonmembership**. **Multinational**. **Description:** Links chemists in developing and industrial countries in collaborative research in the areas of health and agriculture. Organizes laboratory workshops in developing countries to provide chemists hands-on instruction in research techniques. Assists developing countries to build local scientific and entrepreneurial capacity for biodiversity exploration (bioprospecting). **Working Groups:** Biotic Exploration Fund; Books for International Development; Environmental Analytical Chemistry; Medicinal Chemistry; Plant Chemistry; Tropical Diseases. **Affiliated With:** International Union of Pure and Applied Chemistry.

6685 ■ International Society of India Chemists and Chemical Engineers (ISICCE)
c/o Dr. Dayal T. Meshri, Pres.
Advanced Res. Chemicals
1110 W Keystone Ave.
Catoosa, OK 74015
Ph: (918)266-6789
Fax: (918)266-6796
E-mail: sales@fluoridearc.com
Contact: Dr. Dayal T. Meshri, Pres.
Founded: 1982. **Members:** 450. **Description:** Chemists and chemical engineers from India. Goal is to bring together Indians in the chemical profession who live in the U.S. Aids members in securing jobs in their fields. Provides consultation to industries in India and helps individuals to start their own chemical companies in the U.S. Provides a forum for the exchange of social and technical issues. Plans to organize symposia, short courses, and exchange program. Compiles statistics. **Awards: Type:** recognition. **Formerly:** (1985) India Chemists and Chemical Engineers Club. **Publications:** *Directory of India Chemists and Chemical Engineers*, periodic ● Newsletter, bimonthly. **Conventions/Meetings:** competition ● semiannual conference.

6686 ■ International Union of Pure and Applied Chemistry (IUPAC)
c/o Dr. John W. Jost, Exec. Dir.
PO Box 13757
Research Triangle Park, NC 27709-3757
Ph: (919)485-8700
Fax: (919)485-8706
E-mail: secretariat@iupac.org
URL: http://www.iupac.org
Contact: Dr. John W. Jost, Exec. Dir.
Founded: 1919. **Members:** 45. **Staff:** 6. **Multinational. Description:** Fosters worldwide communications in the chemical sciences and unites academic, industrial and public sector chemistry in a common language. Specializes in chemical nomenclature, terminology, standardized methods for measurement, atomic weights and many other critically evaluated data. Establishes a wide range of conferences and projects designed to promote and stimulate modern developments in chemistry. Assists in aspects of chemical education and the public understanding of chemistry. **Computer Services:** database, chemical information. **Committees:** Chemical Research Applied to World Needs; Chemistry and Industry; Chemistry Education; Evaluation; Printed and Electronic Publications. **Divisions:** Analytical Chemistry; Chemical Nomenclature and Structural Representation; Chemistry and Human Health; Chemistry and the Environment; Inorganic Chemistry; Organic and Biomolecular Chemistry; Physical and Biophysical Chemistry; Polymer. **Publications:** *Chemistry International*, bimonthly. Magazine. **Price:** 99.00. **Circulation:** 8,000. **Advertising:** accepted. Alternate Formats: online ● *Pure and Applied Chemistry*, monthly. Journal. **Conventions/Meetings:** biennial general assembly, with symposia.

6687 ■ Iranian Chemists' Association of the American Chemical Society (ICA-ACS)
c/o Dr. Ali R. Banijamali, Dir. of Membership
35 Meadowbrook Ln.
Woodbury, CT 06798
Ph: (203)573-3220
Fax: (203)573-3660
E-mail: banijamali@ica-acs.org
URL: http://www.ica-acs.org
Contact: Dr. Zahra Afrasiabi, Chair
Membership Dues: regular, $20 (annual) ● student/post-doctoral, $10 (annual). **Description:** Encourages and enhances the interchange and sharing of scientific knowledge and friendship among chemists and chemistry-related professionals of Iranian descent. Provides opportunities for members to assist each other in pursuit of academic and professional development and growth. Promotes awareness of scientific contributions made by Iranian scientists. **Publications:** *Journal of the Iranian Chemical Society*. Proliferates and disseminates scholarly research results in the chemical sciences. Also Cited As: *JICS*.

6688 ■ National Mole Day Foundation
PO Box 602
Millersport, OH 43046
Ph: (740)928-8455
Fax: (740)928-8455
E-mail: mole@avolve.net
URL: http://www.moleday.org
Founded: 1991. **Members:** 3,900. **Membership Dues:** general, $10 (annual). **Staff:** 2. **Description:** Individuals interested in the mole concept, chemistry, and Avogadro's number (the number 6.023 x 10 to the 23rd power, indicating the number of atoms or molecules in a mole of any substance.) Promotes the importance and awareness of chemistry in everyday life. Originates activities for school chemistry clubs; celebrates Mole Day (October 23). **Awards:** George R. Hague Travel Award. **Frequency:** biennial. **Type:** monetary. **Recipient:** for young chemistry instructor ● Maury Award. **Frequency:** annual. **Type:** monetary. **Recipient:** for science teacher ● National Mole of the Year. **Frequency:** biennial. **Type:** monetary. **Recipient:** for member who has contributed the most in furthering the cause of Mole Day and chemistry education. **Publications:** Newsletter, periodic. **Price:** included in membership dues. **Circulation:** 1,500 ● Also offers an annual Idea Kit included in membership dues. **Conventions/Meetings:** biennial meeting, held at the Chem Ed Conferences (exhibits).

6689 ■ National Organization for the Professional Advancement of Black Chemists and Chemical Engineers (NOBCChE)
PO Box 77040
Washington, DC 20013
Free: (800)776-1419
Fax: (202)667-1705
E-mail: president@nobcche.org
URL: http://www.nobcche.org
Contact: Victor McCrary PhD, Pres.
Founded: 1972. **Members:** 4,000. **Membership Dues:** regular, $75 (annual) ● associate, $40 (annual) ● student, $10 (annual). **Staff:** 1. **Budget:** $280,000. **Regional Groups:** 5. **Local Groups:** 60. **Description:** Black professionals in science and chemistry. Seeks to aid black scientists and chemists in reaching their full professional potential; encourages black students to pursue scientific studies and employment; promotes participation of blacks in scientific research. Provides volunteers to teach science courses in selected elementary schools; sponsors scientific field trips for students; maintains speakers' bureau for schools. Conducts technical seminars in Africa. Sponsors competitions; presents awards for significant achievements to individuals in the field. Maintains placement service; compiles statistics. **Libraries: Type:** reference. **Holdings:** archival material, books. **Subjects:** chemistry, Science, black history. **Computer Services:** database, records file. **Affiliated With:** American Association for the Advancement of Science; American Chemical Society; American Institute of Chemical Engineers; Chemical Heritage Foundation. **Formerly:** (1989) National Organization of Black Chemists and Chemical Engineers. **Publications:** *Newsmagazine*, quarterly. Newsletter. **Price:** free. **Circulation:** 4,000. **Advertising:** accepted. Alternate Formats: online ●

Proceedings of Annual Meeting. **Conventions/Meetings:** annual conference (exhibits) - always March/April.

6690 ■ North American Alliance of Chemical Engineers (NAAChE)
3 Park Ave.
New York, NY 10016
E-mail: naacheinfo@aiche.org
URL: http://www.naache.org
Contact: Roberto Andrade Cruz, Pres.
Founded: 2000. **Description:** Provides a North American platform to promote collaboration and establish influence for the benefit of chemical engineers and society. Facilitates education and training of the chemical engineering workforce to meet the common needs of chemical engineers. Encourages and improves the mobility of chemical engineers in North America. **Programs:** Education.

6691 ■ North American Chinese Clinical Chemists Association (NACCCA)
c/o Run-Zhang Shi, PhD, Treas.
Medical Coll. of Wisconsin
Dept. of Pathology
8701 Watertown Plank Rd.
Milwaukee, WI 53226
Ph: (414)805-1524
Fax: (414)805-6980
E-mail: rzhangshi@mail.mcw.edu
URL: http://www.naccca.org
Contact: Run-Zhang Shi PhD, Treas.
Members: 500. **Membership Dues:** regular, $15 (annual) ● regular, $25 (biennial). **Multinational. Description:** Fosters academic, developmental, and service excellence in the practice of clinical laboratory medicine. **Publications:** *NACCA Newsletter*. Alternate Formats: online ● Membership Directory. **Conventions/Meetings:** annual meeting.

6692 ■ Organic Reactions Catalysis Society (ORCS)
c/o Michael L. Prunier, Chm.
Lilly Corporate Ctr.
DC 1940
Indianapolis, IN 46285
Ph: (317)433-0372
Fax: (317)433-0533
E-mail: chairman@orcs.org
URL: http://www.orcs.org
Contact: Michael L. Prunier, Chm.
Founded: 1966. **Members:** 230. **Membership Dues:** individual, $150 (biennial). **Staff:** 1. **Description:** Industrial and academic synthetic organic chemists interested in the use of catalysts in synthetic operations. Fosters discussions on catalytic reactions of organic compounds; provides opportunities for members to present and discuss their work; disseminates information on chemical catalyses. **Awards:** Murray Raney Award. **Frequency:** biennial. **Type:** monetary. **Recipient:** for outstanding contribution to the use of Raney type catalysts ● Paul Rylander Award. **Frequency:** annual. **Type:** monetary. **Recipient:** for outstanding contribution to the field of catalysis. **Affiliated With:** North American Catalysis Society. **Publications:** *Catalysis in Organic Reactions*, biennial. Proceedings. **Price:** $62.00. **Conventions/Meetings:** biennial conference (exhibits).

6693 ■ Societe de Chimie Industrielle, American Section
44 Deanna Dr., Ste.128
Hillsborough, NJ 08844
Ph: (212)725-9539
E-mail: mail@societe.org
URL: http://www.societe.org
Contact: John E. Roberts, Pres.
Founded: 1918. **Members:** 700. **Membership Dues:** individual, $60 (annual) ● corporate, $300 (annual). **Budget:** $100,000. **Description:** Serves as professional society of industrialists, chemists, chemical engineers, and molecular scientists. Promotes international cooperation in the chemical and life sciences communities. **Libraries: Type:** reference. **Holdings:** artwork, books, periodicals. **Subjects:** chemical, pharmaceutical, industrial. **Awards:** Gold Medal Award. **Frequency:** annual. **Type:** medal. **Recipient:** for an outstanding individual in the world of chemical heritage ● International Palladium Medal. **Frequency:** biennial. **Type:** medal. **Recipient:** to an outstanding international chemical industrialist ● Perkin Medal. **Frequency:** annual. **Type:** medal. **Recipient:** for outstanding work in applied chemistry ● Winthrop-Sears Award. **Frequency:** annual. **Type:** recognition. **Recipient:** for outstanding individuals in the chemical industry. **Affiliated With:** Chemical Heritage Foundation. **Conventions/Meetings:** biennial International Palladium Medal Dinner ● monthly luncheon, includes speakers dealing with pertinent topics to the industry - always in New York City ● triennial meeting, includes international profit center managers - always in Paris, France.

6694 ■ Society for Biomolecular Sciences (SBS)
36 Tamarack Ave., No. 348
Danbury, CT 06811
Ph: (203)743-1336
Fax: (203)748-7557
E-mail: email@sbsonline.org
URL: http://www.sbsonline.org
Contact: Christine Giordano CAE, Exec. Dir.
Founded: 1994. **Members:** 2,100. **Membership Dues:** student, retired, $75 (annual) ● individual, $175 (annual). **Staff:** 12. **Budget:** $3,500,000. **Multinational. Description:** Aims to advance the science of drug discovery by uniting industrial and academic chemists, biochemists, pharmacologists, cellular/molecular biologists, genomics/proteomics, computer and information specialists, automation and instrumentation manufacturers. Has created four microplate standards recognized by ANSI; works to standardize liquid handling devices; role is to provide networking opportunities to promote the exchange of information, provide professional development through educational opportunities and engage in advocacy for the pharmaceutical discovery industry. **Awards:** SBS Accomplishment Award. **Frequency:** annual. **Type:** monetary. **Recipient:** to a member with a significant technical accomplishment ● SBS Achievement Award. **Frequency:** triennial. **Type:** monetary. **Recipient:** for outstanding achievements in research and innovation ● SBS Award for Innovation in HTS and Lead Discovery. **Frequency:** annual. **Type:** monetary ● SBS PolyPops Foundation Award for the Best Conference Presentation. **Frequency:** annual. **Type:** monetary. **Recipient:** for the best conference presentation at the annual meeting ● SBS PolyPops Foundation Award for the Best Innovation in Microplate Design or Application. **Frequency:** annual. **Type:** monetary. **Recipient:** to a member for the best innovation in microplate design or application ● SBS Small Grants Program. **Frequency:** annual. **Type:** monetary. **Committees:** Academic Outreach; Awards; Conference; Education; Endowment; Microplate Standards Development; Partners in Commerce. **Special Interest Groups:** Assay Design; Compound Management; Data & Information Technology; Standards in Automation; TOX/ADME. **Formerly:** (2006) Society for Biomolecular Screening. **Publications:** *Journal of Biomolecular Screening*, bimonthly. Contains information on biomolecular drug discovery. **Advertising:** accepted. Alternate Formats: online ● *SBS News*, quarterly. Newspaper. Chronicles the professional achievements of SBS membership. **Price:** free for members. **Conventions/Meetings:** triennial Biobay View of Drug Discovery - regional meeting (exhibits) ● quarterly board meeting ● annual conference and trade show (exhibits) ● regional meeting.

6695 ■ Society of Cosmetic Chemists (SCC)
120 Wall St., Ste.2400
New York, NY 10005-4088
Ph: (212)668-1500
Fax: (212)668-1504
E-mail: scc@scconline.org
URL: http://www.scconline.org
Contact: Theresa Cesario, Exec. Dir.
Founded: 1945. **Members:** 4,000. **Membership Dues:** general, national affiliate status, $120 (annual) ● retired, junior, $60 (annual) ● student, $30 (annual). **Staff:** 4. **Budget:** $1,200,000. **Regional Groups:** 4. **Local Groups:** 18. **Description:** Serves a professional society of scientists involved in the cosmetic industry. Sponsors educational institution support programs to stimulate growth of cosmetic science-related programs. Maintains placement service. **Awards:** Chapter Awards. **Type:** recognition. **Recipient:** for excellent papers ● Lifetime Service Award. **Type:** recognition. **Recipient:** for an individual's extraordinary service ● Literature Award. **Frequency:** annual. **Type:** recognition. **Recipient:** for authors of scientific papers in basic research ● Maison G. de Navarre Medal Award. **Frequency:** annual. **Type:** medal. **Recipient:** for outstanding contributions to cosmetic science ● Merit Award. **Frequency:** annual. **Type:** recognition. **Recipient:** for outstanding service and leadership ● Young Scientists Award. **Frequency:** annual. **Type:** recognition. **Recipient:** for new cosmetic scientists. **Telecommunication Services:** electronic mail, tcesario@scconline.org. **Affiliated With:** International Federation of Societies of Cosmetic Chemists. **Publications:** *Journal of Cosmetic Science*, bimonthly. **Price:** $200.00 straight subscribers; $180.00 agency. **Circulation:** 4,200. **Advertising:** accepted ● Newsletter, semiannual ● Monographs. Alternate Formats: online. **Conventions/Meetings:** annual meeting - always December in New York City ● annual seminar, scientific.

6696 ■ Society of Flavor Chemists
3301 Rte. 66, Bldg. C, Ste.205
Neptune, NJ 07753
Ph: (732)922-3393
Fax: (732)922-3590
E-mail: administrator@flavorchemist.org
URL: http://www.flavorchemist.org
Contact: Ms. Eileen Brady, Pres.
Membership Dues: regular, $50 (annual) ● affiliate, $90 (annual). **Description:** Works to advance the field of flavor technology and related sciences. Encourages the exchange of ideas and personal contacts among flavor chemists. **Committees:** Arrangements; Employment; Historian; Library; Midwest Meeting; Program; Publicity; Symposium. **Publications:** Newsletter, quarterly. Alternate Formats: online.

6697 ■ U.S. National Committee for the International Union of Pure and Applied Chemistry (USNC/IUPAC)
The Natl. Academies
Keck Center
500 5th St. NW
Washington, DC 20001
Ph: (202)334-2807
Fax: (202)334-2231
E-mail: iupac-us@nas.edu
URL: http://www7.nationalacademies.org/usnc-iupac
Contact: Katherine Browman, Program Off.
Founded: 1919. **Members:** 45. **Description:** Represents chemists from academia, government, and industry. Investigates and makes recommendations for action on chemical matters of international importance that need regulation, standardization, or codification. Cooperates with other organizations on topics concerning chemicals; promotes cooperation among chemists. Maintains the Chemical Research Applied to World Needs Committee. **Affiliated With:** American Chemical Society. **Publications:** *Pure and Applied Chemistry*, monthly. Journal ● Directory, biennial. **Conventions/Meetings:** biennial congress (exhibits) ● biennial International General Assembly of Pure and Applied Chemistry.

Chinese

6698 ■ Association of Chinese Scientists and Engineers - U.S.A. (ACSE)
PO Box 59715
Schaumburg, IL 60159
E-mail: info@acse.org
URL: http://acse.org
Contact: Chunlai Yang, Pres.
Membership Dues: individual (employed), $25 (annual) ● couple (employed), $40 (annual) ● individual

(student/unemployed), $10 (annual) ● couple (student/unemployed), $15 (annual) ● corporation, $250 (annual) ● life, $500. **Languages:** Chinese, English. **Multinational. Description:** Promotes friendship and fellowship among its members and the Chinese community. Advances the exchange of professional information and experiences to help the career development, growth and success of members. Fosters and develops exchange and cooperation between the United States and China in the areas of science, technology, culture, education and business. **Publications:** Newsletter. Alternate Formats: online.

Civil Engineering

6699 ■ Civil Engineering Forum of Innovation (CEFI)
c/o American Society of Civil Engineers
1801 Alexander Bell Dr., Ste.630
Reston, VA 20191
Ph: (703)295-6314
Fax: (703)295-6315
E-mail: sskemp@asce.org
URL: http://content.asce.org/cefi/HomePage.html
Contact: Ms. Susan Skemp, Exec. VP
Founded: 1989. **Staff:** 55. **Description:** Focuses on constructing an efficient and renewable future. Operates innovative technology programs to speed the use of innovation into practice in the areas of transportation, public works, energy systems and applications, and the environment. Strives to bring about market transformation and move institutions toward a sustainable future through training and technical assistance, financial analysis, policy advocacy, and project demonstrations. **Awards:** CERF Charles Pankow Award for Innovation. **Frequency:** annual. **Type:** recognition. **Recipient:** for industry leaders who have worked collaboratively to move innovation into practice ● Henry L. Michel Award for Industry Advancement of Research. **Frequency:** annual. **Type:** recognition. **Recipient:** for an individual who has gave an exemplary support to research and development efforts. **Formerly:** (2001) Civil Engineering Research Foundation; (2006) CERF/IIEC.

6700 ■ International Geosynthetics Society (IGS)
PO Box 347
Easley, SC 29641
Ph: (864)855-0504
Fax: (864)859-1698
E-mail: igssec@aol.com
URL: http://www.geosyntheticssociety.org
Contact: Daniele Cazzuffi, Pres.
Founded: 1983. **Members:** 2,097. **Membership Dues:** individual, $45 (annual) ● corporate, $1,000 (annual). **National Groups:** 27. **Multinational. Description:** Promotes the scientific and engineering development of geosynthetics and associated technologies. Collects and disseminates knowledge on matters relevant to geotextiles, geomembranes, and related products. Improves the communication and understanding of geosynthetics and their applications. **Committees:** Asian Activities; Education; European Activities; International Liaison; North American Activities; South American Activities; Strategy; Technical. **Publications:** *Geosynthetics International*, bimonthly. Journal. Alternate Formats: online ● *Geotextiles and Geomembranes*. Journal. **Price:** $154.00 for hard copy subscriptions. Alternate Formats: online ● *IGS News*, 3/year. Newsletter. Alternate Formats: online. **Conventions/Meetings:** annual international conference.

6701 ■ North American Geosynthetics Society (NAGS)
PO Box 12063
Albany, NY 12212-2063
Ph: (518)869-2917
Fax: (518)869-2917
E-mail: ldavidalbany@aol.com
URL: http://www.nags-igs.org
Contact: Y. Grace Hsuan PhD, Pres.
Membership Dues: regular, in U.S., $75 (annual) ● regular, in Canada, in Mexico, overseas, $85 (annual). **Multinational. Description:** Promotes the scientific and engineering development of geotextiles, geomembranes, related products, and other associated technologies. Provides leadership in advancing the education and research of geosynthetics. Improves the communication and understanding of geosynthetics and their applications. **Computer Services:** database, expertise directory. **Conventions/Meetings:** annual conference.

Coal

6702 ■ American Coal Council (ACC)
2980 E Northern Ave., Ste.B5
Phoenix, AZ 85028
Ph: (602)485-4737
Fax: (602)485-4847
E-mail: info@americancoalcouncil.org
URL: http://www.americancoalcouncil.org
Contact: Janet Gellici, Exec. Dir.
Founded: 1982. **Members:** 140. **Membership Dues:** corporate, $1,500 (annual) ● fully owned subsidiary, $500 (annual). **Staff:** 3. **Budget:** $650,000. **Description:** Coal, utility, transportation, terminal and coal support services companies. Aims to advance the development and utilization of U.S. coal as an economic, abundant and environmentally sound energy fuel source. Provides CoalMart, an electronic yellow pages directory of utility-coal industry equipment suppliers and service providers. Maintains clearinghouse database of coal, utility power marketing, transportation, shipping and professional service industry contacts. **Computer Services:** Information services, of upcoming events, industry news, and important issues. **Formerly:** (2003) Western Coal Council Mission. **Publications:** *American Coal*, annual. Magazine. Contains listing of western utility-coal resources. **Circulation:** 5,000. **Advertising:** accepted ● *American Coal Advisory*, quarterly. Newsletter. Features member companies and U.S. coal issues. **Price:** included in membership dues. **Circulation:** 3,000. **Advertising:** accepted. Alternate Formats: online ● *Short Lists*, quarterly. Newsletter. Contains listing of western utility-coal resources. **Price:** included in membership dues. **Circulation:** 3,000. Alternate Formats: online ● Membership Directory. Alternate Formats: online. **Conventions/Meetings:** annual Coal Strategies - conference, industry forum on strategic issues (exhibits) ● annual Coal Trading Conference, to keep current on emerging trends and industry developments (exhibits) - every winter ● annual Mercury and Multi-Emissions Compliance Seminar - spring ● annual PRB Coal Use Seminar - summer ● annual Spring Coal Forum - conference, to keep current on emerging trends and industry developments (exhibits).

Coatings

6703 ■ Association for Finishing Processes of the Society of Manufacturing Engineers (AFP/SME)
1 SME Dr.
PO Box 930
Dearborn, MI 48121
Ph: (313)271-1500
Free: (800)733-4763
Fax: (313)425-3401
E-mail: service@sme.org
URL: http://www.sme.org/cgi-bin/communities.pl?/communities/afp/afphome.htm&&&SME
Contact: Mark Tomlinson, Exec. Dir./Gen. Mgr.
Founded: 1975. **Members:** 1,550. **Membership Dues:** individual, $125 (annual). **Staff:** 3. **Regional Groups:** 5. **Description:** Promotes the technology, process, and management aspects of the cleaning and coating of metal or plastic manufactured products and trade organizations concerned with the dissemination of knowledge related to industrial finishing. Conducts clinics and expositions. Offers professional certification. Maintains placement service with free listings for members. **Libraries: Type:** reference. **Awards:** Eli Whitney Productivity Award. **Frequency:** annual. **Type:** recognition. **Recipient:** for distinguished accomplishments in improving capability within the broad concept of orderly production ● Joseph A. Siegel Service Award. **Frequency:** annual. **Type:** recognition. **Recipient:** to a member for significant and unique contributions that benefit the society. **Computer Services:** database, technical referral. **Publications:** *Finishing Line*, quarterly. Newsletter. Contains technical information. **Price:** free for members; $85.00 /year for nonmembers. **Circulation:** 3,000 ● *Finishing Systems Design and Implementation*. Book ● *Lean Directions*, monthly. Newsletter. Features articles on principles and news about using lean techniques. **Price:** free. Alternate Formats: online ● *Managing a Paint Shop*. Book ● *Paint and Powder Coatings*. Video ● *TMEH, Volume 3: Materials, Finishing and Coating*. Book ● *Users Guide to Powder Coating, 3rd Ed.*. Book. **Conventions/Meetings:** biennial Automotive FINISHING - conference (exhibits) - even numbered years.

6704 ■ Federation of Societies for Coatings Technology (FSCT)
492 Norristown Rd.
Blue Bell, PA 19422-2350
Ph: (610)940-0777
Fax: (610)940-0292
E-mail: fsct@coatingstech.org
URL: http://www.coatingstech.org
Contact: Fred Anwari, Chm., Bylaws Committee
Founded: 1922. **Members:** 7,300. **Membership Dues:** full, $79 (annual) ● educator, $20 (annual) ● student, $20 (annual). **Staff:** 15. **Budget:** $3,000,000. **Local Groups:** 26. **Multinational. Description:** Represents chemists, chemical engineers, technologists, and supervisory production personnel in the decorative and protective coatings industry and allied industries. Works to gather and disseminate practical and technical facts, data, and standards fundamental to the manufacturing and use of paints, varnishes, lacquers, related protective coatings, and printing inks. **Awards: Type:** grant. **Recipient:** for colleges and universities' training persons in paint technology. **Committees:** ASTM; Corrosion; Educational; Manufacturing; National Association of Corrosive Engineers; Technical Advisory. **Councils:** Inter-Society Color. **Formerly:** (1960) Federation of Paint and Varnish Production Clubs; (1975) Federation of Societies for Paint Technology. **Publications:** *Coatings Encyclopedic Dictionary* ● *Federation of Societies for Coatings Technology—Yearbook*, annual. Membership Directory. **Price:** included in membership dues; $20.00 for nonmembers. **Circulation:** 7,300. **Advertising:** accepted ● *Infrared Spectroscopy Atlas for the Coatings Industry* ● *Journal of Coatings Technology*, monthly. Includes practical and technical papers on paint and decorative coatings technology and manufacture. **Price:** included in membership dues. ISSN: 0361-8773. **Circulation:** 9,000. **Advertising:** accepted ● *Pictorial Standards of Coatings Defects*. **Conventions/Meetings:** annual conference (exhibits).

6705 ■ International Society of Coating Science and Technology (ISCST)
146 Dewberry Dr.
Hockessin, DE 19707
Ph: (530)752-8780
Fax: (530)752-1039
E-mail: bghiggins@ucdavis.edu
URL: http://www.iscst.org
Contact: Brian G. Higgins, Pres.
Founded: 1996. **Multinational. Description:** Represents academic and industrial engineers who are active in the many aspects of coating technology. Encourages technology transfer, professional development, and networking of scientists who are engaged in the coating process sciences. Provides forums for presenting advances in the mechanisms and technologies used in the preparation, application, solidification, and microstructuring of coated films. Provides continuing educational programs in coating process science and technology. **Awards:** John A. Tallmadge Award for Contributions to Coating Technology. **Frequency:** biennial. **Type:** recognition. **Recipient:** for significant contributions to the

understanding or improvement of the technology of the coating of continuous webs ● L.E. Scriven Young Investigator Award. **Frequency:** biennial. **Type:** recognition. **Recipient:** for outstanding achievements or one-time breakthroughs in the area of continuous liquid film coating science and technology. **Publications:** Papers. **Price:** $30.00 per copy. **Conventions/ Meetings:** biennial symposium - 2008 Sept. 9-13, Marina del Rey, CA.

6706 ■ Surface Engineering Coating Association (SECA)
Univ. of Buffalo Tech. Center
1576 Sweet Home Rd., Ste.102
Amherst, NY 14228
Ph: (716)791-8100
Fax: (716)278-8768
E-mail: fred@surfaceengineering.org
URL: http://www.surfaceengineering.org
Contact: Frederick J. Teeter, Managing Dir.

Founded: 1999. **Members:** 15. **Staff:** 3. **Description:** Companies that apply coatings to cutting tools, forming tools, molds, precision components and decorative fixtures. Promotes the image of the surface engineering industry as a provider of coating services vital to all industry. Collects, compiles and distributes information with respect to matters relating to the industry. Confers and cooperates with government agencies and other official bodies in the interest of the public and the industry.

Color

6707 ■ Eiseman Center for Color Information and Training (ECCIT)
c/o Pantone, Inc.
590 Commerce Blvd.
Carlstadt, NJ 07072-3013
Ph: (201)935-5500
Fax: (201)896-0242
E-mail: leiseman@colorexpert.com
URL: http://www.pantone.com
Contact: Leatrice Eiseman, Exec. Dir.

Founded: 1985. **Staff:** 6. **Description:** Aims to study the psychology of color. Conducts research and disseminates information on the psychology of color, societal and cultural trends relating to color, color and personality, consumer color preferences, color trends, and the functions of color in fashion, marketing, advertising, interior, graphic, and industrial design. Conducts seminars; provides consultation services. **Additional Websites:** http://www.colorexpert.com. **Programs:** Color Design Training. **Formerly:** (1991) Pantone Color Institute. **Publications:** *Alive with Color*. Book ● *Color Answer Book* ● *Colors for Your Every Mood*. Book ● *Pantone Book of Color* ● *Pantone Guide to Communicating with Color*. Book.

6708 ■ Inter-Society Color Council (ISCC)
11491 Sunset Hills Rd.
Reston, VA 20190
Ph: (703)318-0263
Fax: (703)318-0514
E-mail: isccoffice@cs.com
URL: http://www.iscc.org
Contact: Dr. Robert Buckley, Pres.

Founded: 1931. **Members:** 800. **Membership Dues:** student, retired, $10 (annual) ● individual, $75 (annual) ● organization, $200 (annual) ● sustaining, $750 (annual). **Budget:** $25,000. **Description:** Represents national societies and individuals interested in color. Focuses on the practical application of color description and specification to color problems in science, art, and industry. Maintains biographical archives and Speaker's Bureau; organizes seminars. **Awards:** Godlove. **Frequency:** biennial. **Type:** recognition. **Recipient:** for lifetime contributions to the field of color ● Macbeth. **Frequency:** biennial. **Type:** recognition. **Recipient:** for recent outstanding accomplishments in the field of color ● Nickerson Service. **Frequency:** periodic. **Type:** recognition. **Recipient:** for special service to the council. **Computer Services:** Mailing lists, educational institutes. **Publications:** *ISCC News*, bimonthly. Newsletter. Includes book reviews, calendar of events, and obituaries. **Price:** included in membership dues; $90.00 for libraries (hardcopy); $15.00 for retired (hardcopy); $100.00 overseas (hardcopy). **Circulation:** 950. **Advertising:** accepted. Alternate Formats: online ● *Membership List*, annual. Membership Directory ● Books ● Papers ● Reports. **Conventions/Meetings:** periodic congress ● annual meeting ● annual Williamsburg Conference - convention, small group format (exhibits).

Combustion

6709 ■ Combustion Institute (CI)
5001 Baum Blvd., Ste.635
Pittsburgh, PA 15213-1851
Ph: (412)687-1366
Fax: (412)687-0340
E-mail: office@combustioninstitute.org
URL: http://www.combustioninstitute.org
Contact: Sue Steiner Terpack, Exec. Admin.

Founded: 1954. **Members:** 3,500. **Membership Dues:** individual in U.S., $40 (biennial) ● student in U.S., $10 (biennial). **Staff:** 3. **National Groups:** 25. **Description:** Professional society of physicists, chemists, and engineers engaged in combustion research. Seeks to promote science and application of combustion and to disseminate knowledge in this field. **Publications:** *Combustion and Flame*, monthly. Journal. Contains experimental and theoretical investigations of combustion phenomena and closely allied matters. **Price:** $57.00/year; EUR 48.00/year. ISSN: 0010-2180 ● *Symposia Proceedings*, biennial. **Conventions/Meetings:** biennial International Symposium - 2008 Aug. 3-8, Montreal, QC, Canada.

Communications

6710 ■ American Communication Association (ACA)
c/o Dale Cyphert, PhD, Treas.
The Univ. of Northern Iowa
Coll. of Bus. Admin.
1227 W 27th St.
Cedar Falls, IA 50614-0125
Ph: (319)273-6150
E-mail: dale.cyphert@uni.edu
URL: http://www.americancomm.org
Contact: Ann Rosenthal PhD, Pres.

Founded: 1993. **Languages:** English, Portuguese, Spanish. **Multinational. Description:** Works to enable the effective use of new and evolving technologies to facilitate communication instruction, research and criticism. Offers a technologically supportive venue for people who study the ways in which humans communicate. Fosters research and scholarship in all areas of human communication behavior. Provides a voice in communication law and policy. Provides evaluation and certification services for academic programs in communication study. **Telecommunication Services:** electronic mail, ann.rosenthal@bakeru.edu. **Publications:** *American Communication Journal*. Contains analysis and criticism of significant communicative artifacts. Alternate Formats: online. Also Cited As: *ACJ*. **Conventions/ Meetings:** annual Communication Conference of the Americas, held in conjunction with several Latin American universities throughout Central and South America.

6711 ■ International Association of Messaging Professionals (IAMP)
1501 Harkness St.
Manhattan Beach, CA 90266
Ph: (816)414-4972
E-mail: kyle.honadel@capgemini.com
URL: http://www.iampro.org
Contact: Kyle Honadel, Pres.

Membership Dues: company, vendor, $100 (annual). **Multinational. Description:** Provides information to members focusing on unified communications and messaging of all types including voicemail, e-mail, fax and instant messaging. Focuses on messaging technologies in multiple mediums. Facilitates a forum for messaging professionals. **Publications:** Newsletter. Alternate Formats: online.

6712 ■ International Society for Gesture Studies (ISGS)
Dept. of Commun. Stud.
The Univ. of Texas at Austin
1 Univ. Sta.
Austin, TX 78712-0115
E-mail: adamk@dca.net
URL: http://www.gesturestudies.com
Contact: Adam Kendon, Honorary Pres.

Founded: 2002. **Membership Dues:** regular, $50 (annual) ● student, $25 (annual). **Multinational. Description:** Promotes gesture studies worldwide. Facilitates dialogue among researchers, professionals, and the interested public, across disciplinary and institutional boundaries. Integrates the study of gesture with investigations into a diverse range of forms of cognitive, communicative, and cultural life of human groups. **Publications:** *Manufacts*. Newsletter. Contains news and updates from the society and the community of gesture research. Alternate Formats: online.

6713 ■ Markle Foundation
10 Rockefeller Plz., 16th Fl.
New York, NY 10020-1903
Ph: (212)713-7600
Fax: (212)765-9690
E-mail: info@markle.org
URL: http://www.markle.org
Contact: Zoe Baird, Pres.

Founded: 1927. **Staff:** 12. **Description:** Promotes the development of communications industries that address public needs. Pursues goals through activities including analysis, research, public information, and the development of innovative media products and services. **Programs:** Information Technologies for Better Health; Interactive Media for Children; Policy for a Networked Society.

6714 ■ MPLS and Frame Relay Alliance
39355 California St., Ste.307
Fremont, CA 94538
Ph: (510)608-5910
Fax: (510)608-5917
E-mail: info@mplsforum.org
URL: http://www.mplsforum.org
Contact: Alexa Morris, Exec. Dir.

Membership Dues: large company principal, $12,000 (annual) ● small company principal, $6,000 (annual) ● auditing, $4,000 (annual) ● user, $1,000 (annual) ● non-profit, $5,000 (annual). **Multinational. Description:** Networking and telecommunication companies focused on advancing the deployment of multi-vendor multi-service label switching networks and associated applications. **Formed by Merger of:** (2003) Frame Relay Forum; (2003) MPLS Forum. **Conventions/Meetings:** MD&E Committee - meeting, teleconferences ● quarterly Technical Committee - general assembly.

6715 ■ National Association of Communication Systems Engineers (NACSE)
18029 E Dorado Ave.
Centennial, CO 80015
Ph: (720)269-4777
Fax: (720)269-4756
E-mail: rkile@nacse.com
URL: http://www.nacse.com
Contact: Bob Kile, Exec. Dir.

Membership Dues: corporate, $2,400-$6,000 (annual) ● regular, $125 (annual) ● educational partner, $250-$500 (annual). **Description:** Promotes and supports best practices and professional standards that address a broad range of IT disciplines. Advances the technical professionalism, business ethics and personal integrity of communication system engineers. **Publications:** Newsletter, monthly. Alternate Formats: online.

6716 ■ United States Connected Communities Association (US-CCA)
1901 Pennsylvania Ave. NW, 5th Fl.
Washington, DC 20006
E-mail: thenderson@us-cca.org
URL: http://www.us-cca.org
Contact: Tom Henderson, Managing Dir./Co-Founder
Founded: 2005. **Membership Dues:** community, $1,000-$2,000 (annual) ● vendor (publicly-traded company), $40,000 (annual) ● vendor (privately-traded company), $10,000 (annual) ● other, $1,000 (annual). **Description:** Helps communities understand and manage their communications future. Provides economic, planning, and standards models. Fosters research and development. Systematizes and standardizes wiring standards for new construction. Promotes dialog, education and advancement of productive community communications assets. **Libraries: Type:** open to the public; reference. **Holdings:** articles. **Subjects:** connected community. **Publications:** Newsletter.

Compensation Medicine

6717 ■ Hospitality Information Technology Association (HITA)
c/o Corliss Rodgers, Sec.-Treas.
450 S Quinn St., No. 8
Mesa, AZ 85206
Ph: (928)523-0393 (480)423-6637
E-mail: corliss.rodgers@nau.edu
URL: http://www.hitaworld.org
Contact: Corliss Rodgers, Sec.-Treas.
Founded: 1992. **Members:** 150. **Membership Dues:** student, $30 (annual) ● individual, $90 (annual) ● corporate discounted, $250 (annual) ● corporate, $750 (annual). **Staff:** 5. **Budget:** $15,000. **Regional Groups:** 1. **Description:** Works to improve the technology and quality of education of information technology (IT). Develops IT curriculum; disseminates information; acts as a forum for exchange of information and networking among members; develops and adopts standards; sponsors research. **Awards: Type:** scholarship. **Publications:** *Information Technology in Hospitality*. Journal. **Price:** included in membership dues ● Brochure. **Conventions/Meetings:** annual conference.

Computer Science

6718 ■ American Computer Scientists Association (ACSA)
c/o Andrew Vanoceur, Chm.
Gen. Delivery Box ACSA
Los Alamos, NM 87544-9999
Ph: (908)272-0016
Free: (866)836-1932
E-mail: info@acsa2000.net
URL: http://www.acsa.net
Contact: Andrew Vanoceur, Chm.
Founded: 1993. **Members:** 5,980,000. **Membership Dues:** individual, $35 (annual). **Staff:** 14. **Description:** Charitable research and public advocacy foundation combining computer scientists and the general public. **Libraries: Type:** not open to the public. **Holdings:** 2,000,000. **Subjects:** electronic resources, science and technology. **Awards:** Best New Computer System of CPU Idea. **Frequency:** annual. **Type:** recognition ● Best Operating System. **Frequency:** annual. **Type:** recognition ● Computer Scientist of the Year. **Frequency:** annual. **Type:** recognition. **Subgroups:** American Computer Industry Association. **Also Known As:** ACSA. **Publications:** *Advances*. Contains online news, research, and public issues; real-time updating, translatable into 35 languages. **Price:** free. **Advertising:** accepted. Alternate Formats: online; CD-ROM. **Conventions/Meetings:** annual conference.

6719 ■ American Society for Cybernetics (ASC)
2033 K St. NW, Ste.230
Washington, DC 20052
Ph: (202)994-1642
Fax: (202)994-5284
E-mail: rhibit@msn.com
URL: http://www.asc-cybernetics.org
Contact: Mehdi Majidi, Sec.
Founded: 1964. **Members:** 250. **Membership Dues:** regular, fellow, $80 (annual) ● affiliate/student, $35 (annual) ● life, $600. **Local Groups:** 4. **Description:** Represents persons with professional standing or interest in the field of cybernetics. Fosters projects in theoretical and applied cybernetics by means of multidisciplinary scientific research programs; publishes and disseminates results of studies in cybernetics. Encourages education in cybernetics in schools and universities; fosters public understanding of cybernetics, its benefits and implications. Sponsors symposia and workshops. **Publications:** *Conference Proceedings*, annual ● *Cybernetic*, quarterly ● *Glossary of Cybernetics and Systems Theory* ● Newsletter, monthly ● Videos. **Price:** $35.00 in North America; $40.00 outside North America ● Monographs ● Papers. **Price:** $4.25 in North America; $6.00 outside North America. **Conventions/Meetings:** semiannual conference (exhibits).

6720 ■ Applied Voice Input/Output Society (AVIOS)
PO Box 20817
San Jose, CA 95160
Ph: (408)323-1783
Fax: (408)323-1782
E-mail: info@avios.org
URL: http://www.avios.com
Contact: K.W. Scholz, Pres.
Founded: 1981. **Members:** 470. **Membership Dues:** individual, $125 (annual) ● corporate, $800 (annual). **Multinational. Description:** Represents academics, researchers, management personnel, vendors, and engineers; corporations. Seeks to: facilitate communication among potential users of voice technology and the developers and suppliers of this technology; offer information to researchers, technologists, and users on current and future voice input/output technology and its applications. (Voice input/output technology is concerned with the applications of voice recognition and synthesis with and through computers.) Provides information to current and potential users through demonstrations of practical applications of voice systems; offers users opportunities to meet with voice technology researchers, technologists, and service and product providers. **Awards: Type:** recognition. **Recipient:** for unique application of voice input/output technology. **Publications:** *AVIOS Conference Proceedings*, annual ● *AVIOS Journal*, annual. **Conventions/Meetings:** seminar ● annual Speech Developers Conference and Expo.

6721 ■ Association for Computer Aided Design in Architecture (ACADIA)
PO Box 218171
Columbus, OH 43221
Ph: (419)596-6095
E-mail: president@acadia.org
URL: http://www.acadia.org
Contact: Dr. Wassim Jabi, Pres.
Founded: 1980. **Members:** 200. **Membership Dues:** regular in North America, retired outside North America, library in North America, $100 (annual) ● student in North America, $50 (annual) ● student outside North America, $80 (annual) ● library outside North America, $110 (annual) ● retired in North America, $70 (annual) ● regular outside North America, $130 (annual). **Staff:** 20. **Multinational. Description:** Educators, students, and professionals. Works to promote communication and critical thinking regarding the use of computers in architecture, planning and building science; conducts annual national conference, publications, competitions, and exchange with international sister organizations. **Computer Services:** database ● mailing lists. **Publications:** *ACADIA Bits*, 2 or more per year. Newsletter. Alternate Formats: online ● *International Journal of Architectural Computing*. **Price:** $10.00. Alternate Formats: online ● Proceedings, annual. Contains peer reviewed papers about computing in architecture and architectural education. **Price:** included in membership dues. Alternate Formats: online. **Conventions/Meetings:** annual conference (exhibits).

6722 ■ Association for Information Systems (AIS)
PO Box 2712
Atlanta, GA 30301-2712
Ph: (404)651-0348
Fax: (404)651-4938
E-mail: emclean@cis.gsu.edu
URL: http://www.aisnet.org
Contact: Dr. Ephraim McLean, Exec. Dir.
Founded: 1995. **Members:** 4,000. **Membership Dues:** academic, $95 (annual) ● retired academic, $47 (annual) ● student, $60 (annual) ● institutional, $1,750 (annual) ● AIS-SIM joint institutional, $3,000 (annual). **Staff:** 3. **Description:** Academics engaged in the study of information systems and related fields. Represents and promotes members' interests; encourages research and study in information systems and management. Conducts continuing education programs for members; establishes and maintains standards for research and practice in information systems. **Libraries: Type:** reference. **Holdings:** articles. **Awards:** AIS Fellow Award. **Frequency:** annual. **Type:** recognition. **Recipient:** for outstanding contribution to the IS discipline in terms of research, teaching, and service ● Leo Award for Lifetime Exceptional Achievement in Information Systems. **Frequency:** annual. **Type:** recognition. **Recipient:** for outstanding individuals, both academics and practitioners, who have made exceptional contributions to research in and/or the practice of information systems. **Committees:** AISWorld Oversight; Leo Award; Nominating; Organization and Bylaws; Publications; Research Conduct; Technology Innovation. **Subcommittees:** CSAB Accreditation Board Representative. **Publications:** *Communications of the Association for Information Systems*, periodic. Journal. **Price:** included in membership dues; $40.00 /year for nonmembers; $135.00 /year for libraries. Alternate Formats: online ● *Journal of the Association for Information Systems*, periodic. **Price:** included in membership dues; $40.00 /year for nonmembers; $135.00 /year for libraries. Alternate Formats: online ● Proceedings. Alternate Formats: online. **Conventions/Meetings:** annual Americas Conference on Information Systems (exhibits) - always August ● annual International Conference on Information Systems (exhibits) - always December.

6723 ■ CompactFlash Association (CFA)
PO Box 51537
Palo Alto, CA 94303
Ph: (650)843-1220
Fax: (650)493-1871
E-mail: billfrank@compactflash.org
URL: http://www.compactflash.org
Contact: Bill Frank, Contact
Founded: 1995. **Membership Dues:** executive, $5,000 (annual) ● affiliate, $2,500 (annual). **Description:** Encourages the worldwide adoption of CompactFlash (CF) disk drive and CF technology as an open industry standard. Seeks to drive acceptance of the CF specification as an industry standard across platforms and markets internationally. Ensures compatibility for users of CF products, and works to evolve the approved CF standard over time while ensuring backward compatibility.

6724 ■ Computer Measurement Group (CMG)
PO Box 1124
151 Fries Mill Rd., Ste.104
Turnersville, NJ 08012
Ph: (856)401-1700
Free: (800)436-7264
Fax: (856)401-1708
E-mail: cmghq@cmg.org
URL: http://www.cmg.org
Contact: Barbara Yakubovsky, Office Mgr./Sr. Conference Coor.
Founded: 1969. **Members:** 3,000. **Membership Dues:** general, $175 (annual). **Staff:** 4. **Regional Groups:** 30. **Description:** Represents data processing professionals committed to the measurement and management of computer systems, primarily con-

cerned with performance evaluation of existing systems to maximize performance (e.g. response time, throughput, etc.) and with capacity management where planned enhancements to existing systems or the design of new systems are evaluated to find the necessary resources required to provide adequate performance at a reasonable cost. **Awards:** A.A. Michelson Award. **Frequency:** annual. **Type:** recognition. **Recipient:** to an individual outstanding in the field ● Graduate Fellowship Award. **Frequency:** annual. **Type:** fellowship. **Recipient:** to graduate student in computer science ● J. William Mullen Award. **Frequency:** annual. **Type:** recognition. **Recipient:** to an individual who exhibits both technical excellence and an engaging presentation style. **Publications:** *CMG Bulletin*, 3/year. Newsletter ● *CMG Journal*, 3/year. **Price:** $15.00 for members in U.S. and Canada; $20.00 for members outside U.S. and Canada; $30.00 for nonmembers in U.S. and Canada; $40.00 for nonmembers outside U.S. and Canada ● *CMG Proceedings*, annual. **Price:** $60.00 for members in U.S.; $70.00 for members in U.S. and Canada; $80.00 for members outside U.S. and Canada; $120.00 for nonmembers in U.S. **Conventions/Meetings:** annual international conference (exhibits) - always December. 2008 Dec. 7-12, Las Vegas, NV; 2009 Dec. 6-11, Reno, NV; 2010 Dec. 5-10, Orlando, FL; 2011 Dec. 4-9, Reno, NV.

6725 ■ Computing Research Association (CRA)

1100 Seventeenth St. NW, Ste.507
Washington, DC 20036-4632
Ph: (202)234-2111
Fax: (202)667-1066
E-mail: info@cra.org
URL: http://www.cra.org
Contact: Daniel A. Reed, Chm.

Founded: 1972. **Members:** 185. **Membership Dues:** academic department in U.S., $620-$7,100 (annual) ● academic department outside U.S., $332-$2,367 (annual) ● laboratory or center, $14,200 (annual) ● standard laboratory or center for small organization (based on research funding), $1,775-$7,100 (annual) ● sponsoring, $50,000 (annual) ● sustaining, $30,000 (annual) ● supporting, $20,000 (annual) ● standard associate, $13,000 (annual). **Staff:** 7. **Description:** Computer science and computer engineering academic departments, industrial laboratories. Seeks to strengthen research and education in the computing fields, expand opportunities for women and minorities, and educate the public and policy makers on the importance of computing research. Represents the computing research community; advocates on behalf of the community in science and technology policy-making; conducts employment studies and educational programs. **Awards:** CRA Distinguished Service. **Type:** recognition. **Recipient:** for contribution to the computing research community ● Nico Haberman. **Type:** recognition. **Recipient:** for contribution to members of underrepresented groups. **Computer Services:** database, CRA Women's ● mailing lists, professional opportunity announcements. **Telecommunication Services:** electronic mail, members@cra.org. **Formerly:** (1985) Computer Science Board; (1990) Computing Research Board. **Publications:** *Computing Research News*, bimonthly. Newsletter. **Circulation:** 6,000. Alternate Formats: online ● *CRA Bulletin*. Features news and other information of interest to the computing research community. Alternate Formats: online ● *CRA Forsythe List*. Contains listing of PhD-granting and Computer Science and Engineering programs. ● *CRA Taulbee Survey*, annual. Contains information on the production and employment of PhDs and faculty. **Conventions/Meetings:** biennial conference - 2008 July 13-15, Snowbird, UT ● biennial Grace Hopper Celebration of Women in Computing - conference ● periodic seminar.

6726 ■ Embedded Linux Consortium (ELC)

3760 Cross Creek Rd.
Santa Rosa, CA 95403
Ph: (707)576-0111
Fax: (707)576-1944
E-mail: murry@embedded-linux.org
URL: http://www.embedded-linux.org
Contact: Dr. Inder Singh, Chm.

Membership Dues: corporate executive, $24,000 (annual) ● corporate counselor, $10,000 (annual) ● corporate affiliate, $2,500 (annual) ● non-corporate, $150 (annual). **Description:** Works for the advancement, promotion, and standardization of Linux throughout embedded, applied and appliance computing markets to make Linux the operating system of choice for developers designing embedded systems. **Computer Services:** database, resource catalog.

6727 ■ IEEE Computer Society (CS)

1730 Massachusetts Ave. NW
Washington, DC 20036-1992
Ph: (202)371-0101
Fax: (202)728-9614
E-mail: help@computer.org
URL: http://www.computer.org
Contact: Angela R. Burgess, Exec. Dir.

Founded: 1946. **Members:** 90,000. **Membership Dues:** individual, $113 (annual). **Staff:** 110. **Budget:** $36,000,000. **Local Groups:** 323. **Multinational. Description:** Computer professionals. Promotes the development of computer and information sciences and fosters communication within the information processing community. Sponsors conferences, symposia, workshops, tutorials, technical meetings, and seminars. Operates Computer Society Press. Presents scholarships; bestows technical achievement and service awards and certificates. **Libraries: Type:** reference. **Holdings:** periodicals. **Awards:** Award for Software Process Achievement. **Frequency:** annual. **Type:** monetary. **Recipient:** for outstanding achievement in improving the software process ● Computer Entrepreneur Award. **Frequency:** annual. **Type:** recognition. **Recipient:** for managers and leaders who are responsible for the growth of some segment of the computer industry ● Computer Pioneer Award. **Frequency:** annual. **Type:** recognition. **Recipient:** for significant contributions to concepts and developments in the Electronic Computer field which have clearly advanced the state of the art in computing ● Conference Outstanding Paper Awards. **Frequency:** annual. **Type:** monetary. **Recipient:** for the most outstanding contribution to the state of the art within the scope of a Computer Society sponsored or cosponsored conference ● Eckert-Mauchly Award. **Frequency:** annual. **Type:** monetary. **Recipient:** for outstanding contributions to the field of computer architecture ● Hans Karlsson Award. **Frequency:** annual. **Type:** recognition. **Recipient:** for team leadership and achievement through collaboration in the field of computing standards ● K.S. Fu Memorial Best Paper Award. **Frequency:** annual. **Type:** monetary. **Recipient:** for the best paper in the proceedings of the annual conference on pattern recognition ● Lance Staffor Larson Memorial Award. **Frequency:** annual. **Type:** monetary. **Recipient:** for student members who are authors of papers on computer related subjects ● Periodical Outstanding Paper Awards. **Frequency:** annual. **Type:** monetary. **Recipient:** for the most outstanding contribution to the state of the art within the scope of the Computer Science Magazine or IEEE Transactions on Computers ● Richard E. Merwin Award for Distinguished Service. **Frequency:** annual. **Type:** monetary. **Recipient:** for outstanding service to the profession at large ● Sidney Fernbach Memorial Award. **Frequency:** annual. **Type:** monetary. **Recipient:** for outstanding contributions in the application of high performance computers using innovative approaches ● Software Engineering Best Paper Award. **Frequency:** annual. **Type:** monetary. **Recipient:** for the best paper presented at the Software Engineering Annual Conference. **Computer Services:** Mailing lists, of members. **Telecommunication Services:** electronic mail, ombudsman@computer.org. **Committees:** Complexity in Computing; Computational Medicine; Computer and System Packaging; Computer Architecture; Computer Communications; Computer Elements; Computer Generated Music; Computer Graphics; Computer Languages; Data Engineering; Design Automation; Digital Libraries; Distributed Processing; Electronics and the Environment; Engineering of Computer Based Systems; Fault-Tolerant Computing; Mass Storage Systems; Mathematical Foundations of Computing; Microprocessors and Microcomputers; Microprogramming and Microarchitecture; Multimedia Computing; Multiple-Valued Logic; Operating Systems Applications and Environments; Parallel Processing; Pattern Analysis and Machine Intelligence; Real-Time Systems; Security and Privacy; Simulation; Software Engineering Technical; Supercomputing Applications; Test Technology; VLS1. **Programs:** Accreditation (CSAB); Awards; Chapter Tutorials. **Affiliated With:** Institute of Electrical and Electronics Engineers. **Publications:** *Computer*, monthly. Magazine. Covers the major trends in computer science and engineering. **Price:** included in membership dues. **Circulation:** 97,000. **Advertising:** accepted. Alternate Formats: online ● *Computing in Science and Engineering*, bimonthly. Magazine ● *IEEE Annals of the History of Computing*, quarterly. Journal ● *IEEE Computer Graphics and Applications*, bimonthly. Magazine ● *IEEE Design and Test of Computers*, quarterly. Magazine ● *IEEE Intelligent Systems*, bimonthly. Magazine ● *IEEE Internet Computing*, bimonthly. Magazine ● *IEEE Micro*, bimonthly. Magazine ● *IEEE MultiMedia*, quarterly. Magazine ● *IEEE Pervasive Computing*, quarterly. Magazine. **Advertising:** accepted ● *IEEE Security & Privacy*, bimonthly. Magazine. **Advertising:** accepted ● *IEEE Software*, bimonthly. Magazine ● *IEEE Transactions on Computers*, monthly. Journal ● *IEEE Transactions on Knowledge and Data Engineering*, bimonthly. Journal ● *IEEE Transactions on Parallel and Distributed Systems*, monthly. Journal ● *IEEE Transactions on Pattern Analysis and Machine Intelligence*, monthly. Journal ● *IEEE Transactions on Software Engineering*, quarterly. Journal ● *IEEE Transactions on Visualization and Computer Graphics*, quarterly. Journal ● *IT Professional*, bimonthly. Magazine. **Advertising:** accepted ● Also publishes technical reports, papers, newsletters, proceedings, and books. **Conventions/Meetings:** conference and symposium.

6728 ■ IEEE Systems, Man, and Cybernetics Society (SMCS)

c/o IEEE Admission and Advancement Department
3 Park Ave., 17th Fl.
New York, NY 10016-5997
Ph: (212)419-7900
Free: (800)678-4333
Fax: (212)752-4929
E-mail: lohall@ieee.org
URL: http://www.ieeesmc.org
Contact: Lawrence O. Hall, Pres.

Members: 3,895. **Membership Dues:** regular, $12 (annual). **Local Groups:** 25. **Multinational. Description:** A society of the Institute of Electrical and Electronics Engineers. Serves as a forum on the theoretical and practical considerations of systems engineering, human machine systems, and cybernetics—with a particular focus on synthetic and natural systems involving humans and machines. **Awards:** Andrew P. Sage Best Transactions Paper Award. **Frequency:** annual. **Type:** monetary. **Recipient:** to the authors of the best paper published annually in the IEEE Transactions on Systems, Man and Cybernetics (SMC) ● Joseph Wohl Award. **Frequency:** annual. **Type:** monetary. **Recipient:** for outstanding professional contributions to systems engineering concepts, methodology, design, education, or management ● Norbert Wiener Award. **Frequency:** annual. **Type:** monetary. **Recipient:** for significant contributions to research in systems, human factors, and cybernetics. **Committees:** Technical. **Affiliated With:** Institute of Electrical and Electronics Engineers. **Publications:** *IEEE Transactions on Systems, Man, and Cybernetics, Part A: Systems and Humans*, bimonthly. Journal ● *IEEE Transactions on Systems, Man, and Cybernetics, Part B: Cybernetics*, bimonthly. Journal. Publishes papers on cybernetics. ● *IEEE Transactions on Systems, Man, and Cybernetics, Part C: Application and Reviews*, bimonthly. Journal. Publishes applications and reviews in the area of systems, human-machine systems and cybernetics. **Conventions/Meetings:** annual IEEE International

Conference on Systems, Man and Cybernetics, high quality International technical meeting in areas of Systems, Human-Machine Systems and Cybernetics.

6729 ■ IMAGE Society
PO Box 6221
Chandler, AZ 85246-6221
E-mail: image@asu.edu
URL: http://www.public.asu.edu/~image
Founded: 1987. **Membership Dues:** individual in U.S., $50 (annual) ● individual outside U.S., $65 (annual) ● student in U.S., $25 (annual) ● student outside U.S., $40 (annual). **Description:** Individuals and organizations interested in the technological advancement and application of real-time visual simulation (medical, virtual reality, telepresence, aeronautical, and automotive) and other related virtual reality technologies. **Special Interest Groups:** Database Development; Display Systems; Ground Vehicle Simulation; Human Interaction and Training Technologies; Networked Simulation; PC Simulation; Sensors. **Publications:** *Conference Proceedings*, annual. **Price:** $100.00 for printed copy; $125.00 for PDF file on CD. Alternate Formats: CD-ROM ● *IMAGES*, semiannual. Newsletter. Offers society technical news. **Circulation:** 1,000. **Conventions/Meetings:** annual conference (exhibits).

6730 ■ International Association for Artificial Intelligence and Law (IAAIL)
c/o Carole D. Hafner, Sec.-Treas.
Coll. of Cmpt. and Info. Sci.
Northeastern Univ.
202 WVH
Boston, MA 02115
Ph: (617)373-5116
E-mail: info@iaail.org
URL: http://www.iaail.org
Contact: Carole D. Hafner, Sec.-Treas.
Founded: 1992. **Members:** 120. **Staff:** 7. **Multinational. Description:** Computer science and law academics and professionals. Promotes research and development in the field of artificial intelligence and law. **Awards:** Donald H. Berman Award for Best Student Paper. **Frequency:** biennial. **Type:** grant. **Publications:** Newsletter ● Journal ● Proceedings. **Conventions/Meetings:** biennial conference.

6731 ■ International Association for Mathematics and Computers in Simulation (IMACS)
c/o Robert Vichnevetsky, Honorary Pres.
Rutgers Univ. - Bush Campus
Dept. of Cmpt. Sci.
Hill Center
Brett Rd.
New Brunswick, NJ 08903
Ph: (732)445-2081
Fax: (732)443-0537
E-mail: vichneve@cs.rutgers.edu
URL: http://www.research.rutgers.edu/~imacs
Contact: Prof. Robert Beauwens, Pres.
Founded: 1955. **Members:** 1,100. **Membership Dues:** regular, $40 (annual) ● regular, EUR 30 (annual). **State Groups:** 10. **Description:** Professionals and engineers specializing in scientific computation; industrial firms, scientific associations, and government agencies. Facilitates exchange of scientific information among specialists, builders, and users interested in applied mathematics, scientific computation, and simulation; organizes international meetings and exhibits. Conducts symposia. **Telecommunication Services:** electronic mail, rvichnevetsky@aol.com. **Committees:** Direction. **Publications:** *Applied Numerical Mathematics*, monthly. Journal. Provides a forum for high quality research and tutorial papers in computational mathematics. **Price:** $2,039.00 /year for institutions in all countries except Europe and Japan; 242,000.00 /year for institutions in Japan; EUR 1,821.00 /year for institutions in European countries. ISSN: 0168-9274 ● *Computational Acoustic, Vol. 15*, quarterly. Journal. Provides an international forum for the dissemination of the state-of-art information in the field of Computational Acoustics. **Price:** $489.00 /year for institutions (electronic and print); $177.00 /year for individuals (print only); $465.00 /year for institutions (electronic only). ISSN: 0218-396X. Alternate Formats: online ● *Mathematics and Computers in Simulation*, monthly. Journal. Provides an international forum for the dissemination of up-to-date information in the fields of mathematics and computers. **Price:** $2,180.00 /year for institutions in all countries except Europe and Japan; 258,700.00 /year for institutions in Japan; EUR 1,948.00 /year for institutions in European countries. ISSN: 0378-4754 ● Directory, periodic. **Conventions/Meetings:** annual Applications of Computer Algebra - conference (exhibits) ● triennial congress (exhibits) - 2009 July 13-17, Cairns, QL, Australia.

6732 ■ International Disk Drive Equipment and Materials Association (IDEMA)
470 Lakeside Dr., Ste.A
Sunnyvale, CA 94085-4720
Ph: (408)991-9430
Fax: (408)991-9434
E-mail: jweiss@idema.org
URL: http://www.idema.org
Contact: Dr. Joel Weiss, Pres.
Founded: 1986. **Members:** 832. **Membership Dues:** industry leader, $5,000-$30,000 (annual) ● core technology provider, $6,250-$12,500 (annual) ● partner, $1,000-$2,000 (annual) ● university, individual, $300 (annual). **Staff:** 12. **Budget:** $4,000,000. **Multinational. Description:** Corporations, individuals, and universities with an interest in data storage technologies. Promotes the technological, manufacturing, marketing, and business progress of the data storage industry. **Computer Services:** Mailing lists ● online services. **Publications:** *INSIGHT*, bimonthly. Magazine. Features articles on the latest market trends, technical advancements and business issues related to the data storage industry. **Price:** free. **Circulation:** 20,000. **Advertising:** accepted. Alternate Formats: online ● Membership Directory. **Conventions/Meetings:** annual DISKCON USA - trade show and dinner (exhibits) ● periodic Information Storage Week - trade show and dinner (exhibits).

6733 ■ International Game Developers Association (IGDA)
19 Mantua Rd.
Mount Royal, NJ 08061
Ph: (856)423-2990
Fax: (856)423-3420
E-mail: contact@igda.org
URL: http://www.igda.org
Contact: Jason Della Rocca, Exec. Dir.
Founded: 1995. **Members:** 1,400. **Membership Dues:** regular, $48 (annual) ● student, $30 (annual) ● developing country, $35 (annual). **Staff:** 25. **Multinational. Description:** Individuals with a professional interest in the interactive entertainment, educational software, and multimedia industries. Promotes development of new entertainment programs and media. Facilitates exchange of information among members; conducts promotional activities. **Awards: Frequency:** annual. **Type:** recognition. **Computer Services:** Mailing lists, of members. **Telecommunication Services:** information service, IGDA Forums. **Committees:** Women in Game Development. **Publications:** *CCGDA Report*, periodic. **Price:** free for members. **Circulation:** 1,300. **Advertising:** accepted. Alternate Formats: online ● Membership Directory, periodic. Alternate Formats: online ● Newsletter, monthly. Updates members on the events of the association and industry news. Alternate Formats: online. **Conventions/Meetings:** annual conference (exhibits).

6734 ■ International Society of Parametric Analysts (ISPA)
527 Maple Ave. E, Ste.301
Vienna, VA 22180
Ph: (703)938-5090
Fax: (703)938-5091
E-mail: ispa@sceaonline.net
URL: http://www.ispa-cost.org
Contact: Madeline Ellis, Deputy Chair
Founded: 1979. **Members:** 300. **Membership Dues:** student, $30 (annual) ● individual, $55 (annual) ● life, $550. **Staff:** 1. **Budget:** $150,000. **Regional Groups:** 9. **Multinational. Description:** Engineers, designers, statisticians, estimators, and managers in industry, the military, and government who develop and use computerized, parametric cost-estimating models. Conducts educational activities to promote usage of parametric modeling techniques for purposes of cost estimating, risk analysis, and technology forecasting. Sponsors placement service. **Libraries: Type:** reference. **Subjects:** parametric analysis, cost estimating. **Awards: Type:** recognition. **Committees:** Cost Credibility; Education and Technical. **Formerly:** (1978) PRICE Users Association. **Publications:** *International Society of Parametric Analysts—Conference Proceedings*, annual. Monograph. Provides papers on parametrics presented at the society's conference; includes a speakers index. **Price:** included in conference registration; $40.00/copy for non-attendees. **Circulation:** 400. **Advertising:** accepted. Alternate Formats: CD-ROM ● *ISPA Directory*, annual. Membership Directory. **Price:** included in membership dues. **Advertising:** accepted ● *Journal of Parametrics*, semiannual. Reports on parametric analysis in cost modeling, risk analysis, design-to-cost, life-cycle cost analysis, design analysis, and technology forecasting. **Price:** included in membership dues; $60.00 /year for nonmembers. ISSN: 1015-7891. **Circulation:** 400. **Advertising:** accepted ● *Parametric World*, quarterly. Newsletter. **Price:** included in membership dues. **Circulation:** 500. **Advertising:** accepted. **Conventions/Meetings:** annual conference, held in conjunction with SCEA (exhibits) - always May or June ● conference (exhibits) ● seminar ● workshop.

6735 ■ International Training and Simulation Alliance (ITSA)
2111 Wilson Blvd., Ste.400
Arlington, VA 22201-3061
Ph: (703)247-9471
E-mail: prowe@ndia.org
URL: http://itsalliance.org
Multinational. Description: Promotes understanding of the importance of training and simulation technology. Increases the value of training and simulation systems to users and producers.

6736 ■ Korea Information Technology Network (KIN)
3003 N First St.
San Jose, CA 95134
Ph: (408)432-5006
Fax: (408)432-5056
E-mail: heather@koreait.org
URL: http://www.koreait.org
Contact: Sung Park, Chm./Pres.
Founded: 2001. **Multinational. Description:** Works to develop an international network of information technology professionals, companies and investors, both within and outside of Korea. Provides Korean-related and non-Korean entities with access to opportunities, resources, ideas, financing and perspective on current global trade and technology issues affecting the IT industry worldwide.

6737 ■ Manufacturing Integration Tech Group of the Society of Manufacturing Engineers
PO Box 930
One SME Dr.
Dearborn, MI 48121
Ph: (313)271-1500
Free: (800)733-4763
Fax: (313)425-3400
E-mail: techcommunities@sme.org
URL: http://www.sme.org/cgi-bin/communities.pl?/communities/casa/casahome.htm
Contact: Mark Tomlinson, Exec. Dir.
Founded: 1975. **Members:** 7,000. **Staff:** 2. **Multinational. Description:** Sponsored by Society of Manufacturing Engineers; automation implementation professionals, manufacturers, consultants, vendors, academics, and students in 70 countries. Promotes computer automation and enterprise integration for the advancement of research, design, installation, operation, maintenance, and communication in manufacturing. Focuses on integration of and data sharing between manufacturing and design pro-

cesses, performance monitoring, SCADA, and improvement of systems with predictive maintenance. Acts as liaison between industry, government, and academia to identify areas that need further technological development. Encourages companies to develop completely integrated manufacturing facilities. Conducts seminars and workshops on automated manufacturing. **Libraries: Type:** reference. **Holdings:** books, periodicals. **Awards:** CASA/SME Industry and University LEAD Awards. **Frequency:** annual. **Type:** recognition. **Recipient:** for leadership and excellence in application and development of enterprise wide integrated manufacturing. **Computer Services:** Information services. **Affiliated With:** Society of Manufacturing Engineers. **Formerly:** (1975) Computer and Automated Systems Association; (2007) Computer and Automated Systems Association of Society of Manufacturing Engineers. **Publications:** *CIM Implementation Guide* ● *How to Implement Concurrent Engineering and Improve Your Time to Market*. Audiotape ● *Management Guide to CIM* ● *The New Manufacturing Enterprise Wheel*. Booklet ● *SME Blue Book Series*. **Conventions/Meetings:** annual AUTOFACT (Automated, Integrated Factory) Conference and Exposition (exhibits) - always November.

6738 ■ National Training and Simulation Association (NTSA)
2111 Wilson Blvd., Ste.400
Arlington, VA 22201-3061
Ph: (703)247-9471
Fax: (703)243-1659
E-mail: prowe@ndia.org
URL: http://www.trainingsystems.org
Contact: Patrick Rowe, Dir. of Membership Services
Founded: 1988. **Members:** 700. **Membership Dues:** individual, $125 (annual) ● corporate (sustaining), $5,000 (annual) ● corporate (regular; based on number of employees), $1,250-$3,750 (annual) ● corporate (associate), $500 (annual). **Staff:** 3. **Budget:** $2,000,000. **Description:** Represents the business interests of manufacturers of simulation systems, computer-based training systems, and training support systems; providers of contract training and other related training support services. Promotes the growth, development, and application of military training systems, products, and services. Seeks to contribute to the operational readiness and combat effectiveness of the armed forces of the U.S. and its allies; assist in fulfilling the training requirements of related federal agencies; enhance public education and training; increase understanding and appreciation of training systems technologies and services. Fosters communication between government and industry regarding requirements and procurement issues and policies; promotes responsibility and integrity among members. Compiles statistics; conducts research and educational programs. **Libraries: Type:** reference. **Awards:** I/ITSEC Scholarship. **Frequency:** annual. **Type:** monetary. **Computer Services:** database. **Affiliated With:** National Defense Industrial Association. **Publications:** *NTSA Membership Directory*, bimonthly. Alternate Formats: online ● *NTSA Training Industry News*, bimonthly. Newsletter. Includes information on government procurement activities, new product developments, and program updates. **Price:** included in membership dues; $100.00 /year for nonmembers ● *NTSA Training 2010*, biennial. Survey. Serves as a training and simulation industry market survey. **Price:** $250.00 for members; $995.00 for nonmembers. Alternate Formats: CD-ROM ● *NTSA Yearbook*, annual. **Advertising:** accepted ● Reports. **Conventions/Meetings:** annual conference (exhibits) ● monthly Forums for Industry - symposium - usually in Washington, DC ● annual Training and Simulation Industry - symposium - 2008 June 17, Orlando, FL.

6739 ■ Network Professional Association (NPA)
1401 Hermes Ln.
San Diego, CA 92154
Free: (888)672-6720
Fax: (888)672-6720
E-mail: npa@npa.org
URL: http://www.npa.org
Contact: James Belasco, Contact
Founded: 1990. **Members:** 1,000. **Membership Dues:** individual, $175 (annual) ● corporate, $1,000 (annual) ● student, $35 (annual). **Staff:** 5. **Budget:** $500,000. **Local Groups:** 100. **Description:** Advocates for the international network computing professional. **Awards:** Best Networking Professional Career Achievement Award. **Frequency:** annual. **Type:** recognition. **Recipient:** for professionalism and work ethics ● Professional Excellence and Innovation Award. **Frequency:** annual. **Type:** recognition. **Recipient:** for a project with significant contribution to the association.

6740 ■ North American Computational Social and Organization Sciences (NAACSOS)
c/o Janice Kusmierek
Carnegie Mellon Univ., ISRI
Wean Hall 1325
5000 Forbes Ave.
Pittsburgh, PA 15213
Ph: (412)268-3163
E-mail: prietula@bus.emory.edu
URL: http://www.casos.cs.cmu.edu/naacsos/index.php
Contact: Michael Prietula, Pres.
Membership Dues: general, $100 (annual) ● student, $50 (annual). **Multinational. Description:** Represents the interests of researchers from the fields of mathematics, medicine, sociology, public health, business, economics, computer science, engineering, physics, anthropology, and psychology. Seeks to apply computational models to theoretical development and empirical analysis in the study of collectives. **Awards:** NAACSOS Award. **Frequency:** annual. **Type:** recognition. **Recipient:** for best paper presented. **Publications:** *Computational and Mathematical Organization Theory*. Journal. **Price:** included in membership dues.

6741 ■ North American Fuzzy Information Processing Society (NAFIPS)
c/o Dr. Bill Tastle, Treas.
Ithaca Coll.
Scholarship of Bus.
424 Smiddy Hall
Ithaca, NY 14850
Ph: (607)274-3669
Fax: (607)274-1152
E-mail: tastle@ithaca.edu
URL: http://nafips.ece.ualberta.ca
Contact: Dr. Bill Tastle, Treas.
Founded: 1981. **Members:** 400. **Membership Dues:** regular, $19 (annual). **Description:** Civil and electrical engineers, systems scientists, mathematicians, operations researchers, computer scientists, knowledge engineers, and logicians. Promotes scientific study and dissemination of applications and theories of fuzzy sets, logic, and measures. **Awards:** King Sun Fu Award. **Frequency:** annual. **Type:** recognition. **Recipient:** for service to the society and promoting the study and use of fuzzy sets. **Computer Services:** Electronic publishing. **Committees:** Civil Engineering; Decision Making; Expert Systems/AI; Expert Systems/Bio-Med; Information Retrieval/Learning; Information Retrieval/Math; Information Retrieval/Medicine; Neural Network/Parallelism; Operations Research and Simulation. **Publications:** *International Journal of Approximate Reasoning*, quarterly. **Price:** $19.00 each. Alternate Formats: online. **Conventions/Meetings:** annual symposium.

6742 ■ Personal Computer Memory Card International Association (PCMCIA)
2635 N First St., Ste.218
San Jose, CA 95134
Ph: (408)433-2273
Fax: (408)433-9558
E-mail: office@pcmcia.org
URL: http://www.pcmcia.org
Contact: Mr. Patrick Maher, Exec. Dir.
Founded: 1989. **Members:** 150. **Membership Dues:** affiliate, $2,500 (annual) ● executive, $4,500 (annual). **Staff:** 3. **Multinational. Description:** Computer industry professionals, including manufacturers of computers, peripherals and components. Promotes technological development and market adoption of ExpressCard technology and PC Card technology (credit card sized peripheral devices that add capabilities such as memory, mass storage, and I/O to computers). Sets standards and defines technical specifications. Sponsors educational events, research programs, and speakers' bureau. **Libraries: Type:** not open to the public. **Subjects:** PC-related industries. **Committees:** Marketing; Technical. **Publications:** *ExpressCard Standard*, biennial. Book. Contains technical specifications for electrical and mechanical aspects of ExpressCard technology. **Price:** included in membership dues; $2,500.00 for nonmembers. Alternate Formats: online ● *PC Card Standard*. Book. Contains the physical, electrical, and software specifications for the PC card technology. **Price:** $50.00 for members; $499.00 for nonmembers. Alternate Formats: CD-ROM ● *PCMCIA Update Newsletter*, quarterly. **Price:** free. **Circulation:** 5,000. **Conventions/Meetings:** quarterly General Membership Meeting ● monthly meeting.

6743 ■ SD Card Association
2400 Camino Ramon, Ste.375
San Ramon, CA 94583
Ph: (925)275-6687
Fax: (925)275-6691
E-mail: president@sdcard.org
URL: http://www.sdcard.org
Contact: Paul Reinhardt, Exec. Dir.
Founded: 2000. **Membership Dues:** executive, $4,500 (annual) ● general, $2,000 (annual). **Description:** Promotes wide acceptance for the SD Memory Card in digital applications. Aims to establish the technical and specification standards for SD Memory Card applications. Encourages the development of digital A/V, wireless communication and digital networking products. **Publications:** Newsletter.

6744 ■ Society for Computers in Psychology (SCiP)
c/o Kay Livesay, Sec.-Treas.
Dept. of Psychology
Linfield Coll.
900 SE Baker St.
McMinnville, OR 97128
Ph: (503)883-2708
Fax: (503)883-2566
E-mail: klivesa@linfield.edu
URL: http://home.scip.ws
Contact: Kay Livesay, Sec.-Treas.
Founded: 1971. **Membership Dues:** student, $30 (annual) ● regular, $50 (annual). **Description:** Researchers and students interested in the application of computers to psychology. Works to "increase and diffuse knowledge of the use of computers in psychological research." Assists psychologists in using microcomputers in teaching and research. **Awards:** Castellan Award for Outstanding Student Paper. **Frequency:** annual. **Type:** recognition. **Computer Services:** Mailing lists. **Formerly:** (1982) Society for the Use of On-Line Computers in Psychology. **Conventions/Meetings:** annual conference, held the day before the Psychonomic Society meeting (exhibits).

6745 ■ Society for Information Display (SID)
610 S 2nd St.
San Jose, CA 95112-5710
Ph: (408)977-1013
Fax: (408)977-1531
E-mail: office@sid.org
URL: http://www.sid.org
Contact: Jenny Needham, Data Mgr.
Founded: 1962. **Members:** 6,000. **Membership Dues:** student, $5 (annual) ● associate, senior, individual, $75 (annual) ● sustaining, $950 (annual). **Staff:** 2. **Budget:** $1,500,000. **Regional Groups:** 26. **Multinational. Description:** Represents scientists, engineers, students, others, and business firms dealing with information display problems. Encourages scientific, literary, and educational advancement of information display and its allied arts and sciences, including the disciplines of display theory, display device and systems development, and the psycho-

logical and physiological effects of display systems on the human senses. Plans to establish central repository for information and to develop definitions and standards in the field. Maintains speakers' bureau. **Libraries: Type:** reference. **Holdings:** 4,800. **Awards:** Display Material or Component of the Year Award. **Frequency:** annual. **Type:** recognition. **Recipient:** for materials or components that are making, or are expected to make, significant improvements in display performance, manufacturability, economics, usability, or marketability ● Display of the Year Award. **Frequency:** annual. **Type:** recognition. **Recipient:** for products whose focus is the display itself ● Display Product of the Year Award. **Frequency:** annual. **Type:** recognition. **Recipient:** for products that are characterized by their innovative use of a display, even though the display itself may not be particularly new or unusual ● Fellows of the SID. **Frequency:** annual. **Type:** recognition. **Recipient:** for SID member of outstanding qualification and experience as a scientist or engineer in the field of information display ● Jan Rajchman Prize. **Frequency:** annual. **Type:** monetary. **Recipient:** for an outstanding scientific or technical achievement in, or contribution to, research on flat panel displays ● Johann Gutenburg Prize. **Frequency:** annual. **Type:** monetary. **Recipient:** for an outstanding technical achievement in, or contribution to, printer technology ● Karl Ferdinand Braun Prize. **Frequency:** annual. **Type:** monetary. **Recipient:** for an outstanding technical achievement in, or contribution to, display technology ● Lewis and Beatrice Winner Award for Distinguished Service. **Frequency:** annual. **Type:** recognition. **Recipient:** to a member for exceptional and sustained service to SID ● Otto Schade Prize in Display Performance and Image Quality. **Frequency:** periodic. **Type:** recognition. **Recipient:** for an outstanding scientific or technical achievement in, or contribution to, the advancement of functional performance and/or image quality of information displays ● Special Recognition Awards. **Frequency:** annual. **Type:** recognition. **Recipient:** for distinguished and valued contributions to the information display field. **Committees:** Academic; Archives; Bylaws; Chapter Formation; Conventions; Display of the Year; Honors and Awards; Inter-Society; Long Range Planning; Publications; Publicity; Standards. **Publications:** *Information Display*, monthly. Magazine. Includes advertisers index, new product and publications information, calendar of events, chapter news, book reviews, and industry directory. **Price:** included in membership dues; $55.00 /year for nonmembers in U.S.; $85.00 /year for nonmembers outside U.S. ISSN: 0362-0972. **Circulation:** 13,500. **Advertising:** accepted ● *Journal of the Society for Information Display*, quarterly. **Price:** included in membership dues; $200.00 /year for nonmembers. ISSN: 0734-1768. **Circulation:** 4,000. Alternate Formats: online ● *Society for Information Display International Symposium Digest of Technical Papers*, annual. Book. Includes author index. **Price:** $85.00 for members; $100.00 for nonmembers. ISSN: 0097-966X. Alternate Formats: CD-ROM ● *Society for Information Display—Seminar Lecture Notes*, annual. Papers. Includes two-volume collection of papers presented at the seminar. **Price:** $90.00 for members; $100.00 for nonmembers. ISSN: 0887-915X. **Circulation:** 2,500 ● Membership Directory, annual. **Price:** included in membership dues. **Circulation:** 4,000. **Conventions/Meetings:** annual meeting ● annual symposium - 2009 May 31-June 5, San Antonio, TX; 2010 May 23-28, Seattle, WA.

6746 ■ Society for Modeling and Simulation International (SCS)

PO Box 17900
San Diego, CA 92177-7900
Ph: (858)277-3888
Fax: (858)277-3930
E-mail: info@scs.org
URL: http://www.scs.org
Contact: Stephen Branch, Exec. Dir.

Founded: 1952. **Members:** 2,000. **Membership Dues:** individual, $55 (annual) ● professional, $95 (annual) ● student, $22 (annual) ● premier, $195 (annual) ● basic (institutional), $1,000 (annual) ● bronze (institutional), $2,500 (annual) ● silver (institutional), $5,000 (annual) ● gold (institutional), $10,000 (annual) ● platinum (institutional), $25,000 (annual). **Staff:** 9. **Budget:** $1,000,000. **Regional Groups:** 8. **Description:** Persons professionally engaged in simulation, particularly through the use of computers and similar devices that employ mathematical or physical analogies. Maintains speakers' bureau. **Libraries: Type:** reference. **Telecommunication Services:** electronic mail, sbranch@scs.org. **Committees:** Standards; Summer Computer Simulation Conference; Western Simulation Conference. **Also Known As:** Simulation Councils, Inc. **Formerly:** (1987) Society for Computer Simulation. **Publications:** *Proceedings of the Summer Computer Simulation Conference*, annual. Contains reviews of papers presented at the conference. **Price:** $180.00. ISSN: 0094-7474 ● *Proceedings of the Winter Simulation Conference*, annual. Reviews papers on discrete simulation. ● *Simulation: Transactions of the Society for Modeling and Simulation International*, monthly. Journal. Contains computer simulation-related papers, application-oriented feature articles, and association and industry news. **Price:** included in membership dues; $195.00 for nonmembers. ISSN: 0037-5497. **Circulation:** 4,000. **Advertising:** accepted. Alternate Formats: microform ● *Transactions of the Society for Computer Simulation*, quarterly. Journal. Presents papers that deal with theoretical and practical applications of simulation and modeling. Contains papers deemed to be of archival value. **Price:** $40.00 /year for members; $160.00 /year for nonmembers. ISSN: 0740-6797. **Conventions/Meetings:** annual European Simulation Multiconference - meeting - always June ● annual International Modeling and Simulation Multiconference - meeting ● annual Summer Computer Simulation Conference (exhibits) - always July ● annual Western Simulation Multiconference - meeting - always January ● annual Winter Simulation Conference - meeting - always December.

6747 ■ Special Interest Group for Architecture of Computer Systems (SIGARCH)

c/o Doug Burger, Information Dir.
Univ. of Texas at Austin
Dept. of Cmpt. Sci.
1 Univ. Sta. C0500
Austin, TX 78712-0233
Ph: (512)471-9795
Fax: (512)232-1413
E-mail: infodir_sigarch@acm.org
URL: http://www.sigarch.org
Contact: Doug Burger, Information Dir.

Members: 5,000. **Membership Dues:** individual, $28 (annual) ● student, $14 (annual). **Description:** Serves as special interest group of the Association for Computing Machinery (see separate entry). Represents computer professionals interested in the architecture of computers. (Computer architecture is the study of the arrangement of physical resources of computer systems, their partitioning, and the organization of a processor). Disseminates technical information on the architecture of computer systems. Sponsors educational and research programs. **Awards:** Eckert-Mauchley Award. **Frequency:** annual. **Type:** recognition. **Recipient:** for an individual with great contribution to computer and digital systems architecture ● Maurice Wilkes Award. **Frequency:** annual. **Type:** recognition. **Recipient:** for an individual with outstanding contributions to computer architecture ● Student Travel Grant to ISCA and ASPLOS. **Frequency:** annual. **Type:** grant. **Recipient:** for an individual member who attends ISCA or ASPLOS conference. **Telecommunication Services:** electronic mail, dburger@cs.utexas.edu. **Publications:** *Computer Architecture News*, quarterly. Newsletter. **Conventions/Meetings:** annual symposium (exhibits).

6748 ■ Special Interest Group for Computers and Society (SIGCAS)

c/o Association for Computing Machinery
PO Box 30777
New York, NY 10087-0777
Ph: (212)626-0500
Free: (800)342-6626
Fax: (212)944-1318
E-mail: chair_sigcas@acm.org
URL: http://www.sigcas.org
Contact: Florence Appel, Chair

Members: 1,289. **Membership Dues:** professional, $20 (annual) ● student, $10 (annual). **Staff:** 1. **Budget:** $60,000. **Description:** Serves as a special interest group of the Association for Computing Machinery. Represents computer and physical scientists, professionals, and other individuals interested in issues and applications of computers in society. Informs the public of issues concerning computers and society. Conducts computer literacy symposia. **Awards:** Making a Difference Award. **Frequency:** annual. **Type:** recognition. **Recipient:** for an individual who is nationally recognized for his/her work related to the interaction of computers and society ● Outstanding Service Award. **Frequency:** annual. **Type:** recognition. **Recipient:** to a member with outstanding service. **Telecommunication Services:** electronic mail, appel@sxu.edu ● electronic mail, vc_sigcas@acm.org. **Publications:** *Computers and Society*, quarterly. Magazine. **Advertising:** accepted. Alternate Formats: online. **Conventions/Meetings:** Educational Computer Conference ● semiannual meeting.

6749 ■ Special Interest Group for Design Automation (SIGDA)

c/o Prof. Diana Marculescu, Chair
Carnegie Mellon Univ.
Dept. of Elecl. and Cmpt. Engg.
Pittsburgh, PA 15213-3890
Ph: (412)268-1167
Fax: (412)268-2859
E-mail: dianam@acm.org
URL: http://www.sigda.org
Contact: Prof. Diana Marculescu, Chair

Founded: 1965. **Members:** 1,200. **Membership Dues:** regular, $25 (annual) ● student, $15 (annual). **Description:** Serves as a special interest group of the Association for Computing Machinery (see separate entry). Represents professionals interested in the application of computers to engineering design function, especially in the electronic engineering field. Areas of concern include: theoretic, analytic and heuristic methods for performing and assisting in design tasks; use of computer techniques, algorithms and programs to provide design documentation, control manufacturing processes, evaluate design through simulation, and facilitate communication between designers and design tasks. Holds panel and technical meetings. **Awards:** Outstanding New Faculty Award. **Frequency:** annual. **Type:** recognition. **Recipient:** for junior faculty member who demonstrates outstanding potential as an educator and/or researcher in the field of electronic design automation ● Outstanding PhD Dissertation Award in Electronic Design Automation. **Frequency:** annual. **Type:** recognition. **Recipient:** for outstanding PhD dissertation that makes the most substantial contribution to the theory and/or application in the field of electronic design automation. **Publications:** *Design Automaton TechNews*, biweekly. Newsletter. Alternate Formats: online ● Newsletter, 3/year. **Conventions/Meetings:** annual Design Automation Conference - always June ● annual International Conference on Computer-Aided Design - meeting - always November.

6750 ■ Special Interest Group on Management of Data (SIGMOD)

c/o Mary Fernandez, Sec.-Treas.
180 Park Ave., Bldg. 103, E277
Florham Park, NJ 07932-0971
Ph: (973)360-8679
Free: (800)342-6626
E-mail: online@sigmod.acm.org
URL: http://www.sigmod.org
Contact: Mary Fernandez, Sec.-Treas.

Founded: 1970. **Members:** 4,000. **Membership Dues:** regular, $25 (annual) ● student, $13 (annual). **Staff:** 1. **Budget:** $100,000. **Local Groups:** 5. **Description:** A special interest group of the Association for Computing Machinery. Individuals interested in the state of research, development, and application of database technology on a full range of computer organizations. Aims to provide a forum for information exchange on the theoretical foundations for building database management systems, engineering techniques for building database management systems and database access tools and application development tools that accompany database systems, challenging new applications that may demand advances in the field, engineering techniques for building database management systems on newly emerging computer organizations (e.g. client-server architecture, parallel computers, and distributed network architecture), and large-scale user experiences with database management systems. **Awards:** SIGMOD Edgar F. Codd Innovations Award. **Frequency:** annual. **Type:** recognition. **Recipient:** for innovative and highly significant contributions of enduring value to the development, understanding, or use of database systems and databases. **Computer Services:** Online services, research funding information, abstracts of articles, conference information, and jobs postings. **Formerly:** Special Interest Group on Data Communication. **Conventions/Meetings:** annual conference.

6751 ■ Special Interest Group on Measurement and Evaluation (SIGMETRICS)

c/o Vishal Misra
512 CSC
1214 Amsterdam Ave., MC 0401
New York, NY 10027-7003
Ph: (212)939-7061
Fax: (212)666-0140
E-mail: misra@cs.columbia.edu
URL: http://www.sigmetrics.org
Contact: Vishal Misra, Contact
Members: 1,886. **Membership Dues:** professional, $20 (annual) ● student, $10 (annual). **Description:** A special interest group of the Association for Computing Machinery (see separate entry). Individuals interested in the problems related to measuring and evaluating computer system performance, including applying and adapting existing methods and developing new ones. Provides a forum for discussion of the role of simulation, design, and interpretation of benchmarks (standards by which systems are measured); analysis of hardware and software monitor output; development of suitable analytical models. **Awards:** ACM SIGMETRICS Achievement Award. **Type:** recognition. **Recipient:** for an individual who has made long-lasting influential contributions to the practice of computer/communication system performance evaluation. **Publications:** *Performance Evaluation Review*, periodic. **Conventions/Meetings:** annual international conference (exhibits).

6752 ■ Special Interest Group on Security, Audit and Control (SIGSAC)

c/o Prof. Virgil D. Gligor, Chm.
Univ. of Maryland
Dept. of Elecl. and Cmpt. Engg.
2405 A.V. Williams Bldg.
College Park, MD 20742
Ph: (301)405-3647
E-mail: gligor@eng.umd.edu
URL: http://www.sigsac.org
Contact: Prof. Virgil D. Gligor, Chm.
Founded: 1980. **Members:** 1,120. **Membership Dues:** professional, $27 (annual) ● student, $11 (annual). **Description:** A special interest group of the Association for Computing Machinery (see separate entry) composed of security personnel; auditors; accountants and computer technicians. Develops high levels of skill and awareness regarding technology and practice in the fields of computer security, audit, and control. Examines issues including control of access to resources, identity verification, risk analysis, logging of transactions, data reduction, analysis and certification of programs, and architectural foundations for security systems. **Awards:** SIGSAC Outstanding Contribution Award. **Frequency:** annual. **Type:** monetary. **Recipient:** for promising individuals ● SIGSAC Outstanding Innovation Award. **Frequency:** annual. **Type:** monetary. **Recipient:** for outstanding individuals in the field of computer and communication security. **Conventions/Meetings:** annual Conference on Computer and Communication Security ● Information Computer and Communications Security - symposium.

6753 ■ Special Interest Group on Simulation (SIGSIM)

c/o Association for Computing Machinery
2 Penn Plz., Ste.701
New York, NY 10036-5701
Ph: (212)626-0500
Free: (800)342-6626
Fax: (212)944-1318
E-mail: sigsim@acm.org
URL: http://www.sigsim.org
Contact: Simon J.E. Taylor, Chm.
Founded: 1965. **Members:** 2,074. **Membership Dues:** regular, $22 (annual) ● student, $9 (annual). **Description:** A special interest group of Association for Computing Machinery (see separate entry). Researchers and practitioners in computer simulation including professionals in business and industry. Holds technical meetings at annual conference of ACM. Promotes research and conducts surveys on topics such as the type of computer simulation courses being offered at colleges and universities. Researches the application of simulation principles and theory to sub disciplines of computer science. **Computer Services:** Mailing lists, of members and non members. **Publications:** *Simulation Digest*, quarterly. Newsletter. **Price:** included in membership dues ● Annual Reports, annual. Alternate Formats: online. **Conventions/Meetings:** annual Simulation Conference - always winter.

6754 ■ Storage Networking Industry Association (SNIA)

500 Sansome St., Ste.504
San Francisco, CA 94111
Ph: (415)402-0006 (978)203-0442
Fax: (415)402-0009
E-mail: leo.leger@snia.org
URL: http://www.snia.org
Contact: Leo Leger, Exec. Dir.
Founded: 1997. **Membership Dues:** individual, $300 (annual) ● large voting vendor ($500M/year and above revenue), $40,000 (annual) ● medium voting vendor (between $10M and $500M/year revenue), $14,500 (annual) ● small voting vendor (less than $10M/year revenue), $8,500 (annual) ● large non-voting vendor ($500M/year and above revenue), $11,500 (annual) ● medium non-voting vendor (between $10 and $500/year revenue), $8,500 (annual) ● small non-voting vendor (less than $10M/year revenue), $3,500 (annual) ● customer company, $1,000 (annual) ● channel, $2,000-$11,500 (annual). **Staff:** 17. **Description:** Developers, integrators, and information technology professionals. Works to bring reliable storage solutions to the marketplace. Promotes the use of highly evolved, widely accepted storage network systems across the IT community. Accelerates the development and evolution of standards. **Computer Services:** Mailing lists, of members. **Publications:** *SNIA Net*, bimonthly. Newsletter. Alternate Formats: online.

6755 ■ Transaction Processing Performance Council (TPC)

PO Box 29920
San Francisco, CA 94129-0920
Ph: (415)561-6272
Fax: (415)561-6120
E-mail: info@tpc.org
URL: http://www.tpc.org
Contact: Omri Serlin, Co-Founder
Founded: 1988. **Members:** 25. **Membership Dues:** full, $15,000 (annual) ● associate, $1,500 (annual). **Multinational. Description:** Represents computer hardware and software companies, computer users and vendors, and industry organizations. Defines transaction processing and database benchmarks. Disseminates objective, verifiable TPC performance data to the industry. Conducts activities such as Benchmark development and maintenance, publication and dissemination of TPC results. **Libraries: Type:** not open to the public; open to the public. **Holdings:** archival material, articles, business records, clippings, papers, reports. **Computer Services:** database. **Committees:** Public Relations; Steering; Technical Advisory. **Publications:** *Benchmark Status Report*, bimonthly. Features updates on benchmark development and maintenance/update work. **Price:** free. **Circulation:** 5,000. Alternate Formats: online. Also Cited As: *BSR* ● *Complete Listing of TPC Results*. **Price:** $75.00. Alternate Formats: online ● *TPC Background* ● *TPC Benchmark Specifications*. **Conventions/Meetings:** bimonthly meeting, for working committee and general council.

6756 ■ World Wide Web Consortium (W3C)

c/o Massachusetts Institute of Technology
Lab. for Cmpt. Sci. and Artificial Intelligence
32 Vassar St., Rm. 32-G515
Cambridge, MA 02139
Ph: (617)253-2613
Fax: (617)258-5999
E-mail: susan@w3.org
URL: http://www.w3.org
Contact: Susan Westhaver, Admin.
Founded: 1994. **Members:** 430. **Staff:** 72. **Multinational. Description:** Works for the development of interoperable technologies, particularly, specifications, guidelines, software and tools, to lead the Web to full potential; acts as a forum for information, commerce, communication, and collective understanding for the industry. **Computer Services:** database, working group ● mailing lists. **Subgroups:** Architecture; Interaction; Technology and Society; Web Accessibility. **Publications:** *W3C Weekly News*. Newsletter. Describes the week's publications, events and announcements. Alternate Formats: online ● Reports. Technical reports. **Conventions/Meetings:** Carto.net Developers Conference ● semiannual executive committee meeting.

6757 ■ XML.org

c/o OASIS
PO Box 455
Billerica, MA 01821
Ph: (978)667-5115
Fax: (978)667-5114
E-mail: info@oasis-open.org
URL: http://www.xml.org
Contact: Scott McGrath, Contact
Founded: 1999. **Description:** Seeks to advance worldwide utilization and adoption of XML by providing open and nonprofit industry portal. **Computer Services:** Mailing lists, XML-DEV. **Telecommunication Services:** electronic mail, scott.mcgrath@oasis-open.org. **Publications:** *XML.org Daily Newslink*. Newsletter. Alternate Formats: online.

Computer Security

6758 ■ International Information Systems Security Certification Consortium (ISC2)

2494 Bayshore Blvd., Ste.201
Dunedin, FL 34698
Ph: (727)738-8657
Free: (888)333-4458
Fax: (727)738-8522
E-mail: infoisc2@isc2.org
URL: http://www.isc2.org/cgi-bin/index.cgi
Contact: John Colley CISSP, Pres.
Founded: 1989. **Multinational. Description:** Certifies industry professionals and practitioners in an international standard. Maintains a common database for information security. Provides training and certification examinations and ensures credentials are maintained, primarily through continuing education. **Awards:** Harold F. Tipton Award. **Frequency:** annual. **Type:** recognition. **Recipient:** for an individual's life long contributions to the improvement of the information systems security profession. **Computer Services:** Information services, security resources ● online services, study guides, training, assessment. **Committees:** Common Body Knowledge; Common Body Knowledge Review and Training. **Publications:** *Information Systems Security*, bimonthly. Journal.

Alternate Formats: online ● *Official Guide to the CISSP Exam.* Handbook. Serves as the official study guide for the CISSP exam. **Price:** $65.00 each ● *2004 Resource Guide for Today's US Government Information Security Professional*, annual. Manual. Serves as a source of information for the information security community. Alternate Formats: online.

Computer Software

6759 ■ Acacia North American User Group (ANAUG)

Address Unknown since 2007
URL: http://www.ssaglobalusers.org/
Founded: 1983. **Description:** Exchange and provide access to information and ideas concerning the implementation and use of the PRMS, Warehouse BOSS, and QRE software. Works to influence the future direction of this software.

6760 ■ AppleWorks Users Group (AWUG)

PO Box 701010
Plymouth, MI 48170
Ph: (734)454-1969
Fax: (734)454-1965
URL: http://www.awug.org
Founded: 1991. **Members:** 15,000. **Membership Dues:** regular, $39 (annual). **Multinational. Description:** Commits to assist AppleWorks and ClarisWorks users. **Libraries: Type:** open to the public; reference. **Holdings:** books. **Computer Services:** Mailing lists, of members ● online services, technical support. **Telecommunication Services:** information service, AppleWorks News Service. **Programs:** Members Helping Members. **Publications:** *AppleWorks Journal*, 10/year. Newsletter. **Price:** included in membership dues. ISSN: 1059-6542. **Circulation:** 15,000. **Advertising:** accepted. Alternate Formats: CD-ROM; online ● *AWUG Public Domain Library Catalog.* Lists hundreds of templates, enhancements and utilities useful in AppleWorks. **Price:** $6.00 includes postage ● *Getting Started with AppleWorks Databases.* Book. Features seven easy-to-follow lessons about AppleWorks Database. **Price:** $19.95 includes CD ● *Getting Started with AppleWorks Spreadsheets.* Book. Features ten lessons about AppleWorks Spreadsheet. **Price:** $19.95 includes CD.

6761 ■ Association of Esko-Graphics' Users (AEG)

c/o Michael D. Meyer, Chm.
622 High St.
New London, WI 54961
Ph: (920)540-2103
E-mail: mdmeyer@bemis.com
URL: http://www.aegusers.com
Contact: Michael D. Meyer, Chm.
Founded: 1992. **Members:** 120. **Staff:** 2. **Budget:** $200,000. **Description:** Open to companies using BARCO Graphics systems. Provides information about the use of this system. **Formerly:** (2003) BARCO Graphics User Association. **Conventions/Meetings:** annual meeting.

6762 ■ Association of Shareware Professionals (ASP)

c/o Mr. Richard Holler, Exec. Dir.
PO Box 1522
Martinsville, IN 46151
Ph: (765)349-4740
Fax: (765)349-4744
E-mail: execdir@asp-shareware.org
URL: http://www.asp-shareware.org
Contact: Mr. Richard Holler, Exec. Dir.
Founded: 1987. **Members:** 600. **Membership Dues:** standard, $100 (annual) ● supporting, $250 (annual). **Description:** Contains information for computer software developers and distributors, providing resources, aid, and assistance in improving their products and their business operations. **Publications:** *ASPects*, monthly. Newsletter. **Price:** free, for members only. **Circulation:** 1,300. **Advertising:** accepted. Alternate Formats: online; CD-ROM.

6763 ■ Association for Software Testing (AST)

c/o Computer Sciences Department
Florida Inst. of Tech.
150 W Univ. Blvd.
Melbourne, FL 32901
Ph: (317)709-2419
E-mail: president@associationforsoftwaretesting.org
URL: http://www.associationforsoftwaretesting.org
Contact: Michael Kelly, Pres.
Founded: 2004. **Membership Dues:** regular, $50 (annual) ● student, $25 (annual). **Description:** Advances the understanding and practice of software testing. Serves a community of scholars, students, and software development practitioners. Encourages, facilitates, and coordinates partnerships between testing practitioners and testing researchers. Supports the teaching of software testing. **Publications:** *Journal of the Association for Software Testing.* Publishes materials of archival value that advance the understanding and practice of software testing. Also Cited As: *JAST.* **Conventions/Meetings:** annual conference.

6764 ■ CAD Society

8220 Stone Trail Dr.
Bethesda, MD 20817-4556
Ph: (301)365-4585
E-mail: info@cadsociety.org
URL: http://www.cadsociety.org
Contact: Brad Holtz, Chm.
Description: Provides framework that fosters ties and open communications among consultants, press, CAD users and vendors, and those who make a living in the CAD industry. **Awards:** Community Award. **Frequency:** annual. **Type:** recognition. **Recipient:** for outstanding work in improving communication and developing community within the CAD industry ● Leadership Award. **Frequency:** annual. **Type:** recognition. **Recipient:** for outstanding technical and business leadership in the CAD industry ● Lifetime Award. **Frequency:** annual. **Type:** recognition. **Recipient:** for outstanding technical and business contributions to the CAD Industry.

6765 ■ Educational Software Cooperative (ESC)

127 The Ranch Rd.
Del Valle, TX 78617
E-mail: information@edu-soft.org
URL: http://www.edu-soft.org
Contact: Ben Weintraub, Pres.
Founded: 1992. **Membership Dues:** regular, in North America, $35 (annual) ● regular, outside North America, $40 (annual) ● contributing, $50 (annual) ● supporting, $100 (annual) ● life, $1,000. **Multinational. Description:** Supports and encourages the development of educational software. Advances the mutual benefit of authors, publishers, dealers, and distributors of educational software. Provides information on the benefits, uses, and availability of educational software. **Awards:** Outstanding Achievement in Educational Software. **Frequency:** periodic. **Type:** recognition. **Recipient:** for software developers chosen by ESC board of directors ● People's Choice. **Frequency:** annual. **Type:** recognition. **Recipient:** for software developers who received the most number of online ballots received from the public. **Computer Services:** Online services, forums ● online services, software downloads.

6766 ■ Entertainment Software Association (ESA)

575 7th St. NW, Ste.300
Washington, DC 20004
Ph: (202)223-2400
E-mail: esa@theesa.com
URL: http://www.theesa.com
Contact: Michael D. Gallagher, Pres.
Founded: 1994. **Members:** 26. **Description:** Represents the interactive entertainment software publishing industry. Established an autonomous rating board to rate interactive entertainment software. Established a program to combat piracy in the United States and around the world. Represents members on industry issues at the federal and state level. Provides market research and information. **Publications:** none. **Formerly:** (2004) Interactive Digital Software Association. **Conventions/Meetings:** annual Electronic Entertainment Expo - E3 - trade show, with workshops and luncheons; open to industry professionals only (exhibits).

6767 ■ Free Software Foundation (FSF)

51 Franklin St., 5th Fl.
Boston, MA 02110-1301
Ph: (617)542-5942
Fax: (617)542-2652
E-mail: info@fsf.org
URL: http://www.fsf.org
Contact: Richard M. Stallman, Pres.
Founded: 1985. **Membership Dues:** contributing, $500 (annual) ● above and beyond, $240 (annual) ● associate, $120 (annual) ● student, $60 (annual). **Staff:** 10. **Languages:** English, French, Mandarin Dialects, Spanish. **Multinational. Description:** Promotes computer users' right to use, study, copy, modify, and redistribute computer programs; development and use of free (as in freedom) software, particularly the GNU operating system and free (as in freedom) documentation; promotes ethical and political issues of freedom in the use of software. **Awards:** Award for the Advancement of Free Software. **Frequency:** annual. **Type:** recognition. **Telecommunication Services:** electronic mail, membership@fsf.org. **Also Known As:** GNU Project. **Publications:** *GNU Service Directory*, semiannual. Lists people who offer support and other consulting services with regard to software. **Price:** free. Alternate Formats: online ● *GNU's Bulletin*, annual. Newsletter. Contains news about the GNU Project. ● Manual.

6768 ■ Information Technology Association of America (ITAA)

1401 Wilson Blvd., Ste.1100
Arlington, VA 22209
Ph: (703)522-5055 (703)284-5340
Fax: (703)525-2279
E-mail: pbond@itaa.org
URL: http://www.itaa.org
Contact: Phil Bond, Pres./CEO
Founded: 1982. **Members:** 306. **Membership Dues:** associate, $1,030-$6,080 (annual) ● full, $1,000-$46,680 (annual). **Staff:** 30. **Budget:** $4,500,000. **Description:** A division of the Information Technology Association of America; software companies involved in the development or marketing of software for personal, midrange, and mainframe computers. Promotes the software industry and addresses specific problems of the industry. Represents the industry before various governmental units; provides educational programs to members; conducts research and makes available legal services. Develops standards. **Awards:** Customer Support Quality Award. **Frequency:** annual. **Type:** recognition ● Documentation/Training Materials Quality Award. **Frequency:** annual. **Type:** recognition ● Total Quality Award. **Frequency:** annual. **Type:** recognition. **Recipient:** for significant quality achievement by computer software companies. **Committees:** Computer and Network Security; Conference Planning; Export Controls; Federal Procurement; Financial Practices; Image; Industry Statistics; Liaison; Quality Management; Taxation; Technology Information Service. **Projects:** Contracts; Domestic Business Practices; Education and Image; Intellectual Property; International Business Practices; Piracy; Software Protection; Software Support; Standards. **Task Forces:** Issues. **Formerly:** (1988) Microcomputer Software Association - of ADAPSO; (1991) Software Industry Division of ADAPSO. **Publications:** *The Criteria of Quality: A Strategic Approach to ISO 9,000 Compliance for Information Technology Companies.* Report ● *Financial Operating Ratios for Software Companies.* Book ● *ITAA Software Industry Briefing Book.* Report ● *Quality Goes Global: An ITAA Guide to ISO 9,000 Standard Series for Information Technology Companies.* Newsletter ● *Software Industry Executive Newsletter*, bimonthly. **Price:** free. **Conventions/Meetings:** biennial conference.

6769 ■ International Association of Microsoft Certified Partners (IAMCP)
346 Brigham St.
Marlborough, MA 01752
E-mail: bill.breslin@insource.com
URL: http://www.iamcp.org
Contact: Bill Breslin, Pres.
Multinational. Description: Seeks to maximize business opportunities for Microsoft Certified Partners through local networking; aligned with the Microsoft Go To Market campaigns. **Publications:** Newsletter, quarterly. Alternate Formats: online. **Conventions/Meetings:** quarterly conference.

6770 ■ International Association of Software Architects (IASA)
PO Box 204253
Austin, TX 78720
Free: (866)399-4272
Fax: (512)331-4589
E-mail: contact@iasahome.org
URL: http://www.iasahome.org
Contact: Paul Preiss, Pres./Founder
Multinational. Description: Represents individuals dedicated to the advancement and sharing of issues related to software architecture in the enterprise, product, education and government sectors. Encourages research and standards that advance the understanding of software architecture. Provides forums for peer networking. Advocates the views of architects. **Publications:** *Perspectives of the IASA*, bimonthly. Newsletter. Alternate Formats: online ● Brochures. Alternate Formats: online.

6771 ■ International .NET Association (INETA)
PO Box 6713
Bellevue, WA 98008-0713
Ph: (401)885-4943
E-mail: info@ineta.org
URL: http://www.ineta.org
Contact: Chris Pels, Pres.
Multinational. Description: Provides educational and promotional support to user groups interested in the Microsoft .NET platform. Promotes the concept of user groups in Microsoft developer technologies. Offers assistance and provides resources to community groups. **Publications:** Newsletter, monthly. Contains news and articles about the association and its members. Alternate Formats: online.

6772 ■ Internet Systems Consortium (ISC)
950 Charter St.
Redwood City, CA 94063
Ph: (650)423-1300
Fax: (650)423-1355
E-mail: info@isc.org
URL: http://www.isc.org
Contact: Paul Vixie, Pres.
Founded: 1994. **Multinational. Description:** Dedicated to the development and maintenance of production quality open source reference implementations of core Internet protocols. **Formerly:** (2004) Internet Software Consortium.

6773 ■ Oracle Applications Users Group (OAUG)
3525 Piedmont Rd. NE, Bldg. 5, Ste.300
Atlanta, GA 30305
Ph: (404)240-0897
Fax: (404)240-0998
E-mail: info@oaug.org
URL: http://www.oaug.org
Contact: Steven R. Hughes, Exec. Dir.
Founded: 1990. **Members:** 2,300. **Membership Dues:** user, $595 (annual) ● associate, $1,195 (annual) ● individual, $325 (annual). **Staff:** 14. **Description:** International networking Association that represents the interests of a global community of Oracle Applications users. Provides a forum that promotes communication, education, and the exchange and expression of ideas among users. **Special Interest Groups:** Advanced Pricing; Aerospace and Defense; Archive and Purge; Assets; Business Intelligence/Data Warehouse; Change Management; Collaboration Suite; Contracts. **Publications:** *Insight*, quarterly. Magazine ● *OAUG e-News*, bimonthly. Newsletter. Alternate Formats: online ● *OAUG Forum*, semiannual. Magazine. **Conventions/Meetings:** annual COLLABORATE: Technology and Applications Forum for the Oracle Community - conference - in North America ● annual Connection Point - conference and trade show (exhibits) - in Europe, Asia.

6774 ■ Oracle Development Tools User Group (ODTUG)
3208 Oleander Dr., Ste.C
Wilmington, NC 28403
Ph: (910)452-7444
Fax: (910)815-4189
E-mail: odtug@odtug.com
URL: http://www.odtug.com
Contact: John Jeunnette, Pres.
Members: 2,900. **Membership Dues:** individual in U.S., $125 (annual) ● corporate (1-5 members, plus $15 surcharge/member), $495 (annual) ● corporate (6-10 members, plus $15 surcharge/member), $950 (annual) ● individual in Canada, Mexico, $140 (annual) ● individual outside U.S. and Canada, Mexico, $160 (annual). **Description:** Provides assistance in delivering reliable, high-quality information systems. Shares a common interest in Oracle's Internet Developer Suite, methodology, software process management, analysis and modeling, data warehousing, business process design, and web development. Provides education, training, and networking opportunities for members' professional growth and expertise in the marketplace. **Awards:** Oracle Contributor of the Year Award. **Frequency:** annual. **Type:** recognition. **Recipient:** to an Oracle employee who contributes a tremendous amount of time and information to help educate and support ODTUG and its efforts ● Volunteer of the Year Award. **Frequency:** annual. **Type:** recognition. **Recipient:** to an individual who has donated his/her time and expertise to ODTUG. **Publications:** *ODTUG Technology Journal*, quarterly. Alternate Formats: online. **Conventions/Meetings:** annual conference (exhibits).

6775 ■ Society for Software Quality (SSQ)
PO Box 86958
San Diego, CA 92138-6958
E-mail: pete.miller@baesystems.com
URL: http://www.ssq.org
Contact: Mr. Pete Miller, Pres.
Founded: 1984. **Members:** 50. **Membership Dues:** student, $20 (annual) ● individual in U.S., $45 (annual) ● individual outside U.S., $45 (annual). **Budget:** $3,000. **Regional Groups:** 3. **Local Groups:** 1. **Description:** Software professionals. Seeks to advance the art, science, and technology of software quality assurance. Promotes professional development of members and encourages high standards in the field. Fosters communication between the public and the industry. Assists colleges and universities in developing and implementing curricula in quality evaluation and methodologies. Operates Speaker's Bureau. **Libraries: Type:** reference. **Awards:** Dusty Rhodes Memorial Scholastic Grant. **Frequency:** annual. **Type:** grant. **Committees:** Human Factors; Nominating; Publications. **Divisions:** Education; Measurement; Standards; Testing. **Conventions/Meetings:** Achieving Quality Software - conference, with debate (exhibits) ● workshop.

6776 ■ Software Defined Radio Forum (SDR Forum)
1616 17th St., Ste.264
Denver, CO 80202
Ph: (303)628-5461
Fax: (303)374-5403
E-mail: info@sdrforum.org
URL: http://www.sdrforum.org
Contact: Allan Margulies, Exec. Dir.
Members: 100. **Membership Dues:** large company (with revenues over $100M), $8,500 (annual) ● medium company (with revenues of $10M-$100M), $5,000 (annual) ● small company (with revenues less than $10M), $2,500 (annual) ● government, nonprofit organization, $2,500 (annual). **Multinational. Description:** Aims to advance proliferation of software defined radio technologies in wireless networks to support civil, commercial, and military sectors. **Awards: Frequency:** annual. **Type:** recognition. **Telecommunication Services:** electronic mail, asm@sdrforum.org. **Committees:** Regulatory Advisory. **Programs:** Awards. **Publications:** *Current Happenings*. Newsletter ● *Market/Industry*. Survey ● *Meeting Report* ● Brochure. **Conventions/Meetings:** periodic External Affairs Initiatives and Seminars - seminar and workshop ● meeting - 5/year ● annual Technical Conference & Product Exposition.

6777 ■ Software in the Public Interest (SPI)
PO Box 501248
Indianapolis, IN 46250-6248
E-mail: president@spi-inc.org
URL: http://www.spi-inc.org
Contact: Bdale Garbee, Pres.
Founded: 1997. **Description:** Formulates and provides software systems for use by the general public without charge. Supports, encourages and promotes the creation and development of software. Increases access to software systems available to the general public. Provides classes, seminars and workshops on the proper use and application of computers and computer systems. **Telecommunication Services:** electronic mail, officers@spi-inc.org ● electronic mail, board@spi-inc.org. **Conventions/Meetings:** monthly board meeting - usually held on the third Tuesday.

6778 ■ Software Testing Institute (STI)
PO Box 831056
Richardson, TX 75083-1056
Ph: (972)680-8507
Fax: (972)680-8905
E-mail: sarcher@metronet.com
URL: http://www.softwaretestinginstitute.com
Contact: Susan Archer, Dir.
Founded: 1995. **Members:** 50. **Description:** Software development and testing professionals. Works to provide members with expertise to work more productively and efficiently. Provides access to industry publications and research; offers online services; conducts educational programs; compiles statistics. **Libraries: Type:** reference. **Holdings:** software. **Subjects:** testing and testers. **Computer Services:** database ● electronic publishing ● mailing lists ● online services. **Publications:** *Automated Testing Handbook*. **Price:** $29.95 for nonmembers ● *Software Testing Institute Buyer's Guide*, annual. Book. **Price:** $29.95 for nonmembers; free for members ● *Software Testing Newsletter*, quarterly. **Price:** $69.95 for nonmembers; free for members ● *STI Resource Guide*, annual. Booklet. **Price:** $7.95 for nonmembers; free for members.

6779 ■ Special Interest Group on Software Engineering (SIGSOFT)
c/o Association for Computing Machinery
2 Penn Plz., Ste.701
New York, NY 10121-0701
Ph: (212)626-0613
Free: (800)342-6626
Fax: (212)302-5826
E-mail: ignatoff@acm.org
URL: http://www.sigsoft.org
Contact: William G. Griswold, Chm.
Founded: 1976. **Multinational. Description:** Serves as a special interest group of the Association for Computing Machinery (see separate entry). Represents computer professionals interested in the technology of software creation and evolution. Promotes exchange of ideas and information. **Awards:** Distinguished Service Award. **Frequency:** annual. **Type:** recognition ● Outstanding Research Award. **Frequency:** annual. **Type:** recognition. **Publications:** *Software Engineering Notes*, bimonthly. Newsletter. Alternate Formats: online. **Conventions/Meetings:** annual International Symposiums on the Foundations of Software Engineering - conference.

6780 ■ Systems and Software Consortium, Inc. (SSCI)
2214 Rock Hill Rd.
Herndon, VA 20170-4227
Ph: (703)742-8877
Free: (800)827-4772
Fax: (703)742-7347
E-mail: ask-ssci@systemsandsoftware.org
URL: http://www.software.org
Contact: Dr. Jim Kane, Pres./CEO
Multinational. **Description:** Acts as provider of reduced-to-practice technology for development of systems and software. **Boards:** Technical Advisory. **Formerly:** (2006) Software Productivity Consortium.

Computer Users

6781 ■ AFCOM
742 E Chapman Ave.
Orange, CA 92866
Ph: (714)997-7966
Fax: (714)997-9743
E-mail: afcom@afcom.com
URL: http://www.afcom.com
Contact: William L. DiBella, Pres.
Founded: 1980. **Members:** 2,900. **Membership Dues:** individual, $255 (annual) ● site, $585 (annual) ● corporate (5 members can be at different sites), $866 (annual) ● additional site/corporate, $175 (annual). **Staff:** 17. **Local Groups:** 13. **Description:** Data center, networking and enterprise systems management professionals from medium and large scale mainframe, midrange and client/server data centers worldwide. Works to meet the professional needs of the enterprise system management community. Provides information and support through educational events, research and assistance hotlines, and surveys. **Awards:** AFCOM Scholarship Fund at NTID. **Frequency:** annual. **Type:** scholarship. **Recipient:** for hearing impaired high school graduates interested in pursuing Associate's Degree in data processing ● Enterprise Systems Manager of the Year Award. **Frequency:** annual. **Type:** recognition ● NTID Scholarship. **Frequency:** annual. **Type:** scholarship. **Recipient:** for graduates of NTID working in the computer operations field. **Formerly:** (1997) Association for Computer Operations Management; (2000) Association for Data Center, Networking and Enterprise Systems. **Publications:** *AFCOM's Fall Program Proceedings*, annual. **Price:** $40.00/copy. ISSN: 1077-3223 ● *Annual Survey of Data Processing Operations Salaries*, annual. **Price:** included in membership dues; $40.00 for nonmembers. ISSN: 1077-2812. **Circulation:** 2,900 ● *The Communique*, monthly. Newsletter. Contains news items, product announcements, information requests from members, and classified ads. **Price:** included in membership dues. ISSN: 1077-2677. **Circulation:** 2,900. Alternate Formats: online ● *DCM Magazine*, bimonthly. Features columns written by industry professionals. **Advertising:** accepted ● *Digest of Conference Sessions*, annual. Proceedings. **Price:** $40.00/copy. ISSN: 1077-3231 ● *Enterprise Management Issues*, bimonthly. Magazine. Contains feature articles and columns. **Price:** included in membership dues. ISSN: 1061-1401. **Circulation:** 4,000. **Advertising:** accepted ● Also prepares articles for publication in general computer publications. **Conventions/Meetings:** semiannual Educational Conference - conference and trade show (exhibits) - usually March and October ● annual Focus on Enterprise Systems - conference (exhibits) - usually March or April.

6782 ■ Arizona Macintosh Users Group (AMUG)
4331 E Baseline Rd., Ste.B-105
PMB 445
Gilbert, AZ 85234
E-mail: sales@amug.org
URL: http://www.amug.org
Contact: Alex Podressoff, Pres.
Founded: 1984. **Members:** 1,650. **Membership Dues:** in U.S., $39 (annual) ● outside U.S., $89 (annual). **Staff:** 2. **Description:** Macintosh users. Promotes education and assistance of members in the use of Macintosh computers, iconic interfaces, and related products. Provides forum for computer users to share ideas and resources. Operates Resource Center for members and vendors. **Libraries: Type:** reference. **Holdings:** 10,000; software. **Computer Services:** Mailing lists ● online services, training classes, repairs. **Telecommunication Services:** electronic bulletin board, AMUG Preferred ● electronic bulletin board, AMUG I ● electronic bulletin board, AMUG Preferred BBS. **Publications:** *AMUG News*, bimonthly. Newsletter. Contains a collection of public domain software featuring selections from AMUG Disk Library and bulletin boards. **Price:** $3.00/disk for members; $6.00/disk for nonmembers. **Circulation:** 1,650. **Advertising:** accepted. **Conventions/Meetings:** monthly Vendor Presentation - meeting.

6783 ■ Association for Computing Machinery (ACM)
2 Penn Plz., Ste.701
New York, NY 10121-0701
Ph: (212)869-7440 (212)626-0500
Free: (800)342-6626
Fax: (212)944-1318
E-mail: acmhelp@acm.org
URL: http://www.acm.org
Contact: John R. White PhD, CEO/Exec. Dir.
Founded: 1947. **Members:** 80,000. **Membership Dues:** professional, $99 (annual) ● student, $19 (annual). **Multinational**. **Description:** Biological, medical, behavioral, and computer scientists; hospital administrators; programmers and others interested in application of computer methods to biological, behavioral, and medical problems. Works to advance the art, science, engineering, and application of information technology. Serves both the professionals and the public by fostering the open interchange of information and by promoting the highest professional and ethical standards. **Awards:** A.M. Turing Award. **Frequency:** annual. **Type:** recognition. **Recipient:** to an individual selected for contributions of a technical nature made to the computing community ● ACM-AAAI Allen Newell Award. **Frequency:** annual. **Type:** recognition. **Recipient:** to an individual selected for career contributions that have breadth within computer science and other disciplines ● ACM Fellows Program. **Frequency:** annual. **Type:** recognition. **Recipient:** for outstanding achievements in computer science and information technology and significant contributions to the mission of the ACM ● Doctoral Dissertation Award. **Frequency:** annual. **Type:** recognition. **Recipient:** to the author(s) of the best doctoral dissertation(s) in computer science and engineering ● Eugene L. Lawler Award for Humanitarian Contributions within Computer Science and Informatics. **Frequency:** biennial. **Type:** recognition. **Recipient:** to an individual or a group who has made a significant humanitarian contribution through the use of computing technology ● Grace Murray Hopper Award. **Frequency:** annual. **Type:** recognition. **Recipient:** for an outstanding young computer professional ● Karl V. Karlstrom Outstanding Educator Award. **Frequency:** annual. **Type:** recognition. **Recipient:** for an outstanding educator ● Outstanding Contribution to ACM. **Frequency:** annual. **Type:** recognition. **Recipient:** to individuals who are selected on the value and degree of service to ACM ● Paris Kanellakis Theory and Practice Award. **Frequency:** annual. **Type:** recognition. **Recipient:** for specific theoretical accomplishments. **Computer Services:** database, digital library. **Telecommunication Services:** electronic mail, white@acm.org. **Formed by Merger of:** Biomedical Computing Society; Special Interest Group for Biomedical Information Processing. **Formerly:** (1997) Special Interest Group on Biomedical Computing. **Supersedes:** Biological Information Processing Organization. **Publications:** *Ubiquity*. Magazine. Contains information on the IT industry. ● Newsletter, quarterly. **Conventions/Meetings:** annual conference (exhibits).

6784 ■ Association of Minicomputer Users (AMU)
Address Unknown since 2007
Founded: 1978. **Members:** 1,000. **Membership Dues:** corporate, $125 (annual). **Staff:** 7. **Description:** Firms and individuals who use or are interested in using small computer systems for internal applications. Provides speakers on small computer applications; conducts annual review and research and educational programs on trends in the field; compiles statistics. **Libraries: Type:** reference. **Holdings:** 7,000. **Computer Services:** database, vendors and users. **Telecommunication Services:** electronic bulletin board, www Home page. **Committees:** Small Computer; Vendor Relations. **Divisions:** Business Applications; Governmental; Industrial; Microcomputer Users. **Programs:** Client/Server Systems; Decision Support Systems; Departmental Computing; Effective Use and Application of Small Computers. **Publications:** *Client/Server Software Directory*, annual. **Price:** $375.00/year ● *Departmental Computing Analyzer*, bimonthly. Guide to using computers in departmental settings. **Price:** $96.00/year ● *Mini-Beacon*, bimonthly. Newsletter. Contains industry news. **Price:** available to members only ● *Minicomputer Applications Analyzer* ● *Minicomputer Software Analyzer*, annual. Monograph. Covers software reviews and evaluation. **Price:** $135.00/year ● *New Computing Trends*, bimonthly. **Price:** $55.00/year. **Advertising:** not accepted. **Conventions/Meetings:** seminar - 8/year.

6785 ■ Association of Personal Computer User Groups (APCUG)
3155 E Patrick Ln., Ste.1
Las Vegas, NV 89120-3481
Free: (800)558-6867
E-mail: tos@apcug.net
URL: http://www.apcug.net
Contact: Jay Ferron, Pres.
Founded: 1986. **Members:** 400. **Membership Dues:** associate, full, $50 (annual) ● new, $75. **Description:** Umbrella organization of user groups worldwide. Fosters communication among members, hardware manufacturers, and software publishers. Sponsors educational programs; compiles statistics. Conducts charitable activities. **Awards:** REACH Award. **Frequency:** annual. **Type:** recognition. **Recipient:** for community service by a personal computer user group. **Computer Services:** database, computer user groups worldwide. **Telecommunication Services:** electronic bulletin board, via web page. **Publications:** *APCUG Reports*, quarterly. **Price:** free, for members only. **Circulation:** 1,000.

6786 ■ Association for Women in Computing (AWC)
41 Sutter St., Ste.1006
San Francisco, CA 94104
Ph: (415)905-4663
Fax: (415)358-4667
E-mail: info@awc-hq.org
URL: http://www.awc-hq.org
Contact: Mary DiFiore Crowe, Pres.
Founded: 1978. **Members:** 1,006. **Membership Dues:** chapter, $42 (annual) ● independent, $25 (annual). **Local Groups:** 18. **Description:** Individuals interested in promoting the education, professional development, and advancement of women in computing. **Awards:** Augusta Ada Lovelace Award. **Frequency:** annual. **Type:** recognition. **Recipient:** for contributions to the industry and to women ● President's Award. **Frequency:** annual. **Type:** recognition. **Recipient:** for contributions to AWC. **Computer Services:** Mailing lists, email discussion and announcement lists, with pointers to articles of interest. **Telecommunication Services:** electronic mail, president@awc-hq.org. **Committees:** Chapters; Corporate Relations; Finance; Lovelace Awards; Past Presidents; Public Relations; Student Relations; Website. **Publications:** *Source*, annual. Journal. Contains articles written by members and other authors. **Price:** free for members. **Circulation:** 1,000. Alternate Formats: online ● Membership Directory, annual, in January. Contains a complete list of national officers and chapters. **Price:** free for members. **Conventions/Meetings:** board meeting, any member may attend - 3/year.

6787 ■ The Association for Work Process Improvement (TAWPI)
75 Fed. St., Ste.901
Boston, MA 02110

Ph: (617)426-1167
Fax: (617)521-8675
E-mail: fmoran@tawpi.org
URL: http://www.tawpi.org
Contact: Mr. Francis Moran, Pres./CEO
Founded: 1970. **Members:** 1,200. **Membership Dues:** individual, $225 (annual) ● affiliate, $1,195 (annual). **Staff:** 10. **Budget:** $1,800,000. **Regional Groups:** 6. **Description:** Seeks to enhance the performance of organizations and strengthen the value of professionals that employ emerging technologies in mail, remittance, and forms processing. **Libraries: Type:** reference. **Subjects:** technical presentations made at past conferences. **Awards:** TAWPI Hall of Fame. **Frequency:** annual. **Type:** recognition. **Recipient:** for outstanding service to the association and to the industry. **Telecommunication Services:** electronic mail, smcneil@tawpi.org. **Formed by Merger of:** (1993) DEMA, The Association for Input Technology and Management; Recognition Technologies Users Association, OCR/Scanner/ Fax Association. **Publications:** *Buyer's Guide*, annual. Contains information on products and services in information capture and management. **Price:** free. **Circulation:** 70,000. **Advertising:** accepted. Alternate Formats: online ● *TAWPI Membership Directory*, annual ● *Work Process Improvement TODAY*, bimonthly. Magazine. Contains news and information on new products, personnel changes, research updates, and case studies in industry. **Price:** included in membership dues. ISSN: 1073-2233. **Advertising:** accepted. **Conventions/Meetings:** annual Work Process Improvement Forum and Exposition - conference, business automation technologies, applications and supplies; education sessions (exhibits).

6788 ■ Capital PC User Group (CPCUG)
19209 Mt. Airey Rd.
Brookeville, MD 20833
Ph: (301)762-9372 (703)554-8078
Fax: (301)760-3303
E-mail: admin@cpcug.org
URL: http://www.cpcug.org
Contact: Dennis Courtney, Pres.
Founded: 1982. **Members:** 3,500. **Membership Dues:** individual, $42 (annual). **Budget:** $100,000. **Description:** An educational and support group for users of IBM personal computers and compatible computers. Objectives are to: provide a forum for members of the IBM PC and compatible equipment; increase understanding and utilization of the personal computer; encourage experimentation and research on current and potential uses of personal computers; exchange information and experience for the benefit of all concerned; provide an opportunity for both formal and informal education in computer applications and hardware and software technologies. Provides speakers, instructors, materials, and experienced consultants to local educational institutions and nonprofit groups. Conducts charitable program. Sponsors special interest groups. Although it operates primarily in the Washington, DC, area, membership is international. **Libraries: Type:** reference. **Holdings:** 3,000; books, periodicals, software. **Subjects:** computers. **Awards: Type:** recognition. **Recipient:** for use of computers in local school projects. **Telecommunication Services:** hotline, (301)738-9060. **Publications:** *Monitor*, monthly. Magazine. Includes hardware and software reviews, special interest and user group news, advertisers and author/ subject index, and calendar of events. **Price:** included in membership dues. ISSN: 1070-2792. **Circulation:** 3,800. **Advertising:** accepted. **Conventions/Meetings:** monthly meeting - usually second Monday, Bethesda, MD ● monthly seminar.

6789 ■ Center for Computer-Assisted Legal Instruction (CALI)
565 W Adams St.
Chicago, IL 60661-3691
Ph: (312)906-5307
Fax: (312)906-5280
E-mail: jmayer@cali.org
URL: http://www2.cali.org
Contact: John Mayer, Exec. Dir.
Founded: 1982. **Membership Dues:** individual, $250 (annual) ● law school, $4,000 (annual). **Description:** Law schools in the U.S. and interested law schools outside of the U.S; affiliates are law firms and continuing legal education organizations. Seeks to: coordinate distribution and use of computerized instructional exercises in law; establish standards for hardware, software, and courseware; support authors in the development of new instructional programs; to sponsor research for advancing the quality and effectiveness of computerized exercises in legal education. Provides members with computer-based instructional exercises on various subjects including trial advocacy, civil procedure, torts, professional responsibility, evidence, and insurance. Exercises are operational on most microcomputers that use MS DOS and Apple II and MacIntosh microcomputers. Gives advice and consultation to law schools planning to use computer lessons; provides information for potential authors and users of legal exercises. **Libraries: Type:** reference. **Publications:** *The CALI Report*, semiannual. **Price:** free for members; $25.00 /year for nonmembers. **Conventions/Meetings:** annual Conference for Law School Computing Professionals.

6790 ■ Christian Macintosh User Group (CMUG)
2190 Bristolwood Ln.
San Jose, CA 95132
E-mail: cmugdave@earthlink.net
URL: http://www.cmug.org
Contact: David Lang, Content Ed.
Founded: 1987. **Members:** 2,000. **Membership Dues:** in U.S., $15 ● in Canada and Mexico, $20 ● other country, $35. **Local Groups:** 12. **Description:** Facilitates the use of Macintosh computer systems among Christians. Maintains speakers' bureau. Conducts charitable and educational programs. **Libraries: Type:** reference. **Holdings:** audiovisuals, books, periodicals, software. **Subjects:** Macintosh. **Programs:** Research. **Publications:** *The Servant*, monthly. **Circulation:** 2,000. **Advertising:** accepted.

6791 ■ Common-A Users Group
5515 N Cumberland Ave., Ste.810
Chicago, IL 60656
Ph: (312)279-0192
Free: (800)777-6734
Fax: (312)279-0227
E-mail: common@common.org
URL: http://www.common.org
Contact: Ralph Gervasi, Exec. Dir.
Founded: 1960. **Members:** 5,400. **Membership Dues:** corporate/user group, $395 (annual) ● individual, $125 (annual). **Staff:** 20. **Budget:** $4,500,000. **Description:** Represents individuals and organizations united to advance the effective use of equipment among users of IBM computers and data processing machines. Promotes the free interchange of information about the machines and their installation and usage. Maintains liaison with IBM in an effort to improve customer services and hardware and software operation. **Libraries: Type:** reference. **Telecommunication Services:** electronic mail, ralph_gervasi@common.org. **Divisions:** Industry/Applications; Management; Systems. **Formerly:** (2000) Common. **Publications:** *Common.Connect*. Magazine. Alternate Formats: online ● *NewsCOM*, quarterly. Newsletter. **Price:** included in membership dues. **Circulation:** 5,000 ● Also publishes agendas, update booklet, and new member publications. **Conventions/Meetings:** semiannual conference (exhibits).

6792 ■ ENCOMPASS
401 N Michigan Ave., Ste.2200
Chicago, IL 60611
Ph: (312)321-5151
Free: (877)354-9887
Fax: (312)673-4609
E-mail: information@encompassus.org
URL: http://www.encompassus.org
Contact: Christopher Hansen, Exec. Dir.
Founded: 1961. **Members:** 12,000. **Membership Dues:** individual, $90 (annual) ● international individual, $135 (annual) ● corporate, $400 (annual) ● international corporate, $600 (annual). **Staff:** 15. **Budget:** $5,000,000. **Regional Groups:** 15. **Local Groups:** 46. **Description:** Information Technology professionals interested in the products, services, and technologies of Hewlett Packard and related vendors. Promotes the unimpeded exchange of information, with the goal of helping its members and their organizations to be more successful. Provides each member with means to enhance their professional development, forums for technical training, mechanisms for obtaining up-to-date information, advocacy programs, and opportunities for informal disclosure and interaction with professional colleagues of like interests. **Libraries: Type:** reference. **Holdings:** 1,000; software. **Awards:** Lifetime Achievement Awards. **Type:** recognition. **Telecommunication Services:** electronic mail, christopher.hansen@encompassus.org. **Boards:** Directors. **Publications:** *Encompass Points*, monthly. Newsletter. Features articles on industry trends, product updates, and "how-tos" from experienced users. **Price:** free for members. **Circulation:** 12,000. **Advertising:** accepted. Alternate Formats: online. **Conventions/Meetings:** annual symposium and seminar, provides training and product demonstrations (exhibits).

6793 ■ Epicor Users Group
PO Box 10368
Lancaster, PA 17605-0368
Ph: (717)209-7177
Fax: (717)209-7189
E-mail: info@epicorusers.org
URL: http://www.epicorusers.org
Contact: Steve Petska, Pres.
Founded: 1994. **Membership Dues:** general, $360 (annual). **Staff:** 1. **Description:** Represents organizations, institutions, or individuals who own or use Data Flo, ManFact, Avante or InfoFlo; Epicor Software personnel; other interested individuals. Aims to: advance effective utilization of Epicor software; promote the interchange of information and ideas; advance the art of computation through mutual education; establish standards and provide channels to facilitate exchange of computer programs. Provides feedback to Epicor Software on equipment, software, and related problems and suggestions; sponsors special interest groups; conducts demonstrations and question-and-answer sessions. **Telecommunication Services:** electronic mail, steve.petska@metsteco.com ● electronic mail, mshroyer@miltex.com. **Committees:** Data Management; Manufacturing; Marketing, Customer Service, and Financials; Training/ Implementation. **Formerly:** (1998) Dataworks Users Alliance; (2003) DUAL. **Publications:** *Dual Connection*, quarterly. Newsletter. **Price:** free for member companies. **Advertising:** accepted ● *The Prospector*. Newsletter. Alternate Formats: online. **Conventions/Meetings:** semiannual conference (exhibits).

6794 ■ HUG International - HTE Users' Group (HUG)
c/o Tino Anthony, Pres.
PO Box 490630
Leesburg, FL 34749-0630
Ph: (352)728-9703
Fax: (352)728-2594
E-mail: tino.anthony@leesburgflorida.gov
URL: http://www.huginc.org
Contact: Tino Anthony, Pres.
Founded: 1981. **Members:** 84. **Membership Dues:** organization, $195 (annual). **Budget:** $292,000. **Description:** Users of Hogan Systems and IBM Financial Application Software. Facilitates the dissemination of information among members. Promotes sound and professional practices between members. Communicates the needs of members to Hogan Systems Inc. and IBM Corporation, and advises these companies with respect to product refinements and enhancements. **Formerly:** (1988) HUG. **Publications:** *Hug E-Newsletter*. Alternate Formats: online ● Journal, quarterly. **Conventions/Meetings:** annual conference (exhibits) - 2009 June 15-18, Las Vegas, NV; 2010 June 6-10, Orlando, FL.

6795 ■ INTEREX
Address Unknown since 2007
Founded: 1973. **Multinational. Description:** Users of Hewlett-Packard (HP) computers and related

equipment. Promotes the exchange of information between HP computer users and HP. Provides members with the opportunity to constructively influence the design and development of these systems, including HP-UX, MPE, RTE, and workstations. **Computer Services:** direct mail service and list rental ● database ● mailing lists ● online services. **Also Known As:** The International Association of Hewlett-Packard Computing Professionals. **Publications:** *HP World*, monthly. Newsletter. Contains information for HP professionals. **Price:** included in membership dues. **Circulation:** 42,000. **Advertising:** accepted. Alternate Formats: online ● *HP World News*, weekly. Newsletter. E-newsletter with up-to-date stories, important issues, and latest products. **Price:** included in membership dues. **Circulation:** 13,000. Alternate Formats: online ● *HP World Solutions Directory*, semiannual. Directory of software, hardware, services, consulting and training for Open View, HP-UX, MPE, NonStop, OpenVMS, Linux, and Windows Systems. **Price:** included in membership dues. **Circulation:** 42,000. **Advertising:** accepted. Alternate Formats: online ● *HP World Tech Journal*, monthly. Newsletter. E-newsletter with compilation of relevant technical articles from a wide variety of select publications. **Price:** for members only, included in membership dues. **Advertising:** not accepted. Alternate Formats: online ● *Inside HP*, biweekly. Newsletter. Online resource for HP watchers, HP staff and executives, financial analysts, and journalists. **Price:** included in membership dues. **Circulation:** 10,000. Alternate Formats: online ● *INTEREXPress*, weekly. Newsletter. Provides information about the association, including LUG and SIG activities. **Price:** for members only, included in membership dues. **Advertising:** not accepted. Alternate Formats: online. **Conventions/Meetings:** annual HP e3000 Solutions Symposium-West, with training sessions (exhibits) ● annual HP World Conference & Expo, with training sessions (exhibits) ● annual InterWorks Conference and Expo, with training sessions (exhibits).

6796 ■ International Oracle Users Group (IOUG)

401 N Michigan Ave., 22nd Fl.
Chicago, IL 60611-4267
Ph: (312)245-1579
Fax: (312)527-6785
E-mail: ioug@ioug.org
URL: http://www.ioug.org
Contact: Carol McGury, Exec. Dir.

Founded: 1993. **Members:** 14,000. **Membership Dues:** individual, $150 (annual) ● individual, $225 (biennial) ● individual, $275 (3/year) ● premier, $1,750 (annual) ● corporate, $595 (annual) ● vendor, $850 (annual) ● academic, $150 (annual). **Staff:** 17. **Budget:** $3,500,000. **Local Groups:** 100. **Multinational. Description:** Provides communications, networking, and education forum for all users of products and services in the Oracle environment and strives to influence Oracle Corporation in its product direction by being the channel for an integrated voice for the Oracle professionals. **Awards:** Chris Wooldridge Award. **Frequency:** annual. **Type:** recognition. **Recipient:** to outstanding volunteer ● Oracle Recognition Award. **Frequency:** annual. **Type:** recognition. **Recipient:** to individual at Oracle promoting the advancement of IOUG ● Select Editor's Award. **Frequency:** annual. **Type:** recognition. **Recipient:** for best article. **Formerly:** (2002) International Oracle Users Group - Americas. **Publications:** *SELECT Journal*, quarterly. Magazine. Contains technical information. **Price:** $125.00/year. **Circulation:** 5,000. **Advertising:** accepted. Alternate Formats: online ● Reports. **Conventions/Meetings:** annual conference (exhibits) - always spring.

6797 ■ International Tandem Users' Group (ITUG)

401 N Michigan Ave., Ste.2200
Chicago, IL 60611-4267
Ph: (312)321-6851
Fax: (312)245-1064
E-mail: cnestor@itug.org
URL: http://www.itug.org
Contact: Colleen Nestor, Exec. Dir.

Founded: 1973. **Members:** 2,000. **Membership Dues:** individual, $150 (annual) ● organizational/corporate, $500 (annual) ● associate, $100 (annual) ● vendor, $750 (annual). **Staff:** 14. **Budget:** $2,000,000. **Regional Groups:** 27. **Description:** Tandem computer owners and operators. Fosters communication between user groups, Tandem Computers, Inc., and international organizations. Conducts educational programs. **Libraries: Type:** reference. **Holdings:** software. **Awards:** Excellence Awards. **Type:** recognition. **Recipient:** for outstanding service. **Telecommunication Services:** electronic mail, jharmon@itug.org. **Publications:** *Tandem Connection*, bimonthly. Journal. Covers user applications; also includes region/division news. **Price:** included in membership dues. **Circulation:** 2,000. **Advertising:** accepted. Alternate Formats: online. **Conventions/Meetings:** annual Summit - convention and trade show (exhibits).

6798 ■ NAQP Computer Users Group (NAQP-CUG)

c/o PrintImage International
2250 E Devon Ave., Ste.245
Des Plaines, IL 60018
Ph: (847)298-8680
Free: (800)234-0040
Fax: (847)298-8705
E-mail: info@printimage.org
URL: http://www.printimage.org
Contact: Steven D. Johnson, Pres./CEO

Members: 500. **Membership Dues:** gold, $465 ● platinum, $995 ● division, $350 ● supplier (1-24 employees), $969 ● supplier (25-150 employees), $1,200 ● supplier (more than 150 employees), $2,700 ● international, $300 ● educational, $225. **Staff:** 1. **Budget:** $40,000. **Regional Groups:** 7. **Description:** Printers and printer suppliers interested in manual and computerized management systems for purposes such as accounting; estimating inventory and production control, database management, and desktop publishing and typesetting. Established to inform members of current management system developments involving computers, word processors, typesetters, and telecommunications. Provides speakers; compiles statistics. Special interest group of the National Association of Quick Printers (see separate entry). **Formerly:** (1984) NAQP Computer Users Group; (1987) NAQP Management Systems Group. **Publications:** *Quick-Bytes*, monthly. **Conventions/Meetings:** annual conference (exhibits) - always July/August ● annual conference - always February.

6799 ■ Network and Systems Professionals Association (NASPA)

7044 S 13th St.
Oak Creek, WI 53154
Ph: (414)908-4945 (414)768-8000
Fax: (414)768-8001
E-mail: helpdesk@netstream.net
URL: http://www.naspa.com
Contact: Radi Shourbaji, Pres.

Founded: 1986. **Members:** 31,000. **Membership Dues:** faculty, student, retired, $20 (annual) ● subscriber, $40 (annual) ● gold, $45 (annual) ● platinum, $95 (annual) ● life, $995. **Staff:** 12. **Budget:** $2,000,000. **Regional Groups:** 34. **Multinational. Description:** Technicians and technical management personnel in 90 countries who work in corporate data processing. Works to enhance the level of technical education among members through publications, public domain software, electronic information sharing, job and career assistance, and scholarships and grants. Conducts charitable and educational programs; maintains speakers' bureau and placement service; compiles statistics. **Libraries: Type:** reference. **Holdings:** 300; archival material, books. **Subjects:** computing. **Awards:** Member of the Year. **Frequency:** annual. **Type:** recognition. **Computer Services:** Mailing lists. **Formerly:** NaSPA, Inc.; (1986) National Systems Programmers Association; (1997) Association for Corporate Computing Technical Professionals. **Publications:** *Technical Support*, monthly. Magazine. Serves as a technical "How To" magazine for technical manager. **Price:** included in membership dues. **Circulation:** 40,000. **Advertising:** accepted. Alternate Formats: online. **Conventions/Meetings:** annual conference (exhibits).

6800 ■ Personalization Consortium

Address Unknown since 2008

Founded: 2000. **Membership Dues:** executive, $15,000 (annual) ● associate, $5,000 (annual). **Multinational. Description:** Promotes the responsible use of one-to-one marketing technology and practices on the Internet.

6801 ■ Regis System Users' Group

11 Spring St.
Hallowell, ME 04347
Ph: (207)395-4837
E-mail: regispeople@juno.com
Contact: Ron Kley, Coor.

Founded: 1988. **Members:** 135. **Staff:** 2. **Description:** Museum staff members who use the REGIS system for computerized information management; supported by Museum Research Associates. Provides forum for exchange of information and computer software. Develops databases for museum inventory and membership management. Maintains speakers' bureau. **Publications:** *REGIS Users' Newsletter*, bimonthly. **Price:** free for members ● Reports. **Conventions/Meetings:** periodic workshop.

6802 ■ SAS Global Forum

c/o SAS Institute Inc.
100 SAS Campus Dr.
Cary, NC 27513-2414
Ph: (919)531-5000 (919)946-8928
Fax: (919)677-4444
URL: http://support.sas.com/events/sasglobalforum/index.html
Contact: Warren E. Stinson, Conference Chm.

Founded: 1976. **Regional Groups:** 6. **Local Groups:** 300. **Description:** Data processors, scientists, statisticians, econometricians, administrative assistants, and other professionals working with SAS software and products of SAS. Serves as an independent group of the Institute, although it receives its administrative support from the company. Aims to share information with SAS users; set priorities for development efforts; exchange ideas with the SAS staff. **Libraries: Type:** open to the public. **Holdings:** 27. **Subjects:** SAS programming. **Awards: Frequency:** annual. **Type:** recognition. **Recipient:** for best papers on computer performance evaluation and systems software, statistics, graphics, information systems, database systems, econometrics, operations research, qualify control, and training and user support services. **Formerly:** (2006) SAS Users Group International. **Publications:** Proceedings, annual. Contains author and keyword index. **Price:** included in conference fee. Alternate Formats: CD-ROM. **Conventions/Meetings:** annual conference.

6803 ■ Special Interest Group on Accessible Computing (SIGACCESS)

c/o Vicki Hanson, Chair
IBM T.J. Watson Res. Center
19 Skyline Dr.
Hawthorne, NY 10532
Ph: (914)784-6603
Fax: (914)784-7279
E-mail: chair_sigaccess@acm.org
URL: http://www.sigaccess.org
Contact: Vicki Hanson, Chair

Founded: 1970. **Members:** 453. **Membership Dues:** student, $6 (annual) ● regular, $15 (annual). **Staff:** 1. **Description:** Promotes the professional interests of computing personnel with physical disabilities and the application of computing and information technology in solving relevant disability problems. Works to educate the public to support careers for the disabled. **Divisions:** Vice Chair for the Blind; Vice Chair for the Deaf; Vice Chair for the Motor Impaired. **Also Known As:** SIGCAPH. **Formerly:** (1978) Special Interest Committee for Computers and the Physically Handicapped; (2005) Special Interest Group for Computers and the Physically Handicapped. **Publications:** *Accessibility and Computing*. Newsletter. Alternate Formats: online ● *SISCAPH Newsletter*, 3/year.

Price: free for members ● Annual Report, annual. Alternate Formats: online. **Conventions/Meetings:** periodic workshop.

6804 ■ Special Interest Group on Data Communications of the Association for Computing Machinery (ACM SIGCOMM)
c/o Mark Crovella, Chm.
Boston Univ.
U.S. Department of of Cmpt. Sci.
111 Cummington St.
Boston, MA 02215
Ph: (617)353-8923
Fax: (517)353-6457
E-mail: crovella@cs.bu.edu
URL: http://www.sigcomm.org
Contact: Mark Crovella, Chm.
Description: Serves as professional forum for the discussion of topics in the field of communications and computer networks, including technical design and engineering, regulation and operations and the social implications of computer networking. Promotes systems engineering and architectural questions of communication. **Awards:** ACM SIGCOMM Award. **Frequency:** annual. **Type:** recognition. **Recipient:** for outstanding lifetime technical achievement in the field of data and computer communications ● ACM SIGCOMM Student Award. **Frequency:** annual. **Type:** recognition. **Recipient:** for outstanding paper whose main author is a student ● Test of Time Award. **Frequency:** annual. **Type:** recognition. **Recipient:** for outstanding paper published in the past 10 to 12 years that still maintains relevancy in the present year. **Publications:** *Computer Communication Review*, quarterly. Magazine. Contains articles and new ideas or visions in the field data and computer communications. Alternate Formats: online.

6805 ■ UniForum Association
PO Box 3177
Annapolis, MD 21403
Ph: (410)715-9500
Free: (800)333-8649
Fax: (240)465-0207
E-mail: dmurray@uniforum.org
URL: http://www.uniforum.org
Contact: Deb Murray, VP for Training
Founded: 1981. **Members:** 7,500. **Membership Dues:** general, $95 (annual). **Staff:** 19. **Regional Groups:** 33. **Multinational. Description:** Vendor-independent association for computer developers, vendors, and end users. Promotes the exchange of information about Open Systems and related hardware, software, applications, and standards. **Awards:** UniForum Open Award. **Frequency:** annual. **Type:** recognition. **Recipient:** for information architects (and their organizations) who design, develop, and manage custom client/server solutions in an open systems environment to solve a business problem. **Computer Services:** Mailing lists. **Boards:** Editorial Advisory. **Committees:** Technical Steering. **Working Groups:** Realtime; Security. **Also Known As:** International Association of Open Systems Professionals. **Publications:** *The Collected MOSES Whitepapers*. **Price:** included in membership dues ● *Electronic Mail Demystified*. **Price:** included in membership dues ● *Internationalization Explored*. **Price:** included in membership dues ● *Network Applications*. **Price:** included in membership dues ● *Network Substrata*. **Price:** included in membership dues ● *Open Systems Products Directory*, annual. **Price:** included in membership dues. **Advertising:** accepted. Alternate Formats: online; CD-ROM ● *Open Systems Standards*. **Price:** included in membership dues ● *POSIX Explored: Shell and Utilities*. **Price:** included in membership dues ● *POSIX Explored: System Interface*. **Price:** included in membership dues ● *The Systems Administrators Guide to World Wide Web Servers*. **Price:** included in membership dues ● *Uniforum Monthly*. Magazine. **Circulation:** 40,000. **Advertising:** accepted ● *UniNews*, biweekly. Newsletter. Alternate Formats: online ● *Your Guide to POSIX*. **Price:** included in membership dues. **Conventions/Meetings:** annual conference.

6806 ■ USENIX Association
2560 9th St., Ste.215
Berkeley, CA 94710
Ph: (510)528-8649
Fax: (510)548-5738
E-mail: office@usenix.org
URL: http://www.usenix.org
Contact: Ellie Young, Exec. Dir.
Founded: 1975. **Members:** 10,000. **Membership Dues:** individual, $120 (annual) ● corporate, $495 (annual) ● educational, $255 (annual) ● student, $45 (annual) ● supporting, $2,500 (annual). **Staff:** 14. **Budget:** $7,000,000. **Description:** Individuals (7200) with an interest in Advanced Computing Systems in a professional or technical capacity; and (commercial computer firms) institutions, colleges and universities, and research institutes (1700). Promotes innovation in advanced computing systems; fosters the development of research and technological information pertaining to advanced computer systems. **Libraries: Type:** open to the public. **Subjects:** technical proceedings of various workshops, technical conferences. **Awards:** Student Grants. **Type:** scholarship. **Recipient:** to individuals for each workshop and conference. **Computer Services:** Mailing lists. **Special Interest Groups:** SAGE. **Also Known As:** System Administrators Guild. **Publications:** *Login*, 8/year. Journal. **Price:** $60.00/year; $14.00/issue. **Circulation:** 5,000. Alternate Formats: online ● Magazine, bimonthly. **Advertising:** accepted. Alternate Formats: online ● Proceedings. Provides information from workshops and technical conferences. Alternate Formats: online. **Conventions/Meetings:** annual conference and workshop, technical conferences (exhibits) - 2008 June 22-27, Boston, MA; 2009 June 14-19, San Diego, CA; 2010 June 20-25, Boston, MA.

6807 ■ Vivit
PO Box 18510
Boulder, CO 80308
Ph: (646)414-9895
Fax: (212)937-2366
E-mail: information@vivit-worldwide.org
URL: http://www.vivit-worldwide.org
Contact: Donna Farmer, Exec. Dir.
Founded: 1993. **Membership Dues:** individual, $150 (annual). **Staff:** 10. **Multinational. Description:** Represents the interests of Hewlett-Packard Open View users and developers. Provides an expansive body of practical knowledge and experience. **Formerly:** (2007) OpenView Forum International. **Conventions/Meetings:** semiannual HP Software Forum - conference.

6808 ■ XyUser Group (XYUG)
c/o Bob Carr, Exec. Dir.
12310 129th St. N
Largo, FL 33774
Ph: (727)595-9240
Fax: (727)596-1543
E-mail: bob.carr@xyug.org
URL: http://www.xyug.org
Contact: Bob Carr, Exec. Dir.
Founded: 1983. **Members:** 130. **Membership Dues:** corporate, $675 (annual) ● consultant, $750 (annual) ● vendor, $1,200 (annual). **Staff:** 1. **Budget:** $98,000. **Regional Groups:** 1. **Multinational. Description:** Commercial typesetters, design houses, printers, and commercial companies with in-house typesetting or document production facilities such as insurance companies, software producers, and packaging and manufacturing organizations. Assists Xyvision with the development of its products. Shares information to improve use of Xyvision system; remain informed about the current features and capabilities of Xyvision products. **Libraries: Type:** reference. **Holdings:** audiovisuals. **Subjects:** graphic arts production. **Awards: Type:** recognition. **Computer Services:** database. **Committees:** Publishing Advisory; Strategic Advisory; Technical Advisory. **Formerly:** (1990) XyVision Users Group. **Publications:** *Guide to Using the XyUsers Group BBS*. Manual ● *User Assist Directory*, annual. Lists users and areas of expertise. **Conventions/Meetings:** quarterly board meeting ● annual conference (exhibits) ● quarterly regional meeting and seminar.

Computers

6809 ■ Association of Computer Support Specialists (ACSS)
c/o Edward J. Weinberg, Pres.
333 Mamaroneck Ave., No. 129
White Plains, NY 10605
Ph: (917)438-0865
Fax: (914)713-7227
E-mail: edw@acss.org
URL: http://www.acss.org
Contact: Edward J. Weinberg, Pres.
Membership Dues: individual, $100 (annual) ● company, $200 (annual). **Description:** Promotes awareness of computer support as a profession. **Publications:** *The Floppy Desk*. Newsletter. Alternate Formats: online. **Conventions/Meetings:** monthly meeting, with speakers.

6810 ■ Association of Macintosh Trainers (AMT)
112 Britt Ct.
Chapel Hill, NC 27514
Ph: (919)370-3071
E-mail: webmaster@mactrainers.com
URL: http://www.mactrainers.com
Contact: Jimmy Davies, Contact
Founded: 1991. **Membership Dues:** regular, $40 (annual). **Multinational. Description:** Promotes the importance of quality Macintosh computer training and support. Provides an international support network of Macintosh trainers, instructors, and educators so that computer end users can have easy access to quality Apple Macintosh OS support and assistance. Maintains speakers' bureau. **Publications:** *AMT News Bulletin*. Alternate Formats: online.

6811 ■ Chinese American Computer Association (CCA)
5027 Merrill St.
Torrance, CA 90503
E-mail: membership@ccausa.com
URL: http://www.ccausa.com
Contact: Edward Y. Chang, Dir.
Founded: 1981. **Membership Dues:** regular, $30. **Description:** Works to further technological advances and promote business opportunities between the U.S. and other countries.

6812 ■ International Webmasters Association (IWA)
119 E Union St., Ste.F
Pasadena, CA 91103
Ph: (626)449-3709
Fax: (626)449-8308
URL: http://www.iwanet.org
Contact: Richard S. Brinegar, Exec. Dir.
Members: 22,000. **Membership Dues:** full, $49 (annual). **Description:** Web professionals. Works to provide educational programs to include Certified Web Professional programs, support a global network of official IWA chapters, and provide members with professional networking opportunities at all levels. Maintains universal standards on ethical and professional practices for all Web professionals. **Programs:** Web Design Training.

6813 ■ Internet Corporation for Assigned Names and Numbers (ICANN)
4676 Admiralty Way, Ste.330
Marina del Rey, CA 90292
Ph: (310)823-9358
Fax: (310)823-8649
E-mail: icann@icann.org
URL: http://www.icann.org
Contact: Peter Dengate Thrush, Chm.
Founded: 1998. **Languages:** English, French, Italian, Portuguese, Spanish. **Description:** Coordinates and assigns identifiers, including Internet domain names, IP address numbers, protocol parameters and port numbers.

6814 ■ IVI Foundation
PO Box 1016
Niwot, CO 80544-1016
Ph: (303)652-2585
Fax: (303)652-1444
E-mail: info@ivifoundation.org
URL: http://www.ivifoundation.org
Contact: Fred Bode, Admin.
Founded: 1998. **Membership Dues:** sponsor, $7,500 (annual) ● general, $1,500 (annual) ● associate, $750 (annual). **Description:** Promotes specifications for programming test instruments that simplify interchangeability, provide better performance, and reduce cost of program development and maintenance. **Also Known As:** Interchangeable Virtual Instruments.

6815 ■ League of Professional System Administrators (LOPSA)
15000 Commerce Pkwy., Ste.C
Mount Laurel, NJ 08054
Ph: (856)439-0500
Free: (800)285-2141
Fax: (856)439-0525
E-mail: info@lopsa.org
URL: http://lopsa.org
Contact: Sam Albrecht, Exec. Dir.
Founded: 2005. **Membership Dues:** individual/founding, $50 (annual) ● student, $25 (annual). **Multinational. Description:** Aims to advance the practice of system administration. Supports, recognizes, educates, and encourages practitioners of system administration. Serves the public through education and outreach on system administration issues.

6816 ■ Mobile Payment Forum
401 Edgewater Pl., Ste.600
Wakefield, MA 01880
Ph: (781)876-8840
Fax: (781)224-1239
E-mail: info@mobilepaymentforum.org
URL: http://www.mobilepaymentforum.org
Contact: Simon Pugh, Pres.
Founded: 2001. **Membership Dues:** principal, $12,500 (annual) ● associate, $4,000 (annual) ● emerging, $2,000 (annual). **Multinational. Description:** Works to create a framework for standardized, secure, and authenticated mobile commerce using payment card accounts.

6817 ■ Open Geospatial Consortium (OGC)
35 Main St., Ste.5
Wayland, MA 01778-5037
Ph: (508)655-5858
Fax: (508)655-2237
E-mail: jburnett@opengeospatial.org
URL: http://www.opengeospatial.org
Contact: Jeffrey Burnett, VP/Chief Financial Off.
Members: 260. **Membership Dues:** principal, $55,000 (annual) ● technical committee, $11,000 (annual) ● associate: commercial/national government organization, $4,400 (annual) ● associate: government-sub national (province, state), $1,100 (annual) ● associate: government-local (county, municipality), associate: university/research center, $500 (annual) ● associate: small company, $2,200 (annual). **Multinational. Description:** Promotes benefits from geographic information and services made available across any network, application, or platform. **Formerly:** (2006) Open GIS Consortium. **Conventions/Meetings:** quarterly meeting.

6818 ■ PCI Industrial Computer Manufacturers Group (PICMG)
c/o Virtual, Inc.
401 Edgewater Pl., Ste.600
Wakefield, MA 01880
Ph: (781)246-9318
Fax: (781)224-1239
E-mail: info@picmg.org
URL: http://www.picmg.org
Contact: Joe Pavlat, Pres./Chm.
Founded: 1994. **Members:** 600. **Membership Dues:** affiliate, $850 (annual) ● associate, $1,750 (annual) ● executive, $2,500 (annual). **Multinational. Description:** Represents and promotes companies who collaboratively develop open specifications for high performance telecommunications and industrial computing applications. **Telecommunication Services:** electronic mail, pavlat@picmg.org ● electronic mail, picmg@virtualmgmt.com. **Special Interest Groups:** PCI.

6819 ■ PlanetMUG
PO Box 1264
Fremont, CA 94538-0126
E-mail: webmaster@planetmug.org
URL: http://www.bmug.org
Membership Dues: individual (3 hours access/day to the Planet BBS), $25 (annual) ● family (per account), $20 (annual). **Description:** Creates an online community providing access to Internet accessible bulletin board system called The Planet BBS, for use in helping people with MAC operating systems. **Formerly:** BMUG - Berkeley Macintosh Users Group. **Publications:** Brochure. Alternate Formats: online.

6820 ■ PXI Systems Alliance (PXISA)
c/o Bode Enterprises, LLC
PO Box 1016
Niwot, CO 80544
Ph: (619)297-1212 (303)652-2585
Fax: (303)652-1444
E-mail: bhelsel@pxisa.org
URL: http://www.pxisa.org
Contact: Mr. Bob Helsel, Exec. Dir.
Founded: 1995. **Members:** 65. **Membership Dues:** associate, $375 (annual) ● sponsor, $3,000 (annual) ● executive, $1,500 (annual). **Multinational. Description:** Promotes the PCI extensions for Instrumentation (PXI) standard, ensures interoperability, and maintains the PXI specification.

6821 ■ SIGAPP - Special Interest Group on Applied Computing
c/o ACM
2 Penn Plz., Ste.701
New York, NY 10121-0701
Ph: (212)869-7440
Free: (800)342-6626
Fax: (212)944-1318
E-mail: bryant@cis.uab.edu
URL: http://www.acm.org/sigapp
Contact: Barrett R. Bryant, Chair
Description: Promotes development of new computing applications and applications areas as well as transfer of computing technology to new problem domains. **Publications:** *Applied Computing Reviews*, semiannual. Newsletter. **Price:** included in membership dues.

6822 ■ SpamCon Foundation (SCF)
829 14th St.
San Francisco, CA 94114
Ph: (415)552-2557
E-mail: comments@spamcon.org
Contact: Dan Birchall, Exec. Dir.
Founded: 2001. **Membership Dues:** regular, $50 (annual) ● sponsor, $100 (annual) ● super sponsor, $250 (annual) ● benefactor, $500 (annual) ● director's circle, $1,000 (annual) ● friend, $25 (annual). **Multinational. Description:** Protects email as a viable communication and commerce medium by supporting measures to reduce the amount of unsolicited email that crosses private networks, while ensuring that valid email reaches its destination. **Publications:** Newsletter, monthly. Contains news about spam, strategies to improve email practices, and news and trivia. Alternate Formats: online.

6823 ■ Special Interest Group on Design of Communication (SIGDOC)
c/o Association for Computing Machinery
2 Penn Plz., Ste.701
New York, NY 10121-0701
Ph: (212)626-0605
Fax: (212)302-5826
E-mail: brad_m@unity.ncsu.edu
URL: http://www.sigdoc.org
Contact: Brad Mehlenbacher, Pres.
Founded: 1997. **Membership Dues:** professional, $99-$198 (annual) ● student, $19-$62 (annual). **Description:** Represents and promotes senior communication professionals who create documentation in the computer community. **Awards:** Diana Award. **Frequency:** annual. **Type:** recognition. **Recipient:** to an organization that has collectively made an impact on the field ● Graduate Student Competition. **Type:** recognition ● SIGDOC Rigo Award. **Frequency:** annual. **Type:** recognition. **Recipient:** to an individual for a lifetime of significant work in the design of communication ● Undergraduate Scholarship. **Type:** scholarship. **Recipient:** to a young student who is pursuing an established degree program in an area related to the design of communication. **Telecommunication Services:** electronic mail, chair_sigdoc@acm.org. **Formerly:** (2006) Special Interest Group for Documentation. **Publications:** *Communications of the ACM*. Magazine. **Price:** included in membership dues ● *Conference Proceedings* ● *SIGDOC Newsletter*, quarterly. Includes lists of members, activities, interesting items and the job market. **Price:** included in membership dues. Alternate Formats: online ● Annual Report, annual. **Conventions/Meetings:** annual conference, with panels and workshops.

6824 ■ Special Interest Group on Management Information Systems (SIGMIS)
c/o Janice C. Sipior, Chair
Coll. of Commerce and Finance
Villanova Univ.
800 Lancaster Ave.
Villanova, PA 19085
Ph: (610)519-4347
E-mail: janice.sipior@villanova.edu
URL: http://www.sigmis.org
Contact: Janice C. Sipior, Chair
Founded: 1961. **Membership Dues:** individual, $29 (annual) ● student, $19 (annual). **Description:** Promotes information systems and technologies for management, and management of these systems and technologies. **Absorbed:** (2003) Special Interest Group for Computer Personnel Research. **Publications:** *Conference Proceedings* ● *Data Base*, quarterly. Journal. Contains articles of practical research significance and relating experiences in the area of business. **Price:** included in membership dues. **Advertising:** accepted ● *SIGMIS: Management Information Systems*, quarterly. Journal. Contains articles of practical research in area of business uses of information systems. **Price:** $49.00 for nonmembers; $29.00 for members; $19.00 for students; $29.00 for SIG members only. ISSN: 0095-0033 ● *Transaction on Information Systems*, quarterly. Journal. **Price:** $170.00 for nonmembers; $41.00 for members; $36.00 for students; $170.00 for SIG members only ● *Transactions on Information System Online*, quarterly. Journal. **Price:** $204.00 for nonmembers (print and online copies); $49.00 for members (print and online copies); $43.00 for students (print and online copies); $204.00 for SIG members only (print and online copies). ISSN: 1046-8188 ● Annual Report ● Videos. **Price:** $136.00 for nonmembers; $33.00 for members; $29.00 for students; $136.00 for SIG members only. Alternate Formats: online. **Conventions/Meetings:** annual conference, with workshops - November ● annual CPR Conference ● annual European Conference on Information Systems - June ● annual International Conference on Information Systems (In-Coop) - December.

6825 ■ Special Interest Group on Mobility of Systems Users, Data, and Computing (SIGMOBILE)
c/o Fran Spinola, Program Coor.
2 Penn Plz., Ste.701
New York, NY 10121-0701
Ph: (212)626-0603
Fax: (212)302-5826
E-mail: spinola@hq.acm.org
URL: http://www.sigmobile.org
Contact: Prof. David B. Johnson, Chm.
Founded: 1996. **Membership Dues:** professional, $30 (annual) ● student, $20 (annual). **Multinational. Description:** Promotes research in theory and practice of mobility of systems, users, data, and computing. **Awards:** Best Paper Award. **Frequency:**

annual. **Type:** recognition. **Recipient:** the best paper submitted to annual conference ● Distinguished Service Award. **Frequency:** periodic. **Type:** recognition. **Recipient:** for services to the mobile computing and wireless communications community ● MobiCom Best Student Paper Award. **Frequency:** annual. **Type:** recognition. **Recipient:** for the best paper submitted by a student ● Outstanding Contribution Award. **Frequency:** periodic. **Type:** recognition. **Recipient:** to an individual who has made a significant contribution to the research on mobile computing and communications and wireless networking. **Publications:** *Mobile Computing and Communications Review*, quarterly. Journal. Contains academic and industrial research contributions on the design of new generations of information and communications technologies. **Advertising:** accepted. Also Cited As: *MC2R* ● Annual Report, annual. Alternate Formats: online. **Conventions/Meetings:** annual international conference ● annual meeting.

6826 ■ Special Interest Group on Multimedia (SIGMM)
c/o Association for Computing Machinery
2 Penn Plz., Ste.701
New York, NY 10121-0701
Ph: (212)869-4770
Free: (800)342-6626
Fax: (212)944-1318
E-mail: acmhelp@acm.org
URL: http://www.sigmm.org
Contact: Ramesh Jain, Chm.
Membership Dues: professional, $20 (annual). **Description:** Represents professionals in all aspects of multimedia computing, communication, storage and applications. **Computer Services:** Online services, research in multimedia addresses. **Telecommunication Services:** electronic mail, jain@ics.uci.edu. **Publications:** *Conference Proceedings*. **Price:** included in membership dues ● Annual Report, annual ● Video. Alternate Formats: online. **Conventions/Meetings:** annual conference ● workshop.

6827 ■ U.S. Internet Council (USIC)
Address Unknown since 2008
Founded: 1996. **Description:** Non-partisan educational resource for state and federal policy makers. Works to provide reliable information and analysis on Internet policy issues.

6828 ■ Web3D Consortium
325 Sharon Park Dr., Ste.623
Menlo Park, CA 94025
Ph: (248)342-7662
Fax: (650)854-0168
E-mail: anita.havele@web3d.org
URL: http://www.web3d.org
Contact: Anita Havele, Exec. Dir.
Founded: 1994. **Membership Dues:** professional, $100 (annual) ● small academic/student (organizational), $1,500 (annual) ● standard company (organizational), $3,500 (annual) ● large company (organizational), $9,500 (annual) ● small academic/student, standard company (directing), $5,500 (annual) ● large company (directing), $15,000 (annual). **Description:** Works to create open standards for Web3D specifications, and to accelerate the worldwide demand for products based on these standards. **Computer Services:** Mailing lists, of members. **Working Groups:** CAD; DIS-XML; GeoSpatial; H-Anim; Medical; VizSim (XMSF); X3D Conformance Program; X3D Shaders. **Publications:** *Developer Survey*. Alternate Formats: online.

6829 ■ Wi-Fi Alliance
3925 W Braker Ln.
Austin, TX 78759
Ph: (512)305-0790
Fax: (512)305-0791
E-mail: info@wi-fi.org
URL: http://www.wi-fi.org
Contact: Frank Hanzlik, Managing Dir.
Founded: 1999. **Members:** 300. **Membership Dues:** regular, $15,000 (annual) ● adopter, $5,000 (annual). **Multinational. Description:** Advocates for the adoption of a single worldwide-accepted standard for high-speed wireless local area networking. Develops universal specifications and conducts rigorous testing and Wi-Fi certification of wireless devices. Provides Wi-Fi users with the information they need to make decisions about today's Wi-Fi systems. **Publications:** Annual Report. Alternate Formats: online.

6830 ■ X.Org Foundation
c/o Steve Swales, Chm.
SUN Microsystems
4150 Network Cir.
Santa Clara, CA 95054
Free: (800)555-9SUN
E-mail: xorg_info@x.org
URL: http://www.x.org
Contact: Steve Swales, Chm.
Founded: 2004. **Multinational. Description:** Provides stewardship of X Window System standards and technology for distributors, developers, users. Dedicated to maintaining the existing X Window System code base and engineering appropriate enhancements driven by current and future market requirements. Periodically provides official X Window System update releases to the general public free of charge. Governs the evolution of the X11R6 specifications, working with appropriate groups to revise and post updates to the standard as required. **Formerly:** X.Org.

Conservation

6831 ■ Society for Conservation GIS (SCGIS)
PO Box 7183
Redlands, CA 92375
E-mail: scgis@scgis.org
URL: http://www.scgis.org
Contact: Rankin Holmes, Pres.
Founded: 1997. **Membership Dues:** standard, $35 (annual) ● basic (student, senior, low-budget), $20 (annual) ● supporter, $100 (annual) ● sustaining, $250 (annual) ● sponsor, $50 (annual) ● life, $1,000. **Multinational. Description:** Provides knowledge and supports individuals using Geographic Information Systems (GIS) and science for the conservation of natural resources and cultural heritage. Assists conservationists worldwide in using GIS through communication, networking, scholarships and training. **Telecommunication Services:** electronic mail, membership@scgis.org. **Publications:** Newsletter. Contains committee reports, news and regular features. Alternate Formats: online.

Construction

6832 ■ American Concrete Institute (ACI)
PO Box 9094
Farmington Hills, MI 48333-9094
Ph: (248)848-3700
Fax: (248)848-3701
E-mail: bill.tolley@concrete.org
URL: http://www.aci-int.org
Contact: William R. Tolley, Exec. VP
Founded: 1904. **Members:** 16,000. **Membership Dues:** individual, $208 (annual) ● organizational, $911 (annual) ● junior, $117 (annual) ● student in U.S. and Canada, $38 (annual) ● student outside U.S. and Canada, $75 (annual) ● sustaining, $3,081 (annual). **Staff:** 90. **Budget:** $11,000,000. **Multinational. Description:** Technical and educational society of engineers, architects, contractors, educators, and others interested in improving techniques of design construction and maintenance of concrete products and structures. Offers certification program. **Libraries: Type:** not open to the public. **Holdings:** 2,000. **Awards: Frequency:** annual. **Type:** recognition ● **Frequency:** annual. **Type:** scholarship. **Additional Websites:** http://www.concrete.org. **Telecommunication Services:** electronic mail, ward.malisch@concrete.org. **Formerly:** (1913) National Association of Cement Users. **Publications:** *ACI Materials Journal*, bimonthly. Describes research on materials and concrete; properties, use, and handling of concrete; and related ACI standards and committee reports. **Price:** $60.00 for members in U.S.; $65.00 for members outside U.S.; $29.00 for students in the Western Hemisphere; $35.00 for students outside the Western Hemisphere. ISSN: 0889-325X. **Circulation:** 11,700 ● *ACI Structural Journal*, bimonthly. Presents technical papers on structural design and analysis of concrete structures and elements. **Price:** $60.00 for members in U.S.; $65.00 for members outside U.S.; $29.00 for students in the Western Hemisphere; $35.00 for students outside the Western Hemisphere. ISSN: 0889-3241. **Circulation:** 17,400 ● *American Concrete Institute—Directory*, every 2-3 years. Membership Directory. **Advertising:** accepted ● *Concrete International*, monthly. Magazine. Covers institute and chapter news and industry personnel promotions and changes. Includes meetings calendar and new products and services. **Price:** included in membership dues; $104.00 /year for nonmembers. ISSN: 0162-4075. **Circulation:** 20,000. **Advertising:** accepted ● Also publishes technical reports and monographs, reports on symposia, standards, and bibliographies. **Conventions/Meetings:** semiannual convention - usually spring and fall ● seminar and conference.

6833 ■ American Institute of Constructors (AIC)
PO Box 26334
Alexandria, VA 22314
Ph: (703)683-4999
Fax: (703)683-5480
E-mail: admin@aicnet.org
URL: http://www.aicnet.org
Contact: Steve Byrne FAIC, Pres.
Founded: 1971. **Members:** 1,200. **Membership Dues:** student (academic year), $20 (annual) ● candidate (one-time registration), $100 ● associate, $139 (annual) ● affiliate, $290 (annual) ● constructor, $215 (annual) ● fellow, $265 (annual). **Staff:** 2. **Budget:** $250,000. **Local Groups:** 14. **Description:** Professionals engaged in construction practice, education, and research. Serves as the certifying body for the professional constructor. Promotes the study and advances the practice of construction. Facilitates the exchange of information and ideas relating to construction. Conducts educational programs. **Libraries: Type:** reference. **Holdings:** books. **Awards:** Walter Nashert, Sr. Award. **Frequency:** annual. **Type:** recognition. **Recipient:** for professionals in construction who contribute to the industry and maintain a reputation for integrity and fair dealing. **Computer Services:** Mailing lists. **Commissions:** Constructor Certification. **Committees:** Ethics; Inter-Industry Liaison; Membership Services; Professional Standards; Programs and Education; Public Relations; Publications. **Publications:** *American Professional Constructor*, biennial. Journal. Contains general interest and technical articles of use to those in the management of the construction process. **Price:** $100.00 subscription in North America; $125.00 subscription outside North America; $50.00/issue. Also Cited As: *AIC Journal* ● *Constructor Certification Exam Study Guide Level II*. Manual. **Price:** $100.00 for members; $110.00 for nonmembers ● *Ethics Manual*. **Price:** $30.00 for members; $35.00 for nonmembers ● *Roster of Members*, annual. Membership Directory. **Price:** included in membership dues; $100.00 for nonmembers. **Advertising:** accepted ● Newsletter, quarterly. **Price:** included in membership dues. **Circulation:** 1,800. **Advertising:** accepted. **Conventions/Meetings:** biennial board meeting and conference (exhibits) - March/October ● board meeting and workshop - September/October.

6834 ■ American Institute of Steel Construction (AISC)
1 E Wacker Dr., Ste.700
Chicago, IL 60601-1802
Ph: (312)670-2400
Fax: (312)670-5403
E-mail: ferch@aisc.org
URL: http://www.aisc.org
Contact: Roger E. Ferch, Pres.
Founded: 1921. **Members:** 3,000. **Membership Dues:** active, $550 (annual) ● associate, $1,500-

$5,000 (annual) ● affiliate/professional, $135-$1,000 (annual) ● retiree, $65 (annual). **Staff:** 60. **Budget:** $6,500,000. **Description:** Fabricators who erect structural steel for buildings and bridges. Sponsors research cooperatively with other industry groups and independently at engineering colleges. Program includes studies on welded and bolted connections, composite design, allowable stress and load factor design in steel, buckling problems, and techniques of painting structural steel. Collects and releases market data and statistics; develops specifications and standard practice codes. Conducts technical lecture program. Assembles photographic exhibits of steel structures. **Libraries:** **Type:** reference. **Holdings:** audiovisuals, films. **Awards:** Prize Bridge Awards & Architectural Awards of Excellence. **Frequency:** biennial. **Type:** recognition. **Recipient:** for the most beautiful steel bridges and buildings ● **Type:** scholarship. **Recipient:** for undergraduate and graduate students ● Theodore R. Higgins. **Frequency:** annual. **Type:** recognition. **Recipient:** for the best paper on new steel developments. **Telecommunication Services:** electronic mail, solutions@aisc.org. **Committees:** Education; Fabrication Operations; Manuals; Software; Specifications; Steel Structural Research. **Publications:** *Engineering Journal*, quarterly ● *Manual of Steel Construction* ● *Modern Steel Construction*, monthly. Manual. **Price:** included in membership dues; $36.00 for nonmembers ● Bibliographies ● Handbooks. **Conventions/Meetings:** annual meeting ● biennial National Symposium on Steel Bridge Construction - meeting ● annual North American Steel Construction Conference - convention, meeting of plenary and break out sessions (exhibits).

6835 ■ Association of Asphalt Paving Technologists (AAPT)
4711 Clark Ave., Ste.G
White Bear Lake, MN 55110-3268
Ph: (651)293-9188
Fax: (651)293-9193
E-mail: aapt@qwest.net
URL: http://www.asphalttechnology.org
Contact: Eugene L. Skok, Sec.-Treas.
Founded: 1924. **Members:** 825. **Membership Dues:** active, associate, $100 (annual) ● junior, $80 (annual). **Staff:** 2. **Budget:** $168,000. **Description:** Represents engineers and chemists engaged in asphalt paving or related fields such as materials and construction equipment. **Libraries:** **Type:** not open to the public. **Holdings:** 71. **Awards:** Emmons. **Frequency:** annual. **Type:** recognition. **Recipient:** for best paper of the year. **Publications:** *Asphalt Paving Technology*, annual. Book. **Price:** $80.00. **Conventions/Meetings:** annual conference ● annual meeting - 2009 Mar. 16-18, Minneapolis, MN.

6836 ■ Construction Specifications Institute (CSI)
99 Canal Center Plz., Ste.300
Alexandria, VA 22314
Ph: (703)684-0300
Free: (800)689-2900
Fax: (703)684-8436
E-mail: csi@csinet.org
URL: http://www.csinet.org
Contact: Edward L. Soenke FCSI, Pres.
Founded: 1948. **Members:** 17,700. **Membership Dues:** professional, industry, associate, $220 (annual) ● intermediate, $100 (annual) ● student, $27 (annual). **Staff:** 57. **Budget:** $10,500,000. **Regional Groups:** 10. **Local Groups:** 142. **Description:** Individuals concerned with the specifications and documents used for construction projects. Membership includes architects, professional engineers, specifiers, contractors, product manufacturers, teachers and research workers in architectural and engineering fields, and building maintenance engineers. Advances construction technology through communication, service, education, and research. Certifies construction specifiers and others involved in construction and allied industries. Maintains 20 committees including Certification, Credentials, Specifications Competition, and Technical Documents. Sponsors competitions; maintains speakers' bureau; offers seminars. **Libraries:** **Type:** reference. **Holdings:** biographical archives. **Subjects:** architecture, construction. **Computer Services:** Mailing lists, technical documents. **Publications:** *The Construction Specifier*, monthly. Magazine. Provides architects, engineers, specifiers, contractors, and others with technical information on construction materials, methods, and products. **Price:** $40.00. ISSN: 0010-6925. **Circulation:** 24,000. **Advertising:** accepted ● *The Editors Journal*, monthly ● *The Newsdigest*, monthly ● Membership Directory, annual ● Also publishes technical documents and monographs. **Conventions/Meetings:** annual convention and show, non-residential construction producers, materials and services (exhibits).

6837 ■ The Masonry Society (TMS)
3970 Broadway, Ste.201-D
Boulder, CO 80304-1135
Ph: (303)939-9700
Fax: (303)541-9215
E-mail: info@masonrysociety.org
URL: http://www.masonrysociety.org
Contact: Phillip J. Samblanet, Exec. Dir.
Founded: 1977. **Members:** 750. **Membership Dues:** student, $35 (annual) ● associate/professional, $125 (annual) ● affiliate, $295 (annual) ● sustaining, $1,250 (annual) ● junior, $65 (annual). **Staff:** 3. **Budget:** $500,000. **Multinational. Description:** Represents individuals interested in the art and science of masonry. Serves as professional, technical and educational association dedicated to the advancement and knowledge of masonry. Gathers and disseminates technical information. **Libraries:** **Type:** reference. **Awards:** Outstanding Masonry Design Award. **Frequency:** triennial. **Type:** recognition. **Computer Services:** Mailing lists, on disk, for members only. **Telecommunication Services:** electronic mail, psamblanet@masonrysociety.org. **Committees:** Architectural Practices; Certification; Codes and Standards; Construction Practices; Design Practices; Education; International; Research; Technical Advisory. **Affiliated With:** Arizona Masonry Guild; Brick Association of the Carolinas; Brick Industry Association; Concrete Masonry Association of California and Nevada; Expanded Shale Clay and Slate Institute; International Masonry Institute; National Concrete Masonry Association; Rocky Mountain Masonry Institute. **Publications:** *ASTM Standards on Masonry - 4th Edition*. **Price:** $75.00 ● *Commentary to Chapter 21, Masonry, of the 1997 Uniform Building Code*. **Price:** $39.00 for members; $52.00 for nonmembers ● *Commentary to Chapter 21, Masonry, of the UBC*, triennial. Book ● *Masonry Codes and Specifications*. **Price:** $30.00 ● *Masonry Designers' Guide*, triennial ● *The Masonry Society Journal*, annual. Provides an emphasis on masonry research. Includes calendar of events, Association and research news, and abstracts of current literature. **Price:** included in membership dues; $50.00 /year for nonmembers ● *MSJC Masonry Building Code Requirements and Specifications for Masonry Construction*. **Price:** $70.00 for members; $94.00 for nonmembers ● *North American Masonry Conference Proceedings*, triennial ● *Northridge Earthquake Report: Performance of Masonry Structure*. **Price:** $15.00 plus $2 for shipping ● *Standard Method for Determining Fire Resistance of Concrete and Masonry Construction Assemblies*. **Price:** $34.00 for members; $59.00 for nonmembers ● *Standard Method for Determining the Sound Transmission Class Rating for Masonry Walls*. **Price:** $20.00 for members; $26.00 for nonmembers ● *TMS News*, quarterly. Newsletter ● *2000 Masonry Codes and Specifications*. **Price:** $30.00 ● Membership Directory. **Conventions/Meetings:** annual meeting, with technical presentations and committee meetings - 2008 Nov. 6-9, Salt Lake City, UT ● quadrennial North American Masonry Conference ● annual Spring TMS Business Meetings ● University Professors' Masonry Workshop.

6838 ■ National Institute of Building Sciences (NIBS)
1090 Vermont Ave. NW, Ste.700
Washington, DC 20005-4950
Ph: (202)289-7800
Fax: (202)289-1092
E-mail: nibs@nibs.org
URL: http://www.nibs.org
Contact: David A. Harris FAIA, Pres.
Founded: 1976. **Members:** 800. **Membership Dues:** industry sector, $150 (annual) ● public interest sector, $75 (annual) ● sustaining, $1,000 (annual) ● contributing organization, $5,000 (annual). **Staff:** 35. **Description:** Individuals and organizations, including architects, engineers, builders, contractors, realtors, universities, and all levels of government interested in the building industry. Works to promote a favorable and coherent building regulatory environment and encourage new technology in the building industry. **Awards:** BSSC Exceptional Service Award. **Frequency:** annual. **Type:** recognition. **Recipient:** to individuals who have made extraordinary contributions to seismic risk reduction through BSSC programs ● BSSC Honor Award. **Frequency:** annual. **Type:** recognition. **Recipient:** to individuals who have made exceptional contributions toward fostering natural hazard reduction through seismic risk mitigation ● NIBS Honor Award. **Frequency:** annual. **Type:** recognition. **Recipient:** for an individual or organization that has made exceptional contributions to the nation and the building community ● NIBS Member Award. **Frequency:** annual. **Type:** recognition. **Recipient:** to a member of the Institute or an Institute council that has made substantial contributions to the Institute's mission ● President's Award. **Frequency:** annual. **Type:** recognition. **Recipient:** for individuals who have substantially improved the building process through exceptional government service. **Councils:** Building Seismic Safety; Construction Metrication; Facility Information; Multihazard Mitigation. **Publications:** *Asbestos Guide Abatement Specifications*, periodic ● *Asbestos Operations and Maintenance Work Practices Manual*, periodic ● *Building Sciences*, bimonthly. Newsletter. **Price:** included in membership dues; $35.00 /year for nonmembers ● *Construction Criteria Base*, annual. Compilation of more than one million pages of technical and regulatory building design and construction documents. **Circulation:** 2,500. Alternate Formats: CD-ROM ● Annual Report, annual. Alternate Formats: online. **Conventions/Meetings:** Spring Symposium - seminar - every spring ● periodic workshop.

6839 ■ Steel Erectors Association of America (SEAA)
2216 W Meadowview Dr., Ste.115
Greensboro, NC 27407
Ph: (336)294-8880
Fax: (413)208-6936
E-mail: executivedirector@seaa.net
URL: http://www.seaa.net
Contact: Bruce Basden, Pres.
Founded: 1972. **Membership Dues:** for steel erector (annual sales volume of 3 million and below), $450 (annual) ● for steel erector (annual sales volume of 3-5 million), $750 (annual) ● for steel erector (annual sales volume of 5-10 million), $1,000 (annual) ● for steel erector (annual sales volume of 10 million and above), $1,250 (annual) ● fabricator, $750 (annual) ● general contractor, $750 (annual) ● supplier and manufacturer, $750 (annual) ● specialty service, $750 (annual) ● service, $750 (annual). **Description:** Promotes the common interests and needs of those engaged in building with steel. Promotes safety through education and training programs for steel erectors. Promotes trade and development of standards. Cooperates with other organizations involved in the commercial construction business. **Committees:** Budget; Detailing; Education; Long-Range Planning; Safety; Steel Joist and Deck; Trade Show. **Programs:** Insurance. **Publications:** *Connector*. Magazine. Showcases construction products. Profiles members of the industry. **Advertising:** accepted ● *Handling Structural Steel* (in English and Spanish). Video. **Price:** $100.00 for members; plus shipping and handling; $125.00 for nonmembers; plus shipping and handling ● *Steel Joist and Steel Girders* (in English and Spanish). Video. Features a comprehensive look at the types of joist, joist designs, and panelization. **Price:** $100.00 for members; plus shipping and handling; $125.00 for

nonmembers; plus shipping and handling ● *Subpart R Compliance Guide*. Handbook. **Price:** $245.00 plus shipping and handling. Alternate Formats: CD-ROM ● *Subpart R Video Training Program* (in English and Spanish). Includes training programs on Fall Hazard, Connecting, Multiple Lift Rigging, and Controlled Deck Zone. **Price:** $995.00 for members; plus shipping and handling; $1,495.00 for nonmembers; plus shipping and handling.

Corrosion

6840 ■ National Association of Corrosion Engineers (NACE)
1440 S Creek Dr.
Houston, TX 77084-4906
Ph: (281)228-6200 (281)228-6223
Free: (800)797-6223
Fax: (281)228-6300
E-mail: firstservice@nace.org
URL: http://nace.org/nace/content/AboutNace/aboutnaceindex.asp
Contact: David Webster, Pres.
Founded: 1943. **Membership Dues:** individual, $130 (annual) ● student, $20 (annual) ● corporate, $500-$5,000 (annual). **Staff:** 50. **Description:** Commits to the study of corrosion. **Awards:** A.B. Campbell Award. **Frequency:** annual. **Type:** recognition. **Recipient:** for the most outstanding manuscript published in Materials Performance or Corrosion during the year by an author(s) who was no older than 35 years of age when the manuscript was submitted for publication consideration ● Distinguished Organization Award. **Frequency:** annual. **Type:** recognition. **Recipient:** for outstanding contributions to the field of corrosion science or engineering over a sustained period of time ● Distinguished Service Award. **Frequency:** annual. **Type:** recognition. **Recipient:** for distinguished service to NACE at section, region, area or association level ● Fellow Honor. **Frequency:** annual. **Type:** recognition. **Recipient:** for distinguished contributions in the fields of corrosion and its prevention ● Frank Newman Speller Award. **Frequency:** annual. **Type:** recognition. **Recipient:** for significant contributions to corrosion engineering ● H.H. Uhlig Young Educator Award. **Frequency:** annual. **Type:** recognition. **Recipient:** for a young educator who has excited students through outstanding and innovative teaching in corrosion ● Presidential Achievement Award. **Frequency:** annual. **Type:** recognition. **Recipient:** for meritorious work by an individual or group and the nominees need not be members of NACE International ● R.A. Brannon Award. **Frequency:** annual. **Type:** recognition. **Recipient:** for outstanding work by a current member of NACE in good standing for activity at the association or Board committee level of the organization ● T.J. Hull Award. **Frequency:** annual. **Type:** recognition. **Recipient:** for outstanding contribution in the field of publications ● Technical Achievement Award. **Frequency:** annual. **Type:** recognition. **Recipient:** for significant technical achievement in corrosion engineering ● W.R. Whitney Award. **Frequency:** annual. **Type:** recognition. **Recipient:** for significant contributions to the science of corrosion. **Computer Services:** database, membership directory. **Committees:** Technical. **Councils:** Press. **Also Known As:** NACE International. **Publications:** *Materials Performance*, monthly. Magazine. **Price:** included in membership dues. **Conventions/Meetings:** annual conference (exhibits).

Cosmology

6841 ■ National Council for GeoCosmic Research (NCGR)
c/o Liane Thomas Wade, Exec. Sec.
531 Main St., No. 1612
New York, NY 10044
Ph: (212)838-6247
E-mail: execsec@geocosmic.org
URL: http://www.geocosmic.org
Contact: Liane Thomas Wade, Exec. Sec.
Founded: 1972. **Members:** 2,300. **Membership Dues:** individual in U.S., $45 (annual) ● life, $750 ● couple in U.S., $65 (annual) ● couple outside U.S., $70 (annual) ● individual in Canada and Mexico, $50 (annual) ● individual in all other countries, $55 (annual). **Staff:** 1. **Budget:** $80,000. **Regional Groups:** 40. **National Groups:** 3. **Languages:** English, French, Russian, Spanish. **Description:** Works to further study of the interaction of man and the universe. Offers regional master's classes, ongoing teaching programs through local chapters, national and regional teaching conferences, and interdisciplinary referrals. Establishes educational standards. **Libraries: Type:** reference. **Holdings:** biographical archives. **Awards: Type:** recognition. **Computer Services:** Mailing lists, of members. **Committees:** Education; Research. **Publications:** *Geocosmic Journal* (in English, French, German, Russian, and Spanish), semiannual. Magazine. **Price:** included in membership dues; $10.00/copy for nonmembers. **Circulation:** 2,300. **Advertising:** accepted ● *National Council for Geocosmic Research—Memberletter*, bimonthly. Newsletter. **Advertising:** accepted ● *National Council for Geocosmic Research—Memberlist*, semiannual. Membership Directory. Includes new and full moon charts; arranged alphabetically and by zip code. **Price:** included in membership dues; $10.00/copy for nonmembers. **Advertising:** accepted. **Conventions/Meetings:** annual conference (exhibits).

Cost Estimation

6842 ■ AACE International
209 Prairie Ave., Ste.100
Morgantown, WV 26501
Ph: (304)296-8444
Free: (800)858-2678
Fax: (304)291-5728
E-mail: info@aacei.org
URL: http://www.aacei.org
Contact: Mr. James Baxter, Exec. Dir.
Founded: 1956. **Members:** 5,200. **Membership Dues:** professional full, professional associate, $130 (annual) ● student, $25 (annual). **Staff:** 13. **Budget:** $1,500,000. **Regional Groups:** 6. **Local Groups:** 74. **Multinational. Description:** Professional society of cost managers, cost engineers, estimators, schedulers and planners, project managers, educators, representatives of all branches of engineering, engineering students, and others. Conducts technical and educational programs. Offers placement service. Compiles statistics. Operates certification program for Certified Cost Engineers (CCE); Certified Cost Consultants (CCC); Interim Cost Consultants (ICC); Planning & Scheduling Professionals (PSP); and Earned Value Professionals (EVP). **Libraries: Type:** reference; lending; open to the public. **Holdings:** 7,000; archival material, books, monographs, periodicals. **Subjects:** all aspects of total cost management. **Awards:** Award of Merit. **Frequency:** annual. **Type:** recognition. **Recipient:** for outstanding service in cost management and engineering. **Computer Services:** Mailing lists ● online services, bookstore, virtual library, meetings, programs, distance learning. **Telecommunication Services:** electronic mail, jbaxter@aacei.org. **Boards:** Certification; Education; Technical. **Committees:** Aerospace; Appraisals; Contract Management; Cost Estimating; Cost Index; Decision/Risk Management; Environmental; Forest Products; General Construction; Government and Public Works; Human Factors; International Standards; Location Factors; Manufacturing; Metrication; Oil/Gas/Chemicals; Parametric Estimating; Planning and Scheduling; Productivity; Profitability; Project and Cost Control; Quality Management; Specialty Industries; Systems Integration; Transportation; Utilities and Energy; Value Engineering and Constructibility. **Also Known As:** The Association for the Advancement of Cost Engineering. **Formerly:** (1992) American Association of Cost Engineers. **Publications:** *AACE International—Resource Guide & Directory of Members*, annual. Membership Directory. Lists members alphabetically and geographically. **Price:** included in membership dues; $10.00 /year for nonmembers. ISSN: 0274-9696. **Circulation:** 6,000. **Advertising:** accepted. Alternate Formats: microform; CD-ROM ● *AACE Transactions*, annual. Contains complete texts of papers presented at the AACE annual meeting. ISSN: 0065-7158. **Advertising:** accepted. Alternate Formats: microform; CD-ROM ● *Cost Engineering*, monthly. Journal. Contains pre-reviewed articles and information of interest to the cost engineer and cost manager. **Price:** $65.00/year, in U.S. **Circulation:** 6,000. **Advertising:** accepted. Alternate Formats: online ● *Cost Engineer's Notebook*, 3/year. Provides technical data for cost engineers, cost estimators, planners, schedulers, and project managers. **Price:** $80.00 for members; $170.00 for nonmembers. **Circulation:** 6,000. Alternate Formats: microform ● Monograph. **Conventions/Meetings:** annual convention and meeting, with technical papers, 12 two-day educational seminars, panel sessions and software fair (exhibits) - usually June or July ● seminar.

Cryogenics

6843 ■ Cryogenic Engineering Conference (CEC)
c/o Dr. Jay C. Theilacker, Sec.
PO Box 500
Batavia, IL 60510-0500
E-mail: tnicol@fnal.gov
URL: http://tdserver1.fnal.gov/nicol/cec
Contact: Dr. Jay C. Theilacker, Sec.
Founded: 1954. **Members:** 4,000. **Budget:** $200,000. **Description:** Represents academic, industrial and governmental researchers, and managers involved in basic and applied work in cryogenics (the branch of physics and engineering dealing with the phenomena of extreme cold). Provides a forum for a four-day presentation of papers and seminars concerning advances in the science and technology of cryogenics in areas such as superconductivity, heat transfer, insulation, instrumentation, aerospace, liquefied gases, cryo-health services, cryobiology, LNG and power generation. **Awards:** Samuel C. Collins Award. **Frequency:** biennial. **Type:** recognition. **Recipient:** for outstanding contributions to cryogenic technology. **Additional Websites:** http://www.cec-icmc.org. **Telecommunication Services:** electronic mail, theilacker@fnal.gov. **Publications:** *Advances in Cryogenic Engineering*, biennial. Proceedings. Contains proceedings of the Cryogenic Engineering Conference. **Price:** $235.00/volume. **Conventions/Meetings:** biennial conference, oral and poster presentations on recent research results in cryogenic engineering (exhibits).

6844 ■ Cryogenic Society of America (CSA)
c/o Laurie Huget, Exec. Dir.
Huget Advt.
218 Lake St.
Oak Park, IL 60302-2609
Ph: (708)383-6220
Fax: (708)383-9337
E-mail: laurie@cryogenicsociety.org
URL: http://www.cryogenicsociety.org
Contact: Laurie Huget, Exec. Dir.
Founded: 1964. **Members:** 500. **Membership Dues:** individual, $63 (annual) ● regular outside U.S., $89 (annual). **Staff:** 2. **Regional Groups:** 2. **Description:** Individuals, firms, associations, and institutions engaged in cryogenic work. Seeks to encourage the dissemination of information on low temperature processes and techniques and increase public awareness of the usefulness of cryogenic technology. Promotes research and development through meetings, professional contacts, and publications. Undertakes information gathering in response to industrial and other needs. **Awards:** Fellow of the Cryogenic Society of America Award. **Frequency:** periodic. **Type:** recognition. **Recipient:** to a person with valuable contributions to the field of cryogenics ● Robert Vance Award. **Frequency:** periodic. **Type:** monetary. **Recipient:** for contribution to the field of cryogenics; fellow status ● Roger Boom Award. **Frequency:** periodic. **Type:** recognition. **Recipient:** for contribution to the field of cryogenics and superconductivity. **Telecommunication Services:** electronic mail,

csa@cryogenicsociety.org. **Divisions:** Space Cryogenics Workshop. **Absorbed:** Helium Society. **Publications:** *Cold Facts*, 5/year. Magazine. Covers general developments in cryogenics. Includes book reviews, event calendar, chapter meeting summaries, technical articles, product news, etc. **Price:** included in membership dues. **Circulation:** 3,400. **Advertising:** accepted. **Conventions/Meetings:** periodic symposium, short courses.

6845 ■ Immortalist Society (IS)
24355 Sorrentino Ct.
Clinton Township, MI 48035
Ph: (586)791-5961
Fax: (586)792-7062
E-mail: cihq@aol.com
URL: http://www.cryonics.org/info.html
Contact: York Porter, Pres.
Founded: 1967. **Members:** 399. **Membership Dues:** associate, $25 (annual) ● full, $75 (annual). **Staff:** 1. **Description:** Scientists and researchers involved in the study of human life extension; interested individuals. Promotes research and education in life extension sciences, particularly cryobiology, cryogenics, and cryonics. (Cryobiology is the study of the effects of extremely low temperatures on biological systems; cryogenics is a branch of physics dealing with the production and effects of very low temperatures; cryonics is the practice of freezing dead human beings in the hope of bringing them back to life at a later date.) A related organization, the Cryonics Institute, practices cryonics on members following their deaths. Provides financial support to research projects in life extension science. Maintains speakers' bureau. **Awards:** Research Grant. **Type:** monetary. **Formerly:** Cryonics Society of Michigan; (1985) Cryonics Association. **Publications:** *Financial Report*, annual ● *Long Life*, bimonthly. Newsletter. Published in conjunction with American Cryonics Society. **Price:** $25.00/year in U.S.; $30.00/year in Canada and Mexico; $52.00/year in Europe; $62.00/year in Asia or Australia. ISSN: 1079-7823. Alternate Formats: online ● Reports. **Conventions/Meetings:** annual meeting - usually September.

6846 ■ International Cryogenic Materials Conference (ICMC)
c/o Centennial Conferences
901 Front St., Ste.130
Louisville, CO 80027
Ph: (303)499-2299
Fax: (303)499-2599
E-mail: cecicmc07@centennialconferences.com
URL: http://www.cec-icmc.org
Contact: Peter Lee, Chm.
Founded: 1975. **Description:** Represents physicists and engineers in the fields of space, cryogenic fluid transport and storage, superconductivity, structural materials research, refrigeration, and superconducting magnets. **Awards:** Best Paper. **Frequency:** biennial. **Type:** recognition. **Affiliated With:** Cryogenic Engineering Conference. **Publications:** *Advances in Cryogenic Engineering-Materials*, biennial. Proceedings ● *Cryogenic Materials Series*, periodic. Proceedings ● *International Cryogenic Materials Conference Series*, periodic. Proceedings. **Conventions/Meetings:** biennial conference (exhibits) ● biennial Non-Metallic Materials and Composites at Low Temperatures - conference.

6847 ■ Society for Cryobiology (SC)
c/o Wendell Q. Sun, Treas.
1 Millennium Way
Branchburg, NJ 08876
Ph: (908)947-1176
Fax: (908)947-1085
E-mail: wsun@lifecell.com
URL: http://www.societyforcryobiology.org
Contact: Wendell Q. Sun, Treas.
Founded: 1964. **Members:** 450. **Membership Dues:** individual, $60 (annual) ● individual (with print subscription), $130 (annual) ● sustaining, $165 (annual) ● student (with print subscription), $40 (annual) ● retired, $45 (annual) ● corporate, $800 (annual) ● institutional, $275 (annual). **Budget:** $100,000. **Multinational. Description:** Basic and applied research in the field of low temperature biology and medicine. Promotes interdisciplinary approach to freezing, freeze-drying, hypothermia, hibernation, physiological effects of low environmental temperature on animals and plants, medical applications of reduced temperatures, cryosurgery, hypothermic perfusion and cryopreservation of organs, cryoprotective agents and their pharmacological action, and pertinent methodologies. Operates charitable program and placement service. **Libraries: Type:** reference. **Holdings:** archival material. **Publications:** *Cryobiology: International Journal of Low Temperature Biology and Medicine*, bimonthly. **Price:** included in membership dues ● *Medicine*, bimonthly ● *News Notes*, semiannual. Newsletter. Includes bibliographic citations. ● Membership Directory, semiannual. **Conventions/Meetings:** annual meeting ● symposium ● workshop.

Cryptology

6848 ■ Beale Cipher Association (BCA)
Address Unknown since 2007
Founded: 1978. **Membership Dues:** general, $25 (annual). **Description:** Persons interested in Beale Ciphers. (The Beale Ciphers are three sets of numbers left by Thomas Jefferson Beale in the early 19th century; one has been decoded; two have not. The decoding of the first resulted in the disclosure of a treasure: 2921 pounds of gold, 5100 pounds of silver, and $13,000 worth of jewels. The remaining codes, if broken, promise to reveal the 30 heirs to the treasure named by Beale, and the exact location of the treasure.) studies the ciphers and their cryptographic, historical, and sociological aspects, and multiple substitution ciphers. Supports research. **Libraries: Type:** reference. **Holdings:** 82; books. **Subjects:** ciphers. **Publications:** *BCA Newsletter*, quarterly. **Price:** Contains news on new findings and discoveries. **Circulation:** 2,200. **Advertising:** not accepted ● Handbook ● Monographs ● Also publishes indexes, handbooks and monographs. **Conventions/Meetings:** annual meeting and symposium, with maps, code variation and complex linear diagrams - always September, Washington, DC; **Avg. Attendance:** 300.

6849 ■ International Association for Cryptologic Research (IACR)
c/o IACR General Secretary
Univ. of California
Santa Rosa Administrative Center
Santa Barbara, CA 93106-6120
E-mail: iacrmem@iarc.org
URL: http://www.iacr.org
Contact: Andrew J. Clark, Pres.
Founded: 1983. **Members:** 5,000. **Membership Dues:** regular, $88 (annual) ● student, $44 (annual). **Description:** Represents mathematicians, computer scientists, electronic engineers, manufacturers, government agencies, and university departments. Works to further research in cryptology (the scientific study of codes and ciphers). **Awards:** IACR Distinguished Lectures. **Frequency:** annual. **Type:** recognition. **Recipient:** for contributions to cryptology research ● IACR Fellows. **Frequency:** annual. **Type:** recognition. **Recipient:** to IACR members for technical and professional contributions for the field. **Computer Services:** Mailing lists. **Publications:** *IACR Conference Proceedings*. Contains conference proceedings. Alternate Formats: online; CD-ROM ● *The Journal of Cryptology*, quarterly. ISSN: 0933-2790. **Advertising:** accepted ● Newsletter, 3/year. Alternate Formats: online. **Conventions/Meetings:** semiannual conference ● annual Theory and Application of Cryptology and Information Security - conference - 2008 Dec. 7-11, Melbourne, VI, Australia.

6850 ■ New York Cipher Society (NYCS)
17 Alfred Rd. W
Merrick, NY 11566
Ph: (516)378-0263
Contact: Louis Kruh, Pres.
Founded: 1945. **Members:** 55. **Description:** Cryptologists, historians, mathematicians, writers, and researchers. Fosters interest in cryptology (the scientific study of codes and ciphers). Serves as a research and reference center for cryptologic matters; attempts to decipher historical documents written in cipher. Presents educational programs to members. Maintains speakers' bureau. The society has no centralized library, however, inquiries are referred to individual members with collections on cryptology. **Publications:** none. **Conventions/Meetings:** monthly meeting - except July and August.

Crystallography

6851 ■ American Association for Crystal Growth (AACG)
25 4th St.
Somerville, NJ 08876-3205
Ph: (908)575-0649
Fax: (908)575-0794
E-mail: aacg@att.net
Contact: Laura A. Bonner, Exec. Admin.
Founded: 1969. **Members:** 600. **Membership Dues:** student, $20 (annual) ● individual, $50 (annual) ● corporate affiliate, $500 (annual). **Staff:** 1. **Budget:** $80,000. **Regional Groups:** 2. **Local Groups:** 6. **Multinational. Description:** Physical scientists (chemists, ceramists, physicists), engineers, educators, technologists, marketing representatives, and students. Seeks to coordinate and foster activities concerned with crystal growth theory and practice. Conducts educational programs. Organize annual technical conferences with vendor exhibits. **Libraries: Type:** reference. **Holdings:** archival material, periodicals. **Awards:** Crystal Growth Award. **Frequency:** triennial. **Type:** recognition. **Recipient:** for outstanding contribution (technical) to the field of crystal growth and epitaxy ● Young Author Award. **Frequency:** triennial. **Type:** recognition. **Recipient:** for young person (below 35 years old) who has shown outstanding achievement in the field crystal growth. **Computer Services:** Mailing lists, available to members only except for co-sponsored conferences. **Committees:** Executive. **Formerly:** (1970) American Committee for Crystal Growth. **Publications:** *AACG Newsletter*, 3/year. Furnishes historical information and updates on current research concerned with crystallography, specifically crystal growth. **Price:** included in membership dues. ISSN: 1527-2389. **Circulation:** 600. **Advertising:** accepted ● *Roster: Corporate Affiliates, Members*, annual. Membership Directory. **Conventions/Meetings:** annual conference (exhibits) - usually July or August.

6852 ■ American Crystallographic Association (ACA)
PO Box 96
Buffalo, NY 14207-0090
Ph: (716)898-8690
Fax: (716)898-8695
E-mail: aca@hwi.buffalo.edu
URL: http://aca.hwi.buffalo.edu
Contact: Marcia J. Colquhoun, Dir. of Admin. Services
Founded: 1949. **Members:** 2,300. **Membership Dues:** regular, $100 (annual) ● student, $24 (annual) ● post doc, $39 (annual) ● retired, $39 (annual) ● corporate, $850 (annual). **Staff:** 3. **Budget:** $100,000. **Multinational. Description:** Chemists, biochemists, physicists, mineralogists, and metallurgists interested in crystallography and in the application of X-ray, electron, and neutron diffraction. Promotes the study of the arrangement of atoms in matter, its causes, its nature, and its consequences, and of the tools and methods used in such studies. Maintains employment clearinghouse for members and employers. **Awards:** A.L. Patterson Award. **Frequency:** triennial. **Type:** recognition. **Recipient:** for an outstanding research ● Bertram E. Warren Diffraction Physics Award. **Frequency:** triennial. **Type:** recognition. **Recipient:** for outstanding contributions to physics ● Charles E. Supper Instrumentation Award. **Type:** recognition. **Recipient:** for exceptional scientists ● Fankuchen Memorial Award. **Frequency:** triennial. **Type:** recognition. **Recipient:** for outstanding teacher

of crystallography ● M.J. Buerger Award. **Frequency:** triennial. **Type:** recognition. **Recipient:** for exceptional scientists ● Margaret C. Etter Early Career Award. **Type:** recognition. **Recipient:** for outstanding achievement in crystallographic research ● Pauling Prize. **Frequency:** annual. **Type:** recognition ● Public Service Award. **Type:** recognition. **Recipient:** for an exceptional non-crystallographer. **Computer Services:** Mailing lists, of members. **Telecommunication Services:** electronic mail, marcia@hwi.buffalo.edu. **Committees:** Communications; Continuing Education; Data, Standards and Computing. **Divisions:** Amorphous Materials; Biological Macromolecular; Fiber Diffraction; General Interest; Materials Science; Neutron Diffraction; Powder Diffraction; Service Crystallography; Small Angle Scattering; Small Molecule; Synchrotron Radiation; Young Scientist. **Affiliated With:** American Institute of Physics; International Union of Crystallography. **Formed by Merger of:** American Society for X-Ray and Electron Diffraction; Crystallographic Society of America. **Publications:** *ACA Newsletter*, quarterly. **Price:** included in membership dues. **Advertising:** accepted. Alternate Formats: online ● *Transactions of the ACA*, annual. Journal. Contains compilation of the proceedings from the annual symposium. **Price:** $20.00 for members; $30.00 for nonmembers. ISSN: 0065-8006 ● Monograph, periodic. **Conventions/Meetings:** annual conference (exhibits) ● annual meeting.

6853 ■ International Liquid Crystal Society (ILCS)
c/o Joseph E. Maclennan
Dept. of Physics
Univ. of Colorado
390 UCB
Boulder, CO 80309-0390
Ph: (303)492-7543
Fax: (303)492-2998
E-mail: jem@colorado.edu
URL: http://www.ilcsoc.org
Contact: Satyendra Kumar, Pres.

Founded: 1990. **Members:** 900. **Membership Dues:** full, affiliate, $25 (annual) ● associate, $15 (annual) ● student, $10 (annual) ● sustaining, $100 (annual) ● life, $312 ● developing country, $5 (annual) ● developing country (life), $62. **Multinational. Description:** Encourages the scientific and educational advancement of liquid crystals and associated phenomena. Provides a forum for individuals and organizations to exchange information and ideas relating to liquid crystals. Serves the needs of the liquid crystal community, including both individual scientists and industry. **Awards:** Glenn H. Brown Prize. **Frequency:** biennial. **Type:** recognition. **Recipient:** for outstanding dissertations in the broad area of liquid crystal science ● Multimedia Prize. **Frequency:** biennial. **Type:** recognition. **Recipient:** for contributions toward the electronic dissemination of liquid crystal research or the development of liquid crystal based technologies. **Telecommunication Services:** electronic mail, skumar@kent.edu. **Publications:** *Liquid Crystals Today*, semiannual. Newsletter. Contains news items and conference announcements. Alternate Formats: online.

Cytology

6854 ■ International Cell Death Society (ICDS)
c/o Zahra Zakeri, PhD, Pres.
Queens Coll. of CUNY
65-30 Kissena Blvd.
Flushing, NY 11367
Ph: (718)997-3417
Fax: (718)997-3429
E-mail: zahra_zakeri@qc.edu
URL: http://www.celldeath-apoptosis.org
Contact: Zahra Zakeri PhD, Pres.

Membership Dues: industry, $125 (annual) ● academia, $75 (annual) ● student, postdoctoral, $35 (annual). **Multinational. Description:** Fosters a better understanding of the mechanisms of cell death and apoptosis. Seeks to establish communication among the different branches of research and the application of research findings in biology and medicine. Facilitates exchange of information and ideas concerning the study of cell death and apoptosis and other related disciplines. **Publications:** Newsletter.

Data Processing

6855 ■ Infrared Data Association (IrDA)
PO Box 3883
Walnut Creek, CA 94598
Ph: (925)943-6546 (925)944-2930
Fax: (925)943-5600
E-mail: information@irda.org
URL: http://www.irda.org
Contact: Ronald Brown, Exec. Dir.

Founded: 1993. **Members:** 100. **Membership Dues:** executive, $8,000 (annual) ● corporate (gross annual revenues equal or greater than $250,000), $4,000 (annual) ● corporate (gross annual revenues less than $250,000), $1,500 (annual). **Staff:** 3. **Budget:** $400,000. **Multinational. Description:** Develops, maintains and promotes global industry standards for interoperable and cordless infrared (IR) digital information transmissions. **Telecommunication Services:** electronic mail, ron@irda.org. **Committees:** Technical, Marketing, Test and Interoperability. **Special Interest Groups:** IrBurst: HighSpeed Data Transmission for Multimedia Content; IrFM: Infrared Financial Messaging for Wireless Proximity Payments; Travel Mobility. **Affiliated With:** Association for Retail Technology Standards. **Publications:** *IrDA Frontline* (in English and Japanese), monthly. Newsletter. Provides updates on standards, applications, meetings, and member activities. **Price:** included in membership dues. **Circulation:** 6,000. **Advertising:** accepted. Alternate Formats: online ● *IrDA Global Market Report*. **Price:** $600.00 for nonmembers. Alternate Formats: online ● *Point and Shoot Usage Model and Application Profile*. **Price:** $85.00 ● *Serial Interface for Transceiver Control Specification*. **Conventions/Meetings:** meeting, general - 3/year - spring, fall, winter ● bimonthly meeting, marketing.

Database Management

6856 ■ International DB2 Users Group (IDUG)
401 N Michigan Ave.
Chicago, IL 60611-4267
Ph: (312)321-6881
Fax: (312)673-6688
E-mail: idug@idug.org
URL: http://www.idug.org
Contact: Bret Kelsey, Exec. Dir.

Multinational. Description: Supports and strengthens the information services community. Promotes education and exchange of technical information concerning the DB2 family of products. Establishes channels for the education and communication of information in the field of information processing. **Publications:** *IDUG e-Bulletin*, monthly. Newsletter ● *IDUG Solutions Journal*, quarterly. Features technical information about DB2 product family. **Conventions/Meetings:** annual conference.

6857 ■ Quest International Users Group
2365 Harrodsburg Rd., Ste.A325
Lexington, KY 40504
Ph: (859)226-4307
Free: (800)225-0517
Fax: (859)226-4321
E-mail: questdirect@questdirect.org
URL: http://www.questdirect.org
Contact: Steve McDowell, Pres.

Members: 50,000. **Membership Dues:** individual, $245 (annual) ● corporate, $995 (annual) ● silver vendor, $1,000 (annual) ● gold vendor, $3,000 (annual) ● platinum vendor, $7,500 (annual). **Description:** Providers of relevant, timely and unbiased information. Creates decision-making tools and networking encounters. Facilitates instant access for people to communicate. Facilitates collaboration among the entire user community, including the many geographically, product- and industry-based groups. Focuses on the issues and priorities of Oracle applications users. **Publications:** *Q&A Magazine*. **Conventions/Meetings:** conference, with presentations.

Defense

6858 ■ Directed Energy Professional Society (DEPS)
2600 Yale Blvd. SE, Ste.139
Albuquerque, NM 87106
Ph: (505)998-4910
Fax: (505)998-4917
E-mail: office@deps.org
URL: http://www.deps.org
Contact: Dr. Samuel M. Blankenship, Exec. Dir.

Founded: 1999. **Members:** 1,018. **Membership Dues:** standard, $75 (annual) ● government employee, $50 (annual) ● educator, student, $10 (annual). **Staff:** 3. **Description:** Fosters research and development of directed energy technology for national defense and civil applications through professional communication and education. Publishes job openings. Recognizes contributions to directed energy. **Awards: Type:** scholarship. **Recipient:** for students in DE-related programs. **Publications:** *DE Journal*. Covers lasers, optics, and microwaves. **Price:** $60.00 for members; $100.00 for nonmembers ● *DEPS Newsletter*, semiannual. Alternate Formats: online ● Proceedings. **Conventions/Meetings:** annual conference - always March in Albuquerque, NM ● annual conference - always August in Albuquerque, NM ● annual DC Workshop ● annual DE Symposia - symposium ● annual Education Workshop - workshop and symposium ● annual Solid State & Diode Laser Technology Review Conference - May/June.

Demography

6859 ■ Carrying Capacity Network (CCN)
2000 P St. NW, Ste.310
Washington, DC 20036-5915
Ph: (202)296-4548
Fax: (202)296-4609
E-mail: carryingcapacity@covad.net
URL: http://www.carryingcapacity.org
Contact: Virginia Abernethy, Dir.

Founded: 1989. **Members:** 10,000. **Membership Dues:** regular, $25 (annual) ● senior/student, $20 (annual) ● sustaining, $40 (annual) ● benefactor, $500 (annual) ● sponsor, $250 (annual) ● patron, $1,000 (annual). **Staff:** 6. **Description:** Functions as a catalyst for information exchange and activism among individuals and environmental organizations. Focuses on sustainable development issues including environmental quality, population stabilization, resource conservation and growth control, monitors legislation; disseminates information on conferences and publications in the environmental field. **Libraries: Type:** reference. **Holdings:** archival material, articles. **Supersedes:** Carrying Capacity. **Publications:** *Clearinghouse Bulletin*, bimonthly. Reports on activities of environmental organizations; includes updates on environmental legislation. **Price:** free for members; $35.00 for nonmembers; $50.00 for group ● *Focus*, quarterly. Provides in-depth coverage of current environmental issues. **Price:** $20.00.

6860 ■ Population Association of America (PAA)
8630 Fenton St., Ste.722
Silver Spring, MD 20910-3812
Ph: (301)565-6710
Fax: (301)565-7850
E-mail: info@popassoc.org
URL: http://www.popassoc.org
Contact: Stephanie D. Dudley, Exec. Dir.

Founded: 1931. **Members:** 3,000. **Membership Dues:** regular, $100 (annual) ● corporate, $275 (annual) ● emeritus, $68 (annual) ● joint, $47 (annual) ● student, $42 (annual). **Staff:** 2. **Budget:** $600,000. **Multinational. Description:** Professional society of individuals interested in demography and its scientific aspects. **Awards:** Clifford C. Clogg Award. **Frequency:** biennial. **Type:** recognition. **Recipient:** for early career achievement ● Mindel C. Sheps Award. **Frequency:** biennial. **Type:** recognition. **Recipient:** for outstanding contributions to mathematical demography ● Robert J. Lapham. **Frequency:** biennial. **Type:** recognition. **Recipient:** for an individual, not a PAA member. **Computer Services:** Mailing lists, of members and subscribers. **Telecommunication Services:** electronic mail, stephanie@popassoc.org. **Publications:** *Applied Demography Newsletter*, semiannual. **Price:** $5.00 for members; $10.00 for nonmembers. **Circulation:** 375 ● *Demography*, quarterly. Journal. **Price:** included in membership dues; $100.00 /year for nonmembers. ISSN: 0070-3370. **Circulation:** 4,000. **Advertising:** accepted ● *PAA Affairs*, quarterly. Newsletter. **Price:** included in membership dues; $5.00 /year for nonmembers. **Circulation:** 3,000. **Advertising:** accepted. **Conventions/Meetings:** annual conference and meeting (exhibits) - 2009 Apr. 30-May 2, Detroit, MI; 2010 Apr. 15-17, Dallas, TX.

6861 ■ Population Reference Bureau (PRB)
1875 Connecticut Ave. NW, Ste.520
Washington, DC 20009-5728
Ph: (202)483-1100
Free: (800)877-9881
Fax: (202)328-3937
E-mail: popref@prb.org
URL: http://www.prb.org
Contact: William P. Butz, Pres./CEO

Founded: 1929. **Members:** 3,000. **Membership Dues:** individual, $50 (annual) ● library, $75 (annual) ● corporation, $300 (annual) ● life, $5,000. **Staff:** 40. **Budget:** $6,200,000. **Multinational. Description:** Gathers, interprets, and disseminates information on the facts and implications of national and world population trends. **Libraries: Type:** reference. **Holdings:** 13,000; books, monographs, periodicals. **Subjects:** demography, population issues, environment, family planning, women. **Computer Services:** Mailing lists, of members. **Divisions:** Demographic and Policy Analysis; International Programs; Population Education Program; Public Information Program; Publications Program; Support Services. **Publications:** *Population Bulletin*, quarterly. Journal. Covers population issues, country/regional studies, and health issues. **Price:** included in membership dues; $7.00/copy for nonmembers. ISSN: 0032-468X. **Circulation:** 4,500. Alternate Formats: microform ● *Population Handbook: A Quick Guide to Population Dynamics for Journalists, Policymakers, Teachers, Students, and Other People Interested in People*, periodic. Contains glossary. **Price:** $10.00/copy ● *World Population Data Sheet: Demographic Data and Estimates for the Countries and Regions of the World*, annual. Wall chart containing data for 200 countries, includes current population estimates and projections, and other demographic information. **Price:** included in membership dues; $4.50/copy for nonmembers. **Circulation:** 4,500 ● Annual Report, annual. Alternate Formats: online.

6862 ■ Society for the Study of Social Biology (SSSB)
c/o Eileen M. Crimmins, Sec.-Treas.
Univ. of Southern California
Andrus Gerontology Ctr.
Los Angeles, CA 90089-0191
E-mail: crimmin@usc.edu
Contact: Eileen M. Crimmins, Sec.-Treas.

Founded: 1926. **Members:** 300. **Membership Dues:** individual, $30 (annual) ● student, emeritus, $20 (annual). **Description:** Geneticists, demographers, psychologists, physicians, psychiatrists, public health workers, educators, and sociologists interested in the study of heredity and population. Seeks to further the discussion, advancement, and sharing of knowledge concerning the biological and socio-cultural forces affecting human populations and their evolution. **Affiliated With:** American Association for the Advancement of Science. **Formerly:** American Eugenics Society. **Publications:** *Social Biology*, semiannual. Journal. **Price:** free for members; $65.00 for nonmembers and institutions. ISSN: 0037-766X. **Circulation:** 1,000. **Conventions/Meetings:** annual meeting.

Design

6863 ■ Interaction Design Association (IxDA)
PO Box 2833
Westport, CT 06880
E-mail: volunteers@ixdg.org
URL: http://www.ixda.org
Contact: Robert Reimann, Pres./Dir.

Founded: 2003. **Members:** 800. **Languages:** Dutch, English. **Multinational. Description:** Serves the needs of the international interaction design community. Promotes awareness of the discipline, craft and value of interaction design among businesses, academia, consumers and colleagues. Advances the discipline of interaction design. Encourages high standards of practice among interaction designers. Establishes standards for academic programs in interaction design.

Ecology

6864 ■ American Ecological Engineering Society (AEES)
PO Box 116350
Gainesville, FL 32611-6350
E-mail: pkangas@umd.edu
URL: http://aeesociety.org
Contact: Pat Kangas, Pres.

Founded: 1999. **Membership Dues:** regular (with journal), $75 (annual) ● regular (without journal), $45 (annual) ● student (with journal), $35 (annual) ● corporate, institution, $300 (annual) ● emeritus (65 years or older and continuous membership since 2002), $50 (annual) ● life, $700. **Description:** Promotes the development of sustainable ecosystems that integrate human society with its natural environment for the benefit of both. Fosters education and outreach to raise the standards of professional development of its members. Encourages original research on ecological engineering. **Publications:** *AEES Technical Notes*, semiannual. Newsletter. ISSN: 1553-684X. Alternate Formats: online ● *Ecological Engineering*, semiannual. Journal. **Price:** $650.00 2 volumes per year.

6865 ■ United States Society for Ecological Economics (USSEE)
PO Box 44326
West Allis, WI 53214
Ph: (414)453-0030
E-mail: president@ussee.org
URL: http://www.ussee.org
Contact: Karin Limburg, Pres.

Founded: 2000. **Members:** 300. **Multinational. Description:** Advances the understanding of the relationship between ecological and economic systems. Promotes the application of ecological economics to the mutual well-being of nature and people. Facilitates a voice for ecological economists in both public policy and academic forums. **Computer Services:** Information services, ecological economics resources. **Committees:** Conference; Policy. **Affiliated With:** International Society for Ecological Economics. **Publications:** Newsletter, quarterly. Alternate Formats: online.

Economic Development

6866 ■ Organization for Economic Cooperation and Development (OECD)
2001 L St. NW, Ste.650
Washington, DC 20036-4922
Ph: (202)785-6323
Free: (800)456-6323
Fax: (202)785-0350
E-mail: washington.contact@oecd.org
URL: http://www.oecdwash.org
Contact: Ms. Sandra Wilson, Hd. of the Washington Center

Founded: 1948. **Multinational. Description:** Committed to building strong economies in its 30 member countries, improve efficiency, improve market systems, expand free trade and to promote development in industrialized and developing countries. **Libraries: Type:** open to the public. **Holdings:** books, monographs, periodicals. **Subgroups:** European Council of Ministers of Transport; International Energy Agency; Nuclear Energy Agency. **Formerly:** Organisation for European Economic Co-operation. **Publications:** *OECD Factbook*, annual. Annual Report. Provides a global overview and 100 indicators. **Price:** $63.00. Alternate Formats: online.

Economics

6867 ■ American Agricultural Economics Association (AAEA)
555 E Wells, Ste.1100
Milwaukee, WI 53202
Ph: (414)918-3190
Fax: (414)276-3349
E-mail: info@aaea.org
URL: http://www.aaea.org
Contact: Ms. Terri Haffner, Interim Exec. Dir.

Founded: 1910. **Members:** 2,800. **Membership Dues:** senior in U.S., $95 (annual) ● senior outside U.S., $110 (annual) ● regular in U.S., $150 (annual) ● regular outside U.S., $165 (annual) ● student in U.S., $75 (annual) ● student outside U.S., $90 (annual) ● family in U.S., $275 (annual) ● family outside U.S., $290 (annual) ● industry in U.S., $400 (annual). **Staff:** 8. **Budget:** $1,200,000. **Multinational. Description:** Professional society of agricultural economists. Serves to enhance the skills, knowledge and professional contribution of those economists who serve society by solving problems related to agriculture, food, resources and economic development. Offers placement service. **Awards:** Distinguished Policy Contribution Award. **Frequency:** annual. **Type:** recognition. **Recipient:** for outstanding contribution to policy decisions or to the advancement of public and human welfare ● Distinguished Teaching Awards. **Frequency:** annual. **Type:** recognition. **Recipient:** for outstanding ability and performance as a teacher of agricultural economics ● Outstanding Doctoral Dissertation Awards. **Frequency:** annual. **Type:** recognition. **Recipient:** for individuals writing doctoral theses in agricultural, natural resource or rural economics ● Outstanding Master's Thesis Awards. **Frequency:** annual. **Type:** recognition. **Recipient:** for individuals writing master's theses in agricultural, natural resource or rural economics. **Computer Services:** Mailing lists, in label format only for one-time user. **Telecommunication Services:** electronic mail, exec@aaea.org. **Committees:** Agribusiness Economics and Management; Awards; Finance; Institutional and Behavioral Economics; Professional Activities; Senior; Teaching, Learning and Communications. **Sections:** Community Economics; Extension; Food and Agricultural Marketing Policy; Food Safety Nutrition; Graduate Students; International; National Association of Agricultural Economics Administrators; Opportunities and Status of Blacks in Agricultural Economics; Student; Women in Agricultural Economics. **Formerly:** (1918) American Farm Management Association; (1968) American Farm Economic Association. **Publications:** *American Journal of Agricultural Economics*, 5/year, February, May, August, November, and December ● *Choices*. Magazine. Covers agricultural and economic policies in the United States and abroad. Alternate Formats: online ● *The Exchange*, bimonthly. Newsletter. **Price:** $12.00 ● *Review of Agricultural Economies*, semiannual. Journal. **Price:** $20.00/individual copy ● Directory, annual. **Conventions/Meetings:** annual conference and meeting (exhibits) - 2008 July 27-30, Orlando, FL - **Avg. Attendance:** 1600.

6868 ■ American Economic Association (AEA)
2014 Broadway, Ste.305
Nashville, TN 37203
Ph: (615)322-2595
Fax: (615)343-7590
E-mail: aeainfo@vanderbilt.edu
URL: http://www.vanderbilt.edu/AEA
Contact: John J. Siegfried, Sec.-Treas.

Founded: 1885. **Members:** 18,000. **Membership Dues:** regular (based on annual income), $64-$90 (annual) ● student, $32 (annual) ● family, $13 (annual). **Staff:** 20. **Description:** Educators, business executives, government administrators, journalists, lawyers, and others interested in economics and its application to present-day problems. Encourages historical and statistical research into actual conditions of industrial life and provides a nonpartisan forum for economic discussion. **Computer Services:** Information services, DIALOG. **Committees:** Audit; Census Advisory; Economic Education; Economic Statistic; Electronic Publishing; Honors and Awards; Nominating; Status Minority. **Publications:** *American Economic Review*, quarterly. Journal. **Price:** $315.00 /year for institutions in U.S.; $345.00 /year for institutions outside U.S. **Circulation:** 27,000. **Advertising:** accepted ● *Index of Economic Articles* ● *Job Openings for Economists*, 10/year. **Price:** $25.00/year ● *Journal of Economic Literature*, quarterly. Includes reviews of current economic literature. **Price:** included with *American Economic Review*. **Circulation:** 27,000 ● *Journal of Economic Perspectives*, quarterly. **Price:** included with *American Economic Review*. **Circulation:** 27,000 ● *Survey of Members*, quadrennial. **Conventions/Meetings:** annual meeting (exhibits).

6869 ■ American Institute for Economic Research (AIER)
PO Box 1000
Great Barrington, MA 01230
Ph: (413)528-1216
Fax: (413)528-0103
E-mail: info@aier.org
URL: http://www.aier.org
Contact: Charles Murray, Pres./CEO

Founded: 1933. **Members:** 8,000. **Membership Dues:** sustaining, $59 (annual). **Staff:** 33. **Description:** Through research and publications, provides "information on economic and financial subjects that is useful and completely independent of special interests". Sponsors a fellowship program for graduate study of economics at the institute and in absentia. **Libraries: Type:** open to the public. **Holdings:** 10,000. **Subjects:** economics, finance, banking. **Publications:** *Economic Education Bulletin*, monthly. Contains academic reports; includes statistics and personal economics. **Price:** included in membership dues; $25.00 /year for nonmembers. ISSN: 0424-2769 ● *Research Reports*, semimonthly. Newsletter. Includes statistics. **Price:** included in membership dues; $2.00/copy for nonmembers. ISSN: 0034-5407. **Circulation:** 8,000. Alternate Formats: online.

6870 ■ Association for Comparative Economic Studies (ACES)
c/o Prof. Josef Brada, Exec. Sec.
Arizona State Univ.
Dept. of Economics
PO Box 873806
Tempe, AZ 85287-3806
Ph: (480)965-6524
Fax: (480)965-0748
E-mail: josef.brada@asu.edu
Contact: Prof. Josef Brada, Exec. Sec.

Founded: 1972. **Members:** 600. **Membership Dues:** regular, $40 (annual). **Staff:** 1. **Budget:** $25,000. **Description:** Economists and other social scientists from universities, government, and business. Studies comparative economic systems and economic planning and examines the impact of political and social actions as they impinge upon economic systems. Cooperates with other professional societies in arranging meetings for presentation of papers within the scope of comparative economics and economic planning. Sponsors panels jointly with American Economic Association and Allied Social Science Associations meetings. **Libraries: Type:** open to the public. **Holdings:** 44. **Subjects:** comparative economic studies. **Computer Services:** Mailing lists, on diskette, $150-$200 depending on size of requested item(s). **Formed by Merger of:** Association for the Study of Soviet-Type Economies; Association for Comparative Economics. **Publications:** *Comparative Economic Studies*, quarterly. Journal. **Price:** $60.00 domestic; $65.00 foreign. ISSN: 0888-7233. **Circulation:** 1,000. **Advertising:** accepted ● *Journal of Comparative Economics*, quarterly ● Membership Directory, periodic ● Newsletter. Alternate Formats: online. **Conventions/Meetings:** annual meeting, held in conjunction with ASSA/AEA (exhibits) - always first weekend in January.

6871 ■ Association for Cultural Economics International (ACEI)
c/o Prof. Neil O. Alper, Exec. Sec.-Treas.
Dept. of Economics
Northeastern Univ.
301 Lake Hall
Boston, MA 02115
Ph: (617)373-2839
Fax: (617)373-3640
E-mail: acei@neu.edu
URL: http://www.acei.neu.edu
Contact: Prof. Neil O. Alper, Exec. Sec.-Treas.

Membership Dues: individual, $90 (annual) ● student, $65 (annual). **Description:** Economists and economics educators and students. Seeks to advance cultural economics scholarship and practice. Serves as a clearinghouse on cultural economics; sponsors research and educational programs. **Publications:** *ACEI Newsletter*, semiannual. **Price:** included in membership dues. Alternate Formats: online ● *Journal of Cultural Economics*, quarterly. **Price:** included in membership dues. ISSN: 0885-2545. **Conventions/Meetings:** semiannual conference.

6872 ■ Association for Evolutionary Economics (AFEE)
c/o Office of Sec.-Treas.
Bucknell Univ.
Dept. of Economics
Coleman Hall 154
Lewisburg, PA 17837
Ph: (570)577-3648
Fax: (570)577-2372
E-mail: afee@bucknell.edu
URL: http://www.orgs.bucknell.edu/afee
Contact: Helen M. Sauer, Coor.

Founded: 1963. **Members:** 550. **Membership Dues:** in U.S. (with income below $40,000), $45 (annual) ● outside U.S. (with income below $40,000), $50 (annual) ● in U.S. (with income above $40,000), $55 (annual) ● outside U.S. (with income above $40,000), $60 (annual) ● student, $15 (annual). **Budget:** $75,000. **Description:** Economists, including social scientists, who are involved in sociology, economic history, and anthropology. Fosters the development of economics as an evolutionary and holistic rather than static and atomistic science; engages in economic research and the diffusion of economic information; promotes the development of economic study and of economics as a social science based on the complex interrelationships of man and society; encourages economic study that illustrates the need to join questions of economic theory to questions of economic policy. **Awards:** Essay Prize Award. **Frequency:** annual. **Type:** recognition ● Veblen-Commons Award. **Frequency:** annual. **Type:** recognition. **Publications:** *Journal of Economic Issues*, quarterly. Includes articles on methodology, economic control, and policy problems; contains book reviews and proceedings of annual meetings. **Price:** included in membership dues; $65.00 /year for libraries. ISSN: 0021-3624. **Circulation:** 2,000. **Advertising:** accepted. Alternate Formats: microform; online. **Conventions/Meetings:** annual conference, held in conjunction with Allied Social Science Associations and American Economic Association - always January.

6873 ■ Association for Social Economics (ASE)
c/o Elba K. Brown-Collier, Sec.
Educ. Mgt. Info. Systems
7116 Wandering Oak Rd.
Austin, TX 78749
Ph: (512)288-5988
E-mail: email@edmis.com
URL: http://www.socialeconomics.org
Contact: John Tiemstra, Pres.

Founded: 1941. **Members:** 500. **Membership Dues:** individual, $45 (annual). **Budget:** $40,000. **Regional Groups:** 4. **Description:** Professional society of government, business, and academic economists. Promotes scientific discussion of economic problems requiring a knowledge of both economic science and social philosophy. Normative economics and social policy are the prime orientation of the organization. Maintains bibliographical archives at Marquette University Library. **Awards:** Father Divine Award. **Frequency:** annual. **Type:** recognition. **Recipient:** for outstanding social economist ● Helen Potter Award. **Frequency:** annual. **Type:** recognition. **Recipient:** for best article by a junior faculty to appear in *Review of Social Economy* ● Ludwig Mai Service Award. **Frequency:** annual. **Type:** recognition. **Recipient:** for service to the association ● Thomas F. Divine Award. **Frequency:** annual. **Type:** recognition. **Recipient:** for outstanding contributions to social economics and the social economy. **Telecommunication Services:** electronic mail, tmst@calvin.edu. **Formerly:** Catholic Economic Association. **Publications:** *Forum For Social Economics*, semiannual. Journal. Contains original articles and book reviews. **Price:** included in membership dues; $5.00 /year for individuals; $7.00 /year for institutions. **Circulation:** 600 ● *Review of Social Economy*, quarterly. Journal. Contains articles on issues such as justice, human dignity, social responsibilities, liberty, order, freedom, security, power, and values. **Price:** included in membership dues; $230.00 institutions. ISSN: 0034-6764. **Circulation:** 1,300. **Advertising:** accepted. Alternate Formats: microform ● Directory, periodic. **Conventions/Meetings:** periodic conference ● annual meeting (exhibits) - January ● regional meeting - 5/year.

6874 ■ Atlas Economic Research Foundation (AERF)
2000 N 14th St., Ste.550
Arlington, VA 22201
Ph: (703)934-6969
E-mail: atlas@atlasusa.org
URL: http://www.atlasusa.org
Contact: Alejandro A. Chafuen, Pres./CEO

Founded: 1981. **Membership Dues:** sponsor, $1,000-$4,000 (annual) ● benefactor, $5,000-$10,000 (annual). **Staff:** 6. **Description:** Seeks to improve public understanding of economic issues and their wider social ramifications. Sponsors international workshops for public policy professionals. **Awards:** Freda Utley Prize for Advancing Liberty. **Frequency:** annual. **Type:** recognition. **Recipient:** for efforts of think tanks that are most effective in spreading ideas of freedom ● Sir Anthony Fisher International Memorial Awards. **Frequency:** annual. **Type:** recognition. **Recipient:** for publications by independent participating research institutes ● Templeton Freedom Awards. **Frequency:** annual. **Type:** recognition. **Recipient:** for institutes with exceptional promise. **Publications:** *Atlas Year-In-Review*, annual. Annual Report. Alternate Formats: online ● *Highlights*, quarterly. Newsletter. Covers developments among international network of market-oriented think tanks. Alternate Formats: online. **Conventions/Meetings:** semiannual conference ● periodic International Workshop.

6875 ■ Center for Popular Economics (CPE)
Box 785
Amherst, MA 01004
Ph: (413)545-0743
E-mail: programs@populareconomics.org
URL: http://www.populareconomics.org
Contact: Emily Kawano, Exec. Dir.

Founded: 1979. **Staff:** 3. **Budget:** $200,000. **Languages:** English, French, Spanish. **Description:** Provides popular economics education for activists and educators in community groups, labor unions, and other nonprofit organizations; goals include "combating the corporate onslaught" and furthering development of an alternative approach to economics. Conducts Summer Institute in Popular Economics and leads workshops on a contract basis. Maintains speakers' bureau and develops economic literacy resources. **Publications:** *Building Natural Assets: New Strategies for Poverty Reduction and Environmental Protection.* Booklet ● *The Popular Economist.* Newsletter ● *The Ultimate Field Guide to the U.S. Economy*. Book. **Price:** $16.95 ● *War on the Poor: A Defense Manual.* Book. **Price:** $11.95. **Conventions/Meetings:** annual Summer Institute in Popular Economics - workshop, a weeklong intensive training in economics for activists for economic, social, and environmental justice.

6876 ■ Chinese Economists Society (CES)
733 15th St. NW, Ste.910
Washington, DC 20005
Ph: (202)347-8588
Fax: (202)347-8510
E-mail: ces@vmintl.net
URL: http://www.china-ces.org
Contact: Prof. Jack Lou, Pres.
Founded: 1985. **Members:** 700. **Membership Dues:** individual (with lower than $10000 annual income), $10 (annual) ● individual (with annual income between $10000 to $50000), $30 (annual) ● individual (with annual income higher than $50000), $40 (annual) ● life, $1,000. **Multinational. Description:** Professors, graduate students, and Chinese and American economists. Aims to promote scholarly exchange among its members and contribute to the advancement and dissemination of economics and management sciences in China. Bridges academic exchanges in economics and related areas between the U.S. and China. Promotes economic reforms and open-door policy. Develops modern economic education in China. Welcomes economists from various backgrounds and economic research reflecting different views. **Awards:** Fellow Membership. **Type:** recognition. **Recipient:** for members who have made original contributions to economics, management sciences, Chinese economic studies, and have a good publication record in academic journals ● Gregory Chow Best Paper Award. **Type:** recognition. **Recipient:** for active members and author of an outstanding paper submitted to the CES Chongqing Conference. **Telecommunication Services:** electronic mail, office@china-ces.org. **Affiliated With:** Allied Social Science Associations. **Formerly:** (1991) Chinese Young Economists Society. **Publications:** *China Economic Review*, semiannual. Journal. Contains original work on the economy of China and the contiguous region. **Price:** $5.00 for members; $99.00 /year for individuals in U.S.; $418.00 /year for institutions in U.S. ISSN: 1043-951X ● Membership Directory. **Price:** included in membership dues. **Conventions/Meetings:** annual conference.

6877 ■ The Conference Board (TCB)
845 3rd Ave.
New York, NY 10022
Ph: (212)759-0900
Fax: (212)980-7014
E-mail: nick.sutcliffe@conference-board.org
URL: http://www.conference-board.org
Contact: Samuel A. DiPiazza Jr., Chm.
Founded: 1916. **Members:** 3,000. **Staff:** 200. **Multinational. Description:** Corporations, government agencies, libraries, colleges, and universities. Fact-finding institution that conducts research and publishes studies on business economics and management experience. Holds more than 100 conferences, council meetings, and seminars per year in the U.S., Asia, and Europe where members exchange ideas and keep abreast of business trends and developments. Makes research available to secondary schools, colleges, and universities at minimum cost. Disseminates research data to the public. **Libraries: Type:** reference. **Holdings:** 6,000; books, periodicals. **Subjects:** business operations, economics. **Formerly:** (1970) National Industrial Conference Board. **Publications:** *Across the Board*, 10/year. Magazine. **Advertising:** accepted. Alternate Formats: online ● *Business Cycle Indicators*, monthly ● *Consumer Confidence Survey*, monthly. **Price:** $200.00/year; $165.00/year for associates ● *StraightTalk*, monthly. **Price:** $395.00/year; $195.00/year for associates ● Newsletters. Alternate Formats: online. **Conventions/Meetings:** conference.

6878 ■ Conference of Business Economists (CBE)
28790 Chagrin Blvd., Ste.350
Cleveland, OH 44122
Ph: (216)464-2137
Fax: (216)464-0397
E-mail: dwilliams@admgt.com
Contact: David L. Williams Sr., Exec. Dir.
Founded: 1944. **Members:** 50. **Staff:** 2. **Description:** Economists of business and financial organizations united to: bring together economists from the business sector to discuss the economics of their own industries; contribute to mutual understanding of the broader problems concerning business, monetary, and national conditions and policies in which they have a common interest; contribute toward the preservation of the free enterprise system. Membership is by invitation only and meetings are closed.

6879 ■ Economic Affairs Bureau/Dollars and Sense (EAB)
29 Winter St.
Boston, MA 02108
Ph: (617)447-2177
Fax: (617)447-2179
E-mail: dollars@dollarsandsense.org
URL: http://www.dollarsandsense.org
Contact: Amy Gluckman, Co-Ed.
Founded: 1974. **Staff:** 4. **Budget:** $250,000. **Description:** Explains the workings of the U.S. and international economics and provide left perspectives on current economic affairs. Represents economists, journalists, and activists who edited and produced the magazine and are committed to social justice and economic democracy. **Doing business as:** Dollars & Sense Magazine. **Publications:** *Current Economics Issues: Progressive Perspectives from Dollars and Sense.* Book. **Price:** $28.95 ● *Dollars & Sense*, bimonthly. Magazine. **Price:** $18.95 /year for individuals; $42.00 /year for institutions. ISSN: 0012-5245. **Circulation:** 8,000. **Advertising:** accepted. Alternate Formats: microform; CD-ROM ● *Environment in Crisis.* Book ● *Introduction to Political Economy.* Book ● *Real World Banking.* Book ● *Real World Globalization.* Book ● *Real World Macro.* Book ● *Real World Micro.* Book ● *Unlevel Playing Fields: Understanding Wage Inequality and Discrimination.* Book.

6880 ■ Institute for Economic Analysis (IEA)
262 Harvard St., No. 12
Cambridge, MA 02139
Ph: (617)864-9933
Fax: (617)864-9944
E-mail: info@iea-macro-economics.org
URL: http://iea-macro-economics.org
Contact: John S. Atlee PhD, Pres.
Founded: 1974. **Staff:** 2. **Nonmembership. Description:** Seeks to develop tools for macroeconomic analysis and policy that can maintain stable full employment growth, low inflation, low interest rates and equitable distribution of income and wealth. Integrates GDP and financial accounts for more systematic coordination of monetary and fiscal policy. Focuses on federal monetary policy, federal budget deficit/surplus, social security, consumer credit, and world economic recovery. **Libraries: Type:** reference. **Holdings:** 200. **Subjects:** economics. **Publications:** *IEA Pocket Charts.* Includes historical supplement. ● Occasional research and policy reports and analytical charts.

6881 ■ International Association of Agricultural Economists (IAAE)
c/o Dr. Walter J. Armbruster, Sec.-Treas.
1301 W 22nd St., Ste.615
Oak Brook, IL 60523-2197
Ph: (630)571-9393
Fax: (630)571-9580
E-mail: iaae@farmfoundation.org
URL: http://www.iaae-agecon.org
Contact: Dr. Walter J. Armbruster, Sec.-Treas.
Founded: 1929. **Members:** 1,600. **Membership Dues:** income greater than 50,000, $160 ● income in between 20,000 and 50,000, $130 ● income less than 20,000, $75. **Description:** Agricultural economists in 97 countries engaged in research, teaching or administrative work. Fosters development of the science of agricultural economics and furthers the application of the results of economic investigation into agricultural processes to improve economic and social conditions. **Formerly:** (1961) International Conference of Agricultural Economists. **Publications:** *Agricultural Economics.* Journal. **Price:** $105.00 for members ● *International Association of Agriculture Economists—Proceedings of Conferences*, triennial. **Conventions/Meetings:** triennial conference.

6882 ■ International Association for Feminist Economics - USA (IAFFE)
4800 McCullough
Middlebury Coll.
Middlebury, VT 05753
E-mail: iaffe@iaffe.org
URL: http://www.iaffe.org
Contact: Ms. Anne Herman, Coor.
Founded: 1992. **Members:** 650. **Membership Dues:** individual (based upon income level), $25-$135 (annual) ● student, $20 (annual). **Staff:** 1. **Description:** Economists with a feminist point of view. Seeks to advance feminist inquiry into economic issues. Promotes expanded economic opportunities for women. Facilitates communication among members. Works to educate policy makers and the public about feminist views of economics. Encourages inclusion of feminist perspectives in economics curricula. Formulates feminist evaluations for the underlying constructs of economics. **Publications:** *Feminist Economics*, 3/year. Journal. **Price:** included in membership dues. **Advertising:** accepted ● *IAFFE Newsletter*, 3/year. **Conventions/Meetings:** annual conference, presents papers and recent work - 2008 June 19-21, Turin, Italy - **Avg. Attendance:** 200.

6883 ■ International Atlantic Economic Society (IAES)
4949 W Pine Blvd., 2nd Fl.
St. Louis, MO 63108-1431
Ph: (314)454-0100
Fax: (314)454-9109
E-mail: iaes@iaes.org
URL: http://www.iaes.org
Contact: Burton G. Malkiel, Pres.
Founded: 1973. **Members:** 1,500. **Membership Dues:** regular, $67-$100 (annual). **Staff:** 6. **Budget:** $400,000. **Description:** Economists and business specialists from academic, government, and private organizations. Furthers economics and related subjects on both the theoretical and applied levels and increases the exchange of new ideas and research worldwide. **Awards:** AEJ Best Article Award. **Frequency:** annual. **Type:** recognition. **Boards:** Book Review; Editors. **Formerly:** (1998) Atlantic Economic Society. **Publications:** *Atlantic Economic Journal*, quarterly. Features theoretical research articles covering all areas of economics and finance; includes book reviews and shorter research notes. **Price:** free for members; $177.00 /year for institutions. ISSN: 0197-4254. **Circulation:** 1,500. **Advertising:** accepted. Alternate Formats: microform; online ● *International Advances in Economic Research*, quarterly. Journal. Contains economic and political policy-oriented research papers with emphasis on international issues. **Price:** $38.00 for individuals; $138.00 for institutions. ISSN: 1083-0898. **Circulation:** 500. **Advertising:** accepted. Alternate Formats: CD-ROM; online. **Conventions/Meetings:** semiannual International Atlantic Economic Conference, attracts economists from forty-five countries (exhibits) - usually March and October.

6884 ■ International Economics and Finance Society (IEFS)
c/o Prof. Eric W. Bond, Pres.
Vanderbilt Univ.
Dept. of Economics
VU Sta. B, No. 351819
2301 Vanderbilt Pl.
Nashville, TN 37235-1819

Ph: (615)322-3237
Fax: (615)343-8495
E-mail: ksaggi@smu.edu
URL: http://faculty.smu.edu/ksaggi/IEFS
Contact: Prof. Eric W. Bond, Pres.
Membership Dues: life - in U.S., $150 ● life - outside U.S., $165. **Multinational. Description:** Represents academic and professional economists with general interest in international economics, particularly international trade and international finance. Encourages research in international and financial economics. Sponsors research sessions. Promotes professional communication among researchers in these fields. Facilitates cooperation and participation in research efforts among international economists and financial economists in the academic, private and government sectors. **Publications:** Newsletter, monthly. Alternate Formats: online.

6885 ■ International Society for New Institutional Economics (ISNIE)
Washington Univ.
Dept. of Economics, Campus Box 1208
One Brookings Dr.
St. Louis, MO 63130-4899
Fax: (314)935-4156
E-mail: isnie@artsci.wustl.edu
URL: http://www.isnie.org
Contact: Thrainn Eggertsson, Pres.-Elect
Founded: 1997. **Membership Dues:** individual (with a pre-tax income of $35,000 US or less), $40 (annual) ● individual (with a pre-tax income greater than $35,000 US), $60 (annual). **Multinational. Description:** Promotes New Institutional Economics (NIE). Fosters theoretical and empirical investigation of NIE. Encourages participation of scholars and researchers around the world from developing and transitional economies. **Publications:** *ISNIE Newsletter*. **Price:** included in membership dues. Alternate Formats: online ● Proceedings. Alternate Formats: online.

6886 ■ National Association for Business Economics (NABE)
1233 20th St. NW, Ste.505
Washington, DC 20036
Ph: (202)463-6223
Fax: (202)463-6239
E-mail: nabe@nabe.com
URL: http://www.nabe.com
Contact: Susan Doolittle, Exec. Dir.
Founded: 1959. **Members:** 3,500. **Membership Dues:** student, $40 (annual) ● retiree, $100 (annual) ● individual, $140 (annual) ● institution, $600-$2,400 (annual). **Staff:** 4. **Budget:** $500,000. **Regional Groups:** 50. **Description:** Professional society of institutions, businesses, and students with an active interest in business economics and individuals who are employed by academic, private, or governmental concerns in the area of business-related economic issues. Maintains placement service for members; conducts several seminars per year. Maintains speakers' bureau. **Awards:** Abramson Award. **Frequency:** annual. **Type:** recognition. **Recipient:** for an author of article appearing in Business Economics ● **Type:** recognition. **Computer Services:** Mailing lists, of members. **Telecommunication Services:** electronic mail, doolittle@nabe.com. **Committees:** Academic Affairs; Chapter; Education and Training; International and IFABE Liaison; Job Services; Policy Seminar and Statistics; Public Affairs; Publicity; Roundtable. **Divisions:** Corporate Planning; Financial; Health Economics and Manufacturing; International; Manufacturing; Regional/Utility Roundtables. **Affiliated With:** Council of Professional Associations on Federal Statistics; National Bureau of Economic Research. **Formerly:** (1999) National Association of Business Economists. **Publications:** *Business Economics*, quarterly. Journal. Includes articles on applied economics, monetary and fiscal policy, business forecasting, interest rates, and international economics. **Price:** included in membership dues; $60.00 /year for nonmembers in U.S.; $75.00 /year for nonmembers outside U.S.; $20.00/copy. ISSN: 0007-666X. **Circulation:** 4,600. **Advertising:** accepted. Alternate Formats: microform ● *Careers in Business Economics*. Booklet ● *Employment Opportunities for Business Economists*, quarterly. **Price:** free for 1st copy; $1.00 per additional copy ● *NABE News*, bimonthly. Newsletter. Provides information on current economic trends. Contains employment listings, member notes and comments, and chapter news. **Price:** included in membership dues; available to members only. **Circulation:** 3,300. **Advertising:** accepted. Alternate Formats: online ● *NABE Outlook*, quarterly. Survey. Reports on business conditions within the industry and opinions on current economic issues. **Price:** available to members only. Alternate Formats: online ● *NABE Policy Survey*, semiannual. Alternate Formats: online ● *NABE Salary Survey*, biennial. **Price:** free for members; $250.00 /year for nonmembers. **Circulation:** 3,300. Alternate Formats: online. **Conventions/Meetings:** annual meeting (exhibits) - always winter, Washington, DC.

6887 ■ National Bureau of Economic Research (NBER)
1050 Massachusetts Ave.
Cambridge, MA 02138
Ph: (617)868-3900
Fax: (617)868-2742
E-mail: info@nber.org
URL: http://www.nber.org
Contact: Martin Feldstein, Pres./CEO
Founded: 1920. **Staff:** 45. **Budget:** $10,000,000. **Description:** Conducts analyses of economic issues, including economic growth and fluctuations, productivity, financial institutions, money, international economic problems, taxation, government spending, labor studies, health, and American economic history. **Telecommunication Services:** electronic mail, msfeldst@nber.org. **Publications:** *The NBER Digest*, monthly. Newsletter. **Price:** free. **Circulation:** 13,000. Alternate Formats: online ● *NBER Reporter*, quarterly. Reviews broad areas of NBER research and activity. Includes reviews of recent conferences. **Price:** free to academics, journalist, government staff; $20.00/year for other subscribers. Alternate Formats: online ● *NBER Working Papers*, periodic. **Price:** $5.00 each, plus shipping and handling. **Circulation:** 300 ● Books ● Proceedings ● Bulletins. Alternate Formats: online. **Conventions/Meetings:** semiannual board meeting.

6888 ■ National Economic Association (NEA)
c/o Kwabena Gyimah-Brempong, Pres.
Univ. of South Florida
Coll. of Bus. Admin.
4202 E Fowler Ave., BSN 3403
Tampa, FL 33620
E-mail: kgyimah@coba.usf.edu
URL: http://www.neaecon.org/index.htm
Contact: Kwabena Gyimah-Brempong, Pres.
Founded: 1969. **Members:** 200. **Membership Dues:** student, $15 (annual) ● voting, $40 (annual) ● student, $45 (triennial) ● voting, $120 (triennial). **Description:** Purposes are to: promote the professional life of blacks within the economics profession; advance the study and understanding of the economic problems confronting the black community; increase the number of black economists. **Awards:** Samuel Z. Westerfield Award. **Type:** recognition. **Recipient:** for distinguished black economists. **Computer Services:** Online services, listserver. **Formerly:** (1975) Caucus of Black Economists. **Publications:** *Directory of Black Economists*, biennial ● *Job Placement Bulletin*, quarterly ● *National Economic Association Newsletter*. Alternate Formats: online ● *NEA Reports* ● *Review of Black Political Economy*, quarterly. Includes book reviews, annual indexes, manuscripts, and editorial correspondence. **Price:** included in membership dues; $42.00 /year for nonmembers; $45.00/year for Canadian and foreign nonmembers; $76.00 /year for institutions. ISSN: 0034-6446. **Conventions/Meetings:** annual meeting, always held in conjunction with American Economic Association.

6889 ■ National Economists Club (NEC)
PO Box 19281
Washington, DC 20036
Ph: (703)493-8824
E-mail: info@national-economists.org
URL: http://www.national-economists.org
Contact: Anne Vorce, Pres.
Founded: 1968. **Members:** 600. **Membership Dues:** resident, $55 (annual) ● non-resident, $45 (annual) ● under age 30, $35 (annual). **Staff:** 1. **Description:** Professional economists and individuals interested in economic subjects and related fields. Seeks to advance economic science and practice. Organizes lectures, debates, seminars, and meetings. Maintains National Economists Club Education Foundation. **Affiliated With:** National Association for Business Economics. **Publications:** *Calendar of Events*, bimonthly. Newsletter ● *Membership Roster*, annual. Membership Directory. **Advertising:** accepted ● *Summaries*. **Conventions/Meetings:** weekly Educational Economics Forum - luncheon and meeting, features speakers on economic topics of the day.

6890 ■ North American Economics and Finance Association (NAEFA)
c/o Harvey Rosenblum, Exec. Dir.
Fed. Reserve Bank of Dallas
Dallas, TX 75201
Ph: (214)922-5055
Fax: (214)922-5039
E-mail: harvey.rosenblum@dal.frb.org
URL: http://www.naefa.org
Contact: Harvey Rosenblum, Exec. Dir.
Founded: 1971. **Members:** 300. **Membership Dues:** regular, $70 (annual) ● student, $30 (annual) ● life, $500 ● institutional, $300 (annual). **Description:** Economists, financial managers, and international business scholars and practitioners from the government and business sectors of Canada, Mexico, the U.S., and the Caribbean; others interested in economic, financial, and international business issues of the North American and Caribbean nations as well as their interactions. Seeks to encourage joint scholarly research, study, and academic exchange on issues relating to the economies of North America and the Caribbean. Sponsors meetings at which the results of this research are presented and discussed. **Formerly:** North American Economic Studies Association. **Publications:** *Congress Proceedings*, biennial ● *The North American Journal of Economics and Finance*, 3/year. Includes articles on the economic and financial issues facing North American, Caribbean, and Pacific Basin countries. **Price:** $55.00 for individuals; $110.00 for institutions. **Advertising:** accepted. Alternate Formats: microform. **Conventions/Meetings:** annual conference, held in conjunction with American Economic Association ● biennial international conference ● annual meeting - 2009 Jan. 3-5, San Francisco, CA; 2010 Jan. 3-5, Atlanta, GA.

6891 ■ The Other Economic Summit of the U.S. (TOES-USA)
777 UN Plz., Ste.3C
New York, NY 10017
Ph: (212)972-9877
Fax: (212)972-9878
E-mail: tschroye@warwick.net
URL: http://www.ee.upenn.edu/~rabii/toes
Contact: Susan Hunt, VP
Founded: 1987. **Members:** 300. **Membership Dues:** $30 (annual). **Budget:** $60,000. **Regional Groups:** 7. **Description:** Economists, environmentalists, and others interested in building a more just and sustainable society. Promotes education and research in alternative economics. Encourages a positive public view of alternative economic strategies including every seven years a major international gathering on alternative economic, social, and environmental movements to coincide with the G-7 Economic Summit in the United States. Organizes periodic seminars, round tables and other public events. **Committees:** Alternate Vision of New Economics; Regional Coordinating. **Formerly:** (1998) The Other Economic Summit of North America. **Publications:** *Building Sustainable Communities* ● *Chicken Little, Tomato Sauce, and Agriculture* ● *Future Wealth* ● *Greening Cities* ● *The Living Economy* ● *Redefining Wealth and Progress* ● *TOES and Tokyo* ● *What Works* ● *Worker Empowerment*. **Conventions/Meetings:** annual

conference, held in conjunction with the Group of Seven Economic Summit (exhibits).

6892 ■ Pacific Studies Center (PSC)
278 Hope St., No. A
Mountain View, CA 94041-1367
Ph: (650)969-1545
Fax: (650)961-8918
E-mail: lsiegel@cpeo.org
Contact: Lenny Siegel, Dir.
Founded: 1969. **Staff:** 2. **Budget:** $75,000. **Description:** Public interest information center specializing in studies of the social, military, and environmental impact of the production and application of high-technology electronics. Researches the political economics of Asia, the Pacific, the San Francisco Bay area, and particularly the Silicon Valley in California. Works with military toxics network. Maintains resource center for the use of the local community. **Libraries: Type:** reference.

6893 ■ Society for the Advancement of Economic Theory (SAET)
Univ. of Illinois
Dept. of Economics
330 Wohlers Hall
1206 S 6th St.
Champaign, IL 61820
Ph: (217)333-0120
Fax: (217)244-6678
E-mail: aliprantis@mgmt.purdue.edu
URL: http://www.krannert.purdue.edu/centers/saet
Contact: Charambalos D. Aliprantis, Co-Founder
Founded: 1990. **Members:** 170. **Budget:** $1,000,000. **Description:** Individuals interested in theoretical economics. Promotes the advancement of knowledge in theoretical economics; facilitates communication among researchers in economics, mathematics, game theory, and related disciplines. Sponsors research programs; operates speakers' bureau. **Publications:** *Economic Theory*, quarterly. Journal. **Price:** $69.00/year. **Advertising:** accepted ● *Journal of Evolutionary Economics*, quarterly. **Price:** $142.00/year. ISSN: 0936-9937. **Conventions/Meetings:** annual conference.

6894 ■ Society for the Development of Austrian Economics (SDAE)
c/o Joe Salerno, Pres.-Elect
725 Garibaldi Ave.
South Plainfield, NJ 07080
E-mail: jsalerno@pace.edu
URL: http://it.stlawu.edu/sdae
Contact: Randall Holcombe, Pres.
Founded: 1996. **Members:** 100. **Membership Dues:** regular, $20 (annual). **Multinational**. **Description:** Promotes the study of economics using the Austrian approach and influence. Supports the development of an approach to economics that draws upon the insights of Austrian economists such as Carl Menger, Ludwig von Mises, and Friedrich Hayek. Fosters scholarly exchange of ideas and knowledge on Austrian economics, including New Institutional Economics, Evolutionary Economics, Radical Subjectivism, Public Choice Theory, Constitutional Economics or any other related approach. **Telecommunication Services:** electronic mail, sdae@it.stlawu.edu.

6895 ■ Southern Economic Association (SEA)
Univ. of Tennessee at Chattanooga
313 Fletcher Hall, Dept. 6106
615 McCallie Ave.
Chattanooga, TN 37403-2598
Ph: (423)425-4118
Fax: (423)425-5218
E-mail: ashley-harrison@utc.edu
URL: http://www.southerneconomic.org
Contact: J.R. Clark, Sec.-Treas.
Founded: 1927. **Members:** 1,100. **Membership Dues:** regular, $60 (annual) ● student, retired, $20 (annual) ● life, $550. **Staff:** 3. **Budget:** $150,000. **Description:** Professional economists in government, business, and academic institutions. Provides placement service for economists. **Awards:** The Georgescu-Roegen Prize. **Frequency:** annual. **Type:** recognition. **Recipient:** for the best academic article published in the Southern Economic Journal ● Kenneth G. Elzinga Distinguished Teaching Award. **Frequency:** annual. **Type:** recognition. **Recipient:** for one or more faculty members for outstanding contributions to economics education. **Publications:** *Southern Economic Journal*, quarterly, every January, April, July and October. **Price:** $115.00 /year for nonmembers and domestic; $125.00 foreign. **Circulation:** 3,700. **Conventions/Meetings:** annual conference (exhibits) - usually November.

6896 ■ Union for Radical Political Economics (URPE)
URPE Gordon Hall
Univ. of Massachusetts
418 N Pleasant St.
Amherst, MA 01002-1735
Ph: (413)577-0806
E-mail: urpe@labornet.org
URL: http://www.urpe.org
Contact: Hazel Dayton Gunn, Managing Ed.
Founded: 1968. **Members:** 1,500. **Membership Dues:** student/low-income (full), $30 (annual) ● individual (full), $55 (annual) ● individual (with limited benefits), $20 (annual). **Staff:** 2. **Regional Groups:** 4. **Description:** Students and professors; individuals from trade unions, government agencies, progressive political organizations, and community and other nonprofit groups. Utilizes political economics in analysis of social problems. Critiques the capitalist system and "all forms of exploitation and oppression"; works to develop socialist alternatives and create a progressive social policy. Provides a forum for education and debate; sponsors informal study groups. **Publications:** *The Imperiled Economy*, periodic. Provides a comprehensive, critical overview of modern capitalist economies, particularly that of the U.S. ● *Public Sector Crisis Reader* ● *Reading in Radical Political Economics* ● *Review of Radical Political Economics*, quarterly. Journal. Covers topics such as Marxism, institutionalism, the Cambridge approach, patriarchy, social democracy, anarchy, feminism, and Trotskyism. **Price:** included in membership dues; $95.00/issue for institutions; $123.00/issue for individuals. ISSN: 0486-6134. **Circulation:** 2,400. **Advertising:** accepted. Alternate Formats: microform; online ● *Union for Radical Political Economics—Newsletter*, quarterly. Includes calendar of events and book reviews. **Price:** included in membership dues; $15.00 for nonmembers. **Circulation:** 2,400. **Advertising:** accepted. Also Cited As: *URPE Newsletter*. **Conventions/Meetings:** semiannual meeting, held in conjunction with Allied Social Science Associations - always August and December.

6897 ■ Western Economic Association International (WEAI)
7400 Center Ave., Ste.109
Huntington Beach, CA 92647-3039
Ph: (714)898-3222
Fax: (714)891-6715
E-mail: info@weainternational.org
URL: http://www.weainternational.org
Contact: Paul Milgrom, Pres.
Founded: 1922. **Members:** 2,200. **Membership Dues:** regular, $60 (annual) ● student, $25 (annual) ● family, $90 (annual). **Staff:** 5. **Budget:** $400,000. **Description:** Economists working in business, government, research, and academia. Seeks to close the gap between economists in academia and those in the business world or government. Promotes economic research and analysis. **Awards:** Economic Inquiry Article Award. **Frequency:** annual. **Type:** recognition. **Recipient:** chosen by Economic Inquiry editors. **Also Known As:** WEA International. **Formerly:** Pacific Coast Economics Association. **Publications:** *Conference Program*, annual. **Circulation:** 1,200 ● *Contemporary Economic Policy*, quarterly. Journal. Contains information on economic research and analysis of issues significant to business, government, and other decision-makers. **Price:** $226.00/year for academic; $298.00/year for corporate; $71.00 each for academic; $93.00 each for corporate. ISSN: 1074-3529. **Circulation:** 3,000. **Advertising:** accepted. Alternate Formats: microform; online ● *Economic Inquiry*, quarterly. Journal. Contains research on economics. **Price:** $345.00 /year for institutions; $210.00 /year for institutions outside U.S. ISSN: 0095-2583. **Circulation:** 3,400. **Advertising:** accepted. Alternate Formats: microform; online ● Brochures, periodic. **Conventions/Meetings:** annual conference and workshop, with presentations of current research papers in economics - 2008 June 29-July 3, Honolulu, HI; 2009 June 29-July 3, Vancouver, BC, Canada ● biennial Pacific Rim Conference.

Education

6898 ■ Teaching, Learning and Technology Group (TLTG)
1 Columbia Ave.
Takoma Park, MD 20912
Ph: (301)270-8312
Fax: (301)270-8110
E-mail: info@tltgroup.org
URL: http://www.tltgroup.org
Contact: Steven W. Gilbert, Pres.
Founded: 1998. **Multinational**. **Description:** Motivates and enables institutions and individuals to improve teaching and learning with technology, while helping to cope with continual change. Helps provide cost effective teaching and learning techniques through the appropriate use of information technology. **Computer Services:** Information services, resources, news ● online services, discussion group. **Also Known As:** The TLT Group. **Publications:** *FlashLight*, monthly. Newsletter. Contains summaries of formal and informal studies of educational uses of technology. Alternate Formats: online. **Conventions/Meetings:** Cognitive Science Findings and Concept Mapping: Visualizing, Managing and Sharing Conceptual Understandings to Improve Teaching and Learning - workshop, with online workshop.

Education, Alternative

6899 ■ Communication Institute for Online Scholarship (CIOS)
PO Box 57
Rotterdam Junction, NY 12150
Ph: (518)887-2443
Fax: (518)887-5186
E-mail: support@cios.org
URL: http://www.cios.org
Contact: Timothy Stephen, Pres.
Founded: 1990. **Membership Dues:** individual, $50 (annual) ● institution, $300 (annual). **Description:** Individuals and institutions. Strives to support the use of computer technologies in the service of communication scholarship and education. **Computer Services:** database, abstracts available to professional members ● database, journals index service relating to communication literature. **Publications:** *The Electronic Journal of Communication*. Alternate Formats: online.

Electricity

6900 ■ American Electrophoresis Society
1201 Ann St.
Madison, WI 53713
Ph: (608)258-1565
Fax: (608)258-1569
E-mail: matt-aes@tds.net
URL: http://www.aesociety.org
Contact: Matt Hoelter, Exec. Dir.
Founded: 1980. **Members:** 100. **Membership Dues:** full, $75 (annual) ● student, $25 (annual) ● postdoc, $35 (annual) ● emeritus, $35 (annual) ● corporate, $500 (annual) ● platinum sponsor, $2,500 (annual) ● gold sponsor, $1,000 (annual) ● silver sponsor, $500 (annual) ● newsletter sponsor per issue, $300 (annual). **Staff:** 1. **Budget:** $50,000. **Description:** Scientists and technicians using electrophoresis in their work as it relates to the separation and detection of bioproducts. Seeks to further the use of electro-

phoretic methods in biological sciences and to disclose new developments, theories and applications of electrophoretic techniques dealing with all aspects of electrophoresis. **Libraries: Type:** reference. **Holdings:** archival material. **Awards:** Founder Award. **Frequency:** annual. **Type:** recognition. **Computer Services:** Online services. **Formerly:** (1992) International Electrophoresis Society. **Publications:** *Electrophoresis*, semimonthly. Journal. Contains operative approaches from gels through capillaries to chips. ISSN: 0173-0835. Alternate Formats: online ● Newsletter, semiannual. **Price:** included in membership dues. **Circulation:** 5,000. Alternate Formats: online. **Conventions/Meetings:** annual meeting (exhibits) ● symposium ● workshop.

6901 ■ Electric Utility Benchmarking Association (EUBA)
4606 FM 1960 W, Ste.250
Houston, TX 77069-9949
Ph: (281)440-5044
Fax: (281)440-6677
URL: http://www.euba.com
Contact: Mark T. Czarnecki, Exec. Off.
Founded: 1997. **Members:** 4,500. **Staff:** 14. **Budget:** $2,000,000. **Description:** Employees of organizations who produce and/or distribute electricity. Works to identify the best business processes to assist members in delivering excellent services to their customers. Conducts benchmarking studies; supports the use of benchmarking; collects data; provides networking opportunities. **Committees:** Fossil; Hydroelectric; Nuclear; Transmission and Distribution. **Subgroups:** Lines; Power Generation; Power Marketing; Shared Services. **Conventions/Meetings:** annual roundtable and meeting.

6902 ■ IEEE Dielectrics and Electrical Insulation Society (DEIS)
c/o Hulya Kirkici, VP for Admin.
Auburn Univ.
Elecl. and Cmpt. Engg.
200 Broun Hall
Auburn, AL 36849-5201
Ph: (334)844-1822
Fax: (334)844-1809
E-mail: kirkih@eng.auburn.edu
URL: http://tdei.sju.edu/deis
Contact: Mr. W.M. McDermid, Pres.
Founded: 1963. **Members:** 1,980. **Membership Dues:** student, $10 (annual) ● individual, $20 (annual). **Budget:** $978,000. **Local Groups:** 8. **Description:** A society of the Institute of Electrical and Electronics Engineers. Areas of interest include the study of dielectric phenomena and behaviour, and development, charecterization and application of all gaseous, liquid, and solid electrical insulating materials and systems utilized in electrical and electronic equipment. **Libraries: Type:** lending; open to the public; reference. **Holdings:** 2; archival material, articles, reports, video recordings. **Subjects:** Electrical insulation and dielectrics. **Awards:** Dakin Award. **Frequency:** biennial. **Type:** recognition. **Recipient:** for technical achievement ● Forster Award. **Frequency:** annual. **Type:** recognition. **Recipient:** for distinguished service ● Student Fellowship. **Frequency:** annual. **Type:** fellowship. **Recipient:** for students persuing their phd or a major research work as a graduate student. **Computer Services:** Bibliographic search ● information services. **Committees:** Membership Services. **Sections:** Local Chapters. **Working Groups:** Standards Documents Development. **Formerly:** IEEE Electrical Insulation Society. **Publications:** *Electrical Insulation Magazine*, bimonthly. Features articles concerned with the development and characterization of the dielectric. **Circulation:** 5,000. **Advertising:** accepted ● *Transactions on Dielectrics and Electrical Insulation*, bimonthly. Journal. **Price:** included in membership dues. Alternate Formats: online; microform. **Conventions/Meetings:** annual conference.

6903 ■ IEEE Power Engineering Society (IEEEPES)
c/o IEEE Operations Center
445 Hoes Ln.
Piscataway, NJ 08854-1331
Ph: (732)562-3883
Fax: (732)562-3881
E-mail: pes@ieee.org
URL: http://www.ieee.org/portal/site/pes
Contact: Patrick P. Ryan, Exec. Dir.
Members: 21,286. **Local Groups:** 101. **Description:** A society of the Institute of Electrical and Electronics Engineers. Promotes the study of: electrical power system engineering; electrical power generating facilities; fundamental technologies used in the control and conversion of electric power; requirements, planning, analysis, reliability, operation, and economics of electrical generating, transmission, and distribution systems for general industrial, commercial, public, and domestic use. **Publications:** *Power and Energy*, bimonthly. Magazine. **Price:** included in membership dues. **Advertising:** accepted. Alternate Formats: online ● *Power Engineering Review*, monthly ● *Transactions on Energy Conversion*, quarterly. Journal ● *Transactions on Power Delivery*, quarterly. Journal ● *Transactions on Power Electronics*, quarterly ● *Transactions on Power Systems*, quarterly. Journal. **Conventions/Meetings:** annual meeting.

6904 ■ IEEE Solid-State Circuits Society (SSCC)
c/o Katherine Olstein, Admin.
445 Hoes Ln.
Piscataway, NJ 08855-1331
Ph: (732)981-3400 (732)981-3410
Free: (800)672-IEEE
Fax: (732)981-3401
E-mail: sscs@ieee.org
URL: http://www.sscs.org
Contact: Katherine Olstein, Admin.
Founded: 1997. **Members:** 14,300. **Membership Dues:** regular, $22 (annual) ● student, $11 (annual). **Staff:** 2. **Regional Groups:** 10. **Local Groups:** 42. **Description:** Promotes all aspects of solid-state circuits, including the design, testing and application of circuits and subsystems, as well as closely related topics in device technology and circuit theory. **Awards:** IEEE Solid-State Circuits Award. **Frequency:** annual. **Type:** monetary. **Computer Services:** Mailing lists. **Committees:** Awards; Chapters; Education; Meetings; Nominations; Publications. **Formerly:** (1998) IEEE Solid-State Circuits Council. **Publications:** *E-News*. Newsletter. Alternate Formats: online ● *Journal of Solid-State Circuits*, monthly. ISSN: 0018-9200. **Circulation:** 13,500. Alternate Formats: CD-ROM; online. **Conventions/Meetings:** annual meeting (exhibits).

Electronics

6905 ■ Antenna Measurement Techniques Association (AMTA)
c/o Jeff Guerrieri, Sec.
MIST m/s 818.02
325 Broadway
Boulder, CO 80305
E-mail: secretary@amta.org
URL: http://www.amta.org
Contact: Carlo Rizzo, VP
Founded: 1979. **Members:** 400. **Membership Dues:** regular, $50 (annual). **Budget:** $100,000. **Multinational. Description:** Persons from government, private, and institutional laboratories involved in the design, development, and manufacture of antennas and antenna measurement systems. Provides a forum for exchange of information on topics including: advanced measurement techniques such as automatic systems and near field testing; system/equipment interfacing problems and solutions; measurement equipment and techniques; analysis of measurement data; radar cross section instrumentation; antenna range design and evaluations. Encourages presentations that describe the implementation of automatic testing to improve efficiency and data quality. **Libraries: Type:** reference. **Holdings:** archival material. **Subjects:** antenna measurements/RCS measurements. **Awards:** Distinguished Achievement Award. **Frequency:** annual. **Type:** recognition. **Recipient:** for outstanding contributions to antenna measurements techniques or related field. **Publications:** *Call for Papers*, semiannual. **Circulation:** 400 ● *Membership List*, annual. Membership Directory ● *Proceedings of Annual Symposium and Annual Workshop*, annual. **Price:** included in membership dues ● Newsletter, semiannual. **Price:** included in membership dues. **Circulation:** 400. **Conventions/Meetings:** annual symposium, for antenna test equipment vendors (exhibits) - usually fall.

6906 ■ Applied Computational Electromagnetics Society (ACES)
c/o Dr. Richard W. Adler, Exec. Off.
Naval Post Graduate School
ECE Dept.
Code EC/AB
833 Dyer Rd.
Monterey, CA 93943-5121
Ph: (831)646-1111
E-mail: rwa@attglobal.net
URL: http://aces.ee.olemiss.edu
Contact: Dr. Richard W. Adler, Exec. Off.
Founded: 1986. **Membership Dues:** basic, $35 (annual) ● intermediate, $55 (annual) ● expanded in U.S., Canada, and Mexico, $90 (annual) ● institutional, $125 (annual) ● student/retired/unemployed, $20 (annual) ● expanded outside U.S., Canada, and Mexico, $110 (annual). **Description:** Users and developers of electromagnetic modeling codes. Promotes standardization and compatibility in systems of computer modeling and numerical methods applied to electromagnetics. Serves as a clearinghouse in the field of electromagnetics. Analyzes and validates emerging codes and modeling techniques; conducts computational studies; addresses input/output and computer hardware issues. Makes available education and training programs; provides assistance to inexperienced code and model users. Sponsors Code User Groups. **Libraries: Type:** reference. **Holdings:** software. **Committees:** AP-S EM Modeling Software; Industry Relations; Nominations and Elections; Publications; Software; Software Performance Standards. **Publications:** *ACES Journal*, 3/year. Contains scholarly articles in the field of computational electromagnetics. **Price:** free for members. Alternate Formats: online ● *ACES Newsletter*, 3/year. Contains articles on modeling, code, and computer graphics; includes correspondence from members, association news, and bibliographic information. **Price:** free for members. Alternate Formats: online. **Conventions/Meetings:** periodic Benchmark Problem Solution Workshop ● annual conference ● annual meeting ● annual symposium.

6907 ■ Association for Electronics Manufacturing of the Society of Manufacturing Engineers (EM/SME)
c/o Society of Manufacturing Engineers
1 SME Dr.
PO Box 930
Dearborn, MI 48121-0930
Ph: (313)425-3000
Free: (800)733-4763
Fax: (313)425-3400
E-mail: techcommunities@sme.org
URL: http://www.sme.org/cgi-bin/communities.pl?/communities/em/emhome.htm
Contact: Dr. Ismail Fidan, Chm.
Founded: 1932. **Members:** 35,000. **Membership Dues:** regular, $125 (annual). **Staff:** 160. **Multinational. Description:** Promotes an increased awareness of manufacturing engineering. Helps keep manufacturing professionals up to date on leading trends and technologies through its member programs, publications, expositions and professional development resources. **Libraries: Type:** open to the public; reference. **Holdings:** archival material, articles, biographical archives, papers, reports, video recordings. **Subjects:** manufacturing. **Awards:** TEEM Award. **Frequency:** annual. **Type:** recognition. **Recipient:** for extraordinary dedication in the field of electronics manufacturing. **Affiliated With:** Society of Manufacturing Engineers. **Publications:** *Bibliography of Electronics and Electronics Related Technical Papers* ● *Electronics Manufacturing Engineering*, quarterly. Reports on current technology develop-

ments and trends. ● *Electronics Manufacturing Technology Trends Report 2000*. Book ● *Robotics Technology Trends Report 2001*. Booklet ● Videos.

6908 ■ Association of Old Crows (AOC)
1000 N Payne St., Ste.300
Alexandria, VA 22314-1652
Ph: (703)549-1600
Fax: (703)549-2589
E-mail: richetti@crows.org
URL: http://www.crows.org/default.htm
Contact: Don Richetti, Exec. Dir.
Founded: 1964. **Members:** 14,500. **Membership Dues:** individual, corporation, $35 (annual). **Staff:** 11. **Budget:** $2,400,000. **Regional Groups:** 9. **Local Groups:** 65. **National Groups:** 19. **Multinational. Description:** Professional association of scientists, engineers, managers, operators, educators, military personnel, and others engaged in the science of electronic, command, control, and information warfare, and related areas. Works for the advancement of electronic warfare and information superiority; dedicated to national security and a strong defense posture for the U.S. and its allies. Provides a means for communicating and disseminating new developments in electronic warfare technology, training, operations, and doctrines. Conducts studies of special problem areas in conjunction with the Department of Defense. Assists the National and Allied Defense efforts in areas of defense and military requirements, programs, and systems. **Libraries: Type:** reference. **Subjects:** history of electronic warfare. **Awards:** Gold Medal of Electronic Warfare. **Frequency:** annual. **Type:** recognition ● **Type:** scholarship. **Telecommunication Services:** electronic mail, vittoria@crows.org. **Committees:** Awards; Awareness; Education; Historical; National Security Affairs; Technical. **Programs:** Electronic Warfare Educational. **Also Known As:** Electronic Defense Association. **Publications:** *Journal of Electronic Defense*, monthly. **Price:** included in membership dues. ISSN: 0192-429X. **Circulation:** 20,000. **Advertising:** accepted. **Conventions/Meetings:** annual International Electronic Technical Symposium and Convention (exhibits).

6909 ■ Audio Engineering Society (AES)
60 E 42nd St., Rm. 2520
New York, NY 10165-2520
Ph: (212)661-8528
Fax: (212)682-0477
E-mail: hq@aes.org
URL: http://www.aes.org
Contact: Roger Furness, Exec. Dir.
Founded: 1948. **Members:** 11,250. **Membership Dues:** associate, full, $80 (annual) ● student, $30 (annual). **Staff:** 15. **Budget:** $4,500,000. **Local Groups:** 63. **Description:** Engineers, administrators, and technicians who design or operate recording and reproducing equipment for radio, television, motion picture, and recording studios, or who produce, install, and operate disc, magnetic tape, and sound amplifying equipment; educators who use recording in teaching, or who teach acoustics, electronics, and other sciences basic to the recording and reproducing of sound; administrators, sales engineers, and technicians in the sound industry and related fields. Operates educational and research foundation. **Telecommunication Services:** electronic mail, standards@aes.org. **Programs:** Distinguish Speakers. **Publications:** *Directory of the AES*, quadrennial ● *Journal of the Audio Engineering Society: Audio/Acoustics/Applications*, 10/year. Includes book reviews, calendar of events, information on new members, and reviews of acoustical patents. **Price:** included in membership dues; $70.00 /year for nonmembers. **Circulation:** 10,800. **Advertising:** accepted. Alternate Formats: microform. **Conventions/Meetings:** semiannual meeting (exhibits) - always fall in U.S. and early spring in Germany.

6910 ■ Electrical Overstress/Electrostatic Discharge Association (EOS/ESD)
7900 Turin Rd., Bldg. 3
Rome, NY 13440-2069
Ph: (315)339-6937
Fax: (315)339-6793
E-mail: info@esda.org
URL: http://www.esda.org
Contact: Lisa Pimpinella, Operations Mgr.
Founded: 1982. **Members:** 2,000. **Membership Dues:** regular in North America, $60 (annual) ● regular outside North America, $70 (annual). **Staff:** 2. **Local Groups:** 5. **Description:** Works to advance the theory and practice of electrical overstress avoidance, with emphasis on electrostatic discharge phenomena. Focuses on the effects of both material and manmade electromagnetic threats on electronic components, subsystems, and systems. Promotes exchange of technical information and cooperation among members. Develops standards; conducts educational programs. **Computer Services:** Mailing lists, of members. **Committees:** Standards. **Publications:** *EOS/ESD Symposium Proceedings Perfect Bound*, annual. Book. **Price:** $90.00/copy (plus $10 for handling). Alternate Formats: CD-ROM ● *Membership Roster*, annual. Membership Directory. Alternate Formats: online ● *Product Catalog*, periodic. Alternate Formats: online ● *Standards - Technical Documents*, periodic ● *Threshold*, bimonthly. Newsletter. **Conventions/Meetings:** annual symposium, includes tutorials (exhibits) - every September or October. 2008 Sept. 7-11, Tucson, AZ.

6911 ■ Electronic Design Automation Consortium (EDAC)
111 W St. John St., Ste.220
San Jose, CA 95113-1104
Ph: (408)287-3322
Fax: (408)283-5283
E-mail: order@edac.org
URL: http://www.edac.org
Contact: Robert Gardner, Exec. Dir.
Founded: 1989. **Members:** 120. **Membership Dues:** voting, $2,000-$20,000 (annual) ● associate, $1,500-$5,000 (annual) ● individual, $250 (annual). **Staff:** 2. **Budget:** $1,000,000. **Multinational. Description:** Companies engaged in the development, manufacture, sales and services of tools; EDA consultants and other individuals with an interest in EDA and related technologies. Seeks to identify and address common issues. Represents the commercial interests of members; coordinates EDA standards; compiles market statistics; makes available products and services to members. **Awards:** Kaufman Award. **Frequency:** annual. **Type:** recognition. **Recipient:** for an individual who has had demonstrable impact on the field of electronic design. **Committees:** Emerging Companies; Export; Interoperability; Market Statistics; Quality Trade Show. **Conventions/Meetings:** annual conference, design automation (exhibits).

6912 ■ IEEE Aerospace and Electronics Systems Society (AESS)
c/o IEEE Admission and Advancement Department
445 Hoes Ln.
Piscataway, NJ 08854-4141
Ph: (732)981-0060
Fax: (732)981-0225
E-mail: onlinesupport@ieee.org
URL: http://www.ieee-aess.org/default.php
Contact: James V. Leonard, Pres.
Members: 8,502. **Local Groups:** 28. **Description:** A society of the Institute of Electrical and Electronics Engineers. Involved with the development and installation of electronics systems designed to meet the high performance demands of the aerospace industry. Examines the equipment and procedures used by electrical and electronics engineers. **Publications:** *Aerospace and Electronic Systems Magazine*, monthly ● *Transactions on Aerospace and Electronic Systems*, bimonthly. **Conventions/Meetings:** annual meeting.

6913 ■ IEEE Antennas and Propagation Society (APS)
c/o Mike Shields, Sec.-Treas.
MIT Lincoln Lab.
244 Wood St.
Lexington, MA 02421
Ph: (781)981-4919
E-mail: shields@ll.mit.edu
URL: http://www.ieeeaps.org
Contact: Mike Shields, Sec.-Treas.
Members: 7,956. **Local Groups:** 40. **Description:** A society of the Institute of Electrical and Electronics Engineers. Fields of interest include: experimental and theoretical advances in electromagnetic theory; the radiation, propagation, scattering, and diffraction of electromagnetic waves; the devices, media, and fields of application related to these areas, such as antennas, plasmas, and radio astronomy systems. **Publications:** *Antennas and Wave Propagation Letters*, periodic. Newsletter. Contains short, peer-reviewed technical articles. **Price:** free ● *IEEE Antennas and Propagation Magazine*, bimonthly ● *Transactions on Antennas and Propagation*, monthly. Contains peer-reviewed technical articles on antennas, wave propagation and other related subjects. **Advertising:** accepted. **Conventions/Meetings:** annual meeting ● annual symposium.

6914 ■ IEEE Circuits and Systems Society (CSS)
c/o IEEE CASS Executive Office
445 Hoes Ln.
Piscataway, NJ 08854
Ph: (732)465-5821
Fax: (732)981-1769
E-mail: cas-info@ieee.org
URL: http://www.ieee-cas.org
Contact: Ljiljana Trajkovic, Pres.
Members: 13,383. **Membership Dues:** student in U.S., $30 (annual) ● student in Canada, $32 (annual) ● student outside U.S. and Canada, $25 (annual) ● individual in U.S., $156 (annual) ● individual in Canada, $142 (annual) ● individual in Africa, Europe and Middle East, $130 (annual) ● individual in Latin America, $123 (annual) ● individual in Asia and the Pacific, $124 (annual). **Budget:** $150,000. **Local Groups:** 31. **Description:** A society of the Institute of Electrical and Electronics Engineers. Disseminates information on the design and theory of operations involving circuits used in radio and electronics equipment; such information covers methods, algorithms, and man-machine interfaces for physical and logical design. **Libraries: Type:** reference. **Publications:** *IEEE Design and Test of Computers*, bimonthly. Magazine. Focuses on current and near-future practice, and includes tutorials, how-to articles, and real-world case studies. **Price:** $40.00 /year for individuals professional; $20.00/year for student; $71.00 /year for nonmembers. **Advertising:** accepted. Alternate Formats: online ● *Transactions on Circuits and Systems*, monthly. Paper ● *Transactions on Computer-Aided Design of Integrated Circuits and Systems*, bimonthly. Paper. **Conventions/Meetings:** annual conference - always May.

6915 ■ IEEE Components, Packaging, and Manufacturing Technology Society (CPMT)
445 Hoes Ln.
Piscataway, NJ 08854
Ph: (732)562-5529
Fax: (732)981-1769
E-mail: cpmt@ieee.org
URL: http://www.cpmt.org
Contact: Marsha Tickman, Exec. Dir.
Members: 3,800. **Membership Dues:** full, $129-$159 (annual) ● regular (if IEEE member), $12 (annual) ● affiliate, $68 (annual). **Multinational. Description:** A society of the Institute of Electrical and Electronics Engineers. Gathers and disseminates information regarding materials, components, modules including hybrids, and electronic systems. Provides data on selection, assembly, and maintenance of such systems as applied to product design and manufacturing. **Awards:** Best Paper Awards. **Frequency:** annual. **Type:** recognition. **Recipient:** for best paper published ● CPMT Electronics Manufacturing Technology Award. **Frequency:** annual. **Type:** monetary. **Recipient:** for individuals responsible for establishing manufacturing process ● David Feldman Outstanding Contribution Award. **Frequency:** annual. **Type:** monetary. **Recipient:** for IEEE and CPMT members of at least five years ● Exceptional Technical Achievement Award. **Fre-**

quency: annual. **Type:** monetary. **Recipient:** for individuals or group of individuals with exceptional technical achievement. **Committees:** Components and Devices; Core Technologies; Packaging; Process and Manufacturing. **Formerly:** (2000) IEEE Components, Hybrids, and Manufacturing Technology Society. **Publications:** *Transactions on Components, Hybrids, and Manufacturing Technology*, quarterly ● Newsletter, quarterly. Contains information on the various conferences and events of the Society. **Advertising:** accepted. Alternate Formats: online ● Bulletin, monthly. Contains late-breaking news. Alternate Formats: online. **Conventions/Meetings:** annual Electronic Components and Technology Conference (exhibits) ● annual meeting.

6916 ■ IEEE Consumer Electronics Society (CES)

c/o Charlotte Kobert, Sec.
4115 Clendenning Rd.
Gibsonia, PA 15044
E-mail: ckobert@zbzoom.net
URL: http://www.ewh.ieee.org/soc/ces
Contact: Will Lumpkins, Pres.

Founded: 1965. **Members:** 6,874. **Membership Dues:** regular, $15 (annual) ● affiliate, $75 (annual). **Budget:** $363,500. **Local Groups:** 10. **Multinational. Description:** A society of the Institute of Electrical and Electronics Engineers. Gathers and disseminates information regarding the design and manufacture of consumer electronics components and products, particularly those with recreational or educational applications. **Computer Services:** database, consumer electronics standards. **Committees:** Standards; Technical Activities. **Publications:** *Transactions on Consumer Electronics*, quarterly. Contains topics of interest to consumer electronics. ● Newsletter, quarterly. Contains information on topics of current interest. **Conventions/Meetings:** annual conference (exhibits) - always June in Chicago, IL.

6917 ■ IEEE Electromagnetic Compatibility Society (EMCS)

c/o Bruce Archambeault, Awards Chm.
PO Box 12195
Research Triangle Park, NC 27709
Ph: (919)486-0120
E-mail: a.l.drozd@ieee.org
URL: http://www.ewh.ieee.org/soc/emcs
Contact: A.L. Drozd, Pres.

Founded: 1957. **Members:** 5,000. **Membership Dues:** individual, $25 (annual) ● student, $13 (annual). **Staff:** 1. **Budget:** $1,000,000. **Regional Groups:** 10. **Local Groups:** 41. **Description:** A society of the Institute of Electrical and Electronics Engineers. Concerned with the origin, control, and measurement of electromagnetic interference on electronic and Electrical systems. **Awards:** Best Student Paper Award. **Frequency:** annual. **Type:** monetary. **Recipient:** to a student for best paper ● Certificate of Appreciation. **Frequency:** annual. **Type:** recognition. **Recipient:** to a member who has a significant contribution to the administration and overall success of the EMC Society ● Chapter-of-the-Year Award. **Frequency:** annual. **Type:** recognition. **Recipient:** to any EMC chapter for outstanding performance ● Laurence G. Cumming Award for Outstanding Service. **Frequency:** annual. **Type:** recognition. **Recipient:** for a member who has rendered outstanding service to an EMC Society ● Most Improved Chapter Award. **Frequency:** annual. **Type:** recognition. **Recipient:** to any EMC chapter with significantly improved performance ● Richard R. Stoddart Award for Outstanding Performance. **Frequency:** annual. **Type:** monetary. **Recipient:** for a member who has an outstanding performance to an EMC Society ● Technical Achievement Award. **Frequency:** annual. **Type:** recognition. **Recipient:** to a member who has a significant technical accomplishment in the field of Electromagnetic Compatibility ● Transactions Prize Paper Award. **Frequency:** annual. **Type:** monetary. **Recipient:** to an outstanding paper published in the IEEE Transactions on Electromagnetic Compatibility. **Committees:** Education and Student Activities; Representative Advisory; Standards; Technical. **Publications:** Newsletter, quarterly. Alternate Formats: online. **Conventions/Meetings:** annual International Symposium on Electromagnetic Compatibility - symposium and workshop (exhibits) - 2008 Aug. 18-22, Detroit, MI; 2009 Aug. 17-21, Austin, TX.

6918 ■ IEEE Electron Devices Society (EDS)

c/o IEEE Operations Center
445 Hoes Ln.
Piscataway, NJ 08854
Ph: (732)562-3926
Fax: (732)235-1626
E-mail: executivedirector@ieee.org
URL: http://www.ieee.org/portal/pages/society/eds
Contact: Jeffry W. Raynes, Exec. Dir.

Founded: 1951. **Members:** 12,500. **Membership Dues:** in U.S., $165 (annual) ● in Canada (GST included), $156 (annual) ● in Canada (HST included), $162 (annual) ● in Africa, Europe, Middle East, $137 (annual) ● in Latin America, $130 (annual) ● in the Asia Pacific, $131 (annual). **Local Groups:** 33. **Description:** A society of the Institute of Electrical and Electronics Engineers. Concerned with the theory, design, and performance of electron devices, including electron tubes, solid-state devices, integrated electron devices, energy sources, power devices, displays, and device reliability. **Publications:** *Electron Device Letters*, monthly. Journal. Includes theory, design, performance and reliability of electron device. **Price:** $580.00. ISSN: 0741-3106. Alternate Formats: online ● *Journal Electronic Materials*, bimonthly. **Price:** $529.00 ● *Transactions on Electron Devices*, monthly. Journal. **Price:** $985.00 ● *Transactions on Semiconductor Manufacturing*, quarterly. **Conventions/Meetings:** annual meeting.

6919 ■ IEEE Industrial Electronics Society (IES)

c/o Dr. John Y. Hung, Treas.
Elecl. Engg. Dept.
Auburn Univ.
Auburn, AL 36849-5201
Ph: (334)844-1813
Fax: (334)844-1809
E-mail: hungjoh@auburn.edu
URL: http://ieee-ies.org
Contact: Dr. John Y. Hung, Treas.

Founded: 1974. **Members:** 6,000. **Membership Dues:** general, $19 (annual). **Budget:** $1,000,000. **Regional Groups:** 29. **Multinational. Description:** A society of the Institute of Electrical and Electronics Engineers. Studies the application of electronics and electrical sciences to the control of industrial processes. **Awards:** Anthony J. Hornfeck Service Award. **Frequency:** annual. **Type:** monetary. **Recipient:** for outstanding, meritorious services to the IEEE Industrial Electronics Society ● Best Paper Award for the IEEE Transactions on Industrial Electronics. **Frequency:** annual. **Type:** monetary. **Recipient:** for the best paper published in the IEEE Transactions on Industrial Electronics ● Dr.-Ing. Eugene Mittelmann Achievement Award. **Frequency:** annual. **Type:** monetary. **Recipient:** for outstanding contributions to the field of Industrial Electronics. **Publications:** *Industrial Electronic Society Newsletter*, quarterly. ISSN: 0746-1240. **Advertising:** accepted. Alternate Formats: online ● *Journal of Microelectromechanical Systems*, quarterly. Alternate Formats: online ● *Transaction on Mechatronics*, quarterly. Journal. Alternate Formats: online ● *Transactions on Industrial Electronics*, bimonthly. Journal. Discusses the applications of industrial electronics to the industry. **Price:** included in membership dues. **Circulation:** 6,300. Alternate Formats: online ● *Transactions on Industrial Informatics*, quarterly. Journal. Alternate Formats: online ● *Transactions on Mobile Computing*, quarterly. Journal. Alternate Formats: online. **Conventions/Meetings:** annual conference - fall.

6920 ■ IEEE Lasers and Electro-Optics Society (LEOS)

445 Hoes Ln.
Piscataway, NJ 08854-1331
Ph: (732)562-3891 (732)562-3892
Fax: (732)562-8434
E-mail: p.shumate@ieee.org
URL: http://www.ieee.org/portal/site/leos
Contact: Richard Linke, Exec. Dir.

Founded: 1977. **Members:** 8,500. **Membership Dues:** student, $13 (annual) ● individual, full, $25 (annual). **Staff:** 15. **Budget:** $6,700,000. **Local Groups:** 57. **Multinational. Description:** A society of the Institute of Electrical and Electronics Engineers. Serves as a forum for discussion of quantum electronics, photonics, optoelectronic theory, techniques and applications, and the design, development, and manufacture of photonic systems and subsystems (such as lasers and fiber optics). Works to research, develop, design, manufacture, and apply materials, devices and systems for lasers, optical devices, optical fibers and lightwave technology. Involved with information exchange, publications, and conferences in association with laser, optoelectronics, and photonics professional organizations. **Awards:** Aron Kressel Award. **Frequency:** annual. **Type:** recognition. **Recipient:** to individuals or groups who have made important contributions to opto-electronic device technology ● Distinguished Lecturer Awards. **Frequency:** annual. **Type:** recognition. **Recipient:** to excellent speakers who have made technical, industrial or entrepreneurial contributions of high quality to the field of lasers and electro-optics ● IEEE Photonics Field Award. **Frequency:** annual. **Type:** recognition. **Recipient:** for major contributions in the field of photonics ● John Tyndall Award. **Frequency:** annual. **Type:** recognition. **Recipient:** to an individual who has made outstanding contributions in any area of optical-fiber technology ● LEOS Distinguished Service Award. **Frequency:** annual. **Type:** recognition. **Recipient:** to members with exceptional individual contribution of service that had significant benefit to the membership of the IEEE Lasers and Electro-Optics Society as a whole ● LEOS Engineering Achievement Award. **Frequency:** annual. **Type:** recognition. **Recipient:** to an exceptional engineering contribution that had a significant impact on the development of laser or electro-optic technology ● LEOS William Streifer Award. **Frequency:** annual. **Type:** recognition. **Recipient:** to an exceptional single scientific contribution that had a significant impact in the field of lasers and electro-optics in the past 10 years ● Quantum Electronics Award. **Frequency:** annual. **Type:** recognition. **Recipient:** for outstanding technical contributions to quantum electronics, either in fundamentals or applications, or both. **Telecommunication Services:** electronic mail, leos@ieee.org. **Affiliated With:** Institute of Electrical and Electronics Engineers. **Publications:** *IEEE Journal of Quantum Electronics*, monthly. Contains publications reporting latest experimental or theoretical results in all areas of quantum electronics. ISSN: 0018-9197. Alternate Formats: online ● *IEEE Journal of Selected Topics in Quantum Electronics*, bimonthly. Features topical papers within the broad field of science and technology of quantum electronics. ISSN: 1077-260X. Alternate Formats: online ● *IEEE/OSA Journal of Display Technology*, quarterly. Features advances in all aspects of displays and display technologies. ISSN: 1551-319X. Alternate Formats: online ● *IEEE/OSA Journal of Lightwave Technology*, monthly. Contains manuscripts; report original theoretical and/or experimental results that advance the technological base of guided-wave technology. ISSN: 0733-8724. Alternate Formats: online ● *IEEE Photonics Technology Letters*, monthly. Journal. Contains original and significant contributions relating to photonic components and applications. ISSN: 1041-1135 ● *LEOS News*, bimonthly. Newsletter. Contains information and issues about the organization. **Price:** included in membership dues. **Advertising:** accepted. Alternate Formats: online. **Conventions/Meetings:** annual conference and meeting, presents reports, tutorials, and short courses on developments in all areas of lasers, photonics, and electro-optics (exhibits) ● annual Conference on Lasers and Electro-Optics ● annual Optical Fiber Communications Conference - convention and workshop (exhibits) - usually spring.

6921 ■ IEEE Magnetics Society

c/o IEEE Membership Development
445 Hoes Ln.
PO Box 459
Piscataway, NJ 08855-0459

Ph: (908)981-0060
Free: (800)678-4333
Fax: (908)981-0225
E-mail: rahamanmohammed@gmail.com
URL: http://www.ieeemagnetics.org
Contact: Dr. Can E. Korman, Publicity Chair

Founded: 1964. **Members:** 3,500. **Local Groups:** 13. **Description:** A society of the Institute of Electrical and Electronics Engineers (see separate entry) that deals with magnetic phenomena, materials, and devices as applied to electrical engineering. **Awards:** Reynold B. Johnson Data Storage Device Technology Award. **Frequency:** annual. **Type:** recognition. **Recipient:** for outstanding contributions to the advancement of information storage ● Reynold B. Johnson Information Storage Systems Award. **Frequency:** annual. **Type:** recognition. **Recipient:** for outstanding contributions to information storage systems. **Publications:** *IEEE Transactions on Magnetics*, bimonthly. Journal. ISSN: 0018-9464. **Advertising:** accepted ● *Technical Journal.* **Conventions/Meetings:** annual Intermag - conference (exhibits).

6922 ■ IEEE Power Electronics Society (IEEPELS)

c/o Robert Myers, Exec. Dir.
799 N Beverly Glen
Los Angeles, CA 90077
Ph: (310)592-5431
Fax: (310)861-0100
E-mail: bob.myers@ieee.org
URL: http://www.pels.org
Contact: Robert Myers, Exec. Dir.

Founded: 1986. **Members:** 6,200. **Membership Dues:** individual, $20 (annual). **Staff:** 2. **Budget:** $600,000. **Description:** A council of the Institute of Electrical and Electronics Engineers. Serves as a focus for discussion of such subjects as: DC-to-DC converter design; direct off-line switching power supplies, inverters, controlled rectifiers, control techniques, modeling, analysis, and similar techniques; the application of power circuit components (power semiconductors, magnetics, and capacitors); thermal performance of electronic power systems. **Formerly:** (1987) IEEE Power Electronics Council. **Publications:** *Transactions on Power Electronics*, quarterly. **Price:** included in membership dues ● Newsletter, quarterly. **Price:** included in membership dues. **Conventions/Meetings:** annual meeting.

6923 ■ IEEE Professional Communication Society (PCS)

PO Box 6804
Piscataway, NJ 08854-6804
Ph: (732)981-0060
Free: (800)678-4333
Fax: (732)981-0225
E-mail: member.services@ieee.org
URL: http://ewh.ieee.org/soc/pcs
Contact: Luke Maki, Pres.

Members: 2,656. **Membership Dues:** regular, $30 (annual) ● student, $15 (annual). **Local Groups:** 6. **Description:** A society of the Institute of Electrical and Electronics Engineers. Studies, develops, and promotes techniques for the preparation, organization, collection, and dissemination of information in the field of electronics. **Awards:** IEEE Cledo Brunetti Award. **Frequency:** annual. **Type:** monetary. **Recipient:** for outstanding contributions to miniaturization in the electronics arts ● IEEE Components, Packaging and Manufacturing Technology Award. **Frequency:** annual. **Type:** medal. **Recipient:** for meritorious contributions to the advancement of components, electronic packaging or manufacturing technologies ● IEEE Control Systems Award. **Frequency:** annual. **Type:** medal. **Recipient:** to an individual for outstanding contributions to control systems engineering, science or technology ● IEEE Eric Herz Outstanding Staff Member Award. **Frequency:** biennial. **Type:** recognition. **Recipient:** to present and past full time staff members of the IEEE with at least ten years of service ● IEEE Haraden Pratt Award. **Frequency:** annual. **Type:** medal. **Recipient:** to an IEEE senior member or fellow who has rendered outstanding service ● IEEE Richard M. Emberson Award. **Frequency:** annual. **Type:** medal. **Recipient:** to an IEEE member for distinguished service to the development, viability, advancement and pursuit of the technical objectives of the IEEE. **Publications:** *Transactions on Professional Communication*, quarterly. Journal. **Conventions/Meetings:** annual International Professional Communication Conference.

6924 ■ IEEE Reliability Society (RS)

c/o IEEE Corporate Office
3 Park Ave., 17th Fl.
New York, NY 10016-5997
Ph: (212)419-7900
Free: (800)678-4333
Fax: (212)752-4929
E-mail: ieeeusa@ieee.org
URL: http://www.ieee.org
Contact: Leah H. Jamieson, Pres./CEO

Founded: 1949. **Members:** 2,400. **Membership Dues:** regular, in U.S., $161 (annual) ● student outside U.S., $30 (annual). **Staff:** 24. **Budget:** $750,000. **Local Groups:** 22. **Description:** A society of the Institute of Electrical and Electronics Engineers that is concerned with the principles and practices of reliability, maintainability, and product liability relating to electrical and electronic equipment. Operates speakers' bureau. **Publications:** *IEEE Reliability Society Newsletter*, quarterly. Alternate Formats: online ● *IEEE Transactions on Device and Material Reliability*, annual. Journal. Alternate Formats: online ● *Transactions on Reliability*, quarterly. Journal. Alternate Formats: online. **Conventions/Meetings:** quarterly Administrative Committee - meeting ● annual Associate Editors' Meeting ● annual Chapters' Meeting ● annual Technical Operations Committee - meeting.

6925 ■ IEEE Vehicular Technology Society (VTS)

c/o IEEE Admission and Advancement
PO Box 6804
Piscataway, NJ 08855-6804
Ph: (732)981-0225
Free: (800)678-IEEE
Fax: (732)981-0225
E-mail: cbackof@aol.com
URL: http://www.vtsociety.org
Contact: Charlie Backof, Pres.

Members: 5,000. **Local Groups:** 24. **Description:** Serves as society of the Institute of Electrical and Electronics Engineers. Fields of interest include: land, airborne, and maritime mobile services; portable or hand-carried and citizen's communication services, when used with a vehicular system; vehicular electrotechnology, equipment, and automotive systems. **Committees:** Conference; Propagation; Standards. **Publications:** *Transactions on Vehicular Technology*, bimonthly. Journal. **Price:** $22.00 for members. Alternate Formats: online. **Conventions/Meetings:** semiannual Vehicular Technology Conference.

6926 ■ Institute of Electrical and Electronics Engineers (IEEE)

445 Hoes Ln.
Piscataway, NJ 08854
Ph: (732)981-0060
Free: (800)678-4333
Fax: (732)981-1721
E-mail: corporate-communications@ieee.org
URL: http://www.ieee.org
Contact: Prof. Leah H. Jamieson, Pres.

Founded: 1963. **Members:** 370,000. **Staff:** 900. **Regional Groups:** 319. **Local Groups:** 1,676. **Multinational. Description:** Promotes the advancement of technology. Consists of engineers and scientists in electrical engineering, electronics, computer sciences and allied fields. Publishes 30 percent of the world's literature in the electrical and electronics engineering and computer science fields, and has developed nearly 900 active industry standards. **Libraries: Type:** reference. **Holdings:** 132. **Awards:** IEEE Medal of Honor. **Frequency:** annual. **Type:** medal. **Recipient:** for outstanding contribution in science and technology. **Telecommunication Services:** electronic mail, society-info@ieee.org. **Councils:** Intelligent Transportation Systems; Neural Networks; Sensors. **Formed by Merger of:** American Institute of Electrical Engineers; Institute of Radio Engineers. **Publications:** *IEEE Spectrum*, monthly. Magazine ● Proceedings, monthly.

6927 ■ International Coordinating Committee on Solid State Sensors and Actuators Research (ICCSSSAR)

c/o Mr. John Huggins, Exec. Dir.
Berkeley Sensor and Actuator Center
Univ. of California
483 Cory Hall, No. 1774
Berkeley, CA 94720-1774
Ph: (510)643-5663
Fax: (510)643-6637
E-mail: jhuggins@eecs.berkeley.edu
Contact: Mr. John Huggins, Exec. Dir.

Founded: 1981. **Members:** 40. **Membership Dues:** industrial company, $50,000 (annual). **Staff:** 5. **Budget:** $7,500,000. **National Groups:** 3. **Languages:** English, Japanese. **Multinational. Description:** Researchers from 12 countries working in the field of solid-state sensors and actuators. (Sensors are devices such as thermometers or photometers that transmit electrical signals in response to stimuli; actuators are mechanisms such as motors or hydraulic valves that create motion indirectly corresponding to electrical command rather than manually.) Seeks to facilitate communication among members. **Libraries: Type:** open to the public. **Holdings:** 6,000; artwork, papers. **Subjects:** microelectronic. **Awards:** Best Paper Award. **Frequency:** semiannual. **Type:** recognition. **Boards:** Industrial Advisory. **Absorbed:** (1991) International Coordinating Committee on Solid State Transducers Research. **Publications:** *Digest of International Conference on Sensors and Actuators*, biennial. Includes research papers. **Conventions/Meetings:** biennial International Conference on Sensors and Actuators - meeting.

6928 ■ International Engineering Consortium (IEC)

300 W Adams St., Ste.1210
Chicago, IL 60606-5114
Ph: (312)559-4600
Fax: (312)559-4111
E-mail: info@iec.org
URL: http://www.iec.org
Contact: Mr. John R. Janowiak, Exec. Dir./Pres.

Founded: 1944. **Staff:** 50. **Description:** Aims to advance the field of engineering and contribute to the development and dissemination of engineering knowledge; to contribute to the professional development of engineers in practice by providing opportunities for continuing education; to attract and motivate students toward engineering careers; to provide a vehicle for member universities to engage in cooperative programs for their mutual benefit and the benefit of engineering internationally; to promote and develop cooperative programs between member universities and the community, business, industry, government, and professional societies. Conducts educational colloquia. **Libraries: Type:** not open to the public. **Holdings:** 150; books. **Subjects:** telecommunications reports. **Computer Services:** Online services. **Councils:** NEEDHA—National Electrical Engineering Department Heads Association. **Formerly:** National Engineering Consortium; (1978) National Electronics Conference. **Publications:** *Achieving the Triple Play: Technologies and Business Models for Success.* Book. Alternate Formats: CD-ROM ● *Annual Review of Communications*, annual. Journal. Contains papers on switching, lightwave, user issues, tele/CATV networks, telecommunications operations, information systems, and cellular networks. **Price:** $295.00/year. ISSN: 0886-229X. **Circulation:** 3,000. Alternate Formats: microform ● *The Basics of 802.11 Wireless LANs.* Book. Alternate Formats: CD-ROM ● *The Basics of Satellite Communications, 2nd Edition.* Book. Alternate Formats: CD-ROM ● *The Basics of Telecommunications, 5th Edition.* Book. Alternate Formats: CD-ROM ● *The Basics of VOIP.* Book. Alternate Formats: CD-ROM ● *The Broadband Millennium: Communication Technologies and Markets.* Book. Alternate Formats: CD-ROM ● *Design and Test for Multiple Gbps Communication Devices and Systems.* Book. Alternate Formats: CD-ROM ● *The*

Functional Verification of Electronic Systems. Book. Alternate Formats: CD-ROM. **Conventions/Meetings:** Comforum Symposia and Communication Forum - symposium (exhibits) ● workshop.

6929 ■ International Institute of Connector and Interconnection Technology (IICIT)
PO Box 399
Waretown, NJ 08758
Ph: (609)242-2445
E-mail: info@iicit.org
URL: http://www.iicit.org
Contact: Dale Reed, Pres.

Founded: 1958. **Members:** 2,000. **Membership Dues:** individual, $35 (annual) ● corporate, $1,200 (annual). **Staff:** 1. **Budget:** $500,000. **Regional Groups:** 15. **State Groups:** 9. **Description:** Electrical and electronic engineers, designers, technicians, manufacturers, and interconnection users. Objectives are to promote the electronic connector industry and provide for the exchange of technical information. **Libraries: Type:** open to the public. **Holdings:** periodicals. **Subjects:** annual symposium proceedings. **Telecommunication Services:** electronic mail, dreed@stratosintl.com. **Formerly:** Electronic Connector Study Group. **Publications:** *Connector and Interconnection Proceedings*, annual. **Price:** $100. 00. Alternate Formats: CD-ROM ● *Connectors and Interconnections.* Handbook ● Newsletter, quarterly. **Conventions/Meetings:** annual meeting and symposium (exhibits) ● monthly meeting and seminar.

6930 ■ International Microelectronic and Packaging Society (IMAPS)
611 2nd St. NE
Washington, DC 20002-4909
Ph: (202)548-4001 (202)548-8707
Fax: (202)548-6115
E-mail: imaps@imaps.org
URL: http://www.imaps.org
Contact: Michael O'Donoghue, Exec. Dir.

Founded: 1967. **Members:** 9,000. **Membership Dues:** individual, $75 (annual) ● corporate, $600 (annual) ● associate corporate, $250 (annual) ● affiliate corporate, $100 (annual) ● student, retired, $5 (annual). **Staff:** 8. **Regional Groups:** 5. **Local Groups:** 25. **Multinational. Description:** Electronics engineers and specialists in industry, business, and education. Encourages the exchange of information across boundaries of fields of specialization; supports close interactions between the complementary technologies of ceramics, thick and thin films, semiconductor packaging, discrete semiconductor devices, and monolithic circuits. Promotes and assists in the development and expansion of microelectronics instruction in schools and departments of electrical and electronic engineering. Conducts seminars at international, national, regional, and chapter levels. **Libraries: Type:** reference. **Holdings:** 150; articles, books, periodicals. **Subjects:** microelectronics. **Awards: Type:** fellowship ● Hughes Award. **Frequency:** annual. **Type:** recognition ● Tech Achievement Award. **Frequency:** annual. **Type:** recognition. **Telecommunication Services:** electronic mail, modonoghue@imaps.org. **Formerly:** (1997) International Society for Hybrid Microelectronics; (1998) International Microelectric and Packing Society. **Publications:** *Advancing Microelectronics*, bimonthly. Magazine. Includes calendar of events. **Price:** included in membership dues. **Advertising:** accepted. Alternate Formats: online ● *International Symposium Technical Proceedings*, annual ● *Journal of Microelectronics and Electronic Packaging*, quarterly. **Price:** $35.00 /year for members; $100.00 /year for nonmembers. **Conventions/Meetings:** annual International Symposium on Microelectronics - always in United States ● periodic meeting.

6931 ■ Semiconductor Environmental, Safety and Health Association (SESHA)
1313 Dolley Madison Blvd., Ste.402
McLean, VA 22101-3926
Ph: (703)790-1745
Fax: (703)790-2672
E-mail: sesha@burkinc.com
URL: http://seshaonline.org
Contact: Brett Burk, Exec. Dir.

Founded: 1978. **Members:** 2,300. **Membership Dues:** associate, $125 (annual) ● corporate, $300 (annual) ● student, $25 (annual). **Staff:** 2. **Budget:** $450,000. **Regional Groups:** 10. **Description:** Safety, health, and environmental workers in high technology industries. Provides continuing education courses. Maintains placement services. **Awards:** Lifetime Achievement Award. **Frequency:** annual. **Type:** recognition. **Recipient:** for dedication and achievement in advancing environmental, health and safety in the semiconductor industry ● SSA Scholarships. **Frequency:** annual. **Type:** scholarship. **Computer Services:** Mailing lists ● online services, forums. **Formerly:** (2002) Semiconductor Safety Association. **Publications:** *SSA Directory*, annual. **Price:** included in membership dues; $40.00 /year for nonmembers. **Circulation:** 1,500 ● *SSA Journal*, quarterly. **Price:** included in membership dues; $25.00 for nonmembers. **Circulation:** 2,000. **Advertising:** accepted. Alternate Formats: online. **Conventions/Meetings:** annual conference (exhibits) ● annual symposium.

6932 ■ Video Electronics Standards Association (VESA)
860 Hillview Ct., Ste.150
Milpitas, CA 95035
Ph: (408)957-9270
Fax: (408)957-9277
E-mail: info@vesa.org
URL: http://www.vesa.org
Contact: Bob Myers, Chm.

Founded: 1989. **Members:** 165. **Membership Dues:** corporate (based on sales revenue), $1,400-$7,000 (annual). **Staff:** 7. **Budget:** $1,000,000. **Multinational. Description:** Works to promote and establish standards for video electronic manufacturers. Conducts online forums; informs members of technological advances; and creates standards. **Telecommunication Services:** electronic mail, bill@vesa.org. **Committees:** Display Device; Display Systems; Japan; Marketing; Technical Review. **Working Groups:** DisplayID; DisplayPort; EDID; FDMI; MCCS; MDDI; Packet Video. **Publications:** *The VESA Monitor*, monthly. Newsletter. Alternate Formats: online ● *VESA Standards.* **Conventions/Meetings:** semiannual conference and trade show (exhibits).

Email

6933 ■ Coalition Against Unsolicited Commercial Email (CAUCE)
PO Box 727
Trumansburg, NY 14886
Ph: (303)800-6345
E-mail: press@cauce.org
URL: http://www.cauce.org
Contact: Neil Schwartzman, Exec. Dir.

Founded: 1998. **Members:** 15,624. **Staff:** 11. **Description:** Committed to a legislative solution to prohibit junk faxes and junk e-mail; works as the community voice for the anti-spam community. **Computer Services:** Mailing lists, open to nonmembers ● online services, SPAM-L list ● online services, SPAM-LAW list. **Publications:** Newsletter. Alternate Formats: online.

Energy

6934 ■ Alliance to Save Energy (ASE)
1850 M St. NW, Ste.600
Washington, DC 20036-5817
Ph: (202)857-0666
Fax: (202)331-9588
E-mail: info@ase.org
URL: http://www.ase.org
Contact: Kateri Callahan, Pres.

Founded: 1977. **Members:** 1,500. **Staff:** 60. **Multinational. Description:** Coalition of business, government, environmental, and consumer leaders who seek to increase the efficiency of energy use. Promotes energy efficiency worldwide to achieve a healthier economy, a cleaner environment, and a greater energy security. Conducts research, pilot projects, and educational programs. **Awards:** Star of Energy Efficiency. **Frequency:** annual. **Type:** recognition. **Recipient:** for an individual or a company that has demonstrated its commitment to energy efficiency through direct actions. **Telecommunication Services:** electronic mail, newell@ase.org. **Publications:** Annual Report, annual ● Also publishes reports, manuals, computer software, and other materials on energy topics. **Conventions/Meetings:** annual meeting.

6935 ■ Alternative Energy Resources Organization
432 N Last Chance Gulch St.
Helena, MT 59601-5014
Ph: (406)443-7272
Fax: (406)442-9120
E-mail: aero@aeromt.org
URL: http://www.aeromt.org
Contact: Jonda Crosby, Exec. Dir.

Founded: 1974. **Members:** 650. **Membership Dues:** family, $35 (annual) ● individual, $25 (annual) ● patron, $250 (annual) ● group, steward, $50 (annual) ● sustainer, $100 (annual) ● benefactor, $500 (annual). **Staff:** 4. **Budget:** $315,000. **Description:** Promotes sustainable agriculture, resource conservation and transportation choices through community education and citizen representation. Provides current programs that focus on sustainable agriculture, farm improvement clubs, beginning and retiring farmers, smart growth, and a more localized food system for greater community self-reliance. **Libraries: Type:** reference. **Holdings:** 1,500. **Subjects:** sustainable agriculture, gardening, alternative energy, rural communities, transportation and planning. **Awards:** Northern Rockies Sustainable Agriculture Award. **Frequency:** annual. **Type:** recognition. **Recipient:** for outstanding regional contributions in agriculture production and also agriculture researcher, educator, or advisor. **Computer Services:** database, regional sustainable agriculture, renewable energy and conservation, transportation, planning and sustainable development. **Telecommunication Services:** electronic mail, webmaster@aeromt.org. **Formerly:** (1997) Alternative Energy Resources Organization; (2003) AERO. **Publications:** *Abundant Montana*, annual. Directory. Contains a list of Montana growers for consumers to contact and purchase locally grown food. **Price:** free. **Circulation:** 4,000. **Advertising:** accepted ● *AERO Sun-Times*, quarterly. Magazine. **Price:** $15.00/year. ISSN: 1046-0993. **Circulation:** 600. **Advertising:** accepted ● *Big Sky or Big Sprawl Montana at the Crossroads.* Proceedings ● *Montana's Sustainable Agriculture Farming with Foresight.* Includes research results. ● *Sustainable Agriculture Curriculum-Grades 4-6.* Includes research results. **Conventions/Meetings:** annual meeting, gathering of AERO members for education and recreation with keynote speakers and workshops (exhibits) - alternates between summer and fall.

6936 ■ American Association of Blacks in Energy (AABE)
927 15th St. NW, Ste.200
Washington, DC 20005-2321
Ph: (202)371-9530
Free: (800)466-0204
Fax: (202)371-9218
E-mail: aabe@aabe.org
URL: http://www.aabe.org
Contact: Wilton Cedeno, Chm.

Founded: 1977. **Members:** 1,300. **Membership Dues:** individual, $100 (annual) ● student, $20 (annual) ● sustaining, $200 (annual). **Staff:** 3. **Budget:** $325,000. **Regional Groups:** 6. **Local Groups:** 35. **Description:** Seeks to increase the knowledge, understanding, and awareness of the minority community in energy issues by serving as an energy information source for policymakers, recommending blacks and other minorities to appropriate energy officials and executives, encouraging students to pursue professional careers in the energy industry, and advocating the participation of blacks and other minorities in energy programs and policymaking activities. Updates members on key legislation and regulations being developed by the Department of Energy, the Department of Interior, the Department of Commerce, the Small Business Administration, and other federal and state agencies. **Awards:** The Chairman's Cup. **Frequency:** annual. **Type:** recognition. **Recipient:** for exemplary contribution to the organization's growth ● James E. Stewart Award. **Frequency:** annual. **Type:** recognition. **Recipient:** for outstanding leadership in the energy industry. **Computer Services:** database, membership ● mailing lists, of members. **Telecommunication Services:** electronic mail, info@aabe.org. **Affiliated With:** National Association for the Advancement of Colored People; National Bar Association; National Urban League. **Publications:** *AABE Energy News*, quarterly. Newsletter. Contains key energy issues, chapter news, and organization opinions. **Price:** free. **Circulation:** 1,000. **Advertising:** accepted. Alternate Formats: CD-ROM. **Conventions/Meetings:** annual conference and seminar, for minority energy professionals (exhibits).

6937 ■ American Association for Fuel Cells
50 San Miguel Ave.
Daly City, CA 94015
Ph: (650)992-3963
E-mail: dickermn@earthlink.net
Contact: Thomas Dickerman, Chm.

Founded: 1992. **Members:** 20. **Membership Dues:** full, $20 (annual). **Budget:** $300. **Description:** Fuel cell engineers, scientists, and other interested individuals. Promotes public understanding of fuel cells and their environmental benefits. (A fuel cell is an electrical generator that continuously changes chemical energy of hydrogen or other fuel and an oxidant into electric energy, which results in less carbon dioxide emission and heat generation, reducing contribution to global warming and air pollution.) Provides information to the public; conducts educational programs. Provides communication within the fuel cell industry. **Libraries: Type:** not open to the public. **Holdings:** 100. **Subjects:** global warming, fuel cells, pollution, etc. **Formerly:** (2001) Stamps on Stamps - Centenary Unit.

6938 ■ American Council for an Energy-Efficient Economy (ACEEE)
1001 Connecticut Ave. NW, Ste.801
Washington, DC 20036
Ph: (202)429-8873
Fax: (202)429-2248
E-mail: info@aceee.org
URL: http://www.aceee.org
Contact: Steven Nadel, Exec. Dir.

Founded: 1980. **Staff:** 22. **Budget:** $2,500,000. **Description:** Collects, evaluates, and disseminates information to encourage the implementation of energy-efficient technologies and practices. Conducts research on energy conservation and links to environmental and economic issues. Sponsors conferences to facilitate the exchange of information among all interested groups. Provides utilities, federal, state, and local energy officials, private industry, and consumers with information on energy efficiency. **Libraries: Type:** reference. **Holdings:** books, periodicals. **Subjects:** energy efficiency/conservation. **Awards:** ACEEE Champion of Energy Efficiency. **Frequency:** annual. **Type:** recognition. **Recipient:** peer nomination followed by committee selection. **Computer Services:** Mailing lists. **Publications:** *ACEEE Series on Energy Conservation and Energy Policy*. Books ● *ACEEE Summer Study on Energy Efficiency in Buildings*, biennial. Proceedings. Contains conference proceedings and research papers. Also Cited As: *American Council for an Energy Efficient Economy—Proceedings* ● *ACEEE's Green Book*. **Price:** $19.95/year online subscription; $8.95 30 days online subscription. Alternate Formats: online ● *Consumer Guide to Home Energy Savings* ● *The Environmental Guide to Cars and Trucks* ● *Publications Catalog*. **Conventions/Meetings:** biennial Summer Study on Energy Efficiency in Buildings - conference (exhibits) - always even years ● biennial Summer Study on Energy Efficiency in Industry - conference - always summer in odd years ● annual symposium.

6939 ■ American Council on Renewable Energy (ACORE)
PO Box 33518
Washington, DC 20033-3518
Ph: (202)393-0001
Fax: (202)393-0606
E-mail: info@acore.org
URL: http://www.acore.org
Contact: Michael T. Eckhart, Pres.

Founded: 2001. **Membership Dues:** organization (for-profit), $350-$3,000 (annual) ● organization (non-profit), $250-$1,500 (annual). **Description:** Accelerates the adoption of renewable energy technologies into the mainstream of American society. Promotes renewable energy options for the production of electricity, hydrogen, fuels and end-use energy. Promotes renewable energy solutions to the American public through outreach and education. **Boards:** Advisory. **Committees:** Steering. **Publications:** *ACORE News*, quarterly. Newsletter. Alternate Formats: online ● *Renewable Energy in America*, annual. Annual Report. Features renewable energy communities forecast.

6940 ■ American Hydrogen Association (AHA)
2350 W Shangri La Rd.
Phoenix, AZ 85029-4724
Ph: (602)328-4238
E-mail: 123goh2@gmail.com
URL: http://www.clean-air.org
Contact: Roy E. McAlister, Pres.

Founded: 1989. **Members:** 8,000. **Membership Dues:** family, $40 (annual) ● regular, $39 (annual) ● student/senior, $25 (annual) ● sustaining, $100 (annual) ● corporate sponsor, $1,000 (annual) ● life, $1,000. **State Groups:** 9. **Local Groups:** 3. **Multinational. Description:** Individuals interested in renewable natural resources. Advocates a transition from fossil and nuclear energy sources to solar-hydrogen technologies in order to help resolve environmental problems such as global warming, acid rain, ozone depletion, and urban air pollution. Promotes energy alternatives such as the production of hydrogen from sewage and garbage and the generation of electricity from solar power. Sponsors educational and charitable programs. Conducts research; compiles statistics. Operates placement service. Maintains speakers' bureau. **Libraries: Type:** reference. **Holdings:** 4,800. **Subjects:** thermodynamics, physics, chemistry, math, hydrology, wildlife conservation, environmental topics, weather, oceanography. **Awards:** Star of Life Award. **Frequency:** annual. **Type:** recognition. **Recipient:** to students for posters, essays, and projects concerning the quest to overcome dependence upon burning over one million years of fossil accumulations each year. **Additional Websites:** http://www.americanhydrogenassociation.org. **Study Groups:** Brown Cloud Busters. **Publications:** *Fuel from Water: Energy Independence with Hydrogen*. Book ● *Hydrogen Today*. Newsletter. Alternate Formats: online ● *The Philosopher Mechanic*. Book ● *Philosopher Mechanic - Hydrogen Conversion Classnotes*. Book ● *Renewable Engines*. Book ● *Solar Hydrogen Civilization: The Future of Energy is the Future of our Economy*. Book ● *Solar-Hydrogen Economy*. Video. Alternate Formats: CD-ROM ● *The Star of Life*. Book. **Conventions/Meetings:** competition ● annual meeting.

6941 ■ American Society of Gas Engineers (ASGE)
PO Box 66
Artesia, CA 90702
Ph: (949)733-4304
Fax: (949)733-4320
E-mail: asgecge@sbcglobal.net
URL: http://www.asge-national.org
Contact: Jerry Moore CGE, Exec. Dir.

Founded: 1954. **Members:** 280. **Membership Dues:** junior, $30 (annual) ● associate, $35 (annual) ● voting, $50 (annual). **Staff:** 1. **Budget:** $25,000. **Regional Groups:** 6. **State Groups:** 6. **Description:** Serves as professional society of engineers in the field of gas appliances and equipment. **Awards:** Founders Award. **Frequency:** annual. **Type:** recognition. **Formerly:** (1975) Gas Appliance Engineers Society. **Publications:** *ASGE News*, quarterly. Newsletter ● Membership Directory, biennial. **Conventions/Meetings:** annual conference.

6942 ■ Association of Energy Engineers (AEE)
4025 Pleasantdale Rd., Ste.420
Atlanta, GA 30340
Ph: (770)447-5083
Fax: (770)446-3969
E-mail: info@aeecenter.org
URL: http://www.aeecenter.org
Contact: Albert Thumann, Exec. Dir.

Founded: 1977. **Members:** 9,000. **Membership Dues:** individual, affiliate, senior, $165 (annual) ● student, retired, $15 (annual) ● corporate, $1,095 (annual) ● life, $995. **Staff:** 12. **Local Groups:** 63. **Multinational. Description:** Engineers, architects, and other professionals with an interest in energy management and cogeneration; manufacturers and industries involved in energy. Promotes the advancement of the profession and contributes to the professional development of members. Sponsors Cogeneration and Competitive Power Institute, Environmental Engineers and Managers Institute, and Demand-Side Management Society. **Awards: Type:** scholarship. **Recipient:** for outstanding students in energy engineering. **Telecommunication Services:** electronic mail, patty@aeecenter.org. **Councils:** National Energy Policy. **Absorbed:** National Association of Professionals in Energy Conservation; (1984) Total Energy Management Professionals; (1986) Energy Management and Controls Society. **Publications:** *The Cogeneration and Distributed Power Journal*, periodic ● *Energy Engineering Journal*, periodic ● *Energy Insight*. Alternate Formats: online ● *Energy Services Marketing News*, 3/year. Newsletter. Alternate Formats: online ● *Environmental Engineers and Managers Institute News*, 3/year. Newsletter. Contains integrated approach to pollution prevention. Alternate Formats: online ● *Facility Managers Institute News*, 3/year. Newsletter. Contains integrated approach to plant management, security and safety issues, and overall facility management. Alternate Formats: online ● *Renewable Energy Development Institute News*, 3/year. Newsletter. Contains state-of-the-art technological advances in solar, wind, biomass, and other alternative energy resources. Alternate Formats: online ● *Strategic Planning for Energy and the Environment*. Journal. **Conventions/Meetings:** annual GLOBALCON Expo - conference, trade event for latest technologies (exhibits) ● High Performance Facilities Expo - congress (exhibits) ● annual West Coast Energy Management Congress - conference, for business, industrial, and institutional energy users (exhibits) ● World Energy Engineering Congress.

6943 ■ Association of Energy Services Professionals (AESP)
4809 E Thistle Landing Dr., Ste.100
Phoenix, AZ 85044
Ph: (480)704-5900
Fax: (480)704-5905
E-mail: meg@aesp.org
URL: http://www.aesp.org
Contact: Meg Matt, Pres./CEO

Founded: 1989. **Members:** 2,000. **Membership Dues:** individual, $195 (annual) ● group, $2,000-$10,000 (annual). **Staff:** 3. **Budget:** $700,000. **Regional Groups:** 3. **Description:** Advances the professional interests of individuals working to provide value through energy services and energy efficiency by sharing ideas, information, and experience. Conducts training courses. **Computer Services:** database ● online services. **Formerly:** (2000) Association of Energy Services Professionals. **Publications:** *Strategies*, monthly. Newsletter. Covers case studies, updates on ongoing issues, notes on personnel changes in the field, and updates on the latest technologies. **Price:** free for members. **Advertising:** accepted. Alternate Formats: online ● Membership Directory, weekly. Lists the names, addresses, and telephone numbers of members. Alternate Formats: online ● conference proceedings and various reports. **Conventions/Meetings:** annual National Energy Services Conference - meeting and conference (exhibits) - every December.

6944 ■ Association of Professional Energy Managers (APEM)
3916 W Oak St., Ste.D
Burbank, CA 91505
Ph: (818)972-2159
Fax: (818)972-2863
E-mail: buschre@earthlink.net
URL: http://www.apem.org
Contact: Mark Martinez, Chm.
Founded: 1982. **Members:** 600. **Membership Dues:** regular, $125 (annual). **Regional Groups:** 6. **Description:** Seeks to further the understanding and practice of sound energy management principles. Conducts professional seminars and special events to encourage professional networking and information exchange. Provides access to ideas, individuals, and technologies that impact the energy management profession. **Computer Services:** Mailing lists, of members. **Telecommunication Services:** 24-hour hotline, (213)700-9171. **Publications:** *Association of Professional Energy Managers Membership Directory*, annual ● *Professional Energy Manager*, bimonthly. Newsletter. Covers energy management strategies and technologies. Includes Association news, calendar of events, member profiles, and chapter news. **Price:** $18.00/year. **Advertising:** accepted. **Conventions/Meetings:** annual conference - always fall ● annual meeting - always spring.

6945 ■ Association of State Energy Research and Technology Transfer Institutions (ASERTTI)
c/o Sherry Benzmiller, Admin.
455 Sci. Dr., Ste.200
Madison, WI 53711
Ph: (608)238-4601
E-mail: sbenzmiller@ecw.org
URL: http://www.asertti.org
Contact: David Terry, Exec. Dir.
Description: Promotes the research, development, demonstration, and deployment (RDD&D) of advanced energy technologies that can contribute to economic growth, environmental quality and energy security and reliability in the US. Facilitates collaboration and the development of working relationships with state, federal, and private partners to serve the public interest in energy. Provides technical and operational information among members and associates. **Telecommunication Services:** electronic mail, dterry@statelineenergy.org.

6946 ■ Biomass Energy Research Association (BERA)
901 D St. SW, Ste.100
Washington, DC 20024
Ph: (847)381-6320
Free: (800)247-1755
Fax: (847)382-5595
E-mail: beraorg2@excite.com
URL: http://www.bera1.org/indexnorm.html
Contact: Ms. Joan Pellegrino, Acting Pres./Treas./Dir.
Founded: 1982. **Members:** 200. **Membership Dues:** individual, $30 (annual) ● corporate or company, $300 (annual) ● individual, $50 (biennial) ● non-profit society, college/university, $200 (annual). **Staff:** 12. **Description:** Corporations and individuals from universities, public utilities, industries, and research laboratories with a common interest in encouraging biomass and waste-to-energy and fuels research and commercialization. Facilitates technology transfer, information exchange, and education in biomass energy research; promotes international cooperation in biomass energy research. Maintains speakers' and consultants' bureau. Provides proposal and publication review services. Develops recommendations on budgets to congressional committees. **Libraries: Type:** reference. **Awards:** BERA Award. **Type:** monetary. **Recipient:** for outstanding biomass research or commercialization activities. **Telecommunication Services:** electronic mail, bera1@excite.com. **Publications:** Directory. Lists commercial suppliers and systems. ● Reports, annual ● Papers ● Also maintains affiliation with *Bioresource Technology* (journal). **Conventions/Meetings:** annual board meeting ● bimonthly luncheon.

6947 ■ Center for Energy Policy and Research (CEPR)
c/o New York Institute of Technology
Dept. of Energy Mgt.
Harry Schure Hall, Rm. 116
Old Westbury, NY 11568-8000
Ph: (516)686-7578
E-mail: ramundse@nyit.edu
URL: http://iris.nyit.edu/energymanagement
Contact: Dr. Robert N. Amundsen, Dir.
Founded: 1975. **Staff:** 5. **Description:** Established by the New York Institute of Technology as a major facility designed to disseminate information and conduct research into energy utilization and conservation, and to assist public, quasi-public, and private sector organizations in the practical use of present and future findings in the energy field. Conducts Master of Science in Energy Management and specialized professional certificate programs through NYIT's School of Engineering and Technology to provide interdisciplinary training in the technological, economic, sociological, and administrative skills required to implement new approaches to energy conversion and utilization. **Publications:** none. **Conventions/Meetings:** seminar.

6948 ■ Clean Energy Group (CEG)
50 State St., Ste.1
Montpelier, VT 05602
Ph: (802)223-2554
Fax: (802)223-4967
E-mail: lmilford@cleanegroup.org
URL: http://www.cleanegroup.org
Contact: Lewis Milford, Pres./CEO/Founder
Founded: 1998. **Description:** Promotes the use of cleaner energy technologies, such as fuel cells and solar, in newly restructed energy markets. Provides information, advocacy and analysis to develop market opportunities for clean energy. Promotes policies and programs that support replacement of the existing electricity generation system with new, less polluting clean energy technologies in the U.S. and abroad. **Publications:** Reports. Alternate Formats: online.

6949 ■ Clean Energy States Alliance (CESA)
c/o Clean Energy Group
50 State St., Ste.1
Montpelier, VT 05602
Ph: (802)223-2554
Fax: (802)223-4967
E-mail: lmilford@cleanegroup.org
URL: http://www.cleanenergystates.org
Contact: Lewis Milford, Exec. Dir.
Founded: 2003. **Description:** Aims to increase the quality and quantity of clean energy deals to greatly expand the clean energy market. Promotes clean energy technologies. Provides information and technical services to its members and works with them to build and expand clean energy markets in the United States. Collects and disseminates information and analysis, conducts original research, and helps to coordinate activities of the state funds. **Publications:** Report, biennial. Alternate Formats: online. **Conventions/Meetings:** monthly conference - every 3rd Friday except August.

6950 ■ Electric Power Supply Association (EPSA)
1401 New York Ave. NW, 11th Fl.
Washington, DC 20005-2110
Ph: (202)628-8200
Fax: (202)628-8260
URL: http://www.epsa.org
Contact: John E. Shelk, Pres./CEO
Founded: 1997. **Members:** 98. **Membership Dues:** associate, $40,000 (annual) ● supporting, $12,000 (annual) ● state/regional partner, $500 (annual). **Staff:** 19. **Budget:** $4,400,000. **Description:** Represents competitive power suppliers, including generators and power marketers. Provides reliable, competitively priced electricity from environmentally responsible facilities serving global power markets. Seeks to bring the benefits of competition to all power customers. **Committees:** Environment; Ethics; Legislative Affairs; Public Affairs; Regulatory Affairs; Renewables; State Issues. **Formed by Merger of:** (1997) Electric Generation Association; (1997) National Independent Energy Producers. **Publications:** *EPSA Report*, quarterly. Newsletter. **Price:** free. **Circulation:** 2,600. Alternate Formats: online.

6951 ■ Energy Efficiency and Renewable Energy Information Center (EERE)
Dept. of Energy
Mail Stop EE-1
Washington, DC 20585
Ph: (202)586-9220
Free: (877)337-3463
E-mail: eere.ba@ee.doe.gov
URL: http://www.eere.energy.gov
Contact: Alexander Karsner, Asst. Sec.
Founded: 1976. **Staff:** 10. **Languages:** English, Spanish. **Description:** Provides information and technical assistance on energy efficiency and renewable energy technologies; operated by NCI Information Systems, Inc., for the U.S. Department of Energy, Office of Energy Efficiency and Renewable Energy, under contract to the National Renewable Energy Laboratory. **Convention/Meeting:** none. **Libraries: Type:** not open to the public. **Holdings:** 6,000. **Subjects:** passive and active solar energy, energy efficiency, wind, small-scale hydroelectric. **Computer Services:** database ● information services ● online services, copies of some fact sheets and description of services. **Programs:** Biomass; Building Technologies; Federal Energy Management; FreedomCAR and Vehicle Technologies; Geothermal Technologies; Hydrogen, Fuel Cells and Infrastructure Technologies; Industrial Technologies; Wind and Hydropower Technologies. **Formed by Merger of:** (1994) Conservation and Renewable Energy Inquiry and Referral Service; (1994) National Appropriate Technology Assistance Service. **Formerly:** (1981) National Solar Heating and Cooling.

6952 ■ Energy Future Coalition
1800 Massachusetts Ave. NW, Ste.400
Washington, DC 20036
Ph: (202)463-1947
Fax: (202)887-9021
E-mail: info@energyfuturecoalition.org
URL: http://www.energyfuturecoalition.org
Contact: Reid Detchon, Exec. Dir.
Founded: 2002. **Description:** Seeks to bridge the differences among business, labor, and environmental groups. Aims to bring about changes to U.S. energy policy. Addresses the economic, security and environmental challenges related to the production and use of fossil fuels.

6953 ■ EPRI
3420 Hillview Ave.
Palo Alto, CA 94304
Ph: (650)855-2121 (650)855-2000
Free: (800)313-3774
Fax: (704)595-2871
E-mail: askepri@epri.com
URL: http://www.epri.com/default.asp
Contact: Mr. Steven R. Specker, Pres./CEO
Founded: 1973. **Members:** 1,000. **Staff:** 850. **Description:** All sectors of the electric utility industry. Aims to conduct a broad economically and environmentally acceptable program of research and development in technologies for electric power production, transmission, distribution, and utilization. Focuses on advanced power systems, coal combustion systems, electrical systems, energy analysis and environment, energy management and utilization, and nuclear power. **Libraries: Type:** reference; not open to the public. **Computer Services:** database, summaries of ongoing and completed research in the electric power industry. **Formerly:** (1998) Electric Power Research Institute. **Publications:** *EPRI Online Journal*. Contains continuous and updated summary of energy

R&D for technical and lay audiences. **Price:** free for members. Alternate Formats: online.

6954 ■ Fusion Power Associates (FPA)
2 Professional Dr., Ste.249
Gaithersburg, MD 20879
Ph: (301)258-0545
Fax: (301)975-9869
E-mail: fpa@compuserve.com
URL: http://www.fusionpower.org
Contact: Stephen O. Dean, Pres.
Founded: 1979. **Members:** 400. **Membership Dues:** institutional, $1,800 (annual) ● small business affiliate, $500 (annual) ● institutional affiliate, $1,000 (annual) ● individual affiliate, $60 (annual) ● student affiliate, $15 (annual). **Staff:** 2. **Multinational. Description:** Industry, utility, university, and laboratory groups and others interested in the development of fusion energy. (Fusion energy is created by heating deuterium and tritium atoms to over 100 million degrees. The atomic nuclei, driven into each other, fuse and release energy that can be used for a variety of applications, including the generation of electricity.) Seeks to encourage and promote the development of fusion power as a viable energy option for the future. Fosters cooperation in fusion research and development among public and private organizations; works to establish increased public awareness and understanding of the potential of fusion energy. Sees fusion energy as an "inexhaustible, cost-effective, environmentally safe energy source." Presents testimony at congressional authorization and appropriations hearings on fusion budgets; provides information to Executive Branch review committees; testifies before platform committees; presents addresses and survey papers at professional, scientific, and engineering society meetings. Conducts research programs aimed at assisting the technical progress of fusion development, especially fusion reactor design studies. **Awards:** Distinguished Career. **Frequency:** annual. **Type:** recognition ● Excellence in Fusion Engineering. **Frequency:** annual. **Type:** recognition. **Recipient:** for persons who have shown outstanding technical accomplishment and leadership potential ● Leadership. **Frequency:** annual. **Type:** recognition. **Recipient:** for those who have made major contributions to the development of fusion energy. **Subgroups:** Coalition for Plasma Science; Education. **Publications:** *Executive Newsletter*, bimonthly. Contains current events in fusion research. **Price:** $50.00 /year for individuals; $250.00 /year for libraries. **Circulation:** 1,500 ● *Fusion Power Report*, bimonthly. Newsletter. **Price:** $795.00/year. **Circulation:** 50 ● *Fusion Program Notes*, periodic. Bulletin. Features email notes on breaking news. **Price:** $60.00. **Circulation:** 500 ● Also disseminates audiovisual information. **Conventions/Meetings:** annual meeting and symposium, discusses status of fusion program for program managers ● symposium, for persons involved with fusion research.

6955 ■ Institute for Energy and Environmental Research (IEER)
6935 Laurel Ave., Ste.201
Takoma Park, MD 20912
Ph: (301)270-5500
Fax: (301)270-3029
E-mail: ieer@ieer.org
URL: http://www.ieer.org
Contact: Arjun Makhijani PhD, Pres.
Description: Works to bring scientific excellence to public policy issues to promote the democratization of science and a safer, healthier environment. **Projects:** Global Outreach. **Publications:** *Atomic Audit*. Book. **Price:** $40.00 plus shipping and handling ● *Climate Change and Transnational Corporations: Analysis and Trends*. Book. **Price:** $10.00 plus shipping and handling ● *Ecology and Genetics*. Book. **Price:** $8.95 plus shipping and handling. Alternate Formats: online ● *Fissile Materials in a Glass, Darkly*. Book. **Price:** $12.00 plus shipping and handling ● *High-Level Dollars, Low-Level Sense*. Book. **Price:** $15.00 plus shipping and handling ● *Manifesto for Global Democracy*. Book. **Price:** $21.95 plus shipping and handling ● *Mending the Ozone Hole*. Book. **Price:** $55.00 plus shipping and handling ● *The Nuclear Power Deception*. Book. **Price:** $19.95 plus shipping and handling ● *Nuclear Wastelands*. Book. **Price:** $52.00 plus shipping and handling ● *Plutonium: Deadly Gold of the Nuclear Age*. Book. **Price:** $10.00 plus shipping and handling ● *Rule of Power or Rule of Law?*. Book. **Price:** $21.95 plus shipping and handling ● *Science for Democratic Action*, quarterly. Newsletter. Alternate Formats: online ● Reports. Alternate Formats: online.

6956 ■ International Association for Energy Economics (IAEE)
28790 Chagrin Blvd., Ste.350
Cleveland, OH 44122-4630
Ph: (216)464-5365
Fax: (216)464-2737
E-mail: iaee@iaee.org
URL: http://www.iaee.org
Contact: David L. Williams, Exec. Dir.
Founded: 1977. **Members:** 3,400. **Membership Dues:** individual, $65 (annual) ● institution/company, $1,250 (annual) ● full-time student, $35 (annual). **Staff:** 2. **Budget:** $200,000. **Regional Groups:** 34. **State Groups:** 10. **Local Groups:** 10. **Description:** Individuals employed by consulting and research organizations, government, universities, and the energy industries that are professionally interested in energy economics. Provides a forum for professional communication and exchange of experience among energy economists from different countries. Maintains Energy Economics Educational Foundation. **Awards: Frequency:** annual. **Type:** recognition. **Recipient:** for outstanding contributions to the energy economics profession, energy economics literature, and written journalism on topics relating to energy economics. **Formerly:** (1988) International Association of Energy Economists. **Publications:** *Conference Proceedings*, biennial ● *Energy Journal*, quarterly. **Price:** $175.00 in U.S.; $200.00 outside U.S. **Circulation:** 4,000. **Advertising:** accepted ● *The IAEE Newsletter*, quarterly. Announces coming events, gives details of chapter news, and contains articles on a wide range of energy economics issues. **Advertising:** accepted ● Membership Directory, annual. Lists members around the world noting their affiliation, specialization, address, and telephone/fax numbers. **Price:** $109.95. **Circulation:** 3,500. **Advertising:** accepted. **Conventions/Meetings:** semiannual meeting (exhibits).

6957 ■ International Association for Hydrogen Energy (IAHE)
5783 SW 40 St., No. 303
Miami, FL 33155
Ph: (305)284-4666
Fax: (305)284-4792
E-mail: ayfer@iahe.org
URL: http://www.iahe.org
Contact: T. Nejat Veziroglu, Pres.
Founded: 1974. **Members:** 2,500. **Membership Dues:** fast service country, $160 (annual) ● regular service country, $90 (annual) ● fast service country (associate), $110 (annual) ● regular service country (associate), $70 (annual) ● fast service country (emeritus), $80 (annual) ● regular service country (emeritus), $45 (annual) ● fast service country (institutional), $1,100 (annual) ● regular service country (institutional), $700 (annual). **Staff:** 4. **Budget:** $150,000. **National Groups:** 10. **Multinational. Description:** Scientists, engineers, students, educational institutions, professional societies, and corporate groups involved with the use of hydrogen as an energy carrier. Promotes discussion and publication of ideas furthering realization of a clean, inexhaustible energy system based on hydrogen. Organizes independent and joint research projects, short courses, and conferences on various aspects of hydrogen energy. **Libraries: Type:** not open to the public. **Holdings:** 300; books, periodicals. **Subjects:** hydrogen energy system. **Awards: Frequency:** biennial. **Type:** recognition. **Recipient:** for distinguished individual in Hydrogen Energy Field. **Boards:** Advisory; Directors; Editorial; Emeritus; Honorary Editorial. **Publications:** *Hydrogen Energy technologies*, published as necessary. Book. Includes overview of technologies for hydrogen production, storage, transportation and utilization. **Price:** $30.00 for nonmembers; $21.00 for members (booksellers). Alternate Formats: online ● *International Journal of Hydrogen Energy*, monthly. Publishes scientific papers in hydrogen energy. **Price:** free for members; $1,026.00 for libraries. ISSN: 0360-3199. **Circulation:** 2,500. **Advertising:** accepted ● *Solar Hydrogen Energy*, published as necessary. Book. **Price:** $30.00 for nonmembers; $21.00 for members. Alternate Formats: online. **Conventions/Meetings:** biennial World Hydrogen Energy Conference (exhibits) - even years. 2008 June 15-19, Brisbane, QL, Australia; 2010 May 16-21, Essen, Germany ● biennial World Hydrogen Technologies Convention - odd years.

6958 ■ International Institute for Energy Conservation (IIEC)
10005 Leamoore Ln., No. 100
Vienna, VA 22181
Ph: (703)281-7263
Fax: (703)938-5153
E-mail: iiecdc@iiec.org
URL: http://www.iiec.org
Contact: Nitin Pandit PhD, Pres.
Founded: 1984. **Staff:** 50. **Budget:** $3,000,000. **Multinational. Description:** Works to encourage, implement, and improve energy efficiency in developing countries. Facilitates the acquisition of energy conserving technologies and policies. Disseminates information; conducts training and education programs. **Libraries: Type:** open to the public. **Holdings:** 6,000. **Subjects:** energy conservation, transportation, climate change. **Publications:** *E-Notes*, quarterly. Newsletter. Contains news on innovative approaches to energy efficiency, climate change, and sustainable transport throughout the world. **Price:** free. **Circulation:** 5,000. Alternate Formats: online ● Also produces many publications on topics related to energy efficiency in developing countries.

6959 ■ Interstate Renewable Energy Council (IREC)
PO Box 1156
Latham, NY 12110-1156
Ph: (518)458-6059
Fax: (518)458-6059
E-mail: info@irecusa.org
URL: http://www.irecusa.org
Contact: Jane Weissman, Exec. Dir.
Founded: 1980. **Membership Dues:** corporate, government agency (state, local, county, federal), $500 (annual) ● non-profit organization, $250 (annual) ● community (school, faith-based, etc.), $75 (annual) ● individual, $50 (annual) ● sponsoring, $1,000 (annual) ● sustaining, $1,500 (annual). **Staff:** 13. **Description:** Works to advance the sustainable use of renewable energy sources and technologies in and through state and local government and community activities. **Awards:** Innovation Awards. **Frequency:** annual. **Type:** recognition. **Recipient:** for state and local governments, schools, nonprofit and community groups that have implemented innovative projects ● Renewable Energy Recognition Awards. **Frequency:** annual. **Type:** recognition. **Programs:** Community Outreach; Database of State Incentives for Renewable Energy; Going Solar; Schools Going Solar Initiative; Workshop-in-a-Box. **Projects:** Certification; Connecting to the Grid; PV National Consumer. **Publications:** *IREC Interconnection*, monthly. Newsletter. **Price:** free. Alternate Formats: online ● *IREC/MSR Community Outreach E-Newsletter*. **Price:** free. Alternate Formats: online ● *Small Wind Energy E-Newsletter*, bimonthly. **Price:** free. Alternate Formats: online ● Videos.

6960 ■ National Association of Energy Service Companies (NAESCO)
1615 M St. NW, Ste.900
Washington, DC 20036-3224
Ph: (202)822-0950
Fax: (202)822-0955
E-mail: info@naesco.org
URL: http://www.naesco.org
Contact: Donald Gilligan, Pres.
Founded: 1983. **Members:** 115. **Membership Dues:** energy service company (with gross revenues of

more than $25 million), $13,500 (annual) ● energy service affiliate, $6,000 (annual) ● associate energy service affiliate (with less than $1 million annual revenue) and international, $3,000 (annual) ● public sector, $250 (annual) ● energy service company (with gross revenues between $15-25 million), $6,000 (annual) ● energy service company (with gross revenues less than $15 million), $9,000 (annual). **Staff:** 4. **Description:** Firms involved in the design, manufacturing, financing, and installation of energy efficiency equipment and the provision of energy services in the public and private sectors. Provides industry representation at all government levels. Seeks to inform the public regarding performance contracting and financing of alternative energy and energy conservation programs. Promotes the development, growth, and status of the energy service industry. Serves as an information clearinghouse.

6961 ■ National Energy Management Institute (NEMI)
601 N Fairfax St., Ste.250
Alexandria, VA 22314
Ph: (703)739-7100
Free: (800)458-6525
Fax: (703)683-7615
E-mail: tkuczynski@sheetmetal_iti.org
URL: http://www.nemionline.org
Contact: Ted Kuczynski, Exec. Admin.
Founded: 1981. **Members:** 200. **Staff:** 40. **State Groups:** 11. **Description:** Seeks to eliminate barriers to energy efficiency. Offers building owners and managers a warranty program that guarantees energy cost savings will pay for the cost of their retrofit project (processes for making structures more energy efficient) and no comfort or aesthetic variables will be diminished. Operates an indoor air quality program, which analyzes the air quality of buildings. State groups sponsor seminars on energy. **Affiliated With:** Sheet Metal and Air Conditioning Contractors' National Association. **Publications:** *TABB Talk*, quarterly. Newsletter.

6962 ■ National Energy Services Association (NESA)
6430 FM 1960 W, No. 213
Houston, TX 77069
Ph: (713)856-6525
Fax: (713)856-6199
E-mail: tcummins@nesanet.org
URL: http://www.nesanet.org
Contact: Tracy Cummins, Contact
Members: 2,300. **Membership Dues:** individual, $100 (annual). **Description:** Individuals employed in the natural gas, electrical power, and financial services industries. Seeks to improve the delivery of energy services throughout the United States. Facilitates communication and cooperation among members; assists in the development and implementation of public and private energy systems; encourages adherence to high standards of ethics and practice by members; develops energy delivery standards. Conducts educational and technical training programs. **Committees:** Education; Energy Expo; Planning; Publications; Technology. **Publications:** *NESA Energy Journal*, periodic ● Membership Directory, annual ● Newsletter, periodic. **Conventions/Meetings:** annual Houston Energy Expo - trade show ● annual meeting - always in September ● periodic regional meeting.

6963 ■ National Food and Energy Council (NFEC)
PO Box 309
Wilmington, OH 45177-0309
Ph: (937)383-0001
Fax: (937)383-0003
E-mail: info@nfec.org
URL: http://www.nfec.org
Contact: Richard S. Hiatt PE, Pres./Exec. Mgr.
Founded: 1957. **Members:** 250. **Membership Dues:** general, $550-$2,100 (annual) ● statewide association, $600 (annual) ● equipment supplier, $375 (annual) ● group, $3,100 (annual) ● holding company, $4,000 (annual). **Staff:** 4. **Budget:** $250,000. **State Groups:** 15. **Description:** Electric power suppliers (companies, cooperatives, and power districts); electrical equipment manufacturers and distributors. Works to inform and educate consumers regarding the critical interdependence of energy and food and the heavy inter-reliance of the food and energy industries. Encourages wise conservation, prudent management, and logical substitution of available energy supplies for future food production and processing. **Awards:** Distinguished Service Award. **Frequency:** annual. **Type:** recognition. **Recipient:** for an individual who has contributed to customer education and rural community ● Silver Switch Award. **Frequency:** annual. **Type:** recognition. **Recipient:** for well organized programs. **Computer Services:** Online services, computerized interactive wiring programs. **Formerly:** (1962) Inter-Industry Farm Electric Utilization Council; (1976) Farm Electrification Council; (1982) Food and Energy Council. **Publications:** *Agricultural Wiring Handbook* ● *Current Marketing Newsletter*, bimonthly. Covers energy management and marketing programs, new technologies, and electrical farm applications of interest to electric power suppliers. **Price:** included in membership dues; $35.00 for nonmembers ● *Electrical Wiring for Livestock and Poultry Structures* ● *National Food and Energy Council—News and Notes*, bimonthly. Newsletter. Covers the Council's energy management/marketing educational efforts on behalf of agriculture and the electricity supply industry. **Price:** included in membership dues. **Advertising:** accepted ● Booklets. **Conventions/Meetings:** annual conference (exhibits).

6964 ■ National Hydropower Association (NHA)
One Massachusetts Ave. NW, Ste.850
Washington, DC 20001
Ph: (202)682-1700
Fax: (202)682-9478
E-mail: help@hydro.org
URL: http://www.hydro.org
Contact: Linda Church Ciocci, Exec. Dir.
Founded: 1983. **Members:** 140. **Membership Dues:** supporting, $1,428 (annual) ● equipment and service provider/generator (leadership level), $9,286 (annual) ● equipment and service provider (contributing level), $4,432 (annual) ● generator (contributing level), $4,642 (annual). **Staff:** 6. **Budget:** $1,000,000. **Languages:** English, Italian, Spanish. **Description:** Represents hydrodevelopers, dam site owners, manufacturers, utilities and municipalities, individuals from the financial community (such as bankers, brokers, and investors), civil contracting firms, architects, engineering firms, and others actively involved in the promotion and development of hydropower. Promotes the development of hydroelectric energy. Participates in the regulatory process on issues such as simplified licensing procedures, purchase power rates, removal of regulatory barriers, and timely implementation of previously adopted legislation. Informs the government about the potential of hydropower and also monitors and drafts new legislation to government regulatory and legislative bodies. **Awards:** Henwood Award. **Frequency:** annual. **Type:** recognition ● Industry Achievement Award. **Frequency:** annual. **Type:** recognition. **Recipient:** for achievement in one of four categories. **Committees:** Hydraulic Power; International Affairs; Legal; Legislative Affairs; Public Education; Regulatory Affairs; Research and Development. **Publications:** *NHA Today*, bimonthly. Newsletter. Contains the latest information on regulatory and legislative policy, regional concerns and issues on the horizon. **Price:** free for members. **Circulation:** 150. Alternate Formats: online ● Also publishes legislative alerts. **Conventions/Meetings:** annual conference (exhibits) - always April.

6965 ■ National Old Timers' Association of the Energy Industry (NOTAEI)
Address Unknown since 2007
Founded: 1926. **Members:** 1,000. **Staff:** 1. **Description:** Current or past officers and presidents with a minimum of ten years' participation in a national or regional association in the energy industry. Objectives are: to explore new areas of education and interleadership in the energy industry; to promote greater coordination on joint projects; to work with governmental agencies to develop new trends in training programs. Activities include: printing manuals for educational distribution to trade schools; maintaining a speakers' bureau on technical subjects; serving on governmental agency advisory councils to make recommendations; working within trade associations on research and development. Maintains Hall of Flame. Plans to establish a national oil heating industry museum. **Awards:** Distinguished Service. **Frequency:** annual. **Type:** recognition ● Hall of Flame Award. **Type:** recognition ● Public Service Award. **Frequency:** annual. **Type:** recognition ● Service - Manager Award. **Type:** recognition. **Committees:** Air Pollution; Awards; Consumers Coordination; Educational; Energy Conservation; Engineering; Public Education; Research; Who's Who. **Formerly:** (1974) Old Timers' Club of the Oilburners Industry. **Publications:** *Hour Glass*, bimonthly. Newsletter ● *Hydraulic Systems Committees Voluntary Standards and Procedures of Fuel Oil Delivery* ● *National Old Timers' Association of the Energy Industry—Newsletter*, quarterly. Reports on current programs and technology in the energy industry. **Price:** included in membership dues. **Circulation:** 1,000 ● *Technical Manual*, 5/year ● *Who's Who in Energy Industry*, quinquennial. **Conventions/Meetings:** semiannual meeting.

6966 ■ NextGen Energy Council
350 Indiana St., Ste.640
Golden, CO 80401
Ph: (303)577-4611
Fax: (303)496-0334
E-mail: info@nextgenenergy.org
URL: http://www.nextgenenergy.org
Contact: Bob Hanfling, Chm.
Description: Supports continuing efforts to improve the efficiency and environmental performance of all advanced energy technologies. Educates the public about the need for balanced energy policies. Maintains and expands consumer access to reliable, affordable and diverse energy resources.

6967 ■ North American Board of Certified Energy Practitioners (NABCEP)
Saratoga Tech. Energy Park
10 Hermes Rd., Ste.400
Malta, NY 12020
Ph: (518)899-8186
Fax: (518)899-1092
E-mail: info@nabcep.org
URL: http://www.nabcep.org
Contact: Peter Sheehan, Exec. Dir.
Description: Promotes renewable energy. Aims to support and work with the renewable energy and energy efficiency industries, professionals and stakeholders to develop and implement quality credentialing and certification programs for practitioners. **Telecommunication Services:** electronic mail, psheehan@nabcep.org.

6968 ■ Northeast Sustainable Energy Association (NESEA)
50 Miles St.
Greenfield, MA 01301
Ph: (413)774-6051
Fax: (413)774-6053
E-mail: nesea@nesea.org
URL: http://www.nesea.org
Contact: David Barclay, Exec. Dir.
Founded: 1974. **Membership Dues:** student, $25 (annual) ● basic, $55 (annual) ● NESEA/ASES, $94 (annual) ● supporting, $95 (annual) ● sustaining, $250 (annual) ● life, $1,500 ● business (based on membership level), $100-$1,000 (annual). **Staff:** 9. **Description:** Promotes energy conservation, nonpolluting and renewable energy technologies. **Affiliated With:** American Solar Energy Society. **Publications:** *Northeast Sun*, semiannual. Magazine. **Price:** included in membership dues. **Advertising:** accepted. Alternate Formats: online. **Conventions/Meetings:** conference ● workshop.

6969 ■ Nuclear Energy Institute (NEI)
1776 I St. NW, Ste.400
Washington, DC 20006-3708
Ph: (202)739-8000
Fax: (202)785-4019
E-mail: webmasterp@nei.org
URL: http://www.nei.org
Contact: John W. Rowe, Chm./CEO

Founded: 1953. **Members:** 250. **Staff:** 125. **Budget:** $34,000,000. **Description:** Represents Electric utilities, manufacturers, industrial firms, research and service organizations, educational institutions, labor groups, and governmental agencies engaged in development and utilization of nuclear energy, especially nuclear-produced electricity, and other energy matters. Maintains speakers' bureau; compiles statistics and public attitude data. **Libraries: Type:** reference. **Holdings:** 12,000; archival material, audiovisuals, books, periodicals. **Subjects:** nuclear science, energy, radioactive waste, environment, climate change. **Awards:** TIP Awards. **Frequency:** annual. **Type:** recognition. **Computer Services:** Online services, Nexis/Lexis; Westlaw. **Absorbed:** Atomic Industrial Forum. **Formed by Merger of:** U.S. Council for Energy Awareness; American Nuclear Energy Council; Nuclear Management and Resources Council; EEI—Nuclear Division. **Publications:** *Nuclear Energy Insight*, monthly. Newsletter. Alternate Formats: online ● *Nuclear Energy Overview*, weekly. Newsletter ● Annual Report, annual. **Conventions/Meetings:** annual Nuclear Energy Assembly - conference.

6970 ■ Renewable Energy Policy Project - Center For Renewable Energy and Sustainable Technology (REPP-CREST)
1612 K St. NW, Ste.202
Washington, DC 20006
Ph: (202)293-2898
Fax: (202)293-5857
E-mail: gsterzinger@repp.org
URL: http://www.crest.org
Contact: George Sterzinger, Exec. Dir.

Founded: 1994. **Staff:** 1. **Description:** Promotes renewable energy, energy efficiency and sustainability; provides information via the Internet. **Publications:** Reports. **Conventions/Meetings:** seminar.

6971 ■ Renewable Fuels Association (RFA)
One Massachusetts Ave. NW, Ste.820
Washington, DC 20001
Ph: (202)289-3835
Fax: (202)289-7519
E-mail: info@ethanolrfa.org
URL: http://www.ethanolrfa.org
Contact: Bob Dinneen, Pres./CEO

Founded: 1981. **Members:** 75. **Staff:** 5. **Regional Groups:** 40. **State Groups:** 3. **Local Groups:** 7. **Description:** Serves as a national trade association for the U.S. fuel ethanol industry. **Telecommunication Services:** electronic mail, jdavies@ethanolrfa.org. **Publications:** *Ethanol Industry Outlook*, annual. Annual Report ● *The Ethanol Report*, bimonthly. Newsletter. Alternate Formats: online. **Conventions/Meetings:** annual conference - February/March.

6972 ■ Society for Energy Education (SEE)
2526 Van Hise Ave.
Madison, WI 53705
Ph: (608)246-6487
E-mail: richard@asktheenergydoctor.com
URL: http://www.asktheenergydoctor.com
Contact: Dr. Richard Shaten, Ed.

Membership Dues: organization, $180 (annual) ● individual, $65 (annual) ● student, $35 (annual). **Description:** Promotes the understanding of the production and consumption of energy resources and their impact on the economy and the environment. Increases public awareness of energy production and consumption issues. **Computer Services:** database, expert speakers. **Publications:** *The Journal of Energy Education*, annual. Features articles supporting the mission of the Society. **Price:** free for members; $16.00 for nonmembers.

6973 ■ Southface Energy Institute
241 Pine St. NE
Atlanta, GA 30308
Ph: (404)872-3549
Fax: (404)872-5009
E-mail: info@southface.org
URL: http://www.southface.org
Contact: Dennis Creech, Exec. Dir./Co-Founder

Founded: 1978. **Membership Dues:** student, $25 (annual) ● individual, $50 (annual) ● family/couple, $75 (annual) ● supporting, $250 (annual) ● contributing, $500 (annual) ● friend, $125 (annual) ● partner, $1,500 (annual) ● patron, $2,500 (annual) ● sustaining, $5,000 (annual). **Staff:** 39. **Description:** Promotes sustainable homes, workplaces, and communities through education, research, advocacy in energy, building science, environmental technologies. **Libraries: Type:** reference; open to the public. **Holdings:** books, periodicals. **Subjects:** commercial green building, residential green building, alternative energy, environmental technologies, solar energy, high performance homes and buildings. **Awards:** Argon Award. **Frequency:** annual. **Type:** recognition. **Recipient:** for success in sustainability in recognition of a significant commitment to environmental stewardship. **Telecommunication Services:** electronic mail, dcreech@southface.org ● hotline, Radon hotline, (800)745-0037. **Councils:** U.S. Green Building. **Divisions:** Southface Commercial Green Building Services; Southface Home Performance with ENERGY STAR; Southface Residential Green Building Services. **Programs:** EarthCraft House; Internships and Fellowships; Media; speakers' bureau. **Publications:** *A Builder's Guide to Energy Efficient Homes in Georgia*, periodic, published as necessary. Manual. Details building science concepts and prescriptive measures for energy and resource efficient residential building, suitable for mixed climates. Alternate Formats: online ● *EarthCraft House Technical Guidelines*, periodic, published as necessary. Handbook. Features technical guidelines for builders in the EarthCraft House green building program. Includes illustrations of building details. **Price:** $10.00. **Circulation:** 1,000. Alternate Formats: online ● *Southface Annual Report*, annual. Alternate Formats: online ● *Southface Journal of Sustainable Building*, quarterly. Provides information on upcoming activities and practical advice on sustainable energy. **Circulation:** 3,000. **Conventions/Meetings:** annual Environmental Living - conference ● annual Greenprints Conference ● Home Energy Clinics - meeting ● Residential Energy Code - workshop - 3/year ● monthly Sustainable Atlanta - roundtable.

6974 ■ United States Association for Energy Economics (USAEE)
28790 Chagrin Blvd., Ste.350
Cleveland, OH 44122
Ph: (216)464-2785
Fax: (216)464-2768
E-mail: usaee@usaee.org
URL: http://www.usaee.org
Contact: Mr. David L. Williams, Exec. Dir.

Founded: 1994. **Members:** 1,000. **Membership Dues:** individual, $65 (annual) ● sustaining/organization, $1,000 (annual) ● student, $35 (annual). **Staff:** 5. **Budget:** $100,000. **State Groups:** 10. **National Groups:** 10. **Description:** Economists, engineers, geologists, environmentalists, consultants, journalists, corporate planners, and researchers. Provides a forum for the exchange of ideas, experience, and issues among professionals interested in energy economics. **Libraries: Type:** reference. **Holdings:** 1. **Awards:** Adelman Frankle Award. **Frequency:** annual. **Type:** recognition. **Recipient:** to an individual or organization for an innovative contribution to the field of energy economics ● Senior Fellow Award. **Frequency:** annual. **Type:** recognition. **Recipient:** to individuals with distinguished service to the field of energy economics. **Affiliated With:** International Association for Energy Economics. **Publications:** *Dialogue*, 3/year. Newsletter. Features articles about the association and upcoming events, conferences and other news relating to USAEE and the energy field. **Price:** included in membership dues. **Circulation:** 1,000. **Advertising:** accepted. Alternate Formats: online ● Membership Directory. **Advertising:** accepted. **Conventions/Meetings:** annual North American Conference (exhibits) - usually fall. 2008 Dec. 3-5, New Orleans, LA.

6975 ■ U.S. Energy Association (USEA)
1300 Pennsylvania Ave. NW, Ste.550
Mailbox 142
Washington, DC 20004-3022
Ph: (202)312-1230
Fax: (202)682-1682
E-mail: kgrover@usea.org
URL: http://www.usea.org
Contact: Barry K. Worthington, Exec. Dir.

Founded: 1924. **Members:** 160. **Membership Dues:** energy company, trade association, manufacturer, engineering company, $2,000-$5,000 (annual) ● professional society, federal government agency, professional service firm, $1,000 (annual) ● university, educational organization, state government agency, $325 (annual). **Staff:** 28. **Budget:** $7,000,000. **Description:** One of 100 national committees representing the energy interests of industry, government, professional and technical societies, educational institutions, and legal and other professional service organizations. Supports World Energy Council objectives, which are: to provide for broad consideration of energy resources, policy, management, technology, use, and conservation as they relate to the total energy picture of the U.S. and the world; to publish data on energy resources and their utilization; to hold conferences and forums for those concerned with surveying, developing, or using energy resources. Conducts special energy seminars. **Awards:** U.S. Energy Award. **Frequency:** annual. **Type:** recognition. **Recipient:** for lifetime achievement in the energy sector. **Committees:** Energy Efficiency; Environment Protection; Research and Development; Utilities. **Publications:** *Annual Assessment of U.S. Energy Policy and Prospects*, annual. Report. **Price:** free. **Circulation:** 5,000 ● *National Energy Data Profiles* ● *U.S. Energy Association Annual Report*, annual. Alternate Formats: online ● *USEA Report*, monthly. Newsletter. **Price:** free. **Circulation:** 2,000 ● Proceedings. Alternate Formats: online ● Reports. Alternate Formats: online. **Conventions/Meetings:** annual general assembly ● triennial World Energy Congress.

6976 ■ US Fuel Cell Council (USFCC)
1100 H St. NW, Ste.800
Washington, DC 20005
Ph: (202)293-5500
Fax: (202)785-4313
E-mail: info@usfcc.com
URL: http://www.usfcc.com
Contact: Robert Rose, Exec. Dir.

Founded: 1998. **Membership Dues:** executive, $10,000 (annual) ● associate, non-profit, government, $5,000 (annual). **Description:** Fosters the commercialization of fuel cells in the United States. Promotes public understanding of fuel cells and their environmental benefits. **Libraries: Type:** reference. **Holdings:** articles, books, reports. **Subjects:** fuel cells and related issues. **Working Groups:** Codes and Standards; Education and Marketing; Government Affairs; Materials and Components; Portable Power; Power Generation; Sustainability; Transportation. **Publications:** *Fuel Cell Catalyst*, quarterly. Newsletter. Features articles contributed by leading experts in the fuel cell industry. **Price:** free for members. Alternate Formats: online ● *Fuel Cell Connection*, monthly. Newsletter. Includes contract awards, funding opportunities, university fuel cell activities and regulations affecting the technology. **Price:** free for members. Alternate Formats: online.

6977 ■ Women's Council on Energy and the Environment (WCEE)
PO Box 33211
Washington, DC 20033
Ph: (703)351-7850
Fax: (202)318-2506

E-mail: info@wcee.org
URL: http://www.wcee.org
Contact: Christine Tezak, Pres.
Founded: 1981. **Members:** 200. **Membership Dues:** student, $40 (annual) ● tier (based on the annual income), $65-$90 (annual). **Staff:** 1. **Budget:** $30,000. **Description:** Represents individuals, primarily women, who work for the federal government, consulting firms, private industry, and the environmental community and are involved in educating the public about national policy issues. Works to facilitate networking among members on public issues, particularly those concerning energy and the environment. Promotes the professional development of women interested in energy and environmental issues. Advocates informed decision-making on such issues by business and government officials. Maintains speakers' bureau. Sponsors monthly public programs that include roundtable and panel discussions and lectures. **Awards:** Champion Award. **Frequency:** annual. **Type:** recognition. **Recipient:** to a man who champions woman professionals ● Woman of the Year. **Frequency:** annual. **Type:** recognition. **Recipient:** to a woman who has shown consistent leadership and accomplishment in her chosen profession. **Committees:** Professional Development; Special Interest. **Publications:** *WCEE Newsletter*, monthly. **Price:** included in membership dues. **Circulation:** 200 ● Membership Directory, annual. **Conventions/Meetings:** annual meeting - fall.

6978 ■ World Energy Efficiency Association (WEEA)
1101 15th St. NW, Ste.1100
Washington, DC 20005
Ph: (202)778-4942
Fax: (202)463-7241
E-mail: info@weea.org
URL: http://www.weea.org
Contact: Eliane D. Lomax, Contact
Founded: 1993. **Multinational. Description:** Assists developing and reindustrializing countries in accessing information on energy efficiency. Serves as a clearinghouse for information on energy efficiency programs, technologies and measures. Promotes international cooperation efforts in energy efficiency. **Computer Services:** database, directories. **Publications:** Annual Report ● Papers. Alternate Formats: online.

Engineering

6979 ■ ABET
111 Market Pl., Ste.1050
Baltimore, MD 21202
Ph: (410)347-7700
Fax: (410)625-2238
E-mail: info@abet.org
URL: http://www.abet.org
Contact: George D. Peterson, Exec. Dir.
Founded: 1932. **Members:** 30. **Staff:** 35. **Budget:** $2,630,500. **Description:** Serves as umbrella organization for professional and technical societies representing over 1 million applied scientists, computer scientists, engineers, and technologists. Accredits college and university programs in applied science, computing, engineering, and technology areas. **Awards:** ABET Fellow Award. **Frequency:** annual. **Type:** recognition ● Linton E. Grinter Distinguished Service Award. **Frequency:** annual. **Type:** recognition. **Commissions:** Engineering Accreditation; Related Accreditation; Technology Accreditation. **Affiliated With:** American Institute of Chemical Engineers; American Society of Agricultural and Biological Engineers; American Society for Engineering Education; American Society of Mechanical Engineers; Institute of Electrical and Electronics Engineers. **Also Known As:** ABET Inc. **Formerly:** (1980) Engineers' Council for Professional Development; (2004) Accreditation Board for Engineering and Technology - ABET. **Publications:** *Accreditation Yearbook*, annual. Directory ● *Criteria for Accrediting Programs in Computing*, annual. Manual. **Price:** $5.00/piece ● *Criteria for Accrediting Programs in Engineering in the United States*, annual ● *Criteria for Accrediting Programs in Engineering Technology*, annual. Manual. **Price:** $5.00/piece ● Annual Report, annual ● Proceedings, annual. **Conventions/Meetings:** annual conference - always October.

6980 ■ ACEC Research and Management Foundation (ACEC/RMF)
1015 15th St. NW, 8th Fl.
Washington, DC 20005-2605
Ph: (202)347-7474
Fax: (202)898-0068
E-mail: acec@acec.org
URL: http://www.acec.org
Contact: David A. Raymond, Pres.
Founded: 1974. **Staff:** 2. **Budget:** $600,000. **Description:** A research and educational subsidiary of the American Consulting Engineers Council. Established to engage in charitable research and educational opportunities in the public interest in the disciplines practiced by consulting engineers. **Awards: Frequency:** annual. **Type:** scholarship. **Recipient:** for a U.S. citizen pursuing a Bachelor's degree in an accredited engineering program or in an accredited land-surveying program. **Publications:** *RMF Newsletter*, quarterly ● Books ● Reports. **Conventions/Meetings:** annual convention - 2009 Apr. 26-29, Washington, DC; 2010 Apr. 25-28, Washington, DC ● periodic seminar and conference ● annual conference - 2008 Oct. 19-22, Montreal, QC, Canada; 2009 Oct. 7-10, Palm Springs, CA; 2010 Oct. 17-20, Fajardo, PR; 2011 Oct. 3-6, Las Vegas, NV.

6981 ■ Airlines Electronic Engineering Committee (AEEC)
c/o ARINC Inc.
2551 Riva Rd.
Annapolis, MD 21401-7435
Ph: (410)266-2982 (410)266-4000
Free: (800)633-6882
Fax: (410)266-2329
E-mail: flightops@arinc.com
URL: http://www.arinc.com/aeec
Contact: Roy T. Oishi, Chm.
Founded: 1949. **Members:** 27. **Staff:** 12. **Description:** Airline and other transport aircraft electronics and electrical engineers. Develops voluntary standards for air transport avionics equipment and systems. Monitors legislation concerning regulatory matters; acts as a representative for the airline engineering community. Provides technical support. Operates subcommittees. **Libraries: Type:** not open to the public. **Holdings:** 300. **Subjects:** aircraft systems. **Computer Services:** Mailing lists, of members. **Publications:** *AeroLine*, monthly. Newsletter. Contains summary of activities related to committee and avionic manufacturers. **Price:** included in membership dues. **Circulation:** 3,000. Alternate Formats: online ● Reports. Alternate Formats: online ● Also publishes airline standards. **Conventions/Meetings:** annual conference (exhibits).

6982 ■ American Academy of Environmental Engineers (AAEE)
130 Holiday Ct., Ste.100
Annapolis, MD 21401
Ph: (410)266-3311
Fax: (410)266-7653
E-mail: info@aaee.net
URL: http://www.aaee.net
Contact: Lawrence C. Pencak, Exec. Dir.
Founded: 1955. **Members:** 2,600. **Membership Dues:** individual, $75 (annual) ● specialty certification, $85 (annual). **Staff:** 5. **Budget:** $500,000. **Description:** Environmentally oriented registered professional engineers certified by examination as Diplomates of the Academy. Seeks to improve the standards of environmental engineering. Certifies those with special knowledge of environmental engineering. Furnishes lists of those certified to the public. Maintains speakers' bureau. Recognizes areas of specialization: Air Pollution Control; General Environmental; Hazardous Waste Management; Industrial Hygiene; Radiation Protection; Solid Waste Management; Water Supply and Wastewater. Requires written and oral examinations for certification. Works with other professional organizations on environmentally oriented activities. Identifies potential employment candidates through Talent Search Service. **Awards:** Edward J. Cleary Award. **Frequency:** biennial. **Type:** recognition. **Recipient:** for outstanding achievement in environmental engineering ● Excellence in Engineering Awards. **Frequency:** annual. **Type:** recognition. **Recipient:** for design, operations/management, planning, research, small projects, and university research ● Gordon Maskew Fair Award. **Frequency:** annual. **Type:** recognition. **Recipient:** for outstanding service to the environmental engineering profession ● Stanley Kappe Award. **Frequency:** annual. **Type:** recognition. **Recipient:** for service to the academy. **Computer Services:** database ● mailing lists. **Committees:** Admissions; Affiliates; Audit; Awards; Bylaws; Development and Upgrading of Examinations; Engineering Education; Excellence in Environmental Engineering Award; Executive; Finance; Membership; Nominating; Planning; Publications; Re-certification. **Affiliated With:** Air and Waste Management Association; American Institute of Chemical Engineers; American Public Health Association; American Public Works Association; American Society of Civil Engineers; American Society for Engineering Education; American Society of Mechanical Engineers; American Water Works Association; National Society of Professional Engineers; Solid Waste Association of North America; Water Environment Federation. **Absorbed:** (1973) Environmental Engineers Intersociety Board. **Formerly:** Roster of Certified Engineers of the ASEIB; (1966) American Academy of Sanitary Engineers. **Publications:** *Environmental Engineer*, quarterly. Magazine. **Price:** $20.00/year in U.S. and Canada; $30.00/year outside U.S. and Canada. ISSN: 1068-4654. **Advertising:** accepted ● *Environmental Engineering P.E. Examination Guide and Handbook* ● *Environmental Engineering Selection Guide* ● *Practice Problems for the P.E. Examination in Environmental Engineer* ● *Who's Who in Environmental Engineering*. **Conventions/Meetings:** annual meeting.

6983 ■ American Association of Engineering Societies (AAES)
1620 I St. NW, Ste.210
Washington, DC 20006
Ph: (202)296-2237
Free: (888)400-2237
Fax: (202)296-1151
E-mail: dbateson@aaes.org
URL: http://www.aaes.org
Contact: Dan Bateson, Dir., Engineering Workforce Commission
Founded: 1979. **Members:** 28. **Staff:** 9. **Budget:** $1,500,000. **Description:** Coordinates the efforts of the member societies in the provision of reliable and objective information to the general public concerning issues which affect the engineering profession and the field of engineering as a whole; collects, analyzes, documents, and disseminates data which will inform the general public of the relationship between engineering and the national welfare; provides a forum for the engineering societies to exchange and discuss their views on matters of common interest; and represents the U.S. engineering community abroad through representation in WFEO and UPADI. **Awards:** Chairman's Award. **Type:** recognition ● Kenneth Andrew Roe Award. **Type:** recognition ● National Engineering Award. **Type:** recognition ● Palladium Medal. **Type:** recognition. **Telecommunication Services:** electronic mail, wsalmon@aaes.org. **Councils:** Engineering Affairs; Public Affairs. **Affiliated With:** World Federation of Engineering Organisations. **Supersedes:** Engineers Joint Council. **Publications:** *Directory of Engineering Societies*, biennial ● *Engineering and Technology Degrees*, annual. Book. **Price:** $179.00 for members; $295.00 for nonmembers. Alternate Formats: CD-ROM ● *Engineering and Technology Enrollments*, annual. Book. **Price:** $149.00 for members; $245.00 for nonmembers. Alternate Formats: CD-ROM ● *Engineers*, quarterly. Bulletin. Contains information of careers in Engineering. **Price:** $105.00/year ● *Engineers Salaries: Special Industry Report*, annual. Survey. **Price:** $209.00 for members; $345.00 for nonmem-

bers ● *Professional Income of Engineers*, annual. Survey ● *The Role of Engineering in Sustainable Development*. Selected readings and references for the profession. ● *Who's Who in Engineering*, biennial.

6984 ■ American Council of Engineering Companies (ACEC)
1015 15th St., 8th Fl. NW
Washington, DC 20005-2605
Ph: (202)347-7474
Fax: (202)898-0068
E-mail: acec@acec.org
URL: http://www.acec.org
Contact: David A. Raymond, Pres.
Founded: 1973. **Members:** 5,700. **Staff:** 43. **Budget:** $12,000,000. **Regional Groups:** 51. **Description:** Represents consulting engineering firms engaged in private practice. Conducts programs concerned with public relations, business practices, governmental affairs, international practice and professional liability. Compiles statistics on office practices, insurance, employment, insurance clients served and services provided. Holds professional development seminars. Conducts educational programs; maintains Speaker's Bureau. **Libraries: Type:** reference. **Holdings:** 800. **Subjects:** business. **Awards:** Engineering Excellence Award. **Frequency:** annual. **Type:** recognition. **Recipient:** for innovation, expertise and ingenuity in engineering achievement. **Telecommunication Services:** electronic mail, draymond@acec.org. **Committees:** Awards; Federal Agencies/Procurement Advocacy; Government Affairs; Institute for Business Management; International; Political Action. **Affiliated With:** International Federation of Consulting Engineers. **Formed by Merger of:** American Institute of Consulting Engineers; Consulting Engineers Council. **Publications: Circulation:** *Engineering Inc.*, bimonthly. Magazine. **Circulation:** 45,000. **Advertising:** accepted ● *The Last Word*, weekly. Newsletter. Alternate Formats: online. **Conventions/Meetings:** competition ● semiannual meeting.

6985 ■ American Engineering Alliance (AEA)
Bowling Green Sta.
PO Box 1446
New York, NY 10274-1446
Ph: (212)606-4053
E-mail: comunellil@aol.com
URL: http://www.aeaworld.org
Contact: Louis Comunelli PE, Sec.
Founded: 1995. **Membership Dues:** regular, $20 (annual) ● student, $10 (annual) ● life, $300. **Description:** Works for the betterment of the social and economic status of engineers. Promotes the unity and common interests of all engineers, regardless of circumstances of employment or field of practice. Educates engineers and the public on the proper role of engineering in the society. Promotes the ethical practice of engineering.

6986 ■ American Engineering Association (AEA)
4116 S Carrier Pkwy., Ste.280-809
Grand Prairie, TX 75052
Ph: (201)664-6954
E-mail: info@aea.org
URL: http://www.aea.org
Contact: Mr. Richard F. Tax, Pres.
Founded: 1979. **Membership Dues:** individual, associate, $30 (annual) ● retired, academic, $20 (annual) ● student, $15 (annual) ● life, $1,000. **Description:** Members consist of Engineers and engineering professionals. Purpose to advance the engineering profession and U.S. engineering capabilities. Issues of concern include age discrimination, immigration laws, displacement of U.S. Engineers by foreign workers, trade agreements, off shoring of U.S. Engineering and manufacturing jobs, loss of U.S. manufacturing and engineering capability, and recruitment of foreign students. Testifies before Congress. Holds local Chapter meetings. **Libraries: Type:** open to the public; reference. **Holdings:** archival material, articles, papers. **Telecommunication Services:** electronic mail, aea@aea.org. **Committees:** Engineering Manpower. **Sections:** Local Chapters. **Publications:** *American Engineer*, quarterly. Newsletter. **Price:** included in membership dues. Alternate Formats: online.

6987 ■ American Indian Science and Engineering Society (AISES)
PO Box 9828
Albuquerque, NM 87119-9828
Ph: (505)765-1052
Fax: (505)765-5608
E-mail: info@aises.org
URL: http://www.aises.org
Contact: Shirley LaCourse, Deputy Dir.
Founded: 1977. **Members:** 2,700. **Membership Dues:** professional, $65 (annual) ● college student, $25 (annual) ● life (Sequoyah), $1,000. **Staff:** 9. **Budget:** $2,000,000. **Local Groups:** 140. **Description:** Represents American Indian and non-Indian students and professionals in science, technology, and engineering fields; corporations representing energy, mining, aerospace, electronic, and computer fields. Seeks to motivate and encourage students to pursue undergraduate and graduate studies in science, engineering, and technology. Sponsors science fairs in grade schools, teacher training workshops, summer math/science sessions for 8th-12th graders, professional chapters, and student chapters in colleges. Offers scholarships. Adult members serve as role models, advisers, and mentors for students. Operates placement service. **Libraries: Type:** reference. **Telecommunication Services:** electronic mail, shirley@aises.org. **Affiliated With:** American Association of Engineering Societies. **Publications:** *Indian Biographies* ● *Winds of Change*, quarterly. Magazine. **Price:** $24.00 /year for nonmembers; included in membership dues. **Circulation:** 80,000. **Advertising:** accepted ● Catalog, annual. **Price:** $1.00 ● Annual Report, annual. **Price:** free. **Conventions/Meetings:** annual Expanding the Circle - conference (exhibits) ● Student Leadership Conference.

6988 ■ American Institute of Engineers (AIE)
4630 Appian Way, Ste.206
El Sobrante, CA 94803-1875
Ph: (510)758-6240
Fax: (510)758-6240
E-mail: aie@members-aie.org
URL: http://www.members-aie.org
Contact: Engr. Martin S. Gottlieb, Pres.
Founded: 1990. **Members:** 1,300. **Membership Dues:** individual, fellow, honorary, $100 (annual) ● life, $1,000 ● supporting, $300 (annual) ● sponsoring, $500 (annual). **Staff:** 2. **Budget:** $60,000. **Local Groups:** 7. **Description:** Professional association for engineers, scientists, and mathematicians. Multidisciplined, non-technical association who aims to improve the stature and image of engineers, scientists, and mathematicians. Provides endorsements, awards and opportunities for small business start-ups within the AIE Councils. Sponsors "LA Engineer", a comedy-drama television series; produces annual "Academy Hall of FAME (TV)". **Libraries: Type:** reference. **Holdings:** business records, clippings, periodicals. **Awards:** FIST Awards TV. **Frequency:** annual. **Type:** recognition. **Recipient:** for science, engineering, mathematics, and business accomplishments ● Seal of Approval Awards. **Frequency:** periodic. **Type:** recognition. **Computer Services:** database, membership. **Committees:** Awards; Endorsements; Lobbying; Political Action. **Publications:** *AIE Member's Directory*. Membership Directory. Includes biographical information of members. **Price:** $75.00. **Advertising:** accepted ● *AIE Perspectives Newsmagazine*, monthly. **Price:** included in membership dues. **Circulation:** 2,500. **Advertising:** accepted. Alternate Formats: online ● *Alumni Statistical Directory by University, by Year, by Discipline, by Degree* ● *Geographical Statistical Directory by U.S. County, by Discipline*. **Conventions/Meetings:** biennial Summit - general assembly, participation by invitees, engineers, scientists, mathematicians, educators, executives, and politicians (exhibits).

6989 ■ American Lebanese Engineering Society (ALES)
PO Box 585
Norwood, MA 02062
Ph: (617)642-7185
E-mail: ales@alesonline.org
URL: http://www.alesonline.org
Contact: Mr. Salim A. Ayas, Pres.
Founded: 1991. **Members:** 125. **Membership Dues:** regular, $50 (annual) ● associate, $35 (annual). **Description:** Professional engineers united to serve as role models in the American Lebanese community and to advance the science and profession of engineering. **Awards: Frequency:** annual. **Type:** scholarship. **Telecommunication Services:** electronic mail, sayass@aol.com. **Publications:** *ALES News*, quarterly. Newsletter. **Price:** available to members only. **Conventions/Meetings:** annual convention - always May.

6990 ■ American Society of Agricultural and Biological Engineers (ASABE)
2950 Niles Rd.
St. Joseph, MI 49085-8607
Ph: (269)429-0300 (269)428-6322
Free: (800)371-2723
Fax: (269)429-3852
E-mail: hq@asabe.org
URL: http://www.asabe.org
Contact: M. Melissa Moore, Exec. VP
Founded: 1907. **Members:** 9,000. **Staff:** 29. **Budget:** $3,000,000. **Local Groups:** 41. **Multinational. Description:** International professional and technical organization of individuals interested in engineering and technology for agriculture, food and biological systems. Publishes textbooks and journals. Develops engineering standards used in agriculture, food and biological systems. Sponsors technical meetings and continuing education programs. Maintains biographical archives and placement services. Sponsors competitions and special in-depth conferences. Maintains over 200 committees. **Awards: Frequency:** annual. **Type:** medal. **Computer Services:** Mailing lists, labels. **Divisions:** Biological Engineering; Ergonomics, Safety and Health; Food and Process Engineering; Information and Electrical Technology; Power and Machinery; Soil and Water (includes Drainage, Hydrology, Irrigation, and Soil Erosion Groups); Structures and Environment. **Affiliated With:** Council for Agricultural Science and Technology. **Also Known As:** The Society for Engineering in Agriculture, Food and Biological Systems. **Formerly:** (2005) American Society of Agricultural Engineers. **Publications:** *Applied Engineering in Agriculture*, bimonthly. Journal. Reports on solutions for engineering problems related to food and fiber production and processing; includes research reports. **Price:** $65.00 /year for members; $127.00 /year for nonmembers. ISSN: 0883-8542. **Circulation:** 500. Alternate Formats: online ● *ASABE Standards Book*, annual. Contains general agricultural standards, and standards on machines, equipment, electronics, structures, livestock, environment, and soil and water. **Price:** $105.00/copy for members; $290.00/copy for nonmembers. ISSN: 8755-1187. Alternate Formats: CD-ROM; online. Also Cited As: *Agricultural Engineers Yearbook of Standards* ● *Journal of Agricultural Safety and Health*, quarterly. Contains peer-reviewed articles and abstracts on issues related to farm safety and health. **Price:** $59.00 /year for members; $117.00 /year for nonmembers. ISSN: 1074-7583. **Circulation:** 200. Alternate Formats: online ● *Resource: Engineering and Technology for a Sustainable World*, 8/year. Journal. Contains calendar of events, employment opportunities, information on new products and publications, and technical highlights. **Price:** $86.00 /year for nonmembers. **Circulation:** 7,000. **Advertising:** accepted. Alternate Formats: online. Also Cited As: *Agricultural Engineering Magazine* ● *Transactions of the ASABE*, bimonthly. Journal. Includes reports on agricultural machinery, irrigation, drainage, electronics, robotics, food and process engineering, and energy. **Price:** $118.00 /year for members; $361.00 /year for nonmembers. ISSN: 0001-2351. **Circulation:** 800. Alternate Formats: online ● Also publishes books on history of tractors and grain harvesters, directories, indexes, proceedings, and technical papers. **Conventions/Meetings:** Agricultural Equipment Technology Conference (AETC) - workshop ● annual international conference (exhibits).

6991 ■ American Society of Certified Engineering Technicians (ASCET)
PO Box 1536
Brandon, MS 39043
Ph: (601)824-8991
Fax: (913)890-1021
E-mail: general-manager@ascet.org
URL: http://www.ascet.org
Contact: Russel E. Freier CET, Chm.
Founded: 1964. **Members:** 2,500. **Membership Dues:** associate, $30 (annual) ● certified, regular, registered, $50 (annual). **Budget:** $75,000. **Regional Groups:** 7. **Local Groups:** 20. **Description:** Represents certified and non-certified engineering technicians and technologists. Works to obtain recognition of the contribution of engineering technicians and engineering technologists as an essential part of the engineering-scientific team. Cooperates with engineering and scientific societies. Improves the utilization of the engineering technician and technologist. Assists the educational, social, economic, and ethical development of the engineering technician and technologist. Conducts triennial survey among members to determine employer support, pay scales, and fringe benefits. Offers referral service. **Awards:** Student Financial Aid Grant Program. **Frequency:** annual. **Type:** grant. **Recipient:** for student members enrolled in an engineering technology degree program ● Technician/Technologist of the Year Award. **Frequency:** annual. **Type:** recognition. **Committees:** Administrative Study; Certification Study; Chapter Development and Activities; Education; Ethics; Honors, Awards, and Resolutions. **Programs:** Student Financial Aid Grant. **Affiliated With:** American Concrete Institute; American Society for Nondestructive Testing; American Society for Quality; American Welding Society; International Association for Radio, Telecommunications and Electromagnetics; National Association of Industrial Technology; National Institute for Certification in Engineering Technologies. **Publications:** *Certification and the Engineering Team*. Brochure ● *Certified Engineering Technician Magazine*, bimonthly. ISSN: 0746-6641. **Advertising:** accepted. Alternate Formats: online ● *The Engineers and Engineering Technology Spectrum*. Article ● *Information for Employers of Engineering Technicians and Technologists*. Brochure ● *The Voice of Engineering Technicians and Technologists*. Brochure. **Conventions/Meetings:** annual board meeting, with technical equipment and training (exhibits) - always June.

6992 ■ American Society of Civil Engineers (ASCE)
1801 Alexander Bell Dr.
Reston, VA 20191-4400
Ph: (703)295-6300
Free: (800)548-2723
Fax: (703)295-6222
E-mail: webmaster@asce.org
URL: http://www.asce.org
Contact: W.F. Marcuson III, Pres.
Founded: 1852. **Members:** 120,000. **Membership Dues:** regular, $25-$103 (annual) ● fellow, $120 (annual). **Staff:** 203. **Budget:** $36,000,000. **Regional Groups:** 21. **State Groups:** 78. **Local Groups:** 145. **National Groups:** 224. **Description:** Enhances the welfare of humanity by advancing the science and profession of engineering. Offers continuing education courses and technical specialty conferences. Develops technical codes and standards. Works closely with Congress, the White House and federal agencies to build sound national policy on engineering issues. Supports research of new civil engineering technology and material. Informs the public about various engineering-related topics. **Libraries: Type:** reference. **Holdings:** archival material, reports. **Awards:** Achievement Awards. **Frequency:** annual. **Type:** recognition. **Recipient:** for exceptionally meritorious achievement in the engineering profession ● Honorary Membership Award. **Frequency:** annual. **Type:** recognition. **Recipient:** for members with great contributions in some branch of engineering or in the arts and science related thereto ● Outstanding Projects and Leaders (OPAL). **Frequency:** annual. **Type:** recognition. **Recipient:** for civil engineers whose contributions have greatly enhanced the health, safety and economy of its nation and the world. **Computer Services:** Bibliographic search, 80,000 records of more than 20 years of civil engineering publications ● mailing lists, of members. **Subgroups:** Geo-Institute; Structural Engineering Institute. **Publications:** *ASCE News*, monthly. Newsletter. Contains news about ASCE activities and civil engineering positions available. **Price:** included in membership dues; $36.00 /year for nonmembers. ISSN: 0197-4076. **Circulation:** 120,000. **Advertising:** accepted ● *ASCE Publications Information*, bimonthly. Brochure. Features index and abstracts of ASCE publications. ● *Civil Engineering*, monthly. Magazine. Features articles on various civil engineering projects and issues, and ASCE activities. **Price:** included in membership dues; $105.00 /year for nonmembers. ISSN: 0885-7024. **Circulation:** 120,000. **Advertising:** accepted ● *Emerging Technology*, bimonthly. Newsletter. Features new materials, methods, equipment, processes and software just out of the lab and ready for industry use. ● *Manuals and Reports on Engineering Practice*, periodic ● *Official Register*, annual. Contains information on all ASCE activities. ● *Transactions*, annual. Contains abstracts of journals and Civil Engineering magazine articles. ● *Worldwide Projects*, quarterly. Magazine. Covers international projects and business issues. ● Journals. Contains new findings and information on various civil engineering topics. Alternate Formats: CD-ROM ● Also available: Engineer owner and construction related contract documents, forms of agreement, and conference proceedings. **Conventions/Meetings:** annual conference (exhibits) - always October/November.

6993 ■ American Society of Danish Engineers (ASDE)
Address Unknown since 2007
Founded: 1930. **Members:** 200. **Description:** Engineers of Danish birth or descent residing in the U.S. or Canada. **Publications:** Membership Directory, annual ● Newsletter, 5/year. **Conventions/Meetings:** meeting - 3/year.

6994 ■ American Society for Engineering Management (ASEM)
PO Box 820
Rolla, MO 65402-0820
Ph: (573)341-2101
Fax: (573)364-3500
E-mail: asemmsd@rollanet.org
URL: http://www.asem.com
Contact: Kellie Davis, Member Support Department Mgr.
Founded: 1979. **Members:** 2,000. **Membership Dues:** regular, $90 (annual) ● graduate student, $45 (annual) ● undergraduate student, $20 (annual). **Staff:** 1. **Budget:** $100,000. **Regional Groups:** 6. **Local Groups:** 12. **Description:** Persons with management experience in engineering, production, technical marketing, or related activities, or who hold a degree in engineering management. Seeks to advance engineering management science in theory and practice; to promote development of the profession; and to maintain high professional standards. Provides forum for professional contact and discussion; operates speakers' bureau; conducts educational and research programs. **Awards:** Engineering Manager of the Year Award. **Frequency:** annual. **Type:** recognition. **Recipient:** to a manager of engineering or technical program. **Publications:** *ASEM's Publisher's Periodical*, quarterly. Newsletter ● *Engineering Management Journal*, quarterly. Contains engineering management developments. **Price:** $120.00/year for libraries and companies; $8.00 for individual (minimum). **Circulation:** 3,000. **Advertising:** accepted. Also Cited As: *EMJ* ● *Proceedings of the American Society of Engineering Management*, annual. **Conventions/Meetings:** annual conference, with book publishers, software (exhibits).

6995 ■ American Society of Heating, Refrigerating and Air-Conditioning Engineers (ASHRAE)
1791 Tullie Cir. NE
Atlanta, GA 30329
Ph: (404)636-8400
Free: (800)527-4723
Fax: (404)321-5478
E-mail: ashrae@ashrae.org
URL: http://www.ashrae.org
Contact: Jeff Littleton, Sec.
Founded: 1894. **Members:** 55,000. **Membership Dues:** individual, associate, $165 (annual) ● affiliate, $40 (annual) ● student, $16 (annual). **Staff:** 103. **Budget:** $18,000,000. **Regional Groups:** 13. **Local Groups:** 160. **Multinational. Description:** Represents Technical society of heating, ventilating, refrigeration, and air-conditioning engineers. Sponsors numerous research programs in cooperation with universities, research laboratories, and government agencies on subjects such as human and animal environmental studies, effects of air-conditioning, quality of inside air, heat transfer, flow, and cooling processes. Conducts professional development seminars. Writes method of test standards and other standards addressing energy conservation in buildings, indoor air quality, and refrigerants. Publishes extensive literature and electronic products. **Libraries: Type:** reference. **Awards: Frequency:** semiannual. **Type:** recognition. **Committees:** Admissions and Advancements; Chapter Technology Transfer; Chapters Regional; Electronic Communications; Environmental Health; Handbook; Historical; Honors and Awards; Meeting Arrangements; Membership Promotion; Professional Development; Publications; Refrigeration; Research Administration; Resource Promotion; Society Program; Special Publications; Standards; Student Activities; Technical Activities. **Councils:** Members; Publishing and Education; Technology. **Sections:** Air Conditioning and Refrigerating System Components; Building Applications; Building Performance; Environmental Quality; Fundamentals and General; Heating Equipment, Heating and Cooling Systems, and Applications; Load Calculations and Energy Requirements; Materials and Processes; Refrigerating Systems; Ventilation and Air Distribution. **Formed by Merger of:** (1959) American Society Heating and Air-Conditioning Engineers; (1959) American Society of Refrigerating Engineers. **Publications:** *ASHRAE Handbook*, annual. Contains reference source in four volumes: Fundamentals, Refrigeration, HVAC Systems and Equipment, HVAC Applications. **Price:** $155.00 available to members only. **Circulation:** 60,000. Alternate Formats: CD-ROM ● *ASHRAE Insights*, monthly. Newsletter. Contains society and chapter news. **Price:** available to members only. Alternate Formats: online ● *ASHRAE Journal*, monthly. Covers research, development, and progress in heating, air-conditioning, ventilating, and refrigerating engineering. **Price:** included in membership dues; $79.00 /year for nonmembers in U.S.; $149.00 /year for nonmembers outside U.S. **Advertising:** accepted ● *ASHRAE Transactions*, semiannual. Proceedings. Covers environmental control, new applications, design and operating techniques, and summarizes investigations by private and public institutions. **Price:** $185.00/issue for members; $235.00/issue for nonmembers ● *IAQ Applications*, quarterly. Magazine. Provides practical, reliable information on indoor air quality. **Price:** $39.00 for members; $59.00 for nonmembers ● *International Journal of HUAC&R Research*, quarterly. Serves as a reference source available in four volumes: Fundamentals, Refrigeration, HVAC Systems and Equipment, HVAC Applications. **Price:** $99.00 for members domestic; $160.00 for nonmembers domestic. **Circulation:** 60,000. Alternate Formats: CD-ROM ● Also publishes standards and guidelines. **Conventions/Meetings:** annual International Air Conditioning, Heating, Refrigerating Exposition - meeting and convention, for HVAC&R equipment and services (exhibits) - 2008 June 21-25, Salt Lake City, UT; 2009 June 20-24, Louisville, KY ● annual convention (exhibits) - always winter. 2009 Jan. 24-28, Chicago, IL; 2010 Jan. 23-27, Orlando, FL; 2011 Jan. 29-Feb. 2, Las Vegas, NV.

6996 ■ American Society of Plumbing Engineers (ASPE)
8614 Catalpa Ave., Ste.1007
Chicago, IL 60656-1116

Ph: (773)693-2773
Fax: (773)695-9007
E-mail: info@aspe.org
URL: http://www.aspe.org
Contact: Stanley M. Wolfson, Exec. Dir.

Founded: 1964. **Members:** 7,500. **Membership Dues:** full, affiliate, special, governmental, $185 (annual) ● associate, $165 (annual) ● student, $25 (annual). **Staff:** 12. **Budget:** $3,000,000. **Regional Groups:** 5. **Local Groups:** 62. **Description:** Represents engineers and designers involved in the design and specification of plumbing systems; manufacturers, governmental officials, and contractors related to the industry may become members on a limited basis. Seeks to resolve professional problems in plumbing engineering; advocates greater cooperation among members and plumbing officials, contractors, laborers, and the public. Code committees examine regulatory codes pertaining to the industry and submit proposed revisions to code writing authorities to simplify, standardize, and modernize all codes. Sponsors American Society of Plumbing Engineers Research Foundation; operates certification program. **Awards:** ASPE Honor Roll of Employers. **Frequency:** biennial. **Type:** recognition ● ASPE Industry Award. **Frequency:** biennial. **Type:** recognition ● George W. Runkle Award of Merit. **Frequency:** biennial. **Type:** recognition. **Committees:** Code; Education; Technical. **Publications:** *Data Book*, annual ● *Plumbing Systems and Design Magazine*, bimonthly. **Price:** included in membership dues. **Circulation:** 25,000. **Advertising:** accepted ● Handbooks. Contains technical information. **Conventions/Meetings:** biennial Convention and Engineered Plumbing Exposition - meeting, for engineers and specifiers (exhibits) - usually October or November, even years ● biennial Technical Symposium - usually October or November, odd years.

6997 ■ American Society for Precision Engineering (ASPE)

PO Box 10826
Raleigh, NC 27605-0826
Ph: (919)839-8444
Fax: (919)839-8039
E-mail: ddevitt@newwayairbearings.com
URL: http://www.aspe.net
Contact: Andrew J. Devitt, Pres.

Founded: 1986. **Membership Dues:** sustaining, $150 (annual) ● regular, $85 (annual) ● student, $40 (annual) ● corporate sponsor, $1,500 (annual) ● sustaining corporate sponsor, $2,000 (annual). **Description:** Promotes research and development, design, manufacture and measurement of high accuracy components and systems. **Awards:** Lifetime Achievement. **Frequency:** annual. **Type:** recognition. **Recipient:** for individuals who have made significant contributions to the field of Precision Engineering. **Publications:** *Precision Engineering*, quarterly. Journal. **Price:** included in membership dues ● *Precision Engineering: An Evolutionary View*. Book. **Price:** $60.00 ● Proceedings, annual. Alternate Formats: CD-ROM ● Videos. **Price:** $30.00. **Conventions/Meetings:** annual meeting ● annual Spring Topical - meeting ● annual Summer Topical - meeting.

6998 ■ American Society of Swedish Engineers (ASSE)

780 3rd Ave.
King of Prussia, PA 19406
Ph: (610)265-4352
Fax: (610)265-4608
E-mail: information@asse-usa.org
URL: http://www.asse-usa.org
Contact: Bengt Nestell, Pres.

Founded: 1888. **Members:** 150. **Membership Dues:** general, $50 (annual). **Regional Groups:** 1. **Languages:** English, Swedish. **Description:** Serves as professional society of engineers of Swedish birth or Swedish extraction. Maintains biographical archives and placement service. **Awards:** John Ericsson Gold Medal. **Frequency:** annual. **Type:** medal. **Recipient:** for outstanding achievements in science or technology. **Committees:** Award; John Ericsson Medal. **Publications:** Membership Directory, annual. **Price:** free for members. **Circulation:** 200. **Advertising:** accepted ● Newsletter, periodic. Alternate Formats: online. **Conventions/Meetings:** annual meeting - usually January.

6999 ■ APEC - Automated Procedures for Engineering Consultants

Address Unknown since 2007

Founded: 1966. **Members:** 200. **Staff:** 3. **Budget:** $500,000. **Description:** Engineers, engineer/architects, utilities, manufacturers, governmental agencies, universities, and other organizations interested in application of up-to-date computer technology to building design. Members work together in cooperative efforts to develop computer programs for the design of environmental systems for buildings. Holds programs and in-house workshops. Bestows honorary membership and fellowships. **Committees:** Program Development. **Also Known As:** Automated Procedures for Engineering Consultants, Inc. **Publications:** *Abstracts and Documentations*, monthly ● *APEC—Membership Directory*, annual. Lists over 200 engineering and architectural firms, utility companies, and manufacturers interested in application of computer technology. **Price:** included in membership dues. **Advertising:** not accepted ● Brochures. **Conventions/Meetings:** annual meeting - always November.

7000 ■ Applied Technology Council (ATC)

201 Redwood Shores Pkwy., Ste.240
Redwood City, CA 94065
Ph: (650)595-1542 (703)351-5052
Fax: (650)593-2320
E-mail: atc@atcouncil.org
URL: http://www.atcouncil.org
Contact: Christopher Rojahn, Exec. Dir.

Founded: 1972. **Members:** 300. **Membership Dues:** national, $35 (annual) ● international, $50 (annual). **Staff:** 6. **Description:** Directors appointed by the American Society of Civil Engineers, the Structural Engineers Association of California, and the Western States Council of Structural Engineers Association. Seeks to help structural and earthquake engineers keep abreast of current technological changes in the field so that research performed by university groups and others can be more beneficial to the public. Encourages research and develops consensus opinions on structural engineering issues. Sponsors projects to compile resource documents needed for development of guidelines, manuals, codes, standards, specifications, and other materials useful to practicing engineers. **Libraries: Type:** reference. **Holdings:** 150. **Affiliated With:** American Society of Civil Engineers. **Publications:** Reports. **Conventions/Meetings:** seminar, for structural engineers and other professionals (exhibits) ● workshop.

7001 ■ ASME International Gas Turbine Institute (IGTI)

5775-C Glennridge Dr., No. 115
Atlanta, GA 30328
Ph: (404)847-0072
Fax: (404)847-0151
E-mail: igti@asme.org
URL: http://www.asme.org/igti
Contact: Michael Ireland, Managing Dir.

Founded: 1947. **Staff:** 9. **Budget:** $2,000,000. **Multinational. Description:** Engineers with an interest in gas turbine engines. Seeks to advance gas turbine technology. Serves as a clearinghouse on gas turbines; sponsors research and educational programs. **Libraries: Type:** reference. **Holdings:** archival material. **Awards:** Aircraft Engine Technology Award. **Frequency:** annual. **Type:** recognition ● Gas Turbine Award. **Type:** recognition ● John P. Davis Award. **Type:** recognition ● Tom Sawyer Award. **Type:** recognition. **Affiliated With:** American Society of Mechanical Engineers. **Formerly:** Gas Turbine Division; (1986) International Gas Turbine Institute. **Publications:** *Global Gas Turbine News*, semiannual. Newsletter ● *Journal of Engineering for Gas Turbines and Power* ● *Journal of Turbomachinery*, quarterly. **Price:** $50.00 for members. **Conventions/Meetings:** annual Turbo Expo and Technical Conference - conference and symposium (exhibits).

7002 ■ Asociacion de Ingenieros Cubanos (AIC)

PO Box 557575
Miami, FL 33255-7575
E-mail: president@a-i-c.org
URL: http://www.a-i-c.org
Contact: Gerardo B. Fernandez, Pres.

Founded: 1961. **Members:** 300. **Membership Dues:** individual, $50 (annual) ● student, $10 (annual). **Regional Groups:** 4. **Languages:** English, Spanish. **Description:** Cuban-American engineers. Raises funds for Cuban-American engineering students. Offers networking opportunities for Cuban-American professional engineers. **Awards:** ACESF Scholarships. **Frequency:** annual. **Type:** scholarship. **Recipient:** for Cuban-American students ● Engineer of the Year Award. **Frequency:** annual. **Type:** recognition. **Recipient:** for outstanding Cuban engineers. **Computer Services:** database, statistical information ● mailing lists, of members. **Publications:** *The ACE Reporter* (in English and Spanish), bimonthly. Newsletter. **Circulation:** 300. **Advertising:** accepted. **Conventions/Meetings:** annual Dia del Ingeniero - meeting (exhibits).

7003 ■ Association for Facilities Engineering (AFE)

12100 Sunset Hills Rd., Ste.130
Reston, VA 20190
Ph: (703)234-4066
E-mail: mail@afe.org
URL: http://www.afe.org
Contact: Ms. Gabriella Jacobs, Communications Mgr.

Founded: 1954. **Members:** 4,000. **Membership Dues:** individual, $235 (annual) ● student, $15 (annual) ● corporate, $4,000 (annual). **Staff:** 8. **Budget:** $1,800,000. **Regional Groups:** 9. **Local Groups:** 142. **Description:** Professional society of plant engineers and facilities managers engaged in the management, engineering, maintenance and operation of industrial, institutional, and commercial facilities. Compiles statistics. Offers three certification programs, Certified Plant Engineer (CPE), Certified Plant Maintenance Manager (CPMM), and Certified Plant Supervisor. **Libraries: Type:** not open to the public. **Computer Services:** Mailing lists. **Telecommunication Services:** electronic mail, gjacobs@afe.org. **Formerly:** American Institute of Plant Engineers. **Publications:** *Facilities Engineering Journal*, bimonthly. Magazine. **Circulation:** 10,000. **Advertising:** accepted. Also Cited As: *AFE Facilities*.

7004 ■ Association of International Motion Engineers (AIME)

Western Michigan Univ. - Kohrman Hall
1903 W Michigan Ave.
Kalamazoo, MI 49008
Ph: (269)337-7650
Fax: (269)345-4393
E-mail: info@aime.net
URL: http://www.aime.net

Membership Dues: individual, $50 (annual). **Multinational. Description:** Represents and supports the needs of users of motion control solutions. Strives to be user driven by helping the users of motion products and systems find appropriate solutions. Works to provide educational and support systems. Facilitates selection of motion solutions. Identifies and encourages an industry focus on strategic technology development. Promotes advanced technological solutions. Aims to meet these objectives through educational programs targeted both at the user and supplier of motion control solutions.

7005 ■ Association of Muslim Scientists and Engineers (AMSE)

PO Box 38
Plainfield, IN 46168
Ph: (517)947-6338
Fax: (517)947-6338
E-mail: amse@amseweb.org
URL: http://amseweb.org
Contact: Khurshid Qureshi PhD, Pres.

Founded: 1969. **Members:** 640. **Membership Dues:** student in U.S., $15 (annual) ● student outside U.S.,

$30 (annual) ● regular in U.S., $25 (annual) ● regular outside U.S., $40 (annual). **Staff:** 1. **Budget:** $75,000. **Multinational. Description:** International organization of Muslims who are graduates of three-year, post-high school programs in engineering or in the natural, life, or mathematical sciences. Works to channel the talents of Muslim scientists and engineers into providing the Muslim community with assistance and guidance and to improve the gathering, distribution, and dissemination of technical information and scientific knowledge through publications, meetings, and other media. Provides encouragement and guidance to members in their education and careers. **Libraries: Type:** reference. **Divisions:** Agricultural Sciences; Engineering and Technology; Life Sciences; Mathematical Sciences; Natural Sciences. **Affiliated With:** Islamic Society of North America. **Publications:** *AMSE News*, monthly. Newsletter. Alternate Formats: online ● *Chronological and Subject-Wise Index*, annual ● *Directory of Muslim Scientists and Engineers*, annual ● *International Journal of Science and Technology*, biennial ● *Proceedings of Conference*, annual ● *Publication Index Annual*, annual ● Reprints ● Also publishes educational guide. **Conventions/Meetings:** annual conference (exhibits) ● periodic symposium and seminar.

7006 ■ Association of Professional Model Makers (APMM)

PO Box 165
Hamilton, NY 13346
Free: (877)663-2766
Fax: (877)765-6950
E-mail: info@modelmakers.org
URL: http://www.modelmakers.org
Contact: Samanthi Martinez, Exec. Dir.

Founded: 1993. **Members:** 800. **Membership Dues:** student, $25 (annual) ● professional, $125 (annual) ● professional group (per individual), $100 (annual) ● model shop, $600 (annual) ● education, $500 (annual). **Staff:** 3. **Budget:** $100,000. **Regional Groups:** 9. **State Groups:** 51. **Local Groups:** 1. **Description:** Promotes model making as a highly skilled profession integral to the design process. Promotes members' continued learning and achievement of professional goals. **Libraries: Type:** reference; not open to the public. **Holdings:** articles. **Awards:** Student and Professional Model Making Contests. **Frequency:** annual. **Type:** scholarship. **Committees:** Awards; Communications; Conference; Education; Marketing and Promotion; Vendor. **Publications:** *Leading Edge*, quarterly. Newsletter. **Price:** included in membership dues. **Circulation:** 1,500. **Advertising:** accepted. Alternate Formats: CD-ROM; online; diskette ● *Membership Directory and Model Maker's Source Book* ● Also publishes technical papers. **Conventions/Meetings:** annual conference and trade show (exhibits) ● periodic seminar and workshop.

7007 ■ California Engineering Foundation (CEF)

2700 Zinfandel Dr.
Rancho Cordova, CA 95670-4827
Ph: (916)853-1914
Fax: (916)853-1921
E-mail: cef@innercite.com
Contact: Dr. Robert J. Kuntz, Pres.

Founded: 1974. **Members:** 100. **Membership Dues:** organization, corporate, $5,000 (annual) ● associate, personal, $200 (annual). **Staff:** 2. **Budget:** $200,000. **State Groups:** 2. **National Groups:** 2. **Description:** Individuals from academia, government, and industry. Promotes a positive policy environment for an industrial-based economy. Provides a forum for business, government, and academic leaders to analyze and implement private, academic, and public policy with regard to technology, science, and economic development and competitiveness. Promotes long-term investment in a new technological infrastructure in the U.S. Areas of interest include: technology and industrial management; earthquake hazard mitigation; technical education; transportation; venture development; systemic reform of engineering education; crisis in the aerospace industry; and space junk. Conducts research and convenes policy development conferences. **Libraries: Type:** reference. **Holdings:** 1,000; archival material, books, business records, clippings, periodicals. **Subjects:** engineering education, technology transfer, scientific/technical policy, transportation policy, defense conversion, economic development, competitiveness, earthquake hazard mitigation, aerospace. **Awards:** Outstanding Service Award. **Frequency:** periodic. **Type:** recognition. **Recipient:** for outstanding service. **Task Forces:** Benign Design; Communications; Defense/Space; Dual Use Conversion; Earthquake; Earthquake Hazard Mitigation; Engineering Education; Mission Aerospace; Mission America; Technical Education; Telecommunication/Electronics; Toxics Engineering; Transportation. **Publications:** *Earthquake Hazard Mitigation Strategies: The Human Resource Element*. **Price:** $5.00 ● *Federal Technology Transfer Forum*. **Price:** $22.90 ● *Global Relevance: A Necessity for Survival*. **Price:** $5.00 ● *Manufacturing the Future Engineer*. Papers ● *Mission America* ● *Reindustrialization of America*. Videos. **Price:** $20.00 ● *Science, Technology and Reindustrialization—An Economic Imperative*. **Price:** $5.00 ● *Technology for Tomorrow's Transportation*. Report. **Price:** $23.30 ● *Transportation Redefined*. **Price:** $22.90 ● Reports ● Reports. Includes topics on policy development. **Conventions/Meetings:** periodic conference - usually October or November ● annual retreat, strategic planning - usually September or October ● periodic workshop, on policy development.

7008 ■ Chinese American Association of Engineering (CAAE)

PO Box 869
New York, NY 10268
Ph: (718)591-6012
URL: http://www.caae.org
Contact: Weihua Jin PhD, Pres.

Founded: 1995. **Multinational. Description:** Serves as a bridge for cooperation between China and the United States in engineering and related fields. Provides assistance in setting up business or launching programs to advertise new techniques, products and equipment in both countries. Offers professional consultation and service to US and China enterprises or individuals. Provides a forum for members to exchange and share professional experience.

7009 ■ Computational Intelligence Society (CIS)

c/o James Keller, VP for Publications
Univ. of MO-Columbia
Elecl. and Cmpt. Engg. Dept.
217 Engg. Bldg. W
Columbia, MO 65211
Ph: (573)882-7339
Fax: (573)882-0397
E-mail: kellerj.@missouri.edu
URL: http://ieee-nns.org
Contact: Vincenzo Piuri, Pres.

Multinational. Description: Scientific, literary, and educational neural networks. Promotes the theory, design, application and development of biologically and linguistically motivated computational paradigms that underscore neural networks, including connectionist systems, genetic algorithms, evolutionary programming, fuzzy systems, and hybrid intelligent systems. **Awards:** Outstanding Papers Awards. **Type:** recognition ● Pioneer Awards. **Type:** recognition ● Service Awards. **Type:** recognition. **Committees:** Awards; Regional Interest; Standing; Technical. **Formerly:** (2004) IEEE Neural Networks Council. **Conventions/Meetings:** conference.

7010 ■ Council of Engineering and Scientific Society Executives (CESSE)

c/o Corie Dacus
PO Box 130656
St. Paul, MN 55113
Ph: (952)838-3268
Fax: (651)765-2890
E-mail: info@cesse.org
URL: http://www.cesse.org
Contact: Patrick Natalie, VP

Founded: 1950. **Members:** 150. **Membership Dues:** CEO, $75 (annual) ● student, $35 (annual). **Description:** Works to advance, in the public interest, the arts and sciences of the management of engineering and scientific societies. **Committees:** Audit; Meetings Policy; Membership Credentials; Nominations and Awards; Strategic Planning; Surveys. **Conventions/Meetings:** annual meeting - 2008 July 15-18, Detroit, MI; 2009 July 21-24, Orlando, FL; 2010 July 13-16, Pittsburgh, PA; 2011 July 19-22, Vancouver, BC, Canada.

7011 ■ Electrical and Computer Engineering Department Heads Association (ECEDHA)

300 W Adams, Ste.1210
Chicago, IL 60606-5114
Ph: (312)559-3724 (312)559-4100
Fax: (312)559-3329
E-mail: information@ecedha.org
URL: http://www.ecedha.org
Contact: Mr. John Janowiak, Exec. Dir.

Founded: 1985. **Members:** 290. **Membership Dues:** individual, institution, $350 (annual). **Staff:** 2. **Regional Groups:** 6. **Description:** Electrical and computer engineering department heads. Works to advance the fields of electrical and computer engineering through development and dissemination of engineering knowledge. Provides a forum for members to exchange ideas and information on improving the educational process. Fosters communication between members and the electrical engineering profession, related industries, academic institutions, and governmental agencies. **Awards:** Innovative Program Award. **Frequency:** annual. **Type:** recognition. **Recipient:** to a department or individual that has developed and demonstrated an innovative program in EE, ECE, EECS education ● Outstanding Leadership and Service Award. **Frequency:** annual. **Type:** recognition. **Recipient:** to a member or former member who has provided substantial leadership and service to the association. **Computer Services:** Mailing lists, electrical and computer engineering departments. **Formerly:** (2002) National Electrical Engineering Department Heads Association. **Publications:** *ECEDHA Newsletter*, annual. **Conventions/Meetings:** annual meeting - always March.

7012 ■ Engineering Society of Detroit (ESD)

2000 Town Ctr., Ste.2610
Southfield, MI 48075
Ph: (248)353-0735
Fax: (248)353-0736
E-mail: esd@esd.org
URL: http://esd.org
Contact: Richard J. Haller, Pres.

Founded: 1895. **Members:** 6,000. **Membership Dues:** professional, $94 (annual) ● student, $24 (annual) ● retired, $36 (annual). **Staff:** 12. **Description:** Engineers from all disciplines; scientists and technologists. Conducts technical programs and engineering refresher courses; sponsors conferences and expositions. Maintains speakers' bureau; offers placement services; although based in Detroit, MI, society membership is international. **Awards:** Outstanding Student Engineer of the Year Award. **Frequency:** annual. **Type:** recognition. **Recipient:** for outstanding undergraduate ESD members ● Outstanding Young Engineer of the Year. **Frequency:** annual. **Type:** recognition. **Recipient:** for outstanding contributions of an engineer below 35 years old. **Committees:** E-Construction; Facility; Program; Publications; Society Awards; Solid Waste; Southfield Schools; Student and Young Engineer Awards. **Publications:** *ESD News*, 8/year. Newsletter. Alternate Formats: online ● *ESD Technology Roster Issue*, annual. Includes calendar of events, industrial directory, products and services guide, and roster of members and consultants. ISSN: 8750-7811. **Advertising:** accepted ● *Technology Century*, bimonthly. Magazine. Contains calendar of events, directory of corporate/sustaining members, and departmental news concerning construction, controls, and materials. **Price:** included in membership dues; $25.00 /year for nonmembers. ISSN: 8750-7811. **Advertising:** accepted. **Conventions/Meetings:** quarterly conference.

7013 ■ Engineering Workforce Commission (EWC)

1620 I St. NW, Ste.210
Washington, DC 20006

Ph: (202)296-2237
Free: (888)400-2237
Fax: (202)296-1151
E-mail: dbateson@aaes.org
URL: http://www.ewc-online.org
Contact: Dan Bateson, Dir.
Founded: 1950. **Members:** 125. **Membership Dues:** academic, $1,260 (annual) ● sustaining, $2,520 (annual) ● senior, $6,000 (annual) ● patron, $12,000 (annual). **Staff:** 3. **Budget:** $500,000. **Description:** Represents commissioners appointed by member societies of the American Association of Engineering Societies (see separate entry) to engage in studies and analyses of the supply, demand, use and remuneration of engineering and technical personnel. Provides representation to government groups dealing with professional manpower policy; consults with industry. Gathers and disseminates information on the engineering profession. Conducts surveys of engineering school enrollments, degrees, and salaries; monitors federal labor statistics. **Committees:** Associates; Publications. **Affiliated With:** American Association of Engineering Societies. **Formerly:** (1993) Engineering Manpower Commission. **Publications:** *Engineering and Technology Degrees*, annual. Report. Contains information on U.S. engineering and engineering technology degrees awarded. **Price:** $179.00 for members (book); $191.00 for members (CD-ROM); $295.00 for nonmembers (book); $315.00 for nonmembers (CD-ROM). ISSN: 0071-0393. Alternate Formats: CD-ROM ● *Engineering and Technology Enrollments*, annual. Report. Contains information on U.S. fall enrollment in engineering and engineering technology. **Price:** $149.00 for members (book); $191.00 for members (CD-ROM); $245.00 for nonmembers (book); $315.00 for nonmembers (CD-ROM). Alternate Formats: CD-ROM ● *Engineers*, quarterly. Bulletin. Reports on all aspects of engineering careers and compensation. **Price:** $105.00/year. ISSN: 1079-7211 ● *Engineers' Salaries: Special Industry Report*, annual. Provides statistics on the salaries of engineers in industry and government. **Price:** $209.00 for members; $345.00 for nonmembers ● *Salaries of Engineers in Education*, biennial. Report. Details median, quartile, decile, and mean salaries of engineers in institutions of education, quantified by academic rank and length of contract. **Price:** $95.00 for members; $155.00 for nonmembers. **Conventions/Meetings:** semiannual Full Commission Meeting - always March and September.

7014 ■ IEEE Engineering Management Society (EMS)
c/o IEEE Admission and Advancement
445 Hoes Ln.
PO Box 6804
Piscataway, NJ 08855-6804
Ph: (732)981-0025 (732)981-9667
Free: (800)678-4333
Fax: (732)981-1721
E-mail: i.engelson@ieee.org
URL: http://www.ewh.ieee.org/soc/ems
Contact: Mr. Gerard Gaynor, Exec. VP
Founded: 1950. **Members:** 6,550. **Membership Dues:** regular, $30 (annual) ● student, $15 (annual). **Local Groups:** 35. **Description:** Encompasses the management sciences applicable to individuals and organizations engaged in or overseeing the management of engineering and technology. Topics of interest include but are not limited to: technology policy development, assessment, and transfer; strategic management and strategic planning; issues related to research, development, design, evaluation, production, and operations; innovation and entrepreneurship; program and project management; education and training related to engineering and technology management; transitioning to management; socioeconomic impact of engineering and technology management. **Awards:** Engineering Manager of the Year. **Frequency:** annual. **Type:** monetary. **Recipient:** for outstanding contributions in the discipline of engineering and technology management ● **Type:** recognition. **Committees:** Chapters; Education; History; Nominations; Professional Activities. **Formerly:** (1958) IRE Management Engineering Group. **Publications:** *Engineering Management*, quarterly. Newsletter. Includes articles and announcements related to engineering and technology management and general society announcements and comments. **Price:** $1.00 for nonmembers; included in membership dues. ISSN: 1066-212X. **Circulation:** 6,000. Alternate Formats: online ● *Engineering Management Review*, quarterly. Journal. Features the needs of managers coping with the problems and opportunities related to improving productivity. ● *Transactions on Engineering Management*, quarterly. Journal. Features research related to engineering and technology management. **Conventions/Meetings:** annual conference (exhibits).

7015 ■ Institute of Electrical and Electronics Engineers - USA (IEEE-USA)
1828 L St. NW, Ste.1202
Washington, DC 20036-5104
Ph: (202)785-0017
Free: (800)701-IEEE
Fax: (202)785-0835
E-mail: ieeeusa@ieee.org
URL: http://www.ieeeusa.org
Contact: Linda Hall, Office Admin. Mgr.
Founded: 1973. **Staff:** 16. **Description:** Recommends policies and implements programs specifically intended to serve and benefit members, the profession, and the public in the U.S. in appropriate professional areas of economic, ethical, legislative, social, and technology policy concern. **Telecommunication Services:** electronic mail, l.hall@ieee.org. **Committees:** Awards and Recognition; Career and Workforce Policy; Communications; Nominations and Appointments. **Publications:** *The Institute*, quarterly. Newspaper. Contains IEEE activities, member profiles, conference information, election news, and career guidance. **Price:** free for members. Alternate Formats: online ● Newsletters. Contains technology careers, society news and issues of interest to local or geographic regions. **Price:** free for members. Alternate Formats: online.

7016 ■ Institute of Industrial Engineers (IIE)
3577 Parkway Ln., Ste.200
Norcross, GA 30092
Ph: (770)449-0460 (770)449-0461
Free: (800)494-0460
Fax: (770)441-3295
E-mail: execoffice@iienet.org
URL: http://www.iienet2.org/Default.aspx
Contact: Don Greene, Exec. Dir.
Founded: 1948. **Members:** 15,000. **Membership Dues:** professional, senior, international (individual), $125 (annual) ● retired, first-year graduating individual, $62 (annual) ● student, $30 (annual). **Staff:** 31. **Budget:** $5,000,000. **Local Groups:** 325. **Multinational. Description:** Serves as professional society of industrial engineers. Concerned with the design, improvement, and installation of integrated systems of people, materials, equipment, and energy. Draws upon specialized knowledge and skill in the mathematical, physical, and social sciences together with the principles and methods of engineering analysis and design, to specify, predict, and evaluate the results obtained from such systems. Maintains technical societies and divisions. **Libraries: Type:** reference. **Holdings:** 3,000. **Awards:** IIE Honors and Awards Program. **Frequency:** annual. **Type:** recognition ● IIE Scholarship and Fellowship Program. **Frequency:** annual. **Type:** scholarship. **Committees:** Special Productivity Projects. **Programs:** Career Guidance. **Absorbed:** (1992) Industrial Management Society. **Formerly:** (1981) American Institute of Industrial Engineers. **Publications:** *Engineering and Management Press Book Catalog* ● *The Engineering Economist*, quarterly. Journal. **Price:** $69.00 /year for individuals; $129.00 /year for institutions ● *IIE Solutions*, monthly. Magazine. For all engineers and managers who are concerned with reducing operating costs, increasing efficiency, and boosting productivity. **Price:** $152.00 included in membership dues; $66.00 /year for nonmembers in U.S.; $85.00 /year for nonmembers outside U.S. ISSN: 1085-1259. **Circulation:** 30,000. **Advertising:** accepted ● *IIE Transactions*, monthly. Journal. **Price:** $252.00 /year for individuals; $796.00 /year for institutions ● *Industrial Management*, bimonthly. Journal. **Price:** free for members; $65.00 for nonmembers in U.S.; $81.00 for nonmembers outside U.S. ● Reports. **Conventions/Meetings:** annual conference (exhibits) ● seminar.

7017 ■ Insulated Cable Engineers Association (ICEA)
PO Box 1568
Carrollton, GA 30112
Ph: (770)830-0369
Fax: (770)830-8501
E-mail: support@icea.net
URL: http://www.icea.net
Founded: 1925. **Members:** 100. **Membership Dues:** professional engineer, $1,800 (annual). **Staff:** 4. **Budget:** $90,000. **Description:** Serves as professional society of insulated cable engineers. Promotes the reliability of insulated conductors for the transmission and distribution of electric energy, control and instrumentation of equipment, and communications. Principal activity is the development of standards for insulated wire and cable. Conducts research programs. **Libraries: Type:** reference. **Holdings:** 50. **Subjects:** standards for insulated and F.O. cables. **Committees:** Technical Advisory. **Sections:** Communications Cable; Control and Instrumentation Cable; Portable Cable; Power Cable. **Formerly:** Insulated Power Cable Engineers Association. **Conventions/Meetings:** annual conference.

7018 ■ International Alliance for Interoperability (IAI)
1090 Vermont Ave. NW, Ste.700
Washington, DC 20005-4905
Ph: (202)289-7800
Fax: (202)289-1092
E-mail: ekennett@nibs.org
URL: http://www.iai-na.org
Contact: Norbert W. Young Jr., Chm.
Members: 40. **Membership Dues:** product manufacturer, hardware and software vendor, contractor, $1,000-$10,000 (annual) ● research institution, trade and professional association, government agencies, $1,000 (annual) ● professional firm, $1,000-$5,000 (annual) ● building owner and operator, $10,000 (annual). **Staff:** 6. **National Groups:** 9. **Multinational. Description:** Develops a standard universal framework that enables and encourages information sharing and interoperability throughout all phases of the whole building life cycle. Promotes effective means of exchanging information among all software platforms and applications serving the construction community by adopting a single Building Information Model (BIM). **Computer Services:** Information services, technical information resources ● online services, news. **Committees:** Architecture; Building Services; Facilities Management; Library. **Working Groups:** aecXML Catalogs; aecXML Design Scheduling and Cost; aecXML Facilities Management; aecXML Procurement. **Publications:** *Interoperability and IAI*. Pamphlet. Alternate Formats: online. **Conventions/Meetings:** periodic meeting.

7019 ■ International Council on Systems Engineering (INCOSE)
2150 N 107th St., Ste.205
Seattle, WA 98133-9009
Ph: (206)361-6607
Free: (800)366-1164
Fax: (206)367-8777
E-mail: info@incose.org
URL: http://www.incose.org
Contact: Paul Robitaille, Pres.
Founded: 1990. **Members:** 7,600. **Membership Dues:** student, $20 (annual) ● individual, $105 (annual) ● corporate (initial fee), $10,000 ● corporate, $2,000 (annual) ● developing country, $53 (annual) ● senior, $55 (annual). **Budget:** $400,000. **Regional Groups:** 52. **Multinational. Description:** Encourages use of the systems engineering approach to solving large-scale problems in industry, academia, and government. Aims to uphold professional standards of systems engineers. Disseminates information on systems engineering; promotes education and research related to systems engineering. **Librar-**

ies: Type: reference. **Holdings:** papers, periodicals, reports. **Subjects:** systems engineering. **Awards:** Chapter Awards. **Frequency:** annual. **Type:** recognition. **Recipient:** for valuable contributions of individual chapter ● Outstanding Journal Paper Award. **Frequency:** annual. **Type:** recognition. **Recipient:** for outstanding paper from Systems Engineering. **Computer Services:** database ● mailing lists. **Committees:** Communications; Symposium; Ways and Means. **Publications:** *eNote*, published every two to four weeks. Newsletter. Contains news, event announcements and items of interest to members. Alternate Formats: online ● *Insights*, quarterly, in January, April, July and October. Newsletter. **Price:** included in membership dues. **Circulation:** 1,600. **Advertising:** accepted ● *Systems Engineering*, quarterly. Journal ● Proceedings, annual. **Price:** $60.00 in U.S. Alternate Formats: CD-ROM ● Annual Report. **Conventions/Meetings:** annual symposium (exhibits).

7020 ■ International Society of Explosives Engineers (ISEE)
30325 Bainbridge Rd.
Cleveland, OH 44139-2295
Ph: (440)349-4400
Fax: (440)349-3788
E-mail: isee@isee.org
URL: http://www.isee.org
Contact: Jeffrey L. Dean CAE, Exec. Dir./Gen. Counsel
Founded: 1974. **Members:** 4,500. **Membership Dues:** individual, associate, $75 (annual) ● individual with foundation contribution, $85 (annual) ● corporate, $395 (annual) ● student, $20 (annual) ● life, $850. **Staff:** 11. **Budget:** $1,500,000. **Regional Groups:** 36. **State Groups:** 33. **Description:** Persons engaged in, or who have been engaged in, explosives engineering; interested persons and organizations, including those involved in the fields of construction, quarrying, mining, demolition, geophysical prospecting, vibration control, drilling and blasting, and the use and handling of explosives in general. Offers services in matters affecting the manufacture, transportation, storage, and use of explosives and related equipment. Acts as a repository for all information, both inside and outside of the U.S., on explosives engineering. Promotes standardization of terminology in explosives engineering and develops standard methods. Encourages inclusion of explosives engineering instruction in engineering curricula. Maintains information bureau and placement service. **Libraries: Type:** reference. **Holdings:** articles, audio recordings, books, periodicals, video recordings. **Subjects:** explosives and blasting, blast vibrations. **Awards:** Blasters Leadership Award. **Frequency:** annual. **Type:** recognition. **Recipient:** for distinguished service to the explosives industry ● President's Award. **Frequency:** annual. **Type:** recognition. **Computer Services:** Mailing lists, of members. **Telecommunication Services:** electronic mail, chafe@explosives.org. **Sections:** Drilling. **Subgroups:** Fragblast; Seismograph. **Absorbed:** American Blasting Association. **Formerly:** (1991) Society of Explosives Engineers. **Publications:** *Explosives Reference Database on CD-ROM*, annual. Alternate Formats: CD-ROM ● *ISEE Blasters' Handbook*, annual ● *Journal of Explosives Engineering*, bimonthly. **Price:** $50.00 in U.S.; $70.00 outside U.S. **Advertising:** accepted ● *Membership Directory and Desk Reference*, annual ● *Proceedings of Annual Conference on Explosives and Blasting Technique*, annual. **Conventions/Meetings:** annual Best in the West Drill and Blast Conference ● annual Blasters Training Seminar, one-day technical training ● annual Conference on Explosives and Blasting Technique - 2009 Feb. 8-11, Denver, CO ● Explosives and Blasting Regulatory Conference.

7021 ■ International Society of Offshore and Polar Engineers (ISOPE)
PO Box 189
Cupertino, CA 95015-0189
Ph: (650)254-1871
Fax: (650)254-2038
E-mail: info@isope.org
URL: http://www.isope.org
Contact: Dr. Jin S. Chung, Exec. Dir.
Founded: 1989. **Members:** 950. **Membership Dues:** full, associate, $90 (annual) ● student, $50 (annual). **Staff:** 3. **Multinational. Description:** Strives to advance arts and sciences and promote technological progress in the fields of offshore, ocean and Arctic and Antarctic engineering, science and environment through international cooperation and participation. **Awards:** Best Paper Award. **Frequency:** annual. **Type:** monetary. **Recipient:** for the best paper(s) of archival value presented at the annual International Offshore and Polar Engineering Conference ● Best Student Paper Award. **Frequency:** annual. **Type:** monetary. **Recipient:** to archival value paper evaluated and selected from annual ISOPE conference ● C.H. Kim Award. **Frequency:** annual. **Type:** monetary. **Recipient:** to those who made outstanding achievements in floating body hydrodynamics ● ISOPE Award. **Frequency:** annual. **Type:** monetary ● ISOPE EUROMS Award. **Frequency:** biennial. **Type:** recognition ● ISOPE OMS Award. **Frequency:** biennial. **Type:** recognition. **Recipient:** for outstanding organization in the ISOPE Ocean Mining Symposium ● ISOPE PACOMS Award. **Frequency:** biennial. **Type:** recognition. **Recipient:** for outstanding organization in the Asia Pacific Offshore Mechanics Symposium ● Jin S. Chung Award. **Frequency:** annual. **Type:** recognition. **Recipient:** for exceptional innovation or professional lifetime achievements in the fields of ocean, offshore, arctic or related engineering or science ● Neptune Award. **Frequency:** annual. **Type:** recognition. **Recipient:** for selfless dedication to and leadership in the establishment and growth of the society ● Offshore Mechanics Scholarship. **Frequency:** annual. **Type:** scholarship ● Session Organizer of the Year Award. **Frequency:** annual. **Type:** monetary. **Recipient:** to the session organizer who invited the largest number of papers or introduced a new emerging technical field of high significance to the annual ISOPE conference. **Boards:** Directors; Editors. **Committees:** Technical. **Programs:** Conference, Symposium and Workshop. **Working Groups:** Deep-Ocean Mining. **Publications:** *International Journal of Offshore and Polar Engineers*, quarterly. **Price:** $135.00 for nonmembers; $90.00 for members. ISSN: 1053-5381. **Circulation:** 1,050. **Advertising:** accepted. Alternate Formats: online; CD-ROM. Also Cited As: *Engineering Index* ● *International Offshore and Polar Engineering Conference and Exhibition*, annual. Proceedings. **Price:** $220.00 hardcopy/CD-ROM. ISSN: 1053-5381. **Advertising:** accepted. Alternate Formats: CD-ROM; online. **Conventions/Meetings:** biennial European Offshore Mechanics Symposium ● biennial Ocean Mining Symposium ● biennial Pacific/Asia Offshore Mechanics Symposium (exhibits).

7022 ■ International Society for Productivity Enhancement (ISPE)
c/o Dr. Biren Prasad, Managing Dir./Managing Ed.
CERA Inst.
PO Box 3882
Tustin, CA 92781-3882
Ph: (714)505-0662 (714)389-2662
Fax: (714)389-2662
E-mail: prasadb1@cox.net
URL: http://www.ceraj.com
Contact: Dr. Biren Prasad, Managing Dir./Managing Ed.
Founded: 1984. **Members:** 1,000. **Membership Dues:** corporate, $100 (annual). **Staff:** 2. **Budget:** $5,000. **Regional Groups:** 4. **State Groups:** 6. **Local Groups:** 1. **National Groups:** 2. **Multinational. Description:** Represents concurrent engineering and productivity. **Libraries: Type:** reference. **Holdings:** 10; articles, books, periodicals. **Subjects:** concurrent engineering, productivity. **Awards:** Best Paper. **Frequency:** annual. **Type:** recognition. **Recipient:** for best papers published in CERA Journal, previous year. **Additional Websites:** http://www.ispe-org.net. **Committees:** Concurrent Engineering. **Publications:** *Concurrent Engineering: Research and Applications*, quarterly. Journal. **Price:** $595.00. ISSN: 1063-293X. **Circulation:** 500. **Advertising:** accepted. Alternate Formats: CD-ROM. Also Cited As: *CERA*. **Conventions/Meetings:** annual conference (exhibits).

7023 ■ International Systems Security Engineering Association (ISSEA)
c/o Dana McCulloch, Relations Coor.
13873 Park Center Rd., Ste.200
Herndon, VA 20171
Ph: (703)478-7615
Fax: (703)478-7654
E-mail: dmcculloch@ewa.com
URL: http://www.issea.org
Contact: Dana McCulloch, Relations Coor.
Founded: 1999. **Membership Dues:** student, $25 (annual) ● individual, $80 (annual) ● student, $40 (biennial) ● individual, $150 (biennial) ● sustaining (based on classes), $500-$5,000 (annual). **Multinational. Description:** Promotes and enhances the Systems Security Engineering Capability Maturity Model. Provides educational and networking opportunities to the systems security engineering community. Promotes mature security capability among system and software developers, service providers, operations managers and risk management professionals. **Conventions/Meetings:** annual conference.

7024 ■ Korean-American Scientists and Engineers Association (KSEA)
1952 Gallows Rd., Ste.300
Vienna, VA 22182
Ph: (703)748-1221
Fax: (703)748-1331
E-mail: admin@ksea.org
URL: http://www.ksea.org
Contact: Ashley Kim, Admin. Mgr.
Founded: 1971. **Members:** 10,000. **Membership Dues:** regular/international, $35 (annual) ● graduate, $15 (annual). **Staff:** 15. **State Groups:** 55. **Languages:** English, Korean. **Multinational. Description:** Represents scientists and engineers holding single or advanced degrees. Promotes friendship and mutuality among Korean and American scientists and engineers; contributes to Korea's scientific, technological, industrial, and economic developments; strengthens the scientific, technological, and cultural bonds between Korea and the U.S. Sponsors symposium. Maintains speakers' bureau, placement service, and biographical archives. Compiles statistics. **Libraries: Type:** reference. **Holdings:** 100; books. **Subjects:** scientific handbooks and yearbooks in Korean. **Awards:** KSEA Scholarship. **Frequency:** annual. **Type:** scholarship. **Recipient:** for outstanding students with Korean heritage who have excelled in academics and community services. **Telecommunication Services:** electronic mail, sejong@ksea.org. **Committees:** Contest; Election; Fund Management; Honors and Awards; Long-range Planning; Nomination; Rules; Scholarship. **Formerly:** (2005) Korean Scientists and Engineers Association in America. **Publications:** *KSEA Newsletter*, bimonthly ● Membership Directory, triennial. **Conventions/Meetings:** annual conference and meeting - always September in Washington, DC.

7025 ■ Machining and Material Removal Community
PO Box 930
Dearborn, MI 48121
Ph: (313)271-1500
Free: (800)733-4763
Fax: (313)425-3400
E-mail: techcommunities@sme.org
URL: http://www.sme.org/mta
Contact: Mark Tomlinson, Exec. Dir./Gen. Mgr.
Founded: 2003. **Membership Dues:** regular, $125 (annual) ● student, $20 (annual). **Description:** Coordinates technical groups that discuss, explore, and advance ideas related to cutting processes and machining systems. **Libraries: Type:** reference. **Holdings:** articles, books, papers. **Subjects:** technology. **Awards:** Best Paper Awards. **Type:** recognition. **Computer Services:** database, puts SME members in touch with other manufacturing professionals ready to address technology problems specific questions, comments, or problems. **Formerly:** (2004) Machining Technology Association of SME. **Publications:** *Com-*

munity News, quarterly. Newsletter. Contains up-to-date information on the associations' activities. ● *Journal of Manufacturing Processes*, semiannual. **Price:** $499.00 in U.S. and Canada, Mexico. Also Cited As: *JMP* ● *Journal of Manufacturing Systems*, quarterly. **Price:** $499.00 in U.S. and Canada, Mexico. Also Cited As: *JMS* ● *Machining Technology*, quarterly. Newsletter. Alternate Formats: online ● *Manufacturing Engineering*. Magazine. **Price:** included in membership dues.

7026 ■ Malayalee Engineers Association in North America (MEANA)
6807 Fieldstone Dr.
Burr Ridge, IL 60527
Ph: (630)851-1690
E-mail: ajit.chandran@bankofamerica.com
URL: http://www.meanausa.org
Contact: Ajit Chandran, Contact
Founded: 1992. **Members:** 250. **Membership Dues:** student, $25 (annual) ● life, $100. **Multinational. Description:** Represents the interests of Malayalee engineers in North America. Promotes cultural interaction and professional development of its members through technical meetings, networking and information sharing. Aims to help the state of Kerala by promoting and encouraging engineering education. **Awards:** Malayalee Engineer of the Year. **Frequency:** annual. **Type:** recognition. **Recipient:** to distinguished engineers from Kerala ● MEANA Project-100 Scholarship Program. **Frequency:** annual. **Type:** scholarship. **Recipient:** for engineering students in Kerala. **Publications:** Newsletter.

7027 ■ NACE International: The Corrosion Society
1440 S Creek Dr.
Houston, TX 77084-4906
Ph: (281)228-6200
Free: (800)797-6223
Fax: (281)228-6300
E-mail: firstservice@nace.org
URL: http://www.nace.org
Contact: Tony Keane, Exec. Dir.
Founded: 1943. **Members:** 15,800. **Membership Dues:** individual, $130 (annual) ● senior, $65 (annual) ● student, $20 (annual) ● corporate, $500-$5,000 (annual). **Staff:** 58. **Budget:** $10,000,000. **Regional Groups:** 8. **Local Groups:** 82. **Multinational. Description:** Serves as professional technical society dedicated to reducing the economic impact of corrosion, promoting public safety, and protecting the environment by advancing the knowledge of corrosion engineering and science. Conducts programs for technical training, sponsors technical conferences, and produces standards, publications, and software. Maintains certification program for engineers, technicians, and coating inspectors. **Libraries: Type:** reference. **Holdings:** 5,000; articles, books, periodicals. **Subjects:** corrosion and materials. **Awards:** A.B. Campbell Award. **Type:** recognition. **Recipient:** for an outstanding manuscript ● Distinguished Service Award. **Type:** recognition. **Recipient:** for an elected or appointed member ● Fellow Honor. **Type:** recognition. **Recipient:** for outstanding NACE members ● Frank Newman Speller Award. **Type:** recognition. **Recipient:** for significant contributions to corrosion engineering ● H.H. Uhlig Award. **Type:** recognition. **Recipient:** for young educators ● Presidential Achievement Award. **Type:** recognition. **Recipient:** for an individual or group ● R.A. Brannon Award. **Type:** recognition. **Recipient:** for outstanding work by a current member of NACE ● T.J. Hull Award. **Type:** recognition. **Recipient:** for outstanding contribution to NACE in the field of publications ● Technical Achievement Award. **Type:** recognition. **Recipient:** for technical achievement in corrosion engineering ● W.R. Whitney Award. **Type:** recognition. **Recipient:** for an individual who has made a major contribution to corrosion science. **Computer Services:** database, contains abstracts on corrosion, metals, microbiology, and sulphuric acid; consultants directory; subject indexes. **Telecommunication Services:** electronic mail, tony.keane@nace.org. **Committees:** Corrosion Coordinating. **Subgroups:** Aerospace; Aqueous Environments; Corrosion of Military Equipment; Corrosion Oil and Gal Well Equipment; Corrosion Problems in the Process Industries; Energy Technology; Pipe Line Corrosion; Protective Coatings; Refining Industry Corrosion; Transportation; Utilities. **Formerly:** (1993) National Association of Corrosion Engineers; (1999) NACE International. **Publications:** *Corrosion*. Journal. **Price:** $95.00 for members in U.S.; $170.00 for nonmembers in U.S.; $220.00 for members outside U.S.; $320.00 for libraries in U.S. ISSN: 0010-9312 ● *Materials Performance*, monthly. Journal. Includes topics on corrosion and prevention technology. **Price:** included in membership dues. **Circulation:** 17,000. **Advertising:** accepted. Alternate Formats: CD-ROM; diskette. **Conventions/Meetings:** annual conference - usually fall. 2008 Oct. 19-22, Montreal, QC, Canada; 2009 Oct. 7-10, Palm Springs, CA ● annual Corrosion - conference (exhibits) - usually March or April ● periodic regional meeting.

7028 ■ National Academy of Engineering (NAE)
500 Fifth St. NW
Washington, DC 20001
Ph: (202)334-3200 (202)334-3677
Fax: (202)334-2290
E-mail: ldavis@nae.edu
URL: http://www.nae.edu
Contact: Lance Davis, Exec. Off.
Founded: 1964. **Members:** 2,389. **Staff:** 30. **Budget:** $15,000,000. **Description:** Private, honorary organization whose members are elected in recognition of their distinguished and continuing contributions to engineering. With the National Academy of Sciences, advises the federal government through the National Research Council. Promotes public understanding of the role engineering plays in technological fields. Sponsors programs aimed at meeting national needs in the field; encourages research. **Awards:** Arthur M. Bueche Award. **Frequency:** annual. **Type:** recognition. **Recipient:** for statesmanship in technology ● Bernard M. Gordon Prize. **Frequency:** annual. **Type:** recognition. **Recipient:** for innovation in engineering and technology education ● Charles Stark Draper Prize. **Frequency:** annual. **Type:** recognition. **Recipient:** for engineering achievements ● Founders Award. **Frequency:** annual. **Type:** recognition. **Recipient:** for outstanding engineering accomplishments ● Fritz J. and Dolores H. Russ Prize. **Frequency:** biennial. **Type:** recognition. **Recipient:** for biotechnology/bioengineering achievements ● **Type:** recognition. **Publications:** *The Bridge*, quarterly. Journal. Reports on academy activities. **Price:** free. **Circulation:** 5,000. Alternate Formats: online ● Proceedings ● Reports. **Conventions/Meetings:** annual meeting.

7029 ■ National Association of County Engineers (NACE)
25 Massachusetts Ave. NW, Ste.580
Washington, DC 20001-1430
Ph: (202)393-5041
Fax: (202)393-2630
E-mail: nace@naco.org
URL: http://www.countyengineers.org
Contact: Anthony R. Giancola PE, Exec. Dir.
Founded: 1956. **Members:** 1,900. **Membership Dues:** voting (associate), $130 (annual) ● voting (affiliate), $120 (annual) ● corporate (bronze), $500 (annual) ● corporate (silver), $750 (annual) ● corporate (gold), $1,000 (annual) ● corporate (platinum), $5,000 (annual) ● corporate (diamond), $2,500 (annual) ● corporate (platinum), $5,000 (annual). **Staff:** 3. **Budget:** $400,000. **Regional Groups:** 5. **State Groups:** 30. **Description:** Professional organization of engineers and road managers employed by county agencies. Others related to the field. Objectives are: to advance county engineering by providing a forum for the exchange of ideas and information; to stimulate the growth of individual state organizations of county engineers; to improve relations between county engineers and other agencies; to monitor national legislation affecting county transportation/public works departments and through NACo, provide NACE's legislative opinions. Conducts contract research with Federal Highway Administration to produce county highway operational manuals and instruction seminars. Holds annual meeting and technical conference. **Libraries: Type:** open to the public. **Holdings:** 43; books, video recordings. **Subjects:** engineering, road related topics. **Awards:** Urban and Rural County Engineer Award. **Frequency:** annual. **Type:** recognition. **Computer Services:** Mailing lists, of members ● online services, directory of members. **Committees:** Data and Information; Legislative; State Affiliate Development. **Programs:** Technical Transfer. **Affiliated With:** National Association of Counties. **Publications:** *County Action Guide Series* ● *NACE Newsletter*, monthly. **Price:** free for members. **Circulation:** 1,900 ● *Training Guide Series* ● Membership Directory, annual. **Price:** $100.00 for nonmembers; included in membership dues. **Advertising:** accepted. Alternate Formats: CD-ROM; online. **Conventions/Meetings:** annual Management and Technical Conference, with technical sessions on management, technology and transportation (exhibits).

7030 ■ National Association of Engineering Student Councils (NAESC)
c/o National Society of Professional Engineers
1420 King St.
Alexandria, VA 22314-2794
Ph: (480)231-8054
E-mail: president@naesc.org
Contact: Mr. Aric Reutlinger, Pres.
Founded: 1983. **Membership Dues:** individual, $75 (annual). **Regional Groups:** 5. **Description:** Serves engineering student councils by facilitating communication among member councils. Promotes engineering education and organizes programs and events for the benefit of members. Provides a resource of information about engineering student activities, and serves as a collective voice of Engineering Student Councils. **Computer Services:** Information services, wiki links ● online services, forum. **Boards:** Advisory. **Affiliated With:** National Council of Examiners for Engineering and Surveying; National Society of Professional Engineers. **Publications:** Handbook, annual. Provides a summary of the organization and serves as a reference for engineering councils. Alternate Formats: online. **Conventions/Meetings:** annual conference.

7031 ■ National Council of Examiners for Engineering and Surveying (NCEES)
280 Seneca Creek Rd.
PO Box 1686
Clemson, SC 29633-1686
Ph: (864)654-6824
Free: (800)250-3196
Fax: (864)654-6033
E-mail: pfenno@ncees.org
URL: http://www.ncees.org
Contact: Jerry Carter, Exec. Dir.
Founded: 1920. **Members:** 70. **Staff:** 35. **Budget:** $7,000,000. **Regional Groups:** 4. **State Groups:** 70. **Description:** Service organization for engineering and land surveying registration boards. Works to promote uniform standards of registration and to coordinate interstate registration of engineers. Maintains 17 standing and 5 special committees; operates speakers' bureau; compiles statistics. **Libraries: Type:** reference. **Formerly:** (1967) National Council of State Boards of Engineering Examiners; (1989) National Council of Engineering Examiners. **Publications:** *Handbook for Structural Engineers*. Contains samples of typical examination questions. **Price:** $33.00 ● *Land Surveying Candidate Handbook*. **Price:** $33.00 ● *National Council of Examiners for Engineering and Surveying; Volume I, II, & III*. Handbook. Covers fundamentals, principles and practice of engineering. ● *PE Sample Problems: Chemical, Civil, Electrical, Environmental and Mechanical*. Pamphlet ● *Principals and Practice of Engineering, Sample Problems and Solutions*. Book. Contains chemical, civil, electrical, environmental, and mechanical test samples. **Price:** $23.00 ● *Registration Bulletin*, quarterly.

7032 ■ National Council of Structural Engineers Associations (NCSEA)
645 N Michigan Ave., Ste.540
Chicago, IL 60611

Ph: (312)649-4600
Fax: (312)649-5840
E-mail: office@ncsea.com
URL: http://www.ncsea.com
Contact: Jeanne M. Vogelzang, Exec. Dir.

Founded: 1993. **Members:** 10,000. **Membership Dues:** associate (non-commercial organization), $500 (annual) ● associate (commercial organization), $1,000 (annual) ● affiliate, $500 (annual) ● sustaining, $200 (annual). **Staff:** 3. **Budget:** $350,000. **State Groups:** 40. **Description:** State organizations of licensed structural engineers. Seeks to advance the study, teaching, and practice of structural engineering. Provides support and assistance to members; coordinates members' activities and sponsors educational and continuing professional development programs. **Libraries: Type:** not open to the public. **Holdings:** periodicals. **Subjects:** bridges, high-rises, building codes. **Awards:** Outstanding Project Award for Bridge & Transportation Structures over 150 ft. singlespan, or any multiple span. **Frequency:** annual. **Type:** recognition ● Outstanding Project Award for Bridge & Transportation Structures up to 150 ft. simple span. **Frequency:** annual. **Type:** recognition ● Outstanding Project Award for Buildings 5 million to 25 million. **Frequency:** annual. **Type:** recognition ● Outstanding Project Award for Buildings Less than 5 million. **Frequency:** annual. **Type:** recognition ● Outstanding Project Award for Buildings Over 25 million. **Frequency:** annual. **Type:** recognition. **Telecommunication Services:** electronic mail, execdir@ncsea.com. **Committees:** Advocacy; Code Advisory; Member Organization Development; Publications. **Publications:** *STRUCTURE*, monthly. Magazine. **Price:** $35.00 student in U.S.; $65.00 for nonmembers in U.S.; $90.00 for nonmembers in U.S. and Canada; $125.00 for nonmembers other countries. ISSN: 1536-4283. **Circulation:** 32,000. **Advertising:** accepted. Alternate Formats: online ● *Structure Connection*, quarterly. Newsletter. Alternate Formats: online. **Conventions/Meetings:** annual conference (exhibits) - 2008 Oct. 23-25, Cleveland, OH ● annual Winter Institute - meeting (exhibits).

7033 ■ National Institute for Certification in Engineering Technologies (NICET)

1420 King St.
Alexandria, VA 22314-2794
Ph: (703)548-1518
Free: (888)IS-NICET
Fax: (703)682-2756
E-mail: test@nicet.org
URL: http://www.nicet.org
Contact: Michael A. Clark, Gen. Mgr.

Founded: 1961. **Staff:** 17. **Budget:** $3,000,000. **Nonmembership. Description:** Grants and issues certificates to engineering technicians and technologists who voluntarily apply for certification and satisfy competency criteria through examinations and verification of work experience. Requirements for certification involve work experience in terms of job task proficiency and length of progressively more responsible experience. Levels of certification are Technician Trainee, Associate Engineering Technician, Engineering Technician, Senior Engineering Technician, Associate Engineering Technologist, and Certified Engineering Technologist. **Convention/Meeting:** none. **Telecommunication Services:** additional toll-free number, (800)828-1120. **Formed by Merger of:** (1981) Institute for the Certification of Engineering Technicians; (1981) Engineering Technologist Certification Institute. **Publications:** *NICET Newsletter*, semiannual. For technicians and technologists who have obtained NICET certification. **Price:** included in annual certification fee ● *Program Detail Manual*. Series of manuals each explaining a particular certification program.

7034 ■ National Society of Black Engineers (NSBE)

205 Daingerfield Rd.
Alexandria, VA 22314
Ph: (703)549-2207
Fax: (703)683-5312
E-mail: info@nsbe.org
URL: http://national.nsbe.org
Contact: Ainsley A. Stewart Jr., Chm.

Founded: 1975. **Members:** 18,000. **Membership Dues:** student, $5-$10 (annual) ● alumni/professional, $50 (annual). **Staff:** 25. **Budget:** $5,800,000. **Regional Groups:** 6. **State Groups:** 320. **Local Groups:** 220. **National Groups:** 2. **Multinational. Description:** Engineering and science students. Seeks to increase the number of minority graduates in engineering and technology. Works to increase the number of Black culturally responsible engineers and scientists who excel academically and professionally, while positively impacting the community. Sponsors seminars and workshops geared toward preparing students for careers, the industry, and leadership roles. **Awards:** Golden Torch Awards. **Frequency:** annual. **Type:** recognition. **Recipient:** for individuals, corporations, and academic institutions that espouse the mission of the organization ● NSBE Academic Scholarships. **Frequency:** annual. **Type:** scholarship. **Recipient:** for members. **Computer Services:** database, engineering students with 3.2 GPA or higher ● online services, resume distribution service (RDDS). **Telecommunication Services:** electronic mail, membership@nsbe.org. **Publications:** *Alumni Update*, quarterly. Newsletter. **Price:** included in membership dues. **Circulation:** 2,000 ● *Bridge Magazine*. **Price:** $5.00/year. **Circulation:** 100,000. **Advertising:** accepted ● *Career Engineer*, monthly. Magazine. **Price:** $5.00/year. **Circulation:** 10,000. **Advertising:** accepted ● *NSBE Bulletin*, bimonthly. Newsletter. **Circulation:** 3,500. **Advertising:** accepted ● Magazine, quarterly. **Price:** $5.00/year. **Circulation:** 15,000. **Advertising:** accepted ● Newsletter, weekly. Alternate Formats: online. **Conventions/Meetings:** annual Learning From the Past to Engineer Our Future - convention (exhibits).

7035 ■ National Society of Professional Engineers (NSPE)

1420 King St.
Alexandria, VA 22314-2794
Ph: (703)684-2800
Free: (888)285-6773
Fax: (703)836-4875
E-mail: memserv@nspe.org
URL: http://www.nspe.org
Contact: Robert S. Miller III, Pres.

Founded: 1934. **Members:** 60,000. **Membership Dues:** licensed/recent graduate, $220 (annual) ● student, $20 (annual). **Staff:** 48. **Budget:** $6,000,000. **Regional Groups:** 6. **State Groups:** 54. **Local Groups:** 535. **Description:** Represents professional engineers and engineers-in-training in all fields registered in accordance with the laws of states or territories of the U.S. or provinces of Canada; qualified graduate engineers, student members, and registered land surveyors. Is concerned with social, professional, ethical, and economic considerations of engineering as a profession; encompasses programs in public relations, employment practices, ethical considerations, education, and career guidance. Monitors legislative and regulatory actions of interest to the engineering profession. **Awards:** Distinguished Service Award. **Frequency:** annual. **Type:** recognition. **Recipient:** for exceptional technical contributions to the engineering profession ● Engineering Education Excellence Award. **Frequency:** annual. **Type:** recognition. **Recipient:** for engineering educators ● Federal Engineer of the Year Award. **Frequency:** annual. **Type:** recognition. **Recipient:** to an engineer employed by a federal agency ● Mentor of the Year Award. **Frequency:** annual. **Type:** recognition. **Recipient:** for a member who best exemplifies the ideal image of a mentor ● NSPE Award. **Frequency:** annual. **Type:** recognition. **Recipient:** for outstanding contributions to the engineering profession ● NSPE Fellow Membership Grade. **Frequency:** annual. **Type:** recognition. **Recipient:** for licensed members who have demonstrated exemplary service ● Young Engineer of the Year Award. **Frequency:** annual. **Type:** recognition. **Recipient:** for outstanding contributions. **Telecommunication Services:** additional toll-free number, (800)417-0348. **Committees:** Political Action. **Departments:** Communications; Education and Professional Development; Ethics and Legal; Government Relations; Licensure; Policy and Headquarters Operation; Professional Engineers in Construction; Professional Engineers in Education; Professional Engineers in Government; Professional Engineers in Industry; Professional Engineers in Private Practice; Professional Relations; Society Development. **Absorbed:** (1966) American Association of Engineers. **Publications:** *Engineering Licensure Laws Manual and CD*. **Price:** $125.00 for members; $325.00 for nonmembers ● *Engineering Times*, quarterly. Newspaper. Covers matters of importance to engineering educators and students. **Price:** included in membership dues; $50.00 for nonmembers. **Advertising:** accepted. Alternate Formats: online ● *Income and Salary Survey*. Report. Printed report and CD. **Price:** $150.00 for members; $250.00 for nonmembers. Alternate Formats: diskette ● *NSPE Update*, monthly. Newsletter. Alternate Formats: online. **Conventions/Meetings:** annual convention (exhibits) - always July.

7036 ■ North America Taiwanese Engineers' Association (NATEA)

PO Box 360776
Milpitas, CA 95036
E-mail: hq@natea.org
URL: http://www.natea.org
Contact: Tom H. Chang, Pres.

Founded: 1991. **Regional Groups:** 10. **Multinational. Description:** Promotes technological knowledge and its applications. Provides professional development for Taiwanese Americans. Facilitates technology development, entrepreneurship and job opportunities. Increases community awareness of the achievements of Taiwanese American engineers and scientists. Encourages and provides assistance to Taiwanese American youth to pursue scientific or engineering careers. **Publications:** *NATEA Journal*. **Advertising:** accepted ● *Overseas Taiwanese Science and Technology Newsletter*. **Advertising:** accepted. Alternate Formats: online. Also Cited As: *OTSTN*.

7037 ■ Refrigerating Engineers and Technicians Association (RETA)

PO Box 1819
Salinas, CA 93902
Ph: (831)455-8783
Fax: (831)455-7856
E-mail: info@reta.com
URL: http://www.reta.com
Contact: Don Tragethon, Exec. Dir.

Founded: 1910. **Members:** 3,185. **Membership Dues:** individual, $90 (annual). **Staff:** 4. **Budget:** $600,000. **Regional Groups:** 32. **Local Groups:** 32. **Description:** Focuses on the professional development of industrial refrigeration operators and technicians. Offers self-study and on-line training courses on industrial refrigeration. Offers a nationally-recognized certification program for operators and technicians on two levels of understanding and knowledge. **Formerly:** National Association Practical Refrigerating Engineers. **Publications:** *RETA Breeze*, bimonthly. Newsletter. **Price:** free for members. Alternate Formats: online. **Conventions/Meetings:** annual convention, supported by more than 80 exhibiting manufacturers and contractors (exhibits) - 2008 Sept. 23-26, Hershey, PA; 2009 Oct. 13-16, Monterey, CA ● annual meeting (exhibits).

7038 ■ Reliability Engineering and Management Institute/Reliability Testing Institute (REMI/RTI)

1130 N Mountain Ave., Bldg. No. 119
PO Box 210119, Rm. N517
Tucson, AZ 85721-0119
Ph: (520)297-2679 (520)621-6120
Fax: (520)621-8191
E-mail: dimitri@u.arizona.edu
URL: http://www.u.arizona.edu/~dimitri
Contact: Dr. Dimitri B. Kececioglu PhD, Dir.

Founded: 1963. **Members:** 37,000. **Staff:** 6. **Budget:** $300,000. **Local Groups:** 1. **Languages:** English, French, German, Greek. **For-Profit. Description:** Publicizes all aspects, particularly implementation and management of Reliability Engineering, Availability and Maintainability Engineering, Reliability Testing, and Mechanical Reliability Engineering. Puts on two institutes each year, and conducts conferences and training seminars on mentioned subject areas. **Libraries: Type:** reference. **Holdings:** 3,000; articles, books, periodicals. **Subjects:** reliability engineering, reliability testing, maintainability engineering. **Awards: Type:** recognition. **Recipient:** for expert lecturers. **Computer Services:** database, reliability engineers worldwide ● mailing lists. **Formerly:** (2004) Reliability Engineering and Management Institute. **Publications:** *Burn-In Testing: Its Quantification and Optimization.* Book. Provides comprehensive list of burn-in terminology and acronyms. ● *Environmental Stress Screening: Its Quantification, Optimization and Management.* Book. Covers the primary approaches in modern industry to precipitate and eliminate latent or hidden defects in products. ● *Maintainability, Availability and Operational Readiness Engineering Handbook.* Provides all the practical tools of designing for ease of maintenance and quantifying. ● *Proceedings of the Reliability Engineering and Management Institute*, annual. Contains summary of presentations on reliability, maintainability, availability, software, mechanical reliability, and reliability growth. **Price:** $55.00/copy. **Circulation:** 250 ● *Proceedings of the Reliability Testing Institute*, annual. Contains compendium of presentations on reliability, maintainability, availability, software reliability, and reliability growth. **Price:** $55.00/copy. **Circulation:** 250 ● *Reliability Engineering Handbook.* Covers early chance and wear out reliability as experienced in the three life periods of components, equipment and systems. ● *Reliability & Life Testing Handbook.* Covers the latest techniques in reliability data acquisition, reduction and analysis. **Conventions/Meetings:** annual Reliability Engineering and Management Institute - conference - always in Tucson, AZ ● annual Reliability Testing Institute - conference - always in Tucson, AZ.

7039 ■ Silicon Valley Chinese Engineers Association (SCEA)

PO Box 612283
San Jose, CA 95161
E-mail: info@scea.org
URL: http://www.scea.org/web/index.asp
Contact: Wei Wang, Chair

Founded: 1989. **Members:** 4,000. **Membership Dues:** regular, $20 (annual). **Staff:** 11. **Multinational. Description:** Represents professional engineers of Chinese heritage. **Computer Services:** Mailing lists, open to non-members ● online services, forums. **Telecommunication Services:** electronic mail, karen_cai@scea.org. **Publications:** Newsletter, weekly. Alternate Formats: online. **Conventions/Meetings:** conference ● meeting ● seminar ● workshop.

7040 ■ Society of Cable Telecommunications Engineers (SCTE)

140 Philips Rd.
Exton, PA 19341-1318
Ph: (610)363-6888
Free: (800)542-5040
Fax: (610)363-5898
E-mail: scte@scte.org
URL: http://www.scte.org
Contact: John D. Clark Jr., Pres./CEO

Founded: 1969. **Members:** 15,000. **Membership Dues:** retired, student, $29 (annual) ● regular, foreign, $58 (annual) ● sustaining, $350 (annual). **Staff:** 40. **Regional Groups:** 75. **Languages:** English, Spanish. **Description:** Persons engaged in engineering, construction, installation, technical direction, management, or administration of cable telecommunications and broadband communications technologies. Also eligible are students in communications, educators, government and regulatory agency employees, and affiliated trade associations. Dedicated to the technical training and further education of members. Provides technical training and certification and is an American National Standards Institute (ANSI) approved Standards Development Organization for the cable communications industry. **Libraries: Type:** reference. **Holdings:** archival material. **Formerly:** (1995) Society of Cable Television Engineers. **Publications:** *Interval*, monthly. Newsletter. Features society news. **Price:** included in membership dues. ISSN: 0164-677X. Alternate Formats: online ● *Technical Monograph*, periodic ● *Videotape Programs*, periodic ● Reports ● Also publishes management guidelines.

7041 ■ Society of Engineering Science (SES)

c/o Prof. Judith A. Todd, Sec.
Pennsylvania State Univ.
Dept. of Engineering Science and Mechanics
212 EES Bldg.
University Park, PA 16802
E-mail: jtodd@psu.edu
URL: http://www.sesinc.org
Contact: Prof. Judith A. Todd, Sec.

Founded: 1963. **Members:** 300. **Membership Dues:** regular, $50 (annual). **Description:** Individuals with at least a baccalaureate degree who are engaged in any aspect of engineering science or in other pursuits that contributes to the advancement of engineering science. Fosters and promotes the interchange of ideas and information among the various fields of engineering science and among engineering science and the fields of theoretical and applied physics, chemistry, and mathematics. Is dedicated to the advancement of interdisciplinary research and to the establishment of a bridge between science and engineering. **Awards:** A.C. Eringen Medal. **Frequency:** annual. **Type:** medal. **Recipient:** for outstanding achievements in Engineering Science. **Publications:** *Abstracts of Annual Meeting*, annual ● Newsletter, periodic. **Conventions/Meetings:** annual conference (exhibits).

7042 ■ Society of Hispanic Professional Engineers (SHPE)

5400 E Olympic Blvd., Ste.210
Los Angeles, CA 90022
Ph: (323)725-3970
Fax: (323)725-0316
E-mail: shpenational@shpe.org
URL: http://oneshpe.shpe.org/wps/portal/national
Contact: Diana Gomez, Pres.

Founded: 1974. **Members:** 8,000. **Membership Dues:** student, $5 (annual) ● associate, $35 (annual) ● regular/professional, $45 (annual) ● life-associate, $400 ● life-regular/professional, $500. **Staff:** 5. **Regional Groups:** 6. **State Groups:** 40. **Local Groups:** 33. **Languages:** English, Spanish. **Description:** Represents engineers, student engineers, and scientists. Aims to increase the number of Hispanic engineers by providing motivation and support to students. Sponsors competitions and educational programs. Maintains placement service and speakers' bureau; compiles statistics. **Telecommunication Services:** electronic mail, membership@shpe.org. **Committees:** Advancing Careers in Engineering; Entrepreneurship; Foreign Affairs; Human Resources; Leadership Development; Professional Chapters; Scholarships; Socials and Nominations; Student Affairs. **Publications:** *SHPE National Newsletter*, bimonthly. **Price:** included in membership dues. **Circulation:** 8,000. **Advertising:** accepted ● Magazine, quarterly. **Price:** included in membership dues. **Circulation:** 15,000. **Advertising:** accepted. Alternate Formats: online. **Conventions/Meetings:** annual Career Conference (exhibits).

7043 ■ Society of Mexican American Engineers and Scientists (MAES)

11500 Northwest Fwy., Ste.200V
Houston, TX 77092
Ph: (281)557-3677
Fax: (832)202-2699
E-mail: questions@maes-natl.org
URL: http://www.maes-natl.org
Contact: Michael Acosta, Natl. Pres.

Founded: 1974. **Members:** 3,000. **Membership Dues:** student, $10 (annual) ● professional, $50 (annual) ● life, $1,000. **Budget:** $100,000. **Local Groups:** 11. **Multinational. Description:** Represents Mexican-American engineers, scientists, and persons in administrative positions directly related to the engineering or scientific fields; college students in engineering or science. Increases opportunities and recognition of Latinos in engineering and science. Promotes placement of Latinos in professional engineering and the academic and professional communities to improve educational and employment opportunities for Latino engineers and scientists. **Awards:** MAES Gold Medal Awards. **Frequency:** annual. **Type:** medal. **Recipient:** to Latinos who have contributed to the advancement of Latinos in science and engineering. **Telecommunication Services:** electronic mail, secretary@maes-natl.org. **Committees:** Education; Government Communication Service; Professional Development; Scholarships. **Formerly:** (1989) Mexican-American Engineering Society. **Publications:** *Annual National Symposium Proceedings*, annual ● *National Newsletter*, monthly ● Magazine, quarterly. **Conventions/Meetings:** annual National Leadership Conference ● annual symposium, includes career fair (exhibits).

7044 ■ Society of Motion Picture and Television Engineers (SMPTE)

3 Barker Ave.
White Plains, NY 10601
Ph: (914)761-1100
Fax: (914)761-3115
URL: http://www.smpte.org
Contact: Robert B. Kisor, Pres.

Founded: 1916. **Members:** 8,000. **Membership Dues:** active, $135 (annual) ● student, $35 (annual) ● sustaining, $750 (annual) ● bronze, $2,500 (annual) ● silver, $5,000 (annual) ● gold, $7,500 (annual) ● platinum, $25,000 (annual) ● sponsor, 9, $1,250 (annual). **Staff:** 13. **Regional Groups:** 9. **State Groups:** 27. **Description:** Professional engineers and technicians in motion pictures, television, motion imaging and allied arts and sciences. Advances engineering technology, disseminates scientific information, and sponsors lectures, exhibitions, and conferences, advances the theory and practice of engineering. Develops standards for motion pictures and television and sponsors standards promulgated by the American National Standards Institute (see separate entry), promotes interchangeability and provides operating efficiency and standards subscription service. Makes available visual and sound test films for use as standardized measuring tools. **Awards: Frequency:** annual. **Type:** recognition. **Recipient:** for outstanding contributions to motion pictures and television. **Computer Services:** Mailing lists, of members. **Committees:** Audio Recording and Reproduction Technology; Film Technology; Hybrid Technology; Motion Picture Laboratory Services Technology; Motion Picture Projection Technology; Television Production Technology; Television Recording and Reproduction Technology; Television Signal Technology. **Publications:** *News and Notes*, monthly ● *SMPTE Journal, Engineering Documents and Industry News*, monthly. Books. **Price:** $125.00 /year for nonmembers; included in membership dues ● Directory, annual ● Journal, monthly ● Reports. **Conventions/Meetings:** annual Advanced Motion Imaging Conference - always January or February ● annual Technical Conference and Exhibition (exhibits) - usually fall, October or November.

7045 ■ Society of Piping Engineers and Designers (SPED)

9105 W Sam Houston Pkwy. N, Ste.700-193
Houston, TX 77064
Ph: (832)286-3404
E-mail: spedexec@spedweb.com
URL: http://www.spedweb.org
Contact: Dr. William G. Beazley, Exec. Dir./Treas.

Founded: 1980. **Members:** 400. **Membership Dues:** student, $20 (annual) ● single, $70 (annual) ● corporation (based on number of employees), $500-$1,000 (annual). **Staff:** 3. **Description:** Works to promote excellence and quality in piping design and engineering. Offers professional development courses and Professional Piping Designer certification program. **Libraries: Type:** reference. **Holdings:** video recordings. **Subjects:** process plant layout/ piping design, ASME B31-3 petrochemical and refinery piping. **Publications:** Newsletter, quarterly. **Advertising:** accepted.

7046 ■ Society of Reliability Engineers (SRE)
c/o Mr. Russell Chicoine
PO Box 2
Bloomfield, CT 06002-0002
Ph: (860)243-7473
Fax: (860)243-7499
E-mail: webmaster@sre.org
URL: http://www.sre.org
Contact: Dr. Robert Loomis, Pres.
Founded: 1966. **Members:** 1,000. **Description:** Represents reliability, component, and maintainability engineers. Seeks to develop and advance techniques effective in the application of reliability principles. Promotes reliability programs through education fund. Sponsors competitions. Local chapters sponsor symposia and seminars. **Awards:** SRE Stan Ofsthun Award. **Frequency:** annual. **Type:** recognition. **Recipient:** for the best technical paper. **Committees:** Education; Technical Paper Award. **Publications:** *Lambda Notes*, quarterly. Newsletter. Provides chapter news and papers on reliability and related subjects. Includes book reviews. **Price:** included in membership dues. Alternate Formats: online.

7047 ■ Society of Tribologists and Lubrication Engineers (STLE)
840 Busse Hwy.
Park Ridge, IL 60068
Ph: (847)825-5536
Fax: (847)825-1456
E-mail: information@stle.org
URL: http://www.stle.org
Contact: Edward Salek CAE, Exec. Dir.
Founded: 1944. **Members:** 4,400. **Membership Dues:** individual, $115 (annual) ● student, $15 (annual) ● corporate, $875 (annual). **Staff:** 11. **Budget:** $1,700,000. **Local Groups:** 40. **Description:** Represents engineers and others united to: advance the science of lubrication tribology and related arts and sciences; stimulate the study and development of lubrication tribology techniques; accumulate and disseminate information; promote higher standards in the field. Sponsors joint committees, councils and several courses held in conjunction with the annual meeting. Courses include: Basic Lubrication; Bearings; EHD; Hydraulics; Metalworking; Seals; Solid Lubrication; Synthetic Lubricants; Tribology Ceramics. **Awards:** Awards for Excellence in Technical Publishing. **Frequency:** annual. **Type:** recognition. **Recipient:** for papers in the field ● Outstanding Section Awards. **Frequency:** annual. **Type:** recognition. **Recipient:** for local section whose performance during the prior year warrants special recognition ● P.M. Ku Award. **Frequency:** annual. **Type:** recognition. **Recipient:** for a member who typifies the dedicated spirit and hardworking attitude of the late P.M. Ku ● STLE International Award. **Frequency:** annual. **Type:** recognition. **Recipient:** for outstanding contributions to tribology, lubrication engineering or other allied fields ● Vic Joll Award. **Frequency:** annual. **Type:** recognition. **Recipient:** for outstanding and selfless contributions by a member of an STLE section ● Walter D. Hodson Award. **Frequency:** annual. **Type:** recognition. **Recipient:** for lead author of the best paper written by a member 35 years of age or younger. **Committees:** Bearings and Bearing Lubrication; Ceramics and Composites; Computers in Tribology; Condition Monitoring; Engine and Drivetrain Lubrication; Fluids for Metalworking; Gear and Gear Lubrication Grease; Hydraulics and Machine Tool; Lubricant Conservation and Disposal; Lubrication Equipment and Practices; Lubrication Fundamentals; Seals; Solid Lubricants; Synthetic Lubricants; Wear. **Councils:** Aerospace; Environmental Resources; Food, Drug and Cosmetic; Forest and Paper; Mining; National Railroad; Nonferrous Metals; Petroleum and Chemicals; Power Generation; Steel Industry. **Formerly:** (1987) American Society of Lubrication Engineers. **Publications:** *Bound Preprint Volume*, semiannual ● *Individual Technical Papers*, semiannual ● *Membership Roster*, annual. Membership Directory. **Price:** $35.00 for members; $135.00 for nonmembers ● *STLE Tribology Transactions*, quarterly. Journal. Includes research and theory oriented technical papers. **Price:** $125.00 /year for members in U.S.; $145.00 /year for members outside U.S.; $274.00 /year for nonmembers. ISSN: 0569-8197 ● *Tribology and Lubrication Technology (TLT)*, monthly. Journal. Includes technical papers and articles related to lubrication and tribology. **Price:** $155.00 /year for nonmembers in U.S.; $215.00 /year for nonmembers outside U.S.; included in membership dues. ISSN: 0024-7154. **Advertising:** accepted ● Brochures ● Handbook ● Proceedings. **Conventions/Meetings:** annual meeting (exhibits) - always May ● annual Tribology Conference - always October.

7048 ■ Society of Turkish American Architects, Engineers and Scientists (MIM)
821 United Nations Plz., Turkish Ctr., 2nd Fl.
New York, NY 10017
Ph: (646)312-3366
E-mail: oalpoge@m-i-m.org
URL: http://www.m-i-m.org
Contact: Dr. Abdullah Uz Tanzel, Pres.
Founded: 1970. **Members:** 1,000. **Membership Dues:** student, $10 (annual) ● regular/associate, $40 (annual). **Staff:** 15. **Budget:** $10,000. **Languages:** English, Turkish. **Description:** Architects, engineers, scientists, and others who possess at least a bachelor's degree in the positive and technical sciences; associate members are individuals who possess associate or bachelor's degrees in social sciences; student members are post-graduate students of architecture, engineering, and science schools. Encourages and fosters the unity, professional collaboration, networking and mutual cooperation of Turkish American architects, engineers and scientists. Works to develop, establish, and maintain programs designed to foster the professional advancement of members and to initiate and develop collaboration with other scientific organizations. **Computer Services:** database, membership directory. **Telecommunication Services:** electronic mail, membership@m-i-m.org. **Committees:** Forum. **Affiliated With:** Assembly of Turkish American Associations; Federation of Turkish American Associations. **Formerly:** (2002) Society of Turkish Architects, Engineers and Scientists in America. **Publications:** *MIM Bulletin* (in English and Turkish), monthly. Magazine. **Price:** free. **Circulation:** 1,500. **Advertising:** accepted ● Membership Directory, periodic ● Newsletter. **Conventions/Meetings:** monthly board meeting - usually third Friday ● quarterly conference and symposium ● semiannual dinner ● annual general assembly and meeting.

7049 ■ Society of Women Engineers (SWE)
230 E Ohio St., Ste.400
Chicago, IL 60611-3265
Ph: (312)596-5223
Free: (877)SWE-INFO
Fax: (312)596-5252
E-mail: hq@swe.org
URL: http://www.swe.org
Contact: Betty A. Shanahan, Exec. Dir./CEO
Founded: 1950. **Members:** 18,000. **Membership Dues:** individual, student, $20 (annual) ● professional, associate, affiliate, $100 (annual) ● professional (retired), $50 (annual) ● joint, $130 (annual) ● life, $2,000 ● corporate, $3,000 (annual). **Staff:** 12. **Budget:** $1,800,000. **Regional Groups:** 10. **Local Groups:** 100. **Description:** Educational and service organization representing both students and professional women in engineering and technical fields. **Libraries: Type:** reference. **Holdings:** archival material. **Awards:** Achievement Award. **Frequency:** annual. **Type:** recognition. **Recipient:** for outstanding contribution over a significant period of time ● Distinguished Engineering Educator Award. **Frequency:** annual. **Type:** recognition. **Recipient:** for excellence in teaching, scholarship and contribution to the engineering profession ● Entrepreneur Award. **Frequency:** annual. **Type:** recognition. **Recipient:** to a member who started and/or maintained her own engineering-based business ● Resnik Challenger Medal. **Frequency:** annual. **Type:** medal. **Recipient:** for specific engineering breakthrough ● SWE Emerging Leaders Award. **Frequency:** annual. **Type:** recognition. **Recipient:** to a woman engineer who has demonstrated outstanding technical excellence ● Upward Mobility Award. **Frequency:** annual. **Type:** recognition. **Recipient:** for outstanding contribution in the field of engineering. **Committees:** Career Guidance; Membership; Professional Development; Section Vitality; Strategic Planning; Student Activities. **Affiliated With:** American Association of Engineering Societies. **Publications:** *Engineering*. Pamphlets. Covers career guidance. ● *National Survey of Women and Men Engineers* ● Magazine, quarterly. Features achievements and accomplishments of women engineers. **Price:** $30.00 /year for nonmembers. ISSN: 1070-6232. **Circulation:** 18,000. **Advertising:** accepted. Alternate Formats: online. **Conventions/Meetings:** annual convention (exhibits) - 2008 Nov. 6-8, Baltimore, MD ● annual Student Conference (exhibits) - always last week in June.

7050 ■ Ukrainian Engineers' Society of America (UESA)
2 E 79th St.
New York, NY 10021
Fax: (630)839-6014
E-mail: webmaster@uesa.org
URL: http://www.uesa.org
Contact: Andrij Wowk, Pres.
Founded: 1948. **Members:** 900. **Membership Dues:** student, $15 (annual) ● professional/associate, $50 (annual) ● retired professional, $30 (annual). **Local Groups:** 11. **Description:** Serves graduate engineers, architects, and economists of Ukrainian descent. Promotes the study of science and engineering; sponsors lectures. Compiles statistics; maintains hall of fame and special education program. **Libraries: Type:** reference. **Holdings:** 400; archival material, biographical archives. **Committees:** New Technology in the Ukraine. **Sections:** Computer Standards; Economic Development of the Ukraine. **Formerly:** Society of Ukrainian Engineers in America. **Publications:** *Ukrainian Engineering News*, quarterly. **Price:** $12.00. **Circulation:** 1,000. **Advertising:** accepted ● Bulletin, semiannual ● Newsletter, quarterly. Covers local and national organizational news and occasional technical articles. Alternate Formats: online ● Also publishes monographs, scientific papers, and dictionaries. **Conventions/Meetings:** annual Scientific Engineering Conference and General Meeting - conference and meeting.

7051 ■ United Engineering Foundation (UEF)
PO Box 70
Mount Vernon, VA 22121-0070
Ph: (973)244-2328
Fax: (973)882-5155
E-mail: engfnd@aol.com
URL: http://www.uefoundation.org
Contact: Dr. David L. Belden, Exec. Dir.
Founded: 1904. **Staff:** 3. **Budget:** $591,000. **Description:** Federation of 5 major national engineering societies: American Institute of Chemical Engineers; American Institute of Mining, Metallurgical and Petroleum Engineers; American Society of Civil Engineers; American Society of Mechanical Engineers; Institute of Electrical and Electronics Engineers. Supports research in engineering and advances the engineering arts and sciences through its conference program. **Libraries: Type:** reference. **Holdings:** 500,000. **Awards:** Engineering Foundation Grants. **Frequency:** annual. **Type:** grant. **Formerly:** (1930) United Engineering Society; (1998) United Engineering Trustees. **Publications:** Annual Report, annual. Alternate Formats: online.

7052 ■ Value Engineering Society International (VESI)
PO Box 930
Ligonier, PA 15658
Fax: (720)554-7678
E-mail: info@vesociety.com
URL: http://vesociety.com
Membership Dues: individual, associate, government, educator, $59 (annual) ● consultant, trainer, $129 (annual) ● vendor, $89 (annual). **Multinational. Description:** Advances the promotion of value engineering, analysis and management in both public

and private enterprises. **Libraries: Type:** reference. **Subjects:** value engineering. **Computer Services:** database, professional records ● mailing lists ● online services, forums, surveys, and discussion ● online services, program reporting and monitoring systems. **Publications:** Newsletter, periodic ● Membership Directory.

7053 ■ Visual Indicators Council (VIC)
188 Rte. 10, Ste.307
East Hanover, NJ 07936
Ph: (973)884-1668
Free: (800)755-2201
Fax: (973)884-1699
URL: http://www.testandmeasurement.com/storefronts/vic.html

Founded: 1999. **Members:** 7. **Description:** Strives to disseminate information on and promote the use of non-electronic visual sensors throughout the engineering and scientific community. **Libraries: Type:** not open to the public. **Holdings:** articles, clippings.

7054 ■ World Scientific and Engineering Academy and Society (WSEAS)
c/o Yodvadee Hudak
10650 N Central Expy.
Dallas, TX 75231
E-mail: info@wseas.org
URL: http://www.worldses.org
Contact: Prof. Charles A. Long, Pres.

Founded: 1996. **Membership Dues:** individual, EUR 100 (annual) ● company/institution, EUR 200 (annual). **Multinational. Description:** Promotes the development and the unified consideration of new mathematical methods and computational techniques as well as their applications in science and engineering. Supports the research and the diffusion of the scientific and engineering knowledge, especially in the areas of mathematics, computer science and electrical engineering. Carries out autonomous scientific/engineering research and collaborates with universities and state or private research centers and institutions. **Libraries: Type:** reference. **Holdings:** audio recordings, books, periodicals. **Subjects:** electrical engineering, applied mathematics, computer science, biology, economics, acoustic, music, mechanics. **Telecommunication Services:** electronic mail, usa@worldses.org. **Publications:** *WSEAS Transactions*. Journal. Alternate Formats: online ● Newsletter. Alternate Formats: online ● Proceedings. Alternate Formats: online ● Monographs. **Conventions/Meetings:** annual conference.

Engines

7055 ■ Turbine Inlet Cooling Association (TICA)
427 Prairie Knoll Dr., Ste.102
Naperville, IL 60565
Ph: (630)357-3960
Fax: (630)357-1004
E-mail: dpunwani@avalonconsulting.com
URL: http://www.turbineinletcooling.org
Contact: Dennis Halsey, Pres.

Founded: 2001. **Membership Dues:** GT owner (commercial/industrial), GT OEM, $750 (annual) ● GT owner (non-profit organization), consultant (with 6 or more people), $375 (annual) ● TIC OEM/contractor, GT EPC contractor, component supplier to OEM, $1,500 (annual) ● consultant (with 5 or less people), $187 (annual) ● student, individual from an organization that owns GT, qualified non-profit organization, $75 (annual). **Description:** Promotes turbine inlet cooling as a cost-effective, energy efficient and environmentally beneficial means to enhance power generation and capacity. Aims to increase the global market demand for turbine inlet cooling through demonstration of the economic and environmental benefits of this technology to combustion turbine plant users and government entities. Maintains a database of turbine inlet cooling installations by its members.

Entomology

7056 ■ Acarological Society of America (ASA)
c/o Norman J. Fashing, Sec.-Treas.
PO Box 8795
Williamsburg, VA 23185-8795
Ph: (757)221-2221
Fax: (757)221-6483
E-mail: njfash@wm.edu
URL: http://www.wm.edu/biology/mites
Contact: Ronald Ochoa, Pres.-Elect

Membership Dues: active, $20 (annual) ● student, $5 (annual) ● sustaining, $25 (annual). **Multinational. Description:** Represents individuals devoted to furthering all aspects of the knowledge of mites and ticks. Aims to advance studies in the field of acarology. Facilitates the collaboration and exchange of information among members. **Awards:** Joseph A. Camin Fellowship. **Frequency:** annual. **Type:** fellowship. **Recipient:** to support graduate students interested in research on the systematics of mites and ticks ● Outstanding Student Paper Award. **Frequency:** annual. **Type:** recognition. **Recipient:** for the best paper submitted by a student ● Student Travel Award. **Frequency:** annual. **Type:** monetary. **Recipient:** to an outstanding graduate student. **Telecommunication Services:** electronic mail, rochoa@sel.barc.usda.gov. **Publications:** Newsletter. **Price:** included in membership dues.

7057 ■ Association of Indian Entomologists in North America (AIENA)
c/o Seemanti Chakrabarti, Treas.
123 W Waters Hall
Dept. of Entomology
Kansas State Univ.
Manhattan, KS 66506
E-mail: seemanti@ksu.edu
URL: http://www.oznet.ksu.edu/aiena
Contact: Seemanti Chakrabarti, Treas.

Founded: 2002. **Membership Dues:** student, $10 (annual) ● faculty, post-doc, executive, $20 (annual). **Multinational. Description:** Brings together individuals of Indian origin interested in Entomological issues. Promotes exchange of information pertaining to the science of Entomology. Serves as a link for collaborative work between Entomologists in India and North America. Promotes awareness about the contribution of Indian entomologists. Promotes interdisciplinary research of the overall growth of the science of Entomology.

7058 ■ Association for Tropical Lepidoptera (ATL)
c/o Peter J. Eliazar, Sec.-Treas.
PO Box 141210
Gainesville, FL 32614-1210
Ph: (352)846-2000
Fax: (352)373-3249
E-mail: jdtatl@gmail.com
URL: http://www.troplep.org
Contact: Dr. Jon D. Turner, Exec. Dir.

Founded: 1989. **Members:** 1,250. **Membership Dues:** regular, $95 (annual) ● student, $50 (annual) ● life, $2,500. **Description:** Sponsors annual photo contest; conducts scientific and educational programs. **Publications:** *Holarctic Lepidoptera*, semiannual. Journal. Contains peer-reviewed scientific articles on northern species of lepidoptera. **Price:** $40.00 each. ISSN: 1070-4140. **Circulation:** 700 ● *Tropical Lepidoptera*, semiannual. Journal. Contains peer-reviewed scientific articles on tropical species lepidoptera. **Price:** $40.00 each. **Circulation:** 1,200 ● *Tropical Lepidoptera News*, quarterly. Newsletter. **Price:** $5.00. **Advertising:** accepted ● Also publishes books. **Conventions/Meetings:** annual symposium (exhibits) - always April.

7059 ■ Coleopterists Society (CS)
c/o Norman E. Woodley, Treas.
15703 Quince Orchard Rd.
North Potomac, MD 20878-4742
Ph: (202)382-1802
Fax: (866)783-2951
E-mail: coleoptreas@gmail.com
URL: http://www.coleopsoc.org
Contact: Norman E. Woodley, Treas.

Founded: 1949. **Members:** 800. **Membership Dues:** individual, $40 (annual) ● institution, $80 (annual). **Description:** Professionals and amateurs with an interest in Coleoptera (beetles). Promotes the advancement of the science of coleopterology. Conducts field expeditions. **Awards:** J.T. Lacordaire Prize, Youth Incentive Award. **Frequency:** annual. **Type:** monetary. **Recipient:** for outstanding paper of the year. **Computer Services:** database, Colepterists Bulletin bibliography searchable. **Publications:** *Coleopterists Bulletin: An International Journal Devoted to the Study of Beetles*, quarterly. Provides annual indexes of authors, article titles, and new taxa- or taxonomic names; contains book reviews and literature notices. **Price:** included in membership dues; $80.00 /year for libraries and institutions. ISSN: 0010-065X. **Circulation:** 800. **Conventions/Meetings:** annual seminar - usually early December ● workshop.

7060 ■ Council of Entomology Department Administrators (CEDA)
c/o James Harper
North Carolina State Univ.
Dept. of Entomology
Box 7613
Raleigh, NC 27695-7613
Ph: (919)515-2746
Fax: (919)515-7746
E-mail: james_harper@ncsu.edu
URL: http://www.ceda-group.org
Contact: Dr. Gary Brewer, Chm.

Multinational. Description: Represents academic entomology administrators and national program leaders. Promotes the science of entomology in the United States and Canada. Develops initiatives pertaining to insect science and other entomological issues. **Telecommunication Services:** electronic mail, gbrewer2@unl.edu.

7061 ■ Dragonfly Society of the Americas (DSA)
c/o Jerell J. Daigle
2067 Little River Ln.
Tallahassee, FL 32311-9400
Ph: (850)878-8787
E-mail: jdaigle@nettally.com
URL: http://www.odonatacentral.org/index.php/PageAction.get/name/DSAHomePage
Contact: Nick Donnelly, Contact

Founded: 1989. **Members:** 400. **Membership Dues:** individual, $20 (annual) ● institutional, sustaining, $25. **Description:** Promotes the study and conservation of Odonata (dragonflies) and their wetland and aquatic habitats. **Libraries: Type:** reference. **Holdings:** archival material, audiovisuals, books, business records, monographs, periodicals. **Subjects:** Odonata and odonatology. **Formerly:** (1997) Dragonfly Society of America. **Publications:** *Argia*, quarterly. Journal. Includes articles on Odonata and odonatologists. **Price:** $15.00. ISSN: 1061-8503. **Circulation:** 400. Alternate Formats: online ● *Bulletin of American Odonatology*. Journal. Includes research on Odonata. **Price:** $15.00/year. ISSN: 1061-3781. **Circulation:** 200. **Conventions/Meetings:** annual meeting (exhibits).

7062 ■ Entomological Society of America (ESA)
10001 Derekwood Ln., Ste.100
Lanham, MD 20706-4876
Ph: (301)731-4535
Fax: (301)731-4538
E-mail: esa@entsoc.org
URL: http://www.entsoc.org
Contact: Ann Kenworthy, Interim Exec. Dir.

Founded: 1953. **Members:** 5,700. **Membership Dues:** regular, $130 (annual) ● student, $31 (annual) ● family, $197 (annual) ● President's Circle, $260 (annual) ● emeritus, student transition-1 year, $65 (annual) ● emeritus gold, $35 (annual) ● student transition-2 years, $97 (annual) ● sustaining associate-contributor, $500 (annual) ● sustaining associate-bronze, $1,000 (annual) ● sustaining associate-silver, $2,000 (annual) ● sustaining associate-gold, $3,000 (annual) ● youth, $10 (annual). **Staff:** 7. **Budget:** $2,300,000. **Regional Groups:** 5. **Multinational. Description:** Represents the interests of entomologists and others interested in the study of insects. Administers two certification programs. Compiles job opportunities. Publishes journals. Produces one national annual meeting and five geographically based annual meetings. **Libraries: Type:** reference; not open to the public. **Holdings:** archival material. **Awards:** Certification Student Award. **Frequency:** annual. **Type:** monetary. **Recipient:** to outstanding entomology graduate students with interest in the mission of the society certification program ● Distinguished Achievement Award in Extension. **Frequency:** annual. **Type:** monetary. **Recipient:** for outstanding contributions to extension entomology ● Distinguished Achievement Award in Horticultural Entomology. **Frequency:** annual. **Type:** monetary. **Recipient:** to an entomologist who has contributed greatly to the American horticulture industry ● Distinguished Achievement Award in Teaching. **Frequency:** annual. **Type:** monetary. **Recipient:** to the member of the Society deemed to be the most outstanding teacher of the year ● Distinguished Service Award to the Certification Program. **Frequency:** annual. **Type:** monetary. **Recipient:** for outstanding contributions to the society certification program and the professionalism of entomology ● Fellow. **Frequency:** annual. **Type:** recognition. **Recipient:** to individuals who have made outstanding contributions to entomology ● Founders Memorial Award and Lecture. **Frequency:** annual. **Type:** monetary. **Recipient:** for scientists who have made contributions to entomology ● Honorary Member. **Frequency:** annual. **Type:** recognition. **Recipient:** for members who have served the field of entomology with distinction and participated actively in the affairs of the Society ● John Henry Comstock Graduate Student Awards. **Frequency:** annual. **Type:** monetary. **Recipient:** to promote interest in entomology at the graduate level and to stimulate interest in attending the society annual meeting; includes paid trip ● Linnaean Games. **Frequency:** annual. **Type:** medal. **Recipient:** for university-sponsored student teams ● Recognition Award in Entomology. **Frequency:** annual. **Type:** recognition. **Recipient:** to entomologists who have made significant contributions to agriculture ● Recognition Award in Insect Physiology Biochemistry and Toxicology. **Frequency:** annual. **Type:** monetary. **Recipient:** for innovative research in insect physiology, biochemistry and toxicology ● Student Activity Award. **Frequency:** annual. **Type:** monetary. **Recipient:** to a student for outstanding contributions to ESA, his/her academic department, and the community, while still achieving academic excellence ● Student Competition for the Presidents Prize. **Frequency:** annual. **Type:** monetary. **Recipient:** to students who give exceptional presentations of their research at the Society annual meeting. **Computer Services:** database, membership directory ● electronic publishing, journal subscriptions ● mailing lists, available for rental ● online services, electronic balloting. **Committees:** Awards; Common Names of Insects; Education and Youth; Ethics; Fellows; Founders' Memorial; Honorary Membership; International Affairs; Membership; Program; Rules; Strategic Planning; Student Affairs. **Sections:** Biochemistry, Toxicology, and Molecular Biology; Systematics, Morphology, and Evolution. **Affiliated With:** American Association for the Advancement of Science; American Institute of Biological Sciences; Council of Scientific Society Presidents. **Absorbed:** (1992) American Registry of Professional Entomologists. **Formed by Merger of:** American Association of Economic Entomologists and Entomological Society of America. **Publications:** *American Entomologist*, quarterly. Magazine. Covers topics of interest to biologists, including research, professional trends, and Society activities. **Price:** included in membership dues; $42.00 /year for nonmembers; $81.00 /year for institutions. ISSN: 1046-821X. **Advertising:** accepted. Alternate Formats: online ● *Annals of the Entomological Society of America*, bimonthly. Journal. Reports studies on basic aspects of the biology and physiology of insects, including morphology, histology, biochemistry, and behavior. **Price:** included in membership dues; $101.00 /year for nonmembers; $206.00 /year for institutions. ISSN: 0013-8746. **Advertising:** accepted. Also Cited As: *Annals of the ESA* ● *Environmental Entomology*, bimonthly. Journal. Covers studies on insects and their interaction with the biological, chemical, and physical components of their environment. **Price:** $116.00 /year for nonmembers; $109.00 /year for members; $221.00 /year for institutions. ISSN: 0046-225X. **Advertising:** accepted ● *Journal of Economic Entomology*, bimonthly. Covers the systematics and biology of insects, acarines, and other arthropods of public health and veterinary significance. **Price:** $116.00 for nonmember individuals; $246.00 for nonmember institutions; $206.00 /year for institutions. ISSN: 0022-0493. **Advertising:** accepted ● *Journal of Medical Entomology*, bimonthly. Covers the systematics and biology of insects, acarines, and other arthropods of public health and veterinary significance. **Price:** $101.00 /year for nonmembers; $206.00 /year for institutions. ISSN: 0022-2585. **Advertising:** accepted ● *Newsletter of the Entomological Society of America*, monthly. Contains Society news, employment listings, meeting announcements, member profiles, and notices of grants and awards. **Price:** included in membership dues; $28.00 /year for nonmembers; $43.00 /year for institutions. ISSN: 0046-225X. **Advertising:** accepted. Alternate Formats: online. **Conventions/Meetings:** annual conference, features submitted papers, posters and seminars on the latest research in entomology; career center; exhibits (exhibits) - 2008 Nov. 16-19, Reno, NV; 2009 Dec. 13-17, Indianapolis, IN.

7063 ■ International Union for the Study of Social Insects (IUSSI)

c/o Stan Schneider, Sec.-Treas.
Univ. of North Carolina
Dept. of Biology
9201 Univ. City Blvd.
Charlotte, NC 28223
Ph: (704)687-4053
Fax: (704)687-3128
E-mail: sschnedr@email.uncc.edu
URL: http://iussi.bees.net
Contact: Stan Schneider, Sec.-Treas.

Founded: 1952. **Members:** 800. **Membership Dues:** regular, $15 (annual) ● student, $7 (annual). **Regional Groups:** 11. **Languages:** English, French, German, Russian, Spanish. **Description:** Scientists involved in the study, use, and control of social insects. Organizes educational programs; conducts symposia. **Affiliated With:** International Union of Biological Sciences. **Publications:** *Insectes Sociaux*, quarterly. Journal. Covers the biology and evolution of social insects and other presocial arthropods; includes research papers and reviews. ISSN: 0020-1812. Also Cited As: *Social Insects*. **Conventions/Meetings:** quadrennial congress ● quadrennial meeting ● periodic meeting, European congress.

7064 ■ North American Forensic Entomology Association (NAFEA)

c/o Rebecca O'Flaherty Bullard, Treas.
Univ. of California
Dept. of Entomology
One Shields Ave.
Davis, CA 95616
E-mail: john.wallace@millersville.edu
URL: http://www.nafea.net
Contact: Dr. John R. Wallace, Pres.

Membership Dues: regular, $15 (annual) ● associate, $10 (annual). **Multinational. Description:** Promotes the development of forensic entomology throughout North America. Encourages cooperation with other similar international bodies. Provides a cooperative arena for forensic entomologists to interact and collaborate in ways that enhance the science of forensic entomology. **Publications:** Newsletter. Alternate Formats: online.

7065 ■ Orthopterists' Society

c/o Dr. Charles Bomar, Exec. Dir.
Univ. of Wisconsin - Stout
Biology Dept.
203A Sci. Wing
Menomonie, WI 54751
Ph: (715)232-2562
Fax: (715)232-2129
E-mail: bomar@uwstout.edu
URL: http://www.orthoptera.org
Contact: Dr. Charles Bomar, Exec. Dir.

Founded: 1976. **Members:** 330. **Membership Dues:** active, sponsored, institutional, $20 (annual) ● sustaining, $60 (annual) ● student, $10 (annual). **Staff:** 9. **National Groups:** 43. **Multinational. Description:** Promotes all aspects of biology of orthoptera and related organisms, from ecology and taxonomy to physiology, endocrinology, cytogenetics, and control measures. **Awards:** Best Yellow Pages Advertisement Award. **Type:** monetary ● Community Service Award. **Type:** monetary ● Environmental Improvement Award. **Type:** monetary ● Fitzgibbon Scholarship Award. **Type:** scholarship ● Picture Perfect Lawn Award. **Type:** monetary. **Computer Services:** Online services, bulletin board. **Formerly:** Pan-American Acridological Society. **Publications:** *Journal of Orthoptera Research*, semiannual. **Price:** $30.00/volume ● *Metaleptea*, 2-4/year. Newsletter. Contains articles, news items and announcements. **Price:** included in membership dues. Alternate Formats: online ● *Publications on Orthopteran Diversity*, periodic. Includes Daniel Otte's seven volumes of the "Orthoptera Species File" and his "Crickets of Hawaii" and more. ● Papers, periodic. Contains single issue by P.M. Pener. **Conventions/Meetings:** triennial international conference ● annual symposium, held at the Entomological Society of America meeting.

7066 ■ Young Entomologists' Society (YES)

6907 W Grand River Ave.
Lansing, MI 48906-9131
Ph: (517)886-0630
Fax: (517)886-0630
E-mail: yesbugs@aol.com
URL: http://members.aol.com/yesbugs/bugclub.html
Contact: Gary A. Dunn, Dir./Webmaster

Founded: 1965. **Members:** 750. **Membership Dues:** youth, $12 (annual) ● adult, $15 (annual) ● family, $18 (annual) ● educator, $20 (annual) ● kit (junior bugologist, bugologist), $35 (annual) ● educator's kit/supporter, $50 (annual) ● benefactor, $100 (annual) ● patron, $500 (annual) ● sponsor, $1,000 (annual). **Staff:** 2. **Budget:** $90,000. **Description:** Adults and youths interested in studying insects and spiders. Provides a forum to aid in the exchange of insects and information. Conducts educational programs; makes available children's services; operates referral service. Maintains speakers' bureau. Operates Minibeast Zooseum and Education Center. **Libraries: Type:** reference. **Holdings:** 2,000; articles, books, periodicals. **Computer Services:** database, of members, teachers, entomological suppliers and organizations, children's books on insects, mail order sales of books, kits. **Formerly:** (1984) Teen International Entomology Group. **Publications:** *Bug Club Leader Guide*. Manual. Provides instructions for running bug club meetings. ● *Buggy Books: A Guide to Juvenile and Popular Books on Insects and Their Relatives*. Manual ● *Caring for Insect Livestock: An Insect Rearing Manual*. Provides complete information and "tips" for keeping 60 different insects and related anthropods in captivity. ● *The Insect Identification Guide*. Directory ● *Minibeast e-Magazine*, monthly. Includes minibeast information, trivia, project and activity ideas, interactive bug quiz, and humor. **Price:** $10.00 for members; $15.00 for nonmembers. Alternate Formats: online ● *Minibeast World*, bimonthly. Magazine. Contains insect lore, stories, poetry, trivia, puzzles, and activity ideas. **Price:** $35.00 for nonmembers; $15.00 for members. ISSN: 1043-6057. **Circulation:** 300 ● *YES NewsBulletin*. Newsletter. Contains information on society's business and happenings, special events and enrichment opportunities, and new products and services. **Conventions/Meetings:** competition, with essays.

Environment

7067 ■ National Council for Science and the Environment (NCSE)

1707 H St. NW, Ste.200
Washington, DC 20006-3918

Ph: (202)530-5810
Fax: (202)628-4311
E-mail: info@ncseonline.org
URL: http://www.ncseonline.org
Contact: Richard E. Benedick, Pres.
Founded: 1990. **Staff:** 13. **Description:** Seeks to improve the scientific basis for environmental decisions. Provides a role in defining questions and setting priorities for those studying, managing and affected by environmental problems as well as for policymakers. **Conventions/Meetings:** annual Energy for a Sustainable and Secure Future - conference.

Environmental Health

7068 ■ The Pesticide Stewardship Alliance (TPSA)
PO Box 5204
Takoma Park, MD 20913
Free: (877)920-6772
Fax: (877)922-6772
E-mail: contact@tpsalliance.org
URL: http://www.npsalliance.org
Contact: Carol Ramsay, Pres.
Founded: 2000. **Membership Dues:** student, $25 (annual) ● retired, $35 (annual) ● individual, $75 (annual) ● organization (up to 3 members), $200 (annual). **Description:** Seeks to increase the effectiveness, efficiency and longevity of various pesticide stewardship efforts. Serves as a clearinghouse for technical information, data and expertise concerning pesticide stewardship programs and issues. Fosters pesticide stewardship and recycling programs. **Awards:** Award for Program Innovation. **Frequency:** annual. **Type:** recognition. **Recipient:** for demonstrating unique and effective pesticide stewardship ● Career Achievement Award. **Frequency:** annual. **Type:** recognition. **Recipient:** for significant career achievements in promoting the goals of the alliance ● Leadership in Product Stewardship Award. **Frequency:** annual. **Type:** recognition. **Recipient:** for a private sector organization, company or member that has been a leader in product stewardship ● Member Contribution Award. **Frequency:** annual. **Type:** recognition. **Recipient:** for significant contributions to the alliance and its growth ● President's Award. **Frequency:** annual. **Type:** recognition. **Recipient:** for dedicated service to the alliance. **Telecommunication Services:** electronic mail, ramsay@wsu.edu ● electronic mail, info@tpsalliance.org ● electronic mail, membership@tpsalliance.org. **Publications:** Newsletter. Alternate Formats: online.

Ethics

7069 ■ Foundation for Ethics and Meaning
5445 Mariner St., Ste.314
Tampa, FL 33609
Free: (888)LETS-CARE
Fax: (813)251-0492
E-mail: institute@meaning.org
URL: http://www.meaning.org
Contact: Bruce Novak, Sec.
Founded: 1995. **Membership Dues:** basic, $25 ● supporter, $50 ● sustainer, $100 ● patron, $250 ● benefactor, $500. **Local Groups:** 9. **Description:** Seeks to "reawaken and foster the simple yet transformative belief that people are yearning for meaningful connection to others and to a purpose greater than themselves." Aims to challenge the prevailing cultural emphasis on material self-interest by encouraging a spirit of caring and a process of mutual recognition that will nourish inclusive, sustainable and just communities. Works to develop the ideas and philosophy underlying the politics of meaning, developed by Michael Lerner and Peter Gabel out of experience working as activists, theorists, and therapists involved in the anti-war, women's liberation, and labor movements during the 1960 to 1980. **Telecommunication Services:** electronic mail, bjnovak@midway.uchicago.edu. **Task Forces:** Arts; Behavioral Health; Community Support Circles; Education; Environment; Health/Healthcare; Legal Reform; Media Watch; NGO/Coalition-Building; People-Centered Globalization; Religion/Spirituality; Work Issues/Labor/Corporate Responsibility. **Publications:** *Meaning Matters*. Newsletter. Alternate Formats: online.

7070 ■ Institute for Global Ethics (IGE)
PO Box 563
Camden, ME 04843
Ph: (207)236-6658
Free: (800)729-2615
Fax: (207)236-4014
E-mail: ethics@globalethics.org
URL: http://www.globalethics.org
Contact: Rushworth M. Kidder, Pres.
Founded: 1990. **Membership Dues:** regular, $60 (annual) ● student/senior, $35 (annual) ● organization, donor, $100 (annual) ● patron, $250 (annual) ● sustainer, $500 (annual) ● sponsor, $1,000 (annual) ● gift, $45 (annual). **Multinational. Description:** Promotes ethical behavior in individuals, institutions, and nations through global research and education. **Councils:** International Advisory. **Publications:** *Ethical Connections*. Newsletter. Contains latest news on the Institute's works in education, public policy, and corporate services. **Price:** included in membership dues. Alternate Formats: online ● *Ethics Newsline TM*, weekly. Newsletter. Contains current ethics news stories with commentary. **Price:** free. Alternate Formats: online ● *Moral Courage*. Paper. **Price:** $21.50 for members ● Annual Reports, annual. Alternate Formats: online ● Books.

Evaluation

7071 ■ American Evaluation Association (AEA)
16 Sconticut Neck Rd., No. 290
Fairhaven, MA 02719
Ph: (508)748-3326 (814)863-1755
Free: (888)232-2275
Fax: (508)748-3158
E-mail: info@eval.org
URL: http://www.Eval.org
Contact: Ms. Susan Kistler, Exec. Dir.
Founded: 1986. **Members:** 4,900. **Membership Dues:** individual, $80 (annual) ● full-time student, $30 (annual) ● joint CES, $60 (annual). **Regional Groups:** 23. **Multinational. Description:** Represents individuals from university, government, research, consulting, corporate education, and industrial research settings who represent various disciplines including psychology, education, public administration, marketing, social work, and policy analysis. Works to improve evaluation theory, practice, training programs, professional competencies, and evaluation utilization. Compiles a directory of training programs in evaluation. Supports professional standards for evaluation. Conducts multiple professional development workshops and seminars. **Libraries: Type:** reference. **Subjects:** evaluation practice, new directions for evaluation. **Awards:** Range of awards. **Frequency:** annual. **Type:** recognition. **Recipient:** for outstanding theory, practice, and service ● **Type:** recognition. **Telecommunication Services:** electronic mail, susan@eval.org. **Formed by Merger of:** Evaluation Network; Evaluation Research Society. **Publications:** *American Journal of Evaluation*, quarterly. **Advertising:** accepted. Alternate Formats: online ● *New Directions for Evaluation*, quarterly. Journal. **Conventions/Meetings:** annual conference (exhibits) - usually November.

Evolution

7072 ■ Institute of Human Origins (IHO)
Arizona State Univ.
PO Box 874101
Tempe, AZ 85287-4101
Ph: (480)727-6580
Fax: (480)727-6570
E-mail: iho@asu.edu
URL: http://www.asu.edu/clas/iho
Contact: Donald C. Johanson PhD, Dir.
Founded: 1981. **Members:** 1,500. **Membership Dues:** individual, $35 (annual). **Staff:** 6. **Budget:** $1,000,000. **Description:** Scientists, educators, students, volunteers, and other individuals carrying out or supporting research on human evolution. Utilizes the expertise and knowledge of many disciplines to establish when, where, and how the human species originated. Promotes laboratory and field research. Provides a base from which research can be pursued from the planning stages to the dissemination of results. Offers specialized training to scientists and students; maintains repository and data center of photos, slides, casts, field notes, and comparative collections. **Libraries: Type:** reference. **Holdings:** 20,000; archival material, audiovisuals, books, monographs, periodicals. **Subjects:** anthropology, evolution, geology. **Awards:** IHO Fellowship in Paleoanthropology. **Frequency:** 3/year. **Type:** fellowship. **Computer Services:** database, human fossils. **Telecommunication Services:** electronic mail, johanson.iho@asu.edu. **Publications:** *Ancestors: In Search of Human Origins*. Book ● *Institute of Human Origins Newsletter*, semiannual. **Price:** included in membership dues. Alternate Formats: online.

7073 ■ Society for the Study of Evolution (SSE)
c/o Dale Clayton, Sec.
Univ. of Utah
257 S 1400 E
Salt Lake City, UT 84112
Ph: (781)388-8599
Free: (800)835-6670
E-mail: clayton@biology.utah.edu
URL: http://www.evolutionsociety.org
Contact: Don Waller, Pres.
Founded: 1946. **Members:** 3,000. **Membership Dues:** student in U.S., emeritus (print and electronic), regular (electronic only), $40 (annual) ● student outside U.S. (print and electronic), $50 (annual) ● student, emeritus, K-12 educator (electronic only), $20 (annual) ● regular, in U.S. (print and electronic), $75 (annual) ● regular, outside U.S. (print and electronic), $90 (annual) ● life, in U.S., $1,500 ● life, outside U.S., $1,800 ● institution, in U.S., $400 (annual) ● institution, outside U.S., $450 (annual). **Budget:** $200,000. **Description:** Professional society of biologists concerned with organic evolution. **Awards:** Dobzhansky Prize. **Frequency:** annual. **Type:** recognition. **Recipient:** for the accomplishments and future promise of an outstanding young evolutionary biologist ● R.A. Fisher Prize. **Frequency:** annual. **Type:** recognition. **Recipient:** for the best PhD dissertation paper published in the Evolution Journal during a given calendar year. **Telecommunication Services:** electronic mail, jgurvtch@life.bio.sunysb.edu. **Committees:** Education. **Formed by Merger of:** Committee on Common Problems of Genetics, Paleontology and Systematics of National Research Council; Society for the Study of Speciation. **Publications:** *Evolution*, bimonthly. Journal. **Price:** $170.00. ISSN: 0014-3820. **Circulation:** 4,500. **Advertising:** accepted. Alternate Formats: online ● Membership Directory, periodic. **Conventions/Meetings:** annual meeting (exhibits) - always June. 2008 June 20-24, Minneapolis, MN.

Exploration

7074 ■ American Alpine Club (AAC)
710 10th St., Ste.100
Golden, CO 80401
Ph: (303)384-0110
Fax: (303)384-0111
E-mail: getinfo@americanalpineclub.org
URL: http://www.americanalpineclub.org
Contact: Mr. Phil Powers, Exec. Dir.
Founded: 1902. **Members:** 7,000. **Membership Dues:** regular, $75 (annual) ● junior (age 28 and under), $40 (annual) ● senior (age 66 and older), $50 (annual) ● life, $1,750 ● joint, $125 (annual).

Staff: 11. **Budget:** $1,200,000. **Regional Groups:** 13. **Description:** Persons who have made mountain ascents, conducted explorations in the Arctic or Antarctic tracts, or contributed to the literature or science of mountaineering, to recent glaciology, or to alpine art. Conducts scientific studies and explorations. Encourages safety in mountaineering and disseminates information concerning mountains and mountaineering. Maintains museum of alpine memorabilia and art. **Libraries: Type:** reference; open to the public. **Holdings:** 18,000; archival material, articles, books, books, periodicals, video recordings. **Subjects:** mountaineering, trekking, climbing. **Awards:** Angelo Heilprin Citation. **Frequency:** annual. **Type:** recognition. **Recipient:** for exemplary service ● David Brower Conservation Award. **Frequency:** annual. **Type:** recognition. **Recipient:** to a person who has made important contributions to the protection of mountain environments ● **Type:** grant. **Recipient:** for expeditions and research ● Robert and Miriam Underhill Award. **Frequency:** annual. **Type:** recognition. **Recipient:** to a person who has demonstrated the highest level of skill in the mountaineering arts. **Committees:** Alaska; American Mountaineering Center Fundraising and Design; Conservation-Domestic; Expeditions; Grand Teton Climbers' Ranch; International Climbing Exchanges; Library; Medical; Mountaineering Fellowship; Museum Design; Museum Fundraising Leadership; Public and Governmental Policy; Publications; Research; Safety; Zack Martin Fund. **Publications:** *Accidents in North American Mountaineering*, annual. Book. **Price:** $45.00 for nonmembers. ISSN: 0065-082X ● *American Alpine Journal*, annual. **Price:** $35.00 for nonmembers; free for members. Alternate Formats: online ● *American Alpine News*, quarterly. Newsletter. **Advertising:** accepted. Alternate Formats: online ● Books ● Also publishes guidebooks. **Conventions/ Meetings:** annual convention (exhibits) - always first weekend of December ● annual meeting.

7075 ■ Circumnavigators Club (CC)
24 E 39th St.
New York, NY 10016-2555
Ph: (201)612-9100
Fax: (201)612-9595
E-mail: info@circumnavigatorsclub.org
URL: http://www.circumnavigatorsclub.org/index.php
Contact: William P. Holm, Pres.

Founded: 1902. **Members:** 1,000. **Membership Dues:** regular, $150 (annual). **Staff:** 1. **Description:** Individuals who have crossed all meridians of longitude, thus completing a global circumnavigation, and who have more than a superficial interest in other countries. Strives to extend points of friendly contact among those who go to the ends of the earth in the cause of commerce, research, exploration, military news, maritime or government service, or for the simple pleasure of travel. **Libraries: Type:** reference. **Holdings:** papers, reports. **Publications:** *The Log*, bimonthly. Alternate Formats: online.

7076 ■ Explorers Club (EC)
46 E 70th St.
New York, NY 10021
Ph: (212)628-8383
Fax: (212)288-4449
E-mail: president@explorers.org
URL: http://www.explorers.org
Contact: Daniel A. Bennett, Pres.

Founded: 1904. **Members:** 3,000. **Membership Dues:** fellow resident, $380 (annual) ● fellow national, $210 (annual) ● fellow international, $130 (annual) ● friend of the club resident, $1,000 (annual) ● friend of the club national, $350 (annual) ● friend of the club international, $250 (annual) ● international, $223 (annual) ● emeritus, corresponding, $35 (annual) ● resident, $570 (annual) ● national, $310 (annual). **Staff:** 8. **Multinational. Description:** International organization of explorers and scientists. Promotes exploration and disseminates information about scientific exploration. Maintains reports and artifacts from expeditions. Conducts public lectures. **Libraries: Type:** reference; open to the public. **Holdings:** 20,000; biographical archives, books, films, maps. **Subjects:** science, exploration. **Awards:** Exploration Grant. **Frequency:** annual. **Type:** grant. **Recipient:** for originality, enthusiasm and project potential. **Computer Services:** Mailing lists, of members. **Telecommunication Services:** electronic mail, membership@explorers.org. **Committees:** Conservation; Education; Exploration Fund; Flag and Honors; Lecture. **Projects:** Central Park BioBlitz; Explorers Club Oral History; Partnership with Reach the World. **Absorbed:** (1913) Arctic Club. **Publications:** *Explorers Journal*, quarterly. Covers scientific research/expeditions. **Price:** $24.95 /year for nonmembers; $6.50 each for nonmembers; free for members, fellows and friends. **Circulation:** 4,000. **Advertising:** accepted ● Newsletter, quarterly ● Reports. Alternate Formats: online. **Conventions/ Meetings:** annual convention and dinner (exhibits) - usually March, in New York City.

Explosives

7077 ■ International Association of Bomb Technicians and Investigators (IABTI)
PO Box 160
Goldvein, VA 22720-0160
Ph: (540)752-4533
Fax: (540)752-2796
E-mail: admin@iabti.org
URL: http://www.iabti.org
Contact: Marge Yarbrough, Dir.

Founded: 1973. **Members:** 3,600. **Membership Dues:** regular, $50 (annual). **Staff:** 1. **Budget:** $367,000. **Regional Groups:** 7. **Local Groups:** 27. **Description:** Seeks to: increase professionalism and training of bomb technicians and investigators; foster an exchange of ideas and information within the field of explosives, both technical and investigative; encourage friendship and cooperation among technical and investigative personnel; stimulate research and the development of new techniques within the field of explosives. **Telecommunication Services:** electronic mail, members@iabti.org. **Publications:** *Detorator*, bimonthly. Newsletter. **Advertising:** accepted ● Brochures ● Membership Directory, annual ● Pamphlets. **Conventions/Meetings:** annual conference (exhibits).

Fibers

7078 ■ Fiber Society (FS)
North Carolina State Univ.
Coll. of Textiles
Raleigh, NC 27695-8301
Ph: (919)513-0143 (919)515-6555
Fax: (919)515-4556
E-mail: sbatra@unity.ncsu.edu
URL: http://www.thefibersociety.org
Contact: Dr. Subhash Batra, Sec.

Founded: 1941. **Members:** 400. **Membership Dues:** full, $60 (annual) ● student, $20 (annual). **Staff:** 1. **Multinational. Description:** Chemists, physicists, engineers, biologists, mathematicians, and other scientists conducting research in fibers, fiber-based products, and fibrous materials. Sponsors lecture program. Sponsors conferences. **Awards:** Distinguished Achievement Award. **Frequency:** annual. **Type:** recognition ● Emeritus Membership. **Frequency:** periodic. **Type:** recognition ● Founders Award. **Frequency:** periodic. **Type:** recognition ● Honorary Membership. **Frequency:** periodic. **Type:** recognition ● Student Paper Competition. **Frequency:** biennial. **Type:** recognition. **Telecommunication Services:** electronic mail, ylhsieh@ucdavis.edu. **Formerly:** (1945) Industrial Fiber Society. **Publications:** *Journal of Engineered Fibers and Fabrics*, quarterly. Accepts and publishes manuscripts covering basic research on fibers, fabrics, and related materials and applications. Alternate Formats: online. Also Cited As: *JEFF* ● Membership Directory, annual ● Newsletters, biennial. Alternate Formats: online. **Conventions/Meetings:** semiannual convention and symposium, on fiber structure and textile materials ● semiannual meeting, on biomaterials/biotextiles - always spring and fall. 2008 Oct. 1-3, Boucherville, QC, Canada.

7079 ■ North American Industrial Hemp Council (NAIHC)
PO Box 259329
Madison, WI 53725-9329
Ph: (608)835-0428
Fax: (608)835-0428
E-mail: info@naihc.org
URL: http://www.naihc.org
Contact: Erwin A. Sholts, Chm.

Founded: 1995. **Members:** 110. **Membership Dues:** individual, $100 (annual) ● individual government agency, non-profit organization, $500 (annual) ● business and industry (based on total annual sales), $250-$2,500 (annual). **Budget:** $20,000. **Description:** Works to re-establish and expand the use of industrial hemp. **Awards:** Honorary Membership. **Frequency:** annual. **Type:** recognition. **Recipient:** for members who have given outstanding assistance and support for the organization. **Computer Services:** Bibliographic search, informational on industrial hemp. **Conventions/Meetings:** annual meeting - late October or early November.

Fire Protection

7080 ■ International Association for Fire Safety Science
c/o Society of Fire Protection Engineers
7315 Wisconsin Ave., Ste.620E
Bethesda, MD 20814
Ph: (301)718-2910
Fax: (301)718-2242
E-mail: sfpehqtrs@sfpe.org
URL: http://www.sfpe.org
Contact: Dr. David D. Evans PE, Exec. Dir.

Founded: 1985. **Membership Dues:** regular, $20 (annual). **Description:** Engineers and scientists working in the fields of fire research and safety. Encourages research in the prevention and mitigation of the adverse effects of fire; serves as a forum for exchange of research results among members. **Libraries: Type:** open to the public. **Holdings:** 5. **Telecommunication Services:** electronic mail, devans@sfpe.org. **Publications:** *International Fire Safety Science*, triennial. Proceedings. **Price:** $100. 00. **Conventions/Meetings:** triennial symposium.

7081 ■ International FireStop Council (IFC)
17209 Bradgate Ave.
Cleveland, OH 44111
Free: (877)241-3769
E-mail: info@firestop.org
URL: http://www.firestop.org
Contact: Sarah Brewer, Pres.

Founded: 1990. **Membership Dues:** associate, $350-$2,500 (annual) ● voting (based on relative size of company), $4,000-$16,550 (annual) ● government, $50 (annual). **Staff:** 5. **Description:** Manufacturers, distributors and users of fire protective materials. Works to promote fire containment technology in building construction. Conducts educational and research programs; and develops safety standards and codes. **Publications:** *Inspecting Firestop for Compliance*. Video ● *Inspection Manual for Firestopped Through Penetrations, Joints and Perimeter Fire Barrier Systems* ● Newsletter, quarterly. Alternate Formats: online. **Conventions/Meetings:** quarterly meeting.

7082 ■ Society of Fire Protection Engineers (SFPE)
7315 Wisconsin Ave., Ste.620E
Bethesda, MD 20814
Ph: (301)718-2910 (301)661-5982
Fax: (301)718-2242
E-mail: devans@sfpe.org
URL: http://www.sfpe.org
Contact: David D. Evans PE, Exec. Dir.

Founded: 1950. **Members:** 4,150. **Membership Dues:** individual, associate, affiliate, $195 (annual) ●

allied professional group, $97 (annual). **Staff:** 5. **Budget:** $1,000,000. **Local Groups:** 47. **Multinational. Description:** Multinational professional society of fire protection engineers. Objectives are to advance the science and practice of fire protection engineering; to maintain a high ethical standard among members and to foster fire protection engineering education. Offers short courses and conferences. Sponsors SFPE Educational and Scientific Foundation. **Awards:** Arthur B. Guise Medal. **Frequency:** annual. **Type:** medal ● Fire Protection Man/Woman of the Year Award. **Frequency:** annual. **Type:** recognition. **Telecommunication Services:** electronic mail, eandracsek@sfpe.org. **Committees:** Engineering Education; Engineering Licensing; Ethics; Fire Service; Honors; Qualifications; Research; Strategic Planning. **Publications:** *Fire Protection Engineering Magazine*, quarterly. Contains technical articles and case studies. **Price:** included in membership dues. **Circulation:** 10,000. **Advertising:** accepted ● *Journal of Fire Protection Engineering*, quarterly. Contains peer reviewed technical papers. **Price:** $230.00/year. ISSN: 1042-3915. **Circulation:** 4,150 ● *SFPE Today*, bimonthly. Newsletter. Contains chapter and member news and society's activities. **Price:** included in membership dues. **Circulation:** 4,150 ● Books ● Proceedings ● Reports. **Conventions/Meetings:** annual meeting, with engineering seminars and short courses - always fall ● seminar ● symposium ● workshop.

Firearms

7083 ■ Association of Firearm and Tool Mark Examiners (AFTE)
c/o Michelle N. Kuehner, Membership Sec.
Forensic Lab-Firearms Sect.
10 County Office Bldg.
542 Forbes Ave.
Pittsburgh, PA 15219
Ph: (412)350-3732 (301)772-4613
Fax: (412)350-3861
E-mail: mkuehner@county.allegheny.pa.us
URL: http://www.afte.org
Contact: Carlo Rosati, Pres.
Founded: 1969. **Members:** 500. **Membership Dues:** provisional, $135 (annual). **Description:** Firearm and tool mark examiners of law enforcement agencies and private laboratories; private consultants; others in related industries. Works to provide a ready means of communication among members concerning industry products, laboratory procedures, and techniques. Advances the profession. **Libraries: Type:** reference. **Holdings:** archival material. **Awards: Type:** recognition ● **Frequency:** annual. **Type:** scholarship. **Recipient:** for students seeking a career in Forensic Science. **Computer Services:** database, trigger pull. **Telecommunication Services:** electronic mail, rosativa@aol.com. **Publications:** *Association of Firearm and Tool Mark Examiners—Journal*, periodic. **Price:** included in membership dues; $125.00 /year for nonmembers in U.S.; $155.00 /year for nonmembers outside North America. **Conventions/Meetings:** annual seminar.

Fluid Power

7084 ■ International Fluid Power Society (IFPS)
PO Box 1420
Cherry Hill, NJ 08034-0054
Ph: (856)489-8983
Free: (800)303-8520
Fax: (856)424-9248
E-mail: info@ifps.org
URL: http://www.ifps.org
Contact: Bob Kraft, Pres.
Founded: 1960. **Members:** 2,650. **Membership Dues:** professional, $75 (annual) ● student, $35 (annual) ● corporate, $2,500-$10,000 (annual). **Staff:** 6. **Budget:** $900,000. **Local Groups:** 24. **Description:** Persons interested in all phases of fluid power and related motion control and its uses. Concerned with research, development, design, installation, operation, maintenance, education, and application to industry, aviation, marine, mobile, material handling, and agricultural equipment. Maintains speakers' bureau. Operates certification programs and placement service for fluid power mechanics, technicians, specialists, and engineers. **Awards:** Outstanding Fluid Power Educator. **Frequency:** annual. **Type:** recognition ● Outstanding Fluid Power Student. **Frequency:** annual. **Type:** recognition ● Professional Chapter of the Year. **Frequency:** annual. **Type:** recognition ● Professional Member of the Year. **Frequency:** annual. **Type:** recognition ● Student Chapter of the Year. **Frequency:** annual. **Type:** recognition. **Committees:** Certification; Chapter Activities; Education; Membership; Public Relations/Marketing. **Absorbed:** (1960) Industrial Hydraulics Training Association. **Formerly:** (2005) Fluid Power Society. **Publications:** *Certification Directory*, annual. **Price:** $100.00. **Circulation:** 3,000. **Advertising:** accepted ● *Fluid Power Journal*, 9/year. **Price:** $79.95 outside U.S. **Advertising:** accepted. Alternate Formats: online ● Brochures. Contains information on certification and membership. ● Manuals ● Membership Directory, annual. **Price:** $250.00. **Circulation:** 3,000. **Advertising:** accepted. **Conventions/Meetings:** board meeting ● periodic competition ● annual Professional and Student Member Leadership Workshop and Meeting.

7085 ■ National Conference on Fluid Power (NCFP)
3333 N Mayfair Rd., Ste.211
Milwaukee, WI 53222-3219
Ph: (414)778-3344
Fax: (414)778-3361
E-mail: nfpa@nfpa.com
URL: http://www.nfpa.com
Contact: Sue Chase, Sec.
Founded: 1953. **Members:** 240. **Staff:** 13. **Budget:** $1,800,000. **Description:** Individuals active in engineering education and in the field of fluid power. Provides a forum for dissemination of technical advances and information in fluid power, and a focus for communication regarding problems to the fluid power industry and to the academic community. Supports educational and research activities. **Conventions/Meetings:** Hannover Fair - trade show.

7086 ■ WaterJet Technology Association (WJTA)
906 Olive St., Ste.1200
St. Louis, MO 63101-1448
Ph: (314)241-1445
Fax: (314)241-1449
E-mail: wjta@wjta.org
URL: http://www.wjta.org
Founded: 1983. **Members:** 500. **Membership Dues:** individual in U.S. and Canada and Mexico, $60 (annual) ● individual (in other countries), $80 (annual) ● corporate in U.S. and Canada and Mexico, $400 (annual) ● corporate (in other countries), $460 (annual). **Description:** Works to provide a means of cooperation between government, industry, university, and research institutions on matters of fluid jets in the manufacturing, mining, construction, and process industries. Fosters domestic and international trade, promotes the study and advancement of the sciences connected with jet cutting and industrial cleaning. **Awards:** Best Paper. **Frequency:** biennial. **Type:** recognition ● Pioneer. **Frequency:** biennial. **Type:** recognition ● Safety. **Frequency:** biennial. **Type:** recognition ● Technology. **Frequency:** biennial. **Type:** recognition. **Publications:** *American Water Jet Conference Proceedings*, biennial. Includes a compilation of papers and abstracts presented at the conference. ● *Jet News*, semimonthly. Newsletter ● Membership Directory. **Conventions/Meetings:** biennial American Waterjet Conference - conference and trade show (exhibits) - always odd years.

Food

7087 ■ American Association of Candy Technologists (AACT)
175 Rock Rd.
Glen Rock, NJ 07452
Ph: (201)652-2655
Fax: (201)652-3419
E-mail: aactinfo@gomc.com
URL: http://www.aactcandy.org
Contact: Allen R. Allured, Treas.
Founded: 1948. **Members:** 780. **Membership Dues:** in U.S., $60 ● in Canada, $65 ● outside U.S. and Canada, $105. **Description:** Candy technologists who seek to further the education of the technical community of the confectionery industry. **Awards: Type:** recognition ● **Type:** scholarship. **Conventions/Meetings:** seminar.

7088 ■ American Meat Science Association (AMSA)
1111 N Dunlap Ave.
Savoy, IL 61874
Ph: (217)356-5368
Fax: (217)398-4119
E-mail: information@meatscience.org
URL: http://www.meatscience.org
Contact: Thomas Powell, Exec. Dir.
Founded: 1964. **Members:** 850. **Membership Dues:** professional, $155 (annual) ● graduate student, $70 (annual) ● undergraduate student, $25 (annual). **Staff:** 6. **Budget:** $700,000. **Description:** Persons engaged in meat research, extension, and education in universities, industry, government, and organizations. Facilitates exchange of ideas and information; fosters education, research, and development in the field of meat science. Conducts placement service. **Libraries: Type:** reference. **Holdings:** archival material. **Awards:** AMSA Awards. **Frequency:** annual. **Type:** recognition. **Recipient:** for seven categories. **Telecommunication Services:** electronic mail, tpowell@meatscience.org. **Formerly:** (1964) Reciprocal Meat Conference. **Publications:** *AMSA Newsletter*, quarterly ● *Directory of Members*, biennial. Membership Directory ● *Meat Science*. Journal. **Price:** $125.00 /year for members ● *Proceedings of Reciprocal Meat Conference*, annual. **Price:** $75.00. **Circulation:** 1,500 ● Journal, periodic. **Conventions/Meetings:** annual Reciprocal Meat Conference (exhibits).

7089 ■ American Society of Sugar Beet Technologists (ASSBT)
800 Grant St., Ste.300
Denver, CO 80203-2944
Ph: (303)832-4460
Fax: (303)832-4468
E-mail: tom@bsdf-assbt.org
URL: http://www.bsdf-assbt.org
Contact: Thomas K. Schwartz, Exec. VP
Founded: 1937. **Members:** 300. **Regional Groups:** 1. **Description:** Professional society of persons interested in research on sugar beet production and processing. **Libraries: Type:** by appointment only. **Holdings:** archival material, articles, books, papers, periodicals. **Awards:** 40-Year Veteran Award. **Type:** recognition ● Honorary Membership Award. **Type:** recognition ● Meritorious Service Award. **Type:** recognition. **Telecommunication Services:** electronic mail, aa@bsdf-assbt.org. **Sections:** Agronomy; Chemistry and Factory Operation; Entomology and Plant Pathology; Genetics and Variety Improvement; Physiology. **Publications:** Journal, semiannual. **Conventions/Meetings:** biennial meeting.

7090 ■ Association for the Study of Food and Society (ASFS)
c/o Jonathan Deutsch, Sec.
Kingsborough Community Coll., CUNY
Dept. of Tourism and Hospitality (TOU)
2002 Oriental Blvd.
Brooklyn, NY 11235
E-mail: jdeutsch@kbcc.cuny.edu
URL: http://www.food-culture.org
Contact: Jonathan Deutsch, Sec.
Founded: 1986. **Members:** 110. **Membership Dues:** individual, $55 (annual) ● student, $30 (annual). **Description:** Explores complex relationships among food, culture and society. **Publications:** *ASFS Newsletter*, semiannual. **Price:** $7.00 /year for nonmembers. **Circulation:** 141 ● *Food, Culture and Society: An International Journal of Multidisciplinary Research*,

3/year. **Price:** $60.00 for nonmembers; included in membership dues. **Advertising:** accepted. Alternate Formats: online. Also Cited As: *Journal for the Study of Food and Society*. **Conventions/Meetings:** annual Joint Meeting of the Association for the Study of Food and Society and the Agriculture, Food and Human Values Society - conference (exhibits).

7091 ■ Beef Improvement Federation (BIF)
c/o Dr. Twig Marston, Exec. Dir.
222 Weber Hall
Manhattan, KS 66506
Ph: (785)532-5428
Fax: (785)532-7059
E-mail: twig@ksu.edu
URL: http://www.beefimprovement.org
Contact: Chris Christensen, Pres.
Founded: 1967. **Members:** 82. **Membership Dues:** breed association, $100-$600 (annual) ● state/provincial/national organization, associate, $100 (annual) ● sustaining, $50 (annual). **Budget:** $50,000. **State Groups:** 32. **National Groups:** 50. **Description:** Representatives from state, national, and Canadian organizations formed to coordinate beef performance testing programs. Seeks to improve the quality of beef through research and testing and standardize national guidelines. Collects and disseminates information to find answers to problems affecting the industry. **Telecommunication Services:** electronic mail, chrishei@sbtc.net. **Committees:** Biotechnology; Central Test and Growth; Genetic Prediction; Live Animal and Carcass Evaluation; Reproduction; Systems. **Publications:** *Guidelines for Uniform Beef Improvement Programs* ● *Proceedings of BIF Research Symposium and Annual Meeting Update*, bimonthly. Alternate Formats: online ● *25 Year History - Ideas Into Action*. **Conventions/Meetings:** annual convention (exhibits).

7092 ■ Chinese American Food Society (CAFS)
c/o Dr. Vivian Wu, Treas.
Univ. of Maine
5735 Hitchner Hall 101A
Orono, ME 04469-5735
E-mail: ymlo@umd.edu
URL: http://www.cafsnet.org
Contact: Dr. Martin Lo, Pres.
Founded: 1975. **Members:** 350. **Membership Dues:** student, $10 (annual) ● active, associate, $20 (annual) ● life, $300 ● corporate, $250 (annual). **Regional Groups:** 3. **Description:** Represents Chinese-American scientists, engineers, and managers involved in food and food-related industries; university students and professors; research personnel of public and private research institutes. Works advance food science and technology and to promote Chinese cultural and ethnic interests. Operates placement service and charitable program. **Awards:** Student and Professional. **Frequency:** annual. **Type:** monetary. **Recipient:** for academic and scientific achievements. **Computer Services:** Mailing lists, job listings ● online services, membership directory. **Committees:** Employment; Long Term Planning; Public Relations; Workshop/Consultation. **Formerly:** (1983) Association of Chinese Food Scientists and Technologists in America. **Publications:** *CAFS Membership Directory*, annual ● *CAFS Newsletter* (in Chinese and English), quarterly. **Price:** available to members only. **Advertising:** accepted. Alternate Formats: online ● *CAFS Science and Technology Monograph Series*, periodic. **Price:** $5.00 each. **Conventions/Meetings:** annual conference, includes forum (exhibits) ● seminar ● workshop.

7093 ■ Food Distribution Research Society (FDRS)
c/o Denise Mainville, Membership VP
315 Hutcheson Hall
Blacksburg, VA 24061
Ph: (540)231-5774
Fax: (540)231-7417
E-mail: mainvill@vt.edu
URL: http://fdrs.ag.utk.edu
Contact: Denise Mainville, Membership VP
Founded: 1967. **Members:** 225. **Membership Dues:** professional in U.S., $40 (annual) ● junior in U.S., $10 (annual) ● company/business in U.S., $135 (annual) ● life, in U.S., $400 ● junior in Canada and Mexico, $22 (annual) ● professional in Canada and Mexico, $52 (annual) ● company/business in Canada and Mexico, $147 (annual) ● life, in Canada and Mexico, $412 ● professional inside Europe and South America, $66 (annual) ● junior inside Europe and South America, $36 (annual) ● company/business inside Europe and South America, $161 (annual) ● life, in Europe and South America, $426 ● professional in Asia and Pacific Rim, $72 (annual) ● junior in Asia and Pacific Rim, $42 (annual) ● company/business in Asia and Pacific Rim, $167 (annual) ● life, in Asia and Pacific Rim, $432. **Description:** Individuals from the industry and the academic community who have research interests in food distribution. Aims to: gain recognition for food distribution research; attract leaders in the field, provide an atmosphere wherein ideas, methods, and technical developments can be freely discussed. Encourages research by defining problems in the industry; provides guidelines and directions for developing and implementing food distribution research. Serves as an information clearinghouse. **Awards:** Applebaum Award. **Frequency:** annual. **Type:** monetary. **Recipient:** for outstanding PhD level paper or dissertation ● Frank Panyko Award for Distinguished Service. **Frequency:** annual. **Type:** recognition. **Recipient:** for members with outstanding service and leadership ● **Type:** monetary. **Recipient:** for outstanding master of science paper or thesis ● Presidential Award for Emerging Leadership. **Frequency:** annual. **Type:** recognition. **Recipient:** for individuals who have demonstrated evidence of continued involvement in FDRS leadership ● Presidential Award for Excellence in Research and Communication. **Frequency:** annual. **Type:** recognition. **Recipient:** for outstanding article by journal editors' choice. **Committees:** Audit; Budget; Communications; Nominating; Program; Research and Communication Awards; Service Awards; Student Case Study Competition. **Publications:** *Food Distribution Research Society Newsletter*, semiannual. **Price:** included in membership dues. **Circulation:** 225. Alternate Formats: online ● *Journal of Food Distribution Research*, semiannual. Provides information on problems in food distribution research. **Price:** included in membership dues. ISSN: 0047-245X. Alternate Formats: online. **Conventions/Meetings:** annual conference, for industry issues; academic papers.

7094 ■ Institute of Food Technologists (IFT)
525 W Van Buren, Ste.1000
Chicago, IL 60607
Ph: (312)782-8424 (312)604-0256
Free: (800)438-3663
Fax: (312)782-8348
E-mail: info@ift.org
URL: http://www.ift.org
Contact: Dennis R. Heldman, Pres.
Founded: 1939. **Members:** 28,000. **Membership Dues:** regular, professional, $165 (annual) ● student, $35 (annual). **Staff:** 50. **Budget:** $10,000,000. **Regional Groups:** 55. **Description:** Scientific educational society of technical personnel in food industries, production, product development, research, and product quality. Promotes application of science and engineering to the evaluation, production, processing, packaging, distribution, preparation, and utilization of foods. Aids educational institutions in developing curricula for training in this area. **Libraries: Type:** reference. **Holdings:** reports. **Awards: Type:** fellowship. **Recipient:** for outstanding research in food science and technology ● **Frequency:** annual. **Type:** recognition ● **Type:** scholarship. **Recipient:** for outstanding undergraduate students. **Computer Services:** Mailing lists. **Committees:** Annual Meeting; Awards; Career Guidance; Constitution and By-Laws; Continuing Education; Membership and Professional Affairs; Research; Scientific Lectureship. **Divisions:** Biotechnology; Carbohydrates; Citrus Products; Dairy Technology; Education; Extension; Food Chemistry; Food Engineering; Food Microbiology; Food Packaging; Foodservice; Fruits and Vegetables; International Muscle Foods; Nutrition; Quality Assurance; Refrigerated and Frozen Foods; Sensory Evaluation; Toxicology and Safety Evaluation. **Publications:** *Food Technology*, monthly. Magazine. Provides information on the development of new and improved food sources, news, and regulatory and legislative developments. **Price:** included in membership dues; $122.00 /year for nonmembers in U.S. and Canada, Mexico; $132.00 /year for nonmembers outside North America. ISSN: 0015-6639. **Circulation:** 27,000. **Advertising:** accepted. Alternate Formats: microform ● *IFT Membership Directory*, annual. **Price:** included in membership dues ● *IFT Program and Directory*, annual. **Advertising:** accepted ● *Journal of Food Science*, bimonthly. Contains research articles on all aspects of food science. Includes graphs, charts, tables, and index of authors. **Price:** $70.00 /year for members; $275.00 /year for nonmembers in U.S., Canada, and Mexico; $300.00 /year for nonmembers outside North America. ISSN: 0022-1947. **Circulation:** 10,500. Alternate Formats: microform; online ● *Journal of Food Science Education*. Alternate Formats: online ● Newsletter, weekly. Alternate Formats: online. **Conventions/Meetings:** annual conference and convention, includes food exposition (exhibits) ● annual meeting (exhibits) - 2008 June 28-July 2, New Orleans, LA; 2009 June 6-10, Anaheim, CA.

7095 ■ Milling and Baking Division of AACC International
3340 Pilot Knob Rd.
St. Paul, MN 55121
Ph: (651)454-7250
Fax: (651)454-0766
E-mail: aacc@scisoc.org
Contact: Susan Kohn, Membership Dir.
Founded: 1974. **Members:** 1,000. **Staff:** 10. **Description:** Encourages research, discussion, and the dissemination of information on all phases of milling and baking-related activities including the chemistry, development, and processing of cereals. Subgroup of AACC International. **Publications:** none. **Affiliated With:** AACC International. **Formerly:** (2005) Milling and Baking Division of American Association of Cereal Chemists. **Conventions/Meetings:** annual conference and symposium.

7096 ■ Research and Development Associates for Military Food and Packaging Systems (R&DA)
16607 Blanco Rd., Ste.1506
San Antonio, TX 78232
Ph: (210)493-8024
Fax: (210)493-8036
E-mail: hqs@militaryfood.org
URL: http://www.militaryfood.org
Contact: LTC James F. Fagan, Exec. Dir.
Founded: 1946. **Members:** 750. **Membership Dues:** industrial, $400 (annual) ● consultant, $125 (annual) ● institutional, individual, $50 (annual) ● associate, $100 (annual) ● student, $10 (annual). **Staff:** 3. **Budget:** $450,000. **Description:** Represents industrial firms, educational institutions, and related groups. Engaged in food, food service, distribution, and container research and development. Assists in the solution of government food and container problems; such solutions often lead to developments used in the civilian sector. **Libraries: Type:** reference. **Holdings:** 600. **Awards:** Colonel Merton Singer Award. **Frequency:** annual. **Type:** recognition. **Recipient:** for outstanding contributions to the R&DA mission ● Colonel Rohland A. Isker Award. **Frequency:** annual. **Type:** recognition. **Recipient:** for outstanding contributions to national preparedness. **Telecommunication Services:** electronic mail, jfagan@militaryfood.org. **Working Groups:** Dehydrated Food Products; Emerging Technologies; Food Safety; Foodservice Operational; Irradiated Foods; Packaging; Rations/Mobilization; Specification Review. **Formerly:** (1969) Research and Development Associates. **Publications:** *The Link*, quarterly. Newsletter. Covers military food service and packaging systems. Includes research reports, calendar of events, and new members. **Price:** $40.00. **Circulation:** 11,000. Alternate Formats: online ● *Membership Roster*, periodic. Membership Directory. **Price:** $50.00 ● *Minutes of Work Group Meetings*, annual. Report ●

Research and Development Associates for Military Food and Packaging Systems—Activities Report, annual. Booklets. Includes meeting proceedings; author index and research reports. **Price:** $80.00 /year for nonmembers. ISSN: 0198-0181. **Circulation:** 4,000. Also Cited As: *Activities Report of the R&D Associates* ● Newsletter, quarterly. Covers technical information. ● Reports, quarterly. Covers technical information. **Conventions/Meetings:** semiannual Exposition - conference and meeting (exhibits) ● annual meeting (exhibits) - usually spring and fall.

7097 ■ Sugar Industry Technologists (SIT)
164 N Hall Dr.
Sugar Land, TX 77478
Ph: (281)494-2046
Fax: (281)494-2304
E-mail: sit@sucrose.com
URL: http://www.sucrose.com/sit
Contact: Mr. Leon Anhaiser, Exec. Dir.
Founded: 1941. **Members:** 600. **Membership Dues:** corporate, allied, $450 (annual) ● associate, $40 (annual) ● affiliate, $60 (annual). **Staff:** 2. **Budget:** $80,000. **Multinational. Description:** Cane sugar refinery technical engineers, bacteriologists, chemists, processors, production workers, equipment suppliers, research scientists and administrators. Serves the professional interests of members by disseminating information on scientific and other technical aspects of sugar refining and by encouraging original research. **Awards:** Crystal Award. **Frequency:** annual. **Type:** recognition. **Recipient:** to individuals who have contributed to the technological advancement of the sugar refining industry ● Frank Chapman Memorial Award. **Frequency:** annual. **Type:** recognition. **Recipient:** for best poster presentation at the annual technical sessions ● George and Eleanore Meade Award. **Frequency:** annual. **Type:** recognition. **Recipient:** for best paper presented at the annual technical sessions ● Joe Harrison Sr. Memorial Award. **Frequency:** annual. **Type:** scholarship. **Recipient:** to a student attending the Cane Sugar Refiners Institute Course at Nicholls State University. **Telecommunication Services:** electronic mail, exedirsit@aol.com. **Publications:** *Roster*, annual. Proceedings. Includes technical proceedings. ● *Sugar Industry Technologists—Proceedings of Annual Meeting*. **Price:** included in membership dues; C$50.00 /year for nonmembers. **Conventions/Meetings:** annual meeting - usually May.

Forensic Sciences

7098 ■ International Society of Environmental Forensics (ISEF)
150 Fearing St., Ste.21
Amherst, MA 01002
Ph: (413)549-5170
Fax: (413)549-0579
E-mail: clanglois@aehs.com
URL: http://www.environmentalforensics.org
Contact: Cindy Langlois, Managing Dir.
Membership Dues: regular (with electronic subscription to journal), $95 (annual) ● regular (with hard copy subscription to journal), $195 (annual) ● student (with electronic subscription to journal), $50 (annual). **Multinational. Description:** Addresses the environmental contamination issues subjected to law, public debate or formal argumentation. Seeks to investigate the source, fate, transport and identification of environmental contaminants. Encourages the development of technical courses that focus on scientific and technical information, data and critical analysis. **Publications:** *Environmental Forensics*, quarterly. Journal. Covers scientific studies that explore the source, fate, transport and ecological effects of contamination. **Price:** included in membership dues. ISSN: 1527-5922. Alternate Formats: online.

Forestry

7099 ■ Forest Products Society (FPS)
2801 Marshall Ct.
Madison, WI 53705-2295
Ph: (608)231-1361 (662)325-3056
Fax: (608)231-2152
E-mail: info@forestprod.org
URL: http://www.forestprod.org
Contact: Ms. Carol Lewis, Exec. VP
Founded: 1947. **Members:** 2,500. **Membership Dues:** voting, $125-$135 (annual) ● student, $25-$60 (annual) ● retired, $15-$55 (annual) ● contributing, $400 (annual) ● supporting, $800 (annual) ● sustaining, $1,200 (annual) ● developing country, $35 (annual) ● student - developing country, $15 (annual). **Staff:** 9. **Budget:** $1,500,000. **Regional Groups:** 14. **Multinational. Description:** Individuals interested in wood industry research, development, production, utilization, and distribution, from logging operations through finished products and utilization of residue as by-products. Maintains 30 technical committees. **Libraries: Type:** not open to the public. **Holdings:** 100. **Awards:** Fred W. Gottschalk Memorial Award. **Frequency:** annual. **Type:** recognition. **Recipient:** for an individual member ● L.J. Markwardt Wood Engineering Award. **Frequency:** annual. **Type:** recognition. **Recipient:** for an outstanding research paper in the field of wood as an engineering material ● Wood Award. **Frequency:** annual. **Type:** recognition. **Recipient:** for outstanding research in the field of wood and wood products. **Telecommunication Services:** electronic mail, carol@forestprod.org. **Divisions:** Fundamental Disciplines; Management; Processes; Solid Wood Products; Wood Engineering. **Formerly:** (1993) Forest Product Research Society. **Publications:** *Forest Products Journal*, monthly. Contains peer-reviewed research articles related to forest products. Includes yearbook. **Price:** included in membership dues. **Circulation:** 3,000. **Advertising:** accepted ● *Sawing, Edging, and Training Hardwood Lumber: Putting Theory Into Practice*. Manual. Covers all aspects of sawing, resawing, edging, trimming and grading hardwood lumber. **Price:** $35.00 for members; $50.00 for nonmembers ● *Wood Handbook: Wood as an Engineering Material*. Includes an expanded and updated glossary. **Price:** $39.00 for individuals; $19.95 for full-time students ● *Woodframe Housing Durability and Disaster Issues*. Proceedings. Provides information on problems and solutions related to woodframe housing and disaster issues. **Price:** $55.00 for members; $85.00 for nonmembers ● Proceedings. **Conventions/Meetings:** periodic conference, technical ● annual convention - always June. 2008 June 23-25, St. Louis, MO; 2009 June 22-24, Boise, ID.

7100 ■ Society of Wood Science and Technology (SWST)
1 Gifford Pinchot Dr.
Madison, WI 53726-2398
Ph: (608)231-9347
Fax: (608)231-9592
E-mail: vicki@swst.org
URL: http://www.swst.org
Contact: Vicki L. Herian, Exec. Dir.
Founded: 1958. **Members:** 400. **Membership Dues:** full, $75 (annual) ● student, $25 (annual) ● retiree, $40 (annual). **Staff:** 2. **Description:** Wood scientists and technologists in the forest products industry, research, or education; student members are college juniors, seniors, or graduate students in wood science and technology curricula. Sponsors Visiting Scientist Program for colleges offering wood science and technology courses. **Libraries: Type:** open to the public. **Holdings:** 38; periodicals. **Subjects:** wood and fiber science. **Awards:** George Marra Award. **Frequency:** annual. **Type:** recognition. **Recipient:** for excellence in writing and research ● International Visiting Scientist Award. **Frequency:** annual. **Type:** recognition. **Recipient:** for travel; to benefit the society ● Student Poster Competition. **Type:** recognition. **Recipient:** for the first and second place winners in the annual student poster competition. **Committees:** Accreditation; Critical Issues. **Formerly:** (1960) American Institute of Wood Engineering. **Publications:** *Career Opportunities in Applied Science and Engineering*. Brochure ● *Exploring a Profession in Forest Products*. Video ● *SWST Newsletter*, bimonthly. Alternate Formats: online ● *Wood and Fiber Science*, quarterly. Journal. **Price:** $250.00 /year for individuals; $240.00/year for agencies ● Proceedings. Alternate Formats: online ● Survey. Alternate Formats: online ● Handbooks. Alternate Formats: online. **Conventions/Meetings:** annual meeting - always June.

7101 ■ Tree-Ring Society (TRS)
Univ. of Arizona
Lab. of Tree-Ring Res., Bldg. 58
Tucson, AZ 85721
Ph: (520)621-1608
Fax: (520)621-8229
E-mail: pmb@rmtrr.org
URL: http://www.treeringsociety.org
Contact: Peter Brown, Pres.
Founded: 1935. **Members:** 333. **Membership Dues:** individual, $40 (semiannual) ● institution, $50 (semiannual) ● student, $20 (semiannual). **Description:** Scientists and research workers interested in dendrochronology, which is the determination of dates and time intervals by comparative study of the sequence of rings of growth in trees and aged wood. **Convention/Meeting:** none. **Libraries: Type:** reference. **Holdings:** books, periodicals. **Subjects:** dendrochronology, climatology, hydrology, geoscience, ecology. **Publications:** *Tree-Ring Research*, annual. Journal. Contains the study of dendrochronology and related sciences. ISSN: 0041-2198. **Circulation:** 333. Alternate Formats: online.

Future

7102 ■ Association of Professional Futurists (APF)
681 Main St., Ste.324
Waltham, MA 02451
E-mail: info@profuturists.org
URL: http://www.profuturists.org
Contact: Mr. John B. Mahaffie, Chm.
Founded: 2002. **Members:** 200. **Membership Dues:** full, provisional, $195 (annual) ● student, $50 (annual). **Multinational. Description:** Promotes professional excellence in the futures field by developing standards, identifying best practices, and innovating new techniques for understanding the future. Facilitates network and community building. Acts as an advocate for professional futurists by promoting the profession and conducting media outreach to help them understand the nature and significance of futures thinking. **Publications:** *Compass*, bimonthly. Newsletter.

7103 ■ Earthrise
2151 Michelson Dr., Ste.258
Irvine, CA 92612
Ph: (949)623-0980
Free: (800)949-7473
Fax: (949)623-0990
E-mail: lina@earthrise.com
URL: http://www.earthrise.com
Founded: 1982. **Description:** Researchers, educators, and design professionals interested in long-range global trends. Demonstrates simulation games and presents slide lectures. Distributes Global Futures Game, a simulation of the world in terms of population, food, technology, education, and relative growth rates to the year 2020.

7104 ■ Institute for Alternative Futures (IAF)
100 N Pitt St.
Alexandria, VA 22314-3134
Ph: (703)684-5880
Fax: (703)684-0640
E-mail: futurist@altfutures.com
URL: http://www.altfutures.com
Contact: Clement Bezold PhD, Founder/Chm.
Founded: 1977. **Staff:** 10. **Budget:** $1,500,000. **Nonmembership. Multinational. Description:** A public interest organization. Works to enable individuals and organizations to create the preferred future for themselves and society. Conducts Foresight Seminars for congressional staff members and state and local governments. Provides futures research, vision, goals and strategy development assistance to

various organizations. Owns AFA, a consulting firm which provides futures research and training to large corporations. **Libraries: Type:** reference. **Holdings:** 1,000. **Subjects:** health issues, futures, political science, citizen goals, environment, technology, futures projects in U.S. **Projects:** Associations; Education; Environment; Government; Health. **Supersedes:** Center for Adaptive Learning. **Publications:** *Alternative Futures*, monthly. Newsletter. Includes emerging issues, intriguing ideas and shared learning. **Price:** free. Alternate Formats: online. **Conventions/Meetings:** periodic Foresight Seminars on Health and Innovation.

7105 ■ Institute for the Future (IFTF)
124 Univ. Ave., 2nd Fl.
Palo Alto, CA 94301
Ph: (650)854-6322
Fax: (650)854-7850
E-mail: info@iftf.org
URL: http://www.iftf.org
Contact: Mr. Sean Ness, Business Development Mgr.
Founded: 1968. **Membership Dues:** technology horizons program, $65,000 (annual) ● health horizons program, $65,000 (annual) ● ten-year forecast program, $15,000 (annual). **Staff:** 25. **Budget:** $3,000,000. **Languages:** English, French, Norwegian, Spanish. **Multinational. Description:** Assists organizations, businesses, industry, and the government in conducting long-term futures research. Promotes practical application of information techniques for improved management and productivity. Services include consultation, forecasting and strategic planning, teleconferencing and office systems, videotex, home information assistance, and health care. **Libraries: Type:** not open to the public. **Publications:** *Ten-Year Forecast*, annual ● Also publishes books, papers, and research reports.

7106 ■ International Institute of Forecasters (IIF)
c/o Ms. Pamela Stroud, Business Mgr.
53 Tesla Ave.
Medford, MA 02155
Ph: (781)234-4077
Fax: (509)357-5530
E-mail: forecasters@forecasters.org
URL: http://www.forecasters.org
Contact: Ms. Pamela Stroud, Business Mgr.
Founded: 1981. **Members:** 500. **Membership Dues:** regular, $120 (annual) ● student, $55 (annual). **Budget:** $100,000. **National Groups:** 2. **Languages:** English, French. **Multinational. Description:** Forecasters, decision makers, and researchers from 41 countries involved with forecasting in the management, social, engineering, and behavioral sciences. Objectives are to: promote forecasting as a professional multidisciplinary activity; bridge the gap between the theory and practice of forecasting; make forecasting useful and relevant. Facilitates communication among members. Disseminates information on new forecasting methods, data sources and computer programs, assessments of forecasting methods, and uses and abuses of forecasting. **Awards:** Best Paper. **Frequency:** biennial. **Type:** monetary. **Publications:** *FORESIGHT: The International Journal of Applied Forecasting*, 3/year. **Price:** $95.00 for nonmembers. ISSN: 1555-9068. **Circulation:** 600. **Advertising:** accepted. Alternate Formats: online ● *International Journal of Forecasting*, quarterly. Covers forecasting in the management, social, engineering, and behavioral sciences. Includes book and software reviews. **Price:** included in membership dues; $406.00 /year for nonmembers and institutions. ISSN: 0169-2070. **Circulation:** 700 ● *Oracle*, quarterly. Newsletter. **Price:** included in membership dues. **Circulation:** 500. **Advertising:** accepted. Alternate Formats: online. **Conventions/Meetings:** annual International Symposium on Forecasting (exhibits).

7107 ■ World Future Society (WFS)
7910 Woodmont Ave., Ste.450
Bethesda, MD 20814
Ph: (301)656-8274
Free: (800)989-8274
Fax: (301)951-0394
E-mail: info@wfs.org
URL: http://www.wfs.org
Contact: Ms. Susan Echard, VP of Membership/Conference Operations
Founded: 1966. **Members:** 25,000. **Membership Dues:** individual, $49 (annual) ● professional, $135 (annual) ● student (full-time, under 25), $20 (annual) ● comprehensive professional, $245 (annual) ● regular (life), $750 ● professional (life), $1,950 ● comprehensive professional (life), $2,950 ● institution (non-profit), $325 (annual) ● institution (business), $500 (annual). **Staff:** 11. **Budget:** $1,500,000. **Local Groups:** 80. **Multinational. Description:** Helps individuals, organizations, and communities see, understand, and respond appropriately and effectively to change. Raises awareness of change and encourages development of creative solutions through media, meetings, and dialogue among its members. Serves as a neutral forum for exploring possible, probable, and preferable futures. **Libraries: Type:** not open to the public. **Holdings:** 10,000; archival material, artwork, audio recordings, books. **Subjects:** business, creative thinking, ecology, economics, education, future studies, health, information society, leadership, management, planning, public policy, resources, science, society, technology, values and lifestyles, work, world affairs. **Publications:** *Future Survey: A Monthly Abstract of Books, Articles, and Reports Concerning Forecasts, Trends, and Ideas About the Future*. Newsletter. Focuses on current technological, environmental, economic, and social trends and events likely to influence the future. Includes subject index. **Price:** $109.00 /year for individuals; $165.00 /year for libraries. ISSN: 0190-3241. **Circulation:** 2,300 ● *Futures Research Quarterly*. Journal. Promotes public understanding of the methods and uses of the field. Includes calendar of events and book reviews. **Price:** $77.00 /year for individuals; $99.00 /year for libraries. ISSN: 0049-8092. **Circulation:** 1,200. Alternate Formats: microform ● *The Futurist*, bimonthly. Journal. Covers developments, trends, alternative scenarios, and ideas about the future. **Price:** included in membership dues; $59.00 /year for libraries and nonmember institutions. ISSN: 0016-3317. **Circulation:** 25,000. **Advertising:** accepted. Alternate Formats: microform ● Books. **Conventions/Meetings:** annual conference, brings together futurists from around the world to share ideas and vital information about the trends that will affect the world of tomorrow.

Gases

7108 ■ American Association of Radon Scientists and Technologists (AARST)
PO Box 2109
Fletcher, NC 28732
Free: (866)772-2778
Fax: (828)890-8071
E-mail: office@aarst.org
URL: http://www.aarst.org/home.html
Contact: Patrick Hendrick, Exec. Dir.
Founded: 1986. **Members:** 1,100. **Membership Dues:** individual, $125 (annual) ● organization, $500 (annual) ● associate, $75 (annual) ● student, $25 (annual) ● company, $250 (annual) ● executive, $1,000 (annual). **Staff:** 2. **Budget:** $190,000. **Regional Groups:** 16. **Description:** Scientists and tradespeople engaged in radon gas testing and remediation and advocacy on behalf of radon lung cancer victims. Works for policy changes at local, state and federal level to implement the 1988 Indoor Radon Abatement Act. Seeks to improve members' skills and effectiveness; conducts international educational and research programs; maintains speakers' bureau; compiles statistics. **Libraries: Type:** reference. **Awards: Type:** recognition. **Publications:** *Annual Proceedings International Radon Symposium*, annual. Journal. **Price:** $25.00/copy. Alternate Formats: CD-ROM ● *Radon Reporter*, quarterly. Newsletter. **Price:** included in membership dues. **Circulation:** 1,500. **Advertising:** accepted. **Conventions/Meetings:** annual International Radon Symposium - conference (exhibits) - 2008 Sept. 14-17, Las Vegas, NV.

7109 ■ International Ozone Association (IOA)
PO Box 28873
Scottsdale, AZ 85255
Ph: (480)529-3787
Fax: (480)473-9068
E-mail: info3zone@io3a.org
URL: http://www.int-ozone-assoc.org
Contact: Mr. Robert Jarnis, Exec. Dir.
Founded: 1973. **Members:** 800. **Membership Dues:** individual, academic, $100 (annual) ● manufacturer A, $600 (annual) ● manufacturer B, corporate, $360 (annual) ● consulting firm, $240 (annual) ● student, $35 (annual). **Staff:** 3. **Budget:** $150,000. **Regional Groups:** 3. **Description:** Individuals, companies, consulting engineering firms, service/support organizations that design, sell, service, or use ozone equipment, manufacturers, municipal services, institutions, and cooperating organizations. Works to advance the positive applications of ozone; furthers ozone technology through scientific and educational means. **Libraries: Type:** not open to the public. **Holdings:** 20. **Subjects:** ozone technology. **Awards:** Harvey M. Rosen Award. **Frequency:** annual. **Type:** recognition. **Formerly:** (1978) International Ozone Institute. **Publications:** *Ozone News*, bimonthly. Newsletter. Monitors developments in ozone technology and applications. Includes research updates. **Price:** included in membership dues; $150.00 for nonmembers. ISSN: 1065-5905. **Circulation:** 1,500. **Advertising:** accepted ● *Ozone Science and Engineering*, bimonthly. Journal. Covers various aspects of ozone technology. **Price:** included in membership dues; $225.00 for nonmembers. **Circulation:** 1,500 ● Proceedings. Contains information from world congresses, conferences, and symposiums. **Conventions/Meetings:** biennial congress (exhibits) ● symposium ● workshop.

7110 ■ Methanol Institute (MI)
4100 N Fairfax Dr., Ste.740
Arlington, VA 22203
Ph: (703)248-3636
Free: (888)275-0768
Fax: (703)248-3997
E-mail: mi@methanol.org
URL: http://www.methanol.org
Contact: John E. Lynn, Pres./CEO
Founded: 1989. **Members:** 16. **Staff:** 3. **Multinational. Description:** Serves as "the voice of the global methanol industry." Member companies include the principal producers of methanol, as well as methanol distributors, industry suppliers and consumers. Supports the greater use of methanol as a clean energy source for various environmentally beneficial uses. Promotes the use of methanol as a hydrogen carrier for vehicle, stationary and portable power fuel cell technology applications. Issues fact sheets, reports, and press releases, and gives presentations at numerous conferences. **Telecommunication Services:** electronic mail, jlynn@methanol.org. **Formerly:** (2001) American Methanol Institute. **Publications:** Reports.

Genetics

7111 ■ American Genetic Association (AGA)
PO Box 257
Buckeystown, MD 21717-0257
Ph: (301)695-9292
Fax: (301)695-9292
E-mail: agajoh@mail.ncifcrf.gov
URL: http://www.theaga.org
Contact: Dr. Stephen J. O'Brien, Ed.
Founded: 1903. **Members:** 750. **Description:** Represents biologists, zoologists, geneticists, botanists, and others engaged in basic and applied research in genetics. Explores transmission genetics of plants and animals. **Awards:** Stephen J. O'Brien Award. **Frequency:** annual. **Type:** monetary. **Recipient:** for the best student paper published in the Journal of

Heredity. **Formerly:** (1913) American Breeders Association. **Publications:** *Journal of Heredity*, bimonthly. **Advertising:** accepted. **Conventions/Meetings:** annual meeting.

7112 ■ American Institute for Medical and Biological Engineering (AIMBE)
1901 Pennsylvania Ave. NW, Ste.401
Washington, DC 20001
Ph: (202)496-9660
Fax: (202)466-8489
E-mail: info@aimbe.org
URL: http://www.aimbe.org
Contact: Jennifer L. Ayers MPA, Exec. Dir.
Founded: 1991. **Members:** 800. **Staff:** 2. **Budget:** $300,000. **Description:** Represents individuals with an interest in medical and biological engineering. Fosters exchange of ideas and information among members; works to establish a clear identity for the field and improve public awareness of members' activities; serves as liaison between members and government agencies. Conducts educational programs; promotes public interest in science and science education. **Awards: Type:** recognition. **Recipient:** for individual and group achievements in medical and biological engineering. **Publications:** *The AIMBE News*, quarterly. Newsletter. Alternate Formats: online. **Conventions/Meetings:** annual meeting.

7113 ■ American Society of Human Genetics (ASHG)
9650 Rockville Pike
Bethesda, MD 20814-3998
Ph: (301)634-7300
Free: (866)HUM-GENE
Fax: (301)634-7079
E-mail: society@ashg.org
URL: http://www.ashg.org
Contact: Elaine Strass, Exec. Dir.
Founded: 1948. **Members:** 7,500. **Membership Dues:** regular, $150 (annual) ● affiliate outside U.S., $160 (annual) ● trainee (with journal), $65 (annual) ● trainee (without journal), $25 (annual) ● trainee outside U.S., $75 (annual) ● husband/wife, $200 (annual). **Staff:** 12. **Description:** Professional society of physicians, researchers, genetic counselors, and others interested in human genetics. **Awards:** Award for Excellence in Human Genetics Education. **Type:** monetary. **Recipient:** for outstanding contributions to human genetics education ● C.W. Cotterman Award. **Frequency:** annual. **Type:** monetary. **Recipient:** for the best paper published in the journal ● Stern Award. **Frequency:** annual. **Type:** recognition. **Recipient:** for outstanding scientific achievements in human genetics ● Student Awards. **Type:** recognition. **Recipient:** for student presentations ● William Allan Award. **Frequency:** annual. **Type:** recognition. **Recipient:** for exceptional contribution to human genetics. **Computer Services:** Mailing lists, labels (one time use only). **Committees:** Database; Information and Education; Public Policy; Social Issues. **Publications:** *American Journal of Human Genetics*, monthly. **Price:** $1,025.00 /year for institutions and nonmembers in U.S.; $1,120.75 /year for institutions and nonmembers in Canada; $1,080.00 /year for institutions and nonmembers outside U.S.; $91.00/copy, for institutions and nonmembers. Alternate Formats: online ● *Supplement to Journal*, annual ● Membership Directory, biennial. **Conventions/Meetings:** annual convention (exhibits) - usually October ● annual meeting - 2008 Nov. 12-15, Philadelphia, PA; 2009 Oct. 20-24, Honolulu, HI; 2010 Nov. 2-6, Washington, DC.

7114 ■ Eugenics Special Interest Group (ESIG)
PO Box 138
East Schodack, NY 12063-0138
Ph: (518)732-2390
E-mail: willardh2@juno.com
Contact: Willard J. Hoyt, Coor.
Founded: 1982. **Membership Dues:** regular, $6 (annual). **Description:** Persons interested in human genetics and population. Seeks to study how people can band together so that children can be born healthy, long lived, and in such numbers as the world can best support. Aims to set a pattern that can be adopted by the whole human race. **Publications:** Bulletin, periodic.

7115 ■ Genetics Society of America (GSA)
9650 Rockville Pike
Bethesda, MD 20814-3998
Ph: (301)634-7300
Free: (866)486-GENE
Fax: (301)530-7079
E-mail: society@genetics-gsa.org
URL: http://www.genetics-gsa.org
Contact: Allan C. Spradling, Pres.
Founded: 1931. **Members:** 4,100. **Membership Dues:** regular, $120 (annual) ● graduate student, $65 (annual) ● regular affiliate, $60 (annual) ● graduate student (journal online access only), $40 (annual) ● husband/wife, $190 (annual) ● postdoctoral, $90 (annual) ● emeritus, $50 (annual). **Staff:** 10. **Budget:** $1,150,000. **Description:** Individuals and organizations interested in any field of genetics. Provides facilities for association and conferences of students in heredity; encourages communication among workers in genetics and those in related sciences. **Libraries: Type:** reference. **Awards:** GSA Medal. **Frequency:** annual. **Type:** medal. **Recipient:** for contributions over the past 15 years ● Thomas Hunt Morgan Medal. **Frequency:** annual. **Type:** medal. **Recipient:** for lifetime contribution to genetics. **Computer Services:** Mailing lists, of members. **Publications:** *Genetics*, monthly. Journal ● *Solving the Puzzle—Careers in Genetics*. Brochure ● Membership Directory, biennial. Alternate Formats: online ● Newsletter. **Conventions/Meetings:** annual Drosophila Research - conference (exhibits) - 2009 Mar. 4-8, Chicago, IL; 2010 Apr. 7-11, Washington, DC; 2011 Mar. 30-Apr. 3, San Diego, CA.

7116 ■ International Society for Phylogenetic Nomenclature (ISPN)
c/o Nico Cellinese, Treas.
Florida Museum of Natural History
Univ. of Florida
PO Box 117800
Gainesville, FL 32611-7800
Ph: (352)392-1721
E-mail: ncellinese@flmnh.ufl.edu
URL: http://www.phylonames.org
Contact: Nico Cellinese, Treas.
Membership Dues: regular, $40 (annual) ● regular family, $10 (annual) ● student, $20 (annual) ● student family, $5 (annual) ● sustaining, $80 (annual) ● life, $1,000 ● life family, $250. **Multinational. Description:** Encourages the use of, and communication about, phylogenetic nomenclature. Promotes and supports the development of phylogenetic nomenclature. Facilitates cooperation and communication among members.

7117 ■ Middle East Genetics Association (MEGA)
c/o Mohammad Rafi, PhD, Pres.
Dept. of Neurology
Jefferson Medical Coll.
1020 Locust St., JAH394
Philadelphia, PA 19107
Ph: (215)503-5715
Fax: (215)923-7747
E-mail: mohammad.rafi@mail.tju.edu
URL: http://info.med.yale.edu/genetics/clinical/lab_services/mega
Contact: Mohammad Rafi PhD, Pres.
Multinational. Description: Promotes education and research in the fields of human and non-human genetics, primarily pertaining to the area of the Middle East broadly defined. **Conventions/Meetings:** periodic meeting.

7118 ■ National Council on Gene Resources (NCGR)
1738 Thousand Oaks Blvd.
Berkeley, CA 94707
Ph: (510)524-8973
Fax: (510)526-3092
Contact: Dr. David Kafton, Exec. Dir.
Founded: 1980. **Staff:** 15. **Description:** Supporters are industrial, scientific, conservation, and professional organizations, and individuals interested in the management, conservation, and use of the world's genetic resources. Seeks to make gene resource conservation a priority national issue and to provide the information, technical assistance, and funding needed to safeguard the diversity of genetic resources, including the many animals, plants, and microorganisms required to meet society's basic needs. Conducts research on problems, issues, and needs related to the management, conservation, and use of genetic resources. Believes that if destruction of genetic resources continues, the U.S. faces serious hardships affecting the economy and the quality of life because of increased problems in the agricultural, forestry, pharmaceutical, and fishing industries. Sponsors educational programs, including the production of slides, and radio and television presentations. Plans to initiate statewide and regional gene resource conservation programs. **Committees:** Anadromous Salmonid Gene Resources; Barley Gene Resources; Douglas-Fir Genetic Resources; Strawberry Gene Resources. **Programs:** California Gene Resources.

7119 ■ Proteome Society
PO Box 197
Ross, CA 94957-0197
Ph: (415)459-2266
Fax: (415)581-6411
E-mail: info@proteome.org
URL: http://www.proteome.org
Contact: Cara Wykowski, Exec. Dir.
Founded: 1997. **Membership Dues:** individual, $25 (annual). **Multinational. Description:** Aims to provide worldwide opportunities for education, networking, and information exchange. Provides a public forum for panel discussions and scientific posters, seminars and electronic debates as well as a venue for expressing opinions. Serves as a general information resource to all interested parties concerning proteomic sciences and innovation.

Geography

7120 ■ American Geographical Society (AGS)
120 Wall St., Ste.100
New York, NY 10005
Ph: (212)422-5456
Fax: (212)422-5480
E-mail: ags@amergeog.org
URL: http://www.amergeog.org
Contact: Mary Lynne Bird, Exec. Dir.
Founded: 1851. **Members:** 1,000. **Membership Dues:** fellow, $57 (annual) ● institutional, $69 (annual). **Staff:** 10. **Budget:** $700,000. **Multinational. Description:** Professional geographers, educators, and others interested in all phases of geography. Devotes itself to encouraging research in geography and to the dissemination of geographic knowledge. Sponsors research projects. Operates travel and educational programs. **Libraries: Type:** open to the public. **Holdings:** 3,500. **Subjects:** anything related to geography. **Awards:** Honorary Fellowships and 8 Medals. **Frequency:** quadrennial. **Type:** recognition. **Recipient:** for scholarship or service to the discipline ● McColl Family Fellowship. **Frequency:** annual. **Type:** fellowship. **Recipient:** for field research resulting in an article for focus on geography magazine. **Publications:** *Focus on Geography*, quarterly. Magazine. Includes maps, photographs, graphics, wine column, and suggested readings; written for general audience. **Price:** $37.00/year for AGS fellows; $57.00/year for institutional fellows; $44.00 /year for individuals; $66.00 /year for institutions. ISSN: 0015-5004. **Circulation:** 5,000. **Advertising:** accepted. Alternate Formats: microform ● *Geographical Review*, quarterly. Journal. Includes book reviews for geographers. **Price:** $63.00/year for AGS fellows; $114.00/year for institutional fellows; $76.00 /year for individuals; $126.00 /year for institutions. ISSN: 0016-

7428. **Circulation:** 2,900. **Advertising:** accepted. Alternate Formats: microform ● *Ubique*, 3/year. Newsletter. Includes association news, reviews of travel literature, obituaries, and honors and awards announcements. **Price:** included in membership dues; $3.00/issue, for nonmembers. **Conventions/ Meetings:** lecture ● symposium.

7121 ■ Association of American Geographers (AAG)
1710 16th St. NW
Washington, DC 20009-3198
Ph: (202)234-1450
Fax: (202)234-2744
E-mail: gaia@aag.org
URL: http://www.aag.org
Contact: Douglas Richardson, Exec. Dir.
Founded: 1904. **Members:** 9,800. **Membership Dues:** corporate, $5,000 (annual) ● individual (based on gross professional income), $62-$173 (annual) ● life, $2,460 ● life (retired), $1,230 ● fulltime student, $50 (annual) ● undergraduate, $36 (annual) ● partner, $18 (annual) ● retired, $53 (annual). **Staff:** 15. **Budget:** $3,000,000. **Regional Groups:** 9. **Description:** Professional society of educators and scientists in the field of geography. Seeks to further professional investigations in geography and to encourage the application of geographic research in education, government, and business. Conducts research; compiles statistics. **Computer Services:** Mailing lists, of members. **Committees:** Affirmative Action and Minority Status; Archives and Association History; Census Advisory; Community Colleges; Constitution and Bylaws; Employment Opportunities and Career Development; Global Change Research; International Research and Scholarly Exchange; Research Grants; Scientific Freedom and Responsibility; Standards for Geographic Data; Status of Women in Geography. **Publications:** *AAG Newsletter*, monthly. ISSN: 0275-3995. **Circulation:** 7,000. **Advertising:** accepted ● *Annals*, quarterly ● *Guide to Programs in Geography in the U.S. and Canada*, annual. Directory ● *The Professional Geographer*, quarterly. Journal. Contains articles on academic or applied geography. **Conventions/Meetings:** annual meeting (exhibits).

7122 ■ International Biogeography Society (IBS)
c/o Glen M. MacDonald, PhD
2133 Basswood Ct.
Westlake Village, CA 91361
E-mail: funkv@si.edu
URL: http://www.biogeography.org
Contact: Vicki Funk, Pres.
Membership Dues: practicing biogeographer, $40 (annual) ● student, $30 (annual). **Multinational. Description:** Promotes biogeographical science and improves communication and collaboration among biogeographers. Raises the public awareness of the importance of biogeographical science. Ensures the appropriate use of biogeographical science in environmental decision-making. Enhances the communication between the biogeographical community and policy-makers. **Publications:** Newsletter, quarterly. Alternate Formats: online.

7123 ■ National Geographic Society (NGS)
1145 17th St. NW
Washington, DC 20036
Ph: (202)857-7000
Free: (800)647-5463
E-mail: askngs@nationalgeographic.com
URL: http://www.nationalgeographic.com
Contact: John Fahey Jr., Pres./CEO
Founded: 1888. **Members:** 9,000,000. **Membership Dues:** individual, $29 (annual). **Staff:** 1,500. **Description:** Persons interested in increasing and diffusing geographic knowledge. Sponsors expeditions and research in geography, natural history, archaeology, astronomy, ethnology, and oceanography; sends writers and photographers throughout the world; disseminates information through its magazines, maps, books, television documentaries, films, educational media, and information services for media. Maintains National Geographic Society Geography Education Program to enhance geographic education in grades K-12; also maintains Explorers Hall museum. **Convention/Meeting:** none. **Libraries: Type:** reference. **Holdings:** 56,000. **Subjects:** map titles, geography. **Awards:** Grosvenor Medal. **Type:** medal ● Hubbard Medal. **Type:** medal. **Recipient:** for outstanding achievement in geography. **Telecommunication Services:** electronic mail, ngsline@customersvc.com ● hotline, for Canada and other country, (813)979-6845. **Committees:** National Geographic Ventures; Research and Exploration. **Councils:** Expeditions. **Publications:** *National Geographic* (in Chinese, Danish, English, French, German, Greek, Italian, Japanese, Norwegian, Portuguese, Spanish, and Swedish), monthly. Magazine. Serves as an educational and scientific journal for general readership. Other languages include Finnish, Norwegian, Korean, Polish, Thai, and Turkish. **Price:** $19.00. ISSN: 0027-9358. **Circulation:** 9,000,000. **Advertising:** accepted ● *National Geographic Adventure*, bimonthly. Magazine. **Price:** $14.95/year ● *National Geographic Kids*. Magazine. **Price:** $19.95/year ● *National Geographic Traveler*, bimonthly. Magazine. Provides travel articles and tips. Includes book list. **Price:** $12.00. ISSN: 0747-0932. **Circulation:** 700,000. **Advertising:** accepted ● *National Geographic World*, monthly. Magazine. Serves as an educational general interest magazine for children ages 8-14. **Price:** $17.95/year for junior society members. ISSN: 0361-5499. **Circulation:** 1,100,000 ● Also publishes books, maps, and globes and produces audiovisual, videodisc, CD-ROM, and computer programming materials for schools and television programming and videos.

7124 ■ Society of Woman Geographers (SWG)
415 E Capitol St. SE
Washington, DC 20003
Ph: (202)546-9228
Fax: (202)546-5232
E-mail: swghq@verizon.net
URL: http://www.iswg.org
Contact: Kimberly A. Crews, Pres.
Founded: 1925. **Members:** 525. **Membership Dues:** active, associate group, $75 (annual) ● at-large, corresponding, associate individual, $50 (annual) ● student, $15 (annual). **Staff:** 1. **Regional Groups:** 1. **Local Groups:** 6. **Multinational. Description:** Women in the fields of geography, anthropology, geology, biology, archaeology, oceanography and ecology. Seeks to further geographical work, spread geographical knowledge, and encourage research. Works to bring together women whose works have involved extensive travel in their investigations. Conducts educational programs. **Libraries: Type:** reference; open to the public; by appointment only. **Holdings:** 1,200; articles, artwork, audiovisuals, books, clippings, periodicals. **Subjects:** geography, travel, archaeology, anthropology. **Awards:** Gold Medal. **Frequency:** triennial. **Type:** recognition. **Recipient:** for outstanding individuals ● Outstanding Achievement. **Frequency:** annual. **Type:** fellowship. **Recipient:** for young women working towards advanced degrees in geography or allied sciences. **Publications:** *Bulletin*, 3-4/year. Newsletter. Alternate Formats: online. **Conventions/Meetings:** board meeting and convention ● triennial meeting.

Geology

7125 ■ American Association of Petroleum Geologists (AAPG)
1444 S Boulder Ave.
Tulsa, OK 74119
Ph: (918)584-2555
Free: (800)364-2274
Fax: (918)560-2665
E-mail: postmaster@aapg.org
URL: http://www.aapg.org
Contact: Willard R. Green, Pres.
Founded: 1917. **Members:** 33,000. **Membership Dues:** active in North America, $80 (annual) ● active outside North America, $90 (annual) ● associate in North America, $40 (annual) ● associate outside North America, $50 (annual) ● student in North America, $10 (annual) ● student outside North America, $20 (annual). **Staff:** 60. **Description:** Professional society of geologists teaching at the college level and engaged in exploration for hydrocarbons research. Conducts Distinguished Lecture Series and a continuing education program. Compiles statistics. **Libraries: Type:** reference. **Holdings:** 4,000. **Subjects:** petroleum geology. **Awards:** Best Paper Award. **Frequency:** annual. **Type:** recognition ● Best Poster Award. **Frequency:** annual. **Type:** recognition ● Certificates of Merit. **Frequency:** annual. **Type:** recognition ● Distinguished Founders Award. **Frequency:** annual. **Type:** recognition ● Distinguished Service Awards. **Frequency:** annual. **Type:** recognition ● Foundation Grants-in-Aid. **Type:** grant ● George C. Matson Memorial Award. **Frequency:** annual. **Type:** recognition ● J.C. "Cam" Sproule Memorial Award. **Frequency:** annual. **Type:** recognition ● Journalism Award. **Frequency:** annual. **Type:** recognition ● Jules Braunstein Memorial Award. **Frequency:** annual. **Type:** recognition ● Life Membership Award. **Frequency:** annual. **Type:** recognition ● Michel T. Halbouty Human Needs Award. **Frequency:** annual. **Type:** recognition ● Past President's Award. **Frequency:** annual. **Type:** recognition ● President's Excellence in Presentation Award. **Frequency:** annual. **Type:** recognition ● Public Service Awards. **Frequency:** annual. **Type:** recognition ● Robert H. Dott, Sr. Memorial Award. **Frequency:** annual. **Type:** recognition ● Sydney Powers Memorial Award. **Frequency:** annual. **Type:** recognition ● Wallace E. Pratt Memorial Award. **Frequency:** annual. **Type:** recognition. **Committees:** Academic Liaison; Association Group Insurance; Astrogeology; Corporate Liaison; Development Geology; Distinguished Lecture; Education; Geological Computing; Geophysics; Grants-in-Aid; International Liaison; Investments; Marine Geology; Public Information; Student Chapters; Youth Activities. **Divisions:** Energy Minerals; Environmental Geosciences; Professional Affairs. **Programs:** Visiting Geologists. **Formerly:** (1917) Southwest Association of Petroleum Geologists. **Publications:** *Explorer*, monthly. Newspaper ● *Memoir Series*, 3-4/year ● *Special Publications Catalog* ● *Studies in Geology*, 2-3/year ● Bulletin, monthly. **Advertising:** accepted ● Handbooks ● Membership Directory, annual ● Reprints ● Videos. **Conventions/Meetings:** annual conference (exhibits) ● annual convention.

7126 ■ American Geological Institute (AGI)
4220 King St.
Alexandria, VA 22302-1502
Ph: (703)379-2480
Fax: (703)379-7563
E-mail: agi@agiweb.org
URL: http://www.agiweb.org
Contact: Ms. Leigh Sutherland, Exec. Asst.
Founded: 1948. **Members:** 44. **Membership Dues:** academic geosciences department, $175 (annual). **Staff:** 60. **Budget:** $6,000,000. **Multinational. Description:** Federation of national scientific and technical societies in the Earth sciences. Seeks to: stimulate public understanding of Geological sciences; improve teaching of the geological sciences in schools, colleges, and universities; maintain high standards of professional training and conduct; work for the general welfare of members. Provides career guidance program. **Libraries: Type:** not open to the public; reference. **Holdings:** articles, books, maps, papers, periodicals, reports. **Awards:** AGI Award. **Frequency:** annual. **Type:** recognition. **Recipient:** for outstanding contribution to public understanding of the geosciences ● AGI Medal in Memory of Ian Campbell. **Frequency:** annual. **Type:** medal. **Recipient:** for contribution to the profession of geology ● Marcus Milling Legendary Geoscientist Medal. **Frequency:** annual. **Type:** medal. **Recipient:** to a person with significant scientific achievement and who has sustained service to the geosciences throughout their career ● William B. Heroy, Jr. Award. **Frequency:** annual. **Type:** recognition. **Recipient:** for distinguished service to AGI. **Computer Services:** database, GeoRef, a reference file of worldwide geological literature. **Committees:** Communications; Education Publications; Government Affairs; Human

Resources. **Programs:** Minority Participation Scholarship. **Affiliated With:** American Association for the Advancement of Science. **Publications:** *Directory of Geoscience Departments*, annual. Identifies more than 13,000 geoscientists in the U.S., Canada, and Mexico by institution, rank and specialty. Includes contact information. **Price:** $40.00. ISSN: 0364-7811. **Advertising:** accepted ● *Geotimes*, monthly. Magazine. Covers geologic events, research, scientific meetings, education developments, government policies, and activities. **Price:** $26.00 for members; $43.00 for nonmembers; $14.95/year for students; $85.00 /year for institutions. ISSN: 0016-8556. **Circulation:** 10,000. **Advertising:** accepted ● Annual Report, annual. Alternate Formats: online ● Also publishes bibliographies, reports, dictionaries, guides, and technical books. **Conventions/Meetings:** meeting.

7127 ■ American Institute of Professional Geologists (AIPG)
1400 W 122nd Ave., Ste.250
Westminster, CO 80234
Ph: (303)412-6205
Fax: (303)253-9220
E-mail: aipg@aipg.org
URL: http://www.aipg.org
Contact: William J. Siok, Exec. Dir.
Founded: 1963. **Members:** 5,000. **Membership Dues:** certified professional geologist, $120 (annual) ● associate, $60 (annual) ● student, $15 (annual) ● individual, $80 (annual). **Staff:** 4. **Budget:** $500,000. **State Groups:** 35. **Description:** Geologists. Provides certification to geologists attesting to their competence and integrity. Represents the geologic profession before government bodies and the public. **Libraries: Type:** reference. **Awards:** Ben H. Parker Memorial Medal. **Frequency:** annual. **Type:** medal. **Recipient:** for individuals who have long records of distinguished and outstanding service to the profession ● Martin Van Couvering Memorial Award. **Frequency:** annual. **Type:** recognition ● Public Service Award. **Frequency:** annual. **Type:** recognition. **Formerly:** (1976) American Institute of Professional Geologists; (1979) Association of Professional Geological Scientists. **Publications:** *The Citizens Guide to Geologic Hazards*. Features fifty slides depicting geologic hazards throughout the world. **Price:** $22.46 for members; $24.95 for nonmembers; $65.00 slide set ● *Education for Professional Practice*. Monograph ● *Home Buyers' Guide to Geologic Hazards*. Monograph. **Price:** $8.10 for members; $9.00 for nonmembers ● *Organization and Content of a Typical Geologic Report*. Monograph ● *The Professional Geologist*, annual. Membership Directory. **Price:** $50.00. **Circulation:** 6,000. **Advertising:** accepted ● *Professional Geologist*, monthly. Journal. **Price:** $30.00 for members outside U.S.; $40.00 for nonmembers outside U.S. Alternate Formats: online ● *The Professional Geologist as Expert Witness*. Monograph. **Price:** $8.10 for members; $9.00 for nonmembers ● *Program of Cooperative Evaluation of Geology Departments*. Monograph ● Also publishes guide and an issues and answers series. **Conventions/Meetings:** annual meeting (exhibits).

7128 ■ American Society of Forensic Geologists (ASFG)
c/o Jeffrey C. Reid, PhD, Pres.
8401 Summerspring Ln.
Raleigh, NC 27615-3015
Ph: (919)618-0810
E-mail: jreid@forensicgeology.com
Contact: Jeffrey C. Reid PhD, Pres.
Founded: 1999. **Members:** 45. **Membership Dues:** regular, $20 (annual) ● associate, $15 (annual) ● student, $10 (annual). **Staff:** 3. **Description:** Geologists and scientists who practice the specialized study of forensic geology. Promotes the study and utilization of forensic geology in criminal and civil investigations. Makes its members available to federal, state, and local law enforcement agencies. Conducts research on new approaches and techniques for forensic geology. **Awards:** Murray and Tedrow Award. **Frequency:** annual. **Type:** fellowship. **Recipient:** for significant contributions to the field of forensic geology. **Affiliated With:** Geological Society of America. **Publications:** Newsletter, monthly. **Conventions/Meetings:** annual convention.

7129 ■ Association of American State Geologists (AASG)
c/o Chacko J. John, Pres.
Louisiana State Univ.
3079 Energy, Coast and Environment Bldg.
Baton Rouge, LA 70803
Ph: (225)578-5320
Fax: (225)578-3662
E-mail: cjohn@lsu.edu
URL: http://www.stategeologists.org
Contact: Chacko J. John, Pres.
Founded: 1908. **Members:** 51. **Budget:** $50,000. **Regional Groups:** 3. **Description:** State geologists, or equivalent officials from each state, who direct and conduct research in geology and mineral resources (including ground water). Stimulates exchange of scientific and administrative information; seeks to improve coordination of work with federal agencies and other state agencies. **Awards:** Ian Campbell Medal. **Type:** medal. **Recipient:** for singular performance in and contribution to the profession of geology ● John C. Frye Memorial Award. **Type:** recognition. **Recipient:** for scientific paper on environmental geology. **Committees:** Affairs; Energy Resources and Policy; Environmental Affairs and Policy; Geological Hazards and Policy; Geoscience Data Preservation; Mapping and Surveys; Mineral Resources and Policy; Professional Affairs; Water Resources and Policy. **Affiliated With:** American Geological Institute; Geological Society of America. **Publications:** *State Geological Survey Factbook*, annual. Report ● *The State Geological Surveys - A History*. Book ● *State Geologists Journal*, annual. Summarizes the programs of the 50 state geological surveys. Includes directory of member surveys, minutes of annual meeting, and obituaries. **Price:** $10.00/year ● Directory. Lists principal program activity contacts and telephone numbers. **Price:** $15.00/copy. **Conventions/Meetings:** annual conference and meeting - always spring ● annual meeting, held in conjunction with the Geological Society of America - mid-year.

7130 ■ Association of Environmental and Engineering Geologists (AEG)
PO Box 460518
Denver, CO 80246
Ph: (303)757-2926
Fax: (303)757-2969
E-mail: aeg@aegweb.org
URL: http://www.aegweb.org
Contact: Becky Roland, Chief Staff Exec.
Founded: 1957. **Members:** 3,100. **Membership Dues:** full, $105 (annual). **Staff:** 3. **Budget:** $500,000. **Regional Groups:** 25. **Local Groups:** 6. **Description:** Represents graduate geologists and geological engineers; full members must have five years experience in the field of engineering geology. Promotes professional success by providing leadership, advocacy, and applied research in environmental and engineering geology. Seeks to provide a forum for the discussion and dissemination of technical and scientific information. Encourages the advancement of professional recognition, scientific research, and high ethical and professional standards. Compiles information on engineering geology curricula of colleges and universities. Promotes public understanding, health, safety and welfare, and acceptance of the engineering geology profession. Conducts technical sessions, symposia, abstracts, and short courses; cosponsors seminars and conferences with other professional and technical societies and organizations. **Libraries: Type:** reference. **Holdings:** 25. **Subjects:** engineering geology, environmental geology, hydrogeology. **Awards:** AEG Publication Award. **Frequency:** annual. **Type:** recognition. **Recipient:** to the author of the most outstanding paper published in any AEG publication during the fiscal year ● Claire P. Holdredge Award. **Frequency:** annual. **Type:** recognition. **Recipient:** for the exceptional publication by AEG members within the 5 previous years that has left an outstanding contribution to the engineering geology profession ● Douglas R. Piteau Outstanding Young Member Award. **Frequency:** annual. **Type:** recognition. **Recipient:** to the outstanding member who excels in either one or in combination of the following areas: technical accomplishment; service to the association; and service to the engineering geology profession ● Floyd T. Johnston Service Award. **Frequency:** annual. **Type:** recognition. **Recipient:** for the outstanding member with an active and faithful service to the association over a minimum period of 9 years ● Honorary Member. **Frequency:** annual. **Type:** recognition. **Recipient:** to individuals whose careers have exemplified the ideals of AEG ● Marliave Scholar Award. **Frequency:** annual. **Type:** grant. **Recipient:** for the outstanding individuals in the field of engineering geology and geological engineering ● Norman R. Tilford Field Study Scholarships. **Frequency:** annual. **Type:** scholarship. **Recipient:** to a graduate and a post-graduate student conducting field research and an undergraduate student attending a field camp ● The Outstanding Environmental and Engineering Geologic Project Award. **Frequency:** annual. **Type:** recognition. **Recipient:** for an exceptional project that displays national or international significance and demonstrates the application of the principles of environmental and engineering geology to the solution of a problem affecting the public ● Outstanding Section Award. **Frequency:** annual. **Type:** recognition. **Recipient:** for the most outstanding section of the association ● Outstanding Student Chapter Award. **Frequency:** annual. **Type:** recognition. **Recipient:** for outstanding AEG student chapter in a given year ● Richard H. Jahns Distinguished Lecturer in Engineering Geology Award. **Frequency:** annual. **Type:** monetary. **Recipient:** for publication of outstanding paper dealing with engineering geology ● Student Professional Paper. **Frequency:** annual. **Type:** monetary. **Recipient:** for exceptional student members in undergraduate and/or graduate divisions. **Computer Services:** Mailing lists. **Committees:** Academic and Student Affairs; Building Codes and Industrial Safety; Continuing Education; Employment Opportunity; Geology of Cities; Individual and Small Practice; Legislative and Regulatory Affairs; Professional Practice and Ethics; Professional Registration for Engineering Geologists; Professional Registration for Geological Engineers; Public Information; Technical Information. **Subcommittees:** Downhole Inspection and Logging; Rock Logging; Tunnel Mapping. **Subgroups:** Computer Utilization; Dams; Engineering Geology Standards; Ground Water; Hazardous Waste Management; Landslides; Radioactive Waste Management; Remote Sensing; Rock Mechanics; Seismic Safety; Subsidence; Tunneling. **Publications:** *Environmental and Engineering Geoscience*, quarterly. Journal. **Price:** included in membership dues; $125.00 /year for nonmembers ● Directory, annual. **Advertising:** accepted ● Newsletter, quarterly. Includes calendar of events and research updates. **Price:** included in membership dues; $20.00 /year for nonmembers. ISSN: 0514-9142. **Circulation:** 3,200 ● Also publishes technical papers and field trip guidebook. **Conventions/Meetings:** annual conference and seminar (exhibits) - always fall.

7131 ■ Computer Oriented Geological Society (COGS)
Address Unknown since 2008
Founded: 1982. **Members:** 1,000. **Membership Dues:** student, $15 (annual) ● individual, $25 (annual). **Description:** Geologists who make use of computers in their professional undertakings. Promotes increased and improved applications of computers and computer techniques in the study of geology. Serves as a clearinghouse of methods, software, and datasets of interest to members. Produces computer software. **Telecommunication Services:** electronic bulletin board, (303)697-5850. **Publications:** *COGSletter*, periodic. Newsletter. **Price:** included in membership dues. **Advertising:** accepted.

7132 ■ Geological Society of America (GSA)
PO Box 9140
Boulder, CO 80301-9140
Ph: (303)357-1000
Free: (888)443-4472

Fax: (303)357-1070
E-mail: gsaservice@geosociety.org
URL: http://www.geosociety.org
Contact: John W. Hess, Exec. Dir.

Founded: 1888. **Members:** 19,500. **Membership Dues:** professional scientist, $65 (annual) ● student, teacher, affiliate, senior, $30 (annual). **Staff:** 53. **Budget:** $8,000,000. **Regional Groups:** 6. **Description:** Serves as professional society of earth scientists. Promotes the science of geology. Maintains placement service. **Awards:** Penrose Medal. **Type:** medal ● Public Service Award. **Type:** recognition ● Research Grants. **Frequency:** annual. **Type:** grant. **Recipient:** for geologists and graduate students in geology ● Young Scientist Award. **Type:** recognition. **Committees:** Annual Program; Audit; Budget; Education; External Awards; Finance; Geology and Public Policy; Honorary Fellows; Investment; Membership; Minorities and Women in the Geosciences; Nominations; Penrose Conferences; Penrose Medal; Professional Development; Programmatic Overview; Public Service Award; Research Grants; Treatise on Invertebrate Paleontology; Young Scientist Award. **Divisions:** Archaeological Geology; Coal Geology; Engineering Geology; Geobiology and Geomicrobiology; Geophysics; Geoscience Education; History of Geology; Hydrogeology; International; Limnogeology; Planetary Geology; Quaternary Geology and Geomorphology; Sedimentary Geology; Structural Geology and Tectonics. **Affiliated With:** American Association of Petroleum Geologists; American Association of Stratigraphic Palynologists; American Institute of Professional Geologists; Association of Earth Science Editors; Association of Environmental and Engineering Geologists; Association for Women Geoscientists; Geochemical Society; Society of Economic Geologists. **Publications:** *Geological Society of America—Abstracts with Programs*, periodic. Papers. Contains abstracts of all scientific papers to be presented at each of the 6 annual GSA Section and the annual GSA meetings. **Price:** $96.00 for members; $135.00 for nonmembers in U.S., Canada and Mexico; $145.00 foreign. **Circulation:** 7,500. **Advertising:** accepted. Alternate Formats: CD-ROM ● *Geological Society of America—Bulletin*, bimonthly. Journal. Contains scientific papers from around the world presenting results of major research from all earth science disciplines. **Price:** $82.00 /year for members in U.S.; $560.00 /year for nonmembers in U.S. (print only); $710.00 /year for nonmembers in U.S. (online/print); $87.00 /year for members outside U.S. ISSN: 0016-7606. **Circulation:** 5,000. **Advertising:** accepted. Alternate Formats: online; CD-ROM. Also Cited As: *GSA Bulletin* ● *Geology*, monthly. Journal. Contains short articles on current geological issues and investigations worldwide. **Price:** $42.00 /year for members; $560.00 /year for nonmembers in U.S. (print only); $710.00 for nonmembers in U.S. (online/print); $725.00 for nonmembers outside U.S. (online/print). ISSN: 0091-7613. **Circulation:** 7,000. **Advertising:** accepted. Alternate Formats: online; CD-ROM ● *GSA Today*, monthly. Newsletter. Includes employment listings, meeting announcements, new member information, and general earth science data. **Price:** included in membership dues; $75.00 /year for nonmembers in North America; $85.00 /year for nonmembers outside North America. ISSN: 1052-5173. **Circulation:** 18,000. **Advertising:** accepted. Alternate Formats: CD-ROM; online ● *Hydrogeology Journal*. **Price:** $89.00 for members ● *Reviews in Engineering Geology*, periodic ● Membership Directory, annual ● Also publishes division newsletters, map and chart series, and monograph series (including memoirs and special papers). **Conventions/Meetings:** annual convention (exhibits) ● periodic Penrose Conference and Field Forums ● annual meeting - 2008 Oct. 5-9, Houston, TX; 2009 Oct. 18-21, Portland, OR; 2010 Sept. 30-Oct. 3, Denver, CO.

7133 ■ National Association of State Boards of Geology (ASBOG)

PO Box 11591
Columbia, SC 29211-1591
Ph: (803)739-5676
Fax: (803)739-8874
E-mail: asbog@asbog.org
URL: http://www.asbog.org
Contact: Sam Christiano, Exec. Dir.

Description: Serves as a link between individual state geologic registration licensing boards for the planning and preparation of uniform procedures and coordination of geologic protective measures for the public; develops standardized written examinations. **Publications:** *Professional Geologists Candidate Handbook*. Covers the format and outline for the exam. Alternate Formats: online. **Conventions/Meetings:** annual meeting.

7134 ■ Society of Economic Geologists (SEG)

7811 Shaffer Pkwy.
Littleton, CO 80127
Ph: (720)981-7882
Fax: (720)981-7874
E-mail: seg@segweb.org
URL: http://www.segweb.org
Contact: Brian G. Hoal, Exec. Dir.

Founded: 1920. **Members:** 3,600. **Membership Dues:** standard, $95 (annual) ● student, $10 (annual) ● couple, $25 (annual) ● electronic, $75 (annual) ● student (with print journal), $50 (annual). **Staff:** 10. **Description:** Professional society of economic geologists. Advances the science of economic geology through the investigation of mineral deposits and mineral resources, exploration, mineral resource appraisal, mining and mineral extraction endeavors, through educational programs; disseminates basic and applied scientific information through publications, meetings, and lectures. **Awards:** Brian J. Skinner Award. **Frequency:** annual. **Type:** recognition. **Recipient:** for outstanding paper published in Economic Geology ● Distinguished Lectureships. **Frequency:** annual. **Type:** recognition. **Recipient:** for applied geology and geologic research ● Marsden Award. **Frequency:** annual. **Type:** recognition. **Recipient:** for outstanding service to the organization ● Penrose Medal. **Frequency:** annual. **Type:** medal ● Silver Medal. **Frequency:** annual. **Type:** medal ● Waldemar Lindgren Award. **Frequency:** annual. **Type:** recognition. **Recipient:** for outstanding contributions to the science of economic geology. **Committees:** Lecture; Program; Research; Student Affairs. **Publications:** *Economic Geology*, 8/year. Journal. **Price:** included in membership dues; $195.00 /year for nonmembers ● *Economic Geology Monograph 9: Mineral Deposits of Alaska*. **Price:** $45.00 for nonmembers; $36.00 for members ● *SEG Newsletter*, quarterly. **Advertising:** accepted. Alternate Formats: online ● Membership Directory, biennial ● Special publications and field trip guidebooks. **Conventions/Meetings:** semiannual meeting, held with the Geological Society of America (GSA) (exhibits) - always November.

7135 ■ Society of Independent Professional Earth Scientists (SIPES)

4925 Greenville Ave., Ste.1106
Dallas, TX 75206
Ph: (214)363-1780
Fax: (214)363-8195
E-mail: sipes@sipes.org
URL: http://www.sipes.org
Contact: Diane Finstrom, Exec. Dir.

Founded: 1963. **Members:** 1,400. **Membership Dues:** individual, $75 (annual). **Staff:** 2. **National Groups:** 14. **Description:** Geologists, geophysicists, paleontologists, petroleum engineers, and other earth scientists who operate independently or as consultants. Seeks to improve the status of independent earth scientists within the mining and petroleum industries; works to improve the public image of such scientists and to protect the public from unqualified persons representing themselves as consultants. Sponsors specialized education programs; disseminates scientific and technical information. **Libraries:** **Type:** reference. **Holdings:** archival material. **Awards:** Outstanding Service Award. **Frequency:** annual. **Type:** recognition. **Committees:** Education; National Energy: Professional Development. **Publications:** *SIPES Newsletter*, quarterly. Alternate Formats: online ● Membership Directory, annual. **Price:** $10.00. **Circulation:** 1,500. **Advertising:** accepted. Alternate Formats: CD-ROM. **Conventions/Meetings:** annual meeting (exhibits).

Geoscience

7136 ■ American Geophysical Union (AGU)

2000 Florida Ave. NW
Washington, DC 20009-1277
Ph: (202)462-6900
Free: (800)966-2481
Fax: (202)328-0566
E-mail: service@agu.org
URL: http://www.agu.org
Contact: A.F. Spilhaus Jr., Exec. Dir.

Founded: 1919. **Members:** 41,000. **Membership Dues:** individual, associate, $20 (annual) ● student, $7 (annual). **Staff:** 150. **Budget:** $23,000,000. **Description:** Individuals professionally associated with the field of geophysics; supporting institutional members are companies and other organizations whose work involves geophysics. Promotes the study of problems concerned with the figure and physics of the earth; initiates and coordinates research that depends upon national and international cooperation and provides for scientific discussion of research results. Sponsors placement service at semiannual meeting. **Awards:** **Type:** recognition. **Committees:** Audit and Legal Affairs; Budget and Finance; Education and Human Resources; Fellows; History of Geophysics; International Participation; Mineral and Rock Physics; Public Affairs; Publications; Tellers. **Sections:** Atmospheric Chemistry; Atmospheric Physics and Climate; Biocleosciences; Biological Oceanography; Geodesy; Geomagnetism and Paleomagnetism; Geophysics; Hydrology; Maine Geochemistry; Marine Geology and Geophysics; Physical Oceanography; Planetary Sciences; Seismology; Space Physics and Aeronomy; Tectonophysics; Volcanology, Geochemistry and Petrology. **Publications:** *Antarctic Research Series*. Book. Presents detailed scientific results from Antarctic fieldwork. ● *Coastal and Estuarine Studies*. Monographs. Focuses on coastal regions and environmental issues. ● *Earth in Space*, 9/year. Magazine. For teachers and students. **Price:** $12.00/year plus postage, outside U.S. ISSN: 1040-3124 ● *Earth Interactions*. Journal. **Price:** $45.00. ISSN: 1087-3562. Alternate Formats: online ● *EOS*, weekly. Newspaper. Contains meeting reports, book reviews, calendar of events, and announcement of grants, fellowships, and employment opportunities. **Price:** included in membership dues; $369.00 /year for institutions outside U.S., plus postage. ISSN: 0096-3941. **Advertising:** accepted. Alternate Formats: microform ● *International Journal of Geomagnetism and Aeronomy*, bimonthly. Contains research conducted in Russia and elsewhere in the world. **Price:** $350.00 /year for institutions outside U.S., plus postage. ISSN: 1091-6539 ● *Journal of Geophysical Research*. Contains original contributions on the physics and chemistry of the earth, its environment, and the solar system. **Price:** $5,290.00 for nonmembers outside U.S., plus postage; $65.00/issue for individual section. ISSN: 0148-0227. Alternate Formats: microform ● *Paleoceanography*, bimonthly. Journal. Presents papers covering the marine sedimentary record from the present ocean basins and margins and from exposures of ancient marine sediments. **Price:** $75.00 /year for members outside U.S., plus postage; $38.00/year for students outside U.S., plus postage; $329.00 /year for nonmembers outside U.S., plus postage; $55.00/issue for institutions outside U.S., plus postage. ISSN: 0883-8305. Alternate Formats: microform ● *Radio Science*, bimonthly. Journal. Contains papers on all applications of electromagnetic and optical fields including physical problems. **Price:** $69.00 /year for members outside U.S., plus postage; $45.00/year for students outside U.S., plus postage; $65.00/issue for nonmembers outside U.S., plus postage; $455.00 /year for nonmembers outside U.S., plus postage. ISSN: 0048-6604. Alternate Formats: microform ● *Reviews of Geophysics*, quarterly. Journal. Provides summaries of research in all earth sciences, enabling readers to be kept informed on subjects outside their own specialties. **Price:** $35.00 /year for members outside U.S., plus postage; $18.00/year for students; $280.00 /year for nonmembers outside U.S., plus postage; $55.00/issue for institutions outside U.S., plus postage. ISSN: 8755-1209. Alternate Formats: microform ● *Water Resources Research*, monthly. Journal. Contains original contributions on physical, chemical, biological, and social aspects of water science, as well as water law. **Price:** $135.00 /year for members outside U.S., plus postage; $68.00/year for students outside U.S., plus postage; $845.00 /year for nonmembers outside U.S., plus postage; $65.00/issue for institutions outside U.S. ISSN: 0043-1397. Alternate Formats: microform; online. **Conventions/Meetings:** semiannual conference (exhibits) ● annual meeting ● semiannual Ocean Sciences Meeting - conference (exhibits) - always May ● annual Western Pacific Geophysics Meeting - conference.

7137 ■ ASFE

8811 Colesville Rd., Ste.G106
Silver Spring, MD 20910
Ph: (301)565-2733 (504)456-0966
Fax: (301)589-2017
E-mail: info@asfe.org
URL: http://www.asfe.org
Contact: Mr. John P. Bachner, Exec. VP

Founded: 1969. **Members:** 300. **Membership Dues:** firm - minimum (based on gross annual receipts), $550 (annual) ● firm - maximum (based on gross annual receipts), $10,500 (annual). **Staff:** 6. **Budget:** $1,100,000. **Description:** Consulting firms that specialize in geotechnical (soil and foundation), geoenvironmental and civil engineering. Develops and conducts programs geared to help members better manage their professional liability, human resources, and other risks, while enhancing client relations and profitability. Conducts two national and 15 regional seminars each year. Maintains Speaker's Bureau. **Awards:** Founders Award. **Frequency:** annual. **Type:** recognition. **Computer Services:** Mailing lists, of members. **Telecommunication Services:** electronic mail, rose@asfe.org ● electronic mail, john@asfe.org. **Committees:** Business Practice; Emerging Trends and Issues; Information Technology; Legal Affairs; Member Services and Marketing; Peer Review; Practice Education; Program. **Formerly:** (1975) Associated Soil and Foundation Engineers; (1988) Association of Soil and Foundation Engineers; (1993) ASFE/The Association of Engineering Firms Practicing in the Geosciences; (1999) ASFE: Professional Firms Practicing in the Geosciences. **Publications:** *ASFE—Membership Directory*, annual. Contains firm names arranged by state. **Price:** $5.00. **Circulation:** 1,500. Alternate Formats: online ● *ASFE Newslog*, bimonthly. Newsletter. Includes cumulated index for members of geoprofessional, environmental, and civil engineering. **Price:** included in membership dues; $150.00 /year for nonmembers. **Circulation:** 1,500 ● *ASFE—Publications Directory*, annual. **Conventions/Meetings:** semiannual meeting - every spring and fall. 2008 Oct. 4-7, San Francisco, CA.

7138 ■ Association for Efficient Environmental Energy Systems

Address Unknown since 2007
URL: http://www.aeees.org

Founded: 1987. **Members:** 51. **Membership Dues:** individual, $100 (annual) ● supporting, $500 (annual) ● sustaining, $1,000 (annual). **Staff:** 3. **Budget:** $250,000. **Description:** Provides education and training for those interested in geothermal heat pumps and building energy efficiency on the West coast. **Libraries: Type:** reference. **Holdings:** 200; books, periodicals. **Subjects:** geothermal, heat pumps. **Awards:** Best of Show Award. **Frequency:** annual. **Type:** recognition ● Most Informative Award. **Frequency:** annual. **Type:** recognition. **Recipient:** for trade show exhibitors. **Telecommunication Services:** electronic mail, info@aeees.org. **Conventions/Meetings:** annual conference (exhibits); **Avg. Attendance:** 150.

7139 ■ Association for Women Geoscientists (AWG)

PO Box 30645
Lincoln, NE 68503-0645
Ph: (402)489-8122
E-mail: office@awg.org
URL: http://www.awg.org
Contact: Janelle Gerry, Office Mgr.

Founded: 1977. **Members:** 1,000. **Membership Dues:** joint, student, $15 (annual) ● reduced income, retired, unemployed, $25 (annual) ● professional, $50 (annual) ● sustaining, $75 (annual) ● institutional, $100 (annual) ● corporate, $500 (annual) ● life, $1,600. **Staff:** 3. **Budget:** $50,000. **Regional Groups:** 16. **Description:** Represents men and women geologists, geophysicists, petroleum engineers, geological engineers, hydrogeologists, paleontologists, geochemists, and other geoscientists. Aims to encourage the participation of women in the geosciences. Exchanges educational, technical, and professional information. Enhances the professional growth and advancement of women in the geosciences. Provides information through web site on opportunities and careers available to women in the geosciences. Sponsors educational booths and programs at geological society conventions. Operates charitable program. Maintains speaker's bureau, and Association for Women Geoscientists Foundation (educational arm). **Awards:** AWG Minority Scholarship. **Type:** scholarship. **Recipient:** for young minority women ● AWG Winifred Goldring Award. **Type:** scholarship. **Recipient:** for graduate or undergraduate students ● Chrysalis Scholarship. **Frequency:** annual. **Type:** recognition. **Recipient:** for outstanding students in the geosciences ● Outstanding Educator Award. **Frequency:** annual. **Type:** recognition. **Recipient:** for excellent teachers, motivators, and mentors of young women ● Penelope Hanshaw Scholarship. **Frequency:** annual. **Type:** scholarship. **Recipient:** for graduate or undergraduate geoscience majors ● Puget Sound Chapter Scholarship. **Frequency:** annual. **Type:** scholarship. **Recipient:** to an undergraduate woman pursuing a career in geoscience ● William Rucker Greenwood Scholarship. **Frequency:** annual. **Type:** scholarship. **Recipient:** for outstanding minority women geoscience students. **Computer Services:** database, women geoscientists ● mailing lists. **Committees:** Career Development; Education; Field Trips; Public Affairs. **Affiliated With:** American Geological Institute; Geological Society of America. **Formerly:** (1982) Association of Women Geoscientists. **Publications:** *Gaea*, bimonthly. Newsletter. **Price:** $50.00/year. ISSN: 1099-1999. **Circulation:** 1,100. **Advertising:** accepted. **Conventions/Meetings:** semiannual meeting, for board of directors ● workshop and seminar, on job hunting techniques, management skills, and career and professional development.

7140 ■ Environmental and Engineering Geophysical Society (EEGS)

1720 S Bellaire, Ste.110
Denver, CO 80222-4303
Ph: (303)531-7517
Fax: (303)820-3844
E-mail: staff@eegs.org
URL: http://www.eegs.org
Contact: Kathie Barstnar, Exec. Dir.

Founded: 1992. **Members:** 630. **Membership Dues:** individual, $90 (annual) ● student with journal, $50 (annual) ● student without journal, $20 (annual) ● corporate benefactor, $3,500 (annual) ● corporate partner, $1,800 (annual) ● corporate associate, $2,000 (annual) ● corporate donor, $650 (annual). **Staff:** 3. **Budget:** $250,000. **Multinational. Description:** Corporations, students, and others interested in geophysics or related sciences. Seeks to foster and encourage the application of geophysical techniques for environmental and engineering application, and to foster education and research in these areas. Promotes sound geophysical practices and provides a link between the geophysical community and the environmental and engineering industry as a whole. Offers symposiums, workshops, and short courses to provide a forum for the exchange of technical information. **Libraries: Type:** reference. **Subjects:** past proceedings of symposiums. **Awards:** Alan J. Witten Scholarship. **Frequency:** annual. **Type:** scholarship. **Recipient:** to individuals who are full-time, regularly enrolled in the School of Geology and Geophysics ● Dr. Frank C. Frishknect Leadership Award. **Frequency:** annual. **Type:** recognition ● The Gold Medal Distinguished Service Award. **Frequency:** annual. **Type:** recognition. **Publications:** *FastTimes*, quarterly. Newsletter. **Advertising:** accepted. Alternate Formats: online ● *Journal of Environmental and Engineering Geophysics*, quarterly. **Price:** $140.00/year in U.S.; $215.00/year outside U.S. ISSN: 1083-1363. **Advertising:** accepted ● *Near-Surface Seismology (1998 Short Course Handbook)*. **Price:** $10.00 for members; $15.00 for nonmembers ● Directory. **Conventions/Meetings:** annual Symposium on the Application of Geophysics to Environmental and Engineering Problems - meeting (exhibits) ● trade show.

7141 ■ Geochemical Society (GS)

Washington Univ.
E&PS Bldg., Rm. 334
One Brookings Dr., CB 1169
St. Louis, MO 63130-4899
Ph: (314)935-4131
Fax: (314)935-4121
E-mail: gsoffice@geochemsoc.org
URL: http://gs.wustl.edu
Contact: Mr. Seth M. Davis, Business Mgr.

Founded: 1955. **Members:** 2,800. **Membership Dues:** professional, $30 (annual) ● student, $10 (annual) ● senior, $12 (annual). **Staff:** 1. **Budget:** $80,000. **Multinational. Description:** Professional society of geochemists, chemists, geologists, physicists, biologists, oceanographers, mathematicians, meteorologists, and other scientists interested in the application of chemistry to the solution of geological and cosmological problems. The Organic Geochemistry Division focuses on biogeochemistry and organic processes at the Earth's surface and subsurface. **Awards:** Alfred Treibs Medal. **Frequency:** biennial. **Type:** medal. **Recipient:** for lifetime achievement in organic geochemistry ● C.C. Patterson Medal. **Frequency:** annual. **Type:** medal. **Recipient:** for breakthroughs in environmental geochemistry ● F.W. Clarke Medal. **Frequency:** annual. **Type:** medal. **Recipient:** for early career scientist, single accomplishment in geochemistry ● Geochemistry Fellow. **Frequency:** annual. **Type:** recognition. **Recipient:** to scientists for lifetime achievement in geochemistry ● V.M. Goldschmidt Medal. **Frequency:** annual. **Type:** medal. **Recipient:** for lifetime achievement in geochemistry. **Divisions:** Organic Geochemistry. **Publications:** *Elements: An International Magazine of Mineralogy, Geochemistry, and Petrology*, quarterly. **Price:** included in membership dues. ISSN: 1811-5209. **Circulation:** 10,000. **Advertising:** accepted. Alternate Formats: online. Also Cited As: *Elements Magazine* ● *Geochemical News*, quarterly. Newsletter. Covers news, events, announcements, people and activities in the field of geochemistry. **Price:** included in membership dues. ISSN: 0016-7010. **Circulation:** 2,800. **Advertising:** accepted. Alternate Formats: online ● *Geochimica et Cosmochimica Acta*, biweekly. Journal. Peer-reviewed journal published by Elsevier Science with the assistance of the Geochemical Society and the Meteoritical Society. **Price:** $145.00 /year for members (professional); $80.00 /year for members (student and senior). ISSN: 0016-7037. Alternate Formats: online. Also Cited As: *GCA* ● Special publication series 5 volume sets, reviews in mineralogy and geochemistry series. **Conventions/Meetings:** annual V.M. Goldschmidt Conference, discusses about the developments in the geosciences (exhibits) - 2008 July 13-18, Vancouver, BC, Canada - **Avg. Attendance:** 1600.

7142 ■ Geoscience Information Society (GSIS)

c/o Andrea Twiss-Brooks, Sec.
Univ. of Chicago
John Crerar Library
5730 S Ellis Ave.
Chicago, IL 60637

Ph: (773)702-8777
Fax: (773)702-3317
E-mail: pyocum@umich.edu
URL: http://www.geoinfo.org
Contact: Ms. Patricia B. Yocum, Pres.

Founded: 1965. **Members:** 225. **Membership Dues:** personal, $55 (annual) ● institutional, $100 (annual) ● sustaining, $135 (annual) ● student, retired, $20 (annual). **Multinational. Description:** Facilitates the exchange of information in the geosciences through cooperation among librarians, editors, cartographers, educators, scientists, and information professionals. **Awards:** Best Guidebook Award. **Frequency:** annual. **Type:** recognition. **Recipient:** to an outstanding author, editor, or publisher ● Best Paper Award. **Frequency:** annual. **Type:** recognition. **Recipient:** to the best paper published in the field of geosciences information during the previous year ● Best Website Award. **Frequency:** annual. **Type:** recognition. **Recipient:** to a website that exemplified outstanding standards of content, design, organization, and overall site effectiveness ● Mary B. Ansari Best Geosciences Reference Book Award. **Frequency:** annual. **Type:** recognition. **Recipient:** for the best reference work ● Mary B. Ansari Distinguished Service Award. **Frequency:** annual. **Type:** recognition. **Recipient:** for significant contributions to the geosciences information profession. **Computer Services:** Mailing lists, geonet-L listserv. **Committees:** Archives; Best Paper Award; Best Reference Work Award; Collection Development Issues; Distinguished Service Award; Electronic Resources; Exhibits; Guidebooks; International Initiatives; Membership; Nominating; Preservation; Website Advisory. **Affiliated With:** American Geological Institute; Geological Society of America. **Publications:** *Directory of Geoscience Libraries: North America 1997, 5th Edition*. **Price:** $35.00 ● *Geoscience Information Society Proceedings*, annual. ISSN: 0072-1409 ● *GSIS Membership Directory*, annual. **Price:** included in membership dues ● *GSIS Newsletter*, bimonthly. Covers geosciences libraries and information retrieval services, facilitating an exchange of information in the field. **Price:** $40.00 /year for nonmembers in U.S. and Canada; $45.00 /year for nonmembers outside U.S. and Canada. ISSN: 0046-5801. **Circulation:** 300. **Advertising:** accepted. Alternate Formats: online ● *Science Editing and Information Management*. Monograph. **Price:** $25.00. **Conventions/Meetings:** annual conference and meeting, held in conjunction with the Geological Society of America.

7143 ■ Geothermal Resources Council (GRC)

PO Box 1350
Davis, CA 95617
Ph: (530)758-2360
Fax: (530)758-2839
E-mail: grclib@geothermal.org
URL: http://www.geothermal.org
Contact: Curt Robinson PhD, Exec. Dir.

Founded: 1972. **Members:** 850. **Membership Dues:** student in U.S., $40 (annual) ● individual in U.S., retired outside U.S., $100 (annual) ● benefactor in U.S., $180 (annual) ● company in U.S., $500 (annual) ● supporting in U.S., $1,000 (annual) ● sustaining in U.S., $1,750 (annual) ● patron in U.S., $2,500 (annual) ● retired in U.S., $50 (annual) ● individual outside U.S., $150 (annual) ● student outside U.S., $90 (annual) ● benefactor outside U.S., $230 (annual) ● patron outside U.S., $2,550 (annual) ● company outside U.S., $550 (annual) ● supporting outside U.S., $1,050 (annual) ● sustaining outside U.S., $1,800 (annual). **Staff:** 3. **Budget:** $700,000. **Description:** Encourages research, exploration, and development of geothermal energy; promotes establishment of criteria for the development of geothermal resources compatible with the natural environment. Provides information for the public and encourages the collection and dissemination of geothermal information and data. Cooperates and communicates with national and international governmental, institutional, and private agencies. Holds technical training workshops and annual meeting. Maintains largest geothermal technical library in existence. **Libraries: Type:** reference; open to the public. **Holdings:** 34,000; audiovisuals, books, monographs, periodicals. **Subjects:** geothermal information, power plants. **Awards:** Joseph Aidlin Award. **Frequency:** annual. **Type:** recognition. **Recipient:** for outstanding contributions to geothermal development ● Pioneer Award. **Frequency:** annual. **Type:** recognition. **Recipient:** for outstanding achievement and lasting contributions in the development of geothermal resources ● Special Achievement Award. **Frequency:** annual. **Type:** recognition. **Recipient:** for outstanding achievement in all aspects of geothermal development and related areas. **Computer Services:** database, geothermal information. **Committees:** Business; Foundation; Technical Standards. **Publications:** *Geothermal Resources Council—Bulletin*, bimonthly. Covers developments in geothermal research and council activities. Includes new publications, meeting notices, and annual membership roster. **Price:** included in membership dues; $90.00 /year for nonmembers in U.S.; $125.00 /year for nonmembers outside U.S. ISSN: 0160-7782. **Circulation:** 900. **Advertising:** accepted ● *Geothermal Resources Council—Transactions*, annual. Covers geothermal topics addressed at the annual meeting. Includes statistics. ISSN: 0193-5933 ● *Special Reports*, periodic. ISSN: 0149-8991. **Conventions/Meetings:** annual conference (exhibits) ● workshop.

7144 ■ IEEE Geoscience and Remote Sensing Society (GRSS)

c/o IEEE Admission and Advancement Department
PO Box 6804
Piscataway, NJ 08854-6804
Ph: (206)685-7537
Fax: (732)981-0225
E-mail: tsang@ee.washington.edu
URL: http://www.grss-ieee.org
Contact: Dr. Leung Tsang, Pres.

Founded: 1962. **Members:** 2,130. **Membership Dues:** full, $157 (annual) ● student, $44 (annual) ● affiliate, $63 (annual). **Local Groups:** 7. **Description:** A society of the Institute of Electrical and Electronics Engineers. Examines the theory, concepts, and techniques of science and engineering involved in the remote sensing of the earth, oceans, atmosphere, and space. Processes, interprets, and disseminates information. **Publications:** *IEEE Geoscience and Remote Sensing Society Newsletter*, quarterly. ISSN: 0161-7869. Alternate Formats: online ● *IEEE Transactions on Geoscience and Remote Sensing*, monthly. Journal. ISSN: 0196-2892. Alternate Formats: online. **Conventions/Meetings:** annual meeting and symposium (exhibits).

7145 ■ International Flat Earth Research Society

Address Unknown since 2007

Founded: 1800. **Members:** 3,500. **Membership Dues:** associate, $25 (annual). **Description:** Individuals whose outlook is "Zetetic," or characterized by a seeking for truth and the denial of "imaginary" theories. Members rely only on "provable" knowledge and consequently believe that the "spinning ball" theory regarding the earth is absurd, and that, in reality, the earth is flat and infinite in size. Members maintain that Australia is not under the world, Australians do not hang by their feet head down, nor do ships sail over the edge of the world to get there; they also assert that continental drift is really the result of the earth and water being "shaken asunder by God." The society gathers information, disseminates results of its research, and generally seeks to "push forth the frontiers of knowledge in geophysical matters.". **Libraries: Type:** not open to the public. **Holdings:** 1,000; articles, books, periodicals. **Awards:** Seeker for Truth. **Frequency:** periodic. **Type:** recognition. **Recipient:** for an honest person who persists with an unpopular view. **Also Known As:** Flat Earthers; The Zetetics. **Formerly:** (1932) Universal Zetetic Society of America and Great Britain. **Publications:** *Flat Earth News*, quarterly. Newsletter. Tabloid containing articles decrying modern science for providing a false view of the world. **Price:** included in membership dues; $25.00 for nonmembers. ISSN: 8756-0313. **Circulation:** 3,000. **Advertising:** accepted ● *The Last Iconoclast*, periodic ● *Plane Truth*, periodic. Tabloid concerned with showing the Ten Commandments as a "logical and reasonable means to a better life". **Price:** free. **Advertising:** not accepted. **Conventions/Meetings:** periodic conference (exhibits).

7146 ■ International Landslide Research Group (ILRG)

c/o Earl E. Brabb, Emeritus Pres./Ed.
4377 Newland Heights Dr.
Rocklin, CA 95765
E-mail: ebrabb@earthlink.net
URL: http://ilrg.gndci.cnr.it
Contact: Dorian E. Kuper, Pres.

Founded: 1983. **Members:** 350. **Staff:** 3. **Regional Groups:** 3. **Multinational. Description:** Persons interested in landslides. Works to keep members informed about landslide research worldwide. Conducts educational and research programs; maintains speakers' bureau. **Libraries: Type:** reference; open to the public; by appointment only. **Holdings:** 16; archival material. **Subjects:** back issues of newsletters with information on landslides. **Awards:** Distinguished Leadership for Landslide Research. **Frequency:** periodic. **Type:** recognition. **Recipient:** for a leader in landslide research. **Publications:** *ILRG Newsletter*, periodic. Features landslide articles and information about people. **Price:** free. Alternate Formats: online. **Conventions/Meetings:** triennial meeting, in conjunction with International Conference and Field Trip on Landslides.

7147 ■ International Society of Soil Mechanics and Geotechnical Engineering (ISSMGE)

c/o Geo-Institute of the ASCE
1801 Alexander Bell Dr.
Reston, VA 20191-4400
Ph: (703)295-6350 (703)295-6352
Free: (800)548-2723
Fax: (703)295-6351
E-mail: cbowers@asce.org
URL: http://www.geoinstitute.org/static/issmge.cfm
Contact: Carol W. Bowers, Dir.

Founded: 1936. **Members:** 2,450. **Membership Dues:** individual, $95 (annual) ● organization, $600 (annual). **Description:** Geotechnical engineers who are members of the Geo-Institute of the American Society of Civil Engineers. Fosters information exchange between geotechnical engineers in the United States and abroad. Represents the U.S. in affairs of the International Society for Soil Mechanics and Geotechnical Engineering. **Telecommunication Services:** electronic mail, lbayer@asce.org. **Affiliated With:** International Society for Soil Mechanics and Geotechnical Engineering. **Formerly:** (1998) U.S. National Society for the International Society of Soil Mechanics and Foundation Engineering; (2004) U.S. National Society for the International Society of Soil Mechanics and Geotechnical Engineering. **Publications:** *Geo-Strata*, bimonthly. Magazine. Geo-Strata, the official bi-monthly magazine of the Geo-Institute, features articles written by and for engineering professionals. **Price:** included in membership dues. **Circulation:** 10,000. **Advertising:** accepted ● *Geotechnical News*, quarterly. Magazine. Geotechnical News serves as an informative and reliable communications tool for issues of interest to the geotechnical profession. **Price:** $25.00 for members. **Advertising:** accepted. **Conventions/Meetings:** quadrennial conference (exhibits).

7148 ■ Meteoritical Society (MetSoc)

c/o Jeffrey N. Grossman, Sec.
US Geological Survey
954 Natl. Ctr.
Reston, VA 20192
Ph: (703)648-6184
Fax: (703)648-6252
E-mail: secretary@meteoriticalsociety.org
URL: http://www.meteoriticalsociety.org
Contact: Jeffrey N. Grossman, Sec.

Founded: 1933. **Members:** 850. **Membership Dues:** regular, $110 (annual) ● student, retired, $55 (annual). **Budget:** $220,000. **Multinational. Description:** Professional and amateur meteoriticists, educators, and students throughout the world. Promotes the study of meteorites and other samples of extraterrestrial matter, and their relation to the origin and history of the solar system. Additional areas of interest include the investigation of meteors, micrometeorites, impact features, tektites, and planetary surfaces. **Awards:** Barringer Medal. **Frequency:** annual. **Type:** medal. **Recipient:** for outstanding work on impact craters and related phenomena ● Leonard Medal. **Frequency:** annual. **Type:** medal. **Recipient:** for outstanding work in fields of meteoritics and planetary science ● Nier Prize. **Frequency:** annual. **Type:** monetary. **Recipient:** for research excellence by a scientist under age 35 ● Pellas-Ryder Award. **Frequency:** annual. **Type:** monetary. **Recipient:** for the best paper in planetary sciences published by a student; jointly sponsored by the Geological Society of America ● Service Award. **Frequency:** annual. **Type:** recognition. **Recipient:** to a society doing service other than scientific research. **Committees:** Barringer Medal and Prize; Joint Publications (with Geochemical Society); Leonard Medal; Meteorite Nomenclature; Pellas-Ryder Award; Society Publications. **Affiliated With:** Geochemical Society. **Formerly:** (1946) Society for Research on Meteorites. **Publications:** *Geochimica et Cosmochimica Acta*, semimonthly. Journal. Covers research in geochemistry and cosmochemistry. Includes book reviews and membership lists. **Price:** $145.00/year for regular members (online and hardcopy); $80.00/year for regular members (online only); $80.00/year for students/retired (online and hardcopy); $40.00/year for students/retired (online only). ISSN: 0016-7037. Alternate Formats: microform; online ● *Meteoritical Bulletin*, annual. Contains announcements of newly described meteorites. Alternate Formats: online ● *Meteoritics and Planetary Science*, monthly. Journal. Describes research on meteorites, lunar samples, interplanetary dust, impact processes, asteroids and meteors. **Price:** included in membership dues; $700.00 /year for institutions. **Circulation:** 1,200 ● Membership Directory, annual. **Conventions/Meetings:** annual conference, scientific meeting with parallel sessions of oral presentations plus posters (exhibits) ● annual meeting - 2008 July 28-Aug. 1, Matsue, Japan; 2009 July 1-31, Nancy, France; 2010 July 1-31, Toronto, ON, Canada.

7149 ■ Society of Exploration Geo-physicists (SEG)
PO Box 702740
Tulsa, OK 74170-2740
Ph: (918)497-5500 (918)497-5554
Fax: (918)497-5557
E-mail: mfleming@seg.org
URL: http://www.seg.org
Contact: Mary Fleming, Exec. Dir.

Founded: 1930. **Members:** 18,700. **Membership Dues:** active, associate, $75 (annual) ● student, $17 (annual) ● corporate, $1,000 (annual). **Staff:** 47. **Budget:** $7,000,000. **National Groups:** 38. **Description:** Individuals having eight years of education and experience in exploration geophysics or geology. Promotes the science of geophysics, especially as it applies to the exploration for petroleum and other minerals. Encourages high professional standards among members; supports the common interests of members. Maintains SEG Foundation, which receives contributions from companies and individuals and distributes them in the form of scholarships to students of geophysics and related subjects. Offers short continuing education courses to geophysicists and geologists. Maintains 37 committees, including: Development and Production; Engineering and Groundwater Geophysics; Mining and Geothermal; Offshore Exploration and Oceanography. **Awards:** Distinguished Achievement Award. **Type:** recognition ● Maurice Ewing Medal. **Type:** medal ● Reginald Fessenden Award. **Type:** recognition. **Recipient:** for major contribution to the advancement of geophysics ● Virgil Kauffman Gold Medal. **Type:** medal. **Formerly:** (1935) Society of Petroleum Geophysicists. **Publications:** *Geophysics*, monthly. Journal. Contains articles and papers on the latest developments in petroleum and mineral exploration and technological advances in the earth sciences. **Price:** included in membership dues; $500.00 /year for nonmembers in U.S. (print and online); $550.00 /year for nonmembers outside U.S. (print and online); $2,700.00/year for corporations in U.S. (print and online). ISSN: 0016-8033. **Circulation:** 15,000. **Advertising:** accepted. Alternate Formats: microform; online ● *The Leading Edge*, monthly. Journal. Emphasizes practical applications of geophysics, minimizing mathematical formulas. Includes seismic crew surveys and calendar of events. **Price:** included in membership dues; $125.00 /year for nonmembers in U.S. (print and online); $155.00 /year for nonmembers outside U.S. (print and online); $690.00/year for corporations in U.S. (print and online). ISSN: 0732-989X. **Circulation:** 16,700. **Advertising:** accepted. Alternate Formats: online ● *Roster*, annual. Membership Directory ● Monographs ● Annual Report, annual. Alternate Formats: online ● Yearbook, annual. **Conventions/Meetings:** annual Offshore Technology - conference ● annual meeting (exhibits) - 2008 Oct. 26-31, Dallas, TX; 2009 Oct. 25-30, Houston, TX; 2010 Oct. 17-21, Denver, CO.

Glass

7150 ■ Glass Technical Institute (GTI)
12653 Portada Pl.
San Diego, CA 92130
Ph: (858)481-1277
Fax: (858)481-6771
E-mail: docdrake@worldnet.att.net
Contact: Dr. Robert A. Drake, Pres.

Founded: 1984. **Staff:** 4. **For-Profit. Description:** Provides technical, management and design consultation to companies, suppliers, and engineering firms serving the glass industry. Works to promote and improve the glass industry. Offers environmental regulation counseling, engineering and technical services, research and development, and product design consulting services. Conducts presentations. **Awards: Type:** recognition. **Computer Services:** database, environmental, energy, design, operation procedures, and quality assurance. **Committees:** Design; Financial; Legislative Affairs; Technical. **Publications:** *Glass Factory*, periodic. Directory ● *Glass Manufacturing Handbook* ● Article, monthly. Appears in *Glass Industry Magazine*. ● Manuals. **Conventions/Meetings:** annual international conference ● periodic seminar.

Government

7151 ■ Digital Government Society of North America (DGSNA)
c/o Priscilla Rasmussen
209 N Eighth St.
Stroudsburg, PA 18360
Ph: (570)476-8006
Fax: (570)476-0860
E-mail: info@dgsociety.org
URL: http://www.dgsociety.org
Contact: Sharon Dawes, Pres.

Founded: 2006. **Membership Dues:** regular, $75 (annual) ● student, $40 (annual). **Multinational. Description:** Serves the interests of a community of scholars and managers interested in the development and impacts of digital government. Promotes digital or electronic government that fosters the use of information and technology. Equips its members with a professional support network focused on both scholarship and effective practices. Encourages practitioner-researcher exchanges at local, regional, national, and international levels. **Libraries: Type:** reference. **Holdings:** reports. **Subjects:** digital government. **Telecommunication Services:** electronic mail, sdawes@ctg.albany.edu. **Also Known As:** (2006) DG Society. **Publications:** *dgOnline*, monthly. Newsletter. Alternate Formats: online.

Graphics

7152 ■ American Design Drafting Association (ADDA)
105 E Main St.
Newbern, TN 38059
Ph: (731)627-0802
Fax: (731)627-9321
E-mail: cadboss@comcast.net
URL: http://www.adda.org
Contact: Terry Schultz, Pres.

Founded: 1948. **Members:** 2,000. **Membership Dues:** professional in U.S., $85 (annual) ● professional outside U.S., $115 (annual) ● professional in group, $76 (annual) ● professional educational, $75 (annual) ● associate, $45 (annual) ● former student, $35 (annual) ● student-at-large, $30 (annual) ● student in chapters, $25 (annual) ● institutional, $215 (annual) ● business, $250 (annual) ● corporate sponsor, $500 (annual). **Staff:** 5. **Budget:** $200,000. **State Groups:** 3. **Multinational. Description:** Designers, drafters, drafting managers, chief drafters, supervisors, administrators, instructors, and students of design and drafting. Encourages a continued program of education for self-improvement and professionalism in design and drafting and computer-aided design/drafting. Informs members of effective techniques and materials used in drawings and other graphic presentations. Evaluates curriculum of educational institutions through certification program; sponsors drafter certification program. **Awards:** Annual Drafting Contest. **Frequency:** annual. **Type:** recognition. **Recipient:** for students enrolled in a drafting design or graphic arts program ● Annual Poster Contest. **Frequency:** annual. **Type:** recognition. **Recipient:** to the best poster design for use with the annual conference. **Telecommunication Services:** electronic mail, national@adda.org. **Commissions:** Accreditation. **Committees:** Curriculum Certification; Drafter Certification; Drafting Standards; Metrics. **Formerly:** (1960) Association of Professional Draftsman; (1989) American Institute for Design and Drafting. **Publications:** *Compensation Survey*, biennial ● *Design Drafting News*, bimonthly. Newsletter. **Price:** included in membership dues. **Advertising:** accepted ● *Guidelines for Position Classifications and Descriptions for Drafters and Designers*. **Conventions/Meetings:** annual National Design Drafting - conference and competition (exhibits) - always spring.

7153 ■ Guild of Natural Science Illustrators (GNSI)
PO Box 652
Ben Franklin Sta.
Washington, DC 20044-0652
Ph: (301)309-1514
Fax: (301)309-1514
E-mail: gnsihome@his.com
URL: http://www.gnsi.org
Contact: Gretchen Kai Halpert, Pres.

Founded: 1968. **Members:** 1,100. **Membership Dues:** regular in U.S., $85 (annual) ● regular outside U.S., $105 (annual). **Staff:** 3. **Regional Groups:** 5. **Description:** Scientific and medical illustrators and graphic and fine artists interested in natural science illustration; scientists, doctors, universities, natural science libraries, and biological supply houses. Promotes the profession; encourages and assists those entering the profession; promotes better understanding of the field; encourages high standards of competence and ethics. Compiles statistics. **Libraries: Type:** reference. **Holdings:** archival material. **Awards: Type:** recognition. **Committees:** Journal Editors; Newsletter Editors. **Affiliated With:** National Artists Equity Association. **Publications:** *The Guild Handbook of Scientific Illustration*. **Price:** $115.00 for members; $150.00 for nonmembers ● *Guild of Natural Science Illustration—Journal*, annual. **Price:** included in membership dues. **Circulation:** 1,000 ● *Guild of Natural Science Illustrators—Membership Directory*, annual. Includes alphabetical and geographic listings of members. **Price:** included in membership dues ● *Guild of Natural Science Illustrators—Newsletter*, 10/year. **Price:** included in membership dues. **Circulation:** 1,000 ● *Scientific Illustration Courses and Books*. Bibliography. **Price:** $10.00 for members; $15.00 for nonmembers ● Brochures ● Membership Directory ● Papers. **Conventions/Meetings:** monthly meeting ● annual workshop - always summer.

7154 ■ IPA The Association of Graphic Solutions Providers
7200 France Ave. S, Ste.223
Edina, MN 55435
Ph: (952)896-1908
Free: (800)255-8141
Fax: (952)896-0181
E-mail: info@ipa.org
URL: http://www.ipa.org
Contact: Steven Bonoff, Pres.

Founded: 1897. **Members:** 500. **Membership Dues:** regular - minimum (based on total pre-media production employees), $800 (annual) ● regular - maximum (based on total pre-media production employees), $8,000 (annual) ● supplier, $2,000 (annual) ● international, $500 (annual) ● educational, consultant, $400 (annual) ● student, $30 (annual). **Staff:** 7. **Budget:** $1,000,000. **Multinational. Description:** Provides management and technical resources that help companies build, manage and enhance an integrated graphics workflow, from creative to output. **Awards:** Holzinger Award. **Type:** recognition. **Recipient:** for contributions to graphic arts industry. **Committees:** Management Info; Management Programs; Marketing; Packaging; Standards; Technical Services. **Absorbed:** (1987) Graphics Preparatory Association. **Formed by Merger of:** American Photoplatemakers Association; Platemakers Educational and Research Institute. **Formerly:** (1984) International Association of Photoplatemakers; (2004) International Prepress Association. **Publications:** *IPA Bulletin*, bimonthly. Magazine. Provides information for management and technical personnel of companies producing prepress materials for graphic art industry. **Price:** included in membership dues; $20.00 /year for nonmembers in U.S.; $25.00 /year for nonmembers outside U.S. ISSN: 8750-2224. **Circulation:** 1,500. **Advertising:** accepted ● *IPA News*, monthly. Newsletter. Provides industry updates to the prepress graphic arts industry. Includes new members and calendar of events. **Price:** included in membership dues. **Circulation:** 450 ● *SWOP 10th Edition*. Booklet. Provides information on the use and handling of digital files. **Price:** $20.00. **Conventions/Meetings:** annual Business Development - conference ● annual meeting ● seminar ● annual Technical Seminar - meeting (exhibits).

7155 ■ Technical Association of the Graphic Arts (TAGA)
200 Deer Run Rd.
Sewickley, PA 15143
Ph: (412)259-1706
Free: (800)910-4283
Fax: (412)741-2311
E-mail: cmeyers@piagatf.org
URL: http://www.gain.net
Contact: Tony Stanton, Pres.

Founded: 1948. **Members:** 800. **Membership Dues:** student, retired, $40 (annual) ● corporate sponsor, $1,500 (annual) ● individual, $125 (annual). **Staff:** 2. **Budget:** $200,000. **Multinational. Description:** Professional society of individuals interested in or engaged in research or technical control of graphic arts processes or related industries. Promotes advanced technical study and research in the graphic arts. **Libraries: Type:** not open to the public. **Holdings:** 55. **Subjects:** graphic arts. **Awards:** TAGA Honors Award. **Frequency:** annual. **Type:** recognition. **Recipient:** for outstanding contributions to TAGA and/or to the graphic arts industry. **Telecommunication Services:** electronic mail, stanton@andrew.cmu.edu. **Committees:** Education; International Relations; Student Chapters. **Subgroups:** Color Management; Digital Printing; Ink, Paper, and Press. **Formerly:** (1950) Technical Association of the Lithographic Industry. **Publications:** *Technical Association of the Graphic Arts—Proceedings*, annual. Contains research and development papers presented at annual conference. Includes index for 1949-2003. **Price:** $105.00/year. **Circulation:** 1,200. Alternate Formats: CD-ROM ● Newsletter, quarterly. Reports on industry technical issues and association news; conference announcements and reports. **Price:** included in membership dues. **Circulation:** 1,200. **Conventions/Meetings:** annual conference, with technical R&D presentations.

7156 ■ Type Directors Club (TDC)
127 W 25th St., 8th Fl.
New York, NY 10001
Ph: (212)633-8943
Fax: (212)633-8944
E-mail: director@tdc.org
URL: http://www.tdc.org
Contact: Carol Wahler, Exec. Dir.

Founded: 1946. **Members:** 700. **Membership Dues:** student, $50 (annual) ● outside NY, associate, $125 (annual) ● individual outside U.S., $140 (annual) ● regular, $150 (annual) ● sustaining, $400 (annual). **Staff:** 1. **Budget:** $250,000. **Multinational. Description:** Serves as a professional society of typographic designers, type directors, and teachers of typography; sustaining members are individuals with interests in typographic education. Seeks to stimulate research and disseminate information. Provides speakers, classes and offers presentations on history and new developments in typography. **Libraries: Type:** open to the public; by appointment only; reference. **Holdings:** 1,800; books, video recordings. **Subjects:** typography. **Awards: Frequency:** periodic. **Type:** medal. **Recipient:** to an individual with distinguished achievement in the art of type design or typographic usage ● TDC Scholarship. **Frequency:** annual. **Type:** scholarship. **Recipient:** for the use of typography in design. **Computer Services:** Mailing lists. **Publications:** *Letterspace*, quarterly. Newsletter. **Circulation:** 15,000. **Advertising:** accepted ● *Typography Annual*, annual. Lists competition winners. **Conventions/Meetings:** monthly meeting (exhibits) ● seminar.

Hazardous Material

7157 ■ Hazardous Materials Training and Research Institute (HMTRI)
PO Box 2068
Cedar Rapids, IA 52406
Ph: (319)398-5678
Free: (800)GOH-MTRI
Fax: (319)398-1250
E-mail: hmtri@kirkwood.edu
URL: http://www.hmtri.org/hmtri/index_hmtri.htm
Contact: Doug Feil, Admin.

Founded: 1987. **Description:** Recognized as a national center of excellence by several federal agencies; promotes environmental health and safety education and training. Promotes worker protection and the maintenance of a clean and safe environment. **Programs:** Community and College Consortium for Health and Safety Training; Environmental Health and Safety Training; Environmental Technology Online Training and Resources.

Herpetology

7158 ■ American Society of Ichthyologists and Herpetologists (ASIH)
c/o Maureen A. Donnelly, Sec.
Dept. of Biological Sciences
Coll. of Arts and Sci.
Florida Intl. Univ.
11200 SW 8th St.
Miami, FL 33199
Ph: (305)348-1235
Fax: (305)348-1986
E-mail: asih@fiu.edu
URL: http://www.asih.org
Contact: Maureen A. Donnelly, Sec.

Founded: 1913. **Members:** 3,600. **Membership Dues:** student, $45 (annual) ● individual (no journals), $50 (annual) ● regular, $85 (annual) ● sustaining, $100 (annual) ● associate, $20 (annual) ● life, $2,125. **Staff:** 3. **Regional Groups:** 1. **Description:** Scientists, educators, students, and others. Interested in the study of reptiles, amphibians, and fishes. **Awards:** Gaige Fund. **Frequency:** annual. **Type:** recognition. **Recipient:** based upon submission of research proposal ● Raney Fund. **Frequency:** annual. **Type:** recognition. **Recipient:** based upon submission of research proposal ● Robert H. Gibbs, Jr. Memorial. **Frequency:** annual. **Type:** recognition. **Recipient:** based upon nomination ● Storer Award. **Frequency:** annual. **Type:** recognition. **Recipient:** for best student paper (poster) at annual meeting ● Stoye Award. **Frequency:** annual. **Type:** recognition. **Recipient:** for best student paper (oral) at annual meeting. **Computer Services:** Mailing lists, of members. **Telecommunication Services:** electronic mail, asih@allenpress.com. **Committees:** Conservation; Editorial Policy; Endowment Fund; Environmental Quality; Equal Participation; Graduate Student Participation; Ichthyological and Herpetological Collections; Names of Fishes; Publications Policy; Special Publications; Student Awards. **Affiliated With:** American Association for the Advancement of Science; American Fisheries Society; Herpetologists' League; IUCN - The World Conservation Union; Natural Science Collections Alliance; Society for the Preservation of Natural History Collections; Society for the Study of Amphibians and Reptiles. **Publications:** *Copeia*, quarterly. Journal. **Price:** included in membership dues; $135.00 for libraries and institutions. ISSN: 0045-8511. **Circulation:** 3,700 ● Pamphlets. Contains information on career opportunities in ichthyology and herpetology. **Conventions/Meetings:** annual meeting (exhibits) - 2008 July 23-28, Montreal, QC, Canada.

7159 ■ Herpetologists' League (HL)
c/o Dr. Lora Smith, Treas.
Joseph W. Jones Ecological
Research Center, Rte. 2, Box 2324
Newton, GA 39870
Ph: (229)734-4706
E-mail: hleague@bellsouth.net
URL: http://www.herpetologistsleague.org
Contact: Dr. Lora Smith, Treas.

Founded: 1936. **Members:** 2,000. **Membership Dues:** regular, $50-$75 (annual) ● student, $35-$60 (annual) ● family, $60-$85 (annual) ● sustaining, $75-$100 (annual) ● contributing, $100-$125 (annual) ● patron, $1,000 (annual) ● life, $1,500 ● institutional, $250-$330 (annual). **Description:** Persons interested in the study of amphibians and reptiles. **Awards: Type:** recognition. **Recipient:** for student papers. **Computer Services:** Mailing lists, of members. **Publications:** *Herpetologica*, quarterly. Journal. Features scientific reports. ISSN: 0018-0831 ● *Herpetological Monographs*, annual ● *HL Communications*, semiannual. Newsletter ● *Index to Herpetologica*. **Conventions/Meetings:** annual conference, with scientific presentations (exhibits).

7160 ■ Society for the Study of Amphibians and Reptiles (SSAR)
c/o Roy McDiarmid, Pres.
PO Box 37012
Washington, DC 20013
Ph: (540)231-5728
Fax: (540)231-9307
E-mail: dgates@allenpress.com
URL: http://www.ssarherps.org
Contact: Roy McDiarmid, Pres.

Founded: 1958. **Members:** 2,700. **Membership Dues:** regular, $60 (annual) ● plenary, $80 (annual) ● sustaining (minimum), $100 (annual) ● contributing (minimum), $200 (annual) ● patron (minimum), $500 (annual) ● CAAR, $20 (annual) ● plenary (life), $1,600 ● regular (life), $1,200 ● CAAR (life), $400. **Budget:** $150,000. **Description:** Purposes are education, conservation, and research. Participates in conservation funding. **Awards:** Henri Seibert Award. **Frequency:** annual. **Type:** recognition. **Recipient:** for the best student paper ● **Type:** recognition. **Recipient:** for papers on herpetology. **Computer Services:** Mailing lists. **Formerly:** (1968) Ohio Herpetological Society. **Publications:** *Herpetological Circulars*, annual. Pamphlets. Provides a general review of a specific topic in herpetology. ● *Herpetological Review*, quarterly. Journal. Provides semi and non-technical articles related to herpetology and amphibians; includes institutional and regional society news. **Price:** included in membership dues; $28.00

/year for nonmembers. ISSN: 0018-084X. **Circulation:** 2,500. **Advertising:** accepted. Also Cited As: *Herp Review* ● *Journal of Herpetology*, quarterly. Contains research on the biology of amphibians and reptiles. Includes annual index. **Price:** included in membership dues. ISSN: 0022-1511. **Circulation:** 2,400 ● Brochures ● Reprints. **Conventions/Meetings:** annual meeting (exhibits).

Historic Preservation

7161 ■ National Center for Preservation Technology and Training (NCPTT)
645 Univ. Pkwy.
Natchitoches, LA 71457
Ph: (318)356-7444
Fax: (318)356-9119
E-mail: ncptt@nps.gov
URL: http://www.ncptt.nps.gov
Contact: Kirk A. Cordell, Exec. Dir.
Description: Promotes and enhances the preservation and conservation of prehistoric and historic resources in the U.S. by: researching, developing and distributing preservation and conservation techniques, technologies and training; researching and developing the transfer of technologies and techniques from disciplines beyond preservation and conservation; coordinating distribution of preservation information and technologies among government agencies, universities and research institutions and professional organizations; and, partnering with national and international preservation organizations towards exchanging information and technologies and collaborating on projects. **Programs:** Archeology and Collections; Architecture and Engineering; Heritage Education; Historic Landscape; Materials Research. **Publications:** *NCPTT Product Catalog*. Contains a partial listing of products available through NCPTT. Alternate Formats: online ● Annual Report, annual. Outlines the accomplishments, goals, and research priorities of the organization. Alternate Formats: online.

7162 ■ Recent Past Preservation Network (RPPN)
PO Box 100505
Arlington, VA 22210
Ph: (434)293-2872
E-mail: info@recentpast.org
URL: http://www.recentpast.org
Contact: Christine Madrid-French, Pres.
Founded: 2001. **Members:** 200. **Membership Dues:** student, $5 (annual) ● general, $15 (annual) ● patron/institutional, $30 (annual) ● benefactor, $75 (annual) ● corporate, $200 (annual) ● life, $250. **Budget:** $5,000. **State Groups:** 30. **Multinational. Description:** Promotes preservation education, assistance, and activism through new technologies to encourage understanding of modern built environment. **Telecommunication Services:** electronic mail, president@recentpast.org ● electronic mail, madrid-french@mission66.com.

Human Development

7163 ■ World Transhumanist Association (WTA)
PO Box 128
Willington, CT 06279
Ph: (860)297-2376
Fax: (860)297-4136
E-mail: secretary@transhumanism.org
URL: http://transhumanism.org
Contact: James Hughes PhD, Sec./Exec. Dir.
Founded: 1998. **Members:** 3,775. **Membership Dues:** supporting (employed and in a developed country), $50 (annual) ● supporting (unemployed/student/retired or living in a less developed country), $20 (annual) ● sustaining, $250 (annual). **Languages:** Chinese, English, French, German, Spanish. **Multinational. Description:** Advocates the ethical use of technology to expand human capacities. Supports the development of and access to new technologies that enable everyone to enjoy better minds, better bodies and better lives. Fosters communication and cooperation among members. **Publications:** Newsletter.

Human Engineering

7164 ■ Human Factors and Ergonomics Society (HFES)
PO Box 1369
Santa Monica, CA 90406-1369
Ph: (310)394-1811
Fax: (310)394-2410
E-mail: info@hfes.org
URL: http://www.hfes.org
Contact: Lynn Strother, Exec. Dir.
Founded: 1957. **Members:** 4,800. **Membership Dues:** individual, $190 (annual) ● contributing, $285 (annual) ● supporting, $380 (annual) ● student, $35 (annual). **Staff:** 7. **Budget:** $1,400,000. **Local Groups:** 57. **Description:** Professional association of psychologists, engineers, industrial designers, and other related scientists and practitioners who are concerned with the use of human factors and ergonomics in the development of systems and devices of all kinds. Promotes the discovery and exchange of knowledge concerning human characteristics that apply to the design of systems and devices intended for human use and operation. Disseminates current literature on ergonomics to concerned professionals in the scientific community. **Committees:** Relations with Industry and Education; Relations with Other Professional Organizations; Technical Standards. **Formerly:** (1993) Human Factors Society. **Publications:** *Ergonomics in Design: The Magazine of Human Factors Applications*, quarterly. Contains feature articles, interviews, debates, and software and book reviews on a wide range of industries and systems. **Price:** included in membership dues; $60.00 /year for nonmembers. ISSN: 1064-8046. **Circulation:** 5,400. **Advertising:** accepted ● *HFES Bulletin*, 11/year. **Price:** $42.00 /year for nonmembers; included in membership dues ● *Human Factors*, quarterly. Journal. Contains original papers covering basic and applied research, methodology, and applications regarding people in relation to machines and environments. **Price:** included in membership dues; $253.00 /year for nonmembers individuals (print or online); $295.00 /year for institutions (print or online); $534.00 /year for institutions (print plus online). Alternate Formats: online ● *Human Factors and Ergonomics Society—Bulletin*, monthly. Newsletter. Contains news of the field and the society, calendar of events, and calls for papers. **Price:** $383.00 /year for nonmembers individuals (print plus online). ISSN: 0018-7208. **Circulation:** 6,200. Alternate Formats: microform; online ● *Human Factors and Ergonomics Society—Directory and Yearbook*. Membership Directory. Lists members' information arranged alphabetically and geographically. **Price:** included in membership dues; $42.00 /year for nonmembers. ISSN: 0438-1629. **Circulation:** 4,800. **Advertising:** accepted ● *Proceedings of the Human Factors and Ergonomics Society Annual Meeting*. Contains papers presented in technical sessions and symposia. Includes author and keyword index. **Price:** included in membership dues; $75.00/copy for nonmembers. **Circulation:** 5,200. **Advertising:** accepted. **Conventions/Meetings:** annual conference (exhibits) - usually October. 2008 Sept. 22-26, New York, NY.

7165 ■ MTM Association for Standards and Research (MTM)
1111 E Touhy Ave.
Des Plaines, IL 60018
Ph: (847)299-1111
Fax: (847)299-3509
E-mail: webmaster@mtm.org
URL: http://www.mtm.org
Contact: Dirk J. Rauglas, Exec. Dir.
Founded: 1951. **Members:** 1,000. **Membership Dues:** corporate, $1,000 (annual) ● individual, $75 (annual). **Staff:** 25. **Budget:** $1,500,000. **Description:** Persons interested in the fields of industrial engineering, industrial psychology, and human engineering. Conducts research at accredited institutions on human motion (the physical movement of body and limb), with emphasis on examining: internal velocity, acceleration, tension, and control characteristics of a given motion under several conditions; external regularities of given groups of motion as they vary under several conditions of performance; the proper use of motion information in measuring, controlling, and improving manual activities. Also studies ergonomics and the effects of workplace environment on productivity. Provides information on fatigue, optimum methods of performance, the effect of practice on motion performance, and the use of motion information for determining allowances and predicting total performance time. Has developed computer programs for the application of Methods Time Measurement (MTM) and MTM-based work measurement systems. Conducts training courses and testing for certification of practitioners and instructors in all Association MTM Systems. Develops and makes available specialized productivity management services. **Awards: Frequency:** annual. **Type:** recognition. **Committees:** Technical Services for Practitioners and Instructors. **Also Known As:** Methods Time Measurements Association for Standards and Research. **Conventions/Meetings:** annual conference.

7166 ■ National Association of Professional Organizers (NAPO)
4700 W Lake Ave.
Glenview, IL 60025
Ph: (847)375-4746
Fax: (877)734-8668
E-mail: hq@napo.net
URL: http://www.napo.net
Contact: Standolyn Robertson, Pres.
Founded: 1985. **Members:** 3,400. **Membership Dues:** provisional, $180 ● active, $200 (annual) ● associate, $550 (annual) ● branch associate, $150 (annual) ● local associate, $250 (annual). **Staff:** 2. **Budget:** $582,000. **Regional Groups:** 13. **Description:** Professional organizers providing organization, time management, or productivity improvement services; persons in related fields such as organizational product sales and organizational development. Works to promote and educate the public about the profession and to offer support, education, and networking opportunities to members. **Awards:** Founders. **Frequency:** annual. **Type:** recognition. **Recipient:** for excellence in business, education, family, and the professions ● Friend of NAPO. **Frequency:** annual. **Type:** recognition. **Recipient:** for individual ● Organizer's Choice. **Frequency:** annual. **Type:** recognition. **Recipient:** for company ● Organizing Excellence. **Frequency:** annual. **Type:** recognition. **Recipient:** for individual or group ● President's Award. **Frequency:** annual. **Type:** recognition. **Recipient:** for members ● Service to NAPO. **Frequency:** annual. **Type:** recognition. **Recipient:** for member. **Computer Services:** database ● mailing lists. **Committees:** Audit; Awards and Recognition; Certification; Media. **Formerly:** (1986) Association of Professional Organizers. **Publications:** *NAPO Directory*, annual. Includes member listings and specialties that enable NAPO members to easily locate and contact their peers. **Price:** included in membership dues. **Advertising:** accepted ● *NAPO Newsletter*, bimonthly. Includes information about the organizing industry, organizational techniques, current trends and upcoming events. **Price:** included in membership dues. **Advertising:** accepted. Alternate Formats: online. **Conventions/Meetings:** annual conference, with expo (exhibits).

7167 ■ Operations Management Education and Research Foundation (OMER)
Address Unknown since 2008
Founded: 1979. **Description:** Participants are individuals concerned or involved with planning, implementing, managing, or adjusting office, factory, and other physical structures, internal or external environments, applied hardware products, furniture fixtures, and related services. Dedicated to the open exchange of ideas, information, and assistance in all

areas of office environment and operational development. Seeks to provide a research and educational nucleus for the profession. Brings together specialists from all disciplines associated with office planning/design, operations resources management, and end-user concerns. Conducts educational programs relating to operations management. Compiles statistics; maintains speakers' bureau. Plans to establish technical research library and develop telephone referral and computerized services. **Awards: Type:** recognition. **Departments:** Education; Research. **Formerly:** (1984) Organization of Facility Managers and Planners. **Publications:** Also publishes educational materials. **Conventions/Meetings:** seminar, for training relating to operations management.

7168 ■ Project on Technology, Work and Character (PTWC)
c/o The Maccoby Group
4825 Linnean Ave. NW
Washington, DC 20008
Ph: (202)895-8922
Fax: (202)895-8923
URL: http://www.maccoby.com/PTWC
Contact: Dr. Michael Maccoby, Pres.
Founded: 1977. **Staff:** 2. **Description:** Participants include anthropologists, psychologists, and labor management experts. Sponsors anthropological and psychological research and writing on technology as it relates to human character and work. Seeks to identify factors that make work both satisfying and productive for laborers, professionals, and managers. Consults with labor and management groups.

Ichthyology

7169 ■ American Fisheries Society (AFS)
5410 Grosvenor Ln., Ste.110
Bethesda, MD 20814-2199
Ph: (301)897-8616
Fax: (301)897-8096
E-mail: main@fisheries.org
URL: http://www.fisheries.org
Contact: Gus Rassam, Exec. Dir.
Founded: 1870. **Members:** 9,000. **Membership Dues:** individual in North America, $76 (annual) ● international individual, $88 (annual) ● student, $19 (annual) ● young professional, retired, $38 (annual) ● international young professional, retired, $44 (annual) ● life (fisheries only), $1,000-$1,200 ● individual from developing countries (no print copy of fisheries), $5 (annual) ● individual from developing countries (with print copy of fisheries), $25 (annual) ● international student, $22 (annual). **Staff:** 20. **Budget:** $2,500,000. **Regional Groups:** 4. **Local Groups:** 54. **Multinational. Description:** International scientific organization of fisheries and aquatic science professionals, including fish culturists, fish biologists, water quality scientists, fish health professionals, fish technologists, educators, limnologists, and oceanographers. Promotes the development of all branches of fishery science and practice, and the conservation, development, and wise utilization of fisheries, both recreational and commercial. Strengthens professional standards by certifying fisheries scientists, stressing professional ethics, and providing forums for the exchange of scientific and management information. Represents members through written and verbal testimony before legislative and administrative bodies concerning aquatic environmental issues. Maintains over 30 committees. **Awards: Type:** recognition. **Computer Services:** Mailing lists. **Telecommunication Services:** electronic mail, membership@fisheries.org. **Sections:** Bioengineering; Canadian Aquatic Resources; Computer Users; Early Life History; Education; Equal Opportunities; Estuaries; Fish Culture; Fish Health; Fisheries Administrators; Fisheries History; Fisheries Law; Fisheries Management; Genetics; International Fisheries; Introduced Fish; Marine Fisheries; Native Peoples Fisheries; Physiology; Socioeconomics; Water Quality. **Publications:** *AFS Membership Directory and Handbook*, annual. Lists members' information arranged alphabetically and geographically. **Price:** included in membership dues. **Circulation:** 9,400. **Advertising:** accepted. Alternate Formats: online ● *Career Guidance*. Brochures ● *Fisheries*, monthly. Magazine. Contains articles on fisheries administration, economics, education, management, philosophy, and professional responsibilities. Includes book reviews. **Price:** included in membership dues. ISSN: 0363-2415. **Circulation:** 9,400. **Advertising:** accepted ● *Journal of Aquatic Animal Health*, quarterly. Contains research papers on the causes, effects, treatments, and prevention of diseases of fish and shellfish. **Price:** $38.00. ISSN: 0899-7659 ● *North American Journal of Aquaculture*, quarterly. **Price:** $38.00 ● *North American Journal of Fisheries Management*, quarterly. Provides original research on finfish and shellfish in the ocean and fresh waters. Includes management briefs. **Price:** $43.00. ISSN: 0275-5947. **Circulation:** 3,330 ● *Transactions of the American Fisheries Society*, quarterly. Journal. Contains original research on fisheries science including biology, ecology, genetics, physiology, and population dynamics. Contains book reviews. **Price:** $43.00. ISSN: 0002-8487. **Circulation:** 4,040 ● Books ● Monographs. **Conventions/Meetings:** annual meeting (exhibits) - 2008 Aug. 17-21, Ottawa, ON, Canada.

7170 ■ American Institute of Fishery Research Biologists (AIFRB)
c/o Dr. Linda Jones, Pres.
14931 73rd Ave. NE
Kenmore, WA 98028
E-mail: linda.jones@noaa.gov
URL: http://www.aifrb.org
Contact: Dr. Linda Jones, Pres.
Founded: 1956. **Members:** 700. **Membership Dues:** student associate, emeritus, $20 (annual) ● professional, $40 (annual). **Budget:** $15,000. **Regional Groups:** 7. **State Groups:** 14. **Description:** Professional scientific and educational organization formed to: advance the theory and practice of fishery science in pursuit of greater scientific understanding of living marine and freshwater natural resources, their habitat, their biological and physical environment, and their fisheries; support the education of students and the general public, and the professional development and recognition of researchers, practitioners, and institutions in fishery science and related areas of natural resource management public policy, and public affairs; and foster the application of scientific knowledge to the sustainable use, conservation and sound management of living aquatic resources and their allied human applications (having commercial, recreational, subsistence, and aesthetic or intrinsic value to society). **Libraries: Type:** open to the public. **Awards:** AIFRB Distinguished Service Award. **Frequency:** annual. **Type:** recognition. **Recipient:** for an individual's outstanding and sustained service to the AIFRB ● AIFRB Outstanding Achievement Award (Group). **Frequency:** annual. **Type:** recognition. **Recipient:** to an organization or group that has established an outstanding record of contributions to the management living aquatic resources, the fisheries, and the advancement of fisheries science and the profession ● AIFRB Outstanding Achievement Award (Individual). **Frequency:** annual. **Type:** recognition. **Recipient:** to individuals who have demonstrated outstanding contributions to the field of fisheries and the profession ● AIFRB Research Assistance Award. **Frequency:** annual. **Type:** grant. **Recipient:** to student associate members for an original paper or research at scientific meetings; or for conducting research at distant study sites ● W.F. Thompson Best Paper. **Frequency:** annual. **Type:** monetary. **Recipient:** for best paper written and published while in AIFRB student associate status. **Telecommunication Services:** electronic mail, vickie@aifrbregister.org. **Publications:** *BRIEFS*, bimonthly. Newsletters. Contains information on the activities of the Institute, its districts and members; and other matters of importance to the fishery community. **Price:** $40.00 for nonmembers. **Circulation:** 700. **Advertising:** accepted. Alternate Formats: online ● Membership Directory, periodic. **Conventions/Meetings:** annual Board of Control - board meeting, in association with American Fisheries Society.

7171 ■ Aquatic Research Institute (ARI)
2242 Davis Ct.
Hayward, CA 94545
Ph: (510)782-4058
Fax: (510)784-0945
E-mail: rofen@prado.com
Contact: Dr. Robert R. Rofen, Dir.
Founded: 1962. **Description:** Provides research materials on fish, fisheries, and aquaculture, aquatic sciences, and technology. Conducts research projects on fish nutrition, disease, and aquaculture. **Libraries: Type:** reference. **Holdings:** 20,000; books, monographs. **Subjects:** aquatic sciences and technology. **Also Known As:** (2002) Aquatic Research Interactive. **Publications:** *Aquatica*, irregular. Journal ● *Special Reports*, periodic.

7172 ■ Environmental and Contamination Research Center
U.S. Geological Survey
4200 New Haven Rd.
Columbia, MO 65201
Ph: (573)875-5399
Fax: (573)876-1896
E-mail: sculley@usgs.gov
Contact: Michael Mac, Dir.
Staff: 80. **Description:** Ecosystem scientists for large rivers and other aquatic ecosystems in the Central Region of the U.S. Geological Survey, Biological Resources Division. Conducts aquatic ecological investigations, inventory and monitoring programs that focus on the effects of a broad spectrum of environmental stressors. Works through partnerships to provide information on biological diversity, habitat loss, introduction of non-native species, degradation of water quality and other topics of concern, especially those related to large rivers such as the Lower Missouri. Promotes national expertise in ecotoxicology and environmental chemistry. **Libraries: Type:** reference. **Holdings:** 8,000; books, periodicals, reports. **Subjects:** aquatic toxicology, contaminants, chemical analysis, global warming, water quality. **Formerly:** (1978) Fish Pesticide Research Laboratory; (1986) Columbia National Fisheries Research Laboratory; (1994) National Fisheries Contaminant Research Center; (1998) Midwest Science Center.

7173 ■ Federation of American Aquarium Societies (FAAS)
c/o Pat Smith, Membership Chm.
109 Bucknell Rd.
West Sayville, NY 11796
Ph: (217)359-6707
E-mail: jmont@insightbb.com
URL: http://www.faas.info
Contact: Jerry Montgomery, Pres.
Founded: 1973. **Membership Dues:** society (within North, Central and South America), $30 (annual) ● affiliate (societies outside the geographical boundaries of FAAS, non-voting), $15 (annual) ● individual, $15 (annual). **Multinational. Description:** Represents American aquarium societies. **Awards:** Breeders Award Program. **Type:** recognition. **Recipient:** to individual society members who breed fish ● Horticulture Award Program. **Type:** recognition. **Recipient:** to individual society members who propagate aquarium plants ● Photo Award Program. **Type:** recognition. **Recipient:** for excellence in photography ● Publication Award Program. **Type:** recognition. **Recipient:** for society editors and writers. **Publications:** *The Federation Report*, bimonthly. Contains reports from delegates, news and information, and advice on how to run an aquarium society. **Price:** free for members.

7174 ■ International Association of Astacology (IAA)
c/o Bill Daniels, Sec.
Auburn Univ.
Dept. of Fisheries and Allied Aquaculture
Rm. 123, Swingle Hall
Auburn University, AL 36849-5419
Ph: (334)844-9123
Fax: (334)844-9208

E-mail: daniewh@auburn.edu
Contact: Bill Daniels, Sec.
Founded: 1972. **Members:** 300. **Membership Dues:** regular, $40 (biennial) ● student, $20 (biennial) ● business, $80 (biennial). **Staff:** 1. **Budget:** $6,500. **Description:** Individuals from industry, academia, and state and federal government wildlife agencies. Promotes the scientific study and cultivation of freshwater crayfish. Sponsors 8 working groups in areas such as biology, ecology, and zoogeography. **Awards:** Honorary Life Membership. **Frequency:** periodic. **Type:** recognition. **Recipient:** for service to society and the development of crayfish services. **Committees:** Transplantations. **Publications:** *Freshwater Crayfish, A Journal of Astacology*, biennial. Contains compilation of referred papers presented at biennial meetings. **Circulation:** 200 ● *Freshwater Crayfish: IAA Newsletter*, quarterly. ISSN: 1023-8174 ● Membership Directory, biennial. **Conventions/Meetings:** biennial congress ● symposium.

7175 ■ North American Native Fishes Association (NANFA)
c/o Christopher Scharpf, Ed./Membership Coor.
1107 Argonne Dr.
Baltimore, MD 21218
Ph: (410)243-9050 (256)824-6992
E-mail: info@nanfa.org
URL: http://www.nanfa.org
Contact: Bruce Stallsmith, Pres.
Founded: 1972. **Members:** 450. **Membership Dues:** regular, in U.S., $20 (annual) ● regular, in U.S., Canada, Mexico, $25 (annual) ● regular, outside North America, $34 (annual). **Regional Groups:** 19. **Description:** Brings together anyone with an interest in the native fishes of North America: increases and disseminates knowledge about these fishes; promotes practical programs for their conservation and the protection/restoration of their native habitats; advances captive husbandry and the educational, scientific and conservation benefits it affords; encourages the legal, environmentally responsible collection of native fishes for private aquaria as a valid use of a natural resource; and provides a forum for fellowship and camaraderie among its members. **Libraries: Type:** reference. **Awards:** Gerald C. Corcoran Education Grant. **Frequency:** annual. **Type:** grant. **Recipient:** for proposals reviewed by special committee (membership required) ● NANFA Conservation Grant. **Frequency:** annual. **Type:** grant. **Recipient:** for proposals reviewed by special committee (membership required). **Telecommunication Services:** electronic mail, ichthos@comcast.net. **Publications:** *American Currents*, quarterly. Journal. Contains articles, news, and reviews on the collection, identification, conservation, biology, and captive husbandry of North American native fishes. **Price:** included in membership dues. ISSN: 1070-7352. **Circulation:** 450. **Advertising:** accepted ● Bibliographies. Covers native fish research sources. **Conventions/Meetings:** annual meeting and convention, with lectures, native fish displays, and a book, artwork, and merchandise auction ● periodic regional meeting.

7176 ■ Pacific Ocean Research Foundation (PORF)
PO Box 4800
Kailua-Kona, HI 96740
Ph: (808)329-6105
Fax: (808)329-1148
URL: http://holoholo.org/porf
Founded: 1977. **Members:** 800. **Membership Dues:** platinum circle, $1,000 ● gold circle, $500 ● silver circle, $250 ● bronze circle, $100 ● regular, $50 ● associate, $25. **Staff:** 2. **Budget:** $225,000. **Description:** Companies, corporations, clubs, and individuals interested in furthering the knowledge, conservation, and management of Pacific game fish, with particular emphasis on billfish and tuna. Maintains laboratory facilities for research in areas including fish physiology, fishery biology, oceanography, and marine ecology. Sponsors scientists conducting basic research worldwide on projects including tagging and monitoring Pacific game fish to further the study of their habits. Coordinates efforts of conservation-minded groups in major fishing areas of the Pacific Basin, particularly the standardization of statistics on fish data collection. Gathers data on biology, physiology, and ecology of Pacific game fish including tuna, mahi-mahi, and marlin. **Libraries: Type:** reference. **Holdings:** archival material. **Formerly:** (1985) Pacific Gamefish Research Foundation. **Publications:** *Research Newsletter*, 3-4/year. **Conventions/Meetings:** quarterly executive committee meeting ● annual meeting - usually August, Kailua-Kona, HI.

7177 ■ Society for the Protection of Old Fishes (SPOOF)
c/o Dr. Alan J. Mearns, Pres.
20315 92nd Ave. W
Edmonds, WA 98020
Ph: (425)774-9069 (206)526-6336
Fax: (206)526-6329
E-mail: alan.mearns@noaa.gov
Contact: Dr. Alan J. Mearns, Pres.
Founded: 1967. **Members:** 200. **Membership Dues:** student, $15 (annual) ● student outside U.S., $10 (annual). **Multinational. Description:** Scientists, artists, poets, and other professionals interested in advancing knowledge in all scientific disciplines, especially in the study of old (primitive) fishes. Seeks to develop means by which rare fish and other sea life may be obtained for scientific and educational purposes; is concerned especially with the coelacanth, a fish described as a "living fossil" which was discovered by scientists in 1938, and thought to be extinct for 60 to 70 million years. Relatives of the coelacanth, such as sharks, rays, lungfish, hagfish, and skates are also of particular interest. Provides research specimens; disseminates information; produces slides and movies on fish topics. Operates speakers' bureau and placement service. **Libraries: Type:** reference. **Holdings:** audiovisuals, books, clippings. **Subjects:** fish, conservation. **Awards: Frequency:** periodic. **Type:** recognition. **Committees:** Dissection; Education; Library; Membership. **Publications:** *SPOOF Newsletter*, periodic. Reports on the protection of "sea life of all kinds from overexploitation," especially the coelacanth. Includes book and journal reviews. **Price:** included in membership dues. **Circulation:** 200. **Conventions/Meetings:** annual banquet - every 3rd Thursday of October ● annual seminar and meeting.

Imaging Media

7178 ■ DICOM Standards Committee (DICOM)
1300 N 17th St., Ste.1752
Rosslyn, VA 22209
Ph: (703)841-3285
Fax: (703)841-3385
E-mail: hclark@medicalimaging.org
URL: http://dicom.nema.org
Contact: Mr. Howard Clark PhD, Sec.
Founded: 1983. **Members:** 45. **Membership Dues:** manufacturer, vendor, consulting company, $5,000 (annual) ● member of NEMA, COCIR, JIRA, $1,000 (annual) ● biomedical professional organization, $2,500 (annual). **Staff:** 2. **Multinational. Description:** Seeks to create and maintain international standards of communication of biomedical diagnostic and therapeutic information in areas using digital images and associated data. **Computer Services:** Information services, organization's programs, processes, and products. **Telecommunication Services:** electronic bulletin board, preliminary work products. **Also Known As:** Digital Imaging and Communications in Medicine.

Industrial Design

7179 ■ Association of Women Industrial Designers (AWID)
PO Box 468
Old Chelsea Sta.
New York, NY 10011
E-mail: info@awidweb.com
URL: http://www.awidweb.com
Contact: Erika Doering, Co-Founder
Founded: 1992. **Members:** 120. **Membership Dues:** student, $20 (annual) ● professional, $50 (annual). **Regional Groups:** 2. **Description:** Women design professionals; industrial design students. Promotes professional and economic advancement of members. Facilitates communication among members; conducts research and educational programs; sponsors competitions; maintains speakers' bureau. **Computer Services:** Mailing lists ● online services. **Publications:** *Goddess in the Details - Product Design by Women*. Book. **Price:** $10.95/copy ● Newsletter, periodic ● Newsletter, quarterly. Contains design articles, member's news, and events. **Price:** included in membership dues. **Circulation:** 120. Alternate Formats: online. **Conventions/Meetings:** periodic board meeting, with networking and a working meeting ● periodic lecture ● monthly regional meeting (exhibits) ● periodic symposium.

7180 ■ Industrial Designers Society of America (IDSA)
45195 Bus. Ct., Ste.250
Dulles, VA 20166-6717
Ph: (703)707-6000
E-mail: cooperw@idsa.org
URL: http://www.idsa.org
Contact: Cooper C. Woodring, Exec. Dir.
Founded: 1965. **Members:** 3,500. **Membership Dues:** professional, affiliate, international, $315 (annual) ● 1-5 years after graduation, $100-$227 (annual) ● student, $100 (annual). **Staff:** 13. **Budget:** $1,800,000. **Local Groups:** 27. **National Groups:** 12. **Description:** Professional society of industrial designers. Represents the profession in its relations with business, education, government, and international designers; promotes the industrial design profession. Conducts research, educational, and charitable programs. Compiles statistics. **Awards:** Industrial Design Excellence Awards. **Frequency:** annual. **Type:** recognition. **Recipient:** for designs. **Computer Services:** Mailing lists, of members. **Committees:** Education; Ethics; Fellowship and Awards; History and Archives. **Special Interest Groups:** Design Management; Environment; Exhibits; Furniture; Housewares; Human Factors; International; Materials and Processes; Medical; Universal Design; Visual Interface; Women's. **Affiliated With:** International Council of Societies of Industrial Design. **Formed by Merger of:** (1965) Industrial Design Education Association; Industrial Designers Institute. **Publications:** *Compensation Studies 2000*, biennial. Survey. Covers industrial design compensation. **Price:** $125.00 for members; $250.00 for nonmembers ● *Consultant Operating Studies 2000*, triennial. **Price:** $199.00 for members; $200.00 for nonmembers ● *Corporate Operating Study 1999*, triennial. Surveys. **Price:** $199.00 for members; $249.00 for nonmembers ● *Design Perspectives*, monthly. Newsletter. **Price:** $35.00 in U.S.; $50.00 outside U.S. **Circulation:** 3,100. **Advertising:** accepted ● *IDSA Directory of Industrial Designers*, annual. Membership Directory. **Price:** $99.00. **Advertising:** accepted ● *Innovation*, quarterly. Magazine. **Price:** $50.00/year in U.S.; $95.00/year outside U.S. ISSN: 0731-2334. **Circulation:** 3,400. **Advertising:** accepted. **Conventions/Meetings:** annual conference (exhibits) ● annual Design Your Life - conference.

Industrial Engineering

7181 ■ APICS - The Association for Operations Management
5301 Shawnee Rd.
Alexandria, VA 22312-2317
Ph: (703)354-8851
Free: (800)444-2742
Fax: (703)354-8106
E-mail: service@apics.org
URL: http://www.apics.org
Contact: Joseph F. Shedlawski CPIM, Pres.
Founded: 1957. **Members:** 60,000. **Membership Dues:** professional in North America, $110 (annual)

● professional outside North America, $130 (annual) ● student, $25 (annual). **Staff:** 100. **Budget:** $27,000,000. **Local Groups:** 270. **Multinational. Description:** Provides professional certifications, educational programs and publications for manufacturing and service industry professionals across the entire supply chain. Administers the certification programs, Certified in Production and Inventory Management and Certified in Integrated Resource Management; distributes more than 800 business management publications and educational materials. **Libraries: Type:** not open to the public. **Holdings:** 800; articles, books, periodicals. **Subjects:** inventory management. **Awards:** Corporate Awards of Excellence. **Frequency:** annual. **Type:** recognition. **Computer Services:** database, enterprise software ● mailing lists, 60,000 APICS members, by business environment, department, title, geographic region. **Formerly:** American Production and Inventory Control Society; (2005) APICS — The Educational Society for Resource Management. **Publications:** *APICS Conference Proceedings*, annual ● *APICS Dictionary*, triennial. Book. Alternate Formats: CD-ROM ● *APICS Educational Materials Catalog*, annual ● *APICS, The Performance Advantage*, 10/year. Magazine. Covers information on the latest resource management principles and practices. **Price:** included in membership dues; $65.00 /year for nonmembers in U.S.; $77.00 /year for nonmembers in Canada and Mexico; $93.00 /year for nonmembers outside U.S., Canada and Mexico. ISSN: 0274-9874. **Circulation:** 66,000. **Advertising:** accepted ● *Production and Inventory Management Journal*, quarterly. Evaluates systems and technology and chronicles their applications and development. **Price:** included in membership dues; $110.00 /year for nonmembers. **Conventions/Meetings:** annual conference (exhibits) ● symposium ● workshop.

7182 ■ Completion Engineering Association (CEA)

c/o Darrell Hebert, Sec.-Treas.
PO Box 1330
Houston, TX 77251-1330
Ph: (832)636-4804
E-mail: darrell_hebert@anadarko.com
Contact: Darrell Hebert, Sec.-Treas.

Description: Seeks to advance well completion technology by providing a forum to aid in developing future industry sponsored projects. **Awards: Frequency:** annual. **Type:** scholarship. **Recipient:** for Junior or Senior Petroleum Engineering students.

7183 ■ IEEE Industry Applications Society (IAS)

799 N Beverly Glen
Los Angeles, CA 90077
Ph: (310)446-8280
Fax: (310)446-8390
E-mail: bob.myers@ieee.org
URL: http://ewh.ieee.org/soc/ias
Contact: Bob Meyers, Admin.

Members: 11,355. **Membership Dues:** student, $30 (annual) ● regular, $161 (annual) ● affiliate, $37 (annual). **Local Groups:** 60. **Description:** Serves as society of the Institute of Electrical and Electronics Engineers. Studies the application of electrical systems, apparatus, devices, and control to the processes and equipment of industry and commerce. **Publications:** *IEEE Industry Applications Magazine*, bimonthly. **Advertising:** accepted. Alternate Formats: online ● *Transactions on Industry Applications*, bimonthly. **Conventions/Meetings:** annual meeting - 2008 Oct. 5-9, Edmonton, AB, Canada.

7184 ■ Miles Value Foundation (MVF)

5505 Connecticut Ave. NW, No. 149
Washington, DC 20015-2601
Ph: (202)253-5550 (832)445-0030
Fax: (775)522-0547
E-mail: mvf@valuefoundation.org
URL: http://www.valuefoundation.org
Contact: Donald E. Parker, Pres.

Founded: 1977. **Members:** 35. **Membership Dues:** citizen, $25 (annual) ● contributing, $50 (annual) ● donor, $100 (annual) ● sustaining, $500 (annual) ● patron, $1,000 (annual). **Description:** Individuals within the government and private sector in the U.S. and overseas. Works to improve use of the manpower supply, finances, and resources, including energy, through value analysis and value engineering. Value engineering involves analyzing the function of a product or service with the purpose of achieving the required function at the lowest overall cost consistent with requirements for performance. **Libraries: Type:** reference. **Subjects:** value engineering. **Awards: Type:** recognition ● Scholarship Award. **Frequency:** annual. **Type:** monetary. **Recipient:** for the best student who conducted value engineering study performed in an undergraduate value engineering class. **Telecommunication Services:** electronic mail, bllenzer@aol.com. **Programs:** Value Analysis; Value Engineering; Value Management and Related Methodology. **Affiliated With:** SAVE International. **Formerly:** (1987) Value Foundation. **Publications:** *Basic Value Analysis*. Book ● *Management Application of Value Engineering for Business and Government*. Book ● *Value Analysis*. Book ● *Value Engineering Theory*. Book ● Makes available *Principles of Value Analysis/Value Engineering* (videotape) and correspondence course. **Conventions/Meetings:** annual meeting - always in May.

7185 ■ SAVE International

136 S Keowee St.
Dayton, OH 45402
Ph: (937)224-7283 (703)875-6369
Fax: (937)222-5794
E-mail: info@value-eng.org
URL: http://www.value-eng.org
Contact: Kim Fantaci, Exec. Dir.

Founded: 1959. **Members:** 1,200. **Membership Dues:** individual, $125 (annual) ● regular (corporate), $350 (annual) ● sustaining (corporate), $1,000 (annual) ● additional (corporate), $75 (annual). **Staff:** 10. **Budget:** $260,000. **Regional Groups:** 9. **State Groups:** 39. **Description:** Value engineers and analysts. Works to promote advancement of value engineering and value analysis and its application to the research, design, development, test, evaluation, engineering, production, purchasing and distribution phases in government, private industry, and commerce. Sponsors competitions. **Awards: Frequency:** annual. **Type:** recognition. **Recipient:** for members' contributions to the value profession. **Telecommunication Services:** electronic mail, bethanykf@state.gov. **Committees:** Awards and Professional Development; Historical. **Formerly:** (1997) Society of American Value Engineers. **Publications:** *Interactions*, monthly. Newsletter ● *Proceedings of the Annual Meeting*, annual ● *Value World*, quarterly. Journal ● Directory, annual. **Conventions/Meetings:** annual conference (exhibits).

7186 ■ SOLE - The International Society of Logistics (SOLE)

8100 Professional Pl., Ste.111
Hyattsville, MD 20785-2229
Ph: (301)459-8446
Fax: (301)459-1522
E-mail: solehq@erols.com
URL: http://www.sole.org
Contact: Sarah R. James, Exec. Dir.

Founded: 1966. **Members:** 8,000. **Membership Dues:** regular new, $140 ● regular, $130 (annual) ● retired new, $85 ● retired, young logistician, $75 (annual) ● student, $40 (annual). **Staff:** 4. **Budget:** $1,300,000. **Regional Groups:** 26. **Local Groups:** 150. **Multinational. Description:** Represents corporate and individual management and technical practitioners in the field of logistics, including scientists, engineers, educators, managers, and other specialists in commerce, aerospace, and other industries, government, and the military. (Logistics is the art and science of management engineering and technical activities concerned with requirements, and designing, supplying, and maintaining resources to support objectives, plans, and operations.) Covers every logistics specialty, including reliability, maintainability, systems and equipment maintenance, maintenance support equipment, human factors, training and training equipment, spare parts, overhaul and repair, handbooks, field site activation and operation, field engineering, facilities, packaging, supply chain management, materials handling, and transportation. Sponsors on-line job referral service; conducts specialized education programs. **Libraries: Type:** reference; by appointment only; open to the public. **Holdings:** books, periodicals. **Awards:** Eccles Medal. **Frequency:** annual. **Type:** medal. **Recipient:** for individual and institution with outstanding achievements in the development or administration of logistics education ● Field Awards. **Frequency:** annual. **Type:** recognition. **Recipient:** for outstanding services and contributions of individuals in specialty areas of the broad field of logistics ● **Frequency:** annual. **Type:** scholarship. **Recipient:** for individuals currently matriculating in logistics studies and/or related fields. **Committees:** Awards; Education. **Divisions:** Commercial Logistics Application; Defense Logistics Application; Event Logistics Application; Humanitarian and Disaster Relief Logistics Application; Medical Logistics Application; Space Logistics Application. **Formerly:** (1996) Society of Logistics Engineers. **Publications:** *Logistics Spectrum*, quarterly. Journal. Contains technical and non-technical articles for logisticians in industry, military, and education. Includes annual and advertisers indexes. **Price:** included in membership dues; $105.00 for nonmembers. ISSN: 0024-5852. **Circulation:** 10,500. **Advertising:** accepted ● *SOLEtech*, periodic. Newsletter. Includes profiles of current and new members, obituaries, and calendar of events. **Price:** free. ISSN: 0747-623X. **Circulation:** 10,500. **Advertising:** accepted. Alternate Formats: online ● Proceedings. **Conventions/Meetings:** periodic International Logistics Congress ● periodic workshop, three-day workshop for government and industry on logistics standards (exhibits) - in fall.

Information Management

7187 ■ Alliance of Information and Referral Systems (AIRS)

11240 Waples Mill Rd., Ste.200
Fairfax, VA 22030
Ph: (703)218-2477 (402)522-7930
Fax: (703)359-7562
E-mail: info@airs.org
URL: http://www.airs.org
Contact: Jamie Moore, Pres.

Founded: 1973. **Members:** 967. **Membership Dues:** basic, $50 (annual) ● enhanced, $500 (annual) ● standard (agency with budget less than $75,000), $250 (annual) ● standard (agency with budget over $75,000), $350 (annual) ● premium, $750 (annual). **Staff:** 4. **Budget:** $650,000. **Regional Groups:** 2. **State Groups:** 22. **Multinational. Description:** Information and referral service agencies that serve the public under the auspices of public libraries, United Way agencies, government, and independent nonprofit corporations. Aims to enhance standards of information and referral service delivery and to conduct national, regional, and state forums. Provides referral service. **Awards:** Distinguished Service Award. **Frequency:** annual. **Type:** recognition ● George McKinney Memorial Award. **Frequency:** annual. **Type:** scholarship. **Computer Services:** database, listing of information and referral services in the U.S. and Canada. **Telecommunication Services:** electronic mail, moayadzahralddin@airs.org. **Committees:** Accreditation; Advanced Technology; Certification; Marketing; Standards and Accreditation; State and Regional Associations. **Publications:** *Alliance of Information and Referral Systems—Newsletter*, bimonthly. **Circulation:** 1,000. **Advertising:** accepted ● *Information and Referral: The Journal of the AIRS*, annual. Covers practical and theoretical issues related to the impact of information and referral systems on the design and delivery of human services. **Price:** free to premium, enhanced, and standard members; $30.00 /year for nonmembers; $20.00/year for basic members. ISSN: 0278-2383 ● *Out of the Shadows*. Booklet. **Price:** $3.00 ● *Standards for Professional Information and Referral*. **Price:** $8.00 for members; $12.00 for nonmembers. **Con-**

ventions/Meetings: annual conference, education and training (exhibits).

7188 ■ American Society for Information Science and Technology (ASIS&T)
1320 Fenwick Ln., Ste.510
Silver Spring, MD 20910
Ph: (301)495-0900
Fax: (301)495-0810
E-mail: asis@asis.org
URL: http://www.asis.org
Contact: Richard B. Hill, Exec. Dir.
Founded: 1937. **Members:** 4,000. **Membership Dues:** individual, $140 (annual) ● student, $40 (annual) ● corporate patron, $800 (annual) ● institutional affiliate, $650 (annual) ● retired, $70 (annual). **Staff:** 6. **Budget:** $1,000,000. **Local Groups:** 26. **National Groups:** 21. **Description:** Information specialists, scientists, librarians, administrators, social scientists, and others interested in the use, organization, storage, retrieval, evaluation, and dissemination of recorded specialized information. Seeks to improve the information transfer process through research, development, application, and education. Provides a forum for the discussion, publication, and critical analysis of work dealing with the theory, practice, research, and development of elements involved in communication of information. Members are engaged in a variety of activities and specialties including classification and coding systems, automatic and associative indexing, machine translation of languages, special librarianship and library systems analysis, and copyright issues. Sponsors National Auxiliary Publications Service, which provides reproduction services and a central depository for all types of information. Maintains placement service. Sponsors numerous special interest groups. Conducts continuing education programs and professional development workshops. **Awards:** ASIST Award for Research in Information Science. **Frequency:** annual. **Type:** recognition. **Recipient:** for an outstanding research contribution in the field of information science ● Special Award. **Frequency:** periodic. **Type:** recognition. **Recipient:** for long term contributions of a government or industry leader to the advancement of information science and technology ● Student Chapter-of-the-Year Award. **Frequency:** annual. **Type:** recognition. **Recipient:** for outstanding student chapters. **Affiliated With:** American Library Association; National Information Standards Organization. **Formerly:** (1968) American Documentation Institute. **Publications:** *Annual Review of Information Science and Technology*, annual ● *Handbook and Directory*, annual ● *Jobline*, monthly ● *Journal of the American Society for Information Science and Technology*, monthly ● Bulletin, bimonthly. **Advertising:** accepted ● Monographs ● Proceedings, annual. **Conventions/Meetings:** semiannual conference (exhibits) - always fall ● annual meeting - always spring. 2008 Oct. 24-29, Columbus, OH; 2009 Nov. 6-9, Vancouver, BC, Canada.

7189 ■ Association of Information and Dissemination Centers (ASIDIC)
PO Box 3212
Maple Glen, PA 19002-8212
Ph: (215)654-9129
Fax: (215)654-9129
E-mail: info@asidic.org
URL: http://www.asidic.org
Contact: Donald Hawkins, Contact
Founded: 1968. **Members:** 85. **Membership Dues:** full, $495 (annual) ● associate, $250 (annual). **Staff:** 1. **Budget:** $25,000. **Description:** Information centers representing industry, government, and educational institutions in the United States and other countries. Members offer current awareness (selective dissemination of information) and/or retrospective searches processed by computer for databases from a variety of sources. Promotes applied technology of information storage and retrieval as related to large databases containing bibliographic, textual, and factual information; recommends standards for data elements, formats, and codes; promotes research and development for more efficient use of varied databases. Sponsors meetings, seminars, and workshops. Provides a forum for communication among information users and database suppliers and vendors. **Committees:** Executive; Planning; Program; Publications; Standards. **Formerly:** (1976) Association of Information and Dissemination Centers. **Publications:** *ASIDIC Newsletter*, semiannual. Contains meeting proceedings. **Price:** included in membership dues. **Circulation:** 115. **Conventions/Meetings:** semiannual conference - always spring and fall.

7190 ■ Association of Public Data Users (APDU)
c/o APB Associates
28300 Franklin Rd.
Southfield, MI 48034-1562
Ph: (248)354-6520
Fax: (248)354-6645
E-mail: info@apdu.org
URL: http://www.apdu.org
Contact: Patricia Becker, Admin.
Founded: 1975. **Members:** 350. **Membership Dues:** organizational (includes 3 representative), $375 (annual) ● group of 3 additional representative, $100 (annual) ● individual, $200 (annual). **Staff:** 2. **Description:** Academic institutions, private corporations, planning agencies, research institutes, and local, state, and federal governments; individuals. Purposes are: to facilitate the utilization of public data through sharing of information about files and applicable software, exchange of documentation, and joint purchasing of data; to increase knowledge of members concerning new sources of information; to increase the awareness of federal agencies of the needs of data users. **Working Groups:** Census Products; Survey of Income and Program Participation. **Publications:** *APDU Membership Directory*, annual. Describes member products, services, and areas of interest. **Price:** included in membership dues ● *APDU Newsletter*, 10/year. Offers articles focusing on the availability of public data in print and machine-readable formats. **Price:** included in membership dues. Alternate Formats: online ● *APDU Telephone Contacts for Federal Agencies with Significant Statistical Programs*, annual. Contains address and telephone list of federal agencies for users of public data. **Price:** included in membership dues. **Conventions/Meetings:** annual conference.

7191 ■ Coalition for Networked Information (CNI)
21 Dupont Cir., Ste.800
Washington, DC 20036
Ph: (202)296-5098
Fax: (202)872-0884
E-mail: info@cni.org
URL: http://www.cni.org
Contact: Dr. Clifford A. Lynch, Exec. Dir.
Founded: 1990. **Members:** 210. **Membership Dues:** institutional, $6,400 (annual). **Staff:** 6. **Description:** Joint project of the Association of Research Libraries and EDUCAUSE, that works to advance the transformative promise of networked information technology for the advancement of scholarly communication and the enrichment of intellectual productivity. **Awards:** Paul Evan Peters Award. **Frequency:** biennial. **Type:** recognition. **Recipient:** for achievements in the creation and innovative use of information resources and services ● Paul Evan Peters Fellowship. **Frequency:** annual. **Type:** fellowship. **Recipient:** for students pursuing graduate studies in the information sciences and librarianship. **Computer Services:** Mailing lists. **Telecommunication Services:** electronic mail, clifford@cni.org. **Conventions/Meetings:** semiannual Task Force Meetings - every spring and fall.

7192 ■ Council of Regional Information Technology Associations (CRITA)
50 Public Sq., Ste.200
Cleveland, OH 44113
Ph: (216)592-2295
E-mail: info@crita.org
URL: http://www.crita.org
Contact: Joan Myers, Pres./CEO
Membership Dues: association (based on annual budget), $360-$720 (annual). **Multinational. Description:** Facilitates information, visibility, networking, and services for information technology-focused, not-for-profit business organizations in the United States and Canada. Promotes and recognizes information technology issues affecting its members through sustained public relations efforts. Supports public policy consistent with sustained growth of IT-intensive industries. **Telecommunication Services:** electronic mail, jmyers@nc-tech.org.

7193 ■ Data Management Association International (DAMA)
19239 N Dale Mabry Hwy., No. 132
Lutz, FL 33548
Ph: (813)448-7786
Fax: (614)455-3138
E-mail: info@dama.org
URL: http://www.dama.org
Contact: Mr. John Schley, Pres.
Multinational. Description: Represents and promotes data resource management professionals. **Awards:** Academic Achievement Award. **Frequency:** annual. **Type:** recognition. **Recipient:** to a member of the academia for outstanding research or theoretical contributions in the area of IRM/DRM ● DAMA Community Award. **Frequency:** annual. **Type:** recognition. **Recipient:** to a member of the DAMA community who has gone beyond the call of volunteer service to enhance the efforts of providing exceptional benefits to the DAMA membership ● Government Achievement Award. **Frequency:** annual. **Type:** recognition. **Recipient:** to a member of the leadership populace for instituting the inclusion and adherence to DRM/IRM principles ● Professional Achievement Award. **Frequency:** annual. **Type:** recognition. **Recipient:** to a member from the industry (business, discipline, specialist) who has made significant, demonstrable contributions to the IRM/DRM. **Publications:** *DAMA News Bulletin*. Alternate Formats: online. **Conventions/Meetings:** conference ● annual symposium.

7194 ■ Electronic Privacy Information Center (EPIC)
1718 Connecticut Ave. NW, Ste.200
Washington, DC 20009
Ph: (202)483-1140
Fax: (202)483-1248
E-mail: rotenberg@epic.org
URL: http://www.epic.org
Contact: Marc Rotenberg, Pres./Exec. Dir.
Founded: 1994. **Staff:** 10. **Budget:** $1,000,000. **Description:** Interested individuals. Advocates for electronic privacy, free expression, public voice. Sponsors educational and research programs; compiles statistics; conducts litigation. **Libraries: Type:** reference. **Awards: Type:** recognition. **Computer Services:** Mailing lists ● online services, electronic library and archive. **Publications:** *EPIC Alert*, biweekly. Newsletter. Covers issues related to privacy and civil liberties in the information age. **Price:** free. Alternate Formats: online ● Reports ● Annual Report, annual. Alternate Formats: online ● Books. **Conventions/Meetings:** semiannual Technologies of Surveillance - conference.

7195 ■ Information Technology Professionals Association of America (ITPAA)
PO Box 7912
Wilmington, DE 19803
E-mail: info@itpaa.org
URL: http://www.itpaa.org
Contact: Scott Kirwin, Founder
Founded: 2003. **Description:** Aims to discuss, formulate, and pursue solutions for issues pertinent to information technology professionals. Works toward the following goals: 1. Encourages the employment of IT resources within the United States and its territories. 2. Works with companies to enhance profits and strengthen corporate ties to the United States by recognizing the efficiency, flexibility, intelligence and skills of the American IT professional. 3. Educates Americans on how outsourcing and government involvement in immigration through an "open door" policy "undermines the invisible hand of the market." 4. Assists and educates the public in the

organization's efforts to promote a vibrant and secure technology sector in the United States. 5. Stops the turning of IT professionals into "commodities.".

7196 ■ Institute for Computer Capacity Management (ICCM)

c/o Joanne Decker, Chief Financial Off.
9148 Bonita Beach Rd., Ste.210
Bonita Springs, FL 34135-4265
Ph: (239)261-8945
Fax: (239)261-5456
E-mail: sales@demandtech.com
URL: http://www.demandtech.com
Contact: Joanne Decker, Chief Financial Off.

Founded: 1975. **Members:** 110. **Staff:** 7. **Budget:** $650,000. **For-Profit. Description:** Assists industries, government agencies, and military installations in applying effective computer capacity management and performance techniques through specialized education courses, seminars, publications and a virtual community on the web. Maintains speakers' bureau. **Libraries: Type:** open to the public. **Holdings:** 6. **Subjects:** storage, Windows NT, DASD, RAID. **Computer Services:** Online services. **Telecommunication Services:** electronic mail, info@demandtech.com. **Publications:** *Capacity Planning & Alternative Platforms*. Report. **Price:** $75.00 ● *Capacity Planning Techniques and Experiences*. Report. **Price:** $75.00 ● *IS Performance/Capacity Management*. Proceedings. **Price:** $100.00 ● *Managing Customer Service*. Report. **Price:** $75.00 ● *Storage Management*. **Price:** $495.00/year in U.S.; $545.00/year outside U.S.

7197 ■ International Association for Information and Data Quality (IAIDQ)

19239 N Dale Mabry Hwy., No. 137
Lutz, FL 33548
Ph: (813)343-2163
E-mail: lisa.dodson@iaidq.org
URL: http://www.iaidq.org
Contact: Lisa Flint Dodson, Pres.

Founded: 2004. **Membership Dues:** professional, $25-$85 (annual) ● student, $25 (annual) ● corporate, $400-$1,600 (annual). **Multinational. Description:** Advances and improves information and data quality. Cultivates information excellence throughout the data and information lifecycle. Supports learning and sharing of knowledge among information consumers. **Publications:** Newsletter, quarterly. Alternate Formats: online.

7198 ■ International Society for Ethics and Information Technology (INSEIT)

c/o Philosophy Documentation Center
PO Box 7147
Charlottesville, VA 22906-7147
Ph: (414)229-3973
Fax: (414)229-6699
E-mail: inseit@sois.uwm.edu
URL: http://www.uwm.edu/Dept/SOIS/cipr/inseit.html
Contact: James H. Moor, Pres.

Founded: 2000. **Membership Dues:** student, $25 (annual) ● regular, $60 (annual). **Multinational. Description:** Promotes Information Technology (IT). Addresses ethical issues in and surrounding IT. Promotes and facilitates scholarship, education, discussion and debate, and other activities on the ethical issues about information technology. **Telecommunication Services:** electronic mail, james.h.moor@dartmouth.edu. **Publications:** *INSEIT Newletter*, quarterly. Newsletter. Alternate Formats: online.

7199 ■ International Society of Information Fusion (ISIF)

c/o Dr. Erik Blasch, Pres.
2393 Fieldstone Cir.
Fairborn, OH 45324
Ph: (937)255-2632
Fax: (937)255-1100
E-mail: erik.blasch@wpafb.af.mil
URL: http://www.isif.org
Contact: Dr. Erik Blasch, Pres.

Founded: 1998. **Members:** 500. **Membership Dues:** regular, $20 (annual) ● student, $10 (annual). **Staff:** 3. **Multinational. Description:** Dedicated to advancing the knowledge, theory and applications of information fusion. **Libraries: Type:** reference. **Holdings:** 6. **Subjects:** fusion. **Computer Services:** database, fusion information. **Publications:** *International Journal of Multisensor Information Fusion* ● *Journal of Advances in Information Fusion*, semiannual. Alternate Formats: online ● Proceedings, annual. Contains information from the Annual Conference on Information Fusion. **Conventions/Meetings:** annual FUSION - conference (exhibits) - 2008 June 30-July 3, Cologne, Germany ● Information, Decision and Control - conference, co-sponsored by ISIF and IEEE ● Multisensor Fusion and Integration for Intelligent Systems - conference ● Networked Control Systems and Sensor Fusion/Integrated Systems - symposium and convention (exhibits).

7200 ■ Ithaka

151 E 61st St.
New York, NY 10021
Ph: (212)500-2600
Fax: (212)500-2366
E-mail: info@ithaka.org
URL: http://www.ithaka.org
Contact: Paul A. Brest, Chm.

Founded: 2004. **Multinational. Description:** Seeks to accelerate the productive uses of information technologies for the benefit of higher education. Incubates projects with a goal of creating sustainable non-profit enterprises. Conducts research to support the cost recovery goals of affiliated entities and to inform the higher education community about the impact of electronic technologies. Provides administrative and technological services that can be shared by affiliated entities. Provides advisory services to organizations not directly affiliated with Ithaka. **Projects:** Aluka; E-Archive; NITLE.

7201 ■ Latinos in Information Sciences and Technology Association (LISTA)

500 W 37th St., 4th Fl.
New York, NY 10018
Ph: (347)632-4542
E-mail: info@a-lista.org
URL: http://www.a-lista.org
Contact: Jose A. Marquez Leon, Natl. Pres./CEO

Membership Dues: individual, $100 (annual). **Description:** Represents individuals committed to supporting Latinos who focus in Science, Mathematics, Information Sciences and Technology sectors. Promotes the utilization of these sectors for the empowerment of the Latino community. Facilitates communication and cooperation among members. **Publications:** *Punto y Aparte Newsletter*. Alternate Formats: online.

7202 ■ Media Resource Service (MRS)

PO Box 13975
Research Triangle Park, NC 27709
Ph: (919)547-5259
Free: (800)223-1730
Fax: (919)549-0090
E-mail: mediaresource@sigmaxi.org
URL: http://www.mediaresource.org
Contact: Martin Baucom, Contact

Founded: 1980. **Description:** Serves as program of SigmaXi, the Scientific Research Society (see separate entry). Provides free referral services to print, radio, television and online journalists in need of accurate information or expertise on scientific subjects. Maintains a web site with links to science stories of current interest as well as online scientific resources for journalists.

7203 ■ National Association for Public Health Information Technology (NAPHIT)

c/o Yvonne Claudio, Exec. Dir.
1 Res. Ct., Ste.450
Rockville, MD 20850-6222
Ph: (301)216-3825
Fax: (301)438-7681
E-mail: info@naphit.org
URL: http://www.naphit.org
Contact: David Taylor, Pres.

Founded: 2001. **Membership Dues:** student, $50 (annual) ● individual/consultant, health department individual (non-voting), $200 (annual) ● non-profit, $300 (annual) ● corporate (bronze level), $1,500 (annual) ● corporate (silver level), $3,000 (annual) ● corporate (gold and platinum level), $5,000-$1,000 (annual) ● state public health department (voting, with 3 members), $500 (annual) ● health department individual (voting), $200 (annual) ● local public health department (voting, based on members), $75-$500 (annual). **Description:** Provides a forum for leaders in public health information technology to exchange ideas and experiences, discuss and shape current public health information policy and learn about tools and technologies that help them better support public health. Aims to improve quality and reduce the costs of public health information systems and information technology. Promotes a strategic approach to managing information technology solutions that support public health programs. **Telecommunication Services:** electronic mail, yclaudio@naphit.org.

7204 ■ National Association of Regional Media Centers (NARMC)

Oneida Herkimer Co. BOCES
Box 70, Middle Settlement Rd.
New Hartford, NY 13413
Ph: (315)793-8566
Fax: (315)793-8652
E-mail: kford@oneida-boces.org
URL: http://www.oneida-boces.org
Contact: Kenneth M. Ford, Dir. of Information and Technology

Members: 299. **Regional Groups:** 3. **State Groups:** 16. **Description:** Regional media centers. Supports the goals of RMCs, which usually constitute statewide networks that provide instructional resources and services not technically or financially feasible at the individual system level. Acts as clearinghouse for information exchange in such areas as liaison with industry, state and national legislative programs, and financial patterns and structures; develops operational guidelines and standards in areas such as data collection and standardization, operational surveys, budget, quality criteria, and state reporting; establishes professional training and certification programs in areas such as professional guidelines, training sessions, workshops, seminars, work-study programs, accreditation, and certification. Promotes public and professional awareness of media functions; examines techniques to improve the efficiency and effectiveness of RMCs. Maintains library of brochures, reports, videotapes, slides, and booklets; compiles statistics. **Committees:** Clearinghouse; ESTAR/Photogard; Research Proposal. **Affiliated With:** Association for Educational Communications and Technology. **Publications:** *ETIN*, bimonthly ● *Highlights*, bimonthly. Contains state reports. ● *Regional Media Center Data File*, periodic ● Membership Directory, annual ● Also publishes brochures and project reports and has produced a film. **Conventions/Meetings:** annual conference, held in conjunction with AECT and International Communications Industries Association (exhibits).

7205 ■ National Federation of Abstracting and Information Services (NFAIS)

1518 Walnut St., Ste.1004
Philadelphia, PA 19102-3403
Ph: (215)893-1561
Fax: (215)893-1564
E-mail: nfais@nfais.org
URL: http://www.nfais.org
Contact: Bonnie Lawlor, Exec. Dir.

Founded: 1958. **Members:** 52. **Staff:** 3. **Budget:** $500,000. **Multinational. Description:** Represents major abstracting and indexing service organizations, online vendors, CD-ROM vendors, and related organizations. Aims to improve the extent and quality of the documentation and use of the world's literature through research programs, publications, and seminars. Works to develop communications, cooperation, and coordination among all segments of the information processing and dissemination community, including primary publishers, libraries, commercial and industrial abstracting and indexing services, data analysis centers, information dissemination centers, and people teaching or undertaking research in the abstracting and indexing field. Serves as a communication forum for its members through meetings, workshops, committee activities, and formal publications. Provides programs that are designed to: facilitate communication among members; conduct research projects useful to the abstracting and indexing community; provide educational programs for the information-science community; act as a collective voice for member services. Compiles statistics. **Awards:** Ann Marie Cunningham Memorial Award. **Frequency:** annual. **Type:** recognition. **Recipient:** for volunteer efforts on behalf of NFAIS ● Miles Conrad Memorial Lecturer Award. **Frequency:** annual. **Type:** recognition. **Telecommunication Services:** electronic mail, blawlor@nfais.org. **Boards:** Editorial Advisory. **Committees:** Best Practices; Conferences and Meetings; Information Policy; Library Education; Membership; PR and Marketing; Standards. **Roundtables:** Humanities. **Formerly:** (1972) National Federation of Science Abstracting and Indexing Services; (1982) National Federation of Abstracting and Indexing Services. **Publications:** *Beyond Boolean: New Approaches to Information Retrieval.* Reprint. **Price:** $75.00 ● *BIOSIS - Championing the Cause: The First 75 Years* ● *Careers in Electronic Information.* **Price:** $39.00 ● *Computer Support to Indexing.* **Price:** $235.00 ● *Customer Services and User Training.* **Price:** $50.00 ● *Document Delivery in an Electronic Age.* **Price:** $75.00 ● *Effective Exhibiting: A Practical Guide.* **Price:** $50.00 ● *Guide to Careers in Abstracting and Indexing.* **Price:** $29.00 ● *Guide to Database Distribution.* Handbook. **Price:** $75.00 ● *Impacts of Charging Production Technologies.* **Price:** $75.00 ● *Indexing and Searching in Perspective.* **Price:** $50.00 ● *Metadiversity: The Call for Community.* Proceedings. **Price:** $39.00 ● *NFAIS Newsletter*, bimonthly. Provides news and opinions on the information industry. Includes calendar of events, book reviews and profiles of individual organizations. **Price:** $120.00/year in U.S.; $135.00/year outside U.S. ISSN: 0090-0893. **Circulation:** 200 ● *Partnering in the Information Industry.* **Price:** $75.00 ● *Report Series*, periodic ● Handbooks ● Papers. **Conventions/Meetings:** annual conference.

7206 ■ National Information Standards Organization (NISO)

1 N Charles St., Ste.1905
Baltimore, MD 21201
Ph: (301)654-2512
Free: (866)957-1593
Fax: (301)654-1721
E-mail: nisohq@niso.org
URL: http://www.niso.org
Contact: Todd Carpenter, Managing Dir.

Founded: 1939. **Members:** 85. **Membership Dues:** voting (based on gross revenue/operating expenses), $1,325-$9,950 (annual) ● ARL library, $995 (annual) ● other library, $495 (annual). **Staff:** 2. **Budget:** $500,000. **Description:** Identifies, develops, maintains, and publishes technical standards to manage information in the changing environment used by libraries, publishers, and information services. Supports open access to NISO standards. Standards available at website. **Awards:** NISO Fellow. **Type:** recognition. **Computer Services:** Mailing lists, of members ● online services, NISO-L forum. **Committees:** Standards Development. **Affiliated With:** American National Standards Institute; International Organization for Standardization. **Formerly:** (1939) American National Standards Committee - Z39; (1984) National Information Standards Organization - Z39. **Publications:** *Information Standards Quarterly.* Newsletter. Includes reports on standards action; lists new members. **Price:** included in membership dues; $92.00 /year for nonmembers in U.S.; $134.00 /year for nonmembers outside U.S.; $40.00 for back issues. ISSN: 1041-0031. **Circulation:** 700 ● *National Information Standards Series*, periodic. Report. ISSN: 1041-5653 ● *Technical Report*, periodic. ISSN: 1081-8006. **Conventions/Meetings:** annual meeting ● workshop.

7207 ■ National MIS User Group (NUG)

c/o Mary Prolux, Chair
23 Bank St.
Lebanon, NH 03766
Ph: (603)520-5327
Fax: (727)545-7590
E-mail: mary.proulx@behvioralis.org
URL: http://www.nugmis.org
Contact: Mary Prolux, Chair

Description: Increases understanding and use of the CMHC software and other products. Promotes information exchange about CMHC products. Represents users in areas of common interest with CMHC and other vendors.

7208 ■ NiUG International (NiUG)

208 Eagle Valley Mall, No. 124
East Stroudsburg, PA 18301
Ph: (908)459-7889
Free: (866)301-NIUG
Fax: (775)257-1661
E-mail: membership@niug.org
URL: http://www.niug.org
Contact: David Cook, Pres.

Membership Dues: regular, $100 (annual) ● associate, $250 (annual). **Multinational. Description:** Advocates, educates, and connects users of the iMIS product. Represents users and voices out suggestions for improvements and changes in the iMIS product. Assists in implementing, troubleshooting, and maintaining iMIS installation. **Awards:** Great Things. **Type:** recognition. **Recipient:** to customers who demonstrate that they have used iMIS to achieve great things ● John Howarth Memorial. **Frequency:** annual. **Type:** recognition. **Recipient:** for outstanding contribution to iMIS community.

7209 ■ ODF Alliance

1090 Vermont Ave. NW, 6th Fl.
Washington, DC 20005
Ph: (202)789-4450
E-mail: info@odfalliance.org
URL: http://www.odfalliance.org
Contact: Marino Marcich, Managing Dir.

Founded: 2006. **Multinational. Description:** Enables the public sector to have greater control over and direct management of their own records, information and documents. Seeks to promote and advance the use of OpenDocument Format (ODF) as the primary document format for governments. Educates policymakers, IT administrators and the public on the benefits and opportunities of the OpenDocument Format. **Telecommunication Services:** electronic mail, mmarcich@odfalliance.org. **Publications:** Newsletter. Provides the latest developments concerning ODF from around the world. **Price:** free. Alternate Formats: online.

7210 ■ Panel on World Data Centers (WDC)

325 Broadway
Boulder, CO 80305
Fax: (303)497-6478
E-mail: susan.mclean@noaa.gov
URL: http://www.ngdc.noaa.gov/wdc/wdcmain.html
Contact: Susan McLean, Contact

Founded: 1968. **Description:** A committee of the International Council for Science. Seeks to insure efficient operation of scientific data centers worldwide.

7211 ■ Society of Competitive Intelligence Professionals (SCIP)

1700 Diagonal Rd., Ste.600
Alexandria, VA 22314
Ph: (703)739-0696
Fax: (703)739-2524
E-mail: info@scip.org
URL: http://www.scip.org
Contact: John L. Fiegel, Interim Exec. Dir.

Founded: 1986. **Members:** 7,000. **Membership Dues:** individual, $295 (annual) ● student, $25 (annual). **Staff:** 11. **Budget:** $2,500,000. **Local Groups:** 50. **Multinational. Description:** Acts as a forum for the exchange of news and ideas among professionals involved in competitive intelligence and analysis. Addresses legal and ethical concerns; provides opportunities for improving professional expertise. Conducts programs of interest to members. **Awards:** Catalyst Award. **Frequency:** annual. **Type:** recognition. **Recipient:** for important contributions to SCIP ● Faye Brill Award. **Frequency:** annual. **Type:** recognition. **Recipient:** for individuals who gave direct support to SCIP ● Fellows Award. **Frequency:** annual. **Type:** recognition. **Recipient:** for outstanding efforts to promote both the SCIP and the CI profession ● Meritorious Award. **Frequency:** annual. **Type:** recognition. **Recipient:** for meritorious contribution to the CI profession. **Telecommunication Services:** electronic mail, jfiegel@scip.org. **Formerly:** Society of Competitor Intelligence Professionals. **Publications:** *CI Review.* Journal. **Price:** $10.00 for members ● *Competitive Intelligence Magazine*, bimonthly ● *Journal of Competitive Intelligence and Management*, quarterly. Includes publication reviews. **Price:** included in membership dues. ISSN: 1040-9645. **Circulation:** 4,000. **Advertising:** accepted. Alternate Formats: online ● *SCIP Online*, biweekly. Newsletter. **Advertising:** accepted. Alternate Formats: online ● *SCIP.ORG In-box*, weekly. Newsletter. **Price:** included in membership dues. **Advertising:** accepted. Alternate Formats: online ● Audiotape ● Books ● Monographs ● Proceedings ● Also publishes proceedings documents and books. **Conventions/Meetings:** annual conference (exhibits).

7212 ■ Special Interest Group on Information Retrieval (SIGIR)

c/o Elizabeth D. Liddy, Chair
Syracuse Univ.
School of Info. Stud.
Center for Natural Language Processing
335 Hinds Hall
Syracuse, NY 13210
Ph: (315)443-5484
E-mail: chair_sigir@acm.org
URL: http://www.sigir.org
Contact: Elizabeth D. Liddy, Chair

Founded: 1966. **Members:** 1,845. **Membership Dues:** basic, $30 (annual) ● student, $15 (annual). **Description:** Serves as a special interest group of the Association for Computing Machinery (see separate entry). Represents computer professionals interested in information storage and retrieval. Promotes research; sponsors educational programs. **Publications:** *SIGIR Forum*, 3/year. Newsletter. Alternate Formats: online. **Conventions/Meetings:** annual international conference.

7213 ■ Technology Resource Consortium (TRC)

Address Unknown since 2007

Founded: 1987. **National Groups:** 1. **Description:** An affinity group of the Alliance for Nonprofit Management providing education about and access to information technology to private and public nonprofit organizations. Promotes increased awareness of, and access to, information technologies. Facilitates collaboration among members; encourages the formation of new technology assistance provider services; works to improve members' ability to support "the effective use of information technology by nonprofit organizations and government agencies.".

7214 ■ Unicorn Users Group International (UUGI)

c/o Old Colony Library Network
220 Forbes Rd., Ste.401
Braintree, MA 02184
E-mail: exec@uugi.org
URL: http://www.uugi.org
Contact: Mark J. Andrews, Chm.

Membership Dues: regular, $100 (annual). **Multinational. Description:** Educates and assists current and potential users of Unicorn information management systems. Disseminates and exchanges information about Unicorn information management systems. Provides information and recommendations for the future development of Sirsi Corporation.

7215 ■ Urban and Regional Information Systems Association (URISA)

1460 Renaissance Dr., Ste.305
Park Ridge, IL 60068
Ph: (847)824-6300
Fax: (847)824-6363

E-mail: info@urisa.org
URL: http://www.urisa.org
Contact: Susan Johnson, Pres.
Founded: 1963. **Members:** 3,000. **Membership Dues:** professional, $187 (annual) ● corporate, $2,500 (annual) ● student, $25 (annual) ● business, $625 (annual). **Staff:** 9. **Budget:** $1,400,000. **Regional Groups:** 24. **Description:** Represents professionals using Geographic Information Systems (GIS) and other information technologies to solve challenges in state and local government agencies. Produces a number of educational conferences and publications. **Awards:** Barbara Hirsch Special Service Award. **Frequency:** periodic. **Type:** recognition. **Recipient:** for members or staff who have made special contributions ● Exemplary Systems in Government. **Frequency:** annual. **Type:** recognition ● Horwood Distinguished Service Award. **Frequency:** periodic. **Type:** recognition. **Recipient:** for significant contributions ● Leadership Award. **Frequency:** annual. **Type:** recognition. **Recipient:** for members who have demonstrated creativity, innovation and dedicated support of programs ● Outstanding Chapter Award. **Frequency:** annual. **Type:** recognition. **Recipient:** for a chapter that has sponsored particularly effective activities ● Service Award. **Frequency:** annual. **Type:** recognition. **Recipient:** for members who have demonstrated faithful service. **Computer Services:** database, chapter leaders ● online services, virtual exhibit. **Publications:** *Conference Proceedings*, annual. **Circulation:** 4,000. **Advertising:** accepted. Alternate Formats: CD-ROM ● *URISA Journal*, quarterly. **Price:** $295.00 /year for libraries; free for members ● *URISA Marketplace*, monthly. Contains classified job listings. ● *URISA News*, bimonthly. Newsletter. **Conventions/Meetings:** biennial Caribbean GIS - regional meeting ● annual conference (exhibits) ● annual Geospatial Integration for Public Safety - conference ● annual Integrating GIS and CAMA - conference ● biennial IT/GIS in Public Works - conference ● annual Public Participation GIS - conference.

7216 ■ Zangle National Users' Group (ZNUG)
c/o John Getchell, Treas.
4653 Majestic Dr.
Bellingham, WA 98226
E-mail: treasurer@znug.org
URL: http://znug.org
Contact: Mike Webben, Pres.
Description: Helps schools, districts, and other agencies with the use of the Zangle Student Information Software. Promotes information exchange about Zangle Student Information Software. Represents users in areas of common interest with Zangle Student Information Software.

Innovation

7217 ■ Engineering and Science Network on Thinking (ESNETT)
154 Hamilton Blvd.
Struthers, OH 44471-1446
Ph: (330)755-2710
Contact: David L. Diciccio, Exec. Dir.
Founded: 1988. **Staff:** 4. **Description:** Engineers, scientists, technicians, and others interested in the development and application of creative thinking, problem-solving, and idea presentation skills in engineering and science. Acts as a clearinghouse for programs and instructional materials. Conducts research and educational programs. **Publications:** *Thinking Changes*, 5/year. Journal. Includes case studies of creative thinking and problem-solving in engineering and science and descriptions of thinking tools and techniques. **Price:** included in membership dues; $10.00/issue for nonmembers. **Advertising:** accepted. **Conventions/Meetings:** annual workshop - always late June.

7218 ■ National Collegiate Inventors and Innovators Alliance (NCIIA)
100 Venture Way, 3rd Fl.
Hadley, MA 01035
Ph: (413)587-2172
Fax: (413)587-2175
E-mail: info@nciia.org
URL: http://www.nciia.org
Contact: Philip J. Weilerstein, Exec. Dir.
Founded: 1995. **Members:** 200. **Membership Dues:** college, $300 (annual) ● university, $500 (annual). **Description:** Supports and encourages invention, innovation and entrepreneurship education at institutions of higher learning throughout the United States. Offers resources and provides networking opportunities to members. **Awards:** **Frequency:** semiannual. **Type:** grant. **Recipient:** to institutions for the purpose of strengthening existing programs ● **Frequency:** semiannual. **Type:** grant. **Recipient:** for E-Teams needing support for an innovative product or prototype. **Computer Services:** Online services, NCIIA resources. **Publications:** *NCIIA News*, semiannual. Newsletter. Alternate Formats: online.

Instrumentation

7219 ■ IEEE Instrumentation and Measurement Society (IMS)
c/o Ruth A. Dyer, PhD, VP of Membership
Kansas State Univ.
106 Anderson Hall
Manhattan, KS 66506
Ph: (785)532-6224
Fax: (785)532-6507
E-mail: rdyer@ksu.edu
URL: http://www.ieee-ims.org/site/index.php
Contact: Ruth A. Dyer PhD, VP of Membership
Founded: 1950. **Members:** 6,100. **Membership Dues:** individual in U.S., $167 (annual) ● individual outside U.S., $156 (annual) ● individual (in Europe, Middle East, and Africa), $144 (annual) ● individual (in Latin America), $137 (annual) ● individual (in Asia and Pacific), $138 (annual). **Staff:** 2. **Budget:** $500,000. **Local Groups:** 14. **Description:** Serves as society of the Institute of Electrical and Electronics Engineers. Studies measurement and instrumentation utilizing electrical and electronic techniques. **Awards:** IEEE Joseph F. Keithley Award in Instrumentation and Measurement. **Frequency:** annual. **Type:** recognition. **Recipient:** for fundamental contributions to electrical measurements, with particular emphasis on the development of impedance bridges and standards, and the application of microprocessors to impedance measurement science ● Instrumentation and Measurement Society Award. **Frequency:** annual. **Type:** recognition. **Recipient:** for outstanding contributions to the theory and practice of robot sensing and perception ● Instrumentation and Measurement Society Award Young Engineer Award. **Frequency:** annual. **Type:** recognition. **Recipient:** for studies on robustness and application level synthesis of embedded information processing systems. **Publications:** *Instrumentation and Measurement*, quarterly. Magazine. **Advertising:** accepted. Alternate Formats: online ● *Sensors Journal*, bimonthly. Alternate Formats: online ● *Transactions on Instrumentation and Measurement*, quarterly. Alternate Formats: online. **Conventions/Meetings:** annual conference.

7220 ■ ISA - Instrumentation, Systems, and Automation Society
c/o Mr. Pat Gouhin, Exec. Dir.
67 Alexander Dr.
PO Box 12277
Research Triangle Park, NC 27709
Ph: (919)549-8411
Fax: (919)549-8288
E-mail: info@isa.org
URL: http://www.isa.org
Contact: Mr. Thad S. Lee, Dir.
Founded: 1945. **Members:** 30,000. **Membership Dues:** regular, $85 (annual) ● student, $10 (annual) ● virtual student, $5 (annual). **Staff:** 70. **Budget:** $13,000,000. **Regional Groups:** 13. **Local Groups:** 180. **Multinational. Description:** Sets the standard for automation by helping over 30,000 worldwide members and other professionals solve difficult technical problems, while enhancing their leadership and personal career capabilities. Develops standards; certifies industry professionals; provides education and training; publishes books and technical articles; and hosts the largest conference and exhibition for automation professionals in the Western Hemisphere. Is the founding sponsor of The Automation Federation. **Libraries: Type:** not open to the public. **Holdings:** 2,500. **Subjects:** automation, measurement, control topics. **Awards:** Albert F. Sperry Founder Award. **Frequency:** annual. **Type:** monetary. **Recipient:** for outstanding technical, educational, or philosophical contributions to science and technology ● Arnold O. Beckman Founder Award. **Frequency:** annual. **Type:** monetary. **Recipient:** for significant technological contributions to conception and implementation of a new principle of design, development, or application ● Distinguished Society Service Award. **Frequency:** annual. **Type:** recognition. **Recipient:** for long standing devoted service and contributions to the ISA ● Donald P. Eckman Education Award. **Frequency:** annual. **Type:** monetary. **Recipient:** for contributions to education and training in science, engineering, and technology ● Douglas H. Annin Award. **Frequency:** annual. **Type:** monetary. **Recipient:** for outstanding achievements in design or development of an automatic control system ● E.G. Bailey Award. **Frequency:** annual. **Type:** monetary. **Recipient:** for excellence in design, development, or application in instrumentation and control systems in utilities and process control industries ● Excellence in Documentation Award. **Frequency:** annual. **Type:** monetary. **Recipient:** for an outstanding article, paper, or document published by the ISA ● Golden Achievement Award. **Frequency:** annual. **Type:** recognition. **Recipient:** for long, dedicated service to the ISA ● Honorary Member. **Frequency:** annual. **Type:** recognition. **Recipient:** for contributions to arts and science of instrumentation ● Section Performance Award. **Frequency:** annual. **Type:** monetary. **Recipient:** for recognized achievement within the section recognition program or for outstanding accomplishment in a particular area of section activity ● Standards and Practices Award. **Frequency:** annual. **Type:** monetary. **Recipient:** for outstanding contributions to the ISA S&P program ● UOP Technology Award. **Frequency:** annual. **Type:** monetary. **Recipient:** for contribution to instrumentation and/or control in one or more of the technological areas included in the scope of the Society's Automation and Technology Department. **Departments:** Automation and Technology; Industries and Sciences. **Divisions:** Aerospace Industries; Analysis; Automatic Control Systems; Chemical and Petroleum Industries; Computer Technology; Construction/Design; Food and Pharmaceutical Industries; Glass and Ceramics; Management; Mining and Metals Industries; Power Industry; Process Measurement and Control; Pulp and Paper Industry; Robotics and Expert Systems; Safety; Telemetry and Communications; Test Measurement; Textile; Water and Waste Water Industries. **Formerly:** Instrument Society of America; (1939) American Society of Instrument Engineers; (1944) American Society for Measurement Control. **Publications:** *InTech*, monthly. Journal. Provides practical technology information for automation professionals in all industries. **Price:** included in membership dues; $90.00 /year for nonmembers. ISSN: 0192-303X. **Circulation:** 70,000. **Advertising:** accepted. Alternate Formats: microform; online ● *ISA Directory of Automation*, annual. Lists over 2,400 manufacturers and over 1,000 manufacturers representatives and services. Includes product specifications and trade names. **Price:** included in membership dues; $100.00/copy for nonmembers. ISSN: 0272-8141. **Circulation:** 42,000. **Advertising:** accepted. Alternate Formats: online; CD-ROM ● *ISA Transactions*, annual. Annual Reports. Contains transactions of papers on instrumentation and measurement in control engineering. **Price:** $39.00 for members; $49.00 for nonmembers; $335.00 for institutions in U.S. ISSN: 0019-0578 ● *Standards and Practices for Automation*, annual. Annual Reports. Contains industry practices for automation technologies and applications. Alternate Formats: CD-ROM ● Books. Lists over 100 titles available on measurement and control topics. ● Videos. **Conventions/Meetings:** annual convention, for automation professionals to see new technology and applications (exhibits).

Insurance

7221 ■ National InStar Users Group (NIUG)
PO Box 41368
Raleigh, NC 27629
Free: (800)549-2515
E-mail: hq@instarusers.org
URL: http://www.instarusers.org
Contact: Elaine Christian, Exec. Dir.
Membership Dues: agency, $180 (annual). **Description:** Promotes the efficient and productive use of InStar insurance agency management software. Provides evaluation of day-to-day InStar software operations. Gives networking opportunities and exchange of information with other users. **Publications:** Newsletter. Contains information about upcoming events, important issues, trips and tricks about InStar software. Alternate Formats: online. **Conventions/ Meetings:** annual conference.

Internet

7222 ■ Web Analytics Association (WAA)
2300 M St., Ste.800
Washington, DC 20037
Free: (800)349-1070
E-mail: info@webanalyticsassociation.org
URL: http://www.webanalyticsassociation.org
Contact: Bryan Eisenberg, Chm.
Membership Dues: academic, $39 (annual) ● professional, $129 (annual) ● premier corporation (based on annual sales), $2,500-$5,000 (annual). **Description:** Fosters the interests of industry practitioners, vendors, consultants and educators who use, sell, install, implement, consult, teach or train in the field of web analytics. Seeks to advance the study of web analytics through educational programs and research. Provides networking opportunities to members. **Publications:** Newsletter, monthly. **Price:** included in membership dues. Alternate Formats: online.

Interspecies Communication

7223 ■ Interspecies
301 Hidden Meadow
Friday Harbor, WA 98250
E-mail: beluga@interspecies.com
URL: http://www.interspecies.com
Contact: Jim Nollman, Dir.
Founded: 1978. **Members:** 1,000. **Membership Dues:** $35 (annual). **Budget:** $50,000. **Multinational. Description:** Sponsors artists to interact with wilderness and nature. Develops techniques for communication between humans and other animals. Conducts research with scientists and artists to better determine the potential for communication between humans and animals. Methods of communication have been mainly acoustic and musical. Sponsors design and construction of underwater acoustical research equipment. Conducts annual Orca Project and Beluga Peace Project. Maintains Speaker's Bureau. **Libraries: Type:** reference. **Subjects:** human/animal communication, shamanism, cetaceans. **Formerly:** (2001) Interspecies Communication. **Publications:** *The Beluga Cafe, The Charged Border.* Book. **Price:** $18.00 ● *The Interspecies DVD.* Video. **Price:** $20.00. Alternate Formats: CD-ROM ● *The Interspecies Newsletter*, quarterly. Includes book reviews, research updates, and articles on philosophy. **Price:** included in membership dues. **Circulation:** 500 ● *Orca's Greatest Hits.* **Price:** $18.00 plus shipping and handling. Alternate Formats: CD-ROM.

Inventors

7224 ■ Affiliated Inventors Foundation (AIF)
Address Unknown since 2007
Founded: 1975. **Members:** 400. **Staff:** 3. **Budget:** $300,000. **Description:** Offers encouragement and assistance to independent inventors. Supplies members with sufficient information on each phase of their invention. Provides free information and low-cost attorney. **Affiliated With:** Technology Transfer Society.

7225 ■ American Association of Inventors (AAI)
2309 State St.
Saginaw, MI 48602
Ph: (989)793-5319 (989)692-0780
Fax: (989)793-9280
E-mail: denlin310@cs.com
Contact: Dennis Ray Martin, Pres.
Founded: 1879. **Members:** 12,803. **Membership Dues:** general, $45 (annual). **Staff:** 12. **Budget:** $91,000. **Regional Groups:** 8. **State Groups:** 43. **Local Groups:** 379. **National Groups:** 28. **For-Profit. Multinational. Description:** Founded by Richard Jordan Gatling (inventor of the Gatling Gun) in 1879. Membership includes education by patent attorneys and patent agents and related professionals. Seminars are designed to assist inventors in patent process, best practices and cutting edge solutions, featuring critical topics of patent law information, and providing skills needed to succeed and protect the patent application. Provides a unique networking opportunity, lessons and experiences, loans (including small business loans), investors, and grants. **Libraries: Type:** open to the public. **Holdings:** 988; articles, books, periodicals. **Subjects:** annual survey - 30 questions of varying complexity, helping AAI hear from leaders in your field who will tell you what to expect. **Awards:** Golden Eagle Award. **Frequency:** annual. **Type:** monetary ● Inventor of the Year. **Frequency:** annual. **Type:** monetary. **Recipient:** for an individual who has contributed a significant invention that has helped fellow men, the United States of America, and is a vital contribution to the country. **Computer Services:** database ● online services. **Subgroups:** Regional. **Publications:** *Modern Inventor*, bimonthly. Newsletter. Reader service. **Price:** included in membership dues. **Circulation:** 12,803. **Advertising:** accepted. Alternate Formats: CD-ROM; online; magnetic tape. **Conventions/Meetings:** annual American Assembly of Inventors - convention and workshop (exhibits).

7226 ■ American Society of Inventors (ASI)
PO Box 58426
Philadelphia, PA 19102
Ph: (215)546-6601
E-mail: info@asoi.org
URL: http://www.asoi.org
Contact: Henry Skillman, Treas.
Founded: 1953. **Members:** 150. **Membership Dues:** individual, $49 (annual). **Budget:** $3,000. **Local Groups:** 1. **Description:** Engineers, scientists, businessmen, and others who are interested in a cooperative effort to serve both the short- and long-term needs of the inventor and society. Works with government and industry to improve the environment for the inventor. Aims to encourage invention and innovation; help the independent inventor become self-sufficient. Establishes a networking system for inventors and businessmen to solve problems. Sponsors educational programs. **Affiliated With:** United Inventors Association of the U.S.A. **Publications:** *ASI Informer*, bimonthly. Newsletter. Includes calendar of events. **Price:** included in membership dues. **Circulation:** 200 ● *Inventors Digest*, annual. Magazine. **Price:** $27.00 for members. **Conventions/Meetings:** bimonthly meeting - every third Wednesday.

7227 ■ Invent America! (IA)
PO Box 26065
Alexandria, VA 22313
Ph: (703)942-7121
Fax: (703)461-0068
E-mail: inquiries@inventamerica.org
URL: http://www.inventamerica.org
Contact: Nancy Metz, Exec. Dir.
Founded: 1984. **Description:** Aims to stimulate American inventiveness and productivity. Seeks to enhance public awareness of American inventions, both past and present. Works to recover many patent models of the 19th century, most of which were sold at public auction by the U.S. Patent Office in 1925; plans to donate these models to the Smithsonian Institution. (Patent models are working replicas of devices for which patents are sought.) Provides training seminars for teachers involved in the program. Develops curriculum materials. Compiles statistics. **Awards:** Invent America! Student Invention Contest. **Frequency:** annual. **Type:** monetary. **Recipient:** for the best invention based on creativity, usefulness, illustration, communication of ideas and research performed. **Formerly:** (1989) U.S. Patent Model Foundation. **Publications:** *Invent America! Creative Resource Guide* ● Newsletter, quarterly. **Conventions/Meetings:** annual conference (exhibits) ● Educational Conference - meeting - 3/year.

7228 ■ Inventors Assistance League (IAL)
1053 Colorado Blvd.
Los Angeles, CA 90041
Ph: (818)246-6546
Free: (877)433-2246
Fax: (818)244-1882
E-mail: rustyr@earthlink.net
URL: http://www.inventions.org
Contact: Rusty Ruscetta, Dir. of Operations
Founded: 1963. **Members:** 6,942. **Budget:** $60,000. **Description:** Inventors and manufacturers. Helps inventors get their products into the marketplace and assists manufacturers in finding new products to make and market. Brings together inventors and manufacturers for mutual benefit. Maintains speakers' bureau, small museum, and hall of fame. **Libraries: Type:** reference. **Holdings:** 1,600. **Affiliated With:** National Inventors Foundation. **Formerly:** (1993) Invention Marketing Institute. **Publications:** *Inventor's Advisory.* Report. **Price:** free for members.

7229 ■ Inventors Clubs of America (ICA)
524 Curtis Rd.
East Lansing, MI 48823
Ph: (517)332-3561
Fax: (404)846-0980
Contact: Carl Preston, Contact
Founded: 1935. **Members:** 6,000. **Membership Dues:** full, $200 (annual) ● associate, $50 (annual). **Staff:** 3. **Budget:** $50,000. **Regional Groups:** 4. **Local Groups:** 1. **Description:** Clubs of inventors, scientists, manufacturers, and others involved in problem-solving and inventing. Stimulates inventiveness and helps inventors in all phases of their work, including patenting, development, manufacturing, marketing, and advertising. Seeks to prevent abuses of the individual inventor, such as theft of ideas. Works to create new industry and lower the tax rate. Conducts research and educational programs. Sponsors children's services and professional training. Resources include international hall of fame and museum. Operates charitable program and speakers' bureau. **Libraries: Type:** reference. **Holdings:** archival material. **Awards:** International Hall of Fame Awards. **Frequency:** annual. **Type:** recognition. **Recipient:** for inventions, entrepreneurs, arts, technical. **Computer Services:** database. **Committees:** Evaluation; Financial Aid; Marketing. **Publications:** *How to Keep a Journal.* **Price:** included in membership dues ● *How to Protect an Idea Before Patent* ● *How to Shape an Idea Into an Invention* ● *Inventors News*, monthly. Newsletter. **Price:** available to members only. **Circulation:** 6,000. **Advertising:** accepted ● *Mistakes Inventors Make.* **Conventions/Meetings:** annual International Hall of Fame Awards - competition and seminar, to honor inventors, entrepreneurs, related creative projects (art, music, etc.) for community services (exhibits) - first weekend in May.

7230 ■ National Congress of Inventors Organizations (NCIO)
8306 Wilshire Blvd., Ste.391
Beverly Hills, CA 90211
Ph: (323)878-6952
E-mail: ncio@inventionconvention.com
URL: http://inventionconvention.com/ncio
Contact: Stephen Paul Gnass, Exec. Dir.
Founded: 1982. **Members:** 63. **Membership Dues:** regular, $200. **Staff:** 6. **Regional Groups:** 57. **State Groups:** 20. **Local Groups:** 1. **Description:** Repre-

sents inventors' groups. Coordinates information relating to inventor education and programs such as wanted and available inventions and credible organizations offering development and marketing assistance. Offers children's services and educational programs. Maintains speakers' bureau. **Libraries: Type:** reference. **Holdings:** books. **Subjects:** invention, innovation, marketing, idea development and protection. **Committees:** Educational; High Tech; Publicity; Young Students. **Publications:** *America's Inventor*, quarterly. Newsletter. **Price:** $200.00/year. **Circulation:** 250 ● *How to Determine Royalty Fees* ● *NCIO Bulletin*, periodic ● *NCIO Membership Directory*, annual ● *NCIO Newsletter*, quarterly ● *NCIO Proceedings*, annual ● *Successful Inventing*. Book. **Conventions/Meetings:** competition ● National Innovation Workshop, held in conjunction with National Bureau of Standards.

7231 ■ National Inventors Foundation (NIF)
c/o Inventors Assistance League
1053 Colorado Blvd.
Los Angeles, CA 90041
Ph: (818)246-6546
Free: (877)433-2246
Fax: (818)244-1882
E-mail: rustyr@earthlink.net
URL: http://www.inventions.org
Contact: Ted DeBoer, Founder/Pres.

Founded: 1963. **Members:** 10,071. **Staff:** 17. **Budget:** $300,000. **Regional Groups:** 2. **Local Groups:** 1. **National Groups:** 2. **Description:** Independent inventors united to educate individuals regarding the protection and promotion of inventions and new products. Instructs potential inventors on patent laws and how to protect their inventions through methods developed by the foundation. Teaches advertising, sales and marketing techniques to get ideas into the marketplace to determine their commercial value. Assists individuals throughout the U.S. and in 44 other countries. Maintains speakers' bureau, hall of fame, and museum. **Convention/Meeting:** none. **Libraries: Type:** not open to the public. **Holdings:** 1,800. **Subjects:** patents, copyrights, trademarks, sales, advertising and marketing. **Affiliated With:** Inventors Assistance League. **Publications:** *Advisory* (in English, Russian, and Spanish), quarterly. Newsletter. **Price:** free. **Circulation:** 9,000.

7232 ■ United Inventors Association of the U.S.A. (UIAUSA)
c/o Carol Oldenburg, Admin.
999 Lehigh Sta. Rd.
Henrietta, NY 14467
Ph: (585)359-9310
Fax: (585)359-1132
E-mail: uiausa@aol.com
URL: http://www.uiausa.org
Contact: Carol Oldenburg, Admin.

Founded: 1990. **Members:** 3,000. **Membership Dues:** individual in U.S., $97 (annual) ● group in U.S., $225 (annual) ● professional, $325 (annual). **Staff:** 2. **Local Groups:** 60. **Description:** Inventors' organizations and providers of services to inventors. Seeks to facilitate the development of innovation conceived by independent inventors. Provides leadership and support services to inventors and inventors' organizations; makes available referral services. **Telecommunication Services:** electronic mail, bgkaake@biz-consult.com. **Affiliated With:** Academy of Applied Science. **Publications:** *The Inventor's Journal*. Book ● *The Inventor's Master Plan*. Book ● *Inventors' Resource Guide*, periodic. Booklet ● *Starting a Group for Inventors*. Book ● Newsletter, monthly. **Advertising:** accepted. **Conventions/Meetings:** bimonthly board meeting.

Irrigation

7233 ■ International Network on Participatory Irrigation Management (INPIM)
333 1/2 Pennsylvania Ave. SE, 3rd Fl.
Washington, DC 20003
Ph: (202)546-7005
Fax: (202)318-0215
E-mail: info@inpim.org
URL: http://www.inpim.org
Contact: Mr. Salah Darghouth, Chm.

Founded: 1995. **Members:** 1,000. **Multinational. Description:** Seeks to make irrigation systems sustainable by supporting institutional reforms that promote greater involvement and increased capacity of farmers, water users associations and other private stakeholders. Acts as the central resource center for participatory irrigation management. **Computer Services:** Online services, discussion forums. **Programs:** Capacity Building. **Publications:** Newsletter. Alternate Formats: online.

Laboratory

7234 ■ American Association for Laboratory Accreditation (A2LA)
5301 Buckeystown Pike., Ste.350
Frederick, MD 21704
Ph: (301)644-3248 (301)644-3212
Fax: (301)662-2974
E-mail: info@a2la.org
URL: http://www.a2la.org
Contact: Peter Unger, Pres.

Founded: 1978. **Members:** 500. **Membership Dues:** individual, $50 (annual) ● organizational, $200 (annual) ● institutional, $100 (annual). **Staff:** 30. **Budget:** $6,000,000. **Description:** Represents individuals, associations, corporations, universities, laboratories, research institutes and government agencies interested in improving the quality of laboratories. Accredits testing laboratories, certifies laboratory reference materials and registers quality systems. **Computer Services:** database, accredited laboratories ● database, suspensions and withdrawals ● mailing lists, of members. **Programs:** Accreditation for Reference Material Producers; Inspection Body Accreditation; Laboratory Testing; Proficiency Testing Provider. **Publications:** *A2LA Directory*, annual. Lists laboratories accredited and laboratories registered by the association. **Price:** $40.00. ISSN: 1040-9181. **Circulation:** 3,000 ● *A2LA News*, bimonthly. Newsletter. Lists recent accreditations, registrations and summarizing association activities. **Price:** free. ISSN: 1040-9157. Alternate Formats: online ● Annual Report, annual. **Price:** free. ISSN: 1043-0121. Alternate Formats: online. **Conventions/Meetings:** annual meeting ● seminar, covers quality assurance and laboratory assessment.

7235 ■ American Board of Bioanalysis (ABB)
906 Olive St., Ste.1200
St. Louis, MO 63101-1434
Ph: (314)241-1445
Fax: (314)241-1449
E-mail: abb@abbcert.org
URL: http://www.aab.org/abb%20home%20page.htm

Founded: 1968. **Membership Dues:** sustaining, $1,000 (annual) ● supporting, $350 (annual) ● owner, director, $225 (annual) ● affiliate, $100 (annual) ● manager, supervisor, $75 (annual) ● student, $35 (annual). **Description:** Certifying agency consisting of scientists, educators, and recognized authorities in the clinical laboratory field. Certifies clinical laboratory directors at two levels depending on qualifications, including High Complexity or Moderate Complexity Clinical Laboratory Director. Also certifies Technical Consultants, two levels of supervisor (Technical and General), and Bioanalyst Laboratory Manager (BLM). **Affiliated With:** American Association of Bioanalysts. **Formerly:** (2004) American Board of Bioanalysts.

7236 ■ American Council of Independent Laboratories (ACIL)
1629 K St. NW, Ste.400
Washington, DC 20006-1633
Ph: (202)887-5872
Fax: (202)887-0021
E-mail: info@acil.org
URL: http://www.acil.org
Contact: Eddie Van Aken, Deputy Dir./Acting Exec. Dir.

Founded: 1937. **Members:** 350. **Membership Dues:** corporate regular (based on annual revenues), $725-$9,000 (annual) ● corporate new (based on annual revenues), $365-$4,500 ● adjunct, associate, affiliate (based on number of employees), $500-$1,000 (annual). **Staff:** 8. **Budget:** $1,000,000. **Regional Groups:** 4. **Description:** Independent firms doing testing, certification, scientific analysis, inspection and applied research for manufacturers, insurance and financial companies, importers and exporters, architects, engineers and the federal government. Promotes the interests of independent laboratories and quality testing services. **Libraries: Type:** reference. **Holdings:** books, clippings, periodicals. **Subjects:** management, trade. **Awards:** ACIL Scholarship. **Frequency:** annual. **Type:** scholarship. **Recipient:** for college juniors majoring in engineering or sciences practiced by member companies ● Lewis E. Harris Fellow Award. **Frequency:** periodic. **Type:** recognition. **Recipient:** for outstanding contributions to the organization and to the industry ● Preston Millar Award. **Frequency:** annual. **Type:** recognition. **Recipient:** for individuals who have made special contributions to the success of the association over the past years ● Roger Truesdail Award for Outstanding Service. **Frequency:** annual. **Type:** recognition. **Recipient:** for significant contributions to the betterment of the independent scientific, engineering and testing community. **Computer Services:** Online services, searchable directory. **Telecommunication Services:** electronic mail, evanaken@acil.org. **Committees:** Business Practices; Civil Engineering; Conformity Assessment; Environmental Sciences; Government Relations; Insurance; Microbiology/Analytical Chemistry; Tax-Favored Competition. **Affiliated With:** Independent Laboratories Institute. **Formerly:** (1953) American Council of Commercial Laboratories; (1994) American Council of Independent Laboratories; (1997) Association of Independent Scientific Engineering and Testing Firms; (2000) ACIL. **Publications:** *ACIL Newsletter*, monthly. Covers industry issues, laboratory accreditation, legislative and tax matters and news of members. **Price:** included in membership dues. **Circulation:** 1,400. **Advertising:** accepted. **Conventions/Meetings:** annual convention and meeting, for CEOs and top level executives and managers ● Mid-Winter Meeting - conference.

7237 ■ Analytical Laboratory Managers Association (ALMA)
2019 Galisteo St., Bldg. I-1
Santa Fe, NM 87505
Ph: (505)989-4683
Fax: (505)989-1073
E-mail: alma@labmanagers.org
URL: http://www.labmanagers.org
Contact: David W. Green, Exec. Dir.

Founded: 1980. **Members:** 300. **Membership Dues:** individual, $80 (annual) ● corporate, $500 (annual) ● organizational, $1,000 (annual). **Description:** Represents managers and staff of analytical service laboratories in universities, industry and government. Facilitates the exchange of information regarding the operation of an analytical facility. Other goals include: rating laboratories; identifying problems and suggesting solutions; promoting effective post instrument sales service; developing new instrument guidelines. Conducts educational programs. **Awards:** Distinguished Service Award. **Frequency:** annual. **Type:** recognition. **Recipient:** for outstanding performance and service to the profession of analytical laboratory management. **Telecommunication Services:** electronic mail, green@labmanagers.org. **Formerly:** (1982) University Laboratory Managers Association. **Publications:** *Bulletin of the Analytical Laboratory Managers Association*, 3/year. Reports on association news and promotes lab management networking for members. Includes employment listings. **Price:** included in membership dues. **Conventions/Meetings:** annual conference - usually late October.

7238 ■ Association of Biomolecular Resource Facilities (ABRF)
2019 Galisteo St., Bldg. I
Santa Fe, NM 87505
Ph: (505)983-8102
Fax: (505)989-1073
E-mail: abrf@abrf.org
URL: http://www.abrf.org
Contact: Jay W. Fox, Pres.
Founded: 1988. **Members:** 850. **Membership Dues:** voting, $85 (annual) ● associate, $75 (annual) ● student, $35 (annual). **Staff:** 3. **Description:** Biomolecular laboratories and other research facilities. Works to advance the study in the biomolecular sciences, and to improve biotechnical capabilities of laboratories and research centers. Facilitates communication and cooperation among members. Sponsors surveys and studies in the field of biotechnology. Conducts educational programs for biochemists, molecular biologists, and other individuals interested in biomolecular science and biotechnology. **Libraries: Type:** open to the public. **Computer Services:** Mailing lists ● online services, discussion forum. **Telecommunication Services:** electronic mail, shardin@visigenbio.com. **Publications:** *Journal of Biomolecular Techniques*, quarterly. **Price:** included in membership dues. **Advertising:** accepted ● Directory, annual. **Price:** included in membership dues. **Conventions/Meetings:** annual Bioinformatics and Biomolecular Technologies - convention (exhibits).

Lakes

7239 ■ International Association for Great Lakes Research (IAGLR)
2205 Commonwealth Blvd.
Ann Arbor, MI 48105
Ph: (734)665-5303
Fax: (734)741-2055
E-mail: office@iaglr.org
URL: http://www.iaglr.org
Contact: Wendy L. Foster, Business Mgr.
Founded: 1967. **Members:** 1,000. **Membership Dues:** regular (minimum), $70 (annual) ● student (minimum), $37 (annual) ● retiree (minimum), $25 (annual) ● library, institution, $300 (annual) ● sustaining, $1,500 (annual). **Multinational. Description:** Represents scientists, engineers, and others primarily in the U.S. and Canada actively interested in research on the Great Lakes and their basins, or in research directly applicable to the understanding or management of large lakes. Disseminates research findings through publications and annual conference. **Awards:** Anderson-Everett Award. **Frequency:** annual. **Type:** medal. **Recipient:** for outstanding contributions to the association ● Chandler Misener Award. **Frequency:** annual. **Type:** medal. **Recipient:** for best paper in *Journal of Great Lakes Research* ● Hydrolab Student Award. **Frequency:** annual. **Type:** monetary. **Recipient:** for best oral paper and best poster presentation at the annual meeting ● Norman S. Baldwin Fishery Science Scholarship. **Frequency:** annual. **Type:** monetary. **Recipient:** for graduate students who have evaluated on scientific merit and have given potential contribution to sustainable management of fisheries ● Paul W. Rodgers Scholarship. **Frequency:** annual. **Type:** scholarship. **Recipient:** for student who wishes to pursue a future in large lake research; evaluated on basis of academic excellence, record of involvement in Great Lakes issues and candidate's statement. **Computer Services:** database, Journal of Great Lakes Research back issues. **Committees:** Awards; Conference; Endowment; Nominations; Outreach; Publications. **Publications:** *Conference on Great Lakes Research Abstracts*, annual. **Price:** included with institutional memberships ● *Journal of Great Lakes Research*, quarterly. **Price:** included in membership dues. ISSN: 0380-1330. **Conventions/Meetings:** annual conference (exhibits) - always late spring.

7240 ■ International Association of Theoretical and Applied Limnology (IATAL)
c/o Dr. William M. Lewis, Jr., Acting Gen. Sec.-Treas.
Univ. of North Carolina at Chapel Hill
School of Public Hea.
Dept. of Environmental Sciences and Engg.
124 Rosenau Hall, CB No. 7431
Chapel Hill, NC 27599-7431
Ph: (336)376-9362
Fax: (336)376-8825
E-mail: lewis@spot.colorado.edu
URL: http://www.limnology.org
Contact: Dr. William M. Lewis Jr., Acting Gen. Sec.-Treas.
Founded: 1922. **Members:** 3,250. **Membership Dues:** institutional, $165 (annual) ● student, $35 (annual) ● ordinary, $70 (annual). **Staff:** 1. **Budget:** $450,000. **Languages:** English, French, German. **Multinational. Description:** Promotes the study of all aspects of limnology (freshwater research). Encourages scientific discourse among those pursuing academic research and those concerned with practical fishery, pollution, and water supply problems. Organizes lectures, excursions, and symposia. **Awards:** Kilham Memorial Lecture. **Frequency:** triennial. **Type:** recognition. **Recipient:** to individuals who inspired through his innovative ideas and research ● Naumann Thienemann Medal. **Frequency:** triennial. **Type:** medal. **Recipient:** for outstanding scientific contributions to limnology. **Computer Services:** Mailing lists. **Telecommunication Services:** electronic mail, likensg@ecostudies.org. **Committees:** International. **Also Known As:** Societes Internationales Limnologiae Theoreticae et Applicatae. **Publications:** *Mitteilungen*, periodic. Monograph. Consists of accounts of methods, reviews, and the proceedings of symposia. **Price:** included in membership dues. **Circulation:** 3,500 ● *Verhandlungen*, triennial. Proceedings. Provides a summary of current research in the field of fresh water biology. Includes membership directory. **Price:** included in membership dues. **Circulation:** 3,500. **Conventions/Meetings:** triennial International Congress (exhibits).

7241 ■ North American Lake Management Society (NALMS)
PO Box 5443
Madison, WI 53705-0443
Ph: (608)233-2836
Fax: (608)233-3186
E-mail: info@nalms.org
URL: http://www.nalms.org
Contact: Ken Wagner CLM, Pres.
Founded: 1980. **Members:** 2,000. **Membership Dues:** lake leader, $55 (annual) ● lake leader non-North American, $70 (annual) ● professional (with journal), $100 (annual) ● professional non-North American (with journal), $110 (annual) ● emeritus, $45 (annual) ● emeritus (with journal), $90 (annual) ● corporate (with journal), $500 (annual) ● non-profit organization (with journal), $250 (annual). **Staff:** 3. **Regional Groups:** 12. **State Groups:** 24. **Local Groups:** 250. **Description:** Limnologists, researchers, academics, professionals, and government personnel; lake managers and property owners; lake and private sector associations; corporations, institutions, and organizations committed to environmentally sound lake management; interested individuals. Promotes education and furthers understanding of lakes, ponds, reservoirs, impoundments, and their watersheds as ecological units, and advances their protection, restoration, and management. Identifies needs regarding lake management and encourages research for lake ecology and watershed management. Facilitates the exchange of information on the technical and administrative aspects of lake management and offers guidance to public and private agencies. Fosters public awareness of lake ecosystems and encourages support for national, state, provincial, and local conservation programs. Improves the professional status of persons in the field. Fosters the development of lake organization coalitions; sponsors surveys. Monitors and reports on subjects concerning weed control, water pollution, and water quality standards; also reports on legislative activity affecting lake management. Sponsors slide and tape presentation. Has compiled a list of states' needs for the Environmental Protection Agency. Conducts research programs; sponsors internships. **Libraries: Type:** reference. **Holdings:** archival material. **Awards:** Corporate Award. **Frequency:** annual. **Type:** recognition ● **Frequency:** annual. **Type:** grant. **Recipient:** for travel ● Outstanding Scientific Merit. **Type:** recognition ● Secchi Disk Award. **Type:** recognition. **Computer Services:** database, expertise. **Committees:** Canadian Affairs; Chapters; Education; Fund Raising; Government Affairs; Industrial Relations; International; Latin American Affairs; Membership; Policy; Political Action; Publications; Scholarship; Science Advisory; Technology Transfer; Volunteer Monitoring. **Publications:** *Lake and Reservoir Management*, quarterly. Journal. Contains peer-reviewed papers on lake and reservoir management. **Price:** included in membership dues ● *Lake Line*, quarterly. Magazine. Carries news and how-to ideas, reports on lake associations, jobs, and meetings. ISSN: 0743-7978. **Advertising:** accepted ● *Managing Lakes and Reservoirs*. Handbook ● *Your Lake and You*. Brochures ● Bibliographies ● Booklets ● Membership Directory, annual ● Monographs. **Conventions/Meetings:** annual Regional Meeting ● seminar ● annual symposium, for photo, student paper, and student poster (exhibits) ● workshop, regional management.

Language

7242 ■ Cantonese Language Association (CLA)
c/o Prof. Dana Bourgerie, Gen. Sec.
Brigham Young Univ.
4064 JKHB
Provo, UT 84602
Ph: (801)378-4952
Fax: (801)378-4649
E-mail: bourgerie@byu.edu
URL: http://asiane.byu.edu/cla
Contact: Prof. Dana Bourgerie, Gen. Sec.
Founded: 1994. **Membership Dues:** general, $8 (annual). **Description:** Works to facilitate communication among teachers and scholars of Cantonese; promotes study and research in Cantonese language, both Standard Cantonese and Yue dialects. **Publications:** Membership Directory ● Newsletter. **Price:** included in membership dues. Alternate Formats: online. **Conventions/Meetings:** annual meeting, in conjunction with the CLTA and AAS annual meetings.

7243 ■ International Association of Chinese Linguistics (IACL)
c/o Audrey Li, Treas.
East Asian Languages and Cultures
THH 356M
Univ. of Southern California
Los Angeles, CA 90089-0357
Fax: (213)740-9295
E-mail: iacl@usc.edu
URL: http://www.iacling.org
Contact: Prof. Hongming Zhang, Exec. Sec.
Founded: 1992. **Members:** 16. **Membership Dues:** regular, $30 (annual) ● student, $15 (annual) ● life, $300. **Multinational. Description:** Promotes scientific research on Chinese languages and their dialects. **Awards:** Mantaro J. Hashimoto Award. **Frequency:** annual. **Type:** scholarship. **Recipient:** to young scholars who wish to devote themselves to the study of Chinese historical phonology. **Telecommunication Services:** electronic mail, hzhang6@facstaff.wisc.edu. **Publications:** Newsletter, 3/year. Alternate Formats: online.

7244 ■ International Association for Dialogue Analysis (IADA)
c/o Lawrence N. Berlin, PhD, Sec.
Northeastern Illinois Univ.
5500 N St. Louis Ave.
Chicago, IL 60625
Ph: (773)442-5493
E-mail: iada2004@neiu.edu
URL: http://www.uni-muenster.de/Ling/iada
Contact: Lawrence N. Berlin PhD, Sec.
Founded: 1990. **Membership Dues:** regular, EUR 30 (annual) ● student, EUR 20 (annual). **Multinational. Description:** Represents linguists, literary scholars, philosophers, sociologists, psychologists, and scholars from various disciplines interested in dialogic issues. Promotes and undertakes research

focusing on a dialogic view of language use. Supports the publication of substantial pieces of work pertaining to dialogic issues.

Lasers

7245 ■ International Committee on Ultra-High Intensity Lasers (ICUIL)
c/o Christopher P.J. Barty, Co-Chm.
PO Box 808
Livermore, CA 94551
Ph: (925)423-8486
Fax: (925)423-9242
E-mail: barty1@llnl.gov
URL: http://www.icuil.org
Contact: Christopher P.J. Barty, Co-Chm.
Founded: 2003. **Multinational. Description:** Represents individuals concerned with international aspects of ultra-high intensity laser science, technology and education. Provides a venue for discussions among representatives of high-intensity laser facilities and members of user communities. Promotes unity and coherence in the field.

7246 ■ Laser and Electro-Optics Manufacturers Association (LEOMA)
123 Kent Rd.
Pacifica, CA 94044
Ph: (650)738-1492
Fax: (650)738-1769
E-mail: info@leoma.com
URL: http://www.leoma.com
Contact: John Ambroseo, Pres.
Founded: 1986. **Membership Dues:** company, $200-$22,000 ● associate, $660. **Staff:** 1. **Description:** Laser industry companies involved with laser technology. Aims to collectively represent members' interests through industrial services and government/legislative advocacy, particularly at the federal level. Provides interface between the laser industry and government with regard to matters of training, safety standards, imports and exports, and new technologies. Works to promote the use of laser technology in new markets and industries. Advises members on financing and licensing procedures. Sponsors educational programs. **Formerly:** (1990) Laser Association of America. **Publications:** Newsletter, periodic. **Conventions/Meetings:** seminar ● trade show.

7247 ■ Laser Institute of America (LIA)
13501 Ingenuity Dr., Ste.128
Orlando, FL 32826
Ph: (407)380-1553
Free: (800)345-2737
Fax: (407)380-5588
E-mail: lia@laserinstitute.org
URL: http://www.laserinstitute.org
Contact: Bill Shiner, Pres.
Founded: 1968. **Members:** 2,000. **Membership Dues:** individual, $100 (annual) ● corporate ($1 million and under revenues), corporate institutional, $350 (annual) ● corporate ($1-$10 million revenues), $650 (annual) ● corporate ($10 million and above revenues), $850 (annual) ● student, retired, $50 (annual) ● life, $1,000. **Staff:** 17. **Budget:** $900,000. **Description:** Laser scientists, researchers, and manufacturers; educational and governmental institutions; associated individuals and businesses. Assists in the establishment of laser health and safety standards, definitions, and methods of measurements; seeks to advance the state of laser application technology. Sponsors short courses related to lasers. **Awards:** Arthur L. Schawlow Award. **Frequency:** annual. **Type:** recognition. **Committees:** Education; Inspection, Measurement and Control; Materials Processing; Medical and Biology; Safety. **Formerly:** (1974) Laser Industry Association. **Publications:** *Guide for the Selection of Eyewear* ● *Journal of Laser Applications*, quarterly. Contains refereed papers on applications of lasers and electro-optics, including safety standards and education. Includes membership news. **Price:** included in membership dues; $360.00 /year for nonmembers in U.S.; $385.00 /year for nonmembers in Canada, Mexico, Central and South America; $410.00 /year for nonmembers in Europe, Asia, Middle East, Africa, Oceania. ISSN: 1042-346X. **Circulation:** 1,600. **Advertising:** accepted ● *Laser Materials Processing*, annual. Proceedings. **Price:** $160.00 ● *Laser Safety Guide*, bimonthly. Newsletter. **Price:** $80.00/year. **Circulation:** 10,000. **Advertising:** accepted ● *LIA Today*, bimonthly. Newsletter. **Price:** $80.00/year. **Circulation:** 10,000. **Advertising:** accepted ● Monographs ● Proceedings ● Also publishes technical course notes. **Conventions/Meetings:** annual International Congress on Applications of Lasers and Electro-Options (exhibits) ● biennial International Laser Safety Conference.

Lepidopterology

7248 ■ Butterfly Lovers International (BLI)
Address Unknown since 2007
Founded: 1975. **Staff:** 2. **Description:** Individuals interested in butterflies. Promotes education regarding the habits, habitats, and characteristics of various types of butterflies and the protection of endangered butterflies. Collects arts and crafts featuring butterflies, including books, photographs, and artifacts. Fosters butterfly gardens. **Libraries: Type:** by appointment only. **Holdings:** 500. **Subjects:** every aspect of butterflies.

7249 ■ North American Butterfly Association (NABA)
4 Delaware Rd.
Morristown, NJ 07960
Ph: (973)285-0907
Fax: (973)285-0936
E-mail: naba@naba.org
URL: http://www.naba.org
Contact: Jeffrey Glassberg, Pres.
Founded: 1992. **Members:** 4,500. **Membership Dues:** regular in U.S., $30 (annual) ● family, in North America, $40 (annual) ● regular outside U.S., $60 (annual) ● family, outside North America, $80 (annual). **Regional Groups:** 30. **Local Groups:** 32. **Description:** Individuals interested in butterflies. Seeks to promote butterfly conservation and recreational, non-consumptive butterfly appreciation. Conducts educational programs; holds the 4th of July Butterfly Counts. **Publications:** *American Butterflies*, quarterly. Magazine. Contains photography, articles, and information on butterflies. **Price:** included in membership dues. ISSN: 1087-450X. **Circulation:** 8,500. **Advertising:** accepted ● *Butterfly Gardener*, quarterly. Newsletter. **Price:** included in membership dues ● *Fourth of July Butterfly Count*. Annual Report. **Price:** $6.00 for members; $10.00 for nonmembers. **Conventions/Meetings:** biennial meeting - 2008 June 26-29, Kernville, CA.

Lighting

7250 ■ Illuminating Engineering Society of North America (IESNA)
120 Wall St., 17th Fl.
New York, NY 10005-4001
Ph: (212)248-5000
Fax: (212)248-5017
E-mail: iesna@iesna.org
URL: http://www.iesna.org
Contact: William Hanley, Exec. VP
Founded: 1906. **Members:** 9,000. **Membership Dues:** individual/associate in U.S., Canada, and Mexico, $170 (annual) ● individual outside U.S., Canada, and Mexico, $150 (annual) ● student, $20 (annual) ● individual (subscriber), $350 (annual). **Staff:** 20. **Budget:** $3,000,000. **Regional Groups:** 9. **State Groups:** 85. **National Groups:** 12. **Description:** Technical society whose members include engineers, architects, lighting designers, educators, students, contractors, distributors, utility personnel, scientists, and manufacturers dealing with the art, science, or practice of illumination. Provides speakers, referrals, and assistance with technical problems. Maintains liaison with schools and colleges. Offers basic and advanced IES Lighting Courses through local sections and in cooperation with other organizations. Conducts: area symposia and seminars; workshops and lighting exhibitions; slide presentations. Sponsors lighting design competitions. Maintains over 38 committees including: Energy Management; Lighting and Thermal Environment; Photobiology; Quality and Quantity of Illumination. **Awards:** International Illumination Design Award. **Frequency:** annual. **Type:** recognition. **Computer Services:** Mailing lists, of members. **Committees:** Aviation Lighting; Centennial; Computer; Conference; Daylighting; Educational Materials; Educational Seminars. **Publications:** *Journal of the IES*, semiannual. **Price:** $195.00/year. ISSN: 0099-4480. **Circulation:** 9,000 ● *LD and A*, monthly. Magazine. **Price:** $44.00/year; $85.00/2 years; $110.00/3 years. ISSN: 0360-6325 ● Booklets ● Reports ● Also publishes standards, reports, booklets, and guides. **Conventions/Meetings:** annual conference (exhibits) ● annual Lightfair International - trade show (exhibits).

7251 ■ Lighting Research Office
c/o Philip F. Keebler, Proj. Mgr.
Elec. Power Res. Inst.
942 Corridor Park Blvd.
Knoxville, TN 37932
Ph: (865)218-8015
Fax: (865)218-8001
E-mail: pkeebler@epri.com
URL: http://www.epri.com/LRO
Contact: Philip F. Keebler, Proj. Mgr.
Founded: 1982. **Description:** A service of the Electric Power Research Institute. Determines priorities for research on lighting as it affects human behavior in varying conditions and environments. Conducts studies on prediction methodology and criteria for lighting application. Cooperates with scientific, technical, and design disciplines that may provide input into the examination of the effect of lighting and productivity, safety, health preservation, human and electrical energy effectiveness, and the creation of pleasant environments. Makes available research findings to continuing education programs for those in the lighting field. **Formerly:** (2003) Lighting Research Institute. **Supersedes:** Illuminating Engineering Research Institute. **Publications:** *1st International Symposium on Glare: October 1991* ● *Light and Human Health - 2002*. Proceedings. Includes discussions of 22 presented and 7 poster papers. **Price:** free. Alternate Formats: CD-ROM ● *Lighting and Human Performance II - Beyond Visibility Models Toward a Unified Human Factors Approach to Performance - 2001*. Report. Describes vision research that links visibility, photobiology and psychological factors into the performance equation. **Price:** free. Alternate Formats: CD-ROM ● *Lighting for Aging Vision and Health - 1995*. Proceedings. Includes full text and discussions of current research. **Price:** free. Alternate Formats: CD-ROM ● *Visibility and Luminance in Roadway Lighting - 1993*. Proceedings. Includes full text and discussions of 16 presented papers on current research. **Price:** free. Alternate Formats: CD-ROM ● *Vision at Low Light Levels - 1999*. Proceedings. Includes 27 research papers and discussions. **Price:** free. Alternate Formats: CD-ROM ● Papers ● Proceedings ● Reprints. Includes articles on research.

7252 ■ U.S. National Committee of the International Commission on Illumination (CIE/USA)
c/o James Sultan, Treas.
11410 NE 124th St.
PMB 325
Kirkland, WA 98034-4305
Ph: (206)284-3417
E-mail: jsultan@studiolux.com
URL: http://cie-usnc.org
Contact: Dr. Ronald B. Gibbons, Sec.
Founded: 1913. **Members:** 260. **Membership Dues:** regular, $75 (annual) ● contributing organization, $450 (annual) ● constituent society, $900 (annual). **Budget:** $50,000. **Description:** U.S. committee of the International Commission on Illumination organized to promote international cooperation and

exchange of information on matters relating to the art and science of lighting. Goals are: to represent the interests and viewpoints of the U.S. committee in affairs and activities of the CIE; to keep the U.S. informed of proceedings and recommendations of the CIE. (The acronym CIE is derived from the French title of the International Commission on Illumination, Commission Internationale de l'Eclairage). **Libraries: Type:** reference. **Holdings:** 100. **Subjects:** illumination. **Telecommunication Services:** electronic mail, gibbons@vtti.vt.edu. **Committees:** Liaison; Publicity. **Councils:** Technical. **Affiliated With:** International Commission on Illumination. **Publications:** *CIE Standards and Reports*, quarterly. Newsletter. **Price:** free for members. **Circulation:** 5,000. Alternate Formats: online ● *Technical Report*, periodic. Alternate Formats: online ● Also distributes CIE publications in the U.S. **Conventions/Meetings:** quadrennial meeting, technical session and business meeting.

Lubricants

7253 ■ International Council for Machinery Lubrication (ICML)
3015 E Skelly Dr., Ste.443F
Tulsa, OK 74105
Ph: (918)742-2950
Fax: (918)742-2075
E-mail: info@lubecouncil.org
URL: http://www.lubecouncil.org
Contact: Suzy Jamieson, Contact
Membership Dues: individual, $60 (annual) ● sustaining, $2,000 (annual). **Languages:** English, Portuguese, Spanish. **Multinational. Description:** Aims to facilitate growth and development of machine lubrication as a technical field of endeavor. Promotes the development and transfer of knowledge related to machinery lubrication by funding applied research activities. Offers skill certification testing for individuals in the fields of machine condition monitoring, lubrication, and oil analysis. **Awards:** Augustus H. Gill Award. **Frequency:** annual. **Type:** recognition. **Recipient:** to organizations that have exhibited excellence in the application of used oil analysis in machine and lubricant condition monitoring ● John R. Battle Award for Excellence in Machinery Lubrication. **Frequency:** annual. **Type:** recognition. **Recipient:** to organizations that have demonstrated excellence in the application of machinery lubrication. **Telecommunication Services:** electronic mail, suzya@lubecouncil.org. **Publications:** Newsletter, quarterly. Contains recent events, activities, and other pertinent subjects regarding the organization and industry. **Price:** included in membership dues.

Malacology

7254 ■ American Malacological Society (AMS)
c/o Dr. Dawn E. Dittman, Treas.
Tunison Lab. of Aquatic Sci.
3075 Gracie Rd.
Cortland, NY 13045
E-mail: ddittman@usgs.gov
URL: http://www.malacological.org
Contact: Dr. Dawn E. Dittman, Treas.
Founded: 1931. **Members:** 300. **Membership Dues:** student, $20 (annual) ● regular, affiliate, $60 (annual) ● sustaining, $85 (annual). **Local Groups:** 19. **Description:** Scientists, museum curators, biology teachers, fishery researchers, U.S. Public Health Service workers and hobbyists interested in mollusks. Promotes the science of malacology and furthers the interests of students and collectors. **Awards:** Student Research Grants. **Frequency:** annual. **Type:** grant. **Committees:** Conservation; Constitution/Bylaws; Endowment; Nominating; Publications; Resolutions and Recognition; Student Awards; Systematics. **Formerly:** (1999) American Malacological Union. **Publications:** *American Malacological Bulletin*, semiannual. Contains peer-reviewed contributed articles and symposium papers. ● *American Malacological Bulletin Supplement*, periodic ● *AMS News*, semiannual. Newsletter. Includes membership list. Alternate Formats: online. **Conventions/Meetings:** annual meeting and symposium (exhibits).

7255 ■ National Shellfisheries Association (NSA)
c/o Linda Kallansrude
14 Carter Ln.
East Quogue, NY 11942
Ph: (631)653-6327 (856)785-0074
Fax: (631)653-6327
E-mail: biomkk@hofstra.edu
URL: http://www.shellfish.org
Contact: David Bushek, Pres.
Founded: 1909. **Members:** 900. **Membership Dues:** student, $45 (annual) ● regular, $85 (annual). **Budget:** $150,000. **Description:** Biologists, hydrographers, public health workers, shellfish producers, and fishery administrators. Encourages research on mollusks and crustaceans, with emphasis on those forms of economic importance known as shellfish. **Awards:** David Wallace Award. **Type:** recognition. **Recipient:** to a member who had significant contribution to the study of shellfish, aquaculture, and conservation programs. **Telecommunication Services:** electronic mail, bushek@hsrl.rutgers.edu. **Formerly:** National Association of Shellfish Commissioners; National Association of Fisheries Commissioners. **Publications:** *Journal of Shellfish Research*, semiannual. Covers aspects of shellfish research including biology, ecology, physiology, biochemistry, aquaculture, and taxonomy. **Price:** included in membership dues. ISSN: 0077-5711. **Circulation:** 1,200. Also Cited As: *Proceedings of National Shellfisheries Association*. **Conventions/Meetings:** annual meeting (exhibits).

7256 ■ Society for Experimental and Descriptive Malacology (SEDM)
Address Unknown since 2008
Founded: 1967. **Members:** 600. **Languages:** English, Spanish. **Description:** Scientists, especially malacologists, invertebrate zoologists, and paleontologists interested in mollusks. Promotes research, particularly on mollusks; sponsors seminars and symposia on the biology of mollusks. **Convention/Meeting:** none. **Publications:** *A Dissection Guide, Field and Laboratory Manual*. Book ● *A Review of the Genera of the Aquatic Gastropod Subfamily Cochliopinae*. Book ● *Freshwater Snails of Taiwan*. Book ● *Malacological Review*, annual. Journal. Contains research and review articles on mollusks. Includes book reviews, employment opportunities, obituaries, and abstracts. **Price:** $42.00 /year for individuals, add $3.00 for non-USA addresses; $72.00/yfs, add $3.00 for non-USA addresses. **Circulation:** 600 ● *The Mekong Schistosome*. Book ● *Prosobranch Phylogeny*. Book ● *Walkerana—Transactions of the POETS Society*, periodic. Journal. Contains research and review articles on mollusks. **Price:** $20.00/yfi, add $3.00 for non-USA addresses; $40.00/yfs, add $3.00 for non-USA addresses. **Circulation:** 200.

7257 ■ Western Society of Malacologists (WSM)
c/o Victor Smith, Sec.-Treas.
53 Woodbine Dr.
Mill Valley, CA 94941
E-mail: lgroves@nhm.org
URL: http://biology.fullerton.edu/orgs/wsm
Contact: Victor Smith, Sec.-Treas.
Founded: 1968. **Members:** 300. **Membership Dues:** regular, $20 (annual) ● student, $8 (annual). **Description:** Represents professionals and amateurs interested in promoting the study of malacology (the branch of zoology dealing with mollusks) and invertebrate zoology through research, lectures, and publications. **Awards:** Student Grant Award. **Frequency:** biennial. **Type:** grant. **Recipient:** for full time student in a formal graduate or undergraduate degree program. **Committees:** Conservation; Displays; Student Participation. **Publications:** Annual Report, annual. Contains abstracts and proceedings of conference; also includes directory. **Price:** included in membership dues; $15.00 /year for nonmembers; $17.00/year for families; $6.00/year for students. ISSN: 0361-1175 ● Papers. **Conventions/Meetings:** annual conference.

Mammalogy

7258 ■ American Cetacean Society (ACS)
PO Box 1391
San Pedro, CA 90733-1391
Ph: (310)548-6279
Fax: (310)548-6950
E-mail: info@acsonline.org
URL: http://www.acsonline.org
Contact: Patty Geary, Pres.
Founded: 1967. **Members:** 1,500. **Membership Dues:** active, $35 (annual) ● family/foreign, $45 (annual) ● senior, student, teacher, $25 (annual) ● supporting, $75 (annual) ● contributing, $250 (annual) ● patron, $500 (annual) ● life, $750. **Staff:** 1. **Budget:** $300,000. **Regional Groups:** 6. **Description:** Marine biologists, laypeople, students, and teachers interested in cetaceans (whales, dolphins, and porpoises), and their environment. Attempts to broaden knowledge through research and education. Supports a policy of conservation and protection of cetaceans, other marine mammals, and the natural environments that support them. Compiles annual census of eastern Pacific gray whale population during migration, and behavioral studies of cetaceans in their natural environment. Conducts trips for school children. **Libraries: Type:** open to the public. **Holdings:** 2,000; articles, books, periodicals. **Subjects:** cetaceans, marine. **Committees:** Conservation; Education; Expeditions; Research; Scientific Studies. **Publications:** *A Guide to the Photographic Identification of Individual Whales*. Book. **Price:** $12.95 ● *A Sea Guide to Marine Mammals*. Book. **Price:** $5.95 ● *Spyhopper*, semiannual. Newsletter. Covers current whale research, conservation, and education. Includes society news, reading list, species profile, and Washington report. **Price:** included in membership dues. **Circulation:** 2,000. Alternate Formats: online ● *Whalewatcher*, annual. Journal. Contains scholarly articles on whale research and conservation activities worldwide. Includes book reviews and profiles of individuals in the field. **Price:** included in membership dues. **Circulation:** 2,000. **Advertising:** accepted. Alternate Formats: online. **Conventions/Meetings:** biennial Learning from Whales: Education, Inspiration and Action - conference, with speakers, art show, silent auctions, contributed papers and poster sessions (exhibits).

7259 ■ American Society of Mammalogists (ASM)
PO Box 1897
Lawrence, KS 66044-8897
Ph: (785)843-1235
Free: (800)627-0629
Fax: (785)843-1274
E-mail: asm@allenpress.com
URL: http://www.mammalsociety.org
Contact: Robert M. Timm, Pres.
Founded: 1919. **Members:** 4,500. **Membership Dues:** regular, $45 (annual) ● student, $35 (annual) ● regular/student (online only), $30 (annual) ● developing country, $20 (annual) ● life, $1,125 ● patron, $5,000. **Description:** Serves as scientific society of mammalogists, educators and conservationists. **Awards:** C. Hart Merriam Award. **Frequency:** annual. **Type:** recognition. **Recipient:** for outstanding contributions to mammals through research, teaching and service ● Jackson Award. **Frequency:** annual. **Type:** recognition. **Recipient:** for persons who have given long and outstanding service to the society ● Joseph Grinnell Award. **Frequency:** annual. **Type:** recognition. **Recipient:** for individuals who have made outstanding and sustained contributions to education in mammalogy over a period of at least 10 years ● Latin American Student Field Research Award. **Frequency:** annual. **Type:** monetary. **Recipient:** for field projects by Latin American graduate students ● Oliver P. Pearson Award. **Frequency:** annual. **Type:** monetary. **Recipient:** for young professional who holds an academic

position in a Latin American institution within 5 years of receiving a PhD ● **Frequency:** annual. **Type:** recognition. **Recipient:** for three outstanding papers. **Telecommunication Services:** electronic mail, btimm@ku.edu. **Committees:** Animal Care and Use; Conservation of Land Mammals; Education and Graduate Students; Grants-in-Aid; Information Retrieval; International Relations; Legislation and Regulation; Mammal Side Library; Marine Mammals; Nomenclature; Public Education; Systematic Collections. **Publications:** *Journal of Mammalogy*, bimonthly. **Price:** $205.00 for nonmembers in U.S.; included in membership dues. ISSN: 0022-2372. **Circulation:** 3,500. **Advertising:** accepted ● *Mammalian Species*, annual. **Price:** $80.00 ● Also publishes special publications. **Conventions/Meetings:** annual conference (exhibits) - always June.

7260 ■ Center for Whale Research (CWR)
PO Box 1577
Friday Harbor, WA 98250-1577
Ph: (360)378-5835
Fax: (360)378-5954
E-mail: info@whaleresearch.com
URL: http://www.whaleresearch.com
Contact: Kenneth C. Balcomb III, Exec. Dir.
Founded: 1986. **Members:** 1,000. **Membership Dues:** regular, $20 (annual). **Staff:** 5. **Budget:** $100,000. **Description:** Volunteers who perform support and assistance roles in field research on whales and dolphins. **Libraries: Type:** reference; not open to the public. **Holdings:** 600; articles, books, papers. **Subjects:** whale biology. **Publications:** *Killer Whales: A Catalogue of Identified Individuals*, quinquennial. Book. **Price:** $25.00. **Circulation:** 5,000 ● *Southern Resident Killer Whale ID Guide*. Catalog. **Price:** $40.00.

7261 ■ Dolphin Research Center (DRC)
58901 Overseas Hwy.
Grassy Key, FL 33050-6019
Ph: (305)289-1121 (305)289-0002
Fax: (305)743-7627
E-mail: drc@dolphins.org
URL: http://www.dolphins.org
Contact: Jayne Shannon Rodriguez, Pres.
Founded: 1984. **Members:** 3,000. **Membership Dues:** individual, $40 (annual) ● family, $75 (annual) ● sponsor, $150 (annual) ● keep-in-touch, adopt-a-dolphin gift dolfriend, $25 (annual) ● gray cross, $85 (annual) ● adopt-a-dolphin e-friend, $15 (annual) ● adopt-a-dolphin parent, $240 (annual) ● dolfriend, $50 (annual) ● pod pal, $100 (annual). **Staff:** 77. **Budget:** $2,200,000. **Description:** Conducts noninvasive research on dolphin cognition, behavior, their learning ability and biology. Offers Dolphinlab, an educational program that provides hands-on experience in the fields of dolphin husbandry, behavior, training, research, communications, and biology. Provides walking tours, 1/2-day programs. Offers therapy to children with special needs. **Awards:** Terri L. Renner Memorial. **Frequency:** annual. **Type:** scholarship. **Recipient:** for highly motivated educator and student. **Formerly:** (1958) Santini's Porpoise School; (1984) Institute for Delphinid Research. **Publications:** *Dolphin Society*, bimonthly. Newsletter. **Price:** included in membership dues. **Circulation:** 3,000 ● *Gray Cross Update*, quarterly. Newsletter. **Price:** included in membership dues.

Manufacturing

7262 ■ Association for Manufacturing Technology (AMT)
7901 Westpark Dr.
McLean, VA 22102-4206
Ph: (703)893-2900 (703)827-5276
Free: (800)524-0475
Fax: (703)893-1151
E-mail: amt@amtonline.org
URL: http://www.amtonline.org
Contact: John B. Byrd III, Pres.
Founded: 1902. **Members:** 375. **Membership Dues:** regular (less than $2500 annual global shipments), $400 (annual) ● regular ($2500 or above annual global shipments), $1,300-$9,500 (annual). **Staff:** 75. **Budget:** $20,000,000. **Multinational. Description:** Supports and enhances the activities of American manufacturers. Strives to be an effective spokesman for the industry; provides members with the latest information on technical developments, training methods, economic issues, and trade and marketing opportunities; encourages higher safety and technical standards; and gathers and disseminates information about world markets. **Additional Websites:** http://www.imts.org. **Telecommunication Services:** electronic mail, jbyrd@amtonline.org. **Formerly:** (1992) NMTBA (National Machine Tool Builders' Association). **Publications:** *AMT News*, monthly. Newsletter. Alternate Formats: online ● *Directory of Machine Tools and Manufacturing Equipment*, annual. Helps buyers locate manufacturing machinery and equipment. **Price:** free. **Conventions/Meetings:** biennial International Manufacturing Technology Show - trade show (exhibits) - usually in September.

7263 ■ Institute for Molecular Manufacturing (IMM)
555 Bryant St., Ste.354
Palo Alto, CA 94301
Ph: (650)917-1120
Fax: (650)917-1120
E-mail: admin@imm.org
URL: http://www.imm.org
Contact: David Forrest, Pres.
Founded: 1991. **Membership Dues:** associate, $250 (annual) ● fellow, $500 (annual) ● colleague, $1,000 (annual) ● associate, $5,000 (quinquennial). **Description:** Promotes development of molecular manufacturing (molecular nanotechnology, or MNT), as well as guidelines to minimize risk from accidental use or abuse. **Awards:** IMM Prizes in Computational Nanotechnology. **Type:** recognition. **Publications:** *Foresight Update*. Newsletter. Alternate Formats: online ● Reports. Contains reports on molecular manufacturing.

7264 ■ Integrated Manufacturing Technology Initiative (IMTI)
PO Box 5296
Oak Ridge, TN 37830
Ph: (865)862-5667
Fax: (865)862-5697
E-mail: imti@imti21.org
URL: http://www.imti21.org
Contact: Richard Neal, Exec. Dir.
Founded: 2000. **Membership Dues:** full (less than $50M annual revenue), $10,000 (annual) ● full (more than $50M annual revenue), $25,000 (annual) ● associate, academic partner, $5,000 (annual). **Description:** Seeks to bring together industry, academic, and government entities to support and strengthen the nation's manufacturing community. Assists U.S. manufacturing to achieve excellence through manufacturing science and technology. Offers solutions to achieve the future success of manufacturing enterprises and the national manufacturing infrastructure. **Publications:** *IMTI Update*, quarterly. Newsletter. Contains updates on the state of manufacturing science and technology in the country. **Price:** free. Alternate Formats: online.

7265 ■ International Electronics Manufacturing Initiative (iNEMI)
2214 Rock Hill Rd., Ste.110
Herndon, VA 20170-4214
Ph: (703)834-0330 (703)834-2087
Fax: (703)834-2735
E-mail: info@inemi.org
URL: http://www.inemi.org
Contact: Robert C. Pfahl Jr., VP for Operations/Treas.
Founded: 1996. **Members:** 70. **Staff:** 7. **Budget:** $1,000,000. **Multinational. Description:** Works to promote sustained growth of the electronics manufacturing in North America. Provides a forum for electronics manufacturers to come together and share information and knowledge. Conventions/Meetings: none. **Formerly:** (2007) National Electronics Manufacturing Initiative. **Publications:** *Technology Roadmap*, biennial. Report. **Price:** $250.00. Alternate Formats: CD-ROM; online.

7266 ■ North American Manufacturing Research Institution of the Society of Manufacturing Engineers (NAMRI/SME)
1 SME Dr.
PO Box 930
Dearborn, MI 48121-0930
Ph: (313)271-1500
Free: (800)733-4763
Fax: (313)425-3401
E-mail: techcommunities@sme.org
URL: http://www.sme.org/cgi-bin/communities.pl?/communities/namri/namrihome.htm&&&SME&
Contact: Mark Stratton, Community Relations Mgr.
Founded: 1973. **Members:** 180. **Membership Dues:** regular, $99 (annual) ● student, $20 (annual). **Staff:** 1. **Description:** A division of the Society of Manufacturing Engineers. Represents individuals engaged in manufacturing research and technology development. Works to promote and stimulate research, writing, publication, and dissemination of new manufacturing technology; works to coordinate efforts and cooperate with counterpart organizations worldwide; works to provide a forum for the active community of researchers whose work contributes to the furtherance of manufacturing technology and productivity. **Libraries: Type:** reference. **Holdings:** archival material, books, clippings, periodicals. **Subjects:** manufacturing technology and research. **Awards:** Best Paper Award. **Type:** recognition. **Recipient:** for the best paper ● Founders Lecture Award. **Type:** recognition. **Computer Services:** database, INTIME. **Committees:** Organizing; Scientific. **Affiliated With:** Society of Manufacturing Engineers. **Publications:** *Special Index Volume of the North American Manufacturing Research Institute of SME 1973-1992* ● *Transactions of the North American Manufacturing Research Institution of SME*, annual. **Price:** $96.00 each. **Conventions/Meetings:** annual North American Manufacturing Research Conference - always May.

7267 ■ Rapid Technologies and Additive Manufacturing Community (RTAM/SME)
c/o SME
PO Box 930
Dearborn, MI 48121
Ph: (313)271-1500
Free: (800)733-4763
Fax: (313)425-3401
E-mail: techcommunities@sme.org
URL: http://www.sme.org/rpa
Contact: Jane Wellington, Community Relations Mgr.
Description: Design engineers, product engineers, tool engineers, and manufacturing engineers. Promotes the manufacturing community's capabilities through interactive education of advanced rapid product development technologies, focusing on technologies and processes that result in new products. **Awards:** RTAM/SME Dick Aubin Distinguished Paper Award. **Frequency:** annual. **Type:** recognition. **Recipient:** for the author of an individual paper for the innovative application of rapid prototyping processes, techniques and the contribution of ideas and information to the industry through a technical paper. **Publications:** *RTAM Community News*, quarterly. Newsletter. **Price:** free for members. Alternate Formats: online.

7268 ■ Society of Manufacturing Engineers (SME)
PO Box 930
Dearborn, MI 48121
Ph: (313)271-1500 (313)425-3000
Free: (800)733-4763
Fax: (313)425-3401
E-mail: service@sme.org
URL: http://www.sme.org
Contact: Mark Tomlinson, Exec. Dir./Gen. Mgr.
Founded: 1932. **Members:** 50,000. **Membership Dues:** regular, $125 (annual) ● student, $20 (annual). **Staff:** 300. **Regional Groups:** 14. **Local Groups:** 300. **Description:** Professional society of manufacturing engineers, practitioners and management executives concerned with manufacturing

technologies for improved productivity. Seeks to advance the science of manufacturing through the continuing education of manufacturing engineers, practitioners and management. Conducts expositions, international seminars and clinics. **Awards:** Award of Merit. **Frequency:** annual. **Type:** recognition. **Recipient:** for members who have made valued and balanced contributions to the Society's professional activities and growth ● Donald C. Burnham Manufacturing Management Award. **Frequency:** annual. **Type:** recognition. **Recipient:** for exceptional success in the integration of the infrastructure and process manufacturing ● Eli Whitney Productivity Award. **Frequency:** annual. **Type:** recognition. **Recipient:** for distinguished accomplishments in improving capability within the broad concept of orderly production ● Joseph A. Siegel Service Award. **Frequency:** annual. **Type:** recognition. **Recipient:** for significant and unique contributions that benefit the society ● Outstanding Young Manufacturing Engineer Award. **Frequency:** annual. **Type:** recognition. **Recipient:** for young manufacturing engineers age 35 years old or younger ● SME Albert M. Sargent Progress Award. **Frequency:** annual. **Type:** recognition. **Recipient:** for technical accomplishments in the field of manufacturing processes, methods or systems ● SME Education Award. **Frequency:** annual. **Type:** recognition. **Recipient:** for an educator most respected for the development of manufacturing-related curricula ● SME Frederick W. Taylor Research Medal. **Frequency:** annual. **Type:** medal. **Recipient:** for significant published research leading to a better understanding of materials, facilities, principles, operations and their application to improve manufacturing processes ● SME Gold Medal. **Frequency:** annual. **Type:** medal. **Recipient:** for outstanding service to the manufacturing engineering profession. **Computer Services:** database, INTIME. **Committees:** Organizing; Scientific. **Councils:** Manufacturing Enterprise. **Affiliated With:** Association for Electronics Manufacturing of the Society of Manufacturing Engineers; Association for Finishing Processes of the Society of Manufacturing Engineers; Composites Manufacturing Association of the Society of Manufacturing Engineers; Machine Vision Association of the Society of Manufacturing Engineers; Machining and Material Removal Community of the Society of Manufacturing Engineers; Manufacturing Integration Tech Group of the Society of Manufacturing Engineers; North American Manufacturing Research Institution of the Society of Manufacturing Engineers; Robotics Tech Group of the Society of Manufacturing Engineers. **Formerly:** (1960) American Society of Tool Engineers; (1969) American Society of Tool and Manufacturing Engineers. **Publications:** *Composites in Manufacturing*, quarterly. Journal. Covers composite materials in manufacturing. Includes calendar of events. **Price:** $60.00 /year for nonmembers ● *Electronics Manufacturing: SME's Quarterly on Electronics Manufacturing Technology.* Contains calendar of events. **Price:** $60.00 /year for nonmembers ● *Finishing Line: AFP/SME's Quarterly on Finishing and Coatings Technology.* Newsletter. Covers topics related to industrial finishes, such as powder coating, radiation curing, high solids, wood finishing, and coating and finishing. **Price:** included in membership dues; $60.00 /year for nonmembers. **Circulation:** 3,000 ● *Journal of Manufacturing Systems*, quarterly. Includes reviewed papers on manufacturing systems application methodologies, book reviews, and case studies. **Price:** $72.00 /year for members; $78.00 /year for nonmembers. ISSN: 0278-6125 ● *Manufacturing Engineering*, monthly. Magazine. Provides technical information for manufacturing engineers, managers, and technicians to assist in their efforts to improve efficiency. **Price:** included in membership dues; $64.00 /year for nonmembers. ISSN: 0361-0853. **Circulation:** 135,000. **Advertising:** accepted ● *SME News*, bimonthly. Newsletter. Contains society and member news. Includes calendar of events and chapter and regional news. ● *Vision: SME's Quarterly on Vision Technology.* Includes calendar of events and articles on machine vision applications. **Price:** $60.00 /year for nonmembers ● Brochures ● Also publishes Forming and Fabricating. **Conventions/Meetings:** annual conference, includes exposition.

Marine

7269 ■ American Littoral Society - Northeast Region (ALS)

28 W 9th Rd.
Broad Channel, NY 11693
Ph: (718)318-9344
Fax: (718)318-9345
E-mail: driepe@nyc.rr.com
URL: http://www.alsnyc.org
Contact: Don Riepe, Dir.

Founded: 1961. **Members:** 7,000. **Membership Dues:** individual, family, $35 (annual) ● library, $40 (annual) ● outside U.S., $55 (annual) ● sustaining, club, $50 (annual) ● supporting, $100 (annual) ● advocate, $250 (annual) ● donor, $500. **Regional Groups:** 4. **Description:** Marine biologists, teachers, naturalists, divers, anglers, and others. Encourages the study of shore life by direct observation of the occurrence and ways of fish and other marine animals, birds, and habitats. Disseminates records of observations; assists in the solving of problems of scientific study, identification, and description; and fosters public interest in shore life and the need for conservation. Sponsors field trips. **Publications:** *Littorally Speaking*, quarterly. Newsletter. Fosters public interest in shore life and the need for conservation. **Price:** included in membership dues. **Circulation:** 7,000. Alternate Formats: online ● *Oystercatcher*, quarterly. Newsletter. Fosters public interest in shore life and the need for conservation. **Price:** included in membership dues. **Circulation:** 7,000. Alternate Formats: online ● *Underwater Naturalist*, quarterly. Annual Reports. Documents observations of fish and other marine animals and conservation issues. **Price:** included in membership dues; $1.00 for nonmembers. Alternate Formats: microform. **Conventions/Meetings:** annual meeting, three two-day weekend field trips - usually early fall ● symposium, with topics on marine mammals, commercial fishing, and ocean pollution.

7270 ■ American Society of Naval Engineers (ASNE)

1452 Duke St.
Alexandria, VA 22314-3458
Ph: (703)836-6727
Fax: (703)836-7491
E-mail: asnehq@navalengineers.org
URL: http://www.navalengineers.org
Contact: Capt. Dennis K. Kruse CAE, Exec. Dir.

Founded: 1888. **Members:** 6,000. **Membership Dues:** associate, $50-$110 (annual) ● spouse, $20 (annual) ● student, emeritus, $35 (annual). **Staff:** 9. **Budget:** $1,800,000. **Regional Groups:** 6. **Local Groups:** 22. **Description:** Professional civilian and Navy engineers interested in naval engineering including ordnance, navigation, aeronautics, propulsion, hull, electrical and electronic, naval architecture, ocean engineering, space systems, logistics, and related subjects. **Libraries: Type:** not open to the public; reference. **Holdings:** 1,000; books, papers. **Subjects:** naval engineering. **Awards:** ASNE Scholarship Program. **Frequency:** annual. **Type:** scholarship. **Recipient:** for senior undergraduate and graduate students pursuing careers in naval engineering ● Claud A. Jones Award. **Frequency:** annual. **Type:** recognition. **Recipient:** for a fleet or field engineer who has made a significant contribution for improving operational engineering or material readiness of the maritime forces during the past three years ● Frank G. Law Award. **Frequency:** annual. **Type:** recognition. **Recipient:** to an individual whose long time dedication and service to the society is deemed worthy of special recognition ● Gold Medal Award. **Frequency:** annual. **Type:** recognition. **Recipient:** for an individual who has made a significant contribution to naval engineering in the past five years ● Harold E. Saunders Award. **Frequency:** annual. **Type:** recognition. **Recipient:** for an individual whose reputation in naval engineering spans a long career of notable achievement and influence ● Jimmy Hamilton Award. **Frequency:** annual. **Type:** recognition. **Recipient:** for the authors of the best original technical paper published in Naval Engineers Journal during the year ● **Frequency:** annual. **Type:** scholarship ● Solberg Award. **Frequency:** annual. **Type:** recognition. **Recipient:** for an individual who has made a significant contribution to naval engineering through personal research during the past three years. **Telecommunication Services:** electronic mail, dkruse@navalengineers.org. **Committees:** Audit; Awards; Combat Systems; Environmental Engineering; Fleet Maintenance; Logistics; Professional Development; Publicity; Scholarship; Sections; Ways and Means. **Publications:** *American Society of Naval Engineers—Membership Directory*, biennial. Includes advertisers' index. **Price:** included in membership dues. **Circulation:** 7,500. **Advertising:** accepted. Alternate Formats: CD-ROM ● *ASNET*, bimonthly. Newsletter ● *Naval Engineers Journal*, quarterly. **Price:** $20.00 in U.S. and Canada; $25.00 outside U.S. and Canada ● *Naval Engineers Journal Cumulative Index, 1889-1979.* **Conventions/Meetings:** annual conference and meeting, technical (exhibits) ● annual meeting and symposium - always in Washington, DC ● symposium, provides information on combat systems and ship design.

7271 ■ Estuarine Research Federation (ERF)

PO Box 510
Port Republic, MD 20676
Ph: (410)326-7467
Fax: (410)326-7466
E-mail: webmaster@erf.org
URL: http://erf.org
Contact: Robert Christian, Pres.

Founded: 1971. **Members:** 1,650. **Membership Dues:** individual, $120 (annual) ● sponsoring, $600 (annual) ● student, $55 (annual) ● associate, $70 (annual) ● sustaining, $200 (annual) ● family, emeritus, $35 (annual). **Description:** Acts as a forum for persons actively engaged in all research and management issues of estuarine and coastal environments. Maintains a student endowment fund support program. **Awards:** Distinguished Service. **Frequency:** biennial. **Type:** recognition. **Recipient:** for student presentations. **Computer Services:** Online services, job services. **Committees:** Awards; Education; Nominations; Public Outreach; Publications. **Formerly:** (1994) Atlantic Estuarine Research Society. **Publications:** *ERF Newsletter*, quarterly. Informs members on federation happenings, programs and upcoming conferences. Alternate Formats: online ● *Estuaries*, bimonthly. Journal. Contains manuscripts on original research findings on physical, chemical, geological and biological systems. Alternate Formats: online. **Conventions/Meetings:** biennial conference (exhibits).

7272 ■ Marine Board (MB)

c/o Keck Center of the National Academies
500 5th St. NW
Washington, DC 20001
Ph: (202)334-3119 (202)334-2167
Fax: (202)334-2030
E-mail: jcambridge@nas.edu
URL: http://www.trb.org/Activities/MarineBoard/MarineBoard.asp
Contact: Joedy W. Cambridge, Dir.

Founded: 1965. **Members:** 20. **Staff:** 4. **Budget:** $250,000. **Description:** Works as a unit of the National Research Council of the National Academies and operates under the Transportation Research Board. Acts as a study unit for information on U.S. marine engineering and maritime transportation activities; concerned with engineering and technology as it affects: coastal and offshore resources development and operations; navigation and commerce of seas and waterways; related human resources and onshore activities including development of public policy. Identifies opportunities and needs for engineering capabilities and for development of new technologies; makes recommendations; promotes multidisciplinary communication and cooperation; acts as a professional forum for the national and international maritime community. **Libraries: Type:** reference. **Holdings:** books, periodicals. **Subjects:** marine transportation, engineering, finance. **Absorbed:** (1982) Maritime Transportation Research Board. **Publications:** *Project Report*, periodic ● Annual

Report, annual ● Proceedings, periodic. **Conventions/Meetings:** semiannual meeting.

7273 ■ Marine Technology Society (MTS)
5565 Sterrett Pl., Ste.108
Columbia, MD 21044
Ph: (410)884-5330
Fax: (410)884-9060
E-mail: mtsmbrship@erols.com
URL: http://www.mtsociety.org
Contact: Bruce Gilman, Pres.

Founded: 1963. **Members:** 2,500. **Membership Dues:** individual, associate, $75 (annual) ● student, $25 (annual) ● patron, $100 (annual) ● life, $1,000 ● emeritus, $40 (annual) ● corporate (Fortune 500), $2,000 (annual) ● corporate (non-Fortune 500), $1,000 (annual) ● business, institutional, $550 (annual). **Staff:** 4. **Budget:** $500,000. **Description:** Scientists, engineers, educators, and others with professional interest in the marine sciences or related fields; includes institutional and corporate members. Disseminates marine scientific and technical information, including institutional, environmental, physical, and biological aspects; fosters a deeper understanding of the world's seas and attendant technologies. Maintains 13 sections and 29 professional committees. Conducts tutorials. **Libraries: Type:** reference. **Holdings:** 500; periodicals. **Awards:** Compass Achievement. **Frequency:** annual. **Type:** recognition. **Recipient:** for major contributions in marine science or engineering ● Compass Industrial. **Frequency:** annual. **Type:** recognition. **Recipient:** for major corporate contributions in marine science or engineering ● Compass International. **Frequency:** annual. **Type:** recognition. **Recipient:** for major contributions in marine science or engineering by a non-U.S. individual organization ● Lockheed-Martin Technology. **Frequency:** annual. **Type:** recognition. **Recipient:** for major contributions in marine engineering and technology. **Committees:** Autonomous Underwater Vehicles; Buoy Technology; Cables and Connectors; Coastal Zone Management; Diving; Dynamic Positioning; Education; Manned Undersea Vehicles; Marine Geodesy; Marine Law and Policy; Marine Living Resource; Marine Materials; Marine Mineral Resources; Marine Recreation; Marine Salvage and Towing; Marine Security; Moorings; Ocean Economic Potential; Ocean Energy; Ocean Pollution; Oceanographic Instrumentation; Oceanographic Ships; Offshore Structures; Physical Oceanography and Meteorology; Ropes and Tension Members; ROVs; Satellite and Aircraft Remote Sensing; Seafloor Engineering; Underwater Imagining. **Absorbed:** (1971) American Society for Oceanography. **Publications:** *Currents*, bimonthly. Newsletter. **Price:** free for members. **Advertising:** accepted. Alternate Formats: online ● Journal, quarterly. Includes book reviews and peer-reviewed articles. **Price:** $80.00/year in U.S.; $94.00/year outside U.S. ISSN: 0025-3324. **Circulation:** 3,400. **Advertising:** accepted. Alternate Formats: microform ● Proceedings. **Conventions/Meetings:** annual competition (exhibits) ● annual conference (exhibits) - always fall.

7274 ■ National Association of Marine Laboratories (NAML)
c/o Dr. Anthony Michaels, Pres.
Wrigley Inst. for Environmental Stud.
Univ. of Southern California
PO Box 5069
Avalon, CA 90704-5069
Ph: (213)740-6780
Fax: (213)740-7620
E-mail: tony@usc.edu
URL: http://www.naml.org
Contact: Dr. Anthony Michaels, Pres.

Founded: 1980. **Members:** 120. **Description:** Works to improve the quality and effectiveness of ocean, coastal and Great Lakes research, education and outreach. Promotes and supports basic and applied research of the highest quality from the unique perspective of coastal laboratories. Encourages wise utilization and conservation of marine and coastal habitats and resources using ecosystem-based management approaches.

7275 ■ National Association of Marine Surveyors (NAMS)
PO Box 9306
Chesapeake, VA 23321-9306
Ph: (757)638-9638
Free: (800)822-6267
Fax: (757)638-9639
E-mail: nationaloffice@nams-cms.org
URL: http://www.nams-cms.org
Contact: Ghulam Suhrawardi, Pres.

Founded: 1962. **Members:** 400. **Membership Dues:** associate, $250 (annual) ● full/certified, $450 (annual) ● apprentice, $125 (annual). **Staff:** 1. **Budget:** $140,000. **Regional Groups:** 14. **Description:** Professional marine surveyors united to promote the profession. Encourages cooperation and provides for communication among members; assists in the exchange of information concerning the latest approved and recommended practices, new materials and their application to the marine field. Conducts specialized education programs. **Libraries: Type:** reference. **Awards:** Honorary Membership Award. **Type:** recognition. **Computer Services:** database, marine surveyors. **Committees:** Ethics; Insurance; Qualification and Certification; Technical. **Formerly:** (1960) Corresponding Surveyors to the Yacht Safety Bureau. **Publications:** *Membership List*, annual. Membership Directory. Alternate Formats: diskette ● *NAMS News*, semiannual. Newsletter. Provides information to marine surveyors, underwriters, and adjusters. **Price:** included in membership dues; $25.00 /year for nonmembers. **Circulation:** 600. Alternate Formats: online. **Conventions/Meetings:** annual conference.

7276 ■ Sea Grant Association (SGA)
c/o Paul S. Anderson, Pres.
Univ. of Maine
5784 York Complex
Orono, ME 04469
Ph: (207)581-1435
Fax: (207)581-1426
E-mail: panderson@maine.edu
URL: http://www.sga.seagrant.org
Contact: Paul S. Anderson, Pres.

Founded: 1970. **Members:** 39. **Membership Dues:** regular, $3,000 (annual). **Description:** Colleges, universities, institutions, and industries interested in the National Sea Grant Program. Purposes are: to further the optimal development, use, and conservation of oceanic and coastal resources (including those of the Great Lakes) and to encourage increased accomplishment in related areas; to increase the effectiveness of member institutions in their work on oceanic and coastal resources (including those of the Great Lakes); to stimulate cooperation and unity of effort among members. Compiles statistics; conducts workshops; sponsors Sea Grant Week activities. **Awards:** Student Research Award. **Frequency:** annual. **Type:** recognition. **Committees:** Ad Hoc on Presentation to Meetings; Ad Hoc on Roles and Relationships with Agencies; Ad Hoc SG International; Audit; Awards; External Relations; Federal Relations; Nominating; Program Mission; Resources and Finances; Special Events; Standards and Ethics. **Formerly:** (1975) Association of Sea Grant Program Institutions. **Publications:** Brochure ● Papers. Alternate Formats: online ● Also publishes fact sheets. **Conventions/Meetings:** annual Sea Grant Week - conference.

7277 ■ Women's Aquatic Network (WAN)
PO Box 4993
Washington, DC 20008
E-mail: info@womensaquatic.net
URL: http://www.womensaquatic.net
Contact: Nicole Le Boeuf, Vice Chair

Founded: 1985. **Members:** 350. **Membership Dues:** professional, $30 (annual) ● student, senior, $15 (annual) ● family, $40 (annual) ● life, $500 ● patron, $100 (annual). **Budget:** $5,000. **Description:** Individuals and institutions concerned with fresh water and marine affairs; persons involved in all areas/sectors related to aquatic affairs. Focuses on policy issues related to marine and aquatic topics; promotes the importance of women taking an active part in this field. Serves as information clearinghouse. Conducts monthly forum. **Awards:** WAN Achievement Award. **Frequency:** periodic. **Type:** recognition. **Recipient:** to members and non-members who have greatly influenced and presented the role of women in aquatic affairs ● WAN Volunteer of the Year Award. **Frequency:** periodic. **Type:** recognition. **Recipient:** to a member with outstanding contributions and efforts to further the objectives of the organization. **Formerly:** (1984) Women's Network in Aquatic and Marine Affairs. **Publications:** Newsletter, monthly. Covers issues of concern to the marine community. Includes calendar of events, employment opportunities and legislative updates. **Price:** included in membership dues. **Circulation:** 250. **Advertising:** accepted ● Directory, periodic ● Also publishes brochure. **Conventions/Meetings:** monthly meeting.

Marine Biology

7278 ■ American Elasmobranch Society (AES)
c/o Julie A. Neer, Treas.
NOAA Fisheries
3500 Delwood Beach Rd.
Panama City, FL 32408
Ph: (850)234-6541
E-mail: jcarrier@albion.edu
URL: http://www.flmnh.ufl.edu/fish/organizations/aes/aes.htm
Contact: Jeff Carrier, Pres.

Founded: 1983. **Members:** 497. **Membership Dues:** student, $25 (annual) ● foreign, $40 (annual) ● regular, $50 (annual) ● family, $60 (annual) ● associate, $100 (annual) ● sponsor, $250 (annual) ● patron, $500 (annual) ● benefactor, $1,000 (annual) ● corporate, $5,000 (annual). **Description:** Advances the scientific study of living and fossil sharks, skates, rays, and chimaeras. Promotes education, conservation, and wise utilization of natural resources. **Committees:** Conference Planning; Conservation; Finance; Grant Fund; Henry Mollet Fund; Shark Attack File; Student Affairs; Student Award. **Publications:** Newsletter, quarterly. **Conventions/Meetings:** annual meeting.

7279 ■ Aquatic Animal Life Support Operators (AALSO)
PO Box 690067
Orlando, FL 32869-0067
Ph: (407)363-2587
E-mail: info@aalso.org
URL: http://www.aalso.org
Contact: Henry Johnson, Pres.

Membership Dues: individual, $10 (annual) ● vendor, $100 (annual). **Description:** Aims to advance the science of aquatic animal life support system operations. Strives to enhance the environments of marine animals and other zoological specimens. Serves as a resource of information on maintenance and care of marine animals and the systems that support these animals. **Telecommunication Services:** electronic mail, henry.johnson@seaworld.com. **Publications:** Newsletter. **Price:** included in membership dues.

Marketing

7280 ■ CPExchange
c/o IDEAlliance
100 Daingerfield Rd.
Alexandria, VA 22314
Ph: (703)837-1066
E-mail: dsteinhardt@idealliance.org
URL: http://www.idealliance.org/cpexchange
Contact: David Steinhardt, Contact

Membership Dues: regular, $2,500 (annual) ● network, working group, $15,000 (annual). **Description:** Develops an open standard to facilitate exchange of privacy-enabled customer information across enterprise applications.

Materials

7281 ■ Federation of Materials Societies (FMS)

910 17th St. NW, Ste.800
Washington, DC 20006
Ph: (202)296-9282
Fax: (202)833-3014
E-mail: betsyhou@ix.netcom.com
URL: http://www.materialsocieties.org
Contact: Betsy Houston, Exec. Dir.

Founded: 1972. **Members:** 14. **Staff:** 3. **Budget:** $50,000. **Description:** Organizations seeking to enhance materials science and engineering, improve the efficacy of use and application of materials, provide a forum and focus for materials, coordinate and stimulate intersociety activities and cooperation, and provide technical studies for the federal government, including Congress. Conducts educational programs, manpower studies, seminars on national materials policy, and programs on information sources, dissemination, needs, conservation of critical resources, and impact upon energy and environment. **Awards:** National Materials Advancement Award. **Frequency:** annual. **Type:** recognition. **Committees:** Communications; International Affairs. **Publications:** *Conference Proceedings/Materials*, biennial ● Newsletter, quarterly. **Conventions/Meetings:** biennial conference - usually May of even-numbered years in Washington, DC area.

7282 ■ Materials Handling and Management Society (MHMS)

8720 Red Oak Blvd., Ste.201
Charlotte, NC 28217
Ph: (704)676-1190
Fax: (704)676-1199
E-mail: jnofsinger@mhia.org
URL: http://www.mhia.org/PS/PS_MHMS_Home.cfm
Contact: John B. Nofsinger, CEO

Founded: 1949. **Members:** 1,500. **Staff:** 2. **Regional Groups:** 7. **Local Groups:** 15. **Description:** Professional society of engineers, educators, and executives from 4 countries. Advances the theory and practice of material management and material handling systems in manufacturing, distribution, warehousing, transportation, and health care operations. Conducts educational activities; maintains Speaker's Bureau. Provides placement service. **Boards:** Directors. **Committees:** Chapter Presidents. **Formerly:** (1966) American Material Handling Society; (1991) International Material Management Society. **Publications:** *Materials Handling and Management Courses*, quarterly. Highlights correspondence courses. **Price:** $295.00 for members ● *Materials Handling and Management Society—Outlook*, bimonthly. Newsletter. Contains technical papers and news of society activities. **Price:** included in membership dues. **Circulation:** 1,500 ● *MHMS Membership Directory*, annual. **Conventions/Meetings:** annual meeting, membership - 2008 Sept. 7-11, Scottsdale, AZ; 2009 Oct. 4-8, Amelia Island, FL ● annual meeting - every spring. 2009 Mar. 30-Apr. 1, Charlotte, NC.

7283 ■ Materials Research Society (MRS)

506 Keystone Dr.
Warrendale, PA 15086-7573
Ph: (724)779-3003
Fax: (724)779-8313
E-mail: info@mrs.org
URL: http://www.mrs.org
Contact: John B. Ballance, Exec. Dir.

Founded: 1973. **Members:** 14,000. **Membership Dues:** student, retired, unemployed, $30 (annual) ● regular, $105 (annual). **Staff:** 45. **Regional Groups:** 8. **Local Groups:** 33. **Description:** Represents the interests of materials researchers from academia, industry, and government that promotes communication for the advancement of interdisciplinary materials research to improve the quality of life. Fosters interaction among researchers working on different classes of inorganic and organic materials and to promote interdisciplinary basic research on materials. Provides forum for industry, government, and university cooperation; conducts technical conferences, tutorial lectures. Maintains speakers' bureau. **Awards:** Arthur Von Hippel Award. **Frequency:** annual. **Type:** recognition ● Graduate Student Award. **Frequency:** biennial. **Type:** recognition ● MRS Medal Award. **Frequency:** annual. **Type:** medal ● Outstanding Young Investigator Award. **Frequency:** annual. **Type:** recognition ● Turnbull Lectureship Award. **Frequency:** annual. **Type:** recognition. **Computer Services:** Online services, membership directory. **Committees:** Information Services; Membership; Public Affairs; Technical Program. **Publications:** *Journal of Materials Research*, monthly. Includes research articles on advanced materials preparation, processing, characterization, and properties. Also includes occasional review articles. **Price:** $140.00 /year for members in U.S.; $180.00 /year for members outside U.S. ISSN: 0884-2914. **Advertising:** accepted. Alternate Formats: microform; CD-ROM ● *MRS Bulletin*, monthly. Covers news, issues, and technical developments in materials research; includes news of the society. Includes information on new products. **Price:** included in membership dues; $230.00 /year for nonmembers in U.S.; $285.00 /year for nonmembers outside U.S. ISSN: 0883-7694. **Circulation:** 14,000. **Advertising:** accepted ● *MRS Symposium Proceedings*, periodic. Contains scientific papers on materials research. Includes subject and author index. ISSN: 0272-9172 ● Books ● Monographs ● Videos. **Conventions/Meetings:** semiannual meeting (exhibits) - 2008 Dec. 1-5, Boston, MA.

7284 ■ National Materials Advisory Board (NMAB)

c/o The National Academies
500 5th St. NW, Keck WS938
Washington, DC 20001
Ph: (202)334-3505
Fax: (202)334-3718
E-mail: nmab@nas.edu
URL: http://www7.nationalacademies.org/nmab
Contact: Gary Fischman, Dir.

Founded: 1951. **Members:** 22. **Staff:** 10. **Description:** Represents members of the board and its committees and panels appointed by the chairman of the National Research Council (see separate entry); industry, universities, research institutes, and government. Promotes the advancement of materials science and engineering in the national interest. Conducts studies on materials problem, potential approaches, and policy issues. **Telecommunication Services:** electronic mail, gfischman@nas.edu. **Committees:** Development of Technologies for Improved Aviation Security; High Performance Structural Fibers or Advanced Polymer Matrix Composites; Materials Research for Defense; Next Generation Materials and Processes for Advanced Hybrid Power Systems; Small Business Innovative Research Supporting Aging Aircraft; Technical Strategies for Adaptation of Commercial Standards in Defense Procurement. **Formerly:** (1969) Materials Advisory Board. **Publications:** *NMAB News*, annual. Newsletter ● Catalog. Lists selected NMAB reports. **Conventions/Meetings:** semiannual board meeting - usually April and October in Washington, DC.

7285 ■ Society for the Advancement of Material and Process Engineering (SAMPE)

1161 Park View Dr., Ste.200
Covina, CA 91724
Ph: (626)331-0616
Free: (800)562-7360
Fax: (626)332-8929
E-mail: sampeibo@sampe.org
URL: http://www.sampe.org
Contact: Gregg B. Balko, Exec. Dir.

Founded: 1944. **Members:** 5,000. **Membership Dues:** student, $20-$50 (annual) ● professional, associate, $99-$113 (annual) ● retiree, $39 (annual). **Staff:** 13. **Budget:** $2,400,000. **Regional Groups:** 42. **Multinational. Description:** Material and process engineers, scientists, and other professionals engaged in development of advanced materials and processing technology in airframe, missile, aerospace, propulsion, electronics, life sciences, management, and related industries. International and local chapters sponsor scholarships for science students seeking financial assistance. Provides placement service for members. **Libraries: Type:** open to the public. **Awards: Frequency:** annual. **Type:** scholarship. **Computer Services:** Mailing lists. **Committees:** Career Development; Chapter Relations; Editorial and Publicity; Education; Government Liaison; History; Membership Recognition; National Advertising; Space Manufacturing. **Formerly:** (1960) Society of Aircraft Material and Process Engineers; (1972) Society of Aerospace Material and Process Engineers. **Publications:** *SAMPE Journal*, bimonthly. Contains technical papers on materials and composites and covers association news. Includes advertisers index and subject and author indexes. **Price:** included in membership dues; $85.00 /year for nonmembers. ISSN: 0091-1062. **Circulation:** 5,000. **Advertising:** accepted ● *SAMPE Journal of Advanced Materials*, quarterly. Contains technical papers; includes annual subject and author indexes. **Price:** $70.00 /year for nonmembers; $30.00 /year for members. ISSN: 1070-9789. **Circulation:** 4,500 ● Also publishes symposium and technical conference proceedings. **Conventions/Meetings:** annual conference (exhibits) ● annual meeting and conference, for companies that manufacture materials and test equipment, machinery and software for aerospace, aircraft, sporting equipment, and electronics industries (exhibits).

Mathematics

7286 ■ American Mathematical Society (AMS)

201 Charles St.
Providence, RI 02904-2213
Ph: (401)455-4000
Free: (800)321-4AMS
Fax: (401)331-3842
E-mail: ams@ams.org
URL: http://www.ams.org
Contact: Dr. John Ewing, Exec. Dir.

Founded: 1888. **Members:** 30,000. **Membership Dues:** regular introductory rate, $60 ● affiliate, $16 (annual) ● student, unemployed, $40 (annual) ● retired, $60 (annual) ● regular (based on annual income), $80-$160 (annual) ● reciprocity (reside outside US), $80 (annual) ● reciprocity (reside inside US - based on annual income), $120-$160 (annual) ● contributing, $240 (annual) ● life (based on age), $800-$2,400. **Staff:** 150. **Budget:** $22,000,000. **Description:** Professional society of mathematicians and educators. Promotes the interests of mathematical scholarship and research. Holds institutes, seminars, short courses, and symposia to further mathematical research; awards prizes. Offers placement services; compiles statistics. **Libraries: Type:** reference. **Holdings:** biographical archives. **Computer Services:** database, MathSci on SilverPlatter(-TM) ● database, MathSciNet ● database, 2003 subscription information for mathematics reviews and MR database Products ● electronic publishing, MathSciNet, e-Math, Ams preprint server ● information services ● mailing lists, of various groupings available for rent on Cheshire, pressure sensitive, magnetic tape or 3.5 inch floppy disk. **Telecommunication Services:** electronic mail, jhe@ams.org. **Committees:** Institutes and Symposia; Prizes and Awards; Status of Profession. **Formerly:** (1894) New York Mathematical Society. **Publications:** *Abstracts of Papers Presented to the AMS*, quarterly. Journal. Contains abstracts of papers presented for annual and sectional meetings. **Price:** $67.00/year for individual member, plus shipping and handling; $90.00/year for member institution, plus shipping and handling; $112.00 /year for nonmembers, plus shipping and handling; $43.00/back issue. ISSN: 0192-5857 ● *Bulletin (New Series) of the American Mathematical Society*, quarterly. Journal. **Price:** $428.00/back issue (institutional members); $286.00 for institution members, plus shipping and handling; $357.00 /year for nonmembers, plus shipping and handling; $214.00 for individual members, plus shipping and handling. ISSN: 0273-0979 ● *Conformal Geometry & Dynamics: An Electronic Journal of the*

AMS. Available at no charge to subscribers of Journal of the AMS, Mathematics of Computation, Proceedings of the AMS or Transactions of the AMS. **Price:** $25.00 each. ISSN: 1088-4173. **Advertising:** accepted. Alternate Formats: microform; online ● *Current Mathematical Publications*, every 3 weeks. Journal. **Price:** $470.00 for institutional member, plus shipping and handling; $353.00 for individuals, plus shipping and handling. ISSN: 0361-4794. **Advertising:** accepted. Alternate Formats: online ● *Electronic Research Announcements of the AMS*. Journal. **Price:** free. ISSN: 1079-6762. Alternate Formats: online ● *Employment Information in the Mathematical Sciences*, 5/year. **Price:** $111.00 /year for individuals; $185.00 /year for nonmembers; $45.00/year for students or unemployed. ISSN: 0163-3287. Alternate Formats: online ● *Journal of the American Mathematical Society*, quarterly. Contains research articles in all areas of pure and applied mathematics. **Price:** $133.00 /year for members; $177.00 /year for institutions; $221.00 /year for nonmembers. ISSN: 0894-0347. Alternate Formats: online ● *Mathematical Review Sections*. Contains reviews of current published work in an area of interest. **Price:** $143.00 for individuals (class 1); $95.00 for reviewers (class 1); $114.00 for individuals (class 2); $76.00 for reviewers (class 2) ● *Mathematical Reviews*, monthly. Journal. Includes abstracts. **Price:** $501.00 plus shipping and handling; $6,509.00 for electronic database; $5,207.00 for electronic database (institutional member). ISSN: 0025-5629. Alternate Formats: online ● *Mathematics of Computation*, quarterly. Journal. **Price:** $222.00 /year for members; $247.00 /year for members (print); $329.00 /year for institutions (print); $411.00 /year for nonmembers (print). ISSN: 0025-5718. Alternate Formats: online ● *Memoirs of the AMS*, bimonthly. Journal. **Price:** $555.00 list; $444.00/year for member institutions. ISSN: 0065-9266. Alternate Formats: microform; online ● *Notices of the AMS*. Journal. **Price:** $382.00 /year for nonmembers; $229.00 /year for members. ISSN: 0002-9920. **Advertising:** accepted. Alternate Formats: online ● *Proceedings of the AMS*, monthly. Journal. Contains English translations of papers presented to the Mathematical Society of Japan. **Price:** $818.00 list; $654.00 institutional; $491.00 individual. ISSN: 0002-9939. Alternate Formats: microform; online ● *Representation Theory: An Electronic Journal of the AMS*. Dedicated to research in the field of representation theory. **Price:** $25.00 individual. ISSN: 1088-4165 ● *St. Petersburg Mathematical Journal*, bimonthly. Contains English translations of papers presented to the Mathematical Society of Japan. **Price:** $1,472.00 list; $1,178.00 institutional. ISSN: 1061-0022. Alternate Formats: online ● *Sugaku Expositions*, semiannual. Journal. Contains English translations of papers presented to the Mathematical Society of Japan. **Price:** $165.00 list; $132.00 institutional; $99.00 individual. ISSN: 1061-022X. Alternate Formats: online ● *Theory of Probability and Mathematical Statistics*, semiannual. Journal. **Price:** $451.00/year for member institutions; $564.00 /year for nonmembers. ISSN: 0009-9000 ● *Transactions of the Moscow Mathematical Society*, monthly. Journal. **Price:** $1,490.00 /year for nonmembers (paper & electronic); $1,073.00 /year for institutions (electronic); $1,341.00 /year for nonmembers (electronic); $1,192.00 /year for institutions (paper & electronic). ISSN: 0002-9947. Alternate Formats: online. **Conventions/Meetings:** annual Joint Mathematics - conference (exhibits) - always January.

7287 ■ Association for Symbolic Logic (ASL)

Vassar Coll.
124 Raymond Ave.
PO Box 742
Poughkeepsie, NY 12604
Ph: (845)437-7080
Fax: (845)437-7830
E-mail: asl@vassar.edu
URL: http://www.aslonline.org
Contact: Charles I. Steinhorn, Sec.-Treas.

Founded: 1936. **Members:** 1,550. **Membership Dues:** individual, $76 (annual) ● student, unemployed, $38 (annual) ● institution, $625 (annual) ● individual (outreach), $18 (annual) ● institutional (outreach), $130 (annual) ● corporate, $3,000 (annual). **Staff:** 4. **Budget:** $545,894. **Multinational. Description:** Serves as professional society of mathematicians, computer scientists, linguists, philosophers, and others interested in formal or mathematical logic and related fields. Promotes research in symbolic logic and provides for the exchange of ideas within the mathematical community of logicians. **Awards:** Karp Prize. **Frequency:** quinquennial. **Type:** monetary ● Sacks Prize. **Frequency:** annual. **Type:** monetary ● Student Travel Awards. **Type:** monetary. **Computer Services:** Mailing lists, of members. **Publications:** *ASL Newsletter*, quarterly. Alternate Formats: online ● *Bulletin of Symbolic Logic*, quarterly. Journal. Contains articles and communications of interest to logic community. **Price:** included in membership dues. ISSN: 1079-8986. **Circulation:** 2,500. **Advertising:** accepted. Alternate Formats: online ● *Journal of Symbolic Logic*, quarterly. Contains original scholarly work in symbolic logic, research papers, and expository articles. **Price:** included in membership dues. ISSN: 0022-4812. **Circulation:** 2,500. **Advertising:** accepted. **Conventions/Meetings:** annual Logic Colloquium - meeting - always summer ● annual meeting - usually spring ● annual meeting, held in conjunction with the Joint Mathematical Meetings - held in winter ● annual meeting.

7288 ■ Association for Women in Mathematics (AWM)

11240 Waples Mill Rd., Ste.200
Fairfax, VA 22030
Ph: (703)934-0163
Fax: (703)359-7562
E-mail: awm@awm-math.org
URL: http://www.awm-math.org
Contact: Cathy Kessel, Pres.

Founded: 1971. **Members:** 4,500. **Membership Dues:** student, unemployed, $20 (annual) ● part-time employed, retired, $30 (annual) ● individual, $55 (annual) ● academic institutional (minimum), $150 (annual) ● institutional sponsor (minimum), $1,000 (annual). **Staff:** 3. **Budget:** $40,000. **Description:** Represents mathematicians employed by universities, government, and private industry; students. Seeks to improve the status of women in the mathematical profession, and to make students aware of opportunities for women in the field. Membership is open to all interested individuals, regardless of sex. **Awards:** Alice T. Schafer Mathematics Prize. **Frequency:** annual. **Type:** recognition. **Recipient:** for an undergraduate woman, for excellence in mathematics ● **Type:** grant. **Recipient:** for women doing postdoctoral research ● Louise Hay Award. **Frequency:** annual. **Type:** recognition. **Recipient:** for contributions to mathematics education. **Computer Services:** Mailing lists, AWM-Net electronic mail forum. **Committees:** Education. **Funds:** Anniversary Endowment; General. **Formerly:** (1973) Association of Women Mathematicians. **Publications:** *Association for Women in Mathematics—Newsletter*, bimonthly. Contains articles by and about women in mathematics on topics such as employment, education, discrimination, law, mathematics, and biography. **Price:** included in membership dues; $50.00 /year for nonmembers in U.S.; $58.00 /year for nonmembers outside U.S. **Circulation:** 4,000. **Advertising:** accepted ● *Careers That Count: Opportunities in the Mathematical Sciences*. Brochure. **Price:** $1.50 each; $1.00 each (for 10 or more copies) ● *Combined Membership List*. Membership Directory ● *Profiles of Women in Mathematics: The Emmy Noether Lectures*. Booklet. Features profiles of women who have presented Noether Lectures since 1980. **Price:** $1.50 each; $1.00 each (for 10 or more copies). **Conventions/Meetings:** annual meeting, held in conjunction with AMS-MAA.

7289 ■ Conference Board of the Mathematical Sciences (CBMS)

1529 18th St. NW
Washington, DC 20036
Ph: (202)293-1170
Fax: (202)293-3412
E-mail: rosier@georgetown.edu
URL: http://www.cbmsweb.org
Contact: Ronald C. Rosier, Admin. Off.

Founded: 1960. **Members:** 16. **Description:** Presidents of: American Mathematical Association of Two-Year Colleges; American Mathematical Society; American Statistical Association; Association of State Supervisors of Mathematics; Association for Symbolic Logic; Association for Women in Mathematics; Institute for Operations Research and the Management Sciences; Institute of Mathematical Statistics; Mathematical Association of America; National Council of Supervisors of Mathematics; National Council of Teachers of Mathematics; Society of Actuaries; Society for Industrial and Applied Mathematics; National Association of Mathematicians. **Telecommunication Services:** electronic mail, lkolbe@maa.org. **Conventions/Meetings:** semiannual meeting - always May and December.

7290 ■ International Linear Algebra Society (ILAS)

c/o Jeffrey L. Stuart, Sec.-Treas.
Pacific Lutheran Univ.
Dept. of Mathematics
Tacoma, WA 98447
E-mail: jeffrey.stuart@plu.edu
URL: http://www.math.technion.ac.il/iic/ILAS.html
Contact: Jeffrey L. Stuart, Sec.-Treas.

Founded: 1989. **Members:** 400. **Membership Dues:** individual, $20 (annual). **Budget:** $5,000. **Multinational. Description:** Promotes activities in linear algebra. **Awards:** Hans Schneider Prize in Linear Algebra. **Frequency:** triennial. **Type:** recognition. **Recipient:** for research, contribution & achievements. **Computer Services:** Information services, ILAS-NET. **Committees:** Education. **Formerly:** International Matrix Group. **Publications:** *Electronic Journal of Linear Algebra*, 2 volumes/year. Features articles of high standards contributing to new info and insights to matrix analysis and various aspects of linear algebra and application. **Price:** $16.00 for members, plus shipping and handling (vol. 1-4); $20.00 for members, plus shipping and handling (vol. 5-7); $20.00 for nonmembers, plus shipping and handling (vol. 1-4); $25.00 for nonmembers, plus shipping and handling (vol. 5-7). ISSN: 1081-3810. Alternate Formats: online. Also Cited As: *ELA* ● *IMAGE*, semiannual. Bulletin. **Advertising:** accepted. Alternate Formats: online. **Conventions/Meetings:** annual meeting - 2008 June 16-20, Cancun, QR, Mexico - **Avg. Attendance:** 200.

7291 ■ International Society for Bayesian Analysis (ISBA)

c/o Prof. Bruno Sanso, Treas.
Dept. of Applied Mathematics and Statistics
School of Engg.
Univ. of California
1156 High St., MS: SOE2
Santa Cruz, CA 95064
Ph: (831)459-1484
Fax: (831)459-4829
E-mail: bruno@ams.ucsc.edu
URL: http://www.bayesian.org
Contact: Prof. Bruno Sanso, Treas.

Founded: 1992. **Membership Dues:** regular, $25 (annual) ● reduced rate (student, resident of selected countries), $10 (annual). **Multinational. Description:** Promotes the development and application of Bayesian analysis in the solution of theoretical and applied problems in science, industry, and government. Fosters interest in the study of Bayesian analysis and its applications. Serves as a resource of information pertaining to all aspects of the study of Bayesian analysis. **Awards:** Founders Award. **Frequency:** periodic. **Type:** recognition. **Recipient:** for outstanding contribution to the research and advocacy on the Bayesian method. **Publications:** *Bayesian Analysis*. Journal. Contains articles, reviews and case studies pertaining to all aspects of the Bayesian method. Alternate Formats: online ● Newsletter, quarterly. **Price:** included in membership dues ● Proceedings, periodic. Alternate Formats: online.

7292 ■ International Society of Difference Equations (ISDE)
c/o Saber Elaydi, Pres.
Trinity Univ.
Dept. of Mathematics
Marrs-McLean Sci. Bldg., Rm. 115-D
One Trinity Pl.
San Antonio, TX 78212-7200
Ph: (210)999-8246
Fax: (210)999-8264
E-mail: selaydi@trinity.edu
URL: http://web.umr.edu/~isde
Contact: Saber Elaydi, Pres.

Founded: 2001. **Members:** 500. **Membership Dues:** sponsoring, $100 (annual). **Multinational. Description:** Promotes difference equations and discrete dynamical systems as two of the fundamental subjects in Mathematics. Promotes discrete models as models of premiere mathematical importance in the natural sciences, engineering, and economics. Coordinates activities in the area of difference equations. Lends support to researchers. Promotes the publication of books, monographs, lecture notes and expository articles in the area of difference equations. Publishes the Journal of Difference Equations and Applications (12 issues per year) and proceedings of its annual conferences. **Awards:** Best Paper award. **Frequency:** annual. **Type:** monetary. **Recipient:** for the best paper in difference equations and discrete dynamical systems, published in the Journal of Difference Equations and Applications. **Publications:** *Journal of Difference Equations and Applications*, monthly. **Price:** $125.00. **Advertising:** accepted. Alternate Formats: online. Also Cited As: *JDEA*.

7293 ■ Mathematical Association of America (MAA)
1529 18th St. NW
Washington, DC 20036-1358
Ph: (202)387-5200 (202)319-8465
Free: (800)741-9415
Fax: (202)265-2384
E-mail: maahq@maa.org
URL: http://www.maa.org
Contact: Tina H. Straley, Exec. Dir.

Founded: 1915. **Members:** 27,000. **Membership Dues:** regular, $144-$231 (annual) ● regular discounted, $115-$185 (annual) ● graduate student, unemployed, $59-$131 (annual) ● retired, $65-$92 (annual) ● life (based on age), $1,472-$3,170 ● regular (corporate), $550 (annual) ● corporate (sponsoring), $1,100 (annual) ● institutional, $300-$450 (annual). **Staff:** 30. **Budget:** $3,200,000. **State Groups:** 29. **Description:** College mathematics teachers; individuals using mathematics as a tool in a business or profession. Sponsors annual high school mathematics contests and W.L. Putnam Competition for college students. Conducts faculty enhancement workshops and promotes the use of computers through classroom training. Offers college placement test program; operates speakers' bureau. **Awards:** Beckenbach Book Prize. **Frequency:** annual. **Type:** recognition ● Carl Allendoerfer Award. **Frequency:** annual. **Type:** recognition. **Recipient:** for distinguished expository writing in mathematics ● Chauvenet Prize. **Frequency:** annual. **Type:** recognition ● George Polya Award. **Frequency:** annual. **Type:** recognition. **Recipient:** for distinguished expository writing in mathematics ● L.R. Ford Award. **Frequency:** annual. **Type:** recognition. **Recipient:** for distinguished expository writing in mathematics ● **Frequency:** annual. **Type:** recognition. **Recipient:** for distinguished service to mathematics. **Computer Services:** Mailing lists, of members. **Telecommunication Services:** electronic mail, tstraley@maa.org. **Committees:** Continuing Education; High School Contests; Placement Examinations; Teaching of Undergraduate Mathematics; Undergraduate Program in Mathematics; Visiting Lecturers and Consultants. **Publications:** *American Mathematical Monthly*, 10/year. Journal ● *College Mathematics Journal*, 5/year ● *Focus*, 9/year. Newsletter. Includes association news and calendar of events. **Price:** included in membership dues. ISSN: 0731-2040. **Circulation:** 19,000 ● *Mathematics Magazine*, 5/year ● *Membership List*, annual. Membership Directory ● Also publishes monographs, studies, papers, and guides. **Conventions/Meetings:** annual MathFest - festival (exhibits) - always August. 2008 July 31-Aug. 2, Madison, WI; 2009 Aug. 6-8, Portland, OR; 2010 Aug. 5-7, Pittsburgh, PA ● annual meeting (exhibits) - always January. 2009 Jan. 7-10, Washington, DC; 2010 Jan. 6-9, San Francisco, CA; 2011 Jan. 5-8, New Orleans, LA.

7294 ■ Society for Industrial and Applied Mathematics (SIAM)
3600 Market St., 6th Fl.
Philadelphia, PA 19104-2688
Ph: (215)382-9800
Free: (800)447-SIAM
Fax: (215)386-7999
E-mail: siam@siam.org
URL: http://www.siam.org
Contact: James Crowley, Exec. Dir.

Founded: 1952. **Members:** 9,100. **Membership Dues:** regular, $181 (annual) ● postgraduate, $90 (annual) ● student, $37 (annual) ● life, $605 ● reciprocal, $84 (annual) ● corporate/institutional, $5,185 (annual) ● outreach, $10 (annual). **Staff:** 60. **Budget:** $4,100,000. **Regional Groups:** 10. **Local Groups:** 15. **Description:** Mathematicians, engineers, computer scientists, physical scientists, bioscientists, educators, social scientists, and others utilizing mathematics for the solution of problems. Purposes are to: promote research in applied mathematics and computational science; further the application of mathematics to new methods and techniques useful in industry and science; provide for the exchange of information between the mathematical, industrial, and scientific communities. Conducts workshops; offers courses; supports sections and university chapters. **Awards:** George B. Dantzig. **Frequency:** triennial. **Type:** recognition. **Recipient:** for outstanding contributions to the field of mathematics and programming ● George David Birkhoff. **Frequency:** quinquennial. **Type:** recognition ● George Polya Prize. **Frequency:** biennial. **Type:** recognition. **Recipient:** for notable contributions in application of combinatorial theory ● German and Dahlquist Prize. **Frequency:** biennial. **Type:** recognition ● I.E. Block Community Lecture. **Frequency:** annual. **Type:** recognition. **Recipient:** for contributions to future trends in the mathematical sciences ● James H. Wilkinson Prize in Numerical Analysis and Scientific Computing. **Frequency:** quadrennial. **Type:** recognition ● Morgan Prize. **Frequency:** annual. **Type:** recognition. **Recipient:** for undergraduate student research in mathematics ● Norbert Wiemer Prize. **Frequency:** quinquennial. **Type:** recognition ● Richard C. DiPrima Prize. **Frequency:** biennial. **Type:** recognition. **Recipient:** for outstanding research in applied mathematics by a younger student ● SIAM Activity Group on Linear Algebra Prize. **Frequency:** triennial. **Type:** recognition ● SIAM Activity Group on Optimization Prize. **Frequency:** triennial. **Type:** recognition ● SIAM Award in the Mathematical Contest in Modeling. **Frequency:** annual. **Type:** recognition ● SIAM Prize for Distinguished Service to the Profession. **Frequency:** triennial. **Type:** recognition. **Recipient:** for applied mathematician who has made distinguished contributions to applied mathematics at the national level ● SIAM Student Paper Prize. **Frequency:** annual. **Type:** recognition ● Theodore von Karman Prize. **Frequency:** quinquennial. **Type:** recognition. **Recipient:** for notable application of mathematics to mechanics and/or engineering sciences ● Von Neuman Lecture Award. **Frequency:** annual. **Type:** recognition ● W.T. and Idalia Reid Prize. **Frequency:** biennial. **Type:** recognition. **Recipient:** for research or other contributions to differential equations and control theory. **Computer Services:** Electronic publishing, for members. **Telecommunication Services:** electronic mail, jcrowley@siam.org. **Committees:** Awards; Committees and Appointments; Education; Human Rights of Mathematical Scientists; Major Awards; Nominating; Programs; Science Policy; Section Activities; Technology Transfer. **Affiliated With:** American Association for the Advancement of Science; Commission on Professionals in Science and Technology; Computing Research Association; Conference Board of the Mathematical Sciences; Council of Scientific Society Presidents. **Publications:** *Classics in Applied Mathematics and Proceedings*, 2-3/year ● *Monographs on Discrete Mathematics and Applications* ● *Monographs on Mathematics Modelling and Computation*, 3/year ● *Proceedings in Applied Mathematics*, quarterly. Journal. Contains proceedings of SIAM conferences and other conferences of interest to SIAM membership. ● *SIAM Journal on Applied Mathematics*, bimonthly. Provides information on the application of mathematical methods to the biological, engineering, medical, and physical sciences; includes author index. **Price:** $96.00 /year for members (US, Canada, Mexico); $102.00 /year for members (overseas). ISSN: 0036-1399. **Circulation:** 2,164. **Advertising:** accepted ● *SIAM Journal on Computing*, bimonthly. Contains articles on the application of mathematics to the problems of computer science and the non-numerical aspects of computing. **Price:** $96.00 /year for members (US, Canada, Mexico); $102.00 /year for members (overseas). ISSN: 0097-5397. **Circulation:** 1,711. **Advertising:** accepted ● *SIAM Journal on Control and Optimization*, bimonthly. Includes articles on the mathematics and applications of control theory and optimization. **Price:** $96.00 /year for members (US, Canada, Mexico); $102.00 /year for members (overseas). ISSN: 0363-0129. **Circulation:** 1,675. **Advertising:** accepted ● *SIAM Journal on Discrete Mathematics*, quarterly. Contains research articles on a broad range of topics including graph theory, discrete optimization and operations research, etc. **Price:** $70.00 /year for members (US, Canada, Mexico); $74.00 /year for members (overseas). ISSN: 0895-4801. **Circulation:** 1,078. **Advertising:** accepted ● *SIAM Journal on Mathematical Analysis*, bimonthly. Contains articles on those parts of classical and modern analysis that have direct or potential application to engineering and the natural sciences. **Price:** $96.00 /year for members (US, Canada, Mexico); $102.00 /year for members (overseas). ISSN: 0036-1410. **Circulation:** 1,309. **Advertising:** accepted ● *SIAM Journal on Matrix Analysis and Applications*, quarterly. Contains research articles on linear algebra with emphasis on applications and numerical procedures. **Price:** $86.00 /year for members (US, Canada, Mexico); $90.00 /year for members (overseas). ISSN: 0895-4798. **Circulation:** 1,212. **Advertising:** accepted ● *SIAM News*, 10/year. Journal. Contains articles on applied mathematics and related technologies. Includes book reviews, educational, employment, and funding opportunities. **Price:** included in membership dues; $42.00 for nonmembers in U.S., Canada, and Mexico; $50.00 for nonmembers overseas. **Circulation:** 11,833. **Advertising:** accepted ● *SIAM Review*, quarterly. Journal. Contains expository and survey papers on applied or computational mathematics. Includes author, index, book reviews, classroom notes, case studies. **Price:** included in membership dues; $314.00 for nonmembers in U.S., Canada, and Mexico; $376.00 for nonmembers overseas. ISSN: 0036-1445. **Circulation:** 10,223. **Advertising:** accepted. **Conventions/Meetings:** biennial conference - always June ● triennial conference - always June ● triennial conference ● annual Conference on Applications of Dynamical Systems (exhibits) ● biennial Conference on Applied Linear Algebra ● triennial Conference on Control and Its Applications ● biennial Conference on Discrete Method ● biennial Conference on Geometric Design ● annual Symposium on Discrete Algorithms - symposium and meeting (exhibits).

7295 ■ Society for Natural Philosophy (SNP)
c/o Prof. Anna Vainchtein, Treas.
Dept. of Mathematics
Univ. of Pittsburgh
301 Thackeray Hall
Pittsburgh, PA 15260
E-mail: annav@euler.math.pitt.edu
URL: http://www.ms.uky.edu/~snp
Contact: T.J. Healey, Chm.

Founded: 1963. **Members:** 300. **Membership Dues:** individual, $25 (annual). **Description:** Scientists interested in foundations of mathematical sciences; formed by a group of persons interested primarily in rational continuum mechanics, together with specialists in analysis, statistical mechanics, and electromagnetism. Aims to foster specific research aimed at the unity of mathematical and physical science and to recognize and promote high quality work. Operates through organization of selective meetings of topics of common interest to small groups of mathematicians, physicists, chemists, and engineers. **Publications:** none. **Conventions/Meetings:** annual symposium.

7296 ■ Special Interest Group for Symbolic and Algebraic Manipulation (SIGSAM)
c/o Daniel Lichtblau, Treas.
Kernel Technology Gp.
Wolfram Research, Inc.
100 Trade Center Dr.
Champaign, IL 61820
E-mail: chair_sigsam@acm.org
URL: http://www.acm.org/sigsam
Contact: Mark Giesbrecht, Chm.

Founded: 1967. **Members:** 2,000. **Membership Dues:** individual, $29 (annual) ● student, $9 (annual). **Description:** A special interest group of the Association for Computing Machinery (see separate entry). Scientists interested in symbolic and algebraic computation; scope of interests includes design, analysis and application of algorithms, data structures, systems and languages. **Awards:** ISAAC Award. **Frequency:** annual. **Type:** recognition. **Recipient:** to authors of ISAAC papers who have displayed excellence in algebraic computation, symbolic-numeric computation, system design and implementation. **Telecommunication Services:** electronic mail, danl@wolfram.com ● electronic mail, treasurer_sigsam@acm.org. **Publications:** *Proceedings of Symposia*, annual ● *SIGSAM Bulletin*, quarterly. **Conventions/Meetings:** annual International Symposium on Symbolic Algebraic Computation - meeting and symposium - 2008 July 20-23, Linz, Austria.

Mechanics

7297 ■ American Academy of Mechanics (AAM)
c/o Rohan Abeyaratne, Pres.
Massachusetts Inst. of Technology
77 Massachusetts Ave.
Cambridge, MA 02139-4307
Ph: (617)253-2201
Fax: (617)258-6156
E-mail: rohan@mit.edu
URL: http://www.aamech.org
Contact: Rohan Abeyaratne, Pres.

Founded: 1969. **Members:** 1,300. **Membership Dues:** professional, $52 (annual) ● student, $30 (annual) ● retired, $15 (annual). **Staff:** 1. **Budget:** $40,000. **Regional Groups:** 4. **Description:** Individuals recognized for their contributions to the science and profession of mechanics; affiliates are firms and companies interested in advancing the field of mechanics. Criteria for membership include authorship of at least two published articles in books or periodicals that are recognized by the board of directors as significant in the field of mechanics. Promotes the science and profession of mechanics; provides a forum wherein engineers, mathematicians, scientists, and others active in mechanics can meet to pursue their common interests. Maintains placement service. **Libraries: Type:** reference; not open to the public. **Holdings:** periodicals. **Awards:** AAM Outstanding Service Award. **Frequency:** annual. **Type:** recognition ● Junior Award. **Frequency:** periodic. **Type:** recognition. **Publications:** *Mechanics*, bimonthly. Newsletter. Provides news in the field of theoretical and applied mechanics. Alternate Formats: online ● Directory, semiannual. **Conventions/Meetings:** periodic Canadian Congress of Applied Mechanics.

7298 ■ American Society of Mechanical Engineers (ASME)
3 Park Ave.
New York, NY 10016-5990
Ph: (973)882-1170
Free: (800)THE-ASME
Fax: (973)882-1717
E-mail: infocentral@asme.org
URL: http://www.asme.org
Contact: Virgil R. Carter, Exec. Dir.

Founded: 1880. **Members:** 125,000. **Membership Dues:** regular, $51-$129 (annual) ● affiliate, fellow, $129 (annual) ● retired, $64 (annual) ● student, $25 (annual). **Staff:** 380. **Regional Groups:** 12. **Local Groups:** 260. **Description:** Technical society of mechanical engineers and students. Conducts research; develops boiler, pressure vessel, and power test codes. Develops safety codes and standards for equipment. Conducts short course programs, and Identifying Research Needs Program. Maintains 19 research committees and 38 divisions. **Libraries: Type:** reference. **Holdings:** 180,000. **Awards:** Society Achievement Award. **Type:** recognition. **Computer Services:** Online services, forum. **Telecommunication Services:** electronic bulletin board, MechEng ● electronic mail, execdirector@asme.org. **Publications:** *Applied Mechanics Reviews*, monthly. Journal. Includes review articles, abstracts and database access. **Price:** $95.00 for members in U.S.; $120.00 for members outside U.S.; $560.00 for nonmembers in U.S.; $585.00 for nonmembers outside U.S. ● *Applied Mechanics Transactions*, quarterly. Journal. **Price:** $60.00 for members in U.S.; $110.00 for members outside U.S.; $430.00 for nonmembers in U.S.; $480.00 for nonmembers outside U.S. ● *ASME News*, monthly. Newsletter ● *Biomechanical Engineering Transactions*, quarterly. Journal. **Price:** $60.00 for members in U.S.; $100.00 for members outside U.S.; $430.00 for nonmembers in U.S.; $480.00 for nonmembers outside U.S. ● *Dynamic Systems, Measurement and Control Transactions*, quarterly. Journal. **Price:** $60.00 for members in U.S.; $100.00 for members outside U.S.; $430.00 for nonmembers in U.S.; $480.00 for nonmembers outside U.S. ● *Electronic Packaging Transactions*, quarterly. Journal. **Price:** $50.00 for members in U.S.; $80.00 for members outside U.S.; $350.00 for nonmembers in U.S.; $385.00 for nonmembers outside U.S. ● *Energy Resources Technology Transactions*, quarterly. Journal. **Price:** $50.00 for members in U.S.; $70.00 for members outside U.S.; $284.00 for nonmembers in U.S.; $304.00 for nonmembers outside U.S. ● *Engineering for Gas Turbines and Power Transactions*, quarterly. Journal. **Price:** $50.00 for members in U.S.; $90.00 for members outside U.S.; $344.00 for nonmembers in U.S.; $384.00 for nonmembers outside U.S. ● *Engineering for Industry Transactions*, quarterly. Journal ● *Engineering Materials and Technology Transactions*, quarterly. Journal. **Price:** $50.00 for members in U.S.; $75.00 for members outside U.S.; $294.00 for nonmembers in U.S.; $319.00 for nonmembers outside U.S. ● *Fluids Engineering Transactions*, quarterly. Journal. **Price:** $80.00 for members in U.S.; $135.00 for members outside U.S.; $545.00 for nonmembers in U.S.; $600.00 for nonmembers outside U.S. ● *Heat Transfer Transactions*, quarterly. Journal. **Price:** $80.00 for members in U.S.; $135.00 for members outside U.S.; $545.00 for nonmembers in U.S.; $600.00 for nonmembers outside U.S. ● *Mechanical Design Transactions Journal*, quarterly. **Price:** $80.00 for members in U.S.; $135.00 for members outside U.S.; $545.00 for nonmembers in U.S.; $600.00 for nonmembers outside U.S. ● *Mechanical Engineering*, monthly. **Price:** $123.00. ISSN: 0025-6501. **Circulation:** 130,000. **Advertising:** accepted ● *Offshore Mechanics and Arctic Engineering Transactions*, quarterly. Journal. **Price:** $50.00 for members in U.S.; $65.00 for members outside U.S.; $256.00 for nonmembers in U.S.; $276.00 for nonmembers outside U.S. ● *Pressure Vessel Technology Transactions*, quarterly. Journal. **Price:** $50.00 for members in U.S.; $75.00 for members outside U.S.; $289.00 for nonmembers in U.S.; $314.00 for nonmembers outside U.S. ● *Solar Energy Engineering Transactions*, quarterly. Journal. **Price:** $50.00 for members in U.S.; $75.00 for members outside U.S.; $263.00 for nonmembers in U.S.; $288.00 for nonmembers outside U.S. ● *Tribology Transactions*, quarterly. Journal. **Price:** $50.00 for members in U.S.; $90.00 for members outside U.S.; $322.00 for nonmembers in U.S.; $362.00 for nonmembers outside U.S. ● *Turbomachinery Transactions*, quarterly. Journal. **Price:** $50.00 for members in U.S.; $85.00 for members outside U.S.; $328.00 for nonmembers in U.S.; $363.00 for nonmembers outside U.S. ● *Vibration and Acoustics Transactions Journal*, quarterly. **Price:** $60.00 for members in U.S.; $95.00 for members outside U.S.; $355.00 for nonmembers in U.S.; $390.00 for nonmembers outside U.S. **Conventions/Meetings:** competition ● annual International Mechanical Engineering Congress and Exposition - conference - always November.

7299 ■ American Society of Mechanical Engineers Auxiliary (ASMEA)
3 Park Ave., 23rd Fl.
New York, NY 10016-5990
Ph: (212)591-7846
Fax: (212)591-7739
E-mail: persaudl@asme.org
URL: http://www.asme.org
Contact: Leila Persaud, Mgr.

Founded: 1923. **Members:** 450. **Membership Dues:** associate, member-at-large, $10 (annual) ● life, $100. **Staff:** 2. **Budget:** $75,000. **Regional Groups:** 8. **State Groups:** 5. **Description:** Members of the American Society of Mechanical Engineers (see separate entry) and their immediate families. Cooperates with officers and committees of the ASME. Operates a scholarship and student loan fund. **Publications:** none. **Awards:** Berna Lou Cartwright Scholarship. **Frequency:** annual. **Type:** scholarship. **Recipient:** for U.S. citizens completing their final year of undergraduate studies ● Elisabeth M. and Winchell M. Parsons Scholarship. **Type:** scholarship. **Recipient:** for a citizen of the U.S. working toward a doctorate in mechanical engineering ● Marjorie Roy Rothermel Scholarship. **Frequency:** annual. **Type:** scholarship. **Recipient:** for a citizen of the U.S. working toward a master's degree in mechanical engineering ● Rice-Cullimore Scholarship. **Type:** scholarship. **Recipient:** for non-U.S. students coming to the U.S. for one year's maintenance ● Sylvia W. Farny Scholarship. **Frequency:** annual. **Type:** scholarship. **Recipient:** for final year of undergraduate study. **Affiliated With:** American Society of Mechanical Engineers. **Formerly:** (1978) Woman's Auxiliary to the American Society of Mechanical Engineers. **Conventions/Meetings:** annual board meeting ● semiannual meeting.

7300 ■ U.S. Association for Computational Mechanics (USACM)
PO Box 8137
Austin, TX 78713
Ph: (512)529-7333
E-mail: info@usacm.org
URL: http://www.usacm.org
Contact: Mr. Gregory Hulbert, Pres.

Founded: 1988. **Members:** 530. **Membership Dues:** $25 (annual). **Budget:** $13,250. **Description:** Scientists, researchers, institutions, and corporations involved in computational mechanics. Promotes research and commercial and academic activities in computational mechanics; represents U.S. interests in the field through the International Association of Computational Mechanics; coordinates conferences, colloquia, symposia, and other technical meetings. **Awards:** John von Neumann Medal. **Frequency:** biennial. **Type:** medal. **Recipient:** to individuals who have made outstanding, sustained contributions in the field of computational mechanics. **Publications:** Newsletter, bimonthly. **Conventions/Meetings:** biennial meeting.

7301 ■ U.S. National Committee on Theoretical and Applied Mechanics (USNC/TAM)
Bd. on Intl. Sci. Organizations
The Natl. Academies
500 Fifth St. NW, W541
Washington, DC 20001
Ph: (202)334-2807
Fax: (202)334-2231

E-mail: biso@nas.edu
URL: http://www7.nationalacademies.org/usnctam
Contact: Lois Peterson, Program Off.
Founded: 1947. **Members:** 35. **Staff:** 1. **Description:** Coordinating body of scientific and professional societies interested in promoting theoretical and applied mechanics in the U.S. Represents U.S. organizations in the International Union of Theoretical and Applied Mechanics. **Telecommunication Services:** electronic mail, lpeterso@nas.edu. **Subcommittees:** Research Direction in Mechanics. **Affiliated With:** National Research Council. **Publications:** *Research Directions in Mechanics*. **Conventions/Meetings:** quadrennial U.S. National Congress.

7302 ■ Vibration Institute (VI)
6262 S Kingery Hwy., Ste.212
Willowbrook, IL 60527
Ph: (630)654-2254
Fax: (630)654-2271
E-mail: vibinst@att.net
URL: http://www.vibinst.org
Contact: Dr. Ronald L. Eshleman, Dir.
Founded: 1972. **Members:** 3,000. **Membership Dues:** regular in U.S., $60 (annual) ● regular outside U.S., $75 (annual) ● corporate, $500 (annual). **Staff:** 6. **Budget:** $500,000. **Regional Groups:** 34. **Description:** Represents technicians and engineers; manufacturers and users of mechanical equipment. Promotes the exchange of practical information about vibration technology. Organizes seminars on specific topics that include: balancing, rotor/bearing dynamics, torsional vibrations, turbomachinery blading, and shaft vibrations. Provides on-site courses pertaining to specific vibration technology; participates in national and international standards work. Conducts library searches. **Libraries: Type:** reference. **Holdings:** 500; books, periodicals. **Formerly:** (1973) Vibration Foundation. **Publications:** *Vibration Institute—Proceedings of Annual Meeting*. Contains practical aspects of machinery vibration monitoring and analysis. **Price:** $68.00 ● *Vibrations*, quarterly. Magazine. Includes advertisers index, book reviews, and case histories. **Price:** included in membership dues; $65.00 /year for nonmembers; $70.00 /year for nonmembers overseas. **Circulation:** 3,000. **Advertising:** accepted ● Catalog. **Conventions/Meetings:** annual meeting (exhibits).

Media

7303 ■ Digital Media Device Association (DMDA)
14752 Beach Blvd., No. 103
La Mirada, CA 90638
Ph: (714)736-9774
E-mail: info@dmda.org
URL: http://www.dmda.org
Contact: Tom White, Exec. Dir.
Members: 40. **Membership Dues:** sustaining, $7,500 (annual) ● general, $2,000 (annual) ● associate, $500 (annual). **Description:** Promotes implementation of technology and applications for portable and connected digital devices. **Working Groups:** Interoperability. **Publications:** Reports. Alternate Formats: online. **Conventions/Meetings:** monthly meeting.

7304 ■ DVD Association (DVDA)
2250 E Tropicana Ave., Ste.19-435
Las Vegas, NV 89119
Ph: (702)948-0443
Fax: (702)953-8965
E-mail: president@dvda.org
URL: http://www.dvda.org
Contact: Bruce Nazarian, Pres.
Membership Dues: subscribing, $100 (annual) ● student, $50 (annual) ● small business, $500 (annual) ● government, $1,000 (annual) ● silver corporate sponsor, $5,000 (annual) ● gold corporate sponsor, $10,000 (annual) ● platinum corporate sponsor, $25,000 (annual) ● corporate, $1,500 (annual) ● premium, $150 (annual). **Multinational. Description:** Represents members specializing in creation of multimedia programs for training, education, presentations, and entertainment using DVD platform. **Libraries: Type:** reference. **Holdings:** 2,000; software. **Subjects:** multimedia programs on DVD. **Awards:** DVDA Excellence Awards. **Frequency:** annual. **Type:** recognition. **Recipient:** for outstanding work on DVDs ● Hall of Fame. **Frequency:** annual. **Type:** recognition. **Recipient:** to individuals who have made a difference in the DVD industry and the association. **Publications:** *Directory of Resources*. **Conventions/Meetings:** conference.

7305 ■ MultiMediaCard Association (MMCA)
3855 SW 153rd Dr.
Beaverton, OR 97006
Ph: (503)619-0691
Fax: (503)644-6708
E-mail: admin@mmca.org
URL: http://www.mmca.org
Contact: Scott Herbert, Exec. Dir.
Founded: 1998. **Members:** 210. **Membership Dues:** executive, $10,000 (annual) ● affiliate, $2,500 (annual). **Multinational. Description:** Promotes worldwide adoption of storage media and peripheral I/O devices designed especially for mobile phones and digital imaging devices. Strives to ensure a high level of compliance of multimedia card products to the multimedia card specification in order to achieve broad market acceptance. Provides a global forum for memory card and semiconductor component suppliers, software vendors, and manufacturers of mobile electronic devices. **Publications:** *MMCA Newsletter*. Alternate Formats: online ● Brochure. Alternate Formats: online.

Medical Technology

7306 ■ Medical Equipment and Technology Association (META)
220 S Bus. Park Dr., Ste.A-1
Oostburg, WI 53070
Ph: (804)693-3916
E-mail: contact@mymeta.org
URL: http://www.mymeta.org
Contact: Mary Coker, Pres.
Membership Dues: individual, associate, $15 (annual) ● student, $15 (biennial). **Description:** Represents professionals that service and support equipment in the healthcare industry. Aims to enhance healthcare delivery through the development and improvement of the personnel, processes, and techniques related to the management and support of healthcare technology. Serves as the focal point for resources, networking, and activities that will promote the growth and unity for the biomedical technical profession. **Publications:** *META Newsletter*. Alternate Formats: online.

Membrane Science

7307 ■ North American Membrane Society (NAMS)
c/o Chemical and Environment Engineering
Univ. of Toledo
Mail Stop 305
Toledo, OH 43606-3390
Ph: (419)530-8088
Fax: (419)530-8086
E-mail: nams@eng.utoledo.edu
URL: http://www.che.utexas.edu/nams/NAMSHP.html
Contact: Prof. Glenn G. Lipscomb, Managing Ed./Sec.
Founded: 1985. **Members:** 600. **Membership Dues:** student, $20 (annual) ● individual in U.S., $50 (annual) ● individual outside U.S., $60 (annual) ● retiree, $25 (annual) ● corporate/library, $100 (annual). **Budget:** $40,000. **Description:** Academicians, graduate students, scientists, engineers, and corporate executives interested in promoting the advancement of membrane technology. Serves as an educational and technical information center regarding the research and development of synthetic membrane materials and products. **Awards:** International Travel Awards. **Frequency:** annual. **Type:** monetary. **Recipient:** for outstanding individuals who are near the start of their careers in membrane science and technology ● NAMS Annual Meeting Student Travel Awards. **Frequency:** annual. **Type:** recognition. **Recipient:** to outstanding young individuals with beginning work in the membrane area ● NAMS Travel Award. **Frequency:** annual. **Type:** monetary. **Recipient:** for undergraduates, technicians, and graduate students within the first two years of their graduate program ● Undergraduate Research Fellowship. **Frequency:** annual. **Type:** fellowship. **Recipient:** for outstanding undergraduates who wish to pursue a research experience in synthetic membrane science and technology at a university or government faculty in North America. **Computer Services:** database, membrane experts. **Publications:** *Membrane Quarterly*. Newsletter. **Price:** included in membership dues. **Circulation:** 600. **Advertising:** accepted ● Also publishes fliers and circulars. **Conventions/Meetings:** annual conference and symposium (exhibits).

Merchant Marine

7308 ■ Marine Engineers' Beneficial Association (MEBA)
444 N Capitol St., Ste.800
Washington, DC 20001
Ph: (202)638-5355
Free: (800)811-6322
Fax: (202)638-5369
E-mail: mebahq@d1meba.org
URL: http://www.d1meba.org
Contact: Ron Davis, Pres.
Founded: 1875. **Staff:** 8. **Description:** Engineers, deck officers. Works to enhance legislation that promotes maritime industry. **Publications:** *Telex Times*, weekly. Newsletter. Alternate Formats: online.

Metallurgy

7309 ■ American Bureau of Metal Statistics (ABMS)
PO Box 805
Chatham, NJ 07928
Ph: (973)701-2299
Fax: (973)701-2152
E-mail: info@abms.com
URL: http://www.abms.com
Contact: Patricia T. Foley, Exec. Dir.
Founded: 1920. **Members:** 5. **Staff:** 3. **Description:** Nonferrous metal statistics. Collects, compiles, and publishes nonferrous metal statistics. **Formed by Merger of:** American Bureau of Metal Statistics; Copper Institute; United States Copper Association. **Publications:** *American Bureau of Metal Statistics—Statistical Reports*, monthly. Contains statistical data on the aluminum, cadmium, copper, gold, lead, silver, and zinc industries. ● *Industry Reports*, monthly ● *Non-Ferrous Metal Yearbook*, annual. Provides worldwide data on copper, lead, zinc, aluminum, silver, gold, antimony, cadmium, magnesium, molybdenum, cobalt, nickel, and other metals. **Price:** $425.00/copy; $25.00 for copy on diskette. Alternate Formats: diskette.

7310 ■ APMI International
105 Coll. Rd. E
Princeton, NJ 08540-6692
Ph: (609)452-7700
Fax: (609)987-8523
E-mail: apmi@mpif.org
URL: http://www.mpif.org/apmi/index_frame.html
Contact: Christopher T. Adam PMT, Pres.
Founded: 1959. **Members:** 2,500. **Membership Dues:** individual in U.S., Canada, and Mexico, $95 (annual) ● overseas, $110 (annual) ● students (full time only), $20 (annual) ● overseas student, $35 (annual). **Staff:** 15. **Budget:** $655,000. **Local Groups:** 13. **Description:** Technical society for powder metallurgists and others interested in powder metallurgy and particulate materials, and their ap-

plications. Maintains speakers' bureau and placement service. **Libraries: Type:** reference. **Holdings:** 1,500. **Subjects:** powder metallurgy technology. **Awards:** Metallography Competition Award. **Frequency:** annual. **Type:** fellowship. **Affiliated With:** Metal Powder Industries Federation. **Formerly:** (1994) American Powder Metallurgy Institute. **Publications:** *International Journal of Powder Metallurgy*, bimonthly. Includes calendar of events, book reviews, and U.S. patent abstracts. **Price:** included in membership dues; $95.00 for individuals; $175.00 for institutions. ISSN: 0361-3488. **Circulation:** 3,400. **Advertising:** accepted ● *Who's Who in P/M*, annual. Membership Directory. Joint membership directory of APMI and the Metal Power Industries Federation. Includes advertisers' index. **Price:** included in membership dues; $85.00 /year for nonmembers. ISSN: 0361-6304. **Circulation:** 3,000. **Advertising:** accepted. **Conventions/Meetings:** annual International Conference on Powder Metallurgy and Particulate Materials - congress (exhibits).

7311 ■ ASM International (ASM)

9639 Kinsman Rd.
Novelty, OH 44073-0002
Ph: (440)338-5151
Free: (800)336-5152
Fax: (440)338-4634
E-mail: customerservice@asminternational.org
URL: http://www.asminternational.org
Contact: Dr. William W. Scott FASM, Managing Dir./Sec.

Founded: 1920. **Members:** 43,000. **Membership Dues:** professional (basic), $107 (annual) ● student, $15 (annual) ● material advantage student, $25 (annual). **Staff:** 125. **Budget:** $20,000,000. **Regional Groups:** 280. **Description:** Metallurgists, materials engineers, executives in materials producing and consuming industries; teachers and students. Disseminates technical information about the manufacture, use, and treatment of engineered materials. Offers in-plant, home study, and intensive courses through Materials Engineering Institute. Conducts career development program. Established ASM Foundation for Education and Research. **Libraries: Type:** reference. **Holdings:** 10,000. **Subjects:** metals and other materials. **Awards: Type:** recognition. **Recipient:** to teachers of materials science ● **Type:** recognition. **Recipient:** for achievements in the field. **Divisions:** Aerospace; Composites; Electronic Materials and Processing; Energy; Heat Treating; Highway/Off-Highway Vehicle; Joining; Materials Science; Materials Testing and Quality Control; Society of Carbide and Tool Engineers; Specialty Materials; Surface Engineering; Thermal Spray. **Formed by Merger of:** American Steel Treaters' Society; Steel Treating Research Society. **Formerly:** (1934) American Society for Steel Treating; (1986) American Society for Metals. **Publications:** *ASM Handbook* ● *ASM News*, monthly. Newspaper ● *Guide to Engineered Materials*, annual ● *International Materials Reviews*, bimonthly. Contains surveys on the theory and practice of extraction, production, fabrication, and behavior of metals to actual usage. **Price:** $152.00 /year for members; $345.00 /year for nonmembers ● *Journal of Materials Engineering and Performance*, bimonthly. Contains materials science information for solving engineering challenges. **Price:** $184.00 /year for members (print); $1,243.00 /year for nonmembers (print); $349.00 /year for members (print and online); $1,492.00 /year for nonmembers (print and online). **Advertising:** accepted. Alternate Formats: online ● *Journal of Phase Equilibria and Diffusion*, bimonthly. Contains articles on critically evaluated phase diagram data. **Price:** $261.00 /year for members (print); $1,799.00 /year for nonmembers (print); $496.00 /year for members (print and online); $2,159.00 /year for nonmembers (print and online). Alternate Formats: online ● *Metallurgical Transactions A*, monthly. Journal. Contains information on mechanical behavior, alloy phases and structures, transformations, environmental interactions, and optical materials. **Price:** $120.00 /year for members (print); $2,160.00 /year for nonmembers (print); $228.00 for members (print and online); $2,593.00 for nonmembers (print and online). **Advertising:** accepted. Alternate Formats: online ● *Metallurgical Transactions B*, bimonthly. Journal. Contains information on extraction and process metallurgy. **Price:** $96.00 /year for members (print); $1,555.00 /year for nonmembers (print); $183.00 /year for members (print and online); $1,866.00 /year for nonmembers (print and online). **Advertising:** accepted. Alternate Formats: online ● *UPDATE Newsletter*, quarterly. Reports on association's activities in International Data Program for Alloy Phase Diagram Data; includes calendar of events, news, and recent research. **Price:** free ● Also publishes over 150 texts on metals and materials. **Conventions/Meetings:** lecture ● annual Materials Science and Technology - conference (exhibits).

7312 ■ Association for Iron and Steel Technology (AIST)

186 Thorn Hill Rd.
Warrendale, PA 15086
Ph: (724)776-6040
Fax: (724)776-1880
E-mail: info@aist.org
URL: http://www.aistech.org
Contact: Ron Ashburn, Exec. Dir.

Founded: 1974. **Members:** 9,000. **Membership Dues:** professional, $115 (annual) ● young professional (age 25 or younger), $57 (annual) ● material advantage student, $25 (annual). **Staff:** 22. **Budget:** $4,300,000. **Local Groups:** 14. **Description:** Member society of the American Institute of Mining, Metallurgical and Petroleum Engineers (see separate entry). Individuals in the field of iron and steel processing and technology. Seeks to provide a medium of communication and cooperation among those interested in any phase of ferrous metallurgy and materials science and technology. Encourages interest in and the advancement of education in metallurgical and materials science and engineering related to the iron and steel industry. Conducts short continuing education courses. **Libraries: Type:** open to the public. **Holdings:** books, periodicals. **Subjects:** technical information relevant to iron and steelmaking as well as historical educational information. **Awards:** Benjamin Fairless Scholarship. **Frequency:** annual. **Type:** scholarship. **Recipient:** for college students ● Charles E. Slater Scholarship. **Frequency:** annual. **Type:** scholarship. **Recipient:** for college students ● ISS Foundation Scholarship. **Frequency:** annual. **Type:** scholarship. **Recipient:** for college students ● Ronald E. Lincoln Scholarship. **Frequency:** annual. **Type:** scholarship. **Recipient:** for college students ● Willy Korf Scholarship. **Frequency:** annual. **Type:** scholarship. **Recipient:** for college students. **Computer Services:** Online services, membership forums. **Additional Websites:** http://www.aist.org. **Divisions:** Electric Furnace; Ironmaking; Mechanical Working and Steel Processing; Process Technology; Steelmaking. **Affiliated With:** American Institute of Mining, Metallurgical, and Petroleum Engineers. **Formed by Merger of:** (2003) Iron and Steel Society; (2003) Association of Iron and Steel Engineers. **Formerly:** (1974) Iron and Steel Division of the Metallurgical Society of AIME. **Publications:** *Electric Furnace Conference Proceedings*, annual. Contains technical papers focusing on current technology. **Price:** $63.00 for members; $90.00 for nonmembers. **Circulation:** 1,000. Alternate Formats: CD-ROM ● *Iron and Steelmaker*, annual. Membership Directory ● *Iron and Steelmaker*, monthly. Journal. Covers ferrous metallurgy for managers, engineers, and researchers involved in the steel industry. Includes news items and calendar of events. **Price:** $5.00/issue. **Circulation:** 10,000. **Advertising:** accepted ● *Ironmaking Conference Proceedings*, annual. **Price:** $63.00 for members; $90.00 for nonmembers. Alternate Formats: CD-ROM ● *Mechanical Working and Steel Processing Conference Proceedings*, annual. **Price:** $77.00 for members; $110.00 for nonmembers. Alternate Formats: CD-ROM ● *Process Technology Division Proceedings*, annual. **Price:** $69.00 for members; $99.00 for nonmembers. Alternate Formats: CD-ROM ● *Steelmaking Proceedings*, annual. **Price:** $63.00 for members; $90.00 for nonmembers. Alternate Formats: CD-ROM. Also Cited As: *SM Proceedings* ● *Transactions of the Iron and Steel Society*, annual. Papers. Covers research and engineering advances in ironmaking and steelmaking technology with emphasis on effective operational techniques. **Price:** $27.00 for members; $52.00 for nonmembers ● Also publishes reference texts on ferrous metallurgy processes. **Conventions/Meetings:** annual conference (exhibits).

7313 ■ Ductile Iron Society (DIS)

28938 Lorain Rd., Ste.202
North Olmsted, OH 44070
Ph: (440)734-8040
Fax: (440)734-8182
E-mail: jhall@ductile.org
URL: http://www.ductile.org
Contact: Joe Farrar, Pres.

Founded: 1958. **Members:** 495. **Membership Dues:** foundry (minimum), $900 (semiannual) ● foundry (maximum), $8,000 (annual) ● associate, $880 (semiannual) ● research patron, $3,600 (annual). **Staff:** 3. **Budget:** $200,000. **Description:** Conducts metallurgical research and product development and promotion. Sponsors research at engineering schools. **Libraries: Type:** reference. **Holdings:** reports. **Awards: Frequency:** annual. **Type:** recognition. **Recipient:** for outstanding leadership and technical accomplishment in ductile iron industry. **Computer Services:** Online services, membership directory. **Telecommunication Services:** electronic bulletin board, meeting notices, career/wanted. **Committees:** Awards; By-laws; College and University Relations; Ductile Iron Marketing; Nominating; Programs and Publications; Quality Assurance and Specification; Research. **Subcommittees:** Process; Properties. **Publications:** *Ductile Iron News*, 3/year. Newsletter. **Price:** free. **Advertising:** accepted. Alternate Formats: online ● Membership Directory, annual ● Reports. Alternate Formats: online ● Also publishes research reports and bulletins of papers presented at meetings. **Conventions/Meetings:** semiannual Technical and Operating Conference.

7314 ■ Forging Industry Educational and Research Foundation (FIERF)

25 Prospect Ave. W, Ste.300
Cleveland, OH 44115
Ph: (216)781-5040
Fax: (216)781-0102
E-mail: info@forgings.org
URL: http://www.forgings.org
Contact: Karen Lewis, Exec. Dir.

Founded: 1961. **Budget:** $350,000. **Description:** Seeks to enhance knowledge and application of forged products throughout the industry; provides industry a medium for pooling resources to address issues, improve products, methods and productivity. **Awards:** Charles W. Finkl Scholarship. **Type:** scholarship. **Recipient:** to junior university students majoring in engineering ● **Type:** fellowship. **Recipient:** to post graduate university research ● Finkl Challenge Grants. **Type:** grant. **Recipient:** for undergraduate university research. **Telecommunication Services:** electronic mail, karen@forging.org. **Publications:** *Technical Conference*, every 18 months. Proceedings. Alternate Formats: CD-ROM. **Conventions/Meetings:** conference (exhibits) - every 18 months.

7315 ■ International Copper Association (ICA)

260 Madison Ave., 16th Fl.
New York, NY 10016-2401
Ph: (212)251-7240
Fax: (212)251-7245
E-mail: info@copperinfo.com
URL: http://www.copperinfo.com
Contact: Francis J. Kane, Pres.

Founded: 1960. **Members:** 37. **Staff:** 12. **Budget:** $30,000. **Description:** Copper producing and fabricating companies. Conducts market development and research on uses for copper through contracts with commercial, institutional, and university organizations. **Committees:** Environmental; Program Review. **Formerly:** Copper Products Development Association; (1989) International Copper Research Association. **Publications:** *ICA Update*, quarterly. Newsletter. **Circulation:** 800 ● Annual Report, annual.

Conventions/Meetings: semiannual conference ● semiannual Program Review - meeting - always spring and fall ● seminar.

7316 ■ International Lead Zinc Research Organization (ILZRO)
2525 Meridian Pkwy., Ste.100
Durham, NC 27713
Ph: (919)361-4647
Fax: (919)361-1957
E-mail: rputnam@ilzro.org
URL: http://www.ilzro.org
Contact: Jerome F. Cole, Pres.
Founded: 1958. **Members:** 77. **Staff:** 16. **Budget:** $5,000,000. **Description:** Seeks to develop new applications for lead and zinc. Improves current uses of lead and zinc; compiles technical information on these metals. Directs approximately 150 research programs through its contracts with universities, governments, independent laboratories, industrial companies, and member companies. Research and development projects deal with die castings, wrought zinc, alloys, galvanized steel, plating, welding, lead and zinc chemistry, environmental studies, batteries, lead for architectural uses, and other subjects. Acts as a Research organization sponsored by major producers, smelters, and refiners of lead and/or zinc from 15 countries. **Libraries: Type:** reference. **Holdings:** 1,500. **Subjects:** metals. **Committees:** Chemical; Electrochemical; Environmental Health; Metallurgical - Lead and Zinc; Program Review - Lead and Zinc. **Publications:** *R&D Focus and Environmental Update*, periodic. Report ● Articles ● Manuals ● Also publishes data sheets and contractors' reports. **Conventions/Meetings:** annual ALABC - conference - March, April or May ● annual board meeting - usually October ● semiannual Program Planning and Funding - meeting, planning sessions - usually spring and fall.

7317 ■ International Organization on Shape Memory and Superelastic Technologies (SMST)
c/o Sarina Pastoric, Admin., Affiliate Societies Customer Ser. Dept.
9639 Kinsman Rd.
Novelty, OH 44073
Ph: (440)338-5151
Fax: (440)338-4634
E-mail: sarina.pastoric@asminternational.org
URL: http://www.smst.org
Contact: James L. Proft, Pres.
Founded: 1993. **Membership Dues:** regular, $50 (annual). **Multinational. Description:** Promotes the use of shape memory alloys in new applications of emerging materials-related technologies. Disseminates technical education on shape memory and superelastic alloys that are particularly important to the medical devices industry. Provides an online forum for its members to exchange information pertaining to new technologies and trends in shape memory and superelastic technology. **Affiliated With:** ASM International. **Publications:** Newsletter. Alternate Formats: online.

7318 ■ International Precious Metals Institute (IPMI)
5101 N 12th Ave., Ste.C
Pensacola, FL 32504
Ph: (850)476-1156
Fax: (850)476-1548
E-mail: mail@ipmi.org
URL: http://www.ipmi.org
Contact: Dr. Larry Manziek, Exec. Dir.
Founded: 1976. **Members:** 1,000. **Membership Dues:** student, $20 (annual) ● patron, $2,000 (annual) ● sustaining, $750 (annual) ● professional association, trade organization, $500 (annual) ● nonprofit institution, $250 (annual) ● university, individual/qualified, $90 (annual). **Staff:** 5. **Budget:** $450,000. **Regional Groups:** 3. **Local Groups:** 3. **Multinational. Description:** Miners, refiners, research scientists, educators, users, producers, mercantilists, government personnel, and persons with interests in precious metals. Encourages the exchange of information and technology. Collects and publishes data and statistics; conducts educational meetings; enhances the efficient use of precious metals. Conducts various courses in high activity precious metal areas and research studies. Organizes study groups, task forces, and committees to develop a better understanding of problems, technical data use, and future development possibilities. **Libraries: Type:** reference. **Subjects:** precious metals. **Awards:** Distinguished Achievement Award. **Frequency:** annual. **Type:** recognition. **Recipient:** for lifetime achievement in the industry ● Henry J. Albert-Engelhard Award. **Frequency:** annual. **Type:** recognition. **Recipient:** for technical achievement. **Councils:** Security. **Publications:** *Buyers Guide*, annual. **Circulation:** 2,500. **Advertising:** accepted ● *Conference Proceedings*, annual ● *Precious Metals News and Review*, monthly. Newsletter. Includes meetings calendar, new publications, and statistics. **Price:** included in membership dues; $30.00 /year for nonmembers. ISSN: 0730-1901. **Circulation:** 1,400 ● *Seminar Proceedings*, periodic ● Membership Directory, annual. **Conventions/Meetings:** annual conference - 2009 June 13-16, Orlando, FL; 2010 June 12-15, Tucson, AZ ● periodic seminar and workshop, covers fundamental aspects of the precious metals industry.

7319 ■ Materials Properties Council (MPC)
PO Box 1942
New York, NY 10156
Ph: (216)658-3847
Fax: (216)658-3854
E-mail: mprager@forengineers.org
URL: http://foreng1.securesites.net/mpc
Contact: Dr. Martin Prager, Exec. Dir.
Founded: 1966. **Members:** 800. **Staff:** 3. **Budget:** $1,000,000. **Description:** Sponsored by American Society of Mechanical Engineers, ASM International, ASTM, American Welding Society, and Engineering Foundation. Objectives are to identify major unfulfilled needs for reliable data on the engineering properties of metals and alloys; to evolve, plan, and conduct programs for collecting, generating, and evaluating such data so it may be useful; to arrange for making such data promptly available through reports, publications, correspondence, and other means; to keep informed of and to utilize the results of related activities, both national and international, in order to avoid duplication of effort. Conducts research and testing programs. Founded National Materials Properties Data Network. **Committees:** Technical Advisory. **Subcommittees:** Electric Power; Petroleum and Chemical; Welding and Fabrication. **Formerly:** (1986) Metal Properties Council. **Publications:** Annual Report, annual. **Conventions/Meetings:** quarterly meeting, technical committee meeting ● periodic symposium and workshop.

7320 ■ Minerals, Metals, and Materials Society (TMS)
184 Thorn Hill Rd.
Warrendale, PA 15086-7514
Ph: (724)776-9000
Free: (800)759-4867
Fax: (724)776-3770
E-mail: tmsgeneral@tms.org
URL: http://www.tms.org
Contact: Warren H. Hunt Jr., Sec./Exec. Dir.
Founded: 1957. **Members:** 8,000. **Membership Dues:** professional/associate, $105 (annual) ● life, $1,500 ● corporate, $500 (annual) ● supporting (corporate), $2,500 (annual) ● sustaining (corporate), $5,000 (annual) ● student, $25 (annual) ● recent graduate, $52 (annual). **Staff:** 32. **Budget:** $5,300,000. **Description:** A member society of American Institute of Mining, Metallurgical and Petroleum Engineers (see separate entry). Professional society of metallurgists, metallurgical engineers, and materials scientists. Maintains 39 committees. **Computer Services:** Mailing lists, of members. **Divisions:** Electronic, Magnetic, and Photonic Materials; Extraction and Processing; Light Metals; Materials Processing and Design; Structural Materials. **Formerly:** (1988) The Metallurgical Society. **Publications:** *JOM*, monthly. Journal. Covers metallurgy and materials science. Contains articles on mineral characterization, and extractive and physical metallurgy engineered materials. **Price:** included in membership dues; $90.00 /year for nonmembers. ISSN: 0148-6608. **Circulation:** 14,000. **Advertising:** accepted. Alternate Formats: online ● *Journal of Electronic Materials*, monthly. Reports developments in the electronics field as well as traditional uses of semiconductors, magnetic alloys, and insulators. ISSN: 0361-5235 ● *Metallurgical Transactions B*, bimonthly. Journal. Reports on developments in extractive and process metallurgy in the areas of mineral preparation, pyrometallurgy, and hydrometallurgy. ISSN: 0360-2141. **Advertising:** accepted ● Monographs ● Proceedings ● Also publishes textbooks. **Conventions/Meetings:** annual convention (exhibits) ● annual meeting (exhibits).

7321 ■ National Institute for Metalworking Skills (NIMS)
3251 Old Lee Hwy., Ste.205
Fairfax, VA 22030
Ph: (703)352-4971
Fax: (703)352-4991
E-mail: smandes@nims-skills.org
URL: http://www.nims-skills.org
Contact: Stephen C. Mandes, Exec. Dir.
Founded: 1995. **Members:** 6,000. **Description:** Supports the development of a skilled workforce for the metalworking industry by training, validating and maintaining the skill standards for each industry. Maintains accredited training programs for workers to meet quality standards. Forms partnerships with schools, companies, and local governments to implement the skill standards, achieve program certification and provide credentials to trainees and workers.

7322 ■ Society of Carbide and Tool Engineers (SCTE)
c/o Pittsburgh Chapter No. 10
PO Box 77
McKeesport, PA 15135
Ph: (724)352-5151
E-mail: bill_shipley@pennunited.com
URL: http://www.scte10.org
Contact: Bill Shipley, Chm.
Founded: 1947. **Members:** 700. **Membership Dues:** individual, $102 (annual). **Staff:** 1. **Budget:** $50,000. **Regional Groups:** 3. **Local Groups:** 3. **Description:** Industrial engineers, machine operators, sales personnel, and others whose work is concerned with metal removal techniques, particularly by use of carbide. Conducts elementary course, advanced course, and in-plant training program in carbide engineering. Chapters conduct local educational programs and/or annual tool show. **Computer Services:** Mailing lists, of members. **Affiliated With:** ASM International. **Formerly:** (1976) Society of Carbide Engineers.

7323 ■ Wire Association International (WAI)
PO Box 578
Guilford, CT 06437
Ph: (203)453-2777
Fax: (203)453-8384
E-mail: ljacobs@wirenet.org
URL: http://www.wirenet.org
Contact: Steven J. Fetteroll, Exec. Dir.
Founded: 1930. **Members:** 4,700. **Membership Dues:** individual, $95 (annual) ● chapter affiliation, $15 (annual). **Staff:** 20. **Budget:** $3,700,000. **Languages:** English, French, German, Italian, Spanish. **Multinational. Description:** Represents society of operating executives, plant superintendents, engineers, chemists, metallurgists, and others in 57 countries concerned with production in wire mills and insulated wire plants that make bars, rods, strip, wire, wire products, fasteners, fiber-optic, and electrical wire and cable. Promotes industry contacts. Studies production methods, new materials, and applications for existing materials; provides advisory service on technical and operating problems. **Libraries: Type:** not open to the public. **Awards:** Donnellan Memorial Award. **Frequency:** annual. **Type:** recognition. **Recipient:** to a WAI member who made outstanding contributions to the association ● Mordica Memorial Award. **Frequency:** annual. **Type:** recognition. **Re-**

cipient: for extraordinary contributions to the advancement and welfare of the wire and cable industry. **Computer Services:** database, technical and general information. **Telecommunication Services:** electronic mail, tmoran@wirenet.org. **Committees:** Bylaws; Conference Programming; Education; Exhibition Planning; Membership Relations; Nominating; Oversight. **Subgroups:** Technical Advisors. **Formerly:** Wire Association. **Publications:** *Connection*, semimonthly. Newsletter ● *Ferrous Wire* ● *Nonferrous Wire Handbook* ● *Wire Association International—Annual Conference Proceedings*. Transcript of technical papers presented at all meetings. ● *Wire Journal International*, monthly. Serves as the official publications of Wire Association International. **Circulation:** 10,000. **Advertising:** accepted ● *Wire Journal International-Reference Guide*, annual. **Price:** free for members; $60.00/copy for nonmembers. ISSN: 0277-4275. **Circulation:** 13,000. **Advertising:** accepted ● Reports. **Conventions/Meetings:** annual Interwire - meeting (exhibits) ● annual Wire Expo - convention (exhibits).

Meteorology

7324 ■ American Association of State Climatologists (AASC)

c/o Paul Knight, Pres.
Pennsylvania State Climatologist
Dept. of Meteorology
503 Walker Bldg.
University Park, PA 16802
E-mail: info@stateclimate.org
URL: http://www.stateclimate.org
Contact: Paul Knight, Pres.

Founded: 1976. **Members:** 105. **Description:** State-supported climatologists and university-related research climatologists. Promotes applied climatology and climatological services in the U.S. Compiles statistics. **Libraries: Type:** reference. **Holdings:** biographical archives. **Subjects:** climatology. **Telecommunication Services:** electronic mail, knight@mail.meteo.psu.edu. **Committees:** Computer; Education; Goals; Instrumentation and Data Standards; Regional. **Publications:** *State Climatologist*, quarterly. **Conventions/Meetings:** annual conference and meeting (exhibits).

7325 ■ American Meteorological Society (AMS)

45 Beacon St.
Boston, MA 02108-3693
Ph: (617)227-2425 (617)227-2426
Fax: (617)742-8718
E-mail: amsinfo@ametsoc.org
URL: http://www.ametsoc.org
Contact: Keith L. Seitter, Exec. Dir.

Founded: 1919. **Members:** 11,000. **Membership Dues:** associate, $55 (annual) ● associate (pre-college student), individual (with student privileges), student, $15 (annual) ● associate (K-12 teacher), $40 (annual) ● sustaining corporation and institutional, $5,000 (annual) ● regular corporation and institutional, $1,000 (annual) ● small business corporation, $350 (annual) ● publication corporation and institutional, $600 (annual) ● regular, $80 (annual). **Staff:** 54. **Budget:** $9,500,000. **Local Groups:** 81. **Description:** Professional meteorologists, oceanographers, and hydrologists; interested students and nonprofessionals. Develops and disseminates information on the atmospheric and related oceanic and hydrospheric sciences; seeks to advance professional applications. Activities include guidance service, scholarship programs, career information, certification of consulting meteorologists, and a seal of approval program to recognize competence in radio and television weathercasting. Issues statements of policy to assist public understanding on subjects such as weather modification, forecasting, tornadoes, hurricanes, flash floods, and meteorological satellites. Provides abstracting services. Prepares educational films, filmstrips, and slides for a new curriculum in meteorology at the ninth grade level. Issues monthly announcements of job openings for meteorologists. **Libraries: Type:** reference. **Subjects:** historical meteorology. **Awards: Frequency:** annual. **Type:** recognition. **Recipient:** for contributions to meteorology and allied fields. **Computer Services:** database, meteorological and geoastrophysical abstracts. **Telecommunication Services:** electronic mail, kseitter@ametsoc.org. **Boards:** Broadcast Meteorology; Certified Consulting Meteorologists; Meteorological and Oceanographic Education in Universities; Operational Government Meteorologists; Private Sector Meteorology; School and Popular Meteorological and Oceanographic Education; Women and Minorities. **Commissions:** Education and Manpower; Professional Affairs; Scientific and Technological Activities. **Committees:** Agricultural and Forest Meteorology; Applied Climatology; Atmospheric and Oceanic Waves and Stability; Atmospheric Chemistry; Atmospheric Electricity; Biometeorology and Aerobiology; Climate Variation; Cloud Physics; Hydrology; Interaction of the Sea and Atmosphere; Judges for Undergraduate Awards; Laser Atmospheric Studies; Layers and Turbulence; Measurements; Mesoscale Processes; Meteorological Aspects of Air Pollution; Meteorological Aspects of Aviation and Aerospace Vehicles; Meteorology of the Coastal Zone; Middle Atmosphere; Mountain Meteorology; Planned and Inadvertent Weather Modification; Polar Meteorology and Oceanography; Probability and Statistics; Radar Meteorology; Radiation Energy; Satellite Meteorology and Oceanography; Severe Local Storms; Southern Hemisphere; Tropical Meteorology and Tropical Cyclones; Weather Forecasting and Analysis. **Publications:** *AMS Newsletter*, periodic. Contains brief reports on the affairs of government, industry, schools, and national and international bodies as they affect meteorological sciences. Alternate Formats: online ● *Bulletin of the American Meteorological Society*, monthly. Contains calendar of events, chapter news, book reviews, new publications, member news, employment reports, professional directory, and obituaries. **Price:** included in membership dues; $80.00 /year for nonmembers. ISSN: 0003-0007. **Advertising:** accepted ● *Journal of Applied Meteorology*, monthly. Contains research articles concerned with the application of the atmospheric sciences to operational and practical goals. **Price:** $50.00 /year for members; $335.00 /year for nonmembers. ISSN: 0894-8763 ● *Journal of Atmospheric and Oceanic Technology*, bimonthly. Includes original research and survey papers related to instrument-system descriptions, exploratory measurement techniques, and calibration methods. **Price:** $45.00 /year for members; $240.00 /year for nonmembers. ISSN: 0739-0572 ● *Journal of Climate*, monthly. Contains articles on climate data and analysis, long-term atmospheric variability, and climate change and its impact on society. **Price:** $60.00 /year for members; $395.00 /year for nonmembers. ISSN: 0894-8755 ● *Journal of Physical Oceanography*, monthly. Contains original research and survey papers on the physics and chemistry of the oceans and of the processes coupling the sea to the atmosphere. **Price:** $55.00 /year for members; $405.00 /year for nonmembers. ISSN: 0022-3670 ● *Journal of the Atmospheric Sciences*, semimonthly. Contains original research papers and critical surveys related to the atmosphere of the earth and other planets. **Price:** $75.00 /year for members; $495.00 /year for nonmembers. ISSN: 0022-4928 ● *Meteorological and Geoastrophysical Abstracts*, monthly. Journal. Contains abstracts of current world literature in meteorology, climatology, aeronomy, planetary atmospheres, and solar-terrestrial relations. **Price:** $1,010.00/year. ISSN: 0026-1130. Alternate Formats: CD-ROM ● *Monthly Weather Review*. Journal. Contains research articles concerned with weather analysis and forecasting, observed and modeled circulations. **Price:** $60.00 /year for members; $445.00 /year for nonmembers. ISSN: 0027-0644 ● *Weather and Forecasting*, quarterly. Journal. Contains original research and survey papers related to operational forecasting or weather events significant to operational forecast problems. **Price:** $35.00 /year for members; $140.00 /year for nonmembers. ISSN: 0882-8156 ● Also publishes conference reprints, translations, and a glossary of meteorology. **Conventions/Meetings:** annual meeting (exhibits).

7326 ■ Commercial Weather Services Association (CWSA)

c/o Steven Root, CCM, Chm.
WeatherBank, Inc.
1015 Waterwood Pkwy.
Edmond, OK 73034
E-mail: feedback@weatherindustry.org
URL: http://www.weatherindustry.org
Contact: Steven Root CCM, Chm.

Founded: 1987. **Members:** 44. **Membership Dues:** associate, $100 (annual) ● corporate (based on number of employees), $300-$6,750 (annual). **Staff:** 2. **Budget:** $40,000. **Description:** Private weather service companies and firms that provide weather forecasting data to public and private sector clients. Serves as a coordinated voice for the industry on legislative and regulatory issues; provides information on the industry. Seeks to develop a partnership with the government concerning the delivery of weather forecasting services and products. **Committees:** External Affairs; Government Affairs; Legislative Affairs. **Affiliated With:** American Meteorological Society. **Formerly:** (1989) Association of Private Weather Related Companies. **Publications:** *CWSA Washington Report*, monthly. Newsletter ● *Issue Analysis*, periodic. Reports on public policy issues. ● *Legislative Alert*, periodic. **Conventions/Meetings:** semiannual meeting, held in conjunction with American Meteorological Society - usually January and June in Washington, DC.

7327 ■ National Weather Association (NWA)

228 W Millbrook Rd.
Raleigh, NC 27609-4304
Ph: (919)845-1546
Fax: (919)845-1546
E-mail: exdir@nwas.org
URL: http://www.nwas.org
Contact: Steve Harned, Exec. Dir.

Founded: 1975. **Members:** 2,900. **Membership Dues:** regular, $42 (annual) ● full-time student, retiree, $21 (annual) ● corporate, $125 (annual). **Staff:** 2. **Budget:** $140,000. **Local Groups:** 15. **Description:** Individuals and groups interested in operational meteorology and related activities. Promotes professionalism in practical meteorology; develops solutions to problems faced by people working in daily weather forecasting activities; acts as a voice for persons in meteorology. Encourages exchange of information and ideas among meteorologists. **Awards:** Broadcaster of the Year. **Frequency:** annual. **Type:** recognition. **Recipient:** for a member radio or TV weathercaster who has excelled in the delivery of information to the public ● Larry R. Johnson Award. **Frequency:** annual. **Type:** recognition. **Recipient:** for recognition of unique events or accomplishments related to operational meteorology ● Member of the Year Award. **Frequency:** annual. **Type:** recognition. **Recipient:** to forecasters, corporations, and nonprofessional individuals for excellence in and contributions to the field and the NWA ● Operational Achievement Award (Individual and Group). **Frequency:** annual. **Type:** recognition. **Recipient:** for a member whose accurate forecast of some significant weather event has made an impact on life and property ● Public Education Award. **Frequency:** annual. **Type:** recognition. **Recipient:** for an individual or organization providing significant contributions to increase the public's weather awareness ● T. Theodore Fujita Research Achievement Award. **Frequency:** annual. **Type:** recognition. **Recipient:** for a member whose research has made a significant contribution to operational meteorology ● Walter J. Bennett Public Service Award. **Frequency:** annual. **Type:** recognition. **Recipient:** for an individual or organization directly assisting the meteorological community in public service. **Committees:** Analysis and Forecasting; Aviation; Broadcast Meteorology; Editorial; Education; Hydrology; Local Chapters; Marine; Remote Sensing; Training. **Publications:** *A Comprehensive Glossary of Weather Terms for Storm Spotters*. Monograph. Contains definitions used in storm spotting, analysis, forecasting, and broadcasting. **Price:** $6.00 for members; $9.00 for nonmembers ● *The Cloud Chart 1, 2, and 3*. **Price:** $7.50 for members; $9.50 for nonmembers ● *National Weather*

Digest, semiannual. Journal. Covers weather-related subjects such as forecasting, satellites, radar, severe weather, hurricanes, agriculture, and aviation. Includes book reviews. **Price:** included in membership dues; $29.00 /year for institutions. ISSN: 0271-1052. **Circulation:** 3,400. **Advertising:** accepted ● *NWA Monthly Newsletter.* Includes employment opportunities, member news; local chapter news; significant items regarding operational meteorology and related activities. **Price:** included in membership dues; $18.00/year. ISSN: 0271-1044. **Circulation:** 3,100 ● *Polar Orbiter Satellite Imagery Interpretation.* Contains 76 33mm slides and script addressing worldwide examples of polar orbiter satellite imagery. **Price:** $70.00 for members; $84.00 for nonmembers. **Conventions/Meetings:** annual conference and workshop, with presentations, training and education opportunities (exhibits) - always mid-October.

7328 ■ North American Meteor Network (NAMN)

c/o Mark Davis, Coor.
101 Margate Cir.
Goose Creek, SC 29445
E-mail: namn@namnmeteors.org
URL: http://www.namnmeteors.org
Contact: Mark Davis, Coor.

Founded: 1995. **Multinational. Description:** Represents individuals dedicated to the coverage of sporadic meteor shower activity. Promotes astronomy and related sciences. Recruits and trains new observers in the methods of meteor observation. Coordinates North American observations. **Telecommunication Services:** electronic mail, meteors@comcast.net. **Publications:** *Meteor Showers and Their Observation: A North American Meteor Network Guide.* Handbook. Serves as the basic instruction manual for new observers of the NAMN. Alternate Formats: online ● *NAMN Notes*, monthly. Newsletter. Highlights the latest news and views from the world of meteor observing. Alternate Formats: online.

7329 ■ University Corporation for Atmospheric Research (UCAR)

PO Box 3000
Boulder, CO 80307-3000
Ph: (303)497-1000
E-mail: kkd@ou.edu
URL: http://www.ucar.edu
Contact: Kelvin Droegemeier, Chm.

Founded: 1960. **Members:** 68. **Staff:** 1,360. **Description:** Consortium of universities with doctoral programs in the atmospheric sciences and related fields; institutions offering B.S. or M.S. degrees in atmospheric or related sciences are academic affiliate members; international institutions offering degrees and conducting research in atmospheric or related sciences are international affiliate members. Conducts research and fosters the development of facilities and related services for the international academic community concerned with research in the atmospheric, oceanic, and related sciences, including societal impacts and global change research. Operates the National Center for Atmospheric Research under contract with the National Science Foundation (see separate entry). **Committees:** Scientific Programs Evaluation; University Relations. **Affiliated With:** American Astronomical Society; American Geophysical Union; American Meteorological Society. **Publications:** *Highlights Documents*, biennial ● *UCAR Quarterly Newsletter.* Covers atmospheric research including meteorology, oceanography, climatology, earth sciences, and solar-terrestrial research. **Price:** free. **Circulation:** 3,000. Alternate Formats: online ● Reports. Alternate Formats: online. **Conventions/Meetings:** annual meeting - always October in Boulder, CO.

7330 ■ Weather Modification Association (WMA)

PO Box 26926
Fresno, CA 93729-6926
Ph: (559)434-3486
Fax: (559)434-3486
E-mail: wxmod@comcast.net
URL: http://www.weathermodification.org
Contact: Hilda Duckering, Exec. Sec.-Treas.

Founded: 1950. **Members:** 200. **Membership Dues:** individual, $75 (annual) ● corporate, $300 (annual) ● associate, $2,000 (annual) ● retired, $30 (annual) ● student, $20 (annual). **Staff:** 1. **Description:** Individuals and organizations interested in weather modification problems; universities and non-profit research institutes; public utilities, power and water companies, and districts; private meteorological firms, government agencies, and foreign organizations; and other groups and firms. Encourages scientific research; coordinates efforts of different weather modification projects and encourages standardization of weather modification recording procedures. Renders technical assistance in developing legislation pertaining to weather modification. **Libraries: Type:** open to the public. **Holdings:** 32. **Subjects:** weather modification and research. **Awards:** Schaefer Award. **Frequency:** annual. **Type:** recognition. **Recipient:** for outstanding individual with scientific and technological discoveries that has constituted a major contribution to the advancement of weather modification ● Thunderbird Award. **Frequency:** annual. **Type:** recognition. **Recipient:** for outstanding individual with continuing contributions to the art and science of weather modification. **Committees:** Certification; Insurance; Legislative; Publicity. **Formerly:** (1967) Weather Control Research Association. **Publications:** *Facts About Weather Modification.* Brochure. **Price:** $1.50. **Circulation:** 350. **Advertising:** accepted ● *Journal of Weather Modification*, annual. Includes weather modification (cloud seeding), cloud physics, and atmospheric sciences. Also includes cumulative author and published papers index. **Price:** included in membership dues. ISSN: 0739-1781. **Circulation:** 350. **Advertising:** accepted. Alternate Formats: CD-ROM ● *Weather Modification Association Newsletter*, semiannual. **Conventions/Meetings:** annual meeting, with keynote speakers, banquet, panel discussion, and session.

Microbiology

7331 ■ Puerto Rico Society of Microbiologists (PRSM)

PO Box 360175
San Juan, PR 00936-0175
Ph: (787)751-3057
Fax: (787)759-8559
E-mail: smpr50@gmail.com
URL: http://www.asm.org/branch/brpr/index.html
Contact: Miguel Urdaneta, Pres.

Founded: 1957. **Membership Dues:** regular, $25 (annual) ● student, $12 (annual). **Description:** Professionals in the field of microbiology. Aims to promote scientific interest in microbiology and to aid in the development and progress of professionals in the field. Organizes conferences, workshops, symposiums and conventions, sponsors student chapters. **Publications:** *PRSM-News.* Bulletin. Contains articles on recent topics in microbiology and on upcoming activities. **Conventions/Meetings:** conference ● convention ● symposium ● workshop.

Microscopy

7332 ■ American Microscopical Society (AMS)

c/o Dr. Stephen L. Gardiner, PhD, Sec.
Bryn Mawr Coll.
Dept. of Biology
101 N Merion Ave.
Bryn Mawr, PA 19010
Ph: (610)526-5094
Fax: (610)526-5086
E-mail: sgardine@brynmawr.edu
URL: http://www.amicros.org
Contact: Dr. Stephen L. Gardiner PhD, Sec.

Founded: 1878. **Members:** 550. **Budget:** $35,000. **Description:** Serves as professional society of microscopical biologists and microscopists. Fosters biological research, which employs the microscope and invertebrates. **Awards:** American Microscopical Society Student Research Fellowship. **Frequency:** annual. **Type:** fellowship. **Recipient:** for research on invertebrate animals ● The Ralph and Mildred Buchsbaum Prize for Excellence in Photomicrography. **Frequency:** annual. **Type:** recognition. **Committees:** 80-Year Index; Reprinting Back Numbers. **Publications:** *Invertebrate Biology*, quarterly. Journal. Includes book reviews, meeting announcements and research reports. **Price:** included in membership dues. ISSN: 0003-0023. **Conventions/Meetings:** annual seminar ● annual symposium (exhibits) - early January.

7333 ■ International Federation of Societies for Microscopy (IFSM)

c/o Prof. C. Barry Carter, Gen. Sec.
Dept. of Chem. Engg. & Materials Sci.
151 Amundson Hall
421 Washington Ave. SE
Minneapolis, MN 55455
Ph: (612)625-8805
Fax: (612)626-7246
E-mail: carter@cems.umn.edu
URL: http://www.ifsm.umn.edu
Contact: Prof. C. Barry Carter, Gen. Sec.

Founded: 1951. **Regional Groups:** 3. **National Groups:** 40. **Multinational. Description:** National and international societies of electron microscopists. Seeks to advance standards of training and practice in the field. Facilitates communication and cooperation among electron microscopists worldwide. **Formerly:** (2004) International Federation of Societies of Electron Microscopy. **Conventions/Meetings:** quadrennial International Congress on Electron Microscopy - conference and trade show - August/September. 2008 Sept. 1-5, Aachen, Germany.

7334 ■ Microbeam Analysis Society (MAS)

c/o Mr. Louis Ross, Membership Chm.
Univ. of Missouri
Veterinary Sciences Bldg.
Electron Microscopy Core Fac.
W136 Veterinary Medicine Bldg.
Columbia, MO 65211
Ph: (573)882-4777
Free: (800)462-7636
Fax: (573)884-2227
E-mail: rosslm@missouri.edu
URL: http://www.microprobe.org
Contact: Mr. Louis Ross, Membership Chm.

Founded: 1967. **Members:** 400. **Membership Dues:** regular, $25 (annual) ● student, $5 (annual) ● corporate, $300 (annual). **Regional Groups:** 23. **Description:** Works to advance and diffuse knowledge concerning the principles and applications of microbeam instruments or related instrumentation. Provides continuity, advanced planning, and a financing mechanism for annual meetings. Maintains an online newsletter, a national tour speaker program, affiliated regional societies, a software and audiovisual library. Hosts topical meetings. **Libraries: Type:** open to the public. **Holdings:** audiovisuals, software. **Awards:** Birks Award. **Frequency:** annual. **Type:** recognition. **Recipient:** for best contributed paper at the annual meeting ● Castaing Award. **Frequency:** annual. **Type:** recognition. **Recipient:** for best student paper ● Cosslett Award. **Frequency:** annual. **Type:** recognition. **Recipient:** for best invited paper to the annual meeting ● Distinguished Scholar Award. **Frequency:** annual. **Type:** monetary. **Recipient:** for best presentation or poster at the annual meeting ● K.F.J. Heinrich Award. **Frequency:** annual. **Type:** recognition. **Recipient:** for the best young scientist under 30 ● Macres Award. **Frequency:** annual. **Type:** recognition. **Recipient:** for best instrumentation or software paper at the annual meeting. **Formerly:** Electron Probe Analysis Society of America. **Publications:** *Microscopy and Microanalysis*, monthly. Journal. Includes meeting announcements and society news; for those interested in electron microscopy and microanalysis in general. **Price:** included in membership dues; $15.00 for nonmembers in U.S.; $38.00 for nonmembers outside U.S. **Advertising:** accepted.

Conventions/Meetings: annual Microscopy and Microanalysis - meeting (exhibits).

7335 ■ Microscopy Society of America (MSA)
230 E Ohio St., Ste.400
Chicago, IL 60611
Ph: (312)644-1527
Free: (800)538-3672
Fax: (312)644-8557
E-mail: businessoffice@microscopy.org
URL: http://www.microscopy.org
Contact: Michael A. O'Keefe, Pres.
Founded: 1942. **Members:** 4,000. **Membership Dues:** student in North America, $15 (annual) ● student outside North America, $33 (annual) ● regular in North America, $50 (annual) ● regular outside North America, $68 (annual) ● sustaining in North America, $375 (annual) ● sustaining outside North America, $393 (annual). **Staff:** 3. **Budget:** $1,000,000. **Local Groups:** 30. **Description:** Persons interested in the microscope, including medical, biological, metallurgical, and polymer research scientists and technicians, as well as physicists interested in instrument design and improvement. Seeks to increase and disseminate information concerning microscopes and related instruments and results obtained through their use. Maintains traveling scientific exhibit. **Libraries: Type:** reference. **Holdings:** video recordings. **Subjects:** EM techniques. **Awards:** Burton Award. **Frequency:** annual. **Type:** recognition. **Recipient:** for a scientist under 40 years of age ● Distinguished Scientists. **Frequency:** annual. **Type:** recognition. **Recipient:** for outstanding scientific contributions in physical and biological fields ● Presidential Student Award. **Frequency:** annual. **Type:** recognition. **Recipient:** for college/university students. **Computer Services:** Mailing lists, rental use. **Committees:** Certification of EM Technicians; Education. **Affiliated With:** American Association for the Advancement of Science; American Institute of Physics. **Formerly:** (1993) Electron Microscopy Society of America. **Publications:** *Microscopy and Microanalysis*, bimonthly. Journal. Contains articles pertaining to developing trends in microscopy, society's business news, review articles, and invited series. **Price:** included in membership dues. ISSN: 1062-9785. **Circulation:** 6,000. **Advertising:** accepted. Alternate Formats: online ● *Microscopy Today*, bimonthly. Magazine ● *Proceedings of Annual Meeting*, annual ● *Videotape Catalogue*, annual. **Conventions/Meetings:** annual Microscopy and Microanalysis - meeting and symposium (exhibits) - 2009 Aug. 3-6, Baltimore, MD.

7336 ■ New York Microscopical Society (NYMS)
30 N Mountain Ave.
Montclair, NJ 07042
Ph: (973)744-0043
Fax: (973)744-0043
E-mail: dkoleary@verizon.net
URL: http://www.nyms.org
Contact: Mr. Donald O'Leary, Curator
Founded: 1877. **Members:** 426. **Membership Dues:** life, $300 ● individual, $30 (annual) ● supporting, $60 (annual) ● corporate, $175 (annual) ● junior (under 18 years old), $5 (annual). **Budget:** $20,000. **Description:** Works to promote theoretical and applied microscopy. Sponsors educational programs. **Libraries: Type:** reference. **Holdings:** 3,000. **Subjects:** microscopy. **Awards:** Abbe Award. **Frequency:** annual. **Type:** recognition. **Recipient:** for outstanding scientific achievement in the field of microscopy ● Ashby Award. **Type:** recognition ● Bernard Friedman Memorial Workshop Scholarship. **Type:** recognition ● Ernst Abbe Memorial Award. **Type:** recognition ● **Type:** fellowship. **Publications:** *Glossary of Microscopical Terms and Definitions* ● *The Microscopium*, periodic ● *NYMS News*, monthly. Newsletter. **Conventions/Meetings:** monthly lecture.

Microwaves

7337 ■ IEEE Microwave Theory and Techniques Society (MTTS)
c/o IEEE Corporate Office
3 Park Ave., 17th Fl.
New York, NY 10016-5997
Ph: (212)705-7900
Free: (800)678-4333
Fax: (212)752-4929
E-mail: soc.mtt@ieee.org
URL: http://mtt.org/index.html
Contact: J. Stevenson Kenney, Pres.
Members: 9,000. **Local Groups:** 80. **Description:** A society of the Institute of Electrical and Electronics Engineers that is concerned with microwave theory, techniques, and applications relevant to components, devices, circuits, and systems that involve the generation, transmission, and detection of microwaves. **Publications:** *Microwave*, quarterly. Magazine. **Price:** included in membership dues; $20.00 for nonmembers ● *Microwave and Wireless Components Letters*, monthly. Journal ● *Transactions on Microwave Theory and Techniques*, monthly. **Conventions/Meetings:** annual meeting.

7338 ■ International Microwave Power Institute (IMPI)
7076 Drinkard Way
Mechanicsville, VA 23111
Ph: (804)559-6667
Fax: (804)559-4087
E-mail: info@impi.org
URL: http://www.impi.org
Contact: Kimberly D. Thies, Exec. Dir.
Founded: 1966. **Members:** 600. **Membership Dues:** student, $50 (annual) ● professional, $160 (annual) ● corporate, $1,500 (annual). **Staff:** 2. **Budget:** $250,000. **Multinational. Description:** Scientists from 31 countries interested in microwave power for non-communications purposes, particularly in its applications to industrial heating processes, biomedicine, and microwave cooking and ovens. Promotes university research; provides speakers to public affairs conferences and government organizations. Offers short courses. **Libraries: Type:** reference. **Holdings:** books, papers. **Subjects:** microwave power. **Telecommunication Services:** electronic mail, execdir@impi.org. **Committees:** Education; Standards. **Publications:** *Journal of Microwave Power and Electromagnetic Energy*, quarterly. **Price:** free for members; $250.00 for nonmembers ● *Transactions*, annual. **Conventions/Meetings:** annual Microwave Power Symposium - meeting and symposium (exhibits).

Mineralogy

7339 ■ American Federation of Mineralogical Societies (AFMS)
PO Box 302
Glyndon, MD 21071-0302
Ph: (410)833-7926
E-mail: central_office@amfed.org
URL: http://www.amfed.org
Contact: Steve Weinberger, Central Office Admin.
Founded: 1947. **Members:** 50,000. **Staff:** 1. **Regional Groups:** 7. **Local Groups:** 600. **Description:** Aims to further the earth sciences and the education of the public regarding earth sciences. **Awards: Type:** recognition. **Computer Services:** Mailing lists, for officers and chairpersons, regional federation officers and chairpersons, officers of each member local club or society. **Subgroups:** California Federation of Mineralogical Societies; Eastern Federation of Mineralogical & Lapidary Societies; Midwest Federation of Mineralogical & Geological Societies; Northwest Federation of Mineralogical Societies; Rocky Mountain Federation of Mineralogical Societies; South Central Federation of Mineral Societies; Southeast Federation of Mineralogical Societies. **Publications:** *AFMS Uniform Rules*, annual. Booklet. Alternate Formats: online ● *American Federation Newsletter*, 9/year. Provides information for earth science clubs. Reports on forthcoming regional shows, committee activities, education programs, and scholarships. **Price:** $4.50/year. **Circulation:** 2,200. Alternate Formats: online. Also Cited As: *AFMS Newsletter* ● *Approved Lists of Lapidary, Mineral & Fossil Names*, periodic. Manuals ● *Guidelines for Bulletin Editors*. Booklet. Contains information for editors of gem and mineral club newsletters. ● *Lewis & Clark: Rockhounding on the Way to the Pacific*. Booklet. Alternate Formats: online ● Also publishes lists for members use. **Conventions/Meetings:** annual convention, with business meeting held in conjunction with a local club gem & mineral show (exhibits).

7340 ■ Circum-Pacific Council for Energy and Mineral Resources (CPC)
c/o Ms. Nancy Zeigler, Sec.
12201 Sunrise Valley Dr., MS-917
Reston, VA 20192
Ph: (703)648-6645
Fax: (703)648-4227
E-mail: nzeigler@usgs.gov
URL: http://www.circum-pacificcouncil.org
Contact: Ms. Nancy Zeigler, Sec.
Founded: 1972. **Members:** 38. **Staff:** 1. **Multinational. Description:** Countries bordering the Pacific Ocean; scientific organizations; governmental agencies. Supports members' cooperative efforts in the study of energy and mineral resources in the Pacific region; assists independent programs that examine Pacific geologic phenomena and resources; strengthens and facilitates communication and cooperation among members, as well as among organizations and programs. **Conventions/Meetings:** annual conference.

7341 ■ Clay Minerals Society (CMS)
3635 Concorde Pkwy., Ste.500
Chantilly, VA 20151-1125
Ph: (703)652-9960
Fax: (703)652-9951
E-mail: cms@clays.org
URL: http://www.clays.org
Contact: Ms. Michelle Johnson, Office Mgr.
Founded: 1963. **Members:** 720. **Membership Dues:** subscribing, $85 (annual) ● student, $20 (annual) ● non-subscribing, $40 (annual). **Staff:** 1. **Multinational. Description:** Professionals concerned with clay mineralogy and technology in industry, university research, and government. Includes students of mineralogy, geology, soil science, astronomy, physics, geochemistry, and engineering, and representatives of such firms as oil companies, instrument makers, and clay mining companies. Seeks to stimulate research and disseminate information relating to all aspects of clay science and technology. Provides a forum for exchange of information and ideas. Maintains quantities of Source and Special Clays at the Source Clays Repository. **Libraries: Type:** not open to the public; reference. **Holdings:** 54; books, periodicals. **Subjects:** clay science. **Awards:** Brindley Lecture Award. **Frequency:** annual. **Type:** recognition ● Jackson Award. **Frequency:** annual. **Type:** recognition ● Marilyn and Sturges W. Bailey Distinguished Member Award. **Frequency:** annual. **Type:** recognition ● Pioneer Lecture Award. **Frequency:** annual. **Type:** recognition. **Committees:** Awards; Budget and Finance; Continuing Education; Contribution and Membership; Electronic Community; International Liaison; Nomenclature; Nomination; Policy and Administration; Program Development; Publications; Regulatory Issues; Research Grants; Society History; Source Clay Minerals. **Supersedes:** Committee on Clay Minerals of the National Academy of Sciences—National Research Council. **Publications:** *Clay-Water Interface and Its Rheological Implications*. Book. **Price:** $23.00 ● *Clays and Clay Minerals*, bimonthly. Journal. Includes author index, book reviews, and meeting announcements. **Price:** $70.00 /year for members; $235.00 /year for libraries and institutions; $250.00/year outside U.S. ISSN: 0009-8604 ● *Computer Applications in X-Ray Powder Diffraction Analysis of Clay Minerals*. Book. **Price:** $23.00 ● *Electrochemical Properties of Clays*. Book. **Price:** $26.00 ● *Electron-Optical Methods in Clay Science*. Book. **Price:** $26.00 ● *Kaolin Genesis and Utilization*. Book. **Price:** $30.00 ● *Layer Charge Characteristics of 2:1 Silicate Clay Minerals*. Book. **Price:** $20.00 ● *Molecular Modeling of Clays and Mineral Surfaces*. Book. **Price:** $26.00 ● *Organic Pollutants in the Environment*. **Price:** $23.00 ● *Scanning Probe Microscopy of Clays*. Book. **Price:** $26.00

● *Synchrotron X-ray Methods in Clay Science*. Book. **Price:** $23.00 ● *Teaching Clay Science*. Book. **Price:** $26.00. **Conventions/Meetings:** annual conference and workshop.

7342 ■ Fluorescent Mineral Society
PO Box 572694
Tarzana, CA 91357-2694
E-mail: questions@uvminerals.org
URL: http://www.uvminerals.org
Contact: Jan Wittenberg, Interim Pres.
Founded: 1971. **Members:** 525. **Membership Dues:** regular, in U.S., $25 (annual) ● regular, outside U.S., $28 (annual). **State Groups:** 43. **Multinational. Description:** Individuals in 13 countries interested in the collection and study of fluorescent minerals. Acts as a clearinghouse and a forum for exchange of information on fluorescent minerals. Encourages trading of minerals between members. Provides membership lists. Conducts research programs. **Libraries: Type:** reference. **Holdings:** books. **Subjects:** fluorescence. **Committees:** Executive. **Publications:** *The Henkel Glossary of Fluorescent Minerals*. Book. Contains special edition of 1988-89 Journal of the F.M.S. **Price:** $18.50 postpaid; $21.50 postpaid outside U.S. ● *Journal of the Fluorescent Mineral Society*, annual or biennial. Includes illustrations and diagrams. ● *U.V. Waves*, bimonthly. Newsletter. **Conventions/Meetings:** monthly meeting - 3rd Tuesday, Pasadena, CA.

7343 ■ Mineral Information Institute (MII)
505 Violet St.
Golden, CO 80401-6714
Ph: (303)277-9190
Fax: (303)277-9198
E-mail: mii@mii.org
URL: http://www.mii.org
Contact: Nelson Fugate, Pres.
Founded: 1980. **Staff:** 4. **Budget:** $250,000. **Description:** Provides teaching materials about the importance of mineral and energy resources in everyday life. **Publications:** *Update*, periodic. Newsletter. Covers association activities. **Price:** free. **Circulation:** 50,000. **Conventions/Meetings:** annual meeting - always January.

7344 ■ Mineralogical Society of America (MSA)
3635 Concorde Pkwy., Ste.500
Chantilly, VA 20151-1125
Ph: (703)652-9950
Fax: (703)652-9951
E-mail: business@minsocam.org
URL: http://www.minsocam.org
Contact: Barbara L. Dutrow, Pres.
Founded: 1919. **Members:** 2,200. **Membership Dues:** professional, $55 (annual) ● student, $5 (annual) ● sustaining, $205 (annual) ● life, $2,875. **Staff:** 5. **Budget:** $900,000. **Description:** Professional mineralogists, petrologists, crystallographers, geochemists, educators, students, and others with an avocational interest in mineralogy and the related fields of crystallography and petrology. Provides for the continuing education of professionals through symposia and courses. Disseminates information and encourages the preservation of mineral collections, displays, mineral localities, type minerals, and scientific mineralogical data. Conducts research programs; maintains Speaker's Bureau. **Libraries: Type:** not open to the public. **Holdings:** 500; books, periodicals. **Subjects:** mineralogy. **Awards:** Crystallography Research Grant. **Frequency:** annual. **Type:** grant. **Recipient:** for research in crystallography by someone between 25 and 36 years ● Distinguished Public Service Award. **Frequency:** periodic. **Type:** recognition. **Recipient:** for individuals who have made important contributions to furthering the vitality of the geological sciences ● Minerological Society of America Award. **Frequency:** annual. **Type:** recognition. **Recipient:** for stellar publications, or series of publications before age 35 or within 7 years of the PhD ● MSA Grant for Student Research in Mineralogy and Petrology. **Frequency:** annual. **Type:** grant. **Recipient:** for research in mineralogy or petrology by graduate or undergraduate students ● Roebling Medal. **Frequency:** annual. **Type:** medal. **Recipient:** for lifetime achievement. **Telecommunication Services:** electronic mail, dutrow@geol.lsu.edu. **Publications:** *American Mineralogist*, 8/year. Journal. Features research in the general fields of mineralogy; covers descriptive mineralogy, properties of minerals, and experimental mineralogy. **Price:** $40.00 for members; $650.00 /year for institutions. ISSN: 0003-004X. **Circulation:** 3,200 ● *Geological Materials Research*, periodic. Journal. Contains articles on mineralogy that require the capability of computer presentation. ● *Lattice*, quarterly. Newsletter. Includes calendar of events. **Advertising:** accepted ● *Reviews in Mineralogy*, periodic. Books. Covers reviews of the literature and advances in earth and planetary materials. ISSN: 0275-0279. **Conventions/Meetings:** annual convention, held in conjunction with the Geological Society of America (exhibits).

7345 ■ Society of Mineral Analysts (SMA)
PO Box 404
Lewiston, ID 83501
Ph: (208)799-3286
E-mail: secretary@sma-online.org
URL: http://www.sma-online.org
Contact: Patrick Braun, Managing Sec.
Founded: 1986. **Members:** 300. **Membership Dues:** individual, $25 (annual). **Staff:** 1. **Description:** Assayers, chemists, and metallurgists involved in mineral analysis; suppliers and vendors serving the mineral analysis industry. Promotes discussion relating to chemical and physical analysis of minerals and mineral products; encourages mutual cooperation in the industry. Acts as a clearinghouse for technical information and the introduction of new technical equipment. Maintains speakers' bureau and placement service. Sponsors exhibits and mine tours. **Libraries: Type:** not open to the public. **Holdings:** 16. **Subjects:** proceedings, methods manuals. **Awards:** Technician of the Year. **Frequency:** annual. **Type:** monetary ● Vendor of the Year. **Frequency:** annual. **Type:** monetary. **Committees:** Methods; Round Robin Assay Exchange. **Publications:** *Alchemists Digest*, quarterly. Newsletter. **Advertising:** accepted ● *Membership List*, periodic ● *Methods Manual*, annual ● *SMA Directory*, semiannual ● Also publishes reports of proceedings. **Conventions/Meetings:** annual conference (exhibits).

Mining

7346 ■ American Institute of Mining, Metallurgical, and Petroleum Engineers (AIME)
PO Box 270728
Littleton, CO 80127-0013
Ph: (303)948-4255
Fax: (303)948-4260
E-mail: aime@aimehq.org
URL: http://www.aimehq.org
Contact: J. Rick Rolater, Exec. Dir.
Founded: 1871. **Members:** 100,000. **Staff:** 2. **Budget:** $500,000. **Multinational. Description:** Seeks to advance and disseminate through the programs of the member societies, knowledge of engineering and the arts and sciences involved in the production and use of minerals, metals, energy sources and materials for the benefit of humankind, and to represent association and member societies within the larger engineering community. **Awards:** Douglas Rand McConnell Distinguished Service. **Frequency:** annual. **Type:** recognition ● Environmental Conservation. **Frequency:** annual. **Type:** recognition ● Mineral Industry Education. **Frequency:** annual. **Type:** recognition ● Raymond Awards. **Frequency:** annual. **Type:** recognition. **Telecommunication Services:** electronic mail, rolater@aimehq.org. **Affiliated With:** Association for Iron and Steel Technology; Minerals, Metals, and Materials Society; Society for Mining, Metallurgy, and Exploration; Society of Petroleum Engineers. **Formerly:** (1957) American Institute of Mining and Metallurgical Engineers. **Conventions/Meetings:** annual board meeting.

7347 ■ Mining and Metallurgical Society of America (MMSA)
476 Wilson Ave.
Novato, CA 94947-4236
Ph: (415)897-1380
Fax: (415)897-1380
E-mail: info@mmsa.net
URL: http://www.mmsa.net
Contact: Robert W. Schafer, Pres.
Founded: 1908. **Members:** 375. **Staff:** 1. **Regional Groups:** 4. **Description:** Works for the conservation of mineral resources, the advancement of mining and metallurgical industries, the better protection of mine investors and mine workers, the increase of scientific knowledge, and the encouragement of high professional ideals and ethics. **Awards: Frequency:** annual. **Type:** recognition. **Recipient:** for outstanding service to the mineral industries ● **Frequency:** annual. **Type:** recognition. **Recipient:** for mineral economics papers. **Committees:** D.C. Jacking Fund; Education; Ethical Practices. **Publications:** Newsletter, quarterly ● Booklet ● Bulletin, periodic. **Conventions/Meetings:** annual meeting, held in conjunction with American Institute of Mining, Metallurgical and Petroleum Engineers.

7348 ■ National Mine Rescue Association (NMRA)
c/o Robert Gross, Pres.
145 High St.
Waynesburg, PA 15370
E-mail: avigue@msha.gov
URL: http://www.miningorganizations.org/nmra.htm
Contact: Robert Gross, Pres.
Description: Works to the advancement of the science and engineering practices related to the prevention and control of mine fires and explosions. **Libraries: Type:** reference. **Holdings:** reports. **Committees:** Auditing; Banquet; By-Laws; Coal Mine Fire and Explosions Questions and Answers - Preparation; Coal Mine Fire and Explosions Questions and Answers - Revision; Coordinating; Issues; Nominating; Program; Publicity; Ticket. **Publications:** Newsletter. Alternate Formats: online ● Reports. **Conventions/Meetings:** annual meeting and dinner.

7349 ■ Society for Mining, Metallurgy, and Exploration (SME)
8307 Shaffer Pkwy.
Littleton, CO 80127-4102
Ph: (303)973-9550 (303)948-4210
Free: (800)763-3132
Fax: (303)973-3845
E-mail: cs@smenet.org
URL: http://www.smenet.org
Contact: Dave Kanagy, Exec. Dir.
Founded: 1871. **Members:** 17,000. **Membership Dues:** associate, $120 (annual) ● student, $21 (annual) ● registered, $195 (annual). **Staff:** 26. **Budget:** $6,800,000. **Regional Groups:** 6. **Local Groups:** 74. **Description:** A member society of the American Institute of Mining, Metallurgical and Petroleum Engineers (see separate entry). Persons engaged in the finding, exploitation, treatment, and marketing of all classes of minerals (metal ores, industrial minerals, and solid fuels) except petroleum. Promotes the arts and sciences connected with the production of useful minerals and metals. Offers specialized education programs; compiles enrollment and graduation statistics from schools offering engineering degrees in mining, mineral, mineral processing/metallurgical, geological, geophysical, and mining technology. Provides placement service and sponsors charitable programs. **Libraries: Type:** reference. **Holdings:** books. **Subjects:** mining. **Awards:** Merit Scholarship. **Frequency:** annual. **Type:** scholarship. **Recipient:** for achievement in mineral-related areas. **Computer Services:** Electronic publishing ● mailing lists, available for rental ● online services. **Divisions:** Coal; Environmental; Industrial Minerals; Mineral and Metallurgical Processing; Mining and Exploration. **Affiliated With:** American Institute of Mining, Metallurgical, and Petroleum Engineers. **Formerly:** (1957) Mining Branch, American Institute of Mining, Metallurgical and Petroleum Engineers; (1989) Society of Mining Engineers. **Publications:** *Minerals and Metal-*

lurgical Processing, quarterly. Journal. Documents new technological information on the processing of minerals, metals, and fossil fuels. Includes annual index. **Price:** $70.00 /year for members; $90.00 /year for nonmembers. ISSN: 0747-9182. **Circulation:** 750. **Advertising:** accepted. Alternate Formats: microform ● *Mining Engineering*, monthly. Journal. Includes association news, annual index, book reviews, calendar of events, employment opportunities, new products, and obituaries. **Price:** included in membership dues; $110.00 /year for nonmembers. ISSN: 0026-5187. **Circulation:** 17,000. **Advertising:** accepted. Alternate Formats: microform ● *SME Resource Guide*, annual, in March. Membership Directory. **Price:** free for members. **Advertising:** accepted ● *Transactions*, annual ● Also publishes handbooks and other materials on mining. **Conventions/Meetings:** competition ● annual meeting (exhibits).

Minorities

7350 ■ National Network for Minority Women in Science (MWIS)
1200 New York Ave. NW
Washington, DC 20005
Ph: (202)326-6670
Fax: (202)371-9849
Description: Provides a communication and support network for minority women in science and engineering. Promotes research and writing, public speaking, local intervention and service programs.

Mycology

7351 ■ International Mycological Association (IMA)
c/o Mycological Society of America
PO Box 7065
Lawrence, KS 66044
Free: (800)627-0629
Fax: (785)843-1274
E-mail: trond.schumacher@bio.uio.no
URL: http://www.ima-mycology.org
Contact: Pedro Crous, Pres.
Founded: 1971. **Members:** 2,500. **Membership Dues:** sustaining, $400 (annual) ● individual, $20 (quadrennial) ● organization, $60 (annual). **Regional Groups:** 4. **Description:** Represents 20,000 mycologists from 80 countries who promote the study of mycology (a branch of botany dealing with fungi) in all its aspects. Constitutes the Section for General Mycology within the International Union of Biological Sciences. **Committees:** Development of Mycology in African Countries; Development of Mycology in Asian Countries; Development of Mycology in European Countries; Development of Mycology in Latin American Countries. **Foreign language name:** Association Internationale de Mycologie. **Publications:** *Fungal Morphogenesis*. Book. **Price:** $43.00 ● *IMA News*, periodic. Newsletter ● *Plants and Fungi: Multicelled Life*. Book. **Price:** $8.50 ● *Yeast Stress Responses*. Book. **Price:** $129.00. **Conventions/Meetings:** quadrennial International Mycological Congress (exhibits) ● periodic regional meeting.

7352 ■ Mycological Society of America (MSA)
PO Box 1897
Lawrence, KS 66044-8897
Ph: (785)843-1235
Free: (800)627-0326
Fax: (785)843-1274
E-mail: msa@allenpress.com
URL: http://www.msafungi.org
Contact: Gregory M. Mueller, Pres.
Founded: 1932. **Members:** 1,200. **Membership Dues:** student, associate, $50 (annual) ● affiliate, individual (additional $20 for spouse), regular, $98 (annual) ● life, $1,500 ● sustaining, $278 (annual). **Description:** Researchers, industrial and medical mycologists, plant pathologists, students, and others interested in the study of fungi through research, teaching, and industrial application. Maintains placement service. **Awards:** Alexopoulos Prize. **Frequency:** annual. **Type:** recognition. **Recipient:** for the most promising member of the society ● Distinguished Mycologist Award. **Frequency:** annual. **Type:** recognition. **Recipient:** for individual who has established an outstanding mycological career ● **Type:** fellowship. **Recipient:** for graduate fellowships in mycology to MSA members, also student travel awards to MSA members ● William H. Weston Award. **Frequency:** annual. **Type:** recognition. **Recipient:** for outstanding teacher of mycology at the undergraduate and or graduate levels. **Computer Services:** Mailing lists, of members. **Committees:** Ecology; Endowment; Medical Mycology; Nomenclature; Phytopathology; Teaching. **Affiliated With:** International Mycological Association. **Formerly:** Mycological Section, Botanical Society of America. **Publications:** *Inoculum*, bimonthly. Newsletter. Includes information on fungi, society news, calendar of events, and employment opportunity listings. ISSN: 0541-4938. **Circulation:** 1,450 ● *MSA Directory*, periodic ● *Mycologia*, bimonthly ● *Mycologia Memoirs*, periodic. **Conventions/Meetings:** annual conference and meeting (exhibits) - 2008 Aug. 10-13, State College, PA; 2009 July 25-30, Snowbird, UT; 2010 June, Lexington, KY.

7353 ■ North American Mycological Association (NAMA)
c/o Judy Roger, Exec. Sec.
6615 Tudor Ct.
Gladstone, OR 97027-1032
Ph: (503)657-7358
E-mail: execsec@namyco.org
URL: http://www.namyco.org
Contact: Ike Forester, Pres.
Founded: 1959. **Members:** 1,600. **Membership Dues:** student in North America, $15 (annual) ● regular, in North America, $35 (annual) ● regular, outside North America, $40 (annual) ● sustaining, $60 (annual) ● life, $500. **Staff:** 1. **Budget:** $32,000. **Regional Groups:** 35. **State Groups:** 25. **Local Groups:** 40. **Description:** Amateur and professional mycologists, mycophagists, devotees of mushroom lore, students, and botanists. Promotes amateur mycology (the study of fungi, such as mushrooms, puffballs, molds, rusts, and smuts); sponsors field trips. Professional taxonomists assist members in classifying specimens. Conducts biennial course in mycology. Sponsors school programs; rents audiovisual sets on mycology. Compiles statistics. **Awards:** Contributions to Amateur Mycology. **Frequency:** annual. **Type:** recognition. **Recipient:** for contribution to amateur mycology ● Harry and Elsie Knighton Service Award. **Frequency:** annual. **Type:** recognition. **Recipient:** for service to a local club. **Telecommunication Services:** electronic mail, webmaster@namyco.org. **Committees:** Awards; Cultivation; Dyeing; Editorial; Education; Forays; Literature; Mycophagy; Photography; Toxicology. **Formerly:** (1967) People to People Committee on Fungi. **Publications:** *McIlvainea*, annual. Journal. Includes research reports. **Price:** included in membership dues. ISSN: 0099-8400. **Circulation:** 2,200 ● *The Mycophile*, bimonthly. Newsletter. Covers the collection, study, and scientific description of wild mushrooms and fungi. Includes calendar of events, research news, and book reviews. **Price:** included in membership dues. ISSN: 0027-5549. **Circulation:** 2,000 ● *North American Mycological Association Directory*, annual. **Conventions/Meetings:** annual convention (exhibits) - varies by year and location, depending on mushroom season ● annual seminar and workshop, covers taxonomic and mycological issues - usually in September.

7354 ■ North American Truffling Society (NATS)
PO Box 296
Corvallis, OR 97339
Ph: (541)752-2243 (541)929-8165
E-mail: rawlinsonpat@hotmail.com
URL: http://www.natruffling.org
Contact: Pat Rawlinson, Ed.
Founded: 1978. **Members:** 335. **Membership Dues:** individual, $10 (annual) ● additional family, $5. **Description:** Individuals interested in collecting scientific information on North American truffles. (Truffles are the reproductive bodies of certain species of mycorrhizal fungi that grow and mature in the soil. Although related and similar to mushrooms in their edibility, truffles depend solely upon animals for spore dispersal, whereas mushroom spores can be carried by moving air.) Conducts research and records data on the location, identification, classification, plant associations, seasonality, and edibility of truffles and truffle-like fungi. Sponsors forays and field trips to collect truffles. Develops culinary information on the use of truffles. Participates in exhibits and fungi shows. Maintains speakers' bureau. Sponsors charitable programs; compiles statistics. **Libraries: Type:** reference. **Awards: Type:** recognition. **Computer Services:** database. **Committees:** Awards; Library. **Publications:** *The Cookbook of North American Truffles*. **Price:** $5.00 ● *NATS Current News*, bimonthly. Newsletter. Contains truffle findings, foray locations, and information on membership activities. ● *NATS Field Guide to North American Truffles*. Book. **Price:** $20.00 ● *The North American Truffler: Journal of the North American Truffling Society*. Newsletter. Alternate Formats: online. **Conventions/Meetings:** annual dinner ● monthly meeting.

Natural Disasters

7355 ■ Natural Hazards Research and Applications Information Center
Univ. of Colorado
482 UCB
Boulder, CO 80309-0482
Ph: (303)492-6818
Fax: (303)492-2151
E-mail: hazctr@colorado.edu
URL: http://www.colorado.edu/hazards
Contact: Kathleen Tierney, Dir.
Founded: 1977. **Staff:** 7. **Description:** Advances and communicates knowledge on hazards mitigation and disaster preparedness, response, and recovery. Fosters information sharing and integration of activities among researchers, practitioners, and policy makers from around the world; supports and conducts research; and provides educational opportunities for the next generation of hazards scholars and professionals. **Libraries: Type:** reference; by appointment only. **Holdings:** 28,000; articles, books, periodicals, reports. **Subjects:** economic, social, and behavioral aspects of natural hazards and extreme events. **Awards:** Mary Fran Myers. **Frequency:** annual. **Type:** scholarship. **Recipient:** to people whose program-related activities, advocacy efforts, or research had made a lasting, positive impact in reducing hazards vulnerability for women and girls. **Computer Services:** Mailing lists. **Publications:** *Disaster Research*, biweekly. Newsletter. **Circulation:** 2,600. Alternate Formats: online ● *Environment and Behavior Monograph Series*, periodic. **Price:** $20.00 plus shipping and handling. **Circulation:** 400 ● *Natural Hazards Observer*, bimonthly. Newsletter. Provides research information. Includes legislative news; project reports, and schedule of events. **Price:** free for members; $24.00 for nonmembers outside U.S. ISSN: 0737-5425. **Circulation:** 15,000. Alternate Formats: online ● *Natural Hazards Working Papers Series*, periodic. **Price:** $9.00 plus shipping and handling. Alternate Formats: online ● *Quick Response Research Reports Series*, periodic. **Price:** $5.00 plus shipping and handling. Alternate Formats: online ● *Special Publications Series*, periodic. Includes proceedings and special reports. **Price:** $20.00 plus shipping and handling ● *Topical Bibliographies Series*, periodic. **Conventions/Meetings:** annual Hazards Research and Applications Workshop - always July, Boulder, CO. 2008 July 12-15, Boulder, CO.

Natural Sciences

7356 ■ Academy of Natural Sciences (ANS)
1900 Benjamin Franklin Pkwy.
Philadelphia, PA 19103

Ph: (215)299-1000 (215)299-1022
Free: (800)732-0999
Fax: (215)405-1541
E-mail: wbrown@ansp.org
URL: http://www.ansp.org
Contact: Dr. William Brown, Pres.

Founded: 1812. **Members:** 10,000. **Membership Dues:** Partner Club, $250-$499 (annual) ● supporting, $150 (annual) ● family, $70 (annual) ● family plus, $80 (annual) ● individual, $50 (annual) ● Founder's Club, $500-$999 (annual). **Staff:** 260. **Budget:** $16,900,000. **Multinational. Description:** Undertakes research and public education that focuses on the environment and its diverse species. Expands knowledge of nature through discovery and inspires stewardship of the environment. Features four floors of family-oriented exhibitions drawn from the world-renowned research collections of 23 million animal and plant specimens. Exhibits include dinosaur mounts, live butterflies, live animals, and historic dioramas. Conducts variety of educational, interactive shows daily. Provides special educational programs for schoolchildren and teens, plus traveling opportunities for members. Focuses on Scientific research and applications about aquatic ecology and biodiversity. **Libraries: Type:** open to the public. **Holdings:** 338,300; archival material, books, papers, periodicals. **Awards:** Day Medal. **Type:** medal. **Recipient:** for scientific achievement ● Gold Medal. **Type:** medal. **Recipient:** for achievement in natural history art ● Hayden Medal. **Type:** medal. **Recipient:** for scientific achievement ● Leidy Medal. **Type:** medal. **Recipient:** for scientific achievement. **Computer Services:** database, includes general info about all aspects of academy's operations plus science research. **Telecommunication Services:** electronic mail, webmaster@ansp.org. **Departments:** Aquatic Ecology; Biodiversity; Education; Exhibition. **Divisions:** Estuarine Research Center. **Publications:** *Discover*, quarterly. Newsletter. **Price:** included in membership dues. **Circulation:** 12,500 ● Proceedings, periodic ● Also publishes catalogs and monographs. **Conventions/Meetings:** annual meeting - usually May.

7357 ■ American Museum of Natural History (AMNH)

Central Park W at 79th St.
New York, NY 10024-5192
Ph: (212)769-5100 (212)769-5606
Fax: (212)769-5427
E-mail: members@amnh.org
URL: http://www.amnh.org
Contact: Ellen V. Futter, Pres.

Founded: 1869. **Members:** 520,000. **Membership Dues:** individual, $70 (annual) ● dual, $90 (annual) ● family, $115 (annual) ● contributor, $195 (annual) ● supporter, $400 (annual) ● sponsor, $800 (annual) ● friend, $1,000 (annual). **Staff:** 737. **Budget:** $51,000,000. **Description:** Persons interested in the natural sciences. Promotes the study of evolutionary biology. Serves as a research, education, and exhibition center for the study of the zoological, anthropological, and mineralogical sciences. Maintains the Naturemax Theater and permanent exhibits on meteorites, minerals and gems, birds, mammals, reptiles and amphibians, dinosaurs (early and late), the biology of invertebrates, ocean life, American Indians, and the peoples of Asia, Africa, Mexico, the Pacific region, and South and Central America; also prepares temporary exhibitions of international significance several times a year. Operates the American Museum-Hayden Planetarium, which offers courses in astronomy and navigation and maintains collection of meteorites; also operates a Natural Science Center and a People Center. Sponsors many programs and exhibits for school children. Maintains numerous grants and fellowship funding arms, including: Post Doctoral Fellowship Fund; Theodore Roosevelt Memorial Fund; Frank M. Chapman Memorial Fund; Lerner-Gray Fund for Marine Research. Research station programs include: Archbold Biological Station, Florida; Great Gull Island, NY; Southwestern Research Station, Arizona; and St. Catherines Island, GA. **Libraries: Type:** reference. **Holdings:** 420,000; archival material, films, photographs. **Departments:** Anthropology; Astronomy; Education; Entomology; Herpetology and Ichthyology; Invertebrates; Library; Mammalogy; Mineral Sciences; Ornithology; Vertebrate Paleontology. **Publications:** *American Museum Novitates*, periodic. Includes monographs and research papers on systematic and evolutionary studies. ISSN: 0003-0082. **Circulation:** 800. Alternate Formats: microform; online ● *Anthropological Papers of the American Museum of Natural History*, periodic ● *Bulletin of the American Museum of Natural History*, periodic ● *Curator*, quarterly. Journal. Covers topics on museum management and maintenance for museum personnel and administrators. Includes book reviews. **Price:** $25.00 /year for individuals; $45.00/year for organizations. ISSN: 0011-3069. **Circulation:** 1,300 ● *James Arthur Lecture on the Evolution of the Human Brain*, periodic. **Circulation:** 1,000 ● *Natural History*, monthly. Magazine. Covers all aspects of natural history from anthropology to zoology. Includes illustrations, color photographs, and book reviews. **Price:** included in membership dues. ISSN: 0028-0712. **Circulation:** 520,000. **Advertising:** accepted. Alternate Formats: microform ● *Recent Publications in Natural History*, quarterly. Lists monographs on natural sciences, including anthropology and astronomy. **Price:** $17.00/year; $20.00/year for overseas. ISSN: 0738-0925. **Circulation:** 300 ● Annual Report, annual ● Journal, quarterly. **Price:** $50.00 /year for individuals; $110.00 /year for institutions. ISSN: 0026-2803. **Circulation:** 1,000. Alternate Formats: microform.

7358 ■ American Nature Study Society (ANSS)

c/o Pocono Environmental Education Center
RR 2, Box 1010
Dingmans Ferry, PA 18328
E-mail: anssonline@aol.com
URL: http://www.hometown.aol.com/anssonline

Founded: 1908. **Members:** 500. **Membership Dues:** life, $350 ● sponsor, organization, $50 (annual) ● regular, library, $30 (annual) ● student/retiree, $18 (annual). **Budget:** $15,000. **Description:** Professional and amateur naturalists, conservationists, teachers, and others concerned with nature and environmental education. Conducts field excursions and assists in training nature leaders. **Awards:** Eva L. Gordon Award. **Frequency:** annual. **Type:** recognition. **Recipient:** for outstanding children's science literature. **Affiliated With:** American Association for the Advancement of Science; Nature Canada. **Publications:** *ANSS Newsletter*, semiannual. Regards information/content-education, science, and nature. **Price:** included in membership dues. **Circulation:** 1,000 ● *City Critters, Holy Earth*. Book ● *Nature Study*, quarterly. Journal. Covers environmental and nature education. **Price:** $30.00 /year for individuals; $50.00 /year for institutions; $30.00 /year for libraries. ISSN: 0028-0860. **Circulation:** 850. **Advertising:** accepted ● *Nature Study Tips*. Reprint ● Membership Directory, periodic. **Conventions/Meetings:** annual meeting and workshop, programs regarding nature study (exhibits).

7359 ■ American Quaternary Association (AMQUA)

c/o Cary Cock, Treas.
Dept. of Geography
Univ. of South Carolina
Columbia, SC 29208
Ph: (803)777-1211 (217)782-7475
Fax: (803)777-4972
E-mail: treasurer@amqua.org
URL: http://www.amqua.org
Contact: Eric Grimm, Pres.

Founded: 1969. **Members:** 750. **Membership Dues:** student, retired, $10 (annual) ● professional, $20 (annual) ● professional, $50 (triennial). **Budget:** $35,000. **Description:** Represents natural scientists (earth scientists, biologists, geographers, anthropologists, palynologists, and meteorologists). Aims to increase and exchange information on the history of the environment, biota, and climate during the last two million years. **Awards:** Denise Guadreau Award. **Frequency:** biennial. **Type:** monetary. **Recipient:** for excellence in quaternary studies ● Distinguished Career Award. **Frequency:** annual. **Type:** recognition. **Recipient:** for individuals who have made outstanding contributions to the advancement of Quaternary science. **Affiliated With:** Geological Society of America. **Publications:** *American Quaternary Association—Program and Abstracts*, biennial. Proceedings. Contains schedule of the biennial AMQUA meeting and abstracts of all papers to be presented. Include author index. **Price:** included in membership dues. **Circulation:** 1,000 ● *Quaternary Times*. Newsletter. Covers membership activities. Includes calendar of events and book reviews. **Price:** included in membership dues. **Advertising:** accepted. **Conventions/Meetings:** biennial conference (exhibits).

7360 ■ American Society of Naturalists (ASN)

c/o University of Chicago Press
PO Box 37005
Chicago, IL 60637
Ph: (773)753-3347
Free: (877)705-1878
Fax: (773)753-0811
E-mail: subscriptions@press.uchicago.edu
URL: http://www.amnat.org
Contact: Dr. Robert D. Holt, Pres.

Founded: 1883. **Members:** 1,835. **Membership Dues:** individual, $49 (annual). **Description:** Professional society of biologists and others engaged in some area of natural history. Seeks to advance and disseminate information concerning broad biological principles including organic evolution, and to promote conceptual unification of the biological sciences. **Awards:** E.O. Wilson Naturalist Award. **Type:** recognition. **Recipient:** to an active investigator who has made significant contributions to the knowledge of a particular ecosystem or group of organisms ● Presidential Award. **Type:** recognition. **Recipient:** for the best paper published in The American Naturalist during the calendar year ● **Type:** recognition. **Recipient:** to an active investigator in mid-career who has made significant contributions to the knowledge of a particular ecosystem or group of organisms ● Sewall Wright Award. **Type:** recognition. **Recipient:** for senior investigator who has made major contributions that relate to the goals of the society ● Young Investigator's Prize. **Type:** recognition. **Recipient:** for outstanding and promising work by investigators who have received their doctorates in the three years preceding the application deadline or who are in their final year of graduate school. **Telecommunication Services:** electronic mail, asn@press.uchicago.edu. **Affiliated With:** American Association for the Advancement of Science. **Publications:** *The American Naturalist*, monthly. Journal. **Price:** $499.00 institution in U.S.; $75.00 individual in U.S.; $49.00 student, family in U.S. ISSN: 0003-0147 ● *Records of the American Society of Naturalists*, triennial. **Conventions/Meetings:** annual meeting - 2008 June 20-24, Minneapolis, MN.

7361 ■ Big Bend Natural History Association (BBNHA)

PO Box 196
Big Bend National Park, TX 79834-0196
Ph: (432)477-2236
Fax: (432)477-2234
E-mail: anita_johnson@nps.gov
URL: http://www.bigbendbookstore.org
Contact: Mike Boren, Exec. Dir.

Founded: 1956. **Members:** 550. **Membership Dues:** individual, $50 (annual) ● associate, joint, friend, $100 (annual) ● life, family, $500 ● benefactor, $1,000 (annual) ● corporate, $500 (annual). **Staff:** 4. **Budget:** $500,000. **Description:** Promotes the historic and scientific value of the Big Bend area and the Amistad National Recreation Area of Texas. Cooperates with the National Park Service. Sponsors educational programs. **Publications:** *Big Bend of the Rio Grande*. Book. **Price:** $16.95 ● *Big Bend Paisano*, 3/year. Newsletter ● Also publishes geologic camping, hiking, and river guides and maps. **Conventions/Meetings:** semiannual board meeting ● annual meeting, state of the association report to members.

7362 ■ John Burroughs Association (JBA)
c/o Lisa Breslof, Sec.
15 W 77th St.
New York, NY 10024-5192
Ph: (212)769-5169
E-mail: breslof@amnh.org
URL: http://www.johnburroughs.org
Contact: Lisa Breslof, Sec.
Founded: 1921. **Members:** 232. **Membership Dues:** regular, $25 (annual) ● life, $500 ● student/senior, $15 (annual) ● family, $35 (annual) ● patron, $50 (annual) ● benefactor, $100 (annual). **Staff:** 4. **Description:** Scientists, naturalists, writers, and others interested in natural history. Named for John Burroughs (1837-1921), naturalist and writer. Encourages writing in natural history and maintains noted places associated with Burroughs' life and writings such as Slabsides, Burroughs' cabin in West Park, NY. Organizes nature walks and other educational programs. Offers public and school programs and services. Maintains exhibit at the American Museum of Natural History in New York City. **Libraries: Type:** reference. **Holdings:** archival material, artwork, books, business records, clippings, periodicals. **Subjects:** nature, natural history. **Awards:** John Burroughs Book List Award. **Type:** recognition ● John Burroughs Bronze Medal. **Frequency:** annual. **Type:** recognition. **Recipient:** for distinguished piece of contemporary nature writing ● John Burroughs Periodical Essay Award. **Type:** recognition. **Computer Services:** database, book awards ● database, children's book list ● database, periodical essay award ● mailing lists. **Additional Websites:** http://research.amnh.org/burroughs. **Committees:** Awards; Constitution and Bylaws; Exhibition/Education; Finance; Library; Membership; Nomination; Pond House; Publications; Sanctuary; Slabsides. **Formerly:** (1985) John Burroughs Memorial Association. **Publications:** *John Burroughs List of Nature Books for Young Readers*, annual. Provides a list of children's book author winners. Alternate Formats: online ● *Wake-Robin*, 3/year. Newsletter. Includes membership activities and nature articles. **Price:** included in membership dues. **Circulation:** 232. **Conventions/Meetings:** annual John Burroughs Literary Awards - meeting, with lunch - usually first Monday of April, New York City ● semiannual Open House - meeting - always third Saturday of May and first Saturday of October, West Park, NY.

7363 ■ National Association for Interpretation (NAI)
PO Box 2246
Fort Collins, CO 80522
Ph: (970)484-8283
Free: (888)900-8283
Fax: (970)484-8179
E-mail: naiexec@aol.com
URL: http://www.interpnet.com
Contact: Tim Merriman, Exec. Dir.
Founded: 1988. **Members:** 4,200. **Membership Dues:** basic, standard (student), $20-$30 (annual) ● standard (student), $55 (annual) ● basic, standard (professional), $55-$75 (annual) ● basic, standard (family), $65-$85 (annual) ● basic, standard (senior professional), $35-$45 (annual) ● associate, $35-$45 (annual) ● life, $1,350 ● basic, standard (commercial), $275-$500 (annual). **Staff:** 4. **Budget:** $900,000. **Regional Groups:** 10. **National Groups:** 9. **Languages:** English, Spanish. **Description:** Specialists who prepare exhibits and conduct programs at information centers maintained by public and private institutions; persons engaged in educational programs at museums, zoos, parks, arboretums, botanical gardens, historical sites, schools, and camps. Seeks to advance education and develop skills in interpreting the natural, historical, and cultural environment by establishing educational, professional, and ethical standards; and by developing and maintaining lines of communication among related professionals and the public. Provides national training opportunities through the Interpretation Management Institute. Supports the preservation of areas that have significant natural, aesthetic, or historical value. Promotes pre-service and in-service educational programs; encourages research and disseminates results of investigations that will improve the profession; furthers the establishment of interpretation programs to serve the public welfare. **Libraries: Type:** open to the public. **Holdings:** 6. **Subjects:** interpretation, education. **Awards:** Fellow. **Frequency:** annual. **Type:** recognition ● Honorary. **Type:** recognition ● Meritorious Service. **Type:** recognition. **Telecommunication Services:** electronic mail, membership@interpnet.com. **Committees:** Affiliations; Awards; Editorial; Education and Curriculum; Legacy Trust Fund. **Councils:** American Indian Interpretation; Federal Interagency. **Formed by Merger of:** (1988) Association of Interpretive Naturalists; Western Interpreters Association. **Publications:** *Interpnews*, quarterly. Newsletter ● *The Interpreter*, bimonthly. Magazine ● *Interpretive Sourcebook*. Proceedings ● *Legacy*, bimonthly. Magazine. Includes association news, regional reports, book reviews, and research papers. **Price:** included in membership dues; $30.00 for nonmembers. **Circulation:** 3,300. **Advertising:** accepted. Also Cited As: *Journal of Interpretation Research* ● *NAI News*. Newsletters ● Booklets ● Membership Directory, annual. **Price:** $35.00/year. **Conventions/Meetings:** annual conference ● annual National Interpreters Workshop - convention and workshop, five-day training and field trips (exhibits) - 2008 Nov. 11-15, Portland, OR; 2009 Nov. 17-21, Hartford, CT.

7364 ■ Society for Northwestern Vertebrate Biology (SNVB)
c/o Julie Grialou, Treas.
18304 Hwy. 20
Winthrop, WA 98862
Ph: (509)996-2402 (360)902-2544
Fax: (360)902-2946
E-mail: jgrialou@gmail.com
URL: http://www.snwvb.org
Contact: Tara Chestnut, Pres.
Founded: 1920. **Members:** 400. **Membership Dues:** student, $15 (annual) ● regular, $25 (annual) ● contributing individual, $35 (annual) ● sustaining individual, $50 (annual) ● institutional (domestic and foreign), $60 (annual) ● life, $325. **Regional Groups:** 4. **Description:** Ornithologists, mammalogists, herpetologists, ichthyologists, and other persons with an interest in natural history of the Pacific Northwest of the United States, Western Canada, and Alaska. Promotes close working relationships between the ornithologists, mammalogists, ichthyologists, and herpetologists in the region, and to encourage an interest in the scientific study of the region's birds, mammals, reptiles, fish, and amphibians. **Libraries: Type:** open to the public. **Holdings:** 81; books, periodicals. **Subjects:** Northwestern vertebrate biology. **Formerly:** (1988) Pacific Northwest Bird and Mammal Society. **Publications:** *Northwestern Naturalist: Journal of Vertebrate Biology*, 3/year. Provides information on the biology of birds, mammals, reptiles, and amphibians of the Pacific Northwest. Includes book reviews. **Price:** included in membership dues; $50.00 /year for institutions. ISSN: 0027-3716. **Advertising:** accepted. Also Cited As: *The Murrelet*. **Conventions/Meetings:** annual meeting.

7365 ■ Western National Parks Association (WNPA)
12880 N Vistoso Village Dr.
Tucson, AZ 85755
Ph: (520)622-1999
Free: (888)910-9672
Fax: (520)623-9519
E-mail: info@wnpa.org
URL: http://www.wnpa.org
Contact: LeAnn Simpson, Exec. Dir./CEO
Founded: 1938. **Members:** 2,800. **Membership Dues:** individual, $25 (annual) ● life, $1,000 ● family, $45 (annual) ● individual, $45 (biennial) ● family, $80 (biennial). **Staff:** 135. **Budget:** $10,200,000. **Description:** Seeks to aid in the preservation and interpretation of Western features of national interest: specifically, 65 national parks and monuments in 12 Western states. Sponsors research projects related to increasing knowledge and understanding of the history and natural history of National Park System areas in the West. Produces interpretive publications and products for sale or free distribution to park visitors. Operates bookstore sales outlets in national park visitor centers. **Libraries: Type:** reference. **Holdings:** archival material, reports. **Awards:** Western National Parks Association Research Grant. **Frequency:** annual. **Type:** grant. **Recipient:** for researchers working in one or more WNPA-affiliated national parks for scientific research. **Telecommunication Services:** electronic mail, members@wnpa.org ● additional toll-free number, (888)569-SPMA. **Committees:** Donation; Publishing; Research. **Affiliated With:** Museum Store Association; National Parks Conservation Association; Trail of Tears Association. **Formerly:** (1969) Southwestern Monuments Association; (2003) Southwest Parks and Monuments Association. **Publications:** *Publications Catalog*, annual. Lists books published by the association. ● Books.

7366 ■ Western Society of Naturalists (WSN)
Dept. of Biology
San Diego State Univ.
5500 Campanile Dr.
San Diego, CA 92182
E-mail: secretariat@wsn-online.org
URL: http://www.wsn-online.org
Contact: Ralph Larson, Pres.
Founded: 1911. **Members:** 2,100. **Membership Dues:** student, $15 (annual) ● regular, $35 (annual). **Description:** College and university faculty and students; marine scientists; interested laypeople. Seeks to increase interest, knowledge, and integration in the biological sciences and to provide opportunities for the presentation and discussion of problems of common interest, especially in Marine Biology/Ecology. **Libraries: Type:** reference. **Holdings:** archival material. **Awards:** Outstanding Paper Award. **Frequency:** annual. **Type:** monetary. **Recipient:** for the highest quality student paper presented at the annual meeting ● Travel Award. **Type:** monetary. **Recipient:** for students. **Telecommunication Services:** electronic mail, odonnell@msi.ucsb.edu. **Affiliated With:** American Association for the Advancement of Science. **Publications:** *Abstracts of Contributed Papers*, annual ● *Program of Annual Meeting* ● Newsletter, semiannual ● Proceedings. **Conventions/Meetings:** periodic International Symposia - symposium ● annual meeting - usually on the Pacific Coast between December 27-30.

7367 ■ Yosemite Association (YA)
PO Box 230
El Portal, CA 95318
Ph: (209)379-2646 (209)379-2317
Fax: (209)379-2486
E-mail: info@yosemite.org
URL: http://www.yosemite.org
Contact: David Guy, CEO
Founded: 1923. **Members:** 10,000. **Membership Dues:** regular, $35 (annual) ● supporting, $60 (annual) ● contributing, $125 (annual) ● sustaining, $250 (annual) ● patron, $500 (annual) ● benefactor, $1,000 (annual) ● international, $50 (annual) ● joint/family, $40 (annual). **Staff:** 15. **Budget:** $2,250,000. **Description:** Educational organization for individuals, families, and corporations interested in Yosemite National Park. Cooperates with the National Park Service. Provides financial support and services in support of the NPS's educational mission, by publishing books for visitors, operating visitor center bookstores, coordinating volunteer services, offering outdoor field seminars to the public, and managing a membership program. **Awards: Type:** grant. **Recipient:** must benefit Yosemite National Park. **Telecommunication Services:** electronic mail, smedley@yosemite.org. **Formerly:** (1925) Yosemite Museum Association; (1985) Yosemite Natural History Association. **Publications:** *Yosemite*, quarterly. Newsletter. Contains natural history articles, and member information. **Price:** included in membership dues; $30.00 /year for nonmembers. **Circulation:** 8,000. Also Cited As: *Yosemite Nature Notes* ● Natural history, history, Native American, and other books published on an intermittent basis. **Conventions/Meetings:** annual meeting - usually fall ● annual Spring Forum - meeting - always spring in Yosemite National Park, CA.

Naval Engineering

7368 ■ Society of Naval Architects and Marine Engineers (SNAME)
601 Pavonia Ave.
Jersey City, NJ 07306
Ph: (201)798-4800 (201)499-5054
Free: (800)798-2188
Fax: (201)798-4975
E-mail: director@sname.org
URL: http://www.sname.org
Contact: Philip Kimball, Exec. Dir.
Founded: 1893. **Members:** 10,598. **Membership Dues:** affiliate, $50-$150 (annual) ● associate, individual, $125 (annual) ● student, $35 (annual) ● fellow, $150 (annual) ● reciprocal, $35-$150 (annual). **Staff:** 20. **Budget:** $2,500,000. **Regional Groups:** 17. **Description:** Naval architects and marine and ocean engineers. Seeks to advance the art, science, and practice of naval architecture, shipbuilding, marine engineering, and all fields. Aims to: exchange information and ideas among its members; disseminate the results of research, experience, and information; promote the professional integrity and status of its members and advancement in their knowledge; further education in naval architecture, marine, and ocean engineering; encourage and sponsor research and other inquiries important to the advancement of the art. Conducts Technical and Research Program to investigate the design, production, maintenance, and operation of ships, submersibles, small craft, offshore and ocean bottom structures, hydrofoils, and surface effect ships. Maintains 21 standing committees and 8 technical and research committees including: Hull Structure; Hydrodynamics; Offshore; Ship Design; Ship Production; Ship Technical Operations; Ships' Machinery; Small Craft; Steering. **Libraries: Type:** reference. **Holdings:** 1,000; articles, papers. **Awards:** Blakely Smith Medal. **Frequency:** annual. **Type:** medal. **Recipient:** for outstanding accomplishment in ocean engineering ● Captain Joseph H. Linnard Prize. **Frequency:** annual. **Type:** recognition. **Recipient:** for the best paper appearing in the Transactions of the Society ● David W. Taylor Medal. **Frequency:** annual. **Type:** medal. **Recipient:** for notable achievement in naval architecture and/or marine engineering ● Davidson Medal. **Frequency:** annual. **Type:** medal. **Recipient:** for outstanding scientific accomplishment in ship research ● Distinguished Service Award. **Frequency:** annual. **Type:** recognition. **Recipient:** for dedicated personal service and/or technical contributions ● Elmer L. Hann Award. **Frequency:** annual. **Type:** recognition. **Recipient:** for the best paper on ship production ● Student Paper Award. **Frequency:** annual. **Type:** recognition. **Recipient:** for outstanding papers contributed to a meeting of the society or one of its sections ● Vice Admiral E.L. Cochrane Award. **Frequency:** annual. **Type:** recognition. **Recipient:** for the best paper delivered before a section ● Vice Admiral "Jerry" Land Medal. **Frequency:** annual. **Type:** medal. **Recipient:** for outstanding accomplishment in the marine field ● Webb Medal. **Frequency:** annual. **Type:** medal. **Recipient:** for outstanding contributions to education in naval architecture, marine, or ocean engineering ● William M. Kennedy Award. **Frequency:** annual. **Type:** recognition. **Recipient:** for outstanding service and contribution in the development of systems and planning applying to ship building and repair. **Telecommunication Services:** electronic mail, ldavis@sname.org. **Publications:** *Biennial Directory and Information Book*, annual ● *Index to SNAME Publications*, periodic. Facilitates access to the large volume of technical information published by the organization since 1893. ● *Journal of Ship Production*, quarterly. Contains a selection of technical papers relevant to ship professionals, including written discussions and author's closures. **Price:** $280.00 for nonmembers in U.S.; $310.00 for nonmembers outside U.S.; $60.00 for members in U.S.; $75.00 for members outside U.S. ● *Journal of Ship Research*, quarterly. Contains technical papers on applied research in hydrodynamics, propulsion, ship motions, structures, and vibrations. **Price:** $65.00 for members in U.S.; $80.00 for members outside U.S.; $280.00 for nonmembers in U.S.; $310.00 for nonmembers outside U.S. ● *Marine Technology*, quarterly. Journal. Includes member news. **Price:** free for members; $280.00 for nonmembers in U.S.; $310.00 for nonmembers outside U.S. ● *Publications Catalog*, annual ● *Transactions*, annual. Contains technical papers and discussions. ● *Workshop Proceedings* ● Booklet ● Books ● Reports ● Newsletter, semimonthly. **Conventions/Meetings:** European Community of Maritime Research Meeting ● annual meeting ● annual Meeting and International Maritime Exposition - conference (exhibits) ● regional meeting and symposium.

Navigation

7369 ■ Institute of Navigation (ION)
3975 Univ. Dr., Ste.390
Fairfax, VA 22030
Ph: (703)383-9688
Fax: (703)383-9689
E-mail: membership@ion.org
URL: http://www.ion.org
Contact: Lisa Beaty, Dir. of Operations
Founded: 1945. **Members:** 4,000. **Membership Dues:** corporate (class I), $700 (annual) ● corporate (class II), $350 (annual) ● professional in U.S., $55 (annual) ● retired in U.S., student outside U.S., $30 (annual) ● student in U.S., $20 (annual) ● professional outside U.S., $65 (annual) ● retired outside U.S., $40 (annual). **Staff:** 5. **Budget:** $1,110,000. **Regional Groups:** 3. **Local Groups:** 5. **Description:** Members of armed services and maritime service, astronomers, cartographers, meteorologists, educators, scientists engaged in research and development in navigation and related sciences, and practicing navigators. Promotes advancement of navigation in air, space, surface, underseas, and global positioning systems. Coordinates the exchange of information with navigation societies in other countries. **Libraries: Type:** reference. **Holdings:** articles. **Awards:** Burka Award. **Frequency:** annual. **Type:** recognition. **Recipient:** for outstanding achievement in the preparation of papers contributing to the advancement of navigation and space guidance ● Early Achievement Award. **Frequency:** annual. **Type:** recognition. **Recipient:** for individuals who have made a significant achievement (35 years or younger in the year of the achievement) ● Hays Award. **Frequency:** annual. **Type:** recognition. **Recipient:** for individuals engaged in management of the military services, civil government, or industry ● Superior Achievement Award. **Frequency:** annual. **Type:** recognition. **Recipient:** for individuals cited for outstanding performance as a practicing navigator ● Thurlow Award. **Frequency:** annual. **Type:** recognition. **Recipient:** for individuals with outstanding invention or design of equipment which applies to the science of navigation; with outstanding method developed for use in navigation; with outstanding research or study relating to navigation ● Tycho Brahe Award. **Frequency:** annual. **Type:** recognition. **Recipient:** for individuals making overall contributions to the science of space navigation, whose actions have benefited civilization in any form such as scientific, technical, engineering or theoretical writing ● Weems Award. **Frequency:** annual. **Type:** recognition. **Recipient:** for individuals making continuing contributions to the advancement of navigation over a period of years. **Computer Services:** Mailing lists, of members. **Committees:** Awards; Awards Policy; Education; Satellite. **Publications:** *Navigation*, quarterly. Journal. Includes institute news, annual index, book reviews, obituaries, and calendar of events. **Price:** included in membership dues. ISSN: 0028-1522. **Circulation:** 4,000. **Advertising:** accepted ● Newsletter, quarterly ● Proceedings, triennial. **Conventions/Meetings:** annual meeting (exhibits) ● annual National Technical Meeting - conference - always January ● annual conference (exhibits) - always September. 2008 Sept. 16-19, Savannah, GA; 2009 Sept. 22-25, Savannah, GA; 2010 Sept. 21-24, Portland, OR; 2011 Sept. 20-23, Portland, OR.

7370 ■ International Loran Association (ILA)
741 Cathedral Pointe Ln.
Santa Barbara, CA 93111
Ph: (805)967-8649
Fax: (805)967-8471
E-mail: ila@loran.org
URL: http://www.loran.org
Contact: Langhorne Bond, Pres.
Founded: 1972. **Members:** 500. **Membership Dues:** regular, $50 (annual) ● associate, $150 (annual) ● corporate, $250-$500 (annual) ● life, $300. **Description:** Individuals and corporations involved in the design, operation, and use of Loran, a high precision, long-range radio navigation system. Established to: promote Loran; facilitate the exchange of ideas and information; recognize advances and contributions; document the history of Loran. **Libraries: Type:** reference. **Holdings:** archival material, articles, books, business records, papers. **Awards:** Medal of Merit. **Frequency:** annual. **Type:** recognition. **Recipient:** for significant contribution to ILA and the art and science of LORAN. **Formerly:** (1994) Wild Goose Association. **Publications:** *Loran Lines*, quarterly. Newsletter. Contains news of navigation systems. **Price:** included in membership dues. **Circulation:** 500. **Advertising:** accepted ● *Symposium Proceedings*, annual. **Price:** $45.00 for members; $65.00 for nonmembers. **Conventions/Meetings:** annual Technical Symposium - meeting (exhibits).

Nematology

7371 ■ Society of Nematologists (SON)
PO Box 311
Marceline, MO 64658
Ph: (660)256-3331 (505)646-2321
Fax: (660)256-3331
E-mail: son@hughes.net
URL: http://www.nematologists.org
Contact: An E. MacGuidwin, Pres.
Founded: 1961. **Members:** 650. **Membership Dues:** regular, $60 (annual) ● student, $30 (annual) ● sustaining associate, $500 (annual). **Budget:** $123,500. **Description:** Persons interested in basic or applied nematology (a branch of zoology which deals with nematodes, also called roundworms). Seeks to advance the science of nematology in both its fundamental and its economic aspects. Offers placement service. **Awards:** Fellows Award. **Frequency:** periodic. **Type:** recognition ● Honorary Award. **Type:** recognition. **Telecommunication Services:** electronic mail, aem@plantpath.wisc.edu. **Committees:** Biological Control; Computers in Nematology; Ecology; Education; Entomological Nematodes; Extension; Industry; Molecular Biology; Plant Resistance to Nematodes; Regulatory Nematology; Systematic Resources. **Publications:** *Journal of Nematology*, quarterly ● *Nematology Newsletter*, quarterly. Includes book reviews, calendar of events, placement news, and research updates. **Price:** included in membership dues. **Circulation:** 700 ● Books ● Directory, biennial. **Conventions/Meetings:** annual congress (exhibits) - 2008 July 13-18, Brisbane, QL, Australia ● annual meeting (exhibits) ● symposium.

Networking

7372 ■ 10 Gigabit Ethernet Alliance
Address Unknown since 2007
Members: 80. **Description:** Works to facilitate and accelerate the introduction of 10 Gigabit Ethernet into the networking market. **Publications:** *10 Gigabit Ethernet News*. Summary and news update. **Conventions/Meetings:** conference.

7373 ■ Caucus-Association of High Tech Procurement Professionals
Drawer 2970
Winter Park, FL 32790-2970
Ph: (407)740-5600
Fax: (407)740-0368
E-mail: member_services@caucusnet.com
URL: http://www.caucusnet.com
Founded: 1994. **Members:** 1,900. **Membership Dues:** individual, $495 (annual) ● corporate, $2,195

(annual). **Staff:** 5. **Regional Groups:** 27. **For-Profit. Multinational. Description:** Serves the specialized needs of the high tech procurement executive—the person responsible for negotiating and managing contracts with suppliers of advanced technology products and services. Includes disciplines such as procurement, finance, information technology, contract management, and legal. **Libraries: Type:** reference. **Holdings:** articles.

Neuroscience

7374 ■ American Society for Neurochemistry (ASN)

9037 Ron Den Ln.
Windermere, FL 34786-8328
Ph: (407)876-0750 (216)445-2680
Fax: (407)876-0750
E-mail: amazing@iag.net
URL: http://www.asneurochem.org
Contact: Wendy Macklin, Pres.

Founded: 1969. **Members:** 1,018. **Membership Dues:** ordinary, corresponding, $125 (annual) ● postdoc, $50 (annual) ● student, $30 (annual). **State Groups:** 49. **Description:** Represents investigators in the field of neurochemistry and scientists who are qualified specialists in other disciplines and are interested in the activities of the society. Aims to advance and promote the science of neurochemistry and related neurosciences and to increase and enhance neurochemical knowledge; to facilitate the dissemination of information concerning neurochemical research; to encourage the research of individual neurochemists. Conducts roundtables; distributes research communications. Maintains placement service. **Libraries: Type:** reference. **Holdings:** archival material. **Awards:** Bernard Haber Award. **Frequency:** annual. **Type:** recognition. **Recipient:** for members ● Jordi Folch-Pi Award. **Frequency:** annual. **Type:** recognition. **Recipient:** to an outstanding young investigator who has demonstrated a high level of research competence and originality ● Marian Kies Memorial Award. **Frequency:** annual. **Type:** recognition. **Recipient:** to a junior scientist for outstanding research conducted during graduate training. **Telecommunication Services:** electronic mail, mackliw@ccf.org. **Committees:** Advancement and Encouragement of Neurochemistry in Latin America; Basic Neurochemistry; Bernard Haber Award; Electronic Communication; Jordi Folch-Pi Award; Nominating; Presidential Advisory; Public Policy; Publications and Education; Standing Rules. **Affiliated With:** International Society for Neurochemistry. **Publications:** *Basic Neurochemistry*. Book ● *Neurochemistry of Cholinergic Receptors*. Book ● *Transactions*, annual. Abstract volume. ● Newsletter, semiannual. Alternate Formats: online ● Survey. **Conventions/Meetings:** annual meeting (exhibits) ● symposium.

7375 ■ Global Association for Interpersonal Neurobiology Studies (GAINS)

PO Box 3605
Santa Monica, CA 90408
Ph: (949)645-0828
Fax: (949)650-2198
E-mail: bonniebadenoch@mac.com
URL: http://www.mindgains.org
Contact: Dr. Bonnie Badenoch PhD, Pres.

Membership Dues: regular, $100 (annual) ● student, $75 (annual) ● international, $150 (annual). **Multinational. Description:** Promotes and supports the application of the science of interpersonal neurobiology to the art of human relationships in the service of individuals, families and communities. Explores the science of interpersonal neurobiology. Enhances mindsight in the society and nurtures compassion within the modern culture. **Telecommunication Services:** electronic mail, gainsboard@yahoogroups.com. **Publications:** *Connections and Reflections*, quarterly. Newsletter. **Price:** $25.00 per back issue. Alternate Formats: online.

7376 ■ International Society for the History of the Neurosciences (ISHN)

c/o Laurie Swan, Sec.
15518 87th Ave. E
Puyallup, WA 98375
Ph: (253)209-7837
Fax: (253)471-0931
E-mail: laurieswan@comcast.net
URL: http://www.ishn.org
Contact: Laurie Swan, Sec.

Founded: 1995. **Membership Dues:** full (in all countries except in UK and Republic of Ireland), $110 (annual) ● full (in UK and Republic of Ireland), 66 (annual). **Multinational. Description:** Seeks to improve communication between individuals and groups interested in the history of neuroscience. Promotes research in the history of neuroscience. Promotes education in and stimulates interest for the history of neuroscience. **Awards:** Award for Outstanding Article in the History of the Neurosciences. **Frequency:** biennial. **Type:** recognition. **Recipient:** to the author or authors of an article published in the Journal of the History of the Neurosciences ● Award for Outstanding Book in the History of the Neurosciences. **Frequency:** biennial. **Type:** recognition. **Recipient:** to the author or authors of an exceptional book in the history of the neurosciences ● Award for Outstanding Student Essay in the History of the Neurosciences. **Frequency:** biennial. **Type:** recognition. **Recipient:** for younger scholars or recent entrants into the profession ● Lifetime Contribution to the History of the Neurosciences. **Frequency:** biennial. **Type:** recognition. **Recipient:** for outstanding contribution to the history of the neurosciences. **Publications:** *Journal of the History of the Neurosciences: Basic and Clinical Perspectives*, quarterly. Covers all aspects of modern neurology and roots of the neurosciences in the more distant past. **Price:** included in membership dues. ISSN: 0964-704X. Alternate Formats: online. Also Cited As: *JHN*.

7377 ■ International Society of Motor Control (ISMC)

c/o Slobodan Jaric, Sec.
Univ. of Delaware
Human Performance Lab, Rm. 146
547 S Coll. Ave.
Newark, DE 19716
E-mail: jaric@udel.edu
URL: http://www.i-s-m-c.org
Contact: Slobodan Jaric, Sec.

Founded: 2002. **Membership Dues:** regular, $50 (annual) ● student, $25 (annual). **Multinational. Description:** Represents individuals with professional reputations in any of the sub-areas of motor control. Promotes basic and applied research in the area of control of movements of biological systems. Provides a forum for the exchange of scientific information on the control of human movement across the lifespan. Facilitates communication and cooperation among members. **Awards:** Bernstein Award. **Frequency:** biennial. **Type:** recognition. **Recipient:** to an individual who has made an exceptional contribution to the development of the area of motor control. **Publications:** *Motor Control*, quarterly. Journal. Features multidisciplinary examination of human movement and issues related to motor disorders. **Price:** $65.00 /year for individuals (print); $260.00 /year for institutions; $43.00 per year for student; $78.00 /year for individuals (electronic). Alternate Formats: online. Also Cited As: *MC*. **Conventions/Meetings:** biennial Progress in Motor Control - meeting.

7378 ■ The Monroe Institute (TMI)

365 Roberts Mountain Rd.
Faber, VA 22938-2318
Ph: (434)361-1252 (434)263-8692
Free: (866)881-3440
Fax: (434)361-1237
E-mail: monroeinst@aol.com
URL: http://www.monroeinstitute.com
Contact: Skip Atwater, Pres./Exec. Dir.

Founded: 1971. **Members:** 1,900. **Staff:** 27. **Description:** Physicians, psychologists, training specialists, and other professionals. Works to assist individuals in the development and exploration of human consciousness and to enhance the understanding of human potential through "Hemi-Sync" technology and its application to everyday life. (Hemi-Sync is "a state of EEG coherence in which both the right and left sides of the brain have virtually identical electrical patterns"). The institute is named for Robert Monroe, who utilized the Frequency Following Response technique and a system of binaural beat stimulation to enhance specific brain states and effect highly focused attention within each state. Investigates applications of these techniques to areas such as pain control, stress/tension reduction, stroke recovery, and terminal illness. Conducts research in Hemi-Sync and consciousness processes; collects and disseminates information. Sponsors educational programs. **Libraries: Type:** reference. **Holdings:** reports. **Telecommunication Services:** electronic mail, interstate@hemi-sync.com. **Programs:** Gateway Experience; Gateway Voyage; Guidelines; Human-Plus; Lifeline. **Formerly:** (1986) Monroe Institute of Applied Sciences. **Publications:** *Far Journeys*. Book ● *Hemi-Sync Journal*, quarterly. Contains research information on the application of Hemi-Sync technology. **Circulation:** 2,000. Also Cited As: *Monroe Institute—Breakthrough* ● *Journeys Out of the Body*. Book ● *The Monroe Institute—Focus*, quarterly. Newsletter. Contains schedule of events, and program and new products information. **Price:** included in membership dues. **Circulation:** 1,500 ● *Ultimate Journey*. Book. **Conventions/Meetings:** annual Professional Seminar - meeting.

7379 ■ Organization for Human Brain Mapping (OHBM)

5841 Cedar Lake Rd., Ste.204
Minneapolis, MN 55416
Ph: (952)646-2029
Fax: (952)545-6073
E-mail: info@humanbrainmapping.org
URL: http://www.humanbrainmapping.org
Contact: Rainer Goebel, Chm.

Membership Dues: full, $100 (annual) ● student, $50 (annual). **Description:** Advances the understanding of the anatomical and functional organization of the human brain. Provides an educational forum for the exchange of up-to-the-minute and ground breaking research on human brain mapping. **Computer Services:** database, presenters directory. **Committees:** Local Organizing; Meetings; Nominating; Program. **Conventions/Meetings:** annual meeting - 2008 June 15-19, Melbourne, VI, Australia.

7380 ■ Society for Neuroscience (SfN)

1121 14th St. NW, Ste.1010
Washington, DC 20005
Ph: (202)962-4000 (202)962-4943
Fax: (202)962-4941
E-mail: info@sfn.org
URL: http://www.sfn.org
Contact: Martin Saggese, Exec. Dir.

Founded: 1969. **Members:** 36,000. **Membership Dues:** regular, affiliate, $145 (annual) ● student, $45 (annual) ● undergraduate student, $25 (annual). **Staff:** 60. **Budget:** $16,000,000. **Local Groups:** 104. **Description:** Scientists engaged in research relating to the nervous system. Seeks to advance understanding of nervous systems, including their relation to behavior, by bringing together scientists of various backgrounds and by facilitating research at all levels of biological organization. Maintains central source of information on interdisciplinary curricula and training programs in the neurosciences. Produces nontechnical reports on the results and implications of current research. **Awards:** Albert and Ellen Grass Foundation Lecture. **Frequency:** annual. **Type:** recognition. **Recipient:** for distinguished neuroscientists ● Donald B. Lindsley Prize in Behavioral Neuroscience. **Frequency:** annual. **Type:** recognition. **Recipient:** for the most outstanding PhD thesis in the general area of behavioral neuroscience ● Jacob P. Waletzky Memorial Award for Innovative Research in Drug Addiction and Alcoholism. **Frequency:** annual. **Type:** recognition. **Recipient:** to a young scientist who has received an advanced degree of either a PhD or MD within the past fifteen years ● Peter Gruber International Research Award in Neuroscience. **Frequency:**

annual. **Type:** recognition. **Recipient:** to a young scientist who has demonstrated international collaboration based on the best science ● Society for Neuroscience Young Investigator Award. **Frequency:** annual. **Type:** recognition. **Recipient:** to an outstanding neuroscientist who has received an advanced professional degree within the past 10 years. **Computer Services:** database, Neuroscience Gateway. **Telecommunication Services:** electronic mail, membership@sfn.org. **Committees:** Animals in Research; Chapters; Communications and Chapters; Development of Women's Careers in Neuroscience; Education; Finance; Governmental and Public Affairs; History of Neuroscience; International Affairs; Investment; Minority Education, Training, and Professional Advancement; Neuroinformatics; Neuroscience Literacy; Program; Public Information; Publications; Social Issues; Women in Neuroscience. **Programs:** Minority Neuroscience Fellowship; Neuroscience Scholars. **Publications:** *Abstracts Volume*, annual. Contains neuroscience-related abstracts written by members. **Price:** included in membership dues; $50.00 for nonmembers. ISSN: 0190-5295. **Circulation:** 30,000. Alternate Formats: online; CD-ROM ● *Brain Backgrounders*. Articles. Alternate Formats: online ● *Brain Briefings*. Newsletter ● *Brain Facts*. Booklet. Serves as a primer on the brain and nervous system. ● *The Journal of Neuroscience*, weekly. **Price:** included in membership dues. Alternate Formats: online ● *Neuroscience Nexus*, bimonthly. Newsletter. **Price:** included in membership dues; $50.00 /year for nonmembers. Alternate Formats: online ● *Neuroscience Training Programs in North America*. Alternate Formats: online ● *Neuroscience 2000 Video*. **Price:** $60.00 ● Membership Directory. Alternate Formats: online ● Annual Report. Alternate Formats: online ● Books. **Conventions/Meetings:** annual meeting, for neuroscientists and secondary school biology teachers and students (exhibits) - 2008 Nov. 15-19, Washington, DC; 2009 Oct. 24-28, Chicago, IL.

7381 ■ Whitehall Foundation
PO Box 3423
Palm Beach, FL 33480
Ph: (561)655-4474
Fax: (561)655-1296
E-mail: email@whitehall.org
URL: http://www.whitehall.org

Description: Promotes basic research in neurobiology, defined as follows: invertebrate and vertebrate (excluding clinical) neurobiology, specifically investigations of neural mechanisms involved in sensory, motor, and other complex functions of the whole organism as these relate to behavior; the overall goal should be to better understand the behavioral output or brain mechanisms of behavior. **Awards:** Grants-in-Aid. **Frequency:** periodic. **Type:** grant. **Recipient:** for researchers at the assistant professor level ● Research Grants. **Frequency:** periodic. **Type:** grant. **Recipient:** to assist in scholarly research.

Noise Control

7382 ■ Institute of Noise Control Engineering (INCE)
210 Marston Hall
Ames, IA 50011-2153
Ph: (515)294-6142
Fax: (515)294-3528
E-mail: ibo@inceusa.org
URL: http://www.inceusa.org
Contact: Joseph M. Cuschieri, Exec. Dir.

Founded: 1971. **Members:** 1,150. **Membership Dues:** student, $20 (annual) ● domestic, $50 (annual) ● regular, outside U.S., $75 (annual). **Budget:** $250,000. **Description:** Professionals in the field of noise control engineering. Seeks to develop the technology of noise control with emphasis on engineering solutions to environmental noise problems. **Awards:** INCE Education Award. **Frequency:** quinquennial. **Type:** recognition ● Student Award. **Frequency:** annual. **Type:** recognition. **Committees:** Active Control; Community Noise Technical; Industrial Noise Control; Instrumentation and Measurement Techniques; Passive Control; Perception and Effects of Noise; Sources and Propagation; Transportation Noise Technology. **Publications:** *Noise Control Engineering Journal*, bimonthly. **Price:** included in membership dues. ISSN: 0736-2501 ● *Noise/News International*, quarterly. **Price:** included in membership dues. **Advertising:** accepted ● Proceedings, annual. Contains proceedings of national and international conferences. ● Brochure. Alternate Formats: online ● Books. **Conventions/Meetings:** triennial Inter-Noise Convention - meeting (exhibits) ● annual Noise Conference (exhibits) - 2008 July 27-30, Dearborn, MI ● annual seminar.

7383 ■ National Association of Noise Control Officials (NANCO)
c/o Edward J. DiPolvere, Admin.
53 Cubberley Rd.
West Windsor, NJ 08550-3400
Ph: (609)586-2684
Fax: (609)588-5253
Contact: Edward J. DiPolvere, Admin.

Founded: 1978. **Members:** 70. **Description:** State and local officials working to control environmental and industrial noise; interested individuals from government, science, industry, education, and citizens' groups. Aims to: engage in discussion and cooperative study of problems confronting members; promote laws to control noise; sponsor the use of the most effective methods for noise measurement and analysis; encourage adequate labeling of noise sources and noise control devices; cooperate with industry and the scientific community to reduce excessive and unnecessary noise. **Libraries: Type:** reference. **Awards: Type:** recognition. **Affiliated With:** National Environmental Health Association. **Absorbed:** (1982) Community Industrial Noise Control Association. **Publications:** *Noise Effects Handbook: A Desk Reference to Health and Welfare Effects of Noise* ● *Proceedings of Annual Meeting Technical Sessions*, quarterly ● *Vibrations*, monthly. Newsletter ● Manuals. **Conventions/Meetings:** annual conference, held in conjunction with National Environmental Health Association.

Nuclear

7384 ■ American Glovebox Society (AGS)
PO Box 9099
Santa Rosa, CA 95405
Free: (800)530-1022
Fax: (707)578-4406
E-mail: ags@gloveboxsociety.org
URL: http://www.gloveboxsociety.org
Contact: Fidel Vigil, Pres.

Founded: 1986. **Members:** 280. **Membership Dues:** regular, $125 (annual) ● sustaining, $575 (annual). **Staff:** 2. **Description:** Engineers, scientists, teachers, workers, and corporate executives working in the field of glovebox engineering and production. (Gloveboxes are enclosures, which sometimes incorporate radiation-resistant gloves, used in the nuclear, biomedical, semiconductor, and other industries dealing with substances which must be confined to or from the biosphere using differential pressure.) Promotes safety and quality in the design and production of gloveboxes; serves as a forum for the exchange of ideas and information among members, and facilitates technological exchange between glovebox users. Gathers and disseminates information on the design, production, and use of gloveboxes; recommends standards and guidelines for glovebox technologies. **Libraries: Type:** open to the public. **Holdings:** 86; papers. **Subjects:** glovebox-isolation technology. **Computer Services:** database. **Subgroups:** Standards. **Publications:** *The Enclosure*, quarterly. Newsletter. **Circulation:** 2,500. **Advertising:** accepted ● *Guideline for Gloveboxes*. Book. **Price:** $150.00 for members; $200.00 for nonmembers. **Conventions/Meetings:** annual conference and symposium (exhibits) ● periodic symposium.

7385 ■ American Nuclear Society (ANS)
555 N Kensington Ave.
La Grange Park, IL 60526
Ph: (708)352-6611
Free: (800)323-3044
Fax: (708)352-0499
URL: http://www.ans.org
Contact: Harry A. Bradley, Exec. Dir.

Founded: 1954. **Members:** 11,000. **Membership Dues:** professional in U.S., $65-$130 (annual) ● professional outside U.S., $122-$187 (annual) ● student in U.S., $26 (annual) ● student outside U.S., $83 (annual) ● life, $500-$1,800 ● emeritus/fellow emeritus in U.S., $65 (annual) ● emeritus/fellow emeritus outside U.S., $122 (annual). **Staff:** 54. **Regional Groups:** 50. **Local Groups:** 84. **Description:** Physicists, chemists, educators, mathematicians, life scientists, engineers, metallurgists, managers, and administrators with professional experience in nuclear science or nuclear engineering. Works to advance science and engineering in the nuclear industry. Disseminates information; promotes research; conducts meetings devoted to scientific and technical papers; works with government agencies, educational institutions, and other organizations dealing with nuclear issues. **Libraries: Type:** reference. **Holdings:** 3,000; books. **Subjects:** nuclear engineering, business management. **Divisions:** Accelerator Applications; Biology and Medicine; Decommissioning, Decontamination & Reutilization; Education and Training; Environmental Sciences; Fuel Cycle and Waste Management; Fusion Energy; Human Factors; Isotopes and Radiation; Materials Science and Technology; Mathematics and Computation; Nuclear Criticality Safety; Operations and Power; Radiation Protection and Shielding; Reactor Operations; Reactor Physics; Robotics and Remote Systems; Thermal-Hydraulics. **Publications:** *ANS News*, monthly. Newsletter. **Price:** included in membership dues ● *ANS Topical Meeting*. Manual. Alternate Formats: online ● *ANS Topical Meeting Proceedings*, quarterly. **Price:** $145.00 in North America; $175.00 outside North America ● *Fusion Science and Technology*, 8/year. Journal. **Price:** $155.00 in North America; $235.00 outside North America ● *Nuclear News*, monthly. Newsletter. Covers worldwide developments in nuclear field. **Advertising:** accepted ● *Nuclear Science and Engineering*, 9/year. Journal. **Price:** $135.00 in North America; $171.00 outside North America ● *Nuclear Standards News*, monthly. Newsletter ● *Nuclear Technology*, monthly. Journal. **Price:** $145.00 in North America; $193.00 outside North America ● *Radwaste Solution*, bimonthly. Magazine. **Price:** $42.00 in North America; $72.00 outside North America ● *Re-actions*, 3/year. Newsletter. Provides information for educators interested in learning and teaching about the peaceful uses of nuclear science. **Price:** free ● *Transactions*, semiannual. Journal. **Price:** $145.00 in North America; $165.00 outside North America. **Conventions/Meetings:** annual meeting (exhibits) - 2009 June 14-18, Atlanta, GA; 2010 June 13-17, San Diego, CA.

7386 ■ IEEE Nuclear and Plasma Sciences Society (NPSS)
445 Hoes Ln.
PO Box 6801
Piscataway, NJ 08855
Ph: (212)419-7900
Fax: (732)981-0225
E-mail: larsen@slac.stanford.edu
URL: http://ewh.ieee.org/soc/nps
Contact: Jane M. Lehr, Pres.

Members: 3,008. **Local Groups:** 10. **Description:** A society of the Institute of Electrical and Electronics Engineers. Areas of interest include: nuclear science and engineering; instrumentation for research, detection, and measurement of radiation; nuclear biomedical applications; plasma science and engineering; magnetofluid dynamics and thermionics; plasma dynamics; gaseous electronics and arc technology; controlled thermonuclear fusion; space plasmas; plasma chemistry; and colloidal and solid-state plasmas. **Publications:** *Transactions on Nuclear Science*, bimonthly ● *Transactions on Plasma Science*, bimonthly. **Conventions/Meetings:** annual International Conference on Plasma Science ● annual Nuclear Science Radiation Effects Conference ● annual Nuclear Science Symposium/Medical Imaging.

7387 ■ Institute of Nuclear Materials Management (INMM)
60 Revere Dr., Ste.500
Northbrook, IL 60062
Ph: (847)480-9573
Fax: (847)480-9282
E-mail: inmm@inmm.org
URL: http://www.inmm.org
Contact: Nancy Jo Nicholas, Pres.
Founded: 1958. **Members:** 800. **Membership Dues:** regular, senior, fellow, $50 (annual) ● emeritus, student, $20 (annual) ● sustaining (based on the number of employees), $250-$750 (annual). **Budget:** $250,000. **Description:** Representatives of government, industry, academic institutions, Euratom, utilities, transportation organizations, insurance agencies, and private consultants in the nuclear field. Promotes the application of principles of chemistry; chemical, nuclear, and electronic engineering; accounting; auditing; and statistics to nuclear materials management. Sponsors educational courses in nuclear materials control and safeguards. Sponsors American National Standards Institute (see separate entry) committee and Standards for the Control of Nuclear Materials. Maintains speakers' bureau. **Awards:** Distinguished Service Award. **Type:** recognition ● Meritorious Service Award. **Type:** recognition. **Affiliated With:** American National Standards Institute. **Publications:** *INMM Spent Fuel Storage Seminar*, annual. Proceedings. Contains complete text and indexing of papers presented at the annual seminar. **Price:** free to meeting attendees; $200.00/copy for nonmembers ● *Institute of Nuclear Materials Management—Annual Meeting Proceedings Issue.* Includes papers on topics such as nuclear materials management and safeguards, materials control and accounting, waste management and transportation. **Price:** included in membership dues; $175.00 /year for nonmembers; free to meeting participants. **Circulation:** 2,000 ● *Journal of Nuclear Materials Management*, quarterly. Provides information on nuclear materials management and safeguards, including physical protection and materials control and accounting. **Price:** included in membership dues; $100.00 /year for nonmembers. ISSN: 0362-0034. **Circulation:** 8,000. **Advertising:** accepted. **Conventions/Meetings:** annual meeting (exhibits).

7388 ■ National Organization of Test, Research, and Training Reactors (TRTR)
c/o Steve Reese, Chm.
Oregon State Univ.
Radiation Center
Corvallis, OR 97331
Ph: (541)737-2341
Fax: (541)737-0480
E-mail: steve.reese@oregonstate.edu
URL: http://www.trtr.org
Contact: Steve Reese, Chm.
Founded: 1972. **Members:** 100. **Description:** Individuals involved in the operation of nonpower nuclear reactors. Serves as forum on the utilization and operation of nonpower nuclear reactor facilities. Conducts information exchange programs for members. Studies government rules and regulations concerning nonpower facilities. Monitors funding for university reactors. Maintains speakers' bureau; compiles statistics. **Computer Services:** Mailing lists, of members. **Publications:** Directory, periodic ● Reports. Alternate Formats: online. **Conventions/Meetings:** annual conference - always fall.

7389 ■ Nuclear Information and Records Management Association (NIRMA)
10 Almas Rd.
Windham, NH 03087-1105
Ph: (603)432-6476
Fax: (603)432-3024
E-mail: jnirma@nirma.mv.com
URL: http://www.nirma.org
Contact: Jane Hannum, Exec. Dir.
Founded: 1978. **Members:** 600. **Membership Dues:** individual, $100 (annual) ● corporate (silver), $1,000 (annual) ● corporate (gold), $3,000 (annual) ● corporate (platinum), $6,000 (annual). **Staff:** 1. **Description:** Individuals involved in nuclear records responsibilities in utilities, architectural engineering, Nuclear Steam System Supply vending, and industrial consulting. Advances the theory and practices of management of corporate records primarily pertaining to nuclear facilities through research, preparation of papers, and reports on practices in the collection, storage, maintenance, and retrieval of nuclear records. Committees conduct research on a continuing basis. **Libraries: Type:** reference. **Holdings:** papers. **Committees:** Configuration Management; Regulations; Technology Integration & Implementation; Training; Vendor Manual and Information. **Formerly:** Nuclear Records Management Association. **Publications:** Newsletter, quarterly. **Price:** included in membership dues ● Papers. Alternate Formats: online ● Report. Alternate Formats: online. **Conventions/Meetings:** annual conference (exhibits) ● annual meeting and symposium.

7390 ■ Nuclear Suppliers Association (NSA)
PO Box 2038
Springfield, VA 22152
Ph: (703)451-1912
Fax: (703)451-2334
E-mail: nsanews@aol.com
URL: http://www.nuclearsuppliers.org
Contact: Jimmy Orr, Pres.
Founded: 1983. **Members:** 66. **Membership Dues:** regular, $150 (annual). **Description:** Companies involved in the manufacture or distribution of products and services for the nuclear industry. Promotes nuclear power and the interests of the nuclear industry. **Awards: Frequency:** annual. **Type:** scholarship. **Committees:** Standards. **Conventions/Meetings:** annual meeting and symposium (exhibits).

7391 ■ Professional Reactor Operator Society (PROS)
PO Box 484
Byron, IL 61010-0484
Ph: (815)234-8140
Fax: (815)234-8140
E-mail: pres@nucpros.com
URL: http://nucpros.com
Contact: Steve Turin, Pres.
Founded: 1981. **Members:** 500. **Membership Dues:** regular, $35 (annual). **Staff:** 1. **Budget:** $20,000. **Regional Groups:** 5. **Description:** Plenary members are licensed and certified nuclear reactor operators; associate members include equipment manufacturers and utility companies. Aims to develop a communication network between nuclear reactor operators and government agencies, Congress, and industry in order to promote safety and efficiency in nuclear facilities. Believes that the education, experience, and training of nuclear facility operators have not been fairly considered in the formation of regulations, guidelines, and decisions that affect their careers. Areas of concern include educational requirements and job stress. Plans to survey the views and concerns of members and other involved parties; also plans personal presentations of members' views, supported by scientific data, to persons in the decision-making process. Offers direct mailing service to members from advertisers and placement agencies. Compiles statistics. **Publications:** *Professional Reactor Operator Society—Communicator*, quarterly. Newsletter. Provides current technical information to nuclear reactor operators. **Price:** included in membership dues; $35.00/year (corporate rate); $10.00/year (for each additional copy). **Circulation:** 600. **Advertising:** accepted ● Papers. **Conventions/Meetings:** annual meeting.

Nuclear Energy

7392 ■ Institute of Nuclear Power Operations (INPO)
c/o U.S. Department of Energy
1000 Independence Ave. SW
Washington, DC 20585
Ph: (202)586-5575 (202)586-5000
Free: (800)DIA-LDOE
Fax: (202)586-4403
E-mail: ed.blackwood@hq.doe.gov
URL: http://www.hss.energy.gov/csa/csp/inpo
Contact: Ed Blackwood, Dir.
Founded: 1979. **Members:** 45. **Staff:** 350. **Budget:** $61,000,000. **Description:** Electric utilities operating nuclear power plants. Aids in the evaluation of plant operations and develops criteria. Operates the National Academy for Nuclear Training. Conducts workshops and conferences for various levels of operations staff and management. Provides scholarships and fellowships through schools of engineering. Maintains library of 10,000 volumes on standards, regulations, and reports relating to operations of nuclear power plants. **Computer Services:** database, nuclear network ● database, nuclear plant system ● database, training support. **Publications:** *Nuclear Professional*, quarterly. Magazine ● *Review*, semiannual. Magazine.

Oceanography

7393 ■ American Society of Limnology and Oceanography (ASLO)
5400 Bosque Blvd., Ste.680
Waco, TX 76710-4446
Ph: (254)399-9635
Free: (800)929-ASLO
Fax: (254)776-3767
E-mail: business@aslo.org
URL: http://www.aslo.org
Contact: Helen S. Lemay, Business Mgr.
Founded: 1948. **Members:** 3,800. **Membership Dues:** regular, $55 (annual) ● student, $25 (annual). **Staff:** 10. **Budget:** $1,000,000. **Multinational. Description:** Persons interested in scientific study of fresh waters and oceans, including their physical, chemical, and biological aspects. Conducts scientific aquatic and oceanographic studies. **Libraries: Type:** open to the public. **Holdings:** 46; periodicals. **Subjects:** oceanography, limnology. **Awards:** G.E. Hutchinson Award. **Frequency:** annual. **Type:** recognition. **Recipient:** for excellence in aquatic research ● R. Lindeman Award. **Type:** recognition. **Recipient:** for excellence in an aquatic publication by a young scientist. **Formed by Merger of:** Oceanographic Society of the Pacific; Limnology Society of America. **Publications:** *American Society of Limnology and Oceanography—Membership Directory*, triennial ● *Limnology and Oceanography*, bimonthly. Journal ● *Limnology and Oceanography Bulletin*, quarterly. Newsletter ● *Limnology and Oceanography: Methods*, annual. Journal. Contains manuscripts whose primary focus is methodological. Alternate Formats: online. **Conventions/Meetings:** biennial Aquatic Sciences - meeting, all aquatic sciences (exhibits) - 2009 Jan. 25-30, Nice, France.

7394 ■ Center for Oceans Law and Policy (COLP)
Univ. of Virginia
School of Law
580 Massie Rd.
Charlottesville, VA 22903
Ph: (434)924-7441
Fax: (434)924-7362
E-mail: ddg@virginia.edu
URL: http://www.virginia.edu/colp
Contact: Ms. Donna Ganoe, Exec. Admin.
Founded: 1976. **Staff:** 8. **Description:** Assists in promoting rational choices and policies for the oceans and coastal and polar areas through teaching, research, and dissemination of information, and the assembly of archival material. Holds forums on current oceans issues; presents lectures in Washington, DC, by leading authorities; co-sponsors an annual international conference on aspects of oceans law and policy. **Libraries: Type:** reference. **Holdings:** 18,000; archival material. **Subjects:** law of the sea. **Telecommunication Services:** electronic mail, colp@virginia.edu. **Projects:** Commentary. **Publications:** *Center for Oceans Law and Policy Proceed-*

ings, annual. Includes collection of papers dedicated to a particular aspect of ocean's law. ● *Director's Report*, biennial. **Conventions/Meetings:** annual conference ● annual meeting and symposium ● seminar.

7395 ■ The Coastal Society (TCS)
c/o Judy Tucker, CAE, Exec. Dir.
PO Box 3590
Williamsburg, VA 23187-3590
Ph: (757)565-0999
Fax: (757)565-0299
E-mail: coastalsoc@aol.com
URL: http://www.thecoastalsociety.org
Contact: Judy Tucker CAE, Exec. Dir.

Founded: 1975. **Members:** 300. **Membership Dues:** individual, $35 (annual) ● library in U.S., $50 (annual) ● corporate/agency, $250 (annual) ● student, $15 (annual). **Staff:** 1. **Budget:** $50,000. **Description:** Represents individuals primarily from universities, government, and private industry who are concerned with problems relating to coastal areas. Aims to: foster improved interdisciplinary cooperation and communications among scientists, engineers, lawyers, managers, government officials and public-interest groups concerned with coastal environments; improve their effectiveness in the promotion of the use of coastal resources consistent with the dynamic natural processes of coastal environments; and improve public understanding and appreciation of the importance of and the need for science, effective management programs, and clear policy and law in all decisions affecting coastal environments. **Awards:** Thomas A. Bigford Award. **Frequency:** biennial. **Type:** monetary. **Recipient:** for the winner of the student paper presentation. **Publications:** *Coastal Management*, quarterly. Journal. **Price:** $40.00 /year for members; $559.00 /year for institutions; $216.00 /year for individuals ● *TCS Bulletin*, quarterly. Newsletter. **Price:** $35.00. **Circulation:** 300. Alternate Formats: online ● Proceedings, biennial ● Annual Report, annual. Alternate Formats: online. **Conventions/Meetings:** biennial conference - 2008 June 29-July 2, Los Angeles, CA.

7396 ■ Coastal States Organization (CSO)
Hall of States
444 N Capitol St. NW, Ste.322
Washington, DC 20001
Ph: (202)508-3860
Fax: (202)508-3843
E-mail: cso@sso.org
URL: http://www.coastalstates.org
Contact: Katherine Andrews, Exec. Dir.

Founded: 1970. **Members:** 35. **Staff:** 4. **Budget:** $375,000. **Description:** Governor-appointed delegates representing the 35 states, commonwealths, and territories that have an ocean, gulf, or Great Lakes boundary; member states with federally approved coastal management programs collectively govern 95&percent; of the U.S. coastline. Identifies marine and coastal resource problems of concern to U.S. coastal states, commonwealths, and territories. Represents interests before Congress and other public policy forums on behalf of U.S. coastal states; advocates protection, responsible development, and management of federal and state marine and shoreline resources; and encourages dialogue and cooperation among member states and federal and local governments on ocean and coastal policies and issues. Conducts comprehensive legislative research and issues analyses; and serves as information clearinghouse. Represents members' collective views in the formulation, development, and implementation of national marine and coastal resources and policies. **Telecommunication Services:** electronic mail, sarah.cooksey@state.de.us. **Committees:** Coastal Hazards; Coastal Water Quality; Coastal Zone Management Act Reauthorization; Island Affairs; Ocean Policy. **Affiliated With:** National Governors Association. **Publications:** *The CSO Weekly Report*, every Friday. Newsletter. Alternate Formats: online ● Papers ● Reports. **Conventions/Meetings:** conference ● workshop.

7397 ■ IEEE Oceanic Engineering Society (OES)
c/o Kenneth Ferer
114 S Fork Ct.
Hertford, NC 27944
Ph: (252)426-1226
Fax: (252)426-5135
E-mail: kferrer@ieee.org
URL: http://www.oceanicengineering.org
Contact: James T. Barbera, Pres.

Founded: 1973. **Members:** 2,230. **Membership Dues:** student, $14 (annual) ● life, $40. **Regional Groups:** 9. **Local Groups:** 4. **Description:** A society of the Institute of Electrical and Electronics Engineers. Promotes understanding of the oceanic environment and seeks to utilize electrical and electronics engineering to further this understanding. **Publications:** *Journal of Oceanic Engineering*, quarterly. ISSN: 0364-9059. Alternate Formats: online; CD-ROM ● Newsletter. Alternate Formats: online. **Conventions/Meetings:** annual conference (exhibits).

7398 ■ International Association for the Physical Sciences of the Oceans (IAPSO)
c/o Dr. Fred E. Camfield, Sec. Gen.
PO Box 820440
Vicksburg, MS 39182-0440
Ph: (601)636-1363
Fax: (601)629-9640
E-mail: camfield@vicksburg.com
URL: http://www.iugg.org/iapso
Contact: Dr. Fred E. Camfield, Sec. Gen.

Founded: 1919. **Budget:** $25,000. **Description:** Member association of the International Union of Geodesy and Geophysics. Promotes the mathematical, physical, and chemical study of problems relating to the ocean and interactions taking place at its boundaries. Coordinates research and encourages discussion, comparison, and publication of results. **Commissions:** Groundwater Seawater Interactions; Mean Sea Level and Tides; Sea Ice. **Affiliated With:** International Union of Geodesy and Geophysics. **Formerly:** (1929) Section of Physical Oceanography of the International Union of Geodesy and Geophysics; (1948) Association of Physical Oceanography; (1967) International Association of Physical Oceanography. **Publications:** *Proces-Verbaux*, quadrennial. Proceedings. Contains proceedings of the general assembly; an electronic publication of Abstract books. Alternate Formats: online ● *Publications Scientifiques* ● *Reports and Abstract of Communications*. **Conventions/Meetings:** periodic assembly, held in conjunction with other associations (exhibits) ● biennial general assembly, held in conjunction with IUGG (exhibits).

7399 ■ International Oceanographic Foundation (IOF)
Address Unknown since 2008

Founded: 1953. **Members:** 1,200. **Membership Dues:** regular, $24 (annual) ● in Canada, $34 (annual) ● outside U.S. and Canada, $44 (annual). **Staff:** 3. **Description:** Individuals interested in the sea. Encourages the protection and exploration of oceans. Topics include: game and food fish; other creatures of sea and shore; ocean currents; geology, chemistry, and physics of the sea and sea floor; submarine detection; industrial applications of oceanography. **Publications:** *IOF Frontiers*, quarterly. Magazine. Covers the ocean. Includes book reviews. **Price:** included in membership dues. ISSN: 0886-9448. **Circulation:** 50,000. **Advertising:** accepted ● *Ocean Life* ● *Training and Careers in Marine Science* ● Newsletter. Alternate Formats: online.

7400 ■ National Ocean Industries Association (NOIA)
1120 G St. NW, Ste.900
Washington, DC 20005
Ph: (202)347-6900
Fax: (202)347-8650
E-mail: mkearns@noia.org
URL: http://www.noia.org
Contact: Tom Fry, Pres.

Founded: 1972. **Members:** 300. **Membership Dues:** professional service, $2,600 (annual) ● company - minimum (based on gross sales), $1,200 (annual) ● company - maximum (based on gross sales), $40,300 (annual). **Staff:** 7. **Budget:** $1,000,000. **Description:** Corporations organized to promote the common business interests of the offshore and ocean-oriented industries by: increasing public understanding of the ocean's use and its relation to the economy; encouraging interest in industrial, scientific, recreational, research, and educational activities in the field of ocean enterprise; encouraging the development and use of the resources of the ocean consistent with environmental practices and safeguards; encouraging compatible use of ocean resources; improving communication between industry and the federal government. Supports legislation and other governmental action favorable to the offshore and ocean industry and counsels against such action when it is not favorable. Seeks to expand the role of the free enterprise system in the development of ocean resources. **Awards:** NOIA Award for Excellence in Environmental Conservation. **Type:** recognition ● Safety in Seas Award. **Frequency:** annual. **Type:** recognition. **Recipient:** for individuals who have contributed to improving the safety of life offshore. **Committees:** Government Affairs; Health, Safety, Security and Environment; Legislative Strategy; Public Affairs and Education; Technology Policy. **Formerly:** (1972) National Oceanography Association. **Publications:** *Washington Report*, bimonthly. Alternate Formats: online ● Membership Directory, annual. Alternate Formats: online ● Brochure. Alternate Formats: online ● Papers. Alternate Formats: online. **Conventions/Meetings:** annual meeting - always fall. 2008 Oct. 16-18, Las Vegas, NV; 2009 Oct. 8-10, Colorado Springs, CO ● semiannual regional meeting.

7401 ■ Ocean Society
441 Ridgewater Dr.
Marietta, GA 30068-4071
Ph: (770)977-1838
Free: (877)61-OCEAN
Fax: (770)971-9419
E-mail: info@oceansociety.org
URL: http://www.oceansociety.org
Contact: David L. Mattingly, Founding Pres.

Founded: 1988. **Staff:** 10. **Budget:** $30,000. **Description:** Supports research, education, and conservation of the ocean and marine animals. Conducts environmental education programs. **Libraries: Type:** not open to the public. **Holdings:** 100. **Subjects:** marine conservation, research, education. **Awards:** John H. Prescott National Marine Education Award. **Frequency:** annual. **Type:** monetary. **Recipient:** for writing, science activities for students K-12 ● William E. Schultz National Marine Education Award. **Frequency:** annual. **Type:** monetary. **Recipient:** for writing, science activities for students K-12. **Publications:** *Marine Education Program*, annual. Contains four-module education program for K-12. **Price:** $95.00 schools. **Circulation:** 500.

7402 ■ Oceanic Society (OS)
Quarters 35 N, Ft. Mason
San Francisco, CA 94123
Ph: (415)441-1106
Free: (800)326-7491
Fax: (415)474-3395
E-mail: office@oceanic-society.org
URL: http://www.oceanic-society.org
Contact: Birgit Winning, Exec. Dir.

Founded: 1969. **Members:** 40,000. **Membership Dues:** individual (with newsletter subscription), $35 (annual) ● individual (with newsletter and society's illustrated field guide), $50 (annual). **Budget:** $330,000. **Regional Groups:** 5. **Description:** A special project of Friends of the Earth. Works to the protection and wise use of the oceans and the marine environment through public education and awareness programs and conservation activities. Sponsors public policy, policy analysis, and conferences. Performs research concerning key marine issues. Sponsors speakers on marine educational programs and research expeditions through regional chapters and expeditions. **Programs:** Adopt-A-Dolphin; Adopt-an-Atoll; Student Caribbean Coral Reef Ecology.

Projects: Bottlenose Dolphin; Coral Reef Health Monitoring; Dolphin; Giant Otter; Gray Whale. **Publications:** *Whale*, biennial. Journal. **Price:** included in membership dues ● Newsletter, periodic ● Also publishes public policy reports and symposia proceedings.

7403 ■ The Oceanography Society (TOS)
PO Box 1931
Rockville, MD 20849-1931
Ph: (301)251-7708
Fax: (301)251-7709
E-mail: info@tos.org
URL: http://www.tos.org
Contact: Jennifer Ramarui, Exec. Dir.
Founded: 1988. **Members:** 1,300. **Membership Dues:** student, $30 (annual) ● regular, $60 (annual) ● sponsor, $110 (annual) ● corporate, institutional, $500 (annual). **Staff:** 1. **Budget:** $100,000. **Multinational. Description:** Oceanographers, scientists, and engineers active in ocean-related fields or persons who have advanced oceanography by management or other public service. Disseminates knowledge of oceanography and its applications. Works to promote communication among oceanographers and to provide a constituency for consensus-building across all disciplines of the field. Conducts educational and research programs. **Publications:** *Oceanography*, quarterly, every March, June, September and December. Magazine. Contains articles, essays and reviews on ocean science community. **Price:** included in membership dues. **Circulation:** 1,500. **Advertising:** accepted. **Conventions/Meetings:** annual Ocean Sciences Meeting, scientific program.

7404 ■ Seafloor Geosciences Division (SGD)
Address Unknown since 2008
URL: http://www.nrlssc.navy.mil
Founded: 1976. **Staff:** 31. **Description:** Employees of the Seafloor Sciences Branch of the Naval Research Laboratory actively engaged in marine geology and geophysics including geomorphology, acoustic stratigraphy and structure, and sedimentation, marine geophysics, and seismology; marine geotechnology including mass physical/mechanical properties of sediments. Conducts basic and military applied research in deep-ocean and shallow-water environments directed at understanding the geologic process which accounts for the observed character of the ocean floor and subfloor and the effects of the sea floor on Navy systems and operations. **Sections:** Geoacoustics/Geotechniques; Geology/Geophysics. **Formerly:** Global Ocean Floor Analysis and Research Center; (1976) Ocean Floor Analysis Division (of U.S. Naval Oceanographic Office); (1993) Sea Floor Division. **Conventions/Meetings:** annual meeting and symposium.

Oils and Fats

7405 ■ International Society for Fat Research (ISF)
c/o American Oil Chemists' Society
PO Box 3489
Champaign, IL 61826-3489
Ph: (217)359-2344
Fax: (217)351-8091
E-mail: jeanwills@isfnet.org
URL: http://www.isfnet.org
Contact: Dr. Jean Wills, Exec. Dir.
Founded: 1954. **Members:** 25. **Multinational. Description:** Serves as a forum for the international exchange of information about fats, oils and related materials and products by organizing periodic World Congresses on fat science and technology. Encourages the development of national or multinational regional associations related to the field. **Awards:** Kaufmann Memorial Lecture Award. **Frequency:** periodic. **Type:** recognition. **Recipient:** for individuals who have contributed substantial research in the field of international fats and oils science. **Computer Services:** Information services, member meetings calendar. **Conventions/Meetings:** annual convention (exhibits).

Operations Research

7406 ■ Military Operations Research Society (MORS)
1703 N Beauregard St., Ste.450
Alexandria, VA 22311-1717
Ph: (703)933-9070
Fax: (703)933-9066
E-mail: morsoffice@mors.org
URL: http://www.mors.org
Contact: Brian D. Engler, Exec. VP
Founded: 1966. **Members:** 3,000. **Membership Dues:** regular, in U.S., $75 (annual) ● regular, outside U.S., $100 (annual). **Staff:** 5. **Budget:** $800,000. **Description:** Works to improve the quality and effectiveness of military operations research. Sponsors colloquia; facilitates exchange of information and peer criticism among students, theoreticians, practitioners, and users of military operations research. Does not make or advocate official policy nor attempts to influence policy formulation. **Awards:** Barchi Prize. **Frequency:** annual. **Type:** recognition. **Recipient:** for best paper presented at annual symposium ● Graduate Research Prize. **Frequency:** semiannual. **Type:** recognition. **Recipient:** for students ● Rist Prize. **Frequency:** annual. **Type:** recognition. **Recipient:** for best study in response to annual call for entries ● Thomas Award. **Frequency:** annual. **Type:** recognition. **Recipient:** for outstanding performance as practitioner of military operations research ● Wanner Award. **Frequency:** annual. **Type:** recognition. **Recipient:** for service to the military operations research field. **Publications:** *Careers in Military Operations Research*. Brochure ● *Military Operations Research*, quarterly. Journal. **Price:** $70.00/year in U.S.; $135.00/year outside U.S. ● *PHALANX*, quarterly. Bulletin. Includes articles on personalities, organizations, and applications of operations research techniques in the field. **Price:** included in membership dues or meeting fees; $30.00 /year for nonmembers. ISSN: 0195-1920 ● *World of MORS*. Brochure ● Monographs ● Also publishes indexes and other materials. **Conventions/Meetings:** annual symposium - always June.

Optics

7407 ■ Optical Society of America (OSA)
2010 Massachusetts Ave. NW
Washington, DC 20036-1023
Ph: (202)223-8130
Fax: (202)223-1096
E-mail: info@osa.org
URL: http://www.osa.org
Contact: Elizabeth A. Rogan, Exec. Dir.
Founded: 1916. **Members:** 15,000. **Membership Dues:** regular/fellow, $100 (annual) ● regular/fellow residing in economically developing nation, graduate student, $40 (annual) ● corporate (based on annual sales volume), $500-$3,125 (annual) ● student, $30 (annual) ● teacher, $25 (annual) ● life, $1,950. **Staff:** 125. **Budget:** $14,000,000. **Local Groups:** 25. **Description:** Persons interested in any branch of optics: research, instruction, optical applications, manufacture, distribution of optical equipment, and physiological optics. Sponsors topical meetings. **Awards:** Charles Hard Townes Award. **Frequency:** annual. **Type:** recognition. **Recipient:** to individuals for outstanding experimental or theoretical work, discovery or invention in the field of quantum electronics ● David Richardson Medal. **Frequency:** annual. **Type:** medal. **Recipient:** for individuals who have made significant contributions to optical engineering, primarily in the commercial and industrial sector ● Esther Hoffman Beller Medal. **Frequency:** annual. **Type:** medal. **Recipient:** for individuals with outstanding contributions to optical science and engineering education ● John Tyndall Award. **Frequency:** annual. **Type:** recognition. **Recipient:** to an individual who has made pioneering, highly significant, or continuing technical or leadership contributions to fiber optics technology ● Joseph Fraunhofer Award/ Robert M. Burley Prize. **Frequency:** annual. **Type:** recognition. **Recipient:** for individuals with significant accomplishments in the field of optical engineering ● Max Born Award. **Frequency:** annual. **Type:** recognition. **Recipient:** to a person who has made outstanding contributions to physical optics, theoretical or experimental. **Computer Services:** Online services, InfoBase ● online services, OpticsNet. **Publications:** *Applied Optics*, 3/month. Journal. Covers applied optics in lasers, electro-optics, atmospheric optics, optical engineering, thin films, detectors, and holography. **Price:** $3,125.00 /year for institutions in U.S.; $3,270.00 /year for institutions in North America; $3,460.00 /year for institutions outside North America; $2,660.00 /year for institutions in all other countries (online only). ISSN: 0003-6935. **Advertising:** accepted. Alternate Formats: microform ● *Journal of Lightwave Technology*, monthly. Includes research papers on fiber and cable technologies, active and passive guided wave components, and integrated optics and optoelectronics. **Price:** $1,210.00 /year for institutions in U.S., Canada, Mexico, South America, PUAS; $1,335.00 /year for institutions in all other countries. ISSN: 0733-8724. Alternate Formats: microform; online ● *Journal of Optical Networking*, monthly. Covers tapes in the optical networking community. **Price:** $1,440.00 /year for institutions (online only). ISSN: 1536-5379. Alternate Formats: online ● *Journal of Optical Technology*, monthly. Covers optical instrument design as well as the physical properties of optical materials. **Price:** $2,400.00 /year for institutions in U.S.; $2,440.00 /year for institutions in Canada, Mexico, South America, PUAS; $2,205.00 /year for institutions for all countries (online only); $2,505.00 /year for institutions in all other countries. ISSN: 1070-9762. Alternate Formats: microform ● *Journal of the Optical Society of America A: Optics and Image Science*, monthly. Includes original research papers on atmospheric optics, image processing, scattering and coherence theory, machine vision, and physiological optics. **Price:** $1,760.00 /year for institutions in U.S.; $1,810.00 /year for institutions in Canada, Mexico, South America; $1,875.00 /year for institutions in all other countries; $1,500.00 /year for institutions in all countries (online only). ISSN: 1084-7529. Alternate Formats: microform; online ● *Journal of the Optical Society of America B: Optical Physics*, monthly. Covers modern quantum optics, optical physics, laser physics, and the optical properties of solids and interfaces. Also includes annual index. **Price:** $1,760.00 /year for institutions in U.S.; $1,800.00 /year for institutions in Canada, Mexico, PUAS and South America; $1,865.00 /year for institutions in all other countries; $1,500.00 /year for institutions in all countries (online only). ISSN: 0740-3224. Alternate Formats: microform; online ● *Optics and Photonics News*, monthly. Magazine. Reports on the optics industry and research for scientists, engineers, and business executives. Contains research reports and book reviews. **Price:** $100.00 /year for institutions in U.S.; $120.00 /year for institutions in Canada, Mexico, PUAS and South America; $130.00/year in other countries. ISSN: 1047-6938. **Circulation:** 11,000. **Advertising:** accepted ● *Optics and Spectroscopy*, monthly. Translation of *Optika i Spektroskopiya*, the spectroscopic journal published by the Soviet Academy of Sciences, covering basic research. **Price:** $2,850.00/year in U.S.; $2,888.00/ year in Canada, Mexico and South America; $2,949. 00/year in other countries; $2,280.00/year in all countries (online only). ISSN: 0030-400X. Alternate Formats: online ● *Optics Letters*, semimonthly. Journal. Covers optical research, instruction, applications, manufacturing, and equipment. Contains supplies information on developments. **Price:** $1,795.00 /year for institutions in U.S.; $1,860.00 /year for institutions in Canada, Mexico, PUAS and South America; $1,945.00 /year for institutions in other countries; $1,530.00 /year for institutions in all countries (online only). ISSN: 0146-9592. Alternate Formats: online ● *The Science of Color*. Book ● Monographs ● Proceedings ● Also publishes proceedings, collections of papers, and monographs. **Conventions/Meetings:** periodic conference (exhibits) ● annual meeting (exhibits).

7408 ■ SPIE - The International Society for Optical Engineering (SPIE)
PO Box 10
Bellingham, WA 98227-0010

Ph: (360)676-3290
Free: (888)504-8171
Fax: (360)647-1445
E-mail: customerservice@spie.org
URL: http://www.spie.org
Contact: Dr. Eugene G. Arthurs, CEO

Founded: 1955. **Members:** 14,630. **Membership Dues:** regular/fellow, $95 (annual) ● retired, $45 (annual) ● student, $20 (annual) ● corporate (based on annual sales volume), $449-$2,299 (annual) ● institutional, nonprofit organization, $699 (annual). **Regional Groups:** 1. **Description:** Advances scientific research and engineering applications of optical, photonic, imaging and optoelectronic technologies through meetings, education programs and publications. **Libraries: Type:** reference. **Subjects:** optics, optoelectronics and related fields, published by SPIE. **Awards:** BACUS Scholarship. **Frequency:** annual. **Type:** scholarship. **Recipient:** for a full time student in the field of microlithography ● Director's Award. **Frequency:** annual. **Type:** recognition. **Recipient:** for an individual who has rendered significant service of outstanding benefit to the society ● Educator Award. **Frequency:** annual. **Type:** recognition. **Recipient:** for outstanding contributions to optics education by an instructor or an educator in the field ● President's Award. **Frequency:** annual. **Type:** recognition. **Recipient:** for unique and meritorious service to the society ● Student Travel Contingency Grant. **Frequency:** periodic. **Type:** grant. **Recipient:** for selected students in need of travel support to present an accepted paper at any of SPIE's meetings ● Young Investigator Award. **Frequency:** annual. **Type:** recognition. **Recipient:** for a young researcher who has graduated within 5 years of the conference. **Formerly:** (1964) Society of Photographic Instrumentation Engineers; (1981) Society of Photo-Optical Instrumentation Engineers. **Publications:** *Journal of Biomedical Optics*, bimonthly. **Price:** $90.00 for members (print); $45.00 for members (online); $565.00 for nonmembers in U.S. (print and online); $625.00 for nonmembers outside U.S. (print and online) ● *Journal of Electronic Imaging*, quarterly. **Price:** $90.00 for members (print); $45.00 for members (online); $390.00 for nonmembers in U.S. (print and online); $430.00 for nonmembers outside U.S. (print and online) ● *OE Reports*, monthly. Newsletter ● *Optical Engineering*, monthly. Journal. **Price:** $90.00 for members (print); $45.00 for members (online); $785.00 for nonmembers in U.S. (print and online); $865.00 for nonmembers outside U.S. (print and online) ● *SPIE Publications Catalog*, quarterly ● *Technology Directories*, annual. Directory ● *Working Group Newsletters* ● Membership Directory, annual ● Proceedings, 200/year. **Conventions/Meetings:** annual Photonics West - symposium (exhibits) ● periodic Topical Conferences.

Organization Development

7409 ■ Chaordic Commons

875 Island Dr., No. 243
Alameda, CA 94502-6781
Ph: (415)457-3670
Fax: (415)457-3625
E-mail: frontporch@chaordic.org
URL: http://www.chaordic.org
Contact: Jennifer Almstrong, Contact

Founded: 1999. **Description:** "Develops and disseminates new concepts of organization that result in equitable sharing of power and wealth, improved health, and greater compatibility with the human spirit and the biosphere". **Libraries: Type:** reference. **Computer Services:** database, owning member ● information services, chaordic resources. **Projects:** Geodata Organizational Initiative; Northwest Atlantic Marine Alliance; Society for Organizational Learning; United Religions Initiative. **Publications:** Newsletter, semiannual. Alternate Formats: online.

Ornithology

7410 ■ The Amazona Society (TAS)

c/o Shari L. Beaudoin, Pres.
13000 Aldrich Ave. S
Burnsville, MN 55337
Ph: (952)928-9985 (952)769-7049
Fax: (952)928-9129
E-mail: aoratrix@yahoo.com
URL: http://www.amazonasociety.org
Contact: Shari L. Beaudoin, Pres.

Founded: 1984. **Membership Dues:** in U.S., $30 (annual) ● outside U.S., $36 (annual). **Staff:** 4. **Multinational. Description:** Disseminates scientific and avicultural information on Amazon Parrots through a website, member forum and the Amazona Quarterly Magazine. Provides programs benefiting Amazon Parrots both as companion parrots and conservation efforts for those in their wild habits. **Libraries: Type:** reference. **Subjects:** Amazona parrots. **Publications:** *Amazona Quarterly*. Journal. **Advertising:** accepted. **Conventions/Meetings:** annual convention - always August.

7411 ■ American Birding Association (ABA)

4945 N 30th St., Ste.200
Colorado Springs, CO 80919
Ph: (719)578-9703
Free: (800)850-2473
Fax: (719)578-1480
E-mail: member@aba.org
URL: http://www.americanbirding.org
Contact: Richard H. Payne, Pres./CEO

Founded: 1969. **Members:** 21,000. **Membership Dues:** student in U.S., $25 (annual) ● individual in U.S., $45 (annual) ● individual outside U.S., $55 (annual) ● joint in U.S., $52 (annual) ● joint outside U.S., $63 (annual) ● library/corporate in U.S., $60 (annual) ● library/corporate outside U.S., $70 (annual) ● century club, $100-$2,500 (annual) ● student outside U.S., $35 (annual). **Staff:** 23. **Budget:** $2,000,000. **Multinational. Description:** Promotes the enjoyment and protection of wild birds. **Libraries: Type:** reference. **Holdings:** 1,000; archival material, books, business records, monographs, periodicals. **Subjects:** birds. **Awards:** ABA Claudia Wilds Award. **Type:** recognition. **Recipient:** for distinguished service to American Birding Association ● ABA Roger Tory Peterson Award. **Type:** recognition. **Recipient:** for promoting the interests of birding ● America Birding Association Chandler Robbins Award. **Frequency:** biennial. **Type:** recognition. **Recipient:** for conservation/education ● American Birding Association Scholarships. **Frequency:** annual. **Type:** scholarship. **Recipient:** for young people who are interested in birds to attend summer camps, workshops, training programs ● Ludlow Griscom Award. **Frequency:** biennial. **Type:** recognition. **Recipient:** for outstanding ornithological publication. **Computer Services:** Mailing lists, of members. **Committees:** Checklist; Conservation; Development; Education; Finance and Administration; Publications; Rules. **Departments:** ABA Sales; Birders' Exchange and Conservation; Conferences and Convention; Fundraising, Memorials and Wills; General Birding and Endorsed Tours; IFO and Education; Membership and Circulation; Website. **Programs:** Institute for Field Ornithology. **Affiliated With:** American Bird Conservancy. **Publications:** *A Bird's Eye View*, bimonthly. Newsletter. Aimed at teenagers; contains stories about birdwatching and birds. **Price:** included in membership dues. **Circulation:** 2,000 ● *ABA Series of Bird-Finding Guides* ● *ABA Series of Monographs* ● *Big Day Report and List Report*, annual. Alternate Formats: online ● *Birding*, bimonthly. Magazine. Contains major bird-finding and identification articles and book and equipment reviews. **Price:** included in membership dues. ISSN: 0161-1836. **Circulation:** 18,000. **Advertising:** accepted. Alternate Formats: online ● *Checklist of Birds of North America*, periodic ● *North American Birds*, quarterly. Journal. Contains regional reports on bird distribution and rarities. **Price:** $30.00 /year for members in U.S.; $35.00 /year for members outside U.S.; $32.00 /year for nonmembers in U.S.; $60.00 /year for libraries in U.S. ISSN: 15253708. **Circulation:** 4,500. **Advertising:** accepted ● *Volunteer Directory*, annual ● *Winging It*. Newsletter. Contains bird-finding articles, rare bird sightings, and current news in the birding community. **Price:** included in membership dues. ISSN: 1042-511X. **Circulation:** 18,000. **Advertising:** accepted ● Membership Directory, annual. **Conventions/Meetings:** annual convention, with optics, tours, publishers (exhibits) - 2008 June 23-29, Snowbird, UT ● regional meeting and conference.

7412 ■ American Ornithologists' Union (AOU)

1313 Dolley Madison Blvd., Ste.402
McLean, VA 22101
Ph: (703)790-1745
Fax: (703)790-2672
E-mail: aou@aou.org
URL: http://www.aou.org
Contact: Mr. Scott Gillihan, Exec. Off.

Founded: 1883. **Members:** 3,500. **Membership Dues:** regular, $80 (annual) ● life, $2,400 ● student, emeritus, family, $26 (annual). **Staff:** 1. **Budget:** $500,000. **Multinational. Description:** Aims to work on the scientific study of birds. Represents ornithologists, conservationists, game managers, educators, bird banders, students, zoologists, and persons with professional or avocational interest in birds. **Awards:** AOU Conservation Award. **Frequency:** annual. **Type:** recognition. **Recipient:** to an individual or small team for extraordinary scientific contributions to the conservation, restoration, or preservation of birds and/or their habitats ● AOU Research Awards. **Frequency:** annual. **Type:** grant. **Recipient:** to undergraduate or graduate students, or other members without access to funds from major granting agencies ● Elliott Coues Award. **Frequency:** annual. **Type:** medal. **Recipient:** to individuals for extraordinary contributions to ornithological research ● Marion Jenkinson AOU Service Award. **Frequency:** annual. **Type:** recognition. **Recipient:** to an individual who has performed continued extensive service to the AOU ● Ned K. Johnson Young Investigator Award. **Frequency:** annual. **Type:** recognition. **Recipient:** for outstanding and promising work by a researcher early in his/her career in any field of ornithology ● William Brewster Memorial Award. **Frequency:** annual. **Type:** medal. **Recipient:** to the authors or co-authors of the most meritorious body of work on birds of the western hemisphere published during the previous 10 calendar years. **Computer Services:** Mailing lists, of members. **Committees:** Bird Collections; Bylaws; Classification and Nomenclature; Conservation; Development; Historical Records; International Affairs; Local Arrangements; Memorials; Nominations; Public Responsibilities; Publications; Research Awards; Scientific Awards; Scientific Program; Special Affairs; Student Affairs; Student Awards; Web Site. **Affiliated With:** Ornithological Societies of North America. **Publications:** *The Auk*, quarterly. Journal. Contains original, scientific studies of birds and book reviews. **Price:** included in membership dues; $80.00 /year for nonmembers and institutions. **Advertising:** accepted ● *Check-List of North American Birds*, periodic. **Price:** $49.95 for nonmembers; $39.95 for members ● *Ornithological Monographs*, periodic. Includes papers on avian research. **Advertising:** accepted ● *Series in Ornithology*, periodic. Book. **Conventions/Meetings:** annual meeting (exhibits) - 2008 Aug. 6-9, Portland, OR.

7413 ■ Association of Field Ornithologists (AFO)

c/o Cecilia M. Riley, Pres.
103 West Hwy.
Lake Jackson, TX 77566
Ph: (979)480-0999
Fax: (979)480-0777
E-mail: criley@gcbo.org
URL: http://www.afonet.org
Contact: Cecilia M. Riley, Pres.

Founded: 1922. **Members:** 2,400. **Membership Dues:** regular, $21 (annual) ● supporting, $50 (annual) ● student, $15 (annual) ● family, $25 (annual) ● life, $650 ● patron, $1,000. **Languages:** English, Spanish. **Description:** Professional and amateur ornithologists. Dedicated to the study and conservation of birds and their natural habitats, especially through bird banding and the dissemination of information thereon. **Awards:** E. Alexander Bergstrom Memorial Research Award. **Frequency:** annual. **Type:** grant. **Recipient:** to students for ornithological projects ● Pamela and Alexander F. Skutch

Research Award. **Frequency:** annual. **Type:** grant. **Recipient:** to amateur and professional ornithologists of any nationality. **Additional Websites:** http://www.blackwellpublishing.com. **Committees:** Amateur Research; Awards; Conservation; Latin American Research. **Formerly:** (1986) Northeastern Bird-Banding Association. **Publications:** *AFO Afield*, 3/year. Newsletter. Includes news, future plans and AFO activities. **Price:** included in membership dues ● *Journal of Field Ornithology*, quarterly. Contains articles on field research techniques, and on the life history, distribution, ecology, behavior, and migration of birds. **Price:** $45.00/year. ISSN: 0043-5643. **Circulation:** 1,400. **Advertising:** accepted. **Conventions/Meetings:** annual conference (exhibits) - usually fall.

7414 ■ Avicultural Society of America (ASA)
c/o Helen Hanson, Membership Sec.
PO Box 5516
Riverside, CA 92517-5516
Ph: (951)780-4102
Fax: (951)789-9366
E-mail: info@asabirds.org
URL: http://www.asabirds.org
Contact: Helen Hanson, Membership Sec.

Founded: 1927. **Members:** 1,000. **Membership Dues:** individual, $25 (annual) ● student, $12 (annual) ● sustaining, $50 (annual) ● benefactor, $250 (annual) ● contributor, $100 (annual) ● patron (life), $1,000. **Multinational. Description:** Bird breeders, retailers, wholesalers, and hobbyists, zoologists and veterinarians. Works to study foreign and native birds, excepting domestic poultry and pigeons. Disseminates information on the care, breeding, and feeding of birds in captivity. Attempts to preserve species of birds threatened with extinction. Conducts seminars and programs; shows monthly films. Compiles statistics; maintains biographical archives and library of magazines and papers. **Libraries: Type:** open to the public. **Holdings:** periodicals. **Subjects:** birds. **Awards:** First Breeding in U.S. **Type:** recognition. **Committees:** First Breeding Award. **Affiliated With:** American Federation of Aviculture. **Publications:** *ASA Bulletin*, bimonthly. Journal. Contains information on the care, feeding, and breeding of birds in captivity. **Price:** included in membership dues. ISSN: 0567-2856. **Circulation:** 1,000. **Advertising:** accepted. **Conventions/Meetings:** monthly meeting - always first Sunday.

7415 ■ Cooper Ornithological Society (COS)
c/o Eileen M. Kirsch, Sec.
Upper Midwest Environmental Sciences Center
2630 Fanta Reed Rd.
La Crosse, WI 54603
Ph: (608)781-6226
Fax: (608)783-6066
E-mail: eileen_kirsch@usgs.gov
URL: http://www.cooper.org
Contact: Thomas E. Martin, Pres.

Founded: 1893. **Members:** 2,200. **Membership Dues:** regular, $40-$80 (annual) ● special country, student (online Condor only), $25 (annual) ● family, $20 (annual) ● life, $1,000 ● emeritus, $30 (annual) ● student (print and online Condor), $55 (annual) ● patron, $1,000 (annual). **Budget:** $100,000. **Multinational. Description:** Professional society of ornithologists, students, and others interested in birds. Promotes the observation and cooperative study of birds, and the conservation of birds. **Awards:** A. Brazier Howell Award. **Frequency:** annual. **Type:** recognition. **Recipient:** for the best paper presented at the Annual Meeting ● Board of Directors Awards. **Frequency:** annual. **Type:** recognition. **Recipient:** to students who present worthy papers or posters at the Annual Meeting ● Frances F. Roberts Award. **Frequency:** annual. **Type:** recognition. **Recipient:** for an outstanding paper presented at the Annual Meeting ● Joseph Grinnell Student Research Awards. **Frequency:** annual. **Type:** recognition. **Recipient:** for PhD graduate students ● Mewaldt-King Student Research Awards. **Frequency:** annual. **Type:** recognition. **Recipient:** for research studies. **Committees:** Annual Meeting; Archives; Awards; Bylaws; Conservation-Resolutions; History; Nominating for Honorary Membership; Publications; Student Participation and Travel. **Affiliated With:** American Ornithologists' Union; Wilson Ornithological Society. **Formerly:** (1952) Cooper Ornithological Club. **Publications:** *Condor*, quarterly. Journal. **Price:** included in membership dues. **Advertising:** accepted. Alternate Formats: online ● *The Flock*, every 2-3 years. Membership Directory. Alternate Formats: online ● *Pacific Coast Avifauna*. Monograph ● *Studies in Avian Biology*, periodic. Monograph. **Conventions/Meetings:** annual conference (exhibits).

7416 ■ Cornell Laboratory of Ornithology (CLO)
159 Sapsucker Woods Rd.
Ithaca, NY 14850
Ph: (607)254-2473 (607)254-2425
Free: (800)843-2473
Fax: (607)254-2415
E-mail: cornellbirds@cornell.edu
URL: http://www.birds.cornell.edu
Contact: Dr. John Fitzpatrick, Dir.

Founded: 1957. **Members:** 30,000. **Membership Dues:** supporting, $40 (annual) ● family, $50 (annual) ● contributing, $75 (annual) ● guardian, $100 (annual) ● patron, $250 (annual) ● sponsor, $500 (annual) ● benefactor, $1,000 (annual). **Staff:** 178. **Description:** Works to conserve the earth's biological diversity through research, education, and citizen science focused on birds. **Libraries: Type:** reference. **Holdings:** 3,500; archival material, audio recordings, books, periodicals, photographs, video recordings. **Subjects:** conservation, technology development, ornithology, bird watching, nature education. **Awards:** Arthur A. Allen. **Frequency:** annual. **Type:** recognition. **Recipient:** to an individual who is distinguished in the field of ornithology and who has popularized the science. **Computer Services:** Online services, Project FeederWatch, Urban Birds Studies, The Birdhouse Network, ebird, Great Backyard Bird Count, Birds in Forested Landscapes. **Formerly:** (1989) Cornell University Laboratory of Ornithology. **Publications:** *Audio Guides*. Consists of bird songs and other animal sounds. ● *BirdScope*, quarterly. Newsletter. Covers laboratory news and research findings. **Price:** included in membership dues. **Circulation:** 42,000. Alternate Formats: online ● *Living Bird*, quarterly. Magazine. Contains articles and photos on bird biology, behavior, conservation, art, and travel; includes reviews of books, equipment, and birding gear. **Price:** included in membership dues. **Circulation:** 32,000. **Advertising:** accepted.

7417 ■ Eastern Bird Banding Association (EBBA)
c/o Don Mease, Treas.
2366 Springtown Hill Rd.
Hellertown, PA 18055
E-mail: measede@enter.net
URL: http://www.frontiernet.net/~bpbird/index.htm
Contact: Don Mease, Treas.

Founded: 1923. **Members:** 450. **Membership Dues:** active, $25 (annual) ● sustaining, $30 (annual) ● student, $15 (annual) ● institution, $35 (annual) ● non-subscribing, $5 (annual) ● family (fee additional to any category), $2 (annual) ● life, $350. **Description:** Persons licensed by the federal government to band birds for the purpose of studying their population dynamics. Promotes conservation and environmental education. Assists banders in standardizing methods and procedures. Disseminates findings of banding studies. **Awards:** Memorial Grant. **Frequency:** annual. **Type:** grant. **Recipient:** for avian research using bird banding. **Committees:** Conservation; Education; Memorial Grant; Net. **Publications:** *Banders Information Resource Data*. Manual. **Price:** $5.00 ● *Introduction to Statistics for Banders*. Manual. **Price:** $4.00 ● *North American Bird Bander*, quarterly. Journal. Published in conjunction with Inland Bird Banding Association and Western Bird Banding Association. **Price:** included in membership dues. **Circulation:** 2,000. **Advertising:** accepted ● *Relationships Among Body Mass, Fat, Wing Length, Age and Sex for 170 Species Banded at Powdermill Nature Reserve*. Monograph. **Price:** $18.00. **Conventions/Meetings:** annual conference and workshop, weekend featuring bird banding and research using bird banding, keynote speakers, paper session, poster session, workshops, field trips, banding equipment, books (exhibits) - usually in April.

7418 ■ Hawk Migration Association of North America (HMANA)
c/o John Weeks, Membership Sec.
51 Pheasant Run
North Granby, CT 06060
E-mail: aerie.john@cox.net
URL: http://www.hmana.org
Contact: John Weeks, Membership Sec.

Founded: 1974. **Members:** 800. **Membership Dues:** individual, $25 (annual) ● family, $40 (annual) ● club, $50 (annual) ● benefactor, $100 (annual) ● life, $500 ● corporate, $250 (annual). **Regional Groups:** 17. **Description:** Professional conservationists, research scientists, bird-watchers, and bird banders. Works to advance the knowledge of raptor migrations across continents; helps establish rational bases for future monitoring of raptor populations; provides, through use of standard reporting forms and procedures, a data bank on migration in preparation for the use of professional and amateur ornithologists. Provides specialized education and research programs, and children's services. Compiles statistics. **Awards:** Hawk Migration Association of North America Research Award. **Frequency:** annual. **Type:** monetary. **Recipient:** for innovative research on raptor migration. **Computer Services:** Mailing lists, of members ● online services, HMANA Raptors. **Committees:** Education; Nominating-Elections; Publicity; Scientific Research. **Projects:** A New Forecasting Tool for Raptor Migration: BLIPMAP; Olympic Vulture Study; Raptor Population Index. **Publications:** *Hawk Migration Studies*, semiannual. Journal. Contains migration observations, general information about hawkwatching. **Price:** $12.50/copy. **Advertising:** accepted ● *Proceedings of the North American Hawk Migration Conference*, periodic. Contains more than 20 articles, including a discussion of major problems in field identification. ● Brochures ● Also makes available slide programs on raptors. **Conventions/Meetings:** periodic Hawk Migration Conference (exhibits).

7419 ■ Hawkwatch International (HWI)
1800 S West Temple, No. 226
Salt Lake City, UT 84115-5801
Ph: (801)484-6808
Free: (800)726-4295
Fax: (801)484-6810
E-mail: hwi@hawkwatch.org
URL: http://www.hawkwatch.org
Contact: Caroline Goldman, Exec. Dir.

Founded: 1986. **Members:** 4,000. **Membership Dues:** student/senior, $20-$34 (annual) ● sustaining, $35-$99 (annual) ● Falcon Club, $100-$249 (annual) ● Hawk Club, $250-$499 (annual) ● Peregrine Club, $500-$999 (annual) ● Golden Eagle Club, $1,000 (annual). **Staff:** 11. **Budget:** $900,000. **State Groups:** 2. **Description:** Research scientists, raptor biologists, field biologists, educators, and other individuals interested in conservation of raptor populations, ecosystems, and environmental education. Conducts long-term raptor population monitoring and migration research at sites in western North America in addition to large-scale raptor banding studies for determination of population trends, origins and destinations of birds. Also actively addresses threats to raptors such as habitat loss, lead poisoning, and power line electrocutions. Sponsors Adopt-A-Hawk Program which provides funding for programs. Analyzes and publishes data. Maintains speakers' bureau. **Libraries: Type:** reference. **Formerly:** (1991) Western Foundation for Raptor Conservation. **Publications:** *Adopt-A-Hawk*. Brochure ● *Gift Catalog*, annual ● *Patterns and Recent Trends in Counts of Migrant Hawks in Western North America*. Monograph ● *RaptorWatch*, quarterly. Newsletter. Includes description of activities, calendar of events, research findings, conservation news, and activities for children. **Price:** included in membership dues. **Circulation:** 5,000 ● Annual Report, annual ● Brochure. **Conventions/Meetings:** tour ● workshop, to educate students about birds of prey and environmental issues.

7420 ■ Inland Bird Banding Association (IBBA)
c/o James Ingold, Pres.
Dept. of Biology Sci.
Louisiana State Univ.
Shreveport, LA 71115
Ph: (318)797-5236
Fax: (318)797-5222
E-mail: james.ingold@lsus.edu
URL: http://www.aves.net/inlandBBA/ibbamain.htm
Contact: James Ingold, Pres.
Founded: 1922. **Membership Dues:** student, $10 (annual) ● regular, $20 (annual) ● sustaining, $30 (annual) ● inactive, $5 (annual) ● life, $400. **Description:** Represents ornithologists, conservationist, educators, government biologists, and persons with a vocational or avocational interest in birds. Promotes, through banding and other scientific work, the study of wild birds of the central and Mississippi Flyways (the area in the U.S. between the states of Ohio and Alabama, and North Dakota and Texas; and in Canada, the provinces of Manitoba and Saskatchewan). **Awards:** The Inland Bird Banding Association Avian Research Fund. **Frequency:** annual. **Type:** grant. **Recipient:** to individuals conducting research that involves the banding or marking of native wild birds ● Paul Stewart Avian Research Fund. **Frequency:** annual. **Type:** grant. **Recipient:** to individuals conducting research that involves native wild birds. **Committees:** Endowment Fund. **Publications:** *North American Bird Bander*, quarterly ● Reports ● Papers. **Conventions/Meetings:** annual conference and workshop.

7421 ■ North American Banding Council (NABC)
c/o Linda L. Long
USFS Redwood Sci. Lab.
1700 Bayview Dr.
Arcata, CA 95521
Ph: (707)825-2947
Fax: (707)825-2901
E-mail: cjr2@humboldt.edu
URL: http://www.nabanding.net/nabanding/index.htm
Contact: C. John Ralph, Chm.
Multinational. Description: Represents organizations whose members utilize bird banding as a tool. Promotes sound and ethical banding principles and techniques. Develops bander training and certification program to set standards of knowledge, experience and skills at levels of assistant, bander and trainer. **Committees:** Education; Evaluation and Certification; Outreach; Policy.

7422 ■ Nuttall Ornithological Club (NOC)
c/o Museum of Comparative Zoology
26 Oxford St.
Harvard Univ.
Cambridge, MA 02138
Ph: (617)495-2471
URL: http://www.nuttallclub.org
Contact: Peter Alden, Pres.
Founded: 1873. **Members:** 130. **Local Groups:** 1. **Description:** Represents educators and others interested in the scientific study of birds. **Awards:** Blake Grants. **Frequency:** annual. **Type:** monetary. **Recipient:** for ornithological research projects only. **Additional Websites:** http://www.mcz.harvard.edu/Publications/nuttall.htm. **Publications:** *Memoirs of Nuttall Ornithological Club*, periodic. Monographs. Features ornithological research. ● *Publication of Nuttall Ornithological Club*, periodic. Monographs ● *Publications*. Books.

7423 ■ Ornithological Societies of North America (OSNA)
5400 Bosque Blvd., Ste.680
Waco, TX 76710
Ph: (254)399-9636 (515)294-6391
Fax: (254)776-3767
E-mail: info@osnabirds.org
URL: http://www.osnabirds.org
Contact: Helen Schneider Lemay, Exec. Dir.
Founded: 1979. **Description:** Comprises of societies promoting ornithology; is a joint billing and membership service of the American Ornithologists' Union, the Association of Field Ornithologists, the Cooper Ornithological Society, the Raptor Research Foundation, The Waterbird Society, and the Wilson Ornithological Society. **Telecommunication Services:** electronic mail, execdir@osnabirds.org. **Affiliated With:** American Ornithologists' Union; Association of Field Ornithologists; Cooper Ornithological Society; Raptor Research Foundation; Wilson Ornithological Society. **Publications:** *The Flock*, biennial. Membership Directory ● *The Ornithological Newsletter*, bimonthly. Provides members with organization news, positions and opportunities available and meeting announcements. **Price:** $3.50 for members in North America; $5.00 for members outside North America. ISSN: 0274-564X. Alternate Formats: online.

7424 ■ Wilson Ornithological Society (WOS)
c/o OSNA Business Office
5400 Bosque Blvd., Ste.680
Waco, TX 76710
Ph: (254)399-9636
Fax: (254)776-3767
E-mail: dwatt@saintmarys.edu
URL: http://www.ummz.umich.edu/birds/wos/index.html
Contact: Dr. Doris J. Watt, Pres.
Founded: 1888. **Members:** 2,250. **Membership Dues:** student, $15 (annual) ● active, $21 (annual) ● family, $25 (annual) ● sustaining, $30 (annual) ● patron, $1,000 (annual) ● life, $500. **Budget:** $100,000. **Description:** Represents professional ornithologists, biologists, avian hobbyists, and libraries interested in scientific field studies of birds and their habits; named after Alexander Wilson (1766-1813), early American ornithologist. Provides annual summary of major wildlife conservation programs. Sponsors field trips and program of scientific papers dealing with ornithology at annual meeting. Maintains exchanges with 200 ornithological magazines. **Libraries: Type:** reference; lending; not open to the public. **Holdings:** 7,700; books, monographs, periodicals. **Subjects:** birds. **Awards:** Alexander Wilson Student Presentation Award. **Frequency:** annual. **Type:** recognition. **Recipient:** for best student paper given at meeting ● Edwards Prize. **Frequency:** annual. **Type:** recognition. **Recipient:** for best article published in *Wilson Bulletin* ● George A. Hall/Harold F. Mayfield Award. **Frequency:** annual. **Type:** grant. **Recipient:** for researchers and amateurs with no access to institutional support; for avian field research ● Louis Agassiz Fuertes Award. **Frequency:** annual. **Type:** grant. **Recipient:** for avian field research ● Paul A. Stewart Awards. **Frequency:** annual. **Type:** grant. **Recipient:** for avian research using banded birds or economic ornithology. **Committees:** Archives, History and Memorials; Conservation; Library; Publications; Research Awards; Resolutions. **Councils:** WOS. **Formerly:** (1902) Chapter of Agassiz Association; (1955) Wilson Orthological Club. **Publications:** *Manual of Field and Laboratory Exercises for Ornithology* (in English and Spanish). Alternate Formats: online ● *The Wilson Journal of Ornithology*, quarterly. Provides original studies on birds and general information that describes observations of interest to members. Includes book reviews. **Price:** included in membership dues; $40.00 /year for nonmembers. ISSN: 0043-5643. **Circulation:** 3,000. Alternate Formats: microform; online. Also Cited As: *The Wilson Bulletin*. **Conventions/Meetings:** annual meeting (exhibits) - spring.

Packaging

7425 ■ Center for Electronic Packaging Research (CEPR)
c/o Department of Electrical and Computer Engineering
Univ. of Arizona
PO Box 210104
1230 E Speedway Blvd.
Tucson, AZ 85721-0104
Ph: (520)621-2434
Fax: (520)621-8076
E-mail: office@ece.arizona.edu
URL: http://www.ece.arizona.edu/ececenters.php
Contact: Prof. Steven Dvorak, Contact
Description: Performs funded research in the areas of electrical and thermal characteristics of electronic device packages and interconnected devices, particularly the modeling and simulation of electrical and thermal characteristics of Level 1 and Level 2 packaging and experimental verification of the modeling results; provides software tools.

7426 ■ Institute of Packaging Professionals (IoPP)
1601 Bond St., Ste.101
Naperville, IL 60563
Ph: (630)544-5050
Fax: (630)544-5055
E-mail: info@iopp.org
URL: http://www.iopp.org
Contact: Edwin Landon, Exec. Dir.
Founded: 1989. **Members:** 5,200. **Membership Dues:** professional, international, $150 (annual) ● student, $15 (annual) ● retired, $25 (annual). **Staff:** 15. **Budget:** $1,800,000. **Local Groups:** 39. **National Groups:** 9. **Description:** Practicing professionals in the fields of packaging and handling. Holds annual Packaging Design Competition. Offers professional certification and continuing education programs; has 10 standing technical committees and several technical task force groups; maintains speakers' bureau and bookstore. Provides employment referral services; makes available executive placement listings. Offers mail order book purchasing services. **Awards:** AmeriStar Package Awards. **Frequency:** annual. **Type:** recognition. **Recipient:** for innovation, performance and marketing in packaging ● College of Fellows. **Frequency:** annual. **Type:** recognition. **Recipient:** for special and outstanding contributions and service to the field of packaging ● Honorary Life Member. **Frequency:** annual. **Type:** recognition. **Recipient:** for special and outstanding contributions and service to the institute ● Member of the Year. **Frequency:** annual. **Type:** recognition. **Recipient:** to a person who has made outstanding contributions to the institute and to the profession ● Pi Alpha Kappa Award. **Frequency:** annual. **Type:** recognition. **Recipient:** for outstanding active participation and service to a chapter or committee. **Committees:** Drug and Pharmaceutical; Packaging Adhesives and Adhesion; Packaging Equipment and Performance; Technical. **Councils:** Packaging Consultants. **Programs:** Certification; Educational. **Task Forces:** Food and Beverage Packaging. **Formed by Merger of:** Packaging Institute International; SPHE - The Society of Packaging Professionals. **Publications:** *Institute of Packaging Professionals Journal of Packaging*. Serves the entire packaging community's educational needs. Alternate Formats: online ● *IoPP Update*, biweekly. Newsletter. Alternate Formats: online ● *Who's Who in Packaging*, annual. Membership Directory. Lists executive placement firms, packaging consultants and contract packaging companies, and packaging-related periodicals. **Price:** included in membership dues; $295.00/copy for nonmembers; $30.00 additional copy for members. **Circulation:** 7,000. **Advertising:** accepted. **Conventions/Meetings:** periodic conference ● annual seminar.

7427 ■ National Institute of Packaging, Handling and Logistics Engineers (NIPHLE)
177 Fairsom Ct.
Lewisburg, PA 17837-6844
Ph: (570)523-6475
Free: (866)464-7453
Fax: (570)523-0606
E-mail: niphle@dejazzd.com
URL: http://www.niphle.org
Contact: Richard D. Owen, Exec. Dir.
Founded: 1956. **Members:** 700. **Description:** Engineers, chemists, managers, consultants, and executives in preservation, packaging, handling, storage, distribution, and transportation fields. Provides a forum for exchange of ideas and problem-solving. Sponsors placement service. **Awards:** John C. Wilford Memorial Award. **Frequency:** annual. **Type:** recognition ● Packaging, Handling, and Logistics

Person of the Year. **Frequency:** annual. **Type:** recognition. **Committees:** Awards; Publicity; Special Activities; Technical Services. **Publications:** *NIPHLE Membership Directory*, annual ● *PHL Bulletin*, monthly ● Annual Report. **Conventions/Meetings:** annual conference, a meeting of industry and government members including speakers in the areas of packaging, handling and logistics (exhibits) ● annual Packaging Design - competition.

Paleontology

7428 ■ Cushman Foundation for Foraminiferal Research (CFFR)

c/o Jennifer Jett, Sec.-Treas.
Smithsonian Inst.
Washington, DC 20013-7012
Ph: (202)633-1333
Fax: (202)786-2832
E-mail: jettje@si.edu
URL: http://www.cushmanfoundation.org
Contact: Jennifer Jett, Sec.-Treas.

Founded: 1950. **Members:** 600. **Membership Dues:** fellow, $70 (annual) ● library, institution, $150 (annual) ● regular, $60 (annual) ● patron, $120 (annual) ● student, $25 (annual). **Description:** Represents professional geologists, paleontologists, and biological oceanographers interested in the foraminifera (group of marine rhizopods with shells). **Awards:** The Joseph A. Cushman Award for Excellence in Foraminiferal Research. **Frequency:** annual. **Type:** recognition. **Recipient:** for researchers who have made outstanding contributions in the field of foraminiferology ● Joseph A. Cushman Award for Student Research. **Frequency:** annual. **Type:** grant. **Recipient:** for master's and doctoral student who conducts research projects dealing with the systematics, biostratigraphy, paleoecology, and ecology of fossil or living foraminifera ● Loeblich and Tappan Student Research Award. **Frequency:** annual. **Type:** grant. **Recipient:** for undergraduate and graduate student who conducts research on any aspect of living or fossil foraminifera or other protists ● William V. Sliter Research Award. **Frequency:** annual. **Type:** grant. **Recipient:** for a graduate student who conducts research on Mesozoic and Cenozoic foraminifera. **Publications:** *Journal of Foraminiferal Research*, quarterly. **Price:** $60.00 /year for individuals; $150.00 /year for institutions. ISSN: 0096-1191. **Circulation:** 600 ● *Special Publications of the Cushman Foundation*, periodic. **Conventions/Meetings:** annual meeting.

7429 ■ Paleontological Research Institution/Museum of the Earth (PRI)

1259 Trumansburg Rd.
Ithaca, NY 14850
Ph: (607)273-6623
Fax: (607)273-6620
E-mail: info@museumoftheearth.org
URL: http://www.priweb.org
Contact: Dr. Warren D. Allmon, Dir.

Founded: 1932. **Members:** 930. **Membership Dues:** family, $60 (annual) ● individual, $35 (annual) ● student/senior, $25 (annual) ● charter, $100 (annual) ● friend, $250 (annual) ● donor, $500 (annual) ● partner, $1,000 (annual) ● sponsor, $2,500 (annual) ● patron, $5,000 (annual). **Staff:** 18. **Budget:** $750,000. **For-Profit. Description:** Represents the interests of professional and amateur paleontologists, geologists, conchologists, and allied scientists or persons interested in the promotion of natural history. Receives, collects, preserves, and makes accessible to students and scientists paleontological and geological type specimens and exhibits; makes and conducts scientific explorations, research, investigations, and experiments; collects and preserves scientific data, reports, graphs, maps, documents, and publications. Sponsors lectures and conducts education programs for schools. Maintains Speaker's Bureau; operates museum. **Libraries: Type:** reference. **Holdings:** 60,000; archival material, books, maps, monographs, periodicals. **Subjects:** paleontology, geology, malacology, history of science. **Awards:** Axel Olsson Award. **Frequency:** annual. **Type:** recognition. **Recipient:** for promotion of earth science education ● Gilbert D. Harris Award. **Frequency:** annual. **Type:** recognition. **Recipient:** for excellence in contributions to systematic paleontology ● Katherine Palmer Award. **Frequency:** annual. **Type:** recognition. **Recipient:** to an individual who is not a professional paleontologist for the excellence of their contributions to the field ● Student Award In Systematic Paleontology. **Frequency:** annual. **Type:** recognition. **Recipient:** to a graduate student pursuing research in any area of systematic paleontology. **Affiliated With:** Natural Science Collections Alliance. **Publications:** *American Paleontologist*, quarterly. Magazine. Contains articles about paleontology and earth science. **Price:** free for members (family; individual, student). **Circulation:** 2,200. **Advertising:** accepted. Alternate Formats: online ● *Bulletins of American Paleontology*, semiannual ● *Palaeontographica Americana*, periodic. Books ● Also issues special publications. **Conventions/Meetings:** annual meeting, for members.

7430 ■ Paleontological Society (PS)

c/o Prof. Roger D.K. Thomas, Sec.
PO Box 3003
Lancaster, PA 17604-3003
Ph: (717)291-4135
Fax: (717)291-4186
E-mail: roger.thomas@fandm.edu
URL: http://paleosoc.org
Contact: Prof. Roger D.K. Thomas, Sec.

Founded: 1908. **Members:** 1,523. **Membership Dues:** student (without J. Paleontology), $25 (annual) ● student (including J. Paleontology), $45 (annual) ● retired (professional), $83 (annual) ● regular (professional), $95 (annual). **Staff:** 1. **Regional Groups:** 6. **Multinational. Description:** Represents the interests of professional paleontologists, academics, consultants, science editors, earth-science teachers, museum specialists, land managers, students, and amateur collectors and enthusiasts. Works to advance the science of paleontology. **Awards:** Charles Schuchert Award. **Frequency:** annual. **Type:** recognition. **Recipient:** for person under 40 years old; work reflects excellence and promise in the science of paleontology ● Harrell L. Strimple Award. **Frequency:** annual. **Type:** recognition. **Recipient:** for contributions to paleontology by an amateur ● Paleontological Society International Research Program Sepkoski Grants. **Frequency:** annual. **Type:** monetary ● Paleontological Society Medal. **Frequency:** annual. **Type:** medal. **Recipient:** for a person whose eminence is based on advancement of knowledge in paleontology ● Stephen J. Gould Student Research Grants. **Frequency:** annual. **Type:** monetary. **Divisions:** Cordilleran; North-Central; Northeast; Rocky Mountain; South-Central; Southeast. **Affiliated With:** American Association for the Advancement of Science; American Geological Institute; Geological Society of America. **Publications:** *Journal of Paleontology*, bimonthly. **Price:** included in membership dues; $9.00 /year for institutions. ISSN: 0022-3360. **Circulation:** 2,800. **Advertising:** accepted ● *Paleobiology*, quarterly. Journal. Contains short papers covering topics in paleobiology. **Price:** $80.00 /year for institutions; $23.00/year for student members; $46.00 /year for nonmembers; $41.00 /year for members. ISSN: 0094-8373. **Circulation:** 2,100. **Advertising:** accepted ● *Paleontological Society Memoirs*, periodic. Monographs. **Price:** $30.00 /year for nonmembers (student); included in membership dues. ISSN: 0094-8373. **Circulation:** 2,100. **Advertising:** accepted ● *Paleontological Society Papers in Paleontology*, periodic. **Circulation:** 2,800 ● *Priscum*, semiannual. Newsletter. Includes book reviews, calendar of events, and employment opportunities. **Price:** included in membership dues. **Circulation:** 1,500. **Conventions/Meetings:** annual convention, features reports on results of recent research, held in conjunction with Geological Society of America (exhibits).

7431 ■ Paleopathology Association (PPA)

c/o Ann L.W. Stodder, Treas.
Dept. of Anthropology
Univ. of Wisconsin Milwaukee
PO Box 413
Milwaukee, WI 53201
Fax: (414)229-5848
E-mail: stodder@uwm.edu
URL: http://www.paleopathology.org
Contact: Ann L.W. Stodder, Treas.

Founded: 1973. **Members:** 550. **Membership Dues:** regular, $30 (annual) ● student, $20 (annual). **Description:** Scientists from more than 40 countries interested in disease in ancient times. Serves as a forum for the exchange of ideas, information, and published materials among members. **Awards:** Bioanthropology Foundation Prize. **Frequency:** biennial. **Type:** monetary. **Recipient:** for best poster at the biennial European meeting ● Cockburn Student Award. **Frequency:** annual. **Type:** monetary. **Recipient:** for best student paper or poster at the annual meeting. **Formerly:** Paleopathology Club. **Publications:** *Paleopathology Newsletter*, quarterly. **Price:** included in membership dues. ISSN: 0148-4737. **Circulation:** 550. **Conventions/Meetings:** biennial European Meeting - 2008 Aug. 25-27, Copenhagen, Denmark ● annual meeting and workshop (exhibits).

7432 ■ Society for Sedimentary Geology (SEPM)

6128 E 38th St., Ste.308
Tulsa, OK 74135-5814
Ph: (918)610-3361
Free: (800)865-9765
Fax: (918)621-1685
E-mail: hharper@sepm.org
URL: http://www.sepm.org
Contact: Dr. Howard Harper, Exec. Dir.

Founded: 1926. **Members:** 4,000. **Membership Dues:** full, associate, $80 (annual) ● sustaining, $300 (annual) ● spouse, $30 (annual) ● student, $25 (annual). **Staff:** 5. **Budget:** $1,200,000. **Regional Groups:** 9. **National Groups:** 10. **Description:** Scientific society of geologists interested in sedimentary geology, paleontology, and allied disciplines. Sponsors continuing education courses; K-12 earth science education; conducts technical sessions, geological workshops, research conference, and field trips; sponsors books and journals to institutions and individuals in developing countries. **Libraries: Type:** reference. **Holdings:** books, periodicals. **Subjects:** sedimentary geology, paleontology. **Awards:** Best Paper in Journal of Sedimentary Research. **Frequency:** annual. **Type:** recognition ● Best Paper in PALAIOS. **Frequency:** annual. **Type:** recognition ● Honorary Membership. **Frequency:** annual. **Type:** recognition ● James Lee Wilson Award. **Frequency:** annual. **Type:** recognition. **Recipient:** for excellence in sedimentary geology by a young scientist ● Moore Medal. **Frequency:** annual. **Type:** medal. **Recipient:** for excellence in paleontology ● Pettijohn Medal. **Frequency:** annual. **Type:** medal. **Recipient:** for excellence in sedimentology and stratigraphy ● Shepard Medal. **Frequency:** annual. **Type:** medal. **Recipient:** for excellence in marine geology ● Twenhofel Medal. **Frequency:** annual. **Type:** medal. **Recipient:** for career excellence in sedimentary geology. **Computer Services:** Electronic publishing, both CD and online access ● mailing lists, of members. **Committees:** Awards; Meetings; Publications; Research. **Affiliated With:** American Association of Petroleum Geologists; American Geological Institute; American Institute of Biological Sciences; Geological Society of America. **Formerly:** (1989) Society of Economic Paleontologists and Mineralogists. **Publications:** *Journal of Sedimentary Research*, bimonthly. **Price:** included in membership dues; $315.00 /year for nonmembers (online with CD); $350.00 /year for nonmembers in U.S. (print and online with CD); $360.00 /year for nonmembers outside U.S. (print and online with CD). ISSN: 1073-130X. **Circulation:** 6,000. **Advertising:** accepted. Alternate Formats: online; CD-ROM. Also Cited As: *Journal of Sedimentary Petrology* ● *Palaios*. Annual Reports. Contains information on paleontology. **Price:** $200. 00. ISSN: 0883-1351. **Circulation:** 1,700. Alternate Formats: CD-ROM; online ● *The Sedimentary Record*, quarterly. Magazine ● Book and CD Series (Special Publications, Concepts in Sedimentology and Paleontology, Concepts in Hydrogeology, Short Course Notes, Photo CD and Slide Sets, and Miscellaneous). **Conventions/Meetings:** annual conference, offers technical session, short courses, field trips, and other special events (exhibits).

7433 ■ Society of Vertebrate Paleontology (SVP)
60 Revere Dr., Ste.500
Northbrook, IL 60062
Ph: (847)480-9095
Fax: (847)480-9282
E-mail: svp@vertpaleo.org
URL: http://www.vertpaleo.org
Contact: Catherine Badgley, Pres.
Founded: 1940. **Members:** 2,100. **Membership Dues:** regular, $105 (annual) ● student, $50 (annual) ● associate, $30 (annual) ● sustaining, $250-$599 (annual) ● partner, $600-$1,199 (annual) ● patron, $1,200 (annual) ● spouse/second, $25 (annual). **Staff:** 1. **Multinational. Description:** Serves the common interests of persons concerned with the history, evolution, comparative anatomy and taxonomy of vertebrate animals, as well as the field occurrence, collection and study of fossil vertebrates and the stratigraphy of the beds in which they are found. **Awards:** A.S. Romer-G.G. Simpson Medal. **Frequency:** annual. **Type:** recognition. **Recipient:** for sustained and outstanding excellence and service to the discipline of vertebrate paleontology ● Alfred Sherwood Romer Prize. **Frequency:** annual. **Type:** monetary. **Recipient:** for best student presentation ● Bryan Patterson Award. **Frequency:** annual. **Type:** monetary. **Recipient:** for students studying vertebrate paleontology ● John J. Lanzendorf PeleoArt Award. **Type:** recognition. **Recipient:** for outstanding achievements in scientific illustrations and naturalistic art in paleontology ● Joseph T. Gregory Award. **Frequency:** annual. **Type:** recognition. **Recipient:** for an individual member's contribution to the welfare of the society ● Morris F. Skinner Award. **Frequency:** annual. **Type:** recognition. **Recipient:** for excellence and sustained effort in the practice of field collection of fossil vertebrates ● Postdoctoral Fellowship. **Type:** scholarship. **Recipient:** to promote career in vertebrate paleontology ● Richard Estes Award. **Frequency:** annual. **Type:** monetary. **Recipient:** for graduate students in studies of vertebrates other than mammals ● SVP Student Poster Award. **Type:** monetary. **Recipient:** to fund vertebrate paleontology fieldwork in China. **Computer Services:** Information services, paleontology resources ● mailing lists, of members. **Committees:** Auction; Development; Education and Outreach; Government Liaison; Host; Media; Meetings and Program; Student Liaison. **Publications:** *Bibliography of Fossil Vertebrates*, annual. Provides references to publications on vertebrate paleontology and related disciplines. **Price:** $60.00 for members; $100.00 for nonmembers. ISSN: 0272-8869 ● *Journal of Vertebrate Paleontology*, quarterly. Covers the theoretical and applied aspects of paleontology of chordates, including origins, evolution, anatomy, taxonomy, and biostratigraphy. **Price:** $80.00 for members; $270.00 for nonmembers in U.S.; $300.00 for nonmembers outside U.S. ISSN: 0272-4634 ● *The News Bulletin*, semiannual. Includes official business, committee reports, news from members and various meeting announcements. **Price:** $25.00/year (electronic); $40.00/year (paper copy). Alternate Formats: online ● *Society of Vertebrate Paleontology—Address Directory*, every 2-3/ years. **Conventions/Meetings:** annual meeting (exhibits) - always October or November. 2008 Oct. 15-18, Cleveland, OH.

Palynology

7434 ■ American Association of Stratigraphic Palynologists (AASP)
c/o Dr. Thomas D. Demchuk, Sec.-Treas.
PO Box 2197
Houston, TX 77252-2197
E-mail: tdemchuk@swbell.net
URL: http://www.palynology.org
Contact: Dr. Thomas D. Demchuk, Sec.-Treas.
Founded: 1967. **Members:** 600. **Membership Dues:** individual, $45 (annual) ● institutional, $100 (annual) ● retired, $15 (annual) ● student, $30 (annual). **Staff:** 10. **Budget:** $25,000. **Multinational. Description:** Persons engaged or interested in research in all aspects of palynology (the branch of science dealing with pollen, spores, and other organic-walled microfossils); institutions and companies that sponsor research in palynology. Promotes the science of palynology as related to stratigraphic applications, paleoecology, paleoclimatology, and biostratigraphy. Sponsors meetings, symposia, and field trips. **Awards:** AASP Student Scholarships. **Frequency:** annual. **Type:** scholarship. **Recipient:** to support studies in palynology. **Committees:** Audit; Awards; Ballot; Nominating. **Affiliated With:** American Geological Institute; Geological Society of America. **Publications:** *AASP Newsletter*, quarterly. Provides information on palynological research and applications. **Price:** included in membership dues. ISSN: 0732-6041 ● *American Association of Stratigraphic Palynologists—Contribution Series*, periodic. Monograph. Contains monographs and collections of papers covering specific palynological subjects. ● *American Association of Stratigraphic Palynologists—Membership Directory*, biennial. **Price:** included in membership dues. ISSN: 0192-7280 ● *Palynology*, annual. Journal. **Price:** included in membership dues. ISSN: 0191-6122. **Conventions/Meetings:** annual conference (exhibits) - 2008 Aug., Bonn, Germany.

Paper

7435 ■ Institute of Paper Science and Technology (IPST)
500 10th St. NW
Atlanta, GA 30332-0620
Ph: (404)894-5700 (404)894-9550
Fax: (404)894-4778
E-mail: jim.frederick@ipst.gatech.edu
URL: http://www.ipst.gatech.edu
Contact: Jim Frederick, Dir.
Founded: 1929. **Members:** 55. **Staff:** 209. **Budget:** $23,000,000. **Multinational. Description:** Corporations engaged in the manufacture of paper products. Seeks to advance the science and technology of paper making. Serves as a clearinghouse on the commercial manufacture of paper products. Provides multidisciplinary educational courses for paper mill personnel; conducts and fosters research; identifies and evaluates emerging paper making technologies. Offers Masters and Ph.D.s in paper science and technology. **Libraries: Type:** reference. **Holdings:** 80,000; archival material, books, business records, clippings, periodicals, video recordings. **Subjects:** science and engineering, pulp and paper trade and manufacture, paper making techniques and technologies. **Awards: Frequency:** periodic. **Type:** scholarship. **Recipient:** for outstanding graduate student in science. **Computer Services:** Online services, research reports and technical papers from 1940 to present. **Also Known As:** Institute of Paper Chemistry. **Publications:** *Technical Papers on Research*, monthly. Contains research summaries. Alternate Formats: online. **Conventions/Meetings:** annual Paper Industry Executive Conference, features review of industry research directions and programs - May.

7436 ■ Pulp and Paper Safety Association (PPSA)
1370 N Nealon Dr.
Portage, IN 46368
Ph: (219)764-4787
Fax: (219)764-4307
E-mail: ppsa.org@verizon.net
URL: http://www.ppsa.org
Contact: Pamela Cordier, Exec. Dir.
Founded: 1942. **Members:** 310. **Membership Dues:** vendor, $200 (annual) ● location (based on number of employees), $100-$300 (annual). **Staff:** 1. **Budget:** $75,000. **Description:** Represents technical safety and health advisers to manufacturers and converters of pulp, paper, paperboard, woodlands, plywood, and sawmills. Conducts technical safety activities by exchanging ideas on accident prevention, studying causes of accidents, and disseminating safety information. Sponsors courses in basic and advanced safety and in noise control. Compiles statistics. **Awards:** Best Record. **Frequency:** annual. **Type:** recognition. **Recipient:** to a location with a best safety record ● Executive Eagle. **Frequency:** annual. **Type:** recognition. **Recipient:** for an executive ● Most Improved. **Frequency:** annual. **Type:** recognition. **Recipient:** for the location with the greatest improvement over the previous year ● No Lost Work Day. **Frequency:** annual. **Type:** recognition. **Recipient:** to any member location working the previous calendar year without a lost workday injury. **Formerly:** (1991) Southern Pulp and Paper Safety Association. **Publications:** *Pulp and Paper Safety Association—Statistical Report*, quarterly ● *Quarterly Review*. Magazine. Contains safety statistics as submitted by each member location for the preceding quarter as well as year-to-date. **Price:** included in membership dues. **Conventions/Meetings:** annual conference (exhibits) - always second week of June.

Paranormal

7437 ■ American Association for Critical Scientific Investigation into Claimed Hauntings (ACSICH)
PO Box 22772
Denver, CO 80222-0772
Ph: (720)837-6565
E-mail: info@aacsich.org
Founded: 2002. **Description:** Searches for the "real truth on claimed haunted locations (houses, outdoor areas, etc.)". Incorporates science, logical deduction, and skepticism when searching for the truth. **Conventions/Meetings:** lecture and meeting.

7438 ■ American Ghost Society (AGS)
15 Forest Knolls Estates
Decatur, IL 62521
Ph: (217)422-1002
Free: (888)446-7859
URL: http://www.prairieghosts.com/ags.html
Membership Dues: active, $45 (annual) ● investigator, $60 (annual) ● researcher, $110 (annual) ● deluxe investigator, $105 (annual) ● deluxe researcher, $170 (annual). **Description:** Seeks out and authenticates evidence of ghosts. Conducts investigations into paranormal activities. Assists those who are experiencing problems with the paranormal. **Computer Services:** Information services, ghost hunting resources. **Publications:** Articles. Alternate Formats: online.

Parapsychology

7439 ■ Academy of Psychic Arts and Sciences (APA&S)
3523 McKinney Ave., No. 505
PO Box 191129
Dallas, TX 75219-8129
Ph: (214)219-2020
E-mail: contact@psychic2020.com
URL: http://www.psychic2020.com
Contact: Timothy D. Latus DPMP, Founder/Pres.
Founded: 1970. **Membership Dues:** client, $39 (annual) ● professional, $75 (annual). **Staff:** 5. **For-Profit. Description:** Persons and organizations interested in psychic phenomena, parapsychology, metaphysics, and "new age" spiritual issues of personal growth, self-responsibility, and creative living. Promotes a professional approach to the study and practice of parapsychology and metaphysics. Facilitates research and the exchange of ideas and experiences in the field. Certifies practitioners; makes referrals to practitioners. Maintains speakers' bureau and hall of fame; compiles statistics. Conducts seminars and training program. **Computer Services:** database, members, organizations and inquiries. **Telecommunication Services:** hotline, quick questions psychic service, (214)497-1710 ● hotline, (214)-388-8737. **Programs:** Meta Mentor. **Publications:** *Directory of Professional Members*, annual. Member-

ship Directory. **Advertising:** accepted ● *Insighters Quarterly Client Member Newsletter.* **Advertising:** accepted ● *Insighters Quarterly Professional Newsletter.* **Advertising:** accepted ● *Reach For Your Best Self*, annual. Catalog ● *The Timothy Letter*, monthly. Newsletter. **Price:** $120.00/year ● Also publishes study courses, books, and other instructional materials; produces audio- and videocassettes. **Conventions/Meetings:** annual symposium.

7440 ■ Academy of Spirituality and Paranormal Studies, Inc. (ASPSI)

PO Box 614
Bloomfield, CT 06002-0614
Ph: (860)242-4593
E-mail: bateyb@infionline.net
URL: http://www.lightlink.com/arpr
Contact: Mr. Boyce Batey, Exec. Dir.

Founded: 1972. **Members:** 200. **Membership Dues:** patron, $100 (annual) ● academic, $50 (annual) ● supporting, $40 (annual). **Staff:** 1. **Budget:** $25,000. **Multinational. Description:** Works to encourage dialogue, exchange of ideas, and cooperation between clergy, academics in philosophy and religion, and researchers and scientists in parapsychology and related fields in the area where religion and psychical research interface; to conduct an educational program for such scholars and the public with the goal of providing reliable information and stimulation to their spiritual life. **Committees:** Fund-Raising; Program; Publication; Research. **Affiliated With:** Spiritual Frontiers Fellowship International. **Formerly:** (2006) Academy of Religion and Psychical Research. **Publications:** *The Journal of Spirituality and Paranormal Studies*, quarterly. Focuses on the interface of religion, spirituality and paranormal experience with articles and book reviews. **Price:** $20.00 for libraries. ISSN: 1731-2148. **Circulation:** 230 ● *The Searchlight*, quarterly. Newsletter. Contains interface between spirituality, religion, and paranormal events with articles, interviews and book reviews. **Price:** $2.00 for nonmembers; included in membership dues. **Circulation:** 200. **Conventions/Meetings:** annual conference.

7441 ■ American Association for Parapsychology (AAP)

Box 225
Canoga Park, CA 91305
Ph: (818)883-0887
E-mail: info@parapsychologydegrees.com
URL: http://www.parapsychologydegrees.com
Contact: William Saunders PhD, Exec. Off.

Founded: 1971. **Description:** Encourages interest in the expanding field of parapsychology; promotes exchange of information between the public and those in the field; bridges the gap between academic parapsychology and the experimental ESP participation among laymen; stimulates interest in scientific research and encourages public involvement in future research. Offers a complete course in parapsychology including basic theories, principles, and histories of phenomena involving telepathy, clairvoyance, hypnosis, sensory awareness, psychometry, psychokinesis, and the human aura. Maintains consultation and advisory service. Awards certificate after completion of prescribed course of study in the advancement of psychical research and human understanding. **Formerly:** (1986) American Parapsychological Research Association. **Publications:** Publishes outlines and research guides.

7442 ■ American Society for Psychical Research (ASPR)

5 W 73rd St.
New York, NY 10023
Ph: (212)799-5050
Fax: (212)496-2497
E-mail: aspr@aspr.com
URL: http://www.aspr.com
Contact: Patrice Keane, Exec. Dir.

Founded: 1885. **Members:** 2,000. **Membership Dues:** individual, $70 (annual) ● joint, $75 (annual) ● fellow, $100 (annual) ● student/senior citizen, $45 (annual) ● fellow (life), $2,500 ● patron (life), $5,000 ● founder, $10,000 ● benefactor, $50,000. **Staff:** 6. **Budget:** $300,000. **Description:** Investigates and disseminates information about exceptional human abilities such as extended perception, telepathy, precognition, psychokinesis (mind over matter), automatic writing and other forms of automatism, psychometry, psychic healing, dreams, clairvoyance, clairaudience, mediumship and survival, and other unclassified parapsychological phenomena. Works to collect, classify, study, and publish firsthand reports of these phenomena. Maintains speakers' bureau. Conducts specialized education programs. **Libraries: Type:** reference. **Holdings:** 10,000; archival material, books, photographs. **Subjects:** psychical research, mind/body healing, parapsychology, borrowing. **Awards:** Gardner Murphy Memorial Lecture. **Frequency:** annual. **Type:** monetary. **Computer Services:** Online services, catalogue of books, audiotapes and videotapes ● online services, library. **Programs:** Dynamics of Healing Series; Gardner Murphy Memorial Lecture Series; Psi, Psychiatry and Psychotherapy. **Publications:** *ASPR Newsletter*, quarterly. Contains articles about research into exceptional human abilities and related areas of interest. Also lists conferences, lectures, etc. **Price:** included in membership dues. **Circulation:** 2,000 ● *Journal of the American Society for Psychical Research*, quarterly. Covers parapsychological, psychical research and other topics dealing with exceptional human abilities. **Price:** included in membership dues; $60.00 /year for nonmembers. ISSN: 0003-1070. **Circulation:** 2,000. **Conventions/Meetings:** lecture ● seminar and conference ● workshop.

7443 ■ Association for Research and Enlightenment (ARE)

215 67th St.
Virginia Beach, VA 23451-2061
Ph: (757)428-3588
Free: (800)333-4499
Fax: (757)422-6921
E-mail: are@edgarcayce.org
URL: http://www.edgarcayce.org
Contact: Charles Thomas Cayce PhD, Pres./Exec. Dir.

Founded: 1931. **Members:** 35,000. **Membership Dues:** general in U.S. and Canada, $48 (annual) ● general outside U.S. and Canada, $70 (annual) ● life, $2,400. **Staff:** 100. **Languages:** Chinese, English, French, Spanish. **Multinational. Description:** Seeks to give physical, mental, and spiritual help through investigation of the 14,305 "readings" left by Edgar Cayce (1877-1945), a clairvoyant diagnostician who was known as "the sleeping prophet" and "the father of holistic medicine". Also available: worldwide tours, youth camp, regional activities, local study groups, health center, conferences and visitors center, open all year. Offers professional, accredited training in massage therapy and related modalities. Also associated with Atlantic University, offering an at-distance Master's Degree program in Transpersonal Studies. **Libraries: Type:** open to the public. **Holdings:** 65,000; audiovisuals, books, periodicals. **Subjects:** metaphysics, psychic phenomena, holistic health, comparative religion, Eastern philosophy. **Computer Services:** Online services, chat. **Programs:** Travel; Volunteer. **Study Groups:** International Study Group Network. **Also Known As:** Edgar Cayce Foundation. **Publications:** *A.R.E. Press Catalog*, quarterly. Book. Alternate Formats: online ● *Ancient Mysteries*, monthly. Newsletter. Focuses on readings given by Cayce; includes book reviews and general information on metaphysical and paranormal ideas and subjects. **Price:** included in membership dues. **Circulation:** 8,500 ● *Personal Spirituality*, monthly. Newsletter. **Price:** included in membership dues. **Circulation:** 16,000 ● *True Health*, monthly. Newsletter. **Price:** included in membership dues. **Circulation:** 8,500 ● *Venture Inward*, bimonthly. Magazine. Focuses on readings given by Cayce; includes book reviews and general information on metaphysical and paranormal ideas and subjects. **Price:** included in membership dues. **Circulation:** 35,000 ● Books. **Conventions/Meetings:** annual meeting (exhibits) - always June in Virginia Beach, VA.

7444 ■ Committee for the Scientific Investigation of Claims of the Paranormal (CSICOP)

PO Box 703
Amherst, NY 14226
Ph: (716)636-1425 (716)636-1426
Free: (800)634-1610
Fax: (716)636-1733
E-mail: info@csicop.org
URL: http://www.csicop.org
Contact: Paul Kurtz, Chm.

Founded: 1976. **Members:** 150. **Membership Dues:** associate, $20 (annual). **Staff:** 18. **Regional Groups:** 3. **Description:** Psychologists, philosophers, astronomers, science writers and others interested in the field of the paranormal, including UFOs, astrology, and psychic phenomena, and in controversies in science. Is concerned about biased, pseudoscientific media presentations of claims of paranormal occurrences, fearing that the ready acceptance of such claims erodes the spirit of scientific skepticism and opens the populace to gullibility in other areas. Encourages evaluative research in the paranormal and provides a "dissenting scientific point of view" through aggressive challenge. **Libraries: Type:** reference. **Holdings:** 20,000; audiovisuals, books, clippings, periodicals. **Subjects:** science, fringe science, paranormal. **Awards:** In Praise of Reason Award. **Frequency:** annual. **Type:** recognition. **Recipient:** for application of reason and scientific evidence in solving social problems ● Responsibility in Journalism Award. **Frequency:** annual. **Type:** recognition. **Recipient:** for fair reporting of paranormal claims. **Subcommittees:** Astrology; Electronic Communications; Health Claims; Parapsychology; UFO. **Publications:** *Skeptical Briefs*, quarterly. Newsletter. **Circulation:** 4,000 ● *Skeptical Inquirer*, bimonthly. Magazine. Critical investigations into science and fringe science claims. **Price:** $19.95/year in U.S.; $22.95/year outside U.S. ISSN: 0194-6730. **Circulation:** 50,000. **Conventions/Meetings:** annual conference ● seminar - 4-6/year.

7445 ■ International Society for the Study of Ghosts and Apparitions (ISSGA)

Penthouse N
29 Washington Sq. W
New York, NY 10011-9180
Ph: (212)533-5018
E-mail: theghostpost@yahoo.com
URL: http://www.phantasm.mynetcologne.de/issga.html
Contact: Dr. Jeanne Keyes Youngson, Pres./Founder

Founded: 1985. **Staff:** 3. **Budget:** $25,000. **Description:** Professional ghost hunters; individuals interested in ghosts and apparitions. Provides information on ghosts, apparitions, and other phenomena. Sponsors private tours in Greenwich Village, NY, led by the president of the society. Compiles statistics; conducts research. **Libraries: Type:** reference; by appointment only. **Holdings:** archival material. **Telecommunication Services:** electronic mail, jeannekey@aol.com. **Also Known As:** Headquarters for Ghost Investigations. **Publications:** Publishes flyers and announcements for special events. **Conventions/Meetings:** lecture and regional meeting.

7446 ■ MetaScience Foundation (MSF)

c/o MetaScience Annual
Box 32
Kingston, RI 02881
Contact: Marc Seifer, Dir.

Founded: 1976. **Members:** 1,600. **Membership Dues:** $25 (annual). **Staff:** 6. **Description:** Public and university libraries, parapsychologists, doctors, physicists, and New Age laypersons. Explores and develops, by use of scientific methods, all areas usually neglected by mainstream science. These areas of study include futurology, telepathy, precognition, psychokinesis, synchronicity, UFOs, holistic medicine, astrology, graphology, tarot, the multidimensionality of time, and the quantum physics of consciousness. Conducts seminars. Maintains library of 200 parapsychology journals, texts, and biographical data entries. **Libraries: Type:** reference. **Holdings:** 500; books, periodicals. **Subjects:** parapsychology, graphology, consciousness. **Committees:** Parapsychology; Quantum Physics and Consciousness. **Formerly:** (1979) Occult Studies Foundation. **Publications:** *Journal of Occult Studies*, periodic ● *MetaScience Annual*, annual. Includes index. ● *Nikola Tesla: Psychohistory of a Forgotten Inventor*. Monograph ● Also publishes books on Nikola Tesla. **Conventions/Meetings:** annual meeting - always January, Narragansett, RI.

7447 ■ Mind Development Association/U.S. Psi Squad
PO Box 21741
St. Louis, MO 63109
E-mail: uspsisquad@aol.com
URL: http://www.uspsisquad.com
Contact: Raymond G. Jaegers, VP
Founded: 1972. **Members:** 150. **Regional Groups:** 2. **State Groups:** 2. **Local Groups:** 2. **National Groups:** 4. **For-Profit. Description:** Devoted to the study of human cognitive abilities and the learned skills of Psi and Remote Viewing. Seeks to teach, examine, study and practice those abilities of the human mind which were once considered 'psychic' or 'paranormal'. **Libraries: Type:** not open to the public. **Holdings:** 300. **Subjects:** PSI, ESP, remote viewing. **Computer Services:** Online services, bulletin board Q & A. **Committees:** The Guardians; The Skills Group; US Psi Squad. **Formerly:** American Institute of Mind Development and Control; (1974) Psychic Rescue Squad; (1998) Mind Development and Control Association; (2001) Mind Development Association. **Publications:** *PSI Squad News*, periodic. Newsletter. Explains operations, services and procedures. Free through website signup. **Circulation:** 350. Alternate Formats: online. **Conventions/Meetings:** lecture, slides, books, and under auspices of IRVA (exhibits) ● annual Remote Viewing Conference - conference and seminar.

7448 ■ Mind Science Foundation (MSF)
117 W El Prado Dr.
San Antonio, TX 78212
Ph: (210)821-6094
Fax: (210)821-6199
E-mail: info@mindscience.org
URL: http://www.mindscience.org
Contact: Joseph Dial, Exec. Dir.
Founded: 1958. **Members:** 600. **Membership Dues:** individual/student, $30 (annual) ● friend, $60 (annual) ● research sponsor, $250 (annual) ● research partner, $1,000 (annual) ● research circle, $2,500 (annual) ● research pioneer, $500 (annual). **Staff:** 3. **Budget:** $350,000. **Description:** Conducts research and sponsors educational programs on the human mind, with emphasis on the mind/body connection, creativity, human potential, mental "fitness" and parapsychology. **Libraries: Type:** reference. **Holdings:** 3,500; audio recordings, books, video recordings. **Subjects:** human mind and the science of consciousness. **Awards:** Imagineer Awards. **Frequency:** annual. **Type:** recognition. **Recipient:** for creative visionaries who have made a difference in the local community of San Antonio, Texas ● Tom Slick Research Awards in Consciousness. **Frequency:** annual. **Type:** grant. **Recipient:** to support research focused on the brain/mind and human consciousness. **Publications:** *Mind Science Foundation—News*, quarterly. Newsletter. Includes calendars of events, lecture schedule, and brief updates. **Price:** $10.00/year. **Circulation:** 600.

7449 ■ Parapsychological Association (PA)
1390 N McDowell Blvd., Ste.G-208
Petaluma, CA 94954
Fax: (202)318-2364
E-mail: business@parapsych.org
URL: http://www.parapsych.org
Contact: Rex G. Stanford PhD, Pres.
Founded: 1957. **Members:** 300. **Membership Dues:** full, associate, affiliate, $65 (annual) ● student affiliate, $50 (annual). **Multinational. Description:** Full members are persons in the U.S. and foreign countries who hold a PhD degree or its equivalent and who are actively engaged in advancing parapsychology as a branch of science; associates are students or research workers not qualified for full membership; affiliates are scientists or students in other fields. Encourages parapsychological research; disseminates information of scientific findings and their relationship to other branches of science; collaborates with other research societies that serve the interests of a professional and lay membership. **Awards:** Gertrude Schmeidler Student Award. **Frequency:** annual. **Type:** recognition. **Recipient:** for an outstanding paper or presentation by a student ● Outstanding Achievement Award. **Frequency:** annual. **Type:** recognition. **Recipient:** for exceptional scientific, scholarly, or service advancements in parapsychology ● Outstanding Career Award. **Frequency:** annual. **Type:** recognition. **Recipient:** for sustained, exceptional achievements in science, scholarship or service in the discipline of parapsychology ● Parapsychological Association Research Endowment. **Frequency:** annual. **Type:** grant. **Recipient:** to encourage parapsychological research by students and other researchers. **Affiliated With:** American Association for the Advancement of Science. **Publications:** *Proceedings of Annual Convention*, annual. Covers current research, theory and other scholarly treatments of parapsychology. **Price:** $30.00 domestic; $35.00 overseas. **Circulation:** 500 ● Reports. **Conventions/Meetings:** annual conference - always August.

7450 ■ Parapsychology Foundation (PF)
PO Box 1562
New York, NY 10021-0043
Ph: (212)628-1550
Free: (800)537-6727
Fax: (212)628-1559
E-mail: info@parapsychology.org
URL: http://www.parapsychology.org
Contact: Lisette Coly, Exec. Dir.
Founded: 1951. **Membership Dues:** general, $35 (annual) ● initial material fee, $15. **Staff:** 3. **Multinational. Description:** Furthers scientific research in extrasensory perception (telepathy, clairvoyance, precognition) and psychokinesis through university groups and individuals. Encourages and supports impartial scientific inquiry into the psychical aspects of human nature. **Libraries: Type:** reference. **Holdings:** 12,000; audio recordings, books, clippings, monographs, periodicals, video recordings. **Subjects:** parapsychology, anomalies, spiritualism, psychology, altered states of consciousness, anthropology, religion, popular culture, biography, history. **Awards:** D. Scott Rogo Award for Parapsychological Literature. **Frequency:** annual. **Type:** monetary. **Recipient:** for writers with a book project in parapsychology ● Eileen J. Garrett Scholarship. **Frequency:** annual. **Type:** scholarship. **Recipient:** for undergraduate and graduate students who are completing parapsychology degree programs or conducting parapsychological research ● General Scholarly Incentive Awards. **Frequency:** annual. **Type:** grant. **Recipient:** for students, researchers and scholars who need additional funding to complete degree programs or projects in parapsychology ● Parapsychology Scholarly Incentive Awards. **Frequency:** annual. **Type:** grant. **Recipient:** for individuals traveling to the annual convention of the Parapsychological Association to present papers. **Computer Services:** Bibliographic search, collection search and other bibliographic materials. **Additional Websites:** http://www.pflyceum.org, http://www.psychicexplorers.org, http://www.psi-mart.com. **Programs:** International Affiliates; Member Organizations; Outreach; Student Affiliates. **Publications:** *Helix Press*, periodic. Books. Contains trade paperbacks on parapsychological topics, reprints of classic works in parapsychology. ● *International Journal of Parapsychology*, semiannual. Alternate Formats: CD-ROM ● *Parapsychological Monographs*, periodic ● *Parapsychology Foundation Now*, annual. Newsletter ● *Parapsychology Foundation Pamphlet Series* (in Chinese, English, Japanese, and Spanish), periodic. Pamphlets. Features information on parapsychology. **Price:** $10.00 ● *Perspectives Lecture Series*, periodic. Videos ● *PF Lyceum Courses*, periodic. Videos ● *PF Lyceum Forums*, periodic. Videos ● *PF Lyceum So You Want to Be*, periodic. Videos ● *Proceedings of International Conferences*, periodic. Features library-bound scholarly proceedings. **Conventions/Meetings:** periodic conference.

7451 ■ Parapsychology Institute of America (PIA)
PO Box 5442
Babylon, NY 11707
Ph: (631)321-9362 (631)981-4270
Fax: (631)321-9362
E-mail: piavrc@go.com
Contact: Roxanne S. Kaplan, Exec. Dir.
Founded: 1971. **Members:** 72. **Staff:** 9. **Description:** Psychics, psychic researchers, and students of parapsychology. Investigates ghosts, psychic phenomena, and other aspects of parapsychology. Conducts research and investigations of ghosts, haunted houses, and related parapsychological phenomena. Offers educational programs; compiles statistics; maintains speakers' bureau and hall of fame; operates charitable program. Provides advisers on parapsychology to television programs. **Libraries: Type:** not open to the public. **Holdings:** 5,000. **Subjects:** aspects of psychic, unexplained and paranormal phenomena. **Awards: Type:** recognition. **Recipient:** for best and worst practitioners in the field of parapsychological phenomena. **Publications:** *Amityville Horror Conspiracy*. Book. Tells the true story of the original investigator called into the "Amityville Horror" house, Dr. Stephen Kaplan and his wife, Roxanne. **Price:** $12.95 ● *Tales of the Unknown II: Beyond Reality*. Book ● *True Tales of the Unknown: Beyond Reality III*. Book ● *True Tales of the Unknown I*. Book ● *True Tales of the Unknown II: The Uninvited*. Book. **Conventions/Meetings:** annual meeting (exhibits).

7452 ■ Rhine Research Center - Institute for Parapsychology
2741 Campus Walk Ave., Bldg. 500
Durham, NC 27705
Ph: (919)309-4600
Fax: (919)309-4700
E-mail: admin@rhine.org
URL: http://www.rhine.org
Contact: Rhoda Bailey, Contact
Founded: 1962. **Members:** 300. **Membership Dues:** professional, $100 (annual) ● regular, $50 (annual) ● benefactor, $500 (annual) ● friend, $250 (annual). **Staff:** 4. **Description:** Institution "devoted to advancing the understanding of the human individual, particularly to the scientific discovery of what it is that distinguishes him as a person". Sponsors the Parapsychology Press. Conducts research programs. Offers summer study program which includes lectures, discussions, and participation in research meetings and projects, and an advanced program giving students intensive training in experimental methods. **Libraries: Type:** open to the public. **Holdings:** 3,000; books, periodicals. **Subjects:** scientific parapsychology, foreign language. **Computer Services:** Mailing lists, for members. **Formerly:** Foundation for Research on the Nature of Man. **Supersedes:** Parapsychology Laboratory of Duke University. **Publications:** *Journal of Parapsychology*, quarterly. Reports on research and theory in parapsychology. Includes book reviews and glossary. **Price:** included in membership dues; $65.00 /year for nonmembers in U.S.; $75.00 /year for nonmembers outside U.S. and institutions in U.S.; $85.00 /year for institutions outside U.S. ISSN: 0022-3387. **Circulation:** 900. **Advertising:** accepted. Alternate Formats: microform; CD-ROM.

7453 ■ Survival Research Foundation (SRF)
1000 Island Blvd., No. 512
Aventura, FL 33160
Ph: (305)936-1408
E-mail: s5rf@aol.com
Contact: Arthur S. Berger, Pres.
Founded: 1971. **Members:** 100. **Description:** Individuals interested in the investigation of postmortem survival or life after death. Conducts studies and research on death, near-death experiences, immortality, hauntings, apparitions, poltergeists, reincarnation, mediumship, and out-of-body experiences. Presents

results of investigations through publications and lectures to universities and the public. Conducts programs for the terminally ill and bereaved. Conducts long-range survival research experimental program based on ciphers. **Libraries: Type:** reference. **Holdings:** 200.

7454 ■ U.S. Psychotronics Association (USPA)
409 Marquette Dr.
Louisville, KY 40222
Ph: (502)429-6600
Fax: (502)429-4924
E-mail: uspa@aol.com
URL: http://www.psychotronics.org
Contact: Mr. Peter Moscow, Pres.

Founded: 1975. **Members:** 800. **Membership Dues:** general, affiliate in North America, $30 (annual) ● family, $40 (annual) ● general, $75 (triennial) ● general, $125 (quinquennial) ● family, $90 (triennial) ● family, $150 (quinquennial) ● student, $20 (annual) ● life - individual, $300 ● life - senior (over 65), $175 ● affiliate outside North America, $35 (annual) ● life - family, $400. **Staff:** 25. **Budget:** $45,000. **Local Groups:** 15. **National Groups:** 10. **Description:** Represents the interests of persons interested in the study of psychotronics (the science of mind-body-environment relationships, concerned with the interactions of matter, energy, and consciousness), psychic phenomena, free energy systems, radionics, and alternative health methodologies. Provides a forum for the exchange of current research developments in psychotronics. Seeks to maintain high standards of ethical, humanitarian, and scientific practices in the study and application of psychotronics. Promotes standardization in investigating, testing, reporting, and evaluating psychotronics; preserves the history of the field. Fosters continuing education and training of members; presents members' views to the government, the public, and other organizations. Disseminates information. **Libraries: Type:** not open to the public. **Holdings:** 1,500. **Subjects:** new age. **Awards:** Hieronymus - Posthumos. **Frequency:** annual. **Type:** recognition. **Recipient:** for lifetime contributions ● J.G. Gallimore. **Frequency:** annual. **Type:** recognition. **Recipient:** for research ● Margel Vogel. **Frequency:** annual. **Type:** recognition. **Recipient:** for service. **Programs:** Agri-Radionics; Alternative Health; Anti-Gravity; Free Energy; Psychic Detectors; Psychic Instrumentation (hardware types); Radionics; Tens Units; Tesla Waves. **Formerly:** (1976) U.S. Radionics Association. **Publications:** *USPA Newsletter*, quarterly. Reports on association activities and research developments in the field. Includes book reviews and calendar of events. **Price:** included in membership dues. **Circulation:** 1,000. Alternate Formats: online ● Proceedings, annual. **Price:** $35.00 /year for members; $45.00 /year for nonmembers. **Conventions/Meetings:** annual conference, bookstore, alternative health instrumentation, health products (exhibits).

7455 ■ Vampire Information Exchange (VIE)
PO Box 290328
Brooklyn, NY 11229-0328
E-mail: vieheld@aol.com
Contact: Eric S. Held, Ed.

Founded: 1977. **Members:** 500. **Membership Dues:** subscription, $20 (annual). **Description:** Individuals interested in vampires, including the portrayal of vampires in fiction. Distributes information on vampirism; encourages the exchange of information among members. Compiles statistics. **Convention/Meeting:** none. **Libraries: Type:** reference. **Holdings:** 78; archival material, books, periodicals. **Subjects:** vampires in fact and fiction. **Affiliated With:** The Vampire Empire. **Publications:** *Vampire Information Exchange Newsletter*, 5/year. Provides information on vampirism, including book and movie reviews, news releases, and trading and selling information. **Price:** $4.00/sample; $20.00 for 5 issues. **Circulation:** 500. **Advertising:** accepted ● *VIE Bibliography*, annual. Complete listings and descriptions of vampire related fiction and non-fiction books. **Price:** $10.00 ● *VIE Calendar*, annual. Includes dates in vampire history along with articles. **Price:** $7.00.

Pattern Recognition

7456 ■ Classification Society of North America (CSNA)
c/o Stanley L. Sclove, Sec.-Treas.
IDS Dept., (MC 294)
Univ. of Illinois - Chicago
601 S Morgan St.
Chicago, IL 60607-7100
Ph: (312)996-2676 (312)996-2681
Fax: (312)413-0385
E-mail: slsclove@uic.edu
URL: http://www.cs-na.org
Contact: Stanley L. Sclove, Sec.-Treas.

Founded: 1964. **Members:** 160. **Membership Dues:** individual, $80 (annual) ● retired regular, $60 (annual) ● student, $20 (annual) ● journal affiliate, $60 (annual). **Budget:** $18,000. **Multinational. Description:** Statisticians, computer and information scientists, anthropologists, biologists, geologists, library scientists, linguists, psychologists, and other individuals interested in classification. Promotes cooperation and interchange of views and information on the principles and practice of pattern classification in any discipline. **Publications:** *Classification Literature Automated Search Service*, annual. Bibliographies. Alternate Formats: CD-ROM; online ● *Journal of Classification*, semiannual. **Conventions/Meetings:** annual conference (exhibits).

7457 ■ Pattern Recognition Society (PRS)
c/o National Biomedical Research Foundation
3900 Reservoir Rd. NW
Washington, DC 20007
Ph: (202)687-2121
Fax: (202)687-1662
E-mail: ledley@nbrf.georgetown.edu
URL: http://pir.georgetown.edu/nbrf/pr.html
Contact: Dr. Robert S. Ledley, Pres.

Founded: 1966. **Members:** 550. **Description:** Represents scientists and engineers who are interested and working in pattern recognition. Considers pattern recognition, in a broad sense of interest to persons in high energy physics, target recognition, biological taxonomy, meteorology, space science, oceanography, character recognition, optical instrumentation, industrial applications, neuron physiology, and many other fields. Attempts to clarify and standardize terminology used in pattern recognition; assists students in the field. **Convention/Meeting:** none. **Awards: Type:** recognition. **Publications:** *Pattern Recognition*, monthly. Journal ● *Pictorial Pattern Recognition: Proceedings of the Symposium on Automatic Photointerpretation, 1968.*

Peace

7458 ■ World Peace Through Technology Organization (WPTTO)
150 Folsom St.
San Francisco, CA 94105
Ph: (415)371-8706
Fax: (415)348-0762
E-mail: info@peacetour.org
URL: http://www.peacetour.org
Contact: Brad Olsen, Exec. Dir.

Multinational. Description: Strives to educate and motivate the public into world peace through technological means. **Also Known As:** (2005) Peace Tour.

Peat

7459 ■ United States National Committee of the International Peat Society (USNCIPS)
c/o Mr. Donald N. Grubich, Sec.-Treas.
10105 White City Rd.
Britt, MN 55710
Ph: (218)741-2813
Fax: (218)741-2813
E-mail: dgrubich@cpinternet.com
URL: http://www.peatsociety.fi
Contact: Mr. Donald N. Grubich, Sec.-Treas.

Founded: 1968. **Members:** 70. **Membership Dues:** company, $100 (annual) ● individual, $30 (annual). **Description:** Represents the interests of peat producers, researchers and representatives from universities and industries that furnish materials and technical engineering expertise to the peat industry. Fosters utilization of peat in the fields of horticulture, energy development, research, conservation, agriculture and chemical research. Conducts educational programs; compiles statistics. **Committees:** Bog Cultivation and Afforestation; Chemistry, Physics, Biochemistry, and Microbiology; Classification and Formation; Harvesting, Storage, and Transportation; Terminology. **Publications:** *Proceedings of the International Peat Congress*, annual. Journal. **Advertising:** accepted. **Conventions/Meetings:** annual dinner ● quadrennial International Peat Congress - convention, includes machinery, products, research posters (exhibits) - 2012 June 3-8, Stockholm, Sweden.

Petroleum

7460 ■ American Association of Drilling Engineers (AADE)
PO Box 940069
Houston, TX 77094
Ph: (281)293-9800
Fax: (281)293-9800
E-mail: bfreeman@smith.com
URL: http://www.aade.org
Contact: Bob Freeman, Exec. Dir.

Founded: 1978. **Membership Dues:** Dallas and Forth Worth chapter, Houston chapter, $20 (annual) ● West Coast chapter, Permian Basin chapter, Anchorage Alaska chapter, $15 (annual) ● Lafayette chapter, New Orleans chapter, $15 (annual) ● Denver chapter, Mid continent chapter, $25 (annual). **Description:** Provides a forum for the dissemination and exchange of practical drilling technology to those employed or interested in the drilling industry. **Conventions/Meetings:** National Technical Conference and Exhibition, with speakers (exhibits).

7461 ■ Association for the Study of Peak Oil and Gas - USA (ASPO-USA)
PO Box 371438
Denver, CO 80237
Ph: (303)759-1998
E-mail: sbandrews@att.net
URL: http://www.aspo-usa.com
Contact: Steve Andrews, Contact

Membership Dues: benefactor, $10,000 (annual) ● patron, $5,000 (annual) ● founding, $1,500 (annual) ● corporate, $1,000 (annual) ● individual, $250 (annual) ● nonprofit, $150 (annual) ● student/other, $50 (annual). **Description:** Encourages prudent energy management, constructive community transformation and cooperative initiatives in an era of depleting petroleum resources. Encourages a positive endorsement of practical solutions concerning the cultural, economic and ecological impacts of petroleum depletion. Promotes international cooperation in the development, production and consumption of the earth's energy resources. **Publications:** *Peak Oil News*, daily. Newsletter. Covers news, commentary and analysis relating to peak oil and gas. ● *Peak Oil Review*, weekly. Newsletter. Contains news summaries that highlight price trends, depletion numbers, supply completion and substitute fuel issues. ● Proceedings, annual.

7462 ■ Energy Policy Research Foundation, Inc. (EPRINC)
1031 31st St. NW
Washington, DC 20007-4401
Ph: (202)944-3339
Fax: (202)944-9830

E-mail: yulang@eprinc.org
URL: http://www.eprinc.org
Contact: Darius W. Gaskins Jr., Chm.
Founded: 1944. **Staff:** 5. **Description:** Conducts economic research and disseminates information concerning the oil industry. **Libraries: Type:** not open to the public. **Holdings:** 5,000. **Subjects:** petroleum, energy. **Formerly:** (2007) Petroleum Industry Research Foundation. **Publications:** Reports. Alternate Formats: online.

7463 ■ The Society for Organic Petrology (TSOP)

c/o Paul Hackley
U.S. Geological Survey
956 Natl. Ctr.
Reston, VA 20192
Ph: (703)648-6458
Fax: (703)648-6419
E-mail: phackley@usgs.gov
URL: http://www.tsop.org
Contact: Paul Hackley, Contact
Founded: 1984. **Membership Dues:** regular, $30 (annual) ● institution, $75 (annual) ● student, $15 (annual). **Multinational. Description:** Scientists and engineers involved with coal petrology, kerogen petrology, organic geochemistry, and related disciplines. Promotes interest and research in petrology, state-of-the-art technologies; aims to develop acceptable classifications for all types of sedimentary organic matter; provides forum, disseminates information, provides educational opportunities to members; organizes research projects. **Publications:** Newsletter, quarterly. ISSN: 0743-3816 ● Reports. Alternate Formats: online. **Conventions/Meetings:** annual meeting.

7464 ■ Society of Petroleum Engineers (SPE)

222 Palisades Creek Dr.
PO Box 833836
Richardson, TX 75083-3836
Ph: (972)952-9393
Free: (800)456-6863
Fax: (972)952-9435
E-mail: spedal@spe.org
URL: http://www.spe.org
Contact: Abdul-Jaleel Al-Khalifa, Pres.
Founded: 1922. **Members:** 55,000. **Membership Dues:** group 1 country (age 30 and above), $80 (annual) ● group 1 country (under age 30), $50 (annual) ● group 2 country (age 30 and above), $10-$80 (annual) ● group 2 country (under age 30), $10-$50 (annual) ● student (based on country group), $10-$14 (annual). **Staff:** 100. **Regional Groups:** 14. **Local Groups:** 151. **Multinational. Description:** Worldwide technical society of engineers, scientists, managers, and operating personnel in the upstream petroleum industry Offers distance learning, continuing education short courses, and distinguished lecturer program; sponsors contests; offers placement service and Internet Career Center. **Libraries: Type:** reference. **Holdings:** 35,000; papers. **Awards:** Anthony F. Lucas Gold Medal. **Frequency:** annual. **Type:** medal. **Recipient:** for distinguished achievement in improving the technique and practice of finding and producing petroleum ● Cedrik K. Ferguson Medal. **Frequency:** annual. **Type:** medal. **Recipient:** for significant contributions to the permanent technical literature of the profession by a member under age 33 ● DeGoyler Distinguished Service Medal. **Frequency:** annual. **Type:** medal. **Recipient:** for distinguished and outstanding service to SPE, the professions of engineering and/or geology, and to the petroleum industry ● Distinguished Achievement Award for Petroleum Engineering Faculty. **Frequency:** annual. **Type:** recognition. **Recipient:** for superiority in classroom teaching, excellence in research, significant contributions to the petroleum engineering profession and/or special effectiveness in advising and guiding students ● Distinguished Service Award. **Frequency:** annual. **Type:** recognition. **Recipient:** for contributions to the Society that exhibit such exceptional devotion of time, effort, thought, and action as to set them apart from other contributions ● Drilling and Completion Award. **Frequency:** annual. **Type:** recognition. **Recipient:** for outstanding achievements in or contributions to the advancement of this engineering discipline or field ● Formation Evaluation Award. **Frequency:** annual. **Type:** recognition. **Recipient:** for outstanding achievements in or contributions to the advancement of this engineering discipline or field ● Health, Safety and Environment Award. **Frequency:** annual. **Type:** recognition. **Recipient:** for outstanding achievements in or contributions to the advancement of this engineering discipline or field ● John Franklin Carll Award. **Frequency:** annual. **Type:** recognition. **Recipient:** for contributions of technical application and professionalism in petroleum development and recovery ● Lester C. Uren Award. **Frequency:** annual. **Type:** recognition. **Recipient:** for distinguished achievement in petroleum engineering technology by a member who made the contributions before age 45 ● Production and Operations Award. **Frequency:** annual. **Type:** recognition. **Recipient:** for outstanding achievements in or contributions to the advancement of this engineering discipline or field ● Public Service Award. **Frequency:** annual. **Type:** recognition. **Recipient:** for distinguished public service to a country, state, community, or the public through excellence in leadership, service, or humanitarianism ● Reservoir Description and Dynamics Award. **Frequency:** annual. **Type:** recognition. **Recipient:** for outstanding achievements in or contributions to the advancement of this engineering discipline or field ● Young Member Outstanding Service Award. **Frequency:** annual. **Type:** recognition. **Recipient:** for contributions to and leadership in public and community matters, the Society, the petroleum engineering profession, and/or the petroleum industry. **Computer Services:** Information services, online library. **Telecommunication Services:** electronic mail, service@spe.org. **Formerly:** (1957) Petroleum Branch of AIME. **Publications:** *Journal of Petroleum Technology*, monthly. Covers engineering and management reports on oil and gas exploration, drilling, production, and reservoir description and management. **Price:** $45.00 /year for nonmembers; included in membership dues. ISSN: 0149-2136. **Circulation:** 52,000. **Advertising:** accepted. Alternate Formats: microform ● *SPE Drilling and Completion*, quarterly. Journal. Covers engineering and management reports on drilling and completion technologies in the oil and gas industry. **Price:** $90.00 /year for nonmembers (online); $165.00 /year for nonmembers outside U.S. (print); $30.00 /year for members (online); $50.00 /year for members (print). ISSN: 1064-6671. **Circulation:** 5,500. **Advertising:** accepted. Alternate Formats: microform; online ● *SPE Journal*, quarterly. Provides reports on fundamental research developments in petroleum science and engineering. **Price:** $240.00 /year for nonmembers in U.S. (print); $255.00 /year for nonmembers outside U.S. (print); $80.00 /year for members (print); $60.00 /year for members (online). **Circulation:** 1,300. Alternate Formats: online ● *SPE Production and Facilities*, quarterly. Journal. Provides engineering and management reports on oil and gas field operations, including fracturing, acidizing, perforating, and cementing. **Price:** $90.00 /year for nonmembers in U.S.; $105.00 /year for nonmembers outside U.S.; $30.00 for members. ISSN: 1064-668X. **Circulation:** 4,000. **Advertising:** accepted. Alternate Formats: microform ● *SPE Reservoir Evaluation and Engineering*, bimonthly. Journal. Provides engineering and management reports on oil and gas reservoir evaluation and engineering. **Price:** $180.00 /year for nonmembers in U.S. (print); $195.00 /year for nonmembers outside U.S. (print); $50.00 /year for members (print); $40.00 /year for members (online). ISSN: 0885-9248. **Circulation:** 4,300. **Advertising:** accepted. Alternate Formats: microform; online ● Monographs ● Books. Alternate Formats: online. **Conventions/Meetings:** conference ● annual meeting - 2008 Sept. 21-24, Denver, CO ● annual Technical Conference and Exhibition - convention (exhibits) - always September or October.

7465 ■ Society of Petroleum Evaluation Engineers (SPEE)

1001 McKinney, Ste.801
Houston, TX 77002
Ph: (713)651-1639
Fax: (713)951-9659
E-mail: bkspee@aol.com
URL: http://www.spee.org
Contact: B.K. Buongiorno, Exec. Sec.
Founded: 1962. **Description:** Petroleum Evaluation Engineers. Seeks to provide educational and other services to its members and to the oil and gas industry, and to promote the profession of petroleum evaluation engineering. **Publications:** Newsletter, quarterly. Alternate Formats: online. **Conventions/Meetings:** annual meeting.

7466 ■ Society of Petrophysicists and Well Log Analysts (SPWLA)

8866 Gulf Fwy., Ste.320
Houston, TX 77017
Ph: (713)947-8727
Fax: (713)947-7181
E-mail: info@spwla.org
URL: http://www.spwla.org
Contact: Vicki J. King, Exec. Dir.
Founded: 1959. **Members:** 3,000. **Membership Dues:** regular, $60 (annual). **Staff:** 2. **Budget:** $150,000. **Regional Groups:** 32. **Description:** Engineers and geologists who evaluate sedimentary beds by electrical, nuclear, acoustic, lithological, or other means to determine the presence of gas, oil, and other naturally occurring substances. Works to investigate new logging tools and interpretation techniques and promote research in the field. Maintains speakers' bureau; conducts specialized education programs. **Awards: Type:** recognition. **Committees:** Technological. **Formerly:** (2003) Society of Professional Well Log Analysts. **Publications:** *Annual Logging Symposium Transactions*, annual. Papers. Covers the subject of log well formation evaluation. **Price:** $100.00. **Circulation:** 1,200 ● *Petrophysics*, bimonthly. Journals. **Price:** $105.00. **Circulation:** 3,000. **Advertising:** accepted ● Also publishes glossary. **Conventions/Meetings:** annual Logging Symposium (exhibits).

Pharmaceuticals

7467 ■ American Association of Pharmaceutical Scientists (AAPS)

2107 Wilson Blvd., Ste.700
Arlington, VA 22201-3042
Ph: (703)243-2800
Fax: (703)243-9650
E-mail: mays@aaps.org
URL: http://www.aapspharmaceutica.com
Contact: John Lisack Jr., Exec. Dir.
Founded: 1986. **Members:** 13,000. **Membership Dues:** regular, $125 (annual) ● full time student, postdoctoral fellow, $30 (annual) ● retired, $50 (annual) ● e-subscriber, $55 (annual). **Staff:** 45. **Budget:** $10,000,000. **Regional Groups:** 10. **Description:** Pharmaceutical scientists. Provides a forum for exchange of scientific information; serves as a resource in forming public policies to regulate pharmaceutical sciences and related issues of public concern. Promotes pharmaceutical sciences and provides for recognition of individual achievement; works to foster career growth and the development of members. Offers placement service. **Awards: Frequency:** periodic. **Type:** recognition. **Computer Services:** Mailing lists ● online services, publication. **Committees:** Awards; Education; Finance; Nominations; Publications. **Sections:** Analysis and Pharmaceutical Quality; Biotechnology; Clinical Sciences; Drug Design and Discovery; Economic, Marketing, and Management Sciences; Pharmaceutical Technologies; Pharmaceutics and Drug Delivery; Pharmacokinetics, Pharmacodynamics, and Drug Metabolism; Regulatory Sciences. **Publications:** *AAPS Newsmagazine*, monthly. **Price:** included in membership dues. ISSN: 1099-3606. **Circulation:** 13,000. **Advertising:** accepted. Alternate Formats: online ● *AAPS PharmSci*, monthly. Journal. Features original research reports and authoritative reviews on pharmaceutical and biomedical analysis. ISSN: 1522-1059. Alternate Formats: online ● *AAPS PharmSciTech*, monthly. Journal. Focuses on the use of

pharmaceuticals in health care, with particular emphasis on drug marketing and management. **Price:** free. ISSN: 1530-9932. **Circulation:** 500. Alternate Formats: online ● *Journal of Pharmaceutical and Biomedical Analysis*, monthly. Features original research reports and authoritative reviews on pharmaceutical and biomedical analysis. **Price:** $95.00 /year for members. ISSN: 0731-7085. **Circulation:** 2,000. **Advertising:** accepted ● *Journal of Pharmaceutical Marketing and Management*, quarterly. Focuses on the use of pharmaceuticals in health care, with particular emphasis on drug marketing and management. **Price:** $36.00 in U.S.; $50.00 outside U.S. ISSN: 0883-7597. **Circulation:** 500 ● *Pharmaceutical Research*, monthly. Journal. Reports on applied and basic research in the pharmaceutical-biomedical sciences; includes research reports. **Price:** $116.50 /year for members; $1,377.00 /year for institutions; $229.00 /year for nonmembers. ISSN: 0724-8741. **Circulation:** 2,000. **Advertising:** accepted. **Conventions/Meetings:** annual Pharmaceutical Technologies Conference ● annual regional meeting ● periodic workshop ● annual meeting (exhibits) - 2008 Nov. 16-20, Atlanta, GA; 2009 Nov. 8-12, Los Angeles, CA; 2010 Nov. 14-18, New Orleans, LA.

7468 ■ International Society for Pharmaceutical Engineering (ISPE)
3109 W Dr. Martin Luther King Jr. Blvd., Ste.250
Tampa, FL 33607
Ph: (813)960-2105
Fax: (813)264-2816
E-mail: customerservice@ispe.org
URL: http://www.ispe.org
Contact: Robert Best, CEO/Pres.

Founded: 1980. **Members:** 23,000. **Membership Dues:** individual, $200 (annual) ● public authority/government, academic institution, $30 (annual) ● student, $15 (annual). **Staff:** 56. **Description:** Worldwide volunteer society of technical professionals who apply their practical knowledge in the life science industries. Committed to the advancement of the educational and technical efficiency of its members through forums for the exchange of ideas and practical experience. **Libraries: Type:** reference. **Holdings:** 50; archival material, articles, papers, periodicals, reports. **Subjects:** GAMP, IMPG, clinical material, good practice guides, packaging, labeling and warehousing, baseline guides, pharmaceutical engineering, good engineering guides. **Formerly:** (1990) International Society of Pharmaceutical Engineers. **Publications:** *ISPE By-Laws and Membership*, annual. Membership Directory. Lists members arranged alphabetically by name, by country, and by company. **Price:** included in membership dues. **Advertising:** accepted ● *Pharmaceutical Engineering*, bimonthly. Journal. Includes regulatory, association, industry and membership news. Also contains new product information, buyers' directory, and research reports. ISSN: 0273-8139. **Circulation:** 13,000. **Advertising:** accepted ● Brochures, monthly ● Also, publishes GAMP4: Baseline Guide Series, GAMP Good Practice Guides, ISPE Good Practice Guides. **Conventions/Meetings:** annual conference (exhibits).

Phenomena

7469 ■ American Association of Electronic Voice Phenomena (AA-EVP)
PO Box 13111
Reno, NV 89507
E-mail: aaevp@aol.com
URL: http://aaevp.com
Contact: Sarah Estep, Founder

Founded: 1982. **Members:** 450. **Membership Dues:** individual/international, plus $8 if not receiving NewsJournal via email, $30 (annual) ● sustaining, $100 (annual). **Staff:** 2. **Budget:** $6,000. **Multinational. Description:** Engineers, physicists, and other individuals interested in evidence of postmortem survival, particularly verbal communication from the deceased through tape recorders, televisions, computers and other electronic equipment. Investigates evidence that suggests postmortem survival of individual consciousness. Encourages research and development of equipment used in members' work. Focuses on EVP, which members and researchers believe come from other dimensions; these voices are tape-recorded and members claim varied success with soliciting answers to direct questions. Members are available to speak and give demonstrations to local groups. Increases activity in Video Instrumental TransCommunications. Promotes increasing emphasis on members learning to use EVP to continue relationship with loved ones on the other side. **Computer Services:** Online services, document archive for members only. **Formerly:** (2002) American Association - Electronic Voice Phenomena. **Publications:** *AA-EVP NewsJournal*, quarterly. Newsletter. Includes news of members, recording techniques, EVP/ITC examples, news about related concepts and Viewpoint of the Directors. **Price:** included in membership dues. **Circulation:** 450. Alternate Formats: online ● *American Association-Electronic Voice Phenomena—Membership List*, quarterly. Membership Directory. **Price:** included in membership dues. **Circulation:** 180.

7470 ■ American Society of Dowsers (ASD)
PO Box 24
Danville, VT 05828
Ph: (802)684-3417
Fax: (802)684-2565
E-mail: asd@dowsers.org
URL: http://www.dowsers.org
Contact: Tipi Halsey, Pres.

Founded: 1961. **Members:** 4,800. **Membership Dues:** individual, $40 (annual) ● family, $60 (annual) ● individual outside U.S., $48 (annual) ● family outside U.S., $68 (annual) ● junior, $20 (annual) ● library, $35 (annual) ● supporting, $88 (annual) ● contributing, $175 (annual) ● life (based on age), $200-$1,000. **Regional Groups:** 85. **Description:** Amateur and professional dowsers and others interested in locating water, oil, mineral deposits, and various objects and information with or without the use of forked sticks, pendulums, and rods. Promotes fellowship and the teaching of dowsing skills. Informs the public on the significance and uses of dowsing. Society holds no corporate views on the nature of dowsing phenomena and has adopted no standard technique. Conducts research. **Publications:** *The American Dowser*, quarterly. Journal. **Price:** included in membership dues ● *Dowsers Network*, quarterly. Newsletter ● *Membership List*, annual. Membership Directory. **Price:** available to members only ● Also publishes indexes. **Conventions/Meetings:** annual Central ASD Conference and Dowsing School - workshop (exhibits) ● annual conference, various themes and locations ● annual convention ● annual meeting and workshop (exhibits) - always July, August, or September ● Mid-South Conference and Dowsing School - regional meeting ● periodic regional meeting ● South-West Conference.

7471 ■ Borderland Sciences Research Foundation (BSRF)
PO Box 6250
Eureka, CA 95502
Ph: (707)445-2247
Fax: (707)445-1401
E-mail: info@borderlands.com
URL: http://www.borderlands.com

Founded: 1945. **Members:** 1,000. **Staff:** 3. **Description:** Individuals who take an active interest in the "borderland between the visible and invisible manifestations of reality", including the fields of parapsychology, the occult, psychic research, hypnosis, dowsing, radiesthesia, radionics, flying saucers, electricity and the evolving soul, hollow earth mysteries, telepathy, and other phenomena. Explores phenomena which orthodox science cannot or will not investigate. Offers recognition, understanding, and encouragement to individuals who are having unusual experiences of the borderland type or are conducting research in the occult. **Convention/Meeting:** none. **Libraries: Type:** reference. **Holdings:** 1,000. **Subjects:** occult science. **Publications:** *The Journal of Borderland Research*, annual. An information nexus for scholars on the frontiers of science. **Price:** $30.00/year. ISSN: 0897-0394. **Circulation:** 2,000 ● Also publishes paperbacks and research titles, catalog available.

7472 ■ Center for Bigfoot Studies (CBS)
10926 Milano Ave.
Norwalk, CA 90650-1638
Ph: (909)509-2951
E-mail: perez@worldnet.att.net
URL: http://bigfoottimes.net
Contact: Daniel Edward Perez, Founder

Founded: 1984. **Members:** 575. **Membership Dues:** individual, $11 (annual). **Staff:** 2. **Budget:** $5,000. **Description:** Seeks to establish the physical reality of Bigfoot. (Sometimes called "Sasquatch", Bigfoot is a large, manlike creature reputedly inhabiting wilderness regions of North America). Works to solicit support of interested scientists and other Bigfoot researchers. Conducts field investigations. **Libraries: Type:** not open to the public. **Subjects:** Bigfoot. **Computer Services:** database, bibliographic information. **Additional Websites:** http://www.bigfootmuseum.com. **Telecommunication Services:** electronic mail, perez952@sbcglobal.net. **Formerly:** (1984) Southwestern Bigfoot Research Team. **Publications:** *Big Footnotes, 1988*. Book. Features bibliography on subject matter. **Price:** $16.00 post paid ● *Bigfoot Times*, monthly. Newsletter. **Price:** $11.00/year in U.S. and Canada; $13.00/year outside U.S. and Canada. **Conventions/Meetings:** annual Sasquatch Symposium - conference and lecture, with slides, photos, casts (exhibits).

7473 ■ Citizens Against UFO Secrecy (CAUS)
PO Box 2443
Sedona, AZ 86339
Ph: (520)203-0567
E-mail: ufolawyer@msn.com
URL: http://www.v-j-enterprises.com/caus.html
Contact: Peter A. Gersten, Founder/Exec. Dir.

Founded: 1978. **Members:** 100. **Description:** Volunteer researchers specializing in the acquisition and analysis of documentation by local, state, and federal agencies concerning unidentified flying objects. Promotes greater freedom of official UFO information and to demand full accountability thereof. **Publications:** *Update Bulletin*, periodic ● Also publishes findings and recommendations.

7474 ■ Fund for UFO Research (FUFOR)
PO Box 7501
Alexandria, VA 22307
E-mail: fufor@fufor.com
URL: http://www.fufor.com
Contact: Don Berliner, Chm.

Founded: 1979. **Members:** 15. **Budget:** $50,000. **Description:** Reviews research proposals; approves those that promise to advance scientific knowledge and public understanding of UFO phenomena. Disseminates information; grants interviews to news media. Conducts research on the U.S. government's involvement with UFOs, the abduction phenomenon, and case investigations. **Awards:** Donald E. Keyhoe Journalism Award. **Frequency:** annual. **Type:** recognition. **Recipient:** for best reporting on UFOs by print and audiovisual news media ● **Type:** grant. **Recipient:** for UFO research and public education ● Isabel Davis Award. **Frequency:** annual. **Type:** recognition. **Recipient:** for long-term excellence and accomplishments in UFO research. **Publications:** *Fund for UFO Research—Quarterly Report*. Newsletter. Covers activities of the association and major UFO events. Includes list of current publications for sale. **Price:** $15.00/year. **Circulation:** 1,000 ● *Government UFO Documents* ● *Research Reports* ● Books. **Conventions/Meetings:** periodic conference ● periodic workshop.

7475 ■ Ghost Research Society (GRS)
PO Box 205
Oak Lawn, IL 60454-0205
Ph: (708)425-5163
Fax: (708)425-3969

E-mail: dkaczmarek@ghostresearch.org
URL: http://www.ghostresearch.org
Contact: Dale Kaczmarek, Pres.
Founded: 1977. **Members:** 160. **Membership Dues:** associate, $25 (annual) ● patron, $50 (annual) ● life, $200 ● sustaining, $35 (annual). **Staff:** 11. **Description:** Individuals interested in supernatural or preternatural phenomena. Seeks to substantiate claims that man exists after death and that ghosts inhabit the earth. Investigates ghosts, haunting, and poltergeists; analyzes alleged spirit photographs; conducts expeditions to "haunted" sites; compiles data and statistics. Sponsors lectures, speaking engagements, psychic discussions, and "ghost tours". Maintains Speaker's Bureau. **Libraries: Type:** reference. **Subjects:** parapsychology, ghosts, haunting, poltergeists, ghost lights, spirit photography, civil war ghosts, spirit communication. **Formerly:** (1977) Ghost Trackers Club. **Publications:** *Bibliography of Ghost Movies*, annual. Directory. Lists feature films and videos relating to ghosts. **Price:** $7.00 ● *Catalog of Occult Bookstores*. **Price:** $7.00 ● *Dictionary of Occult Terminology*. Newsletter. **Price:** $7.00 ● *Ghost Trackers' Newsletter*, quarterly ● *Ghostly Websites Directory*, annual. **Price:** $7.00. **Advertising:** accepted ● *Greater Chicagoland and NW Indiana Psychic Directory*, annual. **Price:** $7.00 ● *International Directory of Psychic Sciences*, annual. Lists over 240 groups, organizations, and individuals involved in parapsychology and the occult. **Price:** $7.00/copy ● *The Journal*, 3/year. Newsletters. **Price:** $35.00. **Circulation:** 25. **Advertising:** accepted ● *National Register of Haunted Locations*, annual. Directory. **Price:** $28.00. **Advertising:** accepted ● *Occult Publications Directory*, annual. **Price:** $7.00. **Conventions/Meetings:** bimonthly Ghost Trackers Exhibition - conference and meeting (exhibits) - every 3rd Saturday, in odd-numbered months.

7476 ■ International Association for Near-Death Studies (IANDS)

PO Box 502
East Windsor Hill, CT 06028-0502
Ph: (860)882-1211
Fax: (860)882-1212
E-mail: office@iands.org
URL: http://www.iands.org
Contact: Yolaine Stout BA, Pres.
Founded: 1981. **Members:** 900. **Membership Dues:** general, $45 (annual) ● professional, $95 (annual) ● sustaining, $125 (annual). **Staff:** 2. **Budget:** $50,000. **Local Groups:** 40. **Languages:** English, French. **Multinational. Description:** Medical, academic, and health care professionals; laypersons; individuals who have undergone near-death experiences (phenomena which occur to people who are very close to physical death or who pass into a temporary state of clinical death). Encourages, promotes, and supports the scientific study of Near-Death Experiences (NDE) and fosters the exchange and communication of ideas among persons who have conducted or are conducting research on the topic. Collects information for educational material to be dispersed to the public and popular media; relates information emerging from research to appropriate settings, including hospitals and nursing homes. Serves as fraternal organization for those who have experienced such phenomena. **Libraries: Type:** reference. **Holdings:** archival material, audio recordings. **Subjects:** near-death experiences. **Awards:** Bruce Greyson Research Award. **Type:** recognition. **Recipient:** for significant contributions to the field of near-death studies ● **Type:** grant. **Recipient:** for graduate students and academic researchers in the field of near-death experiences. **Computer Services:** database, research. **Special Interest Groups:** Local. **Supersedes:** Association for the Scientific Study of Near Death Phenomena. **Publications:** *Journal of Near-Death Studies*, quarterly. Provides original scholarly reports on near-death experiences and comparable phenomena. **Price:** included in membership dues. **Circulation:** 700 ● *Near-Death Experiences: Index to the Periodical Literature*, updated every few years. Bibliography. Analyzes all scholarly and many non-scholarly articles by 135 near-death-related topics. **Price:** $95.00 for nonmembers; $200.00 for institutions. Alternate Formats: CD-ROM ● *Vital Signs*, quarterly. Newsletter. Includes association news, near-death experience accounts, and original articles. **Price:** included in membership dues. **Circulation:** 1,200. **Conventions/Meetings:** annual conference ● periodic regional meeting ● seminar ● symposium ● workshop.

7477 ■ International Fortean Organization (INFO)

PO Box 50088
Baltimore, MD 21210
E-mail: fortfest99@yahoo.com
URL: http://www.forteans.com
Contact: Phyllis Benjamin, Pres./Fortfest Chm.
Founded: 1965. **Membership Dues:** regular, $25 (annual) ● contributing, $50 (annual) ● patron, $150 (annual) ● life, $250 ● Supporting Inner Circle, $75 (annual). **Staff:** 11. **Regional Groups:** 1. **Languages:** English, French, German, Hebrew, Italian, Japanese, Spanish. **Description:** Scientists, scholars, and laypeople from 20 countries concerned with new and unusual scientific discoveries and philosophic problems pertaining to the criteria of scientific theories and validity. Sponsors investigative teams; provides research services and educational programs. Maintains Speaker's Bureau. Named after Charles Hoy Fort (1874-1932), an American author who researched and documented unusual and unexplained natural phenomena. **Libraries: Type:** reference. **Holdings:** 5,000; books, clippings, periodicals. **Subjects:** physical, biological, and psychological sciences. **Committees:** Cryptozoology; Education; Investigations; Research. **Supersedes:** Fortean Society. **Publications:** *INFO Journal*, 3/year. Contains information on new members, publication reviews, and original research papers. **Price:** included in membership dues. ISSN: 0019-0144. **Circulation:** 800. Alternate Formats: microform ● *INFO Journal Index to Issues 1-50*. **Price:** $12.95 plus $3.50 postage and handling ● *INFO Occasional Papers*, periodic. **Circulation:** 800. **Conventions/Meetings:** annual FortFest and FortNight - conference and lecture, with books, magazine and video sales (exhibits).

7478 ■ International UFO Museum and Research Center at Roswell, New Mexico (IUFOMRC)

114 N Main St.
Roswell, NM 88203
Free: (800)822-3545
Fax: (575)625-1907
E-mail: iufomrc@iufomrc.com
URL: http://www.roswellufomuseum.com
Contact: Stanton Friedman, Contact
Multinational. Description: Promotes public awareness of Roswell, New Mexico sightings of Unidentified Flying Objects and informs the public about the 1947 incident now known as "The Roswell Incident". Preserves written, audio, and visual formats of that and other related phenomena related to UFO research. **Telecommunication Services:** electronic mail, iufomrc@dfn.com. **Divisions:** International UFO Museum. **Publications:** Newsletter. Alternate Formats: online. **Conventions/Meetings:** annual Roswell UFO Festival.

7479 ■ J. Allen Hynek Center for UFO Studies (CUFOS)

2457 W Peterson Ave., Ste.6
Chicago, IL 60659
Ph: (773)271-3611
E-mail: infocenter@cufos.org
URL: http://www.cufos.org
Contact: Dr. Mark Rodeghier, Scientific Dir.
Founded: 1973. **Members:** 700. **Membership Dues:** $25 (annual). **Staff:** 2. **Budget:** $35,000. **Description:** Individuals throughout the U.S. and abroad who are involved in personal research on UFO subjects; and others who wish to be kept informed of the latest research. Collects and studies UFO sighting reports. Promotes public distribution of information on UFOs through publications by researchers and other writers throughout the world. **Libraries: Type:** open to the public; by appointment only. **Holdings:** 6,000. **Computer Services:** database, listings of UFO sightings and reference to source of sighting details. **Absorbed:** National Investigation Committee on Aerial Phenomena. **Formerly:** (1986) Center for UFO Studies. **Publications:** *International UFO Reporter*, quarterly. Magazine. Provides news and commentary on all aspects of UFO phenomena. Includes book reviews. **Price:** included in membership dues. ISSN: 0720-174X. **Circulation:** 800. **Advertising:** accepted ● *Journal of UFO Studies*, periodic. Covers scientific research on the UFO phenomenon.

7480 ■ Michigan/Canadian Bigfoot Information Center (MCBIC)

152 W Sherman
Caro, MI 48723
Ph: (989)673-2715
Contact: Wayne W. King, Dir.
Founded: 1970. **Members:** 4. **Description:** Covers northern and midwestern U.S. and eastern Canada. Assists persons having a sincere desire for information about the "sasquatch," or "bigfoot" (large, hairy, manlike creature reputedly inhabiting various regions of North America); seeks to obtain sasquatch specimen. Conducts overnight vigils in classified areas. Receives cooperative assistance from anthropologists, wildlife pathologists, and Department of Natural Resources affiliates. Maintains transcript and tape collection as well as file and indexing system. Compiles statistics; maintains research program. **Computer Services:** database. **Formerly:** Michigan Bigfoot Information Center.

7481 ■ Mutual UFO Network (MUFON)

c/o James Carrion, Intl. Dir.
PO Box 279
Bellvue, CO 80512-0279
Free: (888)817-2220
Fax: (866)466-9173
E-mail: hq@mufon.com
URL: http://www.mufon.com
Contact: James Carrion, Intl. Dir.
Founded: 1969. **Members:** 4,000. **Membership Dues:** regular, in U.S., $45 (annual) ● regular, outside U.S., $55 (annual) ● additional family, $10 (annual) ● donor, $100 (annual) ● professional, $250 (annual) ● patron, $500 (annual) ● benefactor, $1,000 (annual) ● student (18 years and under), $35 (annual). **Staff:** 6. **Budget:** $190,000. **Regional Groups:** 4. **State Groups:** 50. **Local Groups:** 60. **National Groups:** 15. **Description:** Scientists, engineers, doctors, psychologists, technicians, military personnel, computer programmers, pilots and others. Seeks to resolve the enigma of unidentified flying objects and investigate UFO sighting reports worldwide. Compiles information on UFO sightings worldwide. Operates one amateur radio network which receives and disseminates UFO sighting reports and current UFO information. Maintains file on UFO sighting reports, arranged chronologically by state, province and country. Compiles statistics; provides speakers' bureau; offers research and educational programs. Has computer networks, CompuServe and the Internet. **Libraries: Type:** reference. **Holdings:** 700; artwork, books, clippings, monographs, periodicals. **Subjects:** unidentified flying objects, astronomy, Bigfoot, animal mutilations, crop circles. **Computer Services:** database, case files ● database, UFO ● mailing lists, of members. **Committees:** Abduction; Amateur Radio Network; Animal Mutilations; Astronomy; Computer Net; Humanoid Study Group; Landing Traces; Public Relations and Education; UFO News Clipping Service; UFO Telephone Hot Line. **Formerly:** (1973) Midwest UFO Network. **Publications:** *MUFON Field Investigators Manual*, 5/year. Contains detailed instructions to investigate UFO sighting. **Price:** $28.50 includes postage and handling, for members. **Circulation:** 4,000 ● *MUFON International UFO Symposium Proceedings*, annual. Includes statistics, research reports and case investigations. **Circulation:** 500 ● *MUFON UFO Journal*, monthly. Magazine. Contains statistics, research reports, book reviews and information on UFO sightings. **Price:** $45.00. ISSN: 0270-6822. **Circulation:** 2,900. **Advertising:** accepted. Alternate Formats: microform ● *UFO Crash/Retrieval Syndrome: Status Report II*, periodic. Monographs. Cov-

ers the reported recovery by the U.S. government of UFOs and alien bodies. Includes research reports. **Price:** $5.00/copy ● *UFO Crash/Retrievals: Amassing the Evidence, Status Report III.* Monographs. **Price:** $10.00 ● *UFO's MJ-12 and the Government.* **Price:** $19.00. **Conventions/Meetings:** annual International UFO Symposium, photo exhibits, books, video, and publication sales (exhibits).

7482 ■ National Investigations Committee on Unidentified Flying Objects (NICUFO)
21601 Devonshire St., Ste.217
Chatsworth, CA 91311-8415
Ph: (818)882-0052
Fax: (818)882-0047
E-mail: info@nicufo.org
URL: http://www.nicufo.org
Contact: Dr. Frank E. Stranges, Pres./Founder
Founded: 1967. **Members:** 600. **Membership Dues:** individual in U.S., $30 (annual) ● individual outside U.S., $35 (annual). **Staff:** 5. **Regional Groups:** 15. **Local Groups:** 1. **Multinational. Description:** Provides education and research concerning space, science, UFOs and associated phenomena. Probes UFO reports and relates findings to associates, subscribers, governmental agencies and the public via the press, audiotapes, videotapes, books, booklets and newsletters. Conducts educational and charitable programs. Compiles statistics. Provides free materials to schools, prisons and children. **Libraries: Type:** reference. **Holdings:** 2,500; books, periodicals. **Subjects:** religion, UFOs, space, science. **Awards:** President's Award. **Frequency:** annual. **Type:** recognition. **Recipient:** for level of support and participation in the purposes of the organization. **Telecommunication Services:** electronic mail, nicufo@earthlink.net. **Study Groups:** Inner Circle; Royal Order of Melchizedek. **Also Known As:** NICUFO. **Publications:** *Dead Sea Scrolls Mysteries Vol. 1, Vol. 2, and Vol. 3.* Video. **Price:** $25.00 ● *How I Met Commander Val Thor at Pentagon.* Video. **Price:** $35.95 ● *Interspace Link Confidential Newsletter*, monthly. **Price:** $10.00/sample; $100.00/year in U.S.; $125.00/year outside U.S. **Circulation:** 1,000 ● *Mysteries of Mastership.* Video. **Price:** $35.95 ● *UFO Journal*, quarterly. Newsletter. Provides accounts of sightings of UFOs worldwide; includes book reviews and articles on miscellaneous space/science phenomena. **Price:** included in membership dues; $30.00/year for associates in U.S.; $35.00/year for associates outside U.S. **Advertising:** accepted ● Audiotapes ● Books ● Booklets. **Conventions/Meetings:** semiannual Inner Circle - seminar, space, science and spirituality with emphasis on spiritual elements of life and alleged space visitors/encounters; inner circle membership required - June and November in Las Vegas, NV.

7483 ■ Project Blue Book (PBB)
6214 Carthage St.
Fort Smith, AR 72903
Ph: (479)484-7512
E-mail: bandrpitts@aol.com
Contact: Bill Pitts, Dir.
Founded: 1986. **Members:** 148. **Staff:** 1. **Description:** Active and retired military or federal investigative personnel who conduct probes into alleged sightings of UFOs. (Begun in 1949 by the U.S. Air Force but is no longer a government project.) Provides speakers; and guests for television show; conducts research and educational programs. **Publications:** none.

7484 ■ Sasquatch Investigations of Mid-America (SIA)
2726 NW 34
Oklahoma City, OK 73112
Ph: (405)942-5161
Fax: (405)942-5161
E-mail: hhewufo@cox.net
Contact: Hayden C. Hewes, Dir. of Research
Founded: 1976. **Members:** 1,200. **Staff:** 2. **Regional Groups:** 9. **State Groups:** 50. **National Groups:** 28. **Description:** Individuals interested in the scientific study of the "sasquatch" (also known as "Bigfoot"), a large, hairy, nocturnal creature sighted in thickly wooded regions throughout the world. Sasquatches are reportedly about eight feet tall, walk upright, and appear to be intelligent and peaceful. About 1000 reports of sasquatch sightings have been documented in the U.S. Collects and evaluates data on Bigfoot and releases findings to the public through lectures and radio and television programs. Maintains library of 300 books and magazines pertaining to Bigfoot. Members investigate and report sightings in their areas. **Libraries: Type:** reference. **Holdings:** 300. **Publications:** *Sasquatch News*, annual. Newsletter. **Conventions/Meetings:** annual symposium.

7485 ■ Society for Scientific Exploration (SSE)
PO Box 7065
Lawrence, KS 66044
Free: (800)627-0326
Fax: (785)843-1274
E-mail: jse@allenpress.com
URL: http://www.scientificexploration.org
Contact: Marty Cawthon, Information Off.
Founded: 1982. **Members:** 900. **Membership Dues:** associate, $75 (annual) ● full, $95 (annual) ● student, $35 (annual) ● emeritus, $65 (annual). **Multinational. Description:** Scientists and scholars from a wide range of disciplines united to study unusual phenomena regarding cryptozoology, parapsychology, unidentified flying objects, geophysical anomalies, and related areas. Maintains speakers' bureau; compiles statistics. **Awards:** Dinsdale Award. **Frequency:** semiannual. **Type:** recognition. **Publications:** *Journal of Scientific Exploration*, quarterly. Contains peer-reviewed reports on anomalous phenomena. **Price:** included in membership dues; $65.00 for nonmembers; $125.00 for institutions. ISSN: 0892-3310 ● *Society Directory*, annual ● Brochure. **Conventions/Meetings:** annual conference (exhibits).

7486 ■ UFO Information Retrieval Center (UFOIRC)
3131 W Cochise Dr., No. 158
Phoenix, AZ 85051-9511
Ph: (602)284-5427
E-mail: ideas@ufohelp.com
URL: http://www.ufohelp.com
Contact: Thomas M. Olsen MS, Contact
Founded: 1966. **Languages:** English, German, Italian, Japanese, Norwegian, Russian, Spanish. **Multinational. Description:** Collects, analyzes, publishes, and disseminates information on reports of unidentified flying objects. Compiles statistics; conducts research programs; sponsors photo exhibits; provides children's and students' services; operates speakers' bureau and referrals. **Libraries: Type:** reference. **Holdings:** 495; audio recordings, books, periodicals, photographs, video recordings. **Subjects:** UFO phenomenon. **Computer Services:** database, CUFOS and MUFON. **Publications:** *Recent and Worthwhile UFO Media List.* Bibliography. Lists media such as books, CD-ROMs, and commercial databases with contact information. **Price:** $5.00 postage paid ● *Reference for Outstanding UFO Sighting Reports*, periodic ● *Sighting Alerts.* **Price:** $5.00 ● *UFO Info Packet.* Catalog. Contains source material on UFO information including news of conventions, media list, and museums. **Price:** $38.00/issue in U.S.; $39.65 outside U.S., surface mail; $46.95 outside U.S., air mail ● Proceedings ● UFO Info Help Disk: IBM PC-compatible 3.5 inch floppy disc with frequently-asked questions (FAQ) on the UFO phenomenon and expert answers; hypertext; graphics;(same information as available at Website) $7 ppd; $8.50 ppd. outside of USA.

Philosophy

7487 ■ Association for the Advancement of Philosophy and Psychiatry (AAPP)
c/o Prof. Jerome L. Kroll, MD, Pres.
Univ. of Minnesota Medical School
Community-University Hea. Care Clinic
2201 Bloomington Ave. S
Minneapolis, MN 55404
E-mail: kroll001@umn.edu
URL: http://www3.utsouthwestern.edu/aapp
Contact: Prof. Jerome L. Kroll MD, Pres.
Founded: 1989. **Members:** 520. **Membership Dues:** regular, $95 (annual) ● student, $32 (annual). **Staff:** 2. **National Groups:** 20. **Multinational. Description:** Works to encourage interdisciplinary activity in philosophy and psychiatry. Promotes research and facilitates understanding in both fields. **Special Interest Groups:** Continental Philosophy and Psychiatry. **Publications:** *Philosophy, Psychiatry and Psychology*, quarterly. Journal. **Price:** included in membership dues. **Advertising:** accepted. **Conventions/Meetings:** annual convention and meeting.

7488 ■ Camus Studies Association (CSA/SEC)
c/o Prof. Raymond Gay-Crosier
Univ. of Florida
Dept. of Romance Languages and Literatures
Gainesville, FL 32611
Fax: (352)392-5679
E-mail: gaycros@rll.ufl.edu
URL: http://www.clas.ufl.edu/users/gaycros/Camus.htm
Contact: Prof. Raymond Gay-Crosier, Contact
Founded: 1982. **Members:** 420. **Membership Dues:** active, $25 (annual) ● founding, $30 (annual) ● student, $10 (annual). **Multinational. Description:** Promotes worldwide communication and research on the life and work of Albert Camus (1913-1960). Sponsors sessions at regional and national professional meetings. **Computer Services:** Bibliographic search, critical (updated periodically). **Also Known As:** (2003) Societe des Etudes Cauvsiennes. **Publications:** *Bulletin de la Societe des Etudes Camusiennes*, 3/year.

7489 ■ Concerned Philosophers for Peace (CPP)
c/o David Boersema, Treas.
Dept. of Philosophy
Pacific Univ.
2043 Coll. Way
Forest Grove, OR 97116
URL: http://benezet.org/phpnuke
Contact: David Boersema, Treas.
Founded: 1981. **Members:** 500. **Membership Dues:** regular, $20 (annual) ● student, low income, $5 (annual). **Description:** Professional and non-professional philosophers. Commits in philosophical exploration of peace and its many related topics; seeks to apply philosophy to urgent questions of modern times. **Publications:** *Concerned Philosophers for Peace Newsletter*, semiannual. **Price:** included in membership dues. ISSN: 1062-9114. **Circulation:** 500. Alternate Formats: online. Also Cited As: *CPP Newsletter* ● *Philosophy of Peace (POP) Special Series*, periodic. Books. **Price:** EUR 42.00. **Conventions/Meetings:** annual conference.

7490 ■ Internet Infidels
PO Box 142
Colorado Springs, CO 80901-0142
Fax: (877)501-5113
E-mail: infidels@infidels.org
URL: http://www.infidels.org/infidels/index.shtml
Contact: Jeff Lucas, Treas.
Founded: 1995. **Nonmembership. Description:** Works to defend and promote Metaphysical Naturalism, the belief "that nature is all there is, a closed system in no need of an explanation and sufficient unto itself.". **Libraries: Type:** reference. **Holdings:** periodicals. **Publications:** *Secular Web.* Dedicated to the growth and maintenance of a comprehensive freethought Web site. ● Books ● Papers ● Articles.

7491 ■ Michael Oakeshott Association (MOA)
c/o Timothy Fuller
Political Sciences Dept.
Colorado Coll.
14 E Cache La Poudre St.
Colorado Springs, CO 80903

E-mail: mjrabin@rogers.com
URL: http://www.michael-oakeshott-association.org
Contact: Jeff Rabin PhD, Sec.-Treas.

Founded: 2001. **Members:** 500. **Multinational. Description:** Works on the promotion and critical discussion of the work of British philosopher Michael Oakeshott (1901-1990). **Conventions/Meetings:** biennial conference - odd-numbered years.

7492 ■ Society for Philosophy and Psychology (SPP)
c/o Thomas W. Polger, Sec.-Treas.
Univ. of Cincinnati
Dept. of Philosophy
206 McMicken Hall
Cincinnati, OH 45221
Ph: (513)556-6328
Fax: (513)556-2939
E-mail: sppsectreas@gmail.com
URL: http://www.hfac.uh.edu/cogsci/spp/spphp.html
Contact: Thomas W. Polger, Sec.-Treas.

Founded: 1974. **Membership Dues:** regular, $25 (annual) ● student, $5 (annual). **Description:** Promotes interaction between philosophers, psychologists and cognitive scientists on issues of common interest. **Awards:** Stanton Award. **Frequency:** annual. **Type:** recognition. **Recipient:** for significant contributions to interdisciplinary research ● William James Prize. **Frequency:** annual. **Type:** recognition. **Recipient:** for the best contributed paper by a graduate student. **Computer Services:** Information services, list server. **Conventions/Meetings:** annual meeting - usually on first Thursday-Sunday of June.

7493 ■ Society for Skeptical Studies (SSS)
c/o Dr. Richard Greene, Exec. Dir.
Weber State Univ.
Dept. of Political Sci. and Philosophy
1203 Univ. Cir.
Ogden, UT 84408-1203
E-mail: rgreene@weber.edu
URL: http://departments.weber.edu/sss
Contact: Dr. Richard Greene, Exec. Dir.

Founded: 2000. **Multinational. Description:** Dedicated to philosophical discussion and research on any topic related to skepticism, including the history of skeptical thought, skepticism regarding mental content, skepticism regarding self-knowledge, and moral skepticism, and traditional topics in skepticism. **Publications:** Newsletter ● Videos. **Conventions/ Meetings:** annual meeting and lecture.

7494 ■ Southern Society for Philosophy and Psychology (SSPP)
c/o Hajime Otani, Pres.-Elect
Central Michigan Univ.
Dept. of Psychology
Mount Pleasant, MI 48859
Ph: (517)774-6494
E-mail: hajime.otani@cmich.edu
URL: http://www.soci.niu.edu/~sspp
Contact: Hajime Otani, Pres.-Elect

Founded: 1904. **Members:** 600. **Membership Dues:** full, $35 (annual) ● associate, $15 (triennial). **Description:** Promotes exchange of ideas regarding the philosophy and psychology in the southern section of the United States by those engaged in these fields of inquiry; advances investigation by fostering the educational function of philosophy and psychology; aims to improve the academic status of the topics. **Awards:** Griffith Award. **Frequency:** annual. **Type:** recognition. **Recipient:** for the best paper in each discipline by an author who has held the PhD less than 5 years or who has not yet received the PhD ● Travel Grant Awards. **Type:** monetary. **Recipient:** for graduate students to attend annual meeting. **Committees:** Local Arrangements; Program. **Publications:** Newsletter, 3/year. Alternate Formats: online ● Membership Directory. Contains names, addresses, phone numbers, and email addresses of members. **Conventions/Meetings:** annual meeting, with awards - held Thursday through Saturday of Easter weekend.

Photogrammetry

7495 ■ ASPRS - The Imaging and Geospatial Information Society
5410 Grosvenor Ln., Ste.210
Bethesda, MD 20814-2160
Ph: (301)493-0290
Fax: (301)493-0208
E-mail: asprs@asprs.org
URL: http://www.asprs.org
Contact: Jesse Winch, Program Mgr.

Founded: 1934. **Members:** 7,800. **Membership Dues:** active, in U.S., $120 (annual) ● associate, in U.S., $80 (annual) ● student, in U.S., $45 (annual) ● active, in Canada, $170 (annual) ● associate, in Canada, $127 (annual) ● student, in Canada, $90 (annual) ● active, foreign, $180 (annual) ● associate, foreign, $140 (annual) ● student, foreign, $105 (annual) ● sustaining - corporate company (without subsidiary), $1,200 (annual) ● sustaining - corporate company (based on subsidiaries), $1,825-$3,850 (annual). **Staff:** 10. **Budget:** $2,100,000. **Regional Groups:** 17. **Description:** Firms, individuals, government employees and academicians engaged in photogrammetry, photointerpretation, remote sensing, and geographic information systems and their application to such fields as archaeology, geographic information systems, military reconnaissance, urban planning, engineering, traffic surveys, meteorological observations, medicine, geology, forestry, agriculture, construction and topographic mapping. Mission is to advance knowledge and improve understanding of these sciences and to promote responsible applications. Offers voluntary certification program open to persons associated with one or more functional area of photogrammetry, remote sensing and GIS. Surveys the profession of private firms in photogrammetry and remote sensing in the areas of products and services. **Libraries: Type:** reference. **Holdings:** periodicals. **Awards:** Paul R. Wolf Memorial Scholarship. **Frequency:** annual. **Type:** scholarship. **Recipient:** for graduate students currently enrolled in a college or university in the United States ● Robert E. Altenhofen Memorial Scholarship. **Frequency:** annual. **Type:** scholarship. **Recipient:** for college students with exceptional interest and ability in the theoretical aspects of photogrammetry ● Space Imaging Award for Application of High Resolution Digital Satellite Imagery. **Frequency:** annual. **Type:** grant. **Recipient:** for undergraduate or graduate students at an accredited college or university with image processing facilities appropriate for conducting the proposed work ● Ta Liang Memorial Award. **Frequency:** annual. **Type:** grant. **Recipient:** for graduate students ● William A. Fischer Memorial Scholarship. **Frequency:** annual. **Type:** scholarship. **Recipient:** for graduate students whose career goals are directed towards new and innovative uses of remote sensing data/techniques ● Z/I Imaging Scholarship. **Frequency:** annual. **Type:** recognition. **Recipient:** for student who is currently pursuing graduate-level studies. **Computer Services:** Mailing lists, of members. **Telecommunication Services:** electronic mail, jwinch@asprs.org. **Committees:** Awards and Scholarships; Convention Planning and Policy; Data Preservation and Archiving; Education and Professional Development; Electronic Communication; Evaluation for Certification; External Affairs; Journal Policy; Membership; Professional Conduct. **Divisions:** Geographic Information Systems; Photogrammetric Application; Primary Data Acquisition; Professional Practice; Remote Sensing Applications. **Subcommittees:** Aerial Photography Guidelines; Archaeology/Anthropology; Classification Standards; Coordinate Measurement Systems; Data Processing; Digital Image Processing; Display; Earth Science; Environmental Factors; Government Practice; GPS Photogrammetry; Hydraulic Sciences; Hydrospheric Sciences; Image Quality; Knowledge-Based Expert Systems; National Photogrammetrist Recognition; Plant Sciences; Platforms and Navigation; Private Practice; Reproduction; Sensor Systems; Softcopy Photogrammetry; Standards; Transportation Surveys; Visual Image Interpretation. **Affiliated With:** International Society for Photogrammetry and Remote Sensing. **Formerly:** (1985) American Society of Photogrammetry; (2001) American Society for Photogrammetry and Remote Sensing. **Publications:** *Photogrammetric Engineering and Remote Sensing*, monthly. Journal. Provides technical information about the applications of photogrammetry, remote sensing, and geographic information systems. **Price:** included in membership dues; $120.00 /year for nonmembers. ISSN: 0099-1112. **Circulation:** 10,000. **Advertising:** accepted. Also Cited As: *PE & RS* ● Proceedings. **Conventions/Meetings:** annual conference (exhibits) ● symposium.

7496 ■ Management Association for Private Photogrammetric Surveyors (MAPPS)
1760 Reston Pkwy., Ste.515
Reston, VA 20190
Ph: (703)787-6996
Fax: (703)787-7550
E-mail: info@mapps.org
URL: http://www.mapps.org
Contact: John Palatiello, Exec. Dir.

Founded: 1982. **Members:** 160. **Membership Dues:** firm (based on the number of employees), $1,000-$7,000 (annual) ● associate firm (based on annual sales), $1,250-$3,000 (annual) ● platinum sustaining, $1,000 (annual) ● gold sustaining, $500 (annual) ● silver sustaining, $250 (annual). **Staff:** 4. **Budget:** $500,000. **Description:** Firms engaged in photogrammetry, computer-based geographic information systems and the manufacturing and/or supplying of photogrammetric equipment; consulting firms. Compiles capability study of member firms. Conducts programs on markets for surveying and mapping services. Lobbies Congress. **Telecommunication Services:** electronic mail, john@mapps.org. **Supersedes:** Legislative Council for Photogrammetry. **Publications:** *Capital Coverage*, bimonthly. Newsletter. **Circulation:** 400. Alternate Formats: online ● *Flightline*, bimonthly. Newsletter. Covers MAPPS activities and member firms; provides industry information and legislative, business and management updates. **Price:** included in membership dues. **Circulation:** 750. Alternate Formats: online ● *MAPPS Member Firms Capability Survey*, periodic. Alternate Formats: online ● *MAPPS Standard Photogrammetric Contract*. **Conventions/Meetings:** annual Federal Programs Conference - meeting and conference, private professional photogrammetrists who exchange information and technical expertise - March ● annual meeting - usually January or July ● workshop.

Photography

7497 ■ Society for Imaging Science and Technology (IS&T)
7003 Kilworth Ln.
Springfield, VA 22151
Ph: (703)642-9090
Fax: (703)642-9094
E-mail: info@imaging.org
URL: http://www.imaging.org
Contact: Suzanne E. Grinnan, Exec. Dir.

Founded: 1947. **Members:** 2,000. **Membership Dues:** regular (domestic), $95 (annual) ● regular (outside U.S.), $105 (annual) ● student, $25 (annual) ● corporate (donor), $750 (annual) ● corporate (supporting), $2,500 (annual) ● corporate (sustaining), $5,000 (annual). **Staff:** 8. **Budget:** $1,300,000. **Regional Groups:** 17. **Description:** Individuals who apply photography and imaging to science, engineering and industry. Sponsors International Congress on Advances in Digital Printing Technologies. Offers placement service. **Libraries: Type:** reference. **Holdings:** 500. **Awards:** Chester F. Carlson Award. **Frequency:** annual. **Type:** recognition. **Recipient:** for outstanding work in the science or technology of electrophotography ● Edwin H. Land Medal. **Frequency:** biennial. **Type:** medal. **Recipient:** for an individual who has demonstrated pioneering entrepreneurial creativity that has had a major public impact ● Kosar Memorial Award. **Frequency:** annual. **Type:** recognition. **Recipient:** for outstanding contributions in the area of unconventional photography or imaging ●

Lieven Gevaert Medal. **Frequency:** annual. **Type:** medal. **Recipient:** for outstanding contributions in the field of silver halide photography ● President's Citation. **Frequency:** periodic. **Type:** recognition. **Recipient:** for outstanding long-term contributions and dedication to the achievement of the society's objectives ● Raymond Davis Scholarship. **Frequency:** annual. **Type:** scholarship. **Recipient:** for students of imaging science or engineering. **Telecommunication Services:** electronic mail, suzanne.grinnan@imaging.org. **Formerly:** (1956) Society of Photographic Engineering; (1992) Society of Photographic Scientists and Engineering. **Publications:** *Journal of Electronic Imaging*, quarterly ● *Journal of Imaging Science and Technology*, bimonthly ● Proceedings. **Conventions/Meetings:** annual Digital Printing Technology International Congress (exhibits) - usually October.

Physics

7498 ■ American Center for Physics (ACP)

1 Physics Ellipse
College Park, MD 20740
Ph: (301)209-3100 (301)209-3636
E-mail: webmaster@acp.org
URL: http://www.acp.org

Founded: 1994. **Description:** Works to unify the field of physics and the many programs of physics societies. **Libraries: Type:** reference. **Holdings:** archival material, photographs, reports. **Subjects:** physics. **Affiliated With:** American Association of Physicists in Medicine; American Association of Physics Teachers; American Physical Society.

7499 ■ American Institute of Physics (AIP)

1 Physics Ellipse
College Park, MD 20740
Ph: (301)209-3000
Fax: (301)209-3133
E-mail: brodsky@aip.org
URL: http://www.aip.org
Contact: H. Frederick Dylla PhD, Exec. Dir.

Founded: 1931. **Staff:** 560. **Description:** Consists of ten national societies in the fields of physics, astronomy and related disciplines with a total of 100,000 members, 17 affiliated societies, 47 corporate associates and 7,500 student members. Seeks to assist in the advancement and diffusion of the knowledge of physics and its application to human welfare. Publishes scientific journals devoted to physics and related sciences; provides secondary information services and online electronic journals; serves the public by making available to the press and other channels of public information reliable communications on physics and its progress; carries on extensive career services activities; maintains projects directed toward providing information about physics education to students, physics teachers and physics departments; encourages and assists in the documentation and study of the history of recent physics; cooperates with local, national and international organizations devoted to physics; and fosters the relations of the science of physics to other sciences and to the arts and industry. Provides placement service; compiles statistics; maintains biographical archives and Niels Bohr Library of History of Physics. **Awards:** Abraham Pais Award for the History of Physics. **Frequency:** annual. **Type:** recognition. **Recipient:** for outstanding scholarly achievement in the history of physics ● Andrew Gemant Award. **Frequency:** annual. **Type:** recognition. **Recipient:** for physics and humanities ● Dannie Heineman Prize for Astrophysics. **Frequency:** annual. **Type:** recognition. **Recipient:** for outstanding achievement in astrophysics ● Dannie Heineman Prize for Mathematical Physics. **Frequency:** annual. **Type:** recognition. **Recipient:** outstanding achievement in mathematical physics ● John T. Tate International Medal. **Frequency:** biennial. **Type:** recognition. **Recipient:** for distinguished service to physics by a non-us scientist ● Karl T. Compton Award. **Frequency:** quadrennial. **Type:** recognition. **Recipient:** for outstanding statesmanship in physics ● Marsh W. White Awards. **Frequency:** annual. **Type:** recognition. **Recipient:** for outreach to the public ● Outstanding SPS Chapter Advisory Award. **Frequency:** annual. **Type:** recognition. **Recipient:** for distinguished service ● The Prize for Industrial Applications of Physics. **Frequency:** biennial. **Type:** recognition. **Recipient:** for industrial applications of physics ● Sigma Pi Sigma Undergraduate Research Awards. **Frequency:** annual. **Type:** recognition. **Recipient:** for outstanding undergraduate physics research projects ● SPS Scholarships. **Frequency:** annual. **Type:** scholarship. **Recipient:** outstanding academic performance ● William F. and Edith R. Meggers Project Award. **Frequency:** biennial. **Type:** recognition. **Recipient:** for high school physics projects. **Computer Services:** database, searchable physics information notices ● information services, citation. **Publications:** *AIP History of Physics Newsletter*, semiannual. Summarizes current work of institutions in the field of physics; reports on the history and philosophy of physics and astronomy. **Price:** free for members. **Circulation:** 3,500 ● *Applied Physics Letters*, weekly. Journal. Provides brief reports on new developments in applied physics on topics such as semiconductors, superconductors, lasers and optics. **Price:** $145.00 /year for members of AIP and its affiliates; $1,900.00 /year for nonmembers. ISSN: 0003-6951. Alternate Formats: microform ● *Current Physics Index*, quarterly. Journal. Contains abstracts of articles published in the primary journals of the AIP in the past quarter, classified by subject. **Price:** $215.00 /year for members of AIP and its affiliates; $1,190.00 /year for nonmembers. ISSN: 0098-9819 ● *Journal of Applied Physics*. **Price:** $220.00 /year for members of AIP and its affiliates; $2,185.00 /year for nonmembers. ISSN: 0021-8979. Alternate Formats: microform ● *Journal of Chemical Physics*, 48/year. Contains research papers relevant to both physics and chemistry. **Price:** $250.00 /year for members of AIP and its affiliates; $3,175.00 /year for nonmembers. ISSN: 0021-9606. Alternate Formats: microform ● *Journal of Mathematical Physics*, monthly. Contains articles and papers on branches of mathematics that are currently or potentially useful for the development of theoretical physics. **Price:** $95.00 /year for members of AIP and its affiliates; $1,535.00 /year for nonmembers. ISSN: 0022-2488. Alternate Formats: microform ● *Journal of Optical Technology*, monthly. English translation of the Soviet journal *Optiko-Mekhanischeskaya Promyshlennost*. **Price:** $1,635.00 /year for nonmembers. ISSN: 1070-9762. Alternate Formats: microform ● *Journal of Physical and Chemical Reference Data*, quarterly. Provides physical and chemical property data; includes annual index. **Price:** $98.00 /year for members of the AIP or affiliates; $615.00 /year for nonmembers. ISSN: 0047-2689. Alternate Formats: microform ● *Low Temperature Physics*, monthly. Journal. Provides an English translation of the Soviet journal *Fizika Nizkikh Temperatur*, which presents the latest experimental results. **Price:** $2,070.00/year. ISSN: 1063-777X. Alternate Formats: microform ● *Physics of Fluids*, monthly. Journal. Contains original papers on fluid dynamics including kinetic theory, statistical mechanics and structure. **Price:** $105.00 /year for members; $1,310.00 /year for nonmembers. ISSN: 0031-9171. Alternate Formats: microform ● *Review of Scientific Instruments*, monthly. Journal. Contains articles concerning new and improved scientific instruments and apparatus for physics and related disciplines, such as chemistry. **Price:** $90.00 /year for members of AIP and its affiliates; $1,030.00 /year for nonmembers. ISSN: 0034-6748. **Advertising:** accepted. Alternate Formats: microform ● Also publishes 16 journals, programs, and bulletins for its member organizations; newsletters, and conference proceedings. **Conventions/Meetings:** annual Industrial Physics Forum - conference, meeting of scientific leaders from industry & academia.

7500 ■ American Physical Society (APS)

One Physics Ellipse
College Park, MD 20740-3844
Ph: (301)209-3200 (301)209-3269
Fax: (301)209-0865
E-mail: exoffice@aps.org
URL: http://www.aps.org
Contact: Ken Cole, Special Asst. to the Exec. Off.

Founded: 1899. **Members:** 42,000. **Membership Dues:** regular, $112 (annual) ● junior, senior, $56 (annual) ● student, $28 (annual) ● life - regular, $1,680. **Staff:** 165. **Budget:** $30,000,000. **Regional Groups:** 7. **Description:** Scientists worldwide, dedicated to the advancement and the diffusion of the knowledge of physics. Publishes some of the leading international physics journals, organizes major scientific meetings and provides strong outreach programs in physics education and in international and public affairs. **Awards:** David A. Bouchet Award. **Frequency:** annual. **Type:** recognition. **Recipient:** for Black, Hispanic or Native American who has made significant contributions to physics research ● Hans A. Bethe Prize. **Frequency:** annual. **Type:** monetary. **Recipient:** for outstanding work in theory, experiment or observation in the areas of astrophysics, nuclear physics or closely related fields ● John Wheatley Award. **Frequency:** biennial. **Type:** recognition. **Recipient:** for physicists who have made contributions to the development of physics in Third World countries ● Joseph A. Burton Forum Award. **Frequency:** annual. **Type:** recognition. **Recipient:** for contributions to the public understanding or resolution of issues involving the interface of physics and society ● LeRoy Apker Award. **Frequency:** annual. **Type:** recognition. **Recipient:** for outstanding achievements in physics by undergraduate students ● Shock Compression Science Award. **Frequency:** biennial. **Type:** recognition. **Recipient:** for contributions to understanding condensed matter and nonlinear physics through shock compression. **Computer Services:** Mailing lists, of members. **Divisions:** Astrophysics; Atomic, Molecular, and Optical Physics; Biological Physics; Chemical Physics; Computational Physics; Condensed Matter Physics; Fluid Dynamics; High Polymer Physics; Laser Science; Materials Physics; Particles and Field Physics; Physics of Beams; Plasma Physics. **Special Interest Groups:** Few-Body Systems and Multiparticle Dynamics-Gravitation; Instrument and Measurement Science; Magnetism and Its Application; Plasma Astrophysics; Precision Measurement and Fundamental Constants; Shock Compression of Condensed Matter; Statistical and Nonlinear Physics. **Study Groups:** Education; History of Physics; Industrial and Applied Physics; International Physics; Physics and Society. **Publications:** *APS Newsletter*, 11/year. **Price:** included in membership dues. **Circulation:** 42,000. Alternate Formats: online ● *Bulletin of the American Physical Society*, monthly. Includes meeting programs and abstracts of meetings. ● *Physical Review*, monthly. Journal. Features scholarly articles on physics. **Price:** $35.00 ● *Physical Review Letters*, weekly. Journal. Contains short scholarly articles on physics. **Price:** $300.00 in U.S.; $490.00 outside U.S. ● *Reviews of Modern Physics*, quarterly. Contains major reviews of physics topics. **Price:** $85.00 in U.S.; $105.00 outside U.S. ● Membership Directory, biennial. **Conventions/Meetings:** annual meeting (exhibits) - always April ● annual meeting - always March. 2009 Mar. 16-20, Pittsburgh, PA; 2010 Mar. 21-25, Dallas, TX.

7501 ■ Institute of Physics

c/o Institute of Physics Publishing
The Public Ledger Bldg.
150 S Independence Mall W, Ste.929
Philadelphia, PA 19106
Ph: (215)627-0880
Fax: (215)627-0879
E-mail: info@ioppubusa.com
URL: http://www.iop.org
Contact: Steve Moss, Chief Operating Off.

Founded: 1970. **Multinational. Description:** Promotes physics education research and understanding of other scientists. **Computer Services:** Online services, search service, information portal. **Publications:** *Physics World*, monthly. Magazine. **Price:** $520.00/year for library and corporate. Alternate Formats: online.

7502 ■ International Union of Pure and Applied Physics - USA (IUPAP)

c/o Jackie Beamon-Kiene
Amer. Physical Soc.
One Physics Ellipse
College Park, MD 20740-3844
Ph: (301)209-3269

Fax: (301)209-0865
E-mail: beamon@aps.org
URL: http://www.iupap.org
Contact: Alan Astbury, Pres.
Founded: 1922. **Members:** 48. **Staff:** 1. **Budget:** $370,000. **Languages:** English, French. **Description:** National physics committees or groups of physicists from 48 countries. Aims to stimulate and promote international cooperation in physics and the use of international symbols, units, nomenclature, and standards; provides assistance in organizing committees and meetings; encourages research and publication of papers and tables. Fosters free circulation of scientists. **Commissions:** Astrophysics; Atomic and Molecular Physics and Spectroscopy; Biological; Computational Physics; Cosmic Rays; Development; International Commission for Acoustics; International Commission for Optics; International Commission on General Relativity and Gravitation; Low Temperature Physics; Magnetism; Mathematical Physics; Nuclear Physics; Particles and Fields; Physics Education; Plasma Physics; Quantum Electronics; Semiconductors; Statistical Physics; Structure and Dynamics of Condensed Matter; Symbols, Units Nomenclature, Atomic Masses and Fundamental Constants. **Publications:** *General Report*, triennial ● *News-Bulletin*, periodic. **Conventions/Meetings:** triennial general assembly.

7503 ■ JILA
c/o University of Colorado
Box 440 UCB
Boulder, CO 80309-0440
Ph: (303)492-7789
Fax: (303)492-5235
E-mail: reception.desk@jila.colorado.edu
URL: http://jilawww.colorado.edu
Contact: Julia Bachinski, Exec. Off.
Founded: 1962. **Members:** 225. **Budget:** $7,500,000. **Description:** Serves as interdisciplinary institute for research and graduate education in the physical sciences. Operates in conjunction of CU and the National Institute of Standards and Technology (NIST). Engages in ultra-low-temperature atomic collisions, including Bose Einstein condensation; the chemistry of small molecules; laser physics and precision measurements; spectroscopy and spectral line broadening; solar physics; and astrophysical observation and measurements.

7504 ■ National Society of Black Physicists (NSBP)
6704G Lee Hwy.
Arlington, VA 22205
Ph: (703)536-4207
Fax: (703)536-4203
E-mail: conference.info@nsbp.org
URL: http://www.nsbp.org
Contact: Peter Delfyett, Pres.-Elect
Founded: 1977. **Membership Dues:** undergraduate student, $10 (annual) ● professional, $85 (annual) ● graduate student, $20 (annual). **Local Groups:** 10. **Description:** Individuals interested in promoting the well being of African Americans in physics. Addresses the needs of black physicists; works to create opportunities for minorities in the field. Sponsors mentor program and lectures on research findings. Disseminates information. **Libraries: Type:** reference. **Holdings:** archival material. **Awards:** Career Achievement Award. **Frequency:** annual. **Type:** recognition ● Graduate Dissertation Award. **Frequency:** annual. **Type:** monetary ● **Frequency:** annual. **Type:** scholarship. **Recipient:** for undergraduate students. **Affiliated With:** American Association of Physics Teachers. **Publications:** Newsletter, periodic. **Conventions/Meetings:** annual conference.

7505 ■ National Society of Hispanic Physicists (NSHP)
c/o David J. Ernst, Admin. Exec. Off.
Vanderbilt Univ.
Physics and Astronomy Dept.
1807 Sta. B
Nashville, TN 37235
Ph: (615)343-0483
E-mail: david.j.ernst@vanderbilt.edu
URL: http://www.hispanicphysicists.org
Contact: David J. Ernst, Admin. Exec. Off.
Founded: 1995. **Membership Dues:** student, retired, $10 (annual) ● regular, $25 (annual) ● life, $200 ● institutional, $100 (annual) ● life - institutional, $1,000. **Description:** Promotes the professional well-being and recognizes the accomplishments of Hispanic physicists within the scientific community of the United States. Seeks to develop and support efforts to increase opportunities for Hispanics in physics. Seeks to increase the number of practicing Hispanic physicists. Promotes the study of physics among Hispanic students. **Publications:** *The Hispanic Physicist*. Newsletter. **Price:** included in membership dues. Alternate Formats: online.

7506 ■ Neutron Scattering Society of America (NSSA)
c/o Dr. Greg S. Smith, Membership Sec.
PO Box 2008, MS6393
Oak Ridge, TN 37831-6393
Ph: (865)241-1742
E-mail: smithgs1@ornl.gov
URL: http://www.neutronscattering.org
Contact: Dr. Greg S. Smith, Membership Sec.
Founded: 1992. **Members:** 1,000. **Description:** Represents the interests of individuals dedicated to the advancement of neutron scattering research in the United States. Promotes and broadens the use of neutron scattering in science, engineering and technology. Seeks to bring together the neutron scattering community of the USA. Provides a forum to discuss scientific issues, major facilities and instrumentation needed for research in neutron scattering. **Awards:** Clifford G. Shull Prize in Neutron Science. **Frequency:** biennial. **Type:** recognition. **Recipient:** for outstanding research in neutron science and leadership promoting the North American neutron scattering community ● NSSA Prize for Outstanding Student Research. **Frequency:** biennial. **Type:** recognition. **Recipient:** for outstanding research in the field of neutron scattering that has been performed as part of a thesis or degree ● NSSA Science Prize. **Frequency:** biennial. **Type:** recognition. **Recipient:** for the most significant scientific contribution within the last five years ● NSSA Sustained Research Prize. **Frequency:** biennial. **Type:** recognition. **Recipient:** for sustained contribution to a scientific subfield or subfields, using neutron scattering techniques.

7507 ■ Overseas Chinese Physics Association (OCPA)
c/o Sun-Yiu Fung, Treas.
PO Box 8743
Newport Beach, CA 92658
Ph: (949)721-8812 (217)244-6039
Fax: (949)721-8812
E-mail: fung@ucr.edu
URL: http://www.ocpaweb.org
Contact: Jen-Chieh Peng, Pres.
Founded: 1990. **Membership Dues:** regular, $20 (annual) ● regular (Mainland Chinese), junior, $10 (annual) ● life, $300 ● life (Mainland Chinese), $150 ● junior (Mainland Chinese), $5 (annual). **Description:** Promotes international understanding and mutual awareness of scientific achievements by physicists all over the world. Promotes physics research and the dissemination of physics and related knowledge through seminars, lectures, professional meetings, workshops and publications. Raises awareness of the achievements of Chinese scientists in physics and related fields. **Awards:** Achievement in Asia Award. **Frequency:** annual. **Type:** recognition. **Recipient:** to a Chinese physicist working in Asia who has made outstanding contributions in physics ● Outstanding Young Researcher Award. **Frequency:** annual. **Type:** recognition. **Recipient:** for a young researcher's contributions in physics. **Telecommunication Services:** electronic mail, jcpeng@uiuc.edu ● electronic mail, fung@earthlink.net. **Publications:** Newsletter, semiannual.

7508 ■ Scientific Committee on Solar Terrestrial Physics (SCOSTEP)
c/o Gang Lu, Scientific Sec.
HAO-NCAR
3080 Center Green
Boulder, CO 80301
Ph: (303)497-1591 (303)497-1554
Fax: (303)497-1589
E-mail: hanchett@ucar.edu
URL: http://www.scostep.ucar.edu
Contact: Prof. M.A. Geller, Pres.
Founded: 1967. **Members:** 400. **Membership Dues:** regular (with 1 unit), $400 (annual) ● regular (with 50 units), $20,000 (annual). **Staff:** 3. **Budget:** $130,000. **National Groups:** 40. **Description:** Countries interested in promoting and coordinating international scientific programs in solar terrestrial physics, the study of the relationship between the sun and earth. **Computer Services:** database, member listing. **Affiliated With:** International Council for Science. **Formerly:** Inter-Union Commission on Solar Terrestrial Physics. **Publications:** *International SCOSTEP NL*, quarterly. Proceedings. Features scientific program activities. **Circulation:** 5,000. Alternate Formats: online ● *STP Newsletter*, annual. Features scientific program activities. **Circulation:** 5,000. Alternate Formats: online. **Conventions/Meetings:** meeting ● quadrennial symposium.

7509 ■ Society of Physics Students (SPS)
c/o American Institute of Physics
One Physics Ellipse
College Park, MD 20740-3843
Ph: (301)209-3007
Fax: (301)209-0839
E-mail: sps@aip.org
URL: http://www.spsnational.org
Contact: Dr. Gary White, Dir.
Founded: 1968. **Members:** 4,500. **Membership Dues:** individual in U.S., $20 (annual) ● individual outside U.S., $30 (annual). **Staff:** 9. **Regional Groups:** 18. **Local Groups:** 590. **Description:** Students and others interested in physics. Promotes educational activities for all students interested in physics through participation in professional physics societies, regional meetings, special programs and encouragement of student research activities. **Awards:** Blake Lilly Prize. **Frequency:** annual. **Type:** recognition. **Recipient:** for feedback from physics outreach programs ● Herbert Levy Memorial Scholarship. **Frequency:** annual. **Type:** recognition. **Recipient:** for a member in any year of undergraduate study ● Marsh W. White Award. **Frequency:** annual. **Type:** recognition. **Recipient:** for projects that popularize physics ● Outstanding Chapter Advisor Award. **Frequency:** annual. **Type:** recognition. **Recipient:** for a chapter advisor who has been nominated by chapter student members ● Outstanding Student Award for Undergraduate Research. **Frequency:** annual. **Type:** recognition. **Recipient:** for members ● Sigma Pi Sigma Undergraduate Research Award. **Frequency:** annual. **Type:** grant. **Recipient:** for physics research projects ● SPS Allied Award. **Type:** recognition. **Recipient:** for chapters supporting physics research projects ● SPS Leadership Scholarships. **Frequency:** annual. **Type:** scholarship. **Recipient:** for students. **Telecommunication Services:** electronic mail, gwhite@aip.org. **Affiliated With:** American Institute of Physics. **Publications:** *Journal of Undergraduate Research in Physics*, semiannual. Contains undergraduate physics research papers. **Price:** included in membership dues. ISSN: 0731-3764. **Circulation:** 10,000 ● *SPS Information Book*, annual. Lists SPS chapter contacts in the United States and Canada. **Price:** free for SPS Chapters; $10.00/year for others. ISSN: 0197-6761. **Circulation:** 700 ● *SPS Observer*, 5/year. Newsletter. Includes meeting calendar, articles on employment, available fellowships and society news. **Price:** free. **Circulation:** 6,000. **Conventions/Meetings:** annual meeting.

Physiology

7510 ■ American Physiological Society (APS)
9650 Rockville Pike
Bethesda, MD 20814-3991

Ph: (301)634-7164
Fax: (301)634-7241
E-mail: mfrank@the-aps.org
URL: http://www.the-aps.org
Contact: Martin Frank PhD, Exec. Dir.

Founded: 1887. **Members:** 10,500. **Membership Dues:** regular, $120 (annual) ● student, $20 (annual) ● affiliate, $75 (annual) ● sustaining associate, bronze level, $750 ● sustaining associate, silver level, $1,500 ● sustaining associate, gold level, $3,000 ● sustaining associate, platinum level, $4,500. **Staff:** 75. **Budget:** $15,000,000. **State Groups:** 6. **Description:** Disseminates information to the scientific community and to the public. Promotes excellence and innovation in physiological research and education. **Libraries: Type:** reference. **Holdings:** archival material. **Awards:** Arthur C. Guyton Award for Excellence in Integrative Physiology. **Frequency:** annual. **Type:** recognition. **Recipient:** for an individual who has demonstrated outstanding research ● Lazaro J. Mandel Young Investigator Award. **Frequency:** annual. **Type:** recognition. **Recipient:** for an individual with outstanding research program in renal physiology ● Ray G. Daggs Award. **Frequency:** annual. **Type:** recognition. **Recipient:** for a physiologist who provides distinguished service to APS ● Shih-Chun Wang Young Investigator Award. **Frequency:** annual. **Type:** recognition. **Recipient:** for an individual with outstanding research program in physiological sciences. **Computer Services:** Mailing lists, mailing list of members. **Committees:** Animal Care and Experimentation; Career Opportunities in Physiology; Education; International Physiology; Liaison with Industry; Porter Physiology Development; Public Affairs; Senior Physiologists. **Sections:** Cardiovascular; Cell and Molecular Physiology; Central Nervous System; Comparative Physiology; Endocrinology and Metabolism; Environmental and Exercise Physiology; Gastrointestinal and Liver Physiology; Neural Control and Autonomic Regulation; Renal; Respiration; Teaching of Physiology; Water and Electrolyte Homeostasis. **Affiliated With:** American Association for the Advancement of Science; Association of American Medical Colleges; Association for Assessment and Accreditation of Laboratory Animal Care International; Federation of American Societies for Experimental Biology; International Union of Physiological Sciences. **Publications:** *Advances in Physiology Education*, annual. Journal. Addresses issues of education in physiology through essays on the direction and scope of physiology training and practical aids to teaching. **Price:** included in membership dues; $30.00 for nonmembers. ISSN: 1043-4046. **Circulation:** 11,000. **Advertising:** accepted. Alternate Formats: online ● *American Journal of Physiology: Cell Physiology*, monthly. Covers normal and abnormal cell function and contemporary and innovative study of cell and general physiology. Includes semiannual index. **Price:** $175.00 for members; $430.00 for nonmembers. ISSN: 0363-6143. **Circulation:** 2,700. **Advertising:** accepted. Alternate Formats: online ● *American Journal of Physiology Consolidated*, monthly. Contains comprehensive coverage of the latest research. **Price:** $860.00 for members; $2,325.00 for nonmembers. ISSN: 0002-9513. **Circulation:** 1,600. **Advertising:** accepted. Alternate Formats: online ● *American Journal of Physiology: Endocrinology and Metabolism*, monthly. Contains the results of original investigations on endocrine and metabolic systems. Includes semiannual index. **Price:** $120.00 for members; $310.00 for nonmembers. ISSN: 0193-1849. **Circulation:** 2,650. **Advertising:** accepted. Alternate Formats: online ● *American Journal of Physiology: Gastrointestinal and Liver Physiology*, monthly. Covers original research on the normal and abnormal function of the alimentary canal and its accessory organs. Includes semiannual index. **Price:** $120.00 for members; $325.00 for nonmembers. ISSN: 0193-1857. **Circulation:** 2,650. **Advertising:** accepted. Alternate Formats: online ● *American Journal of Physiology: Heart and Circulatory Physiology*, monthly. Reports original investigations of the physiology of the heart, blood vessels, and lymphatics; includes experimental and theoretical studies. **Price:** $240.00 for members; $600.00 for nonmembers. ISSN: 0363-6135. **Circulation:** 2,900. **Advertising:** accepted. Alternate Formats: online ● *American Journal of Physiology: Lung Cellular and Molecular Physiology*, monthly. Contains investigative and theoretical papers addressing the molecular, cellular, and morphological aspects of cells. **Price:** $115.00 for members; $295.00 for nonmembers. ISSN: 1040-0605. **Circulation:** 2,650. Alternate Formats: online ● *American Journal of Physiology: Regulatory, Integrative, and Comparative Physiology*, monthly. Covers the relationships between organ systems and the control of physiological processes in the whole organism and on comparative physiology. **Price:** $150.00 for members; $415.00 for nonmembers. ISSN: 0363-6119. **Circulation:** 2,550. **Advertising:** accepted. Alternate Formats: online ● *American Journal of Physiology: Renal, Fluid and Electrolyte Physiology*, monthly. Covers a broad range of topics related to the kidney, urinary tract, and epithelial cell layers as well as the control of body fluid volume. **Price:** $140.00 for members; $310.00 for nonmembers. ISSN: 0363-6127. **Circulation:** 2,800. **Advertising:** accepted. Alternate Formats: microform ● *FASEB Directory*, annual. **Advertising:** accepted. Alternate Formats: online ● *Journal of Applied Physiology*, monthly. Covers the normal and abnormal function of the respiratory system. **Price:** $315.00 for members; $740.00 for nonmembers. **Circulation:** 2,400. **Advertising:** accepted. Alternate Formats: online ● *Journal of Neurophysiology*, monthly. Covers the function of the nervous system. Includes semiannual index; cumulative index available separately. **Price:** $315.00 for members; $840.00 for nonmembers. ISSN: 0161-7567. **Circulation:** 1,600. **Advertising:** accepted. Alternate Formats: online ● *The Nervous System*. Handbooks. Covers physiology and clinical physiology. **Price:** $126.25 for members; $194.25 for nonmembers ● *Physiological Genomics*, quarterly. Journal. Covers a wide variety of studies from human and from information model systems with technique linking genes and pathways to physiology. **Price:** $85.00 for members; $180.00 for nonmembers. **Circulation:** 2,200. **Advertising:** accepted. Alternate Formats: online ● *Physiological Reviews*, quarterly. Journal. Includes annual index with cumulative indexes available separately. **Price:** $120.00 for members; $285.00 for nonmembers. ISSN: 0031-9333. **Circulation:** 2,400. **Advertising:** accepted. Alternate Formats: online ● *The Physiologist*, bimonthly. Journal. Contains book reviews, employment opportunities, obituaries, statistics, and abstracts of annual meetings. **Price:** included in membership dues; $60.00 for nonmembers. ISSN: 0031-9376. **Circulation:** 11,500. **Advertising:** accepted. Alternate Formats: online ● *Physiology*, bimonthly. Journal. Includes brief reviews, news of meetings, symposia, and annual index. **Price:** included in membership dues; $160.00 for nonmembers. ISSN: 0886-1714. **Circulation:** 11,500. **Advertising:** accepted. Alternate Formats: online. **Conventions/Meetings:** annual conference ● annual Experimental Biology - meeting (exhibits) - always April.

7511 ■ Society of General Physiologists (SGP)

PO Box 257
Woods Hole, MA 02543-0257
Ph: (508)540-6719
Fax: (508)540-0155
E-mail: sgp@mbl.edu
URL: http://www.sgpweb.org
Contact: Ms. Susan Shephard, Exec. Sec.

Founded: 1946. **Members:** 1,000. **Membership Dues:** regular, $55 (annual) ● young investigator, $27 (annual). **Description:** Represents biologists interested in fundamental physiological principles and phenomena. **Awards:** Paul F. Cranefield Award. **Frequency:** annual. **Type:** recognition. **Recipient:** for a young investigator who published an outstanding article in the journal for the preceding calendar year ● **Frequency:** annual. **Type:** recognition. **Recipient:** for the best paper in JGP for which the first author was a postdoc, a student-graduate, or undergraduate. **Publications:** *Directory of Members*, annual. Membership Directory. Contains contact information for SGP members, past symposium topics, past officers, and organization bylaws. **Price:** free for members. **Circulation:** 1,000 ● *Journal of General Physiology*, monthly ● *Synapses*, semiannual. Newsletter. Alternate Formats: online. **Conventions/Meetings:** annual symposium - always September in Woods Hole, MA.

Pipes

7512 ■ Intervention and Coiled Tubing Association (ICoTA)

PO Box 1082
Montgomery, TX 77356
Ph: (936)520-1549
Fax: (832)201-9977
E-mail: ababin@icota.com
URL: http://www.icota.com
Contact: Allison Babin, Sec./Admin.

Founded: 1994. **Membership Dues:** corporate, $1,000 (annual) ● individual, $50 (annual). **Multinational. Description:** Seeks to enhance communication, technical expertise and safety, training, competency and industry-accepted practices within the well intervention and coiled tubing industries. Serves as a means of supporting, communicating, and promoting rapid technological advances within the coiled tubing industry. Encourages participation of manufacturers, suppliers, service providers, and end-users of coiled tubing and associated technologies. **Libraries: Type:** open to the public; reference. **Holdings:** archival material, articles, papers, reports. **Subjects:** coiled tubing, drilling, well control, surface equipment. **Telecommunication Services:** electronic mail, jholmes@icota.com.

Plastics

7513 ■ Plastics Institute of America (PIA)

600 Suffolk St.
CVIP, 2nd Fl. S
Lowell, MA 01854
Ph: (978)934-3130 (978)934-2575
Fax: (978)458-4141
E-mail: contactus@plasticsinstitute.org
URL: http://www.plasticsinstitute.org
Contact: Dr. Aldo Crugnola, Exec. Dir.

Founded: 1961. **Members:** 50. **Staff:** 6. **Description:** Serves as an educational and research organization supported on a cooperative basis by companies in the plastics and allied industries. Conducts fundamental research in plastics science and engineering. Carry on educational activities at the graduate school level in these fields. Provides comprehensive technical information to its members. Conducts a graduate level program of education for plastics scientists and engineers, in cooperation with major U.S. universities and colleges involved in polymer science and engineering. **Awards: Type:** fellowship. **Recipient:** for graduate students involved in research projects. **Telecommunication Services:** electronic mail, apanos@plasticsinstitute.org. **Publications:** *Catalog of Polymer Science*, biennial ● *Proceedings of ConstructionPlas '92* ● *Proceedings of FoodPlas Conferences*, annual ● *Proceedings of RecyclingPlas Conferences*, annual ● Annual Report. **Conventions/Meetings:** periodic international conference ● quarterly meeting - always in New York City area.

7514 ■ Society of Plastics Engineers (SPE)

14 Fairfield Dr.
PO Box 403
Brookfield, CT 06804-0403
Ph: (203)775-0471
Fax: (203)775-8490
E-mail: info@4spe.org
URL: http://www.4spe.org
Contact: Susan Oderwald, Exec. Dir.

Founded: 1942. **Members:** 25,000. **Membership Dues:** individual, $125 (annual) ● student, $28 (annual). **Staff:** 41. **Budget:** $8,000,000. **Multinational. Description:** Professional society of plastics scientists, engineers, sales professionals, educators, students and others interested in the design, development, production and utilization of plastics materials, products and equipment. Conducts seminars. Maintains 98 sections. **Libraries: Type:** reference; open to the public. **Holdings:** 1,000; books. **Subjects:** plastics. **Awards:** Founder's Medallion. **Frequency:** annual. **Type:** medal. **Recipient:** for a member who has spearheaded the founding of a new section or division ● Fred O. Conley Award. **Frequency:** annual. **Type:** monetary. **Recipient:** for fundamental contributions to the technology of polymer science and engineering ● John W. Hyatt Award. **Frequency:** annual. **Type:** monetary. **Recipient:** for outstanding achievement in plastics that benefit mankind ● Membership Award. **Frequency:** annual. **Type:** recognition. **Recipient:** for sections or divisions that have achieved the largest membership growth in the past year ● President's Cup. **Frequency:** annual. **Type:** recognition. **Recipient:** for outstanding service to the society ● Research Award. **Frequency:** annual. **Type:** monetary. **Recipient:** for outstanding achievement in plastics research. **Telecommunication Services:** electronic mail, seoderwald@4spe.org. **Committees:** Award; Conference; Credentials; Education; Education Seminar; International Relations; Management Involvement; Membership; New Technology; Plastics Education Foundation; Public Interest; Technical Program; Technical Volumes. **Divisions:** Automotive; Blow Molding; Color and Appearance; Composites; Decorating and Assembly; Electrical and Electronics; Engineering Properties and Structure; European Thermoforming; Extrusion; Injection Molding; Marketing and Management; Medical Plastics; Mold Making and Mold Design; Plastics Analysis; Plastics Environmental; Polymer Modifiers and Additives; Product Design and Development; Rotational Molding; Thermoforming; Thermoplastics Materials and Foams; Thermoset; Vinyl Plastics. **Publications:** *Journal of Vinyl and Additive Technology*, quarterly. Covers problem solving and use of vinyl polymers in plastics; includes graphs, tables and charts. **Price:** $145.00 /year for members; $336.00 /year for nonmembers; $570.00 /year for institutions. ISSN: 1083-5601. **Circulation:** 530 ● *Plastics Engineering*, monthly. Magazine. **Price:** included in membership dues; $160.00 /year for nonmembers. **Advertising:** accepted ● *Polymer Composites*, bimonthly. Journal. Covers developments in reinforced plastics and polymer composites; includes graphs, tables and charts. **Price:** $280.00 /year for members; $610.00 /year for nonmembers; $1,095.00 /year for institutions in U.S., Canada and Mexico; $1,209.00 /year for institutions - international. ISSN: 0272-8397. **Circulation:** 420 ● *Polymer Engineering and Science*, monthly. Journal. Contains symposium papers and translations of foreign technical papers dealing with polymers. **Price:** $330.00 /year for members; $675.00 /year for nonmembers; $1,195.00 /year for institutions. ISSN: 0032-3888 ● *Preprint Volumes*. Book. **Conventions/Meetings:** annual ANTEC - conference, technical (exhibits).

Polar Studies

7515 ■ American Polar Society (APS)

PO Box 300
Searsport, ME 04974
E-mail: icechip@prexar.com
URL: http://www.oaedks.net/amerpolr.html
Contact: Charles Lagerbom, Membership Chm.

Founded: 1934. **Members:** 1,100. **Membership Dues:** in U.S., $15 (annual) ● outside U.S., $17 (annual) ● corporate, $100 (annual) ● life, in U.S., $250 ● life, outside U.S., $270. **Staff:** 1. **Budget:** $16,000. **Multinational. Description:** Individuals in 30 countries interested in the history and exploration of the Arctic and Antarctic regions. Seeks to: act as a clearinghouse of polar information; aid organizers and members of polar expeditions; spread knowledge of the Polar Regions. Keeps abreast of polar expeditions and persons and institutions interested in polar matters. Presents honorary memberships to leaders of polar expeditions. **Libraries: Type:** reference. **Holdings:** 800; books, maps, photographs. **Subjects:** polar regions. **Awards:** Honorary Membership. **Frequency:** periodic. **Type:** recognition. **Publications:** *The Polar Times*, semiannual. Magazine. Contains polar information. **Price:** included in membership dues. **Circulation:** 2,000. **Advertising:** accepted. **Conventions/Meetings:** periodic symposium, polar information (exhibits).

7516 ■ Antarctic and Southern Ocean Coalition (ASOC)

1630 Connecticut Ave. NW, 3rd Fl.
Washington, DC 20009
Ph: (202)234-2480
Fax: (202)387-4823
E-mail: info@asoc.org
URL: http://www.asoc.org
Contact: Jim Barnes, Exec. Dir.

Founded: 1978. **Members:** 244. **Membership Dues:** organization, $100-$10,000 (annual) ● regular, $35 (annual) ● senior citizen, student, $25 (annual) ● family, $100 (annual) ● sustaining, $1,000 (annual). **Staff:** 3. **National Groups:** 26. **Languages:** English, Spanish. **Multinational. Description:** Works to preserve Antarctica by monitoring all activities to ensure minimal environmental impact, and consulting with key users of Antarctica, including scientists, tourists, and governments. Conducts legal and policy research and analysis; produces educational materials; focuses international and scientific community on globally significant research. The Antarctica Project is secretariat to Antarctic and Southern Ocean Coalition, composed of 244 conservation groups in 44 nations. **Libraries: Type:** reference. **Holdings:** archival material, photographs. **Subjects:** Antarctica. **Telecommunication Services:** electronic mail, jimbo0628@mac.com. **Affiliated With:** The Antarctica Project. **Publications:** *ECO*, quarterly. Newsletter. Includes information on current political topics concerning the Antarctic Treaty System. **Price:** $30.00/year. **Circulation:** 1,000 ● Annual Reports, annual. Alternate Formats: online.

7517 ■ The Antarctica Project (TAP)

c/o Antarctic and Southern Ocean Coalition
1630 Connecticut Ave. NW, 3rd Fl.
Washington, DC 20009
Ph: (202)234-2480
Fax: (202)387-4823
E-mail: info@asoc.org
URL: http://www.asoc.org
Contact: Jim Barnes, Exec. Dir.

Founded: 1982. **Members:** 310. **Membership Dues:** regular, $35 (annual) ● senior, student, $25 (annual) ● organization (minimum), family, $100 (annual) ● sustaining, $1,000 (annual) ● organization (maximum), $10,000 (annual). **Staff:** 3. **Regional Groups:** 214. **Description:** Works to preserve Antarctica by monitoring all activities to ensure minimal environmental impact, and consulting with key users of Antarctica, including scientists, tourists, governments. Conducts legal and policy research and analysis; produces educational materials; focuses international and scientific community on globally significant research. Serves as secretariat to Antarctic and Southern Ocean Coalition, composed of 214 conservation groups in 44 nations. **Convention/Meeting:** none. **Libraries: Type:** reference. **Holdings:** archival material, articles, books, photographs. **Subjects:** Antarctica, Southern Ocean. **Affiliated With:** Antarctic and Southern Ocean Coalition. **Publications:** *ECO Newspaper*, 3-4/year. Includes information on current political topics concerning the Antarctic Treaty System. ● Newsletter, quarterly. **Price:** included in membership dues. **Circulation:** 1,500 ● Books ● Videos ● Also publishes briefing materials and other educational items; produces slide shows and posters.

7518 ■ U.S. Antarctic Program (USAP)

Off. of Polar Programs
Natl. Sci. Found.
4201 Wilson Blvd., Rm. 755
Arlington, VA 22203
Ph: (703)292-5111 (703)292-8014
Free: (800)281-8749
Fax: (703)292-9081
E-mail: dfriscic@nsf.gov
URL: http://www.nsf.gov
Contact: Mr. David Friscic, Technical Information Specialist

Founded: 1959. **Staff:** 50. **Budget:** $254,950,000. **Description:** Works to award funds and operational support to scientists at U.S. institutions for research and education in aeronomy, astronomy, astrophysics, biology, medicine, geology, geophysics, glaciology, medicine, meteorology, and ocean sciences. Studies may be conducted at home institutions or in Antarctica and the Southern Ocean at three year-round stations (two coastal, one at the geographic South Pole), at field locations throughout the region, and aboard two ice-capable research ships. **Convention/Meeting:** none. **Libraries: Type:** reference. **Holdings:** 60,000. **Subjects:** Antarctic titles. **Awards:** Antarctic Research. **Frequency:** annual. **Type:** grant. **Recipient:** for intellectual merit, broader impacts. **Additional Websites:** http://www.usap.gov. **Supersedes:** Antarctic Program of the International Geophysical Year. **Publications:** *Antarctic Research NSF 03-551*, annual.

Political Science

7519 ■ Academy of Political Science (APS)

475 Riverside Dr., Ste.1274
New York, NY 10115-1274
Ph: (212)870-2500
Fax: (212)870-2202
E-mail: aps@psqonline.org
URL: http://www.psqonline.org
Contact: Demetrios James Caraley, Pres.

Founded: 1880. **Members:** 8,000. **Membership Dues:** individual, $49 (annual) ● institution, $309 (annual) ● student, $35 (annual). **Staff:** 5. **Description:** Individual members, libraries and institutions. Promotes the cultivation of political science and its application to the solution of political, social, and economic problems. **Libraries: Type:** reference. **Holdings:** archival material. **Computer Services:** Mailing lists. **Publications:** *Political Science Quarterly*. Journal. Provides analysis of contemporary and historical aspects of government, politics, and public affairs. Contains annual article index and book reviews. **Price:** included in membership dues; $13.00/copy for nonmembers. ISSN: 0032-3195. **Circulation:** 8,000. **Advertising:** accepted. Alternate Formats: microform; online. **Conventions/Meetings:** periodic meeting.

7520 ■ American Academy of Political and Social Science (AAPSS)

3814 Walnut St.
Philadelphia, PA 19104-6197
Ph: (215)746-6500 (215)746-7321
Fax: (215)573-3003
E-mail: phyllis.kaniss@sas.upenn.edu
URL: http://www.aapss.org
Contact: Dr. Phyllis Kaniss, Exec. Dir.

Founded: 1889. **Members:** 2,000. **Membership Dues:** individual, $91 (annual) ● student, $52 (annual). **Staff:** 3. **Description:** Professionals and laymen concerned with the political and social sciences and related fields. Promotes the progress of political and social science through publications and meetings. The academy does not take sides in controversial issues, but seeks to gather and present reliable information to assist the public in forming an intelligent and accurate judgment. **Awards:** Fellows. **Frequency:** annual. **Type:** recognition. **Recipient:** for outstanding contributions to the social sciences ● Graduate Fellows. **Frequency:** annual. **Type:** recognition. **Recipient:** for the achievements and promises of tomorrow's outstanding social scientists ● Junior Fellows. **Frequency:** annual. **Type:** recognition. **Recipient:** for undergraduates who have displayed a command of their disciplines' methods and theories, a commitment to improving the human condition, and the promise of making outstanding contributions to social science research in the future ● Undergraduate Research Awards. **Frequency:** annual. **Type:** recognition. **Recipient:** for outstanding scholars among junior fellows. **Telecommunication Services:** electronic mail, jodland@sas.upenn.edu. **Publications:** *The Annals*, bimonthly. Journal. **Price:** $71.00/year; $20.00/single issue. ISSN: 0002-7162. **Advertising:** accepted. **Conventions/Meetings:** annual conference - always spring.

7521 ■ American Political Science Association (APSA)
1527 New Hampshire Ave. NW
Washington, DC 20036-1206
Ph: (202)483-2512
Fax: (202)483-2657
E-mail: apsa@apsanet.org
URL: http://www.apsanet.org
Contact: Michael Brintnall, Exec. Dir.
Founded: 1903. **Members:** 15,000. **Membership Dues:** family, $24 (annual) ● high school teacher, student, unemployed, targeted international, $40 (annual) ● associate, $52 (annual) ● retired (based on income), $35-$57 (annual) ● professional (based on income), $84-$208 (annual) ● life, $3,000. **Staff:** 25. **Budget:** $4,000,000. **Multinational. Description:** College and university teachers of political science, public officials, research workers, and businessmen. Encourages the impartial study and promotes the development of the art and science of government. Develops research projects of public interest and educational programs for political scientists and journalists; seeks to improve the knowledge of and increase citizen participation in political and governmental affairs. Serves as clearinghouse for teaching and research positions in colleges, universities, and research bureaus in the U.S. and abroad and for positions open to political scientists in government and private business; conducts Congressional Fellowship Program. Conducts Committee on Professional Ethic, and Rights and Freedom. Offers placement service. **Libraries: Type:** reference. **Holdings:** articles, reports. **Computer Services:** Mailing lists. **Telecommunication Services:** electronic mail, membership@apsanet.org. **Publications:** *American Political Science Review*, quarterly. Journal. Covers all aspects of political science. **Price:** included in membership dues. ISSN: 0003-0554. **Advertising:** accepted. Alternate Formats: microform ● *Personnel Service*, monthly. Newsletter. Contains lists of job openings at colleges and universities. ● *Perspectives on Politics*, quarterly. Journal. Contains integrative and review essays and book reviews. **Price:** included in membership dues. **Advertising:** accepted ● *PS: Political Science and Politics*, quarterly. Journal. Covers political ideas and professional news. **Price:** included in membership dues. **Advertising:** accepted. **Conventions/Meetings:** annual conference ● annual meeting (exhibits) - always August or September.

7522 ■ Association for Politics and the Life Sciences (APLS)
Utah State Univ.
Political Sci. Dept.
Logan, UT 84322-0725
Ph: (435)797-8104
Fax: (435)797-3751
E-mail: dgoetze@hass.usu.edu
Contact: Dr. David Goetze, Exec. Dir.
Founded: 1980. **Members:** 450. **Membership Dues:** student, $40 (annual) ● non-student, $75 (annual) ● non-student, $145 (biennial) ● non-student, $215 (triennial). **Description:** Individuals and libraries interested in the interaction of human biology and public policy. Promotes exchange of ideas and information among members. Emphasizes study of behavioral biology as it relates to political science and the legal and public policy implications of advances in biotechnology and biomedical technology. **Awards:** Graduate Student Paper Award. **Frequency:** annual. **Type:** recognition. **Recipient:** for the best paper by a graduate student on a topic related to both politics or public policy and one or more of the life sciences. **Telecommunication Services:** electronic mail, peritorep@missouri.edu. **Publications:** *The APLS Directory*, annual. **Price:** included in membership dues; $25.00 for nonmembers; $40.00 for mailing labels ● *APLS News*. Newsletter. **Price:** included in membership dues ● *Politics and the Life Sciences*, semiannual, in March and September. Journal. **Price:** included in membership dues. Alternate Formats: online. Also Cited As: *PLS*. **Conventions/Meetings:** annual meeting - in August or early September.

7523 ■ Caucus for a New Political Science (CNPS)
c/o Meredith Reid Sarkees
4802 Wyoming Way
Crystal Lake, IL 60012-2037
Ph: (815)444-0692
Fax: (815)444-0692
E-mail: sarkees@sbcglobal.net
URL: http://www.apsanet.org/~new
Contact: Christine Kelly PhD, Chair
Founded: 1967. **Members:** 500. **Membership Dues:** professional, $20 (annual). **Budget:** $12,000. **Description:** Students, teachers, researchers, and organizers committed to create a democratic, egalitarian society. Aims to advance critical and alternative political science and to protect members' interests. Seeks to join forces with the broader social movement in America. Maintains speakers' bureau. **Libraries: Type:** reference. **Holdings:** archival material. **Awards:** Charles A. McCoy Distinguished Career Award. **Frequency:** annual. **Type:** recognition. **Recipient:** for progressive political scientist who, has a long career as a writer, teacher and activist ● Christian Bay Award. **Frequency:** annual. **Type:** monetary. **Recipient:** for writer of the best section paper, presented at annual meeting of American Political Science Association ● Frances Fox Piven and Richard Cloward Activism Award. **Frequency:** annual. **Type:** monetary. **Recipient:** to a community group in the region of the annual meeting that exemplifies the commitment of the new political science section to make political science relevant to the struggle for a better world ● Michael Harrington Book Award. **Frequency:** annual. **Type:** monetary. **Recipient:** for best book, presented at annual meeting of American Political Science Association. **Computer Services:** Mailing lists, listserv for political discussions. **Telecommunication Services:** electronic mail, kellyc@wpunj.edu. **Boards:** Editorial. **Committees:** Awards Program; Executive; Journal. **Also Known As:** New Political Science. **Publications:** *New Political Science*, quarterly. Journal. Includes scholarly articles and book reviews. **Price:** $30.00 for members; $220.00 for institutions; $60.00 for nonmembers. ISSN: 0739-3148. **Circulation:** 250. **Advertising:** accepted. **Conventions/Meetings:** annual conference, in conjunction with the American Political Science Association (exhibits) - late August or early September.

7524 ■ Conference for the Study of Political Thought (CSPT)
c/o Prof. Sharon Snowiss, Sec.-Treas.
Pitzer Coll.
Dept. of Political Sci.
1050 N Mills Ave.
Claremont, CA 91711
Ph: (212)854-3955 (909)607-3178
Fax: (909)621-8481
E-mail: cspt.chair@columbia.edu
URL: http://www.columbia.edu/cu/polisci/cspt
Contact: David Johnston, Chair
Founded: 1968. **Members:** 350. **Membership Dues:** untenured, $18 (annual) ● tenured, $30 (annual) ● graduate student, $12 (annual). **Local Groups:** 27. **Description:** Professors and graduate students of political philosophy; political theorists, philosophers, and historians. Holds conferences that provide a continuous forum for discussion of theory and leading works, and presentation and criticism of papers. Facilitates graduate student participation; takes measures to help unemployed scholars remain in the discipline. **Libraries: Type:** reference. **Holdings:** archival material. **Awards:** Kelly Prize. **Frequency:** annual. **Type:** recognition ● Spitz Prize. **Frequency:** annual. **Type:** recognition. **Telecommunication Services:** electronic mail, cspt.treas@columbia.edu. **Publications:** *CSPT International Newsletter*, semiannual. Provides information on programs and conferences and chapter news. Includes listing of awards, lectures, fellowships, and book reviews. **Price:** included in membership dues ● *Proceedings of Annual Conference*, annual. **Conventions/Meetings:** annual conference - always April ● regional meeting and workshop.

7525 ■ Inter-University Consortium for Political and Social Research (ICPSR)
Univ. of Michigan Inst. for Social Res.
PO Box 1248
Ann Arbor, MI 48106-1248
Ph: (734)647-5000 (734)647-2200
Fax: (734)647-8200
E-mail: netmail@icpsr.umich.edu
URL: http://www.icpsr.umich.edu
Contact: Myron P. Gutmann, Dir.
Founded: 1962. **Members:** 400. **Membership Dues:** associate/community college, $1,600 (annual) ● specialized institution, BA university, $2,000 (annual) ● master's comprehensive I and II, $6,500 (annual) ● doctoral research (intensive), $9,000 (annual) ● doctoral research (extensive), $15,000 (annual). **Staff:** 100. **Budget:** $5,000,000. **Multinational. Description:** Cooperative partnership among institutions of higher education represented by libraries and departments of political science, history, sociology, and related disciplines concerned with the systematic study of political and social behavior. Seeks to facilitate research in the social sciences by: developing a major data repository providing access to basic research materials; conducting an advanced training program providing formal course work in methodology, research techniques, and substantive fields for advanced graduate students and faculty; stimulating new research projects; consulting in computer support needs. Makes available technical facilities to scholars from member institutions. Data repository holdings include survey, election, census, and roll call data, representing nations throughout the world. **Awards:** Warren E. Miller Award. **Frequency:** annual. **Type:** recognition. **Recipient:** for distinguished service to the social sciences ● William H. Flanigan Award. **Frequency:** annual. **Type:** recognition. **Recipient:** for distinguished contributions as part of ICPSR. **Computer Services:** Online services, web-based data retrieval service. **Telecommunication Services:** electronic mail, membership@icpsr.umich.edu. **Formerly:** (1975) Interuniversity Consortium for Political Research. **Publications:** *Handbook for Official Representatives* ● *Summer Program Brochure*, annual ● Annual Report, annual ● Bulletin, semiannual ● Also publishes codebooks and summaries that document and outline content of data collections. **Conventions/Meetings:** biennial Meeting of Official Representatives - always fall, Ann Arbor, MI.

7526 ■ Joint Center for Political and Economic Studies (JCPES)
1090 Vermont Ave. NW, Ste.1100
Washington, DC 20005-4928
Ph: (202)789-3500
Fax: (202)789-6390
E-mail: general@jointcenter.org
URL: http://www.jointcenter.org
Contact: Ralph B. Everett, Pres./CEO
Founded: 1970. **Staff:** 40. **Budget:** $6,500,000. **Description:** Conducts research and analyses on public policy issues of concern to African Americans and other minorities, promotes their involvement in the governance process, and operates programs that create coalitions within minority, business, and other diverse communities. Headquartered in Washington, DC, with offices in Johannesburg, South Africa, the Center focuses on politics and elections, social issues, economic policy issues, minority business and international affairs. Founded in 1970 by black intellectuals, professionals and elected officials, and established in South Africa in 1993. **Departments:** Information Resources; Research. **Affiliated With:** National Black Caucus of Local Elected Officials. **Formerly:** (1990) Joint Center for Political Studies. **Publications:** *Black Elected Officials: A Statistical Summary*, annual ● *Focus*, monthly. Magazine. **Circulation:** 18,000 ● Annual Report ● Also publishes

analyses of public policy issues, statistical studies, and monographs. **Conventions/Meetings:** annual dinner.

7527 ■ Public Choice Society (PCS)
c/o Jo Ann S. Burgess
George Mason Univ.
Buchanan House MSN 1E6
4400 Univ. Dr.
Fairfax, VA 22030-4444
Ph: (703)993-2337
Fax: (703)993-2334
E-mail: pubchsoc@gmu.edu
URL: http://www.pubchoicesoc.org
Contact: Randall G. Holcombe, Pres.
Founded: 1965. **Members:** 1,300. **Membership Dues:** professor, $30 (annual) ● student, $15 (annual). **Staff:** 2. **Description:** Professors and other academicians in the fields of economics, political science, sociology and law. Seeks the application of economic ideas, concepts, and methods in political science and political economy. **Libraries: Type:** reference. **Holdings:** archival material. **Awards:** Duncan Black Prize. **Frequency:** annual. **Type:** monetary. **Recipient:** for best article in Public Choice Journal. **Formerly:** (1967) Committee on Non-Market Decision Making. **Publications:** *Public Choice*, quarterly. Journal. **Conventions/Meetings:** annual meeting.

7528 ■ Walter Bagehot Research Council on National Sovereignty (WBRC)
Address Unknown since 2008
Founded: 1972. **Members:** 450. **Staff:** 2. **Budget:** $25,000. **Description:** Individuals, libraries, organizations, and political groups supporting the ideal of nationhood - "of enforceable, deeply felt national unity, culminating in government by discussion." Walter Bagehot (1826-77), British economist after whom the council is named, is considered the ideal's most enlightened advocate in the English-speaking world. Functions as an educational foundation studying past, present, and possible future status of nation-state international relations. Promotes regional groups, especially on university campuses. Plans to form speakers' bureau and present annual awards. **Libraries: Type:** reference. **Holdings:** 10,000; archival material, articles, books, monographs, papers, video recordings. **Subjects:** art, history, literature, politics, philosophy, drama. **Awards:** The Walter Bagehot/Henry Paolucci Annual Book Award. **Frequency:** annual. **Type:** monetary. **Also Known As:** The Bagehot Council. **Publications:** *State of the Nation*, periodic. Newsletter. **Price:** $25.00. **Circulation:** 2,000 ● Publishes panel proceedings and special publications.

7529 ■ Women's Caucus for Political Science (WCPS)
c/o Ronnee Schreiber, Treas.
SDSU Dept. of Political Sci.
5500 Campanile Dr.
San Diego, CA 92182
Ph: (803)777-7442
E-mail: rschreib@mail.sdsu.edu
URL: http://www.cas.sc.edu/poli/caucus/main.html
Contact: Laura Woliver, Pres.
Founded: 1969. **Members:** 900. **Budget:** $12,000. **Regional Groups:** 5. **Description:** Women professionally trained in political science. Purposes are to: upgrade the status of women in the profession of political science; promote equal opportunities for women political scientists for graduate admission, financial assistance in such schools, and in employment, promotion, and tenure. Advances candidates for consideration for APSA offices and committees. **Awards:** Alice Paul Dissertation Award. **Frequency:** annual. **Type:** monetary. **Recipient:** for the best dissertation proposal by a woman ● Mary Lepper Award. **Frequency:** annual. **Type:** monetary. **Recipient:** for a nonacademic political scientist ● Mentor Awards. **Frequency:** triennial. **Type:** recognition. **Recipient:** for outstanding mentor to women in political science. **Telecommunication Services:** electronic mail, woliver@sc.edu. **Committees:** Alize Paul; Archives; Assessment of Progress in the Profession; Barnett Award; Chilly Climate; Graduate Student; Legal Defense; Lepper Award; Mentor Award; Nominating; Textbook; Women of Color. **Publications:** *WCPS Quarterly*. Newsletter. Includes information about the association and employment opportunities. **Price:** included in membership dues. **Advertising:** accepted. **Conventions/Meetings:** annual meeting, held in conjunction with the American Political Science Association.

Portuguese

7530 ■ American Portuguese Engineering and Architecture Society (APEAS)
56 Cong. St.
Newark, NJ 07105
Ph: (973)344-9224
Fax: (973)344-9225
E-mail: contact@apeas.org
URL: http://www.apeas.org
Membership Dues: regular, $120 (annual) ● associate, $60 (annual) ● student, $20 (annual). **Description:** Protects, promotes and enhances professional integrity and solidarity among engineers and architects of Portuguese heritage residing in the USA. Develops and supports technical and commercial activities among its members. Provides a forum for social, professional, economic and political empowerment of architects and engineers of Portuguese heritage. **Publications:** Newsletter, published following a general meeting. Contains information about the meeting agenda, meeting location and other related information. **Conventions/Meetings:** monthly meeting - every 3rd week.

Power

7531 ■ Electric Power Research Institute (EPRI)
3420 Hillview Ave.
Palo Alto, CA 94304
Ph: (650)855-2121
Free: (800)313-3774
E-mail: orders@epri.com
URL: http://www.epri.com
Contact: Jeffry E. Sterba, Chm.
Founded: 1973. **Staff:** 750. **Multinational. Description:** Organizations involved in power generation, delivery, sales or related services worldwide. Works to create solutions to benefit members, customers, and society. **Programs:** Business Critical Technology; Proprietary Ventures. **Formerly:** (2002) Electronic Power Research Institute. **Publications:** *EPRI Journal*, quarterly. Magazine. Offers insights on issues of importance to the electric power industry. Alternate Formats: online.

7532 ■ National Association of Power Engineers (NAPE)
1 Springfield St.
Chicopee, MA 01013
Ph: (413)592-6273
Fax: (413)592-1998
E-mail: napenatl@verizon.net
URL: http://www.powerengineers.com
Contact: Michael H. Kaplan, Pres.
Founded: 1882. **Members:** 3,500. **Membership Dues:** individual, $80 (annual) ● life, $1,500. **Staff:** 5. **Regional Groups:** 9. **State Groups:** 10. **Local Groups:** 100. **Description:** Professional society of power and stationary engineers; associate members are sales engineers and teachers of any phase of engineering. Areas of interest include air conditioning, compressed air, electric power, refrigeration, steam, and water. Promotes education in the power engineering areas. Secures and enforces engineers' license laws to prevent the destruction of life and property in the generation and transmission of power and for the conservation of fuel resources of the nation. **Libraries: Type:** open to the public. **Subjects:** power engineering. **Awards:** Henry D. Cozens Scholarship. **Frequency:** annual. **Type:** scholarship. **Recipient:** for a member or a son/daughter of member. **Computer Services:** Mailing lists, of members. **Committees:** License Law; Scholarship. **Publications:** *National Engineer*, bimonthly. **Price:** $25.00/year; $3.00/issue; $70.00/3 years. **Advertising:** accepted ● Also publishes pamphlets and educational material. **Conventions/Meetings:** annual convention - always July.

Primates

7533 ■ Gorilla Foundation (GF)
PO Box 620530
Woodside, CA 94062
Ph: (650)216-6450
Free: (800)634-6273
Fax: (650)365-7906
E-mail: contactus@koko.org
URL: http://www.koko.org
Contact: Dr. Francine Patterson, Pres./Research Dir.
Founded: 1976. **Members:** 25,000. **Membership Dues:** individual, $25 (annual). **Staff:** 20. **Budget:** $2,000,000. **Description:** Promotes conservation, propagation, and behavioral study of apes, particularly gorillas. Currently researching in the area of inter-species communication and the acquisition of sign language potential in gorillas. Aims to create an ape sanctuary and research center in Maui. **Libraries: Type:** reference. **Holdings:** 200; books, periodicals. **Subjects:** gorillas' natural history and cognitive development (primates) language. **Also Known As:** (1999) Koko.org. **Publications:** *Gorilla*, semiannual. Journal. Covers interspecies communication and primates; includes verbatim conversations with the signing gorillas Koko and Michael. **Price:** included in membership dues; $25.00 /year for nonmembers. **Circulation:** 35,000 ● *Koko's Kitten* (in English and French). Video. **Price:** $15.95 ● Newsletters.

Professionals

7534 ■ International Society of Six Sigma Professionals (ISSSP)
10446 N 74th St., Ste.140
Scottsdale, AZ 85258
Ph: (480)368-7083
Fax: (480)585-0640
E-mail: info@isssp.com
URL: http://www.isssp.com
Contact: Roxanne O'Brasky, Pres.
Founded: 1997. **Membership Dues:** regular, $200 (annual). **Multinational. Description:** Promotes the adoption, advancement and integration of Six Sigma in business. Encourages advocacy and awareness efforts and professional recognition and development. Serves as an information and referral source. **Publications:** *iSixSigma Magazine*. **Price:** included in membership dues.

Programming Languages

7535 ■ FORTH Interest Group (FIG)
c/o John Rible, Treas.
317 California St.
Santa Cruz, CA 95060-4215
Ph: (831)458-0399 (650)757-3113
E-mail: pres@forth.org
URL: http://www.forth.org
Contact: George Perry, Pres.
Founded: 1978. **Members:** 1,200. **Staff:** 2. **Local Groups:** 40. **Description:** Represents individuals interested in learning and/or programming in the computer language FORTH. (FORTH is a threaded interpretative computer language that allows the operator programming flexibility.) Promotes the utilization and modification of FORTH. Conducts specialized education programs. **Telecommunication Services:** electronic mail, geoperry@gmail.com ● electronic mail, treas@forth.org. **Committees:** FORTH Modification Lab. **Publications:** *Conference Proceedings*, annual ● *FORTH Dimensions*, bimonthly. **Conventions/Meetings:** annual conference ● periodic meeting (exhibits).

7536 ■ League for Programming Freedom (LPF)
PO Box 9171
1 Kendall Sq., No. 143
Cambridge, MA 02139
Ph: (617)243-4091
E-mail: lpf@lpf.ai.mit.edu
URL: http://lpf.ai.mit.edu
Contact: Jack Larsen, Pres.
Founded: 1989. **Members:** 700. **Membership Dues:** professional, $42 (annual) ● student, $10 (annual) ● organization, $100 (annual) ● individual, $21 (annual). **Description:** Professors, students, business personnel, programmers, software companies, and computer users. Works to protect the freedom to write computer software, which the group feels is threatened by certain interface copyright lawsuits and by software patents. **Computer Services:** database, software patents. **Publications:** *Programming Freedom*, bimonthly. Book. **Price:** free for members; $21.00 for nonmembers. **Circulation:** 700. Alternate Formats: online.

7537 ■ Rexx Language Association (RexxLA)
PO Box 14472
Research Triangle Park, NC 27709-4472
E-mail: president@rexxla.org
URL: http://www.rexxla.org
Contact: Lee Peedin, Pres.
Founded: 1990. **Membership Dues:** full, $24 (annual) ● student, $12 (annual). **Multinational. Description:** Represents individuals interested in Rexx programming language. Promotes the use and understanding of the Rexx programming language. Facilitates networking and collaboration among members. Works to serve the needs of the Rexx community. **Telecommunication Services:** electronic mail, vicepresident@rexxla.org. **Conventions/Meetings:** annual symposium.

7538 ■ Special Interest Group on Ada (SIGAda)
c/o Dr. John W. McCormick, Chm.
Univ. of Northern Iowa
Cmpt. Sci. Dept.
Cedar Falls, IA 50614-0507
Ph: (319)273-6056
Fax: (319)273-7123
E-mail: mccormic@cs.uni.edu
URL: http://www.sigada.org
Contact: Dr. John W. McCormick, Chm.
Founded: 1981. **Members:** 3,707. **Description:** Special interest group of the Association for Computing Machinery made up of computer professionals. Disseminates information about Ada (a programming language) including its usage, environment, standardization, and implementation. **Publications:** *Ada Letters*, bimonthly. Newsletter. **Conventions/Meetings:** annual conference (exhibits).

7539 ■ Special Interest Group on Algorithms and Computation Theory (SIGACT)
c/o Richard Ladner, Chm.
Univ. of Washington
Dept. of Cmpt. Sci. and Engg.
Box 352350
Seattle, WA 98195
Ph: (206)543-9347
Fax: (206)543-2969
E-mail: ladner@cs.washington.edu
URL: http://sigact.acm.org
Contact: Richard Ladner, Chm.
Founded: 1969. **Members:** 2,242. **Membership Dues:** ACM, $15 (annual) ● non ACM, $18 (annual). **Budget:** $96,000. **Description:** Individuals interested in theories of computer sciences and analysis of algorithms (step-by-step procedures for solving mathematical problems). Focuses with automata and formal languages and their applications, formal semantics of programming languages, theories of computing and computational models, computational complexity, and theoretical principles of programming language design and implementation. **Awards:** Best Student Paper Award. **Frequency:** annual. **Type:** recognition ● SIGACT Godel Prize. **Frequency:** annual. **Type:** recognition. **Recipient:** for outstanding papers in the area of theoretical computer science. **Formerly:** Special Interest Group on Automata and Computability Theory; (2001) Special Interest Group on Algorithms Computability Theory. **Publications:** *SIGACT News*, quarterly. Newsletter. Alternate Formats: online. **Conventions/Meetings:** annual Computational Geometry - conference ● annual POPL: Principles of Programming Languages - convention ● annual STOC: Symposium on the Theory of Computing - convention.

7540 ■ Special Interest Group on the APL and J Languages (SIGAPL)
c/o Association for Computing Machinery
1515 Broadway
New York, NY 10036
Ph: (212)869-7440 (212)626-0500
Free: (800)342-6626
Fax: (212)944-1318
E-mail: chair_sigapl@acm.org
URL: http://www.sigapl.org
Contact: Guy R. Larocque, Chm.
Founded: 1960. **Members:** 1,500. **Membership Dues:** regular, $30 (annual) ● student, $15 (annual). **Local Groups:** 7. **Description:** Serves as special interest group of the Association for Computing Machinery. Represents computer professionals including users and developers interested in the programming language APL. Promotes and provides for the exchange of information on APL. **Awards:** Kenneth E. Iverson for Outstanding Contribution to APL. **Frequency:** annual. **Type:** recognition. **Recipient:** to individuals who have worked to further the role of APL. **Telecommunication Services:** electronic mail, guy.larocque@nrcan.gc.ca. **Publications:** *APL Quote Quad*, quarterly. Newsletter. **Advertising:** accepted ● Also publishes conference proceedings. **Conventions/Meetings:** annual international conference (exhibits).

7541 ■ Special Interest Group on Programming Languages (SIGPLAN)
c/o Kathleen S. Fisher, Chair
1 River Oaks Pl.
San Jose, CA 95134
E-mail: kfisher@research.att.com
URL: http://www.sigplan.org
Contact: Kathleen S. Fisher, Chair
Founded: 1966. **Members:** 4,000. **Membership Dues:** student, $15-$40 (annual) ● regular, $25-$50 (annual). **Staff:** 1. **Local Groups:** 1. **Description:** Serves as s special interest group of the Association for Computing Machinery (see separate entry). Represents computer professionals. Promotes the advancement of the state of the art in computer programming languages. Areas of interest include: programming methodology; programming language definition; principles and techniques of compiler implementation; general purpose and application oriented languages; programming language design; teaching of programming languages; standards. **Awards:** Most Influential PLDI Paper Award. **Frequency:** annual. **Type:** recognition. **Recipient:** for the best paper ● Most Influential POPL Paper Award. **Frequency:** annual. **Type:** recognition. **Recipient:** for the best paper ● SIGPLAN Distinguished Service Award. **Frequency:** annual. **Type:** monetary. **Recipient:** for value and degree of service to the programming language community ● SIGPLAN Doctoral Dissertation Award. **Frequency:** annual. **Type:** recognition. **Recipient:** for outstanding doctoral dissertations ● SIGPLAN Programming Languages Achievement Award. **Frequency:** annual. **Type:** monetary. **Recipient:** for significant and lasting contribution to the field of programming languages. **Publications:** *SIGPLAN Notices*, monthly. Newsletter. **Price:** $57.00. **Conventions/Meetings:** periodic conference.

Property Rights

7542 ■ Consumer Project on Technology (CPT)
1621 Connecticut Ave. NW, No. 500
Washington, DC 20009
Ph: (202)332-2670
Fax: (202)332-2673
E-mail: james.love@cptech.org
URL: http://www.cptech.org
Contact: James Love, Dir.
Founded: 1995. **Staff:** 6. **Description:** Provides advocacy work that focuses on intellectual property rights and health care, electronic commerce, and competition policy. **Computer Services:** Mailing lists.

Psychology

7543 ■ Association for Research in Personality (ARP)
c/o R. Chris Fraley, Sec.-Treas./Webmaster
Dept. of Psychology
Univ. of Illinois
603 E Daniel St.
Champaign, IL 61820
Ph: (217)333-3486
Fax: (217)244-5876
E-mail: rcfraley@uiuc.edu
URL: http://www.personality-arp.org
Contact: R. Chris Fraley, Sec.-Treas./Webmaster
Founded: 2001. **Membership Dues:** regular, $40 (annual) ● graduate student, post-doctoral, $30 (annual). **Description:** Aims to advance research and the scientific study of personality development, structure and dynamics. Seeks to bring together the diversity of scholars whose research contributes to the understanding of personality structure, development and dynamics. Serves as an integrative forum for different scientific disciplines in research. **Publications:** *Journal of Research in Personality*, bimonthly. Features articles, brief reports and reviews concerning significant issues relating to personality. **Price:** included in membership dues. ISSN: 0092-6566.

7544 ■ International Society for Dialogical Science (ISDS)
c/o Prof. Vincent W. Hevern
Le Moyne Coll.
Psychology Dept.
1419 Salt Springs Rd.
Syracuse, NY 13214
E-mail: hevern@lemoyne.edu
URL: http://web.lemoyne.edu/~hevern/ISDS/index.htm
Contact: Prof. Vincent W. Hevern, Contact
Founded: 2002. **Multinational. Description:** Furthers the development of dialogical self theory and other theories which deal directly with the relationship between self and dialogue. Promotes the development of scientific methods for assessment, promotion and evaluation of dialogical processes in connection to the development of the self. Stimulates and facilitates interaction between researchers and practitioners. **Publications:** *International Journal of Dialogical Science*. Alternate Formats: online. **Conventions/Meetings:** annual International Conference on the Dialogical Self - 2008 Aug. 26-29, Cambridge, United Kingdom.

7545 ■ International Society for Ecological Psychology (ISEP)
c/o William M. Mace
Dept. of Psychology
300 Summit St.
Hartford, CT 06106-3100
Ph: (860)297-2343
Fax: (860)297-2538
E-mail: william.mace@trincoll.edu
URL: http://www.trincoll.edu/depts/ecopsyc/isep
Contact: William M. Mace, Contact
Founded: 1981. **Members:** 330. **Membership Dues:** regular, $80 (annual) ● student/reduced income, $24 (annual). **National Groups:** 7. **Multinational. Description:** Promotes ecological psychology. **Publications:** *Ecological Psychology*, quarterly. Journal. **Price:** included in membership dues. ISSN: 1040-7413. **Circulation:** 550. Alternate Formats: online ● *Resources for Ecological Psychology*. Books. **Conventions/Meetings:** biennial International Conference on Perceiving and Action - meeting (exhibits) - late July or August.

7546 ■ International Society for Self and Identity (ISSI)
c/o Jennifer Crocker, Pres.
Univ. of Michigan
Dept. of Psychology
530 Church St.
Ann Arbor, MI 48109-1043
E-mail: jcrocker@umich.edu
URL: http://www.psych.neu.edu/ISSI
Contact: Jennifer Crocker, Pres.

Members: 600. **Membership Dues:** professional, $35 (annual) ● student, $25 (annual). **Multinational. Description:** Represents social and behavioral scientists. Promotes the scientific study of the human self. Facilitates communication and collaboration among researchers who study Self and Identity. **Awards:** Early Career Award. **Frequency:** annual. **Type:** recognition. **Recipient:** to a researcher who has made such contributions within 10 years of obtaining a PhD ● Lifetime Career Award. **Frequency:** annual. **Type:** recognition. **Recipient:** to a researcher who has made a sustained contribution to the understanding of self and identity. **Publications:** *Self & Identity*, quarterly. Journal. Brings together work on self and identity undertaken by researchers across different subdisciplines within psychology. ISSN: 1529-8868. Alternate Formats: online.

7547 ■ Society for Chaos Theory in Psychology and Life Sciences (SCTPLS)
PO Box 484
Pewaukee, WI 53072
Fax: (414)288-5333
E-mail: ivelisselazzarini@creighton.edu
URL: http://www.societyforchaostheory.org
Contact: Ivelisse Lazzarini, Pres.

Founded: 1991. **Members:** 365. **Membership Dues:** regular, $75 (annual) ● student, $60 (annual). **Staff:** 23. **Multinational. Description:** Researchers, theoreticians, and practitioners. Examines the application of "dynamical systems theory, far-from-equilibrium thermodynamics, self-organization, neural nets, evolutionary computation, fractals, cellular automata, related forms of chaos, catastrophes, bifurcations, nonlinear dynamics, and complexity theories to psychology and the life sciences". **Awards:** Humanitarian Award. **Frequency:** periodic. **Type:** recognition. **Recipient:** for the application of nonlinear science to a socially relevant purpose ● Outstanding Service to the Society. **Frequency:** periodic. **Type:** recognition. **Recipient:** to a society member who has made outstanding contributions to the society's goals and functioning capabilities. **Committees:** Conference-related; Education; Membership; Publications. **Publications:** *Nonlinear Dynamics, Psychology, and Life Sciences*, quarterly. Journal. **Price:** $220.00 /year for institutions. Alternate Formats: online ● Newsletter, quarterly. Contains SCTPLS news, news from members and other news in nonlinear science of possible interest to the members. **Circulation:** 365. **Advertising:** accepted ● Books. **Conventions/Meetings:** annual international conference, scientific and business meeting - 2008 Aug. 8-10, Richmond, VA.

7548 ■ Society for the History of Psychology (SHP)
c/o Deborah F. Johnson, Pres.-Elect
PO Box 9300
Portland, ME 04104-9300
E-mail: djohnson@mail.maine.edu
URL: http://shp.yorku.ca
Contact: Deborah F. Johnson, Pres.-Elect

Membership Dues: regular, $35 (annual) ● student, $25 (annual). **Multinational. Description:** Promotes the scholarly approach to the history of psychology. Seeks to extend the awareness and appreciation of the history of psychology as an aid to understanding contemporary psychology, psychology's relation to other scientific fields and its role in society. Supports programs intended to improve scholarly communication on the origins of psychology. **Awards: Frequency:** annual. **Type:** recognition. **Recipient:** for best student paper ● **Frequency:** annual. **Type:** recognition. **Recipient:** for best paper published. **Affiliated With:** American Psychological Association. **Publications:** *History of Psychology*, quarterly. Journal. Contains scholarly articles on the history of psychology. **Price:** included in membership dues.

7549 ■ Society for Personality and Social Psychology (SPSP)
c/o Christie Marvin, Office Mgr.
Dept. of Psychology
Cornell Univ.
239 Uris Hall
Ithaca, NY 14853
Ph: (607)254-5416
Fax: (607)255-8433
E-mail: spsp@stolaf.edu
URL: http://www.spsp.org
Contact: Harry Reis, Pres.

Founded: 1974. **Members:** 4,000. **Membership Dues:** regular, $38 (annual) ● student, retired, $25 (annual). **Description:** Represents social and personality psychologists. Conducts and disseminates research on social and personality psychology. Sponsors Diversity Programs. **Awards:** The Donald T. Campbell Award. **Frequency:** annual. **Type:** recognition. **Recipient:** for distinguished contributions in social psychology ● The Henry A. Murray Award. **Frequency:** annual. **Type:** recognition. **Recipient:** for distinguished contributions to the study of lives ● The Jack Block Award. **Frequency:** annual. **Type:** recognition. **Recipient:** for distinguished contributions in personality psychology ● Student Publication Award. **Frequency:** annual. **Type:** recognition. **Recipient:** for excellence in research; to the best student-authored paper published in an SPSP journal ● Theoretical Innovation Prize. **Frequency:** annual. **Type:** recognition. **Recipient:** for the most theoretically innovative article, book chapter, or unpublished manuscript of the year. **Computer Services:** database, social psychology network. **Publications:** *Dialogue*, semiannual. Newsletter. Contains constructive exchange of views and informs members about current developments in the field particularly about the activities of the society. **Price:** included in membership dues. **Circulation:** 3,700. **Advertising:** accepted ● *The Forum*, quarterly. Newsletter. Includes interview with a randomly selected student from the listserv. Alternate Formats: online ● *Personality and Social Psychology Bulletin*, monthly. Journal. Contains original empirical papers in all areas of personality and social psychology. **Price:** $575.00 for regular institution; $50.00 each, for regular institution; $102.00 /year for nonmembers; $11.00 each, for nonmembers ● *Personality and Social Psychology Review*, quarterly. Journal. Contains original theoretical papers and conceptual review articles in personality and social psychology. **Price:** $126.00 /year for nonmembers outside U.S.; included in membership dues; $50.00 /year for individuals in U.S. and Canada; $170.00 /year for institutions in U.S. and Canada. ISSN: 1088-8683. **Conventions/Meetings:** annual conference.

7550 ■ Society for Psychological Anthropology (SPA)
c/o Thomas Weisner, Pres.
Departments of Psychiatry and Anthropology
Univ. of California
760 Westwood Blvd.
Los Angeles, CA 90024-1759
Ph: (310)794-3632 (808)956-7343
Fax: (310)794-6297
E-mail: tweisner@ucla.edu
URL: http://www.aaanet.org/SPA
Contact: Thomas Weisner, Pres.

Founded: 1977. **Membership Dues:** current member of American Anthropological Association, $45 (annual) ● student, $20 (annual). **Description:** Promotes cultural, psychological, and social interrelations at all levels. **Awards:** Boyer Prize for Contributions to Psychoanalytic Anthropology. **Frequency:** annual. **Type:** recognition. **Recipient:** for outstanding published contribution to the field of psychoanalytic anthropology ● Condon Prize for Best Student Essay in Psychological Anthropology. **Frequency:** annual. **Type:** recognition. **Recipient:** for the best student's essay in psychological anthropology ● Lifetime Achievement Award. **Frequency:** biennial. **Type:** recognition. **Recipient:** for career-long contributions to psychological anthropology that have substantially influenced the field and its development ● Stirling Prize for Best Published Work in Psychological Anthropology. **Frequency:** biennial. **Type:** recognition. **Recipient:** to a previously published work that made an outstanding contribution to any area of psychological anthropology. **Computer Services:** Mailing lists, email distribution. **Affiliated With:** American Anthropological Association. **Publications:** *Ethos*, quarterly. Journal. **Price:** $50.00 /year for individuals; $71.00 /year for institutions ● *Leadership Handbook* ● Annual Report, annual. **Conventions/Meetings:** biennial meeting.

7551 ■ Society for Vocational Psychology (SVP)
c/o Rasheed Ali, Communications Off.
Univ. of Iowa
Div. of Psychological and Quantitative Foundations
361 Lindquist Ctr.
Iowa City, IA 52242
Ph: (319)335-5495
E-mail: saba-ali@uiowa.edu
URL: http://www.div17.org/vocpsych
Contact: Rasheed Ali, Communications Off.

Founded: 1996. **Description:** Encourages, promotes and facilitates contributions to research, teaching, practice and public interest in vocational psychology and career interventions. Promotes quality research and practice of vocational psychology and career counseling. Supports the diversity of characteristics, work settings, roles and activities of counselling psychologists involved in vocational psychology and career intervention. **Awards: Frequency:** annual. **Type:** recognition. **Recipient:** for outstanding contributions of members. **Affiliated With:** American Psychological Association. **Publications:** *Vocational Psychology News*. Newsletter. Contains news and updates about the organization and its activities. **Price:** free. Alternate Formats: online.

Quality Control

7552 ■ American Society for Quality (ASQ)
PO Box 3005
Milwaukee, WI 53201-3005
Ph: (414)272-8575
Free: (800)248-1946
Fax: (414)272-1734
E-mail: help@asq.org
URL: http://www.asq.org
Contact: Paul E. Borawski, Exec. Dir./Chief Strategic Off.

Founded: 1946. **Members:** 121,000. **Membership Dues:** regular, $119 (annual) ● associate, $69 (annual) ● forum/division, $29 (annual) ● student, $25 (annual). **Staff:** 215. **Budget:** $40,000,000. **Local Groups:** 251. **Description:** Individuals and organizations dedicated to the ongoing development, advancement, and promotion of quality concepts, principles, and technologies. Through its Education Development Department, offers courses in quality engineering, reliability engineering, managing for quality, management of quality costs, quality audit-development and administration, management of the inspection function, probability and statistics for engineers and scientists, and product liability and prevention. Offers personnel listing service. **Libraries: Type:** reference. **Holdings:** books, periodicals. **Subjects:** quality. **Awards:** Brumbaugh Award. **Frequency:** annual. **Type:** recognition ● E.J. Lancaster Award. **Frequency:** annual. **Type:** recognition ● E.L. Grant Award. **Frequency:** annual. **Type:** recognition ● Edwards Medal. **Frequency:** annual. **Type:** medal ● Ishikawa Medal. **Frequency:** annual. **Type:** medal ● Shewhart Medal. **Frequency:** annual. **Type:** medal. **Computer Services:** Mailing lists, labels. **Boards:** Auditing; Awards; Bylaws; Financial Advisory; International Cooperation; Nominating; Professional Ethics and Qualifications; Research Advisor; Staff Compensation and Benefits; Strategic Planning; Technology Advisory. **Committees:** Community Quality; Product Safety and Liability Prevention; Public Sector Quality

Improvement Network. **Divisions:** Architectural/Engineering and Construction; Automotive; Aviation, Space, and Defense; Biomedical; Chemical and Process Industries; Customer-Supplier; Education; Electronics; Energy and Environmental Quality; Food, Drug, and Cosmetic; Health Care; Human Resources; Inspection; Measurement Quality; Quality Audit; Quality Management; Reliability; Service Industries; Software; Statistics; Textile and Needle Trades. **Formerly:** (1997) American Society for Quality Control. **Publications:** *Journal of Quality Technology*, quarterly. Covers the technical aspects of quality control, reliability and related disciplines. **Price:** $30.00 /year for members in U.S.; $49.00 /year for members outside U.S.; $45.00 /year for nonmembers in U.S.; $100.00 /year for institutions in U.S. ● *Quality Engineering*, quarterly. Journal. Examines in-depth, practical applications of quality technology for engineers. **Price:** $34.75 /year for members in U.S.; $51.25 /year for members outside U.S. ● *Quality Management Journal*, quarterly. **Price:** $50.00 /year for members in U.S.; $74.00 /year for members outside U.S.; $75.00 /year for nonmembers in U.S.; $130.00 /year for institutions in U.S. ● *Quality Progress*, monthly. Magazine. Features in-depth articles describing the application of innovative methods. **Price:** included in membership dues; $80.00 /year for nonmembers in U.S.; $110.00 /year for nonmembers outside U.S.; $120.00 /year for institutions in U.S. **Advertising:** accepted ● *Technical Congress Transactions*, annual ● *Technometrics*, quarterly. Journal. Focuses on statistics for the physical, chemical and engineering sciences. **Price:** $30.00 /year for members. **Conventions/Meetings:** annual Quality Congress (exhibits) - always May.

7553 ■ International Academy for Quality (IAQ)

c/o ASQ Global Development
600 N Plankinton Ave.
PO Box 3005
Milwaukee, WI 53201
Ph: (414)272-8575
Fax: (414)765-8671
E-mail: tborzon@asq.org
URL: http://iaq.asq.org
Contact: Tito Conti, Pres.

Founded: 1972. **Members:** 69. **Languages:** English, French. **Description:** Elected academicians with experience in managing the quality control or reliability activities of an enterprise, specialists in quality control and reliability techniques, and experts in management in 25 countries. Promotes research into the philosophy, theory, and practice of achieving quality and reliability of both products and services. Works to improve the use of world resources and to develop international understanding. Fosters discussion. Serves as a coordinating body for technical activities; provides information service. **Committees:** Policy; Public Relations. **Publications:** *The Best on Quality IAQ-Bookseries*, annual. Includes membership directory. **Price:** $50.00 for members ● *Index of Periodical Literature on Quality Control and Reliability*, quarterly ● Also publishes a quarterly index of periodical literature on quality control and reliability. **Conventions/Meetings:** annual meeting, in conjunction with the ASQ Quality Conference ● annual meeting, in conjunction with the European Organization for Quality annual conference ● annual regional meeting.

7554 ■ Statistical Process Controls (SPC)

5908 Toole Dr., Ste.C
Knoxville, TN 37919
Ph: (865)584-5005
Free: (800)545-8602
Fax: (865)588-9440
E-mail: fwheeler@spcpress.com
URL: http://www.spcpress.com
Contact: Dr. Donald J. Wheeler, Founder

Founded: 1982. **Staff:** 5. **Nonmembership. For-Profit. Multinational. Description:** Individuals and companies interested in implementing statistical process control to optimize their efficiency and product quality. (Statistical process control entails the measurement of the elements of a process in order to reduce variation in its execution.) Seeks to reestablish U.S. industry in competitive world markets. Provides research and technical assistance to members; works to enhance professionalism among members by granting certification in statistical process control; serves as a forum for the exchange of information and ideas. Offers referral resources; conducts surveys, plant tours, problem identification and alternatives in statistical process control. Examines candidates for operational and facilitator certification. Operates speaker's bureau; compiles statistics. **Libraries: Type:** reference. **Holdings:** 250. **Awards:** Federal Quality Award. **Type:** recognition ● Malcolm Baldridge Award. **Type:** recognition. **Telecommunication Services:** electronic mail, spcservice@spcpress.com. **Committees:** Education and Certification Operator and Facilitator; Publicity; Training. **Affiliated With:** Society of Manufacturing Engineers. **Formerly:** (2005) Statistical Process Control Society. **Publications:** *SPC INK*, monthly. Newsletter. Contains news and information about books, products, seminars, and articles. **Price:** free. **Conventions/Meetings:** annual conference (exhibits) ● monthly meeting, for chapters ● seminar ● symposium.

7555 ■ Team and Workplace Excellence Forum

PO Box 3005
Milwaukee, WI 53201-3005
Ph: (414)272-1734
Free: (800)248-1946
Fax: (414)272-1734
E-mail: help@aqp.org
URL: http://www.asq.org/teamwork
Contact: Paul E. Burawski, Exec. Dir./Chief Strategic Off.

Founded: 1977. **Members:** 4,000. **Staff:** 20. **Budget:** $3,100,000. **Local Groups:** 30. **Description:** Works to promote the ideas of involvement, empowerment and workplace democracy. Disseminates information to members through the internet, publications, conferences and educational events. **Libraries: Type:** open to the public. **Holdings:** 6,000; articles, books, periodicals. **Subjects:** participation, employee involvement, teams, quality. **Awards:** National Team Excellence Award. **Frequency:** annual. **Type:** recognition. **Computer Services:** Mailing lists, of members and topical searches for related information on web site. **Telecommunication Services:** electronic mail, info@apq.org. **Formerly:** Association for Quality and Participation; (1987) International Association of Quality Circles. **Publications:** *Annual Spring Conference Transactions*. Books. Alternate Formats: online; CD-ROM ● *The Journal for Quality and Participation*, quarterly. Discusses improving and expanding the knowledge and practice of quality circles and employee involvement processes; includes products/services guide. **Price:** included in membership dues; $45.00 /year for nonmembers in U.S., with online membership; $70.00 /year for nonmembers outside U.S., with online membership; $65.00 /year for nonmembers in Canada. ISSN: 1040-9602. **Circulation:** 5,000. **Advertising:** accepted. Also Cited As: *Quality Circles Journal* ● *News for A Change*, 9/year. Newsletter. Concerns employee involvement, quality circles, and self-managed teams in improving quality, productivity, and motivation. **Price:** included in membership dues; $45.00 for nonmembers. **Circulation:** 5,000. **Advertising:** accepted ● *Transactions of the AQP Annual Conference and Resource Mart* ● Books ● Newsletters ● Surveys ● Videos ● Also publishes training materials. **Conventions/Meetings:** annual Spring Conference and Resource Mart (exhibits) - always spring.

Radiation

7556 ■ Council on Ionizing Radiation Measurements and Standards (CIRMS)

PO Box 1238
Duluth, GA 30096
Ph: (770)622-0026
Fax: (770)622-0026
E-mail: knardi@cirms.org
URL: http://www.cirms.org
Contact: Ms. Katy Nardi, Exec. Sec.

Founded: 1991. **Membership Dues:** corporate sponsor, $500 (annual) ● government sponsor, non-profit organization sponsor, $250 (annual) ● individual, $50 (annual). **Description:** Promotes advancement in radiation measurements and related standards. Seeks to address all issues concerning ionizing radiation. Provides an open forum for dialogue on all aspects of ionizing radiation. **Awards:** Student Awards. **Frequency:** annual. **Type:** recognition. **Recipient:** to students who will be presenting their work at the annual meeting. **Publications:** *National Needs in Ionizing Radiation Measurements and Standards*, triennial. Report. **Price:** $30.00 per copy, plus shipping and handling. Alternate Formats: CD-ROM ● Newsletter. Alternate Formats: online.

7557 ■ Radiation Research Society (RRS)

PO Box 7050
Lawrence, KS 66044
Free: (800)627-0326
Fax: (785)843-1274
E-mail: info@radres.org
URL: http://www.radres.org
Contact: Mark W. Dewhirs PhD, Pres.

Founded: 1952. **Members:** 1,600. **Membership Dues:** active, $140 (annual) ● associate, $125 (annual) ● scholar-in-training, $25 (annual) ● institutional, $1,000 (annual) ● corporate, $1,250 (annual). **Description:** Professional society of biologists, physicists, chemists, and physicians contributing to knowledge of radiation and its effects. Promotes original research in the natural sciences relating to radiation; facilitates integration of different disciplines in the study of radiation effects. **Publications:** *Radiation Research*, monthly. Journal. Reports original research in the natural sciences relating to radiation. **Price:** $68.00 for members; $720.00 /year for institutions in U.S. and Canada; $820.00 /year for institutions outside U.S. and Canada. ISSN: 0033-7587. **Advertising:** accepted ● *rrNEWS*, quarterly. Newsletter. Alternate Formats: online ● Membership Directory, annual. **Conventions/Meetings:** annual congress (exhibits).

7558 ■ RadTech International North America

7986 Old Georgetown Rd., Unit 8D
Bethesda, MD 20814
Ph: (240)497-1242
Fax: (240)209-2340
E-mail: uveb@radtech.org
URL: http://www.radtech.org
Contact: Petra L'Abbe, Pres.

Founded: 1986. **Members:** 800. **Membership Dues:** major corporate supplier, $7,450 (annual) ● expanding corporate supplier, $3,950 (annual) ● growing corporate supplier, $1,950 (annual) ● developing corporate supplier, $950 (annual) ● individual corporate supplier, $75 (annual) ● corporate end user, $1,000 (annual) ● individual end user, $200 (annual) ● individual affiliate, $85 (annual). **Staff:** 5. **Budget:** $500,000. **Description:** Individuals and organizations involved in the use of Ultraviolet (UV) and Electron Beam (EB) technology; suppliers of equipment and chemicals used in processing. Promotes the use and improvement of UV/EB technology. Serves as an international forum for the exchange of ideas and technological advancements. Encourages the use of UV/EB technology to increase productivity, save energy and decrease pollution. Conducts educational seminars. **Computer Services:** Online services. **Committees:** EHS; Marketing; RadTech Editorial; Technical; UV Measurement. **Publications:** *Conference Proceedings*, biennial ● *Introductory UV/EB Primer Book* ● *RadTech Regulatory News*, quarterly. Newsletter. Reports the latest developments on regulations affecting the UV and EB industry. **Price:** included in membership dues ● *RadTech Report*, bimonthly. Journal. Includes technical papers, articles, and industry news. **Price:** included in membership dues; $60.00 /year for nonmembers; $95.00 /year for nonmembers outside U.S. ISSN: 1056-0793. **Circulation:** 2,000. **Advertising:** accepted ● Books. **Conventions/Meetings:**

biennial RadTech Conference and Exhibition, world's largest UV/EB conference and exhibition (exhibits).

Religion

7559 ■ Anabaptist Sociology and Anthropology Association (ASAA)
c/o James P. Hurd, Chm.
Bethel Univ.
Dept. of Anthropology and Sociology
3900 Bethel Dr.
St. Paul, MN 55112
Ph: (651)638-6329 (315)267-2041
E-mail: hurd@bethel.edu
URL: http://cas.bethel.edu/dept/anthropology/asaa
Contact: James P. Hurd, Chm.
Membership Dues: regular, $20 (annual) ● benefactor, $50 (annual) ● sustaining, $100 (annual). **Description:** Represents sociologists and anthropologists who either embrace or study the several Christian movements descended from the Anabaptist movement of the 16th century. Facilitates communication and fellowship among persons with affiliation or interest in the Anabaptist tradition, and whose work involves the application of sociological and anthropological perspectives. **Committees:** Steering. **Publications:** *ASAA Newsletter*, semiannual.

Research

7560 ■ American Institutes for Research (AIR)
1000 Thomas Jefferson St. NW
Washington, DC 20007
Ph: (202)403-5000
Free: (877)334-3499
Fax: (202)403-5001
E-mail: inquiry@air.org
URL: http://www.air.org
Contact: Sol H. Pelavin, Pres./CEO
Founded: 1946. **Staff:** 1,000. **Multinational. Description:** Promotes analyses based on methods of the behavioral and social sciences, focusing on education, health, individual and organizational performance, and quality of life. **Programs:** Education and Human Development; Education Assessment; Health; International Development. **Publications:** Newsletter, quarterly. Alternate Formats: online ● Reports. Alternate Formats: online ● Annual Report, annual. Alternate Formats: online.

7561 ■ Association for Applied Community Researchers (ACCRA)
PO Box 100127
Arlington, VA 22210
Ph: (703)522-4980
Fax: (703)522-4985
E-mail: sam@accra.org
URL: http://www.accra.org
Contact: Kenneth E. Poole PhD, Exec.Dir.
Founded: 1961. **Members:** 500. **Membership Dues:** research, $250 (annual) ● organizational, $500 (annual). **Staff:** 2. **Budget:** $400,000. **Description:** Aims to promote excellence in community and economic research by working to improve data availability, enhance data quality, and foster learning about regional economic analytic methods through professional networks, training, advocacy, research, and delivering innovative products and services. **Libraries: Type:** reference. **Holdings:** 1,700; archival material, articles, books, monographs, papers, reports. **Subjects:** economic development research. **Awards:** Council for Community and Economic Research Award. **Frequency:** annual. **Type:** recognition. **Recipient:** for excellence in research. **Computer Services:** Mailing lists ● online services. **Formerly:** (1995) American Chamber of Commerce Researchers Association. **Publications:** *ACCRA Cost of Living Index*, quarterly. **Circulation:** 2,500 ● *Applied Research in Economic Development*, biennial. Journal. Contains peer-reviewed articles in applied research. **Price:** $35.00. **Circulation:** 150. **Advertising:** accepted. Alternate Formats: online ● *Research in Review*. Newsletter. Provides tips on research applications and methods. **Conventions/Meetings:** annual conference (exhibits) - June.

7562 ■ Association of Independent Research Institutes (AIRI)
c/o DAI Management, Inc.
PO Box 844
Westminster, MD 21158
Ph: (410)751-8900
Fax: (410)751-2662
E-mail: hq@airi.org
URL: http://www.airi.org
Contact: David Issing, Contact
Founded: 1975. **Members:** 89. **Membership Dues:** institute (with less than $2 million annual research revenues), $500 (annual) ● institute (with less than $6 million annual research revenues), $1,200 (annual) ● institute (with less than $10 million annual research revenues), $2,400 (annual) ● institute (with less than $20 million annual research revenues), $3,600 (annual) ● institute (with $20 million or more annual research revenues), $4,800 (annual). **Staff:** 3. **Description:** Works to conduct independent scientific investigation in biomedical science. Provides mutual assistance for common problems; apprises members of federal government issues affecting research institutes. **Publications:** none.

7563 ■ Association of Research Directors (ARD)
c/o Stephen H. Kolison, Jr., Chm.-Elect
Tennessee State Univ.
3500 John A. Merritt Blvd.
Nashville, TN 37209-1561
Ph: (615)963-2194
Fax: (615)963-5532
E-mail: skolison@tnstate.edu
URL: http://www.umes.edu/ard
Contact: Alfred L. Parks, Chm.
Founded: 1972. **Members:** 50. **Membership Dues:** general, $65 (annual). **Description:** Works to coordinate most of the food and agricultural research activities among the 1890 Land-Grant Colleges and Universities and USDA, and other federal and state agencies and private industry. Coordinates research program planning and budgeting together with the Experiment Station Committee on Organization and Policy (ESCOP), USDA and OMB. Develops and monitors legislation and cooperates with the appropriate national bodies. **Committees:** Budget; Marketing and Advocacy; Planning; Regional Research. **Publications:** Membership Directory, annual. **Conventions/Meetings:** monthly meeting - always in New York City area.

7564 ■ Carnegie Institution of Washington
1530 P St. NW
Washington, DC 20005
Ph: (202)387-6400 (202)387-6404
Fax: (202)387-8092
E-mail: president@ciw.edu
URL: http://www.carnegieinstitution.org
Contact: Richard A. Meserve, Pres.
Founded: 1902. **Staff:** 200. **Description:** Conducts fundamental research and pre-doctoral and postdoctoral training in the fields of plant biology, astronomy, developmental biology and the earth and planetary sciences at: the Observatories, Pasadena, CA; Las Campanas Observatory, Chile; Geophysical Laboratory, Washington, DC; Department of Terrestrial Magnetism, Washington, DC; Department of Plant Biology and Global Ecology, Stanford, CA; and Department of Embryology, Baltimore, MD. **Libraries: Type:** reference. **Holdings:** 1,200; books. **Subjects:** basic science. **Awards:** In-Resident Fellowships. **Type:** fellowship. **Recipient:** for postdoctoral and pre-doctoral residents. **Publications:** *Carnegie Institution of Washington Yearbook*, annual ● *Carnegie Science*, 3/year. Newsletter ● *Monographs Series*, periodic ● *Perspectives in Science*, periodic.

7565 ■ Center for Ergonomic Research
Benton Hall, Miami Univ.
Oxford, OH 45056
E-mail: dainofmj@muohio.edu
URL: http://www.units.muohio.edu/psychology/cogsci/ergocenter
Contact: Marvin Dainoff PhD, Dir.
Founded: 1983. **Description:** Conducts research and educational programs on ergonomics. **Conventions/Meetings:** periodic meeting.

7566 ■ Council of American Overseas Research Centers (CAORC)
PO Box 37012
Washington, DC 20013-7012
Ph: (202)633-1599
Fax: (202)786-2430
E-mail: caorc@caorc.org
URL: http://www.caorc.org
Contact: Dr. Mary Ellen Lane, Exec. Dir.
Founded: 1981. **Members:** 19. **Budget:** $3,250,000. **Multinational. Description:** Consortium of American centers of advanced research in Cyprus, Italy, Pakistan, Egypt, Jordan, Israel, Greece, Tunisia, Turkey, Senegal, Morocco, Mexico, Bangladesh, Cambodia, India, Iran, Sri Lanka, West Bank/Gaza and Yemen. Mediates the exchange of scholarly and operational information; encourages joint research projects among the centers and between the centers and host countries; provides publicity for the centers and achievements; acts as a voice of support in government and private sectors; assists in founding new centers. Plans to provide support for conferences, publications, and interregional studies. **Awards:** Multi-Country Research Fellowship Program. **Frequency:** annual. **Type:** grant. **Recipient:** for U.S. Doctoral candidates and PhD scholars. **Telecommunication Services:** electronic mail, lane.maryellen@caorc.org. **Publications:** Newsletter, quarterly. Alternate Formats: online.

7567 ■ Executive Search Roundtable (ESR)
PO Box 3565
Grand Central Sta.
New York, NY 10163
Ph: (212)439-4630
E-mail: info@executivesearchroundtable.org
URL: http://executivesearchroundtable.org/ESR
Contact: Carol Purcell, Pres.
Founded: 1979. **Members:** 500. **Membership Dues:** individual, $125 (annual). **Staff:** 9. **Multinational. Description:** Recruiting professionals from executive search, corporate recruiting, and independent consultants, dedicated to research and search execution. Provides perspective on knowledge and skills of executive search execution and research, as well as best practices, professional development and networking opportunities. **Awards:** ESRA Award. **Frequency:** annual. **Type:** recognition. **Recipient:** for excellence in research. **Publications:** *Directory of Research and Search Consultants*, annual. Contains independent contract search services. **Price:** $100.00 for members; $150.00 for nonmembers ● *On Target*, quarterly. Newsletter. **Conventions/Meetings:** monthly board meeting and meeting, with education, training sessions, industry speakers and vendors serving search community exhibits ● annual meeting.

7568 ■ Industrial Research Institute (IRI)
2200 Clarendon Blvd., Ste.1102
Arlington, VA 22201
Ph: (703)647-2580
Fax: (703)647-2581
E-mail: bernstein@iriinc.org
URL: http://www.iriinc.org
Contact: Edward Bernstein, Pres.
Founded: 1938. **Members:** 285. **Membership Dues:** company, $5,600 (annual). **Staff:** 12. **Budget:** $3,000,000. **Description:** Manufacturers and industrial firms maintaining industrial research laboratories. Identifies and promotes effective techniques for the organization and management of research, development, and engineering in support of technological innovation. **Awards:** IRI Achievement Award. **Frequency:** annual. **Type:** recognition. **Recipient:** for individual innovation and creativity ● IRI Medal. **Frequency:** annual. **Type:** medal. **Recipient:** for leadership of technological innovation ● Maurice Holland Award. **Frequency:** annual. **Type:** recognition. **Re-**

cipient: for the best paper in research technology management. **Committees:** Advanced Programs; Federal Science and Technology; International; Plans and Policies; Pre-College Education; Research-on-Research; Seminar; Study Groups for Innovation Leaders; University Relations. **Publications:** *Industrial Research Institute—Annual Report*. Includes information about member companies and their representatives. **Price:** free ● *Research-Technology Management*, bimonthly. Journal. Includes book reviews. **Price:** $65.00 /year for individuals; $150.00 /year for institutions. **Conventions/Meetings:** annual conference ● semiannual meeting.

7569 ■ Inner Light Foundation
PO Box 750265
Petaluma, CA 94975
Ph: (707)765-2200
E-mail: bettyilf@aol.com
URL: http://www.innerlight.org
Contact: Betty Bethards, Contact
Founded: 1969. **Description:** "Strives to bring about positive changes in the world." Offers a free meditation technique. **Publications:** Newsletter. **Circulation:** 14,000. Alternate Formats: online. **Conventions/Meetings:** semiannual convention.

7570 ■ Institute of Environmental Sciences and Technology (IEST)
5005 Newport Dr., Ste.506
Rolling Meadows, IL 60008-3841
Ph: (847)255-1561 (847)981-0100
Fax: (847)255-1699
E-mail: iest@iest.org
URL: http://www.iest.org
Contact: Julie Kendrick CAE, Exec. Dir.
Founded: 1953. **Members:** 1,000. **Membership Dues:** senior, active, $165 (annual) ● full-time student, $30 (annual). **Staff:** 9. **Budget:** $900,000. **Local Groups:** 25. **Multinational. Description:** Technical engineers, scientists, and educators that serves members and the industries they represent (simulating, testing, controlling, and teaching the environments of earth and space), through education and the development of recommended practices and standards. **Computer Services:** Mailing lists. **Divisions:** Contamination Control; Design, Test-and Evaluation; Product Reliability. **Absorbed:** (1973) American Association for Contamination Control. **Formed by Merger of:** (1994) Institute of Environmental Engineers; Society of Environmental Engineers. **Formerly:** (1999) Institute of Environmental Sciences. **Publications:** *Institute of Environmental Sciences and Technology—Proceedings*, annual ● *Journal of the Institute of Environmental Sciences and Technology*, annual. **Advertising:** accepted ● *Recommended Practices* ● Monographs. **Conventions/Meetings:** annual ESTECH - meeting and conference (exhibits).

7571 ■ International Association for Relationship Research (IARR)
c/o Rebecca Adams, Ed.
PO Box 26170
Greensboro, NC 27402-6170
Ph: (336)334-3578
Fax: (336)334-5283
E-mail: personal_relationships@uncg.edu
URL: http://www.iarr.org
Contact: Rebecca Adams, Ed.
Members: 700. **Membership Dues:** regular, $90 (annual) ● student, $60 (annual) ● associate, domestic partner, $30 (annual). **Multinational. Description:** Represents individuals who are engaged in various disciplines including communication, counseling, education, family studies and child development, gerontology, human sciences, psychology, anthropology, sociology, and philosophy. Seeks to stimulate and support the scientific study of personal relationships. Encourages the application of research findings concerning personal relationships. **Publications:** *Journal of Social and Personal Relationships*, bimonthly. **Price:** included in membership dues ● *Personal Relationships*, quarterly. Journal. **Price:** included in membership dues ● Newsletter, semiannual. **Price:** included in membership dues. Alternate Formats: online ● Membership Directory. **Price:** free for members. Alternate Formats: online. **Conventions/Meetings:** biennial conference - 2008 July 17-20, Providence, RI.

7572 ■ International Society for Presence Research (ISPR)
c/o Matthew Lombard, Pres.
Temple Univ.
Dept. of Broadcasting, Telecommunications, and Mass Media
Annenberg Hall (011-00)
Philadelphia, PA 19122
Ph: (215)204-7182
Fax: (215)204-5402
E-mail: ispr@ispr.info
URL: http://ispr.info
Contact: Matthew Lombard, Pres.
Founded: 2002. **Multinational. Description:** Aims to advance the study of telepresence and promote the importance of its emerging technological applications. Supports academic research related to the concept of telepresence, commonly referred to as a sense of 'being there' in a virtual environment. Serves as a resource of information on all matters pertaining to the concept of presence. **Telecommunication Services:** electronic mail, lombard@temple.edu.

7573 ■ Qualitative Research Consultants Association (QRCA)
1000 Westgate Dr., Ste.252
St. Paul, MN 55114
Ph: (651)290-7491
Free: (888)674-7722
Fax: (651)290-2266
E-mail: inquiries@qrca.org
URL: http://www.qrca.org
Contact: Sharon Livingston, Pres.
Founded: 1983. **Members:** 930. **Membership Dues:** individual, $270 (annual). **Staff:** 6. **Budget:** $2,000,000. **Regional Groups:** 18. **Multinational. Description:** Represents principals and employees of independent market and social Research companies who design, analyze, and conduct qualitative research. Strives to enhance the professional stature of qualitative research; promotes high professional standards in the field; seeks to heighten awareness and appreciation of the merit of research methods and applications used in the trade. Conducts workshops on issues of relevance to members and their clients; directs research to assess impressions and usage of qualitative research. **Libraries: Type:** reference. **Holdings:** audio recordings, video recordings. **Subjects:** qualitative research. **Committees:** By-Laws; Conference; Field Practices; Library; Membership; Newsletter; Professional Standards; Public Relations; Research Methodology; Website. **Publications:** *Facilities and Service Directory*, annual ● *Membership Roster*, annual. Membership Directory ● *QRCA Connections*, monthly. Newsletter. Alternate Formats: online ● *QRCA VIEWS*, quarterly. Magazine. Features ideas and tools for qualitative research. **Advertising:** accepted. Alternate Formats: online. **Conventions/Meetings:** annual conference (exhibits) - in October.

7574 ■ Research Program at Earthwatch Institute
3 Clock Tower Pl., Ste.100
PO Box 75
Maynard, MA 01754
Ph: (978)461-0081
Free: (800)776-0188
Fax: (978)461-2332
E-mail: info@earthwatch.org
URL: http://www.earthwatch.org/research
Contact: Whitney L. Johnson, Chm.
Founded: 1971. **Membership Dues:** individual, $35 (annual) ● dual, $60 (annual) ● sustaining, $250 (annual) ● life, $1,000. **Multinational. Description:** Reviews, recommends, and arranges financial support for research investigators who can constructively use non-specialist field assistants. Prospective assistants collectively finance the projects in return for the opportunity to participate in field research teams. Support is not limited by geographical area; the Program considers proposals for field research in any recognized academic discipline and invites scholars of all nationalities to apply for support; favors postdoctoral research. Sponsored by Earthwatch. **Awards:** Field Research Grants. **Frequency:** annual. **Type:** grant. **Affiliated With:** Earthwatch Institute. **Formerly:** (2003) Center for Field Research at Earthwatch Institute. **Publications:** *Annual Grants List*, annual. Contains listings of all funded projects. Alternate Formats: online ● *Earthwatch Journal*, 3/year. **Price:** included in membership dues. **Conventions/Meetings:** annual Earthwatch - conference (exhibits) - held in November in Cambridge, MA.

7575 ■ ResearchChannel
Univ. of Washington
17 Kane Hall
Box 353090
Seattle, WA 98195-3090
Free: (877)616-7265
Fax: (206)616-0819
E-mail: info@researchchannel.org
URL: http://www.researchchannel.org
Contact: Amy Philipson, Exec. Dir.
Founded: 1996. **Membership Dues:** basic, $100 (annual) ● scholar, $250 (annual) ● lecturer, $500 (annual) ● mentor, $1,000 (annual) ● fellow, $2,500 (annual) ● researcher, $5,000 (annual). **Description:** Aims to connect researchers and academic institutions with the public through creation of accessible and high-quality video resources using advanced streaming and broadband technology programming. Acts as a technology testbed and innovator for new methods of global distribution and interaction. Promotes the works of researchers and academic institutions by making them available to the public. **Telecommunication Services:** electronic mail, amy@researchchannel.org. **Publications:** *Inside ResearchChannel*, quarterly. Newsletter. **Price:** included in membership dues.

7576 ■ Society of Research Administrators (SRA)
1901 N Moore St., Ste.1004
Arlington, VA 22209
Ph: (703)741-0140 (703)741-0158
Fax: (703)741-0142
E-mail: info@srainternational.org
URL: http://www.srainternational.org
Contact: Christopher D. Daniels MPA, Exec. Dir.
Founded: 1967. **Members:** 3,200. **Membership Dues:** individual, institutional, $165 (annual) ● student, retired, $40 (annual) ● affiliate, $20 (annual). **Staff:** 6. **Budget:** $1,200,000. **Regional Groups:** 5. **Local Groups:** 17. **Multinational. Description:** Advances the profession and improving the efficiency and effectiveness of research administration. Serves a diverse mix of research administrators from a wide range of fields in business and industry, academia, medicine, government, nonprofit organizations, among others. Goals include: to provide state-of the art professional development and education opportunities for research administrators at all stages of their careers; to enhance the diversity of membership through support of divisions, sections, chapters, and interest groups; and to advance the public's understanding of the value and importance of research and research administration. **Awards:** Distinguished Contribution to Research Administration Award. **Frequency:** annual. **Type:** recognition ● Excellence Award. **Frequency:** annual. **Type:** recognition ● Hartford-Nicholsen Award. **Frequency:** annual. **Type:** recognition ● Rod Rose Award. **Frequency:** annual. **Type:** recognition. **Recipient:** for best article published in journal. **Computer Services:** Mailing lists, of members ● online services, membership directory. **Committees:** Annual Meeting; Awards; Bylaws; Development and Finance; Education; Electronic Research Administration; External Relations; History and Archives; International; Publications; Strategic Planning. **Divisions:** Commercial; Educational; Not-for-Profit Research Organization. **Publications:** *Journal of the Society of Research Administrators*, 3/year. Presents articles that advance the efficiency and effectiveness of research administration. Includes annual cumulative title index and book reviews. **Price:**

$40.00/year. ISSN: 0038-0024. **Circulation:** 3,600. **Advertising:** accepted. Also Cited As: *SRA Journal* ● *Society of Research Administrators—Membership Directory*, annual. **Price:** included in membership dues. **Advertising:** accepted. Alternate Formats: online ● *SRA eNews*, monthly. Newsletter. Includes employment opportunities listings and legislative updates. **Price:** included in membership dues. **Circulation:** 3,200. **Advertising:** accepted. **Conventions/Meetings:** annual meeting (exhibits) - always fall, October. 2008 Oct. 9-13, Washington, DC; 2009 Oct. 17-21, Seattle, WA.

7577 ■ Universities Research Association (URA)
1111 19th St. NW, Ste.400
Washington, DC 20036
Ph: (202)293-1382
E-mail: info@ura.nw.dc.us
URL: http://www.ura-hq.org
Contact: Frederick M. Bernthal, Pres.
Founded: 1965. **Members:** 90. **Regional Groups:** 7. **Multinational. Description:** Functions through a Council of Presidents in which each member university is represented by its chief executive. Provides a forum for cooperation among universities and other research organizations, U.S. government, and other organizations. Seeks to support and use laboratories, machines, and other research facilities, and develop knowledge in the physical sciences. Currently under contract to the Department of Energy to operate the Fermi National Accelerator Laboratory in Illinois. **Boards:** Overseers. **Committees:** Fermilab; Fermilab Accelerator Advisory; Fermilab Physics Advisory. **Projects:** Pierre Auger Observatory. **Publications:** Annual Report. Alternate Formats: online ● Brochure. Alternate Formats: online. **Conventions/Meetings:** annual Council of Presidents Meeting and Policy Forum - usually last Friday in February.

7578 ■ World Association for Case Method Research and Application (WACRA)
23 Mackintosh Ave.
Needham, MA 02492-1218
Ph: (781)444-8982
Fax: (781)444-1548
E-mail: wacra@rcn.com
URL: http://www.wacra.org
Contact: Dr. Hans E. Klein, Exec. Dir.
Founded: 1984. **Members:** 2,100. **Membership Dues:** regular, $75 (annual) ● organization, $390 (annual) ● sustaining, $550 (annual) ● associate/advanced student, $60 (annual) ● retired, $35 (annual). **National Groups:** 4. **Languages:** Chinese, Czech, English, French, German, Spanish. **Multinational. Description:** Promotes the use of the case method in teaching, training, and planning. Encourages research using the case method and coordinates case writing and case application activities. Includes games, simulations, and other interactive learning and teaching methods as parallels to cases. Offers educational and charitable programs. **Awards: Frequency:** annual. **Type:** recognition ● **Frequency:** annual. **Type:** scholarship. **Subgroups:** ACT-Academy for Creative Teaching; BACRA Baltic ASSN For Case Method Research And Application; CZACRA CZECH Association for Case Method Research And Application; JACRA ASSN For Case Method Research And Application; NACRA North American Case Research Association. **Publications:** *International Journal of Case Method Research and Application*, quarterly. Contains 18 volumes; international refereed journal. ISSN: 1554-7752. **Circulation:** 2,000. **Advertising:** accepted. Alternate Formats: online ● *WACRA News*, semiannual. Newsletter. Contains announcements, managerial column and featured events of the society. Alternate Formats: online. **Conventions/Meetings:** annual international conference, case method research and application, includes interactive methods, distance education, creative teaching (exhibits) - 2008 June 29-July 2, Glasgow, United Kingdom ● workshop (exhibits) - several per year.

Rheology

7579 ■ Society of Rheology (SOR)
c/o A. Jeffrey Giacomin, Sec.
Rheology Res. Center
Univ. of Wisconsin
Madison, WI 53706
Ph: (608)262-7473
Fax: (608)265-2316
E-mail: giacomin@wisc.edu
URL: http://www.rheology.org/sor
Contact: A. Jeffrey Giacomin, Sec.
Founded: 1929. **Members:** 1,700. **Membership Dues:** student, $25 (annual) ● individual, $40 (annual). **Staff:** 1. **Description:** Professional society of chemical engineers, chemists, physicists, biologists, and others interested in the theory and precise measurement of the deformation and flow of matter and application of the physical data in fields such as biology, food, high polymers and plastics, metals, petroleum products, rubber, paint, printing ink, ceramics and glass, starch, floor preparations, and cosmetics. **Awards:** Bingham Award. **Frequency:** annual. **Type:** recognition. **Recipient:** for outstanding contributions to science of rheology or meritorious service to the society. **Computer Services:** Mailing lists, of members. **Affiliated With:** American Institute of Physics; U.S. National Committee on Theoretical and Applied Mechanics. **Publications:** *Journal of Rheology*, bimonthly. **Price:** $550.00 for nonmembers in U.S.; $560.00 for nonmembers in North and South America; $575.00 for nonmembers outside North and South America. ISSN: 0148-6055. **Advertising:** accepted. Alternate Formats: online; CD-ROM ● *Rheology Bulletin*, semiannual. Newsletter. Contains society and professional news. **Price:** included in membership dues. **Conventions/Meetings:** annual meeting (exhibits) - 2008 Aug. 3-8, Monterey, CA; 2009 Oct. 18-22, Madison, WI; 2010 Oct. 24-28, Santa Fe, NM.

Robotics

7580 ■ Association for Unmanned Vehicle Systems International (AUVSI)
2700 S Quincy St., Ste.400
Arlington, VA 22206
Ph: (703)845-9671
Fax: (703)845-9679
E-mail: info@auvsi.org
URL: http://www.auvsi.org
Contact: Daryl Davidson, Exec. Dir.
Founded: 1972. **Members:** 2,700. **Membership Dues:** individual, $50 (annual) ● individual, $100 (triennial) ● individual, outside North America, $60 (annual) ● senior, student, $15 (annual) ● academic, $500 (annual) ● corporate (bronze), $750 (annual) ● corporate (silver), $1,500 (annual) ● corporate (gold), $2,500 (annual) ● corporate (platinum), $5,000 (annual). **Staff:** 5. **Local Groups:** 9. **Multinational. Description:** Represents the interests of government, industry, and academia and is the principal organization promoting unmanned vehicle system technologies. **Formerly:** (1977) National Association for Remotely Piloted Vehicles; (1998) Association for Unmanned Vehicle Systems. **Publications:** *Proceedings on Annual Technical Conference and Other Meetings*, annual. Contains unmanned systems 2000-present. **Advertising:** accepted. Alternate Formats: CD-ROM ● *Unmanned Systems*, bimonthly. Magazine. **Price:** included in membership dues; $300.00 /year for nonmembers. **Advertising:** accepted. **Conventions/Meetings:** annual Unmanned Systems Conference and Exhibition - meeting and symposium (exhibits) - 2009 Aug. 10-13, Washington, DC.

7581 ■ Automated Imaging Association (AIA)
PO Box 3724
Ann Arbor, MI 48106
Ph: (734)994-6088
Free: (800)994-6099
Fax: (734)994-3338
E-mail: dwhalls@robotics.org
URL: http://www.machinevisiononline.org
Contact: Dana Whalls, Managing Dir.
Founded: 1984. **Members:** 238. **Membership Dues:** supplier (based on gross sales), $800-$2,500 (annual) ● user, $600 (annual) ● affiliate, $350 (annual). **Staff:** 13. **Budget:** $1,000,000. **Multinational. Description:** Represents manufacturers of machine vision components and systems, users, system integrators, universities and non-profit research groups, and financial firms that track the machine vision industry. Promotes the use and understanding of image capture and analysis technology. **Awards:** Automated Imaging Achievement Awards. **Frequency:** annual. **Type:** recognition. **Recipient:** for contributions in leadership, technology development, industrial application, and scientific application. **Committees:** Education; Standards; Trade Shows. **Affiliated With:** Robotic Industries Association. **Formerly:** (1984) Vision Group of the Robotic Industries Association; (1989) Automated Vision Association. **Publications:** *Machine Vision Industry Directory*, annual ● *Machine Vision Market Study and Forecast*, annual ● *Machine Vision Online*, monthly. Newsletter. Alternate Formats: online. **Conventions/Meetings:** biennial International Robots and Vision Show - conference and trade show - 2009 June 9-11, Rosemont, IL ● annual The Vision Show - conference and trade show (exhibits).

7582 ■ IEEE Robotics and Automation Society (IEEE-RAS)
c/o Ms. Rosalyn Graham Snyder, Admin.
3603 Octavia St.
Raleigh, NC 27606
Ph: (919)851-3603
Fax: (919)882-9734
E-mail: r.g.snyder@ieee.org
URL: http://www.ieee-ras.org
Contact: Ms. Rosalyn Graham Snyder, Admin.
Founded: 1984. **Members:** 6,300. **Membership Dues:** full, $22 (annual) ● student, $11 (annual). **Staff:** 1. **Budget:** $3,000,000. **Local Groups:** 59. **Multinational. Description:** A society of the Institute of Electrical and Electronics Engineers (IEEE). Society members must also be members of IEEE. Acts as a forum on the theory and application of automation and robot technology in the areas of: robot dynamics and control; robot languages, locomotion, and vision and other sensory interfaces; simulation of robots and manufacturing systems; management of multirobot systems; manipulator design; computer-assisted design methods; robotic and automation task planning and expert systems; hardware and software implementation of robotic systems. Conducts technical workshops. **Awards:** Best IEEE TASE Paper Award. **Frequency:** annual. **Type:** monetary. **Recipient:** for the authors of the most significant paper published in the IEEE Transactions on Automation Science and Engineering ● Googol New Application Paper Award. **Frequency:** annual. **Type:** monetary. **Recipient:** for the best paper in IEEE T-Automation Science and Engineering describing a new application ● ICRA Conference Awards. **Frequency:** annual. **Type:** monetary. **Recipient:** for outstanding papers and videos presented at IEEE International Conference on Robotics and Automation; six awards in various categories ● IEEE/IFR Invention and Entrepreneurship Award. **Frequency:** annual. **Type:** monetary. **Recipient:** for commercialization of ideas into actual products nominations ● IEEE Inaba Technical Award for Innovation Leading to Production. **Frequency:** annual. **Type:** monetary. **Recipient:** for original innovative research and concepts ● IEEE-RAS Distinguished Service Award. **Frequency:** annual. **Type:** monetary. **Recipient:** for outstanding service to the society ● K.S. Fu Memorial Best TRO Paper Award. **Frequency:** annual. **Type:** monetary. **Recipient:** for the authors of the most significant paper published in the IEEE Transactions on Robotics ● RAS Chapter of the Year Award. **Frequency:** annual. **Type:** monetary. **Recipient:** for the most active IEEE-RAS local chapter ● RAS Most Active Distinguished Lecturer Award. **Frequency:** annual. **Type:** monetary. **Recipient:** for most active IEEE-RAS distinguished lecturer ● RAS Most Active Technical Committee Award. **Frequency:** annual. **Type:** monetary. **Recipient:** for the most active technical committee of the society ● RAS Pioneer Award. **Frequency:** annual. **Type:** monetary. **Recipient:** for outstanding contributions to the field of robotics and automation. **Telecommunication Services:** electronic bulletin board, IEEE-RAS WIKI; for members only. **Affiliated With:** Institute of Electrical and Electronics Engineers. **Publications:** *IEEE/*

ASME Journal on Microelectromechanical Systems, bimonthly. Covers Microsensing, Microactuation, Micromechanics, Microdynamics, and Microelectromechanical Systems (MEMS). **Price:** $495.00. ISSN: 1057-7157 ● *IEEE/ASME Transactions on Mechatronics*, bimonthly. Journal. Encompasses all practical aspects of the theory and methods of mechatronics. **Price:** $650.00. ISSN: 1083-4435 ● *IEEE Transactions on Industrial Informatics*, quarterly. Journal. Focuses on knowledge-based factory automation as a means to enhance industrial fabrication and manufacturing processes. **Price:** $475.00. ISSN: 1551-3203. Alternate Formats: online ● *Robotics and Automation Magazine*, quarterly. Deals with prototyping, demonstration and evaluation, and commercialization of robotic and automation technology and systems. **Price:** included in membership dues; $71.00/copy for nonmembers. ISSN: 1070-9932. **Circulation:** 6,893. **Advertising:** accepted. Also Cited As: *RAM* ● *Transactions on Automation Science and Engineering*, quarterly. Journal. Deals with prototyping, demonstration and evaluation, and commercialization of robotic and automation technology and systems. **Price:** $15.00 for members; $8.00 for student members; $385.00 for institutions. ISSN: 1545-5955. Also Cited As: *T-ASE* ● *Transactions on Robotics*, bimonthly. Journal. Includes theory and applications on topics including: kinematics, dynamics, control, and simulation of robots and intelligent machines and systems. ISSN: 1552-3098. Also Cited As: *IEEE Robotics and Automation Journal.* **Conventions/Meetings:** annual conference, with workshops (exhibits) - 2008 Sept. 22-26, Nice, France ● annual conference, international technical conference (exhibits).

7583 ■ Machine Vision Association of the Society of Manufacturing Engineers (MVA/SME)

PO Box 930
Dearborn, MI 48121-0930
Ph: (313)271-1500
Free: (800)733-4763
Fax: (313)425-2861
E-mail: service@sme.org
URL: http://www.sme.org/mva
Contact: Nancy S. Berg, Exec. Dir./Gen. Mgr.

Founded: 1984. **Members:** 1,600. **Description:** A division of the Society of Manufacturing Engineers (see separate entry). Engineers, managers, manufacturers, and students in 35 countries. Promotes individual professional development to effectively use machine vision technology (the use of devices for optical non-contact sensing to automatically receive and interpret an image of a real scene in order to obtain information and control machines or processes). Offers professional certification. **Libraries: Type:** reference. **Awards: Type:** recognition. **Telecommunication Services:** electronic mail, leadership@sme.org. **Publications:** *Machine Vision Industry Directory*, annual ● *Vision*, quarterly. Newsletter. Alternate Formats: online ● Books ● Catalog ● Videos. **Conventions/Meetings:** biennial conference ● workshop and seminar.

7584 ■ Robotic Industries Association (RIA)

PO Box 3724
Ann Arbor, MI 48106
Ph: (734)994-6088
Fax: (734)994-3338
E-mail: ria@robotics.org
URL: http://www.roboticsonline.com
Contact: Jeff Burstein, Exec. VP

Founded: 1974. **Members:** 250. **Membership Dues:** supplier, $1,000-$10,000 (annual) ● user, $150-$1,000 (annual) ● researcher, $350 (annual) ● consultant/agent (based on number of employees), $400-$800 (annual) ● integrator, $1,500-$3,000 (annual). **Staff:** 12. **Description:** Only trade group in North America organized specifically to serve the robotics industry. Member companies include robot manufacturers, users, system integrators, component suppliers, research groups, and consulting firms. Sponsors the biennial International Robots and Vision Show, develops the ANSI/RIA national robot safety standard, collects and reports robotics industry statistics. **Awards:** Joseph F. Engelberger Robotics Award. **Frequency:** annual. **Type:** monetary. **Recipient:** for outstanding contributions in application, education, technology development, and industry leadership. **Committees:** Conferences; Expositions; Marketing; Safety; Standards; Workshops. **Affiliated With:** Automated Imaging Association. **Formerly:** (1984) Robot Institute of America. **Publications:** *Robotics Industry Directory*, annual. **Price:** free (within U.S.) ● *Robotics Online*, monthly. Newsletter. Alternate Formats: online. **Conventions/Meetings:** biennial International Robots and Vision Show - conference and trade show (exhibits) - 2009 June 9-11, Rosemont, IL.

7585 ■ Robotics Tech Group of the Society of Manufacturing Engineers (RI/SME)

PO Box 930
Dearborn, MI 48121
Ph: (313)271-1500 (313)425-3000
Free: (800)733-4763
Fax: (313)425-3404
E-mail: techcommunities@sme.org
URL: http://www.sme.org/cgi-bin/communities.pl?/communities/ri/rihome.htm&&&SME&
Contact: Mr. Mark Tomlinson, Exec. Dir.

Founded: 1980. **Members:** 6,000. **Multinational. Description:** Represents engineers, managers, educators, and government officials in 50 countries working or interested in the field of robotics. Promotes efficient and effective use of current and future robot technology. Serves as a clearinghouse for the industry trends and developments. Includes areas of interest such as: aerospace; assembly systems; casting and forging; education and training; human factors and safety; human and food service; material handling; military systems; nontraditional systems; research and development; small shop applications; welding. Offers professional certification. Operates placement service; compiles statistics. Maintains speakers' bureau. **Affiliated With:** Society of Manufacturing Engineers. **Formerly:** (2005) Robotics International of the Society of Manufacturing Engineers. **Publications:** *Affordable Automation for Small & Medium Facilities.* Video ● *Assembly Automation.* Book ● *Assembly Automation and Product Design, Second Edition.* Book. **Price:** $139.95 for nonmembers; $125.95 for members ● *Automation Encyclopedia* ● *Design of Automatic Machinery.* Book. **Price:** $139.95 for nonmembers; $125.95 for members ● *Developing and Applying End of Arm Tooling* ● *Flexible Assembly Systems - Insights based on Experience.* Booklet ● *Fundamentals of Manufacturing.* Book ● *Getting Factory Automation Right (the first time).* Book ● *Handbook of Design, Manufacturing & Automation* ● *Handbook of Industrial Automation.* **Price:** $225.00 for nonmembers; $202.50 for members ● *Industrial Robotics.* Video ● *Machine Vision & Error Proofing.* Video ● *Manufacturing Engineering*, periodic. Magazine ● *Robotics Quarterly.* Newsletters. Alternate Formats: online ● *Successful Assembly Automation.* Book ● *TMEH Volume 9: Material and Part Handling in Manufacturing.* Book. **Price:** $125.00 for nonmembers; $99.00 for members.

Safety

7586 ■ American Society of Safety Engineers (ASSE)

1800 E Oakton St.
Des Plaines, IL 60018
Ph: (847)699-2929
Fax: (847)768-3434
E-mail: customerservice@asse.org
URL: http://www.asse.org
Contact: Fred J. Fortman, Exec. Dir./Sec.

Founded: 1911. **Members:** 32,000. **Membership Dues:** regular, in U.S., Saudi Arabia, Kuwait, Middle East, $120 (annual) ● all other international address, $120 (annual) ● student, $120 (annual). **Staff:** 50. **Budget:** $8,000,000. **Regional Groups:** 8. **Local Groups:** 135. **Description:** Professional society of safety engineers, safety directors, and others concerned with accident prevention, environmental protection and safety and health programs. Sponsors National Safety Month and conducts research and educational programs. Develops/publishes ANSI safety-related standards and other technical literature. Compiles statistics; maintains job placement service. **Libraries: Type:** reference. **Holdings:** 4,200; articles, books, periodicals. **Subjects:** safety, health, accident prevention, environment. **Awards:** Safety Professional of the Year. **Frequency:** annual. **Type:** recognition. **Recipient:** for an outstanding member whose contributions have significantly advanced the profession and demonstrated leadership in the establishment and maintenance of technical or Society programs. **Computer Services:** Online services, member and chapter services. **Boards:** Editorial. **Committees:** Academic Accreditation; Admissions; Awards and Honors Review; Ethics/Professional Conduct; Fellow Review; Government Affairs; Intersociety Relations; Professional Development Conference Planning; Professional Paper Awards; Public Affairs; Standards Development; Student Member Activities; Technical Publications. **Divisions:** Construction; Consultants; Engineering; Environmental; Healthcare; Industrial Hygiene; International; Management; Mining; Public Sector; Risk Management/Insurance; Transportation. **Publications:** *Crane Hazard, and Their Prevention* ● *CSP Refresher Guide* ● *Illustrated Guide to Electrical Safety, 3rd Edition* ● *Introduction to Fall Protection, 2nd Edition* ● *Product Safety Management and Engineering, 2nd Edition* ● *Professional Safety*, monthly. Journal. Covers developments in the research and technology of accident prevention for safety specialists including engineers and health professionals. **Price:** included in membership dues; $60.00 /year for nonmembers. ISSN: 0099-0027. **Circulation:** 32,000. **Advertising:** accepted ● *Safety Engineering, 2nd Edition* ● *Safety Profession Year 2000* ● *Safety, Work and Life - An International View* ● *Society Update*, monthly. Newsletter. Includes Society events, new products and services, articles, and special recognitions. **Circulation:** 34,000. Alternate Formats: online. **Conventions/Meetings:** annual Professional Development - conference (exhibits) - 2009 June 28-July 1, San Antonio, TX.

7587 ■ Board of Certified Safety Professionals (BCSP)

208 Burwash Ave.
Savoy, IL 61874
Ph: (217)359-9263
Fax: (217)359-0055
E-mail: bcsp@bcsp.org
URL: http://www.bcsp.org
Contact: Roger L. Brauer PhD, Exec. Dir.

Founded: 1969. **Members:** 11,000. **Membership Dues:** certification board, $100 (annual). **Staff:** 15. **Budget:** $2,000,000. **Description:** Grants the Associate Safety Professional designation and Certified Safety Professional certification to individuals involved in the field of safety who pass a series of examinations and meet educational and experience criteria. Conducts research in the evaluation of competency for those in the safety, health, and environmental practice. **Libraries: Type:** reference. **Holdings:** 1,800; periodicals. **Subjects:** regulations, consensus codes and standards, training manuals covering safety, health, and environmental management and engineering, human resources development, training, professional conduct and ethics. **Affiliated With:** American Industrial Hygiene Association; American Society of Safety Engineers; Institute of Industrial Engineers; National Safety Council; Society of Fire Protection Engineers; System Safety Society. **Publications:** *BCSP Directory and International Registry of Certified Safety Professionals.* Lists all persons with the Certified Safety Professional or Associate Safety Professional designations. **Price:** $100.00 for searchable CD-ROM; free online. **Circulation:** 10,000. Alternate Formats: CD-ROM; online ● *BCSP Newsletter*, semiannual. Describes the operational and financial activities of BCSP. **Circulation:** 15,000. Alternate Formats: online ● *BCSP Salary Survey of Safety Professionals*, biennial. Describes salaries of safety professionals, based on comprehensive, diverse survey results of respondents' salaries, positions, industries, etc. **Price:** $300.00 ● *Career Guide to the Safety Profession*, biennial. Describes the safety career. Circulated mainly to colleges, universities, membership organizations, and trade schools.

7588 ■ University of Iowa Injury Prevention Research Center (IPRC)
c/o John A. Lundell, MA, Deputy Dir.
158 IREH Oakdale Res. Campus
Iowa City, IA 52242-5000
Ph: (319)335-4458 (319)335-4895
Fax: (319)335-4631
E-mail: john-lundell@uiowa.edu
URL: http://www.public-health.uiowa.edu/iprc
Contact: John A. Lundell MA, Deputy Dir.

Founded: 1990. **Staff:** 20. **Budget:** $950,000. **Description:** University-based medical research center. Seeks to reduce and prevent injuries. Provides educational and research programs. **Libraries: Type:** lending; reference; not open to the public. **Holdings:** books, monographs, periodicals, reports. **Awards:** Training Program. **Frequency:** annual. **Type:** grant. **Recipient:** for student research support. **Telecommunication Services:** electronic mail, corinne-peek-asa@uiowa.edu. **Publications:** *Midwest Inquiry Control*, semiannual. Newsletter. Contains various injury control articles of interest primarily to Midwest. **Price:** free. **Circulation:** 1,300. Alternate Formats: online ● *Workplace Violence*. Report. Alternate Formats: online. **Conventions/Meetings:** conference (exhibits) - 1-2/year.

Sanitation

7589 ■ AIDIS-USA Section
PO Box 7737
McLean, VA 22106-7737
Ph: (703)734-0367
E-mail: info@aidis-usa.org
URL: http://www.aidis-usa.org

Founded: 1946. **Members:** 200. **Membership Dues:** individual, $60 (annual) ● Peace Corp volunteer, student, $12 (annual) ● corporate, institution, $180 (annual). **Staff:** 1. **Budget:** $12,000. **Regional Groups:** 7. **Local Groups:** 1. **National Groups:** 30. **Languages:** English, Portuguese, Spanish. **Multinational. Description:** Sanitary engineers in government, private business, and educational institutions throughout the Western Hemisphere. Promotes study and solution of sanitary engineering and environmental problems as a necessary condition for economic and social development in the Americas and for advancing understanding; establishes uniform standards for permanent protection of health of all Western Hemisphere inhabitants. Maintains 30 sections. **Awards: Type:** recognition. **Also Known As:** Asociacion Interamericana de Intenieria Sanitaria; Asociacao Interamericana de Engenharia Sanitaria; Inter-American Association of Sanitary and Environmental Engineering. **Formerly:** (1962) Inter-American Association of Sanitary Engineers; (1977) Inter-American Association of Sanitary Engineering; (1980) Inter-American Association of Sanitary Engineering and Environment; (1994) Inter-American Association of Sanitary Engineering and Environmental Sciences. **Publications:** *AIDIS-USA Newsletter*, quarterly. **Conventions/Meetings:** Bolivarian Congress on Environmental and Sanitary Engineering and Exhibit on Water Quality and Environment Technology (exhibits) ● Central American Congress of AIDIS ● Congress of the Brazilian Association of Sanitary and Environmental Engineering ● Inter-American Congress on Environmental and Sanitary Engineering of AIDIS ● North America and Caribbean Congress of AIDIS.

7590 ■ American Society of Sanitary Engineering (ASSE)
901 Canterbury, Ste.A
Westlake, OH 44145
Ph: (440)835-3040
Fax: (440)835-3488
E-mail: info@asse-plumbing.org
URL: http://www.asse-plumbing.org
Contact: Shannon Corcoran, Exec. Dir./Standards Coor.

Founded: 1906. **Members:** 3,000. **Staff:** 7. **Regional Groups:** 22. **Local Groups:** 32. **Description:** Plumbing officials, sanitary engineers, plumbers, plumbing contractors, building officials, architects, engineers, designing engineers, physicians, and others interested in health. Conducts research on plumbing and sanitation, and develops performance standards for components of the plumbing system. Sponsors disease research program and other studies of waterborne epidemics. **Libraries: Type:** open to the public. **Holdings:** articles, books, periodicals. **Subjects:** backflow, medical gas, graywater legionnaires. **Awards:** Henry B. Davis Award. **Frequency:** annual. **Type:** recognition. **Recipient:** for outstanding contribution to the industry. **Computer Services:** database ● mailing lists ● online services. **Committees:** Code; Energy and Water Conservation; Hospital Plumbing Research; International Studies Coordination; Legionnaires Disease Research; Plumbing Design Correspondence Course; Plumbing Testing Laboratory; Refresher Course; Research; Standard (Product); Standards, Seal Approval; Technical. **Formerly:** American Society of Inspectors of Plumbing and Sanitary Engineering. **Publications:** *Cross-Connection Control Booklet* ● *Performance Standards* ● *Plumbing Dictionary* ● *Plumbing Inspection Manual* ● *Plumbing Standards*, quarterly. Magazine ● Newsletter, monthly ● Yearbook, annual. **Conventions/Meetings:** annual meeting and seminar (exhibits) - 2008 Nov. 19-23, Orlando, FL; 2009 Nov. 17-21, San Antonio, TX.

Satellite Dishes

7591 ■ Mobile Satellite Users Association (MSUA)
1350 Beverly Rd., Ste.115-341
McLean, VA 22101
Ph: (650)839-0376
Fax: (650)839-0375
E-mail: msua@msua.org
URL: http://www.msua.org
Contact: Tim Farrar, Pres.

Founded: 1992. **Membership Dues:** corporate, $1,800 (annual) ● associate, $500 (annual) ● personal, $150 (annual) ● individual end user, $25 (annual). **Multinational. Description:** Promotes the interests of users of mobile satellite communications worldwide. **Telecommunication Services:** electronic mail, president@msua.org. **Publications:** *MSUA Link*, monthly. Newsletter ● *Weekly Mobile Satellite Headline News*. Newsletter. **Price:** free. Alternate Formats: online. **Conventions/Meetings:** annual conference (exhibits).

Science

7592 ■ Academy of Applied Science (AAS)
24 Warren St.
Concord, NH 03301
Ph: (603)228-4530
Fax: (603)228-4730
E-mail: admin@aas-world.org
URL: http://www.aas-world.org
Contact: Robert Rines, Pres.

Founded: 1963. **Members:** 300. **Staff:** 7. **Local Groups:** 11. **Description:** Scientific and educational organization dedicated to the advancement and recognition of scientific creativity. Membership includes persons who have made a significant and creative contribution in applied science, engineering, technological management, or administration; persons interested in applied science and engineering, or in advancing and encouraging scientific and technological creativity; and firms, agencies, organizations, or institutions that are engaged in, or interested in, the advancement of applied science, creative engineering, and management. Sponsors Junior Science and Humanities Symposia in 47 regions throughout the U.S. Special projects include underwater and Loch Ness research. Sponsors Cow-Power Television Network in New Hampshire. Sponsors competitions. Offers specialized education and research programs. **Awards: Type:** recognition. **Programs:** Research Engineering and Apprenticeship. **Conventions/Meetings:** periodic conference.

7593 ■ Advocates for Women in Science, Engineering, and Mathematics (AWSEM)
c/o Saturday Academy
PO Box 8728
Portland, OR 97207
Ph: (503)725-2330 (503)725-2338
Fax: (503)725-2335
E-mail: awsem@saturdayacademy.org
URL: http://www.awsem.org
Contact: Sadie Kenzler, Coor.

Founded: 1994. **Description:** Members includes scientists, educators, parents, and other individuals with an interest in the scientific education of women. Seeks to encourage young women to pursue study of the sciences. Creates opportunities for young women to meaningfully interact with professional women in scientific fields; develops model science education programs for young women. Provides an interactive digital handbook with curriculum and instructions on how to run a club.

7594 ■ African Scientific Institute (ASI)
PO Box 12153
Oakland, CA 94604
Ph: (510)653-7027
E-mail: asi@quixnet.net
URL: http://www.asi-org.net
Contact: Mr. Lee O. Cherry, Pres./CEO

Founded: 1967. **Membership Dues:** constituent, $25 (annual). **Budget:** $250,000. **Description:** Encourages minority youth to pursue careers in science and engineering. Serves as a forum for the exchange of technical information and expertise. Sponsors Science and Technology Awareness Program, to assist people in feeling comfortable with science and technology; the African Relief Fund, to ameliorate the crises of drought and famine in Africa by utilizing available technology, conducting research on Africa's resources, and encouraging coordinated efforts between other groups concerned with Africa. Compiles statistics. Maintains placement service and speakers' bureau. Sponsors and cosponsors conferences and seminars relating to scientific and technological development. Maintains networking among scientists and technologists throughout the United States and Africa. **Awards:** ASI Fellow. **Frequency:** periodic. **Type:** recognition. **Recipient:** for accomplished black persons in the areas of science and technology. **Programs:** ASI Fellows. **Formerly:** (1967) Dignity Institute of Technology. **Publications:** *Blacks in Science Calendar*, annual. **Price:** $9.65/copy, plus shipping and handling ● *SciTech: Developments in Science and Technology*, quarterly. Newspaper. Contains calendar of events, individual and organization profiles, and development reports from Africa. **Price:** free to targeted markets. **Circulation:** 24,890. **Advertising:** accepted. **Conventions/Meetings:** semiannual conference (exhibits).

7595 ■ Alliance for Science and Technology Research in America (ASTRA)
Othmer Bldg., Rm. 320
1155 16th St. NW
Washington, DC 20036
Ph: (202)872-6160
URL: http://www.aboutastra.org
Contact: Robert Spurrier Boege, Exec. Dir.

Founded: 2001. **Members:** 3,400. **Description:** Promotes better understanding of the physical and mathematical sciences and engineering. Develops primary and secondary research about science funding. Fosters the growth of coalitions and other forms of organization in promoting the science enterprise. Conducts education and advocacy on topics related to adequate research funding. **Publications:** *ASTRA Briefs*. Newsletter. Alternate Formats: online.

7596 ■ American Association for the Advancement of Science (AAAS)
1200 New York Ave. NW
Washington, DC 20005
Ph: (202)326-6400 (202)326-6640
Fax: (202)371-9526
E-mail: membership@aaas.org
URL: http://www.aaas.org
Contact: Dr. John Holdren, Chm.
Founded: 1848. **Membership Dues:** professional, K-12 teacher (with 6 issues of Science Books and Films plus online access), $142 (annual) ● postdoctoral/resident, K-12 teacher (with online only access to Science Books and Films), $99 (annual) ● NPA postdoctoral, $119 (annual) ● student, $75 (annual) ● patron, $310 (annual) ● emeritus, $110 (annual). **Staff:** 300. **Budget:** $44,000,000. **Description:** Represents all fields of science. Membership includes more than 137,000 individuals and 296 scientific societies, professional organizations, and state and city academies (many of which sponsor junior academies of science). Objectives are to further the work of scientists to facilitate cooperation among them, to foster scientific freedom and responsibility, to improve the effectiveness of science in the promotion of human welfare, to advance education in science, and to increase public understanding and appreciation of the importance and promise of the methods of science in human progress. **Awards:** AAAS-Philip Hauge Abelson Prize. **Type:** recognition ● AAAS Prize for Behavioral Science Research. **Type:** recognition ● AAAS Scientific Freedom and Responsibility Award. **Type:** recognition ● AAAS-Westinghouse Award for Public Understanding of Science and Technology. **Type:** recognition ● AAAS-Westinghouse Science Journalism Award. **Type:** recognition ● Newcomb-Cleveland Award. **Type:** recognition. **Committees:** Arid Lands; Climate; Opportunities in Science; Population, Resources, and the Environment; Public Understanding of Science and Technology; Science, Arms Control, and National Security; Science, Engineering and Public Policy; Scientific Freedom and Responsibility. **Sections:** Agriculture; Anthropology; Astronomy; Atmospheric and Hydrospheric Sciences; Biological Sciences; Chemistry; Dentistry; Education; Engineering; Geology and Geography; History and Philosophy of Science; Industrial Science; Information, Computing and Communication; Mathematics; Medical Sciences; Pharmaceutical Sciences; Physics; Psychology; Social, Economic, and Political Sciences; Societal Impacts of Science and Engineering; Statistics. **Publications:** *AAAS Report: Research and Development*, annual. Monographs. Provides information on the proposed federal research and development budget for the upcoming fiscal year. **Price:** $14.35/copy for members; $17.95/copy for nonmembers. Alternate Formats: microform ● *Science*, weekly. Journal. Contains research reports, book reviews, editorial, news, and comments. **Price:** $130.00 in U.S.; $197.95 in Canada; $185.00 in Mexico/Caribbean; $215.00 in all other countries. **Advertising:** accepted ● *Science Books and Films*, 9/year. Newsletter. Provides critical reviews of science books, films, and videos for children and adults. **Price:** $45.00. ISSN: 0098-342X. **Circulation:** 4,500. **Advertising:** accepted ● *Science Education News*, quarterly. Newsletter. Discusses the efforts to increase public understanding of science. **Price:** included in membership dues ● *This Year in School Science*, annual ● Also publishes compendia from *Science*, symposium volumes, and general reference works. **Conventions/Meetings:** annual meeting (exhibits) ● annual symposium.

7597 ■ American Committee for the Weizmann Institute of Science (ACWIS)
633 3rd Ave.
New York, NY 10017
Ph: (212)895-7900
Free: (800)242-2947
Fax: (212)895-7999
E-mail: info@acwis.org
URL: http://www.weizmann-usa.org
Contact: Martin Kraar, Exec. VP
Founded: 1944. **Staff:** 90. **Regional Groups:** 10. **Description:** Works to establish the Weizmann Institute of Science in Rehovot, Israel, and to raise funds in the United States for its development as an institution for fundamental basic scientific research addressed to the progress of mankind. **Publications:** *Encounters*, annual. Annual Report ● *Interface*, semiannual. Magazine ● *WeizmannNow*, annual. Magazine.

7598 ■ American Philosophical Society (APS)
104 S 5th St.
Philadelphia, PA 19106-3387
Ph: (215)440-3400
Fax: (215)440-3436
E-mail: mmdunn@amphilsoc.org
URL: http://www.amphilsoc.org
Contact: Baruch S. Blumberg, Pres.
Founded: 1743. **Members:** 920. **Staff:** 65. **Description:** Members are elected for their scholarly and scientific accomplishments in all fields of learning, including: mathematical and physical sciences; biological and medical sciences; social sciences; humanities; the arts, professions and public affairs. **Libraries: Type:** reference. **Holdings:** 300,000; archival material, papers, photographs. **Subjects:** history of science in America and its European background, American history before the Civil War. **Awards:** Daland Fellowships. **Type:** fellowship. **Recipient:** to applicants with 8 years beyond date of MD degree ● Franklin Research Grants. **Type:** grant. **Recipient:** for research in the humanities, and a SHEAR grant for research in American history in the early national period ● **Type:** grant. **Recipient:** for individuals in the field of humanities, social sciences, North American Indian linguistics and ethno history, jurisprudence, history of science, clinical medicine, library science, and science ● Lewis and Clark Fund for Exploration and Field Research. **Type:** grant. **Recipient:** to support the cost of travel and equipment in field research of young scholar ● **Type:** recognition. **Recipient:** for individuals in the field of sciences, humanities, public service, jurisprudence, and navigation. **Committees:** Awards; Library; Meetings; Publications; Research. **Publications:** *Memoirs*, 6-8/year. Monograph ● *The Slave Systems of Greek and Roman Antiquity*. Book. Features a memoir of W.L. Westermann. **Price:** $15.00 ● *Transactions*, 7/year ● Newsletter, 3/year ● Proceedings, quarterly ● Yearbook. Contains a list of members, reports of meetings and committees. **Conventions/Meetings:** annual meeting - always April. 2009 Apr. 23-25, Philadelphia, PA; 2010 Apr. 22-24, Philadelphia, PA ● annual meeting - always November. 2008 Nov. 13-15, Philadelphia, PA; 2009 Nov. 12-14, Philadelphia, PA; 2010 Nov. 11-13, Philadelphia, PA.

7599 ■ Annals of Improbable Research (AIR)
PO Box 380853
Cambridge, MA 02238
Ph: (617)491-4437
Fax: (617)661-0927
E-mail: marc@improbable.com
URL: http://www.improb.com
Contact: Marc Abrahams, Ed.
Description: Individuals with interest in sciences. Seeks to debunk poorly conducted scientific research and other unprovable claims. Serves as a clearinghouse on pseudoscientific research. **Formerly:** (2005) Academy of Improbable Research. **Publications:** *mini-AIR*, monthly. Newsletter. **Price:** free for members. Alternate Formats: online ● Magazine, bimonthly. **Price:** $33.00 /year for individuals.

7600 ■ Armenian Engineers and Scientists of America (AESA)
417 W Arden Ave., Ste.112C
Glendale, CA 91203-4046
Ph: (818)547-3372
Fax: (818)574-3372
E-mail: office@aesa.org
URL: http://www.aesa.org
Contact: Shant Kenderian PhD, Pres.
Founded: 1983. **Membership Dues:** general, $80 (annual) ● student, $10 (annual). **Staff:** 160. **Languages:** Armenian, English. **Description:** Armenian scientists and engineers living in the United States. Promotes advancement of science and engineering and related disciplines and technologies in Armenia. Encourages and facilitates communication between members and their counterparts in Armenia; conducts continuing professional education programs and provides technical, voluntary, and financial assistance to educational institutions in Armenia. **Conventions/Meetings:** monthly lecture.

7601 ■ Association of Orthodox Jewish Scientists
c/o Yossi Bennett, Exec. Dir.
1011 Moss Pl.
Lawrence, NY 11559
Ph: (718)969-3669
Fax: (718)554-3069
E-mail: info@aojs.org
URL: http://www.aojs.org
Contact: Yossi Bennett, Exec. Dir.
Founded: 1947. **Members:** 2,000. **Membership Dues:** individual, $50 (annual). **Staff:** 2. **Local Groups:** 12. **Description:** Orthodox Jews engaged in the natural, medical, and behavioral sciences. Obtains and disseminates information pertinent to the interaction between the Jewish traditional way of life (Halacha) and scientific developments. Facilitates constructive incorporation of scientific knowledge and thinking into a Torah way of life and to serve the Jewish community. A medical-dental group conducts discussions and seminars on the problems faced by the orthodox Jewish physician. Maintains speakers' bureau. Works with affiliated organizations in Great Britain and Israel. **Committees:** Common Child Abuse; Social/Political Issues; Soviet Jewry. **Sections:** Behavioral Science and Mental Health; Physical, Life, and Computer Sciences; Rephael Society. **Also Known As:** AOJS. **Publications:** *Intercom*, quarterly. Journal. **Price:** free for members; $2.00 for nonmembers. **Advertising:** accepted ● Membership Directory, periodic ● Proceedings, annual. **Conventions/Meetings:** semiannual seminar and convention (exhibits) - every August and February in New York and Florida.

7602 ■ Association for Women in Science (AWIS)
1200 New York Ave. NW, Ste.650
Washington, DC 20005
Ph: (202)326-8940 (703)934-1223
Free: (866)657-AWIS
Fax: (202)326-8960
E-mail: awis@awis.org
URL: http://www.awis.org
Contact: Janet Bandows Koster, Exec. Dir.
Founded: 1971. **Members:** 5,200. **Membership Dues:** regular, $65 (annual) ● student, retired, $25 (annual) ● sustaining, $150 (annual) ● patron, $500 (annual) ● benefactor, $1,000 (annual). **Staff:** 6. **Budget:** $350,000. **Local Groups:** 75. **Description:** Professional women and students in life, physical, and social sciences and engineering; men are also members. Promotes equal opportunities for women to enter the scientific workforce and to achieve their career goals; provides educational information to women planning careers in science; networks with other women's groups; monitors scientific legislation and the status of women in science. Provides advice and support to women involved in equal opportunity legislation; assists local chapters with programming and support services. Promotes appreciation of past accomplishments of women scientists. **Libraries: Type:** not open to the public. **Holdings:** 600; articles, books, periodicals, video recordings. **Subjects:** women and girls in science, scientific topics, equity. **Awards:** AWIS Educational Foundation Pre-doctoral Award. **Frequency:** annual. **Type:** scholarship. **Recipient:** for women pursuing pre-doctoral studies in any area of science, usually at dissertation level ● AWIS Educational Foundation Undergraduate Award. **Frequency:** annual. **Type:** scholarship. **Recipient:** for undergraduate women with intent on majoring in the sciences. **Committees:** Affirmative Action; Awards; Chapter Relations; Constitution and Bylaws; Development; Education; Election Nominations; Government Relations; Grants and Contracts; Industry Relations; International; Leadership Initiative; Long-Range Planning; Magazine; Media Relations;

Membership. **Publications:** *A Hand Up: Women Mentoring Women in Science*, periodic. Book. **Price:** $29.95 for members; $34.95 for nonmembers. **Circulation:** 5,000. **Advertising:** accepted ● *AWIS Magazine*, quarterly. Features analytical articles on the status of women in science; includes book reviews and chapter news. **Price:** included in membership dues; $7.00/issue for nonmembers. ISSN: 0160-256X. **Circulation:** 5,000. **Advertising:** accepted ● *Gender and Science* ● *Grants-At-A-Glance* ● *Mentoring Means Future Scientists* ● *Resources for Women in Science Series*, periodic ● *Taking the Initiative: Report on a Leadership Conference for Women in Science and Engineering.* **Conventions/Meetings:** periodic meeting, held in conjunction with the American Association for the Advancement of Science.

7603 ■ Bulletin of the Atomic Scientists

6042 S Kimbark Ave.
Chicago, IL 60637
Ph: (773)702-2555 (773)702-0077
Free: (866)584-0009
Fax: (773)702-0725
E-mail: kbenedict@thebulletin.org
URL: http://www.thebulletin.org
Contact: Kennette Benedict, Exec. Dir.

Founded: 1945. **Staff:** 10. **Budget:** $1,500,000. **Nonmembership. Multinational. Description:** Promotes study and public engagement about science, technology, and global security. **Awards:** Leonard Rieser Fellowship. **Frequency:** annual. **Type:** grant. **Recipient:** for undergraduate research projects on science, technology, and global security ● Ruth Salzman Adams Award. **Frequency:** annual. **Type:** grant. **Recipient:** for emerging authors and communicators on science, technology and global security issues. **Formerly:** (2003) Educational Foundation for Nuclear Science. **Publications:** Magazine, bimonthly. Serves as a major source on science, technology, and global security issues, with emphasis on nuclear weapons and nuclear energy. **Price:** $18.00/year in U.S.; $20.00/year in Canada and Mexico; $25.00/year in other countries. ISSN: 0096-3402. **Circulation:** 10,000. **Advertising:** accepted. Alternate Formats: online; microform; CD-ROM. **Conventions/Meetings:** semiannual board meeting.

7604 ■ Commission on Professionals in Science and Technology (CPST)

1200 New York Ave. NW, Ste.113
Washington, DC 20005
Ph: (202)326-7080
Fax: (202)842-1603
E-mail: info@cpst.org
URL: http://www.cpst.org
Contact: Lisa Frehill, Exec. Dir.

Founded: 1953. **Members:** 700. **Membership Dues:** individual, $50 (annual) ● non-profit academic patron, $1,600 (annual) ● non-profit academic, $700 (annual) ● corporate, $1,000 (annual) ● corporate patron, $3,000 (annual). **Staff:** 3. **Budget:** $500,000. **Description:** A participating organization of the American Association for the Advancement of Science (AAAS). Professional societies, corporations, academic institutions and individuals interested in the training, recruitment and deployment of scientific, engineering and technical personnel. Seeks to aid the development of U.S. scientific resources; promotes scientific and technical training; encourages proper use of scientific and technical personnel by educational institutions, industry and government. Collects, analyzes and disseminates data pertaining to the scientific and technical workforce. Functions as liaison with all branches of government dealing with scientific human resources; cooperates with Engineering Workforce Commission and American Association of Engineering Societies (see separate entries). Compiles statistics. Provides policy analysis. **Telecommunication Services:** electronic mail, lfrehill@cpst.org. **Affiliated With:** American Association for the Advancement of Science; American Association of Engineering Societies. **Formerly:** (1985) Scientific Manpower Commission. **Publications:** *CPST Comments*, 8/year. Features current developments affecting the recruitment, training and utilization of scientists, engineers and technologists. **Price:** included in membership dues; $75.00 /year for nonmembers. ISSN: 0036-0768. **Circulation:** 1,200. Alternate Formats: online ● *Professional Women and Minorities: A Total Human Resource Data Compendium*, biennial. Report. Contains breakdowns by sex and/or minority status; includes data on enrollments and degrees arranged by subject index. **Price:** $325.00 print version and online table downloads; $90.00 for members, plus shipping and handling; $121.50 for nonmembers, plus shipping and handling. ISSN: 0190-1796. **Circulation:** 1,000. Alternate Formats: online ● *Salaries of Scientists, Engineers, and Technicians: A Summary of Salary Surveys*, biennial. Report. Presents detailed information from more than 50 salary surveys on salaries in industry, government and educational institutions. **Price:** $64.00 for members, plus shipping and handling; $150.00 print version and online table downloads; $80.00 for nonmembers, plus shipping and handling. ISSN: 0156-5015. **Circulation:** 750. Alternate Formats: online. **Conventions/Meetings:** annual Commissioners Meeting - meeting and workshop - mostly in Washington, DC.

7605 ■ Council of Scientific Society Presidents (CSSP)

1155 16th St. NW
Washington, DC 20036
Ph: (202)872-6230 (202)872-4452
Fax: (202)872-4079
E-mail: cssp@acs.com
URL: http://www.cssp.us
Contact: Martin A. Apple PhD, Pres.

Founded: 1973. **Members:** 65. **Staff:** 6. **Budget:** $500,000. **Description:** Presidents (or equivalent elected officers) of national science federations and professional scientific societies. Serves as National Science Leadership Development Center and Science Policy Development Center. Provides a network for the membership to work jointly on matters of common concern; provides a forum for developing science policy. Maintains science leadership development institute. Disseminates information on broad problems or policies affecting science and science education on a national or international basis. Responds to requests for advice by Congress, the White House, and national organizations. **Libraries: Type:** reference. **Holdings:** books, clippings, monographs. **Subjects:** science, education, science policy. **Awards:** Award for Support of Science. **Frequency:** annual. **Type:** recognition. **Recipient:** for dedicated support of science ● Educational Research. **Frequency:** annual. **Type:** recognition ● Leadership Citation. **Frequency:** semiannual. **Type:** recognition. **Recipient:** for leadership achievement in science during the prior year ● Public Understanding of Science Award. **Frequency:** annual. **Type:** recognition. **Committees:** Alumni; Awards; Environment, Population & Energy; Ethical & Social Issues in Science; Government and Public Policy; Information Technology; International Science; Public Appreciation of Science; Research Vice Presidents; Science and Math Education; Science/Math Careers. **Formerly:** (1977) Committee of Scientific Society Presidents. **Publications:** *Bridging the Communication Gap: Strengthening Relationships Between Scientists and Journalists.* Report ● *Creating a Strategy for Science-Based National Policy: Addressing Conflicting Views on the Health Risks of Low-Level Ionizing Radiation.* Report ● *CSSP Congressional Sourcebook*, annual. Handbook. Provides updates on structure and function of Congress and staff. **Price:** $20.00/issue. **Circulation:** 1,550. Alternate Formats: online ● *CSSP News-Online.* Report. **Circulation:** 1,550. Alternate Formats: online ● *Public Understanding of Science.* Report ● *Research to Practice: Improving the Learning and Teaching of Science and Mathematics*, annual. Report ● *Translating & Using Research for Improving Teacher Education in Science & Mathematics*, annual. Report. Provides updates on structure and function of Congress and staff. **Price:** $20.00/issue ● Directory, annual. **Conventions/Meetings:** semiannual Council of Presidents - general assembly - usually May and December in Washington, DC.

7606 ■ Institute for Axiomatic Knowledge and Education (IAKE)

208-G Victor Pkwy.
Annapolis, MD 21403
Ph: (410)974-9012
Fax: (410)974-9012
E-mail: drudin@radix.net
Contact: Donald O. Rudin, Pres.

Founded: 2002. **Members:** 2. **Membership Dues:** individual, $100 (annual). **Staff:** 2. **Budget:** $5,000. **Regional Groups:** 1. **Multinational. Description:** Professional society of scientists, philosophers, educators, grammarians and engineers, students and others with an interest in axiomatic world theory. Promotes study of foundations of the world, theory of knowledge and axiomatic world theory and all fields needed to gain broadest perspective. Conducts special research programs on reasons for declining educational achievement, and methods of disseminating the theory behind the axiomatic theory. Proposes a model of the world as a thermodynamic fabricating computer. **Libraries: Type:** reference. **Holdings:** 2. **Subjects:** history of science and mankind, causes of conflict and war, social placebo effect, Axiomatic-Combinatorial-Hamiltonian-Recursive program with harmony and completability (ACHR-HC program). **Formerly:** (2002) International Academy for Axiomatic Knowledge, Science and Education; (2004) Institute for Axiomatic Knowledge and Systematic Core Education. **Publications:** *Destiny of Man.* **Price:** $49.95.

7607 ■ Institute of Medicine (IOM)

500 5th St. NW
Washington, DC 20001
Ph: (202)334-2352
Fax: (202)334-1412
E-mail: iomwww@nas.edu
URL: http://www.iom.edu
Contact: Dr. Harvey V. Fineberg, Pres.

Founded: 1970. **Members:** 1,543. **Staff:** 100. **Budget:** $14,000,000. **Description:** Identifies, studies, and reports on the nation's major problems in medicine and the health sciences; recognizes outstanding achievements in the field. Operated under the auspices of the National Academy of Sciences. **Libraries: Type:** reference; lending; not open to the public. **Holdings:** archival material, books, monographs, periodicals. **Awards:** Leinhard Award. **Frequency:** annual. **Type:** monetary. **Recipient:** to contact organization for information ● Rhoda and Bernard Sarnat Award. **Frequency:** annual. **Type:** monetary. **Recipient:** for outstanding achievement in improving mental health. **Boards:** African Science Academy Development; Children, Youth and Families; Food and Nutrition; Global Health; Health Care Services; Health Sciences Policy; Population Health and Public Health Practice. **Affiliated With:** National Academy of Sciences. **Formerly:** (1970) Board on Medicine of the National Academy of Sciences. **Publications:** *Conference and Workshop Proceedings*, periodic ● *Membership List*, annual. Directory ● *Scholarly Reports.* Reprint ● Monographs ● Reports. **Conventions/Meetings:** annual meeting - October. 2008 Oct. 12-14, Washington, DC.

7608 ■ International Association for Science, Technology and Society (IASTS)

c/o Franz Foltz, Treas.
Rochester Inst. of Tech.
One Lomb Memorial Dr.
Rochester, NY 14623-5603
E-mail: fafgsh@rit.edu
URL: http://www.iasts.org
Contact: Franz Foltz, Treas.

Founded: 1988. **Members:** 350. **Membership Dues:** full, $40 (annual) ● patron, $80 (annual) ● institutional, $200 (annual) ● student, $25 (annual). **Staff:** 2. **Budget:** $14,000. **Description:** Teachers, educators, scientists, engineers, science and technology policymakers; clergy and religious groups; public interest groups; print and broadcast professionals; philosophers and historians of science, technologists, interested others. Promotes and provides a forum for examination and understanding of the impact of science and technology on society and the environment and the roles of citizens can take in guiding technology. Promotes methods of increasing technological literacy. Examines topics such as global climate change, workplace technology, alternative health care, toxic waste, and role of religion and ethics. **Awards:** Honorary Member. **Frequency:** annual. **Type:** recognition. **Recipient:** for distinguished service to STS. **Task Forces:** Issues. **Formerly:** National Association for Science, Technology and Society. **Publications:** *Bulletin of Science, Technology and Society*, bimonthly. Journal. **Price:** $35.00 /year for nonmembers; $30.00 /year for members. **Circulation:** 500 ● *STS Today*, quarterly. Newsletter. Includes articles, conference program and announcement. **Conventions/Meetings:** annual National STS Meeting - conference, for interdisciplinary thinkers concerned about the impact of science and technology on society (exhibits) - late February, in Baltimore/ Washington DC area.

7609 ■ International Federation of Nonlinear Analysts (IFNA)
c/o Dr. V. Lakshmikantham, Ed.-in-Chief
Florida Inst. of Tech.
150 W Univ. Blvd.
Melbourne, FL 32901
Ph: (321)674-7412
Fax: (321)674-7412
E-mail: sellings@fit.edu
URL: http://cos.fit.edu/math/ifna
Contact: Dr. V. Lakshmikantham, Ed.-in-Chief
Founded: 1991. **Members:** 400. **Membership Dues:** regular, $65 (annual). **Staff:** 1. **Multinational. Description:** Professional society promoting common understanding of related nonlinear problems and approaches to solutions from all disciplines. Hosts forums for the dissemination of information at a high level of technical detail, but without narrow focus. **Publications:** *Nonlinear Analysis Series B: Real World Applications*, quarterly. Journal. Attempts to understand, model, experiment, compute, predict and provide basic theories for analyzing and solving problems. **Price:** $40.00/year. ISSN: 0362-546X ● *Nonlinear Studies*. Journal. Contains scholarly research and coverage of developments concerning activities of IFNA and Regional Federations. **Conventions/Meetings:** quadrennial World Congress of Nonlinear Analysts - convention.

7610 ■ International Humic Substances Society (IHSS)
c/o Dr. Dan Olk, Natl. Coor.
Natl. Soil Tilth Lab.
2110 Univ. Blvd.
Ames, IA 50011-3120
Ph: (515)294-8412
Fax: (515)294-8125
E-mail: dan.olk@ars.usda.gov
URL: http://www.ihss.gatech.edu
Contact: Dr. Dan Olk, Natl. Coor.
Founded: 1981. **Members:** 900. **Membership Dues:** regular, $25 (annual) ● student/retired, $12 (annual). **Multinational. Description:** Promotes the study and public understanding of humic substances. Encourages the advancement of humic substances research. Fosters the scientific education and research of humic substances. Maintains the collection of standard and reference samples of humic substances. **Conventions/Meetings:** biennial conference.

7611 ■ International Society of African Scientists (ISAS)
PO Box 9209
Wilmington, DE 19809
E-mail: info@internationalsocietyofafricanscientists.org
URL: http://internationalsocietyofafricanscientists.org
Contact: Dr. Cyril E. Broderick, Pres.
Founded: 1982. **Members:** 100. **Membership Dues:** regular, $40 (annual) ● student, $10 (annual) ● associate, $25 (annual) ● life, $1,000. **Description:** Represents scientists and engineers of African descent. Provides a means by which members can use their professional expertise in solving the technical problems facing African and Caribbean nations; updates members on technical developments throughout the world, specifically in Africa and the Caribbean; fosters better communication and cooperation among scientists, engineers, and scientific organizations. Compiles and maintains a list of experts; provides a database of technical information. **Publications:** *ISAS Transactions of Annual Technical Conference*, annual. Proceedings ● Newsletter, quarterly. **Advertising:** accepted. **Conventions/Meetings:** annual Technical Conference, with Genetic Engineering: Technology for Sustainable Development, the Implications and Regulation of its use in Africa.

7612 ■ International Society for Bioluminescence and Chemiluminescence (ISBC)
c/o Erika Hawkins, Treas./Membership Sec.
2800 Woods Hollow Rd.
Madison, WI 53711
Ph: (608)274-4330
Fax: (608)277-2601
E-mail: erika.hawkins@promega.com
URL: http://www.isbc.unibo.it
Contact: Erika Hawkins, Treas./Membership Sec.
Founded: 1994. **Membership Dues:** student, $25 (annual) ● regular, $50 (annual) ● corporate, $1,000 (annual). **Multinational. Description:** Promotes the fundamental and applied sciences of bioluminescence and chemiluminescence throughout the world. Promotes and supports public understanding of science by organizing and supporting education and natural history initiatives. Fosters conservation of luminous species throughout the world. Encourages natural history projects providing new information on their distribution and biology. Provides a forum to facilitate interactions between academics of different disciplines and industry for research in bioluminescence and chemiluminescence. **Awards:** Marlene DeLuca Prize. **Frequency:** biennial. **Type:** recognition. **Recipient:** for young researchers. **Publications:** *Luminescence*, bimonthly. Journal. Publishes details of forthcoming meetings, information on new products, and book reviews. **Price:** $1,275.00 individual; $1,700.00 institutional (print only); $1,870.00 institutional (combined print with online access). ISSN: 1522-7235. **Advertising:** accepted. Alternate Formats: online ● Proceedings. Alternate Formats: online.

7613 ■ International Society of Iraqi Scientists (ISS)
PO Box 4445
Dearborn, MI 48126
Ph: (248)538-9121 (313)340-4341
Fax: (248)538-6034
E-mail: iss@issiraq.org
URL: http://www.issiraq.org
Contact: Prof. Hikmet Jamil MD, Pres.
Founded: 2000. **Membership Dues:** regular, adjunct, $50 (annual) ● corporate, $500 (annual) ● library, $100 (annual). **Multinational. Description:** Establishes and maintains collaborations among Iraqi scientists all over the world. Facilitates the exchange of knowledge in various fields among Iraqi scientists, regardless of locality. Advances the development of research and education in various communities. Contributes scientific support to different organizations within communities. Enhances Iraqi cultural awareness in the international community. **Telecommunication Services:** electronic mail, hjamil@med.wayne.edu. **Publications:** Newsletter, quarterly. **Price:** included in membership dues.

7614 ■ International Society for Nanoscale Science, Computation and Engineering (ISNSCE)
c/o Natasha Jonoska, Treas.
Dept. of Mathematics
Univ. of South Florida
4202 E Fowler Ave., PHY 114
Tampa, FL 33620-5700
E-mail: contactisnsce@isnsce.org
URL: http://www.isnsce.org
Contact: Natasha Jonoska, Treas.
Founded: 2004. **Membership Dues:** student, $25 (annual) ● regular, $60 (annual) ● corporation, $500 (annual). **Multinational. Description:** Promotes the study of the control of the arrangement of the atoms in matter. Unites fields of nanoscale computation with nanoscale science and engineering. Provides an official scientific forum for recognizing the most notable contributions in the area. **Telecommunication Services:** electronic mail, isnsce@chem.udel.edu ● electronic mail, jonoska@math.usf.edu. **Publications:** Newsletter. Alternate Formats: online.

7615 ■ Minority Women In Science (MWIS)
c/o American Association for the Advancement of Science
Directorate for Educ. and Human Resources Programs
1200 New York Ave. NW
Washington, DC 20005
Ph: (202)326-7019 (202)326-6670
Fax: (202)371-9849
E-mail: ygeorge@aaas.org
Contact: Yolanda George, Proj. Coor.
Founded: 1978. **Members:** 250. **Regional Groups:** 1. **Description:** A national network group of the American association for the Advancement of Science (AAAS), Education and Human Resources Directorate. The objectives of this group are: to identify and share information on resources and programs that could help in mentoring young women and minorities interested in science and engineering careers, and to strengthen communication among women and minorities in science and education. **Awards: Frequency:** annual. **Type:** recognition. **Recipient:** for new program ideas, community work to advance science. **Formerly:** National Network of Minority Women in Science. **Publications:** *Girls and Science Newsletter*. **Price:** free ● For orders call 1-800-222-7809. Collaboration for Equity; Fairness in Science and Math Education. Bibliography/Resources (96-23S). Striving for Gender Equity; National Programs to increase student engagement with Math and Science (96-25S); Environmental Checklist (96-29S). **Conventions/Meetings:** annual meeting and breakfast, held in conjunction with American Association for the Advancement of Science (exhibits).

7616 ■ National Academy of Sciences (NAS)
500 Fifth St. NW
Washington, DC 20001
Ph: (202)334-2000
Fax: (202)334-2158
E-mail: webmailbox@nas.edu
URL: http://www.nasonline.org
Contact: Ralph J. Cicerone, Pres.
Founded: 1741. **Members:** 1,637. **Description:** Private, honorary organization dedicated to the furtherance of science and engineering; members are elected in recognition of their distinguished and continuing contributions to either of the two fields. Founded by an act of Congress to serve as official adviser to the federal government on scientific and technical matters. **Awards:** Gilbert Morgan Smith Medal. **Frequency:** biennial. **Type:** medal. **Recipient:** for published research on marine or fresh water algae ● Henry Draper Medal. **Frequency:** periodic. **Type:** medal. **Recipient:** for investigations in astronomical physics ● J. Lawrence Smith Medal. **Frequency:** periodic. **Type:** medal. **Recipient:** for investigations of meteoric bodies ● James Craig Watson Medal. **Frequency:** periodic. **Type:** medal. **Recipient:** for contributions to the science of astronomy ● Jessie Stevenson Kovalenko Medal. **Frequency:** periodic. **Type:** medal. **Recipient:** for important contributions to the medical sciences ● John J. Carty Award for the Advancement of Science. **Frequency:** periodic. **Type:** medal. **Recipient:** for noteworthy and distinguished accomplishments in any field of science ● NAS Award for Behavioral Research Relevant to the Prevention of Nuclear War. **Frequency:** periodic. **Type:** recognition. **Recipient:** for outstanding research on the problems and issues relating to the risk of nuclear war ● Troland Research Awards. **Frequency:** annual. **Type:** recognition. **Recipient:** for the outstanding research on the relationships of consciousness and the physical world. **Affiliated With:** Institute of Medicine; National Academy of Engineering; National Research Council. **Publica-**

tions: *Biographical Memoirs.* Bibliography ● *Organization and Members Directory*, annual. Membership Directory ● *Proceedings of the National Academy of Sciences*, bimonthly. **Conventions/Meetings:** annual meeting - always last week of April.

7617 ■ National Association of Academies of Science (NAAS)

c/o Dr. Michael Strauss, Pres.
4918 King Richard Dr.
Annandale, VA 22003
Ph: (703)323-7810
E-mail: michael_strauss1@hotmail.com
URL: http://astro.physics.sc.edu/naas
Contact: Dr. Michael Strauss, Pres.

Founded: 1926. **Members:** 44. **Regional Groups:** 44. **Description:** Represents state and regional academies of science. Provides an organization for the promotion, through mutual cooperation, of the common aims of the various academies and of the American Association for the Advancement of Science. Aids all academies in their common purposes and accomplishments. Sponsors the American Junior Academy of Science for outstanding high school students. **Awards:** Distinguished Service Award. **Frequency:** annual. **Type:** recognition. **Recipient:** for outstanding service to the NAAS and/or to an individual academy. **Committees:** American Junior Academy of Science. **Affiliated With:** American Association for the Advancement of Science. **Formerly:** (1969) Academy Conference; (1979) Association of Academies of Science. **Publications:** *Directory and Proceedings*, annual. Handbook. Alternate Formats: online ● *NAAS Newsletter*, quarterly. Alternate Formats: online. **Conventions/Meetings:** annual meeting, in conjunction with AAAS (exhibits).

7618 ■ National Council of Black Engineers and Scientists (NCBES)

1525 Aviation Blvd., Ste.C-424
Redondo Beach, CA 90278
Ph: (213)896-9779
Contact: Chris Hammonds, Pres.

Founded: 1986. **Description:** Represents the interests of black engineers and scientists. Aims to increase minority participation in technical professions.

7619 ■ National Hydrogen Association (NHA)

1211 Connecticut Ave. NW, Ste.600
Washington, DC 20036-2705
Ph: (202)223-5547
Fax: (202)223-5537
E-mail: info@hydrogenassociation.org
URL: http://www.hydrogenassociation.org
Contact: Karen Hall, VP, Technical Operations

Founded: 1989. **Members:** 100. **Membership Dues:** sustaining, $15,600 (annual) ● industry (based on annual gross revenues), $6,200-$8,000 (annual) ● small business, government, nonprofit, $2,100 (annual) ● university/education, $1,100 (annual) ● regular, $300 (annual) ● student/teacher, $25 (annual). **Staff:** 7. **Description:** Represents industry, university, research, and small business members who are interested in fostering the development of hydrogen technologies, and their utilization in industrial and commercial applications. Strives to promote the transition role of hydrogen in the energy field. **Committees:** Codes and Standards; Implementation Plan; Policy. **Publications:** *H2 Digest*, quarterly. Newsletter ● *NHA News*, quarterly. Newsletter ● Also publishes technical documents and meeting proceedings, and maintains an active website. **Conventions/Meetings:** annual conference, hydrogen-related products and services (exhibits).

7620 ■ National Organization of Gay and Lesbian Scientists and Technical Professionals (NOGLSTP)

PO Box 91803
Pasadena, CA 91109
Ph: (626)791-7689
Fax: (626)791-7689
E-mail: office@noglstp.org
URL: http://www.noglstp.org
Contact: Rochelle Diamond, Chair

Founded: 1979. **Members:** 290. **Membership Dues:** individual, $35 (annual) ● student, $10 (annual). **Budget:** $2,500. **Regional Groups:** 1. **Description:** Gay and lesbian individuals employed or interested in high-technology or scientific fields; interested organizations. Works to: educate the public, especially the gay and scientific communities; improve members' employment and professional environment; provide role models through mentoring and recognition awards; interact with professional organizations; foster intercity contacts among members. **Affiliated With:** American Association for the Advancement of Science. **Supersedes:** (1980) Lesbian and Gay Associated Engineers and Scientists. **Publications:** *NOGLSTP Bulletin*, quarterly. Includes discussion of issues relevant to the gay and scientific communities. Alternate Formats: online ● *Queer Scientists of Historical Note*. Pamphlet. **Conventions/Meetings:** annual Forum/Reception - meeting, held in conjunction with American Association for Advancement of Science Annual Convention.

7621 ■ National Research Council (NRC)

c/o National Academy of Sciences
500 5th St. NW
Washington, DC 20001
Ph: (202)334-2000
URL: http://www.nationalacademies.org/nrc
Contact: Ralph J. Cicerone, Chm.

Founded: 1916. **Staff:** 1,100. **Budget:** $180,000,000. **Description:** Scientists, engineers, and other professionals serving pro bono on approximately 900 study committees. Serves as an independent adviser to the federal government on scientific and technical questions of national importance; is jointly administered by the National Academy of Sciences, National Academy of Engineering, and Institute of Medicine. Carries out objectives through conferences, technical committees, surveys, collection and analysis of scientific and technical data, and administration of public and private funds for research projects and fellowships. **Libraries: Type:** not open to the public. **Subgroups:** Division on Behavioral and Social Sciences and Education; Division on Earth and Life Studies; Division on Engineering and Physical Sciences; Institute of Medicine; Policy and Global Affairs Division; Transportation Research. **Publications:** *The National Academies InFocus*, 3/year. Magazine. Covers the activities of the NAS, NAE, IOM, and NRC and the studies of their respective units. Includes book reviews. **Price:** $10.00/year in U.S.; $12.00/year outside U.S. **Circulation:** 20,000. Alternate Formats: online ● Newsletters ● Reports.

7622 ■ National Science Foundation (NSF)

4201 Wilson Blvd.
Arlington, VA 22230
Ph: (703)292-5111 (703)292-8000
Free: (800)877-8339
E-mail: info@nsf.gov
URL: http://www.nsf.gov
Contact: Dr. Arden L. Bement Jr., Dir.

Founded: 1950. **Staff:** 1,200. **Budget:** $5,300,000,000. **Description:** Independent agency in the Executive Branch concerned primarily with the support of basic and applied research and education in the sciences and engineering. Funds scientific research in mathematical, physical, biological, computer, engineering, social and other sciences, including unclassified research activities in matters relating to international cooperation; fosters the interchange of scientific information; supports the development and use of computers and other scientific methods and technologies. Administers U.S. Antarctic Research Program (see separate entry), Arctic Research Program, and Office of Polar Program. Supports: National Center for Atmospheric Research, Boulder, CO; National Optical Astronomy Observatory, Tucson, AZ; National Radio Astronomy Observatory, Green Bank, WV; and National Astronomy and Ionosphere Center, Arecibo, PR. **Convention/Meeting:** none. **Libraries: Type:** open to the public. **Holdings:** 15,000. **Computer Services:** Online services, STIS. **Telecommunication Services:** TDD, (703)292-5090 ● TDD, (800)281-8749. **Divisions:** Advanced Scientific Computing; Astronomical Sciences; Atmospheric Sciences; Bioengineering and Environmental Systems; Biological Instrumentation and Resources; Chemical and Transport Systems; Chemistry; Civil and Mechanical Structures; Computer and Computation Research; Cross-Disciplinary Activities; Design, Manufacture, and Industrial Innovation; Earth Sciences; Educational Systematic Reform; Electrical and Communications Systems; Elementary, Secondary, and Informal Education; Engineering Education and Centers; Environmental Biology; Graduate Education and Research Development; Industrial Innovation Interface; Information; Integrative Biology and Neuroscience; International Programs; Materials Research; Mathematical Sciences; Mechanical and Structural Systems; Microelectronic Information Processing Systems; Molecular and Cellular Biosciences; Networking and Communications Research and Infrastructure; Ocean Sciences; Physics; Polar Programs; Research, Evaluation, and Communications; Robotics, and Intelligent Systems; Science and Technology Infrastructure; Science Resources Studies; Social, Behavioral, and Cognitive Sciences; Systemic Reform; Undergraduate Education. **Subgroups:** Biological Sciences; Computer and Information Science and Engineering; Education and Human Resources; Engineering; Geosciences; Mathematical and Physical Sciences; Social, Behavioral, and Economic Sciences. **Publications:** *Guide to Programs*, annual ● *Science Indicators*, biennial ● Bulletin, 10/year. Alternate Formats: online ● Report, annual.

7623 ■ New York Academy of Sciences (NYAS)

7 World Trade Ctr.
250 Greenwich St., 40th Fl.
New York, NY 10007-2157
Ph: (212)298-8600 (212)298-8640
Free: (800)843-6927
Fax: (212)298-3650
E-mail: membership@nyas.org
URL: http://www.nyas.org
Contact: John E. Sexton, Chm.

Founded: 1817. **Members:** 26,000. **Membership Dues:** national, $95 (annual) ● international, $115 (annual) ● student in U.S., $35 (annual) ● student outside U.S., $50 (annual) ● patron, $200 (annual) ● associate, $60 (annual) ● affiliate, $30 (annual). **Staff:** 80. **Budget:** $11,300,000. **Description:** Commits to advance science, technology, and society worldwide. Initiatives include: disseminating scientific information, advancing scientific education, protecting the human rights of scientist, and applying science and technology to achieve social and economic goals. **Committees:** Development; Educational Advisory; Human Rights of Scientists; International Cooperation in Research; New York / New Jersey Harbor; Technology-in-Economic Development. **Sections:** Anthropology; Atmospheric and Geologic Sciences; Biochemistry; Biological; Biomedical; Biophysics; Chemical; Computer and Information; Economics; Engineering; Environmental; Geological; History and Philosophy of Science; Inorganic Chemistry and Catalytic; Linguistics; Mathematics; Microbiology; Neuroscience; Physics and Astronomy; Polymer; Psychology; Science and Public Policy; Science Education; Women in Science. **Publications:** *Annals of the New York Academy of Sciences*, 28/year. Proceedings. Features a scholarly compilation of research papers from conferences. **Price:** $145.00/ volume. ISSN: 0077-8923. Alternate Formats: online ● *Intersections*, monthly. **Circulation:** 9,000 ● *The Sciences*, bimonthly. Magazine. Includes topics in science. **Price:** $23.00 for nonmembers; included in membership dues. **Circulation:** 65,000. **Advertising:** accepted ● *Update*, bimonthly. Magazine. Contains news about the academy, members and programs. **Price:** free. **Circulation:** 26,000. Alternate Formats: online ● Proceedings. **Conventions/Meetings:** conference, discusses research-oriented topics with social and economic implications - 10/year ● workshop.

7624 ■ North American Catalysis Society (NACS)

c/o John N. Armor, Pres.
7201 Hamilton Blvd.
Allentown, PA 18195-1501
Ph: (610)481-5792
E-mail: armorjn@apci.com
URL: http://www.nacatsoc.org
Contact: John N. Armor, Pres.

Founded: 1956. **Members:** 2,000. **Membership Dues:** individual, $5 (annual) ● student, $1 (annual). **Local Groups:** 14. **Description:** Works to promote and encourage the growth and development of the science of catalysis. Offers educational services; provides a forum for the exchange of information; acts as a liaison with foreign catalysis societies. **Awards:** Eugene Houdry Award in Applied Catalysis. **Frequency:** biennial. **Type:** recognition ● F.G. Ciapetta Lectureship in Catalysis. **Frequency:** biennial. **Type:** recognition ● Paul H. Emmett Award in Fundamental Catalysis. **Frequency:** biennial. **Type:** recognition ● Robert Burwell Lectureship in Catalysis. **Frequency:** biennial. **Type:** recognition. **Formed by Merger of:** (1995) Catalysis Society. **Publications:** *North American Catalysis Society Newsletter*, quarterly. **Circulation:** 2,000. Alternate Formats: online. **Conventions/Meetings:** biennial conference, forum for the discussion of relevant technological issues and state of the art research (exhibits).

7625 ■ Oak Ridge Associated Universities (ORAU)

PO Box 117
Oak Ridge, TN 37831-0117
Ph: (865)576-3146
Fax: (865)241-2923
E-mail: phillipc@orau.gov
URL: http://www.orau.org
Contact: Carla Phillips, Contact

Founded: 1946. **Members:** 87. **Staff:** 500. **Budget:** $70,000,000. **Description:** Represents private, not-for-profit corporations and a consortium of 91 doctoral-granting colleges and universities. Serves the government, academia, and the private sector in important areas of science and technology. Manages and operates the Oak Ridge Institute for Science and Education (ORISE) for the U.S. Department of Energy. ORISE undertakes national and international programs in education, training, health, and the environment. **Libraries: Type:** reference. **Telecommunication Services:** electronic mail, carla.phillips@orau.org. **Departments:** Business Support Operations; General Counsel, Human Resources; Office of Partnerships. **Divisions:** Independent Environmental Assessment and Verification; National Security and Emergency Management; Occupational Exposure and Worker Health; Professional and Technical Training; Radiation Emergency Medicine; Science Education Programs; Scientific and Technical Resource Integration. **Affiliated With:** American Association for the Advancement of Science; Council for Advancement and Support of Education. **Formerly:** (1966) Oak Ridge Institute of Nuclear Studies. **Publications:** Annual Report, annual. **Circulation:** 2,000 ● Also publishes technical reports and policy studies related to the medical sciences, energy, the environment, education, and training.

7626 ■ Pacific Science Association (PSA)

c/o Bishop Museum
1525 Bernice St.
Honolulu, HI 96817
Ph: (808)848-4124 (808)944-7245
Fax: (808)847-8252
E-mail: psa@bishopmuseum.org
URL: http://www.pacificscience.org
Contact: John Burke Burnett, Exec. Sec.

Founded: 1920. **Members:** 100. **Membership Dues:** individual, $40 (annual) ● associate scientific association, $50 (annual) ● corporate associate, $100 (annual). **Staff:** 1. **Description:** Countries within or bordering the Pacific Ocean; scientists, scientific societies, institutions, and corporations. Initiates and promotes the study of scientific problems relating to the Pacific region; encourages cooperation among scientists of all Pacific countries. **Awards:** Honorary Life Fellows. **Frequency:** biennial. **Type:** fellowship. **Recipient:** for service to the Pacific area and the PSA. **Telecommunication Services:** electronic mail, burnett@bishopmuseum.org. **Publications:** *International Fax Directory for Biologists* ● *Pacific Science*, quarterly. Journal ● Proceedings, periodic. **Conventions/Meetings:** quadrennial Inter-Congress ● quadrennial Pacific Science Congress (exhibits).

7627 ■ Science for the People (SFTP)

Address Unknown since 2007

Founded: 1969. **Members:** 2,000. **Regional Groups:** 3. **Local Groups:** 7. **Description:** Scientists and others concerned about the social implications of science and technology. Promotes science as a potential method of meeting human needs for general well-being, but maintains that the potential of science is not realized in a "society that puts profits before people and military expansion before real security." Working to demystify science and technology. Investigates and exposes connections among the government, the military, industry, and universities; provides technical assistance to progressive organizations and oppressed peoples. Committed to the development of an organization without racism, sexism, classism, or homophobia. Operates Research Conversion program to effect a change in research priorities from military to civilian needs. Conducts science education programs addressing both the technical and social context of science. Plans to implement Women's Access to Technology and Science program. **Working Groups:** Computers; Disarmament; Energy; Food and Agriculture; Philosophy of Science and Sociobiology; Toxic Chemicals; Women in Science. **Formerly:** SESPA (Scientists and Engineers for Social and Political Action). **Publications:** Articles ● Books ● Newsletter, periodic ● Pamphlets ● Also distributes back issues of *Science for the People Magazine*.

7628 ■ Science Service (SS)

1719 N St. NW
Washington, DC 20036
Ph: (202)785-2255
Fax: (202)785-1243
E-mail: webmaster@sciserv.org
URL: http://www.sciserv.org
Contact: Elizabeth Marincola, Pres.

Founded: 1921. **Staff:** 45. **Budget:** $10,000,000. **Languages:** English, Spanish. **Nonmembership. Multinational. Description:** Aims to enhance public understanding of science. Informs the scientist and nonscientist of developments in science and its applications; encourages young people to engage in scientific efforts such as laboratory research and the communication of scientific results. Places special emphasis on increasing opportunities for populations traditionally underrepresented in the sciences. Sponsors science writing intern program; administers the annual Intel International Science and Engineering Fair (ISEF), which brings together 1400 student participants from the United States, its territories, and over 40 countries; conducts annual Intel Science Talent Search to identify U.S. high school seniors talented in science, mathematics, and engineering; and administers the Discovery Channel Young Scientist Challenge, a competition challenge program for middle school students. **Computer Services:** database, subscriber list. **Publications:** *Science News*, weekly. Magazine. **Price:** $54.50/year. ISSN: 0036-8423. **Circulation:** 150,000. **Advertising:** accepted. Alternate Formats: online. **Conventions/Meetings:** annual Discovery Channel Young Scientist Competition, a week in which 40 middle school students, nominated by their local science fairs and selected by a national panel of judges, participate in multidisciplinary challenges as part of teams ● annual Intel International Science and Engineering Fair - competition, nationwide high school science fair ● annual Intel Science Talent Search - competition, a week in which 40 high school seniors, selected on the basis of their research projects, come to Washington, DC, to be judged for scholarships and to interact with renowned scientists.

7629 ■ Skeptics Society

PO Box 338
Altadena, CA 91001
Ph: (626)794-3119
Fax: (626)794-1301
E-mail: skepticsociety@skeptic.com
URL: http://www.skeptic.com
Contact: Dr. Michael Shermer, Exec. Dir.

Founded: 1992. **Members:** 40,000. **Membership Dues:** individual, $30 (annual) ● in Canada and Mexico, $40 (annual) ● other country, $50 (annual). **Staff:** 25. **Budget:** $2,000,000. **Description:** Scholars, scientists, and historians. Promotes the use of scientific methods to scrutinize such non-scientific traditions as religion, myth, superstition, mysticism, new age beliefs, and cults. Adheres to the posture of 17th century Dutch philosopher Baruch Spinoza, who said "I have made a ceaseless effort not to ridicule, not to bewail, not to scorn human actions, but to understand them." Investigates claims by scientists, pseudoscientists, and others on theories and conjectures about such topics as: life after death, the quest for immortality, differences between science and pseudoscience, magic and the paranormal, medical and psychiatric claims, and the use and abuse of theory and statistics in science. Conducts children's services, research, and educational programs; maintains speakers' bureau. **Libraries: Type:** not open to the public. **Holdings:** 10,000; articles, books, periodicals. **Subjects:** science, pseudoscience, history of science, history, psychology, philosophy, evolution, creationism, paranormal events. **Awards:** Dumbth Award. **Frequency:** annual. **Type:** recognition ● Randi Award. **Frequency:** annual. **Type:** recognition. **Recipient:** to the Skeptic of the year. **Computer Services:** database ● mailing lists ● online services. **Publications:** *eSkeptic*, weekly. Newsletter. **Price:** free for members. Alternate Formats: online ● *Skeptic*, quarterly. Magazine. Contains articles, essays, reviews, and letters on the history of science, magic, superstition, and skepticism. **Price:** included in membership dues; $30.00 for nonmembers in U.S.; $40.00 for nonmembers in Canada and Mexico; $50.00 for nonmembers in other country. ISSN: 1063-9330. **Circulation:** 40,000. **Advertising:** accepted. Alternate Formats: online ● Audiotapes. **Conventions/Meetings:** annual Lecture Series at Caltech - conference - usually June.

7630 ■ Society for Advancement of Chicanos and Native Americans in Science (SACNAS)

PO Box 8526
Santa Cruz, CA 95061-8526
Ph: (831)459-0170
Free: (877)722-6271
Fax: (831)459-0194
E-mail: info@sacnas.org
URL: http://www.sacnas.org
Contact: Judith Camacho, Exec. Dir.

Founded: 1973. **Members:** 1,700. **Membership Dues:** regular, $65 (annual) ● student, $24 (annual) ● K-12 teacher/postdoc, $45 (annual) ● life, $500 ● friend, $1,000 (annual). **Staff:** 14. **Description:** College professors, science professionals, undergraduate and graduate science students, and K-12 science teachers. Seeks to increase the participation of Latinos and Native Americans in the sciences. Promotes graduate science education in the minority community. **Libraries: Type:** open to the public. **Awards:** Financial Scholarships. **Frequency:** annual. **Type:** monetary. **Recipient:** for conference attendee. **Affiliated With:** American Association for the Advancement of Science. **Publications:** *SACNAS News*, 3/year. Journal. **Price:** included in membership dues. **Circulation:** 15,000. **Advertising:** accepted. Alternate Formats: online. **Conventions/Meetings:** annual conference and symposium, includes recruiters from graduate schools, summer programs, internships, fellowships, employers, and publishers (exhibits) - usually October. 2008 Oct. 9-12, Salt Lake City, UT ● workshop, science teaching ● workshop, for students.

7631 ■ Society for Amateur Scientists (SAS)

5600 Post Rd., Ste.114-341
East Greenwich, RI 02818
Ph: (401)398-7001
Fax: (401)398-7002

E-mail: info@sas.org
URL: http://www.sas.org
Contact: Shawn Carlson PhD, Exec. Dir./Founder
Founded: 1994. **Members:** 20,000. **Membership Dues:** individual, $35 ● student, $25 ● family, $50 ● Friends Circle, $100-$999 ● Franklin Circle, $1,000-$10,000. **Budget:** $300,000. **Description:** Educates and encourages people with a passion for science to take part in scientific adventures. Supports and mentors amateur scientists. **Awards:** Benjamin Franklin Citizen Science Award. **Frequency:** annual. **Type:** recognition. **Recipient:** for extraordinary scientific contributions of citizen scientists. **Projects:** LABRats. **Publications:** *The Citizen Scientist*, biweekly. Newsletter. Contains science news, ideas, techniques, and articles for amateur scientists. Alternate Formats: online.

7632 ■ Society of Automotive Engineers (SAE)
400 Commonwealth Dr.
Warrendale, PA 15096-0001
Ph: (724)776-4970 (724)776-4841
Free: (877)606-7323
Fax: (724)776-0790
E-mail: customerservice@sae.org
URL: http://www.sae.org
Contact: Richard Schaum, Pres.
Founded: 1905. **Members:** 85,000. **Membership Dues:** professional, $100 (annual) ● student, $10 (annual). **Staff:** 280. **Budget:** $52,000,000. **Multinational. Description:** Represents engineers, business executives, educators, and students from more than 97 countries who come together to share information and exchange ideas for advancing the engineering of mobility systems. Serves as a major source of technical information and expertise used in designing, building, maintaining and operating self-propelled vehicles, whether land-, sea-, air-, or space-based. Collection, organization, storage and dissemination of information on cars, trucks, aircraft, space vehicles, off-highway vehicles, marine equipment, and engines of all types. Produces technical publications, conducts numerous meetings, seminars and educational activities, and fosters information exchange among the worldwide automotive and aerospace communities. **Libraries: Type:** reference. **Holdings:** papers. **Awards:** Aerospace Chair Award. **Frequency:** annual. **Type:** recognition. **Recipient:** for outstanding leadership demonstrated by chairs of committees under the Aerospace Council and Air & Space Group ● Ambassadors Club. **Frequency:** annual. **Type:** recognition. **Recipient:** for outstanding contributions to the advancement of SAE membership ● Max Bentele Award for Engine Technology Innovation. **Frequency:** annual. **Type:** recognition. **Recipient:** to a member whose work has furthered innovation in the manufacture, design and improvement of engine technology for ground, air or space vehicles ● Vincent Bendix Automotive Electronics Engineering Award. **Frequency:** annual. **Type:** recognition. **Recipient:** for the best paper(s) relating to automotive electronics engineering. **Publications:** *Aerospace Engineering*, 11/year. Magazine. **Price:** $75.00 /year for nonmembers in U.S., Canada and Mexico; $135.00 /year for nonmembers outside North America. **Advertising:** accepted. Alternate Formats: online ● *Automotive Engineering International*, monthly ● *Off-Highway Engineering*, 7/year ● *Papers, Books, Standards* ● *SAE Show Daily* ● *SAE Update*, monthly ● *Worldwide Automotive Supplier Directory*, annual. **Price:** $329.00. Alternate Formats: online ● Newsletters. Alternate Formats: online ● Magazines. Alternate Formats: online ● Annual Report, annual. Alternate Formats: online ● Papers ● Brochures. Alternate Formats: online. **Conventions/Meetings:** annual congress, with 1300 technical presentations and 1200 exhibitors from around the world (exhibits) ● annual meeting.

7633 ■ Society for Social Studies of Science (4S)
c/o Dr. Wesley Shrum, Sec.
Louisiana State Univ.
Dept. of Sociology
126 Stubbs Hall
Baton Rouge, LA 70803
Ph: (225)578-5311
Fax: (225)578-5102
E-mail: shrum@lsu.edu
URL: http://www.4sonline.org
Contact: Dr. Wesley Shrum, Sec.
Founded: 1975. **Members:** 800. **Membership Dues:** professional, $45 (annual) ● student, scholar from non-OECD country, $22 (annual). **Description:** Individuals from academic, governmental, and industrial settings in fields such as sociology, anthropology, economics, history, information science, philosophy, political science, psychology, and natural science. Objectives are to facilitate interdisciplinary communication among those interested in social studies of science and technology. **Libraries: Type:** reference. **Holdings:** books, films. **Awards:** John Desmond Bernal Award. **Frequency:** annual. **Type:** recognition ● Ludwik Fleck Prize. **Frequency:** annual. **Type:** recognition ● Rachel Carson Award. **Frequency:** annual. **Type:** recognition. **Affiliated With:** American Association for the Advancement of Science. **Publications:** *Science, Technology, and Human Values*, bimonthly. Journal. Contains book reviews. **Price:** included in membership dues; $30.00 /year for nonmembers; $15.00/year for students ● *Technoscience Updates*, monthly. Newsletter. **Conventions/Meetings:** annual conference (exhibits).

7634 ■ U.S. Federation of Scholars and Scientists (USFSS)
c/o Prof. Roger Dittmann, PhD, Pres.
California State Univ. at Fullerton
Dept. of Physics
Fullerton, CA 92834-6866
Ph: (714)278-3421 (714)758-9150
Fax: (714)278-5810
E-mail: rdittmann@fullerton.edu
URL: http://faculty.fullerton.edu/rdittmann
Contact: Prof. Roger Dittmann PhD, Pres.
Founded: 1938. **Members:** 200. **Membership Dues:** affiliation, $100 (annual) ● individual, $50 (annual). **Staff:** 4. **Budget:** $2,000. **Regional Groups:** 2. **Local Groups:** 3. **Description:** Scholars and scientists concerned with the national and international relations of science and society and with organizational aspects of science. Maintains regular communication and contact with scholars and scientists all over the world. **Computer Services:** database ● mailing lists. **Subgroups:** California Peace Academy; Southern California Federation of Scientists. **Formerly:** (1988) American Association of Scientific Workers; (1989) U.S. Federation of Scientists and Scholars. **Publications:** *The Concerned Scholar*, bimonthly. Newsletter. **Price:** free for members. **Conventions/Meetings:** annual board meeting.

7635 ■ Women in Science and Engineering (WISE)
c/o National Academy of Science
500 5th St. NW
Washington, DC 20001
Ph: (202)334-2063
E-mail: tbrown@nas.edu
URL: http://www7.nationalacademies.org/wise
Contact: Tenecia Brown, Chair
Founded: 1993. **Description:** Works to increase awareness and recognition of women's contributions to the sciences, engineering, and medical professions, and to enhance and mentor women. **Conventions/Meetings:** quarterly Book Club - meeting ● bimonthly Brownbag Seminars ● annual Career Day - conference - fall ● Lecture Series.

Scientific Cooperation

7636 ■ Turkish American Scientists and Scholars Association (TASSA)
1526 18th St. NW
Washington, DC 20036
Free: (800)620-4120
E-mail: info@tassausa.org
URL: http://www.tassausa.org
Contact: Suleyman Gokoglu PhD, Pres.
Founded: 2004. **Membership Dues:** regular, $75 (annual) ● overseas, $35 (annual) ● student, $25 (annual). **Multinational. Description:** Promotes friendship and fellowship among Turkish-American professionals engaged in engineering, natural life and social sciences. Enhances the professional status of Turkish-American professionals. Promotes educational and scientific cooperation between the USA and Turkey. **Computer Services:** Online services, forum. **Telecommunication Services:** electronic mail, president@tassausa.org. **Committees:** Annual Conference; Bylaws and Elections; Fundraising; Visiting Scholars; Web Development. **Subgroups:** Engineering and Applied Sciences; Health and Biomedical Sciences; Natural Sciences.

Security

7637 ■ United States Industry Coalition (USIC)
1525 Wilson Blvd., Ste.150
Arlington, VA 22209
Ph: (703)526-9447
Free: (800)339-8742
Fax: (703)526-0928
E-mail: hpeterson@usic.net
URL: http://www.usic.net
Contact: Mr. Charles H. Peterson, Gen. Counsel
Founded: 1994. **Membership Dues:** individual/company/other organization, $100 (annual) ● small business, $500 (annual) ● consortia of non-profit business, university/college, $2,000 (annual) ● large business, consortia of for-profit business, $5,000 (annual). **Multinational. Description:** Represents American businesses, associations and academic institutions who are actively engaged in technology commercialization. Facilitates technology commercialization in favor of national security, nonproliferation and global peace. Progresses global security by forming commercial partnerships with scientists and engineers previously engaged in weapons of mass destruction development. **Libraries: Type:** reference. **Holdings:** photographs, reports. **Publications:** *E-Notes*. Newsletter. Alternate Formats: online ● Annual Report, annual. Alternate Formats: online.

Seismology

7638 ■ Earthquake Engineering Research Institute (EERI)
499 14th St., Ste.320
Oakland, CA 94612-1934
Ph: (510)451-0905
Fax: (510)451-5411
E-mail: eeri@eeri.org
URL: http://www.eeri.org
Contact: Susan K. Tubbesing, Exec. Dir.
Founded: 1949. **Members:** 2,500. **Membership Dues:** student, $40 (annual) ● active, $231 (annual) ● affiliate, $154 (annual) ● retired, young professional, $115 (annual) ● institution, $462 (annual) ● reduced e-student, $25 (annual). **Staff:** 8. **Budget:** $1,300,000. **Regional Groups:** 3. **Description:** Professionals interested in earthquake hazard reduction, particularly with regard to the built environment. Operates 22 committees. Maintains annual student paper competition; conducts seminars and workshops, provides 2 fellowships. **Libraries: Type:** reference. **Holdings:** reports. **Awards:** Graduate Fellowship. **Frequency:** annual. **Type:** fellowship ● Housner Medal. **Frequency:** annual. **Type:** medal ● Outstanding Paper Award. **Frequency:** annual. **Type:** recognition ● Professional Fellowship. **Frequency:** annual. **Type:** fellowship. **Telecommunication Services:** electronic mail, juliane@eeri.org. **Affiliated With:** Seismological Society of America. **Publications:** *Earthquake Spectra*, quarterly. Journal. **Price:** $205.00 /year for institutions; $145.00 /year for nonmembers; free for members. **Circulation:** 2,800 ● *EERI Newsletter*, monthly. ISSN: 0270-8337. **Circulation:** 2,600. Alternate Formats: online ● *Roster of Members*, annual. Directory ● Also publishes catalog, monographs, conference proceedings, and reports.

Conventions/Meetings: annual meeting (exhibits) ● quadrennial National Conference on Earthquake Engineering.

7639 ■ International Association of Seismology and Physics of the Earth's Interior (IASPEI)

c/o Prof. Thorne Lay
Univ. of California - Santa Cruz
Earth Sci. Dept.
Santa Cruz, CA 95064
Ph: (831)459-3164
Fax: (831)459-3074
E-mail: thorne@pmc.ucsc.edu
URL: http://www.iaspei.org
Contact: Prof. Thorne Lay, Contact

Membership Dues: individual, $20 (annual). **Multinational. Description:** Promotes scientific study of issues related to earthquakes and other seismic sources, propagation of seismic waves, and Earth's internal structure, properties and processes. **Commissions:** Asian Seismological; Earth Structure and Geodynamics; Earthquake Hazard, Risk and Strong Ground Motion; Earthquake Sources - Prediction and Modelling; Education and Outreach; European Seismological; Seismological Observation and Interpretation; Tectonophysics and Crustal Structure. **Publications:** *IASPEI Manual of Seismological Observatory Practice*. Alternate Formats: online ● *International Handbook of Earthquake and Engineering Seismology*. Alternate Formats: CD-ROM ● Annual Report ● Brochure. Alternate Formats: online. **Conventions/Meetings:** periodic general assembly ● biennial general assembly - 2009 Jan. 10-16, Pretoria, Republic of South Africa ● periodic symposium.

7640 ■ International Tsunami Information Center (ITIC)

737 Bishop St., Ste.2200
Honolulu, HI 96813
Ph: (808)532-6423 (808)532-6422
Fax: (808)532-5576
E-mail: l.kong@unesco.org
URL: http://www.tsunamiwave.info
Contact: Dr. Laura Kong, Dir.

Founded: 1965. **Members:** 25. **Staff:** 2. **Multinational. Description:** Maintained by the National Oceanic and Atmospheric Administration, National Weather Service, member states, and by the Intergovernmental Oceanographic Commission (see separate entry). Consists of scientists interested in tsunamis ("extensive and often very destructive ocean waves caused by violent submarine earthquake; erroneously called 'tidal waves'"); affiliated members are various countries and dependencies belonging to the Intergovernmental Oceanographic Commission who are involved in the Tsunami Warning Services in the Pacific. Insures the dissemination of tsunami warnings and collects tsunami information; encourages research; promotes exchange of scientific and technical personnel. Conducts specialized education and research programs. **Libraries: Type:** open to the public. **Holdings:** 4,500; reports. **Subjects:** tsunami, earthquake, coastal engineering. **Telecommunication Services:** electronic mail, itic.tsunami@unesco.org. **Publications:** *International Tsunami Information Center - Newsletter*, quarterly. Covers oceanography, geophysics, seismology, volcanology, geology, and other topics related to tsunami. **Price:** free. **Circulation:** 400. Alternate Formats: online. Also Cited As: *Tsunami Newsletter*. **Conventions/Meetings:** biennial Meeting of the International Coordination Group for the Tsunami: Warning Systems in the Pacific - assembly and meeting.

7641 ■ National Information Service for Earthquake Engineering (NISEE)

Univ. of California, Berkeley
1301 S 46th St.
RFS 453
Richmond, CA 94804-4698
Ph: (510)665-3419
E-mail: eerclibrary@berkeley.edu
URL: http://nisee.berkeley.edu
Contact: Chuck James, Information Systems Mgr.

Founded: 1971. **Description:** Serves as public service project and technical library that collects and disseminates technical information on earthquake structural and geotechnical engineering and engineering seismology. Provides researchers with engineering software, technical reports, research studies and data. Maintains the Steinbrugge Earthquake Engineering slide collection and other visual resource materials. **Convention/Meeting:** none. **Libraries: Type:** reference; lending; open to the public. **Holdings:** 48,000; audiovisuals, books, periodicals, photographs, reports. **Subjects:** earthquake engineering, seismology, disaster planning, soil dynamics. **Computer Services:** database, Earthquake Engineering Abstracts ● online services, Archive in Earthquake Engineering. **Publications:** *EERC Reports*, periodic ● *PEER Reports*, 20/year. **Price:** $500.00/year domestic (2003 series); $500.00/year international (2003 series); $375.00/year domestic (2002 series); $45.00/copy.

7642 ■ Seismological Society of America (SSA)

201 Plaza Professional Bldg.
El Cerrito, CA 94530
Ph: (510)525-5474 (510)559-1782
Fax: (510)525-7204
E-mail: info@seismosoc.org
URL: http://www.seismosoc.org
Contact: Susan B. Newman, Exec. Dir.

Founded: 1906. **Members:** 1,950. **Membership Dues:** student (with electronic BSSA), $25 (annual) ● student, $35 (annual) ● regular (with electronic BSSA), $110 (annual) ● regular in North America, $120 (annual) ● regular outside North America, $130 (annual). **Staff:** 5. **Budget:** $1,300,000. **Regional Groups:** 1. **Multinational. Description:** Seismologists, geophysicists, other earth scientists and engineers concerned with earthquakes. Promotes research and disseminates information on seismology, the scientific investigation of earthquakes and related phenomena. Works to promote research and public safety by publishing research journals, holding conferences and advising policy makers. **Awards:** Charles F. Richter Early Career Award. **Frequency:** annual. **Type:** recognition. **Recipient:** for outstanding contributions to the goals of the society by a member early in her or his career ● Distinguished Service Award. **Frequency:** periodic. **Type:** recognition. **Recipient:** for individuals who have made outstanding contributions to the work of the society ● Frank Press Public Service Award. **Frequency:** periodic. **Type:** recognition. **Recipient:** for outstanding work that serves the profession of seismology or the advancement of public safety or public information relating to seismology ● Harry Fielding Reid Medal. **Frequency:** annual. **Type:** medal. **Recipient:** for outstanding scientists in seismology, geophysics, and earthquake engineering. **Telecommunication Services:** electronic mail, snewman@seismosoc.org. **Publications:** *Bulletin of the Seismological Society of America*, bimonthly. Journal. Covers advanced research in seismology, earthquake engineering, and related fields. **Price:** included in membership dues; $360.00 /year for nonmembers in North America; $370.00 /year for nonmembers outside North America. ISSN: 0037-1106. **Circulation:** 2,800. Alternate Formats: microform. Also Cited As: *BSSA* ● *Seismological Research Letters*, bimonthly. Journal. Features articles on topics of broad seismological and earthquake engineering interest, earthquake and strong motion reports, and opinion pieces. **Price:** included in membership dues; $115.00 /year for nonmembers in U.S., Canada and Mexico; $125.00 /year for nonmembers outside North America. ISSN: 0012-8287. **Circulation:** 2,200. **Conventions/Meetings:** annual conference and meeting, presentation of research papers in seismology, geophysics, earthquake engineering, and related subjects (exhibits) ● annual Eastern Section - meeting and conference.

7643 ■ Vibration Isolation and Seismic Control Manufacturers Association (VISCMA)

994 Old Eagle School Rd., Ste.1019
Wayne, PA 19087-1866
Ph: (610)971-4850
Fax: (610)971-4859
E-mail: info@viscma.com
URL: http://www.viscma.com
Contact: Robert H. Ecker, Exec. Dir.

Founded: 1999. **Members:** 10. **Staff:** 2. **Budget:** $100,000. **Description:** Represents manufacturers of seismic restraint, vibration isolation and noise isolation equipment. **Projects:** Anchor Bolt Ratings; Industry Standards; Roof Curb Installation; Uniform Testing and Rating Procedures. **Publications:** *Installing Seismic Restraints for Mechanical Equipment, Electrical Equipment, Duct and Pipe* ● *Seismic Installation and Inspection Manual*. Assists field personnel. **Conventions/Meetings:** semiannual meeting - always Saturday of January and June.

Semiotics

7644 ■ Semiotic Society of America (SSA)

c/o Terry J. Prewitt, Exec. Dir.
Univ. of West Florida
Box 32009
Pensacola, FL 32514
Ph: (850)474-2186 (713)942-3449
Fax: (713)942-3452
E-mail: tprewitt@uwf.edu
URL: http://www.uwf.edu/tprewitt/SSA.htm
Contact: Terry J. Prewitt, Exec. Dir.

Founded: 1975. **Members:** 600. **Membership Dues:** individual, $50 (annual) ● student, $25 (annual) ● institutional, $100 (annual). **Description:** Individuals, students, and institutions interested in semiotics (the scientific study of signs and sign functions). Aims are to foster research, teaching, and other forms of information dissemination in the field. Maintains offprint files. **Libraries: Type:** reference. **Holdings:** 200. **Telecommunication Services:** electronic mail, nhouser@iupui.edu. **Committees:** Local Arrangements. **Publications:** *American Journal of Semiotics*, quarterly. Covers semiotics including the analyses of texts, events, groups, and cultural and natural objects. Includes book reviews. **Price:** included in membership dues. ISSN: 0277-7126. **Circulation:** 600 ● *Semiotics*, annual. **Conventions/Meetings:** annual conference and meeting (exhibits).

Social Sciences

7645 ■ Allied Social Science Associations (ASSA)

2014 Broadway, Ste.305
Nashville, TN 37203
Ph: (615)322-2595
Fax: (615)343-7590
E-mail: aeainfo@vanderbilt.edu
URL: http://www.vanderbilt.edu/AEA
Contact: Edda R. Leithner, Admin. Dir.

Description: Joint annual meeting of social science-oriented associations, including American Agricultural Economics Association, Association for Social Economics, Industrial Relations Research Association, American Finance Association, American Economic Association (see separate entries), Econometric Association, other associations, students, and interested individuals. **Conventions/Meetings:** annual meeting - always January.

7646 ■ Association of Muslim Social Scientists (AMSS)

PO Box 5502
Herndon, VA 20172
E-mail: s.khan@wayne.edu
URL: http://www.amss.net
Contact: Dr. Rafik Beekun, Pres.

Founded: 1972. **Members:** 1,000. **Membership Dues:** student, $15 (annual) ● professional, $45 (annual) ● associate student, $10 (annual) ● associate, $35 (annual). **Staff:** 1. **Budget:** $80,000. **Regional Groups:** 3. **Description:** Professors and graduate students in the social sciences and humanities. Encourages members to conduct studies and research in their areas of specialization; assists in developing Islamic positions on contemporary issues and applying them to studies and research; generates Islamic thought through critical and scientific inquiry and disseminates it through various means; aids in the professional development. Holds writing competition for graduate students. Sponsors research projects; maintains speakers' bureau. **Libraries: Type:** reference. **Holdings:** archival material, papers. **Awards:** Mustagur Rahman Graduate Student Award. **Frequency:** annual. **Type:** monetary. **Recipient:** for the best graduate paper presented at Annual Convention. **Computer Services:** Mailing lists. **Telecommunication Services:** electronic mail, beekun@unr.nevada.edu. **Councils:** Art and Literature; Arts and Library Science; Business Administration and Management; Communications; Economics; Education; Geography; History; Law; Linguistics; Philosophy and Religion; Political Science; Psychology; Religion; Sociology. **Publications:** *American Journal of Islamic Social Sciences*, quarterly. **Price:** $45.00 /year for institutions; $30.00 /year for individuals. ISSN: 0742-6763. **Advertising:** accepted. Alternate Formats: online. Also Cited As: *AJISS* ● *AMSS Bulletin*. Alternate Formats: online ● *Proceedings of Seminars*, annual ● Monographs. **Conventions/Meetings:** annual Islam and Society - conference - always October.

7647 ■ Center for Pacific Northwest Studies (CPNWS)
Goltz-Murray Archives Bldg.
Western Washington Univ.
Bellingham, WA 98225-9123
Ph: (360)650-7747
Fax: (360)650-3323
E-mail: cpnws@wwu.edu
URL: http://www.acadweb.wwu.edu/cpnws
Contact: Chris Friday, Dir.
Founded: 1971. **Staff:** 2. **Description:** Seeks to further the research on all aspects of the Pacific Northwest. Covers cultural, demographic, economic, political, and social issues. **Libraries: Type:** reference. **Holdings:** archival material, books, business records, monographs, periodicals. **Subjects:** history, geography, economy of the Pacific Northwest. **Publications:** *The Lyric Singer: A Biography of Ella Higginson*. Book. **Price:** $9.95/copy ● *Pacific Northwest Themes: Historical Essays in Honor of Keith A. Murray*. Booklet. **Price:** $5.95/copy ● *Washington: A Centennial Atlas*. Booklet. Details Washington's progress during its first century of statehood. **Price:** $20.00. **Conventions/Meetings:** periodic conference.

7648 ■ Center for the Study of Group Processes (CSGP)
Univ. of Iowa
Dept. of Sociology
Iowa City, IA 52242-1401
Ph: (319)335-2503
Fax: (319)335-2509
E-mail: michael-lovaglia@uiowa.edu
URL: http://www.uiowa.edu/~grpproc
Contact: Michael Lovaglia, Dir.
Founded: 1992. **Description:** Works to promote research in the field of group processes to enhance the professional development of faculty and graduate students in the social sciences. Maintains a laboratory for research; stimulates cross cultural exchanges; attracts visiting faculty from the U.S. and abroad; conducts educational programs. **Publications:** *Current Research in Social Psychology*. Journal. **Price:** free. ISSN: 1088-7423. Alternate Formats: online. **Conventions/Meetings:** conference ● workshop.

7649 ■ Consortium of Social Science Associations (COSSA)
1522 K St. NW, Ste.836
Washington, DC 20005
Ph: (202)842-3525
Fax: (202)842-2788
E-mail: cossa@cossa.org
URL: http://www.cossa.org
Contact: Dr. Howard J. Silver, Exec. Dir.
Founded: 1981. **Members:** 110. **Staff:** 4. **Budget:** $500,000. **Description:** Supported by over 110 professional associations, scientific societies, universities, and research institutes and centers. Aims to inform and educate members of Congress, congressional staff, and officials in the administration and in federal agencies about recent research in the social and behavioral sciences. Stresses the importance of such research and the need for maintaining adequate financial support. Monitors the research budgets and research policy issues of federal agencies; disseminates information on legislative actions and federal policies to social and behavioral scientists. Conducts briefings on current and emerging research, particularly in areas of congressional interest and responsibility. **Telecommunication Services:** electronic mail, silverhj@cossa.org. **Publications:** *COSSA Washington Update*, biweekly. Newsletter. Reports on developments in Congress and in federal agencies that affect funding for social and behavioral science research. ISSN: 0749-4394. **Circulation:** 1,600. **Conventions/Meetings:** annual meeting - always in Washington, DC ● seminar.

7650 ■ Institute for Social Research (ISR)
Univ. of Michigan
PO Box 1248
Ann Arbor, MI 48106-1248
Ph: (734)764-8354
Fax: (734)647-4575
E-mail: isr-info@isr.umich.edu
URL: http://www.isr.umich.edu
Contact: James Jackson, Dir.
Founded: 1948. **Staff:** 1,000. **Budget:** $31,500,000. **Description:** Social science research professionals and supportive staff engaged in social science research on a national and an international basis. Conducts research on a broad range of subjects utilizing four constituent research centers: Survey Research Center is concerned primarily with the study of large populations, organizations, and special segments of society and generally utilizes interview surveys; Research Center for Group Dynamics is concerned with the development of the basic science of behavior in groups, as well as social factors in human cognition, perception, and development; Center for Political Studies investigates a variety of political behavior, focusing on national politics in many countries, and maintains a data archive with a collection of election and other social science data. Other activities and services include: intercenter programs and special projects; international research, education, and consultation. Offers computerized services. **Councils:** National Advisory. **Publications:** *ISR Sampler*. Newsletter. Includes digestible information about the current research activities as well as news about ISR and the people who make it work. Alternate Formats: online ● *ISR Update*. Newsletter. Highlights research findings of public interest and policy relevance on wide range of topics. Alternate Formats: online.

7651 ■ International Network for Social Network Analysis (INSNA)
c/o Tom Valente
Univ. of Southern California
Dept. of Preventive Medicine
1000 Fremont Ave., Unit No. 8, Bldg. A, Rm. 5133
Alhambra, CA 91803
Ph: (626)457-6678
Fax: (626)457-6699
E-mail: tvalente@usc.edu
Contact: Tom Valente, Contact
Founded: 1977. **Members:** 600. **Membership Dues:** regular, $100 (annual). **Staff:** 1. **Multinational. Description:** Individuals in the social sciences, mathematics, and statistics interested in social network analysis in 25 countries. (Network analysis examines the structure of social systems and how these structures organize and constrain behavior, such as the interlocking ties between corporate, financial, and government organizations.) Maintains clearinghouse for network analysts. Organizes conferences and summer institutes. **Awards:** Freeman Young Investigator Award. **Frequency:** annual. **Type:** monetary. **Computer Services:** database, articles and books. **Telecommunication Services:** electronic mail, insna@sfu.ca. **Also Known As:** Reseau International pour l'Analyse des Reseaux Sociaux. **Publications:** *Connections*, semiannual. Bulletin. **Price:** included in membership dues. **Advertising:** accepted ● *Social Networks*, quarterly. Journal ● Directory, biennial ● Also publishes papers, do-it-yourself guide, critique, and network/health research review. **Conventions/Meetings:** European Conference on Social Network Analysis ● annual International Sunbelt Social Network Conference - always February.

7652 ■ International Society for the Comparative Study of Civilizations (ISCSC)
c/o Dr. Lee Daniel Snyder, Pres.
New Coll. of Florida
Dept. of History
Sarasota, FL 34243
Ph: (941)359-4482 (941)355-4513
Fax: (941)359-4475
E-mail: lldsnyder@aol.com
URL: http://www.iscsc.net
Contact: Dr. Lee Daniel Snyder, Pres.
Founded: 1961. **Members:** 575. **Membership Dues:** individual, $50 (annual) ● retiree, $40 (annual) ● student, $30 (annual) ● joint, $75 (annual) ● sustaining, $150 (annual) ● institutional, $60 (annual). **Description:** Scholars in all disciplines concerned with comparative and civilizational studies. Works to promote individual and cooperative efforts in the comparative study of civilizations and to develop methods for studying any significant problem in the humanities or the social sciences from a comparative civilizational perspective. (A comparative civilizational perspective involves the use of evidence from more than one civilization, employs a method shedding new light on the processes and structures of civilizations, and involves incorporation of perspectives, questions, and methods of both the humanities and social sciences). **Libraries: Type:** reference. **Holdings:** 44; articles, biographical archives. **Awards:** Quigley Award. **Frequency:** annual. **Type:** recognition. **Recipient:** for excellence in scholarship. **Computer Services:** database ● mailing lists. **Telecommunication Services:** electronic mail, aroan@ncf.edu. **Publications:** *Comparative Civilizations Review*, semiannual. Journal. Publishes analytic studies and interpretive essays concerned with the comparison of civilizations. Includes book reviews. **Price:** included in membership dues; $35.00 /year for nonmembers in U.S.; $55.00 /year for nonmembers outside U.S. ISSN: 0733-4540. **Circulation:** 600 ● *ISCSC Newsletter*. Alternate Formats: online. **Conventions/Meetings:** annual conference (exhibits).

7653 ■ Russell Sage Foundation (RSF)
112 E 64th St.
New York, NY 10021
Ph: (212)750-6000
Fax: (212)371-4761
E-mail: info@rsage.org
URL: http://www.russellsage.org
Contact: Eric Wanner, Pres.
Founded: 1907. **Description:** Social scientists and interested others. Promotes the improvement of social and living conditions in the United States of America. Analyzes and interprets social science information; conducts studies of social conditions; formulates and advances "practicable measures aimed at improvement" of living conditions in the U.S. **Libraries: Type:** reference. **Holdings:** books, business records. **Subjects:** foundation activities, reports. **Publications:** *Lone Pursuit: Distrust and Defensive Individualism Among the Black Poor*. Book. **Price:** $32.50 ● *Russell Sage Foundation News*. Newsletter. Alternate Formats: online ● Reports, periodic.

7654 ■ Social Science History Association (SSHA)
c/o Journals Department, Duke University Press
PO Box 90660
Durham, NC 27708
URL: http://www.ssha.org
Contact: William C. Block, Exec. Dir.
Founded: 1974. **Members:** 1,100. **Membership Dues:** regular, $60 (annual) ● student, $15 (annual) ● regular, in Canada, $76 (annual). **Staff:** 1. **Budget:** $20,000. **Description:** Social scientists and historians employing historical perspective to study societies of

the past and present. Promotes the cooperation of historians and social scientists in creating interdisciplinary approaches. Conducts educational programs. **Awards:** Allan Sharlin Memorial Award. **Frequency:** annual. **Type:** recognition. **Recipient:** for outstanding book in social science history published in the previous year ● President's Book Award. **Frequency:** annual. **Type:** monetary. **Recipient:** for beginning scholars. **Publications:** *Social Science History*, quarterly. Journal. **Price:** $50.00. ISSN: 0145-5532. **Circulation:** 2,000. **Advertising:** accepted. Alternate Formats: online. **Conventions/Meetings:** annual conference (exhibits) - 2008 Oct. 23-26, Miami, FL; 2009 Nov. 12-15, Long Beach, CA.

7655 ■ Social Science Research Council (SSRC)

810 7th Ave.
New York, NY 10019-5818
Ph: (212)377-2700
Fax: (212)377-2727
E-mail: info@ssrc.org
URL: http://www.ssrc.org
Contact: Dr. Mary Byrne McDonnell, Exec. Dir./Program Dir.

Founded: 1923. **Staff:** 60. **Budget:** $19,000,000. **Description:** Seeks to improve the quality of publicly available knowledge around the world. Works to advance social science research and education, to enhance communication among scholars and to bring useful knowledge to public attention. Sponsors research, conference and summer training institutes; facilitates scholarly exchange. **Libraries: Type:** reference. **Holdings:** articles, biographical archives. **Awards:** Abe Fellowships. **Frequency:** annual. **Type:** fellowship. **Recipient:** designed to encourage international multidisciplinary research on topics of pressing global concern ● ACLS/SSRC/NEH International and Area Studies Fellowships. **Type:** grant. **Recipient:** for humanistic research in area studies ● Berlin Program for Advanced German and European Studies. **Type:** fellowship. **Recipient:** for anthropologists, economists, political scientists, sociologists and all scholars in germane social science and cultural studies fields, including historians working on the period since the mid-19th century ● Central Asia, Louis Dupree Prize for Research. **Type:** recognition. **Recipient:** for the most promising dissertation involving field research in Central Asia, including Afghanistan, Azerbaijan, Kirghizia, Mongolia, Turkmenistan, Tajikistan, Uzbekistan, and culturally related contiguous areas of Iran, Pakistan, Kazakhstan and China ● East European Language Training Grants. **Type:** grant. **Recipient:** to US institutions willing to offer intensive summer course instruction in Albanian, Bulgarian, Czech, Hungarian, Macedonian, Polish, Romanian, Serbo-Croatian, Slovak or Slovene ● **Type:** fellowship. **Recipient:** for research on the Russian Empire, the Soviet Union and the New Independent States ● International Dissertation Research Fellowships. **Type:** fellowship. **Recipient:** for graduate students in the humanities and social sciences conducting dissertation research outside the United States ● International Migration Summer Institute and Fellowships. **Type:** fellowship. **Recipient:** for advanced doctoral candidates currently involved in research or writing for their dissertations and recent PhDs revising their dissertations for publication or initiating new research ● Japan Society for the Promotion of Science Fellowship Program. **Type:** fellowship. **Recipient:** for US researchers who wish to conduct cooperative research under the leadership of a host researcher ● Mellon Predoctoral Research Grant. **Type:** grant ● Research Fellowship on African Youth in a Global Age. **Type:** fellowship. **Recipient:** for field research and participation in pre and post-fieldwork workshops ● Sexuality Research Fellowships. **Type:** fellowship. **Recipient:** for scholars conducting research in the United States. **Telecommunication Services:** electronic mail, exec@ssrc.org. **Publications:** *The Development Imperative: Toward a People-Centered Approach*. Book. Alternate Formats: online ● *Items & Issues*, quarterly. Newsletter. Features research and council updates. **Price:** free. **Circulation:** 8,500. Alternate Formats: online ● *Working Paper Series: On Building Intellectual Capacity for the 21st Century*, periodic. Papers. **Conventions/Meetings:** competition ● seminar ● workshop.

7656 ■ Social Sciences Services and Resources

PO Box 153
Wasco, IL 60183
Ph: (630)897-5345
Contact: Jack F. Kinton, Exec. Dir.

Founded: 1973. **Membership Dues:** regular, $30 (annual) ● senior, $35 (annual). **Staff:** 3. **Budget:** $15,000. **Regional Groups:** 3. **State Groups:** 8. **National Groups:** 2. **Languages:** English, French, German. **Description:** Represents consulting associates in social sciences. Advances the teaching, consulting, and practice of the social sciences basic disciplines including sociology, anthropology, political science, geography, history, economics, and their applied disciplines: social research and survey agencies, social work, community development, planning, and public administration and management (regional, bi-state, county, city, village). Serves as: a center for dissemination of current and comprehensive social research findings. Provides social sciences and science bibliographic materials to the professional communities, educational institutions, and governmental and public libraries, and a publication of annuals on funds granted, which cover topics such as police professionalization, ethnic cultural life, neighborhood revitalization, curriculum development, crime prevention, youth development, and family styles. Provides consultants for citizen groups, community projects, and governmental units on written request. Upon request from colleges, school boards, and citizens groups, conducts in-service workshops on teaching, consulting, and new developments in the social sciences. Provides consultant evaluation services for small colleges throughout the U.S. Maintains speakers' bureau and placement information service. Conducts research programs upon grants and requests from public, semi-private and private foundations and organizations. **Libraries: Type:** reference. **Holdings:** 2,500; archival material, audio recordings, books, photographs. **Subjects:** U.S. social sciences, European and North American influences, theorists, researchers, professors, leaders, ASA, AAA, APA, U.S. presidents and families since 1950. **Awards: Frequency:** annual. **Type:** recognition. **Recipient:** for the best secondary and college student school paper on community economic development and neighborhood renewal ● SSSR Community Leadership Award. **Frequency:** annual. **Type:** recognition ● 21st Century Social Science Development Award. **Frequency:** annual. **Type:** monetary. **Recipient:** for the best undergraduate papers on community innovations, community renewal, and innovative delinquency prevention programs. **Computer Services:** Mailing lists. **Publications:** *American Communities Tomorrow: Applied Analyses and Case Studies for the 21st Century* (in English and French), annual. Journal. **Price:** $30.00. **Circulation:** 250. **Advertising:** accepted. Alternate Formats: CD-ROM; diskette ● *Best Books in the Social Sciences*, quarterly, February, May, August, November. **Price:** $15.00/year; $30.00 for three years ● Also publishes newsletters, working and evaluating bibliographies, dissertations and reports as professionally requested. **Conventions/Meetings:** conference and general assembly, for developing a sense of community and community leadership among high school and college age students - offered upon request by county officials (exhibits).

7657 ■ Western Social Science Association (WSSA)

c/o Larry Gould, Exec. Dir.
Northern Arizona Univ.
Coll. of Social and Behavioral Sciences
Box 15700
Flagstaff, AZ 86011
Ph: (928)523-9508
Fax: (928)523-6777
E-mail: larry.gould@nau.edu
URL: http://wssa.asu.edu
Contact: Larry Gould, Exec. Dir.

Founded: 1958. **Members:** 600. **Membership Dues:** individual, $40 (annual) ● student, retired, spouse, $25 (annual) ● joint, $50 (annual). **Budget:** $60,000. **Description:** College and university professors; interested individuals. Seeks to foster professional study, advance research, and promote the teaching of the social sciences; works to provide an alternative to what the association calls the modern tendency toward parochial scholarship; offers a forum for communication. Employs a diversity of methods to examine human social action; areas of interest include American Indian studies, anthropology, borderland studies, Canadian studies, Chicano studies, criminal justice, environmental policy and natural resource management, geography, history, mass communications, political science, public administration, rural studies, Slavic studies, social psychology, sociology, urban studies, and women's studies. Solicits conference papers; sponsors student paper competitions. **Awards:** Best Student Papers. **Frequency:** annual. **Type:** recognition. **Recipient:** for outstanding graduate and undergraduate student papers. **Computer Services:** database, conference participant list ● database, membership records. **Affiliated With:** Association for Arid Lands Studies; Association for Borderlands Studies. **Formerly:** (1975) Rocky Mountain Social Science Association. **Publications:** *Annual Conference Paper Abstracts*. **Price:** included in conference fee. **Advertising:** accepted ● *Annual Conference Program*. Journal ● *Social Science Journal*, quarterly. **Price:** included in membership dues ● *WSSA Newsletter*, 3/year. Contains information and items of professional interest. **Price:** included in membership dues. Alternate Formats: online. **Conventions/Meetings:** annual conference, with sessions, panels, and business meeting (exhibits).

Sociology

7658 ■ American Sociological Association (ASA)

1307 New York Ave. NW, Ste.700
Washington, DC 20005
Ph: (202)383-9005
Fax: (202)638-0882
E-mail: executive.office@asanet.org
URL: http://www.asanet.org
Contact: Sally T. Hillsman, Exec. Off.

Founded: 1905. **Members:** 13,000. **Membership Dues:** regular (based on gross annual income), $23-$171 (annual) ● associate, emeritus, $41 (annual) ● student, $18 (annual). **Staff:** 25. **Budget:** $3,600,000. **Description:** Sociologists, social scientists, and others interested in research, teaching, and application of sociology; graduate and undergraduate sociology students. Compiles statistics. Operates the ASA Teaching Resources Center, which develops a variety of materials useful in teaching sociology. Sponsors Minority Fellowship and Professional Development Programs and Teaching Project. Maintains 44 sections including: Aging; Criminology; Medical; Population. **Libraries: Type:** reference. **Holdings:** archival material. **Awards:** Dissertation Award. **Frequency:** annual. **Type:** recognition. **Recipient:** for the best PhD dissertation ● Distinguished Career Award for the Practice of Sociology. **Frequency:** annual. **Type:** recognition. **Recipient:** for outstanding contributions to sociological practice ● Distinguished Contributions to Teaching Award. **Frequency:** annual. **Type:** recognition. **Recipient:** for outstanding contributions to undergraduate and/or graduate teaching of sociology ● Distinguished Scholarly Publication Award. **Frequency:** annual. **Type:** recognition ● DuBois-Johnson-Frazier Award. **Frequency:** annual. **Type:** recognition. **Recipient:** for sociologist and academic institution ● Jessie Bernard Award. **Frequency:** annual. **Type:** recognition. **Recipient:** for scholarly work that has enlarged the horizons of sociology to encompass fully the role of women in society ● W.E.B. Dubois Career of Distinguished Scholarship Award. **Frequency:** annual. **Type:** scholarship. **Recipient:** for scholars who have shown outstanding commitment to the profession of sociology. **Telecommunication Services:** electronic mail, customer@asanet.org ● TDD, (202)638-0981. **Committees:**

Awards Selection; Freedom of Research and Teaching; National Statistics; Professional Ethics; Regulation; Research; Status of Racial and Ethnic Minorities in Sociology; Status of Women in Sociology; Teaching; World Sociology. **Affiliated With:** American Association for the Advancement of Science; American Council of Learned Societies. **Formerly:** American Sociological Society. **Publications:** *American Sociological Association—Annual Meeting Proceedings*. **Price:** $3.00/issue. **Advertising:** accepted ● *American Sociological Association—Directory of Departments*, semiannual. Includes highest degree offered and geographical listing of departments. **Price:** $5.00 /year for members; $10.00 /year for nonmembers and institutions. **Circulation:** 2,000 ● *American Sociological Association—Directory of Members*, biennial. Membership Directory. Lists membership of special interest sections; includes appendix containing name listings by geographical location. **Price:** $5.00/issue for members; $10.00/issue for nonmembers and institutions. **Circulation:** 12,000 ● *American Sociological Association—Employment Bulletin*, monthly. Contains current position vacancy listings in academic, applied, and fellowship settings. **Price:** $20.00/year ● *American Sociological Association—Footnotes*, 9/year. Newsletter. Covers departmental news, activities of the ASA and the executive office, and developments in Washington. Features award news. **Price:** included in membership dues; $40.00 /year for nonmembers and institutions. **Circulation:** 13,000. **Advertising:** accepted. Alternate Formats: online ● *American Sociological Review*, bimonthly. Journal. Includes theoretical developments, results of research and methodological innovations. **Price:** $40.00 /year for members; $196.00 /year for institutions; $25.00/year for students. ISSN: 0003-1224. **Advertising:** accepted. Alternate Formats: online ● *Contemporary Sociology: A Journal of Reviews*, bimonthly. Features reviews and critical discussions of recent works in sociology and related disciplines. **Price:** $40.00 /year for members; $196.00 /year for institutions; $25.00/year for students. ISSN: 0094-3061. **Circulation:** 8,000. **Advertising:** accepted. Alternate Formats: online ● *Guide to Graduate Departments of Sociology*, annual. Directory. Lists 240 departments of sociology offering Masters and/or PhD degrees. Includes name, rank, highest degree, institution and date of degree. **Price:** $5.00 for members and students; $10.00 for nonmembers and institutions. **Circulation:** 2,200 ● *Journal of Health and Social Behavior*, quarterly. Presents reports of empirical studies, theoretical analyses, and synthesizing reviews that employ a sociological perspective. **Price:** $35.00 /year for members; $164.00 /year for institutions; $25.00/year for students. ISSN: 0022-1465. **Advertising:** accepted. Alternate Formats: online ● *Rose Monograph Series*, periodic. Monographs ● *Social Psychology Quarterly*. Journal. **Price:** $35.00 /year for members; $164.00 /year for institutions; $25.00/year for students. ISSN: 0190-2725. **Circulation:** 3,500. **Advertising:** accepted. Alternate Formats: online ● *Sociological Methodology*, annual. Journal. Disseminates material that advances empirical research in sociology and related disciplines. **Price:** $50.00 /year for members; $40.00/year for students; $226.00 /year for institutions. ISSN: 0081-1750 ● *Sociological Theory*, semiannual. Journal. Presents papers in all areas of sociological theory, including new substantive theories, history, metatheory, and formal theory. **Price:** $35.00 /year for members; $25.00/year for students; $232.00 /year for institutions. ISSN: 0735-2751. **Advertising:** accepted. Alternate Formats: online ● *Sociology of Education*, quarterly. Journal. Presents papers on educational processes and human development. Research focuses on the individual, institutions, and structural arrangements. **Price:** $35.00 /year for members; $164.00 /year for institutions; $25.00/year for students. ISSN: 0038-0407. **Advertising:** accepted. Alternate Formats: online ● *Teaching Sociology*, quarterly. Journal. Features research articles, teaching tips, and reports on teaching sociology. **Price:** $35.00 /year for members; $164.00 /year for institutions; $25.00/year for students. ISSN: 0092-055X. **Circulation:** 2,000. **Advertising:** accepted. Alternate Formats: online. **Conventions/Meetings:** annual The Question of Culture - meeting - 2008 Aug. 1-4, Boston, MA.

7659 ■ Association of Black Sociologists (ABS)

4200 Wisconsin Ave. NW
PMB 106-257
Washington, DC 20016-2143
Ph: (202)365-1759 (212)772-5641
Fax: (781)723-6527
E-mail: info@blacksociologists.org
URL: http://www.blacksociologists.org
Contact: Juan Battle, Pres.

Founded: 1968. **Members:** 400. **Membership Dues:** active, $25 (annual) ● emeritus, $40 (annual) ● full, $42-$75 (annual) ● associate, $42-$65 (annual) ● life, $500-$2,000. **Description:** Promotes the professional interests of black sociologists; promotes an increase in the number of professionally trained sociologists; helps stimulate and improve the quality of research and the teaching of sociology; provides perspectives regarding black experiences as well as expertise for understanding and dealing with problems confronting black people; protects professional rights and safeguards the civil rights stemming from executing the above objectives. Conducts research programs. **Awards: Frequency:** annual. **Type:** recognition. **Recipient:** for a black graduate student for excellence in scholarly work. **Telecommunication Services:** electronic mail, alemelle@blacksociologists.org. **Committees:** Awards. **Formerly:** (1976) Caucus of Black Sociologists. **Publications:** *Roster of Membership*, annual. Membership Directory ● Newsletter, quarterly. Includes professional and career development information, announcements, and updates. **Advertising:** accepted ● Journal. **Conventions/Meetings:** annual conference (exhibits).

7660 ■ Association for Humanist Sociology (AHS)

c/o Kathy McMahon-Klosterman, VP of Membership
Dept. of Educational Psychology
1256 Robert Dickey Pkwy.
Kettering, OH 45409
Ph: (505)538-6824
E-mail: lynchjm@muohio.edu
URL: http://www.altrue.net/site/humanist/
Contact: Gina Petonito, Pres.

Founded: 1976. **Members:** 200. **Membership Dues:** student, $12 (annual) ● regular (based on annual income), $24-$100 (annual) ● sponsor, $150 (annual). **Budget:** $15,000. **Description:** Sociologists, social scientists, social workers, and other persons interested in humanistic sociology. Provides a forum for sociologists concerned with the value-related aspects of sociological theory, research, and professional life. Seeks to extend the boundaries of humanist sociology by exploring connections between sociology and other disciplines. **Awards:** AHS Book Award. **Frequency:** biennial. **Type:** recognition. **Recipient:** for the best book. **Telecommunication Services:** electronic mail, petonig@muohio.edu. **Publications:** *The Humanist Sociologist*, quarterly. Newsletter. **Price:** included in membership dues. **Circulation:** 200 ● *Humanity and Society*, quarterly. Journal. **Conventions/Meetings:** annual conference.

7661 ■ Association for the Sociology of Religion (ASR)

618 SW 2nd Ave.
Galva, IL 61434-1912
Ph: (309)932-2727
Fax: (309)932-2282
E-mail: bill4329@hotmail.com
URL: http://www.sociologyofreligion.com
Contact: Dr. William H. Swatos Jr., Exec. Off.

Founded: 1938. **Members:** 800. **Membership Dues:** constituent, $35 (annual) ● student, low income (under 10,000 a year), $15 (annual) ● individual, $30 (annual) ● institution, $75 (annual). **Staff:** 1. **Budget:** $115,000. **Description:** Sociologists, educators, and others interested in the sociological study of religion. Works to encourage study and research in the sociology of religion and to promote the highest professional and scientific standards for research and publication in the sociology of religion. **Awards:** Fichter Research Award. **Frequency:** annual. **Type:** monetary ● McNamara Award. **Frequency:** annual. **Type:** monetary. **Recipient:** for students. **Computer Services:** database ● mailing lists. **Formerly:** (1971) American Catholic Sociological Society. **Publications:** *News & Announcements*, quarterly. Newsletter. **Price:** included in membership dues. **Circulation:** 785. **Advertising:** accepted. Alternate Formats: online ● *Sociology of Religion*, quarterly. Journal. **Price:** $70.00. ISSN: 1069-4440. **Circulation:** 1,533. **Advertising:** accepted. Alternate Formats: CD-ROM; diskette; online. Also Cited As: *Sociological Analysis*, *American Catholic Sociological Review*. **Conventions/Meetings:** annual conference, held in conjunction with the American Sociological Association (exhibits) - always August.

7662 ■ Christian Sociological Society (CSS)

c/o Paul J. Serwinek
2385 Learmonth
Milford, MI 48381
Ph: (248)363-5746
Fax: (248)363-9554
E-mail: pserwinek@comcast.net
URL: http://www.christiansociology.com
Contact: Thomas Hood, Coor.

Founded: 1979. **Members:** 300. **Regional Groups:** 1. **Description:** Christian sociologists and related professionals. Seeks to enable members to "integrate their sociological academic background with their Christian faith." Facilitates networking among members; sponsors research and student activities. **Publications:** *The Christian Sociologist*, periodic. Newsletter. Includes book reviews, news of other Christian sociologists, their experiences and current projects. **Price:** free for members. **Circulation:** 500. Alternate Formats: online. **Conventions/Meetings:** semiannual meeting, in conjunction with the Southern Sociological Society and American Sociological Association.

7663 ■ International Institute of Sociology (IIS)

c/o Prof. Karen S. Cook, Gen. Sec.-Treas.
Stanford Univ.
Dept. of Sociology
Stanford, CA 94305
E-mail: iisoc@post.tau.ac.il
URL: http://www.tau.ac.il/~iisoc
Contact: Prof. Karen S. Cook, Gen. Sec.-Treas.

Founded: 1893. **Membership Dues:** regular, $100 (annual) ● low income country, $50 (annual). **Languages:** English, French. **Description:** Students, educators, researchers, and social scientists active in the field of sociology. Seeks to advance sociological research and study. Facilitates exchange of information among members; sponsors research and educational programs.

7664 ■ International Rural Sociology Association (IRSA)

c/o David O. Hansen, RSS, Sec.-Treas.
Ohio State Univ.
Intl. Prog. for Agriculture
2120 Fyfe Rd.
Columbus, OH 43085
Ph: (614)292-7252
Fax: (614)292-1757
E-mail: hansen.4@osu.edu
URL: http://www.irsa-world.org
Contact: Alessandro Bonanno RSS, Pres.

Founded: 1976. **Members:** 1,600. **Multinational. Description:** Professionals and paraprofessionals working in rural communities. Seeks to foster the development of the science of sociology and further the application of sociological research to the improvement of the quality of life of rural populations. Facilitates discussion and information exchange between rural sociologists and other social scientists concerned with rural life. Sponsors professional interest networks and special projects worldwide. Organizes joint conferences with other international associations with common interests. Maintains International Register of Rural Sociologists and archives lodged in the University of Missouri library. **Affiliated With:** Rural Sociological Society. **Publications:** *Congress Program*, quadrennial ● *IRSA Items*, annual ● Membership Directory, annual ● Proceedings, quadrennial. **Conventions/Meetings:** quadrennial congress.

7665 ■ National Council of State Sociological Associations (NCSSA)
c/o Susan Webb, Pres.
PO Box 261954
Conway, SC 29528-6054
Ph: (843)349-2933
Fax: (843)349-2857
E-mail: sewebb@coastal.edu
URL: http://www.statesociologicalassociations.org
Contact: Susan Webb, Pres.
Description: Promotes and facilitates communication among established state associations. Shares common concerns and contributes to the effective development of state sociological associations. Assists emerging state associations in the establishment of new state associations. **Telecommunication Services:** electronic mail, webmaster@statesociologicalassociations.org.

7666 ■ North American Society for the Sociology of Sport (NASSS)
c/o Dean A. Purdy, Treas.
PO Box 291
Bowling Green, OH 43403
Ph: (419)352-1928 (419)372-6927
Fax: (419)354-2957
E-mail: treasurer@nasss.org
URL: http://www.nasss.org
Contact: Nancy Spencer, Pres.
Founded: 1980. **Members:** 300. **Membership Dues:** professional, $75 (annual) ● sustaining, $85 (annual) ● student/retired/unemployed (without journal), $15 (annual) ● student/retired/unemployed (with journal), $40 (annual) ● institutional, $185 (annual). **Description:** Brings together scholars, including instructors and researchers, involved in the study of the sociology of sport. **Awards:** Barbara Brown Student Paper Award. **Frequency:** annual. **Type:** recognition. **Recipient:** to the best student-authored, non-published paper ● Distinguished Service Award. **Frequency:** annual. **Type:** recognition. **Recipient:** for distinguished service ● Minority Scholarship. **Frequency:** annual. **Type:** scholarship. **Recipient:** for a graduate student who is a member of a racial or ethnic minority group ● NASSS Outstanding Book Award. **Frequency:** annual. **Type:** recognition. **Recipient:** to the author of the most outstanding book published in the previous calendar year ● Sociology of Sport Journal Outstanding Article Award. **Frequency:** annual. **Type:** recognition. **Recipient:** to the author of the best article published in SSJ from the previous calendar year. **Telecommunication Services:** electronic mail, nspencr@bgsu.edu. **Committees:** Distinguished Service Award; Diversity and Conference Climate; Elections; Outstanding Book Award. **Publications:** *NASSS Newsletter*, 3/year. Alternate Formats: online ● *Sociology of Sport Journal*, quarterly. **Circulation:** 700. **Advertising:** accepted. Alternate Formats: online. Also Cited As: *SSJ*. **Conventions/Meetings:** annual conference and symposium, with paper presentations - 2008 Nov. 5-8, Denver, CO.

7667 ■ Rural Sociological Society (RSS)
Univ. of Missouri
104 Gentry Hall
Columbia, MO 65211-7040
Ph: (573)882-9065 (573)882-4350
Fax: (573)882-1473
E-mail: ruralsoc@missouri.edu
URL: http://www.ruralsociology.org
Contact: Edie Pigg, Business Mgr.
Founded: 1937. **Members:** 1,050. **Membership Dues:** professional, $80-$100 (annual) ● student, $35 (annual) ● emeritus, $50 (annual) ● international associate, $55 (annual) ● sustaining, $150 (annual) ● new professional, $50 (annual) ● life, $1,000. **Staff:** 1. **Budget:** $170,000. **Description:** Educators and others employed in the field of rural sociology. Promotes the development of rural sociology through research, teaching, and extension work. **Awards:** Distinguished Rural Sociologist. **Frequency:** annual. **Type:** recognition. **Recipient:** to members who have made superior career contributions to the field of rural sociology ● Distinguished Service to Rural Life. **Frequency:** annual. **Type:** recognition. **Recipient:** for outstanding contribution to the enhancement of rural life and rural people. **Computer Services:** Mailing lists, labels/disks. **Telecommunication Services:** electronic mail, naomi.krogman@ualberta.ca. **Committees:** Development; Diversity; Endowment; Nominations; Professional Communications; Program. **Formerly:** Rural Section of the American Sociological Society. **Publications:** *The Rural Sociologist*, quarterly. **Price:** $22.00 /year for nonmembers. **Advertising:** accepted ● *Rural Sociology*, quarterly. Journal. **Price:** $125.00 /year for nonmembers; $188.75/year for agencies. **Advertising:** accepted ● Brochures ● Proceedings. Alternate Formats: online ● Also publishes Rural Studies Series. **Conventions/Meetings:** annual meeting (exhibits).

7668 ■ Society for Applied Sociology (SAS)
c/o Association for Applied and Clinical Sociology
712 Pray-Harrold
Dept. of Sociology
Eastern Michigan Univ.
Ypsilanti, MI 48197
Ph: (734)487-0012
Fax: (734)487-7010
E-mail: sacs_aacs@emich.edu
URL: http://www.appliedsoc.org
Contact: Fonda Martin, Admin.
Founded: 1984. **Members:** 425. **Membership Dues:** regular, $80 (annual) ● student, $35 (annual) ● life, $1,150 ● organizational, $195 (annual) ● retired, $45 (annual) ● international regular, $100 (annual). **Staff:** 1. **Budget:** $50,000. **Description:** Represents sociologists interested in facilitating and promoting the application of sociological practice and research to specific issues, problems, and topics. **Awards:** Alex Boros Award for Distinguished Contribution to SAS. **Frequency:** annual. **Type:** recognition. **Recipient:** for members who meet the standards of excellence of the founding members ● Lester F. Ward Award. **Frequency:** annual. **Type:** recognition. **Recipient:** for persons who made a significant contribution to applied sociology over a long period of time ● Sociological Practice Award. **Frequency:** annual. **Type:** recognition. **Recipient:** for sociologist made a direct contribution to the understanding of social problems in the society. **Publications:** *Applied Sociology Teaching Handbook*. Includes sample syllabus sets for undergraduate and graduate courses in applied sociology. **Price:** $10.00 for nonmembers; $7.00 for members ● *Journal of Applied Sociology*, annual. Contains articles on current research and policy. **Price:** included in membership dues; $42.00 to libraries; $4.00 for nonmembers. **Advertising:** accepted ● *Social Insight*, annual. Magazine. **Price:** free to current members; $5.00 for members; $10.00 for nonmembers. **Advertising:** accepted ● *The Useful Sociologist*, semiannual. Newsletter. **Price:** included in membership dues. ISSN: 0749-0232. **Circulation:** 500. **Advertising:** accepted. **Conventions/Meetings:** annual Pioneering Applied Sociology in New Practice Frontiers - conference (exhibits) - always October.

7669 ■ Society for the Study of Symbolic Interaction (SSSI)
c/o Leslie Wasson, Treas.
Social Sciences
Chapman Univ.
530 Kings County Dr., Ste.102
Hanford, CA 93230
Ph: (559)587-3445 (217)333-0795
E-mail: lesliewasson@usa.net
URL: http://www.espach.salford.ac.uk/sssi/index.php
Contact: Leslie Wasson, Treas.
Founded: 1975. **Members:** 600. **Description:** College instructors, students, and others interested in symbolic interaction (which holds that people act toward things according to the meanings attached to them and that these symbols are created out of social interaction, which is in constant flux). Promotes knowledge and scholarship of symbolic interaction through educational meetings and publications. **Awards:** Charles Horton Cooley Award. **Frequency:** annual. **Type:** recognition ● Distinguished Lecturer Award. **Frequency:** annual. **Type:** recognition ● Feminist Mentor Award. **Frequency:** annual. **Type:** recognition ● George Herbert Mead Award. **Frequency:** annual. **Type:** recognition ● Herbert Blumer Award. **Frequency:** annual. **Type:** recognition. **Publications:** *SSSI Notes*, quarterly. Newsletter. Alternate Formats: online ● *Symbolic Interaction*, quarterly. Journal. **Price:** $235.00/year. **Advertising:** accepted. Alternate Formats: online. **Conventions/Meetings:** annual conference and symposium, concurrent with American Sociological Association (exhibits) ● Couch-Stone Symposium.

7670 ■ Sociological Practice Association (SPA)
c/o Ross Koppel, PhD, Pres.
Social Res. Corp.
PO Box 15
Wyncote, PA 19095
Ph: (215)576-8221
Fax: (215)576-8346
E-mail: rkoppel@sas.upenn.edu
URL: http://www.socpractice.org
Contact: Ross Koppel PhD, Pres.
Founded: 1978. **Members:** 300. **Membership Dues:** regular, $70 (annual) ● organizational, $150 (annual) ● low income, $35 (annual) ● student, $20 (annual). **Staff:** 1. **Description:** Promotes the application of sociology to individual and social change and advances theory, research, and methods to this end; develops opportunities for the employment and use of clinically trained sociologists; provides a common ground for sociological practitioners, allied professionals, and interested scholars and students. Promotes training and educational opportunities to further sociological practice. Sponsors sessions and programs in clinical and applied sociology at national and regional meetings of other sociological associations. Has conducted a survey on skills, licenses, education, and experience of members. Conducts national certification program. **Libraries:** **Type:** reference. **Holdings:** 22. **Subjects:** clinical sociology from 1978-2002. **Awards:** Alex Buros Award. **Frequency:** annual. **Type:** recognition. **Recipient:** for contributions to the association ● Frank Ward Award. **Frequency:** annual. **Type:** recognition. **Recipient:** for contributions to the discipline ● Roberta Ezra Park Award. **Frequency:** annual. **Type:** recognition. **Recipient:** for contributions to clinical sociology and sociological practice ● W.F. White Award. **Frequency:** annual. **Type:** recognition. **Recipient:** for contributions to the discipline. **Committees:** Accreditation; Certification; Curriculum; Ethics; Training. **Formerly:** (1986) Clinical Sociology Association. **Publications:** *Journal of Applied Social Science*, annual. Covers theory and practice of clinical sociology; includes book reviews. **Price:** included in membership dues; $40.00 /year for nonmembers. ISSN: 0730-840X. **Circulation:** 300. **Advertising:** accepted ● *Sociological Practice*, annual. Journal. Focuses on one theme per issue. **Circulation:** 100 ● *Using Sociology: An Introduction from the Clinical Perspectives* ● Membership Directory, periodic ● Newsletter. Alternate Formats: online. **Conventions/Meetings:** conference and workshop - 3-4/year ● annual meeting and conference.

7671 ■ Sociological Research Association (SRA)
c/o American Sociological Association
1307 New York Ave. NW, Ste.700
Washington, DC 20005
Ph: (202)383-9005
Fax: (202)638-0882
URL: http://www.asanet.org
Contact: Sally Hillsman, Exec. Off.
Founded: 1928. **Budget:** $25,000. **Description:** Persons, elected from membership of the American Sociological Association (see separate entry), "who have made significant contributions to sociological research, other than a doctoral dissertation, and who maintain an active interest in the advancement of sociological knowledge". **Conventions/Meetings:** annual meeting and dinner, held in conjunction with ASA.

Soil

7672 ■ Association of Women Soil Scientists (AWSS)

c/o Kelly Counts, Sec.-Treas.
USDA-NRCS Soil Survey
621 W Fetterman St.
Buffalo, WY 82834
Ph: (951)369-4820
Fax: (951)342-4962
E-mail: kelly.counts@wy.usda.gov
URL: http://www.awss.org
Contact: Kelly Counts, Sec.-Treas.

Founded: 1981. **Members:** 180. **Membership Dues:** student, $10 (annual) ● professional, $15 (annual). **Description:** Women and men who are soil scientists, soil conservationists, soil agriculturists, research scientists, professors, and students. Identifies women in the field and provides them with communication opportunities, technical and career information, assistance, and encouragement. **Libraries: Type:** open to the public. **Holdings:** articles. **Publications:** *AWSS Newsletter*, 3/year ● Membership Directory, biennial. **Conventions/Meetings:** periodic meeting.

7673 ■ Soil and Plant Analysis Council (SPAC)

300 Speedway Cir., Ste.2
Lincoln, NE 68502
Ph: (402)476-0300 (541)567-8321
Fax: (402)476-0302
E-mail: bvaughan@agsource.com
URL: http://www.spcouncil.com
Contact: Byron Vaughan, Sec.-Treas.

Founded: 1970. **Members:** 350. **Membership Dues:** individual, $80 (annual) ● laboratory, $260 (annual) ● sustaining, company/corporate, $400 (annual). **Budget:** $50,000. **Description:** Individuals, business firms, laboratories, researchers, and practitioners interested in soil testing and plant analysis. Promotes uniform soil test and plant analysis methods, use, interpretation, and terminology; encourages research on the calibration and use of soil testing and plant analysis; serves as an information clearinghouse for those interested in soil testing and plant analysis; provides a forum for the exchange of information between individuals and groups from industry, public institutions, and independent laboratories. Compiles statistics; advises on proposed federal legislation and regulations topics. **Awards:** J. Benton Jones, Jr. Award. **Frequency:** biennial. **Type:** recognition. **Affiliated With:** Council for Agricultural Science and Technology. **Formerly:** (1993) Council on Soil Testing and Plant Analysis. **Publications:** *Soil-Plant Analyst*, quarterly. Newsletter. Covers current developments in soil testing and plant analysis; includes reports in abstract form and association news. **Price:** included in membership dues. **Circulation:** 350 ● Newsletter. **Conventions/Meetings:** biennial conference and symposium, usually in conjunction with American Society of Agronomy or American Society for Horticultural Science (exhibits) ● semiannual workshop (exhibits) ● workshop.

7674 ■ Soil Science Society of America (SSSA)

677 S Segoe Rd.
Madison, WI 53711
Ph: (608)273-8080 (608)268-4979
Fax: (608)273-2021
E-mail: headquarters@agronomy.org
URL: http://www.soils.org
Contact: Ellen G.M. Bergfeld, CEO

Founded: 1936. **Members:** 6,200. **Membership Dues:** sustaining, $510 (annual) ● active, $63 (annual) ● graduate/doctoral (non-US, add $4), $27 (annual) ● undergraduate, $10 (annual) ● active (non-US, add $10), $82 (annual). **Staff:** 37. **Budget:** $800,000. **Description:** Professional soil scientists, including soil physicists, soil classifiers, land use and management specialists, chemists, microbiologists, soil fertility specialists, soil cartographers, conservationists, mineralogists, engineers, and others interested in fundamental and applied soil science. **Libraries: Type:** open to the public. **Telecommunication Services:** electronic mail, ebergfeld@agronomy.org. **Committees:** Soil Mineralogy; Soil Testing and Plant Analysis; Soils-Geomorphology; Terminology; Training of Soil Scientists. **Divisions:** Fertilizer Management and Technology; Forest and Range Soils; Soil and Water Management and Conservation; Soil Chemistry; Soil Fertility and Plant Nutrition; Soil Genesis, Morphology, and Classification; Soil Microbiology and Biochemistry; Soil Mineralogy; Soil Physics; Soils and Environmental Quality; Wetland Soils. **Affiliated With:** American Society of Agronomy; Crop Science Society of America. **Formed by Merger of:** American Soil Survey Association; Soils Section of American Society of Agronomy. **Publications:** *Journal of Environmental Quality*, bimonthly. Reports research on environmental quality in nature and in agricultural ecosystems. Includes book reviews. **Price:** $50.00 /year for members; $615.00 /year for nonmembers and institutions. ISSN: 0047-2425. **Circulation:** 3,709. **Advertising:** accepted. Alternate Formats: online; CD-ROM ● *110-Year Indices*, periodic. Arranged by author and subject. ● *Soil Science Society of America—Journal*, bimonthly. Presents original soil science research; includes annual meeting reports. **Price:** $50.00 /year for members; $615.00 /year for nonmembers and institution. ISSN: 0361-5995. **Circulation:** 6,967. **Advertising:** accepted. Alternate Formats: online; CD-ROM ● *Soil Survey Horizons*, quarterly. Journal. Reports on soil research. **Price:** $18.00 /year for nonmembers and institutions. **Circulation:** 1,000. Alternate Formats: online; CD-ROM ● *Vadose Zone Journal*, quarterly. Contains original research reports and review articles on the vadose zone. **Price:** $50.00 for members; $310.00 for nonmembers and institution. **Circulation:** 800. **Advertising:** accepted. Alternate Formats: online; CD-ROM. **Conventions/Meetings:** annual convention, held in conjunction with the American Society of Agronomy and the Crop Science Society of America (exhibits) - 2008 Oct. 5-9, Houston, TX; 2009 Nov. 1-5, Pittsburgh, PA; 2010 Oct. 31-Nov. 4, Long Beach, CA.

7675 ■ United States Permafrost Association (USPA)

PO Box 750141
Fairbanks, AK 99775-0141
Ph: (302)831-0852
Fax: (302)831-6654
E-mail: info@uspermafrost.org
URL: http://www.uspermafrost.org
Contact: Jon E. Zufelt, Pres.

Founded: 2000. **Membership Dues:** regular, $20 (annual) ● student, $10 (annual) ● corporate, institution, $100 (annual) ● sustaining, $250 (annual) ● life, $1,000. **Description:** Encourages scientific and engineering investigations in permafrost related topics. Disseminates results related to permafrost research. Encourages sharing of knowledge and data in permafrost science. Promotes awareness of permafrost among the public and training of new generations of scientists and engineers to work in fields related to permafrost science and engineering. **Publications:** Newsletter. **Price:** included in membership dues. **Conventions/Meetings:** annual meeting - 2008 June 29-July 3, Fairbanks, AK.

Solar Energy

7676 ■ American Solar Energy Society (ASES)

2400 Central Ave., Ste.A
Boulder, CO 80301
Ph: (303)443-3130
Fax: (303)443-3212
E-mail: ases@ases.org
URL: http://www.ases.org
Contact: Bradley D. Collins, Exec. Dir.

Founded: 1970. **Members:** 4,000. **Membership Dues:** corporate, $500 (annual) ● basic, $39 (annual) ● professional, $89 (annual) ● student, $35 (annual) ● senior, $45 (annual) ● life, $1,200 ● senior (life), $600 ● supporting, $125 (annual) ● contributing, small business, $250 (annual) ● non-profit, $200 (annual) ● library, $175 (annual). **Staff:** 4. **Regional Groups:** 26. **Description:** Professional energy society organized to promote a wide utilization of solar energy through the application of science and technology. Encourages basic and applied research and development. Conducts workshops; organizes forums inviting researchers, policymakers, practitioners and consumers for discussion, analysis, and debate. Promotes education by compiling and disseminating information to schools, universities, and the community. **Libraries: Type:** reference. **Holdings:** 3,000. **Awards:** Charles Greeley Abott Award. **Frequency:** annual. **Type:** recognition. **Recipient:** for significant contribution to the American Solar Energy Society or to the field of solar energy ● Fellows of the Society. **Frequency:** annual. **Type:** fellowship. **Recipient:** for longtime ASES members who have provided exceptional service to the society ● Hoyt Clarke Hottel Award. **Frequency:** annual. **Type:** recognition. **Recipient:** for significant contribution to solar technology in any area ● John and Barbara Yellott Award. **Frequency:** annual. **Type:** recognition. **Recipient:** for graduate student and current member of the American Solar Energy Society concentrating his or her program in the field of solar energy ● Passive Pioneer Award. **Frequency:** annual. **Type:** recognition. **Recipient:** for men and women pioneering in the field of passive solar design ● Rebecca Vories Award. **Frequency:** annual. **Type:** recognition. **Recipient:** for special contributions to the American Solar Energy Society ● Women in Solar Energy Award. **Frequency:** annual. **Type:** recognition. **Recipient:** for woman who has created change toward promoting the use of solar energy. **Telecommunication Services:** electronic mail, bcollins@ases.org. **Committees:** Awards; Business and Industry Liaison. **Divisions:** Education; Solar Buildings; Solar Electric; Solar Fuels; Solar Thermal; Sustainability. **Affiliated With:** International Solar Energy Society. **Formerly:** (1982) American Section of the International Solar Energy Society; (2001) American Solar Energy Association. **Publications:** *Advances in Solar Energy*, annual. Book ● *National Passive Conference Proceedings*, annual ● *Solar Today*, bimonthly. Magazine. Reports on the solar energy industry; includes information on new technologies and products. Contains calendar of events and product updates. **Price:** included in membership dues; $29.00 /year for nonmembers. **Circulation:** 4,800. **Advertising:** accepted ● Membership Directory. Alternate Formats: online ● Manuals. **Conventions/Meetings:** annual National Passive Solar Conference ● annual National Solar Conference (exhibits).

7677 ■ Renew the Earth

1900 Oracle Way, Ste.717
Reston, VA 20190
Ph: (703)689-4670
E-mail: information@renew-the-earth.org
URL: http://www.renew-the-earth.org
Contact: Ms. Debbie Reed, Exec. Dir.

Founded: 1989. **Members:** 2,000. **Staff:** 3. **Budget:** $350,000. **Multinational. Description:** Individuals and groups working toward a sustainable future by promoting a safe and healthy environment. Coordinates National Awards for Environmental Sustainability program to recognize positive environmental programs. Operates the Environmental Success Index, a clearinghouse of more than 1600 working environmental projects available to community groups, the media, businesses, policy makers, and individuals dedicated to implementing and promoting positive environmental change. Moving toward developing an international program. **Libraries: Type:** reference. **Holdings:** video recordings. **Subjects:** community-based environmental success stories. **Awards:** National Award for Environmental Sustainability. **Frequency:** annual. **Type:** recognition. **Computer Services:** database, 1600 community-based environmental programs. **Telecommunication Services:** electronic mail, thayer@renew-the-earth.org. **Councils:** National Awards Council for Environmental Sustainability. **Formerly:** (1987) Fund for Renewable Energy and the Environment; (2001) Renew America. **Supersedes:** Center for Renewable Resources; Solar Lobby. **Publications:** *Environmen-*

tal Success Index, annual. Directory. Lists of environmental programs. Includes contact names, addresses, and phone numbers. **Circulation:** 5,000. Alternate Formats: online.

7678 ■ Solar Electric Power Association (SEPA)
805 15th St. NW, Ste.510
Washington, DC 20005
Ph: (202)857-0898
Fax: (202)682-0559
E-mail: info@solarelectricpower.org
URL: http://www.solarelectricpower.org
Contact: Julia Judd, Exec. Dir.
Membership Dues: general (based on annual revenues), $750-$6,000 (annual). **Description:** Facilitates the use and integration of solar electric power by utilities, electric service providers and their customers. Fosters business to business networking. Provides information on solar electric technologies, applications and programs. Reports on policies, regulations and legislation. **Publications:** Newsletter, biweekly. **Price:** included in membership dues. Alternate Formats: online ● Membership Directory, annual. **Price:** included in membership dues. Alternate Formats: online. **Conventions/Meetings:** annual Solar Power - conference - 2008 Oct. 13-17, San Diego, CA.

7679 ■ Solar Energy Industries Association (SEIA)
805 15th St. NW, Ste.510
Washington, DC 20005
Ph: (202)682-0556
Fax: (202)682-0559
E-mail: info@seia.org
URL: http://www.seia.org
Contact: Rhone Resch, Pres.
Founded: 1974. **Members:** 500. **Membership Dues:** business (with revenues of less than $200,000-$500,000), $300-$500 (annual) ● business (with revenues of $500,001-$10,000,000), $1,000-$10,000 (annual) ● business (with revenues of greater than $10,000,001), $25,000 (annual) ● manufacturer (minimum), $2,000 (annual) ● financial institution (minimum), $7,500 (annual). **Staff:** 3. **Budget:** $300,000. **State Groups:** 12. **Description:** Manufacturers, installers, distributors, contractors, and engineers of solar energy systems and components. Aims to accelerate and foster commercialization of solar energy conversion for economic purposes. Maintains Solar Energy Research and Education Foundation. Compiles statistics; offers computerized services. **Libraries:** **Type:** not open to the public. **Holdings:** 1,000. **Awards:** Renewable Leadership Awards (Congressional). **Frequency:** annual. **Type:** recognition. **Computer Services:** database, sales lead referral and member list. **Telecommunication Services:** electronic mail, jstrnad@seia.org. **Committees:** Awards and Honors; Ethics; Government Affairs; International Trade; Statistics. **Councils:** Chapters; Suppliers; Users; Utilities. **Divisions:** Active Heating and Cooling; Photovoltaics; Solar Thermal Power. **Affiliated With:** Alliance to Save Energy; American Council for an Energy-Efficient Economy; American Solar Energy Society; Business Council for Sustainable Energy; Environmental and Energy Study Institute; Sustainable Buildings Industry Council; US Green Building Council. **Publications:** *Statistical Survey of Solar Collector Manufacturers and Suppliers*, quarterly. Provides industry statistics including total production by category of device, analyzes production figures, and forecasts future trends. **Price:** for current edition free for members; $50.00 for previous edition, plus shipping and handling ● Also publishes congressional hearing testimony, consumer guides, and market analyses, position papers, presentation materials and press releases. **Conventions/Meetings:** annual Soltech - conference and trade show, co-located with American Solar Energy Society - always spring.

7680 ■ Solar Energy International (SEI)
PO Box 715
Carbondale, CO 81623
Ph: (970)963-8855
Fax: (970)963-8866
E-mail: sei@solarenergy.org
URL: http://www.solarenergy.org
Contact: Johnny Weiss, Co-Founder/Exec. Dir.
Membership Dues: sunbeam, $25 (annual) ● friend, $50 (annual) ● supporting, $75 (annual) ● community, $100 (annual) ● family, $250 (annual) ● business, $500 (annual) ● sustaining, $1,000 (annual). **Staff:** 13. **Multinational. Description:** Aims to provide education and technical assistance to empower others to use renewable energy technologies. **Funds:** Youth Camp Scholarship. **Programs:** International Project Development and Management; Renewable Energy Education; Renewable Energy Training Programs for Women; Technology Transfer. **Publications:** *Adobe and Rammed Earth Building*. **Price:** $25.00 plus shipping and handling ● *Cooking With the Sun*. **Price:** $10.00 ● *Heaven's Flame*. **Price:** $15.00 ● *Home Power*. Magazine. **Price:** included in membership dues (except student/senior membership) ● *Homemade Money*. **Price:** $20.00 plus shipping and handling ● *Humanure Handbook*. **Price:** $20.00 ● *La Energia Solar*. **Price:** $25.00 ● *The Natural House*. **Price:** $35.00 plus shipping and handling ● *The New Solar Electric Home*. **Price:** $20.00 plus shipping and handling ● *The Passive Solar House*. **Price:** $25.00 plus shipping and handling ● *Photovoltaic Design Manual*. **Price:** $40.00 plus shipping and handling ● *Residential Micro-Hydro Power*. Video. **Price:** $40.00 ● *Residential Solar Electricity*. Video. **Price:** $40.00 ● *Residential Wind Power*. Video. **Price:** $40.00 ● *Rural Energy Services*. **Price:** $20.00 ● *SEI Journal*. Newsletter. **Price:** included in membership dues ● *Serious Straw Bale*. **Price:** $30.00 plus shipping and handling ● *Solar Water Pumping*. Video. **Price:** $40.00 ● *Storage Batteries*. Video. **Price:** $40.00 ● Videos. Contains five-title video set. **Price:** $170.00. **Conventions/Meetings:** Renewable Energy Youth Camp - meeting ● workshop, renewable energy education.

7681 ■ Solar Rating and Certification Corporation (SRCC)
c/o FSEC
1679 Clearlake Rd.
Cocoa, FL 32922-5703
Ph: (321)638-1537
Fax: (321)638-1010
E-mail: srcc@fsec.ucf.edu
URL: http://www.solar-rating.org
Contact: Les Nelson, Exec. Dir.
Founded: 1980. **Members:** 40. **Staff:** 3. **Description:** Serves as a rating and certification board for domestic solar hot water and pool heating panels and systems. **Libraries:** **Type:** open to the public. **Subjects:** directory of certified solar equipment. **Committees:** Consumer Advisory; Design Review; Laboratory Accreditation; Standards; Technical Compliance. **Publications:** *Directory of SRCC Certified Solar Collector and Water Heating System Ratings*, periodic. Features a list of rated products. **Price:** free for members. Alternate Formats: online. **Conventions/Meetings:** annual meeting.

7682 ■ Sustainable Buildings Industry Council (SBIC)
1112 16th St. NW, Ste.240
Washington, DC 20036
Ph: (202)628-7400 (212)564-5800
Fax: (202)393-5043
E-mail: sbic@sbicouncil.org
URL: http://www.sbicouncil.org
Contact: Helen English, Exec. Dir.
Founded: 1980. **Members:** 100. **Membership Dues:** individual, $100 (annual) ● small business, $350 (annual) ● regular (association, non-profit, labor union, professional), $750 (annual) ● regular (business with gross annual revenues of $2 million - $100 million), $1,000 (annual) ● regular (business with gross annual revenues of $100 million - $1 billion), $3,000 (annual) ● regular (business with gross annual revenues over $1 billion), $5,000 (annual). **Staff:** 3. **Budget:** $450,000. **Description:** Works to advance the design, affordability, energy performance, and environmental soundness of commercial, institutional, and residential buildings nationwide. Offers professional training, consumer education, and energy analysis tools. Provides accurate, easy-to-use guidelines, software, and general information about energy conservation measures, energy efficient equipment and appliances, daylighting, and sustainable architecture. Active in presenting workshops and seminars geared toward improving building energy performance in cities and towns throughout the nation. **Libraries:** **Type:** reference. **Holdings:** 2,000. **Subjects:** passive solar subjects, renewable resources, energy. **Computer Services:** database, technical literature and passive solar research information. **Telecommunication Services:** electronic mail, henglish@sbicouncil.org. **Committees:** Government Relations; Technical. **Publications:** *Buildings: Inside and Out*, periodic. Newsletter ● *Passive Solar Design Strategies: Guidelines for Home Builders*. Book. **Price:** $50.00 ● *Savings From the Sun* ● Also publishes other literature for planning, designing, and constructing passive solar buildings. **Conventions/Meetings:** annual meeting ● periodic workshop.

Space

7683 ■ Mars Society
11111 W 8th Ave., Unit A
Lakewood, CO 80215
Ph: (303)984-9653
E-mail: info@marssociety.org
URL: http://www.marssociety.org
Contact: Dr. Robert Zubrin, Founder/Pres.
Founded: 1998. **Members:** 2,000. **Membership Dues:** $50 (annual). **Budget:** $200,000. **State Groups:** 55. **Languages:** English, French, German, Spanish. **Description:** Seeks to further the goals of "exploring and settling Mars, the Red Planet". Conducts public outreach programs to "instill the vision of pioneering Mars". **Awards:** Hakluyt Prize. **Frequency:** annual. **Type:** scholarship. **Recipient:** for letter writing contest winner. **Computer Services:** Mailing lists, special bulletins to 6000 names. **Task Forces:** E-Commerce; Education; Graphics and Production; Marketing; Mars Arctic Research Station; Mars Civilization and Culture; Political and Public Outreach; Technical. **Publications:** *Proceedings of Annual Conference*, annual. Book. **Price:** $75.00. **Conventions/Meetings:** annual convention and lecture, features presentations, task force meetings.

7684 ■ Moon Society
PO Box 940825
Plano, TX 75094-0825
E-mail: info@moonsociety.org
URL: http://www.moonsociety.org
Contact: Peter Kokh, Pres.
Multinational. Description: Works to further scientific study and development of the moon. **Computer Services:** Mailing lists. **Telecommunication Services:** electronic mail, kokhmmm@aol.com. **Publications:** *Moon Miners' Manifesto*, monthly. Newsletter. **Price:** included in membership dues ● *Moon Miners' Review*. **Price:** included in membership dues. **Conventions/Meetings:** conference ● monthly meeting - first and third Wednesday.

7685 ■ Space Access Society (SAS)
5515 N 7th St., No. 134-348
Phoenix, AZ 85014
Ph: (602)431-9283
Fax: (602)431-9283
E-mail: space.access@space-access.org
URL: http://www.space-access.org
Contact: Henry Vanderbilt, Exec. Dir.
Membership Dues: regular, $30 (annual). **Description:** Dedicated to routine, reliable, and less expensive access to space. **Publications:** Newsletter. **Conventions/Meetings:** annual conference.

7686 ■ Space Frontier Foundation
16 1st Ave.
Nyack, NY 10960
Ph: (818)985-7367
Free: (800)787-7223

E-mail: press@space-frontier.org
URL: http://www.space-frontier.org
Contact: Jeff Krukin, Exec. Dir.

Founded: 1988. **Membership Dues:** individual, $25 (annual). **Multinational. Description:** Works to open the Space Frontier to human settlement as quickly as possible; aims to protect the Earth's biosphere. **Awards: Type:** recognition. **Boards:** Advisors. **Publications:** *NewSpace News*, monthly. Newsletter. Alternate Formats: online. **Conventions/Meetings:** annual meeting, held in conjunction with annual conference ● annual NewSpace - conference - 2008 July 17-19, Crystal City, VA.

7687 ■ Space Studies Board

c/o National Research Council
500 Fifth St. NW, 10th Fl.
Washington, DC 20001
Ph: (202)334-3477
Fax: (202)334-3701
E-mail: ssb@nas.edu
URL: http://www.nationalacademies.org/ssb
Contact: Marcia S. Smith, Dir.

Description: Provides an independent, authoritative forum for information and advice on all aspects of space science and applications. Conducts advisory studies and program assessments, facilitates international research coordination, and promotes communications on space science and science policy among the research community, federal government, and the interested public. **Committees:** Astronomy and Astrophysics; Earth Studies; Microgravity Research; Origins and Evolution of Life; Planetary and Lunar Exploration; Solar and Space Physics; Space Biology and Medicine. **Programs:** Space Internship. **Publications:** *Space Studies Board News*, quarterly. Newsletter. Alternate Formats: online ● Reports. Alternate Formats: online ● Annual Report, annual. Alternate Formats: online.

Spectroscopy

7688 ■ American Society for Mass Spectrometry (ASMS)

2019 Galisteo St., Bldg. I-1
Santa Fe, NM 87505
Ph: (505)989-4517
Fax: (505)989-1073
E-mail: office@asms.org
URL: http://www.asms.org
Contact: Judith A. Sjoberg, Exec. Dir.

Founded: 1969. **Members:** 5,500. **Membership Dues:** regular, in North America, $65 (annual) ● regular, outside North America, $75 (annual) ● student in North America, $40 (annual) ● student outside North America, $50 (annual). **Description:** Promotes and publicizes knowledge of mass spectrometry and allied topics primarily through sponsorship of an annual conference. Two-day courses are taught in conjunction with the annual conference. **Libraries: Type:** not open to the public. **Awards:** Biemann Medal. **Frequency:** annual. **Type:** grant ● Research Award. **Frequency:** annual. **Type:** grant. **Recipient:** for a young investigator. **Computer Services:** database, membership white pages ● mailing lists, of members ● online services, forum. **Telecommunication Services:** electronic mail, judith@asms.org. **Affiliated With:** American Association for the Advancement of Science. **Publications:** *Proceedings of Annual Conference*, annual. **Price:** $70.00 ● *What is Mass Spectrometry?*. Booklet. **Price:** $3.00. **Conventions/Meetings:** annual conference - 2009 May 31-June 4, Philadelphia, PA; 2010 May 23-27, Salt Lake City, UT.

7689 ■ Coblentz Society (CS)

c/o Mary W. Carrabba, PhD, Pres.
508 Gold Terr.
Rogue River, OR 97537
Ph: (541)582-2399 (410)822-1220
Fax: (410)822-7526
E-mail: carrabba@rrslabs.com
URL: http://www.coblentz.org
Contact: Mary W. Carrabba PhD, Pres.

Founded: 1954. **Members:** 600. **Membership Dues:** student, $10 (annual). **Multinational. Description:** Represents scientists (primarily chemists) interested in vibrational spectroscopy and its applications. **Awards:** Coblentz Award. **Frequency:** annual. **Type:** recognition. **Recipient:** to a spectroscopist under the age of 35; for significant contribution to the field ● Coblentz Student Award. **Frequency:** annual. **Type:** recognition ● Williams-Wright Award. **Frequency:** annual. **Type:** recognition. **Recipient:** for outstanding achievement by active industrial spectroscopist. **Computer Services:** database, infrared spectral. **Telecommunication Services:** electronic mail, rlarsensdt@aol.com. **Committees:** Booth; Collection of Infrared Spectra; Infrared Analytical Methods; Legal Review. **Affiliated With:** Society for Applied Spectroscopy. **Publications:** Newsletter, quarterly. **Conventions/Meetings:** annual conference.

7690 ■ Society for Applied Spectroscopy (SAS)

201B Broadway St.
Frederick, MD 21701-6501
Ph: (301)694-8122 (513)627-2840
Fax: (301)694-6860
E-mail: office@s-a-s.org
URL: http://www.s-a-s.org
Contact: Bonnie A. Saylor, Exec. Dir.

Founded: 1958. **Members:** 3,000. **Membership Dues:** regular, $70 (annual) ● regular, outside U.S., $110 (annual) ● student/retired, $20 (annual). **Staff:** 3. **Budget:** $1,000,000. **Local Groups:** 32. **Description:** Professional society of persons interested in all phases of spectroscopy. Conducts educational programs. Maintains 14 committees. **Awards:** Allied Spectroscopy William F. Meggers. **Frequency:** annual. **Type:** recognition. **Recipient:** to the author(s) of outstanding paper appearing in Allied Spectroscopy ● Distinguished Service. **Frequency:** annual. **Type:** recognition. **Recipient:** for long time service to the society ● Lester W. Strock. **Frequency:** annual. **Type:** medal. **Recipient:** to author or authors of series of papers that are collectively outstanding ● Lippincott. **Frequency:** annual. **Type:** medal. **Recipient:** for significant contributions to vibrational spectroscopy ● SAS Graduate Student. **Frequency:** annual. **Type:** recognition. **Recipient:** for outstanding research in the area of spectroscopy ● William Poehlman. **Frequency:** annual. **Type:** recognition. **Recipient:** to a local section of the Society. **Telecommunication Services:** electronic mail, exdir@s-a-s.org. **Committees:** Award; Local and Technical Section Affairs; Long Range Planning; Publicity. **Affiliated With:** Coblentz Society; Federation of Analytical Chemistry and Spectroscopy Societies. **Publications:** *Applied Spectroscopy*, monthly. Journal. Covers analytical chemistry and spectroscopy. **Price:** $45.00 /year for libraries. ISSN: 0003-7028. **Circulation:** 6,000. **Advertising:** accepted. Alternate Formats: microform; online ● Newsletter, quarterly. **Conventions/Meetings:** annual meeting, held in conjunction with Federation of Analytical Chemistry and Spectroscopy Societies (exhibits).

Speleology

7691 ■ Association for Mexican Cave Studies (AMCS)

PO Box 7672
Austin, TX 78713
E-mail: editor@amcs-pubs.org
URL: http://www.amcs-pubs.org
Contact: Bill Mixon, Ed.

Founded: 1963. **Staff:** 6. **Languages:** English, French, Spanish. **Nonmembership. Description:** Promotes the exploration, study, and conservation of caves in Mexico, primarily through publications. **Libraries: Type:** by appointment only; open to the public; reference. **Holdings:** 500; archival material, books, maps, papers, periodicals, photographs. **Subjects:** Mexican caves, cave biology, cave geology, cave archaeology, some caving periodicals from other countries. **Affiliated With:** National Speleological Society. **Publications:** *AMCS Activities Newsletter*, annual. Papers. Contains report on all significant original explorations and research in the caves of Mexico. **Circulation:** 150 ● *AMCS Bulletins* (in English and Spanish), periodic. Monographs. Includes monographs on cave areas in Mexico or topics concerning the caves of Mexico. **Circulation:** 150 ● *AMCS Reprint Series* (in English and Spanish), periodic. Reprints. Contains reprints of books originally from other publishers that pertain to the caves of Mexico.

7692 ■ Cave Research Foundation (CRF)

c/o Bob Hoke, Treas.
6304 Kaybro St.
Laurel, MD 20707-2621
E-mail: bob@hoke.net
URL: http://www.cave-research.org
Contact: Scott House, Pres.

Founded: 1957. **Members:** 135. **Description:** Represents individuals elected by fellowship to honor their contribution to the study, conservation, and interpretation of caves; persons who are active participants, selected to take part in field programs. Works to: support research and exploration in caves; assist in the interpretation of caves and karst features for the public; aid in the conservation of caves. Conducts extensive field programs in cartography and research support in the Mammoth Cave Region of Kentucky, the Guadalupe Mountains area of New Mexico and Texas, the Buffalo National River in Arkansas, and the Kings Canyon Karst in California. Supports scientific projects in archaeology, biology, ecology, geology, mineralogy, geography, and history. Operates field stations in Mammoth Cave, Carlsbad Caverns, and Kings Canyon National Parks. Maintains survey data on the Flint Mammoth Cave System, Carlsbad Caverns, Beauty Cave, and Lilburn Cave. **Awards:** Karst Research Fellowship. **Frequency:** annual. **Type:** fellowship. **Recipient:** for graduate thesis research in the biological, social, economic, or earth sciences. **Telecommunication Services:** electronic mail, scott_house@semo.net. **Committees:** Cartography; Computer; Conservation; Interpretation and Information; Science. **Absorbed:** (1972) Guadalupe Cave Survey. **Publications:** Report, annual ● Monographs ● Newsletter, quarterly ● Also publishes results of studies and theses. **Conventions/Meetings:** semiannual board meeting.

7693 ■ National Speleological Society (NSS)

2813 Cave Ave.
Huntsville, AL 35810-4431
Ph: (256)852-1300
Fax: (256)851-9241
E-mail: nss@caves.org
URL: http://www.caves.org
Contact: William Tozer, Pres.

Founded: 1941. **Members:** 12,000. **Membership Dues:** regular, $36 (annual) ● associate, $25 (annual) ● institutional, $75 (annual) ● sustaining, $108 (annual) ● conservation, $100 (annual) ● life, $720 ● limited, $15 (annual) ● family (regular, associate), $7 (annual) ● family sustaining, $43 (annual) ● life (family), $360. **Staff:** 3. **Budget:** $500,000. **Description:** Biologists, geologists, geophysicists, mineralogists, and other scientists whose fields are related to: the study of caves and related phenomena; persons interested in caves and their exploration; libraries and scientific educational organizations; commercial caves. Investigates, collects, compiles, preserves, and publishes information on caves and their contents. Seeks to prevent vandalism, pollution, and exploitation of caves. **Libraries: Type:** reference. **Holdings:** 24,000; archival material, audiovisuals, films. **Subjects:** biology, geology, meteorology, mineralogy, paleontology, folklore, artifacts, saltpeter mining, state cave surveys, speleological investigations of foreign countries. **Awards:** Certificates of Merit. **Frequency:** annual. **Type:** recognition ● Ralph W. Stone Graduate Fellowship. **Frequency:** annual. **Type:** monetary. **Recipient:** to a member currently pursuing graduate studies ● Research Grant. **Type:** grant ● Young Investigator. **Frequency:** annual.

Type: monetary. **Recipient:** to a member under 22 years old. **Committees:** Cave Files; Conservation; Legal; Library; Photo-Salon; Visual Aids. **Sections:** Biology; Cave Diving; Geological; Spelean History. **Affiliated With:** American Association for the Advancement of Science; American Geological Institute; Bat Conservation International. **Formerly:** District of Columbia Speleological Society. **Publications:** *Cave Mapping*. Book. Tells how to map and survey caves. **Price:** $4.00 ● *Caving Basics*. **Price:** $11.00 ● *Cumberland Caverns*. Journal. **Price:** $9.95 ● *Journal of Cave and Karst Studies*, 3/year. Contains information about caves. **Price:** included in membership dues; $18.00 /year for nonmembers. ISSN: 1090-6924. **Circulation:** 10,000. **Advertising:** accepted ● *National Speleological Society—Membership List*, periodic. Membership Directory. **Price:** available to members only ● *NSS News*, monthly. Newsletter. Covers caves, caving, caving equipment, accident reports, safety hints, conservation concerns, and regional and national caving activities. **Price:** included in membership dues; $18.00 /year for nonmembers. ISSN: 0027-7010. **Advertising:** accepted ● *On Rope*. **Price:** $32.00 ● *On Station*. **Price:** $17.00 ● *Speleo-Digest*, annual. Compilation of articles appearing in local grotto newsletters on caves, cave science, cave equipment, and cave humor. **Price:** available to members only ● *U.S. Cave Rescue*. Manual. **Price:** $15.00. **Conventions/Meetings:** annual convention - 2008 Aug. 11-15, Lake City, FL; 2009 July 19-26, Kerrville, TX; 2010 July 12-17, Essex Junction, VT.

Standards

7694 ■ American Measuring Tool Manufacturers Association (AMTMA)

8652 E Ave.
Mentor, OH 44060
Ph: (440)974-6829
Fax: (440)974-6828
E-mail: amtma@amtma.com
URL: http://www.amtma.com
Contact: Mr. Norm Leduc, Co-Pres.

Founded: 1973. **Members:** 93. **Membership Dues:** associate, $613 (annual) ● regular (based on the size of the company), $613-$1,712 (annual). **Staff:** 4. **Budget:** $100,000. **Description:** Promotes the interests of manufacturers of measuring tools. Supports standardization of sizes, dimensions, tolerances and simplify the same in cooperation with national and international engineering bodies. **Publications:** *The Gage*, semiannual. Newsletter. **Price:** included in membership dues. Alternate Formats: online ● *Searching for Zero*. Booklet. **Price:** $3.50/copy for members (for 1 to 4 copies); $10.00/copy for nonmembers (for 1 to 4 copies). **Conventions/Meetings:** semiannual meeting - spring and fall.

7695 ■ Dozenal Society of America (DSA)

472 Village Oaks Ln.
Babylon, NY 11702-3123
Ph: (631)669-0273 (215)923-6167
E-mail: contact@dozenal.org
URL: http://www.Dozenal.org
Contact: Jay Schiffman, Ed.

Founded: 1935. **Members:** 144. **Membership Dues:** student, $3 (annual) ● regular, $12 (annual). **Description:** Conducts research and educates the public on the advantages of using base 12 in numeration, mathematics, computer I/O, weights and measures, and other branches of pure and applied science. Conducts research programs; offers specialized education programs and speakers' bureau. **Libraries: Type:** open to the public; reference; lending. **Holdings:** 170; archival material, articles, biographical archives, books, periodicals. **Subjects:** base twelve; other bases; history of DSA and the base twelve movement; biographies of movement's founders and leaders. **Awards:** Ralph Beard Award. **Frequency:** annual. **Type:** recognition. **Committees:** Awards; Bibliography; Electronic Calculator; Weights and Measures. **Formerly:** (1979) Duodecimal Society of America. **Publications:** *Duodecimal Bulletin*, semiannual. Provides information on base 12 arithmetic and other number systems; includes society news and book reviews; indexed every 12 issues. **Price:** included in membership dues. ISSN: 0046-0826. **Circulation:** 144. **Advertising:** accepted ● Manual of the Dozen System, Excursion in Numbers reprint, The Dozenal Society of America pamphlet. **Conventions/Meetings:** annual meeting.

7696 ■ Manufacturing Skill Standards Council (MSSC)

5020 Overlook Rd. NW
Washington, DC 20036
Ph: (202)237-2300
Fax: (202)237-2322
E-mail: info@msscusa.org
URL: http://www.msscusa.org
Contact: Leo Reddy, CEO

Founded: 1998. **Description:** Develops a national skill standards system for manufacturing in response to industry's growing need to find skilled workers. Provides assessments and certifications to manufacturers that serve as a yardstick for measurement and improvement. **Committees:** Assessment and Documentation; Framework and Systems-building; Standards. **Publications:** *A Blueprint for Workforce Excellence: Core and Concentration Skill Standards for Manufacturing*. Manual. **Price:** $80.00 with discount to NCAM members. Alternate Formats: CD-ROM.

7697 ■ National Standards Educators Association (NSEA)

PO Box 773
Placentia, CA 92871
Ph: (909)930-3835
E-mail: ansi2000@earthlink.net
Contact: Walter J. McGee, Exec. Dir.

Founded: 1987. **Members:** 100. **Staff:** 3. **Description:** Industrial executives and managers, engineers, technicians, educators, and students. Promotes the significance and teaching of standards within American industry. Advances the concept of Management By Accountability (MBA) that imposes the use of detailed certifications, accreditations, registrations, and licensures to combat standards illiteracy. Seeks to institute testing of the American industrial workforce based on standards common to various fields. Maintains that such testing can effect a positive cultural change to bring the United States into a "true state of economic competitiveness." Is currently developing initial testing programs in conjunction with the American Society of Mechanical Engineers. **Committees:** Certification; Government Liaison; Seminar/Training. **Affiliated With:** American Society of Mechanical Engineers. **Publications:** *NSEA Bulletin*, periodic ● *NSEA News*, quarterly. Newsletter ● Also publishes white papers; plans to issue technical materials. **Conventions/Meetings:** annual meeting.

7698 ■ NCSL International

2995 Wilderness Pl., Ste.107
Boulder, CO 80301-5404
Ph: (303)440-3339 (650)493-3955
Fax: (303)440-3384
E-mail: info@ncsli.org
URL: http://www.ncsli.org
Contact: Jack Ferris, Pres.

Founded: 1961. **Members:** 1,531. **Membership Dues:** corporate, educational institution, $400 (annual) ● associate, $200 (annual) ● individual, $100 (annual) ● student, $50 (annual). **Staff:** 5. **Budget:** $100,000. **Regional Groups:** 13. **Multinational. Description:** Representatives of measurements standards and calibration laboratories; organizations with related interests. Seeks cost reduction or solution of problems, both technical and administrative, that besiege all measurement activities in the physical sciences, engineering, and technology. Conducts conferences and meetings for presentation of papers and discussions pertaining to technical and managerial problems, operating practices, and policies for measurement standards laboratories. Works with educational organizations to develop programs for training technical personnel and professional metrologists. **Libraries: Type:** reference. **Holdings:** video recordings. **Subjects:** training aids. **Telecommunication Services:** electronic mail, cgulka@ncsli.org. **Committees:** Automatic Test and Calibration Systems; Biomedical and Pharmaceutical Metrology; Calibration Laboratory Automation; Calibration Systems Management; Education and Training; Electronics; Honors and Awards; Information and Directory; Laboratory Evaluation; Measurement Assurance; National Measurement Requirements; Product and Design Specification; Recommended Practices. **Formerly:** (2000) National Conference of Standards Laboratories. **Publications:** *Conference Proceedings*, annual ● *NCSL Newsletter*, quarterly. Includes calendar of events; lists new members. **Price:** $15.00/year; $5.00 single copy. ISSN: 0194-5149. **Circulation:** 2,300. **Conventions/Meetings:** annual workshop and symposium, about metrology's impact on products and services (exhibits) - 2008 Aug. 3-7, Orlando, FL; 2009 July 26-30, San Antonio, TX.

7699 ■ Society of Allied Weight Engineers (SAWE)

c/o Mr. Ronald L. Fox, Exec. Dir.
2131 Tevis Ave.
Long Beach, CA 90815-3352
Ph: (562)596-2873 (817)777-5171
Fax: (562)596-2874
E-mail: exdirector@sawe.org
URL: http://www.sawe.org
Contact: Mr. Ronald L. Fox, Exec. Dir.

Founded: 1939. **Members:** 800. **Membership Dues:** academic, active, $45 (annual) ● company, $450 (annual) ● student, $10 (annual) ● retired, $25 (annual). **Budget:** $70,000. **Regional Groups:** 22. **Description:** Represents engineers interested in both theoretical and applied mass properties analyses used in the design, development, manufacturing, and testing of air, land, sea and space vehicles and their systems/subsystems, as well as mass properties measurement and control. Cooperates with the Department of Defense, Federal Aviation Administration, airlines, the automobile industry, and marine and scientific societies worldwide on matters of weight reduction, weight estimation, mass distribution, standard weights of raw stock and hardware, and standard methods of mass properties measurement. Collaborates with governmental agencies to produce related recommended practices for practitioners. **Libraries: Type:** reference. **Holdings:** 2,500. **Subjects:** mass properties prediction, control, measurement, advanced design, aircraft design, advanced materials, computer applications, missile design, spacecraft design, surface transportation, marine engineering. **Awards:** Ed Payne Award. **Frequency:** annual. **Type:** recognition. **Recipient:** to young engineers, under the age of 35, who have made significant contributions to the SAWE or the mass properties engineering profession ● Fellow Award. **Frequency:** annual. **Type:** fellowship. **Recipient:** to persons who have achieved distinction in the field of mass properties engineering ● Honorary Fellow Award. **Frequency:** annual. **Type:** fellowship. **Recipient:** to persons who have achieved eminence in mass properties engineering ● L.R. "Mike" Hackney Award. **Frequency:** annual. **Type:** recognition. **Recipient:** to the author or authors of the best technical paper ● Presidents' Award. **Frequency:** annual. **Type:** recognition. **Recipient:** for significant achievement or exceptional merit in service to the society ● SAWE Scholarship. **Frequency:** annual. **Type:** scholarship. **Recipient:** for engineering studies. **Formerly:** Society of Aeronautical Weight Engineers, Inc. **Publications:** *SAWE Newsletter*, quarterly. **Price:** included in membership dues. **Circulation:** 1,000. **Advertising:** accepted. Alternate Formats: online ● *SAWE Operational Manual*. Alternate Formats: online ● *Weight Engineering*, 3/year. Journal. Contains technical articles and society information. **Price:** included in membership dues; $35.00 /year for nonmembers. **Circulation:** 1,000. **Advertising:** accepted ● *Weight Engineer's Handbook*, periodic. **Price:** $50.00 for nonmembers; $25.00 for members. Alternate Formats: CD-ROM ● Papers ● Also publishes technical papers from annual International Conference. **Conventions/Meetings:** annual Mass Properties Engineering International Conference (exhibits) - usually May.

7700 ■ Standards Engineering Society (SES)
13340 SW 96th Ave.
Miami, FL 33176
Ph: (305)971-4798
Fax: (305)971-4799
E-mail: admin@ses-standards.org
URL: http://www.ses-standards.org
Contact: H. Glenn Ziegenfuss, Exec. Dir.
Founded: 1947. **Members:** 425. **Membership Dues:** individual in U.S. and Canada, $85 (annual) ● organization in U.S. and Canada, $600 (annual) ● individual outside U.S. and Canada, $130 (annual) ● organization outside U.S. and Canada, $700 (annual). **Staff:** 1. **Budget:** $85,000. **Regional Groups:** 1. **Multinational. Description:** Engineers, teachers, executives, and scholars interested in practicing standardization. Seeks to further standardization as a means of enhancing general welfare and to promote knowledge and use of approved standards issued by regularly constituted standardizing bodies. **Libraries: Type:** reference. **Holdings:** archival material. **Awards:** Fellow. **Frequency:** annual. **Type:** fellowship. **Recipient:** for outstanding contribution to standards and standardization ● Honorary Life. **Frequency:** annual. **Type:** recognition. **Recipient:** for outstanding accomplishment in the field of standardization ● Leo B. Moore Medal. **Frequency:** annual. **Type:** medal. **Recipient:** for outstanding contribution to the field of standardization ● Lorne K. Wagner Memorial Award. **Frequency:** annual. **Type:** recognition. **Recipient:** for contribution or service to the growth and development of SES ● Robert J. Painter Memorial Award. **Frequency:** annual. **Type:** recognition. **Recipient:** for special service in the field of standardization through a company program, managerial support or educational research ● World Standards Day Paper Competition. **Frequency:** annual. **Type:** recognition. **Recipient:** for outstanding contribution to standards and standardization. **Committees:** Awards; Conference; Metrication; Professional Education; Professional Relations; Publications; Standards; Web. **Affiliated With:** American National Standards Institute. **Formerly:** (1980) Standards Engineers Society. **Publications:** *Standards Engineering*, bimonthly. Journal. Covers topics of interest to members including standards education. **Price:** $12.00/copy; $45.00/year in U.S. and Canada; $70.00/year outside U.S. and Canada. ISSN: 0038-9668. **Circulation:** 400. **Advertising:** accepted ● Membership Directory, biennial ● Newsletter, periodic. **Conventions/Meetings:** annual conference.

7701 ■ U.S. Metric Association (USMA)
10245 Andasol Ave.
Northridge, CA 91325-1504
Ph: (818)363-5606 (909)792-5297
Fax: (818)363-5606
E-mail: hillger@cira.colostate.edu
URL: http://www.metric.org
Contact: Valerie Antoine, Exec. Dir.
Founded: 1916. **Members:** 1,000. **Membership Dues:** individual, $30 (annual) ● company, agency, $150 (annual) ● full-time student, $15 (annual) ● foreign, $35 (annual) ● life, $500 ● individual, $58 (biennial) ● individual, $85 (triennial). **Staff:** 2. **Budget:** $40,000. **Regional Groups:** 3. **Description:** Scientists, engineers, teachers, government and industry personnel, students, and laymen interested in promoting greater use of the metric system of measurement; appointed by the U.S. Department of Commerce to represent the private sector on government metric committees. Aids teachers, consumers, government, and industry in implementing the metric system. Maintains a Certified Metrication Specialist Board which is responsible for screening qualified applicants to work with metric system units. Distributes educational fliers on the metric system. Compiles statistics. **Libraries: Type:** reference. **Holdings:** archival material, articles. **Subjects:** metrication. **Awards:** Fellow Award. **Frequency:** annual. **Type:** fellowship. **Recipient:** for outstanding service in promoting metrication and correct metric system unit usage. **Telecommunication Services:** electronic mail, valerie.antoine@verizon.net. **Committees:** Certified Metrication Specialist; Consumer; Education; Industrial Sector; Metric Practice; Public Relations; Science Fair Coordination. **Affiliated With:** American Association for the Advancement of Science. **Formerly:** (1975) Metric Association. **Publications:** *Metric Today*, bimonthly. Newsletter. Covers metric developments in the U.S. and abroad. Provides data on new metric literature and metric activities. Includes book reviews and obituaries. **Price:** included in membership dues; $30.00 /year for nonmembers. ISSN: 1050-5628. **Circulation:** 1,000 ● *SI Metric System Guide*. Book ● Also publishes a series of educational fliers regarding the metric system of measurement.

Statistics

7702 ■ American Statistical Association (ASA)
732 N Washington St.
Alexandria, VA 22314-1943
Ph: (703)684-1221
Free: (888)231-3473
Fax: (703)684-2037
E-mail: asainfo@amstat.org
URL: http://www.amstat.org
Contact: William B. Smith, Exec. Dir.
Founded: 1839. **Members:** 16,000. **Membership Dues:** individual (limited), $90 (annual) ● senior/retired, $25 (annual) ● corporate, $1,100 (annual) ● institutional, $595 (annual) ● K-12 school, family, $50 (annual) ● post graduate, economically developing country resident, $40 (annual) ● individual (regular), $110 (annual) ● college, $150 (biennial) ● student, $10 (annual). **Staff:** 43. **Budget:** $6,000,000. **Local Groups:** 78. **Description:** Professional society of persons interested in the theory, methodology, and application of statistics to all fields of human endeavor. **Telecommunication Services:** electronic mail, williambsmith@amstat.org ● electronic mail, memdept@amstat.org. **Sections:** Bayesian Statistical Science; Biometrics; Biopharmaceutical; Business and Economic Statistics; Education; Epidemiology; Government Statistics; Health Policy Statistics; NonParametric Statistics; Physical and Engineering Sciences; Quality and Productivity; Risk Analysis; Social Statistics; Statistical Computing; Statistical Consulting Education; Statistical Graphics; Statistics and the Environment; Statistics in Marketing; Statistics in Sports; Survey Research Methods; Teaching of Statistics in the Health Sciences. **Publications:** *The American Statistician*, quarterly. Journal. **Price:** $15.00 ● *AMSTAT News*, 11/year. Newsletter. Includes calendar of events. **Price:** included in membership dues. ISSN: 0163-9617. **Circulation:** 19,000 ● *Chance*, quarterly. Magazine. **Price:** $26.00 ● *Current Index to Statistics*, annual. **Price:** $25.00 ● *Directory of Statisticians*, periodic ● *Journal of Agricultural, Biological, and Environmental Statistics Quarterly*. **Price:** $48.00 for members; $86.00 for nonmembers ● *Journal of ASA*, quarterly. **Price:** $45.00 for members; $10.00 for student members; $480.00 for nonmembers ● *Journal of Business and Economic Statistics*, quarterly. **Price:** $56.00 for members; $14.00 for student members; $135.00 for nonmembers ● *Journal of Computational and Graphical Statistics*, quarterly. **Price:** $55.00 for members; $10.00 for student members; $90.00 for nonmembers ● *Journal of Educational and Behavioral Statistics*, quarterly. **Price:** $25.00 in U.S.; $34.00 outside U.S. ● *Journal of Official Statistics*, quarterly. **Price:** $42.00 ● *STATS: The Magazine for Students of Statistics* ● *Survey Methodology*, semiannual, June/December ● *Technometrics*, quarterly. Journal. **Price:** $24.00. **Conventions/Meetings:** annual Joint Statistical Meeting - conference (exhibits) - 2008 Aug. 3-7, Denver, CO; 2009 Aug. 2-6, Washington, DC; 2010 Aug. 1-5, Vancouver, BC, Canada.

7703 ■ Caucus for Women in Statistics (CWS)
c/o Anna Nevius, Treas.
7732 Rydal Terr.
Rockville, MD 20855-2057
Ph: (301)827-0170 (301)258-0565
Fax: (301)827-6661
E-mail: anna.nevius@fda.hhs.gov
URL: http://caucusforwomeninstatistics.com
Contact: Tena I. Katsaounis, Pres.
Founded: 1970. **Members:** 320. **Membership Dues:** regular (individual), $25 (annual) ● sustaining (individual), $40 (annual) ● associate, $5 (annual) ● regular (couple), regular (individual) in Canada, $30 (annual) ● sustaining (couple), $50 (annual) ● regular (couple) in Canada, $35 (annual) ● sustaining (individual) in Canada, $47 (annual) ● sustaining (couple) in Canada, $60 (annual) ● associate in Canada, $6 (annual) ● Canadian section, $1 (annual) ● Canadian section (in Canada), $2 (annual). **Regional Groups:** 1. **State Groups:** 1. **Multinational. Description:** Individuals, primarily statisticians, united to improve employment and professional opportunities for women in statistics. Conducts technical sessions concerning statistical studies related to women. Maintains biographical archives. **Telecommunication Services:** electronic mail, katsaounis.1@osu.edu. **Committees:** Employment. **Affiliated With:** American Statistical Association. **Publications:** *Caucus for Women in Statistics Directory*, annual ● *Caucus for Women in Statistics—Newsletter*, quarterly. Contains book reviews; lists employment opportunities. **Price:** included in membership dues. **Circulation:** 300. **Conventions/Meetings:** annual meeting.

7704 ■ Committee of Presidents of Statistical Societies (COPSS)
c/o Dr. Joseph Ibrahim
Dept. of Biostatistics
Harvard School of Public Hea. and Dana Farber CancerInstitute
44 Binney St.
Boston, MA 02115
Ph: (617)632-2472
E-mail: copss@copssnet.org
Contact: Marvin Zelen, Chm.
Founded: 1961. **Members:** 18. **Description:** Informal group comprising representatives from the American Statistical Association, the International Biometric Society, the Institute of Mathematical Statistics, and the Statistics Society of Canada. **Awards:** Elizabeth L. Scott Award. **Frequency:** biennial. **Type:** recognition. **Recipient:** for an individual who helped foster opportunities in statistics for women ● George W. Snedecor Award. **Frequency:** biennial. **Type:** recognition. **Recipient:** for an individual who became an instrument in the development of statistical theory in biometry ● Presidents' Award. **Frequency:** annual. **Type:** recognition. **Recipient:** for outstanding contribution to the profession of statistics ● R.A. Fisher Lectureship. **Frequency:** annual. **Type:** recognition. **Recipient:** to an eminent statistician for outstanding contributions to the theory and applications of statistics ● **Type:** recognition. **Committees:** AAAS Coordinating; Elizabeth Scott Award; George Snedecor Award; Presidents' Award; R.A. Fisher Lecturer and Award; Visiting Lecturer Program. **Affiliated With:** American Statistical Association; Casualty Actuarial Society; Institute of Mathematical Statistics; International Biometric Society; International Biometric Society, Eastern North American Region; International Biometric Society, Western North American Region; Society of Actuaries. **Publications:** *Careers in Statistics*. Brochure ● *Committee of Presidents of Statistical Societies—Directory of Statisticians*, periodic. Membership Directory. **Price:** included in membership dues. **Advertising:** accepted. **Conventions/Meetings:** semiannual meeting.

7705 ■ Econometric Society (ES)
New York Univ.
Dept. of Economics
19 W 4th St., 6th Fl.
New York, NY 10012
Ph: (212)998-3820 (609)258-4768
Fax: (212)995-4487
E-mail: sashi@econometricsociety.org
URL: http://www.econometricsociety.org
Contact: Claire Sashi, Gen. Mgr.
Founded: 1930. **Members:** 7,000. **Membership Dues:** ordinary, $45 (annual) ● student, $30 (annual).

Staff: 2. **Multinational. Description:** Economists, statisticians, and mathematicians. Promotes studies that are directed towards unification of the theoretical and empirical approaches to economic problems and advancement of economic theory in its relation to statistics and mathematics. **Publications:** *Econometrica*, bimonthly. Journal. Covers statistical and mathematical economic theory; includes membership news. **Price:** included in membership dues; $214.00 /year for libraries and institutions. ISSN: 0012-9682. **Circulation:** 7,000. **Advertising:** accepted. **Conventions/Meetings:** Australasian Meeting - 2008 July 9-11, Wellington, New Zealand ● Latin American Meeting ● semiannual meeting - always summer and winter ● annual North American Summer Meeting - held in summer. 2008 June 19-22, Pittsburgh, PA ● North American Winter Meeting ● annual regional meeting ● quinquennial World Congress.

7706 ■ Institute of Mathematical Statistics (IMS)

PO Box 22718
Beachwood, OH 44122
Ph: (216)295-2340 (301)634-7029
Fax: (216)295-5661
E-mail: ims@imstat.org
URL: http://www.imstat.org
Contact: Cindy Christiansen, Exec. Sec.

Founded: 1935. **Members:** 3,300. **Membership Dues:** individual, $75 (annual) ● institutional, $680 (annual) ● corporate, $850 (annual) ● reduced/retired, $30 (annual) ● life, $900 ● life-retired, $240 ● first-year graduate, $25 (annual) ● second-year graduate, $50 (annual). **Staff:** 2. **Budget:** $1,000,000. **Description:** Professional society of mathematicians and others interested in mathematical statistics and probability theory. Seeks to further research in mathematical statistics and probability. **Telecommunication Services:** electronic mail, erg@imstat.org ● electronic mail, staff@imstat.org. **Publications:** *Annals of Applied Probability*, quarterly, in February, May, August, and November. Journal. Features traditional areas of applied probability. **Price:** $186.00 /year for nonmembers. ISSN: 1050-5164. **Circulation:** 2,200. **Advertising:** accepted. Alternate Formats: microform. Also Cited As: *Ann App Probab* ● *Annals of Probability*, bimonthly, in January, March, May, July, September and November. Journal. Publishes contributions to the theory of probability and its application. **Price:** $270.00 /year for nonmembers. ISSN: 0091-1798. **Circulation:** 2,700. **Advertising:** accepted. Alternate Formats: microform. Also Cited As: *Ann. Probab* ● *Annals of Statistics*, bimonthly, in February, April, June, August, October, and December. Journal. Publishes contributions to the theory of statistics and its application. **Price:** $270.00 /year for nonmembers. ISSN: 0090-5364. **Circulation:** 4,300. **Advertising:** accepted. Alternate Formats: microform. Also Cited As: *Ann Statist* ● *Current Index to Statistics* ● *IMS Lecture Notes*. Monographs. Features series on statistics and probability. ● *Institute of Mathematical Statistics Bulletin*, bimonthly. Contains meeting programs, calendar of events, faculty recruitment advertising, book reviews, and abstracts of printed papers. **Price:** $50.00 /year for institutions. ISSN: 0146-3942. **Circulation:** 4,200. **Advertising:** accepted. Alternate Formats: microform. Also Cited As: *IMS Bulletin* ● *Statistical Science*, quarterly, in February, May, August, and November. Journal. For practitioners, teachers, researchers, and students of statistics and probability, presenting contemporary statistical thought. **Price:** $140.00 /year for nonmembers. ISSN: 0883-4237. **Circulation:** 4,700. **Advertising:** accepted. Alternate Formats: microform. Also Cited As: *Statist Sci*. **Conventions/Meetings:** annual meeting, publishers of scholarly texts (exhibits) - 2008 July 14-19, Singapore, Singapore; 2009 Aug. 2-6, Washington, DC.

7707 ■ International Biometric Society (IBS)

1444 I St. NW, Ste.700
Washington, DC 20005
Ph: (202)712-9049
Fax: (202)216-9646
E-mail: ibs@bostrom.com
URL: http://www.tibs.org
Contact: Claire Shanley, Exec. Dir.

Founded: 1947. **Members:** 5,300. **Staff:** 2. **Budget:** $473,000. **Regional Groups:** 30. **State Groups:** 2. **Description:** Biologists, statisticians, and others interested in applying statistical techniques to research data. Works to advance subject-matter sciences through the development of quantitative theories and the development, application, and dissemination of effective mathematical and statistical techniques. Compiles statistics. **Computer Services:** Mailing lists. **Boards:** Editorial Advisory. **Committees:** Conference Advisory; Finance. **Funds:** Awards. **Formerly:** The Biometric Society. **Publications:** *Biometric Bulletin* (in English and French), quarterly. Includes membership information, announcements, abstracts, and calendar of events. **Price:** included in membership dues; $17.00/year for associate members. ISSN: 8750-0434. **Circulation:** 6,400. **Advertising:** accepted. Alternate Formats: online ● *Biometrics*, quarterly. Journal. Emphasizes the role of statistics and mathematics in the biological sciences. Includes book reviews and annual index. **Price:** included in membership dues. ISSN: 0006-341X. **Circulation:** 8,500. **Advertising:** accepted. Alternate Formats: microform ● *Journal of Agricultural, Biological and Environmental Statistics*. **Advertising:** accepted. Alternate Formats: online ● *Manual for the Organization of International Biometric Conferences*. Alternate Formats: online. **Conventions/Meetings:** biennial International Biometric Conference (exhibits).

7708 ■ International Biometric Society, Eastern North American Region (ENAR)

12100 Sunset Hills Rd., Ste.130
Reston, VA 20190
Ph: (703)437-4377
Fax: (703)435-4390
E-mail: enar@enar.org
URL: http://www.enar.org
Contact: Kathy Hoskins, Exec. Dir.

Founded: 1947. **Members:** 2,600. **Membership Dues:** regular, $90 (annual) ● student, $27 (annual) ● associate, $40 (annual) ● supporting, $30 (annual). **Regional Groups:** 15. **Description:** Biologists, mathematicians, statisticians, and others interested in the applications of biometry. Promotes advancement of quantitative biological science through the development of quantitative theories and the application, development, and discrimination of effective mathematical and statistical techniques. Sponsors competitions. **Libraries: Type:** reference. **Affiliated With:** American Statistical Association; International Biometric Society, Western North American Region. **Publications:** *Biometric Bulletin*, quarterly. Newsletter. Contains news about membership activities, letters to the editor, and membership and editorial commentaries. **Price:** included in membership dues (regular members) ● *Biometrics*, quarterly. Journal. Promotes and extends the use of mathematical and statistical methods in various subject-matter disciplines. **Price:** included in membership dues (regular members) ● *Journal of Agricultural, Biological and Environmental Statistics*. **Conventions/Meetings:** annual meeting ● annual meeting - always spring. 2009 Mar. 15-18, San Antonio, TX.

7709 ■ International Biometric Society, Western North American Region

c/o Cancer Research and Biostatistics
1730 Minor Ave., Ste.1900
Seattle, WA 98101-1468
E-mail: wnar@crab.org
URL: http://www.wnar.org
Contact: Christine McLaren, Pres.-Elect

Founded: 1948. **Members:** 650. **Membership Dues:** regular, $85 (annual) ● family, emeritus, $23 (annual) ● supporting, $25 (annual). **Description:** Biologists, mathematicians, statisticians, and others interested in the advancement of biological science through the development of quantitative theories and the application, development, and dissemination of effective mathematical and statistical techniques. **Awards:** Student Paper Award. **Type:** recognition. **Formerly:** (1997) Biometric Society, Western North American Region. **Publications:** *Biometrics*, quarterly. **Conventions/Meetings:** annual meeting (exhibits) - usually late June. 2008 June 22-25, Davis, CA ● annual regional meeting.

7710 ■ International Society of Statistical Science (IS-SS)

536 Oasis Dr.
Santa Rosa, CA 95407
Ph: (707)575-3529
Fax: (707)575-3529
E-mail: shvyrkov@juno.com
Contact: Vladislav V. Shvyrkov, Chm.

Founded: 1982. **Members:** 100. **Membership Dues:** $15 (annual). **Staff:** 2. **Budget:** $5,000. **Regional Groups:** 7. **National Groups:** 21. **Multinational. Description:** Statisticians, economists, and econometricians in 21 countries. Seeks to create a union of statisticians and economists in order to clarify statistical applications and promote the development of statistical science on the basis of three axioms. Provides statistical training and education for economists. Sponsors research programs on the improvement of statistical methods; compiles statistics; offers computerized services. **Libraries: Type:** not open to the public. **Holdings:** 500. **Formerly:** (1992) International Society of Statistical Science in Economics. **Publications:** *International Society of Statistical Science in Economics—Directory*, annual ● *The Mystery of Statistical Science*, annual. Books. Covers topics on new methods of research, forecasting, and teaching. **Price:** $35.55 ● *Quantity and Quality in Economic Research: The Latest Developments in Statistics*, annual. Proceedings. Covers statistical and mathematical applications in the field of economics. **Price:** free for members; $35.00 /year for nonmembers. **Circulation:** 300. **Advertising:** accepted. Alternate Formats: microform ● Newsletter, quarterly ● Proceedings, annual. **Conventions/Meetings:** periodic International Conference on Problems of Statistical Science (exhibits) ● seminar.

7711 ■ National Institute of Statistical Sciences (NISS)

PO Box 14006
19 T.W. Alexander Dr.
Research Triangle Park, NC 27709-4006
Ph: (919)685-9300
Fax: (919)685-9310
E-mail: admin@niss.org
URL: http://www.niss.org
Contact: Alan F. Karr, Dir.

Founded: 1991. **Description:** Conducts cross-disciplinary research projects involving statistics and other sciences. Offers research findings. **Convention/Meeting:** none. **Awards:** Jerome Sacks Award For Cross-Disciplinary Research. **Frequency:** annual. **Type:** monetary. **Recipient:** for a high-quality cross-disciplinary research involving the statistical sciences ● NISS Distinguished Service Award. **Frequency:** annual. **Type:** recognition. **Recipient:** to individuals with commendable service that significantly advances NISS and its mission. **Projects:** Cross-Disciplinary Research. **Publications:** Reports, periodic. Contains technical information and research findings. **Price:** available upon request ● Newsletter, quarterly, in January, April, July and October. Alternate Formats: online.

Stress Analysis

7712 ■ Research Council on Structural Connections (RCSC)

c/o Rex Owen, Chm.
7269 S Sundown Cir.
Littleton, CO 80120
Ph: (303)797-1956
E-mail: rex.owen@comcast.net
URL: http://www.boltcouncil.org
Contact: Rex Owen, Chm.

Founded: 1946. **Members:** 56. **Membership Dues:** corporation, trade/technical association, $500 (annual). **Description:** Structural engineers, engineering societies, trade associations, government agencies, and universities are sponsors. Conducts research on behavior of bolted joints in engineering structures under all types of loading conditions. **Libraries: Type:** reference. **Holdings:** articles, reports. **Committees:** Editorial; Education; Membership and Funding; Nominating; Organizational Liaison; Research; Specifications. **Formerly:** (1980) Research Council on Riveted and Bolted Structural Joints. **Publications:** *The Effect of Burrs on the Shear Capacity of Bolted Connections*. Bulletin ● *Factors Meriting Special Attention by the Engineer*. Bulletin ● *Project Specifications for High Strength Bolts*. Bulletin ● *Recommendations for Purchasing, Receiving and Storing A325 and A490 Bolts*. Bulletin ● *Recommended Erection and Field Inspection Procedures for High-Strength Bolts in Structural Steel Assemblies*. Bulletin ● *Specifications for Structural Joints Using ASTM A325 or A490 Bolts*. **Conventions/Meetings:** annual meeting.

7713 ■ Society for Experimental Mechanics (SEM)
7 School St.
Bethel, CT 06801
Ph: (203)790-6373
Fax: (203)790-4472
E-mail: sem@sem1.com
URL: http://sem.org
Contact: Thomas W. Proulx, Exec. Dir.

Founded: 1943. **Members:** 2,100. **Membership Dues:** individual, $72 (annual) ● student, $24 (annual). **Staff:** 7. **Budget:** $800,000. **Local Groups:** 21. **National Groups:** 5. **Multinational. Description:** Consists of international members from academia, government, and industry that are committed to interdisciplinary application, research and development, education, and active promotion of experimental methods to: (a) increase the knowledge of physical phenomena; (b) further the understanding of the behavior of materials, structures and systems; and (c) provide the necessary physical basis and verification for analytical and computational approaches to the development of engineering solutions. **Awards: Type:** recognition. **Telecommunication Services:** electronic mail, director@sem1.com. **Formerly:** (1984) Society for Experimental Stress Analysis. **Publications:** *Experimental Mechanics*, bimonthly. Journal ● *Experimental Techniques*, bimonthly. Magazine ● *Proceedings of the Society for Experimental Mechanics*, annual. **Price:** $150.00 ● Handbooks ● Makes available back issues of conference proceedings. **Conventions/Meetings:** annual Conference and Exposition on Experimental & Applied Mechanics (exhibits) - 2009 May 31-June 3, Albuquerque, NM ● annual IMAC Conference and Exposition on Structural Dynamics - meeting, modal analysis, structural dynamics, vibration, noise - 2009 Feb. 5-8, Orlando, FL ● quadrennial International Congress on Experimental Mechanics.

7714 ■ Structural Stability Research Council (SSRC)
301 Butler Carlton Hall
Rolla, MO 65409-0030
Ph: (573)341-6610
Fax: (573)341-4476
E-mail: ssrc@umr.edu
URL: http://campus.umr.edu/ssrc
Contact: Christina Stratman, Admin.

Founded: 1944. **Members:** 400. **Membership Dues:** member-at-large, $50 (annual) ● Winter Society, $100-$249 (annual) ● Johnston Society, $750-$1,999 (annual) ● Shanley Society, $500-$749 (annual) ● Euler Society (minimum), $2,000 (annual) ● student, $20 (annual) ● Beedle Society, $250-$499 (annual). **Staff:** 4. **Budget:** $100,000. **Description:** Engineers interested in the stability of metal and composite metal and concrete structures and their components. Seeks to: provide a forum for discussion of stability problems; digest world literature on stability; organize and administer cooperative research; stimulate, aid, and guide research; apply research results to design procedures; promote the adoption of improved design procedures; disseminate original research information. Maintains collection of reports of theoretical and experimental research on stability. **Libraries: Type:** reference. **Awards:** Beedle Award. **Frequency:** annual. **Type:** recognition. **Recipient:** for outstanding contribution to SSRC ● Vinnakota Award. **Frequency:** annual. **Type:** recognition. **Recipient:** for the best paper presented at the Annual Stability Conference. **Telecommunication Services:** electronic mail, seaster@vt.edu. **Task Forces:** Beams; Bracing Members; Centrally Loaded Columns; Composite Members and Systems; Computer Applications; Connection Restraint Characteristics; Doubly Curved Shells and Shell-Like Structures; Frame Stability and Columns as Frame Members; Horizontally Curved Girders; International Cooperation on Stability Studies; Plate and Box Girder; Second Order Inelastic Analysis for Frame Design; Stability of Angle Struts; Stability Under Seismic Loading; Test Methods; Thin-Walled Metal Construction; Tubular Members. **Affiliated With:** Aluminum Association; American Bureau of Shipping; American Institute of Steel Construction; American Iron and Steel Institute; American Petroleum Institute; American Society of Civil Engineers; American Society of Mechanical Engineers; Canadian Society for Civil Engineering; Institute of the Ironworking Industry; International Conference of Building Officials; Metal Building Manufacturers Association; National Science Foundation; Steel Joist Institute. **Formerly:** (1976) Column Research Council. **Publications:** *Annual Report and Register*, annual. **Price:** $10.00 ● *Guide to Stability Design Criteria for Metal Structures*, periodic ● *Stability of Metal Structures: A World View*, periodic. Proceedings ● Proceedings, annual. **Conventions/Meetings:** annual conference.

Subterranean Construction

7715 ■ American Underground Construction Association (AUA)
3001 Hennepin Ave. S, Ste.D202
Minneapolis, MN 55408
Ph: (212)465-5541
Fax: (212)631-3787
E-mail: underground@auca.org
URL: http://www.auca.org/aua
Contact: Raymond W. Henn, Pres.

Founded: 1975. **Members:** 700. **Membership Dues:** individual - in U.S., $85 (annual) ● individual - outside U.S., $95 (annual) ● student, $35 (annual) ● corporate - in U.S., $650 (annual) ● corporate - outside U.S., $700 (annual) ● sustaining, $1,200 (annual). **Staff:** 2. **Description:** Corporations, engineers, architects, policymakers, builders, suppliers, planners, and other individuals interested in the development and use of underground space (facilities constructed below ground). Goals are to: promote recognition of the potential of underground space; provide a forum for the exchange of information among the disciplines involved; further analysis, research, and distribution of information on technical, environmental, legal, economic, social and political aspects of underground space use. Promotes professional competency and good practices in all aspects of underground facilities; recognizes persons with a professional interest in the field. **Libraries: Type:** reference. **Holdings:** audiovisuals, books, periodicals. **Awards:** Earth Shelter and Architecture Merit Award. **Type:** recognition ● Ken Lane Prize. **Frequency:** annual. **Type:** monetary. **Recipient:** for the best article by a member published in AUA News or Tunneling and Underground Space Technology ● Planning and Development Merit Award. **Type:** recognition ● Tunnels and Deep Space Merit Award. **Type:** recognition. **Computer Services:** Mailing lists, of members. **Telecommunication Services:** electronic mail, rhenn@lymanhenn.com. **Committees:** Contractual Sharing of Risk; Direct and Indirect Advantages of Underground Space; Equipment and Material Suppliers; Health and Safety; Mechanical Excavation; North American Cooperation; Subsurface Planning and Development; Tunnel Demand Forecast/Markets. **Formerly:** (1978) American Underground Association; (1995) American-Underground-Space Association. **Publications:** *American Underground-Space Association—Directory of Members*, annual. Membership Directory. Lists individual, corporate, and sustaining members; includes expanded information on corporate and sustaining members. **Price:** included in membership dues. **Advertising:** accepted ● *AUA News*, quarterly. Journal. Includes North American tunnel demand forecast and calendar of events. **Price:** included in membership dues. **Advertising:** accepted ● *Groundworks: North American Underground Projects 1980-1989*. Book ● *Insiders*, bimonthly. Bulletin ● *Tunneling and Underground-Space Technology*, quarterly. Journal. Contains articles on the development of new uses of underground space and the results of research, geoinvestigation, design, construction, operation. **Price:** included in membership dues. ISSN: 0886-7798. Alternate Formats: microform ● Reprints. **Conventions/Meetings:** biennial conference (exhibits) - always spring.

Surveying

7716 ■ American Association for Geodetic Surveying (AAGS)
c/o Ronnie Taylor, Sec.
Natl. Geodetic Survey/NOAA
2905 Carnaby Ct.
Tallahassee, FL 32308
Ph: (850)245-2606 (303)653-1437
Fax: (240)632-1321
E-mail: aagsmo@acsm.net
URL: http://www.aagsmo.org
Contact: Karen Meckel, Dir.

Members: 1,500. **Membership Dues:** full, $175 (annual) ● associate, $124 (annual) ● student, $28 (annual). **Description:** Member organization of the American Congress on Surveying and Mapping (see separate entry). Professionals, preprofessionals, technicians, and students in geodetic surveying and related fields. Objectives are: to promote the understanding of geodesy as a science; to create appreciation of the value of geodetic surveys and encourage greater use of such surveys. Promotes geodetic surveys by government and private organizations; fosters adoption of uniform standards and procedures for geodetic surveys; promotes geodetic survey data and information and encourages use of geodetic surveys and the state plane coordinate system in establishing public land survey corners. Supports educational programs. **Awards: Type:** fellowship. **Telecommunication Services:** electronic mail, karen@colomtnsurveys.com. **Affiliated With:** American Congress on Surveying and Mapping. **Formerly:** (1981) Control Surveys Division of the American Congress on Surveying and Mapping. **Conventions/Meetings:** semiannual meeting - always March/April and September/October.

7717 ■ American Congress on Surveying and Mapping (ACSM)
6 Montgomery Village Ave., Ste.403
Gaithersburg, MD 20879
Ph: (240)632-9716 (703)964-1240
Fax: (240)632-1321
E-mail: curtis.sumner@acsm.net
URL: http://www.acsm.net
Contact: Curtis W. Sumner, Exec. Dir.

Founded: 1941. **Members:** 5,500. **Membership Dues:** sustaining, $1,200 (annual) ● student, $28 (annual). **Budget:** $700,000. **Regional Groups:** 10. **State Groups:** 55. **Description:** Professionals, technicians, and students in the field of surveying and mapping including surveying of all disciplines, land and geographic information systems, cartography, geodesy, photogrammetry, engineering, geophysics, geography, and computer graphics; American Association for Geodetic Surveying, American Cartographic Association, and National Society of Professional Surveyors (see separate entries). Objectives are to: advance the sciences of surveying and mapping; promote public understanding and use of surveying and mapping; speak on the national level as the collective voice of the profession; provide publications to serve the surveying and mapping community. Member organizations encourage improvement of university and college curricula for surveying and mapping. **Libraries: Type:** reference. **Holdings:** archival material. **Awards: Type:** recognition. **Computer Services:** Electronic publishing, of academic journals and professional magazine ● online services, membership, subscription renewals, bookstore. **Additional Websites:** http://www.acsm-congress.org. **Telecommunication Services:** electronic mail, trisha.milburn@acsm.net. **Affiliated With:** American Association for Geodetic Surveying; Cartography and Geographic Information Society; National Society of Professional Surveyors. **Formerly:** (1942) National Congress on Surveying and Mapping. **Publications:** *ACSM Bulletin*, bimonthly. Magazine. **Price:** $90.00 in U.S.; $110.00 outside U.S. **Circulation:** 6,000. **Advertising:** accepted ● *Cartography and Geographic Information Science*, quarterly. Journal. Includes high-end cartographic and geographic research. **Price:** $115.00 in U.S.; $130.00 outside U.S. ISSN: 1523-0406. **Circulation:** 1,500. Alternate Formats: online. Also Cited As: *American Cartographer* ● *Surveying and Land Information Science*, quarterly. Journal. **Price:** $115.00 in U.S.; $130.00 outside U.S. ISSN: 1538-1242. **Circulation:** 5,500. **Advertising:** accepted. Alternate Formats: online. Also Cited As: *Surveying and Land Information Systems*. **Conventions/Meetings:** annual conference (exhibits).

7718 ■ The Hydrographic Society of America (THSOA)
PO Box 732
Rockville, MD 20848-0732
Ph: (301)460-4768
Fax: (240)209-0795
E-mail: mail@thsoa.org
URL: http://www.thsoa.org
Contact: Andy Armstrong, Pres.
Founded: 1984. **Members:** 500. **Membership Dues:** individual, $20 (annual) ● individual (local chapter), $30 (annual) ● retired, $10 (annual) ● student, $5 (annual) ● corporate, $100 (annual). **Local Groups:** 3. **Description:** Promotes education and understanding of hydrography. Represents individuals or organizations interested in surveying afloat. **Publications:** *The Seahorse*, 3/year. Newsletter. Contains news, announcements and information about the activities of the organization. **Price:** included in membership dues. Alternate Formats: online.

7719 ■ National Society of Professional Surveyors (NSPS)
6 Montgomery Village Ave., Ste.403
Gaithersburg, MD 20879-3557
Ph: (240)632-9716 (586)254-9577
Fax: (240)632-1321
E-mail: curtis.sumner@acsm.net
URL: http://www.nspsmo.org
Contact: Curtis W. Sumner, Exec. Dir.
Members: 7,500. **Membership Dues:** regular, $228 (annual) ● associate, $150 (annual) ● student, $28 (annual). **Budget:** $180,000. **Description:** A member organization of the American Congress on Surveying and Mapping (see separate entry). Professional surveyors, preprofessionals, technicians, and students. Encourages members to adopt and adhere to standards of ethical and professional behavior and to provide a professional service to the public. Maintains liaison with other professional societies; promotes public confidence in services rendered by members; monitors laws and regulations affecting the profession; helps to develop curricula for teaching surveying. **Awards:** Surveying Excellence Award. **Type:** recognition. **Recipient:** for surveying excellence, projects of the year by students and excellence in professional journalism. **Telecommunication Services:** electronic mail, trisha.milburn@acsm.net. **Committees:** Awards; Education; External Affairs; Government Practice; Land Data Systems; Legislative Liaison; Mine and Mineral Surveying; Photogrammetry; Political Action; Private Practice; Professional Ethics; Professional Liability Insurance Advisory; Public Relations; Publications/Communications; Standards; Youth Outreach. **Publications:** *Surveying and Land Information Systems*, quarterly. Journal ● Membership Directory, periodic. **Conventions/Meetings:** semiannual meeting.

7720 ■ Society of Accredited Marine Surveyors (SAMS)
4605 Cardinal Blvd.
Jacksonville, FL 32210
Ph: (904)384-1494
Free: (800)344-9077
Fax: (904)388-3958
E-mail: samshq@marinesurvey.org
URL: http://www.marinesurvey.org
Contact: Mary Stahler, Exec. Dir.
Founded: 1987. **Members:** 970. **Staff:** 2. **Regional Groups:** 7. **Multinational**. **Description:** Accredited marine surveyors, surveying associates, and other individuals working in related fields. Seeks to advance the craft and profession of marine surveying. Serves as a forum for the exchange of information among members and between members and other marine professionals and industries; provides technical assistance to marine organizations; suggests technical standards for the practice of marine surveying. **Conventions/Meetings:** annual meeting.

7721 ■ U.S. Surveyors Association (USSA)
13430 McGregor Blvd.
Fort Myers, FL 33919
Free: (800)245-4425
E-mail: navsurvey@aol.com
URL: http://www.navsurvey.com
Contact: Lori Brooks, Webmaster
Founded: 1987. **Members:** 300. **Staff:** 3. **Budget:** $60,000. **Description:** Works to maintain high training and ethical standards and provide inspection of vessels according to U.S. Coast Guard requirements. Conducts educational and research programs; maintains speakers' bureau. **Libraries: Type:** reference; open to the public. **Holdings:** 500; archival material, articles, audiovisuals, books, periodicals. **Subjects:** nautical, safety education, surveyor accreditation. **Awards:** Surveyor of the Year. **Frequency:** annual. **Type:** recognition. **Recipient:** for professionalism and integrity. **Computer Services:** database ● mailing lists ● online services ● record retrieval services. **Publications:** *U.S. Surveyor News*, periodic. Newsletter. **Circulation:** 200 ● Bulletin ● Brochure ● Directory. **Conventions/Meetings:** annual board meeting and trade show (exhibits).

Technical Consulting

7722 ■ Manufacturing Enterprise Solutions Association International (MESA)
107 S Southgate Dr.
Chandler, AZ 85226
Ph: (480)893-6883
Fax: (480)893-7775
E-mail: info@mesa.org
URL: http://www.mesa.org
Contact: Karsten Newbury, Chm.
Membership Dues: student, $20 (annual) ● individual manufacturing user, $85 (annual) ● solution provider, $5,500 (annual) ● individual solution provider, $995 (annual) ● manufacturer, $495 (annual) ● solution provider (additional division), $3,500 (annual). **Multinational**. **Description:** Helps manufacturers, systems integrators and vendors achieve manufacturing leadership by deploying practical solutions that include a combination of information, business, manufacturing and supply chain technologies. **Computer Services:** database ● online services, discussion forums.

Technology

7723 ■ Alliance for Public Technology (APT)
919 18th St. NW, Ste.900
Washington, DC 20006
Ph: (202)263-2970
Fax: (202)263-2960
E-mail: apt@apt.org
URL: http://www.apt.org
Contact: Sylvia Rosenthal, Exec. Dir.
Membership Dues: individual, $15 (annual) ● sponsor, $45 (annual) ● local nonprofit, $50 (annual) ● national nonprofit, $100 (annual). **Description:** Public interest groups and individuals. Fosters increased "access to affordable and useful information and communication services technologies by all people." Works to put policies in place that encourage deployment of advanced telecommunications technologies to underserved communities, including the elderly, minorities, people with low incomes, people in rural areas and people with disabilities. **Publications:** *Broadband Initiatives: Enhancing Lives and Transforming Communities*. Report. Alternate Formats: online.

7724 ■ American Filtration and Separations Society (AFS)
7608 Emerson Ave. S
Richfield, MN 55423
Ph: (612)861-1277
Fax: (612)861-7959
E-mail: afs@afssociety.org
URL: http://www.afssociety.org
Contact: Suzanne Sower, Exec. Mgr.
Founded: 1987. **Members:** 800. **Membership Dues:** individual, $95 (annual) ● manufacturer, $1,000 (annual) ● corporate sponsor, $2,000 (annual) ● international, $155 (annual) ● retiree, $60 (annual) ● student, $50 (annual). **Staff:** 4. **Budget:** $500,000. **Local Groups:** 9. **Description:** Marketing and distribution engineers, scientists, technologists, product designers, consultants, academicians, and government officials in all areas of the fluid/separation field. Seeks to provide a forum for exchange of information among members. Offers educational programs. **Publications:** *Filtration Journal*, quarterly. Offers a global interface to researchers, clinicians and manufacturers involved in the rapidly expanding field of therapeutic filtration. **Price:** $245.00 /year for individuals (in North America); $145.00 /year for individuals (rest of the world); $821.00 /year for institutions (in North America); $475.00 /year for institutions (rest of the world). **Advertising:** accepted ● Newsletter, monthly. **Conventions/Meetings:** annual Topical Conference, presenting specific topics of filtration and separation (exhibits).

7725 ■ American Supplier Institute (ASI)
38705 7 Mile Rd., Ste.345
Livonia, MI 48152
Ph: (734)464-1395
Free: (800)462-4500
Fax: (734)464-1399
E-mail: asi@asiusa.com
URL: http://www.amsup.com
Contact: Mr. Shin Taguchi, Pres.
Founded: 1981. **Members:** 5,000. **Staff:** 13. **National Groups:** 7. **Languages:** English, French, German, Korean, Portuguese, Spanish, Swedish. **Description:** Seeks to encourage change in U.S. industry through development and implementation of advanced manufacturing and engineering technologies such as Taguchi Methods, Quality Function Deployment, Statistical Process Control, and Total Quality Management. Offers educational courses, training seminars, and workshops to improve quality, reduce cost, and enhance competitive position of U.S. products. Maintains international network of affiliates for developing training specialists and technologies curriculum. Provides training services to government supplier companies. **Awards:** Taguchi Award. **Frequency:** annual. **Type:** recognition. **Recipient:** for best case study presented at symposium. **Committees:** Executive. **Publications:** *ASI Press*, periodic. Catalog. **Circulation:** 25,000. **Conventions/Meetings:** annual Total Product Development - symposium.

7726 ■ CDMA Development Group (CDG)
575 Anton Blvd., Ste.560
Costa Mesa, CA 92626
Ph: (714)545-5211
Free: (888)800-CDMA

Fax: (714)545-4601
E-mail: cdg@cdg.org
URL: http://www.cdg.org
Multinational. **Description:** Promotes the adoption and evolution of CDMA wireless systems worldwide.

7727 ■ CommerceNet
169 Univ. Ave.
Palo Alto, CA 94301
Ph: (650)289-4040
Free: (888)255-1900
Fax: (650)289-4041
E-mail: info@commerce.net
URL: http://www.commerce.net
Contact: Allan Schiffman, Exec. Dir./Board Member
Founded: 1994. **Description:** Works to advance an open network of business services, comprised of real-time, collaborative business processes. **Publications:** Papers. Alternate Formats: online ● Reports. Alternate Formats: online.

7728 ■ CompuMentor
435 Brannan St., Ste.100
San Francisco, CA 94107
Ph: (415)633-9300
Free: (800)659-3579
Fax: (415)633-9400
E-mail: realperson@compumentor.org
URL: http://www.compumentor.org
Contact: Daniel Ben-Horin, Founder/Pres.
Founded: 1987. **Description:** Helps non-profit organizations and schools use technology more effectively to achieve their goals. Offers technology planning, implementation and support services. Focuses on working with small to medium-sized nonprofit organizations and schools serving low-income and underserved populations. Emphasizes fair compensation, continual learning and skill enhancement.

7729 ■ ControlNet International (CI)
2370 E Stadium Blvd., No. 1005
Ann Arbor, MI 48104-4811
Ph: (734)922-0025
Fax: (734)922-0027
E-mail: controlnet@controlnet.org
URL: http://www.controlnet.org
Contact: Katherine Voss, Exec. Dir./Sec.
Membership Dues: regular (depends on company's number of employees), $1,000-$15,000 (annual) ● associate, $500 (annual). **Multinational**. **Description:** Manages ControlNet technology for vendors and users of ControlNet products. **Libraries: Type:** reference. **Subjects:** ControlNet. **Special Interest Groups:** Conformance; Physical Layer; System Architecture; Technical Review Board/System. **Task Forces:** Marketing. **Publications:** *Conformance Testing: Putting the Interoperability Back in Open Systems*. Paper. Alternate Formats: online ● *ControlNet Insider*. Newsletter ● Catalog, 2-3/year. **Advertising:** accepted. Alternate Formats: online.

7730 ■ Electrocoat Association
PO Box 541083
Cincinnati, OH 45254-1083
Ph: (816)496-2308
Free: (800)579-8806
Fax: (816)496-2309
E-mail: kmcglothlin@electrocoat.org
URL: http://www.electrocoat.org
Contact: Ms. Karen McGlothlin, Exec. Dir.
Founded: 1997. **Membership Dues:** corporate, $500-$6,000 (annual) ● individual, $25-$75 (annual) ● educational, $100 (annual) ● student, $30 (annual). **Description:** Promotes the use of electrocoating. Works to communicate the economic and environmental benefits of electrocoating technology to manufacturers, consumers and the finishing industry. **Publications:** *Conference Proceedings*. **Price:** $85.00 for members; $95.00 for nonmembers. Alternate Formats: CD-ROM.

7731 ■ Electronic Frontier Foundation (EFF)
454 Shotwell St.
San Francisco, CA 94110-1914
Ph: (415)436-9333
Fax: (415)436-9993
E-mail: information@eff.org
URL: http://www.eff.org
Contact: Ms. Shari Steele, Exec. Dir.
Founded: 1990. **Members:** 3,000. **Membership Dues:** student, $15 (annual) ● advocate, $25 (annual) ● pathfinder, $65 (annual) ● pioneer, $100 (annual) ● trailblazer, $250 (annual) ● guardian, $500 (annual) ● defender, $1,000 (annual). **Staff:** 13. **Description:** Promotes the creation of legal and structural approaches to help ease the assimilation of new technologies by society. Seeks to: help policymakers develop a better understanding of issues underlying telecommunications; increase public understanding of the opportunities and challenges posed by computing and telecommunications fields. Fosters awareness of civil liberties issues arising from the advancements in new computer-based communications media and supports litigation to preserve, protect, and extend First Amendment rights in computing and telecommunications technology. Maintains speakers' bureau; conducts educational programs. Encourages and supports the development of tools to endow nontechnical users with access to computer-based telecommunications. **Awards:** Pioneer Award. **Frequency:** annual. **Type:** recognition. **Telecommunication Services:** electronic mail, ask@eff.org. **Publications:** *Effector*, biweekly. Newsletter. Includes issues important to internet users. **Price:** free. ISSN: 1062-9424. **Circulation:** 75,000. Alternate Formats: online. **Conventions/Meetings:** monthly meeting and seminar, for San Francisco Bay-Area members and supporters; includes educational presentations.

7732 ■ Financial Services Technology Consortium (FSTC)
44 Wall St., 12th Fl.
New York, NY 10005
Ph: (212)461-7116
Fax: (646)349-3629
E-mail: fstcadmin@fstc.org
URL: http://www.fstc.org
Contact: Dan Schutzer, Exec. Dir.
Founded: 1993. **Membership Dues:** principal or associate (based on assets), $1,000-$27,500 (annual) ● associate (based on assets), $5,000-$27,500 (annual) ● associate (not-for-profit), $8,250 (annual) ● advisory (based on number of employees), $1,000-$2,750 (annual). **Staff:** 6. **Description:** Represents financial institutions, technology vendors, independent research organizations and government agencies. Aims to advance interoperable, open-standard technologies providing critical infrastructures for the financial services industry. **Telecommunication Services:** electronic mail, zachary.tumin@fstc.org. **Committees:** Business Continuity; Payments; Security and Infrastructure. **Special Interest Groups:** Biometric; Branch Automation; Check Truncation; Web Services; Wireless. **Conventions/Meetings:** semiannual meeting - spring/fall.

7733 ■ Foresight Institute (FI)
PO Box 61058
Palo Alto, CA 94306
Ph: (650)289-0860
Fax: (650)289-0863
E-mail: foresight@foresight.org
URL: http://www.foresight.org
Contact: Pearl Chin, Pres.
Founded: 1986. **Members:** 1,100. **Membership Dues:** student, $25 (annual) ● general, $50 (annual) ● senior associate, $250 (annual) ● patron, $500 (annual) ● colleague, $1,000 (annual) ● friend, $5,000 (annual) ● benefactor, $10,000 (annual). **Staff:** 3. **Budget:** $500,000. **Description:** Science and technology professionals and interested others. Promotes better understanding of emerging technologies through the dissemination of information. Studies technologies including nanotechnology (a projected technology allowing control of the structure of matter) and hypertext (a computer service which links information that is conceptually related). Conducts research and educational programs. Maintains speakers' bureau. **Awards:** Feynman Grand Prize in Nanotechnology. **Type:** monetary. **Recipient:** for specified R&D accomplishments ● Feynman Prizes in Nanotechnology. **Frequency:** annual. **Type:** monetary. **Recipient:** for theoretical and experimental research which most furthers nanotechnology during the year. **Computer Services:** Mailing lists. **Publications:** *Foresight Update*, quarterly. Newsletter. Features news on nanotechnology and other anticipated technologies. **Price:** $45.00. ISSN: 1078-9731. **Circulation:** 1,500. Alternate Formats: online. **Conventions/Meetings:** annual Foresight Conference on Molecular Nanotechnology, features lectures, demonstrations, and discussion on nanotechnology and enabling sciences (exhibits) - always fall in Silicon Valley, CA or in East Coast, USA (alternating).

7734 ■ Global Spatial Data Infrastructure Association (GSDI Association)
946 Great Plain Ave.
PMB 194
Needham, MA 02492-3030
Ph: (508)720-0325
Fax: (703)852-7917
E-mail: mgallant@gsdi.org
URL: http://www.gsdi.org
Contact: Harlan Onsrud, Interim Exec. Dir.
Founded: 2002. **Membership Dues:** full (government agency or organization), $1,000-$9,000 (annual) ● full (private company or for-profit industry organization), $500-$9,000 (annual) ● full (academic organization, professional/non-profit organization), $200-$1,500 (annual) ● associate (private company), $50-$5,000 (annual) ● associate (government agency), $50-$1,000 (annual) ● associate (not-for-profit organization), $50-$500 (annual) ● individual (based on gross national income), $25-$100 (annual). **Budget:** $200,000. **Regional Groups:** 4. **Multinational**. **Description:** Promotes international cooperation and collaboration in support of local, national and international spatial data infrastructure developments. Serves as a point of contact and voice for those in the global community involved in developing, implementing and advancing spatial data infrastructure concepts. Fosters spatial data infrastructures that support sustainable social, economic, and environmental systems integrated from local to global scales. Advances the informed and responsible use of geographic information and spatial technologies. **Publications:** Newsletters, annual. Reviews organization progress, activities, and upcoming events. Alternate Formats: online ● Brochure. Alternate Formats: online. **Conventions/Meetings:** conference (exhibits) - every 12-18 months. 2009 June 15-19, Rotterdam, Netherlands - **Avg. Attendance:** 600.

7735 ■ GlobalPlatform
1515 Cordilleras Rd.
Redwood City, CA 94062
E-mail: secretariat@globalplatform.org
URL: http://www.globalplatform.org
Contact: Kevin Gillick, Exec. Dir.
Founded: 1999. **Members:** 50. **Membership Dues:** full (initial), $50,000 ● full, $25,000 (annual) ● participating, $20,000 (annual) ● observer, $10,000 (annual) ● public entity, $5,000 (annual). **Multinational**. **Description:** Promotes interoperable technical specifications for smart cards, acceptance devices and systems infrastructure. **Computer Services:** Mailing lists. **Committees:** Card; Device; Marketing Center; Planning Unit; Systems. **Programs:** Compliance. **Publications:** *Corporate Overview* (in English, Japanese, and Spanish). Brochure. Alternate Formats: online ● *Deploying Specifications* (in English, Japanese, and Spanish). Brochure. Alternate Formats: online ● *Implementation Overview* (in English, Japanese, and Spanish). Brochure. Alternate Formats: online ● *Membership* (in English, Japanese, and Spanish). Brochure. Alternate Formats: online ● *Overview of GlobalPlatform Technology* (in English, Japanese, and Spanish). Brochure. Alternate Formats: online ● *Specifications Overview* (in English, Japanese, and Spanish). Brochure. Alternate Formats: online ● Newsletter, quarterly, March, June, September, December. Contains committee updates, calendar of events and news of the association. **Price:** free. Alternate Formats: online.

7736 ■ IDB Forum
43588 Wild Ginger Terr.
Lansdowne, VA 20176-8439
Ph: (571)333-1394
Fax: (703)991-5553
E-mail: arlan.stehney@idbforum.org
URL: http://www.idbforum.org
Contact: Arlan Stehney, Exec. Dir./Sec.-Treas.
Membership Dues: associate (not-for-profit organization or academic institution), $1,000 (annual) ● organization (less than $10M gross revenues), $2,000 (annual) ● organization ($10-100M gross revenues), $6,000 (annual) ● organization (over $100M gross revenues), $12,000 (annual). **Description:** Promotes global integration of IDB networking into vehicles, consumer electronics, and automotive electronics. **Task Forces:** Automotive Message Set; Graphical Display Profiles Specification; System and Interoperability Layer; System Power Management. **Working Groups:** Aerospace and Military 1394; Automotive Wireless; 1394 Joint Automotive; Technology Enabling. **Conventions/Meetings:** conference ● meeting ● trade show.

7737 ■ IEEE Society Social Implications of Technology (SSIT)
c/o IEEE Corporate Office
445 Hoes Ln.
Piscataway, NJ 08855-0459
Ph: (732)981-0060
Fax: (732)981-1721
E-mail: perusich@sbcglobal.net
URL: http://www.ieeessit.org
Contact: Mr. Karl Perusich PhD, Pres.
Members: 2,000. **Membership Dues:** regular, $26 (annual) ● student, $13 (annual) ● affiliate (non-IEEE), $83 (annual). **Local Groups:** 7. **Description:** A society of the Institute of Electrical and Electronics Engineers. Concerns itself with: the history of social aspects of electrontechnology; the impact of electrical and electronics technology on society and the engineering profession; professional, social, and economic responsibility in the practice of engineering and related technology. **Committees:** Publications. **Publications:** *Technology and Society Magazine*, quarterly. **Conventions/Meetings:** annual International Symposium on Technology and Society - meeting - 2008 June 26-28, Fredericton, NB, Canada.

7738 ■ INCITS - InterNational Committee for Information Technology Standards (INCITS)
c/o Information Technology Industry Council
1250 Eye St. NW, Ste.200
Washington, DC 20005-5977
Ph: (202)737-8888
Fax: (202)638-4922
E-mail: incits@itic.org
URL: http://www.ncits.org
Contact: Patrick Morris, Exec. Dir.
Founded: 2001. **Membership Dues:** business (based on annual revenues), $9,500-$35,000 (annual) ● government agency, SDO major, $35,000 (annual) ● SDO minor, $8,000 (annual) ● technical/task group, $1,200 (annual) ● academic institution, $1,000 (annual) ● user group, consortium, $10,000 (annual). **Multinational. Description:** Promotes standardization in the field of information and communications technologies, encompassing storage, processing, transfer, display, management, organization, and retrieval of information. **Awards:** INCITS Award for Exceptional International Leadership. **Frequency:** annual. **Type:** recognition. **Recipient:** for no more than two participants for their exceptional leadership of an international committee ● INCITS Chairman's Annual Award. **Frequency:** annual. **Type:** recognition. **Recipient:** for an INCITS participant who has provided outstanding service to the INCITS organization through committee work or duties ● INCITS Gene Milligan Award for Effective Committee Management. **Frequency:** annual. **Type:** recognition. **Recipient:** for no more than four INCITS members holding an officer position within an INCITS subgroup ● INCITS Merit Award. **Frequency:** annual. **Type:** recognition. **Recipient:** for no more than four participants who have demonstrated continuous support for the work of INCITS ● INCITS Service Award. **Frequency:** annual. **Type:** recognition. **Recipient:** for no more than two participants who have provided outstanding service to the INCITS organization through committee work or duties ● INCITS Technical Excellence. **Frequency:** annual. **Type:** recognition. **Recipient:** for no more than four participants in recognition of their technical contributions and dedication to the technical program of work. **Computer Services:** database. **Committees:** B11 Optical Digital Data Disks; B5 Flexible Magnetic Media and Formats; B9 Paper Forms/Layout; B10 Identification Cards and Related Devices; J4 Programming Language COBOL; J1 Programming Language PL/I; J3 Programming Language Fortran. **Programs:** Speakers Bureau. **Formerly:** (1996) Accredited Standards Committee X3, Information Technology; (2001) Accredited Standards Committee NCITS, National Committee for Information Technology Standards. **Publications:** Brochure ● Books. **Price:** $18.00/copy.

7739 ■ International Association for Impact Assessment (IAIA)
1330 23rd St. S, Ste.C
Fargo, ND 58103
Ph: (701)297-7908 (701)297-7912
Fax: (701)297-7917
E-mail: info@iaia.org
URL: http://www.iaia.org
Contact: Rita R. Hamm, CEO
Founded: 1981. **Members:** 2,500. **Membership Dues:** individual, $100 (annual) ● joint, $110 (annual) ● student, $50 (annual) ● institutional, $1,400 (annual) ● sponsoring organization, $3,000 (annual). **Staff:** 3. **Budget:** $175,000. **Regional Groups:** 3. **National Groups:** 10. **Description:** Corporate planners and managers; government planners, administrators, and policy makers; public interest spokespersons; teachers; students; researchers; consultants and policy analysts; individuals who assess environmental, social, and technological impact. Promotes the study and practical application of impact assessment to anticipate the consequences of new technology. Works to: improve techniques of analysis; promote high quality performance in the field; advance training of impact assessors; provide for peer review. Fosters information exchange; conducts research and organizes research networks for members. **Libraries: Type:** open to the public. **Holdings:** periodicals. **Subjects:** various fields of impact assessments. **Awards:** IAIA Rose Hulman Award. **Frequency:** annual. **Type:** recognition. **Recipient:** for outstanding achievement in the field of impact assessment. **Computer Services:** database, listserv discussion groups ● database, membership; with links to associated agencies ● database, training courses. **Telecommunication Services:** electronic mail, jen@iaia.org. **Committees:** Affiliates; Awards; Board Nominations; Conferences; Publications; Training and Professional Development. **Publications:** *Impact Assessment and Project Appraisal*, quarterly. Journal. Contains scholarly articles on environmental impact, risk, social impact, technology, and other topics. Includes book reviews. **Price:** included in membership dues. ISSN: 0734-9165. **Circulation:** 1,700. **Advertising:** accepted. Alternate Formats: online. Also Cited As: *Impact Assessment* ● Also publishes IAIA Newsletter. **Conventions/Meetings:** annual Ethics and Quality Assurance in Impact Assessment - conference, for environmental professionals (exhibits).

7740 ■ International Association for the Management of Technology (IAMOT)
PO Box 248294
Coral Gables, FL 33124-8294
Ph: (305)284-2344
Fax: (305)284-4040
E-mail: iamot@miami.edu
URL: http://www.iamot.org
Contact: Tarek Khalil, Pres.
Membership Dues: regular, associate, $50 (annual) ● student, $25 (annual). **Multinational. Description:** Encourages education in the field of Management of Technology. Facilitates the exchange of information about the Management of Technology with other individuals and organizations. Establishes research priorities in Technology Management on the basis of current and future needs. **Publications:** *Technovation*, monthly. Journal. Contains a variety of topics on the process of technological innovation. **Price:** $1,583.00 /year for individuals (except in Japan, Europe and Iran); EUR 1,416.00 /year for individuals (in Europe and Iran). **Conventions/Meetings:** annual international conference.

7741 ■ International Association of Nanotechnology (IANT)
1290 Parkmoor Ave.
San Jose, CA 95126
Ph: (408)277-3071
Fax: (408)293-9057
E-mail: info@ianano.org
URL: http://www.nanotechcongress.com
Contact: Ms. Alisha White, Outreach Rep.
Membership Dues: industry (individual), $295 (annual) ● government and non-profit organization (individual), $245 (annual) ● academic (individual), $195 (annual) ● retired professional, $55 (annual) ● student, $45 (annual) ● special student, $25 (annual) ● corporate gold, $2,995 (annual) ● corporate silver, $1,595 (annual) ● corporate, $995 (annual). **Multinational. Description:** Fosters scientific research and business development in the areas of Nanoscience and Nanotechnology for the benefit of the society. Conducts education and training in community colleges and universities worldwide about safety, regulation, ethics, and the environmental and societal aspects of Nanotechnology. Promotes friendship, equality and cooperation among members around the world. **Additional Websites:** http://www.ianano.org. **Telecommunication Services:** electronic mail, info@atsicnt.org. **Publications:** *Nanotech Newsletter*. **Price:** included in membership dues.

7742 ■ International Association for Structural Mechanics in Reactor Technology (IASMIRT)
c/o Bonnie Diaz
Center for Nuclear Power Plants Structures, Equip and Piping
Campus Box 7908
North Carolina State Univ.
Raleigh, NC 27695-7908
Ph: (919)515-7736 (919)515-5277
Fax: (919)515-5301
E-mail: bdiaz@eos.ncsu.edu
URL: http://www.iasmirt.org
Contact: Rauno Rintamaa, Pres.
Founded: 1968. **Members:** 200. **National Groups:** 3. **Languages:** English, German. **Multinational. Description:** Scientists and engineers in 16 countries. Organizes conference on structural mechanics in reactor technology. **Libraries: Type:** reference. **Holdings:** archival material. **Awards:** Jaeger Prize. **Frequency:** biennial. **Type:** recognition. **Recipient:** for the best paper by a young author. **Computer Services:** Information services, proceedings from previous conferences. **Subgroups:** American Association for Structural Mechanics in Reactor Technology. **Publications:** *Conference Proceedings*, biennial. Alternate Formats: CD-ROM ● *Transactions of Structural Mechanics in Reactor Technology*, biennial. Proceedings. Alternate Formats: CD-ROM ● Also publishes *Nuclear Engineering and Design*. **Conventions/Meetings:** biennial conference, plenary sessions, paper and panel sessions (exhibits).

7743 ■ International Biometric Industry Association (IBIA)
1666 K St. NW
Washington, DC 20006
Ph: (202)293-8133
Fax: (202)872-1431
E-mail: ibia@ibia.org
URL: http://www.ibia.org
Contact: Walter Hamilton, Chm.
Founded: 1998. **Membership Dues:** class I (developer, manufacturer, integrator), $3,750-$15,000 (annual) ● class II (government agency, consulting firm, nonprofit organization, end user), $200-$1,500 (annual) ● class III (individual), $200 (annual). **Multinational. Description:** Represents international inter-

ests of the biometric industry. **Working Groups:** Global Policy and Advocacy; International Markets and Liaison; Marketing and Education; Standards and Technology. **Publications:** *Biometrics Advocacy Report*. Newsletter.

7744 ■ International Technology Institute (ITI)
PO Box 23166
San Diego, CA 92193-3166
Ph: (858)279-0483
Fax: (858)279-0493
E-mail: itihq@aol.com
URL: http://www.itiworld.org
Contact: Dr. I.S. Tuba, Exec. Dir./Founder

Founded: 1976. **Membership Dues:** student in U.S., $25 (annual) ● student outside U.S., $35 (annual) ● individual in U.S., $75 (annual) ● individual outside U.S., $100 (annual) ● local chapter, $15-$50 (annual) ● patron outside U.S., $200 (annual) ● fellow outside U.S., $150 (annual) ● life, $1,000. **Regional Groups:** 3. **Description:** Professionals working for corporations, universities, and economic development groups; individuals active in research and development. Promotes the transfer and exchange of technology among academic, governmental, industrial, and international groups and corporations. Maintains Hall of Fame for Engineering, Science, and Technology. **Awards:** Remember Hungary 1956 Memorial Medal. **Frequency:** periodic. **Type:** medal. **Recipient:** to advocators of the universal ideology of economics ● The Walter J. Zable Medal. **Frequency:** annual. **Type:** medal. **Recipient:** for excellence in technology ● Willard F. Rockwell, Jr. Award. **Frequency:** annual. **Type:** recognition. **Recipient:** for excellence in technology. **Computer Services:** Mailing lists. **Divisions:** Center for Health and Human Services Technologies; Hall of Fame for Engineering, Science and Technology; Hungarians International; Intellectual Systems Society; Internationally Registered Technology Specialists; Technology Transfer. **Publications:** *Advanced International Program in Engineering Administration - Catalog*, periodic ● *Hall of Fame for Engineering, Science and Technology*. Alternate Formats: online ● *International Technology*, bimonthly. Newsletter. Covers membership information, institute activities, and developments in technology transfer. **Price:** available to members only. **Advertising:** accepted ● *Proceedings of International Congress on Technology and Technology Exchange*, annual. Includes reprints of papers presented at the congress. **Price:** $100.00. ISSN: 1045-585X. **Advertising:** accepted ● *TechnoMart*. Alternate Formats: online ● *TechnoTimes*. Alternate Formats: online ● Brochures. **Conventions/Meetings:** annual International Congress on Technology and Technology Exchange - congress and symposium ● seminar.

7745 ■ Joint Venture: Silicon Valley Network
84 W Santa Clara St., Ste.440
San Jose, CA 95113-1820
Ph: (408)271-7213
Fax: (408)271-7214
E-mail: info@jointventure.org
URL: http://www.jointventure.org
Contact: Russell Hancock, Pres./CEO

Founded: 1993. **Staff:** 9. **Description:** Seeks to find solutions to problems impacting all high-technology sectors of the Silicon Valley region, focusing on innovative economy, livable environment, inclusive society, and regional stewardship. **Computer Services:** Mailing lists. **Publications:** *Internet Cluster Analysis 1999*. **Price:** $3.00. Alternate Formats: online ● *Internet Cluster Analysis 2000*. **Price:** $3.00. Alternate Formats: online ● *Joint Venture Way: Lessons Learned Vol. 1*. **Price:** $3.00. Alternate Formats: online ● *Joint Venture Way: Lessons Learned Vol. 2* ● *1999 Workforce Report* ● *2000 Index of Silicon*. **Price:** $3.00. Alternate Formats: online ● *2001 Index of Silicon Valley*. **Price:** $3.00. Alternate Formats: online ● *2003 Index of Silicon Valley*. **Price:** $3.00. Alternate Formats: online ● *2002 Index of Silicon Valley*. **Price:** $3.00. Alternate Formats: online ● *2002 Workforce Study Report*. **Price:** $3.00. Alternate Formats: online.

7746 ■ The Keystone Center (TKC)
1628 St. John Rd.
Keystone, CO 80435
Ph: (970)513-5800 (970)513-5837
Fax: (970)262-0152
URL: http://www.keystone.org
Contact: Peter S. Adler PhD, Pres.

Founded: 1975. **Staff:** 30. **Budget:** $3,500,000. **Description:** Center for environmental dispute resolution and education. Conducts national policy dialogues on environmental, energy, natural resources, health and science/technology issues. Assists in environmental decision making and regulatory negotiations. Provides environmental mediation services and training and organizational development services in environmental conflict resolution. Operates a year-round residential environmental education center for children and adults in Keystone, CO. **Libraries: Type:** open to the public. **Holdings:** 65. **Subjects:** science, public policy issues. **Awards:** The Keystone Center Leadership Awards. **Frequency:** annual. **Type:** recognition. **Recipient:** to individuals who have demonstrated outstanding leadership through consensus building and creative problem solving. **Formerly:** (1990) Keystone Center for Continuing Education. **Publications:** *Consensus Newsletter*, semiannual ● Annual Report, annual. Alternate Formats: online ● Also publishes reports on public policy dialogue issues.

7747 ■ Machining and Material Removal Community of the Society of Manufacturing Engineers (MMR/SME)
c/o Society Of Manufacturing Engineers
PO Box 930
Dearborn, MI 48121-0930
Ph: (313)425-3000
Free: (800)733-4763
Fax: (313)425-3400
E-mail: leadership@sme.org
URL: http://www.sme.org/mmr
Contact: Mr. Mark Tomlinson, Exec. Dir./Gen. Mgr.

Founded: 1990. **Members:** 3,500. **Staff:** 1. **Description:** A division of the Society of Manufacturing Engineers. Professionals, students, and corporations in the field of machining technology. Promotes individual professional development and the effective use of machining technology for productivity improvement. Analyzes and evaluates the status of machining technology; assists the manufacturing community in incorporating new technology into the manufacturing process. Develops educational programs and materials. **Awards:** Best Paper Awards. **Type:** recognition. **Publications:** *Machining Technology*, quarterly. Newsletter. Alternate Formats: online ● Books ● Videos. **Conventions/Meetings:** periodic Advanced Productivity Exposition - meeting ● periodic International Machining and Grinding Conference.

7748 ■ Metro Ethernet Forum (MEF)
19900 MacArthur Blvd., Ste.810
Irvine, CA 92612
Ph: (949)250-7188
Fax: (949)250-7136
E-mail: manager@metroethernetforum.org
URL: http://www.metroethernetforum.org
Contact: Nan Chen, Pres./Dir.

Founded: 2001. **Members:** 80. **Membership Dues:** regular, $15,000 (annual). **Multinational. Description:** Represents service providers, local exchange carriers, network equipment vendors and other networking companies that share an interest in metro Ethernet. Facilitates implementation of existing and new standards, Ethernet service definition, test procedures and technical specifications to allow delivery of Ethernet services and make Ethernet-based metro networks carrier-class. Enhances worldwide awareness of the benefits of Ethernet services and Ethernet-based metro transport networks. **Awards:** Asia Pacific Carrier Ethernet Service Provider of the Year. **Frequency:** annual. **Type:** recognition. **Recipient:** for Asian service provider ● European Carrier Ethernet Service Provider of the Year. **Frequency:** annual. **Type:** recognition. **Recipient:** for European service provider. **Publications:** Brochure. Alternate Formats: online.

7749 ■ Monte Jade Science and Technology Association
c/o Judy Chu, Exec. Sec.
2870 Zanker Rd., Ste.140
San Jose, CA 95134
Ph: (408)428-0388
Fax: (408)428-0378
E-mail: judychu@montejade.org
URL: http://www.mjglobal.org
Contact: Judy Chu, Exec. Sec.

Founded: 1989. **Membership Dues:** individual, $25 (annual) ● corporate, $250 (annual) ● student, $10 (annual). **Multinational. Description:** Provides community with resources to start up high technology businesses in the information and technology, biotechnology, space sciences, engineering, telecommunications, environmental sciences, business development and management sectors. **Publications:** Newsletter. **Conventions/Meetings:** bimonthly seminar ● trade show ● workshop.

7750 ■ NanoBusiness Alliance
4901 Searle Pkwy., Ste.Q2608
Skokie, IL 60077
Ph: (847)568-8415
Free: (866)809-0690
Fax: (419)818-3312
E-mail: info@nanobusiness.org
URL: http://www.nanobusiness.org
Contact: Alisa Kronshage, Sr. Coor.

Membership Dues: corporate (based on organization type), $1,000-$20,000 (annual) ● foundation, $50,000 (annual). **Multinational. Description:** Aims to advance the emerging business of nanotechnology and microsystems. Seeks to create a collective voice for the small technology industry and develop a range of initiatives to support and strengthen the nanotechnology business community. Promotes the nanotechnology industry by launching public awareness campaigns. **Libraries: Type:** reference. **Holdings:** 500; papers, reports. **Subjects:** nanotechnology. **Telecommunication Services:** electronic mail, alisa@nanobusiness.org. **Publications:** *Carbon Nanotubes: US Markets, Applications and Forecasts*. Report. Contains information on applications and market forecast for carbon nanotubes. ● *NanoBusiness News*, semimonthly. Newsletter. Covers the latest technology news, profiles on companies, and other related topics pertaining to nanotechnology. **Price:** included in membership dues. **Circulation:** 45,000 ● *Quantum Dot and Semiconductor Nanocrystal Patent Survey*. Report. Provides information on quantum dot technologies patents, insights, statistics, and commentary. ● *Sensors: US Markets, Applications and Forecasts*. Report. Provides an overview of the sensors market in the U.S. and outlines its current applications and future prospects. ● *Tools and Instrumentation: US Markets, Applications and Forecasts*. Report. Covers topics on advancement in and market for tools and instruments used in nanotechnology.

7751 ■ National Center For Advanced Technologies (NCAT)
1000 Wilson Blvd., Ste.1700
Arlington, VA 22209-3901
Ph: (703)358-1000 (813)899-4545
Fax: (703)358-1012
E-mail: ncat@ncat.com
URL: http://www.ncat.com
Contact: Stan Siegel, Pres.

Description: Provides a bridge between government, industry, and academia; encourages cooperative efforts on technology development. Offers consulting services. **Telecommunication Services:** electronic mail, stan@aia-aerospace.org. **Programs:** Defense Research; Education & IPPD. **Publications:** *Interactive Video Course*. Provides training in integrated product and process development. ● *Technology For Affordability*. Report. Alternate Formats: online.

7752 ■ National Technical Association (NTA)
1200 G St. NW, Ste.800
Washington, DC 20005
Ph: (216)289-4682 (832)498-1778
Fax: (216)289-4683
E-mail: pres@ntaonline.org
URL: http://www.ntaonline.org
Contact: Willie B. Williams, Pres.

Founded: 1926. **Members:** 1,500. **Membership Dues:** professional, $100 (annual) ● student, $15 (annual) ● life, $1,350 ● trailblazer, $45 (annual) ● sustaining, $200 (annual) ● associate, $60 (annual). **Regional Groups:** 10. **State Groups:** 60. **Local Groups:** 1. **Description:** Persons who have attained proficiency in engineering, architecture, mathematics, and natural sciences. Seeks to: develop and integrate the minority technical input into the total scientific process; give minorities an awareness of their technical contribution to the establishment of the world's societies; provide for technical interchange among minorities; disseminate career opportunity information to minorities; motivate minority youth to consider technical careers; remove barriers against minorities entering into and advancing in technical professions. Compiles statistics; maintains speakers' bureau. Conducts national junior and senior high school scientific and technical career awareness programs, student technical symposia, and 3-T National Mentor Program. **Awards:** High School Application/Credentials Competition. **Frequency:** annual. **Type:** monetary ● National Science Fair Competition. **Frequency:** annual. **Type:** monetary ● NTA Science Research Scholar-of-the-Year Award. **Frequency:** annual. **Type:** monetary ● SNTA Application/Credentials Competition. **Frequency:** annual. **Type:** monetary. **Telecommunication Services:** electronic mail, tres@ntaonline.org. **Publications:** Journal, quarterly ● Newsletter, quarterly. **Conventions/Meetings:** annual meeting - always summer.

7753 ■ National Technical Services Association (NTSA)
Address Unknown since 2007

Founded: 1961. **Members:** 250. **Staff:** 4. **Budget:** $1,000,000. **Regional Groups:** 23. **Description:** Contract technical services firms that provide a variety of technical services including engineering, designing, and drafting to both industry and government. Goals are to increase understanding of the technical services industry and the role it plays in supplying engineers, draftsmen, and other contract personnel to American industry. Encourages programs in such areas as public relations, ethics, informing potential users of services provided by members, personnel classification and recruitment, technical personnel training and development, and effective utilization of technical manpower. Maintains speakers' bureau and hall of fame; conducts research programs; compiles statistics. **Libraries: Type:** reference. **Holdings:** archival material. **Awards:** NTSA Chapter Achievement Award. **Type:** recognition. **Formerly:** (1961) Technical Services Industry Association. **Publications:** *Membership Roster*, annual ● *NTSA Reporter*, monthly. **Price:** free to members. **Advertising:** accepted. **Conventions/Meetings:** annual meeting (exhibits) - always September ● seminar.

7754 ■ National Urban Technology Center (Urban Tech)
80 Maiden Ln., Ste.606
New York, NY 10038
Ph: (212)528-7350
Free: (800)998-3212
Fax: (212)528-7355
E-mail: info@urbantech.org
URL: http://www.urbantech.org
Contact: Patricia Bransford, Exec. Dir./Founder

Founded: 1995. **Description:** Works to help underserved communities to participate in information age technology. **Computer Services:** Online services, life skills curriculum, promotes positive social and emotional skills for teens and young adults. **Programs:** SEEDTECH; Youth Leadership Academy.

7755 ■ One Economy (OE)
1220 19th St. NW, Ste.610
Washington, DC 20036
Ph: (202)393-0051
Fax: (202)393-7260
E-mail: mail@one-economy.com
URL: http://www.one-economy.com
Contact: Rey Ramsey, CEO

Founded: 2000. **Description:** Serves as a catalyst for innovation and change. Helps bring access to technology into the homes of low-income people around the country. Maximizes the potential of technology to help low-income people improve their lives and join the economic mainstream. Uses technology to connect low-income people to information and tools that help them improve their lives.

7756 ■ Organization for the Advancement of Structured Information Standards (OASIS)
PO Box 455
Billerica, MA 01821
Ph: (978)667-5115
Fax: (978)667-5114
E-mail: info@oasis-open.org
URL: http://www.oasis-open.org
Contact: Scott McGrath, Sr. Dir. of Member Services

Founded: 1998. **Members:** 600. **Membership Dues:** foundational sponsor (academic institution, government, association), $44,000 (annual) ● foundational sponsor (organization employing less than 100 people), $46,000 (annual) ● foundational sponsor (organization employing 100-500 people), $48,000 (annual) ● foundational sponsor (organization employing more than 500 people), $50,000 (annual) ● contributor (based on the number of employees), $1,100-$8,000 (annual) ● individual, associate, $300 (annual). **National Groups:** 100. **Multinational. Description:** Seeks to advance the development, convergence, and adoption of e-business standards. **Computer Services:** Online services, cover page. **Telecommunication Services:** electronic mail, scott.mcgrath@oasis-open.org. **Committees:** Computing Management; Document-Centric; e-Commerce; ebXML; Law and Government; Security; Supply Chain; Web Services. **Formerly:** SGML Open. **Publications:** *Cover Pages*, weekly. Newsletter. Provides a summary for feature stories featured on the website during the previous week. Alternate Formats: online ● *Oasis News* (in English and Japanese), weekly. Newsletter. Contains updates of activities and accomplishments of OASIS.

7757 ■ Programmers Guild
PO Box 1250
Summit, NJ 07902-1250
E-mail: info@programmersguild.org
URL: http://www.programmersguild.org
Contact: Mr. Kim Berry, Pres.

Membership Dues: employed, $35 (annual) ● unemployed, $1 (annual). **Description:** Seeks to advance the interests of technical and professional workers in information technology fields. Strives to improve the work and the workplaces of technical professionals across the spectrum of information technology fields and disciplines. **Publications:** Newsletter, periodic. Alternate Formats: online.

7758 ■ Progressive Technology Project (PTP)
2801 21st Ave. S, Ste.132E
Minneapolis, MN 55407
Ph: (612)724-2600
Free: (866)298-6463
E-mail: info@progressivetech.org
URL: http://www.progressivetech.org
Contact: Mark Sherman, Exec. Dir.

Founded: 1998. **Description:** Seeks to raise the scope and scale of technology resources available to grassroots organizing groups. Provides training, technical assistance and grants to develop the capacity of grassroots organizing groups through the use of information technology. **Publications:** *Community Organizing Resource Network*. Newsletter. Contains news, tips and techniques to help grassroots community groups. Alternate Formats: online. Also Cited As: *CORN*.

7759 ■ RDMA Consortium
c/o Joseph Mouhanna
Microsoft Corp.
1 Microsoft Way
Redmond, WA 98052
Ph: (425)706-7421
Fax: (425)936-7329
E-mail: josephmo@microsoft.com
URL: http://www.rdmaconsortium.org
Contact: Joseph Mouhanna, Contact

Description: Seeks to advance the growing memory bandwidth, CPU processing demands. **Publications:** *Membership Roster*. Directory. Alternate Formats: online.

7760 ■ Simulation Interoperability Standards Organization (SISO)
c/o Van Lowe
3280 Progress Dr.
Orlando, FL 32826
Ph: (407)882-1348
Fax: (407)658-5059
E-mail: vlowe@ist.ucf.edu
URL: http://www.sisostds.org
Contact: Sam Knight, Pres.

Founded: 1989. **Members:** 1,400. **Membership Dues:** regular, $45 (annual). **Description:** Dedicated to facilitating simulation interoperability across a wide spectrum. **Libraries: Type:** reference. **Computer Services:** database. **Committees:** Conference; Elections; Standards Activity. **Publications:** *Simulation Technology*. Magazine. Alternate Formats: online ● Reports. Alternate Formats: online. **Conventions/Meetings:** semiannual workshop.

7761 ■ Smart Card Alliance
191 Clarksville Rd.
Princeton Junction, NJ 08550
Free: (800)556-6828
E-mail: info@smartcardalliance.org
URL: http://www.smartcardalliance.org
Contact: Randy Vanderhoof, Exec. Dir.

Founded: 2001. **Members:** 185. **Membership Dues:** Leadership Council, $12,000 (annual) ● general, $5,000 (annual) ● government, university, $1,750 (annual) ● associate, $1,200 (annual). **Description:** Promotes acceptance of multiple application smart cards for banking, financial services, telecommunications, technology, healthcare, retail, and entertainment industries. **Telecommunication Services:** electronic mail, rvanderhoof@smartcardalliance.org. **Councils:** Healthcare; Physical Access. **Sections:** Educational Institute. **Working Groups:** Digital Initiative; Market Research; Telecommunications Advocacy; Transportation. **Absorbed:** (2002) Smart Card Industry Association. **Publications:** *Smart Card Talk*, monthly. Newsletter. Contains news about the activities of the Alliance and information on industry events around the world. **Price:** free for members. Alternate Formats: online. **Conventions/Meetings:** conference ● annual meeting.

7762 ■ Technology Transfer Society (T2S)
2005 Arthur Ln.
Austin, TX 78704
Ph: (512)447-4409 (979)845-8762
Fax: (512)447-1814
E-mail: t2s@t2s.org
URL: http://www.t2society.org
Contact: Dr. Donald Siegel, Pres.

Founded: 1975. **Members:** 650. **Membership Dues:** individual, $125 (annual) ● individual outside U.S., $150 (annual) ● full-time student, retired, $65 (annual) ● organization, $320 (annual) ● not-for-profit organization, $300 (annual) ● for-profit organization, $600 (annual). **Staff:** 2. **Budget:** $180,000. **Local Groups:** 8. **Description:** Individuals, institutions, and other professional societies involved in the process of technology transfer. Encourages development of technology assessment, transfer, utilization, and forecasting techniques; disseminates information on these new techniques. Seeks to develop an environment for and promote the enhancement of professional competence in the field. Establishes standards and ethics; defines terms. Acts as a liaison among disciplines within the technological community such as scientific, management, engineering, and other professional societies. Provides a nonprofit capability to accept charitable contributions, contracts, and grants for the performance of pilot technological transfer programs that will aid the nation. **Libraries: Type:** reference. **Holdings:** 100. **Awards:** Justin Morrill. **Frequency:** annual. **Type:** recognition. **Recipient:** for outstanding contributions ● Lang-Rosen. **Frequency:** annual. **Type:** recognition. **Recipient:** for outstanding contribution ● Thomas Jefferson. **Frequency:** annual. **Type:** recognition. **Recipient:** for outstanding contributions. **Computer Services:** database, membership. **Telecommunication Services:** electronic mail, kaufmb@rpi.edu. **Committees:** Awards; Conference; Publications; Strategic Planning. **Councils:** Chapter Presidents. **Publications:** *Journal of Technology Transfer*, triennial. Contains information on technology transfer, assessment, and forecasting; includes case studies. **Price:** free for members; $100.00 /year for nonmembers. **Circulation:** 800 ● *Roundtable on Technology Transfer Metrics*. Proceedings. Features a documented presentation of the three-hour dialogue among national technology transfer leaders and audience participants. **Price:** $10.00 includes postage; $5.00 those who bought 1997 Metrics Summit Proceedings ● *Technology Transfer Society—International Symposium Proceedings*, annual. Contains original papers on technology transfer, assessment, forecasting, commercialization, financing, case studies, and history. **Price:** $50.00/year. **Circulation:** 600 ● *T'Squared*, bimonthly. Newsletter. Features updates on the latest technology transfer changes. Contains information on the activities and conferences of the association and its members. Alternate Formats: online ● Directory, annual. Includes names, addresses of members by professional categories. **Price:** included in membership dues. **Conventions/Meetings:** annual conference (exhibits) ● annual meeting (exhibits) - July.

7763 ■ Technology Without Borders (TWB)
PO Box 445
The Plains, VA 20198
Ph: (703)220-7327
E-mail: info@technologywithoutborders.org
URL: http://www.technologywithoutborders.org
Contact: Dean E. Bedford, Exec. Dir.
Founded: 2001. **Staff:** 3. **Description:** Develops information management systems for non-profit organizations and educational institutions. Creates a capacity that establishes a foundation for social and economic progress. Applies technology to humanitarian and educational initiatives. Fosters commitment to community service. **Computer Services:** database, design ● information services, technology resources ● online services, survey. **Projects:** Project Manager; V3-CRM System; W3 Website CMS.

7764 ■ Women in Technology International
13351-D Riverside Dr., No. 441
Sherman Oaks, CA 91423
Ph: (818)788-9484
Fax: (818)788-9410
E-mail: eve@corp.witi.com
URL: http://www.witi.com
Contact: Carolyn Leighton, Founder/Chair
Founded: 1989. **Members:** 6,000. **Membership Dues:** individual, $250 (annual) ● life, $1,000 ● student, $175 (annual). **Staff:** 10. **Regional Groups:** 35. **Multinational. Description:** Aims to empower women worldwide to achieve possibilities and transformations through technology, leadership and economic prosperity. Consists of women in technology. Expansion includes the development of vertical markets, such as women in biotechnology, women in business, women in law, as well as innovative programs, web based tools, and other products and services. **Awards:** WITI Hall of Fame and CEO Award. **Frequency:** annual. **Type:** recognition. **Formerly:** (1998) International Network of Women in Technology. **Publications:** *WITI Fasttrack*, quarterly. Magazine. **Advertising:** accepted. Alternate Formats: online. **Conventions/Meetings:** Professional Women's Summit - conference and seminar (exhibits) - 3/year.

Technology Education

7765 ■ Link Foundation
c/o Binghamton University Foundation
PO Box 6005
Binghamton, NY 13902-6005
URL: http://www.binghamton.edu/home/link/link.html
Contact: Cheryl Dimick, Contact
Founded: 1953. **Description:** Strives to foster advanced-level study in simulation and training research. **Awards:** Doctoral Student Award. **Frequency:** 5/year. **Type:** grant. **Recipient:** to qualified doctoral students in academic institutions. **Publications:** *Link Foundation Fellowships Newsletter*. Alternate Formats: online.

Telecommunications

7766 ■ American TeleEdCommunications Alliance (ATAlliance)
c/o Clancy DeLong
1500 W High St.
Mount Pleasant, MI 48858
Free: (888)870-8677
Fax: (989)772-3239
E-mail: ataservice@mictaservice.com
URL: http://www.atalliance.org
Contact: Clancy DeLong, Contact
Founded: 2001. **Membership Dues:** FTE employee, $100-$200 (annual). **Description:** Provides technology products and services. Works to address the rapidly expanding use of technology in the public and nonprofit sectors. Promotes the broad availability of advanced technology acquisition programs. **Telecommunication Services:** electronic mail, membership@mictaservice.com ● additional toll-free number, (866)-216-0006.

7767 ■ Association of Federal Communications Consulting Engineers (AFCCE)
c/o Tom Cox, Sec.
3221 Foothill St.
Clear Channel Radio
Escondido, CA 92025
Ph: (703)780-4824
Fax: (703)780-4214
E-mail: afcce@cuenet.com
URL: http://www.afcce.org
Contact: Michael D. Rhodes, Pres.
Founded: 1948. **Members:** 260. **Membership Dues:** full, $180 (annual) ● associate, $140 (annual) ● government full/associate, $50 (annual) ● life, $20. **Description:** Consulting radio engineers working for the Federal Communications Commission in engineering and allocation matters. Works to assist and advance the proper federal administration and regulation of the engineering and technical phases of radio communication. **Awards: Type:** scholarship. **Recipient:** for undergraduate engineering students. **Telecommunication Services:** electronic mail, j.w.reiser@ieee.org. **Committees:** Nominations. **Conventions/Meetings:** annual meeting.

7768 ■ IEEE Broadcast Technology Society (IEEE/BTS)
c/o Kathy Colabaugh, Admin.
445 Hoes Ln.
PO Box 1331
Piscataway, NJ 08854
Ph: (732)562-3906
Fax: (732)981-1769
E-mail: k.colabaugh@ieee.org
URL: http://www.ieee.org/organizations/society/bt
Contact: William T. Hayes, Pres.
Founded: 1884. **Members:** 3,023. **Membership Dues:** affiliate, $76 (annual). **Local Groups:** 9. **Description:** A society of the Institute of Electrical and Electronics Engineers. Disseminates information on broadcast transmission systems engineering, including the design and utilization of broadcast equipment. **Libraries: Type:** reference. **Awards:** Broadcast Technology Society Special Service. **Frequency:** annual. **Type:** recognition. **Recipient:** for individuals ● Clyde M. Hunt Memorial. **Frequency:** periodic. **Type:** recognition. **Recipient:** for the best student paper ● Matti M. Siukola Memorial. **Frequency:** annual. **Type:** recognition. **Recipient:** for the best paper presented at the annual IEEE Broadcast Symposium ● Scott Helt Memorial. **Frequency:** annual. **Type:** recognition. **Recipient:** for the best paper printed in Transactions on Broadcasting. **Committees:** Advanced Television Systems; Awards; Communications and Information Policy; Education; Historian; Man and Radiation; Nominations; Publicity. **Publications:** *Transactions on Broadcast Technology*, quarterly. **Price:** included in membership dues ● Newsletter, quarterly. **Price:** included in membership dues. Alternate Formats: online. **Conventions/Meetings:** annual Multimedia - symposium ● annual symposium - always late September, in Washington, DC.

7769 ■ IEEE Communications Society (COMSOC)
3 Park Ave., 17th Fl.
New York, NY 10016
Ph: (212)705-8900
Fax: (212)705-8999
E-mail: society@comsoc.org
URL: http://www.comsoc.org
Contact: Jack Howell, Exec. Dir.
Founded: 1952. **Members:** 55,000. **Membership Dues:** regular, in U.S., $167 (annual) ● affiliate, $49 (annual). **Staff:** 23. **Regional Groups:** 10. **Local Groups:** 130. **Multinational. Description:** Industry professionals with a common interest in advancing all communications technologies. Seeks to foster original work in all aspects of communications science, engineering, and technology and encourages the development of applications that use signals to transfer voice, data, image, and/or video information between locations. Promotes the theory and use of systems involving all types of terminals, computers, and information processors; all pertinent systems and operations that facilitate transfer; all transmission media; switched and unswitched networks; and network layout, protocols, architectures, and implementations. Advances developments toward meeting new market demands in systems, products, and technologies such personal communications services, multimedia communications systems, enterprise networks, and optical communications systems. **Awards:** Career Awards. **Frequency:** annual. **Type:** recognition. **Recipient:** for a member of the Communications Society ● Paper Awards. **Frequency:** annual. **Type:** recognition. **Recipient:** for publication of an original paper ● Service Awards. **Frequency:** annual. **Type:** recognition. **Recipient:** for exemplary service to the society. **Publications:** *IEEE/ACM Transactions on Networking*, bimonthly. Journal. Reflects the multi-disciplinary nature of communications. **Price:** $38.00. **Circulation:** 10,000 ● *IEEE Communications Letters*, monthly. Journal. Provides researchers with the ideal venue for sharing their most current results and developments. **Price:** $29.00 print and electronic; $15.00 electronic only. Alternate Formats: online ● *IEEE Communications Magazine*, monthly. Reports on all fields of voice, data, and multi-media communications. **Price:** $23.00 print and electronic; $15.00 electronic only. ISSN: 0163-6804. **Circulation:** 55,000. **Advertising:** accepted ● *IEEE Network, The Magazine of Global Information Exchange*, bimonthly. **Price:** $25.00. **Circulation:** 14,000. **Advertising:** accepted ● *IEEE Personal Communications: The Magazine of Wireless Communications and Networking and Computing*, bimonthly. **Price:** $25.00. **Circulation:** 11,000. **Advertising:** accepted ● *Journal on Selected Areas in Communications*, monthly. Focuses in depth attention on critical aspects of one specific communications topic. **Price:** $33.00 print and electronic; $19.00 electronic only. **Circulation:** 8,000. Alternate Formats: online ● *Transactions on Communications*, monthly. Journal. Covers all aspects of communications from telephony to communication theory. **Price:** $33.00 print and electronic; $19.00 electronic only. **Circulation:** 10,000. Alternate Formats: online. **Conventions/Meetings:** annual conference, all aspects of communication technology (exhibits).

7770 ■ IEEE Information Theory Group (ITG)
c/o IEEE Corporate Office
3 Park Ave., 17th Fl.
New York, NY 10016-5997
Ph: (212)419-7900
Free: (800)678-4333
Fax: (212)328-8599
E-mail: customer-service@ieee.org
Contact: Dan Senese, Gen. Mgr.
Members: 4,977. **Budget:** $200,000. **Local Groups:** 18. **Description:** A society of the Institute of Electrical and Electronics Engineers. Fields of interest includes processing, transmission, storage, and use of information; theoretical and certain applied aspects of coding, communications and communications networks, complexity and cryptography, detection and estimation, learning, Shannon Theory, and stochastic processes. **Formerly:** (1987) IEEE Information Theory Society. **Publications:** *Transactions on Information Theory*, bimonthly. **Conventions/Meetings:** annual symposium.

7771 ■ IMS Forum
211 Summit Pl., No. 292
Silverthorne, CO 80498
Ph: (970)262-6100
Fax: (407)641-9595
E-mail: info@imsforum.org
URL: http://www.imsforum.org
Contact: Michael Khalilian, Pres./Chm.
Membership Dues: company (based on annual revenues), $3,500-$15,000 (annual) ● educational, governmental institution, not for profit organization, $3,500 (annual). **Multinational. Description:** Accelerates the adoption of IP Multimedia Subsystem by creating a community for discussion and resolution of real-world implementations and interoperability. Provides consultancy to the industry, service providers, and vendors on best practices and approaches for IMS rollouts and interconnectivity. **Libraries: Type:** reference. **Subjects:** next-generation switching technologies and innovations. **Formerly:** (2006) International Packet Communications Consortium. **Publications:** Newsletter.

7772 ■ Institute for Global Communications (IGC)
PO Box 29047
San Francisco, CA 94129-0047
E-mail: support@igc.apc.org
URL: http://www.igc.org
Contact: Shirley Strong, Exec. Dir.
Founded: 1987. **Members:** 20,000. **Staff:** 35. **Multinational. Description:** Provides computer networking tools for international communications and information exchange. Maintains 4 networks—EcoNet, PeaceNet, LaborNet and WomensNet—that promote environmental preservation, human rights, sustainable development, peace, and social justice. **Convention/Meeting:** none. **Publications:** *NetNews*, monthly. Newsletter. **Price:** free to subscribers. **Circulation:** 9,000. Alternate Formats: online.

7773 ■ International Association for Radio, Telecommunications and Electromagnetics (iNARTE)
167 Village St.
Medway, MA 02053
Ph: (508)533-8333 (814)466-6559
Free: (800)89-NARTE
Fax: (508)533-3815
E-mail: narte@narte.org
URL: http://www.narte.org
Contact: Brian Lawrence, Exec. Dir.
Founded: 1982. **Members:** 5,175. **Staff:** 4. **Budget:** $310,000. **Description:** Provides certification in telecommunications, Electrostatic Discharge Control and Electromagnetic Compatibility engineers and technicians. Designated and accredited by the Federal Communications Commission as a Commercial Operators License Examination Manager. Objectives are to: foster professionalism; develop and implement guidelines for certification; promote telecommunications, and EMC/ESD education in colleges and universities. **Awards:** Marconi-Bell Award. **Frequency:** annual. **Type:** recognition. **Recipient:** to an engineer/technician for outstanding contribution in his/her respective field ● National Service Award. **Frequency:** annual. **Type:** recognition. **Recipient:** to a recipient of the National Service Award who in turn allocates to a college/university of choice. **Telecommunication Services:** electronic mail, lawrence@narte.org. **Also Known As:** NARTE Inc. **Formerly:** (2007) National Association of Radio and Telecommunications Engineers. **Publications:** *NARTE News*, quarterly. Newsletter. **Price:** included in membership dues. **Circulation:** 6,000. **Advertising:** accepted. Alternate Formats: CD-ROM; online. **Conventions/Meetings:** annual conference and meeting - held in June or October.

7774 ■ International Disaster Recovery Association (IDRA)
c/o BWT Associates
PO No. 4515
Shrewsbury, MA 01545
Ph: (508)845-6000
Fax: (508)842-9003
E-mail: bwt@bwt.com
URL: http://www.idra.com
Contact: Benjamin W. Tartaglia, Exec. Dir.
Founded: 1990. **Members:** 300. **Membership Dues:** professional/associate, $100 (annual) ● corporate, $1,500 (annual) ● sponsoring, $2,500 (annual) ● sustaining, $5,000 (annual). **Staff:** 5. **For-Profit. Description:** Disaster recovery, MIS, security, notification and warning, contingency planning, and emergency preparedness professionals with special interest in telecommunications. Focuses on telecommunications aspects of contingency planning, business continuation, disaster recovery, and restoration of service. Conducts research and survey studies. Organizes educational events and acts as informational clearinghouse. Fosters the professionalism of individuals in the disaster recovery/telecommunications field. Operates speakers' bureau. Consulting services are available. Contingency plan creation; review and audit services provided. **Libraries: Type:** reference. **Holdings:** books, clippings, monographs, periodicals, video recordings. **Awards:** Achievement Award. **Frequency:** annual. **Type:** recognition. **Recipient:** for achievement in disaster recovery, contingency planning and business continuation using telecommunications. **Subgroups:** Member Advisory Panel. **Affiliated With:** National Emergency Number Association; U.S. Internet Industry Association. **Also Known As:** IDRA - International Disaster Recovery Association. **Publications:** *ACK-NAK News*, quarterly. Newsletter. Covers various organizational topics on contingency planning, business continuation and disaster recovery. **Price:** free for members. **Advertising:** accepted ● *IDRA Membership Directory*, periodic. **Price:** free, for members only ● Reports ● Also publishes membership flyers and white papers. **Conventions/Meetings:** annual Disaster Recovery Using Telecommunications - conference, presentations and exhibits focus on telecommunications disaster recovery and contingency planning (exhibits) - spring ● periodic seminar and workshop, covers various topics pertaining to contingency planning, infrastructure, convergence, homeland security, business continuation and disaster recovery.

7775 ■ International Multimedia Telecommunications Consortium (IMTC)
2400 Camino Ramon, Ste.375
San Ramon, CA 94583
Ph: (925)275-6600
Fax: (925)275-6691
E-mail: secretary@imtc.org
URL: http://www.imtc.org
Contact: Jim Polizotto, Sec.
Founded: 1994. **Membership Dues:** corporate, $7,500 (annual) ● university/non-profit, $1,000 (annual). **Multinational. Description:** Promotes standards that enable real-time, rich-media communications worldwide.

7776 ■ International Nortel Networks Users Association (INNUA)
401 N Michigan Ave., Ste.2200
Chicago, IL 60611
Ph: (312)673-6102 (312)673-4834
Free: (877)446-6684
Fax: (312)673-6718
E-mail: info@innua.org
URL: http://www.innua.org
Contact: Victor Bohnert, Exec. Dir.
Founded: 1980. **Members:** 6,000. **Membership Dues:** end user, $100 (annual) ● associate, $200 (annual). **Staff:** 17. **Budget:** $2,300,000. **Multinational. Description:** Works to educate, develop, and inform members on trends and developments in all areas of telecommunications, with an emphasis on the Nortel Networks Meridian product line. Provides opportunities for individuals with concerns pertaining to telecommunications. **Special Interest Groups:** Audio Conferencing; Avotus Users; Contact Center; Customer Owned and Maintained Systems; Education; EMEA Contact Center; Government; Health Care. **Formerly:** International Nortel Networks Meridian Users Group. **Publications:** *Cyber Report*, bimonthly. Newsletter. Contains latest news in the telecommunications industry. Alternate Formats: online ● *INNTouch*, bimonthly. Newsletter. Offers insight into the Nortel systems and the telecommunications industry. Alternate Formats: online. **Conventions/Meetings:** annual Global Connect - meeting, for technical user group (exhibits).

7777 ■ International Telecommunications Satellite Organization (ITSO)
3400 Intl. Dr. NW
Washington, DC 20008-3006
Ph: (202)243-5096 (202)243-5092
Fax: (202)243-5018
E-mail: itsomail@itso.int
URL: http://www.itso.int
Contact: Ahmed Toumi, Dir. Gen./CEO
Founded: 1964. **Members:** 148. **Languages:** English, French, Spanish. **Description:** Governments that adhere to 2 international telecommunications agreements. Each government designates a telecommunications entity, either public or private, as its signatory to the INTELSAT Operating Agreement. Seeks to unify the design, development, construction, establishment, maintenance, and operation of the space segment of the global communications satellite system; the space segment provides overseas telecommunications services and live television, enables a number of domestic communications systems, and includes communication satellites and the telemetry, control, command, monitoring, and related facilities and equipment required to support satellite operations. As of January 1998 there were 19 satellites in geosynchronous orbit. **Libraries: Type:** not open to the public; reference. **Holdings:** 10,000; archival material. **Subjects:** international telecommunication, satellite communication. **Committees:** Advisory. **Subgroups:** Executive Organ; Panel of Legal Experts. **Publications:** Annual Report, annual ● Brochures ● Reports, quarterly ● Also publishes services materials. **Conventions/Meetings:** biennial Assembly of Parties, for member country representatives.

7778 ■ National Association of Black Telecommunications Professionals (NABTP)
2020 Pennsylvania Ave. NW
Box 735
Washington, DC 20006
Free: (877)349-8869
Fax: (877)349-8869
E-mail: office@nabtp.org
URL: http://www.nabtp.org
Contact: Brenda F. Lowe, Pres.
Founded: 1990. **Membership Dues:** regular, $50 (annual). **Description:** Represents African-American professionals in the telecommunications sector. **Awards:** Evelyn Hamm Arthur Award. **Type:** recognition. **Recipient:** for dedicated volunteers ● Granville T. Woods Award for Outstanding CEO. **Frequency:** annual. **Type:** recognition. **Recipient:** for African American CEO of an African American owned business ● Mickey Leland Award for Excellence in Diversity. **Type:** recognition. **Recipient:** for outstanding individual who has demonstrated his or her embrace of diversity in the telecommunications

industry ● The NABTP Collegian. **Frequency:** annual. **Type:** scholarship. **Recipient:** for a student who studies telecommunications or a related field of study ● Patrice Johnson Award for Excellence. **Type:** recognition. **Recipient:** to a member of the judicial, legislative or executive branch of government. **Committees:** Awards and Recognition; Bylaws; Convention/Program; Education; Public Policy; Public Relations; Resolutions; Technology; Ways and Means.

7779 ■ North American Association of Telecommunications Dealers (NATD)
131 NW 1st Ave.
Delray Beach, FL 33444
Ph: (561)266-9440 (480)556-8202
Fax: (561)266-9017
E-mail: joemarion@natd.com
URL: http://www.natd.com
Contact: Joseph Marion, Exec. Dir.
Founded: 1985. **Membership Dues:** regular, vendor, $1,050 (annual) ● company outside U.S., $800 (annual). **Staff:** 16. **Description:** Represents the interests of companies that provide voice and data communications products and services. Provides access to information, resources, business leaders, and opportunities. **Conventions/Meetings:** annual meeting.

7780 ■ OASIS PKI Member Section
c/o OASIS
PO Box 455
Billerica, MA 01821
Ph: (978)667-5115
Fax: (978)667-5114
E-mail: info@oasis-open.org
Contact: June Leung, Chair, Steering Committee
Founded: 1999. **Description:** Fosters standards-based, interoperable public-key infrastructure (PKI) as a foundation for secure transactions in e-business applications. **Telecommunication Services:** electronic mail, june.leung@fundserv.com. **Formerly:** (2002) PKI Forum. **Publications:** Papers.

7781 ■ Open Mobile Alliance (OMA)
4275 Executive Sq., Ste.240
La Jolla, CA 92037
Ph: (858)623-0742
Fax: (858)623-0743
E-mail: snewberry@omaorg.org
URL: http://www.openmobilealliance.org
Contact: Seth Newberry, Gen. Mgr.
Founded: 2002. **Membership Dues:** sponsor, $130,000 (annual) ● full, $39,000 (annual) ● associate, $9,000 (annual) ● supporter, $600 (annual). **Multinational. Description:** Promotes growth in mobile services industry, including digital mobile phones, pagers, personal digital assistants, and other wireless terminals. **Sections:** Speakers' Bureau. **Formerly:** WAP Forum; Open Mobile Architecture Initiative.

7782 ■ Pacific Telecommunications Council (PTC)
2454 S Beretania St., Ste.302
Honolulu, HI 96826-1524
Ph: (808)941-3789
Fax: (808)944-4874
E-mail: info@ptc.org
URL: http://www.ptc.org
Contact: Sharon Nakama, Exec. Dir.
Founded: 1980. **Members:** 700. **Membership Dues:** nonprofit (based on number of employees), $250-$675 (annual) ● affiliate (non-voting), $250 (annual) ● individual, $150 (annual) ● for-profit (based on number of employees), $250-$3,600 (annual) ● student (in developing country), $25 (annual) ● student (in developed country), $65 (annual). **Staff:** 15. **Budget:** $2,800,000. **Multinational. Description:** Organizations and professionals involved as providers, users, policymakers, and analysts in telecommunications development in the Americas, Oceania, and Asia. Provides a forum for discussion between governments, academia, and telecommunications users, planners, and providers of equipment and services. Organizes conferences and seminars to exchange views and information on telecommunication services and systems in the Pacific region. Addresses immediate and future-oriented telecommunications, information services/systems and broadcasting/multimedia issues. Conducts workshops on telecommunications skills; conducts research programs. **Libraries: Type:** reference. **Awards:** PTC Essay Prize. **Frequency:** annual. **Type:** recognition. **Recipient:** for a student or graduate within the last 5 years. **Computer Services:** Mailing lists. **Publications:** *Pacific Telecommunications Council—Membership Directory*, annual. Contains listing of members of PTC and public relations representatives of associated firms. **Price:** available to members only. **Circulation:** 1,400. Alternate Formats: diskette ● *Pacific Telecommunications Review*, quarterly. Reports. Reports on council activities and provides academic articles about telecommunications in the Pacific. Covers international policy issues. **Price:** included in membership dues; $35.00 for nonmembers in North America; $50.00 for nonmembers outside North America. ISSN: 0894-8143. **Circulation:** 2,500. **Advertising:** accepted. Also Cited As: *PTR* ● *PTC Proceedings*, annual. **Price:** $225.00 for nonmembers; $125.00 for members. Alternate Formats: CD-ROM ● *PTC Wire*, monthly. Bulletin. Contains membership activities. **Price:** available to members only. **Circulation:** 1,400. Alternate Formats: online. **Conventions/Meetings:** annual From Convergence to Emergence - conference and seminar (exhibits) ● annual Pacific Telecommunications Conference (exhibits).

7783 ■ Radio Amateur Satellite Corporation (AMSAT)
850 Sligo Ave., Ste.600
Silver Spring, MD 20910-4787
Ph: (301)589-6062
Free: (888)322-6728
Fax: (301)608-3410
E-mail: martha@amsat.org
URL: http://www.amsat.org
Contact: Ms. Martha Saragovitz, Mgr.
Founded: 1969. **Members:** 7,000. **Membership Dues:** regular, in U.S., $44 (annual) ● regular, in Canada and Mexico, $50 (annual) ● international, $55 (annual) ● club, school, society, $80 (annual) ● life, $880. **Staff:** 1. **Description:** Licensed amateur radio operators and others interested in communicating through a series of satellites. Provides satellites for amateur radio communication and experimentation by suitably equipped amateur radio stations worldwide on a nondiscriminatory basis. Participates in data collection, extensive modifications, fabrication, spacecraft design, testing, licensing, and launch arrangements for satellite projects throughout the world. Encourages the development of skills and the fostering of specialized knowledge in the art and practice of amateur radio communications and space science. Promotes international goodwill and cooperation through joint experimentation and study and through the widespread noncommercial participation of radio amateurs in these activities. Facilitates emergency communication by means of amateur satellites. Advocates more effective and extensive use of higher frequency amateur bands. Carries out communications and experimental activities and disseminates resulting operational, scientific, and technical information. Encourages publication of this information in technical and trade journals, theses, and treatises. Works to develop long-life spacecraft and instruments designed for geostationary, near-synchronous, or high-altitude elliptical orbits, providing a new resource for emergency communication and making further experimentation possible. Assists and participates in the activities of other world groups dealing in space communications; presents papers at amateur, professional, and technical meetings. Provides schools of physical science with reviews and advice on curricula dealing with the use of amateur satellite terminals. Sponsors OSCAR (Orbiting Satellite Carrying Amateur Radio), through which a series of communications satellites have been designed, built, and launched. Maintains speakers' bureau. **Libraries: Type:** reference. **Holdings:** archival material. **Publications:** *AMSAT Journal*, bimonthly. **Conventions/Meetings:** annual meeting - always fall.

7784 ■ Radio and Television Research Council (RTRC)
c/o Management Solutions for Associations
234 5th Ave., Ste.417
New York, NY 10001
Ph: (212)481-3038
Fax: (212)481-3071
E-mail: mgmtoffice@aol.com
Contact: Rosemarie Sharpe, Contact
Founded: 1941. **Members:** 200. **Membership Dues:** individual, $75 (annual). **Description:** Individuals actively engaged in radio or television research who have recognized professional standing in the field. Aims to provide members with presentations and discussions of radio and television research problems and of techniques used to study each as an advertising medium and as a means of social communication. Seeks to improve research methods through discussion. **Conventions/Meetings:** meeting - always the third Monday, September-June, New York City.

7785 ■ United States National Committee of the International Union of Radio Science (USNC-URSI)
c/o Piergiorgio L.E. Uslenghi, Chm.
Univ. of Illinois at Chicago
1120 Sci. and Engg. Offices
851 S Morgan St.
Chicago, IL 60607-7053
Ph: (312)996-6059
Fax: (312)996-8664
E-mail: uslenghi@eecs.uic.edu
URL: http://www.usnc-ursi.org
Contact: Piergiorgio L.E. Uslenghi, Chm.
Founded: 1919. **Members:** 30. **Staff:** 3. **Description:** Works under the auspices of the National Academy of Sciences. Represents scientists working in: electromagnetic measurement methods, including radio standards; biological interactions with electromagnetic fields; electromagnetic theory, including antennas and waveguides; scientific developments in telecommunications, including radio electronics and microwave sources; information theory, signal processing, and computing; communications systems and system theory; electromagnetic noise and interference; radio astronomy; remote sensing; wave phenomena in non-ionized media, including radiometeorology and radio-oceanography; and wave phenomena in ionized media, particularly in the earth's ionosphere, including ionospheric soundings and radio communications. Purposes are: to promote the scientific study of radio communications; to participate in radio research requiring cooperation on an international scale; to facilitate agreement upon common methods of measurement and the standardization of measuring instruments; to stimulate and coordinate studies of the scientific aspects of telecommunications using electromagnetic waves. **Awards:** Henry Booker Award and Howard Dellinger Medal. **Frequency:** triennial. **Type:** recognition. **Recipient:** for radio science research ● U.S. Student Paper Prize. **Frequency:** annual. **Type:** recognition. **Telecommunication Services:** electronic mail, rahmat@ee.ucla.edu. **Commissions:** Bioelectromagnetics; Electromagnetic Metrology; Electromagnetic Noise and Interference; Electronic and Optical Devices and Applications; Fluids and Waves; Ionospheric Radio and Propagation; Radio Astronomy; Remote Sensing and Wave Propagation; Signals and Systems; Waves in Plasmas. **Affiliated With:** National Academy of Sciences. **Publications:** *U.S. National Committee for the International Union of Radio Science—Program and Abstracts*, annual. **Price:** $5.00/copy. **Conventions/Meetings:** annual National Radio Science Meeting.

Telemetry

7786 ■ International Foundation for Telemetering (IFT)
5959 Topanga Canyon Blvd., Ste.150
Woodland Hills, CA 91367

E-mail: admin2007@telemetry.org
URL: http://www.telemetry.org
Contact: Norm Lantz, Pres.
Founded: 1964. **Description:** Works to advance the theory and practice of telemetering. Promotes unity, effectiveness, and ethical conduct among those professionals concerned within the field (Telemetry, used in rocketry and space studies, is the science of measuring physical phenomena such as temperature or radiation at some remote point and transmitting, especially by radio, the values obtained to a distant indicator, recorder, or observer). **Also Known As:** ITC/USA/2003. **Publications:** *ITC Proceedings*, annual. Contains information about annual conference. ISSN: 0884-5123. **Conventions/Meetings:** annual International Telemetering Conference - conference and trade show, includes short courses, technical papers (exhibits).

Testing

7787 ■ American Society for Nondestructive Testing (ASNT)
PO Box 28518
Columbus, OH 43228-0518
Ph: (614)274-6003 (509)210-2331
Free: (800)222-2768
Fax: (614)274-6899
E-mail: wholliday@asnt.org
URL: http://www.asnt.org
Contact: Wayne Holliday, Exec. Dir.
Founded: 1941. **Members:** 11,000. **Membership Dues:** individual, $75 (annual) ● student, $15 (annual) ● military (grade E-5 or lower), $30 (annual) ● corporate partner, $410 (annual). **Staff:** 50. **National Groups:** 84. **Description:** Metallurgists, quality control specialists, welding engineers, industrial management personnel, technicians, educators, and suppliers of equipment and services. Promotes education and techniques in methods of nondestructive testing utilizing penetrating radiations, magnetics, electricity, sound, heat, penetrants and visual-optics for the aerospace, airframe, automotive, marine, railroad, chemical, petroleum, electronics, nuclear, materials-joining, ordnance, and utilities industries. **Libraries: Type:** reference. **Holdings:** 2,000; books, periodicals. **Subjects:** materials science, nondestructive testing. **Awards:** Engineering Undergraduate Award. **Frequency:** annual. **Type:** recognition. **Recipient:** to engineering undergraduate students enrolled in engineering programs accredited by ABET or its equivalent ● Faculty Grant. **Frequency:** annual. **Type:** grant. **Recipient:** to an engineering faculty that is accredited by ABET ● Fellow Award. **Frequency:** annual. **Type:** fellowship. **Recipient:** to an individual member of society who has demonstrated outstanding professional distinction ● Fellowship Award. **Frequency:** annual. **Type:** fellowship. **Recipient:** to an educational institution accredited by ABET or its equivalent ● Philip D. Johnson Honorary Member Award. **Frequency:** annual. **Type:** recognition. **Recipient:** for an honorary member of acknowledged eminence in the domain covered by the Society or one who has been recognized as a benefactor to the Society through services such as being an officer in the national society ● Robert B. Oliver Scholarship. **Frequency:** annual. **Type:** scholarship. **Recipient:** to the student who submits the best original manuscript on non-destructive testing. **Telecommunication Services:** electronic mail, jocelyn@sigmatx.com. **Formerly:** (1964) American Industrial Radium and X-Ray Society; (1967) Society for Nondestructive Testing. **Publications:** *ASNT Publications Catalog*, annual. Lists publications available from the group. ● *Materials Evaluation*, monthly. Journal. Covers materials evaluation testing methods; includes ASNT news. Contains research reports, buyers' guide, and calendar of events. **Price:** $105.00/year. ISSN: 0025-5327. **Circulation:** 12,000. **Advertising:** accepted. Alternate Formats: online ● *Nondestructive Testing Handbook*. Covers all major methods of nondestructive testing. ● *Research in Nondestructive Evaluation*, quarterly. Journal. Covers experimental and theoretical investigations dealing with the scientific and engineering bases of NDE. **Price:** $55.00/year (print or online); $35.00 for overseas airmail delivery; $75.00/year (both print and online). Alternate Formats: online. Also Cited As: *RNDE*. **Conventions/Meetings:** semiannual conference and trade show, technical sessions (exhibits) - always spring and fall ● annual symposium, research (exhibits) - 2008 Nov. 10-14, Charleston, SC.

7788 ■ American Society of Test Engineers (ASTE)
PO Box 389
Nutting Lake, MA 01865-0389
E-mail: aste@earthlink.net
URL: http://www.astetest.org
Contact: Michael E. Keller, Exec. Dir./Ed.-in-Chief/ Acting Treas.
Founded: 1981. **Members:** 500. **Membership Dues:** individual, $40 (annual) ● corporate, $400 (annual) ● life (individual), $1,000 ● life (corporate), $5,000 ● full-time student, $15 (annual). **Description:** Companies involved in the electronic testing industry and instrumentation are corporate members; engineers who work in test engineering related fields are regular members. Seeks to foster improved communication among individuals and companies in the testing industry. Offers job referral service. **Awards: Type:** recognition. **Telecommunication Services:** electronic mail, mfreeman@broadcom.com. **Publications:** Newsletter, quarterly ● Proceedings, annual.

7789 ■ American Society for Testing and Materials (ASTM)
PO Box C700
West Conshohocken, PA 19428-2959
Ph: (610)832-9500 (610)832-9585
Fax: (610)832-9555
E-mail: jthomas@astm.org
URL: http://www.astm.org
Contact: James Thomas, Pres.
Founded: 1898. **Members:** 30,000. **Membership Dues:** informational, participating, $75 (annual) ● organization, $400 (annual). **Staff:** 170. **Budget:** $28,000,000. **Description:** Engineers, scientists, managers, professionals, academicians, consumers, and skilled technicians holding membership as individuals in or representatives of business firms, government agencies, educational institutions, and laboratories. Establishes standards for materials, products, systems, and services; has 129 technical committees (each having five to 50 subcommittees); new committees are organized periodically to keep pace with technological advances. Develops more than 11,000 standard test methods, specifications, classifications, definitions, and recommended practices now in use. **Telecommunication Services:** electronic mail, dfranco@astm.org. **Formerly:** (1902) American Section, International Association for Testing Materials. **Publications:** *Annual Book of ASTM Standards*, annual. Contains 75 volumes containing all current ASTM standards. Alternate Formats: CD-ROM ● *Cement, Concrete, and Aggregates Journal*, semiannual ● *Composites Technology and Research*, quarterly. Journal ● *Geotechnical Testing Journal*, quarterly ● *Journal of Testing and Evaluation*, bimonthly ● *Standardization News*, monthly. Magazine ● Reports. **Conventions/Meetings:** symposium - 20/year.

7790 ■ Controlled Environment Testing Association (CETA)
1500 Sunday Dr., Ste.102
Raleigh, NC 27607
Ph: (919)861-5576
Fax: (919)787-4916
E-mail: info@cetainternational.org
URL: http://www.cetainternational.org
Contact: Carl Labella, Pres.
Founded: 1992. **Members:** 275. **Membership Dues:** affiliate, $100 (annual) ● individual, $250 (annual) ● corporate (includes 3 reperesentatives; add $50/additional representative), $575 (annual). **Staff:** 3. **Description:** Certifiers, safety professionals, industrial hygienists, facility engineers, and a quality control personnel. Devoted to promoting and developing quality assurance within the controlled environment testing industry. Promotes environmental safety and occupational health. Develops standards; works with government and regulatory agencies; conducts continuing educational programs. **Committees:** Annual Conference Program; Education; Emerging Technologies; Performance Review; Spec Guide. **Subcommittees:** Bleedthrough; Troubleshooting; USP 797. **Publications:** *Performance Review*, 3/year. Journal. Provides technical articles and a forum for the free exchange of opinions and information. **Price:** included in membership dues; $60.00 /year for nonmembers ● Membership Directory. **Conventions/Meetings:** annual conference.

7791 ■ International Test and Evaluation Association (ITEA)
4400 Fair Lakes Ct., Ste.104
Fairfax, VA 22033-3801
Ph: (703)631-6220 (703)631-6222
Fax: (703)631-6221
E-mail: itea@itea.org
URL: http://www.itea.org
Contact: Lori Tremmel Freeman, Exec. Dir.
Founded: 1980. **Members:** 2,000. **Membership Dues:** individual, $45 (annual) ● foreign, $65 (annual) ● corporate, $745 (annual). **Staff:** 5. **Budget:** $500,000. **Regional Groups:** 5. **State Groups:** 24. **National Groups:** 3. **Description:** Test and evaluation professionals in 4 countries. Seeks to improve test and evaluation processes by applying managerial and technological techniques. Increases the effectiveness of tests and evaluations. Conducts technical symposia and educational seminars. **Awards:** Cross Award. **Frequency:** annual. **Type:** recognition. **Recipient:** for significant contributions to teaching, administration and research of testing and evaluation education ● Matthews Award. **Frequency:** annual. **Type:** recognition. **Recipient:** for contributions to testing and evaluation. **Telecommunication Services:** electronic mail, lfreeman@itea.org ● electronic mail, membership@itea.org. **Committees:** Awards; Corporate Development; Education; Events; Publications. **Divisions:** Facilities; Management/Policy; Technology/Methodology. **Publications:** *Corporate Newsletter*, quarterly. **Price:** free for corporate members ● *International Test and Evaluation Association—Symposia Proceedings*, annual. **Price:** free for attendees. **Circulation:** 300 ● *ITEA Journal of Test and Evaluation*, quarterly. Covers technical test and evaluation subjects, legislative developments, and association news; includes workshop synopsis. **Price:** included in membership dues; $60.00 /year for institutions. ISSN: 1054-0229. **Circulation:** 2,800. **Advertising:** accepted. **Conventions/Meetings:** annual meeting and symposium (exhibits) - 2008 Nov. 10-14, Atlantic City, NJ.

7792 ■ National Association for Proficiency Testing (NAPT)
8100 Wayzata Blvd.
St. Louis Park, MN 55426
Ph: (763)525-1488
Fax: (305)425-5728
E-mail: napt@proficiency.org
URL: http://www.proficiency.org
Contact: Chuck Ellis, Managing Dir.
Founded: 1996. **Description:** Provides professional management and program administration, coordination, data processing and reporting for interlaboratory comparisons, proficiency testing and round robins. Fosters development and dissemination of advanced technical knowledge in the metrology and testing community. Promotes improvement in measurement processes through increased knowledge and data integrity.

7793 ■ VXIbus Consortium
c/o Bob Helsel, Exec. Dir.
PO Box 1016
Niwot, CO 80544-1016
Ph: (303)652-2585
Fax: (303)652-1444
E-mail: bob.helsel@comcast.net
URL: http://www.vxibus.org
Contact: Bob Helsel, Exec. Dir.
Founded: 1987. **Membership Dues:** sponsor, $2,500 (annual). **Multinational. Description:** Pro-

motes VXIbus, the open standard platform for commercial ATE systems.

Textiles

7794 ■ American Association of Textile Chemists and Colorists (AATCC)
PO Box 12215
Research Triangle Park, NC 27709-2215
Ph: (919)549-8141 (919)549-3522
Fax: (919)549-8933
E-mail: danielsj@aatcc.org
URL: http://www.aatcc.org
Contact: John Y. Daniels, Exec. VP

Founded: 1921. **Members:** 5,000. **Membership Dues:** senior, associate, $100 (annual) ● senior, associate (in developing country), $50 (annual) ● corporate, $300-$4,800 (annual) ● student, $25 (annual) ● student (in developing country), $10 (annual). **Staff:** 22. **Budget:** $2,100,000. **Regional Groups:** 5. **Local Groups:** 13. **Multinational. Description:** Professional association for textile design, processing and testing. Works as an authority for industry standard test methods and evaluation procedures. **Libraries: Type:** open to the public. **Holdings:** articles, books, periodicals. **Subjects:** dyeing, finishing, Colour Index International. **Awards:** Millson Award for Invention. **Frequency:** annual. **Type:** recognition. **Recipient:** for significant invention in wet processing technology ● The Olney Medal. **Frequency:** annual. **Type:** medal. **Recipient:** for outstanding achievement in textile chemistry. **Telecommunication Services:** electronic mail, pattyb@aatcc.org. **Committees:** Technology and Research. **Programs:** Education. **Publications:** *AATCC Review*, monthly. Magazine. Contains information on textile design, processing and testing. **Price:** included in membership dues; $180.00 /year for nonmembers in U.S.; $210.00 /year for nonmembers outside U.S.; $25.00 single copy, for nonmembers in U.S. ● *AATCC Technical Manual*, annual ● *Buyer's Guide*, annual. Alternate Formats: online ● *IC&E Proceedings*, annual. Includes papers from International Conference and Exhibition. Alternate Formats: CD-ROM ● *Symposium Papers*, periodic ● Membership Directory, annual. Alternate Formats: online. **Conventions/Meetings:** annual international conference (exhibits).

7795 ■ American Society of Knitting Technologists (ASKT)
Address Unknown since 2007

Founded: 1960. **Members:** 135. **Description:** Knitting technologists in the outerwear, underwear, and hosiery industries. Fosters and encourages the development of knitting technology in both the weft and warp knitting fields; stimulates creativity of the knitting art; promotes knitting science through research. Provides a medium for the exchange of ideas. Acts as a liaison with similar organizations of knitting technologists overseas and analyzes and develops solutions to technological problems. Conducts seminars. Serves as the U.S. section of the International Federation of Knitting Technologists (see separate entry, *International Organizations*). **Committees:** Education; Publicity. **Affiliated With:** National Knitwear and Sportswear Association. **Publications:** *Directory of Members*, biennial. Membership Directory ● Newsletter, quarterly ● Also publishes knitting texts.

Thermal Analysis

7796 ■ Calorimetry Conference (CC)
c/o Michael Frenkel, Chm.
Natl. Inst. of Standards and Tech.
Thermodynamics Res. Center
Physical and Chem. Properties Div. 838
325 Broadway, Rm. 2-1010
Boulder, CO 80308-3328
Ph: (303)497-3952 (732)445-3958
Fax: (303)497-5044
E-mail: frenkel@boulder.nist.gov
URL: http://www.rmc.ca/academic/conference/CalConf/index.html
Contact: Michael Frenkel, Chm.

Founded: 1947. **Members:** 250. **Description:** Scientists interested in calorimetry (the measurement of heat), thermodynamics, and thermochemistry. Promotes improvement of presentation of calorimetric data, better instrumentation, purer samples, better thermometry, newer applications of calorimetry, and computer processing of calorimetric data. **Awards:** Hugh M. Huffman Memorial Award. **Frequency:** annual. **Type:** recognition. **Recipient:** for lifelong research accomplishments and contributions of 51 premier scientists to the field of thermodynamics ● James J. Christensen Award. **Type:** recognition. **Recipient:** for contributions to thermochemistry and thermodynamics ● Stig Sunner Memorial Award. **Type:** recognition. **Recipient:** to individuals 40 years of age or younger for the research contributions to thermodynamics and thermochemistry ● William F. Giangue Travel Award. **Frequency:** annual. **Type:** monetary. **Recipient:** for student participation in the conference. **Telecommunication Services:** electronic mail, cminetti@rci.rutgers.edu. **Committees:** Standards; Symbols and Nomenclature for Thermodynamic Functions. **Formerly:** (1950) Low Temperature Calorimetry Conference. **Conventions/Meetings:** annual conference (exhibits) - always summer.

7797 ■ North American Thermal Analysis Society (NATAS)
c/o Lois Hall, Staff Management Dir.
Thermal Anal. Lab.
Western Kentucky Univ.
Center for Res. and Development
2413 Nashville Rd.
Bowling Green, KY 42101
Ph: (270)745-2220 (302)427-4017
Fax: (270)745-2221
E-mail: natas@wku.edu
URL: http://www.natasinfo.org
Contact: Sima Chervin, Pres.

Founded: 1968. **Members:** 750. **Membership Dues:** full, $60 (annual) ● student, $10 (annual). **Description:** Professional society of thermal analysts. Seeks to improve communication among scientists and engineers using thermoanalytical methods and to provide a base for the dissemination of information pertaining to thermal analysis. Maintains speakers' bureau and placement service. **Awards: Frequency:** annual. **Type:** fellowship. **Recipient:** for members who have established outstanding achievements in the field of thermal analysis ● Mettler Outstanding Service Award. **Type:** recognition. **Recipient:** for individuals who have performed outstanding works in the utilization or creation of thermal techniques ● Outstanding Service Award. **Type:** recognition. **Recipient:** for members of at least three years and are neither past or present Chairs of the society ● PerkinElmer Student Award. **Type:** recognition. **Recipient:** for student papers. **Telecommunication Services:** electronic mail, rblaine@tainst.com. **Committees:** Awards; Education; Long Range Planning; Membership; NATAS Notes; Publicity/Marketing; Technical Program; Vendor Relations. **Affiliated With:** International Confederation for Thermal Analysis and Calorimetry. **Publications:** *NATAS Notes*, quarterly. Newsletter. Includes book reviews, calendar of events, and employment opportunities. **Price:** included in membership dues. **Advertising:** accepted. Alternate Formats: online ● *North American Thermal Analysis Society—Conference Proceedings*, annual. Reports on new applications of thermal methods and advances in instrumentation and automation. **Price:** $20.00/copy; $20.00 for nonmembers who attend conference ● *North American Thermal Analysis Society—Membership Directory*, annual. **Price:** included in membership dues. **Circulation:** 1,000. **Conventions/Meetings:** annual conference, for scientists and engineers (exhibits) ● annual meeting (exhibits).

Tires

7798 ■ Tire Society
PO Box 1502
Akron, OH 44309-1502
Ph: (330)929-5238
Fax: (330)929-3576
E-mail: tiresociety@neo.rr.com
URL: http://www.tiresociety.org
Contact: Howard Snyder, Office Mgr.

Membership Dues: full time student, $50 (annual) ● non-employed/retired, $100 (annual) ● full, $250 (annual). **Multinational. Description:** Promotes the science and technology of tires. **Libraries: Type:** not open to the public; reference. **Holdings:** 33; biographical archives, papers. **Subjects:** tire science and technology. **Awards:** Best Professional Paper Award. **Frequency:** annual. **Type:** recognition. **Recipient:** for best presentation of conference paper ● Student Paper Award. **Frequency:** annual. **Type:** monetary. **Recipient:** for best student paper presented at conference. **Publications:** *Tire Science and Technology*, quarterly. Journal. **Price:** included in membership dues; $125.00 for nonmembers; $50.00/back issue. Alternate Formats: online. **Conventions/Meetings:** annual conference, with meetings, presentations of papers and lecture - 2008 Sept. 15-16, Akron, OH.

Toxicology

7799 ■ American Board of Toxicology (ABT)
PO Box 30054
Raleigh, NC 27622-0054
Ph: (919)841-5022
Fax: (919)841-5042
E-mail: info@abtox.org
URL: http://www.abtox.org

Founded: 1979. **Staff:** 2. **Multinational. Description:** Certifies toxicologists. Administers annual certification and recertification exams. **Publications:** *Directory of Diplomates*, annual. Includes alphabetical listing of certified toxicologists. **Price:** $50.00.

7800 ■ American College of Toxicology (ACT)
9650 Rockville Pike
Bethesda, MD 20814
Ph: (301)634-7840
Fax: (301)634-7852
E-mail: ekagan@actox.org
URL: http://www.actox.org
Contact: Ms. Carol L. Lemire, Exec. Dir.

Founded: 1977. **Members:** 900. **Staff:** 2. **Multinational. Description:** Individuals interested in toxicology and related disciplines such as analytical chemistry, biology, pathology, teratology, and immunology. Addresses toxicological issues. Disseminates information and provides a forum for discussion of approaches to problems in the field in order to advance toxicological science and better serve society. **Libraries: Type:** open to the public. **Awards:** Arthur Furst Award. **Frequency:** annual. **Type:** recognition. **Recipient:** for best student paper presented at the annual meeting ● **Type:** recognition. **Telecommunication Services:** electronic mail, clemire@actox.org. **Publications:** *The International Journal of Toxicology*, bimonthly. Contains peer-reviewed papers in toxicology. **Advertising:** accepted ● Membership Directory, annual. **Price:** included in membership dues. **Circulation:** 900. **Conventions/Meetings:** annual meeting (exhibits) - 2008 Nov. 9-12, Tucson, AZ ● workshop.

7801 ■ CIIT Centers for Health Research
PO Box 12137
Research Triangle Park, NC 27709-2137
Ph: (919)558-1200 (919)558-1331
Fax: (919)558-1300
E-mail: ciitinfo@ciit.org
URL: http://www.ciit.org
Contact: William F. Greenlee PhD, Pres.

Founded: 1974. **Staff:** 150. **Budget:** $17,000,000. **Nonmembership. Description:** Chemical and pharmaceutical companies. Aims to develop the scientific data required for evaluation of the potential health risks of chemicals, pharmaceuticals, and consumer products. Works to: understand human health risk from occupational or environmental exposures; improve species extrapolations used in product safety evaluations; update the existing toxicological testing and investigation of commodity chemicals; develop improved testing methods; train professional toxicologists; serve health and environmental needs of the public through research in toxicology. Maintains scientific advisory panel. Provides fellowships for graduate and postdoctoral toxicological training. Conducts workshops. **Libraries: Type:** reference. **Holdings:** 25,000. **Awards:** Founders Award. **Frequency:** annual. **Type:** recognition. **Recipient:** for scientists making significant contributions to the field of toxicology ● **Type:** grant. **Formerly:** (2003) Chemical Industry Institute of Toxicology. **Publications:** *CIIT Activities*, monthly. Newsletter. Reviews research at CIIT. **Price:** free for investors. ISSN: 8755-4259. **Circulation:** 7,000. Alternate Formats: online.

7802 ■ Genetic Toxicology Association (GTA)
c/o Leon Stankowski, Treas.
Covance Labs.
9200 Leesburg Pike
Vienna, VA 22182
Ph: (302)366-6322
E-mail: leon.stankowski@covance.com
URL: http://www.gta-us.org
Contact: Ofelia Olivero, Chair
Founded: 1975. **Members:** 250. **Membership Dues:** full, $40 (annual) ● student, $20 (annual). **Description:** Academic, industrial, and governmental genetic toxicologists. (Genetic toxicology is the study of the mutagenic properties of substances; mutagenicity is the capacity to induce mutations.) Seeks to keep members abreast of recent developments in genetic toxicology. Sponsors tutorials on research findings. Conducts placement service. **Libraries: Type:** reference. **Holdings:** archival material. **Awards:** EMS Student Travel Award. **Frequency:** annual. **Type:** monetary. **Recipient:** for best EMS poster from Mid-Atlantic region student. **Telecommunication Services:** electronic mail, maria.donner@usa.dupont.com. **Publications:** Newsletter, semiannual. Contains meeting notices, upcoming workshops and news of interest to the membership. **Conventions/Meetings:** semiannual meeting (exhibits) - every spring and fall (usually the 3rd Thursday of May and October).

7803 ■ International Endotoxin and Innate Immunity Society (IEIIS)
c/o Nancy Pollman
3777 Eastside Hwy.
Stevensville, MT 59870
E-mail: info@ieiis.org
URL: http://www.ieiis.org
Contact: Nancy Pollman, Contact
Membership Dues: active, associate, $60 (annual) ● active, associate (plus journal subscription), $170 (annual) ● student, $15 (annual) ● student (plus journal subscription), $125 (annual). **Multinational. Description:** Promotes scientific knowledge on all aspects of endotoxin research. Seeks to propose endotoxin related nomenclatures and standardized abbreviations. Serves as an information center for the exchange of visiting scientists at pre- or postdoctoral or visiting professor levels. Provides an environment where all researchers will benefit from the exchange of data, views and experiences. **Awards:** Young Investigator Award. **Frequency:** biennial. **Type:** recognition. **Recipient:** for outstanding young investigator in the field of endotoxin research. **Telecommunication Services:** electronic mail, membership@ieiis.org. **Publications:** *Endotoxin Newsletter*, quarterly. Contains news about members and meetings, special articles, and other pertinent information. **Price:** included in membership dues. **Advertising:** accepted. Alternate Formats: online ● *Journal of Endotoxin Research*. Contains research articles, brief definitive reports, and mini-reviews. Alternate Formats: online. Also Cited As: *JER* ● Membership Directory. **Price:** included in membership dues. Alternate Formats: online.

7804 ■ Society of Toxicology (SOT)
1821 Michael Faraday Dr., Ste.300
Reston, VA 20190
Ph: (703)438-3115
Free: (800)826-6762
Fax: (703)438-3113
E-mail: sothq@toxicology.org
URL: http://www.toxicology.org
Contact: George B. Corcoran, Pres.
Founded: 1961. **Members:** 5,200. **Membership Dues:** full, associate, $135 (annual) ● postdoctoral, student, $20 (annual). **Staff:** 13. **Budget:** $4,500,000. **Regional Groups:** 18. **Multinational. Description:** Persons who have conducted and published original investigations in some phase of toxicology and who have a continuing professional interest in this field. (Toxicology is the quantitative study of materials that may or may not adversely affect the health of humans, animals, and/or the environment.). **Awards:** Achievement Award. **Frequency:** annual. **Type:** recognition. **Recipient:** for member who has made significant contribution to toxicology ● Arnold J. Lehman Award. **Frequency:** annual. **Type:** recognition. **Recipient:** for an individual who has made a contribution to risk assessment and/or the regulation of chemical agents. **Computer Services:** database, membership list. **Telecommunication Services:** electronic mail, corcoran@wayne.edu. **Boards:** Publications. **Committees:** Animals in Research; Awards; Continuing Education; Education; Finance; K-12 Education; Membership; Minority Initiatives; Nominating; Placement; Program; Regulatory/Legislative; Student Advisory; WWW Advisory. **Publications:** *Society of Toxicology—Membership Directory*, annual. Includes corporate member list and calendar of events; arranged by name, specialty, geographical location, and employer. **Price:** included in membership dues ● *Society of Toxicology—Newsletter*, quarterly. Includes calendar of events, chapter news, legislative news, obituaries, classified ads, and publications list. **Price:** included in membership dues ● *Toxicological Sciences*, monthly. Journal. Contains current research in the field of toxicology as it relates to pharmacology; includes book reviews. **Price:** included in membership dues; $264.00/year for U.S. and Canadian nonmembers; $313.00/year for overseas nonmembers. ISSN: 0272-0590. **Conventions/Meetings:** annual conference, with continuing education program (exhibits) ● annual meeting - 2009 Mar. 15-19, Baltimore, MD.

7805 ■ Toxicological History Society (THiS)
5757 Hall St. SE
Grand Rapids, MI 49546-3845
Ph: (616)391-9099
E-mail: venomous@iserv.net
Contact: John H. Trestrail III, Sec.
Founded: 1990. **Members:** 100. **Staff:** 1. **Description:** Individuals interested in the researching and documentation of the history of poisons, antidotes, and the impact of toxicology on events in world history. Maintains speakers' bureau; has compiled bibliography. **Libraries: Type:** reference. **Holdings:** 1,000; archival material, books. **Subjects:** toxicology, poisons. **Computer Services:** database, Index Toxicologicum-toxicology references published before 1960. **Absorbed:** Venomological Artifact Society. **Publications:** *Mithridata*, semiannual. Newsletter. **Price:** available to members only. **Circulation:** 100. **Conventions/Meetings:** annual North American Congress of Clinical Toxicology - conference (exhibits).

7806 ■ Toxicology Forum (TF)
1300 Eye St. NW, Ste.1010 E
Washington, DC 20005
Ph: (202)659-0030
Fax: (202)789-0905
E-mail: info@toxforum.org
URL: http://www.toxforum.org
Contact: Dr. David Longfellow PhD, Pres./COO
Founded: 1975. **Members:** 127. **Membership Dues:** individual, $70 (annual) ● associate, $1,400 (annual) ● corporate, $5,000-$15,000 (annual). **Staff:** 4. **Budget:** $200,000. **Description:** Represents corporations and individuals interested in toxicology and representing industry, government, universities, and laboratories throughout the world. Seeks to facilitate communication among scientific decision-makers. Aids to develop safety assessments and establishing regulations concerning toxicology. Areas of study and research reflect concerns of membership and the public, and have dealt with subjects such as epidemiology, biotechnology, genetics, carcinogens, saccharine, and caffeine. Maintains archives. **Libraries: Type:** reference. **Holdings:** archival material. **Awards:** George H. Scott Memorial Award. **Frequency:** annual. **Type:** recognition. **Recipient:** to an individual for an outstanding role in developing and applying the science of toxicology ● Philippe Shubik Distinguished Scientist Award. **Frequency:** annual. **Type:** recognition. **Recipient:** to an individual who has had a long and distinguished career and who has made outstanding contributions to the field of toxicology. **Telecommunication Services:** electronic mail, crytkonen@toxforum.org. **Publications:** *20XX European Toxicology Forum*, annual. Proceedings. Contains a direct transcription of the meeting proceedings. **Price:** $150.00 plus shipping and handling ● *20XX Summer Toxicology Forum*, annual. Proceedings. Contains a direct transcription of the meeting proceedings. **Price:** $150.00 plus shipping and handling. Alternate Formats: CD-ROM ● *20XX Winter Toxicology Forum*, annual. Survey. Contains a direct transcription of the meeting proceedings. **Price:** $150.00 plus shipping and handling. **Conventions/Meetings:** annual conference.

Translation

7807 ■ Association for Machine Translation in the Americas (AMTA)
c/o Priscilla Rasmussen, Business Mgr.
209 N 8th St.
Stroudsburg, PA 18360
Ph: (570)476-8006
Fax: (570)476-0860
E-mail: business@amtaweb.org
URL: http://www.amtaweb.org
Contact: Priscilla Rasmussen, Business Mgr.
Membership Dues: student, $50 (biennial) ● individual, $130 (biennial). **Multinational. Description:** Educates the public on important scientific techniques and principles involved in machine translation (MT). Provides opportunities for commercial developers, users, casual MT users and research scientists to meet and share ideas. **Affiliated With:** Asia-Pacific Association for Machine Translation; European Association for Machine Translation. **Publications:** *Compendium of Translation Software*, semiannual. Directory ● *MT Yellow Book*. Catalog. **Price:** included in membership dues. Alternate Formats: online.

Transportation

7808 ■ Advanced Transit Association (ATRA)
c/o Stan Young, Sec.
Box 220249
Boston, MA 02122-0013
Ph: (617)825-2318
E-mail: membership@advancedtransit.org
URL: http://www.advancedtransit.org
Contact: Bob Dunning, Pres.
Founded: 1976. **Members:** 100. **Membership Dues:** regular, $35 (annual) ● retired, $25 (annual) ● student, $15 (annual). **Description:** Engineers, planners, legislators, managers, consultants, property owners, policy analysts, professors, and other individuals interested in practical concepts for improving cost and service effectiveness of urban transportation. Established for education in the analysis, design, planning, and implementation of advanced transit systems. Conducts regional workshops on advanced transit issues and developments. **Libraries: Type:** reference. **Holdings:** articles. **Telecommunication Services:** electronic mail, webcommittee@advancedtransit.org. **Committees:** Technical. **Publications:** *ATRA Updates*, periodic. Newsletter ● *Journal of Advanced Transportation*, quarterly. **Conventions/Meetings:** periodic international conference ● annual meeting (exhibits).

7809 ■ Eno Transportation Foundation (ETF)
1634 I St. NW, Ste.500
Washington, DC 20006

Ph: (202)879-4700 (202)879-4718
Fax: (202)879-4719
E-mail: tdowns@enotrans.com
URL: http://www.enotrans.com
Contact: Tom Downs, Pres./CEO
Founded: 1921. **Staff:** 8. **Budget:** $1,700,000. **Description:** Seeks to educate the public and disseminate information about transportation in the U.S. Fosters careers in the field. Conducts research, educational programs, and policy forums; maintains museum; compiles statistics. Financed by an endowment made by William Phelps Eno. **Libraries: Type:** reference. **Holdings:** archival material, books, business records, clippings, monographs, periodicals. **Subjects:** transportation. **Telecommunication Services:** electronic mail, janet.abrams@enotrans.com. **Formerly:** (1968) Eno Foundation for Highway Traffic Control; (1991) Eno Foundation for Transportation. **Publications:** *Managing National Transportation Policy*. Book. **Price:** $20.00 ● *National Transportation Organizations*, biennial. Report. **Price:** $55.00 ● *Parking*. Book. Provides background on current practices in functional design, layout, and operation of parking facilities. **Price:** $35.00 ● *Parking for Institutions and Special Events*. Book. Provides information that is helpful in planning and designing cost-effective parking for institutions and special events. **Price:** $15.00 ● *Transportation in America*, annual. Analyzes traffic and costs of commercial and private freight and passenger transportation of all types in the U.S. **Price:** $55.00/year; $44.00 /year for libraries and bookstores. **Circulation:** 1,000 ● *Transportation Quarterly*. Journal. Reports on transportation planning, design, operation, and regulation. Includes tables, charts, graphs, and annual conference report. **Price:** $45.00/year in U.S.; $65.00/year outside U.S.; $16.25/issue in U.S.; $18.75/issue outside U.S. ISSN: 0278-9434. **Circulation:** 6,000. Alternate Formats: microform; online. **Conventions/Meetings:** annual Leadership Development Conference ● Management Conference - meeting - 5/year.

7810 ■ High Speed Ground Transportation Association (HSGTA)

1666 K St. NW, Ste.1100
Washington, DC 20006-1215
Ph: (202)261-6020
Fax: (202)496-4349
E-mail: info@hsgta.com
URL: http://peyser.com/hsgta
Contact: Charles Quandel, Chm.
Founded: 1983. **Members:** 800. **Membership Dues:** individual/organization (based on revenue), $300-$7,800 (annual). **Description:** Individuals, corporations, and agencies with an interest in high-speed rail transportation. Promotes development of safe and cost-effective high-speed rail passenger and freight services as an addition to existing transportation networks. "Provides connections to government and industry professionals interested in the application of advanced high-speed ground technologies." Serves as a clearinghouse on high-speed rail technologies and related fields; sponsors research and educational programs. **Conventions/Meetings:** annual conference.

7811 ■ Human Powered Vehicle Association (HPVA)

PO Box 1307
San Luis Obispo, CA 93406-1307
Ph: (805)772-5888
Free: (877)333-1029
Fax: (360)323-1384
E-mail: office@ihpva.org
URL: http://www.ihpva.org/hpva/index.html
Contact: Carole Leone, Sec.-Treas.
Founded: 1976. **Members:** 700. **Membership Dues:** regular in U.S., Canada and Mexico, $32 (annual) ● regular outside U.S., Canada and Mexico, $37 (annual). **Budget:** $30,000. **National Groups:** 3. **Multinational. Description:** Engineers, academic researchers, bicycling enthusiasts, and others representing over 30 countries interested in human-powered vehicles. Seeks to further the development of land, water, submarine and air varieties of human-powered vehicles of unrestricted design. Sanctions competitions and records set by human-powered vehicles. **Committees:** Air; All-Terrain; Land; Submarine; Water. **Formerly:** (1999) International Human Powered Vehicle Association. **Publications:** *HPV News*, quarterly. Newsletter. Includes calendar of events. **Price:** included in membership dues. ISSN: 0898-6894. **Circulation:** 800. **Advertising:** accepted ● *Human Power*, periodic. Journal. Includes technical articles on human-powered vehicles. **Price:** included in membership dues; $5.00 for nonmembers. ISSN: 0898-6908. **Circulation:** 800 ● Proceedings. **Conventions/Meetings:** annual International Human Powered Speed Championship - competition.

7812 ■ Institute of Transportation Engineers (ITE)

1099 14th St. NW, Ste.300 W
Washington, DC 20005-3438
Ph: (202)289-0222
Free: (800)982-4683
Fax: (202)289-7722
E-mail: ite_staff@ite.org
URL: http://www.ite.org
Contact: Earl E. Newman, Intl. Pres.
Founded: 1930. **Members:** 17,000. **Membership Dues:** student, $20 (annual) ● associate, $179-$193 (annual) ● individual, $210 (annual) ● retired, $105 (annual) ● institute (affiliate), $145 (annual) ● fellow, $240 (annual) ● life, $1,450 ● agency - minimum (based on number of professional employees), $925 (annual) ● agency - maximum (based on number of professional employees), $31,250 (annual). **Staff:** 24. **Budget:** $4,300,000. **Regional Groups:** 10. **State Groups:** 60. **Local Groups:** 93. **National Groups:** 5. **Multinational. Description:** Transportation engineers and professionals. Enables engineers and other professionals with knowledge and competence in transportation and traffic engineering to contribute individually and collectively toward meeting human needs for mobility and safety. Promotes professional development of members by the support and encouragement of education, stimulation of research, development of public awareness, exchange of professional information, and maintenance of a central point of reference and action. **Awards: Frequency:** annual. **Type:** fellowship. **Telecommunication Services:** electronic mail, sdollins@ite.org. **Committees:** Application of Control Devices; Design of Equipment; Geometric Design; Professional Standards and Education; Transportation Characteristics; Transportation Operations Measures; Transportation Planning. **Councils:** Consultants; Educators; Expert Witness; Industry; Intelligent Transportation Systems; Safety; Traffic Engineering; Transit; Transportation Demand Management. **Formerly:** (1976) Institute of Traffic Engineers. **Publications:** *ITE Journal*, monthly. Provides information on the planning, design, operation, and maintenance of surface transportation facilities. **Price:** included in membership dues; $65.00 /year for nonmembers. ISSN: 0162-8178. **Circulation:** 15,000. **Advertising:** accepted. Alternate Formats: online ● *Technical Papers from Annual Meeting* ● *Technical Standards and Recommended Practices* ● Also publishes handbooks, textbooks, technical reports, and technical bulletins. **Conventions/Meetings:** annual meeting (exhibits) - 2008 Aug. 17-20, Anaheim, CA; 2009 Aug. 9-12, San Antonio, TX; 2010 Aug. 8-11, Vancouver, BC, Canada.

7813 ■ Transportation Alternatives (TA)

127 W 26th St., Ste.1002
New York, NY 10001
Ph: (212)629-8080
Fax: (212)629-8334
E-mail: info@transalt.org
URL: http://www.transalt.org
Contact: Paul S. White, Exec. Dir.
Founded: 1973. **Members:** 5,500. **Membership Dues:** individual, $30 (annual) ● household, $50 (annual). **Staff:** 10. **Budget:** $800,000. **Local Groups:** 2. **Description:** Grassroots membership organization in New York City, primarily bicyclists and environmentalists united to support alternatives to the automobile, including walking, bicycling, and mass transit. Conducts research, lobbying, specialized education, and public relations programs; compiles statistics. Organizes direct events publishing traffic calming guide. Founder of Neighborhood Streets Network, a coalition of neighborhood-based organizations seeking safer streets through traffic calming and lower speed limits. Also founded Recycle A Bicycle program in local New York City schools. **Libraries: Type:** reference. **Subjects:** bicycling, environment, traffic calming. **Telecommunication Services:** electronic mail, volunteer2@transalt.org. **Publications:** *City Cyclist*, quarterly. Magazine. Includes Cycling News, Features and Editorial. **Price:** free. **Advertising:** accepted ● *Transportation Alternatives Magazine*, quarterly. Contains informative and provocative news and opinion on TA's campaigns and auto-free movements around the country and globe. **Price:** $30.00/year; $3.95 for members. **Circulation:** 6,500. **Advertising:** accepted. Alternate Formats: online.

7814 ■ Transportation Research Board (TRB)

c/o Keck Center of the National Academies
500 Fifth St. NW
Washington, DC 20001
Ph: (202)334-2934 (202)334-3213
Fax: (202)334-2003
E-mail: lwatson@golynx.com
URL: http://www.trb.org
Contact: Linda S. Watson, Chair
Founded: 1920. **Members:** 5,600. **Staff:** 132. **Budget:** $45,327,822. **Description:** A unit of the National Research Council. Encourages research and provides a national clearinghouse and correlation service for research activities and information on transportation technology. Studies all factors pertinent to the understanding, devising, and functioning of transportation systems and their interrelationships with other aspects of society. Is concerned with: the planning, design, construction, operation, maintenance, and safety of transportation systems and their components; the economics, financing, and administration of the systems; the interactions of these systems with the physical, economic, legal, and social environment they are designed to serve. Maintains 426 technical committees, task forces, and panels. Develops and maintains Transportation Research Information Services. **Libraries: Type:** reference. **Holdings:** 17,000; reports. **Subjects:** transportation. **Awards: Frequency:** annual. **Type:** recognition. **Recipient:** for distinguished service and outstanding papers in the field. **Computer Services:** database, transportation research. **Subcommittees:** Design and Construction of Transportation Facilities; Intergroup Resources and Issues; Legal Resources; Operation, Safety, and Maintenance of Transportation Facilities; Transportation Systems Planning and Administration. **Formerly:** (1974) Highway Research Board. **Publications:** *National Cooperative Highway Research Program* ● *Reports and Syntheses* ● *TR News*, bimonthly. Magazine. Includes research reviews, books reviews, calendar of events, and member profiles. **Price:** $55.00 in North America; $78.00 outside North America. **Circulation:** 9,000 ● *Transit Cooperative Research Program* ● *Transportation Research Board—Directory*, annual. Includes lists of committee members and TRB awards and recipients. ISSN: 0360-5078 ● *Transportation Research Board—Publications Catalog*, annual. Contains list of in-print publications; arranged by subject and series. ● *Transportation Research Board—Special Reports*, 5/year. Contains proceedings of transportation-related conferences, workshops, and research or policy studies on transportation issues. ISSN: 0360-859X. **Circulation:** 3,400 ● *Transportation Research Circular*. Reprints. ISSN: 0097-8515. **Circulation:** 3,400 ● *Transportation Research Record*, 40-50/year. Contains peer-reviewed papers on transportation research covering all models and aspects of transportation. **Price:** $1,960.00 in North America (hardcopy and CD-ROM); $680.00 in North America (CD-ROM); $2,150.00 outside North America (hardcopy and CD-ROM). ISSN: 0361-1981. **Circulation:** 3,400. Alternate Formats: CD-ROM. **Conventions/Meetings:** annual meeting - always January, Washington, DC.

7815 ■ Transportation Research Forum (TRF)

PO Box 5074
Fargo, ND 58105

Ph: (701)231-7767 (701)231-7718
Fax: (701)231-1945
E-mail: info@trforum.org
URL: http://www.trforum.org
Contact: John Wells, Pres.

Founded: 1960. **Members:** 400. **Membership Dues:** regular, $120 (annual) ● retired, $45 (annual) ● student, $30 (annual) ● library, $55 (annual) ● supporting, $175 (annual) ● sustaining, $325 (annual) ● sponsor, $1,000 (annual). **Description:** Individuals from government, industry, and academia interested in transportation research. Objectives are to: provide a forum for discussing new approaches to economic, managerial, and public policy problems involving transportation; promote the exchange of ideas and research techniques. **Awards:** Distinguished Transportation Researcher Award. **Frequency:** annual. **Type:** recognition. **Recipient:** for annual accomplishments ● Student Paper Awards. **Frequency:** annual. **Type:** recognition. **Recipient:** for three college students for outstanding research papers. **Publications:** *Journal of the Transportation Research Forum*, quarterly. Contains refereed papers. **Price:** included in membership dues. **Circulation:** 1,000 ● *Transportation Research Forum—Membership Directory*, annual. Lists TRF and Canadian Transportation Research Forum members. **Price:** included in membership dues. **Circulation:** 1,000 ● Proceedings, annual. Contains papers submitted at the Annual Meeting. **Price:** $20.00. Alternate Formats: CD-ROM ● Newsletter, quarterly. Includes calendar of events and award news. **Price:** included in membership dues. **Circulation:** 1,000. **Conventions/Meetings:** annual conference ● annual meeting - every spring.

Tropical Studies

7816 ■ Organization for Tropical Studies (OTS)
North Amer. Off.
Box 90630
Durham, NC 27708-0630
Ph: (919)684-5774 (919)684-6969
Fax: (919)684-5661
E-mail: ots@duke.edu
URL: http://www.ots.duke.edu
Contact: Elizabeth Losos, Pres./CEO

Founded: 1963. **Members:** 64. **Membership Dues:** institutional, $8,800 (annual) ● student, senior, $30 (annual). **Staff:** 160. **Budget:** $6,000,000. **Languages:** English, Spanish. **Multinational. Description:** Universities with established graduate-level programs in tropical studies and research institutions with tropical focus. Seeks to promote understanding of tropical environments and to provide a basis for intelligent use and conservation of the tropics. Offers field-oriented graduate-level courses in areas such as tropical ecology and wild lands management. Courses are taught in English, Spanish and Portuguese by visiting professors from universities and other institutions throughout the Americas. Although application is open to students from all colleges and universities, students from member institutions have preference. Offers science-based undergraduate study abroad program. Encourages individual investigators and research groups conducting similar studies. Takes advantage of the facilities located in diverse tropical environments. Operates in Costa Rica, Brazil, and Peru. Maintains three field stations and fleet of vehicles for rent. **Libraries: Type:** reference. **Holdings:** 4,000; articles, books. **Subjects:** tropical biology, natural resources. **Awards:** OTS fellowships. **Frequency:** semiannual. **Type:** grant. **Recipient:** for scientific merit. **Additional Websites:** http://www.ots.ac.cr. **Telecommunication Services:** electronic mail, elosos@duke.edu. **Also Known As:** (2000) Organizacion para Estudios Tropicales. **Publications:** *Liana*, semiannual. Newsletter. **Price:** $35.00/year. **Circulation:** 2,000. **Conventions/Meetings:** annual Assembly of Delegates - meeting and symposium, science topics - always spring in San Jose, Costa Rica.

Unions

7817 ■ Council of Engineers and Scientists Organizations (CESO)
c/o Charles Bofferding, Exec. Dir.
SPEEA, IFPTE Local 2001
15205 52nd Ave. S
Seattle, WA 98188
Ph: (206)433-0991
E-mail: ceso@usa.net
URL: http://www.cesounions.org
Contact: Charles Bofferding, Exec. Dir.

Founded: 1949. **Members:** 100,000. **Description:** Federation of engineering labor unions. **Publications:** *Sentinel*, periodic. Newsletter. Alternate Formats: online.

Utilities

7818 ■ American Backflow Prevention Association (ABPA)
PO Box 3051
Bryan, TX 77805-3051
Ph: (979)846-7606
Fax: (979)846-7607
E-mail: shane@abpa.org
URL: http://abpa.org
Contact: Rich Koenig, Pres.

Founded: 1984. **Membership Dues:** individual, $50 (annual). **Multinational. Description:** Represents the interests of individuals who have a common interest in protecting drinking water from contamination through cross-connections. Advances all aspects of backflow prevention for the continued protection of all water users. Provides educational programs and technical assistance in the field of backflow prevention to all water consumers. **Awards:** ABPA Meritorious Service Awards. **Frequency:** annual. **Type:** recognition. **Recipient:** for outstanding achievement and contribution to the backflow prevention and cross-connection control industry ● Golden Eagle Awards. **Frequency:** annual. **Type:** recognition. **Recipient:** for an individual who contributed to the success of his or her chapter, region or the national association ● Presidential Award for Chapter Excellence. **Frequency:** annual. **Type:** recognition. **Recipient:** for chapters. **Computer Services:** Online services, discussion forum.

7819 ■ North American Society for Trenchless Technology (NASTT)
1655 N Ft. Myer Dr., Ste.700
Arlington, VA 22209
Ph: (703)351-5252
Fax: (703)739-6672
E-mail: jhemphill@nastt.org
URL: http://www.nastt.org
Contact: John G. Hemphill, Exec. Dir.

Founded: 1990. **Members:** 820. **Membership Dues:** individual, $200 (annual) ● governmental/educational institution, $300 (annual) ● corporate/organizational, $1,000 (annual). **Staff:** 3. **Budget:** $750,000. **Regional Groups:** 4. **Description:** Public utilities, engineers, contractors, regulators, educators, researchers, manufacturers, suppliers, and students interested in technology relating to the installation and rehabilitation of water, sewage, gas, telecommunications, and electrical services without using trenching operations. Promotes the transfer of technology; develops guidelines and specifications; represents the interests of members. Conducts research and educational programs. **Committees:** Cable, Gas, Sewer, Water; Directional Drilling; Education/Public Relations; Horizontal Earth Boring; Membership; Microtunneling; Pipe Jacking; Safety. **Affiliated With:** International Society for Trenchless Technology. **Publications:** *Membership List*, periodic. Membership Directory ● *No-Dig International Magazine*, monthly ● *Standards*, periodic ● *Trenchless Technology Magazine*, monthly ● *Trenchless Times*, bimonthly. Newsletter. **Conventions/Meetings:** annual NO-DIG - conference (exhibits).

7820 ■ UCA International Users Group (UCAlug)
10604 Candler Falls Ct.
Raleigh, NC 27614
Ph: (919)847-2241
Fax: (919)869-2700
E-mail: kay@ucausersgroup.org
URL: http://sharepoint.ucausersgroup.org
Contact: Kay Clinard, Pres.

Membership Dues: individual, $250 (annual) ● company, utility, vendor, university, trade association, $1,000-$5,000 (annual). **Multinational. Description:** Represents utility user and supplier companies. Promotes the integration and interoperability of electric/gas/water utility systems through the use of international standards-based technology. Provides a forum for stakeholders of utility industry. **Telecommunication Services:** electronic mail, jack@ucausersgroup.org.

7821 ■ United States Combined Heat and Power Association (USCHPA)
Natl. HQ
218 D St. SE
Washington, DC 20003
Ph: (202)544-4565
Fax: (202)544-0043
E-mail: uschpa-hq@admgt.com
URL: http://www.uschpa.org
Contact: John Jimison, Exec. Dir./Gen. Counsel

Founded: 1999. **Membership Dues:** corporate (based on gross annual revenues), $750-$7,500 (annual) ● associate, $2,000 (annual) ● user (based on gross annual revenues), $500-$1,000 (annual) ● individual, $225 (annual) ● student, $25 (annual). **Description:** Promotes the use of clean and efficient Combined Heat and Power (CHP) as a major source of electric power and thermal energy in the United States. Educates the public about CHP. Creates opportunities for members to network with each other and participate in federal programs.

Vacuum Technology

7822 ■ AVS Science and Technology Society (AVS)
120 Wall St., 32nd Fl.
New York, NY 10005
Ph: (212)248-0200
Free: (800)888-1021
Fax: (212)248-0245
E-mail: yvonne@avs.org
URL: http://www.avs.org
Contact: Neal D. Shinn, Pres.

Founded: 1953. **Members:** 5,500. **Membership Dues:** student, $25 (annual) ● full, $95 (annual) ● post doc, $45 (annual). **Staff:** 6. **Local Groups:** 20. **Description:** Scientists, engineers, and others interested in vacuum science and engineering. Promotes education and research in vacuum technology; establishes standards for nomenclature, measuring techniques, and such items as flanges and fittings on vacuum equipment. Sponsors short courses in basic vacuum technology. Presents honorary memberships. **Awards:** Albert Nerken Award. **Frequency:** annual. **Type:** recognition. **Recipient:** for outstanding contributions to the solution of technological problems ● AVS Graduate Research Awards. **Frequency:** annual. **Type:** recognition. **Recipient:** for graduate studies in the field of sciences and technologies ● Gaede-Langmuir Award. **Frequency:** annual. **Type:** recognition. **Recipient:** for outstanding discoveries and inventions in sciences and technologies ● George T. Hanyo Award. **Frequency:** annual. **Type:** recognition. **Recipient:** for outstanding performance in technical support of research or development ● John A. Thorton Memorial Award and Lecture. **Frequency:** annual. **Type:** recognition. **Recipient:** for outstanding research or technological innovation, with emphasis on the fields of thin films, plasma processing and related topics ● Medard W. Welch Award in Vacuum Science. **Frequency:** annual. **Type:** recognition. **Recipient:** for outstanding research in the fields of interest to the AVS ● Nellie Yeoh Whetten

Award. **Frequency:** annual. **Type:** recognition. **Recipient:** for excellence by women in graduate studies in the sciences and technologies ● Peter Mark Memorial Award. **Frequency:** annual. **Type:** recognition. **Recipient:** for outstanding theoretical or experimental work by a young scientist or engineer ● Russell and Sigurd Varian Fellowship. **Frequency:** annual. **Type:** fellowship. **Recipient:** for excellence in continuing graduate studies in the sciences and technologies ● Welch Foundation Scholarship. **Frequency:** annual. **Type:** scholarship. **Recipient:** to researchers working for one year in a country in which they have not previously studied. **Telecommunication Services:** electronic mail, membership@avs.org. **Divisions:** Advanced Surface Engineering; Applied Surface Science; Electronic Materials and Processing; Nanometer Scale Science and Technology; Plasma Science and Technology Surface Science; Thin Film; Vacuum Metallurgy; Vacuum Technology. **Affiliated With:** American Institute of Physics. **Formerly:** Committee on Vacuum Technology; American Vacuum Society. **Publications:** *Journal of Vacuum Science and Technology A*, bimonthly. **Advertising:** accepted. Alternate Formats: online; CD-ROM ● *Journal of Vacuum Science and Technology B*, bimonthly ● *Surface Science Spectra*, quarterly. Journal. **Conventions/Meetings:** annual International Symposium - meeting (exhibits).

Water Resources

7823 ■ American Institute of Hydrology (AIH)

300 Village Green Cir., Ste.201
Smyrna, GA 30080
Ph: (770)384-1634 (573)308-3679
Free: (800)970-4244
Fax: (770)438-6172
E-mail: aihydro@aol.com
URL: http://www.aihydro.org
Contact: Ms. Cathryn Seaburn, Gen. Mgr.

Founded: 1981. **Members:** 1,200. **Membership Dues:** organizational (large), $250 (annual) ● organizational (small), $135 (annual). **Staff:** 2. **Budget:** $150,000. **State Groups:** 48. **Multinational. Description:** Professional hydrologists and hydrogeologists. Seeks to enhance and strengthen the standing of hydrology as a profession. Certifies and registers professionals in all fields of hydrological sciences. Establishes standards and procedures to certify qualified individuals. Conducts educational programs. **Libraries: Type:** reference. **Holdings:** 20. **Subjects:** hydrology. **Awards:** C.V. Theis Award. **Frequency:** annual. **Type:** recognition. **Recipient:** for outstanding contribution in ground water hydrology ● Ray K. Linsley Award. **Frequency:** annual. **Type:** recognition. **Recipient:** for outstanding contribution in surface water hydrology. **Computer Services:** Mailing lists. **Telecommunication Services:** electronic mail, ecwitt@usgs.gov. **Boards:** Certification and Editorial. **Committees:** Continuing Education; Examination; Institute Development; Inter-Society; International. **Publications:** *Advances in Ground-Water Hydrology: A Decade of Progress*. Book. **Price:** $35.00 ● *American Institute of Hydrology—Bulletin*, quarterly. **Price:** included in membership dues. **Circulation:** 1,000. **Advertising:** accepted ● *First USA/USSR Joint Conference on Environmental Hydrology and Hydrogeology*. Book. **Price:** $25.00 ● *Gambling with Ground Water*. Book. **Price:** $50.00 ● *Hydrological Sciences and Technology*, quarterly. Journal. **Price:** $24.00 /year for members; $80.00 /year for nonmembers; $100.00 /year for libraries. ISSN: 0887-686X ● *Hydrology and Hydrogeology in the '90s*. Book. **Price:** $25.00 ● *Hydrology and Hydrogeology of Urban and Urbanizing Areas*. Book. **Price:** $55.00 ● *Industrial and Agricultural Impacts on the Hydrologic Environment*. Book. **Price:** $85.00 ● *Interdisciplinary Approaches in Hydrology and Hydrogeology*. Book. **Price:** $20.00 ● *Minimizing Risk to the Hydrologic Environment*. Book. **Price:** $20.00 ● *Recent Advances in Ground-Water Hydrology*. Book. **Price:** $25.00 ● *Registry of Professional Hydrologists and Hydrogeologists*, annual. **Price:** included in membership dues; $125.00 /year for nonmembers ● *Third USA/CIS Joint Conference on Environmental Hydrology and Hydrogeology*. Book. **Price:** $55.00 ● *Toxic Substances and the Hydrologic Sciences*. Book. **Price:** $35.00 ● *Urban and Urbanizing Areas: Hydrology and Hydrology*. Book. **Price:** $55.00 ● *US EPA WHPAS Model, Version 2.0 - A Modular Semi-Analytical Model for the Delineation of Wellhead Protection Areas* ● *Water Resources at Risk*. Book. **Price:** $55.00. **Conventions/Meetings:** annual conference (exhibits).

7824 ■ American Membrane Technology Association (AMTA)

2409 SE Dixie Hwy.
Stuart, FL 34996
Ph: (772)463-0820
Fax: (772)463-0860
E-mail: admin@amtaorg.com
URL: http://www.amtaorg.com
Contact: Janet L. Jaworski, Admin. Dir.

Founded: 1973. **Members:** 400. **Membership Dues:** public agency/manufacturer/supplier/consultant/engineering (with less than 50 employees), $350 (annual) ● public agency/manufacturer/supplier/consultant/engineering (with 50 or more employees), $675 (annual) ● individual, university/college professor, $200 (annual) ● library, student, $50 (annual) ● affiliate, $125 (annual). **Staff:** 4. **Budget:** $350,000. **Regional Groups:** 1. **Multinational. Description:** Water supply agencies; manufacturers of desalting equipment, design and construction companies, advanced water sciences and technologies consultants; individuals, academicians, and librarians. Advances research and development programs in desalination, wastewater reclamation, and other water sciences; promote programs of water supply and urban environment improvement. Sponsors training of water treatment plant operators. Sponsors seminars and workshops. **Awards:** Conference Best Paper Award. **Frequency:** biennial. **Type:** recognition ● Conference Best Poster Presentation Award. **Frequency:** biennial. **Type:** recognition ● Distinguished Service Award. **Frequency:** biennial. **Type:** recognition ● Lifetime Achievement Award - Hall of Fame Award. **Type:** recognition ● Outstanding Member Award. **Frequency:** biennial. **Type:** recognition ● Presidential. **Frequency:** biennial. **Type:** recognition. **Recipient:** to more than 1 person ● Robert O. Vernon Award. **Frequency:** biennial. **Type:** recognition ● Water Quality Person of the Year. **Frequency:** biennial. **Type:** recognition. **Committees:** Annual Meeting; Audit; Awards; Bylaws; Concentrate Disposal; Executive; Finance; Government Programs; International Liaison; Membership; Nominating; Program/Biennial Conference; Publications; Regional Affiliation; Regulatory Permitting Guidelines; Technology Transfer. **Affiliated With:** International Desalination Association; Southeast Desalting Association; WateReuse Association. **Formerly:** (1993) National Water Supply Improvement Association; (2003) American Desalting Association. **Publications:** *Conference Proceedings*, biennial. **Advertising:** accepted. Alternate Formats: CD-ROM ● *Membrane Source Sheet* ● Membership Directory. **Conventions/Meetings:** biennial conference (exhibits) ● seminar - 3/year ● annual workshop.

7825 ■ American Rainwater Catchment Systems Association (ARCSA)

4065 Broadway
San Antonio, TX 78209
E-mail: president@arcsa-usa.org
URL: http://www.arcsa-usa.org
Contact: Heather Kinkade-Levario, Pres.

Membership Dues: individual, $30 (annual) ● business, $60 (annual) ● student, $15 (annual) ● life (individual), $150 ● life (business), $300. **Regional Groups:** 5. **Description:** Promotes rainwater catchment systems in the United States. Provides networking between people with experience in rainwater catchment systems and people who need technical and professional assistance in developing catchment systems. Creates a forum for discussion of new methods, techniques and materials pertaining to rainwater catchment systems. Establishes treatment method for harvested rainwater. **Publications:** Newsletter. Alternate Formats: online ● Proceedings. **Price:** $50.00 for members; $60.00 for nonmembers.

7826 ■ American Society of Irrigation Consultants (ASIC)

125 Paradise Ln.
PO Box 426
Rochester, MA 02770
Ph: (508)763-8140 (816)842-8999
Fax: (508)763-8102
E-mail: info@asic.org
URL: http://www.asic.org
Contact: Norman F. Bartlett, Exec. Dir.

Founded: 1970. **Members:** 270. **Membership Dues:** professional, associate, $330 (annual) ● affiliate, $220 (annual) ● allied, student, $55 (annual) ● apprentice, $110 (annual). **Budget:** $175,000. **Regional Groups:** 5. **Description:** Irrigation consultants, landscape architects, manufacturers, and equipment suppliers. Advances the field of irrigation design and consultation; promotes ethical practices in the profession. Monitors licensing. **Awards:** Roy Williams Memorial Award. **Frequency:** annual. **Type:** recognition ● Sam Tobey Lifetime Achievement Award. **Type:** recognition. **Telecommunication Services:** electronic mail, normanb@asic.org. **Committees:** Uniform Standards. **Affiliated With:** Irrigation Association. **Publications:** *Irrigation Design Standards* ● *Membership Roster*, annual. Membership Directory ● *The Waterfront*, quarterly. Newsletter. **Advertising:** accepted. Alternate Formats: online. **Conventions/Meetings:** annual conference (exhibits).

7827 ■ American Water Resources Association (AWRA)

PO Box 1626
Middleburg, VA 20118-1626
Ph: (540)687-8390 (256)650-0701
Fax: (540)687-8395
E-mail: info@awra.org
URL: http://www.awra.org
Contact: Kenneth D. Reid CAE, Exec. VP

Founded: 1964. **Members:** 3,000. **Membership Dues:** regular, $150 (annual) ● corporate, $425 (annual) ● institutional, $325 (annual) ● student, $30 (annual) ● retired, $75 (annual) ● international, $25 (annual). **Staff:** 7. **Budget:** $1,000,000. **State Groups:** 20. **Multinational. Description:** Engineers; natural, physical, and social scientists; other persons engaged in any aspect of the field of water resources; business concerns and other organizations; students in water resources. Includes members from 62 nations. Seeks to advance water resources research, planning, development, and management. Endeavors to collect and disseminate ideas and information relative to water resources science and technology via scientific journal, newsletter, conferences and symposia and published proceedings. **Awards:** A. Ivan Johnson Outstanding Young Professional Award. **Frequency:** annual. **Type:** recognition. **Recipient:** for young professionals as the future leaders of water resources research ● Fellow Member Award. **Frequency:** annual. **Type:** fellowship ● Henry P. Caulfield, Jr. **Frequency:** annual. **Type:** recognition ● Honorary Member Award. **Frequency:** annual. **Type:** recognition ● Icko Iben Award. **Frequency:** annual. **Type:** recognition ● Mary H. Marsh Medal. **Frequency:** annual. **Type:** medal ● Sandor C. Csallany Award. **Frequency:** annual. **Type:** recognition ● William C. Ackermann Medal. **Frequency:** annual. **Type:** medal. **Computer Services:** database ● mailing lists. **Telecommunication Services:** electronic mail, ken@awra.org. **Publications:** *Journal of the American Water Resources Association*, bimonthly. Contains peer-reviewed research papers, book reviews, information on litigation and legislation, meetings calendar, and corporate membership list. **Price:** included in membership dues; $385.00 /year for nonmembers. ISSN: 0043-1370. **Circulation:** 4,300. Alternate Formats: online ● *Proceedings of AWRA's Symposia*, 3/year. Alternate Formats: online; CD-ROM ● *Water Resources IMPACT*, bimonthly. Magazine. Provides information on water-related topics. Includes meetings calendar. **Price:** included in membership dues; $75.00 /year for nonmembers in U.S.; $90.00 /year for nonmembers outside U.S. **Cir-**

culation: 4,200. **Advertising:** accepted. Alternate Formats: online. **Conventions/Meetings:** annual American Water Resources Conference (exhibits) ● annual AWRA Spring Specialty Conference (exhibits) ● annual AWRA Summer Specialty Conference.

7828 ■ Association of Ground Water Scientists and Engineers - A Division of National Ground Water Association (AGWSE)
601 Dempsey Rd.
Westerville, OH 43081-8978
Ph: (614)898-7791
Free: (800)551-7379
Fax: (614)898-7786
E-mail: smasters@ngwa.org
URL: http://www.ngwa.org/agwse/index.aspx
Contact: Sandy Masters, Contact
Founded: 1963. **Members:** 11,000. **Membership Dues:** individual, $110 (annual) ● company, $290 (annual) ● additional company employee, $85 (annual) ● student, $25 (annual) ● international electronic, international student, $40 (annual) ● individual international, $125 (annual) ● company international, $305 (annual) ● additional company employee international, $100 (annual). **Staff:** 37. **Description:** A technical division of the National Ground Water Association. Hydrogeologists, geologists, hydrologists, civil and environmental engineers, geochemists, biologists, and scientists in related fields. Seeks to: provide leadership and guidance for scientific, economical, and beneficial groundwater development; promote the use, protection, and management of the world's groundwater resources. Conducts educational programs, seminars, short courses, symposia, and field research projects. Maintains speakers' bureau and museum; offers placement service; sponsors competitions; compiles statistics. **Libraries: Type:** reference. **Holdings:** 40,000. **Awards:** John Hem Award. **Frequency:** annual. **Type:** recognition ● Keith E. Anderson Award. **Frequency:** annual. **Type:** recognition ● Life Member Award. **Frequency:** annual. **Type:** recognition ● M. King Hubbert Award. **Frequency:** annual. **Type:** recognition. **Computer Services:** database, bibliographic on groundwater literature ● database, legislative on water-related licensing and construction standards throughout the US. **Committees:** Aquifer Protection; Certification; Regulatory. **Formerly:** (1985) Ground Water Technology Division of the National Water Well Association. **Publications:** *Association of Ground Water Scientists and Engineers—Membership Directory*, triennial ● *Ground Water*, bimonthly. Journal. Contains peer-reviewed scientific articles on pertinent ground water subjects. **Price:** included in membership dues; $260.00 /year for nonmembers. ISSN: 0017-467X. **Circulation:** 12,000. Also Cited As: *Journal of Ground Water* ● *Ground Water Monitoring & Remediation*, quarterly. Journal. Focuses on the protection and restoration of groundwater. Includes advertisers index and equipment news. **Price:** included in membership dues; $92.00 /year for nonmembers. ISSN: 0277-1926. **Circulation:** 12,000. **Advertising:** accepted ● *Newsletter of the Association of Ground Water Scientists and Engineers*, bimonthly. Includes items of interest to members. **Price:** included in membership dues. **Circulation:** 11,000. **Conventions/Meetings:** annual meeting, held in conjunction with NGWA (exhibits).

7829 ■ Groundwater Management Caucus (GMC)
PO Box 905
Colby, KS 67701-0905
Ph: (785)462-3915 (785)443-2642
Fax: (785)462-2693
E-mail: wab@gmd4.org
URL: http://www.gmd4.org
Contact: Wayne Bossert, Mgr.
Founded: 1974. **Members:** 156. **Membership Dues:** individual, $20 (annual) ● affiliate, $90 (annual) ● organizational, $150 (annual) ● district, $200 (annual). **Staff:** 1. **Budget:** $10,000. **Regional Groups:** 133. **State Groups:** 6. **Description:** A unit of the National Water Resources Association. Directors and staff members of water and natural resource districts; members of related institutions and organizations; universities. Provides a forum for the exchange of information concerning groundwater management and conservation technology and research. Encourages members to actively participate in related legislative activities. Current emphasis is on energy conservation and efficiency in groundwater management. **Libraries: Type:** reference. **Subjects:** groundwater management, conservation. **Awards:** GMDA Promoter of the Year. **Frequency:** annual. **Type:** recognition ● Honorary Life Member. **Frequency:** annual. **Type:** recognition ● Water Resource Person of the Year. **Frequency:** annual. **Type:** recognition. **Affiliated With:** National Water Resources Association. **Formerly:** (1985) Groundwater Management Districts Association. **Publications:** Newsletter. Alternate Formats: online. **Conventions/Meetings:** annual conference, held in conjunction with NWRA (exhibits) ● annual meeting.

7830 ■ International Association of Hydrogeologists (IAH-USNC)
c/o Todd Halihan, Sec.-Treas.
105 NRC, School of Geology
Oklahoma State Univ.
Stillwater, OK 74078
Ph: (405)372-8611
E-mail: halihan@okstate.edu
URL: http://www.iah.org
Contact: Todd Halihan, Sec.-Treas.
Founded: 1956. **Members:** 300. **Membership Dues:** student, $39 (annual) ● regular, $79 (annual) ● corporate, $425 (annual). **Description:** Hydrogeologists. United States chapter of the IAH. Works to promote international cooperation among hydrogeologists; to advance the science of hydrogeology worldwide; and to facilitate the international exchange of information on groundwater. Affiliated with the International Union of Geological Sciences and participates in the International Hydrological Programme of UNESCO. Conducts charitable programs. **Computer Services:** Mailing lists. **Publications:** *Hydrogeology Journal*, bimonthly. ISSN: 1431-2174. **Advertising:** accepted. Alternate Formats: online.

7831 ■ International Desalination Association (IDA)
PO Box 387
Topsfield, MA 01983
Ph: (978)887-0410
Fax: (978)887-0411
E-mail: info@idadesal.org
URL: http://www.idadesal.org
Contact: Mr. Jose Antonio Medina, Pres.
Founded: 1985. **Members:** 1,000. **Membership Dues:** corporation/utility, $750 (annual) ● small company, $500 (annual) ● individual, $55-$85 (annual) ● student, non-profit library, $25 (annual). **Staff:** 4. **Regional Groups:** 5. **Multinational. Description:** Users and suppliers of desalination equipment; water reuse and reclamation consultants. Seeks to develop and promote worldwide application of desalination and desalination technology in maintaining water supplies, controlling water pollution, and purifying, treating, and reusing water. Disseminates information on desalination-related subjects and water reuse. Encourages the establishment of standards, specifications, procedures, and the efficient use of water for energy. Conducts seminars and workshops. **Libraries: Type:** reference. **Holdings:** archival material, periodicals. **Awards: Frequency:** biennial. **Type:** recognition ● **Type:** scholarship. **Formed by Merger of:** International Desalination and Environmental Association; Water Supply Improvement Association. **Publications:** *Conference Proceedings*, biennial ● *IDA Desalination and Water Reuse Quarterly*. Magazine. **Price:** $71.00 for nonmembers. **Circulation:** 6,000. **Advertising:** accepted ● *IDA Membership Directory*, annual ● *IDA Newsletter*, bimonthly ● Monographs ● Also publishes inventories and produces computer software. **Conventions/Meetings:** biennial World Congress on Desalination and Water Reuse - meeting (exhibits).

7832 ■ International Rainwater Catchment Systems Association (IRCSA)
c/o Trisha Macomber
UH-CTAHR-NREM
875 Komohana St.
Hilo, HI 96720
E-mail: orojessie@yahoo.com
URL: http://www.ircsa.org
Contact: Dr. Jessica C. Salas, Pres.
Founded: 1989. **Membership Dues:** individual, $20 (annual) ● student, $10 (annual) ● individual with spouse, $30 (annual) ● institutional, $200 (annual) ● life, $150. **Multinational. Description:** Promotes the rainwater catchment system technology with respect to planning, development, management, science, technology, research and education. Establishes an international forum for individuals concerned with rainwater catchment systems. Drafts international guidelines for rainwater catchment system technology. **Computer Services:** Information services, factsheets on rainwater harvesting ● mailing lists.

7833 ■ International Rivers Network (IRN)
1847 Berkeley Way
Berkeley, CA 94703
Ph: (510)848-1155
Fax: (510)848-1008
E-mail: info@irn.org
URL: http://www.irn.org
Contact: Martha Belcher, Chair
Founded: 1985. **Members:** 3,000. **Membership Dues:** regular, $35-$250 (annual) ● low-income/student, $20 (annual). **Staff:** 20. **Budget:** $1,000,000. **Languages:** Chinese, English, French, German, Portuguese, Spanish. **Multinational. Description:** Environmental and human rights nongovernmental organizations and activists; water professionals. Primary purpose is to update and foster development of water policy worldwide by providing a means of communication between members. Publicizes problems with and alternatives to large water projects. Assists in local efforts to stop what the group consider large, destructive dam projects, particularly in the Third World. Promotes research and disseminates information about solutions to social and environmental problems. Campaigns against World Bank funding of water projects that are destructive to the environment. Believes that unless action is taken, most of the world's major rivers will be dammed within the next 25 years, and that modern dams precipitate environmental problems including relocation and cultural destruction, increases in hunger and disease, loss of endangered species, and destruction of rain forests. Maintains speakers' bureau. **Libraries: Type:** reference. **Holdings:** archival material, books, clippings, periodicals, photographs, video recordings. **Subjects:** rivers, water, energy, environment, human rights, dams, hydropower. **Computer Services:** Mailing lists. **Telecommunication Services:** electronic mail, irn@irn.org. **Affiliated With:** Friends of the Earth International. **Formerly:** (1986) International Dams Newsletter. **Publications:** *River Revival*, monthly. Bulletin. Alternate Formats: online ● *World Rivers Review*, bimonthly. Newsletter. **Price:** $35.00 for members; $50.00 for nonmember organizations; $100.00 for nonmember institutions. Alternate Formats: online ● Annual Report, annual. Alternate Formats: online ● Books ● Videos ● Also publishes mail alerts and flyers.

7834 ■ International Water Resources Association (IWRA)
c/o Southern Illinois University
4535 Faner Hall
Carbondale, IL 62901-4516
Ph: (618)453-6021 (618)453-5138
Fax: (618)453-6465
E-mail: iwra@iwra.net
URL: http://www.iwra.net
Contact: Ben Dziegielewski, Exec. Dir.
Founded: 1972. **Members:** 2,000. **Membership Dues:** regular (developed country), $75 (annual) ● student (developed country), $35 (annual) ● regular (developing country), $40 (annual) ● student/retiree (developing country), $25 (annual) ● retiree (developed country), regular (developed country, online only), $45 (annual) ● student/regular/retiree (developed country, online only), $25 (annual) ● fellow (developed country), $85 (annual) ● fellow (developing country), $50 (annual) ● institution, $270 (annual) ● corporation, $430 (annual) ● student/retiree (developing country, online only), $15 (annual). **Staff:**

4. **Description:** Individuals and organizations interested in water resources development. Seeks to: advance the planning, development, management, education, and research of water resources; establish an international forum for those concerned with water resources; encourage international programs in the field of water resources; cooperate with other organizations of common interest. **Libraries: Type:** open to the public. **Holdings:** 27. **Awards:** The Best Paper Award. **Frequency:** annual. **Type:** recognition. **Recipient:** to the author of the most outstanding paper published in *Water International* during the year ● Chow Memorial Endowed Lecturer. **Type:** recognition. **Recipient:** to an internationally acclaimed expert in a water resources field in recognition of his or her exemplary service to science and humanity ● Crystal Drop Award. **Frequency:** triennial. **Type:** recognition. **Recipient:** to individuals or organizations in recognition of their long-term contribution to improving the world's water situation ● IWRA Distinguished Lecturer. **Frequency:** annual. **Type:** recognition. **Recipient:** for ingenuity and resourcefulness in adapting water resources technology in a water management program. **Computer Services:** Mailing lists, of members ● online services, membership expertise directory. **Telecommunication Services:** electronic mail, benedykt@siu.edu. **Committees:** Dispute Resolution; Geographical; Water for the 21st Century. **Publications:** *IWRA Update*, quarterly. Newsletter. **Price:** included in membership dues. **Circulation:** 1,000. Alternate Formats: online ● *Water International*, quarterly. Journal. Covers Association's news, activities, and events in the international water resources field. Includes research reports, and calendar of events. **Price:** included in membership dues; $95.00 /year for nonmembers in US/Canada/ Mexico; $115.00 /year for nonmembers in Europe/ Western Hemisphere; $120.00 /year for nonmembers in Asia/Pacific Rim. ISSN: 0250-8060. Alternate Formats: online ● Brochures. Alternate Formats: online. **Conventions/Meetings:** annual conference (exhibits) ● annual symposium.

7835 ■ National Environmental Development Association/Resource Conservation and Recovery Act Project (NEDA/RCRA)
Address Unknown since 2007
Founded: 1985. **Members:** 14. **Staff:** 5. **Description:** Coalition of industry, agriculture, and labor companies. Seeks to ensure a fair balance is maintained between environmental and economic issues in the reauthorization of the U.S. federal government's Resource Conservation and Recovery Act. **Formerly:** (1991) National Environmental Development Association/Ground Water Project. **Conventions/Meetings:** annual conference ● monthly meeting.

7836 ■ National Institutes for Water Resources (NIWR)
c/o Dr. Anders Andren, Pres.-Elect
Water Resources Inst.
1975 Willow Dr., 2nd Fl.
The Univ. of Wisconsin - Madison
Madison, WI 53706-1177
Ph: (608)262-0591
Fax: (608)262-0905
E-mail: awandren@aqua.wisc.edu
URL: http://niwr.montana.edu
Contact: Dr. Paul Godfrey, Exec. Sec.-Treas.
Founded: 1973. **Members:** 54. **Membership Dues:** state, $2,700 (annual). **Staff:** 1. **Regional Groups:** 8. **State Groups:** 54. **Description:** Directors of university-based water resources institutes. Provides a forum for communication among members and their institutes; promotes the programs and activities of member institutes; participates in technical meetings of related organizations. Provides water resources research referrals, referral programs, and funding sources; offers educational programs. **Libraries: Type:** reference; open to the public. **Subjects:** water resources. **Awards: Frequency:** annual. **Type:** recognition. **Recipient:** for service to the organization. **Formerly:** (1992) National Association of Water Institute Directors. **Publications:** *Executive Summary*, annual. Booklet. **Conventions/Meetings:** annual convention.

7837 ■ National Water Center (NWC)
5473 Hwy. 23 N
Eureka Springs, AR 72631
Ph: (479)253-9431
E-mail: peace@ipa.net
URL: http://www.nationalwatercenter.org
Contact: Barbara Harmony, Pres.
Founded: 1979. **Members:** 300. **Membership Dues:** general, $10 (annual). **Staff:** 1. **Description:** Individuals interested in the maintenance and conservation of water resources. Seeks to increase public awareness of the need to protect clean water; disseminates information on compost toilets and encourages new ways of looking at water. Offers consulting services to individuals and communities interested in protecting water resources. Maintains speakers' bureau. **Libraries: Type:** reference. **Holdings:** 100. **Formerly:** (1991) National Water Center; (2003) Water Center. **Publications:** *Aqua Terra Meta Ecology and Culture*. **Price:** $10.00. ISSN: 0962-0034 ● *Aqua Terra: Water Concepts for the Ecological Society*, periodic. Journal. Covers water metaphysics. **Price:** $6.00. ISSN: 1048-3934. **Circulation:** 3,000 ● *We All Live Downstream: A Guide to Waste Treatment That Stops Water Pollution*. Book. **Price:** $10.00. ISSN: 0962-0034.

7838 ■ National Water Resources Association (NWRA)
3800 N Fairfax Dr., Ste.4
Arlington, VA 22203
Ph: (703)524-1544
Fax: (703)524-1548
E-mail: nwra@nwra.org
URL: http://www.nwra.org
Contact: W.E. West Jr., Pres.
Founded: 1932. **Members:** 4,800. **Staff:** 4. **State Groups:** 17. **Description:** Officers of irrigation districts, canal companies, businesses, and others interested in the development, control, conservation, and utilization of water resources in the reclamation states (17 western states). Conducts legislative tracking and provides updates. **Awards: Type:** recognition. **Telecommunication Services:** electronic mail, kpolly@nwra.org. **Caucuses:** Groundwater Management; Municipal. **Committees:** Energy Issues; Environmental; Groundwater; Project Development and Finance; Resolutions; Small Projects; Water Quality; Water Rights. **Councils:** Professional Services. **Formerly:** (1970) National Reclamation Association. **Publications:** *Groundwater Report*, monthly ● *National Water Resources Association Directory and Handbook*, biennial ● *National Waterline*, monthly ● *Water Report*, biweekly ● *Water Writes*, monthly. **Conventions/Meetings:** annual conference and seminar (exhibits) - 2008 Nov. 28-Dec. 1, San Diego, CA.

7839 ■ New Water Supply Coalition
1750 H St. NW, Ste.600
Washington, DC 20006
Ph: (202)737-0700
Fax: (202)737-0455
E-mail: newwatersupply@newwatersupply.org
URL: http://www.newwatersupply.org
Contact: Hal Furman, Exec. Dir.
Membership Dues: voting, $35,000 (annual) ● associate, $7,500 (annual). **Description:** Represents public water agencies and utilities throughout the United States. Encourages the development of coastal seawater and inland brackish groundwater desalination plants, water recycling projects and groundwater contamination clean-up projects. Raises the level of awareness in Congress concerning the urgent need to make the development of new water supply sources a national priority. **Publications:** Newsletter.

7840 ■ Passaic River Coalition (PRC)
94 Mt. Bethel Rd.
Warren, NJ 07059
Ph: (908)222-0315
Fax: (908)222-0357
E-mail: prc@passaicriver.org
URL: http://passaicriver.org
Contact: Ella F. Filippone PhD, Exec. Dir.
Founded: 1971. **Members:** 2,500. **Membership Dues:** individual, $25 (annual). **Staff:** 7. **Budget:** $225,000. **Regional Groups:** 60. **State Groups:** 30. **Local Groups:** 25. **Description:** Represents organizations, foundations, corporations, municipalities, and individuals concerned with environmental quality in the Passaic River Watershed. (The Passaic River Watershed is an urban river system in New York and New Jersey that provides water to three and a half million people.) Seeks to resolve the problems of an urban river system focusing on explosive population growth, water pollution, water supply, flood control, sewage and garbage disposal, and urban decay. Conducts research into land use, water quality and supply, wildlife and vegetation, flood control, historic preservation, water testing, and solid waste recovery. Sponsors environmental education at elementary through university levels; and offers citizen awareness education. Provides information and assistance to interested persons and groups. Has received grants for special studies and projects. Accepts college interns seeking professional experience. Maintains speakers' bureau. Compiles statistics. **Libraries: Type:** reference. **Holdings:** 9,000. **Subjects:** environment. **Awards:** Award of Achievement. **Frequency:** annual. **Type:** recognition. **Recipient:** for outstanding contribution to the improvement of the Passaic River Watershed. **Committees:** Flood Plain Watch; Passaic River Restoration; Passaic Valley Ground Water Protection; Surface Water Study; Watershed Preservation. **Divisions:** Education; Public Service; Research. **Programs:** Streamside. **Publications:** *Citizen Alerts* ● *Groundwater Sentinel*, quarterly ● *Passaic River Coalition Land Trust*. Pamphlets ● *Passaic River Restoration Newsletter*, quarterly ● *Passaic River Review*, biennial. Articles. **Circulation:** 2,000. **Advertising:** accepted ● *Vibes from the Libe*, annual ● *Watershed News*, bimonthly ● Reports ● Also publishes inventory. **Conventions/Meetings:** annual meeting - always June in Basking Ridge, NJ ● annual meeting - always fall.

7841 ■ Rural Community Assistance Partnership (RCAP)
1522 K St. NW, Ste.400
Washington, DC 20005-1255
Ph: (202)408-1273 (303)545-0964
Free: (800)321-7227
Fax: (202)408-8165
E-mail: info@rcap.org
URL: http://www.rcap.org
Contact: Mr. Robert Stewart, Exec. Dir.
Founded: 1973. **Staff:** 5. **Budget:** $10,000,000. **Regional Groups:** 6. **Nonmembership. Description:** Serves as alliance of private, non-profit, regionally based organizations engaged in facilitating, through development and establishment of water and wastewater systems, the delivery of adequate and affordable drinking water and wastewater disposal services to low-income rural areas in the United States. Conducts research and provides technical assistance and training. **Libraries: Type:** reference. **Holdings:** reports. **Subjects:** Census Information Center. **Computer Services:** database, Census Information Center. **Telecommunication Services:** electronic mail, rstewart@rcap.org. **Commissions:** WSOS Community Action. **Programs:** Community Resource Group; Midwest Assistance; Rural Community Assistance Corporation; Solutions, Inc.; Southeast Rural Community Assistance. **Formerly:** (1987) National Demonstration Water Project; (2004) Rural Community Assistance Program. **Publications:** *Rural Matters*, quarterly. Magazine. **Price:** free. **Circulation:** 5,000. **Advertising:** accepted. Alternate Formats: online ● *Still Living Without the Basics in the 21st Century*. Report. **Price:** free. **Circulation:** 1,000. Alternate Formats: online ● Annual Report, annual. Alternate Formats: online ● Also publishes policy manuals, management guides, and technical manuals. **Conventions/Meetings:** biennial Bringing Rural Issues to Washington, DC - conference (exhibits).

7842 ■ U.S. Committee on Irrigation and Drainage (USCID)
1616 17th St., No. 483
Denver, CO 80202

Ph: (303)628-5430 (559)297-9134
Fax: (303)628-5431
E-mail: stephens@uscid.org
URL: http://www.uscid.org
Contact: Larry D. Stephens, Exec. VP
Founded: 1952. **Members:** 500. **Membership Dues:** individual, $90 (annual) ● institution, $300 (annual) ● library, $150 (annual) ● corporate, $600 (annual) ● life, $1,080 ● associate, $75 (annual) ● senior, $50 (annual) ● student, $20 (annual). **Staff:** 2. **Budget:** $100,000. **Description:** Engineers, scientists, and others interested in irrigation and drainage. Promotes the planning, design, construction, operation, and maintenance of irrigation, drainage, and flood control works. Keeps members informed of developments in agricultural economics, water law, and environmental and social issues affecting irrigated agriculture. **Awards:** USCID/Summers Engineering Scholarship. **Frequency:** annual. **Type:** scholarship. **Recipient:** for a student enrolled in a college or university program related to irrigation, drainage or flood control. **Telecommunication Services:** electronic mail, jayars@cvip.net. **Committees:** Capacity Building, Training and Education; Competing Interests in Water Resources; Comprehensive Approaches to Flood Management; Development and Management of Irrigation Systems; Integrated Land and Water Resources; Irrigated Agriculture Under Drought and Water Scarcity; On-Farm Irrigation Systems; Sustainable Use of Natural Resources for Crop Production. **Affiliated With:** International Commission on Irrigation and Drainage - India. **Formerly:** (1965) U.S. National Committee, International Commission on Irrigation and Drainage; (1984) U.S. Committee on Irrigation, Drainage and Flood Control. **Publications:** *A Guide to Acquiring a Computer System for the Management of Water Resources*. **Price:** $33.00 ● *Automation of Canal Irrigation Systems*. **Price:** $28.00. Also Cited As: *L'Automatisation des Reseaux d'Irrigation en Canaux* ● *Guidelines on the Construction of Horizontal Subsurface Drainage Systems*. **Price:** $32.00 ● *USCID Newsletter*, 3/year. Includes calendar of events and list of new members. **Price:** included in membership dues. **Advertising:** accepted. Alternate Formats: online ● Proceedings. **Conventions/Meetings:** triennial International Congress.

7843 ■ United States Society on Dams (USSD)

1616 17th St., No. 483
Denver, CO 80202-1277
Ph: (303)628-5430
Fax: (303)628-5431
E-mail: stephens@ussdams.org
URL: http://www.ussdams.org
Contact: Larry D. Stephens, Exec. Dir.
Founded: 1928. **Members:** 1,150. **Membership Dues:** regular, $85 (annual) ● life, $1,020 ● associate/senior, $45 (annual) ● student, $20 (annual) ● organizational, $650 (annual) ● sustaining, $2,800 (annual). **Staff:** 2. **Budget:** $150,000. **Description:** Individuals and organizations interested in the planning, design, construction, and maintenance of large dams. Takes part in the activities of the International Commission of Large Dams, which provides a forum for discussion, study tours, and publication of technical research related to cans and water resources. **Awards:** USCOLD Scholarship. **Frequency:** annual. **Type:** monetary. **Recipient:** for graduate students. **Committees:** Concrete; Construction and Rehabilitation; Dam Decommissioning; Dam Safety and Dam Security; Earthquakes; Environment; Foundations; Hydraulics of Dams; Materials for Embankment Dams; Methods of Numerical Analysis of Dams; Monitoring of Dams and Their Foundations; Public Awareness; Register of Dams; Reservoir Slope Stability; Tailings Dams; Technical Activities. **Affiliated With:** International Commission on Large Dams. **Formerly:** (2000) United States Committee on Large Dams. **Publications:** *ICOLD Congress Transactions*, triennial ● *ICOLD Symposium Transactions*, biennial ● Books ● Bulletins ● Membership Directory ● Newsletter, 3/year. **Conventions/Meetings:** triennial international conference and congress ● annual meeting and lecture.

7844 ■ Universities Council on Water Resources (UCOWR)

c/o Southern Illinois University Carbondale
1000 Faner Dr., Rm. 4543
Carbondale, IL 62901-4526
Ph: (618)536-7571 (618)453-6020
Fax: (618)453-2671
E-mail: ucowr@siu.edu
URL: http://ucowr.siu.edu
Contact: Dr. Christopher L. Lant, Exec. Dir.
Founded: 1964. **Members:** 87. **Membership Dues:** student, $20 (annual) ● regular, $70 (annual) ● academic organization, $450 (annual) ● non-academic organization (based on number of employees), $450-$4,000 (annual). **Description:** Eighty-seven U.S. universities and 3 foreign affiliates. Academic institutions with established programs in water resources education and research. Seeks to extend and strengthen these programs through united action. Issues explored have included: manpower, internship programs, awards, research needs, water institutions and legislation, federal water policy, international programs, water rights, federal agency activities and reorganization, water resources planning, public participation in water resources, and graduate and undergraduate water resources education. Activities have included: definition of water resources research and educational needs, visiting scientists program, seminars, workshops and special studies. **Awards:** Friends of UCOWR Award. **Frequency:** annual. **Type:** recognition. **Recipient:** for individuals who have made outstanding contributions to the organization and to water related projects ● PhD Dissertation Award. **Frequency:** annual. **Type:** recognition. **Recipient:** for outstanding PhD dissertations on water issues ● Warren A. Hall Medal. **Frequency:** annual. **Type:** recognition. **Recipient:** for unusual accomplishments and distinction of an individual in the water resources field. **Computer Services:** database, water resources expertise directory. **Telecommunication Services:** electronic mail, clant@siu.edu. **Committees:** Education and Public Service; International Programs; Policy, Legislation and Administration; Research. **Formerly:** (1964) Universities Council on Hydrology. **Publications:** *Graduate Studies in Water Resources* ● *Journal of Contemporary Water Research and Education*, quarterly. **Price:** $35.00/year, in U.S.; $55.00/year, outside U.S.; $15.00/copy, in U.S.; $20.00/copy, outside U.S. Alternate Formats: online. Also Cited As: *Water Resources Update* ● *Proceedings of Annual Meetings* ● *Water Resources Course Listings* ● Brochures. Alternate Formats: online ● Also publishes brochures, reports, and proceedings of workshops and seminars. **Conventions/Meetings:** annual conference.

7845 ■ Western Snow Conference (WSC)

c/o Randall Osterhuber, Documents Mgr.
PO Box 810
Soda Springs, CA 95728
Ph: (530)426-0318
E-mail: randall@sierra.net
URL: http://www.westernsnowconference.org/WSC.htm
Contact: Randall Osterhuber, Documents Mgr.
Founded: 1939. **Members:** 900. **Membership Dues:** regular, $25 (annual). **Regional Groups:** 4. **Description:** Individuals and corporations. United to share developments and research in the nonrecreational uses of snow. Focuses inquiries on utilizing snow as a source of water for irrigation and hydroelectric power; also studies methods of controlling floods, preventing avalanches, and forecasting water supplies. **Libraries: Type:** reference. **Holdings:** 70; archival material, business records, periodicals. **Subjects:** hydrology, snow science, water supply forecasting. **Awards:** JE Church Award. **Frequency:** annual. **Type:** recognition. **Recipient:** for research in snow or hydrologic sciences at the university level within conference area. **Computer Services:** database, membership. **Committees:** North Continental; North Pacific; South Continental; South Pacific; Wilderness. **Affiliated With:** American Geophysical Union. **Publications:** *Proceedings of Western Snow Conference*, annual. Covers scientific exchange. **Price:** $35.00. ISSN: 0161-0589. **Circulation:** 2,000. **Conventions/Meetings:** annual general assembly, exhibit includes snow and climate instrumentation (exhibits).

Welding

7846 ■ American Council of the International Institute of Welding (ACIIW)

550 NW LeJeune Rd.
Miami, FL 33126
Ph: (305)443-9353
Free: (800)443-9353
Fax: (305)443-5951
E-mail: adavis@aws.org
Contact: Andrew Davis, Managing Dir.
Founded: 1948. **Members:** 200. **Membership Dues:** organization, $400 (annual). **Staff:** 2. **Budget:** $40,000. **Languages:** English, French. **Description:** Jointly sponsored by American Welding Society and Welding Research Council. The council and 35 other member-countries of the International Institute of Welding study and exchange information on research, development, and applications of welding. Carries out research by the council's commissions. Provides supporting members with consultation on international welding problems and a review of international welding standards. **Libraries: Type:** reference. **Holdings:** 5,000. **Commissions:** Arc Welding; Behavior of Metals Subjected to Welding; Fatigue Behavior of Welded Components; Flux and Gas Shielded Electrical Welding Processes; Fundamentals of Design and Fabrication for Welding; Health and Safety; Joining, Cutting, Surfacing by Thermal Processes; Pressure Vessels, Boilers, and Pipelines; Residual Stresses and Stress Relieving, Brittle Fracture; Resistance Welding; Special Welding Processes; Terminology; Testing, Measurement, and Control of Welds; Welding Instruction; Welding Research Strategy and Collaboration. **Affiliated With:** American Welding Society; Welding Research Council. **Publications:** Also distributes international publications and reference radiographs from IIW. **Conventions/Meetings:** annual assembly.

7847 ■ American Welding Society (AWS)

550 NW Le Jeune Rd.
Miami, FL 33126
Ph: (305)443-9353 (814)474-3052
Free: (800)443-9353
Fax: (305)443-5647
E-mail: info@aws.org
URL: http://www.aws.org
Contact: Ray W. Shook, Exec. Dir.
Founded: 1919. **Members:** 50,000. **Membership Dues:** individual, $80 (annual) ● student in U.S. and Canada, $15 (annual) ● student outside U.S. and Canada, $50 (annual) ● sustaining company in U.S. and Canada, $800 (annual) ● sustaining company outside U.S. and Canada, $900 (annual) ● supporting company, $400 (annual) ● welding distributor, $500 (annual) ● affiliate company, $150 (annual) ● educational institution, $240 (annual). **Staff:** 105. **Regional Groups:** 22. **Local Groups:** 171. **Multinational. Description:** One of several sponsors of the Welding Research Council and the Materials Properties Council. Professional engineering society in the field of welding. Sponsors seminars. Maintains over 130 technical and handbook committees, 171 sections, educational committees, and task forces. **Awards:** Fellow and Extraordinary Welding. **Frequency:** annual. **Type:** grant. **Recipient:** for members. **Computer Services:** Online services, welding portal. **Telecommunication Services:** electronic mail, rshook@aws.org. **Committees:** Brazing and Soldering Manufacturer's; Welding Equipment Manufacturer's. **Publications:** *Directory of Technical Council Committees*, annual ● *Welding Handbook*, biennial ● *Welding Journal*, monthly. Covers developments in welding technology, the industry, and the society. Includes book reviews, calendar of events, and employment listings. **Price:** included in membership dues; $90.00 /year for nonmembers. ISSN: 0043-2296. **Circulation:** 50,000. **Advertising:** accepted. Alternate Formats: online ● Books. Covers

welding. ● Also publishes codes, standards, and specifications. **Conventions/Meetings:** annual meeting (exhibits).

7848 ■ Edison Welding Institute (EWI)
1250 Arthur E. Adams Dr.
Columbus, OH 43221-3585
Ph: (614)688-5000 (614)688-5005
Fax: (614)688-5001
E-mail: info@ewi.org
URL: http://www.ewi.org
Contact: Dr. Henry J. Cialone, Pres./CEO
Founded: 1984. **Members:** 350. **Staff:** 150. **Description:** Dedicated to materials joining and related technologies; provides technology solutions to more than 3,000 customers and federal agencies, including the U.S. Navy, for which it operates the Navy Joining Center. **Libraries: Type:** reference. **Computer Services:** database, accessed via DIALOG, including Metadex and Weldasearch information services, a reference system that contains abstracts of material related to welding. **Boards:** Industry Advisory. **Departments:** Arc Welding and Automation; Engineering; Laser and Materials Processing; Materials; Microjoining; Non-Destructive Evaluation. **Subgroups:** Aerospace; Automotive; Electronics/Electrical; Heavy Manufacturing; Medical Products; Petrochemicals; Plastics; Power Generation; Primary Metals; Welding Equipment. **Publications:** *Insights*, quarterly. Newsletter. Contains current issues and activities of the organization. **Circulation:** 10,000. Alternate Formats: online ● *Research Reports* ● Brochures ● Catalog. **Conventions/Meetings:** semiannual conference (exhibits).

7849 ■ United States Microscopic Welding Association (USMWA)
c/o Lee R. Gilbert
145 Sabin St.
Pawtucket, RI 02860
Ph: (401)722-6942
Fax: (401)722-7071
E-mail: info@usmwa.com
URL: http://www.usmwa.com
Contact: Lee R. Gilbert, Contact
Founded: 2001. **Membership Dues:** regular, $125. **Description:** Seeks to improve the support industry of mold repair and maintenance. Promotes the advancement of Precision Microscopic Tig and Laser Welding for mold, tool and die repair and maintenance. Provides high quality products, precision training and ongoing technical support to the microscopic welding industry.

7850 ■ Welders Without Borders
c/o Arizona Western College
PO Box 929
Yuma, AZ 85366-0929
Ph: (928)344-7699
Fax: (928)344-7543
E-mail: welderswithoutborders@yahoo.com
URL: http://www.welderswithoutborders.com
Contact: Prof. Samuel Colton Sr., Founder
Founded: 2000. **Multinational. Description:** Represents welders around the world dedicated to the advancement of the welding industry. Aims to create opportunities for members of the welding community to share their experiences with students of welding. Builds understanding between people through the advancement of metals technology. **Telecommunication Services:** electronic mail, samuel.colton@azwestern.edu.

7851 ■ Welding Research Council (WRC)
PO Box 1942
New York, NY 10156
Ph: (216)658-3847 (216)658-3854
Fax: (216)658-3854
E-mail: mprager@forengineers.org
URL: http://www.forengineers.org/wrc
Contact: Dr. Martin Prager, Contact
Founded: 1935. **Members:** 400. **Budget:** $1,300,000. **Description:** Established by the Engineering Foundation under the sponsorship of the major engineering societies to conduct needed cooperative research in welding and closely allied fields, to disseminate research information, to promote welding research in the universities, and to provide a means for cooperation with similar agencies abroad. Activities include administration of large projects by specific committees, as well as sponsorship of small grants-in-aid by the University Research Committee to foster interest in welding research in universities. The council is guided by 24 corporation executives who establish broad policies and prepare overall budgets for its projects. In itself, or through its committees, the Council is considered the welding research arm of eight engineering societies and six trade associations. In addition, it acts in an advisory capacity to the public utility industry, aerospace industry, and the Atomic Energy Commission. Financed by subscriptions from corporations, associations, and government departments; it has more than 900 scientists affiliated with its work, which is carried out in some 45 laboratories. Acts as one of the two sponsor body representatives of the American Council of the International Institute of Welding. **Telecommunication Services:** electronic mail, bulletinsales@forengineers.org. **Committees:** Aluminum Alloys; Brazing; High Alloy; Interpretative Reports; Pressure Vessel Research; Reactive and Refractory Metals; Resistance Welding; Structural Steel; University Research; Utilities Advisory; Weldability; Welding Procedures. **Publications:** *Welding Research Abroad*, 10/year. Journal. Reports on welding research in England, Germany, France, Japan, the Union of Soviet Socialist Republics, and other countries. ● *Welding Research Council—Research Bulletins*, 10/year. Newsletter. Provides information on the results of research projects and technical reports in the welding industry. ● *Welding Research Council Yearbook*. Lists the objectives and long-range plans of the Council and committee membership. ● *Welding Research News*, quarterly. Newsletter. Highlights current developments in welding research. ● *WRC Progress Report*, bimonthly. Covers progress of research being conducted in the welding industry. ● Also publishes books, monographs, and bibliographies produced by its committees, and literature reviews or interpretive reports summarizing existing information in a proposed research area.

Wind Energy

7852 ■ American Wind Energy Association (AWEA)
1101 14th St. NW, 12th Fl.
Washington, DC 20005
Ph: (202)383-2500
Fax: (202)383-2505
E-mail: windmail@awea.org
URL: http://www.awea.org
Contact: Randall Swisher, Exec. Dir.
Founded: 1974. **Members:** 500. **Membership Dues:** advocate, $65 (annual) ● associate, $1,200 (annual) ● academic/non-profit, $250 (annual) ● utility (based on installed wind capacity), $1,500-$8,000 (annual) ● corporate - minimum (based on company revenues), $1,700 (annual) ● corporate - maximum (based on company revenues), $150,000 (annual). **Staff:** 14. **Budget:** $4,000,000. **Description:** Wind energy equipment manufacturers; project developers and dealers; individuals from industry, government, and academia; interested others. Works to: advance the art and science of using energy from the wind for human purposes; encourage the use of wind turbines and wind power plants as alternatives to current energy systems that depend on depletable fuels; facilitate the widespread use of wind as a renewable, non-polluting energy source by fostering communication within the field of wind energy and between the technical community and the public. Provides federal and state legislators with information on wind as an energy source; offers consultation to federal, state, and local government and private industry. Promotes exportation of U.S. manufactured wind energy equipment. **Libraries: Type:** reference. **Holdings:** books, periodicals. **Subjects:** wind energy. **Awards: Type:** recognition. **Committees:** Communications; Export; Legislative; Political Action; Research and Development; Strategic Planning. **Also Known As:** AWEA. **Publications:** *Wind Energy Weekly*. Newsletter. Contains detailed and up-to-date information on the world of wind energy. **Price:** $595.00/year. ISSN: 0747-5500. **Circulation:** 700. **Advertising:** accepted. Alternate Formats: online ● *Windletter*, monthly. Newsletter. Recaps the month's most significant wind energy news and includes interesting information for wind energy enthusiasts. Alternate Formats: online ● *Windpower Conference Proceedings*, annual. **Conventions/Meetings:** annual Windpower - conference (exhibits) - 2009 June 7-10, Minneapolis, MN.

7853 ■ Windustry
2105 1st Ave. S
Minneapolis, MN 55404
Ph: (612)870-3461
Free: (800)946-3640
Fax: (612)813-5612
E-mail: info@windustry.org
URL: http://www.windustry.com
Contact: Lisa Daniels, Exec. Dir.
Membership Dues: student/senior, $25 ● individual, $50 ● non-profit/government, $100 ● family, $150 ● business, $200 ● sustaining business, $500. **Description:** Seeks to increase wind energy opportunities for rural landowners and communities. Responds to barriers to wind energy by building collaborations with rural landowners, local communities and utilities, as well as state, regional and non-profit organizations. Promotes family farms, rural communities and ecosystems through advocacy, research and education and science and technology. **Publications:** Newsletter, quarterly. Contains updates on the state of the wind energy industry in the country. **Price:** included in membership dues. Alternate Formats: online.

7854 ■ Women of Wind Energy (WoWE)
c/o Windustry
2105 First Ave. S
Minneapolis, MN 55404
Ph: (612)870-3461
Free: (800)946-3640
E-mail: womenofwindenergy@windustry.org
URL: http://www.windustry.org/womenofwindenergy
Contact: Lisa Daniels, Contact
Founded: 2005. **Description:** Represents women in the field of wind energy. Supports and encourages the participation and advancement of professional women in the wind energy industry. Works to advance the art and science of using energy from the wind for human purposes. **Awards:** The Rudd Mayer Memorial Sponsorship. **Frequency:** annual. **Type:** scholarship. **Recipient:** to any woman who is interested in a career in the wind energy industry ● Woman of the Year Award. **Frequency:** annual. **Type:** recognition. **Recipient:** to a woman who has contributed to the expansion and improvement of the wind energy industry. **Telecommunication Services:** electronic mail, lisadaniels@windustry.org.

Zoological Gardens

7855 ■ American Association of Zoo Keepers (AAZK)
3601 SW 29th St., Ste.133
Topeka, KS 66614-2054
Ph: (785)273-9149
Free: (800)242-4519
Fax: (785)273-1980
E-mail: aazkoffice@zk.kscoxmail.com
URL: http://www.aazk.org
Contact: Ed Hansen, Exec. Dir.
Founded: 1967. **Members:** 2,700. **Membership Dues:** professional, $40 (annual) ● affiliate, associate, $35 (annual) ● contributing, $65 (annual) ● regular, outside U.S., $55 (annual) ● institution, $125 (annual). **Staff:** 3. **Budget:** $150,000. **Local Groups:** 80. **Description:** Professional members are zookeepers and aquarists; affiliate members are other zoo employees and volunteers; associate members are students and other interested persons. Disseminates

information about the care of wild animals, birds, reptiles, and marine life found in captivity; fosters a professional attitude in animal keepers by encouraging them to become actively involved in the professional teams at zoos and aquariums. Maintains speakers' bureau. Conducts specialized education and research programs; compiles statistics. **Libraries: Type:** reference. **Awards:** Excellence in Exhibitry. **Frequency:** annual. **Type:** recognition. **Recipient:** for exhibit design ● Excellence in Zookeeping Award. **Frequency:** annual. **Type:** recognition. **Recipient:** for professionals who have made exemplary work in animal care ● Meritorious Achievement. **Frequency:** annual. **Type:** recognition. **Recipient:** for enrichment. **Committees:** Animal Data Transfer Forms and Enrichment Data Transfer Forms; Book Review; Conservation, Preservation and Restoration; Enrichment; International Affairs; Legislative; Research Grants. **Publications:** *Animal Keepers' Forum*, monthly. Journal. Includes records of births and hatchings, calendar of events, book reviews, employment listings, and animal husbandry. Contains annual index. **Price:** included in membership dues. ISSN: 0164-9531. **Circulation:** 2,875. **Advertising:** accepted ● *Conference Proceedings*, annual ● *Crisis Management in Zoos and other Animal Care Facilities*. Book ● *Handbook of Zoonotic Diseases*. **Conventions/Meetings:** annual conference (exhibits).

7856 ■ Aquarium and Zoo Facilities Association (AZFA)

1901 N Roselle Rd., Ste.920
Schaumburg, IL 60195
Ph: (847)885-7400
Fax: (847)885-8393
E-mail: support@azfa.org
URL: http://www.azfa.org
Contact: Gary Norman, Pres.

Membership Dues: professional, $25 (annual) ● associate, $20 (annual) ● student, $15 (annual) ● organizational, commercial, $100 (annual). **Description:** Seeks to increase understanding and appreciation of all life forms, with emphasis on conservation of all plants, animals, and natural resources. Fosters business and educational relations of its members. Engenders cooperation among the construction and maintenance staff members of zoos, parks, aquariums, and similar organizations. **Publications:** *The Outlet*. Newsletter. **Price:** included in membership dues.

7857 ■ Association of Zoos and Aquariums (AZA)

8403 Colesville Rd., Ste.710
Silver Spring, MD 20910-3314
Ph: (301)562-0777
Fax: (301)562-0888
E-mail: g.e.n.e.r.a.l.i.n.q.u.i.r.y@aza.org
URL: http://www.aza.org
Contact: Kris Vehrs JD, Exec. Dir.

Founded: 1924. **Members:** 6,500. **Membership Dues:** associate, $60 (annual) ● professional (affiliate), $85 (annual) ● professional (fellow), $175 (annual) ● commercial, $1,725 (annual) ● conservation partner, $435 (annual). **Staff:** 30. **Budget:** $3,000,000. **Description:** Zoological park and aquarium personnel; individuals interested in promoting zoos and aquariums for educational and scientific interpretation of nature and animal conservation and for public recreation and cultural pursuits. **Libraries: Type:** not open to the public. **Awards:** R. Marlin Perkins Award. **Frequency:** annual. **Type:** recognition. **Recipient:** for outstanding service. **Committees:** Accreditation; Animal Health; Conference; Conservation; Development/Marketing; Honors and Awards; Legislation; Public Relations; Scientific; Zoo and Aquarium Accreditation. **Formerly:** (1998) American Association of Zoological Parks and Aquariums; (2007) American Zoo and Aquarium Association. **Publications:** *Anti-venom Index*. **Price:** $20.00 for members; $30.00 for nonmembers ● *AZA Annual Conference Proceedings*, annual. Contains compilation of papers presented at the AZA annual conference. **Price:** $45.00/copy for members; $80.00/copy for nonmembers; $50.00/copy for educational facilities. **Circulation:** 400 ● *AZA Communique*, monthly. Newsletter. Covers conservation issues, legislation affecting wildlife, and news of zoos and aquariums including new exhibits and births in captivity. **Price:** included in membership dues. **Advertising:** accepted ● *AZA Membership Directory*, annual. Lists members, member institutions, government agencies, and commercial and animal suppliers. **Price:** $45.00/copy for members; $100.00/copy for nonmembers; $75.00/copy for educational facilities. **Advertising:** accepted ● *AZA Regional Conference Proceedings*, annual. Covers the three annual regional conferences of the AZA. **Price:** $45.00/copy for members; $80.00/copy for nonmembers; $50.00/copy for educational facilities. **Conventions/Meetings:** annual conference (exhibits) - always September. 2008 Sept. 12-18, Milwaukee, WI; 2009 Sept. 12-18, Portland, OR.

7858 ■ Friends of the National Zoo (FONZ)

PO Box 37012
Washington, DC 20013-7012
Ph: (202)633-4271 (202)633-4800
Fax: (202)673-4890
E-mail: member@fonz.org
URL: http://nationalzoo.si.edu/default.cfm
Contact: Robert J. Lamb, Exec. Dir.

Founded: 1958. **Members:** 34,000. **Membership Dues:** individual, young professional, $40 (annual) ● household, $55 (annual) ● senior, $35 (annual) ● ZooGoer, $30 (annual) ● contributing, $100 (annual) ● sustaining, $150 (annual) ● patron, $250 (annual) ● sponsor, $500 (annual) ● benefactor, $1,000 (annual) ● Director's Circle, $2,500 (annual) ● Conservation Circle, $5,000 (annual) ● Wildlife Society, $10,000 (annual). **Staff:** 100. **Budget:** $18,000,000. **Description:** Dedicated to supporting the joint mission of the Smithsonian's National Zoo to celebrate, study and protect the diversity of animals and their habitats. **Publications:** *Wildlife Adventures*, bimonthly. Newsletter. Lists all classes, trips, and activities for members, as well as any announcements of interest. **Price:** included in membership dues. **Circulation:** 34,000 ● *ZooGoer*, bimonthly. Magazine. Contains articles on animals, biological research, and wildlife conservation. Includes calendar. **Price:** included in membership dues. ISSN: 0163-416X. **Advertising:** accepted. Alternate Formats: online. **Conventions/Meetings:** annual meeting - always October.

Zoology

7859 ■ American Association for Zoological Nomenclature (AAZN)

c/o Eric Hoberg, Treas.
USDA Agricultural Res. Ser.
BARC E No. 1180
10300 Baltimore Ave.
Beltsville, MD 20705
E-mail: ehoberg@anri.barc.usda.gov
URL: http://www.iczn.org/AAZN.htm
Contact: Al Gardner, Pres.

Founded: 1983. **Members:** 250. **Membership Dues:** individual, $20 (annual). **Description:** Comprised of persons in academic institutions, museums, industry, and government interested in systematics of living and fossilized animals. Aims to: promote recognition of the importance of nomenclature and taxonomy in zoology; help support the work of the International Commission on Zoological Nomenclature as the international body in the field. **Publications:** *AAZN Newsletter*, 2-3/year. **Price:** included in membership dues. **Conventions/Meetings:** annual meeting.

7860 ■ Animal Behavior Management Alliance (ABMA)

3650 S Pointe Cir., No. 205
Laughlin, NV 89029
E-mail: susan.rubino@yale.edu
URL: http://www.theabma.org
Contact: Sue Rubino, Pres.

Membership Dues: institutional, $300 (annual) ● commercial, $500 (annual) ● professional, $55 (annual) ● active, emeritus, $50 (annual) ● associate, student, $45 (annual) ● life, $450. **Description:** Represents animal care professionals and individuals who are interested in enhancing animal care through training and enrichment. Seeks to advance animal behavior management to enhance the husbandry and welfare of animals. Works to serve trainers, handlers, and keepers of animals, with information and assistance in behavior management of their charges. **Conventions/Meetings:** annual conference.

7861 ■ Animal Behavior Society (ABS)

Indiana Univ.
2611 E 10th St.
Bloomington, IN 47408-2603
Ph: (812)856-5541
Fax: (812)856-5542
E-mail: aboffice@indiana.edu
URL: http://www.animalbehavior.org
Contact: Gerald Wilkinson, Pres.

Founded: 1964. **Members:** 3,000. **Membership Dues:** student, $18 (annual) ● student with journal, $40 (annual) ● regular, $30 (annual) ● regular with journal, $57 (annual) ● developing nation, $19 (annual) ● developing nation with journal, $24 (annual) ● emeritus with journal, $42 (annual). **Staff:** 3. **Budget:** $200,000. **Description:** Professionals and students engaged in the scientific study of animal behavior. Promotes and encourages the biological study of animal behavior, including studies using both descriptive and experimental methods under natural and controlled conditions. **Awards:** ABS Film Award. **Frequency:** annual. **Type:** recognition. **Recipient:** for best film presented by a commercial filmmaker ● Cetacean Behavior Conservation Award. **Frequency:** annual. **Type:** monetary. **Recipient:** to ABS graduate student conducting research on cetacean behavior or conservation ● Developing Nation Research Award. **Frequency:** annual. **Type:** monetary. **Recipient:** to ABS member conducting animal behavior research in developing nation ● E.O. Wilson Conservation Award. **Frequency:** annual. **Type:** monetary. **Recipient:** for student research with a significant conservation slant ● Jack Ward Memorial Film Award. **Frequency:** annual. **Type:** recognition. **Recipient:** for best film presented by an amateur ● Student Research Award. **Frequency:** annual. **Type:** monetary. **Recipient:** for ABS graduate student research on animal behavior ● Warder Clyde Allee Award. **Frequency:** annual. **Type:** recognition. **Recipient:** for best student paper. **Computer Services:** Mailing lists, of members. **Committees:** Animal Care; Conservation; Education; Film; Professional Certification; Public Affairs. **Affiliated With:** American Institute of Biological Sciences; Society for Integrative and Comparative Biology. **Publications:** *Animal Behavior Society Newsletter*, quarterly. Includes business information for the society. **Price:** $10.00 for nonmembers; free for members. **Circulation:** 2,200. Alternate Formats: online ● *Animal Behaviour*, monthly. Journal. Contains animal behavior research articles and reviews. **Price:** $57.00 available only to members. ISSN: 0003-3472. **Circulation:** 5,000. **Advertising:** accepted. Alternate Formats: online ● *Graduate Programs in Animal Behavior*, periodic. Annual Reports. Includes list of programs accepting graduate students in animal behavior. **Price:** $8.00. Alternate Formats: online. **Conventions/Meetings:** annual conference (exhibits).

7862 ■ Center for the Study of Natural and Historical Anomalies

Address Unknown since 2008

Founded: 1992. **Membership Dues:** subscriber, $15 (annual). **Staff:** 1. **Description:** Investigates reports of animals of unexpected size or occurrences of animals well outside of their normal range. Researches sightings of animals that have been proclaimed extinct. Interested in information on pre-Columbian explorations of North America, by old World cultures. Compiles statistics, disseminates information, coordinates investigators with other researchers. Also researches Legends of Lost Mines and Treasures. **Libraries: Type:** reference; not open to the public. **Holdings:** 3,000; articles, books, periodicals, video recordings. **Subjects:** history and natural science. **Computer Services:** database. **Affiliated With:** Gungywamp Society; International

Society of Cryptozoology. **Formerly:** (1996) Center for the Study of Scientific and Historical Anomalies. **Publications:** *Anomalies*, bimonthly. Newsletter. Examines recent reports and issues. **Price:** available to members only. **Advertising:** accepted. **Conventions/Meetings:** Anomalous Historical & Natural Events - conference (exhibits) - 6-10/year.

7863 ■ The Crustacean Society (TCS)
PO Box 7065
Lawrence, KS 66044-7065
Ph: (785)843-1221
Free: (800)627-0326
Fax: (785)843-1274
E-mail: tcs@allenpress.com
URL: http://www.vims.edu/tcs
Contact: Mary Belk, Treas.
Founded: 1980. **Members:** 850. **Membership Dues:** student, $65 (annual) ● patron, $125 (annual) ● individual, $35-$95 (annual). **Budget:** $95,000. **Multinational. Description:** Institutions, organizations, and individuals interested in crustaceans. Seeks to advance the study of crustacean biology and improve the exchange of information among members. **Awards:** Best Student Paper. **Frequency:** annual. **Type:** recognition. **Recipient:** for best student paper presented at meetings ● Research Excellence Award. **Frequency:** annual. **Type:** recognition. **Recipient:** for lifetime achievement. **Telecommunication Services:** electronic mail, dbelk@texas.net. **Committees:** Awards; Conservation; Editorial. **Publications:** *The Ecdysiast*, semiannual. Newsletter. Lists sources of information on crustacean biology. Contains employment listings. **Price:** included in membership dues. **Circulation:** 850. Alternate Formats: online ● *Journal of Crustacean Biology*, quarterly. Contains papers dealing with crustacean biology and notices of business transacted at meetings of the society. **Price:** $20.00/year for associate members; $55.00 /year for members; $100.00/year for sustaining members; $150.00/year for patron members. ISSN: 0278-0372. **Circulation:** 1,100. **Conventions/Meetings:** annual meeting, held in conjunction with The Society of Integrative and Comparative Biology (exhibits) - winter ● annual meeting - summer.

7864 ■ International Association of Animal Behavior Consultants (IAABC)
505 Timber Ln.
Jefferson Hills, PA 15025
E-mail: info@iaabc.org
URL: http://www.iaabc.org
Contact: Lynn Hoover MSW, Pres./Founder
Founded: 2004. **Membership Dues:** associate, $65 (annual) ● certified, $85 (annual) ● affiliate/professional affiliate, $45 (annual). **Multinational. Description:** Assists and educates owners and handlers of companion animals. Seeks to prevent problems and to interrupt the cycle of inappropriate punishment, rejection, and euthanasia of animals with behavior problems that are resolvable. Advances the profession and the practice of animal behavior consulting. Promotes the common professional interests of animal behavior consultants. **Publications:** *Animal Behavior Consulting: Theory & Practice*. Journal. Covers dog behavior consulting theory and clinical practice, qualitative and quantitative research, and training. **Price:** included in membership dues. Alternate Formats: online.

7865 ■ International Society of Cryptozoology (ISC)
Address Unknown since 2008
Founded: 1982. **Members:** 1,000. **Membership Dues:** regular, $42 (annual) ● joint, $47 (annual). **Staff:** 2. **Description:** Biological scientists and other individuals interested in animals of unexpected size, form, or occurrence in time or location. Investigates and discusses reports of animals such as giant octopuses (spanning 150 feet or more); "lake monsters" in Loch Ness, Scotland, and other lakes; large, long-necked animals in Central African swamps that resemble Mesozoic sauropod dinosaurs, and large, unknown hominoids. Disseminates cryptozoological information among biological scientists, including information on cryptozoological claims, and analyses of evidence such as photographs, sonar tracks, footprint casts, and tissue and hair samples. Serves as a forum for public discussion and education; provides information to authorities and the news media. **Telecommunication Services:** electronic mail, rgreenwell@thewildlifemuseum.org. **Publications:** *Cryptozoology*, annual. Journal. Provides information on cryptozoology. Includes review articles, book reviews, field reports, and research reports. **Price:** included in membership dues. ISSN: 0736-7023. **Circulation:** 1,000. **Advertising:** accepted ● *ISC Newsletter*, quarterly. **Price:** included in membership dues. ISSN: 0741-5362. **Circulation:** 1,000. **Conventions/Meetings:** annual conference.

7866 ■ International Society of Protistologists (ISOP)
Dept. of Biological Sciences
Univ. of Alabama
Box 870344
Tuscaloosa, AL 35487
Ph: (205)348-1830
Fax: (205)348-1786
E-mail: hsmithso@ua.edu
URL: http://www.uga.edu/~protozoa
Contact: Harriett Smith-Somerville, Sec.
Founded: 1947. **Members:** 1,000. **Membership Dues:** regular in U.S., $87 (annual) ● student, emeritus in U.S., $43 (annual) ● corresponding in U.S., $26 (annual) ● regular in Europe, EUR 84 (annual) ● regular (rest of the world), 57 (annual) ● student, emeritus in Europe, EUR 47 (annual) ● student, emeritus (rest of the world), 31 (annual) ● corresponding in Europe, EUR 21 (annual) ● corresponding (rest of the world), 14 (annual). **Budget:** $100,000. **Regional Groups:** 6. **Description:** Persons interested in the study of protozoa and all types of protozoological research. Conducts occasional refresher courses. **Awards:** John O. Corliss Systematics Award. **Frequency:** annual. **Type:** recognition. **Recipient:** for outstanding paper in ciliate systematics ● Seymour H. Hutner Prize. **Frequency:** annual. **Type:** recognition. **Recipient:** for outstanding scientist in the field of protozoology who is recognized on international level ● Theodore L. Jahn and Eugene C. Bovee Award. **Frequency:** annual. **Type:** recognition. **Recipient:** for a graduate student who presented the best paper or poster at the annual meeting ● William Trager Award. **Frequency:** annual. **Type:** recognition. **Recipient:** for the best paper published in the journal. **Formerly:** (2006) Society of Protozoologists. **Publications:** *The Abstracts*, annual ● *Illustrated Guide to the Protozoa*. Book ● *Journal of Eukaryotic Microbiology*, bimonthly ● *Protocols in Protozoology*. Book ● Membership Directory, annual ● Newsletter, 3/year. **Conventions/Meetings:** annual meeting, scientific (exhibits).

7867 ■ Society for Integrative and Comparative Biology (SICB)
1313 Dolley Madison Blvd., Ste.402
McLean, VA 22101-3926
Ph: (703)790-1745
Free: (800)955-1236
Fax: (703)790-2672
E-mail: sicb@burkinc.com
URL: http://www.sicb.org
Contact: Brett J. Burk, Exec. Dir.
Founded: 1902. **Members:** 2,300. **Membership Dues:** full, $100 (annual) ● student, $36 (annual) ● postdoctoral, $45 (annual) ● emeritus (with journal), $70 (annual) ● emeritus (without journal), $60 (annual) ● life, $1,000 ● postdoctoral (family), $60 (annual) ● graduate student (family), $59 (annual) ● full (family), $140 (annual). **Budget:** $750,000. **Description:** Professional animal biologists. Maintains career opportunities desk at Annual Meeting; conducts educational programs. **Awards:** Best Student Paper Program. **Frequency:** annual. **Type:** monetary. **Recipient:** for a student member. **Computer Services:** Mailing lists, of members. **Telecommunication Services:** electronic mail, bburk@burkinc.com. **Committees:** Education; Endowment; Public Affairs; Student Support. **Divisions:** Animal Behavior; Comparative Endocrinology; Comparative Physiology and Biochemistry; Developmental and Cell Biology; Ecology and Evolution; History and Philosophy of Biology; Invertebrate Zoology; Systematic and Evolutionary Biology; Vertebrate Morphology. **Absorbed:** American Morphological Society. **Formerly:** (1996) American Society of Zoologists. **Publications:** *Careers in Animal Biology*. Brochures ● *Integrative and Comparative Biology*, bimonthly. Journal. Papers presented at SICB-sponsored symposia; each issue covers a specific topic. Includes book reviews. **Price:** $240.00 /year for individuals in U.S.; $255.00 /year for individuals in Canada and Mexico; $270.00 /year for individuals outside North America; $578.00 /year for institutions in U.S. (print and online). ISSN: 0003-1569. **Circulation:** 3,000. **Advertising:** accepted. Alternate Formats: microform. Also Cited As: *American Zoologist.* **Conventions/Meetings:** annual meeting, manufacturers of scientific instruments, academic and textbook publishers (exhibits).

7868 ■ Society of Systematic Biologists (SSB)
c/o Keith A. Crandall, Exec. VP
Brigham Young Univ.
Dept. of Zoology
574 Widtsoe Bldg.
Provo, UT 84602-5555
E-mail: keith_crandall@byu.edu
URL: http://systbiol.org
Contact: Keith A. Crandall, Exec. VP
Founded: 1948. **Members:** 1,550. **Membership Dues:** regular, $50 (annual) ● student, $25 (annual) ● sustaining, $70 (annual) ● life, $1,000 ● emeritus with journal, $15 (annual). **Regional Groups:** 1. **Description:** Serves as professional society of persons interested in classification of animals or other aspects of taxonomy, phylogenetics or systematics. Promotes study of biodiversity, living and fossilized, and all aspects of systematic biology. **Awards:** Ernst Mayr Award. **Frequency:** annual. **Type:** recognition ● Mini-PEET Awards. **Frequency:** annual. **Type:** recognition ● **Frequency:** annual. **Type:** recognition. **Recipient:** for best student paper ● Travel Awards. **Frequency:** annual. **Type:** recognition. **Committees:** Education. **Affiliated With:** American Association for the Advancement of Science. **Formerly:** (1991) Society of Systematic Zoology. **Publications:** *Systematic Biology*, quarterly. Journal. Covers the theory, principles, methodology, and practice of zoology. **Price:** $25.00 /year for members; $40.00 /year for nonmembers; $12.50/year for students. ISSN: 0039-7989. **Circulation:** 2,500. **Conventions/Meetings:** annual meeting - 2008 June 20-24, Minneapolis, MN.

Academic Freedom

7869 ■ American Council of Trustees and Alumni (ACTA)
1726 M St. NW, Ste.802
Washington, DC 20036-4525
Ph: (202)467-6787
Free: (888)258-6648
Fax: (202)467-6784
E-mail: info@goacta.org
URL: http://www.goacta.org
Contact: Ms. Anne Neal, Pres.
Founded: 1995. **Nonmembership. Description:** Works through college trustees and alumni to ensure that genuine intellectual diversity, academic excellence, and common sense standards are restored and protected at America's college campuses. **Awards:** Philip Merrill Award for Outstanding Contributions to Liberal Arts Education. **Frequency:** annual. **Type:** recognition. **Recipient:** for individuals who have made an extraordinary contribution to the advancement of liberal arts education, core curricula, and the teaching of Western Civilization and American history. **Publications:** *Inside Academe*, quarterly. Newsletter. Alternate Formats: online. **Conventions/Meetings:** annual ATHENA Roundtable, meeting of trustees, alumni, and others concerned with reforming higher education.

7870 ■ Coalition for Student and Academic Rights (CO-STAR)
PO Box 491
Solebury, PA 18963
Ph: (215)862-9096
Fax: (215)862-9557
E-mail: info@co-star.org
URL: http://www.co-star.org
Contact: Atty. C.L. Lindsay III, Exec. Dir./Founder
Description: Students, professors, administrators, attorneys, and volunteers. Provides information on academic rights at the college and university level. **Funds:** Advocacy. **Publications:** *CO-STAR Newsletter.* Features up-to-date news and information about academic freedom and student rights. ● *The College Student's Guide to the Law.* Book.

Academic Placement

7871 ■ Independent Educational Consultants Association (IECA)
3251 Old Lee Hwy., Ste.510
Fairfax, VA 22030-1504
Ph: (703)591-4850
Free: (800)808-IECA
Fax: (703)591-4860
E-mail: info@iecaonline.com
URL: http://www.iecaonline.com
Contact: Mark Sklarow, Exec. Dir.
Founded: 1976. **Members:** 750. **Membership Dues:** associate, $300 (annual) ● professional, $600 (annual) ● institutional, $185 (annual) ● student, $60 (annual). **Staff:** 5. **Budget:** $1,000,000. **Regional Groups:** 3. **State Groups:** 2. **Multinational. Description:** Represents the interests of established educational consultants. Brings family the knowledge and skills of an experienced professional. Gives advice to students with special circumstances such as learning or physical disabilities, emotional or behavioral issues. Helps members update knowledge and maintain skills through meetings, workshops, training programs, and information exchanges with colleges, schools, programs, and other consultants. Members are required to maintain the highest standards of ethical practice. **Computer Services:** database ● mailing lists. **Formerly:** (1987) Independent Educational Counselors Association. **Publications:** *IECA Insights*, bimonthly. Newsletter. **Circulation:** 1,200. **Advertising:** accepted ● Directory, annual. Lists national and international consultants available to families. **Price:** free. **Circulation:** 13,000 ● Also publishes brochures for parents on college admission, boarding schools, and learning disabilities. **Conventions/Meetings:** semiannual conference (exhibits) - always spring and fall ● workshop, for aspiring consultants.

Accreditation

7872 ■ Accreditation Council for Graduate Medical Education (ACGME)
515 N State St., Ste.2000
Chicago, IL 60610-4322
Ph: (312)755-5000
Fax: (312)755-7498
E-mail: dcl@acgme.org
URL: http://www.acgme.org
Contact: David C. Leach MD, Exec. Dir.
Founded: 1974. **Staff:** 65. **Budget:** $10,000,000. **Description:** Representatives from the American Board of Medical Specialties, American Hospital Association, American Medical Association, Association of American Medical Colleges, and Council of Medical Specialty Societies. Accredits postgraduate medical education programs; recommends and conducts studies aimed at improving programs in postgraduate medical education; reviews and approves proposals for new programs in graduate medical education; provides information to the public and government relating to the evaluation and accreditation of graduate medical education programs. Maintains 25 residency review committees including: Allergy and Immunology; Anesthesiology; Colon and Rectal Surgery; and Dermatology. **Formerly:** (1981) Liaison Committee on Graduate Medical Education. **Publications:** *ACGME Bulletin*, quarterly. Includes meeting dates. **Price:** free for members. Alternate Formats: online ● *ACGME Report* ● *Manual of Policies and Procedures for Graduate Medical Education Review Committees.* **Conventions/Meetings:** meeting - 3/year, always in IL.

7873 ■ Accrediting Commission of Career Schools and Colleges of Technology (ACCSCT)
2101 Wilson Blvd., Ste.302
Arlington, VA 22201
Ph: (703)247-4212 (703)247-4518
Fax: (703)247-4533
E-mail: info@accsct.org
URL: http://www.accsct.org
Contact: Elise Scanlon, Exec. Dir.
Founded: 1993. **Staff:** 31. **Description:** Career schools and colleges of technology. Seeks to "maintain educational excellence and integrity in America's postsecondary career schools". Formulates standards of ethics, curricula, and practice for colleges of technology and career schools; examines and accredits qualifying institution; and sponsors educational programs. **Telecommunication Services:** electronic mail, escanlon@accsct.org. **Publications:** *ACCSCT Directory*, periodic ● Bulletins. Alternate Formats: online. **Conventions/Meetings:** periodic workshop.

7874 ■ Accrediting Council for Independent Colleges and Schools (ACICS)
750 1st St. NE, Ste.980
Washington, DC 20002-4241
Ph: (202)336-6780
Free: (866)510-0746
Fax: (202)842-2593
E-mail: info@acics.org
URL: http://www.acics.org
Contact: Sheryl Moody, Exec. Dir.
Founded: 1912. **Description:** Postsecondary educational institutions offering programs in business and related fields. Seeks to ensure the quality and effectiveness of business education programs. Examines and accredits postsecondary business education programs; serves as a clearinghouse on business studies. **Publications:** *The Criterion*, 3/year. Newsletter. Alternate Formats: online.

7875 ■ American Association of Christian Schools (AACS)
Natl. Off.
602 Belvoir Ave.
East Ridge, TN 37412
Ph: (423)629-4280
Fax: (423)622-7461
E-mail: national@aacs.org
URL: http://www.aacs.org
Contact: Dr. Charles Walker, Exec. Dir.
Founded: 1972. **Members:** 1,050. **Staff:** 10. **Budget:** $1,200,000. **State Groups:** 36. **Description:** Maintains teacher/administrator certification program and placement service. Participates in school accreditation program. Sponsors National Academic Tournament. Maintains American Christian Honor Society. Compiles statistics; maintains speakers' bureau and placement service. **Telecommunication Services:** electronic mail, cwalker@aacs.org. **Divisions:** Accreditation. **Publications:** *AACS Capitol Comments*, quarterly. Magazine. Provides information on developments in the Christian school movement and covers the activities and services of the association. Monitors legislation. **Price:** included in membership dues. **Circulation:** 2,500. **Advertising:** accepted ● *Administrative Leadership: A Christian Perspective*, semiannual. Magazine. Provides information to pastors and administrators. **Price:** included in membership dues.

Circulation: 3,000. **Advertising:** accepted ● *American Association of Christian Schools—Directory*, annual ● *Journal for Christian Educators*, quarterly. Magazine. Includes educational articles for the Christian school teacher, principal, and pastor. **Price:** $15.00/year. **Circulation:** 15,000. **Advertising:** accepted ● *Washington Flyer*, weekly. Newsletter. **Conventions/Meetings:** annual conference (exhibits) - always September ● annual National Education Conference - convention - always February.

7876 ■ International Christian Accrediting Association (ICAA)
2448 E 81st St.
Tulsa, OK 74137
Ph: (918)493-8880
Fax: (918)493-8041
E-mail: icaa@oru.edu
URL: http://www.icaa.us
Contact: Dr. Tom Agnew, Exec. Dir.

Founded: 1987. **Members:** 180. **Membership Dues:** accredited school, $800 (annual) ● provisional school, $800 (annual) ● candidate school, $800 (annual) ● applicant school, $250 (annual). **Staff:** 4. **Budget:** $200,000. **State Groups:** 38. **Description:** Christian schools that share common purposes and goals in such areas as administrative standards, faculty and support staff, educational programs, facilities and support services, and institutional design. Dedicated to the recognition and support of excellence in Christian education. Seeks to instill enthusiasm in member schools to be leaders in the field of education and promote academic, professional, administrative, and spiritual excellence. Accredits Christian schools that meet ICAA standards of excellence. Supports Christian Bible institutes, schools, and colleges. Trains qualified individuals to serve on site visit committees (site visit committees examine, observe, and make recommendations to schools that wish to become accredited). Assists institutions in developing Christian preschool programs. Conducts workshops; compiles statistics. **Committees:** Site Visit. **Divisions:** Bible School/College; Elementary/Secondary; Preschool. **Publications:** *ICAA Accreditation Manual for Postsecondary/Bible Schools*. Book. **Price:** $75.00 ● *ICAA Accreditation Manual for Preschool/Elementary/Secondary Schools*. Book. **Price:** $75.00. **Conventions/Meetings:** annual meeting (exhibits) - 2008 June 16, Tulsa, OK.

7877 ■ National Accrediting Commission of Cosmetology Arts and Sciences (NACCAS)
4401 Ford Ave., Ste.1300
Alexandria, VA 22302
Ph: (703)600-7600
Fax: (703)379-2200
E-mail: webinfo@naccas.org
URL: http://www.naccas.org
Contact: Christopher Walck, Exec. Dir.

Founded: 1969. **Staff:** 32. **Budget:** $3,000,000. **Description:** Accrediting body for schools of cosmetology; presently there are 1030 accredited schools. Objectives are to: raise standards of cosmetology schools throughout the country; encourage use of modern educational methods and techniques; stimulate self-improvement by the schools. Sponsors standards and professional team training workshops. **Formed by Merger of:** Accrediting Commission for Cosmetology Education; National Accrediting Commission for Cosmetology Schools. **Formerly:** (1981) Cosmetology Accrediting Commission. **Publications:** *Directory of Accredited Cosmetology Schools*, annual. **Price:** $12.95 ● *Job Demand in the Cosmetology Industry*, semiannual. **Price:** $19.95 ● *NACCAS Review*, 3/year. **Price:** $65.00/year. **Circulation:** 4,000. **Advertising:** accepted ● Handbook, annual. **Price:** $14.95.

7878 ■ National Association of Private Catholic and Independent Schools (NAPCIS)
2640 3rd Ave.
Sacramento, CA 95818
Ph: (916)451-4963
E-mail: info@napcis.org
URL: http://www.napcis.org
Contact: Most Rev. Raymond L. Burke, Ecclesiastical Advisor

Founded: 1995. **Members:** 62. **Membership Dues:** active, provisional, associate, $125 (annual). **Description:** Provides accreditation for private Catholic and independent schools. Works toward solidarity, strength, and security of small schools teaching the Catholic faith. **Computer Services:** Online services, educational resources and networking opportunities. **Publications:** *Feasibility Packet*. Features an overview of what to consider when starting a private Catholic and Independent school. ● *Manual of Administration*, annual. Contains a listing of NAPCIS member schools: addresses, contacts, and school programs. ● Membership Directory. **Conventions/Meetings:** annual Independent Schools in Service to the Church - conference.

7879 ■ National Council for Accreditation of Teacher Education (NCATE)
2010 Massachusetts Ave. NW, Ste.500
Washington, DC 20036
Ph: (202)466-7496
Fax: (202)296-6620
E-mail: ncate@ncate.org
URL: http://www.ncate.org
Contact: Arthur E. Wise, Pres.

Founded: 1954. **Members:** 575. **Staff:** 20. **Description:** Representatives from constituent colleges and universities, state departments of education, school boards, teacher, and other professional groups. Voluntary accrediting body devoted exclusively to: evaluation and accreditation of institutions for preparation of elementary and secondary school teachers; preparation of school service personnel, including school principals, supervisors, superintendents, school psychologists, instructional technologists, and other specialists for school-oriented positions. **Computer Services:** Mailing lists, of members. **Committees:** Complaint Review; Process and Evaluation; Professional Standards; Review Panel. **Publications:** *How Professional Development Schools Make a Difference: A Review of Research*. Monograph. **Price:** $20.00 ● *Quality Teaching*, semiannual. Newsletter. Alternate Formats: online ● *Standards, Procedures, and Policies for the Accreditation of Professional Education Units*. **Price:** $20.00 ● Handbooks ● Papers. **Conventions/Meetings:** semiannual meeting, with work session.

7880 ■ National Council for Private School Accreditation (NCPSA)
PO Box 13686
Seattle, WA 98198-1010
Ph: (253)874-3408
Fax: (253)874-3409
E-mail: ncpsaexdr@aol.com
URL: http://www.ncpsa.org
Contact: Dr. Don D. Petry, Exec. Dir.

Founded: 1993. **Members:** 16. **Staff:** 10. **Description:** Serves as a national review panel for the standards and review procedures of private school accrediting associations. **Commissions:** Infant and Early Childhood Education; Standard and Review; State and National Relations.

Administration

7881 ■ ACE Fellows Program
c/o American Council on Education
1 Dupont Cir. NW
Washington, DC 20036-1193
Ph: (202)939-9300 (202)939-9420
Fax: (202)785-8056
E-mail: fellows@ace.nche.edu
URL: http://www.acenet.edu/AM/Template.cfm?Section=Fellows_Program1
Contact: Marlene Ross, Dir.

Founded: 1965. **Members:** 1,400. **Staff:** 4. **Description:** Service arm of the American Council on Education to strengthen leadership in American postsecondary education by identifying and preparing individuals who have shown promise for responsible positions in higher education administration. Objectives are: to encourage and prepare individuals making higher education administration their professional career; to provide opportunities for planned observation and experience in decision-making; to identify and develop potential leaders. Arranges internships whereby senior faculty and administrators are given the opportunity to study higher education leadership as an intern at a host institution. The stipulations are that the fellow will do certain assigned reading in higher education administration, focus on a strategic learning project and serve at the home institution for the academic year following the internship. Provides services for alumni of the program. **Formerly:** (1976) Academic Administration Internship Program. **Publications:** *Council of Fellows Directory*, annual ● *Council of Fellows Newsletter*, semiannual. Alternate Formats: online ● *Photobrochure of ACE Fellows*, annual ● Papers. **Conventions/Meetings:** meeting - 3/year ● seminar.

7882 ■ American Association of School Administrators (AASA)
801 N Quincy St., Ste.700
Arlington, VA 22203
Ph: (703)528-0700
Fax: (703)841-1543
E-mail: info@aasa.org
URL: http://www.aasa.org
Contact: Paul D. Houston, Exec. Dir.

Founded: 1865. **Members:** 14,000. **Membership Dues:** active, $387 (annual) ● associate, $361 (annual) ● college professor, $194 (annual) ● aspiring school system leader, $55 (annual) ● retired, $60 (annual) ● allied, $1,000 (annual). **Staff:** 40. **Budget:** $10,000,000. **State Groups:** 54. **Description:** Professional association of administrators and executives of school systems and educational service agencies; school district superintendents; central, building, and service unit administrators; presidents of colleges, deans, and professors of educational administration; placement officers; executive directors and administrators of education associations. Sponsors numerous professional development conferences annually. **Awards:** American Education Award. **Type:** recognition ● Leadership for Learning. **Type:** recognition ● National Superintendent of the Year. **Frequency:** annual. **Type:** recognition. **Computer Services:** Online services, legislative updates, job listings. **Absorbed:** County Intermediate Unit Superintendents (of NEA). **Formerly:** (1870) National Association of School Superintendents; (1907) Department of School Superintendents of the National Education Association; (1937) Department of Superintendents of the National Education Association. **Publications:** *The School Administrator*, 11/year. Magazine. Contains feature articles, abstracts, book reviews, and legislative news for school superintendents, principals, and other central administrators. **Price:** included in membership dues. ISSN: 0036-6439. **Circulation:** 15,500. **Advertising:** accepted. **Conventions/Meetings:** annual National Conference on Education (exhibits) - always February or March. 2009 Feb. 19-22, San Francisco, CA; 2010 Feb. 11-14, Phoenix, AZ.

7883 ■ American Association of School Personnel Administrators (AASPA)
533-B N Mur-Len Rd.
Olathe, KS 66062
Ph: (913)829-2007
Fax: (913)829-2041
E-mail: aaspa@aaspa.org
URL: http://www.aaspa.org
Contact: Dr. Jody Shelton EdD, Exec. Dir.

Founded: 1940. **Members:** 1,900. **Membership Dues:** individual/business, $150 (annual) ● associate, $75 (annual) ● retired, $50 (annual) ● institutional, $325 (annual). **Staff:** 5. **Budget:** $650,000. **Regional Groups:** 50. **Multinational. Description:** Represents persons employed in school personnel administration in the U.S., Canada, and beyond. Establishes acceptable school personnel standards, techniques, and practices. Conducts research. **Awards:** Leon Bradley Scholarship Award. **Fre-**

quency: annual. **Type:** scholarship. **Recipient:** to a minority college student in the field of education ● **Frequency:** annual. **Type:** recognition. **Recipient:** for exemplary personnel practices. **Computer Services:** database ● mailing lists. **Committees:** Professional Development. **Formerly:** (1959) American Association of Examiners and Administrators of Educational Personnel. **Publications:** *AASPA Perspective*, quarterly. Newsletter. **Price:** included in membership dues. **Advertising:** accepted. Alternate Formats: online ● *Best Practices*, annual. Magazine. **Price:** $5.00 included in membership dues. **Advertising:** accepted. Alternate Formats: online. **Conventions/Meetings:** annual conference (exhibits) - 2008 Oct. 15-18, Seattle, WA; 2009 Oct. 13-16, Hartford, CT.

7884 ■ American Association of University Administrators (AAUA)
PO Box 630101
Little Neck, NY 11363
Ph: (347)235-4822
Fax: (718)225-0565
E-mail: dking@aaua.org
URL: http://www.aaua.org
Contact: Dan L. King, Gen. Sec.
Founded: 1970. **Members:** 900. **Membership Dues:** student, $35 (annual) ● associate, $75 (annual) ● active, $100 (annual) ● sponsor, $250 (annual) ● sustaining, $150 (annual) ● emeritus, $55 (annual) ● institution (based on number of members), $500-$2,000 (annual) ● group associate (based on number of associate members), $375-$1,500 (annual). **Staff:** 35. **Budget:** $88,000. **Description:** Promotes excellence in the administration of higher education and assists career administrators in continuing their professional growth. Conducts periodic professional development program. **Awards:** Distinguished Service Award. **Frequency:** annual. **Type:** recognition. **Recipient:** for excellence in the administration of higher education ● Eileen M. Tosney Award. **Frequency:** annual. **Type:** recognition. **Recipient:** for excellence in the administration of higher education ● John L. Blackburn Award. **Frequency:** annual. **Type:** recognition. **Recipient:** for excellence in the administration of higher education. **Committees:** Awards; Development Administrator; Diversity; Exemplary Models Competition; Insurance; International Liaison; Newcomers; Professional Standards. **Publications:** *College and University Administrator*, semiannual. Magazine. Contains information on higher education, educational research, and legal developments affecting administrators and institutions of higher learning. **Price:** included in membership dues. **Circulation:** 1,200. **Advertising:** accepted ● *Communique*, quarterly. Newsletter. Alternate Formats: online. **Conventions/Meetings:** annual assembly (exhibits) - always June ● periodic seminar, regional.

7885 ■ American Conference of Academic Deans (ACAD)
1818 R St. NW
Washington, DC 20009
Ph: (202)884-7419
Fax: (202)265-9532
E-mail: rzepka@acad-edu.org
URL: http://www.acad-edu.org
Contact: Laura Rzepka, Admin. Dir.
Founded: 1945. **Members:** 600. **Membership Dues:** individual (first member from an institution), $95 (annual) ● international, emeritus, $55 (annual) ● group, $80 (annual). **Staff:** 1. **Budget:** $75,000. **Description:** Academic administrators and chief academic officers of two and four-year colleges and universities. **Libraries: Type:** open to the public. **Holdings:** papers. **Subjects:** past proceedings of annual meetings. **Computer Services:** Online services, discussion group for deans and chief academic officers. **Affiliated With:** Association of American Colleges and Universities. **Publications:** *Resource Handbook for Academic Deans*. **Price:** $20.00. Alternate Formats: online. **Conventions/Meetings:** annual meeting, held in conjunction with Association of American Colleges and Universities (exhibits) ● annual meeting - every January. 2009 Jan. 21-24, Seattle, WA; 2010 Jan. 20-23, Washington, DC.

7886 ■ American Federation of School Administrators (AFSA)
1101 17th St. NW, Ste.408
Washington, DC 20036
Ph: (202)986-4209
Free: (800)354-AFSA
Fax: (202)986-4211
E-mail: afsa@admin.org
URL: http://www.admin.org
Contact: Jill Levy, Intl. Pres.
Founded: 1971. **Members:** 12,000. **Staff:** 6. **Budget:** $600,000. **Regional Groups:** 4. **State Groups:** 4. **Local Groups:** 85. **Description:** Principals, vice-principals, directors, supervisors, and administrators involved in pedagogical education. Purposes are to: achieve the highest goals in education; maintain and improve standards, benefits, and conditions for personnel without regard to color, race, sex, background, or national origin; obtain job security; protect seniority and merit; cooperate with all responsible organizations in education; promote understanding, participation, and support of the public, communities, and agencies; be alert to resist attacks and campaigns that would create or entrench a spoils system; promote democratic society by supporting full educational opportunities for every child and student in the nation. **Awards: Type:** recognition. **Affiliated With:** AFL-CIO. **Formerly:** (1976) School Administrators and Supervisors Organizing Committee. **Publications:** *The Administrator*. Newsletter. Alternate Formats: online ● *AFSA News*, monthly. **Advertising:** accepted. **Conventions/Meetings:** triennial conference.

7887 ■ Association of College Administration Professionals (ACAP)
PO Box 1389
Staunton, VA 24402
Ph: (540)885-1873
Fax: (540)885-6133
E-mail: acap@cfw.com
URL: http://www.acap.org
Founded: 1995. **Members:** 3,000. **Membership Dues:** individual, $75 (annual) ● institutional, $195 (annual). **Staff:** 3. **Budget:** $300,000. **Description:** Works to provide professional assistance to college administrators. Conducts educational programs. **Telecommunication Services:** electronic bulletin board. **Publications:** *The Bulletin of Higher Education Administration*, monthly. Newsletter. **Conventions/Meetings:** annual conference (exhibits) ● workshop - 8/year. 2009 Mar. 13-18, Memphis, TN; 2009 Mar. 28-30, San Diego, CA.

7888 ■ Association of College and University Auditors (ACUA)
342 N Main St., Ste.301
West Hartford, CT 06117-2507
Ph: (860)586-7561
Fax: (860)586-7550
E-mail: info@acua.org
URL: http://www.acua.org
Contact: Karen R. Hinen CAE, Exec. Dir.
Founded: 1958. **Members:** 800. **Membership Dues:** institutional, corporate, $350 (annual) ● individual, $150 (annual). **Staff:** 2. **Budget:** $320,000. **Multinational. Description:** Represents universities, colleges, and affiliated organizations with an interest in internal auditing. Promotes productive performance of internal auditors by means of continuing research, professional training, and establishment of internal auditing courses in colleges and universities. **Libraries: Type:** not open to the public. **Subjects:** internal audit in colleges and universities. **Awards:** ACUA Scholarships. **Frequency:** annual. **Type:** scholarship. **Recipient:** for pursuing careers in internal audit. **Committees:** Accounting Principles; Audit; Best Practices; Government Affairs; Information and Technology; Professional Education; Publications. **Publications:** *College and University Auditor*, 3/year. Journal. **Price:** $150.00. **Circulation:** 600. **Advertising:** accepted ● *NCAA Audit Guide* ● *Quality Assurance Review Manual* ● *Software - Control Assessment Tool*. **Conventions/Meetings:** annual conference and seminar (exhibits).

7889 ■ Association of Governing Boards of Universities and Colleges (AGB)
1 Dupont Cir., Ste.400
Washington, DC 20036
Ph: (202)296-8400
Free: (800)356-6317
Fax: (202)223-7053
E-mail: info@agb.org
URL: http://www.agb.org
Contact: Richard D. Legon, Pres.
Founded: 1921. **Members:** 34,000. **Membership Dues:** institution (based on total enrollment), $1,950-$9,250 (annual) ● two-year community college, separately incorporated foundation, advisory or quasi-governing board, governing board, $1,950 (annual). **Staff:** 32. **Budget:** $5,500,000. **Description:** Members are governing boards of public and private 2- and 4-year colleges and universities; constituents include regents, trustees, presidents, and other high-level administrators of colleges and universities. Addresses the problems and responsibilities of trusteeship in all sectors of higher education and the relationships of trustees and regents to the president, the faculty, and the student body. Operates Zwingle Resource Center; conducts the National Conference on Trusteeship. Conducts research programs and the Robert L. Gale Fund for the Study of Trusteeship. **Libraries: Type:** reference. **Awards:** Distinguished Service Award on Trusteeship. **Type:** recognition. **Computer Services:** Mailing lists, of members. **Formerly:** (1963) Association of Governing Boards of State Universities and Allied Institutions. **Publications:** *Centerforgovernance.net*. Newsletter. Alternate Formats: online ● *Priorities*. Report. Alternate Formats: online ● *Trusteeship*, bimonthly. Magazine. Includes reports on issues and trends in higher education. **Price:** included in membership dues; $65.00 /year for nonmembers. **Circulation:** 32,000. Alternate Formats: online. Also Cited As: *AGB Reports*. **Conventions/Meetings:** annual National Conference on Trusteeship - 2009 Apr. 18-21, San Diego, CA ● seminar ● workshop.

7890 ■ Association of Graduate Schools in Association of American Universities (AGS)
1200 New York Ave. NW, Ste.550
Washington, DC 20005
Ph: (202)408-7500
Fax: (202)408-8184
E-mail: matt_owens@aau.edu
URL: http://www.aau.edu
Contact: M. Matthew Owens, Asst. Dir. of Federal Relations
Founded: 1948. **Members:** 61. **Description:** Deans of graduate studies in the 61 universities comprising the Association of American Universities (see separate entry). Works to consider matters of common interest relating to graduate study and research. **Publications:** Newsletter, periodic. **Conventions/Meetings:** annual meeting.

7891 ■ Association of International Education Administrators (AIEA)
c/o Dr. Darla K. Deardorff, Exec. Dir.
Duke Univ.
Campus Box 90404
Durham, NC 27708-0404
Ph: (919)668-1928
Fax: (919)684-8749
E-mail: aiea@duke.edu
URL: http://www.aieaworld.org
Contact: Dr. Darla K. Deardorff, Exec. Dir.
Founded: 1981. **Members:** 450. **Membership Dues:** institutional/organizational, $400 (annual) ● individual, $100 (annual). **Staff:** 1. **Budget:** $85,000. **Description:** Senior-level institutional leaders engaged in advancing the international dimensions of higher education. **Awards:** Charles Klasek Award. **Frequency:** annual. **Type:** recognition. **Recipient:** for long term and outstanding service in the field of international education administration ● **Frequency:** annual. **Type:** grant. **Recipient:** application and selection ● Harold Josephson Award. **Frequency:**

annual. **Type:** recognition. **Recipient:** for promising leadership in international education ● Timothy J. Rutenber Award. **Frequency:** annual. **Type:** recognition. **Recipient:** for outstanding service to the association. **Publications:** *Journal of Studies in International Education*, quarterly. Contains current research in the international education field. **Price:** $75.00 for nonmembers; free for members ● An Organization Dealing with international education affairs. Membership is from universities and related organizations. **Conventions/Meetings:** annual conference, internationalizing higher education; challenges and opportunities - 2010 Feb. 14-18, Washington, DC.

7892 ■ Association of School Business Officials International (ASBO)

11401 N Shore Dr.
Reston, VA 20190-4200
Ph: (703)478-0405 (703)708-7063
Free: (866)682-2729
Fax: (703)478-0205
E-mail: asboreq@asbointl.org
URL: http://www.asbointl.org
Contact: John D. Musso, Exec. Dir.

Founded: 1910. **Members:** 5,800. **Membership Dues:** emeritus, $40 (annual) ● active, $135 (annual) ● associate, $200 (annual) ● publication, student, $85 (annual) ● life, $2,700 ● corporate associate, $495 (annual). **Staff:** 18. **Budget:** $2,500,000. **State Groups:** 56. **Multinational. Description:** School business managers; assistant superintendents in charge of business; supervisors of accounting; directors of transportation, maintenance, food service, data processing, and operations; office managers; school business officials, school board members, and others interested in school business management. Business associates are vendors providing products and/or services to schools. Promotes improvement and advancement of school business management. Provides a forum for the exchange of information and ideas among professionals; keeps legislative bodies, governmental agencies, and members of the educational community informed of key issues relating to the administration of educational facilities. Maintains professional registration program, insurance and continuing education program, certificate of excellence program in financial reporting and meritorious budget awards program. Maintains 17 committees. **Libraries: Type:** not open to the public. **Holdings:** 68. **Subjects:** school business administration. **Awards:** Pinnacle Award. **Frequency:** annual. **Type:** recognition. **Recipient:** for individuals who have created outstanding practices, proposals or publications. **Computer Services:** database, of experts in areas of school management. **Telecommunication Services:** electronic mail, jmusso@asbointl.org. **Committees:** Certificate of Excellence; Editorial Board; Environmental Aspects; Exhibits Advisory; Human Resource and Labor Relations; Information Systems; Legal Aspects; Legislative Affairs. **Absorbed:** (1922) National Association of School Building Officials; (1973) School Facilities Council of Architecture, Education and Industry. **Formerly:** (1918) National Association of School Accounting Officers; (1922) National Association of School Accounting and Business Officials of Public Schools; (1943) National Association of School Business Officials; (1951) Association of School Business Officials; (1985) Association of School Business Officials of the United States and Canada. **Publications:** *ASBO Accents*, monthly. Newsletter. Covers association news and developments affecting educational growth. Includes book reviews, calendar of events, and job listings. **Price:** included in membership dues. **Circulation:** 5,800. Alternate Formats: online ● *Journal of Education Finance*. Provides research and cogent analyses essential to policy studies and decision-making. Alternate Formats: online ● *Scholastic Administrator*, 8/year. Magazine. Contains information, covering topics such as funding and uses for technology, best practices, and online learning. Alternate Formats: online ● *School Business Affairs*, monthly. Magazine. Covers regulatory and legislative developments affecting education. Also covers association news, book reviews, and calendar of events. **Price:** included in membership dues. **Circulation:** 6,300. **Advertising:** accepted. Alternate Formats: online ● Also publishes books on school business management. **Conventions/Meetings:** annual convention, educational programs, discussion groups, product showcases, vendor and architectural exhibits, microcomputer lab, social events (exhibits) ● meeting.

7893 ■ Association of Schools of Journalism and Mass Communication (ASJMC)

234 Outlet Pointe Blvd.
Columbia, SC 29210-5667
Ph: (803)798-0271
Fax: (803)772-3509
E-mail: aejmchq@aol.com
URL: http://www.asjmc.org
Contact: Jennifer H. McGill, Exec. Dir.

Founded: 1917. **Members:** 197. **Membership Dues:** school, $350-$700 (annual) ● individual, $50 (annual). **Staff:** 8. **Description:** Administrators of departments, divisions, and schools of journalism and mass communications. Compiles journalism education statistics. **Computer Services:** Mailing lists. **Absorbed:** (1984) American Society of Journalism School Administrators. **Formerly:** (1954) Association of Accredited School and Departments of Journalism; (1982) American Association of Schools and Department of Journalism. **Publications:** *ASJMC Administrator*, 3/year. Newsletter. Alternate Formats: online ● *ASJMC Insights*, semiannual. Journal. Features topics that focus on administrative issue or concern in JMC education. Alternate Formats: online. **Conventions/Meetings:** annual convention (exhibits).

7894 ■ College and University Computer Users Association (CUMREC)

c/o EDUCAUSE
4772 Walnut St., Ste.206
Boulder, CO 80301-2538
Ph: (303)449-4430
Fax: (303)440-0461
E-mail: info@cumrec.org
URL: http://www.cumrec.org
Contact: Scott D. McGill, Gen. Chm.

Founded: 1956. **Members:** 800. **Description:** Users of data processing equipment for administrative or management purposes at colleges and universities. Seeks to develop a forum for the exchange of ideas and information; promotes increased and improved use of computers for administrative data processing in higher education. **Awards:** Best Presentation Award. **Frequency:** annual. **Type:** monetary. **Recipient:** for individual who gave a presentation at the conference ● The Frank Martin Service Award. **Frequency:** annual. **Type:** recognition. **Recipient:** for individual with exemplary service to the college and university information technology. **Committees:** Communications; Development; Preconference Seminar; Program. **Formerly:** (1989) College and University Machine Records Conference; (1992) College and University Computer Users Conference. **Publications:** *Directory of Attendance*, annual ● Proceedings, annual ● Newsletter, quarterly. **Conventions/Meetings:** annual conference (exhibits) - always May.

7895 ■ Educational Research Service (ERS)

1001 N Fairfax St., Ste.500
Alexandria, VA 22314-1587
Ph: (703)243-2100 (703)248-6220
Free: (800)791-9308
Fax: (703)243-1985
E-mail: ers@ers.org
URL: http://www.ers.org
Contact: John M. Forsyth PhD, Pres./Dir.

Founded: 1973. **Members:** 2,800. **Staff:** 30. **Budget:** $3,000,000. **Description:** School systems, educational service agencies, state departments of education, associations of school administrators and school boards, university departments of education administration, college libraries, and related agencies interested in school management and policy. Provides school administrators and school boards with objective, reliable, and timely research and information essential to effective decision-making for both long-range and day-to-day operations. Serves as a national source and clearinghouse for research. Offers customized information services for subscribing agencies. **Libraries: Type:** reference. **Holdings:** 20,000; articles, books, periodicals. **Subjects:** education. **Telecommunication Services:** electronic mail, k.mclane@ers.org. **Publications:** *ERS Spectrum*, quarterly. Journal. Contains articles on local school district research. ISSN: 0740-7874 ● *The Informed Educator*, bimonthly. Contains research summary. **Price:** included in membership dues; $10.00 for nonmembers. **Circulation:** 2,600 ● Bulletin, biweekly. Summarizes recent reports on education topics. **Price:** included in membership dues. ISSN: 1076-1497. **Circulation:** 2,600. Alternate Formats: online ● Also publishes studies, reports, monographs, Focus On, relevant research for school decisions, executive summaries of research, What We Know About Series, and Concerns in Education series.

7896 ■ Jesuit Association of Student Personnel Administrators (JASPA)

c/o JASPA Newsletter Ed.
2500 California Plz.
Omaha, NE 68178
Ph: (402)280-2717
Fax: (402)280-1275
E-mail: waynejr@creighton.edu
URL: http://jaspa.creighton.edu
Contact: Jacqueline Peterson, Pres.

Founded: 1954. **Members:** 750. **Regional Groups:** 3. **Description:** Represents administrators of student personnel programs in 28 Jesuit colleges and universities in the United States. Sponsors institutes and seminars for personnel in Jesuit colleges. Cooperates with Catholic and non-Catholic educational associations in various projects. Maintains placement service and conducts workshops. Operates organizational archives and compiles statistics. **Awards:** Ignatian Medal for an Outstanding Campus Program. **Frequency:** annual. **Type:** recognition. **Recipient:** for an institution with outstanding programs and services ● Ignatian Medal for Outstanding Achievement in Jesuit Student Affairs Work. **Frequency:** annual. **Type:** recognition. **Recipient:** for significant accomplishments in the field ● Ignatian Medal for Outstanding Service. **Frequency:** annual. **Type:** recognition. **Recipient:** for distinguished contributions on the programs and services of the JASPA ● Ignatian Medal for the Outstanding New Professional in Jesuit Student Affairs. **Frequency:** annual. **Type:** recognition. **Recipient:** for individuals with excellent growth and improvement at early stage of their career ● Rev. Victor R. Yanitelli, S.J. Award. **Frequency:** annual. **Type:** recognition. **Recipient:** for outstanding service in Jesuit higher education. **Telecommunication Services:** electronic mail, jpeterso@holycross.edu. **Affiliated With:** Association of Jesuit Colleges and Universities. **Formerly:** (1981) Conference on Jesuit Student Personnel Administrators. **Publications:** *The Ignatian Perspective: The Role of Student Affairs in Jesuit Higher Education*. Monograph ● *Jesuit Association of Student Personnel Administrators—Newsletter*, quarterly. Covers membership activities. **Price:** free. **Circulation:** 500 ● Directory, annual. **Conventions/Meetings:** annual conference - always spring.

7897 ■ National Association of College and University Business Officers (NACUBO)

1110 Vermont Ave. NW, Ste.800
Washington, DC 20005
Ph: (202)861-2500 (202)861-2517
Free: (800)462-4916
Fax: (202)861-2583
E-mail: john.walda@nacubo.org
URL: http://www.nacubo.org
Contact: John Walda, Pres./CEO

Founded: 1950. **Members:** 2,500. **Staff:** 52. **Budget:** $7,000,000. **Regional Groups:** 4. **Description:** Colleges, universities, and companies that are members of a regional association. Develops and maintains national interest in improving the principles and practices of business and financial administration in higher education. Sponsors workshops in fields such as cash management, grant and contract maintenance, accounting, investment, student loan administration, and costing. Conducts research and information exchange programs between college and university personnel; compiles statistics. **Libraries: Type:** reference. **Holdings:** reports. **Awards:** Daniel D. Robinson Award. **Frequency:** annual. **Type:** recognition. **Recipient:** for an outstanding NACUBO volunteer ● Distinguished Business Officer Award. **Frequency:** annual. **Type:** recognition. **Recipient:** for outstanding business officers ● Higher Education Awards Program. **Frequency:** annual. **Type:** recognition ● Rodney H. Adams Award. **Frequency:** annual. **Type:** recognition. **Recipient:** for outstanding individuals. **Committees:** Membership and Member Services; Professional Development; Public Policy; Small Colleges and Minority Institutions; Two-Year Colleges. **Councils:** Accounting Principles; Awards; Comprehensive Colleges and Universities; Higher Education Awards; Research and Doctoral Universities. **Task Forces:** Taxation. **Affiliated With:** National Association of Independent Schools. **Absorbed:** American Association of College Business Officers; (1967) American Association of College and University Business Officers. **Formerly:** (1962) National Federation of College and University Business Officers Associations. **Publications:** *Business Officer*, monthly. Magazine. Covers business and financial news affecting college and university management; includes association news and meetings schedule. ISSN: 0147-877X. **Circulation:** 22,000. **Advertising:** accepted. Alternate Formats: online ● *Financial Accounting and Reporting Manual*, bimonthly ● *NACUBO Membership Directory*, annual ● *National Association of College and University Business Officers—Annual Report*. Provides association information including publications, research projects, professional development workshops, and committees. **Circulation:** 19,500 ● *National Association of College and University Business Officers—Special Action and Advisory Reports*. Covers developments in the higher education administration field, primarily in the area of federal policies and programs. **Price:** included in membership dues. **Circulation:** 2,300 ● *Student-Centered Financial Services: Innovations That Succeed*. Book. **Price:** $54.95 for members; $70.00 for nonmembers. **Conventions/Meetings:** annual conference (exhibits) - always July.

7898 ■ National Association of Educational Office Professionals (NAEOP)
PO Box 12619
Wichita, KS 67277-2619
Ph: (316)942-4822
Fax: (316)942-7100
E-mail: naeop@naeop.org
URL: http://www.naeop.org
Contact: Sharon Daggett Manner, Exec. Dir.

Founded: 1934. **Members:** 5,000. **Membership Dues:** retired, $25 (annual) ● active, associate, $45 (annual) ● corporate, $55 (annual) ● institutional, $80 (annual). **Staff:** 4. **Regional Groups:** 250. **Description:** Secretaries, stenographers, administrative assistants, bookkeepers, receptionists, and other office workers employed by schools, colleges and universities, educational associations, and county and state departments of education. Conducts professional standards program to measure the services of office personnel in education and awards certificates for achievements on five levels of education, experience, and professional activity. Maintains speakers' bureau. **Awards:** National Educational Administrator of the Year Award. **Frequency:** annual. **Type:** recognition ● National Educational Office Professional of the Year Award. **Frequency:** annual. **Type:** recognition. **Committees:** Awards; Field Service; Professional Growth; Professional Responsibility; Professional Standards; Scholarship Awards (in-house only). **Affiliated With:** American Association of School Administrators; National Association of Elementary School Principals. **Formerly:** (1952) National Association of School Secretaries; (1980) National Association of Educational Secretaries; (1992) National Association of Educational Office Personnel. **Publications:** *A Guide to Organizing an Association*. Booklet. **Price:** $2.00 ● *A Winning Team*. Booklet. **Price:** $2.00 ● *Dynamic Leadership*. Booklet. **Price:** $2.00 ● *Effective Educational Office Professional*. Booklet. **Price:** $2.00 ● *File It Right and Find It*. Booklet. **Price:** $5.00 ● *Goal Setting*. Booklet. **Price:** $2.00 ● *Installation Ceremonies*. Booklet. **Price:** $5.00 ● *Membership: Recruiting and Retaining*. Booklet. **Price:** $2.00 ● *NES Connector*, quarterly. **Price:** included in membership dues; $20.00 for nonmembers ● *Office Management*. Booklet. **Price:** $2.00 ● *Public Relations*. Booklet. **Price:** $2.00 ● *Publications/Newsletter Editing*. Booklet. **Price:** $2.00 ● *Time Management*. Booklet. **Price:** $2.00 ● Also publishes textbooks and instructors' manuals. **Conventions/Meetings:** annual conference, includes institute (exhibits) - always July ● meeting, in conjunction with the American Association of School Administrators - 1-2/year.

7899 ■ National Association of Educational Procurement (NAEP)
5523 Res. Park Dr., Ste.340
Baltimore, MD 21228
Ph: (443)543-5540
Fax: (443)543-5550
E-mail: ceo@naepnet.org
URL: http://www.naepnet.org
Contact: Doreen Murner, CEO

Founded: 1921. **Members:** 2,200. **Membership Dues:** institutional (maximum; based on number of students FTE), $2,528 (annual) ● associate, $468 (annual) ● business affiliate (based on number of representatives), $995-$1,295 (annual). **Staff:** 10. **Regional Groups:** 19. **Description:** Purchasing officials for colleges and universities. Stimulates exchange of purchasing and business management information; maintains liaison with government agencies; holds institutes. Works with the Educational and Institutional Cooperative Service. **Awards:** Bert C. Ahrens Achievement Award. **Frequency:** annual. **Type:** recognition. **Recipient:** for individuals who have demonstrated continued loyalty and dedication to the association ● Distinguished Service Award. **Frequency:** annual. **Type:** recognition. **Recipient:** for individuals who have provided extraordinary service to their institutions. **Committees:** Editorial; Nominating; Professional Development; Public Relations. **Programs:** Advanced Purchasing Institute; Data Processing Institute; Furniture Procurement Institute; Hazardous Waste Removal. **Formerly:** (1947) Educational Buyers Association; (2006) National Association of Educational Buyers. **Publications:** *NAEB Journal*, quarterly. **Price:** $25.00/issue for nonmembers. **Advertising:** accepted. Alternate Formats: online ● *Purchasing Link*, monthly. Bulletin. **Circulation:** 15,000. **Advertising:** accepted. Alternate Formats: online ● Also publishes guides. **Conventions/Meetings:** annual conference (exhibits).

7900 ■ National Association of Federal Education Program Administrators (NAFEPA)
c/o Bobby Burns, Pres.
PO Box 2084
Anniston, AL 36202
Ph: (256)741-7453
Fax: (256)237-5332
E-mail: bburns@calhoun.k12.al.us
URL: http://www.nafepa.org
Contact: Bobby Burns, Pres.

Founded: 1974. **Members:** 1,000. **Membership Dues:** individual, $100 (annual). **Staff:** 1. **Description:** Administrators of state and federal programs in local and county school districts, state departments of education, and institutions of higher learning throughout the U.S. Acts as liaison to federal education decision-makers in Washington, DC. Supplies members with current information relative to compensatory, supplementary, and exemplary programs, changes in rules, regulations, and funding requirements. **Awards:** Ralph Steffek Award. **Frequency:** annual. **Type:** recognition. **Recipient:** for outstanding service to the organization ● **Frequency:** annual. **Type:** scholarship. **Recipient:** for students pursuing a career or degree in education. **Formerly:** National Association of Administrators of State and Federal Education Programs; (1984) National Association of Federal Program Administrators. **Publications:** Newsletter, monthly. Alternate Formats: online. **Conventions/Meetings:** annual conference (exhibits) ● seminar.

7901 ■ National Association of Hebrew Day School Administrators (NAHDSA)
Address Unknown since 2007

Members: 400. **Description:** Administrators of schools affiliated with Torah Umesorah - National Society for Hebrew Day Schools (see separate entry). Sponsors degree programs for active and prospective administrators of day schools. Associated with the Institute for Professional Enrichment which offers undergraduate and graduate degree programs for the benefit of the Torah community through its affiliation with accredited universities. Presently inactive. **Libraries: Type:** reference. **Holdings:** 2,500. **Subjects:** management and personnel relations. **Publications:** *Personal Code* ● Directory, periodic.

7902 ■ National Association of Pupil Services Administrators (NAPSA)
Box 113
Williamsport, PA 17701
Ph: (570)323-2050
Fax: (570)323-2051
E-mail: napsa@comcast.net
URL: http://www.napsa.com
Contact: Wayne D. Fausnaught, Exec. Dir.

Founded: 1966. **Members:** 700. **Membership Dues:** student, $55 (annual) ● associate, $70 (annual) ● regular, $110 (annual) ● retired, $5 (annual) ● institutional, $500 (annual). **Budget:** $80,000. **State Groups:** 12. **Description:** System-wide administrators of pupil services including guidance and counseling, child welfare and attendance, social services, health services, psychological services, speech and hearing services, and special education. Promotes pupil personnel services programs in school systems so the needs of children and youth may be met more effectively; provides a means of communication and professional growth for pupil services administrators; seeks to create an awareness of the role and function of pupil services and the pupil services administrator. **Computer Services:** database ● mailing lists. **Committees:** Legal Update Services; Public Policy; Training, Certification, and Accreditation. **Formerly:** (1989) National Association of Pupil Personnel Administrators. **Publications:** *Administering Pupil Services in Third Millennium*, annual. Monograph. Pertains to pupil services administration. ● *NAPSA News*, quarterly. Newsletter ● Membership Directory, biennial ● Pamphlets. Discusses pupil services administration. **Conventions/Meetings:** annual conference (exhibits).

7903 ■ National Association of Student Affairs Professionals (NASAP)
c/o Dr. Terrance D. Smith, Financial Sec.
Fort Valley State Univ.
1005 State Univ. Dr.
Fort Valley, GA 31030
E-mail: smith0@fvsu.edu
URL: http://www.nasap.net
Contact: Dr. Terrance D. Smith, Financial Sec.

Founded: 1954. **Membership Dues:** institution, $300 (annual) ● professional/associate, $40 (annual) ● student, $12 (annual). **Description:** Student affairs personnel at historically black colleges. Seeks to foster a unified spirit among student affairs personnel at predominantly black universities, colleges, and educational institutions. Works to improve the delivery of student services at black colleges and institutions. Serves as a professional agency for the collection of information and the discussion of scientific studies and problems pertaining to student services administration. Provides professional development for student affairs personnel. Designs projects in accordance with trends in postsecondary education. Monitors legislation that impacts student affairs programs and services. **Committees:** Governmental Relations; Regional Organization; Scholarship; Time and Place. **Formerly:** National Association of Personnel Workers. **Publications:** Newsletter, quarterly ● Journal, quarterly. **Conventions/Meetings:** annual conference.

7904 ■ National Association of Student Personnel Administrators (NASPA)
1875 Connecticut Ave. NW, Ste.418
Washington, DC 20009

Ph: (202)265-7500
Fax: (202)797-1157
E-mail: office@naspa.org
URL: http://www.naspa.org
Contact: Gwendolyn Jordan Dungy, Exec. Dir.

Founded: 1919. **Members:** 8,000. **Membership Dues:** affiliate (professional, faculty), $59 (annual) ● affiliate (student), $35 (annual) ● affiliate (associate, non-profit), $196 (annual) ● affiliate (emeritus), $47 (annual) ● for profit, $563 (annual) ● institution, $354-$1,630 (annual). **Staff:** 14. **Budget:** $3,000,000. **Regional Groups:** 7. **Description:** Representatives of degree-granting institutions of higher education which have been fully accredited. Works to enrich the educational experience of all students. Serves colleges and universities by providing leadership and professional growth opportunities for the senior student affairs officer and other professionals who consider higher education and student affairs issues from an institutional perspective. Provides professional development; improves information and research; acts as an advocate for students in higher education. Maintains career service and conducts the Richard F. Stevens Institute. Supports minority undergraduate fellows program. **Awards:** Fred Turner Award. **Frequency:** annual. **Type:** recognition. **Recipient:** for members with 10 or more years of continuous membership in NASPA ● Melvene D. Hardee Dissertation of the Year Award. **Frequency:** annual. **Type:** recognition. **Recipient:** for outstanding doctoral student ● Mid-Level Student Affairs Professional Award. **Frequency:** annual. **Type:** recognition. **Recipient:** for individuals with outstanding commitment to their profession ● Outstanding Contribution to Higher Education Award. **Frequency:** annual. **Type:** recognition. **Recipient:** for those with excellent contributions in higher education ● Outstanding Contribution to Literature or Research Award. **Frequency:** annual. **Type:** recognition. **Recipient:** for those who demonstrated professional commitment to student affairs administration ● President's Award. **Frequency:** annual. **Type:** recognition. **Recipient:** for a college or university president ● Robert H. Shaffer Award. **Frequency:** annual. **Type:** recognition. **Recipient:** for academic excellence as a graduate faculty member ● Scott Goodnight Award. **Frequency:** annual. **Type:** recognition. **Recipient:** for outstanding performance as a dean. **Formerly:** (1951) National Association of Deans and Advisers of Men. **Publications:** *Career Services Bulletin*, annual ● *The Leadership Exchange*, quarterly. Magazine. Serves as a management magazine for senior-level decision-makers. ● *NASPA Journal*, quarterly. Contains in-depth examinations of student affairs and higher education issues. **Price:** included in membership dues; $35.00 /year for nonmembers. ISSN: 0027-6014. **Circulation:** 8,000 ● *NetResults*. Magazine. Alternate Formats: online ● *Online NASPA Forum*, bimonthly. Newsletter. Contains calendar of events, new resources, and research updates. **Price:** included in membership dues. ISSN: 0271-1672. **Circulation:** 8,000. Alternate Formats: online ● Monographs ● Papers ● Books. **Conventions/Meetings:** annual conference (exhibits).

7905 ■ National Center for Higher Education Management Systems (NCHEMS)

3035 Center Green Dr., Ste.150
Boulder, CO 80301-2251
Ph: (303)497-0301
Fax: (303)497-0338
E-mail: info@nchems.org
URL: http://www.nchems.org
Contact: Dennis Jones, Pres.

Founded: 1969. **Membership Dues:** institution, $300 (annual). **Staff:** 15. **Description:** Devoted exclusively to research, development, education, and direct assistance aimed at improving management in higher education. Serves colleges, universities, state-level agencies, national and regional associations, and other research, development, and service organizations. Seeks to achieve a better understanding of colleges and universities as organizations of a distinct kind; develop, test, and promote the adoption of improved approaches to planning and financing colleges and universities; provide expert consultants; develop educational programs that meet the needs of administrators trying to enhance their management ability; create opportunities for higher education executives to exchange ideas regarding management issues. Conducts research; compiles statistics. Holds institutes and forums designed to improve the management skills of administrators in higher education. **Libraries: Type:** reference. **Holdings:** 20,000. **Computer Services:** database, statistics on finance, enrollment, and degrees. **Publications:** Books ● Catalogs ● Monographs ● Reports. **Conventions/Meetings:** quarterly Management Seminar, covers management issues.

7906 ■ National Council of State Education Associations (NCSEA)

1201 16th St. NW
Washington, DC 20036-3290
Ph: (202)833-4000
Fax: (202)822-7974
URL: http://www.nea.org
Contact: Mel Myler, Dir.

Founded: 1966. **Members:** 130. **Staff:** 3. **Budget:** $185,000. **Description:** Executive directors, presidents, vice-presidents, and secretary/treasurers of state education associations and of the National Education Association (see separate entry). **Formed by Merger of:** National Association of Secretaries of State Teachers Associations; National Council of State Association Presidents. **Publications:** *Information Service Report*, semiannual ● *Profiles*, annual. Directory. **Conventions/Meetings:** annual conference.

7907 ■ National Orientation Directors Association (NODA)

c/o University of Michigan
375 Univ. Center
Flint, MI 48502-1950
Ph: (810)424-5513
Fax: (810)762-3023
E-mail: nodahomeoffice@umflint.edu
URL: http://www.nodaweb.org
Contact: Charlie Andrews, Pres.

Founded: 1947. **Members:** 1,100. **Membership Dues:** student, $30 (annual) ● professional/faculty, $100 (annual) ● associate, $1,500 (annual). **Staff:** 2. **Budget:** $85,000. **Regional Groups:** 9. **Description:** Personnel workers from colleges and universities who deal with the orientation program for their campuses. Seeks advancement in orientation philosophy, techniques, programming and training of student workers in various institutions. Sponsors research in orientation. **Awards:** Norman K. Russell Scholarship. **Frequency:** annual. **Type:** scholarship. **Recipient:** for graduate students who have demonstrated a strong commitment to orientation, retention and transition ● Outstanding Contributions to the Orientation Profession Award. **Frequency:** annual. **Type:** recognition. **Recipient:** for contributions and/or publications in the field of orientation, retention and transition ● Outstanding New Professional Award. **Frequency:** annual. **Type:** recognition. **Recipient:** for a professional who has demonstrated service to the association ● Outstanding Orientation Professional Award. **Frequency:** annual. **Type:** recognition. **Recipient:** for outstanding contributions to the orientation, retention and transition profession ● Outstanding Research Award. **Frequency:** annual. **Type:** recognition. **Recipient:** for graduates and doctoral students ● Outstanding Service Award. **Frequency:** annual. **Type:** recognition. **Recipient:** for a student or professional who has provided outstanding service to the association. **Computer Services:** database, regions ● information services, peer resources ● mailing lists. **Telecommunication Services:** electronic mail, andrewsc@fiu.edu. **Committees:** Data Bank; Mentoring; Regional Conferences; Scholarships; Special Projects and Grants; Sponsored Research. **Formerly:** Orientation Directors Conference; (1977) National Orientation Directors Conference. **Publications:** *Journal of College Orientation & Transition*, biennial ● *NODA Data Bank*, biennial. Survey. Features a statistical survey reporting information on orientation programming. Includes such information as school size and student populations. **Price:** included in membership dues; $30.00/copy for nonmembers ● *NODA Membership Directory*, annual. Focuses on common factors in college/university orientation programs. Provides directors training and planning models. **Price:** included in membership dues; $10.00/copy for nonmembers ● *Orientation Director's Manual*, biennial. Focuses on common factors in college/university orientation programs. Provides directors training and planning models. **Price:** included in membership dues; $30.00/copy for nonmembers ● *The Orientation Review*, quarterly. Newsletter. **Price:** included in membership dues; $1.25/copy for nonmembers. **Conventions/Meetings:** annual The First-Year Experience - conference (exhibits).

7908 ■ National Staff Development Council (NSDC)

5995 Fairfield Rd., Ste.4
Oxford, OH 45056
Ph: (513)523-6029
Free: (800)727-7288
Fax: (513)523-0638
E-mail: nsdcoffice@nsdc.org
URL: http://www.nsdc.org
Contact: Stephanie Hirsh, Exec. Dir.

Founded: 1969. **Members:** 10,500. **Membership Dues:** teacher leader introductory, $49 (annual) ● principal leader, system leader, teacher leader, $99 (annual) ● comprehensive, $129 (annual) ● organizational, $179 (annual). **Staff:** 18. **State Groups:** 37. **Description:** Provides assistance and support to local school district personnel whose primary responsibility is the administration, supervision, and coordination of staff development programs. Promotes public policy favorable to the development of comprehensive district-based staff development programs. Provides information on effective staff development programs, new models of staff development, theories of adult learning, planning and funding of district-based staff development programs, and relevant research. Sponsors regional workshops on topics such as conducting effective staff development programs. **Awards:** Best Dissertation Research. **Frequency:** annual. **Type:** recognition. **Recipient:** for research that demonstrates the impact of staff development on student performance ● Best Evaluation of Staff Development. **Frequency:** annual. **Type:** recognition. **Recipient:** for outstanding staff development evaluation ● Shirley Havens Support and Classified Staff Development. **Frequency:** annual. **Type:** recognition. **Recipient:** for an individual or organization ● Staff Development Book of the Year. **Frequency:** annual. **Type:** recognition. **Recipient:** for a book that makes a significant contribution to the field of staff development ● Susan Loucks-Horsley Award. **Frequency:** annual. **Type:** recognition. **Recipient:** for members. **Projects:** Amplifying Positive Deviance; Online Learning; Results-Based Staff Development; School-Based Staff Developers; 12 Under 12. **Task Forces:** NCLB. **Publications:** *Connect with NSDC*, monthly. Newsletter. Alternate Formats: online ● *Journal of Staff Development*, quarterly. **Price:** $69.00 /year for members. **Advertising:** accepted ● *The Learning Principal*, 8/year. Newsletter. Focuses on the important and unique work of school principals. **Price:** $49.00 /year for members ● *The Learning System*, 8/year. Newsletter. **Price:** $49.00 /year for members ● *Results*, 8/year. Newsletter ● *Teachers Teaching Teachers*, 8/year. Newsletter. Contains information on how the NSDC Standards for Staff Development applies to work. Alternate Formats: online ● *Tools for Schools*, quarterly. Newsletter. **Price:** $49.00 /year for members. **Conventions/Meetings:** annual conference (exhibits) - 2008 Dec. 6-10, Washington, DC; 2009 Dec. 5-9, St. Louis, MO; 2010 Dec. 4-8, Atlanta, GA; 2011 Dec. 2-6, Anaheim, CA.

7909 ■ University Council for Educational Administration (UCEA)

1 Univ. Sta. D5400
Dept. of Educational Admin.
Univ. of Texas at Austin
Austin, TX 78712-0374
Ph: (512)475-8592
Fax: (512)471-5975

E-mail: michelleyoung@austin.utexas.edu
URL: http://www.ucea.org
Contact: Michelle D. Young PhD, Exec. Dir.
Founded: 1959. **Members:** 70. **Membership Dues:** full, $2,000 (annual) ● partner, $500 (annual). **Staff:** 3. **Budget:** $350,000. **Description:** Consortium of departments of educational administration in universities. Promotes and disseminates information on the improvement of pre-service and in-service training of school and higher education administrators. Conducts research and development in educational administration through inter-university cooperation. Operates placement service. **Awards:** Jack A. Culbertson Award. **Frequency:** annual. **Type:** recognition. **Recipient:** for outstanding junior professor in the first decade of his/her career ● Roald F. Campbell Award. **Frequency:** annual. **Type:** recognition. **Recipient:** for outstanding senior professors ● William J. Davis Memorial Award. **Frequency:** annual. **Type:** recognition. **Recipient:** for best article in Educational Administration Quarterly. **Computer Services:** Mailing lists, of members. **Publications:** *Building Bridges: UCEA's First Two Decades*. **Price:** $26.95 ● *Educational Administration Quarterly*. Journal. **Price:** $36.00 /year for members; $42.00 /year for nonmembers. **Circulation:** 1,500. **Advertising:** accepted ● *UCEA Journal of Cases*, 3/year. Alternate Formats: online ● *UCEA Review*, 3/year. Newsletter. Covers news, innovations within the field, and other topics relating to teaching school administration. **Price:** free for members; $5.00 /year for nonmembers. **Circulation:** 5,000. **Advertising:** accepted ● Monographs. **Conventions/Meetings:** annual conference (exhibits) ● convention.

Admissions

7910 ■ American Association of Collegiate Registrars and Admissions Officers (AACRAO)

1 Dupont Cir. NW, Ste.520
Washington, DC 20036
Ph: (202)293-9161
Fax: (202)872-8857
E-mail: info@aacrao.org
URL: http://www.aacrao.org
Contact: Paul Aucoin, Pres.
Founded: 1910. **Members:** 9,300. **Membership Dues:** institutional (based on the number of members), $390-$1,365 (annual) ● corporate, $2,000-$4,000 (annual) ● organizational partner (add $195/additional partner representative), $557 (annual). **Staff:** 24. **Budget:** $3,500,000. **Regional Groups:** 5. **State Groups:** 32. **Description:** Degree-granting postsecondary institutions, government agencies, and higher education coordinating boards, private educational organizations, and education-oriented businesses. Promotes higher education and furthers the professional development of members working in admissions, enrollment management, institutional research, records, and registration. **Libraries: Type:** reference. **Awards:** State and Regional Professional Activity Award. **Frequency:** annual. **Type:** monetary ● Workshop and Professional Development Grants. **Frequency:** annual. **Type:** grant. **Computer Services:** Mailing lists, of members. **Formerly:** American Association of Collegiate Registrars. **Publications:** *AACRAO Data Dispenser*, 10/year. Newsletter. Reports on trends and events affecting higher education. Contains calendar of events. **Price:** free for members. ISSN: 1040-8924. **Circulation:** 9,300. **Advertising:** accepted ● *AACRAO Member Guide*, annual. Membership Directory. **Price:** first copy free for members; $40.00 for members; $75.00 for nonmembers. **Circulation:** 9,700. **Advertising:** accepted ● *College and University*, quarterly. Journal. **Price:** free for members; $50.00 /year for nonmembers in U.S.; $60.00 /year for nonmembers outside U.S. **Circulation:** 10,000. **Advertising:** accepted ● Books ● Handbooks ● Reports. **Conventions/Meetings:** annual conference ● annual meeting (exhibits) ● annual Strategic Enrollment Management Conference, premier educational forum for enrollment managers in the SEM discipline ● annual workshop and conference (exhibits) ● annual meeting - 2009 Mar. 1-4, Chicago, IL; 2010 Apr. 22-25, New Orleans, LA; 2011 Apr. 17-20, Reno, NV.

7911 ■ American College and Career Counseling Center (ACACCC)

2401 Pennsylvania Ave., Ste.10-C-51
Philadelphia, PA 19130
Ph: (215)235-5855
Contact: Dr. Henry Klein, Pres.
Founded: 1962. **Staff:** 2. **Description:** Provides individual, personalized educational and career counseling to youths and adults. Gives information on college admissions and careers to national media. **Formerly:** (1964) American College Admissions Advisory Center; (1977) American College Admissions Center. **Publications:** *College in Your Future*. Book. **Price:** $12.95 ● Provides articles to local and national publications.

7912 ■ National Association for College Admission Counseling (NACAC)

1631 Prince St.
Alexandria, VA 22314-2818
Ph: (703)836-2222
Free: (800)822-6285
Fax: (703)836-8015
E-mail: info@nacac.com
URL: http://www.nacacnet.org/memberportal
Contact: Mary Lee Hoganson, Pres.
Founded: 1937. **Members:** 9,800. **Membership Dues:** college/university, $285 (annual) ● individual, $60 (annual) ● individual from a nonmember secondary school, college/university, $90 (annual) ● secondary school, provisional secondary school, $160 (annual) ● student, $55 (annual) ● independent counselor, $215 (annual) ● organization/agency (voting), $315 (annual) ● organization or agency nonvoting associate, $375 (annual) ● organization/agency (nonvoting), $180 (annual) ● secondary school district, $235 (annual). **Staff:** 37. **Budget:** $8,000,000. **Regional Groups:** 9. **State Groups:** 14. **Description:** Public, parochial, and independent secondary schools; school systems; public and private two-year colleges, four-year colleges, and universities; independent counselors and educational organizations concerned with secondary school guidance, college admission, and financial aid. Seeks to establish and maintain high professional standards in college admission guidance; develop useful and efficient college guidance programs and materials; foster and expand the relationships between and among secondary schools and colleges. Conducts state and regional conferences, seminars and workshops, and research projects. Sponsors National College Fairs for colleges and other post secondary institutions, students, and parents in 35 major cities each year. **Awards:** Excellence in Education Award. **Frequency:** annual. **Type:** recognition. **Recipient:** for contributions to education ● Executive Board Award. **Frequency:** annual. **Type:** recognition ● Gayle C. Wilson Award. **Frequency:** annual. **Type:** recognition. **Recipient:** to an outstanding counselor ● Human Relations Award. **Frequency:** annual. **Type:** recognition ● John B. Muir Editor's Award. **Frequency:** annual. **Type:** recognition. **Recipient:** for editorial/authorship contribution to the profession ● Margaret Addis Award. **Frequency:** annual. **Type:** recognition. **Recipient:** for an outstanding member of the executive board ● Rising Star Award. **Frequency:** annual. **Type:** recognition. **Recipient:** for individuals and programs that exemplify excellence and dedication to serving the needs of students. **Computer Services:** Mailing lists, of members. **Formerly:** (1969) Association of College Admissions Counselors; (1985) National Association of College Admissions Counselors; (1997) National Association of College Admission Counselors. **Publications:** *Journal of College Admission*, quarterly. Includes research and demographic information. **Price:** included in membership dues; $65.00 /year for nonmembers in U.S.; $75.00 /year for nonmembers outside U.S.; $16.00/copy for nonmembers. **Circulation:** 7,000 ● *NACAC Bulletin*, 10/year. Newsletter. Includes executive board annual reports, book reviews, calendar of events, research reports, and statistics. **Price:** included in membership dues; $50.00 /year for nonmembers in U.S.; $60.00 /year for nonmembers outside U.S. **Circulation:** 7,000. **Advertising:** accepted. Alternate Formats: online ● *Space Availability Survey*. Brochures ● *Steps to College*, 5/year. Surveys. Contains information for college-bound juniors and seniors. ● Membership Directory, annual. **Price:** $30.00 for members only ● Journal ● Surveys ● Annual Report. Alternate Formats: online ● Also publishes studies. **Conventions/Meetings:** annual conference, professional development seminars (exhibits) - 2008 Sept. 25-27, Seattle, WA; 2009 Sept. 24-26, Baltimore, MD; 2010 Sept. 30-Oct. 2, St. Louis, MO.

7913 ■ National Association of Graduate Admissions Professionals (NAGAP)

c/o Mr. Michael P. Flanagan, Exec. Dir.
PO Box 14605
Lenexa, KS 66285-4605
Ph: (913)895-4616
Fax: (913)895-4652
E-mail: info@nagap.org
URL: http://www.nagap.org
Contact: Mr. Michael Flanagan, Exec. Dir.
Founded: 1987. **Members:** 1,500. **Membership Dues:** individual, $125 (annual) ● institutional, affiliate, $125 ● retired, $50. **Regional Groups:** 4. **State Groups:** 2. **Local Groups:** 2. **Description:** Represents individuals working in graduate and professional student recruitment, admissions, and enrollment management. **Awards:** Award for Promotional Excellence. **Frequency:** annual. **Type:** monetary. **Recipient:** to a member in graduate admissions for excellence in promotion of a graduate program or graduate school. **Computer Services:** Mailing lists, networking. **Formerly:** New England Association of Graduate Admissions Professionals. **Publications:** *Graduate Enrollment Trends Survey*, annual ● *Membership and Salary Survey*, biennial ● *NAGAP eNewsletter*, monthly. Alternate Formats: online ● *Perspectives: A Newsmagazine for Graduate Admissions Professionals*, quarterly. Journal. **Price:** free for members. **Conventions/Meetings:** annual conference - spring ● annual Executive Institute for Graduate Admissions Professionals - workshop - spring ● annual Summer Institute for New Graduate Admissions - workshop (exhibits) - July ● annual Winter Institute for Advanced Graduate Admissions - workshop - January/February.

7914 ■ North American Coalition for Christian Admissions Professionals (NACCAP)

c/o Chant Thompson, Exec. Dir.
PO Box 5211
Huntington, IN 46750-5211
Ph: (260)356-5211
Free: (888)423-2477
Fax: (260)359-0101
E-mail: chant@naccap.org
URL: http://www.naccap.org
Contact: Dale Seipp, Pres.
Description: Aims to develop the professionalism, skill and knowledge of admissions personnel. Mobilizes members to promote enrollment at Christ-centered colleges and universities. **Publications:** *The Ambassador*. Newsletter. Alternate Formats: online.

Adult Education

7915 ■ Adult Higher Education Alliance (AHEA)

c/o Sue Currey, Dir. of Membership
PACE Organizational Commun.
St. Edward's Univ.
3001 S Cong. Ave.
Austin, TX 78704
Ph: (512)428-1333
E-mail: tessa.mcdonnell@granite.edu
URL: http://www.ahea.org
Contact: Tessa McDonnell, Pres.
Membership Dues: institutional, $100 (annual) ● individual, $40 (annual) ● student, emeritus, $20 (an-

nual). **Description:** Seeks to serve professionals and institutions offering alternative undergraduate and graduate degree programs for adults. Aims to help institutions of higher education develop and sustain learning environments and programs suitable for adults. Serves as a vehicle for cooperative consultation and collaboration among professionals in the field. Supports the professional development of members. **Awards:** AHEA International Graduate Student Award. **Frequency:** annual. **Type:** scholarship. **Recipient:** for graduate students who are studying in the field of adult higher education ● AHEA International Professional Award. **Frequency:** annual. **Type:** scholarship. **Recipient:** for professional educators who are working in adult higher education ● AHEA International Scholarships. **Frequency:** annual. **Type:** scholarship. **Recipient:** to applicants residing outside the United States of America who wish to attend the conference ● The Eugene Sullivan Award for Leadership. **Frequency:** annual. **Type:** monetary. **Recipient:** for a person who has devoted his or her career to adult higher education ● Larry Murphy Scholarship. **Frequency:** annual. **Type:** scholarship. **Recipient:** for a professional educator new to the profession who will be attending their first alliance conference. **Publications:** Newsletter, quarterly. Contains information on association activities and developments in adult education. Alternate Formats: online.

7916 ■ Association for Non-Traditional Students in Higher Education (ANTSHE)
c/o Gabe DeGabriele, Consultant
315 Grand View Park Dr.
Grand Junction, CO 81503
Ph: (970)210-3159
Free: (866)887-9940
E-mail: gabe@wic.net
URL: http://www.antshe.org
Contact: Tina Lloyd, Pres.
Founded: 1996. **Membership Dues:** student, $20 (annual) ● alumnus, academic professional, friend, $50 (annual) ● institutional, $250 (annual) ● organizational, $200 (annual). **Multinational. Description:** Seeks to improve services for non-traditional students in higher education. Encourages and coordinates support, education, and advocacy for the adult learning community. Offers networking with other non-traditional students and professionals in the field of higher education. **Awards:** Marius DeGabriele Scholarship. **Frequency:** periodic. **Type:** scholarship. **Recipient:** for a graduate student with an emphasis in higher education. **Telecommunication Services:** electronic mail, president@antshe.org ● electronic mail, tina_lloyd_psych@yahoo.com. **Publications:** *The Nontrad Journal*, quarterly. Newsletter. Alternate Formats: online.

7917 ■ National Adult Education Professional Development Consortium (NAEPDC)
c/o Dr. Lennox L. McLendon, Exec. Dir.
444 N Capitol St. NW, Ste.422
Washington, DC 20001
Ph: (202)624-5250
Fax: (202)624-1497
E-mail: lmclendon@naepdc.org
URL: http://www.naepdc.org
Contact: Dr. Lennox L. McLendon, Exec. Dir.
Founded: 1990. **Members:** 53. **Staff:** 4. **Description:** Aims to serve state staff in adult education; provides professional development, policy analysis, and a visible presence in Washington, DC; disseminates information to state staff in adult education. Conducts surveys; offers an Executive Development Program. **Committees:** National Programs; Policy; Professional Development; Research. **Publications:** Annual Report ● Newsletter, bimonthly. **Conventions/Meetings:** periodic regional meeting, with consultants.

7918 ■ World Education (WEI)
44 Farnsworth St.
Boston, MA 02210
Ph: (617)482-9485
Fax: (617)482-0617
E-mail: wei@worlded.org
URL: http://www.worlded.org
Contact: Janet Barry, Development Dir.
Founded: 1951. **Description:** Addresses the needs of poor populations in developing countries and people who lack basic skills. Provides professional assistance by designing programs, developing curricula and instructional materials, training trainers, and helping local NGOs to operate more effectively. Maintains that learning is most effective when educational opportunities relate to the priority need of the learners. **Libraries: Type:** reference. **Holdings:** archival material, books, clippings, monographs, periodicals. **Subjects:** development, education, health, family planning. **Computer Services:** Mailing lists. **Divisions:** Africa; Asia; Domestic (USA); Special Projects. **Affiliated With:** PACT. **Absorbed:** (2002) Institute for Development Research. **Formerly:** (1957) World Literacy, Inc. **Publications:** *Adventures in Assessment*, annual. Journal. Serves as a field-based journal in which practitioners of adult education write and reflect about their experiences with learner-centered approaches. **Price:** $10.00 ● *Bright Ideas*. Newsletter. Provides adult education practitioners in Massachusetts a place to share innovative practices, new resources, and information. **Price:** $8.00/copy; free to Massachusetts' practitioners. Alternate Formats: online ● *Faidika!*. Manual. Aims to help village groups develop businesses that profit the whole community. **Price:** $20.00 ● *From the Field: Tested Participatory Activities for Trainers*. Book. Includes exercises from actual training workshops by trainers in health, nutrition, agricultural, community development, and non-formal education. **Price:** $15.50 plus postage.

Advertising

7919 ■ American Academy of Advertising (AAA)
c/o Dr. Donald W. Jugenheimer, Exec. Dir.
Coll. of Mass Communications
Texas Tech Univ.
Box 43082
Lubbock, TX 79409-3082
Ph: (806)742-3385
Fax: (806)742-1085
E-mail: donald.jugenheimer@ttu.edu
URL: http://www.aaasite.org
Contact: Dr. Donald W. Jugenheimer, Exec. Dir.
Founded: 1958. **Members:** 675. **Membership Dues:** individual, $65 (annual) ● retired, $40 (annual) ● student, $35 (annual). **Description:** Serves as a professional organization for college and university teachers of advertising. **Awards:** Distinguished Service Award. **Frequency:** periodic. **Type:** recognition. **Recipient:** for outstanding contributions to advertising education ● Fellow of the American Academy of Advertising Award. **Frequency:** periodic. **Type:** fellowship ● Journal of Advertising Best Article Award. **Frequency:** annual. **Type:** recognition. **Recipient:** for the best article ● Outstanding Contribution to Research Award. **Frequency:** annual. **Type:** grant. **Recipient:** for outstanding contribution to advertising research. **Committees:** Awards; Executive; Finance; Industry Relations; International Advertising Education; Membership; Nominating; Program; Publications; Research. **Publications:** *AAA Newsletter*, quarterly. **Price:** free for members. **Circulation:** 675. Alternate Formats: online ● *Journal of Advertising*, quarterly. Includes book reviews. **Price:** $40.00/year in U.S.; $45.00/year outside U.S.; $65.00/year - airmail. **Circulation:** 1,400. **Advertising:** accepted ● *Proceedings of the Conference of the American Academy of Advertising*, annual. **Price:** $25.00/year in U.S.; $35.00/year outside U.S. ISSN: 0883-2404. **Circulation:** 850. Alternate Formats: online ● *Roster of Members*, annual. Membership Directory. **Conventions/Meetings:** annual conference (exhibits) - always spring.

Aerospace

7920 ■ Aerospace Department Chairman's Association (ADCA)
c/o Helen L. Reed, Chair
710 H.R. Bright Bldg.
Texas A&M Univ.
3141 TAMU
College Station, TX 77843
Ph: (979)458-2158
Fax: (979)845-6051
E-mail: helen.reed@tamu.edu
URL: http://adca.tamu.edu
Contact: Helen L. Reed, Chair
Founded: 1968. **Members:** 79. **Description:** Chairmen or heads of aerospace/aeronautical engineering departments; associate members are persons interested in the field who are invited for membership. Works to improve and promote aerospace engineering education and research and to stimulate the growth of the aerospace profession and related fields. Facilitates discussion of issues among members; formulates resolutions and recommendations for submission to other persons or organizations. Compiles statistics. **Publications:** *So You Want to Be an Aeronautical or Aerospace Engineer?*. **Conventions/Meetings:** annual meeting.

7921 ■ Aviation Technician Education Council (ATEC)
2090 Wexford Ct.
Harrisburg, PA 17112
Ph: (717)540-7121
E-mail: info@atec-amt.org
Contact: Dr. Richard Dumaresq, Exec. Dir.
Founded: 1961. **Members:** 167. **Membership Dues:** individual, $25 (annual) ● institutional, international education, $210 (annual) ● industry, $325 (annual). **Staff:** 2. **Description:** Federal Aviation Administration certified aviation maintenance technicians' schools; associated airlines and manufacturers. Purpose is to further professional aviation maintenance education and to promote mutually beneficial relations with all industry and government agencies. Operates Speaker's Bureau. **Awards:** Ivan Livi Outstanding Aviation Maintenance Instructor. **Frequency:** annual. **Type:** recognition. **Recipient:** for individuals who have made outstanding contributions to the field of aviation education ● James Rardon Aviation Maintenance Technician Student of the Year Award. **Frequency:** annual. **Type:** recognition. **Recipient:** for outstanding achievement of Aviation Maintenance Technician students. **Committees:** Training Materials and Resources. **Publications:** *ATEC Journal*. ISSN: 1068-5901. Alternate Formats: online ● *ATEC Newsletter*, quarterly. Provides information on aviation maintenance practice and training. Includes employment opportunities. **Price:** included in membership dues. **Circulation:** 750. **Conventions/Meetings:** annual conference (exhibits).

7922 ■ Space Foundation
310 S 14th St.
Colorado Springs, CO 80904
Ph: (719)576-8000
Free: (800)691-4000
Fax: (719)576-8801
URL: http://www.spacefoundation.org
Contact: Mr. Elliot G. Pulham, Pres./CEO
Founded: 1983. **Members:** 30. **Staff:** 25. **Budget:** $4,500,000. **Description:** Aims "to vigorously advance civil, commercial and national security space endeavors and educational excellence." Hosts the National Space Symposium, the premiere annual space event featuring the Space Technology Hall of Fame Awards Dinner; the International Space Symposium, "Where Space Means Business"; "Space Discovery" summer graduate courses; year-round "Teaching With Space" in-services. **Libraries: Type:** reference. **Awards:** Douglas S. Morrow Public Outreach. **Frequency:** annual. **Type:** recognition. **Recipient:** for individual or organization ● General James E. Hill Lifetime Space Achievement. **Frequency:** annual. **Type:** recognition. **Recipient:** for outstanding individuals who have distinguished

themselves through lifetime contributions to the space industry ● Space Achievement. **Frequency:** annual. **Type:** recognition. **Recipient:** for individuals or organizations that demonstrate lifetime achievement, breakthrough space technology, or program or product success ● Space Technology Hall of Fame. **Frequency:** annual. **Type:** medal. **Recipient:** for an innovator who has transformed technology originally developed for space use into commercial products. **Formerly:** (2000) United States Space Foundation. **Publications:** *Symposium Proceedings*, annual. Contains text and video clippings of symposium speeches. **Price:** $200.00 all others; $25.00 registrants of symposium. **Advertising:** accepted. Alternate Formats: CD-ROM ● *Symposium Program*, semiannual. **Conventions/Meetings:** annual Florida Space - convention, serves Florida's diverse space community, including civil, commercial, national security and education (exhibits) ● annual National Space Symposium - meeting and symposium (exhibits) ● annual Strategic Space and Defense - convention, conducted in support of America's strategic forces (exhibits).

7923 ■ Students for the Exploration and Development of Space (SEDS)
77 Massachusetts Ave.
MIT Rm. W20-401
Cambridge, MA 02139
Ph: (847)987-3879
E-mail: seds@seds.org
URL: http://www.seds.org
Contact: Ms. Elizabeth Bozek, Exec. Chair

Founded: 1980. **Membership Dues:** chapter, $25 (annual) ● student, $12 (annual) ● individual, $20 (annual). **Local Groups:** 40. **Multinational. Description:** High school and college students organized to promote and increase student awareness and involvement in space studies. Seeks to develop and implement academic programs that will provide students with direct experience and aid in the improvement of space-related education in high schools and colleges. Works to establish a pioneering role for students in the exploration of space. Provides a forum through which students can discuss space-related issues. Maintains Space Topic Education Program, which publishes materials on space-related topics; operates Space Program Series, which designs and develops educational programs. Bestows the Arthur C. Clarke Award for Space Education to an individual or group for outstanding contributions in education aimed at the peaceful use of space. Offers scholarships to students pursuing careers in space studies. Individual chapters conduct seminars, lectures, space-related trips, job fairs, exhibits, tours, workshops, and planning sessions. **Computer Services:** database, SEDS members ● mailing lists. **Funds:** Endowment. **Affiliated With:** American Astronautical Society; Society of Satellite Professionals International; Space Studies Institute; Young Astronaut Council. **Publications:** *SEDS NOVA*, quarterly. Newsletter. Contains chapter news and editorials. **Price:** included in membership dues. **Advertising:** accepted. **Conventions/Meetings:** annual international conference (exhibits).

7924 ■ University Aviation Association (UAA)
3410 Skyway Dr.
Auburn, AL 36830
Ph: (334)844-2434
Fax: (334)844-2432
E-mail: uaa@auburn.edu
URL: http://www.uaa.aero
Contact: Carolyn Williamson, Exec. Dir.

Founded: 1947. **Members:** 800. **Membership Dues:** associate, professional, $60 (annual) ● corporate, $475 (annual) ● institution, $425 (annual) ● student, $20 (annual). **Staff:** 3. **Budget:** $280,000. **Description:** Professional organization of educators, industry representatives, institutions and corporations interested in promoting aviation education at the higher education level. Fosters exchange and dissemination of information among colleges and governmental and industrial organizations in the aerospace field. Supports aerospace-oriented teacher education. Sponsors research programs and compiles statistics. **Libraries:** **Type:** reference. **Holdings:** 600; articles, books, periodicals. **Subjects:** aviation. **Awards:** Gene S. Kropf Scholarship. **Frequency:** annual. **Type:** scholarship. **Recipient:** for students enrolled in an aviation related curriculum ● Joseph Frasca Excellence in Aviation Scholarship. **Type:** scholarship. **Recipient:** for students currently enrolled at a UAA member college or university ● Paul A. Whelan Aviation and Aerospace Scholarship. **Type:** scholarship. **Recipient:** for men and women pursuing an education and future in aviation ● Serving Others Scholarship. **Type:** scholarship. **Recipient:** for outstanding university students who are completing aviation-related degrees ● Wheatley, Laursen, Estridge, and Sorenson Awards. **Frequency:** annual. **Type:** recognition. **Computer Services:** Mailing lists, of members. **Committees:** ATC Education; Aviation Education; Awards; Bylaws; Distance Education; Flight Education; Membership; Nominations; Political Liaison; Publications; Scholarship; Technical Education; Test Advisory. **Publications:** *Collegiate Aviation Guide*, approximately every 4 years. Directory. Identifies colleges and universities that offer aviation programs. **Price:** $24.95 for members; $29.95 for nonmembers. **Advertising:** accepted ● *Collegiate Aviation Scholarship Listing*, semiannual. Booklet. Lists types of aid, methods for applying, and scholarships arranged by broad classifications. **Price;** $14.95 for members; $19.95 for nonmembers. Alternate Formats: CD-ROM ● *University Aviation Association—Newsletter*, quarterly. Provides information on association activities and projects, other aviation organizations, and the impact of collegiate aviation education. **Price:** included in membership dues; $42.00 /year for nonmembers. **Circulation:** 800. Alternate Formats: online ● Proceedings, annual. **Conventions/Meetings:** annual Fall Education Conference - meeting and workshop (exhibits) - always fall.

7925 ■ Young Astronaut Council (YAC)
5200 27th St. NW
Washington, DC 20015
Ph: (301)617-0923
Fax: (301)776-0858
E-mail: youngastronauts@aol.com
URL: http://www.youngastronauts.org
Contact: T. Wendell Butler, Pres./CEO

Founded: 1984. **Members:** 650,000. **Membership Dues:** individual, $60 (annual). **Staff:** 10. **Budget:** $1,000,000. **Local Groups:** 25,000. **Description:** Administers the Young Astronaut Program, an educational program intended to encourage pre-school, elementary, and junior high school students to study science, mathematics, and technology, using the space program as a motivator. Provides updated information on the space program; develops and distributes curricular materials and other educational products. Sponsors essay, art, math, and science competitions. Operates the program in foreign countries. Maintains speakers' bureau. Offers Space School, a live interactive young Astronaut television course for grades 4-6 available to school districts throughout the country via Satellite Learning Networks and the Internet. **Libraries:** **Type:** reference. **Subjects:** space. **Publications:** *Earth Search* ● *Mission: Science*. Contains information about science education. ● *Space Station Alpha: The Encounter*. Alternate Formats: CD-ROM ● *Space3*. **Conventions/Meetings:** annual conference (exhibits).

African

7926 ■ African University Foundation
3737 N Meridian St., Ste.204
Indianapolis, IN 46208
Ph: (317)926-2175
Fax: (317)926-2176
E-mail: webmaster2@aufoundation.org
URL: http://www.aufoundation.org
Contact: Baiyee-Mbi Agbor-Baiyee PhD, Pres./CEO

Founded: 1994. **Staff:** 1. **Multinational. Description:** Works to cultivate international support to establish African University in Tali, Cameroon, a new and different model of higher education in Africa.

7927 ■ American Institute for Maghrib Studies (AIMS)
Center for Middle Eastern Stud.
Marshall Bldg., Rm. 477
845 N Park Ave.
PO Box 210158-B
Tucson, AZ 85721-0158
Ph: (520)626-6498
Fax: (520)621-9257
E-mail: aimscmes@u.arizona.edu
URL: http://aimsnorthafrica.org
Contact: Kerry Adams, Exec. Dir.

Founded: 1984. **Members:** 220. **Membership Dues:** student, $40 (annual) ● regular, $55 (annual) ● institution, $500 (annual) ● library, $75 (annual). **Staff:** 25. **Budget:** $300,000. **Languages:** Arabic, English, French. **Description:** Individuals and institutions interested in the advancement of the study of the Maghrib (the region between Morocco and Libya). Facilitates research and encourages the exchange of information on North Africa. Administers the Center for Maghrib Studies in Tunis (CEMAT), which houses a collection of works and journals on the region and serves as a liaison office for research contacts and for relations with Tunisian scholars and institutions. Awards research grants annually. Also administers the Tangier American Legation Museum (TALM), which houses a specialized research library on the region and serves as a museum and conference center. **Libraries:** **Type:** open to the public. **Holdings:** 9,000; articles, books, periodicals. **Subjects:** North Africa. **Awards:** CEMAT/TALM Fellowships. **Type:** fellowship ● Pre-Dissertation Grants. **Type:** grant ● Short & Long Term Grants. **Frequency:** annual. **Type:** grant. **Recipient:** for quality proposal in any discipline for research in North Africa ● Tangler Summer Arabic Fellowships. **Type:** fellowship. **Affiliated With:** Middle East Studies Association of North America; National Council on U.S.-Arab Relations. **Publications:** *Journal of the North African Studies*, 3/year. **Price:** included in membership dues; $45.00 for nonmembers ● *La Femme et le Developpement au Maghreb*. Book ● *L'Environnement Maghrebin en Danger*. Book ● *Les Experiences d'Integration Regionale*. Book ● *Les Mechanismes d'Articulation au Maghrib*. Book ● *Technologie et Societe au Maghreb*. Book ● Newsletter, biennial. Contains research project summaries and related activities in the U.S. and North Africa. **Price:** free for members. **Circulation:** 600. **Conventions/Meetings:** annual conference and seminar (exhibits) - always November.

7928 ■ Association of African Studies Programs (AASP)
c/o Gail Vernazza
Dartmouth Coll.
Dept. of History
6107 Carson Hall
Hanover, NH 03755-3506
E-mail: ademontrichard@fivecolleges.edu
URL: http://www.dartmouth.edu/~aasp
Contact: Alexandra de Montrichard, Chair

Founded: 1972. **Members:** 80. **Membership Dues:** national resource center in African studies, $100 (annual) ● formally constituted program, $50 (annual) ● informal grouping of African studies scholar, $25 (annual). **Description:** African studies programs, departments, and committees at universities and colleges. Works to promote, develop, and further African studies in the U.S. and Africa. Represents the interests of African studies programs before funding agencies, universities, and state and federal authorities. **Awards:** Francois Manchuella Award. **Frequency:** annual. **Type:** recognition. **Recipient:** for outstanding work in expanding the domain of African studies at undergraduate and/or K-12 levels and for promoting effective outreach initiatives to American communities regarding Africa. **Conventions/Meetings:** semiannual conference and meeting, held in conjunction with the African Studies Association - always spring and fall, Washington, DC.

7929 ■ Association for the Study of the Worldwide African Diaspora (ASWAD)
c/o Prof. Barbara Krauthamer, Treas.
NYU Dept. of History
53 Washington Sq. S, 7th Fl.
New York, NY 10012-1018
E-mail: admin@aswadiaspora.org
URL: http://www.aswadiaspora.org
Contact: Michael A. Gomez, Dir.
Membership Dues: general, full academic - in North America and Europe, $50 (annual) ● general, full academic - outside North America, $10 (annual) ● student, retiree - in North America and Europe, $15 (annual) ● institutional, $100 (annual) ● life in North America and Europe, $1,000 ● life outside North America, $100. **Multinational. Description:** Furthers understanding of the African Diaspora through research and information. Encourages the highest caliber of scholarship regarding the African Diaspora. Helps educate the public and provides a forum where scholars can exchange ideas and information. **Publications:** *Diasporic Africa: A Reader*, Published as necessary. Book. Presents recent research on African people outside the continent of Africa. **Price:** $23.00 per copy.

7930 ■ Sudan Studies Association (SSA)
c/o Dr. Richard Lobban, Exec. Dir.
Rhode Island Coll.
Dept. of Anthropology
600 Mt. Pleasant Ave.
Providence, RI 02908
Ph: (401)456-8784
Fax: (401)461-0907
E-mail: rlobban@ric.edu
URL: http://www.sudanstudies.org
Contact: Dr. Richard Lobban, Exec. Dir.
Founded: 1981. **Membership Dues:** regular, non-profit organization, $30 (annual) ● for-profit organization, $150 (annual) ● life, $200. **Multinational. Description:** Promotes Sudanese studies and scholarship. **Publications:** *Sudan Studies Association Newsletter*, quarterly. Alternate Formats: online. **Conventions/Meetings:** annual meeting.

African-American

7931 ■ National Association of African American Studies (NAAAS)
PO Box 6670
Scarborough, ME 04070-6670
Ph: (207)839-8004
Fax: (207)839-3776
E-mail: naaasconference@earthlink.net
URL: http://www.naaas.org
Contact: Dr. Lemuel Berry Jr., Exec. Dir.
Founded: 1991. **Members:** 468. **Membership Dues:** individual, $125 (annual) ● institutional, $500 (annual) ● student, sustaining, $100 (annual) ● life, $3,000. **Staff:** 15. **Budget:** $50,000. **Regional Groups:** 6. **State Groups:** 21. **Local Groups:** 40. **Languages:** English, Spanish. **Description:** Seeks to further the cause of research in African American studies and promote acquaintanceship among those interested in the field. Provides information and support for researchers; serves as a forum for research and artistic endeavors; conducts educational programs. Maintains speakers' bureau. **Libraries: Type:** reference. **Holdings:** archival material. **Subjects:** African Americans. **Awards:** Executive Directors Award. **Frequency:** annual. **Type:** recognition. **Recipient:** for service ● NAAAS National Award to Outstanding Scholar. **Frequency:** annual. **Type:** scholarship. **Recipient:** for service. **Computer Services:** database, membership lists ● electronic publishing. **Publications:** *Monograph Series*, annual ● *NAAAS-Together We Can Make a Difference*, quarterly. Newsletter. Features book reviews, position announcements and areas of interest. **Price:** $43.50. **Circulation:** 12,000. **Advertising:** accepted ● *Network: Journal of Intercultural Disciplines* (in English and Spanish), biennial. **Price:** $30.00 /year for individuals; $50.00 /year for libraries; $18.00 each. **Circulation:** 500. **Advertising:** accepted. **Conventions/Meetings:** annual conference, with books and educational materials (exhibits) - every February.

7932 ■ Thurgood Marshall Scholarship Fund (TMSF)
80 Maiden Ln., Ste.2204
New York, NY 10038
Ph: (212)573-8888
Free: (877)690-8673
Fax: (212)573-8497
E-mail: bcolbert@tmsf.org
URL: http://www.thurgoodmarshallfund.org
Contact: Mr. Dwayne Ashley, Pres./CEO
Founded: 1987. **Members:** 40. **Staff:** 24. **Description:** Colleges, universities. Provides scholarships to students attending the nation's historically Black public colleges and universities. **Awards:** TMSF Scholarship. **Frequency:** semiannual. **Type:** scholarship. **Recipient:** for students with a demonstrated financial need. **Programs:** Corporate Mentor. **Projects:** Gates Marshall Redesign. **Publications:** *The Scholar*, quarterly. Newsletter. Contains information on students, alumni, and corporate partnerships.

Agricultural Education

7933 ■ American Association for Agricultural Education (AAAE)
c/o Tim Murphy, Treas.
Rm. 229 Scoates Hall
Campus Mail 2116
Texas A&M Univ.
College Station, TX 77843-2116
Ph: (979)862-3419
E-mail: tmurphy@tamu.edu
URL: http://www.aaaeonline.org
Contact: Jacque Deeds, Pres.-Elect
Founded: 1959. **Members:** 300. **Membership Dues:** regular, $80 (annual) ● student, $20 (annual) ● associate, $30 (annual) ● life, $1,600. **Budget:** $47,500. **Regional Groups:** 3. **State Groups:** 50. **Description:** Represents university faculty in agricultural education and related fields. **Awards:** AAAE Fellow. **Frequency:** annual. **Type:** fellowship. **Recipient:** for outstanding contributions on one or more areas of specialization ● Alan A. Kahler Outstanding Dissertation Award. **Frequency:** annual. **Type:** recognition. **Recipient:** for doctoral student who has completed the most outstanding dissertation ● Early Member Award. **Frequency:** annual. **Type:** recognition. **Recipient:** for outstanding young member ● Life Membership Award. **Type:** recognition. **Recipient:** for retiring members ● Outstanding Agricultural Educator Award. **Frequency:** annual. **Type:** recognition. **Recipient:** for outstanding contributions over the years to agricultural education ● Special Award. **Frequency:** annual. **Type:** recognition. **Recipient:** for individuals outside the AAAE membership. **Computer Services:** Mailing lists, of members. **Committees:** Southern Regional Research. **Affiliated With:** Association for Career and Technical Education; National Association of Agricultural Educators; National Association of Supervisors of Agricultural Education. **Formerly:** Teacher Trainers Section of the Agricultural Division of the Association for Career and Technical Education; (1990) American Association of Teacher Educators in Agriculture. **Publications:** *Agricultural Education Directory*, periodic. Alternate Formats: online ● *Agricultural Education Newsletter*, semiannual, every fall and spring. Alternate Formats: online ● *History and AAAE Lectures*, periodic. **Circulation:** 300 ● *Journal of Agricultural Education*, quarterly. Alternate Formats: online. **Conventions/Meetings:** annual convention - in May.

7934 ■ Association for International Agricultural and Extension Education (AIAEE)
c/o Thomas Bruening, PhD, Treas.
Penn State Univ.
Dept. of Agricultural and Extension Educ.
335 Agricultural Admin. Bldg.
University Park, PA 16802
Ph: (814)863-7420
Fax: (814)863-4753
E-mail: tbruening@psu.edu
URL: http://www.aiaee.org
Contact: Thomas Bruening PhD, Treas.
Founded: 1984. **Members:** 200. **Membership Dues:** individual, $30 (annual) ● individual (from developing country), $15 (annual). **Multinational. Description:** Professionals interested in agricultural and extension education. (Agricultural and extension education refers to traditional and nontraditional educational courses and programs.) Promotes continued professional development of individuals working or seeking to work in international agricultural and extension education programs. Acts as a clearinghouse of information on international research and development in the field of agricultural and extension education. Maintains speakers' bureau. **Awards:** Outstanding Leadership and Service. **Frequency:** annual. **Type:** recognition. **Recipient:** for meritorious contribution, peer recognition, dedication, resourcefulness, sustained effort, cooperation, personal commitment, interpersonal relations, self-improvement, achievement, excellence, and prominence. **Committees:** Awards/Recognition; Legislative; Policy and Research; Scholarly Activities. **Formerly:** (1986) Association for International Agricultural Education. **Publications:** *The Informer*, 3/year. Newsletter. Includes announcements and reports, and information on events and activities. **Price:** included in membership dues. **Circulation:** 250. Alternate Formats: online ● *Journal of International Agricultural and Extension Education*, semiannual. **Price:** $30.00 /year for individuals - hardcopy; $45.00 /year for individuals - online; $75.00 /year for libraries - hardcopy. Alternate Formats: online ● *Program of Activities*, annual. Lists board directors, committee chairpersons, and proposed activities. **Circulation:** 200. **Conventions/Meetings:** annual conference and seminar (exhibits) ● semiannual meeting, held in conjunction with American Vocational Association.

7935 ■ Association for International Agriculture and Rural Development (AIARD)
c/o Joy C. Odom, Sec.-Treas.
Dept. of Agricultural Economics
Mississippi State Univ.
PO Box 5187
Mississippi State, MS 39762
Ph: (662)325-0549 (662)325-2752
Fax: (662)325-8777
E-mail: odom@agecon.msstate.edu
URL: http://aiard.org
Contact: Joy C. Odom, Sec.-Treas.
Founded: 1964. **Members:** 242. **Membership Dues:** regular, $35 (annual) ● student, $15 (annual) ● corporate, $500 (annual) ● public sector, $250 (annual) ● bronze (sustaining), $50-$99 (annual) ● silver (sustaining), $100-$249 (annual) ● gold (sustaining), $250-$499 (annual) ● platinum (sustaining), $500-$999 (annual) ● life (sustaining), $1,000. **Multinational. Description:** Professionals and practitioners in international development from universities, private voluntary organizations, commercial firms, consulting companies, trade associations, governmental and donor agencies, and foundations in the U.S. and overseas. Provides information dealing with current and emerging issues concerning global poverty, food security, and related environmental matters, particularly as they relate to international agriculture and development. **Affiliated With:** National Association of State Universities and Land-Grant Colleges. **Formerly:** (1980) Association of U.S. University Directors of International Agricultural Programs. **Publications:** *Annual Meeting Proceedings*, annual ● Also publishes occasional papers. **Conventions/Meetings:** annual Capitol Hill Forum - meeting - January/February, Washington, DC ● annual conference - first week in June.

7936 ■ Council for Agricultural Science and Technology (CAST)
4420 W Lincoln Way
Ames, IA 50014-3447
Ph: (515)292-2125
Fax: (515)292-4512

E-mail: info@cast-science.org
URL: http://www.cast-science.org
Contact: John M. Bonner, Exec. VP
Founded: 1972. **Members:** 4,000. **Membership Dues:** century club, $100 (annual) ● friend, $250 (annual) ● president's club, $500 (annual) ● millennium club, $1,000 (annual) ● life, $2,500 ● individual, $60 (annual) ● retired, $30 (annual) ● student, $25 (annual) ● associate society/organization, $200 (annual). **Staff:** 7. **Budget:** $950,000. **National Groups:** 34. **Description:** Scientific societies, associate societies, individuals, corporations, foundations, and trade associations. Promotes science-based information on food, fiber, agricultural, natural resource, and related societal and environmental issues. **Libraries: Type:** reference. **Subjects:** CAST publications, agricultural science and technology, environment, food safety. **Awards:** Charles A. Black Award. **Frequency:** annual. **Type:** recognition. **Recipient:** for persons communicating benefits of agricultural science and technology. **Publications:** *Comments*, periodic ● *Issue Papers*, periodic ● *NewsCAST*, quarterly. Newsletter. **Price:** included in membership dues. Alternate Formats: online ● *Special Publications*, periodic ● *Task Force Reports*, periodic ● Annual Report. Alternate Formats: online. **Conventions/Meetings:** annual board meeting - always spring, Washington, DC ● semiannual meeting.

7937 ■ Farm-Based Education Association (FBEA)

Minuteman Natl. Historic Park
174 Liberty St.
Concord, MA 01742
Ph: (978)318-7827
E-mail: info@farmbasededucation.org
URL: http://www.farmbasededucation.org
Contact: Brooke G. Redmond, Exec. Dir.
Founded: 2006. **Membership Dues:** student, $35 (annual) ● individual, $50 (annual) ● organization, $140 (annual). **Description:** Aims to inspire, nurture and promote farm-based education. Serves as a resource for professional development, networking, education and facility management. Supports and reinforces member's farm-based educational practices. Promotes the growth and enhances the visibility of farm-based education. **Awards:** Farm-Based Education Program of the Year. **Frequency:** annual. **Type:** recognition. **Recipient:** for farm program that has made significant contribution to the community ● Teacher Farmer of the Year. **Frequency:** annual. **Type:** recognition. **Recipient:** to farm educator who has made significant contribution to the success of farm program and the farm community. **Publications:** Newsletter, quarterly. **Price:** included in membership dues. Alternate Formats: online.

7938 ■ National Association of Agricultural Educators (NAAE)

Univ. of Kentucky
300 Garrigus Bldg.
Lexington, KY 40546-0215
Ph: (859)257-2224
Fax: (859)323-3919
E-mail: naae@uky.edu
URL: http://www.naae.org
Contact: Dr. Jay Jackman CAE, Exec. Dir.
Founded: 1948. **Members:** 8,000. **Membership Dues:** associate, retired, $35 (annual) ● active, $60 (annual) ● life - associate, $420 ● life - active, $720 ● organizational, $750 (annual) ● student, $10 (annual). **Staff:** 4. **Budget:** $600,000. **Regional Groups:** 6. **State Groups:** 49. **Description:** Middle school, secondary, postsecondary, and adult education teachers of agricultural education; state supervisory and teacher education personnel. **Awards:** Ideas Unlimited. **Frequency:** annual. **Type:** recognition ● Lifetime Achievement. **Frequency:** annual. **Type:** recognition ● New Freshman and Upper Division Student. **Frequency:** annual. **Type:** scholarship ● Outstanding Cooperation. **Frequency:** annual. **Type:** recognition ● Outstanding Middle/Secondary Program. **Frequency:** annual. **Type:** recognition ● Outstanding Post-Secondary/Adult Program. **Frequency:** annual. **Type:** recognition ● Outstanding Service Citation. **Frequency:** annual. **Type:** recognition ● Outstanding Teacher. **Frequency:** annual. **Type:** recognition ● Outstanding Young Member. **Frequency:** annual. **Type:** recognition ● Teacher Mentor. **Frequency:** annual. **Type:** recognition ● Teachers Turn the Key. **Frequency:** annual. **Type:** scholarship. **Formerly:** (1998) National Vocational Agricultural Teachers Association. **Publications:** *News and Views*, quarterly. Newsletter. **Price:** included in membership dues. **Advertising:** accepted. Alternate Formats: online ● Annual Report, annual. Alternate Formats: online. **Conventions/Meetings:** annual convention, held in conjunction with American Vocational Association (exhibits) - usually December.

7939 ■ National Association of Supervisors of Agricultural Education (NASAE)

c/o Dr. Jay Jackman, CAE, Exec. Treas.
300 Garrigus Bldg.
Univ. of Kentucky
Lexington, KY 40546-0215
Ph: (859)257-2224
Free: (800)509-0204
Fax: (859)323-3919
E-mail: jjackman.naae@uky.edu
URL: http://www.teamaged.org/stateleaders
Contact: Dr. Jay Jackman CAE, Exec. Treas.
Founded: 1962. **Members:** 150. **Membership Dues:** active (state), associate, $35 (annual) ● active (regular), $60 (annual). **Regional Groups:** 4. **State Groups:** 50. **Description:** Statewide supervisors/coordinators of agricultural education. Provides a better understanding of school-based agricultural education and opportunity for discussing plans and policies of the U.S. Department of Education Office of Vocational and Adult Education (OVAE). Keeps members informed of the trends, plans, and policies of the Association for Career and Technical Education (see separate entry) and their implications for the development of school-based agricultural education. **Awards:** Outstanding NASAE Member Award. **Frequency:** annual. **Type:** recognition. **Recipient:** for outstanding contributions over the years to agricultural education state supervision. **Publications:** *Letter to Members*, periodic. **Conventions/Meetings:** annual meeting - always November or December.

7940 ■ National FFA Organization (NFFA)

PO Box 68960
Indianapolis, IN 46268-0960
Ph: (317)802-6060
Free: (800)772-0939
Fax: (317)802-6061
E-mail: bstagg@ffa.org
URL: http://www.ffa.org
Contact: Travis Jett, Natl. Pres.
Founded: 1928. **Members:** 476,732. **Membership Dues:** collegiate, $5 (annual). **Staff:** 75. **Budget:** $10,000,000. **State Groups:** 52. **Local Groups:** 7,312. **Languages:** English, German, Spanish. **Multinational. Description:** Students of agriculture/agribusiness in public schools. Organized under the National Vocational Education Act to foster character development, agricultural leadership, and responsible citizenship and to supplement training opportunities for students preparing for over 200 careers in agriculture. National FFA Alumni Association is supportive group affiliated with the U.S. Department of Education. **Awards:** American Star Farmer. **Frequency:** annual. **Type:** monetary. **Recipient:** for one outstanding FFA member ● American Star in Agribusiness Award. **Frequency:** annual. **Type:** monetary. **Recipient:** for one outstanding FFA member ● American Star in Agricultural Placement. **Frequency:** annual. **Type:** monetary. **Recipient:** for one outstanding FFA member ● American Star in Agriscience. **Frequency:** annual. **Type:** monetary. **Recipient:** for one outstanding FFA member ● Honorary Awards. **Frequency:** annual. **Type:** recognition. **Recipient:** for teachers, individuals and companies. **Divisions:** Alumni; FFA Unlimited (supply service). **Programs:** Agri-Entrepreneurship; American FFA Degrees; FFA Global; New Century Farmer. **Absorbed:** (1965) New Farmers of America. **Formerly:** Future Farmers of America; (1998) National FFA; (2003) National FFA. **Publications:** *FFA Advisors Making a Difference*, bimonthly. Newsletter. **Price:** free. **Circulation:** 13,500. **Advertising:** accepted. Alternate Formats: online ● *FFA New Horizons Magazine*, bimonthly. Profiles members who have made outstanding contributions to the farming industry. Covers new developments and trends in agriculture and agribusiness. **Price:** free for members; $5.00 /year for nonmembers. ISSN: 0027-9315. **Circulation:** 445,000. **Advertising:** accepted ● *National FFA Convention Proceedings*, annual. **Price:** free. **Circulation:** 12,000 ● *National FFA Organization—Update*, monthly. Newsletter. Includes calendar of events. **Price:** free. **Circulation:** 850. Alternate Formats: online ● Also publishes instructional materials. **Conventions/Meetings:** annual Career Show - convention (exhibits).

7941 ■ National Postsecondary Agricultural Student Organization (PAS)

PO Box 68960
Indianapolis, IN 46278-1370
Ph: (317)802-4214
Fax: (317)802-5214
E-mail: eschilling@nationalpas.org
URL: http://www.nationalpas.org
Contact: Eric Schilling, Exec. Dir.
Founded: 1979. **Members:** 1,270. **Membership Dues:** individual, $15 (annual) ● chapter affiliation, $50 (annual). **Staff:** 2. **Budget:** $100,000. **National Groups:** 53. **Description:** Agriculturally-related student organization; provides opportunity for individual growth, leadership and career preparation. Promotes development of leadership abilities through employment programs, course work, and organization activities. **Awards:** Agricultural Machinery Service Technician Award. **Type:** recognition. **Recipient:** for outstanding performance in the agricultural service technician programs ● Career Planning. **Type:** recognition. **Recipient:** for cooperative efforts between students, educational institutions, and agricultural businesses and industry ● Career-Progress. **Type:** recognition ● College Bowl. **Type:** recognition ● Dairy Specialist. **Frequency:** annual. **Type:** recognition ● Employment Interview. **Frequency:** annual. **Type:** recognition ● Equine Specialist. **Frequency:** annual. **Type:** recognition ● Livestock Specialist. **Frequency:** annual. **Type:** recognition ● National Crops Specialist. **Frequency:** annual. **Type:** recognition ● Ornamental Horticulture/Floriculture. **Frequency:** annual. **Type:** recognition ● Soil Science Specialist. **Frequency:** annual. **Type:** recognition. **Recipient:** for outstanding accomplishment in the soil science and natural resources industry ● Speakers for Agriculture. **Frequency:** annual. **Type:** recognition. **Telecommunication Services:** electronic mail, info@nationalpas.org. **Publications:** *National PAS Handbook*, annual ● *PAStimes*, 3/year. Newsletter. **Conventions/Meetings:** annual board meeting (exhibits) ● annual conference (exhibits) - March.

7942 ■ North American Colleges and Teachers of Agriculture (NACTA)

c/o Marilyn B. Parker, Sec.-Treas.
151 W 100 S
Rupert, ID 83350
Ph: (208)436-0692
Fax: (208)436-1384
E-mail: nactasec@pmt.org
URL: http://www.nactateachers.org
Contact: Marilyn B. Parker, Sec.-Treas.
Founded: 1955. **Members:** 800. **Membership Dues:** institutional active, $70 (annual) ● graduate student, $15 (annual) ● life, $500. **Staff:** 4. **Budget:** $40,000. **Description:** Professionals from two-year and four-year colleges, public and private. Professional society that focuses on promotion and recognition of excellence in teaching agriculture and related disciplines at the postsecondary level. **Libraries: Type:** reference. **Holdings:** 44. **Awards:** E.B. Knight Journal Award. **Frequency:** annual. **Type:** recognition ● Outstanding Teacher Award. **Frequency:** annual. **Type:** recognition. **Recipient:** to a member who has previously received the NACTA Teacher Fellow Award. **Telecommunication Services:** electronic mail, zimmerman.7@osu.edu. **Committees:** Improve-

ment of Teaching; Instructional Media and Book Reviews Boards; International Programs; Teacher Recognition and Evaluation. **Formerly:** (1963) National Association of College Teachers of Agriculture; (2003) National Association of Colleges and Teachers of Agriculture. **Publications:** *NACTA Journal*, quarterly. ISSN: 0149-4910. Alternate Formats: online. **Conventions/Meetings:** annual conference - always June.

Aikido

7943 ■ Aikido Yoshokai Association of North America (AYANA)
Genyokan Dojo
749 Airport Blvd., Ste.4
Ann Arbor, MI 48108
Ph: (734)662-4686
URL: http://www.aikidoyoshokai.org
Contact: Sensei Takashi Kushida, Founder/Chm.
Founded: 1991. **Multinational. Description:** Promotes the teaching and practice of Yoshokai Aikido. Educates the general public about Aikido in particular and Japanese Budo in general. Assists in the formation of new clubs and organizes special classes.

Alternative Education

7944 ■ American Association for Collegiate Independent Study (AACIS)
c/o Lisa Bourlier, Pres.
PO Box 888400
Lincoln, NE 68588-8400
Ph: (402)472-4338
Fax: (402)472-1901
E-mail: lbourlier2@unl.edu
URL: http://www.aacis.org
Contact: Lisa Bourlier, Pres.
Founded: 1993. **Membership Dues:** regular, $25 (annual). **Description:** Provides and promotes professional development opportunities and increased collegiality among independent study professionals and others interested in the field of independent study. Fosters and promotes improved understanding and appreciation of independent study within the higher education community. Provides information and service to the membership. **Awards:** Dale Huffington Leadership Award. **Frequency:** annual. **Type:** recognition. **Recipient:** for an individual who excels at administrative activities and inspires his or her staff to feel a part of the independent study mission ● Ed Map Course Developer Award. **Frequency:** annual. **Type:** recognition. **Recipient:** to an individual who has contributed greatly to the field of Independent Study ● Helen Williams Award for Excellence in Collegiate Independent Study. **Frequency:** annual. **Type:** recognition. **Recipient:** for both the author and primary editor/developer of the most outstanding independent study college-level credit course ● Monty McMahon Award for Excellence in Pre-Collegiate Independent Study. **Frequency:** annual. **Type:** recognition. **Recipient:** to both the author and primary editor/developer of the outstanding independent study pre-collegiate level (K-12) course ● Roger G. Young Professional Achievement Award. **Frequency:** annual. **Type:** recognition. **Recipient:** to an active member for outstanding and permanent contributions to the field of collegiate independent study ● Specialty Books Excellence in Research Award. **Frequency:** annual. **Type:** recognition. **Recipient:** for individuals responsible for conducting an outstanding research project on any area directly related to independent study ● Student Services Award. **Frequency:** annual. **Type:** recognition. **Recipient:** for workers who consistently provide individualized support to students. **Publications:** *The Study Guide*. Newsletter. Alternate Formats: online ● Brochure. Alternate Formats: online.

7945 ■ International Association for Learning Alternatives (IALA)
449 Desnoyer Ave.
St. Paul, MN 55104-4946
Ph: (651)644-2805
Fax: (651)644-2020
URL: http://www.learningalternatives.net
Contact: Wayne Jennings, Chair
Membership Dues: individual, $20 (annual). **Multinational. Description:** Represents the interests of learning alternatives and choice options practitioners. Seeks to promote and support learning alternatives in education. Provides a forum for professional growth, technical and educational support, networking opportunities and dissemination of best practices in learning alternatives.

7946 ■ National Association for Legal Support of Alternative Schools (NALSAS)
PO Box 2823
Santa Fe, NM 87504
Ph: (505)474-0300
E-mail: nalsas@msn.com
URL: http://www.nalsas.org
Contact: Ed Nagel, Coor.
Founded: 1973. **Members:** 234. **Membership Dues:** school or educational program, $60 (annual). **Staff:** 2. **Description:** Parents, teachers, educators, lawyers, and nonpublic schools. National information and legal service center designed to research, coordinate, and support legal actions involving nonpublic educational alternatives. Seeks and distributes information on suits that establish statewide and/or national precedents. Helps organizations and individuals locate, evaluate, and create viable alternatives to traditional schooling approaches. Maintains speakers' bureau. **Convention/Meeting:** none. **Libraries: Type:** reference. **Holdings:** 690. **Divisions:** Accreditation. **Publications:** *National Coalition News*, quarterly. Newsletter. Provides information on accreditation, certification, home school, correspondence schools, resource materials, and directories. **Price:** $20.00/year. **Circulation:** 1,000.

7947 ■ National Association of Private, Nontraditional Schools and Colleges (NAPNSC)
182 Thompson Rd.
Grand Junction, CO 81503
Ph: (970)243-5441
Fax: (970)242-4392
E-mail: director@napnsc.org
URL: http://www.napnsc.org
Contact: Dr. H. Earl Heusser EdD, Exec. Dir.
Founded: 1974. **Members:** 28. **Staff:** 3. **Budget:** $100,000. **Description:** Private, freestanding institutions at all levels of education devoted to nontraditional performance through alternative delivery systems, highly developed academic performance objectives and assessment modes, diverse learning resources, and flexible time-space provisions. Supports the concept of alternative approaches to learning in which one develops the same knowledge, skills, attitudes, and competencies as those commonly known in, and represented by, traditional school, college, and university certificates and degrees; develops equivalent levels and kinds of assessable learning in emerging disciplines for which there are established needs. This philosophy may reduce the need for centralized, traditional classrooms and significantly reduce the length of required resident, in-class instruction, or eliminate the need for resident study altogether. Develops, publishes, and implements criteria and standards, and thereby evaluates and accredits the performance of private, innovative, experimental, and nontraditional schools, colleges, and universities. Offers consultation for newly-founded, developing member institutions. Conducts research. **Libraries: Type:** reference. **Committees:** Standards. **Divisions:** Accrediting Commission for Higher Education; The Association. **Formerly:** (1977) National Association of Schools and Colleges. **Publications:** *Accreditation Fact Sheet*, periodic. **Price:** $6.00 ● *Eligibility and Accrediting Criterion Compliance Check/Comment Sheets*. Handbook ● *Evaluating Team Member Guidelines and Duties* ● *Handbook for Accreditation: Guidelines for Accreditation by Contract, Vols. 1 and 2*, periodic ● *Index of the Incorporated Council on Postsecondary Accreditation-Kellogg Project Findings*, semiannual. Newsletter. **Price:** free. **Circulation:** 100 ● *Information & Accreditation*, periodic. Brochures. **Price:** $6.00 ● *Information Brochure*, periodic ● *Lists of Member Institutions & Programs*. Membership Directory ● *NAPNSC Accrediting History* ● *NAPNSC Current Events and Comments*, semiannual. Newsletter. **Price:** free. **Circulation:** 100 ● *NAPNSC Founding History* ● *Review Committee/Commission Member/Staff Member Guidelines/Duties* ● *Supplementary Guidelines and Examples* ● *Validity and Reliability Review and Assessment Systems* ● Also publishes lists of member institutions and certificate and degree programs. **Conventions/Meetings:** annual Commission's Decision Making Meeting ● seminar, for training evaluation team members.

7948 ■ National Coalition of Alternative Community Schools (NCACS)
PO Box 6009
Ann Arbor, MI 48106-6009
Ph: (734)483-7040
Free: (888)771-9171
Fax: (734)482-1867
E-mail: ncacs1@earthlink.net
URL: http://ncacs.org
Contact: Mary Ellen Bowen, Co-Chair
Founded: 1978. **Members:** 250. **Membership Dues:** student (1-150), $75-$250 (annual) ● associate, $65 (annual) ● affiliate, $20 (annual). **Budget:** $130,000. **Regional Groups:** 4. **Multinational. Description:** Membership network of schools, homeschooling programs, families, resources, publishers, and researchers supporting participant-controlled learning programs which work to foster social justice. **Publications:** *National Coalition News*, semiannual. Newsletter. **Price:** included in membership dues; $30.00 for nonmembers in U.S.; $40.00 for nonmembers outside U.S. ● *National Directory of Alternative Schools*, biennial. **Price:** $21.50 for members in U.S.; $27.50 for nonmembers in U.S.; $30.00 for members outside U.S.; $36.00 for nonmembers outside U.S. Also Cited As: *Annual Directory of Alternative Schools*. **Conventions/Meetings:** annual conference - usually April/May.

7949 ■ North American Council for Online Learning (NACOL)
1934 Old Gallows Rd., Ste.350
Vienna, VA 22182-4040
Ph: (703)752-6216
Free: (888)956-2265
Fax: (703)752-6201
E-mail: info@nacol.org
URL: http://www.nacol.org
Contact: Susan Patrick, Pres./CEO
Founded: 2003. **Membership Dues:** educator, $60 (annual) ● associate (non-profit organization)/institutional, $500 (annual) ● corporate (based on membership level), $5,000-$25,000 (annual). **Multinational. Description:** Promotes online learning as a viable option to acquire quality education. Aims to increase educational opportunities by providing collegial expertise and leadership in K-12 online teaching and learning. Facilitates collaboration, advocacy and research to enhance quality K-12 online learning. Provides its members a web-based forum for information exchange. **Publications:** *NACOL News*, quarterly. Newsletter. Contains news and articles about all aspects of online learning. Alternate Formats: online. **Conventions/Meetings:** annual Virtual School - symposium, highlights the cutting-edge work in K-12 online education across the world (exhibits) - 2008 Oct. 26-28, Phoenix, AZ - **Avg. Attendance:** 1200.

7950 ■ Parents' Rights Organization (PRO)
9333 Clayton Rd.
St. Louis, MO 63124-1511
Ph: (314)997-6361
Fax: (314)997-6321
E-mail: citedfree@educational-freedom.org
URL: http://www.educational-freedom.org
Contact: Mae Duggan, Pres.
Founded: 1967. **Members:** 3,000. **Membership Dues:** individual, $25 (annual) ● family, $35 (annual) ● group, $50 (annual) ● organization, $100 (annual).

Staff: 4. **Description:** Parents who seek an alternative to the public schools; teachers, school administrators, groups, churches, and students seeking freedom of choice in education. Seeks to secure legal recognition for the right of parents to direct and control the education of their children; secure true freedom of choice for parents in the education of their children, including an alternative to the government-established school system; undertake and support court action to achieve these goals; publish literature and other materials to awaken the public to the denial of the human rights of the family in education. Conducts research and educational programs. **Awards:** Parents Rights in Education Award. **Frequency:** annual. **Type:** recognition. **Recipient:** for contribution to better understanding of the rights of parents in education. **Committees:** Lawyers Advisory. **Affiliated With:** Citizens for Educational Freedom. **Formerly:** (1986) Parents Rights, Inc. **Publications:** *Parents Rights Digest*, periodic. Newsletter. **Price:** $15.00/year. **Circulation:** 3,000 ● *Parents Rights Newsletter*, quarterly. Includes legal and legislative developments, book reviews, home education resource lists, and research reports. **Price:** $15.00/year. **Circulation:** 3,000 ● *Public Schools Teach Religion Without God*. Books. **Price:** $5.00/copy ● Monographs ● Papers ● Video-Scholastic Vouchers. **Conventions/Meetings:** annual conference (exhibits).

Anatomy

7951 ■ Human Anatomy and Physiology Society (HAPS)
c/o Shanan Molnar
PO Box 2945
LaGrange, GA 30241-2945
Free: (800)448-4277
Fax: (706)883-8215
E-mail: admin@hapsweb.org
URL: http://www.hapsweb.org
Contact: Mark Bolke, Sec.
Founded: 1989. **Members:** 1,000. **Membership Dues:** regular (full-time faculty), $65 (annual) ● adjunct (part-time faculty), student, $50 (annual) ● president emeritus, retired faculty, $45 (annual) ● international regular, $75 (annual) ● international (virtual), $37 (annual) ● retiree, $45 (annual). **Description:** Human anatomy and physiology teachers. Works to promote communication among teachers in colleges, universities, and related institutions. Hosts workshops and conferences. **Awards: Type:** grant ● **Type:** scholarship. **Computer Services:** Mailing lists, listserv. **Conventions/Meetings:** annual convention (exhibits).

Anglican

7952 ■ Colleges and Universities of the Anglican Communion (CUAC)
815 2nd Ave., No. 315
New York, NY 10017-4594
Ph: (212)716-6148
Fax: (212)986-5039
E-mail: office@cuac.org
URL: http://www.cuac.org
Contact: Rev. Dr. Donald Thompson, Gen. Sec.
Founded: 1993. **Membership Dues:** institution (with 2,000 students or more), $2,100 (annual) ● institution (with 1,500-2,000 students), $1,575 (annual) ● institution (with 1,000-1,500 students), $1,050 (annual) ● institution (with 500-1,000 students), $525 (annual) ● institution (with 250-500 students), $265 (annual) ● institution (with less than 250 students), $135 (annual) ● individual, $105 (annual). **Multinational. Description:** Supports and represents Anglican colleges and universities of higher education. **Telecommunication Services:** electronic mail, dthompson@cuac.org ● electronic mail, cuacaec@aol.com. **Projects:** Cross-Cultural Collaboration. **Publications:** *The Communicator*, monthly. Newsletter. Alternate Formats: online ● *Compass Points*, semiannual. Newsletter. Alternate Formats: online ● *Prologue*, annual. Magazine. Alternate Formats: online ● Journals ● Bulletins.

Anthropology

7953 ■ National Association of Student Anthropologists (NASA)
c/o American Anthropological Association
2200 Wilson Blvd., Ste.600
Arlington, VA 22201
Ph: (703)528-1902
Fax: (703)528-3546
E-mail: kapu0004@umn.edu
URL: http://www.aaanet.org/nasa
Contact: Karen Kapusta-Pofahl, Pres.
Founded: 1985. **Membership Dues:** student, $80 (annual) ● joint, $95 (annual) ● associate, $120 (annual) ● retired, $140 (annual) ● regular, $175 (annual) ● life, $4,000. **Description:** Anthropology graduate and undergraduate students. Promotes the interests and involvement of students as anthropologists-in-training; provides a network of students for finding jobs, attending graduate school or field programs, networking, and more. **Telecommunication Services:** electronic bulletin board. **Publications:** *Anthropology News*. Newsletter. **Price:** free, free, for members only.

7954 ■ Society for Anthropology in Community Colleges (SACC)
c/o Laura Gonzalez, VP for Membership and Development
Miramar Coll.
Dept. of Anthropology
10440 Black Mountain Rd.
San Diego, CA 92126
Ph: (619)388-7534
E-mail: lagonzal@sdccd.edu
URL: http://webs.anokaramsey.edu/sacc
Contact: Laura Gonzalez, VP for Membership and Development
Founded: 1978. **Members:** 257. **Membership Dues:** individual, $25 (annual). **Description:** Serves as section of the American Anthropological Association. Represents anthropologists and anthropology teachers. Promotes public awareness of anthropology; encourages teaching of anthropology at the collegiate and precollegiate levels. **Computer Services:** Mailing lists. **Publications:** *SACC Bulletin*, periodic. **Conventions/Meetings:** annual meeting, held in conjunction with AAA ● annual meeting and seminar.

7955 ■ Society for the Anthropology of Consciousness (SAC)
c/o American Anthropological Association
2200 Wilson Blvd., Ste.600
Arlington, VA 22201
Ph: (703)528-1902
Fax: (703)528-3546
E-mail: sglaz1234@aol.com
URL: http://sacaaa.org
Contact: Mr. John R. Baker PhD, Pres.
Description: A section of the American Anthropological Association. Works to study the consciousness phenomena in cultures worldwide. **Telecommunication Services:** electronic mail, johnbaker@vcccd.net. **Publications:** *Anthropology of Consciousness*, semiannual. Journal. **Price:** included in membership dues; $38.00 /year for nonmembers; $56.00 /year for institutions. **Conventions/Meetings:** annual meeting - spring.

Aquatics

7956 ■ Aquatic Resources Education Association (AREA)
c/o Amanda Wuestefeld, Treas.
Indiana Division of Fish and Wildlife
Natural Resources Educ. Ctr.
Ft. Harrison State Park
5785 Glenn Rd.
Indianapolis, IN 46216-1066
Ph: (317)549-0206
Fax: (317)562-0790
E-mail: gofishin@dnr.in.gov
URL: http://www.areanet.org
Contact: Marc Sommer, Chm.
Membership Dues: regular, $25 (biennial) ● student, $10 (biennial) ● sponsor, $100 (biennial). **Description:** Represents the interests of State, Federal, industry, fisheries and educational professionals involved in aquatic resource education programs. Fosters, promotes and encourages aquatic education. Serves as a liaison between agencies, industry and state aquatic resource education coordinators. Supports aquatic resource management programs. **Telecommunication Services:** electronic mail, jbarnett@agfc.state.ar.us. **Conventions/Meetings:** biennial conference.

Arab

7957 ■ Thought and Education Club (TEC)
Address Unknown since 2007
URL: http://www.angelfire.com/id/multicultural/kadi.html
Founded: 1996. **Multinational. Description:** Promotes contemporary Islamic and Arab discourse that tolerates and understands differences in a civilized manner. **Libraries: Type:** reference. **Holdings:** audio recordings, books. **Subjects:** Islam. **Publications:** *Anticipated Role of Islam* (in Arabic and English). Book. Twelve scholars forecast the role of Islam in the 21st Century worldwide. **Price:** $15.00 ● *Dialogue & Democracy in the Middle East* (in Arabic and English). Book. Eleven scholars show ways Arabs and Muslims perceive Democracy and how they are trying to promote dialogue in the Middle East. ● *For Better Ethics in the 21st Century* (in Arabic and English). Book. Eleven scholars elaborate on ethics perception and call for better international moral and ethics worldwide. **Conventions/Meetings:** seminar.

Arabic

7958 ■ American Association of Teachers of Arabic (AATA)
Dept. of Modern Languages and Literatures
Coll. of William and Mary
PO Box 8795
Williamsburg, VA 23187-8795
Ph: (757)221-3145
Fax: (757)221-3637
E-mail: aata@wm.edu
URL: http://www.wm.edu/aata
Contact: John Eisele, Exec. Dir.
Founded: 1963. **Members:** 120. **Membership Dues:** individual, $30 (annual) ● institution, $200 (annual) ● student, $15 (annual). **Languages:** Arabic, English. **Description:** College and university teachers, scholars, and students in the fields of Arabic studies, language, linguistics, and literature. **Computer Services:** database, bibliographic, including articles on Arabic language linguistics and pedagogy. **Telecommunication Services:** electronic mail, jceise@wm.edu. **Publications:** *Al-Arabiyya* (in Arabic and English), annual. Journal. Includes book reviews. **Price:** included in membership dues. ISSN: 0889-8731. **Circulation:** 300. **Advertising:** accepted ● *An Annotated Bibliography of American Doctoral Dissertations on Arabic Language, Literature, and Culture, 1967-87*. Monograph ● *The Teaching of Arabic as a Foreign Language: Issues and Directions*. Monograph. **Conventions/Meetings:** annual meeting, held in conjunction with the Middle East Studies Association of North America.

Architecture

7959 ■ Association of Collegiate Schools of Architecture (ACSA)
1735 New York Ave. NW, 3rd Fl.
Washington, DC 20006
Ph: (202)785-2324

Fax: (202)628-0448
E-mail: info@acsa-arch.org
URL: http://www.acsa-arch.org
Contact: Michael J. Monti PhD, Exec. Dir.
Founded: 1912. **Members:** 4,500. **Membership Dues:** student, $45 (annual) ● basic, $90 (annual) ● contributor, $170 (annual) ● sustaining, $290 (annual) ● sponsor, $500 (annual) ● patron, $2,500 (annual) ● life, $5,000 ● donor, $1,000 (annual). **Staff:** 7. **Budget:** $14,000,000. **Description:** Full members are architectural schools; affiliate members are foreign schools or schools without professional architectural programs; participating members are individuals. **Awards:** Collaborative Practice Award. **Frequency:** annual. **Type:** recognition. **Recipient:** for the best practices in school-based community outreach programs ● Creative Achievement Award. **Frequency:** annual. **Type:** recognition. **Recipient:** to an individual for his/her creative achievement in teaching, design, scholarship, research, or service that advances architectural education ● Distinguished Professor Award. **Frequency:** annual. **Type:** recognition. **Recipient:** for sustained creative achievement in the advancement of architectural education through teaching, design, scholarship, research, or service ● Topaz Award. **Frequency:** annual. **Type:** recognition. **Recipient:** to an individual for his/her lifelong achievement in teaching, creative work, and service for the advancement of architectural education. **Computer Services:** database, faculty. **Publications:** *ACSA News*, monthly, during academic year (September through June). Newsletter. Contains information on summer programs, conferences, design competitions for students of architecture, and employment opportunities. **Price:** included in membership dues; $58.00 in America; EUR 56.00 in Europe; 37.00 rest of the world. ISSN: 0149-2446. **Circulation:** 3,500. **Advertising:** accepted ● *Architecture Schools: Special Programs*, annual. **Price:** $12.95 ● *Guide to Architecture Schools*, quinquennial. Directory. Describes member schools. **Price:** $22.95 ● *Journal of Architectural Education*, quarterly. Contains articles on architectural design education, theory, and practice. Includes book reviews. **Price:** included in membership dues. ISSN: 1046-4883. **Circulation:** 3,500. **Advertising:** accepted. Alternate Formats: microform ● *Proceedings of the ACSA Annual Meeting*. **Price:** $30.00 ● Monographs ● Handbooks. **Conventions/Meetings:** annual international conference (exhibits) - always May ● annual meeting (exhibits) - March.

7960 ■ Building Research Council (BRC)
c/o School of Architecture
Univ. of Illinois at Urbana-Champaign
Coll. of Fine and Applied Arts
117 Temple Hoyne Buell Hall
611 Lorado Taft Dr., MC-621
Champaign, IL 61820
Ph: (217)333-1330 (217)333-1801
Free: (800)336-0616
Fax: (217)244-2900
E-mail: brc@uiuc.edu
URL: http://brc.arch.uiuc.edu
Contact: James Anderson, Chm.
Founded: 1944. **Staff:** 16. **Description:** Works to improve the quality of buildings in the United States. Sponsors building research and studies on public housing; analyzes procedures for evaluating office environments; conducts research on gender and race-based obstacles to advancement in architecture; develops teaching methods and multimedia courseware. **Libraries: Type:** reference; open to the public. **Holdings:** articles, books, clippings, periodicals. **Subjects:** technical and social building practices. **Telecommunication Services:** electronic mail, jimand@uiuc.edu. **Departments:** Publication. **Programs:** Lead Paint; Technical. **Publications:** *From Roof to Foundation*. Video. Features actual home inspection with housing experts. **Price:** $29.95 ● *Home Owners Catalog*. Contains listing of publications. ● Booklets ● Reports.

7961 ■ Frank Lloyd Wright Association (FLWA)
Taliesin W
PO Box 4430
Scottsdale, AZ 85261-4430
Ph: (480)860-2700
Fax: (480)391-4009
E-mail: fllwfdn@franklloydwright.org
URL: http://www.franklloydwright.org
Contact: Pauline Moleski, Contact
Founded: 1990. **Members:** 5,500. **Membership Dues:** individual, $45 (annual) ● family, $75 (annual) ● contributor, $125 (annual) ● donor, $250 (annual) ● sponsor, $500 (annual). **Description:** Seeks to perpetuate architectural principles of American architect Frank Lloyd Wright (1867-1959). Operates the Frank Lloyd Wright School of Architecture at Spring Green, WI (Taliesin) and Scottsdale, AZ (Taliesin West). Conducts research Wright's work. Maintains Frank Lloyd Wright Archives. **Libraries: Type:** reference. **Holdings:** artwork, biographical archives, books, clippings, monographs, periodicals. **Subjects:** Frank Lloyd Wright. **Formerly:** (1932) Frank Lloyd Wright Foundation. **Publications:** *Frank Lloyd Wright Quarterly*. Magazine. Contains stories about Wright's life and work, book reviews, national calendar of Wright events and exhibits. **Price:** included in membership dues. **Circulation:** 10,000. **Conventions/Meetings:** annual Educational Conference.

7962 ■ National Architectural Accrediting Board (NAAB)
1735 New York Ave. NW
Washington, DC 20006
Ph: (202)783-2007
Fax: (202)783-2822
E-mail: info@naab.org
URL: http://www.naab.org
Contact: Sharon C. Matthews AIA, Exec. Dir.
Founded: 1940. **Staff:** 4. **Nonmembership. Description:** Formed by the American Institute of Architects, Association of Collegiate Schools of Architecture, and National Council of Architectural Registration Boards (see separate entries) to stimulate the improvement of architectural education. Conducts continuing program of accreditation of programs of architecture. Compiles statistics; maintains library of 100 volumes of descriptions and self-evaluations of architecture schools. **Publications:** *Conditions and Procedures*, biennial. Handbook ● *List of Accredited Programs in Architecture*, annual ● *NAAB Statistical Report*, annual. Annual Report. Alternate Formats: online. **Conventions/Meetings:** semiannual board meeting - usually July, October.

7963 ■ Van Alen Institute: Projects in Public Architecture
30 W 22nd St.
New York, NY 10010
Ph: (212)924-7000
Fax: (212)366-5836
E-mail: vanalen@vanalen.org
URL: http://www.vanalen.org
Contact: Adi Shamir, Exec. Dir.
Founded: 1894. **Members:** 350. **Membership Dues:** student, $25 (annual) ● regular, $50-$99 (annual) ● contributor, $100-$249 (annual) ● sustaining, $250-$499 (annual) ● benefactor, $500-$999 (annual) ● sustaining benefactor, $1,000 (annual). **Staff:** 5. **Description:** Architects, educators, and others interested in promoting the inquiry into the process and production of the public realm and architecture's evolving role in its design and implementation. **Awards:** John Dinkeloo Bequests/American Academy in Rome. **Frequency:** semiannual. **Type:** fellowship ● Lloyd Warren Fellowship/Paris Prize. **Frequency:** annual. **Type:** fellowship ● Van Alen Fellowship in Public Architecture. **Frequency:** biennial. **Type:** fellowship. **Telecommunication Services:** electronic mail, ashamir@vanalen.org. **Formerly:** (1941) Society of Beaux-Arts Architects; (1956) Beaux-Arts Institute of Design; (1995) National Institute for Architectural Education. **Publications:** *Van Alen Report*, quarterly. Magazine.

Armenian

7964 ■ Armenian National Education Committee (ANEC)
c/o The Armenian Prelacy
138 E 39th St.
New York, NY 10016
Ph: (212)689-7810
Fax: (212)689-7168
E-mail: anec@armenianprelacy.org
URL: http://www.armenianprelacy.org
Contact: Mrs. Nayri Balanian, Acting Dir.
Founded: 1958. **Staff:** 2. **Budget:** $38,000. **Languages:** Arabic, English, French. **Description:** Advisory body of Armenian schools and institutions in the U.S. and Canada. Serves as a clearinghouse of texts, educational materials, and programs to Armenian schools. Sponsors competitions. Maintains speakers' bureau. **Libraries: Type:** reference. **Subjects:** Armenia. **Awards:** Setian Award. **Frequency:** annual. **Type:** recognition ● Teacher and Administrator of the Year Award. **Frequency:** annual. **Type:** recognition. **Committees:** Comprehensive Cultural Offerings; History; Language; Music. **Affiliated With:** Armenian Relief Society of Eastern USA. **Publications:** *A Course in Modern Western Armenian*. Book. Two-volume work aimed at students learning Armenian as a second language or as a review text for advanced or intermediate speakers. **Price:** $40.00 for volume I; $20.00 for volume II ● *ANEC Newsletter*, 3/year ● *Armenia in Ancient and Medieval Times*. **Price:** $10.00/copy ● *Armenian Dictionary in Transliteration*. **Price:** $10.00/copy ● *Historical Atlas of Armenia*. **Conventions/Meetings:** annual assembly, exhibits of educational texts and related materials (exhibits) - always May ● semiannual seminar and workshop.

Art History

7965 ■ Native American Art Studies Association (NAASA)
Arizona State Univ.
School of Art
Tempe, AZ 85287-1505
E-mail: kate.duncan@asu.edu
URL: http://www.nativearts.org
Contact: Kate Duncan, Pres.
Membership Dues: regular, $35 (biennial) ● sustaining, $50 (biennial) ● patron, $100 (biennial). **Multinational. Description:** Promotes and reviews new research in the field of North American native art history, north of the Rio Grande to the Arctic. **Publications:** Newsletter, quarterly. Alternate Formats: online. **Conventions/Meetings:** biennial conference.

Arts

7966 ■ Arts Education Partnership (AEP)
1 Massachusetts Ave. NW, Ste.700
Washington, DC 20001-1431
Fax: (202)408-8081
E-mail: aep@ccsso.org
URL: http://aep-arts.org
Contact: Richard J. Deasy, Dir.
Founded: 1995. **Members:** 140. **Staff:** 4. **Description:** Promotes the arts in the learning and development of children and in improving the nation's schools. **Affiliated With:** Council of Chief State School Officers; National Assembly of State Arts Agencies; National Education Association. **Formerly:** Goals 2000 Arts Education Partnership. **Publications:** *The Arts and Education: New Opportunities for Research*. Report. Proposes opportunities for future research on the arts and education. **Price:** $5.00 plus shipping and handling. Alternate Formats: online ● *Critical Links: Learning in the Arts and Student Academic and Social Development*. Report. Summarizes and discusses 62 research studies that examine the effects of arts learning on students' social and academic skills. **Price:** $25.00 plus shipping and handling. Alternate Formats: online ● Reports. Alternate Formats: online. **Conventions/Meetings:** meeting.

7967 ■ Association of Arts Administration Educators (AAAE)
c/o Andrew Taylor, Pres./Dir.
Bolz Center for Arts Admin.
975 Univ. Ave.
Madison, WI 53706

Ph: (608)263-4161
Fax: (608)265-2735
E-mail: ataylor@bus.wisc.edu
URL: http://www.artsadministration.org
Contact: Andrew Taylor, Pres./Dir.
Founded: 1975. **Members:** 160. **Membership Dues:** full, $275 (annual) ● associate, $125 (annual) ● affiliate, $50 (annual) ● student, $25 (annual). **Description:** Full members are directors or representatives of graduate and undergraduate level arts administration programs; associate members are other arts management training programs and academic departments planning arts management curricula; affiliate members are individuals who by profession, avocation, interest or other reason wish to affiliate with the Association and students are individuals who are registered in college or university arts administration degree programs or in other degree programs. Works to enhance the quality of arts administration education, preparing students for careers in visual, performance, literary, media, and arts service organizations. Assesses the expansion of programmatic goals to include cooperative projects with national arts service organizations and other professional and academic groups. **Publications:** *Guide to Arts Administration Training and Research*, biennial. Directory. Lists graduate and undergraduate arts administration and management programs in the United States, Canada, and Europe. **Price:** $12.95/copy. ISSN: 7990-3105. Alternate Formats: online. **Conventions/Meetings:** annual conference - usually spring or summer.

7968 ■ Association of Performing Arts Presenters

1112 16th St. NW, Ste.400
Washington, DC 20036
Ph: (202)833-2787
Free: (888)820-2787
Fax: (202)833-1543
E-mail: info@artspresenters.org
URL: http://www.artspresenters.org
Contact: Sandra Gibson, Pres./CEO
Founded: 1957. **Members:** 1,600. **Membership Dues:** presenting organization, artist or artist manager/agent, $150-$2,462 (annual) ● support organization, $475 (annual) ● vendor, consultant, $450 (annual) ● student, $60 (annual) ● individual associate, $95 (annual). **Staff:** 19. **Budget:** $2,500,000. **Description:** Arts organizations involved in presentation of the professional performing arts; artists and artist management companies. Explores the roles, responsibilities, and opportunities for presenters, artists' managers, and artists, in order "to enable and celebrate the rich and diverse presenting field in its service to the public." Administers Lila Wallace/Reader's Digest Arts Partners regranting program. **Awards:** Fan Taylor Distinguished Service Award. **Frequency:** annual. **Type:** recognition. **Recipient:** for exemplary service to the field of professional presenting ● William Dawson Award for Programmatic Excellence. **Frequency:** annual. **Type:** recognition. **Recipient:** for the quality, innovation, and vision of program design, audience building and community efforts. **Computer Services:** database, information on presenting arts organizations. **Boards:** Editorial Advisory. **Committees:** Conference; Executive; Government Affairs; Membership; Planning and Evaluations; Professional Development. **Formerly:** Association of College and University Concert Managers; Association of College, University and Community Arts Administrators. **Publications:** *Inside Arts*, bimonthly. Magazine. Features articles from the perspective of the presenter, manager, and artists. **Price:** included in membership dues; $36.00 /year for nonmembers. **Circulation:** 2,000. **Advertising:** accepted ● *Membership List/Labels*, annual. Directory. **Price:** $205.00 for nonmembers; included in membership dues ● *Presenters' Reports*, 10/year. Contains review of performances including audience response and quality of management information sent to presenters in advance; includes 2 indexes. ● Also sells a variety of books and studies on performing arts administration and specific disciplines. Members receive discounts on publications. **Conventions/Meetings:** annual conference - always January in New York City ● Presenting the Performing Arts - seminar and workshop, includes professional development information on all aspects of the performing arts.

7969 ■ College Art Association (CAA)

275 7th Ave., 18th Fl.
New York, NY 10001
Ph: (212)691-1051
Fax: (212)627-2381
E-mail: nyoffice@collegeart.org
URL: http://www.collegeart.org
Contact: Linda Downs, Exec. Dir.
Founded: 1911. **Members:** 15,000. **Membership Dues:** individual (based on annual income), $55-$175 (annual) ● institution (primary, library/department/museum, academic/corporate), $300-$750 (annual) ● full-time student, $45 (annual) ● sustaining, $210 (annual) ● sponsoring, $300 (annual) ● patron, $500 (annual) ● associate, $75 (annual) ● retired, $55 (annual) ● life, $5,000. **Staff:** 20. **Budget:** $3,200,000. **Description:** Professional organization of artists, art historians and fine art educators, museum directors, and curators. Seeks to raise the standards of scholarship and of the teaching of art and art history throughout the country. **Awards:** Alfred H. Barr, Jr., Award. **Frequency:** annual. **Type:** recognition. **Recipient:** for the author(s) of a especially distinguished catalogue in the history of art ● Art Journal Award. **Frequency:** annual. **Type:** recognition. **Recipient:** for the author of the most distinguished contribution published in the Art Journal ● Arthur Kingsley Porter Prize. **Frequency:** annual. **Type:** recognition. **Recipient:** for a distinguished article published in The Art Bulletin ● Artist Award for a Distinguished Body of Work. **Frequency:** annual. **Type:** recognition. **Recipient:** to an artist for exceptional work through exhibitions, presentations, or performances ● Charles Rufus Morey Book Award. **Frequency:** annual. **Type:** recognition. **Recipient:** for especially distinguished book in the history of art ● Distinguished Artist Award for Lifetime Achievement. **Frequency:** annual. **Type:** recognition. **Recipient:** for an artist who has demonstrated particular commitment to his or her work throughout a long career and has had an important impact nationally and internationally on the field ● Distinguished Teaching of Art Award. **Frequency:** annual. **Type:** recognition. **Recipient:** for an individual who has been actively engaged in teaching art for most of his/her career ● Distinguished Teaching of Art History Award. **Frequency:** annual. **Type:** recognition. **Recipient:** for an individual who has been actively engaged in teaching art history for most of his/her career. **Committees:** Advocacy; Art Historians; Diversity Practices; Education; Intellectual Property; International; Museum; Professional Practices; Services to Artists; Student and Emerging Professionals; Women in the Arts. **Absorbed:** (1968) Committee for the Development of Art in Negro Colleges. **Formerly:** (1989) College Art Association of America. **Publications:** *The Art Bulletin*, quarterly. Journal. **Price:** included in membership dues. **Advertising:** accepted ● *Art Journal*, quarterly. **Price:** included in membership dues; $50.00 /year for individuals; $75.00 /year for institutions. **Advertising:** accepted. Alternate Formats: microform ● *CAA News*, bimonthly. Newsletter. **Advertising:** accepted. Alternate Formats: online ● *Careers*, bimonthly ● *Monographs on the Fine Arts* ● Also publishes directories of PhD programs in art history, MFA programs in the visual arts, and terminal master degree programs in art history and related areas, and a series of monographs on archaeology and fine arts. **Conventions/Meetings:** annual conference and trade show, with sessions on art and art history, book show, placement service, and members' exhibition (exhibits) - every February. 2009 Feb. 25-28, Los Angeles, CA.

7970 ■ Council for Art Education (CFAE)

PO Box 479
Hanson, MA 02341-0479
Ph: (781)293-4100
Fax: (781)294-0808
E-mail: sarahs@acminet.org
URL: http://www.acminet.org/cfae.htm
Contact: Deborah M. Fanning CAE, Exec. VP
Founded: 1984. **Staff:** 2. **Description:** Promotes increased public funding for art education; seeks to publicize the value of art education and improve the quality of school art programs. Sponsors National Youth Art Month each March. **Awards:** Youth Art Month State Report Awards. **Frequency:** annual. **Type:** recognition. **Recipient:** for state Youth Art Month chairpersons. **Publications:** *YAM News*, quarterly. Newsletter.

7971 ■ Council of Colleges of Arts and Sciences (CCAS)

PO Box 8795
Williamsburg, VA 23187-8795
Ph: (757)221-1784
Fax: (757)221-2184
E-mail: ccas@wm.edu
URL: http://www.ccas.net
Contact: Joe Cow, Pres.
Founded: 1965. **Members:** 467. **Membership Dues:** institution (based on number of BA/BS Degrees awarded), $195-$595 (annual). **Staff:** 2. **Budget:** $300,000. **Description:** Represents the interests and needs of arts and sciences deans of public and private colleges and universities. **Publications:** *CCAS Newsletter*, bimonthly. **Circulation:** 1,450. Alternate Formats: online ● Membership Directory, annual. **Conventions/Meetings:** annual meeting - always November.

7972 ■ International Arts Medicine Association (IAMA)

714 Old Lancaster Rd.
Bryn Mawr, PA 19010
Ph: (610)525-3784
Fax: (610)525-3250
E-mail: iamaorg@aol.com
URL: http://members.aol.com/iamaorg
Contact: Karen L. Barton MSS, Exec. Dir.
Founded: 1985. **Nonmembership. Multinational. Description:** Provides a forum for interdisciplinary, international communication between arts and health professionals. Represents medical personnel, educators, researchers and artists who have an interest in the many aspects of relationship between arts and health.

7973 ■ International Council of Fine Arts Deans (ICFAD)

c/o Liz Cole, Exec. Dir.
8725 SR 70 E, Ste.127
Bradenton, FL 34211
Ph: (941)753-0080
Fax: (941)756-4585
E-mail: colee@icfad.org
URL: http://www.icfad.org
Contact: Liz Cole, Exec. Dir.
Founded: 1964. **Members:** 366. **Membership Dues:** institutional, $350 (annual) ● associate, $100 (annual) ● affiliate, $200 (annual) ● emeritus, $50 (annual). **Staff:** 2. **Budget:** $90,000. **Multinational. Description:** Deans of university-level fine arts schools in 15 countries united to exchange ideas, information, and techniques involved in the academic and professional administration of schools encompassing 2 or more arts disciplines. Acts as a voice for faculties, students, and support staffs of such institutions. Conducts advanced training programs addressing career-entry issues faced by artists in the performing and visual arts. Compiles statistics. **Committees:** Annual Conference; Arts in Education; By-Laws; Development and Fund-Raising; Diversity and Inclusion; Executive Development/Leadership; International Initiatives; Nominating; Technology. **Publications:** *International Exchanges in the Arts: A Handbook*. **Price:** included in membership dues; $20.00 for nonmembers, plus shipping and handling ● *Membership Roster*, annual. Membership Directory ● *Update*, quarterly. Newsletter ● Also publishes brochure. **Conventions/Meetings:** annual conference - 2008 Oct. 21-25, Portland, OR; 2009 Oct. 21-24, Salt Lake City, UT.

7974 ■ International Network of Schools for the Advancement of Arts Education

173 Ridge View Dr.
Berkeley Springs, WV 25411
Ph: (304)258-1799

Fax: (304)258-0839
E-mail: execdir@artsschoolsnetwork.org
URL: http://www.artsschoolsnetwork.org
Contact: Roy Fluhrer, Pres.
Founded: 1982. **Members:** 350. **Membership Dues:** individual, $100 (annual) ● corporate, association, $200 (annual) ● institutional, $300 (annual). **Staff:** 3. **Budget:** $150,000. **Description:** Strives to inspire and promote excellence in arts education. Promotes the development of instructional programs and new schools of the arts. Provides leadership in arts education through advocacy, professional development and communication. **Formerly:** (2005) International Network of Performing and Visual Arts Schools. **Publications:** *Membership List*, annual. Directory ● *NETWORK News*, quarterly. Newsletter. **Price:** free for members; $5.00 for nonmembers. **Circulation:** 2,500. **Advertising:** accepted. **Conventions/Meetings:** annual conference.

7975 ■ Kennedy Center Alliance for Arts Education Network (KCAAEN)

John F. Kennedy Center for the Performing Arts
2700 F St. NW
Washington, DC 20566
Ph: (202)416-8817
Fax: (202)416-8802
E-mail: kcaaen@kennedy-center.org
URL: http://www.kennedy-center.org/education/kcaaen
Contact: Barbara Shepherd, Dir.
Founded: 1973. **Staff:** 2. **Budget:** $950,000. **State Groups:** 46. **Description:** Represents the interests of coalition of statewide, non-profit organizations working in partnership with the Kennedy Center to support policies, practices, and partnerships, which ensures that the arts are integral to K-12 American education. Represents the state Alliances for Arts Education (one per state). Brings together the educators, community leaders, arts organizations and concerned citizens to plan and implement programs and activities that address state and local issues and concerns surrounding arts education. Develops partnerships with national arts and education organizations working on school improvement. **Awards:** Creative Ticket National Schools of Distinction Award. **Frequency:** annual. **Type:** recognition. **Recipient:** for up to 5 individual schools for doing an outstanding job of making the arts an essential part of their students' education ● Kennedy Center Alliance for the Arts Education Network and National School Board Association Award. **Frequency:** annual. **Type:** recognition. **Recipient:** for a school board that has demonstrated support for, and commitment to high quality arts education in its school district, community, state, or special jurisdiction. **Committees:** Kennedy Center Alliance for Arts Education Network National Governance. **Formerly:** (1993) Alliance for Arts Education. **Publications:** *A Community Audit for Arts Education*. Report. **Price:** $1.75. Alternate Formats: online ● *The Arts Beyond the School Day: Extending the Power*. Report. **Price:** $1.75. Alternate Formats: online. **Conventions/Meetings:** annual conference and meeting - always July in Washington, DC.

7976 ■ Midori and Friends

352 7th Ave.
New York, NY 10001
Ph: (212)767-1300
Fax: (212)767-0018
E-mail: music@midoriandfriends.org
URL: http://www.gotomidori.com/english/index.html
Contact: Alan Fischer, Chm.
Founded: 1992. **Description:** Individuals concerned in arts education and cultural exchange. Seeks to develop activities that will address the absence of arts education, particularly programs that focus on classical music, in the public school curricula worldwide. Provides children with knowledge, understanding, and acceptance of other cultures as well as their own roots. Promotes better harmony and communication between peoples of different cultures and socioeconomic backgrounds. Provides free lecture-concerts by Japanese violinist Midori and other artists in schools and other venues; establishes musical programs at selected schools; develops a series of musical education/appreciation videos for use in schools. **Additional Websites:** http://www.midoriandfriends.org. **Committees:** Advisory. **Formerly:** Midori Foundation.

7977 ■ National Art Education Association (NAEA)

1916 Assn. Dr.
Reston, VA 20191-1502
Ph: (703)860-8000
Fax: (703)860-2960
E-mail: info@naea-reston.org
URL: http://www.naea-reston.org
Contact: Deborah B. Reeve, Exec. Dir.
Founded: 1947. **Members:** 18,500. **Membership Dues:** student, $20-$40 (annual) ● active, associate, $50-$80 (annual) ● retired, $30-$55 (annual) ● professional, $40-$60 (annual) ● institutional, $170-$250 (annual). **Staff:** 15. **Budget:** $2,000,000. **Regional Groups:** 4. **State Groups:** 50. **Multinational. Description:** Teachers of art at elementary, middle, secondary, and college levels; colleges, libraries, museums, and other educational institutions. Studies problems of teaching art; encourages research and experimentation. Serves as a clearinghouse for information on art education programs, materials, and methods of instruction. Sponsors special institutes. Cooperates with other national organizations for the furtherance of creative art experiences for youth. **Libraries: Type:** reference. **Subjects:** art education. **Awards:** Distinguished Service. **Frequency:** annual. **Type:** recognition. **Recipient:** for outstanding achievement, contribution, and service in previous years to the field of art education and to national and state/province associations ● Manuel Barkan Memorial Award. **Frequency:** annual. **Type:** recognition. **Recipient:** to an individual who, through his/her published work, has contributed a product of scholarly merit to the field ● Marion Quin Dix Leadership Award. **Frequency:** annual. **Type:** recognition. **Recipient:** for outstanding contributions and service to the profession by a state/province association officer ● National Art Educator Award. **Frequency:** annual. **Type:** recognition. **Recipient:** to a member for outstanding achievements and service of national significance during the previous years ● National Division Art Educator Award. **Frequency:** annual. **Type:** recognition. **Recipient:** to an outstanding member from each of the six divisions for outstanding service and achievement of national significance during the previous years ● Regional Art Educator Award. **Frequency:** annual. **Type:** recognition. **Recipient:** for excellence in the development and publication of a state/province association or Special Issues Groups newsletter ● Regional Division Art Educator Award. **Frequency:** annual. **Type:** recognition. **Recipient:** to an outstanding member from each of the 6 divisions within each of the four geographic regions ● State/Province Art Educator Award. **Frequency:** annual. **Type:** recognition. **Recipient:** to an outstanding member from each state/province for service and contributions to art education that merits recognition and acclaim. **Telecommunication Services:** electronic mail, dreeve@naea-reston.org. **Divisions:** Elementary; Higher Education; Middle; Museum Education; Secondary; Supervision and Administration. **Publications:** *Art Education*, bimonthly. Journal. Reports on current issues, problems, and approaches in visual art education, including curriculum, teaching strategies and innovative programs. **Price:** included in membership dues; $50.00 /year for nonmembers. ISSN: 0004-3125. **Circulation:** 24,000. **Advertising:** accepted. Alternate Formats: microform ● *NAEA Newsletter*, bimonthly. Reports on national and state activities, events, and policies of the association. **Price:** included in membership dues; $50.00 /year for nonmembers. ISSN: 0160-6395. **Circulation:** 24,000. **Advertising:** accepted ● *Studies in Art Education*, quarterly. Journal. Provides empirical, historical, and philosophical research in art education; includes book reviews. **Price:** $15.00 /year for members; $25.00 /year for nonmembers. ISSN: 0039-3541. **Circulation:** 4,000 ● Bibliographies ● Books ● Monographs ● Pamphlets. **Conventions/Meetings:** annual conference and workshop (exhibits) - always March or April. 2009 Apr. 17-21, Minneapolis, MN; 2010 Mar. 25-29, Washington, DC.

7978 ■ National Association of Schools of Art and Design (NASAD)

11250 Roger Bacon Dr., Ste.21
Reston, VA 20190-5248
Ph: (703)437-0700
Fax: (703)437-6312
E-mail: info@arts-accredit.org
URL: http://nasad.arts-accredit.org
Contact: Samuel Hope, Exec. Dir.
Founded: 1944. **Members:** 268. **Membership Dues:** institutional, $1,358-$2,246 (annual) ● individual, $65 (annual). **Staff:** 12. **Description:** Serves as the accrediting agency for educational programs in the visual arts and design. Aims to: establish a national forum to stimulate the understanding and acceptance of the educational disciplines inherent in the creative arts in higher education in the U.S; develop reasonable standards in areas of budget, faculty qualifications, faculty-student ratios, class time requirements, and library and physical facilities; evaluate, through the process of accreditation, schools of art and design and programs of studio art instruction in terms of the quality and results they achieve; assure students and parents that accredited art and design programs provide competent teachers, adequate equipment, and sound curricula; assist schools in developing their programs and encourage self-evaluation and continuing self-improvement. **Awards:** Citation. **Frequency:** annual. **Type:** recognition. **Recipient:** for distinguished career in the visual arts or art/design education. **Commissions:** Accreditation. **Committees:** Research. **Formerly:** (1948) National Conference of Schools of Design; (1961) National Association of Schools of Design; (1981) National Association of Schools of Art. **Publications:** *NASAD Directory*, annual. Contains listing of accredited member institutions. **Price:** $15.00 ● *NASAD Handbook*, biennial. **Price:** $15.00. Alternate Formats: online ● Brochures. Alternate Formats: online. **Conventions/Meetings:** annual conference and meeting - always October. 2008 Oct. 10-12, Seattle, WA; 2009 Oct. 15-17, Pittsburgh, PA; 2010 Oct. 14-16, Cincinnati, OH.

7979 ■ National Guild of Community Schools of the Arts (NGCSA)

520 8th Ave., Ste.302
New York, NY 10018
Ph: (212)268-3337
Fax: (212)268-3995
E-mail: info@nationalguild.org
URL: http://www.nationalguild.org
Contact: Jonathan Herman, Exec. Dir.
Founded: 1937. **Members:** 400. **Membership Dues:** full (based on operating expenses), $200-$2,500 (annual) ● education affiliate (based on operating expenses), $175-$2,000 (annual) ● business affiliate, $250 (annual) ● basic, $100 (annual). **Staff:** 4. **Budget:** $750,000. **Regional Groups:** 13. **Description:** Schools; interested individuals. A nationwide service and educational organization that fosters the growth and development of non-profit, nondegree-granting community schools offering instruction in the performing and visual arts to students of all ages and backgrounds. Special emphasis is placed on providing its constituency with broad-based support and promoting the interests of the community arts field worldwide. Programs include: communications, research, advocacy, and professional development for trustees, administrators, and faculty; assistance for starting schools; technical assistance, consultancy, referral services, and replication of model arts education programs. **Awards:** President's Award. **Frequency:** annual. **Type:** recognition. **Recipient:** for exceptional service to the National Guild and to the community school movement ● Rosenbaum Award. **Frequency:** annual. **Type:** recognition. **Recipient:** for exemplifying and promoting the ideals to which the National Guild and its membership are dedicated ● Young Composers Award. **Frequency:** annual. **Type:** recognition. **Recipient:** to junior and senior high school students. **Boards:** Honorary Trustees; Trustees. **Committees:** Advocacy; Devel-

opment; Governance; School Directors. **Councils:** National Advisory. **Affiliated With:** National Music Council. **Formerly:** (1973) National Guild of Community Music Schools. **Publications:** *Community Schools of the Arts: An Arts Education Resource for Your Community*. Monograph. Includes profiles of five schools that demonstrate the wide range of institutional models and describe how these schools serve their communities. **Price:** $6.00 for members; $8.00 for nonmembers ● *Guild Notes*, bimonthly. Newsletter. **Price:** included in membership dues. **Circulation:** 2,000. Alternate Formats: online ● Membership Directory, annual. **Price:** free for members; $20.00 for nonmembers ● Brochure ● Handbook ● Reports ● Surveys. **Conventions/Meetings:** annual conference, attracts school directors, staff, faculty and trustees from around the country with speakers, panel discussions and interactive group sessions (exhibits) - every November.

7980 ■ United States Society for Education Through Art (USSEA)
c/o Dr. Nanyoung Kim, Treas./Chair
East Carolina Univ.
Jenkins Fine Arts Ctr.
Greenville, NC 27858-4353
Ph: (252)328-1298
Fax: (252)328-6441
E-mail: kimn@mail.ecu.edu
URL: http://www.public.asu.edu/~ifmls/usseafolder/usseа.html
Contact: Dr. Nanyoung Kim, Treas./Chair
Founded: 1977. **Members:** 200. **Membership Dues:** individual, $25 (annual) ● student/associate/retired, $15 (annual) ● library/institution/organization, $30 (annual). **Budget:** $7,000. **Regional Groups:** 4. **State Groups:** 50. **Description:** Art educators, schoolteachers, and artists. Promotes the enhancement of multicultural programs in the U.S. and the improvement of public appreciation of multicultural arts. Serves as a forum for the exchange of ideas and information among members; facilitates exchange of student art exhibits worldwide. **Libraries: Type:** open to the public. **Holdings:** 13; periodicals. **Subjects:** multicultural and cross-cultural research in art education. **Awards:** Edwin Ziegfeld International Award. **Frequency:** annual. **Type:** recognition. **Recipient:** for international contribution to international concerns in education in the areas of teaching, service, or research ● Edwin Ziegfeld National Award. **Frequency:** annual. **Type:** recognition. **Recipient:** for national contribution to international concerns in education in the areas of teaching, service, or research. **Computer Services:** Mailing lists, newsletter. **Affiliated With:** National Art Education Association. **Formerly:** United States Society for Education Through Art. **Publications:** *Journal of Cultural Research in Art Education*, annual. Contains research articles, essays, and book reviews. **Price:** $15.00/year. ISSN: 0740-1833. **Circulation:** 250. **Advertising:** accepted ● *USSEA Newsletter*, semiannual. Covers association news; includes reviews of publications. **Circulation:** 200. **Advertising:** accepted. **Conventions/Meetings:** conference - every 2-3 years ● annual convention and meeting, held in conjunction with NAEA (exhibits) - March/April, varies yearly.

Asian

7981 ■ Asian Cinema Studies Society (ACSS)
c/o Dr. John A. Lent, Chm./Ed.
669 Ferne Blvd.
Drexel Hill, PA 19026
Ph: (215)204-8348
E-mail: yomi@u.washington.edu
URL: http://astro.temple.edu/~jlent/ACSS
Contact: Dr. John A. Lent, Chm./Ed.
Founded: 1984. **Members:** 250. **Membership Dues:** individual, $30 (annual) ● institutional, $40 (annual). **Regional Groups:** 7. **National Groups:** 3. **Multinational. Description:** Works to serve scholars, practitioners and aficionados of Asian cinema. **Publications:** *Asian Cinema*, semiannual. Journal. Contains articles, profiles, interviews, reviews and news. **Price:** included in membership dues; $25.00/volume (back issues). **Circulation:** 300. **Advertising:** accepted. **Conventions/Meetings:** biennial conference (exhibits).

7982 ■ Association for Asian American Studies (AAAS)
Cornell Univ.
420 Rockefeller Hall
Ithaca, NY 14853-2502
Ph: (607)255-3320
Free: (800)548-1784
Fax: (607)254-4996
E-mail: aaasconference@cornell.edu
URL: http://www.aaastudies.org
Contact: Rajini Srikanth, Pres.
Founded: 1979. **Members:** 780. **Membership Dues:** student, $35 (annual) ● regular (based on income), $40-$95 (annual) ● associate, $30 (annual). **Staff:** 1. **Regional Groups:** 7. **Description:** Researchers, teachers, and students in higher education. Seeks to advance high professional standards of teaching and research in the field. Works to promote understanding and closer ties between and among various subcomponents within Asian American studies. Sponsors professional activities and events; advocates and represents the interests of Asian American studies and Asian Americans; facilitates communication and scholarly exchange among participants in Asian American studies; educates the public about the history of Asian Americans. **Awards:** Book Award. **Frequency:** annual. **Type:** scholarship ● Service Award. **Frequency:** annual. **Type:** recognition. **Computer Services:** database ● mailing lists ● online services. **Telecommunication Services:** electronic mail, ssh13@cornell.edu. **Publications:** *Journal of Asian American Studies*, 3/year. Features selected papers from the annual conference. Solicited manuscripts and book reviews. ISSN: 1097-2129. Also Cited As: *JAAS* ● *Occasional Papers*, quarterly. Newsletter. **Conventions/Meetings:** annual conference and regional meeting (exhibits).

7983 ■ Association for Asian Studies (AAS)
1021 E Huron St.
Ann Arbor, MI 48104
Ph: (734)665-2490
Fax: (734)665-3801
E-mail: jwilson@aasianst.org
URL: http://www.aasianst.org
Contact: Michael Paschal, Exec. Dir.
Founded: 1941. **Members:** 7,500. **Membership Dues:** life, patron, $1,500 ● student, $35 (annual) ● associate, $25 (annual) ● gross income of $15,000 or under, $35 (annual) ● gross income of $16,000-$30,000, $50 (annual) ● gross income of $31,000-$45,000, $70 (annual) ● gross income of $46,000 - $60,000, $80 (annual) ● gross income of $61,000-$75,000, $95 (annual) ● gross income of $76,000 or over, $105 (annual). **Staff:** 10. **Regional Groups:** 9. **Multinational. Description:** Educators, students, government officials, and others interested in the study of Asia. Sponsors research through conferences; administers special projects; maintains placement service. Maintains 28 committees. **Awards:** AAS CIAC Small Grants. **Frequency:** annual. **Type:** grant. **Recipient:** to scholars ● Book Prizes. **Frequency:** annual. **Type:** monetary. **Recipient:** for English-language, scholarly works on Asian studies ● Korean Studies Scholarship Program. **Frequency:** annual. **Type:** scholarship. **Recipient:** for graduate students majoring in Korean studies in North America. **Computer Services:** Mailing lists, of Asian studies, programs, centers, institutes ● mailing lists, of members ● mailing lists, of subscribers. **Telecommunication Services:** electronic mail, mpaschal@aasianst.org. **Committees:** Asian Law; Buddhist Studies; Language; Women in Asian Studies. **Councils:** China and Inner Asia; Conferences; Northeast Asia; South Asia; Southeast Asia. **Affiliated With:** American Council of Learned Societies. **Formerly:** (1957) Far Eastern Association. **Publications:** *Asian Studies Newsletter*, quarterly. **Price:** $30.00 /year for nonmembers in U.S.; $40.00 /year for nonmembers outside U.S.; free for members. **Circulation:** 8,500. **Advertising:** accepted ● *Bibliography of Asian Studies*. **Price:** $75.00 for members; $125.00 for nonmembers. Alternate Formats: online ● *Education About Asia*, 3/year. Journal. **Price:** $15.00 for members in U.S.; $25.00 for members outside U.S.; $31.00 organization in U.S.; $38.00 organization outside U.S. **Circulation:** 5,000. **Advertising:** accepted ● *Journal of Asian Studies*, quarterly. Concerned with the scholarly study of Asia. Contains annual index and book reviews. **Price:** included in membership dues; $70.00 /year for institutions in U.S.; $80.00 /year for institutions outside U.S. ISSN: 0021-9118. **Circulation:** 10,500. **Advertising:** accepted. Alternate Formats: microform; online ● *Mailing Labels*. Specialized selections of mailing labels. ● Membership Directory, semiannual. **Price:** $20.00 for members; $35.00 for nonmembers ● Monographs ● Also publishes scholarly research. **Conventions/Meetings:** annual conference and meeting, includes placement services (exhibits) - always March or April. 2009 Mar. 26-29, Chicago, IL; 2010 Mar. 25-28, Philadelphia, PA ● annual regional meeting.

7984 ■ China Times Cultural Foundation
PO Box 1234
Flushing, NY 11352
Ph: (718)460-4900
Fax: (718)479-4900
Contact: Sophia Hsieh, Contact
Founded: 1985. **Multinational. Description:** Provides scholarships for doctoral dissertation research in Chinese studies. **Awards:** China Times Young Scholar Award. **Frequency:** annual. **Type:** scholarship. **Recipient:** for humanities or social sciences doctoral candidates with approved dissertation prospectus.

7985 ■ Institute for the International Education of Students (IES)
33 N LaSalle St., 15th Fl.
Chicago, IL 60602-2602
Ph: (312)944-1750
Free: (800)995-2300
Fax: (312)944-1448
E-mail: info@iesabroad.org
URL: http://www.iesabroad.org
Contact: Dr. Mary Dwyer PhD, Pres.
Founded: 1950. **Members:** 165. **Membership Dues:** institutional, $350 (annual). **Staff:** 75. **Budget:** $65,000,000. **Multinational. Description:** Provides programs in 32 locations in 15 countries throughout Europe, Asia, Australia, New Zealand, and South America. Consists of more than 60,000 alumni and enrolls more than 4,500 undergraduate college students each year from its academic consortium, which is comprised of more than 160 top U.S. colleges and universities. Programs are offered for semester, academic year, or summer. Short-term, faculty-led Customized Programs are also available. Offers its students up to nearly $2 million in scholarships and financial aid. **Formed by Merger of:** (1988) Institute of European Studies; (1994) Institute of Asian Studies. **Formerly:** (1998) Institute of European and Asian Studies. **Publications:** *Announcements*, annual. Catalog ● *IES Exchange*, semiannual. Newsletter. Alternate Formats: online. **Conventions/Meetings:** annual meeting ● seminar, for faculty.

7986 ■ International Association of Asian Studies (IAAS)
PO Box 6670
Scarborough, ME 04070-6670
Ph: (207)839-8004
Fax: (207)839-3776
E-mail: naaasconference@earthlink.net
URL: http://www.naaas.org
Contact: Dr. Lemuel Berry Jr., Exec. Dir.
Founded: 1998. **Members:** 123. **Membership Dues:** individual, $125 (annual) ● institutional, $500 (annual) ● student, sustaining donor, $100 (annual) ● life, $3,000. **Staff:** 3. **Regional Groups:** 4. **Description:** Postsecondary educational institutions offering Asian studies programs; academics, students, and other individuals with an interest in Asian studies. Seeks to advance the field of Asian studies. Provides a forum for the presentation of research results; conducts educational programs; maintains speakers'

bureau. **Computer Services:** Mailing lists. **Affiliated With:** National Association of African American Studies; National Association of Hispanic and Latino Studies. **Publications:** *Affiliate News*, 3/year. Newsletter. **Price:** included in membership dues. **Advertising:** accepted. Alternate Formats: online ● *Journal of Intercultural Disciplines*, annual. **Price:** $46.50 /year for nonmembers; included in membership dues. **Circulation:** 1,000. **Advertising:** accepted. **Conventions/Meetings:** annual conference (exhibits).

7987 ■ Malaysia/Singapore/Brunei Studies Group of the Southeast Asia Council Association for Asian Studies
c/o Greg Felker, Chm.
Dept. of Politics
Willamette Univ.
900 State St.
Salem, OR 97301
Ph: (503)370-6261
Fax: (503)370-6720
E-mail: gfelker@willamette.edu
Contact: Greg Felker, Chm.
Founded: 1976. **Members:** 200. **Membership Dues:** regular, $20 (annual). **Multinational. Description:** Supports research and study of Malaysia, Singapore, and Brunei. Promotes interest in the region. Acts as a clearinghouse for information on Southeast Asia. **Libraries: Type:** reference. **Holdings:** 26. **Publications:** *Berita*, 3/year. Newsletter. **Price:** $20.00 /year for individuals; $20.00 /year for institutions. **Circulation:** 150 ● *Berita Bulletin*, quarterly. Magazine. **Price:** $34.02. **Conventions/Meetings:** periodic general assembly ● annual meeting.

7988 ■ National Association for Asian and Pacific American Education (NAAPAE)
PO Box 280346
Northridge, CA 91328-0346
Ph: (818)677-2500 (818)677-6853
Fax: (818)366-2714
E-mail: naapae@naapae.net
URL: http://www.naapae.net
Contact: Clara Park, Pres.
Founded: 1977. **Members:** 500. **Membership Dues:** regular, $30 (annual) ● student, senior citizen, $20 (annual) ● organization, $100 (annual). **Description:** Asian/Pacific-Americans and others in bilingual/multicultural education. Works to enhance awareness of the multicultural structure of America and to unify Asian/Pacific-American communities through educational opportunities. Promotes inclusion of Asian and Pacific-American culture and history in school curricula; advocates bilingual, multicultural, and other programs. Encourages research on related educational topics; works to increase awareness of the educational needs, concerns, and contributions of Asian and Pacific-Americans. Supports the increased participation of Asian/Pacific-Americans in diverse educational roles. Operates bilingual education workshops and service projects. Sponsors competition. **Awards: Frequency:** annual. **Type:** recognition ● **Frequency:** annual. **Type:** scholarship. **Recipient:** to high school seniors, college juniors and seniors. **Publications:** *Contemporary Perspectives on Asian and Pacific American Education: A Resource Guide for Asian Pacific American Students* ● Directory, triennial ● Monographs, periodic ● Newsletter, quarterly. Alternate Formats: online. **Conventions/Meetings:** annual conference (exhibits) - always May or April.

7989 ■ Permanent International Altaistic Conference (PIAC)
Indiana Univ.
GoodBody Hall 157
Bloomington, IN 47405-7005
Ph: (812)855-0959
Fax: (812)855-7500
E-mail: sinord@indiana.edu
Contact: Prof. Denis Sinor, Sec.Gen.
Founded: 1957. **Members:** 600. **Languages:** English, French, German, Russian. **Multinational. Description:** Represents scholars interested in Altaic or Inner Asian studies. Encourages information exchange and public reading of scholarly papers of common interest. **Awards:** Indiana University Prize for Altaic Studies Gold Medal. **Frequency:** annual. **Type:** medal. **Recipient:** for committee of peers. **Publications:** Newsletter, periodic. **Circulation:** 600. **Advertising:** accepted. **Conventions/Meetings:** annual conference.

Asian Studies

7990 ■ Council of Teachers of Southeast Asian Languages (COTSEAL)
PO Box 3798
Arlington, VA 22203-0798
E-mail: bact@calmail.berkeley.edu
Contact: Bac Hoai Tran, Pres.
Founded: 1984. **Membership Dues:** associate, $15 (annual) ● individual, $20 (annual) ● institution, $25 (annual). **Description:** Professional organization for teachers of Southeast Asian Languages. **Computer Services:** Mailing lists, of members. **Publications:** *COTSEALetter*, 3/year. Newsletter. Alternate Formats: online ● *The Journal of Southeast Asian Language Teaching*, annual. Contains articles on second-language acquisition, methodology and linguistics. ● *SEALTEACH*. Membership Directory. Contains electronic mailing list of members. Alternate Formats: online. **Conventions/Meetings:** annual Southeast Asian Language Teaching and Applied Linguistics - conference, teaching and technology.

7991 ■ South Asian Language Teachers Association (SALTA)
Univ. of Pennsylvania
820 Williams Hall
Philadelphia, PA 19104-6305
Ph: (215)898-7475
Fax: (215)573-2138
E-mail: sgambhir@sas.upenn.edu
URL: http://ccat.sas.upenn.edu/salta
Contact: Dr. Surendra Gambhir, Contact
Membership Dues: regular, $5 (annual). **Description:** Professional organization of language educators at university and college level. Encourages cooperation among instructors and educators of South Asian languages, linguistics, and literature in institutions of higher studies, particularly colleges and universities in North America. Aims at developing a national 'architecture' of programs in South Asian languages in terms of national needs, program designs, competency levels, curricular resources, and instructional methodologies. **Publications:** *South Asia Language Teaching and Research*. Newsletter. Alternate Formats: online.

Automotive Education

7992 ■ National Automotive Technicians Education Foundation (NATEF)
101 Blue Seal Dr. SE, Ste.101
Leesburg, VA 20175
Ph: (703)669-6650
Fax: (703)669-6125
E-mail: webmaster@natef.org
URL: http://www.natef.org
Contact: Mr. Bill Kersten, Pres.
Founded: 1983. **Staff:** 4. **Description:** Encourages the development of automotive technical education and the maintenance of national standards set by the automotive industry for secondary and postsecondary educational facilities. Evaluates and reviews the structure and resources of automobile, collision repair and refinish, truck and CNG/LGP training programs in areas such as learning resources, student services, instruction, and facilities. Makes recommendations that lead to program certification by the National Institute of Automotive Service Excellence.

7993 ■ North American Council of Automotive Teachers (NACAT)
PO Box 80010
Charleston, SC 29416
Ph: (843)556-7068
Fax: (843)556-7068
E-mail: office@nacat.com
URL: http://www.nacat.com
Contact: Mr. Dan Perrin, Exec. Mgr.
Founded: 1974. **Members:** 725. **Membership Dues:** individual, $50 (annual) ● individual, $135 (triennial) ● individual, $225 (quinquennial). **Staff:** 1. **State Groups:** 1. **Description:** Provides support for automotive educators, secondary, post-secondary, and industry. Enhances technical training opportunities, peer interaction and resources sharing. Represents automotive teachers on councils and committees where automotive teachers' interests are involved. **Awards:** NACAT Scholarship Awards. **Frequency:** annual. **Type:** monetary. **Recipient:** for students. **Sections:** State, Provincial and Regional Chapters. **Subgroups:** NACAT/SC, NACAT/GA; State and Provincial Chapters. **Formerly:** National Association of College Automotive Teachers. **Publications:** *NACAT News*, 3/year. Newsletter. Contains articles on automobile-related topics. **Price:** free. **Circulation:** 1,000. **Advertising:** accepted. Alternate Formats: online. **Conventions/Meetings:** annual conference (exhibits) - always 3rd week of July. 2008 July 21-25, Williamsport, PA - **Avg. Attendance:** 300; 2009 July 20-24, Charlotte, NC.

Aviation

7994 ■ National Aviation and Space Education Alliance (NASEA)
23 Nutmeg Dr.
Enfield, CT 06082
Ph: (505)774-0029
E-mail: mail@nasea.org
URL: http://www.nasea.org
Contact: Joseph Murtari, Pres.
Description: Collaborates with aviation groups in support of aviation and space education. Forms alliances with representatives of other statewide aviation and space education groups to share information and develop new resources to support similar programs. Fosters communication among organizations engaged in aviation and space education activities.

7995 ■ National Coalition for Aviation Education (NCAE)
c/o M.A. Thomson, Member of the Board
3146 Valentino Ct.
Oakton, VA 22124
E-mail: webmaster@aviationeducation.org
URL: http://www.aviationeducation.org
Contact: Rol Murrow, Treas.
Founded: 1993. **Membership Dues:** regular, $100-$300 (annual) ● associate, $275 (annual). **Description:** Promotes aviation and space education while supporting schools' initiatives at the local, state and national levels. Works with aviation educators, government officials and industry representatives to marshal education resources and use aviation to train America's young people. **Computer Services:** database, career resources ● database, member organizations ● database, teaching resources.

Bangladeshi

7996 ■ American Institute of Bangladesh Studies (AIBS)
c/o Prof. Guy Welbon, PhD, Pres.
South Asia Ctr.
820 Williams Hall
36th & Spruce St.
Univ. of Pennsylvania
Philadelphia, PA 19104-6305
Ph: (215)898-7475 (212)854-5416
Fax: (215)573-2138
E-mail: gwelbon@ccat.sas.upenn.edu
URL: http://www.aibs.net
Contact: Prof. Guy Welbon PhD, Pres.
Founded: 1989. **Members:** 15. **Membership Dues:** college and university, $250 (annual). **Staff:** 4. **Description:** Promotes the study of the history and culture of Bangladesh. **Awards: Frequency:** annual.

Type: grant. **Recipient:** for study in Bangladesh. **Conventions/Meetings:** annual meeting.

Behavioral Sciences

7997 ■ International Society for Quality-of-Life Studies (ISQOLS)
1800 Kraft Dr., Ste.111
Blacksburg, VA 24060-6370
Ph: (540)231-5110
Fax: (540)961-4162
E-mail: sirgy@vt.edu
URL: http://www.isqols.org
Contact: M. Joseph Sirgy, Exec. Dir.

Founded: 1995. **Members:** 300. **Membership Dues:** regular, $75 (annual) ● student and retired, $50 (annual) ● institutional/charter, $125 (annual) ● institutional/charter - life, $300. **Staff:** 2. **Multinational. Description:** Seeks to stimulate research in quality of life studies by linking researchers with a listserv to enhance communication among members; provides publication outlets for research by enhancing network opportunities through conferences and workshops and by building bibliographies and other related reference materials. Conducts research and educational programs. **Awards:** Annual JOHS Paper Award. **Frequency:** annual. **Type:** recognition. **Recipient:** for the best paper in the last year of JOHS ● Award for the Betterment of Humanity. **Frequency:** annual. **Type:** recognition. **Recipient:** for an organization that has developed quality of life measures and implemented those measures to guide public policy for the purpose of enhancing the quality of life of a specific population ● Award for the Betterment of the Human Condition. **Frequency:** annual. **Type:** recognition. **Recipient:** for significant accomplishment of an organization to the development and use of QOL measures in serving its constituency ● Best Annual SIR Paper Award. **Frequency:** annual. **Type:** recognition. **Recipient:** for the best paper ● Best Dissertation Award. **Frequency:** annual. **Type:** recognition. **Recipient:** for the author of the best dissertation related to quality of life studies ● Distinguished Quality of Life Researcher Award. **Frequency:** annual. **Type:** recognition. **Recipient:** for distinguished and long term record of scholarly quality of life research ● Distinguished Service Award. **Frequency:** annual. **Type:** recognition. **Recipient:** to an individual for outstanding service to the society in a leadership position ● Fellow Quality of Life Researcher Award. **Frequency:** annual. **Type:** recognition. **Recipient:** for researchers who have made significant contributions to quality of life research ● Social Indicators Research Best Paper Award. **Frequency:** annual. **Type:** recognition. **Recipient:** for authors who have published in Social Indicators Research, provided that this article has made a significant contribution to the development of the field of quality of life research. **Publications:** *Journal of Business Ethics*, 9/year. **Price:** $241.50 /year for members ● *Journal of Happiness Studies*, quarterly. Features both cognitive evaluations of life and affective enjoyment of life. **Price:** $55.00 /year for members; $318.00 /year for nonmembers ● *Journal of Macromarketing*, quarterly. Contains information about the QOL studies in marketing. ● *Social Indicators Network News*, quarterly. Newsletter. Affiliated with Social Indicators Research and The Journal of Happiness Studies. **Price:** included in membership dues. **Circulation:** 300. **Advertising:** accepted. **Conventions/Meetings:** annual conference, with scholarly book exhibits (exhibits).

Bilingualism

7998 ■ Intercultural Development Research Association (IDRA)
5835 Callaghan Rd., Ste.350
San Antonio, TX 78228-1190
Ph: (210)444-1710
Fax: (210)444-1714
E-mail: contact@idra.org
URL: http://www.idra.org
Contact: Maria Robledo Montecel PhD, Exec. Dir.

Founded: 1973. **Budget:** $4,000,000. **Description:** Professionals who have extensive field, research, and development-based experience in education, especially bilingual minority education and dropout prevention programs. Dedicated to the principle that all children are entitled to an equal educational opportunity. Strives for the elimination of educational inequities through involvement in the areas of training and technical assistance and research. Organizes and sponsors institutes, and programs on management skills, compliance with state and federal laws, and educational social systems evaluation. Works with school districts and early childhood programs in developing alternate delivery models, and evaluating and redesigning existing programs. Disseminates research reports and information concerning alternative programmatic activities. **Libraries: Type:** reference. **Subjects:** interracial and gender issues, national origin desegregation, testing, evaluation, research, statistical methods. **Computer Services:** database, data processing department for the creation and analysis. **Divisions:** Community and Public Engagement; Institute for Policy and Leadership; Professional Development; Research and Evaluation. **Formerly:** (1974) Texans for Educational Excellence. **Publications:** *Hispanic Families as Valued Partners: Educator's Guide*. Book. **Price:** $21.60 each ● *IDRA Newsletter*, 10/year. **Price:** free. ISSN: 1069-5672. **Circulation:** 8,000 ● *The Undereducation of American Youth* ● Books ● Videos ● Also publishes teaching packets. **Conventions/Meetings:** quarterly board meeting ● conference ● annual seminar ● workshop.

7999 ■ National Association for Bilingual Education (NABE)
1313 L St. NW, Ste.210
Washington, DC 20005
Ph: (202)898-1829
Fax: (202)789-2866
E-mail: nabe@nabe.org
URL: http://www.nabe.org
Contact: Barbara Flores, Pres.

Founded: 1975. **Members:** 3,000. **Membership Dues:** individual, $60 (annual) ● state affiliate, $55 (annual) ● college/university student, paraprofessional, parent, $30 (annual) ● institutional, $125 (annual) ● life, $1,000. **Staff:** 12. **Budget:** $1,500,000. **State Groups:** 25. **National Groups:** 25. **Description:** Devoted to representing both the interests of language-minority students and the bilingual education professionals who serve them. Works to ensure that "learning is a reality for every student, regardless of his or her mother tongue"; and establishes contact with national organizations. **Awards:** Bilingual Instructional Assistant of the Year. **Frequency:** annual. **Type:** recognition. **Recipient:** for outstanding instructional assistants ● Bilingual Teacher of the Year. **Frequency:** annual. **Type:** recognition. **Recipient:** for outstanding teachers. **Computer Services:** Mailing lists, of members. **Telecommunication Services:** electronic mail, members@nabe.org. **Subgroups:** Adult/Vocational Education; Asian/Pacific Islanders; Critical Pedagogy; Early Childhood; Elementary Education; ESL in Bilingual Education; Gifted Education; Global Education; Higher Education; Instructional Technology; Language and Culture Retention; Language Policy; Migrant Education; Parent and Community; Policy Maker; Professional Development; Research and Evaluation; Secondary Education; Special Education. **Publications:** *Bilingual Research Journal*, quarterly. Delivers in-depth coverage of education theory and practice. **Price:** $79.00 /year for nonmembers; $140.00 /year for institutions; $39.00 /year for members. **Circulation:** 3,000. **Advertising:** accepted. Also Cited As: *NABE Journal* ● *Language Learner*, 8/year. Newsletter. **Price:** included in membership dues. **Circulation:** 3,000. **Advertising:** accepted. Alternate Formats: online. **Conventions/Meetings:** competition, writing contest for bilingual students ● annual conference - 2009 Feb. 18-21, Austin, TX; 2010 Feb. 3-6, Denver, CO ● annual International Bilingual/Multicultural Education Conference (exhibits) - always between January and April ● workshop.

Biology

8000 ■ National Association of Biology Teachers (NABT)
12030 Sunrise Valley Dr., Ste.110
Reston, VA 20191
Ph: (703)264-9696
Free: (800)406-0775
Fax: (703)264-7778
E-mail: office@nabt.org
URL: http://www.nabt.org
Contact: Pat L. Waller, Pres.

Founded: 1938. **Members:** 8,000. **Membership Dues:** spouse, $33 (annual) ● student, $39 (annual) ● full (in U.S., Canada, Mexico), $79 (annual) ● foreign, $119 (annual) ● organization, $149 (annual) ● life (age 21-29), $1,250 ● life (age 30-39), $1,000 ● life (age 40-49), $850 ● life (age 50-59), $600 ● life (age 60 and up), $400 ● sustaining organization, $750 (annual) ● comprehensive, $109 (annual). **Staff:** 9. **Budget:** $1,300,000. **Regional Groups:** 10. **State Groups:** 17. **Description:** Professional society of biology and life science teachers and others interested in the teaching of biology at all educational levels. Works to achieve scientific literacy among citizens. Promotes professional growth and development; fosters regional activities for biology teachers; confronts issues involving biology, society, and the future; provides a national voice for the profession. Sponsors summer biology updates. **Libraries: Type:** reference. **Holdings:** archival material. **Awards:** Award for Excellence in Encouraging Equity. **Frequency:** annual. **Type:** recognition. **Recipient:** to a biology educator ● Distinguished Service Award. **Type:** recognition. **Recipient:** to scientists making major contributions to biology education ● Evolution Education Award. **Frequency:** annual. **Type:** recognition. **Recipient:** for innovative classroom teaching and community education efforts to promote an accurate understanding of biological evolution. ● Four-Year College Biology Research/Teaching Award. **Frequency:** annual. **Type:** recognition. **Recipient:** to a four-year college faculty ● Four-Year College Biology Teaching Award. **Frequency:** annual. **Type:** recognition. **Recipient:** to a four-year college faculty member ● Honorary Membership. **Type:** recognition. **Recipient:** to an individual achieving distinction in teaching, research or service in biological sciences ● NABT Biotechnology Teaching Award. **Frequency:** annual. **Type:** recognition. **Recipient:** to a secondary school teacher ● Outstanding Biology Teacher Award. **Frequency:** annual. **Type:** recognition. **Recipient:** to a biology educator, grades 7-12 ● Outstanding New Biology Teacher Achievement Award. **Frequency:** annual. **Type:** recognition. **Recipient:** to a new biology/life science instructor, grades 7-12 ● Two-Year College Biology Teaching Award. **Frequency:** annual. **Type:** recognition. **Recipient:** to a two-year college biology educator. **Committees:** Awards; Teacher Education; Teaching Standards. **Publications:** *American Biology Teacher*, 9/year. Journal. Informs biology teachers of new research and teaching strategies, and contains audiovisual, book, and software reviews. **Price:** $124.00/year in U.S.; $228.00/2 years in U.S.; $337.00/3 years in U.S.; $134.00/year outside U.S. ISSN: 0002-7685. **Circulation:** 10,000. **Advertising:** accepted. Alternate Formats: microform ● *Bioinstrumentation - Tools for Understanding Life*. Book. **Price:** $15.00 for members; $20.00 for nonmembers ● *Biology Labs That Work: The Best of How-to-Do-Its, Vol. II*. Articles. **Price:** $248.00/2 years outside U.S.; $372.00/3 years outside U.S.; $24.00 for members; $28.00 for nonmembers. ISSN: 0002-7685. **Circulation:** 10,000. **Advertising:** accepted. Alternate Formats: microform ● *D'Arcy Thompson's Ice Cream and Other Essays from Biology Today*. Book. **Price:** $15.00 for members; $18.00 for nonmembers ● *Encouraging Student Biological Research*. Monograph. **Price:** $32.00 for members; $37.00 for nonmembers ● *In the Light of Evolution: Science Education on Trial*. Book. **Price:** $16.00 for members; $20.00 for nonmembers ● *Investigating Ecology in the Laboratory.* **Price:** $27.00 for members; $32.00 for nonmembers ● *Investigating Plants: Hands-On, Low-Cost Laboratory Exercises in Plant Science.* **Price:** $3.00 for members; $5.00 for nonmembers ● *Learning Biology with Plant Pathology.* Book. **Price:** $5.00 for members; $7.00 for nonmembers ● *Meet the Microbes Through MicrobeWorld Activities.* Book. **Price:** $5.00 ● *Middle School Idea Book.* **Price:** $8.00 for members; $10.00 for nonmembers ● *The Power of Analogy - Teaching Biology with Relevant Classroom-Tested Activities.* **Price:** $24.00 for members; $27.00 for nonmembers ● *Shoestring Biotechnology - Budget-Oriented High Quality Biotechnology Laboratories for Two-Year College and High School.* Book. **Price:** $36.00 for members; $40.00 for nonmembers. **Conventions/Meetings:** annual conference and convention (exhibits) - 2008 Oct. 15-18, Memphis, TN; 2009 Nov. 11-14, Denver, CO.

Broadcasting

8001 ■ Broadcast Education Association (BEA)

1771 N St. NW
Washington, DC 20036-2891
Ph: (202)429-3935
Free: (888)380-7222
Fax: (202)775-2981
E-mail: beainfo@beaweb.org
URL: http://www.beaweb.org
Contact: Heather Birks, Exec. Dir.

Founded: 1955. **Members:** 1,500. **Membership Dues:** individual, $110 (annual) ● student/emeritus, $30 (annual) ● institution, $120 (biennial) ● BA-granting institution, $170 (annual) ● MA-granting institution, $220 (annual) ● PhD-granting institution, $245 (annual) ● associate, $125 (annual) ● state association, $100 (annual) ● bronze corporate, $1,000-$2,499 (annual) ● silver corporate, $2,500-$4,999 (annual) ● gold corporate, $5,000-$9,999 (annual) ● platinum corporate, $24,999 (annual). **Staff:** 3. **Budget:** $500,000. **Regional Groups:** 8. **Multinational.** **Description:** Universities and colleges; faculty and students; promotes improvement of curriculum and teaching methods, broadcasting research, television and radio production, and programming teaching on the college level. **Awards: Frequency:** annual. **Type:** scholarship ● **Frequency:** annual. **Type:** scholarship. **Divisions:** Broadcast and Internet Radio; Communication Technology; Courses, Curricula and Administration; Documentary; Gender Issues; History; International; Law and Policy; Management and Sales; Multicultural Studies; News; Production Aesthetics and Criticism; Research; Student-Media Advisors; Two-Year/Small Colleges; Writing. **Affiliated With:** National Association of Broadcasters. **Formerly:** (1973) Association for Professional Broadcasting Education. **Publications:** *Feedback*, quarterly. Journal. Covers the teaching of television and radio broadcasting at colleges and universities. **Price:** included in membership dues; $40.00 /year for nonmembers in U.S.; $25.00/year for students at member schools; $50.00 /year for nonmembers outside U.S. ISSN: 0883-8151. Alternate Formats: online ● *Journal of Broadcasting and Electronic Media*, quarterly. Covers the teaching of television and radio broadcasting at colleges and universities. **Price:** included in membership dues; $40.00 /year for nonmembers in U.S.; $25.00/year for students at member schools; $50.00 /year for nonmembers outside U.S. ISSN: 0883-8151 ● *Journal of Radio Studies*, quarterly. **Conventions/Meetings:** annual convention (exhibits) - spring ● annual convention, held in conjunction with NAB (exhibits).

8002 ■ Broadcast Foundation of College/University Students (BROADCAST FOCUS)

89 Longview Rd.
Port Washington, NY 11050
Ph: (516)883-0159
Fax: (516)883-0159
E-mail: rstarleton@aol.com
Contact: Robert S. Tarleton, Exec.Dir.

Founded: 1976. **Members:** 400. **Description:** College students interested in broadcasting and professional broadcasters interested in encouraging practical broadcasting experience in colleges and universities. Conducts annual survey of all professional broadcasting stations for part-time and summer employment for college students. Sponsors job advisory and placement service. **Also Known As:** Broadcast FOCUS. **Publications:** *Broadcast Opportunities*, periodic ● *Interface Abstracts*, periodic. **Conventions/Meetings:** semiannual meeting ● seminar, educational.

8003 ■ Center for Communication (CCI)

110 E 23rd St., Ste.900
New York, NY 10010
Ph: (212)686-5005
Fax: (212)504-2632
E-mail: info@cencom.org
URL: http://www.cencom.org
Contact: Catherine Williams, Exec. Dir.

Founded: 1980. **Staff:** 5. **Description:** Organizes educational forums designed to bring leaders from the field of communications together with young media professionals, university professors and media students interested in the communication industry. Provides e-mail transcripts and videotapes of communications-related discussions with leaders in the industry. Conducts seminars and teleconferences focusing on issues such as: the relationship between the media and human rights; the problems of universal access to the information highway; and the role of minorities in the communications industry. Offers sessions on career counseling. Sponsors 40 symposia per year. **Libraries: Type:** open to the public. **Awards:** Communication Award. **Frequency:** annual. **Type:** recognition. **Recipient:** for an outstanding contributor within the field of communications. **Conventions/Meetings:** annual luncheon.

8004 ■ Intercollegiate Broadcasting System (IBS)

367 Windsor Hwy.
New Windsor, NY 12553-7900
Ph: (845)565-0003
Fax: (845)565-7446
E-mail: ibshq@aol.com
URL: http://www.ibsradio.org
Contact: Fritz Kass, Contact

Founded: 1940. **Members:** 968. **Membership Dues:** radio station, professional associate, $125 (annual). **Staff:** 6. **Budget:** $352,747. **Description:** Radio stations at schools, colleges, and universities. Offers educational, informational, and consulting services. Compiles statistics; conducts research and seminars. **Additional Websites:** http://www.frontiernet.net/~ibs/ibshome.html. **Affiliated With:** Iota Beta Sigma. **Publications:** *Journal of College Radio*, quarterly. Reports on the establishment, management, and programming of school and college radio stations. Includes technical tips. **Price:** included in membership dues. **Advertising:** accepted. Also Cited As: *College Radio* ● *Radio Newsletter*, monthly. Alternate Formats: online ● Also publishes summary reports. **Conventions/Meetings:** annual conference (exhibits) - usually March.

8005 ■ World Communication Association (WCA)

c/o Barbara S. Monfils, Pres.
Univ. of Wisconsin-Whitewater
800 W Main St., Hyer 428
Whitewater, WI 53190-1790
Ph: (262)472-1055
Fax: (262)472-1670
E-mail: monfilsb@uww.edu
URL: http://facstaff.uww.edu/wca
Contact: Barbara S. Monfils, Pres.

Founded: 1983. **Members:** 75. **Membership Dues:** regular, $50 (annual) ● institutional, library, $90 (annual) ● student, $20 (annual) ● life, $1,000. **Regional Groups:** 8. **Multinational.** **Description:** Represents educators, scholars, and students worldwide. Promotes academic phases of communication, particularly radio, television, film, oral, written, and electronic communication. Conducts training programs. **Libraries: Type:** open to the public. **Holdings:** 31. **Subjects:** communication. **Publications:** *WCA Newsletter*, semiannual. Includes reports of communication studies. ISSN: 0882-4096. Alternate Formats: online ● *World Communication*, quarterly. Journal. Covers all forms of human communication, with emphasis on intercultural and international communication. ISSN: 0882-4088. **Conventions/Meetings:** biennial conference - always June in Brisbane, QL, AUS.

Building Industries

8006 ■ Metal Buildings Institute (MBI)

c/o Ray Barbieri, Pres.-Elect
588 Winsted Rd.
Torrington, CT 06790
Ph: (860)496-7503
Fax: (860)482-4541
E-mail: rjbcon@rcn.com
URL: http://metal-building-institute.org
Contact: Ray Barbieri, Pres.-Elect

Founded: 2001. **Description:** Aims to improve the quality of metal building construction. **Committees:** Certification. **Conventions/Meetings:** periodic conference.

Business

8007 ■ American Society for Competitiveness (ASC)

PO Box 1658
Indiana, PA 15705
Ph: (724)357-5928 (724)357-5759
Fax: (724)357-7768
E-mail: aaali@iup.edu
URL: http://www.eberly.iup.edu/asc
Contact: Abbas J. Ali, Exec. Dir.

Founded: 1990. **Members:** 300. **Membership Dues:** individual, $40 (annual) ● institutional, $500 (annual) ● institutional sponsorship, $1,500 (annual). **Staff:** 7. **Description:** Seeks to foster education and knowledge in subjects related to competitiveness by: facilitating exchange of information and ideas among educators, policy makers, and business people, and by encouraging and assisting research activities which advance knowledge of competitiveness practices and increase the available body of teaching and practice materials. Seeks to serve the needs of entrepreneurial scholars and intellectual managers. Specifically through its conferences and publications, intends to effectively serve the needs of academicians interested in the practical application of organizational theory and practicing managers interested in the intellectual development of the discipline. **Awards:** Leadership Award. **Frequency:** annual. **Type:** medal. **Recipient:** for contribution to quality and competitiveness ● Philip Crosby Award. **Frequency:** annual. **Type:** medal. **Recipient:** for contribution to quality and competitiveness ● Quality Award. **Frequency:** annual. **Type:** medal. **Recipient:** for contribution to quality and competitiveness. **Councils:** Advisory. **Publications:** *Advances in Competitiveness Research*, annual. Journal ● *Competition Forum*, biennial. **Price:** $60.00 for individuals in U.S.; $80.00 for individuals outside U.S.; $80.00 for institutions in U.S.; $100.00 for institutions outside U.S. ISSN: 1545-2581 ● *Competitiveness Review.* Journal. **Price:** $40.00 /year for individuals (add $20 if outside U.S.); $120.00 /year for institutions (add $20 if outside U.S.) ● *Journal of Global Competitiveness*, annual. **Price:** $60.00 for individuals in U.S.; $80.00 for individuals outside U.S.; $80.00 for institutions in U.S.; $100.00 for institutions outside U.S. ISSN: 1071-0736. **Conventions/Meetings:** annual conference, for policy makers, executives and scholars ● meeting.

8008 ■ Business-Higher Education Forum (BHEF)

2025 M St. NW, Ste.800
Washington, DC 20036-1193
Ph: (202)367-1189

Fax: (202)367-2269
E-mail: info@bhef.com
URL: http://www.bhef.com
Contact: Brian K. Fitzgerald, Exec. Dir.

Founded: 1978. **Members:** 80. **Staff:** 4. **Description:** Board chairmen and chief executive officers of Fortune 500 corporations; presidents and chancellors of universities and colleges. Addresses issues of interest to American business and higher education institutions such as: tax incentives for university research; worker training and retraining; new links between industry and academia; innovative methods of corporate support for higher education. Seeks to expand public awareness of the concerns of business and academic leaders and to influence policy-making affecting those concerns; to enhance relationships between corporate America and institutions of higher learning. Provides interchange between the business and academic communities. Has recently completed several studies on competitiveness; believes that improving the ability of American industry and workers to compete is essential to all other economic and societal goals. Organizes special task forces for in-depth studies on special issues. Disseminates reports and recommendations to policymakers in the public and private sector. **Libraries: Type:** open to the public. **Holdings:** papers, reports. **Affiliated With:** American Council on Education. **Publications:** *A Commitment to America's Future*. Report. Alternate Formats: online ● *American Potential: The Human Dimension* ● *America's Business School: Priorities for Change* ● *America's Competitive Challenge: The Need for a National Response* ● *The Chairman's Report*, biennial ● *Corporate and Campus Cooperation: An Action Agenda* ● *Crosstalk: The Public, the Experts, and Competitiveness*. Report ● *Export Controls: The Need to Balance National Objectives* ● *The New Manufacturing: America's Race to Automate* ● *Space: America's New Competitive Frontier* ● *Three Realities: Minority Life in the United States*. Report ● Membership Directory. Alternate Formats: online ● Books. **Conventions/Meetings:** semiannual roundtable.

8009 ■ National Business Officers Association (NBOA)

c/o Sarah P. Daignault, Exec. Dir.
PO Box 4576
Boulder, CO 80306-4576
Ph: (720)564-0475
Fax: (720)564-4951
E-mail: nboa@nboa.net
URL: http://www.nboa.net
Contact: Sarah P. Daignault, Exec. Dir.

Membership Dues: associate, international school, $350 (annual) ● corporate sponsor, $1,000 (annual) ● retired business officer, $50 (annual) ● independent school in U.S. (small), $385 (annual) ● independent school in U.S. (large), $2,600 (annual). **Description:** Independent school business officers. Helps members streamline business and strategic operations. **Awards:** Kenneth A. White, Jr. Distinguished Business Officer Award. **Frequency:** annual. **Type:** recognition. **Recipient:** to an individual who has demonstrated outstanding achievement in the field of business and financial management in independent schools. **Computer Services:** Mailing lists ● online services. **Programs:** Purchasing. **Publications:** *Net Assets*. Newsletter. **Price:** included in membership dues ● Newsletter, monthly. **Price:** included in membership dues. Alternate Formats: online. **Conventions/Meetings:** annual symposium.

Business Education

8010 ■ AACSB International - Association to Advance Collegiate Schools of Business (AACSB)

777 S Harbour Island Blvd., Ste.750
Tampa, FL 33602-5730
Ph: (813)769-6500
Fax: (813)769-6559
E-mail: maryjo@aacsb.edu
URL: http://www.aacsb.edu
Contact: Eric Romero, Asst. VP, Research

Founded: 1916. **Members:** 900. **Membership Dues:** educational institution, $2,200 (annual) ● non-profit association, government organization, professional association, $1,000 (annual) ● small corporation, $2,500 (annual) ● large corporation, $5,000 (annual) ● sustaining, $10,000 (annual). **Staff:** 30. **Budget:** $3,000,000. **Multinational. Description:** Institutions offering accredited programs of instruction in business administration and accounting at the college level; non-accredited schools; business firms; governmental and professional organizations; educational institutions and organizations outside the U.S. Provides accreditation for bachelor's, master's, and doctoral degree programs in business administration and accounting. Serves as a professional association for management education. Compiles statistics, conducts research, and conducts professional development programs. **Computer Services:** Mailing lists. **Committees:** Accounting Accreditation; Accreditation Coordinating; Accreditation Quality; Candidacy; Initial Accreditation; Maintenance of Accreditation; Pre-Accreditation. **Programs:** Annual Meeting. **Task Forces:** Centers for International Education and Research; Global Forum Planning; International Partnership Teams for Continuous Improvement; Re-accreditation Process; Regional Representatives. **Absorbed:** Council for Professional Education for Business. **Formerly:** (1973) American Association of Collegiate Schools of Business; (1997) American Assembly of Collegiate Schools of Business; (2001) AACSB-The International Association for Management Education. **Publications:** *AACSB-The International Association for Management Education Membership Directory*, annual. **Price:** $15.00 in U.S.; $20.00 outside U.S. ISSN: 0360-697X ● *Achieving Quality and Continuous Improvement Through Self-Evaluation and Peer Review (Standards for Accreditation)*, annual. Manual. Discusses accreditation standards, guidelines and procedures. **Price:** $10.00 in U.S.; $12.00 outside U.S. ● *BizEd*, bimonthly. Magazine. For management education/business school leaders. **Price:** $72.00/year in U.S.; $82.00/year in Canada; $92.00/year outside U.S. and Canada. **Advertising:** accepted. Alternate Formats: online ● *Business and Management Education Funding Alert*, monthly. Provides funding information for business school faculty; includes monthly "flashes" of late-breaking grant or contract announcements. **Price:** $445.00/year in U.S.; $485.00/year outside U.S. ISSN: 1042-5217 ● *eNewsline*, monthly. Newsletter. Covers developments in the administration of collegiate business schools, legislative news, association activities and trends in management education. **Price:** $15.00/year in U.S.; $20.00/year outside U.S. ISSN: 0360-697X. Alternate Formats: online ● *Ethics Education in Business Schools*. Report. Alternate Formats: online ● *Guide to Doctoral Programs in Business and Management*, periodic. Book. Includes an overview of programs of study, admissions criteria and procedures, expenses, financial assistance, and placement records of graduates. **Price:** $15.00 in U.S.; $20.00 outside U.S. ● *Management Education at Risk*. Report. Alternate Formats: online ● *Salary Survey*, annual. Report. Presents a statistical report of faculty and administrative personnel salaries at U.S. business schools; arranged by subjects taught and position. **Price:** $25.00/year in U.S.; $30.00/year outside U.S. ● *Sustaining Scholarship in Business Schools*. Report. Alternate Formats: online ● Publishes studies, international resource guides, diversity, management of technology, and quality management curriculum guides. Videos are also available. **Conventions/Meetings:** annual meeting and conference (exhibits).

8011 ■ Academy of International Business (AIB)

The Eli Broad Coll. of Bus.
Michigan State Univ.
7 Eppley Center
East Lansing, MI 48824-1121
Ph: (517)432-1452
Fax: (517)432-1009
E-mail: aib@aib.msu.edu
URL: http://aib.msu.edu
Contact: Dr. Tunga Kiyak, Managing Dir.

Founded: 1959. **Members:** 3,095. **Membership Dues:** regular, $100 (annual) ● low income, student, $50 (annual) ● electronic (low income individuals from developing countries - all correspondence in electronic form), $25 (annual) ● institutional, $1,100 (annual). **Staff:** 5. **Budget:** $700,000. **Regional Groups:** 14. **Multinational. Description:** Consists primarily of university professors, doctoral students, researchers, writers, consultants, executives, and policy setters in the international business/trade research and education fields. Facilitates information exchange among people in academia, business, and government and encourages research activities that advance the knowledge of international business operations and increase the available body of teaching materials. Compiles an inventory of collegiate courses in international business, a survey of research projects, and statistics. **Awards:** AIB Dean of the Year. **Frequency:** annual. **Type:** recognition. **Recipient:** to business school deans ● AIB Executive of the Year. **Frequency:** annual. **Type:** recognition. **Recipient:** for an executive ● Haynes Prize. **Frequency:** annual. **Type:** monetary. **Recipient:** for the most promising young scholar in the international business field ● JIBS/Palgrave Macmillan Decade Award. **Frequency:** annual. **Type:** recognition. **Recipient:** for the most influential article published in the journal of international business studies ● Richard N. Farmer Dissertation Award. **Frequency:** annual. **Type:** monetary. **Recipient:** for superior doctoral dissertations in the field of international business ● SAMS Dissertation Proposal Award. **Frequency:** annual. **Type:** monetary. **Recipient:** for the best doctoral dissertation proposal ● Temple/AIB Best Paper Award. **Frequency:** annual. **Type:** monetary. **Recipient:** for the best paper at the AIB annual meetings. **Computer Services:** Mailing lists, of members ● online services, resume and job databanks. **Additional Websites:** http://www.jibs.net. **Formerly:** (1972) Association for Education in International Business. **Publications:** *AIB Annual Conference Proceedings*, annual. Contains abstracts of manuscripts presented at the AIB Annual Conference. **Price:** free for conference attendees. **Circulation:** 1,000. **Advertising:** accepted. Alternate Formats: CD-ROM; online ● *AIB Conference Program*, annual. Booklet. **Price:** free for conference participants. **Circulation:** 1,000. **Advertising:** accepted. Alternate Formats: online ● *AIB Membership Directory*, continuously updated. **Price:** available to members only. Alternate Formats: online ● *AIB Newsletter*, quarterly. Provides information on new business education programs, grants, and association news. Includes employment opportunity listings. **Price:** available to members only. **Circulation:** 3,100. **Advertising:** accepted. Alternate Formats: online ● *Journal of International Business Studies*, bimonthly. Publishes academic papers of significant interest that contribute to the theoretical basis of business and management studies. **Price:** $217.00 institutional in U.S.; 138.00 institutional outside U.S. ISSN: 0047-2506. **Advertising:** accepted. Alternate Formats: online. Also Cited As: *JIBS* ● Brochure. **Conventions/Meetings:** annual conference, academic conference with double-blind reviewed manuscripts being presented; exhibits of publishers, schools, and other educational materials (exhibits) - late June or early July. 2008 June 29-July 2, Milan, Italy; 2009 June 27-30, San Diego, CA ● annual Frontiers Conference - conference and meeting - in the fall.

8012 ■ AIESEC - United States

127 W 26th St., 10th Fl.
New York, NY 10001
Ph: (212)757-3774
Fax: (212)757-4062
E-mail: missys@aiesecus.org
URL: http://www.aiesecus.org
Contact: Jim Kelly, Office Mgr.

Founded: 1948. **Members:** 50,000. **Staff:** 15. **Budget:** $1,000,000. **Local Groups:** 37. **Description:** Students of economics or business and related fields presently studying at affiliated universities worldwide.

Aims to develop an internationally educated managers. Manages the international exchange of students on internships around the world. Conducts training of members in the management of international business operations. **Programs:** Customized International Exchange; International Exchange. **Projects:** Salaam. **Also Known As:** International Association of Students in Economics and Business Management—United States; Association Internationale Des Etudiants en Sciences Economiques et Commerciales. **Publications:** *AIESEC-U.S.—Annual Report*. Lists AIESEC financial supporters, participating companies, member countries, and affiliated American colleges and universities. **Price:** free ● *Linkletter*, quarterly. Newsletter. Covers international student exchange organization activities. Used for marketing the AIESEC program to business students around the world. **Price:** free. **Advertising:** accepted. **Conventions/Meetings:** annual conference (exhibits) - always January.

8013 ■ Association to Advance Collegiate Schools of Business (AACSB)
777 S Harbour Island Blvd., Ste.750
Tampa, FL 33602-5730
Ph: (813)769-6500
Fax: (813)769-6559
E-mail: roxanna@aacsb.edu
URL: http://www.aacsb.edu
Contact: Roxanna Strawn, Asst. VP for Communications
Founded: 1916. **Members:** 1,000. **Membership Dues:** educational, $2,200 (annual) ● not-for-profit/professional/government association, $1,000 (annual) ● small corporation, $2,500 (annual) ● large corporation, $5,000 (annual) ● sustaining, $10,000 (annual). **Staff:** 39. **Multinational. Description:** Promotes advancement of collegiate schools of business. **Task Forces:** Management Education. **Publications:** *BizEd*, bimonthly. Magazine. Contains articles for management education/business school leaders. **Price:** $72.00/year. **Circulation:** 15,000. **Advertising:** accepted ● *eNewsline*, 11/year. Newsletter. Serves as an electronic connection. Alternate Formats: online ● *Ethics Education in B-Schools*. Report ● *Management Education at Risk*. Report. Alternate Formats: online ● *Sustaining Scholarship in Business Schools*. Report. **Conventions/Meetings:** annual conference, with speakers.

8014 ■ Association for Business Communication (ABC)
c/o Dr. Betty S. Johnson, Exec. Dir.
PO Box 6143
Nacogdoches, TX 75962-0001
Ph: (936)468-6280
Fax: (936)468-6281
E-mail: abcjohnson@sfasu.edu
URL: http://www.businesscommunication.org
Contact: Dr. Betty S. Johnson, Exec. Dir.
Founded: 1935. **Members:** 2,000. **Membership Dues:** special student, retired, $30 (annual) ● active, $80 (annual) ● limited publication, $60 (annual) ● sustaining, $100 (annual). **Staff:** 1. **Budget:** $265,000. **Regional Groups:** 9. **Description:** College teachers of business communication; management consultants in business communications; training directors and correspondence supervisors of business firms, direct mail copywriters, public relations writers, and others interested in communication for business. **Awards:** Distinguished Publication on Business Communication. **Frequency:** annual. **Type:** recognition. **Recipient:** for an outstanding book, book chapter, or journal article ● Outstanding Article in Business Communication Quarterly. **Frequency:** annual. **Type:** recognition. **Recipient:** for an outstanding article ● Outstanding Article in The Journal of Business Communication. **Frequency:** annual. **Type:** recognition. **Recipient:** for an outstanding article. **Committees:** Business Practices; Community College; Convention Procedures; Diversity Initiative; Employment Opportunities; Intercultural Communications; International Issues; Nominations. **Formerly:** (1969) American Business Writing Association; (1984) American Business Communication Association. **Publications:** *Business Communication Quarterly*. Journal. Covers teaching of business communication, including course outlines, descriptions of training programs, and problems and solutions. **Price:** included in membership dues; $326.00 /year for institutions. ISSN: 8756-1972. **Circulation:** 2,000. **Advertising:** accepted. Alternate Formats: microform; online. Also Cited As: *Bulletin of the Association for Business Communication* ● *Journal of Business Communication*, quarterly. Includes empirical and theoretically conceptual research results in business communication. **Price:** included in membership dues; $326.00 /year for institutions. ISSN: 0021-9436. Alternate Formats: online. Also Cited As: *JBC* ● *Making Communication Requirements More Explicit in the AACSB Standards for MBA Programs*. Paper. Alternate Formats: online ● Membership Directory. Alternate Formats: online ● Proceedings. Alternate Formats: online. **Conventions/Meetings:** annual convention, textbook publishers (exhibits).

8015 ■ Association for Business Simulation and Experiential Learning (ABSEL)
c/o Annette Halpin, VP/Exec. Dir.
Dept. of Marketing
Arcadia Univ.
450 S Easton Rd.
Glenside, PA 19038
Ph: (215)572-2849 (610)648-3375
Fax: (215)572-4489
E-mail: rplatt@uwf.edu
URL: http://www.absel.org
Contact: Richard G. Platt, Pres.
Founded: 1974. **Members:** 200. **Membership Dues:** individual, $60 (annual). **Multinational. Description:** Business professors and practitioners dedicated to the development and use of experiential teaching techniques, both computerized and noncomputerized, in business education. Assists potential users through informal dialogue with experienced members and through tutorial sessions at annual meetings. **Publications:** *Bernie Keys Library*, annual. Proceedings. Contains all ABSEL publications. Alternate Formats: CD-ROM ● *Developments in Business Simulation and Experiential Exercises*, annual. Proceedings ● *Simulations and Games: An Interdisciplinary Journal of Theory, Practice and Research*, quarterly. **Conventions/Meetings:** annual conference, scholarly papers and workshops (exhibits).

8016 ■ Association for Global Business (AGB)
PO Box 651166
Sterling, VA 20165
Ph: (703)421-7768
Fax: (703)421-7768
E-mail: damanpfx@jmu.edu
URL: http://falcon.jmu.edu/~damanpfx
Contact: Prof. Faramarz Damanpour, Pres./Founder
Membership Dues: regular, $50 (annual) ● joint (husband and wife), $80 (annual) ● student, $35 (annual). **Multinational. Description:** Fosters education in the fields of business, economics, computer information and science, political science and related areas of global concern. Encourages and facilitates an exchange of information, ideas and research activities. Creates a general awareness of the significant accomplishments in the area of global enterprises. **Telecommunication Services:** electronic mail, fdamanpour@msn.com. **Publications:** *Journal of Current Research in Global Business* ● *Journal of Global Business*, semiannual. Contains articles from areas of business, economics, computer information, science, political science and global strategies. ISSN: 1053-7287. Also Cited As: *JGB* ● Newsletter, semiannual ● Proceedings, annual. Alternate Formats: online.

8017 ■ Association Global View (AGV)
PO Box 3324
Chico, CA 95927
Ph: (530)892-9696
E-mail: globalview@earthlink.net
URL: http://www.globalview.org
Contact: Jean Hulsoor, Program Development Admin.
Founded: 1996. **Multinational. Description:** Designs, implements and facilitates educational programs specializing in high technology delivery of curriculum at globally linked sites. Strives to connect educational institutions to create a learning environment. Works to link the academic and business communities in collaborative and beneficial relationships. **Awards:** AGV Awards. **Frequency:** annual. **Type:** recognition. **Recipient:** for best advertising.

8018 ■ ASTD
Box 1443
1640 King St.
Alexandria, VA 22313-2043
Ph: (703)683-8100
Free: (800)628-2783
Fax: (703)683-8103
E-mail: memberservices@astd.org
URL: http://www.astd.org
Contact: Tony Bingham, Pres./CEO
Founded: 1944. **Members:** 70,000. **Membership Dues:** classic/international, $180 (annual) ● senior classic, $90 (annual) ● group, $145-$159 (annual) ● student, $59 (annual) ● online individual, $150 (annual). **Staff:** 100. **Budget:** $20,600,000. **Local Groups:** 138. **Multinational. Description:** Represents workplace learning and performance professionals. **Libraries: Type:** reference; not open to the public. **Holdings:** 5,000. **Subjects:** training and development, workplace performance. **Awards:** ASTD BEST Awards. **Type:** recognition. **Recipient:** for successful organizations ● Awards in the Advancing ASTD's Vision. **Type:** recognition. **Recipient:** for outstanding individuals and teams ● Awards in the Advancing Workplace Learning and Performance. **Type:** recognition. **Recipient:** to individuals' thought leadership and advocacy for the profession ● Excellence in Practice. **Type:** recognition. **Recipient:** for organizations. **Computer Services:** database, TRAINLIT ● online services, store (open to public). **Also Known As:** (2001) American Society for Training and Development. **Formerly:** (1964) American Society of Training Directors. **Publications:** *ASTD Buyer's Guide*, annual. Directory. Lists suppliers who serve the training and development industry. Includes subject and geographical index. **Price:** free for members ● *Info-Line: Tips, Tools, and Intelligence for Trainers*, monthly. Booklet. Offers how-to information for human resource development and training professionals. **Price:** $89.00 /year for members; $129.00 /year for nonmembers. ISSN: 8755-9269 ● *T&D Magazine*, monthly. Reports on current training and development practices. **Price:** included in membership dues; $99.00 /year for nonmembers in U.S.; $165.00 /year for nonmembers outside U.S. ISSN: 1535-7740. **Circulation:** 40,000. **Advertising:** accepted ● Books ● Videos. Devoted to training and development. **Conventions/Meetings:** annual International Exposition - conference (exhibits) ● annual Leaders - conference (exhibits).

8019 ■ CDS International (CDS)
871 United Nations Plz., 1st Ave., 49th St.
New York, NY 10017-1814
Ph: (212)497-3500
Fax: (212)497-3535
E-mail: info@cdsintl.org
URL: http://www.cdsintl.org
Contact: Robert Fenstermacher, Exec. Dir.
Founded: 1968. **Staff:** 20. **Budget:** $3,000,000. **Languages:** English, German, Spanish. **Multinational. Description:** Committed to the advancement of international career training opportunities customized to provide individuals with in-depth practical knowledge of other nations' business practices, cultures, and political traditions. Helps strengthen global cooperation and understanding amongst individuals, businesses, organizations and communities. Annually serves approximately 1,700 individuals from the United States, Germany, Japan, and almost 60 other nations around the globe in a wide variety of internship, fact-finding, and work-study programs. Provides opportunities for individuals to enhance their professional abilities cross-culturally in order to obtain and maintain the skills necessary for successful careers in global economy. Promotes international exchange to help strengthen cooperation between different cultures and nations. **Libraries: Type:** not open to

the public. **Telecommunication Services:** electronic mail, rfenster@cdsintl.org. **Formerly:** (1987) Carl Duisberg Society. **Publications:** *CDSsence*, triennial. Newsletter. Contains articles and information on international exchange programs. **Price:** free. Alternate Formats: online. **Conventions/Meetings:** meeting and seminar - 1-2/year.

8020 ■ Community College Business Officers (CCBO)
PO Box 5565
Charlottesville, VA 22905-5565
Ph: (434)293-2825
Fax: (434)245-8453
E-mail: info@ccbo.org
URL: http://www.ccbo.org
Contact: Dr. Bob Hassmiller CAE, Exec. Dir.
Members: 963. **Membership Dues:** institutional, $350 (annual) ● business partner, $480 (annual) ● individual, $175 (annual). **Staff:** 3. **Regional Groups:** 17. **Description:** Represents business officers. Works to support business officers. **Awards:** Exemplary Practices Award. **Frequency:** annual. **Type:** recognition. **Recipient:** to colleges that provide ideas and benchmarks for the improvement of community colleges ● Outstanding Business Officers. **Frequency:** annual. **Type:** recognition. **Recipient:** to professional staff from state coordinating agencies. **Publications:** *The Bottom Line*, quarterly. Newsletter. Alternate Formats: online. **Conventions/Meetings:** annual international conference and lecture.

8021 ■ Decision Sciences Institute (DSI)
Georgia State Univ.
J. Mack Robinson Coll. of Bus.
Univ. Plz.
Atlanta, GA 30303
Ph: (404)413-7710
Fax: (404)413-7714
E-mail: clatta@gsu.edu
URL: http://www.decisionsciences.org
Contact: Carol J. Latta, Exec. Dir.
Founded: 1969. **Members:** 5,500. **Membership Dues:** regular, institutional, $125 (annual) ● student, $25 (annual) ● emeritus in U.S. and Canada, $33 (annual) ● emeritus international, $37 (annual). **Staff:** 5. **Budget:** $650,000. **Regional Groups:** 6. **Description:** Businesspersons and members of business school faculties. Maintains placement service. **Libraries: Type:** open to the public. **Awards:** Best Application Paper Award. **Frequency:** annual. **Type:** recognition ● Elwood S. Buffa Doctoral Dissertation Award. **Frequency:** annual. **Type:** recognition ● Instructional Innovation Award. **Frequency:** annual. **Type:** recognition. **Recipient:** for outstanding contributions that advance instructional approaches within the decision sciences. **Computer Services:** database, journals, annual meeting, news publications ● online services, job placement service. **Committees:** Development; Doctoral Student Affairs; Fellows; Information Technology; Innovative Education; Investment Advisory; Nominating; Programs and Meetings; Regional Activities; Strategic Planning for International Affairs. **Formerly:** (1986) American Institute for Decision Sciences. **Publications:** *Decision Line*, 5/year. Newsletter. Includes practical and educational feature columns as well as information on members, regions annual meeting events and placement activities. **Price:** $20.00 /year for individuals; $30.00 /year for institutions. **Advertising:** accepted. Alternate Formats: online ● *Decision Sciences Institute—Proceedings*, annual ● *Decision Sciences Journal*, quarterly. **Price:** $17.50/copy, in U.S.; $19.50/copy, outside U.S. ISSN: 0011-7315 ● *Decision Sciences Journal of Innovative Education*, semiannual. Includes teaching tips and news from the front lines of the field, updated on a continual basis. Also Cited As: *DSJIE*. **Conventions/Meetings:** annual meeting (exhibits) - always November. 2008 Nov. 22-25, Baltimore, MD; 2009 Nov. 21-24, New Orleans, LA.

8022 ■ Foundation ICPR Junior College (FIJC)
Address Unknown since 2008
Founded: 1995. **Members:** 10. **Description:** Colleges and junior colleges with curricula in business education (15); interested individuals and honorary members (10). Conducts business education research and seminars. **Formerly:** Fundacion ICPR Junior College. **Conventions/Meetings:** annual conference - always second week in March.

8023 ■ Foundation for Student Communication (FSC)
48 Univ. Pl., Rm. 305
Princeton, NJ 08540-5116
Ph: (609)258-1111
Fax: (609)258-1222
E-mail: michaelk@businesstoday.org
URL: http://www.businesstoday.org
Contact: Michael Kratsios, Pres.
Founded: 1968. **Members:** 218,000. **Staff:** 40. **Budget:** $900,000. **Description:** Student subscribers and conference participants who desire to promote communication among students and businesspersons. Sponsors student/business forums. **Libraries: Type:** reference. **Holdings:** archival material, artwork, books, business records, monographs, periodicals. **Subjects:** business, finance, science. **Departments:** Accounting; Advertising; Magazine; Public Relations. **Publications:** *Business Today: Published for Students by Students*, 3/year. Magazine. Provides articles on careers, university campuses, and opinions of students. Includes employment listings. **Price:** $3.00/issue (for libraries and career service offices). **Circulation:** 200,000. **Advertising:** accepted. **Conventions/Meetings:** annual Business Today International Conference, for business executives, government lenders, and top college students from around the world to discuss important issues facing the world.

8024 ■ International Assembly for Collegiate Business Education (IACBE)
PO Box 3960
Olathe, KS 66063
Ph: (913)631-3009
Fax: (913)631-9154
E-mail: bobroller@iacbe.org
URL: http://www.iacbe.org
Contact: Dr. Bob Roller, Pres.
Founded: 1997. **Members:** 200. **Membership Dues:** institution, $1,850 (annual). **Staff:** 5. **Budget:** $700,000. **Regional Groups:** 9. **Multinational. Description:** Business education professionals. Provides industry information to those in the field of business education. **Awards:** Business Leader of the Year. **Frequency:** annual. **Type:** recognition. **Recipient:** for outstanding corporate leader. **Conventions/Meetings:** annual conference.

8025 ■ International Association for Business and Society (IABS)
c/o Jenn Griffin, Exec. Dir.
2201 G St. NW, Funger 615
George Washington Univ. School of Bus.
Washington, DC 20052
Ph: (202)994-2536
E-mail: iabs@iabs.net
URL: http://www.iabs.net
Contact: Jenn Griffin, Exec. Dir.
Founded: 1990. **Members:** 300. **Membership Dues:** faculty, professional, $80 (annual) ● doctoral student, $40 (annual). **Description:** Seeks to provide an international forum for discussion and scholarship regarding social, business and public policy issues. **Publications:** *Business and Society*, quarterly. Journal. **Conventions/Meetings:** annual conference.

8026 ■ International Association of Jesuit Business Schools (IAJBS)
c/o Dr. Gregory W. Ulferts, Exec. Dir./Corporate Sec.
4001 W McNichols Rd.
Detroit, MI 48221
Ph: (313)993-1219
Fax: (313)993-1673
E-mail: ulfertgw@udmercy.edu
URL: http://www.iajbs.org
Contact: Dr. Gregory W. Ulferts, Exec. Dir./Corporate Sec.
Founded: 1990. **Members:** 476. **Membership Dues:** school, individual, $100 (annual). **Languages:** English, Spanish. **Multinational. Description:** Enhances the ability of members to create and transmit knowledge about, and to prepare persons for the profession and vocation of business leadership in a global economy. Develops and promotes the concept of management as a profession and vocation in various societies and countries. Supports and facilitates the on-going professional development and education of business school administrators, and others. **Libraries: Type:** open to the public. **Holdings:** papers. **Subgroups:** World Regions. **Publications:** Newsletter. Alternate Formats: online. **Conventions/Meetings:** annual international conference - 2008 July 8-13, New York, NY - **Avg. Attendance:** 200.

8027 ■ International Society for Business Education (ISBE)
c/o John Lightle, Gen. Sec.
PO Box 2083
Marion, IN 46952
Ph: (765)654-7753
Fax: (765)651-3110
E-mail: jml@comteck.com
URL: http://www.isbeusa.org
Contact: Bettie Goodman, Pres.
Founded: 1901. **Members:** 2,000. **Membership Dues:** individual, $30 (annual) ● corporate sponsor, $500 (annual) ● current, $100 (annual) ● retired, $75 (annual). **Staff:** 1. **Budget:** 60 SFr. **National Groups:** 23. **Languages:** English, French, German, Italian, Spanish. **Description:** Educators involved in business education; heads of in-company training institutions; firms; schools and universities at various levels. Aims to promote the international exchange of ideas and experiences in business education and to further the education of teachers in business fields. Organizes courses in economic and business education. New members must join National Business Education Association before joining ISBE. **Awards:** SIEC Research Award. **Frequency:** annual. **Type:** monetary. **Recipient:** for individuals; recipient receives $500 to $1,000 based on proposal. **Committees:** Network; Pedagogical. **Affiliated With:** National Business Education Association. **Publications:** *Global Business Education*. Journal ● *International Review for Business Education* (in English, French, German, Italian, and Spanish), semiannual. **Price:** 45.00 SFr. **Circulation:** 2,200. **Advertising:** accepted. **Conventions/Meetings:** annual international conference, includes visits to schools and businesses ● periodic seminar.

8028 ■ Junior Achievement (JA)
1 Educ. Way
Colorado Springs, CO 80906
Ph: (719)540-8000
Fax: (719)540-6299
E-mail: newmedia@ja.org
URL: http://www.ja.org
Contact: Mr. Gerald M. Czarnecki, Pres./CEO
Founded: 1919. **Staff:** 2,100. **Budget:** $128,000,000. **Local Groups:** 144. **Multinational. Description:** Aims to educate students in grades K-12 about entrepreneurship, work readiness, and financial literacy through experiential, hands-on programs. Helps prepare young people for the "real world" by showing them how to generate wealth and effectively manage it, how to create jobs which make their communities more robust, and how to apply entrepreneurial thinking to the workplace. Encourages students to apply lessons into action, and learn the value of contributing to their communities. **Awards:** National Leadership Awards. **Frequency:** annual. **Type:** recognition. **Recipient:** for volunteers. **Programs:** Company (high school students); Economics (high school students); Elementary School (Kindergarten through 6 grades); Middle Grades (7th, 8th, and 9th graders). **Publications:** *Junior Achievement Annual Report*, annual. **Price:** free ● Also publishes promotional brochures and materials for exclusive use of local groups. **Conventions/Meetings:** annual Global Business Hall of Fame Conference, no outside exhibitors (exhibits).

8029 ■ Management Education Alliance (MEA)
c/o Francis J. Aguilar, Exec. Dir.
300 Cumnock Hall
Boston, MA 02163

Ph: (617)495-6494
Fax: (617)495-8736
URL: http://www.mgteducationalliance.org
Contact: Francis J. Aguilar, Exec. Dir.
Founded: 1994. **Description:** Seeks to help business schools that serve African-American and Hispanic-American students to provide the skills and knowledge that will lead to successful careers in management. Fosters the professional growth of faculty members, innovations in curriculum, and development of supporting institutional policies. Communicates and collaborates with business schools and US business corporations. **Publications:** Newsletter. Alternate Formats: online.

8030 ■ My Own Business, Inc. (MOBI)
13181 Crossroads Pkwy. N, Ste.190
City of Industry, CA 91746
Ph: (562)463-1800
Fax: (562)463-1802
E-mail: support@myownbusiness.org
URL: http://www.myownbusiness.org
Contact: Phil Holland, Contact
Founded: 1992. **Description:** Educates entrepreneurs by providing free coursework. Develops, produces, implements, updates and markets educational offerings through multiple delivery channels. Seeks to expand collaborations with schools, the community and other institutions. **Publications:** *FYI Newsletter*, quarterly. Contains articles, columns, success stories and other news. **Price:** free. Alternate Formats: online.

8031 ■ NASBITE International
c/o Mr. Archie Pitsilides, Exec. Dir.
Texas Tech Univ.
Rawls Coll. of Bus.
Box 42101
Lubbock, TX 79409-2101
Ph: (806)742-1827
Fax: (806)742-1826
E-mail: info@nasbite.org
URL: http://www.nasbite.org
Contact: Mr. Archie Pitsilides, Exec. Dir.
Founded: 1987. **Members:** 187. **Membership Dues:** individual, $95 (annual) ● institutional, $285 (annual) ● student, $25 (annual) ● corporate (under 100 million in sales), $500 (annual) ● corporate (100 million to 5 billion in sales), $1,000 (annual) ● corporate (over 5 billion in sales), $2,500 (annual). **Staff:** 2. **Description:** Works to improve global economic competitiveness through effective education and training. **Formerly:** (2000) National Association of Small Business International Trade Educators; (2006) North American Small Business International Trade Educators. **Publications:** Membership Directory, annual. Includes address list. **Conventions/Meetings:** annual international conference - every spring.

8032 ■ National Association for Business Teacher Education (NABTE)
c/o National Business Education Association
1914 Assn. Dr.
Reston, VA 20191-1596
Ph: (703)860-8300
Fax: (703)620-4483
E-mail: nbea@nbea.org
URL: http://www.nbea.org
Contact: Peter F. Meggison, Pres.
Founded: 1927. **Members:** 135. **Membership Dues:** institution, $150 (annual). **Staff:** 9. **Description:** An institutional division of National Business Education Association (see separate entry). Represents colleges and universities with programs for the education of business teachers. Works to improve and advance business teacher education. Operates Business Education Research Foundation. **Affiliated With:** National Business Education Association. **Publications:** *Business Education Forum*, quarterly. Journal. **Price:** $7.50 for members (copies dated 1999 to present); $15.00 for nonmembers (copies dated 1999 to present); $5.00 for members (copies dated 1990-1998); $10.00 for nonmembers (copies dated 1990-1998). ISSN: 0007-6678. **Circulation:** 16,000. **Advertising:** accepted. Alternate Formats: microform; online ● *Keying In*, quarterly. Newsletter. Alternate Formats: online ● *NABTE Review*, annual. Journal. Provides information on business education, including curriculum and instructional implications, internships, and technologies. **Price:** $20.00 for members; $40.00 for nonmembers. **Circulation:** 300 ● *NBEA Yearbook*, annual. Alternate Formats: online. **Conventions/Meetings:** annual convention ● annual meeting, held in conjunction with the NBEA's annual convention (exhibits).

8033 ■ National Association for Community College Entrepreneurship (NACCE)
Bldg. 101-R, 1 Fed. St.
Springfield, MA 01105
Ph: (413)755-6102
Fax: (413)755-6101
E-mail: info@nacce.com
URL: http://www.nacce.com
Contact: Heather Van Sickle, Exec. Dir.
Membership Dues: individual, $150 (annual) ● organizational, $500 (annual). **Description:** Establishes entrepreneurship education as a core offering to foster economic development through community colleges. Focuses on increasing economic development through entrepreneurship education and student business incubation at the community college level. **Publications:** *Community College Entrepreneur*, quarterly. Newsletter. Alternate Formats: online. **Conventions/Meetings:** annual conference.

8034 ■ National Association of Supervisors of Business Education (NASBE)
c/o Colleen Hunt, Treas.
Iowa Dept. of Education
12528 525th St.
Elliott, IA 51532
Ph: (515)281-0319
Fax: (515)281-6544
E-mail: kara.burkett@state.tn.us
URL: http://www.nasbe.us
Contact: Kara B. Burkett, Pres.
Founded: 1955. **Members:** 300. **Membership Dues:** active, associate, $15 (annual). **Description:** Acts as a representative voice for local supervisors of business and office education programs in public and private schools. Supports programs and activities in cooperation with the American Vocational Association (see separate entry) and other business education organizations. **Telecommunication Services:** electronic mail, colleen.hunt@iowa.gov. **Formerly:** (1975) National Association of Supervisors of Business and Office Education. **Publications:** *National Association of Supervisors of Business Education—Newsletter*, semiannual. **Price:** included in membership dues. Alternate Formats: online. **Conventions/Meetings:** annual meeting, held in conjunction with AVA - always December ● annual meeting, held in conjunction with National Business Education Association - always spring.

8035 ■ National Black MBA Association (NBMBAA)
180 N Michigan Ave., Ste.1400
Chicago, IL 60601
Ph: (312)236-2622
Fax: (312)236-0390
E-mail: mail@nbmbaa.org
URL: http://www.nbmbaa.org
Contact: Ms. William W. Wells, Chm.
Founded: 1970. **Members:** 6,000. **Membership Dues:** full, associate, $125 (annual) ● student, $60 (annual) ● collegiate student, $35 (annual) ● life, $1,000. **Staff:** 25. **Budget:** $4,800,000. **Regional Groups:** 5. **State Groups:** 35. **Local Groups:** 35. **Description:** Business professionals, lawyers, accountants, and engineers concerned with the role of blacks who hold advanced management degrees. Works to create economic and intellectual wealth for the black community. Encourages blacks to pursue continuing business education; assists students preparing to enter the business world. Provides programs for minority youths, students, and professionals, and entrepreneurs including workshops, panel discussions, and Destination MBA seminar. Sponsors job fairs. Works with graduate schools. Operates job placement service. **Awards:** H. Naylor Fitzhugh. **Type:** recognition ● MBA of the Year. **Frequency:** annual. **Type:** recognition ● Outstanding Educational Institution Award. **Type:** recognition ● Outstanding Educator. **Type:** recognition ● **Type:** scholarship. **Recipient:** for graduate business students ● Silver Touch. **Type:** recognition. **Publications:** *Black MBA Magazine*. **Price:** $8.00/issue, plus shipping and handling; $20.00/3 issues, plus shipping and handling. **Advertising:** accepted. Alternate Formats: online ● *National Black MBA Association—Newsletter*, monthly. Covers membership activities; includes business news and chapter profiles. **Price:** included in membership dues. **Circulation:** 5,000. **Advertising:** accepted. Alternate Formats: online ● *NBMBAA Program Book*, annual ● Membership Directory. **Circulation:** 5,000. **Advertising:** accepted. **Conventions/Meetings:** competition ● annual conference (exhibits).

8036 ■ National Business Education Association (NBEA)
1914 Assn. Dr.
Reston, VA 20191-1596
Ph: (703)860-8300
Fax: (703)620-4483
E-mail: nbea@nbea.org
URL: http://www.nbea.org
Contact: Dr. Janet M. Treichel, Exec. Dir.
Founded: 1892. **Members:** 15,000. **Membership Dues:** professional, $75 (annual) ● associate, $85 (annual) ● professional (International Society for Business Education), $105 (annual) ● student, $40 (annual) ● retired, $50 (annual). **Staff:** 9. **Budget:** $1,500,000. **Regional Groups:** 5. **State Groups:** 54. **Description:** Teachers of business subjects in secondary and postsecondary schools and colleges; administrators and research workers in business education; businesspersons interested in business education; teachers in educational institutions training business teachers; high school and college students preparing for careers in business. **Libraries: Type:** not open to the public. **Awards:** Award of Merit. **Frequency:** annual. **Type:** recognition. **Recipient:** for students ● Distinguished Service Awards. **Frequency:** annual. **Type:** recognition. **Computer Services:** Online services, membership signup, convention registration, and publication purchase. **Telecommunication Services:** electronic mail, jtreichel@nbea.org. **Absorbed:** National Business Teachers Association. **Formed by Merger of:** Department of Business Education of the National Education Association; National Council for Business Education. **Formerly:** (1962) United Business Education Association. **Publications:** *Business Education Forum*, quarterly. Journal. Covers accounting, business principles and economics, communication, information systems, marketing, international business, and entrepreneurship. **Price:** free for members. ISSN: 0007-6678. **Circulation:** 15,000. **Advertising:** accepted. Alternate Formats: microform ● *Keying In*, quarterly. Newsletter. **Circulation:** 15,000. Alternate Formats: online ● *NBEA Yearbook*, annual. Examines topical business education-related subjects. **Conventions/Meetings:** annual convention (exhibits) - always the week before Easter.

8037 ■ National Certification Commission (NCC)
PO Box 15282
Chevy Chase, MD 20825
Ph: (301)847-0102
Fax: (301)847-0103
E-mail: certification@usa.com
Contact: Richard C. Jaffeson, Exec. Dir.
Founded: 1993. **Members:** 150. **Membership Dues:** association, designation, $100 (annual). **Staff:** 4. **Budget:** $100,000. **Description:** Provides associations with information on improving existing certification programs and developing new programs for professions, occupations, or special interest. Offers credentials for ACA (advanced certification administrators) and BCA (basic certification administrators). Maintains national registration of certification programs and program statistics, educational, and research programs. **Libraries: Type:** reference. **Holdings:** 200; books. **Awards:** Annual Certification

Awards Program. **Frequency:** annual. **Type:** recognition. **Computer Services:** Online services, response to questions and email surveys. **Boards:** National Review. **Publications:** *Certification Commentary, Volume 1; Certification Program Development Guide Book* ● *Certification Communications*, monthly. Newsletter. **Price:** free. **Circulation:** 1,000. Alternate Formats: online ● *Certification Program Development Guide*. Book ● Articles, weekly. **Price:** free. Alternate Formats: online. **Conventions/Meetings:** annual National Certification Conference - meeting (exhibits) - spring.

8038 ■ National Foundation for Teaching Entrepreneurship (NFTE)
120 Wall St., 29th Fl.
New York, NY 10005
Ph: (212)232-3333
Free: (800)367-6383
Fax: (212)232-2244
E-mail: nfte@nfte.com
URL: http://www.nfte.com
Contact: Steve Mariotti, Founder/Pres.

Founded: 1987. **Multinational**. **Description:** Devoted to teaching entrepreneurship education to low-income young people, ages 11 through 18. **Publications:** *NFTE News*, quarterly. Newsletter. Alternate Formats: online.

8039 ■ National Hispanic Business Association (NHBA)
5766 Balcones Dr., Ste.203
Austin, TX 78731
Ph: (512)380-7575
Fax: (512)380-7576
E-mail: external@nhba.org
URL: http://www.nhba.org
Contact: David Pena Jr., Exec. Dir.

Founded: 1993. **Membership Dues:** regular, $15 (annual). **Description:** Fosters diversity, higher education and the improvement of the Hispanic community. Promotes the development of undergraduate Hispanic business students through educational, professional and networking opportunities. Aims to boost its members' potential of becoming future business leaders. **Awards:** National Chapter of the Year. **Frequency:** annual. **Type:** scholarship. **Recipient:** to the most outstanding chapter member ● National Representative of the Year. **Frequency:** annual. **Type:** scholarship. **Recipient:** to outstanding student representatives (by region). **Telecommunication Services:** electronic mail, lguzman@nhba.org. **Publications:** *Hispanic Business Magazine*. **Price:** included in membership dues ● Newsletter, quarterly. Contains upcoming events and ongoing programs of the local chapters. **Price:** included in membership dues. Alternate Formats: online.

8040 ■ Seton Hill University's E-magnify
Box 389F, Seton Hill Univ.
Seton Hill Dr.
Greensburg, PA 15601
Ph: (724)830-4625
Fax: (724)834-7131
E-mail: info@e-magnify.com
URL: http://www.e-magnify.com
Contact: Ms. Jayne H. Huston, Dir.

Founded: 1991. **Description:** Promotes women and business ownership. Offers a variety of entrepreneurial resources, educational programs, advocacy initiatives and networking opportunities to women entrepreneurs. Works "to strengthen the economic impact of women business owners as a collective force and to advance their growth through innovative programming in entrepreneurship and new venture creation." Provides support, education and encouragement essential for the continued growth of women-owned businesses through its services. **Telecommunication Services:** electronic mail, huston@setonhill.edu. **Formerly:** (2006) National Education Center for Women in Business. **Publications:** *E-Magnify Extra!*, weekly. Newsletter. **Price:** included in membership dues. Alternate Formats: online.

8041 ■ Society for Judgement and Decision Making (SJDM)
c/o Bud Fennema, Sec.-Treas.
Florida State Univ.
Colorado of Bus.
PO Box 3061110
Tallahassee, FL 32306-1110
Ph: (850)644-8231
Fax: (850)644-8234
E-mail: bfennema@garnet.acns.fsu.edu
URL: http://www.sjdm.org
Contact: Bud Fennema, Sec.-Treas.

Founded: 1986. **Members:** 700. **Membership Dues:** student, $10 (annual) ● individual, $35 (annual). **Budget:** $35,000. **Multinational**. **Description:** Individuals interested in the study of decision-making. Promotes research and scholarship in the field. Conducts research and educational programs; gathers and disseminates information. Facilitates cooperation between members and researchers and scholars in related fields. **Awards:** Einhorn New Investigator Award. **Frequency:** semiannual. **Type:** recognition. **Recipient:** for a promising new researcher in the field ● Jane Beattie Memorial Scholarship. **Frequency:** annual. **Type:** scholarship. **Recipient:** for a foreign scholar in the area of judgment and broadly defined decision research. **Computer Services:** Bibliographic search ● mailing lists. **Publications:** *Journal of Behavioral Decision Making*, quarterly. **Price:** $75.00/year ● *Organizational Behavior and Human Decision Processes*, monthly. Journal. **Price:** $162.00/year in U.S. and Canada; $188.00/year outside North America ● Membership Directory, periodic. Alternate Formats: online ● Newsletter, periodic. Alternate Formats: online. **Conventions/Meetings:** annual conference, research conference - always November.

8042 ■ Southwest Case Research Association (SWCRA)
c/o Joseph Kavanaugh, PhD, Pres.
Management/Marketing Dept.
Sam Houston State Univ.
Huntsville, TX 77341
Ph: (936)294-1236
Fax: (936)294-4284
E-mail: kavanaugh@shsu.edu
URL: http://www.swcrahome.org
Contact: Joseph Kavanaugh PhD, Pres.

Founded: 1991. **Members:** 50. **Description:** Promotes research, writing, and publication of decision-based cases for graduate and undergraduate business studies. **Publications:** *Journal of Applied Case Research* ● Proceedings, annual. **Conventions/Meetings:** annual meeting - always March.

Canadian

8043 ■ Association for Canadian Studies in the United States (ACSUS)
1220 19th St. NW, Ste.801
Washington, DC 20036
Ph: (202)223-9005
Fax: (202)775-0061
E-mail: info@acsus.org
URL: http://www.acsus.org
Contact: David Archibald, Exec. Dir.

Founded: 1971. **Members:** 800. **Membership Dues:** student, $30 (annual) ● retired, $60 (annual) ● life, $1,500 ● institutional, $140 (annual). **Staff:** 1. **Budget:** $200,000. **Regional Groups:** 4. **Description:** Individuals and institutions including librarians, professors, publishers, students, teachers, and government, business, and corporation officials with an educational interest in Canada. Aims to promote scholarly activities including study, research, teaching, and publication about Canada at all educational levels and in all disciplines in the U.S. Attempts to assist those interested in structuring courses and programs on Canada. **Awards:** Donner Medal. **Frequency:** biennial. **Type:** medal. **Recipient:** for excellence in Canadian studies. **Computer Services:** Mailing lists. **Publications:** *ACSUS News & Notes*, monthly. E-Broadcast. **Price:** included in membership dues ● *The ACSUS Papers*. Monograph. Includes various information about Canada. ● *American Review of Canadian Studies*, quarterly. Journal. Includes book reviews and current research in Canadian studies. **Price:** included in membership dues. ISSN: 0272-2011. **Circulation:** 1,300. **Advertising:** accepted ● *Canadian Studies Update*, semiannual. Newsletter. Provides information on new publications, grants and awards, faculty opportunities, and conference updates. **Price:** included in membership dues. ISSN: 0734-4546. **Circulation:** 1,300. **Advertising:** accepted. Alternate Formats: online ● *Financing Canadian Studies, 1995*. Book. Examines revenues and expenditures in the Canadian studies enterprise. **Price:** $5.00 for members; plus shipping and handling; $7.50 for nonmembers; plus shipping and handling ● *Northern Exposures: Scholarship on Canada in the U.S.*. Book. Seventeen essays that examine the state of Canadian studies scholarship in the United States. **Price:** $15.95 for nonmembers; plus shipping and handling; $9.95 for members; plus shipping and handling. **Conventions/Meetings:** biennial conference, a small ACSUS gathering focusing on a specific theme/topic (exhibits).

8044 ■ Center for the Study of Canada
c/o Christopher Kirkey, PhD, Dir.
Plattsburgh State Univ. of New York
133 Court St.
Plattsburgh, NY 12901
Ph: (518)564-2086 (518)564-2394
Fax: (518)564-2112
E-mail: christopher.kirkey@plattsburgh.edu
URL: http://web.plattsburgh.edu/offices/academic/cesca
Contact: Christopher Kirkey PhD, Dir.

Founded: 1980. **Members:** 500. **Membership Dues:** regular in U.S., $45 (annual) ● regular outside U.S., $51 (annual). **Budget:** $50,000. **Description:** Interdisciplinary programs and publications. Works to promote understanding of Canadian society, culture, politics, economy, geography and history. **Awards:** Green Mountain Power. **Frequency:** biennial. **Type:** recognition. **Recipient:** for best article in Quebec studies ● Prix du Quebec. **Frequency:** biennial. **Type:** monetary. **Recipient:** for contribution to field. **Computer Services:** Mailing lists. **Telecommunication Services:** electronic mail, canada@plattsburgh.edu. **Projects:** CONNECT. **Formerly:** (1998) American Council for Quebec Studies; (2001) Center for Canadian Studies and International Programs. **Publications:** *Focus Canada Series*. Monographs. **Price:** $7.50/volume; $20.00/set ● *O Canada*. Book. **Price:** $35.00/copy ● *Quebec Studies*, semiannual. Newsletter ● *Teaching Canada*, annual. Magazine. **Price:** $10.00/copy. Alternate Formats: online. **Conventions/Meetings:** biennial convention (exhibits).

Career Education

8045 ■ AFNA National Education and Research Fund
117 S 17th St., Ste.1200
Philadelphia, PA 19103
Ph: (215)854-1470
Fax: (215)854-1487
Contact: Samuel L. Evans, Pres./CEO

Founded: 1968. **Staff:** 32. **Description:** Has developed a model for educational programs preparing minority students for professional careers. The model, New Access Routes to Professional Careers, which has been used to implement programs for medicine and law in Philadelphia, PA, and New Orleans, LA, consists of four interlocking educational phases designed to enable students to meet the academic standards of professional schools through one-to-one preceptorships, tutorials, advanced study, and counseling, beginning at the 8th grade and continuing through the completion of professional school. Among the aims of the program are solidification of the student's career identification and self-image and improvement of basic communications and abstract reasoning skills. Compiles statistics. Sponsors African

American Hall of Fame. Programs carried out by American Foundation for Negro Affairs National Education and Research Fund. **Libraries: Type:** reference. **Holdings:** biographical archives. **Awards: Type:** recognition. **Divisions:** Commerce and Finance; Communications; Computer; Engineering and Business; Law; Medicine; Science and Technology. **Formerly:** American Foundation for Negro Affairs. **Publications:** *AFNA Projections to the Year 2000 and Beyond*, biennial. Monograph. **Conventions/ Meetings:** periodic Interdisciplinary Conference.

8046 ■ American Association for Career Education (AACE)

2900 Amby Pl.
Hermosa Beach, CA 90254-2216
Ph: (310)376-7378
Fax: (310)376-2926
Contact: Dr. Pat Nellor Wickwire, Pres.

Founded: 1981. **Members:** 900. **Membership Dues:** regular, $15 (annual) ● sustaining, $100 (annual) ● regular, $25 (biennial) ● sustaining, $150 (biennial). **Description:** Connects careers, education, and work. Supports and promotes workforce preparation; basic skills; employability skills; career awareness, exploration, and decision-making; youth apprenticeships and training; productive and satisfying paid and non-paid work; economic development; and collaboration, cooperation, and partnerships. Offers trend alerts, interest networks, briefs, and distinguished member papers. **Awards:** AACE Citation. **Frequency:** annual. **Type:** recognition. **Recipient:** for career education initiatives. **Publications:** *AACE Bonus Briefs*, quarterly. Papers. Covers information of interest compiled by the members. **Price:** included with newsletter. ISSN: 1524-7244 ● *AACE Careers Update*, quarterly. Newsletter. Includes Distinguished Member series and Bonus Briefs section. **Price:** included in membership dues; $15.00 /year for nonmembers. ISSN: 1074-9551. **Advertising:** accepted ● Also publishes InfoPaks, forum, registry. Career education that works, CareerGram, and Career Education Classics. **Conventions/Meetings:** biennial meeting.

8047 ■ Council on Career for Minorities (CCM)

Address Unknown since 2007

Founded: 1964. **Membership Dues:** institutional, $125 (annual). **Staff:** 2. **Budget:** $350,000. **Description:** Works to heighten the career awareness and employability of African American, Hispanic American, and Native American college students and to improve career counseling and referral services offered to them. Provides programs to help minority students improve test-taking and learning skills. Serves as a consultant to colleges involving government grants. Develops and provides professional development and training seminars, including a new partnership on cross-cultural leadership in the field, as well as the annual institutes designed for new and experienced counselling professionals. These seminars offer training on how to champion the career development role, mission and responsibilities on diverse campuses along with training techniques and theory of career development and current labor market and employment trends. Conducts Corporate Orientation Program which provides sophomore-level minority students with the opportunity to study actual college-to-work transitional business issues and learn factors that affect their employability and upward mobility in the world to work. Offers workshops for college presidents from historically black colleges to improve awareness of the role and importance of career services centers on the college campus. Also offers consultations to advise employers on policies, practices, and strategies for the recruitment and retention of college-trained minorities; provides diversity training for both management and recruiting personnel on minority interviewing and assessment techniques. Sends association representatives to meetings of similar organizations. Maintains Julius A. Thomas Fellowship Program to grant minority students the opportunity for graduate studies in career counseling to increase the pool of practicing professionals in the field. **Awards: Frequency:** annual. **Type:** grant ● Julius A. Thomas Graduate Fellowship. **Frequency:** annual. **Type:** scholarship. **Recipient:** BS degree, commitment to career counseling, member of Afrianc American, Hispanic American or Native American population. **Computer Services:** database, historically black colleges and universities and other educational institutions with large concentration of minority students. **Formerly:** (1984) College Placement Services; (2004) Council on Career Development for Minorities. **Publications:** *CCDM Annual Report*. **Price:** free. **Circulation:** 2,000. **Advertising:** not accepted ● *CCDM Minority Student Recruitment Guide*, biennial. Lists minority fraternities, sororities, honor societies, and professional organizations. Includes database enrollment statistics. **Price:** $200.00/copy; includes S/H. ISSN: 0163-2795. **Circulation:** 5,000. **Advertising:** accepted. Also Cited As: *Handbook for Recruiting Minority College Students* ● *CCDM World*, quarterly. Newsletter. Covers activities of the council and its corporate donors. Includes donor listings. **Price:** free. **Advertising:** accepted ● *Directory of Colleges and Universities*, annual. Covers historically Black institutions an minority schools with 15-80% minority student population. **Price:** $125.00 includes S/H ● *Research Report*, annual ● *Special Report*, periodic ● Also publishes brochures. **Conventions/Meetings:** quarterly Institutes for College Career Counseling Personnel - seminar.

8048 ■ National Association for Industry-Education Cooperation (NAIEC)

235 Hendricks Blvd.
Buffalo, NY 14226-3304
Ph: (716)834-7047
Fax: (716)834-7047
E-mail: naiec@pcom.net
URL: http://www2.pcom.net/naiec
Contact: Dr. Donald M. Clark, Pres./CEO

Founded: 1948. **Members:** 1,180. **Membership Dues:** individual, $35 (annual) ● council/chapter, $45 (annual) ● institution, $100 (annual) ● corporate (under 25MM net earnings), $250 (annual) ● corporate (25-100MM net earnings), $500 (annual) ● corporate (100-250MM net earnings), $750 (annual) ● corporate (over 250MM net earnings), $1,000 (annual). **Staff:** 4. **Budget:** $250,000. **Description:** Representatives of business, industry, education, government, labor, and the professions. Fosters industry-education collaboration in continuous school improvement and workforce preparation in order to develop responsive academic and vocational programs which will more effectively serve the needs of both the students and employers as well as further human resources and economic development. Provides technical assistance to schools implementing industry-education councils, high-performance sustainable education systems and business- or industry-sponsored programs. Promotes improved career and entrepreneurship education and supports school-based job placement. Provides staff development programs to improve instruction and curricula and the efficiency and effectiveness of educational management through use of corporate and volunteer services. Acts as national clearinghouse for information on industry involvement in education; serves as liaison between organizations involved in industry-education cooperation, including American Association for Career Education, National Research Center for Career and Technical, and American Society for Training and Development. Conducts research and policy studies. **Libraries: Type:** not open to the public. **Holdings:** 781. **Subjects:** industry-education cooperation, work force preparation, economic development, school improvement. **Divisions:** Community Resource Workshops; Curriculum (Career, Economic, and Special Education); Economic Development; Education Management; Industry-Education Councils; School-Based Job Placement. **Absorbed:** (1972) Community Resources Workshop Association. **Formerly:** (1964) Business-Industry Section of National Science Teachers Association. **Publications:** Newsletter, bimonthly. Includes book reviews, calendar of events, list of resources, and statistics. **Price:** included in membership dues; $25.00 /year for nonmembers. **Circulation:** 1,000. **Advertising:** accepted ● Handbooks. On industry-education councils, community resources workshops, career education, special needs groups (disabled), and adult and special education. ● Film. Contains information on career education advisory councils. **Conventions/ Meetings:** annual conference (exhibits) ● regional meeting ● seminar ● workshop.

8049 ■ National Consortium for Black Professional Development (NCBPD)

Address Unknown since 2007

Founded: 1974. **Members:** 57. **Membership Dues:** individual, $50 (biennial). **Staff:** 21. **Budget:** $1,200,000. **Description:** Industrial corporations and business firms (32); universities, including schools of business, science, and math, and public school systems (20); affiliates (5). Goal is to increase substantially, by the year 2000, the number of black professionals in business administration, communications, applied and natural sciences, engineering, and law. Sponsors a science and engineering competition for black students and Ph.D. programs in the agricultural sciences and business administration. Maintains clearinghouse and placement bureau for black professionals seeking employment. Provides recruitment service for universities seeking qualified black faculty and students. Services several federal contracts. **Awards:** Minority Professional Award. **Frequency:** annual. **Type:** recognition. **Recipient:** for significant achievement in profession. **Committees:** Annual Science Competition; Program Development; Public Relations. **Publications:** *Journal of Minority Employment*, monthly. Reports employment information concerning Hispanics, Blacks, Native Americans, and Asians. **Price:** $24.00/year. **Circulation:** 60,000. **Advertising:** accepted ● *Science and Engineering Newsletter*, monthly. For grades 4-8. **Conventions/ Meetings:** annual Minority Professional Conference - always held in May, usually the 3rd week; **Avg. Attendance:** 1200.

Caribbean

8050 ■ Caribbean Studies Association (CSA)

c/o Dr. Percy C. Hintzen, Pres.
Univ. of California
660 Barrows Hall, No. 2572
Berkeley, CA 94720
Ph: (510)642-0303
Fax: (510)642-0318
E-mail: phintzen@berkeley.edu
URL: http://www.caribbean-studies.org
Contact: Dr. Percy C. Hintzen, Pres.

Founded: 1974. **Members:** 1,000. **Membership Dues:** individual (inside Caribbean), $50 (annual) ● individual (outside Caribbean), $65 (annual) ● student, $25 (annual). **Staff:** 1. **Budget:** $35,000. **Languages:** English, French, Spanish. **Description:** Scholars and other professionals interested in Caribbean studies. Encourages, supports, and conducts professional, interdisciplinary research on the Caribbean; disseminates information about developments in the Caribbean. **Libraries: Type:** reference. **Holdings:** archival material. **Subjects:** biographical. **Awards:** Caribbean Review Award. **Frequency:** annual. **Type:** recognition. **Recipient:** for an individual who has made outstanding contributions to Caribbean studies; given in collaboration with *Caribbean Review* ● Gordon K. Lewis Book Award. **Frequency:** annual. **Type:** recognition. **Recipient:** for an outstanding book on the Caribbean. **Publications:** *Caribbean Studies* (in English, French, and Spanish), 3/year. Newsletter. Includes Spanish texts, book and research notes, congress and conference news, commentaries on Caribbean current events, and member news. **Price:** included in membership dues; $50.00 /year for institutions. ISSN: 0271-6577. **Circulation:** 1,000 ● *Directory of Caribbeanists*, periodic. **Price:** $8.00 for individuals; $15.00 for institutions ● *Membership List*, annual. Membership Directory. **Conventions/Meetings:** annual conference (exhibits).

Catholic

8051 ■ Association of Catholic Colleges and Universities (ACCU)

1 Dupont Cir., Ste.650
Washington, DC 20036

Ph: (202)457-0650
Fax: (202)728-0977
E-mail: accu@accunet.org
URL: http://www.accunet.org
Contact: Richard A. Yanikoski PhD, Pres./CEO
Founded: 1899. **Members:** 217. **Membership Dues:** college/university in U.S., $425-$9,270 (annual) ● college/university outside U.S., $425 (annual) ● campus ministry center, $200 (annual). **Staff:** 5. **Budget:** $336,000. **Description:** Facilitates exchange among Catholic institutions of higher education and represents these institutions to other national associations of higher education, to the International Federation of Catholic Universities, and federal government agencies. Sponsors the Neylan Commission, which engages in special activities for religious women in higher education. Appoints task forces to report on areas of interest such as Hispanic presence and college and high school articulation. **Libraries: Type:** reference. **Holdings:** books, periodicals. **Subjects:** Catholic and secular higher education, institutions, philanthropy, includes institutional catalogues. **Awards:** Presidents' Distinguished Service Award. **Frequency:** periodic. **Type:** recognition ● Theodore M. Hesburgh, CSC, Award. **Frequency:** annual. **Type:** recognition. **Recipient:** for an individual who has made outstanding contributions to Catholic higher education through teaching, scholarship, administrative excellence or leadership on governing boards. **Computer Services:** database, catholic colleges and universities. **Affiliated With:** International Federation of Catholic Universities. **Formerly:** (1978) College and University Department of the National Catholic Education Association. **Publications:** *Current Issues in Catholic Higher Education*, semiannual. Journal. **Price:** $10.00/issue ● *Update*, quarterly. Newsletter. Contains calendar of events and research updates. **Price:** included in membership dues. **Circulation:** 2,000. Alternate Formats: online ● Also publishes financial and enrollment studies of Catholic colleges. **Conventions/Meetings:** semiannual board meeting - every third Friday and Saturday of June, and second Friday of October ● annual meeting - always late January or early February in Washington, DC.

8052 ■ Association of Jesuit Colleges and Universities (AJCU)
One Dupont Cir. NW, Ste.405
Washington, DC 20036
Ph: (202)862-9893
Fax: (202)862-8523
E-mail: goloughlin@ajcunet.edu
URL: http://www.ajcunet.edu
Contact: Rev. Charles L. Currie SJ, Pres.
Founded: 1970. **Members:** 28. **Staff:** 8. **Budget:** $700,000. **Description:** Represents and serves the 28 Jesuit colleges and universities in the United States. Maintains a small library, conducts research, compiles statistics, and offers information services. Fosters cooperation through the maintenance of over 30 Intercollegiate Conferences, which represent such varied interests as Advancement, Business Deans, Information Technology, International Education and Student Personnel. **Awards:** National Book Award. **Frequency:** annual. **Type:** recognition. **Recipient:** for authors who have made outstanding publishing contributions and achievements. **Absorbed:** Jesuit Research Council of America. **Formerly:** Jesuit Educational Association. **Publications:** *AJCU Directory*, annual. **Price:** $15.00. **Circulation:** 766. Alternate Formats: online ● *Connections*, monthly. Newsletter. Covers activities at Jesuit campuses and in Washington, DC. **Price:** free online. **Circulation:** 1,000. Alternate Formats: online ● *International Education Resource Book* ● *Justice Reports*.

8053 ■ Association of Mercy Colleges (AMC)
c/o Dr. Mary Ann Dillon, RSM, Pres.
Mt. Aloysius Coll.
7373 Admiral Perry Hwy.
Cresson, PA 16630
Fax: (814)886-2978
Contact: Dr. Mary Ann Dillon RSM, Pres.
Founded: 1982. **Members:** 19. **Description:** Colleges and universities sponsored by the Religious Sisters of Mercy. Provides a medium for closer cooperation among members concerning education. Sponsors cooperative grant applications. **Programs:** Student Exchange. **Conventions/Meetings:** annual meeting, in conjunction with the Association of Catholic Colleges and Universities ● Summer Conference for Presidents.

8054 ■ Augustinian Secondary Educational Association (ASEA)
2520 S York Town
Tulsa, OK 74114
Ph: (918)746-2600
Fax: (918)746-2636
Contact: Father Bernard Scianna OSA, Pres.
Founded: 1986. **Members:** 9. **Staff:** 1. **Regional Groups:** 3. **Description:** Secondary educational schools of the Augustinian order. Serves as a forum and vehicle for sharing of resources, advancement of Augustinian ideals in education, promotion of secondary education as a vital ministry, and assuring "authentic Augustinian identity" for the schools in the care of the Order of St. Augustine. Compiles statistics; conducts educational programs. **Awards:** ASEA Teachers Award. **Frequency:** annual. **Type:** recognition. **Conventions/Meetings:** Heads of School Meeting ● annual meeting ● Values Institute - meeting.

8055 ■ Jesuit Secondary Education Association (JSEA)
1616 P St. NW, Ste.400
Washington, DC 20036-1418
Ph: (202)667-3888
Fax: (202)387-6305
E-mail: jsea@jsea.org
URL: http://www.jsea.org
Contact: Ralph E. Metts SJ, Pres.
Founded: 1970. **Members:** 46. **Membership Dues:** institutional, $615 (annual). **Staff:** 6. **Budget:** $700,000. **Regional Groups:** 10. **Description:** Serves Jesuit high schools. Promotes leadership development, teacher development, curriculum planning and school-based research. **Libraries: Type:** not open to the public. **Holdings:** 600; articles, books, periodicals. **Subjects:** Jesuit education, leadership, staff development, organizational development, administration, supervision, teaching. **Awards:** Ignatian Educator. **Frequency:** triennial. **Type:** recognition. **Recipient:** for services with Jesuit secondary education. **Telecommunication Services:** electronic mail, mettsr@jsea.org. **Affiliated With:** Association of Jesuit Colleges and Universities. **Formerly:** Jesuit Educational Association. **Publications:** *AJCU/JSEA Directory*, annual. Lists Jesuit high schools, colleges, and universities. **Circulation:** 800. Alternate Formats: online ● *JSEA Bulletin*, 7/year. Newsletter. Contains articles and information on Jesuit secondary education. Includes alumni news and announcements of JSEA publications and workshops. **Price:** $22.00 /year for members; $24.00 /year for nonmembers. **Circulation:** 2,000. Alternate Formats: online ● *MAGISine*, annual. Journal. Provides in-depth treatment of topics of particular interest to Ignatian educators. **Conventions/Meetings:** triennial Colloquium of Ignatian Education - convention, for administrations, teachers, and trustees of Jesuit High Schools ● conference - 15/year ● bimonthly Seminars in Ignatian Leadership ● biennial symposium.

8056 ■ National Association of Boards, Commissions, and Councils of Catholic Education (NABCCCE)
Natl. Catholic Educational Assn.
1077 30th St. NW, Ste.100
Washington, DC 20007-3852
Ph: (202)337-6232
Fax: (202)333-6706
E-mail: nceaadmin@ncea.org
URL: http://www.ncea.org/departments/nabccce
Contact: Dr. Regina M. Haney EdD, Exec. Dir.
Founded: 1967. **Members:** 5,000. **Membership Dues:** individual, $150 (annual) ● student, $75 (annual) ● diocesan board, $230-$315 (annual) ● regional board, $220-$265 (annual) ● school, parish, private, religious education, total education board, $180-$245 (annual). **Description:** A service department of the National Catholic Educational Association (see separate entry). Provides leadership and support for groups and individuals who are responsible for policy formation and decision-making in Catholic education. Aims to: give practical assistance in organizing new boards and education committees; improve the performance quality of established policy making bodies; assist policy makers in identifying and addressing current educational issues; serve as a forum for the exchange of information on both the parish and diocesan levels. Acts as a clearinghouse on policy statements and maintains clearinghouse file. Offers consultation assistance. Compiles statistics. **Awards:** O'Neil D'Amour Award. **Frequency:** annual. **Type:** recognition. **Recipient:** for an individual who has made outstanding contributions to the boards of Catholic education ● Outstanding Board Award. **Frequency:** annual. **Type:** recognition. **Recipient:** for boards, commissions, or councils of Catholic education with outstanding work. **Committees:** Awards. **Programs:** Chairperson Training. **Formerly:** (1999) National Association of Boards of Education. **Publications:** *A Board Shouldn't Think It Won't Happen Here*. Article. Alternate Formats: online ● *A Primer on Educational Governance in the Catholic Church* ● *Benchmarks of Excellence: Effective Boards of Catholic Education* ● *Building Better Boards*. Video. Alternate Formats: online ● *Ensuring a Future Full of Hope*. Newsletter ● *Issue-Gram*, quarterly. Newsletter. Reports on policy issues for Catholic boards of education or education commissions at regional, diocesan, parish, and school levels. **Price:** included in membership dues. Alternate Formats: online ● *School Board Study Programs, Series I and II*. Audiotapes. **Conventions/Meetings:** annual convention.

8057 ■ National Association of Catholic Homes and Educators (NACHE)
7517 Dogwood Rd.
Sykesville, MD 21784
E-mail: catholichome@nache.org
URL: http://www.nache.org
Contact: Tim Hill, Pres.
Description: Represents Catholic parents concerned with the education and faith of their children and families. Provides spiritual, doctrinal, and practical information to Catholics. Aims to support the faith and formation needs of all families. Serves the Catholic community and assists with other regional Catholic educational conventions. **Telecommunication Services:** electronic mail, advertising@nache.org. **Publications:** *The Catholic Home*, quarterly. Journal. **Advertising:** accepted. Alternate Formats: online.

8058 ■ National Association of Catholic School Teachers (NACST)
1700 Sansom St., Ste.903
Philadelphia, PA 19103
Ph: (215)568-4175
Free: (800)99-NACST
Fax: (215)568-8270
E-mail: nacst.nacst@verizon.net
URL: http://www.nacst.com
Contact: Rita C. Schwartz, Pres.
Founded: 1978. **Members:** 5,000. **Membership Dues:** individual, $60 (annual). **Staff:** 1. **Local Groups:** 25. **Description:** Catholic school teachers. Aims to unify, advise, and assist Catholic school teachers in matters of collective bargaining. Promotes the welfare and rights of Catholic schools and teachers; determines needs of Catholic schools and teachers. Monitors legislation, trends, and statistics concerning Catholic education; promotes legislation favorable to nonpublic schools and Catholic school teachers; offers legal advice and addresses issues such as unemployment compensation; assists teachers in organizing and negotiating contracts. Maintains speakers' bureau. **Telecommunication Services:** electronic mail, rita@nacst.com. **Funds:** Legal Defense. **Publications:** *National Association of Catholic School Teachers—Newsworthy*, quarterly. Newsletter. Includes association and legislative news.

Alternate Formats: online. **Conventions/Meetings:** annual convention.

8059 ■ National Catholic Educational Association (NCEA)
1077 30th St. NW, Ste.100
Washington, DC 20007
Ph: (202)337-6232
Fax: (202)333-6706
E-mail: nceaadmin@ncea.org
URL: http://www.ncea.org
Contact: Karen M. Ristau EdD, Pres.
Founded: 1904. **Members:** 20,000. **Staff:** 43. **Budget:** $7,000,000. **Description:** Aims to advance the educational and catechetical mission of the Church and to provide leadership and service to its members in preschools, elementary and secondary schools, parish catechetical/religious education programs, diocesan offices, colleges, universities and seminaries. Members serve over seven million students. **Libraries: Type:** not open to the public. **Awards:** C. Albert Koob Merit Award. **Frequency:** annual. **Type:** recognition ● Catherine T. McNamee CSJ Award. **Frequency:** annual. **Type:** recognition ● Elizabeth Ann Seton Award. **Type:** recognition ● John F. Meyers Award. **Frequency:** annual. **Type:** recognition ● Leonard DeFiore Award. **Frequency:** annual. **Type:** recognition. **Computer Services:** database, statistics on Catholic education ● mailing lists. **Telecommunication Services:** electronic mail, president@ncea.org. **Commissions:** National Association of Boards, Commissions and Councils of Catholic Education. **Departments:** Chief Administrators; Elementary Schools; Religious Education; Secondary Schools; Seminary. **Affiliated With:** Association of Catholic Colleges and Universities. **Formerly:** (1927) Catholic Education Association. **Publications:** *Data Bank Report*, annual ● *Momentum*, quarterly. Journal. Covers current education issues and innovative programs in Catholic schools. Includes index, book reviews, and research reports. **Price:** included in membership dues; $20.00 /year for nonmembers. ISSN: 0026-914X. **Circulation:** 25,000. **Advertising:** accepted. Alternate Formats: microform ● *NCEA Notes*, 5/year. Newsletter. **Price:** included in membership dues ● *Opt-in*. Newsletter ● *Seminary News*, quarterly. Newsletter. **Price:** included in membership dues. **Circulation:** 400 ● Also publishes audiocassettes, papers, books, and manuals on educational topics ranging from preschool through college. **Conventions/Meetings:** annual convention, membership convention (exhibits) - always Easter week ● annual meeting, for chief administrators of catholic education (exhibits).

8060 ■ Regional Education Board of the Christian Brothers (REB)
c/o Christian Brothers Conference
Hecker Center
3025 Fourth St. NE, Ste.300
Washington, DC 20017
Ph: (202)529-0047
E-mail: kdalmasse@cbconf.org
Contact: Bro. Kevin Dalmasse FSC, Education Dir.
Founded: 1970. **Members:** 12. **Description:** An advisory board of the Christian Brothers Conference. Seeks to discuss and evaluate the problems and development of the Lasallian schools, institutions, and colleges, and to develop effective strategies for sustaining the Lasallian educational mission. Conducts conference for staff members of schools in which the Christian Brothers and their Lasallian partners work. **Awards:** Distinguished LaSallian Educator. **Frequency:** annual. **Type:** recognition. **Formerly:** (1970) Christian Brothers Education Association; (1978) National Education Council of the Christian Brothers; (1985) Regional Education Council of the Christian Brothers; (1988) Regional Education Committee of the Christian Brothers. **Publications:** *Blessed Ambiguity: Brothers in the Church*. Book. Contains 6 articles discussing Blessed Ambiguity: Exploring Foundations, and 6 additional essays developing Blessed Ambiguity: Exploring Futures. **Price:** $10.00/copy. **Conventions/Meetings:** annual conference (exhibits).

Ceramics

8061 ■ Ceramic Educational Council (CEC)
c/o R. Allen Kimel, Sec.-Treas.
Pennsylvania State Univ.
212A Steidle Bldg.
University Park, PA 16802
Ph: (814)865-5397
E-mail: kimel@matse.psu.edu
URL: http://www.acers.org/membership/sdc_pages/sdcdisplay.asp?ItemID=1
Contact: Greg Hilmas, Pres.
Founded: 1938. **Members:** 203. **Membership Dues:** individual, $5 (annual). **Multinational. Description:** Seeks to stimulate, promote, and improve ceramic education. Compiles statistics. Conducts educational programs. **Libraries: Type:** reference. **Awards:** Outstanding Educator of the Year. **Frequency:** annual. **Type:** recognition. **Formerly:** Association of Ceramic Educators. **Publications:** Graduate school survey. **Conventions/Meetings:** competition ● annual meeting, held in conjunction with the American Ceramic Society's annual meeting (exhibits).

Chemistry

8062 ■ Institute for Chemical Education (ICE)
Univ. of Wisconsin
Dept. of Chemistry
1101 Univ. Ave.
Madison, WI 53706-1396
Ph: (608)262-3033 (608)262-1483
Free: (800)991-5534
Fax: (608)265-8094
E-mail: ice@chem.wisc.edu
URL: http://ice.chem.wisc.edu
Contact: Dr. John W. Moore, Dir.
Founded: 1983. **Staff:** 4. **Budget:** $1,000,000. **Regional Groups:** 5. **Description:** Seeks to improve the teaching of science at all levels, elementary through college. Conducts research to assess and improve the effectiveness of laboratory programs in chemistry. Sponsors summer workshops for teachers; offers chemistry camps for middle school students. Develops and distributes educational materials. **Convention/Meeting:** none. **Telecommunication Services:** electronic mail, jwmoore@chem.wisc.edu.

Childbirth

8063 ■ Midwifery Education Accreditation Council (MEAC)
20 E Cherry Ave.
Flagstaff, AZ 86001-4607
Ph: (928)214-0997
Fax: (928)773-9694
E-mail: info@meacschools.org
URL: http://www.meacschools.org
Contact: Mary Ann Baul LM, Exec. Dir.
Founded: 1991. **Description:** Promotes excellence in midwifery education through accreditation. Establishes standards for the education of competent midwives. Provides a process for self-evaluation and peer evaluation for diverse educational programs. **Telecommunication Services:** electronic mail, executivedirector@meacschools.org. **Publications:** *MEAC Accreditation Handbook*. **Price:** $50.00 per copy. Alternate Formats: online.

Childhood Education

8064 ■ Association for Childhood Education International (ACEI)
17904 Georgia Ave., Ste.215
Olney, MD 20832
Ph: (301)570-2111
Free: (800)423-3563
Fax: (301)570-2212
E-mail: headquarters@acei.org
URL: http://www.acei.org
Contact: Gerald C. Odland, Exec. Dir.
Founded: 1892. **Members:** 11,000. **Membership Dues:** professional, $45 (annual) ● retired, $23 (annual) ● student, $29 (annual) ● basic, $22 (annual) ● comprehensive, $144 (annual) ● center, $133 (annual). **Staff:** 14. **Budget:** $1,000,000. **State Groups:** 10. **Local Groups:** 50. **Description:** Promotes and supports in the global community, optimal education and development of children, from birth through early adolescence. Influences the professional growth of educators and the efforts of others who are committed to the needs of children in a changing society. Strives to dedicate to a flexible, child-centered approach to education. Conducts advocacy through a variety of public forums and major coalitions for children and education. **Libraries: Type:** reference. **Holdings:** 100; archival material, articles. **Subjects:** birth, kindergarten/early childhood education, middle childhood/early adolescence education, special needs. **Awards:** Friends of Children Award. **Frequency:** annual. **Type:** recognition. **Recipient:** for nonmembers who work outside the field of education; demonstrated commitment to children on a national or international level ● Mini-Grant. **Frequency:** annual. **Type:** grant. **Recipient:** for members who have outstanding educational experiences with children ● Outstanding Service Awards. **Frequency:** annual. **Type:** recognition. **Recipient:** for members who have outstanding contributions to the betterment of children in the field of education ● Patty Smith Hill. **Frequency:** annual. **Type:** recognition. **Recipient:** for significant contribution to the betterment of ACEI and children ● Student Leadership Award. **Frequency:** annual. **Type:** recognition. **Recipient:** for a college student member. **Computer Services:** database ● mailing lists. **Committees:** Awards; Conference; Diversity Concerns; Heritage; Infancy/Early Childhood; Intermediate/Middle Childhood; International/Intercultural; Membership; Nominating; Professional Standards/Teacher Education; Program Development; Public Affairs; Publications; Research; Retired Members; Student; Technology; Week of the Classroom Teacher. **Formed by Merger of:** International Kindergarten Union; National Council of Primary Education. **Publications:** *ACEI Exchange*, bimonthly. Newsletter. **Circulation:** 12,000. **Advertising:** accepted ● *Childhood Education*, bimonthly. Journal ● *Focus on Elementary*, quarterly. Newsletter ● *Focus on Infants and Toddlers*, quarterly. Newsletter ● *Focus on Middle School*, quarterly. Newsletter ● *Focus on Pre-K and K*, quarterly. Newsletter ● *Focus on Teacher Education*, quarterly. Newsletter. Alternate Formats: online ● *Journal of Research in Childhood Education*, quarterly. **Conventions/Meetings:** annual conference (exhibits) - 2009 Mar. 18-21, Chicago, IL ● annual international conference.

8065 ■ GalaxyGoo
4104 24th St., No. 349
San Francisco, CA 94114
URL: http://www.galaxygoo.org
Contact: Kristin F. Henry, Pres.
Description: Serves as the community of scientists, educators, students, artists, programmers, and professionals committed to providing high quality scientific content and services to students and peers. Promotes science literacy among students and the general public through the development of educational and social software for public benefit. **Computer Services:** Information services, articles, informal notes, resources, news, blogs ● online services, interactive learning tools, forum. **Projects:** The Cell; Flash MathML Reader. **Publications:** *The New Masters of Flash Volume 3*. Handbook. Alternate Formats: online ● Newsletter, periodic. Alternate Formats: online.

8066 ■ GreatSchools
301 Howard St., Ste.1440
San Francisco, CA 94105
Ph: (415)977-0700
Fax: (415)977-0704

E-mail: info@greatschools.net
URL: http://www.greatschools.net
Contact: Bill Jackson, Founder/Pres./CEO
Founded: 1998. **Description:** Seeks to improve K-12 education by inspiring parents to get involved. Utilizes resources to help parents choose schools, support children's education and improve schools in the community. Conducts programs to organize and support parents advocating for education excellence in their communities. **Libraries: Type:** reference. **Holdings:** articles. **Telecommunication Services:** electronic mail, pr@greatschools.net. **Publications:** Newsletters. **Price:** free. Alternate Formats: online ● Articles. Alternate Formats: online.

8067 ■ Hands On Science Outreach (HOSO)
12118 Heritage Park Cir.
Silver Spring, MD 20906
Ph: (301)929-2330
Free: (888)HOSO-888
Fax: (301)929-2334
E-mail: info@hosoprograms.org
Contact: Jose Luis Barata, Exec. Dir.
Founded: 1984. **Multinational. Description:** Aims to spark children's interest in science and mathematics. Seeks to educate the children in science and mathematics in a playful and informal environment. Provides programs for children that are structured to meet the needs of different communities.

8068 ■ Institute for Childhood Resources (INICR)
268 Bush St., Ste.2811
San Francisco, CA 94104
Ph: (415)864-1169 (510)540-0111
Free: (800)551-8697
Fax: (510)540-0171
E-mail: drtoy@drtoy.com
URL: http://www.drtoy.com
Contact: Stevanne Auerbach PhD, Dir.
Founded: 1975. **Description:** Represents consultants, writers, professionals, and parents interested in child growth, development, and education. Provides consultation and instruction to individuals, agencies, organizations, community groups, business and industry, and faculty and administrators involved in the preparation of persons to work in children's services. Conducts educational programs. Conducts parent and professional training programs in toys, play, child care and parenting. **Libraries: Type:** by appointment only. **Holdings:** 2,000. **Subjects:** children, toys, children's products, child care contacts. **Publications:** *Choosing Child Care* ● *Dr. Toy's Smart Play/Smart Toys* ● *The Toy Chest* ● *The Whole Child: A Sourcebook*. **Conventions/Meetings:** periodic seminar and workshop, on parenting education, all aspects of toys and games, children's products, child care, and working parents.

8069 ■ National Association for the Education of Young Children (NAEYC)
1313 L St. NW, Ste.500
Washington, DC 20005
Ph: (202)232-8777
Free: (800)424-2460
Fax: (202)328-1846
E-mail: naeyc@naeyc.org
URL: http://www.naeyc.org
Contact: Mark R. Ginsberg PhD, Exec. Dir.
Founded: 1926. **Members:** 104,000. **Membership Dues:** comprehensive, $95 (annual) ● regular, student, $60 (annual). **Staff:** 125. **Budget:** $12,000,000. **Regional Groups:** 400. **Description:** Teachers and directors of preschool and primary schools, kindergartens, child care centers, and early other learning programs for young childhood; early childhood education and child development educators, trainers, and researchers and other professionals dedicated to young children's healthy development. **Telecommunication Services:** electronic mail, membership@naeyc.org. **Formerly:** (1964) National Association for Nursery Education. **Publications:** *Early Childhood Research Quarterly*. Journal. Provides research and scholarship on early childhood field related to care and education of children from birth to age 8. **Price:** $40.00 for members; $95.00 for individual nonmember; $225.00 institutional. ISSN: 0885-2006 ● *Young Children*, bimonthly. Journal. Covers developments in the practice, research, and theory of early childhood education. Includes book reviews and calendar of events. **Price:** included in membership dues; $30.00 /year for nonmembers and institutions. ISSN: 0044-0728. **Circulation:** 115,000. **Advertising:** accepted ● Booklets ● Videos ● Books ● Also publishes posters. **Conventions/Meetings:** annual conference (exhibits).

8070 ■ Parent Cooperative Preschools International (PCPI)
1401 New York Ave. NW, Ste.1100
Natl. Cooperative Bus. Center
Washington, DC 20005
E-mail: inquiries@preschools.coop
URL: http://www.preschools.coop
Contact: Leta Mach, Pres.
Founded: 1960. **Members:** 12,500. **Membership Dues:** school/group, $50 (annual) ● life, $500 ● individual/library, $40 (annual) ● council, $200 (annual) ● sponsor, $100 (annual). **Budget:** $4,000. **Regional Groups:** 30. **State Groups:** 12. **Local Groups:** 459. **National Groups:** 2. **Description:** Individuals and groups in 6 countries interested in preschool education in non-profit nursery schools operated by parents on a cooperative basis. Provides information and research services for members; collects manuals and educational materials pertaining to parent cooperative preschools; encourages exchange of ideas and experiences among member schools. Promotes standards for programs, practices, and conditions in parent cooperatives and encourages continuing education for teachers and directors. Studies legislation related to the health and well-being of children and families. **Libraries: Type:** reference. **Subjects:** historical information stored at Canadian office. **Awards:** Becky Allen Fund. **Frequency:** annual. **Type:** recognition ● Katharine Whiteside Taylor Bursary. **Frequency:** annual. **Type:** recognition. **Recipient:** to educators and parents with outstanding service. **Telecommunication Services:** electronic mail, d.hatch@telus.com. **Committees:** Awards; Leadership Development; Legislative. **Affiliated With:** National Association for the Education of Young Children; National Cooperative Business Association. **Formerly:** (1964) American Council of Parent Cooperatives. **Publications:** *Cooperatively Speaking*, 3/year. Newsletter. Includes articles on parenting issues, preschools, and daycare. **Price:** $25.00 for nonmembers; included in membership dues. ISSN: 0048-2978. **Circulation:** 800. **Advertising:** accepted. Alternate Formats: online ● *How to Start a Co-Op* ● *Leadership Development—A Facilitator's Handbook* ● *Publications Resource Catalog*, triennial. Lists materials about co-op preschool education and co-op preschool boards. **Price:** included in membership dues ● Directory, annual. **Price:** included in membership dues ● Brochure. Alternate Formats: online. **Conventions/Meetings:** annual conference (exhibits).

8071 ■ World Organization for Early Childhood Education U.S. National Committee (OMEP USNC)
c/o Dr. Cathy Mogharreban, Treas.
PO Box 1436
Fairhope, AL 36533
Ph: (618)453-4246
E-mail: mcowles@bellsouth.net
Contact: Dr. Cathy Mogharreban, Treas.
Founded: 1962. **Members:** 400. **Regional Groups:** 8. **Description:** Early childhood and development educators, social workers, psychologists, and private and public school administrators. Promotes optimum conditions for every child's well-being, development, and happiness in families, institutions, and society; helps to improve early childhood education; supports scientific research that can influence these conditions. Promotes preschool education. Maintains consultative status with United Nations Educational, Scientific and Cultural Organization. **Publications:** *International Journal of Early Childhood*, semiannual ● *OMEP/USNC Directory*, periodic. **Price:** available to members only. **Circulation:** 400 ● *OMEP/USNC Newsletter*, 3/year. **Price:** $3.00/year. **Conventions/Meetings:** annual conference, held in conjunction with the Association for Childhood Education International and the National Association for the Education of Young Children ● triennial international conference and congress.

Children

8072 ■ Association for the Education of Children with Medical Needs (AECMN)
7065 Hillgreen Dr.
Dallas, TX 75214
Ph: (214)456-5930
E-mail: judy.einstein@childrens.com
URL: http://www.aecmn.org
Contact: Richard Lemke PhD, Pres.
Founded: 2003. **Membership Dues:** general, $50 (annual). **Description:** Provides professional support to individuals involved in the education of children with chronic illnesses and medical challenges. Promotes quality education of children with medical needs. Links communities of professional educators, parents, caregivers, healthcare professionals and patients. Increases awareness of the challenges of children with medical needs. **Publications:** Newsletter, quarterly. Contains updates on the organization's activities and other endeavors. **Price:** free. Alternate Formats: online.

8073 ■ Sudan-American Foundation for Education (SAFE)
4141 N Henderson Rd., Ste.1205
Arlington, VA 22203
Ph: (703)525-9045
Fax: (703)351-0782
E-mail: lee.burchinal@verizon.net
URL: http://www.sudan-safe.org
Contact: Dr. Lee G. Burchinal, Exec. Dir.
Founded: 1985. **Multinational. Description:** Seeks to improve educational opportunities for children and youth in the Sudan by delivering donated books, equipment, and other educational materials.

Chinese

8074 ■ American Association for Chinese Studies (AACS)
c/o Prof. Peter C.Y. Chow, Exec. Dir.
The City Coll. - CUNY
NAC R4/116
Convent Ave. and 138th St.
New York, NY 10031
Ph: (212)650-6206 (212)650-8268
Fax: (212)650-8287
E-mail: aacs@mail.com
URL: http://www.ccny.cuny.edu/aacs
Contact: Prof. Peter C.Y. Chow, Exec. Dir.
Founded: 1959. **Members:** 600. **Membership Dues:** individual, institution, $30 (annual) ● student, $15 (annual) ● joint, $50 (annual) ● life, $500. **Staff:** 3. **Description:** Scholars engaged in teaching and research in Chinese language and/or cultural subjects in Chinese societies in Mainland China, Hong Kong and Taiwan American colleges and universities; persons interested in Chinese studies. Promotes cooperation among members, especially in pedagogical matters. Conducts research in teaching of Chinese language and culture, socio-political and economic issues in all Chinese populated societies. **Formerly:** American Association of Teachers of Chinese Language and Culture. **Publications:** *AACS Newsletter*, semiannual. Disseminates articles regarding programs for the annual meetings, minutes of the Association, news and announcements. **Price:** included in membership dues. Alternate Formats: online ● *American Journal of Chinese Studies*, semiannual, April/October. Contains articles, theoretical essays, symposia, book reviews, and commentary on China. **Price:** $30.00/year. ISSN: 0742-5929. Also Cited As: *AJCS* ● *Directory of Members*, periodic ● Monographs ● Also publishes teaching aids. **Conven-**

tions/Meetings: annual conference (exhibits) - always October.

8075 ■ Chinese Language Association of Secondary-Elementary Schools (CLASS)
c/o Chih-Wen Su, Membership Coor.
14 Pebble Ridge Rd.
Amherst, MA 01002
E-mail: classk12@yahoo.com
URL: http://www.classk12.org
Contact: Carol Chen-Lin, Pres.
Founded: 1987. **Membership Dues:** student/retired, $25 (annual) ● regular, $40 (annual) ● international, $50 (annual). **Description:** Promotes the learning and teaching of Chinese in secondary and elementary schools in the United States. Provides a national network for the exchange of information, ideas and curricular resources related to the teaching of Chinese language and culture in the United States. **Telecommunication Services:** electronic mail, cchen-lin@choate.edu. **Affiliated With:** National Council of Less Commonly Taught Languages. **Publications:** *CLASS News Update*, semiannual. Newsletter. Alternate Formats: online.

8076 ■ Chinese Language Teachers Association (CLTA)
c/o Center for Chinese Study
Univ. of Hawaii
Moore Hall No. 416
1890 East-West Rd.
Honolulu, HI 96822
Ph: (808)956-2692
Fax: (808)956-2682
E-mail: cyndy@hawaii.edu
URL: http://clta.osu.edu
Contact: Prof. Cynthia Ning, Exec. Dir.
Founded: 1962. **Members:** 700. **Membership Dues:** regular (based on annual income), $30-$95 (annual) ● life, $900. **Staff:** 1. **Description:** Teachers and scholars of the Chinese language. Promotes the study of Chinese language, linguistics, and literature. Organizes panels; maintains placement service. **Awards:** Walton Memorial Awards. **Frequency:** annual. **Type:** recognition. **Computer Services:** Mailing lists. **Affiliated With:** Association for Asian Studies; Modern Language Association of America. **Publications:** *Chinese Language Pedagogy: Current Perspectives of the Emerging Field*. Monograph. **Price:** $20.00 ● *Chinese Pedagogy: An Emerging Field*. Monograph ● *Functionalism and Chinese Grammar*. Monograph. **Price:** $20.00 ● *Journal of the Chinese Language Teachers Association*, 3/year. Contains articles and reviews. **Price:** free for members; $70.00 for nonmembers. ISSN: 0009-4595. **Circulation:** 700. **Advertising:** accepted ● *Mapping the Course of the Chinese Language Field*. Monograph ● Newsletter (in Chinese and English), 3/year. Contains information on events, programs, and announcements. **Price:** free for members; $20.00 for nonmembers. **Circulation:** 800. **Advertising:** accepted. Alternate Formats: online. **Conventions/Meetings:** annual meeting, held in conjunction with American Council on the Teaching of Foreign Languages (exhibits).

8077 ■ Society for the Study of Early China (SSEC)
c/o Institute of East Asian Studies
Univ. of California
Publications Off.
2223 Fulton St., 6th Fl.
Berkeley, CA 94720-2318
Ph: (510)643-6325
Fax: (510)643-7062
E-mail: easia@uclink.berkeley.edu
Contact: Robin D.S. Yates, Chm./Ed.
Founded: 1975. **Members:** 350. **Membership Dues:** regular, institution, $30 (annual) ● student, $20 (annual). **Description:** Professors, graduate students, and scholars. Promotes scholarship in the study of early Chinese culture. **Formerly:** (1975) Society for the Study of Pre-Han China. **Publications:** *Early China*, annual. Journal. Reports on prehistoric, Shang, Chou, and Han China. Includes abstracts of research in Chinese and English; bibliography; book reviews. **Price:** included in membership dues. **Circulation:** 400. **Advertising:** accepted. Alternate Formats: online ● *Early China Monograph Series*. Monographs. **Price:** included in membership dues, plus shipping and handling ● *Early China News*, periodic. Newsletter. Includes conference reports. **Circulation:** 350. **Advertising:** accepted. **Conventions/Meetings:** annual meeting, held in conjunction with the Association for Asian Studies.

8078 ■ Travel China Roads (TCR)
1719 E Feemster Ct.
Visalia, CA 93292
Ph: (559)562-3409 (559)636-6026
E-mail: info@tchinaroads.com
URL: http://www.tchinaroads.com
Contact: Josh Vance, Pres./Dir.
Founded: 2000. **Budget:** $10,000. **Local Groups:** 1. **Nonmembership**. **Description:** Provides English educational projects and charitable contributions to China. Volunteers receive room and board in China in exchange for teaching English as a second language. **Publications:** *China English Program* (in Chinese and English). Brochure. Alternate Formats: online ● Newsletter. **Advertising:** accepted. Alternate Formats: online.

Chiropractic

8079 ■ Foundation for the Advancement of Chiropractic Education (FACE)
PO Box 1052
Levittown, PA 19058
Free: (800)397-9722
E-mail: info@f-a-c-e.com
URL: http://www.f-a-c-e.com
Contact: Dr. Joseph B. Strauss, Contact
Founded: 1982. **Membership Dues:** individual, $100 (annual). **Description:** Promotes straight chiropractic. Straight chiropractic is the method of correcting vertebral subluxations to enable the innate intelligence of the body to be expressed more fully. **Awards:** Scholarships. **Type:** scholarship. **Recipient:** to chiropractic students, as well as educational materials for chiropractic college libraries. **Publications:** *Journal of Straight Chiropractic*. **Price:** included in membership dues ● *The Pivot Review*, quarterly. Newsletter. Contains philosophical articles and essays relevant to the practice of chiropractic from the objective straight viewpoint. **Price:** free. Alternate Formats: online ● *The Practice Builder*. Newsletter. Contains regular articles filled with great tips and ideas for chiropractor in educating patients. **Price:** free. Alternate Formats: online.

Christian

8080 ■ Association for Biblical Higher Education (ABHE)
5575 S Semoran Blvd., Ste.26
Orlando, FL 32822-1781
Ph: (407)207-0808
Fax: (407)207-0840
E-mail: info@abhe.org
URL: http://abhe.gospelcom.net
Contact: Dr. Ralph E. Enlow Jr., Exec. Dir.
Founded: 1947. **Members:** 111. **Membership Dues:** affiliate institution, $500 (annual) ● college (candidate, accredited), $1,600-$4,000 ● applicant college, $1,200-$4,000 ● branch campus, $250-$1,000 ● institution, $1,000-$1,500. **Staff:** 6. **Budget:** $425,000. **Description:** Serves as the official national accrediting agency for Bible colleges. Promotes the interest of biblical and church-vocational higher education for Christian service through representation in national education organization meetings and through cooperation with other accrediting agencies, both regional and professional. Conducts research programs; provides consultative services to colleges; maintains referral service. **Awards:** Delta Epsilon Chi Academic Awards. **Frequency:** annual. **Type:** recognition. **Recipient:** for academic achievement. **Telecommunication Services:** electronic mail, renlow@abhe.org. **Commissions:** Accreditation. **Committees:** Communications; Ethnic Diversity; Professional Development. **Affiliated With:** National Association of Independent Colleges and Universities. **Formerly:** (1957) Association of Bible Institutes and Bible Colleges; (1973) Accrediting Association of Bible Colleges; (1994) American Association of Bible Colleges; (2004) Accrediting Association of Bible Colleges. **Publications:** *AABC Manual*, annual. Includes conditions of eligibility, principle for accreditation, criteria for accreditation policies and procedures. **Price:** $20.00 for members, plus shipping and handling; $25.00 for nonmembers, plus shipping and handling. ISSN: 1078-1307. **Circulation:** 600 ● *ABHE Statistical Report*. Reports. Alternate Formats: online ● *Accrediting Association of Bible Colleges—Directory*, annual. Lists information on each AABC member. **Price:** $18.00 for members, plus shipping and handling; $20.00 for nonmembers, plus shipping and handling. ISSN: 1070-8065. **Circulation:** 1,300 ● *Accrediting Association of Bible Colleges—Newsletter*, quarterly. Reports on issues in higher education and activities of the association, especially in extending the accreditation of Bible colleges. **Price:** $10.00 /year for members; $15.00 /year for nonmembers. Alternate Formats: online ● *Affiliate Membership Brochure*. Alternate Formats: online. **Conventions/Meetings:** annual meeting (exhibits) - always February.

8081 ■ Association of Christian Schools International (ACSI)
PO Box 65130
Colorado Springs, CO 80962-5130
Ph: (719)528-6906
Free: (800)367-0798
Fax: (719)531-0631
E-mail: info@acsi.org
URL: http://www.acsi.org
Contact: Dr. Ken Smitherman, Pres.
Founded: 1978. **Members:** 5,400. **Staff:** 150. **Budget:** $20,000,000. **Regional Groups:** 17. **Multinational**. **Description:** Seeks to enable Christian educators and schools worldwide to effectively prepare students for life. **Formed by Merger of:** (1975) Western Association of Christian Schools; (1978) National Christian School Education Association; Ohio Association of Christian Schools. **Publications:** *ACSI Prayer Guide*, monthly ● *Board Talk*, semiannual. Pamphlet ● *Christian Early Education*, quarterly. Magazine ● *Christian School Comment*, monthly. Article ● *Christian School Education*, 5/year. Magazine ● *Christian School Employment Opportunities*, monthly. Pamphlet ● *Communique*, semiannual. Pamphlet ● *Early Education Director's Report*, quarterly ● *Legal/Legislative Update*, quarterly. Pamphlet ● *National Notes*, monthly. Newsletter ● *Regional Newsletter*, monthly ● *Touch the World*, semiannual. Newsletter ● *World Report*, quarterly. Newsletter. **Conventions/Meetings:** annual Board/Administrator Conferences ● annual International Institute - conference ● annual Leadership Academy - conference ● annual One-Day Enabler - workshop ● annual Student Leadership Conference ● annual Teachers Convention, at 25 different locations.

8082 ■ Christian College Consortium (CCC)
50 Stark Hwy. S
Dunbarton, NH 03046-4406
Ph: (603)774-6623
Fax: (603)774-6628
E-mail: thenglund@earthlink.net
URL: http://www.ccconsortium.org
Contact: Dr. Thomas H. Englund, Pres.
Founded: 1971. **Members:** 13. **Staff:** 1. **Budget:** $85,000. **Description:** Represents Christian evangelical four-year, accredited liberal arts colleges and universities united to advance higher education that is based on an institutional and personal commitment to Christ. Works for the promotion and articulation of the unique contributions that Christ-centered higher education can make to contemporary society. Major projects include Faith/Learning/Living Institute (seminars for integration of faith, knowledge and daily living); cooperative foreign studies program; professional development seminars, and annual compensation study. **Awards:** Frederic and Dorothy Vechery Scholarships. **Frequency:** annual. **Type:** scholar-

ship. **Recipient:** for academic achievement, leadership, and character development. **Councils:** Senior Academic Officers. **Conventions/Meetings:** semiannual board meeting - always March and October.

8083 ■ Christian Schools International (CSI)
3350 E Paris Ave. SE
Grand Rapids, MI 49512-2907
Ph: (616)957-1070
Free: (800)635-8288
Fax: (616)957-5022
E-mail: info@csionline.org
URL: http://csionline.org
Contact: Mr. David Koetje, Pres./CEO
Founded: 1920. **Members:** 450. **Membership Dues:** regular, associate, $1-$7 (annual) ● affiliate, $136-$630 (annual). **Staff:** 35. **Budget:** $3,000,000. **Description:** Christian elementary and secondary schools enrolling 100,000 pupils and employing 7,800 teachers. Aims to: provide a medium for a united witness regarding the role of Christian schools in contemporary society; promote the establishment of Christian schools; help members function more effectively in areas of promotion, organization, administration, and curriculum; help establish standards and criteria to guide the operation of its members; foster high professional ideals and economic well-being among Christian school personnel; establish and maintain communication with member schools, colleges, churches, government agencies, and the public. Encourages study, research, and writing that embodies Christian theories of education; conducts salary studies, research, and surveys on operating costs; offers expert and confidential analysis of member school programs and operation. Sponsors meetings, workshops, and seminars; offers placement service. Administers the Christian School Pension and Trust Funds, Group Insurance Plans, and Life and Insurance Plans and Trust Funds. **Libraries: Type:** reference. **Holdings:** 1,000; books. **Departments:** Business Administration; Employee Benefits; Publications; School Support Services; Support Services. **Formerly:** (1978) National Union of Christian Schools. **Publications:** *The Agenda*, quarterly. Newsletter. **Price:** free for school board members. **Circulation:** 800 ● *Christian Home and School: A Magazine for Contemporary Christian Families*, bimonthly. Includes book and film reviews. **Price:** $13.95/year in U.S.; $21.50/year in Canada. **Circulation:** 50,000. **Advertising:** accepted ● *Christian School Administrator*, quarterly. Newsletter. Provides information to administrators. **Price:** free. **Circulation:** 500 ● *Christian School Teacher*, quarterly. Magazine. **Price:** $10.00 in U.S.; $15.40 in Canada ● *Christian Schools International—Directory*, annual. **Price:** $10.50 /year for members; $45.00 /year for nonmembers ● Also publishes Christian textbooks for elementary and high school teachers and students. **Conventions/Meetings:** annual conference - every late July or early August.

8084 ■ Council for Christian Colleges and Universities
321 8th St. NE
Washington, DC 20002
Ph: (202)546-8713
Fax: (202)546-8913
E-mail: council@cccu.org
URL: http://www.cccu.org
Contact: Dr. Paul R. Corts, Pres.
Founded: 1976. **Members:** 105. **Membership Dues:** regular (based on undergraduate and graduate enrollment), $4,325-$17,538 (annual) ● affiliate in U.S., $2,500 (annual) ● affiliate in Canada, C$1,600 (annual) ● affiliate outside U.S. and Canada, $450 (annual). **Staff:** 60. **Budget:** $8,500,000. **Description:** Represents professional association of fully-accredited, comprehensive institutions of higher education in North America with curricula rooted in the arts and sciences. Aims to advance the cause of Christ-centered higher education and to help its institutions transform lives by faithfully relating scholarship and service to biblical truth. Coordinates collaborative public relations and marketing efforts on behalf of its members, monitors public policy issues and provides professional development opportunities for trustees, administrators, staff and faculty at its campuses. Offers the student programs. **Formerly:** Christian College Coalition; (1999) Coalition for Christian Colleges and Universities. **Publications:** *The News*, 3/year, in fall, winter and spring. Newsletter. **Circulation:** 6,000. **Advertising:** accepted. **Conventions/Meetings:** annual conference.

8085 ■ Council of Christian Scholarly Societies (CCSS)
c/o Amy Black, Chair
Dept. of Politics and Intl. Relations
Wheaton Coll.
501 Coll. Ave.
Wheaton, IL 60187
Ph: (717)291-4055
E-mail: amy.e.black@wheaton.edu
URL: http://www3.baylor.edu/CCSS
Contact: Amy Black, Chair
Description: Serves as a vehicle for member organizations to provide practical support to each other and share the responsibility to nurture new generations of Christian scholars. Provides a cross-disciplinary forum in which members can address major intellectual issues.

8086 ■ Foundation for American Christian Education (FACE)
PO Box 9588
Chesapeake, VA 23321-9588
Ph: (757)488-6601
Free: (800)352-3223
Fax: (757)488-5593
E-mail: info1828@face.net
URL: http://www.face.net
Contact: Dr. Carole G. Adams, Pres.
Founded: 1965. **Members:** 20,000. **Membership Dues:** supporting, $75 (annual). **Staff:** 10. **Budget:** $750,000. **Description:** Works to research, document, publish and teach the Christian heritage of education and government in the United States. Conducts educational and research programs. **Libraries: Type:** reference; not open to the public. **Holdings:** 10,000; archival material, books. **Subjects:** American history, Christian history, principle approach education curriculum, K-12. **Computer Services:** Mailing lists. **Publications:** *Principle Approach Education*, quarterly. Newsletter. **Circulation:** 26,000 ● *Research Journal*, annual ● Articles. Alternate Formats: online ● Catalog. Alternate Formats: online. **Conventions/Meetings:** periodic conference ● periodic regional meeting.

8087 ■ National Collegiate Association for Research of Principles (NCARP)
481 8th Ave., D-10
New York, NY 10001
Ph: (212)382-2402
Fax: (212)382-3044
E-mail: usa@worldcarp.org
URL: http://www.worldcarp.org
Contact: Mr. Max Nose, Treas.
Founded: 1980. **Members:** 120. **Staff:** 20. **Budget:** $1,000,000. **Regional Groups:** 5. **Local Groups:** 5. **Description:** College students interested in reviving religious spirit, especially Christianity, on campus. Revives moral educational values. Provides training; holds seminars, workshops, and lectures. Conducts research projects. Sponsors World Student Service Corps, a summer internship for students in developing nations. **Publications:** *CARP Perspectives*. Contains research reports. ● Publishes manuals, books, and educational materials such as video tapes and slides. **Conventions/Meetings:** annual meeting.

8088 ■ North American Professors of Christian Education (NAPCE)
2825 Lexington Rd.
Louisville, KY 40280
Ph: (502)649-3726
Fax: (502)339-9692
E-mail: mail@napce.org
URL: http://www.napce.org
Contact: Dr. Dennis E. Williams, Exec. Admin.
Founded: 1947. **Members:** 280. **Membership Dues:** regular, $65 (annual) ● student, $35 (annual). **Staff:** 1. **Description:** Represents teachers, former teachers, and professionals concerned with Christian education and related subjects in institutions of higher learning. Serves as a professional organization for professors of Christian education in colleges and seminaries. Stimulates professional growth and development through fellowship and gives direction to the formulation and clarification of a policy of evangelical Christian education. Conducts research. **Awards:** Research Grant. **Frequency:** annual. **Type:** grant ● Student Scholastic Award. **Frequency:** annual. **Type:** recognition. **Telecommunication Services:** electronic mail, dwilliams@sbts.edu. **Formerly:** (1972) Research Commission of National Sunday School; (1992) National Association of Professors of Christian Education; (2002) North American Association of Professors of Christian Education. **Publications:** *NAPCE Newsletter*, 3/year. Contains association news, brief articles, book reviews, and announcements of educational meetings. **Price:** free. **Circulation:** 600. Alternate Formats: online. **Conventions/Meetings:** annual conference (exhibits) - usually third weekend of October.

8089 ■ Oral Roberts University Educational Fellowship (ORUEF)
Oral Roberts Univ.
7777 S Lewis Ave.
Tulsa, OK 74171
Ph: (918)495-6163
Fax: (918)495-6175
E-mail: oruef@oru.edu
URL: http://www.oru.edu
Contact: Dr. Tom Agnew, Exec. Dir.
Founded: 1983. **Members:** 200. **Membership Dues:** pre-school (based on number of students), $450-$650 (annual) ● kindergarten up to 12th grade (based on number of students), $500-$1,100 (annual) ● preschool up to 12th grade (based on number of students), $750-$1,650 (annual) ● international school, $100 (annual). **Staff:** 4. **Multinational. Description:** Represents Christian schools at the preschool, elementary, secondary, and postsecondary levels. Aims to establish continuous spiritual development, academic credibility, and financial stability for Pentecostal, Full Gospel, and Charismatic Christian schools worldwide. Operates International Christian Accrediting Association, which ensures that Christian schools adhere to high academic standards. Sponsors Christian Honor Student Association, which promotes academic achievement and ethical behavior among Christian school students. Maintains speakers' bureau; offers placement service; compiles statistics. **Awards: Type:** recognition ● **Type:** scholarship. **Committees:** ICAA Accreditation Commissioners; National Finals; Post Secondary/Bible School. **Publications:** *ICAA Accreditation Manual/Elementary/Secondary Schools* ● *ICAA Accreditation Manual for Preschools* ● *ICAA Accreditation Manual/Post Secondary/Bible Schools* ● *ORUEF Christian School Directory*, annual ● *ORUEF National Finals Competition Manual*, annual ● *ORUEF Newsletter*, monthly. **Conventions/Meetings:** Christian School Management Seminar ● annual International Christian School Conference (exhibits) - always July, Tulsa, OK ● annual National Finals Competition, for high school students in areas including academics, music, athletics and the arts ● annual seminar, for administrators.

8090 ■ Probe Ministries International (PMI)
1900 Firman Dr., Ste.100
Richardson, TX 75081
Ph: (972)480-0240
Free: (800)899-PROB
Fax: (214)644-9664
E-mail: info@probe.org
URL: http://www.probe.org
Contact: Dr. Ray Bohlin, Pres.
Founded: 1973. **Staff:** 10. **Budget:** $1,000,000. **Description:** Consists of educators helping to bring the Christian message into education, media, and the marketplace by presenting biblical perspectives on current issues and academic tension points. Aims to bring about fair and positive consideration of the Christian viewpoint. Provides speakers; sponsors

research programs and internships on biblical perspectives of academic and contemporary issues. Conducts a daily five-minute radio program broadcast nationally on over 300 stations. Operates Probe Center for students at the University of Texas at Austin. Conducts "Mind Games" College survival course for high school and college youth and for parents and educators. **Libraries: Type:** not open to the public. **Holdings:** 3,000; books, periodicals. **Subjects:** theology, history, science, arts, humanities. **Telecommunication Services:** electronic mail, rbohlin@probe.org. **Departments:** MIND Games-College Survival Course; Probe Books; Probe Center - Austin, TX; Probe Media. **Publications:** *Probe-alert*. Newsletter. Alternate Formats: online ● *Vanguard*, quarterly. Newsletter. Contains information on academic and contemporary issues from a Christian perspective. Also contains ministry news and updates. ● Also publishes radio program transcripts. **Conventions/Meetings:** Mind Games - seminar, conducted on campuses and in churches for high school and college youth - 20/year.

Civics

8091 ■ National Alliance for Civic Education (NACE)
Inst. for Philosophy and Public Policy
Maryland School of Public Affairs
3111 Van Munching
College Park, MD 20742
E-mail: ghomana6@wam.umd.edu
URL: http://www.cived.net
Contact: Gary Homana, Contact
Founded: 2000. **Members:** 200. **Description:** Helps citizens understand the significance of civic education to democracy. Enhances the professional development of teachers involved in civic education. Offers students opportunities to participate in civic activities of their communities. **Computer Services:** Information services, civic requirement guidelines. **Task Forces:** Liaison To Group Members; Public Support and Advocacy; Research and Outcomes Evaluation. **Publications:** Membership Directory.

8092 ■ Patriotic Education Inc. (PEI)
1926 Hidden Creek Dr.
Kingwood, TX 77339
Ph: (713)906-3649
Free: (800)248-1787
E-mail: pei@patriotic-education.org
URL: http://www.patriotic-education.org
Contact: Brion V. Chabot, Chm.
Founded: 1952. **Budget:** $60,000. **Nonmembership. Description:** Promotes and develops constructive patriotic citizenship through education. Encourages comprehensive teaching of the events and historical context of the founding of the American Republic. Develops, publishes and distributes materials and conducts programs designed to inspire appreciation of America's founding principles. Publications are used by schools, American Legion Boys and Girls States, and veterans, civic and service organizations. **Awards:** Blessings of Liberty. **Type:** recognition. **Recipient:** to organizations for exemplary achievement in citizenship education. **Boards:** Trustees. **Affiliated With:** Military Order of the World Wars. **Publications:** *George Washington, Architect of the Constitution*. Booklet ● *The Key to the Constitution of the United States*. Booklet. **Price:** $4.00/issue ● *Living Freedom: The United States Constitution and Bill of Rights for High School Students*. Booklet. Includes seminar information and teaching guide. **Price:** $5.00/issue ● *The Making of George Washington*. Book. **Price:** $18.00/issue ● Also George Mason: Father of the Bill Of Rights, A Teaching Guide. **Conventions/Meetings:** annual board meeting, patriotic and educational themes (exhibits).

8093 ■ Washington Workshops Foundation (WWF)
3222 N St. NW, Ste.340
Washington, DC 20007
Ph: (202)965-3434
Free: (800)368-5688
Fax: (202)965-1018
E-mail: info@workshops.org
URL: http://www.workshops.org
Contact: Sharon E. Sievers, Pres.
Founded: 1967. **Staff:** 8. **Description:** Educational foundation offering seminars in American national government for junior high, high school, and college students. Junior high and high school students each attend a week of seminars in Washington, DC; college students attend a three-week session, combining seminars with an internship in the U.S. legislature. Offers one week congressional seminar and diplomacy and global affairs seminar. **Awards:** Americanism Award of the Freedoms Foundation of Valley Forge. **Type:** recognition. **Committees:** National Student Advisory. **Councils:** National Advisory. **Divisions:** Advanced Congressional Seminar; Congressional Seminar; Diplomacy and Global Affairs Seminars; Junior High/Middle School Seminar. **Conventions/Meetings:** Diplomacy and Global Affairs Seminar ● Junior High/Middle School Seminars.

Civil Rights and Liberties

8094 ■ Leadership Conference Education Fund (LCEF)
1629 K St. NW, No. 1010
Washington, DC 20006
Ph: (202)466-3311 (202)466-3435
E-mail: comlcef@civilrights.org
URL: http://www.wecaretoo.com/Organizations/DC/lcef.html
Contact: Karen McGill Lawson, Exec. Dir.
Founded: 1969. **Description:** Supports educational activities relevant to civil rights. **Awards:** Summer Internship. **Type:** fellowship. **Publications:** *Conference Reports* ● Reports. **Conventions/Meetings:** conference.

Classical Studies

8095 ■ National Junior Classical League (NJCL)
Miami Univ.
422 Wells Mill Dr.
Oxford, OH 45056
Ph: (513)529-7741
Fax: (513)529-7742
E-mail: president@njcl.org
URL: http://www.njcl.org
Contact: Seher Munivar, Pres.
Founded: 1936. **Members:** 50,000. **Membership Dues:** student, $2 (annual) ● chapter, $10-$20 (annual) ● sponsor, $45 (annual). **Staff:** 5. **Local Groups:** 1,033. **Description:** Represents high school students studying Latin. Sponsored by the American Classical League to encourage an interest in and appreciation of the civilization, language, literature, and art of ancient Greece and Rome and to provide young people with an understanding of the debt American culture owes to classical antiquity. **Formerly:** (2002) Junior Classical League. **Publications:** *Torch: U.S.*, quarterly. **Conventions/Meetings:** annual convention (exhibits).

Colleges and Universities

8096 ■ American Association of State Colleges and Universities (AASCU)
1307 New York Ave. NW, 5th Fl.
Washington, DC 20005-4701
Ph: (202)293-7070 (202)478-4647
Fax: (202)296-5819
E-mail: currisc@aascu.org
URL: http://www.aascu.org
Contact: Dr. Constantine W. Curris, Pres.
Founded: 1961. **Members:** 409. **Staff:** 80. **Description:** Colleges and universities offering programs leading to a degree of bachelor, master, or doctor, that are wholly or partially state supported and controlled. Enables members to express their views on national affairs; works to present the contributions and services of state colleges and universities effectively to the public and to agencies concerned with higher education; works to provide representation of members in national education organizations. Conducts national and regional workshops. Sponsors Servicemembers Opportunity College. **Awards:** Christa McAuliffe Award for Excellence in Teacher Education. **Type:** recognition. **Recipient:** for excellence in college and university teacher education programs ● Distinguished Alumnus Award. **Frequency:** annual. **Type:** recognition. **Recipient:** to an alumnus of a member institution who has made a significant contribution to the public, intellectual, or cultural life of the nation. **Absorbed:** Association of Upper Level Colleges and Universities. **Formerly:** Association of State Colleges and Universities. **Supersedes:** Association of Teachers of Education Institutions. **Publications:** *Membership List*, annual. Membership Directory ● *Memo: To The President*, biweekly. Bulletin. **Price:** included in membership dues. ISSN: 0047-6692. **Circulation:** 1,555. Also Cited As: *AASCU Bulletin* ● Pamphlets ● Videos. **Conventions/Meetings:** annual conference (exhibits) - usually November.

8097 ■ Associated Colleges of the Midwest (ACM)
205 W Wacker Dr., Ste.220
Chicago, IL 60606
Ph: (312)263-5000
Fax: (312)263-5879
E-mail: acm@acm.edu
URL: http://www.acm.edu
Contact: Christopher Welna, Pres.
Founded: 1958. **Members:** 14. **Staff:** 12. **Description:** Small, independent, and coeducational liberal arts colleges united to conduct activities that will enrich their programs and increase their operating efficiency. Primary area of cooperation is in off-campus programs that could not profitably be administrated by one college alone. Sponsors extensive activity in professional development for faculty members. Conducts admissions activities, data sharing, and operational research. **Awards:** Nick Adams Short Story Prize. **Frequency:** annual. **Type:** recognition. **Recipient:** for the best story by an ACM college student in good standing. **Publications:** *ACM Notes*, 3/year. Newsletter ● *Pre-College Planner*, annual. Booklet. Offers tips for high school students preparing to seek college admission. ● Brochures.

8098 ■ Association of American Colleges and Universities (AAC&U)
1818 R St. NW
Washington, DC 20009
Ph: (202)387-3760 (202)884-7435
Free: (800)297-3775
Fax: (202)265-9532
E-mail: cgs@aacu.org
URL: http://www.aacu.org
Contact: Carol Geary Schneider, Pres.
Founded: 1915. **Members:** 1,100. **Membership Dues:** associate, $60 (annual). **Staff:** 45. **Description:** Advances and strengthens liberal learning for all students, regardless of academic specialization or intended career. Functions as a catalyst and facilitator, forging links among presidents, administrators, and faculty members who are engaged in institutional and curricular planning. Aims to reinforce the collective commitment to liberal education at both the national and local levels and to help individual institutions keep the quality of student learning at the core of their work as they evolve to meet new economic and social challenges. **Awards:** Frederic W. Ness Book Award. **Frequency:** annual. **Type:** monetary. **Recipient:** for a book that contributes to the understanding and improvement of liberal education. **Formerly:** (1994) Association of American Colleges. **Publications:** *Diversifying the Faculty, Assessing Campus Diversity Initiatives, General Education*. Monographs ● *Greater Expectations: A New Vision for Learning as a Nation Goes to College*. Reports ● *Liberal Education*, quarterly. Journal. Expresses the voices of educators in colleges and universities who are working to enrich liberal learning. **Price:** $14.00

for nonmembers; $10.00 for members. ISSN: 0024-1822. **Circulation:** 6,000. Alternate Formats: microform ● *Peer Review*, quarterly. Journal. Provides briefing on emerging trends and key debates in undergraduate education. **Price:** $10.00 for nonmembers; $8.00 for members. ISSN: 1541-1389. **Circulation:** 5,000 ● Also publishes project results. **Conventions/Meetings:** annual meeting.

8099 ■ Association of American Universities (AAU)
1200 New York Ave., Ste.550
Washington, DC 20005
Ph: (202)408-7500
Fax: (202)408-8184
E-mail: robert_berdahl@aau.edu
URL: http://www.aau.edu
Contact: Robert M. Berdahl PhD, Pres.

Founded: 1900. **Members:** 62. **Membership Dues:** institutional, $72,500 (annual). **Staff:** 22. **Budget:** $5,000,000. **Description:** Executive heads of universities; membership is determined by appraisal of breadth and quality of a university's research and education efforts. Conducts activities to encourage cooperative consideration of major issues concerning research universities, and to enable members to communicate effectively with the federal government. **Publications:** *CFR Weekly Wrap Up*. Newsletter. **Conventions/Meetings:** semiannual meeting - every April and October.

8100 ■ Association of College and University Clubs (ACUC)
1733 King St.
Alexandria, VA 22314-2720
Ph: (703)739-4288
Fax: (703)299-0925
E-mail: acuc@acuclubs.org
URL: http://www.acuclubs.org
Contact: Sara Pietrzak, Managing Dir.

Founded: 1978. **Members:** 100. **Membership Dues:** active, associate, $325 (annual) ● affiliate, $400 (annual). **Multinational. Description:** Promotes global awareness of the services provided by university clubs and campus hosts. **Awards:** Friend Award. **Frequency:** periodic. **Type:** recognition. **Recipient:** to individuals retiring from club management who have made significant contributions of time and talent in service to the Association of College and University Clubs ● Shrader Scholarship. **Frequency:** annual. **Type:** scholarship. **Programs:** Scholarship. **Publications:** *The Globe*, quarterly. Newsletter. **Price:** included in membership dues. Alternate Formats: online ● *Management Resource Directory*. **Conventions/Meetings:** annual conference.

8101 ■ Association of Collegiate Business Schools and Programs (ACBSP)
7007 Coll. Blvd., Ste.420
Overland Park, KS 66211
Ph: (913)339-9356
Fax: (913)339-6226
E-mail: info@acbsp.org
URL: http://www.acbsp.org
Contact: Douglas Viehland, Exec. Dir.

Founded: 1988. **Members:** 500. **Membership Dues:** regular, $1,250 (annual) ● accredited school, $1,850 (annual). **Staff:** 5. **Budget:** $998,000. **Regional Groups:** 8. **Description:** Seeks to enhance and support higher business education. Holds competitions; conducts educational programs; maintains Hall of Fame. **Awards:** Hall of Fame's Teaching Excellence. **Frequency:** annual. **Type:** recognition. **Recipient:** for outstanding teachers. **Computer Services:** database ● mailing lists. **Publications:** *Update*, quarterly. Newsletter. Contains information on recent and upcoming events on the association. **Advertising:** accepted. Alternate Formats: online ● Directory, annual ● Brochure. **Conventions/Meetings:** biennial board meeting - October/February ● annual conference - 2008 June 20-23, New Orleans, LA; 2009 June 26-29, San Antonio, TX.

8102 ■ British Schools and Universities Foundation (BSUF)
575 Madison Ave., Ste.1006
New York, NY 10022-2511
Ph: (212)662-5576
Fax: (212)815-8570
E-mail: info@bsuf.org
URL: http://www.bsuf.org
Contact: John Tepper Marlin, Treas.

Founded: 1961. **Members:** 300. **Membership Dues:** associate, $100 (annual) ● fellow, $250 (annual) ● sustaining, $500 (annual) ● life, $5,000. **Staff:** 1. **Budget:** $1,150,000. **Description:** Makes grants and interest-free loans to schools, colleges, universities, and other educational, scientific, or literary institutions for buildings, facilities, equipment, and other projects in the British Commonwealth. **Awards: Frequency:** quarterly. **Type:** grant. **Recipient:** for institutions. **Computer Services:** database. **Committees:** Grants; Investment. **Publications:** Annual Report, annual. **Circulation:** 300. **Conventions/Meetings:** annual meeting, for members.

8103 ■ College Consortium for International Studies (CCIS)
2000 P St. NW, Ste.503
Washington, DC 20036
Ph: (202)223-0330
Free: (800)453-6956
Fax: (202)223-0999
E-mail: info@ccisabroad.org
URL: http://www.ccisabroad.org

Members: 135. **Description:** Public and private accredited colleges and universities in the U.S. Promotes study abroad programs and professional development designed to enhance international/intercultural perspectives within the academic community.

8104 ■ Committee on Institutional Cooperation (CIC)
1819 S Neil St., Ste.D
Champaign, IL 61820-7271
Ph: (217)333-8475 (217)244-9240
Fax: (217)244-7127
E-mail: cic@staff.cic.net
URL: http://www.cic.uiuc.edu
Contact: Barbara McFadden Allen, Dir.

Founded: 1958. **Members:** 12. **Staff:** 17. **Description:** Voluntary organization of research universities (Chicago, Illinois, Indiana, Iowa, Michigan, Michigan State, Minnesota, Northwestern, Ohio State, Pennsylvania State, Purdue, and Wisconsin). Encourages cooperative ventures among member institutions; identifies specialized areas of teaching, research, public service and university operations in which inter-institutional cooperation may be desirable; seeks means for improving quality and efficiency of university education through shared resources, faculty exchange, and free movement of graduate students among institutions. CIC faculty and administrative committees in 40 different disciplines and major echelons of administration work on various aspects of institutional cooperation. **Awards: Type:** grant. **Recipient:** to faculty groups for conferences and research planning meetings. **Publications:** Annual Report, annual. Includes financial statement. **Price:** free.

8105 ■ Consortium for the Advancement of Private Higher Education (CAPHE)
c/o The Council of Independent Colleges
1 Dupont Cir. NW, Ste.320
Washington, DC 20036-1142
Ph: (202)466-7230
Fax: (202)466-7238
E-mail: rekman@cic.nche.edu
URL: http://www.cic.edu/caphe
Contact: Antoine M. Garibaldi, Chair

Founded: 1983. **Staff:** 4. **Description:** An operating unit of the Council of Independent Colleges. Aims to: provide financial and technical assistance, through foundations and corporations, to private colleges and universities; develop and document model solutions to institutional problems; and disseminate these findings to help private colleges and universities adapt to the future needs of students and society. **Awards:** Davies-Jackson Scholarship. **Frequency:** biennial. **Type:** scholarship. **Recipient:** for students with exceptional academic records ● Heuer Award. **Frequency:** annual. **Type:** recognition. **Recipient:** for outstanding achievement in undergraduate science education. **Computer Services:** database, information for corporate and foundation giving programs. **Funds:** FIHE/UPS Venture. **Programs:** Davies-Jackson Scholarship; Engaging Communities and Campuses. **Publications:** *Assessing Institutional Effectiveness: Redirecting the Self-Study Process*. Book. Includes a set of practical recommendations for administrators. **Price:** $16.95 ● *Building Partnerships with College Campuses: Community Perspectives*, periodic. Monograph. Provides technical assistance for college improvement projects. Alternate Formats: online ● *Marketing Higher Education: Handbook for College Administrators*. Provides theoretical models and nuts-and-bolts information on how to evaluate research and target markets. **Price:** $18.00. **Conventions/Meetings:** annual conference, for grantees.

8106 ■ Great Lakes Colleges Association (GLCA)
535 W William St., Ste.301
Ann Arbor, MI 48103
Ph: (734)661-2350 (734)661-2332
Fax: (734)661-2349
E-mail: detweiler@glca.org
URL: http://www.glca.org
Contact: Richard A. Detweiler, Pres.

Founded: 1962. **Members:** 12. **Staff:** 9. **Budget:** $700,000. **Description:** Independent, liberal arts and sciences colleges in Indiana, Michigan, and Ohio. Seeks to enable members to collaborate on activities that are more effectively done as a group, including off-campus study programs for students, professional development programs for faculty and administrators, sharing management data, and instructional technology. Sponsors women's studies and black studies conferences. **Awards:** New Writers Award. **Frequency:** annual. **Type:** recognition. **Recipient:** for the best fiction and poetry by a first-published author. **Committees:** Institutional Commitment to Educational Equity; International and Off-Campus Education; Technology Advisory Group; Women's Studies. **Councils:** Academic; Deans'. **Affiliated With:** Associated Colleges of the Midwest. **Publications:** *The Beacon*, monthly. Newsletter. ISSN: 0738-3622. Alternate Formats: online ● *Great Lakes Colleges Association—Faculty Newsletter*, quarterly. Includes calendar of events. **Price:** included in membership dues. ISSN: 0738-3622.

8107 ■ Hispanic Association of Colleges and Universities (HACU)
8415 Datapoint Dr., Ste.400
San Antonio, TX 78229
Ph: (210)692-3805
Fax: (210)692-0823
E-mail: hacu@hacu.net
URL: http://www.hacu.net
Contact: Dr. Antonio R. Flores PhD, Pres./CEO

Founded: 1986. **Members:** 450. **Membership Dues:** Hispanic-serving institution (based on number of students enrolled), $2,690-$9,820 (annual) ● associate (based on number of students enrolled), $1,860-$6,710 (annual) ● partner (based on number of students enrolled), $1,820-$6,610 (annual) ● international institution (based on number of students enrolled), $2,010 (annual) ● Hispanic-serving school district (based on number of students enrolled), $500-$2,000 (annual) ● faculty/staff at non-member institution, $200 (annual) ● faculty/staff at HACU member institution, $175 (annual). **Staff:** 45. **Description:** Colleges and universities with a large number of students of Hispanic descent. Seeks to improve access to postsecondary education for Hispanic students; promotes advancement of colleges and universities with significant Hispanic enrollment. Facilitates communication and cooperation among members; works to strengthen members' ties to the business community; serves as a clearinghouse on postsecondary education for Hispanics. **Publica-**

tions: *The Voice*, quarterly. Magazine. **Circulation:** 2,000. **Advertising:** accepted. **Conventions/Meetings:** annual Championing Hispanic Higher Education Success: Strengthening the Nation's Prosperity and Opportunity - conference (exhibits) - 2008 Oct. 11-13, Denver, CO; 2009 Oct. 31-Nov. 2, Orlando, FL; 2010 Sept. 18-20, San Diego, CA; 2011 Oct. 29-31, San Antonio, TX.

8108 ■ LASPAU: Academic and Professional Programs for the Americas
25 Mt. Auburn St.
Cambridge, MA 02138-6095
Ph: (617)495-5255 (617)495-0555
Fax: (617)495-8990
E-mail: ned_strong@harvard.edu
URL: http://www.laspau.harvard.edu
Contact: Ned D. Strong, Exec. Dir.
Founded: 1964. **Staff:** 35. **Budget:** $2,000,000. **Languages:** English, French, Portuguese, Spanish. **Description:** Designs, develops, and implements academic exchange programs on behalf of individuals and institutions in the United States, Canada, Latin America, and the Caribbean. (Most of these academic exchange programs are devoted to graduate-level exchanges, but undergraduate and professional non-degree programs are also part of organization's activities.) Evaluates scholarship and loan candidates selected by participating Latin American and Caribbean institutions; selects grantees for advanced training in the United States or in high-caliber institutions elsewhere in the hemisphere. Coordinates grantees' English-language studies when necessary; arranges for their admission to appropriate universities or training programs; and monitors their progress. Administers programs for several sponsors, including the United States Department of State's Bureau of Educational and Cultural Affairs, The Kellogg Foundation, The Organization of American States, the World Bank, and the Inter-American Development Bank. Offers specialized educational consulting services to institutions both within and outside the Americas. **Telecommunication Services:** electronic mail, laspau-info@calists.harvard.edu. **Formerly:** (1995) Latin American Scholarship Program of American Universities. **Publications:** *Fulbright Programs Administered by LASPAU: A Directory of Grantees*, biennial. Lists recipients of Fulbright-LASPAU awards from 1975 to present. **Price:** free (limited distribution) ● *LASPAU Guide for Grantees* (in English and Spanish), annual. Handbook. Provides information on academic exchange programs, preparing for departure from the home country, and adjusting to life in the host country. Alternate Formats: online ● *LASPAU Informativo*, semiannual. Newsletter. Covers program developments at LASPAU and topics relevant to international educational exchanges. Lists grantee achievements. **Price:** free. **Circulation:** 15,000. Alternate Formats: online ● Annual Report, annual. Includes program information and financial statements. **Price:** free. **Circulation:** 5,000. Alternate Formats: online.

8109 ■ National Association for Equal Opportunity in Higher Education (NAFEO)
209 Third St. SE
Washington, DC 20003
Ph: (202)552-3300
Fax: (202)552-3330
URL: http://www.nafeo.org
Contact: Dr. Lezli Baskerville, Pres./CEO
Founded: 1969. **Members:** 118. **Staff:** 26. **Budget:** $2,000,000. **Description:** Provides a unified framework representing historically and predominantly black universities and colleges and similarly situated institutions in their attempt to continue as viable forces in American society. Seeks to build a case for securing increased support from federal agencies, philanthropic foundations, and other sources, and to increase black leadership of educational organizations and membership on federal boards and commissions relating to education. Offers placement service. Maintains biographical data on member colleges/universities and presidents/chancellors. Compiles statistics on black graduates. **Awards:** Distinguished Alumni Citation of the Year. **Frequency:** annual. **Type:** recognition ● Leadership. **Type:** recognition ● Research Achievement. **Frequency:** annual. **Type:** recognition. **Publications:** *Black Excellence*, bimonthly. Magazine. Provides information to college students. **Price:** $15.00/year; $27.00/2 years. **Circulation:** 60,000. **Advertising:** accepted ● *Blacks on White Campuses* ● *Distinguished Alumni of the Historical and Predominantly Black Colleges and Universities*, annual ● *Institutional and Presidential Profiles of the Historical Black Colleges and Universities*, annual. Directory ● *NAFEO Alumni Record*, annual. Brochure ● Brochure, annual. **Conventions/Meetings:** annual conference (exhibits).

8110 ■ National Association of State Universities and Land-Grant Colleges (NASULGC)
1307 New York Ave. NW, Ste.400
Washington, DC 20005-4722
Ph: (202)478-6040
Fax: (202)478-6046
E-mail: mneufville@nasulgc.org
URL: http://www.nasulgc.org
Contact: M. Peter McPherson, Pres.
Founded: 1887. **Members:** 215. **Staff:** 35. **Description:** Educational association representing the principal public universities of the 50 states, U.S. territories, and the District of Columbia, including 76 U.S. land-grant institutions of which 17 are historically black institutions. Seeks to focus public attention on problems of this special segment of higher education and on contributions these institutions have made to the nation. Special areas of interest include legislation at both the federal and state level affecting public higher education, curriculum revision, academic structure, urban involvement, agriculture and extension activities, university scientific and technical research, education of the disadvantaged, enrollment, cost trends, and degree production. Maintains Office for the Advancement of Public Black Colleges and Federal Relations Groups. **Awards:** Edwin Crawford Award for Innovation in State Relations. **Frequency:** annual. **Type:** recognition. **Recipient:** for young professionals. **Commissions:** Food, Environment, and Renewable Resources; Human Resources and Social Change; Information Technologies; International Programs; Kellog Commission on the Future of State and Land-Grant Universities; Outreach and Technology Transfer; Urban Agenda. **Councils:** Academic Affairs; Business Affairs; Extension, Continuing Education and Public Service; Governmental Affairs; 1890 Colleges and Universities; Presidents; Presidents and Chancellors' Spouses; Research Policy and Graduate Education; Student Affairs; University Relations and Development. **Formed by Merger of:** (1963) Association of Land-Grant Colleges and State Universities. **Publications:** *The Land-Grant Tradition*. Booklet ● *NASULGC: People and Programs*, annual. Contains statistics about NASULGC member institutions and historical background about the association. ● *Newsline*, 5/year. Newsletter. Includes information on NASULGC programs and initiatives, and legislative and other items of interest to member colleges and universities. **Circulation:** 8,000. Alternate Formats: online ● *Proceedings of Annual Meeting*, annual. **Circulation:** 700 ● Monographs. **Conventions/Meetings:** annual meeting - always November.

8111 ■ National Consortium of Arts and Letters for Historically Black Colleges and Universities (NCALHBCU)
Address Unknown since 2007
Founded: 1984. **Members:** 38. **Description:** Historically and/or predominantly black colleges and universities; other institutions of higher learning are associate members. Encourages academic excellence with an emphasis on cultural growth. Promotes study of African-American history and culture in the context of the scholarly study of world cultures. Focuses on needs of teaching faculty.

8112 ■ Office for the Advancement of Public Black Colleges of the National Association of State Universities and Land-Grant Colleges (OAPBC)
c/o National Association of State Universities and Land-Grant Colleges
1307 New York Ave. NW, Ste.400
Washington, DC 20005-4722
Ph: (202)478-6040
Fax: (202)478-6046
E-mail: pmcpherson@nasulgc.org
Contact: M.Peter McPherson, Pres.
Founded: 1968. **Members:** 38. **Staff:** 2. **Regional Groups:** 12. **State Groups:** 19. **Description:** Collects, organizes, interprets, and disseminates data on 37 predominantly black public colleges. The colleges, located in 19 states, enroll over 170,000 students. Conducts research programs. Compiles statistics; maintains databases. **Affiliated With:** American Association of State Colleges and Universities; National Association of State Universities and Land-Grant Colleges. **Formerly:** (1984) Office for Advancement of Public Negro Colleges - of the National Association of State Universities and Land-Grant Colleges. **Publications:** *A National Resource*, biennial ● *Key Administrative Personnel*, annual. Directory ● *Profiles in Success*, quarterly ● Newsletter, periodic ● Also publishes books and booklets. **Conventions/Meetings:** annual conference.

8113 ■ Scripps Association of Families (SAF)
Scripps Coll.
1030 Columbia Ave.
Claremont, CA 91711
Ph: (909)607-1542
E-mail: liz.zug@scrippscollege.edu
URL: http://www.scrippscollege.edu/dept/parents
Contact: Liz Zug, Co-Chair
Founded: 1983. **Description:** Seeks to stimulate communication between families and the Scripps College. **Computer Services:** Online services, New Family Survey. **Committees:** Distinguished and Outstanding Recent Alumna Awards; Ellen Browning Scripps Society Award; Graduates of the Last Decade; Senior Class Gift. **Publications:** *A Family's Guide to Scripps College*, annual. Handbook. Alternate Formats: online ● *Scripps*, quarterly. Magazine. Alternate Formats: online ● *Scripps College Alumnae Association's Online Community*. Directory. Alternate Formats: online ● *Scripps College Catalog 2004-2006* ● *Scripps College Directory*. Alternate Formats: online ● *Volunteer Leadership Conference*. Brochure.

8114 ■ Worldwide University Consortium
c/o International House Bellingham
505 N Forest
Bellingham, WA 98227
Ph: (604)689-0905
Fax: (604)689-0905
E-mail: wunicols@vcn.bc.ca
URL: http://www.vcn.bc.ca/wunicols
Contact: Raymond Spencer Rodgers PhD, Pres.
Founded: 1893. **Members:** 18. **Staff:** 2. **Multinational. Description:** University-level colleges worldwide. Promotes effective postsecondary education. Facilitates communication and exchange of information among members. **Additional Websites:** http://www.worldwideuniversity.edu. **Also Known As:** Vancouver University Worldwide. **Formerly:** (1997) World University Colleges; (1998) World University Colleges Consortium; (2001) Worldwide University Colleges Consortium.

Comics

8115 ■ National Association of Comics Art Educators (NACAE)
PO Box 125
White River Junction, VT 05001
E-mail: info@teachingcomics.org
URL: http://www.teachingcomics.org
Contact: James Sturm, Dir.
Description: Seeks to establish a national forum to stimulate the understanding and acceptance of comics art in educational institutions in the United States. Counsels and assists schools in developing comics art programs. **Computer Services:** Information services, facts about comics ● information services, teaching resources ● online services, message board.

Communications

8116 ■ Religious Communication Association (RCA)

c/o Michael E. Eidenmuller, Coor. of Electronic Communication
Univ. of Texas at Tyler
Dept. of Commun.
3900 Univ. Blvd.
Tyler, TX 75799
Ph: (903)566-7093
Fax: (903)566-7287
E-mail: eiden@mail.uttyl.edu
URL: http://www.americanrhetoric.com/rca
Contact: Michael E. Eidenmuller, Coor. of Electronic Communication

Founded: 1973. **Members:** 265. **Membership Dues:** regular, $25 (annual) ● sustaining, $45 (annual) ● institutional, $50 (annual) ● student, $12 (annual) ● life, $250. **Description:** Educators, professional religious workers, college and seminary students, broadcasters, educational institutions, and other scholars and professionals sharing an interest in religious speech, media, and theatre. Promotes the study of religious communication by teachers, practitioners, and scholars. Sponsors scholarly programs and presents papers. **Awards: Frequency:** annual. **Type:** recognition. **Recipient:** for articles and books. **Divisions:** Curriculum and Instruction; Interpersonal/Group Communication; Mass Media/Forum; Performance Studies; Public Address; Theory. **Formerly:** Religious Speech Division of Speech Communication Association; (1998) Religious Speech Communication Association. **Publications:** *Homiletic: A Review of Publications in Religious Communication*, semiannual. Includes lists of conferences, workshops, and seminars. **Price:** included in membership dues; $7.00 /year for nonmembers; $4.00/ issue for nonmembers; $9.00 /year for libraries. **Advertising:** accepted ● *Journal of Communication and Religion*, semiannual. Focuses on the theoretical and practical stimulation of research and writings in the field of religious communication. Includes resource reports. **Price:** $10.00 /year for individuals in U.S.; $8.50/year for agencies in U.S.; $12.00 /year for individuals outside U.S.; $10.25/year for agencies outside U.S. ISSN: 0894-2838. **Circulation:** 500 ● *Religious Speech Communication Association—Newsletter*, 3/year. Contains information on membership activities, convention program, and membership list. **Price:** included in membership dues. **Circulation:** 325. Alternate Formats: online. **Conventions/Meetings:** annual convention, held in conjunction with Speech Communication Association (exhibits).

Community Colleges

8117 ■ American Association of Community Colleges (AACC)

1 Dupont Cir. NW, Ste.410
Washington, DC 20036-1176
Ph: (202)728-0200
Fax: (202)833-2467
E-mail: gboggs@aacc.nche.edu
URL: http://www.aacc.nche.edu
Contact: George R. Boggs, Pres./CEO

Founded: 1920. **Members:** 1,167. **Staff:** 50. **Budget:** $9,000,000. **Description:** Community colleges; individual associates interested in community college development; corporate, educational, foundation, and international associate members. Office of Federal Relations monitors federal educational programming and legislation. Compiles statistics through data collection and policy analysis. Conducts seminars and professional training programs. **Computer Services:** Mailing lists. **Programs:** College/Employer Partnerships; International Education; Minority Education. **Formerly:** (1972) American Association of Junior Colleges; (1992) American Association of Community and Junior Colleges. **Publications:** *AACC Annual*, annual. Book. Contains state by state analysis of key trends and statistics for community colleges. **Price:** $25.00 for members; $32.00 for nonmembers ● *AACC Letter*, biweekly. Newsletter. Monitors trends and issues affecting community colleges. Provides information on materials, funding sources, legislation affecting two-year colleges. ISSN: 0745-0435. Alternate Formats: online ● *AACC Membership Directory*, annual. **Price:** $45.00 for members; $60.00 for nonmembers ● *Community College Journal*, bimonthly. Magazine. Highlights field research, outstanding programs, college leaders, and membership activities. **Price:** $32.00 in U.S.; $39.00 outside U.S. ISSN: 1067-1803. **Advertising:** accepted ● *Community College Times*, biweekly. Newspaper. Covers news, outstanding programs and people in the community college movement, and federal issues affecting community colleges. **Price:** $54.00 in U.S.; $63.00 outside U.S. ISSN: 8711-7189. **Circulation:** 10,000. **Advertising:** accepted. Alternate Formats: online ● Books ● Monographs. **Conventions/Meetings:** annual convention (exhibits) - always spring.

8118 ■ Association of Community College Trustees (ACCT)

1233 20th St. NW, Ste.301
Washington, DC 20036
Ph: (202)775-4667
Free: (866)895-2228
Fax: (202)223-1297
E-mail: acct@acctinfo.org
URL: http://www.acct.org
Contact: J. Noah Brown, Pres./CEO

Founded: 1969. **Members:** 790. **Membership Dues:** associate, $415 (annual) ● regular in U.S. (based on the number of enrollees), $1,110-$4,445 (annual) ● regular in Canada (based on the number of enrollees), $999-$4,000 (annual). **Staff:** 15. **Budget:** $2,500,000. **Description:** Represents Community college or technical college boards or boards of other accredited postsecondary educational institutions that offer courses that leads to degrees or objectives less than a baccalaureate degree; boards of educational institutions of other nations that are considered as being postsecondary. Provides education to trustees in order to improve the governance of the institutions. Aims to unify trustees in order to give direction to the community college movement through the development of resolutions and policies. Promotes the philosophical concept of the community college and technical college. Provides advice through expert trustees. **Awards:** Charles Kennedy Equity Award. **Frequency:** annual. **Type:** recognition. **Recipient:** for individual who has an exemplary commitment in the community that achieves equity in the college's education programs and services ● M. Dale Ensign Trustee Award. **Frequency:** annual. **Type:** recognition. **Recipient:** for an individual who made a significant contribution as lay trustee toward promoting the community college concept ● Marie Y. Martin CEO Award. **Frequency:** annual. **Type:** recognition. **Recipient:** for an individual who has tremendous contributions in the community college chief executive officers ● Professional Board Staff Award. **Frequency:** annual. **Type:** recognition. **Recipient:** for most promising board staff member of the society. **Formerly:** (1972) Council of Community College Boards. **Publications:** *Trustee Quarterly*. Magazine. Includes trustee education articles. **Price:** free for members. ISSN: 0271-9746. **Circulation:** 7,000 ● Books ● Monographs ● Reports. **Conventions/Meetings:** annual National Legislative Seminar, federal advocacy briefings and meetings with members of congress and the administration - always February, Washington, DC ● seminar and regional meeting ● annual convention (exhibits) - usually September, October or November. 2008 Oct. 29-Nov. 1, New York, NY; 2009 Oct. 7-10, San Francisco, CA; 2010 Oct. 20-23, Toronto, ON, Canada.

8119 ■ Community College Baccalaureate Association (CCBA)

PO Box 60210
Fort Myers, FL 33906
Ph: (239)947-8085
Fax: (239)947-8870
E-mail: bhagan7@aol.com
URL: http://www.accbd.org
Contact: Beth Hagan PhD, Exec. Dir./Ed.

Membership Dues: institutional, $500 (annual) ● individual, $125 (annual) ● platinum partner, $10,000 (annual) ● gold partner, $5,000 (annual) ● silver partner, $2,500 (annual). **Description:** Promotes better access to baccalaureate degrees on community college campuses. Encourages the development of baccalaureate degrees conferred by community colleges. Fosters the development of university centers and joint degree programs with universities on community college campuses. **Affiliated With:** American Association of Community Colleges. **Publications:** *Beacon*, quarterly. Newsletter. Alternate Formats: online ● *The Community College Baccalaureate - Emerging Trends and Policy Issues*. Book. Analyzes the emerging trend of the community college baccalaureate degree in the United States and Canada. **Price:** $65.00/copy (cloth); $29.95/copy (paperback) ● Articles. Alternate Formats: online.

8120 ■ League for Innovation in the Community College

4505 E Chandler Blvd., Ste.250
Phoenix, AZ 85048
Ph: (480)705-8200
Fax: (480)705-8201
E-mail: prather@league.org
URL: http://www.league.org
Contact: Dr. Gerardo E. de los Santos, Pres./CEO

Founded: 1968. **Members:** 750. **Membership Dues:** alliance (minimum), $750 (annual). **Staff:** 15. **Budget:** $2,600,000. **Description:** Community colleges experimenting in teaching, learning, student services, and other aspects of community college operations. Seeks to share conceptual planning and learning objectives and to exchange instructional material designed to enhance learning. Provides workshops and conferences for faculty and administrative staff. **Libraries: Type:** reference. **Holdings:** articles, books, periodicals. **Subjects:** community colleges. **Publications:** *Innovator*, quarterly. Newsletter. **Price:** free for members ● *Leadership Abstracts*, monthly. Alternate Formats: online ● Also publishes resource inventories in specialized areas. **Conventions/Meetings:** annual Conference on Information Technology - 2008 Oct. 19-22, Salt Lake City, UT ● annual Innovations - conference.

8121 ■ National Council for Research and Planning (NCRP)

c/o Richard C. Rindone, Membership Coor.
Santa Fe Community Coll.
6401 Richards Ave.
Santa Fe, NM 87508-4887
Ph: (505)428-1658 (410)455-4745
Fax: (505)428-1296
E-mail: ncrp@nmsu.edu
URL: http://www.nmsu.edu/~NCRP/ncrp_revised.html
Contact: Gayle Fink, Pres.

Founded: 1977. **Members:** 256. **Membership Dues:** individual, $40 (annual) ● institutional, $100 (annual). **Regional Groups:** 10. **Description:** A council of the American Association of Community Colleges. Represents directors of research and planning, deans, presidents, and representatives of state and national two-year college organizations. Provides a forum for activities that promotes research and planning in two-year postsecondary institutions. Promotes interest in and professional development for research, planning, and information-based management as an integral part of two-year colleges and postsecondary institutions. Plans conferences, training workshops, and research studies. **Committees:** Communication; Coordination; Liaison; Research. **Affiliated With:** American Association of Community Colleges; Association for Institutional Research. **Publications:** *Community College Resource Review*, biennial ● *e-Parameters*, periodic. Newsletter. Alternate Formats: online ● *The Journal of Applied Research in the Community College*, semiannual. Serves the needs and interests of institutional researchers and planners in the community college. **Price:** $9.00/year ● *New Directions for Two-Year Colleges*, biennial ● Membership Directory, annual. **Conventions/Meetings:** annual meeting, held in conjunction with AACJC and AIR.

8122 ■ National Council of State Directors of Community Colleges
1 Dupont Cir. NW, Ste.410
Washington, DC 20036-1176
Ph: (202)728-0200
Fax: (202)833-2467
URL: http://www.statedirectors.org
Contact: Marc S. Herzog, Chm.
Members: 38. **Description:** Represents officials with state-level responsibility for community/junior colleges. Conducts research programs. **Libraries: Type:** reference. **Holdings:** archival material, reports. **Committees:** Issues and Trends; Legislation; Research. **Conventions/Meetings:** conference - 3/year.

Community Education

8123 ■ Association for Community Based Education (ACBE)
Address Unknown since 2007
Founded: 1976. **Members:** 150. **Staff:** 10. **Description:** Community-based, freestanding alternative colleges and community organizations providing educational opportunities to adults at the postsecondary level; nonformal adult learning centers and community development organizations that have an established educational or training component. Seeks to: promote the organization and development of community-based, freestanding educational institutions; encourage communication and coordination among members; obtain direct funding for community-based educational institutions. Offers technical assistance on planning, management, fundraising, self-evaluation, and program development. Provides professional review and critique of member proposals. Sponsors "minigrant" programs to assist general institutional improvement, to document exemplary educational methods and approaches, to demonstrate new ideas and approaches, and to provide seed money for pilot projects. **Awards: Type:** scholarship. **Formerly:** (1981) Clearinghouse for Community Based Free Standing Educational Institutions; (1982) Association for Community Based Educational Institutions. **Publications:** *CBE Report*, monthly. Newsletter. Provides information on networking opportunities in the field of community-based and social change. Includes book reviews and calendar of events. **Price:** included in membership dues; $30.00/year for nonmembers. **Circulation:** 500 ● *Directory of Community - Based Adult Literacy Providers* ● *Directory of Funding Sources*, annual ● *Directory of Members*, annual ● Manuals ● Report, annual. **Conventions/Meetings:** annual conference - always October.

8124 ■ Association for Community Networking (AFCN)
c/o Michael Maranda, Pres.
1375 E 54th St., No. 2
Chicago, IL 60615
E-mail: mmaranda@afcn.org
URL: http://www.afcn.org
Contact: Michael Maranda, Pres.
Membership Dues: individual, organizational, $25 (annual) ● community network showcase, $100 (annual) ● corporate, $200 (annual). **Multinational. Description:** Provides resources, shared learning and experienced guidance to help communities and organizations use information and communications technologies effectively. Improves the visibility, viability and vitality of community networking.

8125 ■ National Center for Community Education (NCCE)
1017 Avon St.
Flint, MI 48503
Ph: (810)238-0463
Free: (800)811-1105
Fax: (810)238-9211
E-mail: info@nccenet.org
URL: http://www.nccenet.org
Contact: Daniel Cady, Exec. Dir.
Founded: 1968. **Staff:** 11. **Budget:** $3,000,000. **For-Profit. Description:** Works to provide short-term training workshops for persons entering and/or working in the field of community education. Areas of concern include community education, school advisory councils, group facilitating, time and stress management, and decision-making through problem-solving. Provides information and services to university centers and state departments of education. Offers referral services; maintains small resource center; provides information searches. **Publications:** *MOH Exchange, Community Schools Across America*. Magazine. **Price:** free. **Circulation:** 10,000. Alternate Formats: online. **Conventions/Meetings:** meeting - 10/year.

8126 ■ National Community Education Association (NCEA)
3929 Old Lee Hwy., No. 91-A
Fairfax, VA 22030-2421
Ph: (703)359-8973
Fax: (703)359-0972
E-mail: ncea@ncea.com
URL: http://www.ncea.com
Contact: Beth Robertson, Exec. Dir.
Founded: 1966. **Members:** 1,500. **Membership Dues:** associate, $60 (annual) ● individual, $149 (annual) ● institutional, $315 (annual) ● advisory council, $100 (annual) ● student (full-time), $25 (annual) ● corporate, $1,000 (annual) ● state affiliate, $125 (annual). **Staff:** 5. **Budget:** $575,000. **State Groups:** 35. **Description:** Community school directors, principals, superintendents, professors, teachers, students, and laypeople. Promotes and establishes community schools as an integral part of the educational plan of every community. Emphasizes community and parent involvement in the schools, lifelong learning, and enrichment of K-12 and adult education. Serves as a clearinghouse for the exchange of ideas and information, and the sharing of efforts. Offers leadership training. **Libraries: Type:** not open to the public. **Holdings:** 2,500; archival material. **Subjects:** education, community schools, advisory councils, adult education. **Awards:** Citizen Leadership Award. **Frequency:** annual. **Type:** recognition ● Distinguished Service Award. **Frequency:** annual. **Type:** recognition ● Multicultural Leadership and Involvement. **Frequency:** annual. **Type:** recognition ● Outstanding After-School Program Award. **Frequency:** annual. **Type:** recognition ● Outstanding Contributions to Community Education Legislation Award. **Frequency:** annual. **Type:** recognition ● Outstanding Organization. **Frequency:** annual. **Type:** recognition ● Professional Service Award. **Frequency:** annual. **Type:** recognition ● State Association Leadership Award. **Frequency:** annual. **Type:** recognition ● Youth Leadership. **Frequency:** annual. **Type:** recognition. **Computer Services:** database, membership directory ● mailing lists, of members ● online services, The CE Blogger. **Formerly:** (1974) National Community School Education Association. **Publications:** *Community Education: Building Learning Communities* ● *Community Education Journal*, quarterly. **Price:** $25.00/year. ISSN: 0045-7736. **Circulation:** 2,000. **Advertising:** accepted. Alternate Formats: microform ● *Community Education Today*, 9/year. **Price:** $25.00/year. ISSN: 0744-4575. **Circulation:** 3,000. **Advertising:** accepted. Alternate Formats: online ● *Educational Restructuring and the Community Education Process* ● *Grantseeking, Rebuilding the Partnership for Public Education* ● *Reforming Public Schools Through Community Education* ● *School Community Centers: Guidelines for Interagency Planners* ● Membership Directory, annual. **Conventions/Meetings:** annual conference (exhibits) ● Legislative Training - workshop, in-service.

Computer Science

8127 ■ American Computer Science League (ACSL)
PO Box 521
West Warwick, RI 02893
Ph: (401)822-4312
E-mail: info@acsl.org
URL: http://www.acsl.org
Founded: 1978. **Description:** Secondary schools. Seeks to develop computer science education at the secondary school level. Works to provide educational opportunities for computer enthusiasts and motivate students to pursue classroom computer topics in-depth as well as to study computer subjects not covered in school curricula. Administers the annual Invitational Team All-Star Contest for junior and senior high school students; including computers, trophies, and computer-related materials. **Divisions:** Intermediate; Junior; Non-Programming Classroom; Senior. **Publications:** Newsletter, periodic.

8128 ■ Association of Information Technology Professionals (AITP)
401 N Michigan Ave., Ste.2400
Chicago, IL 60611-4267
Ph: (312)245-1070 (312)673-5771
Free: (800)224-9371
Fax: (312)673-6659
E-mail: aitp_hq@aitp.org
URL: http://www.aitp.org
Contact: Eric Hawkinson, Exec. Dir.
Founded: 1951. **Members:** 10,000. **Membership Dues:** individual, $105 (annual) ● student, $35 (annual). **Staff:** 5. **Budget:** $750,000. **Regional Groups:** 10. **Local Groups:** 190. **For-Profit. Description:** Managerial personnel, staff, educators, and individuals interested in the management of information resources. Founder of the Certificate in Data Processing examination program, now administered by an intersociety organization. Maintains Legislative Communications Network. Professional education programs include EDP-oriented business and management principles self-study courses and a series of videotaped management development seminars. Sponsors student organizations around the country interested in information technology and encourages members to serve as counselors for the Scout computer merit badge. Conducts research projects, including a business information systems curriculum for two- and four-year colleges. **Libraries: Type:** open to the public. **Awards:** Distinguished Information Sciences Award. **Frequency:** annual. **Type:** recognition. **Recipient:** for outstanding contribution to the profession. **Computer Services:** Online services, Inforamp. **Committees:** IT Research Community Outreach; New Professional Member Recruitment; Professional Member Retention; Student Member Recruitment and Retention. **Formerly:** (1962) National Machine Accountants Association. **Publications:** *Executive, The AITP Model Curriculum for a Four-Year Undergraduate Degree for the 1990's* ● *Information Executive*, bimonthly. Newsletter. **Price:** $45.00/year. **Circulation:** 7,000. **Advertising:** accepted. Alternate Formats: online ● Manuals. Alternate Formats: online. **Conventions/Meetings:** annual National Collegiate Conference (exhibits) ● annual seminar, for college students; includes computer programming competition.

8129 ■ Association of the Institute for Certification of Computing Professionals (AICCP)
2350 E Devon Ave., Ste.115
Des Plaines, IL 60018-4610
Ph: (847)299-4227
Free: (800)843-8227
Fax: (847)299-4280
E-mail: office@iccp.org
URL: http://www.iccp.org
Contact: John Whitehouse CCP, Dir.
Founded: 1973. **Members:** 50,000. **Staff:** 7. **Budget:** $500,000. **Description:** Exhibits comprehension and knowledge of stringent industry fundamentals. Administers the experience-based and nonvendor specific CCP designation, recognized as the standard for the computing profession worldwide. Furthers its purpose and goals with assistance from 27 worldwide affiliated societies. **Libraries: Type:** not open to the public. **Holdings:** 500. **Subjects:** technical computing. **Computer Services:** Mailing lists, certificate holders. **Committees:** Certification Examination Questions; Ethics; Good Practices; Inter-Society Relations; Local Representatives; Review Courses and Materials. **Affiliated With:** Institute for Certification of Computing Professionals. **Formerly:** Association of the Institute for Certification of Computer

Professionals. **Supersedes:** (1971) Society of Certified Data Pros. **Publications:** *Certification News*, quarterly. Newsletter. **Circulation:** 26,000. **Advertising:** accepted. **Conventions/Meetings:** biennial board meeting.

8130 ■ Computer Science Teachers Association (CSTA)
PO Box 11414
New York, NY 10286-1414
Ph: (212)626-0530 (212)626-0500
Free: (800)342-6626
Fax: (212)944-1318
E-mail: cstahelp@csta.acm.org
URL: http://csta.acm.org
Contact: Chris Stephenson, Exec. Dir.

Membership Dues: individual, $30 (annual) ● institutional, $200 (annual) ● affiliate, $20 (annual). **Description:** Promotes and supports the teaching of computer science and other computing disciplines. Acts as an advocate for a comprehensive computer curricula at all levels. Provides policy recommendations to support computer science in the high school curriculum. Raises awareness that computer science educators are highly qualified professionals who provide quality education to their students. **Telecommunication Services:** electronic mail, cstephenson@csta.acm.org ● additional toll-free number, (800)401-1799. **Publications:** *CSTA Voice*, quarterly. Newsletter. Provides analysis and commentary on issues of K-12 computer science education. **Price:** included in membership dues. ISSN: 1555-2128. Alternate Formats: online ● *The New Educational Imperative: Improving High School Computer Science Education*. Report. Provides a comprehensive look at high school computer science education in the U.S. and around the world. Alternate Formats: online.

8131 ■ Institute for Certification of Computing Professionals (ICCP)
2350 E Devon Ave., Ste.115
Des Plaines, IL 60018-4610
Ph: (847)299-4227
Free: (800)843-8227
Fax: (847)299-4280
E-mail: office@iccp.org
URL: http://www.iccp.org
Contact: John Gensano, Contact

Founded: 1973. **Members:** 50,000. **Membership Dues:** individual, $50 (annual). **Staff:** 5. **Budget:** $1,000,000. **Description:** Professional societies. Promotes the development of computer examinations which are of high quality, directed toward information technology professionals, and designed to encourage competence and professionalism. Individuals passing the exams automatically become members of the Institute for Certification of Computing Professionals and become certified as CCP or ACP. Has developed code of ethics and good practice to which those taking the exams promise to adhere. Maintains speakers' bureau; compiles statistics. **Committees:** Certification; Education; Marketing Advisory. **Absorbed:** Association of the Institute for Certification of Computing Professionals. **Publications:** *Certification News*, quarterly. Newsletter. **Price:** included in membership dues. **Circulation:** 25,000. **Advertising:** accepted ● *Certified Business Intelligence Professional*. Manual. Covers Examination Guides for each of the examinations and provides sample questions, answers, and discussions of the correct and incorrect items. **Price:** $65.00 each ● *Data Resources Management Study Package*. Manual. Contains a set of notes, sample and questions and answers. **Price:** $35.00 each ● *ICCP Complete Guide to Professional Computing (Examination Study Guide)*. Manual. Contains an expanded outline of the Core Examination, Specialty exam and the Programming Language exams. **Price:** $105.00 each ● *ICCP Examinations Review Manual for Conference ExamCram Sessions*. Contains study materials, timed tests, answers and over 200 review questions and statements. **Price:** $25.00 each ● *Official Exam Review Outline*. Manuals. **Conventions/Meetings:** semiannual meeting.

8132 ■ International Association for Computer Information Systems (IACIS)
c/o Dr. G. Daryl Nord, Managing Dir.
Oklahoma State Univ.
220 College of Business
Stillwater, OK 74078
Ph: (405)744-8632
Fax: (405)744-5180
E-mail: dnord@okstate.edu
URL: http://www.iacis.org
Contact: Robert P. Behling, Exec. Dir.

Founded: 1960. **Members:** 700. **Membership Dues:** individual, $50 (annual) ● student, retired, $25 (annual). **Multinational**. **Description:** Educators and computer professionals. Seeks to promote the knowledge, use, and teaching of computers, and technology; dedicated to the improvement of information systems and computer professionals. **Libraries: Type:** reference. **Holdings:** 43; software. **Subjects:** computers, technology, education. **Awards:** Ben Braun Award for Excellence. **Frequency:** annual. **Type:** recognition. **Recipient:** for senior faculty with significant service to profession, university and community ● Computer Educator of the Year. **Frequency:** annual. **Type:** recognition. **Computer Services:** database ● mailing lists ● online services. **Absorbed:** (1975) Society for Automation in Business Education; (1975) Society for Automation in English and the Humanities; (1975) Society for Automation in Fine Arts; (1975) Society for Automation in Professional Education; (1975) Society for Automation in the Social Sciences; (1975) Society for Educational Data Systems; (1975) Society of Educational Programmers and Systems Analysts; (1975) Society of Independent and Private School Data Education. **Formerly:** (1987) Society for Data Educators; (1991) Association for Computer Educators. **Publications:** *IACIS Newsletter*, semiannual. **Price:** included in membership dues ● *Issues in Information Systems*, annual. Journal. Contains information about the annual conference of IACIS. ISSN: 1529-7314. Alternate Formats: online. Also Cited As: *IIS* ● *Journal of Computer Information Systems*, quarterly. Includes statistics, book reviews, and research news. **Price:** included in membership dues; $175.00 for institutions; $50.00 per back issue. ISSN: 0887-4417. **Circulation:** 1,000. **Advertising:** accepted. Alternate Formats: microform. Also Cited As: *JCIS*. **Conventions/Meetings:** annual conference (exhibits) - always fall.

8133 ■ International Association of Computer Investigative Specialists (IACIS)
PO Box 1728
Fairmont, WV 26555
Free: (888)884-2247
URL: http://www.iacis.info
Contact: William Jeitner, Pres.

Founded: 1990. **Membership Dues:** regular, candidate, $65 (annual). **Multinational**. **Description:** Provides education and certification of law enforcement professionals in the field of computer forensic science. Creates and establishes procedures, trains personnel, and certifies forensic examiners in the recovery of evidence from computer systems. Offers professional training in the seizure and processing computer systems. Provides an opportunity to network with other law enforcement officers trained in computer forensics, and to share and learn from others. **Publications:** Newsletter. **Price:** included in membership dues.

8134 ■ International Society for Technology in Education (ISTE)
175 W Broadway, Ste.300
Eugene, OR 97401-3003
Ph: (541)302-3777 (202)861-7777
Free: (800)336-5191
Fax: (541)302-3778
E-mail: iste@iste.org
URL: http://www.iste.org
Contact: Trina Davis, Pres.

Founded: 1979. **Members:** 10,000. **Membership Dues:** student, retired, $54 (annual) ● standard, $79 (annual). **Staff:** 32. **Description:** Teachers, administrators, computer and curriculum coordinators, and others interested in improving the quality of education through the innovative use of technology. Facilitates exchange of information and resources between international policy makers and professional organizations; encourages research and evaluation relating to the use of technology in education. Maintains the Private Sector Council to promote cooperation among private sector organizations to identify needs and establish standards for hardware, software, and other technology-based educational systems, products, and services. **Awards:** Outstanding Teacher/Leader Awards. **Frequency:** annual. **Type:** recognition. **Recipient:** for leader and teacher. **Computer Services:** Mailing lists. **Committees:** Accreditation and Standards; Awards and Recognition; Certification for Computer Using Educators; Ethics and Equity; International Legislative Action; Preview Centers; Software and Copyright Issues. **Formed by Merger of:** International Association for Computing in Education; International Council for Computers in Education. **Publications:** *ISTE Update*, monthly. Newsletter. Includes activities information, news on events in Washington, and conference calendar. Alternate Formats: online ● *Journal of Computing in Teacher Education*, quarterly. Provides articles on in-service training, research in computer education, and certification issues. Alternate Formats: online. Also Cited As: *JCTE* ● *Journal of Research on Computing in Education*, quarterly. Includes articles on research, system or project descriptions and evaluations, and assessments and theoretical positions on educational computing. ● *Learning and Leading with Technology*, 8/year. Journal. Includes information on language arts, logo, science, mathematics, telecommunications, equity, and international connections. **Circulation:** 10,000. **Advertising:** accepted. Alternate Formats: online. Also Cited As: *L&L* ● *SIGTel*. Bulletin. **Conventions/Meetings:** annual National Educational Computing conference (exhibits).

8135 ■ Special Interest Group on Computer Science Education (SIGCSE)
c/o Association for Computing Machinery
2 Penn Plz., Ste.701
New York, NY 10121-0701
Ph: (212)869-7440 (512)863-1513
Free: (800)342-6626
Fax: (212)944-1318
E-mail: sigcse-board@acm.org
URL: http://www.sigcse.org
Contact: Barbara Boucher Owens, Chair

Founded: 1970. **Multinational**. **Description:** A special interest group of the Association for Computing Machinery. Seeks to provide a forum for the solution of problems common to professionals in developing, implementing, and evaluating computer science programs, courses, and materials; to encourage and assist in the development of effective academic programs and courses in computer science; and to promote research in computer science education. Collects and disseminates information concerning courses and programs offered in secondary, associate, undergraduate, and graduate degree programs. Organizes and presents sessions at national meetings and disseminates information to computer science professionals. **Awards:** Outstanding Contributions to Computer Science Education. **Frequency:** annual. **Type:** recognition. **Recipient:** for significant accomplishments in computer science education. **Publications:** *Inroads (SIGCSE Bulletin)*, quarterly. Newsletter. ISSN: 0097-8418. **Circulation:** 2,500. **Advertising:** accepted. **Conventions/Meetings:** annual conference, with academic research presentations (exhibits).

Computer Software

8136 ■ Education Systems Exchange (ESE)
1111 Torrey Pines Rd.
La Jolla, CA 92037-4551
Ph: (858)454-9765
Free: (866)999-3627
Fax: (858)454-9766

E-mail: contact@emaspro.com
URL: http://www.edsysinc.com
Contact: Dr. Alice Hayes, Pres.
Founded: 1996. **Members:** 400. **Description:** Software systems provider to colleges, universities, and agencies. **Publications:** *EMAS Quarterly*. Newsletter. Alternate Formats: online.

Computers

8137 ■ Computers for Children (CFC)
1799 Clinton St.
Buffalo, NY 14206
Ph: (716)823-7248 (716)823-0952
Fax: (716)823-0960
E-mail: cfc@computersforchildren.com
URL: http://www.computersforchildren.com
Contact: Christine Carr, Exec. Dir.
Founded: 1997. **Multinational**. **Description:** Provides advanced learning opportunities for children. Enhances the learning opportunities for school children by increasing their access to computers and information technology. Improves educational opportunities for children in need. **Computer Services:** Online services, message board. **Programs:** Kids Internet Development Community Outreach; Recycling. **Publications:** Newsletter. Alternate Formats: online.

Conflict

8138 ■ CRU Institute
2330 130th Ave. NE, Bldg. C, Ste.102
Bellevue, WA 98005
Ph: (425)869-4041
Free: (800)922-1988
E-mail: cru@cruinstitute.org
URL: http://www.cruinstitute.org
Contact: Nancy Kaplan MSW, Dir.
Founded: 1987. **Languages:** English, Spanish. **Multinational**. **Description:** Works to teach young people effective, peaceful methods to resolve conflict in a multicultural world. **Programs:** School-Wide Conflict Mediation. **Publications:** *CRU for Elementary School Conflict Managers*. Manual. **Price:** $150.00/copy ● *Everyday Conflicts, Creative Solutions*. Video. **Price:** $95.00/copy ● *Family Problem Solving*. Booklets. **Price:** $195.00/complete training package ● *Names*. Video. **Price:** $125.00/copy ● *Rumors, Conflicts, Resolutions*. Video. **Price:** $95.00/copy.

Conflict Resolution

8139 ■ Grace Contrino Abrams Peace Education Foundation (GCAPEF)
1900 Biscayne Blvd.
Miami, FL 33132-1025
Ph: (305)576-5075
Free: (800)749-8838
Fax: (305)576-3106
URL: http://www.peace-ed.org
Founded: 1980. **Members:** 550. **Staff:** 21. **Budget:** $500,000. **Local Groups:** 1. **Description:** Teachers, counselors, and school administrators; clergy and laypersons; interested others. Works to educate students, parents, and teachers on creative and nonviolent methods of resolving conflict. Develops and disseminates grade-specific curricula on nonviolent conflict resolution and mediation for preschool through high school students. Maintains the Training Institute for Conflict Resolution, Mediation, and Peacemaking. Conducts workshops and seminars; maintains speakers' bureau. Sponsors contests. **Libraries: Type:** open to the public. **Holdings:** 1,000; articles, books, periodicals. **Subjects:** peace movement, conflict resolution, mediation. **Awards:** Peace Essay. **Frequency:** annual. **Type:** monetary ● **Frequency:** annual. **Type:** scholarship. **Also Known As:** Peace Education Foundation. **Publications:** *PeaceWorks*, biennial. Newsletter. Includes list of new members, chronology of foundation activities, and events sponsored by other peace groups. **Price:** free. **Circulation:** 150,000 ● *Prepared for Action: Responding Effectively to Crisis in Your School*. Manual. **Price:** $199.95/copy. Alternate Formats: CD-ROM ● Booklets ● Also publishes brochure. **Conventions/Meetings:** annual Peacemakers Conference to Stop the Violence - luncheon and conference, includes students from Dade County Public Schools; students, teachers and parents attend workshops about peer mediation and conflict resolution - always in Miami, FL.

Consciousness Studies

8140 ■ Association for the Scientific Study of Consciousness (ASSC)
PO Box 20393
Greenville, NC 27858
E-mail: ocarter@wjh.harvard.edu
URL: http://www.assc.caltech.edu
Contact: Olivia Carter, Sec.
Membership Dues: individual, $30 (annual) ● life, $250. **Description:** Scientists, philosophers and other scholars. Promotes research within cognitive science, neuroscience and philosophy. Conducts conferences and seminars, promotes smaller conferences, mailing lists and bibliographic resource. **Publications:** *Consciousness and Cognition*. Journal ● *Psyche*. Journal.

Construction

8141 ■ American Council for Construction Education (ACCE)
1717 N Loop 1604 E, Ste.320
San Antonio, TX 78232-1570
Ph: (210)495-6161
Fax: (210)495-6168
E-mail: acce@acce-hq.org
URL: http://www.acce-hq.org
Contact: Prof. Robert O. Segner, Pres.
Founded: 1974. **Members:** 150. **Membership Dues:** individual, $150 (annual) ● organization, $1,500 (annual) ● association, $4,400 (annual). **Staff:** 3. **Budget:** $200,000. **Description:** Represents construction-oriented associations, corporations, and individuals. Promotes and improves construction education at the postsecondary level. Engages in accrediting construction education programs offered by colleges and universities nationwide. Maintains procedures consistent with the accrediting policies of the Council for Higher Education Accreditation and reports the results of its activities and list the colleges and universities with accredited programs of study in construction. Reviews at regular intervals the criteria, standards, and procedures that the council has adopted to evaluate programs in construction education. Provides visiting teams for campus program evaluations; compiles statistics. **Committees:** Accreditation; Development; Finance; Guidance; Long Range Planning; Nominating; Standards. **Programs:** Accredited Baccalaureate. **Publications:** Annual Report, annual ● Newsletter, semiannual. Alternate Formats: online ● Also publishes accreditation standards and accompanying documents on accrediting procedures. **Conventions/Meetings:** semiannual conference - February and July.

8142 ■ American Society of Professional Estimators (ASPE)
2525 Perimeter Place Dr., Ste.103
Nashville, TN 37214
Ph: (615)316-9200 (203)397-0243
Free: (888)EST-MATE
Fax: (615)316-9800
E-mail: info@aspenational.com
URL: http://www.aspenational.org
Contact: Edward B. Walsh, Exec. Dir.
Founded: 1956. **Members:** 2,500. **Membership Dues:** member-at-large, $205 (annual) ● estimator, associate estimator, affiliate, constructor, associate constructor, $190 (annual) ● student (plus chapter dues), $9 (annual). **Staff:** 4. **Budget:** $250,000. **Regional Groups:** 5. **Local Groups:** 1. **Description:** Construction cost estimators. Develops professional and ethical standards in construction estimating. Offers continuing education to established professionals; provides certification for estimators. **Awards:** Estimator of the Year Award. **Frequency:** annual. **Type:** recognition. **Computer Services:** database ● mailing lists, available to members only. **Telecommunication Services:** electronic mail, edwalsh@aspenational.org ● additional toll-free number, (877)-273-5679. **Committees:** Awards and Fellowship; Certification; Education; Organization and Extension; Standards; Technical Documents. **Publications:** *The Estimator*, quarterly. Journal. **Price:** $30.00/year. **Circulation:** 2,500. **Advertising:** accepted ● *Membership Roster and Buyers' Guide*, annual. Book. **Price:** available to members only ● *Standard Estimating Practice Manual*. **Price:** $125.00 for nonmembers. **Conventions/Meetings:** annual board meeting ● annual convention ● annual meeting and seminar.

8143 ■ Associated Schools of Construction (ASC)
c/o Colorado State University
Mfg. Tech. and Constr. Mgt.
102 Guggenheim
Fort Collins, CO 80523
Ph: (970)491-7958
Fax: (970)491-2473
E-mail: david.rogge@orst.edu
URL: http://www.ascweb.org
Contact: David F. Rogge, Pres.
Founded: 1965. **Members:** 119. **Membership Dues:** institution, industry, governmental, $400 (annual) ● associate, personal, $250 (annual). **Staff:** 4. **Budget:** $55,500. **Regional Groups:** 7. **Multinational**. **Description:** Represents colleges and universities offering a program leading to an undergraduate or advanced degree with major emphasis on construction. Aims to establish objectives for the development of construction education and to assist institutions of higher education in establishing construction education and management programs. Compiles statistics. **Awards:** Outstanding Educator. **Frequency:** annual. **Type:** recognition. **Computer Services:** database, faculty member institutions. **Committees:** Graduate Education; Information Technology; Professional Development; Relations with Industry; Research; Undergraduate Education. **Publications:** *International Journal of Construction Education and Research*, triennial. ISSN: 1522-8150. Alternate Formats: online. Also Cited As: *Journal of Construction Education* ● *Proceedings of the Annual Meeting*, annual ● Annual Report, annual. **Conventions/Meetings:** annual conference (exhibits) - always April ● annual Regional and National Student Competition, includes educational program.

8144 ■ National Roofing Foundation (NRF)
10255 W Higgins Rd., Ste.600
Rosemont, IL 60018-5607
Ph: (847)299-9070
Fax: (847)299-1183
E-mail: lreardon@enterpriseroofing.com
URL: http://www.nrca.net/rp/related/nrf
Contact: Larry Reardon, Pres.
Founded: 1970. **Staff:** 1. **Description:** Sponsors programs and projects that support the highest-quality programs for roofing contractors, ensures timely and forward-thinking industry responses to major economic and technological issues, and enhances the long-term viability and attractiveness of the roofing industry. **Awards:** National Roofing Scholarships. **Frequency:** annual. **Type:** scholarship. **Recipient:** for academic record, potential to succeed, leadership and participation in school and community, honors, work experience ● Roofing Industry Scholarship. **Frequency:** annual. **Type:** scholarship. **Recipient:** for an employee or immediate family member of an employee or immediate family member of an NRCA contractor member, who plans to pursue post-secondary education in college and vocational programs ● William C. Cullen Research Fellowship. **Frequency:** annual. **Type:** grant. **Recipient:** for scientific research relating to the advancement of the roofing industry. **Formerly:**

(1979) National Roofing Education Foundation. **Conventions/Meetings:** meeting - 3/year.

Continuing Education

8145 ■ Accrediting Council for Continuing Education and Training (ACCET)

1722 N St. NW
Washington, DC 20036
Ph: (202)955-1113
Fax: (202)955-1118
E-mail: rjwilliams@accet.org
URL: http://www.accet.org
Contact: Roger J. Williams, Exec. Dir.

Founded: 1974. **Members:** 240. **Staff:** 12. **Budget:** $1,950,000. **Description:** Seeks to inspire and promote quality-oriented continuing education and training through the establishment of standards, policies and procedures for the objective and substantive evaluation of organizations seeking accredited status. **Computer Services:** database. **Formerly:** (1978) Continuing Education Council; (1988) Council for Noncollegiate Continuing Education. **Publications:** *Directory of ACCET Accredited Institutions Offering Continuing Education and Training Programs*, periodic. **Conventions/Meetings:** annual conference, workshops and seminars presented by experts in the various functional areas of education and training organizations (exhibits) - October/November.

8146 ■ American Association for Adult and Continuing Education (AAACE)

10111 Martin Luther King, Jr. Hwy., Ste.200C
Bowie, MD 20720
Ph: (301)459-6261
Fax: (301)459-6241
E-mail: aaace10@aol.com
URL: http://www.aaace.org
Contact: Cle Anderson, Mgr.

Founded: 1982. **Members:** 4,000. **Membership Dues:** individual, $85 (annual) ● institutional, $300 (annual) ● affiliate, $250 (annual) ● student, $60 (annual) ● retiree, $35 (annual). **Staff:** 2. **Budget:** $700,000. **Description:** Provides leadership in advancing adult education as a lifelong learning process. Serves as a central forum for a wide variety of adult and continuing education special interest groups. Works to stimulate local, state, and regional adult continuing education efforts; encourages mutual cooperation and support; monitors proposed legislation and offers testimony to congress. **Awards:** Cyril O. Houle Award. **Frequency:** annual. **Type:** recognition. **Recipient:** for outstanding literature in adult education ● Imogene Okes Award. **Frequency:** annual. **Type:** recognition. **Recipient:** for outstanding research in adult education ● Outstanding Adult Learner. **Frequency:** annual. **Type:** recognition ● President's Award. **Frequency:** annual. **Type:** recognition. **Recipient:** for exceptional and innovative leadership in adult and continuing education. **Computer Services:** Electronic publishing ● mailing lists. **Formed by Merger of:** Adult Education Association of the U.S.A.; National Association for Public Continuing Adult Education. **Publications:** *Adult Education Quarterly*. Journal. **Circulation:** 1,500 ● *Adult Learning*, bimonthly. Magazine. Includes book reviews and calendar of events. **Price:** included in membership dues. ISSN: 0739-2915. **Circulation:** 1,500. **Advertising:** accepted ● *Adult Learning Magazine for Practitioners*, bimonthly ● *Freedom Road*. Book ● *Workplace Literacy*. Monographs ● Membership Directory, annual. **Advertising:** accepted ● Reports. **Conventions/Meetings:** annual Adult Education Conference (exhibits) - usually October or November.

8147 ■ American Seminar Leaders Association (ASLA)

2405 E Washington Blvd.
Pasadena, CA 91104
Ph: (626)791-1211
Free: (800)801-1886
Fax: (626)798-0701
E-mail: info@asla.com
URL: http://www.asla.com
Contact: June Davidson, Pres.

Founded: 1988. **Membership Dues:** regular, $447 (annual). **Description:** Seminar and workshop leaders. Seeks to improve the professional skills of members and promotes improved marketing of seminar and workshop products and services. Facilitates exchange of information among members; conducts examinations; and develops and enforces standards of ethics and practice for seminar and workshop leaders. Conducts educational programs; makes available consulting and referral services; and provides discounts on educational programs and advertising to members. **Publications:** *Up Front*, quarterly. Newsletter ● *Who's Who in Seminar Leaders*, annual. Directory. Alternate Formats: online. **Conventions/Meetings:** periodic seminar ● annual Seminar Leaders Success Conference.

8148 ■ Association for Continuing Higher Education (ACHE)

PO Box 118067
Charleston, SC 29423-8067
Ph: (843)574-6658
Free: (800)807-2243
Fax: (803)574-6470
E-mail: irene.barrineau@tridenttech.edu
URL: http://www.acheinc.org
Contact: Ms. Michele D. Shinn, Exec. VP

Founded: 1939. **Members:** 1,900. **Membership Dues:** institutional, affiliate, $350 (annual) ● professional, $80 (annual). **Staff:** 2. **Budget:** $131,000. **Regional Groups:** 11. **Description:** Institutional members are accredited colleges or universities that offer credit and non-credit continuing education; individual members are persons currently or formerly on the faculty or staff of a university continuing education division and those interested in supporting the association's work. Promotes high standards for professional excellence, stimulates faculty leadership in constructive support of continuing higher education programs, and cooperates with other groups and organizations in the achievement of these goals. **Awards:** Creative Use of Technology Award. **Frequency:** annual. **Type:** recognition. **Recipient:** for innovative use of instructional and distance learning technologies in lifelong learning ● Distinguished Program Award. **Frequency:** annual. **Type:** recognition. **Recipient:** for outstanding credit and non-credit programs ● Minority Affairs Award. **Frequency:** annual. **Type:** recognition. **Recipient:** for innovative lifelong learning programs that demonstrate outstanding service to underserved populations. **Computer Services:** Mailing lists. **Committees:** Instructional Technology and Distance Learning. **Formerly:** (1973) Association of University Evening Colleges. **Publications:** *ACHE Membership Directory*, annual. **Price:** included in membership dues. **Circulation:** 1,600 ● *Five Minutes with ACHE*, 10/year. Newsletter. Includes calendar of events, member and association news, and outreach news. **Price:** included in membership dues. **Circulation:** 1,600. Alternate Formats: online ● *Journal of Continuing Higher Education*, 3/year. Reports and exchanges information based on research, observations, and experience. Includes book reviews. **Price:** included in membership dues; $50.00 /year for nonmembers (in U.S., Canada, Mexico); $60.00 /year for nonmembers (in other countries). ISSN: 0737-7363 ● *Proceedings of Annual Conference*, annual. **Price:** $15.00 for nonmembers; included in membership dues. Alternate Formats: online. **Conventions/Meetings:** annual conference (exhibits) - 2008 Nov. 8-11, Nashville, TN; 2009 Nov. 15-18, Philadelphia, PA.

8149 ■ Elderhostel, Inc. (EI)

11 Ave. de Lafayette
Boston, MA 02111-1746
Ph: (617)426-7788 (978)323-4141
Free: (800)454-5768
Fax: (617)426-0701
E-mail: registration@elderhostel.org
URL: http://www.elderhostel.org
Contact: James A. Moses, Pres./CEO

Founded: 1975. **Description:** Educators, leaders from labor and industry, and individuals interested in lifelong learning and the elderly. A network of more than 1,900 colleges, universities, independent schools, folk schools, and other educational institutions in over 90 countries, including the United States, Canada, England, Denmark, Sweden, Finland, Italy, Israel, Australia, and Norway. Offers special, low-cost, short-term residential academic programs for adults 55 years of age and over and their (younger) spouses or companions. Offers a wide range of noncredit liberal arts and science courses taught by college faculty. Believes retirement does not mean withdrawal, and later years can provide an opportunity to enjoy new experiences. Combines the traditions of education and hosteling inspired by youth hostels and folk schools in Europe. Provides financial aid (for U.S. programs only). **Telecommunication Services:** teletype, (877)426-2167. **Publications:** *Elderhostel Catalog*, 8/year. **Price:** free. **Circulation:** 600,000.

8150 ■ International Association for Continuing Education and Training (IACET)

8405 Greensboro Dr., Ste.800
McLean, VA 22102
Ph: (703)506-3275
Fax: (703)506-3266
E-mail: info@iacet.org
URL: http://www.iacet.org
Contact: Sara Meier, Exec. Dir.

Founded: 1968. **Members:** 700. **Membership Dues:** individual, $100 (annual) ● organization, $300 (annual) ● authorized provider, $675 (quinquennial). **Staff:** 5. **Budget:** $460,000. **Languages:** English, French, German, Italian, Russian, Spanish. **Description:** Continuing educational and training organizations, including colleges and universities; professional societies, associations, and corporate training groups; hospitals; individuals. Seeks to: strengthen educational and professional standards in the field of continuing education and training; ensure continuity in the development of the Continuing Education Unit and achieve consistency in its application. The CEU, defined as hours of participation in an organized continuing education activity, offers individuals a documented record of noncredit educational achievements and provides institutions and others a standard measure for gathering information useful in evaluating continuing education programs and determining public policy and legislation. Serves as a forum for policy development and as clearinghouse for CEU developments and methods. Works cooperatively with members and government agencies to promote development and appropriate use of the CEU, and to increase the quality of continuing education and training. Authorizes use of its CEU certification mark to member institutions and organizations following its guidelines. Conducts research and surveys; collects data. Maintains committees to examine problems in noncredit education and identify exemplary applications of the CEU. **Computer Services:** Mailing lists, of members. **Boards:** Directors. **Formerly:** (1989) Council on the Continuing Education Unit. **Publications:** *A Practical Handbook for Assessing Learning Outcomes in Continuing Education and Training*. **Price:** $27.00 ● *CEU Criteria and Guidelines* ● *Principles of Good Practice in Continuing Education* ● *Reporter*, quarterly. Newsletter ● Booklets ● Handbooks ● Reports. **Conventions/Meetings:** How To Become an Authorized Provider - workshop - 3/year.

8151 ■ Learning Resources Network (LERN)

PO Box 9
River Falls, WI 54022
Ph: (715)426-9777
Free: (800)678-5376
Fax: (715)426-9558
E-mail: info@lern.org
URL: http://www.lern.org
Contact: William A. Draves CAE, Pres.

Founded: 1974. **Members:** 5,000. **Membership Dues:** institution, $295 (annual) ● university, private/community college, trade/professional school, private industry, $395 (annual). **Staff:** 23. **Budget:** $2,000,000. **Regional Groups:** 6. **State Groups:** 1. **Description:** Represents college and university affiliated groups, community education organizations, associations, recreation departments, and learning networks; continuing professional educators and individuals interested in lifelong learning. Objectives are: to help people and communities start adult learning programs; to provide technical assistance to existing adult learning organizations; to promote alternative education and social change at the national level. Serves as a national technical assistance network in adult learning and noncredit programming. Provides speakers and technical assistance to members and nonmembers. Sponsors seminars; compiles statistics. **Libraries: Type:** reference; not open to the public. **Holdings:** 50,200; archival material, books, reports. **Subjects:** marketing, finance, customer service, brochure design, retention. **Awards:** Excellence in Practice Awards. **Frequency:** annual. **Type:** recognition ● Lifetime Achievement Award. **Frequency:** annual. **Type:** recognition ● Sam Brightman Award. **Frequency:** annual. **Type:** recognition. **Computer Services:** Online services, courses. **Formerly:** (1981) Free University Network. **Publications:** *Course Trends* ● *Course Trends in Adult Learning*, monthly ● *Front Line Leadership* ● *Marketing Recreation*, monthly ● Magazine ● Also publishes booklets and manuals. **Conventions/Meetings:** annual conference (exhibits) - always fall/winter.

8152 ■ National Council for Continuing Education and Training (NCCET)
PO Box 820062
Portland, OR 97282-1062
Ph: (503)233-1842
Fax: (503)232-1073
E-mail: rprather@valenciacc.edu
URL: http://www.nccet.org
Contact: Ruth Prather, Pres.

Founded: 1969. **Members:** 1,100. **Membership Dues:** individual, $50 (annual) ● institutional, $200 (annual). **Budget:** $85,000. **Description:** Community services and continuing education practitioners, primarily employed with community, technical, and junior colleges supporting life-long learning and workforce training. Aims to: provide a national unified voice to federal and state officials for community services and continuing education in community and junior colleges; foster individual institutional commitment to community services and continuing education; encourage the growth of community services and continuing education in response to community and economic development needs such as those of older adults, low-income groups, and women preparing for new careers. Provides consulting services to members. Maintains Speaker's Bureau. **Awards:** National Leadership Awards. **Frequency:** annual. **Type:** recognition. **Recipient:** for college administrator or staff member that works in the area of community services, continuing education and workforce development. **Computer Services:** Mailing lists, available to corporate partners. **Affiliated With:** American Association of Community Colleges. **Formerly:** (1998) National Council on Community Services and Continuing Education. **Publications:** *Catalyst*, 3/year. Journal. **Price:** included in membership dues; $40.00 /year for libraries. ISSN: 0739-9227. **Circulation:** 1,300. Alternate Formats: online ● *NCCET Abstract*, semiannual ● *NCCET Newsletter*, bimonthly. **Conventions/Meetings:** annual conference (exhibits) - usually October ● Leadership Institute - meeting - usually spring.

8153 ■ Senior Scholars (SS)
c/o Kathy Manos, Dir.
Off. of Continuing Educ.
341 Sears Bldg., CWRU
10900 Euclid Ave.
Cleveland, OH 44106-7116
Ph: (216)368-2090 (216)368-2000
Fax: (216)368-1861
E-mail: kgm2@po.cwru.edu
URL: http://www.case.edu/artsci/conted/senior.htm
Contact: Kathy Manos, Dir.

Founded: 1972. **Members:** 180. **Description:** Academic program for men and women age 50 and older. The program is designed for those who seek college-level work and intellectual stimulation but do not want or need academic credit. Offers an intersession and three 11-week seminars each semester. All programs are faculty led. Members may participate in all or part of each semester's program. **Formerly:** (1979) Institute for Retirement Studies.

8154 ■ University Continuing Education Association (UCEA)
1 Dupont Cir., Ste.615
Washington, DC 20036
Ph: (202)659-3130
Fax: (202)785-0374
E-mail: kjkohl@ucea.edu
URL: http://www.ucea.edu
Contact: Kay J. Kohl, Exec. Dir./CEO

Founded: 1915. **Members:** 435. **Membership Dues:** professional, $50 (annual) ● professional plus, $75 (annual). **Staff:** 9. **Regional Groups:** 6. **Multinational. Description:** Institutions of higher education, both public and private, that offer professional and continuing education programs, both degree and non-degree, to nontraditional students at the pre and post baccalaureate levels. Offers accelerated learning opportunities to practitioners through professional development seminars, modules and conferences. Collects and disseminates data on continuing education programs and trends. Compiles statistics on the field. Only those individuals who work for a member institution are eligible to become professional members. **Awards:** National Awards. **Frequency:** annual. **Type:** recognition. **Recipient:** for continued education programs and individuals in the field ● Outstanding Program Award. **Frequency:** periodic. **Type:** recognition. **Recipient:** for excellence in achieving educational objectives ● Regional Awards. **Frequency:** annual. **Type:** recognition. **Recipient:** for continued education programs and individuals in the field ● UCEA Excellence in Teaching Award. **Type:** recognition. **Recipient:** for individuals who have provided outstanding teaching, course development, mentoring of students, and service to continuing education. **Computer Services:** Mailing lists, of members. **Formerly:** (1981) National University Extension Association; (1996) National University Continuing Education Association. **Publications:** *Continuing Higher Education Review*, annual. Journal. **Price:** $27.00 in U.S.; $35.00 outside U.S. ● *Improving the Fit: How to Use Assessment Data to Connect University Curricula to Workforce Needs.* **Price:** $16.00 for members; $20.00 for nonmembers ● *Infocus: A Newsletter of the University Continuing Education Association*, 10/year. Presents news of legislative and governmental actions pertinent to continuing education, lifelong learning, extension programs, and related education. **Price:** $75.00/year (international); $85.00/year (in Canada); $90.00/year (in other countries). **Circulation:** 2,000 ● *Lifelong Learning Trends: A Profile of Continuing Higher Education*, biennial. **Price:** $31.95 for members; $39.95 for nonmembers ● *Post-Baccalaureate Futures: New Markets, Resources and Credentials.* **Price:** $34.50 ● *Steal These Ideas Please: Great Marketing Ideas for Continuing Education.* Book. **Price:** $35.00 for nonmembers; $25.00 for members ● *UCEA E-NEWS*, monthly. Newsletter. Contains update for members. Alternate Formats: online ● *Who's Who in College and University Professional and Continuing Education* ● Monographs. **Conventions/Meetings:** annual conference (exhibits) ● annual Executive Assembly - general assembly ● Summer Institute for Professionals - meeting.

8155 ■ Values and Visions
15 W 24th St., 10th Fl.
New York, NY 10010
E-mail: brussat@spiritualrx.com
URL: http://www.spiritualityhealth.com
Contact: Mary Ann Brussat, Co-Dir.

Founded: 1969. **Staff:** 3. **Description:** Interested individuals; clergy; religious groups; public librarians; teachers; discussion clubs; retreat centers; continuing education networks; community groups; professional associations of teachers, lawyers, clergy, doctors, family counselors, and citizen activist groups. Encourages spiritual literacy by reviewing and creating resources for people on spiritual journeys. Reviews books, films, videos, and spoken-word audios. **Computer Services:** database, reviews ● online services, review service. **Additional Websites:** http://www.spiritualityandpractice.com. **Telecommunication Services:** electronic bulletin board, Ecunet. **Formerly:** cultural information@svc.

Cooperative Education

8156 ■ Association of Cooperative Educators (ACE)
c/o The Cooperative Foundation
PO Box 64047
St. Paul, MN 55164
Ph: (703)578-1820
Fax: (651)355-5073
E-mail: leslie.mead@verizon.net
URL: http://www.ace.coop
Contact: Leslie Mead, Exec. Admin./Ed.

Membership Dues: professional, $50 (annual) ● associate, $35 (annual) ● organization, $150 (annual). **Multinational. Description:** Aims to strengthen cooperatives and the cooperative movement by promoting innovative educational responses to social and economic changes. Promotes cooperative research and works closely with universities, cooperatives, and supporting organizations for the coordination and collaboration on programs and projects. Provides its members a forum which highlights programs and practices that increase understanding, innovation, and professionalism in cooperative education. **Awards:** ACE Education Program Award. **Frequency:** annual. **Type:** recognition. **Recipient:** for new cooperative education programs that achieved pre-set goals and objectives through a planning and program implementation process ● Outstanding Contribution to ACE by an Organization. **Frequency:** annual. **Type:** recognition. **Recipient:** to recognize an organization providing special support to ACE ● Outstanding Contribution to Cooperative Education and Training Award. **Frequency:** annual. **Type:** recognition. **Recipient:** for development of training materials, publications, or leadership within the cooperative movement ● Professional Contribution Award. **Frequency:** annual. **Type:** recognition. **Recipient:** to a member whose work has contributed to the advancement of the stature of cooperative education and training ● The Reginald J. Cressman ACE Award. **Frequency:** annual. **Type:** recognition. **Recipient:** for a member's exemplary commitment to staff development ● The William Hlushko Award. **Frequency:** annual. **Type:** recognition. **Recipient:** for a young member's outstanding achievement as a cooperative educator. **Publications:** Newsletter, quarterly. Alternate Formats: online ● Brochure. Alternate Formats: online ● Proceedings, annual. Alternate Formats: online.

8157 ■ Cooperative Education and Internship Association (CEIA)
16 Santa Ana Pl.
Walnut Creek, CA 94598
Ph: (925)947-5581
Free: (800)824-0449
Fax: (925)906-0922
E-mail: info@ceiainc.org
URL: http://www.ceiainc.org
Contact: Anita Todd, Pres.

Founded: 1963. **Members:** 1,350. **Membership Dues:** student, $40 (annual) ● individual, $150 (annual) ● organizational (utmost 3 persons), $350 (annual). **Staff:** 5. **Budget:** $500,000. **Regional Groups:** 8. **Description:** Represents College administrators and faculty members, management personnel from business, industry, and government, others interested in cooperative education programs. (Cooperative education programs employ high school or higher education students for specific periods in off-campus work as a part of the student's academic program. The employment is related as closely as possible to the student's academic program and career interest.) Seeks to elevate the standards of cooperative education programs. Conducts specialized education courses; compiles statistics; operates research programs. Plans to maintain biographical archives.

Libraries: Type: reference. **Holdings:** archival material, audiovisuals, books, clippings, monographs, periodicals. **Awards:** Charles F. Kettering Achievement Award. **Frequency:** annual. **Type:** recognition. **Recipient:** to an employer from the industry, business or government who provides outstanding resources and service to the cooperative education field ● Cooperative Education Student Achievement Award. **Frequency:** annual. **Type:** recognition. **Recipient:** to an outstanding student enrolled in a four-year or five-year degree program who has participated in a Cooperative Education ● Dean Herman Schneider Achievement Award. **Frequency:** annual. **Type:** recognition. **Recipient:** to an outstanding educator from the faculty or administration ● James W. Wilson Award. **Frequency:** annual. **Type:** recognition. **Recipient:** for outstanding contributions to the promotion and advocacy of research activity in cooperative education ● Ralph W. Tyler Research Award. **Frequency:** annual. **Type:** recognition. **Recipient:** for outstanding and distinguished research in the field of cooperative education and internships. **Computer Services:** database, of member organizations ● mailing lists. **Committees:** Awards; Marketing & Public Relations; Professional Development; Research; Student Affairs; Two Year Colleges. **Special Interest Groups:** Career Counseling & Development; Community and Junior Colleges; Community Service and Co-op Ed.; Corporate Employers; Curriculum; Disability Issues; Engineering; Federal Employers; High School Co-op; HPBCUs; Information Systems; International Co-op; Placement and Co-op; Small Business Employers. **Formerly:** (2002) Cooperative Education Association. **Publications:** *Directory of CEA Membership*, annual. Membership Directory. **Price:** $110.00 ● *Journal of Cooperative Education and Internships*, 3/year. **Price:** $50.00 in U.S.; $60.00 outside U.S. Alternate Formats: online ● Newsletter, bimonthly. **Price:** included in membership dues. **Conventions/Meetings:** annual conference (exhibits).

8158 ■ Future Problem Solving Program International (FPSPI)
2015 Grant Pl.
Melbourne, FL 32901
Ph: (321)768-0074
Free: (800)256-1499
Fax: (321)768-0097
E-mail: mail@fpsp.org
URL: http://www.fpsp.org
Contact: Ms. Marianne Solomon, Exec. Dir.

Founded: 1974. **Members:** 200,000. **Membership Dues:** affiliate program, $325 (annual). **Staff:** 4. **Budget:** $900,000. **State Groups:** 43. **National Groups:** 3. **Languages:** English, Korean. **Multinational. Description:** Works as a yearlong curriculum project with competitive and non-competitive options involving 250,000 students worldwide. Helps students enlarge, enrich, and make more accurate their images of the future. Engages students in learning. Equips young people with the vision and skills needed to anticipate, and understand and solve the problems of tomorrow. Acts as an interdisciplinary program and its components meet the creative thinking, creative writing, leadership skills, and academic aptitude needs of gifted and traditional students - teaches students how to think not what to think. **Awards:** Beyonder. **Frequency:** annual. **Type:** recognition. **Recipient:** for exemplary community problem solving project ● Champion. **Frequency:** annual. **Type:** recognition. **Recipient:** for team booklet, individual booklet, scenario writing (international and group), CMPS and adult booklets ● John Daughtrey Award. **Frequency:** annual. **Type:** recognition. **Recipient:** for directors, evaluators, or staff the adults may be a part of an organized FPS program, a school, school district, a state education agency, or other support group such as a fraternal organization ● Keith Frampton. **Frequency:** annual. **Type:** recognition. **Recipient:** for outstanding FPS coaches; Keith Frampton was the head of the Burwood teacher's college in Australia and began the first Australia/New Zealand FPS program in 1988 ● Yes. **Frequency:** annual. **Type:** recognition. **Recipient:** for volunteers, administrators, and/or supervisors parents, and supervisors. **Divisions:** Grades 4-6 (Junior); Grades K-3 (Action-Based Problem Solving); Grades 7-9 (Middle); Grades 10-12 (Senior). **Formerly:** (2006) Future Problem Solving Program. **Publications:** *Annotated Readings, Research and Resources*, annual. Manual. **Price:** $30.00. **Circulation:** 2,000 ● *Coaches Handbook*. Handbooks ● *Community Problem Solving*. Video. **Price:** $10.00 ● *FPSP Catalog*, annual. Includes problem solving instructional material for grades 3-12. **Circulation:** 15,000. Alternate Formats: online ● *Future Problem Solving Six-Step Problem Solving Model*. Video. **Price:** $10.00 ● *Opening Doors to the Future*. Brochure. **Conventions/Meetings:** annual International Conference - competition, teams compete to advance to state/country level, then to international level.

8159 ■ National Commission for Cooperative Education (NCCE)
360 Huntington Ave., 384CP
Boston, MA 02115-5096
Ph: (617)373-3770
Fax: (617)373-3463
E-mail: ncce@neu.edu
URL: http://www.co-op.edu
Contact: Dr. Constantine N. Papadakis, Pres.

Founded: 1962. **Staff:** 3. **Description:** Educational institutions and employers. Represents the interests of individuals dedicated to the advancement of quality college cooperative education programs and will provide national leadership to encourage program quality and standards of excellence through: Research Projects, Benchmarking Studies, National Advocacy, Public Awareness Campaigns. Informs administrators, employers, and students about the advantages of cooperative education programs. **Awards:** National Co-op Scholarship. **Frequency:** annual. **Type:** scholarship. **Recipient:** for students with high school GPA of 3.5 (B) or better interested in Science, Math, Engineering and Technology. **Computer Services:** Information services, cooperative education resources. **Publications:** Report. Alternate Formats: online. **Conventions/Meetings:** annual Corporate Symposium, discussions and networking.

Cosmetology

8160 ■ American Association of Cosmetology Schools/Cosmetology Educators of America (AACS/CEA)
15825 N 71st St., Ste.100
Scottsdale, AZ 85254
Ph: (480)281-0431
Free: (800)831-1086
Fax: (480)905-0993
E-mail: jim@beautyschools.org
URL: http://www.beautyschools.org
Contact: Jim Cox, Exec. Dir.

Founded: 1924. **Members:** 1,700. **Membership Dues:** title school, $850 (annual) ● non-title school, $550 (annual) ● educator in nonmember school, $50 (annual). **Staff:** 3. **Description:** Owners and teachers in cosmetology schools. **Awards:** Educator of the Year. **Frequency:** annual. **Type:** recognition. **Committees:** AACS/TSA; Accreditation; ACE Grant; Advisory; Associate Member; Bylaws; CEA; Communications; Convention; Government Relations; Industry Partner Promotion; Membership; Special Events; State Relations. **Formerly:** (1965) Teachers' Division of National Association of Cosmetology Schools; (1985) Teachers' Educational Council - National Association of Cosmetology Schools; (1991) Teachers' Educational Council - National Association of Accredited Cosmetology Schools. **Publications:** *AACS Newsbreak*, quarterly. Newsletter. Updates on Washington and news affecting schools, business building articles, and beauty school news. **Circulation:** 3,000. **Advertising:** accepted ● *CEA Update*, quarterly. Newsletter. Features new trends and techniques to improve teaching skills. **Circulation:** 4,000. **Advertising:** accepted ● *Salon City Star*. Magazine. **Price:** free for members ● *Skin Inc.*. Magazine. **Price:** free for members. **Conventions/Meetings:** annual convention (exhibits) ● annual Spring Management - conference (exhibits).

Cosmology

8161 ■ Alexandria Society and Educational Foundation
Address Unknown since 2007

Description: Fosters the exploration and understanding of the relationships between cosmology, philosophy, myth, and society, and the world's spiritual, intellectual, and cultural traditions. **Divisions:** Concord Grove Educational Center of West Michigan. **Projects:** Sufi Studies Society. **Publications:** *Alexandria: Cosmology, Philosophy, Myth, and Culture*. Journal. Explores the intellectual, spiritual, and cultural traditions of the Western World, and what the humanities can contribute to contemporary life. **Conventions/Meetings:** conference ● workshop.

Counseling

8162 ■ American College Counseling Association (ACCA)
PO Box 791006
Baltimore, MD 21279-1006
Ph: (703)823-9800
Free: (800)347-6647
Fax: (703)461-9260
E-mail: rick.hanson@rockhurst.edu
URL: http://www.collegecounseling.org
Contact: Dr. Rick Hanson, Pres.

Founded: 1991. **Members:** 1,600. **Membership Dues:** professional, regular, $40 (annual) ● student, new professional, $30 (annual). **Budget:** $133,500. **State Groups:** 19. **Multinational. Description:** Works to advance the practice of college counseling. Promotes ethical practice and communication among members; encourages cooperation with other related organizations; provides advocacy for the profession. **Libraries: Type:** open to the public; by appointment only; reference. **Holdings:** articles, periodicals. **Subjects:** college, school, mental health, career counseling. **Awards:** Advocacy for College Counseling. **Frequency:** annual. **Type:** recognition ● College Counseling Research Grants. **Frequency:** annual. **Type:** grant. **Recipient:** for research projects focusing on college counseling ● Emerging Leaders. **Frequency:** annual. **Type:** grant. **Recipient:** for graduate students or new professionals who are interested in pursuing leadership roles within the organization; to attend training at the national conference ● Meritorious Service Award. **Frequency:** annual. **Type:** recognition ● Professional Leadership Award. **Frequency:** annual. **Type:** recognition. **Recipient:** to members. **Committees:** Awards; Budget and Finance; By-Laws; Conference; Corporate Sponsorship; Graduate Students; Media; Professional Advocacy and Public Awareness; Research; State Divisions; Strategic Planning. **Affiliated With:** American Counseling Association. **Publications:** *ACCA Visions*, quarterly. Newsletter. Alternate Formats: online ● *College Counseling Advocacy Booklet*. Alternate Formats: online ● *Journal of College Counseling*, semiannual. Alternate Formats: online. **Conventions/Meetings:** biennial conference (exhibits).

8163 ■ American School Counselor Association (ASCA)
1101 King St., Ste.625
Alexandria, VA 22314
Ph: (703)683-2722
Free: (800)306-4722
Fax: (703)683-1619
E-mail: asca@schoolcounselor.org
URL: http://www.schoolcounselor.org
Contact: Richard Wong, Exec. Dir.

Founded: 1952. **Members:** 17,000. **Membership Dues:** professional, affiliate, $115 (annual) ● student, retired, $60 (annual). **Staff:** 7. **Budget:** $2,500,000. **Regional Groups:** 4. **State Groups:** 51. **Multinational. Description:** Supports school counselors' efforts to help students focus on academic, personal/

social and career development so they not only achieve success in school but are prepared to lead fulfilling lives as responsible members of society; provides professional development, publications and other resources, research and advocacy, governmental and public relations. Serves as liaison among members and counselors in other settings; disseminates educational, professional, and scientific materials. **Computer Services:** Online services, resource center. **Boards:** Governing. **Committees:** Bylaws; Ethics; Nominations and Elections; Position Statements and Resolutions; Public Policy. **Publications:** *ASCA School Counselor*, bimonthly, always January, March, May, July, September and November. Magazine. Provides news about the profession. **Price:** included in membership dues. **Circulation:** 15,000. **Advertising:** accepted ● *Professional School Counseling*, 5/year. Journal. **Price:** included in membership dues; $90.00 /year for nonmembers. ISSN: 1906-2407. **Circulation:** 15,000. **Advertising:** accepted. Alternate Formats: microform ● Books ● Manuals ● Monographs. **Conventions/Meetings:** annual meeting (exhibits) ● annual convention (exhibits) - 2008 June 28-July 1, Atlanta, GA; 2009 June 28-July 1, Dallas, TX; 2010 July 3-6, Boston, MA; 2011 June 25-28, Seattle, WA.

8164 ■ American Schools Association (ASA)

PO Box 577820
Chicago, IL 60657-7820
Free: (800)230-2263
Fax: (773)782-0113
E-mail: asaceu@hotmail.com
URL: http://asaceu.com
Founded: 1914. **Budget:** $200,000. **Description:** Offers continuing education on a home-study basis for license/certificate maintenance for Rehabilitation Professionals, substance abuse counselors, certified counselors, marriage and family therapists, licensed social workers, and registered nurses nationwide. Distributes training videos for vocational rehabilitation purposes. **Convention/Meeting:** none. **Programs:** Home Study. **Publications:** *A Challenge to America: The Americans with Disabilities Act*. Video ● *Changes: Transition Planning for Persons with Disabilities*. Video ● *Choices: Legal Rights of Persons with Disabilities*. Video ● *Directory of College Transfer Information*, biennial ● *Get a Job: Selling, Marketing and Willing Community Employment*. Video ● *Getting Around: Community Travel Training-Methods and Skills*. Video ● *Job Coaching*. Video.

8165 ■ Association for Counselor Education and Supervision (ACES)

c/o Judith C. Durham, APRN, Pres.
St. Joseph College
Dept. of Counselor Education
1678 Asylum Ave.
West Hartford, CT 06117
Ph: (860)231-6778
Free: (800)347-6647
Fax: (860)231-5774
E-mail: jdurham@sjc.edu
URL: http://www.acesonline.net
Contact: Judith C. Durham APRN, Pres.
Founded: 1964. **Members:** 2,494. **Membership Dues:** professional/regular, $151 (annual) ● student, retired, $85 (annual). **Regional Groups:** 5. **Description:** Represents the interests of persons engaged in the professional preparation of counselors or who are responsible for supervising professional counselors in a wide variety of work settings. Works to improve the education, credentialing and supervision of counselors through accreditation and professional development activities. Disseminates information on current and relevant research, practices, ethical standards and problems related to the profession. Maintains archives on counselor education and supervision. **Libraries: Type:** reference. **Holdings:** 5,000. **Subjects:** counseling in all aspects and settings. **Awards:** ACES Research Grants. **Frequency:** annual. **Type:** grant. **Recipient:** to support deserving ACES research ● Certificates of Appreciation. **Frequency:** annual. **Type:** recognition. **Recipient:** to an individual who has rendered worthy service to the association or profession ● Counseling Vision and Innovation Award. **Frequency:** annual. **Type:** recognition. **Recipient:** to an individual who has shown exemplary commitment, vision, creativity and future thinking and championed transformational leadership ● Distinguished Mentor Award. **Frequency:** annual. **Type:** recognition. **Recipient:** to an individual who has been a significant mentor to graduate counseling students, emerging counseling educators, supervisors and counselors ● Distinguished Professional Service Award. **Frequency:** annual. **Type:** recognition. **Recipient:** for outstanding service by a counselor educator and a counselor supervisor ● Outstanding Dissertation Award. **Frequency:** annual. **Type:** recognition. **Recipient:** to a counseling graduate student who is a member of ACES and whose dissertation was successfully defended during the past academic year ● Outstanding Graduate Student Leadership Award. **Frequency:** annual. **Type:** recognition. **Recipient:** to a graduate student who has provided outstanding leadership to counselor education and ACES and the counseling profession ● Outstanding State ACES Division Award. **Frequency:** annual. **Type:** recognition ● Professional Leadership Award. **Frequency:** annual. **Type:** recognition. **Recipient:** for excellence in leadership by an officer, committee person or other leader or major contributor to ACES ● Publication in Counselor Education and Supervision Award. **Frequency:** annual. **Type:** recognition. **Recipient:** for significant publishing effort by an ACES member focusing on the education and supervision of counselors ● Recognition of Retirees and Deceased. **Frequency:** annual. **Type:** recognition. **Recipient:** for retirees and deceased ACES members ● Research in Counselor Education and Supervision Award. **Frequency:** annual. **Type:** recognition. **Recipient:** for significant research project by members of ACES ● Robert Frank Outstanding Counselor Education Program Award. **Frequency:** annual. **Type:** recognition. **Recipient:** for a counselor education program that exemplifies the importance of excellence through standards and innovation ● Robert Stripling Award for Excellence in Standards. **Frequency:** annual. **Type:** recognition. **Recipient:** to a person who has shown commitment to leadership in the advancement of standards for counselor education and supervision. **Committees:** Graduate Students; Publications; Research Grants; Standing. **Affiliated With:** American Counseling Association. **Publications:** *ACES Spectrum Newsletter*, quarterly. Focuses on the accreditation process and professional development activities for counselors. **Price:** included in membership dues ● *Counselor Education and Supervision*, quarterly. **Price:** free for members; $50.00 /year for nonmembers; $70.00 /year for institutions. ISSN: 0011-0035. **Circulation:** 3,926 ● Monographs. **Conventions/Meetings:** biennial convention (exhibits) ● annual meeting, held in conjunction with the ACA (exhibits).

8166 ■ Association for Spiritual, Ethical and Religious Values in Counseling (ASERVIC)

PO Box 161250
Orlando, FL 32816
Free: (800)347-6647
E-mail: erobinso@email.ucf.edu
URL: http://www.aservic.org
Contact: Michele Briggs, Pres.-Elect
Founded: 1955. **Members:** 1,504. **Membership Dues:** professional/regular (includes required ACA membership), $151 (annual) ● student/retired (includes required ACA membership), $85 (annual). **State Groups:** 20. **Description:** A division of American Counseling Association (see separate entry). Represents the interests of counselors and other human development professionals who are convinced that religious, spiritual and other human values are essential to the full development of the person and to the discipline of counseling. Strives to understand and find ways to integrate religious, spiritual and other values in counseling and other developmental processes. **Formerly:** (1958) Catholic Counselors in APGA; (1960) National Conference of Diocesan Guidance Councils; (1962) National Conference of Catholic Guidance Councils; (1976) National Catholic Guidance Conference; (1993) Association for Religious and Value Issues in Counseling. **Publications:** *ASERVIC Interaction*, quarterly. Newsletter. Covers ethical, moral, religious, and spiritual values in counseling and psychotherapy. Includes book reviews and calendar of events. **Price:** included in membership dues; $8.00 /year for nonmembers. ISSN: 0743-0426. **Circulation:** 2,478. Alternate Formats: online ● *Counseling and Values*, 3/year. Journal. **Price:** free for members; $41.00 /year for nonmembers; $50.00 /year for institutions. ISSN: 0160-7960. **Circulation:** 2,478. **Advertising:** accepted. Alternate Formats: microform. **Conventions/Meetings:** annual convention, held in conjunction with ACA (exhibits) - always March or April.

8167 ■ Association for University and College Counseling Center Directors (AUCCCD)

c/o Charles O. Davidshofer, PhD, Treas.
Colorado State Univ.
4112 Attleboro Ct.
Fort Collins, CO 80525
Ph: (970)491-0745
E-mail: cdavidshofer@ucc.colostate.edu
URL: http://www.aucccd.org
Contact: Charles O. Davidshofer PhD, Treas.
Founded: 1951. **Members:** 626. **Membership Dues:** regular, $130 (annual). **Staff:** 12. **Budget:** $35,000. **Description:** Counseling center directors in the U.S., Mexico, Australia, England, and Canada. Provides opportunities for directors of counseling centers to meet and discuss clinical and management issues, trends in student behavior, and ways to improve services. Conducts research; annually prepares database of research findings. **Awards:** Diversity Leadership Scholarship. **Frequency:** annual. **Type:** scholarship. **Recipient:** to individuals who want to become counseling center director ● Lifetime Achievement Award. **Frequency:** annual. **Type:** recognition. **Recipient:** for members with outstanding service to AUCCCD and exemplary leadership. **Computer Services:** database ● mailing lists. **Publications:** *Proceedings of Annual Meeting*, semiannual. Alternate Formats: online ● Newsletter. Alternate Formats: online. **Conventions/Meetings:** annual conference (exhibits) - October or November. 2008 Oct. 17-21, Fort Worth, TX.

8168 ■ Council for Accreditation of Counseling and Related Educational Programs (CACREP)

5999 Stevenson Ave.
Alexandria, VA 22304
Ph: (703)823-9800
Free: (800)347-6647
Fax: (703)823-1581
E-mail: cacrep@cacrep.org
URL: http://www.cacrep.org
Contact: Jack Culbreth, Chm.
Founded: 1981. **Nonmembership**. **Description:** Seeks to promote the advancement of education by establishing and administering a program for the accreditation of graduate programs at colleges and universities in the fields of counseling and related educational programs, and of programs in counselor education and supervision. **Publications:** *The CACREP Connection*. Newsletter. Alternate Formats: online ● *Directory of CACREP Accredited Programs*. Alternate Formats: online.

8169 ■ International Association of Counseling Services (IACS)

101 S Whiting St., Ste.211
Alexandria, VA 22304
Ph: (703)823-9840
Fax: (703)823-9843
E-mail: iacsinc@earthlink.net
URL: http://www.iacsinc.org
Contact: Nancy E. Roncketti, Exec. Off.
Founded: 1972. **Members:** 170. **Membership Dues:** accredited university/college counseling service, $800 (annual). **Staff:** 2. **Budget:** $120,000. **Multinational**. **Description:** Represents accredited university and four-year college counseling services in the U.S., Canada, and Australia. Fosters communications and cooperation among counseling services. **Boards:** University and College Counseling Services Board of

Accreditation. **Formerly:** American Board on Counseling Services; American Board on Professional Standards in Vocational Counseling. **Publications:** *Counseling Services*, quarterly. Newsletter. Alternate Formats: online ● *National Survey of Counseling Center Directors*, annual. **Price:** free. **Conventions/Meetings:** annual board meeting.

8170 ■ National Academic Advising Association (NACADA)
Kansas State Univ.
2323 Anderson Ave., Ste.225
Manhattan, KS 66502-2912
Ph: (785)532-5717 (785)532-7815
Fax: (785)532-7732
E-mail: nacada@ksu.edu
URL: http://www.nacada.ksu.edu
Contact: Roberta Flaherty, Exec. Dir.

Founded: 1979. **Members:** 9,200. **Membership Dues:** individual, allied, $55 (annual) ● retired, $30 (annual) ● student, $20 (annual) ● institutional, $200 (annual). **Staff:** 13. **Budget:** $2,400,000. **Regional Groups:** 10. **Multinational. Description:** Academic program advisors, faculty, administrators, counselors, and others concerned with the intellectual, personal, and career development of students in all types of postsecondary educational institutions. Works to support and promotes professional growth of academic advising and academic advisers. Provides a forum for discussion, debate, and exchange of ideas regarding academic advising. Serves as advocate for standards and quality programs in academic advising. Operates consultants' bureau to assist advising services on college campuses. Maintains placement service, speakers' bureau, and information clearinghouse. **Awards:** Campus Advising Awards. **Frequency:** annual. **Type:** recognition. **Recipient:** for outstanding academic advising, faculty advising, or advising administration ● Electronic Publication Awards. **Frequency:** annual. **Type:** recognition. **Recipient:** for outstanding electronic advising resources ● Outstanding Advising. **Frequency:** annual. **Type:** recognition. **Recipient:** for outstanding individual advisors ● Outstanding Advising Program. **Frequency:** annual. **Type:** recognition. **Recipient:** for outstanding advising programs ● Research Grant. **Frequency:** annual. **Type:** grant. **Recipient:** for a research related to advising ● **Frequency:** annual. **Type:** scholarship. **Recipient:** for graduate study of a member ● Service to NACADA. **Frequency:** annual. **Type:** recognition. **Recipient:** for service to the association ● Virginia N. Gordon Award. **Frequency:** annual. **Type:** recognition. **Recipient:** for contributions to the field of advising. **Computer Services:** Mailing lists, of members. **Commissions:** Advising Administration; Advising Adult Learners; Advising Business Majors; Advising Graduate and Professional Students; Advising Student Athletes; Advising Students with Disabilities; Advising Transfer Students; Advising Undecided/Exploratory Students; Advisor Training and Development; Assessment of Advising; Engineering and Science Advising; ESL and International Student Advising; Faculty Advising; LGBTA; Liberal Arts Advisors; Multicultural Concerns; Small Colleges and Universities; Technology in Advising; Theory and Philosophy of Advising; Two-Year Colleges. **Committees:** Awards; Diversity; Membership; Professional Development; Research. **Special Interest Groups:** Advising Fine Arts Students; Advising High Achieving Students; Canada; Distance Education; First-Generation College Student Advising; Health Professions Advising; High School to College Advising; Native American and Tribal College; New Advising Professionals; Peer Advising and Mentoring; Pre-Law Advising; Probation/Dismissal/Reinstatement Issues; Study Abroad Advising. **Publications:** *Monograph Series on Current Issues*, periodic. **Price:** $40.00 ● *NACADA Academic Advising Today*, quarterly. Newsletter. Covers the advising profession and current issues in advising. Alternate Formats: online ● *NACADA Highlights*, monthly. Newsletter. Discusses association's events and activities. **Price:** included in membership dues. Alternate Formats: online ● *NACADA Journal*, semiannual. Includes book reviews. **Price:** included in membership dues; $50.00 /year for nonmembers. ISSN: 0271-9517. **Circulation:** 9,000. **Advertising:** accepted. Alternate Formats: microform. **Conventions/Meetings:** annual Academic Advising Administrator's Institute - workshop - always January or February ● annual Assessment of Academic Advising Institute - workshop, training in assessment as applies to academic advising ● annual conference, with over 300 sessions addressing issues in academic advising - always September or October. 2008 Oct. 1-4, Chicago, IL ● annual conference, includes ten events on academic advising - always March or May ● annual Summer Institutes - workshop, comprehensive and intensive study of all aspects of academic advising - every summer.

8171 ■ National Association of Academic Advisors for Athletics (N4A)
NC State Univ.
Campus Box 8509
Raleigh, NC 27695
Ph: (919)513-1007 (919)513-1003
Fax: (919)513-0541
E-mail: nfoura_4@ncsu.edu
URL: http://www.nfoura.org
Contact: Phil Hughes, Pres.

Founded: 1975. **Members:** 550. **Membership Dues:** professional, affiliate, $100 (annual) ● student, $50 (annual) ● alumnus, $25 (annual). **Staff:** 1. **Regional Groups:** 5. **Description:** Represents the interests of academic counselors and advisers of student athletes participating in intercollegiate athletics. Aims to promote academic achievement and personal development among student athletes. Seeks to help the student athlete put his/her academic, athletic, and social life in perspective; assists student athletes in maintaining their athletic eligibility and achieving a viable education leading to graduation. Conducts athletic/academic research. **Awards:** Distinguished Service Award. **Frequency:** annual. **Type:** recognition. **Recipient:** to a member who has demonstrated leadership performance in N4A ● Lan Hewlett Award. **Frequency:** annual. **Type:** recognition. **Recipient:** to an advisor who has demonstrated significant contributions to the field through publications or professional involvement/development ● Professional Promise Award. **Frequency:** annual. **Type:** recognition. **Recipient:** to professionals who have outstanding performance as an academic advisor, life skills coordinator or administrator ● Wilma Rudolph Student Athlete Award. **Frequency:** annual. **Type:** recognition. **Recipient:** to student athletes who have overcome personal, academic or emotional odds to achieve academic success while participating in intercollegiate athletics. **Commissions:** Two-Year College. **Committees:** Ethnic Concerns; Learning Disabilities; Legislative Affairs; Life Skills; Research; Student-Athlete Recognition. **Programs:** Mentoring. **Formerly:** (1985) National Association of Academic Advisors. **Publications:** *Academic Athletic Journal*, semiannual. Presents research reports related to athletics and academics in higher education. **Price:** included in membership dues; $5.00 /year for nonmembers. **Circulation:** 300. **Advertising:** accepted ● *The N4A News*, 3/year. Newsletter. Contains articles, committee, regional and membership highlights and resource information. **Price:** included in membership dues. Alternate Formats: online. **Conventions/Meetings:** annual convention (exhibits) ● annual regional meeting.

Crafts

8172 ■ Precious Metal Clay Guild
PO Box 3000
Denville, NJ 07834
Ph: (859)586-0595
Free: (866)315-6487
E-mail: office@pmcguild.com
URL: http://www.pmcguild.com
Contact: Cece Wire, Exec. Dir.

Founded: 1997. **Membership Dues:** regular, in U.S. and Canada, $25 (annual) ● international, $35 (annual) ● regular, in U.S. and Canada, $45 (biennial) ● international, $55 (biennial) ● regular, in U.S. and Canada, $65 (triennial) ● international, $75 (triennial). **Multinational. Description:** Promotes the instruction, research, teaching and exhibition of Precious Metal Clay (PMC). Provides a forum for artists to learn about PMC and to connect with other artists and suppliers. **Telecommunication Services:** electronic mail, cece@pmcguild.com. **Publications:** *Getting Started with PMC*. Booklet. Alternate Formats: online ● *Studio PMC*, quarterly. Magazine. **Price:** included in membership dues. Alternate Formats: online ● Membership Directory. Alternate Formats: online. **Conventions/Meetings:** biennial conference.

Creative Education

8173 ■ Creative Education Foundation (CEF)
289 Bay Rd.
Hadley, MA 01035
Ph: (413)559-6614
Free: (800)447-2774
Fax: (413)559-6615
E-mail: contact@creativeeducationfoundation.org
URL: http://www.creativeeducationfoundation.org
Contact: Victoria Cliche, Exec. Dir.

Founded: 1954. **Membership Dues:** guild, $185 (annual) ● associate, $85 (annual) ● full-time student, $30 (annual). **Staff:** 2. **Budget:** $800,000. **Description:** Aims to advance human fulfillment, to expand the use of deliberate creativity and to inspire worldwide imaginative change for individuals and organizations. Promotes and develops creativity and innovation as it pursues its mission by officer training through public programs such as the Creative Problem Solving Institute. Provides books, periodicals and other publications. Engages networking activities and encourages the overall expansion of knowledge about creativity and innovation. **Programs:** CEF YouthWise. **Publications:** *Creativity In Action*, monthly. Journal. **Price:** $50.00 in U.S.; $55.00 in Canada and Mexico; $60.00 overseas. Alternate Formats: online ● *Journal of Creative Behavior*, quarterly. Features current research in creative thinking. **Price:** $75.00 /year for individuals in U.S.; $105.00 /year for institutions in U.S.; $85.00 /year for individuals outside U.S.; $120.00 /year for institutions outside U.S. ISSN: 0022-0175. **Circulation:** 2,000. **Conventions/Meetings:** annual Creative Problem-Solving Institute - conference - usually 3rd or 4th week of June.

Culinary Arts

8174 ■ The Culinary Trust (TCT)
PO Box 273
New York, NY 10013
Ph: (646)224-6989
Free: (888)345-4666
E-mail: info@theculinarytrust.com
URL: http://www.theculinarytrust.com
Contact: Andrew F. Smith, Chm.

Founded: 1984. **Staff:** 1. **Nonmembership. Multinational. Description:** Celebrates the past and future through scholarship, grant and preservation programs that encourage and enable professionals in the pursuit of the culinary arts. **Awards:** Harry A. Bell Grant for Food Writers. **Frequency:** annual. **Type:** grant. **Recipient:** for a food writer ● International Scholarship Program. **Frequency:** annual. **Type:** scholarship. **Recipient:** for students and career professionals; requires 3.0 grade point average or higher and an application fee ● Linda D. Russo Food Writers Grant. **Frequency:** periodic. **Type:** grant. **Recipient:** for a food writer ● Richard Sax Memorial Hunger Relief Fund. **Frequency:** annual. **Type:** grant. **Recipient:** to a hunger relief organization. **Committees:** Cookbook Preservation; Food Writers Grants; Hunger Relief; Library Research Guide; Scholarship. **Formerly:** (1992) Cooking Advancement Research and Education Foundation; (2004) International Association of Culinary Professionals Foundation. **Publications:** Annual Report, annual. **Circulation:** 4,000. **Conventions/Meetings:** quarterly board meeting ● annual conference - April.

Cultural Exchange

8175 ■ AFS International
71 W 23rd St., 17th Fl.
New York, NY 10010
Ph: (212)807-8686
Free: (800)AFS-INFO
Fax: (212)807-1001
E-mail: info@afs.org
URL: http://www.afs.org
Contact: Francisco Cazal, Pres./CEO

Founded: 1914. **National Groups:** 50. **Multinational. Description:** International student exchange dedicated to providing intercultural learning opportunities to help people develop the knowledge, skills, and understanding to create a more peaceful world. **Awards:** Galatti Award. **Frequency:** annual. **Type:** recognition. **Recipient:** for up to 3 volunteers; for outstanding service and advancing intercultural learning and global friendship in pursuit of a more peaceful world. **Telecommunication Services:** electronic mail, info.center@afs.org. **Formerly:** American Field Service. **Publications:** Annual Report, annual. Alternate Formats: online.

8176 ■ Associates in Cultural Exchange (ACE)
200 W Mercer St., Ste.108
Seattle, WA 98119-3958
Ph: (206)217-9644
Fax: (206)217-9643
E-mail: ace@cultural.org
URL: http://www.cultural.org
Contact: Mr. David B. Woodward, Pres./CEO

Founded: 1973. **Staff:** 152. **Description:** Works to advance international and intercultural understanding through a broad range of programs and services. **Formerly:** (2004) American Cultural Exchange.

8177 ■ Cross Cultural Collaborative (CCC)
45 Auburn St.
Brookline, MA 02446
Ph: (617)277-0482
Fax: (801)912-3830
E-mail: aba@culturalcollaborative.org
URL: http://www.culturalcollaborative.org
Contact: Ellie Schimelman, Pres./Clerk

Multinational. Description: Promotes cultural exchange and understanding. Offers programs that emphasize multigenerational and multicultural collaborations and encourage participants to find rewards in different forms of creativity. Invites artists and scholars from all over the world to work with Ghanaians on collaborative projects that range from mosaic walls to documentary films.

Curriculum

8178 ■ Association for Supervision and Curriculum Development (ASCD)
1703 N Beauregard St.
Alexandria, VA 22311-1714
Ph: (703)578-9600
Free: (800)933-2723
Fax: (703)575-5400
E-mail: member@ascd.org
URL: http://www.ascd.org
Contact: Nancy DeFord, Pres.

Founded: 1943. **Members:** 160,000. **Membership Dues:** premium, $219 (annual) ● comprehensive, $89 (annual) ● basic, $49 (annual) ● student, $25 (annual) ● express, constituent, $29 (annual). **Staff:** 180. **Budget:** $40,000,000. **Multinational. Description:** Provides education information services, offers cutting-edge professional development for effective teaching and learning, and supports activities to provide educational quality for all students. Members reside in 135 countries and include principals, teachers, superintendents, professors of education and other educators. **Libraries: Type:** open to the public. **Holdings:** 1,000; periodicals, reports. **Subjects:** education. **Awards:** Outstanding Young Educator Award. **Frequency:** annual. **Type:** monetary. **Recipient:** for an education professional, 40 years of age or younger, who demonstrates exemplary commitment and exceptional contribution to the profession. **Computer Services:** database ● online services, library. **Telecommunication Services:** electronic mail, ndeford@cox.net. **Programs:** Health in Education; Understanding by Design. **Projects:** Flexible Curriculum; Leadership/Supervision; Policy Analysis; Restructuring the Teaching Profession; Teacher Certification; Urban Education. **Formed by Merger of:** Department of Supervisors and Directors of Instruction (of NEA); Society for Curriculum Development. **Formerly:** (1946) Department of Supervision and Curriculum Development (of NEA). **Publications:** *Association for Supervision and Curriculum Development—Yearbook*, annual. **Price:** included in membership dues. **Circulation:** 79,000. Alternate Formats: microform ● *Education Update*, monthly. Newsletter. Discusses the improvement of curriculum, instruction, and supervision in elementary and secondary education. **Price:** included in membership dues ● *Educational Leadership*, 8/year. Magazine. Contains information about teaching and learning, new ideas and practices relevant to practicing educators. **Price:** $36.00. **Circulation:** 175,000. **Advertising:** accepted. Alternate Formats: online. Also Cited As: *EL* ● *Infobrief*, quarterly. Newsletter. Provides concise information on current education issues to administrators, teachers, policymakers, journalists and others. **Price:** included in membership dues; $12.50 for nonmembers. Alternate Formats: online. Also Cited As: *IFB* ● *Journal of Curriculum and Supervision*, quarterly. Includes abstracts of selected doctoral dissertations. **Price:** $39.00 /year for members; $49.00 /year for nonmembers. **Circulation:** 5,800. Alternate Formats: microform ● Videos ● Audiotapes ● Booklets ● Books. **Conventions/Meetings:** annual conference (exhibits) - 2009 Mar. 14-16, Orlando, FL; 2010 Mar. 6-8, San Antonio, TX; 2011 Mar. 26-28, San Francisco, CA.

8179 ■ Center for Critical Thinking
PO Box 220
Dillon Beach, CA 94929
Ph: (707)878-9100
Free: (800)833-3645
Fax: (707)878-9111
E-mail: cct@criticalthinking.org
URL: http://www.criticalthinking.org
Contact: Dr. Richard Paul, Dir. of Professional Development

Founded: 1980. **Description:** Scholars and educators working to implement high standards of critical thinking instruction at all levels of education. Provides educational programs and staff development services; conducts research programs. **Libraries: Type:** reference. **Holdings:** books, video recordings. **Affiliated With:** American Federation of Teachers; Association for Supervision and Curriculum Development; National Education Association. **Formerly:** (1990) Center for Critical Thinking and Moral Critique. **Conventions/Meetings:** annual International Conference on Critical Thinking, with sales desk of products.

8180 ■ Coalition of Essential Schools (CES)
1814 Franklin St., Ste.700
Oakland, CA 94612
Ph: (510)433-1451 (510)433-1915
Fax: (510)433-1455
E-mail: lcohen@essentialschools.org
URL: http://www.essentialschools.org
Contact: Lewis Cohen, Exec. Dir.

Founded: 1984. **Members:** 350. **Staff:** 13. **Regional Groups:** 24. **Description:** Network of schools and regional centers. Focuses on helping students learn to use their minds. Asserts that teachers should work more as "coaches than as deliverers of information". **Publications:** *Horace*, quarterly. Newsletter. **Price:** $35.00. **Circulation:** 20,000. Alternate Formats: online ● *Membership List*, periodic. Membership Directory ● Brochure. Contains publications list. **Conventions/Meetings:** annual Fall Forum - meeting - November ● seminar, covers topics related to school change and reform.

8181 ■ High/Scope Educational Research Foundation
600 N River St.
Ypsilanti, MI 48198
Ph: (734)485-2000
Free: (800)407-7377
Fax: (734)485-0704
E-mail: info@highscope.org
URL: http://www.highscope.org
Contact: Ms. Kathleen Woodard, Marketing and Communications Dir.

Founded: 1970. **Members:** 1,300. **Membership Dues:** individual, $40 (annual) ● institution, $500 (annual). **Staff:** 68. **Budget:** $6,000,000. **Multinational. Description:** Works to improve the life chances of children and youth by promoting high-quality educational programs. **Programs:** Assessment Training; Computers in Early Childhood Education; Consultative Group on International Early Childhood Care and Development; Elementary Teacher Institutes; IDEAS Institute for Teenagers; In-service Training; Intergenerational; Lead Teacher Training; Movement and Music Workshops; Preschool Teacher Institutes; Youth Development. **Publications:** *Extensions: Newsletter of High/Scope Curriculum*, bimonthly. Contains information for infant/toddler, preschool and kindergarten teachers, trainers, administrators, parents, and day care providers. **Price:** $30.00 /year for nonmembers; included in membership dues. ISSN: 0892-5135. **Circulation:** 1,800 ● *High/Scope ReSource: A Magazine for Educators*, quarterly. Focuses on research and curriculum information for early childhood educators. Includes book reviews, and a catalog of books, recordings, audiovisual. **Price:** included in membership dues. ISSN: 0887-2007. **Circulation:** 200,000 ● Also publishes child observation materials for use in early education programs, books, monographs and videos. **Conventions/Meetings:** annual international conference (exhibits) - always May.

8182 ■ World Council for Curriculum and Instruction (WCCI)
c/o Dr. Estela C. Matriano, Exec. Dir.
Alliant Intl. Univ.
Graduate School of Educ.
10455 Pomerado Rd.
San Diego, CA 92131
Ph: (858)635-4718
Fax: (858)635-4714
E-mail: wcci@alliant.edu
URL: http://www.wcci-international.org
Contact: Dr. Estela C. Matriano, Exec. Dir.

Founded: 1971. **Members:** 900. **Membership Dues:** life, $1,000 ● institutional, $100 (annual) ● individual, $65 (annual) ● individual from developing country, student, $25 (annual) ● life (from developing country), $500 ● full-time student from developing country, $20 (annual). **Staff:** 1. **Budget:** $25,000. **Regional Groups:** 10. **Description:** Aims to advance the achievement of a just and peaceful world community. Promotes a person-to-person contact and professional relationship. Works to collaborate curriculum and instruction projects. Provides dialogue in global educational and social issues. Promotes exchanges of ideas, concerns and solutions to problems. **Libraries: Type:** reference. **Holdings:** articles, books, papers. **Subjects:** peace education, human rights, environmental concerns, culture of peace. **Awards:** Masako Shoji Scholarship. **Frequency:** annual. **Type:** scholarship. **Recipient:** for research on early childhood development ● Shigeka Talumura Scholarship. **Frequency:** annual. **Type:** scholarship. **Recipient:** for research on global education ● Yoneji Ebitani Scholarship. **Frequency:** annual. **Type:** scholarship. **Recipient:** for research on curriculum and instruction. **Publications:** *Newsletter of the World Council for Curriculum and Instruction*, semiannual ● *Persons as Resources*, triennial. Membership Directory ● *WCCI International Journal of Curriculum & Instruction*, annual. **Price:** included in membership dues; $10.00/issue for nonmembers. **Circulation:** 1,000 ● *World Conference Proceedings*, triennial. **Conventions/Meetings:** biennial international conference.

Dance

8183 ■ Cecchetti Council of America (CCA)
23393 Meadows Ave.
Flat Rock, MI 48134
Ph: (734)379-6710
Fax: (734)379-3886
E-mail: info@cecchetti.org
URL: http://www.cecchetti.org
Contact: Gail Choate-Petit, Business Admin./Treas.
Founded: 1939. **Members:** 500. **Membership Dues:** general, $95 (annual). **Regional Groups:** 15. **State Groups:** 1. **Local Groups:** 1. **Description:** Teachers of ballet and ballet dancers. Aims to raise the quality of ballet teaching and to promote the Cecchetti method of ballet training. (Named for Cavalier Enrico Cecchetti, 1850-1928, Italian ballet dancer and teacher.) Uses the teachings and writings of Cecchetti in a sequence of grades measured to the degree of difficulty and physical development; provides a system of accredited examinations to test the student's proficiency within those grades. Holds exams regularly for teachers and students; conducts refresher courses. Maintains close liaison with Cecchetti Society Branch of the Imperial Society of Teachers of Dancing (see separate entry). **Awards:** CCA Virgiline Smith Teacher Scholarship. **Frequency:** annual. **Type:** scholarship. **Recipient:** for three teacher seminars ● **Frequency:** annual. **Type:** scholarship. **Recipient:** for three male students ● Theodore Smith and Gertrude Jory Scholarship. **Frequency:** annual. **Type:** scholarship. **Recipient:** for two students. **Computer Services:** Mailing lists ● online services, discussion forum. **Publications:** *National CCA Newsletter*, semiannual. **Price:** included in membership dues ● Booklets ● Also produces phonograph records and tapes. **Conventions/Meetings:** annual International Summer School - conference and seminar (exhibits) ● workshop.

8184 ■ Dance Educators of America (DEA)
PO Box 607
Pelham, NY 10803-0607
Ph: (914)636-3200
Free: (800)229-3868
Fax: (914)636-5895
E-mail: dea@deadance.com
URL: http://www.deadance.com
Contact: Vickie Sheer, Exec. Dir.
Founded: 1932. **Members:** 3,284. **Membership Dues:** qualified teacher, $150 (annual). **Staff:** 6. **Regional Groups:** 40. **National Groups:** 3. **Languages:** English, Spanish. **Multinational. Description:** Qualified dance teachers who pass an examination and subscribe to a code of ethics and advertising rules and regulations. Works to further and promote the education of teachers in the performing arts and stage arts and of dance in all its forms. Conducts training schools at New York and Las Vegas. **Libraries: Type:** reference. **Subjects:** ballet, tap, jazz, modern, acrobatic. **Publications:** *Dictionary of Acrobatics/Tumbling*. Book ● *To Teach Is To Learn Twice*. Book. Includes ballet syllabus. **Price:** $50.00 ● Brochure, semiannual. **Price:** free. **Circulation:** 40,000. **Advertising:** accepted. **Conventions/Meetings:** annual meeting and seminar (exhibits) - always summer ● seminar, ballet and all stage arts.

8185 ■ Dance Films Association (DFA)
48 W 21st St., No. 907
New York, NY 10010
Ph: (212)727-0764
Fax: (212)727-0764
E-mail: info@dancefilms.org
URL: http://www.dancefilms.org
Contact: Deirdre Towers, Artistic Dir.
Founded: 1956. **Members:** 400. **Membership Dues:** individual in U.S., $50 (annual) ● organization, $85 (annual) ● individual outside U.S., $60 (annual) ● student, $25 (annual) ● patron, $250 (annual) ● sponsor, $100 (annual) ● angel (minimum), $500 (annual). **Staff:** 4. **Budget:** $185,000. **Languages:** English, French, Russian, Spanish. **Multinational. Description:** Producer of Dance On Camera Festival, annual event since 1971; fiscal sponsor for dance filmmakers. **Libraries: Type:** not open to the public. **Holdings:** 500. **Subjects:** dance, film history. **Awards:** Finishing Funds Grant. **Frequency:** annual. **Type:** grant. **Recipient:** for members. **Computer Services:** database, all dance films and videos in circulation. **Formerly:** (1968) Dance Films, Inc. **Publications:** *Dance on Camera: A Guide to Dance Films and Videos*, quinquennial. Book ● *Dance on Camera Journal*, bimonthly. Newsletter. Provides information on filmmakers and videotape producers in the dance field, film festivals in the U.S. and abroad, and new dance films and videos. **Price:** included in membership dues. ISSN: 1098-8084. **Circulation:** 1,000. **Conventions/Meetings:** annual Dance on Camera Festival - festival and competition.

8186 ■ Dance Masters of America (DMA)
c/o Robert Mann, Exec. Sec.
PO Box 610533
Bayside, NY 11361-0533
Ph: (718)225-4013
Fax: (718)225-4293
E-mail: dmamann@aol.com
URL: http://dma-national.org
Contact: Robert Mann, Exec. Sec.
Founded: 1884. **Members:** 2,500. **Membership Dues:** regular, $62 (annual). **Staff:** 3. **Regional Groups:** 27. **State Groups:** 32. **Description:** Dance teachers. Seeks to further the art of teaching dance. Sponsors: Performing Arts Competition Scholarship Auditions, Miss Dance of America Pageant, and Mr. Dance of America Competition during national convention; Junior Miss Dance - Petite Miss Dance, Junior Mr. Dance Master Dance, and Performing Arts Competition and scholarship auditions during chapter and national convention. **Awards:** DMA Annual Award. **Frequency:** annual. **Type:** recognition ● Fergie Award. **Frequency:** annual. **Type:** recognition. **Recipient:** for outstanding member of the dance profession ● Ivy Hall Foundation Award. **Type:** recognition ● Member of the Year. **Frequency:** annual. **Type:** recognition. **Recipient:** for outstanding DMA member ● President's Award. **Type:** recognition. **Departments:** Ballroom; Business Administration; Performing Arts. **Publications:** *DMA Grapevine*, periodic. Newsletter ● *Roster of Members*, periodic. **Price:** free ● Magazine, bimonthly ● Newsletter, bimonthly. **Conventions/Meetings:** annual convention.

8187 ■ Lloyd Shaw Foundation (LSF)
c/o Bob Fuller, Pres.
293 Stone Rd.
Paris, KY 40361
Ph: (813)662-2341
E-mail: lsfpres@aol.com
URL: http://www.lloydshaw.org
Contact: Bob Fuller, Pres.
Founded: 1964. **Members:** 670. **Membership Dues:** individual, $25 (annual) ● couple, family, $40 (annual) ● supporting, $50 (annual) ● patron, $250 (annual) ● life, $1,000. **Staff:** 2. **Description:** Represents individuals and dance groups united to recall, restore, and teach the folk rhythms of the American people in dance, music, song, and allied folk arts as a tribute to the memory of Lloyd Shaw. (Shaw was a pioneer in the field of folk dancing and his institutes and other promotions have done much to popularize this area of dance.) Provides reference service in the field of American folk dance. Conducts university workshops to train teachers and leaders on the use of dance in their educational or recreational programs. Provides mail information and consultation service. **Committees:** Recordings. **Divisions:** Sales. **Publications:** *American Dance Circle*, quarterly. Magazine. Reports on foundation activities; includes dance descriptions and dance history articles. **Price:** included in membership dues. **Circulation:** 1,500. **Advertising:** accepted ● *LFS Catalogue*. Contains tunes for square dances, quadrilles, folk dances, couple dances and contras. Includes a complete glossary, dance history and teaching aids. **Price:** $90.00 plus shipping and handling ● Books ● Brochures ● Pamphlets ● Also publishes course and workshop materials, and produces records, films, and dance curriculum kits. **Conventions/Meetings:** annual Business Meeting - always first week of July.

8188 ■ National Association of Schools of Dance (NASD)
11250 Roger Bacon Dr., Ste.21
Reston, VA 20190-5248
Ph: (703)437-0700
Fax: (703)437-6312
E-mail: info@arts-accredit.org
URL: http://nasd.arts-accredit.org
Contact: Samuel Hope, Exec. Dir.
Founded: 1981. **Members:** 65. **Membership Dues:** individual, $75 (annual) ● institutional, $800-$950 (annual). **Staff:** 12. **Description:** Serves as accrediting agency for educational programs in dance. Provides prospective students with current, accurate information about schools offering instruction in dance. Seeks to establish standards in the field regarding budget, class time requirements, faculty qualifications, faculty-student ratios, and library and physical facilities. Fosters public understanding and acceptance of the educational disciplines inherent in the creative arts in the nation's system of higher education. Encourages high-quality teaching, as well as varied and experimental methods and theories of dance instruction. Provides national representation in matters pertaining to dance and affecting member institutions and their goals. Encourages the collaboration of individuals and professional dance groups in formulating curricula and standards. Offers members general assistance and counseling in program development and encourages self-evaluation and continuing efforts toward improvement. Evaluates dance schools and dance instruction programs through voluntary accreditation processes; assures students and parents that accredited programs offer competent instructors and adequate curricula and facilities. **Commissions:** Accreditation. **Committees:** Ethics; Nominations; Research. **Publications:** *NASD Directory*, annual. Lists accredited institutions and major degree programs. **Price:** $5.00 ● *NASD Handbook*, biennial. Includes NASD standards for degree-granting and non-degree-granting programs. **Price:** $10.00. Alternate Formats: online ● Brochures. **Price:** free. Alternate Formats: online. **Conventions/Meetings:** annual meeting - always 2nd week of September.

8189 ■ National Dance Council of America (NDCA)
c/o Eleanor Wiblin, Registrar
PO Box 22018
Provo, UT 84602-2018
Ph: (801)422-8124
Fax: (801)422-0541
E-mail: registration@ndca.org
URL: http://www.ndca.org
Contact: Eleanor Wiblin, Registrar
Founded: 1948. **Members:** 3,395. **Membership Dues:** amateur student competitor, $20 (annual) ● amateur adult competitor, $35 (annual) ● competing professional, $70 (annual) ● adjudicator, master of ceremony, music director, registrar, scrutineer, $85 (annual) ● dance teacher, $30 (annual). **Description:** Organizations representing interests of the dance profession on a nationwide basis. Seeks establishment and maintenance of high standards in dance education and professional recognition of dance teachers. **Committees:** Competition; Credentials; Legislative; Scrutineering. **Departments:** Ballroom; Performing Arts; Public Affairs. **Affiliated With:** Dance Educators of America. **Formerly:** (1984) National Council of Dance Teacher Organizations. **Publications:** *Dance Events Bulletin*, 3/year ● *Information and Consumer*. Brochure. Contains information about the benefits of professional dance instruction. Alternate Formats: online. **Conventions/Meetings:** semiannual meeting.

8190 ■ National Dance Institute (NDI)
594 Broadway, Rm. 805
New York, NY 10012
Ph: (212)226-0083
Fax: (212)226-0761

E-mail: cgriffin@nationaldance.org
URL: http://www.nationaldance.org
Contact: Cherita Griffin, Admin./Program Asst.
Founded: 1976. **Staff:** 20. **Budget:** $2,500,000. **Description:** Seeks to introduce dance as a catalyst for all the arts as part of the school curriculum to promote individual development and build self-esteem. Teaches weekly dance classes to young children to enable them to experience the challenge and joy of the arts. Conducts classes for inner-city students, and special dance classes for the deaf and hearing impaired, blind and visually impaired, emotionally challenged, and wheelchair bound. Conducts satellite programs and residency programs in New Mexico, Texas, Vermont, Colorado, Louisiana, New York, Mississippi, and France. Conducts teacher training in New York and around the country to preserve and spread the methodology used in the arts education programs. **Programs:** Adopt-A-School; Teacher Training. **Publications:** *Curriculum Guides*, annual. Handbook ● *NDI Event of the Year Program Journal*, annual. **Circulation:** 10,000. **Advertising:** accepted ● *NDI Teacher Training Manual*, annual.

8191 ■ Professional Dance Teachers Association (PDTA)
c/o Hoctor Dance Enterprises
PO Box 38
157 Franklin Tpke.
Waldwick, NJ 07463
Free: (800)462-8679
E-mail: dance@hoctordance.com
URL: http://www.hoctordance.com
Contact: Jerry Rose, Exec. Asst. Dir.
Founded: 1964. **Members:** 1,000. **Staff:** 1. **Regional Groups:** 4. **Description:** Professional modern, jazz, tap and ballet dance teachers who seek to improve teaching techniques. Provides teachers with new dance routines; offers children's scholarships and awards. **Publications:** *Dance Terminology*. Book ● Monographs. Covers dance techniques. **Conventions/Meetings:** competition ● workshop, for dance students and instructors.

8192 ■ World Congress of Teachers of Dancing (WCTD)
Address Unknown since 2007
Founded: 1985. **Members:** 87,648. **Staff:** 18. **Budget:** $2,500,000. **Description:** A division of the United States National Institute of Dance. Colleges, universities, professional dance schools, and teachers of dancing. Seeks to maintain global standards of excellence in dance. Conducts educational programs and examinations; certifies teachers of dancing. Researches and disseminates information on the history and status of dance from local to international levels. Bestows honorary degrees, including Professor of Dance, Companion of Dance, and Danseur/Premier Danseuse Supreme. Maintains placement service and speakers' bureau. **Programs:** Cultural Exchange; Dance and Medicine; Teachers Workshops. **Affiliated With:** United States National Institute of Dance. **Conventions/Meetings:** periodic competition ● annual conference.

Dentistry

8193 ■ American Dental Education Association (ADEA)
1400 K St. NW, Ste.1100
Washington, DC 20005
Ph: (202)289-7201 (202)289-7385
Fax: (202)289-7204
E-mail: valachovicr@adea.org
URL: http://www.adea.org
Contact: Dr. Richard Valachovic, Exec. Dir.
Founded: 1923. **Members:** 15,500. **Membership Dues:** student, $40 (annual) ● individual, $125 (annual) ● institutional (affiliate allied), $945 (annual) ● institutional (affiliate hospital), $984 (annual) ● institutional (affiliate non-hospital), $3,998 (annual) ● institutional (affiliate federal), $3,922 (annual) ● corporate, $3,400 (annual). **Staff:** 47. **Budget:** $14,000,000. **Description:** Individuals interested in dental education; schools of dentistry, advanced dental and allied dental education in the U.S., Canada, and Puerto Rico; affiliated institutions of the federal government and corporations. Works to promote better teaching and education in dentistry and dental research and to facilitate exchange of ideas among dental educators. Sponsors meetings, conferences, and workshops; conducts surveys, studies, and special projects and publishes their results. Maintains 37 sections and 8 special interest groups representing many different aspects of dental education. **Libraries: Type:** not open to the public. **Holdings:** 100. **Telecommunication Services:** electronic mail, adeaweb@yahoo.com. **Councils:** Allied Dental Program Directors; Corporate; Deans; Faculties; Hospitals and Advance Education Programs; Sections; Students. **Formerly:** (2000) American Association Dental Schools. **Publications:** *Bulletin of Dental Education*, monthly. Provides information on grant and fellowship, legislation and members' activities. **Price:** included in membership dues; $18.00 /year for nonmembers in U.S. and Canada; $18.00 /year for nonmembers outside U.S. and Canada. **Advertising:** accepted ● *Directory of Institutional Members*, annual. **Price:** $50.00 for nonmembers; $25.00 for members ● *Journal of Dental Education*, monthly. **Price:** included in membership dues; $75.00 /year for nonmembers in U.S.; $100.00 /year for nonmembers in Canada; $125.00 /year for nonmembers outside U.S. and Canada. **Advertising:** accepted ● *Official Guide to United States and Canadian Dental Schools*, annual. Catalog. Helps students decide on a career in dentistry, and explains how to go about it. **Price:** $35.00. **Advertising:** accepted ● *Opportunities for Minority Students in U.S. Dental Schools*, semiannual. Catalog. **Price:** $10.00 ● Proceedings, annual. **Conventions/Meetings:** annual board meeting ● annual conference (exhibits) - usually March.

8194 ■ American Student Dental Association (ASDA)
211 E Chicago Ave., Ste.700
Chicago, IL 60611-2687
Ph: (312)440-2795
Free: (800)621-8099
Fax: (312)440-2820
E-mail: nancy@asdanet.org
URL: http://www.asdanet.org
Contact: Nancy Honeycutt, Exec. Dir.
Founded: 1971. **Members:** 15,000. **Membership Dues:** predental, associate, $50 (annual) ● predoctoral, $67 (annual) ● international, $75 (annual). **Staff:** 9. **Budget:** $1,000,000. **Local Groups:** 54. **Description:** Predoctoral and postdoctoral dental students organized to improve the quality of dental education and to promote the accessibility of oral health care; additional membership categories include predental, postdoctoral, international and associate. Represents dental students before legislative bodies, organizations, and associations that affect dental students. Disseminates information to dental students. Sponsors advocacy program and "externships" including Washington National Health Policy, Chicago Administrative, State Government Affairs, and Research. **Awards:** Award of Excellence. **Frequency:** annual. **Type:** recognition ● Chapter Journalism Awards. **Type:** recognition ● Ideal ASDA Chapter Awards. **Type:** recognition. **Telecommunication Services:** electronic mail, membership@asdanet.org. **Committees:** Career Guidance Network; Dental Benefit Programs; Education; Ethics; Hospitals; Membership Marketing and Services; Minority Affairs and Foreign Students; National Board Examinations; Political Education Network; Practice Management; Public Health; Research. **Affiliated With:** American Dental Association. **Formerly:** (1971) Student American Dental Association. **Publications:** *ASDA Handbook*, biennial. Contains annual reference volumes, with information on applying to dental school, financial aid, membership benefits, postdoctoral opportunities. **Price:** $30.00/copy. ISSN: 0277-619. **Circulation:** 15,000. **Advertising:** accepted ● *ASDA News*, monthly. Newspaper. Includes association and industry news and chapter events. **Price:** included in membership dues; $55.00 for nonmembers in U.S.; $65.00 for nonmembers outside U.S. ● *Dentistry*, quarterly ● *Mouth*, quarterly. Journal. Includes case reports, book reviews, new product announcements, technical quizzes, news briefs and student perspectives. **Price:** included in membership dues; $10.00 for nonmembers ● Also publishes a series of guides to post-graduate programs in dentistry and reprints of National Board Examinations. **Conventions/Meetings:** annual general assembly (exhibits) - usually September ● annual Leadership Conference - usually November ● annual regional meeting and conference - in winter.

8195 ■ Association for Continuing Dental Education (ACDE)
c/o Lynda Young, Pres.
Univ. of Minnesota
6-406 Moos HS Tower
515 Delaware St. SE
Minneapolis, MN 55455
Ph: (612)625-5499
Fax: (612)624-8159
E-mail: young002@umn.edu
URL: http://www.dent.unc.edu/acde
Contact: Lynda Young, Pres.
Founded: 1991. **Members:** 48. **Multinational. Description:** Aims to advance the art and science of Continuing Dental Education (CDE). Improves the quality and quantity of educational opportunities for all persons providing oral health care. Promotes high standards in CDE courses offered by schools of dentistry. Fosters the improvement of the dental health of the public. **Conventions/Meetings:** annual meeting - 2008 Aug. 2-5, Chicago, IL.

8196 ■ Oral Health America (OHA)
410 N Michigan Ave., Ste.352
Chicago, IL 60611-4211
Ph: (312)836-9900
Free: (800)523-3438
Fax: (312)836-9986
E-mail: liz@oralhealthamerica.org
URL: http://www.oralhealthamerica.org
Contact: Robert J. Klaus, Pres./CEO
Founded: 1955. **Staff:** 7. **Budget:** $1,500,000. **Description:** Raises awareness of oral health importance to overall health. **Telecommunication Services:** electronic mail, robert@oralhealthamerica.org. **Formerly:** (1963) Fund for Dental Education; (1973) American Fund for Dental Education; (1998) American Fund for Dental Health. **Publications:** *Advocate*, quarterly. Newsletter. Alternate Formats: online ● Annual Report, annual. **Conventions/Meetings:** semiannual board meeting ● Oral Health Leadership - conference.

8197 ■ Organization of Teachers of Oral Diagnosis (OTOD)
c/o William Garbee, DDS, Sec.-Treas.
LSU School of Dentistry
1100 Florida Ave., Box 140
New Orleans, LA 70119-2799
E-mail: wgarbe@lsuhsc.edu
Contact: William Garbee DDS, Sec.-Treas.
Founded: 1963. **Members:** 200. **Membership Dues:** active, $90 (annual). **Staff:** 4. **Budget:** $40,000. **Description:** Teachers and university departments of oral diagnosis (oral medicine and oral pathology). Seeks to update techniques, material, and knowledge in oral diagnosis education. Sponsors seminars focusing on current issues and breakthroughs in the field and provides speakers for dental societies and dental education organizations. Promotes the interests of dental educators. Cosponsors the American Board of Oral Medicine. **Computer Services:** database. **Publications:** *American Association of Stomatology*, 3/year. Newsletter. Also Cited As: *AAS* ● *Oral Surgery, Oral Medicine and Oral Pathology*, 3/year. Journal. **Price:** included in membership dues ● *Treatment Planning - Synopsis of 1981 Workshop* ● Membership Directory, annual. **Conventions/Meetings:** annual meeting, held in conjunction with American Association of Dental Schools ● annual meeting - March.

8198 ■ Student National Dental Association (SNDA)
c/o Calysta Beatty, Treas.
1022 Exchange Pl.
Durham, NC 27713
E-mail: cbeatty1908@yahoo.com
URL: http://www.sndaonline.com
Contact: Marvin Baptiste, Pres.
Founded: 1972. **Members:** 9,000. **Membership Dues:** collegiate, $15 (annual) ● student, $40 (annual). **Regional Groups:** 10. **Local Groups:** 46. **Description:** Serves as section of the National Dental Association (see separate entry). Minority dental students. Addresses the needs of minority dental students; strives to expose and eliminate discriminatory practices encountered by its members. Promotes increased minority enrollment in dental schools. Seeks to improve dental health care delivery to all disadvantaged people. Compiles statistics. **Telecommunication Services:** electronic mail, carloss@umich.edu. **Committees:** House of Delegates Political Action. **Publications:** *Convention Bulletin*, annual ● *Help Us to Build Your Dental Career*, annual ● Membership Directory, annual. **Price:** available to members only. **Conventions/Meetings:** annual meeting (exhibits) - always first week of August.

Developmental Education

8199 ■ Lions-Quest
PO Box 304
Annapolis Junction, MD 20701-0304
Ph: (630)571-5466
Free: (800)446-2700
Fax: (240)646-7023
E-mail: info@lions-quest.org
URL: http://www.lions-quest.org
Contact: Mark Bularzik, Mgr.
Founded: 1984. **Members:** 1,400,000. **Staff:** 10. **Budget:** $1,500,000. **Languages:** Danish, Dutch, English, Finnish, French, German, Hindi, Icelandic, Italian, Norwegian, Spanish, Swedish. **Description:** Aids in helping students, parents, and teachers, kindergarten through 12th grade, to learn basic life skills in areas of problem solving, interpersonal communication, increasing self-esteem, prevention of drug and alcohol abuse, and conflict resolution. Sponsors 1-3 day professional development workshops for teachers, counselors, and other professionals to prepare them for classroom implementation and in the community through service learning projects. **Departments:** Accounting; Communications; Creative Services; Distribution; Events Services; Human Resources; International; Office Systems; Partner Relations; Program Development; Program Services; Promotion Services; Research and Evaluation; Training Development; Urban and Minority Programs. **Programs:** Skills for Action; Skills for Adolescence; Skills for Growing. **Formerly:** (1982) Quest, Inc.; (1988) Quest National Center; (2003) Quest International; (2004) Lions-Quest Programs. **Publications:** *A Bright Day For Everyone*. Book. **Price:** $5.95 ● *Ana and Quentin Go To School*. Book. **Price:** $5.95 ● *Changes and Challenges* (in English and Spanish). Book. Serves as a middle school student book, for grades 6-8. **Price:** $3.50 English version; $5.00 Spanish version ● *Exploring the Issues: Teens Alcohol and Other Drugs*. Book. For high school teachers, grades 9-12. ● *Making A Difference*. Magazine. For high school students, grades 9-12. ● *Mariko Wears Her Thinking Cap*. Book. **Price:** $5.95 ● *Michael's Decision*. Book. **Price:** $5.95 ● *Q-Bear's Book of Rhyme and Songs*. **Price:** $5.95 ● *Skills for Action Curriculum*. A high school teacher curriculum kit that covers grades 9-12. ● *Skills for Adolescence Curriculum*. Serves as a middle school teacher curriculum kit, covers grades 6-8. ● *Skills for Growing Curriculum*. An elementary school teacher curriculum kit, separate kits available for each grade level, K-5. ● *The Surprising Years*. Book. Serves as a middle school parent book, corresponds to grades 6-8. **Price:** $3.95 ● *Together Times*. Booklet. For elementary school students, 5 booklets for each grade level, K-5. ● *Turnabout's Fair Play*. Book. **Price:** $5.95 ● Books. Elementary school picture books, primarily for grades K-1. **Conventions/Meetings:** Classroom Discipline: Establishing Responsibility and Respect - seminar, professional development ● Introduction to Service Learning, Implementation and Integration - seminar, professional development ● Managing Anger, Resolving Conflict and Preventing Violence - seminar, professional development ● Re-Quest Refresher Course - seminar, professional development ● SFG/SFA (K-8) Conference Workshops - workshop and seminar, professional development ● Skills for Action (9-12) Workshops - workshop and seminar, professional development ● Teens - Alcohol and Other Drugs - seminar, professional development.

8200 ■ National Association for Developmental Education (NADE)
500 N Estrella Pkwy., Ste.B2
PMB 412
Goodyear, AZ 85338
Free: (877)233-9455
Fax: (623)792-5747
E-mail: office@nade.net
URL: http://www.nade.net
Contact: Carol O'Shea, Exec. Asst.
Founded: 1976. **Members:** 2,400. **Membership Dues:** individual, $50 (annual) ● student, $30 (annual) ● retired, $25 (annual) ● institutional/program, $350 (annual). **Staff:** 1. **Regional Groups:** 29. **Multinational. Description:** Developmental educators. Seeks to improve the theory and practice of developmental education. Serves as a forum for the exchange of information among members; facilitates communication and cooperation between members and individuals and organizations working in related fields. Sponsors research, evaluation, programming, and training programs. **Awards: Frequency:** annual. **Type:** recognition. **Computer Services:** Mailing lists, 400 dollars per set. **Formerly:** National Association for Remedia/Developmental Studies in Postsecondary Education. **Publications:** *NADE Newsletter*, 3/year. **Circulation:** 2,200. **Advertising:** accepted. **Conventions/Meetings:** annual Reaching for the Stars - conference (exhibits) ● periodic workshop.

Disabled

8201 ■ Association on Higher Education and Disability (AHEAD)
107 Commerce Center Dr., Ste.204
Huntersville, NC 28078
Ph: (704)947-7779
Fax: (704)948-7779
E-mail: ahead@ahead.org
URL: http://www.ahead.org
Contact: Stephan J. Smith, Exec. Dir.
Founded: 1977. **Members:** 2,000. **Membership Dues:** full professional, $185 (annual) ● affiliate, additional professional, $135 (annual) ● preprofessional, emeritus, $75 (annual) ● institutional - silver, $225 (annual) ● institutional - gold (includes 3 individuals), $495 (annual) ● institutional - platinum (includes 5 individuals), $750 (annual) ● partner (not-for-profit), $250 (annual) ● partner (for-profit), $500 (annual). **Staff:** 8. **Budget:** $1,000,000. **Regional Groups:** 17. **Multinational. Description:** Individuals interested in promoting the equal rights and opportunities of disabled postsecondary students, staff, faculty, and graduates. Provides an exchange of communication for those professionally involved with disabled students; collects, evaluates, and disseminates information; encourages and supports legislation for the benefit of disabled students. Conducts surveys on issues pertinent to college students with disabilities; offers resource referral system and employment exchange for positions in disability student services. Conducts research programs; compiles statistics. **Awards:** Professional Recognition Award. **Type:** recognition ● Student Recognition Award. **Type:** recognition. **Telecommunication Services:** electronic mail, stephan@ahead.org. **Committees:** Legislative; Marketing; Publicity; Research and Information Services; Special Concerns. **Special Interest Groups:** AIDS; Blind/Visually Impaired; Canadian; Career Services; Community Colleges; Computers; Deafness/Hearing Impaired; Disability Studies; Head Injuries; Historically Underrepresented Populations; Independent Colleges and Universities; Learning Disabilities; TRIO; Women and Disability. **Also Known As:** AHEAD. **Publications:** *ALERT*, bimonthly. Newsletter ● *Journal of Postsecondary Education and Disability* ● Membership Directory. **Conventions/Meetings:** annual conference (exhibits) - always July. 2008 July 14-19, Reno, NV - **Avg. Attendance:** 1000; 2009 July 20-25, Louisville, KY; 2010 July 19-24, Ottawa, ON, Canada; 2011 July 11-16, Seattle, WA.

8202 ■ Family Resource Center on Disabilities (FRCD)
20 E Jackson Blvd., Rm. 300
Chicago, IL 60604
Ph: (312)939-3513
Free: (800)952-4199
Fax: (312)939-7297
E-mail: frcdptiil@ameritech.net
URL: http://www.frcd.org
Contact: Charlotte Des Jardins, Exec. Dir.
Founded: 1969. **Staff:** 15. **Languages:** English, Polish, Spanish. **Description:** Parents, professionals, and volunteers seeking to improve services for all children with disabilities. Originally organized as a result of the 1969 Illinois law mandating the education of all children with disabilities and operates as a coalition to inform and activate parents. Provides information and referral services, individualized support services for low-income Chicago families, transition services, and special education rights training. **Formerly:** Coordinating Council for Handicapped Children. **Publications:** *How to Get Services by Being Assertive*. Manual. **Price:** $10.00 plus shipping and handling ● *How to Organize an Effective Parent/Advocacy Group and Move Bureaucracies*. Manual. **Price:** $10.00 plus shipping and handling ● *Rehabilitation Act Manual*. **Price:** $25.00 plus shipping and handling ● Also publishes pamphlets.

8203 ■ HEATH Resource Center (GWHRC)
George Washington Univ.
2134 G St. NW
Washington, DC 20037-2704
Ph: (202)973-0904
Fax: (202)994-3364
E-mail: askheath@gwu.edu
URL: http://www.heath.gwu.edu
Contact: Donna Martinez, Dir.
Founded: 1977. **Staff:** 5. **Description:** National information Clearinghouse. Works to aid in the postsecondary education of people who are disabled. Provides information on educational support services, procedures, policies, adaptations, campus opportunities, vocational technical schools, adult education programs, and independent living centers. **Publications:** *Fact Sheet*, quarterly. Newsletter ● *Information*, 3/year. Directory ● *Information from HEATH*, quarterly. Newsletter. Alternate Formats: online ● *Resource Directory*, biennial ● Also publishes topical informational materials. **Conventions/Meetings:** annual conference.

8204 ■ National Association for Adults with Special Learning Needs (NAASLN)
c/o Correctional Education Association
8182 Lark Brown Rd., Ste.202
Elkridge, MD 21075-6332
Free: (888)562-2756
Fax: (614)939-4150
E-mail: naasln@aol.com
URL: http://www.naasln.org
Contact: Robyn Rennick, Pres.
Founded: 1989. **Members:** 350. **Membership Dues:** student, $15 (annual) ● individual, $35 (annual) ● organizational, $250 (annual) ● life, $500. **Staff:** 3. **Description:** Works to organize and promote a coalition of individuals interested in educating adults with special learning needs. Fosters development and implementation of educational programs for adults. Promotes unification of adult education professionals. Encourages research and dissemination of information on adult education. Acts as a forum for the

exchange of information on adult education. Seeks to unify adults with special learning needs. **Awards:** Distinguished Service Award. **Frequency:** annual. **Type:** recognition. **Task Forces:** Emotionally Impaired; Hearing Impaired; Homeless; Incarcerated Adults; Learning Disabled; Library Services; Mentally Retarded; Physically Disabled; Visually Impaired. **Publications:** *NAASLN Membership News and Views*, monthly. Newsletter. Alternate Formats: online. **Conventions/Meetings:** annual Lifelong Learning for Adults with Special Learning Needs - conference, for professionals working with adults with special learning needs (exhibits).

8205 ■ STRIDE: Sports and Therapeutic Recreation Instruction/Developmental Education
PO Box 778
Rensselaer, NY 12144
Ph: (518)598-1279
Fax: (518)286-3201
E-mail: stride@capital.net
URL: http://www.stride.org
Contact: Ms. Mary Ellen Whitney, Pres./CEO/Founder
Founded: 1986. **Description:** Improves the lives of children who have disabilities. Provides sports and recreation programs and opportunities for individuals with disabilities or special needs. **Programs:** Bowling; Camp STRIDE; Little League Baseball; Project STRIDE; Sailing; Skiing and Snowboarding; Snowshoeing; Swimming. **Publications:** *Challenges and Champions*, quarterly. Newsletter. Contains news, upcoming events and program information and profiles of students and volunteers. Alternate Formats: online.

Discipline

8206 ■ National Center for the Study of Corporal Punishment and Alternatives (NCSCPA)
Temple Univ.
253 Ritter Annex
Philadelphia, PA 19122
Ph: (215)204-6091
E-mail: ncscpa@blue.vm.temple.edu
URL: http://www.ruaneproductions.com/NCSCPA/about.html
Contact: Dr. Irwin A. Hyman EdD, Dir.
Founded: 1976. **Members:** 300. **Staff:** 3. **Budget:** $2,000. **Description:** Individuals interested in the study of the psychological and educational aspects of school and home discipline and its relation to aggression and violence. Provides legal advocacy to protest the use of corporal punishment and psychological abuse in schools and at home. Provides expert testimony on the psychological effects of corporal punishment and psychological abuse. Conducts research on post-traumatic stress disorders in children as predictors of later violent and antisocial behavior. Maintains extensive collection of articles and news clippings on corporal punishment and other methods of discipline. Presents speeches to organizations, agencies, and institutions, both nationally and internationally; provides in-service training to teachers, psychologists, social workers, and others. Maintains Speaker's Bureau. **Libraries: Type:** reference. **Holdings:** 2,000. **Subjects:** discipline, misbehavior, violence, remediation, prevention, posttraumatic stress disorder, student victimization by school staff, bullying, prevention/intervention. **Computer Services:** Mailing lists, anticorporal punishment advocates. **Publications:** *Discipline*, periodic. Articles. Contains research papers. ● Books ● Papers ● Videos. Features videos of workshops. **Conventions/Meetings:** Teacher Variance Workshop (exhibits).

8207 ■ National Coalition to Abolish Corporal Punishment in Schools (NCACPS)
155 W Main St., No. 1603
Columbus, OH 43215
Ph: (614)221-8829
Fax: (614)221-2110
E-mail: info@stophitting.org
URL: http://www.stophitting.com
Contact: Robert Fathman PhD, Co-Chm.
Founded: 1987. **Members:** 40. **Membership Dues:** silver medal sponsor, $50 ● gold medal sponsor, $100. **Staff:** 1. **State Groups:** 16. **National Groups:** 40. **Description:** A coalition of state and national organizations working together to end corporal punishment in schools. **Publications:** Brochures. Covers corporal punishment in schools and other sites. **Conventions/Meetings:** annual National Conference to Abolish Corporal Punishment (exhibits).

8208 ■ Parents and Teachers Against Violence in Education (PTAVE)
PO Box 1033
Alamo, CA 94507-7033
Ph: (925)831-1661
Fax: (925)838-8914
E-mail: feedback@nospank.net
URL: http://www.nospank.net
Contact: Jordan Riak, Exec. Dir.
Founded: 1978. **Description:** Works to promote universal acceptance of the belief that every child has the right to grow and learn in environments that are violence free. Opposes the use of corporal punishment or other types of violent punitive techniques for the management of children. Conducts outreach programs to public social service agencies, law enforcement, parents, the media and others to foster respect for the fundamental human rights of children. **Publications:** *Plain Talking About Spanking* (in English and Spanish). **Price:** free.

Driver Education

8209 ■ ADED: The Association for Driver Rehabilitation Specialists
711 S Vienna St.
Ruston, LA 71270
Ph: (318)257-5055
Free: (800)290-2344
Fax: (318)255-4175
E-mail: webmaster@driver-ed.org
URL: http://www.driver-ed.org
Contact: Theresa Evans-Hunter MBA, Exec. Dir.
Founded: 1977. **Members:** 600. **Membership Dues:** corporate, $500 (annual) ● individual, $120 (annual) ● mobility equipment dealer, $250 (annual) ● facility (based on the number of persons), $250-$750 (annual). **Staff:** 1. **Budget:** $147,000. **Regional Groups:** 8. **Languages:** English, Spanish. **Multinational. Description:** Drivers' rehabilitation instructors; suppliers of equipment used by handicapped drivers. Serves as a forum for exchange of ideas and information among members; gathers and disseminates information on drivers' education for the disabled. Promotes uniformity in the training and evaluation of disabled drivers. Conducts educational programs. **Libraries: Type:** reference. **Holdings:** archival material. **Awards: Frequency:** annual. **Type:** recognition. **Computer Services:** database, list of ADED members in any area or state. **Additional Websites:** http://www.aded.net. **Boards:** Certification. **Affiliated With:** American Kinesiotherapy Association; American Occupational Therapy Association. **Formerly:** (1998) Association of Driver Educators for the Disabled. **Publications:** *Member Resource Guide* ● *Membership Roster*. Membership Directory ● *News Brake*, quarterly. Newsletter. **Advertising:** accepted. Alternate Formats: online ● Bibliography.

8210 ■ American Driver and Traffic Safety Education Association (ADTSEA)
Highway Safety Center
Indiana Univ. of Pennsylvania
R & P Bldg.
Indiana, PA 15705
Ph: (724)357-4051
Free: (800)896-7703
Fax: (724)357-7595
E-mail: support@hsc.iup.edu
URL: http://adtsea.iup.edu
Contact: Allen Robinson, CEO
Founded: 1956. **Members:** 1,400. **Membership Dues:** state affiliation, institutional, diamond, $100 (annual) ● professional, $50 (annual) ● presidential, $75 (annual) ● corporate (minimum), $600 (annual) ● platinum, $150 (annual). **Budget:** $200,000. **Regional Groups:** 6. **State Groups:** 38. **Description:** Professional organization of teachers and supervisors interested in improving driver and traffic safety education in colleges and secondary and elementary schools. Awards honorary memberships to retired persons distinguished in the field. Provides assistance to state departments of education, colleges and universities, state associations, and local school districts. **Awards: Type:** recognition. **Telecommunication Services:** electronic mail, arrobin@hsc.iup.edu. **Divisions:** Adult Traffic Safety and Driver Improvement; Education of Special Populations; Elementary Traffic Safety; Higher Education Traffic Safety; Secondary Traffic Safety; Traffic Safety Administration and Supervision; Traffic Safety Research. **Formerly:** (1957) American Driver and Safety Education Association; (1963) American Driver Education Association. **Publications:** *Fundamental Statements of Policies and Guidelines*, quinquennial ● *Journal of Traffic Safety Education*, quarterly ● *Washington Wire*, periodic. Newsletter ● Manuals ● Pamphlets ● Also publishes guidelines, public relations guides, and conference planning aids; produces audiovisual materials. **Conventions/Meetings:** annual competition ● annual conference (exhibits) ● seminar.

8211 ■ Driving School Association of the Americas (DSAA)
3090 E Gause Blvd., Ste.425
Slidell, LA 70461
Ph: (985)643-7803
Free: (800)270-DSAA
Fax: (985)649-9877
E-mail: info@thedsaa.org
URL: http://www.thedsaa.org
Contact: Ms. Sheila Varnado, Marketing and Business Relations Mgr.
Founded: 1972. **Members:** 400. **Membership Dues:** driving school owner (based on number of cars), $115-$215 (annual) ● associate, $250 (annual) ● corporate, $1,000 (annual) ● gold partnership, $10,000 (annual) ● silver partnership, $6,000 (annual) ● bronze partnership, $3,000 (annual). **Budget:** $60,000. **State Groups:** 35. **Description:** Owners of licensed professional driving schools in the U.S. and Canada. Conducts safe driver training for high schools and the public; achieves legislation beneficial to driving schools; promotes high ethical standards within the training program. Conducts trade exhibitions of products and services that best service the driving school owner and its consumer. **Libraries: Type:** reference. **Holdings:** 1. **Subjects:** safety industry information for teaching and running business. **Awards:** Cathy Hensel Award. **Frequency:** annual. **Type:** monetary. **Recipient:** to individual who championed the rights of women and who epitomized the highest standards of professional conduct ● George Hensel/Leadership Award. **Frequency:** annual. **Type:** recognition. **Recipient:** to person who most exemplifies the leadership on a local, state or national level ● H.B. Vinson Award. **Frequency:** annual. **Type:** recognition. **Recipient:** to individuals who most typifies the ideas and thoughts of DSAA ● Presidents' Award. **Frequency:** annual. **Type:** recognition. **Recipient:** to member/members who assisted the current president. **Computer Services:** Information services, of membership and products ● mailing lists, of members and non-members. **Committees:** Legislative. **Publications:** *Dual News Magazine*, 3/year, every summer, fall, and spring. Contains articles that discuss educational changes and methods. **Circulation:** 4,900. **Advertising:** accepted. Alternate Formats: online. **Conventions/Meetings:** annual convention (exhibits) - always November ● seminar, on driver education and training and traffic safety - 6/year ● workshop, dealing with problems within driver education programs.

8212 ■ North American Transportation Management Institute (NATMI)
2460 W 26th Ave., Ste.17-C
Denver, CO 80211
Ph: (303)952-4013
Fax: (775)370-4055
E-mail: info@natmi.org
URL: http://www.natmi.org
Contact: Jeff Arnold, Exec. Dir.
Founded: 1944. **Members:** 900. **Membership Dues:** fleet/associate, $250 (annual) ● government/truck driving school, $100 (annual) ● fleet additional/associate additional, $150 (annual). **Staff:** 5. **Budget:** $600,000. **Multinational**. **Description:** Trucking, insurance, and safety organizations; government agencies. Offers motor fleet supervisor training courses nationwide; course subjects include motor fleet safety, effective fleet operation, accident investigation, motor fleet trainers, and motor fleet maintenance management. Certifies those who meet committee's requirements as professional directors of safety, safety supervisors, driver trainers, directors of equipment and maintenance, and fleet maintenance managers. Serves as a clearinghouse for promotional and instructional materials; develops new data and improves old materials on driver selection, training, supervision, and vehicle maintenance management. **Awards:** Outstanding Teacher Award. **Frequency:** annual. **Type:** recognition. **Recipient:** for teaching at least 3 National Committee courses each year, highest rating. **Committees:** Certification and Safety; Editorial; Maintenance and Membership. **Affiliated With:** American Trucking Associations. **Formerly:** (1998) National Committee for Motor Fleet Supervisor Training and Certification. **Publications:** *Accident Investigation Training*. Manual. **Price:** $14.95 for nonmembers; $12.71 for members ● *Guardrail*, quarterly. Magazine. Covers fleet management issues. **Price:** $30.00. **Advertising:** accepted ● *Hazmat Awareness Training*. Manual. **Price:** $14.95 for nonmembers; $12.71 for members ● *Motor Carrier Security Training*, periodic. Handbook. Takes a straightforward look at the processes ad procedures involved in establishing cargo and facility security. **Price:** $24.95 for nonmembers; $21.20 for members ● *Motor Fleet Monthly*. Newsletter. Lists courses offered by the committee. **Price:** available to members only ● *Motor Fleet Safety Supervision - Principles and Practices*. Book. **Price:** $24.99 ● Directory, periodic. **Conventions/Meetings:** annual meeting.

Dyes

8213 ■ Natural Dyes International
Box 21912
El Prado, NM 87529
Ph: (505)751-1596
E-mail: conference@naturaldyes.org
URL: http://www.naturaldyes.org
Contact: Robin Collier, Pres.
Membership Dues: limited income (Alum), $25 (annual) ● basic (Marigold), $40 (annual) ● family/supporting/organization (Madder), $60 (annual) ● fellow (Indigo), $100 (annual) ● patron (Murex Purple), $250 (annual). **Multinational**. **Description:** Works to research natural dyes and pigments and educate the public about their history and use. Engages in educational, charitable and scientific activities for the benefit of the general public. Establishes and operates a facility for research. Conducts workshops, training, classes, internships, and lectures.

Economics

8214 ■ Association for the Study of the Cuban Economy (ASCE)
PO Box 28267
Washington, DC 20038-8267
E-mail: asce@ascecuba.org
URL: http://www.ascecuba.org
Contact: Armando S. Linde, Pres.
Founded: 1990. **Membership Dues:** regular in U.S., $75 (annual) ● regular outside U.S., $85 (annual) ● sponsor, $120-$300 (annual) ● institutional (minimum), $120 (annual) ● benefactor, $300 (annual) ● student in U.S., $20 (annual) ● student outside U.S., $30 (annual). **Languages:** English, Spanish. **Multinational**. **Description:** Promotes the study of the elements and processes involved in the expected transition of Cuba to a free market economy and a democratic society. Encourages scholarly discussion and research on the Cuban economy. Maintains professional contacts with economists inside Cuba. **Awards:** Privatization Award. **Frequency:** periodic. **Type:** monetary. **Recipient:** for original, previously unpublished scholarly papers ● Student Prize Award. **Frequency:** annual. **Type:** monetary. **Recipient:** for the best student papers on interdisciplinary research dealing with Cuba's domestic issues, its foreign relations, or Cuba in a comparative perspective. **Affiliated With:** American Economic Association. **Publications:** Newsletter. Alternate Formats: online.

8215 ■ Estonian American Fund for Economic Education
4 Noyes Ct.
Silver Spring, MD 20910
Ph: (301)587-9115
Fax: (301)587-0730
E-mail: eafund@delphi.com
URL: http://www.sabre.org/books/bookorg/bkdn_eaf.htm
Contact: Mr. Ago Ambre, Pres.
Founded: 1990. **Budget:** $70,000. **Languages:** English, Estonian. **Nonmembership**. **Description:** Aids Estonian organizations in changing to a free market economy. Provides humanitarian aid, equipment, scientific literature and supplies to hospitals and educational institutions; offers technical and medical training; sponsors seminars; brings Estonian speaking professionals in contact with Estonian institutions. **Publications:** Annual Report (in English and Estonian), annual. **Conventions/Meetings:** board meeting - 3/year.

8216 ■ Foundation for Teaching Economics (FTE)
260 Russell Blvd., Ste.B
Davis, CA 95616-3839
Ph: (530)757-4630
Fax: (530)757-4636
E-mail: information@fte.org
URL: http://www.fte.org
Contact: Julie A. Neithercutt, Assoc. Dir. of Development
Founded: 1976. **Staff:** 6. **Budget:** $1,200,000. **Description:** Introduces young individuals, selected for their leadership potential, to an economic way of thinking about national and international issues. Promotes excellence in economic education by helping economics teachers become more effective educators. Sponsors one-week summer programs for economics teachers and students selected for their leadership potential. **Convention/Meeting:** none. **Computer Services:** Information services, discussion guide for members ● information services, lesson plans and curriculum designs ● online services, ways to make contribution to FTE ● record retrieval services, news. **Programs:** Economic Forces in American History; Economic Issues for Teachers; Economics Online for Teachers; Environment and the Economy; The Gillette Company, Economics for Leaders; One Day Economic Issues Seminars; The Right Start in Teaching Economics. **Publications:** Annual Report, annual. Describes aspects of FTE's goal to improve economic education in classrooms around the nation and the world. Alternate Formats: online.

8217 ■ National Council on Economic Education (NCEE)
1140 Ave. of the Americas, 2nd Fl.
New York, NY 10036
Ph: (212)730-7007 (212)730-1063
Free: (800)338-1192
Fax: (212)730-1793
E-mail: rduvall@ncee.net
URL: http://www.ncee.net
Contact: Robert F. Duvall PhD, Pres./CEO
Founded: 1949. **Staff:** 20. **Budget:** $3,600,000. **State Groups:** 50. **Description:** Economists, educators, and representatives from business, labor, and finance dedicated to improving economic education by improving the quality and increasing the quantity of economics being taught in all levels of schools and colleges. Initiates curriculum development and research; experiments with new economics courses and ways to prepare teachers and students; provides updated teacher-pupil materials; coordinates national and local programs in economics education. Provides consulting services to educators; sponsors workshops; tests new methods in practical school situations. **Libraries:** **Type:** not open to the public. **Holdings:** 3,000. **Subjects:** economics education. **Awards:** National Awards for the Teaching of Economics. **Frequency:** annual. **Type:** recognition. **Recipient:** for outstanding contributions to economic literacy and teaching ● **Type:** recognition. **Recipient:** to school districts for excellence in economic education. **Divisions:** Affiliated Centers and Councils; Market/Product Development; Public Information; Research and University Sciences. **Affiliated With:** AACSB International - Association to Advance Collegiate Schools of Business; American Association of Colleges for Teacher Education; American Association of Community Colleges; American Association of School Administrators; American Economic Association; Association for Supervision and Curriculum Development; Council of Chief State School Officers; National Association of Elementary School Principals; National Association of Secondary School Principals; National Business Education Association; National Council for the Social Studies; National School Boards Association. **Formerly:** (1992) Joint Council in Economic Education. **Publications:** *Curriculum Guide* ● *Economic Education Experiences of Enterprising Teachers*, annual. Journal. Describes award-winning projects entered in the National Awards Program for the Teaching of Economics. **Price:** free to NCEE network affiliates; $2.50/copy for nonmembers. **Circulation:** 9,000 ● *Economics for Kids*, quarterly ● *Journal of Economic Education*, quarterly. Features research in economic education, innovations in teaching and expanded coverage of current economic issues. **Price:** $62.00 /year for individuals; $135.00 /year for institutions. ISSN: 0022-0485. **Circulation:** 1,300. **Advertising:** accepted. Alternate Formats: microform ● *National Council on Economic Education—Annual Report*. **Price:** free ● *National Council on Economic Education—Directory of Affiliated Councils and Centers*, annual. Lists the directors, associates, assistants, and field coordinators working within the NCEE affiliated council and center network. **Price:** free ● *National Council on Economic Education—Update: For Friends of Economic Education*, semiannual. Newsletter. Covers activities, programs, and projects related to the JCEE. Includes new product information and notices of upcoming events. **Price:** free. **Circulation:** 30,000 ● *Senior Economist*, quarterly ● Books ● Catalogs ● Also distributes filmstrips and instructional materials. **Conventions/Meetings:** annual conference (exhibits) - always October.

8218 ■ National Schools Committee for Economic Education (NSCEE)
250 E 73rd St., Ste.12G
New York, NY 10021-8641
Ph: (212)535-9534
Fax: (212)535-4167
E-mail: info@nscee.org
URL: http://www.nscee.org
Contact: John E. Donnelly, Exec. Dir.
Founded: 1953. **Budget:** $150,000. **Description:** Teachers, instructors, professors, supervisors, and administrators at the elementary school level. Seeks to maintain a continuous research and development program in ways and means, aids, and materials, to help school teachers teach the basic concepts and principles of the American free enterprise system. Maintains advisory committee of leading businesspeople and evaluation committee of teachers and

leading school administrators. Conducts short institutes for teachers. **Awards:** Certificate for Outstanding Service. **Type:** recognition. **Recipient:** to selected educators. **Publications:** *Freedom and Enterprise*, semiannual. Newsletter. **Price:** free ● Pamphlets. Provides information for teachers. ● Also develops materials for teachers such as texts, filmstrips, posters, charts, and coloring books. **Conventions/Meetings:** annual meeting - always New York City.

Education

8219 ■ Academy for Educational Development (AED)
c/o Stephen F. Moseley, Pres./CEO
1825 Connecticut Ave. NW
Washington, DC 20009-5721
Ph: (202)884-8000 (202)884-8631
Fax: (202)884-8400
E-mail: communicationsmail@aed.org
URL: http://www.aed.org
Contact: Stephen F. Moseley, Pres./CEO
Founded: 1961. **Staff:** 1,600. **Budget:** $248,000,000. **Description:** Seeks to address human resource and economic development needs through education, communication, and the dissemination of information. Works with educational institutions, community organizations, foundations, corporations, policy leaders, non-governmental and community-based organizations, international multilateral and bilateral funders, and governmental and international agencies to increase access to learning, transfer skills and technology, and support the development of educational institutions. Projects and activities are organized in three-program areas: Education and Exchange Services, including basic education and training programs, the Center for Youth Development and Policy Research, the National Institute for Work and Learning, and international exchange programs; Social Development, including health, nutrition, family planning, environment, telecommunications, development information services; and School and Community Services; and Human Resources and Institutional Development, including higher education management services, management development services, computer and systems services, and vocational and technical training programs. **Libraries: Type:** not open to the public. **Programs:** Democracy; Leadership. **Projects:** Education; Energy; Environment; HIV/AIDS; Youth. **Publications:** *A Place to Grow: Evaluation of the New York City Beacons Final Report*. Alternate Formats: online ● *A Toolbox for Building Health Communication Capacity* ● *A World Against AIDS: Communication for Behavior Change* ● *Connections*, semiannual, spring and fall. Newsletter. Includes program updates. **Price:** free. Alternate Formats: online ● *Education for All: A Global Commitment*. Alternate Formats: online ● *Environmental Education and Communication for a Sustainable World: Handbook for International Practitioners*. Alternate Formats: online ● *Handbook for Excellence in Focus Group Research* ● *Handbook for HIV Prevention Communication Planning* ● *Introducing Antiretroviral Therapy (ART) on a Large Scale: Hope and Caution*. Alternate Formats: online ● *Making a Difference in Ghana's Classrooms: Educators and Communities as Partners*. Alternate Formats: online ● *Making Classrooms Talk: Uganda Sustains Its Teacher Improvement and Support System*. Alternate Formats: online.

8220 ■ African Educational Research Network (AERN)
c/o Dr. David Adewuyi, Managing Ed.
Albany State Univ.
Coll. of Educ.
504 Coll. Dr.
Albany, GA 31705
E-mail: kofori-attah@adelphia.net
URL: http://www.africanresearch.org
Contact: Dr. Craig Brookings, Production Ed.
Founded: 1992. **Members:** 200. **Regional Groups:** 2. **Multinational**. **Description:** Academics working in the field of education; Seeks to advance educational research and scholarship; facilitates exchange of information among members; acxsponsors research and educational programs. **Awards:** Research Fellow. **Frequency:** periodic. **Type:** recognition. **Computer Services:** Mailing lists ● online services, publishing. **Committees:** Editorial; Planning. **Publications:** *The African Symposium*, semiannual. Journal. **Circulation:** 4,000. Alternate Formats: online.

8221 ■ Alliance for the Separation of School and State
1071 N Fulton St.
Fresno, CA 93728-3433
Ph: (559)499-1776
Free: (888)325-1776
Fax: (559)499-1703
E-mail: marshall@schoolandstate.org
URL: http://www.schoolandstate.org
Contact: Marshall Fritz, Chm./Founder
Founded: 1994. **Membership Dues:** regular plan for benefactor, $25 (monthly) ● benefactor, $300 (annual) ● sponsor regular plan, $10 (monthly) ● sponsor, $120 (annual) ● individual regular plan, $5 (monthly) ● individual, $60 (annual) ● associate, student, $25 (annual). **Languages:** English, Spanish. **Description:** Promotes family responsibility in education and the separation of school and state. **Publications:** *Honest Ed News*, monthly. Newsletter. Alternate Formats: online.

8222 ■ Alternative Education Resource Organization (AERO)
417 Roslyn Rd.
Roslyn Heights, NY 11577
Ph: (516)621-2195
Free: (800)769-4171
Fax: (516)625-3257
E-mail: info@educationrevolution.org
URL: http://www.educationrevolution.org
Contact: Jerry Mintz, Dir./Founder
Founded: 1989. **Membership Dues:** individual in U.S., $25 (annual) ● organization/school, $32 (annual) ● individual outside U.S., $28 (annual) ● organization/school outside U.S., $35 (annual). **Description:** Seeks to advance learner-centered approaches to education. **Libraries: Type:** reference. **Holdings:** audio recordings, books, video recordings. **Subjects:** alternative education. **Computer Services:** database, over 11,000 educational alternatives in U.S. and worldwide ● online services, listserv for 200 educators worldwide, and more. **Projects:** Alternative Education Action Groups. **Publications:** *Almanac of Education Choices*. Book. **Price:** $19.95 for nonmembers; $6.95 for members ● *Education Revolution*, quarterly. Magazine. **Price:** included in membership dues; $15.00 /year for nonmembers; $30.00/2 years for nonmembers; $45.00/3 years for nonmembers. **Advertising:** accepted. Alternate Formats: online ● *The Education Revolution*, monthly. Newsletter. Alternate Formats: online ● *No Homework and Recess All Day*. Book. **Price:** $14.95 for nonmembers; $9.95 for members. Alternate Formats: online. **Conventions/Meetings:** annual conference - 2008 June 26-29, Troy, NY.

8223 ■ American Academy of Religion (AAR)
825 Houston Mill Rd. NE, Ste.300
Atlanta, GA 30329
Ph: (404)727-3049
Fax: (404)727-7959
E-mail: aar@aarweb.org
URL: http://www.aarweb.org
Contact: John R. Fitzmier, Exec. Dir.
Founded: 1909. **Members:** 11,000. **Membership Dues:** standard, $40-$195 (annual) ● student, $30 (annual) ● international, $15 (annual). **Staff:** 15. **Budget:** $2,000,000. **Regional Groups:** 10. **Multinational**. **Description:** Professional society of scholars and teachers in the field of religion. Encourages scholarship, research, and publications in the study of religion, and stimulates effective teaching. Hosts annual meeting, publishes academic journal, offers research grants and placement services to members; compiles statistics. **Awards:** Best First Book in History of Religions Award. **Frequency:** annual. **Type:** monetary ● Book Awards for Excellence in Religion. **Frequency:** annual. **Type:** monetary. **Recipient:** for new scholarly publications that make significant contributions to the study of religion ● Excellence in Teaching. **Frequency:** annual. **Type:** monetary. **Recipient:** for excellence in teaching religion at the college or university level ● Journalism Awards. **Frequency:** annual. **Type:** monetary. **Recipient:** for best in-depth reporting that advances the public understanding of religion ● Martin E. Marty Public Understanding of Religion Award. **Frequency:** periodic. **Type:** monetary. **Recipient:** for contributions to the public understanding of religion ● Ray L. Hart Service Award. **Frequency:** periodic. **Type:** monetary. **Recipient:** to individuals whose dedication and service have made significant contributions to the AAR's mission of fostering excellence in the field of religions ● Religion in the Arts Award. **Frequency:** annual. **Type:** monetary. **Recipient:** for individuals who have made significant contributions to religion and the arts. **Computer Services:** Mailing lists, of members. **Committees:** Academic Relations; Executive; Graduate Student; International Connections; Nominations; Program; Public Understanding of Religion; Publications; Regions; Status of Racial and Ethnic Minorities in the Profession; Status of Women in the Profession; Teaching and Learning. **Affiliated With:** American Council of Learned Societies; National Humanities Alliance. **Formerly:** (1964) National Association of Biblical Instructors. **Publications:** *Academy Series*, periodic. Monographs ● *Journal of the American Academy of Religion*, quadrennial. Alternate Formats: online ● *Reflection and Theory in the Study of Religion Series*, periodic. Monographs ● *Religion, Culture, and History Series*, periodic. Monographs ● *Religious Studies News*, quadrennial. Newsletter. **Price:** free for members. Alternate Formats: online ● *Teaching Religious Studies Series*, periodic. Monographs ● *Texts and Translations Series*, periodic. Monographs. **Conventions/Meetings:** annual conference (exhibits) - every October or November.

8224 ■ American Council on Education (ACE)
1 Dupont Cir. NW
Washington, DC 20036-1193
Ph: (202)939-9300
Fax: (202)659-2212
E-mail: comments@ace.nche.edu
URL: http://www.acenet.edu
Contact: David Ward, Pres.
Founded: 1918. **Members:** 17,500. **Staff:** 175. **Budget:** $30,000,000. **Description:** A council of colleges and universities, educational organizations, and affiliates. Represents accredited, degree-granting post-secondary institutions directly or through national and regional higher education associations; advocates on their behalf before congress, the federal government, and federal and state courts. Advances education and educational methods through comprehensive voluntary action on the part of American educational associations, organizations, and institutions. Serves as an advocate for adult education and nationally administers the GED (General Education Development) high school equivalency exam. Provides college credit equivalency evaluations for courses taught outside the traditional campus classroom by corporations and the military. Maintains numerous commissions, committees, and councils. **Libraries: Type:** open to the public; by appointment only. **Holdings:** 7,000; books. **Subjects:** higher education and administration. **Divisions:** Advancement; Business-Higher Education Forum; Center for Adult Learning and Educational Credentials (see separate entry); Center for Leadership Development; Governmental Relations; HEATH Resource Center (Higher Education and Adult Training for People with Handicaps); International Education; Labor-Higher Education; Membership; Minorities in Higher Education; Policy Analysis and Research; Public Affairs; Publications; Women in Higher Education. **Programs:** Adult Learner; Fellows. **Publications:** *Accredited Institutions of Higher Education*, annual. Directories. Lists accredited institutions of higher education in the U.S. ● *ACE/Praeger Series on Higher Education*. Books ● *Higher Education and National Affairs Headlines*,

semiweekly. Newsletter. **Price:** free. **Circulation:** 16,500. Alternate Formats: online. Also Cited As: *HENA* ● *The Presidency*, 3/year. Magazine. Provides information on critical issues that affect higher education leaders. **Price:** $36.00 for members; $40.00 for nonmembers. **Circulation:** 1,500. **Advertising:** accepted ● Yearbooks. **Conventions/Meetings:** annual meeting, for higher education's senior leaders (exhibits).

8225 ■ American Council on Schools and Colleges (ACSC)
Address Unknown since 2007
Founded: 1927. **Members:** 15. **Membership Dues:** Institutional, corporate, $300 (annual). **Staff:** 2. **Description:** Private schools, institutes, colleges, seminaries, trade and vocational schools, educational support companies, publishers, and organizations. Promotes ethical business practices and sound educational standards. Unites private educational institutions for mutual benefit, support, and the exchange of information and resources. Works to advance moral and cultural educational concerns. Conducts research on teaching methods. Maintains speakers' bureau; compiles statistics. **Publications:** none. **Awards:** Award of Merit. **Frequency:** periodic. **Type:** recognition. **Recipient:** for superior performance. **Computer Services:** Online services. **Formerly:** (1981) National Association of Colleges and Universities. **Conventions/Meetings:** periodic workshop, member workshops for internal improvements in academic and business functions.

8226 ■ American Councils for International Education
1776 Massachusetts Ave. NW, Ste.700
Washington, DC 20036
Ph: (202)833-7522
Fax: (202)833-7523
E-mail: general@americancouncils.org
URL: http://www.americancouncils.org
Contact: Dr. Dan E. Davidson, Pres./Co-Founder
Founded: 1974. **Members:** 1,650. **Membership Dues:** associate, full professor, non-academic, $35 (annual) ● assistant professor, lecturer, pre-college teacher, independent scholar, $30 (annual) ● student, $10 (annual) ● retired, $25 (annual) ● life, $500. **Staff:** 21. **Budget:** $49,000,000. **Languages:** Armenian, English, Russian, Serbian, Tajiki, Turkic Dialects, Ukrainian. **Multinational. Description:** Fosters independence and democratic development by advancing education and research, cultivating leadership, and empowering individuals and institutions through learning. **Libraries: Type:** open to the public. **Holdings:** reports. **Subjects:** education. **Computer Services:** database, a Russian language resource for teachers, scholars, students and professionals. **Councils:** American Council of Teachers of Russian. **Affiliated With:** American Association of Teachers of Slavic and East European Languages; National Council for Eurasian and East European Research. **Formerly:** (1998) American Council of Teachers of Russian/American Council for Collaboration and Language Study. **Publications:** *ACTR Letter*. Newsletter. Alternate Formats: online ● Directory, annual ● Brochures. Alternate Formats: online ● Reports. Alternate Formats: online.

8227 ■ American Distance Education Consortium (ADEC)
C218 Animal Sci. Bldg.
Univ. of Nebraska
Lincoln, NE 68583-0952
Ph: (402)472-7000
Fax: (402)472-9060
E-mail: jpoley@unl.edu
URL: http://www.adec.edu
Contact: Dr. Janet Poley, Pres.
Members: 65. **Membership Dues:** full, international education institution, contributing, $10,000 (annual) ● partner, $8,250 (annual) ● associate, $6,000 (annual). **Description:** Promotes the creation and provision of high quality, economical distance education programs and services to diverse audiences by the land grant community of colleges and universities through the aid of the most appropriate information technologies available. **Awards:** National Excellence in Distance Education Awards. **Frequency:** annual. **Type:** recognition. **Recipient:** for educational institutions that offer outstanding distance education programs. **Computer Services:** database, program catalog ● information services, distance education and satellite resources ● online services, online courses, multimedia, software tools. **Committees:** Ideal; Principal Contact; Program Panel. **Projects:** Advance Internet Satellite Extension. **Affiliated With:** Council for Agricultural Science and Technology; Global Alliance for Transnational Education; International Council for Open and Distance Education; W.K. Kellogg Foundation. **Publications:** *IDEAL Committee Report: Improving Administrative Infrastructure*. Alternate Formats: online ● Proceedings. Provides abstracts of the conferences of ADEC. Alternate Formats: online.

8228 ■ American Educational Studies Association (AESA)
c/o Rhonda Jeffries, Sec.
Dept. of Instruction and Teacher Educ.
Wardlaw Coll. of Educ.
Univ. of South Carolina
Columbia, SC 29208
Ph: (803)777-5270
Fax: (803)777-3090
E-mail: rjeffries@gwm.sc.edu
URL: http://www3.uakron.edu/aesa
Contact: Steve Tozer, Pres.
Founded: 1968. **Members:** 650. **Membership Dues:** regular, $45 (annual) ● student, $30 (annual) ● emeritus, $35 (annual) ● institutional, $105 (annual). **Multinational. Description:** Teachers and researchers concerned with the comprehensive view of education including the underlying philosophy, history, sociology, and psychology of education. Encourages research and the improvement of teaching in these areas. Promotes academic study of the educative process and the school as a fundamental social institution. **Committees:** Academic Standards and Accreditation; Promotion of the Study of the Humanities in Education. **Affiliated With:** American Association of University Professors; American Educational Research Association; Comparative and International Education Society; Council on Anthropology and Education; History of Education Society; John Dewey Society; Philosophy of Education Society. **Publications:** *AESA News and Comments*, quarterly. Newsletter. **Price:** included in membership dues. Alternate Formats: online ● *Educational Foundations*, quarterly. Journal. **Price:** $50.00 /year for individuals; $80.00 /year for institutions and libraries. ISSN: 1047-8248 ● *Educational Studies*, quarterly. Journal. Includes book reviews, academic papers, media reviews, essay reviews and poetry. **Price:** included in membership dues. **Conventions/Meetings:** annual conference (exhibits) - always October/November ● annual lecture.

8229 ■ American Sports Institute (ASI)
PO Box 1837
Mill Valley, CA 94942
Ph: (415)383-5750
Fax: (415)383-5785
E-mail: info@amersports.org
URL: http://www.amersports.org
Contact: Joel Kirsch, Pres.
Founded: 1985. **Staff:** 4. **Budget:** $480,000. **Description:** Represents educators, administrators, coaches, and other individuals with an interest in education. Promotes improved educational performance through the study and practice of sports; seeks to transfer sports coaching techniques to the classroom. Conducts training programs for teachers. Operates Promoting Achievement in School Through Sports (PASS) program, through which middle and high school students study fundamentals of athletic excellence and apply these to academics. **Programs:** FirstPASS; PASS. **Publications:** *Athlete's View*, quarterly. Newsletter. Contains articles, information, and an overview of the programs and services offered by the institute. Alternate Formats: online ● *PASS*. Brochure.

8230 ■ ASA International
119 Cooper St.
Babylon, NY 11702
Ph: (631)893-4540
Free: (800)766-4656
Fax: (631)587-1582
E-mail: jordan@student-management.com
URL: http://www.asainternational.com
Contact: Dr. Samuel Gibson, Contact
Founded: 1992. **Staff:** 5. **Description:** International high school student exchange. Promotes world peace and understanding by bringing together foreign teens with volunteer US host families. **Formerly:** (2000) American Scholastic Associates International.

8231 ■ ASPIRA Association
1444 Eye St. NW, Ste.800
Washington, DC 20005-2210
Ph: (202)835-3600
Fax: (202)835-3613
E-mail: info@aspira.org
URL: http://www.aspira.org
Contact: Ronald Blackburn-Moreno, Pres./CEO
Founded: 1961. **Staff:** 1,100. **Budget:** $5,000,000. **Regional Groups:** 7. **Description:** Works to provide leadership development and educational assistance to Latino persons, thus advancing the Hispanic community (Aspira is the Spanish word for aspire). Offers educational counseling for high school and college students. Provides a forum for group discussions, workshops, tutoring, and assistance in applying for college admission, scholarships, and loans; establishes high school clubs. Sponsors National Health Careers Program, which works to: improve the quality of health care delivered to the Latino community, partly through an increase in the number of Hispanic health care providers; increase the number of Hispanics completing their medical education; encourage Hispanic doctors to return to the Latino community. Program provides counseling, tutoring, work/study internships, review courses, financial aid counseling, and placement assistance. Also sponsors Aspira Public Policy Leadership Program, which develops and supports the leadership potential of Latino high school youth via workshops, seminars, and internships. Program participants analyze social, economic, and political issues to acquire skills and knowledge necessary to assume leadership roles. Conducts research on at-risk Hispanic youth and dropouts. **Convention/Meeting:** none. **Committees:** Institute for Policy Research. **Councils:** Corporate Advisory; Leadership Advisory; National Health Careers. **Programs:** ASPIRA Alumni Association; ASPIRA Math and Science Academy (MAS) and CASA MAS; ASPIRA National Health Careers; ASPIRA Parents for Educational Excellence Initiative; ASPIRA Youth Leadership Development; Organizational Development Initiative; Youth Ventures Entrepreneurship. **Projects:** Teachers, Organizations, and Parents for Students. **Formerly:** (1987) Aspira of America. **Publications:** *Aspira News*, quarterly. Newsletter. Contains new publications information, statistics, program and legislative updates, and association activities news. **Price:** free. **Circulation:** 2,000 ● *El Legado: A Puerto Rican Legacy*. Film ● *Hispanic Dropouts in Five Cities* ● *Northeast Hispanic Needs: A Call for Action* ● Annual Report, annual ● Brochures ● Reports.

8232 ■ Association for Direct Instruction (ADI)
PO Box 10252
Eugene, OR 97440
Ph: (541)485-1293
Free: (800)995-2464
Fax: (541)868-1397
E-mail: info@adihome.org
URL: http://www.adihome.org
Contact: Bryan Wickman, Exec. Dir.
Founded: 1981. **Members:** 1,500. **Membership Dues:** regular, $40 (annual) ● student, $30 (annual) ● sustaining, $75 (annual) ● institutional, $150 (annual). **Staff:** 2. **Description:** Public school regular and special education teachers and university instructors. Encourages, promotes, and engages in research aimed at improving educational methods. Promotes dissemination of developmental information and skills

that facilitate the education of adults and children. Administers a preschool for developmentally delayed children. Offers educational training workshops for instructors. Maintains speaker's bureau and placement service. **Awards:** Outstanding Administrator. **Frequency:** annual. **Type:** recognition ● Outstanding Researcher. **Frequency:** annual. **Type:** recognition ● Outstanding Teacher. **Frequency:** annual. **Type:** recognition. **Committees:** Preschool; Recognition. **Publications:** *Direct Instruction News*, quarterly. Magazine. **Price:** included in membership dues ● *Journal of Direct Instruction*, quarterly. **Price:** included in membership dues. ISSN: 1068-7378. **Circulation:** 2,000. **Advertising:** accepted ● Also publishes books on theory and instruction. **Conventions/Meetings:** annual conference (exhibits) - always Eugene, OR ● Direct Instruction Training Opportunities - conference.

8233 ■ Association for Moral Education (AME)
c/o Nancy Nordmann, PhD, Sec.
Natl.-Louis Univ.
Psychology Dept.
122 S Michigan Ave.
Chicago, IL 60603
E-mail: nnordmann@nl.edu
URL: http://www.amenetwork.org
Contact: Nancy Nordmann PhD, Sec.
Founded: 1976. **Membership Dues:** regular, $75 (annual) ● student, $60 (annual). **Description:** Provides interdisciplinary forum for professionals interested in moral dimensions of educational theory and practice. **Awards:** Dissertation Award. **Type:** recognition. **Recipient:** for doctoral dissertations in the field of moral development ● Gift-Of-Time Dissertation Grant. **Frequency:** semiannual. **Type:** grant. **Recipient:** for doctoral students ● Kuhmerker Career Award. **Type:** recognition. **Recipient:** for individuals making outstanding contributions to AME and the field. **Publications:** *AME News*, semiannual. Newsletter. **Price:** included in membership dues ● *Journal of Moral Education*. **Price:** included in membership dues ● Membership Directory. **Conventions/Meetings:** annual conference.

8234 ■ Benjamin Franklin Education Foundation (BFEF)
6275 Hazeltine Natl. Dr.
Orlando, FL 32822
Ph: (407)240-8009
Free: (800)331-0461
Fax: (407)240-8333
E-mail: education@pafgraf.org
URL: http://www.pafgraf.org
Contact: Anne Gaither, Dir.
Founded: 1983. **Members:** 600. **Staff:** 14. **Description:** Aims to inform the public about the rapidly expanding graphic communications industry. Conducts educational programs and projects to increase literacy levels of students and the workforce; makes available educational opportunities related to graphic communications. **Awards: Type:** scholarship. **Conventions/Meetings:** annual conference, held in conjunction with Graphics of the Americas (exhibits).

8235 ■ Books for a Better World
PO Box 30848
Mesa, AZ 85275
Ph: (480)628-2300
E-mail: courtklein@hotmail.com
URL: http://www.booksforabetterworld.org
Contact: Courtney Klein, Asst. Dir.
Founded: 2000. **Members:** 172. **Staff:** 1. **Budget:** $50,000. **Languages:** English, Spanish. **Multinational. Description:** Dedicated to the purpose of books for a better world; seeks to enfranchise, empower, and motivate children in developing nations by establishing libraries and scholarship programs. **Libraries: Type:** not open to the public. **Holdings:** books. **Subjects:** stories, tales and legends, biographies, science. **Awards:** Scholarships. **Frequency:** annual. **Type:** scholarship. **Recipient:** for students; based on need and motivation. **Computer Services:** database ● mailing lists.

8236 ■ Breakthrough Collaborative
545 Sansome St., Ste.700
San Francisco, CA 94111
Ph: (415)442-0600
Fax: (415)442-0609
E-mail: info@breakthroughcollaborative.org
URL: http://www.breakthroughcollaborative.org
Contact: Beth C. Porter, Exec. Dir.
Founded: 1991. **Description:** Represents students teaching students. Strives to promote students as dynamic, successful learners, leaders, and teachers. Hosts conferences; coordinates admissions process; provides technical assistance and training. **Telecommunication Services:** electronic mail, bporter@breakthroughcollaborative.org. **Formerly:** (2002) Summerbridge National. **Publications:** *Celebration*, 3/year, January, May, September. Newsletter. Alternate Formats: online ● *Teaching at Breakthrough Handbook*. Alternate Formats: online.

8237 ■ Camille and Henry Dreyfus Foundation
555 Madison Ave., 20th Fl.
New York, NY 10022-3301
Ph: (212)753-1760
E-mail: admin@dreyfus.org
URL: http://www.dreyfus.org
Contact: Mark J. Cardillo, Exec. Dir.
Founded: 1946. **Description:** Strives to provide teacher-scholar awards. **Awards:** Camille and Henry Dreyfus Teacher-Scholar Awards Program. **Frequency:** annual. **Type:** grant. **Recipient:** to talented young faculties in the chemical sciences ● Faculty Start-up. **Frequency:** annual. **Type:** grant. **Recipient:** to a new faculty engaged in scholarly activity ● Senior Scientist Mentor Program. **Frequency:** annual. **Type:** grant. **Recipient:** to a faculty with an emeritus status ● Special Grant in Chemical Sciences. **Frequency:** annual. **Type:** grant. **Recipient:** to institutions with projects that propose to advance science and chemistry. **Programs:** Camille Dreyfus Teacher-Scholar Awards; Henry Dreyfus Teacher-Scholar Awards; New Faculty Awards; Postdoctoral in Environmental Chemistry. **Publications:** *Dreyfus Teacher-Scholars, 1970-1996: A Retrospective*. Book. Compiles biographical sketches of those who have received the Teacher-Scholar Awards. Alternate Formats: online.

8238 ■ Campus Compact
Brown Univ.
PO Box 1975
Providence, RI 02912
Ph: (401)867-3950
Fax: (401)867-3925
E-mail: campus@compact.org
URL: http://www.compact.org
Contact: Maureen F. Curley, Pres.
Founded: 1985. **Members:** 675. **Staff:** 12. **Budget:** $3,000,000. **State Groups:** 22. **Description:** Represents 675 college and university presidents. Promotes student involvement in community service as a necessary part of higher education. Encourages and facilitates development of programs which instill a sense of public purpose among students and integrate community service efforts as a central aspect of undergraduate education. Encourages campuses to be involved in their communities in areas such as research and service. **Awards:** Howard R. Swearer Student Humanitarian Award. **Frequency:** annual. **Type:** grant. **Recipient:** for exemplary student community service ● Thomas Ehrlich Faculty Award for Service Learning. **Frequency:** annual. **Type:** grant. **Recipient:** for faculty integration of service with academic study. **Computer Services:** Mailing lists ● online services. **Publications:** *Assessing Service-Learning and Civic Engagement: Principles and Techniques*. Book. **Price:** $45.00 for nonmembers; $36.00 for members ● *Campus Compact Newsletter*, bimonthly. **Price:** $20.00 /year for nonmembers; free for members. **Circulation:** 3,500 ● *Service Matters: Engaging Higher Education in the Renewal of America's Communities and American Democracy*. **Conventions/Meetings:** annual conference and workshop.

8239 ■ Carnegie Corporation of New York
437 Madison Ave.
New York, NY 10022
Ph: (212)371-3200
Fax: (212)754-4073
URL: http://www.carnegie.org
Contact: Thomas H. Kean, Chm.
Founded: 1911. **Staff:** 80. **Description:** A grant-making educational foundation that awards funds chiefly to colleges, universities, and national or regional organizations to finance "the advancement and diffusion of knowledge and understanding." Objectives are to: avoid nuclear war and improve U.S.-Soviet relations; educate all Americans, especially young people, for a scientifically and technologically based economy; prevent the development of serious problems for children and young teenagers; strengthen human resources in developing countries; fund special projects concerned with strengthening democratic institutions and resolving conflicts. Sponsors Carnegie Commission on Science, Technology, and Government and the Carnegie Council on Adolescent Development. Functions in the U.S. and in the British Commonwealth. **Libraries: Type:** reference. **Holdings:** archival material, reports. **Publications:** *Carnegie Results*, quarterly. Newsletter. Describes corporation supported activities. ● *General Information* ● *List of Grants and Appropriations*, annual. Contains a pre-print from *Annual Report*. ● Annual Report.

8240 ■ Catholic Healthcare Audit Network (CHAN)
231 S Bemiston Ave., Ste.300
Clayton, MO 63105
Ph: (314)802-2000 (314)802-2005
Fax: (314)802-2020
E-mail: dlemoine@chanllc.com
URL: http://www.chanllc.com
Contact: David LeMoine CPA, Pres./CEO
Founded: 1997. **Staff:** 9. **Budget:** $150,000. **Description:** Works to provide continuing professional education in healthcare auditing. Maintains speakers' bureau. **Computer Services:** database ● mailing lists. **Telecommunication Services:** electronic bulletin board. **Formerly:** (1999) Healthcare Audit Network. **Conventions/Meetings:** board meeting ● annual conference ● semiannual Executive Forum - meeting.

8241 ■ Center for Commercial-Free Public Education
1714 Franklin St., Ste.100-306
Oakland, CA 94612
Ph: (510)268-1100
Free: (800)UNPLUG1
Fax: (510)268-1277
E-mail: unplug@igc.org
URL: http://www.ibiblio.org/commercialfree
Contact: Andrew Hagelshaw, Exec. Dir.
Founded: 1993. **Membership Dues:** individual, $35 (annual) ● organization, $30 (annual) ● student, low income, $15 (annual). **Staff:** 5. **Description:** Works to keep advertising, corporate sponsorship, and incentive programs out of public schools. Conducts skills training programs for teachers, parents and students; maintains speakers' bureau. **Programs:** Classroom Integrity Pledge; Community Assistance; Scholl Watch Team; Unplug. **Also Known As:** (1997) Unplug. **Publications:** *Endangered Education*. Reprint. **Price:** $20.00 ● *Hidden Costs of Channel One*. **Price:** $15.00 ● Newsletter, quarterly. **Price:** free. Alternate Formats: online.

8242 ■ Center for School Change (CSC)
Univ. of Minnesota, Twin Cities (West Bank)
Hubert H. Humphrey Inst. of Public Affairs
301 19th Ave. S, Rm. 234
Minneapolis, MN 55455
Ph: (612)626-1834
Fax: (612)625-0104
E-mail: jnathan@umn.edu
URL: http://centerforschoolchange.org
Contact: Joe Nathan, Dir.
Description: Serves as a program of the Humphrey Institute of Public Affairs at the University of Min-

nesota. Works with parents, educators, business people, students, policy-makers and other concerned individuals to increase student achievement; raise graduation rates; improve student attitudes towards learning, school, and community. Reaches these goals by helping to create new, potentially more effective models of communication, increasing knowledge of and support for educational reform, and stimulating change in local, state and federal institutions. **Publications:** *School Change News*, quarterly. Newsletter. Alternate Formats: online.

8243 ■ The Committee for Western Civilization (TCWC)
2615 O St. NW
Washington, DC 20007
Ph: (202)338-3239
Fax: (202)338-3185
E-mail: robert.schadler@tcs.wap.org
URL: http://conservativeclassics.com
Contact: Robert Schadler, Contact
Founded: 1983. **Members:** 1,600. **Staff:** 1. **Budget:** $50,000. **Description:** Promotes educational and cultural programs and publications through social and cultural activities. Most activities are currently in the Washington, DC area. Has sponsored FORA on topics as varied as monasticism and terrorism. Published a CD by composer Frederick Schadler. The Henry Regnery Legacy Project scans out of print books on continuing values and makes them available free of charge on the internet. **Publications:** *Committee Cultural Calendar*, monthly. Provides cultural calendar for Washington, DC and distributed by e-mail. **Price:** free for members. **Circulation:** 1,000. **Conventions/Meetings:** annual Waltz Event - meeting - usually mid-February, Saturday.

8244 ■ Common Destiny Alliance (CODA)
Univ. of Maryland
2110 Benjamin Bldg.
College Park, MD 20742
Ph: (301)405-0639
Fax: (301)405-3573
E-mail: mh267@umail.umd.edu
URL: http://www.education.umd.edu/CODA/index.html
Contact: Walter Allen, Contact
Founded: 1991. **Members:** 77. **Staff:** 2. **Description:** Organizations and scholars interested in working to end prejudice. Fosters the viewpoint that cultural diversity is "a resource that can help the nation attain goals such as improving economic productivity and the academic achievement of all children." Seeks to end racial isolation in schools, neighborhoods, and the work force. Promotes social policies, especially those related to education, that encourage racial and ethnic understanding and cooperation. Conducts research to identify the causes of racism and means to overcome racism. **Libraries: Type:** reference; open to the public. **Subjects:** multicultural education, race relations, postsecondary education, professional development. **Computer Services:** database, organizations, policies, and programs that focus on combating racism. **Committees:** Consensus Partners; Organizational Partners; Research Partners; Steering. **Publications:** *Toward a Common Destiny: Improving Race and Ethnic Relations in America*. Book. Contains a variety of alternative strategies for improving intergroup relations. **Price:** $45.00 plus shipping and handling ● *Tracking, Diversity, and Educational Equity: What's New in the Research?*. Reports. **Price:** $7.00.

8245 ■ Council for Advancement and Support of Education (CASE)
1307 New York Ave. NW, Ste.1000
Washington, DC 20005-4701
Ph: (202)328-2273 (202)478-5673
Free: (800)554-8536
Fax: (202)387-4973
E-mail: memberservicecenter@case.org
URL: http://www.case.org
Contact: John Lippincott, Pres.
Founded: 1974. **Members:** 3,250. **Membership Dues:** professional, $85 (annual) ● alumni association and affiliated foundation (4-year institution), $425-$1,330 (annual) ● alumni association and affiliated foundation (2-year institution), $505-$1,140 (annual). **Staff:** 86. **Budget:** $10,000,000. **Regional Groups:** 8. **Multinational. Description:** Members are colleges, universities, and independent elementary and secondary schools. Individual member representatives serve these institutions as alumni, fundraising, public relations, admissions, government relations, and publications officers. Serves as national clearinghouse for corporate matching gift information. Offers members professional training seminars and publications. Maintains reference library containing case studies, papers, and examples of reports and other campus publications. Conducts occasional research projects. Monitors federal legislation of interest to members. **Libraries: Type:** open to the public; by appointment only. **Holdings:** articles, books, periodicals. **Subjects:** educational institutions development, communications, alumni relations. **Awards:** Chief Executive Leadership Award. **Frequency:** annual. **Type:** recognition. **Recipient:** for outstanding efforts in promoting and supporting education ● Circle of Excellence Award. **Type:** recognition ● James L. Fisher Award for Distinguished Service to Education honor. **Frequency:** annual. **Type:** recognition. **Recipient:** for extraordinary service to education of national or international significance ● John Grenzebach Research Award. **Frequency:** annual. **Type:** recognition. **Recipient:** for outstanding writing about educational fundraising, communications and alumni relations. **Telecommunication Services:** electronic mail, membership@case.org. **Formed by Merger of:** American Alumni Council; American College Public Relations Association. **Publications:** *Currents*, 9/year. Magazine. **Price:** included in membership dues; $125.00 /year for nonmembers in U.S.; $145.00 /year for nonmembers outside U.S. **Circulation:** 22,000. **Advertising:** accepted ● Directory, annual ● Also publishes handbooks on topics of interest to members. **Conventions/Meetings:** annual conference (exhibits) - always July.

8246 ■ Council of Chief State School Officers (CCSSO)
1 Massachusetts Ave. NW, Ste.700
Washington, DC 20001-1431
Ph: (202)336-7000
Fax: (202)408-8072
E-mail: info@ccsso.org
URL: http://www.ccsso.org
Contact: Gene Wilhoit, Exec. Dir.
Founded: 1927. **Members:** 80. **Staff:** 85. **Budget:** $14,800,000. **Description:** Provides leadership, advocacy, and technical assistance on major educational issues. Seeks member consensus on major educational issues and expresses their views to civic and professional organizations, federal agencies, congress, and the public. Assists chief state school officers and their organizations in achieving the vision of an American education system that enables all children to succeed in school, work, and life. **Awards:** Distinguished Service Award. **Frequency:** annual. **Type:** recognition. **Telecommunication Services:** electronic bulletin board, AIDS education ● electronic bulletin board, community education. **Committees:** Connecting School and Employment; International Relations; Learning Technologies; Legislation; National Goals and School Restructuring; Teacher and Student Assessment. **Formerly:** (1954) National Council of Chief State School Officers. **Publications:** *Chiefline*, biweekly. Newsletter. Contains updates of breaking news and pertinent information for chief state school officers. Alternate Formats: online ● *The Council Quarterly*. Newsletter. Covers council activities and news. **Price:** free ● *State-By-State Educational Indicators Report*, annual. Includes demographics, educational policies and practices, and student data in the 50 states. **Price:** $15.00/year (discount available for bulk orders). **Conventions/Meetings:** annual conference - 2008 June 15-18, Orlando, FL ● annual Legislative Conference ● annual Policy Forum - meeting - always fall ● annual Summer Institute - meeting, professional development.

8247 ■ Council for Higher Education Accreditation (CHEA)
1 Dupont Cir. NW, Ste.510
Washington, DC 20036-1135
Ph: (202)955-6126
Fax: (202)955-6129
E-mail: chea@chea.org
URL: http://www.chea.org
Contact: Charles R. Nash, Sec.
Founded: 1996. **Description:** Colleges, universities, regional associations and higher education commissions, national higher education associations headquartered in Washington, DC, national accrediting bodies for special-mission institutions. Serves students and their families, colleges and universities, sponsoring bodies, governments and employers by promoting academic quality through formal recognition of higher education accrediting bodies; and coordinates and works to advance self-regulation through accreditation. **Telecommunication Services:** electronic mail, cnash@uasystem.ua.edu. **Publications:** *The CHEA Chronicle*. Newsletter. Alternate Formats: online ● *CHEA HEA Update*. Newsletter. Alternate Formats: online ● *2004-2005 Directory of CHEA Recognized Organizations*. Alternate Formats: online ● Monographs. Alternate Formats: online ● Papers.

8248 ■ Council on Occupational Education (COE)
41 Perimeter Center East NE, Ste.640
Atlanta, GA 30346
Ph: (770)396-3898
Free: (800)917-2081
Fax: (770)396-3790
E-mail: puckettg@council.org
URL: http://www.council.org
Contact: Dr. Gary Puckett, Exec. Dir.
Founded: 1971. **Members:** 450. **Staff:** 8. **Budget:** $1,200,000. **Description:** Postsecondary education and training institutions. Promotes improvement of education and training among workforce development providers; develops partnerships that increase the success of national, state and local workforce development initiatives and programs. **Computer Services:** database, of member institutions. **Committees:** Accreditation Standards and Conditions; Review. **Publications:** *Handbook of Accreditation*, annual. Manual. Includes standards and conditions for accreditation. Alternate Formats: online; diskette ● *Policies and Rules of the Commission*. Manual. Contains information on the policies, rules and procedures established and implemented by the commission. Alternate Formats: online ● *Self-Study Manual*. Alternate Formats: online. **Conventions/Meetings:** annual meeting (exhibits).

8249 ■ CUMREC
c/o EDUCAUSE
4772 Walnut St., Ste.206
Boulder, CO 80301-2538
Ph: (303)449-4430
Fax: (303)440-0461
E-mail: info@cumrec.org
URL: http://www.cumrec.org
Contact: Robert A. Engmark, Contact
Founded: 1956. **Members:** 1,100. **Description:** Provides a forum for higher education professionals to share their expertise and experiences with computer systems. **Awards:** Frank Martin Service Award. **Frequency:** annual. **Type:** recognition. **Recipient:** for exemplary service to the college and university information technology community. **Telecommunication Services:** electronic mail, rengmark@grcc.edu. **Publications:** Newsletter, quarterly. Alternate Formats: online ● Proceedings. Alternate Formats: online. **Conventions/Meetings:** annual conference.

8250 ■ Danforth Foundation
211 N Broadway, Ste.2390
1 Metropolitan Sq.
St. Louis, MO 63102
Ph: (314)588-1900
Fax: (314)588-0035
E-mail: cambron@muohio.edu
URL: http://www.orgs.muohio.edu/forumscp/index.html
Contact: Dr. Robert Koff, VP
Founded: 1927. **Staff:** 8. **Budget:** $7,000,000. **Description:** Seeks to improve the quality of teaching

and learning at the precollegiate level. Provides grants and funds programs in an effort to provide opportunities for professional development of high school administrators and expand the knowledge, skills, vision, and commitment of policymakers in education. Programs include: Danforth School Administrators Fellowship for professional growth and development opportunities for senior high school principals in selected urban school districts; Danforth Seminars for Federal Judges and Educators, which provides workshops for federal judges and educational leaders to examine issues related to education and the courts; Danforth Program for School Board Members, which provides professional growth and development activities for members of selected boards of large cities; Dorthy Danforth Compton Fellowships for minority doctoral candidates to study in preparation for careers in college and university teaching. Funds projects in St. Louis, MO, that: supports effective partnership between schools, community agencies, businesses, labor groups, and government; improves the learning opportunities of the educationally disadvantaged; facilitates public participation in the decision-making process about public education; serves the development of leadership opportunities for high school-age youth. **Publications:** Annual Report, annual ● Also publishes funding activities booklet.

8251 ■ Editorial Projects in Education (EPE)
6935 Arlington, Ste.100
Bethesda, MD 20814
Ph: (301)280-3100
Free: (800)346-1834
Fax: (301)280-3200
E-mail: kdorko@epe.org
URL: http://www.edweek.org
Contact: Ms. Kathryn Dorko, Library Dir.
Founded: 1959. **Staff:** 90. **Nonmembership. Multinational. Description:** Board of directors is composed of educators, journalists, and foundation administrators in the U.S. Works to disseminate information on education via journalistic means. Maintains collection of materials relating to education primarily from newspapers, books and periodicals. **Libraries: Type:** by appointment only; open to the public. **Holdings:** 3,000; books, periodicals, reports. **Subjects:** education policy K-12. **Computer Services:** Online services. **Publications:** *Diplomas Count*, annual. Annual Report. Serves as an essential guide to high school graduation policy and rates. **Price:** free to Education Week subscribers. ISSN: 0277-4232. **Circulation:** 45,000. **Advertising:** accepted. Alternate Formats: online ● *Education Week*, 44/year. Newspaper. Covers developments affecting the state of American education policy. **Price:** $79. 94. ISSN: 0277-4232. **Circulation:** 47,000. **Advertising:** accepted. Alternate Formats: online ● *Quality Counts*, annual. Annual Report. Features annual rating of states in providing quality elementary and secondary education. **Price:** $10.00. ISSN: 0277-4232. **Circulation:** 52,000. **Advertising:** accepted. Alternate Formats: online.

8252 ■ Education Commission of the States (ECS)
700 Broadway, Ste.1200
Denver, CO 80203-3460
Ph: (303)299-3600
Fax: (303)296-8332
E-mail: ecs@ecs.org
URL: http://www.ecs.org
Contact: Roderick G.W. Chu, Interim Pres.
Founded: 1966. **Staff:** 65. **Budget:** $13,000,000. **Description:** Consists of 7 representatives from each of the member states, the District of Columbia, American Samoa, Puerto Rico, and the Virgin Islands. Includes the governor of the state, others appointed by the governor, and two state legislators. Together with Interstate Compact for Education, is an agreement among the states to join together for the improvement of education by establishing a partnership of political and educational leadership. Provides a forum for the discussion of major education issues; an education, research, and service function to the member states; and a mechanism for interstate cooperation in educational policy formulation and program development. Seeks to encourage state action for the improvement of schools and schooling. Researches education policy issues. **Libraries: Type:** reference. **Holdings:** archival material, books, business records, clippings, monographs, periodicals. **Subjects:** education. **Awards:** ECS Chairman's Award. **Frequency:** annual. **Type:** recognition. **Recipient:** for an ECS commissioner ● ECS Corporate Award. **Frequency:** annual. **Type:** recognition. **Recipient:** to a for-profit corporation or organization ● Frank Newman Award. **Frequency:** annual. **Type:** recognition. **Recipient:** for excellence and innovation of a state ● James Bryant Conant Award. **Frequency:** annual. **Type:** recognition. **Recipient:** for an outstanding contributor in the field of education. **Divisions:** Communications; Higher Education; Policy and Programs; State Relations/Clearinghouse. **Projects:** Higher Education; Investing in Student Achievement; Issues and Innovations; School Reform Efforts; Student Preparation for College and the Workplace; Teacher Education and Professional Development; Urban Initiative. **Publications:** *eClips*, daily. Newsletter. Provides daily education news. Alternate Formats: online ● *eConnection*, weekly. Bulletin. Highlights state policy trends, new reports, upcoming meetings and events, websites, and ECS news. Alternate Formats: online ● *Governance Notes*, bimonthly. Discusses education governance issues. ● *The Progress of Education Reform*, bimonthly. Report ● *State Education Leader*, 3/year. Reports ● Reports. **Conventions/Meetings:** annual meeting - always summer. 2008 June 30-July 3, Austin, TX.

8253 ■ Education Development Center (EDC)
55 Chapel St.
Newton, MA 02458
Ph: (617)969-7100
Fax: (617)969-5979
E-mail: comment@edc.org
URL: http://main.edc.org
Contact: Luther Luedtke, Pres./CEO
Founded: 1958. **Staff:** 850. **Nonmembership. Multinational. Description:** Seeks to build bridges among research, policy and practice; programs and products, developed in collaboration with partners worldwide, consistently advance learning and health development for individuals of all ages; manages 335 projects in 50 countries; works to strengthen nearly every facet of society, including early child development, K-12 education, health promotion, workforce preparation, community development, learning technologies, basic and adult education, institutional reform, and social justice. **Programs:** Center for Applied Ethics and Professional Practice; Center for Children and Families; Center for Children and Technology; Center for Family, School, and Community; Center for Mathematics Learning and Teaching; Center for Science Education; Global Learning Group. **Formed by Merger of:** Educational Services; Institute for Educational Innovation. **Publications:** *EDC Online Report*, quarterly. Newsletter. Alternate Formats: online ● *Mosaic*, 3/year. Journal. **Circulation:** 4,000 ● Annual Report, annual ● Brochures ● Reports.

8254 ■ Educational Research Associates (ERA)
PO Box 8795
Portland, OR 97207-8795
Ph: (503)228-6345
Free: (800)827-2499
Fax: (810)885-5811
E-mail: info@eralearning.com
URL: http://www.eralearning.com
Founded: 1965. **Nonmembership. Description:** Educational researchers. Investigates ways of improving classroom instructional methods and school management in order to serve students, families, and communities more effectively.

8255 ■ Emotional Health Education Association
1949 W Acacia Bluffs Dr.
Green Valley, AZ 85614
Ph: (520)398-5081
Fax: (520)107-2137
E-mail: rbrill@earthlink.net
URL: http://emotionalhonesty.com
Contact: Ronald R. Brill, Dir.
Founded: 1998. **Members:** 78. **Membership Dues:** individual, $50 (annual) ● institution, $125 (annual). **Staff:** 3. **Description:** Schools, teachers, parents, and organizations. Develops programs which address student and parent needs for understanding emotional growth, coping with hurt feelings effectively, developing and maintaining emotional honesty required for emotional resilience and self-acceptance. Conducts National Youth Violence Prevention Week and the world-wide Campaign for Emotional Health Education. **Libraries: Type:** reference; not open to the public. **Holdings:** 50; articles, books, periodicals. **Subjects:** emotional health education, coping skills, recovery from hurt feelings. **Awards:** Coping Skills 4 Kids School Award. **Frequency:** annual. **Type:** recognition. **Working Groups:** Speakers Panel. **Formerly:** (2000) Emotional Education Association. **Publications:** *Emotional Education Perspectives*, quarterly. Newsletter. Contains a compilation of articles, programs and resources for emotional education. **Price:** included in membership dues. **Advertising:** accepted ● *Emotional Honesty & Self-Acceptance*. Book. **Conventions/Meetings:** annual Emotional Education Institute - convention, for information and training.

8256 ■ Federal Government Distance Learning Association (FGDLA)
c/o Dee Olsen, Treas.
13894 Bently Cir.
Fort Myers, FL 33912
E-mail: luis.ramirez@dau.mil
URL: http://www.fgdla.org
Contact: Luis Ramirez, Pres.-Elect
Membership Dues: regular, $25 (annual). **Description:** Promotes the development and application of distance learning. Seeks to develop distance learning strategies that will support a blended media approach to education and training within the federal government. Facilitates the exchange of information and implementation of distance learning. **Awards:** Diamond Award. **Frequency:** annual. **Type:** recognition. **Recipient:** for best practices in the development/ application of emerging technologies ● Hall of Fame Award. **Frequency:** annual. **Type:** recognition. **Recipient:** for career accomplishments and contributions in distance learning in the Federal Government ● Pillar Award. **Frequency:** annual. **Type:** recognition. **Recipient:** for outstanding support to the FGDLA ● Pioneer Awards. **Frequency:** annual. **Type:** recognition. **Recipient:** for breaking new ground, demonstrating leadership and best practices in the developemnt of online learning techniques ● Star Award. **Frequency:** annual. **Type:** recognition. **Recipient:** for breaking new ground in the development or application of performance support technology. **Publications:** *Distance Learning News*. Newsletter. Alternate Formats: online.

8257 ■ Friends of South African Schools Fund (FOSAS)
c/o C. Sean Day
15 E Putnam Ave., No. 245
Greenwich, CT 06830-5424
Ph: (203)422-2402
Fax: (203)422-2411
E-mail: info@saschools.org
URL: http://www.saschools.org
Contact: C. Sean Day, Contact
Founded: 1997. **Description:** Raises money for scholarships for under privileged South African children. **Publications:** Newsletter. Alternate Formats: online.

8258 ■ George Lucas Educational Foundation (GLEF)
PO Box 3494
San Rafael, CA 94912
Ph: (415)662-1600
Fax: (415)662-1532

E-mail: edutopia@glef.org
URL: http://www.edutopia.org
Contact: Milton Chen PhD, Sec./Exec. Dir.
Founded: 1991. **Staff:** 30. **Description:** Works to promote innovative efforts to improve education through incorporating technology with teaching and learning. Advocates current educational strategies; builds support to improve schools; and uses various communications media to disseminate information. **Libraries: Type:** not open to the public. **Holdings:** 5,000; books, periodicals. **Publications:** *Edutopia*. Magazine. **Advertising:** accepted. Alternate Formats: online ● *Edutopia News*, weekly. Newsletter. Alternate Formats: online ● *Edutopia Newsletter* (in English and Spanish), semiannual. **Price:** free for members. **Circulation:** 45,000. Alternate Formats: online ● *Edutopia: Success Stories for Learning in the Digital Age*. Book. **Price:** $20.00. Alternate Formats: CD-ROM; online ● *Learn and Live*. Book. **Price:** $20.00. **Circulation:** 20,000. Alternate Formats: online.

8259 ■ Healthcare Education Association (HCEA)

PO Box 388
Florissant, MO 63032-0388
Free: (888)298-3861
Fax: (314)869-5811
E-mail: membership@hcea-info.org
URL: http://www.hcea-info.org
Contact: Linda Kocent, Pres.
Founded: 1998. **Members:** 350. **Membership Dues:** individual, $95 (annual) ● student, $45 (annual) ● patron, $250 (annual) ● silver corporate, $1,000 (annual) ● gold corporate, $1,500 (annual) ● platinum corporate, $2,500 (annual). **Staff:** 3. **Description:** Supports and mentors healthcare educators. **Awards:** Excellence in Practice Award for Patient/Community Education. **Frequency:** annual. **Type:** recognition. **Recipient:** to a member who has initiated innovative and effective practices, interventions or programs in patient and community education ● Excellence in Practice Award for Staff Development. **Frequency:** annual. **Type:** recognition. **Recipient:** to a member who has initiated innovation and effective practices, interventions or programs in staff development ● Outstanding Research Award. **Frequency:** annual. **Type:** recognition. **Recipient:** for members. **Computer Services:** database ● mailing lists. **Publications:** *HCEA Newsletter*, quarterly. **Price:** included in membership dues. **Circulation:** 400. **Advertising:** accepted. Alternate Formats: online. **Conventions/Meetings:** annual Health Care Education Institute - conference (exhibits).

8260 ■ Hispanic Council for Reform and Educational Options (CREO)

2600 Virginia Ave. NW, Ste.408
Washington, DC 20037
Ph: (202)625-6766
Free: (877)888-2736
Fax: (202)625-6767
E-mail: ralvarez@hcreo.org
URL: http://www.hcreo.org
Contact: Mrs. Rebeca Nieves Huffman, Pres./CEO
Founded: 2001. **Membership Dues:** individual, $10 (annual) ● immediate family (parent/guardian/child), $25 (annual). **Languages:** English, Spanish. **Description:** Aims to improve educational outcomes for Hispanic children by empowering families through parental choice in education. **Programs:** School Choice. **Projects:** CREO. **Publications:** Newsletter, monthly. **Price:** included in membership dues. Alternate Formats: online.

8261 ■ Home and School Institute (HSI)

MegaSkills Educ. Center
1500 Massachusetts Ave. NW
Washington, DC 20005
Ph: (202)466-3633
Fax: (202)833-1400
E-mail: edstaff@megaskills.org
URL: http://www.megaskillshsi.org
Contact: Dr. Dorothy Rich, Pres.
Founded: 1965. **Languages:** English, Spanish. **Description:** Focuses on the educational importance of the home and the community. Develops academic and character development educational strategies for school-family, school-community, and business-family involvement. Designs and researches practical ways for families to strengthen the home learning environment. Offers the MegaSkills Leader Training for Parent Involvement Program and programs focusing on the educational role of the family. (The institute develops MegaSkills as "the habits, behaviors, and attitudes basic for success in school and beyond.") Develops programs for bilingual, disabled, and disadvantaged children. Provides MegaSkills Essentials for the Classroom, a curriculum and training project for teachers in teaching habits and attitudes needed for success in school and beyond. Offers new training in Adult MegaSkills for Teachers: How to Work More Effectively with Parents. Also sponsors special community services and college credit training programs in school and family-community involvement. **Awards:** Dorothy Rich Learning Leaders Awards. **Type:** monetary ● MegaSkills Training Scholarship. **Type:** scholarship. **Recipient:** for school systems and community groups. **Publications:** *MegaSkills: Building Children's Achievement for the Information Age, 3rd Edition*. Describes activities that teach confidence, motivation, effort, responsibility, initiative, teamwork, and problem solving to children. **Price:** $14.00 ● *MegaSkills: The Best Gift You Can Give Your Child, 2nd Edition*. Book. Includes responses from parents and teachers using the workshops/activities, plus sections on readiness to learn and the importance of grandparents. **Price:** $9.00 ● *The New MegaSkills Bond*. Book. Includes practical strategies to build partnerships with families and the community. **Price:** $6.00 ● *Parent Handbook English/Spanish Bilingual Handbook*. Lists activities for families, especially designed for Hispanic parents. **Price:** $6.00 ● *Reading, Writing, Math - Teaching and Mentoring for Student Achievement*. **Price:** $8.00/set of 20 copies ● *Survival Guide for Today's Parents*. Book. Features dozens of activities for home learning. **Price:** $7.00 ● *What Do I Say? What Do I Do?*. Handbook. Provides problem solving practices. **Price:** $2.00 minimum order of twenty ● *What Do We Say? What Do We Do? Vital Solutions for Children's Educational Success*. Book. Explores natural stresses and frustrations of the home/school relationship. Provides situations/activities using children's words, suggests responses. **Price:** $12.95. **Conventions/Meetings:** workshop, instructs teachers and parents how to provide for the guidance and educational needs of children; works with school districts and the business community to build partnerships in education ● workshop, mentor training programs.

8262 ■ IEEE Education Society (ES)

c/o Joseph L.A. Hughes, Pres.
Georgia Inst. of Tech.
777 Atlantic Dr. NW
Atlanta, GA 30332
Ph: (404)894-2975
E-mail: jhughes@ece.gatech.edu
URL: http://www.ewh.ieee.org/soc/es
Contact: Joseph L.A. Hughes, Pres.
Founded: 1963. **Members:** 3,000. **Membership Dues:** individual, $20 (annual) ● student, $10 (annual). **Budget:** $200,000. **Regional Groups:** 6. **Description:** A society of the Institute of Electrical and Electronics Engineers (see separate entry). Concerned with accreditation, educational methods, technology, instructional materials, development programs, history of electrical engineering education, and the impact of research on education and issues pertinent to electrical engineering education. Conducts educational programs. **Awards:** Achievement Award. **Frequency:** annual. **Type:** recognition. **Recipient:** to a member of the IEEE Education Society for outstanding and sustained contributions to engineering education ● Benjamin Dasher Award. **Frequency:** annual. **Type:** recognition. **Recipient:** to the best paper/presentation at the annual Frontiers in Education Conference (FIE) ● Distinguished Member Award. **Frequency:** annual. **Type:** recognition. **Recipient:** for outstanding long term service to the IEEE Education Society and significant contributions in an IEEE Field of Interest ● Hewlett-Packard/Harriet B. Rigas Award. **Frequency:** annual. **Type:** monetary. **Recipient:** for outstanding women engineering faculty who have made a significant contribution to the profession ● IEEE Transactions on Education Best Paper Award. **Frequency:** annual. **Type:** recognition. **Recipient:** to the author(s) of the best paper from the previous year's Transactions on Education ● Mac Van Valkenburg Early Career Teaching Award. **Frequency:** annual. **Type:** monetary. **Recipient:** to members of the IEEE Education Society who have made outstanding contributions to teaching unusually early in their professional careers ● McGraw-Hill/Jacob Millman Award. **Frequency:** annual. **Type:** monetary. **Recipient:** to authors of pedagogically innovative textbooks in the fields of electrical engineering, computer engineering, or related areas ● Meritorious Service Award. **Frequency:** annual. **Type:** recognition. **Recipient:** for outstanding leadership and service to the IEEE Education Society over a sustained period of time. **Committees:** Awards; Chapters; Constitution and By-Laws; FIE Steering; Meetings; Nominating; Publications; Technical Area. **Publications:** *IEEE Transactions on Education*, quarterly. Journal. Features educational methods, technology, and programs; history of technology; impact of evolving research on education. ● *Newsletter of the IEEE Education Society and the ASEE Electrical Engineering Division*, 3/year. **Price:** included in membership dues. **Circulation:** 4,000. **Advertising:** accepted ● *Transactions on Education*, quarterly. Journal. Includes scholarly papers on electrical engineering education. **Price:** included in membership dues. ISSN: 0018-9359. **Circulation:** 4,000. **Conventions/Meetings:** annual Frontiers in Education Conference (exhibits).

8263 ■ Institute for Development of Educational Activities (IDEA)

Address Unknown since 2007
Founded: 1965. **Staff:** 5. **Budget:** $1,000,000. **Description:** Action-oriented research and development organization, originating from the Charles F. Kettering Foundation, established to assist the educational community in bridging the gap that separates research and innovation from actual practice in the schools. Goal is to design and test new responses to problems in education and to create arrangements for their extensive application. Main activities include: developing new and improved processes, systems, and materials; providing information and services that facilitate use of improved methods and materials. **Publications:** */I/D/E/A/ Reporter*, semiannual. Newsletter. **Circulation:** 23,000. **Advertising:** not accepted. **Conventions/Meetings:** annual In-Service Institute - conference and seminar, in-service conference for school administrators - always July ● seminar, three four-day conferences held at different locations depending on topic and interest in geographic area.

8264 ■ Institute for Educational Leadership (IEL)

4455 Connecticut Ave. NW, Ste.310
Washington, DC 20008
Ph: (202)822-8405
Fax: (202)872-4050
E-mail: iel@iel.org
URL: http://www.iel.org
Contact: Elizabeth L. Hale, Pres.
Founded: 1971. **Staff:** 35. **Budget:** $4,000,000. **For-Profit. Description:** Coordinates programs at national, state, and local levels that are designed to support and enhance the capabilities of educators and policymakers. Areas of interest include: leadership development and expanding the talents, skills, and vision of those working in education and related fields; informing and linking policymakers within and across sectors; establishing access to policy and analysis expertise and providing for specialized interests through ongoing networks, research, and communication. Works to identify emerging issues and options for policymakers whose decisions about allocations of resources and priorities affect the quality of education in the U.S. Acts as educational forum for policy and information exchange among governmental, non-profit, and business sectors; sponsors

Washington policy seminars to assist education leaders and managers worldwide, provide training in federal policy processes, and offer seminars on specific aspects of policymaking; conducts state education policy seminars, bringing together key state political and educational leaders to examine policy issues and explore options in a neutral forum. Projects include: Education Policy Fellowship Program, a one-year training program to prepare mid-career individuals to deal effectively with the shaping of public policy. **Publications:** *IELeadership Connections*, bimonthly. Newsletter. **Price:** free. Alternate Formats: online ● Newsletter, triennial ● Also publishes numerous policy reports.

8265 ■ Institute for Educational Services (IES)
108 Johnston St.
Savannah, GA 31405-5605
Ph: (912)355-2259
E-mail: iesgalin@aol.com
Contact: Melvyn P. Galin, Pres./CEO
Founded: 1970. **Nonmembership. Multinational. Description:** Provides support primarily to other not-for-profit and educational institutions and organizations, with a focus on information technology. **Conventions/Meetings:** meeting.

8266 ■ Institute of Near Eastern and African Studies (INEAS)
PO Box 425125
Cambridge, MA 02142
Ph: (617)864-6327
Fax: (617)864-6328
E-mail: ineas@aol.com
URL: http://www.ineas.org
Contact: Wafaa' Al-Natheema, Founder/Dir.
Founded: 1994. **Membership Dues:** individual, $25-$70 (annual) ● family, $40-$120 (annual) ● institution, company, $55-$250 (annual). **Staff:** 4. **Description:** Aims to educate the Arab, African, Middle Eastern, and Muslim communities. Offers different services and informs the media on issues related to the Arab and Islamic worlds, Africa, and the non-Arab Middle East. **Projects:** Iraq Stolen Arts and Project; Translators/Interpreters for Hospitals and Law Firms. **Publications:** *INEAS News*, quarterly. Newsletter. **Price:** included in membership dues. Alternate Formats: online ● Reports. Alternate Formats: online.

8267 ■ Institute for People's Education and Action (IPEA)
73 Willow St.
Florence, MA 01062
Ph: (413)585-8755
E-mail: cspicer@admin.umass.edu
URL: http://www.peopleseducation.org
Contact: Alan Furth, Co-Chair
Founded: 1977. **Description:** Represents individuals and institutions involved with "people's education" (community learning among peers, based in culture and experience, that builds democratic communities through dialogue and action) as exemplified by the Scandinavian folk high schools and study circles, and the Latin American liberatory education experience. **Formerly:** (1978) Folk College Association of America; (1980) Folk-School Association of America; (2004) Folk Education Association of America. **Publications:** *Conversations*, 3/year. Newsletter. Includes features, resources, member highlights, book sales, and international events. **Price:** included in membership dues. **Advertising:** accepted ● *Option*, semiannual. Journal. Covers association's education philosophy and activities; includes book reviews, biographies, and indexes. **Price:** included in membership dues; $8.00 for nonmembers (2 volumes set). **Circulation:** 250. **Advertising:** accepted ● *People's Education Resource Directory*, annual. Lists folk education institutions. **Price:** $10.00. **Advertising:** accepted.

8268 ■ International Boys' Schools Coalition (IBSC)
c/o Christopher Wadsworth, Assoc. Exec. Dir.
PO Box 117
Dennis, MA 02638-0117
Ph: (508)385-4563
Fax: (508)385-4273
E-mail: office@theibsc.org
URL: http://www.theibsc.org
Contact: Christopher Wadsworth, Assoc. Exec. Dir.
Founded: 1993. **Multinational. Description:** Works for the education and development of boys, the professional growth of those who work with them, and the advocacy and the advancement of institutions - primarily schools for boys that serve them. **Affiliated With:** National Association of Independent Schools. **Publications:** Newsletter ● Monograph. Contains information about the education of boys and boys' schools. **Price:** $6.50. **Conventions/Meetings:** annual The Spirit of Boys - meeting.

8269 ■ International Education and Resource Network (IEARN)
475 Riverside Dr., Ste.450
New York, NY 10115
Ph: (212)870-2693
Fax: (212)870-2672
E-mail: iearn@us.iearn.org
URL: http://www.iearn.org
Contact: Dr. Edwin Gragert, Exec. Dir.
Founded: 1988. **Membership Dues:** teacher, $100 (annual) ● school, $400 (annual). **Multinational. Description:** Empowers teachers and young people to work together on different online projects relevant to education and learning using the Internet and other new communications technologies. **Libraries: Type:** reference. **Holdings:** articles. **Subjects:** youth, education, teachers, teaching, learning. **Computer Services:** database, searchable people and project ● information services, educational resources ● online services, interactive forums. **Programs:** Armenia School Connectivity; Building Respect through Internet Dialogue; Feeding Minds, Fighting Hunger; Friendship through Education; Laws of Life; Linking Individuals, Knowledge and Culture; Media Mosaic; School Connectivity for Uzbekistan. **Publications:** *Interaction*. Newsletter. Alternate Formats: online ● Handbook. Contains outlines of some of the steps to getting started in online collaborative project work. Alternate Formats: online ● Annual Report, annual. Alternate Formats: online. **Conventions/Meetings:** annual conference, includes youth summit and workshops.

8270 ■ International Listening Association (ILA)
PO Box 744
River Falls, WI 54022
Ph: (715)425-3377
Free: (800)452-4505
Fax: (715)425-9533
E-mail: ilistening@aol.com
URL: http://www.listen.org
Contact: Jim Pratt, Exec. Dir.
Founded: 1979. **Members:** 400. **Membership Dues:** regular, $95 (annual) ● regular, $170 (biennial) ● emeritus, $45 (annual) ● life, $1,000 ● sustaining, $295 (annual) ● organizational, $535 (annual) ● student, $45 (annual). **Staff:** 1. **Budget:** $80,000. **Regional Groups:** 4. **Description:** Representatives from areas including education, business, industry, and government; other interested individuals. Promotes the study and development of effective listening. Conducts research on listening and how it affects humanity in regard to economic, educational, race, cultural, and international relations. Exchanges information on teaching methods, training experiences, and materials. Sponsors workshops and seminars on such topics as therapeutic and assertive listening. **Libraries: Type:** reference. **Holdings:** 11; biographical archives. **Subjects:** listening. **Awards:** Graduate Thesis/Dissertation Award. **Frequency:** annual. **Type:** recognition. **Recipient:** for any full time graduate student who has completed outstanding research in the form of a thesis or dissertation ● Hall of Fame Award. **Frequency:** annual. **Type:** recognition. **Recipient:** for individuals who are recognized for notable achievements involving listening in academic, business, or other settings and have contributed to the advancement of effective listening over a number of years ● ILA Special Recognition Award. **Frequency:** annual. **Type:** recognition. **Recipient:** for individuals or organizations who have performed outstanding service to the ILA for an extended period of time, or have provided unusual or unique service to the promotion of listening ● Listener of the Year. **Frequency:** annual. **Type:** recognition. **Recipient:** for nationally/internationally prominent listeners who epitomize the highest standard and principles of effective listening ● Listening Research Award. **Frequency:** annual. **Type:** recognition. **Recipient:** for outstanding achievement in research by an ILA member or group ● Undergraduate Research Award. **Frequency:** annual. **Type:** recognition. **Recipient:** for an outstanding research project. **Computer Services:** Bibliographic search; of listening materials ● mailing lists ● online services. **Committees:** Archives; Audit; Awards; Business; Curriculum/Assessment; Elementary/Secondary; International Outreach; Local Arrangements; Membership; Program Planning; Public Relations; Research; Site. **Publications:** *ILA Membership Directory*, annual. **Price:** $15.00 ● *International Journal of Listening*, annual. ISSN: 1090-4018 ● *Listening Post*, quarterly. Newsletter ● *Listening Professional*, annual. **Conventions/Meetings:** annual convention (exhibits) - usually March ● periodic regional meeting and conference (exhibits) ● annual regional meeting, in east, southeast, and mid-west regions.

8271 ■ International Visual Literacy Association (IVLA)
c/o Dr. Constance L. Cassity, Exec. Treas.
Northeastern State Univ.
3100 E New Orleans St.
Broken Arrow, OK 74014
E-mail: trhergert@stcloudstate.edu
URL: http://www.ivla.org
Contact: Tom Hergert, Pres.
Founded: 1968. **Members:** 200. **Membership Dues:** student, retired, $30 (annual) ● full, $60 (annual) ● life, $500. **Description:** Professionals in many countries from the fields of teaching (visual media and early learning), medicine, art, psychology, and television. Promotes exploration and education in the methods of visual communication. **Libraries: Type:** reference. **Holdings:** archival material. **Committees:** Awards; International; Publications. **Affiliated With:** Association for Educational Communications and Technology. **Formerly:** (1973) Conference on Visual Literacy. **Publications:** *Journal of Visual Literacy*, semiannual. **Price:** $18.00/year. Also Cited As: *JVL* ● *Readings from the Annual Conference of the International Visual Literacy Association*. Papers. Contains more than 30 papers on visual literacy. **Price:** $30.00/copy ● *Visual Literacy Review*, quarterly. Newsletter. Covers membership activities; includes book reviews. **Price:** included in membership dues. Alternate Formats: online. **Conventions/Meetings:** annual Vision Quest: Journeys toward Visual Literacy - conference.

8272 ■ John Dewey Society (JDS)
c/o Dr. Robert C. Morris, Sec.-Treas.
Educational Leadership
Univ. of West Georgia
Carrollton, GA 30118
Ph: (678)839-6132
Fax: (678)839-6097
E-mail: rmorris@westga.edu
Contact: Dr. Robert C. Morris, Sec.-Treas.
Founded: 1935. **Members:** 450. **Membership Dues:** retired, student, $30 (annual) ● fellow, $40 (annual) ● institution/library, $50 (annual). **Budget:** $15,000. **Multinational. Description:** Individuals interested in contemporary educational and cultural problems. Sponsors and encourages study of educational and cultural matters of particular concern to teachers. Conducts educational programs. **Libraries: Type:** reference. **Subjects:** educational. **Awards:** John Dewey Society Award. **Frequency:** annual. **Type:** recognition. **Computer Services:** database ● mailing lists. **Committees:** Inquiries into Education and Culture; Insights; John Dewey Lecture and AERA Program; John Dewey Memorial Session Associated; Liaison; NCSS. **Publications:** *Education and Culture*, semiannual. Journal ● *Insights*, semiannual. Mono-

graph ● *John Dewey Society—Directory of Members*, annual. Membership Directory ● *John Dewey Society Lectures*, annual ● Books, annual ● Yearbook, annual ● Also publishes studies and working papers. **Conventions/Meetings:** annual conference, held in conjunction with American Educational Research Association (exhibits) ● annual seminar, held in conjunction with the Association for Supervision and Curriculum Development and the National Council for the Social Studies.

8273 ■ Learning First Alliance
4455 Connecticut Ave., Ste.310
Washington, DC 20008
Ph: (202)296-5220
Fax: (866)218-3759
E-mail: vonzastrowc@learningfirst.org
URL: http://www.learningfirst.org
Contact: Claus von Zastrow, Exec. Dir.
Founded: 1996. **Staff:** 3. **State Groups:** 8. **Description:** Improves student learning in America's public schools. Encourages parents and other community members in helping students achieve high academic expectations. Ensures a safe and supportive place of learning for students. **Publications:** Reports. Alternate Formats: online.

8274 ■ Lewis J. Smith Association
PO Box 30093
Raleigh, NC 27622
Ph: (919)755-3952
Contact: JoAnn Smith, Pres.
Founded: 1980. **Description:** Works to promote history and education. Supports and contributes to the Lewis J. Smith Scholarship fund at Western Carolina University in Cullowhee, NC. **Conventions/Meetings:** annual meeting.

8275 ■ LULAC National Educational Service Centers (LNESC)
2000 L St. NW, Ste.610
Washington, DC 20036
Ph: (202)835-9646
Fax: (202)835-9685
E-mail: lgarrido@lnesc.org
URL: http://www.lnesc.org
Contact: Richard Roybal, Exec. Dir.
Founded: 1973. **Members:** 15. **Staff:** 66. **Regional Groups:** 6. **State Groups:** 60. **Languages:** English, Spanish. **Description:** Educational corporation established by the League of United Latin American Citizens. Seeks to ensure access to higher education for Hispanic students. Offers counseling program to assist students with educational counseling, career planning, and financial aid. Conducts Washington Week Seminar, a three-day educational conference for high school students designed to foster leadership development. Operates LULAC National Scholarship Fund Program. Also sponsors projects aimed at motivating students to study, learn, and explore career options. **Awards:** GE Scholarship. **Frequency:** annual. **Type:** scholarship. **Recipient:** for sophomores at accredited institutions ● GM Scholarship. **Frequency:** annual. **Type:** scholarship. **Recipient:** for bachelors degree students at accredited institutions ● LULAC National Scholarship Fund. **Frequency:** annual. **Type:** scholarship. **Recipient:** for high school senior, undergrad, graduate. **Telecommunication Services:** electronic mail, communications@lnesc.org.

8276 ■ Mid-Atlantic Equity Consortium (MAEC)
5272 River Rd., Ste.340
Bethesda, MD 20816
Ph: (301)657-7741
Fax: (301)657-8782
E-mail: info@maec.org
URL: http://www.maec.org
Contact: Warren Simmons, Exec. Dir.
Founded: 1992. **Description:** Works to assist school systems and other educational organizations to create learning environments free of race, gender, class, ethnic and cultural biases to provide equal opportunity for all students. **Computer Services:** Mailing lists. **Programs:** African American Student Achievement Network; Mid-Atlantic Equity Center; National Origin Specialists Network; Parent Empowerment; Statewide and Schoolwide School Improvement; Student Equity Leadership; Title IX Network. **Projects:** Museum Magnet Schools Evaluation. **Publications:** *Educate America: A Call for Equity in School Reform*. Report. **Price:** $7.50. Alternate Formats: online ● *Excellence And Equity For Language Minority Students: Critical Issues and Promising Practices (1998)*. Articles. **Price:** $10.00 ● *Legal Responsibilities of Educational Agencies Serving Language Minority Students(1995)-Synopsis*. Pamphlet. **Price:** $1.25. Alternate Formats: online.

8277 ■ Middle States Association of Colleges and Schools (MSA)
3624 Market St.
Philadelphia, PA 19104
Ph: (215)662-5600
Fax: (215)662-5501
E-mail: info@msache.org
URL: http://www.middlestates.org
Contact: Sister Mary Reap IHM, Pres.
Founded: 1887. **Members:** 3,700. **Staff:** 38. **Budget:** $4,000,000. **Description:** Serves as a nongovernmental, voluntary organization of colleges and universities, secondary schools, and elementary schools in Panama, Delaware, District of Columbia, Maryland, New Jersey, New York, Pennsylvania, Puerto Rico, and the Virgin Islands, that have been accredited by either the Commission on Higher Education, the Commission on Secondary Schools, or the Commission on Elementary Schools. One of six regional accrediting agencies in the U.S. **Formerly:** (1975) Middle States Association of Colleges and Secondary Schools. **Publications:** *Accredited Membership List*, annual. Membership Directory ● *Commission on Higher Education Newsletter*, quarterly.

8278 ■ Montessori Accreditation Council for Teacher Education (MACTE)
524 Main St., Ste.202
Monument Sq.
Racine, WI 53403
Ph: (262)898-1846
Fax: (262)898-1849
E-mail: information@macte.org
URL: http://www.macte.org
Contact: Gretchen Warner PhD, Exec. Dir.
Founded: 1991. **Membership Dues:** institution/program, $300 (annual) ● additional location, contract location, $250 (annual) ● student, $125 (annual) ● organization/consortium/independent, $350 (annual). **Multinational. Description:** Works as accrediting agency for Montessori teacher education programs. **Publications:** Annual Report, annual. **Conventions/Meetings:** meeting.

8279 ■ Montessori Institute of America (MIA)
3410 S 272nd
Kent, WA 98032
Free: (888)564-9556
Fax: (253)859-1737
E-mail: miaorg@aol.com
URL: http://www.montessoriconnections.com/MIA
Founded: 1960. **Membership Dues:** teacher/director in U.S., parent outside U.S., $40 (annual) ● parent in U.S., $30 (annual) ● teacher/director in U.S., $70 (biennial) ● teacher/director outside U.S., $50 (annual) ● teacher/director outside U.S., $80 (biennial) ● parent outside U.S., $50 (biennial) ● parent in U.S., $55 (biennial). **Description:** Promotes the vision and philosophy of Dr. Maria Montessori; to provide a harmonious, global organization to support the development of the whole child. Aims to: expand teacher preparation programs to other levels of training and advanced degrees; to provide consulting services to members; to enhance online communications and information. **Computer Services:** Online services, communications and information. **Divisions:** Teacher preparation centers. **Programs:** Videotape Training. **Publications:** *MIA Newsletter*. **Price:** included in membership dues ● Membership Directory. **Price:** included in membership dues. **Conventions/Meetings:** seminar ● workshop.

8280 ■ National Academy of Education (NAEd)
500 Fifth St. NW, No. 333
Washington, DC 20001
Ph: (202)334-2341
Fax: (202)334-2350
E-mail: info@naeducation.org
URL: http://www.naeducation.org
Contact: Gregory White, Exec. Dir.
Founded: 1965. **Members:** 150. **Staff:** 3. **Budget:** $2,600,000. **Description:** Honorary society of leaders in education. Offers advice and assistance to the federal government and national foundations. Administers post-doctoral fellowship program to ensure the future of research in education concerning key educational issues. **Awards:** National Academy of Education/Spencer Postdoctoral Fellowship. **Frequency:** annual. **Type:** fellowship. **Recipient:** to recent doctoral recipients working on educational research. **Publications:** *Assessing Student Achievement in the States*. **Price:** $20.00 ● *Assessing Student Achievement in the States: Background Studies*. **Price:** $17.00 ● *Assessment in Transition: Monitoring the Nation's Educational Progress*. **Price:** $32.00 ● *Authors' Rejoinder: Race Differences in Intelligence*. **Price:** $5.00 ● *Comparative Analysis of Systems of Higher Education*. **Price:** $5.00 ● *How Scholars From Abroad View Higher Education in America*. **Price:** $5.00 ● *Images of Education in Kyklios Paideia*. **Price:** $5.00 ● *Improving Education: Perspectives on Educational Research*. **Price:** $5.00 ● *Improving Education Through Standards-Based Reform*. **Price:** $5.00 ● *The International Evaluation of Educational Achievement: Review of International Association for the Evaluation of Educational Achievement*. **Price:** $5.00 ● *Issues in Education Research: Problems and Possibilities*. **Price:** $39.95 ● *The Methodology of International Evaluation of Educational Achievement*. **Price:** $5.00 ● *The Nation's Report Card: Improving the Assessment of Student Achievement*. **Price:** $15.00 ● *New Maps of Development: New Visions of Maturity*. **Price:** $5.00 ● *On Educating the Gifted*. **Price:** $5.00 ● *Proceedings of the National Academy of Education*. Includes 4 separate volumes. **Price:** $18.00/volume ● *Quality and Utility: The 1994 Trial State Assessment in Reading*. **Price:** $25.00 ● *Quality and Utility: The 1994 Trial State Assessment in Reading, Background Studies*. **Price:** $17.00 ● *Race Differences in Tested Intelligence: Important Socially, Obscure Causally*. **Price:** $5.00 ● *The Trial State Assessment: Prospects and Realities*. Reports. **Price:** $27.00. **Conventions/Meetings:** annual meeting.

8281 ■ National Association of Charter School Authorizers (NACSA)
105 W Adams St., Ste.1430
Chicago, IL 60603-6253
Ph: (312)376-2300
Fax: (312)376-2400
E-mail: info@qualitycharters.org
URL: http://www.qualitycharters.org
Contact: Greg Richmond, Pres.
Founded: 2000. **Membership Dues:** associate (institution), $500 (annual) ● associate (resource center and association), $250 (annual). **Description:** Professional membership organization of authorizers and other education leaders who work to achieve quality public charter schools. Provides training, consultation, and policy guidance to authorizers and others interested in using public charter schools to improve student outcomes. Offers individualized assistance, seminars and conferences, web resources, and practical publications to improve the knowledge and skill of the organizations overseeing America's charter schools. **Publications:** *Authorizing Matters*. Report ● *Principles & Standards*. Report ● *Starting Fresh in Low-Performing Schools*. Report.

8282 ■ National Association for Year-Round Education (NAYRE)
PO Box 711386
San Diego, CA 92171-1386
Ph: (619)276-5296
Fax: (858)571-5754

E-mail: info@nayre.org
URL: http://www.nayre.org
Contact: Mr. Sam Pepper, Exec. Dir.
Founded: 1972. **Members:** 900. **Membership Dues:** basic, $45 (annual) ● commercial, $200 (annual) ● retired, $25 (annual) ● institution (based on number of students), $350-$750 (annual) ● life, $250. **Staff:** 5. **Budget:** $600,000. **State Groups:** 12. **Description:** Representatives of school systems, institutions of higher education, civic organizations, and parents. Fosters the study of year-round education as a way to improve educational programs by providing continuous instruction; adapting the school calendar to the community and family living patterns; attaining optimum economic efficiency. Disseminates information. **Libraries: Type:** reference. **Holdings:** books, clippings. **Subjects:** research. **Awards:** Electronic Media, Print Media, Four Seasons, Jensen. **Frequency:** annual. **Type:** recognition. **Recipient:** for outstanding journalism, outstanding service to year round education ● Schools of Merit. **Frequency:** annual. **Type:** recognition. **Recipient:** for innovative year round schools. **Computer Services:** database ● information services ● online services. **Publications:** *From Parent to Parent: A Look at Year-Round Education* (in English and Spanish). Book. **Price:** $11.00 ● *Intersession Handbook* ● *National Association for Year-Round Education—Directory*, annual. Lists school districts in the United States that utilize some form of year-round education. **Price:** included in membership dues; $22.00 for nonmembers ● *Y-R Learning: A Research Synthesis Relating to Student Achievement.* **Price:** $21.00 ● *YRE-FAQ: Frequently Asked Questions.* Book ● Pamphlets ● Also publishes fliers. **Conventions/Meetings:** annual It's About Time - conference (exhibits) - February.

8283 ■ National Center on Education and the Economy (NCEE)
555 13th St. NW, Ste.500 W
Washington, DC 20004
Ph: (202)783-3668
Fax: (202)783-3672
E-mail: info@ncee.org
URL: http://www.ncee.org
Contact: Marc S. Tucker, Pres.
Founded: 1987. **Staff:** 140. **Description:** Dedicated to providing the tools and technical assistance needed to lead the world in education and training. Has 4 main programs: The America's Choice School Design, which provides schools, school systems, and states with the designs, materials and assistance they need to ensure that all students leave high school ready to do rigorous college-level work; the Workforce Development program, which provides the federal government, states and localities designs, assistance, and policy guidance to implement world-class workforce development systems; the National Institute for School Leadership, which draws on the best leadership-training practices in education, business and the military; and the NCEE Policy Forums, which promotes discussion of standards-based reform among the nation's opinion leaders. **Supersedes:** Carnegie Forum on Education and the Economy.

8284 ■ National Center for Education Statistics (NCES)
1990 K St. NW
Washington, DC 20006
Ph: (202)502-7300 (202)502-7434
Fax: (202)502-7466
E-mail: valena.plisko@ed.gov
URL: http://nces.ed.gov
Contact: Valena W. Plisko, Assoc. Commissioner
Members: 115. **Description:** Agency of the U.S. Department of Education. Collects and disseminates statistics and other data related to education in the U.S. **Computer Services:** database, U.S. schools, colleges and libraries ● information services, fast facts, quick tables and figures ● online services, students' classroom. **Programs:** Annual Reports; Assessment Design and Analysis; Assessment Development and Quality Assurance; Data Development; Early Childhood and Household Studies; International Studies; Statistical Standards; Technology Support. **Formerly:** National Center for Education Statistics; (1988) Center for Statistics. **Publications:** *The Condition of Education*, annual. Report. Alternate Formats: online ● *Digest of Education Statistics*, annual. Report. Alternate Formats: online ● *Education Directory, Colleges and Universities*, annual ● *Projections of Education Statistics.* Report. Alternate Formats: online. **Conventions/Meetings:** annual MIS Conference.

8285 ■ National Center for Research on Evaluation, Standards, and Student Testing (CRESST)
UCLA CSE/CRESST
GSE and IS Bldg., 3rd Fl.
300 Charles E. Young Dr. N
Mailbox 951522
Los Angeles, CA 90095-1522
Ph: (310)206-1532
Fax: (310)825-3883
E-mail: dietel@cse.ucla.edu
URL: http://www.cse.ucla.edu
Contact: Ron Dietel, Asst. Dir. of Communications
Description: Focuses on assessment of educational quality, addressing persistent problems in the design and use of assessment systems to serve multiple purposes. **Libraries: Type:** reference. **Holdings:** reports. **Computer Services:** Mailing lists. **Publications:** *CRESST Line.* Newsletter. Alternate Formats: online ● *Guidebook.* Books. Alternate Formats: online ● Reports. Alternate Formats: online ● Articles. Alternate Formats: online.

8286 ■ National Circus Project (NCP)
56 Lion Ln.
Westbury, NY 11590
Ph: (516)334-2123
Fax: (516)334-2249
E-mail: info@nationalcircusproject.com
URL: http://www.nationalcircusproject.com
Contact: Ed Neuwirth, Marketing Dir.
Founded: 1984. **Staff:** 12. **Budget:** $400,000. **Description:** A division of Circus Education Specialists. Promotes circus skills training as a means of attaining physical fitness and improving coordination. Devises and conducts educational outreach programs through which elementary schoolchildren are taught circus skills such as juggling, plate-spinning, and unicycling in their school physical education programs. Establishes a national network of circus education programs. Conducts research. Operates Artist-in-Residence Program, through which circus skills instructors conduct assemblies and workshops in schools, and Lecture/Demonstration Programs, which provide an overview of circus skills programs to conferences of school administrators, physical education teachers, and therapeutic recreation specialists. **Publications:** Brochures.

8287 ■ National Clearinghouse for English Language Acquisition and Language Instruction Educational Programs (NCELALIEP)
2121 K St. NW, Ste.260
Washington, DC 20037
Ph: (202)467-0867
Free: (800)321-6223
Fax: (202)467-4283
E-mail: askncela@ncela.gwu.edu
URL: http://www.ncela.gwu.edu
Contact: Minerva Gorena, Sr. Advisor/Acting Dir.
Description: Identifies, collects, and disseminates information to individuals interested in educating English language learners. Serves as a national clearinghouse for those in the field of education. **Computer Services:** database, provides access to over 20,000 citations and abstracts. **Formerly:** (2002) National Clearinghouse for Bilingual Education. **Publications:** *Newsline*, weekly. Bulletin. Alternate Formats: online.

8288 ■ National Coalition of Girls' Schools (NCGS)
57 Main St.
Concord, MA 01742
Ph: (978)287-4485
Fax: (978)287-6014
E-mail: ncgs@ncgs.org
URL: http://www.ncgs.org
Contact: Whitney Ransome, Exec. Dir.
Founded: 1991. **Members:** 101. **Membership Dues:** school (based on the number of students), $1,700-$6,400 (annual) ● school (with less than 100 students enrolled), $800 (annual) ● individual (international), $500 (annual) ● associate, $500 (annual). **Staff:** 4. **Budget:** $350,000. **Regional Groups:** 3. **State Groups:** 20. **Description:** Boarding, day, private, and public girls' schools within the United States, Canada, New Zealand, Australia, United Kingdom, and South Africa. Works to promote the values and advantages of all girls' schools. Collects and conducts research on gender issues; sponsors national forums for girls' and women's groups; compiles statistics. **Libraries: Type:** open to the public. **Subjects:** education for girls in math, science, physical sciences, and technology. **Awards:** Educator of Achievement. **Type:** recognition ● Woman of Achievement. **Type:** recognition. **Computer Services:** database. **Publications:** *Dads and the Daughters* ● *Financial Literacy for Girls and Women* ● *Girls and Physical Sciences* ● *Girls and Technology* ● *In the News.* Newsletter ● *Math and Science for Girls* ● *Raising Confident Competent Daughters* ● *Why a Girls' School.* Brochure. **Price:** $2.00. **Conventions/Meetings:** annual conference - 2008 June 23-26, Cleveland, OH.

8289 ■ National Coalition of Title I/Chapter 1 Parents (NCTIC1P)
310 Pennsylvania Ave. SE, 3rd Fl.
Washington, DC 20003
Ph: (202)547-3135
Fax: (202)547-3137
E-mail: nctic1p@aol.com
URL: http://www.nceseatip.org
Contact: Carla A. Jones, Admin. Asst.
Founded: 1972. **Members:** 5,000. **Membership Dues:** regular, $10 (annual) ● life, $100 ● sustaining, $25 (annual). **Staff:** 3. **Budget:** $264,000. **Regional Groups:** 10. **Description:** Helps economically disadvantaged parents to develop the necessary skills and abilities needed to make sound decisions that result in improving the quality of their children's education. Administers programs and serves as a clearinghouse for information concerning parent involvement and education for disadvantaged children. Provides training conferences on the local and national levels; workshops on the Title I program with a focus on parent involvement and scholarships to Title I students pursuing postsecondary education. Reauthorized by the Improving America's Schools Act of 1994 and was originally authorized under the Elementary and Secondary Education Act of 1965 as a part of President Lyndon Johnson's War on Poverty. **Committees:** Legislative; Nomination; Scholarship. **Formerly:** (1983) National Coalition of ESEA Title I Parents. **Publications:** *The National Coalition of Title I/Chapter 1 Parents Newsletter*, quarterly. **Price:** free for members. **Circulation:** 5,000. **Advertising:** accepted ● Newsletter, quarterly. **Conventions/Meetings:** National In-service Training Conference - convention, designed by parents to involve parents, teachers, community representatives, federal and local program administrators, and renowned educators in exchanging information on maximizing education.

8290 ■ National Collegiate Honors Council (NCHC)
1100 Neihardt Residence Ctr.
Univ. of Nebraska-Lincoln
540 N 16th St.
Lincoln, NE 68588-0627
Ph: (402)472-9150
Fax: (402)472-9152
E-mail: nchc@unlserve.unl.edu
URL: http://www.nchchonors.org
Contact: Patricia Ann Speelman, Exec. Dir.
Founded: 1966. **Members:** 1,300. **Membership Dues:** institution, $500 (annual) ● individual, professional from member institution, $100 (annual) ● individual, professional from non-member institution, $350 (annual) ● affiliate, $50 (annual) ● student, $35

(annual). **Staff:** 2. **Budget:** $250,000. **Regional Groups:** 6. **Description:** College and university-level institutions, faculty, administrators, and honors students. Provides information on developments in honors education. Offers advice and support to institutions establishing honors programs. Encourages the exchange of learning resources among institutions; fosters curriculum experimentation. Sponsors Honors Semesters, a college credit program that allows students to participate in educational activities conducted in various regions of the U.S. Conducts field studies and research; offers internships. **Libraries: Type:** reference. **Holdings:** archival material. **Awards:** NCHC Consulting Grant. **Frequency:** 3/year. **Type:** grant. **Recipient:** to support the fees of a site visitor to evaluate honors programs ● Portz Grant. **Frequency:** 5/year. **Type:** grant. **Recipient:** for innovative honors programming ● Portz Scholarship. **Frequency:** 3/year. **Type:** monetary. **Recipient:** for outstanding student research papers. **Computer Services:** Mailing lists, of members. **Committees:** Diversity; Honors Semesters; International Education; Large University; Portz Grant; Pre-College Education for the Gifted; Research; Small College; Student Concerns; Two-Year College. **Supersedes:** Inter-University Committee on the Superior Student. **Publications:** *Honors in Practice*, annual. Journal. **Price:** $12.50 for nonmembers; $10.00 for members. **Circulation:** 1,400 ● *Journal of the NCHC*, semiannual. **Price:** $12.50 for nonmembers; $10.00 for members. ISSN: 1559-0151. **Circulation:** 1,400 ● *NCHC Handbook*, periodic. Membership Directory. **Conventions/Meetings:** annual conference (exhibits) ● seminar.

8291 ■ National Dissemination Association (NDA)

c/o Max McConkey, Exec. Dir.
4732 N Oracle Rd., Ste.217
Tucson, AZ 85705
Ph: (602)888-2838
Fax: (602)888-2621
URL: http://www.ed.gov/pubs/EPTW/eptwndas.html
Contact: Max McConkey, Exec. Dir.

Founded: 1981. **Members:** 300. **Membership Dues:** funded institutional, $300 (annual) ● nonfunded institutional, $100 (annual) ● associate, $50 (annual) ● individual, $25 (annual). **Staff:** 2. **Description:** Teachers, program directors, school staff, parents, and district administrators. Supports the dissemination and implementation of effective educational systems, programs and practices. Seeks to provide practitioners with the best available solutions to education problems, enabling educators to take advantage of effective practices at a fraction of the cost of initial development. **Publications:** *Educational Programs that Work*. Catalog. Describes all the educational programs validated by the U.S. Department of Education. ● *The Update*, monthly. Newsletter. **Conventions/Meetings:** periodic workshop and seminar.

8292 ■ National School Development Council (NSDC)

c/o Dr. John R. Sullivan, Jr., Sec.-Treas.
28 Lord Rd., No. 210
Marlborough, MA 01752
Ph: (508)481-9444 (631)360-0800
Fax: (508)481-5655
E-mail: jrsull@nesdec.org
URL: http://www.casdany.org/nsdc/nsdc.html
Contact: Dr. John R. Sullivan Jr., Sec.-Treas.

Founded: 1969. **Members:** 22. **Membership Dues:** Study/Development Council (with a membership income below 25,000), $250 (annual) ● Study/Development Council (with a membership income of 25,000-50,000), $300 (annual) ● Study/Development Council (with a membership income of 50,000 and above), $350 (annual). **Staff:** 1. **Budget:** $10,000. **Description:** School study councils. Promotes school study councils and facilitates the exchange of information and successful programs plans. **Awards:** Cooperative Leadership. **Frequency:** annual. **Type:** recognition. **Recipient:** to a local educator with outstanding leadership qualities ● Executive Secretary Exchange. **Frequency:** annual. **Type:** monetary. **Recipient:** for a director's visit to another council's headquarters for sharing organizational and program experiences. **Publications:** *Catalyst for Change*, semiannual. **Price:** $10.00. **Conventions/Meetings:** annual meeting.

8293 ■ National Society for the Study of Education (NSSE)

Univ. of Illinois at Chicago
Coll. of Educ. (M/C 147)
1040 W Harrison St.
Chicago, IL 60607-7133
Ph: (312)996-4529
Fax: (312)996-8134
E-mail: nsse@uic.edu
URL: http://www.nsse-chicago.org
Contact: Debra Miretzky, Program Coor.

Founded: 1901. **Members:** 2,300. **Membership Dues:** regular, $40 (annual) ● graduate student, retiree, $35 (annual) ● international, $45 (annual). **Staff:** 2. **Budget:** $125,000. **Description:** Professional society of educators, researchers, and policymakers. Promotes the investigation and discussion of educational problems. **Supersedes:** National Herbart Society for the Scientific Study of Education. **Publications:** *National Society for the Study of Education—Yearbook*, annual. **Price:** included in membership dues. ISSN: 0077-5762. **Circulation:** 2,300.

8294 ■ NEA Foundation for the Improvement of Education

1201 16th St. NW
Washington, DC 20036-3207
Ph: (202)822-7840
Fax: (202)822-7779
E-mail: info-neafoundation@list.nea.org
URL: http://www.neafoundation.org
Contact: Harriet Sanford, Pres./CEO

Founded: 1969. **Staff:** 13. **Budget:** $2,100,000. **Description:** Seeks to ensure that all students succeed by improving teaching and learning in public schools, colleges, and universities nationwide through grants, technical assistance, and other resources. Interest includes systemic change, educational innovation, closing the achievement gap, improving professional development for educators, and improving arts education. **Awards:** Innovation Grants. **Frequency:** 3/year. **Type:** grant. **Recipient:** for public education employees only ● Learning and Leadership Grants. **Frequency:** 3/year. **Type:** grant. **Recipient:** for eligible public school employees only. **Affiliated With:** National Education Association. **Formerly:** (2000) National Foundation for the Improvement of Education. **Publications:** *Connecting the Bits: A Reference for Using Technology in Teaching & Learning in K-12 Schools*. Report. Alternate Formats: online ● *Creating a Teacher Mentoring Program*. Paper. Alternate Formats: online ● *Creating Teacher-Led Professional Development Centers*. Paper. Alternate Formats: online ● *Engaging Public Support for Teachers' Professional Development*. Paper. Alternate Formats: online ● *Teachers Take Charge of Their Learning: Transforming Professional Development for Student Success*. Report. **Price:** free; $15.00/copy. Alternate Formats: online ● *Using Data about Classroom Practice and Student Work to Improve Professional Development for Educators*. Alternate Formats: online ● *Using Data to Improve Teacher Induction Programs*. Alternate Formats: online.

8295 ■ NETWORK

136 Fenno Dr.
Rowley, MA 01969-1004
Ph: (978)948-7764
Free: (800)877-5400
Fax: (978)948-7836
E-mail: info@thenetworkinc.org
URL: http://www.thenetworkinc.org
Contact: David P. Crandall, Pres.

Founded: 1969. **Staff:** 3. **Description:** Seeks to enhance learning and improve teaching systems of U.S. schools, public agencies and organizations, businesses, and other institutions. Conducts interactive and mutually supportive research, technical assistance, evaluation, and information dissemination programs designed to produce an approach to school and educational improvement that focuses on learning and learners. Services include: training, individual assistance, and consulting for government education officials at the local, state, and federal levels; research on how to best support school improvement programs; gathering and disseminating information on topics in systemic change, educational equity, urban education, regional collaboration, professional development, school administration and improvement; evaluation assistance to educational systems or institutions contemplating implementation of new programs. Creates and distributes learning simulations in both board game and CD-ROM formats, including Making Change (aka the Change Game), Systems Thinking/Systems Changing (TM) and Improving Student Success: Teachers, Schools and Parents. **Libraries: Type:** reference. **Holdings:** audiovisuals, books, clippings, monographs, monographs, periodicals. **Subjects:** restructuring assessments, at-risk youth curriculum, early childhood, policy, rural and urban education, teacher developments, technology, equity. **Formerly:** Network of Innovative Schools. **Publications:** *Publications Catalog*, periodic. **Conventions/Meetings:** periodic meeting.

8296 ■ New England Association of Schools and Colleges (NEASC)

209 Burlington Rd.
Bedford, MA 01730-1433
Ph: (781)271-0022 (781)541-5406
Fax: (781)271-0950
E-mail: jludes@neasc.org
URL: http://www.neasc.org
Contact: Jacob Ludes III, Exec. Dir./CEO

Founded: 1885. **Members:** 2,000. **Staff:** 41. **Budget:** $6,500,000. **State Groups:** 6. **Description:** Institutions of higher education, public and independent schools, and vocational-technical schools in Connecticut, Maine, Massachusetts, New Hampshire, Rhode Island, and Vermont, accredited on recommendation of the Commission on Institutions of Higher Education, the Commission on Independent Schools, the Commission on Public Secondary Schools, the Commission on Public Elementary and Middle Schools, the Commission on Technical and Career Institutions; the Commission on American and International Schools Abroad, other subscribers are agencies, and individuals. One of six regional accrediting organizations in the U.S. **Awards:** Richard J. Bradley Endowment Fund Award. **Frequency:** annual. **Type:** monetary. **Recipient:** for educator from one of the six New England states whose exemplary work establishes, maintains or advocates high standards of excellence. **Computer Services:** database ● mailing lists. **Committees:** Overseas Schools; School and College Relations. **Formerly:** (1972) New England Association of Colleges and Secondary Schools. **Publications:** *The Report*, semiannual. Newsletter. **Circulation:** 3,500. Alternate Formats: online ● *Roster of Membership*, annual. Membership Directory. Lists member institutions. **Price:** $10.00. **Conventions/Meetings:** annual meeting - always first week of December in Boston, MA.

8297 ■ North Central Association of Colleges and Schools Commission on Accreditation and School Improvement (NCA CASI)

Arizona State Univ.
PO Box 871008
Tempe, AZ 85287-1008
Ph: (480)773-6900
Free: (800)525-9517
Fax: (480)773-6901
E-mail: nca@ncacasi.org
URL: http://www.ncacasi.org
Contact: Dr. Mark Elgart, Exec. Dir.

Founded: 1895. **Members:** 9,000. **Staff:** 25. **State Groups:** 20. **Description:** Accredits over 9000 public and private schools in 19 states, the Navajo Nation, and the Department of Defense schools overseas; accreditation is a voluntary, non-governmental process that requires schools to meet high quality standards and challenges them to continuously improve student performance. **Telecommunication**

Services: electronic mail, melgart@advanc-ed.org. **Formerly:** (2005) North Central Association of Colleges and Schools. **Publications:** *NCA*, 3-4/year. Newsletter ● *NCA Journal of School Improvement*. Provides information on accreditation. ● Also publishes standards for optional and special function schools, secondary schools, junior high/middle schools, elementary schools, college-preparatory schools, and vocational/adult schools. **Conventions/Meetings:** annual meeting - always March or April in Chicago, IL.

8298 ■ Northwest Association of Accredited Schools (NAAS)

1910 Univ. Dr.
Boise, ID 83706-3007
Ph: (208)426-5727
Fax: (208)334-3228
E-mail: northwest@boisestate.edu
URL: http://www.boisestate.edu/naas
Contact: Shelli D. Clemens, Office Mgr.

Founded: 1917. **Members:** 1,643. **Membership Dues:** elementary, $200 (annual) ● middle level, $300 (annual) ● high, K-12, special purpose, distance education, supplemental, $400 (annual) ● foreign school, $1,250 (annual) ● travel study, $1,000 (annual). **Staff:** 4. **Budget:** $600,000. **Regional Groups:** 1. **State Groups:** 7. **Languages:** English, Russian. **Description:** Schools in Alaska, Idaho, Montana, Nevada, Oregon, Utah, and Washington, accredited by appropriate commissions. Seeks to advance the concept of education, develop policies and activities that extend and improve educational opportunities and services, develop criteria of evaluation that will stimulate, evaluate, and accredit vital educational effort, and promote cooperative relationships among colleges and schools. One of six regional organizations in the U.S. recognized by U.S. Dept. of Education. **Awards:** Distinguished Service Award. **Frequency:** annual. **Type:** recognition. **Recipient:** to a retired commissioner ● Northwest Association of Schools. **Frequency:** annual. **Type:** recognition. **Telecommunication Services:** electronic mail, sclemens@boisestate.edu. **Commissions:** Community and Junior Colleges; Independent Schools; Institutions of Higher Education; Public Schools; Secondary Schools; Senior Colleges and Universities; Supplemental Education Schools; Vocational, Technical, Career Institutions. **Committees:** Distance Education; Finance and Personnel; International Affairs and Alternative Education; Member Services; Research; Standards and Policies; Strategic Planning. **Formerly:** (1978) Northwest Association of Secondary and Higher Schools; (1998) Northwest Association of Schools and Colleges; (2004) Northwest Association of Schools and Colleges Commission on Schools. **Publications:** *Administrator, Steering Committee, and Response Team Manual*, annual. Manuals. Contains ideas, suggestions, and outlines the School Improvement Process required of all accredited schools. **Price:** $45.00 ● *Directory of Accredited and Affiliated Institutions*, annual. Proceedings. Lists member schools and colleges. **Price:** $45.00/copy. **Circulation:** 1,500 ● *Northwest Report*, quarterly. Newsletter. **Price:** included in membership dues ● Has also published a history of the association. **Conventions/Meetings:** semiannual meeting, presents an educational opportunity for school and colleges - always summer and winter.

8299 ■ OMNI Learning Institute

135 Verrill Rd.
Poland Spring, ME 04274-5316
Ph: (207)865-1611
E-mail: all4omni@aol.com
Contact: Dr. Gar Roper, Dir./ Founder

Founded: 1975. **Staff:** 7. **Budget:** $375,420. **Description:** Offers modular learning systems that develop new "brain-mind pathways" for innovative solutions to critical organizational problems. Conducts research workshops, and seminars on the development of the intuitive faculty and health; also conducts research on the use of flower essences and essential oils in human wellness. Develops microcomputer educational software and CD courseware. **Libraries: Type:** open to the public. **Holdings:** 2. **Subjects:** esoteric psychology. **Computer Services:** database, wellness and leadership courseware and self-development and breakthrough information ● mailing lists. **Formerly:** (1986) United Focus. **Publications:** *Hidden Grace*. Book. **Price:** $26.95 ● *Intuition Workbook* ● *Multidimensional Healing*. Book ● *The Power of Intuitive Leadership*. Book ● Newsletter, periodic. Alternate Formats: online ● Also makes available audiovisual materials. **Conventions/Meetings:** annual Advances in Energy Medicine - conference, advances in energy medicine.

8300 ■ Per Scholas

1231 Lafayette Ave.
Bronx, NY 10474
Ph: (718)991-8400
Free: (800)877-4068
Fax: (718)991-0362
E-mail: info@perscholas.org
URL: http://www.perscholas.org
Contact: Dr. Plinio Ayala, Pres./CEO

Founded: 1995. **Staff:** 52. **Budget:** $7,500,000. **Description:** Aims to bring technology to children and families at the lowest possible price. Founded by a consortium of foundations and corporations. **Publications:** Brochures.

8301 ■ Phelps-Stokes Fund (PSF)

1400 Eye St. NW, Ste.750
Washington, DC 20005
Ph: (202)371-9544
Fax: (202)371-9522
E-mail: bfoster@psfdc.org
URL: http://www.psfdc.org
Contact: Dr. Badi Foster, Pres.

Founded: 1911. **Staff:** 13. **Multinational. Description:** Works to promote the education of African Americans, Native Americans, and Africans. Sponsors research, educational studies and fellowship programs. **Programs:** Education for Women and Girls; Entrepreneurship Education and Training; International Educational and Cultural Exchanges; Leadership Development in Education.

8302 ■ Plymouth Rock Foundation (PRF)

1120 Long Pond Rd.
Plymouth, MA 02360
Ph: (508)833-1189
Free: (800)210-1620
Fax: (508)833-2481
E-mail: info@plymrock.org
URL: http://www.plymrock.org
Contact: Dr. Charles Wolfe, Exec. Dir./Pres.

Founded: 1970. **Members:** 20,000. **Membership Dues:** regular, $25 (annual). **Staff:** 4. **Budget:** $250,000. **Regional Groups:** 10. **Description:** Advances God's Biblical principles of self and civil government as the only real basis for a society of free people. Helps restore the foundation of the American Christian Republic. Sponsors Christian Freedom Institutes. Maintains Christian Committees of Correspondence as local action/service units. Conducts workshops and seminars for pastors and Christian educators in biblical principles of government and education and America's Christian history. Sponsors annual 4th of July and Thanksgiving Essay and Art Contests for students in grades 9-12; maintains speakers' bureau. Disseminates facts concerning America's Christian origins and heritage. **Libraries: Type:** not open to the public. **Holdings:** 1,500; articles, books, periodicals. **Subjects:** history, religion, current issues. **Awards:** Pilgrim of the Year. **Frequency:** annual. **Type:** recognition. **Recipient:** for outstanding service in community programs. **Publications:** *A Worthy Company*. Book. Lists founding fathers. **Price:** $9.95 ● *American Christian Heritage Series*. Book ● *American Christian Statesmen Series*. Book ● *The Correspondent*, monthly. Newsletter. Provides news of local committee activities and plans, reprints of articles from local units, bulletin board, and biographies of key people. **Price:** included in membership dues. **Circulation:** 5,000 ● *Dating and Courtship*. Book ● *FAC-Sheet*, monthly. Newsletter. Covers current public affairs and social issues from a Christian perspective. **Price:** included in membership dues; $25.00 /year for nonmembers. **Circulation:** 30,000 ● *Faith and Freedom*. Videos ● *Fundamentals for American Christians*. Book ● *Go Ye Therefore and Teach*. Manual. Gives instruction on planning and operating a Christian day school. ● *Letter From Plymouth Rock*, 4-6/year. Newsletter. **Price:** included in membership dues; $25.00 /year for nonmembers. **Circulation:** 30,000 ● *The Pilgrims' Progress*, semiannual. Newsletter. **Price:** included in membership dues ● *Plymouth Rock Foundation—Correspondent*, quarterly. Newsletter. Covers the activities of Committees of Correspondence. **Price:** included in membership dues. **Circulation:** 1,200 ● *Stepping Stones: Letters to Today's Pilgrims*. Audiotape. **Conventions/Meetings:** annual American's Christian Heritage - conference and workshop (exhibits) - 2nd weekend of November.

8303 ■ Quality Education for Minorities Network (QEM)

1818 N St. NW, Ste.350
Washington, DC 20036
Ph: (202)659-1818
Fax: (202)659-5408
E-mail: qemnetwork@qem.org
URL: http://qemnetwork.qem.org
Contact: Dr. Shirley McBay, Pres.

Founded: 1990. **Staff:** 13. **Description:** Created to implement the plan developed by the QEM Project to improve education at all levels for American Indians, African Americans, Mexican Americans, Alaska Natives and Puerto Ricans. Responds to the reality that most minorities are underserved by the educational system and thus disproportionately lack the skills needed to participate effectively in a society increasingly based on high technology. Works with school systems, communities, universities, and public and private sector organizations to insure that minorities in the U.S. have equal access to educational opportunities; facilitates networking and coordination among institutions and organizations involved in the education of minorities; and assists local communities in implementing education programs to benefit minority children with a special focus on science and mathematics, leadership development, and meeting high standards. **Boards:** Directors. **Councils:** January 15th Group; MSE Network; Technical Advisors Group. **Formerly:** (1990) Quality Education for Minorities Project. **Publications:** *QEM Update*, quarterly.

8304 ■ Sloan Consortium (SLOAN-C)

Sloan Ctr.
Franklin W. Olin Coll. of Engg.
Olin Way
Needham, MA 02492-1200
Ph: (781)292-2523
Fax: (781)292-2505
E-mail: info@sloan-c.org
URL: http://www.sloan-c.org
Contact: A. Frank Mayadas PhD, Pres.

Membership Dues: individual, $69 (annual) ● institution, $945 (annual). **Description:** Helps learning organizations continually improve the quality, scale and breadth of their online programs according to their own distinctive missions in order to become accessible and affordable for everyone. Maintains a catalog of degree and certificate programs offered by a wide range of regionally accredited member institutions, consortia, and industry partners. Provides speakers and consultants to help institutions learn about online methodologies. **Awards:** Effective Practice Awards. **Frequency:** annual. **Type:** recognition. **Recipient:** for academic institutions that demonstrated effective improvement in teaching practices ● Excellence in Teaching and Learning Awards. **Frequency:** annual. **Type:** recognition. **Recipient:** for persons or institutions who demonstrated remarkable teaching methodologies in their curriculum. **Computer Services:** database, Sloan-C catalog ● electronic publishing, synthesis of Sloan-C Effective Practices ● information services, distance learning resources ● online services, learning surveys, events information. **Publications:** *ALN Magazine*. Contains reports on uses of technology, experiences with ALN courses, and summaries of activities. Alternate Formats: online ● *Journal of Asynchronous Learning*

Networks, bimonthly. Describes original work in asynchronous learning networks, including experimental results. **Price:** $225.00 /year for nonmembers; $122.50 /year for members. Alternate Formats: online ● *Sloan-C View*, monthly. Newsletter. Provides useful information about online learning, commentaries about the field and pointers to more details about the work of the Sloan Consortium. Alternate Formats: online ● *Sloan Consortium Series*. Book. Peer-reviewed case studies that present inside information about the strategies successful programs are using to improve learning effectiveness. Alternate Formats: online. **Conventions/Meetings:** annual conference, discussion of asynchronous learning.

8305 ■ Society for the Advancement of Education (SAE)

500 Bi-County Blvd., Ste.203
Farmingdale, NY 11735
Ph: (631)293-4343
Free: (866)USA-MAG1
E-mail: infousa@usatodaymagazine.net
URL: http://www.usatodaymagazine.net
Contact: Wayne M. Barrett, Pres.

Founded: 1939. **Members:** 3,000. **Staff:** 5. **Description:** Represents educators, administrators, and other professionals of schools, colleges, and universities. **Publications:** *USA Today: The Magazine of the American Scene*, monthly. Includes video and book reviews. **Price:** included in membership dues. ISSN: 0161-7389. **Circulation:** 254,000. **Advertising:** accepted. Alternate Formats: microform.

8306 ■ Society for Educational Reconstruction (SER)

c/o Dr. David Conrad, Sec.
35 Wilson St.
Burlington, VT 05401
Ph: (802)658-1047
E-mail: david.conrad@uvm.edu
Contact: Dr. David Conrad, Sec.

Founded: 1969. **Members:** 40. **Membership Dues:** individual, $25 (annual) ● family, $35 (annual) ● full-time student, $15 (annual) ● institutional, $50 (annual) ● life, $250. **Description:** Primary mission is to further the understanding and practice of educational reconstruction philosophy. Educators and social service professionals dedicated to personal, social, and political transformation through education. Goals include: social democracy; cooperative power exercised toward moral ends; global order; and the possibility of self-transformation for each individual. Serves as a support network for educators who function as social change activists. Presents at national and regional conferences and seminars; shares curricular resource materials; conducts research and panel discussions on current educational concerns. **Libraries: Type:** open to the public. **Holdings:** archival material, papers, photographs. **Subjects:** philosophy of education, education for social change, educational reconstruction. **Awards:** Gertrude Langsam Educational Reconstruction Award. **Frequency:** annual. **Type:** recognition. **Recipient:** for action in support of the Society for Educational Reconstruction. **Committees:** Executive. **Publications:** *Education as Power*. Book. Reissued version in 2000 of the 1965 book by Theodore Brameld, with forward by Robert J. Nash. ● *Introducing Educational Reconstruction: The Philosophy and Practice of Transforming Society through Education*. Book. **Price:** $14.95 ● *SER in Action*, periodic. Newsletter. Contains book reviews, calendar of events, and research reports. **Price:** included in membership dues. **Circulation:** 200 ● *Theodore Brameld's Educational Reconstruction: An Intellectual Biography*. Book. **Conventions/Meetings:** Theodore Brameld Symposium.

8307 ■ Society of Professors of Education (SPE)

c/o Robert C. Morris, Sec.-Treas.
Univ. of West Georgia
Coll. of Educ.
Dept. of Educational Leadership and Professional Stud.
1600 Maple St.
Carrollton, GA 30118-5160
Ph: (770)836-4426
E-mail: rmorris@westga.edu
URL: http://www.unm.edu/~spe
Contact: Robert C. Morris, Sec.-Treas.

Founded: 1902. **Members:** 274. **Multinational. Description:** Professors of education in colleges and universities. Provides a forum in which specialists in a variety of disciplines represented in teacher education share ideas and discuss common problems. **Formerly:** (1969) National Society of College Teachers of Education. **Publications:** *DeGarmo Lectures*, annual. Monograph ● *Monograph Series*, annual ● *Retrieving the Language of Compassion: The Education Professor in Search of Community* ● *Society of Professors of Education Newsletter*, periodic. Includes publications list. ● *Two Dilemmas of Equal Educational Opportunity* ● Membership Directory, periodic ● Papers ● Reports. **Conventions/Meetings:** annual meeting, held in conjunction with the American Educational Research Association.

8308 ■ Southern Association of Colleges and Schools (SACS)

1866 Southern Ln.
Decatur, GA 30033-4033
Ph: (404)679-4500
Fax: (404)679-4556
E-mail: info@sacscasi.org
URL: http://www.sacs.org
Contact: Dr. John E. Pickelman, Chm.

Founded: 1895. **Members:** 12,651. **Staff:** 55. **Budget:** $4,000,000. **State Groups:** 22. **Description:** Represents colleges, universities, secondary schools, and elementary schools in Alabama, Florida, Georgia, Kentucky, Louisiana, Mississippi, North Carolina, South Carolina, Tennessee, Texas, Virginia, and Latin America, accredited by an appropriate commission. Conducts educational research and development through education improvement program. **Commissions:** Colleges; Elementary Schools; Secondary Schools. **Committees:** Investments; Personnel Policies. **Projects:** Vocational-Technical Education Consortium of States. **Publications:** *Membership List*, annual. Membership Directory. **Price:** $10.00/copy. ISSN: 0038-3813. **Circulation:** 18,300 ● *Proceedings of Annual Meeting*, annual ● Newsletter, quarterly ● Also publishes special project and research reports, standards, policies, and procedures for accreditation. **Conventions/Meetings:** annual conference (exhibits).

8309 ■ Southern Education Foundation (SEF)

135 Auburn Ave. NE, 2nd Fl.
Atlanta, GA 30303
Ph: (404)523-0001
Fax: (404)523-6904
E-mail: info@southerneducation.org
URL: http://www.southerneducation.org
Contact: Lynn Huntley, Pres.

Founded: 1937. **Staff:** 15. **Description:** Improves and extends educational opportunities for Southern youth, with special regard to the needs of minorities. Conducts educational programs. **Computer Services:** Information services, topical briefs, essays. **Programs:** "Education Summer" Intern; Investing in Historically Black Colleges and Universities Leadership; Kresge HBCU Initiative; Science and Technology Education; Teaching and Teacher Testing - "Unintended Consequences". **Projects:** Instructional Technology Assistance; "Miles to Go" - Southern State Education Policies and Practices; New Imperatives for Education and Economic Development. **Publications:** *Miles To Go*. Report. **Price:** $15.00. Alternate Formats: online ● *On the Right Side of History: Jack Greenberg*. Monograph. Addresses the great historic wrong of segregating African-American children in school. **Price:** $15.00. Alternate Formats: online ● *Patterns of Excellence, Policy Perspectives on Diversity in Teaching and School Leadership*. Monograph. **Price:** $15.00. Alternate Formats: online ● *Redeeming the American Promise*. Report. **Price:** $15.00. Alternate Formats: online ● *Southern Education*, semiannual. Newsletter. Covers issues related to minority teachers; also contains annual report and review of educational research publications. **Price:** free. **Circulation:** 3,000 ● *Unintended Consequences*. Report. **Price:** $15.00. Alternate Formats: online.

8310 ■ Telluride Association (TA)

217 West Ave.
Ithaca, NY 14850
Ph: (607)273-5011
Fax: (607)272-2667
E-mail: telluride@cornell.edu
URL: http://www.tellurideassociation.org
Contact: Ellen Baer, Admin. Dir.

Founded: 1911. **Members:** 100. **Description:** Educational association founded by Lucien L. Nunn (1853-1925), educator and pioneer in the high-voltage transmission of alternating current, with extensive mining and real estate interests in and around Telluride, CO. The association evolved from Telluride Institute, an educational experiment begun by Nunn to combine work and study for promising but untrained young men hired by his power enterprises. Members now include young men and women elected as trustees responsible for the management of funds and the planning and administration of educational programs. Operates a Telluride House at Cornell University, Ithaca, NY, and at the University of Michigan, Ann Arbor, where graduate and undergraduate students, as well as faculty guests, live during the academic year. Conducts summer programs for high school students who have completed their junior year, offering six weeks' study on a significant topic in the humanities or social sciences. **Awards: Type:** scholarship. **Recipient:** to students demonstrating high intellectual capacity, idealism, leadership ability, and common sense in practical situations. **Publications:** *Convention Proceedings*, annual ● Directory, annual ● Newsletter, 3/year. **Conventions/Meetings:** annual meeting - always June.

8311 ■ Up With People (UWP)

1600 Broadway, Ste.1460
Denver, CO 80202
Ph: (303)460-7100
Free: (877)264-8856
Fax: (303)225-4649
E-mail: tspaulding@upwithpeople.org
URL: http://www.upwithpeople.org
Contact: Mr. Thomas Spaulding, Pres./CEO

Founded: 1965. **Staff:** 16. **Multinational. Description:** Provides students with a renowned international education and an unmatched passageway to see the world through travel and cultural immersion. Addresses the need for young adults and leaders who have global perspectives, intercultural understanding, knowledge of worldwide social issues, leadership skills and a dedication to community service. Provides students to experience personal growth, leadership training, service learning and performing arts. **Computer Services:** Information services, resources.

8312 ■ Van Andel Education Institute (VAEI)

333 Bostwick Ave. NE
Grand Rapids, MI 49503
Ph: (616)234-5528 (616)234-5000
Fax: (616)234-5529
E-mail: hopeonthehill@vai.org
URL: http://www.vai.org/education.aspx
Contact: David L. Van Andel, Chm./CEO

Description: Represents educators. Works to promote K-12 education. **Special Interest Groups:** Van Andel Educators Institute.

8313 ■ Waters Foundation

6085 N Kolb Rd.
Tucson, AZ 85750
Ph: (503)679-5309 (520)575-1243
Fax: (520)575-1370
E-mail: jyates@fc.cfsd.k12.az.us
URL: http://www.watersfoundation.org
Contact: Joan Yates, Program Coor.

Description: Works to support systems thinking and dynamic modeling in K-12 education and various other educational research.

8314 ■ Western Association of Schools and Colleges (WASC)
c/o Accrediting Commission for Senior Colleges and Universities
985 Atlantic Ave., Ste.100
Alameda, CA 94501
Ph: (510)748-9001
Fax: (510)748-9797
E-mail: wascsr@wascsenior.org
URL: http://www.wascweb.org
Contact: Ralph A. Wolff, Sec.-Treas.
Founded: 1962. **Description:** Serves as educational institutions in California, Hawaii, Guam, and other areas of the Pacific. One of 6 regional organizations in the U.S. **Commissions:** Accrediting Commission for Community and Junior Colleges; Accrediting Commission for Schools; Accrediting Commission for Senior Colleges and Universities. **Publications:** Directory, annual.

8315 ■ WorldTeach
c/o Center for International Development
Harvard Univ.
79 John F. Kennedy St.
Cambridge, MA 02138
Ph: (617)495-5527
Free: (800)483-2240
Fax: (617)495-1599
E-mail: info@worldteach.org
URL: http://www.worldteach.org
Contact: Helen Claire Sievers, Exec. Dir.
Founded: 1986. **Staff:** 40. **Budget:** $1,000,000. **Regional Groups:** 22. **Multinational. Description:** Provides opportunities for individuals to make a meaningful contribution to international education by living and working as volunteer teachers in developing countries. **Publications:** *WorldTeach Dispatch*. Newsletter. Alternate Formats: online.

Education, Alternative

8316 ■ Eta Sigma Alpha National Home School Honor Society
11665 Fuqua St., Ste.A-100
Houston, TX 77034
Ph: (281)922-0478
Fax: (281)922-0504
E-mail: jjuren@hepbookstore.com
URL: http://esa.homeeducationpartnership.com
Contact: Joanne E. Juren BA, Founder/Exec. Dir.
Founded: 1999. **Membership Dues:** chapter, $15 (annual). **Description:** Advocates homeschooling as a viable and successful educational methodology. Seeks to recognize and encourage scholarship among home school students. Provides opportunities for the development of leadership and service. Works to stimulate the exchange of ideas and ideals, foster scholarship, and promote academic excellence. Acts as a liaison for homeschooling to the general public, colleges/universities, and the media.

Education Law

8317 ■ Council on Law in Higher Education (CLHE)
9386 Via Classico W
Wellington, FL 33411
Ph: (561)792-4440
Fax: (561)792-4441
E-mail: info@clhe.org
URL: http://www.clhe.org
Contact: Daren Bakst Esq., Pres.
Founded: 1998. **Members:** 325. **Membership Dues:** institutional/organizational/law firm, $275 (annual) ● school, $125 (annual) ● student, $20 (annual) ● full time faculty, $65 (annual). **Staff:** 3. **Description:** Colleges, universities, and law firms. Dedicated to improving the understanding of higher education law and policy in order to improve compliance and reduce legal risks. **Publications:** *The Campus Privacy Letter*, quarterly. Newsletter. Contains analysis on current privacy issues. Alternate Formats: online ● *CLHE's Legal Wire*. Bulletin. **Price:** free ● *Privacy in the 21st Century*. Book. Contains article on privacy, recent primary cases, legislations and regulations. **Price:** $16.95 for members; $21.95 for nonmembers ● *The Regulatory Advisor*, monthly. Newsletter. Covers a wide range of regulatory area affecting colleges and universities. Alternate Formats: online ● *Student Affairs Law and Policy Weekly*. Newsletter. Features timely articles on policy issues affecting student affairs leaders. Alternate Formats: online.

Education Youth

8318 ■ Educators Serving the Community (EduSerc)
PO Box 2536
Laurel, MD 20709
Ph: (301)498-2899
Fax: (301)498-0944
E-mail: educators@eduserc.org
URL: http://www.eduserc.org
Contact: Brian K. Smith, Exec. Dir.
Founded: 1996. **Membership Dues:** student, $15 (annual) ● individual/educator, $35 (annual) ● college/university/government/military/non-profit organization, $200 (annual) ● corporation/business, $350 (annual) ● affiliate, $500 (annual). **Description:** Advocates for the development and advancement of the youth across the nation. Seeks to strengthen the middle and high school student community by providing the skills and education necessary to compete in mainstream corporate, collegiate and social environments. Motivates youth to pursue their goals. Aids students in linking their interests with particular fields of study. Facilitates interaction among youth, parents, colleges and businesses. **Awards:** Educator Industry Awards. **Frequency:** annual. **Type:** recognition. **Recipient:** for significant educational contributions to the community in a particular industry ● Educator Serving the Community Awards. **Frequency:** annual. **Type:** recognition. **Recipient:** for serving as a role model of excellence and success in yielding exceptional results through community based programs or individual efforts ● EduSerc Image Award. **Frequency:** annual. **Type:** recognition. **Recipient:** for nationally known efforts and achievements in impacting the community and serving as an example for youth and adults to follow ● Most Improved Awards. **Frequency:** annual. **Type:** recognition. **Recipient:** for significant improvements in the classroom, with students yielding high results in key social and academic areas ● Principal Leadership Awards. **Frequency:** annual. **Type:** recognition. **Recipient:** for a principal who showed outstanding leadership to students and faculty during a school year ● Role Model/Mentor Awards. **Frequency:** annual. **Type:** recognition. **Recipient:** for outstanding leadership and positive consistent interaction affecting the lives of the youth. **Publications:** *Young Innovators*, quarterly. Magazine. **Price:** $22.00/year. **Advertising:** accepted.

8319 ■ For Inspiration and Recognition of Science and Technology (FIRST)
200 Bedford St.
Manchester, NH 03101
Ph: (603)666-3906
Fax: (603)666-3907
E-mail: info@usfirst.org
URL: http://www.usfirst.org
Contact: John E. Abele, Chm.
Founded: 1989. **Multinational. Description:** Aims to transform the culture by inspiring young people, schools, and communities to appreciate science and technology. Creates activities that encourage kids to have fun with science and technology. **Publications:** Annual Report, annual. Alternate Formats: online.

8320 ■ Kids Universe, Inc. (KUI)
c/o Janeczka Eberhart, CFO
PO Box 465552
Lawrenceville, GA 30042
Ph: (678)407-1331
Fax: (775)251-7367
E-mail: clee@kidsuniverse.org
URL: http://www.kidsuniverse.org
Contact: Curtis Lee, CEO
Description: Strives to improve the quality of education for all children. Aims to bridge the gap between technology and the socio-economic divide. Develops and creates programs that are designed to ensure that all children and youth have fair and equal opportunities to receive quality education. **Telecommunication Services:** electronic mail, jeberhart@kidsuniverse.org ● electronic mail, kwatkins@kidsuniverse.org.

Educational Advocacy

8321 ■ A Better Chance
240 W 35th St., 9th Fl.
New York, NY 10001-2506
Ph: (646)346-1310
Free: (800)562-7865
Fax: (646)346-1311
E-mail: stimmons@abetterchance.org
URL: http://www.abetterchance.org
Contact: Ms. Sandra E. Timmons, Pres.
Founded: 1963. **Staff:** 25. **Budget:** $3,000,000. **Description:** Identifies, recruits, and places academically talented and motivated minority students into leading independent secondary schools and selected public schools. Students receive need-based financial assistance from member schools. Prepares students to attend selective colleges and universities and encourages their aspirations to assume positions of responsibility and leadership in American society. Conducts research and provides technical assistance on expanded educational opportunities for minority group students in secondary and higher education. **Convention/Meeting:** none. **Libraries: Type:** reference. **Holdings:** biographical archives. **Awards: Type:** recognition. **Computer Services:** Information services, collection of resources. **Programs:** College Preparatory Schools; Community Schools. **Absorbed:** National Public School ABC Program; Educational Policy Center. **Formerly:** Independent Schools Talent Search Program. **Publications:** *Alumni*. Directory. **Price:** $79.00 deluxe edition; $69.00 standard edition ● *Letters to Member Schools*, annual ● Annual Report ● Brochure.

8322 ■ Black Alliance for Educational Options (BAEO)
1710 Rhode Island Ave. NW, 12th Fl.
Washington, DC 20036
Ph: (202)429-2236
Fax: (202)429-2237
E-mail: lawrence@baeo.org
URL: http://www.baeo.org
Contact: Lawrence C. Patrick III, Pres./CEO
Founded: 2000. **Membership Dues:** full-time student, $10 (annual) ● individual, retired, $25 (annual) ● family, $35 (annual) ● life (based on level of membership), $500-$2,500. **Description:** Seeks to empower families and increase quality educational options for children. Educates and informs the general public about parental choice initiatives and efforts to reduce or limit educational options available to parents. Provides information on scholarships and other program initiatives pertaining to educational options. **Publications:** Newsletter. **Price:** included in membership dues ● Report, annual. Alternate Formats: online.

8323 ■ Communities in Schools (CIS)
277 S Washington St., Ste.210
Alexandria, VA 22314
Ph: (703)519-8999 (703)518-2544
Free: (800)CIS4-KIDS
E-mail: cis@cisnet.org
URL: http://www.cisnet.org
Contact: William E. Milliken, Founder/Vice Chm.
Founded: 1977. **Staff:** 65. **Budget:** $12,800,000. **Regional Groups:** 5. **State Groups:** 16. **Local Groups:** 121. **Description:** Works to help kids succeed in school and prepare for life. Champions the connection of needed community resources with

schools to help young people successfully learn, stay in school and prepare for life. **Libraries: Type:** reference. **Holdings:** biographical archives. **Telecommunication Services:** electronic mail, stockinfo@cisnet.org. **Formerly:** (1998) Cities in Schools. **Publications:** *CIS Network News*, quarterly. Newsletter. **Price:** free. ISSN: 1069-966X. Alternate Formats: online ● *Facts You Can Use*, quarterly. Journal. Alternate Formats: online ● *Forward, March!*, quarterly. Newsletter ● Annual Report, annual. Alternate Formats: online ● Brochures ● Manuals. **Conventions/Meetings:** semiannual conference ● annual Seeking Solutions Through Partnerships for Youth - meeting and conference (exhibits).

8324 ■ Council for Opportunity in Education (COE)
1025 Vermont Ave. NW, Ste.900
Washington, DC 20005
Ph: (202)347-7430
Fax: (202)347-0786
E-mail: arnold.mitchem@coenet.us
URL: http://www.coenet.us
Contact: Dr. Arnold L. Mitchem, Pres.
Founded: 1981. **Members:** 900. **Membership Dues:** institution, $1,700 (annual). **Staff:** 15. **Budget:** $5,000,000. **Regional Groups:** 10. **State Groups:** 54. **Description:** Institutions of higher education, administrators, counselors, and teachers. Works to advance educational opportunities for disadvantaged students in colleges and universities. Provides professional development and continuing education. Monitors federal legislation designed to serve disadvantaged students. Provides technical assistance to educational opportunity program personnel. Assists institutions in preparing competitive proposals for federal funding. Conducts workshops and training programs; encourages research. **Libraries: Type:** reference. **Holdings:** clippings, periodicals. **Subjects:** legislation, minorities, federally funded TRIO programs. **Computer Services:** database, services provided to disadvantaged students ● mailing lists, of members. **Telecommunication Services:** phone referral service, information line, (202)347-1724 ● phone referral service, job line, (202)347-1821. **Formerly:** (2000) National Council of Educational Opportunity Associations. **Publications:** *Equality*, quarterly. Newsletter. Contains vital information for professionals who direct, sponsor or support educational opportunity programs in the United States. **Price:** $200.00 for members; $400.00 for nonmembers ● *Opportunity Outlook*, semiannual. Journal ● Directory, annual. Contains listing of TRIO programs. **Price:** $40.00 for members; $80.00 for nonmembers. **Advertising:** accepted ● Monograph, periodic. **Conventions/Meetings:** annual conference (exhibits) - 2008 Sept. 17-20, Washington, DC.

8325 ■ The Education Coalition (TEC)
31 Segovia
San Clemente, CA 92672
Ph: (949)369-3867
Fax: (949)369-3865
E-mail: tecemail@aol.com
URL: http://www.tecweb.org
Contact: Dr. Carla Lane EdD, Exec. Dir.
Founded: 1993. **Description:** Aims to serve the needs of the business and education communities. Promotes systemic educational reform through the use of multiple technologies. Works to create new public educational systems, models and partnerships. Serves as a focus for development, dissemination, research, advocacy and funding related to educational change and the use of technologies. **Publications:** Newsletter. Alternate Formats: online.

8326 ■ International Association for Truancy and Dropout Prevention (IATDP)
c/o Henrietta Pryor, Sec.
812 W 28th St.
Houston, TX 77008
Ph: (713)293-9711
E-mail: hpryor@houstonisd.org
URL: http://www.iatdp.org
Contact: Jimmie Thacker Jr., Exec. Dir.
Founded: 1911. **Members:** 400. **Membership Dues:** regular, $35 (annual) ● library, $30 (annual) ● retired or student, $20 (annual) ● life, $250. **Description:** Professional society of school attendance and pupil personnel workers including school administrators, counselors, attendance officers, visiting teachers, and school social workers. Believes in the premise that all children have the right to an education. Objectives are: to increase the educational competence of pupil personnel; to provide leadership in the development of pupil personnel services, philosophy, theory, practice, and skills; to help administrators, teachers, and parents understand school problems that face children; to provide ways to improve school attendance and behavior; to enforce and support the educational objectives set forth in compulsory attendance laws; to provide new and improved social, employment, and educational opportunities for children; to collect and disseminate information regarding pupil personnel work. Conducts research programs. Monitors related legislative activities. Maintains speakers' bureau and consultant service. **Libraries: Type:** reference. **Holdings:** biographical archives. **Computer Services:** database. **Telecommunication Services:** electronic mail, thackerj1@k12tn.net. **Committees:** Awards; Legislative; Public Relations; Research; School Attendance/Absenteeism. **Formerly:** (1957) National League to Promote School Attendance; (2005) International Association of Pupil Personnel Workers. **Publications:** *The Journal for Truancy and Dropout Prevention*, semiannual. Addresses the problem of student truancy and other school social welfare issues; includes conference proceedings, research reports, and news releases. **Price:** included in membership dues; $35.00 /year for libraries. ISSN: 0020-6016. **Circulation:** 500. Alternate Formats: microform. Also Cited As: *IAPPW Journal* ● Membership Directory, annual. **Conventions/Meetings:** annual conference (exhibits) - always third week in October.

8327 ■ National At-Risk Education Association (NAREA)
Address Unknown since 2007
Founded: 2003. **Members:** 200. **Membership Dues:** ordinary, $29 (annual). **Staff:** 1. **Budget:** $10,000. **Regional Groups:** 1. **State Groups:** 1. **Local Groups:** 1. **National Groups:** 1. **Description:** Works to enhance the quality of education for students at-risk to graduation by promoting the development of professional educators, counselors, psychologists, administrators, parents, students, family members, and advocates, in meeting the quality standards and practices necessary for effective education. **Libraries: Type:** by appointment only. **Holdings:** 200; books, periodicals, reports. **Subjects:** behavior, learning styles, teaching methods, teaching activities, psychological disorders, discipline, grant writing. **Committees:** Convention Planning; Ethics & Standards; Professional Development. **Conventions/Meetings:** annual board meeting and convention (exhibits).

8328 ■ National Coalition of Advocates for Students (NCAS)
Address Unknown since 2007
Founded: 1981. **Members:** 23. **Staff:** 10. **Budget:** $600,000. **State Groups:** 23. **Description:** Organizations united to provide educational advocacy to poor, minority, limited English-proficient, and handicapped students in public schools. Serves as a network for providing information and shared experiences among members and as a catalyst for school reconstruction. Operates immigrant student, school restructuring, and AIDS education programs. **Publications:** *The Good Common School: Creating A Vision That Works.*

8329 ■ National Council of Education Providers (NCEP)
1001 Connecticut Ave. NW, Ste.216
Washington, DC 20036
Ph: (202)822-5076
URL: http://www.educationproviders.org
Contact: Michael Musante, Contact
Description: Advocates for equity, opportunity, innovation and performance in K-12 education. Promotes and supports parents in meeting the demands for quality education. Protects, enhances and furthers the educational opportunities made available to children. Fosters innovation in the structure, approach and content of teaching, learning and parental involvement in the schooling of children.

8330 ■ National Dropout Prevention Center/Network (NDPC/N)
Clemson Univ.
209 Martin St.
Clemson, SC 29631-1555
Ph: (864)656-2599
Free: (800)443-6392
Fax: (864)656-0136
E-mail: ndpc@clemson.edu
URL: http://www.dropoutprevention.org
Contact: Ms. Bonnie Talakte, Chair
Founded: 1986. **Members:** 500. **Membership Dues:** individual, $75 (annual) ● organization, $285 (annual) ● student, $35 (annual) ● international individual, $185 (annual) ● international full package, $375 (annual) ● corporate active, $675 (annual). **Staff:** 12. **Description:** Serves as a research center and resource network for practitioners, researchers, and policymakers to reshape school and community environments to meet the needs of youth in at-risk situations so these students receive the quality education and services necessary to succeed academically and graduate from high school. **Libraries: Type:** reference. **Holdings:** 3,000. **Awards:** Awards of Excellence in Dropout Recovery, Intervention, and Prevention. **Frequency:** annual. **Type:** recognition. **Computer Services:** database, available through internet. **Publications:** *Alternative Schools: Best Practices for Development and Evaluation* ● *The Journal of At-Risk Issues*, quarterly ● *National Dropout Prevention Newsletter*, quarterly. **Circulation:** 3,000 ● *National Dropout Prevention Update*, quarterly. Newsletter. **Price:** $1.00 for nonmembers; free for members. Alternate Formats: online ● *Straight Talk about Discipline.* Monographs ● Also publishes brochures. **Conventions/Meetings:** annual America's At-Risk Youth National Forum - conference (exhibits) ● annual conference.

8331 ■ Plan of Action for Challenging Times (PACT)
635 Divisadero St.
San Francisco, CA 94117
Ph: (415)922-2550
Fax: (415)922-6305
E-mail: info@pactinc.org
URL: http://www.pactinc.org
Contact: Charlene Folsom, Pres./CEO
Founded: 1965. **Description:** Program to benefit first generation and low-income students who are U.S. citizens or permanent residents and who have not, in most cases, utilized their educational potential. Serves the city and county of San Francisco, CA. Provides college admissions, financial aid, and career counseling services; offers assistance with application forms; organizes campus visits, meetings between college recruiters and students, and visits to corporations and public institutions to observe various professions; conducts financial aid workshops; sponsors presentations to organizations, churches, and clubs. Supported by U.S. Department of Education under Educational Talent Search Program. **Convention/Meeting:** none. **Publications:** *Pact Times.* Newsletter. Alternate Formats: online ● Annual Report, annual. Alternate Formats: online.

8332 ■ Project Appleseed: The National Campaign for Public School Improvement
520 Melville Ave.
St. Louis, MO 63130-4506
Ph: (314)225-7757
Fax: (314)725-2319
E-mail: headquarters@projectappleseed.org
URL: http://www.projectappleseed.org
Contact: Kevin S. Walker, Pres./Natl. Dir.
Founded: 1993. **Members:** 3,500. **Membership Dues:** school, school district, $250 (annual) ● PTA, PTO, parent group, $200 (annual) ● individual school, $50 (annual). **Staff:** 6. **Budget:** $1,250,000. **State Groups:** 50. **Local Groups:** 2,000. **Description:** Advocates the improvement in public education by

increasing parental involvement in all of the public school districts in the country. Offers competitions, statistics, educational, research, and charitable programs, and a speakers' bureau. **Libraries: Type:** reference; open to the public. **Holdings:** archival material, articles, books, clippings, periodicals. **Awards:** Johnny Appleseed Parental Involvement Award. **Frequency:** annual. **Type:** recognition. **Recipient:** for the person or organization that best exemplifies good parental involvement in schools. **Computer Services:** database ● electronic publishing ● online services, website clearinghouse. **Telecommunication Services:** electronic mail, projectappleseed@k12mail.com. **Publications:** *Appleseed Today*, quarterly. Newsletter. **Advertising:** accepted. Alternate Formats: online. **Conventions/Meetings:** annual conference - always November.

Educational Facilities

8333 ■ APPA: The Association of Higher Education Facilities Officers (APPA)
1643 Prince St.
Alexandria, VA 22314-2818
Ph: (703)684-1446 (970)472-0491
Fax: (703)549-2772
E-mail: lander@appa.org
URL: http://www.appa.org
Contact: E. Lander Medlin, Exec. VP

Founded: 1914. **Members:** 5,000. **Staff:** 14. **Budget:** $4,000,000. **Regional Groups:** 6. **Multinational. Description:** Supports educational excellence with quality leadership and professional management through education, research, and recognition. Promotes excellence in the administration, care, operation, planning, and development of facilities (buildings, grounds, and power plants) used by colleges and universities. Conducts research programs. Compiles statistics. **Libraries: Type:** reference. **Holdings:** reports. **Awards:** APPA Fellow. **Frequency:** annual. **Type:** scholarship ● Award for Excellence in Facilities Management. **Frequency:** annual. **Type:** recognition. **Recipient:** for outstanding organizational facilities operations ● Effective & Innovative Practices. **Frequency:** annual. **Type:** monetary. **Recipient:** for the best institutional practice ● Meritorious Service Award. **Frequency:** annual. **Type:** recognition ● Pacesetter. **Frequency:** annual. **Type:** recognition. **Recipient:** to a member ● Strategic Business Partner. **Frequency:** annual. **Type:** recognition. **Recipient:** to corporate sector business partner members who have given exemplary support to the association. **Computer Services:** database, International Experience Exchange Database providing facilities management data on member schools. **Telecommunication Services:** electronic mail, colin@appa.org. **Committees:** Educational Programs; Information and Research Service; International Relations; Membership; Professional Affairs. **Formerly:** Association of Physical Plant Administrators; National Association of Physical Administrators of Universities and Colleges; (1948) Association of Superintendents of Buildings and Grounds of Universities and Colleges; (1991) Association of Physical Plant Administrators of Universities and Colleges. **Publications:** *APPA Membership Directory*, annual. **Advertising:** accepted ● *Facilities Core Data Survey*, annual. Contains various data on facilities staffing and operations. **Price:** $150.00 for nonmembers; $95.00 for members. ISSN: 0913-3591. Also Cited As: *Comparative Costs & Staffing Survey* ● *Facilities Management: A Manual for Plant Administration (3rd Edition)*. Books ● *Facilities Manager*, bimonthly. Magazine ● *Facilities Performance Indicators*, annual. Report. Includes findings from the facilities core data survey. Also Cited As: *Comparative Costs & Staffing Report* ● *Resources in Facilities Management*. Catalog ● Also publishes: Successful Funding Strategies for Facility Renewal; The Building Commissioning Handbook; A Foundation to Uphold; Facilities Management Manual; Customer Service; Environmental Compliance Assistance Guide; Field Notes; Custodial Staffing Guidelines; Grounds Maintenance Staffing Guidelines; Maintenance Trades Staffing Guidelines; and Strategic Assessment Model. **Conventions/Meetings:** annual Educational Facilities Leadership Forum - meeting and conference, educational (exhibits) ● semiannual Institute for Facilities Management - meeting - usually September and January.

8334 ■ Community Learning and Information Network (CLIN)
1750 K St. NW, Ste.1200
Washington, DC 20006
Ph: (202)857-2330
Fax: (202)835-0643
E-mail: bpurdy@clin.org
URL: http://www.clin.org
Contact: Brenda Purdy, VP, Operations and Finance

Founded: 1992. **Staff:** 8. **Budget:** $1,200,000. **Description:** Seeks to improve the global competitiveness of U.S. industry through employment of technology-based educational and training programs. Designs and implements model technology-based educational programs. Maintains network of Centers to coordinate technology-based educational programs throughout the United States; works with government agencies and educational organizations to increase availability of technology-based educational programs. **Computer Services:** Online services, publication. **Projects:** National Guard's Distributive Training Technology. **Publications:** *CLINews*, quarterly. Newsletter. Alternate Formats: online. **Conventions/Meetings:** quarterly board meeting (exhibits).

8335 ■ Council of Educational Facility Planners, International (CEFPI)
9180 E Desert Cove Dr., Ste.104
Scottsdale, AZ 85260-6231
Ph: (480)391-0840
Fax: (480)391-0940
E-mail: contact@cefpi.org
URL: http://www.cefpi.org
Contact: Art Gissendaner, Dir.

Founded: 1921. **Members:** 3,300. **Membership Dues:** individual in U.S. and Canada, $245 (annual) ● corporate in U.S. and Canada (based on number of members), $675-$2,700 (annual) ● individual outside U.S. and Canada, $215 (annual) ● corporate outside U.S. and Canada (based on number of members), $595-$2,350 (annual) ● student, $40 (annual) ● institutional in U.S. and Canada, $225 (annual) ● institutional outside U.S. and Canada, $195 (annual) ● institutional group in U.S. and Canada (based on number of members), $610-$2,392 (annual) ● institutional group outside U.S. and Canada (based on number of members), $535-$2,110 (annual). **Staff:** 9. **Budget:** $1,000,000. **Regional Groups:** 7. **Local Groups:** 30. **Multinational. Description:** Individuals and firms who are responsible for planning, designing, creating, maintaining, and equipping the physical environment of education. Sponsors an exchange of information, professional experiences, best practices research results, and other investigative techniques concerning educational facility planning. Activities include publication and review of current and emerging practices in educational facility planning; identification and execution of needed research; development of professional training programs; strengthening of planning services on various levels of government and in institutions of higher learning; leadership in the development of higher standards for facility design and the physical environment of education. Operates speakers' bureau; sponsors placement service; compiles statistics. **Libraries: Type:** reference. **Holdings:** 3,500. **Awards:** James D. MacConnell Award. **Frequency:** annual. **Type:** recognition. **Recipient:** for exemplary planning, design and construction ● Planner of the Year Award. **Frequency:** annual. **Type:** recognition. **Recipient:** for commendable achievement in planning and design. **Formerly:** (1967) National Council on Schoolhouse Construction. **Publications:** *The CEFPI Consultants Directory*, annual. **Price:** $25.00. Alternate Formats: online ● *CEFPI Membership Directory*, annual ● *The Educational Facility Planner*, quarterly. Journal. Publishes articles concerning the latest in school building research and hot topics. **Price:** $60.00/year in U.S.; $70.00/year in Canada; $85.00/year outside U.S. and Canada ● *Guide for Planning Educational Facilities*. Book. Covers planning, design, and construction of educational facilities. **Price:** $60.00 ● *The Guide for School Facility Appraisal*. Book. **Price:** $35.00 for members; $45.00 for nonmembers ● *Preparing Your School Building for Technology*. **Conventions/Meetings:** annual international conference (exhibits) - always September or October.

8336 ■ National Association for the Exchange of Industrial Resources (NAEIR)
560 McClure St.
Galesburg, IL 61401
Ph: (309)343-0704
Free: (800)562-0955
Fax: (309)343-0862
E-mail: donor@naeir.org
URL: http://www.naeir.org
Contact: Mr. Gary Smith, Pres./CEO

Founded: 1977. **Members:** 9,500. **Membership Dues:** regular, $595 (annual) ● affiliate, $250 (annual). **Staff:** 130. **Description:** Seeks to match donated industrial supplies and equipment with schools and nonprofit organizations. Sponsors National Gifts in Kind program. **Computer Services:** Online services, information request. **Publications:** *Gift Catalog*, 5/year. Lists available donated products. ● *Member's Choice Mini-Catalog*, quarterly ● *NAEIR Advantage*, quarterly. Newsletter ● Membership Directory, annual.

8337 ■ National Educational Telecommunications Association (NETA)
PO Box 50008
Columbia, SC 29250
Ph: (803)799-5517
Fax: (803)771-4831
E-mail: skip@netaonline.org
URL: http://www.netaonline.org
Contact: Skip Hinton, Pres.

Members: 94. **Description:** Providers of telecommunications, communications, and computer programming services to educational institutions at all levels. Promotes effective application of telecommunications technology in education. Facilitates communication and cooperation among members; sponsors educational programs. **Computer Services:** database, programs. **Councils:** Communication; Development; Education; Engineering; Outreach; Production; Programming.

Educational Freedom

8338 ■ Citizens for Educational Freedom (CEF)
9333 Clayton Rd.
St. Louis, MO 63124
Ph: (314)997-6361
Fax: (314)997-6321
E-mail: citedfree@educational-freedom.org
URL: http://www.educational-freedom.org
Contact: Mae Duggan, Pres.

Founded: 1959. **Members:** 9,000. **Membership Dues:** individual, $25 (annual) ● family, $35 (annual) ● sponsoring organization, $100 (annual) ● group, $50 (annual). **Regional Groups:** 10. **State Groups:** 15. **Local Groups:** 10. **Description:** Represents nonsectarian organization of parents, individuals and groups. Encourages citizens to attempt to influence the collection and expenditure of their education tax dollars; proclaims the right of parents to choose the types of education they desire for their children. Advocates programs such as tuition vouchers and tax deductions/credits. Maintains speakers' bureau; conducts research programs and conferences. **Boards:** Trustees. **Publications:** *Parents Choice Newsletter* (in English and Spanish), bimonthly. Includes legislative and judicial case histories. **Circulation:** 10,000. **Advertising:** accepted. **Conventions/Meetings:** annual meeting.

8339 ■ Home School Legal Defense Association (HSLDA)
PO Box 3000
Purcellville, VA 20134-9000
Ph: (540)338-5600

Fax: (540)338-2733
E-mail: info@hslda.org
URL: http://www.hslda.org
Contact: J. Michael Smith Esq., Pres.
Founded: 1983. **Members:** 70,000. **Membership Dues:** standard, $115 (annual). **Staff:** 60. **Description:** Families that educate their children at home rather than enrolling them in a public or private school. Provides legal assistance to families whose attempts to educate their children at home are challenged by state government or the local school board. Monitors legal and legislative developments nationwide pertaining to what the group believes is a family's right to educate its children at home. (Legal and moral controversy has arisen in recent years regarding families that wish to educate their children at home.) Current U.S. state laws generally dictate specific home schooling guidelines. **Telecommunication Services:** information service, "Alerts to Action" and other information on home schooling issues for members. **Publications:** *Constitutional Law for Christian Students*. Book ● *Future of Home Schooling*. Book ● *The Home School Court Report*, bimonthly. Magazine. Covers home school law and national legislative developments. **Price:** $15.00 for nonmembers; included in membership dues. **Circulation:** 60,000 ● *The Home-Schooling Father*. Book ● *Home Schooling in the U.S.: A Legal Analysis*. Book. **Price:** $15.00 for members plus shipping and handling; $20.00 for nonmembers plus shipping and handling ● *Home Schooling: The Right Choice*. Book. **Price:** $15.00 for nonmembers plus shipping and handling; $12.00 for members plus shipping and handling ● *How a Man Prepares His Daughters for Life*. Book. **Conventions/Meetings:** annual Leadership Conference, state home school leaders and families.

8340 ■ Parents in Control (PIC)
c/o Jeff Barclay, Interim Exec. Dir.
2511 Jasu Dr.
Lawrence, KS 66046
Ph: (785)749-0083
Fax: (785)749-0580
E-mail: vcsjbarclay@sunflower.com
URL: http://www.parentsincontrol.org
Contact: Jeff Barclay, Interim Exec. Dir.
Founded: 1997. **Staff:** 3. **Budget:** $100,000. **State Groups:** 1. **Local Groups:** 6. **Description:** Promotes and influences education of individuals about need for and implementation of parent control over children. **Libraries: Type:** open to the public. **Computer Services:** database ● mailing lists.

Educational Funding

8341 ■ ACUO
PO Box 65298
Washington, DC 20035
Ph: (202)659-2104
Fax: (240)632-9425
E-mail: webmaster@acuo.org
URL: http://www.acuo.org
Contact: J. Timothy Hanson, Pres.
Founded: 1977. **Membership Dues:** full, $10,000 (annual). **Staff:** 5. **Budget:** $250,000. **For-Profit. Description:** Assists colleges and universities in the pursuit of grants from the federal government and private foundations. Specializes in support for faculty development, faculty research, laboratory instrumentation and modernization, curriculum development, dormitory and academic facility renovation, and partnerships with pre-college institutions. Offers special training programs on budget development and proposal development. **Libraries: Type:** reference. **Subjects:** source materials on grants. **Computer Services:** Information services, government and foundation grant opportunities. **Formerly:** Association of College and University Offices; (1989) Association for Affiliated College and University Offices. **Publications:** *News Notes and Deadlines*, 10/year. Newsletter. **Price:** $80.00/year; $140.00/2 years; $250.00 copyright-waived version. **Conventions/Meetings:** annual conference and workshop - always October ● workshop.

8342 ■ American Education Finance Association (AEFA)
PO Box 117049
Gainesville, FL 32611-7049
Ph: (352)392-2391
E-mail: aefa@coe.ufl.edu
URL: http://www.aefa.cc
Contact: Dr. Jennifer King Rice, Pres.
Founded: 1976. **Members:** 600. **Membership Dues:** regular, $95 (annual) ● student, $45 (annual) ● retired, international student, $65 (annual) ● international, $115 (annual) ● institutional, $1,000 (annual). **Budget:** $60,000. **Description:** State and national teacher organizations, university personnel, school administrators, state educational agency personnel, legislators and legislative staff, federal agency personnel, and interested foundations and students. Facilitates communication among groups and individuals in the field of educational finance including academicians, researchers, and policymakers. Main interests include traditional school finance concepts, public policy issues, and the review and debate of emerging issues of educational finance. Conducts workshop. Compiles statistics. Maintains placement service. **Libraries: Type:** reference. **Holdings:** archival material. **Subjects:** AEFA publications. **Awards:** Outstanding Dissertation Award. **Frequency:** annual. **Type:** recognition. **Recipient:** for exemplary dissertation research in education finance ● Outstanding Service Award. **Frequency:** annual. **Type:** recognition. **Recipient:** for contributions made for public policy development. **Publications:** *Education Finance and Policy*, quarterly. Journal. **Advertising:** accepted ● Newsletter, quarterly. Alternate Formats: online ● Yearbook, annual. **Conventions/Meetings:** annual board meeting and conference (exhibits) ● annual conference - always March or April.

8343 ■ Armenian Educational Foundation (AEF)
600 W Broadway, Ste.130
Glendale, CA 91204
Ph: (818)242-4154
Fax: (818)242-4913
E-mail: aef@aefweb.org
URL: http://www.instantweb.com/a/aef
Contact: Hasmik Keyribarian, Exec. Sec.
Founded: 1950. **Members:** 100. **Membership Dues:** honorary and individual, $500 (annual). **Description:** Renders financial assistance to Armenian schools in Armenia, the United States, and countries friendly to the U.S. Establishes working structures for Armenian education in public schools. Has built schools in Athens, Greece, Beirut, Lebanon, Pico Rivera, CA, and Grashen, Armenia. Sponsors programs for Armenian students in public schools. Supports other schools; sponsors research programs. Has established Endowment for "Modern Armenian History" Chair at UCLA. Sponsors Armenian State University in Yerevan and the Polytechnic of Yerevan in Armenia. **Awards:** Educator of the Year. **Frequency:** annual. **Type:** recognition. **Recipient:** to a preK-12 educator or a higher education leader ● Lifetime Achievement Award. **Frequency:** annual. **Type:** recognition. **Recipient:** to a preK-12 educator or a higher education leader ● Richard R. Tufenkian Memorial Scholarship. **Frequency:** annual. **Type:** scholarship. **Recipient:** for Armenian students attending college or a university. **Additional Websites:** http://www.aefweb.org. **Publications:** Brochure (in Armenian and English), annual. Describes membership activities and responsibilities. ● Brochure (in Armenian and English), annual. Describes the work of the foundation. ● Armenian educational books and textbooks, and teachers' guide books. **Conventions/Meetings:** periodic seminar.

8344 ■ Coalition of Higher Education Assistance Organizations (COHEAO)
1101 Vermont Ave. NW, Ste.400
Washington, DC 20005-3586
Ph: (202)289-3910
Fax: (202)371-0197
E-mail: whuffman@wpllc.net
URL: http://www.coheao.org
Contact: Harrison M. Wadsworth, Exec. Dir.
Founded: 1980. **Members:** 300. **Membership Dues:** institutional, $190-$545 (annual) ● commercial, $3,000 (annual) ● organizational, $1,250 (annual) ● associate, $125 (annual). **Budget:** $100,000. **Description:** Institutions of higher learning and their contracted commercial billers and collectors of student loans; lawyers involved with the collection of unpaid National Direct Student Loans. Aims to build a healthy environment in which members can operate; support student loan programs; monitor regulations and legislative activities. **Awards: Frequency:** annual. **Type:** scholarship. **Recipient:** for undergraduate students. **Computer Services:** database, membership. **Telecommunication Services:** hotline, (800)8COHEAO. **Publications:** *The TORCH*, monthly. Newsletter. **Conventions/Meetings:** semi-annual conference - mid-year ● annual conference, higher education issues, with a focus on the Perkins loan program.

8345 ■ Committee for Education Funding (CEF)
122 C St. NW, Ste.280
Washington, DC 20001
Ph: (202)383-0083
Fax: (202)383-0097
E-mail: ekealy@cef.org
URL: http://www.cef.org
Contact: Dr. Edward R. Kealy PhD, Exec. Dir./Sec.
Founded: 1969. **Members:** 100. **Membership Dues:** institutional, $1,323. **Staff:** 3. **Budget:** $550,000. **Description:** Individuals, institutions, and organizations. Represents elementary, secondary, and higher education associations in their efforts to maintain federal funding of education at all levels. Collects and analyzes budget and appropriations information and advises on the best ways to persuade Congress and the Administration to fully fund educational programs. **Awards:** Bell Outstanding Education Advocacy. **Frequency:** annual. **Type:** recognition ● O'Hara Education Leadership Award. **Frequency:** annual. **Type:** recognition. **Formerly:** (1974) Emergency Committee for Full Funding of Education Programs; (1982) Committee for Full Funding of Education Programs. **Publications:** *Education Budget Alert*, annual. Report. **Price:** $29.00. **Advertising:** accepted ● *Education Funding Update*, quarterly. Newsletter. **Conventions/Meetings:** annual Legislative Conference and Awards Gala - meeting - always September.

8346 ■ Council for Aid to Education (CAE)
215 Lexington Ave., 21st Fl.
New York, NY 10016-6023
Ph: (212)661-5800 (212)217-0700
Fax: (212)661-9766
E-mail: vse@cae.org
URL: http://www.cae.org
Contact: Roger Benjamin PhD, Pres./CEO
Founded: 1952. **Staff:** 8. **Budget:** $1,100,000. **Description:** Works to improve quality and productivity in higher education. Conducts the annual Voluntary Support of Education Survey, the "leading source of data on private giving to education". Conducts research on and promotes policy reforms in higher education. Operates the Collegiate Learning Assessment program, a national effort to assess the quality of undergraduate education in the United States by directly measuring student learning outcomes. The program aims to create a performance-based assessment model and incentive system for continuous improvement, and to develop direct measures of quality that all the major stakeholders-university administrators, faculty, students, parents, employers and policy makers-can use as part of their evaluation of academic programs nationwide. **Libraries: Type:** reference. **Holdings:** archival material. **Awards:** Leaders for Change. **Frequency:** annual. **Type:** recognition. **Recipient:** for outstanding corporate support of education. **Computer Services:** Online services, Data Miner access to analyze VSE survey data. **Programs:** Collegiate Learning Assessment;

Leaders for Change Award. **Affiliated With:** Foundation for Independent Higher Education; National Association of Independent Schools. **Publications:** *Intelligent Giving: Insights and Strategies for Higher Education Donors*. Reports. **Price:** $28.00 paperback; $25.20 discounted web price ● *Voluntary Support of Education*, annual. Report. **Price:** $106.00 non-participating institution; $71.00 survey participant. **Circulation:** 2,000. Alternate Formats: online ● Newsletters. **Conventions/Meetings:** annual Leaders for Change - luncheon - usually January in New York City, NY.

8347 ■ Council for Resource Development (CRD)
1 Dupont Cir. NW, Ste.365
Washington, DC 20036-1176
Ph: (202)822-0750
Fax: (202)822-5014
E-mail: crd@crdnet.org
URL: http://www.crdnet.org
Contact: Polly Binns, Exec. Dir.
Founded: 1972. **Members:** 1,550. **Membership Dues:** professional, emeritus, $195 (annual) ● institutional professional, $585 (annual) ● affiliated, $1,000 (annual). **Regional Groups:** 10. **Description:** Represents presidents and development officers of two-year higher education institutions. Promotes the development of private and public funding sources for member institutions. Aims to establish business and industry partnerships with colleges and foundations for gift solicitations. Sponsors regional workshops. **Affiliated With:** American Association of Community Colleges. **Publications:** *Dispatch*, 3/year. Newsletter. Includes information on legislation. **Price:** free for members. **Circulation:** 1,520. Alternate Formats: online ● *Federal Funding to Two Year Colleges*, annual. Book ● *Fostering Civility on Campus*. Book. **Price:** $30.00 for members; $38.00 for nonmembers ● *Resource Development in the Two-Year College*. Book ● Papers. **Conventions/Meetings:** annual conference (exhibits) - always Washington, DC.

8348 ■ Education Funding Research Council (EFRC)
c/o Thompson Publishing Group, Inc.
Govt. Info. Services
1725 K St. NW, Ste.700
Washington, DC 20006
Ph: (202)872-4000
Free: (800)876-0226
Fax: (800)926-2012
E-mail: service@thompson.com
URL: http://www.grantsandfunding.com
Contact: James E. Finkelstein, Chm.
Founded: 1972. **Description:** Assists education administrators, grant seekers, and community and nonprofit organization leaders in successful fundraising in the public and private sectors. **Libraries: Type:** reference. **Holdings:** books, periodicals. **Subjects:** education. **Computer Services:** Mailing lists. **Publications:** *The New Title I*, annual. Book. Includes all the new Title I guidance and regulations issued through 2005. **Price:** $99.00 each ● *School Administrator's Guide to ESEA Formula Grants*, bimonthly. **Price:** $379.00/year ● *Title I Handbook*, quarterly. Provides information on Title I funding. **Price:** $399.00/year ● *Title I Monitor*, monthly. Newsletter. Focuses exclusively on the federal Title I compensatory education program. **Price:** $299.00/year.

8349 ■ National Association of Federally Impacted Schools (NAFIS)
Hall of States
444 N Capitol St. NW, Ste.419
Washington, DC 20001
Ph: (202)624-5455
Fax: (202)624-5468
E-mail: carolmisa@aol.com
URL: http://www.nafisdc.org
Contact: John Deegan, Pres.
Founded: 1973. **Members:** 600. **Membership Dues:** school, $350 (annual). **Staff:** 5. **Budget:** $1,100,000. **Regional Groups:** 6. **Local Groups:** 1,600. **Description:** Public school districts receiving federal impact aid. Seeks to monitor, influence, explain, and assist in all matters regarding federal reimbursement programs title VIII of PL 103-382, known as Impact Aid. Informs members and congressional representatives concerning issues and philosophies influencing financial and political support of the program. **Awards:** Friends of NAFIS Award. **Frequency:** annual. **Type:** recognition. **Recipient:** for member of congress or federal agency personnel. **Subgroups:** Federal Property Districts; Federal Relations Outreach; Military Impacted Schools Association; National Indian Impacted Schools Association; State Chair. **Publications:** *IMPACT*, monthly. Newsletter. Includes legislative updates and reports on U.S. Department of Education activities. **Price:** included in membership dues. **Circulation:** 2,000 ● *Impact Aid Blue Book*, annual. Manual. Contains the updated laws, regulations and a history of the program, as well as congressional district breakdowns. ● *NAFIS News*, weekly. Newsletter. Alternate Formats: online. **Conventions/Meetings:** semiannual conference, legislative (exhibits) - always spring and fall in Washington, DC ● seminar ● workshop.

8350 ■ National Association of Student Financial Aid Administrators (NASFAA)
1129 20th St. NW, Ste.400
Washington, DC 20036-3453
Ph: (202)785-0453
Fax: (202)785-1487
E-mail: web@nasfaa.org
URL: http://www.nasfaa.org
Contact: Dr. A. Dallas Martin Jr., Pres.
Founded: 1966. **Members:** 2,900. **Membership Dues:** student, $125 (annual) ● institutional, affiliate, $720 (annual) ● constituent (based on annual revenue), $1,326-$6,312 (annual). **Staff:** 37. **Budget:** $6,000,000. **Regional Groups:** 6. **State Groups:** 49. **Description:** Postsecondary institutions, agencies, financial aid administrators, students, and other interested individuals. Seeks to promote the professionalism of student financial aid administrators; serves as the national forum for matters related to student aid; represents the interests and needs of students, faculties, and other persons involved in student financial aid. **Awards:** Committee of the Year. **Frequency:** annual. **Type:** recognition. **Recipient:** to the committee that made some contribution to the advancement of the objectives of the association ● Distinguished Service Award. **Frequency:** annual. **Type:** recognition. **Recipient:** for outstanding achievements in the furtherance of NASFAA goals and significant contributions over a sustained period of time ● Robert P. Huff Golden Quill Award. **Frequency:** annual. **Type:** recognition. **Recipient:** to individual or individuals chosen for their contributions to the literature on student financial aid ● Sponsored Research Grant Program. **Frequency:** annual. **Type:** grant. **Publications:** *Encyclopedia* ● *Encyclopedia of Student Financial Aid* ● *Journal of Student Financial Aid*, 3/year. Alternate Formats: online ● *National Membership Directory*, annual ● *Special Reports* ● *Student Aid Transcript*, 3/year. Magazine. Features articles on student aid management, innovative programs, professional awards, and member ideas. ● *Today's News*, daily. Features articles on program administration, legislation, regulations, appropriations, and association news. **Price:** included in membership dues. **Circulation:** 10,000. Alternate Formats: online ● *Transcript Magazine* ● Newsletter, weekly. Features articles on program administration, legislation, regulations, appropriations, and association news. **Price:** included in membership dues. **Circulation:** 5,600. Alternate Formats: online ● Directory ● Monographs. **Conventions/Meetings:** annual conference (exhibits) - always July.

8351 ■ National Council of Higher Education Loan Programs (NCHELP)
1100 Connecticut Ave. NW, Ste.1200
Washington, DC 20036-4110
Ph: (202)822-2106
Fax: (202)822-2143
E-mail: info@nchelp.org
URL: http://www.nchelp.org
Contact: Brett Lief, Pres.
Founded: 1961. **Description:** Directors of state and private nonprofit corporations that guarantee student loans under the Higher Education Act of 1965 as amended; state secondary markets and state direct lenders. Affiliate members include: lenders, servicers, collectors, and other organizations involved in the Federal Family Education Loan Program (FFELP). Coordinates federal, state, and private functions in the student loan program. **Committees:** Default Management; Electronic Standards; Legal Affairs; Membership Education and Training; Program Operations; Program Regulations. **Formerly:** (1969) National Conference of Executives of Higher Education Loan Plans. **Publications:** Directory, annual. Lists lenders and other organizations involved in FFELP. **Price:** free for members. Alternate Formats: online. **Conventions/Meetings:** annual conference, training (exhibits) ● annual conference, on legislative issues - 2008 Sept. 25-26, Washington, DC ● annual Debt Management - conference (exhibits).

Educational Reform

8352 ■ Accuracy in Academia (AIA)
4455 Connecticut Ave. NW, Ste.330
Washington, DC 20008
Ph: (202)364-3085
Free: (800)787-0429
Fax: (202)364-4098
E-mail: mal.kline@academia.org
URL: http://www.academia.org
Contact: Malcolm A. Kline, Exec. Dir.
Founded: 1985. **Members:** 1,200. **Membership Dues:** individual, $30 (annual). **Staff:** 2. **Budget:** $400,000. **Description:** Seeks accurate use of facts and historical information on college and university campuses. Investigates student reports of inaccurate information being communicated by classroom instructors, either through lectures or required reading materials. Publicizes such reports and cases of intolerance on campuses with respect to guest lecturers, students, and professors. Encourages universities to provide students with accurate descriptions of courses in catalogs. **Libraries: Type:** reference. **Holdings:** audiovisuals, books, clippings, periodicals. **Affiliated With:** Accuracy in Media. **Publications:** *Academic License: The War on Academic Freedom*. Book ● *Campus Report*, monthly. Newspaper. **Price:** $30.00/year. ISSN: 0890-4618. **Circulation:** 5,000. **Advertising:** accepted. Alternate Formats: online ● *Cop Killer - How Mumia Abu-Jamal Conned Millions Into Believing He Was Framed*. Booklet ● *Enemies Within*. Booklet. **Conventions/Meetings:** annual Conservative University - conference (exhibits) - usually summer.

8353 ■ Big Picture Company
325 Public St.
Providence, RI 02905
Ph: (401)752-3528
Fax: (401)752-2652
E-mail: dlittky@bigpicture.org
URL: http://www.bigpicture.org
Contact: Dennis Littky, Co-Founder/Co-Dir.
Founded: 1995. **Description:** Encourages change in the American education system. Promotes and creates personalized education programs that are unique for each student. Designs breakthrough public schools and replicates new designs for education. Trains educators to serve as leaders in their respective schools. **Publications:** Newsletter. Alternate Formats: online.

8354 ■ Center for Occupational Research and Development (CORD)
PO Box 21689
Waco, TX 76702-1689
Ph: (254)772-8756
Fax: (254)772-8972
E-mail: hinckley@cord.org
URL: http://www.cord.org
Contact: Dr. Richard Hinckley, Pres./CEO
Founded: 1979. **Description:** Provides innovative changes in education to prepare students for better chances in career and higher education. Assists educators in secondary schools and colleges through

new curricula, teaching strategies, professional development and partnerships with community leaders. Initiates developments in curriculum design, learning tools and creating applications in educational technology and conducting educational research and evaluation. **Councils:** Community College President's. **Programs:** Career and Technical Education Mathematics Professional Development. **Projects:** Career Cluster Curriculum Development; Curriculum Integrator; Raising Mathematics Achievement Levels in Ohio High Schools; Rescuing Concrete Learners in the Middle School Math Classroom. **Publications:** *Rigor and Relevance: A New Vision for Career and Technical Education*. Report. Contains discussions on the Carl D. Perkins Vocational and Technical Education Act. Alternate Formats: online ● *Teacher Professional Development: It's Not an Event, It's a Process*. Paper. Describes the context, content, and process of high quality teacher professional development. **Price:** $3.50 for each reprint. Alternate Formats: online ● *Teaching Mathematics Contextually*. Booklet. Features concepts that help students discover the relationships between abstract concepts and practical applications. **Price:** $4.00 reprint. Alternate Formats: online ● *Tech Prep: The Next Generation*. Book. Offers a model for strategic planning that addresses the critical elements of a successful Tech Prep program. **Price:** $22.95 hardcover; $14.95 softcover ● *Technology to Improve Texas Education*. Report. Contains recommendations to improve public education in Texas. Alternate Formats: online.

8355 ■ Institute for Learning Technologies (ILT)
c/o John B. Black, Dir.
Columbia Univ.
2960 Broadway
New York, NY 10027-6902
Ph: (212)678-4007
E-mail: jbb21@columbia.edu
URL: http://www.ilt.columbia.edu
Contact: John B. Black, Dir.
Founded: 1986. **Description:** Determines how to use technology and media to increase learning and understanding both in and outside of schools. Conducts research on the effects of current technology and media and develops more effective uses of current and future technology and media for learning and understanding. **Projects:** Aquaponics Remote Lab for Learning; Associating Real and Imaginary Agents; Case Technologies to Enhance Literacy Learning; Handheld Computers Embodied Cognition and Augmented Reality for Transfer; Harlem Live; Integrated Curriculum; Reflective Agent Learning Environment; Technology Integration Partnership; Videogames and Learning Research. **Publications:** *An Interpretation Construction Approach to Constructivism Design*. Paper. Alternate Formats: online ● *Assessing Student Understanding and Learning in Constructivist Study Environments*. Paper. Alternate Formats: online ● *Constructivist Design of Graphic Computer Simulations*. Paper. Alternate Formats: online ● *Imaginary Worlds*. Paper ● *Text and Interactive Panoramic Imagery: Psychological Findings that Affect their Use in Education and Training*. Paper. Alternate Formats: online.

8356 ■ National Academy of American Scholars (NAAS)
PO Box 337380
North Las Vegas, NV 89031-7380
Ph: (760)488-9673
Free: (800)725-7849
E-mail: staff@naas.org
URL: http://www.naas.org
Contact: H. Borgstedt, Contact
Founded: 1988. **Staff:** 20. **Description:** Encourages a national discourse in order to raise the current educational level of pre-college students by setting high academic standards and offering incentives to surpass these standards. Works with local, regional, and national organizations to employ distinguished American scholars in the fields of science, education, and business to serve as role models for college-bound youth. **Awards:** Easley National Scholarship. **Type:** scholarship. **Recipient:** for high school seniors who have exhibited outstanding academic excellence and personal integrity ● NAAS. **Frequency:** annual. **Type:** scholarship. **Recipient:** for high school senior. **Committees:** Data and Statistics; Research; Scholarship. **Publications:** *Scholarship Watch: The Newsletter for Scholarships, Fellowships, Grants and Loans*, quarterly. Includes bibliography. **Price:** free. **Advertising:** accepted. Alternate Formats: online ● Brochure. **Conventions/Meetings:** biennial symposium.

8357 ■ National Paideia Center
400 Silver Cedar Ct., Ste.200
Chapel Hill, NC 27514
Ph: (919)962-3128
Fax: (919)962-3139
E-mail: info@paideia.org
URL: http://www.paideia.org
Contact: Dr. Terry Roberts, Dir.
Founded: 1988. **Description:** Assists schools and school systems to radically improve its services. Hosts educational programs. **Telecommunication Services:** electronic mail, troberts@northcarolina.edu. **Publications:** *Paideia Next Century*, quarterly. Newsletter. **Conventions/Meetings:** annual conference and board meeting - usually held in March.

8358 ■ National Tech Prep Network (NTPN)
PO Box 21689
Waco, TX 76702-1689
Ph: (254)772-5095
Free: (800)518-1410
Fax: (254)776-2306
E-mail: ntpn@cord.org
URL: http://www.cord.org/ntpn
Contact: Dianna Davis, Coor.
Founded: 1991. **Members:** 3,000. **Membership Dues:** individual, $75 (annual) ● institutional, consortium, corporate, $750 (annual) ● institutional, consortium, corporate, $1,500 (annual). **Description:** Represents educators and employers involved in the advancement of Tech Prep and related education reform initiatives. Assists its members in planning, implementing, evaluating, and improving Tech Prep programs by pooling the resources of the country's leading practitioners. Serves as a conduit for timely information and effective partnerships. **Awards:** Daniel M. Hull and Dale P. Parnell Partnership Excellence Award. **Frequency:** annual. **Type:** recognition. **Recipient:** for tech prep/school-to-career initiatives. **Telecommunication Services:** electronic mail, ddavis@cord.org. **Publications:** *Connections*, monthly. Newsletter. Contains the latest Tech Prep news. **Price:** included in membership dues. Alternate Formats: online.

8359 ■ Teaching for Change
PO Box 73038
Washington, DC 20056
Ph: (202)588-7204
Free: (800)763-9131
Fax: (202)238-0109
E-mail: info@teachingforchange.org
URL: http://www.teachingforchange.org
Contact: Alicia Horton, Co-Chair
Founded: 1989. **Staff:** 7. **Budget:** $280,000. **Description:** Promotes social and economic justice through "transformative, quality education for all learners." Seeks to create equitable relationships among families, students, school staff, and communities. Functions as a network linking teachers; makes available educational and cultural resources. **Libraries: Type:** open to the public. **Holdings:** 1,500; books, video recordings. **Subjects:** equity education, Central America, US history. **Projects:** Tellin' Stories. **Formerly:** (2002) Network of Educators on the Americas. **Publications:** Catalog, semiannual. Alternate Formats: online ● Newsletter. Alternate Formats: online ● Annual Report, annual. Alternate Formats: online. **Conventions/Meetings:** periodic Workshop for Equity and Multicultural Education.

Educators

8360 ■ National Association for Alternative Certification (NAAC)
PO Box 5750
Washington, DC 20016
Ph: (202)277-3600
E-mail: info@alternativecertification.org
URL: http://www.alt-teachercert.org
Contact: Judy Corcillo, Contact
Membership Dues: regular, $50 (annual) ● intern/student, $15 (annual). **Description:** Advocates programs for alternative certification/licensure. Improves education and teaching profession. Promotes the professional development of educators. Facilitates funding and sharing research and networking opportunities among educators. Recruits and selects adults to become teachers, principals, administrators and school support personnel. **Telecommunication Services:** electronic mail, jcorcillo@yahoo.com. **Publications:** *Journal of the National Association for Alternative Certification*. **Price:** included in membership dues. Alternate Formats: online. Also Cited As: *JNAAC* ● *NAAC Newsletter*. **Price:** included in membership dues. Alternate Formats: online.

8361 ■ National Council for Workforce Education (NCWE)
410 Oak St., ALU 113
Big Rapids, MI 49307
Ph: (231)591-3534
Free: (800)562-9130
Fax: (231)591-3539
E-mail: ncwe@ncwe.org
URL: http://www.ncwe.org
Contact: Dr. Nancy E. Poppe, Pres.
Founded: 1975. **Members:** 600. **Membership Dues:** individual, $125 (annual) ● institutional (three members), $295 (annual) ● institutional (five or more members), $495 (annual) ● organization (per individual), $150 (annual) ● student, $60 (annual). **Description:** Promotes excellence and growth in workforce education at the post secondary level. Provides a national forum for administrators and faculty in occupational, vocational, technical, and career education as well as representatives of business, labor, military, and government, to affect and direct the future role of two-year and other post-secondary institutions in work-related education. **Formerly:** (2006) National Council for Occupational Education. **Conventions/Meetings:** annual conference (exhibits).

8362 ■ Nature and Environmental Writers - College and University Educators (NEW-CUE)
c/o St. Thomas Aquinas College
125 Rte. 340
Sparkill, NY 10976
Ph: (845)398-4247
Fax: (845)398-4224
E-mail: info@new-cue.org
URL: http://www.new-cue.org
Contact: Dr. Diana Post, Contact
Founded: 2000. **Staff:** 2. **Nonmembership. Multinational. Description:** Dedicated to promoting nature and environment through literature. Encourages nature writers and educators to pursue and develop talents; promotes the writing of Rachel Carson; and supports efforts that ensure the preservation of nature. **Conventions/Meetings:** biennial Writers Conference and Workshop in Honor of Rachel Carson.

8363 ■ Society of Building Science Educators (SBSE)
c/o Judy Theodorson, Sec.-Treas.
PO Box 1495
Spokane, WA 99210
E-mail: jtheodorson@wsu.edu
URL: http://www.sbse.org
Contact: Chris Theis, Pres.
Membership Dues: full, $25 (annual) ● student, $15 (annual). **Description:** Promotes quality instruction and excellence in the teaching of environmental science and building technologies. Supports the institutional needs of technical education within the professional curricula in architecture. Offers a network for the exchange of pertinent information through written, visual, and interpersonal means. **Awards:** Jeffrey Cook Memorial Scholarship. **Frequency:** periodic. **Type:** scholarship. **Recipient:** to a faculty

member from a developing country ● Jeffrey Cook Student Travel Award to PLEA. **Frequency:** annual. **Type:** grant. **Recipient:** to a student who will be attending the PLEA conference ● Student Retreat Scholarship. **Frequency:** annual. **Type:** scholarship. **Recipient:** for students with keen interests in pursuing future teaching positions in environmental control systems or a related area of building science ● Student Travel Scholarship to ASES. **Frequency:** annual. **Type:** scholarship. **Recipient:** for students who will present papers at the annual American Solar Energy Society (ASES) conference. **Telecommunication Services:** electronic mail, decod6@lsu.edu. **Publications:** *SBSE News*, quarterly. Newsletter. **Price:** included in membership dues. Alternate Formats: online.

Electronics

8364 ■ National Coalition for Electronics Education (NCEE)
c/o Ed Clingman
I.S.C.E.T.
3608 Pershing Ave.
Fort Worth, TX 76107
Ph: (817)921-9101
Free: (800)946-0201
E-mail: ed@iscet.org
URL: http://www.ncee-edu.org
Contact: Mike Fabery, Pres.
Description: Seeks to expand training opportunities and to increase the number of trained technicians in the electronics and appliance service industries. Promotes electronics and appliance servicing as a desirable professional career. Works with industry and educational groups to improve electronics training courses. **Telecommunication Services:** electronic mail, mfabery@unitedradio.com.

Employment

8365 ■ Compete America
1341 G St. NW, Ste.1100
Washington, DC 20005
E-mail: info@competeamerica.org
URL: http://www.competeamerica.org
Contact: Eric Thomas, Contact
Description: Represents corporations, educators, research institutions and trade associations committed to ensuring that U.S. has the talent for continued innovation, job creation and economic expansion. Provides education and job training. Establishes a secure and efficient employment-based immigration system.

Engineering

8366 ■ American Society for Engineering Education (ASEE)
1818 N St. NW, Ste.600
Washington, DC 20036-2479
Ph: (202)331-3500 (202)331-3545
Fax: (202)265-8504
E-mail: aseeexec@asee.org
URL: http://www.asee.org
Contact: Frank L. Huband, Exec. Dir.
Founded: 1893. **Members:** 13,000. **Membership Dues:** professional in U.S., $69 (annual) ● retired, $30 (annual) ● student, $20 (annual) ● K-12 educator, $35 (annual) ● global on-line, $39 (annual) ● US/Canadian academic, non-US/Canadian academic, corporate, government, association, $1,000 (annual) ● college affiliate, corporate affiliate, association affiliate, $250 (annual) ● K-12, $125 (annual) ● professional in Canada and Mexico, $84 (annual). **Staff:** 50. **Regional Groups:** 12. **Description:** Professional educational society of college and university engineering deans, administrators, and teachers; practicing engineers; corporate executives; persons interested in engineering education; engineering colleges; technical colleges and institutes; junior colleges; government agencies; industrial organizations. Seeks to advance education and research in engineering, science, and related fields. Administers annual College-Industry Education Conference and Engineering Research Forum; sponsors summer schools, workshops, and effective teaching institutes. Conducts summer faculty fellowship research programs; cosponsors Frontiers in Education Conference. Carries out special research projects; administers institutional development programs; assists in the development of historically black engineering colleges. Presents over 75 honors and awards. Maintains 15 standing committees, four professional interest councils, six institutional councils, and 41 divisions. **Awards:** Best Paper Award. **Frequency:** annual. **Type:** recognition. **Recipient:** for outstanding conference papers at the Annual Conference of the previous year ● Council Awards. **Frequency:** annual. **Type:** recognition. **Recipient:** for engineering education and career ● Fellow Member Honorees. **Frequency:** annual. **Type:** recognition. **Recipient:** for outstanding contributions to engineering technology education ● Zone and Section Awards. **Frequency:** annual. **Type:** recognition. **Recipient:** for an outstanding Zone Campus Representative. **Publications:** *ASEE Annual Conference—Proceedings*, annual. **Price:** included in membership dues; $70.00 for nonmembers ● *ASEE Prism*, monthly. Magazine. Covers engineering and education. **Price:** included in membership dues; $150.00 /year for nonmembers and libraries (in U.S. and Canada); $200.00 /year for nonmembers and libraries (outside U.S. and Canada). ISSN: 1056-8077. **Circulation:** 12,500. **Advertising:** accepted. Alternate Formats: online ● *Chemical Engineering Education*, quarterly. Journal. **Price:** $25.00 for members; $80.00 for nonmembers ● *Civil Engineering Education*, semiannual. **Price:** included in membership dues; $8.00 for American Society of Civil Engineers members; free to libraries ● *CoED Journal*, quarterly ● *College-Industry Education Conference—Proceedings*, annual ● *Computers in Education Division*, quarterly. Journal. **Price:** $15.00/year; $7.50/year for students; $45.00 /year for institutions and libraries ● *Deans and Department Heads Directory*, annual ● *Directory of Graduate Programs in Engineering*, annual. Includes information on graduate degree programs, requirements, tuition, and appointments in over 200 institutions. **Price:** included in membership dues; $75.00 for nonmembers ● *Directory of Undergraduate Programs in Engineering and Engineering Technology*, annual. Focuses on undergraduate programs at over 300 engineering and engineering technology institutions. **Price:** included in membership dues; $75.00 for nonmembers. **Advertising:** accepted ● *Engineering Design Graphics*, 3/year. Journal. **Price:** $1.50 for members; $5.00 for nonmembers ● *The Engineering Economist*, quarterly. Journal. **Price:** $129.00 institution (print); $123.00 institution (online); $69.00 individual. ISSN: 0013-791X. Alternate Formats: online ● *Frontiers in Education Conference—Proceedings*, annual ● *Journal of Engineering Education*, quarterly. Reports on programs and teaching techniques, methods of conducting and funding research, enrollments and degrees. **Price:** included in membership dues; $25.00 single issue, for nonmembers; $150.00 /year for libraries in U.S., Canada, and Mexico; $160.00 /year for libraries elsewhere. ISSN: 1069-4730. **Circulation:** 12,500. Alternate Formats: microform ● *Journal of Engineering Technology*, semiannual. **Price:** $5.00 /year for members; $15.00 /year for nonmembers and libraries ● Also publishes research reports, brochures, reprints, and various division newsletters. **Conventions/Meetings:** annual conference, focuses on current trends in engineering education (exhibits) - 2008 June 22-25, Pittsburgh, PA.

8367 ■ Association for Media-Based Continuing Education for Engineers (AMCEE)
888 N Euclid Ave., No. 302
PO Box 210158
Tucson, AZ 85721
Free: (800)338-9344
Fax: (520)626-3708
E-mail: info@amcee.org
Founded: 1976. **Members:** 22. **Staff:** 2. **Description:** Engineering universities united to increase the international effectiveness of continuing education for engineers, industrial scientists, and technical managers. Promotes continuing education among engineers and technical professionals. Makes available, for rental or purchase, videotapes and CD-ROMs of more than 200 engineering courses in 15 disciplines. **Libraries: Type:** reference. **Holdings:** 250; software, video recordings. **Subjects:** engineering/technical. **Divisions:** CD-ROM; Videotape. **Publications:** *AMCEE Media-Based Courses for Engineers, Scientists, and Technical Managers*, annual. Catalog. Lists courses in engineering available on videotape and CD-ROM from 22 leading American engineering universities, represents 15 academic disciplines. **Price:** free. Alternate Formats: CD-ROM. **Conventions/Meetings:** annual meeting - always October.

8368 ■ Junior Engineering Technical Society (JETS)
1420 King St., Ste.405
Alexandria, VA 22314-2794
Ph: (703)548-5387
Fax: (703)548-0769
E-mail: info@jets.org
URL: http://www.jets.org
Contact: Leann Yoder, Exec. Dir.
Founded: 1950. **Members:** 20,000. **Staff:** 3. **Budget:** $1,000,000. **Description:** Represents high school students interested in mathematics, science, technology, and engineering. **Convention/Meeting:** none. **Absorbed:** (1988) National Engineering Council for Guidance. **Formerly:** Junior Engineering Training for Schools. **Publications:** *Pre-Engineering Times*, monthly. Newsletter. **Price:** free. Alternate Formats: online ● Brochures.

8369 ■ National Action Council for Minorities in Engineering (NACME)
440 Hamilton Ave., Ste.302
White Plains, NY 10601-1813
Ph: (914)539-4010
Fax: (914)539-4032
E-mail: webmaster@nacme.org
URL: http://www.nacme.org
Contact: Dr. John Brooks Slaughter, Pres./CEO
Founded: 1974. **Staff:** 23. **Budget:** $8,000,000. **Nonmembership. Description:** Leads the national effort to increase access to careers in engineering and other science-based disciplines. Conducts research and public policy analysis, develops and operates national demonstration programs at precollege and university levels, and disseminates information through publications, conferences and electronic media. Serves as a privately funded source of scholarships for minority students in engineering. **Libraries: Type:** open to the public. **Holdings:** 2,000; articles, books, periodicals. **Subjects:** access of minorities to engineering. **Awards:** Reginald H. Jones Distinguished Service Award. **Frequency:** annual. **Type:** recognition. **Recipient:** for demonstrating leadership in assuring increased diversity in engineering workforce. **Committees:** Forum; Management Advisory; Minority Engineering Leadership; Secondary School Relations; University Interaction. **Formed by Merger of:** Minority Engineering Education Effort; National Fund for Minority Engineering Students. **Supersedes:** National Advisory Council for Minorities in Engineering. **Publications:** *Academic Gamesmanship: Becoming a Master Engineering Student*. Book. Serves as a guide for student success in engineering. ● *NACME Now*, quarterly. Newsletter. Contains topics, research and statistics for educators, counselors and program directors who participate in minority engineering education. **Price:** free. **Circulation:** 7,500. Alternate Formats: online ● *The Sky's Not the Limit*. Brochure. Serves as a pre-college guide to engineering, with advice on choosing schools and courses. ● Annual Report, annual. **Conventions/Meetings:** annual meeting (exhibits).

8370 ■ National Association of Multicultural Engineering Program Advocates (NAMEPA)
341 N Maitland Ave., Ste.130
Maitland, FL 32751
Ph: (407)647-8839
Fax: (407)629-2502

E-mail: namepa@namepa.org
URL: http://www.namepa.org
Contact: Phil Pyster CAE, Exec. VP
Founded: 1979. **Members:** 450. **Membership Dues:** individual, $250 (annual) ● institutional, small business, $500 (annual) ● corporate partner, $1,500 (annual) ● institutional partner, government agency, nonprofit organization, $1,000 (annual) ● senior corporate partner, $2,500 (annual) ● executive corporate partner, $5,000 (annual). **Staff:** 11. **Budget:** $200,000. **Regional Groups:** 5. **Description:** Administrators of college minority engineering programs; community, corporate, and technical group representatives. Seeks to enhance the recruitment, admission, retention, and graduation of minority engineering students, whom the association believes have traditionally been without representation. Examines the issue of enrollment constraint concerning overcrowding in schools of engineering and the practice of establishing higher enrollment requirements and restricting financial aid for minority students; cooperates in and sponsors studies regarding student retention. Provides assistance to pre-college programs and directors in properly matching potential students with member institutions; offers counseling and guidance services. Acts as liaison among students and industry to facilitate job placement and the development of internship programs. Places administrators as interns in the industry to gain insight into problems faced by students. Sponsors job fairs, internship and in-service training programs, and workshops. **Awards:** National Scholarship Award. **Frequency:** annual. **Type:** scholarship. **Computer Services:** database ● mailing lists ● online services. **Committees:** Research and Evaluation. **Formerly:** (2006) National Association of Minority Engineering Program Administrators. **Publications:** Newsletter, semiannual. **Conventions/Meetings:** annual conference - 2008 July 23-26, Atlanta, GA.

8371 ■ National Association of PreCollege Directors (NAPD)
c/o Dr. Eugene M. Deloatch, Pres.
1818 N St. NW, Ste.600
Washington, DC 20036
Ph: (202)331-3500
Fax: (202)265-8504
E-mail: gmack@eng.morgan.edu
URL: http://www.asee.org
Contact: Dr. Eugene M. Deloatch, Pres.
Description: Increases the pool of students pursuing engineering, mathematics, and technology-based college study. Students are of ethnicities that are historically underrepresented in the science and engineering professions (African American, American Indian, and Hispanic).

8372 ■ National Consortium for Graduate Degrees for Minorities in Engineering and Science (GEM)
1800 K St. NW, Ste.900
Washington, DC 20006
Ph: (202)457-8672
Fax: (202)457-8690
E-mail: info@gemfellowship.org
URL: http://www.gemfellowship.org
Contact: Ms. Michele Lezama, Exec. Dir.
Founded: 1976. **Members:** 140. **Membership Dues:** regular, $1,000 (annual). **Staff:** 6. **Description:** Provides fellowships, programs and materials designed to promote graduate study in engineering and natural sciences to historically underrepresented minority students. GEM's three fellowships include stipends as well as funds for tuition and fees. The fellowships are portable to any of over 90 university Consortium's 50 employer members. Offers mentorship training to business and academia through its National Institute on Mentoring. **Awards:** M.S. Engineering Fellowship. **Frequency:** annual. **Type:** fellowship. **Recipient:** for minority graduate students in engineering ● PhD Engineering Fellowship. **Frequency:** annual. **Type:** fellowship. **Recipient:** for post-masters minority engineering students who are interested in college teaching ● PhD Science Fellowship. **Frequency:** annual. **Type:** fellowship. **Recipient:** for minority students pursuing doctoral degrees in natural, physical, and life sciences. **Computer Services:** database ● mailing lists ● online services. **Formerly:** National Consortium for Graduate Degrees for Minorities in Science and Engineering; (1990) National Consortium for Graduate Degrees for Minorities in Engineering. **Publications:** *Graduate School*. Video. **Price:** $35.00 ● *Making the Grade in Graduate School: Survival Strategy 101*. **Price:** $5.00 ● *Mentoring: An Essential Factor in the Doctoral Process for Minority Students*. **Price:** $5.00 ● *Minority Student Graduate School Information Kit*. **Price:** $8.00 ● *Partners in Progress: The GEM Story*. Video. **Price:** $30.00 ● *Successfully Negotiating the Graduated School Process: A Guide for Minority Students*. **Price:** $5.00 ● *Techniques for Effective Undergraduate Mentoring: A Faculty/Student Guide*. **Price:** $5.00 ● *What Is Graduate School and How Do You Select One*. Video. **Price:** $30.00 ● *Why Graduate School in Science and Engineering*. Video. **Price:** $30.00 ● *Your Internship Is as Good as You Make It: A Practical Guide for Student Internships*. **Price:** $10.00 ● Newsletter, semiannual ● Brochure, annual. **Conventions/Meetings:** board meeting ● annual Selection Meeting - always January.

8373 ■ Society of Manufacturing Engineers Education Foundation
1 SME Dr.
PO Box 930
Dearborn, MI 48121-0930
Ph: (313)425-3300
Free: (800)733-4763
Fax: (313)425-3411
E-mail: foundation@sme.org
URL: http://www.sme.org/cgi-bin/smeefhtml.pl?/foundation/foundation_hp.htm&&&SEF&
Contact: Bart Aslin, Dir.
Founded: 1979. **Staff:** 5. **Budget:** $650,000. **Description:** Dedicated to advancing manufacturing education through student outreach programs, scholarships and fellowships, and college and university grants. Focuses on: introducing young people to careers in manufacturing, engineering, science and technology; providing financial support to undergraduate and graduate students in engineering and manufacturing-related degree programs in the U.S. and Canada; improving the quality and quantity of manufacturing curriculums at colleges and universities. **Libraries: Type:** reference. **Holdings:** books, business records, periodicals. **Awards:** Building the Future Award. **Frequency:** annual. **Type:** monetary. **Recipient:** for a program that promotes engineering career awareness among middle school students ● MEP Collegiate Grants. **Frequency:** annual. **Type:** grant. **Recipient:** for research initiation, capital equipment, and student, faculty, and curriculum developments. **Committees:** Fund Development; Grant Review; Scholarship Review; Youth. **Also Known As:** SME Foundation. **Publications:** *Grant Proposal Package*, annual ● *SME Foundation Grant Summary*, annual. Directory. **Price:** free ● *SME News*. Newsletter. Alternate Formats: online ● Annual Report. **Conventions/Meetings:** semiannual board meeting.

English

8374 ■ Association of Departments of English (ADE)
26 Broadway, 3rd Fl.
New York, NY 10004-1789
Ph: (646)576-5130
Fax: (646)835-4056
E-mail: dlaurence@mla.org
URL: http://www.ade.org
Contact: David Laurence, Dir.
Founded: 1962. **Members:** 750. **Membership Dues:** PhD granting department, $625 (annual) ● BA or MA granting department (19 or more full-time faculty members), $425 (annual) ● BA or MA granting department (18 or fewer full-time faculty members), $225 (annual) ● two-year college, no degree offered, $125 (annual). **Staff:** 3. **Description:** Administrators of college and university departments of English, humanities, rhetoric, and communications. Works to improve the teaching of English and the administration of English departments. Conducts studies and surveys of literature and writing courses. Sponsors sessions at major English conventions and conferences nationwide. Sponsored by Modern Language Association of America (see separate entry). **Awards:** Francis Andrew March Award. **Frequency:** annual. **Type:** recognition. **Recipient:** for exceptional service to the profession of English. **Computer Services:** Mailing lists. **Divisions:** PhD; Private B.A./M.A.; Public B.A./M.A.; Two-Year. **Formerly:** Association of Departments of English in American Colleges and Universities. **Publications:** *ADE Bulletin*, 3/year. Journal. Includes annual membership directory. **Price:** included in membership dues; $27.00 /year for individuals; $30.00 /year for institutions and libraries. **Circulation:** 2,000. **Advertising:** accepted. Alternate Formats: online ● *Job Information List*, quarterly. **Conventions/Meetings:** semiannual Summer Seminar.

8375 ■ College English Association (CEA)
c/o Joe Pestino, Treas.
Nazareth Coll. of Rochester
4245 East Ave.
Rochester, NY 14618-3790
Ph: (585)389-2645
Fax: (585)586-2452
E-mail: jfpestin@naz.edu
URL: http://www2.widener.edu/~cea
Contact: Joe Pestino, Treas.
Founded: 1939. **Members:** 1,200. **Membership Dues:** individual, $40 (annual) ● joint, $50 (annual) ● student, $15 (annual) ● retired, part-time, $25 (annual) ● life - individual (based on age), $250-$350 ● life - joint (based on age), $350-$450. **Staff:** 5. **Budget:** $45,000. **Regional Groups:** 20. **Description:** Members of faculties of English and related disciplines in colleges and universities of the U.S. and Canada. Studies and works actively to enhance the teaching function of scholars in English and related humanities disciplines. **Awards:** CEA Honorary Life Membership. **Frequency:** annual. **Type:** recognition. **Recipient:** to individuals for extraordinary and sustained service to the association and the profession ● CEA Professional Achievement Award. **Frequency:** annual. **Type:** recognition. **Recipient:** to an association member who has significantly contributed to teaching and scholarship at the college level ● Joe D. Thomas (CEA) Distinguished Service Award. **Frequency:** annual. **Type:** recognition. **Recipient:** for service to CEA through contributions to the organization over a period of time ● Outstanding Paper Presented by a Graduate Student at CEA Annual Conference. **Frequency:** annual. **Type:** monetary. **Recipient:** for outstanding paper presented by a graduate student of CEA ● Robert A. Miller Memorial Prize. **Frequency:** annual. **Type:** recognition. **Recipient:** to the best essay and essay writer ● Robert Hacke Scholar-Teacher Award. **Frequency:** annual. **Type:** grant. **Recipient:** for working in a project involving scholarship or pedagogy related to English studies. **Committees:** English in the First Two Years; Nontraditional Student. **Publications:** *The CEA Critic*, 3/year. Journal. Covers interpretation and teaching of literature in college. Includes book reviews. **Price:** included in membership dues. ISSN: 0007-8069. **Circulation:** 1,200. **Advertising:** accepted ● *The CEA Forum*, semiannual. Journal. Describes innovations, changes and advancements in the teaching of college-level English. Includes professional news. **Price:** included in membership dues. ISSN: 0007-8034. **Advertising:** accepted. **Conventions/Meetings:** annual conference (exhibits) - always April.

8376 ■ Conference on College Composition and Communication (CCCC)
1111 W Kenyon Rd.
Urbana, IL 61801-1096
Ph: (217)328-3870
Free: (877)369-6283
Fax: (217)328-9645
E-mail: public_info@ncte.org
Contact: Kristen McGowan, Admin. Liaison Specialist
Founded: 1949. **Members:** 10,000. **Membership Dues:** individual, $40 (annual) ● student, $20 (annual). **Description:** Represents college and university

educators involved in teaching composition and communication. **Awards:** Exemplar Award. **Frequency:** annual. **Type:** recognition. **Recipient:** to an individual who has served or serves as an exemplar to the organization ● James Berlin Memorial Outstanding Dissertation Award. **Frequency:** annual. **Type:** recognition. **Recipient:** to a graduate whose dissertation improves the educational process in composition studies ● Outstanding Book Award. **Frequency:** annual. **Type:** recognition. **Recipient:** to authors or editors of books ● Outstanding Dissertation Award in Technical Communication. **Frequency:** annual. **Type:** recognition. **Recipient:** to an author of the best article published in a journal ● Richard Braddock Award. **Frequency:** annual. **Type:** recognition. **Recipient:** to an author of the best article published in a journal ● Scholars for the Dream Travel Award. **Frequency:** annual. **Type:** monetary. **Recipient:** for originality of research, significance of pedagogical or theoretical contributions to the field. **Committees:** Assessment; Computers in Composition and Communication; Convention Concerns; Intellectual Property; Language Policy; Nominating; Project Mentor; Resolutions; Second Language Writing; Service Learning; Status of Women in the Profession; Technical Communications. **Affiliated With:** National Council of Teachers of English. **Publications:** *College Composition and Communication*, quarterly. Journal. Contains information on the study and teaching of reading and writing at the college level. **Price:** $25.00 /year for members; $75.00 /year for nonmembers; $7.50/year for student; $25.00/year for emeritus. ISSN: 0010-096X. **Advertising:** accepted. Alternate Formats: online. **Conventions/Meetings:** annual convention (exhibits).

8377 ■ Conference on English Education (CEE)

c/o National Council of Teachers of English
1111 W Kenyon Rd.
Urbana, IL 61801-1096
Ph: (217)328-3870
Free: (877)369-6283
Fax: (217)328-9645
E-mail: membership@ncte.org
URL: http://www.ncte.org/groups/cee
Contact: Don Zancanella, Chm.

Founded: 1963. **Members:** 3,000. **Membership Dues:** individual, $40 (annual) ● student, $20 (annual). **Description:** A conference of the National Council of Teachers of English. College teachers specializing in English education; English education department chairs; supervisors of beginning English teachers; state and local supervisors of English. Maintains 7 commissions. **Awards:** CEE Cultural Diversity Grant. **Frequency:** annual. **Type:** grant. **Recipient:** for conference presentation proposal completed by members of historically underrepresented groups ● James Britton Award. **Frequency:** annual. **Type:** recognition. **Recipient:** for inquiry within the English language arts ● James Moffett Award. **Frequency:** annual. **Type:** grant. **Recipient:** for research projects of teachers ● Janet Emig Award. **Frequency:** annual. **Type:** recognition. **Recipient:** for research in English education ● Richard A. Meade Award. **Frequency:** annual. **Type:** recognition. **Recipient:** for research in English education. **Affiliated With:** National Council of Teachers of English. **Publications:** *English Education*, quarterly. Journal. **Price:** $15.00 /year for members; $45.00 /year for nonmembers; $5.00/year, student; $15.00/ year, emeritus. ISSN: 0007-8204. **Circulation:** 3,500. **Advertising:** accepted. **Conventions/Meetings:** annual conference, held in conjunction with NCTE Elementary and Secondary Sections (exhibits).

8378 ■ English Institute (EI)

The Carpenter Center
24 Quincy St.
Harvard Univ.
Cambridge, MA 02138
Ph: (617)496-1006
E-mail: englinst@fas.harvard.edu
Contact: Kelli Costello, Conference Coor.

Founded: 1938. **Members:** 300. **Staff:** 1. **Budget:** $35,000. **Description:** Represents scholars, critics, writers, and teachers of English and the humanities. **Publications:** *English Institute—Essays*, annual. **Price:** included in membership dues. **Conventions/ Meetings:** annual conference.

8379 ■ International Society of Anglo-Saxonists (ISAS)

c/o David F. Johnson, PhD, Exec. Dir.
Florida State Univ.
432 Diffenbaugh
Tallahassee, FL 32306
E-mail: djohnson@english.fsu.edu
URL: http://www.isas.us
Contact: David F. Johnson PhD, Exec. Dir.

Founded: 1983. **Membership Dues:** regular, $50 (biennial) ● student, $35 (biennial). **Description:** Provides scholars who are interested in the languages, literatures, arts, history, and material culture of Anglo-Saxon England with support in their research. Facilitates an exchange of ideas and materials within and between the disciplines. **Conventions/Meetings:** semiannual conference.

8380 ■ National Council of Teachers of English (NCTE)

1111 Kenyon Rd.
Urbana, IL 61801-1096
Ph: (217)328-3870
Free: (800)369-6283
Fax: (217)328-0977
E-mail: public_info@ncte.org
URL: http://www.ncte.org
Contact: Joanne Yatvin, Pres.

Founded: 1911. **Members:** 50,000. **Membership Dues:** individual, $40 (annual). **Staff:** 70. **State Groups:** 50. **Local Groups:** 80. **Description:** Represents teachers of English at all school levels. Works to increase the effectiveness of instruction in English language and literature. Sponsors Conference on College Composition and Communication, Conference on English Education, Conference on English Leadership, Whole Language Umbrella, and Two-Year College English Association. Provides information and aids for teachers involved in formulating objectives, writing and evaluating curriculum guides, and planning in-service programs for teacher education. **Libraries: Type:** reference. **Holdings:** archival material, audio recordings, books, monographs, periodicals. **Subjects:** English/language arts, education. **Awards:** Achievement Award in Writing. **Frequency:** annual. **Type:** recognition. **Recipient:** for excellence in writing by high school juniors ● Promising Young Writers Award. **Frequency:** annual. **Type:** recognition. **Recipient:** for excellence in writing by eighth grade students. **Computer Services:** Electronic publishing. **Committees:** Political Action. **Sections:** College; Elementary; Secondary. **Publications:** *Classroom Notes Plus*, quarterly. Journal. Provides practical teaching ideas for the secondary classroom. **Price:** $20.00 /year for members. ISSN: 1526-5641. **Circulation:** 20,500. **Advertising:** accepted. Alternate Formats: online ● *College Composition and Communication*, quarterly. Journal. Provides information on theory, practice, history, and politics of composition and its teaching at all college levels; includes book reviews. **Price:** $18.00 /year for members. ISSN: 0010-096X. **Circulation:** 10,000. **Advertising:** accepted. Alternate Formats: microform; online ● *College English*, bimonthly. Journal ● *English Education*, quarterly. Journal. Contains pre-service training and in-service education for teachers of English and language arts. **Price:** $15.00 /year for members; $30.00 /year for institutions. ISSN: 0007-8204. **Circulation:** 3,200. **Advertising:** accepted. Alternate Formats: microform; online ● *English Journal*, bimonthly. Contains information on the teaching of literature, language, and composition to middle and high school students. **Price:** $20.00 /year for members; $40.00 /year for institutions. ISSN: 0013-8274. **Circulation:** 53,000. **Advertising:** accepted. Alternate Formats: microform; online ● *English Leadership Quarterly*. Journal. Alternate Formats: online ● *Language Arts*, bimonthly. Journal. Provides practical, classroom-tested ideas for helping children learn to read, write, and speak more effectively. **Price:** $20.00 /year for members; $40.00 /year for institutions. ISSN: 0360-9170. **Circulation:** 20,000. **Advertising:** accepted. Alternate Formats: microform; online ● *Research in the Teaching of English*, quarterly. Journal. Covers research into the teaching and learning of the English language. **Price:** $15.00 /year for individuals; $20.00 /year for institutions. ISSN: 0034-527X. **Circulation:** 4,100. **Advertising:** accepted. Alternate Formats: microform; online ● *School Talk*, quarterly. Journal. Alternate Formats: online ● *Teaching English in the Two-Year College*, quarterly. Journal. Provides ideas and information to English teachers, especially to those teaching at two-year colleges; includes book reviews. **Price:** $15.00 /year for members; $30.00 /year for institutions. ISSN: 0098-6291. **Circulation:** 4,000. **Advertising:** accepted. Alternate Formats: microform; online ● *Voices from the Middle*, quarterly. Journal. Alternate Formats: online ● Also publishes 15-20 books each year. **Conventions/Meetings:** annual convention (exhibits) - 2008 Nov. 20-25, San Antonio, TX - **Avg. Attendance:** 7000.

8381 ■ Society for the Preservation of English Language and Literature (SPELL)

PO Box 321
Braselton, GA 30517
Ph: (770)586-0184
Fax: (770)868-0578
E-mail: spellgang@juno.com
URL: http://www.spellorg.com
Contact: James Wallace, Pres./Exec. Dir.

Founded: 1984. **Members:** 1,900. **Membership Dues:** initially, $15 ● regular, $30 (biennial) ● regular, $20 (annual). **Staff:** 2. **Description:** Promotes the proper use of standard English in schools and the mass media; encourages newspapers to improve their use of the language; strives to eliminate grammatical errors in print and on television and radio. **Convention/Meeting:** none. **Awards:** Stephen H. Manhard Scholarship. **Frequency:** annual. **Type:** monetary. **Recipient:** for high school seniors. **Publications:** *Members Handbook and Guide to Good Usage*. **Price:** included in membership dues ● *Spell/ Binder*, bimonthly. Newsletter. Includes research news, society reports, articles on grammar, usage, and word origins. **Price:** included in membership dues. **Circulation:** 2,000 ● *SPELL Members' Handbook* ● THE WRITE WAY by Richard Dowis and Richard Lederer, published by Pocket Books under the auspices of spell.

8382 ■ Teachers of English to Speakers of Other Languages (TESOL)

700 S Washington St., Ste.200
Alexandria, VA 22314-4287
Ph: (703)836-0774
Free: (888)547-3369
Fax: (703)836-7864
E-mail: info@tesol.org
URL: http://www.tesol.org
Contact: Sandra Briggs, Pres.

Founded: 1966. **Members:** 19,000. **Membership Dues:** individual, $75 (annual) ● joint, $120 (annual) ● student, $30 (annual) ● retired, $51 (annual) ● global-individual, $40 (annual) ● global-electronic, $25 (annual). **Staff:** 22. **Budget:** $3,700,000. **Regional Groups:** 89. **Description:** School, college, and adult education teachers who teach English as a second or foreign language; students and professional people in the field; colleges and schools are institutional members. Aims to improve the teaching of English as a second or foreign language by promoting research, disseminating information, developing guidelines and promoting certification, and serving as a clearinghouse for the field. Offers placement service; operates speakers' bureau. Sponsors annual institute. **Awards:** Albert H. Marckwardt Travel Grants. **Frequency:** annual. **Type:** grant. **Recipient:** to a distinguished member educator ● Ruth Crymes TESOL Academies Fellowships. **Frequency:** annual. **Type:** recognition. **Recipient:** to any TESOL member who is a classroom teacher or teacher trainer/supervisor ● Ruth Crymes TESOL Fellowship for Graduate Study. **Frequency:** annual. **Type:** recognition. **Recipient:** to members who are or have been enrolled within the past year in a TESOL or

TEFL graduate program ● TESOL Professional Development Scholarships. **Frequency:** annual. **Type:** scholarship. **Recipient:** to all current TESOL members. **Computer Services:** Mailing lists. **Committees:** Awards; Membership; Professional Development; Publications; Rules and Resolutions; Sociopolitical Concerns. **Divisions:** Communications and Marketing; Conventions; Education Programs; Field Services; Finance and Administration; Membership and Placement. **Publications:** *Directory of Professional Preparation Programs in TESOL in the U.S.*, semiannual ● *Essential Teacher*, quarterly. Magazine. Contains guidance to mainstream teachers who work with students for whom English is an additional language. ● *TESOL Journal*, quarterly. Includes referred articles on ESL/EFL methodology and techniques, materials/curriculum, design and development, teacher education, and research. **Price:** $16.75 /year for members. **Circulation:** 12,000. **Advertising:** accepted. Alternate Formats: CD-ROM ● *TESOL Matters*, bimonthly. Newspaper. Covers conference and organizational news; includes referred articles and book reviews. Lists TESOL awards and grants. **Price:** included in membership dues. **Circulation:** 19,000. **Advertising:** accepted. Alternate Formats: microform ● *TESOL Quarterly*. Journal. Covers testing and evaluation, professional preparation, bilingual education, adult education, and the psychology and sociology of language learning. **Price:** $45.00 /year for individuals; $360.00 /year for libraries. ISSN: 0039-8322. **Circulation:** 19,000. **Advertising:** accepted. Alternate Formats: microform; CD-ROM ● *Training Program Directory*, biennial. Bibliographies. **Conventions/Meetings:** annual convention (exhibits) - usually March.

Environment

8383 ■ American Society for Environmental History (ASEH)
c/o Interdisciplinary Arts and Sciences Program
Univ. of Washington
Box 358436
Tacoma, WA 98402-3100
E-mail: director@aseh.net
URL: http://www.aseh.net
Contact: Lisa Mighetto, Exec. Dir.
Founded: 1976. **Members:** 1,400. **Membership Dues:** individual, $55 (annual) ● joint (individual), $75 (annual) ● dual (same address), $82 (annual) ● student, $25 (annual) ● joint (student), $32 (annual) ● institutional, $100 (annual) ● library, $130 (annual). **Staff:** 1. **Multinational. Description:** Represents teachers and researchers exploring the relationship between humans and the environment in the past. Membership is primarily university, business and government. **Awards:** Alice Hamilton Prize. **Frequency:** annual. **Type:** recognition. **Recipient:** for best article in a journal other than Environmental History ● George Perkins Marsh Prize. **Frequency:** annual. **Type:** recognition. **Recipient:** for best book in environmental history ● Leopold-Hidy Prize. **Frequency:** annual. **Type:** recognition. **Recipient:** for best article in the Environmental History journal ● Rachel Carson Prize. **Frequency:** annual. **Type:** recognition. **Recipient:** for best dissertation in environmental history. **Affiliated With:** Forest History Society. **Publications:** *Environmental History*, quarterly. Journal. **Price:** $20.00 for students; included in membership dues; $24.00 for nonmembers in U.S.; $32.00 for nonmembers outside U.S. ISSN: 0147-2496. **Advertising:** accepted ● Newsletter, quarterly. Alternate Formats: online. **Conventions/Meetings:** annual conference (exhibits).

8384 ■ Compassionate Kids
PO Box 329
Sunny Side, GA 30284-0329
Ph: (678)447-4269
Fax: (801)720-1498
E-mail: info@compassionatekids.com
URL: http://www.compassionatekids.com
Contact: Kelly Palmatier, Founder
Founded: 2004. **Multinational. Description:** Aims to teach children compassion towards the Earth, animals and people. Strives to instill awareness in children by encouraging them to participate in environment-related activities. Organizes compassion-oriented field trips and community service-related events.

8385 ■ The Cousteau Society (TCS)
710 Settlers Landing Rd.
Hampton, VA 23669-4035
Ph: (757)722-9300
Free: (800)441-4395
Fax: (757)722-8185
E-mail: cousteau@cousteausociety.org
URL: http://www.cousteau.org
Contact: Francine Cousteau, Pres.
Founded: 1973. **Members:** 50,000. **Membership Dues:** individual, $30 (annual) ● family, $40 (annual). **Staff:** 12. **Budget:** $6,000,000. **Languages:** English, French. **Multinational. Description:** Environmental education organization dedicated to the protection and improvement of the quality of life for present and future generations. Aims to educate and evaluate the relationships between humans and nature. **Additional Websites:** http://www.cousteaukids.org. **Telecommunication Services:** electronic mail, fcousteau@cousteau.org. **Also Known As:** (2005) Cousteau Society. **Publications:** *Calypso Log*, quarterly. Magazine. Covers the world's natural environment. Includes news of TCS activities and ecological issues. **Price:** included in membership dues. ISSN: 8756-6354. **Circulation:** 21,000 ● *Cousteau Kids*, bimonthly. Magazine. For children ages seven to 15 covering all areas of science, history, and arts related to the world's water system. **Price:** included in membership dues (family membership). ISSN: 8756-6362. **Circulation:** 20,000 ● Books ● Films.

8386 ■ Educational Communications (EC)
PO Box 351419
Los Angeles, CA 90035-9119
Ph: (310)559-9160
Fax: (310)559-9160
E-mail: ecnp@aol.com
URL: http://www.ecoprojects.org
Contact: Nancy Pearlman, Exec. Dir.
Founded: 1958. **Membership Dues:** $20 (annual). **Staff:** 2. **Languages:** English, Hebrew, Japanese, Russian, Spanish, Swahili, Vietnamese. **Multinational. Description:** Multimedia educational organization focusing its programs on environmental preservation and ecology issues. Produces Environmental Directions international radio series, and ECONEWS national television series, and audio- and videotapes on environmental topics. Maintains speakers' bureau and the Ecology Center of Southern California, a regional conservation organization and environmental resources library. Conducts Project Ecotourism and Earth cultures. Creates ecotourism documentaries. **Libraries: Type:** by appointment only. **Holdings:** 2,500; audio recordings, books, periodicals, video recordings. **Subjects:** environment, ecotourism. **Computer Services:** database ● mailing lists. **Subgroups:** Ecology Center of Southern California. **Publications:** *The Compendium*, bimonthly. Newsletter. Contains radio and television listings, book reviews, editorials and association updates and action alerts. **Price:** $20.00/year. ISSN: 0198-9103. **Advertising:** accepted. Alternate Formats: diskette ● *Directory of Environmental Organizations*, annual ● *ECONEWS*. Videos ● *Environmental Directions*. Audiotapes. **Conventions/Meetings:** annual board meeting - always October.

8387 ■ Environic Foundation International (EFI)
12035 Stonewick Pl.
Glen Allen, VA 23059-7152
Ph: (804)360-9130
Fax: (804)360-9131
E-mail: info@environicfoundation.org
URL: http://www.environicfoundation.org
Contact: Mr. William R. Godfrey, Pres.
Founded: 1970. **Nonmembership. Multinational. Description:** Aims to bring about better environic (social, economic and environmental) conditions on a global scale by providing practical educational programs that balances people, place and priorities. Develops integrated interdisciplinary programs that examine numerous areas of social, economic and environmental conditions for analysis and problem-solving. Employs lessons of real world case studies. Programs are applicable for students, professionals, civic leaders and policy-makers, and are able to be integrated into existing programs at colleges and universities. Conducts Environing workshops, usually in partnership with local projects seeking solutions to existing problems; and examines cross-sector problems and trains participants to prioritize goals and develop successful strategies for sustainable solutions. Organizes and conducts seminars, lectures and demonstrations of environic process. Organization's Board of Trustees and Advisors is drawn from around the world, with experience and expertise in education, environmental science, finance, health and medicine, architecture, business, history, human rights, public policy, planning, journalism, information technology, anthropology, international development, art, transportation, urban design, real estate, law, peace, landscape architecture, and physical sciences. **Libraries: Type:** reference. **Holdings:** 12,000. **Awards:** Frances Humphrey Howard Internship. **Frequency:** annual. **Type:** recognition. **Recipient:** for sustainability issue research. **Publications:** *ENVIRONING*, annual. Annual Report ● Newsletter, periodic. Alternate Formats: online ● Annual Report, annual. Alternate Formats: online. **Conventions/Meetings:** annual meeting and workshop, includes reception - usually spring.

8388 ■ Environmental Careers Organization (ECO)
30 Winter St., 6th Fl.
Boston, MA 02108-4720
Ph: (617)426-4375 (617)426-4783
Fax: (617)423-0998
E-mail: kdoyle@eco.org
URL: http://www.eco.org
Contact: Virginia Meany, Chair
Founded: 1972. **Staff:** 32. **Budget:** $10,000,000. **Regional Groups:** 4. **Description:** Seeks to protect and enhance the environment through the development of professionals, the promotion of careers, and the inspiration of individual action. Offers paid internships, career development educational programs and related publications. Participants in programs are mostly upper-level undergraduate, graduate, and doctoral students, or recent graduates seeking professional experience relevant to careers in the environmental fields. Individual subject areas of placement service include biology, chemistry, community development, hazardous waste, natural resources, pollution, public/occupational health, transportation, and wildlife. **Libraries: Type:** reference. **Subjects:** environment, diversity, job openings, job descriptions, research, consulting. **Awards:** Alumni Citations. **Frequency:** annual. **Type:** recognition ● Environmental Achievement and Founders Awards. **Frequency:** annual. **Type:** recognition ● Founder's Award. **Frequency:** annual. **Type:** recognition. **Boards:** Trustees. **Committees:** Executive. **Formerly:** (1979) Center for Experiential Education; (1984) Center for Environmental Intern Programs; (1992) CEIP Fund. **Publications:** *The Complete Guide to Environmental Careers* ● *Connections*, quarterly. Newsletter. Describes current activities and programs of organization and educational information pertaining to environmental career development. **Price:** free. **Circulation:** 10,000. Alternate Formats: online ● *The ECO Guide to Careers that Make a Difference: Environmental Work for a Sustainable World*. Book. **Price:** $18.95 ● Annual Report, annual. **Price:** free. **Circulation:** 7,500. **Conventions/Meetings:** annual Environmental Workforce Symposium - conference, comprehensive educational program detailing issues, trends and career options pertaining to environmental careers.

8389 ■ Institute for Earth Education (IEE)
Cedar Cove
PO Box 115
Greenville, WV 24945

Ph: (304)832-6404
Fax: (304)832-6077
E-mail: iee1@aol.com
URL: http://www.eartheducation.org
Contact: Jim Kilbane, Office Coor.
Founded: 1974. **Members:** 2,000. **Membership Dues:** individual, $25 (annual) ● professional, $35 (annual) ● affiliate, $50 (annual) ● sponsor, $100 (annual). **Staff:** 3. **Multinational. Description:** Represents individuals and member organizations committed to fostering earth education programs throughout societies; develops and disseminates educational programs to help people build understanding of, appreciation for, and harmony with the earth and its life. **Formerly:** (1984) Acclimatization Experiences Institute. **Publications:** *Conceptual Encounters I and II - Program Building Tools* (in English and German). Book. Features age-specific activities for use in ecological education programs. **Price:** $49.95 for volume 1; $34.95 for volume 2 ● *Earth Education: A New Beginning* (in English, Finnish, and German). Book. Describes earth education as an alternative educational answer to environmental problems. **Price:** $21.95 ● *Earth Education Sourcebook*, periodic. Catalog. Describes earth education programs and materials. **Price:** $21.95 ● *The Earth Speaks*. Book. Contains a collection of writings and images from people who had a good sense of relationship with the natural world. **Price:** $12.95/copy ● *Earthkeepers* (in English, French, German, and Italian). Book. Describes a complete learning adventure for young people aged 10 to 12. **Price:** $12.95/copy ● *Earthwalks: An Introduction to the Wonders of Nature* (in Dutch, English, French, German, and Italian). Book. Contains activities to develop an appreciation of the natural world. **Price:** $14.95/copy ● *Earthwalks: Snow Walks* (in English and French). Book. Contains activities for developing an appreciation of the natural world. **Price:** $9.95/copy ● *Rangers of the Earth: Young People Responding to the Planet's Cry for Help*. Book ● *Sunship III: Perception and Choice for the Journey Ahead*. Book. **Conventions/Meetings:** conference ● international conference.

8390 ■ Kids for Saving Earth (KSE)
PO Box 421118
Minneapolis, MN 55442
Ph: (763)559-1234
Fax: (651)674-5005
E-mail: kseww@aol.com
URL: http://www.kidsforsavingearth.org
Contact: Tessa Hill, Pres.
Founded: 1989. **Members:** 7,000. **Membership Dues:** kid, $7 (annual) ● family, $12 (annual) ● group, $15 (annual). **Staff:** 3. **Budget:** $150,000. **Description:** Works to educate and empower kids to unite and take positive and peaceful action to help protect the Earth's environment. Engages in recycling projects, adopting endangered animals, and creating letters, signs, plays, and petitions. Distributes educational programs and supports local community efforts; free membership is available to instructors and paid memberships provide more in depth materials; formed by individual members and other groups interested in environmental issues. Consists of school, church, scout and other groups. **Awards:** Defender of the Planet Award. **Type:** recognition. **Publications:** *KSE News*, 3/year. Newsletter. **Price:** included in membership dues. **Circulation:** 5,500. **Advertising:** accepted.

8391 ■ National Association of University Fisheries and Wildlife Programs (NAUFWP)
c/o Thomas Franklin, Liaison/Wildlife Policy Dir.
Wildlife Soc.
5410 Grosvenor Ln.
Bethesda, MD 20814
Ph: (301)897-9770
Fax: (301)530-2471
E-mail: tom@wildlife.org
URL: http://www.naufwp.iastate.edu
Contact: Thomas Franklin, Liaison/Wildlife Policy Dir.
Founded: 1991. **Members:** 55. **Membership Dues:** associate, $100 (annual) ● institution, $500 (annual). **Staff:** 4. **Budget:** $25,000. **Regional Groups:** 4. **Description:** Representatives of fishery and wildlife programs at U.S. universities. Promotes enhanced understanding of fisheries and wildlife resources throughout the world. Seeks to improve the quality of university research, teaching, and programs in the field. Communicates with the U.S. Congress, federal government agencies, and the public. Prepares reports. **Computer Services:** Mailing lists, list-serve for electronic document distribution to all members. **Committees:** Academic Programs; International; Research. **Formerly:** (1991) Association of University Fisheries and Wildlife Program Administrators. **Publications:** *Report and Directory*, annual. Lists programs and members. **Price:** free. **Circulation:** 200 ● *Research Report*. **Conventions/Meetings:** annual North American Wildlife and Natural Resources Conference, in conjunction with the annual meeting of the North American Wildlife and Natural Resources Conference (exhibits) - always March.

8392 ■ National Energy Foundation (NEF)
3676 California Ave., Ste.A117
Salt Lake City, UT 84104
Ph: (801)908-5800
Free: (800)616-8326
Fax: (801)908-5400
E-mail: info@nef1.org
URL: http://www.nef1.org
Contact: Ellen Toth, Admin. Asst.
Founded: 1976. **Staff:** 10. **Budget:** $1,700,000. **Description:** Works to stimulate interest and increase knowledge of the current energy situation through nationwide educational programs for teachers and students. Focuses on usage, conservation, economics, renewable energy resources, new sources of energy, projected changes in lifestyle (economic, scientific, social, and political), and creation of dialogue among corporate and educational communities. Creates and distributes economic instruction materials dealing with energy, water, mining, science, technology, conservation, the environment, and other natural resource topics. Sponsors teacher training programs. **Convention/Meeting:** none. **Telecommunication Services:** electronic mail, ellen@nef1.org. **Councils:** Sponsor. **Absorbed:** Energy in Man's Environment. **Publications:** *Internet*, semiannual. Newsletter. **Price:** free ● Also publishes catalog and curriculum materials for teachers and students.

8393 ■ North American Association for Environmental Education (NAAEE)
2000 P St. NW, Ste.540
Washington, DC 20036
Ph: (202)419-0412
Fax: (202)419-0415
E-mail: brian@naaee.org
URL: http://www.naaee.org
Contact: Brian A. Day, Exec. Dir.
Founded: 1971. **Members:** 2,500. **Membership Dues:** professional, $55 (annual) ● student, $35 (annual) ● retired, teacher, $35 (annual) ● institutional, non-profit, educational, government (standard), $150 (annual) ● institutional, non-profit, educational, government (plus), $450 (annual) ● corporate, $1,000-$10,000 (annual) ● commercial (standard), $250 (annual) ● commercial (plus), $550 (annual) ● life (individual), $500. **Staff:** 5. **Budget:** $3,000,000. **Regional Groups:** 3. **State Groups:** 55. **Description:** Represents individuals associated with colleges, schools, nature centers, government agencies, and environmental organizations; associates include students in environmental education and environmental studies. Promotes environmental education programs at all levels. Assists educational institutions in beginning or developing programs of this kind and to serve as a resource to them. Fosters sharing of information about environmental education programs among institutions and individual members. Promotes communication about environmental education and the pooling of information, resources, and activities in connection with such programs. Fosters research and evaluation in connection with environmental education and other study and investigation of such programs. **Libraries: Type:** reference; open to the public. **Holdings:** 500; audio recordings, books, monographs, video recordings. **Subjects:** domestic and international environmental education topics. **Awards:** Jeske Award. **Frequency:** annual. **Type:** recognition. **Recipient:** for leaders in the field of environmental education ● Outstanding Affiliate Award. **Frequency:** annual. **Type:** recognition. **Recipient:** peer review ● Outstanding Individual at the Local Level. **Frequency:** annual. **Type:** recognition. **Recipient:** peer review ● Outstanding Individual at the National/International Level. **Frequency:** annual. **Type:** recognition. **Recipient:** peer review ● Outstanding Organization at the Local Level. **Frequency:** annual. **Type:** recognition. **Recipient:** peer review ● Outstanding Organization at the National/International Level. **Type:** recognition ● President's Award. **Frequency:** annual. **Type:** recognition. **Recipient:** outstanding environmental educators and organizations. **Additional Websites:** http://www.eelink.net. **Programs:** National Project for Excellence in Environmental Education. **Publications:** *EE News Online*, biweekly. Newsletter. Alternate Formats: online ● *Environmental Communicator*, quarterly. **Price:** included in membership dues ● *Environmental Education in the Schools*. Book ● *Grant Funding for Your Environmental Education Program: Strategies and Options*. Book ● *Guidelines for Excellence*. Booklet ● *Partners in Action: Environmental Social Marketing and Environmental Education* ● *Volunteers Teaching Children: A Guide for Establishing Ecology Education Outreach Programs*. Brochure. **Conventions/Meetings:** annual conference (exhibits).

Environmental Education

8394 ■ Earth Share
7735 Old Georgetown Rd., Ste.900
Bethesda, MD 20814
Ph: (240)333-0300
Free: (800)875-3863
Fax: (240)333-0301
E-mail: info@earthshare.org
URL: http://www.earthshare.org
Contact: Kalman Stein, Pres./CEO
Founded: 1988. **Staff:** 11. **State Groups:** 4. **National Groups:** 44. **Description:** Works to promote environmental education and charitable giving through workplace giving campaigns. **Affiliated With:** Earth Share of Missouri; Earth Share of Washington. **Publications:** *Sharing News*, annual. Newsletter. Alternate Formats: online.

8395 ■ National Environmental Education Foundation (NEEF)
4301 Connecticut Ave. NW, Ste.160
Washington, DC 20008
Ph: (202)833-2933
Fax: (202)261-6464
E-mail: dianewood@neefusa.org
URL: http://www.neefusa.org
Contact: Diane W. Wood, Pres.
Founded: 1990. **Description:** Aims to advance environmental literacy in its many forms. Has taken a nontraditional approach to environmental education, moving beyond the K-12 classroom emphasis and targeting professionals who are trusted by and have daily contact with the general public. Provides environmental education and training to those leaders whose occupations give them opportunities to make meaningful, practical environmental connections that in turn can be translated into responsible actions. Seeks to generate more savings and curtail environmental destruction by building an environmentally literate citizenry capable and motivated to care for the environment at home, at work, and in its communities. **Programs:** Business and Environment; Classroom Earth; Earth Gauge; Environment Week; Health and Environment; National Public Lands Day. **Formerly:** (2007) National Environmental Education and Training Foundation.

8396 ■ Trips for Kids (TFK)
138 Sunnyside Ave.
Mill Valley, CA 94941
Ph: (415)458-2986

E-mail: tfkbike@pacbell.net
URL: http://www.tripsforkids.org
Contact: Marilyn Price, Founder/Dir.
Founded: 1988. **Multinational**. **Description:** Provides mountain biking outings and environmental education for children who would not otherwise have these opportunities. **Programs:** Earn-a-Bike/Job Training; Green Cyclers; Mobile; National; Re-Cyclery Bike Shop; Rides. **Publications:** *National News* ● Newsletter. Alternate Formats: online.

Episcopal

8397 ■ Association of Episcopal Colleges (AEC)
c/o Colleges and Universities of the Anglican Communion
815 2nd Ave.
New York, NY 10017-4594
Ph: (212)716-6148 (212)716-6149
Fax: (212)986-5039
E-mail: office@cuac.org
URL: http://www.cuac.org
Contact: Rev. Donald Thompson, Gen. Sec.
Founded: 1962. **Members:** 12. **Membership Dues:** institution (based on number of students), $125-$2,000 (annual) ● individual, $100 (annual). **Staff:** 2. **Budget:** $240,000. **Regional Groups:** 8. **National Groups:** 6. **Multinational. Description:** Accredited Episcopal Church-related colleges. Solicits and receives gifts and bequests for its member colleges, collectively or individually, to strengthen the member colleges and their educational programs. Sponsors the "Learning Through Service" program, which places students from all colleges and faiths as volunteers in service agencies, most church-related, in the U.S. and around the world. Some combine service with academic study for credit. Functions as a chapter of the worldwide association, colleges and universities of the Anglican Community. **Awards:** Charitable Service Scholarship. **Type:** scholarship. **Recipient:** for students at Episcopal colleges to gain experience in service occupations. **Formerly:** (1965) Foundation for Episcopal Colleges; (1966) Fund for Episcopal Colleges. **Publications:** *Compass Points*, semiannual. Newsletter. Includes education, service, and student activities on Episcopal college campuses and in service projects. Includes news about AEC board members. **Price:** free. Alternate Formats: online ● *Guide to the Episcopal Colleges*, periodic. Directory. **Price:** free. **Circulation:** 10,000 ● *Learning Through Service Catalog*, annual. Lists opportunities for college students and recent graduates to volunteer for service programs. Some opportunities include academic credit. **Price:** free ● *Prologue*. Journal. **Price:** $10.00/copy. Alternate Formats: online ● Newsletter, monthly. Alternate Formats: online. **Conventions/Meetings:** triennial conference.

8398 ■ National Association of Episcopal Schools (NAES)
815 2nd Ave., Ste.819
New York, NY 10017-4594
Ph: (212)716-6134
Free: (800)334-7626
Fax: (212)286-9366
E-mail: info@episcopalschools.org
URL: http://www.episcopalschools.org
Contact: Rev. Daniel R. Heischman, Exec. Dir.
Founded: 1964. **Members:** 509. **Membership Dues:** school (based on the total tuition monies received in 2005-2006), $122-$4,260 (annual) ● school exploration committee, $185 (annual). **Staff:** 6. **Budget:** $986,000. **Description:** Represents episcopal day and boarding schools and preschools. Promotes the educational ministry of the Episcopal Church. Provides publications, consultation services and conference focusing on Episcopal identity of schools, worship, religious education, spirituality, leadership development and governance for heads/directors, administrators, chaplains and teachers of religion, trustees, rectors and other church and school leaders. **Libraries: Type:** open to the public. **Holdings:** archival material. **Committees:** Episcopal Identity; Leadership and Governance. **Programs:** Episcopal School Celebration. **Formerly:** (1965) Episcopal School Association. **Publications:** *NAES Directory*, annual, every January. **Advertising:** accepted ● *Network*, 11/year. Newsletter ● Booklets ● Pamphlets. **Conventions/Meetings:** periodic regional meeting ● biennial conference - always fall of even-numbered years. 2008 Nov. 6-8, Tampa, FL; 2010 Nov. 18-20, San Antonio, TX; 2012 Nov. 15-17, Washington, DC.

Equal Education

8399 ■ Association for Gender Equity Leadership in Education (AGELE)
317 S Div.
PMB 54
Ann Arbor, MI 48104
Ph: (734)769-2456
Fax: (734)769-2456
E-mail: agelebusiness@yahoo.com
URL: http://www.agele.org
Contact: Marta Larson, Business Mgr.
Founded: 1979. **Members:** 500. **Membership Dues:** individual, $75 (annual) ● organization, $375 (annual) ● retired (62 and over), student, $25 (annual) ● supporting, $125 (annual). **Description:** Educators, administrators, consultants, authors, and filmmakers, and any individuals working for the advancement of equity in education. Provides leadership and advocacy to restructure education; conducts research and development activities; encourages professional development of members; collaborates with and seeks to influence other organizations. Maintains archives. Awards annual grants from the Barb Landers Fund to members pursuing special gender equity projects. **Computer Services:** Mailing lists. **Telecommunication Services:** electronic mail, businessmgr@agele.org. **Committees:** Communications; Legislative; Planning and Development. **Task Forces:** Computer/Technology; Curriculum Content; Early Childhood; Male Issues; Multicultural; P.E. and Athletics; Sexual Harassment; Sexual Orientation; Teacher/Preparation/Staff Development; Vocational Issues. **Formerly:** (2002) National Coalition for Sex Equity in Education. **Publications:** *AGELE News*, quarterly. Newsletter. Highlights the current news and trends in sex equity in education and its related issues. **Price:** included in membership dues. **Advertising:** accepted ● Directory, annual. **Price:** included in membership dues ● Also publishes article reprints from NCSEE News. **Conventions/Meetings:** annual Training Conference (exhibits).

8400 ■ Educational Equity Center (EEC)
100 5th Ave., 8th Fl.
New York, NY 10011
Ph: (212)243-1110
Fax: (212)627-0407
E-mail: information@edequity.org
URL: http://www.edequity.org
Contact: Merle Froschl, Co-Dir.
Founded: 1982. **Staff:** 6. **Languages:** English, Hebrew, Spanish. **Description:** Promotes equality of opportunity by eliminating bias due to gender, race/ethnicity, disability, and poverty through the development of educational programs and materials, training programs for teachers, and parents, and consultations on promoting bias-free learning. Current programs include "Playtime is Science" an equity-based parent/child science program with modifications for students with disabilities; "After-School Science PLUS" and "After School Math PLUS" inquiry-based curriculums that expand students' views about who does science and math; "Quit It!", a school-wide intervention model to address teasing and bullying; and "Raising and Educating Healthy Boys," an initiative to address the growing crisis in boy's education. **Telecommunication Services:** electronic mail, merle@edequity.org. **Publications:** *After-School Science PLUS Planning and Activity Guide*. Video ● *Breaking Stereotypes: Teens Talk About Raising Children*. Video ● *Bridging the Gap: A National Directory of Services for Women and Girls with Disabilities*, periodic. **Price:** $15.00 for individuals; $25.00 for institutions ● *Building Community: A Manual Exploring Issues of Women and Disability* ● *Including All of Us: An Early Childhood Curriculum About Disability* ● *Playtime Is Science: An Equity-based Parent/child Science Program Chew* ● *Quit It! A Teacher's Guide on Teasing and Bullying for Use with Students in Grades K-3*. **Price:** $20.00 ● *What Will Happen If: Young Children and the Scientific Method* ● Reprints.

8401 ■ Minority Student Achievement Network (MSAN)
1600 Dodge Ave.
Evanston, IL 60204
Ph: (847)424-7185
Fax: (847)424-7192
E-mail: info@msanetwork.org
URL: http://www.msanetwork.org
Contact: Rossi Ray-Taylor, Exec. Dir.
Founded: 1999. **Description:** Aims to discover, develop and implement the means to ensure high academic achievement of minority students. Works to increase knowledge of the processes that contribute to the achievement gap in order to inform policies and practices that will enhance the academic performance of African American and Latino students. Focuses on improving teaching and learning. Conducts collaborative research that informs school practices. Builds stronger relationships between teachers and students. **Telecommunication Services:** electronic mail, rraytaylor@msanetwork.org. **Publications:** *Network News*, 3/year. Newsletter. Alternate Formats: online. **Conventions/Meetings:** annual conference and meeting - every June.

8402 ■ Organization for Equal Education of the Sexes (OEES)
Address Unknown since 2007
Founded: 1978. **Staff:** 1. **Description:** Poster series on women's history, nontraditional careers, and dropout prevention. **Publications:** *Teaching About Women and Girls with Disabilities*. Manual ● *Teaching About Women in American History*. Manual.

Esperanto

8403 ■ American Association of Teachers of Esperanto (AATE)
c/o Sally Lawton
12 Stage Rd.
Westhampton, MA 01027-9603
Ph: (413)527-3579 (314)869-2303
E-mail: rglosso@siue.edu
URL: http://www.tejo.org/aaie
Contact: Mr. Ron Glossop, Pres.
Founded: 1961. **Members:** 80. **Membership Dues:** individual, $30 (annual) ● life, $375. **Languages:** English, Esperanto. **Description:** Individuals who teach or have taught Esperanto; educators interested in Esperanto. Promotes the introduction of Esperanto into American schools. Exchanges pedagogical information of every kind through Esperanto. Compiles statistics on Esperanto classes in the U.S. **Formerly:** (1967) U.S. Society of Esperanto Instructors. **Publications:** *American Association of Teachers of Esperanto—Bulletin* (in English and Esperanto), quarterly. Includes book reviews, calendar of events, listing of educational opportunities, statistics, teaching suggestions, and pen-pal addresses. **Price:** available to members only. ISSN: 0002-7499. **Circulation:** 100. **Conventions/Meetings:** annual meeting, held in conjunction with Esperanto League for North America - usually last week of July.

European

8404 ■ Council for European Studies (CES)
Columbia Univ.
420 W 118th St.
MC 3310
New York, NY 10027
Ph: (212)854-4172
Fax: (212)854-8808

E-mail: ces@columbia.edu
URL: http://www.councilforeuropeanstudies.org
Contact: Michele Lamont, Chm.
Founded: 1970. **Members:** 1,200. **Membership Dues:** institutional (college), $200 (annual) ● institutional (university), $400 (annual) ● individual, $75 (annual) ● student, $40 (annual). **Staff:** 2. **Budget:** $200,000. **Multinational. Description:** Institutional members are universities and colleges with study programs dealing with European society, culture, history, politics, and economy; also offers individual membership. Promotes European studies by encouraging scholarship and research in the social sciences. **Awards:** Fellowship Program. **Frequency:** annual. **Type:** fellowship. **Recipient:** for young scholars' first major research projects in Europe. **Publications:** *European Studies Newsletter*, 3/year. Provides announcements of council programs and activities as well as information on fellowships, grants, conferences, and research resources. **Price:** $40.00/year. ISSN: 0046-2802. **Circulation:** 1,500. **Advertising:** accepted ● *The Fellowship Guide to Western Europe* ● Also publishes guides to the libraries and archives of France, Germany, and Italy. **Conventions/Meetings:** biennial international conference, fosters the development and exchange of knowledge on European research; enables experts from around the world to meet (exhibits).

8405 ■ IES, Institute for the International Education of Students
33 N LaSalle St., 15th Fl.
Chicago, IL 60602-2602
Ph: (312)944-1750
Free: (800)995-2300
Fax: (312)944-1448
E-mail: info@iesabroad.org
URL: http://www.IESabroad.org
Contact: Mary M. Dwyer PhD, Pres.
Founded: 1950. **Members:** 135. **Membership Dues:** regular, $350 (annual). **Staff:** 300. **Budget:** $20,000,000. **Languages:** Chinese, English, French, German, Italian, Japanese, Spanish. **Multinational. Description:** Represents more than 130 highly selective U.S. colleges and universities that contributes to the development of quality study abroad programs for over 2,500 U.S. students each year. The study abroad programs are located in 22 cities across 4 continents and combine the best elements of foreign university offerings and U.S. higher education practices with a focus on learning foreign languages and gaining intercultural competence. In addition to outstanding courses, most programs include homestays, internship opportunities, field trips and field study, and extensive orientation and re-entry programs. **Awards:** Lifetime Achievement Award. **Frequency:** annual. **Type:** monetary ● Professional Development Award. **Frequency:** annual. **Type:** monetary. **Committees:** Curriculum; Institutional Membership; Nominations. **Councils:** Academic. **Formerly:** (1998) Institute for European Studies. **Publications:** *IES Exchange (IES Alumni Newsletter)*, 3/year. Contains alumni news. **Circulation:** 14,000. Alternate Formats: online ● *The IES Financial Aid Brochure*, annual ● *The IES Get Set!*, annual. Brochure ● *The Interculturalist*, semiannual. Newsletter ● *Study Abroad with IES*, annual. Catalog ● Also publishes brochures, orientation bulletins, seminar proceedings, and calendars of special events. **Conventions/Meetings:** annual conference and general assembly, general assembly of IES college consortium members.

Evaluation

8406 ■ Center for Lifelong Learning (CLLL)
c/o American Council on Education
One Dupont Cir. NW
Washington, DC 20036-1193
Ph: (202)939-9486 (202)939-9300
Fax: (202)785-8056
E-mail: susan_robinson@ace.nche.edu
URL: http://www.acenet.edu/AM/Template.cfm?Section=CLLL
Contact: Susan Porter Robinson, VP
Founded: 1942. **Staff:** 55. **Budget:** $15,000,000. **Description:** A division of the American Council on Education (see separate entry). Educators representing colleges and universities, postsecondary education associations, and secondary schools. Evaluates learning acquired in non-collegiate settings; monitors educational credit and credentialing policies and practices for postsecondary education; provides guidance to postsecondary education institutions for developing policies and procedures for evaluating extra institutional learning and awarding credit for it; operates the ACE Registries, which provide a record of an individual's educational accomplishments for which credit is recommended by ACE. Cooperates with postsecondary educational institutions, national and state educational organizations, the Armed Forces, business and industry, accrediting agencies, and the Veterans Administration. **Commissions:** Adult Learning and Educational Credentials. **Committees:** ACE/Army Registry Transcript Service Advisory; College Credit Recommendation Service Advisory. **Programs:** Military (courses and occupations). **Sections:** College Credit Recommendation Service; Military Evaluations (courses and occupations). **Affiliated With:** American Council on Education. **Formerly:** Office on Educational Credit; (1975) Commission on Accreditation of Service Experiences; (1987) Office on Educational Credit and Credentials; (2004) Center for Adult Learning and Educational Credentials. **Publications:** *Center Update*. Newsletter. **Price:** free. ISSN: 1089-4683. **Circulation:** 30,000 ● *CenterPoint*. Magazine. Alternate Formats: online ● *Guide to Educational Credit by Examination, 4th Edition*, annual. Book. Lists all ACE credit recommendations for tests and includes credit recommendations for certification examinations. **Price:** $40.50 for members; $45.00 for nonmembers ● *Guide to the Evaluation of Educational Experiences in the Armed Services*. Book. Contains more than 8,000 courses offered by the U.S. armed services and defense department between January 1990 and the present. **Price:** $99.00 for members; $110.00 for nonmembers ● *National Guide to Educational Credit for Training Programs*. Book. Provides information on thousands of educational courses offered by business, labor unions, schools, training suppliers etc. **Price:** $94.50 for members; $105.00 for nonmembers. **Conventions/Meetings:** annual meeting, for college presidents and other education officials (exhibits) - usually February.

8407 ■ Commission on Certification of Work Adjustment and Vocational Evaluation Specialists (CCWAVES)
300 N Martingale Rd., Ste.460
Schaumburg, IL 60173
Ph: (847)944-1340
Fax: (847)944-1346
E-mail: info@ccwaves.org
URL: http://www.ccwaves.org
Contact: Michelle Hamilton CVE, Chair
Founded: 1981. **Members:** 1,250. **Staff:** 9. **Description:** Certification program for vocational evaluation specialists. **Publications:** *CCWAVES Code of Ethics*. Manual. Alternate Formats: online ● *Wavelengths*. Newsletter.

8408 ■ Institute for Responsive Education (IRE)
Cambridge Colorado School of Educ.
80 Prospect St., 3rd Fl.
Cambridge, MA 02138
Ph: (617)873-0610
Fax: (617)873-0273
E-mail: jorge.cardoso@cambridgecollege.edu
Contact: Jorge Cardoso, Exec. Dir.
Founded: 1973. **Staff:** 10. **Budget:** $1,300,000. **Description:** Studies and assists the process of parent and citizen participation in education. Activities include research, evaluation, participation in national meetings, work with other national organizations, and writing about national issues. Provides technical assistance and training in parent and citizen involvement in education. **Programs:** Achievement Through Partnership; Parent Leadership; Partnering for Student Success; Principal Partnership Institute. **Projects:** Boston Parent Organizing Network; Family Participation in After-school Study; High School Family Center Research; Parent Leadership Exchange. **Absorbed:** (1983) National Commission on Resources for Youth. **Publications:** *New Schools, New Communities*, 3/year. Journal. Covers developments in desegregation, bilingual education, and choice in public schools. Includes book reviews, case studies, and resource summaries. **Price:** $24.00/year. ISSN: 0882-3863. **Circulation:** 1,000. **Advertising:** accepted ● Books ● Handbooks ● Reports. **Conventions/Meetings:** semiannual conference.

8409 ■ National Association of Credential Evaluation Services (NACES)
c/o IERF
PO Box 3665
Culver City, CA 90231-3665
Ph: (310)258-9451
Fax: (310)342-7086
E-mail: information@ierf.org
URL: http://www.naces.org
Contact: Elaine Wheeler, Chair
Founded: 1987. **Members:** 15. **Description:** Independent foreign academic credential evaluation agencies. Seeks to maintain quality in credential evaluation services; promotes cooperation among members involved in international education and exchange; functions as a forum for exchange of information concerning comparative education. **Publications:** *List of Members*, annual. Membership Directory. **Conventions/Meetings:** annual meeting.

8410 ■ National Study of School Evaluation (NSSE)
1699 E Woodfield Rd., Ste.406
Schaumburg, IL 60173-4958
Ph: (847)995-9080
Free: (800)843-6773
Fax: (847)995-9088
E-mail: schoolimprovement@nsse.org
URL: http://www.nsse.org
Contact: Lori Thompson, Dir. of Information Services
Founded: 1933. **Staff:** 16. **Budget:** $3,000,000. **State Groups:** 30. **National Groups:** 3. **Multinational. Description:** Acts as the research and development arm of the regional school accrediting commissions. Provides research-based resources to support the work of schools and school systems as they engage in a continuous process of improvement; development of a comprehensive framework for school and system-wide improvement and knowledge management that assists schools in developing initiatives grounded in the research on high-performing systems of teaching and learning. **Formerly:** (1959) Cooperative Study of Secondary School Standards; (1969) National Study of Secondary School Evaluation.

Experiential Education

8411 ■ Association for Experiential Education (AEE)
3775 Iris Ave., Ste.4
Boulder, CO 80301-2043
Ph: (303)440-8844
Free: (866)522-8337
Fax: (303)440-9581
E-mail: executive@aee.org
URL: http://www.aee.org
Contact: Ms. Patricia Hammond, CEO
Founded: 1972. **Members:** 1,400. **Membership Dues:** individual, $115 (annual) ● student, $55 (annual) ● institutional, $500 (annual) ● family, $145 (annual) ● organizational, $275 (annual). **Staff:** 8. **Budget:** $800,000. **Regional Groups:** 8. **National Groups:** 6. **Description:** Dedicated to experiential education and the students, educators and practitioners who utilize its philosophy. Strives to: connect educators in practical ways so that they have access to the growing body of knowledge that fuels their growth and development; publish and provide access to relevant research, publications and resources; raise the quality and performance of experiential programs through its accreditation program; and increase recognition of experiential education world-

wide. Contributes to making a more just and compassionate world by transforming education. Aims to develop and promote experiential education. Committed to supporting professional development, theoretical advancement and the evaluation of experiential education worldwide. **Libraries: Type:** reference. **Holdings:** 250; articles, audio recordings, books, periodicals. **Subjects:** experiential education, adventure programming, standards of practice, education philosophy, ethics, risk management, experiential activities. **Awards:** Kurt Hahn Award. **Frequency:** annual. **Type:** recognition. **Recipient:** to those who have contributed to the development and advancement of experiential education with the tenacity and conviction that was exemplified by Kurt Hahn. **Computer Services:** Bibliographic search, resources of articles and research for and about experiential education ● database, directory of organizations providing experiential programs and training. **Councils:** Accreditation. **Special Interest Groups:** Elders and Allies; Native, African American, Asian, Latino Americans; Women in Experiential Education. **Subgroups:** Experience Based Training and Development; Outdoor Adventure Programs; Schools and Colleges; Therapeutic Adventure Programs. **Publications:** *Journal of Experiential Education*, 3/year. **Price:** free for members; $50.00 for nonmembers. **Circulation:** 1,000. **Advertising:** accepted. **Conventions/Meetings:** annual international conference and regional meeting, gathering of educators, members, exhibitors, and workshop presenters (exhibits).

8412 ■ Council for Adult and Experiential Learning (CAEL)
55 E Monroe St., Ste.1930
Chicago, IL 60603-5720
Ph: (312)499-2600
Fax: (312)499-2601
E-mail: cael@cael.org
URL: http://www.cael.org
Contact: Pamela Tate, Pres./CEO
Founded: 1974. **Members:** 600. **Membership Dues:** individual, $100 (annual) ● retiree, $60 (annual) ● student, $40 (annual) ● institutional, $370-$670 (annual) ● organizational (for profit), $525 (annual) ● organizational (non-profit), $425 (annual) ● international, $320 (annual). **Staff:** 100. **Regional Groups:** 20. **Description:** Aims to create and manage effective learning strategies for working adults through partnerships with employers, higher education, government and labor. **Awards:** Institutional Service Award. **Frequency:** annual. **Type:** recognition. **Recipient:** to an institution that has shown an outstanding commitment to the expansion of lifelong learning opportunities and for innovative efforts to improve access to and quality in academic programs for adult learners ● Learner of the Year Award. **Frequency:** annual. **Type:** recognition. **Recipient:** to individuals who have overcome multiple barriers and successfully returned to a learning environment ● Morris T. Keeton Adult and Experiential Learning Award. **Frequency:** annual. **Type:** recognition. **Recipient:** for lifelong achievements and dedication to adult learning ● Workforce Chicago 2.0 Exemplary Practices Award. **Frequency:** annual. **Type:** recognition. **Recipient:** to companies in the region that have demonstrated exemplary employee learning and development practices. **Telecommunication Services:** electronic mail, ptate@cael.org. **Boards:** EPCE; NACTEL. **Departments:** Tuition Assistance Management Systems. **Programs:** Adult Learning Focused Institutions Initiative; Career Pathways; Coaching and Advising Services; Prior Learning Assessment; Transition Services. **Projects:** LiLAs; Workforce Innovation In Regional Economic Development Initiative. **Working Groups:** Workforce Chicago 2.0; Workforce Philadelphia 2.0; Workforce St. Louis 2.0. **Formerly:** (1985) Council for the Advancement of Experiential Learning. **Publications:** *CAEL Forum and News*, 3/year. Magazine. **Price:** $15.00 for nonmembers; included in membership dues. Alternate Formats: online ● *NACTEL - Telecom Careers Newsletter*, monthly. Newsletters. Alternate Formats: online ● *SmartWork*, quarterly. Newsletters. Alternate Formats: online ● Also publishes guidebooks and handbooks for faculty, administrators, and students in the field of experiential learning. **Conventions/Meetings:** annual convention (exhibits) ● Prior Learning Assessment - workshop ● seminar.

8413 ■ Earthwatch Institute
3 Clock Tower Pl., Ste.100
Box 75
Maynard, MA 01754-0075
Ph: (978)461-0081
Free: (800)776-0188
Fax: (978)461-2332
E-mail: info@earthwatch.org
URL: http://www.earthwatch.org
Contact: Edward Wilson, Pres./CEO
Founded: 1971. **Members:** 30,000. **Membership Dues:** individual, $35 (annual) ● dual, $60 (annual) ● sustaining, $250 (annual) ● life, $1,000 ● regular, outside North America, $50 (annual). **Staff:** 50. **Budget:** $9,500,000. **Multinational. Description:** Research and educational organization that allows individuals who have an avocational interest in science and the humanities to become working members of research teams led by highly qualified scientists. Maintains speakers' bureau of scientists and members. Provides career training scholarship program for high school students and a fellowship program for secondary school teachers. Provides internships for college students and volunteer opportunities within the U.S. Office. Engages people worldwide in scientific field research and education to promote the understanding and action necessary for a sustainable environment. **Libraries: Type:** open to the public. **Holdings:** 1,000; articles, books, periodicals. **Subjects:** all disciplines of field research. **Awards:** Educator and Student Awards and Fellowships. **Type:** scholarship ● **Frequency:** annual. **Type:** recognition. **Computer Services:** Online services, global classroom. **Telecommunication Services:** electronic mail, sfulmer@earthwatch.org. **Formerly:** (1975) Educational Expeditions International. **Publications:** *Earthwatch Expedition Guide*, annual. **Price:** free sample issue upon request. Alternate Formats: online ● *Member Journal*, 3/year. Magazine. Contains information on current issues and list of expeditions which members may join. **Price:** $35.00 for members. **Conventions/Meetings:** annual conference (exhibits).

8414 ■ National Society for Experiential Education (NSEE)
c/o Talley Management Group, Inc.
19 Mantua Rd.
Mount Royal, NJ 08061
Ph: (856)423-3427
Fax: (856)423-3420
E-mail: nsee@talley.com
URL: http://www.nsee.org
Contact: Dr. Karen Roloff, Pres.
Founded: 1971. **Members:** 1,500. **Membership Dues:** individual, $135 (annual) ● institutional, $450 (annual) ● sustaining, $900 (annual) ● student, $40 (annual) ● retired faculty/staff, $90 (annual). **Staff:** 4. **Budget:** $500,000. **Description:** Represents academic departments and administrators; individuals representing cooperative education, field experience education, internship programs, community service-learning, intercultural experiences, and continuing education departments; career planning personnel; students and interested individuals. Promotes quality programs in experiential and service-learning education and encourages its acceptance as an integral part of education. Acts as a forum for sharing information and ideas on the design and development related to all forms of experiential education. Activities include: offering technical assistance in the establishment and operation of internship programs; conducting research and identifying and disseminating results of innovative projects. Provides consulting services. **Libraries: Type:** reference. **Subjects:** experiential education, community service, program design and administration, research. **Awards:** Experiential Education Community-Based Organizational Leader of the Year. **Frequency:** annual. **Type:** recognition. **Recipient:** for a community-based or non-profit organization ● Experiential Education Corporate/Foundation Leader of the Year. **Frequency:** annual. **Type:** recognition. **Recipient:** for business or corporation ● Experiential Education K-12 Leader of the Year. **Frequency:** annual. **Type:** recognition. **Recipient:** for an active member of NSEE ● Experiential Education Pioneer of the Year. **Frequency:** annual. **Type:** recognition. **Recipient:** for an individual or NSEE member ● Experiential Education Program of the Year. **Frequency:** annual. **Type:** recognition. **Recipient:** for an outstanding K-12 or higher education institution ● Experiential Higher Education Leader of the Year. **Frequency:** annual. **Type:** recognition. **Recipient:** for NSEE higher education member. **Committees:** Arts and Culture; Career Development; Community Colleges; Cooperative Education; Cross-Cultural Learning; Deliberative Public Policy; Ecology/Environmental Studies; Evaluation and Assessment; Faculty; Internship Coordinators; K-12; Learning in the Classroom; Research; Service-Learning; Social Justice. **Formed by Merger of:** (1978) National Center for Public Service Internship Programs; Society for Field Experience Education. **Formerly:** (1992) National Society for Internships and Experiential Education. **Publications:** *Combining Service and Learning: A Resource Book for Community and Public Service*. **Price:** $40.00 for volume 1; $14.00 for volume 3 (bibliography); $35.00 for volume 2 ● *The Internship as Partnership: A Handbook for Campus-Based Coordinators and Advisors*. Includes sample forms. **Price:** $22.00 ● Also publishes resource papers, student guides, and other papers on experiential education. **Conventions/Meetings:** annual conference, national (exhibits) ● periodic regional meeting.

8415 ■ NTL Institute for Applied Behavioral Sciences
300 N Lee St., Ste.300
Alexandria, VA 22314-2630
Ph: (703)548-8840 (703)548-1500
Free: (800)777-5227
Fax: (703)684-1256
E-mail: info@ntl.org
URL: http://www.ntl.org
Contact: Margaret Tyndall PhD, Pres./CEO
Founded: 1947. **Members:** 350. **Membership Dues:** consultant/trainer, $250 (annual). **Staff:** 12. **Budget:** $5,000,000. **Multinational. Description:** Offers training, consultation, research, and publication services. Conducts more than 150 programs annually at locations throughout the country. Participants are individuals and teams from occupational groups and corporations, as well as leaders in schools, colleges, communities, and government at all levels. **Libraries: Type:** not open to the public. **Holdings:** 500; books, periodicals. **Subjects:** training/consulting issues. **Also Known As:** NTL Institute. **Formerly:** National Institute for Applied Behavioral Science; (1954) National Training Laboratory in Group Development; (1959) National Training Laboratories. **Publications:** *Journal of Applied Behavioral Science*, quarterly. Provides research, theory and methodology while informing professionals and their clients of issues in group and organizational dynamics. **Price:** $603.00 /year for institutions (print and online); $591.00 /year for institutions (print); $115.00 /year for individuals (print); $37.00/single print issue for individual ● Books ● Monographs ● Also publishes training materials. **Conventions/Meetings:** annual meeting.

Families

8416 ■ Families for Natural Living (FNL)
PO Box 3653
Williamsburg, VA 23187-3653
Ph: (757)566-9630
Free: (888)365-4777
E-mail: fnlemail@aol.com
URL: http://www.familiesfornaturalliving.org
Contact: Lisa Reagan, Pres./Co-Founder
Founded: 1996. **Membership Dues:** family, $25 (annual) ● circle builder, $65 (annual) ● community builder, $150 (annual) ● dream builder, $500 (annual) ● world regeneration facilitator, $1,000 (an-

nual). **Description:** Empowers parents to make informed choices for their children by facilitating support groups and a clearing house of information. Provides education found by the collection of state, national, and international resources in the organization's archives. Serves as a forum for exchange of information among parents and natural living families. **Libraries: Type:** lending. **Holdings:** audio recordings, books. **Subjects:** health, midwifery, parenting, relationships, vaccines. **Affiliated With:** Alliance for Transforming the Lives of Children. **Publications:** Newsletter, annual. Alternate Formats: online.

8417 ■ Family, Career and Community Leaders of America (FCCLA)
281 Park Ave. S
New York, NY 10010-6102
Ph: (212)358-1250
Fax: (212)358-1256
E-mail: info@amshq.org
URL: http://www.fcclainc.org
Contact: Richard A. Ungerer, Exec. Dir.

Founded: 1945. **Members:** 220,000. **Membership Dues:** individual outside U.S., $25 (annual) ● individual in U.S., $55 (annual). **Staff:** 23. **Budget:** $3,000,000. **State Groups:** 53. **Local Groups:** 10,000. **Description:** Young men and women studying family and consumer sciences and related occupational courses in public and private schools through grade 12 in the U.S., Puerto Rico, and the Virgin Islands. Youth assume social roles in areas of personal growth, family life, vocational preparation, and community involvement. Sponsors STAR (Students Taking Action with Recognition) competitions. Cosponsors, with Youth for Understanding (see separate entry), 8-week summer scholarships to Japan for 10th and 11th graders. **Libraries: Type:** reference; not open to the public. **Awards: Type:** recognition. **Recipient:** for distinguished service ● STAR Events (Students Taking Action with Recognition). **Type:** recognition. **Recipient:** for winners of high challenge, low threat competitions. **Telecommunication Services:** electronic mail, richard@amshq.org. **Absorbed:** (1965) New Homemakers of America. **Formerly:** (2000) Future Homemakers of American. **Publications:** *The Adviser*, semiannual. Newsletter. **Price:** $2.00/issue; $7.00/year. **Circulation:** 10,200. **Advertising:** accepted ● *Co-Curricular Guide for FCCLA Chapters.* Handbook ● *FCCLA is..* Video ● *Guide for Middle Level FCCLA Chapters.* Handbook ● *Publications Catalog*, annual ● *State Advisers' Bulletin*, 11/year ● *Teacher Educator's Guide.* Handbook ● *Teen Times*, quarterly. Magazine. **Price:** $8.00 /year for nonmembers; included in membership dues. **Circulation:** 220,000. **Advertising:** accepted. **Conventions/Meetings:** annual National Leadership Meeting - conference (exhibits) - always July.

8418 ■ Family and Consumer Sciences Education Association (FCSEA)
Dept. of Family & Consumer Sci.
Central Washington Univ.
400 E 8th Univ. Way
Ellensburg, WA 98926-7565
Ph: (509)963-2766
Fax: (509)963-2787
E-mail: hubbards@cwu.edu
URL: http://www.cwu.edu/~fandcs/fcsea
Contact: Jan Bowers, Exec. Dir.

Founded: 1927. **Members:** 1,500. **Membership Dues:** student/retired, $15 (annual) ● active/associate, $25 (annual) ● foreign, $35 (annual). **Staff:** 1. **Budget:** $60,000. **State Groups:** 50. **Description:** Family and consumer sciences educators and interested persons. Dedicated to helping individuals to help themselves through understanding family and community life. Works with other organizations to develop public policy. Conducts educational programs. **Libraries: Type:** not open to the public. **Holdings:** monographs. **Awards:** The FCSEA Educator of the Year. **Frequency:** annual. **Type:** monetary. **Recipient:** for outstanding members with significant contribution in representing and promoting family and consumer sciences education. **Computer Services:** Mailing lists. **Formerly:** (1938) Department of Home Economics (of NEA); (1994) Home Economics Education Association. **Publications:** *Education Reform in Family and Consumer Sciences.* Monograph. **Price:** $10.00 plus shipping and handling ● *The Educator*, semiannual. Newsletter. **Price:** included in membership dues. **Circulation:** 1,200 ● *Implementing Family and Consumer Sciences Standards through Project-Based Learning.* Monograph. **Price:** $10.00 plus shipping and handling ● *The Importance of Reading in Family and Consumer Sciences*, annual. Monograph. **Price:** $10.00 plus shipping and handling ● *Importance of Reading in Family and Consumer Sciences.* Monograph. **Price:** $10.00 plus shipping and handling ● *Positioning Family and Consumer Sciences in the 21st Century.* Monograph. **Price:** $8.00 plus shipping and handling ● *Taking Action to Recruit Family and Consumer Sciences Teachers.* Monograph. **Price:** $8.00 plus shipping and handling. **Conventions/Meetings:** semiannual board meeting and conference, held in conjunction with the American Association of Family and Consumer Sciences in June and held in conjunction with Association for Career and Technical Education in December - always December and June.

8419 ■ Family Learning Association
3925 Hagan St., No. 101
Bloomington, IN 47401
Ph: (812)323-9862
Fax: (812)331-2776
E-mail: canlearn@bloomington.in.us
URL: http://www.kidscanlearn.com
Contact: Dr. Carl B. Smith, Dir.

Founded: 1990. **Members:** 890. **Membership Dues:** general, $18 (annual). **Staff:** 2. **Description:** Provides research, information, grandparent pen-pals and book service, answers and guidance for parents. **Computer Services:** database, Kids Can Learn. **Publications:** *Parent Talk* (in English and Spanish), monthly. Magazine. Contains informative articles for parents. **Price:** $18.00/year. **Circulation:** 3,000. Alternate Formats: online ● Books. Contains information about family, tutoring and reading. ● Videos. Contains information about family, tutoring and reading.

Film

8420 ■ University Film and Video Association (UFVA)
c/o Cheryl Jestis
Univ. of Illinois Press
1325 S Oak St.
Champaign, IL 61820-6903
Ph: (217)244-0626
Free: (866)244-0626
Fax: (217)244-9910
E-mail: journals@uiuc.edu
URL: http://www.ufva.org
Contact: Cheryl Jestis, Contact

Founded: 1947. **Members:** 800. **Membership Dues:** active, $75 (annual) ● student, $30 (annual) ● institutional, $125 (annual) ● sustaining, $275 (annual). **Description:** Professors and video/filmmakers concerned with the production and study of film and video in colleges and universities. Conducts research programs; operates placement service; presents annual grants; bestows scholarships and awards. **Awards:** Carole Fielding Student Grant. **Frequency:** annual. **Type:** grant. **Recipient:** to support research project of a student or faculty member. **Telecommunication Services:** electronic mail, berryks@gwm.sc.edu. **Affiliated With:** University Film and Video Foundation. **Formerly:** (1968) University Film Producers Association; (1982) University Film Association. **Publications:** *Journal of Film and Video*, quarterly. Includes book reviews and author index. **Price:** included in membership dues. Alternate Formats: microform ● *UFVA Digest*, periodic. Newsletter. Contains notices of jobs, festivals, grants, publishing opportunities, member news and upcoming conferences. **Price:** included in membership dues ● Membership Directory, annual. **Price:** included in membership dues ● Also publishes monographs. **Conventions/Meetings:** annual conference (exhibits).

8421 ■ University Film and Video Foundation (UFVF)
c/o William O. Huie, Jr., Pres.
Texas A&M Univ. - Corpus Christi
6300 Ocean Dr.
Unit 5722
Corpus Christi, TX 78412-5503
Ph: (361)825-5750
Fax: (361)825-2250
E-mail: bill.huie@tamucc.edu
Contact: William O. Huie Jr., Pres.

Founded: 1958. **Members:** 25. **Budget:** $6,000. **Description:** Supports the coordination and promotion of university film and video production, the improvement of education for filmmakers and video producers (including provisions for scholarships and fellowships), and the improvement of the motion picture and telecommunications as educational tools and creative arts. Coordinates national and international projects; supports research and educational programs. Refers audiences to appropriate university speakers. Has conducted national surveys of university film and video production facilities and international film and video education. **Awards:** Eastman Scholars Award. **Frequency:** annual. **Type:** grant. **Recipient:** to faculty, nomination by college/university ● Eastman Scholarship Award. **Frequency:** annual. **Type:** scholarship. **Recipient:** to students, nomination by school/university - BA, BFA, MA, MFA. **Committees:** Film/Video Distribution; Scholarships. **Affiliated With:** University Film and Video Association. **Formerly:** (1982) University Film Foundation. **Conventions/Meetings:** annual meeting, held in conjunction with the University Film and Video Association (exhibits) - usually August, often on a University campus.

Finance

8422 ■ American Association of Individual Investors (AAII)
625 N Michigan Ave.
Chicago, IL 60611
Ph: (312)280-0170
Free: (800)428-2244
Fax: (312)280-9883
E-mail: members@aaii.com
URL: http://www.aaii.com
Contact: James B. Cloonan PhD, Chm./Founder

Founded: 1978. **Members:** 180,000. **Membership Dues:** basic, $29 (annual) ● enhanced, $53 (annual) ● life, $290. **Staff:** 40. **Local Groups:** 60. **Description:** Individuals who make their own investment decisions. Assists individuals in becoming effective managers of their own assets through educational programs and research. Programs help individuals develop an investment philosophy and decision-making process based on their objectives, capabilities and attitudes. Offers home-study curriculum on investment topics and a videotape course on investing fundamentals and mutual funds. **Awards:** Best Paper in Investment. **Frequency:** annual. **Type:** grant. **Recipient:** through financial associations. **Publications:** *AAII Journal*, annual. Includes annual index. **Price:** included in membership dues. Alternate Formats: online ● *AAII Year End Tax Strategy Guide*, annual. **Price:** included in membership dues. Alternate Formats: online ● *Computerized Investing Newsletter*, bimonthly. Includes annual index. **Price:** $30.00 for members; $40.00 for nonmembers. Alternate Formats: online ● *Individual Investor's Guide to Computerized Investing*, annual. **Price:** included in subscription to newsletter ● *Individual Investor's Guide to Low-Load Mutual Funds*, annual. **Price:** included in membership dues ● *Stock Investor News*, quarterly. Newsletter. **Price:** $99.00 /year for members. **Conventions/Meetings:** annual conference.

8423 ■ Foundation for the Advancement of Monetary Education (FAME)
PO Box 625
FDR Sta.
New York, NY 10150-0625
Ph: (212)818-1206
Fax: (212)818-1197
E-mail: larryparks@fame.org
URL: http://www.fame.org
Contact: Dr. Lawrence M. Parks, Exec. Dir.
Founded: 1995. **Multinational. Description:** Educates people about the benefits of honest monetary weights and measures and "the harm caused by dishonest fiat money monetary system". **Publications:** *What Does Mr. Greenspan Really Think?*. Book. Alternate Formats: online.

8424 ■ Institute of Consumer Financial Education (ICFE)
PO Box 34070
San Diego, CA 92163-4070
Ph: (619)239-1401
Fax: (619)923-3284
E-mail: icfe@cox.net
URL: http://www.financial-education-icfe.org
Contact: Paul S. Richard RFC, Exec. Dir.
Founded: 2000. **Membership Dues:** sponsorship, $50 (annual). **Staff:** 2. **Budget:** $50,000. **State Groups:** 50. **Description:** Aims to encourage Americans to improve spending, saving, investing, insuring, and financial planning habits to lessen their dependence on Social Security, welfare, or other individuals. Provides financial education courses to junior high and high school. Maintains a resource section of videos, books and home study courses in personal finance. **Formerly:** (1991) National Center for Financial Education. **Publications:** *Do-It-Yourself Credit File Correction Guide* (in English and Spanish) ● *The Money Instruction Book: A Wealth-Building Course in Personal Finance, Revised 2002*.

8425 ■ Investment Education Institute (IEI)
PO Box 220
Royal Oak, MI 48068
Ph: (248)583-6242
Free: (877)275-6242
Fax: (248)583-4880
E-mail: peterb@betterinvesting.org
URL: http://www.better-investing.org
Contact: Bonnie Reyes, Pres./CEO
Founded: 1961. **Membership Dues:** individual (stock and mutual fund), $50-$80 (annual) ● club, $40 (annual) ● club member, $25 (annual) ● youth, $20 (annual) ● life, $875. **Budget:** $100,000. **Description:** Affiliated with the National Association of Investors Corporation (see separate entry) and conducted through various business schools. Seeks to enlarge the scope and quality of investment education, especially through investment clubs. Has held conferences for educators, financial institutions, financial writers, and corporate shareholder relations executives to gain information and to stimulate activity in these groups. Representatives from 50 investment club councils have taken a series of special courses to improve their teaching skills. Individuals and corporations have contributed funds to establish the program. **Awards:** Distinguished Science Award in Investment Education. **Frequency:** annual. **Type:** recognition. **Recipient:** for special or superior contribution to investment education. **Affiliated With:** National Association of Investors Corporation. **Publications:** *BetterInvesting*, monthly. Magazine. Contains investment education articles. **Advertising:** accepted. Alternate Formats: online. **Conventions/Meetings:** annual convention.

Financial Aid

8426 ■ American Indian Graduate Center (AIGC)
4520 Montgomery Blvd. NE, Ste.1B
Albuquerque, NM 87109
Ph: (505)881-4584
Free: (800)628-1920
Fax: (505)884-0427
E-mail: aigc@aigc.com
URL: http://www.aigc.com
Contact: Shenan R. Atcitty, Pres.
Founded: 1969. **Staff:** 10. **Description:** Provides scholarship and fellowship assistance for Native American or Alaska Native students from federally recognized tribes at the graduate and professional school levels. Encourages colleges and universities to cooperate with financial assistance for those Indian students receiving its grants. **Awards:** AIGC Fellowship. **Frequency:** annual. **Type:** fellowship. **Recipient:** for American Indian and Alaska natives. **Computer Services:** database, list of former and current recipients. **Committees:** Fellowship Advisory. **Formerly:** (1989) American Indian Scholarships. **Publications:** *American Indian Graduate*, semiannual. Magazine. Includes educational topics and information for graduate and undergraduate American Indian students. **Circulation:** 10,000. **Advertising:** accepted. Alternate Formats: CD-ROM; online. **Conventions/Meetings:** semiannual board meeting.

8427 ■ Catching the Dream (CTD)
8200 Mountain Rd. NE, Ste.203
Albuquerque, NM 87110
Ph: (505)262-2351
Fax: (505)262-0534
E-mail: nscholarsh@aol.com
URL: http://www.catchingthedream.org
Contact: James Lujan, Pres.
Founded: 1986. **Staff:** 4. **Budget:** $700,000. **Description:** Raises funds to provide Native American students with merit scholarships for university study, primarily in math, engineering, science, business, education, and computers, at undergraduate and graduate levels. Conducts research and educational programs. Maintains speakers' bureau and placement service. Compiles statistics. **Libraries: Type:** reference. **Holdings:** 1,000. **Subjects:** Native American education, college admission. **Awards:** EPIE. **Frequency:** annual. **Type:** monetary. **Recipient:** for best program in Native American education in the U.S. ● MESBEC. **Frequency:** periodic. **Type:** scholarship. **Recipient:** for outstanding students ● NES. **Frequency:** annual. **Type:** monetary. **Recipient:** for schools with increased improvements in education ● RAP. **Frequency:** annual. **Type:** monetary. **Recipient:** for best reading programs. **Computer Services:** Mailing lists, 75000 Native Americans nationwide. **Programs:** Grant; MESBEC Scholarships; Native American Leadership in Education Scholarships; Tribal Business Management Scholarships. **Formerly:** (2000) Native American Scholarship Fund. **Publications:** *Exemplary Institute Proceedings*, annual. **Price:** $69.95/volume; $447.68 for libraries (8 volumes) ● *Exemplary Programs in Indian Education*. Book. **Price:** $39.95 plus shipping and handling. **Circulation:** 500. **Conventions/Meetings:** annual Exemplary Institute - board meeting, teaching exemplary Indian school programs to other Indian schools.

8428 ■ Chinese-American Educational Foundation (CAEF)
Address Unknown since 2007
Founded: 1965. **Members:** 100. **Budget:** $15,000. **Description:** Supported by individuals, churches, and corporations interested in aiding Chinese youth in higher education. Sponsors competitions and educational programs. **Awards: Frequency:** annual. **Type:** scholarship. **Recipient:** for college students graduates ● Youth Award. **Frequency:** annual. **Type:** recognition. **Recipient:** to American high school graduates of Chinese descent. **Subgroups:** Scholarship; Youth Award. **Publications:** *A List of Doctoral Dissertations by Chinese Students in the U.S., 1961-64* (in Chinese and English). Contains information on Confucius' concept of one great harmonious world. **Price:** free. **Advertising:** accepted ● *Letter to Members*, periodic ● Brochure, annual. **Circulation:** 500. **Advertising:** accepted. **Conventions/Meetings:** annual board meeting (exhibits) - June. Chicago, IL - **Avg. Attendance:** 250.

8429 ■ College Savings Plans Network (CSPN)
PO Box 11910
Lexington, KY 40578-1910
Ph: (859)244-8175
Free: (877)277-6496
E-mail: cspn@csg.org
URL: http://www.collegesavings.org
Contact: Jacqueline Williams, Chair
Founded: 1991. **Members:** 125. **Description:** State sponsored savings plans allowing parents to set aside money for their children's postsecondary education. Promotes use of state savings plans to defray postsecondary educational costs. Serves as a clearinghouse on state educational savings plans. **Affiliated With:** National Association of State Treasurers. **Conventions/Meetings:** annual conference, meeting of policy makers, directors, and staff to discuss issues affecting state college savings plans ● annual Management Training Institute for College Savings Plans - conference.

8430 ■ Harry S. Truman Scholarship Foundation (HSTSF)
712 Jackson Pl. NW
Washington, DC 20006
Ph: (202)395-4831
Fax: (202)395-6995
E-mail: office@truman.gov
URL: http://www.truman.gov
Contact: Frederick G. Slabach, Exec. Sec.
Founded: 1975. **Staff:** 5. **Description:** Permanent educational scholarship program whose board selects up to 85 Truman Scholars annually. Honors the memory of the 33rd President by providing opportunities for outstanding students to prepare for careers in government service at the federal, state, and local levels. **Libraries: Type:** reference. **Holdings:** archival material. **Awards:** Harry S. Truman Scholarship. **Frequency:** annual. **Type:** scholarship. **Recipient:** to students pursuing graduate degrees in public service fields. **Publications:** *Bulletin of Information*. Alternate Formats: online ● Annual Report, annual. Alternate Formats: online.

8431 ■ Hispanic Scholarship Fund (HSF)
55 2nd St., Ste.1500
San Francisco, CA 94105
Free: (877)473-4636
Fax: (415)808-2302
E-mail: info@hsf.net
URL: http://www.hsf.net
Contact: Frank D. Alvarez, Pres./CEO
Founded: 1975. **Staff:** 29. **Budget:** $27,000,000. **Languages:** English, Spanish. **Description:** Raises funds; distributes scholarships to Hispanic-American undergraduate and graduate students. **Awards: Frequency:** annual. **Type:** scholarship. **Recipient:** for United States citizens, or permanent residents of Hispanic parentage, who have completed at least 15 units of college work. **Publications:** Annual Reports ● Brochures ● Newsletter, quarterly. **Conventions/Meetings:** annual board meeting, awards reception ● biennial meeting.

8432 ■ National Association of Student Loan Administrators
c/o Paul J. Thornburgh
2401 Intl. Ln.
Madison, WI 53704-3121
Ph: (608)246-1403
Fax: (608)246-1481
E-mail: pthornburgh@glhec.org
Contact: Paul Thornburgh, Contact
Founded: 1998. **Members:** 3. **Description:** Promotes the common business interests of organizations engaged in the administration of student loans.

8433 ■ National Pell Grant Coalition (NPGC)
Address Unknown since 2007
Founded: 1986. **Description:** Seeks to advance financial aid on a national level for Pell Grant recipients and influence funding for full and part-time students.

8434 ■ Sallie Mae Fund
12061 Bluemont Way
Reston, VA 20190
Free: (800)824-7044

Fax: (703)984-5042
URL: http://www.salliemaefund.org
Contact: Kathleen deLaski, Pres.
Founded: 1960. **Description:** Provides financial aid for college students and their parents by guaranteeing and administering low-cost loans. Operates in all 50 states, Puerto Rico, Pacific Trust Territories, and the Virgin Islands. **Libraries: Type:** reference. **Holdings:** reports. **Awards:** The Sallie Mae Fund American Dream. **Frequency:** annual. **Type:** scholarship. **Recipient:** for African-American students who have demonstrated financial need ● The Sallie Mae Fund First in My Family. **Frequency:** annual. **Type:** scholarship. **Recipient:** for Hispanic-American students who are first in their family to attend college ● The Sallie Mae Fund Unmet Need. **Frequency:** annual. **Type:** scholarship. **Recipient:** for an undergraduate whose financial aid packages fall short by 1,000 or more ● The Sallie Mae 911 Education Fund. **Frequency:** annual. **Type:** scholarship. **Recipient:** for children of those who were killed or permanently disabled in the attacks. **Formerly:** (1998) United Student Aid Funds; (2003) USA Group. **Publications:** Annual Report ● Newsletter, quarterly ● Also publishes student aid pamphlets. **Conventions/Meetings:** annual conference and workshop.

8435 ■ Southeastern Regional Office National Scholarship Service and Fund for Negro Students (SERO-NSSFNS)
230 Peachtree St., Ste.530
Atlanta, GA 30303
Ph: (404)522-7260
Fax: (404)525-6226
E-mail: nssfns@nssfns.com
URL: http://www.nssfns.com
Founded: 1969. **Staff:** 31. **Description:** Supported by foundation and corporate grants and individual contributions. Maintains a free college advisory and referral service for interested students and those enrolled in Talent Search and Upward Bound projects. Sponsors annual Student-College Interview Sessions. Participates in professional meetings. **Libraries: Type:** reference. **Holdings:** books, periodicals. **Subjects:** educational awards, college preparations. **Computer Services:** Mailing lists, student mailing lists for higher education institutions. **Departments:** School-College Relations; Special Programs. **Subgroups:** Educational Opportunity Center; Vet Re-Entry Project; Veterans Upward Bound. **Formerly:** (1987) National Scholarship Service and Fund for Negro Students. **Publications:** *EOC Newsletter*. **Price:** free for members ● Annual Report, annual ● Brochure. **Conventions/Meetings:** workshop, for guidance and admissions counselors.

8436 ■ Thanks to Scandinavia (TTS)
165 E 56th St.
New York, NY 10022
Ph: (212)891-1403
Fax: (212)891-1450
E-mail: tts@ajc.org
URL: http://www.thankstoscandinavia.org
Contact: Richard Netter, Pres.
Founded: 1963. **Staff:** 4. **Budget:** $300,000. **Multinational. Description:** Perpetuates recognition of singular acts of humanity and bravery of the Scandinavian people in rescuing Jews from the Holocaust of World War II. Sponsors information programs; provides scholarship in the U.S. and Israel for students from Denmark, Finland, Norway, and Sweden. Provides training opportunities to Scandinavian doctors, nurses, and others involved with health care at American medical institutions. Presents speakers for radio and television programs and before religious organizations to relate the story of the Scandinavian rescue. Conducts research to provide a fuller account of the rescue activities of the Scandinavian countries; has funded books on the Scandinavian rescue. **Libraries: Type:** reference. **Holdings:** archival material. **Awards: Frequency:** annual. **Type:** scholarship. **Recipient:** for Scandinavian students/doctors ● Spirit of Scandinavia Award. **Frequency:** annual. **Type:** recognition. **Recipient:** for ages 12 to 20. **Publications:** *Study Guide to the Legend, the Story of the Danish Rescue as Told by Victor Borge; histories of Jews in Scandinavia during World War II*. Brochure ● *Thanks To Scandinavia—Report*, periodic. Newsletter.

8437 ■ United Negro College Fund (UNCF)
8260 Willow Oaks Corporate Dr.
PO Box 10444
Fairfax, VA 22031-8044
Ph: (703)205-3404 (703)205-3594
Free: (800)331-2244
Fax: (703)205-3575
URL: http://www.uncf.org
Contact: Michael L. Lomax PhD, Pres./CEO
Founded: 1944. **Members:** 39. **Staff:** 249. **Regional Groups:** 26. **Description:** Comprehensive educational assistance organization providing fundraising, educational programs, and technical assistance primarily to its 39 historically black private colleges and universities and graduate and professional schools, all of which are private and fully accredited. The UNCF Department of Educational Services provides information on a broad range of educational and administrative programs to the member schools; conducts Premedical Summer Institute; sponsors college fairs for high school and community college students; administers major corporate and foundation programs. **Awards:** UNCF Scholarships. **Frequency:** annual. **Type:** scholarship. **Recipient:** to undergraduate and graduate students attending UNCF member schools and other schools across the country. **Publications:** *A Mind Is.*, semiannual. Magazine. Contains articles and announcements regarding issues of interest in African-American higher education. **Circulation:** 175,000. **Advertising:** accepted ● *Dare to Dream*, annual. Annual Report ● *Mining Great Minds*. Newsletter ● *Statistical Report*. Reports. Contains information on government affairs, research, and statistics.

8438 ■ Winston Churchill Foundation (WCF)
600 Madison Ave., 16th Fl.
New York, NY 10022-1615
Ph: (212)752-3200
Fax: (212)246-8330
E-mail: info@winstonchurchillfoundation.org
URL: http://www.winstonchurchillfoundation.org
Contact: Peter C. Patrikis, Exec. Dir.
Founded: 1959. **Staff:** 1. **Budget:** $500,000. **Description:** Aims to enhance the training of top-level American men and women, in science and engineering; encourages Anglo-American academic and scientific cooperation; and serves as a tribute to Sir Winston Churchill (1874-1965). Provides scholarships to American students at selected colleges and universities to attend Churchill College, Cambridge University. **Awards:** Churchill Scholarships. **Frequency:** annual. **Type:** scholarship. **Recipient:** to U.S. graduate students at selected institutions for advanced work in the sciences, engineering, and mathematics at Churchill College ● Winston Churchill Award. **Type:** recognition. **Recipient:** to men and women of exceptional achievement. **Formerly:** United States Churchill Foundation.

8439 ■ Woodrow Wilson National Fellowship Foundation (WWNFF)
PO Box 5281
Princeton, NJ 08543-5281
Ph: (609)452-7007
Fax: (609)452-0066
E-mail: communications@woodrow.org
URL: http://www.woodrow.org
Contact: Arthur E. Levine, Pres.
Founded: 1945. **Staff:** 50. **Budget:** $15,000,000. **Description:** Dedicated to excellence in education through the identification of critical needs and the development of effective national programs to address them. Programs include fellowships for graduate study, professional development for teachers, educational opportunities for women and minorities, creating collaborations across educational levels, and relating the academy to society. Areas of concern include A Renaissance for the Liberal Arts, Access and Opportunity, and Teachers as Intellectual Leaders. Program funds are granted by various foundations, agencies, corporations, and individuals. **Awards: Type:** grant ● **Type:** monetary ● **Type:** recognition ● **Type:** scholarship. **Telecommunication Services:** electronic mail, levine@woodrow.org. **Publications:** Newsletter, semiannual. **Circulation:** 18,000. Alternate Formats: online ● Annual Report, annual. Features recent developments from the foundation's programs. Alternate Formats: online ● Brochure. Contains an overview of the foundation's programs. Alternate Formats: online.

Financial Planning

8440 ■ American Savings Education Council (ASEC)
1100 13th St. NW, Ste.878
Washington, DC 20005-4204
Ph: (202)659-0670
Fax: (202)775-6312
E-mail: info@asec.org
URL: http://www.choosetosave.org/asec
Contact: Mr. Dallas Salisbury, Pres./CEO
Founded: 1995. **Members:** 87. **Membership Dues:** corporate, $1,000 (annual). **Description:** Serves as a coalition of public- and private-sector institutions committed to making saving and retirement planning a priority for all Americans. Is a program of the Employee Benefit Research Institute Education and Research Fund (EBRI-ERF). Has driven the financial security mission forward with the collective leadership and efforts of a coalition of major organizations. Brings together public- and private-sector partners to share information on best practices and to collaborate on financial security initiatives. **Programs:** Choose to Save Education. **Affiliated With:** Employee Benefit Research Institute. **Publications:** *ASEC Fact Sheet*.

8441 ■ Financial Management Association International (FMA)
Univ. of South Florida
Coll. of Bus. Admin.
4202 E Fowler Ave., BSN 3331
Tampa, FL 33620-5500
Ph: (813)974-2084
Fax: (813)974-3318
E-mail: fma@coba.usf.edu
URL: http://www.fma.org
Contact: Jonathan Karpoff, Pres.
Founded: 1970. **Members:** 12,600. **Membership Dues:** regular, $70 (annual). **Staff:** 9. **Budget:** $750,000. **Description:** Professors of financial management; corporate financial officers. Facilitates exchange of ideas among persons involved in financial management or the study thereof. Conducts workshops for comparison of current research projects and development of cooperative ventures in writing and research. Sponsors honorary society for superior students at 300 colleges and universities. Offers placement services. **Libraries: Type:** reference. **Holdings:** 26. **Awards: Type:** recognition. **Sections:** Student Chapters. **Publications:** *Careers in Finance*, periodic ● *Financial Management*, quarterly ● *Financial Management Collection*, triennial ● *Journal of Applied Finance*, semiannual. **Conventions/Meetings:** annual conference (exhibits) ● annual meeting (exhibits) - 2008 Oct. 8-11, Grapevine, TX; 2009 Oct. 21-24, Reno, NV.

8442 ■ Native Financial Education Coalition (NFEC)
c/o Joanna Donohoe, Coor.
PO Box 32188
Palm Beach Gardens, FL 33420
Ph: (561)626-9700
Fax: (561)626-4010
E-mail: joanna@donohoeconsulting.com
URL: http://www.nfec.info
Contact: Joanna Donohoe, Coor.
Founded: 2000. **Description:** Promotes financial education in native communities. Increases awareness of the need for adequate personal finance skills in native communities. Seeks to provide financial education curriculum helpful to those setting up financial education programs in native communities.

Promotes financial management skills through information sharing and collaboration.

Firearms

8443 ■ Common Sense about Kids and Guns
1225 I St. NW, Ste.1100
Washington, DC 20005-3914
Ph: (202)546-0200
Free: (877)955-KIDS
Fax: (202)546-6250
E-mail: info@kidsandguns.org
URL: http://www.kidsandguns.org
Contact: Victoria Reggie Kennedy, Pres.
Description: Works to reduce gun-related injuries and deaths to children and teens. **Computer Services:** database ● online services, bulletin board.

Foreign Students

8444 ■ AYUSA International
600 California St., 10th Fl.
San Francisco, CA 94108
Free: (800)727-4540
Fax: (415)674-5232
E-mail: info@ayusa.org
URL: http://www.ayusa.org
Contact: John F. Wilhelm, Pres.
Founded: 1980. **Description:** Fosters international peace and understanding through high school student exchange program. **Awards: Type:** scholarship. **Publications:** *AYUSA Star*, annual. Newsletter. Contains information about the organization.

8445 ■ NAFSA/Association of International Educators (NAFSA)
1307 New York Ave. NW, 8th Fl.
Washington, DC 20005-4701
Ph: (202)737-3699
Fax: (202)737-3657
E-mail: inbox@nafsa.org
URL: http://www.nafsa.org
Contact: Marlene M. Johnson, Exec. Dir./CEO
Founded: 1948. **Members:** 8,500. **Membership Dues:** individual, $275 (annual) ● regular, $315 (annual) ● associate, $105 (annual). **Staff:** 53. **Budget:** $6,000,000. **Regional Groups:** 11. **Description:** Individuals, organizations, and institutions dealing with international educational exchange, including foreign student advisers, overseas educational advisers, credentials and admissions officers, administrators and teachers of English as a second language, community support personnel, study-abroad administrators, and embassy cultural or educational personnel. Promotes self-regulation standards and responsibilities in international educational exchange; offers professional development opportunities primarily through publications, workshops, grants, and regional and national conferences. Advocates for increased awareness and support of international education and exchange on campuses, in government, and in communities. Offers services including: a job registry for employers and professionals involved with international education; a consultant referral service. Sponsors joint liaison activities with a variety of other educational and government organizations to conduct a census of foreign student enrollment in the U.S; conducts workshops about specific subjects and countries. **Libraries: Type:** reference. **Awards: Type:** grant. **Recipient:** for international student enrichment programs ● Life Membership. **Frequency:** annual. **Type:** recognition. **Recipient:** for senior members. **Computer Services:** Online services, NAFSA Gopher. **Sections:** U.S. Students Abroad Administrators and Advisers. **Formerly:** (1964) National Association of Foreign Student Advisors; (1990) National Association for Foreign Student Affairs. **Publications:** *International Educator*, bimonthly. Magazine. Includes articles, interviews, and updates on trends in international education. **Price:** free for members; $35.00 /year for nonmembers; $48.00 /year for nonmembers in Canada and Mexico; $63.00 /year for nonmembers, elsewhere. **Advertising:** accepted ● *NAFSA Newsletter*, bimonthly. Includes book reviews, professional information exchange, and statistics. **Price:** included in membership dues; for members only. ISSN: 0027-5824. **Advertising:** accepted. **Conventions/Meetings:** annual conference, brings together international educators (exhibits).

Forensics

8446 ■ National Organization of Forensic Social Work (NOFSW)
460 Smith St., Ste.K
Middletown, CT 06457
Ph: (860)613-0254
Fax: (860)668-9858
E-mail: pbrady@nofsw.org
Contact: Mr. Paul W. Brady, Exec. Dir.
Membership Dues: full, $75 (annual) ● associate/allied professional, $85 (annual) ● student, $45 (annual). **Description:** Works for the advancement of education in the field of forensic social work. Enhances the professional activities of forensic practitioners, administrators and policy makers. Organizes and implements courses of instruction in the area of social work and the law. Educates the public about the forensic social work field. Stimulates and encourages scientific research in the field. **Publications:** Newsletter, periodic. **Advertising:** accepted.

Free Methodist

8447 ■ Association of Free Methodist Educational Institutions (AFMEI)
PO Box 535002
Indianapolis, IN 46253-5002
Ph: (317)244-3660
Free: (800)342-5531
Fax: (317)241-8897
E-mail: info@freemethodistchurch.org
URL: http://www.freemethodistchurch.org
Contact: Dr. David W. Kendall, Bishop
Members: 19. **Membership Dues:** foundation, $1,000 (annual). **Budget:** $30,000. **Description:** Aims to define and maintain standards of scholarship and discipline in Free Methodist Christian educational institutions. Acts in a cooperative and advisory relationship of the Free Methodist Church of North America. Encourages a close relationship among members; compiles statistics. **Conventions/Meetings:** annual meeting.

French

8448 ■ American Association of Teachers of French (AATF)
Southern Illinois Univ.
Mail Code 4510
Carbondale, IL 62901
Ph: (618)453-5731
Fax: (618)453-5733
E-mail: abrate@siu.edu
URL: http://www.frenchteachers.org
Contact: Jayne Abrate, Exec. Dir.
Founded: 1927. **Members:** 9,500. **Membership Dues:** regular in U.S., $45 (annual) ● regular outside U.S., $55 (annual) ● family in U.S., $67 (annual) ● family outside U.S., $77 (annual) ● student, emeritus in U.S., $22 (annual) ● life, $9,000 ● student, emeritus outside U.S., $32 (annual). **Staff:** 4. **Budget:** $513,000. **Regional Groups:** 9. **Local Groups:** 74. **Languages:** English, French. **Description:** Teachers of French in public and private elementary and secondary schools, colleges and universities. Sponsors National French Week each November to take French out of the classroom and into the schools and community. Conducts National French Contest in elementary and secondary schools and awards prizes at all levels. Maintains Materials Center with promotional and pedagogical materials; National French Honor Society (high school), Placement Bureau, summer scholarships. **Awards:** Dorothy S. Ludwig Excellence in Teaching Awards. **Type:** recognition. **Recipient:** to outstanding teachers: one at each level for demonstrated excellence and commitment in the teaching of French language, culture, and literature ● **Frequency:** annual. **Type:** scholarship. **Recipient:** to teachers for summer study in France. **Computer Services:** Mailing lists. **Telecommunication Services:** electronic bulletin board, for sharing ideas, seeking help, and posting K-12 job openings. **Commissions:** Articulation; Community Colleges; Cultural Competence; FLES; French for Business and International Trade; High Schools; Middle Schools; Professional Teacher Standards; Promotion of French; Student Standards; Telematics and New Technologies; Universities. **Councils:** Executive. **Affiliated With:** International Federation of Teachers of French; Joint National Committee for Languages. **Publications:** *AATF Membership Directory*, annual. **Price:** available to members only ● *AATF National Bulletin* (in English and French), quarterly. Newsletter. Reports on the French language and culture and the problems of teaching French in the United States. **Price:** included in membership dues. **Circulation:** 9,500 ● *French Review*, bimonthly. Journal. **Price:** $38.00 in U.S.; $43.00 outside U.S. ISSN: 0016-111X. **Advertising:** accepted. **Conventions/Meetings:** annual convention, includes French civilization, literature sessions, workshops and post convention excursions (exhibits) - always July.

8449 ■ Club Francais d'Amerique (CFA)
944 Market St., Ste.210
San Francisco, CA 94102
Ph: (415)981-9088
Fax: (415)981-9177
E-mail: info@francetoday.com
Contact: Marie Galanti, Pres.
Founded: 1978. **Members:** 60,000. **Staff:** 10. **Languages:** English, French. **For-Profit. Description:** Subscribers and friends of Le *Journal Francais and France Today* (*The French Newspaper*); individuals interested in the French language and culture. Seeks to assist teachers and students of French in defining practical applications for foreign language ability. Offers nationwide workshops for teachers on the use of foreign language publications in the classroom; sponsors academic contests. **Also Known As:** French Club of America. **Publications:** *France Today*, 10/year. Journal. Contains articles on French travel and culture. **Price:** $39.00/year. ISSN: 0895-3651. **Circulation:** 15,000. **Advertising:** accepted. Alternate Formats: online ● *Le Journal Francais*, monthly. **Price:** $41.00/year. ISSN: 1089-1862. **Circulation:** 20,000. **Advertising:** accepted. Alternate Formats: online. Also Cited As: *Journal Francais d'Amerique*.

8450 ■ Societe des Professeurs Francais et Francophones d'Amerique (SPFFA)
PO Box 6026
FDR Sta.
New York, NY 10150-6026
Fax: (212)750-5644
E-mail: mbom@brooklyn.cuny.edu
URL: http://www.spffa.net
Contact: Gerard Roubichou, Pres.
Founded: 1904. **Members:** 400. **Membership Dues:** individual, $30 (annual) ● student, $20 (annual). **Languages:** English, French. **Description:** Represents French nationals, Americans and other individuals involved in the teaching of French or related subjects at any level. **Awards:** Bourses Etc. (Quebec). **Frequency:** annual. **Type:** scholarship. **Recipient:** for study in Montreal and Quebec, Canada ● Bourses Marandon, Bourse Dufrenoy. **Type:** scholarship. **Recipient:** for research in France/Quebec. **Formerly:** (1981) Societe des Professeurs Francais en Amerique. **Publications:** *Francographies - Bulletin de la Societe des Professeurs Francais, d'Amerique* (in English and French), annual. Journal. Includes directory. **Price:** $15.00 for nonmembers; free for members. **Circulation:** 400. **Conventions/Meetings:** biennial competition and symposium ● annual general assembly - always in New York City.

Friends

8451 ■ Friends Association for Higher Education (FAHE)
1501 Cherry St.
Philadelphia, PA 19102

Ph: (215)241-7116
Fax: (215)241-7278
E-mail: fahe@quaker.org
URL: http://www.earlham.edu/~fahe
Contact: Kori Heavner, Coor.
Founded: 1980. **Members:** 350. **Membership Dues:** student, $10 (annual) ● individual, $50 (annual) ● family, $60 (annual) ● sustainer, $75-$100 (annual). **Staff:** 1. **Budget:** $24,000. **Description:** Provides a supportive relationship and opportunities for fellowship among all who share Society of Friends (Quaker) ideals of higher education, whether on Quaker or non-Quaker campuses. Promotes strengthened Quaker values in higher education; assists Friends colleges in their efforts to deepen their Quaker character. Works to establish a supportive relationship among Friends engaged in higher education on both Quaker and non-Quaker campuses. Fosters a closer relationship among members and between other Friends organizations and the association. **Publications:** *FAHE Newsletter*, quarterly. **Price:** included in membership dues. ISSN: 0741-1545. **Circulation:** 500. Alternate Formats: online. **Conventions/Meetings:** annual Centering on the Edge: Intellect, Spirit & Action - conference, occasionally from Quaker college or related organization (exhibits) - late June.

8452 ■ Friends Council on Education (FCE)
1507 Cherry St.
Philadelphia, PA 19102
Ph: (215)241-7245 (215)241-7289
Fax: (215)241-7299
E-mail: info@friendscouncil.org
URL: http://www.friendscouncil.org
Contact: Irene McHenry, Exec. Dir.
Founded: 1931. **Members:** 82. **Staff:** 3. **Budget:** $310,000. **Description:** Representatives appointed by Friends Yearly Meetings; heads of Quaker secondary and elementary schools and colleges; members-at-large. Acts as a clearinghouse for information on Quaker schools and colleges. Holds meetings and conferences on education and provides in-service training for teachers, administrators and trustees in Friends schools. **Telecommunication Services:** electronic mail, irene@friendscouncil.org. **Committees:** Development; Grants; Nominating; Publications; Quaker Self-Study. **Publications:** *Chronicles of Quaker Education*, 3/year. Newsletter. **Price:** $10.00. **Circulation:** 6,000. Alternate Formats: online ● *Schools, Colleges and Study Centers Under the Care of Friends*, annual ● Pamphlets. **Conventions/Meetings:** annual meeting - October.

Future

8453 ■ Schiller Center
c/o Sherry L. Schiller, PhD, Pres.
801 Duke St.
Alexandria, VA 22314
Ph: (703)684-4735
Fax: (703)684-4738
E-mail: sherry@schillercenter.org
URL: http://www.constructivechange.org
Contact: Sherry L. Schiller PhD, Pres.
Founded: 1985. **Staff:** 3. **Description:** Provides organizational support including training seminars and workshops on topics such as strategic planning and visioning, creativity, decision making and education for the future. Offers information and consulting services on managing change. **Formerly:** The Schiller Center: Catalysts for Managing Change; Center for Constructive Change; (1993) Countdown 2001. **Publications:** *Dispelling the Megatrends Myth: A Leader's Guide to Managing Change.* Book. **Price:** $28.00 ● Newsletter, periodic.

Gaming

8454 ■ International Simulation and Gaming Association (ISAGA)
c/o John F. Lobuts
George Washington Univ.
School of Bus. and Public Mgt.
Monroe Hall
Washington, DC 20052
Ph: (202)994-6918 (202)994-4930
E-mail: lobuts@gwu.edu
URL: http://www.isaga.info
Contact: John F. Lobuts, Contact
Founded: 1968. **Members:** 240. **Regional Groups:** 5. **Multinational. Description:** Individuals interested in any facet of simulation and gaming. Maintains resource lists; conducts specialized education; sponsors workshops, symposia, and research activities. **Publications:** *Conference Proceedings*, annual ● *Simulation and Games: An International Journal of Theory, Design, and Research*, quarterly. Provides a forum for theoretical and empirical papers related to human, human-machine, and machine simulations of social processes. **Price:** $35.00 /year for nonmembers; $70.00 /year for institutions. ISSN: 0037-5500. **Advertising:** accepted. Alternate Formats: microform. **Conventions/Meetings:** annual conference (exhibits) - 2008 July 7-11, Kaunas, Lithuania.

8455 ■ North American Simulation and Gaming Association (NASAGA)
PO Box 78636
Indianapolis, IN 46278
Ph: (317)387-1424
Free: (888)432-GAME
Fax: (317)387-1921
E-mail: info@nasaga.org
URL: http://www.nasaga.org
Contact: Doug Nelson, Chm.
Founded: 1974. **Members:** 200. **Description:** Teachers, trainers, media specialists, faculty, and researchers in various disciplines. Seeks to promote training of specialists in the field of simulation and gaming; facilitate communication between these specialists, policymakers, students, and others; promote the development of better techniques in the field of simulation and gaming. Provides referrals to simulation-gaming consultants; maintains speakers' bureau and gaming archives. (Gaming is the application of experimental techniques to simulated conditions, especially for training or testing purposes.). **Computer Services:** Mailing lists, of members. **Formerly:** (1974) National Gaming Council. **Publications:** *Conference Program*, annual ● *Handbook of Simulation Gaming* ● *Textbook in Simulation Gaming* ● Newsletter, periodic. **Conventions/Meetings:** annual conference - always October or November ● periodic seminar.

Gay/Lesbian

8456 ■ Gay, Lesbian, and Straight Education Network (GLSEN)
90 Broad St., 2nd Fl.
New York, NY 10004
Ph: (212)727-0135
Fax: (212)727-0254
E-mail: glsen@glsen.org
URL: http://www.glsen.org
Contact: Kevin Jennings, Exec. Dir.
Founded: 1995. **Members:** 7,000. **Membership Dues:** ambassador donor, $35 (annual). **Staff:** 30. **Budget:** $5,900,000. **Local Groups:** 40. **Description:** Creates an environment at school in which every member of the school community is valued and respected, regardless of sexual orientation. Addresses homophobia and heterosexism in schools; promotes dialogue with and among schools; develops and distributes training, curricula and other material; helps schools understand how communities which value diversity are healthy ones; and educates the general public on the necessity for addressing gender identity/expression in the educational system. **Libraries: Type:** open to the public; reference. **Holdings:** 50. **Subjects:** education. **Telecommunication Services:** electronic mail, kjennings@glsen.org. **Divisions:** Chapters. **Formerly:** (1998) Gay/Lesbian Straight Teachers Network.

Geography

8457 ■ National Council for Geographic Education (NCGE)
206A Martin Hall
Jacksonville State Univ.
Jacksonville, AL 36265-1602
Ph: (256)782-5293
Fax: (256)782-5336
E-mail: ncge@ncge.org
URL: http://www.ncge.org
Contact: Dr. Michal L. LeVasseur, Exec. Dir.
Founded: 1915. **Members:** 3,900. **Membership Dues:** sustaining, $100 (annual) ● new teacher, student, retired, $30 (annual) ● spouse, $15 (annual) ● library, school, $90 (annual) ● corporate, $110 (annual) ● life, $1,000. **Staff:** 3. **Budget:** $250,000. **Description:** Teachers of geography and social studies in elementary and secondary schools, colleges and universities; geographers in governmental agencies and private businesses. Encourages the training of teachers in geographic concepts, practices, teaching methods and techniques; works to develop effective geographic educational programs in schools and colleges and with adult groups; stimulates the production and use of accurate and understandable geographic teaching aids and materials. **Awards:** Distinguished Service Award. **Frequency:** annual. **Type:** recognition. **Recipient:** for meritorious service to geographic education ● **Frequency:** annual. **Type:** recognition. **Recipient:** for exceptional geographical articles published each year. **Telecommunication Services:** electronic mail, levasseu@isu.edu. **Formerly:** (1955) National Council of Geography Teachers. **Publications:** *Journal of Geography*, bimonthly. **Price:** $65.00. **Circulation:** 4,100. **Advertising:** accepted ● *National Council for Geographic Education—Perspective*, bimonthly. Includes calendar of conventions and meetings. **Price:** $10.00/year. **Circulation:** 3,200 ● *Pathways Book Series.* Books ● Also publishes color slide sets. **Conventions/Meetings:** annual conference and meeting (exhibits).

8458 ■ National Geographic Society Education Foundation (NGSEF)
1145 17th St. NW
Washington, DC 20036-4688
Ph: (202)857-7310
Fax: (202)429-5701
E-mail: foundation@ngs.org
URL: http://www.nationalgeographic.com/foundation/grants_teacher.html
Contact: Barbara A. Chow, Exec. Dir.
Founded: 1988. **Staff:** 3. **Budget:** $3,500,000. **Description:** A foundation of the National Geographic Society. Funds and develops geography programs in U.S. school curricula. Believes that U.S. schools should promote geographic education to help students achieve educational parity with students from other regions in the world. Contends that if society becomes more geographically literate, it can improve public understanding of global issues. Offers teacher training programs and workshops.

Geology

8459 ■ National Association of Geoscience Teachers (NAGT)
31 Crestview Dr.
Napa, CA 94558
Ph: (707)427-8864
Fax: (707)427-8864
E-mail: nagt@gordonvalley.com
URL: http://www.nagt.org
Contact: Dr. Karen Havholm, Pres.
Founded: 1938. **Members:** 1,800. **Membership Dues:** regular, in U.S., $35 (annual) ● regular, outside U.S., $47 (annual) ● student in U.S., $20 (annual) ● student outside U.S., $32 (annual) ● retired, $30 (annual) ● library in U.S., $75 (annual) ● library outside U.S., $87 (annual). **Staff:** 1. **Budget:** $100,000. **Regional Groups:** 11. **Description:** Represents College and university professors, high school and other teachers of geology and the earth sciences. Sponsors summer field training program and distinguished speaker program. **Awards:** Dorothy LaLonde Stout NAGT Professional Development Grants. **Frequency:** annual. **Type:** monetary. **Recipient:** to community college faculty, community college student and K-12 educator ● Jim Shea Award. **Frequency:** annual. **Type:** recognition. **Recipient:** for

outstanding writing or editing in earth science ● Neil Miner Award. **Type:** recognition. **Recipient:** for outstanding college and university teaching ● Outstanding Earth Science Teacher Award. **Frequency:** annual. **Type:** recognition. **Recipient:** for outstanding pre-college teaching ● Summer Field Camp. **Frequency:** annual. **Type:** scholarship. **Committees:** Dorothy Stout; Jim Shea Award; Neil Miner Award; OEST Award; Summer Field Camp Scholarships. **Programs:** Distinguished Speakers. **Affiliated With:** American Association for the Advancement of Science; American Geological Institute; Geological Society of America; National Science Teachers Association. **Formerly:** (1951) Association of Geology Teachers; (1955) Association of College Geology Teachers. **Publications:** *Journal of Geoscience Education, NAGT*, 5/year. **Price:** included in membership dues; $55.00 /year for nonmembers in U.S.; $67.00 /year for nonmembers outside U.S. ISSN: 0022-1368. **Circulation:** 2,700. **Advertising:** accepted ● Membership Directory, periodic. **Conventions/Meetings:** annual meeting, held in conjunction with Geological Society of America (exhibits).

German

8460 ■ American Association of Teachers of German (AATG)

112 Haddontowne Ct., No. 104
Cherry Hill, NJ 08034-3668
Ph: (856)795-5553
Fax: (856)795-9398
E-mail: headquarters@aatg.org
URL: http://www.aatg.org
Contact: Helene Zimmer-Loew, Exec. Dir.

Founded: 1926. **Members:** 6,000. **Membership Dues:** full-time employment, $75 (annual) ● new teacher, full-time student, emeritus/retired, part-time teacher, temporarily unemployed teacher, $35 (annual) ● joint, $10 (annual) ● contributing, $150 (annual) ● sustaining, $200 (annual) ● patron, $250 (annual) ● life, $3,000. **Staff:** 8. **Budget:** $1,100,000. **Regional Groups:** 61. **Languages:** English, German. **Description:** Represents teachers of German at all levels; individuals interested in German language and culture. Offers in-service teacher-training workshops, materials, student honor society, national German examination and stipends/scholarships. **Awards:** National Testing and Awards Program for Secondary Students. **Frequency:** annual. **Type:** recognition. **Recipient:** to outstanding high school students ● Outstanding German Educator Award. **Frequency:** annual. **Type:** recognition. **Recipient:** to an outstanding teacher of German. **Telecommunication Services:** electronic mail, helene@aatg.org. **Programs:** Chapter Projects; Elementary School German Project; German for Business and Engineering; Honor Society for Secondary School Students; Job Information Service (listserver); Materials Center; Professional Development; Travel-Study for Secondary Students. **Publications:** *Die Unterrichtspraxis: For the Teaching of German*, semiannual. Journal. Includes pedagogical articles, reports and teaching tips. Contains some articles in German, book reviews, software reviews and index. **Price:** included in membership dues; $25.00/issue for nonmembers; $50.00 /year for nonmembers. ISSN: 0042-062X. **Advertising:** accepted ● *German Quarterly*. Journal. Covers German literature and language. Includes some articles in German, volume index, book reviews and review essays. **Price:** included in membership dues; $20.00/issue for nonmembers; $75.00 /year for nonmembers. ISSN: 0016-8831. **Advertising:** accepted ● Newsletter, quarterly. Contains news of grants, fellowships and internships. **Price:** included in membership dues; $10.00 /year for nonmembers. **Circulation:** 7,000. **Conventions/Meetings:** annual meeting (exhibits) - usually November.

Gerontology

8461 ■ Association for Gerontology Education in Social Work (AGESW)

c/o Maureen Corley
1416 Fama Dr. NE
Atlanta, GA 30329-3308
Ph: (615)256-1885
E-mail: agesocialwork@gmail.com
URL: http://www.agesocialwork.org
Contact: Sherry Cummings PhD, Pres.

Membership Dues: individual, $40 (annual) ● institutional, $120 (annual) ● student, $20 (annual). **Description:** Provides leadership and assistance to social work professionals. Advocates for the integration of gerontological content in undergraduate and graduate social work education. Promotes the teaching of gerontology to all social workers. **Awards:** Career Achievement Award. **Frequency:** annual. **Type:** recognition. **Recipient:** for significant contribution in gerontological social work education ● Faculty Achievement Award. **Frequency:** annual. **Type:** recognition. **Recipient:** for significant research contribution in gerontological and social work education. **Computer Services:** Mailing lists. **Publications:** *Social Work Agenda*, semiannual. Newsletter. Contains interviews with gerontology experts and information on research opportunities. Alternate Formats: online ● Membership Directory. Includes full listing of members with contact information and research interests.

8462 ■ Association for Gerontology in Higher Education (AGHE)

1220 L St. NW, Ste.901
Washington, DC 20005-4018
Ph: (202)289-9806
Fax: (202)289-9824
E-mail: mariebernard@ouhsc.edu
URL: http://www.aghe.org
Contact: Marie Bernard, Pres.

Founded: 1974. **Members:** 320. **Membership Dues:** university, $620 (annual) ● two-year college, $350 (annual) ● four-year college, organizational affiliate, $475 (annual). **Staff:** 3. **Description:** Represents predominantly Higher education institutions that offer, on a national level, gerontological education and research programs. Promotes and encourages education and training of persons preparing for research or careers in gerontology, and works to increase public awareness of the needs of such training. Provides base for continuing cooperation with public officials, voluntary organizations, national associations, and others interested in aging and education. **Awards:** Clark Tibbitts Award. **Frequency:** annual. **Type:** recognition. **Recipient:** for significant achievements in the advancement of gerontology. **Computer Services:** database, contains programs in gerontology and geriatrics (searchable by region, educational level, etc.). **Committees:** Faculty Development; Program Development; Public Policy. **Publications:** *AGHExchange*, quarterly. Newsletter. Includes program resources, public policy update, research reports, calendar of workshops and seminars, association news, and new member profiles. **Price:** included in membership dues; $25.00 /year for nonmembers; $12.00/year for students and retirees. ISSN: 0890-278X. **Circulation:** 3,500. **Advertising:** accepted ● *Brief Bibliographies*, periodic. Covers 29 different titles. **Price:** $10.00. ISSN: 1045-0157 ● *Determining the Impact of Gerontology Preparation on Personnel in the Aging Network* ● *Diversity and Change in Gerontology, Geriatrics, and Aging Studies Programs in Institutions of Higher Education* ● *Meeting Abstracts*, annual ● *National Directory of Educational Programs in Gerontology and Geriatrics*, biennial. **Price:** included in membership dues; $85.00 /year for nonmembers. ISSN: 0148-4508. **Circulation:** 1,000 ● *Standards and Guidelines for Gerontology Programs*. **Conventions/Meetings:** annual conference (exhibits).

Gifted

8463 ■ American Association for Gifted Children (AAGC)

c/o Duke University
PO Box 90270
Durham, NC 27708-0270
Ph: (919)783-6152
E-mail: megayle@aol.com
URL: http://www.aagc.org
Contact: Margaret Evans Gayle, Exec. Dir.

Founded: 1946. **Membership Dues:** general, $25 (annual). **Staff:** 1. **Description:** Works to help gifted children reach their potential and use their many talents to benefit others. Encourages understanding on the part of the public about the needs and problems of the gifted and talented through a program of cooperation with community and professional groups. **Convention/Meeting:** none. **Publications:** *American Association for Gifted Children Newsletter*, 3/year. **Price:** included in membership dues. **Advertising:** accepted ● Also issues guides for parents, grandparents, and others dealing with gifted children. Also publishes working papers.

8464 ■ American Indian Research and Development (AIRD)

Address Unknown since 2007

Founded: 1982. **Staff:** 19. **Description:** Educational service organization which seeks to improve the quality of education for gifted and talented Native American students. Provides training and technical assistance to local and state education agencies, tribes, and other Native American organizations. Conducts research; develops curriculum and teaching materials, teacher preparation, master degree level. Maintains speakers' bureau; compiles statistics. **Publications:** *American Indian Gifted and Talented Assessment Model* ● *Centering Optimem Youth Opportunities Toward Excellence Catalog* ● *Elementary American Indian Gifted and Talented Assessment Model* ● *Secondary Mentorship Model* ● *Weekend Program Model* ● Also publishes curriculum guides. **Conventions/Meetings:** competition.

8465 ■ The Association for the Gifted (TAG)

c/o Tom Southern, Pres.
Miami Univ.
McGuffey Hall, Rm. 156
Oxford, OH 45056
Ph: (513)529-6634
E-mail: southewt@muohio.edu
URL: http://www.cectag.org
Contact: Tom Southern, Pres.

Founded: 1958. **Members:** 700. **Membership Dues:** professional, $25 (annual) ● student, $10 (annual). **State Groups:** 4. **Multinational. Description:** A division of The Council for Exceptional Children. Focuses on the delivery of information to both professionals and parents about gifted and talented children and their needs. **Awards:** Certificate of Appreciation. **Frequency:** annual. **Type:** recognition ● Certificate of Merit. **Frequency:** annual. **Type:** recognition. **Telecommunication Services:** TDD, (703)620-3660. **Formerly:** Association of Educators of Gifted Children. **Publications:** *Journal for the Education of the Gifted*, quarterly. Contains current research, position papers, literature reviews, historical perspectives, book reviews, and information on classroom materials. **Price:** included in membership dues; $36.00 /year for nonmembers; $48.00 /year for institutions. ISSN: 0162-3532. **Circulation:** 1,800 ● *TAG Update*, quarterly. Newsletter. Features information on TAG activities, upcoming events, workshops and institutes, reports on legislation, and relevant news. **Price:** included in membership dues. **Circulation:** 1,800. **Conventions/Meetings:** annual conference, held in conjunction with CEC (exhibits).

8466 ■ National Association for Gifted Children (NAGC)

1707 L St. NW, Ste.550
Washington, DC 20036
Ph: (202)785-4268
Fax: (202)785-4248
E-mail: nagc@nagc.org
URL: http://www.nagc.org
Contact: Nancy Green CAE, Exec. Dir.

Founded: 1954. **Members:** 8,000. **Membership Dues:** individual/institution in U.S., $65 (annual) ● individual/institution outside U.S., $75 (annual) ● contributor, $100 (annual) ● life, $700 ● parent associate/graduate associate, $25 (annual). **Staff:** 12. **Budget:** $1,700,000. **State Groups:** 50. **Descrip-**

tion: Teachers, university personnel, administrators and parents. Advances interest in programs for the gifted. Seeks to further the education of the gifted and to enhance their potential creativity. Distributes information to teachers and parents on the development of the gifted child. Maintains Speaker's Bureau. **Awards:** A. Harry Passow Classroom Teacher Scholarship. **Frequency:** annual. **Type:** scholarship. **Recipient:** for teachers of grades K-12 who have shown excellence in teaching gifted students ● Administrator Award. **Frequency:** annual. **Type:** recognition. **Recipient:** for a principal or district superintendent who has made a significant contribution to gifted education in his/her school, district or across the nation ● Community Service Award. **Frequency:** annual. **Type:** recognition. **Recipient:** for an individual or group who has made a contribution that benefits the development of gifts and talents in young people ● David W. Belin Advocacy Award. **Frequency:** annual. **Type:** recognition. **Recipient:** for individuals or groups who successfully advocated at the state or federal level to incorporate gifted education into state or federal education policy ● Distinguished Scholar Award. **Frequency:** annual. **Type:** recognition. **Recipient:** for individuals who have made significant contributions to the field of knowledge regarding the education of gifted and talented individuals ● Distinguished Service Award. **Frequency:** annual. **Type:** recognition. **Recipient:** for individuals who have made significant contributions to the field of gifted education and to the development of the organization ● Early Leader Award. **Frequency:** annual. **Type:** recognition. **Recipient:** for individuals who have made significant contributions in leadership and service to the field of gifted education ● Early Scholar Award. **Frequency:** annual. **Type:** recognition. **Recipient:** for individuals who have made significant contributions in conducting and reporting research regarding the education of gifted and talented individuals. **Divisions:** Creativity; Curriculum; Early Childhood; Global Awareness; Guidance and Counseling; Middle Grades; Parent/Community; Professional Development; Research and Evaluation; Special Populations; Special Schools/Programs. **Publications:** *Gifted Child Quarterly*. Journal. **Price:** $50.00. **Circulation:** 7,000. **Advertising:** accepted ● *National Association for Gifted Children—Communique*, quarterly. Newsletter. Covers the educational and familial needs of gifted children. Reports on federal legislative actions that affect gifted children. **Price:** included in membership dues. **Circulation:** 7,000 ● *Parenting for High Potential*, quarterly. Magazine. Helps parents work to bring out their children's best at home, in school and tips on talking to teachers, best in books, software, etc. **Conventions/Meetings:** annual convention, provides training in curriculum planning, program evaluation, and parenting and guidance relevant to gifted children (exhibits) - usually October or November.

8467 ■ World Council for Gifted and Talented Children (WCGTC)
c/o Sandra Kaplan
Univ. of Southern California
School of Educ., Waite
Phillips Hall 1004
Los Angeles, CA 90089-0031
E-mail: worldgt@uwinnipeg.ca
URL: http://www.worldgifted.ca
Contact: Sandra Kaplan, Contact

Founded: 1975. **Members:** 700. **Membership Dues:** silver, $100 (annual) ● individual, $50 (annual) ● life, $1,250 ● graduate student, $40 (annual) ● gold, $250 (annual) ● platinum, $500 (annual). **Description:** Parents, educators, researchers and educational organizations. Aims to: foster international exchange of information on research and programs; promote educational programs for gifted and talented persons; create a climate of acceptance for gifted children. Organizes a consultant service that will assist countries with inadequate provisions for the gifted to develop appropriate programs. Reviews proposals for international comparative research. **Awards:** A. Harry Passow Leadership Award. **Type:** recognition. **Recipient:** for an individual whose life and work have significantly influenced policy and practices in gifted education ● World Council Distinguished Service Award. **Type:** recognition. **Recipient:** for outstanding contributions to gifted education ● World Council International Creativity Award. **Type:** recognition. **Recipient:** for significant contributions in promoting creativity in education. **Committees:** Advocacy; Curriculum; Gifted Child International Network; Global Awareness; Guidance and Counseling Research; Non School Setting; Parenting; Teacher Education. **Publications:** *Connecting the Gifted Community Worldwide*. Proceedings ● *Gifted and Talented: A Challenge for the Near Millennium*. Proceedings ● *Gifted & Talented International*, semiannual. Journal. A peer-reviewed journal. **Price:** $40.00/year; $20.00/copy. ISSN: 0738-7849. **Advertising:** accepted ● *World Gifted*, 3/year. Newsletter. Contains the latest news and information concerning the organization, its membership, and the international gifted education community. **Conventions/Meetings:** biennial World Conference - international conference, publishers and producers of materials appropriate for gifted and talented children, educators and parents (exhibits).

Girls

8468 ■ Girlstart
1400 W Anderson Ln.
Austin, TX 78757
Ph: (512)916-4775
Free: (877)768-4775
Fax: (512)916-4776
E-mail: info@girlstart.org
URL: http://www.girlstart.org
Contact: Rachel Muir, Founder/Exec. Dir.

Founded: 1997. **Description:** Seeks to empower girls in math, science, engineering and technology. Provides hands-on learning in math, science, technology and engineering concepts to a diverse group of girls and their parents. Holds after-school clubs, free Saturday camps, science nights, family math nights, summer camps, and other educational events. **Publications:** Newsletter, monthly. Contains updates on events and programs and other news. Alternate Formats: online.

Graphic Arts

8469 ■ Gravure Education Foundation (GEF)
1200-A Scottsville Rd.
Rochester, NY 14624
Ph: (585)436-2150
Fax: (585)436-7689
E-mail: rbsheridan@gaa.org
URL: http://www.gaa.org/gef/index.htm
Contact: Robert Sheridan, Dir. of Development

Founded: 1979. **Description:** Aims to establish gravure curricula with graphic arts educational facilities at all educational levels; provides financial assistance to students; develops new resources for conducting educational programs; encourages post-graduate projects and research within the graphic arts; provides career orientation at the high school level; provides for internships throughout the gravure industry. Seeks to serve as a catalyst within the framework of established institutions and to provide encouragement to enterprising individuals. **Libraries:** **Type:** reference. **Awards:** Corporate Endowed Scholarships. **Frequency:** annual. **Type:** scholarship. **Recipient:** for students ● GEF Resource Center Scholarships. **Frequency:** annual. **Type:** scholarship. **Recipient:** for fourteen individuals at seven universities designated as GEF Resource Centers ● Gravure Persons of the Year Awards. **Frequency:** annual. **Type:** scholarship. **Recipient:** for outstanding leaders in the gravure industry ● Werner B. Thiele Memorial Scholarship. **Frequency:** annual. **Type:** scholarship. **Recipient:** for undergraduate students. **Funds:** General GEF Scholarship; Memorial Scholarship. **Projects:** Gravure Press Simulators. **Affiliated With:** Gravure Association of America. **Publications:** *Visions*, quarterly. Newsletter. Contains news of interest to members of printing industry. **Circulation:** 2,400. **Conventions/Meetings:** annual meeting, in conjunction with GAA.

8470 ■ International Graphic Arts Education Association (IGAEA)
1899 Preston White Dr.
Reston, VA 20191-4367
Ph: (703)758-0595
E-mail: dw.dailey@eku.edu
URL: http://www.igaea.org
Contact: David W. Dailey, Pres.

Founded: 1923. **Members:** 841. **Membership Dues:** individual, $35 (annual) ● retiree, $12 (annual) ● student, $10 (annual) ● library, $20 (annual) ● sustaining (platinum), $500 (annual) ● sustaining (gold), $300 (annual) ● sustaining (silver), $200 (annual) ● sustaining (bronze), $100 (annual). **Staff:** 9. **Budget:** $40,000. **Regional Groups:** 8. **National Groups:** 2. **Multinational. Description:** Graphic arts and printing teachers. Develops an integrated and comprehensive system of graphic arts education in schools and colleges of the U.S. Assists organizations in arranging lectures or other programs relating to graphic arts. Sponsors annual Graphic Communications Week; Visual Communication Journal; conducts research programs. **Awards:** Earl I. Sundeen Award. **Frequency:** annual. **Type:** recognition. **Recipient:** for leadership in graphic arts education ● Education Council Award for Excellence. **Type:** recognition ● Fred J. Hartman Award. **Frequency:** annual. **Type:** recognition. **Recipient:** to a member who has devoted many years of service to the association ● Frederick D. Kagy Life Achievement Award. **Frequency:** annual. **Type:** recognition. **Recipient:** to individuals for significant contributions to graphic arts education and the graphic arts industry ● Gutenberg Award. **Frequency:** annual. **Type:** recognition. **Recipient:** for individuals with exceptional achievement in the field of graphic arts. **Computer Services:** database, membership and budget accounting. **Committees:** Auditing; Bylaws; Conference Planning; Conference Site; Election; Graphic Communications Week; Gutenberg Awards; History and Archives; Liaison; Planning; Project/Idea Exchange; Publications; Scout Merit Badge. **Formerly:** (1940) National Graphic Arts Guild; (1950) National Graphic Arts Education Association. **Publications:** *The Communicator*, quarterly. Newsletter. Alternate Formats: online ● *Visual Communications Journal*, annual. Provides professional communicative link for educators and industry personnel. Alternate Formats: online ● Membership Directory, annual. **Conventions/Meetings:** annual conference (exhibits) - always summer (July/August).

8471 ■ Tamarind Institute (TI)
108-110 Cornell Dr. SE
Albuquerque, NM 87106
Ph: (505)277-3901
Fax: (505)277-3920
E-mail: tamarind@unm.edu
URL: http://tamarind.unm.edu
Contact: Marjorie Devon, Dir.

Founded: 1960. **Staff:** 10. **Description:** Division of the College of Fine Arts of the University of New Mexico, established to print original lithographs, to train master printers in hand-printing of lithographs from drawings made on stones and metal plates, and to conduct research on all aspects of artists' lithography. Offers custom printing on a limited basis, invitations to selected artists for major projects, and advanced training for those who have the desire and ability to become master printers. **Convention/Meeting:** none. **Formerly:** Tamarind Lithography Workshop. **Publications:** Also publishes announcements of lithographs, pamphlets, catalogs, slides, films, and books.

8472 ■ Vesalius Trust (VT)
c/o Lisa Warren, Exec. Dir.
20751 W Chartwell Dr.
Kildeer, IL 60047
Ph: (847)540-8671
Fax: (847)540-8681

E-mail: vesaliustrust@aol.com
URL: http://www.vesaliustrust.org
Contact: Lisa Warren, Exec. Dir.
Founded: 1988. **Staff:** 1. **Budget:** $50,000. **Nonmembership. Description:** Provides leadership and funding for the advancement of education and research in visual communication for the health sciences. **Awards:** Charlotte S. Holt Fund. **Frequency:** annual. **Type:** scholarship. **Recipient:** for students enrolled in a medical illustration program ● Frank Netter Award. **Frequency:** annual. **Type:** recognition. **Recipient:** to the person or persons who have recently developed visually oriented educational materials with either proven or potential impact on the way health sciences are taught and/or practiced ● Inez Demonet Scholarship. **Frequency:** annual. **Type:** scholarship. **Recipient:** for a student in AMI accredited medical illustration program ● VT Student Research Scholarship. **Frequency:** annual. **Type:** scholarship. **Recipient:** for student in a biocommunications program. **Affiliated With:** Association of Medical Illustrators. **Conventions/Meetings:** annual board meeting - February.

Health

8473 ■ National Consortium on Health Science and Technology Education (NCHSTE)
c/o Michigan Health Council
2410 Woodlake Dr.
Okemos, MI 48864-3997
Ph: (517)347-3332
E-mail: cstacy@mhc.org
URL: http://www.nchste.org
Contact: Carole Stacy, Contact
Founded: 1991. **Membership Dues:** individual, $100 (annual) ● group, $2,500 (annual). **Description:** Ensures a well-prepared health care workforce through health science and technology education.

8474 ■ NEA Health Information Network (NEA HIN)
1201 16th St. NW, Ste.216
Washington, DC 20036
Ph: (202)822-7570
E-mail: info@neahin.org
URL: http://www.neahin.org
Contact: Jerald Newberry, Exec. Dir.
Founded: 1987. **Staff:** 11. **Budget:** $2,500,000. **Description:** Dedicated to improve health, safety, and student achievement by providing school employees with vital, effective and timely health information. **Computer Services:** Mailing lists. **Programs:** Cancer Information; Children's Health Insurance; Environmental Health; Mental Wellness; Parent-Child Communication; Physical Activity and Nutrition; School and Community Safety; Sexual and Reproductive Health. **Affiliated With:** National Education Association. **Formerly:** (2001) Health Information Network. **Publications:** *Exposure to Blood on the Job: What School Employees Need to Know* (in English and Spanish). Booklet. Alternate Formats: online ● *Pointer's Dish*, quarterly. Newsletter. Alternate Formats: online ● *Responding to HIV and AIDS*. Booklet. Alternate Formats: online.

Health Education

8475 ■ International Alliance of Healthcare Educators (IAHE)
11211 Prosperity Farms Rd., Ste.D-325
Palm Beach Gardens, FL 33410
Ph: (561)622-4334
Free: (800)311-9204
Fax: (561)622-4771
E-mail: iahe@iahe.com
URL: http://www.iahe.com
Contact: Kathy Wall, Dir.
Founded: 1996. **Membership Dues:** silver, $25 (annual) ● gold, $50 (annual) ● platinum, $125 (annual). **Description:** Represents health care instructors and curriculum developers; seeks to advance innovative therapies through continuing education. **Conventions/Meetings:** annual workshop, supporting the 20 modalities developed by practitioners.

8476 ■ International Center for the Health Sciences (ICHS)
Address Unknown since 2008
Founded: 1991. **Staff:** 5. **Description:** Works to improve the health of all people through creative health education programs designed to meet the unique needs and capabilities of communities around the world. Sponsors collaborative research; develops and strengthens current preventative and curative care; manages and implements health science education programs in cooperation with US institutions in Central America, Africa and the former Soviet Union; advocates for the health care needs of all people.

Higher Education

8477 ■ Alliance for Higher Education (AHE)
2602 Rutford Ave.
Richardson, TX 75080
Ph: (972)713-8170
Fax: (972)713-8209
E-mail: info@allianceedu.org
URL: http://www.allianceedu.org
Contact: Allan Watson PhD, Pres.
Founded: 1965. **Description:** Comprised of businesses, non-profit organizations, and institutions of higher education. Seeks to "forge a critical link between and among the academic, healthcare, and community service sectors". Facilitates linkage between business and higher education; provides community services; promotes achievement of common goals shared by businesses and community service organizations in areas including education, training, electronic networking, and information management. Maintains Green Education and Information Network. **Councils:** Articulation. **Programs:** Alliance Education and Consulting Institute; Electronic Telecommunications Network; Information Resource Sharing; Joint Purchasing; Off-Campus Study Opportunities; Virtual Classroom. **Formerly:** (1982) Association for Graduate Education and Research; (1992) Association for Higher Education of North Texas. **Publications:** *Advocacy and Media Guide*. Book.

8478 ■ American Association for Higher Education (AAHE)
Address Unknown since 2007
Founded: 1870. **Members:** 7,000. **Membership Dues:** regular, $125 (annual) ● student, $55 (annual) ● retired, $70 (annual). **Staff:** 18. **Description:** Administrators, students, trustees, faculty, public officials, and interested individuals from all segments of postsecondary education. Seeks to clarify and help resolve critical issues in postsecondary education through conferences, publications, and special projects. Conducts Assessment and Faculty Roles and Rewards Forums; maintains Office on School/College Collaboration, and Community Compacts for Student Success. **Formerly:** Association for Higher Education. **Publications:** *AAHE Bulletin*, 10/year. Newsletter. Covers academic affairs, employment, public policy, teaching methods, technology, and testing. Includes book reviews and research updates. **Price:** included in membership dues; $35.00 /year for nonmembers. ISSN: 0162-7910. **Circulation:** 9,000 ● *Change Magazine*, bimonthly ● Also publishes books and reports developed from special projects. **Conventions/Meetings:** Assessment Conference ● annual conference (exhibits) - always March or April ● Conference on Faculty Roles and Rewards ● annual National Conference on Higher Education.

8479 ■ Association for the Advancement of Sustainability in Higher Education (AASHE)
1935 SE 24th Ave.
Portland, OR 97214
Ph: (503)222-7041
Fax: (503)236-3220
E-mail: info@aashe.org
URL: http://www.aashe.org
Contact: Julian Dautremont-Smith, Assoc. Dir.
Membership Dues: 4-year institution (based on FTE student enrollment), $500-$1,500 (annual) ● 2-year institution (based on FTE student enrollment), $250-$500 (annual) ● business partner (based on annual sales), $250-$3,000 (annual) ● NGO/government partner (based on budget), $250-$750 (annual). **Multinational. Description:** Aims to advance sustainability in higher education in the U.S. and Canada. Promotes sustainability in all sectors of higher education through education, communication, research and professional development. Increases collaboration among individuals, institutions and external partners to speed the adoption of sustainability practices. Facilitates member efforts to integrate sustainability into teaching, research and operations. **Awards:** Campus Achievement Award. **Frequency:** annual. **Type:** recognition. **Recipient:** to a member institution that has made a significant progress in implementing sustainable practices on campus ● Student Achievement Award. **Frequency:** annual. **Type:** recognition. **Recipient:** to an undergraduate student from a member institution who has made an outstanding contribution in advancing campus sustainability. **Publications:** *AASHE Bulletin*, weekly. Newsletter. Features campus sustainability news, announcements, resources and opportunities. **Price:** free. Alternate Formats: online ● *AASHE Digest*, annual. Report. Contains a compilation of categorized campus sustainability stories which previously appeared in the AASHE Bulletin of that year. Alternate Formats: online ● *AASHE Update*, bimonthly. Newsletter. Keeps members informed about AASHE activities, programs, new resources and special announcements. ● Annual Report, annual.

8480 ■ Association for Consortium Leadership (ACL)
c/o Virginia Tidewater Consortium for Higher Education
4900 Powhatan Ave.
Norfolk, VA 23508-1836
Ph: (757)683-3183
Fax: (757)683-4515
E-mail: nicolabelt@aol.com
URL: http://www.acl.odu.edu
Contact: Ms. Nicola V. Beltz, Program Mgr.
Members: 65. **Membership Dues:** small consortium, $250 (annual) ● regular consortium, $500 (annual) ● sustaining, $1,000 (annual) ● corporate, $5,000 (annual). **Staff:** 3. **Budget:** $30,000. **National Groups:** 65. **Description:** Higher education professionals involved in cooperative programs. Provides guidance in creating and strengthening partnerships in higher education institutions. Provides in-service opportunities to members.

8481 ■ Association for the Study of Free Institutions (ASFI)
c/o Carson Holloway, Exec. Dir.
Univ. of Nebraska at Omaha
Dept. of Political Sci.
275 Arts and Sciences Hall
Omaha, NE 68182
Ph: (402)554-4862
E-mail: cholloway@mail.unomaha.edu
URL: http://www.freestudies.org
Contact: Carson Holloway, Exec. Dir.
Description: Seeks to revive the study of free institutions and free societies as a major concern of American higher education. Encourages research and discussion on an inter-disciplinary basis. Gathers scholars and programs sharing interest in and appreciation of free institutions.

8482 ■ Association for the Study of Higher Education (ASHE)
Michigan State Univ.
424 Erickson Hall
East Lansing, MI 48824
Ph: (517)432-8805
Fax: (517)432-8806

E-mail: ashemsu@msu.edu
URL: http://www.ashe.ws
Contact: Linda K. Johnsrud, Pres.
Founded: 1972. **Members:** 1,370. **Membership Dues:** regular, $82 (annual) ● student, $52 (annual) ● emeritus, $52 (annual). **Staff:** 5. **Budget:** $100,000. **Description:** Professors, researchers, administrators, policy analysts, graduate students, and others concerned with the study of higher education. Aims to advance the study of higher education and facilitate and encourage discussion of priority issues for research in the study of higher education. **Awards:** ASHE/Lumina Dissertation Fellowship. **Frequency:** 10/year. **Type:** grant. **Recipient:** for dissertations in the areas of student access, success, financial and adult education ● Distinguished Dissertation Award. **Frequency:** annual. **Type:** recognition ● Research Achievement Award. **Frequency:** annual. **Type:** recognition. **Telecommunication Services:** electronic mail, johnsrud@hawaii.edu. **Committees:** Public Policy; Publications. **Councils:** Ethnic Participation. **Formerly:** Association of Professors of Higher Education. **Publications:** *ASHE Newsletter*, periodic. **Price:** included in membership dues. **Circulation:** 1,300. Alternate Formats: online ● *Higher Education Program Directory*. Alternate Formats: online ● *Review of Higher Education*, quarterly. Journal. **Price:** included in membership dues. **Circulation:** 1,300. Alternate Formats: microform; online. **Conventions/Meetings:** annual conference (exhibits) ● seminar, for graduate students.

8483 ■ Association of University Leaders for a Sustainable Future (ULSF)

2100 L St. NW
Washington, DC 20037
Ph: (202)778-6133
Fax: (202)778-6138
E-mail: info@ulsf.org
URL: http://www.ulsf.org
Contact: Richard M. Clugston, Exec. Dir.
Founded: 1992. **Multinational. Description:** Aims to strengthen the capacity of colleges and universities to make sustainability and environmental literacy a major focus of teaching, research, service and operations. Seeks to advance education for sustainability through research, resource development, assessment, membership support, and international partnerships. Serves as the secretariat for signatories of the Talloires Declaration. **Telecommunication Services:** electronic mail, rmclugston@aol.com. **Publications:** *The Declaration*, semiannual. Report. Features articles about current sustainability initiatives at higher education institutions around the world. **Price:** included in membership dues; $6.00 /year for nonmembers in U.S.; $10.00 /year for nonmembers outside U.S. ● *International Journal of Sustainability in Higher Education*, quarterly. Contains articles, book reviews and news pertaining to issues of sustainable development at higher education institutions. **Price:** $1,149.00. ISSN: 1467-6370. Alternate Formats: online.

8484 ■ Australian and New Zealand Studies Association of North American (ANZSANA)

Edward A. Clark Center for Australian and New Zealand Stud.
Harry Ransom Humanities Res. Ctr., Ste.3.362
The Univ. of Texas at Austin
Austin, TX 78713-7219
Fax: (512)471-8869
E-mail: yacker@www.utexas.edu
URL: http://www.utexas.edu/depts/cas/anzsana/index.html
Contact: Frances Cushing, Sec.-Treas.
Membership Dues: individual - in U.S. and Mexico, $25 (annual) ● individual - in Canada, C$35 (annual) ● group/institutional - in U.S., $50 (annual). **Multinational. Description:** Promotes teaching about Australia and New Zealand and the scholarly investigation of Australian and New Zealand topics and issues throughout institutions of higher education in North America. Strengthens and deepens bilateral relationships between Australia/New Zealand and North America. Maximizes the use of existing resources through exchange of information among North American institutions of higher education. Expands the Australian and New Zealand content of curricula and courses in North American colleges and universities and encourages undergraduate and graduate educational exchanges and academic internships. **Telecommunication Services:** electronic mail, jason.pierce@notes.udayton.edu. **Publications:** Newsletter.

8485 ■ College Parents of America

2000 N 14th St., Ste.800
Arlington, VA 22201-2540
Free: (888)761-6702
Fax: (703)875-2199
E-mail: info@collegeparents.org
URL: http://www.collegeparents.org
Contact: James A. Boyle, Pres.
Membership Dues: family, $79 (annual) ● institutional (K-12), $365 (annual) ● institutional (higher education), $495 (annual) ● institutional (international), $650 (annual). **Description:** Aims to make higher education accessible for all Americans. Strives to ensure that parents are informed about and included in the legislative and regulatory debates concerning issues in higher education. Provides its members with vital resources and information pertaining to college savings strategies, financial aid, scholarships, college applications and admissions. **Publications:** *Decade of Decisions*, quarterly. Newsletter. **Price:** included in membership dues. Alternate Formats: online.

8486 ■ College Summit

1763 Columbia Rd. NW, 2nd Fl.
Washington, DC 20009
Ph: (202)319-1763
Free: (866)266-1100
Fax: (202)319-1233
E-mail: info@collegesummit.org
URL: http://www.collegesummit.org
Contact: J.B. Schramm, Founder/CEO
Founded: 1993. **Description:** Aims to increase the college enrollment rate of low-income students. Assists and encourages deserving students to attend college. Conducts summer workshops for low-income youth.

8487 ■ Consortium for North American Higher Education Collaboration (CONAHEC)

c/o Francisco J. Marmolejo, Exec. Dir.
Univ. of Arizona
PO Box 210300
Tucson, AZ 85721-0300
Ph: (520)621-7761
Fax: (520)626-2675
E-mail: fmarmole@email.arizona.edu
URL: http://www.conahec.org
Contact: Francisco J. Marmolejo, Exec. Dir.
Founded: 1994. **Members:** 147. **Membership Dues:** institutional, $1,750 (annual). **Staff:** 7. **Budget:** $1,000,000. **Languages:** English, French, Spanish. **Multinational. Description:** Aims to advance collaboration, cooperation, and community building among higher education institutions in North America. **Publications:** *Understanding the Difference* (in English, French, and Spanish), annual. Papers. Features working papers of comparative higher education analysis. **Conventions/Meetings:** annual North American Higher Education Conference - congress, with participation of key leaders, government representatives and corporations from Canada, U.S. and Mexico (exhibits) - 2008 Oct. 8-10, Monterrey, NL, Mexico - **Avg. Attendance:** 500.

8488 ■ Council of Graduate Schools (CGS)

1 Dupont Cir. NW, Ste.430
Washington, DC 20036-1146
Ph: (202)223-3791
Fax: (202)331-7157
E-mail: general_inquiries@cgs.nche.edu
URL: http://www.cgsnet.org
Contact: Debra W. Stewart, Pres.
Founded: 1960. **Members:** 470. **Membership Dues:** regular (based on graduate students head count), $1,982-$5,987 (annual) ● associate (based on graduate students head count), $1,781-$5,311 (annual) ● corporate partner, $25,000 (annual) ● corresponding associate, $5,000 (annual) ● corresponding affiliate, $3,000 (annual) ● international institution, $750 (annual) ● global affiliate, $3,000 (annual) ● international affiliate, $500 (annual). **Staff:** 17. **Regional Groups:** 5. **Description:** Accredited graduate schools that have conferred at least 30 Master degrees or ten doctoral degrees or a combination thereof, in at least three distinct fields or disciplines, within the three-year period preceding application. Seeks to serve as a representative body through which graduate schools may counsel and act together. Works to improve and advance graduate education, define its needs and improve ways to meet those needs. Collects and disseminates information about U.S. graduate schools; provides a channel of communication between the schools and government agencies and foundations; assists graduate schools in working out new programs and in revision of the process and procedures of graduate education. **Awards:** CGS/Peterson's Award for Promoting an Inclusive Graduate Community. **Frequency:** annual. **Type:** recognition. **Recipient:** for innovative institutional programmatic efforts in the identification, recruitment, retention and graduation of minority graduate students ● CGS/UMI Dissertation Award. **Frequency:** annual. **Type:** recognition. **Recipient:** for an association ● Gustave O. Arlt Award. **Frequency:** annual. **Type:** recognition. **Recipient:** for work in the humanities. **Formerly:** (1987) Council of Graduate Schools in the United States. **Publications:** *Communicator*, 10/year. Newsletter. **Price:** $110.00/year. **Circulation:** 2,500 ● *Policy Statements*, periodic ● Books. Features information on graduate education, faculty, etc. **Conventions/Meetings:** annual meeting (exhibits) - always December ● annual New Deans Institute and Summer Workshop for Graduate Deans (exhibits) - always summer.

8489 ■ Higher Education Information Technology Alliance (HEIT)

c/o Hilary Goldmann, Coor.
1307 New York Ave. NW, 4th Fl.
Washington, DC 20036
Ph: (202)478-6086
Fax: (202)478-6046
E-mail: info@heitalliance.org
URL: http://www.heitalliance.org
Contact: Hilary Goldmann, Coor.
Description: Promotes the collective interests of the higher education and library community in federal information technology policy. Encourages its members and stakeholders to share information and formulate positions on information technology policy issues that impact the higher education and library community. Provides a forum for discussion of establishing the agenda on information technology policy.

8490 ■ National Association of Scholars (NAS)

221 Witherspoon St., 2nd Fl.
Princeton, NJ 08542-3215
Ph: (609)683-7878
Fax: (609)683-0316
E-mail: nasonweb@nas.org
URL: http://www.nas.org
Contact: Stephen H. Balch, Pres.
Founded: 1985. **Members:** 4,400. **Membership Dues:** full-time faculty, administrator, independent scholar, $42 (annual) ● graduate student, $22 (annual) ● life, $500. **Staff:** 7. **Budget:** $1,000,000. **State Groups:** 46. **Description:** College and university faculty members and administrators; graduate students. Provides a forum for the discussion of curricular issues and trends in higher education. Advocates preservation of intellectual standards in scholarship and higher education. Seeks to provide students with an informed understanding and appreciation of "Western intellectual heritage." Is concerned with what the group considers the "politicization of academic life." Conducts panel discussions, research, and outreach programs. Operates academic search service; compiles statistics. **Awards:** Barry R. Gross Award. **Frequency:** periodic. **Type:** recognition. **Recipient:** for distinguished service to the cause of

academic reform ● Peter Shaw Award. **Frequency:** periodic. **Type:** recognition. **Recipient:** for exemplary writing on issues pertaining to higher education and American culture ● Sidney Hook Award. **Frequency:** periodic. **Type:** recognition. **Recipient:** to an individual for distinguished contributions to the defense of academic freedom and the integrity of academic life. **Formerly:** (1987) Campus Coalition for Democracy. **Publications:** *Academic Questions*, quarterly. Journal. Contains information on problems and trends related to the quality of scholarship and teaching and the politicization of academic life. **Price:** included in membership dues; $64.00 /year for nonmembers; $176.00 /year for institutions. ISSN: 0895-4852. **Circulation:** 5,000. **Advertising:** accepted ● *NAS Update*, quarterly. Newsletter. Alternate Formats: online ● *Science Insight*, bimonthly. Features news briefs, book reviews, interviews, bibliographic information, and short essays on topical science issues. Alternate Formats: online. **Conventions/Meetings:** conference and seminar, includes table for literature of other educational organizations (exhibits) - every 18 months.

8491 ■ National Coalition of Independent Scholars (NCIS)

PO Box 838
St. Helena, CA 94574
E-mail: kbogar@earthlink.net
URL: http://www.ncis.org
Contact: Georgia Wright, Pres.

Founded: 1989. **Members:** 250. **Membership Dues:** regular (based on household's total income), $20-$100 (annual) ● patron, $200 (annual) ● benefactor, $500 (annual) ● life, $1,000 ● associate in U.S., $15 (annual) ● associate in Canada, $25 (annual) ● associate outside U.S. and Canada, $30 (annual). **Staff:** 2. **Budget:** $17,000. **Description:** Active scholars, individuals, and groups interested in enhancing the standing of independent scholars. Seeks equal treatment of all qualified scholars by research facilities, funding programs, and professional societies. Serves as fiscal sponsor for grants. Holds national and local conferences. Monitors a listserv for independent scholars through H-Net and maintains a website of scholarly resources. **Publications:** *Handbook of Fellowships and Grants for Independent Scholars*, 1-2/year. Offers information on grants. **Price:** $7.00 ● *The Independent Scholar*, quarterly. Newsletter. **Price:** $6.00/copy; $12.00/year ● Membership Directory, annual. **Price:** $10.00 ● Report, annual. **Price:** $7.00. **Conventions/Meetings:** biennial conference (exhibits).

8492 ■ North American Association of Commencement Officers (NAACO)

1901 N Roselle Rd., Ste.920
Schaumburg, IL 60195
Free: (877)622-2606
Fax: (847)885-8393
E-mail: eilis.courtney@ubc.ca
URL: http://www.naaco.info
Contact: Eilis Courtney, Pres.

Founded: 2001. **Description:** Provides the opportunity to interact within one's own institution, with other institutions, and with corporations specializing in commencement and graduation-related products and services. Develops and disseminates information and research about commencement/convocation. Recognizes the achievements of leaders who have contributed to commencement/convocation policies and practices.

8493 ■ Pathways to College Network

c/o Aimee McCarron, Admin. Asst.
The Educ. Resources Inst.
31 St. James Ave., 4th Fl.
Boston, MA 02116
Ph: (617)535-6829 (617)556-0535
E-mail: coles@teri.org
URL: http://www.pathwaystocollege.net
Contact: Ann Coles, Proj. Dir.

Founded: 2001. **Members:** 38. **Description:** Aims to advance college access and success for underserved students. Seeks to improve the effectiveness of college access marketing campaigns that aim to influence the college-going behavior of underserved students. Encourages early financial aid commitments and early notification programs for underserved students. Pursues ongoing research about how policies and practices can be improved to better serve students. **Publications:** *Financial Aid - A Shared Agenda to Achieve Access and Success for Under-served Students*. Brochure. Alternate Formats: online ● Newsletter, monthly. Alternate Formats: online ● Reports. Alternate Formats: online.

8494 ■ Professional and Organizational Development Network in Higher Education (POD Network)

PO Box 3318
Nederland, CO 80466
Ph: (303)258-9521
Fax: (303)258-7377
E-mail: podnetwork@podweb.org
URL: http://www.podnetwork.org
Contact: Mr. Hoag Holmgren, Exec. Dir.

Founded: 1975. **Members:** 1,600. **Membership Dues:** individual in U.S. and Canada, $80 (annual) ● individual outside U.S. and Canada, $95 (annual) ● student, retired, $40 (annual) ● international - institutional (3 members), $245 (annual) ● domestic - institutional (3 members), $210 (annual). **Staff:** 1. **Budget:** $400,000. **Regional Groups:** 5. **Multinational. Description:** Represents universities, colleges, and other professionals dedicated to advancing post-secondary teaching and learning through faculty, administrative, instructional, and such as: ethics, diversity, pedagogy, research, service, technology, scholarship of teaching and learning, Preparing Future Faculty, and assessment. Seeks to exchange information and ideas; forges supportive relationships; enhances professional skills. **Awards:** Faculty Development Start-up Grant. **Frequency:** annual. **Type:** monetary. **Recipient:** to support new or beginning faculty development initiatives competitive ● POD Innovation Award. **Frequency:** annual. **Type:** recognition. **Recipient:** for participants who have implemented creative ideas for the enhancement of teaching and learning and/or faculty development. **Computer Services:** Mailing lists. **Telecommunication Services:** electronic mail, hoag.holmgren@gmail.com. **Commissions:** Diversity. **Committees:** Awards and Recognition; Electronic Resources and Communications; Governance; Graduate Student Professional Development; Historian; Nominations and Elections; Outreach. **Formerly:** POD Network. **Publications:** *Essays on Teaching Excellence*, semiannual. **Price:** $120.00 for nonmembers; $100.00 for members. Alternate Formats: online ● *POD Network News*, 3/year. Newsletter. **Price:** included in membership dues ● *Teaching Excellence*, 8/year. Includes scholarly essays on teaching excellence. **Price:** $100.00 /year for members; $120.00 /year for nonmembers ● *To Improve the Academy*, annual. Handbook. Offers a range of materials on teaching and learning written by POD members. **Price:** included in membership dues ● Membership Directory, annual. Lists all POD Network members alphabetically by last name and includes complete mailing and contact information. **Price:** available to members only ● Newsletter, quarterly. **Conventions/Meetings:** annual conference - always fall.

8495 ■ Second Nature (SN)

18 Tremont St., Ste.1120
Boston, MA 02108
Ph: (617)224-1610
E-mail: mbegley@secondnature.org
URL: http://www.secondnature.org
Contact: Dr. Anthony D. Cortese ScD, Pres.

Founded: 1993. **Description:** Works to aid institutions in their quest to make sustainability an integral part of the institution. Hosts workshops. **Conventions/Meetings:** workshop.

Hispanic

8496 ■ Latin American Educational Foundation (LAEF)

561 Santa Fe Dr.
Denver, CO 80204
Ph: (303)446-0541
Fax: (303)446-0526
E-mail: info@laef.org
URL: http://www.laef.org
Contact: George Garcia, Pres.

Founded: 1949. **Description:** Hispanics and other interested individuals. Raises money for scholarships for Hispanic students. Works to advance the economic and social status of Hispanics and the Hispanic Community by improving access to higher education through scholarships, leadership development, community collaboration and support programs. **Awards: Frequency:** annual. **Type:** scholarship. **Recipient:** for a Colorado resident of Hispanic descent and/or actively involved in Hispanic community. **Programs:** Colorado Higher Education Partnership; Community Coalition; High School Network; Internship. **Publications:** *LAEF News*, quarterly. Newsletter. **Conventions/Meetings:** monthly meeting.

8497 ■ Mujeres Activas en Letras Y Cambio Social (MALCS)

1404 66th St.
Berkeley, CA 94704
Ph: (510)926-4021
E-mail: lupeg@berkeley.edu
URL: http://malcs.net
Contact: Adriana Ayala, Chair

Founded: 1982. **Members:** 250. **Membership Dues:** regular (based on income), $25-$100 (annual). **Local Groups:** 3. **Description:** Represents Chicana (Mexican-American), Latina, and indigenous women in higher education and related communities who conduct or foster research and writing on Chicanas and Latinas. Seeks to fight race, class, and gender oppression in universities; strives to bridge the gap between intellectual work and active commitment to communities. Develops strategies for social change; works to organize, collect, and disseminate course materials useful to developing and teaching courses on Chicanas. Documents, analyzes, and interprets the Chicana experience in the U.S; is concerned with women's conditions in the home and/or workplace, and their struggle for social and economic justice. **Libraries: Type:** open to the public. **Holdings:** archival material. **Computer Services:** Mailing lists, of registered members ● mailing lists, open to public; interested in Chicana and Latina issues. **Additional Websites:** http://malcs.net/blog. **Caucuses:** Graduate Student; Indigenous/Native American; Lesbian; Undergraduate Student. **Publications:** *Chicana/Latina Studies: The Journal of MALCS*, semiannual. Features review essays, research articles, literary criticism, and creative writing. **Price:** free for members ● *MALCS Noticias*, semiannual. Newsletter. Includes information on educational placements and fellowships. Alternate Formats: online ● *Trabajos Monograficos: Studies in Chicana/Latina Research*, annual. Reports. **Conventions/Meetings:** annual conference - always summer ● periodic regional meeting.

8498 ■ National Association for Chicana and Chicano Studies (NACCS)

PO Box 720052
San Jose, CA 95172-0052
Ph: (408)924-5310
Fax: (408)924-5700
E-mail: naccs@naccs.org
URL: http://www.naccs.org
Contact: Dr. Julia E. Curry Rodriguez, Exec. Dir.

Founded: 1972. **Members:** 500. **Membership Dues:** graduate student, $40 (annual) ● retired, $60 (annual) ● institution, $100 (annual) ● library, $85 (annual) ● income under $20,000, $45 (annual) ● income within $20,000-34,999, $60 (annual) ● income within $35,000-44,999, $70 (annual) ● income within $45,000-54,999, $80 (annual) ● income within $55,000-64,999, $90 (annual) ● income within $65,000-74,999, $100 (annual) ● income $75,000 and over, $125 (annual) ● undergraduate student, $30 (annual) ● life, $2,500. **Staff:** 3. **Budget:** $70,000. **Regional Groups:** 9. **Languages:** English, Spanish. **Description:** Represents faculty, researchers, staff, undergraduate/graduate students, community scholars interested in Chicana and Chicano studies and social and cultural awareness. **Awards:** Frederick A. Cervantes Student Premio. **Frequency:** annual. **Type:** monetary. **Recipient:** for the best graduate and undergraduate research paper ● NACCS Scholar. **Frequency:** annual. **Type:** scholarship. **Recipient:** for life achievement to the development of Chicana and Chicano studies. **Telecommunication Services:** electronic mail, executive_director@naccs.com. **Committees:** Editorial; Policy; Program. **Divisions:** Critical Semiotics; Cultural Production; Gender and Sexuality; Indigenous; Information and Archival; Institutional Impact and Participation; Political Economic; Race/Ethnicity/National Character/Identity; Social and Cultural; Space and Location. **Subgroups:** East Coast; Midwest; Pacific Northwest. **Affiliated With:** REFORMA: National Association to Promote Library Services to the Spanish-Speaking. **Formerly:** (1999) National Association for Chicano Studies. **Publications:** *Beginning a New Millennium of Chicana and Chicano Scholarship*. Proceedings. **Price:** $30.00 ● *Chicano Discourse*. Proceedings ● *The Chicano Struggle: Analyses of Past and Present Effort*. Proceedings ● *Chicano Studies: Critical Connection Between Research and Community*. Proceedings. **Price:** $15.00 ● *Community Empowerment and Chicano Scholarship*. Proceedings. **Price:** $15.00 ● *Conference Proceedings* ● *Directory of Chicana/o, Latina/o, and Latin American Studies Program, Research and Policy Centers*. Alternate Formats: CD-ROM; online ● *Noticias de NACCS*, quarterly. Newsletter. **Price:** included in membership dues. **Circulation:** 550. **Advertising:** accepted. **Conventions/Meetings:** annual conference, includes book publishers, arts, and crafts (exhibits) - always March or April.

8499 ■ Sociedad Honoraria Hispanica (SHH)
PO Box 5318
Buffalo Grove, IL 60089-5318
Ph: (847)550-0455 (847)726-7127
Fax: (847)550-0460
E-mail: sociedad@comcast.net
URL: http://www.sociedadhonorariahispanica.org
Contact: Ms. Judith Park, Natl. Co-Dir.
Founded: 1953. **Membership Dues:** student, emeritus, $25 (annual) ● regular, $60 (annual). **Budget:** $300,000. **Languages:** English, Portuguese, Spanish. **Description:** Secondary school sophomore, junior, and senior students doing superior work in Spanish classes. Sponsors trips abroad. Conducts contests. **Awards:** Joseph Adams Sr. Scholarships. **Frequency:** annual. **Type:** scholarship. **Recipient:** for seniors in high school ● Junior Travel Award. **Frequency:** annual. **Type:** monetary ● Premio de Honor. **Frequency:** annual. **Type:** recognition. **Recipient:** for graduating senior members. **Telecommunication Services:** electronic mail, tlaloc31@comcast.net. **Affiliated With:** American Association of Teachers of Spanish and Portuguese. **Also Known As:** Spanish National Honor Society. **Publications:** *Albricias!*, quarterly. Journal. Contains student contributions, general information, and lists of new chapters and sponsors. **Price:** available to members only. **Conventions/Meetings:** annual competition ● annual conference (exhibits) - always August.

History

8500 ■ American History Forum and Civil War Education Association (AHF & CWEA)
PO Box 78
Winchester, VA 22604
Ph: (540)678-8598
Free: (800)298-1861
Fax: (800)550-1347
E-mail: cwea@earthlink.net
URL: http://www.cwea.net
Contact: Bob Maher, Pres.
Membership Dues: individual, $25 (annual) ● family, $35 (annual) ● student, $10 (annual). **Description:** Enhances the memory of and the understanding of the Civil War and other eras of American history. Supports historic preservation of American history. Conducts fundraising and public awareness programs. **Publications:** *The Color Bearer*, semiannual, in mid-May and mid-November. Journal. Contains history articles and viewpoints. ● *History News and Views*, semiannual, in mid-February and mid-August. Newsletter. Contains project and member news.

8501 ■ American Journalism Historians Association (AJHA)
c/o Carol Sue Humphrey, Admin. Sec.
OBU Box 61201
500 W Univ.
Shawnee, OK 74804-2590
Ph: (405)878-2221
Fax: (405)878-2502
E-mail: carol.humphrey@okbu.edu
URL: http://ajhaonline.org
Contact: Carol Sue Humphrey, Admin. Sec.
Founded: 1981. **Members:** 300. **Membership Dues:** student, retired faculty, $25 (annual) ● faculty, professional, $45 (annual). **Budget:** $12,000. **Description:** Academics, researchers, and business professionals. Devotes efforts to the study of American and international media history. Maintains speaker's bureau. **Libraries: Type:** reference. **Holdings:** archival material. **Awards: Frequency:** annual. **Type:** monetary ● **Frequency:** annual. **Type:** recognition. **Special Interest Groups:** AJHA Women's Research; Early Americans; International; Racial and Ethnic Media; Senior Scholars. **Publications:** *American Journalism*, quarterly. **Price:** included in membership dues. **Circulation:** 500. **Advertising:** accepted ● *Intelligence*. Newsletter. **Price:** included in membership dues ● Membership Directory. Alternate Formats: online. **Conventions/Meetings:** annual convention (exhibits).

8502 ■ AMISTAD America
746 Chapel St., Ste.300
New Haven, CT 06510
Ph: (203)495-1839
Free: (866)264-7823
Fax: (203)495-9647
E-mail: kperry@amistadamerica.org
URL: http://www.amistadamerica.org
Contact: Mr. William Minter, Chm.
Founded: 1996. **Membership Dues:** child, adult full-time student, $20 (annual) ● individual adult, $40 (annual) ● dual adult, $50 (annual) ● household, grandchild under 18, $60 (annual) ● senior, teacher, volunteer, $30 (annual) ● adult family, $45 (annual) ● individual sustaining, $125 (annual) ● dual sustaining, $250 (annual) ● household sustaining, $500 (annual). **Description:** Promotes improved relationships between races and cultures by acknowledging common experiences. Strives to increase multicultural understanding and reduce racial isolation. Educates the public on the inherent lessons and legacies of freedom, justice, perseverance, cooperation and leadership arising form the Amistad Incident of 1839.

8503 ■ Chinese Historians in the United States (CHUS)
c/o George Wei, Pres.
Susquehanna Univ.
Dept. of History
Selinsgrove, PA 17870
Ph: (570)372-4194
E-mail: wei@suqu.edu
URL: http://instructional1.calstatela.edu/pyao/chus
Contact: George Wei, Pres.
Founded: 1987. **Membership Dues:** student, $20 (annual) ● regular, $35 (annual) ● regular, $50 (biennial) ● life, $200. **Multinational. Description:** Aggregates students and scholars of history and anthropology who are Chinese descendants. Aims to advance historical studies both in the United States and in China. Serves as a cultural and academic homebase that provides emotional, spiritual and psychological support for members who reside in the United States, far away from their original homeland and hometown. **Publications:** *The Chinese Historical Review*. Journal. ISSN: 1547-402X. Alternate Formats: online ● Newsletter. Alternate Formats: online.

8504 ■ Economic History Association (EHA)
Santa Clara Univ.
Dept. of Economics
500 El Camino Real
Santa Clara, CA 95053-0385
Ph: (408)554-4348
Fax: (408)554-2331
E-mail: afield@scu.edu
URL: http://eh.net/eha
Contact: Alexander J. Field, Exec. Dir.
Founded: 1940. **Members:** 1,100. **Membership Dues:** student or professor emeritus, $20 (annual) ● regular (annual income under $50,000), $35 (annual) ● regular (annual income over $50,000), $60 (annual). **Staff:** 8. **Budget:** $150,000. **Description:** Represents scholars, teachers and students of economic history. **Awards:** Alexander Gerschenkron Prize. **Frequency:** annual. **Type:** recognition. **Recipient:** for the best doctoral dissertation in economic history on a non-North American topic ● Alice Hanson Jones Prize. **Frequency:** biennial. **Type:** recognition. **Recipient:** for an outstanding book in North American (including Caribbean) economic history ● Allan Nevins Prize. **Frequency:** annual. **Type:** recognition. **Recipient:** for best doctoral dissertation on American economic history ● Arthur H. Cole Grants. **Frequency:** annual. **Type:** grant. **Recipient:** for research in economic history ● Arthur H. Cole Prize. **Frequency:** annual. **Type:** recognition. **Recipient:** for the best article in the journal of economic history during the past year ● Economic History Association Research Grant Awards for Graduate Students. **Frequency:** annual. **Type:** grant. **Recipient:** for predissertation and dissertation fellowships in the area of economic history ● Jonathan Hughes Prize. **Frequency:** annual. **Type:** recognition. **Recipient:** for excellence in teaching economic history ● Ranki Prize. **Frequency:** biennial. **Type:** recognition. **Recipient:** for the best English language book in European economic history. **Computer Services:** database ● online services. **Publications:** *Journal of Economic History*, quarterly. Promotes the scholarly study of economic aspects of the human past from a diversity of perspectives. **Price:** included in membership dues. **Circulation:** 3,300. **Advertising:** accepted. Alternate Formats: online. Also Cited As: *JEH*. **Conventions/Meetings:** annual meeting, with book exhibition (exhibits) - usually September.

8505 ■ Eighteenth-Century Scottish Studies Society (ECSSS)
New Jersey Inst. of Tech.
Newark, NJ 07102-1982
Ph: (973)596-3377
Fax: (973)596-5345
E-mail: sher@njit.edu
URL: http://www.ecsss.org
Contact: Richard B. Sher, Exec. Sec.
Founded: 1986. **Members:** 300. **Membership Dues:** individual in U.S., $20 (annual) ● individual in U.K., 12 (annual) ● institutional in U.S., $30 (annual) ● institutional in U.K., 18 (annual). **Multinational. Description:** Scholars and others interested in the study of 18th-century Scotland. Promotes the study of all aspects of 18th-century Scottish culture and society. **Affiliated With:** American Society for Eighteenth-Century Studies. **Publications:** *ECSSS Studies in Eighteenth-Century Scotland, Vol. 5: William Robertson and the Expansion of Empire*. Book ● *ECSSS Studies in Eighteenth-Century Scotland, Vol. 4: The Glasgow Enlightenment*. Book ● *ECSSS Studies in Eighteenth-Century Scotland, Vol. 1: Scotland and America in the Age of Enlightenment*. Book ● *ECSSS Studies in 18th-Century Scotland, Vol. 7: Scotland and France in the Enlightenment*. Book ● *ECSSS Studies in Eighteenth Century Scotland, Vol. 6: Nation and Province in the First British Empire: Scotland and the Americas, 1600-1800*. Book ● *ECSSS Studies in Eighteenth-Century Scotland, Vol. 3: Sociability and Society in Eighteenth-Century Scotland*. Book ● *ECSSS Studies in Eighteenth-Century Scotland, Vol. 2: Ossian Revisited*, annual. Book. Contains articles, announcements, and book reviews. **Price:** free for members; $10.00 for nonmembers. **Circulation:** 400 ● *Eighteenth-Century Scotland*, annual. Newsletter. Contains articles, announcements,

and book reviews. **Price:** free for members; $10.00 for nonmembers. **Circulation:** 400. **Conventions/Meetings:** annual international conference.

8506 ■ Historians of American Communism (HOAC)
c/o Daniel Leab, Gen. Sec.
PO Box 1216
Washington, CT 06793
Ph: (860)868-7408
Fax: (860)868-0080
E-mail: danleab@earthlink.net
URL: http://www.historians.org/affiliates/hisn_am_communism.htm
Contact: Daniel Leab, Gen. Sec.
Founded: 1982. **Members:** 165. **Membership Dues:** individual, $15 (annual) ● foreign, institution, $20 (annual). **Description:** Individuals interested in the history of American communism. Promotes the history of American communism, American anti-communism, and related topics, and historical research in these issues. **Telecommunication Services:** electronic mail, rcohen@iun.edu. **Affiliated With:** American Historical Association. **Publications:** *American Communist History*, semiannual. Includes bibliographical listings. **Advertising:** accepted ● *Newsletter of the Historians of American Communism*, quarterly.

8507 ■ International Society for the History, Philosophy, and Social Studies of Biology (ISHPSSB)
c/o Dr. Roberta Millstein, Sec.
UC Davis
Dept. of Philosophy
One Shields Ave.
Davis, CA 95616
E-mail: treasurer@ishpssb.org
URL: http://www.ishpssb.org
Contact: Dr. Roberta Millstein, Sec.
Founded: 1982. **Members:** 600. **Membership Dues:** student, $15 (biennial) ● full, $50 (biennial). **Budget:** $20,000. **Multinational. Description:** Scholars from diverse disciplines, including history, philosophy, and social studies of science. Fosters informal, cooperative exchanges, and collaborations. **Awards:** Marjorie Grene Prize. **Frequency:** biennial. **Type:** monetary. **Recipient:** to a graduate student who submitted the best manuscript. **Computer Services:** database, archives ● mailing lists. **Committees:** Education; Local Arrangements; Marjorie Grene Prize; Nominations; Off-Year Workshop; Operations; Program; Student Advisory. **Publications:** Newsletter, semiannual. Includes information about events, conferences, governance, and other items of interest to members. **Price:** included in membership dues. Alternate Formats: online. **Conventions/Meetings:** biennial conference (exhibits).

8508 ■ National Council for History Education (NCHE)
26915 Westwood Rd., Ste.B-2
Westlake, OH 44145
Ph: (440)835-1776
Fax: (440)835-1295
E-mail: nche@nche.net
URL: http://www.nche.net
Contact: Cynthia Stout, Exec. Dir.
Founded: 1990. **Members:** 5,700. **Membership Dues:** partner level, $30 (annual) ● student/retired level, $20 (annual) ● patron level, department, $100 (annual) ● sustaining level, $300 (annual) ● Chairman's club, $1,000 (annual). **Staff:** 8. **State Groups:** 41. **Description:** Elementary and secondary school teachers of history, academic historians, education curriculum policymakers and developers, and historical society and museum personnel. Promotes the formal and informal study of history in schools and society. Maintains speakers' bureau. Conducts teacher education programs: Partnering with Local Education Agencies in writing proposals for Teaching American History Grant projects; and conducting History Colloquium and History Academy professional development programs for K-12 history teachers. Provides services to states and local school districts that are writing and revising their social studies and history curriculum. Assists with staff development in history. **Awards:** The Paul Gagnon Prize. **Frequency:** annual. **Type:** monetary. **Recipient:** for a K-12 history teacher exhibiting exceptional historical scholarship. **Computer Services:** Mailing lists, one-time rental, history. **Formerly:** (1990) Bradley Commission on History in Schools. **Publications:** *Building a History-Centered Curriculum for Kindergarten through Grade Four*, periodic. Booklet. Provides a guideline for teaching history in grades Kindergarten through grade 4. **Price:** $10.00. **Circulation:** 40,000 ● *Building a History Curriculum: Guidelines for Teaching History in Schools*. Bulletins. Provides recommendations for improving the teaching and learning of history in schools K-12 and college. **Price:** $10.00. **Circulation:** 100,000. Alternate Formats: online. Also Cited As: *The Report of the Bradley Commission on History in Schools* ● *Building a United States History Curriculum*, periodic. Booklet. Provides curriculum guidelines for the teaching and learning of U.S. History in grades 5-12. **Price:** $10.00. **Circulation:** 45,000 ● *Building a World History Curriculum*, periodic. Booklet. Provides guidelines for teaching and learning of world history in grades 5-12. **Price:** $10.00. ISSN: 1090-1450. **Circulation:** 30,000 ● *History Matters!*, monthly, September-June. Newsletter. Provides a clearinghouse of information on history education in the U.S. ISSN: 1090-1450. **Circulation:** 15,000 ● Papers, periodic. **Conventions/Meetings:** annual conference, new ideas in history education for K-16 teachers (exhibits).

8509 ■ National History Club (NHC)
The Concord Rev., Inc.
730 Boston Post Rd., Ste.24
Sudbury, MA 01776
Ph: (978)443-0022
Free: (800)331-5007
E-mail: nasson@tcr.org
URL: http://www.tcr.org/nhc/index.htm
Contact: Robert Nasson, Exec. Dir.
Founded: 2002. **Description:** Promotes the reading, writing, discussion and enjoyment of history among secondary students and teachers. Aims to connect secondary school history students of diverse backgrounds and varying abilities in schools across the country. Creates a forum for members to learn about each other's ideas and experiences. **Telecommunication Services:** electronic mail, fitzhugh@tcr.org. **Publications:** Newsletter, semiannual. Contains history knowledge games and quizzes. Features the activities of history clubs around the country. Alternate Formats: online.

8510 ■ National History Day (NHD)
Univ. of Maryland
0119 Cecil Hall
College Park, MD 20742
Ph: (301)314-9739
Fax: (301)314-9767
E-mail: info@nhd.org
URL: http://www.nhd.org
Contact: Cathy Gorn, Exec. Dir.
Founded: 1980. **Staff:** 8. **State Groups:** 50. **Local Groups:** 400. **Nonmembership. Description:** Encourages students in secondary schools to participate in history competitions judged by professional historians at district, state, and national levels. Students must follow an annual theme in their papers, exhibits, performances, or documentary presentations. Conducts 1-week summer institute and workshop for secondary school teachers, which can be used to fill continuing education credit requirements. **Awards:** 1st-2nd-3rd Place Awards. **Frequency:** annual. **Type:** monetary. **Recipient:** to the top three student projects in each division and category at the national contest ● Outstanding History Educator Award. **Frequency:** annual. **Type:** recognition. **Recipient:** for an educator who has made an exceptional contribution to history education through the National History Day program ● Richard M. Farrell Teacher of Merit Award. **Frequency:** annual. **Type:** recognition. **Recipient:** for educators who have used the National History Day program as part of their curriculum ● Special Prizes. **Frequency:** annual. **Type:** monetary. **Recipient:** for outstanding research and achievements in various subject areas to students at the national contest ● University Scholarships. **Frequency:** annual. **Type:** scholarship. **Recipient:** to students at the national contest to case Western Reserve University, University of Maryland College Park, University of Minnesota, and Chaminade University in Hawaii. **Publications:** *Contest Guide, Teacher Theme Supplement and Curriculum Guide*, annual. Newsletter ● *National History Day Annual Report*, annual. Alternate Formats: online ● *National History Day News*, quarterly. Newsletter. **Price:** $25.00 ● *NHD Curriculum Book*, annual. **Circulation:** 40,000. **Advertising:** accepted. **Conventions/Meetings:** annual competition and meeting (exhibits) - always June.

8511 ■ Society for History Education (SHE)
California State Univ., Long Beach
1250 Bellflower Blvd.
Long Beach, CA 90840
Ph: (562)985-2573
Fax: (562)985-5431
E-mail: herrera@thehistoryteacher.org
URL: http://www.thehistoryteacher.org
Contact: Elisa Herrera, Mgr.
Founded: 1967. **Members:** 2,000. **Membership Dues:** individual in U.S., $32 (annual) ● individual in Canada and Mexico, $41 (annual) ● individual outside U.S., Canada and Mexico, $50 (annual) ● student in U.S., $22 (annual) ● student outside U.S., $31 (annual) ● institution in U.S., $63 (annual) ● institution in Canada and Mexico, $72 (annual) ● institution outside U.S., Canada and Mexico, $81 (annual). **Staff:** 15. **Budget:** $70,000. **Description:** Represents high school and college history teachers and libraries. Serves the needs of the historian who is fulfilling his or her role as a teacher at the university, college, community college, and secondary levels of education. **Affiliated With:** American Historical Association. **Supersedes:** History Teachers' Association. **Publications:** *The History Teacher*, quarterly. Journal. Contains articles on historiography, the state of the profession, and classroom techniques. Includes book and audiovisual reviews. **Price:** $22.00 students, retired (with I.D.) in U.S.; $32.00 individuals in U.S.; $63.00 institutions in U.S.; $81.00 institutions outside U.S. **Circulation:** 6,000. **Advertising:** accepted. Alternate Formats: microform. **Conventions/Meetings:** annual conference, presents papers and roundtable discussions on history teaching.

Home Economics

8512 ■ International Federation for Home Economics - USA (IFHE-US)
122 Point Ln.
Ridgeway, SC 29130
E-mail: office.ifhe@t-online.de
URL: http://www.ifhe-us.org
Contact: Dr. Mary Andrews, Pres.
Founded: 1999. **Members:** 370. **Membership Dues:** active, $65 (annual). **Description:** Represents educators, advisors, and extension workers in the field of home economics; government agencies; other interested individuals. Promotes development of home economics programs and curricula. Cooperates with related scientific, professional, and international development organizations.

8513 ■ National Association for Family and Community Education (FCE)
73 Cavalier Blvd., Ste.106
Florence, KY 41042
Ph: (859)525-6401 (937)465-6376
Free: (877)712-4477
Fax: (859)525-6496
E-mail: nafcehq@juno.com
URL: http://www.nafce.org
Contact: Carolyn Ropp, Pres.
Founded: 1936. **Members:** 14,000. **Membership Dues:** individual (national member-at-large), $25 (annual) ● individual (national FCE classification), $13 (annual) ● family (national member-at-large), $35 (annual) ● corporate (national member-at-large),

$100 (annual) ● senior (national FCE classification), $10 (annual) ● family (national FCE classification), $20 (annual). **Staff:** 1. **Budget:** $400,000. **Regional Groups:** 4. **State Groups:** 29. **Languages:** English, Spanish. **Description:** Men and women who are members of state family and community education associations in 28 states, and Puerto Rico. Educational organization assisting individuals and family members in identifying and solving family and community problems, in cooperation with local resources, state land-grant universities, and the United States Department of Agriculture. Educational programs are concerned with children's issues, environmental problems, and literacy. Conducts leadership development programs. Sponsors Family Community Leadership Program. **Awards:** Program Award. **Frequency:** annual. **Type:** recognition. **Recipient:** for best educational programs ● **Type:** recognition. **Recipient:** for outstanding projects in each of the work programs; education, action, leadership. **Committees:** Children and Television; Literacy; Special Projects; Young Families Coordinators. **Programs:** Character Counts; Family ChoicE-TV; Family Community Leadership; The FCE Network; Hearth Fire Series. **Projects:** India; Romania Project and HUNGER, PLUS. **Formerly:** National Home Demonstration Council; (1992) National Extension Homemakers Council. **Publications:** *An Official History: National Extension Homemakers Council 1936-1990, Voices of American Homemakers* ● *Children and Television Project: What About the Children* ● *The Family Action Plan Book: Children's Issues* ● *The Family Action Plan Book: Windows to the World* ● *FCE Today*, quarterly. Newsletter. Includes articles relating to issues of program focus. **Price:** included in membership dues. **Circulation:** 14,000 ● *NAFCE Annual Report*, annual. **Circulation:** 3,000 ● Handbook, annual. **Conventions/Meetings:** annual conference and trade show (exhibits).

8514 ■ National Association of State Administrators for Family Consumer Sciences (NASAFACS)

c/o Robin Harris, Treas.
State Dept. of Educ.
120 SE 10th Ave.
Topeka, KS 66612-1182
Ph: (785)296-4912
Fax: (785)296-2214
E-mail: rharris@ksde.org
Contact: Robin Harris, Treas.

Members: 70. **Membership Dues:** regular, $20 (annual). **Description:** Represents state administrators of family and consumer sciences in each state and members of state family and consumer sciences education staffs whose major responsibilities are to: provide for group expression and group action on problems of national importance to family and consumer sciences education; provide an avenue for disseminating information for strengthening and improving family and consumer sciences education in public schools; serve in an advisory capacity in the interest of family and consumer sciences when requested by organizations and agencies working for common goals; provide supervision and administration for family and consumer sciences education programs. **Computer Services:** Online services, internal listserv (not open to public). **Formerly:** National Association of Home Economics Supervisors; (2001) National Association of State Supervisors of Vocational Home Economics. **Publications:** Membership Directory, annual. Alternate Formats: online. **Conventions/Meetings:** annual conference, held in conjunction with Association of Career and Technical Education (exhibits) - always spring.

8515 ■ National Association of Teacher Educators for Family and Consumer Sciences (NATEFACS)

c/o Debra DeBates, Pres.
College of Family and Consumer Sciences
NFA 305, Box 2275A
South Dakota State Univ.
Brookings, SD 57007
Ph: (605)688-4666
Fax: (605)688-4888
E-mail: dohner.1@osu.edu
URL: http://www.natefacs.org
Contact: Debra DeBates, Pres.

Founded: 1949. **Members:** 100. **Membership Dues:** professional, $20 (annual) ● graduate student, retired professional, $15 (annual). **Staff:** 40. **Description:** Individuals engaged in pre-service and in-service education of family and consumer science teachers. Serves as a forum for discussion of professional concerns and issues confronting family and consumer sciences teacher educators. Assists with research; participates in policy deliberations. Maintains archives and organizational records at Iowa State University. **Awards:** Family and Consumer Sciences Education Graduate Student Fellowship. **Frequency:** annual. **Type:** fellowship. **Recipient:** to doctoral or masteral students in family and consumer sciences. **Affiliated With:** Association for Career and Technical Education. **Formerly:** National Association of Teacher Educators for Home Economics; (1995) National Association of Teacher Educators for Vocational Home Economics. **Publications:** *AVA Connections*, annual. Newsletter. Contains announcements of applications for awards, research presentations and annual meeting events. **Price:** included in membership dues. **Advertising:** accepted ● *Journal of Family and Consumer Sciences Education*, semiannual. Includes research reports. **Price:** included in membership dues; $40.00 /year for nonmembers. **Circulation:** 200. Alternate Formats: online. **Conventions/Meetings:** annual Association of Career and Technical Education - conference (exhibits) - usually second week of December.

Home Study

8516 ■ Christian Home Educators Association of California (CHEA)

PO Box 2009
Norwalk, CA 90651-2009
Ph: (562)864-2432
Free: (800)564-CHEA
E-mail: info@cheaofca.org
URL: http://www.cheaofca.org
Contact: Susan Beatty, Dir.

Founded: 1982. **Members:** 5,500. **Membership Dues:** individual, $35 (annual). **Staff:** 10. **Local Groups:** 275. **Description:** Provides information and support to parents who wish to educate their children at home, especially those who do so for religious reasons. Although active primarily in California, CHEA disseminates information nationwide. Provides referral service. Catalog of Books and Resources. **Awards:** Teen Scholarship. **Frequency:** annual. **Type:** scholarship. **Recipient:** for home-schooled senior students to attend a college or vocational school of their choice; applicants must be a member of CHEA and its support network group. **Affiliated With:** Home School Legal Defense Association. **Also Known As:** CHEA of California; CHEA of CA. **Formerly:** (1998) Christian Home Educators Association. **Publications:** *An Introduction to Home Education*. Handbook. **Price:** $29.00 ● *The California Parent Educator*, bimonthly. Magazine. Features home education news and articles for CHEA members. **Circulation:** 5,500. **Advertising:** accepted ● *The High School Handbook*, bimonthly. **Price:** $22.99 ● *The Parent Educator Ready Reference*. Handbook. **Price:** $16.00 ● Newsletter, quarterly. **Conventions/Meetings:** annual Convention and Area Conventions - convention and assembly, statewide (exhibits).

8517 ■ Distance Education and Training Council (DETC)

1601 18th St. NW
Washington, DC 20009
Ph: (202)234-5100
Fax: (202)332-1386
E-mail: mike@detc.org
URL: http://www.detc.org
Contact: Michael P. Lambert, Exec. Dir.

Founded: 1926. **Members:** 80. **Staff:** 6. **Description:** Represents the interests of home study (correspondence) schools. Establishes standards for the operation of distance education institutions and serves as the accrediting agency for schools meeting these standards. Sponsors independent accrediting commission listed by the U.S. Department of of Education as a nationally recognized accrediting agency. Sponsors workshops and maintains small home study library. **Telecommunication Services:** electronic mail, rachel@detc.org. **Commissions:** Accrediting. **Committees:** Awards and Recognition; Finance, Budget and Audit; Nominating; Standards. **Formerly:** (1994) National Home Study Council. **Publications:** *DETC Accreditation Handbook*, annual. Contains the commission's policies, procedures and standards. **Price:** $30.00/copy. Alternate Formats: online ● *DETC News*, semiannual. Journal. Includes information on accreditation, ethics and standards. Includes council news, book reviews, calendar of events and research. **Price:** free. **Circulation:** 1,800 ● *Directory of Accredited Distance Education Institutions*, annual. Lists schools and their courses accredited by the council. **Price:** free ● *Facts About DETC*. Brochure. **Conventions/Meetings:** annual conference - 2009 Apr. 5-7, Coronado, CA; 2010 Apr. 11-13, Del Mar, CA.

8518 ■ Home Study Exchange (HOSTEX)

PO Box 289
Torreon, NM 87061-0289
Ph: (505)847-2909
Free: (866)703-9375
E-mail: educate@sfcs-homestudy.org
URL: http://www.sfcs-homestudy.org
Contact: Lee Ann Blue, Ed.

Founded: 1979. **Members:** 72. **Membership Dues:** subscription, $10 (annual). **Staff:** 1. **Description:** Publishes newsletter which is written by and for home study students of all ages across the United States and around the world; it gives these students contact with each other and a chance to express themselves creatively. **Libraries: Type:** reference. **Publications:** Newsletter, 5/year. Contains information about home study students; written by home study students. **Price:** $10.00/year; $2.00/sample issue.

8519 ■ National Black Home Educators (NBHE)

c/o Eric Burges, Co-Founder
13434 Plank Rd.
PMB 110
Baker, LA 70714
E-mail: contact@nbhe.net
URL: http://www.nbhe.net
Contact: Eric Burges, Co-Founder

Founded: 2000. **Description:** Empowers parents to teach their children at home. Encourages, supports and offers fellowship to families who are exploring the benefits of home education. Serves families by providing information on parent-directed education and importance of home school. **Formerly:** (2006) National Black Home Educators Resource Association. **Publications:** *The Legacy*. Newsletter. Features an African American homeschooling family. **Price:** $35.00 ● *Teach Me How to Teach My Child: Creating a Learning Atmosphere for Our Children*. Book. **Price:** $15.99.

8520 ■ National Challenged Homeschoolers Associated Network (NATHHAN)

PO Box 310
Moyie Springs, ID 83845
Ph: (208)267-6246
E-mail: nathanews@aol.com
URL: http://www.nathhan.com
Contact: Tom Bushnell, Co-Dir.

Founded: 1992. **Members:** 15,000. **Membership Dues:** ordinary, $25 (annual). **Staff:** 6. **Description:** Christian homeschooling families with special needs children. Promotes more effective home study, with particular emphasis on the education of children with special needs. Serves as a clearinghouse on home study and special needs children; facilitates establishment of networks of families engaged in homeschooling; supports legal and advocacy campaigns protecting the right of families to teach their children at home. **Libraries: Type:** lending; not open to the public. **Holdings:** 800; articles, books. **Subjects:** homeschooling, education of special needs children. **Publications:** *Family Directory*, annual ● *NATHHAN News*, quarterly. Magazine ● Brochures.

8521 ■ National Christian Forensics and Communications Association (NCFCA)
PO Box 212
Mountlake Terrace, WA 98043-0212
Ph: (425)776-3620
E-mail: office@ncfca.org
URL: http://www.ncfca.org
Contact: Mike Larimer, Pres.
Description: Provides a means for home schooled students to learn and exercise analytical and oratorical skills through formal speech and debate, addressing life issues from a Biblical worldview in a manner that glorifies God. Encourages students to pursue forensics as a means to learn the skills necessary to effectively communicate truth to the world. Facilitates qualifying tournaments throughout the country.

8522 ■ National Home Education Research Institute (NHERI)
PO Box 13939
Salem, OR 97309
Ph: (503)364-1490
Fax: (503)364-2827
E-mail: mail@nheri.org
URL: http://www.nheri.org
Contact: Brian D. Ray PhD, Founder/Pres.
Founded: 1990. **Multinational. Description:** Performs data gathering research and serves as an information clearinghouse on the subject of homeschooling (or home education, homeschooling, home-based education.) Works to define and promote understanding of the goals of the home education movement. Provides testimony in court cases and legislation hearings on the relative merits of homeschooling. Maintains speakers' bureau; compiles statistics. **Libraries: Type:** reference. **Holdings:** monographs, periodicals. **Subjects:** home-centered learning, homeschooling, home education, home-based education. **Computer Services:** database, annotated bibliography ● mailing lists, of members. **Publications:** *Home Based Education: The Informed Choice*. Video. **Price:** $19.95 ● *Home Centered Learning Annotated Bibliography*. **Price:** $14.00 ● *Home School Researcher*, quarterly. Journal. **Price:** $25.00 /year for individuals; $40.00/year for organizations. ISSN: 1054-8033. **Circulation:** 500. **Advertising:** accepted ● *Home Schooling on the Threshold: A Survey of Research at the Dawn of the New Millennium*. Report ● *Strengths of Their Own Home Schoolers Across America: Academic Achievement, Family Characteristics, and Longitudinal Traits*. Book. **Price:** $9.95 ● *Worldwide Guide to Homeschooling: Facts and Stats on the Benefits of Home School*. Book. **Price:** $10.99 ● Also publishes research reports, fact sheets, books, audio cassettes, and a video.

8523 ■ United States Distance Learning Association (USDLA)
8 Winter St., Ste.508
Boston, MA 02108
Free: (800)275-5162
Fax: (617)399-1771
E-mail: information@usdla.org
URL: http://www.usdla.org
Contact: John G. Flores PhD, Exec. Dir.
Membership Dues: student, $30 (annual) ● individual, $125 (annual) ● non-profit organization, $500 (annual) ● for-profit organization, $1,000 (annual) ● state chapter initiation fee, $500. **Description:** Serves the needs of the distance learning community by providing advocacy, information and networking opportunities. Provides national leadership in the field of distance learning. Represents the distance learning community before the government and regulatory bodies. **Awards:** Excellence in Distance Learning Programming. **Frequency:** annual. **Type:** recognition. **Recipient:** to organizations with outstanding achievement in distance learning programming ● Excellence in Distance Teaching. **Frequency:** annual. **Type:** recognition. **Recipient:** to individuals with outstanding achievement in distance teaching ● Most Outstanding Achievement by an Individual. **Frequency:** annual. **Type:** recognition. **Recipient:** to individuals with most outstanding achievement in distance teaching ● USDLA Eagle Awards. **Frequency:** annual. **Type:** recognition. **Recipient:** to individuals with excellent achievement in the field of distance teaching. **Publications:** *Electronic Learning Communities: Issues and Practices*. Book. Contains instructional technology issues and practices. **Price:** $39.95 for nonmembers (paperback); $33.95 for members (paperback); $73.25 for nonmembers (hardcover); $64.25 for members (hardcover) ● Annual Reports.

Horses

8524 ■ Equine Guided Education Association (EGEA)
PO Box 337
Valley Ford, CA 94972
Ph: (707)876-1908
Fax: (707)876-1908
E-mail: info@equineguidededucation.org
URL: http://www.equineguidededucation.org
Contact: Ariana Strozzi, Co-Founder
Membership Dues: general, $75 (annual) ● associate, $500 (annual) ● Seabiscuit Circle, $1,250 (annual) ● Spirit Horse Circle, $5,000 (annual). **Description:** Seeks to create a unified discourse involving the interaction of the horse as a respected "guide" in human growth, learning and development. Encourages collaboration and sharing of knowledge among equine-guided education professionals. Increase awareness of the educational opportunities for the incorporation of the horse's natural wisdom and healing presence into various areas of human development and learning. **Publications:** Newsletter. **Price:** included in membership dues.

Hotel Management

8525 ■ International Council on Hotel, Restaurant, and Institutional Education (CHRIE)
2810 N Parham Rd., Ste.230
Richmond, VA 23294
Ph: (804)346-4800
Fax: (804)346-5009
E-mail: kmccarty@chrie.org
URL: http://www.chrie.org
Contact: Kathy McCarty, CEO
Founded: 1946. **Members:** 1,500. **Membership Dues:** educator, $195 (annual) ● institution, $355-$555 (annual) ● corporation/organization/association, $555 (annual) ● premium, $1,000 (annual). **Staff:** 9. **Budget:** $1,000,000. **Regional Groups:** 20. **State Groups:** 9. **Description:** Schools and colleges offering specialized education and training in hospitals, recreation, tourism and hotel, restaurant, and institutional administration; individuals, executives, and students. Provides networking opportunities and professional development. **Awards: Type:** recognition. **Computer Services:** Mailing lists, of members. **Committees:** Awards; Liaison Activities; Nominating; Paper Review; Projects and Research; Strategic Planning; Two-Year Accreditation and Approval. **Sections:** Computer Users; Continuing Education; Convention Management; Culinary Arts; Food Services Management; Graduate Programs; Historically and Predominantly Black Colleges and Universities; Hospitality Financial Management Educators; Hospitality Recruiters; Human Resources Planning and Development; International Exchanges; Internships; Multi-Cultural Management; Professional Development; Quality and Ethics; Travel and Tourism. **Formerly:** In Council on Hotel, Restaurant and Institutional Education; (1959) National Council on Hotel and Restaurant Education. **Publications:** *CHRIE Communique*, monthly. Newsletter. **Advertising:** accepted ● *Guide to Hospitality Education*, semiannual ● *Hosteur Magazine*, biennial ● *The Journal of Hospitality and Tourism Education*, quarterly ● *The Journal of Hospitality and Tourism Research*, 3/year ● *Membership Directory and Research Guide*, annual. **Conventions/Meetings:** annual international conference (exhibits).

Humanistic Education

8526 ■ Association of Waldorf Schools of North America (AWSNA)
337 Oak Grove St.
Minneapolis, MN 55403
Ph: (612)870-8310
Fax: (612)870-8316
E-mail: awsna@awsna.org
URL: http://www.awsna.org
Contact: Frances Kane, Contact
Founded: 1964. **Members:** 143. **Membership Dues:** initiative, $200. **Staff:** 9. **Budget:** $750,000. **Regional Groups:** 3. **Multinational. Description:** Waldorf Schools (also known as Steiner Schools) in Canada, the United States, and Mexico. Promotes the educational ideals of Austrian social philosopher Rudolf Steiner (1861-1925), which address the "full and harmonious development of the child's spiritual, emotional, and physical capacities, so that he may act in life as a self-disciplined and morally responsible human being". Supports and encourages the establishment of Waldorf Schools; offers consulting services to assist established Waldorf Schools. Serves as an information clearinghouse. Publishes books relevant in assisting teacher and schools. **Telecommunication Services:** electronic mail, fkane@awsna.org. **Committees:** Development; Economic; Legal; Multicultural; Public Schools; Publications; Teacher Education. **Publications:** *INFORM*, biennial. Newsletter. Reports on schools and current issues. ● *News Bulletin*, bimonthly. Journal. Distributed to schools for inclusion in local newsletters. ● *Renewal: A Journal for Waldorf Education*, semiannual. Contains articles on many aspects of child development and Waldorf education. **Price:** $21.00 outside U.S.; $12.00 in U.S. **Advertising:** accepted. **Conventions/Meetings:** periodic conference.

8527 ■ Counseling Association for Humanistic Education and Development (C-AHEAD)
c/o American Counseling Association
PO Box 791006
Baltimore, MD 21279-1006
Ph: (703)823-9800
Free: (800)347-6647
Fax: (800)473-2329
E-mail: lleech@gw.mp.sc.edu
URL: http://www.c-ahead.com
Founded: 1951. **Members:** 364. **Membership Dues:** regular, $45 (annual) ● student, new professional, retired, $25 (annual). **Description:** A division of the American Counseling Association (see separate entry). Teachers, educational administrators, community agency workers, counselors, school social workers, and psychologists; others interested in the area of human development. Aims to assist individuals in improving their quality of life. Provides forum for the exchange of information about humanistically-oriented administrative and instructional practices. Supports humanistic practices and research on instructional and organizational methods for facilitating humanistic education; encourages cooperation among related professional groups. **Formerly:** (1974) Student Personnel Association for Teacher Education; (2000) Association for Humanistic Education and Development. **Publications:** *Infochange*, quarterly. Newsletter ● *Journal of Humanistic Counseling, Education and Development*, semiannual. Includes research reports. **Price:** free for members; $42.00 /year for nonmembers (individual); $50.00 /year for nonmembers (institution). ISSN: 0735-6846. **Circulation:** 1,446. **Advertising:** accepted. **Conventions/Meetings:** annual convention, in conjunction with the American Counseling Association (exhibits).

8528 ■ Institute for Humanist Studies (IHS)
48 Howard St.
Albany, NY 12207-1608
Ph: (518)432-7820

Fax: (518)432-7821
E-mail: info@humaniststudies.org
URL: http://humaniststudies.org
Contact: Mr. Matt Cherry, Exec. Dir.
Founded: 1999. **Staff:** 6. **Multinational. Description:** Works to educate the public about humanist beliefs, organizations, and resources. Lobbies New York State Legislature on issues of importance to humanists: i.e. reproductive rights, science education and research, separation of religion and government. Offers free online courses in humanism. Publishes a free weekly ezine and a free monthly podcast with humanist news and views. **Libraries: Type:** by appointment only. **Holdings:** 6,000; articles, audio recordings, books, films, periodicals, video recordings. **Subjects:** humanism, philosophy, atheism, science, government. **Awards:** Institute for Humanist Studies Grant Fund. **Frequency:** annual. **Type:** grant. **Recipient:** to humanist projects. **Computer Services:** Electronic publishing. **Programs:** Continuum of Humanist Education; Humanist Network News Ezine and Podcast. **Projects:** Humanist Internet. **Affiliated With:** International Humanist and Ethical Union. **Publications:** *Humanist Network News*, weekly. Magazine. Contains news, opinion, advice column, and cartoons about humanism. Alternate Formats: online. Also Cited As: *HNN.*

8529 ■ Threefold Educational Foundation and School
260 Hungry Hollow Rd.
Spring Valley, NY 10977
Ph: (845)352-5020
Fax: (845)352-5071
E-mail: info@threefold.org
URL: http://threefold.org
Founded: 1965. **Description:** Supports Waldorf education and anthroposophy, the philosophy of Rudolf Steiner (1861-1925). **Conventions/Meetings:** periodic conference.

Humanities

8530 ■ Community College Humanities Association (CCHA)
c/o Prof. David Berry, Exec. Dir.
Essex County Coll.
303 Univ. Ave.
Newark, NJ 07102
Ph: (973)877-3577
Fax: (973)877-3578
E-mail: dberry@ccha-assoc.org
URL: http://www.ccha-assoc.org
Contact: Prof. David Berry, Exec. Dir.
Founded: 1979. **Members:** 1,200. **Membership Dues:** individual, $40 (annual) ● part-time, $15 (annual) ● institution (based on number of students), $300-$500 (annual). **Staff:** 1. **Budget:** $60,000. **Regional Groups:** 5. **Description:** Faculty and administrators from two-year colleges who promote the teaching of humanities. Conducts national and regional conferences and summer teaching institutes. Offers consulting services. Compiles statistics; operates speakers' bureau. **Awards:** Distinguished Humanities Educator Awards. **Frequency:** annual. **Type:** recognition ● **Type:** recognition. **Computer Services:** Mailing lists, of members. **Committees:** Research and Development; Status and Future. **Affiliated With:** American Association of Community Colleges; American Council of Learned Societies; American Historical Association; National Humanities Alliance; Organization of American Historians. **Publications:** *The Community College Humanist*, 3/year. Newsletter ● *Community College Humanities Review*, annual. Journal ● Proceedings ● Also publishes course syllabi and course modules. **Conventions/Meetings:** competition, literary ● biennial conference ● seminar ● Summer Institutes - meeting.

8531 ■ National Association for Humanities Education (NAHE)
c/o Prof. Fred Thompson, Treas.
Peninsula College
1502 E Lauridsen Blvd.
Port Angeles, WA 98362
E-mail: fredt@pcadmin.ctc.edu
URL: http://www.nahe.org
Contact: Dr. Marcia Green DMA, Exec. Dir.
Founded: 1967. **Members:** 400. **Membership Dues:** individual, $80 (biennial) ● full time student, retired, $40 (biennial) ● joint (two persons, one domicile), $120 (biennial). **Description:** Teachers, educational administrators, museum directors, librarians, independent scholars, and others interested in promoting the cause of interdisciplinary humanities education in K-12, community and junior colleges, universities, museums, libraries and the community. Offers consulting services for institutions, which are planning or revising interdisciplinary humanities programs. Provides forums and conferences; assists in structuring, implementing, and evaluating programs; conducts research. **Awards:** The Darrell Bourque Scholarship Fund for Graduate Student Travel. **Frequency:** biennial. **Type:** scholarship. **Recipient:** for graduate students to attend NAHE conferences ● The NAHE Award. **Frequency:** biennial. **Type:** recognition. **Recipient:** for outstanding contributions to interdisciplinary humanities. **Affiliated With:** Southern Humanities Council. **Publications:** *Interdisciplinary Humanities*, semiannual. Journal. Includes accounts of interdisciplinary programs and courses, book reviews, and scholarly articles on instructional models. **Price:** included in membership dues; $100.00 /year for libraries. ISSN: 1056-6139. **Circulation:** 400. **Advertising:** accepted. Also Cited As: *IH.* **Conventions/Meetings:** biennial conference, interdisciplinary scholarly papers; workshops; panel discussions; poetry readings; fiction readings; music performance (exhibits).

8532 ■ National Humanities Institute (NHI)
PO Box 1387
Bowie, MD 20718-1387
Ph: (301)464-4277
Fax: (301)464-4277
E-mail: mail@nhinet.org
URL: http://www.nhinet.org
Contact: Joseph Baldacchino, Pres.
Founded: 1984. **Staff:** 3. **Budget:** $200,000. **Description:** Promotes and supports the academic study of the humanities. Seeks to educate students about the practical and aesthetic value of humanities study. Provides a forum for discussion of the state of humanities education in the U.S. Organizes internship programs in the U.S. for students from Sweden. **Projects:** Irving Babbitt. **Publications:** *Economics and the Moral Order.* Book. **Price:** $6.00 plus $2 shipping and handling ● *Educating for Virtue.* Book. **Price:** $7.00 ● *Humanitas*, semiannual. Journal. **Price:** $14.00 for individuals; $28.00 for institutions. ISSN: 1066-7210. **Circulation:** 1,500 ● *Literature and the American College.* Book. **Price:** $12.00 plus $2 shipping and handling ● *National Humanities Bulletin*, semiannual. Newsletter ● *The New Jacobinism.* Book.

Hungarian

8533 ■ American Hungarian Educators' Association (AHEA)
c/o Eniko Molnar Basa, Exec. Dir.
4515 Willard Ave., No. 2210
Chevy Chase, MD 20815-3685
Ph: (301)657-4757
Fax: (301)657-4764
E-mail: eniko.basa@verizon.net
URL: http://hungaria.org/hal/ahea
Contact: Eniko Molnar Basa, Exec. Dir.
Founded: 1974. **Members:** 250. **Membership Dues:** individual, $15 (annual) ● couple/joint, $20 (annual) ● retired, student, $10 (annual). **Budget:** $1,000. **National Groups:** 2. **Languages:** English, Hungarian. **Description:** Educators, translators, and librarians who are of Hungarian origin, teach Hungarian or related subjects, or conduct research on Hungarian topics. Seeks to further the study of Hungarian cultural activities by encouraging the inclusion of folk arts, language, literature, folklore, and cultural history instruction in curricula; to facilitate organization of groups and identification of methods to work within members' respective professional organizations; to provide for discussion of common problems; to promote and participate in cooperative scholarly ventures. Provides resources including speakers' bureau and costume and artifact museum of folklore. Produces position papers and supportive research on an ad hoc basis to answer needs and queries; identifies scholars in the field. Conducts research in ethnic history. **Awards: Frequency:** annual. **Type:** grant. **Recipient:** for Hungarian studies. **Computer Services:** database, membership ● mailing lists. **Affiliated With:** American Hungarian Folklore Centrum. **Publications:** *American Hungarian Educators' Association—Directory*, periodic. Features a list of members and their interests. **Price:** included in membership dues ● *The Educator*, 3/year. Newsletter. Covers Hungarian and Hungarian-American studies, ethnic studies, international exchanges, and news of the association. **Price:** included in membership dues; $15.00 /year for nonmembers. ISSN: 0163-0040. **Circulation:** 300 ● Brochure, annual. **Conventions/Meetings:** annual conference (exhibits).

Independent Schools

8534 ■ American Association of Presidents of Independent Colleges and Universities (AAPICU)
Box 7070
Provo, UT 84602
Ph: (801)422-5625 (801)422-5624
Fax: (801)422-0617
E-mail: john_stohlton@byu.edu
Contact: John B. Stohlton, Exec. Dir.
Founded: 1968. **Members:** 180. **Membership Dues:** regular, $200 (annual). **Budget:** $50,000. **Description:** Presidents of independent colleges. Seeks to provide an opportunity for the exchange of views and comparison of experiences. Examines common problems and seek solutions to them. Takes formal action on matters of special concern to independent college presidents. Consults with government agencies about subjects such as Title IX, tax reform, veteran education, and the needs and interests of independent colleges. Files amicus briefs on behalf of member presidents or their institutions threatened by the federal government or one of its agencies. **Committees:** Governmental Relations. **Formerly:** (1969) American Association of Independent College and University Presidents. **Publications:** *The Presidents' Newsletter*, quarterly. Contains columns by executive officers and articles submitted by members. **Price:** free for members. **Conventions/Meetings:** annual conference - always third weekend of February, in Phoenix, AZ.

8535 ■ Council of Independent Colleges (CIC)
1 Dupont Cir., Ste.320
Washington, DC 20036-1142
Ph: (202)466-7230
Fax: (202)466-7238
E-mail: cic@cic.nche.edu
URL: http://www.cic.edu
Contact: Richard H. Ekman, Pres.
Founded: 1956. **Members:** 550. **Membership Dues:** international, associate, $900 (annual) ● affiliate, $295 (annual) ● retired President subscriber, $25 (annual) ● institution (based on full-time equivalent enrollment), $2,277-$7,387 (annual). **Staff:** 21. **Budget:** $3,000,000. **Description:** Independent, 4-year liberal arts colleges and universities. Conducts programs and projects on curriculum development, management practices, student development, and related subjects. Consortium for the Advancement of Private Higher Education (CAPHE) operating unit conducts competitive grants programs for private colleges. **Awards:** Heuer Science Awards. **Frequency:** annual. **Type:** recognition. **Recipient:** to colleges and universities for outstanding achievement in undergraduate science education ● **Frequency:** annual. **Type:** recognition. **Recipient:** for outstanding

service to independent colleges. **Computer Services:** Mailing lists, of members. **Programs:** Engaging Communities and Campuses; Teaching Scholar Partnerships; Tuition Exchange. **Projects:** Survey of Historic Architecture and Design on the Independent College and University Campus. **Absorbed:** (1998) Consortium for the Advancement of Private Higher Education. **Formerly:** (1981) Council for the Advancement of Small Colleges. **Publications:** *A Good Place to Work*. Book. Sourcebook for the Academic Workplace. ● *Building Bridges: Meeting Institutional Needs by Collaboration through Interinstitutional Exchanges*. Monograph. Features needs by collaboration through Interinstitutional Exchanges. **Price:** $7.00 ● *Independent*, quarterly. Newsletter. **Price:** included in membership dues. Alternate Formats: online. **Conventions/Meetings:** annual National Institute for Independent College and University Chief Academic Officers - meeting ● annual President's Institute - conference, for college and university presidents.

8536 ■ Council for Spiritual and Ethical Education (CSEE)
PO Box 19807
Portland, OR 97280
Ph: (706)354-4043
Free: (800)298-4599
Fax: (678)623-5634
E-mail: info@csee.org
URL: http://csee.org
Contact: David Streight, Exec. Dir.

Founded: 1898. **Members:** 400. **Membership Dues:** century, $2,000 (annual) ● school, international, $410 (annual) ● school enrollment under 100, $260 (annual) ● school enrollment 101-1,000, $535-$1,320 (annual) ● school enrollment over 1,000, $1,375 (annual). **Staff:** 5. **Budget:** $620,000. **Regional Groups:** 2. **Description:** Assists independent schools in the spiritual and moral aspects of their programs; acts as professional organization for chaplains and teachers of religion and ethics. Promotes school-based community service. Conducts workshops and conferences for administrators, faculty and staff, and parents and students. **Awards:** National Community Service Network. **Frequency:** annual. **Type:** recognition. **Recipient:** for community service. **Telecommunication Services:** electronic mail, ds@csee.org. **Also Known As:** The Council for Religion. **Formerly:** (1998) Council for Religion in Independent Schools. **Publications:** *CSEE Connections*, 9/year. Newsletter. **Price:** included in membership dues; $25.00 /year for nonmembers. ISSN: 1063-0864. **Circulation:** 1,500. **Advertising:** accepted ● Also publishes curricular materials, syllabi, and over 60 publications in course outlines for the Bible, ethics, values, literature, community service, and world religions. **Conventions/Meetings:** conference, attended by the chaplains, faculty, trustees, and heads of member schools (exhibits).

8537 ■ Foundation for Independent Higher Education (FIHE)
1920 N St. NW, Ste.210
Washington, DC 20036
Ph: (202)367-0333
Fax: (202)367-0334
E-mail: info@fihe.org
URL: http://www.fihe.org
Contact: Dr. William E. Hamm, Pres.

Founded: 1958. **Members:** 36. **Staff:** 3. **Budget:** $700,000. **Description:** National partner in a network of member state and regional fund raising associations; secures financial resources in support of U.S. independent colleges and universities and their students; develops collaborative programs within the network and with other organizations works as primary voice of independent higher education to corporate and philanthropic communities. **Awards:** Distinguished Donor Awards Program. **Type:** recognition. **Recipient:** to corporations for providing volunteer leadership and financial support ● Distinguished Performance Awards Program. **Type:** recognition. **Recipient:** for fundraising efforts of member associations ● GM Liberal Arts Excellence Awards Program. **Type:** grant. **Recipient:** for outstanding liberal arts students intending to pursue careers in business and industry. **Telecommunication Services:** electronic mail, bhamm@fihe.org. **Projects:** Cost Containment in Administrative and Business Centers; Enhancing Pedagogy Through Technology; Professional Development; Research; Student Volunteerism; Technology Resources; Training Tomorrow's Teachers; Undergraduate Research and Enrichment. **Formerly:** Independent College Funds of America. **Publications:** *Directory: Associations of Independent Colleges and Universities*, annual ● Annual Report, annual. **Conventions/Meetings:** annual meeting - always March or April.

8538 ■ Independent Schools Association of the Central States (ISACS)
1165 N Clark St., Ste.311
Chicago, IL 60610
Ph: (312)255-1244
Fax: (312)255-1278
E-mail: rbelding@isacs.org
URL: http://www.isacs.org
Contact: Rick Belding, Pres.

Founded: 1909. **Members:** 221. **Membership Dues:** corporate sponsor, $500 (annual). **Staff:** 5. **Description:** Independent schools including, but not limited to, private prep, special education, boarding, religiously affiliated, and day schools. Strives to foster good relations and communication among member schools and between schools and governmental or public education agencies; promotes the interests and positive public image of independent schools; works to ensure that member schools are serving the public interest; assists member schools in preserving freedoms that enable them to practice their educational philosophies. Maintains and reviews an evaluation/accreditation program (schools are evaluated every seven years). Provides access to other independent school associations and organizations. Monitors relevant federal, state, and regional legislation, regulations, and judicial activity. Maintains speakers' bureau; compiles statistics; sponsors seminars and workshops. **Computer Services:** database. **Affiliated With:** The College Board; Council for American Private Education; National Association of Independent Schools; North Central Association Commission on Accreditation and School Improvement. **Publications:** *Accreditation Guide*. Features a comprehensive description of ISACS Accreditation Program, 7-year cycle, including a full appendix of forms. **Price:** $18.00 for members; $25.00 for nonmembers. Alternate Formats: online ● Membership Directory, annual. Alternate Formats: online. **Conventions/Meetings:** annual Heads of School Conference - always winter. 2008 Nov. 6-7, St. Paul, MN ● annual Leaders and Learners - meeting - always June ● annual Leadership Forum - meeting (exhibits) - always November.

8539 ■ National Association of Independent Colleges and Universities (NAICU)
1025 Connecticut Ave. NW, Ste.700
Washington, DC 20036
Ph: (202)785-8866
Fax: (202)835-0003
E-mail: geninfo@naicu.edu
URL: http://www.naicu.edu
Contact: Dr. David L. Warren, Pres.

Founded: 1976. **Members:** 1,000. **Staff:** 22. **Budget:** $4,600,000. **State Groups:** 39. **National Groups:** 30. **Description:** Independent (private) colleges and universities throughout the United States; 29 national and 38 state associations of such colleges. Serves as a unified voice for independent higher education, by initiating and influencing public policies that will foster the optimum opportunities for higher education to serve the education needs of society; to promote public policies that will assure all students the widest range of choices of institutions and programs that best meet their educational needs; to defend institutional integrity, freedom, and diversity, and work to minimize governmental intrusion into higher education; to support fiscal and tax policies that provide maximum encouragement for charitable giving to independent colleges and universities; to increase public awareness and understanding of the contributions made by independent higher education in meeting public needs through teaching, research, and community service; to coordinate efforts with member institutions and state associations to promote positive actions toward independent higher education at the state and local levels of government; to gather data and provide analysis of public policy issues that concerns the independent sector. **Awards:** Henry Paley Memorial Award. **Frequency:** annual. **Type:** recognition. **Recipient:** for an individual who embodies the spirit of unfailing service toward the students and faculty of independent higher education ● NAICU Award for Advocacy of Independent Higher Education. **Frequency:** annual. **Type:** recognition. **Recipient:** for individuals outside the academe who have championed the cause of independent higher education. **Committees:** Accountability; Policy Analysis and Public Relations; Student Aid; Tax Policy. **Absorbed:** (1995) National Institute of Independent Colleges and Universities. **Formerly:** (1971) Federation of State Associations of Independent Colleges and Universities; (1976) National Council of Independent Colleges and Universities. **Publications:** *Independent Colleges and Universities: A National Profile*, triennial. Booklet. Serves as a case-stating publication for private higher education. ● *Twelve Facts That May Surprise You About America's Private Colleges and Universities*, biennial. Booklet. Includes statistical data on private colleges and universities in the U.S. Alternate Formats: online ● *The Week in Review*, weekly. Newsletter. Covers actions in the legislative, executive, and judicial branches of government that may affect independent institutions. **Price:** included in membership dues. **Circulation:** 1,100. **Conventions/Meetings:** annual conference (exhibits) - always in Washington, DC.

8540 ■ National Association of Independent Schools (NAIS)
1620 L St. NW, Ste.1100
Washington, DC 20036-5695
Ph: (202)973-9700 (202)973-9710
Free: (800)793-6701
Fax: (202)973-9790
E-mail: info@nais.org
URL: http://www.nais.org
Contact: Patrick Bassett, Pres.

Founded: 1962. **Members:** 1,200. **Membership Dues:** full, provisional (per student), $11 (annual). **Staff:** 38. **Budget:** $10,000,000. **Description:** Independent elementary and secondary school members; regional associations of independent schools and related associations. Provides curricular and administrative research and services. Conducts educational programs; compiles statistics. **Libraries: Type:** reference. **Commissions:** Accreditation. **Committees:** Equity and Justice; Governance; Member Services; Public Policy/Government Relations. **Subgroups:** School and Student Service for Financial Aid. **Task Forces:** Global; Strategy and Design. **Formed by Merger of:** Independent Schools Education Board; National Council of Independent Schools. **Publications:** *Audio-Visual Marketing Handbook for Independent Schools*. Includes information on videos and slide tapes as tools of admission and school marketing. **Price:** $12.00 for members; $16.00 for nonmembers ● *Business Management for Independent Schools*. Manual. Includes uniform accounting procedures, understandable financial reporting, managerial uses of accounting data, budgeting and cash management. **Price:** $35.00 for members; $50.00 for nonmembers ● *The Difference It Makes: A Resource Book on Gender for Educators*. Includes information on how schools can establish curricular and noncurricular methods of gender equity. **Price:** $15.00 for members; $20.00 for nonmembers ● *Independent School*, 3/year. Magazine. **Price:** $25.00 for members in U.S.; $35.00 for members outside U.S.; $45.00 for nonmembers outside U.S. ● *Middle School Handbook*. Includes middle school issues and curriculum. **Price:** $15.00 for members; $20.00 for nonmembers ● *The Next Marketing Handbook for Independent Schools*. Features 18 independent school marketing specialists' comments on public relations, morality in enrollment marketing, and multicultural marketing. **Price:** $18.00 for members; $22.00 for nonmembers ● *Paths to New Curriculum*.

Handbook. Offers a model process for evaluation and review of curriculum. **Price:** $15.00 for members; $20.00 for nonmembers ● *Philanthropy at Independent Schools.* Handbook. **Conventions/Meetings:** annual conference (exhibits) - always late February/ March.

Indian

8541 ■ American Institute of Indian Studies (AIIS)
1130 E 59th St.
Chicago, IL 60637
Ph: (773)702-8638
Fax: (773)702-6636
E-mail: aiis@uchicago.edu
URL: http://www.indiastudies.org
Contact: Elise Auerbach, Contact
Founded: 1961. **Members:** 52. **Description:** Universities and colleges supporting South Asian studies in the U.S. Promotes research by American scholars in India. Grants faculty research and dissertation fellowships. Conducts language-training program in India. **Awards:** Fellowships for Senior Scholarly/Professional Development. **Type:** fellowship. **Recipient:** for established scholars who have not previously specialized in Indian studies, and for established professionals who have not previously worked or studied in India ● Junior Research Fellowships. **Type:** fellowship. **Recipient:** for graduate students from all academic disciplines whose dissertation research requires study in India ● Senior Performing Arts Fellowships. **Type:** fellowship. **Recipient:** for accomplished practitioners of the performing arts of India who have demonstrated that studying in India will enhance their skills and develop their capabilities to teach or perform in the US ● Senior Research Fellowship. **Type:** fellowship. **Recipient:** for academic specialists in Indian studies who have possessed a PhD or equivalent. **Committees:** Art and Archaeology; Ethnomusicology; Language; Selection. **Conventions/Meetings:** annual board meeting.

Industrial Education

8542 ■ Association for Skilled and Technical Sciences (ASTS)
c/o Don Eshelby, Exec. Dir.
1931 Mortimer Ct.
Boise, ID 83712
Ph: (703)777-1740
E-mail: asts@mindspring.com
URL: http://www.astsonline.org
Contact: Don Eshelby, Exec. Dir.
Founded: 1974. **Membership Dues:** regular, $25 (annual). **Description:** Educators in trade and industrial education. Works for the promotion, development, and improvement of trade and industrial education. Provides leadership in developing support for greater identity in federal legislation. Supports instructional programs for members to prepare for job entry level and supplementary instruction, apprentice training, adult retraining, and special training for industry. **Awards:** E.M. Smith Memorial Award. **Frequency:** annual. **Type:** recognition. **Affiliated With:** National Association of Industrial and Technical Teacher Educators. **Formed by Merger of:** (2006) National Association for Trade and Industrial Education and National Association of State Supervisors for Trade and Industrial Education. **Publications:** *Improving Vocational Curriculum* ● *NATIE News Notes*, quarterly. Newsletter. Includes book reviews, calendar of events, research updates, and statistics. **Price:** included in membership dues. **Circulation:** 1,500 ● *National Standards for Program Administration* ● *Philosophy and Standards of Excellence* ● *State Supervisors/Consultants of Trade and Industrial Education*, semiannual. Directory ● *Supervision and Implementations* ● *Trade and Industrial Education.* **Conventions/Meetings:** annual meeting, held in conjunction with American Vocational Association and Vocational Industrial Clubs of America ● biennial National Trade and Industrial Ed Conference.

8543 ■ Council on Technology Teacher Education (CTTE)
c/o International Technology Education Association
1914 Assn. Dr.
Reston, VA 20191
Ph: (703)860-2100
E-mail: rseymour@bsu.edu
URL: http://www.teched.vt.edu/ctte
Contact: Dr. Richard Seymour, Pres.
Founded: 1950. **Members:** 560. **Membership Dues:** regular, $40 (annual) ● full-time student, $20 (annual). **Staff:** 5. **Budget:** $20,000. **Multinational. Description:** A division of the International Technology Education Association (see separate entry). College faculty members and other individuals engaged in technology teacher education. Conducts research. **Libraries: Type:** open to the public. **Holdings:** 52. **Subjects:** teacher education. **Awards:** Stimulating Research Award. **Frequency:** annual. **Type:** grant. **Recipient:** for members ● Technology Educator of the Year Award. **Frequency:** annual. **Type:** recognition. **Computer Services:** Mailing lists, of members. **Committees:** Accreditation; College Clubs; Graduate Studies; Plant and Facilities; Professional Development; Publication; Research; Undergraduate Studies; Yearbook Planning. **Affiliated With:** International Technology Education Association. **Formerly:** (1986) American Council on Industrial Arts Teacher Education. **Publications:** *CTTE Newsletter*, semiannual. Contains events and council news. **Price:** $25.00 ● Yearbook, annual ● Also publishes monograph series, standards, and guidelines. **Conventions/Meetings:** annual conference (exhibits).

8544 ■ National Association of Industrial and Technical Teacher Educators (NAITTE)
c/o Danny C. Brown, Pres.
Illinois State Univ.
210E Turner Hall
Campus Box 5100
Normal, IL 61790-5100
Ph: (309)438-2695 (309)438-5874
Fax: (309)438-8626
E-mail: dcbrown@ilstu.edu
URL: http://www.coe.uga.edu/naitte
Contact: Danny C. Brown, Pres.
Founded: 1937. **Members:** 250. **Membership Dues:** regular, $50 (annual) ● regular (international), $60 (annual) ● student, $15 (annual) ● institution, $150 (annual). **Description:** Professional society of teacher educators in technology education, industrial and military training, vocational trade, and industrial and technical education; officials of state industrial education departments and local school industrial educators whose duties include teacher improvement. Promotes professional programs to help teachers and trainers prepare for supervisory and administrative positions; and fosters research on teaching, supervision, and quality of instruction in industrial education. **Committees:** Auditing; Awards; Nominating; Research. **Sections:** Industrial and Military; Technical; Technology Education; Trade and Industrial. **Affiliated With:** Association for Career and Technical Education. **Formerly:** National Association of Industrial Teacher Trainers; (1969) National Association of Industrial Teacher Educators. **Publications:** *Industrial Teacher Education Directory*, annual. **Price:** included in membership dues. Alternate Formats: online ● *Journal of Industrial Teacher Education*, quarterly. Covers industrial and technical teacher education, military training, and industrial training. Includes book reviews and research reports. **Price:** included in membership dues; $50.00 /year for nonmembers in U.S. and Canada; $55.00 /year for nonmembers outside U.S. and Canada; $55.00 /year for libraries in U.S. and Canada. **Circulation:** 270 ● *National Association of Industrial and Technical Teacher Educators—News and Views*, quarterly. Newsletter. **Price:** included in membership dues. **Circulation:** 270 ● *Task Force Reports*, periodic. **Conventions/Meetings:** annual conference, in conjunction with Association for Cancer and Technical Education (exhibits).

8545 ■ National Association of Industrial Technology (NAIT)
3300 Washtenaw Ave., Ste.220
Ann Arbor, MI 48104
Ph: (734)677-0720
Fax: (734)677-0046
E-mail: nait@nait.org
URL: http://www.nait.org
Contact: Mr. Rick Coscarelli, Exec. Dir.
Founded: 1967. **Members:** 1,900. **Membership Dues:** student, retired, $20 (annual) ● professional, $80 (annual) ● organizational, $240 (annual) ● international, $100 (annual). **Staff:** 2. **Budget:** $270,000. **Local Groups:** 15. **Description:** Industrial technology organizations, administrators, industrialists, educators, students, and graduates of industrial technology programs. Provides opportunities for collecting, developing, and disseminating information concerning industrial technology. Promotes research related to the curricula of industrial technology. Acts as an accrediting agency for baccalaureate and associate level industrial technology programs. Provides certification for industrial technologies. **Awards:** Outstanding Industrial Technologists. **Frequency:** annual. **Type:** recognition. **Recipient:** for individuals with exemplary leadership and application of industrial technology practice ● Outstanding Industrial Technology Professor Award. **Frequency:** annual. **Type:** recognition. **Recipient:** to individuals having primary responsibilities in industrial technology programs. **Computer Services:** database, membership ● mailing lists, available to members for professional purposes. **Telecommunication Services:** electronic mail, rcoscarelli@nait.org. **Boards:** Accreditation; Certification. **Committees:** Standards and Accreditation. **Divisions:** Community College and Technical Institute; Electronics, Electricity, and Computer Technology; Graphic Communications; Industry; Manufacturing Systems; Research; Safety; Student; University. **Publications:** *Accreditation Handbook*, triennial. Contains standards and procedures for accreditation. **Price:** free for members; $5.00 for nonmembers ● *Baccalaureate Program Directory*, annual. Contains institution, program and faculty listings of baccalaureate level industrial technology programs. **Price:** $6.00. **Advertising:** accepted ● *Convention Proceedings and Selected Papers*, annual. Contains abstracts of presentations from the Convention and complete text of the 48 selected papers. **Price:** $5.00. Alternate Formats: CD-ROM ● *Convention Program*, annual. **Circulation:** 600. **Advertising:** accepted ● *History of the Baccalaureate Degree in Industrial Technology in the United States* ● *IT Insider*, 3/year. Newsletter. Features industrial technology programs. **Circulation:** 4,000. **Advertising:** accepted ● *Journal of Industrial Technology*, quarterly, always January, April, July and October. Contains articles, research and literature reviews of existing literature. **Price:** free. **Advertising:** accepted. Alternate Formats: online. **Conventions/Meetings:** annual convention (exhibits) - 2008 Nov. 19-22, Nashville, TN; 2009 Nov. 11-14, Louisville, KY.

8546 ■ SkillsUSA
PO Box 3000
Leesburg, VA 20177-0300
Ph: (703)777-8810
Free: (800)321-8422
Fax: (703)777-8999
E-mail: anyinfo@skillsusa.org
URL: http://www.skillsusa.org
Contact: Timothy W. Lawrence, Exec. Dir.
Founded: 1965. **Members:** 264,500. **Membership Dues:** student (high school and college/postsecondary), $8 (annual) ● professional (advisor, partner), $14 (annual). **Staff:** 26. **Budget:** $3,000,000. **State Groups:** 54. **Local Groups:** 13,000. **Description:** Represents the interests of students, teachers and industry. Works to ensure that America has a skilled work force. Provides education experiences for students in leadership, teamwork, citizenship and character development. Builds and reinforces self-confidence, work attitudes and communications skills. Emphasizes total quality at work, high ethical standards, superior work skills, life-long education and pride in the dignity of work. Promotes understanding of the free enterprise system and involvement in community service activities. **Awards:** SkillsUSA Championships. **Frequency:** annual. **Type:** medal. **Recipient:** for the best career and technical students.

Formerly: (1999) Vocational Industrial Clubs of America. **Publications:** *SkillsUSA Champions*, quarterly, during the school year. Magazine. **Price:** $1.30 for members; $15.00 for nonmembers. ISSN: 1040-4538. **Circulation:** 280,000. **Advertising:** accepted ● Also publishes curriculum material, DVDs and posters. **Conventions/Meetings:** annual National and Leadership and Skills Conference, with seminars; attendees include students, business and industry, teachers, educators, staff and general public (exhibits) - 2008 June 23-27, Kansas City, MO ● annual SkillsUSA Championships - competition, a showcase for the best career and technical students in the nation (exhibits).

8547 ■ Technology Student Association (TSA)
1914 Assn. Dr.
Reston, VA 20191-1540
Ph: (703)860-9000
Fax: (703)758-4852
E-mail: general@tsaweb.org
URL: http://www.tsaweb.org
Contact: Mary Jo Patterson, Leadership Services Mgr.

Founded: 1978. **Members:** 200,000. **Membership Dues:** student, $9 (annual) ● chapter affiliation (plus applicable state and local dues), $350 (annual). **Staff:** 10. **Budget:** $1,000,000. **Regional Groups:** 5. **State Groups:** 45. **Local Groups:** 2,000. **Description:** Middle and high school students who are presently enrolled in or have completed technology education courses. Goals are to assist students in making informed occupational choices through experiences in technology programs and to help prepare them for entry into technology-related careers. Provides opportunities for students to meet and work with leaders from industry to gain career information and to adapt learning experiences from other instructional areas. Promotes high standards of technological literacy, leadership, and scholarship in technology education. Offers leadership training for local, state, and national officers. Sponsors Technology Honor Society, projects, and competitions. **Awards:** TSA Technology Honor Society. **Frequency:** annual. **Type:** recognition. **Recipient:** for middle school and high school student member ● William P. Elrod Memorial Scholarship. **Frequency:** annual. **Type:** scholarship. **Recipient:** for a high school senior or student enrolled in an undergraduate program with outstanding service in technology. **Computer Services:** Mailing lists, of members. **Committees:** Community Liaison; Competitive Events; National Service Project; Professional; Public Relations; Publications Review; Social; Special Projects. **Formerly:** (1988) American Industrial Arts Student Association. **Publications:** *Chapter Program Kit* ● *Curricular Resources Guide* ● *School Scene*, quarterly. Newsletter. **Price:** included in membership dues. **Advertising:** accepted ● *TSA Directory* ● Booklets. **Conventions/Meetings:** annual conference (exhibits) - always June. 2008 June 28-July 2, Orlando, FL.

Instructional Media

8548 ■ ACUTA: The Association for Communications Technology Professionals in Higher Education (ACUTA)
152 W Zandale Dr., Ste.200
Lexington, KY 40503
Ph: (859)278-3338
Fax: (859)278-3268
E-mail: jsemer@acuta.org
URL: http://www.acuta.org
Contact: Jeri A. Semer CAE, Exec. Dir.

Founded: 1971. **Members:** 1,200. **Staff:** 9. **Budget:** $2,000,000. **Multinational. Description:** University and college administrators of telecommunications and IT services; persons involved in the educational technologies industry. Works to improve the professional competence of college and university technology administrators. Assists colleges and universities in solving technological problems through members' experience. Alerts the technology industry to the varied and special needs of institutions of higher learning. **Libraries: Type:** reference. **Holdings:** books, monographs, periodicals. **Subjects:** communications technology. **Awards:** Institutional Excellence in Communications Technology. **Frequency:** 3/year. **Type:** trophy. **Recipient:** to an institution for institutional excellence, innovation, exemplary program or project in communications technology ● Ruth A. Michalecki Leadership Award. **Frequency:** annual. **Type:** recognition. **Computer Services:** Mailing lists, of members only. **Telecommunication Services:** electronic bulletin board ● information service. **Special Interest Groups:** Voice Over IP Community of Interest. **Formerly:** ACUTA: The Association of College and University Telecommunications Administrators Inc.; (2003) ACUTA: The Association for Telecommunication Professionals in Higher Education. **Publications:** *ACUTA Membership Directory*, annual. **Price:** free for members. **Advertising:** accepted ● *ACUTA News*, monthly. Newsletter. Covers telecommunications and teleconferencing activities at member institutions. **Price:** $45.00 /year for institutions. Alternate Formats: online ● *Journal of Communications Technology in Higher Education*, quarterly. **Price:** $80.00 /year for nonmembers; $20.00/issue for nonmembers; free for members. **Circulation:** 2,500. **Advertising:** accepted. Alternate Formats: online ● Monographs. **Conventions/Meetings:** Audio Seminars, with sponsorship opportunities - 4-6/year ● annual conference (exhibits) - always in July ● seminar, features two educational tracks on technical or management topics in telecom/communications technology, exhibits, networking events (exhibits) - always January, April, October in various locations.

8549 ■ Agency for Instructional Technology (AIT)
Box A
1800 N Stonelake Dr.
Bloomington, IN 47402-0120
Ph: (812)339-2203
Free: (800)457-4509
Fax: (812)333-4218
E-mail: info@ait.net
URL: http://www.ait.net
Contact: Charles E. Wilson, Exec. Dir.

Founded: 1970. **Staff:** 25. **Budget:** $5,000,000. **Description:** Works to develop, acquire and distribute technology-based resources. Currently offers 160 learning products containing 2,000 titles. Programming includes video, DVD, CD-Rom, software, print, and Internet resources; programs address preschool through adult learners. In addition to traditional curricular areas, products cover career development, early childhood, guidance/mental health, vocational education, and professional development. Licenses collections of digital content and have recently launched The Learning Source, a collection of online streamed video. **Computer Services:** Online services, forums for teacher communication. **Formerly:** (1984) Agency for Instructional Television. **Supersedes:** National Instructional Television Library. **Publications:** Catalog, annual. Available through audiovisual or electronic transmission. Alternate Formats: online ● Reports ● Also publishes teacher's guides. **Conventions/Meetings:** periodic workshop, teacher training activities.

8550 ■ Association of American University Presses (AAUP)
71 W 23rd St., Ste.901
New York, NY 10010-4102
Ph: (212)989-1010
Fax: (212)989-0275
E-mail: info@aaupnet.org
URL: http://www.aaupnet.org
Contact: Peter J. Givler, Exec. Dir.

Founded: 1937. **Members:** 129. **Staff:** 10. **Regional Groups:** 4. **Multinational. Description:** Helps university presses do their work more economically, creatively, and effectively through its own activities in education-training, fundraising and development, statistical research and analysis, and community and institutional relations. **Awards:** Constituency Award. **Frequency:** annual. **Type:** recognition. **Recipient:** for individual who has made an outstanding contribution to the scholarly publishing community. **Computer Services:** Bibliographic search ● database, data collection and analysis ● mailing lists ● online services, job list. **Telecommunication Services:** electronic mail, spatton@aaupnet.org. **Committees:** Admissions and Standards; Annual Meeting; Business Handbook; Business Systems; Copyright; Design and Production; Diversity; Electronic; International; Marketing; Nominating; Professional Development; Scholarly Journals. **Task Forces:** Environmental; Training. **Publications:** *AAUP Book, Jacket, and Journal Show Catalog*, annual. **Price:** $10.00. ISSN: 1064-5470 ● *AAUP Directory*, annual. Includes information on university presses and scholarly publishing. **Price:** $19.00 ● *Advertising and Publicity Resources for Scholarly Books*, biennial. Booklets ● *Exchange*, quarterly. Newsletter ● *University Press Books Selected for Public and Secondary School Libraries*, annual. Booklets. **Price:** free. ISSN: 1055-4173 ● *What is a University Press?*. Brochure. **Conventions/Meetings:** annual meeting (exhibits) - 2008 June 26-29, Montreal, QC, Canada; 2009 June 18-21, Philadelphia, PA ● quarterly regional meeting.

8551 ■ Association for Educational Communications and Technology (AECT)
1800 N Stonelake Dr., Ste.2
Bloomington, IN 47404
Ph: (812)335-7675
Free: (877)677-AECT
Fax: (812)335-7678
E-mail: aect@aect.org
URL: http://www.aect.org
Contact: Dr. Phillip Harris, Exec. Dir.

Founded: 1923. **Members:** 5,000. **Membership Dues:** regular, in U.S., $99 (annual) ● corporate, $400 (annual) ● individual, $95 (annual) ● student, in U.S., $50 (annual). **Staff:** 3. **Budget:** $1,500,000. **Regional Groups:** 9. **State Groups:** 49. **Description:** Instructional technology professionals. Provides leadership in educational communications and technology by linking professionals holding a common interest in the use of educational technology and its application of the learning process. **Libraries: Type:** not open to the public. **Subjects:** technology, education. **Awards:** AECT Annual Achievement Award. **Frequency:** annual. **Type:** recognition. **Recipient:** for the individual who has done the most in the past year to advance the field ● AECT Distinguished Service Award. **Frequency:** annual. **Type:** recognition. **Recipient:** for outstanding leadership in advancing the theory or practice of educational communications and technology ● AECT/SIRS Intellectual Freedom Award. **Frequency:** annual. **Type:** recognition ● AECT Special Service Award. **Frequency:** annual. **Type:** recognition. **Recipient:** for notable service to AECT as a whole or to one of its programs or divisions. **Computer Services:** Mailing lists. **Committees:** Accreditation; Affiliate Relations; Awards; Certification; Conference Evaluation; Continuing Education; Copyright; Curriculum; Definition and Terminology; Distance Education Standards; Electronic Services; Evaluation of Instructional Materials; Evaluation of Media Programs; Governmental Relations; History and Archives; Human Capital Campaign; Intellectual Freedom; Leadership Development; Post-Secondary Guidelines; Program Evaluation and Consultation. **Divisions:** Design & Development; Distance Learning; Educational Media Management; Industrial Training and Education; Instructional Development; Interactive Systems and Computers; International; Learning and Performance Environments; Media Design and Production; Research and Theory; School Media Specialists; Systemic Change in Education; Telecommunications; Trading & Performance. **Affiliated With:** International Visual Literacy Association. **Formerly:** (1932) National Academy of Visual Instruction; (1947) Department of Visual Instruction; (1970) Department of Audiovisual Instruction. **Publications:** *Association for Educational Communications and Technology—Membership Directory*, annual. Lists of those involved in communications media for instruction. **Price:** included in membership dues; $40.00 /year for nonmembers. **Advertising:** accepted. Alternate Formats: CD-ROM ● *Educational Technology Re-*

search and Development, quarterly. Journal. **Price:** $35.00 /year for members in U.S.; $75.00 /year for nonmembers in U.S.; $60.00 /year for members outside U.S.; $100.00 /year for nonmembers outside U.S. ● *Handbook of Research for Educational Communications and Technology*. **Price:** $115.00 plus shipping and handling. Alternate Formats: online ● *TechTrends*, bimonthly. Magazine. Focuses on how developments in new technology affect the way professionals in schools, colleges, and universities perform their jobs. **Price:** included in membership dues; $30.00 /year for nonmembers. **Advertising:** accepted. **Conventions/Meetings:** annual convention (exhibits).

8552 ■ Center for Teaching About China (CTAC)
c/o Kathleen Trescott
1214 W Schwartz St.
Carbondale, IL 62901
Ph: (618)549-1555
Fax: (618)549-9766
E-mail: ctac@uscpfa.org
URL: http://www.uscpfa.org/ctac.html
Contact: Kathleen Trescott, Contact
Founded: 1977. **Members:** 3,000. **Membership Dues:** individual, $25 (annual) ● family, $40 (annual). **Staff:** 4. **Budget:** $1,500. **Regional Groups:** 4. **Local Groups:** 45. **Languages:** Chinese, English. **Description:** Serves as a part of the educational outreach of US-China Peoples Friendship Association; a national clearinghouse for instructional materials on China. Keeps abreast of and evaluates new classroom materials. Supplies display material for and participates in local, regional, and national educational conferences. Sponsors a tour program enabling teachers to visit the People's Republic of China. Provides children's services; operates Speaker's Bureau. Services global education and multicultural educational programs. **Libraries: Type:** reference. **Holdings:** 2,000; artwork, audiovisuals, books, periodicals. **Subjects:** China. **Awards:** Koji Aryoshi Award. **Frequency:** biennial. **Type:** recognition. **Recipient:** for contribution to U.S.-China friendship ● Volunteer Award. **Frequency:** biennial. **Type:** recognition. **Recipient:** for outstanding work for USCPFA. **Boards:** Volunteers. **Affiliated With:** U.S.-China Peoples Friendship Association. **Also Known As:** (2005) US-China Peoples Friendship Association. **Publications:** *China in the Classroom*, annual. Catalog. **Price:** free. **Circulation:** 2,000. **Advertising:** accepted. Alternate Formats: online ● Pamphlets. Contains study series on different subject areas concerning China. **Conventions/Meetings:** biennial seminar and convention (exhibits) - always odd-numbered years.

8553 ■ Computer Assisted Language Instruction Consortium (CALICO)
Texas State Univ.
214 Centennial Hall
601 Univ. Dr.
San Marcos, TX 78666
Ph: (512)245-1417 (512)245-2360
Fax: (512)245-9089
E-mail: info@calico.org
URL: http://calico.org
Contact: Esther Horn, Mgr.
Founded: 1983. **Members:** 900. **Membership Dues:** individual, $65 (annual) ● individual, $125 (biennial) ● individual, $185 (triennial) ● K-12/community college, $50 (annual) ● K-12/community college, $95 (biennial) ● K-12/community college, $140 (triennial) ● senior, student, $40 (annual) ● senior, $75 (biennial) ● senior, $110 (triennial) ● institutional, $105 (annual) ● institutional, $190 (biennial) ● institutional, $275 (triennial) ● corporate, $155 (annual) ● corporate, $290 (biennial) ● corporate, $425 (triennial). **Staff:** 1. **Multinational. Description:** Individuals, corporations, and institutions from the academic, business, research, manufacturing, and government sectors. Seeks to apply primarily computer-related technology to the teaching, learning, and processing of first and second languages. Acts as clearinghouse; facilitates and coordinates information sharing. Conducts software fairs, workshops, and annual conferences on the application of computer-assisted language instruction. **Libraries: Type:** reference. **Holdings:** 20; business records, monographs, periodicals. **Subjects:** educational technology, computer-assisted language learning. **Awards:** Sony Outstanding Article. **Frequency:** annual. **Type:** monetary ● Tandberg Outstanding Graduate Student. **Frequency:** annual. **Type:** monetary. **Computer Services:** database, membership ● mailing lists. **Special Interest Groups:** Computer Mediated Communications; Courseware Development; Foreign Character Fonts/Asian Languages; InSTIL; Intelligent Computer Assisted Language Instruction; Language Acquisition and Technology. **Subgroups:** Editorial Board; Executive Board. **Formerly:** (1998) Computer Assisted Language, Learning and Instruction Consortium. **Publications:** *CALICO Journal*, 3/year. **Price:** included in membership dues; $45.00 /year for nonmembers in U.S.; $45.00 /year for nonmembers in Canada and Mexico; $60.00 /year for nonmembers overseas. ISSN: 0742-7778. **Advertising:** accepted. Alternate Formats: online; CD-ROM; diskette ● *CALICO Monograph Series*. Monographs. Written by professionals; provides in-depth coverage of specific areas of planning and using language learning centers, authoring software, etc. ● *CALICO Resource Guide*. Contains listings of resources, tools, consultants, and graduate programs for language teachers, learners, and those who use educational technologies. Alternate Formats: online. **Conventions/Meetings:** annual conference and symposium (exhibits).

8554 ■ Consortium of College and University Media Centers (CCUMC)
Iowa State Univ.
1200 Communications Bldg.
Ames, IA 50011-3243
Ph: (515)294-1811
Fax: (515)294-8089
E-mail: ccumc@ccumc.org
URL: http://www.ccumc.org
Contact: Jon P. McKamey, Pres.
Founded: 1971. **Members:** 750. **Membership Dues:** student, $55 (annual) ● associate, $325 (annual) ● institutional/corporate (based on number of persons), $325-$795 (annual). **Staff:** 2. **Budget:** $245,000. **Multinational. Description:** University and college media centers; producers and distributors of video programs. Assists in making educational media more accessible, promotes their widespread and most effective use, and recommends optimal standards of service and distribution. Fosters cooperative planning among universities, institutions, agencies, foundations, and organizations in the solving of mutual problems, gathers and disseminates information on improved procedures and new developments, and reports statistics in common terminology. Reduces waste of resources and duplication of effort through open sharing and cooperative exchange among members, develops and provides programs that have real economic benefit for the membership and inspires, generates, and coordinates research and scholarship that may further these purposes and objectives. **Awards:** Research Grant. **Frequency:** annual. **Type:** grant. **Recipient:** for research that increases the accessibility to and utilization of educational media, equipment or technology. **Computer Services:** Mailing lists. **Telecommunication Services:** electronic mail, jon.mckamey@cincinnatistate.edu. **Boards:** Publications Advisory. **Committees:** Awards; Corporate Member; Elections; Executive Office Management; Government Regulations and Public Policy; Program; Research. **Formerly:** (1988) Consortium of University Film Centers. **Publications:** *College and University Media Review*, semiannual, published in fall and spring. Journal. Includes articles that focus on media and technology, related research and instructional development. **Price:** $75.00 /year for nonmembers; $30.00/back issue for nonmembers; included in membership dues. ISSN: 1075-8496. **Circulation:** 850. Alternate Formats: online ● *Leader*, 3/year, published in January, May and September. Newsletter. Reports news, information and events of the Consortium. Alternate Formats: online ● Proceedings, annual. **Price:** included in membership dues ● Annual Report, annual. Provides an organizational profile. ● Membership Directory, annual. **Price:** included in membership dues. **Conventions/Meetings:** annual conference.

8555 ■ Consortium for School Networking (COSN)
1025 Vermont Ave. NW, Ste.1010
Washington, DC 20005
Ph: (202)861-2676
Free: (866)267-8747
Fax: (202)393-2011
E-mail: info@cosn.org
URL: http://www.cosn.org
Contact: Katie Lovett, Chair
Founded: 1992. **Members:** 800. **Membership Dues:** corporate, $3,500 (annual) ● institutional (non-profit organization/association/intermediate service unit), $850 (annual) ● individual, $125 (annual) ● institutional (medium school district), $750 (annual) ● institutional (small school district), $250 (annual) ● institutional (college and university), $500 (annual) ● individual school, $150 (annual) ● institutional (state department of education/state network), $1,500 (annual) ● institutional (large district), $1,000 (annual). **Staff:** 3. **Budget:** $500,000. **For-Profit. Description:** Promotes the use of telecommunications in K-12 classrooms to improve learning. Members represent state and local education agencies, non-profits, companies and individuals who share the organization's vision. **Awards:** Outstanding Achievement Awards. **Frequency:** annual. **Type:** recognition. **Publications:** *A Guide to Handheld Computing in K-12 Schools*. Report. **Price:** $19.95 for members; $24.95 for nonmembers ● *CoSN Compendium*. Monographs. **Price:** free for members ● *TechLearning News*, bimonthly. Newsletter ● *Washington Update*, monthly. **Conventions/Meetings:** annual conference (exhibits).

8556 ■ Education, Training and Research Associates (ETR)
4 Carbonero Way
Scotts Valley, CA 95066-4200
Ph: (831)438-4060
Free: (800)321-4407
Fax: (831)461-9534
E-mail: customerservice@etr.org
URL: http://www.etr.org
Contact: Dr. Robert Keet MD, Pres.
Founded: 1981. **Members:** 5,000. **Staff:** 95. **Description:** Provides family life and sexuality education materials and training programs to school districts, health organizations, and youth-serving agencies. Administers California Tobacco Education Clearinghouse. Conducts surveys and research. **Libraries: Type:** reference. **Subjects:** AIDS, sex education, tobacco. **Divisions:** Publishing; Research and Development; Training. **Programs:** AIDS Education Training; Family Life Education Training. **Publications:** *Family Life Educator*, quarterly. Journal. Reports on news in the field. Includes reviews of books, curricula, media, teaching tools, and journal abstracts. **Price:** $45.00 /year for individuals; $55.00 /year for institutions. ISSN: 0732-9962. **Circulation:** 5,000 ● Books ● Catalog ● Films ● Pamphlets ● Videos.

8557 ■ Education Turnkey Institute (ETI)
256 N Washington St.
Falls Church, VA 22046
Ph: (703)536-2310
Fax: (703)536-3225
E-mail: cblaschke@edturnkey.com
URL: http://edturnkey.com
Contact: Charles Blaschke, Pres.
Founded: 1979. **Staff:** 3. **For-Profit. Description:** Provides technology monitoring service for software publishers, vendors, and state agencies. Conducts market and development research for state and federal agencies on emerging niche markets, adult literacy, at-risk youth, and early childhood. Offers a variety of technology workshops for administrators and teachers who are interested in using computers, in the local educational setting. Offers monthly technology monitoring information service. **Formerly:**

Education Turnkey Systems; (1988) Micro Computer Education Application Network.

8558 ■ EDUCAUSE
4772 Walnut St., Ste.206
Boulder, CO 80301-2538
Ph: (303)449-4430 (303)939-0318
Fax: (303)440-0461
E-mail: info@educause.edu
URL: http://www.educause.edu
Contact: Brian L. Hawkins, Pres./CEO
Founded: 1964. **Members:** 600. **Membership Dues:** corporate, $2,000 (annual) ● association/non-profit/state and federal agency/system office, $1,145 (annual) ● international, $980 (annual). **Staff:** 11. **Budget:** $4,000,000. **Description:** Colleges, universities, and non-profit educational service organizations. Promotes resource sharing among colleges and universities in the application of computing, communications, and information technology in higher education. Conducts research projects; provides a forum for discussion of issues; represents the interests of higher education in the development and application of communications technology. Recent research has focused on computer literacy, computer-intensive environments, national and international computer networking for higher education, telecommunications, computer networks, software contracting, use, development, and distribution, and the use of computer-based models for financial planning. Holds seminars, workshops, and institutes. **Awards:** Leadership Award. **Frequency:** annual. **Type:** recognition. **Recipient:** for prominent leaders that have significant achievements and broad influence to the society. **Telecommunication Services:** electronic mail, bhawkins@educause.edu. **Task Forces:** National Learning Infrastructure Initiative; Networking and Telecommunications. **Formerly:** College and University Systems Exchange. **Publications:** *EDUCOM Review*, bimonthly. Reports on educational software and networking issues, book reviews, members computing projects. **Price:** included in membership dues; $18.00 /year for nonmembers. ISSN: 0424-6268. **Circulation:** 14,000. **Advertising:** accepted ● *Research Report*, periodic. **Conventions/Meetings:** annual conference (exhibits) - 2008 Oct. 28-31, Orlando, FL; 2009 Oct. 3-6, Denver, CO.

8559 ■ EPIE Institute
PO Box 590
Hampton Bays, NY 11946-0509
Ph: (631)728-9100
Free: (888)776-7730
Fax: (516)728-9228
E-mail: kkomoski@epie.org
URL: http://www.epie.org
Contact: P. Kenneth Komoski, Exec. Dir.
Founded: 1967. **Staff:** 8. **Description:** Aims to systematically analyze and collect user data on instructional materials, educational software, and curriculum development. Provides consultation on the selection of instructional materials, focusing on the integration of technology into curricula. **Convention/Meeting:** none. **Computer Services:** database, Curriculum Alignment Services for Educators (CASE) for aligning textbooks, software, and tests with curriculum objectives ● database, TESS software and publisher information. **Also Known As:** Educational Products Information Exchange Institute. **Publications:** *Educational Software Selector TESS*, annual. Directory. **Price:** $29.95. Alternate Formats: CD-ROM.

8560 ■ French American Cultural Exchange (FACE)
972 5th Ave.
New York, NY 10021
Ph: (212)439-1449
Fax: (212)439-1455
E-mail: info@facecouncil.org
URL: http://www.facecouncil.org
Contact: Elisabeth Hayes, Exec. Dir.
Founded: 1955. **Staff:** 3. **Budget:** $200,000. **Languages:** English, French. **Description:** Sells videotapes of French documentaries and CD-ROMs to schools, universities, libraries, museums and educational organizations. **Libraries:** **Type:** not open to the public. **Holdings:** 200; video recordings. **Subjects:** France, Europe. **Awards:** Tournees. **Frequency:** annual. **Type:** grant. **Recipient:** for institutions of higher education. **Telecommunication Services:** electronic mail, tourneesfestival@facecouncil.org. **Formerly:** (2004) Society for French American Cultural Services and Educational Aid. **Publications:** *Eclairage* (in English and French), biennial. Catalog. Contains listings of feature films, documentaries and CD-ROMs. **Circulation:** 5,000. Alternate Formats: online.

8561 ■ Health Sciences Consortium (HSC)
300 Silver Cedar Ct.
Chapel Hill, NC 27514-1696
Ph: (919)942-8731
Fax: (919)942-3689
E-mail: tony.penta@edtsi.com
URL: http://www.healthsciencesconsortium.org
Contact: Tony Penta, Publications Dir.
Founded: 1971. **Members:** 1,000. **Membership Dues:** general, $100 (annual). **Staff:** 2. **Budget:** $2,000,000. **Description:** Cooperative of health science institutions dedicated to publishing effective instructional materials at a low cost. Distributes audiovisual and computer-based instructional programs. **Libraries:** **Type:** reference. **Holdings:** 700; video recordings. **Publications:** *Consortium News*, quarterly. Newsletter. **Price:** free. **Circulation:** 6,000 ● *Medical, Nursing, Dental, Computer-Assisted Instruction, and Allied Health Catalogs*, periodic. Alternate Formats: online; CD-ROM ● Also publishes health education materials.

8562 ■ Institute for Computers in Jewish Life (ICJL)
8170 N McCormick Blvd., Ste.111
Skokie, IL 60076
Ph: (312)533-4240
Fax: (773)583-5456
E-mail: director@icjl.net
Contact: Dr. Irving J. Rosenbaum, Founder
Founded: 1981. **Staff:** 6. **Description:** Researches, develops, and disseminates applications of computer technology to appropriate areas in Jewish life, especially Jewish education. Works to create microcomputer software for classroom and individual use by students; provides consultative services for Jewish educators on preparing and using computers in education and school administration; conducts seminars and training sessions on computer use. Creates a database covering major areas of Jewish scholarship worldwide; conducts searches and prepares summaries and translations; and provides consulting services and assistance in software development for national Jewish organizations, Jewish seminaries, and synagogues.

8563 ■ Institute for the Transfer of Technology to Education (ITTE)
c/o National School Boards Association
1680 Duke St.
Alexandria, VA 22314
Ph: (703)838-6722
Fax: (703)683-7590
E-mail: info@nsba.org
URL: http://www.nsba.org/site/page.asp?TRACKID=&CID=63&DID=195
Contact: Ms. Ann Flynn, Education Technology Dir.
Founded: 1985. **Members:** 360. **Membership Dues:** institutional (public school district and private school), $1,500 (annual). **Staff:** 4. **Budget:** $400,000. **Description:** A program of the National School Boards Association. Seeks to educate policymakers, administrators, educators, manufacturers, and the public about the current status and future potential of technology in schools with the goal of creating a more effective education system. Maintains the Technology Leadership Network, which helps school districts and education service centers share experiences and aggregate their influence in dealing with technology developers. Offers online courses and produces special reports. **Awards:** Technology Leadership Network Salute. **Frequency:** annual. **Type:** recognition. **Recipient:** to K-12 school districts for their effective use of technology across all aspects of district operations. **Publications:** *Leadership and Technology: What School Board Members Need to Know* ● *Plans and Policies for Technology in Education: A Compendium* ● Has published Technology and Schools: Creating Spaces for Learning; Investing in School Technology: Strategies to Meet the Funding Challenge; and Technology for Students with Disabilities: A Decision Makers Guide. **Conventions/Meetings:** annual Technology and Learning - conference, designed for K-12 education leaders to learn about effective implementation across all aspects of district operations (exhibits).

8564 ■ Instructional Systems Association (ISA)
12427 Hedges Run Dr., No. 120
Lake Ridge, VA 22192
Ph: (703)730-2838
Free: (877)533-4914
Fax: (703)730-2857
E-mail: info@isaconnection.org
URL: http://www.isaconnection.org
Contact: Ms. Pamela J. Schmidt, Exec. Dir.
Founded: 1978. **Members:** 150. **Membership Dues:** firm, $6,500 (annual). **Staff:** 4. **Budget:** $500,000. **Description:** Organizations and firms engaged in the design and distribution of instructional systems in the field of human resources and training. Seeks to: enhance the development and success of member firms and improve members' capability to serve clients; expand the influence of the instructional systems industry. Conducts education programs; compiles statistics. **Libraries:** **Type:** reference. **Publications:** *Intercom*, 3/year. Newsletter ● *Newswire*, monthly. Newsletter. Provides timely marketplace information and spotlights trends, member profiles and more. Alternate Formats: online. **Conventions/Meetings:** annual conference and meeting - always March.

8565 ■ Instructional Technology Council (ITC)
1 Dupont Cir. NW, Ste.360
Washington, DC 20036-1143
Ph: (202)293-3110
Fax: (202)822-5014
E-mail: cmullins@itcnetwork.org
URL: http://www.itcnetwork.org
Contact: Christine Mullins, Exec. Dir.
Founded: 1977. **Members:** 600. **Membership Dues:** institution, $450 (annual) ● corporate, $750 (annual). **Staff:** 2. **Budget:** $300,000. **Regional Groups:** 6. **Multinational. Description:** Community colleges or other postsecondary institutions making extensive use of telecommunications and other technologies for independent and distance learning; commercial publishers of video-based instructional materials. Strives to monitor legislative activity and disseminate information concerning technology-enhanced instruction. Encourages collaboration among institutions regarding project development and telecommunications-based curriculum planning. Represents members' interests in seeking to influence policies affecting instructional telecommunication use. Sponsors activities in faculty development and regional professional workshops focusing on the use of telecommunications media. Conducts research; compiles statistics. **Awards:** ITC Award. **Frequency:** annual. **Type:** recognition. **Recipient:** for excellence in Distance Education. **Computer Services:** Mailing lists, of members. **Affiliated With:** American Association of Community Colleges. **Formerly:** Instructional Telecommunications Consortium; (1980) Task Force on Using Mass Media; (2002) Instructional Telecommunications Council. **Publications:** *Faculty Compensation and Support Issues in Distance Education*. Report. Provides benchmarks for comparing institutional compensation and support practices. **Price:** $15.00 for members; $25.00 for nonmembers ● *ITC News*, monthly. Newsletter. **Circulation:** 1,000. **Advertising:** accepted ● *New Connections: A Guide to Distance Education, Second Edition*. Report. Contains discussion on copyright, assessment and compatibility issues with practical advice on new and emergent technologies. **Price:** $25.00 for members; $35.00 for nonmembers ● *Qual-*

ity Enhancing Practices in Distance Education: Student Services. Report. Contains comprehensive orientation, new student assessment and online library services. **Price:** $20.00 each ● *Quality Enhancing Practices in Distance Education: Teaching and Learning.* Report. Contains the use of quality standards. **Price:** $20.00 for members; $30.00 for nonmembers ● Monographs. **Conventions/Meetings:** annual Telelearning - conference (exhibits) - usually spring.

8566 ■ International University Consortium (IUC)
Univ. of Maryland Univ. Coll.
3501 Univ. Blvd. E
Adelphi, MD 20783
Ph: (301)985-7826
Fax: (301)985-7496
E-mail: iuc-info@nova.umuc.edu
URL: http://www.umuc.edu/ide/potentialweb97/sponsors.html
Contact: Dr. Eugene Rubin, Exec. Dir.
Founded: 1980. **Members:** 42. **Staff:** 8. **Description:** Colleges and universities. Distributes and develops television, audio, and other technology-assisted courses that are designed for long-distance adult education and other curricular uses by member institutions. Offers selected courses in the humanities, behavioral and social sciences, management and technology, and general science and mathematics to nonmembers. Offers upper division course materials in addition to general education courses. **Formerly:** (1983) National University Consortium for Telecommunications in Teaching; (1998) International University Consortium for Telecommunications in Learning. **Publications:** *Newsource*, quarterly. Newsletter ● Also makes available courses. **Conventions/Meetings:** annual conference - always spring.

8567 ■ Manpower Education Institute (MEI)
715 Ladd Rd.
Bronx, NY 10471-1203
Ph: (718)548-4200
Fax: (718)548-4202
E-mail: meiready@aol.com
URL: http://www.manpower-education.org
Contact: James J. McFadden, Pres.
Founded: 1966. **Staff:** 10. **Budget:** $150,000. **Description:** Individuals from the fields of business, labor, and education who develop educational film series for the U.S. labor force. Series includes: Ready or Not (pre-retirement planning), Your Future Is Now (high school equivalency programs), Read Your Way Up (reading skills improvement), Out of Work (for the unemployed), If You Don't Come In Sunday, Don't Come In Monday (history of the American labor movement), Plug Us In (to assist workers reentering the labor market), and Where Do I Fit In (new worker orientation). **Publications:** *Promote Yourself With Better Grammar.* Book. **Price:** $10.00/copy ● *Ready or Not Retirement Planning*, annual. Book. **Price:** $15.45 plus shipping and handling ● *Retirement Life*, quarterly. Newsletter. **Conventions/Meetings:** annual conference.

8568 ■ National Association of State Educational Media Professionals (NASTEMP)
c/o Frances Roscello, Pres.
Off. of New York City School and Community Services
New York State Educ. Dept., Rm. 375 EBA
89 Washington Ave.
Albany, NY 12205
Ph: (518)474-8485
Fax: (518)474-7948
E-mail: froscell@mail.nysed.gov
Contact: Frances Roscello, Pres.
Members: 110. **Description:** Educational media professionals employed by state offices of education. Focuses on how best to integrate instruction in the use of new technologies into existing curricula. Seeks to facilitate the exchange of information among members by providing automatic mailing of topical papers. **Affiliated With:** American Association of School Librarians; Association for Educational Communications and Technology. **Formed by Merger of:** (1976) State School Library Media Supervisors Association; Association of Chief State School Audiovisual Officers. **Publications:** Membership Directory, annual ● Newsletter, quarterly ● Also publishes safety bulletins. **Conventions/Meetings:** annual conference, usually in conjunction with American Library Association or American Association of School Librarians.

8569 ■ National Information Center for Educational Media (NICEM)
PO Box 8640
Albuquerque, NM 87198-8640
Ph: (505)998-0800
Free: (800)926-8328
Fax: (505)256-1080
E-mail: mhlava@nicem.com
URL: http://www.nicem.com
Contact: Marjorie Hlava, Pres.
Founded: 1966. **Staff:** 6. **Languages:** English, French, German, Spanish. **For-Profit. Description:** Catalogs and stores, in computerized form, information on audiovisual educational materials such as films, filmstrips, audio and videotapes, recordings, CD ROMs, DVDs and special educational materials which may then be disseminated to school districts, universities, and libraries. Maintains database and has produced a series of master indices describing audiovisual materials available to the educational community. **Convention/Meeting:** none. **Computer Services:** database, NICEM Audiovisual. **Programs:** Media Sleuth.

8570 ■ Playing 2 Win (PTW)
1330 5th Ave.
New York, NY 10026
Ph: (212)369-4077
Fax: (212)369-7046
E-mail: bushell@playing2win.org
URL: http://www.playing2win.org
Contact: Shawna Bu Shell, Dir.
Founded: 1980. **Members:** 550. **Membership Dues:** individual, $35 (annual) ● family, $45 (annual). **Staff:** 9. **Budget:** $650,000. **Description:** Members are participants in local Playing To Win centers. Promotes constructive and informed use of computers by minorities and societally disadvantaged persons. Establishes computer use and resource centers in low-income areas. Offers technical assistance, at minimal cost, to community-based organizations and social service agencies that seek to incorporate educational computing programs into their services. **Formerly:** (2003) Playing to Win.

8571 ■ Society for Applied Learning Technology (SALT)
50 Culpeper St.
Warrenton, VA 20186
Ph: (540)347-0055
Fax: (540)349-3169
E-mail: info@salt.org
URL: http://www.salt.org
Contact: Raymond G. Fox, Pres.
Founded: 1972. **Members:** 300. **Membership Dues:** regular, $55 (annual). **Description:** Senior executives from military, academic, and industrial organizations which design, manufacture, or use training technology, including computer assisted instruction, simulators, trainers, audio-visual instruction delivery devices, and job performance aids. Objectives are to contribute to the development of the highest standards and practices in the application of technology to training; to assist individuals, agencies, and institutions in applying training technology to the definition and solution of social problems; to facilitate the exchange of information and experience; to promote understanding and knowledge in actual and potential uses of technology in the field of training; to provide an effective educational channel among scientists, managers, and users of training technology in the private and public sectors in order to assure adequate skills, understanding, and effective management of training technology. Maintains special interest groups. **Awards: Type:** recognition. **Recipient:** for outstanding contributions to the society. **Computer Services:** Online services, glossary search utility. **Publications:** *Conference Proceedings*, annual ● *Journal of Educational Technology Systems*, quarterly. Contains information that deals with the use of computers as an integral component of education systems. **Price:** $60.00 /year for members ● *Journal of Instruction Delivery Systems*, quarterly. Contains issues, problems, and applications of instructional delivery systems in education, training and job performance. **Price:** $30.00 /year for members; $45.00 /year for nonmembers. **Circulation:** 500. Alternate Formats: online ● *Journal of Interactive Instruction Development*, quarterly. Contains information on design and development of interactive instruction delivery systems. **Price:** $30.00 /year for members; $45.00 /year for nonmembers. **Circulation:** 600. Alternate Formats: online ● Newsletter, quarterly. Alternate Formats: online. **Conventions/Meetings:** annual Conference on New Learning Technologies (exhibits) ● annual Education Technology - conference (exhibits) ● seminar.

8572 ■ University and College Designers Association (UCDA)
199 W Enon Spring Rd., Ste.300
Smyrna, TN 37167
Ph: (615)459-4559
Fax: (615)459-5229
E-mail: info@ucda.com
URL: http://www.ucda.com
Contact: Tadson Bussey, Exec. Dir.
Founded: 1971. **Members:** 1,000. **Membership Dues:** full/educator, $150 (annual) ● affiliate, $200 (annual) ● student, $50 (annual) ● retired, $65 (annual). **Staff:** 3. **Budget:** $350,000. **Multinational. Description:** Represents colleges, universities, junior colleges, or technical institutions that have an interest in visual communication design; individuals who are involved in the active production of such communication design or as teachers or students of these related disciplines. Improves members' skills and techniques in communication and design areas such as graphics, photography, signage, films, and other related fields of communication design. Aids and assists members in their efforts to be professionals in their respective fields through programs of education and information. Maintains placement service. **Awards:** UCDA Design Competition Award. **Frequency:** annual. **Type:** recognition. **Computer Services:** Mailing lists, listserv. **Telecommunication Services:** electronic mail, tadson@ucda.com. **Boards:** Designer; Regional Coordinators; Visual Creativity Workshop. **Committees:** Competition; Conference; Education; Nominations. **Publications:** *Designer*, quarterly. Magazine. **Price:** $75.00 /year for nonmembers; included in membership dues. **Advertising:** accepted ● *The Home Page Newsletter*, monthly ● *UCDA Membership Directory*, annual. **Conventions/Meetings:** annual conference and workshop ● annual conference (exhibits) ● workshop.

8573 ■ Vocational Instructional Materials Section (VIM)
c/o Dr. Dana Tannehill, Dir.
Univ. of Missouri
Instructional Materials Lab.
1400 Rock Quarry Center
Columbia, MO 65211
Ph: (573)882-2883 (573)882-9613
Free: (800)669-2465
Fax: (573)882-1992
E-mail: iml@missouri.edu
URL: http://iml.missouri.edu
Contact: Dr. Dana Tannehill, Dir.
Founded: 1969. **Members:** 85. **Description:** Persons engaged in or interested in the preparation and dissemination of vocational instructional materials. Aims to: facilitate the development of high quality instructional materials; identify and solve problems within the area of materials development; stimulate the interchange of information. Conducts seminars. **Awards:** Outstanding Instructional Materials Award. **Type:** recognition ● Outstanding Member Award. **Type:** recognition ● Outstanding Retiring Member Award. **Type:** recognition. **Committees:** Awards; Competencies for Curriculum Specifications; Legislation. **Affiliated With:** Association for Career and

Technical Education. **Publications:** Newsletter, semiannual. **Conventions/Meetings:** annual meeting.

Insurance

8574 ■ American Risk and Insurance Association (ARIA)

716 Providence Rd.
Malvern, PA 19355-3402
Ph: (610)640-1997
Fax: (610)725-1007
E-mail: aria@cpcuiia.org
URL: http://www.aria.org
Contact: Anthony Biacchi, Exec. Dir.

Founded: 1932. **Members:** 500. **Membership Dues:** professional in U.S., $127 (annual) ● professional in Europe, $153 (annual) ● professional in rest of the world, 102 (annual) ● student/retired in U.S., 53 (annual) ● student/retired in Europe, 56 (annual) ● student/retired in rest of the world, 37 (annual) ● student/retired in U.S. (online only), $27 (annual) ● student/retired in Europe (online only), 27 (annual) ● student/retired in rest of the world (online only), 18 (annual). **Staff:** 2. **Description:** Comprises of insurance educators and others interested in risk management and insurance education and research. **Libraries: Type:** reference. **Awards:** Casualty Actuarial Society Research Award. **Frequency:** annual. **Type:** recognition ● Hedges Scholarship Award. **Frequency:** annual. **Type:** scholarship. **Recipient:** for undergraduate student in insurance and/or risk management to attend the annual meeting ● Kulp-Wright Book Award. **Frequency:** annual. **Type:** recognition. **Recipient:** for book on insurance and/or risk management ● Les B. Strickler Innovation in Instruction Award. **Frequency:** annual. **Type:** recognition. **Recipient:** for outstanding instruction in the field of risk management and insurance ● Presidents' Award. **Frequency:** annual. **Type:** recognition. **Recipient:** for individual's commitment and dedicated service to ARIA ● RMIR Feature Article Award. **Frequency:** annual. **Type:** recognition. **Recipient:** for best feature article in risk management and insurance review ● RMIR Perspectives Article Award. **Frequency:** annual. **Type:** recognition. **Recipient:** for best perspective article in risk management and insurance review ● Robert C. Witt Award. **Frequency:** annual. **Type:** recognition. **Recipient:** for outstanding feature article in Journal of Risk and Insurance ● Robert I. Mehr Award. **Frequency:** annual. **Type:** recognition. **Recipient:** for literature contribution having a ten-year impact in the field of risk and insurance management. **Formerly:** (1960) American Association of University Teachers of Insurance. **Publications:** *Journal of Risk and Insurance*, quarterly. Includes title and author index, book reviews, and quinquennial membership directory. **Price:** $267.00 /year for institutions in U.S.; 206.00 /year for institutions in Europe; $206.00 /year for institutions in other countries. ISSN: 0022-4367. **Circulation:** 1,900. **Advertising:** accepted. Alternate Formats: online ● *Risk Management and Insurance Review*, semiannual. Journal. **Price:** $114.00 /year for institutions (premium online only); $132.00 /year for institutions (print & premium online); $120.00 /year for institutions (print & standard online). Alternate Formats: online. **Conventions/Meetings:** annual meeting.

8575 ■ Insurance Education Foundation (IEF)

3601 Vincennes Rd.
Indianapolis, IN 46268
Ph: (317)876-6046
Free: (800)433-4811
Fax: (317)879-8408
E-mail: info@theiei.org
URL: http://www.ief.org
Contact: Larry L. Forrester, Pres./CEO

Founded: 1988. **Staff:** 4. **Nonmembership. Description:** Sponsors educational programs aimed at high school students and teachers. Works to promote the understanding of how insurance works. **Libraries: Type:** reference. **Holdings:** audiovisuals. **Subjects:** high school teaching materials about insurance. **Awards:** James Osborne Insurance Educator of the Year. **Frequency:** annual. **Type:** monetary. **Recipient:** for individuals who attend one of the institutes or teach insurance. **Publications:** *Choice, Chance, Control, Fast Lanes: Risky Roads*. Newsletter. Teaching kit for high school teachers including teachers guides, lesson plans, activity copymasters and a video. **Price:** $50.00 others; free for educators ● *The Insurance Educator*, semiannual, January and August. Newsletter. **Price:** free. **Circulation:** 25,000 ● Annual Report, annual. Alternate Formats: online ● Brochures. Alternate Formats: online. **Conventions/Meetings:** annual Insurance Education Institutes for High School Teachers - workshop - summer.

8576 ■ Life Underwriter Training Council (LUTC)

7625 Wisconsin Ave.
Bethesda, MD 20814
Ph: (610)526-1000
Free: (888)263-7265
E-mail: otc@theamericancollege.edu
URL: http://www.theamericancollege.edu
Contact: Laurence Barton PhD, Pres./CEO/Prof. of Management

Founded: 1947. **Members:** 29,000. **Staff:** 50. **Description:** Serves the needs of the life insurance and financial services industry nationwide. Develops products designed to meet specific industry needs. **Libraries: Type:** reference. **Holdings:** archival material, periodicals. **Subjects:** staff, board members, guest speakers, insurance industry, other related courses. **Awards:** Edmund L. Zalinski Distinguished Service Award. **Frequency:** annual. **Type:** recognition ● Ernest E. Cragg Ambassador Awards. **Frequency:** annual. **Type:** recognition ● Golden Eagle Award. **Frequency:** semiannual. **Type:** recognition. **Committees:** Agency Head Advisory; Content and Techniques; Education and Evaluation; Exam Board; Field Advisory; Future Directions; International; LUTCF Advisory; Marketing. **Departments:** Administration; Education; International; Marketing. **Affiliated With:** American Council of Life Insurers; LIMRA International; National Association of Insurance and Financial Advisors. **Publications:** *Chairmen's Topics*, periodic. Newsletter. Provides information to LUTC chairmen. **Price:** free for members. **Circulation:** 1,000 ● *Class Notes*, bimonthly. Newsletter. Provides association information of interest to students. **Price:** free for students. **Circulation:** 30,000 ● *Life Lines*, semiannual. Newsletter. Contains membership activities. **Price:** free for members. **Circulation:** 10,000 ● *LUTCF Review*, annual. Newsletter. Provides information to LUTC fellows. **Price:** free for members. **Circulation:** 50,000 ● *Professor's Page*, periodic. Newsletter. Provides information to LUTC moderators. **Price:** free for members. **Circulation:** 3,200 ● Also publishes textbooks. **Conventions/Meetings:** semiannual board meeting - always February and July ● annual Chairmen's Conferences ● semiannual Moderator's Conferences - meeting.

8577 ■ Society of Certified Insurance Counselors (CIC)

3630 N Hills Dr.
Austin, TX 78731-3028
Ph: (512)345-7932
Free: (800)633-2165
Fax: (512)349-6194
E-mail: alliance@scic.com
URL: http://www.scic.com
Contact: William T. Hold PhD, Pres.

Founded: 1969. **Members:** 51,450. **Membership Dues:** academy fellowship, $15 (annual) ● academy associate, $35 (annual). **Staff:** 102. **Description:** Holders of the Certified Insurance Counselor (CIC), Certified Insurance Service Representative (CISR), and Certified Risk Manager (CRM) designation; each are acquired through the successful completion of five courses and accompanying examinations. Licensed agents, brokers, solicitors, corporate risk managers, and members of the insurance faculty of an accredited college or university are eligible for examination and certification; to retain the CIC, CISR, or CRM designation, one must complete an annual update each year. Maintains National Insurance Education Scholarship Program, which directly or in conjunction with other associations grants scholarships covering all institute tuition. Compiles statistics. Co-founded and supports the National Alliance Research Academy, an independent research organization. **Convention/Meeting:** none. **Awards:** National Outstanding Customer Service Representative. **Frequency:** annual. **Type:** recognition ● **Type:** scholarship. **Computer Services:** database, membership, participation, continuing education. **Committees:** National Education. **Publications:** *The Academy —Preliminary Findings*, annual. Newsletter. **Price:** free to affiliates. **Circulation:** 6,000 ● *Resources*, 3/year. Magazine. **Price:** available to members only. **Circulation:** 30,000.

8578 ■ Society of Insurance Trainers and Educators (SITE)

6635 W Happy Valley Rd., Ste.A104-444
Glendale, AZ 85310
Ph: (623)547-6401
Fax: (623)547-6814
E-mail: ed@insurancetrainers.org
URL: http://www.insurancetrainers.org
Contact: Kathy Hodge AIM, Exec. Dir.

Founded: 1953. **Members:** 700. **Membership Dues:** designee, $125 (annual) ● associate, student, $95 (annual) ● retiree, $45 (annual). **Staff:** 1. **Regional Groups:** 5. **Description:** Individuals engaged in education and training within the insurance business; university teachers or others whose primary occupation is the furtherance of insurance education. **Awards:** Distinguished Graduate Award. **Frequency:** annual. **Type:** monetary. **Recipient:** to a graduate of associate management course at AICPCU/IIA ● Distinguished Student Scholarship. **Frequency:** annual. **Type:** monetary. **Recipient:** for distinguished student at Katie School of Insurance. **Formerly:** (1985) Insurance Company Education Directors Society. **Publications:** *InSite: Information for the Society of Insurance Trainers and Educators*, bimonthly. Newsletter. Includes conference schedule. **Price:** available to members only. **Circulation:** 700. **Advertising:** accepted ● *Society of Insurance Trainers and Educators—The Journal*, annual. Includes book reviews. **Price:** available to members only. **Circulation:** 700. **Conventions/Meetings:** annual conference (exhibits) - 2008 June 28-July 2, Savannah, GA; 2009 June 27-July 1, Albuquerque, NM.

8579 ■ Teachers Insurance and Annuity Association (TIAA)

730 3rd Ave.
New York, NY 10017-3206
Ph: (212)490-9000
Free: (800)842-2252
E-mail: trustees@tiaa-cref.org
URL: http://www.tiaa-cref.org
Contact: Stanley O. Ikenberry, Pres.

Founded: 1918. **Members:** 1,500,000. **Description:** Represents active and retired staff members of non-profit colleges, universities, junior colleges, independent schools, foundations, libraries, scientific and research organizations, and teaching hospitals. Aids and strengthens nonproprietary and non-profit colleges, universities, and related non-profit institutions engaged primarily in education and research by providing annuities, individual life insurance/group life, mutual funds, long-term total disabilities insurance, and long-term care insurance suited to the needs of such institutions and of their faculty and staff. **Awards:** Hesburgh Award. **Frequency:** annual. **Type:** recognition. **Recipient:** for faculty development to enhance undergraduate teaching ● Samuelson Award. **Type:** recognition. **Recipient:** for published article or book on retirement. **Affiliated With:** TIAA-CREF. **Publications:** *TIAA-CREF Annual Report*, annual. **Conventions/Meetings:** annual meeting.

8580 ■ University Risk Management and Insurance Association (URMIA)

PO Box 1027
Bloomington, IN 47402-1027
Ph: (812)855-6683

Fax: (812)856-3149
E-mail: urmia@urmia.org
URL: http://www.urmia.org
Contact: Ms. Jenny Whittington, Exec. Dir.
Founded: 1966. **Members:** 700. **Membership Dues:** individual, $250 (annual) ● affiliate, $750 (annual) ● institution (primary member), $325 (annual) ● institution (any deputy members), $50 (annual). **Staff:** 2. **Budget:** $70,000. **Description:** Represents colleges and universities that have an insurance/risk management program of any type and related commercial organizations, such as, insurance companies. Promotes the exchange of concepts and data for sound risk and insurance management. Conducts risk management projects and professional development. **Awards:** Distinguished Risk Manager Award. **Frequency:** annual. **Type:** recognition. **Formerly:** (1976) University Insurance Managers Association; (1980) University Risk and Insurance Managers Association. **Publications:** *URMIA Journal*, annual ● *URMIA Report*, bimonthly. Newsletter. **Price:** included in membership dues ● Directory, annual. **Conventions/Meetings:** annual conference - usually September or October. 2008 Sept. 10-14, Washington, DC; 2009 Sept. 12-16, Nashville, TN ● annual seminar and conference.

Intelligence

8581 ■ International Association for Intelligence Education (IAFIE)
c/o Heather Tate
PO Box 10508
Erie, PA 16514
Ph: (814)824-2131
E-mail: info@iafie.org
URL: http://www.iafie.org
Contact: Tom Shreeve, Chm.
Founded: 2004. **Membership Dues:** full, $100 (annual) ● student, $25 (annual) ● institutional, $500 (annual) ● corporate sponsor, $1,000 (annual). **Multinational. Description:** Expands research, knowledge and professional development in intelligence education. Sets standards, builds resources and shares knowledge in intelligence studies. Provides a forum for the exchange of ideas and information about intelligence education. Fosters relationships and cultivates cooperation among intelligence professionals in academia, business and government. Develops, disseminates and promotes theory, curricula, methodologies and techniques for pure and applied intelligence. **Publications:** Newsletter. **Price:** included in membership dues.

Intercultural Studies

8582 ■ National Association for Multicultural Education (NAME)
5272 River Rd., Ste.430
Bethesda, MD 20816
Ph: (301)951-0022
Fax: (301)951-0023
E-mail: name@nameorg.org
URL: http://www.nameorg.org
Contact: Joyce E. Harris, Exec. Dir.
Founded: 1990. **Membership Dues:** regular, $100 (annual) ● student, community activist, $40 (annual) ● retired, $60 (annual) ● institutional, $225 (annual) ● overseas, $65 (annual). **Staff:** 2. **Regional Groups:** 10. **State Groups:** 22. **Multinational. Description:** Promotes the understanding of unique cultural and ethnic heritage. Aims to eliminate racism and discrimination in society. Establishes a clearinghouse for multicultural education resource materials. Promotes the development of culturally responsible and responsive curricula. **Awards:** Carl A. Grant Multicultural Research Award. **Frequency:** annual. **Type:** recognition. **Recipient:** for significant research contribution to multicultural education ● G. Pritchy Smith Multicultural Educator Award. **Frequency:** annual. **Type:** recognition. **Recipient:** for outstanding contribution in the field of multicultural education. **Computer Services:** Information services, multicultural education resources ● online services, e-mail discussion group. **Committees:** Annual Conference; Awards; Planning and Finance; Publications. **Publications:** *Multicultural Perspectives*, quarterly. Journal. Features articles by multicultural educators. **Advertising:** accepted ● *NAME News*, 3/year. Newsletter. **Advertising:** accepted. **Conventions/Meetings:** annual conference.

Interdisciplinary Studies

8583 ■ Global Studies Association North America (GSA)
c/o Jerry Harris, Sec.
1250 N Wood St.
Chicago, IL 60622
E-mail: gharris234@comcast.net
URL: http://www.net4dem.org/mayglobal
Contact: Jerry Harris, Sec.
Founded: 2002. **Membership Dues:** concessionary, $20 ● senior/junior academic, $50 ● institution, $100. **Multinational. Description:** Seeks to advance the work of scholars and other individuals interested in promoting the creation and dissemination of multi and interdisciplinary knowledge in the social and human sciences concerning global affairs, problems and changes. Encourages worldwide exchanges between people working in all fields of research related to global studies. Facilitates the emergence of a worldwide federation of quasi-independent academic groupings. **Publications:** *Global Networks*. Journal. Publishes articles on global networks, transnational affairs and practices and their relation to wider theories of globalization. **Price:** $29.00 for members ● *Globalizations*. Journal. Features contributions from all regions of the world. **Price:** $29.00 for members. ISSN: 1474-7731.

Interior Design

8584 ■ Council for Interior Design Accreditation
146 Monroe Ctr. NW, Ste.1318
Grand Rapids, MI 49503-2822
Ph: (616)458-0400
Fax: (616)458-0460
E-mail: info@accredit-id.org
URL: http://www.accredit-id.org
Contact: Holly Mattson, Exec. Dir.
Founded: 1970. **Nonmembership. Description:** Formed by Interior Design Educators Council and American Society of Interior Designers (see separate entries). Administers voluntary plan for the special accreditation of interior design education programs offered at institutions of higher learning throughout the U.S. and its possessions and Canada; emphasizes the use of accreditation procedures to assure that the purposes and accomplishments of programs of interior design education meet the needs of society, students, and the interior design profession; recognized by the Council for Higher Education Accreditation as a national accrediting agency for programs in interior design in schools throughout the country. **Committees:** Accreditation; Research; Standards. **Formerly:** (2006) Foundation for Interior Design Education Research. **Publications:** *Directory of Interior Design Programs Accredited by FIDER*, semiannual. Lists professional programs in interior design; accredited programs are listed by state. **Conventions/Meetings:** board meeting - 3/year.

8585 ■ Interior Design Educators Council (IDEC)
7150 Winton Dr., Ste.300
Indianapolis, IN 46268
Ph: (317)328-4437
Fax: (317)280-8527
E-mail: info@idec.org
URL: http://www.idec.org
Contact: Jeffrey Beachum, Exec. Dir.
Founded: 1962. **Members:** 500. **Membership Dues:** professional, $280 (annual) ● associate, $220 (annual) ● retired, graduate, $60 (annual) ● educator affiliate, $125 (annual) ● industry affiliate, $250 (annual). **Budget:** $75,000. **Description:** Interior design educators at universities or schools that have at least a 2-year professional program; other interested individuals. Seeks to develop and improve interior design education and the professional level of interior design practice. Conducts research; compiles statistics. Offers placement services. Maintains Interior Design Education Foundation. **Awards:** Industry Merit Award. **Frequency:** annual. **Type:** recognition. **Recipient:** to an individual or firm with significant contribution to IDEC, interior design education and interior design ● Juried Design Competition Award. **Frequency:** annual. **Type:** recognition. **Recipient:** for design projects and creative work in either interior design or visual arts category ● Merit Award. **Frequency:** annual. **Type:** recognition. **Recipient:** for individuals with sustainable and notable contributions over and above that expected by virtue of appointment or relationship to IDEC ● Presidential Award. **Frequency:** annual. **Type:** recognition. **Recipient:** for meritorious service by an IDEC member or nonmember to the Interior Design Educators Council or interior design education ● Regional Chairs' Award. **Frequency:** annual. **Type:** recognition. **Recipient:** for quality scholarship and presentation skills at the Annual Conference ● Special Project Award. **Frequency:** annual. **Type:** grant. **Recipient:** for individual projects that relate to interior design education and the profession. **Committees:** Bibliography; Career Guidance; Competitions; Educational Innovation and Improvement; Historic Preservation; Placement and Recruitment; Research; Visual Communication. **Affiliated With:** Council for Interior Design Accreditation; International Federation of Interior Architects/Designers; National Council for Interior Design Qualification. **Publications:** *Bibliography for Interior Design* ● *Journal of Interior Design*, semiannual. Covers research, educational, historical, and critical aspects of interior design and allied fields; includes book reviews. **Price:** included in membership dues; $50.00 /year for individuals in U.S.; $80.00 /year for libraries and institutions in U.S.; $25.00/year for students in U.S. ● *RECORD*, periodic. Newsletter. Includes calendar of events, employment opportunities, news of competitions, and reading list. **Price:** $60.00 /year for individuals outside U.S.; $90.00 /year for libraries and institutions outside U.S.; $35.00/year for students outside U.S. ISSN: 0147-0418. **Circulation:** 600. Alternate Formats: online ● Also publishes national conference addresses and workshop abstracts. **Conventions/Meetings:** competition ● annual conference (exhibits).

Internal Medicine

8586 ■ Alliance for Academic Internal Medicine (AAIM)
2501 M St. NW, Ste.550
Washington, DC 20037-1325
Ph: (202)861-9351
Fax: (202)861-9731
E-mail: aaim@im.org
URL: http://www.im.org/aaim
Contact: Tod Ibrahim, Exec. VP
Description: Represents departments of internal medicine from medical schools and teaching hospitals. Aims to advance the study of internal medicine from the perspective of education. Seeks to increase effective communication among executive directors and senior staff of medical schools and teaching hospitals. **Telecommunication Services:** electronic mail, tibrahim@im.org. **Publications:** *AAIM Connection*, weekly. Newsletter. Alternate Formats: online ● *Academic Internal Medicine Insight*, quarterly. Newsletter. Addresses topics such as accreditation issues, member editorials, upcoming association meetings and special projects. **Advertising:** accepted. Alternate Formats: online. **Conventions/Meetings:** annual AAIM Executive Leadership Program - symposium.

8587 ■ Association of Specialty Professors (ASP)
c/o Alliance for Academic Internal Medicine
2501 M St. NW, Ste.550
Washington, DC 20037-1325

Ph: (202)861-9351 (202)861-6900
Fax: (202)861-9731
E-mail: asp@im.org
URL: http://www.im.org/ASP
Contact: Stuart L. Linas MD, Pres.

Membership Dues: departmental, $1,500 (annual) ● divisional, $300 (annual) ● individual, $100 (annual) ● societal, $3,000 (annual). **Multinational. Description:** Promotes specialty internal medicine as a career discipline. Facilitates cooperation within the internal medicine community. Provides training and educational opportunities for internal medicine division chiefs and fellowship training program directors. **Awards:** ASP Eric G. Neilson, MD, Distinguished Professor Award. **Frequency:** annual. **Type:** recognition. **Recipient:** to a physician who has demonstrated outstanding leadership and support of specialty medicine. **Publications:** Membership Directory. **Price:** for members only. Alternate Formats: online.

International Exchange

8588 ■ Academic Travel Abroad (ATA)
1920 N St. NW, Ste.200
Washington, DC 20036
Ph: (202)785-9000
Free: (800)556-7896
Fax: (202)342-0317
E-mail: info@aas-world.org
URL: http://www.academic-travel.com
Contact: David Parry, Pres.

Founded: 1948. **For-Profit. Description:** Seeks to foster intercultural relations and educational cooperation between institutions of higher learning in the United States and in countries throughout the world. Pursues this goal through a comprehensive program of organized and supervised travel for colleges, schools, museums, alumni groups and professional organizations. Promotes interest in international educational travel by conducting conferences and research in cooperation with educational, professional, and civic organizations. Sponsors the Association for Academic Travel Abroad, a non-profit organization that has provided aid to needy students to allow them to participate in ATA programs; however, funds have not been distributed for several years.

8589 ■ AFS Intercultural Programs (AFS)
71 W 23rd St., 17th Fl.
New York, NY 10010-4102
Ph: (212)807-8686
Free: (800)AFS-INFO
Fax: (212)807-1001
E-mail: info@afs.org
URL: http://www.afs.org
Contact: Francisco Cazal, Pres./CEO

Founded: 1914. **Multinational. Description:** Promotes international understanding, primarily through exchange of secondary school students, 16 to 18 years of age. Presents a variety of exchange programs providing family living experiences to fit the needs of the participants. Conducts research into the nature and impact of intercultural experiences, program quality, cultural training, specific cultures, and global education. **Libraries: Type:** reference. **Holdings:** 300; archival material, books. **Awards:** The Galatti Award. **Frequency:** annual. **Type:** recognition. **Recipient:** for volunteers and host families. **Formerly:** (1978) American Field Service. **Publications:** *AFS Orientation Handbook*, annual ● *AFS Research Reports*, periodic ● *Papers in Intercultural Learning*, semiannual. **Conventions/Meetings:** semiannual Volunteer Training Conference (exhibits).

8590 ■ AHA International (AHAI)
221 NW 2nd Ave., Ste.200
Portland, OR 97209
Ph: (503)295-7730 (503)295-3686
Free: (800)654-2051
Fax: (503)295-5969
E-mail: ahamail@uoregon.edu
URL: http://www.aha-intl.org
Contact: Anne Haberkern, Exec. Dir.

Founded: 1957. **Multinational. Description:** Post-secondary educational exchange and study abroad programs. Seeks to "bring people from diverse parts of the world together in mind, body, and spirit". Creates and administers study abroad programs; and facilitates establishment of cooperative exchange arrangements involving U.S. colleges and universities and their counterparts abroad. **Additional Websites:** http://ahastudyabroad.org. **Formerly:** (2003) American Heritage Association International. **Publications:** *Student Handbook for Studying Abroad.* Alternate Formats: online.

8591 ■ Alliance for International Educational and Cultural Exchange
1776 Massachusetts Ave. NW, Ste.620
Washington, DC 20036-1912
Ph: (202)293-6141
Fax: (202)293-6144
E-mail: info@alliance-exchange.org
URL: http://www.alliance-exchange.org
Contact: Michael McCarry, Exec. Dir.

Founded: 1993. **Members:** 77. **Staff:** 4. **Budget:** $300,000. **Description:** Consists of non-governmental organizations comprising the international educational and cultural exchange community in the United States. Aims to formulate and promote public policies that support the growth and well-being of international exchange links between the people of the United States and other nations. **Also Known As:** The Alliance. **Formed by Merger of:** (1993) International Exchange Association; Liaison Group for International Educational Exchange. **Publications:** *International Exchange Locator*, semiannual. Directory. Contains U.S. organizations, federal agencies, and congressional committees in international exchange. **Price:** $25.00.

8592 ■ American Council for International Studies (ACIS)
343 Cong. St., Ste.3100
Boston, MA 02210
Ph: (617)236-2051
Free: (800)888-ACIS
Fax: (617)450-5601
E-mail: info@acis.com
URL: http://www.acis.com
Contact: Joel Cody, Chief Strategy and Marketing Off.

Founded: 1978. **Members:** 30,000. **Staff:** 100. **For-Profit. Description:** Teachers and students in the U.S. who wish to study abroad; foreign students studying in the U.S. Promotes international educational experience for high school teachers and students. Facilitates group travel by teachers and their classes by procuring airline tickets; arranging exchange programs with high schools in Europe, Canada, Central America, and China; providing orientation materials and workbooks. Maintains program centers in London, England and Paris, France. **Awards:** Travel is Education Scholarship. **Frequency:** annual. **Type:** scholarship. **Recipient:** for students. **Publications:** *Travel Talk*, monthly. Newsletter. Alternate Formats: online ● Also publishes books. **Conventions/Meetings:** annual meeting - always January, concurrently in London, England and Paris, France.

8593 ■ American Forum for Global Education (AFGE)
120 Wall St., Ste.2600
New York, NY 10005
Ph: (212)624-1300
Free: (800)813-5056
Fax: (212)624-1412
E-mail: info@globaled.org
URL: http://www.globaled.org

Founded: 1970. **Staff:** 15. **Budget:** $1,100,000. **Description:** Works to prepare American students for "the challenge of responsible national citizenship in a global age". Supports activities of other groups and individuals through network development and cooperative projects which further both conceptualization and implementation efforts. Develops instructional materials for kindergarten through grade 12; encourages professional development and support through in-service and pre-service training programs; works to develop broad public support "to ensure that global perspectives become a permanent feature of our schools". Works with educators and educational agencies at all levels, with national, state, and community organizations, and with media, business, labor, and other interest groups to enhance global perspectives education. Acts as a clearinghouse for resources and information on developmental education and operates speakers' bureau. **Libraries: Type:** reference. **Holdings:** 800. **Awards: Type:** recognition. **Computer Services:** database, global and international educational materials for elementary, secondary, and undergraduate education. **Telecommunication Services:** electronic mail, afglobaled@aol.com. **Divisions:** Communications; Professional Development; Public Education; Public Policy; Research and Development. **Formed by Merger of:** Global Perspectives in Education; National Council on Foreign Language and International Studies. **Formerly:** (1988) American Forum: Education in a Global Age. **Publications:** *An Attainable Global Perspective.* Paper. Contains a clear, concise, and workable definition of global perspective. **Price:** $4.00. Alternate Formats: online ● *Believing is Seeing: Attitudes and Assumptions that Affect Learning about Development.* Book. Contains shared belief in determining how to perceive the world. **Price:** $5.00 ● *Children and Languages: Research, Practice and Rationale for Early Grades.* Paper. Contains a compilation from the first International Conference on Second/Foreign Language Acquisition by Children. **Price:** $10.00 ● *Chinese Identity: Foundations and Structures.* Monographs. Provides teachers with short enrichment materials which will help them re-think how they will talk. **Price:** $10.00. Alternate Formats: online ● *Curricular Package*, bimonthly. Newsletter. Issues in global education. **Price:** $30.00 in U.S.; $36.00 in Canada; $48.00 outside U.S. and Canada. **Circulation:** 500. **Advertising:** accepted. Alternate Formats: online ● *Issues in Global Education*, 6/year, during school year. **Price:** $30.00. **Advertising:** accepted.

8594 ■ American Home Life International (AHLI)
1725A Oregon Pike
Lancaster, PA 17601-4206
Ph: (717)560-2840
Fax: (717)560-2845
E-mail: amhomelife@amhomelife.org
URL: http://amhomelife.org
Contact: Keith Mayer, Pres.

Founded: 1986. **Staff:** 10. **Budget:** $1,000,000. **Languages:** Chinese, English, Japanese, Korean. **Multinational. Description:** Oversees a homestay program where international students are teamed with Christian host families in Lancaster, PA, Tampa, FL and Lancaster, CA. Offers international students educational opportunities at the high school and post high school level as well as cultural, social and sightseeing experiences. **Publications:** Brochures. **Price:** available upon request ● Newsletters. **Price:** available upon request.

8595 ■ American Institute for Foreign Study Foundation (AIFS)
9 W Broad St.
River Plz.
Stamford, CT 06902
Ph: (203)399-5414
Free: (800)322-4678
Fax: (203)399-5593
E-mail: aya.info@aifs.org
URL: http://www.aifsfoundation.org
Contact: Ms. Melanie French, Exec. Dir.

Founded: 1965. **Description:** Promotes intercultural understanding by providing an international academic exchange program, which enables foreign students to reside with American host families. Seeks to increase foreign students' fluency in English as well as their knowledge and understanding of American history and culture. Encourages Americans to become acquainted with foreign countries and peoples through personal contact as well as appreciation of foreign language, culture, and history. Sponsors the Academic Year in America Program which allows foreign high school students to study at an American high school for a semester or academic year while living with a host family. **Awards:** Tony Cook Grants. **Frequency:** annual. **Type:** scholarship. **Recipient:** to schools that showed eagerness to incorporate international education into their curriculum. **Programs:** Au Pair in America. **Formerly:** (1998) American Institute for Foreign Study Scholarship Foundation. **Publications:** *Study Abroad: A 21st Century Perspective*. Booklet. Includes topics such as diversification of study abroad participants, financial aid, technology, safety, and service learning. Alternate Formats: online ● Brochures.

8596 ■ American Intercultural Student Exchange (AISE)
707 Lakehall Rd.
Lake Village, AR 71653
Ph: (870)265-5050
Free: (800)653-2473
Fax: (870)265-5001
E-mail: mail@aise.com
URL: http://www.aise.com
Contact: Judy Scott, Pres.
Founded: 1980. **Description:** Participants are students and host families worldwide. Promotes international student exchanges; serves as a conduit through which students in the U.S. can contact host families in 10 countries, and students from 20 countries can contact host families in the U.S. Host families provide room, board, and, if they choose, travel and other opportunities to their students. **Convention/Meeting:** none. **Publications:** Newsletter. Contains information for students and host families to keep updated on the events of present students as well as former students. Alternate Formats: online.

8597 ■ American University in Moscow (AUM)
1800 Connecticut Ave. NW
Washington, DC 20009
Ph: (202)364-0200
Fax: (202)364-0200
E-mail: russia@russiahouse.org
URL: http://russiahouse.org/aum
Contact: Edward D. Lozansky, Pres.
Founded: 1988. **Staff:** 6. **Budget:** $500,000. **Languages:** English, Russian. **Description:** Scientists, scholars and businessmen. Operates the American University in Moscow, Russia. Provides business contacts for American companies in Russia and Russian companies in the United States. Organizes conferences to promote U.S.-Russian cooperation in business, science, culture, and education. Publishes books, magazines, and newspapers. **Libraries: Type:** reference; not open to the public. **Holdings:** 1,000; books, periodicals. **Subjects:** literature, history, Russian novels (all in Russian language). **Formerly:** (1993) Independent University, Washington-Paris-Moscow. **Publications:** *Foundations of Free Society*, annual. Book ● *Kontinent* (in English and Russian), quarterly. Magazine. **Price:** $12.00/copy; $48.00/year. **Circulation:** 50,000. **Advertising:** accepted ● *Kontinent USA*, weekly. Newspaper. **Conventions/Meetings:** annual conference - always in Washington, DC.

8598 ■ Asian American Curriculum Project (AACP)
529 E 3rd Ave.
San Mateo, CA 94401
Ph: (650)375-8286
Free: (800)874-2242
Fax: (650)375-8797
E-mail: aacpinc@asianamericanbooks.com
URL: http://www.asianamericanbooks.com
Contact: Florence M. Hongo, Pres./Gen. Mgr.
Founded: 1969. **Staff:** 3. **Budget:** $100,000. **Description:** Develops, promotes, and disseminates Asian-American studies and curriculum material to schools, libraries, and Asian-Americans. Sponsors demonstrations when feasible. **Convention/Meeting:** none. **Libraries: Type:** not open to the public. **Holdings:** 1,500. **Formerly:** Japanese American Curriculum Project. **Publications:** *Asian American Curriculum Project—Catalogue*, annual. Lists Asian American books, journals, posters, games, and dolls. Includes index of titles and book reviews. **Price:** $3.00. **Circulation:** 20,000. Alternate Formats: online. Also Cited As: *Asian American Materials Catalogue.*

8599 ■ ASPECT Foundation (ASPECT)
211 Sutter St., 10th Fl.
San Francisco, CA 94108
Free: (800)879-6884
Fax: (415)228-8051
E-mail: exchange@aspectworld.com
URL: http://www.aspectfoundation.org
Contact: Joan Boru, Pres.
Founded: 1985. **Members:** 400. **Staff:** 15. **Regional Groups:** 5. **State Groups:** 50. **Local Groups:** 350. **Description:** Exchanges students from 30 different countries live with volunteer American host families and attend the local public or private high school for a semester or academic year. **Publications:** *The Host Family Informer*, quarterly. **Price:** free for members. **Circulation:** 1,200 ● *The Melting Pot*, bimonthly. Newsletter. **Price:** free for members. **Circulation:** 1,300. Alternate Formats: online ● *The Spectrum*, bimonthly. **Price:** free for members. **Circulation:** 400. **Conventions/Meetings:** annual conference ● annual Training Meeting.

8600 ■ ASSE International Student Exchange Programs
603 High Dr.
Laguna Beach, CA 92651
Ph: (949)497-1699
Free: (800)733-2773
Fax: (949)497-8704
E-mail: asseusawest@asse.com
URL: http://www.asse.com
Contact: Lana Tereshko, Area Rep.
Description: Seeks to provide high quality cultural exchange experiences for students ages 15-18 from Scandinavian countries, Germany, Italy, Great Britain, Holland, Spain, Mexico, France, Poland, Portugal, Japan, the Czech and Slovak Republics, Australia, New Zealand, and the former Soviet Union. **Awards:** Congress-Bundestag Youth Exchange Program. **Frequency:** annual. **Type:** scholarship. **Recipient:** for student in USA, Canada and New Zealand ● Walter Danielson Scholarship. **Frequency:** annual. **Type:** scholarship. **Recipient:** for student in USA, Canada and New Zealand. **Telecommunication Services:** electronic mail, asse@asse.com. **Formerly:** American Scandinavian Student Exchange.

8601 ■ Association for International Practical Training (AIPT)
10400 Little Patuxent Pkwy., Ste.250
Columbia, MD 21044-3519
Ph: (410)997-2200
Fax: (410)992-3924
E-mail: aipt@aipt.org
URL: http://www.aipt.org
Contact: Elizabeth Chazottes, Pres./CEO
Founded: 1950. **Staff:** 40. **Budget:** $4,000,000. **Local Groups:** 5. **Description:** Providers worldwide of on-the-job training programs for students and professionals seeking international career development and life-changing experiences. Arranges workplace exchanges in hundreds of professional fields, bringing employers and trainees together from around the world. Client list ranges from small farming communities to Fortune 500 companies. **Awards:** Jessica King Scholarship Fund. **Frequency:** annual. **Type:** scholarship. **Recipient:** for U.S. citizens who have a degree in the hospitality industry, or currently employed for at least one year in the hospitality industry ● **Frequency:** annual. **Type:** scholarship. **Recipient:** for students based on their academic merit and the quality of their essays, which are submitted with their job selections in February. **Affiliated With:** International Association for the Exchange of Students for Technical Experience. **Formerly:** (1980) International Association for the Exchange of Students for Technical Experience (United States). **Publications:** *AIPT Annual Report*, annual. Includes information on each year's exchanges, participating employers, financial statements and list of officers/directors. **Price:** free. Alternate Formats: online ● *International IAESTE Annual Report*, annual. Includes the results of each year's exchange of students among the 70 IAESTE member countries; also includes national reports and statistics. **Price:** free. **Circulation:** 3,000 ● *Practically Speaking*, semiannual. Magazine. Contains articles on events, trainee exchanges, and industry news. **Advertising:** accepted. Alternate Formats: online. **Conventions/Meetings:** annual board meeting - summer.

8602 ■ Association for World Travel Exchange (AWTE)
c/o International Student Center
38 W 88th St.
New York, NY 10024
Ph: (212)787-7706
Fax: (212)580-9283
E-mail: info@nystudentcenter.org
URL: http://www.nystudentcenter.org
Contact: Suresh Paul, Exec. Dir.
Founded: 1953. **Members:** 12,000. **Staff:** 23. **Multinational. Description:** Sponsors a camp counselor program for foreign student visitors to the United States. Operates the International Student Center (youth hostel) in New York City. Conducts placement service. **Convention/Meeting:** none. **Publications:** none.

8603 ■ Au Pair in America (APIA)
9 W Broad St., River Plz.
Stamford, CT 06902
Ph: (203)399-5000
Free: (800)928-7247
Fax: (203)399-5592
E-mail: aupair.info@aifs.org
URL: http://www.aupairinamerica.com
Contact: William L. Gertz, Pres./CEO
Founded: 1986. **Description:** A program of the American Institute for Foreign Study, Inc. (see separate entry). International youth exchange program organized to promote cross-cultural understanding and cooperation between American families and Western European young adults by providing the opportunity for young people overseas to learn about American culture and family life while living in the U.S. Arranges for foreigners between the ages of 18 and 26 to reside in the U.S. for a year while caring for the children of a host family; participants serve as an "au pair," or equal person, in the host family's household. Has developed a reciprocal program which allows young Americans to travel to Europe. **Additional Websites:** http://www.aifs.org. **Affiliated With:** American Institute for Foreign Study Foundation. **Publications:** Brochure.

8604 ■ Brazilian Studies Association (BRASA)
Vanderbilt Univ.
2301 Vanderbilt Pl.
VU Sta., B 350031
Nashville, TN 37235-0031
Ph: (615)322-2527
Fax: (615)343-6002
E-mail: brasa@vanderbilt.edu
URL: http://www.brasa.org
Contact: Kenneth P. Serbin, Pres.
Founded: 1994. **Members:** 1,200. **Membership Dues:** student, $15 (annual) ● independent scholar, $20 (annual) ● faculty, $50 (annual) ● institution, $70 (annual) ● joint, $60 (annual) ● joint, $160 (triennial). **Staff:** 5. **Budget:** $16,000. **Regional Groups:** 4. **Languages:** English, Portuguese. **Description:** Academics and others interested in the social, cultural, and natural aspects of Brazil. Fosters academic exchange between Brazil and the United States. **Awards:** Roberto Reis BRASA Book Award. **Frequency:** annual. **Type:** recognition. **Recipient:** for 2 books in Brazilian Studies published in English, with significant contribution to the understanding of Brazil. **Computer Services:** database ● mailing lists. **Committees:** Conference Planning; Library and Information Resources; Publications. **Publications:** *BRASAnotes* (in English and Portuguese), annual.

Newsletter. **Advertising:** accepted. Alternate Formats: online ● Proceedings, semiannual. Alternate Formats: online. **Conventions/Meetings:** semiannual international conference (exhibits).

8605 ■ British American Educational Foundation (BAEF)
520 Summit Ave.
Oradell, NJ 07649
Ph: (201)261-4438
URL: http://www.baef.org
Contact: Laurel Zimmermann, Exec. Dir.
Founded: 1966. **Budget:** $100,000. **Description:** Offers selected American secondary school students and graduates an opportunity to spend from one term to a year at an independent boarding school in England.

8606 ■ British Universities North America Club (BUNAC)
PO Box 430
Southbury, CT 06488
Ph: (203)264-0901
Free: (800)462-8622
Fax: (203)264-0251
E-mail: info@bunacusa.org
URL: http://www.bunac.org/USA
Contact: Anna Crew, Dir.
Founded: 1962. **Members:** 19,000. **Description:** Promotes educational and cultural, work/travel, exchange programs between British and North American students and around the world. Coordinates employment opportunities, including camp counseling, in the United States, Canada, and Jamaica plus Ghana, South Africa, Australia, New Zealand and programs to the United States and United Kingdom for New Zealand and Australia participants for British students and in Great Britain, Australia and New Zealand for American students. Offers scholarships to British students studying in North America. **Telecommunication Services:** electronic mail, scusa@bunacusa.org. **Publications:** *BUNAC News*, 2 issues per semester. Newsletter ● *Moneywise Guide to North America*, annual. Handbook. Serves as a guidebook for budget travelers covering the U.S., Canada, and Mexico. Includes background, accommodation, food, and sightseeing information. **Price:** free to program participants. **Circulation:** 13,000. Also Cited As: *Student Guide to North America* ● Also publishes brochures detailing available programs.

8607 ■ Community Colleges for International Development (CCID)
PO Box 2068
Cedar Rapids, IA 52406-2068
Ph: (319)398-1257
Fax: (319)398-7113
E-mail: ccid@kirkwood.edu
URL: http://ccid.kirkwood.cc.ia.us
Contact: Mr. John Halder, Pres./Exec. Dir.
Founded: 1976. **Members:** 100. **Membership Dues:** affiliate (per academic year), $750 (annual). **Staff:** 2. **Multinational. Description:** Provides opportunities for building global relationships that strengthen educational programs and promote economic development. Develops technical training for economic independence and human resource development. Supports curriculum development and programs that encourages global understanding. Facilitates educational exchanges that results in increased global awareness. Initiates and coordinates international linkages to advocate the necessity of global partnerships. Initiates, facilitates and encourages international relationships that enhance global competitiveness. **Libraries: Type:** not open to the public. **Holdings:** 100. **Subjects:** multicultural and multinational education. **Awards:** CCID Presidents' Award. **Type:** recognition. **Recipient:** for sustained excellence in support for CCID programs, chosen by CCID ● Dr. Werner Kubsch Award for Achievement in International Education. **Frequency:** annual. **Type:** monetary. **Recipient:** for sustained superior support to International education ● **Frequency:** annual. **Type:** grant. **Recipient:** for project proposal selected by peer review. **Affiliated With:** American Association of Community Colleges. **Publications:** *CCID International News*, quarterly. Newsletter. **Price:** included in membership dues. **Circulation:** 5,000. Alternate Formats: online. **Conventions/Meetings:** annual board meeting and conference - in February.

8608 ■ Council on International Educational Exchange - USA (CIEE)
7 Custom House St., 3rd Fl.
Portland, ME 04101
Ph: (207)553-7600
Free: (800)407-8839
Fax: (207)553-7699
E-mail: studyinfo@ciee.org
URL: http://www.ciee.org
Contact: Stevan Trooboff, Pres./CEO
Founded: 1947. **Members:** 326. **Membership Dues:** institution, $400 (annual). **Staff:** 400. **Budget:** $100,000,000. **Description:** Provides study abroad programs for university students, 95 programs in 33 countries. Conducts annual reviews, student evaluations, and academic research that are constantly improving existing programs and developing new ones that satisfy the needs and interests of students and educators. Offers academics alongside plentiful opportunities for cultural immersion including excursions, homestays, volunteer opportunities, and internships. Administers teach abroad programs in Chile, China, Spain, and Thailand. **Divisions:** Higher Education Programs; Secondary Education Programs. **Programs:** College and University; Languages and Cultural. **Working Groups:** Teach Abroad Programs. **Absorbed:** Student Services West. **Formerly:** Council on Students Travel. **Conventions/Meetings:** annual Conference on Educational Exchange - November.

8609 ■ Council for International Exchange of Scholars/Institute of International Education (CIES)
3007 Tilden St. NW, Ste.5L
Washington, DC 20008-3009
Ph: (202)686-4000 (202)686-4009
Fax: (202)362-3442
E-mail: apprequest@cies.iie.org
URL: http://www.iie.org/cies
Contact: Jack Bailey, Deputy Exec. Dir.
Founded: 1947. **Staff:** 50. **Multinational. Description:** Comprised of chairman and three representatives each from American Council of Learned Societies, American Council on Education, Social Science Research Council, and National Academy of Sciences (see separate entries). Cooperates with the U.S. Information Agency and the J. William Fulbright Foreign Scholarship Board in administration of the mutual educational exchange program under the Fulbright-Hays Act as it applies to university lecturing and advanced research. Sponsors annual competitions for Americans interested in Fulbright Scholar Awards abroad. Assists with placement of visiting scholars in U.S. colleges and universities and administers scholar-in-residence lecturing program for visiting scholars. Maintains 38 specialist review committees and 33 geographic area review committees. **Convention/Meeting:** none. **Awards:** Fulbright Scholars Program. **Frequency:** annual. **Type:** grant. **Affiliated With:** American Council on Education; American Council of Learned Societies; National Academy of Sciences; Social Science Research Council. **Formerly:** Conference Board of Associated Research Councils; (1974) Committee on International Exchange of Persons Conference Board of Associated Research Councils; (1976) Council for International Exchange of Scholars Conference Board of Associated Research Councils; (1998) Council for International Exchange of Scholars. **Publications:** *Directory of American Fulbright Scholars*, annual. Lists American scholars who have received Fulbright awards for university lecturing and advanced research abroad. **Price:** free. **Circulation:** 6,000 ● *Fulbright Scholar-in-Residence Program: Guidelines for Proposals*, annual. Manual. Provides information for U.S. institutions that wish to host a visiting Fulbright Scholar as a lecturer for a semester or an academic year. **Circulation:** 4,000 ● *Fulbright Scholar Program Grants U.S. for Faculty and Professionals: Research and Lecturing Awards*, annual. Manual. **Price:** free. **Circulation:** 50,000 ● *Visiting Fulbright Scholars and Occasional Lecturers*, annual. Directory. Lists visiting Fulbright scholars arranged by academic field to assist institutions that wish to participate in the Occasional Lecturer Program. **Price:** free. **Circulation:** 12,000.

8610 ■ Council on Standards for International Educational Travel (CSIET)
212 S Henry St.
Alexandria, VA 22314
Ph: (703)739-9050
Fax: (703)739-9035
E-mail: mailbox@csiet.org
URL: http://www.csiet.org
Contact: John Lewis, Chm.
Founded: 1984. **Members:** 320. **Membership Dues:** individual, $65 (annual) ● organization, $400 (annual) ● school, $50 (annual) ● school district (voting), $425 (annual) ● school district (associate), $75 (annual) ● international, $525 (annual). **Staff:** 3. **Budget:** $350,000. **Description:** Educational and international exchange organizations. Aims to establish standards for youth exchange programs. Evaluates and monitors youth exchange programs. **Committees:** Evaluation. **Publications:** *Advisory List of International Educational Travel and Exchange Programs*, annual. Directory. **Price:** $18.00/copy, in U.S.; $23.00/copy, outside U.S. **Circulation:** 30,000. **Advertising:** accepted. **Conventions/Meetings:** annual conference (exhibits) - always October.

8611 ■ EF Foundation for Foreign Study (EF Foundation)
One Educ. St.
Cambridge, MA 02141
Free: (800)44-SHARE
Fax: (617)619-1401
E-mail: foundation@ef.com
URL: http://www.effoundation.org
Contact: Asa Fanelli, Chair
Founded: 1979. **Staff:** 45. **Regional Groups:** 100. **Description:** A network of representatives throughout Europe, Asia, and the Americas, dedicated to international student exchange and education. Aims to encourage cultural awareness and mutual respect between nations. Reaches out to students in 28 countries. Sponsors programs such as High School Year Abroad and High School Year in America. **Affiliated With:** Alliance for International Educational and Cultural Exchange; Council on Standards for International Educational Travel. **Formerly:** EF Educational Foundation for Foreign Study. **Publications:** *The Exchange*, 3/year. Newspaper. Focuses on student, family, and volunteer activities. **Price:** free. **Circulation:** 50,000 ● *Host Families - Open Your Hearts and Home*. Brochures ● *International Exchange Coordinators - Make a Difference!*. Brochures ● *Program Review*, annual. Pamphlet ● *Student Exchange in Your School*. Brochures. **Conventions/Meetings:** annual Regional Coordinator Meeting and Regional Meeting - conference, training (exhibits).

8612 ■ Foundation for International Cooperation (FIC)
1237 S Western Ave.
Park Ridge, IL 60068
Ph: (847)518-0934
Free: (800)890-3543
Fax: (847)518-0934
E-mail: fic1960@att.net
URL: http://www.ficcultureswap.org
Contact: Irene B. Horst, Exec. Dir.
Founded: 1960. **Members:** 500. **Membership Dues:** family, $35 (annual) ● individual, $25 (annual) ● contributing, $50 (annual). **Staff:** 1. **Regional Groups:** 10. **Local Groups:** 12. **Description:** Provides information and services to foreign visitors and students. Provides adult study experiences including short-term home hospitality, lectures, and special visits as well as sightseeing expeditions abroad. Arranges tours and home hospitality in the U.S. for people from abroad. Offers language conversation groups, workshops, and discussion programs; occasionally offers other international cooperation

projects. **Committees:** Adult Study Tour; Chapter II (Young Adult Group); Foreign Student Services; Young Adult Study Tour. **Publications:** *Foundation for International Cooperation—Newsnotes*, quarterly. Newsletter. **Price:** included in membership dues. **Circulation:** 600. **Conventions/Meetings:** annual conference and reunion.

8613 ■ Fulbright Association (FA)
666 11th St. NW, Ste.525
Washington, DC 20001
Ph: (202)347-5543
Fax: (202)347-6540
E-mail: fulbright@fulbright.org
URL: http://www.fulbrightalumni.org/olc/pub/FBA/cpages/about_us/about_us.jsp
Contact: Ms. Jane L. Anderson CAE, Exec. Dir.

Founded: 1977. **Members:** 6,750. **Membership Dues:** student, retired, $25 (annual) ● life (individual), $500 ● individual, associate, $40 (annual) ● couple, $65 (annual) ● institution, $500 (annual). **Staff:** 4. **Budget:** $600,000. **Local Groups:** 47. **Description:** Past participants in the Fulbright program of international exchange; interested others. Coordinates membership support of international educational and cultural exchange programs and public service projects. Local chapters offer hospitality, enrichment, and mentor programs to visiting Fulbright scholars, teachers, and students. **Awards:** J. William Fulbright Prize for International Understanding. **Frequency:** annual. **Type:** monetary. **Recipient:** to an individual who has made outstanding contributions to bringing people, cultures, and nations to greater understanding of each other. **Telecommunication Services:** electronic mail, jane.anderson@fulbright.org. **Task Forces:** Arts; International Education. **Also Known As:** Fulbright Association of Alumni of International Educational and Cultural Exchange. **Publications:** *Fulbright Association Newsletter*, periodic. Covers the Fulbright Program, international exchange, international education, chapter news, available scholarships, alumni achievements and activities. **Price:** included in membership dues. **Circulation:** 10,000. **Advertising:** accepted. **Conventions/Meetings:** annual conference - always fall in Washington, DC.

8614 ■ German Academic Exchange Service (DAAD)
871 United Nations Plz.
New York, NY 10017
Ph: (212)758-3223
Fax: (212)755-5780
E-mail: daadny@daad.org
URL: http://www.daad.org
Contact: Mr. Ulrich Grothus, Dir.

Founded: 1925. **Members:** 220. **Budget:** $220,000,000. **Multinational. Description:** Promotes international relations among institutions of higher education, specifically in the area of academic and scientific exchange. Offers information on German educational systems and administers German government grants for graduate study or research in Germany. Conducts seminars on German language and literature, German and European studies, German law, German-Jewish history, and international education marketing. **Convention/Meeting:** none. **Libraries: Type:** open to the public. **Holdings:** books. **Subjects:** German universities' course offerings. **Awards:** DAAD Conference Funding. **Frequency:** periodic. **Type:** grant. **Recipient:** for assistance with conferences in German studies at American and Canadian universities ● DAAD EMGIP-Bundestag Internship. **Frequency:** annual. **Type:** fellowship. **Recipient:** for international students at Germany's Bundestag (parliament) ● DAAD German Studies Research Grant. **Frequency:** semiannual. **Type:** grant. **Recipient:** for study of cultural, political, historical, economic and social aspects of modern and contemporary German affairs from an inter- and multi-disciplinary perspective ● DAAD Group Study Visit. **Frequency:** periodic. **Type:** grant. **Recipient:** for student groups from North American universities accompanied by faculty ● DAAD High Tech in Old Munich. **Frequency:** annual. **Type:** scholarship. **Recipient:** for juniors or seniors enrolled full time in an engineering program in the US or Canada; involves lectures on language, entrepreneurial culture, and management from a German perspective, in Germany ● DAAD Hochschulsommerkurse. **Frequency:** annual. **Type:** scholarship. **Recipient:** for summer language study in Germany ● DAAD Intensive Language Grant. **Frequency:** annual. **Type:** scholarship. **Recipient:** for graduate students to participate in intensive German language study at private language institutions in Germany including the renowned Goethe Institute Center ● DAAD International Lawyers. **Frequency:** annual. **Type:** fellowship. **Recipient:** for fellows of the eight-month study internship program in international law ● DAAD Learn German in Germany. **Frequency:** annual. **Type:** grant. **Recipient:** for US/Canadian university faculty ● DAAD Research Grant. **Frequency:** semiannual. **Type:** grant. **Recipient:** for doctoral degree students and post-doctoral of North American universities who wish to conduct research in Germany ● DAAD Research Internships in Science and Engineering. **Frequency:** annual. **Type:** fellowship. **Recipient:** for North American undergraduate students in science and engineering fields ● DAAD Research Visit Grant (for Faculty). **Frequency:** semiannual. **Type:** grant. **Recipient:** for American/Canadian university faculty who wish to conduct research at universities, archives, etc. in Germany ● DAAD Short Term Lectureship. **Frequency:** periodic. **Type:** monetary. **Recipient:** for assistance with costs in hosting a German scholar at an American or Canadian university for a guest lectureship ● DAAD Summer Seminar. **Frequency:** annual. **Type:** fellowship. **Recipient:** for university faculty and doctoral students ● DAAD Visiting Professorship. **Frequency:** semiannual. **Type:** grant. **Recipient:** for the hosting of American and Canadian guest lecturers at German higher education institutions ● Germany Today. **Frequency:** annual. **Type:** fellowship. **Recipient:** for American and Canadian VIP's. **Computer Services:** Electronic publishing ● mailing lists. **Also Known As:** Deutscher Akademischer Austausch Dienst. **Publications:** *Grants for Study and Research in Germany* (in English and French), annual. Catalog. Includes annual funding opportunities.

8615 ■ Global Outreach
1920 Lee Blvd.
North Mankato, MN 56003
Ph: (612)333-2353
Fax: (612)395-5206
E-mail: info@globaloutreach.net
URL: http://www.globaloutreach.net
Contact: Jennifer L. Wagner, Exec. Dir.

Founded: 1994. **Staff:** 3. **Multinational. Description:** Assists rural and/or agricultural youth in the development and appreciation of global cultural diversity, and an understanding of the international agricultural economy. Strives to provide international exchange opportunities for individuals studying agriculture or horticulture. Exchange interns are generally placed on agricultural operations or agribusiness in one of their chosen countries. Host businesses provide room and board and a stipend equal to minimum wage. **Publications:** *Host*. Handbook ● *The Outreach*, monthly. Newsletter.

8616 ■ Institute of International Education (IIE)
809 United Nations Plz.
New York, NY 10017-3580
Ph: (212)883-8200 (212)984-5381
Fax: (212)984-5452
E-mail: dkaisth@iie.org
URL: http://www.iie.org
Contact: Mr. Daniela Z. Kaisth, VP, Strategic Development

Founded: 1919. **Members:** 900. **Membership Dues:** college/university, educational, not-for-profit organization, $500. **Staff:** 500. **Budget:** $185,000,000. **Regional Groups:** 5. **Multinational. Description:** Designs and implements over 200 programs of study and training for students, educators and young professionals, with government and private sponsorship. Conducts policy research and provides counseling on international educational opportunities abroad. Maintains 19 offices worldwide and nearly 900 member campuses. Provides educators with a forum for discussion, interaction and networking and a source of expert analytical information and research upon which to build and extend professional practice. **Computer Services:** database, scholarship information for foreign students, grants, events ● online services, search engine for study abroad programs, article archives. **Additional Websites:** http://www.iienetwork.org, http://www.iiebooks.org, http://www.fundingUSstudy.org. **Affiliated With:** Council for International Exchange of Scholars/Institute of International Education. **Publications:** *Academic Year Abroad*, annual. Directory. Features a guide to over 3000 overseas study programs offered by U.S. colleges and universities during the academic year. **Price:** $44.95/copy. **Circulation:** 6,000. **Advertising:** accepted ● *Basic Facts*. Booklet. Provides basic information about selecting an educational opportunity abroad. ● *Financial Resources for International Study*. Directory. Lists sources of financial aid for U.S. students studying abroad. **Price:** $39.95/copy. **Circulation:** 5,000 ● *Funding for U.S. Study*. Directory. Contains lists of sources for financial aid of International students studying in the U.S. **Price:** $39.95/copy. **Circulation:** 15,000 ● *IIENetworker*, semiannual. Magazine. **Price:** free for members. **Advertising:** accepted ● *Institute of International Education—Annual Report* ● *Intensive Language U.S.A.*, biennial. Directory. Lists over 500 intensive English programs for foreign students admitted to U.S. postsecondary schools. **Price:** $59.95/copy. **Circulation:** 2,500. **Advertising:** accepted ● *Open Doors*, annual. Book. Includes reports of annual statistics on foreign students enrolled at U.S. colleges and universities, and U.S. students studying abroad. **Price:** $42.95/copy. **Circulation:** 5,000 ● *Short-Term Study Abroad*, annual. Directory. Serves as a guide to over 2,700 overseas study programs offered to U.S. nationals. **Price:** $146.95/copy. **Circulation:** 6,000. **Advertising:** accepted.

8617 ■ InterExchange
161 6th Ave.
New York, NY 10013
Ph: (212)924-0446
Free: (800)597-1722
Fax: (212)924-0575
E-mail: info@interexchange.org
URL: http://www.interexchange.org
Contact: Uta Christianson, Pres./CEO

Founded: 1968. **Staff:** 38. **Budget:** $9,500,000. **Description:** Promotes the enhancement of international understanding through the development and implementation of affordable intercultural and educational work/training opportunities. **Additional Websites:** http://www.aupairusa.org, http://www.workingabroad.org, http://www.worktravelusa.org. **Affiliated With:** Alliance for International Educational and Cultural Exchange. **Formerly:** (1968) International Student Visitors Service; (1972) U.S. Student Travel Service. **Publications:** *Program Brochures*, periodic. Contains information about exchange programs. ● Also publishes informational and publicity materials.

8618 ■ Interhostel
Univ. of New Hampshire
6 Garrison Ave.
Durham, NH 03824
Ph: (603)862-1147
Free: (800)733-9753
Fax: (603)862-1113
E-mail: interhostel@unh.edu
URL: http://www.unh.edu
Contact: Carol Bense, Mgr.

Founded: 1981. **Staff:** 6. **Description:** Provides opportunities for adults 50 years and older to travel to foreign countries and locations in the U.S. and Canada to study a particular region of the world in detail under the auspices of the University of New Hampshire and participating institutions overseas. **Publications:** *Learning Vacations*, 3/year. Bulletin. **Price:** free. Alternate Formats: online ● Brochure, 3/year. Lists programs for the season. **Conventions/Meetings:** lecture, with field trips ● tour.

8619 ■ International Book Bank (IBB)
PO Box 1662
Baltimore, MD 21203
Ph: (410)362-0334 (410)685-2665
Fax: (410)362-0336
E-mail: info@internationalbookbank.org
URL: http://www.internationalbookbank.org
Contact: Valerie Staats, Exec. Dir.
Founded: 1987. **Staff:** 6. **Budget:** $785,000. **Multinational. Description:** Helps increase literacy and advances education by distributing books and other educational materials to non-governmental and not-for-profit organizations in almost 100 developing countries around the world.

8620 ■ International Book Project (IBP)
Van Meter Bldg.
1440 Delaware Ave.
Lexington, KY 40505
Ph: (859)254-6771
Free: (888)999-2665
Fax: (859)253-2293
URL: http://www.intlbookproject.org
Founded: 1966. **Members:** 2,500. **Staff:** 2. **Budget:** $175,000. **Multinational. Description:** Individuals, civic groups, and churches working to collect funds for the distribution of books to needy institutions such as schools, hospitals, clinics, seminaries, churches, and urban and village libraries in 100 developing countries, including Bahamas, Belize, Ghana, India, Indonesia, Kenya, Liberia, Nigeria, and Philippines. Seeks to provide information to people who do not have access to books and journals. Encourages Americans to become involved with the people and conditions in developing countries through correspondence with people of these countries. Encourages members to send books and journals to these countries; provides mailing tips. Compiles statistics. **Libraries: Type:** open to the public. **Holdings:** 400,000; books, periodicals. **Awards:** Harriet Van Meter Humanitarian Award for International Relations. **Frequency:** annual. **Type:** recognition. **Recipient:** for fostering international relations and global friendships through humanitarian aid or outreach. **Publications:** *Books Abroad*, quarterly. Newsletter. **Circulation:** 2,500. **Conventions/Meetings:** annual meeting.

8621 ■ International Research and Exchanges Board (IREX)
2121 K St. NW, Ste.700
Washington, DC 20037
Ph: (202)628-8188
Fax: (202)628-8189
E-mail: irex@irex.org
URL: http://www.irex.org
Contact: Dr. Mark G. Pomar, Pres.
Founded: 1968. **Staff:** 250. **Description:** Commits to international education in its broadest sense. Efforts encompass academic research, professional training, institution building, technical assistance, and policy programs between the United States and the countries of Eastern Europe, the New Independent States, Asia and the Near East. **Libraries: Type:** reference. **Awards: Type:** grant. **Recipient:** for individual scholars to foster collaboration and exchange ● **Type:** grant. **Recipient:** for American scholars in the social sciences and humanities in Central and Eastern Europe ● Individual Advanced Research Opportunities. **Frequency:** annual. **Type:** fellowship. **Recipient:** for area studies in the U.S. preparatory to exchange participation. **Computer Services:** database ● online services, newsletter, listserv. **Publications:** *About IREX*, annual. Brochure. **Price:** free ● *Grant Opportunities for Foreign Scholars*, annual. Paper. Lists grants and Special Project opportunities available to foreign scholars. **Price:** free ● *Grant Opportunities for U.S. Scholars*, annual. Report. Lists grants and special project opportunities available to American scholars. **Price:** free ● *IREX Frontline*, quarterly. Directory. Covers IREX exchanges and other cooperative activities with the NIS in Central and Eastern Europe. **Price:** free. **Circulation:** 7,000 ● Annual Report, annual. **Price:** free. Alternate Formats: online ● Papers, periodic. Alternate Formats: online. **Conventions/Meetings:** annual Black Sea Regional Symposium, university representatives in conjunction with the American Association for the Advancement of Slavic Studies.

8622 ■ Japan-America Student Conference (JASC)
1819 L St. NW, Ste.LL2
Washington, DC 20036
Ph: (202)289-4231
Fax: (202)789-8265
E-mail: jascinc@jasc.org
URL: http://www.jasc.org
Contact: Ms. Regina McGarvey, Exec. Dir.
Founded: 1934. **Members:** 2,000. **Staff:** 3. **Budget:** $250,000. **Description:** Educational and cultural exchange program between university students (both graduate and undergraduate) from the U.S. and Japan. Promotes mutual understanding, friendship, and trust through an annual month-long summer program (held alternately in the U.S. and Japan) planned by and for top university students. Allows a student to exchange views on such issues as trade, science, politics, minorities, business, environment, education, information technology, and the arts. **Awards: Frequency:** periodic. **Type:** scholarship. **Recipient:** for university student delegates. **Boards:** Directors. **Committees:** American Executive; Japanese Executive; National Advisory. **Publications:** *Conference Brochure*, annual ● *Conference Bulletin*, annual ● *Executive Director's Report*, annual ● *JASC Journal*, semiannual. Newsletter ● *Overall Brochure*, annual ● Also publishes recruitment materials. **Conventions/Meetings:** annual conference - always July/August; alternates between the U.S. and Japan.

8623 ■ Lisle Intercultural
900 County Rd. 269
Leander, TX 78641
Free: (800)477-1538
E-mail: lisle2@io.com
URL: http://www.lisleinternational.org
Contact: Marty Tillman, Pres.
Founded: 1936. **Members:** 1,600. **Staff:** 1. **Budget:** $85,000. **Regional Groups:** 1. **Local Groups:** 4. **Description:** College students and adults of all nationalities, races, and faiths aged 18 and older; includes about 75 participants each year. Seeks to improve the quality of human life through human understanding between persons of similar and different cultures. Conducts experiential educational programs in intercultural human relations in India, Indonesia, Turkey, and the U.S. **Awards:** Marion Wright Edelman Scholarship. **Frequency:** annual. **Type:** scholarship. **Recipient:** for a minority person with experience in working for intellectual understanding. **Also Known As:** Lisle Inc. **Formerly:** Lisle Fellowship. **Publications:** *Aunt Edna: Fifty Years of Memories*. Book. Contains information about the founder Edna Aiken. **Price:** $8.00/copy ● *Lisle Directory*, biennial. **Price:** $20.00/copy ● *Lisle Interaction*, quarterly. Newsletter. **Price:** included in membership dues ● *Tiger By The Tail: The Story of the Lisle Fellowship*. Book. Highlights the history of the Lisle Fellowship as told by the founder. **Price:** $25.00/copy. **Conventions/Meetings:** annual meeting.

8624 ■ Metro International Program Services of New York
285 W Broadway, Ste.450
New York, NY 10013
Ph: (212)431-1195
Fax: (212)941-6291
E-mail: info@metrointl.org
URL: http://www.metrointl.org
Contact: Tracy Snyder, Exec. Dir.
Founded: 1977. **Members:** 80. **Membership Dues:** institutional, $450 ● individual, $150. **Staff:** 8. **Budget:** $700,000. **Description:** Institutions of higher education in the New York City area; foreign students living and studying in the New York City area. Assists foreign students and Fulbright scholars and their families. Provides orientation leadership and enrichment programs. Coordinates community visits during weekends and holidays with local residents; introduces students to the people, neighborhoods, and institutions of New York City. Administers the Global Classroom Program, which places international speakers in local high schools. Hosts social, cultural, and educational activities. Serves as a network for New York City area professionals in the field of international educational exchange. **Telecommunication Services:** electronic mail, tsnyder@metrointl.org. **Publications:** *Help Yourself to Housing in the New York City Area*. Booklet. **Price:** $8.00. **Advertising:** accepted. Alternate Formats: online ● *Inside New York: The International Student Edition*, biennial. Book. **Price:** $12.95. **Advertising:** accepted ● *Metro-Views*, semiannual. Newsletter. Alternate Formats: online ● *Network Directory: Foreign Student Advisors*, annual ● *NewsMemo*, monthly. Newsletter. Alternate Formats: online. **Conventions/Meetings:** annual meeting.

8625 ■ NACEL Open Door
1536 Hewitt Ave.
Box 268
St. Paul, MN 55104
Ph: (651)686-0080
Free: (800)622-3553
Fax: (651)686-9601
E-mail: info@nacelopendoor.org
URL: http://www.nacelopendoor.org
Contact: Dr. Frank Tarsitano, Pres./CEO
Founded: 1963. **Staff:** 14. **Budget:** $6,000,000. **Description:** Serves as an International high school student exchange between high school age students from the U.S. and those from Asia, Australia, Europe, Latin America, and the Middle East; foreign students come to the U.S. for a period of 3, 5, or 10 months, live with a family, and attend a U.S. high school; U.S. students go abroad for a home stay during the summer, school semester, or academic year. **Formerly:** (1998) Open Door Student Exchange. **Publications:** *Keynotes*, semiannual. Newsletter. **Conventions/Meetings:** annual conference ● annual regional meeting and workshop.

8626 ■ National Registration Center for Study Abroad (NRCSA)
PO Box 1393
Milwaukee, WI 53201
Ph: (414)278-0631
Fax: (414)271-8884
E-mail: study@nrcsa.com
URL: http://studyabroad.nrcsa.com/index.jsp
Contact: Renol Ziekle, Dir.
Founded: 1968. **Members:** 3,018. **Budget:** $400,000. **Description:** Consortium of 126 universities, adult education colleges, and foreign language institutions offering programs for study and foreign language/culture immersion training abroad. Offers programs in Argentina, Aruba, Australia, Austria, Bolivia, Brazil, Britain, Canada, Chile, China, Colombia, Costa Rica, Czech Republic, Denmark, Dominican Republic, Ecuador, Egypt, Finland, France, Germany, Greece, Honduras, Hungary, Ireland, Israel, Italy, Japan, Korea, Monaco, Netherlands, New Zealand, Norway, Mexico, Paraguay, Peru, Poland, Portugal, Puerto Rico, Russia, Spain, Switzerland, Sweden, Thailand, United Arab Emirates, Uruguay, and Venezuela as well as multi-country training in Asia, Africa, Europe, and Latin America. Foreign language training for Arabic, Basque, Cantonese, Chinese, Czech, Danish, Dutch, Finnish, French, Gaelic, Garifuna, German, Greek, Guarani, Hebrew, Hungarian, Italian, Japanese, Korean, Latin, Mandarin, Mayan, Miskito, Mixteco, Nahuatl, Norwegian, Papiamentu, Polish, Portuguese, Quechua, Russian, Spanish, Swedish, Thai, Wayuu, and Zapotec. **Publications:** *New Horizons*, quarterly. Newsletter. Describes programs and changes in existing programs. **Price:** $50.00/two-year. **Circulation:** 15,000. **Advertising:** accepted ● Catalog. **Conventions/Meetings:** annual meeting - always second weekend of September in Mexico City, Mexico.

8627 ■ Palestine Center
2425 Virginia Ave. NW
Washington, DC 20037
Ph: (202)338-1290 (202)338-1958
Fax: (202)333-7742

E-mail: info@palestinecenter.org
URL: http://www.thejerusalemfund.org/palestine-center/index.php
Contact: Subhi D. Ali MD, Chm.
Founded: 1991. **Languages:** Arabic, English. **Description:** Dedicated to the study and analysis of the relationship between the U.S. and the Middle East, with particular emphasis on the Palestinian problem and the Arab-Israeli conflict. Seeks to bring into focus the implications of specific U.S. policies with regard to the Palestine question and to provide Palestinian/Arab perspective that will address the political, academic, and media establishments in Washington D.C. Provides information and analysis on matters relating to U.S. policy on Palestine and the Arab-Israeli conflict. Conducts symposiums, educational programs, and a lecture series. Publishes a variety of reports and papers reflecting various programs and activities. **Libraries: Type:** reference. **Holdings:** 5,000; books, video recordings. **Subjects:** Palestinian affairs, Arab-Israeli conflict. **Formerly:** (2004) Center for Policy Analysis on Palestine. **Publications:** Newsletter, bimonthly. Contains information on previous symposiums, conferences, and luncheon meetings. **Price:** free for members; $30.00 /year for nonmembers. **Conventions/Meetings:** annual international conference, focuses on major and timely themes dealing with the Middle East and the U.S. national interest.

8628 ■ Program of Academic Exchange (PAX)
242 King St.
Port Chester, NY 10573
Ph: (914)690-1340
Free: (800)555-6211
Fax: (914)690-0350
E-mail: academicexchange@pax.org
URL: http://www.pax.org
Contact: Libby Cryer, Pres.
Founded: 1990. **Multinational. Description:** Promotes and arranges international student exchange. Fosters the positive development of the world's young people. Supports international peace, friendship and cross-cultural understanding. Provides students from the United States and abroad with opportunities to live with a family in another country and to study and travel abroad.

8629 ■ Project Harmony (PH)
5197 Main St., Unit 6
Waitsfield, VT 05673
Ph: (802)496-4545
Fax: (802)496-4548
E-mail: ann@projectharmony.org
URL: http://www.projectharmony.org
Contact: Lynn Jondahl, Exec. Dir.
Founded: 1985. **Staff:** 20. **Budget:** $700,000. **Multinational. Description:** Seeks to expand communication and cooperation between what is now the former Soviet Union and the United States through student and teacher exchange programs. Provides direct school exchange programs in which American and Russian schools are paired based on specific areas of study including language, music, gymnastics, and art. Conducts educational programs for peer exchange. Operates the teacher exchange program to allow American teachers, administrators, and curriculum developers the opportunity to visit Russian schools. Provides pre-trip orientation and post-trip debriefing. **Telecommunication Services:** electronic mail, donorservices@projectharmony.org. **Programs:** Azerbaijan Women's Leadership; Community Connections Hosting; Internet Access and Training; Junior Achievement; Open World; School Connectivity; Technology Ambassadors; Zang Armenia Legal Socialization. **Publications:** Newsletter, periodic. Alternate Formats: online ● Annual Report, annual. Alternate Formats: online.

8630 ■ Scandinavian Seminar (SS)
24 Dickinson St.
Amherst, MA 01002
Ph: (413)253-9736
Fax: (413)253-5282
E-mail: study@scandinavianseminar.org
URL: http://www.scandinavianseminar.org
Contact: Jacqueline D. Waldman, CEO
Founded: 1949. **Staff:** 7. **Budget:** $8,000,000. **Description:** Seeks to promote life-long learning and cultural exchange. **Libraries: Type:** reference. **Holdings:** 1,000. **Telecommunication Services:** electronic mail, jorgensen@scandinavianseminar.org. **Affiliated With:** Council on International Educational Exchange - USA. **Publications:** Newsletter, periodic.

8631 ■ Stelios M. Stelson Foundation
Address Unknown since 2007
Founded: 1952. **Members:** 100. **Description:** A people-to-people program promoting international friendship by providing free English language books to schools and libraries worldwide. Funded entirely by private donations. Conducts educational programs. **Formerly:** International Friendship Foundation. **Conventions/Meetings:** annual board meeting.

8632 ■ U.S.-China Education Foundation (USCEF)
4140 Oceanside Blvd., Ste.159 - No. 112
Oceanside, CA 92056-6005
Ph: (760)644-0977
E-mail: uscef@sage-usa.net
URL: http://www.sage-usa.net/uscef.htm
Contact: Dr. Joseph B. Kennedy Sr., Pres.
Founded: 1979. **Members:** 3,700. **Staff:** 3. **Budget:** $500,000. **Regional Groups:** 4. **State Groups:** 10. **Local Groups:** 1. **National Groups:** 7. **Languages:** Cantonese, English, Indian Dialects, Mandarin, Spanish. **Description:** Aims to promote the learning of the Chinese languages (including Mandarin, Cantonese, and minority languages such as Mongolian) by Americans, and the learning of English by Chinese. Conducts short-term travel-study program to prepare Americans and Chinese for stays of four, six, or eight months or one to four years in China or the U.S., respectively. Operates teacher placement service and speakers' bureau. A project of The Society for the Development of Global Education (S.A.G.E. Inc.). **Libraries: Type:** reference. **Subjects:** China, Asia, art. **Awards:** Jolene Mumtaz Kennedy International Dance. **Frequency:** annual. **Type:** scholarship. **Recipient:** for students 12 years of age or older who want to study abroad. **Departments:** Cultural Exchange; Development; Scholarships and Grants. **Publications:** *USCEF Update*, 3/year. Published in conjunction with SAGE. **Price:** free. **Conventions/Meetings:** annual meeting - always mid-June in San Francisco, CA.

8633 ■ U.S. Committee for Scientific Cooperation With Vietnam (USCSCV)
1095 Medical Sci. Ctr.
1300 Univ. Ave.
Madison, WI 53706
Ph: (608)263-4150 (608)263-9310
Fax: (608)263-8828
E-mail: jlladins@facstaff.wisc.edu
Contact: Dr. Judith L. Ladinsky, Pres.
Founded: 1978. **Members:** 550. **Membership Dues:** individual, $50 (annual). **Staff:** 50. **Languages:** English, Laotian, Vietnamese. **Multinational. Description:** University professors in medicine, math, social sciences, agriculture, engineering, appropriate technology, chemistry, physics, biology, and geology. Facilitates exchange of scientists and academics between Vietnam and the U.S. Provides consultants to Vietnam and Laos. Makes available medical and scientific journals, medicine, supplies, and equipment. Offers professional training and scientific programs; conducts research in Vietnam; operates charitable programs. **Libraries: Type:** reference. **Holdings:** books, periodicals. **Subjects:** Vietnam, Laos. **Awards:** Kovaleskaia Award. **Frequency:** annual. **Type:** recognition. **Recipient:** for the best woman scientist and female research group in Vietnam ● **Type:** monetary ● Vietnam Educational Exchange Program. **Frequency:** annual. **Type:** fellowship. **Recipient:** for graduate students from Vietnam and Laos ● Women in Science Award. **Frequency:** annual. **Type:** recognition. **Committees:** Agriculture; Chemistry; Culture; Engineering and Appropriate Technology; Environmental Sciences; Health Science; Higher Education; Linguistics; Mathematics; Physics and Other Natural Sciences; Social Sciences; Women in Science. **Publications:** *Bulletin of U.S. Committee*, 3/year. Newsletter. **Price:** included in membership dues. **Circulation:** 1,000. **Advertising:** accepted. **Conventions/Meetings:** annual meeting.

8634 ■ World Heritage
10725 Boston St.
Henderson, CO 80640
Ph: (303)252-8215
Free: (800)888-9040
Fax: (303)252-0629
E-mail: info@world-heritage.org
URL: http://www.world-heritage.org
Founded: 1980. **Staff:** 30. **Budget:** $1,000,000. **Regional Groups:** 10. **Description:** International high school student exchange program involving students from Germany, France, Great Britain, Mexico, Spain, and the United States. Makes arrangements for American students to live with Spanish-speaking families and attend local high schools. Offers a 3-week school-to-school exchange for groups led by an American teacher, a 4-week summer homestay without classes, and a 5-week summer study with classes. Provides placement services. **Computer Services:** database ● mailing lists. **Formerly:** Spanish Heritage-Herencia Espanola; (1981) Spanish Heritage Association. **Publications:** *AYUSA Bulletin*, monthly. **Conventions/Meetings:** annual conference.

8635 ■ World Learning
PO Box 676
Brattleboro, VT 05302-0676
Ph: (802)257-7751
Free: (800)257-7751
Fax: (802)258-3248
E-mail: info@worldlearning.org
URL: http://www.worldlearning.org
Contact: Carol Bellamy, Pres./CEO
Founded: 1932. **Staff:** 453. **Multinational. Description:** Provides individuals and institutions the ability to develop the leadership capabilities and cross-cultural competence needed to function effectively in the global arena. Administers social and economic development activities under U.S. government and international contracts and grants. Offers masters degrees in international and intercultural management leadership and service and in teaching; and study abroad programs for undergraduates. Offers programs in intensive language and culture training to professionals from international corporations, as well as overseas cultural exchange experiences to high school students. Administers projects in international training and development sponsored by government agencies and private foundations. Conducts professional training workshops and educational seminars. **Libraries: Type:** reference. **Holdings:** 30,000. **Awards:** Experiment Citation Award. **Frequency:** annual. **Type:** recognition. **Recipient:** for distinguished service in international education and exchange. **Computer Services:** Mailing lists, of members. **Additional Websites:** http://www.sit.edu. **Departments:** The Experiment in International Living; Language and Intercultural Training for Enterprises; Projects in International Development and Training; School for International Training; SIT Study Abroad. **Affiliated With:** CIVICUS: World Alliance for Citizen Participation; Earthwatch Institute; Interaction/American Council for Voluntary International Action; National Peace Corps Association; Save the Children; World Education. **Formerly:** Experiment in International Living; Experiment in International Living/School for International Training. **Publications:** *SIT Graduate Bulletin, SIT Study Abroad Catalogue, The Experiment in International Living*. Brochures ● *World Learning Odyssey*, semiannual. Newsletter. Contains alumni report, news, class notes, regional events reports and development reports. **Price:** free. **Circulation:** 60,000. Alternate Formats: online ● Annual Report, annual. Alternate Formats: online.

8636 ■ World Pen Pals
PO Box 337
Saugerties, NY 12477

Ph: (845)246-7828
Fax: (845)246-7828
E-mail: worldpenpals@aol.com
URL: http://www.world-pen-pals.com
Contact: Robert Carroll, Dir.
Founded: 1950. **Staff:** 4. **National Groups:** 83. **For-Profit. Multinational. Description:** Promotes international friendship and cultural understanding between students around the world in a penfriend exchange. **Libraries: Type:** not open to the public. **Subjects:** Africa and Asia. **Awards: Type:** recognition. **Affiliated With:** FIOCES; United Nations Educational, Scientific and Cultural Organization. **Publications:** Makes available posters and classroom display materials. **Conventions/Meetings:** seminar.

8637 ■ Yale-China Association (YCA)
442 Temple St., Box 208223
New Haven, CT 06520-8223
Ph: (203)432-0880
Fax: (203)432-7246
E-mail: yale-china@yale.edu
URL: http://www.yalechina.org
Contact: Nancy E. Chapman PhD, Exec. Dir.
Founded: 1901. **Members:** 1,900. **Membership Dues:** friend, $50 (annual) ● associate, $125 (annual) ● sponsor, $250 (annual) ● patron, $500 (annual) ● benefactor, $1,000 (annual) ● student, $25 (annual). **Staff:** 20. **Budget:** $550,000. **Description:** Promotes mutual understanding between the peoples of China and the United States through cultural and education exchange. Sends young American graduates and medical professionals to start up, administer and teach in hospitals and schools in China. Provides scholars from the United States to teach English and American studies to Chinese students; and scholars from China and the United States collaborate on projects involving medical research and care. Provides information and guidance on living, working and studying in China. **Formerly:** (1975) Yale-in-China Association. **Publications:** *Hsiang-Ya Journal* ● *The Yale-China Health Journal*, annual. **Price:** $5.00. Alternate Formats: online ● *Yale-China Review*, semiannual. Magazine. Summarizes events concerning Chinese politics, economics, social issues, Taiwan, international relations, and U.S.-China relations. **Price:** included in membership dues. **Circulation:** 6,000 ● *Yale-in-China - The Mainland, 1901-1950* ● Annual Report, biennial. **Price:** $1.00 for nonmembers; free for members. **Conventions/Meetings:** annual meeting.

8638 ■ YMCA International Camp Counselor Program (ICCP)
5 W 63rd St., 2nd Fl.
New York, NY 10023-9197
Ph: (212)727-8800
Free: (888)477-9622
Fax: (212)727-8814
E-mail: ips@ymcanyc.org
URL: http://www.internationalymca.org/ICCP/home.html
Contact: Amarillis Soler, Dir.
Founded: 1959. **Description:** Serves as a work-travel program designed to introduce international university students and teachers and social workers aged 19-30 to life in America; the students spend 8 to 9 weeks counseling in children's camps across the country, followed by a period of independent or group travel. Sponsors ICCP-Abroad placement service for American university students aged 18-25 wishing to serve as camp counselors in Africa, Asia, Australia, Hungary, New Zealand, and South America. **Telecommunication Services:** electronic mail, asoler@ymcanyc.org. **Publications:** *Camp Director's Manual*. Alternate Formats: online ● *The Globe*. Newsletter. Alternate Formats: online.

8639 ■ Youth For Understanding USA (YFU USA)
6400 Goldsboro Rd., Ste.100
Bethesda, MD 20817
Ph: (240)235-2100
Free: (800)TEENAGE
Fax: (240)235-2104
E-mail: admissions@yfu.org
URL: http://www.yfu-usa.org
Contact: Michael Finnell, Pres.
Founded: 1951. **Staff:** 65. **Budget:** $16,000,000. **Description:** Groups and individuals. Provides educational opportunities for young people and adults who want to learn more about other people, language, and culture through international student exchange. Sponsors teenage exchange program, under auspices of the U.S. Information Agency, through which U.S. students can live in homes abroad and students from foreign countries can live with American families. International Students, 15-18 years of age, spend six months to a year in the U.S; U.S., ages 15-18, spend a summer, semester or year abroad, live with volunteer host families, and attend local high schools in Europe, Latin America, Africa, Australia or Asia. Offers orientation, school placement, insurance, language assistance, and counseling to make the experience successful for all participants. Administers scholarship programs for students in cooperation with other governments, the U.S. Senate, corporations, professional associations, youth groups, and other international and educational organizations. **Telecommunication Services:** additional toll-free number, regional, (866)4YFU-USA. **Formerly:** (2003) Youth For Understanding International Exchange. **Publications:** Brochures ● Manuals ● Newsletters ● Report, annual ● Also publishes orientation and training materials.

International Schools

8640 ■ Association for the Advancement of International Education (AAIE)
PO Box 1500
Sheridan, WY 82801-1500
Ph: (307)674-6446
Fax: (307)674-7205
E-mail: aaiemfritz@sheridan.edu
URL: http://www.aaie.org
Contact: Everett McGlothlin, Pres.
Founded: 1966. **Members:** 600. **Membership Dues:** institution, $350 (annual) ● associate, $95 (annual) ● corporate, $300 (annual). **Staff:** 2. **Budget:** $390,000. **Regional Groups:** 10. **Description:** Acts as service organization for American schools overseas; cooperates with U.S. educational accreditation organizations. Sponsors School-to-School Project. Offers consulting services; engages in research. Provides in-service training for school administrators, teachers, and subject specialists. Maintains hall of fame. **Awards:** Hall of Fame. **Frequency:** annual. **Type:** recognition. **Recipient:** to an individual who has made significant contributions over a period of ten or more years to American/international education and who has furthered the goals of AAIE ● Superintendent of the Year. **Frequency:** annual. **Type:** recognition. **Publications:** *Inter Ed*, quarterly, combined spring/summer edition. Newsletter. Contains news and articles of interest to American international school heads abroad. **Price:** $50.00 /year for nonmembers; included in membership dues. **Circulation:** 600. **Advertising:** accepted. Alternate Formats: online ● Membership Directory, annual. **Conventions/Meetings:** annual conference (exhibits) - always late February/early March ● annual conference (exhibits).

8641 ■ Association of American International Colleges and Universities (AAICU)
1301 S Noland Rd.
Independence, MO 64055
Ph: (816)461-3633
Fax: (816)461-4925
E-mail: tiuf@aol.com
URL: http://www.aaicu.org
Contact: Dr. Erick O. Nielsen, Pres.
Founded: 1973. **Members:** 7,940. **Staff:** 5. **Description:** Individuals (8729), organizations and institutions (26). Promotes international cooperation and understanding; assists in achieving a coordinated program among institutions of higher education to help eliminate ignorance, superstition, disease, and poor communication; develops alternative solutions and institutions of higher education. Maintains a network of scholars and learning centers. Compiles statistics. **Libraries: Type:** reference. **Formerly:** (2001) Association of International Colleges and Universities. **Publications:** *Association of International Colleges and Universities—Directory*, annual. **Price:** available to members only ● *Association of International Colleges and Universities—Newsletter*, quarterly. **Price:** available to members only. **Conventions/Meetings:** annual conference - always London, England ● seminar ● workshop.

8642 ■ Association of American Schools in South America (AASSA)
12333 NW 18th St., Ste.5
Pembroke Pines, FL 33026
Ph: (954)436-4034
Fax: (954)436-4092
E-mail: info@aassa.com
URL: http://www.aassa.com
Contact: Paul Poore, Exec. Dir.
Founded: 1961. **Members:** 40. **Budget:** $325,000. **Multinational. Description:** American-type schools in 20 South American countries. Serves as a cooperative planning and problem-solving structure for member schools; provides staff development programs, workshops, and low-cost services (such as purchasing and shipping) otherwise unavailable to individual members. **Telecommunication Services:** electronic mail, poorep@bellsouth.net. **Publications:** *AASSA Newsletter*, monthly. **Advertising:** accepted ● Annual Report, annual. **Conventions/Meetings:** annual Chief Administrators' Conference ● annual Optimal Match Network Institute - conference ● annual Recruiting Fair - conference ● annual Superintendents Conference (exhibits).

8643 ■ Institute for American Universities (IAU)
1830 Sherman Ave., Ste.402
Evanston, IL 60201
Ph: (847)864-6876
Free: (800)221-2051
Fax: (847)864-6897
E-mail: usa@iaufrance.org
URL: http://www.iaufrance.org
Contact: Dr. Andrea Leskes PhD, Pres.
Founded: 1957. **Members:** 12,000. **Staff:** 13. **Languages:** English, French. **Description:** Provides a program of study abroad for American undergraduates from more than 700 United States universities. Courses of study include French, European Studies, French Civilization, European Business, Economics, Studio Arts, Archaeology and Ancient History, and International Relations. **Libraries: Type:** reference. **Holdings:** 11,000. **Subjects:** European civilization, Mediterranean studies, French language and literature, business, art and art history. **Divisions:** Advanced French Program; European Area Studies; Studio Art. **Also Known As:** Institut Americain Universitaire. **Publications:** *Alumni Newsletter*, annual. **Circulation:** 12,000 ● *La Cigale*, annual ● Bulletin, biennial ● Bulletin, biennial.

8644 ■ International Education Research Foundation (IERF)
PO Box 3665
Culver City, CA 90231-3665
Ph: (310)258-9451
Fax: (310)342-7086
E-mail: info@ierf.org
URL: http://www.ierf.org
Contact: Susan J. Bedil, Exec. Dir.
Founded: 1969. **Staff:** 31. **Budget:** $1,900,000. **Languages:** Arabic, Chinese, English, French, Hebrew, Russian, Spanish, Swedish. **Multinational. Description:** A charter member of the National Association of Credentials Evaluation Services. Evaluates foreign education credentials in terms of U.S. educational equivalence. Provides evaluations for employment purposes, colleges, universities, state licensing agencies, professional organizations, and the armed services. Conducts research and issues books on non-U.S. educational systems. **Libraries: Type:** not open to the public. **Holdings:** 20,000; books, periodicals. **Subjects:** education (foreign countries).

Awards: IERF Grant. **Frequency:** annual. **Type:** monetary. **Publications:** *The Country Index*. Book ● *German Monograph 1989*. Book.

8645 ■ International Educator's Institute (TIE)
PO Box 513
Cummaquid, MA 02637
Ph: (508)790-1990
Free: (877)375-6668
Fax: (508)790-1922
E-mail: tie@tieonline.com
URL: http://www.tieonline.com
Contact: Julianne Thrasher, Dir.
Founded: 1986. **Members:** 3,500. **Staff:** 5. **Budget:** $250,000. **Description:** Facilitates the placement of teachers and administrators in American, British, and international schools. Seeks to create a network that provides for professional development opportunities and improved financial security of members. Offers advice and information on international school news, recent educational developments, job placement, and investment, consumer, and professional development opportunities. Makes available insurance and travel benefits. Operates International Schools Internship Program. **Computer Services:** Mailing lists, of members. **Telecommunication Services:** electronic mail, jthrasher@tieonline.com. **Publications:** *The International Educator*, 5/year. Newspaper. **Price:** $43.00 in U.S. and Canada; $53.00 outside U.S. and Canada; $99.00 for institutions (3 subscriptions). ISSN: 1044-3509. **Circulation:** 13,000. **Advertising:** accepted.

8646 ■ International Schools Association (ISA)
10333 Diego Dr. S
Boca Raton, FL 33428
Ph: (561)883-3854
Fax: (561)483-2004
E-mail: info@isaschools.org
URL: http://www.isaschools.org
Contact: Mr. Clive Carthew, Chm.
Founded: 1951. **Members:** 100. **Staff:** 1. **Languages:** English, French, Spanish. **Multinational. Description:** International schools and other educational institutions. Seeks to establish an interchangeable curriculum and graduation standards for international schools and to advance the recognition of equivalent educational qualifications worldwide. Provides advisory and consultative services; promotes and carries out studies on educational or administrative questions; encourages establishment of new schools; fosters an interest in international affairs in regular schools. Facilitates teacher exchanges; initiated the International Baccalaureate program and the International Baccalaureate Middle Years program. **Committees:** Curriculum Development. **Publications:** *Internationalism in Schools - A Self-Study Guide*. Booklet. **Conventions/Meetings:** annual conference (exhibits).

8647 ■ International Schools Services (ISS)
PO Box 5910
15 Roszel Rd.
Princeton, NJ 08543
Ph: (609)452-0990
Fax: (609)452-2690
E-mail: iss@iss.edu
URL: http://www.iss.edu
Contact: Dan Scinto, Pres.
Founded: 1955. **Staff:** 200. **Description:** Provides educational services for American and international schools overseas. Operates a number of schools on behalf of U.S. industry abroad and recruits and recommends personnel. Offers curricular and administrative guidance; provides procurement, facility planning, and personnel services; conducts chief school officer search; serves as liaison with American educational resources; advises industry concerning schooling for U.S. dependent children overseas; gives consultative visits to individual schools. Conducts feasibility and evaluative studies. Operates four recruitment centers per year in January, February and June. **Formed by Merger of:** Inter-American School Service; International Schools Foundation. **Publications:** *International Schools Services—NewsLinks*, quarterly. Newsletter. Reports on international education. **Price:** free. **Circulation:** 14,000. **Advertising:** accepted ● *The ISS Directory of International Schools*, annual. Includes information on American/international schools overseas, accrediting and regional organizations. **Price:** $45.95/issue. **Circulation:** 3,000. **Advertising:** accepted ● *Newslinks*, quarterly. Newspaper. Features news from different schools, updates on staff and faculty members, trends in education and other current information. **Advertising:** accepted. **Conventions/Meetings:** quarterly International Recruitment Center - meeting, features international and U.S. based educational recruitment centers.

8648 ■ International University Foundation (IUF)
1301 S Noland Rd.
Independence, MO 64055
Ph: (816)461-3633
Free: (800)369-0009
Fax: (816)461-4925
E-mail: admin@tiuf.com
Contact: Dr. John Wayne Johnston, Pres.
Founded: 1973. **Members:** 62,337. **Staff:** 4. **Regional Groups:** 8. **Description:** Individuals and institutions united to advance the free flow of information and personnel between universities worldwide. Encourages international cooperation in higher education as a means of resolving global dilemmas in a rational, informed manner. Attempts to integrate and coordinate the educational efforts of member institutions via communication networks. Sponsors training programs. Maintains museum; compiles statistics. **Libraries: Type:** reference. **Holdings:** 12,885; archival material. **Publications:** *International University Foundation—Directory*, annual. **Price:** available to members only ● *International University Foundation—Report*, annual. **Price:** available to members only ● Books. **Conventions/Meetings:** annual conference ● seminar.

8649 ■ United Board for Christian Higher Education in Asia
475 Riverside Dr., Ste.1221
New York, NY 10115
Ph: (212)870-2600
Fax: (212)870-2322
URL: http://www.unitedboard.org
Contact: Patricia S. Stranahan, Pres.
Founded: 1932. **Staff:** 17. **Budget:** $6,818,485. **Multinational. Description:** Supports the efforts of eighty partner institutions in twelve countries to enhance academic and administrative excellence and promote a commitment to public service. Program emphases include strengthening partner institution's faculties through exchange opportunities in both Asia and America; enabling selected faculty members to pursue higher degrees; fostering active networking on issues of mutual interest among the related colleges; and facilitating support for partner institutions from their alumni in North America. **Libraries: Type:** reference. **Subjects:** Christian Colleges in Asia. **Formerly:** (1945) Associated Boards for Christian Colleges in China; (1955) United Board for Christian Colleges in China. **Publications:** *Quest*, semiannual. Journal. Interdisciplinary journal for Asian Christian scholars. ISSN: 1684-6206. **Conventions/Meetings:** semiannual board meeting.

International Studies

8650 ■ American Association for Ukrainian Studies (AAUS)
1583 Massachusetts Ave.
Cambridge, MA 02138
Ph: (617)495-4053
Fax: (617)495-8097
E-mail: vchernet@fas.harvard.edu
URL: http://www.ukrainianstudies.org
Contact: Vitaly Chernetsky, Acting Sec.-Treas.
Founded: 1989. **Membership Dues:** student/retiree, $20 (annual) ● faculty/professional, $30 (annual) ● joint, $40 (annual). **Multinational. Description:** Advances Ukrainian studies in the United States and other countries. Provides career-building resources to members. Furthers knowledge about Ukraine and related topics. **Publications:** *Harvard Ukrainian Studies*. Journal. **Price:** included in membership dues ● *Visnyk*. Newsletter. **Price:** included in membership dues.

8651 ■ American Council on International Intercultural Education (ACIIE)
Oakton Community Coll.
1600 E Golf Rd.
Des Plaines, IL 60016
Ph: (847)635-2605
E-mail: lkorbel@oakton.edu
URL: http://www.aciie.org
Contact: Linda Korbel, Exec. Dir.
Founded: 1975. **Membership Dues:** institution (US community college), $350-$595 (annual) ● institution (international), $300 (annual) ● individual, $50 (annual) ● affiliate (domestic-four year college and university), $350-$595 (annual). **Description:** Advocates for community colleges in the global arena. Uses its collective expertise to facilitate programs, activities, and linkages in international and intercultural education. **Computer Services:** database, state consortia directory. **Affiliated With:** American Association of Community Colleges. **Publications:** Newsletter, 3/year. Alternate Formats: online. **Conventions/Meetings:** annual conference.

8652 ■ American Institute for Foreign Study (AIFS)
River Plz.
9 W Broad St.
Stamford, CT 06902-3788
Ph: (203)399-5000
Free: (866)906-2437
Fax: (203)399-5590
E-mail: info@aifs.com
URL: http://www.aifs.com
Contact: William L. Gertz, Pres./CEO
Founded: 1964. **Staff:** 150. **Description:** Students and teachers at all levels. Encourages the understanding of foreign countries, and their languages and cultures among American students and teachers. Sponsors courses in Australia, Asia, Europe, and Mexico at renowned universities using local faculty and professors from participating United States institutions. Organizes courses for junior high school through college level students and interested adults, including homestays, internships, and credit courses. **Awards:** Minority Scholarship. **Frequency:** annual. **Type:** scholarship. **Publications:** *Academic Year and Summer Programs Catalog*, annual. Alternate Formats: online ● *American Institute for Foreign Study College Division Catalog*, annual. **Conventions/Meetings:** meeting (exhibits) - 5-10/year.

8653 ■ Association for Borderlands Studies (ABS)
c/o Dr. Manuel Chavez, Pres.
Center for Latin Amer. and Caribbean Stud.
Michigan State Univ.
300 Intl. Center
East Lansing, MI 48824
Ph: (517)353-1960
Fax: (517)432-7475
E-mail: chavezm1@msu.edu
URL: http://www.absborderlands.org
Contact: Dr. Manuel Chavez, Pres.
Founded: 1976. **Members:** 300. **Membership Dues:** regular, $50 (annual) ● student, $20 (annual) ● library, $50 (annual). **Staff:** 6. **Description:** Scholars at academic and governmental institutions representing the Americas, Asia, Africa, and Europe. Dedicated to the systematic interchange of ideas and information relating to international border areas including the United States-Mexico borderlands. Researchers, teachers, policy makers, and activists interested in the interchange of ideas and information relating to boundary line and borderlands areas worldwide. **Computer Services:** Mailing lists. **Publications:** *Journal of Borderlands Studies*, semiannual. Contains research. **Price:** included in membership dues; C$55.00 /year for libraries. Alternate Formats: online

● *La Frontera*, semiannual. Newsletter. Reports on meetings and professional news. **Price:** included in membership dues. Alternate Formats: online. **Conventions/Meetings:** annual conference - late April. 2009 Apr. 15-18, Albuquerque, NM.

8654 ■ Association of Professional Schools of International Affairs (APSIA)
c/o Braden Smith, Exec. Dir.
225 Eggers Hall
Syracuse, NY 13244-1090
Ph: (315)443-2113
Fax: (315)443-9204
E-mail: bsmith@apsia.org
URL: http://www.apsia.org
Contact: Braden Smith, Exec. Dir.
Members: 29. **Multinational. Description:** Works to advance global understanding and cooperation by preparing men and women to assume positions of leadership in world affairs; serves as a source of information on professional international affairs education, represents the interests of professional international affairs education in national and international forums, and coordinates activities among and for its member institutions. **Computer Services:** database, member schools.

8655 ■ Comparative and International Education Society (CIES)
c/o Dr. Hilary Landorf, Treas.
Florida International University
Coll. of Educ.
Dept. of Curriculum and Instruction
347A ZEB Bldg.
Miami, FL 33199
Ph: (305)348-3488 (305)348-2410
Fax: (305)348-1515
E-mail: secretariat@cies.us
URL: http://www.cies.us
Contact: Dr. Hilary Landorf, Treas.
Founded: 1956. **Members:** 2,500. **Membership Dues:** individual, $35 (annual) ● student, $20 (annual) ● institutional, $67 (annual). **Regional Groups:** 4. **Description:** Represents professors of comparative education and related fields, professors of academic subjects, university administrators, governmental and other workers in international comparative education. Promotes the study of comparative and international education in universities. Encourages research projects and cooperates with international educational agencies. **Libraries: Type:** reference. **Holdings:** archival material. **Awards:** Gail Kelly Award. **Frequency:** annual. **Type:** recognition. **Recipient:** for outstanding doctoral dissertation ● George Bereday Award. **Frequency:** annual. **Type:** recognition. **Recipient:** for best CER article. **Formerly:** (1970) Comparative Education Society. **Publications:** *CIES Newsletter*, 3/year. Covers comparative education worldwide. Includes book reviews, employment opportunities, and membership directory. **Price:** included in membership dues. ISSN: 0010-4043. **Circulation:** 2,500. **Advertising:** accepted ● *Comparative Education Review*, quarterly. **Price:** $17.75 /year for individuals; $49.75 /year for institutions; $30.00/year for students in U.S. **Conventions/Meetings:** annual conference (exhibits).

8656 ■ Cordell Hull Foundation for International Education (CHF)
501 5th Ave., 3rd Fl.
New York, NY 10017
Ph: (212)300-2138
E-mail: cordellhull@aol.com
URL: http://www.cordellhull.org
Contact: Marianne Mason Morrison, Exec. Dir.
Founded: 1951. **Members:** 12. **Staff:** 3. **Languages:** English, French, German, Russian, Spanish. **Description:** "Works to develop comity among the United States and the rest of the Hemisphere in the general interest of international education." Named for Cordell Hull (1871-1955), who won the 1945 Nobel Peace Prize as "Father of the UN", a title bestowed by President Franklin Roosevelt. He was the longest-serving U.S. Secretary of State from 1933-1944. **Publications:** Brochure, annual.

8657 ■ Global Alliance for Transnational Education (GATE)
9697 E Mineral Ave.
Englewood, CO 80112
Ph: (303)784-8368 (303)784-8232
Free: (800)525-7002
E-mail: publicrelations@jones.com
URL: http://www.jones.com/gate
Contact: John G. Flores, Contact
Founded: 1995. **Membership Dues:** individual-affiliate, $150 (annual) ● educational institution, agency, corporate-affiliate, $1,000 (annual). **For-Profit. Description:** Global alliance of businesses, postsecondary educational institutions, and government agencies. Seeks to improve the quality and availability of international educational services worldwide. Serves as a clearinghouse on international education, e-learning, and technology-based corporate training; develops and maintains principles of best practice for transnational education and accredits programs and institutions. **Computer Services:** database, of accredited providers of international educational services. **Publications:** *Demand for Transnational Education in the Asia-Pacific*, annual. Published jointly with UNESCO. ● *Higher Education in Europe*, annual. Published jointly with UNESCO. ● *Transnational Education and the New Economy*, annual. Published jointly with UNESCO. ● Newsletter. **Conventions/Meetings:** annual conference.

8658 ■ Global Learning (GL)
22 Mary Ann Dr.
Brick, NJ 08723
Ph: (732)528-0016
Fax: (732)528-1027
E-mail: globallearningnj@comcast.net
URL: http://www.globallearningnj.org
Contact: Jeffrey L. Brown, Exec. Dir.
Founded: 1974. **Staff:** 2. **Budget:** $142,000. **Description:** Seeks to promote concepts of global education in state and local school systems, and train teachers and librarians in global education concepts and teaching strategies. Offers program presentations on energy conservation in schools, global climate change, cutting greenhouse gas emissions, high performance school buildings, sustainable development, nonviolent conflict resolution, war, peace, disarmament, world hunger, and multicultural studies. Trains teachers and students as mediators in the Conflict Mediators Program. Conducts workshops, institutes, in-service courses, on-site school evaluation, and curriculum revision consultations. Also holds workshops for businesses on cross-cultural communications and awareness and conflict resolution skills. **Libraries: Type:** reference. **Holdings:** 1,000; audiovisuals. **Subjects:** elementary, secondary, college curricula, general global education, sustainable development, peer mediation, general teacher-education. **Publications:** *A Sustainable Development Curriculum Framework for World History/Cultures* ● *Decide Tomorrow Today: Libraries Build Sustainable Communities: A Guide for Libraries* ● *Doing Our Share: Greenhouse Gas Reductions Manual for Schools* ● *Making Connections in Middle School: Lessons on the Environment, Development, and Equity* ● *Sustaining the Future: Activities for Environmental Education in American History*. **Conventions/Meetings:** quarterly New Jersey Sustainable Schools Network - meeting.

8659 ■ International Initiatives of the American Council on Education
1 Dupont Cir. NW
Washington, DC 20036-1193
Ph: (202)939-9300
Fax: (202)785-8056
E-mail: comments@ace.nche.edu
URL: http://www.acenet.edu/AM/Template.cfm?Section=International
Contact: Madeleine F. Green, VP/Dir.
Founded: 1979. **Staff:** 4. **Budget:** $250,000. **Description:** Works with the Commission on International Education of the American Council on Education to: identify international education issues of importance to higher education; help shape international education policies at the federal level; assist higher educational institutions in the U.S. to adopt more international activities. Works with overseas institutions and associations. Sponsors Leadership Network for International Education and programs for university leadership development abroad. **Libraries: Type:** open to the public. **Holdings:** 6,500; books, periodicals. **Subjects:** all aspects of higher education, including admissions, administration, adult and continuing education, curriculum, faculty issues, economics and finance, history, instruction, international education, minority concerns, philosophy, policy, students, women's issues. **Telecommunication Services:** electronic mail, madeleine_green@ace.nche.edu. **Publications:** *Beyond September 11: A Comprehensive National Policy on International Education*. Report. Contains an outline of U.S. need for international and foreign language expertise and citizen awareness. **Price:** $10.00 for nonmembers; $9.00 for members. Alternate Formats: online ● *Brave New (and Smaller) World of Higher Education: A Transatlantic View*. Manual. **Price:** $15.00 for nonmembers; $13.50 for members. Alternate Formats: online ● *Brief Guide to U.S. Higher Education*. Manual. Provides an overview of higher education in the United States. **Price:** $15.00 for nonmembers; $13.50 for members. Alternate Formats: online ● *Educating Americans for a World in Flux: Ten Ground Rules for Internationalizing Higher Education*. Manual. Contains a general rationale for international education and recommends specific strategies for internationalizing institutions. **Price:** $8.00 for nonmembers; $7.20 for members ● *Educating for Global Competence: America's Passport to the Future*. Manual. Highlights the importance of international education to nation's economic and political path. **Price:** $10.00 for nonmembers; $9.00 for members ● *Faculty of the Future: A Transatlantic Dialogue*. Manual. **Price:** free ● *Guidelines for College and University Linkages Abroad*. Manual ● *Higher Education-Private Sector Linkages in the USA and Mexico* ● *International Visitors Guide to U.S. Higher Education* ● *Internationalization of U.S. Higher Education: Preliminary Status Report 2000*. Contains reports on the state of international education in the United States, primarily at the undergraduate level. **Price:** $15.00 for nonmembers; $13.50 for members. Alternate Formats: online ● *Internationalizing the Campus: A User's Guide*. Manual. Contains practical guide for higher education administrators and faculty engaged in internationalizing institutions. **Price:** $34.95 for nonmembers; $29.95 for members. Alternate Formats: online ● *Internationalizing the Undergraduate Curriculum: A Handbook for Campus Leaders*. **Price:** $5.00 for nonmembers; $4.50 for members ● *New Demands, Enduring Values: The Challenge of Human Resources (Highlights of a Transatlantic Seminar on Higher Education)*. **Price:** $8.00 for nonmembers; $7.20 for members ● *New Times, New Strategies: Curricular Joint Ventures*. Paper. Contains an exploration of one emerging type of strategic alliance-the curricular joint venture. **Price:** $15.00 for nonmembers; $13.50 for members ● *Next Steps for Languages Across the Curriculum: Prospects, Problems and Promise*. Report. Contains the nature, status, and intellectual potential of languages across the programs by campus participants. **Price:** $10.00 for nonmembers; $9.00 for members ● *One Year Later: Attitudes about International Education since September 11*. Report. Contains an examination of public's attitudes toward international education since September 11, 2001. Alternate Formats: online ● *Policy Roundtable Series*. Reports. Provides issues in higher education and regional and international economic development. **Price:** $4.00 for nonmembers; $3.60 for members. Alternate Formats: online ● *Promising Practices: Spotlighting Excellence in Comprehensive Internationalization*. Contains case study/s done by eight U.S. colleges and universities that are leading the movement to educate a globally competent citizenry. **Price:** $20.00 for nonmembers; $18.00 for members. Alternate Formats: online ● *Public Experience, Attitudes, and Knowledge: A Report on Two National Surveys About International Education*. Contains detailed information about the findings of two surveys related to international education. **Price:** $20.00 for nonmembers; $18.00 for

members ● *Reforming the Higher Education Curriculum: Internationalizing the Campus.*

8660 ■ Maryknoll Mission Center of New England (MMCNE)
Address Unknown since 2008
Founded: 1911. **Description:** A program of the Catholic Foreign Mission Society of America established to increase awareness of the Third World and its problems. Provides presentations to schools, colleges and churches regarding the Third World, current emphasis on globalization, cultures, world religions, social justice and peace. **Libraries: Type:** not open to the public. **Holdings:** 600; video recordings. **Subjects:** U.S. foreign policy, Third World or developing countries, spirituality. **Formerly:** Maryknoll Center for Justice Concerns. **Publications:** *Maryknoll* (in English and Spanish), monthly. Magazine. Covers the Catholic foreign mission. **Circulation:** 800,000 ● *Revista Maryknoll*, monthly. Magazine.

8661 ■ National Model United Nations (NMUN)
3489 Valento Cir.
St. Paul, MN 55127
Ph: (651)493-4404
Fax: (651)484-2531
E-mail: info@nmun.org
URL: http://www.nmun.org
Contact: Erin Kennedy, Sec. Gen.
Founded: 1967. **Members:** 2,600. **Membership Dues:** college, $200 (annual). **Staff:** 75. **Budget:** $150,000. **Description:** Sponsors educational programs and National Model United Nations, which conducts United Nations simulations to teach college students about international diplomacy. **Libraries: Type:** reference. **Holdings:** archival material. **Subjects:** human rights, security, economic development, environment, peacekeeping, nuclear non-proliferation, sanctions, refugees, children. **Awards:** Distinguished Delegation Award. **Frequency:** annual. **Type:** recognition. **Recipient:** for country representation ● Outstanding Delegation Award. **Frequency:** annual. **Type:** recognition. **Telecommunication Services:** electronic mail, eaton@nmun.org. **Committees:** Secretariat Staff. **Formerly:** (1968) National Model United Nations. **Publications:** *Staff Infection*, monthly. Newsletter. **Circulation:** 100. **Advertising:** accepted ● *UN Journal* ● Annual Report, annual. Alternate Formats: online ● Brochure. Alternate Formats: online. **Conventions/Meetings:** annual Model United Nations - competition and conference - always a week before Easter.

International Understanding

8662 ■ Center for Global Education
Augsburg Coll.
2211 Riverside Ave.
Minneapolis, MN 55454
Ph: (612)330-1159
Free: (800)299-8889
Fax: (612)330-1695
E-mail: globaled@augsburg.edu
URL: http://www.augsburg.edu/global
Contact: Orval Gingerich, Dir.
Founded: 1982. **Staff:** 24. **Budget:** $1,300,000. **Description:** Church congregations and church-related agencies; civic leaders and other individuals; local, state, and federal government officials. Seeks to provide opportunities for experiential education regarding the problems of international development and the dynamics of social change. Sponsors educational programs including travel seminars to Central America, Southern Africa, and Mexico. Operates program center in Cuernavaca, Mexico, which offers two semester-long undergraduate programs focusing on gender issues, and the role of the church in social change. Offers two semester programs in Namibia, and a semester program in Central America. Provides consulting on global education. **Absorbed:** (1986) Nicaragua-Honduras Education Project. **Publications:** *Global News and Notes*, quarterly. Newsletter.

8663 ■ Institute of World Affairs (IWA)
1321 Pennsylvania Ave. SE
Washington, DC 20003
Ph: (571)214-5293
Fax: (706)225-6578
E-mail: info@iwa.org
URL: http://www.iwa.org
Contact: Dr. Hrach Gregorian, Pres.
Founded: 1924. **Staff:** 8. **Budget:** $600,000. **Languages:** Armenian, English, Russian. **Description:** Conducts programs and training seminars in the U.S. and abroad designed to enhance professional skills in conflict resolution and infrastructure development. Operates several long-term development and post-conflict reconciliation projects in the Middle East and Eastern Mediterranean. **Libraries: Type:** open to the public. **Holdings:** 2,500; books. **Subjects:** international relations. **Computer Services:** Mailing lists, of members. **Formerly:** (1977) Institute of World Affairs; (1981) American Universities Field Staff -Institute of World Affairs; (1988) Universities Field Staff International -Institute of World Affairs.

8664 ■ InterFuture (IF)
c/o David L. Robbins, Pres.
PO Box 282
State House Sta.
Boston, MA 02133
Ph: (617)573-8267
Fax: (617)573-8513
E-mail: drobbins@acad.suffolk.edu
URL: http://www.interstudios.net/timothy/IF/index.htm
Contact: David L. Robbins, Pres.
Founded: 1969. **Budget:** $70,000. **Description:** Volunteer network of academics, professionals, students, and community leaders in 17 countries. Works to give college students a world perspective on the problems and possibilities of the human future. Selects annually 10-20 undergraduates who design, conduct, and carry out comparative, independent studies in the United States, Europe, and the Third World. Studies may be selected from 3 themes: Individual and Society; Habitat; or Internationalism. After an 8-month preparatory period, students live for 3 months in another country, study with a local expert, and live with local families. After participants return to their home country, they present findings to home institutions for academic credit and share their experiences with their campuses and communities through service projects and organized information centers. Holds seminars, symposia, workshops, and exhibitions. **Awards:** Hugh H. and Mabel M. Smythe International Service Citation Award. **Type:** recognition. **Recipient:** for a distinguished member of the academic, diplomatic, voluntary service, or business community in recognition of longstanding and continuing service to the cause of increased international understanding ● **Frequency:** annual. **Type:** scholarship. **Recipient:** for sophomore students. **Committees:** Awards; Visiting Scholars. **Publications:** *InterFuture Reports*, periodic. Contains project summaries. **Conventions/Meetings:** annual meeting - always in Boston, MA.

8665 ■ Legacy International (LI)
1020 Legacy Dr.
Bedford, VA 24523
Ph: (540)297-5982
Fax: (540)297-1860
E-mail: mail@legacyintl.org
URL: http://www.legacyintl.org
Contact: Shanti Thompson, VP/Dir. of Training
Founded: 1979. **Staff:** 15. **Budget:** $800,000. **Multinational. Description:** Dedicated to strengthen civil society, linking cultures and provides tools for individuals and organizations to build a better tomorrow today. **Telecommunication Services:** electronic mail, thompson@legacyintl.org. **Also Known As:** Institute for Practical Idealism. **Publications:** *Community Connections*, annual. Newsletter. **Price:** free. **Circulation:** 2,000.

8666 ■ Moorhead Kennedy Group
114 Clinton St.
Brooklyn, NY 11201
Ph: (718)858-2528
Fax: (718)625-8064
E-mail: mkgroup@aol.com
Contact: Brenda Repland, Managing Partner
Founded: 1990. **Staff:** 2. **Budget:** $100,000. **Languages:** Arabic, Chinese, English, French, Norwegian, Spanish. **For-Profit. Description:** Practices innovative and interactive mode of training. Deals with corporate and social issues. **Libraries: Type:** not open to the public. **Holdings:** 1,200. **Subjects:** ethics, middle east, corporate policy, Asia, international business, global cultures. **Publications:** *ATOMIC!* ● *The Ayatollah in the Cathedral: Reflections of a Hostage*. Book ● *Death of a Dissident* ● *Fire in the Forest* ● *Focus on Iraq*. Serves as a resource guide. ● *Focus on Russia and the Republics*. Serves as a teaching and resource guide. ● *Grocery Store* ● *Hostage Crisis*.

8667 ■ Society for Intercultural Education, Training and Research U.S.A. (SIETAR-USA)
603 Stewart St., Ste.610
Seattle, WA 98101
Ph: (206)859-4351
E-mail: info@sietarusa.org
URL: http://www.sietarusa.org
Contact: Peggy Pusch, Exec. Dir.
Founded: 1974. **Members:** 400. **Membership Dues:** full, $125 (annual) ● family, $160 (annual) ● institutional, $500 (annual) ● sustaining, $250 (annual) ● student, senior, $70 (annual) ● senior family, $100 (annual). **Budget:** $75,000. **Regional Groups:** 40. **Description:** Promotes and facilitates intercultural education, training, and research through professional exchange. Works to improve intercultural relations, both domestic and global, by supporting the development and diffusion of cross-cultural knowledge and intercultural skills and practices. Encourages highest ethical standards and conduct information clearinghouse, a core support system for professionals, and a reference service for linking resources to needs. Sponsors annual week-long summer institute; works to stimulate research and funding of research. **Computer Services:** Mailing lists, U.S. and Canada addresses. **Subgroups:** SIETAR Australia-Victoria; SIETAR Austria; SIETAR Calgary; SIETAR Cascadia; SIETAR Europa; SIETAR France; SIETAR Germany; SIETAR Houston; SIETAR Israel; SIETAR Japan; SIETAR Metro New Jersey; SIETAR Metro Washington D.C.; SIETAR Netherlands; SIETAR New Zealand; SIETAR Thailand. **Formerly:** (1983) Society for Intercultural Education, Training and Research; (2002) International Society for Intercultural Education, Training and Research. **Publications:** *S-USA News*, quarterly. Newsletter. Includes affiliate news, job listing, articles. **Price:** included in membership dues. **Circulation:** 2,200. **Advertising:** accepted. Alternate Formats: online. **Conventions/Meetings:** annual conference (exhibits) ● annual workshop.

Iranian

8668 ■ Association for the Study of Persianate Societies (ASPS)
c/o Habib Borjian, Sec.-Treas.
118-18 Union Tpke., Apt. 18E
Kew Gardens, NY 11415
E-mail: habibborjian@hotmail.com
URL: http://www.d.umn.edu/cla/persianatesocieties/main/index.php
Contact: Habib Borjian, Sec.-Treas.
Founded: 1996. **Membership Dues:** regular, $35 (annual) ● student, $15 (annual) ● institution, $75 (annual). **Multinational. Description:** Represents scholars and researchers interested in the culture and civilization of Persian societies. Promotes the study of Persian societies and related people in the Iranian civilization area. Upholds a scholarly approach to the culture and civilization of Persian-speaking societies. **Awards:** Travel Fellowship Program. **Type:** fellowship. **Recipient:** for applicants from Iran, Afghanistan and Tajikistan engaged in teaching or research in the social sciences. **Publications:** *Studies on Persianate Societies*, annual. Journal. Contains research articles about Persianate

societies. **Price:** $75.00 /year for individuals ● Newsletter, semiannual. Includes news and updates on the organization's activities, as well as other contributions and announcements. **Price:** free. Alternate Formats: online.

Islamic

8669 ■ Council on Islamic Education (CIE)
PO Box 20186
Fountain Valley, CA 92728-0186
Ph: (714)839-2929
Fax: (714)839-2714
E-mail: info@cie.org
URL: http://www.cie.org
Contact: Munir A. Shaikh, Exec. Dir.
Founded: 1990. **Description:** Aims to strengthen American public education. Seeks to draw inspiration from all aspects of Islamic principles and apply them in ways that are suitable for the American academic society. Strives to employ a contributory approach that affirms the institutional mechanisms that support the American system.

8670 ■ Institute of Islamic and Arabic Sciences in America (IIASA)
8500 Hilltop Rd.
Fairfax, VA 22031
Ph: (703)641-4986 (703)207-3901
Fax: (703)641-4899
E-mail: info@iiasa.org
URL: http://www.iiasa.org
Contact: Nadeem Malik, Contact
Founded: 1988. **Staff:** 50. **Languages:** Arabic, English. **Description:** Promotes the study of Islam and Arabic culture and language. Provides free tuition for undergraduate and graduate education, and continuing education in Islamic and Arabic sciences. Promotes public dialogue and education about Islamic teachings and Muslim culture. Works with American centers and universities interested in Islamic and Arabic studies. Conducts research and educational programs; sponsors seminars, forums, and competitions; offers placement service and children's services; maintains museum and speakers' bureau. **Libraries: Type:** lending; reference; open to the public. **Holdings:** archival material, audio recordings, books, clippings, periodicals, video recordings. **Subjects:** Arabic and Islamic education. **Awards: Type:** monetary ● **Type:** recognition. **Computer Services:** database ● mailing lists ● record retrieval services. **Departments:** Public Relations; Research; Seminar. **Sections:** Language Laboratory. **Publications:** *Manar-as-Sabeel*, monthly. Magazine. **Price:** free. **Advertising:** accepted. Alternate Formats: online. **Conventions/Meetings:** monthly seminar.

8671 ■ Islamic Research Foundation International (IRFI)
7102 W Shefford Ln.
Louisville, KY 40242-6462
Ph: (502)287-6262 (502)423-1988
E-mail: irfi@iname.com
URL: http://www.irfi.org
Contact: Dr. Tajuddin Ahmed, Chm.
Founded: 1988. **Members:** 300. **Membership Dues:** individual, $20 (annual) ● fellow, $30 (annual) ● student, $10 (annual). **Staff:** 1. **Regional Groups:** 12. **Languages:** Arabic, English, Hindi, Kannada, Telugu, Urdu. **Description:** Individuals of the Islamic religion. Promotes the revitalization of Islamic Renaissance. Works to achieve excellence in all branches of knowledge and interpret Qur'an and Hadith in light of modern knowledge. Conducts research, charitable, and educational programs; offers children's services; maintains speakers' bureau. Runs an Islamic school. Awards research grants and scholarships. Establishes centers of higher learning to integrate Islamic and modern education. **Libraries: Type:** lending; reference; open to the public. **Holdings:** 1,988; audio recordings, books, clippings, monographs, periodicals, video recordings. **Subjects:** Qur'an, Hadith, Islamic sciences, Islamic medicine, Islamic renaissance, IJTIHAD. **Awards:** Dr. Tajuddin Ahmed Book Publication Award. **Frequency:** annual. **Type:** recognition. **Recipient:** for an author of a work on the Islamic renaissance, Tafsir of the Qur'an, or understanding of the Qur'an and Hadith in the light of modern knowledge ● Essay Competition. **Frequency:** annual. **Type:** recognition. **Recipient:** for the best essays on how the fundamental scientific and medical discoveries and inventions of Muslim scientists laid the foundation for European Renaissance and paved the way for modern scientific discoveries and technical achievements ● Travel Grants to Students Coming to USA from Developing Countries. **Frequency:** annual. **Type:** recognition. **Computer Services:** Mailing lists ● online services. **Telecommunication Services:** electronic mail, president@irfi.org ● electronic mail, islamicresearch@yahoo.com. **Committees:** Awards & Honors; Fundraising; Membership; Public Relations; Publications. **Also Known As:** (1988) Islamic Research Foundation for Advancement of Knowledge. **Publications:** *AALIM*, quarterly. Newsletter. Includes information, news, book reviews, articles, quotations and calendar. **Price:** free. **Circulation:** 1,000. **Advertising:** accepted. Alternate Formats: diskette ● *International Conference on Islamic Renaissance.* Proceedings. **Conventions/Meetings:** biennial International Conference on Islamic Renaissance (exhibits).

Israel

8672 ■ Unity Coalition for Israel (UCI)
3965 W 83rd St., No. 292
Shawnee Mission, KS 66208
Ph: (913)648-0022
Fax: (913)648-7997
E-mail: voices@israelunitycoalition.org
URL: http://www.israelunitycoalition.org
Contact: Esther Levens, CEO/Founder
Founded: 1991. **Membership Dues:** individual, $36 (annual) ● organization, $100-$1,000 (annual). **Multinational. Description:** Represents the interests of Christian and Jewish organizations across the US. Works to ensure a safe and secure Israel. Gathers information and people to support and preserve Israel. Encourages people to visit Israel and its religious sites. **Publications:** *Today's News Summaries*, daily. Newsletter. **Price:** free. Alternate Formats: online ● Brochure. Alternate Formats: online.

Israeli

8673 ■ American Associates, Ben-Gurion University of the Negev (AABGU)
1430 Broadway, 8th Fl.
New York, NY 10018
Ph: (212)687-7721
Free: (800)962-2248
Fax: (212)302-6443
E-mail: info@aabgu.org
URL: http://www.aabgu.org
Contact: Amos Drory, Exec. VP
Founded: 1972. **Staff:** 25. **Regional Groups:** 11. **Description:** Individuals interested in supporting Ben-Gurion University of the Negev, a major educational and research center of 10,500 students in Israel. Conducts research at the university's Applied Research Institutes, Jacob Blaustein Institute for Desert Research, and Ben-Gurion Institute and Archives. **Libraries: Type:** reference. **Awards:** Donor Recognition Awards. **Type:** recognition. **Committees:** Academic Advisory; Library; Medical. **Formerly:** (1974) American Friends of the University of the Negev. **Publications:** *Impact*, 3/year. Newsletter. **Price:** free. **Circulation:** 20,000. Alternate Formats: online. **Conventions/Meetings:** periodic regional meeting and dinner.

8674 ■ American Committee for Shenkar College
307 7th Ave., Ste.1805
New York, NY 10001
Ph: (212)947-1597
Fax: (212)643-9887
E-mail: shenkarcollege@verizon.net
URL: http://www.shenkarcollege.org
Contact: Bruce Pernick, Pres.
Founded: 1971. **Description:** Provides support and capital funding for Shenkar College in Israel. Conducts educational and research programs. Maintains speakers' bureau. **Libraries: Type:** reference. **Awards: Type:** scholarship. **Publications:** *Shenkar News*, quarterly. Newsletter. **Conventions/Meetings:** quarterly board meeting.

8675 ■ American Friends of the Alliance Israelite Universelle (AFAIU)
15 W 16th St., 6th Fl.
New York, NY 10011-6301
Ph: (917)606-8260
Fax: (212)294-8348
E-mail: afaiu@cjh.org
Contact: Ms. Isabelle Friedman, Pres.
Founded: 1947. **Staff:** 1. **Local Groups:** 2. **Description:** Assists a network of 60 Jewish schools, teacher training seminaries, and remedial programs in Europe, Canada, Israel, and the Middle East and works to familiarize the public in the United States about the educational, cultural, and human rights activities of the Alliance Israelite Universelle. **Publications:** *The Alliance Review*, annual. Magazine. Includes reports on organizations activities and academic articles. **Circulation:** 5,000. **Conventions/Meetings:** annual meeting.

8676 ■ American Friends of The Hebrew University (AFHU)
1 Battery Park Plz., 25th Fl.
New York, NY 10004
Ph: (212)607-8500
Free: (800)567-AFHU
Fax: (212)809-4430
E-mail: info@afhu.org
URL: http://www.afhu.org
Contact: George A. Schieren, Pres.
Founded: 1925. **Description:** Promotes the development and maintenance of The Hebrew University of Jerusalem and other institutes of higher education in Israel and elsewhere. This support has aided Hebrew University in becoming a world leader in research and scholarship in many fields, including technology, medicine, agriculture, and Jewish studies, as well as in making significant contributions to promote peace and pluralism in the Middle East. **Divisions:** Dental; Lawyers; Pharmacy. **Absorbed:** (1965) American Jewish Physicians' Committee. **Publications:** *Scopus*, annual ● Newsletter, semiannual. **Conventions/Meetings:** annual International Board of Governors - international conference ● annual Leadership Engagement Forum - ALEF - seminar ● annual National Leadership - meeting.

8677 ■ American Society for Technion-Israel Institute of Technology (ASTIIT)
55 E 59th St., No. 124
New York, NY 10022-1112
Ph: (212)407-6300
Fax: (212)753-2925
E-mail: info@ats.org
URL: http://www.ats.org
Contact: Melvyn H. Bloom, Exec. VP
Founded: 1940. **Members:** 35,000. **Staff:** 90. **Budget:** $12,319,000. **Regional Groups:** 31. **Local Groups:** 31. **Description:** Supports organization in the United States for the Technion-Israel Institute of Technology. Supports higher education in Israel. Provides financial and technical support to the Institute, maintains speakers' bureau; operates charitable program. **Awards:** Albert Einstein Award. **Type:** recognition. **Recipient:** for exemplary service to the organization. **Committees:** Consulting Service for Israel; New Leadership; Research and Development; Scholarship and Women's Division. **Also Known As:** American Technion Society. **Formerly:** (1952) American Society for Advancement of Haifa Institute of Technology. **Publications:** *American Society for Technion-Israel Institute of Technology—Update Newsletter*, semiannual. Covers information on the group's activities. **Price:** free for members ●

Technion—USA, semiannual. Newsletter. Provides information about technological advances, scientific research, organizational activities and engineering education at the institute. **Price:** included in membership dues. **Circulation:** 25,000. **Conventions/Meetings:** semiannual board meeting - 2008 Oct. 28-Nov. 1, Los Angeles, CA; 2009 Mar. 2-7, Phoenix, AZ.

8678 ■ Ohr Torah Institutions of Israel (OTII)
49 W 45th St., Ste.701
New York, NY 10036-4603
Ph: (212)935-8672
Fax: (212)935-8683
E-mail: jrosengarten@otsny.org
URL: http://www.ohrtorahstone.org.il
Contact: Jayne Rosengarten, Exec. Dir.
Founded: 1972. **Multinational. Description:** Works to develop future Jewish leaders worldwide. Sponsors secular and religious educational programs. **Telecommunication Services:** electronic mail, ohrtorahstone@otsny.org. **Formerly:** (1987) American Committee for the Advancement of Torah Education. **Publications:** *OHR*. Newsletter. Alternate Formats: online. **Conventions/Meetings:** annual Student Reunion.

8679 ■ Tel Aviv University: American Council
39 Broadway, Ste.1510
New York, NY 10006
Ph: (212)742-9070
Free: (800)989-1198
Fax: (212)742-9071
E-mail: info@tauac.org
URL: http://www.tauac.org
Contact: Roni Krinsky, Pres.
Founded: 1955. **Description:** Represents supporters and donors that are interested in the work of the Tel Aviv University. Raises funds to support programs of the Tel Aviv University in Israel. Holds seminars and other educational programs, as well as occasional fundraising events. **Awards: Type:** recognition. **Formerly:** (2007) American Friends of the Tel Aviv University. **Publications:** *Friends Newsletter*, semiannual ● *TAU News*, quarterly. Newsletter. **Conventions/Meetings:** periodic meeting.

Italian

8680 ■ American Association of Teachers of Italian (AATI)
c/o Edoardo Lebano, Exec. Dir.
Indiana Univ.
Dept. of French and Italian
Ballentine 642
Bloomington, IN 47405
Ph: (812)855-2508
Fax: (812)855-8877
E-mail: pgiordan@mail.ucf.edu
URL: http://www.aati-online.org
Contact: Paolo Giordano, Pres.
Founded: 1924. **Members:** 1,500. **Membership Dues:** regular, $45 (annual) ● student/emeritus, $25 (annual) ● professional couple, $50 (annual) ● institution, $60 (annual) ● sustaining, $60-$99 (annual) ● patron, $100-$499 (annual) ● donor, $500-$1,000 (annual). **Budget:** $50,000. **Local Groups:** 14. **Description:** Professional society of college and secondary school teachers and others interested in Italian language and culture. Promotes study of Italian language, literature, and culture in schools. Maintains speakers' bureau; compiles statistics. Works with Italian government and universities to sponsor special seminars and with Italian-American organizations for the promotion of the Italian language in the K-12 schools. **Awards:** Distinguished Service Award. **Frequency:** biennial. **Type:** recognition. **Recipient:** for members. **Computer Services:** Mailing lists, of members. **Committees:** Awards; National College Essay Contest; National Italian Contest for Secondary Schools; Program. **Publications:** *AATI Newsletter* (in English and Italian), semiannual. Publishes information about new publications, forthcoming conferences, events, contests and awards. **Circulation:** 1,500. **Advertising:** accepted. Alternate Formats: online ● *Journal Italica*, quarterly. Includes membership directory. Alternate Formats: online. **Conventions/Meetings:** annual meeting, usually held in conjunction with American Council on the Teaching of Foreign Languages and in Italy, with paper sessions and roundtables ● workshop and seminar.

8681 ■ Society for Italian Historical Studies (SIHS)
c/o Prof. Alan J. Reinerman, Exec. Sec.-Treas.
Boston Coll.
Dept. of History
Chestnut Hill, MA 02467
Ph: (617)552-3814
E-mail: alan.reinerman@bc.edu
URL: http://faculty.valenciacc.edu/ckillinger/sihs
Contact: Prof. Alan J. Reinerman, Exec. Sec.-Treas.
Founded: 1955. **Members:** 350. **Membership Dues:** individual, $10 (annual) ● graduate student, part-time instructor, retiree, unemployed scholar, $5 (annual). **Staff:** 1. **Description:** College and University professors and graduate students. Encourages the study and teaching of Italian history. Aims to promote research and publication of studies dealing with the history of Italy and with relations between the U.S. and Italy; seeks grants for students and scholars. Facilitates exchange of technical and professional information on Italian historical subjects. **Awards:** Best Unpublished Manuscript. **Frequency:** annual. **Type:** recognition. **Recipient:** for scholars ● Career Achievement. **Frequency:** annual. **Type:** recognition. **Recipient:** for Americans making original contributions in the field ● Helen and Howard R. Marraro Prize. **Frequency:** annual. **Type:** recognition. **Recipient:** for the best book or article. **Committees:** Prize Award and Citation. **Councils:** Advisory. **Publications:** *Membership List*, annual. Membership Directory. **Price:** included in membership dues ● *Society for Italian Historical Studies—Newsletter*, annual. Contains information on the society's annual meeting. **Price:** included in membership dues. **Circulation:** 350. **Conventions/Meetings:** annual conference, held in conjunction with American Historical Association - always first weekend of January.

Japanese

8682 ■ Association of Teachers of Japanese (ATJ)
240 Humanities Bldg.
279 UCB
Boulder, CO 80309-0279
Ph: (303)492-5487
Fax: (303)492-5856
E-mail: atj@colorado.edu
URL: http://www.colorado.edu/ealld/atj
Contact: Joan E. Ericson, Pres.
Founded: 1963. **Members:** 1,000. **Membership Dues:** individual in U.S., $45 (annual) ● life, $1,000 ● student/retired faculty, $20 (annual) ● part-time instructor, $35 (annual) ● institution, $60 (annual). **Staff:** 3. **Budget:** $150,000. **Description:** Teachers of Japanese as a foreign language; associate members are students formally enrolled in a graduate school preparing to become teachers of Japanese. Works to meet the common intellectual and academic needs of its members. Sponsors panels on Japanese language research and instruction, linguistics, and literature at the conventions of the Association for Asian Studies (see separate entry). Works on projects that include developing and implementing standards for Japanese language learning, encouraging study abroad in Japan, and promoting professional development projects. **Publications:** *ATJ Newsletter*, quarterly. Covers association activities and regional news about Japanese language education. Includes annual membership list. **Price:** included in membership dues. **Circulation:** 1,500. **Advertising:** accepted. Alternate Formats: online ● *Japanese Language and Literature*, semiannual. Journal. Contains articles on Japanese literature, linguistics, and language pedagogy. Includes book reviews, dissertations and thesis abstracts. **Price:** included in membership dues. **Circulation:** 1,500. **Advertising:** accepted. Alternate Formats: microform ● Directory, annual. **Conventions/Meetings:** annual conference, in conjunction with AAS.

Jewish

8683 ■ Association of Advanced Rabbinical and Talmudic Schools (AARTS)
Address Unknown since 2008
Founded: 1971. **Members:** 59. **Staff:** 3. **Budget:** $293,000. **Description:** Association of major Rabbinical and Talmudic schools concerned with the perpetuation and advancement of American centers of Jewish scholarship. Accredits advanced Rabbinical and Talmudic schools, provides forum for discussion of problems facing Jewish higher education, facilitates cooperation, and encourages inter-school faculty visits. **Formerly:** (1971) Council of Roshei Yeshivos. **Publications:** *Handbook of the Accreditation Commission*, annual. **Conventions/Meetings:** annual meeting.

8684 ■ Association for Jewish Studies (AJS)
15 W 16th St.
New York, NY 10011-6301
Ph: (917)606-8249
Fax: (917)606-8222
E-mail: ajs@ajs.cjh.org
URL: http://www.ajsnet.org
Contact: Rona Sheramy PhD, Exec. Dir.
Founded: 1969. **Members:** 1,500. **Membership Dues:** regular (based on the income level), $70-$130 (annual) ● student, $35 (annual) ● institution (full), $1,000 (annual) ● institution (associate), $500 (annual) ● joint student, $45 (annual). **Staff:** 2. **Multinational. Description:** Promotes the teaching of Jewish studies in colleges and universities. **Publications:** *AJS Perspectives*, semiannual. Magazine. Provides information in the field of Jewish studies. **Price:** included in membership dues. **Circulation:** 1,600. **Advertising:** accepted ● *AJS Review* (in English and Hebrew), semiannual. Journal. **Price:** included in membership dues. ISSN: 0364-0094. **Circulation:** 1,450. **Advertising:** accepted ● Monographs ● Proceedings. **Conventions/Meetings:** annual conference (exhibits).

8685 ■ Association for the Social Scientific Study of Jewry (ASSJ)
c/o Prof. Harriet Hartman, PhD, Pres.
Rowan Univ.
Dept. of Sociology
201 Mullica Hill Rd.
Glassboro, NJ 08028
Ph: (856)256-4500
Fax: (856)256-5610
E-mail: hartman@rowan.edu
URL: http://www.assj.org
Contact: Prof. Harriet Hartman PhD, Pres.
Founded: 1971. **Members:** 150. **Membership Dues:** regular, $50 (annual) ● student, $25 (annual) ● emeritus, $36 (annual). **Description:** Represents college and university professors and administrators, researchers for local and national organizations. Encourages the social scientific study of Jewry. Conducts academic sessions at professional meetings. **Awards:** Graduate Student Travel Awards. **Frequency:** annual. **Type:** grant. **Recipient:** for graduate students; funding for travel to annual meeting of association for Jewish studies; worthy paper for delivery at conference ● Marshall Sklare Distinguished Scholar. **Frequency:** annual. **Type:** recognition. **Recipient:** to a senior scholar who has made a significant scholarly contribution to the social scientific study of Jewry. **Telecommunication Services:** electronic mail, exec@assj.org. **Formerly:** (1992) Association of the Sociological Study of Jewry. **Publications:** *Contemporary Jewry*, annual. Journal. Contains empirical and theoretical articles on the social scientific study of Jewry. **Price:** $36.00. ISSN: 0147-1694. **Circulation:** 300. **Advertising:** accepted. **Conventions/Meetings:** annual conference,

held in conjunction with the Association for Jewish Studies - always December.

8686 ■ B'nai B'rith International's Center for Jewish Identity
c/o B'nai B'rith International
2020 K St. NW, 7th Fl.
Washington, DC 20006
Ph: (202)857-6600
Free: (888)388-4224
E-mail: website@bnaibrith.org
URL: http://bnaibrith.org/programs/jr/index.cfm
Contact: Daniel S. Mariaschin, Exec. VP

Membership Dues: individual, couple (under age 35), $75 (annual) ● individual (under age 35), $37 (annual) ● couple, $112 (annual) ● YLAN individual, $42 (annual) ● YLAN individual, $75 (triennial). **Description:** Represents B'nai B'rith's commitment to providing opportunities and experiences to strengthen Jewish identity. Aims to enhance the transmission of Jewish values, ethics, and knowledge from generation to generation by reaching out to all members of the community, including the intermarried and the unaffiliated. **Affiliated With:** B'nai B'rith International. **Formerly:** (1986) B'nai B'rith International Commission on Adult Jewish Education. **Publications:** Books. **Conventions/Meetings:** annual international conference (exhibits).

8687 ■ Brandeis - Bardin Institute (BBI)
1101 Peppertree Ln.
Brandeis, CA 93064
Ph: (805)582-4450
Fax: (805)526-1398
E-mail: info@thebbi.org
URL: http://www.thebbi.org
Contact: Gary Brennglass, Exec. Dir.

Founded: 1941. **Members:** 1,000. **Staff:** 40. **Description:** Experiential education institution "whose task is to discover ways, methods, and approaches to make Judaism meaningful in one's own life and bring forth an interest and desire to be of service to the community". The institute includes a college institute, a youth camp, and adult weekend institutes. Activities include discussions with Jewish thinkers, religious observances, art, dance, music, and social events. Membership includes 600 House of the Book member households who attend advanced weekend institutes. **Libraries: Type:** reference. **Holdings:** 10,000. **Subjects:** Judaica. **Telecommunication Services:** electronic mail, gbrennglass@thebbi.org. **Formerly:** Brandeis Camp Institute of the West; Brandeis Institute. **Publications:** *Branches*, quarterly. Newsletter. **Circulation:** 15,000. Alternate Formats: online.

8688 ■ Central Organization for Jewish Education (COJE)
770 Eastern Pkwy.
Brooklyn, NY 11213
Ph: (718)953-2353
Contact: Dr. Nissan Mindel, Sec.

Founded: 1943. **Members:** 600,000. **Description:** Educational arm of the Lubavitch Movement (see separate entry). Promotes Jewish education and religious observance as a daily experience for all Jews. Develops curricula that will stimulate concern for and active interest in Jewish education. Operates Chabad Research Center which conducts research on Hasidic philosophy and history. **Libraries: Type:** reference. **Holdings:** 125,000. **Subjects:** Hebraic literature, worldwide network of schools, summer camps, Chabad-Lubavitch houses. **Also Known As:** Merkos L'inyonei Chinuch. **Publications:** Journal, monthly ● Journal, quarterly ● Also publishes books, booklets, and pamphlets. **Conventions/Meetings:** periodic conference.

8689 ■ Coalition for the Advancement of Jewish Education (CAJE)
520 Eighth Ave., North Tower, 2nd Fl.
New York, NY 10018
Ph: (212)268-4210
Fax: (212)268-4214
E-mail: cajeny@caje.org
URL: http://www.caje.org
Contact: Jeffrey Lasday, Exec. Dir.

Founded: 1976. **Members:** 3,800. **Membership Dues:** teacher, other, $100 (annual) ● administrator/rabbi/cantor/lay leader, $125 (annual) ● high school student, $18 (annual) ● college student/graduate school student, $36 (annual) ● life, $1,800 ● partner institution, $250 (annual) ● individual (associated with partner), $60 (annual). **Staff:** 10. **Budget:** $2,200,000. **Description:** Works to transmit the Jewish heritage. Promotes excellence in Jewish education across the spectrum of Jewish life. **Awards:** Abraham A. Spack Fellowship. **Frequency:** annual. **Type:** fellowship. **Recipient:** for Jewish educators. **Subgroups:** Adult Education; Art; Bar/Bat Mitzvah Programming; Computer Network; Dance; Day School Principals; Drama; Early Childhood; Environmental Issues; Family Life Education; Hebrew Language; Holocaust Education; Informal Education; Interfaith Issues in Jewish Education; Intergenerational/Aging; Israel Education; Jewish Spiritual Healing; Jewish Storytelling; Media Resource; Moral Education; Music; Sexual Orientation in Jewish Education; Small/Supplementary Schools; Special Needs; Teacher Resource Centers; Teaching Teens; Tzedakah. **Formerly:** (1988) Coalition for Alternatives in Jewish Education. **Publications:** *CAJE Membership Directory*, annual ● *Hanukat CAJE*, monthly. Pamphlets ● *Jewish Education News*, 3/year. Journal. Includes updates, network news, scholarly articles on issues in Jewish education, and interviews. **Price:** free for members; $5.00/issue for nonmembers. **Advertising:** accepted. Alternate Formats: online. Also Cited As: *JEN* ● *Network Newsletters*, periodic ● Also publishes teacher's guides and curricula covering critical community issues such as teaching terrorism, Jewish environmental education, Jewish civics, Arab-Israeli crises, and educating Jewish children with special needs. **Conventions/Meetings:** annual Conference on Alternatives in Jewish Education, brings together educators to share curricula, programmatic ideas, and scholarship (exhibits) - always August.

8690 ■ Council for Jewish Education (CJE)
11 Olympia Ln.
Monsey, NY 10952
Ph: (845)368-8657
Fax: (845)369-6538
E-mail: mjscje@aol.com
Contact: Dr. Morton Summer, Pres.

Founded: 1926. **Members:** 275. **Membership Dues:** $125 (annual). **Staff:** 2. **Budget:** $50,000. **Description:** Teachers of Hebrew in universities; heads of Bureaus of Jewish Education and their administrative departments; faculty members of Jewish teacher training schools. Seeks to: further the cause of Jewish education in America; raise professional standards and practices; promote the welfare and growth of Jewish educational workers; improve and strengthen Jewish life. Conducts educational programs; cosponsors a Personnel Placement Committee with Jewish Education Service of North America. **Formerly:** (1981) National Council for Jewish Education. **Publications:** *Journal of Jewish Education*, 3/year. Includes editorials, articles, reports on research programs and experiments, and book reviews. **Price:** $36.00 for individuals in U.S.; $65.00 for institutions in U.S.; $51.00 for individuals outside U.S.; $75.00 for institutions outside U.S. **Circulation:** 1,800. **Advertising:** accepted ● Membership Directory, biennial ● Newsletter, quarterly. **Conventions/Meetings:** biennial conference - always in June.

8691 ■ Federated Council of Beth Jacob Schools (FCBJS)
Address Unknown since 2008

Founded: 1940. **Members:** 100. **Staff:** 12. **Description:** Representative for the maintenance of all-day schools for girls providing full Hebrew and English education, recognized by the city boards of education. Operates a summer camp at Woodburn, NY. **Committees:** Camp; Educational.

8692 ■ Jewish Education Service of North America (JESNA)
111 8th Ave., 11th Fl.
New York, NY 10011
Ph: (212)284-6950 (212)284-6888
Fax: (212)284-6951
E-mail: info@jesna.org
URL: http://www.jesna.org
Contact: Dr. Jonathan Woocher, Chief Ideas Off.

Founded: 1981. **Members:** 1,000. **Staff:** 25. **Description:** Widely recognized leader in the areas of research and program evaluation, organizational change and innovative program design and dissemination. Operates the Mandell J. Berman Jewish Heritage Center for Research and Evaluation. Supports the Covenant Foundation, a joint venture with the Crown Family, which makes awards and grants for creativity in Jewish education. **Awards:** Mesorah Award for Jewish Educational Leadership. **Frequency:** annual. **Type:** recognition. **Recipient:** for exceptional service by a lay leader. **Committees:** Joint Placement. **Programs:** Visitors. **Sections:** Community Services; Educational Development; Personnel; Research; Teachers Exchange. **Formerly:** (1981) American Association for Jewish Education. **Publications:** *Agenda: Jewish Education*, semiannual. Journal ● *Research and Information Bulletins*.

8693 ■ Jewish Educators Assembly (JEA)
PO Box 413
Cedarhurst, NY 11516
Ph: (516)569-2537
Fax: (516)295-9039
E-mail: jewisheducators@jewisheducators.org
URL: http://www.jewisheducators.org
Contact: Edward Edelstein, Exec. Dir.

Founded: 1951. **Members:** 450. **Membership Dues:** student, Israeli, retiree, $50 (annual) ● teacher, $75 (annual) ● academic, supporter, $150 (annual). **Staff:** 2. **Budget:** $90,000. **Regional Groups:** 7. **Local Groups:** 1. **Languages:** English, Hebrew. **Multinational. Description:** Educational and supervisory personnel serving Jewish educational institutions. Seeks to: advance the development of Jewish education in the congregation on all levels in consonance with the philosophy of the Conservative Movement; cooperate with the United Synagogue of America Commission on Jewish Education as the policy-making body of the educational enterprise; join in cooperative effort with other Jewish educational institutions and organizations; establish and maintain professional standards for Jewish educators; serve as a forum for the exchange of ideas; promote the values of Jewish education as a basis for the creative continuity of the Jewish people. Maintains placement service and speaker's bureau. **Awards:** JEA Lifetime Achievement. **Frequency:** annual. **Type:** recognition. **Recipient:** for outstanding educator. **Committees:** Ethics; Placement; Research; Scholarship; Welfare. **Affiliated With:** United Synagogue of Conservative Judaism Commission on Jewish Education. **Formerly:** (1981) Educators Assembly of America. **Publications:** *Beineinu*, monthly. Newsletter. **Advertising:** accepted ● *High School Resource*. Book ● *V'Aleh Ha Chadashot/News of the JEA*, quarterly. Newsletter. Includes program summaries and members' information. **Price:** free. **Circulation:** 1,500. **Conventions/Meetings:** annual conference, education materials, media, Judaica, arts and crafts (exhibits).

8694 ■ Jewish Student Press Service (JSPS)
114 W 26th St., Ste.1004
New York, NY 10001
Ph: (212)675-1168
Fax: (212)929-3459
E-mail: editor@newvoices.org
URL: http://www.newvoices.org
Contact: Ilana Sichel, Ed.

Founded: 1970. **Membership Dues:** regular, $18 (annual). **Staff:** 5. **Description:** Publishes New Voices Magazine, written by and for Jewish college students; distributed on over 400 campuses in the United States and covers Jewish politics, culture, campus life, and Israel. Also publishes New Voices WebWire, an online magazine of Jewish campus news from student correspondents across the United States, emailed every 2 weeks. Organizes annual conference for Jewish student journalists and the New York Collective, a year-round series of events bringing student writers together for workshops and seminars on key Jewish and journalistic issues. **Formerly:** (2000) Jewish Student Editorial Projects. **Publications:** *New Voices*, 5/year. Magazine. Covers Jewish politics, culture, campus life, and Israel. **Price:** free for students; $18.00/year for non-student; $25.00 /year for institutions; $36.00 /year for libraries. **Circulation:** 27,000. **Advertising:** accepted ● *New Voices WebWire*, biweekly. Magazine. Alternate Formats: online. **Conventions/Meetings:** annual conference, with workshops and seminars on key Jewish and journalistic issues.

8695 ■ National Association of Professors of Hebrew (NAPH)
Univ. of Wisconsin-Madison
1346 Van Hise Hall
1220 Linden Dr.
Madison, WI 53706-1525
Ph: (608)262-2997
Fax: (608)262-9417
E-mail: naph@mailplus.wisc.edu
URL: http://polyglot.lss.wisc.edu/naph
Contact: Prof. Gilead Morahg, Exec. VP

Founded: 1950. **Members:** 450. **Membership Dues:** regular, $50 (annual) ● retired, $30 (annual) ● student, $15 (annual). **Regional Groups:** 3. **Description:** Professors, students, and others interested in the study of the Bible, Hebrew language, and literature. Provides a forum for the study, research, and teaching of the Bible, Hebrew language, and literature. Sponsors student honor society. **Publications:** *Bulletin of Higher Hebrew Education* ● *Hebrew Higher Education*. Journal ● *Hebrew Studies Journal*, annual ● *Iggeret*, semiannual. Newsletter. **Price:** included in membership dues. **Circulation:** 450. **Conventions/Meetings:** annual convention, held in conjunction with Society of Biblical Literature.

8696 ■ National Committee for the Furtherance of Jewish Education (NCFJE)
c/o Chabad of Mineola, NY
261 Willis Ave.
Mineola, NY 11501
Ph: (516)739-3636
E-mail: rabbi@rabbiperl.com
URL: http://www.rabbiperl.com/ncfje.htm
Contact: Rabbi Anchelle Perl, Program Coor.

Founded: 1940. **Members:** 400. **Membership Dues:** individual, $250 (annual). **Staff:** 27. **Budget:** $4,500,000. **Regional Groups:** 2. **Description:** Works to disseminate the ideals of Torah-true education among the Jewish youth of America, and to strengthen their identity, commitment, and pride. Combats anti-religious and Christian missionary activities. Sponsors camps; Released Time Program for public school children; family and vocational counseling services; Operation Survival (War on Drugs), a drug and alcohol abuse prevention program; and TAG Family Counseling and Early Intervention after school and pre-school. Maintains parochial, elementary, and high schools in Brooklyn and Queens; an Ivy League Torah Study Program, a summer seminar for college men and women. Other charitable programs include Toys for Hospitalized Children, Camp Fund for Underprivileged Children, and Poor and Sick Fund. **Libraries: Type:** not open to the public. **Holdings:** 10,000; books, periodicals. **Subjects:** Jewish jurisprudence, Jewish philosophy, Rabbinic's, ethics, Bible commentary, Talmudic studies. **Awards:** Jacob J. Hecht Memorial Award. **Frequency:** annual. **Type:** recognition. **Recipient:** to carry out legacy of Rabbi J.J. Hecht ● Josef Hirsch Chesed Award. **Frequency:** annual. **Type:** recognition. **Recipient:** for Chesed kindness and philanthropy ● Sara Domb Jewish Education Award. **Frequency:** annual. **Type:** recognition. **Recipient:** for excellence in fostering Jewish ideals. **Divisions:** Anti-Shmad; Camp Emunah; Hadar Hatorah Rabbinical Seminary; Ivy League Torah Study Program Boys; Ivy League Torah Study Program Girls; Machon Chana Women's College; Mesivta Ohr Torah; Toys for Hospitalized Children; Vocational. **Programs:** Torah Teen Summer. **Affiliated With:** Machne Israel. **Publications:** *A Life Full of Giving*. Journal ● *Confessions of a Jewish Cultbustr: Brimstone and Fire*. Journal ● *Focus*. Journal ● *Intermarriage, The Problem, Its Causes, Effects, and Cure*. Journal ● *My First Siddur*. Newsletter ● *Panorama*, quarterly. Newsletter. **Advertising:** accepted ● *Passover Handbook* ● *Seder Guide*. Handbook. **Conventions/Meetings:** annual National Awards Dinner.

8697 ■ National Ramah Commission (NRC)
3080 Broadway
New York, NY 10027
Ph: (212)678-8881
Fax: (212)749-8251
E-mail: ramah@jtsa.edu
URL: http://www.campramah.org
Contact: Rabbi Mitchell Cohen, Dir.

Founded: 1953. **Members:** 45. **Staff:** 10. **Budget:** $600,000. **Regional Groups:** 7. **Description:** Serves as a department of The Jewish Theological Seminary. Operates seven camps for Jewish young people in various parts of the U.S. and Canada, in addition to programs in Israel, to encourage heightened Jewish identification, the study of Jewish tradition and religious observance. Ramah means "heights" in Hebrew. Conducts educational programs. **Libraries: Type:** reference. **Holdings:** archival material, audiovisuals, books, periodicals, photographs. **Subjects:** Jewish education. **Awards:** Ramah Leadership Award. **Frequency:** annual. **Type:** recognition. **Recipient:** for service to the camps. **Publications:** *Kolot Ramah*, annual. Newspaper. **Price:** free. **Circulation:** 15,000. **Advertising:** accepted. Alternate Formats: online. **Conventions/Meetings:** bimonthly board meeting - always in New York City.

8698 ■ North American Association of Jewish High Schools (NAAJHS)
Akiba Hebrew Acad.
223 N Highland Ave.
Merion Station, PA 19066
E-mail: naajhs@akibaweb.org
Contact: Philip D. Field, Pres.

Founded: 1999. **Membership Dues:** school (plus $3 per student up to a maximum of $1,000 per school), $500. **Multinational. Description:** Works for the advancement of Jewish high school education. Serves as a forum for Jewish day high schools to exchange ideas, discuss common concerns and collaborate on educational projects. Sponsors programs, workshops and conferences for professionals and students. **Telecommunication Services:** electronic mail, pdfield@hotmail.com.

8699 ■ Pirchei Agudath Israel (PAI)
Address Unknown since 2008

Founded: 1922. **Members:** 20,000. **National Groups:** 125. **Description:** Children's division of Agudath Israel of America (see separate entry). Educates Orthodox male Jewish children in the traditional Orthodox Jewish way of life and thought, with emphasis on Torah concepts and values. Membership composed mainly of Yeshiva students. Activities include: congregation, Oneg Shabbos, learning groups, Sholosh Seudos, Melave Malkos, Chanukah Spectacular, regional Siyum Mishnayos, interbranch Shabbosim, leaders seminars, leaders Melave Malkos, Talmud Torah Shabbosim, trips, hospital programs and visits, homebound and telephone pals, Saturday Night Learning program, and special Post Bar Mitzvah program. Maintains speakers' bureau. Sponsors annual contests, including: Gemoro; Hasmodo; Hilchos Tefilin; Kedushas Shabbos; Midos Tovos; Mishnayos Bifnim; Mishnayos Lichvod Habarmitzvah; Shnayim Mikro. **Awards:** Best Leader Award. **Frequency:** annual. **Type:** recognition. **Affiliated With:** Agudath Israel of America. **Publications:** *Branch Directory*, annual ● *Darkeinu*, quarterly ● Journal, annual ● Newsletter, periodic ● Also publishes leaders' guides. **Conventions/Meetings:** annual meeting.

8700 ■ Project Genesis
122 Slade Ave., Ste.250
Baltimore, MD 21208
Ph: (410)602-1350
Free: (888)WWW-TORA
Fax: (410)510-1053
E-mail: genesis@torah.org
URL: http://www.torah.org
Contact: Rabbi Yaakov Menken, Dir.

Founded: 1993. **Staff:** 5. **Languages:** English, French, German, Spanish. **Description:** Promotes further Jewish education and awareness of Jewish identity. Works to expand Jewish knowledge and the encourage more involvement with Judaism and the Jewish community. Conducts educational programs, online classes, and campus outreach. Maintains speakers' bureau. **Computer Services:** database ● mailing lists, classes in diverse Jewish topics.

8701 ■ Solomon Schechter Day School Association (SSDSA)
155 5th Ave., 5th Fl.
New York, NY 10010-6802
Ph: (212)533-7800 (646)519-9210
E-mail: abramson@uscj.org
URL: http://www.ssdsa.org
Contact: Dr. Robert Abramson, Dir.

Founded: 1964. **Members:** 76. **Staff:** 6. **Languages:** English, Hebrew. **Description:** A division of the United Synagogue of Conservative Judaism Commission on Jewish Education. Jewish elementary day schools and high schools with a total of over 21,500 students. Named for Solomon Schecher (1850-1915), scholar of Talmud and rabbinical literature at Cambridge and founder of the United Synagogue of America and the Jewish Theological Seminary. Provides visitations and consultations regarding education, governance and administration; publication of advisories and position papers, biennial conferences for lay leaders, annual conferences of the principals council, Shibboley Schechter newsletter, listserves for presidents, School heads, Business managers, and development directors. Also provides dissemination of demographics and statistics, chartering and accreditation of schools, seminars and board training for lay leaders, Schechter website, SHAR"R, 7th and 8th grade trips to Israel, placement service, MaToK-TaNaKH curriculum development project for Solomon Schecter Day schools, residency fellowship program to prepare professional leadership (SREL) and a listing of consultants. **Libraries: Type:** reference; not open to the public. **Telecommunication Services:** electronic mail, ssds-prez@uscj.org ● electronic mail, roshnet@uscj.org ● electronic mail, ssds-business@uscj.org ● electronic mail, ssds-development@uscj.org. **Committees:** Day School Education; Standards. **Affiliated With:** Council for American Private Education. **Publications:** *Shibboley Schechter Newsletter*, 3/year ● *SSDSA Directory*, annual. Lists affiliated day schools. **Price:** free ● Also publishes curricular materials; books, pamphlets, brochures, newsletter and charts; produces videotapes. **Conventions/Meetings:** biennial conference.

8702 ■ United Synagogue of Conservative Judaism Commission on Jewish Education (USCJCOJE)
c/o United Synagogue of Conservative Judaism
155 5th Ave.
New York, NY 10010-6802
Fax: (212)353-9439
E-mail: info@uscj.org
URL: http://www.uscj.org
Contact: E. Temma Kingsley, VP for Development

Members: 39. **Staff:** 6. **Description:** Representatives of five national Jewish organizations. Sets policy, develops courses and objectives, and prepares text materials to implement curricula for Jewish religious schools. **Telecommunication Services:** TDD, (212)260-7442. **Committees:** Day School; Special Education. **Also Known As:** United Synagogue Commission on Jewish Education. **Publications:** *Tov L'Horot*, periodic. Newsletter. Provides information to professionals and lay school leaders. **Price:** free. **Circulation:** 1,000 ● *Your Child*, 3/year. Newsletter. Provides information to the parents of young children. **Price:** $7.00/year. **Circulation:** 3,000. **Conventions/Meetings:** general assembly - 3/year.

Journalism

8703 ■ Accrediting Council on Education in Journalism and Mass Communications (ACEJMC)
Stauffer-Flint Hall
1435 Jayhawk Blvd.
Lawrence, KS 66045-7575
Ph: (785)864-3973
Fax: (785)864-5225
E-mail: sshaw@ku.edu
URL: http://www.ku.edu/~acejmc
Contact: Susanne Shaw, Exec. Dir.
Founded: 1945. **Members:** 23. **Staff:** 3. **Budget:** $188,000. **Description:** Consists of journalism education associations and related industry groups. Encourages cooperation between the mass media and colleges and universities in education for journalism and accredits professional programs in schools and departments of journalism. Approved list currently includes 104 colleges and universities and one university outside the country. **Computer Services:** Electronic publishing, newsletter. **Committees:** Accrediting. **Formerly:** (1945) Joint Committee of Schools of Journalism; (1981) American Council on Education for Journalism. **Publications:** *Accredited Journalism and Mass Communications Education*, annual. Booklet. **Price:** free ● Also publishes accrediting standards. **Conventions/Meetings:** annual meeting, with council and committee meetings - March.

8704 ■ American Press Institute (API)
11690 Sunrise Valley Dr.
Reston, VA 20191-1498
Ph: (703)620-3611
Fax: (703)620-5814
E-mail: info@americanpressinstitute.org
URL: http://www.americanpressinstitute.org
Contact: Drew Davis, Pres./Exec. Dir.
Founded: 1946. **Description:** Provides leadership development opportunities for women and men holding a broad range of news/editorial and business-side assignments across the full range of news media and its enterprises in print, broadcast, Web, cable and wireless, and journalism education. **Telecommunication Services:** electronic mail, adavis@americanpressinstitute.org. **Publications:** Bulletin, annual. **Conventions/Meetings:** seminar, residential, weeklong.

8705 ■ Associated Collegiate Press (ACP)
Univ. of Minnesota
2221 Univ. Ave. SE, Ste.121
Minneapolis, MN 55414
Ph: (612)625-8335
Fax: (612)626-0720
E-mail: info@studentpress.org
URL: http://www.studentpress.org/acp
Contact: Tom E. Rolnicki, Exec. Dir.
Founded: 1921. **Members:** 1,500. **Membership Dues:** in Canada, broadcast station, $69 (annual) ● regular (based on the number of enrollment), $109-$139 (annual). **Staff:** 6. **Budget:** $250,000. **Description:** Conducts annual critique of newspapers and annual critique of magazines and yearbooks. Sponsors competitions. **Awards:** Pacemakers. **Frequency:** annual. **Type:** recognition. **Recipient:** for excellence in design, writing, content and photography. **Affiliated With:** National Scholastic Press Association. **Publications:** *Trends in College Media*, quarterly. Includes book reviews and information on new products, scholarships, and internships. **Price:** $10.00/year. ISSN: 1046-2163. **Conventions/Meetings:** annual meeting (exhibits) - always last weekend of October.

8706 ■ Association for Education in Journalism and Mass Communication (AEJMC)
234 Outlet Pointe Blvd.
Columbia, SC 29210-5667
Ph: (803)798-0271
Fax: (803)772-3509
E-mail: aejmc@aejmc.org
URL: http://www.aejmc.org
Contact: Jennifer H. McGill, Exec. Dir.
Founded: 1912. **Members:** 3,500. **Membership Dues:** regular in U.S. and Canada, associate, $105 (annual) ● graduate student, retired, $45 (annual) ● international, $85 (annual) ● spouse, $25 (annual). **Staff:** 8. **Description:** Professional organization of college and university journalism and communication teachers. Works to improve methods and standards of teaching and stimulate research. Compiles statistics on enrollments and current developments in journalism education. Maintains a listing of journalism and communication teaching positions available and teaching positions wanted, revised bimonthly. **Committees:** Professional Freedom and Responsibility; Research; Status of Minorities; Status of Women; Teaching Standards. **Divisions:** Advertising; Communication Technology and Policy; Communication Theory and Methodology; History; International Communications; Law; Magazine; Mass Communications and Society; Media Management and Economics; Minorities and Communication; Newspaper; PR; Qualitative Studies; Radio-TV; Scholastic Journalism; Visual Communication. **Affiliated With:** Accrediting Council on Education in Journalism and Mass Communications; Association of Schools of Journalism and Mass Communication. **Absorbed:** Council on Communications Research. **Formerly:** (1951) American Association of Teachers of Journalism; (1982) Association for Education in Journalism. **Publications:** *AEJMC News*, bimonthly. Newsletter. Contains news of AEJMC and journalism/communication education. **Price:** $10.00 in U.S.; $20.00 outside U.S. ISSN: 0747-8909. **Circulation:** 4,017. **Advertising:** accepted ● *J&MC Directory*, annual. Membership Directory. Lists more than 400 schools and departments of journalism and mass communication. **Price:** $40.00 individual in U.S.; $55.00 individual outside U.S.; $50.00 institution in U.S.; $65.00 institution outside U.S. ISSN: 0895-6545. **Advertising:** accepted ● *Journalism and Communication Monographs*, quarterly. Presents research on specific topics within journalism and mass communication. **Price:** $55.00 individual in U.S.; $65.00 individual outside U.S.; $90.00 institution in U.S.; $105.00 institution outside U.S. ISSN: 1522-6379. Also Cited As: *J&C Monographs* ● *Journalism and Mass Communication Abstracts*, annual. Contains abstracts of master's theses and doctoral dissertations accepted for graduate degrees. **Price:** free. Alternate Formats: online. Also Cited As: *J&MC Abstracts* ● *Journalism and Mass Communication Educator*, quarterly. Focuses on learning and teaching, curriculum, educational leadership, and related exploration of higher education. **Price:** $55.00 individual in U.S.; $65.00 individual outside U.S.; $90.00 institution in U.S.; $105.00 institution outside U.S. ISSN: 1077-6958. **Advertising:** accepted. Alternate Formats: online. Also Cited As: *J&MC Educator* ● *Journalism and Mass Communication Quarterly*. Focuses on research in journalism and mass communication. **Price:** $80.00 individual in U.S.; $90.00 individual outside U.S.; $140.00 institution in U.S.; $160.00 institution outside U.S. ISSN: 1077-6990. **Advertising:** accepted. Alternate Formats: online. Also Cited As: *J&MC Quarterly*. **Conventions/Meetings:** annual convention (exhibits) - always August. 2008 Aug. 6-9, Chicago, IL; 2009 Aug. 5-8, Boston, MA; 2010 Aug. 4-7, Denver, CO.

8707 ■ Carol Burnett Fund for Responsible Journalism (CBFRJ)
c/o Prof. Tom Brislin, Admin.
Univ. of Hawaii
Scholarship of Communications
2550 Campus Rd.
Honolulu, HI 96822-2217
Ph: (808)956-8881
Fax: (808)956-3441
E-mail: tbrislin@hawaii.edu
URL: http://www2.hawaii.edu/~tbrislin/cbfund.html
Contact: Prof. Tom Brislin, Admin.
Founded: 1981. **Description:** Established by an endowment made by actress Carol Burnett, who won a libel suit against the *National Enquirer*. Supports teaching and student research designed to further high standards of ethics and professionalism in journalism. **Awards:** Carol Burnett Prizes. **Frequency:** annual. **Type:** recognition. **Recipient:** for students at the University of Hawaii who have written the best articles and research papers on ethics ● **Type:** recognition. **Recipient:** for best research papers on ethical issues in journalism by graduate and undergraduate journalism students. **Affiliated With:** Association for Education in Journalism and Mass Communication. **Conventions/Meetings:** annual lecture, on ethics ● workshop, on issues in journalism ethics.

8708 ■ College Media Advisers (CMA)
Univ. of Memphis
Dept. of Journalism
3711 Veterans Ave., Rm. 300
Memphis, TN 38152-6661
Ph: (901)678-2403 (901)754-8112
Fax: (901)678-4798
E-mail: rsplbrgr@memphis.edu
URL: http://www.collegemedia.org
Contact: Ronald E. Spielberger, Exec. Dir.
Founded: 1954. **Members:** 800. **Membership Dues:** individual, associate, $80 (annual) ● individual, $155 (biennial) ● business, institution, $240 (annual). **Staff:** 1. **Budget:** $50,000. **Regional Groups:** 9. **Description:** Professional association serving advisers, directors, and chairmen of boards of college student media (newspapers, yearbooks, magazines, handbooks, directories, and radio and television stations); heads of schools and departments of journalism; and others interested in junior college, college, and university student media. Serves as a clearinghouse for student media; acts as consultant on student theses and dissertations on publications. Encourages high school journalism and examines its relationships to college and professional journalism. Conducts national survey of student media in rotation each year by type: newspapers, magazines, and yearbooks; radio and television stations. Compiles statistics. Maintains placement service and speakers' bureau. **Awards:** Distinguished Advisor Award. **Frequency:** annual. **Type:** recognition. **Recipient:** for outstanding faculty newspaper adviser, yearbook adviser, magazine adviser, and broadcast adviser ● Honor Roll Advisers. **Frequency:** annual. **Type:** recognition. **Recipient:** for media advisers. **Computer Services:** database. **Committees:** Awards and Recognition; High School Relations; Legal Status; Professional Standards for Advisers; Public Relations. **Formerly:** (1983) National Council of College Publications Advisers. **Publications:** *CMA Directory*, periodic. Membership Directory. **Price:** $15.00/copy. **Circulation:** 800 ● *College Media Review*, periodic. **Price:** $15.00/year. **Advertising:** accepted ● *Media College*, 10/year. Newsletter. **Price:** included in membership dues. **Circulation:** 800. Alternate Formats: online. **Conventions/Meetings:** semiannual National College Media Convention (exhibits) - 2008 Oct. 30-Nov. 2, Kansas City, MO.

8709 ■ Collegiate Network (CN)
PO Box 4431
Wilmington, DE 19807
Ph: (302)652-4600
Free: (800)225-2862
Fax: (302)652-1760
E-mail: info@isi.org
URL: http://www.isi.org/cn
Contact: T. Kenneth Cribb Jr., Pres.
Founded: 1978. **Description:** Focuses on the "politicization of American college and university classrooms, curricula and student life and the resulting decline of educational standards" for public awareness. Provides support for alternative student publications across the country. **Awards: Frequency:** annual. **Type:** grant. **Recipient:** for papers that are not self-sufficient ● Incentives to Excellence Awards. **Frequency:** annual. **Type:** grant. **Recipient:** for publications with a track record of improvement, campus focus, contact with the CN and investigative reporting. **Publications:** *Canon*, 3/year, each academic year. Magazine. Features articles to heighten public

awareness of the problems that beset higher education. **Circulation:** 29,000. **Advertising:** accepted. Alternate Formats: online ● *The Intercollegiate Review: A Journal of Scholarship and Opinion*, semiannual. **Price:** included in membership dues; $10.00 4 issues in U.S.; $20.00 4 issues outside U.S. **Circulation:** 50,000. **Advertising:** accepted ● *Modern Age*, annual. Journal. **Price:** $18.00/year in U.S.; $23.00/year outside U.S. **Advertising:** accepted ● *The Political Science Review*, annual. Journal. **Price:** $12.00 in U.S.; $15.00 outside U.S. **Advertising:** accepted.

8710 ■ Community College Journalism Association (CCJA)
c/o Tina Davis, Ed.
163 E Loop Dr.
Camarillo, CA 93010
Ph: (805)389-3744
Fax: (520)438-4886
E-mail: docames@adelphia.net
URL: http://www.ccjaonline.org
Contact: Dr. Steve Ames, Exec. Sec.-Treas.

Founded: 1968. **Members:** 300. **Membership Dues:** voting, associate, affiliate, retired, institutional, $40 (annual) ● combined (CCJA and AEJMC), $140 (annual) ● combined (CCJA and CMA), $190 (annual). **Description:** Two-year college journalism educators. Aims to have two-year journalism programs certified through a self-study and visitation program so instruction offered is equivalent to undergraduate journalism programs at four-year schools. Seeks to accomplish these goals by upgrading community college journalism programs; smoothing articulation between two- and four-year schools for students transferring, and by helping to improve the teaching and programs of two-year college journalism teachers. **Awards:** Distinguished Service Awards. **Frequency:** annual. **Type:** recognition. **Recipient:** for outstanding service ● Hall of Fame. **Frequency:** annual. **Type:** recognition. **Recipient:** for members. **Formerly:** (1974) Junior College Journalism Association. **Publications:** *Community College Journalist*, quarterly. Magazine. Contains items of interest to two-year college journalism educators. Includes book reviews and teaching and news articles. **Price:** included in membership dues; $35.00 /year for nonmembers. **Circulation:** 400. **Advertising:** accepted. Alternate Formats: microform; online. Also Cited As: *CC Journalist*. **Conventions/Meetings:** annual meeting, held in conjunction with Association for Education in Journalism and Mass Communication in the summer, National College Media Convention of the Associated Collegiate Press in the fall.

8711 ■ Dow Jones Newspaper Fund (DJNF)
PO Box 300
Princeton, NJ 08543-0300
Ph: (609)452-2820
Fax: (609)520-5804
E-mail: newsfund@wsj.dowjones.com
URL: http://djnewspaperfund.dowjones.com
Contact: Richard S. Holden, Exec. Dir.

Founded: 1958. **Staff:** 4. **Description:** Established by Dow Jones and Company, publisher of *The Wall Street Journal*, to encourage careers in journalism. Operates newspaper's editing, and Sports Copy Editing Internship Programs for all junior, senior, and graduate level college students interested in journalism. Also offers Business Reporting Intern Program for minority college sophomores and juniors to complete summer internships on daily newspapers as business reporters. Students receive monetary scholarships to return to school in the fall. Offers information on careers in journalism. **Awards:** Centers for Editing Excellence. **Frequency:** annual. **Type:** grant. **Recipient:** for colleges and non-profit organizations ● High School Journalism Workshops for Minorities. **Frequency:** annual. **Type:** grant. **Recipient:** for colleges, schools, and non-profit organizations ● Journalism Teacher of the Year. **Frequency:** annual. **Type:** recognition. **Recipient:** for outstanding journalism teachers ● **Type:** scholarship. **Recipient:** to students of winning teachers. **Formerly:** (1985) Newspaper Fund. **Publications:** *Adviser Update*, quarterly. Newsletter. Tabloid newspaper for scholastic journalism. **Price:** free. **Circulation:** 4,000. **Advertising:** accepted. Alternate Formats: online ● *How to Run A Summer Journalism Workshop for Minority High School Students*, 3/year. Manual. Alternate Formats: online ● *In the Beginning: Reviving Scholastic Journalism, School by School*. Booklet. Features steps to help urban and rural schools start and maintain viable student newspapers. Alternate Formats: online ● *The Journalist's Road to Success: A Career Guide*. Booklet. Contains lists of colleges offering journalism majors. **Price:** free. Alternate Formats: online ● Annual Report, annual. Alternate Formats: online.

8712 ■ Journalism Association of Community Colleges (JACC)
PO Box 18846
Oakland, CA 94619
Ph: (408)864-8588 (408)225-6397
E-mail: grobman@fhda.edu
URL: http://www.jacconline.org
Contact: Prof. Beth Grobman, Sec.

Founded: 1957. **Members:** 70. **Membership Dues:** college, $200 (annual). **Staff:** 3. **Budget:** $20,000. **Description:** Journalism departments of 2-year colleges in California and other states; 4-year colleges and universities or individuals interested in community college journalism. Promotes exchange of ideas and development of the most effective curricula; provides enriching experiences for journalism students. Conducts curriculum studies and research surveys and prepares promotional material on the journalism field for students; holds conferences, competitions and workshops for journalism students. **Awards:** Art Margosian Scholarship. **Frequency:** annual. **Type:** scholarship. **Recipient:** for promising journalism students ● JACC Educational Scholarships. **Frequency:** annual. **Type:** scholarship. **Recipient:** for promising journalism students ● Warren Mack Scholarship. **Frequency:** annual. **Type:** scholarship. **Recipient:** for promising journalism students. **Computer Services:** Mailing lists, of members. **Sections:** Northern California and Southern California. **Formerly:** (1970) Journalism Association of Junior Colleges. **Publications:** *JACC Convention Program*, annual. Brochure. Features programs for the yearly convention. **Price:** $1.00. **Advertising:** accepted ● Membership Directory, annual. **Price:** $1.00 ● Videos, periodic. Contains information on the association. **Price:** $1.00. **Conventions/Meetings:** annual convention, with speakers, tours and competitions (exhibits) ● annual Faculty Conference - usually February or March ● biennial regional meeting, with workshops, speakers and competitions for journalism students (exhibits) - always October.

8713 ■ Journalism Education Association (JEA)
Kansas State Univ.
103 Kedzie Hall
Manhattan, KS 66506-1505
Ph: (785)532-5532 (785)532-7822
Free: (866)532-5532
Fax: (785)532-5563
E-mail: jea@spub.ksu.edu
URL: http://www.jea.org
Contact: Linda S. Puntney, Exec. Dir.

Founded: 1924. **Members:** 2,300. **Membership Dues:** teacher/adviser, associate, $50 (annual) ● student, retired teacher/adviser, $30 (annual) ● institutional, affiliate, sustaining, $55 (annual) ● life - teacher/adviser, $500. **Staff:** 4. **Budget:** $725,650. **State Groups:** 51. **Description:** High school and middle school journalism teachers and advisers of school media; college and university journalism teachers interested in secondary school journalism. Works to improve the quality of scholastic publications and the teaching of media. Provides e-mail service and online bookstore offering discounts to members. **Awards:** Administrator of the Year. **Frequency:** annual. **Type:** recognition. **Recipient:** for school administrators who have shown a dedication to journalism ● Aspiring Young Journalist Award. **Frequency:** annual. **Type:** recognition. **Recipient:** for junior high/middle school students who continue journalistic studies in high school ● Carl Towley Award. **Frequency:** annual. **Type:** recognition. **Recipient:** for exemplary service to JEA and scholastic journalism ● Cornerstone Award. **Frequency:** annual. **Type:** monetary. **Recipient:** for two secondary schools that have shown their students, teachers and administration thoroughly understand the importance of the first amendment ● Diversity Award. **Frequency:** annual. **Type:** recognition. **Recipient:** for scholastic journalism teacher, student media adviser or scholastic journalism group demonstrating a commitment to cultural awareness and encouraging a multicultural approach with its student media staff, media production and/or community ● First Amendment Press Freedom Award. **Frequency:** annual. **Type:** recognition. **Recipient:** for schools that actively support and honor the first amendment through its student publications ● Friend of Scholastic Journalism. **Frequency:** annual. **Type:** recognition. **Recipient:** for support of scholastic journalism ● Future Journalism Teacher Scholarship. **Frequency:** annual. **Type:** scholarship. **Recipient:** for an upper-level or graduate college student who is studying to teach journalism at the high school level ● High School Journalist of the Year/Sister Rita Jeanne Scholarships. **Frequency:** annual. **Type:** scholarship. **Recipient:** for outstanding high school seniors who have been active in student media at least two years and plan to study journalism/mass communications in college ● Lifetime Achievement Award. **Frequency:** annual. **Type:** recognition. **Recipient:** for lifetime achievement in scholastic journalism ● Medals of Merit. **Frequency:** annual. **Type:** medal. **Recipient:** for support of JEA and its programs ● National Yearbook Adviser of the Year. **Frequency:** annual. **Type:** monetary. **Recipient:** for outstanding high school yearbook advisers ● Rising Star Award. **Frequency:** annual. **Type:** recognition. **Recipient:** for advisers with one to five years' journalism teaching/advising experience ● Ryan White Excellence in Journalism Award. **Frequency:** annual. **Type:** monetary. **Recipient:** for high school students who have written or broadcast exemplary health-related stories ● Student Journalist Impact Award. **Frequency:** annual. **Type:** monetary. **Recipient:** for students with outstanding journalistic writing ● Teacher Inspiration Award. **Frequency:** annual. **Type:** monetary. **Recipient:** for journalism teacher who inspired others to pursue journalism teaching as a career and who has made a positive difference in the teaching community. **Commissions:** Certification; Curriculum/Development; Junior High/Middle School; Multicultural; Scholastic Press Rights. **Committees:** Awards; Nominations; Scholarship; Scholastic Journalism Week; Write-off Contest. **Formerly:** (1928) Central Inter-Scholastic Press Association; (1929) National Association of Supervisors and Teachers of High School Journalism; (1935) National Association of High School Teachers of Journalism; (1946) National Association of Journalism Directors. **Publications:** *Communication: Journalism Education Today*, quarterly. **Price:** included in membership dues. **Circulation:** 2,500. **Advertising:** accepted. Alternate Formats: microform. Also Cited As: *C:JET* ● *Extra: A Supplement to Communication: Journalism Education Today*, quarterly. Newsletter. Contains news of local and regional journalism associations as well as national JEA news. **Price:** included in membership dues ● *JEA Bookstore Catalog*, annual ● Also issues commission summaries. **Conventions/Meetings:** semiannual convention and competition, instructional convention with student competition (exhibits) - every spring and fall. 2008 Nov. 13-8, St. Louis, MO.

8714 ■ National Agricultural Communicators of Tomorrow
c/o Deb Dunsford, PhD, Advisor
127 Scoates Hall, MS 2116
Texas A&M Univ.
College Station, TX 77843
E-mail: dunsford@tamu.edu
URL: http://www.gonact.org
Contact: Deb Dunsford PhD, Advisor

Founded: 1970. **Members:** 220. **Membership Dues:** individual, $12 (annual). **Staff:** 1. **Local Groups:** 20. **Description:** College students with professional interest in agricultural communications. Works to bring together members in a learning atmosphere to exchange ideas and better prepare them for careers. Sponsors annual communications critique and contest, internship directory and scholarship. **Libraries: Type:** reference. **Holdings:** archival material. **Subjects:** agricultural communications. **Awards: Type:** scholarship. **Formerly:** (1970) Agricultural College Magazines Associated; (1999) American Association of Agricultural Communicators of Tomorrow. **Publications:** Directory ● Newsletter. **Conventions/Meetings:** annual conference.

8715 ■ National Newspaper Association Foundation (NNAF)
Univ. of Missouri, Columbia
129 Neff Annex
Columbia, MO 65211
Ph: (573)882-5800
Free: (800)829-4NNA
Fax: (573)884-5490
E-mail: briansteffens@nna.org
Contact: Brian Steffens, Exec. Dir.
Founded: 1957. **Budget:** $12,000. **Nonmembership. Description:** Seeks to enhance literacy, print journalism, and the role of community newspapers. **Awards: Type:** scholarship. **Recipient:** for journalism school students. **Formerly:** (1966) National Editorial Foundation; (2001) National Newspaper Foundation. **Conventions/Meetings:** semiannual meeting.

8716 ■ Nieman Foundation (NF)
Harvard Univ.
Lippmann House
1 Francis Ave.
Cambridge, MA 02138
Ph: (617)495-2237 (617)496-5827
Fax: (617)495-8976
E-mail: bob_giles@harvard.edu
URL: http://www.nieman.harvard.edu
Contact: Bob Giles, Curator
Founded: 1938. **Staff:** 7. **Nonmembership. Description:** Alumni (journalists who have been awarded an academic-year Nieman Fellowship to Harvard University). Provides mid-career opportunity for journalists to study and broaden their intellectual horizons. Fellows are free to study in all schools and departments of Harvard, both graduate and undergraduate; no credit is granted for coursework done during the Fellowship year. Fellows also meet with distinguished figures from journalism, public service, the arts, business, education, and science to discuss contemporary issues. Maintains informal book collection, some written by Nieman Fellows. **Convention/Meeting:** none. **Libraries: Type:** by appointment only; open to the public. **Holdings:** 2,016; periodicals. **Subjects:** journalism. **Committees:** Advisory; Selection. **Also Known As:** Nieman Foundation for Journalism. **Publications:** *Nieman Reports*, quarterly. Journal. Provides a forum for the discussion of media-related issues by journalists, educators, and public figures. Includes book reviews. **Price:** $20.00/year; $30.00/year with foreign airmail; $35.00/two years; $55.00/two years with foreign airmail. ISSN: 0028-9817. **Circulation:** 1,350. Alternate Formats: online.

8717 ■ Scripps Howard Foundation
PO Box 5380
Cincinnati, OH 45201
Ph: (513)977-3035
Free: (800)888-3000
URL: http://www.scripps.com/foundation
Contact: Judith Clabes, Pres.
Description: Strives to "advance the cause of a free press through support of excellence in journalism, quality journalism education, and professional development.". **Awards:** Roy W. Howard Award. **Frequency:** annual. **Type:** recognition ● Ted Scripps Memorial Scholarships. **Frequency:** annual. **Type:** scholarship.

8718 ■ Society of Environmental Journalists (SEJ)
PO Box 2492
Jenkintown, PA 19046
Ph: (215)884-8174
Fax: (215)884-8175
E-mail: sej@sej.org
URL: http://www.sej.org
Contact: Beth Parke, Exec. Dir.
Founded: 1990. **Members:** 1,200. **Membership Dues:** regular in U.S., $45 (annual) ● student in U.S., regular in Canada, $35 (annual) ● regular in Mexico, $30 (annual). **Staff:** 5. **Budget:** $500,000. **Description:** Working journalists in all media, educators and students. Programs include national and regional conferences, publications, on-line services. Seeks to improve the quality, accuracy and visibility of environmental reporting. **Awards:** Awards for Reporting on the Environment. **Frequency:** annual. **Type:** monetary. **Computer Services:** Electronic publishing, press releases ● mailing lists ● online services, job postings distribution service. **Telecommunication Services:** electronic bulletin board, press release distribution service. **Publications:** *SEJournal*, quarterly. Newsletter. Includes resources and training covering the environment. **Price:** $200.00 corporate; $80.00 government; $55.00 university; $45.00 individual. ISSN: 1053-7082. **Circulation:** 1,500. **Advertising:** accepted. Alternate Formats: online. **Conventions/Meetings:** annual conference (exhibits).

8719 ■ Washington Journalism Center (BUWJC)
c/o Boston University
2807 Connecticut Ave. NW
Washington, DC 20008
Ph: (202)756-7800
Fax: (202)756-7854
E-mail: washjo@bu.edu
URL: http://www.bu.edu/washjocenter
Contact: Linda Killian, Dir.
Founded: 1965. **Staff:** 3. **Description:** Offers students the chance to spend a semester in Washington, D.C. where they can meet newsmakers, work in the bureaus of national news organizations, report on Congress and the federal government for New England news outlets and study political reporting in the best political city in the world. **Libraries: Type:** reference. **Subjects:** political reporting, journalism internship, print journalism-directed study, broadcast journalism-directed study. **Awards:** Thomas L. Stokes Award. **Frequency:** annual. **Type:** monetary. **Recipient:** for best report, analysis or comment on energy - oil, gas, coal, nuclear, solar or water. **Affiliated With:** National Press Foundation. **Also Known As:** (2005) Boston University Washington Journalism Program. **Conventions/Meetings:** periodic conference - usually in Arlington, VA.

Labor

8720 ■ American Labor Education Center (ALEC)
Address Unknown since 2007
Founded: 1979. **Description:** Participants include labor educators, researchers, and writers. Seeks to help workers develop the necessary skills to solve work-related problems. Produces educational and training materials for workers on occupational safety and health, organizing unions, newsletter production, and other related topics. **Convention/Meeting:** none. **Publications:** *American Labor*, periodic. Newsletter.

8721 ■ Center for Labor Research and Education (CLRE)
c/o Institute of Industrial Relations
2521 Channing Way, No. 5555
Berkeley, CA 94720-5555
Ph: (510)642-0323
Fax: (510)643-4673
E-mail: laborcenter@berkeley.edu
URL: http://laborcenter.berkeley.edu
Contact: Katie Quan, Assoc. Chair
Founded: 1964. **Staff:** 5. **Description:** Works to develop educational programs to meet the needs of unions. Conducts research concerning organized labor and the workforce; offers management training courses; holds computer training workshops; sponsors multi-union conferences on labor issues. Maintains speakers' bureau. **Libraries: Type:** open to the public. **Holdings:** 65,000; artwork, books, periodicals. **Computer Services:** Electronic publishing, educational materials posted on website ● mailing lists ● online services. **Also Known As:** The Labor Center. **Publications:** *California Workers Rights: A Manual of Job Rights, Protections and Remedies, 2nd Edition*. Book. **Price:** $17.95 each. ISSN: 9378-1708 ● *The First Steps to Identifying Sex and Race Based Pay Inequities in a Workplace: A Guide to Achieving Pay Equity*. Book. **Price:** $7.50 each ● *Hey, The Boss Just Called Me Into The Office*. Book. Features the Weingarten Decision and the Right to representation on the job. **Price:** $8.00 each ● *On the Move*, semiannual. Newsletter. Alternate Formats: online ● *Service Contracting in the Bay Area: A Study of Local Government Contracting Out*. Book. **Price:** $10.50 each. **Conventions/Meetings:** quarterly board meeting, advisory board ● conference.

8722 ■ United Association for Labor Education (UALE)
c/o Dennis Serrette, Pres.
501 Third St. NW
Washington, DC 20001
Ph: (202)434-9503
E-mail: dserrette@cwa-union.org
URL: http://www.uale.org
Contact: Dennis Serrette, Pres.
Founded: 2000. **Members:** 500. **Membership Dues:** student, retiree (based on annual income), $25-$100 (annual) ● sustaining, $150 (annual) ● institutional, $300 (annual). **Description:** Universities and colleges with full-time labor education programs; individuals. Formed to: coordinate labor education activities of colleges and universities with the AFL-CIO and other labor organizations; promote the development of labor education. Compiles salary surveys of labor education personnel. **Libraries: Type:** reference. **Subjects:** labor education. **Awards:** Career Achievement Award. **Type:** recognition. **Committees:** Academic Standards and Degree Programs; Black Workers and Labor Educators; Building Trades; Career Achievement; Constitution; Electronic Communications; Institutional Integrity and Academic Freedom; International Labor Education; Legislation; Salary and Benefits; Trade Union Women; Worker Participation. **Affiliated With:** Committee for Education Funding; International Council for Adult Education. **Formerly:** (1975) University Labor Education Association; (2000) University and College Labor Education Association. **Publications:** *Abstracts*, annual. Contains papers and presentations made at conference. ● *Labor Studies Journal*, quarterly. **Price:** $35.00/copy for institutions; $15.00/copy for individuals; $120.00 /year for institutions; $45.00 /year for individuals. ISSN: 0160-449X ● *Research Resource Directory*, annual ● Membership Directory, annual. **Conventions/Meetings:** annual meeting ● quarterly regional meeting.

Labor Studies

8723 ■ Labor and Working Class History Association (LAWCHA)
c/o Max Krochmal, Exec. Sec.
Stanford Indus.
Duke Univ.
Box 90239
Durham, NC 27708-0239
Ph: (919)613-7399
E-mail: lawcha@duke.edu
URL: http://www.lawcha.org
Contact: Max Krochmal, Exec. Sec.
Membership Dues: individual, union, $50 (annual) ● student, $30 (annual). **Description:** Represents scholars, union members, students, and citizens promoting a wider understanding of the history of working-class people, their communities, and their organizations in the United States. Promotes historical study and research in the field of labor and working-class history. Seeks to advance the study of working-class men and women, their lives, their workplaces, communities, organizations, and cul-

tures. Promotes public and scholarly awareness of labor and working-class history through research, writing and organizing. Seeks to develop mutually supportive relationships with existing labor studies and labor history societies, independent labor unions and organizations, and labor history associations. **Awards:** LAWCHA Conference Travel Grants for Graduate Students. **Type:** grant. **Recipient:** to facilitate graduate student participation in labor history conferences ● LAWCHA Minority Graduate Student Conference Travel Award. **Type:** grant. **Recipient:** to support the participation of a minority graduate student in a labor history conference ● LAWCHA - North American Labor History Conference Graduate Research Essay Prize. **Frequency:** annual. **Type:** monetary. **Recipient:** to outstanding research work by a young scholar in the field of labor and working class history. **Publications:** *Labor: Studies in Working-Class History of the Americas*, quarterly. Journal. **Price:** included in membership dues. Alternate Formats: online ● Newsletter. **Price:** included in membership dues.

Landscaping

8724 ■ Council of Educators in Landscape Architecture (CELA)
PO Box 7506
Edmond, OK 73083
Ph: (405)330-4150 (405)341-3643
Fax: (405)330-4150
E-mail: cela@telepath.com
Contact: Janet Singer, Exec. Dir.
Founded: 1920. **Membership Dues:** institution, $1,000 (annual) ● associate institution, $350 (annual) ● affiliate institution, $125 (annual) ● international institution, $100 (annual) ● individual corresponding, $50 (annual). **Description:** Promotes all programs of landscape architecture in the U.S. and Canada. **Publications:** *Conference Proceedings* ● *DesignNet*. Journal. Alternate Formats: online ● *Forum on Education*. Newsletter ● *Landscape Journal*, semiannual. Contains editorial columns, correspondence section and reviews. **Price:** $170.00 /year for libraries and institutions; $50.00 /year for individuals. ISSN: 0277-2426. **Advertising:** accepted. Alternate Formats: online. **Conventions/Meetings:** annual conference - held in fall.

Language

8725 ■ American Association of Teachers of Spanish and Portuguese (AATSP)
900 Ladd Rd.
Walled Lake, MI 48390
Ph: (248)960-2180
Fax: (248)960-9570
E-mail: corporate@aatsp.org
URL: http://www.aatsp.org
Contact: Emily Spinelli, Exec. Dir.
Founded: 1917. **Members:** 13,000. **Membership Dues:** regular, $65 (annual) ● student, $25 (annual) ● life, $1,800. **Staff:** 4. **State Groups:** 53. **Local Groups:** 74. **Languages:** English, Portuguese, Spanish. **Description:** Teachers of Spanish and Portuguese languages and literatures and others interested in Hispanic culture. Operates placement bureau and maintains pen pal registry. Sponsors honor society, Sociedad Honoraria Hispanica and National Spanish Examinations for secondary school students. **Libraries: Type:** open to the public. **Holdings:** periodicals. **Subjects:** literature, pedagogy. **Awards:** AATSP Outstanding Service Award. **Type:** recognition. **Recipient:** to a member who has made outstanding service contributions ● Outstanding Teacher of the Year. **Frequency:** annual. **Type:** recognition. **Recipient:** to teachers of Spanish or Portuguese. **Computer Services:** Mailing lists, of members. **Telecommunication Services:** electronic mail, espinell@umich.edu. **Publications:** *Enlace*, semiannual. Newsletter. Contains timely articles of interest to members, including the annual meeting preliminary program and registration information. ● *Hispania*, quarterly. Journal. Contains critical studies and annotated bibliographies on the literatures and languages of Spain, Portugal, and Latin America. **Price:** included in membership dues; $30.00 /year for libraries. ISSN: 0018-2133. **Circulation:** 13,000. **Advertising:** accepted ● *Portuguese*, semiannual. Newsletter. Features items of interest about the Luso-Brazilian world. ● Membership Directory, annual. Available to members upon request. ● Handbooks. **Conventions/Meetings:** annual meeting (exhibits).

8726 ■ American Classical League (ACL)
Miami Univ.
422 Wells Mills Dr.
Oxford, OH 45056-1694
Ph: (513)529-7741
Fax: (513)529-7742
E-mail: info@aclclassics.org
URL: http://www.aclclassics.org
Contact: Geri Dutra, Admin. Sec.
Founded: 1919. **Members:** 3,500. **Membership Dues:** regular, $45 (annual) ● retired teacher, $25 (annual) ● student, $20 (annual) ● joint, $67 (annual) ● life, $800 ● life (joint), $1,200. **Staff:** 5. **Description:** Teachers of classical languages in high schools and colleges. Works to promote the teaching of Latin and other classical languages. Presents scholarship. Maintains placement service, teaching materials, and resource center at Miami University in Oxford, OH to sell teaching aids to Latin and Greek teachers. **Awards:** Arthur Patch McKinlay Scholarship. **Frequency:** annual. **Type:** scholarship. **Recipient:** for current members ● Ed Phinney Commemorative Scholarship. **Frequency:** annual. **Type:** scholarship. **Recipient:** for current members ● Glenn Knudsvig Memorial Scholarship. **Frequency:** annual. **Type:** scholarship. **Recipient:** for current JCL sponsors ● Maureen V. O'Donnell/Eunice E. Kraft Teacher Training Scholarships. **Frequency:** annual. **Type:** scholarship. **Recipient:** for individuals. **Telecommunication Services:** electronic mail, announcements@aclclassics.org. **Affiliated With:** National Junior Classical League. **Publications:** *Classical Outlook*, quarterly. Journal. **Price:** included in membership dues. **Advertising:** accepted ● Newsletter, 3/year. Publishes news, articles, reviews, and announcements of interest to classicists in North America and abroad. **Conventions/Meetings:** annual meeting (exhibits).

8727 ■ American Council on the Teaching of Foreign Languages (ACTFL)
700 S Washington St., Ste.210
Alexandria, VA 22314
Ph: (703)894-2900
Fax: (703)894-2905
E-mail: headquarters@actfl.org
URL: http://www.actfl.org
Contact: Bret Lovejoy, Exec. Dir.
Founded: 1967. **Members:** 8,000. **Membership Dues:** regular, $75 (annual) ● regular, $140 (biennial) ● regular, $200 (triennial) ● new teacher, $50 (annual) ● retired, student, $25 (annual) ● international/joint, $20 (annual). **Staff:** 10. **Budget:** $2,000,000. **Regional Groups:** 5. **State Groups:** 53. **National Groups:** 21. **Description:** Individuals interested in the teaching of classical and modern foreign languages in schools and colleges throughout America. Included in the structure are state, regional, and national organizations of foreign language teachers and supervisors from all levels of education. Conducts seminars and workshops. **Awards:** ACTFL/FDP - Houghton Mifflin Award for Excellence in Foreign Language Instruction Using Technology with IALL. **Frequency:** annual. **Type:** recognition. **Recipient:** for individuals ● Anthony Papalia Award for Excellence in Teacher Education. **Frequency:** annual. **Type:** recognition. **Recipient:** for teachers, educators and authors ● Edwin Cudecki International Business Award. **Frequency:** annual. **Type:** recognition. **Recipient:** for individuals ● Emma Birkmaier Award for Doctoral Dissertation Research in Foreign Language Education. **Frequency:** annual. **Type:** recognition. **Recipient:** for authors of doctoral dissertation research ● Florence Steiner Award for Leadership in Foreign Language Education. **Frequency:** annual. **Type:** recognition. **Recipient:** for teachers, department chairs and professional speakers ● National Textbook Company Award for Building Community Interest in Foreign Language Education. **Frequency:** annual. **Type:** recognition ● Nelson Brooks Award for Excellence in the Teaching Culture. **Frequency:** annual. **Type:** recognition. **Recipient:** for foreign language educators ● Paul Pimsleur Award for Research in Foreign Language Education. **Frequency:** annual. **Type:** recognition. **Recipient:** for authors of foreign language research. **Telecommunication Services:** electronic mail, blovejoy@actfl.org. **Publications:** *Foreign Language Annals*, quarterly. Journal. Covers teaching methods, educational research and experimentation, and professional concerns. Includes book reviews, calendar, and annual directory. **Price:** included in membership dues; $225.00 /year for libraries and institutions in U.S.; $300.00 /year for libraries and institutions outside U.S. ISSN: 0015-718X. **Circulation:** 8,000. **Advertising:** accepted ● *Foreign Language Education Series*, annual. Book. **Price:** $20.00 each for 1 to 10 copies; $15.00 each for more than 10 copies ● *The Language Educator*, semiannual. Magazine. **Price:** $225.00 /year for libraries and institutions (domestic); $300.00/year for libraries and institutions outside U.S. **Advertising:** accepted. **Conventions/Meetings:** annual Language Learners - convention (exhibits) - always November. 2008 Nov. 21-23, Orlando, FL.

8728 ■ Association of Departments of Foreign Languages (ADFL)
26 Broadway, 3rd Fl.
New York, NY 10004-1789
Ph: (646)576-5140 (646)576-5134
Fax: (646)458-0030
E-mail: adfl@mla.org
URL: http://www.adfl.org
Contact: David Goldberg, Assoc. Dir.
Founded: 1969. **Members:** 1,050. **Membership Dues:** department (based on number of faculty members), $200-$550 (annual) ● joint (each additional department), $150 (annual) ● community college department, $100 (annual). **Staff:** 4. **Description:** College and university foreign language departments. Promotes communication and concerted action on professional and pedagogical matters. Compiles statistics. **Awards:** Award for Distinguished Service in the Profession. **Frequency:** annual. **Type:** recognition. **Recipient:** for outstanding service. **Telecommunication Services:** electronic mail, dgoldberg@mla.org. **Affiliated With:** Modern Language Association of America. **Publications:** *ADFL Bulletin*, 3/year. Journal. Covers curriculum, instruction, methods, career placement, and department objectives. **Price:** included in membership dues; $27.00 /year for nonmembers; $30.00 /year for institutions. ISSN: 0148-7639. **Circulation:** 2,000. **Advertising:** accepted. Alternate Formats: microform ● *Modern Language Association: Job Information List, Foreign Language Editor*, quarterly. Contains list of positions available in universities and colleges, and some business organizations, nationally and abroad. **Price:** included in membership dues; $35.00 /year for nonmembers. **Circulation:** 5,500. **Advertising:** accepted. **Conventions/Meetings:** annual seminar, for foreign language department chairs - always June.

8729 ■ College Language Association (CLA)
c/o Booker T. Anthony, Pres.
Fayetteville State Univ.
Dept. of English and Foreign Languages
1200 Murchison Rd.
Fayetteville, NC 28301
Ph: (910)672-1347
Fax: (910)672-1425
E-mail: banthony@uncfsu.edu
URL: http://www.clascholars.org
Contact: Booker T. Anthony, Pres.
Founded: 1937. **Members:** 800. **Membership Dues:** institutional, $200 (annual) ● regular, $75 (annual) ● student, $50 (annual) ● retiree, $40 (annual) ● life, $500. **Staff:** 2. **Budget:** $40,000. **Languages:** English, French, German, Spanish. **For-Profit. Description:** Teachers of English and modern foreign languages, primarily in historically black colleges and universities. Maintains placement service. **Libraries:**

Type: reference. **Holdings:** archival material, papers, periodicals. **Awards:** CLA Book Award. **Frequency:** annual. **Type:** recognition. **Recipient:** for scholarly publication ● CLA Margaret Walker Alexander Award. **Frequency:** annual. **Type:** recognition. **Recipient:** for meritorious service ● CLA Service Award. **Frequency:** annual. **Type:** recognition. **Recipient:** to students in member colleges for study abroad. **Committees:** Archives; Awards; Black Studies; CLA and HBCUs; CLA and HWCUs; Constitution; Creative Writing; Membership; Nominations; Placement; Research. **Sections:** Curriculum: English; Curriculum: Foreign Language. **Affiliated With:** Modern Language Association of America. **Formerly:** (1937) Association of Teachers of English in Negro Colleges. **Publications:** *CLA Journal*, quarterly. Covers English language and literature and modern foreign languages and literature. **Price:** included in membership dues; $75.00 /year for nonmembers and libraries in U.S.; $77.50/year in Canada; $37.75/copy for nonmembers. ISSN: 0007-8549. **Circulation:** 1,700. **Advertising:** accepted. Also Cited As: *College Language Association Journal* ● *Studies on James Baldwin, Langston Hughes, Jean Toomer and Others* ● Membership Directory, annual, every September. **Conventions/Meetings:** annual convention, books and instructional materials, CLA materials, works or art (exhibits) - usually in April.

8730 ■ ERIC Clearinghouse on Languages and Linguistics (ERIC/CLL)
4646 40th St. NW
Washington, DC 20016-1859
Ph: (202)362-0700
Free: (800)276-9834
Fax: (202)362-3740
E-mail: eric@cal.org
URL: http://www.cal.org/ericcll
Contact: Dr. Craig Packard, User Services Coor.

Founded: 1974. **Staff:** 8. **Budget:** $445,000. **Description:** Collects and disseminates information on current developments in educational research, instructional methods and materials, program design and evaluation, teacher training, and assessment. Topics covered include: foreign languages; English as a second or foreign language; psycholinguistics and sociolinguistics; theoretical and applied linguistics; bilingualism and bilingual education; intercultural communication and cultural education; study abroad and international exchange. Materials are prepared for specialists as well as nonspecialists. Offers workshops for teachers, students, librarians, and other information service providers. ERIC/CLL is one of 16 ERIC educational clearinghouses. **Libraries: Type:** open to the public; by appointment only. **Holdings:** books, periodicals. **Subjects:** languages and linguistics. **Computer Services:** database, computer searches ● database, educational. **Affiliated With:** Center for Applied Linguistics. **Publications:** *ERIC/CLL News Bulletin*, semiannual. Newsletter. Includes information about the ERIC system, new products and services, activities at ERIC/CLL, and topics of current interest. **Price:** free. **Circulation:** 20,000. Alternate Formats: online ● *ERIC Digests*. Reports. Highlights topics in foreign education, ESL, bilingual education, and linguistics. Alternate Formats: online ● *Language in Education: Theory and Practice*, periodic. Monograph.

8731 ■ Foundation for European Language and Educational Centres U.S.A.
101 N Union St., Ste.300
Alexandria, VA 22314
Ph: (703)684-1494
Free: (888)387-6236
Fax: (703)684-1495
E-mail: alx-info@eurocentres.com
URL: http://www.eurocentres.com
Contact: Diane Vespucci, Dir.

Founded: 1958. **National Groups:** 3. **Languages:** English, French, German, Italian, Japanese, Russian, Spanish. **Description:** Division of the Foundation for European Language and Educational Centres. Serves approximately 25,000 students through 30 centers worldwide. Provides instruction in American English for foreigners at several universities in the United States. Makes foreign language study available to Americans at Eurocentres in Europe, Japan, and Russia. **Awards: Type:** scholarship. **Recipient:** for at least 3 months study based on educational standing and economic need. **Also Known As:** EUROCENTRES USA.

8732 ■ International Lexical Functional Grammar Association (ILFGA)
c/o Tracy Holloway King
Palo Alto Res. Ctr.
3333 Coyote Hill Rd.
Palo Alto, CA 94304
Ph: (650)812-4808
Fax: (650)812-4374
E-mail: majordomo@lists.stanford.edu
URL: http://www.stanford.edu/~thking/index.html
Contact: Tracy Holloway King, Contact

Founded: 1998. **Members:** 100. **Multinational. Description:** Individuals for the advancement of LFG based approaches for scientific study of language. Holds annual conferences, business meetings, and Executive Committee meetings. **Computer Services:** Mailing lists. **Committees:** Program. **Publications:** *LFG Bulletin*, quarterly, March, June, September, and December. **Conventions/Meetings:** annual convention ● annual meeting, business; held concurrently with annual convention ● annual meeting, executive committee; held concurrently with annual conference.

8733 ■ Language Materials Project (LMP)
1337 Rolfe Hall
Box 951487
Los Angeles, CA 90095-1487
Ph: (310)267-4720
Fax: (310)267-4722
E-mail: lmp@international.ucla.edu
URL: http://www.lmp.ucla.edu
Contact: Prof. Thomas J. Hinnebusch, Proj. Dir./ Principle Investigator

Founded: 1992. **Description:** Helps locate teaching and learning materials for less commonly taught languages throughout the world. Provides bibliographic information and annotations that describe the content and teaching methodology. **Computer Services:** database.

8734 ■ Less Commonly Taught Languages Project (LCTL)
c/o Center for Advanced Research on Language Acquisition
619 Heller Hall
271 19th Ave. S
Minneapolis, MN 55455
Ph: (612)626-8600 (612)624-9016
Fax: (612)624-7514
E-mail: carla@tc.umn.edu
URL: http://www.carla.umn.edu/lctl
Contact: Louis Janus, Proj. Coor.

Founded: 1993. **Staff:** 2. **Description:** Helps advance the teaching and learning of languages excluding English, French, German, and Spanish. Encourages people to study less commonly taught languages; assists teachers develop high quality teaching materials; helps teachers cooperate and communicate. Provides resources through the Internet. **Awards:** Material Development Mini-Grant. **Frequency:** periodic. **Type:** grant. **Recipient:** for the development and submission of sharable material for teaching LCTL. **Computer Services:** database, of where LCTL is taught in North America ● mailing lists, for teachers of various LCTLs. **Telecommunication Services:** electronic mail, lctl@umn.edu. **Publications:** *The Virtual Picture Album*. Journal. Contains digitized photographs and drawings. Alternate Formats: online ● Papers ● Proceedings.

8735 ■ Modern Language Association of America (MLA)
26 Broadway, 3rd Fl.
New York, NY 10004-1789
Ph: (646)576-5000 (646)576-5102
Fax: (646)458-0300
E-mail: execdirector@mla.org
URL: http://www.mla.org
Contact: Rosemary G. Feal, Exec. Dir.

Founded: 1883. **Members:** 30,000. **Membership Dues:** non-student, $35 (annual) ● graduate student, $20 (annual). **Staff:** 88. **Budget:** $9,000,000. **Regional Groups:** 6. **Description:** Provides opportunities for the members to share their scholarly findings and teaching experiences with colleagues and to discuss trends in the academy. Works to strengthen the study and teaching of language and literature. **Awards:** Aldo and Jeanne Scaglione Prize for Comparative Literary Studies. **Frequency:** annual. **Type:** monetary. **Recipient:** for an outstanding scholarly work by a member in the field of comparative literary studies involving at least two literatures ● Aldo and Jeanne Scaglione Prize for Literary Translation. **Frequency:** annual. **Type:** monetary. **Recipient:** for an outstanding translation into English of a book length literary work ● Aldo and Jeanne Scaglione Prize for Studies in Germanic Languages and Literature. **Frequency:** biennial. **Type:** monetary. **Recipient:** for an outstanding literary work on the linguistics or literatures of the Germanic languages (Danish, Dutch, German, Icelandic, Norwegian, Swedish, Yiddish) ● Aldo and Jeanne Scaglione Prize for Studies in Slavic Languages and Literatures. **Frequency:** biennial. **Type:** monetary. **Recipient:** for an outstanding scholarly work on the linguistics or literatures of the Slavic languages ● Aldo and Jeanne Scaglione Prize in French and Francophone Studies. **Frequency:** annual. **Type:** monetary. **Recipient:** for an outstanding scholarly work by a member in French or francophone linguistic or literary studies ● Howard R. Marraro Prize. **Frequency:** biennial. **Type:** monetary. **Recipient:** for a book or essay length study on Italian literature ● James Russell Lowell Prize. **Frequency:** annual. **Type:** monetary. **Recipient:** for an outstanding book by a member ● Katherine Singer Kovacs Prize. **Frequency:** annual. **Type:** monetary. **Recipient:** for outstanding book published in English in the field of Latin American and Spanish literatures and cultures ● Kenneth W. Mildenberger Prize. **Frequency:** annual. **Type:** monetary. **Recipient:** for an outstanding book or article on teaching foreign language and literature ● Mina P. Shaughnessy Prize. **Frequency:** annual. **Type:** monetary. **Recipient:** for an outstanding book or article on teaching English language and literature ● MLA Prize for a First Book. **Frequency:** annual. **Type:** monetary. **Recipient:** for an outstanding literary or linguistic study, a critical edition of an important work, or a critical biography ● MLA Prize for a Scholarly Edition. **Frequency:** biennial. **Type:** monetary. **Recipient:** for a distinguished scholarly edition in the field of language or literature ● MLA Prize for Independent Scholars. **Frequency:** annual. **Type:** monetary. **Recipient:** for distinguished published research by an independent scholar ● Morton N. Cohen Award. **Frequency:** biennial. **Type:** monetary. **Recipient:** for distinguished edition of letters ● William Riley Parker Prize. **Frequency:** annual. **Type:** monetary. **Recipient:** for an outstanding article. **Computer Services:** Bibliographic search, literature and linguistics. **Telecommunication Services:** electronic mail, governance@mla.org. **Boards:** PMLA Editorial; Texts and Translations Series Editorial. **Committees:** Academic Freedom and Professional Rights and Responsibilities; Community Colleges; Disability Issues in the Profession; Honors and Awards; Information Technology; International Bibliography; Literatures of People of Color in the United States and Canada; New Variorum Edition of Shakespeare; PMLA Advisory; Program; Publications; Radio; Scholarly Editions; Status of Graduate Students in the Profession; Status of Women in the Profession. **Affiliated With:** Association of Departments of English; Association of Departments of Foreign Languages. **Publications:** *Convention Program*, annual ● *MLA International Bibliography*, annual. Lists books and articles on modern languages and literature. **Price:** $1,000.00 for print library edition. Alternate Formats: online ● *MLA Job Information List*, 5/year. Contains information on college teaching positions available in English and foreign language departments; available in two editions respectively. **Price:** $38.00 online; $50.00 print, in U.S. and Canada; $70.00 print, outside U.S. and Canada; $90.00 online and print outside U.S. and Canada. **Circulation:** 4,000. **Advertising:** accepted ● *MLA Newsletter*, quarterly. **Price:** included in membership dues; $8.00 /year for nonmembers in U.S. and Canada; $18.00 /year for nonmembers outside U.S. and Canada. ISSN: 0160-5720. **Circulation:** 32,000. **Advertising:** accepted ● *PMLA: Publications of the Modern Language Association of America*, bimonthly. Journal. **Price:** included in membership dues; $140.00 /year for libraries and institutions - print only. ISSN: 0030-8129. **Circulation:** 35,000. **Advertising:** accepted. Alternate Formats: microform ● *Profession*, annual. Journal. Contains articles on the state of the profession in the language and literature fields. **Price:** one issue included with new membership; $7.50/copy for nonmembers. ISSN: 0740-6959 ● Membership Directory, annual ● Books ● Monographs ● Pamphlets ● Reports. **Conventions/Meetings:** annual convention (exhibits).

8736 ■ National Association of Self-Instructional Language Programs (NASILP)
Critical Languages Prog.
Univ. of Arizona
1717 E Speedway Blvd., Ste.3312
Tucson, AZ 85721-0151
Ph: (520)626-5258
Fax: (520)626-8205
E-mail: nasilp@u.arizona.edu
URL: http://www.nasilp.org
Contact: Dr. Alexander Dunkel, Exec. Dir.
Founded: 1971. **Members:** 125. **Membership Dues:** institutional, $200-$500 (annual). **Staff:** 3. **Budget:** $25,000. **Description:** Academic institutions at the secondary, college, and university levels and other nonacademic organizations that provide foreign language instruction in the self-study format and tutorials. Fosters self-instructional programs in all foreign languages, with special attention given to those less commonly taught. Provides services to aid in the design and operation of self-instructional methodology. Establishes uniform guidelines; provides for external consultants; offers advisory service for institutions planning the inauguration of self-study programs. Sponsors textual materials and orientation multi-media materials development for various languages. Compiles statistics on enrollment and curricular aspects of self-instructional language centers. Maintains speakers' bureau. **Libraries: Type:** reference. **Holdings:** audio recordings, software, video recordings. **Subjects:** less commonly taught languages. **Telecommunication Services:** electronic mail, adunkel@u.arizona.edu. **Committees:** Development; Editorial; Membership; Standards and Guidelines. **Publications:** *NASILP Journal*, annual. Contains association news and articles on methodology and pedagogical techniques for self-instruction. **Price:** included in membership dues. **Circulation:** 350. Also Cited As: *NASILP Bulletin*. **Conventions/Meetings:** annual conference - Friday and Saturday prior to Election Day, Arlington, VA/DC area.

8737 ■ National Council of Less Commonly Taught Languages (NCOLCTL)
c/o Antonia Folarin Schleicher, PhD, Exec. Dir.
Natl. African Language Rsrc. Ctr.
4231 Humanities Bldg.
455 N Park St.
Madison, WI 53706
Ph: (608)265-7905
Fax: (608)265-7904
E-mail: ncolctl@mailplus.wisc.edu
URL: http://www.councilnet.org
Contact: Antonia Folarin Schleicher PhD, Exec. Dir.
Founded: 1990. **Members:** 300. **Membership Dues:** individual, $50 (annual) ● student, $30 (annual). **Staff:** 1. **Budget:** $50,000. **Regional Groups:** 18. **Multinational. Description:** National organization that represents teachers of less commonly taught languages. Addresses the issue of national capacity in the LCTL by facilitating communications among member organizations and with the governmental, private, heritage, and overseas sectors of the language community. Increases the collective impact of LCTL constituencies on America's ability to communicate with peoples from all parts of the world. **Awards:** A. Ronald Walton Award. **Frequency:** annual. **Type:** recognition. **Recipient:** for a career with distinguished service to the LCTL. **Affiliated With:** American Council on Education; American Council on the Teaching of Foreign Languages; Joint National Committee for Languages; National Foreign Language Center. **Formerly:** (2005) National Council of Organizations of Less Commonly Taught Languages. **Publications:** *Journal of the National Council of Less Commonly Taught Languages* ● *NCOLCTL Newsletter*, annual. Contains news on organization, member organization and affiliate organization activities, awards, publications, upcoming events. **Price:** free. **Circulation:** 2,500. Alternate Formats: online ● Reports. Alternate Formats: online. **Conventions/Meetings:** annual conference and assembly (exhibits).

8738 ■ National Council of State Supervisors of Foreign Languages (NCSSFL)
c/o Ryan Wertz, Treas.
1265 Millington Ct.
Columbus, OH 43235
URL: http://www.ncssfl.org
Contact: Jacque Bott Van Houten, Pres.
Founded: 1960. **Members:** 67. **Membership Dues:** regular institution, associate, $40 (annual) ● retired, $20 (annual). **Description:** State supervisors of foreign languages. Aims to increase the effectiveness of state foreign language supervisors by acting as an information service for state programs and experimental studies, and by cooperating with other organizations in the improvement of instruction in modern and classical languages at all levels. **Awards:** State Supervisor of the Year. **Frequency:** annual. **Type:** recognition. **Recipient:** for foreign language supervisory leadership. **Publications:** *Mailing List*, annual. Directory ● Also publishes position papers. **Conventions/Meetings:** annual meeting.

8739 ■ National Federation of Modern Language Teachers Associations (NFMLTA)
c/o Dr. Gerard L. Ervin, Treas.
7841 E Camino Montaraz
Tucson, AZ 85715-3713
Ph: (520)885-2663
Fax: (520)885-2663
E-mail: ervin7841@earthlink.net
Contact: Dr. Gerard L. Ervin, Treas.
Founded: 1916. **Members:** 15. **Staff:** 1. **Budget:** $110,000. **Description:** Federation of national, regional, and state associations of modern foreign language teaching organizations. Encourages research in foreign language education. Commissions articles on special topics of interest to the language teaching profession. **Publications:** *Modern Language Journal*, quarterly. Includes book and computer program reviews. ISSN: 0026-7902. **Circulation:** 4,000. **Advertising:** accepted.

8740 ■ National Foreign Language Center (NFLC)
5201 Paint Br. Pkwy.
Patapsco Bldg., Ste.2132
College Park, MD 20742-6715
Ph: (301)405-9828
Fax: (301)405-9829
E-mail: inquiries@nflc.org
URL: http://www.nflc.org
Contact: Dr. Catherine Ingold, Dir.
Founded: 1986. **Description:** A research institute of the University of Maryland. Focuses on language policy and U.S. needs for competence in languages. Operates as a think tank and also conducts studies for a wide range of clients. Recent activities include the initiation of a web-based database system, customized services to language teachers and language learners, feasibility studies of language programs for advanced language students, evaluations of study abroad, language programs, explorations of K-12 language needs, and testimony before congressional committees. **Computer Services:** database, of foreign languages. **Projects:** Evaluation of Exchange, Language, International and Area Studies System; Language Access Initiative; Recursos para la Ensenanza y el Aprendizaje de las Culturas Hispanas. **Publications:** *A View from Within: A Case Study of Chinese Heritage Community Language Schools*. Magazine. Provides insider's perspective on the issues affecting the Chinese heritage community languages schools. **Price:** $10.95 each ● *The Design of the Alta Langnet Project*. Article. Describes the vision of a customizable language learning program. ● Reports ● Papers.

8741 ■ North American Association for Celtic Language Teachers (NAACLT)
c/o John J. Morrissey, Sec.-Treas.
647 Maybell Ave.
Palo Alto, CA 94306-3817
E-mail: secretary@naaclt.org
URL: http://www.naaclt.org
Contact: John J. Morrissey, Sec.-Treas.
Membership Dues: student/retired, $15 (annual) ● regular, $25 (annual). **Description:** Celtic language teachers and students worldwide. Promotes improved methods of language instruction; facilitates professional development of members. Serves as a forum for the exchange of information among members; strengthens links between members and teachers of other languages. **Publications:** *Journal of Celtic Language Learning*, periodic. **Price:** $10.00 /year for members in North America; $13.00 /year for members outside North America; $12.00 /year for nonmembers in North America; $15.00 /year for nonmembers outside North America. ISSN: 1078-3911 ● *NAACLT News*, quarterly. Newsletter. **Price:** included in membership dues. Alternate Formats: online. **Conventions/Meetings:** annual convention.

8742 ■ Northeast Conference on the Teaching of Foreign Languages (NECTFL)
c/o Dickinson College
PO Box 1773
Carlisle, PA 17013-2896
Ph: (717)245-1977
Fax: (717)245-1976
E-mail: nectfl@dickinson.edu
URL: http://www.dickinson.edu/nectfl
Contact: Rebecca R. Kline, Exec. Dir.
Founded: 1954. **Membership Dues:** Advisory Council, $175 (annual) ● advocate, $100 (annual) ● associate, $200 (annual). **Staff:** 3. **Description:** Sponsored by groups or institutions which have nonprofit educational status and which are actively engaged in teaching. Seeks to further the teaching and learning of foreign languages, classical and modern, in the U.S. **Awards:** Foreign Language Advocate Award. **Frequency:** annual. **Type:** recognition. **Recipient:** for a person outside foreign language teaching ● NECTFL Service. **Frequency:** periodic. **Type:** recognition. **Recipient:** for members ● Nelson H. Brooks Award for Leadership in the Profession. **Frequency:** annual. **Type:** recognition. **Recipient:** for members ● Stephen A. Freeman. **Frequency:** annual. **Type:** recognition. **Recipient:** for the best published articles ● Student Language. **Frequency:** periodic. **Type:** recognition. **Recipient:** for foreign language students and educators ● Vista Higher Learning Graduate Student. **Frequency:** annual. **Type:** scholarship. **Recipient:** for graduate students. **Computer Services:** Mailing lists, foreign language educators. **Publications:** *NECTFL Review*, semiannual. Journal. **Advertising:** accepted. Alternate Formats: online ● *Northeast Conference Reports*, annual. Book. **Price:** $10.95 each. **Conventions/Meetings:** annual conference (exhibits) - 2009 Apr. 16-18, New York, NY; 2010 Mar. 25-27, New York, NY.

Leadership

8743 ■ American Humanics (AH)
1100 Walnut St., Ste.1900
Kansas City, MO 64106
Ph: (816)561-6415
Free: (800)343-6466
Fax: (816)531-3527

E-mail: kstroup@humanics.org
URL: http://www.humanics.org
Contact: Kala M. Stroup PhD, Pres.

Founded: 1948. **Members:** 2,500. **Staff:** 14. **Budget:** $1,400,000. **Description:** Individuals, corporations, and foundations supporting AH work in preparing young people for professional leadership in youth and human service agencies. Provides leadership for co-curricular program on 71 campuses of colleges that feature specialized professional courses that lead to B.A., B.S., or M.A. degrees and prepare graduates to serve professionally with groups such as Boy Scouts of America, Boys and Girls Clubs of America, American Red Cross, Big Brothers/Big Sisters of America, Camp Fire Boys and Girls, Girl Scouts of the U.S.A., Junior Achievement, Young Men's Christian Associations of the United States of America, Young Women's Christian Association of the United States of America, and Girls, Inc., Catholic Charities United States of America, Habitat for Humanity International, National Urban League, Special Olympics, Inc., United Way of America, Volunteers of America. Sponsors field trips, workshops, and special courses; offers counseling, loan assistance, and career placement services to students; operates graduate programs in affiliation with American Humanics at Lindenwood College, Missouri Valley College, Murray State University, and University of Northern Iowa. Conducts research, compiles statistics. **Computer Services:** Online services, profile system. **Committees:** Agency and Institution Review; Business Management; Communications; Student Loan. **Affiliated With:** Hugh O'Brian Youth Leadership. **Formerly:** (1974) American Humanics Foundation. **Publications:** *Connections*, quarterly. Newsletter. Alternate Formats: online ● Annual Report, annual. Alternate Formats: online ● Brochures. **Conventions/Meetings:** annual American Humanics Management Institute - meeting ● annual meeting - always early January.

8744 ■ Association of Leadership Educators (ALE)

233 Human Environmental Sciences Bldg.
Oklahoma State Univ.
Stillwater, OK 74078
Ph: (405)744-6231
Fax: (405)744-2800
E-mail: renee.daugherty@okstate.edu
Contact: Dr. Renee A. Daugherty PhD, Treas.

Founded: 1990. **Members:** 250. **Membership Dues:** open, $50 (annual) ● student, retiree, $25 (annual). **Multinational. Description:** Works to strengthen the leadership skills and competencies of the professional educators who work to develop the leadership capabilities of others; and to strengthen and broaden the knowledge base which supports research, teaching and outreach, student services, consulting, and other programs in leadership. **Awards:** Distinguished Leadership and Service Award. **Frequency:** annual. **Type:** recognition ● Graduate Student Scholarship. **Frequency:** annual. **Type:** scholarship. **Recipient:** for outstanding graduate students who attend and present at the national conference ● Outstanding Leadership Program Award. **Frequency:** annual. **Type:** monetary ● Undergraduate Student Scholarship. **Frequency:** annual. **Type:** scholarship. **Recipient:** for outstanding undergraduate student who attends the national conference. **Computer Services:** Online services, e-mail listserv for members only ● online services, website for public and a member's only section. **Publications:** *FORUM*, quarterly. Newsletter. Alternate Formats: online ● *Journal of Leadership Educators*, biennial. ISSN: 1552-9045. Alternate Formats: online. **Conventions/Meetings:** annual conference (exhibits).

8745 ■ Center for International Initiatives (CII)

c/o American Council on Education
1 Dupont Cir. NW
Washington, DC 20036
Ph: (202)939-9313
Fax: (202)785-8056
E-mail: international@ace.nche.edu
URL: http://www.acenet.edu/AM/Template.cfm?Section=International
Contact: Madeleine F. Green, VP/Dir.

Founded: 1965. **Staff:** 11. **Description:** Offers programs and services that situate U.S. higher education in a global context and enhance internationalization on U.S. campuses. Works with international partners on higher education issues that have a global impact. **Programs:** Leadership Network for International Education; Office of Leadership. **Projects:** Global Learning for All; Sharing Quality Higher Education Across Borders; Where Faculty Live: Internationalizing the Disciplines. **Working Groups:** Assessing International Learning. **Affiliated With:** American Council on Education. **Formerly:** (1981) Institute for College and University Administrators; (1983) Center for Leadership Development and Academic Administration; (2007) Center for Institutional and International Initiatives. **Conventions/Meetings:** annual meeting, with concurrent sessions, plenaries - always February.

8746 ■ Educational Leadership Institute (ELI)

Address Unknown since 2007

Founded: 1980. **Staff:** 4. **Description:** Seeks to improve the quality of educational leadership at all levels through field-level research and training programs, focusing on problems related to special education, multicultural education, legal mandates, demography, and pupil personnel. Conducts research; compiles statistics on education; provides in-service and training programs. University professors and public school administrators participate in research and training activities. **Convention/Meeting:** none. **Libraries: Type:** reference. **Holdings:** 960; books, reports. **Subjects:** general and special education administration, school law, demography. **Divisions:** Inservice Training and Consultation; Research and Publication. **Publications:** Books. **Advertising:** not accepted ● Monograph ● Also publishes research results, tests, and in-service materials.

8747 ■ The Fund for American Studies (TFAS)

1706 New Hampshire Ave. NW
Washington, DC 20009
Ph: (202)986-0384
Free: (800)741-6964
Fax: (202)986-0390
E-mail: info@tfas.org
URL: http://www.tfas.org
Contact: Roger R. Ream, Pres.

Founded: 1967. **Staff:** 19. **Budget:** $4,788,767. **Nonmembership. Multinational. Description:** Promotes and supports the development of campus leadership through academic programs and internships designed to encourage and facilitate the preparation of young people, without regard to race, color, national origin, or religious belief, for the assumption of leadership roles. Programs are built upon the concept that students who confront national and international issues with the assistance of accomplished professionals are those who will be the most qualified leaders. The international programs educate students from Eastern and Central Europe, the Middle East, and Asia about principles of democratic government and free enterprise. Established in honor of Charles Edison (1890-1969), former governor of New Jersey and Secretary of the Navy, son of inventor Thomas Alva Edison. **Awards:** Clark Mollenhoff Award. **Frequency:** annual. **Type:** monetary. **Recipient:** for working student with outstanding investigative reporting ● Excellence in Economic Reporting. **Frequency:** annual. **Type:** recognition. **Recipient:** for magazine or newspaper writer ● **Type:** scholarship. **Recipient:** for student who has attended any of the institutes the organization sponsors ● Thomas L. Phillips Collegiate Journalism. **Frequency:** annual. **Type:** recognition. **Recipient:** for deserving students. **Formerly:** Charles Edison Youth Fund; (1986) Charles Edison Memorial Youth Fund. **Publications:** *Alumni*, monthly. Newsletter. Covers upcoming regional alumni events, news and updates. Alternate Formats: online ● *FASTrack*, quarterly. Magazine. Includes news on programs and information about upcoming events and alumni. ● Annual Report. Provides information on activities of the organization. ● Video. **Conventions/Meetings:** quarterly Weekend Journalism Conferences, with seminars.

8748 ■ Hugh O'Brian Youth Leadership (HOBY)

10880 Wilshire Blvd., Ste.410
Los Angeles, CA 90024
Ph: (310)474-4370
Fax: (310)475-5426
E-mail: hoby@hoby.org
URL: http://www.hoby.org
Contact: Javier LaFianza, Pres./CEO

Founded: 1958. **Staff:** 25. **Budget:** $2,500,000. **Regional Groups:** 15. **State Groups:** 60. **Local Groups:** 91. **Description:** Seeks, recognizes, and develops leadership potential in American and international high school sophomores by sponsoring annual state and international leadership seminars. (The group is named for actor Hugh O'Brian, who founded the organization upon returning from a nine-day visit with Dr. Albert Schweitzer. According to O'Brian, Schweitzer told him, "The most important thing in education is to teach young people to think for themselves." The group resulted from O'Brian's desire to put Schweitzer's words into action.) Encourages and aids young people in their struggle for self-identification and self-development. Serves as a liaison among young potential leaders and recognized leaders in business, education, government, science, and the professions through workshops. Works to create opportunities for participants to demonstrate their leadership abilities for the betterment of their communities and country. Administers the Hugh O'Brian Youth Foundation Alumni Association. **Awards:** Albert Schweitzer Leadership Award. **Frequency:** semiannual. **Type:** recognition. **Recipient:** for youth leadership ● HOBY Alumni Achievement Award. **Frequency:** biennial. **Type:** recognition. **Recipient:** for outstanding alumni who has demonstrated leadership abilities and has used its leadership for the betterment of youth. **Telecommunication Services:** electronic mail, lafianzaj@hoby.org. **Formerly:** (1998) Hugh O'Brian Youth Foundation. **Publications:** *Alumni Directory*, biennial ● *Chairmen's Resource Guide* ● *Corporate Operating Guide* ● *District Directors Manual* ● *Hoby Horizons*, bimonthly ● *Leadership Seminar Chairmen's List* ● *Long Range Plan*, triennial ● Annual Report, annual ● Brochures. **Conventions/Meetings:** annual World Leadership - convention, for alumni - always summer.

8749 ■ INROADS

10 S Broadway, Ste.300
St. Louis, MO 63102
Ph: (314)241-7488
Fax: (314)241-9325
E-mail: info@inroads.org
URL: http://www.INROADS.org
Contact: Mr. Charles H. Cornelius, Pres./CEO

Founded: 1970. **Staff:** 186. **Regional Groups:** 12. **Local Groups:** 48. **Description:** Provides internships for ethnically diverse students which lead to full-time career opportunities for the interns. Aims to develop and place talented Black, Hispanic/Latino, and Native American Indian high school and college students in business and industry and to prepare them for corporate and community leadership. Recruits, trains, and matches over 5000 individuals with paid internships for over 500 business corporations per year. Offers professional training seminars on time management, business presentation skills, team building, and decision making. Provides personal and professional guidance to pre-college and college interns. Operates in the U.S; Mexico City; and Toronto and Saskatchewan, Canada. **Awards:** Conversion Award. **Frequency:** annual. **Type:** recognition. **Recipient:** for corporations who converted the largest number of students to full-time employee ● Corporate Excellence Award. **Frequency:** annual. **Type:** recognition. **Recipient:** for leading corporations who provided the most opportunities for talented minority youth ● Growth Award. **Frequency:** annual.

Type: recognition. **Computer Services:** database. **Publications:** Annual Report, annual. **Conventions/Meetings:** annual Best of Class Conference - convention, leading corporations gather to discuss best practices as it relates to diversity, internships, and the organization ● annual Leadership Development Institute - meeting ● annual Local Awards Banquet - dinner - held in each local market.

8750 ■ Junior State of America (JSA)
400 S El Camino Real, Ste.300
San Mateo, CA 94402
Ph: (650)347-1600 (202)296-7838
Free: (800)334-5353
Fax: (650)347-7200
E-mail: jsa@jsa.org
Contact: Richard T. Prosser, Exec. Dir.
Founded: 1934. **Members:** 20,000. **Staff:** 18. **Budget:** $1,300,000. **Regional Groups:** 7. **Local Groups:** 500. **Description:** Nonpartisan organization of high school student leaders interested in politics and government. Serves as a student opinion forum stressing the development of leadership skills. Conducts educational programs to help high school students gain an understanding of American politics, government, and current issues. Programs are carried out by students with minimal adult assistance. **Formerly:** (1998) Junior Statesmen of America. **Publications:** *Junior Statement*, quarterly. Newspaper. **Circulation:** 25,000. **Conventions/Meetings:** convention - 30/year.

8751 ■ Junior Statesmen Foundation (JSF)
400 S El Camino Real, Ste.300
San Mateo, CA 94402
Ph: (650)347-1600 (202)296-7838
Free: (800)334-5353
Fax: (650)347-7200
E-mail: jsa@jsa.org
URL: http://www.jsa.org
Contact: Richard T. Prosser, Exec. Dir.
Founded: 1934. **Members:** 20,000. **Staff:** 18. **Budget:** $5,500,000. **Description:** Sponsors Junior States of America; also sponsors Junior Statesmen Summer School offering courses in political science, public speaking, and leadership. Encourages nonpartisan study of politics and government by high school students and teachers. **Telecommunication Services:** electronic mail, rprosser@jsa.org. **Affiliated With:** Junior State of America. **Publications:** *Alumni Report*, annual. Magazine. **Circulation:** 10,000. **Conventions/Meetings:** semiannual meeting - always April and November.

8752 ■ Leadership America (LA)
PO Box 191009
Dallas, TX 75219
Ph: (214)397-0900
Fax: (214)954-0712
E-mail: info@leadershipamerica.com
URL: http://www.leadershipamerica.com
Contact: Candace O'Keefe, Exec. Dir.
Founded: 1988. **Membership Dues:** individual, $100 (annual). **Description:** Works to recognize, educate, and connect accomplished and diverse women to increase their individual and collective impact globally.

8753 ■ Leadership Institute (LI)
1101 N Highland St.
Arlington, VA 22201
Ph: (703)247-2000
Free: (800)827-5323
Fax: (703)247-2001
URL: http://www.leadershipinstitute.org
Contact: Morton C. Blackwell, Pres./Founder
Founded: 1979. **Members:** 57,000. **Staff:** 58. **Budget:** $6,000,000. **Description:** Aims to identify, recruit, train and place conservatives in politics, government and media. Provides skills for public policy and personal success. **Formerly:** (1980) Conservative Leadership Youth Foundation. **Publications:** *Building Leadership*, bimonthly. Newsletter. Contains reports on institute programs. **Circulation:** 20,000. Alternate Formats: online.

8754 ■ National Youth Leadership Council (NYLC)
1667 Snelling Ave. N, Ste.D300
St. Paul, MN 55108
Ph: (651)631-3672
Fax: (651)631-2955
E-mail: nylcinfo@nylc.org
URL: http://www.nylc.org
Contact: Dr. James Kielsmeier, Pres./CEO
Founded: 1983. **Staff:** 20. **Regional Groups:** 3. **Description:** Engages young people in communities and schools through innovation in learning, leadership, service and public policy. Develops service-oriented youth leadership programs. Supports individuals, organizations, and communities that encourage youth service and leadership. **Projects:** Growing to Greatness: The State of Service-Learning; Ignition; Outreach to Empower; Pathway to Possibilities: Supporting the Transition of American Indian High School Youth; St. Paul Public Schools; Service-Learning Diversity/Equity; 3M Innovation in Community and Youth Development; Y-RISE: The Service-Learning and HIV/AIDS Initiative. **Publications:** *Getting Started in Service-Learning*. Book. Covers the basic of service-learning, from assessing community needs to reflection strategies. **Price:** $12.00 ● *Growing Hope: Sourcebook on Integrating Youth Service into the School Curriculum*. Contains history of service-learning, its rationale, hands-on ideas, sample program materials, and much more. **Price:** $10.00 ● *Growing to Greatness 2005*. Book. Contains national study of the state of service-learning in kindergarten through 12th grade. **Price:** $18.00 ● *Profiles in Service: A Handbook of Service Learning Program Design Models*. **Price:** $25.00 ● *Route to Reform: Service-Learning and School Improvement*. Book. **Price:** $20.00. **Conventions/Meetings:** annual National Service-Learning Conference (exhibits).

8755 ■ New Leaders for New Schools
30 W 26th St., 2nd Fl.
New York, NY 10010
Ph: (646)792-1070
E-mail: info@nlns.org
URL: http://www.nlns.org/NLWeb/Index.jsp
Contact: Jon Schnur, CEO/Co-Founder
Founded: 2000. **Description:** Ensures high academic achievement for every student through its 'New Leaders for New Schools' program. Aims to build the next generation of outstanding leaders for urban public schools. Forms a partnership with different organizations which are devoted to improving urban schools through effective leadership.

8756 ■ Presidential Classroom (PC)
119 Oronoco St.
Alexandria, VA 22314-2015
Ph: (703)683-5400
Free: (800)441-6533
Fax: (703)548-5728
E-mail: info@presidentialclassroom.org
URL: http://www.presidentialclassroom.org
Contact: Elizabeth A. Sherman PhD, Exec. Dir.
Founded: 1968. **Staff:** 14. **Budget:** $5,000,000. **Description:** High school juniors and seniors. Seeks to provide an in-depth study and an insider's behind-the-scenes look of the U.S. government in Washington, DC to students; enlightens students by personal involvement in government functions. Promotes a dedication to and a greater understanding of the American system of government. Offers volunteer opportunities for undergraduate and graduate students, teachers, civil servants, military personnel, and other interested professionals. Also offers the Future World Leaders Summit program for American and international students to explore international relations, diplomacy and economics in Washington, D.C. **Telecommunication Services:** electronic mail, esherman@presidentialclassroom.org. **Formerly:** (1998) Presidential Classroom for Young Americans. **Publications:** *Outlook*, annual. Book. Contains original articles that supplement students' learning experience in Washington, D.C. **Price:** free ● *Presidential Daily* ● Brochures. Contains information on senior high school program, volunteering, and internships. **Conventions/Meetings:** weekly conference - always January-July ● seminar, includes week-long program for high school students.

Legal Education

8757 ■ Academy of Legal Studies in Business (ALSB)
c/o Prof. Daniel J. Herron, Exec. Sec.
120 Upham Hall - Dept. of Finance
Miami Univ.
Oxford, OH 45056
Fax: (513)523-8180
E-mail: herrondj@muohio.edu
URL: http://www.alsb.org
Contact: Prof. Daniel J. Herron, Exec. Sec.
Founded: 1924. **Members:** 1,300. **Membership Dues:** individual, $60 (annual). **Regional Groups:** 11. **Multinational. Description:** Teachers of business law and legal environment in colleges and universities. Promotes and encourages business law scholarship and teaching outside of the law school environment. **Committees:** Regionals. **Sections:** Alternative Dispute Resolution; Employment/Labor Law; Environment and Business; Ethics; Feminist Legal Jurisprudence; International; Marketing; Technology. **Formerly:** (1992) American Business Law Association. **Publications:** *ALSB Newsletter*, 3/year ● *American Business Law Journal*, quarterly ● *Journal of Legal Studies Education*, semiannual. **Conventions/Meetings:** annual conference (exhibits) - always August.

8758 ■ ALI-ABA Committee on Continuing Professional Education (ALI-ABA)
4025 Chestnut St.
Philadelphia, PA 19104-3099
Ph: (215)243-1600
Free: (800)CLE-NEWS
Fax: (215)243-1664
E-mail: jfranki@ali-aba.org
URL: http://www.ali-aba.org
Contact: Julene Franki, Exec. Dir.
Founded: 1947. **Members:** 25. **Membership Dues:** organization, $400 (annual) ● extra mailing address, $125 (annual). **Staff:** 75. **Budget:** $8,500,000. **Description:** Representatives from American Bar Association and American Law Institute (see separate entries). Assists in the development, organization, and implementation of educational programs for lawyers who have been admitted to practice. Programs run from 1-day institutes to advanced and specialized training courses of 1 or more weeks. **Libraries: Type:** not open to the public. **Holdings:** 6,000; books, periodicals. **Subjects:** law, continuing education. **Awards:** Francis Rawle Award. **Frequency:** annual. **Type:** recognition. **Recipient:** for excellence in the field of continuing legal education ● Harrison Tweed Awards. **Frequency:** annual. **Type:** recognition. **Affiliated With:** American Bar Association; American Law Institute. **Formerly:** (1974) Joint Committee on Continuing Legal Education - of ALI-ABA. **Publications:** *AILTO Insider*, quarterly. Newsletter. Contains articles related to in-house training of attorneys. **Price:** included in membership dues. **Circulation:** 250 ● *ALI-ABA Business Law Course Materials Journal*, bimonthly. Provides articles from ALI-ABA continuing education coursebooks. **Price:** $40.00/year. ISSN: 0145-6342. **Circulation:** 6,500 ● *ALI-ABA CLE Review*, monthly. Journal. **Price:** free. ISSN: 0044-7560. **Circulation:** 89,000 ● *ALI-ABA Estate Planning Course Materials Journal*, bimonthly. Newsletter. Provides articles related to estate planning from ALI-ABA continuing education coursebooks. **Price:** $40.00/year ● *Audio Estate Planner*, quarterly ● *The CLE*. Journal. **Price:** $25.00/year ● *Practical Lawyer*. Magazine. **Price:** $40.00/year ● *Practical Tax Lawyer*. Magazine. **Price:** $35.00/year ● Also publishes course study materials on taxation, trial techniques, business and commercial transactions, labor laws, federal legislation, investments, criminal law, family law, law office management, and the Uniform Commercial Code.

8759 ■ American Association for Paralegal Education (AAFPE)
19 Mantua Rd.
Mount Royal, NJ 08061
Ph: (856)423-2829
Fax: (856)423-3420
E-mail: info@aafpe.org
URL: http://www.aafpe.org
Contact: Hedi Nasheri, Pres.
Founded: 1981. **Members:** 500. **Membership Dues:** institutional, associate, affiliate, $375 (annual) ● sustaining, $400 (annual) ● individual, $100 (annual). **Budget:** $200,000. **Description:** Represents paralegal educators and institutions of higher learning offering paralegal programs. Aims to promote and maintain high standards for paralegal education. Serves as a forum and clearinghouse for information on the professional improvement of paralegal educators and education. Develops guidelines for paralegal education programs in cooperation with the American Bar Association (see separate entry) and other institutional and professional associations. Promotes research and offers consultation services to institutions; maintains speakers' bureau. **Publications:** *Journal of Paralegal Education and Practice*, annual. **Advertising:** accepted ● *The Paralegal Educator*, quarterly. Newsletter. **Advertising:** accepted ● Directory, annual. **Price:** $25.00. **Circulation:** 400. **Advertising:** accepted ● Also publishes model course syllabi. **Conventions/Meetings:** annual conference (exhibits) - 2008 Oct. 15-18, Dallas, TX; 2009 Oct. 28-31, Portland, OR.

8760 ■ Association of American Law Schools (AALS)
1201 Connecticut Ave. NW, Ste.800
Washington, DC 20036-2717
Ph: (202)296-8851
Fax: (202)296-8869
E-mail: aals@aals.org
URL: http://www.aals.org
Contact: Judith C. Areen, Pres.
Founded: 1900. **Members:** 166. **Staff:** 22. **Budget:** $3,200,000. **Description:** Law schools association. Seeks to improve the legal profession through legal education. Interacts for law professors with state and federal government, other legal education and professional associations, and other national higher education and learned society organizations. Compiles statistics; sponsors teacher placement service. Presents professional development programs. **Libraries: Type:** reference. **Holdings:** archival material. **Awards:** Scholarly Papers of New Law Teachers. **Frequency:** annual. **Type:** recognition. **Recipient:** for paper submission. **Computer Services:** Mailing lists, of law professors. **Committees:** Academic Freedom and Tenure; Admissions to the Bar and Lawyer Performance; Clinical Legal Education; Curriculum and Research; Government Relations; Libraries and Technology; Membership Review; Professional Development; Recruitment and Retention of Minority Law Teachers; Sections and Annual Meeting. **Projects:** Equal Justice; Faculty Appointments Register; Pro Bono; Workshops and Conferences for Law Professors. **Affiliated With:** American Association for Higher Education; American Council on Education; American Council of Learned Societies; Consortium of Social Science Associations; International Law Institute; National Association of College and University Attorneys; National Association for Law Placement; National Conference of Bar Examiners; National Humanities Alliance. **Publications:** *AALS Directory of Law Teachers*, annual. **Price:** $250.00 for nonmembers; $100.00 for members ● *Association Handbook*, annual. Provides membership requirements, statements, and committee lists. **Price:** $16.00 for nonmembers; $8.50 for members ● *Journal of Legal Education*, quarterly. **Price:** $38.00 in U.S.; $42.00 outside U.S. ● *Placement Bulletin*, quarterly. Newsletter. Lists faculty and administrative job positions available at law schools. Focuses on openings in the United States. **Price:** $85.00/year; $22.00/issue. **Circulation:** 1,500 ● Newsletter, quarterly. Supports the professional development of law professors and administrators, with information on law education and curriculum. **Price:** $32.00/year; $8.00/issue. **Circulation:** 8,000. Alternate Formats: online ● Proceedings, annual. **Price:** $22.50 for nonmembers; $15.00 for members. **Conventions/Meetings:** annual Faculty Recruitment - conference - usually early November ● annual meeting (exhibits) - always early January. 2009 Jan. 6-10, San Diego, CA.

8761 ■ Association of American Law Schools Section on Sexual Orientation and Gender Identity Issues (AALS-SOGII)
c/o Prof. Mark E. Wojcik, Chm.-Elect
The John Marshall Law School
315 S Plymouth Ct.
Chicago, IL 60604
Ph: (312)987-2391
Fax: (312)427-9974
E-mail: 7wojcik@jmls.edu
URL: http://www.aals.org/services_sections_gl.php
Contact: Prof. Mark E. Wojcik, Chm.-Elect
Founded: 1983. **Members:** 1,150. **Description:** Law teachers concerned with lesbian, gay, bisexual and transgender legal issues. Promotes consideration of legal issues related to sexual orientation and gender identity within the Association of American Law Schools; encourages incorporation of lesbian and gay legal issues in law school curricula; advances professional interests of lesbian and gay people in legal education. Compiles statistics on law school policies concerning sexual orientation and gender identity. **Libraries: Type:** not open to the public. **Holdings:** archival material. **Formerly:** (2007) Section on Gay and Lesbian Legal Issues, Association of American Law Schools. **Publications:** Newsletter, periodic. **Price:** included in membership dues. **Circulation:** 900. **Conventions/Meetings:** annual meeting, held in conjunction with AALS.

8762 ■ Association for Continuing Legal Education (ACLEA)
c/o Donna J. Passons, Exec. Dir.
PO Box 4646
Austin, TX 78765
Ph: (512)453-4340
Fax: (512)451-2911
E-mail: aclea@aclea.org
URL: http://www.aclea.org
Contact: Donna J. Passons, Exec. Dir.
Founded: 1965. **Members:** 600. **Membership Dues:** primary (plus 180 per additional member), $195 (annual). **Staff:** 3. **Budget:** $200,000. **Description:** Professionals and organizations involved in continuing legal education including state and local bar associations, law schools, government agencies, and independents. Seeks to improve the quality of public legal services by providing a forum for the exchange of information and ideas; assists members in curriculum development and problem solving. Aims to develop and promote formal positions on issues relevant to the practice of law as it is affected by continuing legal education. **Libraries: Type:** reference. **Awards:** ACLEA Award of Excellence. **Type:** recognition. **Boards:** Best of ACLEA Editorial; CLE Journal Editorial. **Committees:** Awards; Exhibitors and Sponsors; International; Mandatory CLE; Newsletter Editorial; Public Interest. **Formerly:** Association of Continuing Legal Education Administrators; (1964) Association of Continuing Legal Education Administrators. **Publications:** Handbook ● Newsletter, quarterly. **Conventions/Meetings:** annual meeting (exhibits) - 2008 Aug. 2-5, Vancouver, BC, Canada ● annual meeting (exhibits) - always midyear.

8763 ■ Clinical Legal Education Association (CLEA)
c/o Paula Galowitz, Sec.
New York Univ. School of Law
245 Sullivan St., 5th Fl.
New York, NY 10012
Ph: (212)998-6441
Fax: (212)995-4031
E-mail: clea@cleaweb.org
URL: http://www.cleaweb.org
Contact: Paula Galowitz, Sec.
Founded: 1992. **Membership Dues:** individual, $40 (annual) ● group, $150-$375 (annual). **Description:** Promotes the interests and professional development of clinical teachers. Encourages the expansion and improvement of clinical legal education. Supports clinical research and scholarship. Disseminates information about issues and developments that affect clinical teachers. **Awards:** Excellence in a Public Interest Case or Project. **Frequency:** annual. **Type:** recognition. **Recipient:** for case or project that truly contributes to the public good ● Outstanding Advocate for Clinical Teachers. **Frequency:** annual. **Type:** recognition. **Recipient:** to teachers who have contributed to the advancement of clinical legal education ● Outstanding Student Award. **Frequency:** annual. **Type:** recognition. **Recipient:** to law students who have excelled in a clinical course in law school. **Publications:** *CLEA Newsletter*. Alternate Formats: online.

8764 ■ Council on Legal Education Opportunity (CLEO)
740 15th St. NW, 9th Fl.
Washington, DC 20005
Ph: (202)828-6100
Free: (866)866-4343
Fax: (202)828-1009
E-mail: cleo@abanet.org
URL: http://cleoscholars.com
Contact: William Arthur Blakey, Chm.
Founded: 1968. **Budget:** $2,991,000. **Description:** Federally funded program that assists economically and educationally disadvantaged students gain entrance to American Bar Association approved law schools. Sponsors six-week summer institutes for selected college graduates and provides a 5,000 annual living stipend to those certified summer institute graduates who continue in law school. **Affiliated With:** American Bar Association; Association of American Law Schools; Hispanic National Bar Association; Law School Admission Council; National Bar Association. **Publications:** *CLEO Edge*. Magazine. Alternate Formats: online. **Conventions/Meetings:** biennial board meeting ● semiannual meeting.

8765 ■ Earl Warren Legal Training Program (EWLTP)
99 Hudson St., Ste.1600
New York, NY 10013
Ph: (212)965-2200
E-mail: mbagley@naacp.ldf.org
URL: http://www.naacpldf.org/content.aspx?article=41
Contact: G. Michael Bagley, Dir. of Education
Founded: 1972. **Staff:** 2. **Description:** Serves as special project of the NAACP Legal Defense and Educational Fund (see separate entry). Aims to increase the number of practicing black lawyers in the U.S. Conducts one or more Lawyers Training Institutes each year, which are attended by both experienced and young minority lawyers. Seeks to retain a close personal and professional relationship with program graduates. Offers program on public interest law. **Convention/Meeting:** none. **Awards:** Earl Warren Shearman and Sterling. **Frequency:** annual. **Type:** scholarship. **Recipient:** for academically qualified entering law students in need for the full three years of law school ● **Frequency:** annual. **Type:** scholarship. **Recipient:** for students entering first year of fulltime study. **Affiliated With:** National Association for the Advancement of Colored People Legal Defense and Educational Fund.

8766 ■ Global Alliance for Justice Education (GAJE)
c/o Frank Bloch
Vanderbilt Univ. Law School
131 21st Ave. S
Nashville, TN 37203-1181
Ph: (615)322-4964
Fax: (615)343-6562
E-mail: owner-gaje@list.vanderbilt.edu
URL: http://www.gaje.org
Contact: Frank Bloch, Contact
Founded: 1996. **Multinational. Description:** Seeks to achieve justice through education. Works to advance other forms of socially relevant legal education. Facilitates international information sharing and

collaboration on justice education. Receives and administers funds to support the development of innovative justice education, especially in developing countries. Serves as a clearinghouse of teaching methods and materials. **Telecommunication Services:** electronic mail, frank.bloch@law.vanderbilt.edu. **Publications:** Newsletter, published every even numbered month. Alternate Formats: online.

8767 ■ International Association of Law Schools (IALS)
1201 Connecticut Ave. NW, Ste.800
Washington, DC 20036-2717
Ph: (202)296-8851
Fax: (202)296-8869
URL: http://www.ialsnet.org
Contact: Carl C. Monk, Pres.
Founded: 2005. **Languages:** Arabic, Chinese, English, French, Russian, Spanish. **Multinational. Description:** Works to contribute to the development and improvement of law schools and the conditions of legal education throughout the world. Aims to enhance and strengthen the role of law in the development of societies through legal education. Helps to educate students about diverse legal systems and cultures. Serves as a clearinghouse for information about perspectives on law and legal education, law schools, curriculum issues and pedagogy. **Publications:** Newsletter ● Brochure. Alternate Formats: online.

8768 ■ Law School Admission Council (LSAC)
PO Box 40
Newtown, PA 18940
Ph: (215)968-1001
Fax: (215)968-1119
E-mail: lsacinfo@lsac.org
URL: http://www.lsac.org
Contact: Philip D. Shelton, Pres./Exec. Dir.
Founded: 1948. **Members:** 202. **Staff:** 200. **Multinational. Description:** Law schools in the U.S. and Canada. Develops and administers the Law School Admission Test (LSAT). Provides services to law schools and law school applicants to support the admission process. Holds law school forums. Publishes legal education and test preparation material. **Libraries: Type:** not open to the public. **Subjects:** law school admission. **Awards:** Minority Outreach Grants. **Frequency:** annual. **Type:** grant. **Committees:** Finance and Legal Affairs; Minority Affairs; Services and Programs; Test Development and Research. **Formerly:** Law Services. **Publications:** *Becoming A Lawyer: A Video Collection*. **Price:** $18.00 each. Alternate Formats: CD-ROM ● *The Next 10 Actual, Official PrepTests*. Book. Contains actual, previously administered LSATs (PrepTests 7-16, 18). **Price:** $30.00 each ● *Official Guide to ABA Approved Law Schools*, annual. Book. **Price:** $24.00 direct; in U.S. bookstores; $35.00 in Canada bookstores. ISSN: 0886-3342. **Circulation:** 10,000 ● *The Official LSAT SuperPrep*. Contains three new PrepTests with explanations for each item in all three tests. **Price:** $28.00 each ● *The Official LSAT TriplePrep Plus with Explanations*. **Price:** $19.00 each ● *Official LSAT TriplePrep: Volume 1*. **Price:** $17.00 direct; in U.S. bookstores; $25.00 in Canada bookstores ● *Prep Tests*. Book. **Price:** $8.00 each ● *So You Want to Be a Lawyer: A Practical Guide to Law as a Career*. Book. **Price:** $12.00 direct; $12.00 bookstores ● *Ten Actual, Official LSAT PrepTests*. Book. **Price:** $30.00 direct ● *10 More Actual, Official LSAT PrepTests*. Book. Contains 10 previously administered LSATS (PrepTests 19-28). **Price:** $30.00 each. **Conventions/Meetings:** annual conference, for law school administrators and faculty - May or June.

8769 ■ Law Student Division
c/o American Bar Association
321 N Clark St.
Chicago, IL 60610
Ph: (312)988-5623 (312)988-5624
Free: (800)285-2221
Fax: (312)988-6033
E-mail: abalsd@abanet.org
URL: http://www.abanet.org/lsd
Contact: Michael DePetrillo, Chm.
Founded: 1949. **Members:** 51,000. **Membership Dues:** law student, $20 (annual). **Staff:** 5. **Regional Groups:** 15. **Description:** Seeks to: further academic excellence through participation by law students in the efforts of the organized bar; achieve awareness and promote the involvement of law students in the solutions of problems confronted in today's changing society; promote professional responsibility. Sponsors nationwide Client Counseling Competition, National Appellate Advocacy Competition, and Negotiation Competition. Conducts seminars and workshops. **Boards:** Governors. **Divisions:** Assembly; Liaisons. **Formerly:** (1967) American Law Student Association. **Publications:** *Student Lawyer*, monthly. Magazine. Covers legal education, law practice, and socio-legal topics. **Price:** $22.00/year in U.S.; $31.00/year outside U.S. ISSN: 0039-274X. **Advertising:** accepted. **Conventions/Meetings:** annual conference, held in conjunction with American Bar Association - always August.

8770 ■ National Association for Law Placement (NALP)
1025 Connecticut Ave. NW, Ste.1110
Washington, DC 20036-5413
Ph: (202)835-1001
Fax: (202)835-1112
E-mail: info@nalp.org
URL: http://www.nalp.org
Contact: James G. Leipold, Exec. Dir.
Founded: 1971. **Members:** 2,100. **Membership Dues:** institutional, $825 (annual). **Staff:** 14. **Budget:** $3,500,000. **Multinational. Description:** Brings together law schools, legal employers, and bar associations to share information, research, and professional development opportunities. Works to facilitate legal career counseling and planning, recruitment and retention, and the professional development of law students and lawyers. Aims to cultivate ethical practices and fairness in legal career counseling and planning, recruitment, employment, and professional development; to promote the full range of legal career opportunities and to foster access to legal public interest and public sector employment; and to advocate for diversity in the legal profession and in the membership. **Awards:** Awards of Distinction. **Frequency:** annual. **Type:** recognition. **Recipient:** for outstanding achievement in furthering the mission of the organization ● Pro Bono Publico Award. **Frequency:** annual. **Type:** monetary. **Recipient:** to 2nd/3rd year law student for contributions to the pro bono. **Computer Services:** database, law schools ● database, legal employers ● mailing lists, detailed information on legal employers. **Additional Websites:** http://www.pslawnet.org. **Telecommunication Services:** electronic mail, jleipold@nalp.org. **Committees:** Awards of Distinction; Nominating; PSLawNet; Publications; Recruitment Practices; Research. **Sections:** Canadian; Diversity; Gay/Lesbian/Bisexual/Transgender; Judicial Clerkship; Lawyer Professional Development; LLM; Newer Professionals; Public Service; Student Professional Development. **Working Groups:** Educational Programming. **Publications:** *Associate Salary Survey*, annual. Report. **Price:** $95.00 ● *Directory of Law Schools*, annual. Lists of law school information allowing employers to interpret student resumes, grading systems, and standards for honors recognition. **Price:** $55.00 additional copy for members; $75.00/copy for nonmembers; first copy free for members ● *Directory of Legal Employers*, annual. Includes employer's specialties, salary and benefits, job opportunities and demographic data. **Price:** first copy free for members; $75.00 additional copy for members. Alternate Formats: online ● *Jobs & J.D.s*, annual. Report. Provides data on more than 35,000 law graduates gathered from law school placement offices nationwide and presented in tables by region. **Price:** $55.00 /year for members; $75.00 /year for nonmembers ● *NALP Bulletin*, monthly. Newsletter. **Price:** $125.00 /year for nonmembers; free for members. **Advertising:** accepted ● *Patterns and Practices: Measures of Law Firm Hiring, Leverage & Billable Hours*, annual. Report ● *Public Sector and Public Interest Attorney Salary Report*, biennial. **Conventions/Meetings:** annual Education Conference - meeting (exhibits) - 2009 Apr. 1-4, Washington, DC - **Avg. Attendance:** 1400; 2010 Apr. 28-May 1, San Juan, PR - **Avg. Attendance:** 1300.

8771 ■ National Black Law Students Association (NBLSA)
1225 11th St. NW
Washington, DC 20001-4217
Ph: (202)210-6556
Fax: (866)518-6863
E-mail: chair@nblsa.org
URL: http://www.nblsa.org
Contact: Mr. Eddie L. Koen Jr., Natl. Chm.
Founded: 1968. **Members:** 6,000. **Staff:** 4. **Regional Groups:** 6. **Local Groups:** 200. **Description:** Aims to serve the needs and goals of black law students and "effectuate change" in the legal community. Includes chapters or affiliates in six different countries including the Bahamas, Nigeria, and South Africa. Conducts sessions comprising a program of prominent speakers, seminars, case study analyses, and small group discussions covering concerns, problems, issues, and opportunities in academic administration. **Libraries: Type:** open to the public; reference. **Holdings:** 6; archival material, articles, biographical archives, clippings, photographs. **Awards:** Chapter of the Year. **Frequency:** annual. **Type:** recognition. **Recipient:** for chapters that participate in all programs and goes beyond expectations of the national board ● Frederick Douglass Moot Court Competition Awards. **Frequency:** annual. **Type:** recognition ● International Negotiations Competition Awards. **Frequency:** annual. **Type:** recognition ● Most Improved Chapter. **Frequency:** annual. **Type:** recognition ● Most Improved Region. **Frequency:** annual. **Type:** recognition ● NBLSA Hall of Fame. **Frequency:** annual. **Type:** recognition ● Region of the Year. **Frequency:** annual. **Type:** recognition ● Student of the Year Award. **Frequency:** annual. **Type:** recognition ● Thurgood Marshall Mock Trial Competition Award. **Frequency:** annual. **Type:** recognition. **Computer Services:** database, for search of past officers. **Committees:** College Student; Convention; Education; International; Legislative. **Projects:** Death Penalty Moratorium. **Task Forces:** Law Journal. **Affiliated With:** National Bar Association; National Counsel of Black Lawyers. **Formerly:** (1983) Black American Law Students Association. **Publications:** Reports, quarterly. **Conventions/Meetings:** annual convention (exhibits) ● annual meeting.

8772 ■ National Native American Law Students Association (NNALSA)
c/o Marilyn Phelps, Treas.
UCLA School of Law, 2L
Los Angeles, CA 90095
E-mail: chaluks@gmail.com
URL: http://www.nationalnalsa.org
Contact: Nicole Willis, Pres.
Founded: 1970. **Members:** 160. **Membership Dues:** general/native American law student, $10 (annual) ● associate/non-native law student, $10 (annual) ● alumni/native American law graduate, $10 (annual) ● sponsor/friend of NNALSA, $100 (annual). **Regional Groups:** 6. **Local Groups:** 14. **Description:** American Indian or Native Alaskan law students. Promotes unity, communication, and cooperation among Indian law students; seeks to provide financial aid and summer employment opportunities for members; encourages development of educational opportunities such as tutorial programs, research projects, and curriculum development in Indian law; offers a forum for discussion of legal problems relating to law affecting American Indians. Maintains speakers' bureau of students in the field of Indian law. Does not operate a library; however, members have access to the extensive Indian law collection at the University of New Mexico. **Formerly:** (1990) American Indian Law Students Association; (2003) Native American Law Students Association. **Publications:** Newsletter, periodic. **Conventions/Meetings:** annual confer-

ence, held in conjunction with Federal Bar Association - always in Albuquerque, NM.

8773 ■ North American South Asian Law Student Association (NASALSA)
c/o Shaheen Karolia, Treas.
1901 Minnehaha Ave., Apt. 419
Minneapolis, MN 55404
E-mail: karol008@umn.edu
URL: http://www.nsalsa.org
Contact: Shaheen Karolia, Treas.
Founded: 1997. **Multinational. Description:** Seeks to create a strong network and community among South Asian law students and legal professionals throughout the U.S. and Canada. Promotes education, leadership and community service among South Asian law students. Supports groups aimed at South Asian law students across the U.S. and Canada. **Awards: Frequency:** annual. **Type:** fellowship. **Recipient:** for South Asian law students.

8774 ■ Practising Law Institute (PLI)
810 7th Ave.
New York, NY 10019-5818
Ph: (212)824-5710
Free: (800)260-4754
E-mail: info@pli.edu
URL: http://www.pli.edu
Contact: Victor J. Rubino, Exec. Dir.
Founded: 1933. **Members:** 50,000. **Staff:** 90. **Description:** Provides through publications, videotapes, forums, and live and online seminars, training for lawyers throughout the country in new developments in the law and new legal techniques. Presents over 250 seminars annually. **Telecommunication Services:** electronic mail, victorjrubino-pli@pli.edu. **Publications:** *All-Star Briefing*, weekly. Newsletter ● *Lawyer's Toolbox*, weekly. Newsletter ● *Pocket MBA*, weekly. Newsletter ● Audiotapes ● Books. Includes topics about business, intellectual property, trial practice, federal taxation, and other special areas. ● Handbook. Provides latest information on topics such as corporate practice intellectual property, litigation, and tax. Alternate Formats: CD-ROM ● Videos.

Liberal Arts

8775 ■ American Academy for Liberal Education (AALE)
1050 17th St. NW, Ste.400
Washington, DC 20036
Ph: (202)452-8611
Fax: (202)452-8620
E-mail: charters@aale.org
URL: http://www.aale.org
Contact: Dr. Jeffrey Wallin, Pres.
Description: Acts as an accreditation organization for undergraduates in liberal education. **Libraries: Type:** reference. **Holdings:** reports.

8776 ■ Association for Core Texts and Courses (ACTC)
Saint Mary's Coll. of California
1928 St. Mary's Rd.
Moraga, CA 94556
Ph: (925)631-8597
E-mail: info@coretexts.org
URL: http://www.coretexts.org
Contact: J. Scott Lee, Exec. Dir.
Founded: 1994. **Membership Dues:** individual, $50 (annual) ● community college, $250 (annual) ● 4-year baccalaureate college, $500 (annual) ● university, $1,000 (annual). **Multinational. Description:** Aims to advance liberal education in institutions through the development and promotion of educational programs which integrate core text courses with advanced developments in all aspects of education. Promotes the proliferation of these educational programs in order to strengthen undergraduate education in the United States and Canada. Develops networks to support existing programs. **Publications:** *ACTC Core Newsletter*, annual. **Price:** included in membership dues. Alternate Formats: online.

8777 ■ Association for General and Liberal Studies (AGLS)
c/o Paul Ranieri, Exec. Dir.
Ball State Univ.
English Dept., RB 2109
Muncie, IN 47306
Ph: (765)285-8406 (765)285-2385
Fax: (765)285-2384
E-mail: pranieri@bsu.edu
URL: http://www.agls.org
Contact: Paul Ranieri, Exec. Dir.
Founded: 1961. **Members:** 200. **Membership Dues:** student, $10 (annual) ● institution, $500 (annual) ● adjunct/retiree, $25 (annual) ● faculty/administration, $40 (annual) ● faculty/administration, $70 (biennial) ● faculty/administration, $100 (triennial). **Staff:** 1. **Description:** Persons associated with liberal arts and general education programs in colleges and universities. Serves as a forum for professional people concerned with undergraduate liberal and general education in each of the several disciplines of the curriculum. Maintains speakers' and consultants' bureau. **Awards:** Gaff Faculty Award. **Frequency:** annual. **Type:** recognition ● Katz Award. **Frequency:** biennial. **Type:** recognition. **Recipient:** for excellence in general and liberal studies. **Publications:** *AGLS Newsletter*, 3/year. **Price:** free for members. ISSN: 0890-9792. Alternate Formats: online. **Conventions/Meetings:** annual conference (exhibits) - always October.

8778 ■ Association of Graduate Liberal Studies Programs (AGLSP)
c/o Duke University
Box 90095
Durham, NC 27708-0095
Ph: (919)684-1987
Fax: (919)681-8905
E-mail: info@aglsp.org
URL: http://www.aglsp.org
Contact: Linda Paulson, Pres.
Founded: 1975. **Members:** 150. **Membership Dues:** full, associate, $250 (annual) ● affiliate, $40 (annual). **Staff:** 1. **Multinational. Description:** Members are colleges and universities that have interdisciplinary liberal studies programs at the graduate level (these programs are usually nontraditional and serve part-time, adult learners). Promotes liberal studies on a national basis and provides services for other institutions contemplating graduate liberal studies programs. Compiles information and data, evaluates new programs, publishes manuals, journals, and occasional papers. **Awards:** National Faculty Award. **Frequency:** annual. **Type:** monetary. **Recipient:** for excellence in teaching GLS students. **Publications:** *Curriculum Guides Series*. Manuals. **Price:** $20.00 ● *The Journal of Graduate Liberal Studies*, semiannual. Contains scholarly and creative works of students, faculty, and alumni of graduate liberal studies programs. **Price:** $25.00/year ● Newsletter, periodic. **Conventions/Meetings:** annual conference, features speakers, panels, presentations, breakout sessions on a theme of interest to interdisciplinary graduate programs - typically fall ● annual Conference Workshop, covers topics from administration to curriculum to student recruiting for existing and new programs and institutions considering liberal studies graduate programs.

8779 ■ Educational Leadership Program (ELP)
15 E 91st St., Apt. 2B
New York, NY 10128
Ph: (917)330-0320
Contact: Nicholas Farnham, Pres.
Founded: 2000. **Staff:** 2. **Multinational. Description:** Works to instill and reinforce the skill, philosophy, and motivation required of liberal arts education leaders. Conducts programs and seminars.

Liberal Studies

8780 ■ Modernist Studies Association (MSA)
c/o The Johns Hopkins University Press
PO Box 19966
Baltimore, MD 21211-0966
Free: (800)548-1784
Fax: (410)516-3866
E-mail: ccmiller@pomona.edu
URL: http://msa.press.jhu.edu
Contact: Cristanne Miller, Pres.
Founded: 1998. **Membership Dues:** individual, $60 (annual) ● student/adjunct faculty, $40 (annual). **Description:** Promotes the study of the arts in their social, political, cultural, and intellectual contexts from the later nineteenth through the mid-twentieth century. Seeks to develop an international and interdisciplinary forum to promote exchange among scholars in the field. **Awards:** MSA Book Prize. **Frequency:** annual. **Type:** monetary. **Recipient:** for outstanding book on the field of modernist studies. **Conventions/Meetings:** annual meeting - 2008 Nov. 13-16, Nashville, TN.

Libraries

8781 ■ North American Coordinating Council on Japanese Library Resources (NCC)
c/o Victoria Lyon Bestor, Exec. Dir.
149 Upland Rd.
Cambridge, MA 02140
Ph: (617)945-7294
Fax: (617)812-5854
E-mail: vbestor@fas.harvard.edu
URL: http://www.fas.harvard.edu/~ncc
Contact: Victoria Lyon Bestor, Exec. Dir.
Founded: 1991. **Multinational. Description:** Works to expand and improve access to library resources and other forms of information about Japan within the existing framework of North American library collections. Defines and articulates the common concerns and needs both of libraries and users of Japanese resources. Develops programs and materials to address those needs. Provides coordination between North American libraries and funding agencies. **Publications:** *NCC Newsletter*, annual. Alternate Formats: online ● Reports. Alternate Formats: online.

Library Science

8782 ■ Association for Library and Information Science Education (ALISE)
65 E Wacker Pl., Ste.1900
Chicago, IL 60601-7246
Ph: (312)795-0996
Fax: (312)419-8950
E-mail: contact@alise.org
URL: http://www.alise.org
Contact: Ms. Kathleen Combs, Exec. Dir.
Founded: 1915. **Members:** 450. **Membership Dues:** full-time, $125 (annual) ● part-time/retired, $75 (annual) ● doctoral student, $60 (annual). **Staff:** 3. **Budget:** $171,000. **Description:** Graduate schools offering degree programs in library science and their faculties. Seeks to: promote excellence in education for library and information science as a means of increasing the effectiveness of library and information services; provide a forum for the active interchange of ideas and information among library educators; promote research related to teaching and to library and information science; formulate and promulgate positions on matters related to library education. Offers employment program at annual conference. **Awards:** ALISE Award for Professional Contribution. **Frequency:** annual. **Type:** recognition ● ALISE Award for Teaching Excellence. **Frequency:** annual. **Type:** recognition. **Recipient:** for research ● ALISE Service Award. **Frequency:** annual. **Type:** recognition. **Recipient:** for regular and sustained service to ALISE through the holding of offices and positions within the organization or accomplishing specific responsibilities for the organization. **Computer Services:** Mailing lists, of members. **Committees:** Awards & Honors; Budget & Finance; Conference Program Planning; Governmental Relations; International Relations; JELIS Editorial; Nominating; Organization, Bylaws & Resolutions; Pratt-Severn Award Jury; Publications; Recruitment; Research; Statistical Report Advisory; Tellers; Web. **Councils:** Deans,

Directors, & Program Chairs. **Special Interest Groups:** Archival/Records Management Education; Assistant/Associate Deans & Directors; Continuing Education; Curriculum; Distance Education; Doctoral Students; Gender Issues; Historical Perspectives; International Library Education; Multicultural, Ethnic, and Humanistic Concerns; New Faculty; Part-Time/ Adjunct Faculty; Preservation Education; Research; Teaching Methods; Technical Services Education; Youth Services. **Affiliated With:** American Association of Law Libraries; American Library Association; American Society for Information Science and Technology; ARMA International - The Association of Information Management Professionals; Association of Canadian Archivists; Association for Computing Machinery; Association of Research Libraries; Canadian Association for Information Science; Canadian Association of Law Libraries; Canadian Association of Research Libraries; Canadian Library Association; Council on Library and Information Resources; International Federation of Library Associations and Institutions; Medical Library Association; Society of American Archivists; Special Libraries Association. **Publications:** *ALISE Membership Directory*, annual. **Price:** $40.00 ● *Journal of Education for Library and Information Science*, quarterly. Includes scholarly papers on library and information science, association news, and special columns on continuing education and special education. **Price:** included in membership dues; $150.00 /year for nonmembers in U.S.; $175.00 /year for nonmembers outside U.S. ISSN: 0748-5786. **Circulation:** 1,200. Also Cited As: *JELIS* ● *Library and Information Science Education Statistical Report*, annual. **Price:** $100.00. **Conventions/ Meetings:** annual Community Engagement: Integrating Learning, Research, and Practice - international conference, features juried programs and papers, research poster sessions, job placement, exhibits and informal discussion groups (exhibits).

8783 ■ Council on Library-Media Technicians (COLT)
c/o Margaret Barron, Exec. Dir.
28262 Chardon Rd.
PMB 168
Wickliffe, OH 44092-2793
Ph: (630)257-6541
Fax: (630)257-7737
E-mail: jmhite0@dia.mil
URL: http://colt.ucr.edu
Contact: Jackie Hite, Pres.

Founded: 1967. **Members:** 700. **Membership Dues:** regular in U.S., $45 (annual) ● individual outside U.S., institution in U.S., $70 (annual) ● student, $35 (annual) ● institution outside U.S., $95 (annual). **Description:** Persons involved in two-year associate degree programs for the training of library technical assistants (professional-support workers) and graduates of programs employed as library/media technical assistants (B.A. degree holders without M.L.S. degree). Membership includes junior college deans, librarians, curriculum directors, professors, employers, special libraries, university libraries, library schools, publishers, and library technical assistants. Provides a channel of communication among the institutions and personnel that have developed such training programs; attempts to standardize curriculum offerings; develops educational standards; conducts research on graduates of the programs; represents the interests of library technical assistants and support staff. The council's concerns also include development of clear job descriptions and criteria for employment of technicians and dissemination of information to the public and to prospective students. Sponsors workshops for support staff in areas such as management, supervisory skills, interpersonal communication, business writing, and media center management. Maintains speakers' bureau. Develops a program for certification of library media technicians and a continuing education program for library support staff. **Awards:** Support Staff of the Year. **Frequency:** annual. **Type:** recognition. **Recipient:** for individual ● Supporter of Support of the Year. **Frequency:** annual. **Type:** recognition. **Recipient:** for individual. **Committees:** Constitution; Education and Research; Public Relations and Publications. **Affiliated With:** American Library Association. **Formerly:** Council on Library Technical-Assistants; (1967) Council on Library Technology. **Publications:** *Membership Directory and Data Book*, biennial ● *Mosaic*, monthly ● Newsletter, monthly. **Conventions/Meetings:** annual meeting (exhibits).

8784 ■ International Coalition of Library Consortia (ICOLC)
c/o Tom Sanville
2455 N Star Rd., Ste.300
Columbus, OH 43221
Ph: (614)728-3600
Fax: (614)728-3610
E-mail: info@ohiolink.edu
URL: http://www.library.yale.edu/consortia
Contact: Tom Sanville, Contact

Founded: 1997. **Members:** 150. **Multinational. Description:** Facilitates discussion among consortia on issues of common interest, primarily higher education institutions. **Computer Services:** Online services, consortia listserv.

Literacy

8785 ■ American Literacy Council (ALC)
1441 Mariposa Ave.
Boulder, CO 80302
Ph: (303)440-7385
Free: (800)781-9985
E-mail: support@americanliteracy.com
URL: http://www.americanliteracy.com
Contact: Alan Mole, Pres.

Founded: 1876. **Members:** 110. **Membership Dues:** regular, $25 (annual). **Staff:** 5. **Description:** Individuals interested in simpler literacy through the use of computer technology. Sponsors Sound-Write remedial writing software program that corrects invented spellings and speaks the words that are typewritten, instantly and automatically. Provides a simpler sound spelling that is regularized, easily learned by children and adult illiterates, and compatible with traditional spelling. Offers computer software that enables traditional spelling to be immediately translated into sound spelling and vice versa. Conducts research and provides simpler spelling products and services. **Telecommunication Services:** electronic mail, president@americanliteracy.com. **Formed by Merger of:** (1989) Phonemic Spelling Council; American Language Academy. **Publications:** *ALC Bulletin Board*, monthly. Based on O'Henry's "Gift of the Magi" that provides reading material in a remedial way. **Price:** free for members. **Circulation:** 200. **Advertising:** accepted. Alternate Formats: online ● *Dictionary of Simplified American Spelling*. Book. **Price:** $25.00 ● *The Gift*. Book. Based on O'Henry's "Gift of the Magi" that provides reading material in a remedial way. **Price:** $10.00 ● *Sound-Write*. Presents a multisensory spelling software with instant audiovisual feedback. **Price:** $55.00. **Conventions/Meetings:** periodic meeting.

8786 ■ Barbara Bush Foundation for Family Literacy (BBFFL)
1201 15th St. NW, Ste.420
Washington, DC 20005
Ph: (202)955-6183
Fax: (202)955-5492
E-mail: krichardson@cfncr.org
URL: http://www.barbarabushfoundation.com
Contact: Mrs. Benita Somerfield, Exec. Dir.

Founded: 1989. **Staff:** 4. **Languages:** English, Spanish. **Description:** Establishes literacy as a family value and break the intergenerational cycle of illiteracy in American families. Supports programs that bring parents and children together to develop mutual reading and literacy skills; encourages a home environment that fosters the child's educational development. Provides grants to successful intergenerational literacy efforts and offers seed money for family literacy programs and activities; encourages recognition of volunteers, educators, students, and effective literacy programs. The foundation is named after its founder, First Lady Barbara Bush (1925-). **Awards: Frequency:** annual. **Type:** monetary. **Recipient:** for family literacy programs. **Telecommunication Services:** electronic mail, tbynum@cfncr.org. **Programs:** First Lady's Family Literacy Initiative for Texas; Maine Family Literacy Initiative; Maryland Family Literacy Initiative. **Publications:** *The Barbara Bush Foundation Newsletter*, quarterly. Contains information on the Foundation's latest activities. **Price:** free ● *Barbara Bush's Family Reading Tips* (in English and Spanish). Brochure. **Price:** free for first 20 copies ● *First Teachers: A Family Literacy Handbook for Parents, Policy Makers, and Literacy Providers*. **Price:** $5.50 plus shipping and handling ● *Lessons Learned: A Review of the First Lady's Literacy Initiative for Texas*. Book. **Price:** $7.00 plus shipping and handling ● Also publishes information kit.

8787 ■ Children's Literacy Initiative (CLI)
2314 Market St.
Philadelphia, PA 19103
Ph: (215)561-4676
Fax: (215)561-4677
E-mail: info@clionthe web.org
Contact: Linda Katz, Exec. Dir.

Founded: 1988. **Staff:** 60. **Budget:** $5,700,000. **Languages:** English, Spanish. **Description:** Works to encourage literacy skills of young children by providing training workshops for teachers who serve low-income children in pre-kindergarten through third grade. Offers research-based training in effective literacy practices, including quality books for the classroom. **Libraries: Type:** reference. **Holdings:** clippings. **Subjects:** emergent literacy. **Publications:** *Creating a Literary Environment in Your Classroom*. Handbook. Contains photos and text for pre-K classrooms. ● *News & Views*, 3/year. Newsletter. Alternate Formats: online. **Conventions/Meetings:** periodic Classroom Management for New Teachers - workshop, training for new teachers who serve low-income children.

8788 ■ Christian Literacy Associates (CLA)
541 Perry Hwy.
Pittsburgh, PA 15229-1851
Ph: (412)364-3777
E-mail: drliteracy@aol.com
URL: http://www.christianliteracy.com
Contact: Dr. William E. Kofmehl Jr., Pres.

Founded: 1977. **Members:** 5,200. **Staff:** 3. **Budget:** $125,000. **Local Groups:** 50. **Description:** Christian professionals and para-professionals who prepare basic adult literacy materials for use through churches; volunteers also train tutors and plan literacy campaigns. In the U.S., works with local congregations, councils of churches, denominations, jails and jail ministries, retarded and disabled groups, refugee help groups, and school districts. Outside the U.S., works with local councils of churches, denominations, seminaries, missionary groups, and international ministries. Produces adult basic literacy primers in several languages in cooperation with native speakers. Maintains volunteer staff of professional educators to help design and prepare supplementary reading materials and to train potential tutors. Assists local churches and groups in organizing regional and national basic literacy programs. Conducts training workshops for literacy tutors. Model programs include Christian Literacy Associates of Haiti and the Allegheny County Literacy Council. **Libraries: Type:** reference. **Holdings:** 200. **Subjects:** literacy, reading. **Publications:** *The Christian Literacy Outreach*, quarterly. Newsletter. Contributions newsletter. **Price:** free to contributors ● *Christian Literacy Series "The Light is Coming"*. Book. Features Bible content reading materials for K-6 grade level. Also available in red print on yellow. **Price:** $20.00 black on white; $30.00 red on yellow. Alternate Formats: CD-ROM ● *Comprehension Activity Book*. Handbook. Includes activities using the dictionary, newspaper, and the Holy Bible. **Price:** $10.00 ● *40 Bible Stories for New Readers*. Books. Consists of three books in one set. Uses the 40 most common English words. **Price:** $10.00 ● *The Four R's- Review, Reinforce, Respond, Read*. Handbook. Serves as an activity book for tutor and student. **Price:** $10.00 ● *Guide to Establishing a*

Christian Literacy Outreach. Booklet. Serves as an informational guide for creating a church-centered literacy program. **Price:** $5.00 ● *The Knight Who'd Never Been Taught to Fight: A Play to be Read Aloud*. Booklets. Includes 13 scripts. Suggested for use with the SRC Curriculum Guide & Handbook. **Price:** $30.00 ● *Reading Fun Pack*. Handbook. Includes 16 laminated Word Bingo Game boards, a teacher word list, and dry erase markers. **Price:** $30.00 ● *Reading Is Fun Gamebook*. Handbook. Features a gamebook including word games, word searches, and puzzles. **Price:** $10.00 ● *Summer Reading Camp Curriculum Guide & Handbook*. Serves as an informational guide for creating a SRC using CLA materials. **Price:** $20.00 ● *Summer Reading Camp Staff Training Workshop*. Video. Corresponds with SRC Curriculum Guide & Handbook. Used for training SRC staff. **Price:** $35.00 ● *Textbook Tutor Workshop*. Video. Used for training tutors in the use of Christian Literacy Series and supplementary material. **Price:** $35.00 ● *Writing Journal*. Handbook. Presents a twelve-day daily diary for children or adults. **Price:** $2.50. **Conventions/Meetings:** annual meeting - December.

8789 ■ First Book
1319 F St. NW, Ste.1000
Washington, DC 20004-1155
Ph: (202)393-1222
Fax: (202)628-1258
E-mail: staff@firstbook.org
URL: http://www.firstbook.org
Contact: Kyle Zimmer, Pres./Co-Founder
Founded: 1992. **Staff:** 40. **Description:** Provides children from low-income families the opportunity to read and own their first books. Conducts community-based mentoring, tutoring and family literacy programs. **Computer Services:** Information services, facts on illiteracy. **Boards:** Campus Advisory; Local Advisory.

8790 ■ India Literacy Project (ILP)
PO Box 361143
Milpitas, CA 95035-9998
E-mail: ilp@ilpnet.org
URL: http://www.ilpnet.org
Contact: Ravi Mani, Chm.
Founded: 1990. **Multinational**. **Description:** Promotes literacy as a first step to effective economic development and population control. Provides financial, technical, and other assistance to projects with similar goals. Produces and distributes promotional materials including shirts and greeting cards to increase public awareness of the importance of literacy. **Telecommunication Services:** electronic mail, ravimani66@yahoo.com. **Publications:** *The Beacon*, monthly. Newsletter. **Conventions/Meetings:** monthly meeting - always second Sunday in Milpitas, CA.

8791 ■ Literacy and Evangelism International (LEI)
1800 S Jackson Ave.
Tulsa, OK 74107
Ph: (918)585-3826
Fax: (918)585-3224
E-mail: general@literacyevangelism.org
URL: http://www.literacyevangelism.org
Contact: Rev. Sid Rice, Exec. Dir.
Founded: 1967. **Budget:** $600,000. **Multinational**. **Description:** Provides reading instruction with biblical materials. Provides free assistance with adult literacy material development in needed languages. Conducts five and three-week institutes to train people from the U.S. and other countries to implement and manage their own literacy programs. Organizes literacy conferences. Sends long-term missionaries overseas. Provides English-as-a-Second Language assistance. **Libraries: Type:** reference. **Holdings:** 2,500; archival material, books, periodicals, video recordings. **Subjects:** literacy, world missions, religious subjects. **Awards:** Robert F. Rice Literacy Legacy Award. **Frequency:** annual. **Type:** recognition. **Recipient:** for outstanding service in the U.S.A. or worldwide in the field of adult literacy. **Computer Services:** Electronic publishing, basic adult literacy materials. **Boards:** Trustees. **Committees:** Ministry Coordinating Team; Personnel. **Task Forces:** ILTI. **Affiliated With:** Evangelical Council for Financial Accountability. **Also Known As:** (2001) Literacy International. **Publications:** *Adult Literacy Primer, Bible-content*. Book ● *Adult Literacy Primer in English*. Book ● *Firm Foundations: Basic Literacy for Adults*, periodic. Booklets. Contains information for literacy missionary, trainer and supervisor use. **Price:** $42.00 for entire set ● Passport to the World of English, English-as-a-second language curriculum, manuals and audiotapes, Bible-content. **Conventions/Meetings:** workshop, on adult literacy and to train ESL tutors.

8792 ■ Literacy USA
3131 W Alabama, Ste.110
Houston, TX 77098
Ph: (713)961-3922
Free: (888)269-4902
Fax: (713)961-4775
E-mail: office@literacyusa.org
Contact: Carl Guerriere, Pres.
Founded: 1995. **Membership Dues:** general, $100 (annual). **Description:** Supports local literacy coalitions. Creates a forum for a peer-learning group of coalition leaders across the United States. Serves as a clearinghouse of information on best practices, successes and challenges of urban literacy coalitions. Disseminates resources to the grassroots. Provides technical assistance to emerging coalitions and those in transition or crisis. **Libraries: Type:** reference; lending. **Computer Services:** Information services, literacy issues. **Boards:** Corporate Advisory. **Programs:** Literacy AmeriCorps. **Conventions/Meetings:** annual meeting - always beginning of March.

8793 ■ National Center for Family Literacy (NCFL)
325 W Main St., Ste.300
Louisville, KY 40202-4237
Ph: (502)584-1133
URL: http://www.famlit.org
Contact: Sharon Darling, Pres./CEO
Founded: 1989. **Description:** Promotes family literacy. **Publications:** *Connecting*, quarterly. Magazine. **Price:** included in membership dues ● Annual Report, annual. **Conventions/Meetings:** annual conference.

8794 ■ National Coalition for Literacy (NCL)
PO Box 11592
Washington, DC 20008
Ph: (202)244-0732
Free: (800)228-8813
Fax: (866)738-3757
E-mail: jennifer.maloney@ncldc.net
URL: http://www.national-coalition-literacy.org
Contact: Jennifer Maloney, Dir.
Founded: 1981. **Members:** 44. **Membership Dues:** voting organization, $1,000 (annual) ● nonvoting organization, $300 (annual) ● nonvoting individual, $75 (annual). **Description:** National organizations concerned with adult illiteracy. Seeks to provide a forum for communication among national groups whose primary focus is literacy. Believes that functional illiteracy contributes to incompetent job performance, forgone tax revenues, remedial education in business and the military, welfare, and crime. **Publications:** none. **Formerly:** (1989) Coalition for Literacy. **Conventions/Meetings:** quarterly meeting.

8795 ■ National Jewish Coalition for Literacy (NJCL)
134 Beach St.
Boston, MA 02111
Ph: (617)423-0063
E-mail: mmarcus@njcl.net
URL: http://njcl.net
Contact: Leonard Fein, Dir.
Description: Aims to affect an increase in the organized Jewish community's involvement in the fight against illiteracy and in the number of Jews involved in that fight. Mobilizes volunteer tutors and reader partners for at-risk children in kindergarten through third grade. Strives to help all American children to learn to read by the end of third grade. **Publications:** *LitBits*, semiannual. Newsletter. Alternate Formats: online.

8796 ■ PlanetRead (PR)
26 Manor Dr.
Piedmont, CA 94611
Ph: (510)435-3175 (413)421-0421
Fax: (413)420-9183
E-mail: info@planetread.org
URL: http://www.PlanetRead.org
Contact: Dr. Brij Kothari, Pres.
Founded: 1996. **Members:** 40. **Staff:** 30. **Multinational**. **Description:** Aims to have a "reading planet - a planet where everyone can read and has access to interesting and affordable reading opportunities in native and other language(s)". Contributes to literacy worldwide by innovating and implementing simple, scalable, and cost-effective solutions, especially using mass media and information technologies. **Additional Websites:** http://www.DesiLassi.com, http://www.BookBox.com.

8797 ■ ProLiteracy Worldwide
1320 Jamesville Ave.
Syracuse, NY 13210
Ph: (315)422-9121
Free: (888)528-2224
Fax: (315)422-6369
E-mail: info@proliteracy.org
URL: http://www.proliteracy.org
Contact: Patricia Johnson, Pres.
Founded: 1955. **Members:** 92,250. **Membership Dues:** state organization, council, or organization, $100 (annual) ● individual affiliate, $30 (annual) ● group affiliate, $125 (annual) ● supporting organization, silver, $100 (annual) ● supporting organization, gold, $500 (annual) ● supporting organization, platinum, $1,000-$10,000 (annual). **Staff:** 110. **Budget:** $11,000,000. **State Groups:** 40. **Local Groups:** 1,100. **National Groups:** 1,400. **Multinational**. **Description:** Trains and aids individuals and organizations to tutor adults in basic literacy and English for speakers of other languages. Provides training materials and services on national scale to literacy programs that utilize volunteers. Compiles statistics. Sponsors more than 1400 literacy programs in the U.S. and 71 partner programs in 36 developing countries worldwide. Operates New Readers Press (NRP), a division that publishes educational materials for adults with limited reading skills and resources for teachers and tutors in the U.S. **Libraries: Type:** reference. **Holdings:** 30,000. **Subjects:** adult basic education, volunteer tutoring, nonprofit management, reading, ESL, literacy. **Awards:** National Book Scholarship Fund. **Frequency:** periodic. **Type:** scholarship. **Computer Services:** database, OPAC: public access catalog of the literacy research collection ● online services, in-house catalog. **Telecommunication Services:** additional toll-free number, New Readers Press, (800)448-8878. **Divisions:** International Programs; US Program - ProLiteracy America; US Publishing - New Readers Press. **Formed by Merger of:** (2003) Literacy Volunteers of America; (2003) Laubach Literacy International. **Formerly:** (1972) Literacy Volunteers. **Publications:** *ProLiteracy Worldwide Annual Report*, annual. Alternate Formats: online ● *ProLiteracy Worldwide State of Literacy Report*, annual ● Also publishes literacy skills instructional and training materials. **Conventions/Meetings:** annual conference (exhibits) - 2008 Oct. 1-4, Little Rock, AR.

Literature

8798 ■ African American Literature and Culture Society (AALCS)
c/o Loretta G. Woodard PhD, Pres.
Marygrove Coll.
8425 W McNichols Rd.
Detroit, MI 48221-2599
Ph: (313)927-1452
Fax: (313)927-1345

E-mail: lwoodard@marygrove.edu
URL: http://aalcs.marygrove.edu
Contact: Loretta G. Woodard PhD, Pres.
Founded: 1993. **Membership Dues:** regular, $25 (annual) ● graduate student, retired and independent scholar, $15 (annual) ● charter, $250 (annual). **Description:** Seeks to study the African-American literature within the context of contemporary theory and traditional discourse. Expands the appreciation of African-American literature. Encourages the students' participation in the study of African-American literature and culture. **Boards:** Advisory. **Committees:** Joint Awards. **Projects:** Japan; Langston Hughes National Poetry. **Publications:** Newsletter.

8799 ■ Conference on Christianity and Literature (CCL)
c/o Prof. Paul Contino, Co-Ed.
Pepperdine Univ.
24255 Pacific Coast Hwy.
Malibu, CA 90263-3999
Ph: (310)506-4095
Fax: (310)506-4206
E-mail: tammy.ditmore@pepperdine.edu
URL: http://www.pepperdine.edu/sponsored/ccl
Contact: Prof. Paul Contino, Co-Ed.
Founded: 1956. **Members:** 1,125. **Membership Dues:** student, $20 (annual) ● individual, $25 (annual) ● institutional, $35 (annual). **Staff:** 1. **Regional Groups:** 7. **Multinational. Description:** College and university teachers of English and modern languages; other interested persons. Works to explore the relationships between Christianity and literature. Promotes fellowship and scholarly excellence. **Awards:** Book of the Year Award. **Frequency:** annual. **Type:** recognition ● Lifetime Achievement Award. **Frequency:** annual. **Type:** recognition. **Recipient:** to a person who has exemplified values of conference on Christianity and literature in body of work over number of years ● Student Writing Contest. **Frequency:** annual. **Type:** recognition. **Recipient:** for student's entry in poetry, fiction and nonfiction categories. **Committees:** Book Award; MLA Program; Student Writing Contest. **Affiliated With:** Modern Language Association of America. **Publications:** *Christianity and Literature*, quarterly. Journal. ISSN: 0148-3331. **Circulation:** 1,125. **Conventions/Meetings:** annual regional meeting ● annual Student Writing Contest - meeting.

8800 ■ International Association for the Study of Irish Literatures (IASIL)
c/o Dr. Dawn Duncan, PhD, Exec. Sec.
Concordia Coll.
Dept. of English
901 8th St. S
Moorhead, MN 56562
Ph: (218)299-3961
E-mail: duncan@gloria.cord.edu
URL: http://www.iasil.org
Contact: Dawn Duncan PhD, Exec. Sec.
Founded: 1969. **Members:** 1,200. **Membership Dues:** individual, $40 (annual) ● individual, $110 (triennial) ● couple, $50 (annual) ● couple, $125 (triennial) ● student (with Irish University Review), $25 (annual) ● student (without Irish University Review), $10 (annual). **Staff:** 3. **Budget:** $10,000. **Regional Groups:** 4. **Languages:** English, Irish. **Multinational. Description:** Supports teaching and study of Irish writing in third-level education throughout the world. **Awards:** Student Scholarship for Conference Attendance. **Frequency:** triennial. **Type:** scholarship. **Publications:** *Irish University Review*, 3/year. Journal. Contains essays and reviews on Irish studies. **Price:** $15.00 each. ISSN: 0021-1427. **Conventions/Meetings:** annual conference.

Lutheran

8801 ■ Association of Lutheran Secondary Schools (ALSS)
c/o Dr. Ross Stueber, Exec. Dir.
Concordia Univ. Wisconsin
12800 N Lake Shore Dr.
Mequon, WI 53097-2404
Ph: (262)243-4519 (262)243-4210
Fax: (262)243-2942
E-mail: alss@alss.org
URL: http://www.alss.org
Contact: Dr. Ross Stueber, Exec. Dir.
Founded: 1944. **Members:** 93. **Membership Dues:** school, $450 (annual). **Staff:** 2. **Description:** Represents the Lutheran high schools and administrators. Defines and interprets dynamic models of effective leadership for Lutheran secondary schools and identifies, nurtures, trains, and challenges potential leaders to apply such models to their work. **Awards:** Paul Lange Award. **Frequency:** annual. **Type:** recognition. **Recipient:** for outstanding leadership and service as a Lutheran high school administrator. **Telecommunication Services:** electronic mail, admin@alss.org. **Affiliated With:** Thrivent Financial for Lutherans. **Publications:** *The Leader's E-Compass*, bimonthly, during school year. Reprint. **Circulation:** 300. Alternate Formats: online ● Newsletter. **Conventions/Meetings:** annual conference, with educational resources/fund-raising (exhibits) - always March.

8802 ■ Evangelical Lutheran Education Association (ELEA)
500 N Estrella Pkwy., Ste.B2
Box 601
Goodyear, AZ 85338
Ph: (623)925-1594
Free: (800)500-7644
Fax: (623)882-8770
E-mail: eleanational@cs.com
URL: http://www.eleanational.org
Contact: Gayle Denny, Exec. Dir.
Founded: 1961. **Members:** 500. **Membership Dues:** individual, $97 (annual) ● school/center, $195 (annual). **Staff:** 2. **Budget:** $125,000. **Regional Groups:** 14. **Description:** Congregations that operate Lutheran high schools, elementary schools, and/or preschools. Fosters Christian commitment and in-service experiences; serves as a forum for the exchange of ideas. Provides testing service and inter-school activities; makes available resource materials; operates accreditation program. **Libraries: Type:** not open to the public. **Holdings:** 100; video recordings. **Subjects:** curriculum, child development, parenting. **Formerly:** (1989) American Lutheran Education Association. **Publications:** *ELEA Yearbook*, annual. Contains listing of members and association information. **Price:** free for members; $10.00 for nonmembers. **Advertising:** accepted. Alternate Formats: online; diskette ● *Views and Vision*, quarterly. Newsletter. Contains articles on education and sections for elementary and early childhood educators. **Circulation:** 3,000 ● Various resources for centers and schools. **Conventions/Meetings:** annual conference and convention (exhibits).

8803 ■ Lutheran Education Association (LEA)
7400 Augusta St.
River Forest, IL 60305
Ph: (708)209-3343
Fax: (708)209-3458
E-mail: lea@lea.org
URL: http://www.lea.org
Contact: Jonathan C. Laabs EdD, Exec. Dir.
Founded: 1942. **Members:** 4,000. **Membership Dues:** individual, $99 (annual) ● husband/wife, $125 (annual) ● retired husband/wife, $75 (annual) ● retired, student, $50 (annual). **Staff:** 5. **Budget:** $277,900. **Multinational. Description:** Teachers and administrators in Lutheran schools, pastors and DCEs of Lutheran congregations, and board of education members of Lutheran congregations. Aims to: promote and encourage the interchange of thoughts, practices, and ideas among Lutheran educators; develop and disseminate resources to aid educators in Lutheran ministries; "increase Lutheran educators growing commitment to God's calling in their personal lives and in their involvement with students and staff members". Supports research helpful to Lutheran educators. Maintains archives. **Awards:** Christus Magister Award. **Frequency:** annual. **Type:** recognition. **Recipient:** to selected Lutheran educators who have made outstanding contributions to Lutheran education at any level ● Distinguished Lutheran Early Childhood Administrator. **Frequency:** annual. **Type:** recognition. **Recipient:** for outstanding leadership in a Lutheran preschool ● Distinguished Lutheran Early Childhood Teacher. **Frequency:** annual. **Type:** recognition. **Recipient:** for outstanding teaching in preschool through grade 2 ● Distinguished Lutheran Elementary School Administrator. **Frequency:** annual. **Type:** recognition. **Recipient:** for outstanding leadership in a Lutheran elementary school ● Distinguished Lutheran Elementary Teacher. **Frequency:** annual. **Type:** recognition. **Recipient:** for exemplary accomplishments in teaching grades 3-8 ● Distinguished Lutheran Secondary Educator. **Frequency:** annual. **Type:** recognition. **Recipient:** for outstanding service in a Lutheran high school ● Master DCE. **Frequency:** annual. **Type:** recognition. **Recipient:** for outstanding educational leadership in a Lutheran congregation ● Outstanding New DCE. **Frequency:** annual. **Type:** recognition. **Recipient:** for outstanding educational leadership with three or fewer years in a Lutheran congregation ● Outstanding New Lutheran Early Childhood Teacher. **Frequency:** annual. **Type:** recognition. **Recipient:** for outstanding teaching with three or fewer years of service in a Lutheran preschool ● Outstanding New Lutheran Elementary Teacher. **Frequency:** annual. **Type:** recognition. **Recipient:** for outstanding service as a teacher with three or fewer years teaching grades 3-8 ● Outstanding New Lutheran Secondary Educator. **Frequency:** annual. **Type:** recognition. **Recipient:** for outstanding service with three or fewer years of service in a Lutheran high school. **Telecommunication Services:** electronic mail, jonathan.laabs@lea.org. **Subgroups:** DCE Network; Early Childhood Educators Network; Leadership Network; Lutheran Elementary Teachers Network; Mission Minded Educators Network; Outreach Network; Secondary Network. **Publications:** *Lutheran Education*, quarterly. Journal. **Price:** included in membership dues; $10.00 for nonmembers. ISSN: 0024-7488 ● *Shaping the Future*, quarterly. Magazine. Features by and about Lutheran education. **Price:** included in membership dues. **Circulation:** 4,000 ● Monograph, 3/year ● Also publishes brochures. **Conventions/Meetings:** triennial Convocation - convention, international Lutheran educator conference (exhibits) ● National Administrators Conference, for administrators of Lutheran schools and preschools (exhibits) - non-convocation years ● triennial National DCE Conference.

8804 ■ Lutheran Educational Conference of North America (LECNA)
First Financial Center
110 S Phillips Ave., Ste.306
Sioux Falls, SD 57104
Ph: (605)782-4003 (605)782-4004
Fax: (605)782-4008
E-mail: wagoner@lutherancolleges.org
URL: http://www.lutherancolleges.org
Contact: Dr. Ralph H. Wagoner, Pres.
Founded: 1910. **Members:** 42. **Staff:** 3. **Budget:** $650,000. **Description:** Lutheran colleges, universities, and boards of higher education. Functions as free forum in which representatives of Lutheran institutions of higher education, boards, organizations, and individuals discuss the problems and concerns of Lutheran higher education, collegiate or theological. Assists member institutions with public policy and projects. **Libraries: Type:** not open to the public. **Subjects:** church-related higher education. **Formerly:** (1967) National Lutheran Education Conference. **Publications:** *Lutheran Higher Education Directory*, annual. Lists Lutheran colleges, universities, and seminaries. **Price:** included in membership dues. **Conventions/Meetings:** annual Lutheran College Presidents Meeting - conference.

Management

8805 ■ Academy of Management (AOM)
PO Box 3020
Briarcliff Manor, NY 10510-8020
Ph: (914)923-2607

Fax: (914)923-2615
E-mail: aom@pace.edu
URL: http://www.aomonline.org
Contact: Nancy Urbanowicz, Exec. Dir.
Founded: 1936. **Members:** 17,041. **Membership Dues:** academic, executive/practitioner, $140 (annual) ● student, emeritus, $70 (annual). **Staff:** 12. **Budget:** $1,500,000. **Regional Groups:** 5. **Description:** Professors in accredited universities and colleges who teach management; selected business executives who have made significant written contributions to the literature in the field of management and organization. Offers placement service. **Telecommunication Services:** electronic mail, nurbanowicz@pace.edu. **Publications:** *Academy of Management Journal*, bimonthly. Provides readers with a forecast for new management thoughts and techniques. **Price:** $140.00 /year for individuals and academic libraries (print only); $175.00 /year for individuals and academic libraries (print and electronic); $170.00 for corporate libraries (print only); $205.00 for corporate libraries (print and electronic). ISSN: 0001-4273. **Circulation:** 17,300. Alternate Formats: CD-ROM ● *Academy of Management Learning and Education*, quarterly. Journal. **Price:** $99.00 /year for individuals and academic libraries (print only); $135.00 /year for individuals and academic libraries (print and electronic); $135.00 for corporate libraries (print only); $170.00 for corporate libraries (print and electronic). ISSN: 1537-260X. Alternate Formats: CD-ROM ● *Academy of Management Membership Directory*, periodic. Alternate Formats: online ● *Academy of Management News*, quarterly. Newsletter. Keeps members up-to-date on association announcements and news. ● *Academy of Management Perspectives*, quarterly. Journal. **Price:** $70.00 /year for individuals in U.S. (print only); $100.00 /year for individuals in U.S. (print and electronic); $110.00/year for academic libraries in U.S. (print only); $150.00/year for corporate libraries in U.S. (print only). Alternate Formats: CD-ROM; online ● *Academy of Management Proceedings*, annual. Alternate Formats: CD-ROM ● *Academy of Management Review*, quarterly. Journal. Includes reviews of relevant literature. **Price:** $120.00 /year for individuals in U.S. (print only); $155.00 /year for individuals in U.S. (print and electronic); $140.00/year for academic libraries in U.S. (print only); $170.00/year for corporate librar'es in U.S. (print only). ISSN: 0363-7425. Alternate Formats: CD-ROM. **Conventions/Meetings:** annual conference and meeting (exhibits) - always August. 2008 Aug. 8-13, Anaheim, CA; 2009 Aug. 7-12, Chicago, IL; 2010 Aug. 6-11, Montreal, QC, Canada.

8806 ■ The Consortium
5585 Pershing Ave., Ste.240
St. Louis, MO 63112-4621
Ph: (314)877-5500 (314)877-5520
Free: (888)658-6814
Fax: (314)877-5505
E-mail: arandap@cgsm.org
URL: http://www.cgsm.org
Contact: Peter J. Aranda III, Exec. Dir./CEO
Founded: 1966. **Members:** 13. **Staff:** 17. **Budget:** $15,000,000. **Description:** Represents the interests of leading American business schools and some of the country's top corporation including Dartmouth College, Indiana University, University of Michigan, New York University, University of North Carolina, University of Rochester, University of Southern California, Carnegie Mellon University, Emory University, University of Texas-Austin, University of Virginia, Washington University and University of Wisconsin. Strives to enhance diversity in business education and leadership. Provides tuition for up to two consecutive years of full-time graduate business education. **Also Known As:** (2005) Consortium for Graduate Study in Management. **Formerly:** (1971) Consortium for Graduate Study in Business for Negros. **Publications:** *IN*, 3/year. Magazine. Includes alumni news, student placement statistics, the annual report, conference program and school, corporate and alumni profiles. **Price:** included in membership dues. **Circulation:** 6,000. **Advertising:** accepted. **Conventions/Meetings:** annual Orientation and Alumni Professional Development Program - conference, for fellowship winners beginning management studies (exhibits).

8807 ■ Graduate Management Admission Council (GMAC)
1600 Tysons Blvd., Ste.1400
McLean, VA 22102
Ph: (703)749-0131 (703)245-4222
Free: (866)505-6559
Fax: (703)749-0169
E-mail: webmaster1@gmac.com
URL: http://www.gmac.com
Contact: David A. Wilson, Pres./CEO
Founded: 1970. **Members:** 183. **Staff:** 38. **Multinational. Description:** Graduate schools of management and business administration. Works to establish criteria for use in admission to graduate management programs. Provides professional development for academic administrators and seminars for admissions officers. Maintains Graduate Management Admission Search Service, a program that provides institutions with the names of qualified students with desirable characteristics. Employs Educational Testing Service to develop and administer the Graduate Management Admission Test. Conducts research on student selection issues and political and social issues related to graduate management education. **Libraries: Type:** open to the public. **Holdings:** 3. **Subjects:** graduate management, education, industry. **Formerly:** (1976) Graduate Business Admission Council. **Publications:** *GMAC Directory*, annual. Lists member school representatives; includes photographs. **Price:** included in membership dues. **Circulation:** 800. Alternate Formats: online ● *GMAT Bulletin of Information*, annual. Provides information for people who apply for admission to graduate schools of management that require scores from the GMAT. **Price:** free. **Circulation:** 250,000 ● *Graduate Management News*, quarterly. Newsletter. Includes committee updates and calendar of events. **Price:** included in membership dues. **Circulation:** 300 ● *Selections*, 3/year. Magazine. Provides information on graduate management education. Includes opinions, interviews, research reports, and statistics. ISSN: 0882-0228. **Circulation:** 7,000. **Conventions/Meetings:** annual meeting - always June.

8808 ■ Operation Enterprise (OE)
c/o American Management Association
1601 Broadway
New York, NY 10019-7420
Ph: (212)903-8038
Free: (800)797-7483
Fax: (212)903-8509
E-mail: govops@openterprise.com
URL: http://www.openterprise.com
Founded: 1963. **Staff:** 4. **Budget:** $400,000. **Description:** Gives high school and college students an opportunity to learn about management by working with executives and managers. Learning techniques used include small group discussions, panel forums, a business simulation, and role playing. Sponsors Career Skills program, to encourage development of job skills. Candidates are sponsored in a variety of ways by companies, civic organizations, or individuals. **Awards: Type:** scholarship. **Recipient:** for those participating in the program. **Additional Websites:** http://www.amanet.org/oe. **Affiliated With:** American Management Association. **Formerly:** Youth Adult Program. **Publications:** *Operation Enterprise Newsletter*, semiannual. Covers developments in the programs. Includes speaker, alumni, and sponsor profiles. **Price:** free. **Circulation:** 10,000. **Conventions/Meetings:** seminar - 14/year.

Manufacturing

8809 ■ International Production Planning and Scheduling Association (IPPSA)
PO Box 5031
Incline Village, NV 89450
Ph: (775)833-3922
E-mail: billk@ippsa.org
URL: http://www.ippsa.org
Membership Dues: general, $50 (annual). **Multinational. Description:** Seeks to expand the knowledge of advanced planning and scheduling technology among manufacturing companies. Conducts educational planning and scheduling seminars and integrates Material and Capacity Management in its workshops. **Publications:** *Evaluating Scheduling Performance*. Article. Alternate Formats: online ● *FCS Book Description*. Article. Alternate Formats: online ● *Scheduling Methods that Work*. Article. Alternate Formats: online ● *Seminar Presenters Biography*. Article. Alternate Formats: online.

Marine

8810 ■ National Marine Educators Association (NMEA)
c/o Johnette Bosarge, Admin. Asst.
PO Box 1470
Ocean Springs, MS 39566-1470
Ph: (228)818-8893
Fax: (228)872-4279
E-mail: johnette.bosarge@usm.edu
URL: http://www.marine-ed.org
Contact: Lynn Whitley, Pres.
Founded: 1976. **Members:** 1,200. **Membership Dues:** active, institutional, $40 (annual) ● student, $20 (annual) ● affiliate, $35 (annual) ● associate, $55 (annual) ● family, $65 (annual) ● life, $500 ● corporate, $250 (annual). **Budget:** $30,000. **Regional Groups:** 16. **Description:** Represents active teachers (kindergarten through graduate school) and other interested individuals. Acts as a clearinghouse on marine education. Shares teaching materials and promotes dialogue among those interested in the world of water. **Awards:** Honorary Member. **Frequency:** annual. **Type:** recognition. **Recipient:** to individuals who have demonstrated distinguished career in teaching, research or service in marine education ● James Centorino Award. **Frequency:** annual. **Type:** recognition. **Recipient:** for distinguished performance in marine education ● Marine Education Award. **Frequency:** annual. **Type:** recognition. **Recipient:** for outstanding work in any aspect of marine education at the local or national level ● Ocean Technology Foundation's Scholarship Program. **Frequency:** annual. **Type:** scholarship. **Recipient:** to NMEA member ● Outstanding Teacher Award. **Frequency:** annual. **Type:** recognition. **Recipient:** for effective and innovative classroom teaching at any level ● President's Award. **Frequency:** annual. **Type:** recognition. **Recipient:** for outstanding contributions to NMEA and/or marine education. **Committees:** Aquaria, Museums and Parks; Computers in Marine Education; Curriculum; Minorities and Women in Marine Education; Professional Development; Public Relations. **Formerly:** (1985) National Marine Education Association. **Publications:** *Current: The Journal of Marine Education*, 3-4/year. Features articles on marine education. **Price:** $5.00. **Circulation:** 1,200. **Advertising:** accepted ● *NMEA News*, quarterly. Newsletter. **Conventions/Meetings:** annual conference (exhibits).

8811 ■ Sea Education Association (SEA)
PO Box 6
Woods Hole, MA 02543
Ph: (508)540-3954
Free: (800)552-3633
Fax: (508)457-4673
E-mail: admission@sea.edu
URL: http://www.sea.edu
Contact: John K. Bullard, Pres.
Founded: 1971. **Members:** 71. **Staff:** 60. **Budget:** $5,100,000. **Description:** Runs fully accredited academic programs focusing on the sea. Owns and operates two deep-sea research sailing vessels to increase students' understanding of the oceanic environment; theories learned ashore are put into practice at sea aboard SSV Corwith Cramer, a 134-foot brigantine and Robert C. Seamans, a 134.5 brigantine. Offers Woods Hole semester, a 12-week,

full-credit undergraduate program that provides college students with an intensive, practical, multidisciplinary introduction to the oceans; students and faculty work together toward seamanship, navigation and maritime studies (economics, history, literature and oceanography of the sea). Following the shore component is a subsequent 6-week research cruises on board the Robert C. Seamans or the Corwith Cramer, which focuses on regional oceanography in the North Atlantic Ocean, the Caribbean Sea and the Pacific Ocean. Woods Hole Semester is offered six times a year; students successfully completing the program receive a full semester's credit from Boston University. Offers summer session, an eight-week summer undergraduate program; similar coursework to Woods Hole Semester, but with four weeks ashore and four weeks at sea; also offers three week summer programs ashore and at sea for motivated high school students and summer seminars for teachers K-12. **Libraries: Type:** reference. **Holdings:** artwork, books, periodicals. **Subjects:** marine science, maritime history and literature, navigation, ship operation. **Committees:** Education; External Affairs; Investment, Finance, and Personnel; Legal and Insurance; Marine; Oceanographic; Trustees and Members. **Affiliated With:** American Sail Training Association. **Formerly:** (1975) American Sailing Education Association. **Publications:** *Following SEA*, semiannual. Newsletter. Includes updates on SEA research, staff, and alumni activities. **Price:** free. **Circulation:** 8,500. Alternate Formats: online ● *Sea Education Association—Annual Report*. **Price:** free. **Circulation:** 1,500 ● *Under Full Sail*. Newsletter. **Conventions/Meetings:** semiannual meeting - always November and June in Woods Hole, MA.

Maritime

8812 ■ Grays Harbor Historical Seaport Authority (GHHSA)

712 Hagara St.
PO Box 2019
Aberdeen, WA 98520
Free: (800)200-5239
Fax: (360)533-9384
E-mail: les@historicalseaport.org
URL: http://www.historicalseaport.org
Contact: Capt. Les Bolton, Exec. Dir.

Founded: 1986. **Members:** 200. **Membership Dues:** midshipman (individual), $50 (annual) ● ship's crew (family), $100 (annual) ● first mate, $200 (annual) ● commander, $250 (annual) ● Bulfinch Society, $500 (annual) ● commodore, $1,000 (annual) ● admiral, $2,500 (annual). **Staff:** 8. **Budget:** $396,000. **Description:** Preserves the rich and colorful maritime heritage of the Pacific Northwest and the nation through innovative, experiential, hands-on education programs and activities. Tall Ships Lady Washington and Hawaiian Chieftain introduces young people from Alaska to San Diego to a wide variety of learning experiences ranging from history to math, science, team building, and group problem solving. Seaport Learning Center and fleet of small boats provides vocational and pre-vocational educational opportunities for at-risk and special needs of youth. Features the largest spar makers lathe in North America. **Libraries: Type:** open to the public. **Holdings:** articles, artwork, clippings. **Subjects:** maritime pertaining to Lady Washington and related programs. **Computer Services:** database ● mailing lists. **Publications:** *Currents*, quarterly. Newsletter. **Conventions/Meetings:** semimonthly board meeting - always second and fourth Tuesday.

8813 ■ National Association of Maritime Educators (NAME)

c/o Richard A. Block, Newsletter Ed.
124 North Van Ave.
Houma, LA 70363
Ph: (985)879-3866 (985)851-2134
Fax: (504)879-3911
E-mail: rusty@martinint.com
Contact: Richard A. Block, Newsletter Ed.

Founded: 1987. **Members:** 400. **Staff:** 2. **Description:** Maritime academies, vocational-technical programs, and license-prep schools; allied publishers and support personnel. Aims to further the education, training, and licensing support for U.S. merchant seamen. Presents a collective voice to the U.S. Coast Guard concerning license examinations and preparation training; facilitates exchange of information among members. **Convention/Meeting:** none. **Libraries: Type:** reference. **Holdings:** 1,000. **Subjects:** federal register (1983 to present); maritime. **Awards: Type:** recognition. **Recipient:** for outstanding service of an individual member; awarded plaques. **Telecommunication Services:** electronic mail, namenet@triparish.net. **Formerly:** (1988) National Association of Independent Maritime Educators. **Publications:** Newsletter, periodic. **Price:** free. **Circulation:** 400. Alternate Formats: online.

Marketing

8814 ■ Academy of Marketing Science (AMS)

Univ. of Miami
School of Bus. Admin.
PO Box 248012
Coral Gables, FL 33124-6536
Ph: (305)284-6673
Fax: (305)284-3762
E-mail: ams.sba@miami.edu
URL: http://www.ams-web.org
Contact: Harold W. Berkman, Exec. VP/Dir.

Founded: 1971. **Members:** 1,500. **Membership Dues:** student, $35 (annual) ● corporate sponsor, $100 (annual) ● individual, $75 (annual). **Staff:** 2. **Description:** Marketing academicians and practitioners; individuals interested in fostering education in marketing science. Aims to promote the advancement of knowledge and the furthering of professional standards in the field of marketing. Explores the special application areas of marketing science and its responsibilities as an economic, ethical, and social force; promotes research and the widespread dissemination of findings. Facilitates exchange of information and experience among members, and the transfer of marketing knowledge and technology to developing countries; promotes marketing science on an international level. Provides a forum for discussion and refinement of concepts, methods and applications, and the opportunity to publish papers in the field. Assists member educators in the development of improved teaching methods, devices, directions, and materials. Offers guidance and direction in marketing practice and reviewer assistance on scholarly works. Contributes to the solution of marketing problems encountered by individual firms, industries, and society as a whole. Encourages members to utilize their marketing talents to the fullest through redirection, reassignment, and relocation. Sponsors competitions. **Publications:** *Academy of Marketing Science—News*, quarterly. Newsletter. **Price:** free for members. **Circulation:** 1,500 ● *Academy of Marketing Science Review—Membership Roster*, annual. Membership Directory. **Price:** free for members. **Circulation:** 1,500 ● *Developments in Marketing Science*, annual. Proceedings. **Price:** $30.00/copy for participants of the conference; $30.00/copy for fellows of the AMS; $50.00/copy for libraries. ISSN: 0149-7421. **Circulation:** 500. Alternate Formats: microform. Also Cited As: *Academy of Marketing Science—Proceedings* ● *Index of JAMS*, annual. Article ● *Journal of the Academy of Marketing Science*, quarterly. Includes book reviews and cumulative bibliography of articles. **Price:** included in membership dues. ISSN: 0092-0703. **Circulation:** 2,000. **Advertising:** accepted. Alternate Formats: online ● Also publishes books and monograph series. **Conventions/Meetings:** annual conference, academic book (exhibits) - usually last week of May.

8815 ■ American Collegiate Retailing Association (ACRA)

c/o Robert Robicheaux, Membership Chm.
219 Business-Engineering Complex
1150 10th Ave. S
Birmingham, AL 35294-4460
Ph: (205)934-4648
Fax: (205)934-0058
E-mail: bobr@uab.edu
URL: http://www.acraretail.org
Contact: Robert Robicheaux, Membership Chm.

Founded: 1948. **Members:** 300. **Membership Dues:** regular, $50 (annual). **Budget:** $10,000. **Description:** Administrators and faculty from research-based colleges and universities with specialized curricula in retailing and merchandising. Maintains hall of fame. **Publications:** Membership Directory, annual. **Price:** included in membership dues ● Newsletter, quarterly. Covers positions openings, conference notices, and research notes. Alternate Formats: online. **Conventions/Meetings:** semiannual conference.

8816 ■ Direct Marketing Educational Foundation (DMEF)

1120 Ave. of the Americas
New York, NY 10036-6700
Ph: (212)768-7277
Fax: (212)790-1561
E-mail: dmef@the-dma.org
URL: http://www.the-dma.org/dmef
Contact: Terri L. Bart, Pres.

Founded: 1966. **Members:** 500. **Membership Dues:** student (full-time only), $25 (annual) ● regular in U.S., $50 (annual) ● regular outside U.S., $60 (annual) ● regular outside U.S. (with JIM subscription), $70 (annual). **Staff:** 9. **Description:** Represents individuals, firms, and organizations interested in furthering college-level education in direct marketing. Functions as the collegiate arm of the direct marketing profession. Sponsors a summer internship, programs for students and professors, and campaign competition for students. Provides educational materials and course outlines to faculty members; arranges for speakers for college classes and clubs. Cosponsors academic research competitions. Maintains hall of fame. **Awards:** Academic Awards. **Type:** fellowship. **Recipient:** for college and university faculty members engaged in the instruction of advertising, marketing, business communications, or journalism. **Computer Services:** Online services, research. **Affiliated With:** Direct Marketing Association. **Formerly:** (1972) DMAA Educational Foundation; (1979) Direct Mail Educational Foundation; (1983) Direct Mail/Marketing Educational Foundation. **Publications:** *Journal of Interactive Marketing*, quarterly. Provides a forum for the exchange of ideas and concepts. Includes books and software reviews, abstracts, and editorials. **Price:** $250.00 /year for individuals in U.S., Canada and Mexico; $274.00 /year for individuals outside North America; $920.00 /year for institutions in U.S. (print only); $1,012.00 /year for institutions in U.S. (print and online). **Circulation:** 1,200. **Advertising:** accepted. Alternate Formats: online. Also Cited As: *JIM* ● Newsletters ● Pamphlets. **Conventions/Meetings:** periodic Regional Institute - meeting ● Robert B. Clarke Annual Educators' Conference - always in fall.

8817 ■ Distributive Education Clubs of America (DECA)

1908 Assn. Dr.
Reston, VA 20191
Ph: (703)860-5000
Fax: (703)860-4013
E-mail: ed_davis@deca.org
URL: http://www.deca.org
Contact: Edward L. Davis, Exec. Dir.

Founded: 1946. **Members:** 180,000. **Staff:** 30. **Budget:** $2,500,000. **Local Groups:** 6,000. **Description:** Works to improve education and career opportunities for students interested in the field of marketing, management and distribution (retailing and wholesaling). **Divisions:** Alumni; Collegiate; High School; Junior Collegiate; Professional. **Publications:** *DECA Advisor*, monthly, during school year. Newsletter. Covers teaching aids, surveys, corporation support, scholarships, and special events. Includes teaching guide. **Price:** free for members. **Circulation:** 7,000. **Advertising:** accepted. Alternate Formats: online ● *DECA Guide*, annual. Covers insurance, membership, and competitive events programs; catalog of instructional materials; scholarship information. **Price:** free to DECA chapter advisors. **Circulation:** 6,000.

Advertising: accepted. Alternate Formats: online ● *Dimensions*, quarterly. Magazine. For high school and college students of marketing, merchandising, and management. **Price:** free for members; $5.00 /year for nonmembers. ISSN: 0279-473X. **Circulation:** 165,000. **Advertising:** accepted. **Conventions/ Meetings:** annual Career Development Conference - 2009 Apr. 29-May 2, Anaheim, CA; 2010 Apr. 24-27, Louisville, KY.

8818 ■ Marketing Education Association (MEA)
PO Box 27473
Tempe, AZ 85285-7473
Ph: (602)750-6735 (602)692-8092
Fax: (602)777-7315
E-mail: mea@nationalmea.org
URL: http://www.nationalmea.org
Contact: Dr. Rod Davis, Exec. Dir.
Founded: 1982. **Members:** 500. **Membership Dues:** professional, $56 (annual) ● student, $15 (annual) ● executive, $111 (annual) ● loyalty, $20 (annual). **Description:** Teachers, teacher coordinators, local and state supervisors, teacher educators, researchers, and curriculum specialists. Fosters the development and expansion of education for and about marketing as a discrete, clearly defined profession. Supports professionals responsible for marketing education and training. (Marketing education involves training for retailing, wholesaling, selling, and other occupations). **Committees:** Communications; Editorial and Publications; Merchandise; Nominations; Professional Development; Public Relations; Research; State Relationships. **Formed by Merger of:** National Association of Distributive Education Local Supervisors; National Association for Distributive Education Teachers; National Association of State Supervisors of Distributive Education; Council for Distributive Teacher Education. **Formerly:** (1986) Marketing and Distributive Education Association. **Publications:** *MEAdvocate*, quarterly. Newsletter. **Advertising:** accepted. Alternate Formats: online. **Conventions/ Meetings:** annual conference, leadership development training (exhibits).

Marriage

8819 ■ Commission on Accreditation for Marriage and Family Therapy Education (COAMFTE)
c/o American Association for Marriage and Family Therapy
112 S Alfred St.
Alexandria, VA 22314
Ph: (703)838-9808
Fax: (703)838-9805
E-mail: coamfte@aamft.org
URL: http://www.aamft.org/about/coamfte/about-coamfte.asp
Contact: Donald Kaveny, Dir.
Founded: 1978. **Members:** 97. **Staff:** 2. **Budget:** $320,000. **Multinational. Description:** Specialized accrediting body for master's, doctoral, and post-graduate degree clinical training programs in marriage and family therapy throughout U.S. and Canada. **Programs:** Doctoral Degree; Master's Degree; Post-Graduate Degree Clinical Training. **Publications:** *Manual on Accreditation*.

Martial Arts

8820 ■ Association for Renaissance Martial Arts (ARMA)
5220 Jimmy Lee Smith Pkwy., Ste.104, No. 111
Hiram, GA 30141
E-mail: thearma@comcast.net
URL: http://www.thearma.org
Contact: John Clements, Dir.
Founded: 1992. **Membership Dues:** associate, $30 (annual). **Multinational. Description:** Promotes the study and practice of historical fencing and the Western martial heritage. Focuses on the interpretation and legitimate reconstruction of Medieval and Renaissance combat systems as a modern discipline. Seeks to advance the quality of skills demonstrated with Medieval and Renaissance weaponry. Encourages understanding of historical European combat skills. **Publications:** Articles. Alternate Formats: online.

Mathematics

8821 ■ American Mathematical Association of Two-Year Colleges (AMATYC)
Southwest Tennessee Community Coll.
5983 Macon Cove
Memphis, TN 38134
Ph: (901)333-4643
Fax: (901)333-4651
E-mail: amatyc@amatyc.org
URL: http://www.amatyc.org
Contact: Cheryl Cleaves PhD, Exec. Dir. of Office Operations
Founded: 1974. **Members:** 2,800. **Membership Dues:** individual, $75 (annual) ● associate (full-time student, non-voting), $10 (annual) ● retired, adjunct faculty, $37 (annual) ● life, $1,500. **Staff:** 4. **Budget:** $500,000. **Regional Groups:** 8. **State Groups:** 41. **Description:** Two-year college mathematics and computer science professors; four-year college mathematics professors concerned with lower division mathematics education. Encourages development of effective mathematics programs; allows for the interchange of ideas on the improvement of mathematics education and mathematics-related experiences of students in two-year colleges or at the lower division level. **Awards:** Mathematics Excellence Award. **Frequency:** biennial. **Type:** recognition. **Recipient:** for educators who have made outstanding contributions to mathematics or mathematics education at the two-year college ● Teaching Excellence Award. **Frequency:** biennial. **Type:** recognition. **Recipient:** for educators who have made outstanding contributions to mathematics and shown excellence in teaching. **Computer Services:** Mailing lists. **Telecommunication Services:** electronic mail, ccleaves@amatyc.org. **Committees:** Developmental Mathematics; Distance Learning; Equal Opportunity in Mathematics; Faculty Development; Placement and Assessment; Program/Curriculum Issues; Technical Mathematics; Technology in Mathematics Education. **Publications:** *AMATYC News*, 5/year. Newsletter. **Price:** included in membership dues. ISSN: 0889-3845. **Advertising:** accepted. Alternate Formats: online ● *AMATYC Review*, semiannual. **Advertising:** accepted. Alternate Formats: online ● Also publishes AMATYC history, constitution, and bylaws. **Conventions/Meetings:** annual Summer Institutes in Regional Locations - seminar ● annual Two-Year College Mathematics League Competition - competition and conference (exhibits).

8822 ■ Association of State Supervisors of Mathematics (ASSM)
c/o Diane Schaefer, Pres.
Rhode Island Dept. of Educ.
225 Westminster St.
Providence, RI 02903-3400
Ph: (401)222-8436
E-mail: diane.schaefer@ride.ri.gov
URL: http://smtc.uwyo.edu/assm
Contact: Diane Schaefer, Pres.
Founded: 1959. **Members:** 120. **Description:** Individuals serving on the mathematics education agency staff of any U.S. state or possession, the District of Columbia, the U.S. Department of Education, or any Canadian province or territory. Promotes high standards in the teaching of mathematics; encourages interest in mathematics and its teaching. Facilitates exchange of ideas and information among members; promotes cooperation among education agencies. Identifies the needs of the future and makes recommendations for improving mathematics education. Maintains speakers' bureau. **Affiliated With:** National Council of Teachers of Mathematics. **Publications:** *Resource Guide and Operational Handbook for State-Level Coordinators of the Presidential Awards for Excellence in Mathematics and Science Teaching*. Alternate Formats: online ● Newsletter, quarterly ● Membership Directory, annual. **Conventions/Meetings:** annual meeting.

8823 ■ International Association for Game Education and Research (IAGER)
530 S Lake Ave., Ste.171
Pasadena, CA 91101
E-mail: contact@iager.org
URL: http://www.iager.org
Contact: Dr. Tim Langdell PhD, Pres.
Founded: 2005. **Membership Dues:** educator, researcher, $69 (annual) ● for-profit corporate, $250-$1,000 (annual) ● non-profit corporate, $100 (annual) ● educational institution, $250 (annual) ● student, $30 (annual) ● associate, $49 (annual). **Multinational. Description:** Represents individuals involved in teaching games or games-based curricula or training, or engaged in games education research. Promotes and improves games education through curriculum development, educational research and shared resources. Covers teaching, curriculum questions and education related research. Serves the needs of the game academic community. **Telecommunication Services:** electronic mail, membership@iager.org. **Publications:** *Journal of Game Research*, semiannual. Sets precedence for quality of writing on the topics of game education, curriculum, and game education related research. Also Cited As: *JGER*.

8824 ■ The Madison Project (TMP)
c/o James Madison University
Graduate School of Educ.
800 S Main St.
PO Box 8298
Harrisonburg, VA 22801
E-mail: president@themadisonproject.com
URL: http://www.themadisonproject.com
Contact: Mr. Jeff Chandler, Pres.
Founded: 1957. **Staff:** 9. **Description:** Independent, student-run organization devoted to sharing their love of music through a cappella to the James Madison University community and beyond. As the university's premier a cappella group, they held their first performance in 1997, and has since performed hundreds of shows, released six albums, had over fifty members, traveled all over the East Coast, and visited more than 30 other schools. One of eight a cappella groups on the JMU campus, and one of three all-male groups. **Publications:** *Journal of Mathematical Behavior*, quarterly. **Price:** $70.00 /year for individuals; $195.00 /year for institutions. ISSN: 0732-3123. **Advertising:** accepted.

8825 ■ Math/Science Network
Mills Coll.
5000 MacArthur Blvd.
Oakland, CA 94613
Ph: (510)430-2222
Fax: (510)430-2090
E-mail: msnstaff@mills.edu
URL: http://www.expandingyourhorizons.org
Contact: Stacey Roberts-Ohr, Exec. Dir.
Founded: 1974. **Members:** 275. **Staff:** 2. **Budget:** $112,000. **Description:** Mathematicians, scientists, educators, counselors, parents, community leaders, and representatives from business and industry who are interested in increasing the participation of girls and women in mathematics, science, and technology. Coordinates Expanding Your Horizons in Science and Mathematics career education conferences for 6th-12th grade girls. **Publications:** *Beyond Equals: To Promote the Participation of Women in Mathematics*. Book ● *Broadcast*, quarterly. Newsletter ● *Handbook for Conference Planners* ● Books. **Conventions/Meetings:** annual meeting.

8826 ■ National Council of Supervisors of Mathematics (NCSM)
6000 E Evans Ave., No. 3-205
Denver, CO 80222
Ph: (303)758-9611
Fax: (303)758-9616

E-mail: ncsm@mathforum.org
URL: http://www.ncsmonline.org
Contact: Tim Kanold, Pres.
Founded: 1968. **Members:** 3,000. **Membership Dues:** individual, $75 (annual). **Staff:** 1. **Budget:** $250,000. **Description:** Represents leaders in mathematics education. Supports mathematics education leadership at the school, district, college/university, state/province, and national levels. Membership constitutes an international force, collaborating to achieve excellence in mathematics education. **Awards:** Glenn Gilbert National Leadership Award. **Frequency:** annual. **Type:** recognition. **Recipient:** for members ● Mathematics Student Recognition Program. **Frequency:** annual. **Type:** recognition. **Recipient:** for high school seniors ● **Type:** recognition. **Recipient:** for two high school students who have excelled in mathematics. **Computer Services:** database ● mailing lists, provided on labels only; $500 charge. **Telecommunication Services:** electronic mail, tkanold@district125.k12.il.us. **Publications:** *Future Basics: Developing Numerical Power.* Monograph. **Price:** $10.00 for members ● Membership Directory, annual. **Circulation:** 3,000 ● Newsletter, quarterly. **Circulation:** 3,000 ● Journal, semiannual. **Circulation:** 3,000. Alternate Formats: online. **Conventions/Meetings:** annual conference - 2009 Apr. 20-22, Washington, DC ● annual Leadership Training Academy - meeting - 2009 Apr. 22-25, Washington, DC.

8827 ■ National Council of Teachers of Mathematics (NCTM)
1906 Assn. Dr.
Reston, VA 20191-1502
Ph: (703)620-9840
Free: (800)235-7566
Fax: (703)476-2970
E-mail: inquiries@nctm.org
URL: http://www.nctm.org
Contact: James M. Rubillo, Exec. Dir.
Founded: 1920. **Members:** 100,000. **Membership Dues:** full, individual (includes one school journal), $76 (annual) ● full, individual (includes one research journal), $100 (annual) ● institutional (includes one school journal), $99 (annual) ● institutional (includes one research journal), $156 (annual) ● K-8 school, $135 (annual) ● student, $38 (annual) ● emeritus, $28 (annual) ● e-membership, $48 (annual). **Staff:** 110. **Budget:** $17,000,000. **Regional Groups:** 254. **State Groups:** 52. **Description:** Aims to improve teaching and learning of mathematics. **Awards:** Clarence Olander Grants. **Frequency:** annual. **Type:** grant. **Recipient:** for in-service training ● Dale Seymour Scholarship. **Frequency:** annual. **Type:** scholarship. **Recipient:** for K-12 teachers ● Ernest Duncan Scholarship. **Frequency:** annual. **Type:** grant. **Recipient:** for K-6 teachers ● Future Leaders Annual Meeting Scholarship. **Type:** monetary. **Recipient:** for K-12 teachers ● Implementing NCTM Standards in Your Own Classroom. **Frequency:** annual. **Type:** monetary. **Recipient:** for elementary and secondary school teachers ● Lifetime Achievement Awards. **Frequency:** annual. **Type:** recognition. **Recipient:** to NCTM members who have exhibited a lifetime of achievement in mathematics education. **Telecommunication Services:** electronic mail, orders@nctm.org. **Publications:** *Journal for Research in Mathematics Education*, 5/year. Reports on research, philosophical and historical studies, and theoretical analysis; contains volume index and annual monographs. ISSN: 0021-8251. **Circulation:** 11,233. **Advertising:** accepted. Alternate Formats: online. Also Cited As: *JRME* ● *Mathematics Teacher*, monthly. Journal. Provides information for secondary and two-year college teachers of algebra and calculus; includes information on new concepts. ISSN: 0025-5769. **Circulation:** 48,000. **Advertising:** accepted. Alternate Formats: microform. Also Cited As: *MT* ● *Mathematics Teaching in the Middle School*, monthly. Journal. Contains articles, teaching ideas and features on the improvement of mathematics instruction in junior high and middle schools. ISSN: 1072-0839. **Circulation:** 36,000. **Advertising:** accepted. Also Cited As: *MTMS* ● *National Council of Teachers of Mathematics—Yearbook*. Monograph. Presents scholarly papers on a selected topic. **Price:** $16.00/copy for members; $20.00/copy for nonmembers. ISSN: 0077-4103. Alternate Formats: microform ● *NCTM News Bulletin*, 9/year. Reports on association activities, legislation affecting education, new learning and teaching techniques, and new programs. **Price:** included in membership dues. ISSN: 0277-1365. **Circulation:** 110,000. Alternate Formats: online ● *Teaching Children Mathematics*, 9/year. Journal. Features articles and teaching ideas; covers information of interest to teachers of mathematics in the elementary grades. ISSN: 1073-5836. **Circulation:** 48,000. **Advertising:** accepted. Alternate Formats: microform. Also Cited As: *TCM*. **Conventions/Meetings:** annual meeting and convention (exhibits) - usually April.

8828 ■ Women and Mathematics Education (WME)
c/o Pat Frey, Treas.
PO Box 922
Buffalo, NY 14201
E-mail: freyp@aol.com
URL: http://www.wme-usa.org
Contact: Pat Frey, Treas.
Founded: 1978. **Members:** 300. **Membership Dues:** general, $15 (annual) ● full-time student, retired, unemployed individual, $7 (annual). **Budget:** $4,000. **Description:** Individuals concerned with promoting the mathematical education of girls and women. Serves as a clearinghouse for ideas and resources in the area of women and mathematics. Establishes communications for networks focusing on doctoral students, elementary and secondary school teachers, and teacher educators. Encourages research in the area of women and mathematics, especially research that isolates factors contributing to the dropout rate of women in mathematics. Emphasizes the need for elementary and secondary school programs that help reverse the trend of avoidance of mathematics by females. **Awards:** Dora Helen Skypek Award. **Frequency:** annual. **Type:** recognition. **Recipient:** for the promotion of mathematical education of women. **Telecommunication Services:** electronic mail, mylne@sbcglobal.net ● electronic mail, wiest@unr.edu. **Boards:** Advisory. **Programs:** SummerMath. **Projects:** Northwest Girls Collaborative; PDK Poster. **Affiliated With:** National Council of Teachers of Mathematics. **Formerly:** (1979) Association for the Promotion of the Mathematics Education of Girls and Women. **Publications:** *Women and Mathematics*, biennial. Directory. Contains resource list. **Price:** included in membership dues ● *Women and Mathematics Education—Newsletter*, 3/year. Covers conferences, institutes, programs, and meetings significant to members. Reports on organization activities. **Price:** included in membership dues. **Circulation:** 300. **Conventions/Meetings:** annual convention, held in conjunction with NCTM.

Mechanics

8829 ■ Association of Chairmen of Departments of Mechanics (ACDM)
Virginia Polytechnic Inst. and State Univ.
Dept. of Engg. Sci. and Mechanics
223 Norris Hall - MC 0219
Blacksburg, VA 24061
Ph: (540)231-6651
Fax: (540)231-4574
E-mail: esmhead@vt.edu
URL: http://www.esm.vt.edu
Contact: Prof. Ishwar K. Puri, Contact
Founded: 1969. **Members:** 103. **Membership Dues:** regular, $15 (annual). **Budget:** $325. **Description:** Chairmen of departments of mechanics or mechanics groups at universities. Seeks to enhance the status and teaching of mechanics in universities. Sponsors studies; disseminates information; compiles statistics; maintains advisory services; offers placement assistance. **Publications:** Newsletter, periodic ● Also publishes information papers. **Conventions/Meetings:** semiannual meeting.

Media

8830 ■ Alliance for a Media Literate America (AMLA)
721 Glencoe St.
Denver, CO 80220
Free: (888)775-2652
E-mail: amla@amlainfo.org
URL: http://www.amlainfo.org
Contact: Lynda Berqsma, Pres.
Founded: 2001. **Members:** 400. **Membership Dues:** student, $35-$60 (annual) ● national non-profit organization, $350-$500 (annual) ● academic institution, $300 (annual) ● local/state/regional group, $150 (annual). **Description:** Promotes media literacy education that is focused on critical inquiry, learning and skill-building. Aims to help people to critically analyze and create messages using a wide variety of technological tools now available in and out of school. **Computer Services:** Information services, media literacy resources. **Telecommunication Services:** electronic mail, amlamembership@qwest.net. **Committees:** Communications; Conference; Conference Program; Governance; Membership; Nominations; Program; Resource Development and Fundraising. **Publications:** *Year in Review*, annual. Annual Report. Alternate Formats: online.

8831 ■ Media Ecology Association (MEA)
c/o Stephanie Bennett, PhD, Dir. of Communication
Palm Beach Atlantic University
Gregory Hall 457
West Palm Beach, FL 33401
Ph: (561)803-2617
E-mail: stephanie_bennett@pba.edu
URL: http://www.media-ecology.org
Contact: Janet Sternberg, Exec. Sec.
Membership Dues: student, $30 (annual) ● regular, $60 (annual) ● sustaining, $90 (annual) ● institution, $100 (annual). **Description:** Promotes, sustains, and recognizes excellence in media ecology scholarship, research, criticism, application, and artistic practice. Provides a network for fellowship, contacts, and professional opportunities. Serves as a clearinghouse for information related to academic programs around the world in areas pertinent to the study of media ecology. **Publications:** *Explorations in Media Ecology*, quarterly. Journal. Alternate Formats: online ● *In Media Res*, semiannual. Newsletter. Alternate Formats: online ● *Proceedings*. Article. Alternate Formats: online. **Conventions/Meetings:** annual Communication, Technology and the Sacred - conference - 2008 June 19-22, Santa Clara, CA.

Medical Accreditation

8832 ■ Commission on Accreditation of Allied Health Education Programs (CAAHEP)
1361 Park St.
Clearwater, FL 33756
Ph: (727)210-2350
Fax: (727)210-2354
E-mail: megivern@caahep.org
URL: http://www.caahep.org
Contact: Kathleen Megivern, Exec. Dir.
Founded: 1994. **Members:** 80. **Membership Dues:** organizational, $3,000 (annual). **Staff:** 3. **Budget:** $650,000. **Description:** Serves as a nationally recognized accrediting agency for allied health programs in 18 occupational areas. **Telecommunication Services:** electronic mail, mail@caahep.org. **Formerly:** (1994) Committee on Allied Health Education and Accreditation. **Publications:** *Communique*, quarterly. Newsletter. Alternate Formats: online ● Annual Report, annual. Alternate Formats: online ● Manuals. Alternate Formats: online. **Conventions/Meetings:** annual meeting.

8833 ■ Committee on Accreditation for Educational Programs for the EMS Professions (CoAEMSP)
1248 Hardwood Rd.
Bedford, TX 76021
Ph: (817)283-9403

Fax: (817)354-8519
E-mail: george@coaemsp.org
URL: http://www.coaemsp.org
Contact: George W. Hatch EdD, Exec. Dir.
Founded: 1979. **Members:** 16. **Budget:** $60,000. **Description:** Cooperates with the Committee on Allied Health Education and Accreditation to accredit emergency medical technician-paramedic training programs across the U.S. Establishes national education standards and programs for the EMT-paramedic. Compiles statistics. **Computer Services:** Mailing lists. **Affiliated With:** Commission on Accreditation of Allied Health Education Programs. **Formerly:** (2000) Joint Review Committee on Educational Programs for the EMT-Paramedic. **Publications:** *Annual Report to You*, annual. Newsletter. Alternate Formats: online ● *Chairman's Newsletter*, semiannual. Alternate Formats: online ● Annual Report, annual. Alternate Formats: online. **Conventions/Meetings:** semiannual conference.

8834 ■ Committee on Accreditation for Opthalmic Medical Personnel (CoA-OMP)
2025 Woodlane Dr.
St. Paul, MN 55125-2998
Free: (800)284-3937
Fax: (651)731-0410
E-mail: coa-omp@jcahpo.org
URL: http://www.jcahpo.org/newsite/coaomp.html
Contact: Lisa Rovick, Chair
Founded: 1987. **Members:** 4. **Staff:** 1. **Budget:** $50,000. **Description:** Individuals from collaborating health organizations including the Association of Technical Personnel in Ophthalmology and Joint Commission on Allied Health Personnel in Ophthalmology. Evaluates ophthalmic educational programs applying for accreditation from the Commission on Accreditation of Allied Health Education Programs. Reviews and revises guidelines, maintains policies, and approves processes that comply with standards established for national accrediting agencies. Analyzes self-study reports; provides teams of representatives to conduct site visits of programs. Compiles statistics. **Affiliated With:** Association of Technical Personnel in Ophthalmology; Joint Commission on Allied Health Personnel in Ophthalmology. **Formerly:** (1988) Joint Review Committee for the Opthalmic Medical Assistant; (1989) Joint Review Commission for the Opthalmic Medical Personnel; (1997) Joint Review Committee for Opthalmic Medical Personnel. **Publications:** *Educational Programs for Opthalmic Medical Personnel*, 3/year. Brochure. **Price:** free ● Annual Reports, annual. Alternate Formats: online ● Newsletters. Alternate Formats: online. **Conventions/Meetings:** semiannual meeting.

8835 ■ Council on Accreditation of Nurse Anesthesia Educational Programs (COA)
c/o American Association of Nurse Anesthetists
222 S Prospect Ave.
Park Ridge, IL 60068
Ph: (847)692-7050
Fax: (847)692-6968
E-mail: info@aana.com
URL: http://www.aana.com
Contact: Mr. Jeffery Beutler, Exec. Dir.
Founded: 1975. **Members:** 85. **Staff:** 4. **Budget:** $500,000. **Description:** Nurse anesthesia programs. Provides accreditation and evaluates the education offered by educational institutions and programs. Functions as an autonomous council within the framework of the American Association of Nurse Anesthetists (see separate entry). Conducts on-site reviews and educational workshops. Compiles statistics. **Libraries: Type:** reference. **Awards:** Agatha Hodgins Award. **Frequency:** annual. **Type:** recognition. **Recipient:** for individuals who have shown dedication in art and science of nurse anesthesia ● Alice Magaw Outstanding Clinician Practitioner Award. **Frequency:** annual. **Type:** recognition. **Recipient:** for a Certified Registered Nurse Anesthetics involved in direct patient care, who has made an important contribution to the advancement of nurse anesthesia practice ● Clinical Instructor of the Year. **Frequency:** annual. **Type:** recognition. **Recipient:** for an individual who has made a significant contribution to the teaching of nurse anesthesia students in clinical area ● Didactic Instructor of the Year Award. **Frequency:** annual. **Type:** recognition. **Recipient:** for an individual who has made a significant contribution to the education of student nurse anesthetists in the classroom ● Federal Political Director of the Year Award. **Frequency:** annual. **Type:** recognition. **Recipient:** for an individual who is responsible for coordinating grassroots legislative, lobbying efforts and keeping the state members informed about legislative issues ● Helen Lamb Outstanding Educator Award. **Frequency:** annual. **Type:** recognition. **Recipient:** for a Certified Registered Nurse Anesthetics who has made a significant contribution to the education of nurse anesthetists ● Ira P. Gunn Award. **Frequency:** annual. **Type:** recognition. **Recipient:** for an individual who has made a highly significant contribution to the preservation and advancement of the nurse anesthesia profession through legislative, legal and regulatory effort ● National Health Leadership Award. **Frequency:** annual. **Type:** recognition. **Recipient:** for an individual working at the federal government level who made a significant contribution to the formation of national health policy. **Formerly:** (1999) Council on Accreditation of Nurse Anesthesia Educational Programs/Schools. **Supersedes:** Approval of Schools Committee. **Publications:** *Educational Standards and Guidelines*. Directory ● *List of Accredited Nurse Anesthesia Educational Program/Schools*, annual. Directory ● *Policies and Procedures Manual*. **Conventions/Meetings:** meeting - 3/year, always in Park Ridge, IL.

8836 ■ Council on Medical Education of the American Medical Association (CME-AMA)
515 N State St.
Chicago, IL 60610
Ph: (312)464-4690 (312)464-4649
Free: (800)621-8335
Fax: (312)464-5830
E-mail: barbara.barzansky@ama-assn.org
URL: http://www.ama-assn.org/ama/pub/category/2954.html
Contact: Barbara Barzansky PhD, Sec.
Founded: 1847. **Members:** 12. **Membership Dues:** student, $54 (3/year). **Staff:** 50. **Description:** A council of the American Medical Association. Participates in the accreditation of and provides consultation to medical school programs, graduate medical educational programs, and continuing medical educational programs. Provides information on medical education at all levels. **Libraries: Type:** not open to the public. **Holdings:** archival material, books, papers, periodicals. **Subjects:** medicine. **Awards:** Physicians Recognition Award. **Type:** recognition. **Councils:** Constitution and Bylaws; Ethical and Judicial Affairs; Legislation; Scientific Affairs. **Publications:** *Allied Health Education Directory*, annual ● *Annual Report of Medical Education in the Journal of the AMA* ● *Continuing Education Courses for Physicians Supplement to the Journal of the AMA*, semiannual ● *Directory of Graduate Medical Education Programs*, annual. **Conventions/Meetings:** quarterly meeting.

8837 ■ Joint Review Committee on Education in Diagnostic Medical Sonography (JRCDMS)
2025 Woodlane Dr.
St. Paul, MN 55125-2998
Ph: (651)731-1582
E-mail: jrc-dms@jcahpo.org
URL: http://www.jrcdms.org
Contact: Felicia Toreno PhD, Chair
Founded: 1979. **Members:** 9. **Staff:** 2. **Budget:** $150,000. **Description:** Participants are physicians and medical sonographers. In collaboration with the Commission on Accreditation for Allied Health Education Programs, accredits post-secondary education programs in diagnostic medical sonography. (Sonography utilizes ultrasonic waves to take two-dimensional pictures of internal body structures.) **Convention/Meeting:** none. **Affiliated With:** American College of Cardiology; American College of Obstetricians and Gynecologists; American College of Radiology; American Institute of Ultrasound in Medicine; American Society of Echocardiography; American Society of Radiologic Technologists; Commission on Accreditation of Allied Health Education Programs; Society for Vascular Ultrasound. **Publications:** *JRCDMS News*, semiannual. Newsletter. **Circulation:** 300.

8838 ■ Joint Review Committee on Education in Radiologic Technology (JRCERT)
20 N Wacker Dr., Ste.2850
Chicago, IL 60606-3182
Ph: (312)704-5300
Fax: (312)704-5304
E-mail: mail@jrcert.org
URL: http://www.jrcert.org
Contact: Leslie F. Winter RT, CEO
Founded: 1969. **Members:** 652. **Staff:** 9. **Budget:** $1,300,000. **Description:** Aims to evaluate and accredit educational programs in the radiologic sciences, such as radiography, radiation therapy, magnetic resonance, and medical dosimetry. **Publications:** *JRCERT Review*, semiannual. Newsletter. Includes interpretations of educational standards and summaries of recent Board actions. **Price:** $6.00/year. **Circulation:** 6,000. **Conventions/Meetings:** semiannual meeting, for Board of Directors only.

8839 ■ Liaison Committee on Medical Education (LCME)
c/o American Medical Association
515 N State St.
Chicago, IL 60610
Ph: (312)464-4933
Fax: (312)464-5830
E-mail: lcme@aamc.org
URL: http://www.lcme.org
Contact: Barbara Barzansky PhD, Interim Sec.
Founded: 1942. **Members:** 17. **Staff:** 6. **Description:** Sponsored by the American Medical Association and the Association of American Medical Colleges (see separate entries); membership is drawn from these groups and the Committee on Accreditation of Canadian Medical Schools, as well as two students, and two public members. Principal function is to accredit programs in medical education leading to the M.D. degree. Conducts research on medical education programs; maintains data banks on medical schools in the U.S. and Canada. Compiles statistics. **Telecommunication Services:** electronic mail, barbara.barzansky@ama-assn.org. **Affiliated With:** American Medical Association; Association of American Medical Colleges. **Publications:** *Functions and Structure of a Medical School*. Contains LCME standards of accreditation. **Price:** free. Alternate Formats: online. **Conventions/Meetings:** quarterly meeting.

Medical Education

8840 ■ Academy of Pharmaceutical Physicians and Investigators (APPI)
500 Montgomery St., Ste.800
Alexandria, VA 22314
Free: (866)225-2779
Fax: (703)254-8101
E-mail: andrea@acrpnet.org
URL: http://www.appinet.org
Contact: Andrea Edens, Marketing Mgr.
Founded: 1993. **Members:** 1,200. **Membership Dues:** regular, $300 (annual) ● physician-in-training, $100 (annual). **Staff:** 6. **Budget:** $350,000. **Regional Groups:** 9. **Multinational. Description:** Enhances the proficiency of pharmaceutical physicians and physician investigators and protects the welfare of patients and study subjects. **Awards:** Honorary Membership. **Frequency:** annual. **Type:** recognition. **Recipient:** for contribution to pharmaceutical medicine. **Affiliated With:** Association of Clinical Research Professionals. **Formerly:** (2007) American Academy of Pharmaceutical Physicians Education Foundation. **Publications:** *APPI Bulletin*, monthly. Newsletters. **Conventions/Meetings:** annual conference (exhibits).

8841 ■ Alliance for Continuing Medical Education (ACME)
1025 Montgomery Hwy., Ste.105
Southcrest Bldg.
Birmingham, AL 35216
Ph: (205)824-1355
Fax: (205)824-1357
E-mail: acme@acme-assn.org
URL: http://www.acme-assn.org
Contact: Paul D. Weber MA, Exec. Dir.
Founded: 1978. **Members:** 2,500. **Membership Dues:** active, $345 (annual). **Staff:** 10. **Budget:** $1,700,000. **Description:** Professionals engaged in continuing medical educational programs. Seeks to "educate and support continuing medical education professionals and to promote leadership in the development of continuing medical education to improve health care outcomes and the performance of health care providers". Facilitates exchange of information among members; makes available educational and continuing professional development opportunities; works to "shape and influence policy in the field of continuing medical education". Makes available discounts on product and services to members. **Awards:** Alliance President's Awards. **Frequency:** annual. **Type:** recognition. **Recipient:** for contributions to the Alliance for CME ● Frances M. Maitland Memorial Lecture Award. **Frequency:** annual. **Type:** recognition. **Recipient:** for lifelong commitment, dedication, and significant contributions as a mentor and colleague ● Frances M. Maitland-PACME Award. **Frequency:** annual. **Type:** recognition. **Recipient:** for contribution to the field of CME and to the future of the profession ● William Campbell Felch/Wyeth Award for Research in CME. **Frequency:** annual. **Type:** recognition. **Recipient:** for completed research project in continuing medical education. **Computer Services:** database, continuing medical education ● mailing lists, of members. **Committees:** Governance; International Strategies; Physicians Curriculum; Professional Development Coordinating; Provider Section Relations; State and Regional Organizations. **Publications:** *Almanac*, monthly. Newsletter. **Price:** included in membership dues; $60.00 for nonmembers. **Circulation:** 2,500. **Advertising:** accepted. Alternate Formats: online ● *Evaluating Educational Outcomes Workbook*. **Price:** $35.00 for members; $55.00 for nonmembers. Alternate Formats: online ● *Journal of Continuing Education in the Health Professions*, quarterly. **Price:** $89.25 for nonmembers in U.S. and Canada (individual); $139.75 for nonmembers in U.S. and Canada (institution); $121.50 for nonmembers outside U.S. and Canada (individual); $177.40 for nonmembers outside U.S. and Canada (institution) ● Membership Directory, annual ● Annual Report, annual. Alternate Formats: online. **Conventions/Meetings:** annual conference, education and technology in medical education (exhibits) - 2009 Jan. 28-31, San Francisco, CA; 2010 Jan. 27-30, New Orleans, LA; 2011 Jan. 26-29, San Francisco, CA; 2012 Jan. 25-28, Miami Beach, FL.

8842 ■ American Association of Colleges of Nursing (AACN)
1 Dupont Cir. NW, Ste.530
Washington, DC 20036
Ph: (202)463-6930
Fax: (202)785-8320
E-mail: pbednash@aacn.nche.edu
URL: http://www.aacn.nche.edu
Contact: Geraldine Bednash, Exec. Dir.
Founded: 1969. **Members:** 570. **Membership Dues:** institutional, $3,536 (annual). **Staff:** 34. **Budget:** $1,000,000. **Description:** Institutions offering baccalaureate and/or graduate degrees in nursing. Seeks to advance the practice of professional nursing by improving the quality of baccalaureate and graduate programs, promoting research, and developing academic leaders. Works with other professional nursing organizations and organizations in other health professions to evaluate and improve health care. Conducts educational programs on masters and doctoral nursing education and faculty practice; sponsors executive development series for new and aspiring deans of nursing. **Awards:** CampusRN/AACN Nursing Scholarship Fund. **Frequency:** annual. **Type:** scholarship. **Recipient:** for students pursuing professional nursing education programs ● Sister Bernadette Armiger Award. **Frequency:** biennial. **Type:** recognition. **Recipient:** for significant contributions to nursing and nursing education. **Computer Services:** Mailing lists. **Committees:** Educational Benchmarking Survey Advisory Group; Government Affairs; Journal of Professional Nursing; Nominating. **Subcommittees:** Baccalaureate Education; Dean Mentoring; Doctoral Conference; Executive Development Series. **Publications:** *A Guide to Grassroots Activism*. Handbook. **Price:** $5.00 ● *A Model for Differentiated Nursing Practice*. **Price:** $10.00 ● *Annual State of the Schools*, annual. Annual Report ● *Enrollment and Graduations in Baccalaureate and Graduate Programs in Nursing*, annual. Report. **Price:** $40.00 ● *Essential Clinical Resources for Nursing's Academic Mission*. **Price:** $9.00 for members; $12.00 for nonmembers ● *Essentials of Baccalaureate Education for Professional Nursing Practice*. **Price:** $9.00 for members; $12.00 for nonmembers ● *Essentials of Master's Education for APN*. **Price:** $9.00 for members; $12.00 for nonmembers ● *Faculty Salaries in Baccalaureate and Graduate Programs in Nursing*, annual. Report ● *Issue Bulletin*, 3/year. Examines issues in nursing education and research. ● *Journal of Professional Nursing*, bimonthly ● *Meet the Press.and Succeed: A Handbook for Nurse Educators*. **Price:** $4.75 for members; $5.75 for nonmembers ● *Position Statement on Nursing Research*. **Price:** $3.00 ● *Salaries of Administrative Nursing Faculty in Baccalaureate and Graduate Programs in Nursing*, biennial. Report. **Price:** $50.00 ● *Salaries of Deans in Baccalaureate and Graduate Programs in Nursing*, annual. Report. **Price:** $30.00 ● *Syllabus*, bimonthly. Newsletter. **Advertising:** accepted. **Conventions/Meetings:** annual Baccalaureate Conference - December ● annual Business Officers of Nursing Schools (BONUS) - meeting (exhibits) ● annual Dean's Summer Seminar - usually January in Florida ● annual Doctoral Conference - usually January in Florida ● semiannual Executive Development Series - meeting (exhibits) - usually March and October in Washington, DC ● semiannual Faculty Practice Conference ● Fall Semiannual Meeting (exhibits) - every fall in Washington, DC ● semiannual Hot Topics Conference ● semiannual Master's Education Conference - December ● annual Nursing Advancement Professionals - conference (exhibits) ● Spring Annual Meeting (exhibits) - always held in Washington, DC.

8843 ■ American Medical Association Foundation (AMAF)
515 N State St.
Chicago, IL 60610
Ph: (312)464-4200 (312)464-5852
Free: (800)621-8335
Fax: (312)464-4142
E-mail: maria.maher@ama-assn.org
URL: http://www.ama-assn.org/ama/pub/category/3119.html
Contact: Maria Maher, Interim Exec. Dir.
Founded: 1962. **Description:** Foundation managed by Directors of the American Medical Association (see separate entry). Receives and distributes funds to benefit medical education in U.S. medical schools and to support education, research and service programs within the community of medicine. Foundation funds consist of contributions from physicians, medical societies and auxiliaries, of other foundations, private industry, and the public. Accepts bequests and other gifts for allocation to various projects in medicine. **Convention/Meeting:** none. **Awards:** AMA Foundation Excellence in Medicine Awards. **Type:** recognition. **Recipient:** for the extraordinary efforts of medical students, physicians, and health care organizations ● Audio-Digest Award for Excellence in Continuing Medical Education for a Practicing Physician. **Frequency:** periodic. **Type:** monetary. **Recipient:** for an individual with significant accomplishments in the field of continuing medical education ● Audio-Digest Awards for Excellence in Continuing Medical Education. **Frequency:** periodic. **Type:** recognition. **Recipient:** for an institution that supports Continuing Medical Education (CME) activities ● Award for Health Education. **Frequency:** periodic. **Type:** recognition. **Recipient:** for a physician with outstanding efforts in the field of health education ● Minority Scholars Award. **Frequency:** annual. **Type:** scholarship. **Recipient:** for rising second or third year students with a minority background ● National Scholarship. **Frequency:** periodic. **Type:** recognition. **Recipient:** for rising fourth year medical students with an interest in medical journalism. **Sections:** International Medical Graduates; Medical Schools; Medical Student; Organized Medical Staff; Resident and Fellow; Young Physicians. **Subgroups:** Minority Affairs Consortium; Practice Physicians. **Affiliated With:** American Medical Association. **Formed by Merger of:** American Medical Education Foundation; American Medical Research Foundation. **Formerly:** (1999) American Medical Association Education and Research Foundation. **Publications:** Newsletter. Includes information on education, service and research.

8844 ■ American Medical Student Association (AMSA)
1902 Assn. Dr.
Reston, VA 20191
Ph: (703)620-6600
Free: (800)767-2266
Fax: (703)620-5873
E-mail: amsa@amsa.org
URL: http://www.amsa.org
Contact: Paul R. Wright, Interim Exec. Dir./CEO
Founded: 1950. **Members:** 35,000. **Membership Dues:** medical student (first and second year), $75 (annual) ● medical student (third and fourth year), $55 (annual) ● premedical sustaining/supporting affiliate, $35 (annual) ● international sustaining medical student in U.S. (first and second year), $50 (annual) ● international sustaining medical student in U.S. (third and fourth year), $55 (annual) ● international sustaining medical student outside U.S., $50 (annual) ● resident/alumni, $10. **Staff:** 30. **Budget:** $3,000,000. **Local Groups:** 140. **Description:** Medical students; local, state, and national organizations; premedical students, interns, and residents. Seeks to improve medical education by making it relevant to today's needs and by making the process by which physicians are trained more humanistic. Contributes to the improvement of health care of all people; involves its members in the social, moral, and ethical obligations of the profession of medicine. Serves as a mechanism through which students may actively participate in the fields of community health through various student health programs. Addresses political issues relating to the nation's health care delivery system and other medical and health issues. Maintains action committees and interest groups which publish newsletters, organize educational workshops, and initiate special projects. **Awards:** Paul R. Wright Excellence in Medical Education Award. **Frequency:** annual. **Type:** monetary. **Recipient:** to a medical school for its exemplary achievements in medical education. **Computer Services:** database ● mailing lists, of medical students and members. **Formerly:** (1975) Student American Medical Association. **Publications:** *Alumni Connection*. Newsletter ● *Global Pulse: AMSA's International Health Journal*. Alternate Formats: online ● *The Healer's Voice*, monthly. Journal. Alternate Formats: online ● *The New Physician*, 9/year. Magazine. **Price:** included in membership dues; $28.00 /year for nonmembers in U.S.; $45.00 /year for nonmembers outside U.S. **Circulation:** 28,000. **Advertising:** accepted. **Conventions/Meetings:** annual convention (exhibits) - 2009 Mar. 11-15, Washington, DC.

8845 ■ American Society for Bioethics and Humanities (ASBH)
4700 W Lake Ave.
Glenview, IL 60025-1485
Ph: (847)375-4745
Fax: (877)734-9385
E-mail: info@asbh.org
URL: http://www.asbh.org
Contact: Amy Claver, Exec. Dir.
Founded: 1998. **Members:** 1,500. **Membership Dues:** student, $30 (annual) ● institution/organiza-

tion, $600 (annual) ● individual, $95-$140 (annual). **Description:** Promotes the exchange of ideas and fosters multidisciplinary, interdisciplinary, and interprofessional scholarship, research, teaching, policy development, professional development, and collegiality among people engaged in all of the endeavors related to clinical and academic bioethics and the health-related humanities. **Awards:** Distinguished Service. **Frequency:** annual. **Type:** recognition ● Lifetime Achievement. **Frequency:** annual. **Type:** recognition. **Telecommunication Services:** electronic bulletin board, on-line member only directory and discussion forums. **Boards:** Directors. **Special Interest Groups:** Affinity Groups. **Absorbed:** (1998) Society for Health and Human Values; (1998) Society for Bioethics Consultation. **Formerly:** Society for Bioethics Consultation. **Publications:** *Core Competencies for Health Care Ethics Consultation*. Report. **Price:** $12.00 ● Membership Directory, annual. **Conventions/Meetings:** annual meeting and lecture, includes program, held in conjunction with SHHV (exhibits) ● annual meeting - 2008 Oct. 23-26, Cleveland, OH; 2009 Oct. 15-18, Washington, DC.

8846 ■ Association of American Medical Colleges (AAMC)

2450 N St. NW
Washington, DC 20037-1126
Ph: (202)828-0400
Fax: (202)828-1125
E-mail: aamcpresident@aamc.org
URL: http://www.aamc.org
Contact: Darrell G. Kirch MD, Pres.

Founded: 1876. **Members:** 2,200. **Staff:** 325. **Budget:** $56,000,000. **Description:** Medical schools, graduate affiliate medical colleges, academic societies, teaching hospitals, and individuals interested in the advancement of medical education, biomedical research, and healthcare. Provides centralized application service. Offers management education program for medical school deans, teaching hospital directors, department chairs, and service chiefs of affiliated hospitals. Develops and administers the Medical College Admissions Test (MCAT). Operates student loan program. Maintains information management system and institutional profile system. Compiles statistics. **Libraries: Type:** reference; open to the public; by appointment only. **Holdings:** 2,000; books, periodicals. **Subjects:** medical education, health policy, higher education policy. **Awards:** Abraham Flexner Award. **Frequency:** annual. **Type:** recognition. **Recipient:** to an individual for his/her extraordinary contributions to the medical education community ● David E. Rogers Award. **Frequency:** annual. **Type:** recognition. **Recipient:** to a medical school faculty member who has made major contributions in improving the health and health care of the American people ● Distinguished Research Award. **Frequency:** annual. **Type:** recognition. **Recipient:** for outstanding biomedical research related to health and disease. **Telecommunication Services:** electronic mail, amcas@aamc.org. **Councils:** Academic Societies; Council of Teaching Hospitals; Deans; Organization of Resident Representatives; Organization of Student Representatives. **Publications:** *AAMC Reporter*, monthly. Newsletter. Covers major programs and initiatives at the AAMC and member institutions. **Price:** $30.00 for members; $50.00 for nonmembers. ISSN: 1544-0540. Alternate Formats: online ● *AAMC STAT*, weekly. Newsletter. Offers brief and immediate news bites summarizing the latest AAMC initiatives, policy statements and other activities. **Price:** free. Alternate Formats: online ● *Academic Medicine*, monthly. Journal. Provides scholarly articles on physician education and workforce issues. **Price:** $143.00 /year for individuals in U.S.; $210.00 /year for individuals outside U.S.; $221.00 /year for institutions. ISSN: 1040-2446. **Circulation:** 6,000. **Advertising:** accepted. Also Cited As: *Journal of Medical Education* ● *Directory of American Medical Education*, annual ● *Medical School Admission Requirements*, annual ● Reports, annual ● Reports, semiannual. **Conventions/Meetings:** annual meeting (exhibits) - 2008 Oct. 31-Nov. 5, San Antonio, TX; 2009 Nov. 6-11, Boston, MA.

8847 ■ Association of American Medical Colleges-Women in Medicine Program (AAMC-WIM)

2450 North St. NW
Washington, DC 20037-1126
Ph: (202)828-0521
Fax: (202)828-1125
E-mail: dmagrane@aamc.org
URL: http://www.aamc.org/members/wim/start.htm
Contact: Diane Magrane MD, Assoc. VP

Staff: 4. **Description:** Aims to increase women's leadership in academic medicine. **Awards:** AAMC Women in Medicine Leadership Development Award. **Frequency:** annual. **Type:** recognition. **Recipient:** to advancing women leaders in academic medicine. **Publications:** *Faculty Vitae*, 3/year, fall, winter, spring. Journal. Contains news and professional development opportunities for the academic medical faculty. Alternate Formats: online ● *Women in Medicine Update*, quarterly. Newsletter ● *Women in U.S. Academic Medicine Statistics Report*, annual ● Membership Directory. **Conventions/Meetings:** annual meeting ● seminar - always summer.

8848 ■ Association of Black Nursing Faculty (ABNF)

PO Box 589
Lisle, IL 60532
Ph: (630)969-3809
Fax: (630)969-3895
E-mail: clay@tuckerpub.com
Contact: Sallie Tucker Allen PhD, Ed.

Founded: 1987. **Members:** 127. **Membership Dues:** regular, student, honorary, $75 (annual). **Budget:** $25,000. **State Groups:** 25. **Description:** Black nursing faculty teaching in nursing programs accredited by the National League for Nursing. Works to promote health-related issues and educational concerns of interest to the black community and ABNF. Serves as a forum for communication and the exchange of information among members; develops strategies for expressing concerns to other individuals, institutions, and communities. Assists members in professional development; develops and sponsors continuing education activities; fosters networking and guidance in employment and recruitment activities. Promotes health-related issues of legislation, government programs, and community activities. Supports black consumer advocacy issues. Encourages research. Maintains speakers' bureau and hall of fame. **Libraries: Type:** reference. **Holdings:** archival material. **Subjects:** African American nursing, nurses, students. **Awards:** Dissertation Award. **Frequency:** annual. **Type:** recognition. **Recipient:** for ABNF members who have reached dissertation phase of doctoral studies ● Johnella Banks Award. **Frequency:** annual. **Type:** recognition. **Recipient:** for an ABNF member who has excelled overall ● Lifetime Achievement in Education and Research Award. **Frequency:** annual. **Type:** recognition ● Young Publisher Award. **Type:** recognition ● Young Researcher Award. **Frequency:** annual. **Type:** recognition. **Committees:** Program; Public Policy; Publication/Communications; Research; State Coordinators. **Study Groups:** Alcoholism/Drug Abuse; Black Elderly/Black Family; Black Student/Black Faculty; Family Violence/Suicide; Homeless; Hypertension; Sickle Cell Anemia; Teen-Age Pregnancy; Transculturalism. **Affiliated With:** National League for Nursing. **Publications:** *ABNF Journal*, bimonthly. Includes research reports and scholarly papers. **Price:** $210.00 /year for institutions; $110.00 /year for individuals; $65.00/year for students. ISSN: 1046-7041. **Circulation:** 400. **Advertising:** accepted ● *ABNF Newsletter*, quarterly. Includes member profiles and activities, research abstracts, conference information, job opportunities, and fellowship information. **Price:** $25.00/year. **Advertising:** accepted ● *Membership Directory of the ABNF*, annual. **Conventions/Meetings:** competition (exhibits) ● annual meeting (exhibits).

8849 ■ Association for Medical Education and Research in Substance Abuse (AMERSA)

125 Whipple, 3rd Fl.
Providence, RI 02908
Ph: (401)243-8460
Fax: (877)418-8769
E-mail: admin@amersa.org
URL: http://www.amersa.org
Contact: Ms. Doreen MacLane-Baeder, Co-Dir.

Founded: 1976. **Members:** 300. **Membership Dues:** full, $150 (annual) ● associate, $75 (annual) ● emeritus, $50 (annual) ● corporate, $1,000 (annual). **Description:** Multidisciplinary organization of health care professionals dedicated to improving education in the care of individuals with substance abuse problems. **Awards:** Betty Ford Award. **Frequency:** annual. **Type:** recognition. **Recipient:** to an individual who has played a significant role in the treatment and recovery of drug-dependent individuals, particularly women ● John P. McGovern Lectureship Award. **Frequency:** annual. **Type:** recognition. **Recipient:** to an individual who has made important contributions to substance abuse education and research. **Computer Services:** Mailing lists, of members. **Task Forces:** Assistance for Healthcare Professionals; Physician Education. **Publications:** *AMERSA Newsletter*, quarterly. **Price:** free for members. Alternate Formats: online ● *Substance Abuse*, quarterly. Journal. **Price:** included in membership dues; $40.00 /year for nonmembers. **Conventions/Meetings:** annual conference (exhibits) - 2008 Nov. 6-8, Washington, DC - **Avg. Attendance:** 130.

8850 ■ Association of Minority Health Professions Schools (AMHPS)

100 Edgewood Ave., Ste.1020
Atlanta, GA 30303
Ph: (678)904-4217 (678)904-4389
Free: (877)895-0902
Fax: (678)904-4518
E-mail: fcarpenter@minorityhealth.org
URL: http://minorityhealth.org
Contact: Phyllis R. Champion, Pres./CEO

Founded: 1978. **Members:** 11. **Staff:** 2. **Description:** Predominantly black health professions schools. Seeks to: increase the number of minorities in health professions; improve the health of blacks in the U.S; increase the federal resources available to minority schools and students. Provides information to the U.S. Congress; conducts educational programs. **Libraries: Type:** reference. **Holdings:** reports. **Publications:** *Study of the Health Status of Minorities in the U.S.*, periodic. **Conventions/Meetings:** annual meeting ● meeting - 3/year.

8851 ■ Association of Optometric Educators (AOE)

c/o Northeastern State University
Coll. of Optometry
Optometry Bldg. 124
600 N Grand Ave.
Tahlequah, OK 74464
Ph: (918)456-5511
Free: (800)722-9614
Fax: (918)458-2104
E-mail: nsuopt@nsuok.edu
URL: http://www.nsuok.edu
Contact: Dr. George Foster, Dean

Founded: 1972. **Members:** 100. **Description:** Teachers in schools and colleges of optometry. Works to enhance the professional and academic status and conditions of service of optometric educators and to promote communication among members. Concerned with faculty welfare, faculty-administration relations, faculty-student relations, and faculty-professional relations. **Conventions/Meetings:** annual Scientific and Educational Meeting, held in conjunction with the American Academy of Optometry.

8852 ■ Association of Pediatric Program Directors (APPD)

6728 Old McLean Village Dr.
McLean, VA 22101-3906
Ph: (703)556-9222
Fax: (703)556-8729
E-mail: info@appd.org
URL: http://www.appd.org
Contact: Laura E. Degnon CAE, Exec. Dir.

Founded: 1984. **Members:** 1,024. **Staff:** 3. **Description:** Directors of accredited pediatric residency programs. Seeks to advance the study, teaching, and practice of pediatrics. Facilitates communication and cooperation among members; supports research in clinical medicine as it relates to resident education. **Awards:** Carol Berkowitz Award. **Frequency:** annual. **Type:** recognition. **Recipient:** for lifetime advocacy and leadership in pediatric medical education ● Robert S. Holm, MD Leadership Award. **Frequency:** annual. **Type:** recognition. **Recipient:** to a program director or associate program director who has contributed extraordinary leadership. **Publications:** Newsletters. Alternate Formats: online. **Conventions/Meetings:** annual meeting.

8853 ■ Association of Professors of Medicine (APM)
2501 M St. NW, Ste.550
Washington, DC 20037-1325
Ph: (202)861-9351 (202)861-7700
Fax: (202)861-9731
E-mail: apm@im.org
URL: http://www.im.org/APM
Contact: William J. Bremner MD, Pres.
Founded: 1954. **Members:** 152. **Membership Dues:** institutional in U.S. (based on the size of the department of medicine), $4,000-$6,000 (annual) ● affiliate, $2,000 (annual) ● institutional in Canada, $3,100 (annual) ● affiliate in Canada, $1,500 (annual). **Staff:** 7. **Description:** Represents heads of departments of internal medicine in medical schools. Conducts educational programs; compiles statistics. **Awards:** APM Special Recognition Award. **Frequency:** annual. **Type:** recognition. **Recipient:** to a nonmember who has contributed most to helping the association meet its mission ● Robert H. Williams, MD, Distinguished Chair of Medicine Award. **Frequency:** annual. **Type:** recognition. **Recipient:** to a physician who has demonstrated outstanding leadership as the chair of a department of internal medicine. **Committees:** Communications; Education; Patient Care; Program Planning; Research. **Special Interest Groups:** Community-Based Schools; Research-Intensive Schools; Urban/Public Hospital Schools. **Formerly:** Academic Medicine Club. **Publications:** *The American Journal of Medicine*, monthly. Contains original clinical research of interest to physicians in internal medicine. Alternate Formats: online. Also Cited As: *The Green Journal* ● *APM Update*, quarterly. Newsletter. **Circulation:** 1,500 ● *Federal Health Policy Update*, quarterly. **Circulation:** 1,500 ● Directory, annual. **Conventions/Meetings:** annual meeting - always end of February ● annual symposium - every fall.

8854 ■ Association of Psychology Postdoctoral and Internship Centers (APPIC)
10 G St. NE, Ste.440
Washington, DC 20002
Ph: (202)589-0600
Fax: (202)589-0603
E-mail: appic@aol.com
URL: http://www.appic.org
Contact: Steve McCutcheon PhD, Chm.
Founded: 1968. **Members:** 550. **Membership Dues:** single, $400 (annual) ● combined, $600 (annual) ● regular, $250 (annual). **Staff:** 2. **Budget:** $500,000. **Description:** Veterans administration hospitals, medical centers, state hospitals, university counseling centers, and other facilities that provide internship and postdoctoral programs in professional psychology. Promotes activities that assist in the development of professional psychology training programs. Serves as a clearinghouse to provide Ph.D. candidates with internship placement assistance at member facilities. Conducts workshops and seminars on training procedures in clinical psychology at the PhD level. **Formerly:** (1991) Association of Psychology Internship Centers. **Publications:** *Internship and Postdoctoral Programs in Professional Psychology*, annual. Directory ● Newsletter, semiannual. **Price:** $10.00/issue. Alternate Formats: online. **Conventions/Meetings:** annual conference (exhibits).

8855 ■ Association of Schools of Allied Health Professions (ASAHP)
4400 Jenifer St. NW, Ste.333
Washington, DC 20015
Ph: (202)237-6481
Fax: (202)237-6485
E-mail: thomas@asahp.org
URL: http://www.asahp.org
Contact: Thomas W. Elwood PhD, Exec. Dir.
Founded: 1967. **Members:** 750. **Membership Dues:** institutional, $4,300 (annual). **Staff:** 3. **Description:** National allied health professional membership organizations, clinical service programs, academic institutions, and other institutions and organizations whose interests include the advancement of allied health education, research, and service delivery. Aims to: provide communication among schools and colleges of allied health professions; promote development of new programs; encourage research and provide liaison with other health organizations, professional groups, and educational and governmental institutions. Sponsors short-term institutes for allied health education, administration, and practice. Conducts research programs. **Awards:** Fellows Award. **Frequency:** periodic. **Type:** recognition ● New Investigator's Award. **Frequency:** periodic. **Type:** recognition ● Outstanding Educator Award. **Frequency:** periodic. **Type:** recognition ● Outstanding Researcher Award. **Frequency:** periodic. **Type:** recognition ● Scholarship of Excellence. **Frequency:** periodic. **Type:** scholarship. **Recipient:** to outstanding allied health students who are achieving excellence in their academic programs. **Computer Services:** Mailing lists. **Telecommunication Services:** electronic bulletin board, Special Net. **Committees:** Accreditation; Editorial; Education. **Formerly:** (1974) Association of Schools of Allied Health Professions; (1992) American Society of Allied Health Professions. **Publications:** *Journal of Allied Health*, quarterly. Contains scholarly works related to research and development, feature articles, research abstracts and book reviews. **Price:** $105.00/year in U.S.; $25.00/back issue in U.S.; $122.00/year outside U.S.; $30.00/back issue outside U.S. **Advertising:** accepted. Alternate Formats: online ● *Trends*, monthly. Newsletter. **Price:** $55.00. **Advertising:** accepted. Alternate Formats: online ● Directory, annual. **Conventions/Meetings:** annual conference ● annual meeting - always fall.

8856 ■ Association for Surgical Education (ASE)
SIU School of Medicine
Dept. of Surgery
PO Box 19655
Springfield, IL 62794-9655
Ph: (217)545-3835
E-mail: membershipo@surgicaleducation.com
URL: http://www.surgicaleducation.com
Contact: Susan Kepner MEd, Exec. Dir.
Founded: 1980. **Members:** 850. **Membership Dues:** individual, international, $175 (annual) ● institutional, $400 (annual). **Staff:** 2. **Budget:** $200,000. **Multinational. Description:** Surgeons and individuals involved or interested in undergraduate surgical education. Purpose is to develop and disseminate information on motivation, techniques, research, and applications for presenting curricula in undergraduate surgical education. Acts as forum for research in surgical education; serves as information clearinghouse. Compiles statistics; maintains speakers' bureau. Conducts educational programs. **Libraries: Type:** reference. **Holdings:** audiovisuals, books, periodicals. **Subjects:** surgical education. **Awards:** Best Paper Award. **Frequency:** annual. **Type:** recognition ● Presidential Teaching Award. **Frequency:** annual. **Type:** grant. **Recipient:** for research in surgical education. **Telecommunication Services:** electronic mail, skepner@siumed.edu. **Committees:** Curriculum; Faculty Development; Information Technology; Research in Surgical Education; Testing and Evaluation. **Publications:** *Focus on Surgical Education*, quarterly. Magazine. **Price:** included in membership dues. **Circulation:** 700. Alternate Formats: online. **Conventions/Meetings:** annual conference, mostly educational material; some surgical supplies (exhibits) - always April ● annual meeting.

8857 ■ Association of University Programs in Health Administration (AUPHA)
2000 N 14th St., Ste.780
Arlington, VA 22201
Ph: (703)894-0940
Fax: (703)894-0941
E-mail: aupha@aupha.org
URL: http://www.aupha.org
Contact: Lydia M. Reed MBA, Pres./CEO
Founded: 1948. **Members:** 1,200. **Membership Dues:** full, $2,300-$3,750 (annual) ● associate, $2,000-$3,250 (annual) ● affiliate, international program, $1,000 (annual) ● individual, $100 (annual) ● corporate, $500 (annual) ● international individual, $120 (annual). **Staff:** 7. **Budget:** $900,000. **Description:** Serves as global network of colleges, universities, faculty, individuals and organizations dedicated to the improvement of healthcare delivery through excellence in Health Administration Education. Includes the premier Baccalaureate and Masters degree programs in Health Administration Education in the United States and Canada for membership. **Libraries: Type:** reference. **Holdings:** 2,000; reports. **Subjects:** health services administration. **Awards:** Filerman Prize for Innovation. **Frequency:** annual. **Type:** recognition. **Recipient:** for distinguished service ● John D. Thompson Prize for Young Investigators. **Type:** recognition. **Recipient:** for young investigators. **Projects:** David A. Winston Health Policy Fellowship; Pedagogy Enhancement. **Formerly:** (1973) Association of University Programs in Hospital Administration. **Publications:** *AUPHA Exchange*, bimonthly. Newsletter ● *Health Services Administration Education*, biennial. Directory ● *Healthcare Management Education Directory*. **Price:** $45.00 for nonmembers; $40.00 additional copies for members; free for members ● *Journal of Health Administration Education*, quarterly. **Price:** $100.00 /year for individuals in U.S.; $120.00 /year for individuals outside U.S. ● *Year in Review*, annual. Annual Report. Alternate Formats: online. **Conventions/Meetings:** competition ● annual meeting (exhibits).

8858 ■ Coalition of National Health Education Organizations (CNHEO)
c/o Kathleen M. Conley, PhD, Coor.
Eastern Michigan Univ.
School of Hea. Promotion and Human Performance
318 Porter Bldg.
Ypsilanti, MI 48197
Ph: (734)487-7120 (734)671-5542
Fax: (734)487-2024
E-mail: kconley101@gmail.com
URL: http://www.cnheo.org
Contact: Kathleen M. Conley PhD, Coor.
Founded: 1972. **Members:** 10. **Membership Dues:** organizational, $200 (annual). **Description:** Represents national health education organizations, each represented by a delegate and an alternate. Facilitates coordination, collaboration and communication among the member organizations, to identify and discuss profession wide issues. Formulates recommendations, takes appropriate action, communicates information to the health education field, and serves as a focus for collaborative initiatives. **Conventions/Meetings:** annual meeting, for all delegates ● monthly meeting, conference call with all delegates.

8859 ■ Commission on Collegiate Nursing Education (CCNE)
1 Dupont Cir. NW, Ste.530
Washington, DC 20036
Ph: (202)887-6791
Fax: (202)887-8476
E-mail: jbutlin@aacn.nche.edu
URL: http://www.aacn.nche.edu/accreditation
Contact: Jennifer Butlin, Dir.
Founded: 1996. **Description:** Serves as an autonomous accrediting agency contributing to the improvement of public health. Ensures the quality and integrity of baccalaureate and graduate education programs preparing effective nurses. **Publications:** Annual Report, annual. Alternate Formats: online.

8860 ■ Comprehensive Health Education Foundation (CHEF)
22419 Pacific Hwy. S
Seattle, WA 98198-5106
Ph: (206)824-2907
Free: (800)323-2433

Fax: (206)824-3072
E-mail: info@chef.org
URL: http://www.chef.org
Contact: Larry Clark, Pres./CEO
Founded: 1974. **Staff:** 40. **Description:** Promotes health and quality of life through education, addressing such important topics as drug abuse, violence, HIV/AIDS, smoking, obesity, and other unhealthy behaviors. **Conventions/Meetings:** quarterly board meeting - always in Seattle, WA.

8861 ■ Council on Medical Student Education in Pediatrics (COMSEP)
c/o Robin Deterding, MD, Pres.
Off. of Medical Affairs
Dept. of Pediatrics
1056 E 19th Ave., B395
Denver, CO 80218-1007
Ph: (303)861-6867
Fax: (303)837-2924
E-mail: deterding.robin@tchden.org
URL: http://www.comsep.org
Contact: Robin Deterding MD, Pres.
Founded: 1992. **Description:** Fosters excellence in undergraduate medical education in pediatrics. Promotes the development, dissemination, and evaluation of curricular materials and educational resources. Advocates for research in pediatric medical education. **Publications:** *The Pediatric Educator*, semiannual. Newsletter. Contains task force updates, journal reviews, and organizational updates. Alternate Formats: online. **Conventions/Meetings:** annual meeting.

8862 ■ Global Alliance for Medical Education (GAME)
c/o Celene Chasen, Membership Chair
Off. of Continuing Medical Educ.
Baylor Coll. of Medicine
1709 Dryden Rd., Ste.1218
Houston, TX 77030-2404
Ph: (713)798-4024
Fax: (713)798-6600
E-mail: membership@game-cme.org
URL: http://www.game-cme.org
Contact: James Arnott, Pres.
Membership Dues: regular, $100 (annual). **Multinational. Description:** Represents the interests of medical education professionals. Advances innovation in medical education throughout the world. Provides an international forum where thought leaders network and share innovative ideas in continuing medical education. **Telecommunication Services:** electronic mail, jarnott6@cs.com. **Publications:** Newsletter. **Price:** included in membership dues. Alternate Formats: online.

8863 ■ Health Occupations Students of America (HOSA)
6021 Morriss Rd., Ste.111
Flower Mound, TX 75028
Free: (800)321-HOSA
Fax: (972)874-0063
E-mail: hosa@hosa.org
URL: http://www.hosa.org
Contact: Heather Coggins, Pres.
Founded: 1975. **Members:** 52,000. **Membership Dues:** general, $10 (annual). **Budget:** $750,000. **State Groups:** 36. **Local Groups:** 2,100. **Description:** Secondary and postsecondary students enrolled in health occupations education programs; health professionals and others interested in assisting and supporting the activities of HOSA; alumni of health occupations education programs and individuals who have made significant contributions to the field. Improves the quality of healthcare for all Americans by urging members to develop self-improvement skills. Operates within health occupation education programs in public high schools and postsecondary institutions. Encourages members to develop an understanding of current healthcare issues, environmental concerns, and survival needs worldwide. Conducts programs to help individuals improve their occupational skills and develop leadership qualities. Conducts exhibits, management workshops, and medical facility tours; provides social and recreational activities. Maintains speakers' bureau; compiles statistics. **Computer Services:** database ● mailing lists ● online services, chat rooms. **Committees:** Competitive Events; People Development. **Divisions:** Alumni; Associate; Collegiate; Postsecondary; Professional; Secondary. **Affiliated With:** Association for Career and Technical Education. **Also Known As:** National HOSA. **Publications:** *HOSA E-Magazine*. Alternate Formats: online ● *HOSA Leaders Directory*, annual ● *HOSA Leaders' Update*, quarterly ● *Story of HOSA*. Video ● Brochure ● Handbook. Alternate Formats: online ● Also publishes recruitment package. **Conventions/Meetings:** competition ● annual National Leadership - conference (exhibits) - always third week in June. 2008 June 18-21, Dallas, TX; 2009 June 24-27, Nashville, TN.

8864 ■ Hispanic-Serving Health Professions Schools (HSHPS)
1120 Connecticut Ave. NW, Ste.261
Washington, DC 20036
Ph: (202)293-2701
Fax: (202)293-2704
E-mail: hshps@hshps.org
URL: http://www.hshps.com
Contact: Maria Soto-Greene MD, Pres./CEO
Founded: 1996. **Members:** 22. **Membership Dues:** medical school, $5,000 (annual) ● school of public health, $2,500 (annual). **Staff:** 3. **Description:** Represents 16 medical schools. Seeks to strengthen the nation's capacity to educate and increase the numbers of high-quality Hispanic health care providers to serve and improve the health status of Hispanics and other populations. Develops educational opportunities in health professions schools in curriculum, research, and clinical experiences that will enable Hispanic and non-Hispanic health professions students to provide excellent health care to Hispanic populations. Promotes collaboration at the regional and national levels among educational institutions, communities, and other partners. **Telecommunication Services:** electronic mail, msoto@hshps.org. **Programs:** HSHPS/CDC Student Internship; HSHPS/OMH Research Fellowship. **Projects:** Potential Extramural. **Formerly:** (2003) National Association of Hispanic-Serving Health Professions Schools. **Publications:** *HSHPS News Flash*, biweekly. Newsletter. Contains information on current events within HSHPS. Alternate Formats: online ● *HSPS Newsletter*, semiannual. Contains non-time sensitive information for students, faculty, researchers, and health policy advocates. Alternate Formats: online.

8865 ■ Indians Into Medicine (INMED)
UNDSMHS, Rm. 2101
501 N Columbia Rd., Stop 9037
Grand Forks, ND 58202-9037
Ph: (701)777-3037 (701)777-3039
Fax: (701)777-3277
E-mail: inmed@medicine.nodak.edu
URL: http://www.med.und.edu/depts/inmed/home.html
Contact: Eugene DeLorme JD, Dir.
Founded: 1973. **Staff:** 9. **Description:** Support program for American Indian students. Seeks to: increase the awareness of and interest in healthcare professions among young American Indians; recruit and enroll American Indians in healthcare education programs; place American health professionals in service to Indian communities. Coordinates financial and personal support for students in healthcare curricula. Provides referral and counseling services. Provides summer enrichment sessions at the junior high, high school and pre-medical levels as well as academic year support for college and professional level students. **Libraries: Type:** not open to the public. **Holdings:** 2,000. **Subjects:** medical, cultural, study aids. **Computer Services:** database, financial aid sources. **Publications:** *Serpent, Staff and Drum*, semiannual. Newsletter. **Price:** free for members. Alternate Formats: online ● Also publishes program information and motivational materials. **Conventions/Meetings:** periodic Educational Conference ● annual Summer Academic Enrichment Sessions - meeting.

8866 ■ National Association of Advisors for the Health Professions (NAAHP)
PO Box 1518
Champaign, IL 61824-1518
Ph: (217)355-0063
Fax: (217)355-1287
E-mail: naahpja@aol.com
URL: http://www.naahp.org
Contact: Susan A. Maxwell, Exec. Dir.
Founded: 1974. **Members:** 1,275. **Membership Dues:** regular, $110 (annual) ● full, patron, $350 (annual) ● patron associate, $175 (annual) ● associate (minimum; varies by region), $85 (annual) ● emeritus, $20 (annual). **Staff:** 5. **Budget:** $230,000. **Regional Groups:** 4. **Description:** College and university faculty who advise and counsel students on health careers. Seeks to improve and preserve advisement at all educational levels of the health professions. Fosters and coordinates communication among the health professions and advisers. Marshalls resources; provides services concerning health professions advisement. Aims to provide counseling and proper preparation of student evaluations for the professional schools and participation of advisers in curriculum development. Improves communication, coordination of record keeping, and information exchange among undergraduate schools and local, state, and regional preprofessional programs. Makes available Advisor's Supplementary Student Evaluation Tool software program; conducts surveys. **Libraries: Type:** reference; not open to the public. **Holdings:** 5,000; archival material, audiovisuals, books, clippings, periodicals. **Subjects:** health profession advising. **Awards: Type:** recognition. **Computer Services:** database ● mailing lists. **Committees:** Editorial; Ethics; Public Issues. **Publications:** *Directory of the National Association of Advisors for the Health Professions*, annual. Includes health professional school announcements and order forms. **Price:** $25.00/issue. **Circulation:** 1,200. **Advertising:** accepted ● *Interviewing for Health Professions Schools*. Booklet. **Price:** $4.00 for members; $6.00 for nonmembers ● *National Association of Advisors for the Health Professions—The Advisor*, quarterly. Journal. Focuses on manpower statistics, financial aid, admission procedures, curriculum, advising, recruitment, counseling practice, and ethics. **Price:** included in membership dues. ISSN: 0736-0436. **Circulation:** 1,200 ● *Premedical Advisor's Reference Manual*. **Price:** $25.00/copy for members; $28.00/copy for nonmembers ● *Strategy for Success: A Handbook for Prehealth Students* ● *Write for Success*. **Price:** $10.00 for members; $13.00 for nonmembers. **Conventions/Meetings:** biennial Strengthening Our Connections: Partnerships in the 21st Century - meeting (exhibits) - 2008 June 25-29, Chicago, IL.

8867 ■ National Association of EMS Educators (NAEMSE)
Foster Plz. 6
681 Anderson Dr.
Pittsburgh, PA 15220-2766
Ph: (412)920-4775
Fax: (412)920-4780
E-mail: naemse@naemse.org
URL: http://www.naemse.org
Contact: Joann Freel, Exec. Dir.
Founded: 1996. **Members:** 2,038. **Membership Dues:** individual in U.S., $70-$80 (annual) ● individual outside U.S., $85-$95 (annual). **Staff:** 5. **Budget:** $600,000. **Multinational. Description:** Promotes EMS education, develops and delivers educational resources, and advocates research and life long learning. **Committees:** Distributed Learning; Education; Endorsement; Finance; Membership; Nominating; Program; Publications; Research; Standards and Practices. **Publications:** *Domain3*, quarterly. Journal. Features teaching tips, current research, and educator's toolbox. **Price:** included in membership dues. Alternate Formats: online ● *Educator Update*, monthly. Newsletter. **Advertising:** accepted. Alternate Formats: online. **Conventions/Meetings:** annual EMS Educational Symposium - meeting and symposium, for the EMS trade (exhibits).

8868 ■ National Association of Medical Minority Educators (NAMME)
c/o Dr. Dorothy C. Dobbins, Budget and Finance Chair
East Tennessee State Univ.
Off. of Cultural Affairs
Division of Hea. Sciences
Box 70599
Johnson City, TN 37614-0734
Ph: (423)439-2144
Fax: (423)439-8090
E-mail: dobbinsd@etsu.edu
URL: http://www.nammenational.org
Contact: Dr. Dorothy C. Dobbins, Budget and Finance Chair

Founded: 1975. **Members:** 200. **Membership Dues:** regular, $125 (annual) ● associate, $100 (annual) ● student, $35 (annual). **Regional Groups:** 4. **Description:** Educators, administrators, and practitioners of medicine, osteopathic medicine, dentistry, veterinary medicine, optometry, podiatry, public health, and allied health. Promotes the increase of medical minority personnel; admissions of minority students to health professionals' schools; retention and graduation of minority students in health profession schools; recruitment and development of minority faculty administrators and managerial personnel in the health professions; delivery of quality health care for minority populations; and recruitment, retention, and development of minority students in pre-health profession programs. Sponsors workshops for high school counselors and junior high and high school science teachers; provides training for minority affairs workers and officers. Offers annual student development sessions and recruitment fairs. Conducts research programs and systematic studies. **Libraries: Type:** reference. **Holdings:** archival material. **Awards:** NAMME Scholarship. **Frequency:** annual. **Type:** scholarship. **Recipient:** to underrepresented minority students who have completed the first year of health professions training. **Publications:** *Financing Your Medical Education*, annual. Book ● *James Stills Quarterly - NAMME Edition*. Newsletter. **Conventions/Meetings:** annual conference (exhibits) ● annual regional meeting.

8869 ■ National Association for Practical Nurse Education and Service (NAPNES)
PO Box 25647
Alexandria, VA 22314
Ph: (703)933-1003
Fax: (703)940-4089
E-mail: jbova@napnes.org
URL: http://www.napnes.org
Contact: Mattie P. Marshall LPN, Pres.

Founded: 1941. **Members:** 30,000. **Membership Dues:** student, $25 (annual) ● associate, $35 (annual) ● individual, $75 (annual) ● agency, $100 (annual) ● life, $500. **Staff:** 5. **State Groups:** 20. **Description:** Licensed practical/vocational nurses, registered nurses, physicians, hospital and nursing home administrators, and interested others. Provides consultation service to advise schools wishing to develop a practical/vocational nursing program on facilities, equipment, policies, curriculum, and staffing. Promotes recruitment of students through preparation and distribution of recruitment materials. Sponsors seminars for directors and instructors in schools of practical/vocational nursing and continuing education programs for LPNs/LVNs; approves continuing education programs and awards contact hours; holds national certification courses in post licensure specialties such as pharmacology, long term care and gerontics. **Computer Services:** database, Continuing Education Record Keeping System for LPNs (CERKS). **Committees:** P/VN Educators. **Councils:** Executive Secretaries. **Absorbed:** (1985) National Association of Licensed Practical Nurses. **Publications:** *Journal of Practical Nursing*, quarterly. Contains news of association activities, nursing law, and pending legislation affecting the nursing profession. **Price:** included in membership dues; $25.00 /year for nonmembers in U.S.; $70.00 /year for nonmembers outside U.S. ISSN: 0022-3867. **Circulation:** 10,000. **Advertising:** accepted ● *NAPNES Forum*, 8/year. Journal. Serves as a supplement to the *Journal of Practical Nursing*. ● Also publishes brochures, pamphlets, and reprints. **Conventions/Meetings:** annual convention (exhibits).

8870 ■ National Association of Supervisors and Administrators of Health Occupations Education (NASAHOE)
Address Unknown since 2008
URL: http://www.pen.k12.va.us

Members: 35. **Description:** State administrators and local supervisors of health occupations education. Acts as resource sharing group, particularly in the area of curriculum development. Seeks to develop shared resources for recruitment. **Formerly:** (1988) National Association for State Administrators of Health Occupations Education. **Publications:** *NASAHOE News*, quarterly. Newsletter. **Conventions/Meetings:** annual meeting, held in conjunction with American Vocational Association ● biennial meeting.

8871 ■ National Medical Fellowships (NMF)
5 Hanover Sq., 15th Fl.
New York, NY 10004
Ph: (212)483-8880
Fax: (212)483-8897
E-mail: nmf1@nmfonline.org
URL: http://www.nmfonline.org
Contact: Daniel T. McGowan, Chm.

Founded: 1946. **Staff:** 16. **Regional Groups:** 2. **Description:** Promotes education of minority students in medicine. Provides need-based scholarships, special merit awards, and leadership opportunities to medical students of African American, Native American, Mexican American and mainland Puerto Rican heritage. **Awards:** Aura E. Severinghaus Award. **Frequency:** annual. **Type:** recognition. **Recipient:** to a senior minority student attending Columbia University's College of Physicians and Surgeons ● Hugh J. Andersen Memorial Scholarships. **Frequency:** annual. **Type:** scholarship. **Recipient:** to Minnesota residents enrolled in any accredited U.S. medical school or students attending Minnesota medical schools ● Irving Graef Memorial Scholarship. **Frequency:** annual. **Type:** scholarship. **Recipient:** to a third-year student in recognition of outstanding academic achievement, leadership and community service ● William and Charlotte Cadbury Award. **Frequency:** annual. **Type:** recognition. **Recipient:** to a senior medical student in recognition of outstanding academic achievement, leadership and community service. **Formerly:** (1952) Provident Medical Associates. **Publications:** *NMF Update*, quarterly ● Newsletter ● Annual Report.

8872 ■ National Resident Matching Program (NRMP)
2450 N St. NW
Washington, DC 20037-1118
Ph: (202)828-0566 (202)828-0676
Free: (866)617-5834
Fax: (202)828-4797
E-mail: nrmp@aamc.org
URL: http://www.nrmp.org
Contact: Mona M. Signer MPH, Exec. Dir.

Founded: 1952. **Description:** National clearinghouse for matching the preferences of medical school graduates for medical residencies in the U.S. with the hospitals' choices of applicants. Runs matches for 17 medical sub-specialty fellowships. **Formerly:** (1953) National InterAssociation Committee on Internships; (1968) National Intern Matching Program; (1978) National Intern and Resident Matching Program. **Publications:** *NRMP Data*, annual. Booklet. **Price:** $35.00. **Conventions/Meetings:** semiannual board meeting.

8873 ■ National Student Nurses' Association (NSNA)
45 Main St., Ste.606
Brooklyn, NY 11201
Ph: (718)210-0705
Fax: (718)210-0710
E-mail: nsna@nsna.org
URL: http://www.nsna.org
Contact: Diane J. Mancino EdD, Exec. Dir.

Founded: 1952. **Members:** 50,000. **Membership Dues:** sustaining new graduate, $30 (annual) ● sustaining individual, $50 (annual) ● sustaining local, state, national organization, $250 (annual). **Staff:** 12. **Budget:** $2,500,000. **State Groups:** 48. **Local Groups:** 500. **Description:** Students enrolled in state-approved schools for the preparation of registered nurses. Seeks to aid in the development of the individual nursing student and to urge students of nursing, as future leaders and health professionals, to be aware of and to contribute to improving the health care of all people. Encourages programs and activities in state groups concerning nursing, health, and the community. Provides assistance for state board review, as well as materials for preparation for state RN licensing examination. Cooperates with nursing organizations in recruitment of nurses and in professional, community, and civic programs. Sponsors Foundation of the National Student Nurses' Association in memory of Frances Tompkins. **Awards:** Student Scholarship Program. **Frequency:** annual. **Type:** scholarship. **Recipient:** to student nurses. **Publications:** *Dean's Notes*, 5/year ● *Imprint*, 5/year. Magazine. Features issues and trends of concern to nursing students. **Price:** included in membership dues; $5.00/single copy for nonmembers. **Circulation:** 35,000. **Advertising:** accepted. Alternate Formats: online ● *NSNA News*, semiannual. Newsletter. **Advertising:** accepted. **Conventions/Meetings:** annual conference, features an exhibit hall, keynote speaker and endnote address, and topics that specifically explore specialty nursing areas and career issues for nursing students (exhibits) - every November ● annual convention, with keynote speaker, exhibit hall, focus sessions, awards ceremony, association activity seminars, and an auction (exhibits) - 2009 Apr. 15-19, Nashville, TN.

8874 ■ North American Association of Medical Education and Communication Companies (NAAMECC)
3416 Primm Ln.
Birmingham, AL 35216
Ph: (205)824-7612
Fax: (205)823-2760
E-mail: info@naamecc.org
URL: http://www.naamecc.org
Contact: Karen Overstreet, Pres.

Founded: 2002. **Membership Dues:** organization, $1,200 (annual). **Description:** Provides representation, advocacy and education for its members. Strengthens the understanding between MECCs, commercial supporters, and other types of Continuing Medical Education (CME) providers. Examines ways to elevate the best practices of MECCs. Serves as a forum for discussion of issues, problems and opportunities relevant to MECCs. **Awards:** Best Practice and Exemplary CME Professional Awards. **Frequency:** annual. **Type:** recognition. **Recipient:** to individuals and organizations for exceptional contributions to CME. **Telecommunication Services:** electronic mail, karen.overstreet@indiciaed.com. **Publications:** Manual. Alternate Formats: online.

8875 ■ Society for Academic Continuing Medical Education (SACME)
c/o Prime Management Services
3416 Primm Ln.
Birmingham, AL 35216
Ph: (205)978-7990
Fax: (205)823-2760
E-mail: sacme@primemanagement.net
URL: http://sacme.org
Contact: Craig M. Campbell MD, Chair

Members: 200. **Membership Dues:** general, $425 (annual). **Regional Groups:** 4. **Multinational. Description:** Advances the research, evaluation and development of effective continuing medical education. Improves patient care and increases the competency of physicians. **Awards:** SACME Endowment Council Manning Award. **Frequency:** biennial. **Type:** grant. **Recipient:** for potential contribution in the field of continuing medical education ● SACME Endowment Council Research Grant. **Frequency:** biennial. **Type:** grant. **Recipient:** for a project that advances the current knowledge of continuing medical education. **Computer Services:** database, member directory ● information services, medical and health resources ● mailing lists, members listserv. **Telecommunication Services:** electronic mail, sacme@lists.wayne.edu. **Committees:** Awards; Communications; Program; Research. **Publications:** *Intercom*, 3/year. Newsletter. Features activities and management information. Alternate Formats: online ● *Journal of Continuing Education in the Health Professions*, quarterly. Includes articles relevant to the theory and practice of continuing education in the health sciences. Alternate Formats: online. Also Cited As: *JCEHP*. **Conventions/Meetings:** biennial meeting.

8876 ■ Student National Medical Association (SNMA)
5113 Georgia Ave. NW
Washington, DC 20011
Ph: (202)882-2881
Fax: (202)882-2886
E-mail: snma@snma.org
URL: http://www.snma.org
Contact: Wallace Davenport II, Exec. Dir.
Founded: 1964. **Members:** 6,000. **Membership Dues:** active, $60 (quadrennial) ● associate, $15 (annual) ● physician, patron, $30 (annual) ● institution, $100 (annual) ● corporate, $500 (annual). **Staff:** 3. **Budget:** $500,000. **Regional Groups:** 10. **Local Groups:** 155. **Description:** Medical students, residents, and undergraduates of color. Seeks to help students in recruitment, admission, and retention in medical school and publishes information on problems and achievement in this area. Conducts annual research forum and community service projects. **Awards:** Research Forum Scientific Competition. **Frequency:** annual. **Type:** recognition. **Computer Services:** Mailing lists. **Telecommunication Services:** electronic mail, execdir@snma.org. **Programs:** Health Professions Recruitment Exposure; Tissue and Organ Donation Education and Recruitment; Youth Science Enrichment. **Publications:** *Journal of the Student National Medical Association*, quarterly. Includes topics about medical education, research publication, health advocacy, mentorship, career opportunities and others. **Price:** included in membership dues; $30.00 /year for nonmembers. **Circulation:** 20,000. Alternate Formats: CD-ROM; online; magnetic tape. Also Cited As: *JSNMA* ● *SNMA News*, quarterly. Newsletter. **Circulation:** 5,000. **Advertising:** accepted. Alternate Formats: online. **Conventions/Meetings:** annual Medical Education - conference (exhibits).

Medical Examiners

8877 ■ American Board of Independent Medical Examiners (ABIME)
1338 3rd Ave.
Huntington, WV 25701
Ph: (304)523-1415 (304)523-1416
Free: (877)523-1415
Fax: (304)523-1824
E-mail: info@abime.org
URL: http://www.abime.org
Contact: Prof. Mohammed Ranavaya MD, Pres.
Founded: 1994. **Members:** 2,500. **Membership Dues:** Board of Registry, $185 (annual). **Staff:** 3. **Budget:** $800,000. **Multinational. Description:** Educates and certifies physicians to perform independent medical examinations. Works to improve the quality of independent medical exams by setting and maintaining standards and promoting physicians who meet those standards. **Awards:** Certified Independent Medical Examiner. **Frequency:** 5/year. **Type:** fellowship. **Recipient:** to doctors after accomplishing a satisfactory training and passing a certification exam. **Committees:** Examination; Standards. **Publications:** *ABIME National Directory*. **Price:** $100.00 ● *Disability Medicine*, quarterly. Journal. **Price:** $100.00. **Advertising:** accepted. Alternate Formats: online ● *Lecture Notes for ABIME Exam Review Course*. Handbook. **Price:** $150.00. **Advertising:** accepted.

Mental Health

8878 ■ Association for Advanced Training in the Behavioral Sciences (AATBS)
5126 Ralston St.
Ventura, CA 93003
Ph: (805)676-3030
Free: (800)472-1931
Fax: (805)676-3033
E-mail: info@aatbs.com
URL: http://www.aatbs.com
Description: Aims to produce study materials in order to provide education and training for psychologists, marriage and family therapists, social workers, mental health counselors and alcohol/drug counselors to pass professional exams. **Conventions/Meetings:** workshop, for training.

Methodist

8879 ■ National Association of Schools, Colleges and Universities of the United Methodist Church (NASCUMC)
PO Box 340007
Nashville, TN 37203-0007
Ph: (615)340-7399
Fax: (615)340-7379
E-mail: kbedell@gbhem.org
Contact: Dr. Ken Bedell, Sec.-Treas.
Founded: 1940. **Members:** 123. **Membership Dues:** school, $150 (annual) ● college, $450 (annual) ● university, $550 (annual). **Staff:** 2. **Budget:** $50,000. **Description:** Schools, colleges, and universities related to the United Methodist Church. Sponsors training institutes for college administrators. **Publications:** *Directory of Chief Executive Officers of United Methodist Schools, Colleges, Universities, and Theological Schools*, annual. **Conventions/Meetings:** semiannual conference - usually February and July ● semiannual seminar.

Middle East

8880 ■ Syrian Studies Association (SSA)
c/o Prof. Peter Sluglett, Pres.
Carlson Hall
214 C Hall History
380 S 1400 E, Rm. 211
Salt Lake City, UT 84112
E-mail: sluglett@aol.com
URL: http://www.ou.edu/ssa
Contact: Prof. Peter Sluglett, Pres.
Founded: 1993. **Membership Dues:** regular, $25 (annual) ● regular, $47 (biennial) ● regular, $69 (triennial) ● joint, $35 (annual) ● student, $10 (annual) ● institutional, $100 (annual). **Multinational. Description:** Promotes research and scholarly understanding of Syria in all periods and in all academic disciplines. Fosters high standards of scholarship and instruction. Facilitates communication among its members. Encourages dialogue between Middle Eastern, Western, and all scholars of the Middle East. **Awards:** SSA Prizes for Best Writing on Syria. **Frequency:** annual. **Type:** recognition. **Recipient:** for best written work on Syria. **Affiliated With:** Middle East Studies Association of North America. **Publications:** Newsletter, semiannual. **Price:** included in membership dues. Alternate Formats: online.

Middle Schools

8881 ■ National Middle School Association (NMSA)
4151 Executive Pkwy., Ste.300
Westerville, OH 43081
Ph: (614)895-4730
Free: (800)528-6672
Fax: (614)895-4750
E-mail: info@nmsa.org
URL: http://www.nmsa.org
Contact: Ms. Sue Swaim, Exec. Dir.
Founded: 1973. **Members:** 30,000. **Membership Dues:** individual, $65 (annual) ● institutional, $219 (annual) ● institutional plus, $349 (annual) ● college student, parent, retiree, $40 (annual). **Staff:** 30. **Budget:** $6,000,000. **Regional Groups:** 1. **State Groups:** 48. **National Groups:** 2. **Description:** Educators, families, and community members interested in the education and well-being of young adolescents. Provides forums for the sharing of ideas and innovations; cooperates with organizations and associations with common interests. **Awards:** Distinguished Educator Award. **Frequency:** annual. **Type:** recognition. **Recipient:** for outstanding practitioners in middle level education who have made a significant impact on the lives of young adolescents through leadership, vision, and advocacy ● John H. Lounsbury Award. **Frequency:** periodic. **Type:** recognition. **Recipient:** to an individual who has demonstrated a level of service, integrity, and leadership in middle level education ● Teams That Make a Difference. **Frequency:** annual. **Type:** recognition. **Recipient:** for teams of any kind-teachers, administrators, parents, community members, or any combination of these individuals. **Formerly:** (1973) Midwest Middle School Association. **Publications:** *Middle Ground*, quarterly, every August, October, February, and April. Magazine. Provides a voice and a resource for those committed to the educational and developmental needs of young adolescents. **Price:** included in membership dues. ISSN: 1094-6675. **Circulation:** 30,000. **Advertising:** accepted ● *Middle School Journal*, 5/year. Contains articles based on educational research and promotes middle level education. **Price:** included in membership dues; $40.00 /year for nonmembers. **Circulation:** 34,000. **Advertising:** accepted ● *Research in Middle Level Education*, quarterly. Journal. Alternate Formats: online ● Books ● Monographs. **Conventions/Meetings:** annual conference, attracts over 10,000 attendees; includes over 500 sessions addressing issues relevant to middle level educators (exhibits) - always November ● conference - 10/year.

Military

8882 ■ Association of Graduates (AOG)
U.S. Air Force Acad.
3116 Acad. Dr.
USAF Academy, CO 80840-4475
Ph: (719)472-0300
Fax: (719)333-4194
E-mail: aog@usafa.org
URL: http://www.usafa.org
Contact: Jim Shaw, Pres./CEO
Founded: 1869. **Members:** 59,300. **Membership Dues:** graduate, parent, friend, $50 (annual) ● life (graduate, parent, friend, upper-class cadet), $700 ● life (fourth-class cadet), $600. **Description:** Graduates of the United States Military Academy (West Point); membership currently includes all graduates still living. Promotes the welfare of, and raises money for the academy; helps to improve the education and training of the cadets by providing funds beyond the minimum normal appropriations. Has approximately 120 local and state chapters known as West Point Societies. Compiles statistics; offers career advisory services. **Libraries: Type:** not open to the public. **Holdings:** 1,500; books, periodicals. **Subjects:** historical data on West Point, West Point graduates. **Awards:** Distinguished Graduate Award. **Frequency:** annual. **Type:** recognition. **Recipient:** for a living graduate who exemplifies the West Point motto of Duty, Honor, Country in their life and career ● Sylvanus Thayer Award. **Frequency:** annual. **Type:** recognition. **Recipient:** for an American citizen, not a graduate, who best epitomizes West Point motto of Duty, Honor, Country in his life and career. **Computer Services:** database, addresses and biographical data on United States Military Academy graduates, parents of cadets, friends, widows, and former cadets. **Publi-**

cations: *ASSEMBLY*, bimonthly. Magazine. Includes extensive coverage of class activities, memorial articles, feature articles, and book reviews. **Price:** $40.00/year. ISSN: 1041-2581. **Circulation:** 24,000. **Advertising:** accepted ● *Financial Reports.* Alternate Formats: online ● *Register of Graduates*, annual. Directory. Contains biographies of living graduates, historical data, and feature articles. **Price:** $45.00/ copy. **Circulation:** 14,000. **Advertising:** accepted. **Conventions/Meetings:** board meeting - 3/year.

8883 ■ Association of Military Colleges and Schools of the United States (AMCSUS)
c/o Dr. Rudolph H. Ehrenberg, Jr., Exec. Dir.
3604 Glenbrook Rd.
Fairfax, VA 22031-3211
Ph: (703)272-8406
E-mail: amcsus@cox.net
URL: http://www.amcsus.org
Contact: Dr. Rudolph H. Ehrenberg Jr., Exec. Dir.
Founded: 1914. **Members:** 42. **Staff:** 1. **Description:** Comprises of military colleges and secondary schools. **Awards:** President's Medal. **Frequency:** annual. **Type:** medal. **Recipient:** to one cadet from each member college and school. **Absorbed:** (1972) National Association of Military Schools. **Formerly:** (2003) Association of Military Colleges and Schools of the U.S. **Publications:** *Membership Listing*, annual. Membership Directory. **Conventions/Meetings:** annual conference (exhibits).

8884 ■ Association of NROTC Colleges and Universities
c/o Jennifer Ashbaugh, Admin. Off.
Univ. of Rochester
33A Wallis Hall
PO Box 270041
Rochester, NY 14627-0041
Ph: (585)275-2096
Fax: (585)275-8531
E-mail: jennifer.ashbaugh@rochester.edu
URL: http://www.conferences.rochester.edu/NROTC-constitution.html
Contact: Jennifer Ashbaugh, Admin. Off.
Founded: 1946. **Members:** 63. **Membership Dues:** regular, $200 (annual). **Description:** Representatives from colleges and universities that have Naval Reserve Officers Training Corps units on their campuses. Promotes NROTC training and coordinates the efforts of institutions offering this service. **Formerly:** (1994) Association of Naval ROTC Colleges and Universities. **Conventions/Meetings:** annual conference.

8885 ■ Military Impacted Schools Association (MISA)
1600 Hwy. 370
Bellevue, NE 68005
Ph: (402)293-4000
Free: (800)291-MISA
E-mail: cbellevue@aol.com
URL: http://www.militaryimpactedschoolsassociation.org
Contact: John F. Deegan EdD, Exec. Dir.
Founded: 1986. **Description:** Provides the educational needs of military families, including quality of life initiatives, community and school district support, and aid funding.

Military Families

8886 ■ Military Child Education Coalition (MCEC)
PO Box 2519
Harker Heights, TX 76548-2519
Ph: (254)953-1923
Fax: (254)953-1925
E-mail: mary.keller@militarychild.org
URL: http://www.militarychild.org
Contact: Dr. Mary M. Keller, Exec. Dir.
Membership Dues: individual, $36 ● organization, $75 ● school district/military installation, $750. **Multinational. Description:** Identifies the problems faced by military children and implements programs that deal with such challenges. Aims to level the educational playing field for military children. Shares information in order to develop systems and processes to resolve transition issues for military students. Coordinates with educational institutions for communication and networking. **Awards:** Bernard Brown II Space Camp Scholarship. **Frequency:** annual. **Type:** scholarship. **Recipient:** for military children enrolled in grades 6 to 9 ● Pete Taylor Partnership of Excellence Award. **Frequency:** annual. **Type:** recognition. **Recipient:** for joint-effort projects of a military installation and a school district. **Publications:** *Deployment Booklet.* **Price:** $1.50. Alternate Formats: online ● *Guard and Reserve Booklet.* Contains information about the National Guard and the Reserves. **Price:** $1.50. Alternate Formats: online ● *Military Child Education News.* Newsletter. Contains news and articles on military children and their families. Alternate Formats: online ● *The Military Parents' Guide to No Child Left Behind.* Booklet. Offers an overview of the major provisions of the No Child Left Behind Act. **Price:** $3.50 ● *Preparing for the Journey - Birth through Grade 2.* Book.

Minorities

8887 ■ Center for Advancement of Racial and Ethnic Equity (CAREE)
One Dupont Cir. NW
Washington, DC 20036-1193
Ph: (202)939-9395 (202)939-9300
Fax: (202)785-2990
E-mail: diana_cordova@ace.nche.edu
URL: http://www.acenet.edu
Contact: Diana I. Cordova, Dir.
Founded: 1981. **Description:** Works to provide information on the educational status of minorities. Provides assistance to colleges and universities seeking to improve their recruitment and retention of minority students. **Projects:** ACE's Minority Initiative. **Formerly:** (2005) Office of Minorities in Higher Education. **Publications:** *Status Report on Minorities in Higher Education*, annual. Contains information on minorities in higher education. **Conventions/Meetings:** biennial Educating All of One Nation - conference.

8888 ■ Dialogue on Diversity
1000 Connecticut Ave. NW, Ste.600
Washington, DC 20036
Ph: (703)631-0650
Fax: (703)631-0617
E-mail: dialog.div@prodigy.net
URL: http://www.dialogueondiversity.org
Contact: Ma. Cristina C. Caballero, Pres./CEO
Founded: 1989. **Membership Dues:** benefactor, $10,000 (annual) ● patron platinum, $5,000 (annual) ● patron gold, $2,500 (annual) ● patron silver, $1,000 (annual) ● sponsor, $500 (annual) ● corporate non-profit/associate, $250 (annual) ● advocate, $750 (annual) ● entrepreneur, $150 (annual) ● student, $15 (annual) ● senior, $10 (annual). **Description:** Promotes social and political advancement of women and men from diverse ethnic and national traditions; fosters increased economic empowerment; aims to promote and develop entrepreneurial excellence, technology, networking, and education. **Awards:** **Frequency:** annual. **Type:** recognition. **Committees:** Communications/Newsletter; Elections/Award Nominations; Fundraising; Internship; Membership; Mentorship; Organization Development; Programs/Events; Public Relations; Scholarship. **Publications:** Newsletter. **Price:** included in membership dues. Alternate Formats: online. **Conventions/Meetings:** seminar.

Minority Students

8889 ■ America Council on Education, Center for Advancement of Racial and Ethnic Equity (CAREE)
One Dupont Cir. NW
Washington, DC 20036-1193
Ph: (202)939-9300 (202)939-9395
Fax: (202)785-2990
E-mail: comments@ace.nche.edu
URL: http://www.acenet.edu/AM/Template.cfm?Section=CAREE
Contact: Diana I. Cordova, Dir.
Founded: 1987. **Members:** 1,800. **Staff:** 8. **Description:** Works to improve the status of people of color on campus, in order to increase participation rates and degree attainment by U.S. ethnic minorities. **Formerly:** (2004) America Council on Education, Office of Minorities in Higher Education. **Publications:** *Status Report*, annual. **Price:** $29.95. Also Cited As: *Annual Status Report on Minorities in Higher Education.* **Conventions/Meetings:** biennial Educating All of One Nation - conference (exhibits).

Montessori

8890 ■ American Montessori Consulting (AMC)
PO Box 5062
Rossmoor, CA 90720
Ph: (562)598-2321
E-mail: amonco@aol.com
URL: http://www.amonco.org
Description: Promotes Montessori education; offers consulting services to schools and learning centers. **Publications:** *Montessori Resources.* Book. **Price:** $15.00 ● *Reading, Writing, and Spelling in Spanish I.* Book. **Price:** $19.00 ● Newsletter.

8891 ■ American Montessori Society (AMS)
281 Park Ave. S
New York, NY 10010-6102
Ph: (212)358-1250
Fax: (212)358-1256
E-mail: info@amshq.org
URL: http://www.amshq.org
Contact: Richard A. Ungerer, Exec. Dir.
Founded: 1960. **Members:** 12,000. **Membership Dues:** individual in U.S., $55 (annual) ● individual outside U.S., $65 (annual) ● life, $545. **Staff:** 13. **Budget:** $2,200,000. **Description:** School affiliates and teacher training affiliates; heads of schools, teachers, parents, non-Montessori educators, and other interested individuals dedicated to stimulating the use of the Montessori teaching approach and promoting better education for all children. Seeks to meet demands of growing interest in the Montessori approach to early learning. Assists in establishing schools; supplies information and limited services to member schools in other countries. Maintains school consultation and accreditation service; provides information service; assists research and gathers statistical data; offers placement service. Maintains Montessori and related materials exhibit. **Libraries: Type:** reference. **Holdings:** archival material, books. **Subjects:** education. **Awards:** Outstanding Doctoral Dissertation and Master's Thesis. **Frequency:** annual. **Type:** monetary. **Recipient:** for graduate level work that furthers the public understanding of Montessori ● Teacher Education Scholarships. **Frequency:** annual. **Type:** scholarship. **Recipient:** to Montessori teachers who need financial support. **Computer Services:** Mailing lists ● online services, bulletin board ● online services, research library. **Committees:** Communications; Professional Development; Professional Services; School Accreditation; Teacher Training. **Affiliated With:** Council for American Private Education; National Association of Independent Schools. **Formed by Merger of:** (2006) National Center for Montessori Education and American Montessori Society. **Publications:** *Montessori in the 21st Century.* Video ● *Montessori Life*, quarterly. Magazine. **Price:** $39.00 for nonmembers; included in membership dues. ISSN: 1054-0040. **Advertising:** accepted. Alternate Formats: online ● *Salary & Tuition Surveys*, biennial ● *School Directory*, annual ● Brochures. Contains information related to Montessori education. **Conventions/Meetings:** quarterly Teacher Symposium ● annual conference, educa-

tional (exhibits) - 2009 Feb. 26-Mar. 1, New Orleans, LA; 2010 Mar. 25-28, Boston, MA; 2011 Mar. 24-27, Chicago, IL.

8892 ■ Association Montessori International-U.S.A. (AMI-USA)
410 Alexander St.
Rochester, NY 14607-1028
Ph: (585)461-5920
Free: (800)872-2643
Fax: (585)461-0075
E-mail: ami-usa@montessori-ami.org
URL: http://www.montessori-ami.org
Contact: Virginia McHugh, Exec. Dir.
Founded: 1972. **Members:** 2,300. **Membership Dues:** individual in U.S., $50 (annual) ● life, EUR 1,100 ● individual outside U.S., $70 (annual). **Staff:** 4. **Description:** Individuals interested in the method of education developed by Dr. Maria Montessori (1870-1952), Italian physician and educator. (Montessori schools provide a prepared environment where children are free to respond to their natural drive to work and learn). Promotes authentic Montessori education in the United States through school recognition, teacher training, conferences, institutes, refresher courses, and publications. **Publications:** *AMI International Study Conference Proceedings*, periodic. **Price:** $12.00/copy ● *AMI/USA Directory of Member Schools, Individuals, and Training Centers*, annual. **Price:** $12.00/copy ● *AMI/USA News*, quarterly. Newsletter. **Price:** available to members only. **Circulation:** 1,900 ● *AMI/USA Training Center Brochure* ● *What is Montessori?*. Brochure. Gives an overview of Montessori education through all age levels. **Price:** $17.50 each. **Conventions/Meetings:** annual conference ● quadrennial congress - 2009 Jan. 5-8, Chennai, TN, India ● annual Summer Institute and Refresher Course - meeting.

8893 ■ International Montessori Accreditation Council (IMAC)
c/o Lee Havis
9525 Georgia Ave., No. 200
Silver Spring, MD 20910
Ph: (301)589-1127
Free: (800)301-3131
E-mail: havis@imsmontessori.org
URL: http://imsmontessori.org/imac.htm
Contact: Lee Havis, Contact
Founded: 1994. **Multinational**. **Description:** Umbrella accrediting agency providing accreditation for teacher education throughout the entire Montessori community. **Committees:** Accreditation; Advisory; Generic Review; IMS Review.

8894 ■ International Montessori Society (IMS)
9525 Georgia Ave., No. 200
Silver Spring, MD 20910
Ph: (301)589-1127
Free: (800)301-3131
Fax: (301)589-0733
E-mail: havis@erols.com
URL: http://imsmontessori.org
Contact: Lee Havis, Exec. Dir.
Founded: 1979. **Members:** 700. **Membership Dues:** individual, $30 (annual) ● associate school, $35 (annual) ● Montessori school recognition, $45-$700 (annual). **Staff:** 4. **Multinational. Description:** Recognizes Montessori schools that follow Montessori teaching. Provides individual and associate school membership. Supports the effective practice of Montessori teaching as a scientific approach to bring about true normal being in children throughout the world. Seeks to promote harmony in the Montessori community, raise awareness and better understanding, and the effective use of Montessori technology in education. Conducts teacher education, consultation and publications to provide comprehensive technology for Montessori teaching. **Publications:** *Montessori News*, semiannual. Newspaper. **Price:** included in membership dues. ISSN: 0889-6720 ● *Montessori Observer*, quarterly. Newsletter. **Price:** included in membership dues. ISSN: 0889-5643. **Advertising:** accepted. **Conventions/Meetings:** periodic Creating the New Education - workshop and seminar, discussion format including instruction on Montessori teaching skills.

8895 ■ Montessori Educational Programs International (MEPI)
PO Box 2199
Gray, GA 31032
Ph: (478)986-2768
Fax: (478)986-2768
E-mail: mepi@alltel.net
URL: http://www.mepiforum.org
Contact: Cara Bockholt, Exec. Coor.
Founded: 1995. **Membership Dues:** individual, $35 (annual) ● level I internship site (per program level), $75 (annual) ● level II internship site (per program level), $150 (annual) ● teacher education program (per program level), $100 (annual) ● student certification fee (per program level & student), $175 (annual) ● foreign country level I internship site (per program level), $35 (annual) ● foreign country level II internship site (per program level)/student certification fee (per program level & student), $50 (annual) ● foreign country individual, $15 (annual). **Multinational. Description:** Promotes Montessori excellence through certified schools, professional training, and certified classroom teachers; promotes peace through education. **Awards:** Internships. **Type:** scholarship. **Programs:** Pennies for Peace. **Publications:** *Open Forum*, monthly. Newsletter. Alternate Formats: online ● Directory. Features Montessori individuals and schools associated with MEPI. **Conventions/Meetings:** annual Hands for Peace Conference - workshop (exhibits).

Mortuary Science

8896 ■ American Board of Funeral Service Education (ABFSE)
c/o Dr. Michael Smith, Exec. Dir.
3432 Ashland Ave., Ste.U
St. Joseph, MO 64506
Ph: (816)233-3747 (816)341-2573
Fax: (816)233-3793
E-mail: exdir@abfse.org
URL: http://www.abfse.org
Contact: Dr. Michael Smith, Exec. Dir.
Founded: 1946. **Members:** 57. **Staff:** 2. **Budget:** $320,000. **Description:** Representatives from National Funeral Directors Association, International Conference of Funeral Service Examining Boards of the United States, the National Funeral Directors and Mortuaries Association, and college program representatives and public members. Seeks to: formulate and enforce rules and regulations setting up standards concerning the schools and colleges teaching mortuary science; accredit schools and colleges of mortuary science. Sponsors the National Scholarship for Funeral Service program to provide capable young men and women studying in the field with financial assistance. Compiles statistics. **Awards:** National Scholarship Program of the American Board of Funeral Service Education. **Frequency:** annual. **Type:** scholarship. **Recipient:** for students enrolled in funeral service or mortuary science programs. **Committees:** Accreditation; College and University; Constitution & Bylaws; Curriculum; National Board Exam Liaison; Program; Scholarship. **Formerly:** (1959) Joint Committee on Mortuary Education. **Publications:** *Accredited Colleges of Mortuary Science*, annual ● *Directory of Accredited College Programs in Mortuary Science and Committees of the American Board of Funeral Service Education*, semiannual. Contains listings of member programs, officers and committees of the Board. **Price:** free ● *National Scholarships for Funeral Service*, semiannual, in April and October. **Conventions/Meetings:** annual conference.

Music

8897 ■ Accordionists and Teachers Guild, International (ATG)
c/o Joan Cochran Sommers, Pres.
2312 W 71 Terr.
Prairie Village, KS 66208-3322
Ph: (913)722-5625
E-mail: sommersj@umkc.edu
URL: http://accordions.com/atg
Contact: Joan Cochran Sommers, Pres.
Founded: 1940. **Members:** 100. **Membership Dues:** general, $30 (annual). **Description:** Professional society of accordion teachers, accordionists, and patrons. Conducts research. Sponsors workshops, competitions, and festival concerts. Maintains biographical archives; provides children's services. **Libraries: Type:** reference. **Holdings:** biographical archives. **Committees:** Commissioning of Composers. **Formerly:** (1998) Accordion Teachers' Guild. **Publications:** *Accordion Teachers' Guild—Newsletter*, quarterly. Focuses on accordion teaching and performing. **Price:** included in membership dues. **Circulation:** 180. **Conventions/Meetings:** annual festival and workshop, with music festival and concerts (exhibits) - every last weekend in June, usually Midwest.

8898 ■ American Academy of Teachers of Singing (AATS)
c/o Jan Eric Douglas, Chm.
777 W End Ave.
New York, NY 10025-5551
Ph: (212)666-5951 (212)662-9338
E-mail: info@americanacademyofteachersofsinging.org
URL: http://www.americanacademyofteachersofsinging.org
Contact: Jeannette L. LoVetri, Sec.
Founded: 1922. **Members:** 35. **Membership Dues:** individual, $100 (annual). **Description:** Represents the interests of professional singing teachers. Offers professional advice and guidance to those who teach singing or perform as singers. **Conventions/Meetings:** meeting - 5/year.

8899 ■ American College of Musicians (ACM)
PO Box 1807
Austin, TX 78767
Ph: (512)478-5775
E-mail: ngpt@pianoguild.com
URL: http://www.pianoguild.com
Contact: Gloria Castro, Chair
Members: 14,867. **Membership Dues:** regular, $50 (annual). **Description:** Grants diplomas and degrees to members of the National Guild of Piano Teachers (see separate entry) and other worthy musicians who have passed examinations administered by a board of examiners. Membership includes guild judges and members whose qualifications make them eligible to judge. Grants high school, collegiate, and artist diploma to teachers who present programs in the National Piano Playing Auditions that meet basic requirements of the guild; serves as an examinations board in adjudicating guild members' pupils in the auditions. Grants Certificate of Approval to teachers who have at least 25 pupils attaining national or international membership in the National Fraternity of Student Musicians (see separate entry) and meeting high score standards over a five-year period. **Convention/Meeting:** none.

8900 ■ American Institute of Musical Studies (AIMS)
28 E 69th St.
Kansas City, MO 64113
Ph: (816)268-3657
E-mail: aimsgraz@gmail.net
URL: http://www.aimsgraz.com
Contact: Thomas King, Pres.
Founded: 1969. **Staff:** 5. **Budget:** $850,000. **Languages:** English, German. **Description:** Institute that sponsors The AIMS Graz Experience in Graz, Austria, which includes the Summer Vocal Institute, and the AIMS Festival Orchestra. Launches advanced young singers, pianists and instrumentalists on a professional career by providing experience and emphasizing audition training. Faculty, comprised of over 60 internationally known professional musicians, conducts hands-on training programs. **Libraries: Type:** reference. **Subjects:** vocal and orchestral works. **Awards:** Meistersinger Competition. **Frequency:** annual. **Type:** monetary. **Recipient:** to the selected

registered participants. **Computer Services:** Information services, faculty and staff bios ● information services, Graz resources ● information services, piano curriculum ● information services, vocal curriculum. **Publications:** *AIMS Bulletin*. Includes course listings, program and faculty descriptions. **Price:** free ● *The AIMSer Newsletter*. **Conventions/Meetings:** annual workshop - always July or August, Graz, Austria.

8901 ■ American Matthay Association (AMA)
c/o George Loring, Pres.
232 Pond Brook Rd.
West Chesterfield, NH 03466
E-mail: gloring@aol.com
URL: http://www.matthay.org
Contact: George Loring, Pres.
Founded: 1925. **Members:** 170. **Membership Dues:** active, $40 (annual) ● workshop/friend, $25 (annual) ● student, $20 (annual) ● patron, $500 (annual). **Description:** Seeks to further and perpetuate the understanding of Tobias Matthay (British musician and educator, 1858-1945) and his teaching principles and to encourage a high standard of performance and instruction. Sponsors annual Clara Wells Competition for Young Pianists. **Publications:** *Matthay News*, semiannual. Journal. **Price:** included in membership dues. **Conventions/Meetings:** annual Matthay Festival and Workshop - festival and workshop.

8902 ■ American Recorder Teachers Association (ARTA)
c/o Susan P. Groskreutz, Pres.
1355 Westminster Ln.
Bourbonnais, IL 60914-1633
Ph: (815)937-9936
Fax: (815)937-9858
E-mail: president@arta-recorder.org
URL: http://www.arta-recorder.org
Contact: Susan P. Groskreutz, Pres.
Membership Dues: individual in U.S. and Canada, $25 (annual) ● family in U.S. and Canada, $30 (annual) ● individual outside U.S. and Canada, $30 (annual) ● family outside U.S. and Canada, $35 (annual). **Description:** Provides a support network for recorder teachers. Acts as an advocate and source of information for recorder pedagogy. Encourages professionalism in recorder education by making available current research and ideas to those in the teaching profession. **Telecommunication Services:** electronic mail, suegroskreutz@earthlink.net. **Publications:** *ARTAfacts*, quarterly. Newsletter. Alternate Formats: online ● *Recorder Education Journal*, annual. Also Cited As: *REJ*.

8903 ■ American School Band Directors' Association (ASBDA)
PO Box 696
Guttenberg, IA 52052
Ph: (563)252-2500
E-mail: asbda@alpinecom.net
URL: http://home.comcast.net/~asbda
Contact: Dennis L. Hanna, Office Mgr.
Founded: 1953. **Members:** 1,300. **Membership Dues:** retired, emeritus, past president, $25 (annual) ● associate, $65 (annual) ● active, $75 (annual) ● affiliate, $55 (annual). **Staff:** 25. **Budget:** $50,000. **State Groups:** 46. **Description:** Persons actively engaged in teaching instrumental music at the elementary, junior high or senior high school level; affiliates are persons no longer engaged in active teaching; associates are commercial firms dealing in products used by members. Seeks to improve instruction of instrumental music in the schools, the equipment used in instrumental music, music materials and methods, audiovisual aids, and acoustics of musical instruments used in school instructional programs. **Awards:** ASBDA Dale Harris Exemplary Band Program Award. **Frequency:** annual. **Type:** recognition ● Austin Harding Award. **Frequency:** annual. **Type:** recognition. **Recipient:** for individuals who gave valuable and dedicated service to the bands of America ● Edwin Franko Goldman Award. **Frequency:** annual. **Type:** recognition. **Recipient:** for exceptional contributions to the school band movement ● Outstanding Band Directors. **Frequency:** annual. **Type:** recognition. **Computer Services:** database ● mailing lists. **Committees:** Acoustical Research; Budgets and Salaries; Community Band Participation; Construction and Equipment; Curriculum Study; Exchange of Programs on Concerts; New Band Scores and Original Manuscripts; Outstanding Literature for Concert Band; Public Relations and the School Band; Room Design; Scheduling of Instrumental Music; Solo and Ensemble Materials; Standardization of Instrumentation of Band Publications; Visual Aids and Recordings. **Publications:** *American School Band Directors' Association—Research Committee Report for the Annual Convention* ● *ASBDA Directory and Handbook*, annual. **Price:** available to members only ● *Bandworld*, periodic. Magazine ● Newsletter, bimonthly. **Price:** available to members only. Alternate Formats: online. **Conventions/Meetings:** annual conference and seminar - usually June or July.

8904 ■ American String Teachers Association (ASTA)
4153 Chain Bridge Rd.
Fairfax, VA 22030
Ph: (703)279-2113
Fax: (703)279-2114
E-mail: asta@astaweb.com
URL: http://www.astaweb.com
Contact: Donna Sizemore Hale, Exec. Dir.
Founded: 1946. **Members:** 11,500. **Membership Dues:** professional, $93 (annual) ● student, $42 (annual) ● senior, $66 (annual) ● dual, $130 (annual) ● institutional, $275 (annual) ● String Industry Council, $166-$321 (annual). **Staff:** 8. **Budget:** $1,000,000. **State Groups:** 49. **Description:** Promotes excellence in string and orchestra teaching and playing, together with the National School Orchestra Association. Pursues its mission through: an open sharing of ideas; benefits, services, and activities responsive to the needs of all members; development of strong state leadership and chapters; enhancing the image and visibility of string teaching and study; advocacy for string education; and an inclusive community of string teachers and players. **Libraries: Type:** reference. **Holdings:** video recordings. **Awards:** Artist Teacher Award. **Frequency:** annual. **Type:** recognition ● String Teacher of the Year Award. **Frequency:** annual. **Type:** recognition. **Computer Services:** Mailing lists, labels ● online services, membership; bookstore; request advocacy materials. **Telecommunication Services:** electronic mail, donna@astaweb.com. **Absorbed:** (1998) National School Orchestra Association. **Publications:** *American String Teacher*, quarterly. Journal. Contains feature articles, book and music reviews, chapter news, and conference reports. **Price:** included in membership dues. ISSN: 0003-1313. **Circulation:** 11,500. **Advertising:** accepted ● *ASTA eNews*, monthly. Newsletter. Alternate Formats: online ● *Why Strings? A Career Invitation*. Pamphlets. **Conventions/Meetings:** annual conference (exhibits).

8905 ■ Association for Technology in Music Instruction (ATMI)
312 E Pine St.
Missoula, MT 59802
Ph: (406)721-1152
Fax: (406)721-9419
E-mail: atmi@music.org
URL: http://www.atmionline.org
Contact: Scott Lipscomb, Pres.
Founded: 1975. **Members:** 300. **Membership Dues:** individual, $40 (annual) ● student, $20 (annual). **Staff:** 1. **Description:** University professors, public school teachers, music industry professionals, and research laboratory personnel. Seeks to increase public awareness of computer-based music systems. Provides a forum for publishing research; facilitates the exchange of information among users of computers in music instruction; aids music teachers in implementing computer-based systems in music education. Serves as a research clearinghouse in the field. **Affiliated With:** College Music Society. **Formerly:** (1986) National Consortium for Computer-Based Music Instruction. **Publications:** *ATMI Music Technology Directory*, annual. Alternate Formats: CD-ROM ● *Technology Directory*, annual. Includes annual listing of available computer software and hardware for music education. **Conventions/Meetings:** annual conference, held in conjunction with the College Music Society (exhibits).

8906 ■ College Band Directors National Association (CBDNA)
c/o Thomas Verrier, Sec.
Vanderbilt Univ.
Blair School of Music
2400 Blakemore Ave.
Nashville, TN 37212
Ph: (615)322-7651
Fax: (615)343-0324
E-mail: thomas.verrier@vanderbilt.edu
URL: http://www.cbdna.org
Contact: Thomas Verrier, Sec.
Founded: 1941. **Members:** 1,200. **Membership Dues:** active, $60 (annual) ● institutional, $75 (annual) ● life, $300 ● music industry, $100 (annual) ● professional/professional associate, $50 (annual) ● retired/student, $20 (annual). **Regional Groups:** 6. **Description:** Represents directors of university and college marching and concert bands. **Commissions:** Colors and Contours; Consorts; Olympic Dances; Palace Rhapsody; Scorpio; Songfest; Transitions; Voyage. **Publications:** Directory, biennial ● Journal, semiannual ● Newsletter, 3/year ● Report, quarterly. Contains program reports. Alternate Formats: online ● Proceedings. Contains national conference proceedings. **Conventions/Meetings:** biennial conference.

8907 ■ College Music Society (CMS)
312 E Pine St.
Missoula, MT 59802-4624
Ph: (406)721-9616
Free: (800)729-0235
Fax: (406)721-9419
E-mail: cms@music.org
URL: http://www.music.org
Contact: Robby D. Gunstream, Exec. Dir.
Founded: 1958. **Members:** 9,000. **Membership Dues:** regular, $60 (annual) ● student, $30 (annual) ● retired, $30 (annual) ● joint (regular), $70 (annual) ● joint (student/retired), $40 (annual). **Staff:** 9. **Budget:** $950,000. **Regional Groups:** 10. **Description:** Consortium of college, conservatory, university and independent musicians and scholars interested in all disciplines of music; promotes music teaching and learning, musical creativity and expression, research and dialogue, diversity and interdisciplinary interaction. **Computer Services:** Mailing lists. **Committees:** Advocacy; Career Services; Cultural Inclusion; Mentoring; Professional Development; Professional Life. **Publications:** *College Music Symposium*, annual. Journal. Presents issues in music and higher education. **Price:** $25.00 for nonmembers. ISSN: 0069-5696. **Circulation:** 6,000. **Advertising:** accepted ● *Directory of Music Faculties in Colleges and Universities, U.S. and Canada*, annual. **Price:** $90.00 ● *Monographs and Bibliographies in American Music* ● Newsletter, 5/year. **Advertising:** accepted. **Conventions/Meetings:** annual conference (exhibits) ● biennial international conference.

8908 ■ Council for Research in Music Education (CRME)
School of Music
1114 W Nevada St.
Urbana, IL 61801
Ph: (217)333-1027
Fax: (217)244-8136
E-mail: crme@uiuc.edu
Contact: Gregory DeNardo, Contact
Founded: 1963. **Membership Dues:** regular, $35 (annual). **Staff:** 2. **Description:** International organization of authors who contribute articles to the *Bulletin of the Council for Research in Music Education*. Aims to promote scholarly research in music education. **Awards:** Outstanding Dissertation Award. **Frequency:** triennial. **Type:** monetary. **Publications:** Journal, quarterly. Includes research reports, book reviews and occasional conference papers. **Price:**

$10.00/issue; $35.00 /year for individuals; $45.00 /year for institutions; $50.00 for international subscription. ISSN: 0010-9894. **Circulation:** 800.

8909 ■ Early Music America (EMA)
2366 Eastlake Ave. E, No. 429
Seattle, WA 98102
Ph: (206)720-6270
Fax: (206)720-6290
E-mail: info@earlymusic.org
URL: http://www.earlymusic.org
Contact: Maria V. Coldwell, Exec. Dir.
Founded: 1985. **Members:** 3,000. **Membership Dues:** individual, $55 (annual) ● family, overseas, instrument maker, $65 (annual) ● senior citizen (65 and older), $45 (annual) ● student, $30 (annual) ● organization (income less than $100,000 to $200,000 or more), $85-$150 (annual). **Staff:** 3. **Budget:** $300,000. **Description:** Serves and strengthens the early music community in North America. Compiles statistics. Conducts educational programs. **Libraries: Type:** reference. **Holdings:** 300; books. **Subjects:** historical performance in North America. **Awards:** Early Music Outreach Award. **Frequency:** annual. **Type:** monetary. **Recipient:** for outstanding achievement in education or outreach to adults or children ● Howard Mayer Brown Award. **Frequency:** annual. **Type:** monetary. **Recipient:** for outstanding contributions to the field of early music ● Thomas Binkley Award. **Frequency:** annual. **Type:** monetary. **Recipient:** for outstanding accomplishments by a college or university collegium director. **Publications:** *EMA Bulletin*, quarterly. Newsletter. Alternate Formats: online ● Magazine, quarterly. **Price:** $4.95/copy. ISSN: 1083-3633. **Circulation:** 5,000. **Advertising:** accepted. Alternate Formats: online ● Membership Directory, annual. **Conventions/Meetings:** annual conference and seminar, with symposia ● annual meeting.

8910 ■ Gordon Institute for Music Learning (GIML)
c/o Jennifer McDonel, Exec. Dir.
PO Box 528
Lebanon, OH 45036-0528
Ph: (513)932-0765
Free: (800)442-1358
E-mail: execdir@giml.org
URL: http://www.giml.org
Contact: Jennifer McDonel, Exec. Dir.
Membership Dues: regular, $40 (annual). **Description:** Seeks to advance research in music education pioneered by Edwin E. Gordon. **Publications:** *A Music Learning Theory for Newborn & Young Children*. Book. **Price:** $20.00 ● *Audea*. Magazine ● *Audie: A Game for Understanding & Analyzing Your Child's Music Skills, Ages 3-4*. **Price:** $13.00 complete kit; $2.00 additional game pads ● *Experimental Songs & Chants, Book One*. **Price:** $10.00 ● *Guiding Your Child's Musical Development*. Book. **Price:** $13.00 book and cassette ● *Jump Right In To Listening: Music for Young Children*. Audiotapes. **Price:** $35.00 for 4 cassettes ● *Music Play: The Early Childhood Music Curriculum*. Book. Features a guide for parents, teachers, and caregivers. **Price:** $45.00 book & CD set. **Conventions/Meetings:** workshop.

8911 ■ Institute for Studies in American Music (ISAM)
Brooklyn Coll. of CUNY
2900 Bedford Ave.
Brooklyn, NY 11210-2889
Ph: (718)951-5655
Fax: (718)951-4858
E-mail: isam@brooklyn.cuny.edu
URL: http://depthome.brooklyn.cuny.edu/isam
Contact: Jeff Taylor, Acting Dir.
Founded: 1971. **Members:** 3,900. **Staff:** 5. **Budget:** $85,000. **Description:** Libraries, scholars, teachers, students, and booksellers. Serves as information center encouraging and supporting research in American music studies. Organizes concerts. **Libraries: Type:** reference. **Holdings:** 3,000; audio recordings. **Subjects:** American music, jazz, classical, R&B, folk. **Awards:** Student Composer Awards. **Frequency:** annual. **Type:** fellowship. **Computer Services:** Mailing lists. **Telecommunication Services:** electronic mail, jtaylor@brooklyn.cuny.edu. **Publications:** *Institute for Studies in American Music—Monographs*, periodic. Features a series on American music and composers. ● *Institute for Studies in American Music—Newsletter*, semiannual. Contains news and information, brief research reports, editorials, and reviews. **Price:** free. ISSN: 0145-8396. **Circulation:** 3,900. **Advertising:** accepted. Alternate Formats: online ● Directory, semiannual. **Conventions/Meetings:** periodic conference ● seminar.

8912 ■ International Association for Jazz Education (IAJE)
Box 724
Manhattan, KS 66505
Ph: (785)776-8744
Fax: (785)776-6190
E-mail: info@iaje.org
URL: http://www.iaje.org
Contact: William F. McFarlin, Exec. Dir.
Founded: 1968. **Members:** 8,000. **Membership Dues:** student, $30 (annual) ● active, $68 (annual) ● associate, $240 (annual) ● patron, $1,800 (annual) ● super patron, $7,500 (annual) ● retired, $60 (annual). **Staff:** 10. **Budget:** $1,500,000. **State Groups:** 40. **Multinational. Description:** Music teachers from grade school through college, professional musicians, and others; students from junior high through college; libraries; individuals from the music industry. Fosters and promotes understanding, appreciation, and artistic performance of jazz music; disseminates educational and professional news. Encourages the adoption of curricula that will explore contemporary composition, arrangement, and improvisation; cooperation with all organizations dedicated to the development of musical culture in America. Maintains hall of fame. **Libraries: Type:** reference. **Awards: Frequency:** annual. **Type:** recognition. **Recipient:** for outstanding service to jazz education ● **Type:** scholarship. **Recipient:** for deserving youngsters who study jazz. **Telecommunication Services:** electronic mail, bill@iaje.org. **Divisions:** General Music; String; Vocal; Wind. **Affiliated With:** MENC: The National Association for Music Education. **Formerly:** (1989) National Association of Jazz Educators; (2002) International Association of Jazz Educators. **Publications:** *Jazz Education Journal*, bimonthly. **Advertising:** accepted ● Papers. **Conventions/Meetings:** annual conference (exhibits) ● periodic workshop, traveling jazz clinics.

8913 ■ MENC: The National Association for Music Education (MENC)
1806 Robert Fulton Dr.
Reston, VA 20191
Ph: (703)860-4000
Free: (800)336-3768
Fax: (703)860-1531
E-mail: executive@menc.org
URL: http://www.menc.org
Contact: John J. Mahlmann EdD, Exec. Dir.
Founded: 1907. **Members:** 90,000. **Membership Dues:** individual, $62 (annual). **Staff:** 75. **Budget:** $8,000,000. **Regional Groups:** 6. **State Groups:** 52. **Description:** Comprised of music educators, administrators, supervisors, consultants, and music education majors in colleges. Publishes materials for music educators, presents conferences, compiles statistics. **Libraries: Type:** reference. **Holdings:** archival material. **Awards:** FAME Awards. **Frequency:** annual. **Type:** recognition. **Recipient:** for outstanding contribution to music education. **Telecommunication Services:** additional toll-free number, (800)828-0229. **Councils:** Advisory; Music Teacher Education; Society for General Music; Society for Research in Music Education. **Formerly:** (1934) Music Supervisors National Conference; (1998) Music Educators National Conference. **Publications:** *General Music Today*, 3/year. Journal ● *Journal of Music Teacher Education*, semiannual ● *Journal of Research in Music Education*, quarterly. **Price:** included in membership dues. Alternate Formats: microform ● *Music Educators Journal*, bimonthly. Contains articles on all phases of music education in schools and communities. Features readers' comments, book reviews, and announcements. **Price:** included in membership dues. ISSN: 0027-4321. **Advertising:** accepted. Alternate Formats: microform. Also Cited As: *Music Supervisors Journal* ● *Teaching Music*, bimonthly. Journal. Features practical teaching items for educators. **Price:** included in membership dues ● Also publishes administration, supervision, and teacher education materials; orchestral and band instrument teaching materials, and career information. **Conventions/Meetings:** biennial conference (exhibits).

8914 ■ Mr. Holland's Opus Foundation (MHOF)
15125 Ventura Blvd., Ste.204
Sherman Oaks, CA 91403
Ph: (818)784-6787
Fax: (818)784-6788
E-mail: info@mhopus.org
URL: http://www.mhopus.org
Contact: Doreen Ringer-Ross, Pres.
Founded: 1996. **Staff:** 29. **Description:** Dedicated to partnering with businesses, schools, and communities to provide new and refurbished musical instruments to qualified schools and individual students. **Awards: Frequency:** annual. **Type:** grant. **Recipient:** for students ● Mr. Holland's Opus Foundation Teacher Awards. **Frequency:** annual. **Type:** recognition. **Recipient:** for teachers. **Computer Services:** Mailing lists. **Committees:** Grant. **Councils:** Advisory. **Programs:** Melody; Special Projects. **Publications:** *Opus Notes*. Newsletter.

8915 ■ Music EdVentures
c/o Betty Hoffmann
807 Montana
Deer Lodge, MT 59722
Ph: (406)846-1317
E-mail: bhoff918@aol.com
URL: http://www.musicedventures.org
Contact: Betty Hoffmann, Contact
Founded: 1992. **Members:** 500. **Membership Dues:** patron, $1,000 ● sustaining, $50 ● regular, $25 ● student, $10. **Multinational. Description:** International network of classroom and music educators. Works to search for and practice ways of making music and of interacting with people who preserve and celebrate the dignity of both. Focuses work on educational practices that foster interactive, facilitative learning environments, teaching strategies that empower the learner within the context of music experience and study, and networks that encourage collaboration between diverse disciplines, professionals and interest groups. **Divisions:** SongWorks. **Publications:** Magazine.

8916 ■ Music and Entertainment Industry Educators Association (MEIEA)
c/o Ms. Suzanne Clement, Admin. Asst.
1900 Belmont Blvd.
Nashville, TN 37212-3758
Ph: (615)460-6946
E-mail: office@meiea.org
URL: http://www.meiea.org
Contact: Ms. Suzanne Clement, Admin. Asst.
Founded: 1979. **Members:** 1,100. **Membership Dues:** active, $60 (annual) ● student, $18 (annual) ● educational institution, $150 (annual) ● industry, $150 (annual). **Budget:** $25,000. **Description:** Music educators and leaders in the music and entertainment industries. Seeks to more successfully prepare music and entertainment students. Facilitates collaboration among members to devise innovative music and entertainment curricula and teaching methods; assists educational institutions wishing to develop music industry education programs. **Computer Services:** Online services, member list, job postings, ezine, journal, speakers bureau. **Publications:** *MEIEA E-zine*, monthly. Magazine ● *MEIEA Journal*, annual. **Price:** $25.00 back issues plus shipping and handling. **Conventions/Meetings:** annual conference - every spring.

8917 ■ Music Notation Modernization Association (MNMA)
c/o Thomas Reed, Founder
PO Box 241
Kirksville, MO 63501

Ph: (660)665-8098
Fax: (660)665-8098
E-mail: scott.reed@mnma.org
URL: http://web.syr.edu/~pwmorris/mnma
Contact: Mr. Scott B. Reed, Exec. Dir.
Founded: 1985. **Members:** 60. **Membership Dues:** regular, library and organization, $40 (biennial) ● student and low income, $20 (biennial). **Staff:** 4. **Description:** Seeks to help modernize the current music notation system. **Publications:** *Music Notation News*, quarterly. Newsletter. Discusses new suggestions for simplifying music notation. **Price:** included in membership dues. ISSN: 0258-963X. **Circulation:** 60. **Conventions/Meetings:** periodic conference.

8918 ■ Music Teachers National Association (MTNA)
441 Vine St., Ste.3100
Cincinnati, OH 45202-3004
Ph: (513)421-1420
Free: (888)512-5278
Fax: (513)421-2503
E-mail: mtnanet@mtna.org
URL: http://www.mtna.org
Contact: Dr. Gary L. Ingle, Exec. Dir.
Founded: 1876. **Members:** 24,000. **Staff:** 17. **Budget:** $1,700,000. **Regional Groups:** 7. **State Groups:** 51. **Local Groups:** 580. **Description:** Professional society of independent and collegiate music teachers committed to furthering the art of music through programs that encourage and support teaching, performance, composition, and scholarly research. **Libraries: Type:** reference. **Awards:** Distinguished Composer of the Year. **Frequency:** annual. **Type:** monetary. **Recipient:** for compositions commissioned by affiliated state music teacher associations. **Computer Services:** Mailing lists. **Boards:** Certification. **Committees:** Community Outreach and Education; Competition; Convention; Editorial; Electronic Media; Exhibitors; Membership; Pedagogy. **Publications:** *American Music Teacher*, bimonthly. Journal. Contains association news and topics on American music, chamber music, aesthetics, composition, criticism, musicology, pedagogy, and performance. **Price:** included in membership dues; $22.00 /year for libraries. ISSN: 0003-0112. **Circulation:** 27,000. **Advertising:** accepted. Alternate Formats: microform ● Also publishes guides for communication, music instruction software, tax, and certification for independent music teacher. **Conventions/Meetings:** annual conference (exhibits).

8919 ■ National Association of College Wind and Percussion Instructors (NACWPI)
c/o Dr. Richard K. Weerts, Exec. Sec.-Treas.
308 Hillcrest Dr.
Kirksville, MO 63501
Ph: (660)785-4442
Fax: (660)785-7463
E-mail: dweerts@sbcglobal.net
URL: http://www.nacwpi.org
Contact: Dr. Richard K. Weerts, Exec. Sec.-Treas.
Founded: 1951. **Members:** 1,200. **Membership Dues:** regular, $35 (annual) ● student, $25 (annual) ● retired, $15 (annual) ● associate, $35 (annual). **Regional Groups:** 6. **State Groups:** 48. **Description:** College and university teachers of woodwind, brass, or percussion instruments. Advances wind and percussion instrument playing and teaching. Commissions the composition of wind and percussion music by American composers. Sponsors programs, clinics, concerts, lectures, and workshops at Music Educators National Conference state, divisional, and national conventions. Maintains placement service; conducts research. **Libraries: Type:** reference. **Holdings:** 15,600. **Publications:** *NACWPI Journal*, quarterly. **Price:** included in membership dues; $50.00 /year for libraries and institutions. ISSN: 0027-576X. **Circulation:** 6,000. **Advertising:** accepted ● *Research Library Catalog*. **Conventions/Meetings:** semiannual conference ● semiannual symposium.

8920 ■ National Association of Pastoral Musicians (NPM)
962 Wayne Ave., Ste.210
Silver Spring, MD 20910-4461
Ph: (240)247-3000
Fax: (240)247-3001
E-mail: npmsing@npm.org
URL: http://www.npm.org
Contact: Dr. J. Michael McMahon, Pres.
Founded: 1976. **Members:** 9,000. **Membership Dues:** individual, $58 (annual) ● regular parish (2), $97 (annual) ● parish group (4), $147 (annual) ● single parish, $70 (annual) ● youth and retired/senior, $29 (annual). **Staff:** 11. **Budget:** $1,600,000. **Local Groups:** 75. **National Groups:** 18. **Description:** Fosters the art of musical liturgy. Members serve the Catholic Church in the United States as musicians, clergy, liturgists, and other leaders of prayer. Provides ongoing formation for musicians and clergy through annual conventions, educational institutes, and events in more than 70 diocesan chapters. Also provides certification programs for cantors, organists, and directors of music ministries. **Libraries: Type:** not open to the public. **Holdings:** 300. **Subjects:** Catholic hymnals. **Awards:** Jubilate Deo, Pastoral Musician of the Year. **Frequency:** annual. **Type:** recognition ● NPM Scholarships. **Frequency:** annual. **Type:** scholarship. **Recipient:** for graduate and undergraduate in pastoral music and for parishes and individuals with limited resources to participate in NPM conventions and institutes. **Commissions:** Certification; Education; Music Industry; Operation; Publications. **Supersedes:** National Catholic Music Educators Association. **Publications:** *Catholic Music Educator*, quarterly. Newsletter ● *Clergy Update*, bimonthly. Newsletter ● *The Liturgical Singer*, quarterly. Newsletter. For psalmists, cantors, choir members and directors. ● *Pastoral Music Magazine*, bimonthly. Alternate Formats: online ● *Pastoral Music Notebook*, bimonthly. Newsletter. **Conventions/Meetings:** biennial Western Regional Convention (exhibits).

8921 ■ National Association of Schools of Music (NASM)
11250 Roger Bacon Dr., Ste.21
Reston, VA 20190-5248
Ph: (703)437-0700
Fax: (703)437-6312
E-mail: info@arts-accredit.org
URL: http://nasm.arts-accredit.org
Contact: Samuel Hope, Exec. Dir.
Founded: 1924. **Members:** 610. **Membership Dues:** individual, $65 (annual) ● institutional, non degree-granting institution, community/junior college, $841 (annual) ● baccalaureate degree-granting institution, $1,102 (annual) ● master's degree-granting institution, $1,659 (annual) ● doctoral degree-granting institution, $2,198 (annual). **Staff:** 12. **Description:** Serves as an accrediting agency for music educational programs. Compiles statistics. **Commissions:** Accreditation. **Publications:** Directory, annual. Lists accredited schools and their degrees and programs. **Price:** included in membership dues; $20.00/copy for nonmembers ● Handbook, biennial. Contains accreditation standards for schools and organizational documents of NASM. **Price:** included in membership dues; $20.00/copy for nonmembers ● Proceedings, annual. **Price:** included in membership dues; $20.00/copy for nonmembers. **Circulation:** 1,000 ● Brochures. Contains principles outlined in the NASM Code of Ethics. **Price:** free ● Also publishes special projects. **Conventions/Meetings:** annual meeting - always November. 2008 Nov. 21-25, Seattle, WA; 2009 Nov. 20-24, San Diego, CA.

8922 ■ National Association for the Study and Performance of African-American Music (NASPAAM)
c/o Mark Philips, Financial Sec.
1225 W High St.
Petersburg, VA 23803
Ph: (901)396-2913
Fax: (617)555-1212
E-mail: naspaam@yahoo.com
URL: http://www.naspaam.org
Contact: Frank Suggs, Pres.
Founded: 1972. **Members:** 133. **Membership Dues:** active, $50 (annual) ● retired, $35 (annual) ● corporate, $120 (annual) ● collegiate, $10 (annual) ● life, $500. **Description:** Fosters the creation, study, and promotion of black-derived music in education. Seeks to heighten public awareness of the problems faced by black music educators and students and to increase public understanding of those problems. Provides a forum for the discussion of concerns. Coordinates and disseminates materials concerning black-derived music in order to assist music teachers in teaching black music and students. Encourages blacks to aspire to leadership positions and to demand inclusion in the development and presentation of Music Educators National Conference activities, including participation in MENC's regional conferences. Sponsors collegiate and high school gospel choir competitions. Compiles list of music, books, and related music materials by blacks. **Awards:** National Achievement Awards. **Frequency:** annual. **Type:** recognition. **Recipient:** for educators who are successful in demonstrating values inherent in music education. **Computer Services:** database, black musicians and educators. **Committees:** Achievement Awards/Scholarships; Choral/Instrumental; Exhibits/Awards; Fund Raising and Development; General Music; National Symposiums/Conferences; Research/Publications/Special Projects. **Formerly:** (1997) National Black Music Caucus of the Music Educators National Conference. **Publications:** *Con Brio*, quarterly. Newsletter. Reports on regional conferences, collegiate and high school gospel choir competitions, and activities of members. **Price:** included in membership dues. **Conventions/Meetings:** biennial conference, held in conjunction with MENC ● annual retreat.

8923 ■ National Association of Teachers of Singing (NATS)
9957 Moorings Dr., Ste.401
Jacksonville, FL 32257
Ph: (904)992-9101
Free: (888)262-2065
Fax: (904)262-2587
E-mail: info@nats.org
URL: http://www.nats.org
Contact: Martha Randal, Pres.
Founded: 1944. **Members:** 6,000. **Membership Dues:** individual in U.S., $80 (annual) ● individual outside U.S., $90 (annual). **Staff:** 3. **Budget:** $500,000. **Regional Groups:** 14. **Local Groups:** 79. **Description:** Serves as a professional society of teachers of singing. Encourages the highest standards of the vocal art and of ethical principles in the teaching of singing. Promotes vocal education and research at all levels, both for the enrichment of the general public and for the professional advancement of the talented. **Awards:** NATS Art Song Composition Award. **Frequency:** annual. **Type:** monetary ● NATS Artist Awards Competition. **Frequency:** biennial. **Type:** monetary. **Computer Services:** Mailing lists. **Publications:** *InterNos*, 3/year. Newsletter. **Circulation:** 6,000. Alternate Formats: online ● *The Journal of Singing*, 5/year. **Advertising:** accepted ● Membership Directory, biennial. **Conventions/Meetings:** biennial conference and convention (exhibits) - 2008 June 27-July 1, Nashville, TN ● International Congress ● periodic regional meeting ● periodic workshop, international and summer.

8924 ■ National Fraternity of Student Musicians (NFSM)
c/o American College of Musicians
PO Box 1807
Austin, TX 78767
Ph: (512)478-5775
Fax: (512)478-5843
E-mail: ngpt@pianoguild.com
URL: http://www.pianoguild.com
Contact: Richard Allison, Pres.
Founded: 1927. **Membership Dues:** active, $50 (annual). **Staff:** 12. **Description:** Piano students whose teachers are members of the National Guild of Piano Teachers (see separate entry) and who enter the annual National Piano Playing Auditions sponsored by the guild. Six degrees of membership can be attained based on increasing difficulty of the musical program presented satisfactorily by the student. Awards pins, certificates, diplomas, national honor roll recognition,

and scholarships. **Affiliated With:** American College of Musicians; International Piano Guild.

8925 ■ National Guild of Piano Teachers (NGPT)
c/o American College of Musicians
PO Box 1807
Austin, TX 78767
Ph: (512)478-5775
Fax: (512)478-5843
E-mail: ngpt@pianoguild.com
URL: http://www.pianoguild.com
Contact: Richard Allison, Pres.
Founded: 1929. **Members:** 11,868. **Staff:** 12. **Budget:** $1,000,000. **Local Groups:** 780. **Description:** Serves as a division of the American College of Musicians (see separate entry). Works as a professional society of piano teachers and music faculty. Promotes music education through examinations, auditions, and competitions from coast to coast. Sponsors National Piano Playing Auditions and Van Cliburn International Competition. Maintains library. **Divisions:** Piano and Theory. **Affiliated With:** National Fraternity of Student Musicians. **Publications:** *Piano Guild Notes*, bimonthly. Journal ● *Syllabus*, annual.

8926 ■ National High School Band Directors Hall of Fame (NHSBDHOF)
c/o Dr. Oliver C. Boone, Exec. Dir.
4166 Will Rhoades Dr.
Columbus, GA 31909
E-mail: oboone9007@mchsi.com
Contact: Dr. Oliver C. Boone, Exec. Dir.
Founded: 1985. **Members:** 35. **Staff:** 2. **Budget:** $31,000. **Description:** Recognizes and honors outstanding school band directors. Holds national school concert and marching band music performance contests. **Awards:** Legion of Service Medal. **Frequency:** annual. **Type:** medal ● National High School Band Director of the Year. **Frequency:** annual. **Type:** recognition ● National High School Band of the Year. **Frequency:** annual. **Type:** recognition. **Formerly:** (1988) National High School Band Institute; (1989) National High School Band and Choral Directors Hall of Fame; (1997) National Band and Choral Directors Hall of Fame. **Publications:** Newsletter, quarterly. **Advertising:** accepted. Alternate Formats: online. **Conventions/Meetings:** annual meeting (exhibits).

8927 ■ National Piano Foundation (NPF)
5960 W Parker Rd., Ste.278, No. 233
Plano, TX 75093-7792
Ph: (972)625-0110
Fax: (972)625-0110
E-mail: don@dondillon.com
URL: http://www.pianonet.com
Contact: Donald W. Dillon, Exec. Dir.
Founded: 1962. **Membership Dues:** individual, teacher, technician, $20 (annual) ● publisher, college, retail, $40 (annual). **Description:** Educational arm of the Piano Manufacturers Association International. Seeks to achieve maximum public interest and participation in playing the piano. Works with piano teachers, technicians, publishers, retailers, and performers to promote cooperation and interaction between segments of the music industry. **Publications:** *NPF Piano Notes*, quarterly ● Brochures ● Videos. **Price:** $35.00 plus shipping and handling.

8928 ■ NFHS Music Association
PO Box 690
Indianapolis, IN 46206
Ph: (317)972-6900
Fax: (317)822-5700
E-mail: ksummers@nfhs.org
URL: http://www.nfhs.org
Contact: Kent Summers, Asst. Dir.
Founded: 1983. **Members:** 842. **Membership Dues:** individual, $20 (annual). **Description:** Highschool music directors and judges. Disseminates information regarding the administration of music programs and the judging of music contests. Provides personal liability insurance for members. **Awards:** Outstanding Music Educator Award. **Frequency:** annual. **Type:** recognition. **Recipient:** for outstanding high school music educators. **Affiliated With:** National Federation of State High School Associations. **Formerly:** (1986) National Federation Music Adjudicator Association; (2002) National Federation Interscholastic Music Association. **Publications:** *NFHS Music Association Journal*, semiannual. Contains "how-to" articles and analyses of current styles and techniques in music. **Circulation:** 900 ● *NFHS News*, bimonthly. Newsletter. **Conventions/Meetings:** annual conference.

8929 ■ Organization of American Kodaly Educators (OAKE)
1612 29th Ave. S
Moorhead, MN 56560
Ph: (218)227-6253
Fax: (218)277-6254
E-mail: oakeoffice@oake.org
URL: http://www.oake.org
Contact: Brent Gault, Pres.
Founded: 1973. **Members:** 1,700. **Membership Dues:** active, institutional, $75 (annual) ● student, $20 (annual) ● library, corresponding, $70 (annual) ● life, $1,000 ● retired, $40 (annual) ● sustaining, $125 (annual). **Staff:** 1. **Budget:** $300,000. **Regional Groups:** 8. **State Groups:** 36. **Description:** Represents music educators, students, organizations, schools, and libraries interested in the Kodaly concept of music education. Zoltan Kodaly (1882-1967), Hungarian composer and educator, originated a concept of music education that seeks to develop the sensibilities, intellectual facilities, and skills of children, with the intention of creating a musically educated public. Objectives are: to encourage communication and cooperation among Kodaly educators; to encourage musical and human growth; to provide a forum for comment on the impact of the Kodaly concept; to recognize, identify, and convey the multicultural musical heritage of American society; to contribute to and encourage the aesthetic education of the child. Conducts clinics and other small unit activities. **Libraries: Type:** reference. **Holdings:** 31; archival material. **Subjects:** music education. **Awards: Frequency:** annual. **Type:** grant. **Recipient:** for research and educational programs ● **Type:** recognition. **Computer Services:** Mailing lists. **Affiliated With:** International Kodaly Society; MENC: The National Association for Music Education. **Publications:** *Kodaly Concept of Music Education*. Brochures. Contains information on music education. **Price:** free for members; $1.00 for nonmembers. **Advertising:** accepted ● *Kodaly Envoy*, quarterly. Journal. **Price:** $1.00/copy for members; $2.50/copy for nonmembers. ISSN: 1084-1776. **Advertising:** accepted ● *OAKE Research Collection Vol. 1*. Monograph. Contains multicultural songs, games and dances. ● *The Owl Sings*. Book. Includes a collection of folksongs arranged for young voices. **Price:** $10.50/copy for members; $12.00/copy for nonmembers ● *Sourwood Mountain*. Book. Includes folksongs arranged for children's voices. **Price:** $10.50/copy for members; $12.00/copy for nonmembers ● *Who Was Kodaly: OAKE Monograph No. 1*. **Price:** $6.50/copy for members; $8.00/copy for nonmembers ● The Sounds of Rounds & Canons; Traditional & contemporary rounds/canons from around the world. **Conventions/Meetings:** annual conference, with music education (exhibits) ● workshop.

8930 ■ Society for General Music (SGM)
c/o MENC: The National Association for Music Education
1806 Robert Fulton Dr.
Reston, VA 20191
Ph: (703)860-4000
Free: (800)336-3768
Fax: (703)860-1531
E-mail: info@menc.org
URL: http://www.menc.org
Contact: Mary Jo Ruane, Contact
Founded: 1982. **Members:** 3,100. **Description:** A society of MENC: The National Association for Music Education (see separate entry). Consists of MENC members interested in general music education who are united to provide direction and leadership by uniting general music groups. Provides forum for discussion of different approaches to all levels of general music education. **Telecommunication Services:** electronic mail, maryj@menc.org. **Affiliated With:** MENC: The National Association for Music Education. **Publications:** *General Music Today*, 3/year. Journal. ISSN: 1048-3713. **Conventions/Meetings:** biennial conference, held in conjunction with MENC (exhibits).

8931 ■ Society for Music Teacher Education (SMTE)
c/o MENC: National Association for Music Education
1806 Robert Fulton Dr.
Reston, VA 20191
Ph: (703)860-4000
Free: (800)336-3768
Fax: (703)860-1531
E-mail: dester@bsu.edu
URL: http://smte.us
Contact: Don P. Ester, Chm.
Founded: 1983. **State Groups:** 50. **Description:** College faculty and individuals involved in music education who are members of the Music Educators National Conference (see separate entry). Seeks to improve the quality of music teacher education. Represents members before certification boards, state departments of education and other professional organizations. Conducts professional training seminars. **Telecommunication Services:** additional toll-free number, (800)828-0229. **Formerly:** (1984) Council on Music Teacher Education. **Publications:** *Journal of Music Teacher Education*, semiannual. ISSN: 1057-0837. **Conventions/Meetings:** biennial meeting, held in conjunction with MENC (exhibits).

8932 ■ Suzuki Association of the Americas (SAA)
PO Box 17310
Boulder, CO 80308
Ph: (303)444-0948
Free: (888)378-9854
Fax: (303)444-0984
E-mail: info@suzukiassociation.org
URL: http://www.suzukiassociation.org
Contact: Pamela Brasch, Exec. Dir.
Founded: 1972. **Members:** 8,000. **Membership Dues:** active in U.S., $60 (annual) ● active in Canada, C$70 (annual) ● association in U.S., $32 (annual) ● association in Canada, C$37 (annual). **Staff:** 7. **Budget:** $600,000. **Description:** Represents parents and teachers united to promote the Suzuki Method of music education for children. (The Suzuki Method works on the assumption that children learn music in the same way they learn language: by repetition and imitation. Children play size-appropriate instruments, listen to recordings of music of outstanding quality, and learn to read notes soon after they have experienced the music-making process.) Offers instruction in violin, viola, cello, string bass, harp, flute, guitar, recorder, and piano. **Awards: Frequency:** annual. **Type:** scholarship. **Computer Services:** Mailing lists. **Publications:** *American Suzuki Journal*, quarterly. **Price:** included in membership dues. ISSN: 0193-5372. **Circulation:** 8,200. **Advertising:** accepted ● Pamphlets ● Videos. **Conventions/Meetings:** biennial Teacher Conference (exhibits).

8933 ■ Technology Institute for Music Educators (TI:ME)
305 Maple Ave.
Wyncote, PA 19095
Ph: (617)747-2816
E-mail: jpdunphy@comcast.net
URL: http://www.ti-me.org
Contact: John Dunphy, Exec. Dir.
Founded: 1995. **Membership Dues:** individual, $40 (annual) ● institutional/commercial, $250 (annual) ● student, $20 (annual) ● library, $30 (annual). **Description:** Works to assist music educators in the application of technology to improve music education. **Telecommunication Services:** electronic mail, timemused@ti-me.org. **Conventions/Meetings:** annual conference.

8934 ■ Women Band Directors International (WBDI)
10611 Ridgewood Dr.
Palos Park, IL 60464-2589
Ph: (765)463-1738
Fax: (765)463-1738
E-mail: carolnen@aol.com
URL: http://www.womenbanddirectors.org
Contact: Carol Nendza, Treas./Membership Chair
Founded: 1969. **Members:** 420. **Membership Dues:** professional band director, $30 (annual) ● student, $20 (annual). **Staff:** 1. **Budget:** $6,000. **Regional Groups:** 6. **State Groups:** 30. **Description:** Women band directors. Objectives are: to develop a comprehensive program of musical and educational benefit to women band directors and their subjects; to work with administrators to provide the best music education program possible; to provide for equality of women in the profession; to establish a common meeting ground for an exchange of ideas, methods, and problems peculiar to women band directors. Encourages young women entering the instrumental musical field; recognizes the obligations of the school band to school and community, and encourages reciprocal support. Maintains hall of fame and biographical archives. Holds competitions; offers scholarship. Compiles statistics. **Libraries: Type:** by appointment only. **Holdings:** 32; archival material. **Awards:** Citation of Merit. **Frequency:** annual. **Type:** recognition. **Recipient:** for members who have contributed significantly to WBDNA ● International Golden Rose, Silver Baton, Scroll of Excellence. **Type:** recognition. **Recipient:** for women of national reputation and outstanding achievement in instrumental music ● Music. **Frequency:** quarterly. **Type:** scholarship. **Recipient:** to music students ● **Type:** scholarship. **Recipient:** to 4 college students working toward a degree in music ● Scroll of Excellence. **Frequency:** annual. **Type:** recognition. **Recipient:** for women in instrumental music at the state, national, or international level ● Silver Baton. **Type:** recognition. **Recipient:** for members whose bands have high performance levels or who have made outstanding contributions to the improvement of bands. **Formerly:** (1999) Women Band Directors National Association. **Publications:** *WBDNA Directory*, annual. **Price:** included in membership dues. **Advertising:** accepted ● *Woman Conductor*, quarterly. Journal. Reports on career improvement, conducting techniques, and association news. Features employment opportunities. **Price:** included in membership dues. **Circulation:** 500 ● *Women of the Podium*, periodic. Directory. Contains biographies. **Conventions/Meetings:** semiannual Midwest Band and Orchestra Clinic - workshop, all types of band and orchestra music, instrument, supplies and services (exhibits) - summer and winter.

Native American

8935 ■ American Indian Higher Education Consortium (AIHEC)
121 Oronoco St.
Alexandria, VA 22314
Ph: (703)838-0400
Fax: (703)838-0388
E-mail: ggipp@aihec.org
URL: http://www.aihec.org
Contact: Gerald E. Gipp PhD, Exec. Dir.
Founded: 1972. **Members:** 35. **Staff:** 15. **Description:** Promotes the improvement of post-secondary and higher education institutions for American Indian, Eskimo, and Alaskan Natives. Advocates for tribal colleges located on or near Indian reservations. Conducts training programs for administrators, teachers, and support staffs. Establishes information centers for the dissemination of information. Encourages the continued development of language, culture, and traditions of the American Indian, Eskimo, and Alaskan Natives. **Publications:** *Tribal College: Journal of American Indian Higher Education*, quarterly. **Price:** $14.00 for students; $34.00 for institutions; $24.00 for individuals. ISSN: 1052-5505. **Circulation:** 9,000. **Advertising:** accepted. Alternate Formats: online. Also Cited As: *Tribal College Journal*. **Conventions/Meetings:** quarterly board meeting (exhibits).

8936 ■ Association of Community Tribal Schools (ACTS)
c/o Dr. Roger Bordeaux, Exec. Dir.
5320 Paragon St.
Rocklin, CA 95677
Ph: (916)315-0906
Fax: (916)315-0906
E-mail: acts@acts-tribal.org
URL: http://acts-tribal.org
Contact: Dr. Roger Bordeaux, Exec. Dir.
Founded: 1982. **Members:** 30. **Budget:** $38,000. **Regional Groups:** 2. **Description:** American Indian-controlled schools organized under the Indian Self-Determination and Educational Assistance Act and Tribally Controlled Schools Act; American Indian schools seeking status under these acts; interested individuals and organizations. Advocates Indian self-determination and Indian-controlled school. Provides technical assistance in making self-determination contracts; offers school board training assistance. **Formerly:** (1987) Association of Contract Tribal Schools. **Publications:** Newsletter, quarterly. **Conventions/Meetings:** annual conference and workshop (exhibits) - always spring.

8937 ■ Council for Indian Education (CIE)
1240 Burlington Ave.
Billings, MT 59102-4224
Ph: (406)248-3465 (406)652-7598
Fax: (406)248-1297
E-mail: cie@cie-mt.org
URL: http://www.cie-mt.org
Contact: Dr. Hap Gilliand, Pres./Ed.
Founded: 1970. **Members:** 100. **Membership Dues:** regular, $20 (annual) ● associate, $10 (annual) ● helping, $50 (annual) ● corporate, $75 (annual) ● promoter, $100 (annual) ● sponsor, $300 (annual) ● book sponsor, $1,000 (annual). **Staff:** 3. **Description:** Individuals interested in improving and securing higher standards of education for American Indian children. Promotes quality children's literature on authentic Indian culture. Publishes books about American Indian life, past and present, for use in reading programs. Conducts in-service education of teachers working on Indian reservations. **Formerly:** (1982) Montana Council for Indian Education. **Publications:** Books. For children. ● Also publishes teacher training textbooks. **Conventions/Meetings:** annual meeting, gathering of members, board of directors, and Intertribal Indian Editorial Board - usually January.

8938 ■ Indian Educators Federation (IEF)
2309 Renard Pl. SE, Ste.202
Albuquerque, NM 87106
Ph: (505)243-4088
Free: (888)433-2382
Fax: (505)243-4098
E-mail: secretary@ief-aft.org
URL: http://www.ief-aft.org
Contact: Patrick Carr, Pres.
Founded: 1967. **Members:** 400. **Description:** Professional educators employed in federal schools operated by the Bureau of Indian Affairs. Protects the rights and interests of teachers in Indian education. Promotes quality educational opportunities for Indian students. Maintains speakers' bureau. **Telecommunication Services:** electronic mail, pat@ief-aft.org. **Affiliated With:** AFL-CIO; American Federation of Teachers. **Formerly:** (1994) National Council of BIA Educators. **Conventions/Meetings:** annual meeting.

8939 ■ International Association of Native American Studies (IANAS)
c/o NAAAS and Affiliates
PO Box 6670
Scarborough, ME 04070-6670
Ph: (207)839-8004
Fax: (207)839-3776
E-mail: naaasconference@earthlink.net
URL: http://www.naaas.org
Contact: Dr. Lemuel Berry Jr., Exec. Dir./Founder
Founded: 1998. **Members:** 100. **Membership Dues:** individual, $125 (annual) ● institution, $500 (annual) ● student, sustaining, $100 (annual) ● life, $3,000. **Staff:** 7. **Regional Groups:** 4. **Description:** Post-secondary educational institutions offering Native American studies programs; academics, students, and other individuals with an interest in Native American studies. Seeks to advance the field of Native American studies. Provides a forum for the presentation of research results; conducts educational programs; maintains speakers' bureau. **Publications:** *Journal of Intercultural Disciplines*, semiannual. **Price:** $46.50/year. **Circulation:** 1,000. **Advertising:** accepted. **Conventions/Meetings:** annual conference (exhibits).

8940 ■ National Association of Native American Studies (NANAS)
PO Box 6670
Scarborough, ME 04070-6670
Ph: (207)839-8004
Fax: (207)839-3776
E-mail: naaasconference@earthlink.net
URL: http://www.naaas.org
Contact: Dr. Lemuel Berry Jr., Exec. Dir.
Membership Dues: life, $3,000 ● institution, $500 (annual) ● individual, $125 (annual) ● student and sustaining donor, $100 (annual). **Description:** Promotes and supports the interest of Native Americans. **Publications:** *Journal of Intercultural Disciplines*, semiannual, spring and fall. **Price:** free for members; $30.00 /year for nonmembers; $50.00 /year for libraries, agencies, etc.; $18.00/copy for nonmembers ● Newsletters ● Monographs, annual. Alternate Formats: online.

8941 ■ National Indian Education Association (NIEA)
110 Maryland Ave. NE, Ste.104
Washington, DC 20002
Ph: (202)544-7290
Fax: (202)544-7293
E-mail: niea@niea.org
URL: http://www.niea.org
Contact: Lillian A. Sparks Esq., Exec. Dir.
Founded: 1969. **Members:** 2,000. **Membership Dues:** general, associate, international, $50 (annual) ● student (voting and non-voting), elder, $25 (annual) ● tribal, educational institution, associate organization, federal agency, $400 (annual) ● corporate, $500 (annual). **Staff:** 1. **Budget:** $100,000. **Description:** American Indians, Alaska natives, and associate members are non-Indians. Advocates educational programs to improve the social and economic well-being of American Indians and Alaskan natives. Represents diversity of geographic and tribal backgrounds. Focuses on exchange of ideas, techniques, and research methods among the participants in Indian/native education through an annual fall convention. **Awards:** Community Service Award. **Frequency:** annual. **Type:** recognition. **Recipient:** for natives that exemplify positive role as an individual ● Educator of the Year. **Frequency:** annual. **Type:** recognition. **Recipient:** for native teachers, counselors, or administrators ● Elder of the Year. **Frequency:** annual. **Type:** recognition. **Recipient:** for 60 years or older individuals ● Parent of the Year. **Frequency:** annual. **Type:** recognition. **Recipient:** for native parents with outstanding leadership, commitment, concern and voluntary efforts ● Teacher of the Year. **Frequency:** annual. **Type:** recognition. **Recipient:** for exceptional achievement in teaching AI/AN/NH students. **Publications:** *Indian Education Newsletter*, quarterly. **Conventions/Meetings:** annual meeting (exhibits) - always fall.

8942 ■ Navajo Area School Board Association (NASBA)
PO Box 3719
Window Rock, AZ 86515-0578
Ph: (928)871-5225 (928)871-5223

Fax: (928)871-5148
Contact: Pauline Billie, Exec. Dir.
Founded: 1969. **Members:** 275. **Membership Dues:** school board organization, $1,500 (annual). **Staff:** 10. **Budget:** $336,000. **Local Groups:** 54. **Description:** Elected school board members of Navajo communities authorized by the Navajo National Council to promote and advocate for quality education for the Navajo population. Provides training and technical services for school governance, improvement, and student achievement goals. Maintains speakers' bureau; compiles statistics. **Awards:** School Board Member of the Year. **Frequency:** annual. **Type:** recognition ● School Board of the Year. **Frequency:** annual. **Type:** recognition. **Computer Services:** Online services, school board services; training technical assistance. **Boards:** School. **Publications:** *NASBA News* (in English and Navajo), monthly. Newsletter. Includes education trends and program changes. **Price:** free. **Circulation:** 1,000. **Advertising:** accepted. **Conventions/Meetings:** annual conference, with training on Navajo School Governance (exhibits).

Naturopathy

8943 ■ Association of Accredited Naturopathic Medical Colleges (AANMC)
4435 Wisconsin Ave. NW, Ste.403
Washington, DC 20016
Ph: (202)237-8150
Free: (866)538-2267
Fax: (202)237-8152
E-mail: info@aanmc.org
URL: http://www.aanmc.org
Contact: Coquina Deger, Managing Ed.
Founded: 2001. **Multinational. Description:** Promotes the naturopathic medical profession. Supports the academic efforts of accredited and recognized schools of naturopathic medicine. Fosters collaboration between its members and compatible organizations. Seeks to improve the quality of education, operations, research and patient care. **Publications:** *Explore Naturopathic Medicine.* Brochure. Alternate Formats: online ● *Naturopathic Medical School E-Newsletter.* Alternate Formats: online.

Nepalese

8944 ■ Association of Nepal and Himalayan Studies (ANHS)
c/o Himalaya
Portland State Univ.
Geography Dept.
Box 751
Portland, OR 97207-0751
Ph: (503)725-8044 (503)725-8312
Free: (800)547-8887
Fax: (503)725-3166
E-mail: hrb@pdx.edu
URL: http://www.macalester.edu/~guneratne
Contact: Dr. Arjun Guneratue, Pres.
Founded: 1972. **Members:** 400. **Membership Dues:** individual, $35 (annual) ● institution, library, $75 (annual) ● student, Himalayan national, $20 (annual). **Staff:** 2. **Description:** Scientists, scholars, and development planners; individuals interested in Nepal and the Himalayas; libraries. Seeks to further studies and research on the Himalayas and Nepal and to contribute to international communication among scholars. Promotes panel discussions on Himalayan subjects. **Additional Websites:** http://www.himalayan.pdx.edu. **Telecommunication Services:** electronic mail, guneratne@macalester.edu. **Affiliated With:** Association for Asian Studies. **Formerly:** (2001) Nepal Studies Association. **Publications:** *Himalaya*, semiannual. Journal. Includes scholarly articles, book reviews, and recent conference abstracts. **Price:** available to members only. **Circulation:** 400. **Advertising:** accepted. **Conventions/Meetings:** annual South Asian Conference (exhibits) - usually second week in October, Friday-Sunday.

Nonviolence

8945 ■ Empower Program
Address Unknown since 2008
URL: http://www.empowered.org
Founded: 1992. **Description:** Empowers young people and adults to create safe schools and communities by providing effective prevention strategies to address bullying and other forms of peer aggression. Promotes violence prevention. Seeks to teach girls self-defense as a means of safeguarding them from violence. Provides innovative approaches to dealing with violence. **Telecommunication Services:** electronic mail, bpursell@empowered.org. **Programs:** Owning Up; Reaching Out; Real Young Men; Stepping Up. **Publications:** *Empowered.* Newsletter ● Brochures.

Nursing

8946 ■ International Nursing Coalition for Mass Casualty Education (INCMCE)
c/o Colleen Conway-Welch, PhD, Dir.
Vanderbilt Univ. School of Nursing
461 21st Ave. S
111 Godchaux Hall
Nashville, TN 37240
Ph: (615)343-8876
Fax: (615)292-0158
E-mail: colleen.conway-welch@vanderbilt.edu
URL: http://www.mc.vanderbilt.edu/nursing/incmce
Contact: Colleen Conway-Welch PhD, Dir.
Founded: 2001. **Multinational. Description:** Facilitates the development of sustainable educational policies related to mass casualty events. Increases awareness of all nurses regarding mass casualty incidents. Initiates research efforts designed to improve nursing care and mass casualty incident responses. **Publications:** Proceedings. Alternate Formats: online.

Nutrition

8947 ■ Association of Nutrition Departments and Programs (ANDP)
c/o Dr. Connie M. Weaver, Chair
Purdue Univ., Foods and Nutrition
700 W State St.
West Lafayette, IN 47907-2059
E-mail: weavercm@purdue.edu
URL: http://andpnet.org
Contact: Dr. Connie M. Weaver, Chair
Members: 50. **Description:** Promotes the common interests of academic units of nutrition in colleges and universities which offer or support graduate degree programs in nutrition. Assists with student recruitment for nutrition departments and programs. Addresses policy issues pertaining to nutrition. Acts as a resource for government agencies, legislators, and industry to provide points of contact with experts in nutrition throughout the United States.

Occupational Safety and Health

8948 ■ NATSO Foundation
1737 King St., Ste.200
Alexandria, VA 22314
Ph: (703)549-2100
Free: (888)275-6287
Fax: (703)684-9667
E-mail: foundation@natsofoundation.org
URL: http://www.natsofoundation.org
Contact: Sharon L. Corigliano, Exec. Dir.
Founded: 1989. **Budget:** $400,000. **Description:** Research, educational and public outreach subsidiary of America's Travel Plaza and Truckstop Industry. Offers scholarships and research grants. Administers national blood drive and disaster relief programs. **Libraries: Type:** reference. **Subjects:** transportation, drug/alcohol abuse, environment, freight, fuel, highway development. **Awards:** Bill Moon Scholarship Award. **Frequency:** annual. **Type:** scholarship. **Recipient:** for students' college expenses ● Roadblock Driver of the Year Award. **Frequency:** annual. **Type:** recognition. **Formerly:** (1999) Maryland Truk Stop Foundation.

Orthopedics

8949 ■ Orthopaedic Research and Education Foundation (OREF)
6300 N River Rd., Ste.700
Rosemont, IL 60018
Ph: (847)698-9980 (847)384-4346
Fax: (847)698-7806
E-mail: communications@oref.org
URL: http://www.oref.org
Contact: Mr. Gene Wurth, Pres./CEO
Founded: 1955. **Staff:** 16. **Budget:** $3,200,000. **Description:** Focuses on the advancement of knowledge concerning the prevention and treatment of conditions affecting the musculoskeletal and related systems and the maintenance of the general physical well being of the individual. **Awards:** Career Development Award. **Frequency:** annual. **Type:** monetary. **Recipient:** for scientific research of orthopedic surgeons ● Prospective Clinical Research Grant. **Frequency:** annual. **Type:** grant. **Recipient:** for promising prospective studies in the field of orthopedic surgery ● Research Grant. **Frequency:** annual. **Type:** grant. **Recipient:** for promising research projects.

Outdoor Education

8950 ■ Association of Outdoor Recreation and Education (AORE)
6511 Buckshore Dr.
Whitmore Lake, MI 48189
Ph: (810)299-2782
Fax: (810)299-3436
E-mail: nationaloffice@aore.org
URL: http://www.aore.org
Contact: Jeannette Stawski, Natl. Office Dir.
Founded: 1993. **Members:** 500. **Membership Dues:** student, associate, $35 (annual) ● professional, $75 (annual) ● organizational, $145 (annual) ● vendor, $195 (annual). **Staff:** 1. **Description:** Represents outdoor recreation and education professionals and students. Seeks to advance the field of outdoor recreation and education. **Publications:** *Association News*, quarterly. Newsletter ● *International Conference on Outdoor Recreation & Education (ICORE)*, annual. Proceedings. **Conventions/Meetings:** annual International Conference on Outdoor Recreation and Education, features pre- and post-conference workshops, professional presentations, and presentations by leaders in the field of outdoor recreation and education.

8951 ■ Wilderness Classroom Organization (WCO)
4605 Grand Ave.
Western Springs, IL 60558
Ph: (312)505-9973
E-mail: info@wildernessclassroom.com
URL: http://www.wildernessclassroom.com
Contact: Eric Frost, Founder/Co-Dir.
Description: Strives to engage, excite, and motivate students and teachers using an interactive technology-based learning model. Encourages people to expand and explore their world by fostering an appreciation for wilderness and cultural diversity. Provides curriculum based on state and national standards that will provide the motivation, instruction, and resources necessary to enhance teacher instruction. Fosters an interactive learning environment that turns students into adventurers. Develops lasting relationships between students and their Learning Adventure guides. Introduces children and young adults to the wonders of canoeing, kayaking, skiing, camping, and other forms of wilderness travel.

8952 ■ Wilderness Education Association (WEA)
900 E 7th St.
Bloomington, IN 47405
Ph: (812)855-4095
Fax: (812)855-8697
E-mail: wea@indiana.edu
URL: http://www.weainfo.org
Contact: Scott Jordan, Pres.
Founded: 1977. **Members:** 350. **Membership Dues:** student/associate, $35 (annual) ● library, $16 (annual) ● professional, $75 (annual) ● organization, affiliate, $250 (annual) ● corporate, $1,500 (annual) ● life, $1,000. **Staff:** 3. **Budget:** $100,000. **Regional Groups:** 9. **National Groups:** 49. **Description:** Promotes the professionalization of outdoor leadership. Improves the safety and quality of outdoor trips and enhances the conservation of the wild outdoors. Trains and certifies outdoor leaders; operates in affiliation with 43 colleges, universities, and outdoor programs. Conducts National Standard Program for Outdoor Leadership Certification. Provides national standards for outdoor leadership training. Reduces incidents of environmental harm; teaches basic skills in areas including judgment, leadership, expedition behavior, and environmental ethics to instructors of specialty activities and sports. Sponsors the Steward Program. **Awards:** Frank Lupton Service Award. **Frequency:** annual. **Type:** recognition. **Recipient:** for outstanding service to the WEA ● Kitty Drury Scholarship. **Frequency:** annual. **Type:** scholarship. **Recipient:** for WEA instructor development ● Paul Petzoldt Award. **Frequency:** annual. **Type:** recognition. **Recipient:** for excellence in wilderness education. **Computer Services:** Online services, job referral service for members. **Affiliated With:** American Camp Association; Association for Experiential Education. **Formerly:** (1980) Wilderness Education Association. **Publications:** *The Backcountry Classroom: Lesson Plans for Teaching in the Wilderness*. Book. **Price:** $24.99. **Circulation:** 1,500 ● *The New Wilderness Handbook*. **Price:** $11.95 ● *Trustees and Affiliates Briefing System*. Bulletin ● *WEA Legend*, 3/year. Newsletter. **Price:** included in membership dues. **Advertising:** accepted ● *Wilderness Education Association Affiliate Handbook*, periodic. Includes affiliation membership process, curriculum outline, and outdoor leader evaluation process. ● *Wilderness Educator: WEA Curriculum Guide*. Book. **Price:** $29.95. **Conventions/Meetings:** annual National Conference on Outdoor Leadership (exhibits).

Parents

8953 ■ National Association of Hebrew Day School PTAs
160 Broadway, 4th Fl.
New York, NY 10038
Ph: (212)227-1000
Fax: (212)406-6934
E-mail: umesorah@aol.com
Contact: Bernice Brand, Exec. Sec.
Founded: 1947. **Members:** 300. **Staff:** 2. **Languages:** English, Hebrew. **Description:** Federation of 300 parent-teacher associations of Hebrew elementary and secondary schools. Provides services for members in areas of programming, fundraising, and individual consultation. **Publications:** *National PTA Bulletin*, 3/year ● Manuals. Includes PTA information. ● Pamphlets. Includes fund-raising information.

8954 ■ National PTA - National Congress of Parents and Teachers
541 N Fairbanks Ct., Ste.1300
Chicago, IL 60611-3396
Ph: (312)670-6782
Free: (800)307-4PTA
Fax: (312)670-6783
E-mail: info@pta.org
URL: http://www.pta.org
Contact: Warlene Gary, CEO
Founded: 1897. **Members:** 5,897,934. **Membership Dues:** national, $25 (annual). **Staff:** 65. **Regional Groups:** 8. **State Groups:** 54. **Local Groups:** 26,000. **Description:** Parents, teachers, students, principals, administrators, and others interested in uniting the forces of home, school, and community on behalf of children and youth. Works for legislation benefiting children and youth through its Washington, DC office. Maintains resource center. **Libraries: Type:** not open to the public. **Holdings:** 5,000; archival material, books, periodicals, video recordings. **Subjects:** education, parenting, child advocacy, PTA history. **Awards:** Arts in Education Program: Reflection Program. **Frequency:** annual. **Type:** recognition. **Recipient:** for preschool to grade 12 students in literature musical composition, photography, and visual arts; sponsored by local PTA units ● Parent Involvement Schools of Excellence Certification. **Type:** recognition. **Recipient:** for schools having outstanding parent involvement practices ● Phoebe Apperson Hearst Outstanding Educator of the Year Award. **Frequency:** annual. **Type:** recognition. **Recipient:** for local or national outstanding educators who demonstrate professional excellence and commitment to the objectives of the PTA. **Programs:** Education; Health and Welfare; Leadership; Legislation. **Absorbed:** (1970) National Congress of Colored Parents and Teachers. **Formerly:** (1908) National Congress of Mothers; (1925) National Congress of Mothers and Parent-Teachers Associations; (1976) National Congress of Parents and Teachers. **Publications:** *Annual Resources for PTAs*, annual. Contains resources for PTAs. ● *Our Children*, bimonthly, issued in Sep., Oct., Nov./Dec., Jan./Feb., Mar., Apr./May. Magazine. Provides useful information on parenting, education, and child health and welfare. **Price:** $12.00 /year for members; $20.00 /year for nonmembers. ISSN: 1083-3080. **Circulation:** 36,000. Alternate Formats: microform. Also Cited As: *PTA Today* ● *The PTA Story: A Century of Commitment to Children*. Book. Contains a chronicle of the history of the National PTA. **Conventions/Meetings:** annual National PTA Convention, with workshops, seminars, and leadership training in the fields of education, health, welfare, advocacy and non-profit management (exhibits) ● periodic National PTA Legislative Conference.

8955 ■ National Visiting Teachers Association (NVTA)
Address Unknown since 2008
Founded: 1990. **Members:** 15. **Staff:** 2. **Budget:** $15,000. **Description:** Educators and education professionals. Encourages parents to take an active role in their child's education. Offers information regarding parents' rights and responsibilities in the education of their offspring, and assists parents in their efforts to monitor and reinforce the academic progress of their children. Sponsors youth services geared toward increasing students' awareness of their personal responsibility in educational development. Provides pre-service and ongoing in-service training to teaching staff. Assists educational agencies in developing effective communication strategies. **Publications:** Newsletter, quarterly. **Circulation:** 250. **Conventions/Meetings:** annual workshop.

8956 ■ New Parents Network
PO Box 64237
Tucson, AZ 85728-4237
Ph: (520)327-1451
Fax: (520)884-1854
E-mail: moreinfo@newparentsnetwork.org
URL: http://www.npn.org
Contact: Ms. Paula Dunn, Chair/Pres.
Founded: 1988. **Description:** Provides a windows-based software program for parents and professionals; software is installed on kiosks and the World Wide Web. Provides educational programs and children's services. Contains preventative and health-related parenting information. **Libraries: Type:** open to the public. **Subjects:** parenting. **Computer Services:** database ● online services.

8957 ■ Parent Network
c/o The Montessori Academy
530 E Day Rd.
Mishawaka, IN 46545
Ph: (574)255-1703
Contact: Becky Ludwick, Pres.
Founded: 1988. **Nonmembership. Description:** Parents of primary and secondary school-age children. Works to broaden the role of parents in the educational community. Acts as a forum for the exchange of information and ideas among parents. Promotes "curiosity, creativity and a love of learning in children". Conducts educational programs.

Peace

8958 ■ PeaceJam
5605 Yukon St.
Arvada, CO 80002
Ph: (303)455-2099
Fax: (303)455-3921
E-mail: info@peacejam.org
URL: http://www.peacejam.org
Contact: Beverly Keen, Chair
Founded: 1996. **Multinational. Description:** An international education program built around Nobel Peace Laureates that promotes peace throughout the world and inspires a new generation of peacemakers. Designed for high school youth, high school teachers, youth group leaders, and college-age mentors. Operates in South Africa, India, Guatemala, Costa Rica, United States, Mexico and Canada. **Programs:** Distinguished Speaker Series. **Publications:** *PeaceJam DVD*. Video. **Price:** $25.00 each, plus shipping and handling ● Book. **Price:** $22.00 each, plus shipping and handling.

8959 ■ Worldwide Forgiveness Alliance
20 Sunnyside Ave., Ste.A268
Mill Valley, CA 94941
Ph: (415)381-3372
Fax: (415)332-4003
E-mail: rwplath@forgivenessday.org
URL: http://www.forgivenessday.org
Contact: Robert W. Plath, Founder/Exec. Dir.
Membership Dues: celebration of Forgiveness Day, $20 (annual) ● sustaining, $50 (annual) ● sponsor, $100 (annual) ● patron, $500 (annual) ● president's club, $1,000 (annual) ● director's club, $2,000 (annual). **Multinational. Description:** Dedicated to evoking the healing power of forgiveness worldwide. **Publications:** Articles. Alternate Formats: online. **Conventions/Meetings:** annual International Forgiveness Day - meeting - 1st Sunday of August.

Personal Development

8960 ■ Society for Research on Identity Formation (SRIF)
c/o William M. Kurtines, PhD, Treas.
Florida Intl. Univ.
Dept. of Psychology
11200 SW 8th St.
Univ. Park, DM 269-F
Miami, FL 33199
Ph: (305)348-3941
E-mail: srif@fiu.edu
URL: http://w3.fiu.edu/srif
Contact: William M. Kurtines PhD, Treas.
Founded: 1985. **Members:** 150. **Membership Dues:** regular (includes journal), $75 (annual) ● shared (two voting privileges/one journal), $90 (annual) ● student (includes journal), affiliate (no voting privilege/includes journal), $40 (annual) ● student (no journal), $10 (annual). **Staff:** 1. **Languages:** English, Spanish. **Multinational. Description:** Dedicated to the study of identity issues and development. **Publications:** *Identity: An International Journal of Theory and Research*, quarterly. Also Cited As: *IJTR*. **Conventions/Meetings:** annual conference and convention ● annual meeting.

Personnel

8961 ■ American College Personnel Association (ACPA)
1 Dupont Cir. NW, Ste.300
Washington, DC 20036-1188

Ph: (202)835-2272
Fax: (202)296-3286
E-mail: info@acpa.nche.edu
URL: http://www.acpa.nche.edu
Contact: Vasti Torres, Pres.

Founded: 1924. **Members:** 8,000. **Membership Dues:** student, $25-$30 (annual) ● general, $110 (annual) ● emeritus, $45 (annual) ● transitional, $60 (annual) ● general institutional, $65 (annual) ● associate, $150 (annual) ● institutional, $195-$1,670 (annual). **Staff:** 10. **Budget:** $2,000,000. **State Groups:** 30. **Multinational. Description:** Represents individuals employed in higher education and involved in student personnel work, including administration, counseling, research, and teaching. Fosters student development in higher education in areas of service, advocacy, and standards by offering professional programs for educators committed to the overall development of post-secondary students. Sponsors professional and educational activities in cooperation with other organizations. Offers placement services. **Awards:** Ester Lloyd Jones Professional Service Award. **Frequency:** annual. **Type:** recognition. **Recipient:** for professional commitment to service and leadership or outstanding contributions to a body of knowledge through work such as films, speeches, and publications ● Voice of Inclusion Medallion. **Frequency:** annual. **Type:** recognition. **Recipient:** for individuals with exemplary contributions on campus programs. **Commissions:** Academic Affairs Administrators; Academic Support in Higher Education; Administrative Leadership; Admissions, Orientation, and First Year Experience; Alcohol and Other Drug Issues; Assessment for Student Development; Campus Judicial Affairs and Legal Issues; Career Development. **Formerly:** (1929) National Association of Appointment Secretaries; (1931) National Association of Placement Personnel Officers. **Publications:** *About Campus*, bimonthly. Magazine. **Price:** included in membership dues; $60.00 for nonmembers; $125.00 outside U.S., Canada and Mexico. ISSN: 1086-4822. **Circulation:** 8,500. **Advertising:** accepted ● *Journal of College Student Development*, bimonthly. **Price:** included in membership dues; $60.00 /year for nonmembers (individuals); $120.00 /year for nonmembers (institutions). ISSN: 0021-9789. **Circulation:** 7,500. **Advertising:** accepted. Alternate Formats: online. **Conventions/Meetings:** annual convention (exhibits) - always March/April. 2009 Mar. 28-Apr. 1, Washington, DC ● bimonthly seminar and workshop ● annual workshop, student affairs/development professionals (exhibits).

8962 ■ College and University Professional Association for Human Resources (CUPA-HR)
2607 Kingston Pike, Ste.250
Knoxville, TN 37919
Ph: (865)637-7673
Fax: (865)637-7674
E-mail: abrantley@cupahr.org
URL: http://www.cupahr.org
Contact: Andy Brantley, CEO

Founded: 1946. **Members:** 9,500. **Staff:** 26. **Budget:** $4,000,000. **Regional Groups:** 5. **State Groups:** 28. **Description:** Professional organization made up of colleges and universities interested in the improvement of campus Human Resource administration. Carries out special research projects and surveys, including annual administrative compensation survey for higher education. Sponsors training seminars to meet members' technical, professional, and developmental needs in human resource management. Disseminates information to members regarding federal legislation and regulations affecting higher education institutions. Compiles statistics. **Awards:** Distinguished Service Award. **Frequency:** annual. **Type:** recognition. **Recipient:** for a member who, during the past fiscal year, has given outstanding service through its constituent activities ● Donald E. Dickason Award. **Frequency:** annual. **Type:** recognition. **Recipient:** for outstanding service to CUPA-HR over a sustained period of five or more years ● Kathryn G. Hansen Publication Award. **Frequency:** annual. **Type:** recognition. **Recipient:** for the author or editor of a CUPA-HR publication or videotape that has made a significant contribution in the field of human resource management in the past year ● Quality in Human Resource Practice Award. **Frequency:** annual. **Type:** recognition. **Recipient:** for significant contributions to the practice of human resource management in higher education ● Teaching Excellence Award. **Frequency:** annual. **Type:** recognition. **Recipient:** for a member who, during the past three years, has demonstrated outstanding teaching preparedness, creativity, and recognized excellence and professionalism in higher education human resource management. **Computer Services:** database ● mailing lists. **Committees:** Career Development; Knowledge Center; National Awards; Public Policy; Strategic Planning Advisory. **Councils:** Corporate Advisory. **Task Forces:** Policy Governance. **Formerly:** (2001) College and University Personnel Association. **Publications:** *CUPA-HR Journal*, semiannual. **Price:** included in membership dues. **Advertising:** accepted ● *CUPA-HR News*, monthly. Newsletter. Covers national, legal, and regulatory issues affecting professionals in higher education. Also includes Association news. **Price:** included in membership dues. ISSN: 0892-7855. **Advertising:** accepted. Alternate Formats: online ● Surveys, annual. Contains salary, benefits and benchmarking surveys for administrative positions at higher educational institutions, faculty and other staffs. **Price:** included in membership dues ● Also publishes research reports, books, and monographs. **Conventions/Meetings:** annual conference (exhibits) - 2008 Oct. 12-15, St. Louis, MO; 2009 Oct. 11-14, Portland, OR ● regional meeting - 5/year ● annual seminar.

Pharmacy

8963 ■ Pharmacy Technician Educators Council (PTEC)
c/o Dolores Sewchok, Pres.
Bidwell Training Center, Inc.
1650 Metropolitan St., Ste.200
Pittsburgh, PA 15233
Ph: (412)323-4000
E-mail: dsewchok@mcg-btc.org
URL: http://www.rxptec.org
Contact: Dolores Sewchok, Pres.

Founded: 1991. **Membership Dues:** active, associate, $80 (annual) ● corporate, $500 (annual). **Multinational. Description:** Assists the profession of pharmacy in preparing high quality, well-trained technical personnel through education and practical training. Promotes the profession of pharmacy through professional activities and dissemination of information and knowledge to members, pharmacy organizations, and other specialists and professions. Focuses on the interests and concerns of technician educators. **Awards:** The Phil Naut Award. **Frequency:** annual. **Type:** recognition. **Recipient:** to associate member who has demonstrated a valued contribution to the education and training of pharmacy technicians ● The Roy Kemp Award. **Frequency:** annual. **Type:** recognition. **Recipient:** to a member who has demonstrated a valued contribution to the education of pharmacy technicians. **Publications:** *journal of Pharmacy Technology*. Contains information dedicated to pharmacy technician practice, training, and technology. **Price:** included in membership dues. ISSN: 8755-1225. **Advertising:** accepted. Also Cited As: *jPT* ● Newsletter, monthly. Alternate Formats: online ● Newsletter, quarterly. Alternate Formats: online.

Philosophy

8964 ■ American Association of Philosophy Teachers (AAPT)
c/o Betsy Decyk, Exec. Dir.
Off. of Univ. Ombuds
6300 State Univ. Dr., No. 140
Long Beach, CA 90815
E-mail: bdecyk@csulb.edu
URL: http://aapt-online.org
Contact: Betsy Decyk, Exec. Dir.

Founded: 1979. **Members:** 300. **Membership Dues:** regular, $25 (annual) ● student, emeritus, part-time/adjunct, $15 (annual) ● life, $500. **Staff:** 1. **Description:** Individuals interested in improving the quality of philosophy teaching at all educational levels. Conducts workshops and educational programs; operates speakers' bureau. **Computer Services:** database ● mailing lists. **Committees:** Lenssen Prize; Selection. **Publications:** *AAPT News*, 3/year. Newsletter. Includes articles on teaching, information on conferences and programs, reports, and calendar of events. **Price:** included in membership dues. **Circulation:** 300. **Advertising:** accepted. Alternate Formats: online. **Conventions/Meetings:** meeting, held in conjunction with the American Philosophical Association - 3/year ● biennial Teaching Philosophy - workshop and conference (exhibits) - always August, even-numbered years. 2008 Aug. 6-10, Guelph, ON, Canada.

8965 ■ American Catholic Philosophical Association (ACPA)
Univ. of St. Thomas
Centre for Thomistic Stud.
3800 Montrose Blvd.
Houston, TX 77006
Ph: (713)942-3483
Fax: (713)942-3464
E-mail: osborntm@stthom.edu
URL: http://www.acpaweb.org
Contact: Michael Baur, Natl. Sec.

Founded: 1926. **Members:** 1,600. **Staff:** 3. **Description:** College and university teachers of philosophy; students engaged in research; writers and others interested in philosophical knowledge. **Awards:** ACPA Young Scholar Award. **Frequency:** annual. **Type:** recognition. **Recipient:** for the best paper in philosophy by a young scholar presented at the annual meeting ● Aquinas Medal. **Frequency:** annual. **Type:** medal. **Recipient:** for an outstanding work in philosophy. **Computer Services:** Mailing lists. **Committees:** Call for Papers; International Congress. **Affiliated With:** American Philosophical Association; International Federation of Philosophical Societies. **Publications:** *American Catholic Philosophical Quarterly*. Journal. Covers subjects in philosophy, religion, ethics, cultures, and related fields. Includes book reviews. **Price:** included in membership dues; $25.00 /year for nonmembers. ISSN: 1051-3558. **Circulation:** 2,000. **Advertising:** accepted. Alternate Formats: microform ● *Proceedings of American Catholic Philosophical Association*, annual. **Price:** included in membership dues; $36.00/copy for nonmembers. **Circulation:** 2,000. Alternate Formats: microform. **Conventions/Meetings:** annual convention (exhibits) - always November.

8966 ■ American Nihilism Association
Address Unknown since 2008

Founded: 1914. **Members:** 2,200. **Staff:** 3. **Budget:** $100,000. **Regional Groups:** 4. **State Groups:** 26. **Local Groups:** 91. **Description:** Espouses the philosophy of Friedrich Nietzsche (1844-1900), who "sketched an overall theory of value, in which the human animal invents value mattrices with which to survive within, and perhaps dominate, his physical and psychological environments.". **Awards:** Turgenev Medal. **Frequency:** annual. **Type:** recognition. **Publications:** *Abyss*, quarterly. Journal. Scholarly journal on nihilism and associated issues. **Conventions/Meetings:** annual International Nihilism Conference.

8967 ■ Association for Practical and Professional Ethics (APPE)
Indiana Univ.
618 E 3rd St.
Bloomington, IN 47405-3602
Ph: (812)855-6450
Fax: (812)855-3315
E-mail: appe@indiana.edu
URL: http://www.indiana.edu/~appe
Contact: Dr. Brian Schrag, Exec. Sec.

Founded: 1990. **Members:** 700. **Membership Dues:** regular (under $25K income level), $25 (annual) ● regular ($25K-40K income level), $50 (annual) ● regular ($41K-75K income level), $75 (annual) ● regular ($75K income level), $100 (annual) ● supporting individual, institutional, $150 (annual) ●

sustaining, RCREC organization, $500 (annual) ● RCREC organizational sponsor, $2,000 (annual). **Staff:** 2. **Budget:** $110,000. **Description:** Scholars and professionals interested in practical and professional ethics. Encourages high quality interdisciplinary scholarship and teaching in ethics. Fosters communication and joint ventures among centers, schools, colleges, and individual faculty. Supports efforts to develop curricula and research. **Computer Services:** Mailing lists. **Publications:** *Ethically Speaking*, semiannual. Newsletter. **Price:** included in membership dues; $10.00 /year for nonmembers. **Circulation:** 10,000 ● *Oxford University Press Series in Practical and Professional Ethics*. Books ● *Profiles in Ethics*. Newsletter. Contains profiles of institutional members of the association. **Price:** free for members; $4.00 for nonmembers ● *Research Ethics: Cases and Commentaries, Volumes 1-6*. **Price:** $15.00/copy; $80.00/set ● Books ● Membership Directory. **Conventions/Meetings:** Ethics in the Professions and Practice - workshop ● annual meeting, for members and nonmembers interested in practical and professional ethics issues (exhibits).

8968 ■ International Institute for Field-Being (IIFB)
Fairfield Univ.
Dept. of Philosophy
332 Donnarumma Hall
Fairfield, CT 06824-5195
Ph: (203)254-4000
Fax: (203)254-4074
E-mail: lktong@iifb.org
URL: http://faculty.fairfield.edu/cnaser/iifb
Contact: Prof. Lik Kuen Tong PhD, Founder/Pres.
Founded: 1996. **Membership Dues:** regular, $15 (annual) ● student, $10 (annual) ● life, $1,000. **Multinational. Description:** Promotes and studies the Field-Being modes of thought, especially the philosophical implications of the Field-Being world view, non-substantialism versus Substantialism East and West, and the non-substantialistic turn in the 20th Century thought and philosophy. **Additional Websites:** http://www.iifb.org. **Telecommunication Services:** electronic mail, cnaser@iifb.org. **Affiliated With:** American Academy of Religion; American Philosophical Association. **Publications:** *International Journal for Field-Being*. Promotes the Field-Being philosophy and non-substantialist thought. ● *Uroboros*. Journal. Contains information for experiments and explorations in Field-Being thought. Alternate Formats: online. **Conventions/Meetings:** meeting ● symposium.

8969 ■ Philosophy of Education Society (PES)
c/o Dr. Alexander Sidorkin, Exec. Dir.
Univ. of Northern Colorado
McKee 208
Greeley, CO 80639
Ph: (970)351-2701
Fax: (970)351-1877
E-mail: sasha.sidorkin@unco.edu
URL: http://philosophyofeducation.org
Contact: Dr. Alexander Sidorkin, Exec. Dir.
Founded: 1941. **Members:** 500. **Regional Groups:** 7. **Description:** Professional society of professors and graduate students who teach, write, or otherwise work in the area of philosophy of education. Promotes analysis of educational problems of a philosophic or theoretic nature. **Publications:** *Educational Theory*, quarterly. Journal. Provides information on educational theory. **Price:** included in membership dues; also available to nonmembers ● *Philosophy of Education*, annual. Proceedings. **Price:** included in membership dues; also available to nonmembers. **Circulation:** 500. **Conventions/Meetings:** annual meeting (exhibits).

8970 ■ Society for Philosophy of Religion (SPR)
c/o Frank R. Harrison, III, Sec.-Treas.
Univ. of Georgia
Dept. of Philosophy
Peabody Hall
Athens, GA 30602
Ph: (706)542-2823
Fax: (706)542-2839
E-mail: harrison@uga.edu
Contact: Frank R. Harrison III, Sec.-Treas.
Founded: 1940. **Members:** 125. **Membership Dues:** regular, $20 (annual). **Description:** University, college, and seminary professors; graduate students; others interested in the clarification and advancement of issues in religious philosophy through investigation and discussion. Membership by invitation. **Affiliated With:** Southern Humanities Council. **Publications:** *International Journal for Philosophy of Religion*, bimonthly. Includes book reviews. **Price:** $102.00 for individuals; $108.00 for institutions. **Conventions/Meetings:** annual conference.

8971 ■ Undergraduate Philosophy Association
313 Waggener Hall
Dept. of Philosophy
Univ. of Texas
Austin, TX 78712
Ph: (512)475-9185 (512)475-9184
E-mail: jeff.casey@mail.utexas.edu
URL: http://www.utexas.edu/cola/depts/philosophy/undergraduate/advising/
Contact: Jeff Casey, Contact
Description: Seeks to enhance the quality of undergraduate education and improve quality of community for philosophy majors. **Publications:** *Ex Nihilo*, semiannual. Journal. Alternate Formats: online. **Conventions/Meetings:** weekly Lunch talks - meeting ● weekly meeting - every Friday ● Texas Undergraduate Philosophy Conference.

Photography

8972 ■ International Center of Photography (ICP)
1114 Ave. of the Americas, 43rd St.
New York, NY 10036
Ph: (212)857-0001
Fax: (212)857-0090
E-mail: info@icp.org
URL: http://www.icp.org
Contact: Willis E. Hartshorn, Dir.
Founded: 1974. **Members:** 4,430. **Membership Dues:** senior, $45 (annual) ● senior (double), $60 (annual) ● individual, $70 (annual) ● double, $95 (annual) ● international, $100 (annual) ● family, $150 (annual) ● focus, $275 (annual) ● Photography's Circle, $300 (annual) ● silver card patron, $600 (annual) ● gold card patron, $1,200 (annual) ● benefactor patron, $3,000 (annual). **Staff:** 90. **Multinational. Description:** Works to preserve the past and ensuring the future of the art of photography. Presents exhibitions of the finest works of some of the most talented photographers in the world; features an extensive array of historical and contemporary photographs, revealing the power and diversity of the medium from documentary photography to digital imaging. Fosters study of the history, techniques, aesthetics, and practices of photography in a wide range of programs: continuing education classes; two full-time certificate programs; a Master of Fine Arts program in collaboration with Bard College, Master of Arts and Master of Fine Arts degree programs in conjunction with NYU; Digital Media Program; lectures; and symposia. **Libraries: Type:** reference. **Holdings:** 15,000; archival material, periodicals, photographs. **Awards:** ICP Infinity Awards. **Frequency:** annual. **Type:** recognition. **Recipient:** for contributions of influential photographers; for emerging young talent, acknowledging the widespread impact of photography on contemporary culture. **Councils:** President's. **Departments:** Education; Exhibitions; External Affairs. **Formerly:** (1974) International Fund for Concerned Photography. **Publications:** *Programs Guide (Education)*, quarterly. Bulletin. Contains course catalog and a listing of lectures, exhibitions and other programs. Alternate Formats: online ● Annual Report ● Catalogs ● Books ● Also publishes postcards and posters.

8973 ■ National Photography Instructors Association (NPIA)
1255 Hill Dr.
Eagle Rock, CA 90041
Ph: (323)254-1549
Fax: (323)254-2797
E-mail: easedo@aol.com
Contact: Pierre Odier, Exec. Off.
Founded: 1979. **Languages:** English, French, German. **Description:** Represents photography instructors in America.

8974 ■ Photo Imaging Education Association (PIEA)
c/o Mark Murray, Consultant
Arlington Independent School District
1203 W Pioneer Pkwy.
Arlington, TX 76013
Ph: (817)229-2237
E-mail: consultant@pieapma.org
URL: http://www.pieapma.org
Contact: Prof. Edward Youngman, Pres.
Membership Dues: educator, $35 (annual). **Multinational. Description:** Represents photo imaging education practitioners and students. Builds a network where educators and students can create resources, solve problems and discuss issues relating to photo industry. Inspires members to be successful and to become better teachers of photo imaging. **Telecommunication Services:** electronic mail, president@pieapma.org. **Affiliated With:** PMA - The Worldwide Community of Imaging Associations. **Publications:** *Photo Imaging*. Newsletter. Alternate Formats: online.

8975 ■ Photographic Art and Science Foundation (PASF)
c/o International Photography Hall of Fame and Museum
2100 NE 52nd St.
Kirkpatrick Ctr.
Oklahoma City, OK 73111
Ph: (405)424-4055
Fax: (405)424-4058
E-mail: info@iphf.org
URL: http://www.iphf.org
Contact: Paul Skipworth, Chm.
Founded: 1965. **Members:** 750. **Membership Dues:** student, $20 (annual) ● supporting, $50 (annual) ● exhibitor, $150 (annual) ● elector, $250 (annual) ● patron, sponsor, $500 (annual) ● benefactor, $1,000 (annual) ● donor, $2,500 (annual) ● guardian, $5,000 (annual). **Staff:** 2. **Budget:** $120,000. **Multinational. Description:** Professional photographers and photographic equipment manufacturers interested in photographic education; established by the Professional Photographers of America. Encourages and conducts educational and scientific activities in the art and science of photography by sponsoring lectures, programs, exhibitions, and displays. Maintains International Photography Hall of Fame and Museum in Oklahoma City, OK at the Kirkpatrick Center. **Libraries: Type:** open to the public. **Holdings:** 1,800. **Subjects:** art, photography. **Affiliated With:** Professional Photographers of America. **Publications:** *Photography Hall of Fame Newsletter*, quarterly. Contains original historical material. **Price:** included in membership dues. **Circulation:** 3,100. **Conventions/Meetings:** semiannual board meeting.

8976 ■ Society for Photographic Education (SPE)
Art Crat Bldg., No. 403
2530 Superior Ave.
Cleveland, OH 44114
Ph: (513)529-8328
Fax: (513)529-9301
E-mail: speoffice@spenational.org
URL: http://www.spenational.org
Contact: Virginia Morrison, Exec. Dir.
Founded: 1963. **Members:** 1,800. **Membership Dues:** regular, $90 (annual) ● student, $50 (annual) ● senior, $65 (annual) ● sustaining, $150 (annual) ● collector, $380 (annual) ● institutional, $400 (annual) ● corporate, $600 (annual). **Staff:** 3. **Budget:** $150,000. **Regional Groups:** 8. **Description:** Repre-

sents teachers of photography on both secondary and college level, museum curators of photography, writers, editors, and publishers of photographic publications. Promotes high standards of photographic education; assists members in matters relating to academic freedom, curriculum, and educational teaching aids. Seeks to increase public awareness of the art of photography. **Awards:** Garry B. Fritz Imagemaker Award. **Frequency:** annual. **Type:** monetary. **Recipient:** for a first time imagemaker presenter who demonstrates outstanding achievement as determined by the peer review process ● Jeannie Pearce Award. **Frequency:** annual. **Type:** monetary. **Recipient:** for graduate and undergraduate students majoring/concentrating in photography and working with digital technology ● SPE Student Award. **Frequency:** annual. **Type:** monetary. **Recipient:** for a student attended the national conference. **Computer Services:** Mailing lists. **Affiliated With:** College Art Association. **Publications:** *Exposure*, biennial. Journal. Analyzes photographic issues and education. **Price:** $35.00/year. ISSN: 0098-8863. **Circulation:** 1,800. **Advertising:** accepted ● *Members' SPE Newsletter*, quarterly ● *National Conference Program Guide*, annual. **Advertising:** accepted ● *SPE Resource Guide/Membership Directory*, annual. **Conventions/Meetings:** annual Look Out: Photography and the Worlds of Contemporary Art - conference, for educators, students, artists, curators, critics, art historians and writers interested in the visual arts (exhibits) ● annual Passage - conference (exhibits).

8977 ■ University Photographers Association of America (UPAA)
c/o Jim Dusen, Pres.
SUNY Brockport
350 New Campus Dr.
Brockport, NY 14420-2931
Ph: (585)395-2133
E-mail: jdusen@brockport.edu
URL: http://www.upaa.org
Contact: Jim Dusen, Pres.
Founded: 1961. **Members:** 300. **Membership Dues:** full, $50 (annual) ● associate, $35 (annual) ● student, $25 (annual). **Staff:** 10. **Description:** College and university personnel engaged professionally in photography, audiovisual work, or journalism for universities. Seeks to advance applied photography and the profession through the exchange of thoughts and opinions among its members. Awards fellowship for exceptional work in the advancement of photography. Provides a medium for exchange of ideas and technical information on photography, especially university photographic work. Sponsors exhibits. Provides placement service for members. **Libraries: Type:** reference. **Awards:** Honor Awards. **Type:** recognition. **Computer Services:** database ● online services, listserv. **Committees:** Corporate Relations and Symposium Site Selection; Print Competition; Publicity. **Publications:** *The Contact Sheet*, quarterly. Newsletter. **Price:** included in membership dues. **Conventions/Meetings:** competition ● annual conference.

Physical Education

8978 ■ American Academy of Kinesiology and Physical Education (AAKPE)
c/o Human Kinetics
PO Box 5076
Champaign, IL 61820-2200
Ph: (217)351-5076
Free: (800)747-4457
Fax: (217)351-2674
E-mail: kims@aakpe.org
URL: http://www.aakpe.org
Contact: John Dunn, Pres.-Elect
Founded: 1926. **Members:** 125. **Description:** Honorary organization of physical education leaders. Limited to 150 active members. Encourages and promotes the study and educational applications of the art and science of human movement and physical activity; to honor persons who have made significant contributions to the field. Examines and promotes action in the improvement of existing physical education programs and in the extension of knowledge and recognition of multidiscipline contributions to the study of man. **Awards:** Hetherington Award. **Frequency:** annual. **Type:** recognition. **Recipient:** for career contributions by an Academy fellow ● **Frequency:** periodic. **Type:** recognition. **Recipient:** for excellence in the improvement or development of programs or the extension of knowledge in the field. **Telecommunication Services:** electronic mail, john.dunn@wmich.edu. **Committees:** Accreditation of Programs; Awards; Doctoral Program Review; Documents of Governance; Historian; Memorials. **Affiliated With:** American Alliance for Health, Physical Education, Recreation and Dance. **Formerly:** (1993) American Academy of Physical Education. **Publications:** *The Academy Papers*, annual. Journal. Serves as a special issue of Quest Journal. ISSN: 0033-6297. **Advertising:** accepted. Alternate Formats: online ● Also publishes position statements and studies. **Conventions/Meetings:** annual conference.

8979 ■ American Alliance for Health, Physical Education, Recreation and Dance (AAHPERD)
1900 Assn. Dr.
Reston, VA 20191-1598
Ph: (703)476-3400
Free: (800)213-7193
Fax: (703)476-9527
E-mail: info@aahperd.org
URL: http://www.aahperd.org
Contact: Michael G. Davis, CEO
Founded: 1885. **Members:** 26,000. **Staff:** 70. **Budget:** $6,000,000. **Regional Groups:** 6. **State Groups:** 54. **Description:** Students and educators in physical education, dance, health, athletics, safety education, recreation, and outdoor education. Works to improve its fields of education at all levels through such services as consultation, periodicals and special publications, leadership development, determination of standards, and research. Sponsors placement service. **Awards:** Honor Award. **Type:** recognition ● Luther Halsey Gulick Medal. **Type:** medal ● R. Tait McKenzie Award. **Type:** recognition ● **Frequency:** annual. **Type:** recognition. **Divisions:** American Association of Health Education; National Association for Girls and Women in Sport; National Dance Association; Research Consortium. **Special Interest Groups:** American Association for Active Lifestyles and Fitness; American Association for Leisure and Recreation; National Association for Sport and Physical Education. **Affiliated With:** International Council for Health, Physical Education, Recreation, Sport, and Dance; United States Collegiate Sports Council. **Formerly:** American Alliance for Health, Physical Education, Recreation and Dance; (1885) American Association for Advancement of Physical Education; (1903) American Physical Education Association; (1938) American Association for Health, Physical Education and Recreation; (1974) American Alliance for Health, Physical Education and Recreation. **Publications:** *AAHPERD Update*, bimonthly. Newsletter. **Price:** $4.00 for nonmembers; included in membership dues. **Circulation:** 30,000. **Advertising:** accepted ● *Health Education*, bimonthly. Journal. Includes advertisers' index and book reviews for health educators. **Price:** included in membership dues; $70.00 /year for institutions. ISSN: 0097-0050. **Circulation:** 10,000. **Advertising:** accepted. Alternate Formats: microform ● *Journal of Physical Education Recreation and Dance*, 9/year. **Price:** $80.00 ● *Research Quarterly*. **Price:** $125.00/year ● *Strategies*, bimonthly. **Price:** $40.00. **Circulation:** 9,000 ● Also publishes manuals and handbooks. **Conventions/Meetings:** annual conference (exhibits).

8980 ■ International Association of Physical Education and Sport for Girls and Women (IAPESGW)
Address Unknown since 2008
Founded: 1949. **Members:** 400. **Membership Dues:** $25 (annual). **Description:** Organizations in 61 countries with an interest in physical education for girls and women. Seeks to bring together women working in physical education or sports; cooperate with organizations that encourage women's services; promote the exchange of persons and ideas between member organizations. Conducts research into problems affecting physical education and sport for women. **Affiliated With:** International Council for Health, Physical Education, Recreation, Sport, and Dance; National Council of Women of the United States. **Publications:** *Report Following Congresses*, quadrennial. **Price:** $28.00. **Conventions/Meetings:** quadrennial congress.

8981 ■ International Council for Health, Physical Education, Recreation, Sport, and Dance (ICHPER-SD)
1900 Assn. Dr.
Reston, VA 20191-1598
Ph: (703)476-3486 (703)476-3462
Fax: (703)476-9527
E-mail: ichper@aahperd.org
URL: http://www.ichpersd.org
Contact: Dr. Dong Ja Yang, Pres.
Founded: 1958. **Members:** 1,500. **Membership Dues:** individual (group A), $40 (annual) ● institutional, $100 (annual) ● life, $1,500 ● national organizational, $200-$2,500 (annual) ● international organizational, $200 (annual) ● library, $35 (annual) ● contributing, $1,000 ● perpetual business and educational, $5,000 ● individual (group B), $30 (annual) ● individual (group C), $20 (annual). **Description:** Commits in scholarly pursuit and exchange of knowledge among its individual and organizational members in the field. Fosters the essence of education in HPERSD fields through international understanding and good will, safeguarding peace, and freedom, and respect for human dignity. Organizes its anniversary world congress while encouraging its regional organizations to organize their respective regional congresses. **Awards:** Ainsworth/Troester Founder's Award. **Frequency:** biennial. **Type:** recognition. **Recipient:** for distinguished meritorious service to the professions represented by ICHPER-SD ● ICHPER-SD Biennial Distinguished Scholar Award in Health Education. **Frequency:** biennial. **Type:** recognition. **Recipient:** for outstanding scholars in the field of health education ● ICHPER-SD Biennial Distinguished Scholar Award in Leisure and Recreation. **Frequency:** biennial. **Type:** recognition. **Recipient:** for outstanding scholars in the field of leisure and recreation ● ICHPER-SD Biennial Distinguished Scholar Award in Physical Education. **Frequency:** biennial. **Type:** recognition. **Recipient:** for outstanding scholars in the field of physical education ● ICHPER-SD Biennial Distinguished Scholar Award in Research. **Frequency:** biennial. **Type:** recognition. **Recipient:** for outstanding scholars in the field of research ● ICHPER-SD Biennial Distinguished Scholar in Sport and Olympic Movement. **Frequency:** biennial. **Type:** recognition. **Recipient:** for outstanding scholars in the field of sport and Olympic movement ● ICHPER-SD Biennial Outstanding Administration Award. **Frequency:** biennial. **Type:** recognition. **Recipient:** for individuals and institutional organizations ● ICHPER-SD Biennial Outstanding Contribution and Service Award. **Frequency:** biennial. **Type:** recognition. **Recipient:** for distinguished meritorious contributions and services to ICHPER-SD. **Publications:** *Congress Proceedings*, biennial ● *Journal of the International Council for Health, Physical Education, Recreation, Sport, and Dance*, quarterly. Contains association news, coverage of developments in international athletic competition, and information about new techniques in physical education. **Price:** included in membership dues. ISSN: 1091-2193. **Advertising:** accepted ● Report. Covers physical education and games in curriculum. Published in conjunction with UNESCO. ● Report. Covers teacher preparation for physical education. Published in conjunction with UNESCO. ● Report. Covers the status of teachers in physical education. Published in conjunction with UNESCO. **Conventions/Meetings:** biennial World Congress - meeting (exhibits).

8982 ■ National Association of Collegiate Women Athletics Administrators (NACWAA)
5018 Randall Pkwy., Ste.3
Wilmington, NC 28403

Ph: (910)793-8244
Fax: (910)793-8246
E-mail: jalley@nacwaa.org
URL: http://www.nacwaa.org
Contact: Jennifer Alley, Exec. Dir.

Founded: 1979. **Members:** 1,700. **Membership Dues:** active, $150 (annual) ● associate, $75 (annual) ● institutional (based on number of employees), $500-$1,000 (annual) ● retired/student/intern, $35 (annual) ● affiliate nonprofit, $100 (annual) ● corporate, $275 (annual) ● affiliate institutional nonprofit, $340 (annual) ● affiliate institutional corporate, $1,000 (annual). **Staff:** 5. **Description:** Works to provide educational programs, professional and personal development opportunities, information exchange and support services to enhance college athletes; promotes the growth, leadership and success of women athletics administrators, professional staff, coaches and student athletes. **Awards:** Administrator of the Year. **Frequency:** annual. **Type:** recognition ● Honor Award. **Frequency:** annual. **Type:** recognition. **Recipient:** for outstanding support of women in athletics ● Lifetime Achievement Award. **Frequency:** annual. **Type:** recognition. **Recipient:** for retirees from intercollegiate athletics administration who have rendered meritorious service ● Nell Jackson Award. **Frequency:** annual. **Type:** recognition. **Recipient:** for NACWAA/HERS graduates. **Computer Services:** Information services. **Formerly:** (1991) Council of Collegiate Women's Athletic Administrators. **Publications:** *NACWAA Newsletter*, quarterly. Alternate Formats: online. **Conventions/Meetings:** annual convention and workshop, for women in athletics administration (exhibits) - always fall.

8983 ■ National Association for Girls and Women in Sport (NAGWS)

c/o American Alliance for Health, Physical Education, Recreation and Dance
1900 Assn. Dr.
Reston, VA 20191-1598
Ph: (703)476-3400
Free: (800)213-7193
Fax: (703)476-4566
E-mail: nagws@aahperd.org
URL: http://www.aahperd.org/nagws
Contact: Ms. Pamela Noakes, Exec. Dir.

Founded: 1899. **Members:** 4,000. **Membership Dues:** education, $100 (annual). **Staff:** 3. **Regional Groups:** 6. **State Groups:** 50. **Description:** Represents teachers, coaches, athletic trainers, officials, athletic administrators, and students. Has 4 main structures: Advocacy Coaching Enhancement; Minority Representation; Professional Development Publications, and Student Representation. Supports and fosters the development of quality sports programs that will enrich the lives of all participants. Holds training sessions for leadership development. Conducts research programs. **Awards:** Guiding Woman in Sport. **Frequency:** annual. **Type:** recognition. **Recipient:** for outstanding service in female sports ● Honor Award. **Frequency:** annual. **Type:** recognition. **Recipient:** for exemplary devotion and strong demonstration of leadership in female sport ● Nell Jackson Award. **Frequency:** annual. **Type:** recognition. **Recipient:** for outstanding accomplishment in sports ● Pathfinder Award. **Frequency:** annual. **Type:** recognition. **Recipient:** for remarkable demonstration of advocacy in female sports ● Presidential. **Frequency:** annual. **Type:** recognition ● Rachel Bryant Award. **Frequency:** annual. **Type:** recognition. **Recipient:** for remarkable distinction in the world of female sports. **Affiliated With:** Amateur Softball Association of America; American Alliance for Health, Physical Education, Recreation and Dance; Professional Association of Volleyball Officials; U.S.A. Basketball; USA Gymnastics; U.S.A. Track and Field. **Formerly:** (1971) Division of Girl's and Women's Sports of the American Association of Health, Physical Education, and Recreation. **Publications:** *GWS News*, 3/year. Newsletter ● *Women in Sport and Physical Activity Journal*, biennial. **Price:** $15.00 for members; $25.00 for nonmembers ● Manuals. **Conventions/Meetings:** annual convention (exhibits).

8984 ■ National Association for Kinesiology and Physical Education in Higher Education (NAKPEHE)

c/o Ginny Overdorf, Exec. Sec.-Treas.
William Paterson Univ.
Dept. of Exercise and Movement Sciences
300 Pompton Rd.
Wayne, NJ 07470
Ph: (973)720-2419
Fax: (973)720-2034
E-mail: vgo@prodigy.net
URL: http://www.nakpehe.org
Contact: Ginny Overdorf, Exec. Sec.-Treas.

Membership Dues: faculty, $80 (annual) ● emeritus (all publications), $45 (annual) ● emeritus (chronicle only), $15 (annual) ● graduate student, $30 (annual) ● concurrent, $20 (annual). **Description:** Encourages and promotes the study and educational applications of the art and science of human movement and physical activity. Provides a forum for interdisciplinary ideas, concepts, and issues related to the role of kinesiology and physical education in higher education. Fosters action in the improvement of existing physical education programs. **Publications:** *Chronicle of Kinesiology and Physical Education in Higher Education*. Newsletter ● *Quest*. Journal. Addresses issues and concerns relevant and meaningful to kinesiology and physical education in higher education.

8985 ■ National Association for Physical Education in Higher Education (NAPEHE)

c/o Gail Evans
Dept. of Human Performance
San Jose State Univ.
San Jose, CA 95192-0054
Ph: (765)285-4217
Fax: (765)285-3485
E-mail: gevans@email.sjsu.edu
Contact: Jackie Lund, Exec.Sec.-Treas.

Founded: 1978. **Members:** 500. **Membership Dues:** faculty, $70 (annual). **Staff:** 1. **Budget:** $40,000. **Regional Groups:** 6. **Description:** Serves as professional society of physical educators in colleges and universities. Maintains speakers' bureau. **Computer Services:** Online services, job postings for vacancies in higher education. **Affiliated With:** American Alliance for Health, Physical Education, Recreation and Dance. **Formed by Merger of:** National College Physical Education Association for Men; National Association for Physical Education of College Women. **Publications:** *The Chronicle of Physical Education in Higher Education*, 3/year. Newsletter. Covers membership activities. **Price:** included in membership dues ● *Quest*, 3/year. Journal. Covers exercise science, physical education, athletics, and related topics. **Price:** included in membership dues. **Conventions/Meetings:** annual conference.

8986 ■ National Association for Sport and Physical Education (NASPE)

1900 Assn. Dr.
Reston, VA 20191-1598
Ph: (703)476-3400
Free: (800)213-7193
Fax: (703)476-8316
E-mail: naspe@aahperd.org
URL: http://www.naspeinfo.org
Contact: Charlene R. Burgeson, Exec. Dir.

Founded: 1974. **Members:** 18,000. **Membership Dues:** $125 (annual). **Staff:** 13. **Description:** Men and women professionally involved with physical activity and sports. Seeks to improve the total sport and physical activity experience in America. Conducts research and education programs in such areas as sport psychology, curriculum development, kinesiology, history, philosophy, sport sociology, and the biological and behavioral basis of human activity. Develops and distributes public information materials which explain the value of physical education programs. Supports councils involved in organizing and supporting elementary, secondary, and college physical education and sport programs; administers the National Council of Athletic Training in conjunction with the National Association for Girls and Women in Sport; serves the professional interests of coaches, trainers, and officials. Maintains hall of fame, placement service, and media resource center for public information and professional preparation. Member benefits include group insurance and discounts. **Awards:** Athletic Director of the Year. **Frequency:** annual. **Type:** recognition. **Recipient:** for outstanding athletic director ● Physical Education Teacher of the Year. **Frequency:** annual. **Type:** recognition. **Recipient:** for outstanding physical education teacher. **Councils:** Athletic Training; Coaches; College and University Physical Education; Intramural Sports; Middle and Secondary School Physical Education; Physical Education for Children; School Leadership in Physical Education; Secondary School Athletic Directors; Youth Sports. **Subgroups:** Biomechanics; Curriculum and Instruction; Exercise Physiology; Motor Development; Philosophy; Sport Art; Sport History; Sport Psychology; Sport Sociology. **Affiliated With:** National Association for Girls and Women in Sport; National Council of Athletic Training. **Publications:** *NASPE News*, 3/year. Contains information on operations, reports and other related issues about the association. **Circulation:** 18,000. **Advertising:** accepted ● *Strategies: A Journal for Physical and Sport Educators*, bimonthly. Magazine ● *Update*, bimonthly. Newsletter ● Books ● Manuals ● Also produces audiovisual aids. **Conventions/Meetings:** conference ● annual convention, held in conjunction with American Alliance for Health, Physical Education, Recreation and Dance (exhibits).

8987 ■ National Council of Athletic Training (NCAT)

c/o National Association for Sport and Physical Education
1900 Assn. Dr.
Reston, VA 20191-1598
Ph: (703)476-3410
Free: (800)213-7193
Fax: (703)476-8316
E-mail: naspe@aahperd.org
URL: http://www.aahperd.org/naspe
Contact: Ms. Charlene R. Burgeson, Exec. Dir.

Founded: 1976. **Members:** 2,000. **Staff:** 3. **Description:** Members of the National Association for Girls and Women in Sport, the American Alliance for Health, Physical Education, Recreation and Dance and the National Association for Sport and Physical Education who are involved in or interested in the profession of athletic training. Purposes are to: prepare and disseminate information concerning the profession; provide for coordination of activities in athletic training. Promotes the use of National Athletic Trainers Association certified athletic trainers at all interscholastic, intercollegiate, and international competitions. Has developed: career education information; checklist for safety in sports; coaches first aid kit. **Affiliated With:** National Association for Girls and Women in Sport; National Association for Sport and Physical Education. **Formerly:** (1976) NAGWS Athletic Training Committee; (1986) Athletic Training Council. **Publications:** *Nutritional Supplements for Athletics*. Brochure ● Papers. **Conventions/Meetings:** annual convention, held in conjunction with the American Alliance National Convention (exhibits).

8988 ■ National Council of Secondary School Athletic Directors (NCSSAD)

1900 Assn. Dr.
Reston, VA 20191-1598
Ph: (703)476-3400
Free: (800)213-7193
Fax: (703)476-8316
E-mail: naspe@aahperd.org
URL: http://www.aahperd.org/naspe
Contact: Charlene R. Burgeson, Contact

Founded: 1968. **Members:** 600. **Staff:** 12. **Regional Groups:** 6. **State Groups:** 50. **Description:** A council of the National Association for Sport and Physical Education, which is a division of the American Alliance for Health, Physical Education, Recreation and Dance (see separate entries). Professional athletic directors in secondary schools. Purposes are to improve the educational aspects of interscholastic athletics; to provide for an exchange of ideas; to establish closer working relationships with related professional groups and promote greater unity; to establish and implement standards for the professional preparation of secondary school athletic directors. Provides in-service training programs. Maintains placement service and speakers' bureau. **Awards:** Athletic Director of the Year Award. **Frequency:** annual. **Type:** recognition. **Recipient:** for state, regional and national levels. **Affiliated With:** National Association for Sport and Physical Education. **Publications:** Books ● Pamphlets. **Conventions/Meetings:** annual conference and meeting (exhibits) - always spring ● annual meeting, held in conjunction with AAHPERD.

8989 ■ National Interscholastic Athletic Administrators Association (NIAAA)
9100 Keystone Crossing, Ste.650
Indianapolis, IN 46240
Ph: (317)587-1450
Fax: (317)587-1451
E-mail: niaaainf@nfhs.org
URL: http://www.niaaa.org
Contact: Gerry Durgin, Pres.
Founded: 1977. **Members:** 5,400. **Membership Dues:** regular, associate, $60 (annual) ● retired, $30 (annual) ● life (regular), $600 ● life (retired), $300 ● student, $15 (annual). **Budget:** $250,000. **State Groups:** 50. **Description:** Represents high school athletic directors. Promotes the professional growth and image of interscholastic athletic administrators and state programs. Preserves educational value of athletics and the place of these programs in the school curriculum. Operates leadership and certification programs for athletic administrators. **Awards: Type:** recognition. **Telecommunication Services:** electronic mail, bwhitehead@niaaa.org. **Committees:** Certification; Professional Development. **Affiliated With:** National Federation of State High School Associations. **Publications:** *Athletic Director's Reference Manual* ● *Guide for College-Bound Student-Athletes and their Parents*. Pamphlet. Contains procedures for the NCAA Eligibility Clearinghouse and academic requirements. **Price:** $4.00/copy ● *Interscholastic Athletic Administration*, quarterly. Magazine. Includes membership information and book reviews. **Price:** $12.00 /year for nonmembers; $15.75/year outside U.S. and Canada. **Advertising:** accepted ● *National Conference Proceedings*, annual ● *Profile of Athletic Administration in the 90's*. Pamphlet ● *Speakers' Directory*, periodic ● *State Athletic Director Association*, annual. Directory. **Conventions/Meetings:** annual meeting (exhibits).

8990 ■ North American Society for Sport Management (NASSM)
W Gym 014
Slippery Rock Univ.
Slippery Rock, PA 16057
Ph: (724)738-4812
Fax: (724)738-4858
E-mail: nassm@sru.edu
URL: http://www.nassm.org
Contact: Dr. Carol Barr, Pres.
Founded: 1985. **Members:** 400. **Membership Dues:** student, $45 (annual) ● professional, $100 (annual) ● emeritus with JSM, $50 (annual) ● emeritus without JSM, $20 (annual). **Multinational. Description:** Academics interested or involved in sports administration; students enrolled in sports management university-level programs; sports managers. Encourages study, research, scholarly writing, and professional development in the field, specifically sports exercise, dance, and play. Maintains speakers' bureau. **Awards:** Earle F. Zeigler Honorary Lecturer Award. **Frequency:** annual. **Type:** recognition. **Recipient:** for professional and organizational contributions. **Publications:** *Journal of Sport Management*, quarterly. **Price:** included in membership dues. **Conventions/Meetings:** annual conference, for professionals and students - usually end of May or early June.

8991 ■ PE4life
810 Baltimore, Ste.100
Kansas City, MO 64105-1706
Ph: (816)472-7345
Fax: (816)472-7329
E-mail: info@pe4life.org
URL: http://pe4life.com
Contact: Anne Flannery, Pres./CEO
Founded: 2000. **Membership Dues:** gold, $50 (annual) ● silver, $30 (annual). **Staff:** 5. **Description:** Advances the development of physical education programs for children. Raises awareness of physical inactivity levels of America's youth and the state of physical education across America. Stimulates private and public funding for quality physical education. **Computer Services:** Mailing lists ● online services, discussion list. **Programs:** Center for the Advancement of Physical Education; National P.E. Day; PE4life Institute. **Publications:** Newsletter. Alternate Formats: online.

8992 ■ Society of State Directors of Health, Physical Education and Recreation (SSDHPER)
1900 Assn. Dr., Ste.100
Reston, VA 20191-1599
Ph: (703)390-4599
Fax: (703)476-0988
E-mail: info@thesociety.org
URL: http://www.thesociety.org
Contact: Sharon Murray MHSE, Exec. Dir.
Founded: 1926. **Members:** 180. **Membership Dues:** regular, $70 (annual) ● associate, $50 (annual) ● retired, $35 (annual). **Staff:** 3. **Budget:** $240,000. **Description:** Represents state directors, supervisors, and coordinators of health, physical education, and recreation in state departments of education. Associate members include personnel in other state, federal, and nongovernmental agencies and organizations and interested individuals. Promotes sound school programs of health, physical education, safety, recreation, and athletics. Conducts summer workshops on professional leadership. Presents Certificate of Honor annually, and Distinguished Service Certificate occasionally. **Formerly:** Society of State Directors of Physical and Health Education. **Publications:** *The Society Page*, periodic. Newsletter. Alternate Formats: online ● Directory, annual ● Also publishes statement of basic beliefs. **Conventions/Meetings:** annual conference.

Physics

8993 ■ American Association of Physics Teachers (AAPT)
1 Physics Ellipse
College Park, MD 20740-3845
Ph: (301)209-3300 (301)209-3311
Fax: (301)209-0845
E-mail: aapt-web@aapt.org
URL: http://www.aapt.org
Contact: Toufic M. Hakim, Exec. Off.
Founded: 1930. **Members:** 10,500. **Staff:** 25. **Budget:** $4,400,000. **Regional Groups:** 46. **Description:** Serves as a professional society of teachers of physics in colleges, universities, and secondary schools; undergraduates and graduates with major interest in physics. **Libraries: Type:** reference. **Holdings:** archival material, reports. **Awards: Type:** recognition. **Additional Websites:** http://www.psrc-online.org. **Telecommunication Services:** electronic mail, eo@aapt.org. **Committees:** Apparatus; Astronomy Education; Computers in Physics Education; Instructional Media; International Education; Minorities in Physics; Physics in Graduate Education; Physics in High School; Physics in Two-Year Colleges; Physics in Undergraduate Education; Professional Concerns; Research in Physics Education; Science Education for the Public; Women in Physics, History and Philosophy of Physics. **Publications:** *American Journal of Physics*, monthly. **Price:** included in membership dues; $515.00 /year for nonmembers in U.S.; $540.00 /year for nonmembers outside U.S.; $568.00/year outside U.S. (via airmail). ISSN: 0002-9505. **Circulation:** 7,000. **Advertising:** accepted. Alternate Formats: online. Also Cited As: *AJP* ● *Announcer*, quarterly. Newsletter. Monitors developments in physics of interest to high school and college teachers. Contains calendar of events. **Price:** included in membership dues; $44.00 /year for nonmembers in U.S.; $64.00 /year for nonmembers outside U.S.; $97.00/year outside U.S. (via airmail). ISSN: 0275-5696. **Circulation:** 11,000 ● *The Physics Teacher*, 9/year. Journal. Includes book reviews and articles on physics research, philosophy and development. **Price:** included in membership dues; $309.00 /year for nonmembers in U.S.; $329.00 /year for nonmembers outside U.S.; $362.00/year outside U.S. (via airmail). ISSN: 0031-921X. **Circulation:** 10,000. Alternate Formats: online. **Conventions/Meetings:** annual conference (exhibits) - always winter. 2009 Feb. 12-16, Chicago, IL ● annual conference, for physics teachers - always summer. 2008 July 19-23, Edmonton, AB, Canada ● periodic workshop, for physics teachers.

Placement

8994 ■ American Association for Employment in Education (AAEE)
3040 Riverside Dr., Ste.125
Columbus, OH 43221-2550
Ph: (614)485-1111 (303)387-0555
Fax: (614)485-9609
E-mail: aaee@osu.edu
URL: http://www.aaee.org
Contact: B.J. Bryant, Exec. Dir.
Founded: 1934. **Members:** 1,000. **Membership Dues:** associate (not-for-profit organization), institutional, $200 (annual) ● associate (for-profit organization), $500 (annual). **Staff:** 2. **Budget:** $350,000. **Regional Groups:** 7. **State Groups:** 7. **Description:** Represents colleges, universities, and other post-secondary educational institutions, which are not-for-profit. Prepares teachers and other educational personnel for service in public and private educational institutions, organizations and agencies. Provides information or services relating to career planning, placement, and recruitment activities in education. **Libraries: Type:** reference. **Holdings:** reports. **Awards:** Priscilla A. Scotlan Distinguished Service Award. **Frequency:** annual. **Type:** recognition. **Recipient:** for professional growth, research and service to the association. **Computer Services:** Mailing lists, project connect: service listing vacancies for K-12 and higher education. **Telecommunication Services:** electronic mail, office@aaee.org. **Committees:** Conference; Ethics; Membership; Peer Counseling; Placement Service/Job Fairs; Publications; Recognition and Awards; Relations with Other Groups; Research Grants; Supply and Demand. **Sections:** Educational Career Centers; Human Resource Administrators. **Affiliated With:** Council for the Advancement of Standards in Higher Education; National Association of Colleges and Employers. **Formerly:** (1962) National Institutional Teacher Placement Association; (1996) Association for School, College and University Staffing. **Publications:** *AAEE National Directory for Employment in Education*, annual. **Price:** $10.00/copy, for members; $20.00/copy, for nonmembers ● *Directory of Public School Systems in the U.S.*, annual. Lists nearly 15,000 public schools with the name of the individual responsible for hiring, grade levels, and size of each district. **Price:** $55.00/copy, for members; $80.00/copy, for nonmembers ● *The Job Search Handbook for Educators*, annual. Includes a compilation of articles for teacher candidates to be used as reference when organizing job search. **Price:** $5.00/copy, for members (minimum order of 25); $8.00/copy, for nonmembers ● *The Recruiter's Guide*, annual. Directory. **Price:** $12.00/copy, for members; $20.00/copy, for nonmembers ● *Recruiting the Best: A Guide to Successful Recruitment Strategies in Education*. Book. **Price:** $5.00 for members ● *Teacher Supply and Demand in the U.S.*, annual. Report. **Price:** $25.00/copy, for nonmembers. **Conventions/Meetings:** annual Meeting Current Challenges in Education Employment - conference (exhibits) - usually November. 2008 Nov. 9-12, Denver, CO ● workshop.

8995 ■ National Association of Colleges and Employers (NACE)
62 Highland Ave.
Bethlehem, PA 18017-9481

Ph: (610)868-1421 (610)868-0208
Free: (800)544-5272
Fax: (610)868-0208
E-mail: mmackes@naceweb.org
URL: http://www.naceweb.org
Contact: Marilyn Mackes, Exec. Dir.

Founded: 1956. **Members:** 8,800. **Membership Dues:** college (institutional), $360 (annual) ● employer (organizational), $390 (annual) ● individual, $130 (annual) ● electronic, $80 (annual). **Staff:** 34. **Budget:** $4,600,000. **Description:** Connects more than 5,200 college career services professionals at nearly 2,000 college and universities nationwide, and more than 3,000 HR/staffing professionals focused on college relations and recruiting. Forecasts trends in the job market; tracks legal issues in employment, the job search, and hiring practices; and provides college and employer professionals with benchmarks for their work. Provides research and information to its professional members through website, quarterly surveys of starting salary offers to new college graduates, and surveys of employer and college members. Provides members with primary tools for reaching and educating college students through Job Choices publications. **Awards:** Excellence Awards. **Frequency:** annual. **Type:** recognition. **Recipient:** for outstanding accomplishments in four categories: advance of the vision and future; advancement of the profession; educational programming; information for students ● Kauffman Award. **Frequency:** annual. **Type:** recognition. **Recipient:** for outstanding service to NACE ● NACE Academy of Fellows. **Frequency:** annual. **Type:** recognition. **Recipient:** for individuals who have contributed to the career services and human resources/staffing profession through the advancement of knowledge, leadership, or excellence in professional practice ● NACE/Chevron Award. **Frequency:** annual. **Type:** recognition. **Recipient:** for innovative programs in career services of a college member for the development of a groundbreaking program in the field. **Computer Services:** Mailing lists. **Telecommunication Services:** electronic mail, rbrigham@southwestern.com. **Formerly:** (1995) College Placement Council. **Publications:** *Job Choices Diversity Edition*, annual. Magazine. Includes information about prospective employers, as well as career advice. **Price:** $17.00/copy; $41.00 for 3-volume set. **Circulation:** 156,025. **Advertising:** accepted ● *Job Choices in Business and Liberal Arts Students*, annual. Magazine. Includes information about prospective employers, as well as career advice. **Price:** $17.00 for volume II; $41.00 for 3-volume set. ISSN: 0069-5734. **Circulation:** 423,400. **Advertising:** accepted ● *Job Choices in Science, Engineering & Technology Students*, annual. Magazine. Includes narratives and display pages with information about prospective employers, as well as career advice. **Price:** $17.00/copy; $41.00 for 3-volume set. ISSN: 0069-5734. **Circulation:** 219,600. **Advertising:** accepted ● *NACE Journal*, quarterly, every October, December, March, and May. Includes articles and book reviews. **Price:** included in membership dues; $72.00 /year for nonmembers; $8.50/copy for nonmembers. ISSN: 0884-5352. **Circulation:** 4,100. **Advertising:** accepted ● *NACE—Salary Survey*, quarterly. Reports on average salary offers to college graduates for first-time employment. Includes statistics. **Price:** included in membership dues; $220.00 /year for nonmembers. ISSN: 0196-1004 ● *NACE—Spotlight Online*, biweekly. Newsletter. Covers legal issues, trends, and statistics. Contains calendar of events, employment opportunities, and personnel changes. **Price:** included in membership dues; $72.00 /year for nonmembers. ISSN: 0162-1068. **Circulation:** 8,000. Alternate Formats: online. **Conventions/Meetings:** annual conference (exhibits) - 2009 May 26-29, Las Vegas, NV.

8996 ■ National Student Employment Association (NSEA)

c/o Joan Adams, Office Mgr.
PO Box 23606
Eugene, OR 97402
Ph: (541)484-6935 (801)581-4473
Fax: (541)484-6935
E-mail: nsea@nsea.info
URL: http://www.nsea.info
Contact: Joan Adams, Office Mgr.

Founded: 1976. **Members:** 510. **Membership Dues:** individual, $125 (annual) ● institution, $375 (annual) ● corporation, $750 (annual). **Staff:** 1. **Budget:** $110,000. **Regional Groups:** 4. **Description:** Directors, coordinators, and senior staff personnel of postsecondary educational institutions, including proprietary schools and corporate human resource directors, who are involved in student employment, internships, cooperative and experiential education, federal work-study, job location and development, and student placement. Answers problems associated with the management of student employment programs. Provides financial support for students in higher education. Creates and conducts training and professional development programs for higher education student employment professionals. Sponsors State Work Study Clearinghouse on state sponsored student employment programs. Compiles statistics. Conducts research programs. Provides legislative updates on current issues. **Libraries:** **Type:** reference. **Holdings:** 2; books, periodicals. **Awards:** Frank Adams Founders Award. **Frequency:** annual. **Type:** recognition. **Recipient:** for outstanding members ● Jim Campbell Rookie of the Year Award. **Frequency:** annual. **Type:** recognition. **Recipient:** for a new professional who has made an outstanding or unique contribution to the association during the first three years in the profession ● John R. Griffin Service Award. **Frequency:** annual. **Type:** recognition. **Recipient:** for outstanding members ● Margene Orzalli Memorial Award. **Frequency:** annual. **Type:** recognition. **Recipient:** for outstanding members ● President's Award. **Frequency:** annual. **Type:** recognition. **Recipient:** to an individual who has shown exceptional dedication and made significant contributions ● Student Employee of the Year. **Frequency:** annual. **Type:** recognition. **Recipient:** for students. **Computer Services:** Mailing lists. **Telecommunication Services:** electronic mail, lbolton@sa.utah.edu. **Committees:** Bylaws; Elections; Federal Relations; Grants/Development; Marketing; Minority Concerns; National Conference; Public Relations; Publications; Research. **Formerly:** (1978) National Association on Work and the College Student; (1998) National Association of Student Employment Administrators. **Publications:** *Journal of Student Employment*, annual. Annual Report. Features research in student employment and student services. **Price:** $20.00. **Circulation:** 1,000. **Advertising:** accepted. Alternate Formats: online; diskette ● *Making Your Voice Heard in Washington*, periodic. Newsletter. **Price:** $1.00. **Circulation:** 1,000 ● *NSEA News*, 3/year. Newsletter. Discusses issues such as job development, summer employment, and student financial aid. Includes book reviews. **Price:** free for members. **Circulation:** 750 ● *Policy and Procedures Manual*. Alternate Formats: online ● *The Workbook*. **Price:** $40.00 for members; $50.00 for nonmembers ● Brochure. Alternate Formats: online. **Conventions/Meetings:** quarterly regional meeting ● annual Work and the College Student - conference (exhibits).

Planning

8997 ■ Association for Institutional Research (AIR)

1435 E Piedmont Dr., Ste.211
Tallahassee, FL 32308
Ph: (850)385-4155
Fax: (850)385-5180
E-mail: air@airweb2.org
URL: http://www.airweb.org
Contact: Dr. Terrence R. Russell, Exec. Dir.

Founded: 1965. **Members:** 4,000. **Membership Dues:** individual, $115 (annual) ● graduate student, $30 (annual) ● organization, $315 (annual). **Staff:** 14. **Budget:** $1,200,000. **Regional Groups:** 8. **State Groups:** 32. **National Groups:** 4. **Description:** Represents individuals interested in institutional research or policy analysis in the improvement of planning, management and resource allocation. Fosters research leading to improved understanding, planning and operation of institutions of postsecondary education. Encourages the application of appropriate methodologies and techniques. Publishes and exchanges information concerning institutions of higher learning. **Libraries:** **Type:** reference. **Awards:** John E. Stecklein Distinguished Membership Award. **Frequency:** annual. **Type:** recognition. **Recipient:** for substantial contributions in the field of institutional research ● Outstanding Service Award. **Frequency:** periodic. **Type:** recognition. **Recipient:** for members or former members who have made extraordinary and sustained contributions to the association for a period of at least 5 years ● Research Grants. **Frequency:** annual. **Type:** grant. **Recipient:** for studies using U.S. National Databases. **Formerly:** (1965) National Institutional Research Forum. **Publications:** *Effective Reporting*. Book ● *Electronic Air*, monthly. Newsletter ● *New Directions in Institutional Research*, quarterly. Journal ● *People, Processes and Managing Data*. Book ● *Professional File*, quarterly ● *Research in Higher Education*, bimonthly. Journal ● *Strategies for the Practice of Institutional Research*, annual. Book.

8998 ■ Educational Planning Institute (EPI)

Address Unknown since 2007

Founded: 1971. **Staff:** 23. **Description:** Professional organization of educators, sociologists, and economists experienced in manpower programming, administration, legislative analysis, and all phases of educational and community development. Designed to provide an interdisciplinary approach to manpower/human service programming and to deal with federal agencies, state educational and CDA programs, and local educational institutions. Encourages and develops among schools, manpower, and training agencies a recognition of the need for professional assistance to solve organizational and administrative problems. Responds to specific requests for counsel and programmatic assistance in planning the improvement of and heightening the quality of education, training needs, and manpower development utilization. Spe cializes in the development, design, and implementation of model programs on topics including bilingual clerical work/study, labor market information for youth, part-time employment needs of youths in school, and community resources inventories. Applies its research and special services to school board consultations, job development for youth, input into legislative proposals, community needs assessment, and interpretation of legislative regulations. Adapts programs to local needs; develops participation of community-based organizations and grass roots projects; attempts to bridge the gap between education and the world of work for young people. **Publications:** *Part Time Employment Needs of In-School Youth*.

8999 ■ International Society for Educational Planning (ISEP)

c/o Dr. Walter S. Polka, Superintendent
Lewiston-Porter Central School
4061 Creek Rd.
Youngstown, NY 14174
Ph: (716)878-5028 (716)878-5032
Fax: (716)878-5833
E-mail: bmcinern@purdue.edu
URL: http://web.ics.purdue.edu/~bmcinern
Contact: Dr. Walter S. Polka, Superintendent

Founded: 1970. **Members:** 350. **Membership Dues:** professional, institutional, $35 (annual) ● student, $15 (annual). **Description:** Members are educators at the university level; personnel from federal, state, or local agencies; consulting firms; students; and interested laypersons. Strengthens the professionalism of educational planners. Furthers the knowledge of educational planning. Promotes cooperation and exchange among planners. Maintains biographical archives and speakers' bureau. Conducts workshops for groups. Has formed a research commission. **Awards:** Dissertation of the Year. **Frequency:** annual. **Type:** recognition ● Outstanding Award for School District Planning. **Frequency:** annual. **Type:** recognition. **Committees:** International Programs; Political Action; Training. **Affiliated With:** American

Association for the Advancement of Science. **Formerly:** International Society for Educational Planning; (1993) Educational Planning. **Publications:** *Educational Planning*, quarterly. Journal. **Price:** $35.00 /year for individuals; $45.00 /year for libraries. ISSN: 0315-9388. **Advertising:** accepted ● Directory, annual. **Conventions/Meetings:** annual conference (exhibits) - always October.

9000 ■ Society for College and University Planning (SCUP)
339 E Liberty, Ste.300
Ann Arbor, MI 48104-2205
Ph: (734)998-7832 (734)998-6969
Fax: (734)998-6532
E-mail: info@scup.org
URL: http://www.scup.org
Contact: Jolene Knapp, Exec. Dir.
Founded: 1965. **Members:** 4,500. **Membership Dues:** institutional A, institutional F, small non-institutional, $645 (annual) ● institutional B (3000-5999 FTE), $845 (annual) ● institutional C (6000-11999 FTE), $1,055 (annual) ● institutional D (12000-17999 FTE), $1,295 (annual) ● institutional E (18000 and over FTE), $1,535 (annual) ● non-institutional, $1,295 (annual) ● individual, $285 (annual) ● student, $50 (annual) ● retired, $75 (annual). **Staff:** 15. **Budget:** $2,500,000. **Regional Groups:** 5. **Description:** Maintains the organizing principle that planning is essential to improving and maintaining the fitness, vitality and quality of higher education. Members are university and college presidents, vice presidents, directors, deans, faculty, government agencies, corporations and private consultants interested in higher education planning. **Telecommunication Services:** electronic mail, membership@scup.org. **Boards:** Academic Planning Academy; Directors; Editorial Review; Facilities Planning Academy. **Committees:** Advancement; Awards; Membership; Nominating; Professional Development; Publications Advisory. **Publications:** *A Guide for New Planners*. Book ● *The Best of Planning for Higher Education*. Book ● *Campus Architecture: Building in the Groves of Academe*. Book ● *Campus Planning*. Book ● *Contract Management or Self-Operation*. Book ● *Doing Academic Planning: Effective Tools for Decision Making*. Book ● *Financial Planning Guidelines for Facility Renewal and Adaption*. Book ● *Innovation in Student Services: Planning for Models Blending High Touch/High Tech*. Book ● *Innovation in Student Services: Planning for Models Blending High Touch/High Tech*, quarterly. Video ● *New Forces and Realities Making the Adjustment*. Monograph ● *Planning for Higher Education*, quarterly. Journal ● *Planning for Student Services: Best Practice for the 21st Century*. Book ● *Planning for Student Services: Best Practices for the 21st Century*. Video. Presents a video of 2000 PBS satellite program. ● *Revolutionary Strategy for the Knowledge Age*. Book ● *Technology Driven Planning: Principles to Practice*. Video. Presents a video of 2001 PBS satellite program. ● *Transforming eKnowledge*. Book ● *Transforming Higher Education: A Vision for Learning in the 21st Century*. Book ● *Unleashing the Power of Perpetual Learning*. Book. **Conventions/Meetings:** annual conference (exhibits) - usually in July. 2008 July 19-23, Montreal, QC, Canada; 2009 July 18-22, Portland, OR ● annual January Workshops ● annual Mid Atlantic Regional - conference - usually spring ● annual North Atlantic Regional - conference - usually spring ● annual North Central Regional - conference - usually fall ● annual Pacific Regional - conference - usually spring ● annual Southeast Regional - conference - usually fall.

9001 ■ State Higher Education Executive Officers (SHEEO)
3035 Center Green Dr., Ste.100
Boulder, CO 80301-2251
Ph: (303)541-1600 (303)541-1605
Fax: (303)541-1639
E-mail: sheeo@sheeo.org
URL: http://www.sheeo.org
Contact: Dr. Paul E. Lingenfelter, Pres.
Founded: 1954. **Members:** 58. **Staff:** 10. **Description:** Provides assistance to higher education executives and the states as they seek to develop and sustain excellent systems of higher education. **Libraries: Type:** not open to the public. **Holdings:** 6,000. **Committees:** Nominating; Time and Place. **Projects:** Changing Direction: Integrating Higher Education Financial Aid and Financing Policy; K-16 Professional Development Collaborative; National Commission on Accountability in Higher Education; Pathways to College; SHEEO-NCES Network; State Higher Education Finance. **Publications:** *Compendium of National Data Sources on Higher Education*. Includes a guide to multiple data sources, comparative statistics, and information used by higher education policy makers and researchers. ● *Compendium of Resources on Teacher Mobility*. **Price:** $20.00 ● *SHEEO/NCES Network Newsletter*, quarterly. Alternate Formats: online ● *State Higher Education Finance*. Alternate Formats: online.

Political Science

9002 ■ Jefferson Legacy Foundation (JLF)
PO Box 76
Ripton, VT 05766-0076
Ph: (802)388-7676
Fax: (802)388-1776
E-mail: info@jeffersonlegacy.org
URL: http://www.jeffersonlegacy.org
Contact: Sydney N. Stokes Jr., Chm.
Founded: 1993. **Members:** 23. **Membership Dues:** contributing, $50 (annual) ● sponsoring, $100 (annual) ● sustaining, $250 (annual) ● benefactor, $500 (annual) ● student, $15 (annual) ● individual, $25 (annual). **Staff:** 2. **Budget:** $100,000. **Description:** Encourages people to learn about and from Thomas Jefferson, his time, his philosophy to promote participation in public affairs. **Libraries: Type:** reference. **Holdings:** 3,000. **Subjects:** American Revolution, Jefferson and his contemporaries. **Programs:** Community Garden; Educational Outreach. **Publications:** *Discourse*. Monograph ● *News and Comment*, periodic. Newsletter. **Price:** included in membership dues. Alternate Formats: online.

9003 ■ Robert H. Smith International Center for Jefferson Studies (ICJS)
PO Box 316
Charlottesville, VA 22902
Ph: (434)984-7500
Fax: (434)296-1992
E-mail: icjs@monticello.org
URL: http://monticello.org/icjs
Contact: Ms. Joan Hairfield, Asst. to the Dir.
Founded: 1994. **Nonmembership. Multinational. Description:** Promotes research and education to foster Jefferson scholarship and disseminate findings. **Libraries: Type:** reference. **Holdings:** 12,000; archival material, audio recordings, audiovisuals, papers, periodicals, photographs. **Subjects:** Thomas Jefferson's life, times and legacy, includes original research. **Awards:** Gilder Lehrman Junior Research Fellowships. **Frequency:** annual. **Type:** grant. **Recipient:** to scholars working on Jefferson projects, devoting their time researching on topics directly related to Thomas Jefferson, his times, and legacy ● Short-Term Fellowships. **Frequency:** semiannual. **Type:** fellowship. **Recipient:** to doctoral candidates and postdoctoral scholars from any country working on Jefferson-related projects ● Travel Grants. **Type:** grant. **Recipient:** for scholars and teachers wishing to make short-term visits to Monticello to pursue research or educational projects related to Jefferson. **Computer Services:** database, Thomas Jefferson Portal. **Formerly:** (2004) International Center for Jefferson Studies. **Publications:** *Monticello Monograph Series*. Monographs ● *The Papers of Thomas Jefferson: Retirement Series* ● *Thomas Jefferson Portal*. Catalog. Alternate Formats: online ● Bulletin. Alternate Formats: online. **Conventions/Meetings:** conference ● lecture ● seminar.

Portuguese

9004 ■ American Portuguese Studies Association (APSA)
PO Box 1158
Ames, IA 50014
E-mail: mmapsa@unm.edu
URL: http://www.umassd.edu/apsa
Contact: Margo Milleret, Sec.
Founded: 1996. **Membership Dues:** faculty, $35 (annual) ● faculty, $60 (biennial) ● student, $10 (annual). **Multinational. Description:** Promotes the study of all topics related to the Portuguese-speaking world. Strives to foster the expansion and spreading of knowledge about the languages, peoples and cultures of Portuguese-speaking countries and diasporas. Promotes the development of Portuguese language programs in North America. **Telecommunication Services:** electronic mail, kholton@andromeda.rutgers.edu. **Publications:** *ellipsis*, annual. Journal. Alternate Formats: online.

Presbyterian

9005 ■ Association of Presbyterian Colleges and Universities (APCU)
100 Witherspoon St.
Louisville, KY 40202-1396
Ph: (502)569-5364 (502)569-5509
Free: (888)728-7228
E-mail: apcu@ctr.pcusa.org
URL: http://www.apcu.net
Contact: Gary W. Luhr, Exec. Dir.
Founded: 1983. **Members:** 62. **Staff:** 2. **Budget:** $200,000. **Description:** Colleges and universities officially related to the Presbyterian Church (U.S.A.). Advocates interests of private Presbyterian and Reformed colleges and universities. Conducts educational programs; offers mutual support and publicizes institutions. Compiles statistics. **Awards: Type:** recognition. **Telecommunication Services:** electronic mail, gluhr@ctr.pcusa.org. **Formed by Merger of:** Association of Presbyterian Colleges; Presbyterian College Union. **Conventions/Meetings:** annual Presidents' Conference (exhibits).

Preschool Education

9006 ■ National Head Start Association (NHSA)
1651 Prince St.
Alexandria, VA 22314
Ph: (703)739-0875
Fax: (703)739-0878
E-mail: sgreene@nhsa.org
URL: http://www.nhsa.org
Contact: Sarah M. Greene, Pres./CEO
Founded: 1973. **Members:** 10,000. **Membership Dues:** individual, $1-$40 (annual) ● associate, $100-$350 (annual) ● affiliate, $100 (annual). **Staff:** 24. **Budget:** $4,500,000. **Regional Groups:** 12. **State Groups:** 53. **Local Groups:** 2,033. **Description:** Members of National Head Start Parent Association, National Head Start Directors Association, National Head Start Staff Association, National Head Start Friends Association, and others interested in the Head Start Program. Upgrades the quality and quantity of Head Start Program services. Integrates the activities of the 4 divisions to present cohesive policies, positions, and statements. Conducts seminars and training sessions in early childhood education. Maintains speakers' bureau. **Libraries: Type:** reference. **Holdings:** reports. **Awards:** Edward Zigler Research Award. **Frequency:** annual. **Type:** scholarship. **Recipient:** for a student currently pursuing a PhD in research with an emphasis on psychology, public education or a related discipline ● **Type:** recognition. **Computer Services:** database ● mailing lists. **Telecommunication Services:** electronic mail, ojarvis@nhsa.org. **Committees:** Information and Education; Policy and Regulations; Public Relations; Scholarship. **Publications:** *Children and Families*, quarterly. Magazine ● *NHSA Newsletter*, quarterly. **Price:** included in membership dues; $60.00 for nonmembers. **Advertising:** accepted. **Conventions/Meetings:** annual conference, training, books, educational aids (exhibits) ● annual Parent Training - conference.

9007 ■ National Kindergarten Alliance (NKA)
PO Box 309
Agua Dulce, TX 78330
Ph: (361)998-2240
E-mail: ppillack@aol.com
URL: http://nkateach.org
Contact: Penny Pillack, Pres.
Founded: 2000. **Membership Dues:** individual, $25 (annual). **Description:** Represents the interests of individuals and organizations that share a common goal of ensuring the highest quality education for kindergarten students. Encourages and assists the formation and growth of state organizations. Develops leaders in the field of early childhood education. Seeks to address the major issues facing kindergarten classroom teachers. **Awards:** National Kindergarten Alliance Professional Practices Grant. **Frequency:** annual. **Type:** grant. **Recipient:** for members of the Alliance ● **Frequency:** annual. **Type:** scholarship. **Recipient:** for members pursuing an advanced degree in Early Childhood Education or a closely related field. **Telecommunication Services:** electronic mail, pwarner@winona.edu.

9008 ■ Waldorf Early Childhood Association of North America (WECAN)
285 Hungry Hollow Rd.
Chestnut Ridge, NY 10977
Ph: (845)352-1690
Fax: (845)352-1695
E-mail: info@waldorfearlychildhood.org
URL: http://www.waldorfearlychildhood.org
Contact: Joan Almon, Co-Chair
Founded: 1983. **Members:** 500. **Membership Dues:** individual, $40 (annual) ● full, $125 (annual) ● developing, $150 (annual). **Staff:** 2. **Budget:** $32,000. **Description:** Nursery and kindergarten teachers, daycare providers, parents, professionals, and individuals interested in the Waldorf approach to education. Follows the educational ideals of Austrian social philosopher Rudolf Steiner (1861-1925), which emphasize a concerted development of the child's physical, spiritual, and emotional abilities. Works with all of the Waldorf Kindergartens, Playgroups, and Initiatives in Canada, Mexico, and throughout the United States to create educational programs. **Computer Services:** database ● mailing lists. **Affiliated With:** Anthroposophical Society in America; Association of Waldorf Schools of North America. **Formerly:** (1998) Waldorf Kindergarten Association of North America. **Publications:** *An Overview of the Waldorf Kindergarten and A Deeper Understanding*. Books. Contains a compilation of back issues. ● *First Steps in Natural Dyeing*. Book ● *Gateways*, semiannual. Newsletter. Contains articles on Waldorf early childhood education covering all aspects of the practical work and the principles behind the work. **Price:** included in membership dues ● *Plays for Puppets*. Book ● *Understanding Young Children, Excerpts from Rudolf Steiner*. Newsletter. **Conventions/Meetings:** annual board meeting - always November ● periodic regional meeting and workshop.

Press

9009 ■ Association of Educational Publishers (AEP)
510 Heron Dr., Ste.201
Logan Township, NJ 08085
Ph: (856)241-7772
Fax: (856)241-0709
E-mail: mail@aepweb.org
URL: http://www.edpress.org
Contact: Charlene F. Gaynor, CEO
Founded: 1895. **Members:** 350. **Membership Dues:** independent, freelance, $260 (annual) ● corporate, affiliate, $750 (annual) ● nonprofit, school, $495 (annual) ● student, $50 (annual) ● international, $500-$1,000 (annual). **Staff:** 8. **Budget:** $950,000. **Description:** Print and digital publishers, educational foundations and associations, and the education and trade press, schools and school districts that support the growth of publishing. Supports publishing as a positive impact on learning and teaching. Tracks education and industry information and trends, provides professional development, and promotes quality supplemental materials as essential learning resources. **Awards:** Distinguished Achievement Award. **Frequency:** annual. **Type:** recognition. **Recipient:** for excellence in publishing (educational technology instructional materials) ● Distinguished Marketer Awards. **Type:** recognition ● Golden Lamp Awards. **Type:** recognition. **Recipient:** for highest honor in educational publishing ● Student Publishing Awards. **Type:** recognition. **Computer Services:** database, member directory ● mailing lists, of members. **Telecommunication Services:** electronic mail, cgaynor@aepweb.org. **Formed by Merger of:** (2005) Classroom Publishers Association and Association of Educational Publishers. **Formerly:** (1998) Educational Press Association of America; (2001) EdPress - The Association of Educational Publishers. **Publications:** *EDPRESS Membership Roster and Freelance Directory*, annual. Lists publication information such as type, circulation, frequency, and geographic distribution. **Price:** included in membership dues; $35.00 for nonmembers. Alternate Formats: online ● *Magazines for Kids and Teens*. Directory. Lists magazines published for children aged 2-17. ● Newsletter, biweekly. Covers writing, editing, photography, production, postal matters, new technology, and printing and copyright changes; contains book reviews. **Price:** included in membership dues. **Circulation:** 1,000. Alternate Formats: online. **Conventions/Meetings:** annual New Media Publishing - conference (exhibits) ● annual workshop and conference, editorial (exhibits).

9010 ■ Columbia Scholastic Press Advisers Association (CSPAA)
Columbia Univ.
Mail Code 5711
New York, NY 10027-6902
Ph: (212)854-9400
Fax: (212)854-9401
E-mail: cspa@columbia.edu
URL: http://www.columbia.edu/cu/cspa
Contact: Mary Kay Downes, Pres.
Founded: 1926. **Members:** 1,900. **Membership Dues:** regular, $10 (annual). **Staff:** 4. **Budget:** $20,000. **Description:** Teachers who serve as advisers to student publications at all educational levels. Prepares technical aids and other materials for advisers and student staffs in cooperation with Columbia Scholastic Press Association (see separate entry). Maintains national speakers' bureau. **Libraries: Type:** reference. **Awards:** Honorary Membership. **Frequency:** annual. **Type:** recognition. **Committees:** Convention Planning; Honors and Awards; Judging Standards and Practices. **Affiliated With:** Columbia Scholastic Press Association. **Formerly:** (1927) Columbia School Press Advisers; (1928) Columbia School Press Specialists. **Conventions/Meetings:** annual convention, held in conjunction with CSPA (exhibits) - always March in New York City.

9011 ■ Columbia Scholastic Press Association (CSPA)
Columbia Univ.
Mail Code 5711
New York, NY 10027-6902
Ph: (212)854-9400
Fax: (212)854-9401
E-mail: cspa@columbia.edu
URL: http://www.columbia.edu/cu/cspa
Contact: Mr. Edmund J. Sullivan, Exec. Dir.
Founded: 1925. **Members:** 2,000. **Membership Dues:** regular, $239 (annual) ● associate, $130 (annual) ● professional, $99 (annual). **Staff:** 4. **Budget:** $1,050,000. **Description:** Newspapers, magazines, and yearbooks issued by schools from junior high school level through college and university, with the majority being from secondary schools. Works to promote student writing through the medium of the school publication. Improves publications in all phases. Offers critiques for each regular member. Compiles statistics. Provides consultation and referral services to student publications. **Libraries: Type:** reference; not open to the public. **Holdings:** 350; archival material, books, periodicals. **Subjects:** journalism education in high schools and colleges. **Awards:** Crown Awards. **Frequency:** annual. **Type:** recognition. **Recipient:** for overall excellence in student publications ● Gold Circle Awards. **Frequency:** annual. **Type:** recognition. **Recipient:** to students in writing, cartooning, design and layout ● Gold Key Award. **Frequency:** annual. **Type:** recognition. **Recipient:** to journalism professionals and faculty advisers. **Computer Services:** Electronic publishing, ezine. **Committees:** Judging Standards. **Affiliated With:** Columbia Scholastic Press Advisers Association. **Publications:** Also publishes guide books on the fundamentals of student newspapers, magazines, and yearbooks. **Conventions/Meetings:** annual Fall Conference, for Northeast United States' high schools and middle schools - always November ● annual Scholastic Convention, national event; high schools and middle schools only (exhibits) - always March ● annual Summer Journalism Workshop - always June.

9012 ■ National Elementary Schools Press Association (NESPA)
1345 Hendersonville Rd.
Asheville, NC 28803
Ph: (828)210-9164
Fax: (828)277-8832
E-mail: mlevin@cdschool.org
URL: http://www.nespa.org
Contact: Mark Levin, Dir.
Founded: 1993. **Members:** 660. **Membership Dues:** life, $42. **Staff:** 1. **Budget:** $5,000. **Description:** Elementary and middle schools that produce school newspapers. Promotes effective teaching of journalism and writing skills at the primary and secondary levels. Provides support and assistance to school newspapers and journalism and writing programs. **Libraries: Type:** by appointment only. **Holdings:** books. **Subjects:** educational journalism. **Awards:** Exceptional Product Award. **Frequency:** annual. **Type:** recognition ● Newspaper Rating and Review Award. **Frequency:** annual. **Type:** recognition ● Student Recognition Award. **Frequency:** annual. **Type:** recognition. **Publications:** *Kids in Print*. Handbook ● *Membership Roster*, periodic. Directory ● *NESPAper*, periodic. Newsletter ● *The Reporters Notebook*.

9013 ■ National Scholastic Press Association (NSPA)
2221 Univ. Ave. SE, Ste.121
Univ. of Minnesota
Minneapolis, MN 55414
Ph: (612)625-8335
Fax: (612)626-0720
E-mail: info@studentpress.org
URL: http://www.studentpress.org/nspa
Contact: Logan Aimone, Exec. Dir.
Founded: 1921. **Members:** 3,600. **Membership Dues:** level 1, $109 (annual) ● level 2, $189 (annual) ● broadcast, $69 (annual). **Budget:** $250,000. **Description:** Represents publishers of high school newspapers, yearbooks, and magazines. Offers critical services for newspapers, yearbooks, and magazines. **Awards:** All-American Awards. **Frequency:** annual. **Type:** recognition. **Recipient:** for outstanding school newspapers and yearbooks ● Pacemaker Award. **Frequency:** annual. **Type:** recognition. **Recipient:** for general excellence of newspapers, yearbooks, newsmagazines, and literary magazines. **Affiliated With:** Associated Collegiate Press. **Publications:** *Trends in High School Media*, quarterly. Includes articles on design, editing, illustration, and writing. Contains book reviews and information on new products and scholarships. **Price:** $12.00/year. ISSN: 1046-2155. **Advertising:** accepted. **Conventions/Meetings:** competition ● semiannual convention (exhibits) - always April and November.

Principals

9014 ■ National Association of Elementary School Principals (NAESP)
1615 Duke St.
Alexandria, VA 22314

Ph: (703)684-3345
Free: (800)386-2377
Fax: (703)549-5568
E-mail: naesp@naesp.org
URL: http://www.naesp.org
Contact: Gail Connelly, Exec. Dir.
Founded: 1921. **Members:** 30,000. **Membership Dues:** active, $215 (annual) ● institutional, $260 (annual) ● emeritus, $108 (annual) ● retired, $55 (annual) ● associate, $115 (annual) ● international associate, $145 (annual). **Staff:** 50. **Budget:** $7,700,000. **State Groups:** 51. **Description:** Professional association of principals, assistant or vice principals, and aspiring principals; persons engaged in educational research and in the professional education of elementary and middle school administrators. Sponsors National Distinguished Principals Program, President's Award for Educational Excellence, American Student Council Association. Offers annual national convention and exhibition, on-site and internet professional development workshops throughout the year. Recently expanded professional publications offered through the National Principals' Resource Center. **Awards:** National Distinguished Principals. **Frequency:** annual. **Type:** recognition. **Recipient:** for elementary and middle school principals who set the pace, character, and quality of the education children receive during their early school years. **Telecommunication Services:** electronic mail, membership@naesp.org. **Formerly:** (1970) Department of Elementary School Principals, NEA. **Publications:** *Communicator*, 9/year. Newsletter. **Price:** included in membership dues. **Circulation:** 30,000 ● *Middle Matters*, 5/year. Newsletter. Highlights the special needs of NAESP administrators of schools serving the middle grades, 5-8. **Price:** included in membership dues. **Circulation:** 30,000. **Advertising:** accepted. Alternate Formats: online ● *Principal*, 5/year. Magazine. **Price:** included in membership dues. **Circulation:** 30,000. **Advertising:** accepted. **Conventions/Meetings:** annual convention, largest professional development experience created exclusively for elementary and middle level educators (exhibits).

9015 ■ National Association of Principals of Schools for Girls (NAPSG)

23490 Caraway Lakes Dr.
Bonita Springs, FL 34135-8441
Ph: (239)947-6196 (212)979-5030
Fax: (239)390-3245
E-mail: napsg@mac.com
URL: http://www.napsg.org
Contact: Bruce W. Galbraith, Exec. Dir.
Founded: 1920. **Members:** 600. **Membership Dues:** school, $250 (annual) ● college, $50 (annual) ● affiliate - employed, $25 (annual) ● affiliate - retired, $10 (annual). **Staff:** 1. **Budget:** $150,000. **Description:** Professional organization of principals and deans of private secondary and elementary schools for girls and of coeducational schools; retired heads of these institutions; college admissions officers. Investigates problems bearing upon the organization, administration, and function of private education for girls. **Telecommunication Services:** electronic mail, rlauder@friendsseminary.org. **Publications:** Proceedings, annual. **Price:** available to members only. **Conventions/Meetings:** annual conference, with speakers.

9016 ■ National Association of Secondary School Principals (NASSP)

1904 Assn. Dr.
Reston, VA 20191-1537
Ph: (703)860-0200
Free: (800)253-7746
Fax: (703)860-3422
URL: http://www.principals.org
Contact: Dr. Joseph A. Militello, Pres.
Founded: 1916. **Members:** 33,000. **Membership Dues:** individual/institution, $218 (annual) ● associate, $73 (annual) ● retired, $42 (annual) ● international, $99 (annual). **Staff:** 111. **Budget:** $25,000,000. **State Groups:** 60. **Description:** Middle level and high school principals, assistant principals, and aspiring school leaders, others engaged in secondary school administration and/or supervision; college professors teaching courses in secondary education. Sponsors National Association of Student Councils (NASC), National Honor Society (NHS), and National Junior Honor Society (NJHS). **Awards:** Assistant Principal of the Year. **Frequency:** annual. **Type:** recognition. **Recipient:** for outstanding secondary school assistant principals ● President's Education Awards Program. **Frequency:** annual. **Type:** recognition. **Recipient:** to outstanding students who have achieved high academic goals through their dedication to learning ● Principal of the Year. **Frequency:** annual. **Type:** recognition. **Recipient:** for outstanding middle level and high school principals ● Prudential Spirit of Community Award. **Frequency:** annual. **Type:** recognition. **Recipient:** for students in grades 5 to 12 with exemplary community service. **Committees:** Assistant Principalship; Curriculum; International Programs; Middle Level Schools; Non-Public Schools; Urban Schools. **Task Forces:** No Child Left Behind; Principal Preparation. **Affiliated With:** National Honor Society; National Junior Honor Society. **Publications:** *A Legal Memorandum*, quarterly. Newsletter. Features legal issues of interest to secondary school leaders. ● *Leadership for Student Activities*, monthly. Magazine ● *NASSP Bulletin*, quarterly. Journal. Features a peer-reviewed journal containing a wide range of articles of enduring interest to educators. ● *NewsLeader*, monthly. Newspaper. Encourages principals to act as informed advocates for their schools in their local communities. **Advertising:** accepted ● *Principal Leadership (Middle Level and High School Editions)*, monthly. Magazine. Focuses on school leaders' real needs. **Conventions/Meetings:** annual convention (exhibits).

9017 ■ National Conference of Yeshiva Principals (NCYP)

Address Unknown since 2008
Founded: 1947. **Members:** 1,000. **Membership Dues:** school, $54 (annual). **Staff:** 7. **Description:** Principals in Hebrew day schools. Sponsors School visitations and evaluations. Compiles statistics. Sponsors annual regional teacher training seminar. **Awards: Type:** recognition. **Publications:** *Machberes Hamenahel*, monthly ● Newsletter, monthly ● Also publishes curriculum materials. **Conventions/Meetings:** annual Mid-Winter Principle Conference, Leadership Convention (exhibits) - always May, New York City ● annual National Curriculum Conclave for Principles - meeting - usually January-February.

Private Schools

9018 ■ The Association of Boarding Schools (TABS)

2141 Wisconsin Ave. NW, Ste.H
Washington, DC 20007
Ph: (202)965-8982
Fax: (202)965-8988
E-mail: tabs@schools.com
URL: http://www.schools.com
Contact: Peter Upham, Exec. Dir.
Founded: 1976. **Members:** 290. **Membership Dues:** school (with 90 or fewer boarding enrollment), $1,375 (annual) ● school (per boarder; with 91-226 boarding enrollment), $15 (annual) ● school (with 227 and above boarding enrollment), $3,425 (annual). **Staff:** 4. **Budget:** $1,000,000. **Multinational. Description:** Disseminates information to families and the public about schools with residential facilities. **Computer Services:** Online services. **Affiliated With:** National Association of Independent Schools; Secondary School Admission Test Board. **Formerly:** (1994) Committee on Boarding Schools. **Publications:** *Boarding Schools Directory*, annual. Contains information on members' facilities, programs, and application procedures. **Price:** free. **Circulation:** 40,000. Alternate Formats: online. **Conventions/Meetings:** annual Admission Academy - workshop, for new admissions staff ● annual Boarding Schools Changing Lives - conference, for boarding school professionals, admissions staff, residential/dorm staff ● annual Midwinter Residential Life Seminar, for residential/dorm staff ● annual Residential Life Workshop, for residential/dorm staff.

9019 ■ Association of Private Enterprise Education (APEE)

c/o Dr. J.R. Clark, Sec.-Treas.
The Univ. of Tennessee at Chattanooga
313 Fletcher Hall, Dept. 6106
615 McCallie Ave.
Chattanooga, TN 37403-2598
Ph: (423)425-4118
Fax: (423)425-5218
E-mail: j-clark@utc.edu
URL: http://www.apee.org
Contact: Dr. J.R. Clark, Sec.-Treas.
Founded: 1963. **Membership Dues:** institutional, $250 (annual) ● individual, $70 (annual) ● supporter, $750 (annual) ● sponsor, $1,000 (annual). **Multinational. Description:** Teachers, professors, school administrators involved with private enterprise education or business that want to support efforts to improve economic understanding for employees. Strives to put into action accurate and objective understandings of private enterprise. Aims to teach and research on private enterprise. **Awards:** Adam Smith Award. **Frequency:** annual. **Type:** recognition. **Recipient:** for an individual who has made a sustained contribution to the perpetuation of the ideals of a free market economy ● Distinguished Scholar Award. **Frequency:** annual. **Type:** recognition. **Recipient:** for significant contribution to the research and literature of free market economics ● Herman W. Lay Memorial Award. **Frequency:** annual. **Type:** recognition. **Recipient:** for individuals who have emulated the pattern of success and philanthropy that Herman W. Lay lived ● Thomas Jefferson Award. **Frequency:** annual. **Type:** recognition. **Recipient:** for an individual whose public service has embodied the Jeffersonian ideal. **Publications:** *The Journal of Private Enterprise*, semiannual. **Price:** $10.00/copy for nonmembers; included in membership dues. **Conventions/Meetings:** annual convention.

9020 ■ Council for American Private Education (CAPE)

13017 Wisteria Dr., No. 457
Germantown, MD 20874-2607
Ph: (301)916-8460
Fax: (301)916-8485
E-mail: cape@capenet.org
URL: http://www.capenet.org
Contact: Joseph McTighe, Exec. Dir.
Founded: 1971. **Members:** 17. **Staff:** 2. **State Groups:** 28. **Description:** Coalition of national organizations serving the interests of private schools (kindergarten through 12th grade). Seeks to promote understanding and cooperation between private schools, public schools, and the government at all levels. Encourages the sharing of resources among member organizations and their schools. Stimulates the creation and effectiveness of state and local private school groups. Formulates and disseminates public policy concerning private schools at the national, state, and local levels. Maintains relationships with state and federal governments and with education-related organizations. Follows and participates in relevant court actions. Identifies and works with private school advocates to build support for private education on the local, state, and national levels. **Libraries: Type:** reference. **Holdings:** archival material. **Publications:** *Outlook*, monthly. Newsletter. **Price:** $15.00 /year for individuals - email; $25.00 /year for individuals - regular mail; $100.00/year for schools. **Circulation:** 3,000. **Conventions/Meetings:** semiannual board meeting - every March and October in Washington, DC.

9021 ■ National Association of State Administrators and Supervisors of Private Schools (NASASPS)

c/o Teri Candelaria, Pres.
Arizona State Bd. for Private Postsecondary Educ.
1400 W Washington St., Rm. 260
Phoenix, AZ 85007
Ph: (602)542-5709
Fax: (602)542-1253

E-mail: webmaster@nasasps.com
URL: http://www.nasasps.com
Contact: Teri Candelaria, Pres.
Founded: 1971. **Members:** 45. **Membership Dues:** regular, $25 (annual). **Regional Groups:** 5. **Description:** State administrators and supervisors of post-secondary private schools. Seeks to coordinate state licensing and practices of postsecondary private schools. **Publications:** Newsletter, annual. **Conventions/Meetings:** annual conference.

Professors

9022 ■ American Association of University Professors (AAUP)
1012 14th St. NW, Ste.500
Washington, DC 20005
Ph: (202)737-5900 (510)841-1997
Free: (800)424-2973
Fax: (202)737-5526
E-mail: aaup@aaup.org
URL: http://www.aaup.org
Contact: Cary Nelson, Pres.
Founded: 1915. **Members:** 45,000. **Membership Dues:** faculty (new), $6 (monthly) ● faculty (more than 4 years in service), $12 (monthly). **Staff:** 37. **Budget:** $4,000,000. **State Groups:** 35. **Local Groups:** 500. **Description:** College and university teachers, research scholars, and academic librarians. Purposes are to facilitate cooperation among teachers and research scholars in universities, colleges, and professional schools, for the promotion of higher education and research, and to increase the usefulness and advance the standards, ideals, and welfare of the profession. Compiles statistics. **Telecommunication Services:** electronic mail, membership@aaup.org. **Committees:** Academic Freedom and Tenure; Accrediting of Colleges and Universities; College and University Government; College and University Teaching, Research and Publication; Economic Status of the Profession; Historically Black Institutions; Junior and Community Colleges; Professional Ethics; Relationships of Higher Education to Federal and State Governments; Representation of Economic and Professional Interests; Status of Minorities in the Profession; Status of Women in the Academic Profession. **Publications:** *AAUP Redbook*, quinquennial. **Price:** $18.00/copy for nonmembers; $12.50/copy for members ● *Academe: Bulletin of the AAUP*, bimonthly. Magazine. Covers Association business and issues in higher education. Includes book reviews and information on censured administrations. **Price:** included in membership dues; $62.00 /year for nonmembers. ISSN: 0190-2946. **Circulation:** 46,500. **Advertising:** accepted. Alternate Formats: microform ● *Collective Bargaining Newsletter*, bimonthly. Covers chapter and contract news and legal developments. **Price:** available to members only. **Circulation:** 3,000. **Conventions/Meetings:** annual meeting.

9023 ■ Association of Environmental Engineering and Science Professors (AEESP)
c/o Joanne Fetzner
2303 Naples Ct.
Champaign, IL 61822
Ph: (217)398-6969
Fax: (217)355-9232
E-mail: secretary@aeesp.org
URL: http://www.aeesp.org
Contact: Charlie Werth, Sec.
Founded: 1963. **Members:** 700. **Membership Dues:** student, $15 (annual) ● assistant professor, $40 (annual) ● associate professor, $60 (annual) ● full professor, $75 (annual) ● affiliate, regular, $50 (annual) ● sustaining, $500 (annual). **Staff:** 2. **Description:** Professors and interested individuals. Works to improve education and research programs in the science and technology of environmental protection. Provides information to government agencies and the public; encourages graduate education by supporting research and training for students; maintains speaker's bureau. **Awards:** Masters Thesis. **Frequency:** annual. **Type:** recognition ● PhD Dissertation. **Frequency:** annual. **Type:** monetary. **Recipient:** for the best doctoral dissertation ● **Type:** recognition. **Telecommunication Services:** electronic mail, jfetzner@uiuc.edu. **Formerly:** (1999) Association of Environmental Engineering Professors. **Publications:** *AEESP Newsletter*, 3/year. **Price:** included in membership dues. **Advertising:** accepted ● *Computer Software*. Manual ● *Register of Graduate Programs*, quinquennial. Directory. Contains information on graduate programs for over 100 universities. ● Membership Directory, annual. **Conventions/Meetings:** quinquennial Environmental Engineering Education - conference ● annual meeting ● quinquennial Research Needs in Environmental Engineering - conference.

9024 ■ Society of Chinese American Professors and Scientists (SOCAPS)
c/o Dr. Zuotao Zeng, Treas.
PO Box 5735
Woodridge, IL 60517
E-mail: admin@socaps.org
URL: http://socaps.org
Contact: Guokui Liu, Pres.
Founded: 2003. **Members:** 180. **Membership Dues:** regular, $50 (biennial). **Regional Groups:** 38. **Description:** Advocates for Chinese American academics. Facilitates its members' contributions to the American society through their academic achievements. Advances science and education through academic collaborations and information exchange. **Computer Services:** Online services, public chat. **Committees:** Academic; Communication; Culture Exchange and Development; International Collaboration; Long-Range Planning; Public Affairs; Publication. **Publications:** *Inside SoCAPS*. Newsletter ● Proceedings. Alternate Formats: online.

9025 ■ University Faculty for Life (UFL)
120 New North Bldg.
Georgetown Univ.
Washington, DC 20057
Ph: (202)687-6101
Fax: (202)687-8000
E-mail: bcollett1@msn.com
URL: http://www.uffl.org
Contact: Richard S. Myers, Pres.
Founded: 1989. **Members:** 671. **Membership Dues:** individual, $25 (annual). **Budget:** $15,000. **Regional Groups:** 2. **Local Groups:** 3. **Multinational. Description:** Represents current and former professors at a college or university or seminary. Works to promote research and dialogue among professors concerning abortion, infanticide and euthanasia and the value of human life. Provides education on pro-life issues; disseminates scholarly studies; distributes proceedings. **Telecommunication Services:** electronic mail, francis_beckwith@baylor.edu. **Publications:** *Life & Learning*, annual. Proceedings. **Price:** $10.00/copy. ISSN: 1097-0878. **Circulation:** 800 ● *Pro Vita*, quarterly. Newsletter. **Price:** free for members. **Circulation:** 600. **Conventions/Meetings:** annual convention - always in June.

9026 ■ University Professors for Academic Order (UPAO)
Address Unknown since 2008
Founded: 1970. **Members:** 300. **Membership Dues:** $25 (annual). **Description:** College and university faculty and administrators connected with institutions of higher learning; interested individuals. Purposes are: to foster and maintain the integrity of the academic teaching and research professions; to study and improve the administration of universities and professional schools; to advance and promote the study of legitimate ideals of higher and professional education; to preserve and advance the ideals of the freedom to teach and the freedom to learn; to promote academic standards for universities and professional schools and their teaching and research staffs; to advance the professional and economic interests of teaching and research staffs; to promote cooperation among members of teaching and research staffs. Upholds the function of the university to "impart knowledge, wisdom, and culture rather than serve as a center for political activity and social activism;" believes that persons working for or attending a university should not engage in pursuits against university regulations and/or the laws of the community. Opposes collective bargaining and compulsory unionism for higher education faculties. Maintains a speakers' bureau. **Publications:** *Community in Crisis and Highlights: A Capsule History of UPAO 1970 Present*. **Advertising:** accepted ● *Universitas*, quarterly. Newsletter. **Price:** included in membership dues; $10.00/year for libraries. ISSN: 0146-9061 ● *UPAO VOX*. **Conventions/Meetings:** annual conference, papers presented according to the themes (exhibits) - always December or January.

Property Management

9027 ■ Building Owners and Managers Institute International (BOMI)
1521 Ritchie Hwy.
Arnold, MD 21012
Free: (800)235-2664
Fax: (410)974-1935
E-mail: service@bomi-edu.org
URL: http://www.bomi-edu.org
Contact: Jeff Horn, Pres./CEO
Founded: 1970. **Multinational. Description:** Provides commercial property education. **Publications:** *FM Solutions*. Newsletter ● *Graduate Lookout*, quarterly. Newsletter ● *Student Navigator*, quarterly. Newsletter.

Psychoanalysis

9028 ■ International Federation for Psychoanalytic Education (IFPE)
c/o Stuart Spence, Interim Admin.
8234 McGroarty St.
Sunland, CA 91040
Ph: (818)352-3882
Fax: (818)353-5837
E-mail: ifpe@spence.net
URL: http://www.ifpe.org
Contact: Stuart Spence, Interim Admin.
Founded: 1991. **Membership Dues:** student, $50 (annual) ● individual, $95 (annual) ● organizational, $120 (annual). **Multinational. Description:** Fosters the growth of psychoanalysis. Seeks to advance the study, teaching and practice of psychoanalysis. Encourages alternatives to restrictive psychoanalytic training. Facilitates dialogue with disciplines that can enrich psychoanalysis by broadening its horizons. Provides a forum on psychoanalytic developments for membership and community. **Awards:** Hans W. Loewald Memorial Award. **Frequency:** annual. **Type:** recognition. **Recipient:** for individual's distinguished contribution to psychoanalytic education. **Publications:** Newsletter. Alternate Formats: online.

Psychology

9029 ■ Consciousness-Based Education Association (CBEA)
1100 Univ. Manor Dr., B-24
Fairfield, IA 52556
Free: (888)472-1677
Fax: (641)472-3116
E-mail: info@cbeprograms.org
URL: http://www.cbeprograms.org
Contact: Dr. John Hagelin, Contact
Description: Provides practical, scientifically validated programs to unfold the latent creative intelligence and inner happiness of students and teachers. Seeks to provide the knowledge and technology to make education capable of creating exemplary citizens. Offers distinct support services to provide Consciousness-Based education programs for existing schools, new schools, and after-school educational programs. **Publications:** Brochure. Alternate Formats: online.

9030 ■ Northamerican Association of Masters in Psychology (NAMP)
PO Box 721270
Norman, OK 73070
Ph: (405)329-3030
Free: (800)919-9330
E-mail: namp@att.net
URL: http://www.enamp.org
Contact: Randy Churchill, Pres.
Membership Dues: student, $30 (annual) ● regular, $65 (annual). **Multinational. Description:** Represents the interests of all master level psychologists throughout Canada, the United States and Mexico. Promotes advocacy, affiliation, identity, and communication for psychologists in training or trained at the master's level in the professional, academic, governmental and consumer communities. Encourages legislative recognition of all competent psychologists to increase high quality and affordable psychological services. **Telecommunication Services:** electronic mail, enamp@enamp.org. **Publications:** *Journal of Psychological Practice*, semiannual. Augments the general dissemination of theoretical and empirical knowledge with practical approaches. **Price:** included in membership dues. Alternate Formats: online ● *Master's Advocate*, quarterly. Newsletter. Covers issues that are important to the graduate level psychologist. **Price:** included in membership dues. Alternate Formats: online.

Public Relations

9031 ■ Institute for Public Relations (IPR)
PO Box 118400
Gainesville, FL 32611-8400
Ph: (352)392-0280
Fax: (352)846-1122
URL: http://www.instituteforpr.com
Contact: Frank E. Ovaitt Jr., Pres./CEO
Founded: 1956. **Staff:** 2. **Budget:** $350,000. **Description:** Dedicated to the science beneath the art of public relations. Exists to build and document the intellectual foundations of public relations and to mainstream this knowledge by making it available and useful to all. **Libraries: Type:** reference. **Holdings:** reports. **Awards:** Alexander Hamilton Award. **Frequency:** annual. **Type:** recognition. **Recipient:** for individuals who have made major contributions to the practice of PR ● Ketchum Excellence in Public Relations Research. **Frequency:** annual. **Type:** recognition. **Recipient:** for developing new research methods in public relations ● Master Thesis Award. **Frequency:** annual. **Type:** recognition ● Pathfinder Award. **Frequency:** annual. **Type:** recognition. **Recipient:** for significant contribution to the body of knowledge and practice of PR. **Commissions:** Public Relations Measurement and Evaluation. **Formerly:** Foundation for Public Relations Research and Education; (1999) Institute for Public Relations Research and Education. **Conventions/Meetings:** annual Public Relations Executive Forum - seminar, professional development seminar.

9032 ■ National Council for Marketing and Public Relations (NCMPR)
c/o Becky Olson, Exec. Dir.
PO Box 336039
Greeley, CO 80633
Ph: (970)330-0771
Fax: (970)330-0769
E-mail: bolson@ncmpr.org
URL: http://www.ncmpr.org
Contact: Becky Olson, Exec. Dir.
Founded: 1974. **Members:** 1,600. **Membership Dues:** individual associate, $175 (annual) ● college or district office, educational associate, $350 (annual) ● corporate associate, $650 (annual) ● retired, student, $75 (annual). **Staff:** 2. **Regional Groups:** 7. **Description:** Communications specialists working within community and junior colleges in areas including public, community, media, government, enrollment management and alumni relations, publications, marketing, and coordination of special events. Promotes improved relations and communication between two-year colleges and their communities; seeks to enhance the professionalism and strengthen the positions of communications specialists within two-year college systems. Fosters exchange of information; participates in needs assessments and national surveys concerning the field. **Awards:** Communicator of the Year Award. **Frequency:** annual. **Type:** recognition. **Recipient:** for excellence in public relations efforts ● D. Richard Petrizzo Award. **Frequency:** annual. **Type:** recognition. **Recipient:** for career excellence in public relations efforts ● Pacesetter of the Year Award. **Frequency:** annual. **Type:** recognition ● Paragon Award. **Frequency:** annual. **Type:** recognition. **Recipient:** for excellence in public relations efforts. **Affiliated With:** American Association of Community Colleges. **Formerly:** (1988) National Council for Community Relations. **Publications:** *COUNSEL*, quarterly. Newsletter. Covers membership activities. Includes research reports and statistics. **Price:** included in membership dues.

9033 ■ National School Public Relations Association (NSPRA)
15948 Derwood Rd.
Rockville, MD 20855-2123
Ph: (301)519-0496 (301)519-1225
Fax: (301)519-0494
E-mail: nspra@nspra.org
URL: http://www.nspra.org
Contact: Richard D. Bagin APR, Exec. Dir.
Founded: 1935. **Members:** 1,926. **Membership Dues:** professional, $225 (annual) ● associate, $135 (annual) ● student, $55 (annual) ● retiree, $65 (annual) ● organizational (level 2), $785 (annual). **Staff:** 9. **Budget:** $1,100,000. **State Groups:** 34. **Multinational. Description:** Represents school system public relations directors, school administrators, and others interested in furthering public understanding of the public schools. Has adopted standards for public relations professionals and programs and an accreditation program. **Libraries: Type:** not open to the public. **Holdings:** 1,000. **Subjects:** school communication. **Awards:** Barry Gaskins Mentor Legacy Award. **Frequency:** annual. **Type:** recognition. **Recipient:** for outstanding efforts in mentoring colleagues new to school public relations ● Bob Grossman Leadership in School Communications Award. **Frequency:** annual. **Type:** recognition. **Recipient:** for practicing superintendent of a school or CEO of an education agency ● Gold Medallion. **Frequency:** annual. **Type:** medal. **Recipient:** for excellence in educational public relations programs ● Golden Achievement. **Frequency:** annual. **Type:** recognition. **Recipient:** for exemplary public relations activities, programs and projects ● President's Award. **Frequency:** annual. **Type:** recognition. **Recipient:** for outstanding contributions to the field of public relations education ● Publications and Electronic Media. **Frequency:** annual. **Type:** recognition. **Recipient:** for outstanding education publications and electronic media programs. **Computer Services:** Mailing lists, of members ● online services, catalog. **Telecommunication Services:** electronic mail, rbagin@nspra.org. **Publications:** *Counselor*, periodic. Newsletter. Contains information on crucial emerging trends and issues. **Price:** free for members. Alternate Formats: online ● *Network*, monthly, except for July. Newsletter. **Price:** included in membership dues ● *NSPRA Opportunities*, monthly. Report. Contains new tips, tactics and resources for school-PR practitioners. **Price:** available to members only. Alternate Formats: online ● *Principal Communicator*, monthly. Newsletter. Provides communication information and ideas for use at the school building level. **Price:** included in membership dues. **Circulation:** 2,000 ● Also publishes public relations kits. **Conventions/Meetings:** annual seminar (exhibits) - always July ● workshop.

9034 ■ Public Relations Student Society of America (PRSSA)
33 Maiden Ln., 11th Fl.
New York, NY 10038-5150
Ph: (212)460-1474 (212)460-1466
Fax: (212)995-0757
E-mail: prssa@prsa.org
URL: http://www.prssa.org
Contact: Melissa M. Csuhran, Pres.
Founded: 1967. **Members:** 8,500. **Membership Dues:** associate, $60 (annual) ● regular, $225 (annual). **National Groups:** 233. **Description:** Professionally oriented student association organized to cultivate a favorable and mutually advantageous relationship between students and professional public relations practitioners. Fosters understanding of public relations theories and procedures; encourages students to adhere to high ideals and principles of public relations. **Awards:** National Gold Key Award. **Frequency:** annual. **Type:** recognition. **Recipient:** for members who demonstrate leadership qualities and academic excellence in public relations ● **Frequency:** annual. **Type:** scholarship. **Recipient:** for academic achievement, demonstrated leadership, practical experience and commitment to public relations. **Publications:** *Forum*, quarterly. Newspaper. Alternate Formats: online. **Conventions/Meetings:** annual assembly - always spring ● competition ● annual conference - always fall.

Public Schools

9035 ■ Designs for Change (DFC)
814 S Western Ave.
Chicago, IL 60612
Ph: (312)236-7252
Fax: (312)236-7927
E-mail: info@designsforchange.org
URL: http://www.designsforchange.org
Contact: Dr. Donald R. Moore, Exec. Dir.
Founded: 1977. **Staff:** 10. **Languages:** English, Spanish. **Description:** Conducts research focused on improving public schools at the local level. Assists parents, teachers, principals, students, and others attempting to initiate change in local schools by providing consultation, offering supportive training and advice, disseminating literature, and making referrals. Offers training and information in the areas of child advocacy, staff development, school finance, special education issues, reading instruction, and organizational development. Works to assist in the reform of the public school system in Chicago, IL. **Convention/Meeting:** none. **Libraries: Type:** reference. **Telecommunication Services:** TDD, (312)236-7944. **Publications:** *Building a School Community that Reads: Literacy as the Catalyst for Schoolwide Improvement*. Handbook ● *Chicago's Local School Councils: What the Research Says*. Reports ● *Helping Schools Change: Ideas for Assistance Groups* ● *Rethinking Retention to Help All Students Succeed: A Resource Guide*. Handbook ● *Standing Up for Children: Effective Child Advocacy in the Schools*. Report ● *What Makes These Schools Stand Out: Chicago Elementary Schools with a Seven-Year Trend of Improved Reading Achievement*. Report.

9036 ■ Horace Mann League of the U.S.A. (HML)
c/o Dr. Jack McKay, Exec. Dir.
61D N Chandler Ct.
Port Ludlow, WA 98365
Ph: (360)437-1186
Fax: (360)437-0641
E-mail: jmckay@hmleague.org
URL: http://www.hmleague.org
Contact: Dr. Jack McKay, Exec. Dir.
Founded: 1922. **Members:** 1,100. **Membership Dues:** $50 (annual). **Staff:** 1. **Budget:** $40,000. **Description:** Educators and others interested in perpetuation of the ideas and ideals of Horace Mann (1796-1859). Seeks to strengthen the public school system; supports the belief that public schools should be free, classless, nonsectarian, and open to all children; opposes use of public funds for private schools. **Awards:** Ambassador Award. **Frequency:** annual. **Type:** recognition ● Outstanding Educator Award. **Type:** recognition. **Recipient:** for public educator ● Outstanding Friend of Public Education Award. **Frequency:** annual. **Type:** recognition. **Recipient:** for outstanding contributions to the develop-

ment and preservation of the U.S. system of free public education. **Affiliated With:** American Association of School Administrators. **Publications:** *Strengthening Public Education*, semiannual. Newsletter. Alternate Formats: online. **Conventions/Meetings:** annual meeting, in conjunction with the American Association of School Administrators (exhibits) - 2009 Feb. 21, San Francisco, CA; 2010 Feb. 13, Phoenix, AZ.

9037 ■ National Alliance for Public Charter Schools
1101 14th St. NW, Ste.801
Washington, DC 20005
Ph: (202)289-2700
Fax: (202)289-4009
E-mail: info@publiccharters.org
URL: http://www.publiccharters.org
Contact: Andy Smarick, Chief of Staff
Founded: 2004. **Description:** Aims to increase the number of high-performing charter schools available to all families, particularly low-income and minority families who currently do not have access to quality public schools. Provides assistance to state charter school associations and resource centers. Develops and advocates for improved public policies. **Telecommunication Services:** electronic mail, andy@publiccharters.org.

9038 ■ National Association for Single Sex Public Education (NASSPE)
PO Box 108
Poolesville, MD 20837
Ph: (301)461-5065
Fax: (301)972-8006
E-mail: mail@singlesexschools.org
URL: http://www.singlesexschools.org
Contact: Dr. Leonard Sax, Chm.
Founded: 2002. **Description:** Advocates for the advancement of single-sex public education for both girls and boys. Promotes single-sex public education as a more feasible system of learning as compared to the coeducational system. Serves as a clearinghouse for relevant facts and information about public schools and classrooms in the United States.

9039 ■ National Coalition of Education Activists (NCEA)
Address Unknown since 2008
Founded: 1991. **Members:** 1,000. **Membership Dues:** organization, $100 (annual) ● individual, $40 (annual). **Staff:** 3. **Description:** Parents, community activists, and educators working to improve the quality of public schools throughout the U.S. Conducts educational programs; maintains resource bank and networking service. **Libraries: Type:** by appointment only. **Holdings:** articles, books, clippings, periodicals. **Subjects:** public school issues. **Awards: Type:** grant. **Recipient:** for local and regional activities and gatherings. **Computer Services:** database ● mailing lists. **Telecommunication Services:** phone referral service. **Publications:** *Action for Better Schools*, quarterly. Newsletter. **Price:** included in membership dues. **Circulation:** 4,500. **Advertising:** accepted. Alternate Formats: online. Also Cited As: *Action*. **Conventions/Meetings:** semiannual board meeting ● biennial conference (exhibits) - always summer.

9040 ■ Public Education Network (PEN)
601 13th St. NW, Ste.710 S
Washington, DC 20005
Ph: (202)628-7460
Fax: (202)628-1893
E-mail: pen@publiceducation.org
URL: http://www.publiceducation.org
Contact: Wendy D. Puriefoy, Pres.
Founded: 1988. **Members:** 88. **Membership Dues:** organization (based on budget), $1,000-$3,000 (annual). **Staff:** 20. **Budget:** $8,000,000. **Description:** Promotes improved public education through the development of local education funds (LEFs). Provides information and technical assistance on LEFs to interested parties. Includes services such as affinity groups, conferences and seminars, data and survey information, and materials on LEFs. **Awards:** Crossing The River Jordan. **Frequency:** annual. **Type:** recognition. **Recipient:** for individuals who have made significant contributions to the support and improvement of public education of poor and disadvantaged children ● Wendy D. Puriefoy. **Frequency:** annual. **Type:** recognition. **Recipient:** for distinguished contribution by a local education fund to create conditions of learning that benefit all children. **Publications:** *Connections*, quarterly. Newsletter. **Circulation:** 3,500 ● *Newsblast*, weekly. Article. **Circulation:** 250,000. Alternate Formats: online ● Annual Report, annual. **Conventions/Meetings:** annual conference, national experts and community leaders join in building public/private partnerships to improve teaching and learning for all children - always November ● seminar, for LEF directors - usually July.

Public Speaking

9041 ■ International Public Debate Association (IPDA)
c/o Scott Kuttenkuler, Exec. Sec.
Box 3460
Monticello, AR 71656
E-mail: kuttenkuler@uamont.edu
URL: http://www.ipdadebate.org
Contact: Scott Kuttenkuler, Exec. Sec.
Founded: 1997. **Membership Dues:** program, $35 (annual) ● individual, $20 (annual) ● student, $10 (annual). **Multinational. Description:** Helps serve the needs of students of debate, both traditional and non-traditional, native speakers and those learning English as a second language. Seeks to develop highly effective speaking and argumentation skills for business, law and the professions. Helps serve the needs of forensics educators. Provides economic and academic benefits to the forensic community. **Awards:** Daniel Webster Award. **Frequency:** annual. **Type:** recognition. **Recipient:** to an individual who accumulates the best record of achievement in the open divisions of six tournaments over the course of the forensics season ● Edmund Burke Award. **Frequency:** annual. **Type:** recognition. **Recipient:** to the varsity competitor who accumulates the best record of achievement in six tournaments over the course of the forensics season ● Isocrates Award. **Frequency:** annual. **Type:** recognition. **Recipient:** to educators who have demonstrated a consistent commitment to and excellence in promoting genuine oratorical skills in their debaters ● Mahatma Gandhi Award. **Frequency:** annual. **Type:** recognition. **Recipient:** to the program that accumulates the most varsity division points over the course of the forensics season ● Martin Luther King Award. **Frequency:** annual. **Type:** recognition. **Recipient:** to the program that accumulates the most novice points over the course of the forensics season ● President's Cup. **Frequency:** annual. **Type:** recognition. **Recipient:** to all debaters reaching outrounds ● Protagoras Cup. **Frequency:** annual. **Type:** recognition. **Recipient:** to the top programs ● Susan B. Anthony Award. **Frequency:** annual. **Type:** recognition. **Recipient:** to the novice competitor who accumulates the best record of achievement in six tournaments over the course of the forensics season ● Winston Churchill Award. **Frequency:** annual. **Type:** recognition. **Recipient:** to the program that accumulates the most sweepstakes points in the open divisions of six tournaments over the course of the forensics season. **Publications:** Newsletter.

Reading

9042 ■ College Reading and Learning Association (CRLA)
PO Box 382
El Dorado, KS 67042
Ph: (307)382-1725 (320)308-4742
Fax: (316)322-7369
E-mail: staylor@wwcc.wy.edu
URL: http://www.crla.net
Contact: Sharon Taylor, Pres.
Founded: 1967. **Members:** 1,200. **Membership Dues:** general, $50 (annual). **Staff:** 1. **Budget:** $50,000. **State Groups:** 26. **Description:** Professionals involved in college/adult reading, learning assistance, developmental education, and tutorial services. Promotes communication for the purpose of professional growth. **Awards:** Distinguished Research Award. **Frequency:** annual. **Type:** recognition. **Recipient:** for a significant research article ● Distinguished Teaching Award. **Frequency:** annual. **Type:** recognition. **Recipient:** to a member who exemplifies teaching and learning as a lifelong journey ● Robert Griffin Long and Outstanding Service Award. **Frequency:** annual. **Type:** recognition. **Recipient:** to members who contribute exemplary service and extraordinary talent over many years ● **Type:** scholarship. **Recipient:** for members pursuing graduate education, seeking research assistance or participating in intensive workshops. **Computer Services:** Mailing lists. **Telecommunication Services:** electronic mail, dbonser@buckeye-express.com. **Subgroups:** Cognitive Psychology; College Reading; Computer Technology; Developmental/Basic Writing; Distance Learning; English as a Second Language; Evaluation/Research; Learning and Study Strategies; Learning Assistance Center Management; Learning Disabilities; Mathematics Tutorial; Multicultural Issues; Paired Courses; Peer Tutoring; Teaching Excellence; Workplace Literacy. **Formerly:** Western College Reading Association; Western College Reading and Learning Association. **Publications:** *Journal of College Reading and Learning*, semiannual, every fall and spring. Contains reports of original research and articles linking theory. **Price:** included in membership dues. **Advertising:** accepted ● *Newsnotes*, January, March, August, and November. Newsletter. **Price:** included in membership dues. **Advertising:** accepted. Alternate Formats: online ● Also publishes tutor registry and glossary of terms. **Conventions/Meetings:** annual conference (exhibits) - 2008 Oct. 22-25, Cleveland, OH.

9043 ■ International Reading Association (IRA)
PO Box 8139
Newark, DE 19714-8139
Ph: (302)731-1600 (202)624-8800
Free: (800)336-7323
Fax: (302)731-1057
E-mail: pubinfo@reading.org
URL: http://www.reading.org
Contact: Alan E. Farstrup, Exec. Dir.
Founded: 1956. **Members:** 90,000. **Staff:** 120. **Budget:** $15,000,000. **Languages:** English, French, Spanish. **Multinational. Description:** Represents teachers, reading specialists, consultants, administrators, supervisors, researchers, psychologists, librarians, and parents interested in promoting literacy. Seeks to improve the quality of reading instruction and promote literacy worldwide. Disseminates information pertaining to research on reading, including information on adult literacy, early childhood and literacy development, international education, literature for children and adolescents, and teacher education and professional development. Maintains over 40 special interest groups and over 70 committees. **Libraries: Type:** reference. **Holdings:** 37,000. **Subjects:** reading, (elementary, secondary, college and adult) language arts, children's literature. **Awards:** Advocacy Award. **Frequency:** annual. **Type:** recognition. **Recipient:** for state and provincial councils who demonstrated effective advocacy at the local, state/provincial and/or national level ● Albert J. Harris Award. **Frequency:** annual. **Type:** recognition ● Arbuthnot Award. **Type:** monetary ● Award of Excellence. **Frequency:** annual. **Type:** recognition. **Recipient:** for state and provincial associations that have organized and implemented a wide range of programs and activities that serve and support councils and members, contribute to education, and support programs and goals of the association ● Broadcast Media Award for Television. **Frequency:** annual. **Type:** recognition ● Constance M. McCullough Award. **Frequency:** annual. **Type:** monetary. **Recipient:** for a member who assists in the investigation of reading-related problems and participates in professional development activities that is carried out in countries outside North America ● Developing

Country Grants. **Frequency:** annual. **Type:** grant. **Recipient:** to members of the association residing in developing countries who seek support for literacy projects in their own countries ● Dina Feitelson Research Award. **Type:** monetary. **Recipient:** for exemplary work published in English in a refereed journal that reports on an empirical study investigating aspects of literary acquisition ● Eleanor M. Johnson Award. **Type:** recognition ● Elva Knight Research Grant. **Type:** grant. **Recipient:** for research in reading and literacy that addresses significant questions for the disciplines of literacy research and practice ● Gertrude Whipple Professional Development Grant. **Type:** grant. **Recipient:** for a member who assists in the planning and creation of professional development projects, production of high-quality materials, marketing and scheduling of meetings and workshops and the logistic support for conducting them ● Helen M. Robinson Award. **Frequency:** annual. **Type:** monetary ● Honor Council Program. **Frequency:** annual. **Type:** recognition. **Recipient:** for local and special interest councils that organize and conduct well-rounded programs serving the council members, the community, the state/provincial association or affiliate, and the association ● Institute for Reading Research Fellowship. **Type:** fellowship ● IRA Children's Book Awards. **Frequency:** annual. **Type:** monetary ● IRA John Chorlton Manning Award. **Frequency:** annual. **Type:** monetary. **Recipient:** for integrating teacher preparation, professional development, and related research to improve the work of public schools, classrooms, teachers, and students ● IRA Presidential Award for Reading and Technology. **Type:** recognition. **Recipient:** for educators who have made an outstanding contribution to the field of reading education through the use of technology ● Jeanne S. Chall Research Fellowship. **Type:** fellowship. **Recipient:** for reading research by promising scholars in areas of beginning reading, readability, reading difficulty, stages of reading development, relation of vocabulary to reading, and diagnosing those with limited ability ● Local Council Community Service Award. **Type:** recognition ● Nila Banton Smith Award. **Frequency:** annual. **Type:** monetary. **Recipient:** to a middle or secondary school classroom teacher or reading teacher who has shown leadership in translating theory and current research into practice for developing content area literacy ● Nila Banton Smith Research Dissemination Support Grant. **Type:** grant. **Recipient:** to assist any association member to spend from 2 to 10 months working on a research dissemination activity ● Outstanding Dissertation of the Year Award. **Type:** recognition ● Outstanding Teacher Educator in Reading Award. **Frequency:** annual. **Type:** monetary ● Paul A. Witty Short Story Award. **Type:** monetary ● Print Media Award. **Frequency:** annual. **Type:** recognition ● Reading/Literacy Research Fellowship. **Type:** monetary. **Recipient:** for a researcher residing outside the U.S. or Canada who has experienced exceptional promise in reading research ● Regie Routman Recognition Award. **Type:** monetary. **Recipient:** for an outstanding elementary teacher in Grades K to 6 (ages 5-12) dedicated to improving teaching and learning through reflective writing about his or her teaching and learning ● Ronald W. Mitchell Convention Travel Grant. **Type:** grant. **Recipient:** for teachers of children in grades 4 and 5 (ages 10-11) that might not otherwise have the opportunity to attend an IRA annual convention ● Special Service Award. **Type:** recognition ● Steven A. Stahl Research Grant. **Frequency:** annual. **Type:** monetary. **Recipient:** to individual with at least 3 years teaching experience ● Teacher as Researcher Grant. **Type:** grant. **Recipient:** to support teachers in their inquiries about literacy and instruction ● Travel Grants for Educators. **Type:** grant. **Recipient:** to educators from any country to attend meetings (across continents) ● William S. Gray Citation of Merit. **Frequency:** annual. **Type:** recognition. **Telecommunication Services:** electronic mail, customerservice@reading.org. **Also Known As:** Asociacion Internacional de Lectura. **Formed by Merger of:** (1956) National Association for Remedial Teachers; International Council for the Improvement of Reading and Instruction. **Publications:** *Journal of Adolescent & Adult Literacy*, 8/year. Offers information on the theory and practice of teaching reading and study skills to adolescents and adults. **Price:** $61.00/year. ISSN: 1081-3004. **Circulation:** 17,000. **Advertising:** accepted. Alternate Formats: online ● *Lectura y Vida* (in English and Spanish), quarterly. Journal. Covers reading theory research and practice in Latin America. **Price:** $61.00/year. ISSN: 0325-8637. **Circulation:** 2,100. **Advertising:** accepted. Alternate Formats: microform ● *Reading Research Quarterly*. Journal. Includes original research reports and articles on theory in teaching reading and learning to read. **Price:** $61.00/year. ISSN: 0034-0553. **Circulation:** 11,000. Alternate Formats: online ● *Reading Teacher*, 8/year. Journal. Contains articles on the theory and practice of teaching reading skills to preschool and elementary school children. **Price:** $61.00/year. ISSN: 0034-0561. **Circulation:** 57,000. **Advertising:** accepted. Alternate Formats: online ● *Reading Today*, bimonthly. Provides news on reading education; includes Washington D.C. updates and news for parents. **Price:** included in membership dues. **Circulation:** 86,000. **Advertising:** accepted ● Books ● Catalog ● Monographs. **Conventions/Meetings:** biennial congress ● annual convention, focuses on issues related to reading and literacy (exhibits).

9044 ■ National Reading Conference (NRC)

7044 S 13th St.
Oak Creek, WI 53154
Ph: (414)908-4924 (908)737-3944
Fax: (414)768-8001
E-mail: customercare@nrconline.org
URL: http://www.nrconline.org
Contact: Patricia Edwards, Pres.

Founded: 1950. **Members:** 1,200. **Membership Dues:** regular, $110 (annual) ● student, $40 (annual) ● emeritus, $75 (annual) ● gold regular, $170 (annual) ● platinum regular, $210 (annual) ● silver regular, $140 (annual). **Budget:** $95,000. **Description:** Represents college and university professors interested primarily in research in literacy at the college and adult level. Aims to encourage the study of literacy problems at all educational levels, with special emphasis on college and adult literacy. Stimulates and promotes research in developmental, corrective, and remedial reading and writing. Studies the factors that influence progress in reading and writing. Assists in the development of teacher-training programs; disseminates knowledge helpful in the solution of problems related to reading. **Libraries: Type:** not open to the public. **Awards:** Albert J. Kington. **Frequency:** annual. **Type:** recognition. **Recipient:** for the distinguished service ● Ed Fry Book Award. **Frequency:** annual. **Type:** recognition. **Recipient:** for the outstanding contributions to literacy research and practice ● Oscar Causey. **Frequency:** annual. **Type:** recognition. **Recipient:** for the outstanding contributions to reading research ● Student Outstanding Research Award. **Frequency:** annual. **Type:** recognition. **Recipient:** for an exemplary Student Research Paper presented at the NRC Conference. **Computer Services:** database ● mailing lists. **Telecommunication Services:** electronic mail, slallier@niu.edu. **Publications:** *Annual Program*, annual. **Advertising:** accepted ● *Journal of Literacy Research*, quarterly ● Yearbook ● Newsletter, quarterly ● Also publishes research results. **Conventions/Meetings:** annual conference (exhibits) - always first week in December.

9045 ■ National Right to Read Foundation (NRRF)

PO Box 560
Strasburg, VA 22657
Ph: (540)465-2349
Fax: (540)465-2349
E-mail: info@nrrf.org
URL: http://www.nrrf.org
Contact: Mr. Robert Sweet Jr., Pres.

Founded: 1993. **Staff:** 1. **Nonmembership. Description:** Works to return research-based, explicit, systematic phonics instruction along with good literature to every elementary school in America.

9046 ■ Phonics Institute

PO Box 98785
Tacoma, WA 98498-0785
Ph: (253)588-3436
E-mail: read@readingstore.com
URL: http://www.readingstore.com
Contact: Marian Hinds, Pres.

Founded: 1961. **Membership Dues:** individual, $25 (annual). **Budget:** $50,000. **Description:** Operated by nine trustees with a national advisory council and committees in most states, the District of Columbia, Canada, England, Australia, and the Federal Republic of Germany. Restores the alphabet (phonetics) to its proper place as the basis of elementary reading instruction in English. Acts as a clearinghouse for its state committees; appears before local, state, and federal educational authorities; furnishes speakers for television, radio, and live programs; disseminates information on its activities through circulars, press releases, and correspondence; lists teachers in various states available for phonetic teacher-training workshops. Compiles statistics. **Libraries: Type:** reference. **Holdings:** 200. **Subjects:** contemporary phonetic literature. **Awards:** Watson Washburn Memorial Award. **Frequency:** annual. **Type:** recognition. **Telecommunication Services:** electronic mail, rrf@readingstore.com. **Formerly:** (2000) Reading Reform Foundation. **Publications:** *The Reading Informer*, quarterly ● *The Sounds of Reading*, 8/year. Newsletter. Includes calendar of events. ● *Summary of Conference*, annual ● Also publishes reports; plans to publish newsletter and monographs. **Conventions/Meetings:** annual conference.

9047 ■ Reading Is Fundamental (RIF)

1825 Connecticut Ave. NW, Ste.400
Washington, DC 20009
Ph: (202)536-3400
Free: (877)RIF-READ
Fax: (202)536-3531
E-mail: contactus@rif.org
URL: http://www.rif.org
Contact: Carol H. Rasco, Pres./CEO

Founded: 1966. **Staff:** 75. **Budget:** $29,000,000. **Local Groups:** 4,130. **Nonmembership. Description:** Volunteer groups composed of community leaders, educators, librarians, parents, and service club members who sponsor local grass roots reading motivation programs serving 4,460,000 children nationwide. Aims to involve youngsters, preschool to high school age, in reading activities aimed at showing that reading is fun. Provides services to parents to help them encourage reading in the home. Sponsors book events which emphasize each child's freedom of choice and personal ownership of selected books. Is supported by corporations, foundations, and private citizens and through a federal contract. **Convention/Meeting:** none. **Awards:** Gift of Reading Awards. **Frequency:** annual. **Type:** recognition. **Recipient:** to individuals and organizations whose significant achievements have expanded literacy and educational opportunities for at-risk children. **Computer Services:** Online services, resource about RIF and literacy. **Boards:** Directors. **Councils:** Advisory. **Publications:** *Required Reading*, 3/year. Newsletter. Contains important news about RIF and its programs. **Circulation:** 1,500. Alternate Formats: online ● Annual Report, annual.

9048 ■ Reading Recovery Council of North America (RRCNA)

400 W Wilson Bridge Rd., Ste.250
Worthington, OH 43085-5218
Ph: (614)310-7323
Free: (877)883-READ
Fax: (614)310-7345
E-mail: jjohnson@readingrecovery.org
URL: http://www.readingrecovery.org
Contact: Jady Johnson, Exec. Dir.

Founded: 1995. **Members:** 11,000. **Membership Dues:** student, retired, $40 (annual) ● electronic international, regular, $50 (annual) ● international, $70 (annual) ● supporting, $100 (annual) ● supporting international, $120 (annual) ● associate, $1,500 (annual). **Multinational. Description:** Serves as an advocate for Reading Recovery throughout North America. Works to ensure access to Reading Recovery for every child who needs its support. Provides a network of opportunities for leadership and professional development. Aims to sustain the integrity of Reading Recovery and expand its implementation by increasing the number of individuals who understand, support and collaborate. **Awards:** Geri Stone Memorial Scholarships. **Frequency:** annual. **Type:** scholarship. **Recipient:** for Reading Recovery trainers ● Sue Hundley Memorial Scholarships. **Frequency:** annual. **Type:** scholarship. **Recipient:** for Reading Recovery teacher and teacher leader. **Publications:** *The Journal of Reading Recovery*, semiannual. **Price:** included in membership dues. **Advertising:** accepted. Alternate Formats: online. Also Cited As: *JRR* ● *Literacy Teaching and Learning: An International Journal of Early Reading and Writing*, semiannual. Contains issues related to language acquisition, literacy development, and instructional theory and practice. **Price:** included in membership dues. Alternate Formats: online.

Real Estate

9049 ■ American Real Estate Society (ARES)
c/o Diane Quarles, Membership Services Mgr.
Clemson Univ.
Box 341323
Clemson, SC 29634
Ph: (864)656-1373
Fax: (864)656-3748
E-mail: equarle@clemson.edu
URL: http://www.aresnet.org
Contact: Mr. Marc Louargand PhD, Pres.
Founded: 1985. **Members:** 1,000. **Membership Dues:** academic, $115 (annual) ● professional, $250 (annual) ● student, retired academic, $77 (annual) ● corporate, $500 (annual) ● sponsor, $1,500 (annual) ● regent, $3,000 (annual) ● President's Council, $6,000 (annual) ● academic library, $400 (annual) ● professional library, $450 (annual). **Staff:** 4. **Budget:** $200,000. **Description:** College and university professors; high-level practicing professionals involved in real estate finance, investment, development, valuation, marketing, consulting, management, education, and law; and institutions. Acts as a forum for the exchange of information and research on applied business and individual decision-making within real estate finance, real estate market analysis, investment, valuation, development, and other areas related to real estate in the private sector. Operates ARES Case Clearinghouse, which makes available copies of instructional cases pertinent to real estate practice. Conducts educational programs for real estate professionals. **Awards:** James A. Graaskamp Award. **Frequency:** annual. **Type:** recognition. **Recipient:** for unconventional leadership ● **Frequency:** annual. **Type:** monetary. **Telecommunication Services:** electronic mail, helen_murphy@und.nodak.edu. **Committees:** Doctoral Seminar; Education; Electronic ARES; Fund Raising; Industry Liaison; Institutional Marketing; Membership; Public Relations; Special Projects; Strategic Planning. **Publications:** *ARES Newsletter*, semiannual. **Advertising:** accepted. Alternate Formats: online ● *Journal of Real Estate Literature*, semiannual. **Advertising:** accepted ● *Journal of Real Estate Portfolio Management*, quarterly. **Advertising:** accepted ● *The Journal of Real Estate Research*, bimonthly. **Advertising:** accepted ● *Journal Real Estate Practice and Education*, annual. **Advertising:** accepted ● *Program of Annual Meeting*, annual ● *Real Estate Markets Report*, quarterly. Reprint ● *Real Estate Research Issues*, annual. Book ● *Real Estate Research Studies*, annual. Monographs. **Conventions/Meetings:** annual meeting and seminar, with research presentations and panel discussions (exhibits).

9050 ■ American Real Estate and Urban Economics Association (AREUEA)
PO Box 9958
Richmond, VA 23228
Free: (866)273-8321
Fax: (877)273-8323
E-mail: areuea@areuea.org
URL: http://www.areuea.org
Contact: Michael LaCour-Little, Exec. VP
Founded: 1965. **Members:** 1,260. **Membership Dues:** professional, academic, $100 (annual) ● student, $50 (annual) ● contributing, $500 (annual) ● special contributor, $501-$2,999 (annual) ● contributing sponsor, $3,000-$9,999 (annual) ● partner, $10,000 (annual). **Description:** University faculty, individuals in real estate and related areas, and firms and organizations active in real estate and research. Promotes education and encourages research in real estate, urban land economics, and allied fields; improves communication in real estate and allied matters among college and university faculty who are teaching or conducting research in fields of interest to the association; facilitates the mutual association of academic and research persons in real estate, urban land economics, and allied fields. **Awards:** American Association of Individual Investors/AREUEA Research Prize. **Frequency:** annual. **Type:** monetary. **Recipient:** for best paper in the real estate investment area ● Dissertation Award. **Frequency:** annual. **Type:** monetary. **Recipient:** for best dissertation in the fields of real estate and urban land use ● George Bloom Award. **Frequency:** annual. **Type:** recognition. **Recipient:** for distinguished service ● National Association of Realtors Research Award. **Frequency:** biennial. **Type:** monetary. **Recipient:** for best paper in the field of international real estate. **Publications:** *News Bytes*. Newsletter. Alternate Formats: online ● *Real Estate Economics*, quarterly. Journal. Contains research and scholarly studies of current and emerging real estate issues. **Advertising:** accepted ● Membership Directory, annual. Contains alphabetical and geographical lists of members' addresses, phones, and professional information. **Price:** free for members ● Newsletter, semiannual. Provides news of meetings, past meeting highlights, member activities, and industry news. **Advertising:** accepted. **Conventions/Meetings:** annual international conference - 2008 July 4-8, Istanbul, Turkey ● annual meeting, hosted by the National Association of Home Builders - always May.

Religion

9051 ■ URANTIA Association of the United States (UAUS)
c/o URANTIA Foundation
533 Diversey Pkwy.
Chicago, IL 60614
Ph: (773)525-3319
E-mail: rutabl@aol.com
URL: http://www.urantiausa.com
Contact: Benet Rutenberg, Pres.
Description: Represents and acts as a unifying body bringing together local URANTIA associations on an international level. **Publications:** *UAUS Messenger*. Newsletter. Alternate Formats: online. **Conventions/Meetings:** conference ● international conference.

Religious Studies

9052 ■ National Council On Bible Curriculum In Public Schools (NCBCPS)
PO Box 9743
Greensboro, NC 27429
Ph: (336)272-3799
Free: (877)662-4523
URL: http://www.bibleinschools.net
Contact: Elizabeth Ridenour, Pres.
Description: Serves the public through educational efforts concerning a First Amendment right and religious freedom issue. Aims to bring a state certified Bible course (elective) into the public high schools nationwide. **Computer Services:** Mailing lists. **Publications:** *The Bible in History and Literature*. Book. **Price:** $150.00/copy ● Newsletter. Alternate Formats: online.

Research

9053 ■ American Educational Research Association (AERA)
1430 K St. NW, Ste.1200
Washington, DC 20005
Ph: (202)238-3200
Fax: (202)238-3250
E-mail: webmaster@aera.net
URL: http://www.aera.net
Contact: Felice J. Levine PhD, Exec. Dir.
Founded: 1916. **Members:** 25,000. **Membership Dues:** student, $35 (annual) ● regular (voting), affiliate (non-voting), $120 (annual) ● international affiliate, $100 (annual) ● regular (voting), affiliate (non-voting), $230 (biennial) ● graduate student (voting), student affiliate (non-voting), $35 (annual). **Staff:** 28. **Description:** Represents education researchers and behavioral scientists interested in the development, application, and improvement of education research, from pre-kindergarten to post-secondary education and beyond. Includes members such as: professors, state and local school system research directors, research specialists at think tanks, administrators at federal, state and local education agencies, graduate students of education, and educators in foreign countries. Holds an annual convention that more than half of its members attend. Offers a robust scholarly publishing program, including peer-reviewed journals and books. Offers fellowships and other programs for its members. **Awards:** Distinguished Contributions to Education Research. **Frequency:** annual. **Type:** recognition. **Recipient:** to a meritorious contributor to educational research ● Distinguished Public Service Award. **Frequency:** annual. **Type:** recognition. **Recipient:** to an individual who has worked to enact or implement policies that are well-grounded in education research. **Telecommunication Services:** electronic mail, members@aera.net. **Divisions:** Administration; Counseling and Human Development; Curriculum Studies; Education in the Professions; Educational Policy and Politics; History and Historiography; Learning and Instruction; Measurement and Research Methodology; Postsecondary Education; School Evaluation and Program Development; Social Context of Education; Teaching and Teacher Education. **Formerly:** (1930) National Directors of Educational Research. **Publications:** *American Educational Research Journal*, quarterly. Contains empirical and theoretical studies and analyses in education. **Price:** $48.00 /year for individuals; $140.00 /year for institutions. **Advertising:** accepted ● *Annual Meeting Program Book*, annual. Includes lists of all annual meeting sessions and presentations. **Price:** $15.00/copy ● *Educational Evaluation and Policy Analysis*, quarterly. Book. **Price:** $48.00 /year for individuals; $140.00 /year for institutions ● *Educational Researcher*, 9/year. Journal. **Price:** $48.00 /year for individuals; $150.00 /year for institutions. **Advertising:** accepted ● *Encyclopedia of Educational Research*. Book ● *Handbook of Research on Teaching*, every 10 years. Contains current and sometimes competing schools of thought and presents exciting possibilities for educational research and writing. **Price:** $85.00 for members; $100.00 for nonmembers; $120.00 for institutions ● *Handbook on Curriculum* ● *Journal of Educational and Behavioral Statistics*, quarterly. **Price:** $60.00 /year for individuals; $75.00 /year for institutions. Alternate Formats: online ● *Review of Educational Research*, quarterly. Journal. **Price:** $48.00 /year for individuals; $140.00 /year for institutions. Alternate Formats: online ● *Review of Research in Education*, annual. Journal. **Price:** $48.00 /year for individuals; $67.00 /year for institutions. Alternate Formats: online. **Conventions/Meetings:** annual convention and meeting, with scholarly research presentations in various formats, professional development sessions and exhibitions (exhibits) - always March or April. 2009 Apr. 13-17, San Diego, CA.

9054 ■ Association of University Research Parks (AURP)
6262 Swan Rd., Ste.170
Tucson, AZ 85718
Ph: (520)529-2521
Fax: (520)529-2499
E-mail: info@aurp.net
URL: http://www.aurp.net
Contact: J. Michael Bowman, Pres.
Founded: 1986. **Members:** 300. **Membership Dues:** regular, associate, $750 (annual) ● sustaining, $2,000 (annual). **Staff:** 4. **Budget:** $700,000. **De-**

scription: Representatives of research parks, interested companies, and universities, including park staff members, board members, private company managers, and university officials. (Research parks are property-based ventures in which land is set aside specifically for the building of research and development facilities. These parks are operated by or in association with a university or other institutions of higher education.) Provides information to members regarding the planning, construction, management, and marketing of university-related research parks. Monitors legislative and regulatory measures affecting the development and operation of research parks. Compiles statistics. **Libraries: Type:** reference. **Holdings:** 1,000; archival material. **Awards: Frequency:** annual. **Type:** recognition. **Computer Services:** database, list of members and research parks. **Formerly:** (1986) International Association of University Research Parks; (2002) Association of University Related Research Parks. **Publications:** *AURP Membership Directory*, annual ● *Research Park Forum*, monthly. Newsletter. **Price:** free for members. Alternate Formats: online ● *Worldwide Research and Science Park Directory*, annual. Contains contact and statistical information on worldwide research parks. **Conventions/Meetings:** annual conference (exhibits) - 2008 Dec. 10-12, St. Petersburg, FL ● seminar ● workshop.

9055 ■ College-University Resource Institute (CURI)
Address Unknown since 2008
URL: http://www.curi-inc.org
Founded: 1982. **Description:** Aims to achieve recognition for privately funded university projects that are left unnoticed and are not disseminated. Goals are to pool resources so researchers will be recognized for their work; draw information from as many institutions as possible; facilitate the transfer of technological information among higher learning institutions. **Publications:** *Washington Metropolitan Foundation Directory*, periodic. **Conventions/Meetings:** annual meeting and workshop.

9056 ■ Computer Ethics Institute (CEI)
c/o The Brookings Institution
1775 Massachusetts Ave. NW
Washington, DC 20036
Ph: (202)797-6183
Fax: (202)797-6264
E-mail: itsinfo@brookings.edu
URL: http://www.brook.edu/its/cei/cei_hp.htm
Contact: Cynthia Darling, Sec.
Founded: 1985. **Description:** Includes members of the IT professions, the academic, corporate and public policy communities. Works to provide an advanced forum and resource for identifying, assessing and responding to ethical issues associated with the advancement of information technologies in society. **Publications:** Papers. Alternate Formats: online.

9057 ■ Consortium on Financing Higher Education (COFHE)
238 Main St., Ste.402
Cambridge, MA 02142
Ph: (617)253-5030
Fax: (617)258-8280
E-mail: cofhe@jhu.edu
URL: http://www.cofhe.org
Contact: Dr. Kristine E. Dillon, Pres.
Founded: 1974. **Members:** 31. **Staff:** 6. **Description:** Represents private colleges and universities; membership limited. Conducts comparative research and analysis on issues related to high achieving students, admissions, financial aid, financing of graduate and undergraduate education, and cost and other management studies for members only.

9058 ■ Council on Governmental Relations (COGR)
1200 New York Ave. NW, Ste.750
Washington, DC 20005
Ph: (202)289-6655
Fax: (202)289-6698
URL: http://www.cogr.edu
Contact: Jane Youngers, Chair
Founded: 1948. **Members:** 146. **Staff:** 5. **Description:** Research and academic administrators and business officers of leading research universities concerned with the expanding influence of governmental regulations, policies, and practices on the performance of research by educational institutions. Provides advice and information and makes recommendations to executive government agencies with regard to policies, regulations, and practices that affect university research. **Committees:** Costing Policies; Federal Management Developments; Grant and Contract Policies. **Affiliated With:** National Association of College and University Business Officers. **Conventions/Meetings:** meeting - 5/year.

9059 ■ Council on Undergraduate Research (CUR)
734 15th St. NW, Ste.550
Washington, DC 20005-1013
Ph: (202)783-4810 (309)677-3020
Fax: (202)783-4811
E-mail: cur@cur.org
URL: http://www.cur.org
Contact: Dr. Nancy Henzel, Natl. Exec. Off.
Founded: 1978. **Members:** 4,000. **Membership Dues:** active, $72 (annual) ● post doc, $52 (annual) ● retired, student, $36 (annual). **Staff:** 5. **Budget:** $800,000. **Description:** Promotes high quality undergraduate student-faculty collaborative research and scholarship, including biology, chemistry, geosciences, mathematics and computer science, physics and astronomy, psychology, social sciences, and a division that serves administrators and other disciplines. **Libraries: Type:** reference. **Holdings:** articles, books, periodicals. **Subjects:** undergraduate research. **Awards:** Summer Fellowships. **Frequency:** annual. **Type:** monetary. **Recipient:** for summer student research. **Telecommunication Services:** electronic mail, nancy@cur.org. **Councils:** At-Large; Biology; Chemistry; Geology; Mathematics-Computer Science; Physics-Astronomy; Psychology; Social Sciences. **Publications:** *CUR Quarterly*, September, December, March, June. Journal. Contains articles on scientific research and information on funding sources. **Price:** included in membership dues; $40.00 for nonmembers; $85.00 for libraries. ISSN: 1072-5830. **Circulation:** 3,500. **Advertising:** accepted ● *How to Develop and Administer Institutional Undergraduate Research Programs.* Manual ● *How to Get a Tenure-Track Position at a Predominantly Undergraduate Institution.* Booklet ● *How to Get Started in Research.* Booklet ● *How to Mentor Undergraduates.* Book. **Price:** $12.00 plus shipping and handling ● *Undergraduate Electronic Research Directory.* Alternate Formats: online. **Conventions/Meetings:** semiannual Crossing Boundaries - conference (exhibits) - even-numbered years ● annual CUR Institute - Institutionalizing Undergraduate Research - meeting - always October ● annual CUR Institute - Proposal Writing - meeting - always July ● biennial CUR Institute - The Vital Faculty: Issues After Tenure - meeting - even-numbered years ● annual Undergraduate Research Posters on Capitol Hill - meeting, poster session - always March/April.

9060 ■ International Association of Word and Image Studies (IAWIS)
c/o Dr. Michele Hannoosh, Sec.
Univ. of Michigan
Dept. of Romance Languages and Literature
Modern Languages Bldg.
Ann Arbor, MI 48109
Ph: (734)764-5344
Fax: (734)764-8163
E-mail: hannoosh@umich.edu
URL: http://www.iawis.org
Contact: Dr. Michele Hannoosh, Sec.
Founded: 1987. **Membership Dues:** EUR 80 (triennial) ● EUR 120 (periodic). **Languages:** English, French. **Nonmembership. Multinational. Description:** Members are from the international community. Aims to be an international forum for different disciplines and approaches, where professionals can meet and exchange ideas about the way visual and verbal work and interact. **Publications:** *Interactions* (in English and French), semiannual. Bulletin. Alternate Formats: online ● Proceedings. Contains information from conferences. **Conventions/Meetings:** triennial conference ● triennial international conference - 2008 July 7-11, Paris, France.

9061 ■ Knowledge Alliance
850 Connecticut Ave. NW, Ste.220
Washington, DC 20006
Ph: (202)518-0847
Fax: (202)785-3849
E-mail: kohlmoos@nekia.org
URL: http://www.nekia.org
Contact: Jim Kohlmoos, Pres./CEO
Founded: 1971. **Members:** 24. **Staff:** 3. **Description:** Educational research and development institutions. Aims to advance the development and use of knowledge-based solutions to improve schools and help all students achieve. Believes that equity and excellence should be the foundation for improving teaching and learning, which must also be fully supported by the effective use of knowledge. Commits to rigorous standards of quality and creates new and better approaches to knowledge use to support education programs and policies at the federal, regional, state, tribal, and local levels. **Telecommunication Services:** electronic mail, bannan@nekia.org. **Divisions:** Business Managers; Communicators. **Formerly:** (1998) Council for Educational Development and Research; (2007) National Education Knowledge Industry Association. **Conventions/Meetings:** annual meeting.

9062 ■ National Conferences on Undergraduate Research (NCUR)
c/o Janet Stocks, Chair
Center for Academic and Professional Success
Baldwin-Wallace Coll.
275 Eastland Rd.
201 Bonds
Berea, OH 44017-2088
Ph: (440)826-2379
Fax: (440)826-3577
E-mail: jstocks@bw.edu
URL: http://www.ncur.org
Contact: Janet Stocks, Chair
Founded: 1987. **Description:** Provides a forum for undergraduate students to present the results of research, scholarly activities conducted during the academic year in conjunction with faculty members at their institutions. **Awards:** NCUR. **Type:** grant. **Recipient:** for summer undergraduate research programs that require interdisciplinary interaction among the participants. **Publications:** Proceedings, annual. Contains results of some of the undergraduate research and presentations made at the prior conference. **Price:** $60.00/volume; $135.00/set. Alternate Formats: CD-ROM. **Conventions/Meetings:** annual conference, student postings and artistic exhibits (exhibits) - always March or April.

9063 ■ National Council of University Research Administrators (NCURA)
1225 19th St. NW, Ste.850
Washington, DC 20036
Ph: (202)466-3894
Fax: (202)223-5573
E-mail: info@ncura.edu
URL: http://www.ncura.edu
Contact: Kathleen M. Larmett, Exec. Dir.
Founded: 1959. **Members:** 4,000. **Membership Dues:** individual, $155 (annual). **Staff:** 11. **Budget:** $2,500,000. **Regional Groups:** 7. **Description:** Individuals engaged in the administration of sponsored programs in colleges, universities, teaching hospitals, organizations wholly organized and administered by colleges and universities, or a consortium of colleges and universities. Promotes development of more effective policies and procedures in the administration of sponsored programs to achieve maximum educational potential in academic research. Fosters development of college and university research and sponsored program administration as a professional field. Conducts workshops and placement services.

Computer Services: Mailing lists. **Telecommunication Services:** electronic mail, larmett@ncura.edu. **Committees:** Financial Management; Nominating and Leadership Development; Professional Development. **Publications:** *Cost Accounting Standards*. Handbook. **Price:** $7.00 for members; $8.25 for nonmembers ● *Facilities & Administrative Costs in Higher Education*. Handbook. **Price:** $8.25 for members; $9.75 for nonmembers ● *Research Management Review*, semiannual. Journal. **Price:** included in membership dues ● *The Role of Research Administration*. Handbook. **Price:** $8.75 for members; $10.25 for nonmembers ● Directory. Contains listing of all current members. **Price:** included in membership dues. Alternate Formats: online ● Newsletter, 5/year. **Price:** included in membership dues. **Conventions/Meetings:** annual conference ● annual meeting (exhibits) - always in Washington, DC. 2008 Nov. 2-5, Washington, DC ● monthly seminar.

9064 ■ National Postdoctoral Association (NPA)
1200 New York Ave. NW, Ste.635
Washington, DC 20005
Ph: (202)326-6424
Fax: (202)371-9849
E-mail: info@nationalpostdoc.org
URL: http://www.nationalpostdoc.org
Contact: Alyson Reed, Exec. Dir.
Founded: 2003. **Membership Dues:** postdoctoral/graduate student, $35 (annual) ● non-postdoctoral, $75 (annual) ● postdoctoral association, $500 (annual) ● postdoctoral office/institutional, $500-$1,000 (annual) ● professional society/organization, $250 (annual) ● corporate partner, $2,000 (annual). **Description:** Fosters necessary improvements to the postdoctoral situation in the United States. Advances the U.S. research enterprise by maximizing the effectiveness of the research community and enhancing the quality of the postdoctoral experience for all participants. Seeks to work with all stakeholders to improve the postdoctoral experience in the United States. **Committees:** Diversity; International Postdoctoral; Outreach; Oversight; Policy. **Publications:** *The POSTDOCket*. Newsletter ● Proceedings. **Conventions/Meetings:** annual meeting.

Retirement

9065 ■ National Retired Teachers Association, Division of AARP (NRTA)
c/o American Association of Retired Persons
601 E St. NW
Washington, DC 20049
Ph: (202)434-2560
Free: (888)687-2277
E-mail: member@aarp.org
URL: http://www.aarp.org/about_aarp/nrta
Contact: William D. Novelli, CEO
Founded: 1947. **Members:** 600,000. **Membership Dues:** regular, in U.S., $12 (annual) ● regular, in Canada and Mexico, $17 (annual) ● regular, outside U.S., Canada and Mexico, $28 (annual). **Staff:** 1,200. **State Groups:** 51. **Local Groups:** 2,600. **Description:** Represents active and retired teachers and educators age 50 and older. Became a division of the American Association of Retired Persons (see separate entry) in 1982. **Publications:** *NRTA Edition of Modern Maturity*, bimonthly. **Conventions/Meetings:** biennial meeting.

9066 ■ TIAA-CREF
PO Box 1259
Charlotte, NC 28201
Free: (800)842-2252
Fax: (800)842-5916
E-mail: trustees@tiaa-cref.org
URL: http://www.tiaa-cref.org
Contact: Herbert M. Allison Jr., Chm./CEO
Founded: 1952. **Members:** 1,235,200. **Description:** Provides a nationwide portable pension system for over 2 million employees of some 8,000 colleges, universities, independent schools, and related nonprofit educational and research institutions. **Formerly:** (1998) College Retirement Equities Fund.

Rural Development

9067 ■ Rural School and Community Trust (Rural Trust)
1530 Wilson Blvd., Ste.240
Arlington, VA 22209
Ph: (703)243-1487
Fax: (703)243-6035
E-mail: info@ruraledu.org
URL: http://www.ruraledu.org
Contact: Rachel B. Tompkins, Pres.
Staff: 27. **Description:** Works with a network of schools and community groups striving to improve quality of education and community life and to improve state education. **Publications:** *Rural Policy Matters*, monthly. Newsletter. Provides news for citizens and community groups working on state-level policy issues affecting rural schools. ● *Rural Roots*, monthly. Newsletter. Provides news and information on place-based education for teachers, students, and community members. Alternate Formats: online ● *Why Rural Matters*, biennial. Report. Offers a snapshot of the condition of rural education in each of the 50 states. **Price:** $25.00 print. Alternate Formats: online.

Rural Education

9068 ■ National Rural Education Advocacy Coalition (NREAC)
22 S 22nd St.
Harrisburg, PA 17104
Ph: (717)236-7180
Fax: (717)236-5840
E-mail: info@nreac.org
URL: http://www.nreac.org
Contact: Joseph Bard, Contact
Membership Dues: organization, $2,500-$5,000 (annual). **Description:** Represents organizations concerned about educational opportunities for children who live in the rural areas of the United States. Advocates for the highest quality education for the children of rural America's public schools. Represents the interests of rural public schools in the national forums. Strives to expand the programs and services available to rural public schools. Maintains rural schools as centers for learning and community life for rural America. **Telecommunication Services:** electronic mail, jfbard@comcast.net.

9069 ■ National Rural Education Association (NREA)
c/o Dr. Bob Mooneyham, Exec. Dir.
Univ. of Oklahoma
112 4th St., Box 2
Norman, OK 73019
Ph: (405)325-7959 (785)532-5886
Fax: (405)325-7959
E-mail: bmooneyham@ou.edu
URL: http://www.nrea.net
Contact: Dr. Bob Mooneyham, Exec. Dir.
Founded: 1907. **Members:** 1,200. **Membership Dues:** individual, $100 (annual) ● institution (per member), $75 (annual) ● library, $50 (annual) ● teacher, $75 (annual) ● retired educator, $50 (annual) ● student (non-voting), $15 (annual). **Staff:** 6. **Budget:** $100,000. **State Groups:** 20. **Description:** Rural educators; state, county, district, and local school administrators; teachers, board members, college faculty, representatives of state departments of education; education associations; lay leaders, federal administrators, parents, and others interested in rural and small schools. Seeks to: promote state and regional delivery systems; serve as an advocate and representative for rural education; stimulate discussion, research, and policy developments regarding equal education opportunities for all school children and those living in rural areas; provide coordination for rural education programs and brokering assistance of appropriate agencies and individuals to meet the needs of rural and small schools; encourage colleges and universities to develop materials and resources specifically for rural schools and train personnel to work more effectively in these schools; disseminate information relating to rural education as well as sharing services and resources among educational organizations and agencies; provide leadership for rural education related conferences and workshops. Acts as a forum for all those involved in rural education and stresses the need for public and private agencies to develop educational materials and technology appropriate for children in rural schools. Compiles statistics. **Libraries: Type:** reference. **Awards:** Elementary, Middle/Junior High, High School Essay Awards. **Frequency:** annual. **Type:** monetary ● NREA Hero Award. **Frequency:** annual. **Type:** recognition. **Recipient:** to members of the U.S. House of Representatives and U.S. Senate with exemplified leadership and advocacy to rural education ● NREA/Howard A. Dawson Award. **Frequency:** annual. **Type:** recognition. **Recipient:** for service agencies ● Outstanding Rural Program. **Frequency:** annual. **Type:** recognition. **Recipient:** for the best rural program ● Rural Dissertation Award. **Frequency:** annual. **Type:** recognition. **Recipient:** for doctoral research with significant contribution to rural education and addresses issues of current concern ● Rural Educator of the Year. **Frequency:** annual. **Type:** recognition. **Recipient:** for rural teachers. **Telecommunication Services:** electronic mail, gtgoudar@ou.edu. **Committees:** Awards; Bylaws; Communications; Higher Education; Legislative; Marketing; Nominations/Elections; Research; Site Selection; Teachers; Ways and Means. **Formerly:** (1919) Department of Rural and Agricultural Education; (1970) Department of Rural Education; (1975) Rural Education Association; (1980) Rural/Regional Educational Association; (1986) Rural Education Association. **Publications:** *Directory of Rural Education Programs and Centers*, periodic ● *Rural Education News*, quarterly. Newsletter. Alternate Formats: online ● *The Rural Educator*, 3/year. Journal. **Price:** included in membership dues. Alternate Formats: online. **Conventions/Meetings:** annual convention (exhibits).

Scandinavian

9070 ■ Society for the Advancement of Scandinavian Study (SASS)
Brigham Young Univ.
Box 26118
Provo, UT 84602-6118
Ph: (801)422-5598
E-mail: sass@byu.edu
URL: http://www.scandinavianstudy.org
Contact: Christian D. Nokkentved, Ed.
Founded: 1911. **Members:** 800. **Membership Dues:** regular (in U.S. and Canada), $55 (annual) ● regular (other countries), $70 (annual) ● student, retired, $30-$45 (annual) ● patron, $70-$85 (annual) ● life, $750-$900. **Staff:** 5. **Description:** Scholars, teachers, students, and laymen interested in fostering teaching and research in the Scandinavian languages, literature, culture, and society. Works to promote Scandinavian study and instruction in America; to encourage original research in Scandinavian languages, literature, history, government, and society and to provide for publication of the results of such research; to foster closer relations among persons interested in Scandinavian studies. **Computer Services:** Mailing lists. **Telecommunication Services:** electronic mail, drnok@imsa.edu. **Publications:** *News and Notes*, periodic ● *Scandinavian Studies*, quarterly. **Price:** included in membership dues; $50.00 for nonmembers. ISSN: 0036-5637. **Circulation:** 1,200. **Advertising:** accepted. **Conventions/Meetings:** meeting (exhibits) - always first weekend in May.

Scholarship

9071 ■ Association of African Women Scholars (AAWS)
c/o Dr. Obioma Nnaemeka, Pres.
French and Women's Stud.
Cavanaugh Hall, Rm. 001C
Indiana Univ.
425 Univ. Blvd.
Indianapolis, IN 46202
Ph: (317)278-2038 (317)274-0062
Fax: (317)274-2347
E-mail: aaws@iupui.edu
URL: http://www.iupui.edu/~aaws
Contact: Dr. Obioma Nnaemeka, Pres.
Founded: 1995. **Members:** 327. **Membership Dues:** regular (based on income), $15-$40 (annual) ● associate (based on income), $10-$35 (annual) ● student (outside Africa), $10 (annual) ● resident in Africa, $10 (annual) ● student (in Africa), $5 (annual) ● institutional (outside Africa), $100 (annual) ● institutional (in Africa), $50 (annual) ● life, $1,000 ● associate (life), $900. **Languages:** English, French. **Description:** Individuals. Promotes scholarship among women of African descent worldwide. Seeks to form intellectual links among scholars studying Africa, colonialism, and related topics. Serves as a clearinghouse on African history, culture, economics, and development, particularly as these subjects impact women. Provides information and advice to policy makers; participates in advocacy work. Conducts research and educational programs. **Projects:** African Women Bibliographies; Against Widowhood Practices in Africa. **Publications:** *AAWS Newsletter*, semiannual. **Circulation:** 800. **Advertising:** accepted. **Conventions/Meetings:** semiannual conference.

9072 ■ Association of Marshall Scholars (AMS)
3100 Massachusetts Ave. NW
Washington, DC 20008-3600
Ph: (202)588-7844
Fax: (415)617-1340
E-mail: alumni@marshallscholarship.org
URL: http://www.marshallscholarship.org
Contact: Ted Leinbaugh, Acting Pres.
Founded: 1959. **Members:** 1,300. **Membership Dues:** regular, $25 (annual). **Description:** Provides scholarships named for General George C. Marshall (1880-1959), U.S. Secretary of State and author of the Marshall Plan; the scholarships are offered in gratitude by the United Kingdom for such aid. Selection of scholars is through the British Embassy and the British Consulates General in Atlanta, GA; Boston, MA; Chicago, IL; Los Angeles, CA; New York, NY and San Francisco, CA. **Awards:** Marshall Scholarships. **Frequency:** annual. **Type:** scholarship. **Recipient:** to American graduates for degree study at UK universities. **Telecommunication Services:** electronic mail, apps@marshallscholarship.org. **Formerly:** (1986) Association of Marshall Scholars and Alumnae/i.

9073 ■ International Society for the Scholarship of Teaching and Learning (ISSOTL)
c/o Barbara Cambridge, Pres.
Natl. Coun. of Teachers of English
1410 King St.
Alexandria, VA 22314
Ph: (202)316-6828
E-mail: bcambridge@ncte.org
URL: http://www.issotl.org
Contact: Barbara Cambridge, Pres.
Founded: 2004. **Membership Dues:** administrator, faculty/staff, $40 (annual) ● retired faculty/staff, part-time faculty/staff, $30 (annual) ● student, $25 (annual). **Multinational. Description:** Fosters inquiry and disseminates findings about what improves and articulates post-secondary learning and teaching. Recognizes and encourages scholarly work on teaching and learning in each discipline. Facilitates the collaboration of scholars in different countries. Encourages the integration of discovery, learning and public engagement. Advocates for support, review, recognition, and appropriate uses of the scholarship of teaching and learning. **Publications:** *The International Commons*, 3/year. Newsletter. **Price:** included in membership dues. Alternate Formats: online.

9074 ■ National Scholarship Providers Association (NSPA)
101 Monroe St.
Denver, CO 80206
Ph: (720)941-4498
Fax: (720)941-4492
E-mail: aweinstein@scholarshipproviders.org
URL: http://www.scholarshipproviders.org
Contact: Amy Weinstein, Exec. Dir.
Founded: 1999. **Membership Dues:** scholarship provider, $150-$500 (annual) ● institutional, $250 (annual) ● affiliate, $1,000 (annual). **Multinational. Description:** Advances the collective impact of scholarships. Provides opportunities for professional development and the exchange of best practices among scholarship providers. Facilitates collaboration and communication among scholarship providers.

9075 ■ National Society of Collegiate Scholars (NSCS)
1900 K St. NW, Ste.890
Washington, DC 20006
Ph: (202)265-9000
Free: (800)989-6727
Fax: (202)265-9200
E-mail: loflin@nscs.org
URL: http://www.nscs.org
Contact: Stephen E. Loflin, Exec. Dir.
Founded: 1994. **Membership Dues:** life, $75. **Regional Groups:** 218. **Description:** Nation's only honors organization recognizing outstanding academic achievement among first- and second-year college students. Offers a wide variety of opportunities for involvement on the campus, community, and national levels and encourages members to become involved in community service and leadership activities throughout their college years and beyond. Membership is by invitation only, based on grade point average and class standing. Has more than 450,000 lifetime members at 218 chapters in all 50 states, the District of Columbia and Puerto Rico. Member of the Association of College Honor Societies. **Awards:** Exemplary Scholar. **Frequency:** annual. **Type:** recognition. **Recipient:** to members for their high academic achievement, as well as a demonstrated passion for community service and extra-curricular involvement ● Merit Award. **Frequency:** annual. **Type:** monetary. **Recipient:** for members who exemplify the three pillars of the society ● Scholar Abroad. **Frequency:** annual. **Type:** scholarship. **Recipient:** for students studying abroad ● Scholar at Sea. **Frequency:** annual. **Type:** scholarship. **Recipient:** to students attending the semester at Sea program. **Publications:** *The Collegiate Scholar*, quarterly. Journal. Contains poetry, prose, and photos from members across the country. Alternate Formats: online ● Annual Report, annual. Highlights activities and summarizes finances. Alternate Formats: online. **Conventions/Meetings:** annual convention, for academic and professional development opportunities with employers/partner (exhibits).

9076 ■ National Society of High School Scholars (NSHSS)
1936 N Druid Hills Rd.
Atlanta, GA 30319
Free: (866)343-1800
Fax: (866)282-4634
E-mail: information@nshss.org
URL: http://www.nshss.org
Contact: Mr. Claes Nobel, Chm.
Membership Dues: regular, $45. **Description:** Seeks to recognize academic excellence and to encourage members to apply talents, vision, and potential for the betterment of themselves and the world. **Awards:** Academic Paper Awards. **Frequency:** annual. **Type:** scholarship ● Claes Nobel Academic Scholarships. **Frequency:** annual. **Type:** scholarship ● National Scholar Awards. **Frequency:** annual. **Type:** scholarship ● Partner Scholarships. **Frequency:** annual. **Type:** scholarship. **Recipient:** for members ● Robert P. Sheppard Leadership Award. **Frequency:** annual. **Type:** scholarship. **Recipient:** for a member who has demonstrated outstanding commitment to community service and initiative in volunteer activities. **Telecommunication Services:** electronic mail, scholarships@nshss.org ● electronic mail, studentcouncil@nshss.org ● electronic mail, editor@nshss.org. **Councils:** Student. **Affiliated With:** American Association of School Administrators; American School Counselor Association; Association for the Advancement of International Education; Southern Association of Independent Schools. **Publications:** *Scholar's Journal*, semiannual, winter and summer. Newsletter. Features articles and information to highlight Society and member milestones, announce scholarship winners, provides resources. Alternate Formats: online.

9077 ■ National Valedictorian Society
PO Box 3
Redmond, WA 98073
Ph: (425)836-1000
E-mail: mail@valedictorian.org
Contact: John T. Murdock II, Exec.Dir.
Founded: 1996. **Description:** National organization of scholars dedicated to the advancement of academic excellence. Conducts research and educational programs to improve the quality of teaching and learning. Sponsors the National Valedictorian Honor Society. **Libraries: Type:** reference. **Holdings:** archival material. **Committees:** Achievement and Awards; Archives; Executive; Fundraising; International Outreach; Program Planning; Publications/Communications; Research. **Affiliated With:** National Valedictorian Honor Society.

9078 ■ Society for Academic Achievement (SAA)
Address Unknown since 2008
Founded: 1959. **Members:** 5,148. **Staff:** 2. **State Groups:** 9. **Local Groups:** 39. **Description:** Educational society organized to make available and coordinate two academic honors programs to encourage high school students to achieve academic excellence. To promote, popularize, and reward high academic achievement; to motivate academically talented students to seek advanced education and develop their leadership potential. The programs are sponsored in any accredited high school by one or more community organizations. **Libraries: Type:** reference. **Awards: Type:** recognition. **Recipient:** for high academic achievement. **Divisions:** Editorial Board. **Conventions/Meetings:** quarterly meeting - always January, April, July, and October ● annual meeting.

9079 ■ Underprivileged Students of Anthropological Vocations (USAV)
Address Unknown since 2007
Description: Dedicated to the science of anthropology; provides opportunities for students majoring in anthropology who demonstrate promise, but may not meet the criteria for other scholarship programs. **Awards: Type:** scholarship. **Recipient:** for study at archaeological field schools.

Scholarships

9080 ■ National Association of Fellowships Advisors (NAFA)
c/o John Richardson, Treas.
Univ. of Louisville
Louisville, KY 40292
E-mail: info@nafadvisors.org
URL: http://www.nafadvisors.org
Contact: Beth Powers, Pres.
Founded: 2000. **Membership Dues:** individual, $150 (annual) ● individual, affiliate, $200 (annual). **Description:** Provides members with access to information concerning national undergraduate and graduate grants, scholarships, fellowships and the foundations

that support them. Provides a forum for the exchange of ideas concerning the scholarship process, the foundations and the ethical issues surrounding the advising process. Provides information support for faculty and staff who are assisting students through the process of applying for these awards. **Telecommunication Services:** electronic mail, bpowers@uic.edu. **Publications:** Newsletter, semiannual.

9081 ■ Scholarship America
4960 Viking Dr., Ste.110
Edina, MN 55435
Ph: (952)830-7300
Free: (800)279-2083
E-mail: sponwith@scholarshipamerica.org
URL: http://www.scholarshipamerica.org
Contact: Susan Ponwith, Pres.
Founded: 1958. **Description:** Unites communities, corporations, and adults to assist young people achieve educational goals through scholarships. Sponsors National Scholarship Month. **Programs:** Dollars for Scholars; Honor a Scholar; Scholarship Management Services; ScholarShop. **Formerly:** (2005) Citizens' Scholarship Foundation of America. **Publications:** *Donor Report*. Alternate Formats: online ● Annual Report, annual. Alternate Formats: online.

School Boards

9082 ■ National Association of State Boards of Education (NASBE)
277 S Washington St., Ste.100
Alexandria, VA 22314
Ph: (703)684-4000
Free: (800)220-5183
Fax: (703)836-2313
E-mail: brendaw@nasbe.org
URL: http://www.nasbe.org
Contact: Brenda L. Welburn, Exec. Dir./CEO
Founded: 1958. **Members:** 590. **Membership Dues:** associate, $150 (annual). **Staff:** 18. **Budget:** $2,000,000. **State Groups:** 50. **Description:** Members of state and territorial boards of education. Aims to: study problems of mutual interest and concern, improving communication and cooperation among the state boards; maintain an effective liaison with educator groups; exchange and disseminate information concerning educational programs and activities; coordinate activities and studies toward a nationwide consensus on education. **Committees:** Awards; Governmental Affairs; Nominations; Organization Study Groups; Resolutions; State-Local Relations. **Publications:** *State Board Connection*, 10/year. Annual Report ● *State Education Standard*, quarterly. Journal. **Price:** included in membership dues ● Membership Directory ● Also publishes special reports and issue papers. **Conventions/Meetings:** annual conference ● New State Board Member Institute and Annual Chairman's Leadership Conference.

9083 ■ National School Boards Association (NSBA)
1680 Duke St.
Alexandria, VA 22314-3493
Ph: (703)838-6722
Fax: (703)683-7590
E-mail: info@nsba.org
URL: http://www.nsba.org
Contact: Dr. Anne L. Bryant, Exec. Dir.
Founded: 1940. **Members:** 52. **Staff:** 150. **Budget:** $22,000,000. **Regional Groups:** 5. **State Groups:** 50. **Local Groups:** 2,350. **Description:** Federation of state school boards associations, the Board of Education of the District of Columbia and the Virgin Islands Board of Education. Advocates equity and quality education for primary and secondary public school children through legal counsel, research studies, legislative advocacy programs, and services for members, conferences, and magazines. Provides information on topics affecting K-12 public education and school policy. Maintains library and specialized clearinghouses. **Libraries: Type:** reference. **Holdings:** 4,000; books, periodicals. **Subjects:** K-12 public education. **Awards:** Magna Award. **Frequency:** annual. **Type:** recognition. **Recipient:** for boards distinguished by truly outstanding governance programs. **Telecommunication Services:** electronic mail, csavoie1@cox.net ● electronic mail, abryant@nsba.org. **Caucuses:** Black School Board Members; Hispanic School Board Members. **Councils:** School Attorneys; Urban Boards of Education. **Programs:** National Affiliate. **Subgroups:** Federal Relations Network; Large District Forum; National Education Policy Network Service; Rural and Small District Forum; Technology Leadership Network. **Formerly:** (1948) National Council of State School Boards Association. **Publications:** *The American School Board Journal*, monthly. Reports on school governance and management, policy making, and leadership. Includes articles on academics, computers, and school finance. **Price:** $48.00/year. ISSN: 0003-0953. **Circulation:** 36,750. **Advertising:** accepted ● *Inquiry and Analysis*, bimonthly. Newsletter. Reports on legislation, regulation, and recent court decisions affecting public schools. Features case studies. **Price:** included in membership dues; $75.00 /year for nonmembers. **Circulation:** 3,600 ● *Leadership Insider: Practical Perspectives on School Law and Policy*, bimonthly. Newsletter. Offers educational policy and legal advice for school board members and administrators on topics of current concern. **Price:** free for members. **Circulation:** 3,300 ● *School Board News*, biweekly. Newsletter. Provides information on curriculum developments and legislation and court decisions affecting education and school policy. **Price:** $45.00 /year for nonmembers; free for members. **Advertising:** accepted ● *Urban Advocate*, periodic. Newsletter. Includes information for urban school boards. **Conventions/Meetings:** annual conference (exhibits) - always March or April ● seminar.

School Security

9084 ■ International Association of Campus Law Enforcement Administrators (IACLEA)
342 N Main St., Ste.301
West Hartford, CT 06117-2507
Ph: (860)586-7517 (507)933-8809
Fax: (860)586-7550
E-mail: info@iaclea.org
URL: http://www.iaclea.org
Contact: Peter J. Berry CAE, Chief Staff Off.
Founded: 1958. **Members:** 1,700. **Membership Dues:** professional, $60 (annual) ● affiliate, $100 (annual) ● supporting, $300 (annual) ● retired, $30 (annual). **Regional Groups:** 8. **Description:** Advances public safety for educational institutions by providing educational resources, advocacy, and professional development. Promotes professional ideals and standards in the administration of campus security/public safety/law enforcement. Works to make campus security/public safety/law enforcement an integral part of the educational community. **Awards:** James L. McGovern Scholarship Award. **Frequency:** annual. **Type:** scholarship. **Recipient:** for qualified students. **Telecommunication Services:** electronic mail, pberry@iaclea.org. **Committees:** Government Relations; Professional Development; Public Relations; Standards. **Formerly:** International Association of College and University Security Directors; National Association of College and University Security Directors. **Publications:** *Campus Law Enforcement Journal*, bimonthly. Contains organizational charts and job descriptions for nearly all positions in public safety/security departments. **Price:** included in membership dues; $30.00 /year for nonmembers; $5.00/copy for nonmembers. **Advertising:** accepted ● *Handling Natural Disasters on Campus*. Monograph. **Price:** $35.00 for members; $50.00 for nonmembers ● *IACLEA Membership Directory*, annual. **Price:** $15.00 for members; $60.00 for nonmembers ● *If I Look Confused and Lost, It's Probably Because I am.*. Video. **Price:** $59,00 for members; $69.00 for nonmembers. **Conventions/Meetings:** annual meeting and conference (exhibits) - always late June. 2008 June 28-July 1, Hartford, CT; 2009 June 29-July 2, Quebec, QC, Canada; 2010 June 19-22, St. Louis, MO.

9085 ■ National Alliance for Safe Schools (NASS)
PO Box 290
Slanesville, WV 25444-0290
Ph: (304)496-8100
Fax: (304)496-8105
E-mail: nass@raven-villages.net
Contact: Peter D. Blauvelt, Pres./CEO
Founded: 1977. **Staff:** 2. **Budget:** $200,000. **Description:** Research and information arm of the National Association of School Safety and Law Enforcement Officers. Works to help school administrators and staff improve their methods for maintaining safe and secure learning environments. Designs, tests, and implements crime prevention and disciplinary models for public school systems. Provides assistance with: security assessments of school districts; research into strategies for combating particular problems; technical studies of appropriate security hardware. Offers workshops such as Managing Student Misbehavior, Expanding Security Awareness, and Involving Students in Safety Programs. Has designed and implemented the School Management and Resource Team Program. Compiles statistics. Maintains speakers' bureau. **Computer Services:** database, bibliographic information. **Formerly:** Center for Improved Learning Environments; (1983) Institute for Reduction of Crime. **Publications:** *Making Schools SAFE for Students*. Book. Includes CD-ROM Emergency Management Plan. **Price:** $69.95 print; $59.95 CD-ROM. Alternate Formats: CD-ROM ● Also publishes guides, reports, and articles.

9086 ■ National Association of School Resource Officers (NASRO)
1951 Woodlane Dr.
St. Paul, MN 55125
Ph: (651)209-3153
Free: (888)316-2776
Fax: (651)457-5665
E-mail: kevin.quinn@nasro.org
URL: http://www.nasro.org
Contact: Dr. Dick Caster, Exec. Dir.
Founded: 1989. **Members:** 10,000. **Membership Dues:** general, $40 (annual). **Staff:** 4. **Budget:** $1,000,000. **Regional Groups:** 9. **State Groups:** 11. **Description:** School resource/police officers, school administrators, juvenile detectives, school security officers, and DARE officers. Seeks to build a rapport between law enforcement officers and America's youth, while providing safe and secure learning environments. **Awards:** Floyd Ledbetter Award. **Frequency:** annual. **Type:** recognition. **Recipient:** for officers. **Publications:** *Resourcer*, quarterly. Newsletter. **Price:** included in membership dues. **Circulation:** 14,000. **Advertising:** accepted ● Manuals. **Conventions/Meetings:** annual conference (exhibits) - 2008 July 26-Aug. 1, Phoenix, AZ.

9087 ■ National Association of School Safety and Law Enforcement Officers (NASSLEO)
PO Box 210079
Milwaukee, WI 53221
Ph: (315)529-4858 (414)345-6635
Fax: (877)282-4860
E-mail: nassleo@nassleo.org
URL: http://www.nassleo.org
Contact: Peter Pochowski, Exec. Dir.
Founded: 1970. **Members:** 216. **Membership Dues:** regular/associate, $50 (annual). **Regional Groups:** 6. **Description:** Persons paid by educational institutions and engaged in school security in the U.S. and Canada. Provides a coordinated effort in dealing with increasing violence and property damage in school systems and to assist school officials who have responsibility for the safety and protection of personnel and physical assets within their system. Commits to reduce the personal risk problems and tax dollar losses as a result of: vandalism, burglary, theft, assault, drug abuse, riot, and disturbance. Offers speakers' bureau and consultant service. Compiles statistics. Conducts research programs; maintains placement service. **Awards:** NASSLEO Annual

Scholarship. **Frequency:** annual. **Type:** scholarship. **Recipient:** to students aiming to be law enforcers. **Telecommunication Services:** electronic mail, secretary@nassleo.org. **Committees:** Job Placement; Public Information; Regional Adjustment. **Formerly:** (1973) International Association of School Security Directors; (1992) National Association of School Security Directors. **Publications:** Membership Directory, annual. **Conventions/Meetings:** annual Training Conference (exhibits) - always July.

9088 ■ National School Safety Center (NSSC)
141 Duesenberg Dr., Ste.11
Westlake Village, CA 91362-3480
Ph: (805)373-9977
Fax: (805)373-9277
URL: http://www.schoolsafety.us
Contact: Dr. Ronald D. Stephens, Exec. Dir.
Founded: 1984. **Staff:** 4. **Description:** Focuses national attention on cooperative solutions to problems that disrupt the educational process. Emphasizes efforts to eliminate crime, violence, and drugs from schools and improve student discipline, attendance, achievement, and the school climate. Coordinates a national network of education, law enforcement, and legal professionals to provide school safety leadership training. Provides on-site training and technical assistance programs worldwide. Sponsors America's Safe Schools Week and technical assistance programs worldwide. **Programs:** School Safety Leadership Training. **Conventions/Meetings:** periodic seminar, conducts school safety leadership training.

Schools

9089 ■ Association of Classical and Christian Schools (ACCS)
PO Box 9741
Moscow, ID 83843
Ph: (208)882-6101
Fax: (208)882-9097
E-mail: info@accsedu.org
URL: http://www.accsedu.org
Contact: Patch Blackey, Exec. Dir.
Membership Dues: school (plus $2/student), $150 (annual) ● college, international, $75 (annual) ● associate school (plus $2/student), affiliate - business, $100 (annual) ● affiliate - homeschool/individual, $25 (annual). **Multinational. Description:** Promotes schools committed to a classical approach to education in light of a Christian worldview grounded in the Bible. Seeks to set an educational standard for a unified and directed approach to Classical and Christian learning. **Publications:** *Classis*, bimonthly. Newsletter. Alternate Formats: online. **Conventions/Meetings:** annual conference.

9090 ■ Chinese School Association in the United States (CSAUS)
385 Fox Run
Powell, OH 43065
Fax: (614)863-0685
E-mail: csaus@csaus.org
URL: http://www.csaus.org
Contact: Jason Ma, Pres.
Founded: 1994. **Members:** 300. **Membership Dues:** school, $50 (annual). **Languages:** Chinese, English. **Description:** Provides information, networking and services to member schools in promoting the Chinese language and cultural education. Helps the younger generation to preserve and appreciate the Chinese heritage. Fosters educational and cultural exchanges and friendship between USA and China. Assists member schools in marketing and maximizing organizational efforts. **Telecommunication Services:** electronic mail, jason_ma_yh@yahoo.com ● electronic mail, datamanager@csaus.org. **Publications:** Newsletter, quarterly. **Price:** included in membership dues. Alternate Formats: online.

9091 ■ National Association for Professional Development Schools (NAPDS)
Univ. of South Carolina
College of Educ.
Wardlaw 201
Columbia, SC 29208
Ph: (803)777-1515
Fax: (803)777-3035
E-mail: kinseyw@gwm.sc.edu
URL: http://www.napds.org
Contact: Elliott Lessen, Pres.
Founded: 2003. **Membership Dues:** professional, $75 (annual) ● student, $25 (annual). **Description:** Serves as an advocate for the educational community. Creates and sustains collaborative partnerships between P-12/higher education. Fosters equal representation of, and access for, all educators invested in improving education. Supports teacher leadership in the P-12/higher education community. **Publications:** Proceedings, annual. Alternate Formats: online. **Conventions/Meetings:** annual conference.

9092 ■ National Service-Learning Clearinghouse (NSLC)
c/o ETR Associates
4 Carbonero Way
Scotts Valley, CA 95066
Ph: (831)438-4060
Free: (866)245-7378
Fax: (831)430-9471
E-mail: nslc@servicelearning.org
URL: http://www.servicelearning.org
Contact: Barbara Holland PhD, Dir.
Staff: 7. **Description:** Supports the service learning community in higher education, kindergarten through grade twelve, community-based initiatives and tribal programs. **Libraries: Type:** reference. **Holdings:** articles, books, papers, periodicals, reports, video recordings. **Subjects:** service-learning, education, civic education, youth service, voluntarism, community engagement. **Telecommunication Services:** electronic mail, info@servicelearning.org ● electronic mail, barbarah@etr.org ● TDD, (831)461-0205. **Publications:** *LSA-News*, periodic. Newsletter. Provides timely information and relevant resources on Learn and Serve America programs. **Price:** free. Alternate Formats: online ● *NSLC-Resources*, periodic. Newsletter. Provides timely information and relevant resources on service learning. **Price:** free. Alternate Formats: online.

9093 ■ North Central Association Commission on Accreditation and School Improvement (NCA-CASI)
Arizona State Univ.
PO Box 871008
Tempe, AZ 85287-1008
Ph: (480)773-6900
Free: (800)525-9517
Fax: (480)773-6901
E-mail: communications@advanc-ed.org
URL: http://www.ncacasi.org
Contact: Ms. Jennifer Oliver, VP for Communications
Founded: 1895. **Members:** 9,000. **Description:** Elementary, middle, secondary, college preparatory, vocational/adult, optional/special function, and unit (K-12) schools. Dedicated to accreditation, evaluation, and school improvement; protects the public trust; promotes an educational system that enhances student learning; fosters healthy, creative and innovative human beings; prepares students to exist in an ever-changing, diverse world; provides standards and evaluation services that ensure successful schooling transitions for students. **Libraries: Type:** reference. **Additional Websites:** http://www.advanc-ed.org. **Publications:** *E-News*, bimonthly. Newsletter. Alternate Formats: online ● *Product and Service Catalog*, annual. Alternate Formats: online ● Handbooks. **Conventions/Meetings:** annual meeting (exhibits) - always March or April in Chicago, IL. 2009 Mar. 29-Apr. 1, Chicago, IL ● workshop.

9094 ■ StandardsWork
1001 Connecticut Ave. NW, Ste.840
Washington, DC 20036
Ph: (202)835-2000
Fax: (202)659-4494
E-mail: info@standardswork.org
URL: http://www.standardswork.org
Contact: Barbara Davidson, Pres.
Founded: 1991. **Description:** Collaborates with school districts, state agencies and civic groups around the country to improve student achievement. Helps communities and the schools they support to transform a vision of academic success into a better standard of education for all students. Works for higher education standards and improved results for kids.

Science

9095 ■ Access Research Network (ARN)
PO Box 38069
Colorado Springs, CO 80937-8069
Ph: (719)633-1772
Free: (888)259-7102
E-mail: dwagner@arn.org
URL: http://www.arn.org
Contact: Dennis A. Wagner, Co-Founder/Chm.
Founded: 1977. **Members:** 1,000. **Description:** Gathers and disseminates information in issues pertaining to science, technology, and society. Encourages dialogue between proponents of differing viewpoints. Produces material for science courses in public schools. **Libraries: Type:** reference. **Holdings:** 600. **Committees:** Earth Sciences; Life Sciences; Philosophy; Technical. **Publications:** *Currents*, quarterly ● *Origin and Design*, periodic. Journal. **Price:** $5.00 per back issue (add $1.50 shipping and handling). ISSN: 0748-9919. Alternate Formats: online ● Audiotapes ● Books ● Videos.

9096 ■ Association of Educators in Imaging and Radiologic Sciences (AEIRS)
PO Box 90204
Albuquerque, NM 87199-0204
Ph: (505)823-4740
Fax: (505)823-4740
E-mail: office@aeirs.org
URL: http://www.aeirs.org
Contact: Ms. Valerie Christensen, Exec. Sec.
Founded: 1967. **Members:** 500. **Membership Dues:** individual, $75 (annual). **Staff:** 1. **Multinational. Description:** Radiological science faculty at postsecondary educational institutions and hospitals. Seeks to advance the study and teaching of the radiological sciences. Facilitates exchange of information among members; conducts educational programs; conducts international networking initiatives. **Awards:** AEIRS Fellow. **Frequency:** annual. **Type:** fellowship ● AEIRS Research Grant. **Frequency:** annual. **Type:** monetary. **Recipient:** for AEIRS member for two years; research must focus on some facet of radiologic science education or practice. **Committees:** Bylaws; Nominating; Research. **Task Forces:** Educator Workforce Development. **Formerly:** (1984) Association of University Radiologic Technologists; (2006) Association of Educators in Radiological Sciences. **Publications:** *Radiologic Science and Education*, annual. Journal. **Price:** $25.00 /year for libraries. ISSN: 1078-5450. **Advertising:** accepted ● *Spectrum*, quarterly. Newsletter. **Price:** included in membership dues. **Advertising:** accepted. **Conventions/Meetings:** periodic Instructor Workshop - seminar ● annual meeting.

9097 ■ Association for Multicultural Science Education (AMSE)
c/o Meg Wilder Watson, Sec.
11 Westland St.
Brockton, MA 02301
E-mail: beton@cox.net
URL: http://amse.edhost.org/index.php
Contact: Aurietha M. Hoesing, Pres.
Membership Dues: professional, $25 (annual) ● student, $5 (annual). **Staff:** 5. **Description:** Promotes multicultural science education. **Publications:** *The Multicultural Science Educator Informer*, 3/year. Newsletter. **Advertising:** accepted. Alternate Formats: online.

9098 ■ Coalition for Education in the Life Sciences (CELS)
c/o Dr. Louise W. Liao, Program Dir.
Univ. of Wisconsin - Madison
Center for Biology Educ.
425 Henry Mall
1271 Genetics/Biotechnology Bldg.
Madison, WI 53706
Ph: (608)262-5266
Fax: (608)262-6748
E-mail: cels@macc.wisc.edu
URL: http://www.wisc.edu/cbe/cels
Contact: Dr. Louise W. Liao, Program Dir.
Members: 47. **Description:** Sponsored by the American Institute of Biological Sciences. Scientific and teaching organizations working in the life sciences. Promotes improvement in undergraduate science education. Studies social issues impacting the life sciences, including wellness, genetics, overpopulation, resource use, alteration of natural systems, and functional and dysfunctional behavior. Facilitates communication and cooperation among members; conducts research, educational, and training programs. **Formerly:** (1991) Commission on Undergraduate Education in the Biological Sciences. **Conventions/Meetings:** annual conference.

9099 ■ Committee on Capacity Building Science (CCBS)
FERMILAB
PO Box 500
Batavia, IL 60510-0500
Ph: (630)840-3000
Fax: (630)840-4343
E-mail: treend@fnal.gov
URL: http://www.fnal.gov
Contact: Judy Treend, Contact
Founded: 1993. **Description:** A committee of the International Council of Scientific Unions. Scientists and educators. Promotes more effective science education and increased access to scientific information for policy makers and the public. Plans to develop science education curricula and strategies. **Libraries: Type:** open to the public; reference. **Holdings:** books. **Subjects:** physics. **Publications:** *Fermilab Today*, daily. Newsletter. Contains information for employees. ● *Symmetry*, monthly. Magazine. Contains information about science, people and culture of particle physics.

9100 ■ Council for Elementary Science International (CESI)
c/o Judy Lederman, Pres.
Illinois Inst. of Tech.
3424 S State St., 4th Fl., Rm. 4009
Chicago, IL 60616
Ph: (312)567-3662 (860)465-4532
Fax: (312)567-3659
E-mail: ledermanj@iit.edu
URL: http://www.cesiscience.org
Contact: Judy Lederman, Pres.
Founded: 1920. **Members:** 600. **Membership Dues:** general, $20 (annual) ● retired, student, $10 (annual). **Multinational. Description:** Represents elementary teachers, supervisors, principals, college students, and interested others. Works to stimulate, improve, and coordinate science teaching at all levels of preschool and elementary school. Promotes the improvement of science programs that begin in preschool and develop in a continuous and integrated fashion through grade twelve and beyond. **Awards:** CESI Advocacy Award. **Frequency:** annual. **Type:** recognition ● CESI/CIBA Exemplary Elementary Principal Award. **Frequency:** annual. **Type:** recognition. **Recipient:** for leadership in science education ● CESI/CIBA Exemplary Elementary Science Teaching Award. **Frequency:** annual. **Type:** recognition. **Recipient:** to an elementary teacher who has demonstrated exemplary science teaching performance ● Mary McCurdy International Award. **Frequency:** annual. **Type:** recognition. **Recipient:** for outstanding contributions to elementary science ● Muriel Green Award. **Frequency:** annual. **Type:** recognition. **Recipient:** to outstanding new elementary science teachers or teachers-to-be ● Outstanding New Science Teacher Award. **Frequency:** annual. **Type:** recognition. **Recipient:** to outstanding new science teachers. **Computer Services:** Mailing lists, of members. **Telecommunication Services:** electronic mail, amccorma@mail.sdsu.edu. **Committees:** Futures. **Formerly:** (1958) National Council for Elementary Science. **Publications:** Directory, annual ● Journal, semiannual. **Price:** included in membership dues. **Circulation:** 600. **Advertising:** accepted ● Newsletter, semiannual. Contains information about how to get involve in CESI activities at the regional and national NSTA conventions. **Price:** included in membership dues. **Advertising:** accepted. **Conventions/Meetings:** annual meeting, held in conjunction with National Science Teachers Association ● workshop.

9101 ■ Council of State Science Supervisors (CSSS)
c/o C.J. Evans, Treas.
8816 Manchester Rd., No. 261
Brentwood, MO 63144
Ph: (314)614-7707
E-mail: linda.k.jordan@state.tn.us
URL: http://www.csss-science.org
Contact: Linda Jordan, Exec. Sec.
Founded: 1963. **Members:** 100. **Description:** State science department educators. Promotes science education safety programs to facilitate the teaching of science in a safe atmosphere. Develops curriculum and encourages innovative ideas and suggestions. Serves in advisory capacity as expert witness in legal matters. Offers safety program for laboratory science in conjunction with the National Institute of Safety and Health. Obtains funds for projects through grants; conducts safety workshops. **Telecommunication Services:** electronic mail, jecjevans@charter.net. **Committees:** Critical Issues in Science Education; Laboratory Design; Materials; Safety. **Publications:** Newsletter, periodic. **Conventions/Meetings:** annual meeting - always March or April. 2009 Mar. 18-21, Washington, DC.

9102 ■ Federation for Unified Science Education (FUSE)
Ctr. for Unified Sci.
6529 Sunbury Rd.
Westerville, OH 43082
Ph: (614)895-2252
Fax: (614)895-0583
E-mail: scitech2000@aol.com
Contact: Dr. Victor M. Showalter, Exec. Dir.
Founded: 1966. **Members:** 83. **Staff:** 2. **Description:** Science teachers, college professors, and school administrators united to improve science education. Objectives are to promote unified science education and to facilitate the development of high quality, locally developed unified science programs so that increasing proportions of the public will achieve desirable levels of scientific literacy. Operates the Center for Unified Science with additional support from Capital University. Conducts regional and local workshops for interested educators. Maintains response system to provide information on unified science and useful resources. Maintains speakers' bureau. **Libraries: Type:** reference. **Holdings:** 2,500; articles, books, papers. **Subjects:** science learning activities. **Publications:** *Prism II*, annual. **Circulation:** 100 ● *Proceedings of Annual Conference*, biennial. **Conventions/Meetings:** annual conference, often held in conjunction with National Science Teachers Association.

9103 ■ HOPOS - The International Society for the History of Philosophy of Science
222 Cockefair Hall
Dept. of Philosophy
Univ. of Missouri
5100 Rockhill Rd.
Kansas City, MO 64110-2499
Ph: (816)235-1331
E-mail: sfisher@acls.org
URL: http://scistud.umkc.edu/hopos
Contact: Saul Fisher, Pres.
Membership Dues: $25 (annual). **Description:** Promotes scholarly research on the history of the philosophy of science, including all historical periods, studied through diverse methodologies, including topics in the history of related disciplines such as natural and social sciences, logic, philosophy, and mathematics. **Committees:** External Relations; Nominating & Elections; Program; Publications. **Working Groups:** HOPOS.

9104 ■ International Council of Academies of Engineering and Technological Sciences (CAETS)
3601 N Peary St.
Arlington, VA 22207
Ph: (703)527-5782
Fax: (703)526-0570
E-mail: caets@nae.edu
URL: http://www.caets.org
Contact: William C. Salmon PE, Sec.-Treas.
Founded: 1978. **Members:** 24. **Membership Dues:** national academy (one per country), $3,000 (annual). **Staff:** 1. **Budget:** $72,000. **National Groups:** 24. **Multinational. Description:** Consists of engineering and technological sciences academies prepared to advise governments and international organizations on technical and policy issues related to its areas of expertise. Contributes to the strengthening of engineering and technological activities in order to promote sustainable economic growth and social welfare throughout the world. Fosters a balanced understanding of the applications of engineering and technology by the public. Provides an international forum for discussion and communication of engineering and technological issues of common concern. Fosters cooperative international engineering and technological efforts through meaningful contacts for development of programs of bilateral and multilateral interest. **Formerly:** (2002) Council of Academies of Engineering and Technological Sciences. **Conventions/Meetings:** biennial Convocations - assembly ● annual meeting.

9105 ■ Middle Atlantic Planetarium Society (MAPS)
c/o John Meader
PO Box 302
Fairfield, ME 04937
Ph: (207)453-7668
E-mail: info@northern-stars.com
URL: http://www.maps-planetarium.org
Contact: Gloria Villalobos, Pres.-Elect
Founded: 1965. **Members:** 200. **Membership Dues:** individual, $25 (annual). **Description:** Planetarium educators from Washington, DC, and the states of Connecticut, Delaware, Maine, Maryland, Massachusetts, New Hampshire, New Jersey, New York, Pennsylvania, Rhode Island, Vermont, Virginia, and West Virginia. Provides recommendations on construction to boards of education planning a planetarium; acquaints members with curriculum materials for all grade levels, developed by planetarium educators throughout the country; informs members of new projects, projectors, and audiovisual aids developed by other members. Helps new planetarium teachers, primarily with curriculum materials. Conducts program of planetarium research. **Awards:** Distinguished Service Award. **Frequency:** periodic. **Type:** recognition. **Committees:** Audit; Awards; Education; Nomination and Election; Program; Publications. **Affiliated With:** International Planetarium Society; National Science Teachers Association. **Publications:** *Annual Conference Proceedings*, annual ● *Constellation*, quarterly. Newsletter. **Price:** included in membership dues. **Circulation:** 250. **Advertising:** accepted ● *Under Roof, Dome and Sky*. Manual. Serves as an educator's manual/teacher's guide. **Conventions/Meetings:** annual conference and workshop (exhibits).

9106 ■ National Alliance of State Science and Mathematics Coalitions (NASSMC)
1840 Wilson Blvd., Ste.200
Arlington, VA 22201-3000
Ph: (703)516-5970 (703)516-5973
Fax: (703)516-5979

E-mail: info@nassmc.org
URL: http://www.nassmc.org
Contact: Jim McMurtray, Exec. Dir.
Founded: 1994. **Membership Dues:** regular, $200 (annual). **Description:** Represents state coalitions of business, education, and public policy leaders working to improve science, technology, engineering, and mathematics education for all students. Provides a forum for the discussion of critical issues relevant to the continuous and systemic improvement of mathematics, science, and technology education. Promotes adaptation and implementation of new state standards for school mathematics, science, and technology education. **Telecommunication Services:** electronic mail, jmcmurtray@nassmc.org. **Publications:** *NASSMC News Bulletin*, monthly. Newsletter. Provides articles, news and issues that are of interest to member coalitions. **Price:** free. Alternate Formats: online.

9107 ■ National Association of Health Science Education Partnership (NAHSEP)
c/o Erin Dolan, PhD, Pres.
Biochemistry, Falin Center
Virginia Tech.
West Campus Dr., MC 0346
Blacksburg, VA 24061
Ph: (540)231-2692
Fax: (540)231-7126
E-mail: biooutreach@vt.edu
URL: http://www.nahsep.org
Contact: Erin Dolan PhD, Pres.
Membership Dues: regular, $40 (annual). **Description:** Seeks to improve pre-college health and science education. Promotes and facilitates the dissemination of innovative approaches to K-12 health and science education. Disseminates curricular ideas and partnership models. **Publications:** *NAHSEP News*, quarterly. Newsletter. Shares information about NAHSEP's ongoing activities. **Price:** included in membership dues. Alternate Formats: online.

9108 ■ National Association for Research in Science Teaching (NARST)
12100 Sunset Hills Rd., Ste.130
Reston, VA 20190-3221
Ph: (703)437-4377 (703)234-4138
Fax: (703)435-4390
E-mail: info@narst.org
URL: http://www.narst.org
Contact: Penny J. Gilmer, Pres.
Founded: 1928. **Members:** 1,700. **Membership Dues:** student, emeritus, $50 (annual) ● regular, $100 (annual) ● sustaining, $175 (annual). **Staff:** 2. **Budget:** $300,000. **Description:** Science teachers, supervisors, and science educators specializing in research and teacher education. Promotes and coordinates science education research and interprets and reports the results. **Libraries: Type:** reference. **Holdings:** archival material. **Awards:** Distinguished Contributions to Science Education Through Research Award. **Frequency:** annual. **Type:** recognition. **Recipient:** for contributions to research in science education ● Early Career Research Award. **Frequency:** annual. **Type:** recognition. **Recipient:** to individuals for contributions to science education through research ● JRST Award. **Frequency:** annual. **Type:** recognition. **Recipient:** for best article published in journal ● NARST Award. **Frequency:** annual. **Type:** recognition. **Recipient:** for best research report ● Outstanding Doctoral Dissertation Award. **Frequency:** annual. **Type:** recognition. **Recipient:** for best doctoral dissertation ● Outstanding Paper Award. **Frequency:** annual. **Type:** recognition. **Recipient:** for the best master thesis. **Computer Services:** Mailing lists, of members. **Telecommunication Services:** electronic bulletin board, NARSTNET ● electronic mail, gilmer@chem.fsu.edu. **Committees:** Dissertation Award; Distinguished Contributions Award; Early Career Research Award; Elections; International; JRST Award; Outstanding Paper Award; Program; Research. **Affiliated With:** American Association for the Advancement of Science; National Science Teachers Association. **Publications:** *A Theory of Instruction*. Monograph. **Price:** $6.00/copy ● *Abstracts of Papers Presented to Annual Meeting* ● *Interpretive Research in Science Education*. Monograph ● *Journal of Research in Science Teaching*, 10/year. Contains articles on issues of science teaching and learning, as well as in the broader context of science education policy. ISSN: 0022-4308 ● *Learning Environment Research in Science Classrooms*. Monograph ● *NARST News*, quarterly. Newsletter ● *Research Matter. . . .to the Science Teacher*. Paper. Includes papers developed by NARST members for the science teaching community. ● *World View Theory and Science Education Research*. Monograph. **Conventions/Meetings:** annual conference ● annual meeting, in conjunction with National Science Teachers Association and the American Education Research Association (exhibits).

9109 ■ National Center for Improving Science Education (NCISE)
1840 Wilson Blvd., Ste.201A
Arlington, VA 22201-3000
Ph: (703)875-0496
Fax: (703)875-0479
E-mail: sraizen@wested.org
URL: http://www.wested.org/cs/we/view/pj/445
Contact: Senta A. Raizen, Dir.
Founded: 1987. **Staff:** 6. **Nonmembership. Description:** A division of WestEd. Promotes changes in state and local policies and practices in science education, including curriculum, instruction, assessment of student learning, and professional development of teachers. Provides products and services to educational policy makers and practitioners who work to strengthen science teaching and learning. Carries out evaluation of science education programs. **Libraries: Type:** not open to the public; reference. **Holdings:** 300; archival material, articles, books, papers, periodicals, reports. **Subjects:** science and mathematics education, teacher education. **Publications:** *Assessment in Elementary School Science Education*. **Price:** $15.00 plus shipping and handling ● *Assessment in Science Education: The Middle Years*. Book. **Price:** $15.00 plus shipping and handling ● *Building Scientific Literacy: A Blueprint for Science Education in the Middle Years*. **Price:** $7.00 plus shipping and handling ● *Curriculum Frameworks for Mathematics and Science*. **Price:** $16.95 plus shipping and handling ● *Developing and Supporting Teachers for Elementary School Science Education*. **Price:** $12.00 plus shipping and handling ● *Developing and Supporting Teachers for Science Education in the Middle Years*. **Price:** $15.00 plus shipping and handling ● *Elementary School Science for the 90's*. **Price:** $13.95 plus shipping and handling ● *The Future of Science in Elementary Schools: Educating Prospective Teachers*. **Price:** $26.95 plus shipping and handling ● *Getting Started in Science: A Blueprint for Elementary School Science Education*. **Price:** $7.00 plus shipping and handling ● *The High Stakes of High School Science*. **Price:** $22.50 plus shipping and handling ● *Profiling Student Programs: An Approach to Formative Evaluation* ● *Profiling Teacher Research Participation Program: An Approach to Formation Evaluation* ● *Profiling Teacher Research Participation Programs: An Approach to Formative Evaluation* ● *Science and Technology Education for the Elementary Years: Frameworks for Curriculum and Instruction*. **Price:** $12.00 plus shipping and handling ● *Science and Technology Education for the Middle Years: Frameworks for Curriculum and Instruction*. **Price:** $15.00 plus shipping and handling ● *Technology Education: Understanding the Designed World*. Book ● *What College Bound Students Abroad Are Expected to Know About Biology*. **Price:** $10.00 plus shipping and handling ● *What We Know About Science Teaching and Learning*. **Price:** $9.00 plus shipping and handling.

9110 ■ National Center for Science Education (NCSE)
420 40th St., Ste.2
Oakland, CA 94609-2688
Ph: (510)601-7203
Free: (800)290-6006
Fax: (510)601-7204
E-mail: ncseoffice@ncseweb.org
URL: http://www.ncseweb.org
Contact: Eugenie C. Scott PhD, Exec. Dir.
Founded: 1981. **Members:** 4,500. **Membership Dues:** individual in U.S., $30 (annual) ● individual outside U.S., $37 (annual) ● individual outside U.S. (via air mail), $39 (annual) ● life, $600. **Staff:** 11. **Budget:** $500,000. **Description:** Scientists, teachers, students, clergy, and interested individuals. Seeks to improve science education, specifically the study of evolutionary science; opposes the teaching of creationism as part of public school science curricula. Coordinates, supports, and provides information to individuals and local groups that work to improve science education through counseling school personnel, collecting and disseminating information, monitoring legislation, and sponsoring workshops. Reviews and researches textbooks, publications, and audiovisual materials. Maintains speakers' bureau. **Libraries: Type:** reference. **Holdings:** archival material, audiovisuals, books, clippings, periodicals. **Subjects:** science, evolution/creationism controversy. **Awards:** Clarence Darrow. **Frequency:** annual. **Type:** recognition. **Recipient:** for attorneys/legal professionals who have made a significant contribution to the furtherance of NCSE's goals ● Friend of Darwin. **Frequency:** annual. **Type:** recognition. **Recipient:** for service to NCSE and evolution education. **Computer Services:** Mailing lists, for rental/trade with other non-profit groups. **Committees:** Audio-Visual; Public Information; Teacher Training; Textbook Evaluation and Review. **Affiliated With:** American Association for the Advancement of Science; National Science Teachers Association. **Publications:** *Reports of the National Center for Science Education*, bimonthly. Journal. Contains examination of issues and current events in science education with a focus on evolutionary science, and the evolution/creation controversy. **Price:** $30.00/year in U.S.; $37.00/year outside U.S.; $39.00/year outside U.S. - via air mail. ISSN: 1064-2358. **Circulation:** 4,000. **Advertising:** accepted ● *Reviews of Creationist Books*. **Price:** $10.00 ● *Voices for Evolution*. Books. **Price:** $10.00 ● Brochures ● Monographs. **Conventions/Meetings:** periodic symposium.

9111 ■ National Earth Science Teachers Association (NESTA)
c/o Dr. Roberta Johnson, Exec. Dir.
PO Box 3000
Boulder, CO 80307-3000
Ph: (303)497-2591 (303)530-9795
Fax: (303)497-2598
E-mail: rmjohnsn@ucar.edu
URL: http://www.nestanet.org
Contact: Dr. Roberta Johnson, Exec. Dir.
Founded: 1983. **Members:** 1,000. **Membership Dues:** individual, $20 (annual). **Staff:** 1. **Budget:** $15,000. **Regional Groups:** 11. **Description:** Represents earth science teachers and individuals interested in earth science education. Promotes the advancement and improvement of the field. Provides materials and information sessions at national and regional conferences. **Awards:** Distinguished Service Award. **Frequency:** annual. **Type:** recognition ● Fellow of Association. **Frequency:** annual. **Type:** recognition ● Jan Woerner and Harold Stonehouse Award. **Frequency:** biennial. **Type:** recognition. **Recipient:** for an individual or organization's efforts in promoting earth science education. **Computer Services:** Mailing lists. **Sections:** Ten Regions. **Working Groups:** NESTANet. **Affiliated With:** Triangle Coalition for Science and Technology Education. **Publications:** *The Earth Scientist*, quarterly. Journal. **Price:** included in membership dues. **Circulation:** 1,000. **Advertising:** accepted ● NESTA Slide sets. NESTA E-News. **Conventions/Meetings:** annual conference, held in conjunction with National Science Teachers Association - spring.

9112 ■ National Middle Level Science Teachers' Association (NMLSTA)
c/o Dale Rosene, Founding Pres.
548 N Linden St.
Marshall, MI 49068

E-mail: carlac.johnson@utoledo.edu
URL: http://www.nmlsta.org
Contact: Carla Johnson, Pres.
Membership Dues: professional educator, educational institution, $15 (annual) ● first year educator, $12 (annual) ● student pre-service educator, $10 (annual). **Description:** Aims to stimulate, improve, and coordinate science teaching in the middle level grades. Promotes the continuity of science education by developing and improving programs that begin in preschool or first grade and develop in a continuous fashion through grade twelve and beyond. Recruits and retains qualified individuals to teach science at the middle level. Shares effective teaching activities and the results of educational research useful to middle level science teachers. **Awards:** Paul Dearth Hurd Award. **Frequency:** annual. **Type:** recognition. **Recipient:** for middle level science teaching and leadership ● Vincent J. Market Jr. Award. **Frequency:** annual. **Type:** recognition. **Recipient:** for creative science teaching. **Publications:** *Level Line*, quarterly. Newsletter. Contains short articles written by middle school science teachers. Includes information on middle school science workshops. **Price:** included in membership dues ● Articles. Alternate Formats: online.

9113 ■ National Science Education Leadership Association (NSELA)

2011 Holly Dr.
Prescott, AZ 86305
Ph: (928)771-1030 (480)497-3354
Fax: (480)240-4188
E-mail: susansprague@yahoo.com
URL: http://www.nsela.org
Contact: Susan Sprague, Exec. Dir.
Founded: 1958. **Members:** 900. **Membership Dues:** individual, $45 (annual) ● company, $75 (annual) ● retired, $15 (annual). **Staff:** 1. **Budget:** $50,000. **State Groups:** 33. **Description:** Represents department heads, supervisors, coordinators, consultants, science specialists, administrators, teacher advocates, lead-teachers and others concerned with leadership in science curricula, science education innovations, and science education in general. Seeks to communicate principles and practices of effective science education leadership through new approaches to science and their coordination into varied school systems. Offers summer leadership institutes for members. Offers professional development institute (formerly mini-conference) one day prior to the NSTA annual meeting. **Libraries: Type:** open to the public. **Subjects:** science education and leadership. **Awards:** Kendall Hunt/NSELA Outstanding Administrative Support Award. **Frequency:** annual. **Type:** recognition. **Recipient:** for an outstanding administrator who has supported the science instructional program in his/her school or district ● Outstanding Leadership in Science Education Award. **Frequency:** annual. **Type:** recognition. **Recipient:** for outstanding service to the profession. **Computer Services:** Mailing lists. **Telecommunication Services:** electronic mail, beth@seven-oaks.net. **Affiliated With:** National Science Teachers Association. **Formerly:** National Science Supervisors Association. **Publications:** *Issues in Science Education*, annual. Paper. **Circulation:** 3,000 ● *National Science Education Leadership Association Handbook*, annual. Lists executive committee and membership; includes position statements and policies. **Price:** included in membership dues; $20.00 for nonmembers. **Circulation:** 1,200. **Advertising:** accepted ● *The Navigator*, quarterly. Newsletter. Includes list of award winners, membership and regional updates, and conference schedule. **Price:** included in membership dues. **Circulation:** 1,200. **Advertising:** accepted. Alternate Formats: online ● *Science Educator*, semiannual. Journal. **Advertising:** accepted. **Conventions/Meetings:** annual meeting, membership, with breakfast on Thursday of NSTA annual meeting ● annual Summer Leadership Institute - workshop, for leaders in science.

9114 ■ National Science Teachers Association (NSTA)

1840 Wilson Blvd.
Arlington, VA 22201-3000
Ph: (703)243-7100
Free: (800)722-6782
Fax: (703)243-7177
E-mail: executive@nsta.org
URL: http://www.nsta.org
Contact: Dr. Gerard Wheeler, Exec. Dir.
Founded: 1944. **Members:** 53,000. **Membership Dues:** individual, $74 (annual) ● student, retired, new teacher, $32 (annual) ● joint-individual, $89 (annual) ● joint-student, $37 (annual) ● institutional, $84 (annual) ● international (online), $35 (annual). **Staff:** 110. **Budget:** $10,000,000. **State Groups:** 50. **Description:** Teachers seeking to foster excellence in science teaching. Studies students and how they learn, the curriculum of science, the teacher and his/her preparation, the procedures used in classroom and laboratory, the facilities for teaching science, and the evaluation procedures used. **Awards:** NSTA Distinguished Service to Science Education Awards. **Frequency:** annual. **Type:** recognition. **Recipient:** to members who have made extraordinary contributions to the advancement of education in the sciences and science teaching ● NSTA Distinguished Teaching Award. **Frequency:** annual. **Type:** recognition. **Recipient:** to member teachers who have made extraordinary contributions to the field of science teaching ● NSTA Robert H. Carleton Award. **Frequency:** annual. **Type:** recognition. **Recipient:** to an individual who has made outstanding contributions to, and provided leadership in, science education at the national level. **Telecommunication Services:** electronic mail, membership@nsta.org. **Committees:** Awards and Recognitions; Elementary Through College Level Teaching; International Activities; Member Services and Associated Groups; Multicultural Science Education; Publications; Research; Science Teacher Education; Special Education; Student Programs; Supervision of Science Teaching. **Affiliated With:** American Association for the Advancement of Science. **Publications:** *Journal of College Science Teaching*, bimonthly. Includes information on innovative teaching methods at the college level, research, and problem solving. ISSN: 0047-231X. **Circulation:** 5,600. **Advertising:** accepted ● *NSTA Express*, weekly. Newsletter. Features latest news and information about science education, including legislative updates, member news, and resources. Alternate Formats: online ● *NSTA Reports*, bimonthly. Newsletter. Includes national news, programs for teachers and students and advance notice about programs, conventions and publications. **Price:** included in membership dues. **Circulation:** 53,000 ● *Quantum*, bimonthly. Handbook. **Price:** $18.00/copy. ISSN: 1048-8820. **Circulation:** 10,000. **Advertising:** accepted ● *Science and Children*, 8/year. Journal. Includes reports on innovative teaching methods, experiments, research, and inexpensive teaching materials. **Price:** included in membership dues. ISSN: 0036-8148. **Circulation:** 24,000. **Advertising:** accepted. Alternate Formats: microform ● *Science Class*, monthly. Newsletter. Alternate Formats: online ● *Science Scope*, 7/year. Journal. Reports on innovative teaching methods, experiments, and educational theory. Includes research reports and index of advertisers. **Price:** $15.00/year for subscribers to another NSTA journal. ISSN: 0887-2376. **Circulation:** 16,000. **Advertising:** accepted ● *The Science Teacher*, 9/year. Journal. Includes reports on innovative teaching methods, experiments, research, and inexpensive teaching materials. **Price:** included in membership dues. ISSN: 0036-8555. **Circulation:** 30,000. **Advertising:** accepted. Alternate Formats: microform ● Annual Report, annual. Alternate Formats: online ● Also publishes curriculum development and professional materials, teaching aids, career booklets, and audiovisual aids. **Conventions/Meetings:** annual conference (exhibits) - 2009 Mar. 19-22, New Orleans, LA ● regional meeting - 3-4/year.

9115 ■ School Science and Mathematics Association (SSMA)

c/o Dr. Julie Thomas, Co-Exec. Dir.
Oklahoma State Univ.
College of Education
245 Willard
Stillwater, OK 74078
Ph: (405)744-7396
Fax: (405)744-6290
E-mail: office@ssma.org
URL: http://www.ssma.org
Contact: Dr. Julie Thomas, Co-Exec. Dir.
Founded: 1901. **Members:** 600. **Membership Dues:** regular, in U.S., $50 (annual) ● regular, outside U.S., $60 (annual) ● student, $25 (annual). **Staff:** 1. **Budget:** $180,000. **Multinational. Description:** Science and mathematics teachers at elementary through college levels and persons involved in teacher education. Works to facilitate the dissemination of knowledge in mathematics and the sciences; to encourage critical thinking and use of the scientific method; to emphasize the interdependence of mathematics and the sciences in education, research, writing, and curriculum development; to provide the means for dialogue among teachers of mathematics and the sciences; to identify and help solve problems common to science and mathematics education. Makes available information concerning selection, organization and use of instructional materials and methods in the sciences and mathematics; plans, organizes, administers, and evaluates projects that conform with the aims of science and mathematics education. Works for the improvement of the professional qualifications of teachers in the sciences and mathematics; encourages research in science and mathematics education; informs teachers, administrators, and the public of studies that suggest better ways for students to learn mathematics and science. **Libraries: Type:** reference. **Holdings:** 41. **Awards:** Integration. **Frequency:** annual. **Type:** trophy. **Recipient:** for outstanding contribution to the integration of science and mathematics ● Mallinson. **Frequency:** annual. **Type:** trophy. **Recipient:** for outstanding service to the organization. **Computer Services:** Mailing lists. **Affiliated With:** American Association for the Advancement of Science. **Formerly:** Central Association of Science and Mathematics Teachers. **Publications:** *School Science and Mathematics*, 8/year. Journal. **Price:** $76.00 in U.S.; $90.00 outside U.S. ISSN: 0036-6803. **Advertising:** accepted. **Conventions/Meetings:** annual convention (exhibits).

9116 ■ Triangle Coalition for Science and Technology Education (TCSTE)

1840 Wilson Blvd., Ste.201
Arlington, VA 22201
Ph: (703)516-5960
Free: (800)582-0115
Fax: (703)516-5969
E-mail: tricoal@trianglecoalition.org
URL: http://www.triangle-coalition.org
Contact: Cynthia Howell, Pres.
Founded: 1985. **Members:** 160. **Membership Dues:** organization (based on annual operating budget), $150-$6,000 (annual). **Staff:** 6. **Budget:** $925,000. **Regional Groups:** 25. **State Groups:** 25. **Local Groups:** 35. **National Groups:** 75. **Description:** A consortium of national organizations representing the business sector, scientific and engineering societies, and educational associations. Aims to improve the quality of science and technology education for all students. Collects, organizes, and disseminates information on problems and identifies solutions that will improve science and technology education. Maintains Local Alliance Networking Project, an interactive system of community-based action groups that coordinate activities between schools and local businesses, industry, and government agencies. Operates the Scientific Work Experience Programs for Teachers (SWEPT), which provides technical assistance and printed materials to local programs. Administers an Albert Einstein Distinguished Education Fellowship program for elementary and secondary mathematics, science and technology teachers. **Task Forces:** Congressional Liaison. **Publications:** *A Guide for Planning a Volunteer Program for Science, Mathematics, and Technology Education* ● *Alliances*. Brochure ● *Grants for Mathematics and Science Education: Where to Look and How to Win*. **Price:** $2.50/copy ● *Guide for Building an Alliance for Science, Mathematics, and Technology Education* ● *Reports of the Congressional Liaison Task Force* ● *Scientific Work Experiences for Professional Teach-*

ers. **Price:** $7.00/copy; $10.00/copy (with video) ● *Triangle Coalition Electronic Bulletin*, weekly. **Price:** $100.00/year. **Circulation:** 475 ● *Triangle Coalition Local Directory* ● *Triangle Coalition Network News*, bimonthly. Newsletter. **Circulation:** 3,000 ● *What We Know About Science Teaching and Learning.* **Price:** $5.00/copy.

9117 ■ Tripoli Rocketry Association (TRA)
PO Box 87
Bellevue, NE 68005
Ph: (402)884-9530
Fax: (402)884-9531
E-mail: info@tripoli.org
URL: http://www.tripoli.org
Contact: Paul Holmes, Tripoli Motor Testing Chm.
Founded: 1964. **Members:** 4,000. **Membership Dues:** junior, $30 (annual) ● senior, $70 (annual). **Staff:** 10. **Budget:** $90,000. **Regional Groups:** 105. **Languages:** Chinese, English, French, German, Japanese, Spanish. **Description:** Secondary school and college students; college graduates in both technical and teaching occupations. Devoted to cooperative technology and amateur high-powered rocketry. Conducts research and popular science programs. **Libraries: Type:** not open to the public. **Computer Services:** database. **Committees:** Advanced Projects; Rocket Science; Rocketry; Safety. **Supersedes:** Tripoli Science Association. **Publications:** *Rockets*, bimonthly. Magazine. **Price:** $6.95/copy in U.S.; $8.95/copy in Canada; $10.95/copy in Australia. **Advertising:** accepted ● *Tripoli Report*, periodic. Newsletter. Includes membership communications, board minutes and information on elections. **Price:** included in membership dues. **Circulation:** 4,000. **Conventions/Meetings:** annual conference - always August ● annual convention (exhibits).

Secondary Education

9118 ■ Alliance for Excellent Education
1201 Connecticut Ave. NW, Ste.901
Washington, DC 20036
Ph: (202)828-0828
Fax: (202)828-0821
E-mail: alliance@all4ed.org
URL: http://www.all4ed.org
Contact: Bob Wise, Pres.
Founded: 1999. **Description:** Aims to promote high school transformation to make it possible for every child to graduate prepared for postsecondary education and success in life. Addresses the problems of low literacy skills, poorly prepared teachers, absence of academic and social supports, lack of motivation and other roots of student failure. Advocates to reform America's secondary education system. **Telecommunication Services:** electronic mail, wise@all4ed.org. **Publications:** *Straight A's: Public Education: Policy and Progress*, biweekly. Newsletter. Focuses on education news and events both in Washington, D.C. and around the country. Alternate Formats: online ● Reports. Alternate Formats: online.

Security Training

9119 ■ Academy of Security Educators and Trainers (ASET)
PO Box 802
Berryville, VA 22611-0802
Ph: (540)554-2540
Fax: (540)554-2558
URL: http://www.asetcse.org
Contact: Dr. Richard W. Kobetz CST, Exec. Dir.
Founded: 1980. **Members:** 300. **Membership Dues:** individual, $50 (annual) ● life, $500 ● original application, $55. **Staff:** 1. **Budget:** $20,000. **Languages:** English, Spanish. **Multinational. Description:** Persons supporting security education and training. Promotes and aids in the development of security degree programs and training courses in colleges, universities, and industries. Facilitates dialogue among teachers, trainers, and practitioners; acts as resource for legislative bodies. **Awards:** Certified Security Trainer Award. **Frequency:** annual. **Type:** recognition. **Recipient:** for men and women in the security field ● **Type:** grant. **Recipient:** for research. **Committees:** Certification; Legislation; Research; Technology. **Formerly:** (2004) Academy of Security Educators and Trainees. **Publications:** *ASET Membership*, annual. Membership Directory ● *Bibliography for Security Trainers.* Monograph ● *The Educator*, quarterly. Newsletter ● *Professional Certifications.* Monograph. **Price:** $10.00. **Conventions/Meetings:** annual meeting and symposium (exhibits).

Service

9120 ■ National Service-Learning Partnership (NSLP)
c/o Academy for Educational Development
1825 Connecticut Ave. NW, Ste.800
Washington, DC 20009-5721
Ph: (202)884-8356
E-mail: nslp@aed.org
URL: http://www.service-learningpartnership.org
Contact: Nelda Brown, Exec. Dir.
Founded: 2001. **Members:** 8,500. **Description:** Works to educate, organize, and mobilize service-learning supporters around a strategic agenda that promotes and strengthens the practice of service-learning. Strengthens the impact of service-learning on young people's learning and development, especially their academic and civic preparation. Supports members sharing resources, organizing change, and sponsoring innovation. **Publications:** *Service-Learning Advances*, monthly. Newsletter. Offers information about K-12 service-learning. Alternate Formats: online ● *We Make the Road by Walking*, annual. Annual Report ● Videos. **Price:** free.

Sewing

9121 ■ Sewing Educator Alliance (SEA)
c/o Sewing Dealers Trade Association/Vacuum Dealers Trade Association
2724 2nd Ave.
Des Moines, IA 50313
Free: (800)473-9464
Fax: (515)282-4483
E-mail: mail@vdta.com
URL: http://www.sewingeducators.com
Contact: Cindy Cummins, Contact
Founded: 2003. **Members:** 2,200. **Membership Dues:** regular, $75 (annual). **Description:** Bringing together professional sewing educators. Promotes sewing awareness through education. Seeks to expand personal business, technology and teaching skills, including knowledge of the home sewing industry. Provides networking opportunities to share and learn from other educators in the home sewing industry.

Sexual Freedom

9122 ■ Center For Sex and Culture
c/o Dr. Carol Queen, Founder
2215-R Market St., PMB 455
San Francisco, CA 94114
Ph: (415)255-1155
E-mail: info@centerforsexandculture.com
URL: http://www.sexandculture.org
Contact: Dr. Carol Queen, Founder
Description: Provides non-judgmental, sex-positive sexuality education and support. **Libraries: Type:** reference. **Holdings:** archival material. **Subjects:** sex and culture. **Conventions/Meetings:** workshop.

Sexual Health

9123 ■ National Abstinence Education Association (NAEA)
1701 Pennsylvania Ave. NW, Ste.300
Washington, DC 20006
Ph: (202)248-5420
Fax: (202)580-6559
E-mail: info@abstinenceassociation.org
URL: http://www.abstinenceassociation.org
Contact: Valerie Huber, Exec. Dir.
Founded: 2006. **Membership Dues:** organization, $200 (annual) ● individual, $100 (annual) ● student, $30 (annual). **Description:** Works to serve, support and represent individuals and organizations in the practice of abstinence education. Offers professional development opportunities for abstinence educators. Improves the public understanding and perception of abstinence education. Provides research and initiates studies that impact abstinence education.

Sexuality

9124 ■ International Association for the Study of Sexuality, Culture and Society (IASSCS)
c/o Niels Teunis, Sec.-Treas.
2017 Mission St., No. 300
San Francisco, CA 94110
Ph: (415)437-1473
E-mail: nielsft@sfsu.edu
URL: http://iasscs.sfsu.edu
Contact: Niels Teunis, Sec.-Treas.
Founded: 1997. **Membership Dues:** basic, $25 (annual). **Multinational. Description:** Promotes the study of sexual identity, desire, and experience in the context of specific social and cultural circumstances. Fosters research and educational collaboration across national and ethnic boundaries. Provides a forum for expanding and developing sexuality as a legitimate area of scholarship. **Telecommunication Services:** electronic mail, iasscs@sfsu.edu. **Publications:** *Culture, Health and Sexuality*, bimonthly. Journal. Deals with issues concerning all aspects of sexuality, culture, and health. **Price:** $40.00 developing country; $562.00 institutional; $534.00 institutional online; $233.00 personal. ISSN: 1369-1058. Alternate Formats: online ● Newsletter. Alternate Formats: online.

Slavic

9125 ■ American Association of Teachers of Slavic and East European Languages (AATSEEL)
PO Box 569
Beloit, WI 53512-0569
Ph: (608)361-9697 (610)328-8162
Fax: (608)361-9697
E-mail: aatseel@sbcglobal.net
URL: http://aatseel.org
Contact: Patricia L. Zody PhD, Exec. Dir.
Founded: 1940. **Members:** 1,450. **Membership Dues:** administrator, associate professor, $65 (annual) ● affiliate, $30 (annual) ● assistant professor, non-academic, $55 (annual) ● full professor, $75 (annual) ● independent scholar, retired/emeritus, student, $40 (annual) ● instructor/lecturer, $50 (annual) ● joint, $25 (annual) ● secondary school teacher, $45 (annual) ● sustaining, $200 (annual) ● benefactor - life, $1,000 ● institution, $60-$95 (annual) ● agency, $57-$90 (annual). **Staff:** 2. **Budget:** $100,000. **Local Groups:** 47. **Description:** Professors, researchers, teachers, graduate students, and university libraries. Encourages study of Slavic and East European languages, literature, and culture at the elementary, high school, and college levels. **Awards:** Distinguished Service. **Frequency:** annual. **Type:** recognition. **Recipient:** for outstanding service ● Excellence in Teaching. **Frequency:** annual. **Type:** recognition. **Recipient:** for outstanding teachers ● Outstanding Contribution to Scholarship. **Frequency:** annual. **Type:** recognition. **Recipient:** for outstanding contributions ● Outstanding Contribution to the Profession. **Frequency:** annual. **Type:** recognition. **Recipient:** for outstanding contributions. **Telecommunication Services:** electronic mail, sforres1@swarthmore.edu. **Sections:** College Methodology; High School Methodology; Linguistics; Literature and Literature Discussion. **Publications:** *Slavic and East*

European Journal, quarterly. Contains original research and review essays in the areas of Slavic and East European languages, literatures, cultures, linguistics, and methodology. **Advertising:** accepted ● Newsletter (in English and Russian), quarterly. Reports on study programs, teaching innovations, and association news. Includes calendar of events and list of employment opportunities. **Price:** included in membership dues; $32.00 /year for nonmembers. ISSN: 0001-0251. **Circulation:** 1,400. **Advertising:** accepted. Alternate Formats: online. **Conventions/ Meetings:** annual meeting, in conjunction with the Modern Language Association of America (exhibits).

Social Justice

9126 ■ Educating for Justice (EFJ)
601 Bangs Ave., Ste.601
Asbury Park, NJ 07712
Ph: (732)988-7322
Fax: (732)988-3288
E-mail: info@educatingforjustice.org
URL: http://www.educatingforjustice.org
Contact: Jim Keady, Co-Founder/Co-Dir.
Founded: 2000. **Multinational. Description:** Works to educate and empower people to take action to end social injustice. Develops, produces and distributes justice-oriented programming and content to the educational marketplace. Seeks to raise awareness about issues of justice and sparks efforts for social change. **Telecommunication Services:** electronic mail, jim@educatingforjustice.org. **Publications:** Newsletter, monthly. Alternate Formats: online ● Books ● Pamphlets ● Articles.

Social Studies

9127 ■ Center for Social Studies Education (CSSE)
901 Old Hickory Rd.
Pittsburgh, PA 15243
Ph: (412)341-1967
Fax: (412)341-6533
E-mail: jmstarr@adelphia.net
Contact: Jerold M. Starr, Exec. Off.
Founded: 1984. **Staff:** 2. **Budget:** $30,000. **Description:** Offers a range of materials and services to promote more and better reaching of the Vietnam War, its lessons and legacies. Award winning resources include textbooks, resource guide, teachers' manual with activities, teacher training handbook, teacher trainer videocassette, Vietnam veteran speakers bureaus and master teacher trainers. **Computer Services:** Mailing lists. **Affiliated With:** Citizens for Independent Public Broadcasting. **Publications:** *Lessons of the Vietnam War*. Book ● *Resources for Teaching the Vietnam War: An Annotated Guide*. Book ● *Teacher Trainer Handbook: Professional Development Workshops* ● *Teaching the Vietnam War: Classroom Strategies*. Video.

9128 ■ National Council for the Social Studies (NCSS)
8555 16th St., Ste.500
Silver Spring, MD 20910
Ph: (301)588-1800 (302)644-0546
Free: (800)683-0812
Fax: (301)588-2049
E-mail: ncss@ncss.org
URL: http://www.socialstudies.org
Contact: Susan Griffin, Exec. Dir.
Founded: 1921. **Members:** 25,000. **Membership Dues:** comprehensive - individual, international, $70 (annual) ● comprehensive - institution, $95 (annual) ● regular - individual, international, $59 (annual) ● regular - institution, $79 (annual) ● retired, first year teacher, student, $33 (annual). **Staff:** 17. **Budget:** $2,960,000. **Regional Groups:** 5. **State Groups:** 51. **Local Groups:** 57. **National Groups:** 4. **Description:** Teachers of elementary and secondary social studies, including instructors of civics, geography, history, law, economics, political science, psychology, sociology, and anthropology; interested others. Promotes the teaching of social studies to the best advantage of the student. **Libraries: Type:** not open to the public. **Holdings:** 150. **Subjects:** social studies education, publications, general education statistics. **Awards:** Carter G. Woodson Book Awards. **Frequency:** annual. **Type:** recognition. **Recipient:** for outstanding performance of teachers, researchers, and other worthy individuals and programs ● Christa McAuliffe Reach for the Stars Award. **Frequency:** annual. **Type:** grant. **Recipient:** for members ● Defense of Academic Freedom. **Frequency:** annual. **Type:** recognition. **Recipient:** to the teachers who have distinguished themselves in defending the principles of academic freedom in specific controversies ● Distinguished Career Research in the Social Studies. **Frequency:** annual. **Type:** recognition. **Recipient:** for outstanding research ● Exemplary Dissertation in Social Studies. **Frequency:** biennial. **Type:** recognition. **Recipient:** for the best dissertation ● Exemplary Research in Social Studies Award. **Frequency:** annual. **Type:** recognition. **Recipient:** for substantive scholarly inquiry in social studies education ● Fund for the Advancement of Social Studies Education (FASSE) Demonstration Project. **Frequency:** triennial. **Type:** grant ● Grant for the Enhancement of Geographic Literacy. **Frequency:** annual. **Type:** grant. **Recipient:** for outstanding performance of teachers, researchers, and other worthy individuals and programs ● James A. Michener Prize in Writing. **Frequency:** quinquennial. **Type:** recognition ● Jean Dresden Grambs Distinguished Career Research in Social Studies. **Frequency:** biennial. **Type:** recognition. **Recipient:** to professionals who have made extensive contributions to knowledge concerning significant areas of social studies education ● Outstanding Service. **Frequency:** annual. **Type:** recognition. **Recipient:** to members for outstanding long term service to the local, state, and regional councils ● Spirit of America. **Frequency:** annual. **Type:** recognition. **Computer Services:** Mailing lists, available for rent. **Telecommunication Services:** electronic mail, sgriffin@ncss.org. **Committees:** College and University Faculty Assembly; Council of State Social Studies Supervisors; International Assembly; National Social Studies Supervisors Association. **Publications:** *Expectations of Excellence: Curriculum Standards for Social Studies*, periodic. Book. Presents a model based on 10 thematic strands for achieving excellence in social studies. Explains the purpose, organization, utility of standards. **Price:** $12.75 for members; $15.00 for nonmembers. **Circulation:** 20,000. Also Cited As: *NCSS Curriculum Standards* ● *Social Education*, 7/year. Journal. Contains articles by scholars, curriculum designers, and teachers on all aspects of teaching and learning the social studies. **Price:** included in membership dues; $59.00 for nonmembers and institutions. ISSN: 0037-7724. **Circulation:** 20,000. **Advertising:** accepted ● *Social Studies and the Young Learner*, quarterly. Journal. Provides new and creative classroom activities, content, research, and theory for social studies teaching in grades K-6. **Price:** $20.00 /year for members (institutions); $37.00 /year for nonmembers (institutions). **Circulation:** 5,000 ● *The Social Studies Professional*, bimonthly. Newsletter. Covers council activities and news of the profession. **Price:** included in membership dues. **Circulation:** 21,000. **Advertising:** accepted ● *Teaching Social Issues*, semiannual. Bulletin ● *Theory and Research in Social Education*, quarterly. Journal. Provides scholarly articles and research findings about purposes, conditions, and effects of schooling and education about society. **Price:** $39.00 /year for nonmembers. ISSN: 0093-3104. **Circulation:** 1,000 ● Bulletin, semiannual. **Price:** included in membership dues. **Conventions/Meetings:** annual conference (exhibits) - 2008 Nov. 14-16, Houston, TX - **Avg. Attendance:** 4000; 2009 Nov. 13-15, Atlanta, GA - **Avg. Attendance:** 4000; 2010 Nov. 19-21, Denver, CO - **Avg. Attendance:** 4000.

9129 ■ Social Science Education Consortium (SSEC)
c/o National Council for the Social Studies
8555 16th St., Ste.500
Silver Spring, MD 20910
Ph: (301)588-1800
Free: (800)683-0812
Fax: (301)588-2049
E-mail: jdavis_ssec@msn.com
URL: http://www.socialstudies.org/ssec
Contact: Susan Griffin, Exec. Dir.
Founded: 1963. **Members:** 130. **Membership Dues:** invitational, $40 (annual) ● comprehensive (individual), $70 (annual) ● comprehensive (institution), $95 (annual) ● regular (individual), $59 (annual) ● regular (institution), $79 (annual) ● teacher, student, retired, $33 (annual). **Staff:** 10. **Budget:** $1,000,000. **Description:** Social scientists and educators. Improves the quality of social science education at all grade levels. Offers teacher-training programs in which individuals and groups are trained in social science/history content and innovative training approaches. Maintains a consultation program whereby SSEC staff, for a fee, travel to school districts to train educators. **Libraries: Type:** reference. **Holdings:** 5,000; audiovisuals, books, clippings, periodicals. **Subjects:** social studies education. **Telecommunication Services:** electronic mail, sgriffin@ncss.org. **Publications:** Books, 5/year. Includes curriculum resources for social studies. ● Brochures ● Papers ● Also publishes materials related to social science education, including curriculum units and instructional frameworks. **Conventions/Meetings:** annual conference, for academic papers and discussion groups on social science education.

Social Welfare

9130 ■ Council for Standards in Human Service Education (CSHSE)
PMB 703
1050 Larrabee Ave., Ste.104
Bellingham, WA 98225-7367
Ph: (360)650-3531
E-mail: jrheapes@hacc.edu
URL: http://www.cshse.org
Contact: John Heapes MA, Pres.
Founded: 1976. **Members:** 75. **Membership Dues:** program, $300 (annual). **Regional Groups:** 8. **Description:** Strives to improve the quality of human service education through the self-study and accreditation process. Reviews and accredits educational programs. Maintains National Standards in human service education. Provides access to consultants and technical assistance to members. **Libraries: Type:** reference. **Holdings:** monographs. **Subjects:** series on human services. **Awards:** Mary DiGiovanni Award. **Frequency:** annual. **Type:** recognition. **Recipient:** to exemplary degree-granting program in human services education that is a program accredited with the council. **Publications:** *CSHSE Bulletin*, quarterly. Newsletter. Features current information on trends, new publications, workshops and conferences, and other issues in human service education. ● *National Standards*, periodic ● Directory. Lists human service education programs in the United States. ● Monographs. Explores new developments in human service education and provides guidelines on administrative and program development. **Conventions/Meetings:** workshop, for faculty development in curriculum design, program policymaking, resource development, and program evaluation.

9131 ■ National Organization for Human Services (NOHS)
90 Madison St., Ste.206
Denver, CO 80206
Ph: (303)320-5430
Fax: (303)322-1455
E-mail: info@nationalhumanservices.org
URL: http://www.nationalhumanservices.org
Contact: Ms. Randall Moke, Mgr.
Founded: 1975. **Members:** 875. **Membership Dues:** regular, $95 (annual) ● student, $35 (annual) ● retired, $60 (annual) ● organization ($80 for additional individual), $190 (annual). **Staff:** 1. **Budget:** $100,000. **Regional Groups:** 6. **Description:** Human service professionals, faculty, and students.

Fosters excellence in teaching, research and curriculum planning in the human service area. Encourages and supports the development of local, state, and national human services organizations. Aids faculty and professional members in their career development. Provides a medium for cooperation and communication among members. Maintains registry of qualified consultants in human service education. Conducts professional development workshop. Operates speakers' bureau. **Awards:** David C. Maloney Scholarship. **Frequency:** annual. **Type:** scholarship. **Recipient:** to a current student member ● Lenore McNeer Award. **Frequency:** annual. **Type:** recognition. **Recipient:** for contributions to the field ● Miriam Clubok Award. **Frequency:** annual. **Type:** recognition. **Recipient:** to a member who has demonstrated outstanding leadership ● Outstanding Human Services Student. **Frequency:** annual. **Type:** recognition. **Recipient:** to a student who has demonstrated his/her commitment to the association's goals and to the profession. **Committees:** Awards; Education; Professional Development. **Formerly:** (1985) National Organization of Human Service Educators; (2006) National Organization for Human Service Education. **Publications:** *Human Service Education*, annual. Journal. Includes latest research in the profession. **Price:** $40.00/year. ISSN: 0890-5428. **Advertising:** accepted ● *The Link*, quarterly. Newsletter. Reports on program development, legislation, funding, professional issues, and news. Contains book reviews and calendar of events. **Price:** $100.00 for members; $150.00 for nonmembers. **Circulation:** 800 ● Also publishes brochure. **Conventions/Meetings:** annual conference (exhibits) - always October.

Social Work

9132 ■ Council on Sexual Orientation and Gender Expression (CSOGE)
c/o Council on Social Work Education
1725 Duke St., Ste.500
Alexandria, VA 22314-3457
Ph: (703)683-8080
Fax: (703)683-8099
E-mail: info@cswe.org
URL: http://www.cswe.org/CSWE/about/governance/councils/SOGE.htm
Contact: Michael LaSala PhD, Co-Chm.
Founded: 1980. **Members:** 9. **Description:** Social work students, faculty, and practitioners. Purposes are to: add material to the social work education curriculum on lesbian/gay history, politics, and personality in order to improve social work's effectiveness with regard to homosexuality; provide support to social workers, social work educators, and students, especially when they face antigay bias. Maintains speakers' bureau to address topics such as the change in the response of human service professionals toward homosexual rights and needs. A commission of the Council on Social Work Education (see separate entry). **Formerly:** (1984) Task Force on Lesbian/Gay Issues; (2001) Commission on Gay/Lesbian Issues in Social work Education; (2006) Commission on Sexual Orientation and Gender Expression. **Publications:** *Annotated Bibliography of Lesbian/Gay Reading*. **Conventions/Meetings:** semiannual meeting.

9133 ■ Council on Social Work Education (CSWE)
1725 Duke St., Ste.500
Alexandria, VA 22314-3457
Ph: (703)683-8080 (703)519-2066
Fax: (703)683-8099
E-mail: info@cswe.org
URL: http://www.cswe.org
Contact: Julia M. Watkins PhD, Exec. Dir.
Founded: 1952. **Members:** 3,500. **Membership Dues:** full, associate, $188 (annual) ● student, emeritus, $67 (annual). **Staff:** 32. **Description:** Graduate and undergraduate programs of social work education; national, regional, and local social welfare agencies; libraries and individuals. Formulates criteria and standards for all levels of social work education; accredits graduate and undergraduate social work programs; provides consulting to social work educators on curriculum, faculty recruitment and development, students and admissions, and teaching methods and materials. Conducts research and compiles data on social work education. **Publications:** *Journal of Social Work Education*, 3/year ● *Statistics on Social Work Education*, annual. Report ● Books ● Catalog ● Monographs ● Pamphlets ● Reports ● Also publishes teaching materials. **Conventions/Meetings:** annual convention (exhibits) - 2008 Oct. 29-Nov. 1, Philadelphia, PA - **Avg. Attendance:** 3000.

9134 ■ School Social Work Association of America (SSWAA)
PO Box 2072
Northlake, IL 60164
Ph: (847)289-4527 (847)289-4642
E-mail: sswaa@aol.com
URL: http://www.sswaa.org
Contact: Randy Fisher, Exec. Dir.
Membership Dues: affiliate, retired, $40 (annual) ● associate, full, $75 (annual) ● student, $25 (annual). **Description:** Promotes the profession of School Social Work and the professional development of School Social Workers. Enhances the educational experience of students and their families. Assists school social workers in creating linkages among home, school, and community. Influences public policy and educational issues. **Telecommunication Services:** electronic mail, info@sswaa.org. **Publications:** *SSWAA Bell*. Newsletter.

9135 ■ Society for Social Work and Research (SSWR)
11240 Waples Mill Rd., Ste.200
Fairfax, VA 22030
Ph: (703)352-7797
Fax: (703)359-7562
E-mail: info@sswr.org
URL: http://www.sswr.org
Contact: Jennifer Lewis, Admin. Dir.
Founded: 1993. **Members:** 1,300. **Membership Dues:** full, $100 (annual) ● student, $50 (annual). **Multinational. Description:** Promotes the development and dissemination of high quality research to improve the social welfare of all people. Encourages the design, implementation and dissemination of high quality research that addresses critical social practice and social policy issues. Fosters a support network among researchers conducting research on social work practice and social policy in the United States and around the world. Promotes increased research funding and training programs for social workers. **Awards:** Aaron Rosen Lectureship. **Frequency:** annual. **Type:** recognition. **Recipient:** for members who have accumulated a body of significant and innovative scholarship relevant to practice or effective utilization of research in practice ● Deborah K. Padgett Early Career Achievement Award. **Frequency:** annual. **Type:** recognition. **Recipient:** for individuals who have done innovative work and are making a notable influence in their field and in the profession ● Distinguished Achievement Award. **Frequency:** annual. **Type:** recognition. **Recipient:** to individuals for cumulative career accomplishments ● Doctoral Fellows Award. **Frequency:** annual. **Type:** recognition. **Recipient:** for doctoral students whose proposed dissertation research reflects innovative ideas and methodologies related to social work research, policy, or practice ● Excellence in Research Award/Best Scholarly Contribution. **Frequency:** annual. **Type:** recognition. **Recipient:** for outstanding social work research that advances knowledge with direct applications to practice, policy, and the resolution of social problems ● Outstanding Social Work Doctoral Dissertation Award. **Frequency:** annual. **Type:** recognition. **Recipient:** for dissertations exemplifying high standards in social work research and scholarship. **Telecommunication Services:** electronic mail, lewis@sswr.org. **Publications:** *Research on Social Work Practice*, bimonthly. Journal. **Price:** included in membership dues ● *SSWR News*. Newsletter. **Price:** included in membership dues. Alternate Formats: online.

Space

9136 ■ Federation of Galaxy Explorers (FOGE)
12609 Springloch Ct.
Silver Spring, MD 20904
Free: (877)761-1266
E-mail: info@foge.org
URL: http://www.foge.org
Contact: Mr. Nicholas Eftimiades, Founder/Chm.
Founded: 2002. **Membership Dues:** individual, $20 (annual). **Description:** Seeks to educate and inspire America's youth in space-related science and engineering. Aims to expand the frontiers of science and technology for the exploration and development of space. Establishes collaborative working relationships with different agencies that specialize in space and astronomical related fields. **Publications:** Newsletter, monthly. **Price:** included in membership dues. Alternate Formats: online.

Special Education

9137 ■ American Council on Rural Special Education (ACRES)
Montana Center on Disabilities/MSU-Billings
1500 Univ. Dr.
Billings, MT 59101
Ph: (406)657-2312 (435)797-0697
Free: (888)866-3822
Fax: (406)657-2313
E-mail: inquiries@acres-sped.org
URL: http://www.acres-sped.org
Contact: David Forbush, Chm.
Founded: 1981. **Members:** 200. **Membership Dues:** individual, $75 (annual) ● individual (international), $81 (annual) ● state/regional agency, school building, university, $100 (annual) ● state/regional agency, school building, university (international), $106 (annual) ● student, $25 (annual). **Description:** Represents rural special educators and administrators, parents of students with disabilities, and university and state department personnel. Works to enhance direct services to rural individuals and agencies serving exceptional students and to increase educational opportunities for rural students with special needs; works to develop models for serving at-risk rural students, and a system for forecasting futures for rural special education and to plan creative service delivery alternatives. Provides professional development opportunities; disseminates information on the current needs of rural special education. Conducts task forces on specific rural problems and professional training. **Libraries: Type:** reference. **Holdings:** 22. **Awards:** Exemplary Rural Special Education Program Award. **Frequency:** annual. **Type:** recognition. **Recipient:** must be related to rural special education ● Outstanding Special Educator Award. **Frequency:** annual. **Type:** recognition. **Recipient:** to a person whose contribution to the field of rural special education exemplifies outstanding work for the benefit of those placed in rural areas ● **Frequency:** annual. **Type:** scholarship. **Recipient:** for rural teachers. **Computer Services:** database ● mailing lists. **Telecommunication Services:** electronic mail, davidf@cc.usu.edu. **Publications:** *Rural Special Education Quarterly*. Journal. Contains articles concerning federal and other events relevant to rural individuals with disabilities and progressive service delivery systems. **Price:** $75.00 /year for individuals; $100.00 /year for libraries; $81.00/year (international). ISSN: 8756-8705. **Advertising:** accepted ● *RuraLink*, quarterly. Newsletter. Provides information on improving services to rural individuals with disabilities. Includes book reviews and calendar of events. **Price:** free for members. Alternate Formats: online ● Books. **Conventions/Meetings:** annual A New Idea for Rural Special Education - conference (exhibits) - always March.

9138 ■ AVKO Dyslexia Research Foundation (AVKOEFR)
3084 W Willard Rd., Ste.W
Clio, MI 48420-7801

Ph: (810)686-9283
Free: (866)AVKO-612
Fax: (810)686-1101
E-mail: donmccabe@aol.com
URL: http://www.avko.org
Contact: Don McCabe, Research Dir.

Founded: 1974. **Members:** 500. **Membership Dues:** individual, $25 (annual) ● individual, $50 (biennial) ● institution, $100 (annual) ● institution, $200 (biennial). **Staff:** 5. **Budget:** $200,000. **Description:** Teachers and individuals interested in helping others learn to read and spell and in developing reading training materials for individuals with dyslexia or other learning disabilities using a method involving audio, visual, kinesthetic, and oral (AVKO) techniques. Offers advice on the techniques of tutoring, classroom teaching, diagnosis, and remediation. Conducts research into the causes of reading, spelling, and writing disabilities. Publishes and disseminates information on research. Provides a reading and spelling center where children and adults with educational deficiencies can receive diagnostic attention and remediation. Sponsors adult community education courses to train adults in tutoring their spouses or children in reading and spelling skills. Maintains speakers' bureau; compiles statistics. **Libraries: Type:** reference. **Holdings:** 4,000. **Subjects:** special education, reading, and spelling. **Awards: Type:** recognition. **Telecommunication Services:** electronic mail, avkoemail@aol.com. **Publications:** *AVKO Educational Research Foundation—Newsletter*, quarterly. Covers techniques and materials for teaching reading and spelling to dyslexics and the learning disabled. **Price:** included in membership dues. **Circulation:** 500 ● *If It Is To Be, It Is Up To Me To Do It* ● *The Patterns of English Spelling* ● *Sequential Spelling I-VII* ● *The Teaching of Reading: A Continuum from Kindergarten through College* ● *To Teach A Dyslexic*. **Conventions/Meetings:** annual conference (exhibits).

9139 ■ Council of Administrators of Special Education (CASE)

c/o Dr. Luann L. Purcell, Exec. Dir.
Fort Valley State Univ.
1005 State Univ. Dr.
Fort Valley, GA 31030
Ph: (478)825-7667 (816)537-5534
Free: (800)585-1753
Fax: (478)825-7811
E-mail: lpurcell@bellsouth.net
URL: http://www.casecec.org
Contact: Dr. Luann L. Purcell, Exec. Dir.

Founded: 1951. **Members:** 5,000. **Staff:** 2. **Budget:** $825,000. **State Groups:** 43. **Description:** Current members of Council for Exceptional Children (see separate entry) who are administrators, directors, supervisors, and/or coordinators of programs, schools, or classes of special education for exceptional children; college faculty and graduate students whose major responsibility is the professional preparation of administrators of special education; individuals interested in special education. Promotes professional leadership, provides opportunity for study of problems common to its members, and disseminates information that will develop improved services for exceptional children. Sponsors regional training institutes for special education administrator leadership skill development. Maintains speakers' bureau on topics concerning issues in administration of programs for exceptional, handicapped, and gifted children. **Libraries: Type:** not open to the public; reference. **Holdings:** archival material. **Awards:** Harrie Selznek Outstanding Administrator of the Year. **Frequency:** annual. **Type:** monetary. **Recipient:** for outstanding leadership at the international level with emphasis on involvement at the state/provincial level and national/international level. **Telecommunication Services:** electronic bulletin board, CASE.NEWS ● electronic mail, terryallee@comcast.net. **Publications:** *InCASE*, bimonthly. Newsletter. Covers council activities and news. **Price:** included in membership dues. **Circulation:** 5,300. **Advertising:** accepted ● *Journal of Special Education Leadership*, semiannual. Concerned with programs and developments affecting the special education field. **Price:** included in membership dues. **Circulation:** 5,300. **Advertising:** accepted ● Monographs ● Also publishes special education program management packets. **Conventions/Meetings:** Conference in Special Education (exhibits).

9140 ■ Council for Children with Behavioral Disorders (CCBD)

1110 N Glebe Rd., Ste.300
Arlington, VA 22201-5704
Ph: (703)620-3660 (480)965-6893
Free: (800)224-6830
Fax: (703)264-9494
E-mail: sarup.mathur@asu.edu
URL: http://www.ccbd.net
Contact: Dr. Sarup Mathur, Pres.

Founded: 1962. **Members:** 8,500. **Membership Dues:** professional, $22 (annual) ● student, $15 (annual). **Regional Groups:** 10. **State Groups:** 52. **Description:** A division of The Council for Exceptional Children. Works to promote and facilitate the education and welfare of children and youth with behavioral and emotional disorders, and to promote professional growth and research as a means to better understand the problems of these children. Acts with CEC to improve educational programs for all exceptional children. **Awards:** Carl Fenichel Memorial Research Competition. **Frequency:** annual. **Type:** recognition. **Recipient:** for outstanding graduate student paper ● Outstanding Professional Performance Award. **Frequency:** annual. **Type:** recognition. **Telecommunication Services:** electronic mail, jaime@ccbd.net ● additional toll-free number, membership, (888)232-7733 ● teletype, (703)264-9446. **Publications:** *Behavioral Disorders*, quarterly. Journal. Provides information related to research and issues relevant to students with emotional/behavioral disorders. **Price:** included in membership dues; $20.00 /year for nonmembers; $50.00 /year for institutions; $12.50/copy for nonmembers. ISSN: 0198-7429. **Circulation:** 9,300. **Advertising:** accepted ● *Beyond Behavior*, 3/year. Journal. Focuses on issues faced by direct service providers in the field. **Price:** $25.00 for nonmembers; $40.00 for institutions; included in membership dues. **Circulation:** 8,600. **Advertising:** accepted ● Newsletter, quarterly. Provides information on division activities. Includes convention and conference announcements. **Price:** included in membership dues. **Circulation:** 8,700. Alternate Formats: online ● Handbook, periodic. Provides information and guidance to the officers, standing committee chairs, and other appointees of CCBD to fulfill their duties. **Conventions/Meetings:** annual conference, in conjunction with CEC (exhibits) - always spring ● biennial conference - always fall.

9141 ■ Council for Exceptional Children (CEC)

1110 N Glebe Rd., Ste.300
Arlington, VA 22201-5704
Ph: (703)620-3660 (703)264-9408
Free: (888)232-7733
Fax: (703)264-9494
E-mail: service@cec.sped.org
URL: http://www.cec.sped.org
Contact: Mary Ruth Coleman, Pres.

Founded: 1922. **Members:** 50,000. **Membership Dues:** student, $66 (annual) ● associate, retired, $87 (annual) ● professional, $108-$120 (annual) ● premier, $182-$201 (annual) ● joint, $193-$211 (annual). **Staff:** 90. **State Groups:** 59. **Local Groups:** 1,012. **Description:** Administrators, teachers, parents, and others who work with and on behalf of children with disabilities and/or gifts. Seeks to improve the educational success for individuals with exceptionalities - children, youth, and young adults with disabilities and/or gifts. Advocates for appropriate government policies; provides information to the media. Operates the ERIC Clearinghouse on Disabilities and Gifted Education, and the National Clearinghouse for Professions in Special Education. Develops programs to help teachers, administrators, and related services professionals improve their practice. **Libraries: Type:** reference; open to the public. **Holdings:** articles, books, periodicals. **Subjects:** special education, gifted education. **Awards:** Business Award. **Frequency:** annual. **Type:** recognition. **Recipient:** for businesses/corporations ● Clarissa Hug Teacher of the Year. **Frequency:** annual. **Type:** monetary. **Recipient:** for outstanding teachers ● Elizabeth Wetzel Scholarship. **Frequency:** annual. **Type:** scholarship ● J.E. Wallace Wallin Special Education Lifetime Achievement. **Frequency:** annual. **Type:** monetary ● Joan Wald Baaken Award. **Frequency:** annual. **Type:** recognition ● Outstanding Leadership. **Frequency:** annual. **Type:** recognition ● Outstanding Public Service Award. **Frequency:** annual. **Type:** recognition. **Recipient:** for outstanding service ● Special Education Research. **Frequency:** annual. **Type:** recognition. **Computer Services:** database, ERIC. **Telecommunication Services:** electronic mail, mary_ruth-coleman@unc.edu. **Boards:** Directors. **Formerly:** (1968) Association of Educators for Homebound and Hospitalized Children; (1979) Division on Physically Handicapped, Homebound and Hospitalized; (1993) Division for Physically Handicapped. **Publications:** *Exceptional Child Education Resources*, quarterly. Journal. Includes abstracts of book, non-print media, and journal literature. Alternate Formats: online ● *Exceptional Children*, quarterly. Journal. Covers special education and research. **Price:** included in membership dues; $125.00 /year for nonmembers; $150.00 /year for institutions and libraries; $20.00/copy for nonmembers. Alternate Formats: online ● *SmartBrief*, 3/week. Newsletter. Includes news from hundreds of top sources created for special education professionals. **Price:** free. Alternate Formats: online ● *Teaching Exceptional Children*, bimonthly. Journal. Includes classroom-oriented information about instructional methods, materials, and techniques for students of all ages with special needs. **Price:** included in membership dues; $135.00 /year for nonmembers; $170.00 /year for institutions and libraries; $25.00/copy for nonmembers. Alternate Formats: online ● Audiotapes ● Books ● Films ● Videos ● Also publishes search reprints, other materials relevant to teaching exceptional children, microfilms, and publications catalog. **Conventions/Meetings:** annual conference ● annual convention (exhibits) - always April.

9142 ■ Council of Parent Attorneys and Advocates (COPAA)

PO Box 6767
Towson, MD 21285
Ph: (443)451-5270
Fax: (443)451-2680
E-mail: membership@copaa.org
URL: http://www.copaa.org
Contact: Selene Almazan Esq., Chair

Membership Dues: advocate/parent/other, $50 (annual) ● attorney, $150 (annual) ● organization, $400 (annual). **Description:** Secures high quality educational services for children with disabilities. Enables parents to work more effectively with school personnel, advocates and attorneys to plan and obtain effective educational programs for their children with disabilities. Establishes methods to obtain and exchange necessary information, training and consultation relevant to planning and obtaining effective educational programs. **Computer Services:** Mailing lists. **Committees:** Advocates; Amicus; Awards; Government Relations; Training. **Programs:** Special Education Advocacy Training (SEAT) Grant. **Conventions/Meetings:** annual conference.

9143 ■ Division on Career Development and Transition (DCDT)

c/o Council for Exceptional Children
PO Box 79026
Baltimore, MD 21279-0026
Free: (888)232-7733
Fax: (703)264-9494
E-mail: cathoma@vcu.edu
URL: http://www.dcdt.org
Contact: Colleen Thoma PhD, Pres.

Founded: 1979. **Members:** 2,000. **State Groups:** 25. **Description:** A division of The Council for Exceptional Children. Professionals and paraprofessionals involved in career development and transition of exceptional children, youth, and adults; students training in the field. Promotes professional growth, research, legislation, and information dissemination; encourages interaction among persons and organizations involved in the career development of exceptional individuals. **Awards:** DCDT Employer of the Year. **Frequency:** annual. **Type:** recognition ● DCDT Field Initiated Research Award. **Frequency:** annual. **Type:** recognition ● DCDT Teacher of the Year. **Frequency:** annual. **Type:** recognition ● Donn Brolin Award for State/Province Leadership and Service. **Frequency:** annual. **Type:** recognition ● Marc Gold Award. **Frequency:** annual. **Type:** recognition ● Oliver P. Kolstoe Award. **Frequency:** annual. **Type:** recognition. **Telecommunication Services:** teletype, (703)264-9446. **Formerly:** (1993) Division on Career Development of The Council for Exceptional Children; (1994) Division on Career Development and Transition of the Council for Exceptional Children. **Publications:** *Career Development for Exceptional Individuals*, semiannual. Journal. Covers current research and practice in career development and transition issues for exceptional individuals. **Price:** included in membership dues; $20.00 /year for nonmembers. ISSN: 0885-7288. **Circulation:** 2,800. **Advertising:** accepted ● *DCDT Network*, 3/year. Newsletter. **Price:** included in membership dues. **Circulation:** 2,600. **Conventions/Meetings:** biennial conference - always fall of odd-numbered years ● annual meeting, held in conjunction with CEC (exhibits).

9144 ■ Division for Early Childhood of the Council for Exceptional Children (DEC CEC)

27 Ft. Missoula Rd., Ste.2
Missoula, MT 59804
Ph: (406)543-0872
Fax: (406)543-0887
E-mail: dec@dec-sped.org
URL: http://www.dec-sped.org
Contact: Sarah Mulligan, Exec. Dir.

Founded: 1973. **Members:** 5,000. **Membership Dues:** professional, $25 (annual) ● student, $12 (annual) ● associate, $12. **Staff:** 4. **State Groups:** 30. **Description:** Represents individuals who work with or on behalf of children with special needs, birth through age eight, and their families. Promotes policies and advances evidence-based practices that support families and enhance the optimal development of young children who have or are at risk for developmental delays and disabilities. **Telecommunication Services:** electronic mail, sarah.mulligan@dec-sped.org ● teletype, (703)264-9446. **Publications:** *Journal of Early Intervention*, quarterly. Provides information on current research and practice for individuals who work with young children with special needs. Includes book reviews. **Price:** included in membership dues; $50.00/year for individual nonmembers; $70.00 /year for institutions. ISSN: 0885-3460. **Circulation:** 7,000. **Advertising:** accepted ● *Young Exceptional Children*, quarterly. Magazine. Provides information to teachers, early care and education personnel, administrators, therapists, family members, and others who work with children. **Price:** included in membership dues; $20.00 individual nonmembers; $35.00 for institutions. ISSN: 1096-2506. **Circulation:** 6,700. **Conventions/Meetings:** annual International Early Childhood Conference on Children With Special Needs (exhibits) - always fall ● annual meeting, held in conjunction with CEC (exhibits) - always spring.

9145 ■ Division on Visual Impairments (DVI)

c/o Council for Exceptional Children
1110 N Glebe Rd., Ste.300
Arlington, VA 22201-5704
Ph: (703)620-3660
Free: (800)224-6830
Fax: (703)264-9494
E-mail: ellynross@comcast.net
URL: http://www.cec.sped.org
Contact: Dr. Ellyn Ross PhD, Pres.

Founded: 1954. **Members:** 1,000. **Membership Dues:** professional, $20 (annual) ● student, $5 (annual). **State Groups:** 5. **Description:** Serves as a division of the Council for Exceptional Children. (See Separate Entry.) Teachers, college faculty members, administrators and supervisors, and others concerned with the education and welfare of children and youth with visual impairments. **Awards:** Distinguished Service Award. **Frequency:** annual. **Type:** recognition ● Exemplary Advocate Award. **Frequency:** annual. **Type:** recognition ● Outstanding Dissertation of the Year. **Frequency:** annual. **Type:** recognition ● Outstanding Student of the Year. **Frequency:** annual. **Type:** recognition ● Outstanding Teacher of the Year. **Frequency:** annual. **Type:** recognition. **Recipient:** for excellence in instructing students with blindness/ visual impairment. **Telecommunication Services:** TDD, (703)264-9446 ● additional toll-free number, 888232-7733. **Formerly:** (1976) Council for the Education of the Partially Seeing; (1992) Division for the Visually Handicapped; (1997) Division on Visual Handicaps. **Publications:** *DVI Quarterly*. Newsletter. Covers current developments in education of children and youth with visual impairments, and political action updates. **Price:** included in membership dues. **Circulation:** 1,100. **Advertising:** accepted. **Conventions/Meetings:** annual meeting, held in conjunction with CEC (exhibits) - always spring.

9146 ■ Inter-American Conductive Education Association (IACEA)

PO Box 3169
Toms River, NJ 08756-3169
Ph: (732)797-2566
Free: (800)824-2232
Fax: (732)797-2599
E-mail: info@iacea.org
URL: http://www.iacea.org
Contact: Patrick F. Riley, Pres./CEO

Founded: 1992. **Membership Dues:** interested party, student, $10 (annual) ● professional, organization, parent, grandparent, $25 (annual) ● patron, $50 (annual) ● benefactor, conductive education center, $100 (annual). **Multinational. Description:** Promotes and disseminates the principles of conductive education using the services of parents, conductors, therapists, teachers, and other related health care professionals. Qualifies trained conductors as new professionals to obtain health care, Medicare, Medicaid, and private health insurance reimbursement. Trains and certifies conductive education practitioners working in the United States and Canada. **Telecommunication Services:** electronic mail, patriley@iacea.org. **Publications:** Newsletter. **Price:** included in membership dues.

9147 ■ National Association of Private Special Education Centers (NAPSEC)

1522 K St. NW, Ste.1032
Washington, DC 20005
Ph: (202)408-3338
Fax: (202)408-3340
E-mail: napsec@aol.com
URL: http://www.napsec.org
Contact: Sherry L. Kolbe, CEO/Exec. Dir.

Founded: 1971. **Members:** 300. **Membership Dues:** regular (based on school budget), $960-$2,070 (annual) ● sustaining, $2,163 (annual) ● contributing, $2,472 (annual) ● friend, $2,833 (annual) ● gold, $3,708 (annual) ● platinum, $5,150 (annual). **Staff:** 5. **Budget:** $600,000. **State Groups:** 9. **Description:** Represents over 300 private special programs nationally, and over 600 at the state level, through its Council of Affiliated State Associations. Serves private early intervention services, schools, residential therapeutic centers, and adult living centers. Promotes excellence in educational opportunities for children with disabilities by enhancing the role of private special education as a vital component of the nation's educational system. Strives to educate the public about the education and therapeutic services needed for individuals with disabilities. **Awards:** Educator of the Year. **Frequency:** annual. **Type:** recognition. **Recipient:** for outstanding educators ● Executive of the Year. **Frequency:** annual. **Type:** recognition. **Recipient:** for outstanding executives. **Computer Services:** database, free information of placement options for a student with a disability. **Committees:** Conference Planning; Development; Governmental Affairs; Public Awareness. **Formerly:** (2001) National Association of Private Schools for Exceptional Children. **Publications:** *NAPSEC News*, 3/year. Newsletter. Reports association and member news. **Price:** included in membership dues ● *National Issues Service*, monthly. Newsletter. Contains legislative update and membership news. ● Membership Directory, biennial. **Price:** $20.00/copy. **Conventions/Meetings:** annual conference (exhibits) - always January ● annual Government Affairs - conference and meeting - always spring, Washington, DC.

9148 ■ National Association of Special Education Teachers (NASET)

1250 Connecticut Ave. NW, Ste.200
Washington, DC 20036
Free: (800)754-4421
E-mail: contactus@naset.org
URL: http://www.naset.org
Contact: Dr. Roger Pierangelo, Co-Exec. Dir.

Membership Dues: special education teacher, affiliate, professor, $45 (annual) ● student, $39 (annual) ● international, $49 (annual) ● special education teacher, affiliate, professor, $85 (biennial) ● student, $75 (biennial) ● international, $95 (biennial). **Description:** Provides support and assistance to professionals who teach children with special needs. Fosters exceptional teaching for exceptional children. Seeks to promote standards of excellence and innovation in special education research, practice, and policy. **Libraries: Type:** reference. **Awards:** Certificate of Merit for Excellence in Special Education. **Frequency:** annual. **Type:** recognition. **Recipient:** to schools that have exhibited excellence in the education of exceptional students ● Distinguished Service Award in Special Education. **Frequency:** annual. **Type:** recognition. **Recipient:** to an individual who has made a commitment to educate and advocate for children with disabilities and their families ● Excellence in Special Education Award. **Frequency:** annual. **Type:** recognition. **Recipient:** to organizations who have made a commitment to educate and advocate for children with disabilities and their families ● Exemplary Service Award. **Frequency:** annual. **Type:** recognition. **Recipient:** to members who have distinguished themselves in the field of special education ● Outstanding Graduate Student Performance Award. **Frequency:** annual. **Type:** recognition. **Recipient:** to graduate students who are entering the field of teaching with degrees in special education ● Outstanding Special Education Teacher Award. **Frequency:** annual. **Type:** recognition. **Recipient:** for special education teachers who have demonstrated outstanding achievement as a teacher in the field of special education. **Publications:** *Classroom Management Series*. Articles. Provides teachers with practical guidelines covering a variety of topics and supportive information. Alternate Formats: online ● *The Special Educator e-Journal*, 10/year. Contains current information in the field of special education. **Price:** included in membership dues. Alternate Formats: online.

9149 ■ National Association of State Directors of Special Education (NASDSE)

Address Unknown since 2008

Founded: 1938. **Members:** 211. **Membership Dues:** basic affiliate, $70 (annual) ● enhanced affiliate, $245 (annual). **Staff:** 20. **Budget:** $5,000,000. **Description:** Professional society of state directors; consultants, supervisors, and administrators who have statewide responsibilities for administering special education programs. Provides services to state agencies to facilitate their efforts to maximize educational outcomes for individuals with disabilities. **Telecommunication Services:** TDD, (703)519-7008. **Committees:** Legislation. **Publications:** *Counterpoint*, quarterly. Newspaper. **Price:** $20.00/year. **Advertising:** accepted. **Conventions/Meetings:** annual conference and meeting (exhibits) - always fall.

9150 ■ National Resource Center for Paraprofessionals in Education and Related Services (NRCP)

Utah State Univ.
6526 Old Main Hill
Logan, UT 84322-6526
Ph: (435)797-4242

Fax: (435)797-3572
URL: http://www.nrcpara.org
Contact: Dr. Marilyn Likins, Co-Dir.
Founded: 1979. **Staff:** 4. **Nonmembership. Description:** A resource center for administrators of state and local education agencies and community and four-year colleges and universities. Collects and disseminates information on the training and employment of paraprofessionals working with children and adults with special needs. Provides technical assistance and program evaluation services; conducts training courses for education administrators and policy makers. Maintains speakers' bureau; compiles statistics. **Formerly:** (1990) National Resource Center for Paraprofessionals in Special Education and Related Human Services; (1993) National Resource Center for Paraprofessionals in Education and Related Services. **Publications:** *Employment and Training of Paraprofessional Personnel: A Technical Assistance Manual for Administrators and Staff Developers* ● *New Directions*, quarterly. Newsletter. Covers employment and personnel practices, supervision, and training of paraprofessionals who work in programs for individuals with special needs. **Price:** free. Alternate Formats: online ● *Paraprofessional Bibliography: Training Materials and Resources for Paraprofessionals Working in Programs Serving People With Disabilities* ● Also publishes training materials. **Conventions/Meetings:** annual conference.

Speech

9151 ■ American Debate Association (ADA)

c/o University of Mary Washington
Combs Hall
1301 Colorado Ave.
Fredericksburg, VA 22401
Ph: (540)654-1252
URL: http://www.umw.edu/cas/debate/ada/default.php
Contact: Timothy M. O'Donnell, Dir.
Founded: 1985. **Members:** 100. **Membership Dues:** individual, $10 (annual) ● affiliate, $20 (annual) ● patron, $30 (annual). **Description:** Colleges and universities. Promotes and helps to develop intercollegiate policy debate at all levels. Offers resources to assist in initiating debate programs. Sponsors rules governing debate tournaments. **Awards:** National Tournament Award. **Frequency:** annual. **Type:** recognition. **Recipient:** for the winning debate team or individual. **Affiliated With:** American Forensic Association; National Communication Association. **Publications:** *Extensions*, quarterly. Newsletter. **Price:** included in membership dues. **Circulation:** 100. **Conventions/Meetings:** annual meeting - always in the spring.

9152 ■ American Forensic Association (AFA)

Box 256
River Falls, WI 54022
Ph: (715)425-3198
Free: (800)228-5424
Fax: (715)425-9533
E-mail: amforensicassoc@aol.com
URL: http://www.americanforensics.org
Contact: James W. Pratt, Exec. Sec.
Founded: 1949. **Members:** 900. **Membership Dues:** individual, $75 (annual) ● life, $600 ● student, $20 (annual). **Staff:** 1. **Budget:** $45,000. **Regional Groups:** 4. **Description:** High school and college directors of forensics and debate coaches. Promotes debate and other speech activities. Sponsors annual collegiate National Individual Events Tournament and National Debate Tournament; sells debate ballots; makes studies of professional standards and debate budgets. Supports research grants. **Awards: Frequency:** annual. **Type:** recognition. **Recipient:** for outstanding performance in argumentation and debate. **Committees:** Educational Practices; High School Affairs; Legal Communication; Professional Relations; Research; Two Year Colleges. **Affiliated With:** National Communication Association. **Publications:** *Argumentation and Advocacy: The Journal of the American Forensic Association*, quarterly. Covers debate and speech activities at high schools and colleges, and argumentation theory and practice. **Price:** included in membership dues. ISSN: 1051-1431. **Circulation:** 1,200. **Advertising:** accepted ● *Proceedings of the NCA/AFA Argumentation Conference* ● Newsletter, 3/year, January, June, September. Includes annual directory. **Price:** included in membership dues. **Circulation:** 1,200. **Advertising:** accepted. **Conventions/Meetings:** annual meeting.

9153 ■ American Parliamentary Debate Association (APDA)

401 Alfred Lerner Hall, MC 2602
2920 Broadway
New York, NY 10027
E-mail: president@apdaweb.org
URL: http://www.apdaweb.org
Contact: John Hollwitz, Pres.
Membership Dues: $100 (annual). **Description:** Promotes parliamentary debate.

9154 ■ Association for Communication Administration (ACA)

Address Unknown since 2008
Founded: 1972. **Members:** 300. **Membership Dues:** departmental/university, $75 (annual). **Staff:** 2. **Budget:** $50,000. **Description:** Chairpersons of schools, divisions, or departments of communication, radio-T.V., journalism, theatre, humanities, or English; administrators in higher education. Serves as a forum for the discussion of issues relating to speech as a discipline in higher education; facilitates communication between departmental and higher administrative personnel; collects and disseminates information. Encourages the development of policies relating to staff, departmental, school, and college management, curriculum, assistantship, and fellowships. Compiles statistics. **Libraries: Type:** reference. **Holdings:** periodicals. **Subjects:** communication discipline. **Committees:** Careers; Community College; Departmental Data; Departmental Evaluation; Ethics; Faculty Exchange. **Formerly:** (1975) Association of Departments and Administrators in Speech Communication. **Publications:** Journal, 3/year. Includes research, papers of topical interest, reviews, and surveys. **Price:** included in membership dues. ISSN: 0360-0939. **Circulation:** 400. Alternate Formats: microform; online. **Conventions/Meetings:** annual meeting and seminar (exhibits).

9155 ■ National Association of Urban Debate Leagues (NAUDL)

332 S Michigan Ave., Ste.500
Chicago, IL 60604
Ph: (312)427-0175
Fax: (312)427-6130
E-mail: info@urbandebate.org
URL: http://www.urbandebate.org
Contact: Anthony Jardina, Exec. Asst.
Founded: 1997. **Regional Groups:** 14. **Description:** Uses academic debate as a mechanism for urban education improvement, to increase equity and excellence in urban public schools by helping students become effective advocates, and to improve skills in critical and analytical thinking, oral and written communication, research, computer literacy, and conflict resolution. Promotes equal access and opportunity to participate in debate by increasing the participation of under-represented races and ethnicities, and females. Institutionalizes competitive policy debate programs, particularly in urban high schools, thus bolstering existing and emerging debate circuits. Supports and professionalizes urban high school teachers as the centerpiece of debate programs. **Sections:** Urban Debate Network. **Affiliated With:** National Forensic League; Open Society Institute. **Publications:** Newsletter, quarterly. **Conventions/Meetings:** IdeaFest - conference ● UDL Championship Events - regional meeting - 3/year.

9156 ■ National Catholic Forensic League (NCFL)

c/o Richard Gaudette, Exec. Sec.-Treas.
21 Nancy Rd.
Milford, MA 01757
E-mail: dickgaudette@msn.com
URL: http://www.ncfl.org
Contact: Ms. Lynda Luce, Pres.
Founded: 1952. **Members:** 900. **Membership Dues:** regular, $20 (annual). **Budget:** $40,000. **Regional Groups:** 66. **Description:** Promotes curricular and extracurricular speech and debate in public, parochial, and private secondary schools. **Awards: Frequency:** annual. **Type:** trophy. **Telecommunication Services:** electronic mail, footluce@charter.net. **Publications:** *NCFL Newsletter*, 3/year. Alternate Formats: online. **Conventions/Meetings:** annual Grand National Speech and Debate Tournament - competition, held locally for speaking and debating - held every Memorial Day weekend.

9157 ■ National Communication Association (NCA)

1765 N St. NW
Washington, DC 20036
Ph: (202)464-4622
Fax: (202)464-4600
E-mail: rsmitter@natcom.org
URL: http://www.natcom.org
Contact: Dr. Roger Smitter, Exec. Dir.
Founded: 1914. **Members:** 7,700. **Membership Dues:** regular, $155 (annual) ● sustaining, $250 (annual) ● patron, $330 (annual) ● life, $3,500 ● student, $60 (annual). **Staff:** 14. **Budget:** $1,400,000. **Description:** Elementary, secondary, college, and university teachers, speech clinicians, media specialists, communication consultants, students, theater directors, and other interested persons; libraries and other institutions. Works to promote study, criticism, research, teaching, and application of the artistic, humanistic, and scientific principles of communication, particularly speech communication. Sponsors the publication of scholarly volumes in speech. Conducts international debate tours in the U.S. and abroad. Maintains placement service. **Awards: Frequency:** annual. **Type:** recognition. **Recipient:** for outstanding teaching and professional service. **Commissions:** Basic Course; Communication and Aging; Communication and Law; Communication Apprehension; Communication Assessment; Communication Ethics; Communication Needs of Students at Risk; Experiential Learning in Communication; Freedom of Speech; Spiritual Communicator; Visual Communication. **Committees:** Affirmative Action; Dissertation Awards; Intercollegiate Discussion and Debate; International Discussion and Debate; Intrapersonal Communication Processes; Placement Service; Professional Service Awards. **Divisions:** Argumentation and Forensics; Family Communication; Feminist and Women's Studies; Health Communicator; Instructional Development; International and Intercultural Speech; Interpersonal and Small Group Interaction; Intrapersonal Communicator; Language and Social Interaction; Mass Communication; Organizational Communication; Performance Studies; Political Communication; Public Address; Public Relations; Rhetorical and Communication Theory; Theatre. **Sections:** Applied Communication; Community College; Elementary/Secondary Education; Four-year College/University; Student. **Affiliated With:** American Council of Learned Societies; Consortium of Social Science Associations; National Humanities Alliance. **Formerly:** Private Communications Association; (1970) Speech Association of America; (1998) Speech Communication Association. **Publications:** *Communication Education*, quarterly. Journal. Includes book reviews and research reports. **Price:** included in membership dues. ISSN: 0363-4523. **Circulation:** 3,500. **Advertising:** accepted. Alternate Formats: microform; online ● *Communication Monographs*, quarterly. Journal. Devoted to scientific and empirical investigations of communication processes. ISSN: 0363-7751. **Circulation:** 3,200. Alternate Formats: microform; online ● *Communication Teacher*, quarterly. Journal. Includes teaching strategies and classroom exercises. **Price:** $15.00/year. **Circulation:** 1,500. Alternate Formats: online ● *Critical Studies in Media Communication*, quarterly. Journal. Includes research reports. **Price:** included in membership dues. ISSN: 0739-3180. **Circulation:** 2,700. **Advertising:** accepted. Alternate Formats:

microform; online ● *Free Speech Yearbook*, annual. Contains articles and research reports on freedom of expression. Includes bibliography and book reviews. ● *Journal of Applied Communication Research*, quarterly. **Price:** included in membership dues; $275.00 /year for institutions (print); $261.00 /year for institutions (online); $71.00 /year for individuals (print). ISSN: 0090-9882. Alternate Formats: online. Also Cited As: *JACR* ● *Quarterly Journal of Speech*. Includes book reviews and research reports. **Price:** included in membership dues. ISSN: 0033-5630. **Circulation:** 4,700. **Advertising:** accepted. Alternate Formats: microform; online ● *The Review of Communication*, quarterly. Journal. Includes reviews of communication texts. **Price:** included in membership dues. Alternate Formats: online ● *Spectra*, monthly. Newsletter. Provides information on association news and meetings, conferences, award news, calls for papers, employment opportunities, and new publications. **Price:** included in membership dues; $40.00 /year for nonmembers. **Circulation:** 6,000. **Advertising:** accepted. Alternate Formats: online ● *Text and Performance Quarterly*. Journal. Includes literary studies in drama, poetry, short stories, novels and nonfiction, intercultural studies, and studies of speeches and scripts. **Price:** included in membership dues. **Circulation:** 1,500 ● Directory, annual. Lists regional, state, and related organizations, and selected journals. Also lists related institutions and communication departments. **Circulation:** 7,000. **Advertising:** accepted. **Conventions/Meetings:** annual convention (exhibits) - 2008 Nov. 20-23, San Diego, CA; 2009 Nov. 12-15, Chicago, IL.

9158 ■ National Forensic Association (NFA)

c/o Prof. Larry Schnoor, Pres.
107 Agency Rd.
Mankato, MN 56001-5053
Ph: (507)387-3010
Fax: (507)387-3068
E-mail: lgene9535@aol.com
URL: http://cas.bethel.edu/dept/comm/nfa
Contact: Prof. Larry Schnoor, Pres.

Founded: 1974. **Members:** 300. **Membership Dues:** institution, $40 (annual). **Local Groups:** 300. **Description:** Colleges interested in promoting individual speaking scholarship and competition. Activities include sponsoring academic panels and directing individual events and annual national championship. Compiles statistics. Maintains hall of fame and museum. Operates speakers' bureau. **Libraries: Type:** reference. **Holdings:** biographical archives. **Telecommunication Services:** electronic mail, mdreher@bethel.edu. **Affiliated With:** National Communication Association. **Publications:** *National Forensic Journal*, semiannual. **Advertising:** accepted. Alternate Formats: online ● Newsletter, 3/year. Alternate Formats: online. **Conventions/Meetings:** semiannual meeting.

9159 ■ National Forensic League (NFL)

125 Watson St.
PO Box 38
Ripon, WI 54971
Ph: (920)748-6206
Fax: (920)748-9478
E-mail: nfl@nflonline.org
URL: http://nflonline.org
Contact: J. Scott Wunn, Exec. Sec.

Founded: 1925. **Members:** 1,098,878. **Membership Dues:** student (one time initiation fee), $10 ● affiliate, $99 (annual). **Staff:** 12. **Budget:** $1,300,000. **Regional Groups:** 99. **Description:** High school honor society. Promotes the art of debate, oratory, interpretation, and extemporaneous speaking. Conducts educational and outreach programs; maintains speakers' bureau; maintains hall of fame; compiles statistics. **Awards:** Leading Chapter Awards. **Frequency:** annual. **Type:** recognition. **Recipient:** for leading schools ● National Tournament Awards. **Frequency:** annual. **Type:** recognition. **Recipient:** for winners of National Speech Tournament. **Computer Services:** Mailing lists, of members. **Committees:** Lincoln Douglas Debate Topic Wording. **Publications:** *National Forensic Library*. Videos. Includes lectures and lessons about speech and debate subject matters. **Price:** $17.99/copy ● *Rostrum*, monthly. Magazine. Contains articles for students and teachers about speech and debate. **Price:** $10.00/year; $1.00/copy. **Circulation:** 15,600. **Advertising:** accepted. Alternate Formats: online. **Conventions/Meetings:** annual John C. Stennis National Student Congress - meeting, with Lincoln Financial Group National Speech Tournament (exhibits) ● annual Lincoln Financial Group National Speech Tournament - meeting and competition (exhibits).

9160 ■ National Parliamentary Debate Association (NPDA)

c/o Prof. Brent Northup, Treas.
Carroll Coll.
1601 N Benton
Helena, MT 59625
Ph: (406)447-5400
Fax: (406)447-5476
E-mail: bnorthup@carroll.edu
URL: http://cas.bethel.edu/dept/comm/npda/index.html
Contact: Prof. Brent Northup, Treas.

Founded: 1991. **Membership Dues:** regular, $50 (annual) ● affiliate, $20 (annual) ● individual, $10 (annual). **Description:** Promotes parliamentary debate. Provides collegiate student debaters with opportunities to debate various topics of current importance. Promotes competitive practices that ensure long-term growth and survival of intercollegiate academic and public debate. **Awards:** Season Sweeptakes Award. **Frequency:** annual. **Type:** recognition. **Recipient:** for outstansding schools that participate in sanctioned tournaments. **Publications:** *Parliamentary Debate*. Journal. Provides a forum to stimulate critical thinking and dialogue. **Price:** included in membership dues. Alternate Formats: online.

9161 ■ NFHS Speech, Debate and Theatre Association

PO Box 690
Indianapolis, IN 46206
Ph: (317)972-6900
Fax: (317)822-5700
E-mail: ksummers@nfhs.org
URL: http://www.nfhs.org
Contact: Kent Summers, Asst. Dir.

Founded: 1986. **Members:** 1,162. **Membership Dues:** individual, $20 (annual). **Staff:** 2. **Description:** High school speech, debate and theatre directors, coaches, and sponsors. Coordinates speech, debate and theatre programs at the state and national level. Provides a network of educators who prepare students for contests and festivals. Provides personal liability insurance for members. **Awards:** NFHS Outstanding Speech, Theatre and Debate Educator. **Frequency:** annual. **Type:** recognition. **Recipient:** for outstanding high school speech, theatre, and debate educators. **Affiliated With:** National Federation of State High School Associations. **Formerly:** (2002) National Federation Interscholastic Speech and Debate Association. **Publications:** *Forensic Educator*, annual. Booklet. Contains insights, techniques, information, and teaching strategies for highschool forensics. **Price:** free, for members only. **Circulation:** 1,250 ● *NFHS News*, bimonthly. Newsletter. **Conventions/Meetings:** annual State Speech Directors Conference.

9162 ■ Southern States Communication Association (SSCA)

c/o J. Emmett Winn, Exec. Dir.
Auburn Univ.
Commun. and Journalism
217 Tichenor Hall
Auburn University, AL 36849-5211
Ph: (334)844-2853
Fax: (334)844-4573
E-mail: director@ssca.net
URL: http://www.ssca.net
Contact: J. Emmett Winn, Exec. Dir.

Founded: 1930. **Members:** 1,500. **Membership Dues:** regular, $45 (annual) ● sustaining/emeritus, $85 (annual) ● patron, $185 (annual) ● life, $1,250 ● student, $25 (annual) ● institutional, $100 (annual). **Staff:** 4. **Budget:** $80,000. **Description:** Individuals, institutions, and libraries. Aims to promote the study, criticism, research, teaching, and application of the artistic, humanistic, and scientific principles of communication. Sponsors competitions for top papers. Offers placement services. **Awards:** Teaching, Research, and Service Awards. **Frequency:** annual. **Type:** recognition. **Recipient:** for best papers and association service. **Computer Services:** Mailing lists. **Divisions:** Applied Communication; Communication Theory; Freedom of Speech; Gender Studies; Instructional Communication; Intercultural Communication; Interpersonal Communication; Interpretation; Language and Social Interaction; Mass Communication; Popular Communication; Public Relations; Rhetoric and Public Address; Southern Forensics. **Formerly:** Southern Speech Association; (1988) Southern Speech Communication Association. **Publications:** *Connections*, 3/year. Newsletter. **Price:** $30.00/year. **Circulation:** 1,500. **Advertising:** accepted. Alternate Formats: online ● *Southern Communication Journal*, quarterly. ISSN: 1041-794X. **Circulation:** 2,600. **Advertising:** accepted. **Conventions/Meetings:** annual convention, educational and business professionals (exhibits) - late March to early April.

9163 ■ VoiceCare Network (VCN)

c/o Department of Music
St. John's Univ.
Collegeville, MN 56321
Ph: (320)363-3374
E-mail: info@voicecarenetwork.org
URL: http://www.voicecarenetwork.org
Contact: Axel Theimer, Exec. Dir.

Description: Provides lifespan voice education for choral conductors, music educators, church musicians, singing teachers, singers, and speech pathologists.

Spiritual Understanding

9164 ■ Swedenborg Association

PO Box 9111
Lutherville, MD 21093
Ph: (410)504-1949
E-mail: info@swedenborgproject.org
URL: http://www.swedenborgproject.org
Contact: Kurt Simons, Dir.

Founded: 1937. **Membership Dues:** $20 (annual). **Staff:** 4. **Budget:** $50,000. **Languages:** Albanian, English, French, German, Russian. **Multinational. Description:** Philosophers, theologians and all interested in Swedenborg's writings. Dedicated to the publication, sale and distribution of Swedenborg's theological writings, as well as books on Swedenborgian themes. **Libraries: Type:** open to the public. **Holdings:** 2,000; books, periodicals. **Subjects:** religion, philosophy, art, literature. **Computer Services:** database ● mailing lists ● online services, book catalog, book sales. **Publications:** *Arcana: Inner Dimensions of Spirituality*, quarterly. Journal. Contains articles on comparative religion, spirituality, and Swedenborgian themes. **Price:** $5.00/issue; $15.00/year. ISSN: 1075-2897. **Circulation:** 1,000. **Advertising:** accepted. Alternate Formats: online ● *Visionary Consciousness*. Book. **Price:** $9.95.

Standards

9165 ■ Postsecondary Electronic Standards Council (PESC)

1 Dupont Cir., Ste.520
Washington, DC 20036
Ph: (202)293-7383
E-mail: info@pesc.org
URL: http://www.pesc.org
Contact: Michael Sessa, Exec. Dir.

Founded: 1997. **Membership Dues:** college/university, $500-$4,000 (annual) ● state/federal government agency, bank/lender, non-profit organization, $10,000 (annual) ● commercial organization (based on revenues), $7,500-$10,000 (annual) ●

non-profit association (based on revenues), $3,500-$5,000 (annual). **Description:** Establishes and adopts data exchange standards in education. Seeks to enable the improvement of institutional performance and foster collaboration across educational communities. Promotes and facilitates the use of standards for data sharing. **Awards:** Distinguished Service Award. **Frequency:** annual. **Type:** recognition. **Recipient:** for valuable individual output on higher education. **Publications:** *The STANDARD*, monthly. Newsletter. Provides news and commentary on technology and standards in postsecondary education. Alternate Formats: online ● Brochures. Alternate Formats: online ● Papers. Alternate Formats: online.

Student Services

9166 ■ Association of College Unions International (ACUI)
One City Centre, Ste.200
120 W 7th St.
Bloomington, IN 47404-3925
Ph: (812)245-2284 (812)245-8052
Fax: (812)245-6710
E-mail: acui@acui.org
Contact: Marsha Herman-Betzen, Exec. Dir.

Founded: 1914. **Members:** 950. **Membership Dues:** institutional, $335-$2,779 ● associate plus, $50 ● student, $40 ● associate, $655. **Staff:** 12. **Budget:** $1,000,000. **Regional Groups:** 16. **Description:** Founded on a commitment to the advancement of the educational goals of member colleges and universities. Dedicated to helping student activities and college unions make significant contributions to the total campus environment for learning and to the development of persons who form the academic community. Maintains placement service. Sponsors regional and national tournaments in bowling, billiards, table tennis, and college bowl. **Awards:** Butts-Whiting Award. **Frequency:** annual. **Type:** recognition. **Recipient:** for contributions to the profession and to ACUI ● Education Council Research Grant. **Frequency:** annual. **Type:** grant. **Recipient:** to individuals submitting outstanding research proposals that are germane to the college unions and student activities profession ● Richard D. Blackburn New Professional Award. **Frequency:** annual. **Type:** recognition. **Recipient:** to an individual who demonstrates the potential for excellence in the field of college union. **Computer Services:** database, physical facilities, budgets, and operating practices of member institutions. **Telecommunication Services:** electronic mail, mherman@acui.org. **Committees:** Art Related Activities; College Bowl; Computer and Technology; Education; Gay, Lesbian, Bisexual, and Transgender Concerns; Minority Programs; Outdoor Programs; Recreation; Research; Small College and University Network; Students; Two-Year Colleges; Women's Concerns. **Formerly:** (1961) Association of College Unions. **Publications:** *Association of College Unions International—Bulletin*, bimonthly. Covers college student union activity programming, operations, staffing, student development, and other concerns. Includes book reviews. **Price:** included in membership dues. ISSN: 0004-5659. **Circulation:** 4,500. **Advertising:** accepted. Alternate Formats: microform; online ● *Association of College Unions International—Directory and Catalog*, annual. Membership Directory. Lists institutional and professional members of ACU-I. **Price:** included in membership dues; $100.00 for nonmembers. **Circulation:** 1,800. **Advertising:** accepted ● *College Unions at Work Monograph Series*, periodic. **Price:** priced individually ● *Union Wire Electronic Newsletter*, bimonthly. Provides information on college union and student activities. Contains employment opportunities, personnel changes, and notices of publications. **Price:** included in membership dues ● Books ● Monographs ● Pamphlets ● Reports. Alternate Formats: online ● Annual Report, annual. Alternate Formats: online ● Brochure. Alternate Formats: online. **Conventions/Meetings:** annual conference, association's community gathering (exhibits) ● annual Indiana Professional Development - seminar, on employee supervision, legal issues, ethics, ideal unions, and customer service ● workshop.

9167 ■ Association of College and University Housing Officers International (ACUHO-I)
941 Chatham Ln., Ste.318
Columbus, OH 43221-2416
Ph: (614)292-0099
Fax: (614)292-3205
E-mail: office@acuho-i.org
URL: http://www.acuho-i.org
Contact: Sallie Traxler, Exec. Dir.

Founded: 1951. **Members:** 6,400. **Membership Dues:** institutional in U.S., $216-$1,324 (annual) ● institutional outside U.S., $172-$1,060 (annual) ● sustaining affiliate, $853 (annual) ● faculty affiliate in U.S., $43 (annual) ● faculty affiliate outside U.S., $35 (annual) ● associate affiliate in U.S., $135 (annual) ● associate affiliate outside U.S., $99 (annual) ● student affiliate in U.S., emeritus affiliate in U.S., $39 (annual) ● student affiliate outside U.S., emeritus affiliate outside U.S., $28 (annual). **Staff:** 12. **Budget:** $2,000,000. **Regional Groups:** 11. **Description:** Officials of educational institutions in 13 countries concerned with all aspects of student housing and food service operation. Supports and conducts research. Organizes seminars and workshops. Offers internships. Maintains biographical archives; offers placement service. Compiles statistics. **Awards:** ACUHO-I Award. **Frequency:** annual. **Type:** recognition. **Recipient:** to a member who has made an outstanding contribution to ACUHO-I and the field of housing and food service ● **Type:** grant. **Recipient:** for multimedia ● James A. Hurd Award. **Frequency:** annual. **Type:** recognition. **Recipient:** to a member for outstanding contributions to the association and profession ● James C. Grimm Leadership and Service Award. **Frequency:** annual. **Type:** recognition. **Recipient:** for individuals who have assisted ACUHO-I with dedicated service and outstanding leadership ● Outstanding Corporate Friend Award. **Frequency:** annual. **Type:** recognition. **Recipient:** for corporate individuals who have contributed to the association and profession ● Research and Publication Award. **Frequency:** annual. **Type:** recognition. **Recipient:** to an individual who has made a significant contribution to the body of research and publications related to the housing profession. **Computer Services:** Mailing lists, of members. **Committees:** Academic Initiatives; Apartments; Awards and Recognition; Benchmarking Services; Commissioned Research; Conference Services; Corporate Relations and Exhibits; Educational Programs; Exhibits and Displays; Food Service Internship; Gay, Lesbian, and Bisexual Issues; Host; Housing Facilities; Housing Internship; Housing Marketing Strategies; Information Technology; International Relations; Legislative Issues; Multicultural Affairs; Nominating and Elections; Placement; Professional Standards; Program; Research and Information; Talking Sticks; Time and Place. **Publications:** *Advice for Advisors: The Development of an Effective Residence Hall Association* ● *Campus Housing Construction and Renovation* ● *Contract Management or Self-Operation: A Decision Making Guide for Higher Education* ● *Educational Programming and Student Learning* ● *Journal of College and University Student Housing*, semiannual. Features articles on current research and trends in the housing profession. **Price:** $20.00 for members; $30.00 for nonmembers ● *Planning A Career in College and University Housing* ● *Talking Stick*, 7/year. Magazine. **Price:** $37.00 for members; $45.00 for nonmembers. **Advertising:** accepted ● Membership Directory, annual. **Price:** free for members. **Advertising:** accepted. Alternate Formats: online. **Conventions/Meetings:** annual Apartments Conference - usually fall ● annual Chief Housing Officers Training Institute - conference - usually fall ● annual conference - usually summer ● annual Conference Services Workshop - usually fall ● annual Facilities Workshop - conference, with products or services for college and university student housing facilities (exhibits) - usually fall ● annual Housing Marketing Strategies Workshop - conference - usually fall ● annual Information Technology Conference, with products or services for college and university student housing facilities (exhibits) - usually fall.

9168 ■ Association of College and University Religious Affairs (ACURA)
c/o Rev. Susan Henry-Crowe, Sec.-Treas.
Emory Univ.
Atlanta, GA 30322
Ph: (404)727-6226 (609)258-3049
E-mail: acura@coloradocollege.edu
URL: http://www.emory.edu/rel_life/acura/a.c.u.r.a.htm
Contact: Rev. Deborah Blanks, Pres.

Founded: 1959. **Members:** 125. **Membership Dues:** institutional, $60 (annual) ● individual, $35 (annual). **Budget:** $1,500. **Description:** Universities and those employed by universities for the administration of "religious life"; campus denominational pastors and religious advisers are associate members. Communicates with organizations in the religious and student personnel fields such as denominational and interdenominational chaplaincy groups, American Association for Higher Education, American College Personnel Association (see separate entry), and National Association of College and University Chaplains and Directors of Religious Life. **Telecommunication Services:** electronic mail, dkblanks@princeton.edu. **Formerly:** (1990) Association for the Coordination of University Religious Affairs. **Publications:** *Dialogue on Campus*, 3/year. Newsletter. Covers current developments regarding religion in higher education. Includes book reviews and calendar of events. **Price:** included in membership dues; $5.00 /year for nonmembers. ISSN: 0012-2289. **Circulation:** 200. **Advertising:** accepted ● Monographs. **Conventions/Meetings:** annual conference (exhibits).

9169 ■ National Association for Campus Activities (NACA)
13 Harbison Way
Columbia, SC 29212-3401
Ph: (803)732-6222
Free: (800)845-2338
Fax: (803)749-1047
E-mail: info@naca.org
URL: http://www.naca.org
Contact: Alan Davis, Exec. Dir.

Founded: 1960. **Members:** 2,130. **Membership Dues:** student professional, $20 (annual) ● staff professional, $58 (annual) ● school (based on full time enrollment), $368-$843 (annual) ● regular affiliate, $322 (annual) ● non-profit affiliate, $169 (annual) ● national associate, $632 (annual) ● regional associate, $314 (annual) ● school section, $95 (annual). **Staff:** 25. **Budget:** $4,000,000. **Regional Groups:** 7. **Description:** Institutions of higher education; associate members are firms whose services or products are related to campus activities, events, and programs; professional members. Assists in the educational development of programmers (both student and staff) at member institutions in all areas of extracurricular activities including entertainment, recreation, and the arts; disseminates educational information to members via publications. Maintains hall of fame. Operates career services center. **Libraries: Type:** reference. **Awards:** Founders' Award. **Frequency:** annual. **Type:** recognition. **Recipient:** for an outstanding individual ● Harry Chapin Award for Contributions to Humanity. **Frequency:** periodic. **Type:** recognition. **Recipient:** for an individual or organization in the entertainment industry whose support for a humanitarian cause best reflects the spirit of Harry Chapin and his efforts to relieve world hunger ● Lifetime Membership. **Frequency:** annual. **Type:** recognition. **Recipient:** for school staff members, associate members, or NACA office staff ● NACA Hall of Fame Award. **Frequency:** annual. **Type:** recognition. **Recipient:** for outstanding individual, national or regional in the field of arts ● Patsy Morley Outstanding Programmer Award. **Frequency:** annual. **Type:** recognition. **Recipient:** for outstanding individual in the field of campus activities advisement ● Performing Arts/Program Achievement Award. **Frequency:** annual. **Type:** recognition. **Recipient:** for individuals or groups in the field of arts. **Computer**

Services: database, Cooperative Buying ● database, membership. **Formerly:** (1968) Block Booking Conference; (1976) National Entertainment Conference; (1982) National Entertainment and Campus Activities Association. **Publications:** *Campus Activities Programming*, 8/year. Magazine ● *NACA Membership Directory and Buyers' Guide*, annual. Contains contact information for both school and associate members. Alternate Formats: online ● Monographs. **Conventions/Meetings:** annual competition and convention (exhibits) - every February ● workshop, on concert production, visual arts, programming, student government, fundraising, and leadership development.

9170 ■ National Council on Student Development (NCSD)
c/o Dr. Ron Opp
Univ. of Toledo
Judith Herb Coll. of Educ., MS 921
Dept. of Educational Leadership
2801 W Bancroft St.
Toledo, OH 43606-3390
Ph: (419)530-4947
Fax: (419)530-4912
E-mail: ncsd@ncsdonline.org
URL: http://www.NCSDonline.org
Contact: Dr. Ron Opp, Contact
Founded: 1960. **Members:** 750. **Membership Dues:** individual, $75 (annual) ● institution, $250 (annual) ● graduate student, $25 (annual). **Staff:** 2. **Regional Groups:** 12. **Description:** A council of the American Association of Community Colleges. Professionals at two-year colleges involved in student affairs and student development. Offers direction and input to the AACC in matters pertaining to student development. Provides a forum for members to discuss issues relating to student services and development. Conducts studies on the provision of student services. Conducts educational programs. **Awards:** Achievement of Excellence Award. **Frequency:** annual. **Type:** recognition. **Recipient:** for individuals or groups who have made outstanding achievement towards furthering the aims of student development in the community colleges ● Terry O'Banion Shared Journey Exemplary Practice Award. **Frequency:** annual. **Type:** recognition. **Recipient:** for a community college student. **Computer Services:** Online services. **Publications:** *Membership Brochure*. Brochures. Alternate Formats: online ● *NCSD Newsletter*, semiannual. **Price:** included in membership dues. Alternate Formats: online ● Monographs. **Conventions/Meetings:** annual convention, premiers leading community college student development programs and speakers (exhibits) ● annual Leadership Workshop, to identify and prepare for future leaders in community college student development.

9171 ■ National Student Assistance Association (NSAA)
4200 Wisconsin Ave. NW, Ste.106-118
Washington, DC 20016
Free: (800)257-6310
Fax: (215)257-6997
E-mail: info@nsaa.us
URL: http://www.nasap.org
Contact: Patricia Berry, Pres.
Founded: 1987. **Membership Dues:** regular, $85 (annual) ● a friend of kids, $10 (annual) ● affiliate, $250 (annual) ● partner, $500 (annual) ● sponsor, $1,000 (annual) ● benefactor, $5,000 (annual). **Description:** Professionals working in areas including student substance abuse, violence, and academic underachievement. Promotes increased availability of effective student services; facilitates professional advancement of members. Serves as a forum for the exchange of information among members; conducts continuing professional development programs. **Awards:** Evaluation/Research Award. **Frequency:** annual. **Type:** recognition. **Recipient:** to an evaluation/research study in the Student Assistance Program field that serves as a model for other programs ● Individual Award. **Frequency:** annual. **Type:** recognition. **Recipient:** for an individual who has made significant contributions in the Student Assistance field ● Program Award. **Frequency:** annual. **Type:** recognition. **Recipient:** to a Student Assistance Program that has demonstrated effectiveness in supporting students. **Computer Services:** database, membership. **Formerly:** (1998) National Association of Leadership for Student Assistance Programs; (2003) National Association of Student Assistance Professionals. **Publications:** *Student Assistance Journal*, quarterly. Magazine. Contains articles. ● *Student Assistance Today*. Newsletter. Contains news about the association. **Advertising:** accepted.

9172 ■ National Student Exchange (NSE)
4656 W Jefferson Blvd., Ste.140
Fort Wayne, IN 46804
Ph: (260)436-2634
Fax: (260)436-5676
E-mail: bworley@nse2.org
URL: http://www.nse.org
Contact: Bette Worley, Pres.
Founded: 1967. **Members:** 180. **Membership Dues:** organization, college, university, $650 (annual). **Staff:** 4. **Budget:** $300,000. **Description:** Four-year U.S. colleges and universities; a cooperative program that provides one-year undergraduate exchange opportunities to approximately 3500 students each year at U.S. and Canadian institutions. Allows for the exploration of new geographic settings, academic diversification, cultural awareness, and search for self-identity; provides opportunity for institutions to expand the scope and variety of educational experiences available to students. Services include institutional recruitment, development and distribution of student recruitment posters and brochures, dissemination of information among member campuses, and evaluation of the exchange program; exchange is made through a simplified admissions procedure, with assurance of credit transferability, and at the in-state tuition/fee of either the home or host campus. Conducts in-service training for campus coordinators. **Publications:** Brochure ● Handbook ● Newsletter. **Conventions/Meetings:** annual conference - always March.

9173 ■ School Nutrition Association (SNA)
700 S Washington St., Ste.300
Alexandria, VA 22314
Ph: (703)739-3900
Fax: (703)739-3915
E-mail: servicecenter@schoolnutrition.org
URL: http://www.schoolnutrition.org/Index.aspx?id=1075
Contact: Mary Hill SNS, Pres.
Founded: 1946. **Members:** 55,000. **Membership Dues:** food service/nutrition employee, child care employee, student, retired, $25 (annual) ● food service/nutrition manager, child care manager, $27 (annual) ● other professional, $90 (annual) ● affiliate part-time staff, affiliate retired, $10 (annual) ● industry - corporate, $650 (annual) ● industry - individual, $250 (annual). **Staff:** 49. **Budget:** $8,500,000. **State Groups:** 51. **Local Groups:** 2,500. **Description:** Persons engaged in school food service or related activities in public or private schools, preschools, colleges and universities. Seeks to encourage and promote the maintenance and improvement of the school food and nutrition program. Sponsors National School Lunch Week in October and National School Breakfast week in March. Distributes information on school food and nutrition programs and child nutrition legislation. Holds industry seminar, major city directors and supervisors' meeting, and annual national conference for school food service personnel. Maintains School Food Service Foundation, which conducts research and educational programs relating to child nutrition and encourages professional development of school food service personnel. Maintains hall of fame. Operates political action committee. **Awards:** Heart of the Program Award. **Frequency:** annual. **Type:** recognition. **Recipient:** for school food service and nutrition employees who work with their manager in preparing and serving appetizing meals to children ● Louise Sublette Award. **Frequency:** annual. **Type:** recognition. **Recipient:** for an individual who has taken a special idea, developed it into a goal and used that goal to help the school's nutrition program grow ● Outstanding Director of the Year Award. **Frequency:** annual. **Type:** recognition. **Recipient:** for school food service and nutrition directors who manage effective programs that provide healthful, appetizing and nutritious meals to students ● Schwan's Food Service Scholarship. **Frequency:** annual. **Type:** scholarship. **Recipient:** for members pursuing formal education in school food service-related field. **Computer Services:** database, recipes ● information services, child nutrition ● mailing lists. **Boards:** House of Delegates; Industry; Marketing. **Committees:** Education; Member Services; Nominating; Nutrition; Public Policy and Legislative; Research; Resolutions and Bylaws. **Sections:** College Personnel; District Level Supervisors and Directors; Major City Directors and Supervisors; Single Unit Personnel; State Directors and Supervisors. **Formerly:** (2004) American School Food Service Association. **Publications:** *Journal of Child Nutrition and Management*, semiannual. Contains information in the areas of food service facilities, food quality and production, management, program evaluation, and nutrition standards. **Price:** $25.00 /year for members; $29.00 /year for nonmembers. ISSN: 0160-6271. **Circulation:** 60,000. **Advertising:** accepted. Alternate Formats: online ● *School Food Service and Nutrition*, 11/year. Magazine. Includes legislative and regulatory developments, current news and trends, and articles on management and equipment topics. Contains media reviews. **Price:** included in membership dues; $75.00 /year for nonmembers; $125.00 /year for institutions. ISSN: 0160-6271. **Circulation:** 60,000. **Advertising:** accepted. Also Cited As: *SFS Journal*. **Conventions/Meetings:** annual competition and conference (exhibits) - always July.

Students

9174 ■ American Student Association of Community Colleges (ASACC)
2250 N Univ. Pkwy., Ste.4865
Provo, UT 84604-1510
Ph: (801)863-8620
Free: (888)140-4993
Fax: (801)863-7229
E-mail: info@asacc.org
URL: http://www.asacc.org
Contact: Phil Clegg, Exec. Dir.
Founded: 1982. **Members:** 175. **Membership Dues:** school, $250 (annual) ● district, $200 (annual) ● state, $150 (annual). **Staff:** 3. **Description:** Student governments representing more than 11 million community college students. Seeks to advance the collective interests of members; promotes leadership development among community college students. Serves as the national voice of community college student governments; lobbies at the local, state, and national levels on issues affecting community colleges; functions as a clearinghouse on student assistance and federal financial aid programs. **Publications:** *ASACC Alert*, monthly. Newsletter. Alternate Formats: online. **Conventions/Meetings:** annual National Conference on Student Advocacy - meeting, allows students to learn about issues on a federal level and then meet with their representative in Congress - held in March.

9175 ■ American Student Government Association (ASGA)
412 NW 16th Ave.
Gainesville, FL 32601-4203
Ph: (352)373-6907
Free: (877)275-2742
Fax: (352)373-8120
E-mail: info@asgaonline.com
URL: http://www.asgaonline.com
Contact: W.H. Oxendine Jr., Exec. Dir.
Founded: 2003. **Membership Dues:** student government (based on undergraduate full-time enrollment), $297-$997 (annual) ● institutional individual, $199 (annual) ● student, $179 (annual). **Description:** Promotes the advancement of student governments nationwide. Serves as the voice of student governments in the United States. Provides all student government leaders and advisors with networking,

research, and information resources. **Publications:** Brochures. Alternate Formats: online.

9176 ■ Breakthroughs Abroad
Address Unknown since 2008
Multinational. Description: Provides international community experiences for high school and college students by combining global travel with community service and cultural experience. **Awards: Frequency:** periodic. **Type:** scholarship. **Recipient:** to students with financial need. **Programs:** Community Development in the Fijian Highlands; Conservation/Eco-tourism Project in the Osa Peninsula; Huay Pukaeng Village of the Long Neck Women; Teaching English and Improving Prong-Kae School.

9177 ■ Council for the Advancement of Standards in Higher Education (CAS)
One Dupont Cir. NW, No. 300
Washington, DC 20036-1188
Ph: (202)862-1400
Fax: (202)296-3286
E-mail: phyllismable@aol.com
URL: http://www.cas.edu
Contact: Phyllis Mable, Exec. Dir.
Founded: 1979. **Members:** 37. **Membership Dues:** association, $400 (annual). **Staff:** 1. **Description:** Consortium of international and national professional associations providing guidance for student programs in higher education. Facilitates the development, evaluation, and dissemination of professional standards for higher education services. Works to educate professionals and educators in the use of professional standards for program development, evaluation and staff development. Encourages accrediting bodies to use such standards for accreditation purposes. **Committees:** Standards Publication; Standards Review. **Formerly:** Council for the Advancement of Standards for Student Services/Development Programs. **Publications:** *Book of Professional Standards*, biennial. Includes standards and guidelines for 30 functional areas in higher education. **Price:** $45.00 in U.S. (1-9 books); $35.00 in U.S. (10 or more books); $50.00 outside U.S. (1-9 books); $40.00 outside U.S. (10 or more books). **Circulation:** 8,000. Also Cited As: *CAS Blue Book* ● *CAS Self-Assessment Guides*. Guides for 30 functional areas. **Price:** $20.00 each; $150.00 in U.S. (PC-Mac format); $160.00 outside U.S. (PC-Mac format). Alternate Formats: CD-ROM ● *Frameworks for Assessing Learning and Development Outcomes*. Book. Contains chapters on assessing each one of the sixteen CAS learning and development outcomes.

9178 ■ Education Pioneers
PO Box 28293
San Jose, CA 95159-8293
Ph: (408)315-3986
Fax: (408)904-4873
E-mail: info@educationpioneers.org
URL: http://www.educationpioneers.org
Contact: Scott Morgan, Founder/Pres./Exec. Dir.
Founded: 2004. **Description:** Trains, connects, and inspires education leaders dedicated to transforming the educational system. Seeks to develop a pipeline of talented leaders from multiple disciplines who will significantly improve student outcomes in urban schools. Increases the capacity of existing schools, districts and education ventures to operate as high-performing organizations. **Telecommunication Services:** electronic mail, scott.morgan@educationpioneers.org.

9179 ■ Egyptian Student Association in North America (ESANA)
c/o Hatem Seliem, Pres.
1810 Crossroads Vista Dr., Apt. No. 202
Raleigh, NC 27606
Ph: (919)513-1222 (919)851-9846
Fax: (919)851-9858
E-mail: president@esana.org
URL: http://www.esana.org
Contact: Hatem Seliem, Pres.
Members: 1,500. **Local Groups:** 50. **Multinational. Description:** Represents Egyptian students in North America. Aims to unveil the true civilized and Islamic character of Egypt and propagate the national efforts of the country and the Arab world for peace in front of the international community. Protects the interests of its members. **Telecommunication Services:** electronic mail, hmseliem@ncsu.edu. **Publications:** *Voice of ESA*, periodic. Magazine. Alternate Formats: online. Also Cited As: *VESA* ● Brochure. Alternate Formats: online.

9180 ■ Francena Purchase Applied Liberal Studies Society
PO Box 88304
Kentwood, MI 49518
Ph: (616)285-5568
Contact: Francena Purchase, Pres.
Founded: 1999. **Staff:** 1. **Regional Groups:** 1. **State Groups:** 1. **Local Groups:** 1. **Description:** Professional society of students who have excelled in various areas of study through their education and work experience and continue to be active contributors in communities. **Libraries: Type:** lending; reference; not open to the public. **Holdings:** 2,000; articles, artwork, books. **Awards:** F.P. International Applied Studies Award. **Frequency:** annual. **Type:** recognition. **Recipient:** for academic and community involvement. **Computer Services:** Mailing lists.

9181 ■ International Association for the Exchange of Students for Technology Experience (IAESTE)
10400 Little Patuxent Pkwy., Ste.250
Columbia, MD 21044-3519
Ph: (410)997-3069 (410)997-3068
Fax: (410)997-5186
E-mail: info@iaeste.org
URL: http://www.iaeste.org
Contact: Ms. Pamela Ruiz, Natl. Sec.
Founded: 1948. **Membership Dues:** professional, $50 (annual). **Multinational. Description:** Provides U.S. students with international internships in more than 70 member countries and to supply U.S. companies with qualified technical interns from around the world.

9182 ■ InterVarsity Link
PO Box 7895
Madison, WI 53707-7895
Ph: (608)274-9001
Fax: (608)274-7882
E-mail: information@intervarsity.org
URL: http://www.intervarsity.org/link
Contact: Rebecca D. Stephen, Dir.
Founded: 1983. **Staff:** 54. **Budget:** $2,000,000. **Multinational. Description:** Seeks to link Americans to the International Fellowship of Evangelical Students through the InterVarsity Christian Fellowship/U.S.A. Members are hired as employees of InterVarsity Christian Fellowship/USA, and are required to raise their full annual salary and expense budget through donations. **Affiliated With:** International Fellowship of Christians and Jews.

9183 ■ Leadership Enterprise for a Diverse America (LEDA)
39 Hamilton Terr.
New York, NY 10031
Ph: (212)234-1384
Free: (888)400-LEDA
Fax: (212)234-1385
E-mail: leda@ledascholars.org
URL: http://www.ledascholars.org
Contact: Enrique Foster Gittes, Pres.
Founded: 2003. **Staff:** 12. **Description:** Nurtures the leadership potential of exceptionally promising young people of racial, ethnic and socio-economic backgrounds, which are under-represented in the national "leadership pool". Seeks to address the inequality of educational opportunity based on race or socio-economic status. Aims to increase the number of Black, Latino and Native American students, and of low income students of all races, who are viable candidates for admission to the nation's most selective colleges and universities. **Programs:** LEDA College-Bound Community; LEDA Scholars.

9184 ■ Muslim Students Association of the United States and Canada (MSAUSC)
PO Box 1096
Falls Church, VA 22041
Ph: (703)820-7900
Fax: (703)820-7888
E-mail: manager@msa-national.org
URL: http://www.msa-national.org
Contact: Asma Mirza, Pres.
Founded: 1963. **Languages:** Arabic, English, French. **Multinational. Description:** Muslim students in North America. Seeks to advance the interests of members; works to enable members to practice Islam as a complete way of life. Provides assistance to Islamic programs and projects; facilitates organization of local Muslim student organizations; and coordinates the activities of Muslim student groups in North America. **Computer Services:** database ● mailing lists. **Telecommunication Services:** electronic mail, president@msa-national.org. **Projects:** Downtown. **Task Forces:** Community Service; Compass; Information Technology; Media and Communications; Programs. **Publications:** *MSA Conference Planning Manual*. Alternate Formats: online.

9185 ■ National Association of Graduate-Professional Students (NAGPS)
209 Pennsylvania Ave. SE
Washington, DC 20003
Ph: (202)543-0812
Fax: (202)454-5298
E-mail: office@nagps.org
URL: http://www.nagps.org
Contact: Joel Bellezza, Sec.
Founded: 1986. **Members:** 200. **Membership Dues:** associate affiliate, $200 (annual) ● contributing affiliate, $400 (annual) ● sponsoring affiliate, $800 (annual) ● regular, $500 (annual) ● supporting, $1,000 (annual) ● graduate/alumni, $50 (annual) ● undergraduate, $35 (annual). **Staff:** 1. **Budget:** $200,000. **Regional Groups:** 6. **Description:** Improves the quality of graduate and professional student life. Promotes the interests and welfare of these students in public and private universities, as well as in the public and private agencies. Acts as a clearinghouse for information on graduate and professional student groups at all stages of development. **Awards:** Service Awards. **Frequency:** annual. **Type:** recognition. **Computer Services:** Mailing lists. **Conventions/Meetings:** annual conference, for graduate students, leaders, and educators (exhibits).

9186 ■ National Association of Student Councils (NASC)
1904 Assn. Dr.
Reston, VA 20191-1537
Ph: (703)860-0200
Free: (800)253-7746
Fax: (703)476-5432
E-mail: nasc@nasc.us
URL: http://www.nasc.us
Contact: Rocco Marano, Dir.
Founded: 1931. **Members:** 18,000. **Membership Dues:** school, $75 (annual). **Staff:** 13. **State Groups:** 51. **Description:** Student councils in secondary schools. Works to develop student government; works to improve student-teacher relationships; works to assist in the management of the school; works to provide orderly direction of student activities; works to charter school clubs and other organizations. **Awards:** Prudential Spirit of Community Award. **Frequency:** annual. **Type:** recognition. **Recipient:** to middle level and high school students who have demonstrated exemplary, self-initiated community service ● Warren E. Shull NASC Adviser of the Year. **Frequency:** annual. **Type:** recognition. **Recipient:** for a high school and middle level student council advisers. **Boards:** Executive. **Affiliated With:** National Association of Secondary School Principals. **Publications:** *Leadership for Student Activities*, monthly. Magazine. **Advertising:** accepted ● *Student Council Handbook* ● Monographs. **Conventions/Meetings:** annual conference (exhibits) - always June ● periodic regional meeting ● semiannual workshop.

9187 ■ National Clearinghouse for Commuter Programs (NCCP)
c/o Jennifer Bonnet, Coor.
Univ. of Maryland
0110 Stamp Student Union
College Park, MD 20742
Ph: (301)405-0986
Fax: (301)314-9634
E-mail: jbonnet@umd.edu
URL: http://www.nccp.umd.edu
Contact: Jennifer Bonnet, Coor.
Founded: 1972. **Members:** 300. **Membership Dues:** individual, $35 (annual) ● individual, $60 (biennial). **Staff:** 2. **Description:** Represents professionals in fields related to higher education that work with or are interested in student commuters and related issues. (Commuter refers to students not living on campus.) Serves as a central data bank for the collection and dissemination of information about programs, services, and advocacy on behalf of commuter students in higher education. Encourages and conducts research; sponsors specialized education programs. Offers referral service linking individuals having specific concerns with institutions having tried or established programs in response to those concerns. Maintains files of research studies, information on pertinent issues (such as transportation and materials gathered from institutions), and federal and state governments. Documents demographic changes in student populations in the U.S. and how colleges and universities respond to these changes. **Convention/Meeting:** none. **Libraries: Type:** not open to the public. **Holdings:** 250. **Subjects:** commuters, adult learners, student affairs. **Computer Services:** database, member data and job listings. **Publications:** *Commuter Perspectives*, 3/year. Newsletter. Provides articles on adult students, assessing student needs, campus concerns, and the effect commuting has on learning. **Price:** included in membership dues. **Advertising:** accepted ● *Learning About Commuter Students: Resources Within Reach*, triennial. Serves as a guide to accessing literature on commuter students. **Price:** included in membership dues. **Advertising:** accepted ● *Serving Commuter Students: Examples of Good Practice*, triennial. Directory. Updates high quality commuter programs and services from campuses nationwide. **Price:** included in membership dues. **Circulation:** 300. **Advertising:** accepted.

9188 ■ National Conference on Student Leadership (NCSL)
2718 Dryden Dr.
Madison, WI 53704-3086
Ph: (608)246-3590 (608)227-8111
Free: (800)206-4805
Fax: (608)246-3597
E-mail: conferences@magnapubs.com
URL: http://www.ncslcollege.com
Contact: William Haight, Pres.
Founded: 1978. **Staff:** 3. **Budget:** $400,000. **For-Profit. Description:** College administrators and student government leaders concerned with the non-academic aspects of student life. Seeks to enhance college life by improving the health, social life, entertainment, and race relations among college students. **Libraries: Type:** reference. **Holdings:** 200; video recordings. **Subjects:** student services, diversity. **Telecommunication Services:** additional toll-free number, (888)936-4400. **Formerly:** (2004) National Conference on Student Services. **Publications:** *National On-Campus Report*, biweekly. Newsletter. **Conventions/Meetings:** semiannual National Conference on Student Services - usually April and November.

9189 ■ National Society of Leadership and Success
50 Harrison St., Ste.308
Hoboken, NJ 07030
Ph: (201)222-6544
Free: (800)601-6248
Fax: (201)222-0613
URL: http://www.societyofsuccess.com
Contact: Gary Tuerack, Pres.
Founded: 2001. **Description:** Represents professional motivational speakers who want to truly impact student's lives on a long-term continuous basis. Aims to improve one's ability to successfully attain desired outcomes. Guides individuals in identifying and committing to their personal success. **Also Known As:** (2007) Sigma Alpha Phi.

9190 ■ North American Students of Cooperation (NASCO)
PO Box 7715
Ann Arbor, MI 48107
Ph: (734)663-0889
Fax: (734)663-5072
E-mail: info@nasco.coop
URL: http://www.nasco.coop
Contact: Tom Pierson, Exec. Dir.
Founded: 1968. **Members:** 7,000. **Membership Dues:** housing cooperative, $10 (annual) ● retail and worker cooperative/associate (based on gross revenues), $150-$1,000 (annual) ● low-income, $35 (annual) ● regular, $50 (annual) ● supporting, $51-$150 (annual) ● associate, $150-$1,000 (annual) ● sponsoring, $151-$1,000 (annual). **Staff:** 4. **Budget:** $130,000. **Description:** Supports the formation of student cooperatives and offers technical assistance, training, and education in the field. Provides consultation services and leadership training programs. **Libraries: Type:** reference. **Holdings:** 1,000. **Subjects:** cooperation. **Awards:** Cooperative Hall of Fame. **Frequency:** annual. **Type:** recognition. **Computer Services:** Online services, forums. **Programs:** Internship. **Formerly:** (1978) North American Student Cooperative Organization. **Publications:** *Campus Co-op Directory*, biennial ● *Co-op Voices*, quarterly. Newsletter. **Price:** included in membership dues. Alternate Formats: online ● *Guide to Cooperative Careers* ● *Kitchenbriefs*, 8/year ● Brochures ● Pamphlets ● Papers. **Conventions/Meetings:** annual Cooperative Education and Training Institute - meeting (exhibits).

9191 ■ Student Affiliate Group (SAG)
Univ. of Akron
Dept. of Psychology
Arts and Sciences Bldg.
Akron, OH 44325-4301
Ph: (330)972-7280
Fax: (330)972-5174
E-mail: sag@uakron.edu
URL: http://www3.uakron.edu/sagweb
Contact: Sally Diegelman, Sec.-Treas.
Founded: 1977. **Membership Dues:** individual, $17 (annual). **Description:** Strives to enhance communication between counseling professionals and students in counseling graduate programs. **Publications:** *The Counseling Psychologist*. Journal. **Price:** included in membership dues ● Newsletter.

9192 ■ Student Empowerment Training Project (SET)
c/o Abe Scarr, Proj. Dir.
407 S Dearborn, Ste.701
Chicago, IL 60605
Ph: (312)291-0395
E-mail: abe@trainings.org
URL: http://www.trainings.org
Contact: Abe Scarr, Proj. Dir.
Founded: 1984. **Staff:** 1. **Description:** A project of the Center for Public Interest Research. Offers technical assistance to student government associations. Advocates ways to involve and advance students' interests, and protect students' rights. Provides training sessions and workshops; sponsors speakers. **Publications:** *National Student Government Directory*, annual ● *Student Advocate*, monthly. Includes student news and updates. **Price:** $15.00/year ● Also publishes organizing manuals for student governments.

9193 ■ Student Leadership Network (SLN)
Address Unknown since 2008
Founded: 1991. **Members:** 5,000. **Membership Dues:** student council (basic), $95 (annual) ● student council (platinum), $348 (annual) ● honor society (basic), $55 (annual) ● honor society (gold), $285 (annual). **Staff:** 10. **Budget:** $500,000. **Regional Groups:** 3. **Description:** Offers educational and charitable programs as well as a speakers bureau and statistics. **Awards:** Youth Leadership and Activism Awards. **Frequency:** annual. **Type:** recognition. **Recipient:** for youths aged 14 to 21. **Computer Services:** database ● mailing lists. **Formerly:** (2001) Student Alliance. **Publications:** *Empowerment Pages Newsletter*, quarterly. Includes membership information. **Circulation:** 5,000. **Advertising:** accepted. Alternate Formats: online ● *Youth Yellow Pages*, annual. Brochure. **Circulation:** 10,000. **Conventions/Meetings:** annual conference.

9194 ■ Student Organization of North America (SONA)
c/o Jose Manuel Castellon, Co-Chm.
PO Box 210300
Tucson, AZ 85721-0300
Ph: (520)626-4392
Fax: (520)626-2675
E-mail: joecastellon@hotmail.com
Contact: Jose Manuel Castellon, Co-Chm.
Founded: 1999. **Multinational. Description:** Fosters student awareness and personal involvement in North American regional collaboration. Promotes cross-cultural relations, respect and understanding across Canada, the United States and Mexico. Serves as a framework for student-led cooperation across national boundaries. Promotes opportunities for students to experience our North American Community.

9195 ■ United States Student Association (USSA)
815 16th St. NW, 4th Fl.
Washington, DC 20006
Ph: (202)637-3924
Free: (800)574-4243
Fax: (202)637-3931
E-mail: ussa@usstudents.org
URL: http://www.usstudents.org
Contact: Jennifer Pae, Pres.
Founded: 1946. **Members:** 425. **Staff:** 10. **Description:** Confederation of student bodies at American colleges and universities represented through their democratically-elected student government and statewide student associations. Provides a voice for students before the Department of Education and Congress. Gives expression to student opinion; seeks to increase students' responsibility and contribution to the college community and society; works to strengthen relations between American and foreign students. Works with major educational and civil rights organizations; provides programming aids to members. Member services include credit card programs. **Projects:** Grassroots Organizing Weekends; Recruitment and Retention of Students of Color in Higher Education. **Absorbed:** Women's Leadership Network, National Student Education Fund; (1978) National Student Lobby. **Formerly:** United States National Student Association. **Publications:** *Access: A Student Activists' Guide to the U.S. Congress*, annual. Manual. **Advertising:** accepted ● *Advance: A Retention Organizing Manual* ● *U.S. Student Association—Legislative Update*, monthly. Newsletter. **Price:** included in membership dues. **Conventions/Meetings:** annual Legislative Conference & National Student Lobby Day ● annual National Student Congress - always July or August.

9196 ■ USSA Foundation (USSAF)
c/o United States Student Association
815 16th St. NW, 4th Fl.
Washington, DC 20006
Ph: (202)637-3924
Fax: (202)637-3931
E-mail: ussa@usstudents.org
URL: http://www.usstudents.org
Contact: Jennifer Pae, Pres.
Founded: 1972. **Staff:** 3. **Description:** Educational organization working to increase student access, choice, and success in postsecondary education. Conducts higher education policy research from the student perspective; provides information on issues that affect students; conducts training for student representatives. Has collected and reproduced background material on areas in higher education including educational reform and governance and

Title IX. Provides current resource material on issues such as students, student financial aid problems and developments, educational equity and women's concerns, consumer protection in postsecondary education, educational training, internship opportunities, and developing statewide student lobbies. Offers research and consultation service to institutional, state, and national boards, agencies, and committees; acts as distribution center for materials published by others; provides policy analysis of federal and state educational programs to student organizations; monitors activities of national higher educational associations and inserts a student perspective on programs and issues. **Programs:** International Student Exchange; State Student Association Development. **Projects:** Student of Color Strategy and Policy Department; Student Organizing Training. **Formerly:** (1992) National Student Educational Fund. **Conventions/Meetings:** annual Grassroots-Legislative Conference (exhibits) ● annual National Student Congress - general assembly (exhibits).

Substance Abuse

9197 ■ International Coalition for Addiction Studies Education (INCASE)
PO Box 224
Vermillion, SD 57069-0224
Ph: (480)517-8522
Fax: (480)517-8449
E-mail: kirkbowdenphd@gmail.com
URL: http://incase-edu.net
Contact: Dr. Kirk Bowden PhD, Pres.
Founded: 1990. **Membership Dues:** full, $80 (annual) ● student, $50 (annual). **Multinational. Description:** Seeks to enhance the quality of training and education in addiction studies. Provides a global forum for the examination and debate of issues concerning post-secondary education in addiction studies. Aims to provide professional knowledge and share ideas regarding addiction studies and scholarship in the field of addiction studies. Works to develop standards and implement an accreditation process for addictions studies programs. **Publications:** *Journal of Teaching Addictions*. **Price:** included in membership dues ● *News Notes*, quarterly. Newsletter. **Price:** included in membership dues.

9198 ■ National Association of Substance Abuse Trainers and Educators (NASATE)
6400 Press Dr.
Southern Univ. at New Orleans
New Orleans, LA 70126
Ph: (504)286-5234
E-mail: eharrell@suno.edu
Contact: Evelyn Harrell, Dir.
Founded: 1982. **Members:** 100. **Regional Groups:** 2. **Description:** Accredited colleges and universities offering 12 or more course credit hours in the field of substance abuse. Goal is to provide a network for exchange on courses, student population, degreed and nondegreed programs, and graduate study in chemical dependency training. Acts as a clearinghouse for students interested in substance abuse training programs; assists universities with the development of such programs. Provides for the exchange of information among universities concerning certificates, continuing education units, degrees, and opportunities for transfer and enrollment in undergraduate, graduate, and professional schools. Examines the educational and training needs of students and their career mobility as substance abuse practitioners. **Publications:** *Annual Directory*. **Conventions/Meetings:** annual meeting.

Summer School

9199 ■ Association of University Summer Sessions (AUSS)
c/o Dr. Leslie J. Coyne, Recorder
Maxwell Hall 222
Indiana Univ.
750 E Kirkwood Ave.
Bloomington, IN 47405
Ph: (812)855-5048
Fax: (812)855-3815
Contact: Dr. Leslie J. Coyne, Recorder
Founded: 1925. **Members:** 50. **Description:** Consists of universities having major summer programs for graduates and undergraduates. Serves as a forum for the mutual consideration of matters of educational policy and administration peculiar to university summer sessions. Fosters research and sharing of relevant data. **Formerly:** (1964) Association of Summer Sessions Deans and Directors. **Conventions/Meetings:** annual conference.

9200 ■ North American Association of Summer Sessions (NAASS)
c/o Michael U. Nelson, Exec. Sec.
43 Belanger Dr.
Dover, NH 03820-4602
Ph: (603)740-9880
Fax: (603)742-7085
E-mail: naass@aol.com
URL: http://www.naass.org
Contact: Michael U. Nelson, Exec. Sec.
Founded: 1964. **Members:** 450. **Membership Dues:** institutional, $175 (annual) ● individual, extra-institutional, $45 (annual). **Staff:** 1. **Budget:** $75,825. **Regional Groups:** 5. **Multinational. Description:** Summer session deans and directors and other sponsors of summer programs in colleges and universities. Sponsors research studies; compiles statistical report on summer sessions. **Awards:** Creative and Innovative Award. **Frequency:** annual. **Type:** recognition. **Recipient:** for credit, noncredit and administrative programs. **Computer Services:** Mailing lists. **Committees:** Conference and Program Planning; Creative and Innovative Awards; Finance; Information and Communications; Membership; Nominations and Elections; Quality and Research. **Formerly:** (1964) National Association of College and University Summer Sessions; (1968) National Association of Summer Sessions. **Publications:** *North American Association of Summer Sessions—Membership Directory*, annual. Lists individual and institutional members. **Price:** included in membership dues ● *North American Association of Summer Sessions—Newsletter*, quarterly. Provides association and new membership news. ● *North American Association of Summer Sessions—Proceedings*, annual. Contains abstracts of programs, committee reports, panel discussions, and speeches delivered at association's annual conference. **Price:** included in membership dues. Alternate Formats: online ● *Summer Academe*, biennial. Contains research studies, case studies, and administrative issues. **Conventions/Meetings:** annual conference.

9201 ■ North Central Conference on Summer Schools (NCCSS)
c/o Jon C. Neidy, Pres.
Bradley Univ.
1501 W Bradley Ave.
Peoria, IL 61625
Ph: (309)677-2374
Fax: (309)677-3321
E-mail: neidy@bradley.edu
URL: http://www.nccss.org
Contact: Dr. Roger Swanson, Sec.-Treas.
Founded: 1949. **Members:** 150. **Membership Dues:** institution, $150 (annual) ● individual, $50 (annual). **Budget:** $15,000. **Description:** College and university summer session representatives from the north central states of the U.S. Provides opportunities for members to review pertinent phases of summer school operations, review investigative reports, and exchange information. **Awards:** Honorary Membership Research. **Frequency:** annual. **Type:** recognition. **Committees:** Public Relations; Research, Development, and Statistics. **Publications:** Directory, annual ● Proceedings. Provides information on annual meeting. ● Report, annual. Provides statistical information. **Conventions/Meetings:** annual meeting (exhibits).

Survival

9202 ■ California Wilderness Survival League (CWSL)
395 Rio St.
Redding, CA 96001-3611
Ph: (530)247-0632
Fax: (530)247-0632
E-mail: rmaich@pacbell.net
Contact: Rudy W. Maich, Pres.
Founded: 1984. **Members:** 809. **Staff:** 3. **Description:** Individuals and families who are interested in enhancing and applying wilderness and modern survival skills; others interested in safe campsites and retreat facilities and in fellowship with similar individuals. Seeks to: establish recreation, camping, and retreat grounds and facilities; maintain, stock, and operate such grounds and facilities; promote safety and survival skills; provide information and services to enhance members' safety and ability to survive; encourage friendship among members for their mutual benefit and safety. Conducts research and educational survival and wilderness skills training programs. (Membership is open to individuals and families outside of California and is by invitation only.). **Libraries: Type:** reference; not open to the public. **Holdings:** 8,000. **Subjects:** community and individual survival skills. **Computer Services:** Information services, nuclear alert warning system. **Publications:** *California Wilderness Survival League Newsletter*, quarterly. Reviews current situations in the world and contains calendar of events. **Price:** included in membership dues ● Monographs. **Conventions/Meetings:** annual retreat.

9203 ■ Live-Free, USA (LF/USA)
PO Box 375
Dolton, IL 60419-9998
E-mail: lfinow@aol.com
URL: http://www.live-free.org
Contact: James C. Jones, Pres.
Founded: 1974. **Members:** 730. **Membership Dues:** individual, full, $20 (annual). **Staff:** 6. **Budget:** $4,000. **Regional Groups:** 2. **State Groups:** 2. **Local Groups:** 14. **Description:** Individuals concerned with long-range survival preparation and self-sufficiency; believes that preparedness and self-sufficiency result in freedom. Strives to develop and promote the philosophy and technology of survival. Sponsors seminars on survival methods and field training events; develops survival training programs; conducts semiannual outdoor symposium. Supports operations to open communication channels and to organize network support systems for individuals and groups seeking freedom through emergency preparedness and self-sufficiency. Provides contacts and sources for survival writers, organizers, inventors, and instructors. Sponsors competitions; provides placement services; offers discounts. **Awards:** Life and Freedom Award. **Frequency:** periodic. **Type:** recognition. **Recipient:** to persons who have made outstanding contributions to emergency preparedness and self-reliance education. **Committees:** Civilian Preparedness. **Formerly:** (1990) Live-Free, Inc.; (2005) Live-Free International. **Publications:** *American Survivor*, quarterly. Newsletter. Contains self-reliance information and emergency survival. **Price:** $20.00/year. **Circulation:** 600. **Advertising:** accepted ● *Survival Papers*, periodic. Contains over 80 titles on paper or CD covering a variety of emergency preparedness, survival and self-reliance subjects. **Price:** $20.00. Alternate Formats: CD-ROM.

9204 ■ Outward Bound (OB)
100 Mystery Point Rd.
Garrison, NY 10524
Ph: (845)424-4000
Free: (866)467-7651
Fax: (845)424-4121
E-mail: info@obusa.org
URL: http://www.outwardbound.org
Contact: Arthur M. Blank, Chm.
Founded: 1962. **Budget:** $45,000,000. **Description:** Adventure-education organization that serves and supports four wilderness schools, two urban centers and a primary and secondary school-reform program. Wilderness courses are offered in 20 states as well as internationally and include activities such as backpacking, canoe touring, dogsledding, mountain biking, mountaineering, rock climbing, sailing, sea kayaking, skiing, snowboarding, whitewater activities and multi-activity courses. Wilderness programs

emphasize personal growth through experience and challenge in the wilderness, boardrooms and classrooms in the United States and around the world. Students develop self-reliance, responsibility, teamwork, confidence, compassion, environmental and community stewardship in all of the Outward Bound programs and courses. Has over 500,000 alumni, and serves more than 60,000 young people and adults each year. **Awards: Type:** grant. **Recipient:** for participants; on first come first serve basis ● **Type:** monetary. **Recipient:** for participants; on first come first serve basis ● **Type:** scholarship. **Recipient:** for participants; on first come first serve basis. **Publications:** *Map & Compass*, periodic. Handbook ● *Outward Bound Course Catalog*, annual ● *Outward Bound USA*. Book.

Taiwan

9205 ■ North American Taiwan Studies Association (NATSA)
c/o Huey-Tyng Gau, Treas.
Educ., UW-Madison
4723 Sheboygan Ave., No. 221
Madison, WI 53705
E-mail: hueytynggau001@yahoo.com
URL: http://www.na-tsa.org
Contact: Huey-Tyng Gau, Treas.
Founded: 1994. **Multinational. Description:** Promotes Taiwan studies in North America. Enhances interaction between the academia of Taiwan and North America. Fosters the exchange of information about Taiwan studies. Facilitates communication among graduate students and scholars concerning and conducting Taiwan studies. **Additional Websites:** http://freetaiwan.org/index.html. **Telecommunication Services:** electronic mail, webmaster@na-tsa.org.

Teacher Education

9206 ■ Joseph Campbell Foundation (JCF)
PO Box 36
San Anselmo, CA 94979-0036
Free: (800)330-6984
E-mail: info@jcf.org
URL: http://www.jcf.org
Contact: Robert Walter, Pres.
Founded: 1991. **Description:** Established to preserve, protect, and perpetuate Campbell's pioneering work. **Awards:** Erdman-Campbell Award for Creative Contributions to the Contemporary Mythopoetic Imagination. **Frequency:** periodic. **Type:** grant. **Recipient:** for a pioneer in the creation and exploration of new myths (mythopoesis) who then nominates a next-generation honoree. **Computer Services:** database, publication and resources ● online services, forums. **Roundtables:** Mythological.

Teachers

9207 ■ African Language Teachers Association (ALTA)
Univ. of Wisconsin - Madison
4231 Humanities Bldg.
455 N Park St.
Madison, WI 53706
Ph: (608)265-7902
Fax: (608)265-7904
E-mail: alta@mailplus.wisc.edu
URL: http://lang.nalrc.wisc.edu/alta
Contact: Dr. Antonia Schleicher, Advisor
Membership Dues: regular, $35 (annual) ● retired, student, $20 (annual) ● institutional, $50 (annual). **Description:** Promotes the study and teaching of African languages in the areas of basic research, language pedagogy and literature. Seeks to develop a field of African language teaching where members can share common interests and concerns on the study of African languages. Provides training on pedagogy, computer use, and language program design. **Publications:** *Journal of African Language Learning and Teaching*. Contains original research on African language learning and acquisition. Also Cited As: *JALLT* ● *Journal of the African Language Teachers Association*. Contains selected annual conference presentations. Also Cited As: *JALTA* ● *LUGHA*. Newsletter. **Price:** included in membership dues.

9208 ■ American Association of Colleges for Teacher Education (AACTE)
1307 New York Ave. NW, Ste.300
Washington, DC 20005-4701
Ph: (202)293-2450
Fax: (202)457-8095
E-mail: aacte@aacte.org
URL: http://www.aacte.org
Contact: Dr. Sharon P. Robinson, Pres./CEO
Founded: 1948. **Members:** 760. **Staff:** 35. **Budget:** $2,250,000. **State Groups:** 46. **Description:** Represents colleges and universities concerned with the preparation and development of professionals in education and human resources. Seeks to improve the quality of institutional programs of the education profession. Conducts summer leadership, institutes for department chairs and new deans' institutes. Compiles statistics. Administers short-term task forces to examine issues in the development of professional education. **Awards:** Best Practice Awards. **Frequency:** annual. **Type:** recognition. **Recipient:** for institutions that have demonstrated best practices in achieving AACTE's strategic goals ● Professional Achievement. **Frequency:** annual. **Type:** recognition. **Recipient:** for distinguished research in teacher education and for outstanding contributions to teacher education ● Writing and Research. **Frequency:** annual. **Type:** recognition. **Recipient:** for outstanding dissertation and publication. **Committees:** Advisory Council of State Representatives; Global and International Teacher Education; Governmental Relations; Multicultural Education; Publications and the Journal of Teacher Education; Quality and Accountability; Research and Information; Technology in Teacher Education; Women's Issues. **Affiliated With:** National Council for Accreditation of Teacher Education. **Formed by Merger of:** American Association of Teachers Colleges; National Association of Colleges and Departments of Education; National Association of Teacher Education Institutions of Metropolitan Districts. **Publications:** *AACTE Annual Directory*, annual. Membership Directory. **Price:** $50.00. ISSN: 0516-9313. **Circulation:** 1,000 ● *AACTE Briefs*, 17/year. Newsletter. Contains information on teacher education, federal and state legislation, and association activities. **Price:** included in membership dues; $40.00/year in U.S.; $53.00/year outside U.S.; $20.00/year for students. **Circulation:** 6,600. Alternate Formats: online ● *Journal of Teacher Education*, bimonthly. Includes book reviews and research reports. **Price:** $87.00/copy - institutional; $26.00/copy - individual. ISSN: 0022-4871 ● Books ● Monographs ● Reports. **Conventions/Meetings:** annual conference (exhibits) - usually February.

9209 ■ American Association of Teaching and Curriculum (AATC)
c/o Marcella L. Kysilka, Exec. Sec.
4240 Yorketowne Rd.
Orlando, FL 32812-7958
E-mail: kysilka@bellsouth.net
URL: http://www.aatchome.org
Contact: Marcella L. Kysilka, Exec. Sec.
Founded: 1993. **Membership Dues:** individual, $40 (annual). **Description:** Promotes the study of teaching and curriculum through analytical and interpretive approaches. Conducts discussion, exploration, practice and research for teaching and curriculum. **Awards:** Distinguished Dissertation Awards. **Frequency:** annual. **Type:** recognition. **Recipient:** to doctoral dissertation that represents significant contribution to fostering the understanding of current issues or interests in teaching and curriculum. **Publications:** *AATC Newsletter*. Alternate Formats: online ● *Curriculum and Teaching Dialogue*, semiannual. Journal. Also Cited As: *CTD* ● Brochure. Alternate Formats: online.

9210 ■ Association of Orthodox Jewish Teachers (AOJT)
1577 Coney Island Ave.
Brooklyn, NY 11230
Ph: (718)258-3585
Fax: (718)258-3585
E-mail: aojt@juno.com
Contact: Ruth Stillman, Exec. Dir.
Founded: 1964. **Members:** 5,000. **Membership Dues:** teacher, $20 (annual). **Staff:** 2. **Budget:** $100,000. **Description:** Teachers, guidance counselors, and supervisors employed by the New York City, Philadelphia, PA, and Nassau County, NY, boards of education who are observant Jews. Seeks to provide a forum for discussion of professional problems of Jewish teachers. Provides social and professional activities, promotes the welfare and serves the special needs of its members. Sponsors in-service training and charitable programs. Provides free supplemental educational services to new immigrants and a network of Jewish culture clubs in public schools. **Awards:** AOJT Awards. **Frequency:** annual. **Type:** recognition. **Recipient:** for outstanding work by Jewish and non-Jewish teachers and administrators ● Jewish Heritage Essay Contest. **Type:** recognition. **Recipient:** for all students in the New York City public schools. **Committees:** Akiva Clubs; Community Relations; Jewish Studies; Political Action; Professional Activities; Religious Guidance; Retired Teachers; Seminar in Israel; Teacher Grievance; Tours and Travel; Welfare. **Also Known As:** Association of Orthodox Jewish Teachers of the New York City Public Schools. **Publications:** *AOJT News*, bimonthly. Newspaper. Designed for teachers and administrators in the school system as well as legislative and community leaders. **Price:** included in membership dues; $10.00 /year for nonmembers. ISSN: 1075-4601. **Circulation:** 9,000. **Advertising:** accepted ● Journal, annual. Published in conjunction with annual banquet. **Conventions/Meetings:** annual banquet, includes awards distribution - always March.

9211 ■ Association for Science Teacher Education (ASTE)
c/o Dr. Eugene Wagner, Exec. Sec.
113 Radcliff Dr.
Pittsburgh, PA 15237
Ph: (412)624-2861
E-mail: ewagner@pitt.edu
URL: http://aste.chem.pitt.edu
Contact: Dr. Eugene Wagner, Exec. Sec.
Founded: 1923. **Members:** 800. **Membership Dues:** regular, $85 (annual) ● retired plus, student, $50 (annual) ● sustaining, $200 (annual) ● patron, $400 (annual). **Staff:** 1. **Budget:** $35,000. **Regional Groups:** 7. **Description:** Promotes leadership in, and support for those involved in, the professional development of teachers of science. Serves educators involved in the professional development of teachers of science, including science teacher educators, staff developers, college-level science instructors, education policy makers, instructional material developers, science supervisors/specialists/coordinators, lead/mentor teachers, and all others interested in promoting the development of teachers of science. **Libraries: Type:** reference. **Holdings:** periodicals. **Awards:** Innovation in Teaching Science Teachers. **Frequency:** annual. **Type:** recognition. **Recipient:** for development and dissemination of new designs for courses and curricula, new instructional methods and approaches in education of science teachers ● Outstanding Mentor Award. **Frequency:** annual. **Type:** recognition. **Recipient:** for encouragement of preservice and inservice science teachers and/or new science teacher educators entering the profession ● Outstanding Science Teacher Educator of the Year. **Frequency:** annual. **Type:** recognition. **Recipient:** for individual achievement and contribution in science education. **Computer Services:** Mailing lists ● online services. **Formerly:** (2005) Association for the Education of Teachers in Science. **Publications:** *Journal of Science Teacher Education*, quarterly. Features articles

which suggest ways to improve conditions in classroom methods, in-service workshops, and teacher recruitment and retention. **Conventions/Meetings:** annual convention (exhibits) - always January.

9212 ■ Association of Teacher Educators (ATE)
PO Box 793
Manassas, VA 20113
Ph: (703)331-0911
Fax: (703)331-3666
E-mail: info@ate1.org
URL: http://www.ate1.org
Contact: Terry L. James, Pres.

Founded: 1920. **Members:** 3,800. **Membership Dues:** regular, $90 (annual) ● library, $130 (annual) ● retired, student, $25 (annual) ● life, $1,800. **Staff:** 5. **Budget:** $550,000. **Regional Groups:** 3. **State Groups:** 41. **Description:** Individuals who have a part or an interest in the professional, sociological, psychological, and personal growth and development of those who will be or are teachers; professional associations and learned societies; government agencies. Provides professional growth opportunities for all persons concerned with teacher education; promotes quality teacher education programs. Maintains Speaker's Bureau. **Libraries: Type:** reference. **Holdings:** archival material, books, business records, monographs, periodicals. **Subjects:** teacher education. **Awards:** Distinguished Clinician in Teacher Education. **Frequency:** annual. **Type:** recognition. **Recipient:** for school-based teacher educators ● Distinguished Dissertation in Teacher Education. **Frequency:** annual. **Type:** recognition. **Recipient:** for exemplary doctoral level research ● Distinguished Program in Teacher Education. **Frequency:** annual. **Type:** recognition. **Recipient:** for outstanding teacher education programs ● Distinguished Research in Teacher Education. **Frequency:** annual. **Type:** recognition. **Recipient:** for outstanding investigations influencing teacher education and/or student learning. **Computer Services:** Mailing lists. **Commissions:** Professional Issues; Special Interest Groups. **Formerly:** (1946) National Association of Supervisors of Student Training; (1970) Association for Student Teaching. **Publications:** *Action in Teacher Education*, quarterly. Journal. Features information, ideas, and research related to the improvement of teaching and teacher education at all levels. **Price:** included in membership dues; $15.00 for nonmembers. ISSN: 0162-6620. **Circulation:** 3,300. **Advertising:** accepted ● Newsletter, quarterly. Monitors developments and regulations affecting teacher education. Profiles national award-winning teacher education programs. **Price:** included in membership dues. ISSN: 0001-2718. **Circulation:** 3,500. Alternate Formats: online ● Books ● Reports ● Yearbook, annual. **Conventions/Meetings:** annual Promoting Quality and Professionalism - conference and meeting, professional development speeches and workshops (exhibits) - usually February.

9213 ■ Association of WORKSHOP WAY Consultants (AWWC)
PO Box 850170
New Orleans, LA 70185-0170
Ph: (504)486-4871
Fax: (504)360-8827
Contact: Joan Roosevelt, Contact

Founded: 1987. **Members:** 33. **Membership Dues:** licensed consultant, $35 (annual). **Staff:** 1. **Budget:** $1,650. **Regional Groups:** 4. **Description:** Persons licensed to teach the WORKSHOP WAY educational system. (WORKSHOP WAY concentrates on developing children's personal-based life skills before competency in knowledge-based skills.) Works to develop and enrich the knowledge of members to promote the philosophy and psychology of Workshop Way. Offers consulting services to universities and schools. **Computer Services:** Mailing lists. **Publications:** *Pilon Workshop Way Catalog*, annual. Lists all Workshop Way publications. **Circulation:** 2,000. **Conventions/Meetings:** semiannual conference (exhibits).

9214 ■ Carnegie Foundation for the Advancement of Teaching (CFAT)
51 Vista Ln.
Stanford, CA 94305-8703
Ph: (650)566-5100 (650)566-5162
Fax: (650)326-0278
E-mail: clyburn@carnegiefoundation.org
URL: http://www.carnegiefoundation.org
Contact: Gay Clyburn, Dir. of Communications and Information

Founded: 1905. **Nonmembership. Description:** Conducts and monitors research, analyses, and policy studies on education. **Libraries: Type:** reference. **Holdings:** 9,000. **Subjects:** education, social science. **Publications:** Annual Report, annual. **Price:** free ● Monographs ● Reports ● Videos.

9215 ■ Education Industry Association (EIA)
c/o Steven Pines, Exec. Dir.
5909 Barbados Pl., Ste.20
Rockville, MD 20852
Free: (800)252-3280
Fax: (301)468-3249
E-mail: spines@educationindustry.org
URL: http://www.educationindustry.org
Contact: Deborah M. McGriff, Pres.

Founded: 1990. **Members:** 800. **Membership Dues:** governing (small business), $150 (annual) ● silver governing (corporate), $1,100 (annual) ● gold governing (corporate), $2,600 (annual) ● platinum governing (corporate), $5,300 (annual) ● business, $600 (annual) ● student, $25 (annual) ● individual, $200 (annual). **Staff:** 5. **Description:** Educators in private practice and private educational institutions. Promotes "education reform through entrepreneurship." Facilitates communication and cooperation among members; conducts educational and advocacy activities. **Awards:** AEPP Entrepreneurial Leadership Award. **Frequency:** annual. **Type:** recognition. **Formerly:** (2002) Association of Educators in Private Practice; (2003) Association of Education Practitioners and Provider. **Publications:** *Enterprising Educators*, quarterly. Newsletter. Alternate Formats: online ● Membership Directory, annual. **Conventions/Meetings:** annual EDVentures - conference.

9216 ■ International Council on Education for Teaching (ICET)
c/o National Louis University
1000 Capitol Dr.
Wheeling, IL 60090-7201
Ph: (847)465-0191
Free: (800)443-5522
Fax: (847)465-5629
E-mail: icet@nl.edu
URL: http://myclass.nl.edu/icet
Contact: Dr. Darrell Bloom, Exec. Dir./Treas.

Founded: 1953. **Staff:** 4. **Budget:** $500,000. **Regional Groups:** 6. **Multinational. Description:** Individuals, universities, and organizations concerned with the professional preparation of teachers, school administrators, and specialists. Serves as the voice of teacher education; provides a forum for examination and discussion of issues, trends, problems, and innovations in teacher education. Encourages cooperation in the preparation of educational specialists; conducts cooperative research projects. Training division operates administrative fellowship programs, selects and oversees technical assistance personnel, develops and manages specialized training programs including individually-tailored programs for university administrators. Maintains consultative status with United Nations Educational, Scientific and Cultural Organization. **Awards:** ICET Award for Research in Teacher Education. **Type:** recognition. **Publications:** *Frank W. Klassen Lecture*, annual ● *International Yearbook on Teacher Education*, annual. **Price:** $15.00. Alternate Formats: CD-ROM ● Newsletter, quarterly. Alternate Formats: online ● Pamphlets ● Proceedings, annual. **Conventions/Meetings:** annual World Assembly.

9217 ■ National Alliance of Black School Educators (NABSE)
310 Pennsylvania Ave.
Washington, DC 20003
Ph: (202)608-6310
Free: (800)221-2654
Fax: (202)608-6319
E-mail: lavette@nabse.org
URL: http://www.nabse.org
Contact: Quentin R. Lawson, Exec. Dir.

Founded: 1970. **Members:** 7,000. **Membership Dues:** individual, $100 (annual) ● institutional, $1,000 (annual) ● corporate, $2,000 (annual) ● retired, $25 (annual) ● student, $20 (annual) ● life, $900. **Staff:** 7. **Budget:** $2,200,000. **Regional Groups:** 5. **State Groups:** 4. **Local Groups:** 98. **Description:** Black educators from all levels; others indirectly involved in the education of black youth. Promotes awareness, professional expertise, and commitment among black educators. Goals are to: eliminate and rectify the results of racism in education; work with state, local, and national leaders to raise the academic achievement level of all black students; increase members' involvement in legislative activities; facilitate the introduction of a curriculum that more completely embraces black America; improve the ability of black educators to promote problem resolution; create a meaningful and effective network of strength, talent, and professional support. Sponsors workshops, commission meetings, and special projects. Encourages research, especially as it relates to blacks, and the presentation of papers during national conferences. Plans to establish a National Black Educators Data Bank and offer placement service. **Libraries: Type:** not open to the public. **Holdings:** 100. **Subjects:** education. **Awards:** Hall of Fame. **Frequency:** annual. **Type:** recognition. **Recipient:** for outstanding contributions to education and/or toward improving the quality of life of African-Americans. **Computer Services:** Mailing lists, of members. **Commissions:** District Administration; Governance in Education; Higher Education; Instruction and Instructional Support; Local School Administration; Parent; Program Development, Research and Evaluation; Retired Educators; Special Projects Administration. **Committees:** Legislation; Membership; Resolutions; Strategic Planning. **Formerly:** (1973) National Alliance of Black School Superintendents. **Publications:** *NABSE Annual Conference Program*, annual. Newsletter. Contains news on membership, research, and coming events. **Price:** included in membership dues. **Circulation:** 7,000. **Advertising:** accepted. Alternate Formats: online ● *NABSE Journal* ● *News Briefs*, 3/year. Newsletter. **Price:** free. **Circulation:** 7,000. **Advertising:** accepted. Alternate Formats: online. **Conventions/Meetings:** annual conference, with minority vendors (exhibits) - always November. 2008 Nov. 18-23, Atlanta, GA; 2009 Nov. 16-22, Indianapolis, IN.

9218 ■ National Association for the Advancement of Caring Teachers (NAACT)
c/o Sindi D. Wasserman
PO Box 1282
Chino, CA 91708
E-mail: caringteacher@earthlink.net
URL: http://www.naact.org
Contact: Sindi D. Wasserman, Contact

Description: Promotes national awareness of the accomplishments of teachers. Provides a forum for the identification of and solutions for problems and issues surrounding the field of education. Enhances the educational opportunities of students with special academic, emotional and physical needs. Increases the number of bilingual, multicultural and caring teachers in public schools. **Computer Services:** Online services, forum.

9219 ■ National Association for Beginning Teachers (NABT)
c/o Warren-Walker Upper School
1165 Sandy Ridge Ave.
Henderson, NV 89052
Ph: (702)616-3027
Fax: (702)616-2065
E-mail: jvm68@aol.com
URL: http://www.beginningteachers.org
Contact: Dr. J. Victor McGuire, Founder

Membership Dues: general, $35 (annual). **Description:** Helps new teachers by providing tools to develop skills needed to succeed in the classroom. Offers support to pre-service and beginning teachers. **Computer Services:** Information services, teacher resources. **Telecommunication Services:** electronic mail, shelleyseagle@yahoo.com.

9220 ■ National Association of Blind Teachers (NABT)
c/o American Council of the Blind
1155 15th St. NW, Ste.1004
Washington, DC 20005
Ph: (202)467-5081
Free: (800)424-8666
Fax: (202)467-5085
E-mail: info@acb.org
URL: http://www.acb.org
Contact: Mitch Pomerantz, Pres.
Founded: 1971. **Members:** 81. **State Groups:** 1. **Description:** Public school teachers, college and university professors, and teachers in residential schools for the blind. Promotes employment and professional goals of blind persons entering the teaching profession or those established in their respective teaching fields. Serves as a vehicle for the dissemination of information and the exchange of ideas addressing special problems of members. Compiles statistics. **Libraries: Type:** reference. **Holdings:** archival material. **Telecommunication Services:** electronic mail, mn.dresser@verizon.net. **Committees:** Manual of Methods of Teaching Without Vision. **Affiliated With:** American Council of the Blind. **Publications:** *The Blind Teacher*, quarterly. Newsletter ● *National Directory of Blind Teachers*, periodic. **Conventions/Meetings:** annual conference (exhibits).

9221 ■ National Association of Community College Teacher Education Programs (NACCTEP)
c/o Dr. Cheri St. Arnauld, Exec. Dir.
2411 W 14th St.
Tempe, AZ 85281-6942
Ph: (480)731-8760
Fax: (480)731-8786
E-mail: cheri.st_arnauld@domail.maricopa.edu
URL: http://www.nacctep.org
Contact: Dr. Cheri St. Arnauld, Exec. Dir.
Membership Dues: institutional, educational partner, $300 (annual) ● corporate, $500 (annual) ● individual, $110 (annual) ● student, $35 (annual) ● affiliate, $800 (annual). **Description:** Promotes the community college role in the recruitment, preparation, retention and renewal of diverse Pre K-12 teachers. Advances quality teacher education programs in the community college. Advocates for and represents at the national level the interests of community colleges in teacher preparation. Promotes programs, services, and activities to enhance the role and effectiveness of community college teacher education programs. Provides connections among community college professionals and others interested in teacher preparation. **Affiliated With:** American Association of Colleges for Teacher Education. **Publications:** Newsletter, quarterly. Contains news regarding membership, upcoming events, community college spotlights, and educational issues. **Price:** included in membership dues. **Conventions/Meetings:** annual conference (exhibits).

9222 ■ National Association of Early Childhood Teacher Educators (NAECTE)
c/o Anne Dorsey
1082 Witt Rd.
Cincinnati, OH 45255
E-mail: marjorie.fields@uas.alaska.edu
URL: http://www.naecte.org
Contact: Marjorie Fields, Pres.
Founded: 1977. **Members:** 500. **Membership Dues:** regular, $45 (annual) ● international, $55 (annual). **Regional Groups:** 10. **State Groups:** 22. **Description:** Works to promote the professional growth of early childhood teacher educators. Provides a forum for the discussion of issues and concerns; advocates improvements in early childhood teacher education; cooperates with other national organizations; and disseminates information on research and practice. **Awards:** NAECTE and Merrill-Prentice Hall Outstanding Dissertation of the Year. **Frequency:** annual. **Type:** monetary. **Recipient:** for outstanding dissertation ● NAECTE and Pearson/Allyn and Bacon Early Childhood Teacher Educator of the Year. **Frequency:** annual. **Type:** recognition. **Recipient:** for leadership, professionalism, and mentoring ● NAECTE and Thomson Delmar Learning Outstanding Early Childhood Practitioner of the Year. **Frequency:** annual. **Type:** monetary. **Recipient:** for outstanding DAP practices, mentoring other early childhood professionals. **Computer Services:** Mailing lists, labels can be purchased from VP for membership ● online services, announcements and membership forms, affiliate information. **Telecommunication Services:** electronic mail, chaillec@pdx.edu. **Committees:** Awards; Conference; Long-Range Planning; Policy; Program; Publications. **Publications:** *Journal of Early Childhood Teacher Education*, quarterly. Addresses issues of interest to those teaching early childhood students. **Conventions/Meetings:** semiannual conference and board meeting, early childhood publications of members, held in conjunction with NAEYC (exhibits) - always June and November.

9223 ■ National Association of Professional Educators (NAPE)
900 17th St., Ste.300
Washington, DC 20006
Ph: (202)848-8969
E-mail: acrocke@tenet.edu
Contact: Philip Strittmatter, Dir.
Founded: 1972. **Membership Dues:** $40 (annual). **Regional Groups:** 6. **State Groups:** 17. **Local Groups:** 36. **Description:** Represents professional educators, school personnel, and other interested individuals. Establishes local and state organizations as alternatives to teacher unions. Maintains and ensures citizen control of public school systems. Promotes uninterrupted education of students during the school year. Fosters public confidence in state educational systems. Promotes professional status of compensation for educators and protects educators' individual freedoms. Improves and provides educational opportunities for educators. Monitors and takes part in related legislative activities. Prevents control of certification and decertification of educators by employee organizations. Conducts networking among related groups, legislators, school boards, and citizens. Makes available abstracts from databases on educational research. Drafted a code of ethics for professional educators. **Libraries: Type:** open to the public. **Telecommunication Services:** electronic mail, freebird@mindspring.com. **Committees:** Ethics/Standards. **Publications:** *Professional Educator Newsletter*, 7/year. Keeps educators informed of association activities and current educational issues. Includes list of events and educational opportunities. **Price:** included in membership dues. **Conventions/Meetings:** annual meeting.

9224 ■ National Association of State Directors of Teacher Education and Certification (NASDTEC)
1225 Providence Rd.
PMB 116
Whitinsville, MA 01588
Ph: (508)380-1202
Fax: (508)278-5342
E-mail: rje@nasdtec.com
URL: http://www.nasdtec.org
Contact: Roy Einreinhofer, Exec. Dir.
Founded: 1928. **Members:** 160. **Membership Dues:** agency, $3,500 (annual) ● associate, $400 (annual). **Staff:** 1. **Budget:** $300,000. **Regional Groups:** 1. **State Groups:** 60. **Multinational. Description:** Represents agencies in the states, District of Columbia, Guam, Mariana Islands, Alberta, British Columbia, and Ontario that have major administrative responsibility for the preparation and certification of professional school personnel and professional standards and practices. Seeks to upgrade skills of members and interested persons and to improve teacher preparation programs and certification procedures. **Committees:** Interstate Certification; Professional Practice; Professional Preparation and Continuing Development; Technology. **Publications:** *Directory of State Certification Personnel*. **Price:** $35.00/year. **Circulation:** 2,000. Alternate Formats: online ● *NASDTEC KnowledgeBase*. Manual. **Price:** $96.95/year; $30.00 for 3 months; $12.00 for 1 month trial. **Circulation:** 1,500. Alternate Formats: online. **Conventions/Meetings:** annual conference, with presentations and interactive sessions addressing important topics related to educator preparation, certification, and professional practices (exhibits) - usually June ● annual Professional Practice Institute - conference, with presentations and interactive sessions targeting professional practices in the education profession - usually October/November.

9225 ■ National Board for Professional Teaching Standards (NBPTS)
1525 Wilson Blvd., Ste.500
Arlington, VA 22209
Ph: (703)465-2700
Free: (800)22-TEACH
Fax: (703)465-2715
URL: http://www.nbpts.org
Contact: Dr. Joseph A. Aguerrebere Jr., Pres./CEO
Founded: 1987. **Members:** 64. **Staff:** 30. **Description:** Teachers and state and local officials in the field of elementary and secondary education; leaders from the business community and higher education. Seeks to strengthen the profession of elementary and secondary teaching and thereby raise the quality of education in the U.S; establish high standards of accomplishment for teachers and recognize, through advanced certification, teachers who meet these standards. Through certification, the board hopes to act as a catalyst to transform teaching as a career by enabling states and schools to recognize outstanding teaching professionals, offer them better compensation, provide them with increased responsibilities, and place important decisions about teaching policy and practice in their hands, and thereby attract and retain superior teachers. Conducts a national forum to inform educators, policy makers, and all other interested persons about its activities and to gain feedback from attendees. Operates speakers' bureau. **Computer Services:** database ● mailing lists. **Publications:** *The Professional Standard*, quarterly. Newsletter. Alternate Formats: online ● *Raising the Standard: A 15-Year Retrospective*. Booklet. **Price:** $5.00. Alternate Formats: online ● *Toward High and Rigorous Standards for the Teaching Profession*, annual. **Price:** $8.00 ● *Toward High and Rigorous Standards for the Teaching Profession: A Summary*. Pamphlet ● *Vision of the National Board*. Pamphlet ● Annual Report, annual ● Pamphlets ● Videos. **Conventions/Meetings:** annual conference ● meeting - 3/year.

9226 ■ National Council of Japanese Language Teachers (NCJLT)
PO Box 3719
Boulder, CO 80307-3719
E-mail: ncjlt@japaneseteaching.org
URL: http://www.ncjlt.org
Contact: Miko Foard, Pres./Teacher Award Dir.
Membership Dues: individual, $20 (annual) ● international individual, $25 (annual) ● domestic institution, $35 (annual) ● international institution, $40 (annual) ● corporate, $95 (annual). **Multinational. Description:** Promotes Japanese language teaching at the elementary, secondary, and higher education levels across the United States. Fosters the study of Japanese language and culture at the Pre-K-16 levels. Provides professional development opportunities for Japanese language teachers. **Awards:** NCJLT Teacher Award. **Frequency:** annual. **Type:** recognition. **Recipient:** for outstanding teachers of Japanese. **Telecommunication Services:** electronic mail, ncjltboard@japaneseteaching.org. **Affiliated With:** American Council on the Teaching of Foreign Languages. **Publications:** *Oshirase*, quarterly. Newsletter. Contains news and updates on the organization's activities and other relevant information. **Price:** included in membership dues. Alternate Formats: online ● Brochure. Contains information about the organization's cultural advocacies. **Price:** free. Alternate Formats: online.

Technical Education

9227 ■ American Foundry Society (AFS)

1695 N Penny Ln.
Schaumburg, IL 60173
Ph: (847)824-0181
Free: (800)537-4237
Fax: (847)824-7848
E-mail: jcall@afsinc.org
URL: http://www.afsinc.org
Contact: Gerald G. Call, Contact

Founded: 1896. **Members:** 13,000. **Membership Dues:** personal, $100 (annual) ● corporate affiliate, $65 (annual) ● teaching associate, $60 (annual) ● retired, $20 (annual) ● junior, $15 (annual) ● international technical, $185 (annual). **Staff:** 60. **Budget:** $4,000,000. **Regional Groups:** 53. **State Groups:** 16. **Local Groups:** 52. **Description:** Technical, trade and management association of foundrymen, patternmakers, technologists, and educators. Sponsors foundry training courses through the Cast Metals Institute on all subjects pertaining to the castings industry; conducts educational and instructional exhibits of foundry industry; sponsors 10 regional foundry conferences and 400 local foundry technical meetings. Maintains Technical Information Center providing literature searching and document retrieval service; and Metalcasting Abstract Service involving abstracts of the latest metal casting literature. Provides environmental services and testing; conducts research programs; compiles statistics, provides marketing information. **Libraries: Type:** reference. **Holdings:** 1,000. **Subjects:** metal casting. **Divisions:** Aluminum; Brass and Bronze; Cast Iron; Engineering; Environmental Control; Governmental Affairs; Human Resources; Investment Casting; Lost Foam; Management; Melting Methods and Materials; Molding Methods and Materials; Pattern; Steel. **Absorbed:** (1991) American Cast Metals Association. **Formerly:** (1948) American Foundrymen's Association; (2005) American Foundrymen's Society. **Publications:** *Engineered Casting Solutions*, quarterly. Magazine. **Price:** $99.00/year in North America; $150.00/year outside North America. Alternate Formats: online ● *Modern Casting*, monthly. Magazine. Covers current technology practices and other influences affecting the production and marketing of metal castings. **Price:** included in membership dues; $50.00/year; $85.00/year (airmail). ISSN: 0026-7562. **Circulation:** 22,000. **Advertising:** accepted ● Also publishes engineering manuals and books and computer and management software. **Conventions/Meetings:** annual Metalcasting Congress (exhibits).

9228 ■ American Technical Education Association (ATEA)

c/o North Dakota State College of Science
800 N 6th St.
Wahpeton, ND 58076-0002
Ph: (701)671-2240 (701)671-2301
Fax: (701)671-2260
E-mail: betty.krump@ndscs.edu
URL: http://www.ateaonline.org
Contact: Betty M. Krump, Exec. Dir.

Founded: 1928. **Members:** 2,500. **Membership Dues:** student, $12 (annual) ● retired, $30 (annual) ● individual, $60 (annual) ● institutional, $300 (annual) ● corporate/business, $400 (annual) ● life, $550. **Staff:** 2. **Budget:** $90,000. **Regional Groups:** 12. **Multinational. Description:** Dedicated to excellence in the quality of post-secondary technical education with emphasis on professional development. **Awards:** Outstanding Technical Service Award. **Frequency:** annual. **Type:** recognition. **Recipient:** to an individual who has contributed and achieved prominence in technical education at the local, state, regional, and national levels ● Outstanding Technical Student. **Frequency:** annual. **Type:** recognition. **Recipient:** to an individual who is currently a full-time student in a post-secondary technical program ● Outstanding Technical Teacher. **Frequency:** annual. **Type:** recognition. **Recipient:** to full-time post-secondary technical instructors from anywhere in the nation whose performance and contribution are exceptional ● Silver Star of Excellence Award. **Frequency:** annual. **Type:** recognition. **Recipient:** to a company that is supportive and committed to post-secondary technical education. **Computer Services:** database ● mailing lists. **Formerly:** (1949) American Association of Technical High Schools and Institute. **Publications:** Journal, semiannual. Includes articles on current trends and best practices in technical education in addition to book reviews and employment opportunities. **Price:** included in membership dues. ISSN: 0889-6488. **Circulation:** 2,000. **Advertising:** accepted. **Conventions/Meetings:** annual National Conference on Technical Education, vendors involved with post-secondary technical education (exhibits).

9229 ■ General Society of Mechanics and Tradesmen of the City of New York (GSMT)

20 W 44th St.
New York, NY 10036
Ph: (212)840-1840
Fax: (212)840-2046
E-mail: info@generalsociety.org
URL: http://www.generalsociety.org
Contact: David J. Schneiderman, Exec. Dir.

Founded: 1785. **Members:** 160. **Staff:** 12. **Description:** Operates Mechanics Institute, founded in 1820, which offers free evening classes in architectural drafting, computer aided design, plumbing and sanitation, and industrial electricity. **Libraries: Type:** lending; open to the public; reference. **Holdings:** 150,000; books, periodicals. **Subjects:** history, fiction, biography. **Formerly:** (2002) General Society of Mechanics and Tradesmen. **Publications:** *Library Newsletter*, quarterly.

9230 ■ International Fire Service Training Association (IFSTA)

Oklahoma State Univ.
930 N Willis
Stillwater, OK 74078-8045
Ph: (405)744-5723
Free: (800)654-4055
Fax: (405)744-8204
E-mail: info@ifsta.org
URL: http://www.ifsta.org
Contact: Susan F. Walker, Contact

Founded: 1934. **Staff:** 50. **Nonmembership. Description:** Educational organization formed to develop training materials for the fire service. Committee members are individuals who represent their respective fire-related fields and are considered leaders or innovators. Association committee members meet annually to validate training material for publication, add new techniques and developments, delete outmoded methods and equipment, and upgrade fire service training in general; actual publication is done for the association by Fire Protection Publications of Oklahoma State University. **Libraries: Type:** reference. **Holdings:** 10,000; archival material, books, periodicals, reports, software, video recordings. **Subjects:** fire, rescue, terrorism, emergency medical services, public education, training. **Awards:** Hudiberg Award. **Frequency:** annual. **Type:** recognition. **Recipient:** for outstanding fire training contribution. **Telecommunication Services:** electronic mail, customer.service@osufpp.org. **Publications:** *Fire Protection Training Materials Catalog*, semiannual. Lists publications and training aids available from IFSTA and other publishers. **Price:** free. **Circulation:** 120,000 ● *IFSTA Conference Proceedings*, annual. **Price:** free to conference participants. **Circulation:** 300 ● *Speaking of Fire*, quarterly. Provides information pertinent to the fire protection community. **Price:** free. **Circulation:** 120,000 ● Also publishes 50 fire protection training manuals and training aids. **Conventions/Meetings:** annual conference - always first week of July, Oklahoma.

9231 ■ International Technology Education Association (ITEA)

1914 Assn. Dr., Ste.201
Reston, VA 20191-1539
Ph: (703)860-2100
Fax: (703)860-0353
E-mail: itea@iteaconnect.org
URL: http://www.iteaconnect.org
Contact: Kendall N. Starkweather PhD, Exec. Dir.

Founded: 1939. **Members:** 4,000. **Membership Dues:** professional in U.S., sustaining technical representative, $70 (annual) ● professional in Canada and Mexico, $75 (annual) ● professional outside North America, $80 (annual) ● retired, student, $35 (annual) ● institutional/university, museum, $210 (annual) ● sustaining corporation, $350 (annual) ● elementary school, $140 (annual). **Staff:** 12. **Regional Groups:** 4. **State Groups:** 50. **Multinational. Description:** Technology education teachers and supervisors in elementary, secondary, and higher education. Promotes technological literacy; arranges seminars and special projects. Sponsors national leadership institute. Operates placement services. **Awards:** ITEA and EEA-SHIP. **Frequency:** annual. **Type:** scholarship. **Recipient:** for outstanding undergraduate students ● Teacher Excellence/Program Excellence. **Frequency:** annual. **Type:** recognition. **Recipient:** for outstanding teacher and program excellence in each state and province. **Formerly:** (1985) American Industrial Arts Association. **Publications:** *Advancing Excellence in Technological Literacy: Student Assessment, Professional Development, and Program Standards*. Addresses student assessment of technological literacy, teacher development and program enhancement for K-12. ● *Directory of Universities and Colleges*, periodic ● *Journal of Technology Education*, semiannual. Contains research information related to technology education. **Price:** $12.00 in U.S.; $16.00 foreign. **Circulation:** 2,000 ● *Standards for Technological Literacy: Content for the Study of Technology* ● *Technology and Children*, quarterly. Journal. Contains practical, innovative and creative articles and activities for elementary teachers. **Price:** $35.00 in U.S.; $45.00 foreign. **Advertising:** accepted ● *Technology Teacher*, 8/year. Journal. Includes reports of current trends. **Price:** $80.00 in U.S.; $90.00 foreign. **Advertising:** accepted. Alternate Formats: microform. **Conventions/Meetings:** annual international conference and trade show (exhibits) - 2009 Mar. 25-28, Louisville, KY.

9232 ■ International Technology Education Association - Council for Supervisors (ITEA-CS)

c/o Melvin L. Robinson, Communication Chm.
PO Box 144200
Salt Lake City, UT 84114-4200
Ph: (801)538-7598
Fax: (801)538-7868
E-mail: mrobinson@schools.utah.gov
URL: http://www.iteawww.net/CS
Contact: Melvin L. Robinson, Communications Chm.

Founded: 1951. **Members:** 300. **Membership Dues:** professional, undergrad student, full-time grad student, retired, sustaining technical rep, $30-$70 (annual) ● group, $140-$350 (annual) ● individual (international), $30-$80 (annual) ● passport electronic (international), $45 (annual) ● group (international), $140-$350 (annual). **Regional Groups:** 4. **State Groups:** 50. **Description:** Technology education supervisors from the U.S. Office of Education; local school department chairpersons; state departments of education, local school districts, territories, provinces, and foreign countries. Improves instruction and supervision of programs in technology education. Conducts research; compiles statistics. Sponsors competitions. Maintains speakers' bureau. **Telecommunication Services:** electronic mail, mrobinso@usoe.k12.ut.us. **Committees:** Awards; Council of Chief State School Officers (see separate entry); Legislation; Professional Improvement Plan; Talent Matrix. **Formerly:** (1987) American Council of Industrial Arts Supervisors. **Publications:** *Council for Supervisors Steering Committee Handbook*, annual. Alternate Formats: online ● *SuperLink*, 3/year. Newsletter. Alternate Formats: online ● Also publishes monographs, booklets, and guides; offers videos and software. **Conventions/Meetings:** annual meeting, held in conjunction with International Technology Education Association.

9233 ■ National Association of Trade and Industrial Instructors (NATII)
PO Box 1665
Leesburg, VA 20177
Ph: (703)777-1740
E-mail: info@natie.org
URL: http://www.skillsusa.org/NATIE
Contact: Terry Robinson, Pres.
Founded: 1965. **Members:** 600. **Regional Groups:** 5. **Description:** Represents trade and industrial instructors, primarily at the junior high and high school level. Seeks to improve communication among members and to support the needs of classroom teachers. Holds seminars and workshops. **Publications:** *NATII News*, quarterly. Newsletter. **Price:** included in membership dues. **Conventions/Meetings:** annual conference, held in conjunction with American Vocational Association.

9234 ■ Organizational Systems Research Association (OSRA)
c/o Dr. Donna R. Everett, Exec. Dir.
Morehead State Univ.
150 Univ. Blvd.
Box 2478
Morehead, KY 40351-1689
Ph: (606)783-2718
Fax: (606)783-5025
E-mail: d.everett@moreheadstate.edu
URL: http://www.osra.org
Contact: Dr. Donna R. Everett, Exec. Dir.
Founded: 1982. **Members:** 150. **Membership Dues:** individual, student chapter, $55 (annual) ● corporate, $300 (annual) ● retired, student, $35 (annual). **Staff:** 1. **Budget:** $25,000. **Description:** Faculty members at colleges and universities that offer degrees in an organizational systems area; administrators in business, government, or education in office systems areas; administrators, research directors, consultants, or vendors interested in organizational systems research. Aims to: develop and promote organizational systems as a discipline with a common body of knowledge in the analysis, design, and administration of interrelated administrative support systems; provide funds for study and research in the discipline; provide for the distribution of findings from research and experiences relating to practices and instruction in the discipline. Conducts research programs. **Awards: Type:** recognition. **Recipient:** for an outstanding research in the field of information technology and end-user information systems. **Computer Services:** database, membership. **Committees:** Business Outreach and Research Foundation; Research. **Formerly:** (2000) Office Systems Research Association. **Publications:** *Information Technology, Learning, and Performance Journal*, semiannual. **Price:** $50.00/year. ISSN: 0737-8998. **Circulation:** 250. **Advertising:** accepted. Alternate Formats: online ● *OSRA Newsletter*, quarterly. Includes calendar of events and research notes. **Price:** included in membership dues. **Circulation:** 350. Alternate Formats: online ● Proceedings. Alternate Formats: online. **Conventions/Meetings:** annual Research Conference (exhibits).

9235 ■ Silver Eagles of America (SEA)
PO Box 1336
Flat Rock, NC 28731
Free: (800)801-7090
Fax: (828)698-8564
E-mail: apowell@nths.org
URL: http://www.nths.org
Contact: Allen Powell, Exec. Dir.
Membership Dues: student, $10 ● honorary, $25. **State Groups:** 30. **Description:** Chartered middle, junior, and high schools; students and other interested individuals. Promotes more effective technology and technical education to prepare young people for the modern workplace. Assists schools wishing to build business and industry partnerships to better tailor their curricula to meet changing economic conditions; seeks to advance technology and technical education. **Publications:** *SEA High School and Career Planning Guide*. Handbook.

Technology

9236 ■ Society of International Chinese in Educational Technology (SICET)
c/o Hong Zhan, Sec.-Treas.
7200 E Pioneer Ln.
Prescott Valley, AZ 86314
Ph: (928)523-0408
Fax: (928)523-1929
E-mail: hong.zhan@nau.edu
URL: http://www.sicet.org
Contact: Hong Zhan, Sec.-Treas.
Founded: 2003. **Membership Dues:** regular, $47 (annual) ● student, $25 (annual) ● joint outside U.S., $30 (annual). **Multinational. Description:** Brings together international Chinese scholars and experts in the field of educational technology. Strengthens the academic international connections, exchanges, researches and studies in educational technology for teaching and learning. Promotes the application of educational technology in Chinese education. **Computer Services:** Mailing lists. **Telecommunication Services:** electronic mail, hyang2@oswego.edu. **Affiliated With:** Association for Educational Communications and Technology. **Publications:** *International Journal of Technology in Teaching and Learning*, semiannual. ISSN: 1551-2576. Alternate Formats: online ● Newsletter. Alternate Formats: online ● Brochure. Alternate Formats: online. **Conventions/Meetings:** annual convention, with paper presentation.

Technology Education

9237 ■ Association for the Advancement of Computing in Education (AACE)
PO Box 1545
Chesapeake, VA 23327-1545
Ph: (757)366-5606
Fax: (703)997-8760
E-mail: info@aace.org
URL: http://www.aace.org
Founded: 1981. **Membership Dues:** professional, $95 (annual) ● student, $60 (annual). **Multinational. Description:** Strives to advance the knowledge, theory, and quality of learning and teaching at all levels with information technology. **Libraries: Type:** reference. **Holdings:** 1,000; papers, periodicals. **Subjects:** educational technology, e-learning. **Publications:** *International Journal on E-Learning*, quarterly. Serves as forum on the exchange of information on the theory, research, development and practice of E-Learning in education and training. **Price:** $55.00 for professional members; $40.00 for student members; $165.00 for institutions. ISSN: 1537-2456. Also Cited As: *IJEL* ● *Journal of Computers in Mathematics and Science Teaching*, quarterly. Offers forum for the exchange of information in science, mathematics and computer science. **Price:** $55.00 for professional members; $40.00 for student members; $165.00 for institutions. ISSN: 0731-9258. **Advertising:** accepted. Also Cited As: *JCMST* ● *Journal of Computing in Childhood Education* ● *Journal of Educational Multimedia and Hypermedia*, quarterly. Provides forum on research, development and applications of multimedia and hypermedia in education. **Price:** $55.00 for professional members; $40.00 for student members; $165.00 for institutions. ISSN: 1055-8896. Also Cited As: *JEMH* ● *Journal of Interactive Learning Research*, quarterly. Features papers on the theory, design, implementation, effectiveness and impact on education and training of interactive learning environments. **Price:** $55.00 for professional members; $40.00 for student members; $165.00 for institutions. ISSN: 1093-023X. Also Cited As: *JILR* ● *Journal of Technology and Teacher Education*, quarterly. Serves as forum about the use of information technology in teacher education. **Price:** $55.00 for professional members; $40.00 for student members; $165.00 for institutions. ISSN: 1059-7069 ● Additional journals include: *International Journal of Educational Telecommunications* and *AACE Review*. Also publishes books and CD-ROMs. **Conventions/Meetings:** annual ED-MEDIA - conference - 2008 June 30-July 4, Vienna, Austria.

9238 ■ Fiber Optic Association (FOA)
1119 S Mission Rd., Ste.355
Fallbrook, CA 92028
Ph: (760)451-3655
Fax: (781)207-2421
E-mail: info@thefoa.org
URL: http://www.thefoa.org
Contact: Jim Hayes, Pres./Treas.
Founded: 1995. **Multinational. Description:** Promotes professionalism in the field of fiber optics. Sets standards for and administering technical certification programs. Promotes fiber optics applications and education. **Publications:** *FOA News*. Newsletter. Alternate Formats: online.

9239 ■ National Association for Tech Prep Leadership (NATPL)
c/o KS Board of Regents
1000 SW Jackson St., Ste.520
Topeka, KS 66612-1368
Ph: (785)296-3958
Fax: (785)296-3957
E-mail: info@natpl.org
URL: http://www.natpl.org
Contact: Dennis Fiscus, Pres.-Elect
Founded: 1997. **Membership Dues:** general, $40 (annual). **Regional Groups:** 4. **Description:** Encourages career development, professional involvement and networking among Tech Prep leaders. Increases awareness of the benefits of Tech Prep. Provides opportunities for students to enhance their academic and technical knowledge and skills required for continued education and workforce readiness. **Publications:** Bulletin, quarterly.

9240 ■ National Coalition of Advanced Technology Centers (NCATC)
c/o Moraine Valley Community College
9000 W Coll. Pkwy.
Palos Hills, IL 60465
Ph: (708)326-2509
Fax: (708)326-2511
E-mail: rchinckley@msn.com
URL: http://www.ncatc.org
Contact: Dr. Richard Hinckley, Exec. Dir.
Founded: 1988. **Members:** 130. **Membership Dues:** full, associate, corporate sponsor, $600 (annual) ● individual, $75 (annual). **Multinational. Description:** Serves as a network of higher education resources that advocates and promotes the use of technology applications that enhance economic and workforce development programs and services. Promotes national awareness of technology centers and their positive impact on the competitive ability and economic growth of America.

9241 ■ National Coalition for Technology in Education and Training (NCTET)
c/o Ann M. Dorman
Meetings and Events of Distinction, LLC
2724 Kenwood Ave.
Alexandria, VA 22302
Ph: (703)626-1266
Fax: (703)998-0526
E-mail: adorman@nctet.org
URL: http://www.nctet.org
Contact: Mary Ann Wolf PhD, Exec. Dir.
Description: Represents education associations, corporations, and organizations and individuals with an interest in education technology. Promotes and supports the effective use of technology to improve education and training in America. Acts as a convener, catalyst and resource for relevant and timely information. **Awards:** NCTET Community Builder Award. **Frequency:** annual. **Type:** recognition. **Recipient:** to recognize exemplary effort in advancing the cause of education technology nationally. **Telecommunication Services:** electronic mail, irene@cosn.org.

9242 ■ Open Door Education Foundation
1420 King St., Ste.610
Alexandria, VA 22314
Ph: (703)838-2050
Fax: (703)838-3610
E-mail: susan@keys2it.org
URL: http://www.keys2it.org
Contact: Stephanie Skinner, Pres.
Founded: 1998. **Description:** Serves as the education arm of the National Association of Computer Consultant Businesses. Encourages students, their parents, counselors, and people considering a career shift to the information technology industry. Gives scholarships in communities where donors do business. **Affiliated With:** National Association of Computer Consultant Businesses.

9243 ■ Society for Information Technology and Teacher Education (SITE)
PO Box 1545
Chesapeake, VA 23327-1545
Ph: (757)366-5606
Fax: (703)997-8760
E-mail: info@aace.org
URL: http://www.aace.org/site/default.htm
Contact: Ian Glenn, Pres.
Founded: 1990. **Membership Dues:** professional, $95 (annual) ● professional, non-US, $110 (annual) ● student, $55 (annual) ● student, non-US, $70 (annual). **Description:** Represents individual teacher educators and affiliated organizations. Promotes the creation and dissemination of knowledge about the use of information technology in teacher education and faculty/staff development. Promotes research, scholarship, collaboration, exchange and support among its members. Fosters the development of new national organizations. Aims to integrate instructional technologies into teacher education programs. **Libraries: Type:** reference. **Holdings:** articles, papers, periodicals, reports. **Subjects:** educational technology, e-learning, information technology. **Awards:** Award for Outstanding Service to Digital Equity. **Frequency:** annual. **Type:** recognition. **Recipient:** for outstanding service in the area of digital equity ● National Technology Leadership Initiative Fellowships. **Frequency:** annual. **Type:** fellowship. **Recipient:** for exemplary use of technology in social studies, language arts, science and mathematics teaching ● Outstanding Paper Awards. **Frequency:** annual. **Type:** recognition. **Recipient:** for outstanding paperwork submitted to the organization. **Computer Services:** Online services, discussion forum, job board. **Publications:** *Contemporary Issues in Technology and Teacher Education*. Journal. Includes theoretical discussions of technology and teacher preparation, and snapshots of technology in practice. ISSN: 1528-5804. Alternate Formats: online ● *Journal of Technology and Teacher Education*. Contains information on the use of technology in teacher education. **Price:** included in membership dues; $140.00 /year for libraries and institutions. ISSN: 1059-7069 ● *Membership Brochure: Benefits and Rates*. Alternate Formats: online ● *Statement of Basic Principles and Suggested Actions*. Paper. Alternate Formats: online.

9244 ■ State Educational Technology Directors Association (SETDA)
c/o Mary Ann Wolf, Exec. Dir.
PO Box 10
Glen Burnie, MD 21060
Ph: (410)647-6965
Fax: (309)210-7073
E-mail: mwolf@setda.org
URL: http://www.setda.org
Contact: Tera Daniels, Office Mgr.
Founded: 2001. **Description:** Represents the state directors for educational technology. Aims to improve student achievement through technology. Promotes national leadership in educational technology to support achievement in lifelong learning. Provides professional development for state educational technology directors. Builds partnerships to advance learning opportunities. **Awards:** Leader of the Year. **Frequency:** annual. **Type:** recognition. **Computer Services:** database, member directory ● information services, news, business resources ● mailing lists, general information e-mail list ● online services, SETDA connects, technology courses. **Committees:** Data Collection; Federal and State Policy; Innovations and Partnerships; Membership and Communications; Professional Growth. **Programs:** Technical Assistance Partnership. **Projects:** Data Collection: Common Data Elements. **Affiliated With:** Council of Chief State School Officers; International Society for Technology in Education. **Publications:** *National Leadership Institute Toolkit: States Helping States Implement No Child Left Behind*. Manual. Alternate Formats: online ● *National Trends: Enhancing Education Through Technology Review*. Report. Documents implementation of the formula and competitive grant programs and highlights state programs in alignment with purposes of the association. Alternate Formats: online ● Newsletter. Alternate Formats: online.

9245 ■ Technology Management Education Association (TMEDA)
c/o Chuck Rutledge
71 James Way
Eatontown, NJ 07724
Ph: (973)285-3850
E-mail: info@tmeda.net
URL: http://www.tmeda.net
Contact: Dr. Audrey Curtis, Sec.-Treas.
Description: Seeks to improve awareness, effectiveness and education of technology management education. Provides a forum for the sharing of ideas among technology management professionals. Raises awareness and understanding of the values of technology management. **Awards:** TMEDA Management Education Award. **Frequency:** annual. **Type:** recognition. **Recipient:** for outstanding long time contributions to the field of technology management education. **Telecommunication Services:** electronic mail, acurtis@stevens-tech.edu. **Publications:** Brochure. Alternate Formats: online.

Testing

9246 ■ ACT
PO Box 168
Iowa City, IA 52244-0168
Ph: (319)337-1000
Fax: (319)339-3020
E-mail: mediarelations@act.org
URL: http://www.act.org
Contact: Richard L. Ferguson, CEO/Chm.
Founded: 1959. **Staff:** 1,100. **Budget:** $30,000,000. **State Groups:** 37. **Description:** Provides guidance-oriented assessment and research programs for students, schools, colleges, universities, vocational-technical institutes, and scholarship agencies. ACT Assessment Program, which consists of a profile questionnaire, interest inventory, and four 35-60 minute tests in English, mathematics, reading, and scientific reasoning, is completed by more than 1,700,000 students annually. Provides colleges and universities with information used in admission, placement, and advising. ASSET and COMPASS, placement programs for two-year colleges, are completed by more than 1,600,000 students annually. Also offers eighth grade and tenth grade assessments; Work Keys, the nation's leading work skills testing system; and DISCOVER, an interactive educational and career planning program. Conducts more than 90 other assessment programs on behalf of organizations, and agencies. Conducts research, compiles statistics, and processes federal financial aid applications. **Libraries: Type:** reference. **Holdings:** 25,000; audio recordings, books, periodicals, video recordings. **Subjects:** educational psychology, assessment, measurement, statistics, education. **Computer Services:** database, financial aid administration software. **Divisions:** Business and Finance; Communications; Development; Educational Services; Information Systems; Operations; Professional Development Services; Research; Workforce Delivery Services. **Formerly:** (1996) American College Testing. **Publications:** *ACTivity*, quarterly. Newsletter. Provides accounts of programs, services, and activities. **Price:** free. **Circulation:** 100,000. Alternate Formats: online ● *Research Report Series*, periodic. Alternate Formats: online ● Brochures ● Pamphlets ● Reports. **Conventions/Meetings:** annual general assembly and conference.

9247 ■ Association for Assessment in Counseling and Education (AACE)
c/o American Counseling Association
5999 Stevenson Ave.
Alexandria, VA 22304-3300
Free: (800)347-6647
Fax: (800)473-2329
E-mail: lundberg@ncat.edu
URL: http://aac.ncat.edu
Contact: Dr. Brian Glaser, Pres.
Founded: 1965. **Members:** 995. **Membership Dues:** professional, regular, $35 (annual) ● retired, student, new professional, $25 (annual). **State Groups:** 13. **Description:** A division of the American Counseling Association (see separate entry). School and college counselors, career counselors, rehabilitation counselors, private practice counselors and counselor educators. Supports counselors with information and advice that will help them use assessments appropriately. Provides: information on trends, issues, and advances in assessment; reviews and evaluations of new or revised tests; guidelines and position papers on topics such as responsible test use, application of minimum competency tests, career assessments, and performance assessments. **Libraries: Type:** reference. **Holdings:** 5,000. **Subjects:** counseling in all aspects and settings. **Awards:** Exemplary Practices Award. **Frequency:** periodic. **Type:** recognition. **Recipient:** for outstanding contributions to assessment in counseling ● Student Award. **Frequency:** periodic. **Type:** recognition. **Recipient:** for outstanding contribution to the counseling profession. **Affiliated With:** American Counseling Association. **Formerly:** (1985) Association for Measurement and Evaluation in Guidance; (1992) Association for Measurement and Evaluation in Counseling and Development; (2005) Association for Assessment in Counseling. **Publications:** *Measurement and Evaluation in Counseling and Development*, quarterly. Journal. Contains articles focusing on research and applications in guidance and counseling. Intended for counselors and directors of research. **Price:** included in membership dues; $60.00 /year for nonmembers. ISSN: 0748-1756. **Circulation:** 2,396. **Advertising:** accepted. Also Cited As: *MECD* ● *Newsnotes*, quarterly. Newsletter. Contains state, regional, national, and international news and information. **Price:** included in membership dues. **Conventions/Meetings:** annual convention, held in conjunction with the ACA (exhibits) ● workshop.

9248 ■ The College Board (TCB)
45 Columbus Ave.
New York, NY 10023-6992
Ph: (212)713-8000 (212)713-8050
Free: (866)392-3017
Fax: (212)649-8442
E-mail: publicaffairs@collegeboard.org
URL: http://www.collegeboard.com
Contact: Governor Gaston Caperton, Pres.
Founded: 1900. **Members:** 5,200. **Membership Dues:** secondary/higher education institution, system, non-profit association, $325 (annual). **Staff:** 1,000. **Regional Groups:** 6. **Languages:** English, Spanish. **Description:** Represents the schools, colleges, universities, and other educational organizations that seeks to connect members to success and opportunity. Serves students, parents, high schools, and colleges through major programs and services in college admission, guidance, assessment, financial aid, enrollment, and teaching and learning. **Committees:** Academic Advisory; Advanced Placement Test Development; CLEP Test Development; Research and Development and Academic Affairs; SAT and SAT Subject Test Development. **Councils:** Academic Assembly; College Scholarship Service Assembly; Guidance and Admission Assembly. **Also Known As:** College Entrance Examination Board. **Publications:** *Campus Visits and College Interviews*. Book ● *CLEP Official Study Guide*, annual. Book ● *The College*

Application Essay. Book ● *College Board Book of Majors*, biennial. Handbook ● *College Board College Handbook*, annual. Directory ● *College Board Review*, 3/year. Magazine. Covers fresh, provocative topics. **Price:** $30.00/year; $55.00/2 years; $80.00/3 years ● *College Counseling Sourcebook*, annual. Handbook ● *College Scoop*, biennial. Magazine ● *CollegeEd Family Handbooks* ● *CollegeEd Student Workbooks*. Handbooks ● *CollegeEd Teachers Guides*. Handbooks ● *Getting Financial Aid*, annual. Directory ● *International Student Handbook*, annual ● *Meeting College Costs*. Handbook ● *Official SAT Study Guide*. Book ● *Onboard*. Newsletters. Alternate Formats: online ● *Scholarship Handbook*, annual ● Proceedings, annual. **Conventions/Meetings:** annual College Board Forum - conference and meeting.

9249 ■ Educational Records Bureau (ERB)
220 E 42nd St.
New York, NY 10017
Ph: (212)672-9800
Free: (800)989-3721
Fax: (212)370-4096
E-mail: info@erbtest.org
URL: http://www.erbtest.org
Contact: Dr. David F. Clune, Pres.

Founded: 1927. **Members:** 1,500. **Membership Dues:** independent school, suburban public school district, $295 (annual) ● nursery school, $140 (annual). **Staff:** 15. **Budget:** $11,000,000. **Multinational. Description:** Independent and nonpublic schools, international schools, and suburban public schools. Provides student testing services and research to member schools; ability/achievement test, writing assessment, and independent school admissions program. Plans student testing programs, scores tests, reports results to schools, prepares normative data, conducts research on test results, publishes research reports on testing, and assists schools in using test results in instruction and guidance. **Publications:** *Catalog of Programs and Services*, annual ● *The Evaluator*, quarterly. Newsletter. Highlights issues of educational interest, provides announcements of important upcoming events, and summarizes important developments. Alternate Formats: online. **Conventions/Meetings:** annual conference, with presentations and workshops on testing, admission, and other areas of interest to educators - each October in New York City.

9250 ■ Educational Testing Service (ETS)
Rosedale Rd.
Princeton, NJ 08541
Ph: (609)921-9000
Fax: (609)734-5410
E-mail: etsinfo@ets.org
URL: http://www.ets.org
Contact: Kurt Landgraf, Pres./CEO

Founded: 1947. **Staff:** 2,500. **Description:** Educational measurement and research organization, founded by merger of the testing activities of American Council on Education, Carnegie Foundation for the Advancement of Teaching, and The College Board. Provides tests and related services for schools, colleges, governmental agencies, and the professions; offers advisory services in the sound application of measurement techniques and materials; conducts educational, psychological, and measurement research. Offers a summer program in educational testing for scholars and educators from other countries, continuing education programs, and measurement, evaluation, and other instructional activities. **Libraries: Type:** reference. **Holdings:** 18,000. **Subjects:** measurement, tests. **Awards:** ETS Award for Distinguished Service to Measurement. **Frequency:** annual. **Type:** recognition. **Recipient:** for distinguished service to measurement. **Affiliated With:** American Council on Education; Carnegie Foundation for the Advancement of Teaching; The College Board. **Publications:** *ETS Developments*, quarterly. Newsletter. Covers new products and services. **Price:** free. **Circulation:** 70,000 ● Articles ● Reports. **Conventions/Meetings:** annual conference.

9251 ■ Graduate Record Examinations Board (GRE BOARD)
c/o Educational Testing Service
PO Box 6000
Princeton, NJ 08541-6000
Ph: (609)771-7670 (609)921-9000
Fax: (609)734-5410
E-mail: gre-info@rosedale.org
URL: http://www.ets.org/gre
Contact: Dale Johnson, Chm.

Founded: 1966. **Description:** Participants are appointees of the Association of Graduate Schools in Association of American Universities, the Council of Graduate Schools, and the GRE Board. Has responsibility for the Graduate Record Examinations Program (GRE) to assist in graduate school selection. Seeks to ensure that the program is carried out in the best interests of graduate education, the students, and the schools. Educational Testing Service provides technical advice, research expertise, professional counsel, and administers the GRE. Graduate Record Examinations, first administered in 1937, were initiated as a joint venture of the Carnegie Foundation for the Advancement of Teaching and the graduate school deans of four eastern U.S. universities. The examination and programs in which they were used became the responsibility of ETS when it began operating in 1948, until 1966, when the present structure was formed in order to give broader representation to the graduate education community. **Telecommunication Services:** electronic mail, gre-info@ets.org. **Affiliated With:** Association of Graduate Schools in Association of American Universities; Carnegie Foundation for the Advancement of Teaching; Council of Graduate Schools; Educational Testing Service. **Publications:** *Directory of Graduate Programs*, biennial ● *General Test Practice Book*, every 6 years ● *General Test Preparation Software*, biennial ● *GRE Information Bulletin*, annual ● *Subject Tests Practice Books*, annual. **Conventions/Meetings:** semiannual board meeting.

9252 ■ International Society for Performance Improvement (ISPI)
1400 Spring St., Ste.260
Silver Spring, MD 20910
Ph: (301)587-8570
Fax: (301)587-8573
E-mail: info@ispi.org
URL: http://www.ispi.org
Contact: Richard D. Battaglia, Exec. Dir.

Founded: 1962. **Members:** 10,000. **Membership Dues:** active, $145 (annual) ● student, retired, $60 (annual) ● sustaining, $950 (annual) ● life, $1,500 ● patron, $1,400 (annual). **Staff:** 10. **Budget:** $2,500,000. **National Groups:** 55. **Multinational. Description:** Works to improve productivity and performance in the workplace through the application of performance and instructional technologies. Offers education and employment referral service. Publishes books and periodicals. Offers annual awards competitions. **Awards:** Awards of Excellence. **Frequency:** annual. **Type:** recognition. **Recipient:** for outstanding publications/communications, outstanding performance improvement, outstanding research, chapters of merit. **Computer Services:** database, CPT directory ● mailing lists, of members ● online services, discussion groups. **Telecommunication Services:** electronic mail, rick@ispi.org. **Formerly:** (1973) National Society for Programmed Instruction; (1995) National Society for Performance and Instruction. **Publications:** *Performance Improvement*, 10/year. Journal. Contains how-to instruction, personal viewpoints, guidelines, procedural models, and book reviews. **Price:** $10.00/copy. **Circulation:** 6,000. **Advertising:** accepted. Alternate Formats: microform; diskette ● *Performance Improvement Quarterly*. Journal. Includes research and theory information in performance technology. **Price:** $40.00 /year for members; $50.00 /year for nonmembers, in North America; $70.00 /year for nonmembers, outside North America ● *Performance Improvement Resources and Membership Directory*, annual. Contains Membership listing alphabetical and geographic, ISPI general information, listing of paid advertiser's services. **Price:** $75.00 for nonmembers; included in membership dues. **Circulation:** 6,000. **Advertising:** accepted ● *PerformanceXpress*, monthly. Newsletter. Alternate Formats: online. **Conventions/Meetings:** annual International Performance Improvement Conference: Performance Beyond Borders - international conference, in conjunction with IFTDO (exhibits).

9253 ■ National Assessment of Educational Progress (NAEP)
Assessment Div., 8th Fl.
1990 K St. NW
Washington, DC 20006
Ph: (202)502-7300 (202)502-7321
Free: (800)223-0267
Fax: (202)502-7440
E-mail: peggy.carr@ed.gov
URL: http://nces.ed.gov/nationsreportcard
Contact: Peggy Carr, Assoc. Commissioner

Founded: 1964. **Description:** A program of the Office for Educational Research and Improvement, under contract to Educational Testing Service (see separate entry). Objectives are to: provide census-like data on various educational levels; conduct national assessments of major learning areas; report results to professional public and educational decision-makers; continue ongoing research. Assessments have been conducted in reading, mathematics, science, writing, literature, citizenship, social studies, computer competence, career and occupational development, art, and music; areas are periodically reassessed. Financed through Department of Education. Provides reports on what American students know and can do; compiles statistics. **Libraries: Type:** reference. **Holdings:** 2,000; audiovisuals. **Also Known As:** (2005) Nation's Report Card. **Formerly:** (1968) Exploratory Committee on Assessing the Progress of Education; (1969) Committee on Assessing the Progress of Education; (1986) National Assessment of Educational Progress; (1987) National Assessment of Educational Progress, The Nation's Report Card. **Publications:** Reports. Alternate Formats: online.

9254 ■ National Association of Test Directors (NATD)
c/o Sherry Rose Bond
1091 King Ave.
Columbus, OH 43212
Ph: (614)365-5786
E-mail: srosebond@columbus.k12.oh.us
URL: http://www.natd.org
Contact: Sherry Rose Bond, Pres.

Founded: 1985. **Members:** 300. **Membership Dues:** individual, $20 (annual). **Budget:** $13,000. **Description:** Individuals responsible for educational testing programs, test development, administration, and interpretation primarily in public school systems. Aims to: disseminate information about testing in educational environments; facilitate the appropriate application of educational measurement to students; foster research in educational measurement. Maintains speakers' bureau; compiles statistics. **Awards:** Professional Recognition Award. **Frequency:** annual. **Type:** recognition. **Recipient:** for service relating to national issues of testing. **Publications:** *NATD Newsletter*, quarterly. Alternate Formats: online ● *Symposia Papers*, annual ● Membership Directory, biennial. **Conventions/Meetings:** annual conference and symposium, held in conjunction with American Educational Research Association and National Council on Measurement in Education - always spring.

9255 ■ National Center for Fair and Open Testing
342 Broadway
Cambridge, MA 02139
Ph: (617)864-4810
Fax: (617)497-2224
E-mail: info@fairtest.org
URL: http://www.fairtest.org
Contact: Monty Neill EdD, Exec. Dir.

Founded: 1985. **Membership Dues:** subscriber, $30 (annual) ● sponsor, $100 (annual). **Staff:** 6. **Budget:** $400,000. **Description:** Seeks to ensure that the 100 million standardized tests administered annually are fair, open, and educationally sound. Works to: eliminate racially, culturally, and sexually biased standardized tests, including aptitude tests, intelligence tests, and professional certification exams; replace multiple-choice tests, which the group feels do not adequately measure performance with educationally sound alternatives; prevent non-validated tests from being administered. Supports truth-in-testing requirements that compel test makers to publicly disclose test questions; encourages requiring test companies to publicize statistics about the reliability and validity of their tests. Opposes the use of experimental sections on tests without the test subjects' consent. Encourages withholding of test scores from institutions that misuse them. Holds educational programs. Maintains library and speakers' bureau; compiles statistics. **Libraries: Type:** by appointment only. **Holdings:** 1,000. **Subjects:** detailed files on test skills, university admissions, employment assessments. **Boards:** National Policy Advisory Panel. **Also Known As:** FairTest. **Publications:** *Annotated Bibliography on Assessment of Young Children* ● *Annotated Bibliography on Performance Assessment* ● *Annotated Bibliography on SAT Bias and Misuse*. **Price:** $8.00 ● *Beyond Standardized Tests: Admissions Alternatives That Work* ● *Failing Our Children*. Report. **Price:** $30.00 full report; $10.00 summary. Alternate Formats: online ● *FairTest Examiner*, quarterly. Contains news on the testing reform movement and reports on lawsuits, research, policy changes, new exams, and conferences. **Price:** $30.00 /year for individuals; $45.00 /year for institutions; $5.00 for postage outside U.S. **Circulation:** 4,000. Alternate Formats: online ● *Fallout From the Testing Explosion*. **Price:** $12.00 ● *Implementing Performance Assessments: A Guide to Classroom, School and System Reform*. **Price:** $6.00 each; $25.00 for 5 copies; $40.00 for 10 copies; $75.00 for 25 copies ● *Principles and Indicators for Student Assessment Systems*. **Price:** $10.00 each; $80.00 for 10 copies; $350.00 for 50 copies; $600.00 for 100 copies ● *The SAT Coaching Cover-up*. **Price:** $10.00 ● *Sex Bias in College Admissions Tests: Why Women Lose Out* ● *Standardized Tests and Our Children: A Guide to Testing Reform* (in English and Spanish). **Price:** $4.00 each; $15.00 for 5 copies; $20.00 for 10 copies; $50.00 for 50 copies ● *Standing Up to the SAT* ● *Testing Our Children: A Report Card on State Assessment Systems*. **Price:** $30.00 each; $125.00 for 5 copies. **Conventions/Meetings:** periodic conference ● seminar ● workshop.

9256 ■ National Council on Measurement in Education (NCME)

2810 Crossroads Dr., Ste.3800
Madison, WI 53718
Ph: (608)443-2487
Fax: (608)443-2474
E-mail: info@ncme.org
URL: http://www.ncme.org
Contact: Bruce Wheeler, Exec. Dir.

Founded: 1938. **Members:** 2,300. **Membership Dues:** active, associate, $60 (annual) ● emeritus, student, $30 (annual). **Budget:** $275,000. **Description:** University and test publishers; educational measurement specialists and educators interested in measurement of human abilities, personality characteristics, and educational achievement, and of the procedures appropriate for the interpretation and use of such measurements. **Awards:** Jason Millman Promising Measurement Scholar Award. **Frequency:** annual. **Type:** recognition. **Recipient:** for a promising NCME member. **Computer Services:** Mailing lists. **Formerly:** (1960) National Council on Measurements Used in Education. **Publications:** *Educational Measurement - Issues and Practice*, quarterly. Magazine. Features articles that deal with the practical aspects of testing in educational settings. **Price:** included in membership dues. ISSN: 0731-1745. **Circulation:** 2,600. **Advertising:** accepted ● *Journal of Educational Measurement*, quarterly. Contains original measurement research and provides reviews of measurement publications and reports. **Price:** included in membership dues. ISSN: 0022-0655. Also Cited As: *JEM* ● *NCME Newsletter*, quarterly, always March, June, September, and December. Contains information on events pertinent to research and practice in educational measurement. Alternate Formats: online. **Conventions/Meetings:** annual convention, held in conjunction with American Educational Research Association (exhibits) - always spring.

9257 ■ Secondary School Admission Test Board (SSATB)

CN 5339
Princeton, NJ 08543
Ph: (609)683-4440
Free: (800)442-SSAT
Fax: (609)683-4507
E-mail: info@ssat.org
URL: http://www.ssat.org
Contact: Dr. Regan Kenyon, Pres.

Founded: 1957. **Members:** 700. **Staff:** 17. **Budget:** $3,000,000. **Regional Groups:** 1. **State Groups:** 1. **Local Groups:** 1. **Description:** Administers entrance examinations for 600 independent schools in the U.S. and in foreign countries to 50,000 candidates. The tests are administered at centers throughout the world. Offers professional services and training to educators in admission at independent schools. **Awards:** Everett Gourley Award. **Frequency:** annual. **Type:** recognition. **Recipient:** to an individual whose interest in students and concern for colleagues is an inspiration to those who serve in admission ● William B. Bretnall Award. **Frequency:** annual. **Type:** recognition. **Recipient:** for individual excellence in education. **Additional Websites:** http://www.memberanda.org, http://www.ssatmembers.org. **Publications:** *About Applying* ● *About SSAT* ● *Interpretive Guide to the SSAT*, annual ● *Memberanda Newsletter*, quarterly. Reports on education at independent schools and issues of interest to educators in admission. **Price:** included in membership dues. Alternate Formats: online ● *Preparing And Applying* ● *Professional Services Guide* ● Directory, annual. Contains a listing of school or organization name, educator's name and geographic region. Alternate Formats: online. **Conventions/Meetings:** annual meeting, three-day conference offering a concentrated workshop program - last weekend in September.

Textbooks

9258 ■ American Textbook Council

475 Riverside Dr., Rm. 1948
New York, NY 10115
Ph: (212)870-2760
Fax: (212)870-2720
E-mail: atc@columbia.edu
URL: http://www.historytextbooks.org
Contact: Gilbert T. Sewall, Dir.

Founded: 1989. **Staff:** 3. **Description:** Historians, educators, public officials, and citizens concerned with the quality of history and humanities textbooks in schools. Seeks to improve the content of social studies and curriculum. Conducts textbook reviews and curriculum studies; a program of the Center for Education Studies. **Libraries: Type:** reference. **Holdings:** 500; books. **Subjects:** curriculum, social studies. **Publications:** *History Textbooks: A Standard and Guide*. **Price:** $10.00 ● *History Textbooks at the New Century*. Report. **Price:** $10.00 ● *Learning about Religion, Learning from Religion*. Report. **Price:** $10.00 ● *Religion in the Classroom: What the Textbooks Tell Us*. Report. **Price:** $10.00 ● *World History Textbooks: A Review*. Report.

9259 ■ Educational Research Analysts

PO Box 7518
Longview, TX 75607-7518
Ph: (903)753-5993 (903)753-8424
Fax: (903)753-8424
E-mail: info@textbookreviews.org
URL: http://www.textbookreviews.org
Contact: Mr. Mel Gabler, Co-Founder

Founded: 1961. **Staff:** 3. **Budget:** $100,000. **Description:** Reviews and analyzes public school curricula, programs, and textbooks in order to reveal those that conflict with America's traditional values, including "censorship" of the Judeo-Christian ethic, free-enterprise economics, strict construction of the Constitution, and "scientific" flaws in the theory of evolution. Participates in Texas textbook review process. Identifies science texts that teach both strengths and weaknesses of evolutionary theory, reading programs that are true phonics, and traditional math programs. Rates textbooks and sends results to all Texas school districts and the nationwide mailing list. Maintains files of textbook and program reviews. **Libraries: Type:** reference. **Holdings:** 12,000; articles, books, periodicals. **Subjects:** education. **Formerly:** (1973) The Mel Gablers. **Publications:** *The Mel Gablers' Newsletter*, semiannual. **Price:** donation. **Circulation:** 3,000 ● *Textbooks on Trial* ● *What Are They Teaching Our Children?*. Book.

9260 ■ National Association of State Textbook Administrators (NASTA)

c/o Ann Asbeck, Instructional Resources Consultant
Kentucky Dept. of Educ.
500 Mero St., 17th Fl.
Frankfort, KY 40601
Ph: (502)564-2106
E-mail: ann.asbeck@education.ky.gov
URL: http://www.nasta.org
Contact: Dr. Anita Buckley, Pres.

Description: Promotes the profession of state textbook administrators. **Conventions/Meetings:** annual meeting.

9261 ■ PALTEX - Expanded Textbook and Instructional Materials Program (PALTEX)

525 23rd St. NW
Washington, DC 20037
Ph: (202)974-3451
Fax: (202)974-3658
E-mail: paltex@paho.org
URL: http://www.paho.org/English/PAHEF/PALTEX/paltex-home.htm
Contact: Dr. Mirta R. Periago, Dir.

Members: 23. **Description:** Directors of state educational agencies responsible for the purchase and distribution of textbooks for public schools. Purposes are to: foster cooperation among administrators in the adoption, purchase, and distribution of textbooks; arrange for continued study and review of textbook specifications; authorize special surveys, tests, and studies; initiate action leading to better quality textbooks. Provides a working knowledge of textbook construction; monitors lowest net wholesale prices through the "most favored nations" clause; shares adoption information among member states; identifies trouble spots in content. Holds discussions with publishers and book manufacturers. Provides assistance to any adoption state or any state interested in becoming a textbook adoption state. Works with Association of American Publishers and Book Manufacturers Institute. **Formerly:** National Association of State Textbook Directors; (1998) National Association of State Textbook Administrators; (2003) Internal Administration Textbook Program. **Conventions/Meetings:** semiannual meeting.

Theatre

9262 ■ Association for Theatre in Higher Education (ATHE)

PO Box 1290
Boulder, CO 80306-1290
Ph: (303)530-2167
Free: (888)284-3737
Fax: (303)530-2168
E-mail: info@athe.org
URL: http://www.athe.org
Contact: Susan Burgoyne, Pres.

Founded: 1986. **Members:** 2,200. **Membership Dues:** student, unemployed, $50 (annual) ● individual, $105 (annual) ● organization, $195 (annual) ● retiree, $80 (annual) ● benefactor, $200 (annual) ● patron, $160 (annual) ● donor, $130 (annual). **Staff:** 1. **Budget:** $300,000. **National Groups:** 23. **Description:** Universities, colleges, and professional education programs; artists, scholars, teachers, and other individuals; students. Promotes the exchange of information among individuals engaged in theatre study and research, performance, and crafts. Provides advocacy and support services. Encourages excellence in postsecondary theatre training, production, and scholarship. **Awards:** Lifetime Achievement in Professional and Educational Theatre. **Frequency:** annual. **Type:** recognition ● **Frequency:** annual. **Type:** recognition. **Computer Services:** Mailing lists, of members. **Councils:** Governing. **Study Groups:** Focus. **Supersedes:** University and College Theater Association; American Theatre Association. **Publications:** *ATHE Membership Directory*, annual. **Advertising:** accepted ● *ATHE News*, 6/year. Newsletter. Alternate Formats: online ● *ATHE Outcomes Assessment Guideline for Theatre Programs in Higher Education*. Pamphlet ● *Guidelines for Evaluating Teacher/Artists for Promotion and Tenure* ● *Models for Evaluating Creative Activity* ● *Theatre Journal*, quarterly. ISSN: 0192-2882. Alternate Formats: online ● *Theatre Topics: Dramaturgy, Performance, Studies, and Pedagogy*, semiannual. Journal. ISSN: 1054-8378. Alternate Formats: online. **Conventions/Meetings:** annual Difficult Dialogues: Theatre and The Art of Engagement - conference (exhibits) - 2008 July 31-Aug. 3, Denver, CO.

9263 ■ Association of Theatre Movement Educators (ATME)
c/o Annette Thornton, Sec.
Lawrence Univ.
Dept. of Theatre Arts
PO Box 599
Appleton, WI 54912-0599
E-mail: annette.thornton@lawrence.edu
URL: http://www.atmeweb.org
Contact: Sarah Romersberger, Pres.
Membership Dues: regular, $45 (annual) ● student, $25 (annual). **Multinational. Description:** Promotes and provides information on theatre movement training. Facilitates networks for support and educational exchange. Disseminates information on latest research, skill method integration, and career planning. **Libraries: Type:** reference. **Holdings:** archival material. **Subjects:** creative teaching, theater movement. **Publications:** *ATME News*, semiannual. Newsletter. **Price:** included in membership dues.

9264 ■ Educational Theatre Association (EdTA)
2343 Auburn Ave.
PO Box 632347
Cincinnati, OH 45219
Ph: (513)421-3900
Fax: (513)421-7077
E-mail: info@edta.org
URL: http://www.edta.org
Contact: Michael J. Peitz, Exec. Dir.
Founded: 1929. **Members:** 1,000,000. **Membership Dues:** professional, $75 (annual) ● high school student, $22 (annual) ● thespian, junior thespian troupes, $65 (annual) ● pre-professional, $25 (annual) ● junior thespian, $6 (annual). **Staff:** 26. **Budget:** $3,500,000. **Regional Groups:** 4. **State Groups:** 38. **Local Groups:** 3,925. **Description:** Professional organization for educators and supporters of educational theatre. Works to promote and strengthen theatre in education through grassroots advocacy programs and professional development programs. Runs the International Thespian Society, an honorary organization for high school theatre students that has inducted more than two million members since its founding in 1929, Junior Thespians, a middle school honorary and senior theatre league of America, for senior adults in theatre. Focuses on strengthening advocacy, student development, and teacher training. **Libraries: Type:** not open to the public. **Holdings:** 2,400; books, periodicals. **Subjects:** theatre, dramatic literature, theatre education. **Awards:** Administrator's Award. **Frequency:** annual. **Type:** recognition. **Recipient:** to outstanding school administrators who have demonstrated exemplary support for education theatre ● EdTA Conference Grants. **Frequency:** annual. **Type:** grant. **Recipient:** to K-12 classroom teachers in a public or private school whose employer is financially unable to pay the registration fee ● EDTA Hall of Fame. **Frequency:** annual. **Type:** recognition. **Recipient:** for membership in association and recommendation by peers ● Finney Festival Grants. **Frequency:** annual. **Type:** grant. **Recipient:** to four members of the International Thespian Society who have demonstrated a strong commitment to theatre ● Founder's Award. **Frequency:** annual. **Type:** recognition. **Recipient:** to an individual or group of individuals who have made significant contributions to the growth and development of theatre education, research and practice ● Leadership Grant. **Frequency:** annual. **Type:** grant. **Recipient:** for students who have demonstrated leadership by being a troupe or state Thespian officer ● Lifetime Achievement Award. **Type:** recognition. **Recipient:** to celebrities or group for outstanding contribution to theatre or theatre education ● Outstanding School Awards. **Frequency:** annual. **Type:** recognition. **Recipient:** to 12 high schools (up to 3/region) with theatre programs that exemplify and promote high standards of quality in educational theatre ● President's Award. **Frequency:** annual. **Type:** recognition. **Recipient:** to an individual who has made exceptional contributions to the association, president, governing board, or volunteer leadership ● Standing Ovation Award. **Type:** recognition. **Recipient:** to a corporation or business that has made significant contributions on a regional, national or international level. **Computer Services:** Mailing lists ● online services. **Boards:** EdTA Governing. **Formerly:** International Thespian Society; (1969) National Thespian Society. **Publications:** *Dramatics*, 9/year. Magazine. Includes theatre news, plays, classroom resource materials, profiles, and practical how-to pieces on theatre. **Price:** $24.00/year in U.S.; $34.00/year in Canada. ISSN: 0012-5989. **Circulation:** 36,500. **Advertising:** accepted ● *Teaching Theatre*, quarterly. Journal. Includes an article, a profile, a piece, and a report on current trends or issues in the field. **Price:** $34.00 /year for libraries. **Circulation:** 4,000. **Conventions/Meetings:** annual Conference for Theatre Teachers, features workshops and networking opportunities (exhibits) ● annual International Thespian Festival - festival and workshop (exhibits) - 2008 June 23-28, Lincoln, NE.

9265 ■ National Association of Schools of Theatre (NAST)
11250 Roger Bacon Dr., Ste.21
Reston, VA 20190-5248
Ph: (703)437-0700
Fax: (703)437-6312
E-mail: info@arts-accredit.org
URL: http://www.arts-accredit.org
Contact: Samuel Hope, Exec. Dir.
Founded: 1969. **Members:** 150. **Membership Dues:** individual, $50 (annual) ● institution with graduate degree, $1,302 (annual) ● other institution, $1,085 (annual). **Staff:** 12. **Description:** Accrediting agency for post-secondary educational programs in theatre. Seeks to improve educational practices and maintain high professional standards in theatre education. Counsels and assists institutions in developing their programs, and encourages the cooperation of professional theatre groups and individuals in the formulation of appropriate curricula and standards. Compiles statistics. **Commissions:** Accreditation. **Committees:** Research. **Publications:** Directory, annual. Lists accredited member institutions. **Price:** $10.00 ● Handbook, biennial. Contains standards and guidelines used to make decisions about accredited institutional membership. **Price:** $10.00. Alternate Formats: online. **Conventions/Meetings:** annual meeting - always March/April.

9266 ■ O'Neill National Theater Institute (NTI)
Eugene O'Neill Theater Center
305 Great Neck Rd.
Waterford, CT 06385
Ph: (860)443-7139
Fax: (860)444-1212
E-mail: nti@theoneill.org
URL: http://nti.conncoll.edu
Contact: Jean Routt, Exec. Admin.
Founded: 1970. **Staff:** 25. **Budget:** $600,000. **Description:** Established at the Eugene O'Neill Memorial Theater Center as a resource for colleges and universities throughout the country. Offers a resident semester of concentrated theatre training to college and university students; each student receives a full semester's credit for his or her work at the institute. Program combines liberal arts philosophy of studies with exposure to professional standards of the theatre. Conducts overseas study program. **Libraries: Type:** reference. **Subjects:** theater, criticism, plays, poetry. **Awards:** Tony Awards. **Frequency:** annual. **Type:** recognition. **Computer Services:** database, alumni. **Affiliated With:** Eugene O'Neill Memorial Theater Center. **Formerly:** (2003) National Theatre Institute. **Publications:** *Alumnae Newsletter*, semiannual. **Conventions/Meetings:** annual reunion, for alumni ● workshop, with professional job opportunities in theatre.

9267 ■ Organization of Professional Acting Coaches and Teachers (OPACT)
3968 Eureka Dr.
Studio City, CA 91604
Ph: (323)877-4988
Fax: (323)877-4988
Contact: Lilyan Chauvin, Pres.
Founded: 1980. **Members:** 12. **Languages:** English, French, German, Italian, Russian, Spanish. **Description:** Provides guidelines of professional conduct for acting coaches and teachers. Prepares informative material to enable prospective students to wisely select an acting teacher. Conducts research and educational programs. Maintains speakers' bureau. **Libraries: Type:** reference. **Holdings:** video recordings. **Awards:** Parent's Choice Award. **Type:** recognition. **Affiliated With:** American Association of University Women. **Publications:** *Discover Yourself in Hollywood*. Video. **Price:** $49.95 ● *Hollywood Scams and Survival Tactics*. Book. **Price:** $19.95 ● *Speak the French You Already Know*. Audiotape. **Price:** $25.00 ● *VDO Tapes*. Book.

9268 ■ Society of American Fight Directors (SAFD)
1350 E Flamingo Rd., No. 25
Las Vegas, NV 89119
Free: (800)659-6579
E-mail: payson@41afa.org
URL: http://www.safd.org
Contact: Payson H. Burt, Regional Rep. Coor.
Founded: 1977. **Members:** 400. **Membership Dues:** individual in U.S., $35 (annual) ● individual outside U.S., $40 (annual). **Staff:** 4. **Budget:** $25,000. **Description:** Actors, stage fight choreographers, and other interested individuals. Provides training and certification for qualified stage combat performers and instructors. Promotes historical accuracy and aesthetic merit in staged fights. Seeks to ensure the safety of stage fight participants. **Publications:** *Cutting Edge*, bimonthly. Newsletter. Includes updates on union regulation, society policy, and activity of members. **Price:** included in membership dues ● *The Fight Master*, semiannual. Journal. Includes articles related to fight choreography such as historical, technical, teaching, resources, and reviews. Also includes society news. **Price:** $25.00. **Circulation:** 400. **Advertising:** accepted ● *Parrving Daggers and Poinards*. Monograph. **Conventions/Meetings:** annual meeting, with stage combat workshop ● periodic regional meeting.

9269 ■ University/Resident Theatre Association (URTA)
1560 Broadway, Ste.712
New York, NY 10036
Ph: (212)221-1130
Fax: (212)869-2752
E-mail: info@urta.com
URL: http://urta.com
Contact: Johana Castro, Dir. of Operations
Founded: 1969. **Members:** 45. **Membership Dues:** full, $2,080 (annual). **Staff:** 3. **Budget:** $500,000. **Languages:** English, Spanish. **Description:** Colleges, universities, and professional theatres. Encourages and promotes professionalism among students in member institutions by encouraging training with theatre professionals. Serves as a liaison between

graduate training programs and professional theatres. Holds the National Unified Auditions for college students interested in pursuing graduate studies in theatre. Administers the Contract Management Program, which issues contracts that allow institutions to employ actors, stage managers, directors, choreographers and designers. **Computer Services:** Mailing lists. **Telecommunication Services:** electronic mail, cmp@urta.com. **Publications:** *U/RTA Directory of Member Training Programs and Associated Theatres*, annual. Includes guide to members, services and programs. **Price:** $5.00. **Advertising:** accepted. Alternate Formats: online ● *U/RTA Handbook for Actors and Coaches*, annual ● *U/RTA Update*, semiannual. Newsletter. **Price:** free for members. **Conventions/Meetings:** annual National Unified Auditions/Interviews - meeting - January, New York, NY; February, Chicago, IL; and March, San Francisco, CA.

Theology

9270 ■ Association of Theological Schools in the United States and Canada (ATS)

10 Summit Park Dr.
Pittsburgh, PA 15275-1103
Ph: (412)788-6505
Fax: (412)788-6510
E-mail: ats@ats.edu
URL: http://www.ats.edu
Contact: Daniel O. Aleshire, Exec. Dir.

Founded: 1918. **Members:** 250. **Staff:** 21. **Budget:** $4,000,000. **Description:** Represents Protestant, Roman Catholic, and Orthodox graduate theological schools in the U.S. and Canada. Aims to promote the improvement and enhancement of theological schools for the benefit of communities of faith and the public. **Computer Services:** database. **Commissions:** Accrediting. **Absorbed:** (1965) American Association of Schools of Theological Schools. **Formerly:** (1936) Conference of Theological Seminaries of the United States and Canada; (1975) American Association of Theological Schools. **Publications:** *Colloquy*, 5/year. Newsletter. **Price:** $15.00/year. Alternate Formats: online ● *Fact Book on Theological Education*, annual. Provides statistical data useful for planning by theological institutions. **Price:** $15.00 plus shipping and handling. Alternate Formats: online ● *Faculty Grants Directory*, annual. Lists funding sources with special focus on religion and theology. Alternate Formats: online ● *Handbook of Accreditation*. **Price:** $20.00 for nonmembers. Alternate Formats: online ● *The Papers of the Henry Luce III Fellows in Theology*. **Price:** $14.95/copy, plus shipping and handling; $69.95 complete set ● *Theological Education*, semiannual. Journal. Contains articles on major issues of theological education. **Price:** $10.00 /year for individuals in U.S. and Canada; $11.00 /year for individuals outside U.S. and Canada; $8.00/copy. Alternate Formats: online ● Membership Directory, annual. **Price:** $10.00. Alternate Formats: online ● Newsletters. Alternate Formats: online. **Conventions/Meetings:** biennial meeting - 2008 June 21-23, Atlanta, GA.

9271 ■ Boston Theological Institute (BTI)

210 Herrick Rd.
Newton Centre, MA 02459
Ph: (617)527-4880
Fax: (617)527-1073
E-mail: btioffice@bostontheological.org
URL: http://www.bostontheological.org
Contact: Rev. Dr. Rodney L. Petersen, Exec. Dir.

Founded: 1968. **Members:** 9. **Staff:** 10. **Budget:** $500,000. **Description:** Ecumenical venture working to produce a comprehensive center of resources for theological education. Consists of nine separate theological schools and seminaries working to make possible, the effective cooperation among members. This includes cross-registration; joint curricular planning; faculty exchange; library cooperation; specially designed courses; and a common catalog. Sponsors faculty colloquia and programs on topics such as field education, international missions, race relations, women in theological studies, urban concerns, peace and justice education, and interreligious dialogue. Makes available to approximately 3000 students and 200 full-time faculty members teaching approximately 750 courses. Provides students and faculty with membership in a large ecumenical family of faith and inquiry. **Libraries: Type:** open to the public. **Holdings:** 1,500,000. **Subjects:** theology. **Awards:** Annual Humanitarian Award. **Frequency:** annual. **Type:** recognition. **Recipient:** to an individual who is actively engaged in the field of dying, death and bereavement and hospice care ● Community Restorative Justice Award. **Frequency:** annual. **Type:** recognition. **Recipient:** for restorative justice service to the community. **Affiliated With:** Boston Theological Institute. **Publications:** *BTI Newsletter*, weekly. Alternate Formats: online ● *Bulletin of the Boston Theological Institute*, semiannual, every September and January. Alternate Formats: online ● *Christianity and a Civil Society*. Catalog ● *Creation as Beloved of God*. Booklet ● *Faculty Directory*, annual ● Catalog, annual. Contains collective course offerings.

9272 ■ Catholic Biblical Association of America (CBA)

c/o Catholic University of America
433 Caldwell Hall
Washington, DC 20064
Ph: (202)319-5519
Fax: (202)319-4799
E-mail: cua-cathbib@cua.edu
URL: http://cba.cua.edu
Contact: Rev. Joseph Jensen OSB, Exec. Sec.

Founded: 1936. **Members:** 1,467. **Membership Dues:** active, associate, sustaining, $35 (annual). **Staff:** 4. **Regional Groups:** 4. **Description:** Represents research scholars in the biblical field. **Computer Services:** Mailing lists. **Committees:** Archaeology; Credentials; Episcopal Liaison; Memorial Stipends and CBA Fellowships; Visiting Professors. **Affiliated With:** Council of Societies for the Study of Religion. **Publications:** *Catholic Biblical Quarterly*. Journal. **Price:** $30.00 /year for nonmembers; included in membership dues. ISSN: 0008-7912. **Advertising:** accepted. Alternate Formats: online ● *Catholic Biblical Quarterly Decennial Index* ● *Catholic Biblical Quarterly Monograph Series*. Also Cited As: *CBQMS* ● *Catholic Biblical Quarterly Supplement*, quinquennial. **Price:** $10.00 for nonmembers; free for members ● *Old Testament Abstracts*, 3/year. Journal. **Price:** $26.00/year. **Advertising:** accepted. Alternate Formats: CD-ROM. **Conventions/Meetings:** annual meeting (exhibits) - always August.

9273 ■ College Theology Society (CTS)

c/o Prof. Elena Procario-Foley, Sec.
Iona Coll.
715 North Ave.
New Rochelle, NY 10801
Ph: (914)637-2744
E-mail: eprocariofoley@iona.edu
URL: http://www2.bc.edu/~barciaus/cts.html
Contact: Prof. Elena Procario-Foley, Sec.

Founded: 1954. **Members:** 873. **Membership Dues:** full, $50 (annual). **Description:** Professors of religion in colleges and universities in the U.S. and Canada. Works to improve the quality of the teaching of religion by: stimulating and sharing scholarly research; developing programs of theology that meet the needs and interests of students; exploring, evaluating, and encouraging effective ways to teach. **Awards: Frequency:** annual. **Type:** recognition. **Recipient:** for best book, article, and graduate student paper. **Sections:** Art, Literature and Religion; Contemporary Theologies; History of Christianity; History of Theology; Justice and Peace; Mysticism and Politics; Philosophy of Religion; Symbol, Ritual and Sacrament. **Formerly:** (1967) Society of Catholic College Teachers of Sacred Doctrine. **Publications:** *College Theology Society Annual Volume*, annual. Proceedings ● *Horizons*, semiannual. Journal. **Conventions/Meetings:** annual conference (exhibits) - weekend after Memorial Day.

9274 ■ Council of Societies for the Study of Religion (CSSR)

PO Box 1872
MS-156
Houston, TX 77251-1892
Ph: (713)348-5721
Fax: (713)348-5725
E-mail: russell.mccutcheon@ua.edu
URL: http://www.cssr.org
Contact: Andrew O. Fort PhD, Exec. Dir.

Founded: 1969. **Members:** 6,500. **Staff:** 4. **Budget:** $200,000. **Description:** Represents learned societies concerned with the academic study of religion. Seeks to define an appropriate focus for the field as a whole and develop an effective means of coordinating and extending the work of existing associations. **Computer Services:** Online services, membership roster. **Telecommunication Services:** electronic mail, cssr@rice.edu. **Committees:** Editorial; Liaison. **Formerly:** (1985) Council on the Study of Religion. **Publications:** *Bulletin of CSSR*, quarterly. Newsletter. Promotes communication among the constituent and affiliate societies of the council. Includes constituent and society news and officer directory. **Price:** $30.00 /year for individuals in U.S.; $60.00 /year for individuals outside U.S.; $40.00 /year for libraries in U.S.; $70.00 /year for libraries outside U.S. ISSN: 1060-1635. **Circulation:** 6,500. **Advertising:** accepted ● *Directory of Departments of Religion*, annual. Lists information on more than 1,500 departments and programs that serve the field of religious studies in North America. **Price:** $60.00 hardbound. **Advertising:** accepted ● *Religious Studies Review*, quarterly. Includes major review essays and brief reviews of more than 1,000 titles annually. **Price:** $60.00 /year for individuals in U.S.; $70.00 /year for individuals outside U.S.; $45.00 /year for institutions in U.S.; $30.00/year for students and retired in U.S. ISSN: 0319-485X. **Circulation:** 3,500. **Advertising:** accepted. **Conventions/Meetings:** annual meeting.

9275 ■ Institute for Advanced Studies of World Religions (IASWR)

Address Unknown since 2008
URL: http://www.iaswr.org

Founded: 1970. **Staff:** 9. **Description:** Provides research facilities and information services to individuals, institutions, and organizations interested or engaged in the academic study and social role of world religions. Undertakes the collection, organization, and preservation of religious materials. Administers research fellowships in selected Asian and comparative religious studies. Facilitates contacts among persons and organizations engaged in those fields; fosters translation and publication of Asian religious texts and studies. Conventions/Meetings: none. **Libraries: Type:** reference. **Holdings:** 72,204; audio recordings, films, maps, monographs, periodicals, video recordings. **Subjects:** Buddhism, Confucianism, Hinduism, Islam, Jainism, Shinto, Sikhism, Taoism, Zoroastrianism, other Asian religious systems. **Awards: Type:** fellowship. **Recipient:** for selected Asian and comparative religious studies. **Computer Services:** database, in development; to contain bibliographic information about current research and multilingual publications on Asian and comparative religion subjects. **Departments:** IASWR Library; Information Services; Microform Resources. **Publications:** *IASWR Series*, periodic. Monograph. Contains doctoral dissertations, text translations, and studies on Asian religions. ● Also publishes IASWR library catalogues of Chinese holdings, microfiche editions of Indie materials, Cambodian, Chinese, Sanskrit, Tibetan Buddhist texts, and related language dictionaries.

9276 ■ International Association of Baptist Colleges and Universities (IABCU)

8120 Sawyer Brown Rd., Ste.108
Nashville, TN 37221-1410
Ph: (615)673-1896
Fax: (615)662-1396
E-mail: tim_fields@baptistschools.org
URL: http://www.baptistschools.org
Contact: Thomas E. Corts, Exec. Dir.

Founded: 1915. **Members:** 51. **Staff:** 2. **State Groups:** 18. **Description:** Southern Baptist senior colleges, universities, junior colleges, academies, and Bible schools. Promotes Christian education through literature, faculty workshops, student recruitment, teacher placement, trustee orientation, statistical information, and other assistance to members. **Formerly:** Southern Association of Baptist Colleges and Schools; (2006) Association of Southern Baptist Colleges and Schools. **Publications:** *Directory of Southern Baptist Related Colleges and Schools*, biennial. Lists schools related to Southern Baptist state conventions. **Price:** $3.00 ● *The Southern Baptist Educator*, quarterly. Journal. Covers the philosophy and methods of church-related higher education. Includes campus reports. **Price:** $8.00/year. **Circulation:** 11,000. Alternate Formats: online. **Conventions/Meetings:** annual conference and meeting - always June.

9277 ■ National Association of Baptist Professors of Religion (NABPR)
c/o Danny S. Mynatt, Exec. Sec.-Treas.
PO Box 1123
Anderson Coll.
Anderson, SC 29621
E-mail: dsmynatt@aol.com
URL: http://www.mercer.edu/nabpr
Contact: Danny S. Mynatt, Exec. Sec.-Treas.
Founded: 1927. **Members:** 400. **Membership Dues:** regular (20000-50000 base salary), $20-$50 (annual) ● retired/retired associate, student, $20 (annual). **Description:** Represents teaching professors of religion in colleges, universities, and seminaries. Conducts lectures and discussions. **Formerly:** (1981) Association of Baptist Professors of Religion. **Publications:** *Festschrift Series*, annual ● *NABPR Dissertation Series*, periodic. Monograph ● *NABPR Special Studies Series*, periodic. Monograph ● *NABPRnews*, quarterly. Newsletter. Contains columns or articles by various officers and news of member accomplishments. Alternate Formats: online ● *Perspectives in Religious Studies*, quarterly. Journal. Includes book reviews. **Price:** $18.00 /year for individuals; $25.00/year for churches and libraries. **Conventions/Meetings:** annual meeting, held in conjunction with American Academy of Religion and Society of Biblical Literature.

Timepieces

9278 ■ North American Sundial Society (NASS)
c/o Frederick W. Sawyer, III, Pres./Ed.
8 Sachem Dr.
Glastonbury, CT 06033
E-mail: nass_president@sundials.org
URL: http://sundials.org
Contact: Frederick W. Sawyer III, Pres./Ed.
Founded: 1994. **Membership Dues:** regular in North America, $30 (annual) ● regular in North America, $57 (biennial) ● regular outside North America, $45 (annual) ● regular outside North America, $86 (biennial). **Multinational. Description:** Promotes the study, development, history and preservation of sundials and the art of dialing throughout the continent. Maintains a sundial registry. Encourages and assists in the design and construction of sundials, either for public display or personal use. Provides mechanisms for the exchange of information about sundials and sundial design among members and other sundial societies around the world. **Publications:** *The Compendium*, quarterly. Journal. **Price:** included in membership dues. Alternate Formats: online; CD-ROM.

Travel

9279 ■ My Travel Bug
60 Elm St.
Westerly, RI 02891
E-mail: amanda@mytravelbug.org
URL: http://www.mytravelbug.org
Contact: Amanda O'Neil, Exec. Dir.
Founded: 2001. **Multinational. Description:** Promotes the benefits of international travel. Enhances the cross-cultural awareness, communication skills and tolerance of individuals through international travel. **Awards: Frequency:** annual. **Type:** fellowship. **Recipient:** for financially needy Americans who want to travel abroad. **Programs:** Travel Bug Fellowships. **Publications:** Newsletter, bimonthly.

9280 ■ Visitor Studies Association (VSA)
PO Box 14375
Columbus, OH 43214-4375
Ph: (614)670-7379
Fax: (614)447-2211
E-mail: info@visitorstudies.org
URL: http://www.visitorstudies.org
Contact: Randy Roberts, Mgr.
Founded: 1987. **Members:** 350. **Membership Dues:** basic, $60 (annual) ● full, $100 (annual) ● supporting, $250 (annual) ● sustaining, $500 (annual) ● patron, $1,000 (annual) ● retired, student, $30 (annual) ● institutional, $300 (annual). **Staff:** 1. **Multinational. Description:** Promotes enhancing the experience of visitors in a variety of settings—from zoos and museums to parks and galleries. Conducts educational programs. **Awards:** April Award. **Frequency:** annual. **Type:** grant. **Recipient:** for members only. **Publications:** *Visitor Studies Today*, 3/year. Journal. Contains peer-reviewed papers focusing on the visitor experience in informal learning settings. **Price:** free for members. ISSN: 1064-5578. **Advertising:** accepted. **Conventions/Meetings:** annual conference - 2008 July 15-19, Houston, TX - **Avg. Attendance:** 200.

Trial Advocacy

9281 ■ American Mock Trial Association (AMTA)
2700 Westown Pkwy., Ste.220
West Des Moines, IA 50266-1411
Ph: (515)283-0803
Fax: (515)283-0702
E-mail: amta@dwx.com
URL: http://www.collegemocktrial.org
Contact: Marcus D. Pohlmann, Pres.
Founded: 1985. **Description:** Facilitates the growth of the individual student as a person able to work with and support others as a knowledgeable citizen acquainted with the legal system and as a community leader working for the betterment of humanity. Conducts mediation trainings for professors and mediation tournaments for participating universities and colleges. **Telecommunication Services:** electronic mail, jwagoner@ferreri-fogle.com.

Turkish

9282 ■ American Association of Teachers of Turkic Languages (AATT)
Princeton Univ.
Near Eastern Stud.
110 Jones Hall
Princeton, NJ 08544-1008
Ph: (609)258-1435
Fax: (609)258-1242
E-mail: ehgilson@princeton.edu
URL: http://www.princeton.edu/~turkish/aatt
Contact: Dr. Erika H. Gilson, Exec. Sec.-Treas.
Founded: 1985. **Members:** 200. **Membership Dues:** regular, $20 (annual) ● institutional, $40-$500 (annual) ● student, $10 (annual). **Languages:** Azerbaijani, English, Turkic, Turkish. **Description:** Teachers of the Turkic languages; universities, including language schools in government services; other institutions. Dedicated to the enhancement of study, criticism, and research in the field of Turkic languages, literature, and linguistics. Seeks to improve and advance the teaching of modern and historical Turkic languages. Develops guidelines and standards for proficiency-based teaching of Turkic languages, bibliography of teaching materials, and workshops for teachers. **Libraries: Type:** reference. **Awards:** Redhouse Prize. **Frequency:** annual. **Type:** monetary. **Recipient:** for best progress in Turkish. **Affiliated With:** Middle East Studies Association of North America; Turkish Studies Association. **Formerly:** (1993) American Association of Teachers of Turkish. **Publications:** *AATT Bulletin*, semiannual. **Price:** included in membership dues. ISSN: 1062-6840. **Circulation:** 200. **Advertising:** accepted ● Pamphlet ● Reports ● Also publishes teaching aids. **Conventions/Meetings:** annual conference and workshop, held in conjunction with Middle East Studies Association of North America - always November.

Tutoring

9283 ■ National Tutoring Association (NTA)
PO Box 6840
Lakeland, FL 33807-6840
Ph: (863)529-5206
E-mail: ntatutor@aol.com
URL: http://www.ntatutor.org
Contact: Dr. Sandi Ayaz, Exec. Dir.
Founded: 1991. **Members:** 4,900. **Membership Dues:** program, $80 (annual) ● individual, $45 (annual) ● student, $5 (annual) ● institutional, $400 (annual) ● corporate basic, $650 (annual) ● corporate silver, $1,500 (annual) ● corporate gold, $2,500 (annual). **Budget:** $7,000. **Multinational. Description:** Represents elementary school, middle school, high school, college/university, private practice, faith based and community tutor. Sponsors tutoring programs. **Awards:** Professional Development Award. **Frequency:** annual. **Type:** recognition ● Tutor of the Year, Activity. **Frequency:** annual. **Type:** recognition. **Formerly:** (1993) National Organization of Tutoring and Mentoring Centers; (1998) National Association of Tutoring. **Publications:** *NTA Newsletter*, biennial. Features articles on tutoring elementary and secondary school children. **Price:** $40.00/year. **Circulation:** 600 ● *Teaching Learning Center Handbook* ● Proceedings. **Conventions/Meetings:** annual meeting and conference, presentations and roundtable divisions (exhibits) - 2009 Apr. 4-8, Reno, NV; 2010 Apr. 10-14, Memphis, TN.

United Kingdom

9284 ■ Cambridge in America (CAm)
100 Ave. of the Americas, 4th Fl.
New York, NY 10013
Ph: (212)984-0960 (212)984-0977
Fax: (212)984-0970
E-mail: mail@cantab.org
URL: http://www.cantab.org
Contact: Mr. John Hanselman, Exec. Dir.
Founded: 1967. **Members:** 10,000. **Staff:** 2. **Budget:** $300,000. **Local Groups:** 20. **Description:** Works to raise funds in support of Cambridge University and its constituent colleges. Provides and supports Cambridge Alumni network in America. **Awards:** American Friends Scholarship. **Frequency:** annual. **Type:** scholarship. **Formerly:** (2003) American Friends of Cambridge University. **Publications:** Annual Report, annual ● Newsletter, semiannual. **Conventions/Meetings:** semiannual board meeting.

Urban Affairs

9285 ■ Association of Collegiate Schools of Planning (ACSP)
c/o Donna Dodd, Mgr.
6311 Mallard Trace Dr.
Tallahassee, FL 32312
Ph: (850)385-2054
Fax: (850)385-2084
E-mail: ddodd@acsp.org
URL: http://www.acsp.org
Contact: Donna Dodd, Mgr.
Founded: 1959. **Members:** 1,517. **Membership Dues:** full, $350 ● affiliate, corresponding, $115 ● individual, $85 ● student, $35 ● retired, $50. **Staff:** 1. **Budget:** $130,000. **Description:** Represents schools (117) and faculty (1400) of urban planning at U.S., European, and Canadian colleges and universities. Conducts research programs; compiles statistics. **Awards:** Chester Rapkin Award for Best Paper in

JPER. **Frequency:** annual. **Type:** recognition. **Recipient:** for the best papers published in the Journal of Planning Education and Research ● Distinguished Educator Award. **Frequency:** annual. **Type:** recognition. **Recipient:** for service and contribution to the field of planning ● Edward McClure Award for the Best Master's Student Paper. **Frequency:** annual. **Type:** recognition. **Recipient:** for superior scholarship in a paper prepared by a student in an ACSP-member school ● Paul Dairdiff Award. **Frequency:** biennial. **Type:** recognition. **Recipient:** to a publication that promotes values of participatory democracy and positive social change. **Computer Services:** Mailing lists, planet. **Publications:** *Guide to Graduate Education in Urban and Regional Planning*, semiannual. Alternate Formats: online ● *Guide to Undergraduate Education in Urban and Regional Planning and Related Fields*, semiannual ● *Journal of Planning Education and Research*, quarterly. ISSN: 0739-456X ● *Update*, quarterly. Newsletter. Alternate Formats: online. **Conventions/Meetings:** annual conference (exhibits).

9286 ■ Higher Education Consortium for Urban Affairs (HECUA)
2233 Univ. Ave. W, Ste.210
Wright Bldg.
St. Paul, MN 55114
Ph: (651)646-8832 (651)646-8831
Free: (800)554-1089
Fax: (651)659-9421
E-mail: info@hecua.org
URL: http://www.hecua.org
Contact: Jenny Keyser PhD, Exec. Dir.
Founded: 1971. **Members:** 15. **Staff:** 18. **Budget:** $1,500,000. **Languages:** English, Norwegian, Spanish. **Multinational. Description:** Engages students, faculty and practitioners in exceptional learning opportunities that provide tools and knowledge for community building and social transformation. Represents of 15 member colleges and universities in the upper Midwest. Faculty and students from other nationwide schools also participate. Provides programs that emphasize integrating theoretical frameworks with skills and practices that enable students to see how social change happens and to develop their capacities for effective citizenship. Program sites in Asia, Europe, North America, Central and South America serve as extensions of member campuses that afford consistent opportunities for substantive exchange and study. Works in partnership and supports the development of individuals and institutions, the group is "charting new directions that are enriching higher education and the community". **Awards:** HECUA Fellows Scholarship. **Frequency:** semiannual. **Type:** scholarship. **Recipient:** to a member college faculty ● HECUA Student Scholarship. **Frequency:** semiannual. **Type:** scholarship. **Publications:** *HECUA Newsline*. Newsletter ● *HECUA Off-Campus Study Program Catalog*, annual. Contains program catalog. **Price:** free.

9287 ■ Urban Affairs Association (UAA)
c/o University of Delaware
298 Graham Hall
Newark, DE 19716
Ph: (302)831-1681
Fax: (302)831-4225
E-mail: uaa@udel.edu
URL: http://www.udel.edu/uaa
Contact: Margaret Wilder, Exec. Dir.
Founded: 1969. **Members:** 575. **Membership Dues:** institution, $295 (annual) ● individual, $60 (annual) ● student, $30 (annual). **Staff:** 2. **Budget:** $150,000. **Description:** Represents institutions; urban specialists from private or public universities involved in teaching, research, or public service. Supports the development of university programs in urban affairs. Disseminates information about urbanism and urbanization. Fosters the development of urban affairs as a professional and academic field. Offers technical advice to universities and urban institutes regarding organizational and program development. Develops surveys on topics such as the organization and staffing of centers, enrollment, and student placement. **Awards:** Alma H. Young Emerging Scholars Award. **Frequency:** annual. **Type:** monetary. **Recipient:** for emerging scholars whose work exemplifies outstanding scholarship in urban affairs ● Best in Urban Affairs. **Frequency:** annual. **Type:** monetary ● Best Paper at the UAA Annual Meeting. **Frequency:** annual. **Type:** monetary. **Recipient:** to the author(s) of the paper judged to be the best paper presented at the Urban Affairs Association's (UAA) Annual Meeting ● Best Published Paper in Journal of Urban Affairs. **Frequency:** annual. **Type:** recognition. **Recipient:** to a paper published in the Journal of Urban Affairs, that is considered particularly outstanding as a scholarly contribution to the field of urban affairs. **Computer Services:** Mailing lists. **Formerly:** (1981) Council of University Institutes for Urban Affairs. **Publications:** *Journal of Urban Affairs*, quarterly. Includes book reviews. **Price:** included in membership dues; $110.00 /year for nonmembers in U.S.; $275.00 /year for individuals in U.S.; $163.00 /year for nonmembers outside U.S. ● *Urban Affairs*, 5/year. Newsletter. Provides information on programs, curriculum developments, technical assistance activities and faculty and staff appointments within the field. **Price:** included in membership dues. **Circulation:** 900. Alternate Formats: online. **Conventions/Meetings:** annual conference and meeting (exhibits).

9288 ■ Urban Superintendent's Association of America (USAA)
c/o C. Fred Bateman, Exec. Dir.
PO Box 1248
Chesapeake, VA 23327-1248
Ph: (757)436-1032
E-mail: info@usaa.org
URL: http://www.usaa.org
Contact: C. Fred Bateman, Exec. Dir.
Membership Dues: general, $350 (annual). **Description:** Advances urban education through shared experiences and research. Provides frequent updates on issues that impact daily operations of schools. Serves as a clearing house for expressing urban concerns, recommendations and legislative initiatives. **Conventions/Meetings:** annual conference.

Urban Education

9289 ■ Council of the Great City Schools (CGCS)
1301 Pennsylvania Ave. NW, Ste.702
Washington, DC 20004
Ph: (202)393-2427
Fax: (202)393-2400
E-mail: mcasserly@cgcs.org
URL: http://www.cgcs.org
Contact: Michael D. Casserly, Exec. Dir.
Founded: 1956. **Members:** 64. **Staff:** 17. **Budget:** $4,500,000. **Description:** Large city school districts. Conducts studies of problems shared by urban schools; coordinates projects designed to provide solutions to these problems; uses the findings and recommendations of studies for the improvement of education in the great cities. Provides informational support for legislative activities. Conducts seminars, workshops, and special projects to provide forum for members to share successful projects and to learn new programs. Studies the educational needs of urban children exposed to the effects of discrimination; school financing; teacher preparation for urban schools; more functional approaches to outmoded urban schools; current status and needs in the areas of testing and technology. **Awards:** Queen Smith Award for Commitment to Urban Education. **Frequency:** annual. **Type:** recognition. **Recipient:** to an urban school educator who has made significant contribution to education and to the community ● Richard R. Green Award. **Frequency:** annual. **Type:** recognition. **Recipient:** to a member superintendent or school board member who best represents the group's ideals and commitments. **Committees:** Legislation; Public Advocacy; Research; Special Projects. **Task Forces:** Achievement Gaps; Bilingual, Immigrant and Refugee Education; Leadership, Governance and Management; Professional Development. **Formerly:** Research Council of the Great Cities Program for School Improvement. **Publications:** *Council Directory*, annual ● *Legislative Activity Report*, biweekly. Newsletter ● *Roster of Board of Directors*, periodic ● *Urban Educator*, monthly. Newsletter. Alternate Formats: online ● *Urban Indicator*, bimonthly ● Annual Report, annual. Alternate Formats: online ● Reports. Alternate Formats: online. **Conventions/Meetings:** annual conference - always fall.

9290 ■ National Council of Urban Education Associations (NCUEA)
c/o National Education Association
1201 16th St. NW, Ste.410
Washington, DC 20036
Ph: (202)822-7155
Fax: (202)822-7624
E-mail: ncuea@nea.org
URL: http://www.nea.org/ncueahome
Contact: Susie Jablinske, Pres.
Founded: 1964. **Members:** 201. **Membership Dues:** regular, $300 (annual). **Budget:** $100,000. **Local Groups:** 201. **Description:** Serves as a division of the National Education Association (see separate entry). Resolves urban problems having to do with quality education. Promotes improved relations between local and state authorities. Provides training for members. Provides a forum for sharing mutual problems. Supports urban projects concerning problems such as overcrowding and violence in schools. **Telecommunication Services:** electronic mail, susiej@aol.com. **Publications:** *Backgrounder* ● *NCUEA Guide to NEA/RA*, annual. Serves as a conference guide. **Circulation:** 350 ● *NCUEA Newsletter*, 20/year. Provides information on membership activities. **Circulation:** 700 ● *Q and A*. **Conventions/Meetings:** semiannual conference, held in conjunction with NEA.

9291 ■ National Urban Alliance for Effective Education (NUA)
33 Queens St., Ste.100
Syosset, NY 11791
Ph: (516)802-4192
Free: (800)NUA-4556
Fax: (516)921-0298
E-mail: info@nuatc.org
URL: http://www.nuatc.org
Contact: Dr. Yvette Jackson, CEO
Founded: 1989. **Description:** Promotes the capacity of all children to reach the high levels of learning and thinking demanded by an ever-changing global community. Provides ongoing professional development activities for teachers, principals and other school personnel to improve classroom instruction. Focuses on instructional strategies based on concept and cognitive development, reasoning, thinking and higher-order comprehension skills. **Publications:** Articles. Alternate Formats: online.

Veterans

9292 ■ National Association of Veterans Program Administrators (NAVPA)
2020 Pennsylvania Ave. NW, Ste.1975
Washington, DC 20006-1846
Ph: (480)461-7428
Fax: (480)461-7815
E-mail: navpa@mnstate.edu
URL: http://www.navpa.org
Contact: Giacomo Mordente, Pres.
Founded: 1975. **Members:** 550. **Membership Dues:** institutional; individual, associate, $150 (annual) ● auxiliary, $25 (annual). **Staff:** 25. **Regional Groups:** 8. **Description:** University and college representatives who work with veterans and veterans programs on campus. Assists veterans seeking success in higher education (for example, through full utilization of federal GI bills); also helps resolve veterans' educational problems with the Department of Veterans Affairs. **Awards:** Distinguished Service Award. **Frequency:** annual. **Type:** recognition. **Recipient:** to an individual/organization who has made a significant contribution to veterans programs ● NAVPA Service Award. **Frequency:** annual. **Type:** recognition. **Re-**

cipient: to individuals who have contributed and served veterans and veterans programs ● Ron York Achievement Award. **Frequency:** annual. **Type:** recognition. **Recipient:** to an individual who has made a significant contribution to the purpose and goals of NAVPA and has demonstrated leadership in the profession. **Computer Services:** Mailing lists. **Telecommunication Services:** electronic mail, mordente@scsu.ctstateu.edu. **Committees:** Diversity; Education; Internal Affairs; Internal Audit; Legislative; Membership; Public Relations; Special Recognition; Technology Enhancement. **Publications:** *NAVPA News*, quarterly. Newsletter. Alternate Formats: online ● *NAVPA School Liability Manual* ● *President's Update*, periodic. **Conventions/Meetings:** annual conference - always third week in October.

Veterinary Education

9293 ■ Association of American Veterinary Medical Colleges (AAVMC)
1101 Vermont Ave. NW, Ste.301
Washington, DC 20005
Ph: (202)371-9195
Fax: (202)842-0773
E-mail: leheider@aavmc.org
URL: http://www.aavmc.org
Contact: Dr. Lawrence E. Heider, Exec. Dir.
Founded: 1966. **Members:** 49. **Staff:** 6. **Description:** Coordinates the affairs of the 27 U.S. Veterinary Medical Colleges, 4 Canadian Colleges of Veterinary Medicine, Departments of Veterinary Science and Comparative Medicine, animal medical centers, and 2 international veterinary schools. **Committees:** Academic Affairs; Advancement; Animal Care; Comparative Data; Multicultural Affairs; Strategic Planning. **Formerly:** (1962) Association of Deans of American Colleges of Veterinary Medicine. **Publications:** *Journal of Veterinary Medical Education*, quarterly. **Price:** $100.00 /year for institutions; $100.00 /year for individuals; $25.00/issue. ISSN: 0748-321X. **Advertising:** accepted ● *Veterinary Medical School Admission Requirement*. Handbook ● Newsletter. Alternate Formats: online. **Conventions/Meetings:** annual conference.

9294 ■ Association of Veterinary Technician Educators (AVTE)
c/o Ronald J. Epps, Sec.-Treas.
McLennan Community Coll.
1400 Coll. Dr.
Waco, TX 76708
E-mail: repps@mclennan.edu
URL: http://www.avte.net
Contact: Ronald J. Epps, Sec.-Treas.
Membership Dues: institutional, $150 (annual) ● individual, $25 (annual) ● associate, $10 (annual). **Description:** Promotes quality education in veterinary technology. **Publications:** *AVTE Newsletter*. Alternate Formats: online. **Conventions/Meetings:** board meeting.

9295 ■ World Association of Veterinary Educators (WAVE)
c/o I.H. Siddique, Pres.
School of Veterinary Medicine
Tuskegee Univ.
Tuskegee, AL 36083
Ph: (334)727-8478
Fax: (334)727-8177
E-mail: isidd@acd.tusk.edu
URL: http://www.vet.purdue.edu/bms/intl/international/wave.htmworld
Contact: I.H. Siddique, Pres.
Members: 350. **Membership Dues:** regular, $5 (annual). **Multinational. Description:** Veterinarians and veterinary educators. Strives to improve the exchange between the teaching institutions; aims to upgrade the quality of veterinary training. **Conventions/Meetings:** general assembly and meeting.

Vietnamese

9296 ■ Group of Universities for the Advancement of Vietnamese Abroad (GUAVA)
Univ. of Washington
Southeast Asian Ctr.
JSIS Box 353650
Seattle, WA 98195-3560
Ph: (206)543-9606 (206)616-2113
Fax: (206)685-0668
E-mail: vasi@u.washington.edu
URL: http://www.public.asu.edu/~ickpl/guava
Contact: Ngo Nhu Binh, Outreach Chair
Founded: 1993. **Members:** 8. **Description:** Consortium of institutions of higher learning offering programs of instruction in the Vietnamese language. Promotes the collection and archiving of Vietnamese language teaching materials; the establishment of minimum standards for various levels of Vietnamese language competency to facilitate inter university student exchange; pooling of Vietnamese language teaching experiences at the international level; the dissemination of effective methodologies and curriculum; facilitating international student and faculty exchange in Vietnamese language teaching.

Visually Impaired

9297 ■ Seedlings Braille Books for Children
PO Box 51924
Livonia, MI 48151-5924
Ph: (734)427-8552
Free: (800)777-8552
Fax: (734)427-8552
E-mail: info@seedlings.org
URL: http://www.seedlings.org
Contact: Debra Bonde, Founder/Dir.
Founded: 1984. **Description:** Increases the opportunity for literacy by providing high-quality, low-cost braille books for visually-impaired children. **Computer Services:** Information services, braille resources ● information services, facts on eye conditions and vision. **Projects:** Anna's Book Angel; Rose.

Vocational Education

9298 ■ American Association for Vocational Instructional Materials (AAVIM)
220 Smithonia Rd.
Winterville, GA 30683
Ph: (706)742-5355
Free: (800)228-4689
Fax: (706)742-7005
E-mail: sales@aavim.com
URL: http://www.aavim.com
Contact: Mr. Gary Farmer, Dir.
Founded: 1949. **Members:** 7. **Membership Dues:** state, $3,000 (annual) ● agency, $1,000 (annual). **Staff:** 5. **Budget:** $450,000. **Description:** Serves as an interstate organization of universities, colleges, and divisions of vocational education devoted to the improvement of teaching through better information and teaching aids. Purpose is to provide vocational instructional materials in a manner most useful to both teacher and student. **Formerly:** (1969) American Association for Agricultural Engineering and Vocational Agriculture. **Publications:** Catalogs, annual. Describes materials that have been developed and published. **Price:** free ● Also publishes textbooks and do-it-yourself manuals; prepares and distributes computer software, videos, and textbooks. **Conventions/Meetings:** annual board meeting - always May.

9299 ■ American Board of Vocational Experts (ABVE)
3540 Soquel Ave., Ste.A
Santa Cruz, CA 95062-1769
Ph: (831)464-4890
Fax: (831)576-1417
E-mail: abve@abve.net
URL: http://www.abve.net
Contact: Glenn Zimmermann, Exec. Dir.
Founded: 1980. **Members:** 380. **Membership Dues:** associate, $140 (annual) ● student, $50 (annual). **Staff:** 2. **Budget:** $102,000. **Description:** Psychologists, rehabilitation specialists, social workers, and vocational counselors. Promotes uniform high standards of professional practice among vocational consultants. Provides credentialing reviews and certification examinations. Sponsors educational programs. **Awards:** David S. Frank Lifetime Achievement Award. **Frequency:** annual. **Type:** recognition. **Recipient:** to an active member ● Presidential Citation. **Frequency:** annual. **Type:** recognition. **Recipient:** for a member or nonmember who exhibited dedication and continued support to the organization. **Computer Services:** Mailing lists, members. **Committees:** Continuing Education; Credentialing; Ethics; Nominations; Professional Standards and Ethics; Publications. **Publications:** *Journal of Forensic Vocational Analysis*, biennial. **Price:** $35.00 for nonmembers; plus shipping and handling; $25.00 for members; plus shipping and handling. Alternate Formats: online ● *National Directory of Vocational Experts*, annual. **Advertising:** accepted ● *The Vocational Expert*, quarterly. Newsletter. **Price:** $25.00/year. **Circulation:** 420. **Advertising:** accepted. Alternate Formats: online. **Conventions/Meetings:** semiannual conference (exhibits) - spring and fall. 2008 Oct. 3-5, San Antonio, TX.

9300 ■ Association for Career and Technical Education (ACTE)
1410 King St.
Alexandria, VA 22314
Ph: (703)683-3111
Free: (800)826-9972
Fax: (703)683-7424
E-mail: acte@acteonline.org
URL: http://www.acteonline.org
Contact: Jan Bray, Exec. Dir./Sec.-Treas.
Founded: 1926. **Members:** 35,000. **Membership Dues:** professional, $60 (annual) ● life, $1,200 ● retired, $31 (annual) ● student, $10 (annual) ● international, $60 (annual) ● affiliate organization, $500 (annual) ● associate, $1,200 (annual). **Staff:** 32. **Budget:** $5,000,000. **State Groups:** 57. **Description:** Represents teachers, supervisors, administrators, and others interested in the development and improvement of vocational, Technical, and practical arts education. Areas of interest include: secondary, postsecondary, and adult vocational education; education for special population groups; cooperative education. Works with such government agencies as: Bureau of Apprenticeship in Department of Labor; Office of Vocational Rehabilitation in Department of Health and Human Services; Veterans Administration; Office of Vocational and Adult Education of the Department of Education. Maintains hall of fame. **Awards:** Arch of Fame. **Frequency:** annual. **Type:** recognition. **Recipient:** for contributions and distinguished accomplishments of persons who have been identified with the work and purposes of ACTE ● Award of Merit. **Frequency:** annual. **Type:** recognition. **Recipient:** to individuals or organizations outside the field of career and technical education ● Awards for Excellence, Automotive Service. **Frequency:** annual. **Type:** recognition. **Recipient:** for programs in automotive service that exemplify the highest standards of excellence for career preparation ● Outstanding Service Award. **Frequency:** annual. **Type:** recognition. **Recipient:** for contributions to the improvement, promotion, development and progress of career and technical education ● Policymaker of The Year Award. **Frequency:** annual. **Type:** recognition. **Recipient:** to policymakers who have made a contribution of national significance to career and technical education. **Computer Services:** database, membership list, by vocational field and positions. **Telecommunication Services:** electronic mail, jbray@acteonline.org. **Divisions:** Adult Workforce Development; Agricultural Education; Business Education; Family and Consumer Sciences Education; Guidance; Health Occupations Education; Industrial Arts Education; Marketing Education; New and Related Services; Special Needs; Technology Education; Trade and Industrial Education. **Formed by Merger of:** Vocational Association of the Middle West; National Society for Vocational Education. **Formerly:** (2000) American Vocational Association. **Publications:** *ACTE News*, monthly. Newsletter. Alternate Formats: online ● *Career Tech Update*, semimonthly. Newsletter. **Price:** $139.00 /year for nonmembers. Alternate Formats: online ● *Legislative Alert*, publish as needed with an average of 2/month. Newsletter. Alternate Formats: online ● *National Awards Program*. Booklet. Alternate Formats: online ● *Tech-*

niques, 8/year. Magazine. **Price:** $48.00 /year for nonmembers in U.S.; $81.00 /year for nonmembers outside U.S. **Advertising:** accepted. Alternate Formats: online ● *Vocational Education Journal*, monthly. Contains information about trends affecting the workplace and programs that prepare students for work. Includes advertisers index. **Price:** included in membership dues; $3.00/year for student members; $20.00 /year for nonmembers. ISSN: 0164-9175. **Circulation:** 50,000. **Advertising:** accepted. Alternate Formats: microform ● Newsletter, weekly. Covers legislative and governmental developments affecting vocational education. **Price:** $115.00. **Conventions/Meetings:** annual National Policy Seminar - every spring ● annual convention (exhibits) - 2008 Dec. 4-6, Charlotte, NC; 2009 Nov. 19-21, Nashville, TN; 2010 Dec. 2-4, Las Vegas, NV.

9301 ■ Association for Career and Technical Education Research (ACTER)

c/o Dick Joerger, Pres.
Univ. of Minnesota
320B VoTech Educ. Bldg.
1954 Buford Ave.
St. Paul, MN 55108
Ph: (612)624-4298
Fax: (612)625-2798
E-mail: djoerger@umn.edu
URL: http://www.agri.wsu.edu/acter
Contact: Dick Joerger, Pres.

Founded: 1966. **Members:** 500. **Membership Dues:** student, emeritus, $10 (annual) ● regular, $40 (annual). **Description:** Vocational and other educators interested in supporting or conducting research in vocational education; graduate students in vocational education research. Promotes research and development activities in vocational education; encourages training programs for vocational education researchers. **Libraries: Type:** reference. **Holdings:** archival material. **Awards: Frequency:** annual. **Type:** recognition. **Recipient:** for outstanding research paper. **Committees:** Legislative Information. **Formerly:** (2005) American Vocational Education Research Association. **Publications:** *The Beacon*, quarterly. Newsletter ● *Career and Technical Education Research*, quarterly. Journal. Provides articles about training programs and research and development activities. **Price:** included in membership dues; $57.00 /year for nonmembers. ISSN: 0739-3369. **Circulation:** 750 ● Monographs. **Conventions/Meetings:** annual convention, held in conjunction with American Vocational Association (exhibits) - always December ● annual meeting, with paper sessions.

9302 ■ Business Professionals of America (BPA)

5454 Cleveland Ave.
Columbus, OH 43231-4021
Ph: (614)895-7277
Free: (800)334-2007
Fax: (614)895-1165
E-mail: sdziura@bpa.org
URL: http://www.bpa.org
Contact: Mr. Stephen Dziura, Dir. of Communications

Founded: 1966. **Members:** 54,000. **Membership Dues:** secondary of post-secondary division, $10. **Staff:** 8. **Budget:** $1,607,000. **Local Groups:** 3,300. **Description:** High school and post secondary career and technical, business, and office education students. Seeks to develop leadership abilities, interest in the American business system, and competency in office occupations within the framework of career and technical education. Conducts projects in safety, citizenship, and economic awareness involvement. **Awards: Type:** recognition ● Special Recognition Awards. **Frequency:** annual. **Type:** recognition ● Torch Awards. **Frequency:** annual. **Type:** recognition. **Recipient:** for members in good standing of a secondary, associate, middle school or post secondary chapter of the association. **Computer Services:** Online services, information on membership and conference registration. **Councils:** Classroom Educators Advisory; National Business Advisory; State Association Advisory. **Formerly:** (1987) Office Education Association. **Publications:** *Advisor's Bulletin*, quarterly. Newsletter. **Price:** available to members only ● *Communique*, quarterly. Magazine. Includes chapter news. **Price:** included in membership dues; $7.00 /year for nonmembers. ISSN: 0889-4817. **Circulation:** 55,000. **Advertising:** accepted ● *Competitive Events Guidelines*, annual. **Price:** $7.00 for members. **Circulation:** 3,500. **Conventions/Meetings:** annual conference (exhibits).

9303 ■ Career College Association (CCA)

1101 Connecticut Ave. NW, Ste.900
Washington, DC 20036
Ph: (202)336-6700
Fax: (202)336-6828
E-mail: cca@career.org
URL: http://www.career.org
Contact: Mr. Bruce Leftwich, VP of Government Relations

Founded: 1991. **Members:** 1,400. **Staff:** 25. **Budget:** $3,000,000. **Description:** Represents private postsecondary schools, institutes, colleges and universities that provide career-specific educational programs. **Awards:** Community Service of the Year. **Frequency:** annual. **Type:** recognition ● Hall of Fame. **Frequency:** annual. **Type:** recognition ● Outstanding Allied Member. **Frequency:** annual. **Type:** recognition ● Outstanding State Association. **Frequency:** annual. **Type:** recognition ● Teacher of the Year. **Frequency:** annual. **Type:** recognition. **Committees:** Awards; Communications; Convention; Governmental Relations; Membership Services; Professional Development; State Associations. **Affiliated With:** American Society of Association Executives. **Formerly:** (1992) National Association of Trade and Technical Schools and the Association of Independent Colleges and Schools. **Publications:** *Fact Book*, biennial. Contains research and analysis of important trends in the career college sector of higher education. **Price:** $24.95/copy ● *The Link*, quarterly. Magazine. Contains useful information and news to the career college community. **Circulation:** 1,400. **Advertising:** accepted ● Annual Report, annual. Contains a summary of activities accomplished by the major departments within CCA. **Conventions/Meetings:** annual convention (exhibits).

9304 ■ Center on Education and Training for Employment (CETE)

Ohio State Univ.
1900 Kenny Rd.
Columbus, OH 43210-1016
Ph: (614)292-6991
Free: (800)848-4815
Fax: (614)292-1260
E-mail: chambers.2@osu.edu
URL: http://www.cete.org
Contact: Mr. Ronald Jacobs PhD, Dir.

Founded: 1965. **Staff:** 50. **Description:** Aims to increase the ability of diverse agencies, institutions, and organizations to solve educational problems relating to individual career planning, preparation, and progression. Conducts occupational analyses and staff training programs. Evaluates programs and agencies and provides technical assistance. Researches identified problems or needs. Develops databases, information systems, and occupational curricula. **Libraries: Type:** reference. **Holdings:** 64,000. **Subjects:** research and development in all aspects of adult, career and vocational education. **Formerly:** (1977) Center for Vocational Education; (1988) National Center for Research in Vocational Education. **Publications:** *Centegram*, quarterly. Newsletter. Features news on the center's current works and upcoming events. Alternate Formats: online. **Conventions/Meetings:** workshop, for professional development.

9305 ■ International Association of Jewish Vocational Services (IAJVS)

1845 Walnut St., Ste.640
Philadelphia, PA 19103
Ph: (215)854-0233
Fax: (215)854-0212
E-mail: coheng@iajvs.org
URL: http://www.iajvs.org
Contact: Genie Cohen, Exec. Dir.

Founded: 1939. **Members:** 29. **Staff:** 3. **Budget:** $912,136. **Regional Groups:** 26. **Multinational. Description:** Jewish-sponsored social service agencies in the U.S., Israel, Canada and Argentina. Promotes appropriate and effective delivery of workplace related social services. Provides central coordinating, technical assistance, consultation, professional development tools, and planning services to local member agencies. **Awards:** IAJVS Awards. **Frequency:** annual. **Type:** recognition. **Recipient:** for outstanding service. **Formerly:** (1976) Jewish Occupational Council; (1990) National Association of Jewish Vocational Services. **Publications:** *Conference Proceedings*, periodic ● *E-Lights*. Newsletter. Alternate Formats: online ● *Executive Quarterly Reports*. Newsletter. Alternate Formats: online ● Annual Report, annual. Alternate Formats: online. **Conventions/Meetings:** annual conference ● annual meeting (exhibits).

9306 ■ International Vocational Education and Training Association (IVETA)

c/o Barbara Herrmann, Exec. Sec./Treas.
186 Wedgewood Dr.
Mahtomedi, MN 55115
Ph: (651)770-6719
Fax: (651)305-9600
E-mail: iveta@visi.com
URL: http://www.iveta.org
Contact: Barbara Herrmann, Exec. Sec./Treas.

Founded: 1984. **Members:** 210. **Membership Dues:** individual, $50 (annual) ● student, $25 (annual) ● organization (includes 3 individuals with printed copies of the journal), $300 (annual). **Multinational. Description:** Works for the advancement and improvement of vocational education and skill training; fosters and promotes professional linkages among international educators and trainers. Serves as a forum for the exchange of information; assists in development of the profession; disseminates information. **Awards:** Joel Magisos Exceptional Service Award. **Frequency:** annual. **Type:** recognition. **Recipient:** for significant contributions for the development and growth of the organization ● Robert D. Cain Business/Organization Award. **Frequency:** annual. **Type:** recognition ● Silvius Wolansky Outstanding International Leader in Technical Vocational Education and Training Award. **Frequency:** annual. **Type:** monetary ● Valued Supporter of IVETA. **Frequency:** annual. **Type:** recognition. **Computer Services:** Online services, internet access for nonmembers and a members only section. **Publications:** *International Journal of Vocational Education and Training*, semiannual. **Price:** $50.00/year. ISSN: 1075-2455. **Circulation:** 450. **Advertising:** accepted. Also Cited As: *Iveta Journal* ● *IVETA Newsletter*, quarterly. Contains news of interest to members. Alternate Formats: online. **Conventions/Meetings:** semiannual international conference, sponsored by an IVETA member country based on a conference template (exhibits) ● annual Vocational Education and Training - conference - usually held in late November or early December.

9307 ■ National Association of State Directors of Vocational Technical Education Consortium (NASDVTEC)

444 N Capitol St. NW, Ste.830
Washington, DC 20001
Ph: (202)737-0303
Fax: (202)737-1106
E-mail: kgreen@nasdvtec.org
URL: http://infolit.org/members/nasdvte.htm
Contact: Kimberly Green, Exec. Dir.

Founded: 1920. **Members:** 220. **Staff:** 2. **Budget:** $550,000. **Description:** Serves as a professional society of chief administrative officers for vocational education in each state and/or territory; assistant directors; leaders in occupational education. **Awards:** Outstanding Contribution to Vocational Education. **Frequency:** annual. **Type:** recognition. **Recipient:** for individual, organization, and business categories. **Computer Services:** Mailing lists. **Additional Websites:** http://www.careertech.org. **Affiliated With:** National Vocational Technical Education Foundation. **Publications:** *Technocrat*, monthly. Newsletter. Covers association activities and legislative activities affecting occupational education. **Advertising:** accepted. **Conventions/Meetings:** conference - always spring, fall, and winter.

9308 ■ National Vocational Technical Education Foundation (NVTEF)
Address Unknown since 2008

Founded: 1907. **Staff:** 2. **Budget:** $250,000. **Description:** State education departments. Provides professional development activities such as seminars, workshops, conferences, classes, and tours for staff members of state departments of education and other occupational education leaders. Develops policy and program partnerships at the secondary and postsecondary levels. **Libraries: Type:** reference. **Awards: Type:** recognition. **Recipient:** for individuals who have contributed to the advancement of vocational education. **Computer Services:** database. **Affiliated With:** National Association of State Directors of Vocational Technical Education Consortium. **Formerly:** National Vocational Educational Foundation; (1990) National Vocational Educational Professional Development Foundation. **Publications:** Directory, periodic ● Papers. **Conventions/Meetings:** conference - 3/year, always spring, fall, and winter.

9309 ■ University Economic Development Association (UEDA)
HFR-WCU, Ste.440
Cullowhee, NC 28723
Ph: (828)227-7059
Fax: (828)227-7081
E-mail: mcclure@wcu.edu
URL: http://www.universityeda.org
Contact: Thomas E. McClure, Exec. Dir.

Founded: 1976. **Members:** 160. **Membership Dues:** regular, $350 (annual). **Staff:** 2. **Budget:** $100,000. **Description:** Provides advocacy, information, and a forum to enhance the performance of university-based organizations and their affiliates providing business, economic development, and technical assistance to businesses and communities. **Awards:** Project of the Year. **Frequency:** annual. **Type:** recognition. **Subgroups:** Business Assistance; Economic Development Assistance; Technology Transfer Assistance. **Formerly:** (2004) National Association of Management and Technical Assistance Centers. **Publications:** *Members' Publications Directory*, periodic ● *UEDA Weekly Update*. Newsletter. **Price:** included in membership dues. ISSN: 0892-3256. **Conventions/Meetings:** annual conference - November.

Water

9310 ■ Water Advocates
1506 21st St. NW
Washington, DC 20036
Ph: (202)293-4002
E-mail: info@wateradvocates.org
URL: http://www.wateradvocates.org
Contact: David Douglas, Pres./Treas.

Multinational. Description: Represents individuals dedicated to increasing American support for worldwide access to safe, affordable and sustainable supplies of drinking water and adequate sanitation. Advocates on behalf of those people who lack safe water and basic sanitation. Seeks to increase U.S. public and private funding for efficient drinking water and sanitation systems internationally.

Women

9311 ■ American Association of University Women (AAUW)
1111 16th St. NW
Washington, DC 20036
Ph: (202)785-7700
Free: (800)326-AAUW
Fax: (202)872-1425
E-mail: info@aauw.org
URL: http://www.aauw.org
Contact: Ms. Michele Wetherald, Exec. Dir.

Founded: 1881. **Members:** 130,000. **Membership Dues:** individual (member-at-large), $47 (annual) ● student affiliate, $17 (annual) ● college, university (based on the number of student enrolled), $125-$350 (annual). **Staff:** 90. **Budget:** $4,000,000. **Regional Groups:** 10. **State Groups:** 52. **Local Groups:** 1,500. **Description:** Graduates of regionally accredited 4-year colleges, colleges, and universities. Engages in research and lobbying. Supports local branches involved in community action projects to foster advocation for girls. **Libraries: Type:** reference. **Holdings:** archival material. **Awards:** AAUW Educational Foundation Achievement Award. **Frequency:** biennial. **Type:** recognition. **Recipient:** for a woman of outstanding achievement in an academic or professional field ● AAUW Recognition for Emerging Scholars. **Frequency:** annual. **Type:** recognition. **Recipient:** for an untenured woman scholar who has a record of exceptional early accomplishments and shows promise of future distinction ● Annie Jump Cannon Award in Astronomy. **Frequency:** annual. **Type:** recognition. **Recipient:** to an untenured woman astronomer pursuing significant postdoctoral research in astronomy ● Eleanor Roosevelt Fund Award. **Frequency:** biennial. **Type:** recognition. **Recipient:** for outstanding contributions to equity and education. **Telecommunication Services:** TDD, (202)785-7777. **Committees:** College-University Relations; Educational Foundation Programs; Legislative Programs; Women's Issues. **Affiliated With:** International Federation of University Women - Switzerland. **Formerly:** Association of Collegiate Alumnae. **Publications:** *AAUW Outlook*, periodic. Magazine. Contains articles on issues such as equity in education and the workplace. Includes policy update on current legislative issues. **Price:** included in membership dues; $15.00/4 issues (institutes only). **Circulation:** 150,000. **Advertising:** accepted. Alternate Formats: microform. Also Cited As: *Graduate Woman* ● *American Association of University Women—Action Alert*, periodic. Newsletter. Covers legislative news and other issues, including pay equity, child care, and family law. **Price:** $20.00/year ● Booklets ● Brochures. **Conventions/Meetings:** biennial Shaping the Future - convention (exhibits).

9312 ■ American Association of University Women Educational Foundation (AAUWEF)
1111 16th St. NW
Washington, DC 20036
Ph: (202)728-7602
Free: (800)326-AAUW
Fax: (202)872-1425
E-mail: foundation@aauw.org
URL: http://www.aauw.org/ef/index.cfm
Contact: Barbara O'Connor, Pres.

Founded: 1881. **Members:** 135,000. **Membership Dues:** regular, $40 (annual). **Staff:** 90. **Budget:** $8,000,000. **Regional Groups:** 10. **State Groups:** 51. **Local Groups:** 1,750. **Description:** Serves as an arm of the American Association of University Women (see separate entry). Established to: expand AAUW's primary emphasis on educational work; facilitate the building of endowments for fellowships, research, and public service projects; supplement and further specified areas of concern; assume administrative and managerial responsibilities in the AAUW Educational Center. Sponsors conferences; encourages development of the Educational Center in Washington, DC, as a center for women scholars throughout the world; seeks support from other foundations for research and educational projects; also receives contributions from AAUW members; is especially concerned with women's participation in the community and in higher education. Administers Educational Foundation Library, American and International Fellowships Program, Research and Projects endowment funds, and the Eleanor Roosevelt Fund for Women and Girls Teacher Enrichment Sabbaticals. Enables 35 women from other countries to come to the U.S. for study each year. **Libraries: Type:** reference. **Holdings:** 500. **Awards: Type:** fellowship. **Recipient:** to 85 American women for advanced study ● **Type:** grant. **Recipient:** to member divisions and branches for public service ● **Type:** grant. **Recipient:** to individual women for projects. **Affiliated With:** American Association of University Women. **Publications:** *Outlook*, quarterly. Magazine. **Advertising:** accepted. **Conventions/Meetings:** biennial convention.

9313 ■ American Association for Women in Community Colleges (AAWCC)
PO Box 336603
Greeley, CO 80633-0611
Ph: (970)352-2079
Fax: (970)352-2080
E-mail: aawcc@comcast.net
URL: http://www.aawccnatl.org
Contact: Patricia C. Donohue PhD, Pres.

Founded: 1973. **Members:** 1,300. **Membership Dues:** individual, $75 (annual) ● institutional, $300 (annual). **Staff:** 1. **Budget:** $72,500. **Regional Groups:** 10. **State Groups:** 18. **Local Groups:** 121. **Description:** Women faculty members, administrators, staff members, students, and trustees of community colleges. Objectives are to: develop communication and disseminate information among women in community, junior, and technical colleges; encourage educational program development; obtain grants for educational projects for community college women. Disseminates information on women's issues and programs. Conducts regional and state professional development workshops and forums. Recognizes model programs that assist women in community colleges. An affiliate council of the American Association of Community Colleges (see separate entry). **Awards:** AAWCC Trustees of the Year. **Frequency:** annual. **Type:** recognition ● Carolyn Desjardins President of the Year Award. **Frequency:** annual. **Type:** recognition ● Mildred Bulpitt Woman of Year Award. **Frequency:** annual. **Type:** recognition ● Model Program Awards. **Frequency:** annual. **Type:** recognition. **Recipient:** to outstanding programs at community colleges that championed women. **Computer Services:** database. **Formerly:** (1993) American Association for Women in Community and Junior Colleges. **Publications:** *AAWCC Journal*, in moratorium since 1989. Covers research on women's issues. **Price:** included in membership dues; $25.00 for nonmembers in U.S.; $28.00 for nonmembers in Canada; $33.46 for nonmembers outside U.S. and Canada. **Circulation:** 3,000 ● *AAWCC Quarterly*. Newsletter. Reports on association and regional activities and programs involving women. Includes book reviews, calendar of events, and educational opportunities. **Price:** included in membership dues. **Circulation:** 3,000. **Conventions/Meetings:** semiannual board meeting ● semiannual conference and convention (exhibits).

9314 ■ Association of Black Women in Higher Education (ABWHE)
PO Box 210
Princeton, NJ 08540
Ph: (609)258-5494
E-mail: mclay@princeton.edu
URL: http://www.abwhe.org
Contact: Makeba L. Clay, Pres.

Founded: 1979. **Members:** 350. **Membership Dues:** regular, $50 (annual) ● student, retired, $25 (annual) ● institutional, $175 (annual). **State Groups:** 6. **Local Groups:** 6. **Description:** Represents faculty members, education administrators, students, retirees, consultants, managers, and affirmative action officers. Aims to nurture the role of black women in higher education, and to provide support for the professional development goals of black women. Conducts workshops and seminars. **Awards:** Graduate Scholarships. **Type:** recognition ● Undergraduate Scholarships. **Type:** recognition. **Telecommunication Services:** electronic mail, dbrown@pobox.upenn.edu. **Committees:** Chapter Development; Conference; Nominations and Elections; Programs; Publications. **Publications:** *ABWHE Newsletter*, quarterly. **Conventions/Meetings:** biennial conference (exhibits) - always odd-numbered years.

9315 ■ Center for the Education of Women (CEW)
330 E Liberty St.
Ann Arbor, MI 48104
Ph: (734)998-7080
Fax: (734)998-6203
E-mail: cew.mail@umich.edu
URL: http://www.umich.edu/~cew
Contact: Carol Hollenshead, Dir.
Founded: 1964. **Description:** Offers services, advocacy and research in the area of women's employment, education, leadership, career and life transitions, and women faculty. **Libraries: Type:** open to the public; lending; reference. **Holdings:** articles, books, clippings. **Subjects:** women in the workforce, college financial aid, statistics on women in higher education, resume writing, Internet. **Awards:** Faculty Research Grants. **Type:** grant ● **Type:** scholarship. **Recipient:** to returning women students ● Student Research Grants. **Type:** grant. **Publications:** *Cornerstone*, semiannual. Newsletter.

9316 ■ Educational Foundation for Women in Accounting (EFWA)
c/o Cynthia Hires, Admin.
PO Box 1925
Southeastern, PA 19399-1925
Ph: (610)407-9229
Fax: (610)644-3713
E-mail: info@efwa.org
URL: http://www.efwa.org
Contact: Cynthia Hires, Admin.
Founded: 1966. **Description:** Women in the accounting field. Supports the advancement of women in the accounting profession through funding of education, research, career literature, publications, and other projects. **Awards:** Laurels. **Frequency:** periodic. **Type:** scholarship. **Recipient:** for women who are pursuing a PhD in accounting ● Women in Need. **Frequency:** periodic. **Type:** scholarship ● Women in Transition. **Frequency:** periodic. **Type:** scholarship. **Recipient:** for women returning to school to earn a bachelor's degree in accounting. **Publications:** *The Educator*, semiannual. Newsletter. Alternate Formats: online.

9317 ■ The Feminist Press at the City University of New York (TFPNY)
c/o The Graduate Center, CUNY
365 5th Ave., Ste.5406
New York, NY 10016
Ph: (212)817-7915
Fax: (212)817-1593
E-mail: gjacobs@gc.cuny.edu
URL: http://www.feministpress.org
Contact: Ms. Gloria Jacobs, Exec. Dir.
Founded: 1970. **Staff:** 9. **Budget:** $1,000,000. **Nonmembership. Description:** Works to: eliminate sexrole and social stereotypes in education at all levels; further the rediscovery of the history of women; provide literature "with a broad vision of human potential." Provides texts for college courses and has created syllabi in which women's history and literatures by women are introduced into traditional college courses. Reprints lost or neglected literature by women writers. Maintains Women's Studies International, a network of individuals and institutions that has published a report of its 1985 meeting in Nairobi, Kenya, and held a 1995 meeting in Beijing. **Awards:** The Femmy Awards. **Frequency:** annual. **Type:** recognition. **Recipient:** for outstanding service to the association. **Publications:** *The Feminist Press*, annual. Catalog ● *WSQ*, semiannual. Journal. Combines contemporary developments in feminist theory and scholarship with essays, reviews, poetry, fiction, creative nonfiction, and visual arts. **Price:** $40.00 /year for individuals in U.S.; $60.00 /year for institutions in U.S. **Circulation:** 1,500. **Advertising:** accepted ● Books, 12-16/year. Includes children's literature that is nonsexist, and women's writing. ● Also publishes reprints of works by women authors, original anthologies, original autobiographies, biographies, curricular materials, bibliographies, essays, and directories; makes available books for libraries, bookstores, classrooms, and the public.

9318 ■ Feminist Teacher Editorial Collective (FTEC)
c/o Gail Cohee
Sarah Doyle Women's Center
Brown Univ.
Box 1829
Providence, RI 02912
E-mail: feminist-teacher@uwec.edu
URL: http://www.uwec.edu/wmns/FeministTeacher/editors.htm
Contact: Gail Cohee, Contact
Founded: 1984. **Members:** 5. **Description:** Teachers and students; schools, libraries, archives, and women's organizations. Opposes sexism, racism, and other forms of oppression in the classroom. Encourages innovative teaching practices that challenge traditional, educational, disciplinary, and research methodologies. **Publications:** *Feminist Teacher*, 3/year. Annual Reports. Provides a forum for new ideas in the classroom. Includes feminist teacher network news, information on teaching resources, and book reviews. **Price:** $30.00 /year for individuals in U.S.; $50.00 /year for individuals outside U.S.; $75.00 /year for institutions in U.S.; $95.00 /year for institutions outside U.S. ISSN: 0882-4843. **Circulation:** 500. **Advertising:** accepted.

9319 ■ Foundation for Women's Resources (FWR)
3800 Parry Ave.
Dallas, TX 75226
Ph: (214)421-5566
Fax: (214)421-5576
E-mail: okeefe@leadershiptexas.org
URL: http://www.womensresources.org
Contact: Candace O'Keefe Mathis, Exec. Dir.
Founded: 1973. **Members:** 20. **Staff:** 2. **Budget:** $400,000. **Description:** Develops nonpartisan projects and programs to improve the status of women. Projects include a video documenting women's contributions to the state of Texas, Leadership Texas, the Power Pipeline, and the Women's Museum: An Institute for the Future. **Programs:** Ann Richards Fund; Leadership Texas; Leadership Texas Alumnae Association; Power Pipeline. **Conventions/Meetings:** Leadership Texas - seminar - 5/year. 2008 Aug. 11-13, Amarillo, TX; 2008 Oct. 6-8, Dallas, TX.

9320 ■ National Association of University Women (NAUW)
1001 E St. SE
Washington, DC 20003-2847
Ph: (202)547-3967
Fax: (202)547-5226
E-mail: info@nauw1910.org
URL: http://www.nauw1910.org
Contact: Mrs. Ollie D. Johnson, Chair
Founded: 1923. **Members:** 4,000. **Regional Groups:** 5. **Local Groups:** 92. **Description:** Women college or university graduates. Works to promote constructive work in education, civic activities, and human relations; studies educational conditions with emphasis on problems affecting women; encourages high educational standards and stimulate intellectual attainment among women generally. Theme is Women of Action: Reaching, Risking, Responding. Offers tutoring and sponsors After High School-What? youth development program. Maintains placement service. **Awards: Frequency:** annual. **Type:** fellowship ● **Frequency:** annual. **Type:** scholarship. **Committees:** Literacy Program Development; National and International Affairs; Necrology; Political Awareness; Scholarship; Youth Programs. **Affiliated With:** Leadership Conference on Civil Rights; United Negro College Fund. **Formerly:** (1974) National Association of College Women. **Publications:** *Directory of Branch Presidents and Members*, annual ● *Journal of the National Association of University Women*, biennial ● Bulletin, biennial. **Conventions/Meetings:** biennial convention - usually July 30-August 4.

9321 ■ National Coalition for Women and Girls in Education (NCWGE)
c/o American Association of University Women
1111 16th St. NW
Washington, DC 20036
Ph: (202)785-7745 (202)785-7793
Fax: (202)466-7618
E-mail: maatzl@aauw.org
URL: http://www.ncwge.org
Contact: Liza Maatz, Contact
Founded: 1975. **Members:** 50. **Membership Dues:** national (not-for-profit organization), $200 (annual). **Description:** Works to improve educational opportunities for women. Advocates for the strong enforcement of Title IX and other civil rights law; monitors federal agencies implementation of federal education programs; and provides a valuable forum to share information and strategies to advance educational equity. **Task Forces:** Athletics; Elementary and Secondary Education; Higher Education; Sexual Harassment; Testing; Vocational Education and Workforce Training. **Publications:** *Catching Up: A Review of the Women's Educational Equity Act Program* ● *Documenting the Success of Vocational Equity Programs for Women and Girls* ● *Education for All: Women and Girls Speak Out on the National Education Goals* ● *Exploring America's Families* ● *The Higher Education Act: A Guide for Women* ● *How Does the SAT Score for Women?* ● *Title IX: A Practical Guide to Achieving Sex Equity in Education* ● *Title IX at 30: Report Card on Gender Equity.* Alternate Formats: online ● *Title IX at 25: Report Card on Gender Equity.* Alternate Formats: online ● *Working Toward Equity: A Report on the Implementation of the Sex Equity Provisions of the Carl D. Perkins Vocational Education Act.* **Conventions/Meetings:** monthly meeting - always first Monday ● periodic Press Conference.

9322 ■ National Women Law Students Association (NWLSA)
PO Box 60727
Oklahoma City, OK 73146-0727
Ph: (417)425-7832
E-mail: rmwinka@syr.edu
URL: http://www.okcu.edu/law/NWLSA/index.asp
Contact: Becky Winka, Dir. of Membership
Membership Dues: student, $20 (annual) ● alumni, professional, $40 (annual). **Staff:** 5. **Description:** Strives to assist women in achieving full equality and improve their status in the legal profession and throughout society; establishes an effective coalition of law students from around the world. **Publications:** Newsletter. Alternate Formats: online. **Conventions/Meetings:** conference.

9323 ■ National Women's Studies Association (NWSA)
c/o University of Maryland
7100 Baltimore Ave., Ste.502
College Park, MD 20740
Ph: (301)403-0525 (301)403-0524
Fax: (301)403-4137
E-mail: nwsaoffice@nwsa.org
URL: http://www.nwsa.org
Contact: Loretta Younger, Exec. Admin.
Founded: 1977. **Members:** 2,000. **Membership Dues:** regular (with journal), $70-$180 (annual) ● regular (without journal), $40-$150 (annual) ● joint, $40 (annual) ● student, unemployed, $17 (annual) ● retired, $45 (annual) ● standard department/program, $300 (annual) ● MA-granting department/program, $400 (annual) ● PhD-granting department/program, $475 (annual) ● standard women's center, $250 (annual) ● small program/center, K-12 school, $175 (annual) ● non-profit organization, $225-$500 (annual). **Staff:** 5. **Budget:** $550,000. **Regional Groups:** 12. **Description:** Represents teachers, students, community activists, and interested individuals; academic and community-based programs, projects, and groups interested in feminist education. Works to further the social, political, and professional development of women's studies programs. Supports feminist causes. Compiles statistics. Conducts conferences to address topics such as: new developments and controversies in feminist research and theory in the humanities, social sciences, and sciences; curricular development; political and legal issues and strategies; intersection of race and gender; international women's studies. **Computer Services:** Mailing lists, women's studies programs. **Telecommunication**

Services: electronic mail, loretaat.younger@nwsa.org. **Projects:** Inclusion/Empowerment of Underrepresented Constituencies; Women's Studies Archival. **Publications:** *Bridges on Power: Women's Multicultural Alliances*. **Price:** $11.00 ● *The Courage to Question: Women's Studies and Student Learning*. Features new research on multicultural learning, critical thinking, classroom dynamics, and integrating knowledge into life choice. **Price:** $17.00 ● *Guide to Graduate Work in Women's Studies, 2000 Edition*. Book. Includes addresses, phone numbers, and contact people. **Price:** $15.00 for members; $20.00 for nonmembers ● *National Report on the Women's Studies Major*. Includes program models and makes recommendations for strengthening the major. **Price:** $3.00 each ● *NWSA Directory of Women's Studies Programs, Women's Centers, and Women's Research Centers*. **Price:** $5.00 ● *NWSAction*, semiannual. Magazine. Contains calendar of events, conference reports, fellowship and employment opportunity listings, association news, and resources listings. **Price:** included in membership dues. **Circulation:** 2,000. **Advertising:** accepted ● *Re-membering: NWSA 1977-1987*. Includes personal essays covering the first ten years of the organization. **Price:** $11.00 ● *Students at the Center: Feminist Assessment*. Includes practical advice about how to set up a student-centered, faculty driven assessment project on campus. **Price:** $13.00 ● Also publishes audio and video tapes from previous national conferences. Double audiocassettes are available for $16.00, single audiotapes available for $10.00 and videos available for $40.00. **Conventions/Meetings:** annual conference (exhibits).

9324 ■ Office of Women in Higher Education, American Council on Education
c/o American Council on Education
1 Dupont Cir. NW
Washington, DC 20036
Ph: (202)939-9300 (202)939-9390
Fax: (202)883-5696
E-mail: comments@ace.nche.edu
URL: http://www.acenet.edu
Contact: Donna Burns Phillips PhD, Dir.

Founded: 1973. **Staff:** 4. **State Groups:** 50. **Description:** Provides information and council to constituencies within the higher education community, regarding policies, issues, education and research that influences women's equity, diversity and advancement. Works to improve the status of women. Aims to advance women's leadership by: identifying women leaders nationally in higher education through extensive networks; developing women's leadership abilities through state and national programming; advancing more women into senior-level leadership positions by nominating them and working with search firms on placement; and supporting the tenure of mid-and-senior-level women administrators and presidents throughout their careers. **Awards:** The ACE Network Award for the Advancement of Women in Higher Education. **Frequency:** annual. **Type:** recognition. **Recipient:** for outstanding, visionary and innovative program that has significantly contributed to the advancement and support of women or women's issues in higher education ● Donna Shavlik Award. **Frequency:** annual. **Type:** recognition. **Recipient:** to individual who has demonstrated sustained commitment to advancing women in higher education. **Affiliated With:** American Council on Education. **Formerly:** (1998) National Identification Program for the Advancement in Higher Education Administration; (2001) National Network for Women Leaders; (2001) THE NETWORK. **Publications:** *Breaking the Barriers: A Guidebook of Strategies*. Report. **Price:** $18.00 for members; $20.00 for nonmembers. Also Cited As: *Breaking the Barriers: Presidential Strategies for Enhancing Career Mobility Workbook* ● *Breaking the Barriers: Presidential Strategies for Enhancing Career Mobility*. Report. **Price:** $18.00 for members; $20.00 for nonmembers ● *Women's Perspectives on the Presidency*. Report. **Price:** $13.50 for members; $15.00 for nonmembers. **Conventions/Meetings:** semiannual ACE National Leadership Forum - meeting ● Network Leadership Development Programs - meeting, implemented by the individual State Networks.

9325 ■ PEO International
3700 Grand Ave.
Des Moines, IA 50312
Ph: (515)255-3153
Fax: (515)255-3820
E-mail: glane@peodsm.org
URL: http://www.peointernational.org
Contact: Ann H. Fields, Pres.
Founded: 1869. **Members:** 247,600. **Staff:** 39. **State Groups:** 50. **Local Groups:** 5,640. **Description:** International women's organization seeking to further opportunities for higher education for women. Has established International Peace Scholarship Fund, Educational Loan Fund, Program for Continuing Education, and PEO Scholar Awards. Maintains Cottey Junior College for Women, Nevada, MO. **Formerly:** (1998) PEO Sisterhood. **Publications:** *Directory of Presidents*, annual ● *PEO Record*, bimonthly. Newsletter. ISSN: 0746-5130. **Conventions/Meetings:** biennial meeting.

9326 ■ Public Leadership Education Network (PLEN)
1001 Connecticut Ave. NW, Ste.900
Washington, DC 20036
Ph: (202)872-1585
Fax: (202)872-0141
E-mail: plen@plen.org
URL: http://www.plen.org
Contact: Ms. Marianne Alexander, Pres.
Founded: 1978. **Members:** 19. **Staff:** 3. **Description:** Serves as consortium of women's colleges working together to educate women for public leadership positions. Sponsors public policy conferences, seminars and internships in Washington, D.C. and abroad. **Awards:** Mentor Awards. **Frequency:** annual. **Type:** recognition. **Recipient:** for women public leaders who excel as role models for women students. **Publications:** *Learning to Lead: An Inventory of Leadership Learning Experiences at PLEN Colleges*. Report. **Price:** $15.00 ● *Preparing to Lead: The College Women's Guide to Internships in Washington, DC*. **Price:** $20.00. **Circulation:** 2,000 ● *Wingspread Report: Educating Women for Leadership*. **Conventions/Meetings:** annual Women and Congress Seminar ● annual Women and International Policy Seminar - meeting ● annual Women and Public Policy - seminar ● Women and Public Policy: A Public Leadership Career Conference ● Women and Public Policy Internship Semester - seminar - 3/year.

9327 ■ Wellesley Centers for Women (WCW)
Wellesley Coll.
106 Central St.
Wellesley, MA 02481
Ph: (781)283-2500
Fax: (781)283-2504
E-mail: wcw@wellesley.edu
URL: http://www.wcwonline.org
Contact: Susan McGee Bailey, Exec. Dir.
Founded: 1974. **Nonmembership**. **Description:** Scholars engaged in research, training, analysis and action. Works to shape a better world for women and girls, men and boys. **Publications:** *Research and Action Report*, semiannual. Contains research and action conducted at WCW. Alternate Formats: online.

9328 ■ Women Educators (WE)
c/o Paula Lane, Treas.
Sonoma State Univ.
School of Educ.
1801 E Cotati
Rohnert Park, CA 94928
Ph: (805)893-5356
Fax: (805)893-8736
E-mail: paula.lane@sonoma.edu
URL: http://www.rwesig.net/womeneducators.html
Contact: Paula Lane, Treas.
Founded: 1974. **Members:** 300. **Membership Dues:** basic, $10 (annual) ● activist, $15 (annual) ● sustaining, $20 (annual) ● foundational, $25 (annual). **Description:** Educational researchers and educators in institutions of higher education, school systems, government units, and private research organizations. Promotes equal opportunity for women in educational research. Bestows annual Research on Women in Education Award, Sex-Affirmative Curriculum Materials Award, and Scholar/Activist Award. Received grant from the Women's Educational Equity Act Program for a Project on Sex Stereotyping in Education. **Awards:** Women Educators Awards. **Frequency:** annual. **Type:** recognition. **Recipient:** for outstanding contributions of women who have produced curricular materials, conducted research, or engaged in activism and policy making on behalf of girls and women. **Formerly:** (1975) American Educational Research Association Women's Caucus. **Publications:** *Awards Report*, annual ● *Handbook for Achieving Sex Equity Through Education* ● *Sex Equity Handbook for Scholars* ● Newsletter, periodic. **Conventions/Meetings:** annual meeting, held in conjunction with AERA (exhibits).

9329 ■ Women in Real Estate (WIRE)
c/o Tracy Wood, VP
Architectural Resources Gp.
Pier 9
San Francisco, CA 94111
Ph: (650)365-9226 (415)421-1680
E-mail: vconcello@rcn.com
URL: http://www.womeninrealestate.org
Contact: Valerie Concello, Pres.
Founded: 1983. **Members:** 80. **Membership Dues:** individual, $85 (annual). **Staff:** 5. **Description:** Commercial real estate professionals with a minimum of two years experience in the industry. Provides support for real estate colleagues in the commercial real estate industry. **Publications:** Newsletter, quarterly. Alternate Formats: online.

9330 ■ Women's College Coalition (WCC)
1678 Asylum Ave.
West Hartford, CT 06117
Ph: (860)231-5596
E-mail: colleges@womenscolleges.org
URL: http://www.womenscolleges.org
Contact: Susan E. Lennon, Exec. Dir.
Founded: 1972. **Members:** 58. **Staff:** 2. **Budget:** $200,000. **Description:** Represents women's colleges and universities - public and private, independent and church-related, two-year and four-year - in the United States and Canada whose primary mission is the education and advancement of women. Makes the case for women's education to the higher education community, to policy makers, to the media and to the general public. Collects and disseminates information relating to the education of women and gender equity in education; other priority areas are the issues of recruitment and retention of women in math, science and engineering, and the development of women's leadership. **Affiliated With:** American Council on Education; Council of Independent Colleges; National Association of Independent Colleges and Universities. **Conventions/Meetings:** annual conference.

Women's Studies

9331 ■ Society for the Study of Early Modern Women (SSEMW)
c/o Nancy A. Guttierez, Treas.
Coll. of Arts and Sciences
Univ. of North Carolina at Charlotte
9201 Univ. City Blvd.
Charlotte, NC 28223
Ph: (704)687-3388
Fax: (704)687-3228
E-mail: nguttier@uncc.edu
URL: http://www.ssemw.org
Contact: Nancy A. Guttierez, Treas.
Founded: 1994. **Membership Dues:** sustaining, $50 (annual) ● regular, $25 (annual) ● student, part-time, independent scholar, $15 (annual) ● regular, $75 (triennial). **Description:** Studies women and their contributions to the cultural, political, economic, or social spheres of the early modern period. Furthers

scholarship on early modern women. Promotes the exchange of ideas in the field of early modern women study.

Writing

9332 ■ Association of Teachers of Technical Writing (ATTW)
c/o Journals Subscription Dept.
LEA, Inc.
10 Indus. Ave.
Mahwah, NJ 07430
E-mail: sims@unt.edu
URL: http://cms.english.ttu.edu/attw
Contact: Stuart Selber, Pres.
Founded: 1973. **Members:** 900. **Membership Dues:** student, individual, institution, library, $15 (annual). **Description:** Teachers and students of technical communication at all levels and all types of educational institutions; technical communicators from government and industry. Serves as a forum of communication among technical writing teachers and acts as a liaison with other professional organizations. Provides current bibliographies of teaching/learning materials and reports of current research in the teaching of technical writing. Sponsors meetings and workshops at the annual conventions of the Modern Language Association of America and the Conference on College Composition and Communication. **Awards: Type:** recognition. **Recipient:** for outstanding technical communication educators. **Computer Services:** Mailing lists. **Affiliated With:** Conference on College Composition and Communication; Modern Language Association of America. **Publications:** *ATTW Bulletin*, semiannual. Newsletter. Contains information on programs and trends. **Price:** included in membership dues. **Circulation:** 2,000 ● *Technical Communication Quarterly*. Journal. Contains articles on research, theory, and pedagogical methods in technical communication; includes book reviews and software reviews. **Price:** included in membership dues. **Circulation:** 1,200. **Advertising:** accepted. Alternate Formats: microform ● Brochure ● Also publishes anthologies on teaching technical communication. **Conventions/Meetings:** annual meeting, held in conjunction with the Conference on College Composition and Communication.

9333 ■ Council of Writing Program Administrators (WPA)
c/o Dr. Linda Bergmann, Sec.
Purdue Univ.
English Dept.
Heavilon Hall
West Lafayette, IN 47907-1356
Ph: (765)494-7268
Fax: (765)494-3780
E-mail: lbergmann@purdue.edu
URL: http://www.wpacouncil.org
Contact: Dr. Linda Bergmann, Sec.
Founded: 1977. **Members:** 600. **Membership Dues:** individual, $30 (annual) ● institutional, $40 (annual) ● graduate student, $10 (annual). **Staff:** 1. **Description:** Directors of freshman composition or undergraduate writing programs, coordinators, writing center directors, department chairs, and deans. Seeks to provide opportunities to focus on matters attendant to the administration of college and university writing programs. **Awards:** Best Article in WPA: Writing Program Administration. **Frequency:** biennial. **Type:** recognition. **Recipient:** for author(s) of exemplary article presenting the intellectual work of writing program administration ● WPA Award for Outstanding Book on Writing Program Administration. **Frequency:** biennial. **Type:** recognition. **Recipient:** for author(s) or editor(s) of a book publishing excellent research and scholarship related to writing program administration ● WPA Research Grants Program. **Frequency:** annual. **Type:** grant. **Recipient:** for individuals or teams conducting research projects relevant to writing program administration. **Affiliated With:** Association of American Colleges and Universities; Modern Language Association of America; National Council of Teachers of English. **Formerly:** (2002) National Council of Writing Program Administrators. **Publications:** *WPA: Writing Program Administration*, semiannual. Journal. Contains information about the organization, publishes scholarship and research related to the intellectual work of writing program administration. **Price:** included in membership dues. **Advertising:** accepted. Alternate Formats: online; CD-ROM. **Conventions/Meetings:** annual conference and workshop, weeklong workshop and 3-day conference ● annual workshop and conference - during summer.

9334 ■ National Writing Project (NWP)
Univ. of California
2105 Bancroft Way
Berkeley, CA 94720
Ph: (510)642-0963
Fax: (510)642-4545
E-mail: nwp@nwp.org
URL: http://www.writingproject.org
Contact: Richard Sterling, Exec. Dir.
Founded: 1974. **Members:** 12,402. **Staff:** 65. **Budget:** $21,000,000. **Regional Groups:** 10. **State Groups:** 50. **Local Groups:** 195. **Description:** Provides teachers with the skills necessary to teach students how to write. Believes elementary, high school, and college teachers of all subjects can improve their effectiveness by using writing as a teaching tool; feels that writing should be taught as a process with emphasis upon frequent drafts and revision. Sponsors five-week institutes for elementary, high school, and college teachers to improve their writing skills, develop their skills in the teaching of writing, and share new ideas and methods. Conducts research on writing instruction methods for students and for teacher workshops. Pilots national initiatives that support and strengthen the teaching of writing. **Libraries: Type:** by appointment only. **Holdings:** 2,200; articles, books, monographs, periodicals. **Subjects:** education, teaching, learning of reading and writing. **Boards:** Directors. **Projects:** National Network; Outreach. **Special Interest Groups:** English Language Learners Network; Rural Sites Network; Teacher Inquiry Communities; Technology Liaisons Network; Urban Sites Network. **Working Groups:** Local Site Research Initiative; National Reading Initiative; National Technology Initiative; New-Teacher Initiative; Research Forum. **Publications:** *Briefing*, annual. Papers ● *E-Voice*, bimonthly. Newsletter. **Circulation:** 17,000. Alternate Formats: online ● Annual Report, annual ● Monographs ● Books. Contains 14 titles. **Conventions/Meetings:** annual conference, with writing project teachers from across the U.S. to conduct interactive workshops on teaching writing (exhibits) ● biennial Rural Sites Conference, opportunities and issues facing rural schools - early March ● annual Urban Sites Network Conference - late April.

9335 ■ Teachers and Writers Collaborative (T&W)
520 8th Ave., Ste.2020
New York, NY 10018
Ph: (212)691-6590
Fax: (212)675-0171
E-mail: info@twc.org
URL: http://www.twc.org
Contact: Amy Swauger, Dir.
Founded: 1967. **Membership Dues:** basic, $35 (annual) ● patron, $75 (annual) ● benefactor, $150 (annual). **Staff:** 5. **Description:** Teachers and writers interested in the teaching of imaginative writing. Offers educational programs and children's services. **Convention/Meeting:** none. **Libraries: Type:** reference; open to the public; by appointment only. **Holdings:** archival material, books, periodicals. **Subjects:** education, writing, poetry, belles letters. **Publications:** *Teachers and Writers*, 5/year. Newsletter. ISSN: 0146-3381. Alternate Formats: microform ● *Teachers and Writers Magazine*, quarterly. Contains articles about censorship, nature writing, assessment and creative writing. **Price:** included in membership dues; $20.00 for nonmembers; $40.00 for schools and libraries.

Youth

9336 ■ Global Nomads Group (GNG)
381 Broadway, 4th Fl.
New York, NY 10013
Ph: (212)529-0377
Fax: (917)591-6232
E-mail: info@gng.org
URL: http://www.gng.org
Contact: Mark von Sponeck, Co-Founder/Dir.
Founded: 1998. **Multinational. Description:** Aims to increase children's understanding and appreciation for the world and its people. Fosters dialogue and understanding among students of different cultures and nationalities. Seeks to improve the communication skills, cultural understanding and critical thinking skills of the youth. Provides an educational framework in which students can become active leaders in their own education. **Telecommunication Services:** electronic mail, mark@gng.org. **Publications:** *The Nomad*. Newsletter. Alternate Formats: online ● Videos.

9337 ■ National Association of Street Schools (NASS)
1567 Marion St.
Denver, CO 80218
Ph: (303)830-8213
Free: (877)981-7700
Fax: (303)860-1402
E-mail: info@streetschools.com
URL: http://www.streetschools.com
Contact: Mr. Tom Tillapaugh, Founder/Pres.
Founded: 1996. **Members:** 20. **Membership Dues:** regular, $100 (annual). **Description:** Aims to meet the challenges of at-risk youth by developing a network of schools providing personalized, comprehensive education, a moral code and tools for self-sufficiency. **Publications:** *NASS School Directory*. Alternate Formats: online ● *NASS Times*. Newsletter. Alternate Formats: online. **Conventions/Meetings:** annual conference, with reunion.

9338 ■ Peer Health Exchange (PHE)
1460 Broadway, Ste.5-24D
New York, NY 10036
Ph: (212)735-2844
Fax: (917)777-7008
E-mail: national@peerhealthexchange.org
URL: http://www.peerhealthexchange.org
Contact: Louise E. Davis, Exec. Dir.
Staff: 7. **Description:** Strives to give teenagers the knowledge and skills to make healthy decisions. Trains college students to teach a comprehensive health curriculum in public high schools that lack health education. Encourages college students to foster a commitment in public service.

9339 ■ Project YES
5275 Sunset Dr.
Miami, FL 33143
Ph: (305)663-7195
Fax: (305)663-7197
E-mail: web@yesinstitute.org
URL: http://yesinstitute.org
Contact: Martha Fugate, Dir.
Founded: 1996. **Staff:** 4. **Nonmembership. Description:** Aims to prevent suicide and ensure the healthy development of gay, lesbian, bisexual, transgender and all youth by initiating dialogue, providing education, and creating support systems. Fosters dynamic partnerships with individuals and organizations that have a commitment to creating a safer world for all youth: schools, parent groups, healthcare settings, justice departments, clergy, and nonprofit organizations contact the institute seeking nonconfrontational communication and innovative education and training on gender, orientation, leadership and communication. **Programs:** Community Coalition; God As Love; Speakers' Bureau. **Publications:** *ReVision*, bimonthly. Newsletter. Articles are mostly news of the results of the institute's work during the past 2 months. **Circulation:** 5,200. Alternate Formats: online. **Conventions/Meetings:** annual conference - every January.

Adirondacks

9340 ■ Adirondack Historical Association (AHA)
c/o Adirondack Museum
PO Box 99
Blue Mountain Lake, NY 12812-0099
Ph: (518)352-7311
Fax: (518)352-7653
E-mail: cwelsh@adkmuseum.org
URL: http://www.adkmuseum.org
Contact: Caroline Welsh, Dir.
Founded: 1948. **Members:** 5,500. **Membership Dues:** individual, $30 (annual) ● household, $60 (annual). **Staff:** 33. **Budget:** $5,000,000. **Description:** Preserves and promotes the history of the Adirondack area. Maintains the Adirondack Museum at Blue Mountain Lake, NY. Conducts educational programs. **Libraries: Type:** reference; open to the public. **Holdings:** 9,000; books, photographs. **Subjects:** Adirondack history. **Publications:** *Museum Newsletter*, semiannual. Provides information on current museum events and exhibits, on museum artifacts, and on the Adirondacks. **Price:** included in membership dues. **Circulation:** 5,500 ● Also publishes brochures, monographs, and books. **Conventions/Meetings:** quarterly board meeting.

Aerospace

9341 ■ Apollo Society
PO Box 61206
Honolulu, HI 96839-1206
Ph: (808)473-3316
E-mail: capcom@apollo-society.org
URL: http://apollo-society.org
Contact: Gregory A. Smith, Pres.
Founded: 1983. **Members:** 500. **Membership Dues:** Mercury, $25 (annual) ● Gemini, $50 (annual) ● Apollo, $100 (annual). **Staff:** 3. **Description:** Saves, restores, and preserves the Apollo Launch Tower (used in sending American astronauts to the moon) and transforms it into a showplace of Apollo history. Sponsors the formation of a National Space Monument. **Affiliated With:** National Space Society. **Formerly:** Save the Apollo Launch Tower. **Publications:** *Space Update*. Magazine. Covers current human and robotic space exploration missions. Alternate Formats: online.

9342 ■ MAPS Air Museum - Military Aviation Preservation Society (MAPS)
2260 Intl. Pkwy.
North Canton, OH 44720
Ph: (330)896-6332
E-mail: jchevrauxmaps@neo.rr.com
URL: http://www.mapsairmuseum.org
Contact: Rick Hamlet, Dir.
Founded: 1990. **Members:** 500. **Membership Dues:** individual, $35 (annual) ● family, $40 (annual) ● life, $350 ● corporate, $500 (annual) ● patron, $1,000 (annual) ● senior family, $90 (annual) ● senior individual, $85 (annual) ● student, $20 (annual). **Staff:** 15. **Budget:** $100,000. **Local Groups:** 1. **Description:** Individuals dedicated to preserving historical military aircraft. Restores military aircraft to flying condition for ground and aerial display; provides hangar and building restoration. Maintains museum, hall of fame, and speakers' bureau. Sponsors research and educational programs. **Libraries: Type:** reference. **Holdings:** 3,500; archival material, artwork, books, clippings, periodicals. **Subjects:** aviation, military history. **Awards:** Certificate of Achievement Award. **Type:** recognition. **Computer Services:** Mailing lists, of members. **Formerly:** Military Aviation Preservation Society; (2003) Military Aviation Preservation Society and Museum. **Publications:** *MAPS Briefing*, monthly. Newsletter. **Price:** free. **Circulation:** 950. **Advertising:** accepted. Alternate Formats: online. **Conventions/Meetings:** monthly meeting (exhibits) - always first Wednesday in North Canton, OH.

Afghanistan

9343 ■ Society of Afghan Professionals (SAP)
39155 Liberty St., Ste.D460
Fremont, CA 94538
Ph: (510)574-2183
E-mail: info@sapnet.org
URL: http://www.sapnet.org
Contact: Deana Haya, Pres.
Founded: 1999. **Membership Dues:** professional, $40 (annual). **Description:** Aims to create a strong network of Afghan professionals within the US. Promotes academic and cultural resources of Afghan community through its humanitarian advocacy. **Projects:** Aftaab Camp; Art Shows; Dari Pashto Class; Events; Fundraisers; Humanitarian Aid; Paghman; Seminars.

Africa

9344 ■ Wimbum Cultural and Development Association in the United States of America (WICUDA-USA)
PO Box 3108
Bellaire, TX 77402
E-mail: info@wicuda-usa.org
URL: http://www.wimbum.org
Contact: Mrs. Florence Ngundam, Chair
Founded: 2003. **Description:** Represents the interests of the Mbum People. Promotes the social, educational, developmental, and cultural well-being of the Wimbum people in the Diaspora. Aims to develop Mbumland and to improve the quality of life of its people through education, health care, community development initiatives and the promotion of Mbum cultural values.

African

9345 ■ African Children's Choir
PO Box 29690
Bellingham, WA 98228-1690
Ph: (604)575-4500
Free: (877)532-8651
Fax: (604)575-4511
E-mail: info@africanchildrenschoir.com
URL: http://www.africanchildrenschoir.com
Contact: Ray Barnett, Pres./Founder
Founded: 1984. **Membership Dues:** regular, in UK, $10 (monthly) ● regular, in Canada, $15 (monthly). **Multinational. Description:** Children between seven and twelve years of age from Uganda, Kenya, Rwanda, Nigeria and Ghana. Aims to provide funds necessary for school fees, securing a brighter future for children. Conducts tours worldwide and raises funds from individuals attending concerts. **Publications:** *Between Friends*, periodic. Newsletter. Alternate Formats: online.

9346 ■ African Family Film Foundation (AFFF)
PO Box 630
Santa Cruz, CA 95061-0630
E-mail: friends@africanfamily.org
URL: http://www.africanfamily.org
Contact: Taale Laafi Rosellini, Founder/Exec. Dir.
Founded: 1992. **Staff:** 2. **Description:** Aims to bring inspiring images of African peoples to schools, community groups, and media outlets in the United States and internationally. Produces and distributes films, videos, audio-cassettes, CDs, photographs. Assists African children at risk through the African Family Children's Fund. **Boards:** Advisory. **Funds:** African Family Children's Fund.

9347 ■ African Heritage Center for African Dance and Music (AHCADM)
4018 Minnesota Ave. NE
Washington, DC 20019
Ph: (202)399-5252
Fax: (202)399-5252
E-mail: ahdd@interchange.org
Contact: Melvin Deal, Founding Dir.
Founded: 1973. **Members:** 50. **Membership Dues:** registration, $25 (monthly). **Staff:** 8. **Budget:** $100,000. **Regional Groups:** 2. **State Groups:** 2. **Local Groups:** 4. **National Groups:** 4. **Description:** Serves as a multicultural center for instruction and training in traditional West African dance, music, and dramatic ritualistic forms; also serves as institution for cross-cultural workshops between ethnic groups. Receives traveling artists from abroad for workshops and exchange. Presents concerts; conducts lecture demo-performances. Teaches modern and jazz dance. Provides children's services; sponsors charitable program. **Publications:** none. **Conventions/Meetings:** annual Anniversary & Kwanzaa Celebration - party - always December 26.

9348 ■ African Studies Association (ASA)
c/o Rutgers the State University
Douglass Campus
132 George St.
New Brunswick, NJ 08901-1400
Ph: (732)932-8173
Fax: (732)932-3394
E-mail: asaed@rci.rutgers.edu
URL: http://www.africanstudies.org
Contact: Dr. Carol L. Martin, Exec. Dir.
Founded: 1957. **Members:** 3,000. **Membership Dues:** regular (based on income), $45-$150 (annual) ● faculty, staff, retiree, $65 (annual) ● joint, $45 (annual) ● subscribing institutional, $200 (annual) ● supporting institutional, $600 (annual). **Staff:** 5. **Budget:** $500,000. **Description:** Persons specializing in teaching, writing, or research on Africa including political scientists, historians, geographers, anthropologists, economists, librarians, linguists, and government officials; persons who are studying African subjects; institutional members are universities, libraries, government agencies, and others interested in receiving information about Africa. Seeks to foster communication and to stimulate research among scholars on Africa. Sponsors placement service; conducts panels and discussion groups; presents exhibits and films. **Awards:** Children's Book Award. **Frequency:** annual. **Type:** recognition. **Recipient:** for best children's book on Africa ● Conover-Porter Book Award. **Frequency:** annual. **Type:** recognition. **Recipient:** for outstanding contributions to African List bibliography or reference works ● Distinguished Africanist Award. **Type:** recognition. **Recipient:** for noted contribution to African studies ● Graduate Student Paper Prize. **Frequency:** annual. **Type:** recognition ● Herskovits Award. **Frequency:** annual. **Type:** recognition. **Recipient:** for important publication in African Scholarship for preceding year ● International Visitor Award. **Frequency:** annual. **Type:** monetary ● Text Prize. **Frequency:** biennial. **Type:** recognition. **Recipient:** for best critical edition or translation into English of primary source materials on Africa. **Computer Services:** Mailing lists. **Councils:** Current Issues; Outreach. **Study Groups:** Gays and Lesbians in African Studies. **Working Groups:** Electronic Technology. **Publications:** *African Studies Review*, 3/year. Journal. **Price:** included in membership dues. ISSN: 0002-0206. **Circulation:** 3,700. **Advertising:** accepted ● *ASA News*, 3/year. Newsletter ● *Directory of African and Afro-American Studies in the U.S.*, periodic ● *History in Africa*, annual. Journal ● Also publishes scholarly and bibliographical material. **Conventions/Meetings:** annual meeting, with panel discussion, roundtables, combined exhibits, and vendors (exhibits) - 2008 Nov. 13-16, Chicago, IL; 2009 Nov. 19-22, New Orleans, LA; 2010 Nov. 18-21, San Francisco, CA.

9349 ■ Association for the Study of Classical African Civilizations (ASCAC)
2274 W 20th St.
Los Angeles, CA 90018
Ph: (323)730-1155
Fax: (323)730-0665
E-mail: info@ascac.org
URL: http://www.ascac.org
Contact: Mrs. Nzinga Ratibisha Heru, Intl. Pres.
Founded: 1984. **Members:** 1,000. **Membership Dues:** individual, $50 (annual) ● student, elder, $25 (annual). **Staff:** 8. **Regional Groups:** 5. **Description:** Individuals interested in the study and promotion of African civilization and an African worldview. Promotes the preservation of the ancient African heritage. Conducts research and educational programs; operates museum; maintains library and speakers' bureau. Bestows annual Leo Hansberry Award. **Computer Services:** Mailing lists, of members. **Commissions:** Creative Production; Education; Research; Spiritual Development. **Publications:** *Critical Commentaries*, annual. **Price:** $5.00. **Circulation:** 2,000. **Conventions/Meetings:** annual conference.

9350 ■ Homowo African Arts and Cultures
4839 NE Martin Luther King Blvd., Ste.209
Portland, OR 97211
Ph: (503)288-3025
Fax: (503)331-6688
E-mail: info@homowo.org
URL: http://www.homowo.org
Contact: Susan Addy, Exec. Dir.
Founded: 1986. **Staff:** 3. **Budget:** $300,000. **Local Groups:** 1. **Description:** Promotes African culture through performing arts. Serves as a clearinghouse for information on African performing arts. Sponsors lectures, forums, and concerts. Sponsors Annual African Festival in August. **Telecommunication Services:** electronic mail, susan@homowo.org. **Formerly:** (1999) Homowo Foundation for African Arts and Cultures.

African-American

9351 ■ African American Cultural Alliance (AACA)
PO Box 22173
Nashville, TN 37202
Ph: (615)251-0007
E-mail: aaca1983@bellsouth.net
URL: http://www.africanamericanculturalalliance.com
Contact: Steven Moore, Pres.
Founded: 1983. **Members:** 12. **Membership Dues:** regular, $25 (monthly). **Staff:** 3. **Budget:** $15,000. **Languages:** English, Kiswahili. **Description:** Seeks to promote African culture and increase public awareness of the cultural and historical heritage of people of African descent. Offers educational programs for children through theater, music, dance, history and poetry; conducts research; maintains speakers' bureau, tours of significant sites, official 501C3 designation. **Libraries:** **Type:** reference. **Holdings:** 50. **Computer Services:** database ● mailing lists. **Task Forces:** Advisory. **Publications:** Booklets, annual. **Conventions/Meetings:** annual African Street Festival (exhibits) - September.

9352 ■ African American Museum (AAM)
1765 Crawford Rd.
Cleveland, OH 44106
Ph: (216)000-0000
Fax: (216)000-0000
E-mail: ourstory@aamcleveland.org
URL: http://www.aamcleveland.org
Contact: Nancy Nolan-Jones, Exec. Dir.
Founded: 1953. **Members:** 350. **Membership Dues:** student, $10 (annual) ● senior citizen, $15 (annual) ● individual, $25 (annual) ● Ebony Family, $50 (annual) ● Pyramid, $100 (annual) ● Diamond Pyramid, $250 (annual) ● Golden Pyramid, $500 (annual) ● Dynasty, $1,000 (annual) ● Diamond Dynasty, $2,500 (annual) ● Golden Dynasty, $5,000 (annual). **Staff:** 6. **Budget:** $10,000. **Regional Groups:** 1. **State Groups:** 2. **Local Groups:** 1. **National Groups:** 2. **Description:** Individuals, organizations, and businesses. Seeks to preserve, exhibit, and educate all people about the accomplishments and contributions to society of people of African American origin. Collects, preserves, and exhibits African American artifacts; sponsors educational programs. **Departments:** Education; Special Research. **Formerly:** (1987) Afro-American Cultural and Historical Society. **Publications:** *African American Museum Newsletter*, quarterly. **Price:** free. **Circulation:** 10,000. **Conventions/Meetings:** monthly Life Development Workshop - always 4th Saturday.

9353 ■ Afro-American Historical and Genealogical Society (AAHGS)
PO Box 73067
Washington, DC 20056-3067
E-mail: info@aahgs.org
URL: http://www.aahgs.org
Contact: Khadijah Matin, Pres.
Founded: 1977. **Members:** 1,025. **Membership Dues:** individual, $35 (annual) ● organization, $45 (annual) ● family, $40 (annual) ● life, $1,000. **Regional Groups:** 23. **Description:** Individuals, libraries, and archives. Encourages scholarly research in Afro-American history and genealogy as it relates to American history and culture. Collects, maintains, and preserves relevant material, which the society makes available for research and publication. Conducts seminars and workshops. **Libraries:** **Type:** reference. **Holdings:** 21. **Subjects:** Afro-American family, church history, genealogy. **Awards:** James Dent Walker Award. **Frequency:** annual. **Type:** recognition. **Recipient:** to a person exhibiting distinguished performance. **Telecommunication Services:** electronic mail, khadmatin@earthlink.net. **Committees:** Awards; Conference Planning; Development; Education; Internship; Library; Public Relations; School Education Projects; Special Publications. **Affiliated With:** Federation of Genealogical Societies; National Genealogical Society. **Publications:** *AAHGS News*, bimonthly. Newsletter. Contains a message from the president, news and notes, book reviews, etc. ● *Journal of the Afro-American Historical and Genealogical Society*, semiannual. **Price:** included in membership dues. **Circulation:** 800. **Advertising:** accepted. **Conventions/Meetings:** annual conference, genealogical African American products (exhibits) - always in Washington, DC.

9354 ■ Afro-American Historical Society Museum
c/o Neal E. Brunson, Esq., Dir.
1841 Kennedy Blvd.
Jersey City, NJ 07305
Ph: (201)547-5262
Fax: (201)547-5392
URL: http://www.cityofjerseycity.org/docs/afroam.shtml
Contact: Neal E. Brunson Esq., Dir.
Founded: 1977. **Members:** 307. **Membership Dues:** regular, $500 (annual). **Staff:** 5. **Budget:** $120,000. **Description:** Individuals, corporations, and sororities. Preserves, teaches and exhibits the history and culture of African Americans. Conducts research; organizes exhibits of African American history and culture; conducts charitable fund raising activities. **Libraries:** **Type:** open to the public. **Holdings:** 212,000; articles, audio recordings, books, periodicals, video recordings. **Subjects:** African Diaspora-Focus on New Jersey. **Publications:** Newsletter, quarterly. **Price:** free for members. **Circulation:** 750. **Advertising:** accepted. **Conventions/Meetings:** semiannual Afro-American History and Culture - lecture ● monthly meeting (exhibits).

9355 ■ Association for the Preservation and Presentation of the Arts (APPA)
2011 Benning Rd. NE
Washington, DC 20002
Ph: (202)529-3244
Contact: Bernice Hammond, Pres.
Founded: 1964. **Members:** 500. **Description:** Individuals representing the visual and performing arts; interested others. Serves as a vehicle for the promotion of blacks in the arts. Seeks to increase public awareness and appreciation of the arts and its representation of African American culture. Works on the development of musical and dance productions. Produces children's shows; sponsors lectures. Offers scholarships to children and young people interested in the arts. **Publications:** *Cultural Magnet*, semiannual. Newsletter ● Also publishes pamphlets and information on artists. **Conventions/Meetings:** meeting - 3/year.

9356 ■ Association for the Study of African-American Life and History (ASALH)
CB Powell Bldg.
Howard Univ.
525 Bryant St., Ste.C142
Washington, DC 20059
Ph: (202)865-0053
Fax: (202)265-7920
E-mail: info@asalh.net
URL: http://www.asalh.org
Contact: Sylvia Cyrus-Albritton, Exec. Dir.
Founded: 1915. **Members:** 2,500. **Membership Dues:** general, $65 (annual) ● senior, $45 (annual) ● student, $35 (annual) ● corporate, $1,500 (annual) ● institution, $250 (annual) ● interim life, $200 ● life, $1,000 ● dual, $100 (annual). **Staff:** 5. **Budget:** $200,000. **State Groups:** 30. **Local Groups:** 160. **Description:** Historians, scholars, and students

interested in the research and study of black people as a contributing factor in civilization. Works to promote historical research and writings, collect historical manuscripts and materials relating to black people throughout the world, and bring about harmony among the races by interpreting one to the other. Encourages the study of black history and training in the social sciences, history, and other disciplines. Cooperates with governmental agencies, foundations, and peoples and nations in projects designed to advance the study of ethnic history, with emphasis on black heritage and programs for the future. Maintains Carter G. Woodson home in Washington, DC. Sponsors Afro-American History Month. **Additional Websites:** http://www.dpw-archives.org/asalh.html. **Formerly:** (1975) Association for the Study of Negro Life and History; (2000) Association for the Study of Afro-American Life and History. **Publications:** *Black History Bulletin*, semiannual. Magazine. Describes events in black life and history. **Price:** included in membership dues; $40.00 for individuals; $40.00 for institutions in U.S.; $45.00 for institutions outside U.S. **Advertising:** accepted. Alternate Formats: online. Also Cited As: *BHB* ● *Journal of African American History*, quarterly. **Price:** included in membership dues; $55.00 for individuals; $80.00 for institutions in U.S.; $90.00 for institutions outside U.S. ISSN: 0022-2922. **Advertising:** accepted. Also Cited As: *JAAH* ● Brochures ● Also publishes textbooks and other materials through the Associated Publishers division. **Conventions/Meetings:** annual Carter G. Woodson and the Origins of Multiculturalism - convention (exhibits) - always October. 2008 Oct. 1-5, Birmingham, AL ● annual competition, essay contest for undergraduate and graduate students (exhibits).

9357 ■ Black World Foundation (BWF)

PO Box 22869
Oakland, CA 94609
Ph: (734)213-2400
Fax: (734)213-2657
E-mail: blkschlr@aol.com
URL: http://www.theblackscholar.org
Contact: Robert Chrisman, Ed.-in-Chief/Publisher

Founded: 1969. **Staff:** 5. **Description:** Black professionals and activists united to develop and distribute black educational materials and to develop black cultural and political thought. Offers books in the areas of black literature, history, fiction, essays, political analysis, social science, poetry, and art. **Libraries: Type:** reference. **Publications:** *The Black Scholar*, quarterly. Journal. Features articles on contemporary black thought. **Price:** $30.00 /year for individuals; $6.00/copy for individuals; $85.00 /year for institutions; $20.00/copy for institutions. **Advertising:** accepted ● *Listing of Black Books in Print*, annual ● Books. Contains poetry and information on black sociology. **Advertising:** accepted.

9358 ■ Charles H. Wright Museum of African American History (MAAH)

315 E Warren Ave.
Detroit, MI 48201-1443
Ph: (313)494-5800
Fax: (313)494-5855
E-mail: webmaster@maah-detroit.org
URL: http://www.maah-detroit.org
Contact: Ms. Juanita Moore, Pres./CEO

Founded: 1965. **Members:** 5,000. **Membership Dues:** individual, $35 (annual) ● family, $65 (annual) ● contributor, $150 (annual) ● supporter, $500 (annual) ● partner, $1,000 (annual) ● youth (ages 5-17), $5 (annual) ● senior (ages 62 and over), $15 (annual) ● college student, $25 (annual). **Staff:** 58. **Budget:** $7,000,000. **State Groups:** 1. **Description:** Dedicated to preserving, documenting, interpreting, and exhibiting the cultural heritage of African-Americans and their ancestors. Serves as a learning and resource center; collects and documents contributions of Black people. Offers permanent and traveling exhibits. Conducts workshops, seminars, and lecture series. Sponsors competitions; maintains children's services; offers specialized education program. **Libraries: Type:** reference. **Holdings:** 3,000; audio recordings, books, video recordings. **Subjects:** African-American and African world history, art, culture. **Awards:** Ford Freedom Award. **Frequency:** annual. **Type:** recognition. **Recipient:** for posthumous recognition of excellence in one of five areas, selected by committee. **Affiliated With:** African American Museums Association; American Association of Museums; American Association for State and Local History. **Formerly:** (1969) International Afro-American Museum Committee; (1978) International Afro-American Museum; (1983) Afro-American Museum of Detroit; (2001) Museum of African American History. **Publications:** *African AmericaNews*, quarterly. Newsletter. **Price:** included in membership dues. **Circulation:** 5,000. **Conventions/Meetings:** annual meeting.

9359 ■ Institute for the Advanced Study of Black Family Life and Culture (IASBFLC)

1012 Linden St.
Oakland, CA 94607
Ph: (510)836-3705
E-mail: lgoddard@iasbflc.org
URL: http://www.iasbflc.org
Contact: Wade W. Nobles PhD, Exec. Dir.

Founded: 1980. **Description:** Seeks to reunify African American families and to revitalize the black community. Advocates the reclamation of what the group considers traditional African American culture. Conducts research on issues impacting the black community such as teenage pregnancy, child-rearing practices, mental health support systems, and the effects of alcohol and drugs. Maintains HAWK Federation (High Achievement, Wisdom, and Knowledge Federation), a training program employed in school systems to aid in the character development of young black males. Sponsors in-service training for agencies, school systems, and the juvenile justice system. Develops training curricula for teen parents. Maintains speakers' bureau. **Publications:** *African American Families - Issues, Insights, and Direction*. Book. **Price:** $15.00 ● *African Psychology - Toward Its Reclamation, Re-Ascension and Revitalization*. Book. Responds to innate questions such as: "Why is there a black psychology". **Price:** $15.00 ● *Africanity and the Black Family - The Development of a Theoretical Model*. Book. Provides the student of the Black family with a framework for critiquing the field of Black family scholarship. **Price:** $15.00 ● *To Be African or Not to Be*. Article ● *Understanding the Black Family - A Guide for Scholarship and Research*. Book. Provides set of guidelines for understanding the strengths, weaknesses, capabilities and inabilities of science and research. **Price:** $15.00. **Conventions/Meetings:** annual conference.

9360 ■ Museum of African American History (MAAH)

14 Beacon St., Ste.719
Boston, MA 02108
Ph: (617)725-0022
Fax: (617)720-5225
E-mail: history@afroammuseum.org
URL: http://www.afroammuseum.org
Contact: Marita Rivero, Chair

Founded: 1965. **Members:** 380. **Membership Dues:** Eunice Ross student/senior, $15 (annual) ● Lewis Hayden individual, $25 (annual) ● Susan and Thomas Paul family, $50 (annual) ● Absalom Boston friend, $100 (annual) ● Maria Stewart Society, $500 (annual) ● Frederick Douglas Society, $1,000 (annual) ● National Trust friend, $125 (annual) ● Legacy Society, $5,000 (quinquennial) ● associate, $2,500 (annual) ● benefactor, $5,000 (annual) ● partner, $10,000 (annual) ● leader, $25,000 (annual). **Staff:** 8. **Budget:** $1,540,000. **Description:** Aims to "preserve, conserve and interpret the contributions of people of African descent and those who have found common cause with them in the struggle for liberty, dignity and justice for all Americans." Owns four historic sites, the African Meeting House in Boston, Abiel Smith School in Boston and the African Meeting House on Nantucket and Florence Higginbotham House. The African Meeting House in Boston is the nation's oldest extant Black church. The Abiel Smith School in Boston built in 1835, was the first publicly funded segregated primary and secondary school in the nation. **Libraries: Type:** reference. **Holdings:** 4,000; audiovisuals, books. **Subjects:** Afro-American history and literature. **Awards:** Living Legends Awards. **Frequency:** annual. **Type:** recognition. **Formerly:** (1968) American Museum of Negro History. **Publications:** *The African Meeting House in Boston: A Celebration of History* ● *The African Meeting House in Boston: A Sourcebook*, periodic ● *Black Heritage Trail*, periodic. Brochure ● Also, produces slide-tape programs, videos, curriculum guides.

9361 ■ National Center of Afro-American Artists (NCAAA)

300 Walnut Ave.
Boston, MA 02119
Ph: (617)442-8614
E-mail: bgaither@mfa.org
URL: http://www.ncaaa.org
Contact: Ms. Elma Lewis, Founder

Founded: 1968. **Membership Dues:** student, $20 (annual) ● individual single, $35 (annual) ● family, $55 (annual) ● friend, $85 (annual) ● supporter, $100 (annual) ● donor, $150 (annual) ● contributor, $250 (annual) ● patron, $500 (annual) ● grand patron, $1,000 (annual). **Description:** African American artists; institutions; and interested others. Aims to: promote cultural activities in African American history and culture; encourage the development of artistic and cultural expression within black communities; increase awareness and appreciation of the achievements of black artists. Organizes and conducts cultural events, theatrical productions, and concerts. Sponsors workshops on topics such as 19th Century Black America, Introduction to Africa, and the Caribbean.

9362 ■ San Francisco African American Historical and Cultural Society (SFAAHCS)

762 Fulton St., 2nd Fl.
San Francisco, CA 94102
Ph: (415)292-6172
Fax: (415)440-4231
E-mail: info@sfblackhistory.org
URL: http://www.sfblackhistory.org
Contact: Mr. William E. Hoskins DDS, Exec. Dir.

Founded: 1955. **Members:** 200. **Membership Dues:** senior, student, $10 (annual) ● individual, $25 (annual) ● family, $40 (annual) ● life, $500 ● participating, $75 (annual) ● donor, $275 (annual). **Staff:** 2. **Budget:** $250,000. **Regional Groups:** 1. **State Groups:** 1. **Local Groups:** 1. **Description:** Preserves the history and culture of African and African American people. Collects and disseminates information. Offers educational programs; maintains museum and gallery; sponsors speakers' bureau. Although activities are centered in the San Francisco Bay area, members are nationwide. **Libraries: Type:** reference. **Holdings:** 8,000; archival material, books. **Subjects:** African Americans. **Awards:** Praise Singer Award. **Frequency:** annual. **Type:** recognition. **Computer Services:** Online services. **Committees:** African Affairs, Sanderson Senior History Club. **Publications:** *Praise Singer*, quarterly. Newsletter. **Price:** included in membership dues. **Advertising:** accepted ● *Walking Tour of the Black Presence in San Francisco in the 19th Century*. **Price:** $10.00. **Conventions/Meetings:** semimonthly board meeting ● annual meeting (exhibits) - always second Sunday of October, San Francisco, CA.

9363 ■ Schomburg Center for Research in Black Culture

515 Malcolm X Blvd.
New York, NY 10037-1801
Ph: (212)491-2200
Fax: (212)491-6760
E-mail: scgenref@nypl.org
URL: http://www.nypl.org/research/sc/sc.html
Contact: Howard Dodson, Dir.

Founded: 1926. **Membership Dues:** associate, $35 (annual) ● friend, $50 (annual) ● supporter, $100 (annual) ● patron, $250 (annual) ● sustainer, $500 (annual) ● conservator, $1,000 (annual). **Languages:** Afrikaans, Creole, Dutch, English, French, German, Spanish. **Multinational. Description:** Works to promote the study of the histories and cultures of peoples of African descent and interprets its collections through exhibitions and publications and educational, scholarly, and cultural programs. **Libraries: Type:** open to the public; reference. **Holdings:** 198,000; artwork, audio recordings, books, films, photographs, video recordings. **Subjects:** African-American history and culture, African history, Afro-Caribbean history and culture. **Computer Services:** Online services, catalog, digital images. **Divisions:** Art and Artifacts; General Research and Reference; Manuscripts, Archives, and Rare Books; Moving Image and Recorded Sound; Photographs and Prints. **Programs:** Scholars-in-Residence. **Publications:** *In Motion: The African-American Migration Experience.* Book. Covers four major periods of migration. Contains data-based maps and illustrations. **Price:** $35.00 ● *Jubilee: The Emergence of African-American Culture.* Book. Contains a documentation of the evolution of the African culture. **Price:** $35.00 ● *Standing in the Need of Prayer: A Celebration of Black Prayer.* Book. Contains prayers relevant to black experience. **Price:** $27.50.

Aircraft

9364 ■ Aircraft Engine Historical Society (AEHS)
1019 Old Monrovia Rd. NW, Ste.201
Huntsville, AL 35806
Ph: (256)683-1458
E-mail: information@enginehistory.org
URL: http://www.enginehistory.org
Contact: Kimble D. McCutcheon, Pres.

Founded: 2001. **Membership Dues:** in North America, $35 ● outside North America, $44 ● student in North America, $19. **Description:** Fosters an appreciation of the people, art, and science associated with aircraft engine development, manufacture, and use. Educates students, historians, enthusiasts and the public about the history of aircraft engines. Encourages the restoration and public display of historical aircraft engines. **Publications:** *Torque Meter*, quarterly. Newsletter. **Price:** included in membership dues.

Alleghenies

9365 ■ Council of the Alleghenies (CA)
c/o Dr. Anthony Crosby, Journal Ed.
PO Box 514
Frostburg, MD 21532
Ph: (301)689-8178 (301)687-4889
E-mail: acrosby@frostburg.edu
URL: http://www.councilofthealleghenies.org
Contact: Dr. Anthony Crosby, Journal Ed.

Founded: 1960. **Members:** 180. **Membership Dues:** active, $15 (annual) ● supporting, $25 (annual) ● sustaining, $50 (annual) ● life, $150. **Description:** Individuals and university libraries interested in the welfare of the mountainous regions of Western Pennsylvania, Western Maryland, and northern West Virginia. Preserves, develops, and communicates the rich and meaningful traditions, folklore, history, human values, and resources of the Allegheny Highlands. Encourages regional preservation of historic features; fosters establishment of local archives; seeks to coordinate efforts of local groups by cutting across state and county lines. Sponsors lecture series and tours. **Publications:** *Journal of the Alleghenies*, annual. **Price:** included in membership dues. **Circulation:** 200 ● Monographs ● Also publishes index to all council publications. **Conventions/Meetings:** annual meeting ● symposium.

Amegroid

9366 ■ Amegroid Society of America (ASA)
3 Woodthorne Ct., No. 12
Owings Mills, MD 21117
Ph: (410)363-6187
E-mail: nahbb@msn.com
URL: http://www.nuamericas.org/asa
Contact: Cynthia Brower, Contact

Founded: 1980. **Description:** Amegroids, who define themselves as individuals who are a biological mixture of two or more of the Negroid, Caucasoid, and Mongoloid races; other members include persons who cannot trace their racial heritage beyond America. Promotes recognition and approval of the Amegroid race. Helps to establish the culture, education, and philosophy of the Amegroid people. **Publications:** *Amegroids: The New Native American (An Ethnic and Racial Heritage Book).* **Price:** $21.95. **Conventions/Meetings:** monthly Amegroid Heritage Forums - workshop.

American

9367 ■ American Studies Association (ASA)
1120 19th St. NW, Ste.301
Washington, DC 20036
Ph: (202)467-4783
Fax: (202)467-4786
E-mail: asastaff@theasa.net
URL: http://www.georgetown.edu/crossroads/asainfo.html
Contact: John F. Stephens, Exec. Dir.

Founded: 1951. **Members:** 5,500. **Membership Dues:** regular (based on income), $20-$99 (annual) ● student, emeritus, $20 (annual) ● institutional, $140 (annual) ● affiliate foreign scholar, $35 (annual) ● life, $1,400 ● joint, $15 (annual). **Staff:** 5. **Budget:** $500,000. **Regional Groups:** 13. **Description:** Serves as professional society of persons interested in American literature, American history, sociology, anthropology, political science, philosophy, fine arts, and other disciplines; librarians, museum directors, and government officials. Concerned with any field of study relating to American life and culture, past and present. Members are interested in research and teaching that crosses traditional departmental lines. **Awards:** Annette K. Baxter Awards. **Frequency:** annual. **Type:** recognition. **Recipient:** for excellent graduate student conference papers ● Bode-Pearson Prize. **Frequency:** annual. **Type:** recognition. **Recipient:** for lifetime achievement ● Constance P. Rourke Prize. **Frequency:** annual. **Type:** recognition. **Recipient:** for best article in field ● John Hope Franklin Publication Prize. **Frequency:** annual. **Type:** recognition. **Recipient:** for best book in field ● Lora Romero First Book Publication Prize. **Frequency:** annual. **Type:** recognition. **Recipient:** for excellent graduate student conference papers ● Mary C. Turpie Prize. **Frequency:** annual. **Type:** recognition. **Recipient:** for outstanding teaching and administrative work ● Ralph Henry Gabriel Dissertation Prize. **Frequency:** annual. **Type:** recognition. **Recipient:** for best dissertation in field ● Wise-Susman Prize. **Frequency:** annual. **Type:** recognition. **Recipient:** for best student conference paper. **Committees:** American Studies Programs; Electronic Projects; Ethnic Studies; International; Minority Scholars; Prize; Secondary Education; Students; Women's. **Publications:** *American Quarterly.* Journal. Concerns the study of past and present American culture. **Price:** included in membership dues; $110.00 /year for libraries. ISSN: 0003-0678. **Circulation:** 7,000. **Advertising:** accepted. Alternate Formats: microform; online ● *American Studies Association—Newsletter*, quarterly. Promotes the interdisciplinary study of American culture. Includes employment opportunities and research updates. **Price:** included in membership dues. ISSN: 0742-9290. **Circulation:** 6,000. Alternate Formats: microform; online ● *Guide to American Studies Resources.* **Conventions/Meetings:** annual meeting, with book exhibit (exhibits) - 2008 Oct. 16-19, Albuquerque, NM; 2009 Nov. 5-8, Washington, DC.

9368 ■ Confederate Memorial Association (CMA)
PO Box 6010
Washington, DC 20005
Ph: (202)483-5700
E-mail: hurley@confederate.org
URL: http://www.confederate.org
Contact: John E. Hurley, Chm.

Founded: 1872. **Members:** 2,000. **Membership Dues:** regular, $25 (annual) ● sustaining, $100 (annual) ● life, $1,000 ● patron, $50 (annual) ● benefactor, $500 (annual). **Staff:** 3. **Description:** Individuals interested in the literature, artifacts, and culture of the Southern U.S. and the American Civil War (1861-65). Seeks to preserve Southern culture as part of America's heritage by maintaining the Confederate Memorial Hall museum and library in Washington, DC. Sponsors Confederate Embassy Honor Guard and Confederate Cavalry. Conducts charitable programs. Operates speakers' bureau. **Libraries: Type:** reference. **Holdings:** 1,000; archival material, books, monographs, periodicals. **Awards: Type:** recognition. **Publications:** *Confederate Embassy News*, quarterly. **Price:** free for members. **Circulation:** 2,000. **Conventions/Meetings:** annual Confederate Embassy Ball - meeting ● annual Confederate Hunt - meeting ● periodic Literary Symposium - meeting.

9369 ■ Freedom Alliance
22570 Markey Ct., Ste.240
Dulles, VA 20166
Ph: (703)444-7940
Free: (800)475-6620
Fax: (703)444-9893
URL: http://www.freedomalliance.org
Contact: Thomas P. Kilgannon, Pres.

Founded: 1990. **Description:** Works to promote the American heritage of freedom embodied in the constitution, to defend the sovereignty of the United States, monitor the United Nations, and encourage and honor military service. **Awards:** Edward J. Bronars Defender of Freedom Award. **Frequency:** annual. **Type:** recognition. **Recipient:** to an outstanding individual who exemplifies faith, courage and fidelity in the face of adversity ● Freedom Alliance Scholarship Award. **Frequency:** annual. **Type:** scholarship. **Recipient:** to a dependent child of active duty service member who died or was permanently disabled in the line of duty. **Publications:** *Freedom Alliance Review*, annual. Newsletter. Alternate Formats: online ● *Freedom Alliance Scholarship Fund*, annual. Annual Report. Alternate Formats: online ● *Military Leadership Academy*, annual. Annual Report. Alternate Formats: online ● Newsletter, bimonthly. **Conventions/Meetings:** annual Army-Navy Weekend - dinner, with Defender of Freedom Award Dinner.

9370 ■ Friends of the American Museum in Britain/Halcyon Foundation (FAMB)
100 Park Ave., 20th Fl.
New York, NY 10017
Ph: (212)370-0198
Fax: (212)370-0028
E-mail: halcyonfdn@worldnet.att.net
URL: http://www.americanmuseum.org
Contact: Katherine G. Bursack, Admin.

Founded: 1957. **Members:** 800. **Membership Dues:** individual, $60 (annual) ● family, $100 (annual) ● associate, $250 (annual). **Staff:** 2. **Description:** Represents supporters of the American Museum, Claverton Manor, Bath, England. The museum provides a "living" picture of American domestic life, from the 17th to mid-19th century. Maintains 18 completely furnished rooms with original paneling brought from the U.S., along with complementary galleries and garden exhibits on the grounds of Claverton Manor. Conducts educational programs; operates children's services. **Libraries: Type:** reference. **Holdings:** 9,000. **Subjects:** Americana. **Telecommunication Services:** electronic mail, lynne.erskine@americanmuseum.org. **Publications:** *America in Britain*, semiannual. Magazine.

American Indian

9371 ■ National Indian Wars Association (NIWA)
1707 Bates Ct.
Thousand Oaks, CA 91362

E-mail: ghelms1@verizon.net
URL: http://www.indianwars.org
Contact: Maj. Gen. Gary L. Helms Sr., Contact
Membership Dues: regular, $20 (annual). **Description:** Represents individuals dedicated to preserving and bringing to light the Indian War period of the country's history. Seeks to educate the American public about the Indian War period. Works with other organizations in promoting nationwide interest in the preservation of historic military and Indian landmarks. **Publications:** *The NIWA Dispatch*, quarterly. Newsletter.

American Revolution

9372 ■ American Revolution Round Table (ARRT)
c/o Mr. David W. Jacobs, Chm.
6 Grovedale Rd.
Niantic, CT 06357
Ph: (718)762-2817
E-mail: djacobs01@snet.net
URL: http://www.arrt-ny.org
Contact: Mr. David W. Jacobs, Chm.
Founded: 1958. **Members:** 150. **Membership Dues:** regular, $25 (annual). **Staff:** 2. **Budget:** $3,000. **Local Groups:** 1. **Description:** Represents persons interested in the history of the American Revolution; majority of members are from business and professional fields. Discusses Revolutionary topics, view displays of manuscripts, weapons, and other historical objects, and hear brief addresses by authors and other experts on Revolutionary history. Encourages research and education on this period. Assists in the formation of new roundtables. **Awards:** Best Book of Year on American Revolution. **Frequency:** annual. **Type:** recognition. **Recipient:** for outstanding book on the Revolution. **Publications:** *Broadside*, 5/year. Newsletter. Alternate Formats: online. **Conventions/Meetings:** dinner (exhibits) - 5/year, every first Tuesday of December, February, April, June, October.

9373 ■ H.M. 10th Regiment of Foot, American Contingent
61 Ivan St.
Lexington, MA 02420-1422
Ph: (781)862-2586
E-mail: frommage@comcast.net
URL: http://www.redcoat.org
Contact: Lt. Col. Paul O'Shaughnessy, Commanding Off.
Founded: 1969. **Members:** 40. **Staff:** 8. **Description:** Promotes re-creation of the companies and music of the British 10th Regiment of Foot as it appeared in Boston in 1775. Uniforms are made from wool, linen, cotton, and silk, with no modern fabrics or zippers employed. Regimental members are not allowed to wear beards, moustaches, or long sideburns; modern wristwatches and modern eyeglasses are not permitted nor can any man smoke a cigarette, cigar, or modern pipe when in uniform. Members were officially assigned to serve as Honor Guard for the visit of Queen Elizabeth II during her visit to Boston in July 1976. **Libraries: Type:** reference. **Formed by Merger of:** H. M. 10th Foot in America; 10th Foot Royal Lincolnshire Regimental Association American Contingent Branch. **Publications:** *A Manual of Drills and Commonly Practiced Maneuvers*. Alternate Formats: online ● *A Military Guide* ● *The Springers*, monthly. Newsletter. **Price:** $25.00/year. **Circulation:** 100. Alternate Formats: online ● Informational papers. **Conventions/Meetings:** monthly 18th Century Military Exercise - meeting - always third Wednesday at National Guard Armory, Lexington, MA.

9374 ■ Northwest Territory Alliance (NWTA)
c/o Robin Klepfer, Adjutant Gen.
11405 E 63rd St.
Indianapolis, IN 46236-3925
Ph: (317)823-4556
E-mail: robin12863@excite.com
URL: http://www.nwta.com
Contact: Robin Klepfer, Adjutant Gen.
Founded: 1974. **Membership Dues:** family, $25 (annual) ● single, $20 (annual). **Staff:** 11. **Local Groups:** 47. **Description:** Works to accurately represent the causes and activities of the Revolutionary War. Reproduces the firearms, equipment, and clothing of the period. Fosters education through reenactments and other historical activities; encourages historical research. Supports the activities of local groups. Maintains speakers' bureau. **Libraries: Type:** reference. **Publications:** *Northwest Territory Alliance Courier*, 10/year. Newsletter. Includes organization news, research results, articles on reenactments, and book reviews. **Price:** $5.00 for nonmembers. **Circulation:** 700. **Advertising:** accepted. **Conventions/Meetings:** Regional Events - meeting - 8-15/year.

9375 ■ Valley Forge Historical Society (VFHS)
Address Unknown since 2007
Founded: 1918. **Members:** 700. **Membership Dues:** individual, $25 (annual) ● family, $50 (annual). **Staff:** 6. **Description:** A subsidiary of the National Center for the American Revolution. Individuals interested in preserving the history of Valley Forge. Seeks to perpetuate the patriotic spirit of service and sacrifice associated with Valley Forge through the preservation and exhibition of artifacts, documents, and manuscripts. (George Washington and the Revolutionary Army spent the winter of 1777-78 at this site where many of them suffered from sickness and cold. In 1778 Valley Forge became the first training camp of the U.S. armed forces.). **Libraries: Type:** reference. **Holdings:** 3,500; archival material, books. **Subjects:** Revolutionary history. **Committees:** Education; Museum. **Publications:** *VFHS Perspective*, triennial. Newsletter. **Price:** included in membership dues.

American South

9376 ■ Center for Southern Folklore (CSF)
PO Box 226
Memphis, TN 38101
Ph: (901)525-3655
Fax: (901)544-9965
E-mail: info@southernfolklore.org
URL: http://www.southernfolklore.com
Contact: Judy Peiser, Exec. Dir./Co-Founder
Founded: 1972. **Members:** 500. **Membership Dues:** regular, $35 (annual). **Staff:** 6. **Budget:** $450,000. **Description:** Researches, presents, and interprets indigenous and ethnic traditions of the Southern U.S. Serves educational institutions, libraries, museums, and television networks in the U.S., Canada, and Europe. Operates museum and speakers' bureau; provides children's and consultant services; conducts research and educational programs, festivals of crafts, music, and folk tales. **Libraries: Type:** reference. **Holdings:** 5,000; archival material, biographical archives, photographs. **Telecommunication Services:** electronic mail, queenbee@southernfolklore.com. **Divisions:** Archives and Research; Distribution; Education; Production and Performances. **Publications:** *Brochure of Center Purpose and Activities* ● *Center for Southern Folklore Catalog*. Alternate Formats: online ● *Press Packet*. **Conventions/Meetings:** annual Memphis Music and Heritage Festival, music, crafts, and food relevant to cultural groups that live in area (exhibits) - 3 days; Labor Day weekend.

9377 ■ Institute for Southern Studies (ISS)
PO Box 531
Durham, NC 27707
Ph: (919)419-8311
Fax: (919)419-8315
E-mail: info@southernstudies.org
URL: http://www.southernstudies.org
Contact: Chris Kromm, Exec. Dir.
Founded: 1970. **Members:** 5,000. **Membership Dues:** subscribing, $24 (annual). **Staff:** 4. **Description:** Professors, students, community activists, policymakers, social service agencies, and concerned Southerners. Conducts studies of regional, social and economic conditions, the role of economic institutions in policy formulation, and the interaction of regional and national influences. Fosters a dynamic identity for Southerners by revitalizing the region's rich historical traditions and cultural heritage in popular and formal educational materials. Sponsors annual Southern Journalism Contest. Conducts seminars; provides technical assistance for grassroots community leaders and internships. **Convention/Meeting:** none. **Libraries: Type:** reference. **Holdings:** 31. **Awards:** Southern Journalism Award. **Frequency:** annual. **Type:** monetary. **Computer Services:** Mailing lists. **Telecommunication Services:** electronic mail, chris@southernstudies.org. **Publications:** *Facing South*, biweekly. Newsletter. Covers news and trends in the South. Alternate Formats: online ● *Southern Exposure*, quarterly. Magazine. Covers the culture, politics, history, and current issues regarding the Southern United States. **Price:** included in membership dues; $5.00/copy for nonmembers. ISSN: 0146-809X. **Circulation:** 5,000. **Advertising:** accepted. Alternate Formats: online ● Reports. **Price:** $25.00. Alternate Formats: online.

9378 ■ Southern Historical Association (SHA)
Univ. of Georgia
Dept. of History, Rm. 111A
LeConte Hall
Athens, GA 30602-1602
Ph: (706)542-8848 (713)348-6039
Fax: (706)542-2455
E-mail: jinscoe@arches.uga.edu
URL: http://www.uga.edu/~sha
Contact: Dr. John C. Inscoe, Sec.-Treas.
Founded: 1934. **Members:** 5,000. **Membership Dues:** regular, $40 (annual) ● student, $10 (annual) ● sustaining, family, $50 (annual) ● life, $600 ● institutional, $60 (annual). **Description:** History teachers and students; libraries. Promotes interest and research in Southern history, collection and preservation of the South's historical records, and the encouragement of state and local historical societies in the South. Encourages the study of history in the South, with emphasis on the history of the South. **Libraries: Type:** reference. **Awards:** Charles S. Sydnor Award. **Frequency:** biennial. **Type:** monetary. **Recipient:** for publications on Southern history published in odd numbered years ● Fletcher M. Green and Charles W. Ramsdell Award. **Frequency:** biennial. **Type:** monetary. **Recipient:** for the best article published in the *Journal of Southern History* ● Francis B. Simkins Award. **Frequency:** biennial. **Type:** monetary. **Recipient:** for best first book by an author in the field of Southern history ● Frank L. and Harriet C. Owsley Award. **Frequency:** biennial. **Type:** monetary. **Recipient:** for publications on Southern history published in even numbered years ● H.L. Mitchell Award. **Frequency:** biennial. **Type:** monetary. **Recipient:** for a distinguished book concerning the history of the Southern working class. **Computer Services:** Mailing lists. **Publications:** *Journal of Southern History*, quarterly. Contains scholarly articles, edited documents, historical notes, book reviews, reports of annual meetings, and news of historical interest. **Price:** $20.00 for individuals; $50.00 for institutions; $10.00 for students. ISSN: 0022-4642. **Circulation:** 5,000. **Advertising:** accepted. Alternate Formats: online. Also Cited As: *JSTOR*. **Conventions/Meetings:** annual conference (exhibits) - 2008 Oct. 9-12, New Orleans, LA; 2009 Nov. 5-8, Louisville, KY; 2010 Nov. 4-7, Charlotte, NC.

American West

9379 ■ American Cowboy Culture Association (ACCA)
c/o National Cowboy Symposium and Celebration
PO Box 6638
Lubbock, TX 79493
Ph: (806)787-8871 (806)866-9825

E-mail: cowboysymposium@suddenlink.net
URL: http://www.cowboy.org
Contact: Cherry McCelvey, Contact
Founded: 1989. **Budget:** $100,000. **Description:** Promotes interest in, and appreciation of, elements of Cowboy culture including Western art, cooking, and crafts. Conducts educational programs; participates in charitable activities; sponsor competitions; makes available children's services; maintains museum. **Computer Services:** Mailing lists. **Conventions/Meetings:** annual National Cowboy Symposium & Celebration and Culture Awards Show - conference and symposium, with trade show (exhibits) - always first weekend after Labor Day.

9380 ■ National Association for Outlaw and Lawman History (NOLA)
c/o Paula Miller, Membership Sec.
1917 Sutton Place Trail
Harker Heights, TX 76548-6043
Ph: (254)698-6518 (254)698-2363
E-mail: millrpaula@aol.com
URL: http://www.outlawlawman.com
Contact: Paula Miller, Membership Sec.
Founded: 1974. **Members:** 500. **Membership Dues:** regular in U.S., $35 (annual) ● regular outside U.S., $45 (annual). **Staff:** 3. **Description:** Writers, researchers, memorabilia collectors, photographers, gun collectors, genealogists, historians, and history buffs united to collect, preserve, and share materials on outlaw-lawman history and to preserve historic sites and trails. Promotes historical and genealogical research; compiles statistics; sponsors dedications and memorials; conducts tours; operates speakers' bureau. **Awards:** Friends of NOLA plaques; Literary Award; Research Grants. **Frequency:** annual. **Type:** recognition. **Recipient:** for three to four recipients ● **Type:** grant. **Recipient:** for three to four recipients. **Committees:** Auction; Awards; Editorial; Products; Rendezvous Site Selection. **Publications:** *Index to the NOLA Quarterly, 1975-1998*. Includes a comprehensive index to research articles published in NOLA quarterly journal. **Price:** $20.00/copy, plus $3 postage. **Circulation:** 100 ● *National Association for Outlaw and Lawman History—Newsletter*, bimonthly. **Price:** included in membership dues. **Circulation:** 450. **Advertising:** accepted ● *National Association for Outlaw and Lawman History—Quarterly*. Journal. Features articles on outlaws and lawmen of the American Old West. Includes book reviews. **Price:** included in membership dues. **Advertising:** accepted ● Also publishes rendezvous program and four books. **Conventions/Meetings:** annual NOLA Rendezvous - conference and meeting, annual board meeting, presentation on outlaw-lawmen history, field trip.

9381 ■ National Cowboy and Western Heritage Museum
1700 NE 63rd St.
Oklahoma City, OK 73111
Ph: (405)478-2250
Fax: (405)478-4714
E-mail: info@nationalcowboymuseum.org
URL: http://www.nationalcowboymuseum.org
Contact: Charles P. Schroeder, Exec. Dir.
Founded: 1954. **Members:** 4,000. **Membership Dues:** premium family, $75 (annual) ● Golden Spike Society, $250 (annual) ● Pony Express Society, $500 (annual) ● Grand Canyon Society, $1,000 (annual) ● Prix de West Society, $2,500 (annual) ● American West Society, $5,000 (annual) ● Remington and Russell Society, $10,000 (annual). **Staff:** 90. **Budget:** $2,000,000. **Description:** Persons interested in preserving the heritage of the American West and in honoring the pioneers who developed the West. Maintains Hall of Fame of Great Westerners, Hall of Great Western Performers, Rodeo Hall of Fame, Western Art Exhibition Galleries, "Prosperity Junction", Western Town, American Rodeo Gallery, American Cowboy Gallery, Joe Grandee Museum of the Frontier West, Dickinson Research Center and the Children's Cowboy Corral. Conducts scheduled education programs and workshops for adults and children. **Libraries: Type:** reference. **Holdings:** 25,000; archival material, artwork, audiovisuals, books, clippings, periodicals. **Subjects:** Western history and art, cowboy culture, Western popular culture, rodeo history. **Awards:** Rodeo Hall of Fame. **Frequency:** annual. **Type:** recognition. **Recipient:** for outstanding contribution to rodeo ● Western Heritage Award. **Frequency:** annual. **Type:** recognition. **Recipient:** for valuable contributions to Western heritage. **Affiliated With:** Rodeo Historical Society. **Formerly:** (2000) National Cowboy Hall of Fame and Western Heritage Center. **Publications:** *Bettina Steinke: A Retrospective*. Catalog. Contains reproductions of oil, charcoal, and pastel works of Steinke. **Price:** $10.00 ● *National Academy of Western Art Catalogue 1982*. Includes Western arts greats such as: William Reese, Kent Ullberg, and Conrad Schwiering. **Price:** $5.00 ● *Persimmon Hill*, quarterly. Magazine. Contains historical and contemporary articles on the American West. **Price:** included in membership dues; $30.00 /year for nonmembers. ISSN: 0093-707X. **Circulation:** 12,000 ● *Prix de West*, annual. Catalogs. Features a biography on each artist as well as color reproductions of their art. ● *Rodeo Historical Society Ketchpen*, semiannual. Magazine. **Conventions/Meetings:** annual meeting (exhibits) - always third week of each October, in Oklahoma City, Oklahoma ● annual Prix de West Invitational Art Exhibition and Sale - meeting, includes demonstrations, and seminars (exhibits) - always 2nd weekend of June.

9382 ■ Rodeo Historical Society (RHS)
c/o National Cowboy and Western Heritage Museum
1700 NE 63rd St.
Oklahoma City, OK 73111
Ph: (405)478-2250
Fax: (405)478-2842
E-mail: info@nationalcowboymuseum.org
URL: http://www.nationalcowboymuseum.org
Contact: Judy Dearing, Admin. Asst./Dir.
Founded: 1968. **Members:** 400. **Membership Dues:** individual, $35 (annual) ● museum, $100 (annual). **Staff:** 2. **Description:** Veteran rodeo and "Wild West" show performers; rodeo associations; rodeo producers and managers. Collects and preserves rodeo historical information. Compiles statistics; operates museum and hall of fame. **Libraries: Type:** reference. **Holdings:** archival material. **Awards:** Rodeo Hall of Fame. **Frequency:** annual. **Type:** recognition. **Affiliated With:** National Cowboy and Western Heritage Museum. **Publications:** *Ketch Pen*, semiannual. Magazine. **Conventions/Meetings:** annual meeting - always in Oklahoma City, OK.

9383 ■ Superstition Mountain Historical Society (SMHS)
PO Box 3845
Apache Junction, AZ 85217-3845
Ph: (480)983-4888
E-mail: smhsgold@aol.com
URL: http://www.superstitionmountainmuseum.org
Contact: Kathy Johnson, Exec. Dir.
Founded: 1979. **Members:** 270. **Membership Dues:** prospector, $25 (annual) ● strike-it-rich, life, $500 ● Dutchman family, life, $1,000. **Staff:** 2. **Description:** Individuals, businesses, and families. Seeks to collect and preserve the history and legends of the Superstition Mountain wilderness region and adjacent geographical areas; publish books and papers about the region; develop educational programs for the public; support research involving the region. (Superstition Mountain Wilderness Area encompasses a 160,000-acre mountain range in Central Arizona, believed to contain the richest gold mine in the world.) Operates Superstition Mountain/Lost Dutchman Museum. Maintains Speaker's Bureau; compiles data and statistics. **Libraries: Type:** reference. **Holdings:** 1,250. **Subjects:** lost mines and treasures. **Awards: Type:** recognition. **Computer Services:** database, on the history and legends of lost mines and treasure tales of the American Southwest. **Committees:** Superstition Mountain Museum Guild. **Affiliated With:** Apache Junction Chamber of Commerce. **Publications:** *Lost Dutchman Museum*, annual. Journal. **Price:** $5.00. **Circulation:** 10,000 ● *Superstition Mountain*. Brochures. **Circulation:** 30,000 ● *Superstition Mountain Historical Society Newsletter*, quarterly ● *Superstition Mountain Journal*, annual. **Price:** $5. 00. **Circulation:** 500. **Conventions/Meetings:** annual general assembly and board meeting - usually 3rd Tuesday of February.

9384 ■ Western History Association (WHA)
Univ. of Missouri - St. Louis
152C Univ. Center
1 Univ. Blvd.
St. Louis, MO 63121
Ph: (314)516-7282
Fax: (314)516-7272
E-mail: wha@umsl.edu
URL: http://www.umsl.edu/~wha
Contact: Kevin Fernlund, Exec. Dir.
Founded: 1962. **Members:** 2,000. **Membership Dues:** student, $25 (annual) ● emeritus/retired, $40 (annual) ● individual, $60 (annual) ● joint, $80 (annual) ● sustaining, $125 (annual) ● sponsor institution, $150 (annual) ● patron, $250 (annual) ● donor, $500 (annual). **Staff:** 2. **Description:** Professional historians and others interested in the history of the trans-Mississippi West of the US (from the Mississippi River to the Pacific Coast) and neighboring Mexico, Canada, and Alaska. **Awards:** Arrell M. Gibson Award. **Frequency:** annual. **Type:** monetary. **Recipient:** for the best essay of the year published on the history of Native Americans ● Arrington-Prucha Award. **Frequency:** annual. **Type:** monetary. **Recipient:** for the best article on the history of religion in the West ● Award of Merit. **Frequency:** annual. **Type:** recognition. **Recipient:** for an outstanding service to the field of Western History and to the WHA ● Bert M. Fireman Prize. **Frequency:** annual. **Type:** monetary. **Recipient:** for the best essay in the "Western Historical Quarterly" ● Bolton-Kinnaird Award. **Frequency:** annual. **Type:** recognition. **Recipient:** for the best article published in the previous calendar year in any scholarly journal or edited volume on any phase of the history of Spanish Borderlands ● Caughey Western History Association Award. **Frequency:** annual. **Type:** monetary. **Recipient:** for the best book on the North American West published in the previous calendar year ● Dwight L. Smith Prize. **Frequency:** biennial. **Type:** monetary. **Recipient:** to the creator of a bibliographic or research work serving historians and other person engaged in research on Western History ● Graduate Student Conference Scholarship. **Frequency:** annual. **Type:** monetary. **Recipient:** to graduate student attendees at the WHA Conference ● Honorary Life Membership. **Frequency:** annual. **Type:** monetary. **Recipient:** for members ● Huntington-WHA Martin Ridge. **Frequency:** annual. **Type:** monetary. **Recipient:** for study in Western History ● Indian Student Conference Scholarship. **Frequency:** annual. **Type:** monetary. **Recipient:** to support Indian student attendees at the WHA Conference ● Joan Paterson Kerr Book Award. **Frequency:** biennial. **Type:** monetary. **Recipient:** to the author of the best illustrated book published by a university press on the American West ● John C. Ewers. **Frequency:** biennial. **Type:** monetary. **Recipient:** for the best book on North American Indian Ethnohistory ● Michael P. Malone. **Frequency:** annual. **Type:** monetary. **Recipient:** for best article, essay, or commentary on state, provincial or territorial history in North America appearing in a periodical publication ● Oscar O. Winther Award. **Frequency:** annual. **Type:** monetary. **Recipient:** for the author of the best article to appear in the Western Historical Quarterly ● Ray A. Billington Award. **Frequency:** annual. **Type:** monetary. **Recipient:** for the best article (not published in Western Historical Quarterly) on Western History ● Robert G. Athearn Award. **Frequency:** biennial. **Type:** monetary. **Recipient:** for a published book on the twentieth-century American West ● Robert M. Utley Award. **Frequency:** annual. **Type:** monetary. **Recipient:** for the best book published on the Military History of the West ● Sara Jackson Award. **Frequency:** annual. **Type:** monetary. **Recipient:** for graduate student research ● W. Turrentine Jackson Award. **Frequency:** biennial. **Type:** monetary. **Recipient:** for a beginning professional historian for a first book on any aspect of the American West ● Walter Rundell Graduate Student Award. **Frequency:** annual. **Type:** monetary. **Recipi-**

ent: for a doctoral candidate who has completed comprehensive PhD examinations and is in the process of researching the dissertation subject. **Publications:** *Program Pamphlet*, annual. Includes conference highlights and information on the sessions. ● *Western Historical Quarterly*. Journal. **Circulation:** 2,000. **Advertising:** accepted ● *WHA Newsletter*, periodic. Includes membership activities. ● Association publishes a magazine provided to the members via contract with the Montana Historical Society. **Conventions/Meetings:** annual conference (exhibits).

9385 ■ Westerners International (WI)
1700 NE 63rd St.
Oklahoma City, OK 73111
Free: (800)541-4650
E-mail: wihomeranch@aol.com
URL: http://www.westerners-international.org
Contact: Revere Young, Chm.
Founded: 1944. **Members:** 4,500. **Staff:** 1. **State Groups:** 107. **National Groups:** 30. **Multinational. Description:** Individuals interested in Western American history and folklore. Stimulates interest and publishing related to America's frontier West. **Libraries: Type:** reference. **Holdings:** 500. **Subjects:** history. **Awards:** Co-Founders Best Book Award. **Frequency:** annual. **Type:** recognition. **Recipient:** for members who have written a nonfiction book on western history, a biography or a book of social significance ● Coke Wood Award. **Frequency:** annual. **Type:** recognition. **Recipient:** for the best published monograph or article dealing with Western American History ● Phillip A. Danielson Award. **Frequency:** annual. **Type:** recognition. **Recipient:** for a member with best presentation or program delivered to a corral or posse ● Westerners International Scholarship Award. **Frequency:** annual. **Type:** scholarship. **Recipient:** for graduate student member of Phi Alpha Theta for the Best Doctoral Dissertation in Western History. **Formerly:** (1970) Westerners Foundation. **Publications:** *Buckskin Bulletin*, quarterly. Covers activities of groups and various western history articles. **Price:** included in membership dues; $5.00 /year for nonmembers. **Circulation:** 4,000. **Advertising:** accepted. **Conventions/Meetings:** annual meeting, held in conjunction with Western History Association.

Andean

9386 ■ Institute of Andean Research (IAR)
Address Unknown since 2007
Founded: 1937. **Members:** 25. **Staff:** 1. **Description:** Museum curators and university professors. Sponsors fieldwork on the archaeology, history, and cultural anthropology of the Andean region of South America. **Publications:** Publishes results. **Conventions/Meetings:** annual meeting - always New York City.

9387 ■ Institute of Andean Studies (IAS)
PO Box 9307
Berkeley, CA 94709
Ph: (510)222-6284
E-mail: mwf@berkeley.edu
URL: http://www.instituteofandeanstudies.net
Contact: Madeleine Fang, Sec.
Founded: 1960. **Members:** 290. **Membership Dues:** active, $40 (annual). **Description:** Persons interested in encouraging and supporting research and publication in Andean studies. **Publications:** *Nawpa Pacha* (in English, French, and Spanish), annual. Journal. Includes separate index covering Vols. 1-24, and new publications listing. **Price:** included in membership dues; $15.00 /year for nonmembers. ISSN: 0077-6297. **Circulation:** 500. **Conventions/Meetings:** annual conference - always in Berkeley, CA.

Animation

9388 ■ Animators Unite
525 85th St.
Brooklyn, NY 11209
E-mail: rkohr@animatorsunite.com
URL: http://www.animatorsunite.com
Contact: Robert Kohr, Pres.
Description: Cultivates interest in all forms of animation. Provides educational, informational and promotional services to individuals who are interested in pursuing a career in the animation industry. Provides an online forum for its members to interact and exchange information. **Publications:** Newsletter. Alternate Formats: online.

Antiquities

9389 ■ Saving Antiquities for Everyone (SAFE)
123 Town Square Pl., No. 151
Jersey City, NJ 07310
E-mail: cho@savingantiquities.org
URL: http://www.savingantiquities.org
Contact: Cindy Ho, Exec. Dir.
Founded: 2003. **Members:** 100. **Membership Dues:** student, $25 (annual) ● associate, $50 (annual) ● contributor, $100 (annual) ● patron, $250 (annual) ● benefactor, $500 (annual) ● donor, $700 (annual). **Description:** Raises the public awareness of the importance of preserving cultural heritage worldwide. Seeks to address the destructive effects of the illicit antiquities trade. **Computer Services:** Information services, cultural heritage resources ● online services, forum. **Projects:** Advertising; Advocacy; Conference Organization; Education; Fundraising; Media; Museums. **Publications:** *Save the Past for our Future*. Brochure. Alternate Formats: online.

Appalachian

9390 ■ Appalachian Consortium (AC)
c/o Dr. Patricia D. Beaver, Dir.
Center for Appalachian Stud.
Appalachian State Univ.
ASU Box 32018
Boone, NC 28608
Ph: (828)262-4089
Free: (888)557-8163
Fax: (828)262-4087
E-mail: beaverpd@appstate.edu
URL: http://people.uvawise.edu/appalcon/press.htm
Contact: Dr. Patricia D. Beaver, Dir.
Founded: 1973. **Members:** 195. **Staff:** 1. **Regional Groups:** 1. **Description:** Colleges, universities, government agencies, historical associations, other organizations, and citizens promoting a positive image of the Appalachian region and its people. Seeks to preserve Appalachian heritage, solve current problems, and improve the present and future life in Appalachia by encouraging regional cooperation. Holds symposia, teacher institutes, and workshops; conducts research. Maintains traveling exhibits; sponsors student competitions. **Libraries: Type:** reference. **Holdings:** biographical archives. **Awards:** Laurel Leaves Award. **Frequency:** annual. **Type:** recognition. **Committees:** Administration; Editorial; Folklife; Museum Cooperative; Regional Collections; Regional Cooperation and Development; Regional Education; Regional Health Services. **Programs:** Traveling Exhibits. **Publications:** *Appalachian Consortium Publication Brochure*, annual. Lists books published by Appalachian Consortium. ● *Consortium News*, annual. Newsletter ● *The Curator*, annual. Newsletter ● Books ● Also publishes manuscripts.

9391 ■ Appalachian Studies Association (ASA)
ASA Off.
Marshall Univ.
111 Jenkins Hall
One John Marshall Dr.
Huntington, WV 25755
Ph: (304)696-2904
Fax: (304)696-6221
E-mail: asa@marshall.edu
URL: http://www.appalachianstudies.org
Contact: Ms. Mary K. Thomas, Exec. Dir.
Founded: 1977. **Members:** 750. **Membership Dues:** regular, $50 (annual) ● student, $30 (annual) ● institution/library, $45 (annual). **Staff:** 1. **Description:** Scholars, teachers, activists, artists, writers, and interested individuals. Works to advance the field of Appalachian Studies and promotes scholarship on Appalachia. Provides a network and forum for those interested in the history, development, and culture of the Appalachian region. Holds annual conference and publishes the Journal of Appalachian Studies. **Awards:** Carl A. Ross Student Paper Award. **Frequency:** annual. **Type:** monetary. **Recipient:** to an undergraduate or graduate student ● Cratis D. Williams/James S. Brown Service Award. **Frequency:** annual. **Type:** recognition. **Recipient:** to individuals who made exemplary contributions to Appalachia and/or the association ● Helen M. Lewis Community Service Award. **Frequency:** annual. **Type:** recognition. **Recipient:** for exemplary contribution to Appalachia, through involvement with and service to people and communities ● Jack Spadaro e-Appalachia Award. **Frequency:** annual. **Type:** monetary. **Recipient:** for an outstanding website that provides insight on the Appalachian region, or provides a vital community service to Appalachians ● Jack Spadaro Media Arts Award. **Frequency:** annual. **Type:** monetary. **Recipient:** for the best documentary on Appalachia or its people that recognizes the producer for outstanding work in film, video, television, or radio ● University Press of Kentucky Appalachian Studies Award. **Frequency:** annual. **Type:** recognition. **Recipient:** for the best book manuscript ● Weatherford Award. **Frequency:** annual. **Type:** recognition. **Recipient:** for the author or work of fact, fiction or poetry in the U.S. that best describes and analyzes the challenges, personalities and qualities of the Appalachian South, book length or shorter. **Computer Services:** database ● mailing lists. **Committees:** Steering. **Publications:** *Appalink*, semiannual. Newsletter. **Price:** included in membership dues. **Circulation:** 750. **Advertising:** accepted. Alternate Formats: online ● *Journal of Appalachian Studies*, semiannual. Includes book reviews, annual bibliography. Available to institutions and libraries by subscription. **Price:** included in membership dues; $45.00 /year for institutions and libraries; $50.00 /year for individuals; $30.00/year, student. ISSN: 1082-7161. **Circulation:** 750. **Advertising:** accepted. **Conventions/Meetings:** annual conference, with book sales and author signings (exhibits) ● annual meeting.

Arabic

9392 ■ American Federation of Ramallah, Palestine (AFRP)
27484 Ann Arbor Trail
Westland, MI 48185
Ph: (734)425-1600
Fax: (734)425-3985
E-mail: info@afrp.org
URL: http://www.afrp.org
Contact: Jamal Jubran, Pres.
Founded: 1959. **Description:** Works to perpetuate and enhance ties among all Ramallah people, and to orient the American public with Arab culture and heritage in order to promote understanding.

9393 ■ Arab World and Islamic Resources and School Services (AWAIR)
PO Box 174
Abiquiu, NM 87510
Ph: (505)685-4533 (510)704-0517
Fax: (505)685-4533
E-mail: awair@igc.org
URL: http://www.awaironline.org
Contact: Audrey Shabbas, Exec. Dir.
Founded: 1991. **Staff:** 3. **Budget:** $95,000. **Languages:** Arabic, English. **Description:** Strives to increase awareness and understanding of the Arab World and Islam through educational outreach at the

pre-collegiate level. Seeks to impact how these subjects are taught in schools. Develops curricula on the Arab World and Islam. Conducts teacher training and a summer institute for teachers. **Libraries: Type:** reference. **Holdings:** 1,000; audiovisuals, books, clippings, periodicals, video recordings. **Subjects:** Arab world, Islam, Muslim world, women. **Awards:** Arab and Islamic History Special Award. **Frequency:** annual. **Type:** monetary. **Recipient:** for the winner of the national grade 6 to 12 competition. **Computer Services:** Mailing lists. **Telecommunication Services:** electronic mail, requests@awaironline.org. **Publications:** *A Medieval Banquet in the Alhambra Palace*. Book. **Price:** $29.95 ● *Arab World Notebook For the Secondary School Level*. **Price:** $39.95 ● *The Arabs: Activities for the Elementary School Level*. Book. **Price:** $16.00 ● *AWAIR Catalogue*, annual. Includes educational materials. **Price:** free. **Circulation:** 25,000 ● *Doorways to Islamic Art*. Contains a curriculum kit of 34 slides and a book. **Price:** $49.95. **Advertising:** accepted. **Conventions/Meetings:** weekly Content and Strategies for Teaching About the Arab World and Islam - workshop, for teachers.

9394 ■ Birzeit Society (BZS)
PO Box 1822
Norwalk, CA 90651
Ph: (714)996-3389 (714)991-1943
Fax: (714)996-4507
E-mail: info@birzeitsociety.org
URL: http://www.birzeitsociety.org
Contact: Ramsey Nasir, Natl. Pres.
Founded: 1987. **Regional Groups:** 7. **Multinational. Description:** Works to perpetuate strong ties among members to link communities around the world together with ancestral roots in Palestine. **Awards:** Birzeit Society's Scholarship. **Frequency:** annual. **Type:** scholarship. **Recipient:** for high school and college level Birzeit students. **Committees:** Finance; Medical Fund; Publication; Scholarships. **Publications:** *Birzeit*, quarterly. Newsletter. Features society news, member affairs, cultural coverage, social issues, and general information. **Price:** free for members. **Circulation:** 1,500. **Advertising:** accepted ● Membership Directory, semiannual. Lists members' addresses and phone numbers. **Price:** $5.00 for members. **Advertising:** accepted. **Conventions/Meetings:** semiannual board meeting - January, August ● biennial convention.

9395 ■ Chaldean Federation of America (CFA)
30777 Northwestern Hwy., Ste.300
Farmington Hills, MI 48334
Ph: (248)851-3023
Fax: (248)851-9551
E-mail: info@chaldeanfederation.org
URL: http://www.chaldeanfederation.org
Contact: Joseph T. Kassab, Exec. Dir.
Founded: 1980. **Membership Dues:** student, $10 (monthly) ● individual, $25 (monthly) ● family, $50 ● small business, $100 (annual) ● corporation, $500 (annual). **Staff:** 1. **Description:** Promotes services to the Chaldean community, including language classes. **Telecommunication Services:** electronic mail, jkassab@chaldeanfederation.org.

9396 ■ Council of Lebanese American Organizations (CLAO)
PO Box 661823
Los Angeles, CA 90066
Ph: (919)427-8869
Free: (888)4CL-AO89
E-mail: clao@nc.rr.com
URL: http://www.clao.us/index.html
Contact: Elie Najm, Chm.
Founded: 1989. **Members:** 4,500. **Membership Dues:** individual, $50 (annual) ● organization, $300 (annual). **Staff:** 6. **Regional Groups:** 20. **Languages:** Arabic, English. **Description:** Local, regional, and national groups representing Americans of Lebanese descent. Works for freedom and sovereignty for Lebanon, beginning with the "complete and unconditional withdrawal of all foreign occupation forces from Lebanese territory." Promotes friendship and cooperation between the United States and Lebanon based on the principles of democracy and human rights. Monitors and lobbies Congress. Conducts research, educational, and charitable programs; maintains speakers' bureau; compiles statistics. **Libraries: Type:** reference. **Holdings:** 10,000; archival material, books, clippings, monographs, periodicals. **Subjects:** Lebanon, Lebanese-Americans, Middle East. **Awards:** Cadmus Award. **Frequency:** annual. **Type:** recognition. **Recipient:** for contributions to Lebanon and the Lebanese-American community. **Computer Services:** database, news and analysis. **Committees:** Policy; Political Action. **Publications:** *Adonis*, monthly. Report. Presents a collection of relevant press clippings and international reports on Lebanon. **Price:** $24.00/year. **Circulation:** 25,000. **Advertising:** accepted ● *Lebanon File*, monthly. Newsletter. Includes commentary and researched subjects on Lebanon; primarily intended for Congress, policy makers, politicians, and the media. **Price:** $24.00/year. ISSN: 1059-6097. **Circulation:** 10,000. **Advertising:** accepted ● *Perspective*, periodic. Newsletter. Includes activity reports of member organizations and schedules of upcoming events. **Conventions/Meetings:** annual convention ● quarterly meeting.

9397 ■ Institute for Palestine Studies (IPS)
3501 M St. NW
Washington, DC 20007
Ph: (202)342-3990
Fax: (202)342-3927
E-mail: ipsdc@palestine-studies.org
URL: http://palestine-studies.org
Contact: Ms. Linda Butler, Co-Dir.
Founded: 1963. **Staff:** 8. **Languages:** Arabic, English, French. **Multinational. Description:** Independent private research organization focusing on the Arab-Israeli conflict and Palestinian affairs. Conducts research and documentation programs. Washington, DC office serves as the publication and distribution center for the Institute's English language publications, and the distribution center for its Arabic and French publications in North America. **Computer Services:** Mailing lists, of members. **Committees:** Editorial; Library; Research. **Sections:** Friends of IPS. **Publications:** *Before Their Diaspora: Photographic History of the Palestinians 1876-1948*. Book. **Price:** $35.00 ● *Expulsion of the Palestinians: The Concept of Transfer in Zionist Politics of Thought, 1882-1948*, periodic. Book. **Price:** $11.95 ● *Hamas: Political Thought and Practice*. Book. **Price:** $16.95 ● *Islam and Israel: Muslim Religious Endowments and the Jewish State*. Monographs. **Price:** $12.00 ● *Journal of Palestine Studies: A Quarterly on Palestinian Affairs and the Arab-Israeli Conflict*. Includes bibliographies, book reviews, documents and source materials listings, Occupied Territories' reports and Palestine Chronology. **Price:** $40.00 /year for individuals; $115.00 /year for institutions; $23.00/year for students. ISSN: 0377-919X. **Circulation:** 4,000. **Advertising:** accepted. Alternate Formats: microform ● *Majallat al-Dirasat al-Filastiniyah* (in Arabic), quarterly. Journal. **Advertising:** accepted ● *Revue d'Etudes Palestiniennes* (in French), quarterly. Journal. **Advertising:** accepted ● *U.S. Official Statements Regarding United Nations Resolution 242* ● Books ● Monographs ● Reprints.

Architecture

9398 ■ Walter Burley Griffin Society of America
1152 Center Dr.
St. Louis, MO 63117
Ph: (314)644-4546
E-mail: info@walterburleygriffin.org
URL: http://www.wbgriffinsociety.org
Contact: Peter Burley Griffin, Pres.
Membership Dues: general, $25 (annual). **Description:** Preserves the legacy of architects Walter Burley Griffin and Marion Mahony Griffin. Fosters professionalism and accountability among architects. Promotes design excellence. **Telecommunication Services:** electronic mail, wbgsociety@charter.net. **Publications:** Newsletter, periodic. Contains Society's activities such as lectures, tours, exhibitions and other events related to the Griffins' work. **Price:** included in membership dues.

Archives

9399 ■ Association of Catholic Diocesan Archivists (ACDA)
Address Unknown since 2007
Founded: 1981. **Members:** 250. **Membership Dues:** $25 (annual). **Budget:** $25,000. **Description:** Archivists responsible for the maintenance of diocesan records, archives, and historical materials. Promotes and fosters professional care of diocesan records through meetings and archival theory workshops. Works to establish archival programs in local dioceses; acts as a channel for personal discussions and exchanges among archivists; represents the profession before Catholic associations and laity. Develops guidelines designed to standardize archival procedures and practices. **Awards:** James O'Toole Scholarship. **Frequency:** annual. **Type:** scholarship. **Recipient:** for ACDA member. **Committees:** Finance; Scholarship. **Affiliated With:** United States Conference of Catholic Bishops. **Publications:** *ACDA Bulletin*, 3/year. **Advertising:** accepted ● *Basic Standards for Diocesan Archives: A Guide for Bishops, Chancellors, and Archivists* ● *Guidelines for Access to Diocesan Archives* ● *Preparing for the 90's: Strategies for Diocesan Archivists and Records Managers* ● *Two Hundred Years of Catholic Record Keeping in America: Current Issues and Responsibilities*. **Conventions/Meetings:** annual meeting, held in conjunction with the Society of American Archivists every other year (exhibits).

9400 ■ Black Archives of Mid-America
2033 Vine St.
Kansas City, MO 64108
Ph: (816)483-1300
Fax: (816)483-1341
URL: http://www.blackarchives.org
Contact: Thabit Murarah, Exec. Dir.
Founded: 1974. **Members:** 200. **Membership Dues:** regular, $25 (annual). **Staff:** 4. **Budget:** $148,000. **Description:** Works for the acquisition, preservation, study, display and interpretation of regional African-American history and culture. Maintains a collection of artifacts consisting of photographs, maps, posters, postcards, sound recordings, books, and original artwork. Holds permanent exhibits open to the public. **Convention/Meeting:** none. **Libraries: Type:** reference. **Holdings:** archival material, audio recordings, books, clippings, periodicals, video recordings. **Subjects:** African-American experience. **Awards:** Community Service. **Frequency:** annual. **Type:** recognition ● Personal or Academic Achievement. **Frequency:** annual. **Type:** recognition. **Publications:** *Archival Gridt*, annual. Newsletter. **Price:** free. **Circulation:** 5,000. **Advertising:** accepted.

9401 ■ Midwest Archives Conference (MAC)
c/o Gregory Brooks, Admin./Membership Coor.
4300 S U.S. Hwy. 1, No. 203-293
Jupiter, FL 33477
E-mail: membership@midwestarchives.org
URL: http://www.midwestarchives.org
Contact: Gregory Brooks, Admin./Membership Coor.
Founded: 1972. **Members:** 1,000. **Membership Dues:** individual, $30 (annual) ● institution in U.S., $60 (annual) ● institution in Canada or Mexico, $70 (annual) ● institution outside U.S., Canada or Mexico, $80 (annual). **Budget:** $50,000. **Regional Groups:** 1. **Description:** Represents archivists, genealogists, historians, librarians, local historical society and museum personnel, manuscript curators, oral historians, records managers, and related professionals (membership is international). Promotes cooperation and exchange of information among individuals and institutions interested in the preservation and use of archives and manuscript materials. Disseminates information on research materials and the methodology and theory in current archival practice. Provides

a forum for discussion among members. Awards emeritus status to retired members who have made significant contributions to the profession or the organization. **Libraries: Type:** reference. **Holdings:** archival material. **Awards:** Archie Motley Minority Scholarship Award. **Frequency:** annual. **Type:** scholarship. **Recipient:** to a minority student studying archival methods ● Louisa Bowen Memorial Scholarship Award. **Frequency:** annual. **Type:** scholarship. **Recipient:** to students of archival studies. **Committees:** Education; Local Arrangements; Nominating; Program. **Publications:** *Archival Issues*, semiannual. Journal. Contains issues and problems confronting the contemporary archivist. **Price:** included in membership dues; $16.00/issue for nonmembers. ISSN: 0363-888X. **Circulation:** 1,100. **Advertising:** accepted. Also Cited As: *Midwestern Archivist* ● *MAC Newsletter*, quarterly. Includes employment opportunities, conference reports, financial statements, meeting minutes, news of members, and listing of publications available. **Price:** included in membership dues; $6.00 for nonmembers. ISSN: 0741-0379. **Circulation:** 1,100. Also Cited As: *Midwest Archives Conference Newsletter*. **Conventions/Meetings:** semiannual conference and workshop, for archival vendors (exhibits) - always May and fall, in various locations ● seminar.

9402 ■ National Archives and Records Administration Volunteer Association (NAVA)
8601 Adelphi Rd.
College Park, MD 20740-6001
Ph: (301)837-0482
Free: (866)272-6272
Fax: (301)837-0483
URL: http://www.archives.gov
Contact: Robert Lewis, Pres.

Founded: 1976. **Members:** 328. **Membership Dues:** regular, $3 (annual). **Staff:** 3. **Languages:** English, French, German, Italian, Russian. **Description:** Volunteers at the National Archives (U.S. government housing of public records and historical documents including papers, machine-readable records, motion pictures, sound recordings, still pictures, and maps). Seeks to provide information, administrative service, and public awareness of the National Archives through volunteer participation in: tours of specified areas and its exhibits for the public, school groups, and congressional constituencies; outreach programs for senior citizens, nursing homes, community groups, and classrooms, assistance in genealogical research; assisting the staff working on archival projects. **Libraries: Type:** not open to the public. **Holdings:** 1,850. **Subjects:** history, government, biography, genealogy, foreign affairs. **Awards:** Achievement Award. **Frequency:** annual. **Type:** recognition. **Committees:** Civil War Conservation Corps; Genealogical Aids; Hospitality; Information Aides; Publicity; Resources and Reference; Staff Aides. **Formerly:** (1983) Docent Association; (1984) National Archives and Record Service Volunteer Association. **Publications:** *The Columns*, monthly. Newsletter. **Price:** available to members only. **Conventions/Meetings:** monthly general assembly - always second Wednesday in Washington, DC ● periodic seminar.

9403 ■ Society of American Archivists (SAA)
527 S Wells St., 5th Fl.
Chicago, IL 60607
Ph: (312)922-0140
Fax: (312)347-1452
E-mail: info@archivists.org
URL: http://www.archivists.org
Contact: Nancy Perkin Beaumont, Exec. Dir.

Founded: 1936. **Members:** 3,400. **Membership Dues:** retired, $65 (annual) ● full, $70-$180 (annual) ● associate in U.S., $70 (annual) ● associate outside U.S., $80 (annual) ● student, bridge, $40 (annual) ● regular (institutional), $225 (annual) ● sustaining (institutional), $440 (annual). **Staff:** 12. **Budget:** $1,200,000. **Description:** Individuals and institutions concerned with the identification, preservation, and use of records of historical value. **Awards:** SAA Awards Competition. **Frequency:** annual. **Type:** recognition. **Recipient:** for achievements in writing, public service, and advocacy. **Computer Services:** Mailing lists, of members. **Telecommunication Services:** electronic mail, nbeaumont@archivists.org. **Committees:** Awards; Education and Professional Development; Ethics and Professional Conduct; Goals and Priorities; Institutional Evaluation and Development; International Archival Affairs; Public Information; Regional Archives Activity; Status of Women in the Archival Profession. **Roundtables:** Architectural Records; Archival Educators; Archival History; Archives Management; International Affairs; Local Government Records. **Sections:** Acquisition; Business Archives; College and University Archives; Description; Electronic Records; Government Records; Manuscript Repositories; Museum Archives; Oral History; Preservation; Reference, Access and Outreach; Religious Archives; Visual Materials. **Supersedes:** Public Archives Commission of the American Historical Association. **Publications:** *The American Archivist*, semiannual. Journal. Includes information on new systems and emerging technologies and book reviews. **Price:** included in membership dues; $85.00 /year for nonmembers; $100.00 /year for nonmembers outside North America. ISSN: 0360-9081. **Circulation:** 4,600. **Advertising:** accepted. Alternate Formats: microform ● *Archival Outlook*, bimonthly. Newsletter. Reports regional, national, and international news of relevance to the American archival profession. Includes Association news. **Price:** included in membership dues. ISSN: 1520-3379. **Advertising:** accepted. Alternate Formats: online ● *SAA Employment Bulletin*, bimonthly. Lists of professional opportunities. ● *SAA Publications Catalog*. Includes more than 150 titles. ● *Society of American Archivists—Directory of Individual and Institutional Members*, biennial. Includes institutional affiliation. **Price:** included in membership dues; $50.00/copy for nonmembers. **Circulation:** 5,000. **Advertising:** accepted. **Conventions/Meetings:** annual conference (exhibits) - always September ● annual meeting - 2008 Aug. 23-31, San Francisco, CA; 2009 Aug. 1-9, Austin, TX ● seminar ● workshop.

Armenian

9404 ■ Armenian Assembly of America (AAA)
1140 19th St. NW, Ste.600
Washington, DC 20036
Ph: (202)393-3434
Fax: (202)638-4904
E-mail: info@aaainc.org
URL: http://www.aaainc.org
Contact: Bryan Ardouny, Exec. Dir.

Founded: 1972. **Members:** 1,800. **Membership Dues:** affiliate, $100-$249 (annual) ● contributing, $500-$999 (annual) ● fellow trustee, $1,000-$4,999 (annual) ● associate trustee, $5,000-$19,999 (annual) ● trustee, $20,000 (annual) ● life trustee, $200,000 ● supporting, $250-$499 (annual). **Staff:** 16. **Budget:** $4,000,000. **National Groups:** 3. **Languages:** Armenian, English. **Description:** Works to serve as a forum for the promotion of communication, cooperation, and coordination of activities within the Armenian-American community; to foster an awareness and appreciation of the Armenian cultural heritage and to promote the preservation of significant Armenian cultural materials and monuments; to advance research and data collection and to disseminate accurate information regarding the Armenian people; to provide the means by which the Armenian community can speak effectively on issues of importance and concern; to gather and disseminate information to the Armenian-American community; to promote greater Armenian-American participation in the American democratic process; to assist persons of Armenian ancestry subject to infringement or violation of basic human and civil rights; to engage in charitable, humanitarian, and educational efforts to alleviate human suffering of Armenians. **Libraries: Type:** not open to the public. **Holdings:** archival material, books. **Departments:** Development; Government Relations; Grassroots; Intern Program; Public Affairs; Research and Analysis. **Projects:** Armenia Tree. **Publications:** *The Advocate*, bimonthly. Newsletter. Contains information on congressional actions regarding Armenia and Nagorno Karabakh. Alternate Formats: online ● *Armenia this Week/Assembly this Week*, weekly. Newsletter. Alternate Formats: online ● *Assembly Annual Report*, annual. Alternate Formats: online ● *Financial Aid Directory for Students of Armenian Descent*, annual. Lists scholarships, loans, and grants available to students of Armenian descent. **Price:** free. Alternate Formats: online. **Conventions/Meetings:** annual meeting - usually in March.

9405 ■ Armenian Film Foundation (AFF)
2219 Thousand Oaks Blvd., Ste.292
Thousand Oaks, CA 91362
Ph: (805)495-0717
Fax: (805)379-0667
E-mail: info@armenianfilm.org
URL: http://www.armenianfilm.org
Contact: J. Michael Hagopian PhD, Chm.

Founded: 1979. **Members:** 13. **Staff:** 3. **Budget:** $25,000. **Description:** Board members comprised of community leaders, attorneys, film producers, editors, writers, and other interested professionals. Produces and distributes films on subjects related to Armenians and the Middle East. **Libraries: Type:** reference. **Holdings:** 14; articles, films, video recordings. **Subjects:** Armenia, Armenians, the Middle East. **Computer Services:** Mailing lists, of members. **Telecommunication Services:** electronic mail, affoundation@verizon.net.

9406 ■ National Association for Armenian Studies and Research (NAASR)
395 Concord Ave.
Belmont, MA 02478
Ph: (617)489-1610
Fax: (617)484-1759
E-mail: hq@naasr.org
URL: http://www.naasr.org
Contact: Nancy R. Kolligian, Chair

Founded: 1955. **Members:** 1,200. **Membership Dues:** regular, $50 (annual) ● family, $75 (annual) ● senior citizen, $40 (annual) ● student, $35 (annual) ● supporting, $125 (annual) ● sustaining, $250 (annual) ● sponsor, $500 (annual) ● patron, $1,000 (annual). **Staff:** 3. **Budget:** $200,000. **Regional Groups:** 5. **State Groups:** 15. **Languages:** Armenian, English. **Description:** Supports Armenian studies, research, and publication. Fosters the study of Armenian history, culture, and language on an active, scholarly, and continuous basis in American institutions of higher education. Has established centers of learning, research, and training at Harvard University and the University of California at Los Angeles by endowing permanent Chairs of Armenian Studies. Has a permanent endowment fund for Armenian Studies and other funds to support research grants, fellowships, publications, libraries, conferences, and other programs. Operates Armenian Information, Education, and Documentation Center. Operates Armenian Book Clearing House and Distribution Center dealing primarily in English-language books; over 2,000 titles are available on Armenian and related subjects; makes discounts available to members, schools, libraries, and retailers. Has established Armenian Heritage Press for the publication of popular and scholarly works as well as translations and reprints. Sponsors conferences, seminars, lecture series, courses, book fairs, exhibits, and heritage tours. **Libraries: Type:** reference. **Holdings:** 20,000; archival material, audiovisuals, books, clippings, monographs, periodicals. **Subjects:** Armenian history and related subjects such as art, language, literature, memoirs, reference works. **Awards:** Distinguished Service Award. **Frequency:** periodic. **Type:** recognition. **Recipient:** for extraordinary service in furthering Armenian studies ● 25-Year Award. **Frequency:** annual. **Type:** recognition. **Recipient:** for service in furthering Armenian studies continuously for 25 years. **Committees:** Regional. **Publications:** *Books on Armenia and the Armenians*, annual. Catalog. Lists available books, periodicals, videos, audiotapes, maps, posters, cards through its Armenian book clearing house. **Price:** $3.00 domestic; $4.00 foreign. **Circulation:** 300. **Advertising:** accepted. Alternate

Formats: online ● *Journal of Armenian Studies*, semiannual. Contains scholarly and popular articles on Armenian history, culture, and other related subjects. **Price:** $25.00/year in U.S.; $30.00/year outside U.S. ISSN: 0883-9948. **Circulation:** 1,200. **Advertising:** accepted ● *NAASR Book News*, 3-4/year. Newsletter. **Price:** free. **Circulation:** 1,200. **Advertising:** accepted ● *NAASR Newsletter*, 2-4/year. Includes activity updates, information on programs and developments in Armenian studies, and news of recent publications on Armenian subjects. **Price:** $7.50/year in U.S.; $10.00/year outside U.S. ISSN: 0890-3794. **Circulation:** 1,400. **Advertising:** accepted. **Conventions/Meetings:** annual assembly - usually November at Center and National Headquarters ● biennial conference - always spring or fall in Greater Boston, MA.

9407 ■ Society for Armenian Studies (SAS)
c/o Armenian Studies Program
California State Univ.
5245 N Backer Ave., PB4
Fresno, CA 93740-8001
Ph: (559)278-2669
Fax: (559)278-2129
E-mail: barlowd@csufresno.edu
URL: http://armenianstudies.csufresno.edu/sas/index.htm
Contact: Richard Hovannisian, Pres.

Founded: 1974. **Members:** 221. **Membership Dues:** student, $15 (annual) ● retired, $25 (annual) ● supporting, regular, donor, $40 (annual) ● patron, $100 (annual). **Staff:** 1. **Languages:** Armenian, English. **Description:** Scholars in all disciplines who are directly concerned with Armenology and individuals engaged in research or study in the Armenian field. Promotes the study of Armenia and related geographic areas, as well as issues related to the history and culture of Armenia. Serves as a forum whereby active scholars can exchange information about Armenian studies. **Libraries: Type:** reference. **Holdings:** 5,700; archival material, books. **Subjects:** Armenia, Russia, USSR, Turkey, Middle East, Eastern Europe. **Awards:** Best Graduate Student Article for SAS. **Frequency:** annual. **Type:** monetary ● Best Graduate Student Conference Paper. **Frequency:** annual. **Type:** monetary ● SAS Distinguished Dissertation Award. **Frequency:** biennial. **Type:** recognition. **Recipient:** for outstanding dissertation on a topic related to Armenian studies. **Computer Services:** Mailing lists, of members. **Committees:** Development; Panels. **Affiliated With:** American Historical Association; Middle East Studies Association of North America. **Publications:** *Journal of the Society for Armenian Studies*, annual. **Price:** $20.00 for nonmembers; $10.00 for members. ISSN: 0747-9301. **Advertising:** accepted ● *Roster of the Society for Armenian Studies*, annual. Membership Directory. **Price:** $5.00 ● *SAS Newsletter*, 3/year. **Price:** $5.00 ● Membership Directory, annual. **Price:** $5.00 ● Also publishes occasional papers and a translation series. **Conventions/Meetings:** annual conference, held in conjunction with Middle East Studies Association of North America - always late November or early December ● lecture ● symposium.

Art

9408 ■ 18th Street Arts Complex
1639 18th St.
Santa Monica, CA 90404
Ph: (310)453-3711
Fax: (310)453-4347
E-mail: office@18thstreet.org
URL: http://www.18thstreet.org
Contact: Jan Williamson, Co-Exec. Dir.

Founded: 1978. **Members:** 500. **Membership Dues:** critic, $35 (annual) ● art historian, $75 (annual) ● curator, $150 (annual) ● patron, $300 (annual) ● cultural ambassador, $500 (annual) ● muse, $1,000 (annual). **Staff:** 3. **Budget:** $300,000. **Description:** Provides services to artists and art organizations engaged with contemporary issues of community and diversity. **Libraries: Type:** not open to the public. **Holdings:** books, periodicals. **Subjects:** arts. **Also Known As:** (2005) 18th Street Arts Center. **Formerly:** (1992) Astro Artz. **Publications:** *Traffic Report*, annual. Magazine. **Circulation:** 35,000.

9409 ■ African American Visual Arts Association (AAVA)
3403 Milford Mill Rd.
Baltimore, MD 21244
Ph: (410)521-0660
Fax: (410)521-4053
E-mail: gboone8715@aol.com
URL: http://aavaa.org

Membership Dues: student, $35 (annual) ● family (maximum of 4 members), $55 (annual). **Description:** Promotes public awareness of African-American arts and artists. Preserves African-American history and diaspora through the use of visual arts.

9410 ■ American Academy of Equine Art (AAEA)
c/o Kentucky Horse Park
4089 Iron Works Pkwy.
Lexington, KY 40511
Ph: (859)281-6031
Fax: (859)281-6043
E-mail: shelleyh@aaea.net
URL: http://www.aaea.net
Contact: Shelley Hunter, Dir.

Founded: 1980. **Members:** 80. **Membership Dues:** full in U.S., $350 (annual) ● associate in U.S., $175 (annual) ● associate outside U.S., supporting, $50 (annual) ● full outside U.S., donor, $100 (annual) ● friend, $25 (annual) ● corporate, $500 (annual) ● life, $3,000. **Staff:** 1. **Budget:** $100,000. **Description:** Professional and qualified amateur artists. Establishes standards of excellence and promotes public recognition of equine painting and sculpture. Organizes and presents exhibitions that are coordinated with major equine activities. Certified artists conduct seminars, lectures, demonstrations on equine painting and sculpture. Sponsors competitions. Is interested in art from painting and sculpture on subjects such as horse breeding, training, racing, steeple chasing, fox hunting, polo, and related sports. **Libraries: Type:** reference. **Holdings:** 1,000; books. **Subjects:** horse art. **Awards: Type:** recognition. **Publications:** *AAEA Newsletter*, semiannual. **Circulation:** 3,000. Alternate Formats: online. **Conventions/Meetings:** semiannual meeting (exhibits) - always September and April in Lexington, KY.

9411 ■ American Art Pottery Association (AAPA)
c/o Marie Latta
907 Maurer
Wilton, IA 52778
E-mail: zona@netwtc.net
URL: http://www.amartpot.org
Contact: Marie Latta, Contact

Founded: 1978. **Members:** 1,000. **Membership Dues:** regular, $54 (annual) ● dual, $60 (annual). **Description:** Collectors and dealers of American art pottery. Fosters knowledge about and appreciation of American art pottery and promotes the interests of American art pottery dealers and collectors. **Awards: Frequency:** annual. **Type:** scholarship. **Publications:** *Journal of the American Art Pottery Association*, bimonthly. **Price:** included in membership dues. **Advertising:** accepted ● Membership Directory, biennial. **Conventions/Meetings:** annual conference and show, includes auction, show, banquet and tours (exhibits).

9412 ■ American Color Print Society (ACPS)
c/o Elizabeth MacDonald, Treas./Membership Chair
205 Woodside Ave.
Narberth, PA 19072
E-mail: idwill@patmedia.net
URL: http://www.americancolorprintsociety.org
Contact: Idaherma Williams, Pres.

Founded: 1939. **Members:** 75. **Membership Dues:** non-profit, $30 (annual). **Description:** Color printmaking artists. Conducts annual exhibition of members' works. **Awards:** Hatten Prize. **Type:** monetary ● Otto Lambert Grever Award. **Type:** monetary ● Stella Drabkin Memorial Awards. **Frequency:** annual. **Type:** monetary. **Telecommunication Services:** electronic mail, ehm205@comcast.net. **Publications:** *Color Proof*. Newsletter. Alternate Formats: online.

9413 ■ American Council for Southern Asian Art (ACSAA)
c/o Joan Cummins, Sec.
133 W 17th St., No. 6D
New York, NY 10011
E-mail: joancummins@nyc.rr.com
URL: http://kaladarshan.arts.ohio-state.edu/acsaa/hp.html
Contact: Joan Cummins, Sec.

Founded: 1967. **Members:** 250. **Membership Dues:** regular, $40 (annual) ● institutional, $50 (annual) ● student, unemployed, $15 (annual) ● contributing, $60 (annual) ● sustaining, $100 (annual). **Description:** Scholars, collectors, students, university departments, museums, and other institutions with holdings or programs in South and Southeast Asian art. Supports advancement of knowledge and understanding of the art and archaeology of South and Southeast Asia and related areas by providing research and teaching materials and disseminating information about scholarly and public activity in the field. Conducts biennial symposium. **Committees:** Outreach. **Projects:** Color Slide. **Affiliated With:** Association for Asian Studies; College Art Association. **Formerly:** American Committee for South Asian Art. **Publications:** *ACSAA Newsletter*, semiannual. **Price:** included in membership dues. **Advertising:** accepted. Alternate Formats: online ● *Bibliography on South Asian Art*, biennial. **Price:** $12.00 for members; $15.00 for nonmembers ● *Microfiche Archive of Art*, periodic ● *Slide Set on India*, 5/year ● Also publishes a list of museums with South Asian art. **Conventions/Meetings:** annual meeting (exhibits) - always February/March.

9414 ■ American Guild of Judaic Art (AGJA)
15 Greenspring Valley Rd.
Owings Mills, MD 21117
Ph: (410)902-0411
Fax: (410)581-0108
E-mail: office@jewishart.org
URL: http://www.jewishart.org
Contact: David Ascalon, Pres.

Membership Dues: regular, $90 (annual). **Description:** Promotes education and appreciation of Judaic art. Serves as a forum and resource center for contemporary Jewish artists and the public. Increases public awareness and education of contemporary Judaic craft and fine art. **Publications:** *AGJA Update*, periodic. Newsletter. Contains information about membership networking. ● *Hiddur*, periodic. Newsletter. Features halachic information, book and exhibition reviews, and other articles of interest related to Judaic Art.

9415 ■ American Physician Art Association (APAA)
c/o Dr. Lawrence Travis, MD, Sec.-Treas.
2410 Patterson St., Ste.202
Nashville, TN 37203
Ph: (615)327-4944
Fax: (615)463-7841
E-mail: lwtjr@bellsouth.net
URL: http://www.americanphysiciansartassociation.com
Contact: Dr. Lawrence Travis MD, Sec.-Treas.

Founded: 1936. **Members:** 200. **Membership Dues:** active, $75 (annual). **Staff:** 1. **Description:** Physicians interested in art. Furthers the art interest of the medical profession. Stimulates physician artists to produce works of art in the fields of painting, sculpture, photography, graphic arts, design, and computer art. **Libraries: Type:** open to the public. **Holdings:** photographs. **Awards: Frequency:** annual. **Type:** recognition. **Telecommunication Services:** electronic mail, jking@usouthal.edu. **Conventions/Meetings:** annual conference, held in conjunction with the Southern Medical Association (exhibits) ● annual meeting and show, held with annual meeting of the Southern Medical Association.

9416 ■ American Tapestry Alliance (ATA)
PO Box 28600
San Jose, CA 95159-8600
E-mail: webeditor@americantapestryalliance.org
URL: http://www.americantapestryalliance.org
Contact: Alex Friedman, Dir.
Founded: 1982. **Membership Dues:** individual, $35 (annual) ● circle, $55-$250 (annual) ● student, $25 (annual). **State Groups:** 44. **National Groups:** 15. **Multinational. Description:** Supports the fine arts medium of contemporary hand-woven tapestry. Promotes an awareness of and appreciation for tapestries designed and woven by individual artists. Educates the public about the history and techniques involved in tapestry making. **Libraries: Type:** reference. **Computer Services:** database, artist pages ● online services, discussion forums. **Committees:** Education; Exhibition; Fundraising; Library; Planning; Promotion. **Programs:** Education; Outreach. **Publications:** *Tapestry Topics Online*, quarterly. Newsletter. Alternate Formats: online.

9417 ■ American Watercolor Society (AWS)
47 5th Ave.
New York, NY 10003
Ph: (212)206-8986
Fax: (212)206-1960
E-mail: awshq@verizon.net
URL: http://www.americanwatercolorsociety.com
Contact: Janet Walsh, Pres.
Founded: 1866. **Members:** 500. **Membership Dues:** sustaining associate, $45 (annual). **Description:** Full and sustaining associate members devoted to the advancement of watercolor painting. Awards 13 medals including Gold, Silver, and Bronze Medals of Honor in addition to cash awards. Supports traveling exhibition throughout the United States. **Awards:** Dolphin Medal. **Type:** medal. **Recipient:** for outstanding contributions to art ● **Frequency:** annual. **Type:** scholarship. **Recipient:** for students of watercolor painting. **Publications:** Newsletter, biennial. Includes news about the members of the society and new businesses. ● Also publishes color catalog of the annual art exhibition. **Conventions/Meetings:** annual meeting (exhibits) - always April in New York City.

9418 ■ Aouon Archive (AA)
c/o Michael Rossman, Dir.
1741 Virginia St.
Berkeley, CA 94703
Ph: (510)849-1154
E-mail: mrossman@sbcglobal.net
Contact: Michael Rossman, Dir.
Founded: 1977. **Description:** Maintains 5500 posters and prints from the post-1960 U.S. progressive social and political movement. Sponsors lectures, presentations, and exhibits. Operates speakers' bureau. Compiles statistics. (AOUON stands for All of Us Or None). **Publications:** Bulletin, periodic.

9419 ■ Archives of American Art (AAA)
PO Box 37012
Washington, DC 20013-7012
Ph: (202)633-7940 (202)633-7950
Fax: (202)633-7994
E-mail: driscollj@si.edu
URL: http://www.aaa.si.edu
Contact: John W. Smith, Dir.
Founded: 1954. **Members:** 2,000. **Membership Dues:** sustaining, $65 (annual) ● associate, $125 (annual) ● sponsor, $250 (annual) ● patron, $500 (annual) ● fellow, $1,000 (annual) ● benefactor, $2,500 (annual) ● Chairman's Circle, $5,000 (annual). **Staff:** 35. **Description:** Various levels of membership. Scholars, writers on art, critics, and cultural historians. Seeks to document the art world of the U.S. as a whole. Preserves and makes accessible to scholars the papers of artists and craftsmen of every period of American art, and of collectors, dealers, critics, historians, museums, societies, and institutions of art. Collection comprises original and secondary source material, manuscripts, letters, notebooks, sketchbooks, clippings, exhibition catalogs, publications of societies, rare and out-of-print materials, microfilm, recorded interviews, and photographs of works of art and artists. **Convention/Meeting:** none. **Libraries: Type:** reference. **Holdings:** 16,000,000. **Subjects:** all records/collections related to Art in America. **Awards:** Lawrence A. Fleischman Award. **Frequency:** annual. **Type:** scholarship. **Recipient:** for scholarly excellence in the field of American art history. **Telecommunication Services:** TDD, (202)633-9320. **Sections:** Artists; Collectors; Critics and Historians; Dealers; Museums; Societies and Institutions. **Publications:** *Archives of American Art Journal*, quarterly. Contains fresh and uncommon perspectives on American cultural and social history. **Price:** $50.00 /year for institutions; $25.00 /year for nonmembers (students); $15.00/single copy for nonmembers; included in membership dues. **Circulation:** 3,000 ● Journal, quarterly.

9420 ■ Armenian Rugs Society (ARS)
939 N Amphlett Blvd.
San Mateo, CA 94401
Ph: (650)343-8585
Fax: (650)343-5118
E-mail: info@armenianrugssociety.com
URL: http://www.armenianrugssociety.com
Contact: Levon DerBedrossian, Pres.
Founded: 1979. **Members:** 50. **Membership Dues:** individual, $50 (annual) ● donor, $100 (annual) ● patron, $500 (annual) ● corporate, $100 (annual) ● student, $25 (annual). **Budget:** $70,000. **Regional Groups:** 2. **Description:** Fosters the identification, preservation and dissemination of knowledge of Armenian rugs. Maintains a data bank of hand knotted oriental rugs, carpets, kilims, bags and trappings bearing inscriptions woven in the Armenian alphabet. Organizes symposiums and exhibitions. **Libraries: Type:** reference. **Holdings:** archival material. **Awards:** Kohar Award. **Frequency:** annual. **Type:** recognition. **Recipient:** for stewardship, collecting, maintaining, lecturing and publishing. **Computer Services:** database, inscribed rugs. **Publications:** *ARS Newsletter*, 3-6/year. **Price:** included in membership dues. **Circulation:** 300 ● Catalog, annual. **Conventions/Meetings:** annual Passages - meeting.

9421 ■ Art Alliance for Contemporary Glass (AACG)
PO Box 7022
Evanston, IL 60201
Ph: (847)869-2018
Fax: (847)869-2018
E-mail: george_kaiser@msn.com
URL: http://www.contempglass.org
Contact: George Kaiser, Pres.
Members: 500. **Membership Dues:** general, in U.S., $65 (annual) ● collector/gallery, $100 (annual) ● friend, $250 (annual) ● contributor, $500 (annual) ● general, outside U.S., $80 (annual) ● founder, $1,000 (annual). **Staff:** 6. **Regional Groups:** 8. **Multinational. Description:** Works to advance the development and appreciation of art made from glass. **Awards:** AACG Annual Award. **Frequency:** annual. **Type:** grant. **Recipient:** for contributions to the contemporary glass movement ● AACG Honors. **Frequency:** annual. **Type:** recognition. **Recipient:** for individuals with outstanding accomplishments in the field of contemporary glass art. **Computer Services:** database ● mailing lists, of members. **Programs:** Grants. **Publications:** *Glass Focus*, bimonthly. Newsletter. **Price:** $30.00 for nonmembers; included in membership dues. **Conventions/Meetings:** Glass Weekend Exhibition - meeting.

9422 ■ Art Directors Club (ADC)
106 W 29th St.
New York, NY 10001
Ph: (212)643-1440
Fax: (212)643-4266
E-mail: info@adcglobal.org
URL: http://www.adcglobal.org
Contact: Ami Brophy, Exec. Dir.
Founded: 1920. **Members:** 1,100. **Membership Dues:** professional, associate, $225 (annual) ● student, friend, $75 (annual) ● corporate (agency/firm), $1,500 (annual) ● non-resident, $175 (annual) ● young professional, $100 (annual). **Staff:** 14. **Budget:** $1,200,000. **Multinational. Description:** Art directors of advertising magazines and agencies, visual information specialists, and graphic designers; associate members are artists, cinematographers, photographers, copywriters, educators, journalists, and critics. Promotes and stimulates interest in the practice of art direction. Sponsors Annual Exhibition of Advertising, Editorial and Television Art and Design; International Traveling Exhibition. Provides educational, professional, and entertainment programs; on-premise art exhibitions; portfolio review program. Conducts panels for students and faculty. **Libraries: Type:** reference; not open to the public. **Holdings:** 1,000; books, periodicals, video recordings. **Subjects:** art, advertising, design. **Awards:** Art Directors Awards. **Frequency:** annual. **Type:** recognition. **Recipient:** for winners of annual competition ● Art Directors Club Hall of Fame. **Type:** recognition ● Art Directors Scholarship Foundation. **Frequency:** annual. **Type:** scholarship. **Recipient:** for art schools in New York Metropolitan area that distribute awarded funds to individual students ● Vision Award. **Frequency:** annual. **Type:** recognition. **Computer Services:** Mailing lists. **Committees:** Education; Exhibitions; Portfolio Reviews; Scholarship; Speaker Events. **Programs:** Seminars; Speaker Evenings; Speaker Luncheons; Symposia. **Publications:** *ADC Newsletter*, monthly. **Price:** free for members. **Circulation:** 3,000. Alternate Formats: online ● *Art Directors Annual*, annual. Book. Covers "the best" in national and international advertising, graphic design, and new media. **Price:** $70.00. ISSN: 0735-2026. **Circulation:** 15,000. **Advertising:** accepted. **Conventions/Meetings:** annual meeting - always May or June in New York City ● seminar.

9423 ■ Art Dreco Institute (ADI)
PMB 131
2570 Ocean Ave.
San Francisco, CA 94132
Ph: (415)333-8372
E-mail: director@artdreco.com
URL: http://www.artdreco.com
Contact: Paul Drexler, Founder/Dir.
Founded: 1973. **Members:** 250. **Membership Dues:** individual, $25 (annual). **Description:** Artists, art dealers, collectors, and historians; other individuals interested in Art Dreco. (Dreco is an art form characterized by a total disregard for public taste and fashion.) Also recognizes "found" or utilitarian objects and acknowledges such facets as Sports Dreco, Television Dreco, and Architectural Dreco. Maintains that Art Dreco has existed since the beginning of time, although the late 19th century, 1930s, 1940s, and 1950s have produced it most prolifically. Makes the public more aware of Art Dreco. Gives "bad taste" a higher aesthetic standing than it currently enjoys. Teaches people how to recognize Art Dreco. Conducts lectures and exhibitions; sponsors film festivals featuring selections of "loathsome" movies. Authenticates Dreco objects d'art. Maintains hall of fame and museum. **Libraries: Type:** reference. **Holdings:** archival material. **Subjects:** art dreco. **Awards:** Best in Show from Art Dreco Roadshow. **Type:** recognition. **Publications:** *Art Dreco Catalog*.

9424 ■ Art Information Center (AIC)
Address Unknown since 2008
Founded: 1959. **Staff:** 3. **Description:** Serves as a clearinghouse of information on contemporary fine arts. Assists artists in finding outlets for their work; assists art dealers in finding new talent; aids curators, and collectors. Data collected is donated to the Archives of American Art. **Convention/Meeting:** none. **Formerly:** (1962) Artists' Gallery and Art Information Center.

9425 ■ Art Institute of Light (AIL)
Address Unknown since 2007
Founded: 1930. **Description:** Devoted to research and education in the use of light as an independent art medium. Provides library and laboratory facilities for artists and inventors to solve their individual problems and aid in promoting the artistic use of light. Presently inactive. **Libraries: Type:** reference. **Holdings:** 1,000. **Subjects:** all forms of artistic expression, particularly the use of light. **Conventions/Meet-**

ings: annual meeting - always second Wednesday in June, Gap, PA.

9426 ■ Art Services International (ASI)
1319 Powhatan St.
Alexandria, VA 22314
Ph: (703)548-4554
Fax: (703)548-3305
E-mail: asi@artservicesintl.org
URL: http://www.artservicesintl.org
Contact: Lynn K. Rogerson, Dir./CEO
Founded: 1987. **Staff:** 7. **Budget:** $1,300,000. **Description:** Circulates traveling art exhibitions, borrowed both domestically and internationally, for tours in America and abroad. Has organized exhibitions borrowed from major museums and private collections in America, Europe, and Japan, among them: Gold and Silver Treasures for the Thyssen-Bornemisza Collection and the Harold Samuel Collection. Included are outstanding selections of paintings, drawings, photographs, sculpture, graphic arts, textile, and ceramic arts. Invites noted international scholars to serve as guest curators, select works to be shown, write catalogs, and lecture. Provides accompanying educational and publicity materials. **Convention/Meeting:** none. **Libraries: Type:** not open to the public. **Supersedes:** International Exhibitions Foundation. **Publications:** Catalog. Includes substantive scholarly essays, followed by an individual description of each work of art on view.

9427 ■ Arthur Rackham Society
10 Cameron Pl.
Grosse Pointe, MI 48230
URL: http://www.angelfire.com/ar/ArthurRackhamSociety
Founded: 1984. **Members:** 150. **Membership Dues:** regular in U.S., $20 (annual) ● regular in UK, 15 (annual) ● regular outside U.S., $22 (annual). **Regional Groups:** 2. **Description:** Represents individuals interested in the work of English artist Arthur Rackham (1867-1939), best known for illustrating such works as *Rip van Winkle, Midsummer Night's Dream, Alice in Wonderland,* and *The Wind in the Willows.* Encourages appreciation of Rackham and exchange of information about his works. Provides information to researchers on locations of Rackham materials, particularly items in private collections. Maintains lists of sources of Rackham materials, modern reprints, first editions, and biographical and bibliographical information. Maintains speakers' bureau; conducts educational and research programs; provides information on works suitable for children. **Libraries: Type:** reference. **Holdings:** artwork, audiovisuals, books, clippings, monographs, periodicals. **Subjects:** Arthur Rackham. **Awards:** Rackham Illustration Prize. **Frequency:** annual. **Type:** recognition. **Computer Services:** Mailing lists, of members. **Publications:** *The Journal of the Arthur Rackham Society*, 3/year. **Price:** included in membership dues. ISSN: 1076-8912. **Circulation:** 150 ● *The Newsletter of the Arthur Rackham Society*, periodic. **Conventions/Meetings:** biennial international conference, with visits to library, museum and private collections; lecturers; visits sites associated with Rackham (exhibits) - always odd-numbered years.

9428 ■ Artists for Israel International (AFII)
PO Box 2056
New York, NY 10163-2056
Ph: (212)245-4188 (646)607-0667
E-mail: phil@philglobe.com
URL: http://www.afii.org
Contact: Dr. Phillip Goble, Pres.
Founded: 1980. **Membership Dues:** individual, $40 (annual). **Languages:** Arabic, English, Greek, Hebrew, Spanish, Urdu. **Description:** Bible society; promotes the interpretation and understanding of the Bible through art and commercial media. Sponsors training school. Publishers of The Orthodox Jewish Bible; also filmmakers of Rabbi from Tarsus VHS video production. **Libraries: Type:** reference. **Holdings:** 2,000; books. **Subjects:** Judaism, Islam, Cross-Cultural Communication. **Publications:** *The Orthodox Jewish Bible* (in English, French, Hebrew, Latin, Russian, Spanish, and Yiddish). Book. **Price:** $39.95/copy. Alternate Formats: online ● *The Rabbi From Tarsus.* Video ● Brochure.

9429 ■ Arts and Crafts Society (ACS)
828 SE 34th Ave., Ste.B
Portland, OR 97214
Ph: (503)459-4422
Fax: (503)459-4440
E-mail: info@arts-crafts.com
URL: http://www.arts-crafts.com
Contact: Ms. Lauren Russell, Librarian
Founded: 1995. **Nonmembership. For-Profit. Multinational. Description:** Represents and promotes the present-day arts and crafts movement community. **Libraries: Type:** by appointment only. **Holdings:** archival material, articles, books, papers, periodicals. **Subjects:** House Plans (1900-1960), women's magazines, catalogs of furniture, stencils, lighting, pottery, metalwork instruction in handicraft from the Arts and Crafts era - embroidery, furniture making, metalwork, biographies of architects and artists from the arts and crafts era. **Computer Services:** Bibliographic search, arts and crafts related resources, annotation, images ● online services, forum. **Publications:** *Events Calendar.*

9430 ■ Association for Art History
Indiana Univ.
Henry Radford Hope School of Fine Arts
Fine Arts 124
Bloomington, IN 47405
Fax: (812)855-9556
E-mail: aah@indiana.edu
URL: http://www.indiana.edu/~aah
Contact: Warren Sanderson, Pres.
Description: Represents professionals working in art history; promotes issues concerning art history. **Publications:** Newsletter ● Journal. Features articles and essays by art historians, museum professionals, independent scholars and art critics.

9431 ■ Association of Historians of Nineteenth-Century Art (AHNCA)
c/o Janet Whitmore, Membership Coor.
5614 N Wayne Ave., No. 1
Chicago, IL 60660
E-mail: janetwhitmore@earthlink.net
URL: http://www.arthistory-archaeology.umd.edu/ahnca
Contact: Janet Whitmore, Membership Coor.
Founded: 1993. **Members:** 400. **Membership Dues:** regular, $25 (annual) ● benefactor, $200 (annual) ● patron, $100 (annual) ● supporting, $50 (annual) ● sustaining, $35 (annual). **Multinational. Description:** Fosters dialogue and communication among those who have a special interest in the field of nineteenth-century art and culture. Offers opportunities for younger scholars to present papers related to their doctoral research. **Awards:** AHNCA Prize. **Frequency:** annual. **Type:** recognition. **Recipient:** to the PhD candidate who submits the best conference or symposium paper on a topic related to 19th-century art. **Computer Services:** Mailing lists, listserv. **Affiliated With:** College Art Association. **Publications:** Newsletter, semiannual. Contains information about new books and exhibitions. **Price:** included in membership dues.

9432 ■ Association for Textual Scholarship in Art History (ATSAH)
c/o Dr. Liana De Girolami Cheney, Pres.
112 Charles St.
Beacon Hill
Boston, MA 02114
Ph: (617)367-1679
Fax: (617)557-2962
E-mail: lianacheney@earthlink.net
URL: http://www.uml.edu/Dept/History/ArtHistory/ATSAH
Contact: Dr. Liana De Girolami Cheney, Pres.
Founded: 1990. **Members:** 70. **Membership Dues:** regular, $20 (annual). **Multinational. Description:** Promotes the study and publication of art-historical primary sources, and to facilitate communication among scholars working with art literature. Publishes a newsletter to disseminate information about ongoing scholarship, publications, conferences, and computer programs for textual analysis. Organizes conference sessions, publishes summaries and reviews of important publications and presentations concerning editions, sources, and art-historical literature. Arranges discounts on reprints and facsimile editions for members. **Publications:** Newsletter, semiannual. Contains information about ongoing scholarship, publications, conferences, and computer programs for textual analysis. ISSN: 1089-1293. Alternate Formats: online. **Conventions/Meetings:** conference.

9433 ■ Audubon Artists
47 5th Ave., 3rd Fl.
New York, NY 10003
E-mail: vinart@usamailbox.com
URL: http://www.audubonartists.org
Contact: Vincent J. Nardone, Pres.
Founded: 1940. **Members:** 475. **Membership Dues:** associate, $35 (annual). **Staff:** 16. **Budget:** $75,000. **Description:** Represents artists who work in aquamedia, oil, graphics, or sculpture. Members, associate members, and selected nonmembers hold annual exhibition in New York City of painting, sculpture, and graphic art which is assembled and juried by practicing artists, with awards and $10,000 worth of cash of art techniques prizes presented by Audubon Artists and others; demonstrations are presented in conjunction with the exhibition. **Awards:** Audubon Gold Medal of Honor. **Frequency:** annual. **Type:** medal. **Recipient:** for winners of exhibition ● Audubon Silver Medal of Honor. **Frequency:** annual. **Type:** medal. **Recipient:** for winners of exhibition. **Affiliated With:** Salmagundi Club. **Publications:** *Exhibition Catalog*, annual. Contains national cross section of artwork in four categories; oils, aquamedia, graphics, and sculpture. **Price:** $50.00. **Circulation:** 5,000. **Conventions/Meetings:** quarterly assembly, exhibits once annually (exhibits) ● quarterly board meeting ● annual show (exhibits).

9434 ■ Center for the Study of Political Graphics (CSPG)
8124 W 3rd St., Ste.211
Los Angeles, CA 90048-4340
Ph: (323)653-4662
Fax: (323)653-6991
E-mail: cspgweb@politicalgraphics.org
URL: http://www.politicalgraphics.org
Contact: Mary Sutton, Contact
Founded: 1988. **Membership Dues:** general, $50 (annual) ● student, $25 (annual). **Staff:** 4. **Budget:** $350,000. **Description:** Collects, preserves, documents, and circulates domestic and international political poster art. Offers lectures and workshops on the significance of poster art as an expression of social change. Sponsors more than 20 exhibitions on various human rights and social justice struggles available for rent. **Libraries: Type:** reference; by appointment only. **Holdings:** artwork, books, clippings, periodicals. **Subjects:** political art, posters. **Computer Services:** Mailing lists. **Publications:** *Che Guevara as Icon.* Catalog. **Price:** $30.00 ● *Exhibition Catalogs on the Topics of Los Angeles Protests* ● *Vietnam War Protest Posters.* **Conventions/Meetings:** periodic Public Forum - meeting.

9435 ■ Christian Comic Arts Society (CCAS)
PO Box 254
Temple City, CA 91780
URL: http://www.christiancomicarts.com
Contact: Eric Jansen, Treas.
Founded: 1984. **Members:** 23. **Membership Dues:** individual, $4 (bimonthly). **Description:** Aims to discuss, research, and set forth a Christian perspective on the world of comic books, comic strips, cartooning, and related areas such as fantasy and science fiction; to encourage the development and use of God-given creative talents in the areas of writing and art related to comics and cartooning; to encourage the spiritual growth and sense of community among Christian fans and professionals in the comic related fields. **Publications:** *Alpha-Omega*, bimonthly. Magazine. **Price:** $7.80 for members only, mailing fees 1st class (3 issues); $4.80 for members

only, mailing fees 3rd class (3 issues). **Conventions/Meetings:** regional meeting.

9436 ■ Colored Pencil Society of America (CPSA)
c/o Cynthia L. Haase, Membership Dir.
8156-E S Wadsworth Blvd., No. 184
Littleton, CO 80128
Ph: (303)972-9210
E-mail: secretary@cpsa.org
URL: http://www.cpsa.org
Contact: Betty Sandner, Sec.
Founded: 1990. **Members:** 1,600. **Membership Dues:** regular, in U.S. and Canada, $40 (annual) ● regular, outside U.S. and Canada, $45 (annual) ● life, in U.S., $500 ● life, in Canada, $650 ● life, outside U.S. and Canada, $800. **Regional Groups:** 23. **Multinational. Description:** Represents artists working with colored pencils. **Publications:** *To The Point*, 3/year. Newsletter. **Advertising:** accepted ● Directory. Serves as a networking directory. **Conventions/Meetings:** annual banquet and convention (exhibits) ● annual international conference (exhibits) ● workshop and seminar.

9437 ■ Conservation Center for Art and Historic Artifacts (CCAHA)
264 S 23rd St.
Philadelphia, PA 19103
Ph: (215)545-0613
Fax: (215)735-9313
E-mail: ccaha@ccaha.org
URL: http://www.ccaha.org
Contact: Ingrid E. Bogel, Exec. Dir.
Founded: 1977. **Membership Dues:** institutional (with budget under $1.5M), $150 (annual) ● institutional (with budget over $1.5M), $250 (annual). **Description:** Supports and represents museums, archives, libraries, historical societies, academic institutions, state agencies, cooperative conservation programs and private foundations conserving art and historic artifacts. **Libraries: Type:** reference. **Subjects:** preservation and conservation. **Programs:** Collections Care Training. **Publications:** *Artifacts*, semiannual. Newsletter. Alternate Formats: online ● *Managing a Mold Invasion: Guidelines for Disaster Response* (in English and Spanish). Handbook. **Conventions/Meetings:** workshop.

9438 ■ The Drawing Center (TDC)
35 Wooster St.
New York, NY 10013
Ph: (212)219-2166
Fax: (212)966-2976
E-mail: info@drawingcenter.org
URL: http://www.drawingcenter.org
Contact: Ms. Lisa Gold, Public Relations and Marketing Dir.
Founded: 1976. **Members:** 500. **Membership Dues:** artist, $35 (annual) ● individual, $50 (annual) ● dual, $85 (annual) ● contributor, $150 (annual) ● supporter, $300 (annual) ● associate, $500 (annual) ● donor, $1,000 (annual) ● friend, $2,500 (annual) ● corporate, $5,000 (annual). **Staff:** 12. **Budget:** $1,400,000. **Description:** Seeks to provide opportunities for emerging artists. Demonstrates the significance of diversity of drawings throughout history and stimulates public dialogue on issues of art and culture. **Libraries: Type:** reference; by appointment only. **Holdings:** 2,000; artwork. **Subjects:** Artist Slide Registry. **Computer Services:** database, slide registry index. **Publications:** *Creative Copies: Interpretive Drawings from Michelangelo to Picasso* ● *Drawing Papers*, periodic. Catalogs. **Price:** $15.00 ● *The Drawings of Antonio Gaudi* ● *Drawn from Artists' Collections, 1999* ● *Inigo Jones - Complete Architectural Drawings* ● *Philip Guston's Poem-Pictures* ● *Picasso's "Parade" from Paper to Stage* ● *Pierced Hearts and True Love: A Century of Drawings for Tattoos, 1995.* Catalog ● *Plains Indian Drawings 1865-1935: Pages from a Visual History, 1996.* Catalogs ● *Rajasthani Miniatures: The Welch Collection from the Sackler Museum, Harvard University, 1997.* Catalog ● *Sculptors' Drawings Over Six Centuries* ● *Shadows of a Hand: The Drawings of Victor Hugo, 1998* ● *Tracing Taiwan: Contemporary Works on Paper, 1997.* Catalog ● *Willem de Kooning: Drawing Seeing/Seeing Drawing, 1998* ● Also publishes many other resources on drawing.

9439 ■ Experiments in Art and Technology (EAT)
c/o Dr. Billy Kluver, Co-Founder/Pres.
69 Apple Tree Rd.
Berkeley Heights, NJ 07922
Ph: (212)285-1690
Fax: (908)322-2529
E-mail: kluverb@comcast.net
URL: http://www.fondation-langlois.org/html/e/page.php?NumPage=306
Contact: Dr. Billy Kluver, Co-Founder/Pres.
Founded: 1966. **Staff:** 3. **Description:** Artists, engineers, scientists, composers, dancers, and educators. Works to initiate projects, based on collaboration between scientists and artists, dealing with the aesthetic and cultural components of technological change and adaptation and leading to imaginative application of technology in areas that directly affect human development. **Publications:** *EAT Bibliography 1965-1980* ● *Pavilion.* Books ● Reports.

9440 ■ Franklin Furnace Archive (FF)
80 Arts - The James E. Davis Arts Bldg.
80 Hanson Pl., No. 301
Brooklyn, NY 11217-1506
Ph: (718)398-7255
Fax: (718)398-7256
E-mail: mail@franklinfurnace.org
URL: http://www.franklinfurnace.org
Contact: Martha Wilson, Founding Dir.
Founded: 1976. **Members:** 1,000. **Membership Dues:** Smoke Signal, $30 (annual) ● Pony Express, $60 (annual) ● Carrier Pigeon, $100 (annual) ● Singing Telegram, $300 (annual) ● Princess Phone, $600 (annual) ● Satellite Dish, $3,000 (annual). **Staff:** 8. **Budget:** $400,000. **Description:** Artists, art enthusiasts, art organizations, scholars, and libraries. Maintains international database of contemporary art exhibitions and performances. Mounted historical and thematic exhibitions of published work by artists. Collected books, periodicals, postcards, cassette tapes, and broadsides published by artists as artworks. Curates traveling shows; conducts internship program for college students. Offers literacy program for elementary and high school students and artists' regrant programs. **Convention/Meeting:** none. **Libraries: Type:** reference. **Subjects:** avant-garde expression. **Publications:** Catalogs.

9441 ■ Friends of Fiber Art International
Box 468
Western Springs, IL 60558
Ph: (708)246-9466
Fax: (708)246-9466
URL: http://206.204.3.133/dir_nii/nii_dat_fiber.html
Founded: 1991. **Members:** 800. **Membership Dues:** friend, $35 (annual) ● sponsor, $100 (annual) ● patron, $250 (annual) ● benefactor, $500 (annual). **Staff:** 1. **Budget:** $90,000. **Description:** Collectors, artists, critics, gallery and museum personnel, and interested individuals. Promotes contemporary art in fibrous media. Supports museum exhibitions. Attempts to educate collectors and potential collectors of fiber art. Sponsors educational programs and tours. **Libraries: Type:** not open to the public. **Holdings:** 1,000; books, periodicals. **Subjects:** contemporary fiber art. **Awards:** Friends of Fiber Art Grant. **Frequency:** annual. **Type:** grant. **Recipient:** to groups initiating contemporary fiber art exhibitions that travels to at least three cities and are documented by a catalog. **Computer Services:** Mailing lists, of members. **Publications:** *Fiber Art News*, periodic. Newsletter. Includes international calendar of fiber art exhibitions. **Price:** included in membership dues. ISSN: 1531-7668. **Circulation:** 800. Also Cited As: *Dear Friends.* **Conventions/Meetings:** annual Fiber Art Weekend - meeting, contemporary fiber art (exhibits) - every October ● semiannual Travel and Learn Expedition - meeting, group travels to important international contemporary fiber art exhibitions in Poland and European cities.

9442 ■ Gen Art
133 W 25th St., 6th Fl.
New York, NY 10001
Ph: (212)255-7300
Free: (866)861-8072
Fax: (212)255-7400
E-mail: info@genart.org
URL: http://www.genart.org
Contact: Adam Walden, Pres.
Founded: 1993. **Members:** 2,500. **Membership Dues:** platinum, Collector's Circle, $250 (annual) ● silver, $75 (annual) ● associate producer, $500 (annual). **Staff:** 10. **Budget:** $3,000,000. **Regional Groups:** 5. **Description:** Supports and showcases young emerging talent in film, fashion, and the visual arts. Has various exhibition formats from month-long exhibitions to three-day art fairs. Also showcases emerging fashion designers in group fashion shows and young independent filmmakers in week-long film festivals. Strives to display these different forms of art in an accessible manner so as to help develop new supporters and patrons for the arts. **Awards:** Film Festival Audience Award. **Frequency:** annual. **Type:** monetary. **Recipient:** audience selection ● International Design Competition. **Frequency:** annual. **Type:** monetary. **Recipient:** for judges. **Telecommunication Services:** electronic mail, awalden@genart.org.

9443 ■ Global Alliance for Intelligent Arts (GAIA)
795 S State St. 75
Ukiah, CA 95482
Ph: (413)374-6531
Fax: (413)374-6531
E-mail: gaia@crocker.com
URL: http://www.global-alliance.com
Contact: Michael DiMartino, Contact
Founded: 1994. **Members:** 30. **Membership Dues:** directory, $125 (annual). **Staff:** 12. **Regional Groups:** 1. **State Groups:** 3. **Local Groups:** 1. **Languages:** English, Spanish. **Description:** Promotes human development through the arts. Conducts workshops and performances. Event production and management, cultural tours, audio and video production. Has music and video label and conducts product sales. Has a weekly television show on arts and a worldwide directory. **Libraries: Type:** open to the public. **Holdings:** 250; archival material, audiovisuals, books. **Subjects:** multiculturalism, music, visual, healing arts. **Computer Services:** Mailing lists.

9444 ■ Independent Curators International (ICI)
799 Broadway, Ste.205
New York, NY 10003
Ph: (212)254-8200
Fax: (212)477-4781
E-mail: info@ici-exhibitions.org
URL: http://www.ici-exhibitions.org
Contact: Judith Olch Richards, Exec. Dir.
Founded: 1975. **Staff:** 10. **Budget:** $800,000. **Description:** Traveling exhibition service specializing in contemporary art. Organizes traveling exhibitions which circulate nationally and internationally to museums, university art galleries, and art centers. **Awards:** Leo Award. **Frequency:** biennial. **Type:** recognition. **Recipient:** for outstanding contributions to the contemporary art world. **Telecommunication Services:** electronic mail, richards@ici-exhibitions.org. **Formerly:** (2001) Independent Curators Incorporated. **Publications:** Brochure, annual ● Catalogs. Covers exhibitions.

9445 ■ International Association of Pastel Societies (IAPS)
PO Box 2057
Falls Church, VA 22042
Ph: (703)241-2826
Fax: (703)536-0308
E-mail: susan@pastelinternational.com
URL: http://www.pastelinternational.com
Contact: Urania Christy Tarbet, Founder/Pres.
Founded: 1994. **Members:** 48. **Membership Dues:** society, $100 (annual). **Multinational. Description:** Represents pastel societies uniting for a common

cause. Promotes the validity and quality of pastel as a major fine art painting medium. **Awards:** Convention Cover Award. **Frequency:** biennial. **Type:** recognition. **Recipient:** for winning work of art from competition held during the convention ● Golden Mentor Award. **Frequency:** biennial. **Type:** recognition. **Recipient:** for outstanding individuals who have contributed to the growth of artists and the medium of pastel. **Computer Services:** Online services, showcases. **Telecommunication Services:** electronic mail, president@pastelinternational.com. **Conventions/Meetings:** biennial convention.

9446 ■ International Chain Saw Wood Sculptors Association (ICSWSA)
Address Unknown since 2007
Founded: 1985. **Members:** 30. **Description:** International group of chain saw wood sculptors, artists, and interested others. Works to introduce and promote the art of chain saw sculpting to the public; encourages recycling of tree stumps into works of art. Establishes rules and guidelines for chain saw sculpting. Produces television commercials to promote the art. Organizes periodic exhibitions, with demonstrations; conducts fund-raising events, chain saw events, and competitions. **Publications:** Bulletin, annual.

9447 ■ International Comic Arts Association (ICAA)
533 Johnson Ave.
Morris, IL 60450
Ph: (815)942-1819
E-mail: info@comicarts.org
URL: http://www.comicarts.org
Contact: Erik Enervold, Exec. Dir./Founder
Membership Dues: fan/collector/institutional in North America, $35 (annual) ● fan/collector/institutional outside North America, $50 (annual) ● individual professional in North America, $75 (annual) ● individual professional outside North America, $100 (annual) ● company/group in North America, $350 (annual) ● company/group outside North America, $450 (annual) ● retailer in North America, $150 (annual) ● retailer outside North America, $200 (annual) ● charter in North America, $25 (annual) ● charter outside North America, $40 (annual). **Multinational. Description:** Aims to strengthen and promote the comic art industry through advocacy, education, research, and dissemination of information. Seeks to increase comic book readership and sales through dynamic marketing strategies. Fosters public understanding, recognition and appreciation of the unique values of comics as an art form and its influential contribution to society and popular culture. Collects and preserves a vast collection of comic art works. **Awards:** ICAA Industry Achievement Awards. **Frequency:** annual. **Type:** recognition. **Recipient:** for outstanding achievement in promoting the comic art industry to a wider market. **Telecommunication Services:** electronic mail, director@comicarts.org. **Publications:** *Comic Industry Resource Directory*, annual ● *ComicArts Illustrated*, bimonthly. Journal. Provides in-depth news coverage of the comic art industry, and previews and reviews of upcoming comics and related products. **Price:** included in membership dues ● *ICAA Comic Retailers Marketing Handbook* ● *Live Wire*. Newsletter. Covers up-to-date industry news and events. **Price:** free. Alternate Formats: online ● Membership Directory, annual.

9448 ■ International Council of the Museum of Modern Art
11 W 53rd St.
New York, NY 10019
Ph: (212)708-9400
Fax: (212)708-9740
E-mail: info@moma.org
URL: http://www.moma.org
Contact: Glenn D. Lowry, Dir.
Founded: 1953. **Description:** Art patrons and leaders from the U.S. and abroad actively interested in contemporary art. Seeks to further international understanding through the circulation of exhibitions of paintings, sculpture, drawings, prints, architecture, design, photography, and film, and through other projects.

9449 ■ International Foundation for Art Research (IFAR)
500 5th Ave., Ste.935
New York, NY 10110
Ph: (212)391-6234
Fax: (212)391-8794
E-mail: kferg@ifar.org
URL: http://www.ifar.org
Contact: Dr. Sharon Flescher, Exec. Dir.
Founded: 1969. **Membership Dues:** associate, $100 (annual) ● individual (regular), $250 (annual) ● individual (sustainer), $500 (annual) ● individual (patron), corporate (regular), $1,000 (annual) ● individual (benefactor), corporate (patron), $5,000 (annual) ● corporate (sustainer), $2,500 (annual) ● corporate (benefactor), $10,000 (annual). **Staff:** 3. **Budget:** $300,000. **Description:** Offers impartial and authoritative information on authenticity, ownership, theft, and other artistic, legal, and ethical issues concerning works of art. Serves as a bridge between the public and the scholarly and commercial art communities and as a trusted resource for the art community. Sponsors lectures and symposia, offers an Art Authentication Service, and serves as a repository of information. **Libraries: Type:** reference. **Holdings:** archival material. **Subjects:** art theft, cultural property law, art fraud, connoisseurship. **Councils:** Art Advisory; Law Advisory. **Roundtables:** Collectors'. **Publications:** *IFAR Journal*, quarterly. Reports on art authentications, stolen and recovered art, and related legal and judicial issues affecting the art world. **Price:** $15.00/issue; $65.00/year. ISSN: 1098-1195. **Circulation:** 2,000. **Advertising:** accepted. **Conventions/Meetings:** periodic lecture ● symposium and conference, authentication and Catalogue Raisonne.

9450 ■ International Hajji Baba Society (IHBS)
c/o Virginia Day, Treas.
6500 Pinecrest Ct.
Annandale, VA 22003
Ph: (703)354-4880 (301)565-2079
E-mail: hajji@krauss.ws
URL: http://www.intlhajjirugsociety.org
Contact: Austin Foyle, Pres.
Founded: 1963. **Members:** 500. **Membership Dues:** household, $50 (annual) ● individual, $35 (annual) ● student, $10 (annual). **Staff:** 1. **Description:** Individuals from 15 countries united to: promote interest in oriental rugs and textiles; provide a forum for discussing these fabrics and furthering knowledge in the field; create alliances with countries in which the textiles are made and in areas where there is great interest in them; assist students and new collectors and counsel the more experienced; supply qualified lecturers and assist in producing exhibitions; aid research efforts with financial support and field work. Activities include: selecting and hanging rugs and producing catalogs for exhibitions in museums; supplying lecturers to museums; giving grants for research projects; sponsoring trips to the Middle East. **Formerly:** (1973) Rug Society of Washington, District of Columbia. **Publications:** *Exhibition Catalogues*, periodic. Catalogs ● Newsletter, monthly ● Newsletter. Alternate Formats: online. **Conventions/Meetings:** monthly meeting.

9451 ■ International Society for the Study of Pilgrimage Art
c/o Rita Tekippe, Exec. Ed.
Univ. of West Georgia
Art Dept.
324 Humanities Hall
Carrollton, GA 30118
Ph: (770)836-4532
Fax: (770)836-4392
E-mail: rtekippe@westga.edu
URL: http://peregrinations.kenyon.edu
Contact: Rita Tekippe, Exec. Ed.
Founded: 2000. **Multinational. Description:** Brings together scholars who explore the art and architecture of pilgrimage in the late Middle Ages. Provides a forum for themes and topics related to pilgrimage art. Shares current research in pilgrimage art. **Publications:** *Peregrinations*, 3-4 times per year. Journal. Contains research topics on art and architectural history, medieval history and religion. ISSN: 1554-8678. Alternate Formats: online.

9452 ■ James Renwick Alliance (JRA)
4405 East-West Hwy., Ste.510
Bethesda, MD 20814
Ph: (301)907-3888
Fax: (301)907-3855
E-mail: jraoffice@jra.org
URL: http://www.jra.org
Contact: Anne Mehringer, Pres.
Founded: 1982. **Membership Dues:** guild-participating craft artisan, $50 ● single (Alliance for Renwick Tomorrow; ages 25-40), $70 ● donor, $100 ● sponsor, $250 ● sustainer, $500 ● craft leader caucus (single)/gallery caucus, $1,000 ● craft leader caucus (double), $1,500 ● benefactor, $2,500 ● grand salon patron, $5,000 ● Renwick Society, $10,000. **Description:** Promotes and celebrates the achievements of America's craft artists. Fosters scholarship, education, and public appreciation of craft art. **Publications:** Newsletter, quarterly. **Conventions/Meetings:** Craft Leaders Caucus - meeting ● Craft Weekend - meeting ● lecture ● seminar ● symposium ● Trips and Study Tours ● workshop.

9453 ■ Kinetic Art Organization (KAO)
301 Clematis St., No. 3000
West Palm Beach, FL 33401
Ph: (561)655-2745
Fax: (561)655-4158
E-mail: webmaster@kinetic-art.org
URL: http://www.kinetic-art.org
Contact: Ralf Gschwend, Founder/Pres.
Membership Dues: colleague, $50 (annual). **Multinational. Description:** Promotes kinetic art as a valuable and unique art form. Provides a place for kinetic artists where they can interact with people who are interested in kinetic art and sculptures. Raises public awareness and interest in kinetic art. **Awards:** KAO International Kinetic Art Competition. **Frequency:** annual. **Type:** recognition. **Recipient:** for the best kinetic sculptures or kinetic art works. **Telecommunication Services:** electronic mail, ralfonso@ralfonso.com. **Publications:** Newsletter. **Price:** free. Alternate Formats: online.

9454 ■ Lesbians in the Visual Arts (LVA)
Address Unknown since 2008
Founded: 1990. **Members:** 500. **Membership Dues:** regular, $25-$65 (annual) ● supporter, $25 (annual). **Budget:** $30,000. **Multinational. Description:** Promotes the visibility of lesbians in the visual arts by encouraging and supporting their work and building an international network for the exchange of ideas, techniques, and experiences. **Libraries: Type:** reference; by appointment only. **Holdings:** articles, artwork, books, periodicals. **Subjects:** lesbians and lesbian/gay arts. **Formerly:** (1998) Lesbian Visual Artists. **Publications:** *Pentimenta, Art Journal of LVA*, biennial. Contains interviews, discussions, reviews. **Price:** included in membership. **Circulation:** 1,000. **Conventions/Meetings:** quarterly board meeting (exhibits).

9455 ■ Leslie-Lohman Gay Art Foundation
26 Wooster St.
New York, NY 10013
Ph: (212)431-2609
Fax: (212)431-2666
E-mail: lldirector@earthlink.net
URL: http://www.leslielohman.org
Contact: Wayne Snellen, Dir.
Founded: 1990. **Members:** 100. **Membership Dues:** art lover, $35 (annual) ● domestic partner, $60 (annual) ● art voyager, $150 (annual) ● art patron, $500 (annual) ● art benefactor, $1,000 (annual) ● corporate art benefactor, $1,500 (annual). **Staff:** 2. **Budget:** $78,000. **Description:** Provides forum to further the awareness and appreciation of art by lesbian, gay, bisexual, and transgendered persons. Programs

include a membership program, newsletter, archives, gallery for exhibitions, and a permanent collection of art. **Libraries: Type:** reference. **Holdings:** 200; archival material, books. **Subjects:** artists (gay/lesbian). **Awards:** Founders Purchase Award. **Frequency:** annual. **Type:** monetary. **Recipient:** selected from the current year's exhibitions by the founders. **Computer Services:** database, gay/lesbian artists. **Boards:** Advisory; Directors. **Also Known As:** LLGAF. **Publications:** *The Archive*, quarterly. Journal. Includes review of shows and interviews with artists. **Price:** $2.00 for nonmembers (plus shipping); included in membership dues. **Circulation:** 3,000. **Advertising:** accepted. **Conventions/Meetings:** periodic show and workshop, discussions with artists about their work (exhibits).

9456 ■ Master Drawings Association (MDA)
225 Madison Ave.
New York, NY 10016
Ph: (212)590-0369
Fax: (212)685-4740
E-mail: administrator@masterdrawings.org
URL: http://www.masterdrawings.org
Contact: Ms. Deborah Garwood, Admin.
Founded: 1962. **Description:** Represents museums, colleges, institutions, galleries, and individuals who studies, promotes and preserves European drawings since the Renaissance. **Publications:** *Master Drawings*, quarterly. Journal. Contains 65-75 plates of black-and-white (and occasional color) reproductions. Includes annual index, book reviews, and exhibition reviews. **Price:** $75.00 in U.S.; $85.00 outside U.S. ISSN: 0025-5025. **Circulation:** 1,300. **Advertising:** accepted ● *Thirty-Five Year Cumulation Index (1963-98)*.

9457 ■ National Art Museum of Sport (NAMOS)
Univ. Pl. - IUPUI
850 W Michigan St.
Indianapolis, IN 46202
Ph: (317)274-3627
Fax: (317)274-3878
E-mail: arein@iupui.edu
URL: http://www.namos.iupui.edu
Contact: Ann M. Rein, Admin. Dir.
Founded: 1959. **Staff:** 1. **Budget:** $25,000. **Nonmembership. Description:** Individuals, industrial corporations, and arts support institutions interested in helping to broaden the art tradition by developing the public's knowledge and enthusiasm for sport art. Acquires paintings, prints, sculptures; commissions new works; organizes special exhibits; maintains speakers' bureau and museum. Offers children's services and educational programs. **Libraries: Type:** by appointment only. **Holdings:** 400; archival material, articles, artwork, biographical archives, books. **Subjects:** sport and art. **Committees:** Collection and Acquisitions; Resource Planning and Development. **Publications:** *Score Board*, 3/year. Newsletters. **Price:** free. **Circulation:** 250. **Conventions/Meetings:** tour, for schools, adults, and communities (exhibits).

9458 ■ National Ice Carving Association (NICA)
PO Box 2664
Glen Ellyn, IL 60138
Ph: (630)871-8431
Fax: (630)871-0839
E-mail: nicaexdir@aol.com
URL: http://www.nica.org
Contact: Alice C. Connelly, Exec. Dir.
Founded: 1987. **Members:** 600. **Membership Dues:** business, associate, $250 (annual) ● carver, $75 (annual) ● student, retiree, $35 (annual). **Staff:** 1. **Description:** Ice carvers, students, and interested individuals. Promotes the art of ice sculpture through education, and competitions. Sanctions regional, international, and national ice carving exhibitions and competitions throughout the U.S. and Canada. Develops and reviews competition criteria annually. Holds demonstrations. **Awards:** National Champion. **Frequency:** annual. **Type:** monetary. **Computer Services:** Mailing lists. **Publications:** *On Ice*, monthly. Newsletter. **Price:** included in membership dues. **Advertising:** accepted. **Conventions/Meetings:** competition.

9459 ■ National Oil and Acrylic Painters' Society (NOAPS)
PO Box 676
Osage Beach, MO 65065-0676
Ph: (573)348-1764
E-mail: admin@noaps.org
URL: http://www.noaps.org
Contact: Joe Ray Kelly, Chm.
Founded: 1991. **Members:** 1,400. **Membership Dues:** artist, patron, $50 (annual). **Staff:** 3. **Budget:** $30,000. **Description:** Represents artists and others interested in exhibition and sales of original oil and acrylic paintings. **Awards: Frequency:** annual. **Type:** monetary. **Publications:** *Exhibit Catalog*, annual. Contains information of complete exhibit. **Price:** $4.00. **Circulation:** 1,500 ● *NOAPS Newsletter*, semiannual. Alternate Formats: online. **Conventions/Meetings:** annual executive committee meeting and board meeting (exhibits).

9460 ■ National Park Academy of the Arts (NPAA)
PO Box 608
Jackson Hole, WY 83001
Ph: (307)690-0055
Free: (800)553-2787
Fax: (307)739-1199
E-mail: info@artsfortheparks.com
URL: http://www.artsfortheparks.com
Contact: Abi Garaman, Chm.
Founded: 1987. **Description:** Encourages American artists to portray the beauty and values of the National Park system. Sponsors annual Arts for the Parks competition and collector books and traveling exhibition to help benefit the National Park Foundation. Offers limited edition prints and posters. **Awards:** Award of Merit, Bird Category. **Frequency:** annual. **Type:** monetary ● Award of Merit Wildlife Category. **Frequency:** annual. **Type:** monetary ● Founder's Favorite Winner Award. **Frequency:** annual. **Type:** monetary ● Grand Prize Winner Award. **Frequency:** annual. **Type:** monetary ● Grand Teton Lodge Company Cash Award. **Frequency:** annual. **Type:** monetary. **Recipient:** for a painting that best depicts the beauty and majesty of Grand Teton National Park ● Judges Award of Merit. **Frequency:** annual. **Type:** monetary ● Orion Goe Jillson-Native American Heritage Award. **Frequency:** annual. **Type:** monetary. **Recipient:** for the artwork best depicting Native American heritage ● Three Awards of Merit. **Type:** monetary. **Recipient:** for historical, marine, and landscape art ● Three Regional Winner Awards. **Frequency:** annual. **Type:** monetary ● U.S. Art Magazine Award of Merit. **Frequency:** annual. **Type:** monetary. **Publications:** *Artline*, quarterly. Newsletter ● *Press Release*, periodic ● Also publishes fact sheet and fliers. **Conventions/Meetings:** annual Arts for the Parks Banquet and Awards, with silent auction (exhibits) - September.

9461 ■ National Watercolor Society (NWS)
915 S Pacific Ave.
San Pedro, CA 90731
Ph: (310)831-1099
E-mail: nws-art@hotmail.com
URL: http://www.nws-online.org
Contact: Chris Van Winkle, Pres.
Founded: 1920. **Members:** 1,700. **Membership Dues:** signature, $40 (annual) ● associate, $35 (annual). **Staff:** 15. **Budget:** $100,000. **Regional Groups:** 13. **Description:** Watercolor artists who have been approved by the Jury of Selection are signature members; associate members are other watercolorists; life/signature members are Society past presidents. Encourages interest in watermedia painting by providing exhibitions and acting as an educational channel for providing information programs benefiting artists and the public. Sponsors travel shows in which 30 paintings by members are selected to circulate galleries and museums throughout the U.S. for one year and a Permanent Collection exhibition which also travels. Operates the NWS Artists Referral Program, which provides demonstrations and workshops for students by professionals. Maintains biographical archives; sponsors charitable program. **Libraries: Type:** not open to the public. **Holdings:** 7; articles, periodicals. **Subjects:** society exhibition, watercolor art. **Awards: Frequency:** annual. **Type:** monetary. **Formerly:** (1920) California Water Color Society; (1975) California National Watercolor Society. **Publications:** *All Member Show Brochure*, annual. Contains full color thumbnail photos of all paintings in the exhibition of the All Member Show. ● *Board of Directors Meeting*, quarterly. Newsletter ● *National Watercolor Society Exhibition Catalog*, annual. Contains complete color reproductions from exhibition, photographs of Board of Directors, and color examples of their work. **Price:** $15.00 includes postage; $12.00 back issues. **Circulation:** 4,000 ● *Roster*, biennial. Membership Directory. **Price:** available to members only ● Newsletter, 5/year. **Conventions/Meetings:** annual banquet, connected to annual exhibition ● annual meeting, for business purposes - always January.

9462 ■ Natural Figure Art Association (NFAA)
Address Unknown since 2007
Membership Dues: regular, $30 (annual). **Description:** Seeks to promote the nude human figure in the art of painting, drawing, and photography. Represents members on the internet; offers space to show artists work; conducts painting and sculpting workshops; provides opportunities for networking among artists. **Publications:** Newsletter. **Conventions/Meetings:** workshop.

9463 ■ Pacific Arts Association (PAA)
c/o Hilary Scothorn, Treas.
PO Box 6061-120
Sherman Oaks, CA 91413
E-mail: ivorycs@wsu.edu
URL: http://www.pacificarts.org
Contact: Michael Gunn, Pres.
Founded: 1974. **Members:** 300. **Membership Dues:** professional, institutional, $40 (annual) ● artist, student, retired person, $30 (annual) ● in Europe, $4 (annual). **Budget:** $7,000. **Multinational. Description:** Individuals and institutions in 34 countries interested in the practice, teaching, or development of Pacific Island art. Fosters cooperation and international understanding among individuals, institutions, and nations involved in oceanic arts. Promotes high standards of research, conservation, and preservation; increases interest in teaching oceanic courses; disseminates information to members on recent developments in the field. **Committees:** Editorial. **Publications:** *Exploring the Visual Art of Oceania*. Proceedings. Contains the proceedings of the First International Symposium on the Arts of Oceania. ● *Pacific Arts*, annual. Journal. Contains news and articles on pacific art, anthropology, archaeology, and worldwide exhibition information. **Price:** included in membership dues. ISSN: 1018-4252. **Circulation:** 300 ● *Pacific Arts Association Newsletter*, semiannual. Contains news and events about the association. Alternate Formats: online ● Also publishes papers. **Conventions/Meetings:** quadrennial International Symposium.

9464 ■ Pastel Society of America (PSA)
15 Gramercy Park S
New York, NY 10003
Ph: (212)533-6931
Fax: (212)353-8140
E-mail: pastelny@juno.com
URL: http://www.pastelsocietyofamerica.org
Contact: Barbara Fischman, Pres.
Founded: 1972. **Members:** 900. **Membership Dues:** signature, $60 (annual) ● juried associate, sponsor (minimum), $50 (annual) ● supporting, $40 (annual) ● patron (minimum), $100 (annual) ● donor (minimum), $25 (annual). **Staff:** 2. **Regional Groups:** 32. **Description:** Aims to unite pastel artists in the U.S. and abroad and to encourage young artists by offering scholarships. Focuses attention on the renaissance of pastel and educates the public on its permanence and strength as an art form. Supports the position that, a pastel is a pure medium, it should

be judged separately in all art exhibitions. Facilitates the exchange of news, achievements, and ideas among members. Conducts exhibits and classes. Operates hall of fame. **Libraries: Type:** reference. **Holdings:** 50; biographical archives, video recordings. **Subjects:** demonstrations by outstanding pastel painters. **Awards:** Board of Directors Award. **Frequency:** annual. **Type:** recognition. **Recipient:** for pastel artists ● Hall of Fame Honoree. **Frequency:** annual. **Type:** recognition. **Recipient:** for pastel artists ● Master Pastelist. **Frequency:** annual. **Type:** recognition. **Recipient:** for pastel artists ● **Frequency:** periodic. **Type:** scholarship. **Publications:** *Pastelagram*, semiannual. Newsletter. Covers artists, their work, and the techniques of using pastel. **Price:** included in membership dues. **Circulation:** 900. **Advertising:** accepted ● *PSA Update*, semiannual. Newsletter. **Price:** included in membership dues. **Circulation:** 850. **Conventions/Meetings:** monthly board meeting ● annual International Open Juried Exhibition - show (exhibits) - always September at National Arts Club, New York.

9465 ■ Portrait Society of America
PO Box 11272
Tallahassee, FL 32302
Ph: (850)878-9996
Free: (877)772-4321
Fax: (850)222-7890
E-mail: info@portraitsociety.org
URL: http://www.portraitsociety.org
Contact: Christine Egnoski, Exec. Dir.
Members: 2,000. **Membership Dues:** general (associate/artist), $65 (annual) ● patron, corporate, service, agent, $100 (annual) ● international, $80 (annual). **Description:** Promotes the study and understanding of the practice, techniques and applications of traditional fine art portraiture and figurative works. Increases the aesthetic and technical knowledge for the practicing artist, aspiring amateur, student artist and the general public. Provides educational resources for members and other interested individuals. **Awards:** Gold Medal Award. **Frequency:** annual. **Type:** medal. **Recipient:** for artists of distinction who have produced bodies of work that epitomizes excellence within the discipline. **Publications:** *The Art of the Portrait*, quarterly. Newsletter. **Price:** included in membership dues ● *International Artist*, bimonthly. Magazine. **Price:** included in membership dues. **Conventions/Meetings:** annual conference.

9466 ■ Print Council of America (PCA)
Dept. of Drawings and Prints
The Metropolitan Museum of Art
1000 Fifth Ave.
New York, NY 10025
E-mail: nadine.orenstein@metmuseum.org
URL: http://www.printcouncil.org
Contact: Dr. Nadine M. Orenstein, Pres.
Founded: 1956. **Members:** 200. **Description:** Museum professionals. Fosters the study and appreciation of new and old prints, drawings, and photographs; stimulates discussion. Sponsors educational programs and research publications; offers placement services. **Publications:** *A Census of Fifteenth-Century Prints in Public Collections in the U.S. and Canada*. Survey ● *A Paper Sample Book* ● *Guidelines for The Lending of Works of Art on Paper* ● *Print Council Index to Oeuvre-Catalogues of Prints by European and American Artists*. Catalogs ● Newsletter, annual. **Price:** available to members only. **Conventions/Meetings:** annual meeting - usually May ● periodic symposium.

9467 ■ Professional Picture Framers Association (PPFA)
3000 Picture Pl.
Jackson, MI 49201
Ph: (517)788-8100
Free: (800)762-9287
Fax: (517)788-8371
E-mail: ppfa@ppfa.com
URL: http://www.pmai.org/index.cfm/ci_id/24438/la_id/1.htm
Contact: Ted Fox, Exec. Dir./Sec.
Founded: 1971. **Members:** 3,500. **Membership Dues:** retailer in U.S. (based on sales volume), $149-$1,800 (annual) ● manufacturer/distributor/consulting firm in U.S. (based on number of employees), $210-$1,600 (annual) ● retailer in Australia (based on sales volume), $65-$1,200 (annual) ● manufacturer/distributor/consulting firm in Australia (based on number of employees), $285-$1,745 (annual) ● retailer in Canada (based on sales volume), $60-$985 (annual) ● manufacturer/distributor/consulting firm in Canada (based on number of employees), $270-$965 (annual) ● retailer in New Zealand, $250 (annual) ● supplier in New Zealand (based on number of employees), $300-$450 (annual). **Staff:** 12. **Budget:** $1,200,000. **Local Groups:** 30. **Multinational. Description:** Individuals, firms, or corporations engaged in the picture framing and fine art businesses (art dealers, manufacturers, wholesalers, importers, and publishers). Provides guidance and service in developing quality craftsmanship in the art of picture framing. Sponsors certification program and national consumer marketing program. Provides education and trade show programming. Offers business and insurance services and products. Researches and disseminates information concerning technical and service problems. Maintains hall of fame and bookstore; compiles statistics. **Libraries: Type:** reference. **Holdings:** 1,000; audiovisuals, books, periodicals. **Awards:** Innovation Award. **Frequency:** annual. **Type:** recognition ● Leadership Award. **Frequency:** annual. **Type:** recognition ● Service Award. **Frequency:** annual. **Type:** recognition. **Telecommunication Services:** electronic mail, tfox@pmai.org. **Councils:** Art and Framing. **Programs:** Certified Picture Framer. **Absorbed:** PPFA Guild. **Publications:** *For Members Only*, 10/year. Provides information to industry suppliers. **Price:** included in membership dues. **Circulation:** 3,500. **Advertising:** accepted. Alternate Formats: online ● *Who's Who in Picture Framing and Fine Art Directory*, annual ● Directory, annual. **Conventions/Meetings:** annual convention and trade show.

9468 ■ Recycled Art Association
Address Unknown since 2007
Founded: 2002. **Members:** 48. **Membership Dues:** member, $35 (annual) ● associate, $65 (annual). **Staff:** 3. **Multinational. Description:** Represents and promotes artists and craftspeople using recycled materials. **Publications:** Newsletter, quarterly. Features news, reviews and events for artists.

9469 ■ The Rock Poster Society (TRPS)
PO Box 20309
Oakland, CA 94620-0309
E-mail: mhohncab@comcast.net
URL: http://www.trps.org
Contact: Marty Hohn, Pres.
Founded: 1998. **Membership Dues:** in U.S., $25 (annual) ● foreign, $35 (annual). **Multinational. Description:** Aims to cultivate interest and public awareness of poster art. Seeks to explore the continuing tradition of rock poster art. Promotes the long-standing relationship between music and graphic art. Acts as a hub of information and resources. Fosters fellowship among members and other poster enthusiasts. **Publications:** Newsletter, quarterly. **Price:** included in membership dues.

9470 ■ Saving and Preserving Arts and Cultural Environments (SPACES)
345 White Rd.
Watsonville, CA 95076
Ph: (831)684-0405
Fax: (831)684-0405
E-mail: jfh@cruzio.com
Contact: Jo Farb Hernandez, Dir.
Founded: 1978. **Staff:** 3. **Budget:** $53,000. **Languages:** English, French, Spanish. **Nonmembership. For-Profit. Description:** Works to document and preserve folk art environments. The group defines folk art environments as "handmade personal spaces" having a component of accumulated objects usually discarded by society and not traditionally considered as materials for the production of art. These environments are usually developed organically and without formal plans by persons not generally considered to be artists, and often represent a life's work. Seeks to: identify or develop state or local organizations to assume responsibility for preserving such sites; develop a national clearinghouse for resources on documenting, preserving, restoring, and maintaining folk art environments; establish a reference library of photographs, oral histories, maps, printed materials, and related documents. Provides lectures to interested classes and organizations; conducts exhibits on folk environments and their artists; disseminates information. Is currently conducting a national survey to locate all existing folk art environments. **Libraries: Type:** by appointment only. **Holdings:** 1,600; articles, books, periodicals. **Subjects:** environmental folk, self taught art. **Publications:** *SPACES: Notes on America's Folk Art Environments*, periodic. Newsletter. Concerned with the identification, documentation, and preservation of folk art environments throughout the country. Profiles folk art environments. **Price:** available to members only. ISSN: 0748-8378. **Circulation:** 500 ● Books ● Bulletin, periodic ● Also publishes postcards.

9471 ■ Silvermine Guild Arts Center (SGAC)
1037 Silvermine Rd.
New Canaan, CT 06840-4398
Ph: (203)966-9700
Fax: (203)966-2763
E-mail: sgac@silvermineart.org
URL: http://www.silvermineart.org
Contact: Pamela Davis, Exec. Dir.
Founded: 1922. **Members:** 2,600. **Membership Dues:** single, $45 (annual) ● family, $75 (annual) ● friend, $125-$249 (annual) ● patron, $250-$499 (annual) ● benefactor, $500-$999 (annual) ● apprentice (silvermine conservator), $1,000-$2,499 (annual) ● master (silvermine conservator), $2,500-$4,999 (annual) ● Borglum Circle (minimum; silvermine conservator), $5,000 (annual). **Staff:** 15. **Budget:** $1,600,000. **Description:** Seeks to foster an appreciation of the arts and to provide education in the arts. Operates the Silvermine School of Art, offering courses of instruction in the visual arts and related areas of study. Maintains gallery for the exhibition of paintings, sculpture, prints, photographs, ceramics, weaving, jewelry, and other crafts. Supports and promotes Guild of artists; conducts social events; also conducts a summer chamber music series. **Awards: Type:** recognition. **Recipient:** for national shows; based on artwork. **Committees:** Artist Admissions; Scholarship. **Formerly:** Silvermine Guild Center for the Arts; (1980) Silvermine Guild of Artists. **Publications:** *Art Beat*, semiannual. Newsletter.

9472 ■ Society for Asian Art (SAA)
Asian Art Museum
200 Larkin St.
San Francisco, CA 94102
Ph: (415)581-3701
Fax: (415)861-2358
E-mail: saa@asianart.org
URL: http://www.societyforasianart.org
Contact: Nazneen Spliedt, Pres.
Founded: 1958. **Members:** 1,200. **Membership Dues:** senior, $30 (annual) ● student, $25 (annual) ● teacher, $40 (annual). **Staff:** 2. **Description:** Supports organization for the Asian Art Museum of San Francisco. Membership includes persons interested in Asian art. Encourages the study and appreciation of Asian art and culture. Sponsors morning and evening lecture series, study groups, and symposium; organizes author lectures, studio visits and hands-on workshops. Manages special interest travel programs. **Committees:** Administration; Development; Education; Financial. **Publications:** *Lotus Leaves*, semiannual. Newsletter. Contains scholarly articles. **Advertising:** accepted ● Newsletter, bimonthly. **Conventions/Meetings:** annual meeting.

9473 ■ Society for the Promotion of Japanese Animation (SPJA)
1733 S Douglass Rd., Ste.G
Anaheim, CA 92806
Ph: (714)937-2994

E-mail: press@spja.com
URL: http://www.spja.org
Contact: Marc Perez, Chm.

Founded: 1992. **Members:** 2,000. **Staff:** 200. **Budget:** $75,000. **Regional Groups:** 1. **Description:** Seeks to promote the art of Japanese animation. Conducts educational, charitable and research programs; compiles statistics; holds competitions. **Awards:** SPJA Industry Award. **Frequency:** annual. **Type:** recognition. **Recipient:** for excellence in Japanese and American animation. **Publications:** *Anime Reference Guide*, annual. Book. Features Japanese animation releases. **Price:** $7.95 each. **Circulation:** 4,000. **Advertising:** accepted ● *Online World of Anime and Manga*. Magazine. Features Japanese animation industry on both sides of the Pacific. Alternate Formats: online. **Conventions/Meetings:** annual trade show (exhibits).

9474 ■ Stencil Artisans League, Inc. (SALI)
PO Box 3109
Los Lunas, NM 87031
Ph: (505)865-9119
Fax: (505)865-9119
E-mail: salihelp@aol.com
URL: http://www.sali.org
Contact: Beth Farnsworth, Pres.

Founded: 1983. **Members:** 2,800. **Membership Dues:** business associate, $195 (annual) ● professional, $100 (annual) ● home-based business, $75 (annual) ● individual, $45 (annual). **Multinational. Description:** Seeks to promote and preserve the art of stenciling and related decorative painting. Provides opportunities for artistic and professional growth. **Computer Services:** Information services, SALI certification. **Telecommunication Services:** electronic mail, beth@sali.org. **Committees:** Certification and Awards; Chapter; Education; News Magazine; Public Relations. **Projects:** SALI Philanthropic. **Publications:** *The Artistic Stenciler*. Magazine.

9475 ■ Sumi-e Society of America (SSA)
c/o Ms. Karen Kurka Jensen, Membership Sec.
2523 Zika Ave. NW
Cedar Rapids, IA 52405
Ph: (703)812-8175
E-mail: eagletouch@gmail.com
URL: http://www.sumiesociety.org
Contact: Ms. Karen Kurka Jensen, Membership Sec.

Founded: 1963. **Members:** 450. **Membership Dues:** regular, $40 (annual) ● supporting, $70 (annual) ● sustaining, $100 (annual) ● sponsor, $130 (annual) ● patron, $160 (annual) ● student, $23 (annual). **Staff:** 15. **Budget:** $25,000. **Regional Groups:** 11. **Description:** Artists and others interested in East Asian brush painting. Encourages display of Asian brush paintings in private or public art galleries; sponsors educational programs. **Libraries: Type:** reference; lending; not open to the public. **Holdings:** 10; archival material, books, photographs, video recordings. **Subjects:** Oriental brush painting. **Awards:** Juried Show Award. **Frequency:** annual. **Type:** recognition. **Computer Services:** Mailing lists. **Boards:** Directors/Officers. **Publications:** *Membership List*, biennial. Membership Directory. **Price:** free for members ● *Sumi-e Exhibition*, annual. Catalog ● *Sumi-e Quarterly*. **Price:** free for members. **Conventions/Meetings:** annual Juried Exhibition - meeting, painting demonstration.

9476 ■ Taos National Society of Watercolorists (TNSW)
PO Box 2943
Taos, NM 87571
E-mail: info@taoswatercolor.org
URL: http://www.taoswatercolor.org
Contact: KC Benson, Pres.

Founded: 1992. **Description:** Represents national watercolorists living in Taos. Promotes the production of professional quality watercolor on both local and national levels. Conducts watercolor workshops and exhibitions in Taos.

9477 ■ Thomas Nast Society (TNS)
c/o Morristown-Morris Township Library
1 Miller Rd.
Morristown, NJ 07960
Ph: (973)538-3473
E-mail: jochem@main.morris.org
URL: http://www.jfpl.org/nast.htm
Contact: Christine Jochem, Contact

Founded: 1986. **Members:** 87. **Membership Dues:** sponsor, $30-$99 (annual) ● patron, $100 (annual). **Budget:** $2,500. **Description:** Individuals interested in the political cartoons and book illustrations of Thomas Nast (1840-1902). Seeks to perpetuate the memory and works of Nast. (Nast is recognized as the creator of the Democratic and Republican party symbols and the image of Uncle Sam. As staff cartoonist for Harper's Weekly, he and his scathing cartoons were credited with the overthrow of the "Tweed Ring" in New York City during the years 1869-72 and helping jail corrupt politician William M. Tweed.). **Publications:** *Journal of the Thomas Nast Society*, annual. Includes bibliographic and scholarly articles related to Thomas Nast's work and life. **Price:** included in membership dues. ISSN: 1535-9328. **Conventions/Meetings:** annual Nast Day Celebration - meeting.

Art History

9478 ■ Historians of British Art (HBA)
c/o Anne Helmreich
10900 Euclid Ave.
Cleveland, OH 44106
E-mail: anne.helmreich@case.edu
URL: http://www.case.edu/artsci/arth/hba
Contact: Anne Helmreich, Contact

Founded: 1992. **Membership Dues:** student, $10 ● professional, $15 ● institution, $100. **Multinational. Description:** Promotes the study and sharing of ideas among those engaged in any type of scholarship or other professional endeavor related to British art and architecture of any time period. Fosters communication among its members and other organizations interested in the history of British art. **Awards:** Book Prize. **Frequency:** annual. **Type:** recognition. **Recipient:** for books on British Art ● Travel Award. **Frequency:** annual. **Type:** recognition. **Recipient:** to a graduate student member. **Affiliated With:** College Art Association. **Publications:** Newsletter, semiannual. Includes information about publications, fellowships and opportunities for the organization. **Price:** included in membership dues. Alternate Formats: online.

9479 ■ Historians of Eighteenth-Century Art and Architecture (HECAA)
2507 Foxwood Dr.
Chapel Hill, NC 27514
Fax: (919)932-6186
E-mail: schroder@duke.edu
URL: http://plaza.ufl.edu/mhyde/hecaa
Contact: Dr. Anne Schroder, Pres.

Founded: 1991. **Members:** 125. **Membership Dues:** regular, $20 ● student, $5. **Description:** Promotes knowledge of all aspects of visual culture through the encouragement of research and publication among its members. Encourages graduate training in the visual culture of the eighteenth century. Facilitates communication among its constituents. **Awards:** Dora Wiebenson Graduate Student Prize. **Frequency:** annual. **Type:** recognition. **Recipient:** for the best graduate student paper. **Affiliated With:** American Society for Eighteenth-Century Studies; College Art Association. **Publications:** Newsletter, semiannual.

9480 ■ Japan Art History Forum (JAHF)
c/o Ms. Sarah Thompson, Treas.
Art of Asia, Oceania and Africa
Museum of Fine Arts, Boston
465 Huntington Ave.
Boston, MA 02115
Ph: (617)369-3223
E-mail: jahf@ku.edu
URL: http://www2.ku.edu/~jahf
Contact: Toshio Watanabe, Pres.

Founded: 1997. **Members:** 260. **Membership Dues:** individual, $10 (annual). **Description:** Promotes the study and understanding of Japanese art history, visual and material culture. Coordinates opportunities for interchange and dialogue among members at exhibitions and symposia of Japanese art and at other conferences in North America. Encourages research and dissemination of research. **Telecommunication Services:** electronic mail, tpwatanabe@aol.com ● electronic mail, sthompson162@mindspring.com.

Artifacts

9481 ■ Early American Industries Association (EAIA)
c/o Elton W. Hall, Exec. Dir.
167 Bakerville Rd.
South Dartmouth, MA 02748-4198
Ph: (508)993-9578
Fax: (508)993-9578
E-mail: eaia@comcast.net
URL: http://www.eaiainfo.org
Contact: Elton W. Hall, Exec. Dir.

Founded: 1933. **Members:** 2,500. **Membership Dues:** individual/institutional, $35 (annual) ● individual with spouse, $50 (annual) ● contributing, $60 (annual) ● sustaining, $100 (annual) ● benefactor, $250 (annual) ● corporate, $500 (annual). **Staff:** 1. **Budget:** $100,000. **Description:** Craftspeople, collectors, museum curators, dealers, libraries, and historians. Encourages improved understanding and appreciation of early American industry in the home, on the farm, in the shop, and on the sea. Seeks to discover, identify, classify, preserve, and exhibit old tools, implements, utensils, instruments, vehicles, and mechanical devices. Maintains publications program to study and record for future use the history of industry in America. **Libraries: Type:** reference. **Holdings:** 5,000; audiovisuals, books, periodicals. **Subjects:** tools, technology, industry, mechanical arts. **Awards:** Research Grants. **Frequency:** annual. **Type:** grant. **Recipient:** for projects related to the Association's purpose. **Publications:** *Directory of American Toolmakers*. Provides a listing of toolmakers in North America to 1900. **Price:** $65.00 ● *Early American Industries Association—Chronicle*, quarterly. Journal. Contains information on the history of tools, trades, and mechanical arts. **Price:** included in membership dues. **Circulation:** 2,600 ● *Early American Industries Association—Membership Directory*, annual. **Price:** included in membership dues. **Circulation:** 2,600. **Advertising:** accepted ● *Shavings*, bimonthly. Newsletter. Provides information on early American industry. **Price:** included in membership dues. **Circulation:** 2,600. **Advertising:** accepted. **Conventions/Meetings:** annual meeting (exhibits).

9482 ■ Historical Society of Early American Decoration (HSEAD)
c/o Ann Stewart, Admin. Asst.
PO Box 30
The Farmer's Museum
Cooperstown, NY 13326
Ph: (607)547-5667
Free: (866)304-7323
E-mail: info@hsead.org
URL: http://www.hsead.org
Contact: Ann Stewart, Admin. Asst.

Founded: 1946. **Members:** 900. **Membership Dues:** applicant, $40 (annual) ● associate, $55 (annual) ● benefactor, $3,000 (annual). **Staff:** 1. **Regional Groups:** 16. **Description:** Craftsmen, historians, researchers, and collectors of early American decorated objects. The areas covered are decorated tinware, furniture, and other articles used in early American homes. Decorating techniques are divided into various classifications: stencilling on tin and wood, country painting, metal leaf painting, ornamental glass, freehand bronze, Victorian floral, and Pontypool painting. Formed to honor the late Mrs. Esther Stevens Brazer, who amassed an extensive collection of patterns, artifacts, and research material pertaining to early American decoration. Has developed standards of craftsmanship for execution of techniques in the various categories of decoration; trains judges. Offers teacher certification program which qualifies applicants in both craftsmanship and teaching methods. Conducts workshops; holds semiannual exhibition. **Committees:** Conservation; Historical Research; Photography; Research; Standards; Teacher Certification. **Formerly:** (1948) Esther Stevens Brazer Guild; (1952) Society of Early American Decoration. **Publications:** *American Painted Tinware, Vol. 1 and Vol. 2*. Book. Research on regional shops with illustrations of identifying characteristics. ● *Antique Decoration - 27 Articles by Esther Stevens Brazer*. Book ● *Decorative Arts: 18th-19th Century* ● *The Decorator*, semiannual. Journal. Contains research articles on various aspects of decorative art as well as those of historical interest. **Price:** included in membership dues; $9.00/issue for nonmembers. **Circulation:** 1,100. **Advertising:** accepted ● Newsletter, semiannual.

9483 ■ Midwest Old Settlers and Threshers Association (MOSTA)
405 E Threshers Rd.
Mount Pleasant, IA 52641
Ph: (319)385-8937
Fax: (319)385-0563
E-mail: info@oldthreshers.org
URL: http://www.oldthreshers.org
Contact: Lennis Moore, CEO

Founded: 1950. **Members:** 39,000. **Staff:** 9. **Budget:** $400,000. **Description:** Persons interested in old steam equipment, threshering machines, gas engines, farm tractors, antique automobiles, narrow gauge railroad, working trains, trolley lines, and other artifacts of early agriculture and pioneer days. Develops a log village, which includes a school house, church, general store, and blacksmith shop; an antique machinery museum is open each summer. Offers specialized educational programs, tours, workshops, slide features, illustrated lectures, films, historical books, exhibits, practicums, and Responsible Social Involvement Program with students at Iowa Wesleyan College. Maintains theatre research center for early day tent, folk, and repertory theatre. Operates hall of fame. Conducts children's services and research programs, compiles statistics on reunion attendees. **Libraries: Type:** open to the public. **Holdings:** 2,000; books. **Subjects:** history, agricultural history, technology. **Awards:** Thresher Award. **Type:** recognition. **Computer Services:** database, closed, in-house list. **Committees:** Education; Entertainment. **Publications:** *Threshers Chaff*, quarterly. Newsletter. **Price:** $5.00/year ● *Threshers Review*, semiannual. Covers upcoming year's reunion. ● Also publishes books and historical magazine. **Conventions/Meetings:** annual Old Threshers Reunion - festival, largest steam show and historic agricultural show in America (exhibits).

9484 ■ National Threshers Association (NTA)
c/o David Schramm, Pres.
22343 Lemoyne Rd.
Luckey, OH 43443
Ph: (419)833-6371
E-mail: daveschramm@earthlink.net
URL: http://nationalthreshers.com
Contact: David Schramm, Pres.

Founded: 1945. **Members:** 2,545. **Membership Dues:** regular, $7 (annual). **Description:** Individuals united to exhibit, display, and operate various types of steam and internal combustion powered equipment and machinery. **Libraries: Type:** open to the public. **Holdings:** photographs. **Awards:** Best Restored Engine. **Frequency:** annual. **Type:** trophy. **Publications:** *Steam-O-Gram*, annual. **Conventions/Meetings:** annual reunion (exhibits) - always last weekend of June, in Wauseon, OH.

9485 ■ Society for Commercial Archeology (SCA)
PO Box 45828
Madison, WI 53744-5828
E-mail: office@sca-roadside.org
URL: http://www.sca-roadside.org
Contact: Carrie Scupholm, Pres.

Founded: 1977. **Members:** 750. **Membership Dues:** individual, $35 (annual) ● contributor, $250 (annual) ● family, institution, $50 (annual) ● donor, $100 (annual) ● sponsor, $500 (annual) ● patron, $1,000 (annual). **Budget:** $30,000. **Description:** Recognizes the unique historical significance of the 20th-century commercial built environment and cultural landscapes of North America, emphasizing the impact of the automobile and the commercial process. Promotes public awareness and appreciation of the recent past; encourages and emphasizes preservation of the commercial built environment and its landscapes and highways, including roadside diners, motels, fast food restaurants, shopping centers, neon signs, auto dealerships, bus stations, movie theaters, billboards, and gas stations. **Telecommunication Services:** electronic mail, president@sca-roadside.org ● electronic mail, membership@sca-roadside.org. **Publications:** *Delaware Valley Diner Tour Guide*. Booklet. **Price:** $10.00 ● *Granite Faces and Concrete Critters: Commercial Archeology in Western South Dakota*. Features detailed descriptions of numerous roadside artifacts. **Price:** $7.00 ● *Roadside America: The Automobile in Design and Culture*. Book. **Price:** $39.95 ● *Wildwood Workbook* ● Journal, semiannual. Includes book reviews. **Price:** included in membership dues; $5.00 for nonmembers ● Newsletter, quarterly. Includes news articles. **Price:** included in membership dues; $5.00/volume for nonmembers; $45.00/complete set for nonmembers. ISSN: 1069-0492. **Conventions/Meetings:** annual meeting and conference, with paper sessions and bus tours (exhibits) ● annual Reno or Bust: Sin and the American Roadside - conference and meeting.

Artists

9486 ■ Adolph and Esther Gottlieb Foundation
380 W Broadway
New York, NY 10012
Ph: (212)226-0581
Fax: (212)226-0584
E-mail: shirsch@gottliebfoundation.org
URL: http://www.gottliebfoundation.org
Contact: Ms. Sheila Ross, Grants Mgr.

Founded: 1976. **Nonmembership. Multinational. Description:** Works to support painters and sculptors. **Awards:** Emergency Grant. **Frequency:** periodic. **Type:** grant. **Recipient:** to visual artists who need assistance for a specific catastrophic emergency ● Individual Support Grant. **Frequency:** annual. **Type:** grant. **Recipient:** for visual artists who have dedicated their lives (at least 20 years) to developing their art, regardless of their level of commercial success.

9487 ■ Allied Artists of America (AAA)
15 Gramercy Park S
New York, NY 10003
Ph: (212)582-6411
E-mail: thomasvalenti@alliedartistsofamerica.org
URL: http://www.alliedartistsofamerica.org
Contact: Ron Beuzenburg, VP

Founded: 1914. **Members:** 1,800. **Membership Dues:** associate, $30 (annual). **Budget:** $42,000. **Description:** Represents professional fine artists, sculptors, and painters interested in advancing American art through art exhibitions. Sponsors art slide programs and art demonstrations. **Libraries: Type:** reference. **Holdings:** archival material. **Subjects:** arts. **Awards:** Allied Artist of America Gold Medal of Honor. **Frequency:** annual. **Type:** medal. **Recipient:** to exhibitor with excellent works ● Allied Artist of America Silver Medal of Honor. **Frequency:** annual. **Type:** medal. **Recipient:** to exhibitor with excellent works. **Committees:** Membership; Presidential Advisory. **Publications:** *Exhibition Catalogue*, annual ● Newsletter, annual. **Conventions/Meetings:** competition ● annual National Fine Arts Exhibition - meeting (exhibits) - always in New York City.

9488 ■ American Abstract Artists (AAA)
194 Powers St.
Brooklyn, NY 11211
E-mail: americanabart@aol.com
URL: http://www.americanabstractartists.org
Contact: Don Voisine, Pres.

Founded: 1936. **Members:** 88. **Membership Dues:** individual, $35 (annual). **Description:** Sculptors and painters. Seeks to foster communication among abstract artists and to exhibit their works. Informs the public of the history and development of abstract art through exhibitions and publications. **Publications:** *American Abstract Artists 50th Anniversary Celebration, 1936-1986*. Catalog ● *American Abstract Artists 50th Anniversary Portfolio Prints, 1986-1987* ● *American Abstract Artists/New Work New Members 1987* ● *American Abstract Artists, North Carolina Museum of Art* ● *American Abstract Artists, 1936-66* ● *American Abstract Artists-60th Anniversary Exhibition 1996* ● *The Early Years* ● *The Language of Abstraction* ● *The Persistence of Abstraction* ● *Pioneers of Abstract Art/ American Abstract Artists 1936-1996* ● *60th Anniversary Print Portfolio, 1997*. **Conventions/Meetings:** lecture, studio visits on abstract art - 5/year.

9489 ■ American Artists Professional League (AAPL)
47 5th Ave.
New York, NY 10003
Ph: (212)645-1345
Fax: (212)645-1345
E-mail: aapl@verizon.com
URL: http://www.americanartistsprofessionalleague.org
Contact: Konrad Hansalik, Pres.

Founded: 1928. **Members:** 1,000. **Membership Dues:** regular, $40 (annual). **Staff:** 1. **Description:** Advances the cause of fine arts in America through the promotion of high standards of beauty, integrity and craftsmanship in painting, sculpture and the graphic arts. **Awards:** AAPL Medal of Honor. **Frequency:** annual. **Type:** medal ● American Artists Fund Scholarship. **Frequency:** annual. **Type:** scholarship ● Director's Award. **Frequency:** annual. **Type:** monetary ● Frank C. Wright Memorial Award. **Frequency:** annual. **Type:** monetary ● President's Award. **Frequency:** annual. **Type:** monetary. **Computer Services:** Mailing lists. **Committees:** Awards; Exhibition; Hanging; Selection; Technical. **Publications:** *Grand National Catalog*, annual. Includes names and addresses of exhibitioners and photographs of exhibitors' work. **Price:** included in membership dues ● Newsletter, semiannual. **Price:** included in membership dues ● Also issues special letters. **Conventions/Meetings:** annual Grand National Exhibition - show.

9490 ■ American Impressionist Society (AIS)
856 5th Pl.
Vero Beach, FL 32962
Ph: (772)569-0597
E-mail: info@americanimpressionistsociety.org
URL: http://www.americanimpressionistsociety.org
Contact: Mary Garrish, Pres.

Founded: 1998. **Membership Dues:** regular, $40 (annual). **Description:** Represents impressionist artists dedicated to support Impressionism. Promotes the appreciation of Impressionism through exhibitions, workshops and other media. Serves as a resource for various impressionist art works by providing links to the websites of its members. **Awards:** Exhibition Awards. **Frequency:** annual. **Type:** recognition. **Recipient:** for the outstanding works of impressionist artists. **Telecommunication Services:** electronic mail, mary@marygarrishfineart.com. **Publications:** Newsletter. Alternate Formats: online.

9491 ■ American Society of Artists (ASA)
PO Box 1326
Palatine, IL 60078
Ph: (312)751-2500 (847)991-4748

E-mail: asoa@webtv.net
URL: http://www.americansocietyofartists.com
Contact: Nancy J. Fregin, Pres.
Founded: 1972. **Members:** 10,000. **Description:** Professional artists and craftspeople. Maintains art referral service and information exchange service. Sponsors art and craft festivals and a Lecture and Demonstration Service; the Special Arts Services Division aids disabled individuals to either practice or enjoy the visual arts. Presents demonstrations in visual arts to better acquaint the public with various processes in different media. **Libraries: Type:** reference. **Holdings:** books. **Subjects:** art. **Committees:** Festival. **Divisions:** American Artisans (Crafts); Associateship; International Artists; Lecture and Demonstration; Patronship; Special Arts Services. **Publications:** *Art Lovers Art and Craft Fair Bulletin*, quarterly. Contains list of shows held by different organizations throughout Illinois. ● *ASA Artisan*, quarterly. Includes list of shows and competitions, and member news.

9492 ■ American Society of Botanical Artists (ASBA)

47 5th Ave.
New York, NY 10003
Ph: (212)691-9080
Free: (866)691-9080
Fax: (212)691-9130
E-mail: asba@aol.com
URL: http://huntbot.andrew.cmu.edu/ASBA/asbotartists.html
Contact: Marilyn A. Garber, Pres.
Founded: 1994. **Members:** 1,100. **Membership Dues:** individual in U.S., $60 (annual) ● individual outside U.S., $75 (annual) ● institutional in U.S., contributor, $150 (annual) ● institutional outside U.S., $175 (annual) ● supporter, $250 (annual) ● sponsor, $500 (annual). **Staff:** 1. **Budget:** $95,000. **Description:** Botanical artists and individuals with an interest in contemporary botanical art. Promotes increased public awareness and appreciation of botanical art. Develops and conducts botanical art education programs; sponsors exhibitions; serves as a clearinghouse on botanical art and art history. Grants are available to members for professional development and educational purposes. **Awards:** Award for Excellence in Botanical Art. **Frequency:** annual. **Type:** recognition ● Award for Service to the Field of Botanical Art. **Frequency:** annual. **Type:** recognition. **Computer Services:** database ● mailing lists. **Publications:** *The Botanical Artist*, quarterly. Newsletter. **Price:** included in membership dues. ISSN: 1523-5165. **Circulation:** 1,000. Alternate Formats: online. **Conventions/Meetings:** annual conference and meeting - 2008 Oct. 30-Nov. 1, Pasadena, CA.

9493 ■ American Society of Contemporary Artists (ASCA)

c/o Harriet FeBland
245 E 63rd St., No. 1803
New York, NY 10021
Ph: (212)759-2215
URL: http://www.anny.org/2/orgs/0050/asca.htm
Contact: Harriet FeBland, Contact
Founded: 1917. **Members:** 100. **Description:** Represents professional fine artists, painters, sculptors, and printmakers in New York City and surrounding areas. Members are elected on the basis of their high level of professional distinction. Conducts discussions, slide lectures, and demonstrations. Contributes art to museums. **Convention/Meeting:** none. **Publications:** none. **Formerly:** (1963) Brooklyn Society of Artists.

9494 ■ American Society of Marine Artists (ASMA)

PO Box 369
Ambler, PA 19002
E-mail: asma@icdc.com
URL: http://www.americansocietyofmarineartists.com
Contact: Richard Moore, Pres.
Founded: 1978. **Members:** 640. **Membership Dues:** regular, $45 (annual) ● artist/fellow, $75 (annual) ● supporting, $100 (annual) ● patron, $500 (annual). **Description:** Represents artists, historians, and art collectors; art galleries. Promotes American maritime activities and heritage by publicizing members' artwork. Encourages marine artists to hold the highest professional standards. Sponsors biennial museum exhibition of member artists' work. **Awards:** Iron Man Award. **Type:** recognition. **Recipient:** for a member who contributes most to the society. **Publications:** *ASMA News*, quarterly. Newsletter. Features local and national marine art news and information about art exhibitions and exhibition opportunities. ● Catalogs. Includes museum exhibits. **Conventions/Meetings:** annual conference.

9495 ■ American Society of Portrait Artists (ASOPA)

PO Box 230216
Montgomery, AL 36106
Free: (800)62-ASOPA
E-mail: info@asopa.com
URL: http://www.asopa.com
Contact: Carl Samson, Chm.
Founded: 1987. **Members:** 2,000. **Membership Dues:** contributing patron, $50 (annual) ● sustaining patron, $100 (annual) ● sponsoring patron, $250 (annual). **Staff:** 2. **Description:** Works to advance the art of portraiture and support portrait artists. Provides a forum for artists to exchange ideas and techniques. Holds competitions. **Awards:** John Singer Sargent Award. **Frequency:** annual. **Type:** recognition. **Recipient:** for an outstanding portrait painter. **Computer Services:** database ● mailing lists. **Publications:** *The Portrait Signature*, quarterly. Journal. **Conventions/Meetings:** annual Portrait Arts Festival - convention and seminar, demonstrations, panel discussion computation.

9496 ■ Art Students League of New York

215 W 57th St.
New York, NY 10019
Ph: (212)247-4510
Fax: (212)541-7024
E-mail: info@artstudentsleague.org
URL: http://www.theartstudentsleague.org
Contact: Salvatore Barbieri, Pres.
Founded: 1875. **Membership Dues:** regular, $35 (annual). **Description:** Founding members of the Art Students' League of New York, the New York Architectural League, the Society of American Artists, and other art societies. Provides exhibition space, studios, and offices to members. Sponsors lectures, exhibitions, and related activities. **Libraries: Type:** reference. **Holdings:** books. **Subjects:** arts. **Awards:** The Art Students League Grant. **Frequency:** annual. **Type:** grant. **Recipient:** to all students in full time and part time classes ● The Art Students League Scholarship. **Frequency:** annual. **Type:** scholarship. **Recipient:** to all students in full time and part time classes. **Funds:** Building and Development. **Formerly:** (1998) American Fine Arts Society. **Publications:** *Linea: The Journal of the Arts Students League of New York*, 3/year. Includes news, exhibition reviews and essays written by artists. **Conventions/Meetings:** annual meeting.

9497 ■ Arthur Szyk Society

1200 Edgehill Dr.
Burlingame, CA 94010
Ph: (650)343-9588
Fax: (650)579-6014
E-mail: info@szyk.org
URL: http://www.szyk.org
Contact: Dr. Sander Stadtler, Pres.
Founded: 1991. **Members:** 100. **Membership Dues:** individual, $36 (annual) ● student, $18 (annual) ● institution, $250 (annual) ● donor, $500 (annual) ● sponsor, $2,000 (annual) ● patron, $5,000 (annual) ● sustainer, $10,000 (annual) ● citizen soldier, $20,000 (annual). **Staff:** 2. **Description:** Individuals interested in renewing the popularity of Arthur Szyk (1894-1951), artist, cartoonist, and illustrator. Promotes the values of justice, equality, and freedom that Szyk portrayed in his work. Collects and disseminates information on the artist's life and works. Organizes exhibits; operates speakers' bureau. Future plans to raise public awareness of Szyk's works include publication of a biography, production of a television mini-series and feature film, and a scholarship for young artists. Travels with an exhibition to college campuses. **Libraries: Type:** reference. **Holdings:** 10; archival material, artwork, books, clippings, monographs, periodicals. **Subjects:** the life, art and personal works of Arthur Szyk, Julia Szyk. **Computer Services:** database, images of Szyk's original works of art. **Formerly:** (1994) Historic Art's Arthur Szyk Society. **Publications:** Newsletter, semiannual. **Price:** $50.00/year. **Circulation:** 1,000. **Conventions/Meetings:** semiannual Art Exhibit - meeting.

9498 ■ Artists Helping Artists (Aha!)

300 Redwood Dr.
Santa Cruz, CA 95060
Ph: (831)457-2476
E-mail: ahawonders88@yahoo.com
URL: http://www.artistshelpingartists.org
Contact: Glen Horton, Founder
Membership Dues: Round Table, $20 (annual) ● Creative Vision, $50 (annual) ● Renaissance, $100 (annual). **Multinational. Description:** Works to connect artists, arts leaders and arts organizations to other artists, leaders and organizations. Ignites the imagination and vision of artists and arts leaders. Enhances culture and heals society through art forms and creative innovation. Fosters greater arts community across the world. **Awards:** Creative Vision Award. **Frequency:** quarterly. **Type:** recognition. **Recipient:** to deserving artists, innovative arts leaders and arts humanitarians. **Publications:** *The Creative Bullet*. Magazine. **Price:** included in membership dues. Alternate Formats: online ● *The Creative Line*, semiannual. Magazine. **Circulation:** 50,000.

9499 ■ Artists Space (AS)

38 Greene St., 3rd Fl.
New York, NY 10013
Ph: (212)226-3970
Fax: (212)966-1434
E-mail: info@artistsspace.org
URL: http://www.artistsspace.org
Contact: Benjamin Weil, Exec. Dir.
Founded: 1972. **Members:** 40. **Membership Dues:** best friend, $150 (annual) ● friend, $50 (annual) ● inner space (single), $375 (annual) ● inner space (couple), $500 (annual) ● director's circle, $1,500 (annual). **Staff:** 5. **Budget:** $500,000. **Description:** Responds to diverse needs of emerging artists in New York. Provides exhibition opportunities as well as audience access to current art work. Coordinates bi-monthly exhibitions and events. Maintains photo CD registry of artists who are not represented by galleries; sponsors video programs and film screenings. Offers CV internship that allows students to earn course credit. **Libraries: Type:** reference. **Holdings:** 3,120; audiovisuals, software. **Subjects:** contemporary art. **Awards:** Independent Project Grants. **Frequency:** 3/year. **Type:** grant. **Recipient:** for artists who present their work in non-commercial, non-institutional venues. **Computer Services:** database, artist's file. **Affiliated With:** Media Alliance; National Association of Artists' Organizations. **Formerly:** Committee for the Visual Arts; (1984) Committee for the Visual Arts/Artists Space. **Publications:** *Artists Space Pamphlet*, 5/year. Pamphlets. **Price:** included in membership dues; free for artists. **Circulation:** 9,000 ● *5000 Artists Return to Artist's Space: 25 Years*. Book. **Price:** $25.00 plus tax ● Catalog.

9500 ■ ArtTable

116 John St., Ste.822
New York, NY 10038
Ph: (212)343-1735
Fax: (212)343-1430
E-mail: women@arttable.org
URL: http://www.arttable.org
Contact: Dena Muller, Exec. Dir.
Founded: 1981. **Members:** 1,600. **Staff:** 7. **Budget:** $400,000. **Regional Groups:** 4. **Description:** Invitational organization for women leaders in the visual arts profession. Seeks to create understanding of the field and enrich the cultural life of the society. Creates forums for idea exchange. Sponsors educational programs. **Computer Services:** Mailing lists. **Publi-**

cations: *ArtTable News*, semiannual. Newsletter. **Price:** free, for members only. **Circulation:** 950.

9501 ■ Black Gold Group
c/o Windsor Artworks
123 Cedar Landing Rd.
Windsor, NC 27983
Ph: (252)794-9764
Fax: (252)794-8477
E-mail: info@marvinsin.com
URL: http://www.marvinsin.com
Contact: Marvin Sin, Pres.
Founded: 1989. **Members:** 350. **Description:** African-American artists. Provides support and technical assistance to artists. **Awards: Type:** recognition. **Publications:** *Black Gold National Shoppers' Guide*, biennial. Book ● Directory, biennial. **Conventions/Meetings:** conference ● trade show - 3/year.

9502 ■ Federation of Modern Painters and Sculptors (FMPS)
c/o Anneli Arms
113 Greene St.
New York, NY 10012
Ph: (212)966-4864
Fax: (212)966-4864
E-mail: aarms2001@yahoo.com
Contact: Anneli Arms, Contact
Founded: 1940. **Members:** 50. **Membership Dues:** individual (sponsored by existing members), $30 (annual). **Local Groups:** 1. **Description:** Professional painters and sculptors, working only in the U.S.A., united to promote the individual diversity and cultural interests of artists working in the U.S., facilitate exhibition of their work, and improve their professional status. Holds group exhibitions, and film showings. Is active in legislation and causes for artists' equities. **Libraries: Type:** reference. **Holdings:** archival material. **Publications:** Catalog, 10/year. **Conventions/Meetings:** quarterly lecture ● symposium.

9503 ■ Fractured Atlas
248 W 35th St., Ste.1202
New York, NY 10001
Ph: (212)277-8020
Fax: (212)277-8025
E-mail: helpdesk@fracturedatlas.org
URL: http://www.fracturedatlas.org
Contact: Amy Wrzesniewski, Chair
Membership Dues: single, $75 (annual) ● partner, $125 (annual) ● family, $225 (annual) ● emerging organization, $150 (annual) ● small organization, $300 (annual) ● mid-sized organization, $500 (annual). **Description:** Provides artists with services, tools and resources that enhance fiscal stability and creative autonomy. Provides low-cost healthcare options for artists in need. Assists artists in promoting projects and events. **Publications:** Newsletter, quarterly. Alternate Formats: online.

9504 ■ Friends-in-Art of American Council of the Blind (FIA)
c/o American Council of the Blind
1155 15th St. NW, Ste.1004
Washington, DC 20005
Ph: (202)467-5081
Free: (800)424-8666
Fax: (202)467-5085
E-mail: info@acb.org
URL: http://www.acb.org
Contact: Mitch Pomerantz, Pres.
Members: 200. **Description:** Blind and visually impaired artists and art enthusiasts. Promotes access to the arts by blind and visually impaired persons. **Affiliated With:** American Council of the Blind. **Publications:** *Log of the Bridgetender*, quarterly. Newsletter. **Conventions/Meetings:** annual conference (exhibits).

9505 ■ Graphic Artists Guild (The Guild)
32 Broadway, Ste.1114
New York, NY 10004-1612
Ph: (212)791-3400
Fax: (212)791-0333
E-mail: admin@gag.org
URL: http://gag.org
Contact: Ms. Patricia McKiernan, Admin. Dir.
Founded: 1967. **Members:** 2,400. **Membership Dues:** student, retired, $75 (annual) ● standard associate, $170 (annual) ● professional, $200 (annual). **Staff:** 4. **National Groups:** 8. **Multinational. Description:** Professional graphic artists who work in the disciplines of illustration, graphic design, surface design, computer graphics, and cartoons, and create work for national magazines, newspaper syndicates, books, television, advertising, corporate and promotional materials. Aims to: raise the business and ethical standards in the industry; provide legal and educational services to members; increase public appreciation of graphic artists as professionals. Maintains professional discipline meetings and provides professional education services for each chapter. **Awards: Type:** recognition. **Committees:** Advocacy; Educational Outreach; Membership. **Absorbed:** (1993) Cartoonist Guild of New York. **Formerly:** (1994) National Graphic Artists Guild. **Publications:** *Graphic Artists Guild Handbook: Pricing & Ethical Guidelines*, biennial. Contains information about professional ethics and business standards. **Price:** included in membership dues; $34.95 for nonmembers, plus shipping and handling ● *Guild News*, bimonthly. Newsletter. **Price:** included in membership dues. **Circulation:** 2,400. **Advertising:** accepted. **Conventions/Meetings:** conference and convention.

9506 ■ International Artists Network (IAN)
Address Unknown since 2007
Founded: 1963. **Members:** 18,000. **Description:** Poets, performance artists, graphic artists, painters, photographers, musicians, and artists whose work has been reproduced in book or magazine form. Promotes communication among artists. Develops exhibitions for artists; opposes exhibitions charging entry fees. Forms ad hoc political action committees. Compiles statistics; operates speakers' bureau. **Libraries: Type:** reference. **Holdings:** archival material. **Subjects:** correspondence art, eternal network, mail art, exhibition catalogues, stamp art. **Affiliated With:** National Postal Arts Association. **Formerly:** Eternal Artists Network; (1963) New York Correspondence School. **Publications:** *List exhibitions*. Directories ● Books. **Conventions/Meetings:** periodic conference (exhibits).

9507 ■ International Society of Copier Artists (ISCA)
759 Pres. St., No. 2H
Brooklyn, NY 11215
Ph: (718)638-3264 (845)687-7769
E-mail: isca4art2b@aol.com
Contact: Louise Neaderland, Dir.
Founded: 1981. **Members:** 100. **Staff:** 1. **Budget:** $6,000. **Description:** Artists in Australia, England, Federal Republic of Germany, Finland, Italy, Japan, Netherlands, Philippines, and Switzerland who use the photocopier as a creative tool, alone or with other mediums to create fine prints and artists books. Collectors include libraries, museums, and corporations. Works to establish electrostatic prints, bookwork multiples, and other unique pieces as legitimate and collectible works of art. Arranges international traveling exhibition of xerographic prints and book works. Seeks to introduce the copier to elementary and secondary classrooms. Sponsors workshops, seminars, and speakers' bureau, and traveling exhibition of ISCA graphics. **Libraries: Type:** reference. **Holdings:** artwork, biographical archives. **Computer Services:** Mailing lists. **Publications:** *ISCA Invitational Book Arts Annual & Traveling Exhibition* ● *ISCA Quarterly*. Contains original xerographic prints and bookworks created and printed by member artists. ISSN: 0741-2940. **Circulation:** 150.

9508 ■ Jussi Bjorling Society - USA (JBS-USA)
c/o Laura Homonnay-Demilio
2354 Buena Vista Ave.
Pittsburgh, PA 15218
E-mail: demiliol@upmc.edu
URL: http://www.jussibjorlingsociety.com
Contact: Daniel Shea, Pres.
Membership Dues: individual, $35 (annual) ● family, $50 (annual) ● founder, $100 (annual) ● life, $1,000. **Description:** Collects and disseminates information on the life and career of Swedish opera singer Jussi Bjorling. Fosters understanding and appreciation of Jussi Bjorling's career by promoting vocal music, developing educational programs and offering scholarships. Facilitates sharing and exchange of information with local and international opera groups and other related associations. **Publications:** Journal. **Price:** included in membership dues ● Newsletter. **Price:** included in membership dues.

9509 ■ Landscape Artists International (LAI)
c/o Karl Eric Leitzel, Founder/Dir.
Karl Eric Leitzel Studio
155 Murray School Ln.
Spring Mills, PA 16875
Ph: (814)422-8461
E-mail: karl@keleitzel.com
URL: http://l-a-i.com
Contact: Karl Eric Leitzel, Founder/Dir.
Membership Dues: regular, $20 (annual). **Multinational. Description:** Fosters appreciation of landscape-oriented art. Promotes the careers of its member artists. Encourages communication and cooperation among members.

9510 ■ Midmarch Associates (MA)
300 Riverside Dr.
New York, NY 10025-5239
Ph: (212)666-6990
Fax: (212)865-5510
Contact: Cynthia Navaretta, Exec. Dir.
Founded: 1972. **Staff:** 3. **Budget:** $75,000. **Nonmembership. Description:** Women in the arts, women's studies groups, public and university libraries, and museums. Organizes conferences, exhibitions, and symposia. Sponsors research programs; compiles statistics; publishes books on the arts. **Libraries: Type:** by appointment only. **Holdings:** 300; archival material, articles, books, periodicals, photographs. **Subjects:** women artists. **Affiliated With:** College Art Association; Women's Caucus for Art. **Also Known As:** Midmarch Arts Press. **Publications:** *Artists and Their Cats*. Book. **Price:** $10.00 each, plus shipping and handling ● *Auroras of the Autumn*. Book. **Price:** $22.00 each, plus shipping and handling ● *Camera Fiends & Kodak Girls: Women in Photography (2 Volumes)*. Book. **Price:** $14.90 for volume 1, plus shipping and handling; $18.00 for volume 2, plus shipping and handling ● *Craft and Concept: The Rematerialization of the Art Object*. Book. **Price:** $28.00 each, plus shipping and handling ● *Epicenter: Essays on North American Art*. Book. **Price:** $25.00 each, plus shipping and handling ● *Expanding Circles: Women, Art & Community*. Book. **Price:** $22.00 each, plus shipping and handling ● *The First Wife's Tale: Louise Straus Ernst*. Book. **Price:** $22.00 each, plus shipping and handling ● *Gumbo YaYa: Anthology Contemporary African-American Women Artists*. Book. **Price:** $35.00 each, plus shipping and handling ● *Howardena Pindell: The Heart of the Question*. Book. **Price:** $14.00 each, plus shipping and handling ● *Joanna Frueh: Retrospective - Her Life & Work*. Book. **Price:** $20.00 each, plus shipping and handling ● *The Lady Architects: Howe, Manning & Almy*. Book. **Price:** $11.50 each, plus shipping and handling ● *Michelangelo and Me - Six Years in My Italian Haven*. Book. **Price:** $14.00 each, plus shipping and handling ● *Modernism and Beyond: Women Artists of the Northwest*. Book. **Price:** $15.00 each, plus shipping and handling ● *Mutiny & The Mainstream: Talk That Changed Art*. Book. **Price:** $22.00 each, plus shipping and handling ● *Parallels: 3 Artists/47 Women Poets*. Book. **Price:** $12.00 each, plus shipping and handling ● *Postmodern Heretics: Catholic Imagination in Contemporary Art*. Book. **Price:** $24.00 each, plus shipping and handling ● *Voices From the Past: 1970s Letters From Women Architects*. Book. **Price:** $24.00 each, plus shipping and handling ● *What is Theater: A Novella in Verse*. Book. **Price:** $15.00 each, plus shipping

and handling ● *Whirling Round the Sun*. Book. **Price:** $12.00 each, plus shipping and handling ● *Women Artists of the World*. Book. **Price:** $30.00 each, plus shipping and handling ● Art of the 1930s/Tarnished Silver/Sight Lines. **Conventions/Meetings:** annual conference (exhibits) - usually February ● symposium, held in conjunction with the Women's Caucus for Art.

9511 ■ National Artists Equity Association (NAEA)
c/o Artists Equity
PO Box HG
Pacific Grove, CA 93950
Ph: (831)479-7226
E-mail: duffyart@sbcglobal.net
URL: http://www.artists-equity.org
Contact: Michael Duffy, Contact

Founded: 1947. **Members:** 600. **Membership Dues:** active, $40 (annual). **Staff:** 1. **Local Groups:** 2. **Description:** Professional society of visual artists. Seeks to: promote and protect the interests of visual arts professionals; advocate for appropriate legislation to benefit the profession; safeguard against abuses to the artist in dealings with persons or organizations connected directly or indirectly with the visual arts. The educational and charitable arm of the association is called the Artists Equity Fund. Offers fine art insurance, group health and life insurance. **Convention/Meeting:** none. **Formerly:** (1984) Artists Equity Association.

9512 ■ National Association of Artists' Organizations (NAAO)
308 Prince St., Ste.270
St. Paul, MN 55101
Ph: (651)294-0907
E-mail: info@naao.net
URL: http://www.naao.net
Contact: Sandy Agustin, Exec. Dir.

Founded: 1982. **Members:** 700. **Membership Dues:** individual, organization (income under 30,000), $40 (annual) ● individual, organization (income from 30,000 to 100,000), $60 (annual) ● individual, organization (income from 100,001 to 250,000), $75 (annual) ● individual, organization (income from 250,001 to 500,000), $100 (annual) ● individual, organization (income over 500,000), $150 (annual). **Staff:** 3. **Budget:** $400,000. **Regional Groups:** 6. **Description:** Contemporary art centers and individuals committed to support artists' art works. Serves as clearinghouse for information on legislation and activities of interest to artist organizations. Promotes public awareness of the role of artists organizations; provides technical assistance; conducts networking among artists organizations. **Libraries: Type:** reference. **Holdings:** archival material. **Computer Services:** Mailing lists. **Publications:** *Directory: Organizing Artists*, annual. Contains listings of full and associate members. **Price:** $25.00/copy ● *NAAO Bulletin*, bimonthly ● *NAAO Field Guide*, annual. Journal. **Conventions/Meetings:** periodic conference and workshop (exhibits).

9513 ■ National Association of Independent Artists (NAIA)
72 Douglas St.
Homosassa, FL 34446
E-mail: michaelkopald@naia-artists.org
URL: http://naia-artists.org
Contact: Michael Kopald, Chm.

Founded: 1995. **Membership Dues:** single artist, $95 (annual) ● generous artist, $130-$299 (annual) ● benefactor artist, $300 (annual). **Description:** Enhances the economic well-being of people who exhibit their work at high quality outdoor and indoor art and fine craft shows. Expands public awareness, appreciation and acquisition of fine art and fine craft. **Computer Services:** Information services, arts and artists gallery ● online services, NAIA survey. **Publications:** Newsletter. Alternate Formats: online.

9514 ■ National Association of Women Artists (NAWA)
80 5th Ave., Ste.1405
New York, NY 10011
Ph: (212)675-1616 (212)675-8257
Fax: (212)675-1616
E-mail: office@nawanet.org
URL: http://www.nawanet.org
Contact: Linda Pedersen, Exec. Dir.

Founded: 1889. **Members:** 800. **Membership Dues:** artist, $100 (annual). **Staff:** 3. **Description:** Professional women artists (painters in oil, acrylic, watercolor, and paper works; sculptors; printmakers; computer artists; and photographers). Sponsors art exhibitions and education programs. **Libraries: Type:** open to the public. **Subjects:** miscellaneous. **Awards:** Anna Walinska Memorial Scholarship. **Frequency:** annual. **Type:** scholarship. **Recipient:** for members only. **Committees:** Awards; Oil, Paper Works, Printmaking and Sculpture, Computer Art, Photography; Traveling Painting Exhibitions; Traveling Printmaking Exhibitions. **Formerly:** Association of Women Painters and Sculptors; Women's Art Club of the City of New York. **Publications:** *A View of One's Own*. Brochure ● *The Enduring Figure 1890s-1970s: Sixteen Sculptors from the National Association of Women Artists* ● *MEN*. Brochure ● *National Association of Women Artists—Annual Exhibition Catalog*. Lists members, exhibiting members, and those receiving awards; includes black-and-white reproductions of prize-winning works. **Price:** included in membership dues. **Advertising:** accepted ● *National Association of Women Artists—News*, semiannual. Newsletter. Includes notices of exhibitions, shows, publications, awards, and corporate and museum purchases of members. ● *NAWA News*, semiannual. Newsletter. Includes news, announcements and events of NAWA. Alternate Formats: online ● *One Hundred Years - A Centennial Celebration of the National Association of Women Artists* ● *Works of the National Association of Women Artists in the USA*. **Conventions/Meetings:** semiannual meeting - always spring and fall, in New York City ● annual meeting - always in New York City.

9515 ■ National Cartoonists Society (NCS)
341 N Maitland Ave., Ste.130
Maitland, FL 32751
Ph: (407)647-8839
Fax: (407)629-2502
E-mail: becca@crowsegal.com
URL: http://www.reuben.org
Contact: Jeff Keane, Pres.

Founded: 1946. **Members:** 560. **Membership Dues:** retired, $50 (annual) ● full, $125 (annual) ● associate, $250 (annual). **Staff:** 1. **Regional Groups:** 8. **Description:** Professional society of cartoonists; associate members are editors, writers, and persons with an interest in cartooning and/or cartoonists. Stimulates interest in cartooning by cooperating with established schools and encouraging students. Prepares exhibits of original cartoons for schools and museums; assists governmental and charitable institutions; maintains hall of fame. Provides financial or professional aid to needy, sick, or incapacitated cartoonists. **Awards:** Milton Caniff Lifetime Achievement Award. **Frequency:** annual. **Type:** recognition. **Recipient:** for outstanding contributions to the art form ● Rueben Award. **Frequency:** annual. **Type:** recognition. **Recipient:** to the outstanding cartoonist of the year ● Silver Plaque Award. **Type:** recognition. **Recipient:** to a cartoonist who excels in individual categories of cartooning ● T-Square. **Type:** recognition. **Recipient:** for outstanding dedication or service to the profession. **Committees:** Education; Ethics; Exhibition. **Sections:** Advertising; Animation; Comic Books; Editorial; Gags; Humor Strips; Sports; Story Strips; Syndicated Panels. **Publications:** *The Cartoonist*, periodic. Newsletter. **Price:** available to members only ● *National Cartoonists Society Album*, quadrennial. Contains history of NCS as well as biographies, photographs, and sample art works of member cartoonists. **Price:** included in membership dues; $50.00/copy for nonmembers. **Advertising:** accepted. **Conventions/Meetings:** annual Reuben Awards - meeting - every spring.

9516 ■ National Society of Artists (NSA)
PO Box 1885
Dickinson, TX 77539-1885
Ph: (281)337-4232 (281)309-0239
E-mail: rmorris@houston.rr.com
URL: http://www.nsartists.org
Contact: Ray Morris, Pres.

Founded: 1985. **Members:** 90. **Membership Dues:** individual, $30 (annual) ● life, $150 ● spouse, $5 (annual) ● associate, $10 (annual) ● patron, $50 (annual) ● corporate, $250 (annual). **Staff:** 4. **Description:** Sponsors annual national juried art show, 2 annual judged membership shows, monthly demonstrations and workshops. Maintains library of paintings and photos from previous shows. Conducts educational programs; provides children's services. **Awards:** National Society of Artists Signature Membership Award. **Frequency:** annual. **Type:** recognition. **Recipient:** for members. **Publications:** Newsletter ● Membership Directory. **Conventions/Meetings:** monthly meeting - every 4th Monday, except June, July, and August.

9517 ■ National Society of Mural Painters (NSMP)
450 W 31st St., 7th Fl.
New York, NY 10001
Ph: (212)244-2800
E-mail: info@nationalsocietyofmuralpainters.com
URL: http://nationalsocietyofmuralpainters.com
Contact: Jeff Greene, Pres.

Founded: 1895. **Members:** 117. **Membership Dues:** regular, $45 (annual) ● student, $25 (annual). **Description:** Professional muralists working in mural techniques, including oil, tempera, acrylic on canvas, fresco, mosaic, etched and stained glass, and terrazzo, metal techniques, and sculptured walls. Promotes high standards in mural painting and decoration. Assists architects in incorporating fine mural design into architectural environments. Promotes cooperation and interchange among muralists, as well as national pride in the tradition of art for public space. Encourages education in understanding of mural composition and techniques. Provides information on prices per square foot for various projects, and interior and exterior wall treatments. Sponsors design exhibitions. **Telecommunication Services:** electronic mail, info@evergreene.com. **Committees:** Education and Exhibition; Membership; Professional Practice; Public Relations. **Publications:** *Exhibition Catalogs* ● *National Society of Mural Painters Newsletter*, periodic ● Brochure, quarterly. **Price:** free. **Circulation:** 200. **Advertising:** accepted. **Conventions/Meetings:** Four-Day Symposium and Centennial Exhibition (exhibits) ● quarterly meeting (exhibits) - always in New York City.

9518 ■ National Society of Painters in Casein and Acrylic (NSPCA)
969 Catasauqua Rd.
Whitehall, PA 18052
Ph: (610)264-7472
URL: http://www.bright.net/~paddy-o/art/nspca.htm
Contact: Douglas Wiltraut, Pres.

Founded: 1952. **Members:** 125. **Membership Dues:** associate, $25 (annual). **Description:** Limited to 125 elected professional artists working in casein and acrylics. Provides artists the opportunity to exhibit works regardless of style, "school", or subject matter. **Conventions/Meetings:** annual meeting (exhibits) - usually March.

9519 ■ NURTUREart Non-Profit
910 Grand St.
Brooklyn, NY 11211
Ph: (718)782-7755
E-mail: gallery@nurtureart.org
URL: http://www.nurtureart.org
Contact: Karen Marston, Exec. Dir.

Founded: 1997. **Members:** 350. **Staff:** 15. **Multinational. Description:** Fine artists, curators and volunteers. Strives to support and provide opportunities for visual artists and curators who currently lack the resources to become full-time, self-supporting professionals. Mounts exhibitions and presents educational programs for public and art professionals. **Subgroups:** MUSE FUSE.

9520 ■ Oil Painters of America (OPA)
PO Box 2488
Crystal Lake, IL 60039-2488
Ph: (815)356-5987 (847)934-1721
Fax: (815)356-5987
E-mail: mail@oilpaintersofamerica.com
URL: http://www.oilpaintersofamerica.com
Contact: Kathryn Beligratis, Exec. Dir.
Founded: 1991. **Membership Dues:** associate, signature, supporting, $60 (annual). **Description:** Represents the interests of individuals committed to the preservation of representational art. Promotes understanding and appreciation of art, with emphasis on traditional oil painting. Supports the education process through scholarships, workshops and exhibitions of art. **Publications:** *Brushstrokes*, quarterly. Newsletter. Alternate Formats: online ● Catalogs, annual. Contains pictures of paintings which were featured during the association's national exhibitions. **Conventions/Meetings:** annual show (exhibits) - 2009 May 1-31, Santa Fe, NM.

9521 ■ Pen and Brush (P&B)
16 E 10th St.
New York, NY 10003
Ph: (212)475-3669
Fax: (212)475-6018
E-mail: info@penandbrush.org
URL: http://www.penandbrush.org
Contact: Janice Sands, Exec. Dir.
Founded: 1893. **Members:** 270. **Membership Dues:** resident artist, $275 (annual) ● non-resident artist, $200 (annual) ● junior, $100 (annual) ● associate, $150 (annual). **Staff:** 2. **Budget:** $220,000. **Description:** Represents professional women writers, artists, sculptors, craftspersons, and musicians. Holds exhibitions of paintings, sculpture, and crafts; offers poetry, prose, and playwrighting workshops and readings. Conducts educational seminars, art classes, lectures, demonstrations, conference and concerts. **Libraries: Type:** reference. **Holdings:** 1,200. **Subjects:** women's literature. **Awards: Frequency:** monthly. **Type:** scholarship. **Publications:** *P&B Bulletin*, monthly. **Price:** free. **Circulation:** 500. **Conventions/Meetings:** biennial conference ● Playwriting, Poetry and Prose - workshop (exhibits) - 7/year.

9522 ■ The Print Center (TPC)
1614 Latimer St.
Philadelphia, PA 19103
Ph: (215)735-6090
Fax: (215)735-5511
E-mail: info@printcenter.org
URL: http://www.printcenter.org
Contact: Ashley Peel Pinkham, Asst. Dir.
Founded: 1915. **Members:** 1,500. **Membership Dues:** student, $30 (annual) ● artist/individual, $40 (annual) ● contributing, $75 (annual) ● sustaining, $150 (annual) ● collector, $300 (annual). **Staff:** 4. **Budget:** $415,000. **Multinational. Description:** Artists, collectors, and others interested in printmaking and photography. Encourages contemporary printmaking and photography through educational and service programs. Houses 3 galleries and maintains gallery store. **Computer Services:** Mailing lists. **Formerly:** (1998) Print Club. **Publications:** *Annual Competition Catalog*, annual ● *NewsPrint*, biennial. Newsletter. **Circulation:** 2,000. **Advertising:** accepted.

9523 ■ Professional Association of Comics Entertainment Retailers (PACER)
Address Unknown since 2007
Founded: 1994. **Members:** 100. **Membership Dues:** retailer, $250 (annual). **Description:** Represents comic book store owners and suppliers. **Computer Services:** database ● mailing lists ● online services, BBS. **Telecommunication Services:** electronic bulletin board. **Publications:** *Pacer Newsletter*, monthly. **Conventions/Meetings:** annual board meeting ● annual meeting.

9524 ■ Silk Painters International (SPIN)
6806 Trexler Rd.
Lanham, MD 20706
Ph: (301)474-7347
Fax: (301)441-2395
E-mail: spin@silkpainters.org
URL: http://www.silkpainters.org
Contact: Diane Tuckman, Exec. Dir.
Membership Dues: resident in U.S., $30 (annual) ● supporting in U.S., $60 (annual) ● corporate, sustaining, $150 (annual) ● international, $45 (annual) ● supporting - international, $75 (annual). **Multinational. Description:** Aims to establish silk painting as a recognized art form. Encourages and promotes the collection, display, and production of silk art. Supports eclectic artistic expression on silk painting. **Awards:** SPIN Artist of the Month. **Frequency:** monthly. **Type:** recognition. **Recipient:** for the most outstanding art work by a member. **Publications:** *The Silkworm*, quarterly. Newsletter. **Price:** included in membership dues; $3.00/back issue (in U.S., plus shipping and handling); $4.50/back issue (outside U.S., plus shipping and handling). **Advertising:** accepted ● Articles. Alternate Formats: online.

9525 ■ Society of American Mosaic Artists (SAMA)
PO Box 624
Ligonier, PA 15658
Ph: (724)238-3087
Free: (866)902-SAMA
Fax: (724)238-3973
E-mail: info@americanmosaics.org
URL: http://www.americanmosaics.org
Contact: Ms. Dawnmarie Zimmerman, Exec. Dir.
Membership Dues: general, $45 (annual) ● professional, $65 (annual) ● corporate, $150 (annual) ● patron, $250 (annual). **Description:** Promotes mosaic art and the advancement of mosaic artists through research, education and networking. **Publications:** *Groutline*, quarterly. Newsletter. **Price:** included in membership dues. Alternate Formats: online.

9526 ■ Society of Animal Artists (SAA)
47 5th Ave.
New York, NY 10003
Ph: (212)741-2880
Fax: (212)741-2262
E-mail: admin@societyofanimalartists.com
URL: http://www.societyofanimalartists.com
Contact: Leslie Delgyer, Pres.
Founded: 1960. **Members:** 350. **Membership Dues:** artist, $150 (annual) ● associate, $75 (annual) ● contributing (minimum), $100 (annual). **Staff:** 1. **Budget:** $50,000. **Description:** Artists specializing in painting and modeling animals, birds, and fish; includes sculptors, illustrators, oil and water colorists, and graphic artists. Holds exhibits of members' works at museums and galleries; advises young artists about art schools and suitable textbooks for the study of animal art. Operates speakers' bureau. **Libraries: Type:** reference. **Holdings:** 500; archival material, clippings. **Subjects:** animal life, animal art. **Awards:** Award of Excellence. **Frequency:** annual. **Type:** recognition ● Don Eckleberry Scholarship Award. **Frequency:** annual. **Type:** monetary. **Recipient:** to bird artist ● Donald Miller Interpretive Sculpture Award. **Frequency:** annual. **Type:** monetary. **Recipient:** to sculptor ● Evelyn Haller Interpretive Sculpture Award. **Frequency:** annual. **Type:** monetary. **Recipient:** to sculptor ● Leonard Meiselman Representational Painting Award. **Frequency:** annual. **Type:** monetary. **Recipient:** to painter ● Leonard Meiselman Representational Sculpture Award. **Frequency:** annual. **Type:** monetary. **Recipient:** to sculptor ● Patricia Allen Bott Creative Excellence Award. **Frequency:** annual. **Type:** recognition. **Publications:** *Catalogue of Exhibition*, annual. Illustrated catalog from annual exhibition. **Price:** $25.00 ● *Directory of Artist Members*, annual ● *Society of Animal Artists—Newsletter*, quarterly. Provides information on SAA activities and advice on wildlife art studies. Includes articles written by member artists on how to research a subject. **Price:** included in membership dues. **Circulation:** 450.

9527 ■ Society of Illustrators (SI)
128 E 63rd St.
New York, NY 10021-7303
Ph: (212)838-2560
Fax: (212)838-2561
E-mail: info@societyillustrators.org
URL: http://www.societyillustrators.org
Contact: Terrence Brown, Dir.
Founded: 1901. **Members:** 900. **Membership Dues:** artist resident, $500 (annual) ● artist non-resident, $300 (annual) ● associate resident, $580 (annual) ● associate non-resident, $300 (annual) ● educator resident and non-resident, $580 (annual) ● corporate, $1,500 (annual) ● artist non-resident senior, associate non-resident senior, $150 (annual) ● associate resident young, $290 (annual) ● museum friend, $250 (annual). **Staff:** 9. **Budget:** $750,000. **Multinational. Description:** Professional society of illustrators and art directors. Maintains Museum of American Illustration which sponsors continuous exhibits; holds annual exhibit (February-April) of best illustrations of the year; conducts benefit and sale in gallery in December. Participates in annual U.S. Air Force exhibits. Maintains hall of fame; traveling exhibition. **Libraries: Type:** reference. **Holdings:** biographical archives. **Subjects:** arts and graphics. **Awards:** Hall of Fame. **Frequency:** annual. **Type:** recognition. **Recipient:** for an artist ● **Frequency:** annual. **Type:** scholarship. **Recipient:** for students of accredited college-level art schools. **Committees:** Education; Exhibition; Permanent Collection; Welfare. **Publications:** *Annual of American Illustration*, annual. Book. Contains full-color reproductions of illustrations done by new and established illustrators in the past year. **Price:** $50.00/copy. **Advertising:** accepted. **Conventions/Meetings:** competition ● semiannual lecture.

9528 ■ Society of Tempera Painters
c/o Michael Bergt, Pres.
PO Box 30766
Santa Fe, NM 87592-0766
Ph: (505)473-9654
E-mail: michael@mbergt.com
URL: http://www.eggtempera.com
Contact: Michael Bergt, Pres.
Founded: 1997. **Membership Dues:** general, $35 (annual) ● patron, contributor, $75 (annual). **Multinational. Description:** Aims to improve the art of Tempera painting through exchange of knowledge and experience among its members and fellow tempera painters. Provides a forum for the discussion of tempera-related topics. **Publications:** Newsletter. **Price:** free for members.

9529 ■ Ward Museum of Wildfowl Art, Salisbury University
909 S Schumaker Dr.
Salisbury, MD 21804
Ph: (410)742-4988
Fax: (410)742-3107
E-mail: ward@wardmuseum.org
URL: http://www.wardmuseum.org
Contact: Lora Bottinelli, Interim Dir.
Founded: 1968. **Members:** 2,300. **Membership Dues:** individual, $35 (annual) ● family, $60 (annual) ● sponsor, $150 (annual) ● contributor, $250 (annual) ● Heritage Club, $500 (annual) ● Heritage Club (gold), $1,000 (annual) ● benefactor, $5,000 (annual). **Staff:** 12. **Budget:** $1,000,000. **Description:** Features a collection of decorative and antique decoys available to the public. **Libraries: Type:** reference. **Subjects:** antique. **Awards:** World Championship Wildfowl Carving Competition. **Frequency:** annual. **Type:** monetary. **Computer Services:** database ● mailing lists ● online services. **Formerly:** (2003) Ward Foundation. **Publications:** *Wildfowl Art Journal*, semiannual. **Price:** $5.00. **Circulation:** 6,000. **Advertising:** accepted. **Conventions/Meetings:** annual Ward World Wildfowl Carving Competition - competition and seminar - always April in Ocean City, MD.

9530 ■ Westbeth Corporation (WC)
463 West St.
New York, NY 10014
Ph: (212)691-1500
E-mail: info@westbeth.org
URL: http://www.westbeth.org
Contact: Randy Winston, Mgr.
Founded: 1967. **Description:** Housing project for artists in the New York City area. Jointly sponsored

by J.M. Kaplan Fund and the National Endowment for the Arts. Administered renovation of a 13-story structure, called Westbeth, so that its 383 apartment-studios could be offered for rent to practicing artists. Facilities include theaters, indoor and outdoor exhibition space, public park, and restaurants. Maintains one committee for each arts discipline. **Publications:** *The Artists Community*, annual ● *Westbeth Poets.*

9531 ■ Women's Caucus for Art (WCA)
Canal St. Sta.
PO Box 1498
New York, NY 10013
Ph: (212)634-0007
E-mail: info@nationalwca.com
URL: http://www.nationalwca.org
Contact: Jennifer Colby, Pres.
Founded: 1972. **Members:** 1,500. **Membership Dues:** individual, $30 (annual) ● institutional, $75 (annual) ● life, $500 ● student, subsidized, $25 (annual). **Staff:** 1. **Budget:** $51,000. **Regional Groups:** 6. **National Groups:** 30. **Description:** Professional women in visual art fields: artists, critics, art historians, museum and gallery professionals, arts administrators, educators and students, and collectors of art. Aims to increase recognition for contemporary and historical achievements of women in art. Ensures equal opportunity for employment, art commissions, and research grants. Encourages professionalism and shared information among women in art. Stimulates and publicizes research and publications on women in the visual arts. Conducts workshops, periodic affirmative action research, and statistical surveys. **Awards:** Honor Award. **Frequency:** annual. **Type:** recognition. **Recipient:** to senior women in the visual arts ● Lifetime Achievement. **Frequency:** annual. **Type:** recognition. **Recipient:** for active women who have distinguished themselves by activism in the women's movement and arts. **Telecommunication Services:** electronic mail, president@nationalwca.org ● electronic mail, karin@nationalwca.org. **Committees:** Affirmative Action; Exhibitions; Honors; Networking. **Affiliated With:** College Art Association. **Formerly:** (1974) Women's Caucus of the College Art Association. **Publications:** *Artlines Newsletter*, 3/year. **Circulation:** 1,500. Alternate Formats: online ● *WCA Honor Awards: Honor Awards for Outstanding Achievement in the Visual Arts*, annual. Catalog. Contains biographies of women artists and their works honored at the caucus' national conference. **Price:** $5.00/copy ● *WCA National Directory*, biennial. Lists WCA membership. **Price:** $5.00/copy ● Also publishes syllabi and bibliographies. **Conventions/Meetings:** annual conference - always February ● periodic regional meeting.

9532 ■ YLEM: Artists Using Science and Technology
PO Box 31923
San Francisco, CA 94131-0923
Ph: (415)445-0196
E-mail: info@ylem.org
URL: http://www.ylem.org
Contact: Torrey Nommesen, Contact
Founded: 1981. **Members:** 200. **Membership Dues:** individual, $40 (annual) ● institution, $60 (annual) ● student, senior, $30 (annual) ● donor, $300 (annual) ● life, $500. **Staff:** 1. **Description:** Represents artists, scientists, authors, educators, and art enthusiasts who explore the intersection of the arts and sciences. With science and technology as driving forces in contemporary culture, members strive to bring the humanizing and unifying forces of art in this arena. Members work in new art media such as digital photography, kinetic sculpture, interactive multimedia, holograms, 3-D media, film and video. **Publications:** *YLEM Newsletter*, bimonthly. ISSN: 1057-2031 ● Directory, annual. Provides illustrations of artists' work and contact information. **Conventions/Meetings:** bimonthly meeting, forum - usually first Wednesday of even-numbered months.

Arts

9533 ■ Affiliated Woodcarvers (AWC)
PO Box 104
Bettendorf, IA 52722
Ph: (563)359-9684 (563)355-3787
E-mail: webmaster@awcltd.org
URL: http://www.awcltd.org
Contact: Larry Yudis, Treas.
Founded: 1981. **Members:** 1,000. **Membership Dues:** in U.S., $10 (annual) ● outside U.S., $15 (annual). **Multinational. Description:** Woodcarvers; others interested in collecting and promoting woodcarving. Seeks to advance woodcarving as a fine art rather than a craft. **Committees:** Publicity. **Publications:** *Club Newsletter*, bimonthly. **Price:** included in membership dues. Alternate Formats: online ● *International Woodcarvers Directory* ● *Show Report*, semiannual. Alternate Formats: online. **Conventions/Meetings:** annual International Woodcarvers Congress - meeting and seminar, competitive woodcarving art show (exhibits) - always 3rd full week of June.

9534 ■ All Out Arts (AOA)
c/o CSV Cultural Center
107 Suffolk St.
New York, NY 10002
Ph: (212)477-9945 (212)260-4080
E-mail: clgri@interport.net
URL: http://csvcenter.com
Contact: Paul Nagle, Exec. Producing Dir.
Membership Dues: friend, $15-$49 (annual) ● program, $35 (annual) ● business, $50-$299 (annual) ● organizational, committee of 100 men and women, $300 (annual). **Description:** Dedicated to nurturing the lesbian and gay creative spirit. **Programs:** ArtGroup: for Lesbian and Gay Artists; National Renaissance League: for Playwrights and Producers; OLGAD for Architects and Designers. **Publications:** Newsletter, quarterly. **Price:** included in membership dues.

9535 ■ Alliance for the Arts (AFTA)
330 W 42nd St., Ste.1701
New York, NY 10036
Ph: (212)947-6340
Fax: (212)947-6416
E-mail: info@allianceforarts.org
URL: http://www.allianceforarts.org
Contact: Ashton Hawkins, Chm.
Founded: 1976. **Description:** Dedicated to information services, policy research, and advocacy for the arts. **Libraries: Type:** reference. **Holdings:** reports. **Awards:** Estate Project Grants. **Frequency:** annual. **Type:** grant. **Recipient:** to AIDS service organizations that assist artists. **Projects:** Artists with AIDS. **Formerly:** (1985) Cultural Assistance Center. **Publications:** *The Arts and Business Survey*, periodic. Report. Contains information based on survey. ● *New York City Culture Catalog*, periodic. Contains a cultural guide. **Price:** $12.95/copy ● *NYCkidsARTS*, semiannual. Pamphlet. Features arts education programs at cultural institutions or in schools for children. **Price:** $3.95/copy ● *Who Pays for the Arts?*, periodic. Paper. Features the income trends at New York City's cultural organizations. **Price:** $12.95/copy.

9536 ■ Alliance for Cultural Democracy (ACD)
PO Box 192244
San Francisco, CA 94119-2244
Ph: (415)821-9652 (415)437-2721
E-mail: acd@f8.com
URL: http://f8.com/ACD
Contact: Darnell Johnson, Pres.
Founded: 1976. **Members:** 300. **Membership Dues:** individual, $25 (annual) ● group, $50 (annual) ● institutional, $100 (annual). **Staff:** 1. **Description:** Community-based arts and cultural organizations, public cultural agencies, community artists, arts organizers, educators, and others. Promotes exchange among community cultural groups nationwide; provides information to grassroots arts activists, cultural organization employees, and community organizers. Advocates cultural pluralism; distributes Declaration of Cultural Human Rights. Holds regional workshops. **Libraries: Type:** reference. **Holdings:** 50; archival material, artwork, books, clippings, monographs, periodicals. **Subjects:** cultural democracy, arts activism. **Computer Services:** database, listserv. **Telecommunication Services:** electronic mail, cdemocracy@aol.com. **Formerly:** (1983) Neighborhood Arts Programs National Organization Committee. **Publications:** *ACD National Archive*, periodic. Monographs ● *Alliance for Cultural Democracy—Regional Bulletin*, annual. Includes articles by artists and news on cultural policy. **Price:** included in membership dues. **Circulation:** 400 ● *Cultural Democracy*, quarterly. Magazine. Includes articles written by activist artists about their work, analysis of cultural art policy, theory about culture and cultural democracy. **Price:** included in membership dues; $15.00 /year for nonmembers. ISSN: 0730-9503. **Conventions/Meetings:** semiannual Gathering Our Strength: Cultural Politics at the Millennium - conference (exhibits).

9537 ■ Alpha Omega Association
c/o Harry W. Miller
190 Peach Blossom Ln.
Bowling Green, KY 42103
Ph: (270)843-2300
Contact: Harry W. Miller, Contact
Founded: 1985. **Members:** 30. **Staff:** 5. **Description:** Christian fans and creators of comic books. Promotes publication of comics which advances what the group believes are quality values and aesthetics. Facilitates communication and good fellowship among members. **Libraries: Type:** open to the public. **Affiliated With:** Christian Comic Arts Society. **Publications:** Newsletter, bimonthly. **Circulation:** 35. **Conventions/Meetings:** periodic convention.

9538 ■ American Artists of Chinese Brush Painting (AACBP)
PO Box 4256
Huntington Beach, CA 92605
E-mail: aacbp@purpleweb.com
URL: http://www.aacbp.org
Membership Dues: general, $10 (annual). **Local Groups:** 4. **Description:** Stimulates interest in Chinese brush painting. Enriches the knowledge of members and the public on brush painting. Promotes intercultural understanding.

9539 ■ American Arts Alliance
1112 16th St. NW, Ste.400
Washington, DC 20036
Ph: (202)207-3850
Fax: (202)833-1543
E-mail: info@americanartsalliance.org
URL: http://www.americanartsalliance.org
Contact: Ms. Rachel Lyons, Mgr.
Founded: 1977. **Members:** 4,100. **Staff:** 1. **Description:** Supports America's professional nonprofit arts organizations, artists and their publics before the US Congress and key policy makers. Advocates for national policies that recognize, enhance and foster the contributions the performing arts make to America. Member organizations include: American Symphony Orchestra League, Association of Performing Arts Presenters, Dance/USA, OPERA America, and Theatre Communications Group. **Telecommunication Services:** electronic mail, rlyons@artspresenters.org.

9540 ■ American Cultural Resources Association (ACRA)
PO Box 4020
Ithaca, NY 14852
Ph: (801)394-0013 (607)257-2126
Fax: (801)394-0032
E-mail: scott@hartgen.com
URL: http://www.acra-crm.org
Contact: Mike Polke, Pres.
Founded: 1995. **Members:** 140. **Membership Dues:** student, $25 (annual) ● individual, non-profit, $85 (annual) ● corporate (based on the gross income), $175-$1,250 (annual). **Staff:** 2. **Budget:** $70,000. **Description:** Cultural resources practitioners. Promotes the "professional, ethical and business practices of the cultural resources industry"; seeks to increase public awareness of cultural resources services. Supports the business operations of members; makes available educational and training programs for cultural resources practitioners; sponsors promotional activities. **Awards:** ACRA Award of

Excellence. **Frequency:** annual. **Type:** recognition. **Computer Services:** Mailing lists, of corporate members and cultural resources professionals. **Publications:** *ACRA Edition*, periodic. Newsletter. **Conventions/Meetings:** annual conference ● periodic workshop.

9541 ■ American Federation of Arts (AFA)
305 E 47th St., 10th Fl.
New York, NY 10017
Ph: (212)988-7700
Free: (800)232-0270
Fax: (212)861-2487
E-mail: pubinfo@afaweb.org
URL: http://www.afaweb.org
Contact: Julia Brown, Dir.
Founded: 1909. **Members:** 600. **Membership Dues:** friend, $250 (annual) ● supporting, $500 (annual) ● national patron, $1,500 (annual) ● Benefactor's Circle, $3,000 (annual) ● Founder's Circle, $5,000 (annual). **Staff:** 41. **Budget:** $5,000,000. **Description:** Provides traveling art exhibitions and educational, professional, and technical programs. Seeks to strengthen the ability of museums to "enrich the public's understanding and experience of art". **Absorbed:** (1987) Art Museum Association of America. **Publications:** *Memo to Members*, quarterly. Newsletter ● Books ● Catalogs. Publishes or co-publishes catalogues to accompany AFA fine art exhibitions. ● Videos.

9542 ■ American Fired Arts Alliance (AFAA)
PO Box 202
Iola, WI 54945-0202
Free: (800)331-0038
Fax: (715)445-4053
E-mail: jomar@powercom.net
URL: http://www.jonespublishing.com/afaa
Contact: Mari Loomans, Pres.
Membership Dues: full, $49 (annual) ● basic, $25 (annual). **Multinational. Description:** Brings together artists, studio owners and manufacturers to share talents and experiences with each other while drawing new people into the fired arts. Increases awareness of fired arts through educational programs. Provides a forum for the exchange of information and related ideas about fired arts. Sponsors educational events around the country. **Publications:** *Fired Arts & Crafts*, monthly. Magazine. **Price:** included in membership dues. Alternate Formats: online.

9543 ■ American Friends of the Paris Opera and Ballet (AFPOB)
972 5th Ave.
New York, NY 10021
Ph: (212)439-1426
Fax: (212)439-1455
URL: http://www.afpob.org
Contact: Edward A. Reilly, Pres.
Founded: 1984. **Membership Dues:** regular, $1,000 (annual). **Description:** Corporations, foundations, and individuals who wish to support the Paris, France, opera and ballet companies. Fosters artistic cooperation between French and American artistic communities. Provides financial support for United States tours by the Paris Opera and Ballet companies. **Publications:** Brochures.

9544 ■ American Print Alliance
302 Larkspur Turn
Peachtree City, GA 30269-2210
E-mail: printalliance@mindspring.com
URL: http://www.printalliance.org
Contact: Dr. Carol Pulin, Dir.
Founded: 1992. **Multinational. Description:** Represents the interests of individuals dedicated to educating the public about prints and related contemporary arts while providing resources for artists. Encourages and strengthens contemporary printmaking, papermaking and book arts by helping artists consider conceptual and theoretical issues to improve the quality of their work. Helps artists present and explain their work to scholars and to the general public. **Telecommunication Services:** electronic mail, jandraka@erols.com ● electronic mail, kerslake@ufl.edu ● electronic mail, webmaster@printalliance.org. **Publications:** *Contemporary Impressions*. Journal. **Price:** $37.00 for nonmembers; $30.00 for members; $54.00 for institutions; $15.00 for students.

9545 ■ American Society for Aesthetics (ASA)
Armstrong Atlantic State Univ.
11935 Abercorn St.
Savannah, GA 31419
Ph: (912)921-2124
Fax: (912)921-5740
E-mail: asa@aesthetics-online.org
URL: http://www.aesthetics-online.org
Contact: Dabney Townsend, Sec.-Treas.
Founded: 1942. **Members:** 700. **Membership Dues:** regular, in U.S., $70 (annual) ● emeritus in U.S., $56 (annual) ● joint in U.S., $105 (annual) ● student, unemployed in U.S., $35 (annual) ● emeritus in Canada, $85 (annual) ● joint in Canada, $136 (annual) ● student, unemployed in Canada, $60 (annual) ● regular, in Canada, $102 (annual) ● regular, outside U.S. and Canada, $83 (annual) ● emeritus outside U.S. and Canada, $69 (annual) ● joint outside U.S. and Canada, $124 (annual) ● student, unemployed outside U.S. and Canada, $40 (annual). **Staff:** 1. **Budget:** $100,000. **Regional Groups:** 3. **Multinational. Description:** Persons interested in the study of the arts and related areas from a philosophic, scientific, historical, critical, or educational point of view; includes artists, teachers, philosophers, writers, advanced students, and others interested in the visual arts, architecture, urban aesthetics, music, literature, theatre, dance, and film arts. Monitors and participates in the activities of related organizations such as American Association for the Advancement of Science and American Council of Learned Societies. **Awards:** John Fisher Memorial Prize. **Frequency:** annual. **Type:** monetary. **Recipient:** to winners of the essay competition. **Computer Services:** Mailing lists. **Telecommunication Services:** electronic mail, secretary-treasurer@aesthetics-online.org. **Affiliated With:** American Association for the Advancement of Science; American Council of Learned Societies. **Publications:** *ASA Newsletter*, 3/year ● *Journal of Aesthetics and Art Criticism*, quarterly. **Price:** $60.00/year in U.S.; $71.00/year outside U.S. ISSN: 0021-8529. **Circulation:** 1,500. **Advertising:** accepted. Also Cited As: *JAAC* ● Also publishes cumulative index to volumes 1-35 and 36-40 of journal. **Conventions/Meetings:** annual meeting (exhibits) - always autumn.

9546 ■ Americans for the Arts
1000 Vermont Ave. NW, 6th Fl.
Washington, DC 20005
Ph: (202)371-2830
Free: (800)321-4510
Fax: (202)371-0424
E-mail: webmaster@artsusa.org
Contact: Robert L. Lynch, Pres./CEO
Founded: 1978. **Members:** 5,000. **Staff:** 75. **Budget:** $9,000,000. **Regional Groups:** 8. **Local Groups:** 3,800. **Description:** Dedicated to representing and serving local communities and creating opportunities for every American to participate in and appreciate all forms of the arts. Aims to: foster an environment in which the arts can thrive and contribute to the creation of more livable communities; generate more public- and private-sector resources for the arts and arts education; and build individual appreciation of the value of the arts. Partners with local, state, and national arts organizations; government agencies; business leaders; individual philanthropists; educators; and funders throughout the country in order to achieve its goals. Provides extensive arts industry research, and information and professional development opportunities for community arts leaders via specialized programs and services, including a content-rich website and an annual national convention. **Libraries: Type:** reference. **Holdings:** 6,000. **Subjects:** arts management, arts education, arts giving. **Awards:** Alene Valkanas State Arts Advocacy Award. **Frequency:** annual. **Type:** recognition. **Recipient:** for an individual at the state level who has dramatically affected the political landscape through their arts advocacy efforts ● Arts Education Award. **Frequency:** annual. **Type:** recognition. **Recipient:** to identify the best in arts education program design and execution, as well as leadership and bringing visibility and national recognition to model partnership programs ● Emerging Leader Award. **Frequency:** annual. **Type:** recognition. **Recipient:** for extraordinary work in the arts administration field ● Michael Newton Award. **Frequency:** annual. **Type:** recognition. **Recipient:** for dedication to United Arts Fund Movement ● Public Art Network Award. **Frequency:** annual. **Type:** recognition. **Recipient:** for innovative and creative contributions and/or exemplary commitment and leadership in the field of public art ● Selina Roberts Ottum Award. **Frequency:** annual. **Type:** recognition. **Recipient:** to an individual who has made a meaningful contribution through the arts to their local communities. **Computer Services:** database, of articles on arts policy ● mailing lists, local art agencies and affiliate members. **Boards:** National Policy. **Councils:** Arts Education Network; Emerging Leader; National Patrons; Public Art Network; State Arts Action Network. **Roundtables:** National Arts Policy. **Special Interest Groups:** United Arts Funds; United States Urban Arts Federation. **Formerly:** (1982) National Assembly of Community Arts Agencies; (1988) National Assembly of Local Arts Agencies; (1991) Arts for America, National Assembly of Local Arts Agencies; (2000) American Council for the Arts. **Publications:** *Arts Link*, quarterly. Newsletter. Includes information on employment opportunities and new publications. **Price:** included in membership dues ● *Field Directory*, biennial. Contains in-depth articles about arts programming and activities, arts administration, and trends in the field. **Price:** included in membership dues; $75.00/copy for nonmembers ● Monographs, bimonthly. Contains information on a single topic issue. **Price:** included in membership dues; $75.00/copy for nonmembers. **Conventions/Meetings:** annual Arts Advocacy Day - meeting ● annual Nancy Hanks Lecture on Arts and Public Policy - convention and lecture.

9547 ■ Art in the Public Interest (API)
PO Box 68
Saxapahaw, NC 27340
Ph: (336)376-8404
E-mail: info@apionline.org
URL: http://www.apionline.org
Contact: Linda Frye Burnham, Co-Dir./Ed.
Founded: 1995. **Description:** Serves the information needs of artists and organizations who bring the arts together with the community and social concerns. **Computer Services:** Mailing lists. **Projects:** Community Arts Network. **Publications:** *APInews*, monthly. Newsletter. Covers the field of community-based art. ● *High Performance*, quarterly. Magazine. Alternate Formats: online ● Pamphlets. **Conventions/Meetings:** workshop.

9548 ■ Art Watch International (AWI)
c/o James Beck, Pres.
Columbia Univ.
931 Schermerhorn
New York, NY 10027
Ph: (212)854-4569
Fax: (212)854-7329
E-mail: info@artwatchinternational.org
URL: http://www.artwatchinternational.org
Contact: James Beck, Pres.
Founded: 1992. **Description:** Individuals and organizations with an interest in "the treatment of art objects and cultural institutions that deal with the visual arts." Seeks to insure the quality of art preservation and restoration programs worldwide. Promotes increased public awareness of arts restoration efforts. Monitors and reports on preservation and restoration activities and techniques; conducts educational programs for professional art object restorers and the public. Organizes missions to observe and advise arts restoration projects worldwide. **Conventions/Meetings:** periodic lecture ● periodic symposium.

9549 ■ Artists for a Better World International (AFABW)
4845 Fountain Ave., No. 13
Hollywood, CA 90028

E-mail: info@artistsforabetterworld.com
URL: http://www.artistsforabetterworld.com
Contact: George Alger, Pres.
Founded: 1997. **Multinational. Description:** Aims to "raise awareness of worldwide artists about using their creative powers to benefit mankind by leading the way to a better world and by supporting like-minded public benefit organizations that advocate humanitarian benevolence. Cultivates international artistic participation in constructive, inspirational and creative projects as well as working hand-in-hand with other community advancement organizations.". **Computer Services:** database, artists directory ● information services, art resources. **Publications:** *Art Line*, monthly. Newsletter. Includes news, contests, art, stories and articles for artists and art enthusiasts of all genres. **Price:** free. Alternate Formats: online ● *Notes In The Margins*, monthly. Newsletter. **Price:** free. Alternate Formats: online ● *Performing Artists Update.* Newsletter. Contains news about the monthly AFABW Showcase at Celebrity Centre International in Hollywood. **Price:** free. Alternate Formats: online ● *Singers Unite*, bimonthly. Newsletter. Contains tips, articles and news for vocalists. **Price:** free. Alternate Formats: online.

9550 ■ Arts and Business Council
Address Unknown since 2008
Founded: 1965. **Members:** 250. **Membership Dues:** arts, $100-$250 (annual) ● corporate, $500 (annual) ● individual, $50 (annual). **Staff:** 10. **Budget:** $1,900,000. **Regional Groups:** 25. **Local Groups:** 130. **Description:** Businesses and nonprofit arts organizations. Promotes the mutuality of arts and business partnerships, strengthening the two sectors through programs that serve the fullest diversity of individuals, organizations, and communities. Programs bring expertise, resources, and leadership talent from business to the arts and promote the arts to business. Operates Business Volunteers for the Arts that places specially trained business executives as free management consultants for arts groups, now replicated in 30 U.S. cities and two sites abroad. Sponsors conferences, workshops, publications, internships/fellowships, awards. Coordinates national affiliate network; offers an information center. **Awards:** ENCORE. **Frequency:** annual. **Type:** monetary ● Michael Newton Award. **Frequency:** annual. **Type:** recognition. **Recipient:** for effective, innovative, and creative fundraising techniques; distinctive management style; commitment; and dedication to the UAF movement ● National Arts Awards. **Frequency:** annual. **Type:** recognition. **Recipient:** to an artist, organization or company, or individual who displayed exemplary artistic accomplishments in their field ● Public Art Network Award. **Frequency:** annual. **Type:** recognition. **Recipient:** for innovative and creative contributions and/or exemplary commitment and leadership in the field of public art ● Public Leadership in the Arts. **Frequency:** annual. **Type:** recognition. **Recipient:** to an elected official who works for the advancement of the arts and arts education within his or her community ● Selina Roberts Ottum Award. **Frequency:** annual. **Type:** recognition. **Recipient:** for individuals working in the arts and arts management who made a meaningful contributions to their local communities. **Computer Services:** database, arts to business ● database, listing of resources New York City arts groups can offer business, such as space for rent, artists' services, sponsorship opportunities. **Also Known As:** Business Volunteers for the Arts. **Publications:** *The Arts Guide to Business Sponsorship.* Manual. **Price:** $20.00 ● *Business Volunteers for the Arts: Program Feasibility Guide.* Report ● *Critical Issues and the Arts: Status Reports.* **Conventions/Meetings:** annual conference ● annual Encore Awards Luncheon ● annual Gala Dinner.

9551 ■ Arts International (AI)
770 Broadway, 2nd Fl.
New York, NY 10003-9522
Ph: (212)674-9744
Fax: (212)674-9092
E-mail: info@artsinternational.org
URL: http://web.archive.org/web/20041019074601/www.artsinternational.org
Contact: Noreen Tomassi, Pres./CEO
Founded: 1981. **Staff:** 11. **Budget:** $2,600,000. **Languages:** English, French, Italian, Portuguese, Spanish. **Description:** Encourages the development and support of global cultural interchange in the arts. Creates international projects and partnerships that help to identify, develop and circulate new work across borders worldwide. Develops and administers grant programs that provide support to artists and arts organizations engaged in international work. **Awards:** The Artists Exploration Fund. **Frequency:** semiannual. **Type:** grant. **Recipient:** for international projects by individual U.S. performing artists to promote their creative development ● FACE Croatia. **Type:** grant. **Recipient:** for cultural exchange projects between the U.S. and Croatia, artists must be based in New York, Zagreb or Dubrovnik ● The Fund for U.S. Artists at International Festivals and Exhibitions. **Frequency:** 3/year. **Type:** grant. **Recipient:** for U.S. performing artists, ensembles, and companies invited to perform abroad at international festivals. **Computer Services:** database, sponsors, festivals, competitions, public and private programs, country-specific arts information, and international art service organizations. **Formerly:** (2003) Arts International Program of the Institute of International Education. **Publications:** *American Visions* (in English and Spanish). Book. **Price:** $29.95 plus shipping and handling. Also Cited As: *Visiones de las Americas* ● *Money for International Exchange in the Arts.* Book. Provides information on international sources of funding for projects. **Price:** $14.95 plus shipping and handling. **Conventions/Meetings:** Inroads/Africa - conference.

9552 ■ Asian American Arts Alliance
155 Ave. of the Americas, 6th Fl.
New York, NY 10013
Ph: (212)941-9208
Fax: (212)366-1778
E-mail: a4@aaartsalliance.org
URL: http://www.aaartsalliance.org
Contact: Lillian Cho, Exec. Dir.
Founded: 1983. **Members:** 300. **Membership Dues:** organization, $35 (annual) ● individual artist, $25 (annual). **Staff:** 2. **Budget:** $300,000. **Description:** Works to support, recognize, and appreciate Asian American arts. Provides information, advocacy, and network services through projects such as technical assistance and regnant initiative for New York City Asian American arts groups. **Libraries: Type:** reference. **Subjects:** Asian American art. **Computer Services:** Mailing lists, membership. **Formerly:** Alliance for Asian American Arts and Culture. **Publications:** *Asian American Arts Calendar*, bimonthly. Directory. Lists events and opportunities for artists. **Circulation:** 4,000. **Advertising:** accepted ● *Asian American Arts Organizations and Touring Artists.* Directory. **Price:** $7.00 ● *Dialogue*, semiannual. Magazine. Contains information on Asian American artists. **Price:** $5.00. **Circulation:** 3,000. **Advertising:** accepted.

9553 ■ Asian American Arts Centre (AAAC)
26 Bowery St.
New York, NY 10013
Ph: (212)233-2154
Fax: (212)766-1287
E-mail: aaacinfo@artspiral.org
URL: http://www.artspiral.org
Contact: Robert Lee, Dir.
Founded: 1974. **Membership Dues:** individual (allows member to receive invitation/announcement of events and exhibition only), $35 (annual). **Staff:** 5. **Regional Groups:** 4,500. **National Groups:** 300. **Languages:** Chinese, English, Japanese, Korean. **Multinational. Description:** Supports exhibition of traditional and contemporary Asian and Asian American art. Conducts educational programs. Maintains archive of Asian American artists' slides with 1,000 entries since 1985. **Libraries: Type:** open to the public. **Holdings:** 2,000; archival material, books, periodicals. **Subjects:** visual arts, Asian American ethnic studies. **Subgroups:** Artslam. **Affiliated With:** Asian American Arts Alliance; The Association of American Cultures. **Formerly:** (1986) Asian American Dance Theater. **Publications:** *Artspiral.* Magazine. Alternate Formats: online ● Catalog, annual. Serves as a catalogue of Asian American art for annual show. **Price:** $10.00. **Circulation:** 8,000 ● Also publishes exhibition catalogs and Web magazine. **Conventions/Meetings:** monthly Artslam Series - meeting.

9554 ■ The Association of American Cultures (TAAC)
656 S 2nd Ave.
Yuma, AZ 85364
Ph: (928)783-1757
E-mail: taac@taac.com
URL: http://www.taac.com
Contact: Louis LeRoy, Chm.
Founded: 1985. **Members:** 1,000. **Membership Dues:** senior/student, $45 (annual) ● individual, $60 (annual) ● community organization/business (based on budget), $150-$500 (annual) ● state arts agency-national arts organization, $900 (annual) ● supporter, $300 (annual) ● benefactor, $600 (annual) ● patron, $1,200 (annual) ● silver helping hand, $5,000 ● gold helping hand, $10,000. **Staff:** 3. **Budget:** $250,000. **Description:** Artists and arts administrators of color. Represents culturally diverse arts programs. Promotes public awareness of culturally diverse arts issues. Works for the preservation of cultural identity through the arts. Conducts educational programs. **Awards:** Crystal Stairs Award. **Frequency:** biennial. **Type:** recognition. **Recipient:** for exceptional work as artist of color. **Computer Services:** Mailing lists. **Telecommunication Services:** electronic mail, louis@taac.com. **Publications:** *Open Dialogue*, quarterly. Newsletter. **Price:** $35.00 for members. **Circulation:** 6,000. **Advertising:** accepted. **Conventions/Meetings:** biennial Open Dialogue - conference (exhibits).

9555 ■ Association for the Calligraphic Arts (ACA)
26 Main St.
East Greenwich, RI 02818
E-mail: aca@calligraphicarts.org
URL: http://www.calligraphicarts.org
Contact: Joan Merrell, Pres.
Founded: 1997. **Members:** 800. **Membership Dues:** individual in U.S., $35 (annual) ● individual outside U.S., $45 (annual) ● guild, $65 (annual). **Staff:** 1. **Description:** Promotes the art of calligraphy. **Libraries: Type:** lending; not open to the public. **Holdings:** artwork, books. **Subjects:** calligraphy. **Awards: Frequency:** annual. **Type:** scholarship. **Telecommunication Services:** electronic mail, president@calligraphicarts.org ● electronic mail, newsletter@calligraphicarts.org ● electronic mail, membership@calligraphicarts.org. **Publications:** *The Newsletter*, quarterly. Journal. Brings forth ideas about guild development, fundraising, planning exhibits, profiles of calligraphers and much more. **Advertising:** accepted.

9556 ■ Association of Israel's Decorative Arts (AIDA)
c/o Erika Vogel, Dir.
110 E 59th St., 26th Fl.
New York, NY 10022
Ph: (212)931-0089
E-mail: info@aidaarts.org
URL: http://www.aidaarts.org
Contact: Erika Vogel, Dir.
Founded: 2003. **Multinational. Description:** Fosters the development of contemporary decorative artists from Israel by connecting them to an international audience of galleries, institutions, and collectors. Supports international museum exhibitions presenting the work of artists from Israel. Promotes the exchange of artistic ideas amongst artists from Israel, North America and Europe. Identifies international fellowships, internships and scholarships to provide continuing education to artists from Israel. **Awards:** The Andrea M. Bronfman Prize for the Arts. **Frequency:** annual. **Type:** monetary. **Recipient:** to an Israeli decorative artist for excellence in the fields of ceramics, jewelry, textile or glass.

9557 ■ Atlatl
Address Unknown since 2008
URL: http://www.atlatl.org
Membership Dues: native artist, $25 (annual) ● subscriber, $35 (annual) ● contributor, $50 (annual) ● sponsor, $100 (annual) ● patron, $250 (annual) ●

benefactor, $500 (annual) ● donor, $1,000 (annual). **Description:** Promotes the vitality of contemporary Native American art. Creates an informational network between Native American artists and arts organizations. Provides training and leadership development. Presents Native Arts through local and national art exhibits. **Programs:** Networking; Presenting Native Arts; Training and Leadership Development. **Also Known As:** National Native Arts Network. **Publications:** *Native Arts Journal*, quarterly. **Price:** included in membership dues.

9558 ■ Beaux Arts Alliance
119 E 74th St.
New York, NY 10021
Ph: (212)639-9120
Fax: (212)639-9120
E-mail: sfkforbes@aol.com
URL: http://www.beauxarts.org
Contact: Sally Forbes, Exec. Dir.
Founded: 1995. **Members:** 672. **Membership Dues:** regular, $100 (annual). **Staff:** 2. **Budget:** $50,000. **Languages:** English, French. **Description:** Celebrates the cultural links between the United States and France with lectures, walking tours, trips, exhibitions and publications. **Libraries: Type:** by appointment only. **Subjects:** art, architecture, history, culture. **Awards:** The Beaux Arts Alliance Award. **Frequency:** annual. **Type:** recognition. **Recipient:** for architectural or publication excellence. **Committees:** Preservation. **Councils:** Advisory. **Conventions/Meetings:** monthly lecture and workshop (exhibits).

9559 ■ Beyond Baroque Literary/Arts Center
681 Venice Blvd.
Venice, CA 90291
Ph: (310)822-3006
Fax: (310)827-7432
E-mail: mikealynch@yahoo.com
URL: http://www.beyondbaroque.org
Contact: Frederick Dewey, Exec./Artistic Dir.
Founded: 1968. **Membership Dues:** foundation, $33 (annual) ● supporter, $55 (annual) ● friend, $110 (annual) ● benefactor, $275 (annual) ● sponsor, $550 (annual) ● patron, $1,100 (annual). **Staff:** 3. **Budget:** $200,000. **Description:** Literary arts center. Provides literary arts programming and services, education, and information. Writes workshops and weekly literary readings, film series, music and theater performances, small exhibition space and small-scale publishing. Operates art and literature bookstore and a small press archive. **Libraries: Type:** reference. **Holdings:** 20,000. **Councils:** Artist and Community Advisory; National Advisory. **Formerly:** (1992) Beyond Baroque Foundation. **Publications:** *Calendar*, bimonthly.

9560 ■ Business Committee for the Arts (BCA)
29-27 Queens Plz. N, 4th Fl.
Long Island City, NY 11101
Ph: (718)482-9900
Fax: (718)482-9911
E-mail: info@bcainc.org
URL: http://www.bcainc.org
Contact: Judith A. Jedlicka, Pres.
Founded: 1967. **Members:** 100. **Staff:** 6. **Regional Groups:** 8. **Description:** Encourages business investments in the arts. Conducts research and statistical analysis pertaining to support of the arts; offers consultations, seminars and workshops for businesses to develop new and increased business support for the arts. Sponsors a nationwide public service advertising campaign to increase business interest in arts support. Cosponsors, with *Forbes Magazine*, annual Business in the Arts Awards. **Awards:** Business in the Arts Awards. **Frequency:** annual. **Type:** recognition. **Recipient:** for outstanding support to the arts by a business or business executive. **Publications:** *A Business Guide to Investing in the Arts: Invest A Little, Get a Lot* ● *Art of Leadership: Building Business-Arts Alliances*. Book. **Price:** $65.00 plus shipping and handling ● *BCA Case Studies*. Report. **Price:** $10.00 plus shipping and handling ● *BCA News*, quarterly, March, June, September, December. Newsletter. Features news about business-arts alliances. **Price:** $30.00/year for non-profit in U.S.; $55.00/year for others in U.S.; $65.00/year, international ● *BCA Report: 2004 National Survey of Business Support to the Arts - Executive Summary*. **Price:** $7.00 plus shipping and handling ● *Business in the Arts Award Brochures*. Presents highlights of theatre-support programs developed by businesses receiving the national Business in the Arts Awards. **Price:** $4.00 plus shipping and handling ● *Change the Way You Do Business*. Article. **Price:** $8.00 plus shipping and handling ● *David Rockefeller Lecture Reprints*. Covers the 1998-2002 lectures. **Price:** $4.00 each, plus shipping and handling ● *Invest a Little, Get a Lot*. Paper. **Price:** $5.00 plus shipping and handling ● *Think Small for Big Results*. Paper. **Price:** $5.00 plus shipping and handling ● *2004 National Survey of Business Support to the Arts*. **Price:** $100.00 for nonmembers, plus shipping and handling; $50.00 for members and non-profits ● *2002 Business in the Arts Awards*. Article. **Price:** $4.00 plus shipping and handling. **Conventions/Meetings:** periodic conference ● annual meeting, includes awards presentation.

9561 ■ Cartoonists Northwest (CNW)
PO Box 31122
Seattle, WA 98103
Ph: (425)226-7623 (206)369-2123
Fax: (425)227-0511
E-mail: cartoonistsnw@gmail.com
URL: http://www.cartoonists.net
Contact: Luke Martin, Pres.
Founded: 1981. **Members:** 300. **Membership Dues:** individual, $30 (annual) ● international, $40 (annual). **Staff:** 10. **Budget:** $2,000. **Regional Groups:** 1. **State Groups:** 1. **Local Groups:** 1. **Description:** Cartoonists, writers, publishers, illustrators, agents, and others interested in cartooning. Members are accepted nationwide and internationally. Provides information on all aspects of the cartooning profession to amateur, aspiring, and practicing cartoonists. Promotes cartooning as an art form. Provides networking opportunities and referral services. Conducts educational programs. **Libraries: Type:** reference. **Awards:** Toonie Awards. **Frequency:** annual. **Type:** recognition. **Recipient:** for recognition in 5 or 6 categories. **Formerly:** (1980) Northwest Cartoonists Association. **Publications:** *Penstuff*, monthly. Newsletter. Includes president's column, comic strip reviews, comic book/publishing news, speaker previews and reviews, trivia, and cartoons. **Price:** included in membership dues. **Circulation:** 500. **Advertising:** accepted. **Conventions/Meetings:** monthly meeting - always third Friday, in Seattle, WA.

9562 ■ Catholic Fine Arts Society (CFAS)
Address Unknown since 2008
Founded: 1955. **Members:** 200. **Membership Dues:** $25 (annual). **Staff:** 5. **Regional Groups:** 2. **State Groups:** 10. **National Groups:** 1. **Description:** Professional artists; art teachers at college, high school, and elementary school levels; and others, regardless of religious affiliation, who are engaged in fostering the growth of creativity through art education and personal expression. Works to maintain contact among members and promote the exchange of ideas. Sponsors workshops, field trips, and museum tours. Conducts programs honoring prominent artists and featuring lectures, demonstrations, art films, and exhibitions of the works of members and their students. Offers assistance to classroom teachers with art programs. Members' services available for workshops in schools requested by superintendents and principals. Sponsors competitions and art shows in conjunction with Paul VI Institute for the Arts. **Libraries: Type:** reference. **Holdings:** archival material. **Awards:** Honorary Membership Award. **Frequency:** annual. **Type:** recognition. **Recipient:** for a prominent artist dedicated to liturgical or religious art. **Affiliated With:** Paul VI Institute for the Arts. **Publications:** *CFAS/CAA*, quarterly. Newsletter. Provides information on religious fine arts, membership activities, and exhibition activities. **Price:** included in membership dues. **Circulation:** 400 ● *Membership List*, annual. Membership Directory. **Conventions/Meetings:** biennial meeting.

9563 ■ Christians in the Visual Arts (CIVA)
255 Grapevine Rd.
Wenham, MA 01984-1813
Ph: (978)867-4124 (978)867-4128
Fax: (978)867-4125
E-mail: office@civa.org
URL: http://www.civa.org
Contact: Katherine McClure, Office Mgr.
Founded: 1979. **Members:** 1,300. **Membership Dues:** student, $30 (annual) ● senior, $50 (annual) ● individual, $60 (annual) ● institutional, $150 (annual) ● organizational, $75 (annual) ● supporting institutional, $200 (annual) ● sustaining institutional, $1,000 (annual) ● library, $15 (annual) ● starving artist, $45 (annual). **Staff:** 6. **Budget:** $300,000. **Description:** Christian visual artists and Christian educational institutions offering visual arts programs. Encourages "Christians in the visual arts to develop their particular callings to the highest professional level." Assists members in dealing with "specific problems in the field without compromising either faith or standards of artistic endeavor." Facilitates communication and cooperation among members. Serves as a clearinghouse on Christian artists, galleries, and art exhibitions. Conducts art study tours. **Committees:** Graphic Artists Network; Printmakers Network; Scholars. **Also Known As:** Christians in Visual Arts. **Publications:** *CIVA Member Directory*, biennial. Includes listing of 1300 members. **Price:** $15.00. **Advertising:** accepted ● *SEEN*, semiannual. Journal. **Conventions/Meetings:** biennial conference and workshop - every June in varying locations ● annual Glen Workshop - always in Santa Fe, NM ● annual workshop - every July on the Gordon College Campus, Wenham, MA.

9564 ■ Cowles Charitable Trust
PO Box 219
Rumson, NJ 07760
Ph: (732)936-9826
Contact: Gardner Cowles III, Pres.
Description: Provides grants for arts and culture, education, and social services.

9565 ■ Creative Time (CT)
59 E 4th St. 6E
New York, NY 10003
Ph: (212)206-6674
Fax: (212)255-8467
E-mail: info@creativetime.org
URL: http://www.creativetime.org
Contact: Anne Pasternak, Pres./Artistic Dir.
Founded: 1973. **Staff:** 9. **Budget:** $900,000. **Description:** Presents new works by visual artists, performers, musicians, poets and choreographers in unlikely, unexplored and even abandoned public spaces. Works with artists of all disciplines and believes "that art moves society forward and that artists can be a positive catalyst for change". Encourages artists to use their voices to address cultural, as well as social issues. Roster of artists include: Vito Acconci, Laurie Anderson, Ann Carlson, Philip Glass, Spalding Gray, Red Grooms, Jenny Holzer, Bill T. Jones, Nam June Paik, Martin Puryear, Steve Reich, Alison Saar, Elizabeth Streb, William Wegman, Sonic Youth, Felix Gonzalez-Torres and Takashi Murakami. **Publications:** *Fashion Fabrication-Exposing Meanings in Fashion Theory Presentation*. Book. **Price:** $29.95 ● *Time Capsule: A Concise Encyclopedia By Women Artists*. Book. **Price:** $27.50 plus shipping and handling ● Catalog, biennial. Provides documentation of events and exhibitions.

9566 ■ Dance Theater Workshop (DTW)
219 W 19th St.
New York, NY 10011
Ph: (212)691-6500
Fax: (212)633-1974
E-mail: dtw@dtw.org
URL: http://www.dtw.org
Contact: Andrea Sholler, Interim Exec. Dir.
Founded: 1965. **Members:** 900. **Membership Dues:** artist, company, $65 (annual) ● non-profit organization, $150 (annual). **Staff:** 29. **Budget:** $2,600,000. **Description:** Choreographers, artistic directors, and performing arts companies in related fields. Seeks to create and facilitate performance opportunities for

choreographers, composers, and theater artists and to stimulate the development of new and wider public audiences for the individual artist. Activities include production and sponsorship of 75 artists and companies at the Bessie Schonberg Theater in New York City; preproduction counseling on publicity, promotion, and overall budgetary concerns as well as technical production problems; assistance with specific dance and performance-related administrative questions. Maintains video viewing facilities and archives of the performance work of a wide range of member artists for copyright and historical purposes. Offers mail preparation service and discounts on newspaper advertising. Conducts economic survival seminars; acts as clearinghouse of dance information. Provides children's services. **Awards:** The Bessies: The New York Dance and Performance Awards. **Frequency:** annual. **Type:** monetary ● **Type:** recognition. **Recipient:** for outstanding creative achievement by individual artists. **Computer Services:** Mailing lists, of members. **Programs:** College Partnership; Corporate Partners; Digital Fellows; DTW Presents; Fresh Tracks Performance and Residency; Outerspace. **Projects:** National Performance Network; The Suitcase Fund. **Publications:** *Poor Dancer's Almanac*, quinquennial. Serves as a manual and resource directory for artists of all disciplines. Includes periodic updates. **Price:** $10.00 for members; $15.00 for nonmembers; $12.00 for libraries ● *Poor Dancer's Almanac Newsletter*, 3/year. Contains announcements of special programs, offerings of discounted services, and a forum for articles by members and others. ● *Press Reference List*, annual ● *I'm an artist, how about you?* Dance Theater workshops activity book for kids of all ages. **Conventions/Meetings:** annual meeting - always September in New York City.

9567 ■ Decorative Arts Trust

106 Bainbridge St.
Philadelphia, PA 19147
Ph: (215)627-2859
Fax: (215)925-1144
E-mail: pennyhunt@decorativeartstrust.org
URL: http://www.decorativeartstrust.org
Contact: Jonathan Fairbanks, Pres.

Founded: 1977. **Members:** 1,200. **Membership Dues:** student, $15 (annual) ● individual, $35 (annual) ● joint, $55 (annual) ● sustaining, $75 (annual) ● patron, $100 (annual) ● benefactor, $250 (annual) ● sponsor, $500 (annual) ● corporate, $1,000 (annual). **Description:** Persons interested in all aspects of the decorative arts, including collectors, dealers, and curators. Administers a national speakers' registry intended to help museums, historical societies, and other interested groups and individuals set up lectures and seminars. Provides information to members on sources of identification, preservation, and disposition of decorative art objects. **Awards:** Award of Excellence. **Type:** recognition ● Dewey Lee Curtis Scholarship. **Frequency:** semiannual. **Type:** scholarship. **Recipient:** for a person actively working in the field of American decorative arts. **Publications:** *Decorative Arts Trust Lecturers Registry*, quinquennial. Booklet. Lists all who have spoken at one symposium; listed chronologically by symposium, cross indexed by speakers name and subjects. **Price:** $11.50 ● *Decorative Arts Trust—Newsletter*, quarterly. Includes book and exhibit reviews, calendar of events, reports, listings of exhibits, and information on scholarly opportunities. **Price:** included in membership dues. **Circulation:** 1,500. **Conventions/Meetings:** semiannual meeting and symposium - always spring and fall ● periodic regional meeting.

9568 ■ Friends of the Kennedy Center (FOKC)

c/o John F. Kennedy Center for the Performing Arts
2700 F St. NW
Washington, DC 20566
Ph: (202)416-8301 (202)467-4600
Free: (800)444-1324
Fax: (202)416-8775
E-mail: webmaster@kennedy-center.org
URL: http://www.kennedy-center.org
Contact: Brooks Boeke, Mgr.

Founded: 1965. **Members:** 500. **Staff:** 2. **Description:** Provides volunteer support to the John F. Kennedy Center for the Performing Arts and its national outreach and public service programs. **Libraries: Type:** open to the public. **Subjects:** arts. **Publications:** *Friendscript*, monthly. Newsletter. **Price:** free for volunteers and staff. **Circulation:** 1,000. **Advertising:** accepted.

9569 ■ Getty Grant Program

1200 Getty Center Dr., Ste.800
Los Angeles, CA 90049-1697
Ph: (310)440-7300 (310)440-7320
Fax: (310)440-7703
E-mail: communications@getty.edu
URL: http://www.getty.edu/grants
Contact: Joan Weinstein, Interim Dir.

Founded: 1984. **Staff:** 18. **Multinational. Description:** Works to support institutions and individuals who promote learning and scholarship in the history of the visual arts and the conservation of cultural heritage. **Awards: Type:** grant. **Recipient:** for individuals at postdoctoral and senior scholar levels working in art history. **Telecommunication Services:** electronic mail, info@getty.edu. **Publications:** *Funding Priorities*. Brochure. **Price:** free ● *Grants Awarded*. Booklet. **Price:** free ● *J. Paul Getty Trust*, annual. Annual Report. **Price:** free ● Newsletter, monthly. Contains family program, featuring highlights of exhibitions and events. Alternate Formats: online.

9570 ■ Indo-American Arts Council (IAAC)

118 E 25th St., Third Fl.
New York, NY 10010
Ph: (212)529-2347
Fax: (212)477-4106
E-mail: aroon@iaac.us
URL: http://www.iaac.us
Contact: Aroon Shivdasani, Exec. Dir.

Founded: 1998. **Membership Dues:** friend, $50-$500 ● supporter, $550-$2,000 ● donor, $2,500-$5,000 ● patron, $5,000-$10,000 ● pacesetter, $10,500. **Multinational. Description:** Raises awareness of Indian artistic disciplines in North America. Promotes the creation, production, exhibition, publication and performance of Indian and cross-cultural art forms in North America. Supports all artistic disciplines in the classical, fusion, folk and innovative forms influenced by the arts of India. Fosters an exchange of artists and arts related information between India and the United States. **Telecommunication Services:** electronic mail, iaac@iaac.us. **Publications:** Newsletter. Alternate Formats: online.

9571 ■ Interlochen Center for the Arts (ICA)

PO Box 199
Interlochen, MI 49643-0199
Ph: (231)276-7472 (231)276-7200
Fax: (231)276-7464
E-mail: admissions@interlochen.org
URL: http://www.interlochen.org
Contact: Jeffrey S. Kimpton, Pres.

Founded: 1928. **Staff:** 200. **Budget:** $27,000,000. **Multinational. Description:** Educational center offering two separate programs: the Interlochen Arts Camp and the Interlochen Arts Academy. The Interlochen Arts Camp conducts annual summer educational and camping program for 1800 students who enroll in two-, three-, four- and six-week sessions and students from Michigan who attend special two-week, All-State sessions. Conducts programs in music, visual art, dance, theatre and creative writing. The Interlochen Arts Academy, a college preparatory boarding school, offers intensive study in music, visual art, theatre arts, dance, creative writing, and college-preparatory academics. Maintains the Leland B. Greenleaf collection of historical musical instruments, the Walter Hastings collection of natural history artifacts and photographs, and an art gallery. Operates Interlochen Public Radio, a charter member of National Public Radio. Presents the Interlochen Arts Festival featuring well-known artists and ensembles. **Convention/Meeting:** none. **Libraries: Type:** not open to the public. **Holdings:** 21,000. **Divisions:** High School (students 14-18); Intermediate (students 12-14); Junior (students 8 to 12). **Formerly:** (1990) National Music Camp. **Publications:** *Crescendo*, semiannual. Magazine. Intended alumni and friends of the Interlochen Center for the Arts. Includes obituaries. **Price:** free. **Circulation:** 60,000. Alternate Formats: online ● *IAA Catalog*, annual. Contains information about the fine arts programs of the Interlochen Arts Academy. **Price:** free ● *IAC Catalog*, annual. For recruiting artistically talented young people between 8-18 years old for Interlochen Arts Camp. **Price:** free ● *Performance Programs*, weekly. Report.

9572 ■ International Arts and Artists (IA&A)

9 Hillyer Ct. NW, 2nd Fl.
Washington, DC 20008
Ph: (202)338-0680
Fax: (202)333-0758
E-mail: info@artsandartists.org
URL: http://www.artsandartists.org
Contact: David Furchgott, Pres./CEO

Founded: 1995. **Multinational. Description:** Promotes cross-cultural understanding and exposure to the arts through exhibitions, programs and services to artists, art institutions and the public. **Programs:** USArts International Training.

9573 ■ International Association of Art Critics - United States Section (AICA USA)

333 E 55th St., No. 3B
New York, NY 10022
Ph: (212)838-2475
Fax: (212)838-3789
E-mail: board@aicausa.org
URL: http://www.aicausa.org
Contact: Ms. Phyllis Braff, Pres.

Founded: 1948. **Members:** 400. **Membership Dues:** general, $85 (annual). **Multinational. Description:** Elevates the value of art criticism. Represents the physical and moral defense of artwork. **Awards:** Best Shows Award. **Frequency:** annual. **Type:** recognition. **Computer Services:** database, member directory ● online services, general discussion. **Committees:** Advocacy; Art Critics; Development; Outreach; Professional Issues; Young Critics. **Affiliated With:** United Nations Educational, Scientific and Cultural Organization. **Publications:** Newsletter. Alternate Formats: online.

9574 ■ International Guild of Realism (IGOR)

4400 N Scottsdale Rd., No. 9539
Scottsdale, AZ 85251
E-mail: realismguild@cox.net
URL: http://www.realismguild.com
Contact: Larry Charles, Contact

Founded: 2002. **Membership Dues:** regular, $100 (annual). **Multinational. Description:** Advances realism in fine art and promotes the careers of representational artists. Creates exhibition opportunities in the top art galleries and museums. Provides marketing and technical assistance to members. **Telecommunication Services:** electronic mail, brandranch@worldnet.att.net.

9575 ■ International Society for the Performing Arts (ISPA)

17 Purdy Ave.
PO Box 909
Rye, NY 10580
Ph: (914)921-1550
Fax: (914)921-1593
E-mail: info@ispa.org
URL: http://www.ispa.org
Contact: Horacio Lecona, Sec.

Founded: 1948. **Members:** 700. **Membership Dues:** master, $575-$1,835 (annual) ● affiliate, $275 (annual). **Staff:** 3. **Budget:** $800,000. **Languages:** English, French. **Description:** Executives and directors of concert and performance halls, festivals, performing companies, and artist competitions; government cultural officials; artists' managers; and other interested parties with a professional involvement in the performing arts from more than 50 countries in every region of the world, and in every arts discipline. **Awards:** Angel Award. **Frequency:** annual. **Type:** recognition. **Recipient:** for outstanding leadership, advocacy, philanthropy, innovation, scholarship, or curatorship ● Distinguished Artist Award. **Frequency:** annual. **Type:** recognition. **Recipient:** to performing artists who have made outstanding contribution of talent, artistry, dedication, and service to the world of performing arts ● International Citation of Merit. **Frequency:** annual. **Type:** recognition. **Recipient:** for distinguished service working within the profession ● Patrick Hayes Award. **Frequency:** annual. **Type:** recognition. **Recipient:** to an ISPA member of long standing whose achievements in arts management are deserving of special praise and recognition. **Formerly:** (1994) International Society of Performing Arts Administrators. **Publications:** *Performing Arts Forum*, periodic. Newsletter. Contains information on employment opportunities, member news, and statistics. **Price:** included in membership dues. **Circulation:** 700 ● Membership Directory, annual. Includes detailed information on all members. **Conventions/Meetings:** semiannual conference (exhibits).

9576 ■ International Society for the Performing Arts Foundation (ISPA)

PO Box 909
Rye, NY 10580
Ph: (914)921-1550
Fax: (914)921-1593
E-mail: info@ispa.org
URL: http://www.ispa.org
Contact: Ella Baff, Exec. Dir.

Founded: 1949. **Members:** 600. **Membership Dues:** master (based on annual budget), $575-$1,835 (annual) ● affiliate, $275 (annual). **Staff:** 4. **Multinational. Description:** Executives and directors of concert and performance halls, festivals, performing companies, and artist competitions, government cultural officials, artists' managers. Dedicated to advancing the field of performing arts, nationally and internationally. Strengthens leadership capabilities of member arts institutions; provides support to enrich creative potential and intellectual growth in the field; affirms the importance and necessity of the performing arts. **Awards:** Angel Award. **Frequency:** semiannual. **Type:** recognition. **Recipient:** to an individual or organization that has demonstrated a significant and lasting contribution in support of the performing arts ● Distinguished Artist Award. **Frequency:** semiannual. **Type:** recognition. **Recipient:** to performing artists who made outstanding contributions in the performing arts ● International Citation of Merit. **Frequency:** semiannual. **Type:** recognition. **Recipient:** for unique lifetime achievement that has enriched the international performing arts ● Patrick Hayes Award. **Frequency:** semiannual. **Type:** recognition. **Recipient:** for ISPA member whose achievements in arts management are deserving of special praise and recognition. **Publications:** *Forum*. Newsletter. Contains membership news and articles. **Price:** included in membership dues ● Membership Directory, annual. Includes biographical information and photographs for all members. **Conventions/Meetings:** annual conference - December.

9577 ■ International Society of Phenomenology, Aesthetics, and the Fine Arts

c/o The World Phenomenology Institute
1 Ivy Pointe Way
Hanover, NH 03755
Ph: (802)295-3487
Fax: (802)295-5963
E-mail: info@phenomenology.org
URL: http://www.phenomenology.org
Contact: Louis Houthakker, Contact

Founded: 1997. **Members:** 60. **Staff:** 3. **Budget:** $800. **Multinational. Description:** Represents persons interested in the study of arts and literature from a philosophic, historical, critical, or educational point of view. Fosters communication and exchange among members. **Libraries: Type:** open to the public. **Holdings:** 68; articles, artwork, books, periodicals. **Subjects:** aesthetics, phenomenology, literature. **Awards: Frequency:** periodic. **Type:** scholarship. **Conventions/Meetings:** annual meeting.

9578 ■ Labor Heritage Foundation (LHF)

815 16th St. NW
Washington, DC 20006
Ph: (202)637-3963 (202)639-6204
E-mail: info@laborheritage.org
URL: http://www.laborheritage.org
Contact: Peter Jones, Exec. Dir.

Founded: 1984. **Members:** 3,217. **Staff:** 2. **Budget:** $100,000. **Description:** Labor and arts organizations; trade unionists, academics, artists, and interested individuals. Seeks to revive the tradition of labor music and art and increase its use in local union activities, including rallies, boycotts, and strikes, in order to educate and organize the labor movement and the public. Focuses on artistic and musical works that the foundation feels address the current interests and concerns of working people. Encourages and facilitates communication among artists. Operates as a referral service and information clearinghouse for labor artists and cultural activities. Offers assistance to unions in planning and coordinating activities. Sponsors regional arts/songs exchanges, concerts, and festivals. Conducts fundraising activities. Works closely with the AFL-CIO. **Awards:** Joe Hill Award. **Frequency:** annual. **Type:** recognition. **Recipient:** for lifetime achievement in field of labor culture. **Affiliated With:** AFL-CIO. **Publications:** Audiotapes ● Videos ● Also makes available songbooks, posters, and notecards. **Conventions/Meetings:** Conference on Creative Organizing ● annual Great Labor Arts Exchange Conference - meeting - always last Sunday through Tuesday in June, Silver Spring, MD.

9579 ■ Nashville Entertainment Association (NEA)

Address Unknown since 2007

Founded: 1980. **Members:** 2,000. **Membership Dues:** $45 (annual). **Staff:** 2. **Budget:** $70,000. **Description:** Individuals in the music and entertainment industry. Seeks to: further the growth and recognition of Nashville, TN as a total center for entertainment; act as an industry information clearinghouse; advance and promote a variety of live entertainment performances. Provides educational programs, seminars, and forums. Compiles statistics. **Awards:** Master Award. **Frequency:** annual. **Type:** recognition. **Recipient:** for creators of the Nashville sound. **Computer Services:** membership list. **Committees:** Actors; Film/Video; Music; Musical Arts and Education; Promotion/Publicity. **Formerly:** (1986) Nashville Music Association. **Publications:** *Marquee*, quarterly. Newsletter. **Price:** free, for members only. **Advertising:** accepted. Alternate Formats: online. **Conventions/Meetings:** annual general assembly - always June, Nashville, TN.

9580 ■ National Alliance for Media Arts and Culture (NAMAC)

145 9th St., Ste.250
San Francisco, CA 94103
Ph: (415)431-1391
Fax: (415)431-1392
E-mail: namac@namac.org
URL: http://www.namac.org
Contact: Helen De Michiel, Co-Dir.

Founded: 1980. **Members:** 350. **Membership Dues:** institutional, $75-$450 (annual) ● commercial, $500-$1,000 (annual) ● individual, $75 (annual) ● special, $45 (annual). **Staff:** 4. **Budget:** $450,000. **Description:** Represents diverse member organizations who are dedicated to encouraging film, video, audio and online/multimedia arts, and promoting the cultural contributions of individual media artists. Aims to strengthen media arts organizations as an integral part of the community; facilitates the support of independent media artists from all cultural community and regions; integrates media into all levels of education and advocates for media literacy as an educational goal; promotes humane uses of and individual access to current and future media technologies; encourages media arts that are rooted in local communities, as well as those, which are global in outlook. **Libraries: Type:** not open to the public. **Holdings:** 200; books, periodicals. **Subjects:** telecommunications, public policy, youth media, experimental media, broadcast, community development, distribution, education, media literacy, exhibition, fundraising, leadership, organization development, arts policy, preservation, technology. **Awards:** Capacity Building Support Program. **Frequency:** annual. **Type:** grant. **Recipient:** for media arts organizations and programs. **Computer Services:** Online services, member directory with contact info and profile of over 200 media arts organizations, media advocacy, fleets and activities, listservs, links. **Publications:** *A Closer Look*, annual. Report. Contains case studies. **Price:** included in membership dues; $15.00/copy for nonmembers ● *NAMAC eBULLETin*, biweekly. Newsletter. Features news from the field, convening opportunities, job listings, and more. Alternate Formats: online ● *NAMAC Newsletter*, 3/year. Includes association news, artist profiles, calendar of events, and regional news. **Price:** included in membership dues. ISSN: 0889-8928. **Circulation:** 650. Alternate Formats: online. **Conventions/Meetings:** biennial conference (exhibits).

9581 ■ National Art Exhibitions by the Mentally Ill (NAEMI)

PO Box 350891
Miami, FL 33135
Ph: (954)922-8692
E-mail: naemi@bellsouth.net
URL: http://www.naemi.org

Founded: 1988. **Description:** Aims to reduce the stigma associated with mental illness through the promotion, exhibition and preservation of the art of mentally ill individuals in the U.S. **Conventions/Meetings:** annual Art Exhibition - show (exhibits).

9582 ■ National Arts Foundation

4444 Oakton St.
Skokie, IL 60076
Ph: (847)674-7990
Fax: (847)675-8116
E-mail: info@nafgallery.com
Contact: Arthur Harry Sahagian, Dir.

Founded: 1989. **Members:** 80. **Staff:** 5. **Budget:** $24,000. **Regional Groups:** 3. **State Groups:** 58. **Local Groups:** 11. **Description:** Promotes public awareness and appreciation of the arts in U.S.A. **Libraries: Type:** reference. **Holdings:** 1,600; books. **Subjects:** art enhancement and historical art. **Awards:** Paintings and Books. **Frequency:** weekly. **Type:** recognition. **Computer Services:** Mailing lists. **Publications:** *Reflections of the Century*. Book. Contains pictures of paintings. ● *Sahagian's Armenia* ● *Sahagian's Century*. Book. **Price:** $8.00. **Conventions/Meetings:** monthly board meeting.

9583 ■ National Assembly of State Arts Agencies (NASAA)

1029 Vermont Ave. NW, 2nd Fl.
Washington, DC 20005
Ph: (202)347-6352
Fax: (202)737-0526
E-mail: nasaa@nasaa-arts.org
URL: http://www.nasaa-arts.org
Contact: Jonathan Katz, CEO

Founded: 1968. **Members:** 56. **Membership Dues:** friend (minimum), $50 (annual) ● sustainer (minimum), $100 (annual) ● sponsor (minimum), $250 (annual) ● patron (minimum), $500 (annual) ● Leadership Circle (minimum), $1,000 (annual). **Staff:** 10. **Description:** State arts agencies (governmental units receiving appropriations from their state and designated by their authorizing legislation to receive funding from the National Endowment for the Arts). Enhances the growth of the arts and represent the collective needs and concerns of members. Serves as a liaison between members, federal agencies, and arts organizations. Provides forums for review and development of national arts policies. Compiles statistics; conducts research. **Libraries: Type:** reference. **Computer Services:** Mailing lists, state arts agencies. **Telecommunication Services:** electronic mail, jonathan@nasaa-arts.org ● TDD, (202)347-5948. **Committees:** Advocacy; Communications; Research and Information. **Task Forces:** Cultural Pluralism. **Publications:** *The NASAA Advocate*, quarterly. Compendium of Rationales, Models, Questionnaires and Analysis. **Price:** $7.00/issue ● *NASAA Notes*, monthly. Newsletter. Contains articles clipped from national publications on such subjects as art policy, education, financing, and art. **Price:** available to members only ● *National Assembly of*

State Arts Agencies—Directory, monthly. Lists state arts agencies involved with art policy, education, and financing. **Price:** $10.00/copy ● *1994 State Arts Agency Profile.* Overviews state arts agencies. **Price:** $40.00 ● *Part of the Solution: Creative Alternatives for Youth.* Contains research of examples of how the arts are making a positive difference in the lives of children, especially those most at risk. **Price:** $17.00 ● *Serving the Arts in Rural Areas* ● *The State of the States.* **Conventions/Meetings:** annual conference and meeting - always fall.

9584 ■ National Association of Latino Arts and Culture (NALAC)
1204 Buena Vista St.
San Antonio, TX 78207
Ph: (210)432-3982
Fax: (210)432-3934
E-mail: info@nalac.org
URL: http://www.nalac.org
Contact: Rosalba Rolon, Chair
Founded: 1989. **Members:** 300. **Membership Dues:** individual, $25 (annual) ● family, $40 (annual) ● organization (based on annual budget), $50-$800 (annual). **Description:** Preserves, develops, and promotes the cultural and artistic expressions of the diverse Latino populations of the United States. Provides direct services to the constituency. Collects information about the current needs and challenges for Latino artists and organizations. **Publications:** *El Aviso*, 3/year. Newsletter. **Price:** included in membership dues ● *NALAC e-Boletin* (in English and Spanish), monthly. Bulletin. Alternate Formats: online.

9585 ■ National Endowment for the Arts (NEA)
1100 Pennsylvania Ave. NW
Washington, DC 20004
Ph: (202)682-5400 (202)682-5415
Fax: (202)682-5064
E-mail: webmgr@arts.endow.gov
URL: http://www.arts.gov
Contact: Eileen B. Mason, Sr. Deputy Chair
Description: Seeks to give access to the arts for all Americans. Facilitates the creation and presentation of "artistically excellent work." Supports a lifelong education in the arts for all. Strives to preserve the national heritage. Strengthens and stabilizes arts organizations. Supports the building of community through the arts. **Awards:** Jazz Masters Fellowship. **Frequency:** annual. **Type:** fellowship. **Recipient:** to jazz musicians ● National Heritage Fellowships. **Frequency:** annual. **Type:** fellowship. **Recipient:** to master folk and artists ● National Medal of Arts. **Frequency:** annual. **Type:** medal. **Recipient:** for extraordinary accomplishments of artists. **Telecommunication Services:** teletype, (202)682-5496. **Publications:** *NEA Arts*, bimonthly. Newsletter. Contains information on NEA's programs, awards, grants and upcoming events. Alternate Formats: online.

9586 ■ National Endowment for the Christian Arts (NECA)
13222 Park Ln.
Fort Washington, MD 20744
Ph: (301)203-8789
Fax: (301)203-6708
E-mail: info@theneca.org
URL: http://www.theneca.org
Contact: David M. Wright, Exec. Dir.
Founded: 2000. **Members:** 12,000. **Description:** Promotes Christian works of art created or produced by non-compromising Christian artists in the U.S. **Awards: Type:** grant. **Recipient:** to Christian artists, churches and organizations. **Computer Services:** Online services, chat ● online services, message board. **Publications:** *The Artist Corner.* Newsletter. Alternate Formats: online.

9587 ■ National Foundation for Advancement in the Arts (NFAA)
444 Brickell Ave., P-14
Miami, FL 33131
Ph: (305)377-1140
Free: (800)970-ARTS
Fax: (305)377-1149
E-mail: info@nfaa.org
URL: http://www.nfaa.org
Contact: William H. Banchs, Pres.
Founded: 1981. **Members:** 7,000. **Membership Dues:** high school student (per category), $40 (annual). **Staff:** 19. **Budget:** $2,400,000. **Description:** Aims to identify emerging artists and assist them at critical junctures in their educational and professional development; and to raise appreciation for, and support of, the arts in American society. Conducts main program, which is the youngARTS Program (formerly known as the Arts Recognition and Talent Search) that gives over $525,000 in cash awards to high school seniors in art forms including dance, music, music jazz, music voice, theatre, visual arts, photography, cinematic arts and writing. Serves as the exclusive nominating body for the Presidential Scholars in the Arts program. **Libraries: Type:** not open to the public; reference. **Holdings:** archival material, audio recordings, biographical archives, films, photographs, video recordings. **Subjects:** theatre, musical theatre, dance, world dance, jazz, jazz voice, voice, writing, cinematic arts, photography, visual arts. **Awards:** youngARTS Award. **Frequency:** annual. **Type:** monetary. **Recipient:** for talented individuals in the arts (17-18 years old). **Computer Services:** Mailing lists, of awardees ● mailing lists, of students who register for the ARTS program available to all colleges and arts programs. **Publications:** *YoungARTS*, 3/year. Magazine. **Advertising:** accepted ● Annual Report, annual. **Conventions/Meetings:** annual youngARTS Week - competition, with final auditions for arts finalists to determine their cash awards - second week of January.

9588 ■ National League of American Pen Women (NLAPW)
Pen Arts Bldg.
1300 17th St. NW
Washington, DC 20036-1973
Ph: (202)785-1997
Fax: (202)452-8868
E-mail: nlapw1@verizon.net
URL: http://www.nlapw.org
Contact: Elaine Waidelich, Pres.
Founded: 1897. **Members:** 3,600. **Membership Dues:** national active, associate, international affiliate, regular, $30 (annual). **Staff:** 2. **Budget:** $178,000. **State Groups:** 32. **Local Groups:** 200. **Description:** Writers, composers, artists, professional women in the creative arts. Promotes the professional development of members. Conducts and encourages literary, educational, and charitable activities in the fields of art, letters, and music. Fosters the exchange of ideas and techniques through workshops, discussion groups, and professional lecturers; sponsors art exhibits and contests. Bestows certificates of proficiency; received Literary Hall of Fame Award. **Libraries: Type:** open to the public; by appointment only. **Holdings:** 3,000; biographical archives, books, periodicals. **Subjects:** poetry, fiction, non-fiction, history, travel. **Awards:** Mature Woman Award. **Frequency:** biennial. **Type:** recognition. **Recipient:** for a non-pen woman in art, letters and music ● **Frequency:** biennial. **Type:** scholarship. **Recipient:** for mature women 35 years and over who are not members of the organization. **Computer Services:** database. **Divisions:** Art; Letter; Music. **Publications:** *National League of American Pen Women—Roster*, biennial. Membership Directory. **Price:** included in membership dues. ISSN: 0031-4242. **Circulation:** 5,000. Alternate Formats: online ● *The Pen Woman*, bimonthly. Magazine. Includes book reviews, poetry, essays, fiction, profiles and obituaries. **Price:** included in membership dues; $15.00 /year for nonmembers; $2.00/copy for nonmembers. **Circulation:** 5,000. **Advertising:** accepted. Alternate Formats: online ● Brochures. **Conventions/Meetings:** biennial conference (exhibits).

9589 ■ New Horizons Arts Initiative (NHAI)
Address Unknown since 2008
URL: http://www.artsinitiative.net
Membership Dues: adult, $45 (annual) ● student, $25 (annual) ● professional, $245-$5,045 (annual). **Description:** Represents the interests of individuals dedicated to providing financial support to the arts. Provides members with supplemental income, health and other benefits, grants and scholarships. Creates growth of membership through credits toward annual membership for each member or member organization through sponsorship.

9590 ■ Omega Theatre and the Omega Arts Network
41 Greenough Ave.
Jamaica Plain, MA 02130
Ph: (617)522-8300
E-mail: info@omegatheater.org
URL: http://www.omegatheater.org
Contact: Saphira Linden, Dir.
Founded: 1966. **Members:** 600. **Budget:** $50,000. **Description:** Omega Arts Network encompasses artists of all media involved in sacred, visionary, or transformational artwork that reflects a reverence for the earth, addresses social issues, and promotes unity of humanity. Works to strengthen and support an international community of like-minded artists. Maintains Living Galleries, which provide a forum for artists to share their work with peers and the public. Organizes creative meditation retreats; produces original theatrical works. Omega Theatre is a Transpersonal Drama Therapy certification program through the National Association of Drama Therapists to obtain RDT Credential (Registered Drama Therapist). **Libraries: Type:** reference. **Holdings:** 200; articles, books. **Subjects:** meditation, theater, drama therapy, education. **Computer Services:** database, information on members ● mailing lists, for members. **Affiliated With:** National Association for Drama Therapy. **Formerly:** Omega Arts Network; Theater Workshop Boston. **Publications:** *Drama Therapy: Dramascope*, quarterly. Newsletter ● *Omega Arts Network News*, periodic. Includes calendar of events. ● Membership Directory, periodic ● Also publishes articles in journals and newspapers about transpersonal Drama Therapy.

9591 ■ Paul VI Institute for the Arts
619 10th St. NW
Washington, DC 20001-4532
Ph: (202)347-2714
Fax: (202)347-1401
Contact: Msgr. Michael di Teccia Farina, Pres.
Founded: 1975. **Members:** 2,700. **Staff:** 2. **Description:** Promotes the arts as part of the Catholic church's evangelistic mission and seeks to reestablish and promote the church's role as sponsor of the arts. Assists in developing the talents of young artists and helping young people develop an appreciation of the arts. Conducts educational programs.

9592 ■ Performing Arts Foundation (PAF)
401 N 4th St.
Wausau, WI 54403
Ph: (715)842-0988
Free: (888)239-0421
Fax: (715)842-8715
E-mail: blofstad@grandtheater.org
URL: http://www.onartsblock.org
Contact: James O'Connell, Exec. Dir.
Founded: 1963. **Description:** Seeks to unite and assist young performing artists from around the world. Sponsors ALLNATIONS Dance Company, which presents performances of international dance. **Convention/Meeting:** none. **Formerly:** (1967) International Folk Dance Foundation.

9593 ■ Performing Arts Resources (PAR)
88 E 3rd St., No. 19
New York, NY 10003
Ph: (212)673-6343
Fax: (212)673-1856
E-mail: perfrtrsrc@aol.com
URL: http://members.aol.com/perfrtrsrc
Contact: Donna E. Brady, Exec. Dir.
Founded: 1981. **Membership Dues:** individual, $35 (annual) ● company, $150 (annual). **Staff:** 2. **Description:** Experienced professionals in the fields of production management, lighting design, stage management, tour coordination, general company management, and arts project administration provid-

ing technical and management services to dance and theatre. Acts as clearinghouse offering consultations on general administration, structure, technical issues and practices of companies or projects. Sponsors referral service for dance and theatre companies in need of personnel including technicians, stage managers, designers, and managers. Maintains listings of rental and purchase sources of sound equipment, lighting equipment, drapery, and dance floors. Runs the Set Recycling Hotline. **Libraries: Type:** reference. **Holdings:** archival material, books, clippings, monographs, periodicals. **Subjects:** technical specification sheets on theaters and performing spaces in the U.S. and other countries, dance floors and rehearsal and performance spaces in the New York City area, equipment manuals, reference manuals. **Telecommunication Services:** electronic mail, dbradypar@aol.com. **Affiliated With:** Dance Theater Workshop. **Formerly:** (1981) Technical Assistance Group; (1985) Technical Assistance Project/American Dance Festival; (1987) Technical Assistance Program/American Dance Guild. **Publications:** Newsletter, quarterly. **Price:** included in membership dues. **Advertising:** accepted. **Conventions/Meetings:** annual Fringe U - seminar and workshop, panels - end of August in New York, NY ● workshop.

9594 ■ Professional Arts Management Institute (PAMI)

110 Riverside Dr., No. 4E
New York, NY 10024
Ph: (212)579-2039 (212)344-7447
Fax: (212)579-2049
E-mail: skipreiss@aol.com
Contact: Alvin H. Reiss, Dir.
Founded: 1957. **Staff:** 1. **Description:** Intensive training program designed to supplement the knowledge and skills of both professionals and students interested in or involved in managing cultural institutions and performing arts programs. Conducts one three-day seminar per year; compiles statistics. **Libraries: Type:** reference. **Awards:** Arts Management Awards. **Frequency:** annual. **Type:** recognition. **Recipient:** for service to field. **Telecommunication Services:** electronic mail, aebmedia@column.edu. **Formerly:** (1965) Musical Arena Theatres Association; (1986) Performing Arts Management Institute. **Publications:** *Arts Management*, 5/year. Newsletter. Includes case histories on funding and marketing. **Price:** $22.00 in U.S.; C$23.00 in Canada; $25.00 outside U.S. and Canada. **Advertising:** accepted. **Conventions/Meetings:** annual conference.

9595 ■ P.S.1 Contemporary Art Center

22-25 Jackson Ave.
Long Island City, NY 11101
Ph: (718)784-2084
Fax: (718)482-9454
E-mail: mail@ps1.org
URL: http://www.ps1.org
Contact: Alanna Heiss, Dir.
Founded: 1971. **Staff:** 27. **Languages:** English, French, German, Italian. **Nonmembership. Description:** Offers artists an opportunity to utilize a wider range of spaces in a more flexible manner than counterparts in the museum sector or private gallery system. Maintains the Clocktower Gallery in Manhattan, NY, which presents exhibitions, performances, and related events. Provides a limited number of studios for artists. Sponsors educational programs. **Convention/Meeting:** none. **Libraries: Type:** not open to the public. **Holdings:** 500; articles, books, photographs. **Formerly:** (1988) Institute for Art and Urban Resources; (2002) PSI Institute for Contemporary Art.

9596 ■ Rhizome

210 11th Ave., 2nd Fl.
New York, NY 10001
Ph: (212)219-1288
Fax: (212)431-5328
E-mail: webmaster@rhizome.org
URL: http://www.rhizome.org
Contact: Lauren Cornell, Exec. Dir.
Founded: 1996. **Membership Dues:** individual, $25 ● organization (based on size), $250-$5,000 (annual). **Multinational. Description:** Provides an online platform for the global new media art community. Supports the creation, presentation, discussion and preservation of contemporary art that uses new technologies. **Computer Services:** database, collection of new media artworks from members. **Publications:** *Rhizome Digest*, weekly, every Friday. Newsletter. Presents an original feature piece. Alternate Formats: online ● *Rhizome News*, 3 times a week. Newsletter. Features original writing by artists, curators and critics from around the world. Alternate Formats: online.

9597 ■ Salmagundi Club (SC)

47 5th Ave.
New York, NY 10003
Ph: (212)255-7740
E-mail: info@salmagundi.org
URL: http://www.salmagundi.org
Contact: Claudia Seymour, Pres.
Founded: 1871. **Members:** 650. **Membership Dues:** artist, layperson, $450 (annual). **Description:** Professional art club of painters, sculptors, writers, and artists. Provides exhibition facilities for members' work in all media. Serves as a meeting place for professional artists and persons with artistic interests. Presents seven exhibitions each season in the club's galleries; offers art demonstrations and classes to the public. Maintains: art collection of American impressionists from 1871 to the present; art reference library of several thousand volumes; biographical archives of former and present members; national historic landmark building which is open to the public daily. Bestows art scholarships to talented artists under the age of 30 and awards prizes. Provides specialized education programs; sponsors competitions; the word Salmagundi is taken from the "Salmagundi Papers" of Washington Irving and also the name of a stew served to the members. **Libraries: Type:** by appointment only. **Holdings:** 6,500. **Subjects:** art, architecture, sculpture, fashion. **Committees:** Art; Coast Guard Art Program; Curators. **Publications:** *Salmagundi Roster*, biennial. Directory ● *Salmagundi Stew*, 7/year. Newsletter ● *Salmagundian*, 3/year. Newsletter. **Conventions/Meetings:** bimonthly general assembly - usually October to June.

9598 ■ Saving the Arts

PO Box 4045
Nooksack, WA 98276
E-mail: sta_office@excite.com
URL: http://www.savingthearts.org
Contact: Jeff Sprague, Pres.
Description: Represents the interests of musicians, dancers, actors, teachers, photographers, singers, parents and business owners dedicated to saving the arts in schools and communities throughout the country. Provides funding, awareness and educational links to the arts, while supporting students, educators, communities and schools locally and nationwide. Works closely with communities and sponsorship programs. Provides benefit concerts, special events, fundraising projects, auctions and merchandise sales. **Telecommunication Services:** electronic mail, sta_jeff@excite.com.

9599 ■ Society for the Arts, Religion and Contemporary Culture (ARC)

c/o Nelvin Vos, Exec. Dir.
15811 Kutztown Rd.
Box 15
Maxatawny, PA 19538
Ph: (610)683-7581
Fax: (610)683-7581
E-mail: nlvos@enter.net
URL: http://www.sarcc.org
Contact: Nelvin Vos, Exec. Dir.
Founded: 1961. **Members:** 500. **Membership Dues:** individual, organizational (1-5 persons), $50 (annual) ● organizational (more than 5 persons), $100 (annual). **Staff:** 1. **Budget:** $20,000. **Description:** Scholars, artists, musicians, theologians, scientists, and playwrights. Seeks to build bridges between the arts and religion, the roles of which the society believes are decisive in any culture. **Libraries: Type:** open to the public. **Holdings:** 500; archival material, audio recordings, papers, reports, video recordings. **Subjects:** religion, arts. **Awards:** Fellows of the Society. **Frequency:** annual. **Type:** recognition. **Recipient:** for distinctive achievement in religion and/or the arts. **Formerly:** (1968) Foundation for the Arts, Religion and Culture. **Publications:** *ARC Newsletter*, periodic. Includes articles and program papers on the arts. **Price:** included in membership dues. **Circulation:** 600 ● *Publication of The ARC Story—A Narrative Account of the Society of Arts, Religion and Contemporary Culture*. **Conventions/Meetings:** symposium - always first Saturday of February, May and November in New York City.

9600 ■ Subud International Cultural Association - U.S.A. (SICA)

14019 NE 8th St., Ste.A
Bellevue, WA 98007
Ph: (425)643-1904
Fax: (425)643-2725
E-mail: ahbromley@teleline.es
URL: http://www.subud-sica.org
Contact: Andrew Bromley, Corporate Sec./Office Mgr.
Founded: 1983. **Members:** 2,000. **Staff:** 1. **Regional Groups:** 7. **State Groups:** 40. **Local Groups:** 56. **Description:** Individuals who belong to Subud U.S.A. Coordinates and develops cultural programs and events. Sponsors performing and visual arts programs for youth organizations, schools, and other groups. Conducts educational courses. Operates research and charitable programs. **Libraries: Type:** reference. **Awards: Type:** recognition. **Computer Services:** database ● mailing lists. **Affiliated With:** Subud United States of America. **Formerly:** (1993) Subud International Cultural Association. **Publications:** *Subud USA News*, bimonthly. Newsletter. **Price:** included in membership dues. **Advertising:** accepted. Alternate Formats: online ● Also publishes anthologies. **Conventions/Meetings:** competition ● annual meeting (exhibits) - usually July 4th weekend.

9601 ■ Symphony for United Nations (SUN)

3240 NE 11 St.
Pompano Beach, FL 33062
Ph: (954)782-9703
E-mail: eger@symphonyun.org
URL: http://www.symphonyun.org/home.html
Contact: Maestro Joseph Eger, Founder/Music Dir./Conductor
Founded: 1974. **Members:** 140. **Membership Dues:** regular, $35 (annual) ● student, $20 (annual) ● Conductor's Circle, $100-$500 (annual) ● first chair player, $501-$1,000 (annual) ● concert master, $1,001-$5,000 (annual) ● conductor's associate, $5,001-$10,000 (annual) ● sponsor, $15,000 (annual) ● golden baton, $25,000 (annual) ● patron, $50,000 (annual) ● grand patron, $50,001 (annual). **Staff:** 3. **Budget:** $1,200,000. **State Groups:** 2. **Description:** Promotes music and public education in an effort to improve understanding among people of all nations. Seeks to achieve this goal by giving concerts, playing at and producing festivals, and holding symposia. Provides children's services; conducts charitable and educational programs. **Awards: Type:** recognition. **Committees:** Artistic Advisory; International Advisory. **Formerly:** SUN Symphony Soc. Inc. **Publications:** *Sunspots*, semiannual. Newsletter. **Price:** free. **Circulation:** 2,000. **Advertising:** accepted. Alternate Formats: online; magnetic tape. **Conventions/Meetings:** annual meeting (exhibits).

9602 ■ Wolf Trap Foundation for the Performing Arts (WTFPA)

1645 Trap Rd.
Vienna, VA 22182
Ph: (703)255-1900 (703)255-1942
Free: (877)WOLFTRAP
Fax: (703)255-1905
E-mail: wolftrap@wolftrap.org
URL: http://www.wolf-trap.org
Contact: Terrence D. Jones, Pres./CEO
Founded: 1966. **Membership Dues:** friend, $50 (annual) ● curtain raiser, $125 (annual) ● Silver Society, $250 (annual) ● conductor, $500 (annual) ● director,

$1,250 (annual) ● producer, $3,000 (annual). **Staff:** 55. **Budget:** $15,000,000. **Description:** Presents opera, musical comedy, ballet, theater, modern dance, and classical and pop concerts in the Filene Center, the park's 7,000 person capacity outdoor theater, and in The Barns of Wolf Trap, a 350-seat theater with performances year-round. Committed to the advancement of talented young Americans through the Wolf Trap Opera Company, a group of 13-20 singers selected by audition each year from across the country to participate in an advanced training program at Wolf Trap. Operates the Institute for Early Learning Through the Arts. Provides theater workshops, live theater for children, and master classes. Awards internships. **Convention/Meeting:** none. **Awards:** Catherine Filene Shouse Scholarship. **Frequency:** annual. **Type:** scholarship. **Recipient:** for high school juniors and seniors (piano, voice, strings), selected by audition. **Publications:** Brochures.

9603 ■ Young Audiences (YA)
115 E 92nd St.
New York, NY 10128-1688
Ph: (212)831-8110
Fax: (212)289-1202
E-mail: ya4kids@ya.org
URL: http://64.78.18.246
Contact: Richard Bell, Natl. Exec. Dir.
Founded: 1952. **Staff:** 8. **Budget:** $12,000,000. **Description:** Seeks to have professional ensembles to present live educational programs in music, dance, and theatre to children (grades K-12) during school hours. Works to increase the creative and imaginative capacities of children through listening and participating in live performing arts experiences; to help build future audiences for the performing arts; to develop the performing arts resources of communities by training ensembles in educational techniques. Trains musicians, dancers, and actors to present performances, demonstrations, workshops, and residencies in each of the art forms. Researches and develops new program techniques and concepts for initial exposure and short-term residency programs. **Libraries: Type:** reference. **Holdings:** 200. **Subjects:** arts education, arts administration. **Committees:** Chapter Affiliations; Chapter Relations; Public Relations; Special Events; Staff Development; Technical Assistance Materials in Program Development. **Projects:** Arts Card; Arts Partner; Faces; Family Festival of the Arts; Master Artists Series; Run for the Arts. **Publications:** Annual Report. Includes chapter and funding highlights, annual conference report, listings endowment fund and benefit supporters, and other contributors. ● Booklets ● Newsletter, bimonthly. **Conventions/Meetings:** annual conference.

9604 ■ Youth Education in the Arts (YEA)
601 W Hamilton St.
Allentown, PA 18101
Ph: (610)821-0345
Fax: (610)821-1451
E-mail: hopkins@yea.org
URL: http://www.yea.org
Contact: George Hopkins, Exec. Dir.
Multinational. Description: Supports the development of young people through participation in the performing arts. Provides programs that allow talented performers to participate in pageantry events around the continent. **Computer Services:** Online services, discussion forum. **Programs:** The Cadets; Crossmen; US Scholastic Marching Band Association. **Publications:** Newsletter. Alternate Formats: online.

Arts and Sciences

9605 ■ American Academy of Arts and Sciences (AAAS)
136 Irving St.
Cambridge, MA 02138
Ph: (617)576-5000 (617)576-5010
Fax: (617)576-5050
E-mail: aaas@amacad.org
URL: http://www.amacad.org
Contact: Leslie C. Berlowitz, CEO
Founded: 1780. **Members:** 4,300. **Staff:** 40. **Description:** Honorary society and interdisciplinary studies center. Includes scholars and national leaders in five classes: mathematical and physical sciences; biological sciences; social arts and sciences; humanities; and public affairs, business, and administration. Conducts interdisciplinary studies of current social and intellectual issues. Seeks to bring together scholars and leaders whose research, experience, or knowledge can help to clarify contemporary problems and place them in perspective. **Awards:** Amory Prize. **Type:** recognition. **Recipient:** for individuals who have made a major contribution in reproductive biology ● Emerson-Thoreau Medal. **Type:** medal. **Recipient:** for individuals who have distinguished achievements in the field of literature ● Founders' Award. **Frequency:** annual. **Type:** recognition. **Recipient:** for men, women and institutions that have advanced the ideals of the founders of the academy ● Humanistic Studies Award. **Type:** recognition ● Rumford Prize. **Type:** recognition. **Recipient:** for promising individuals who have contributed in the field of heat and light ● Talcott Parsons Prize. **Type:** recognition. **Recipient:** for individuals who have contributed in the field of social sciences. **Programs:** Education; Humanities and Culture; Science and Global Security; Social Policy and American Institutions. **Publications:** *Daedalus*, quarterly. Journal. Covers a variety of interdisciplinary topics including mathematical and physical sciences, biological sciences, and social arts and sciences. **Price:** $33.00 /year for individuals; $50.00 /year for institutions. ISSN: 0011-5266. **Circulation:** 14,000 ● *Records*, annual ● Bulletin, quarterly. Alternate Formats: online. **Conventions/Meetings:** periodic conference ● seminar.

9606 ■ American Romanian Academy of Arts and Sciences (ARA)
c/o Dr. Nicolae H. Pavel, Sec. Gen.
Ohio Univ.
Dept. of Mathematics
Athens, OH 45701
Ph: (740)593-1267 (740)593-1252
Fax: (740)593-9805
E-mail: iopara@meca.polymtl.ca
URL: http://www.meca.polymtl.ca/ion/ARA-AS/index.htm
Contact: Prof. Ion Paraschivoiu, Pres.
Founded: 1975. **Members:** 250. **Membership Dues:** full, $70 (annual) ● corresponding, $10 (annual). **Languages:** English, French, Romanian. **Description:** Artists and scholars from Romania who live in the U.S; American and European scholars with an interest in Romanian art, culture, and history. Seeks to: foster Romanian cultural traditions; educate the public concerning Romanian spiritual values; strengthen cultural and spiritual ties between the U.S. and Romania. Conducts research, through the ARA Research Institute in any Romanian related topics, and in the fields of mathematics, linguistics, economics, social and political science, history, and literary criticism. **Libraries: Type:** reference. **Holdings:** 5,000; archival material. **Subjects:** literature, history, linguistics, political science, economics, mathematics. **Awards:** ARA Annual Award. **Frequency:** annual. **Type:** recognition. **Recipient:** for renowned scholars and artists contributing to the enhancement of Romanian culture and science. **Computer Services:** Mailing lists. **Telecommunication Services:** electronic mail, npavel@bing.math.ohiou.edu. **Publications:** *ARA Journal* (in English, French, and Romanian), annual. Includes book reviews, obituaries, and scholarly papers. **Price:** included in membership dues. ISSN: 0896-1018. **Circulation:** 500. **Advertising:** accepted ● *ARA Newsletter*, semiannual. **Price:** included in membership dues. **Advertising:** accepted. Alternate Formats: online ● *Clash Over Romania* ● *Homo Religiosus* ● *Ionel Jianu si Opera Lui* ● *Istoria Romanilor* ● *Libertas Mathematica*, annual. **Price:** $30.00 ● *Miron Butariu, O Viata de Om* ● *Nicolas Timiras: Anii Tineretii* ● *Romani in Stinta Si Cultura Occidentala* ● *Romania and the Romanians* ● *Romanian Artists in the West* ● *United States and Romania: Relations in the Twentieth Century*. **Conventions/Meetings:** annual congress, includes discussion groups and panels (exhibits).

9607 ■ Art and Science Collaborations (ASCI)
130 E End Ave. - 1A
New York, NY 10028
Ph: (941)955-5103
E-mail: info@asci.org
URL: http://www.asci.org
Contact: Cynthia Pannucci, Exec. Dir.
Founded: 1988. **Members:** 400. **Membership Dues:** student/senior, $30 (annual) ● artist/scientist, $40 (annual) ● individual, $50 (annual) ● institution/associate (small company, organization, educational institution), $100 (annual) ● friend, $250 (annual) ● donor, $500 (annual) ● patron, $1,000 (annual). **Multinational. Description:** Raises public awareness of using science and technology to explore new forms of creative expression. Seeks to increase communication and collaboration between artists, scientists and technologists. Provides members with opportunities for professional growth, increased public visibility and a supportive community. **Computer Services:** Online services, bulletin board. **Publications:** *ASCI eBulletin*, monthly. Alternate Formats: online.

9608 ■ Chinese-American Arts Council (CAAC)
456 Broadway, 3rd Fl.
New York, NY 10013-5800
Ph: (212)431-9740
Fax: (212)431-9789
E-mail: info@caacarts.org
URL: http://www.caacarts.org
Contact: Alan Chow, Artistic Dir.
Founded: 1975. **Members:** 1,000. **Staff:** 6. **Budget:** $160,000. **Description:** Seeks to: maintain cultural identity of new immigrants and cultural heritage of American-born Asians; deepen children's cultural identity through the arts; provide opportunities for Asian-American artists; provide opportunities for the general public to enjoy cultural events; maintain an international communication network for Asian-American artists. Hosts performances, including modern and traditional dramas, dances, martial arts, and vocal and instrumental concerts. Sponsors several visual art exhibitions and an international travelling exhibition; provides services for artists including staging, costuming, publishing, public relations, and funding; coordinates and presents Asian-American cultural events by request. Offers children's services; conducts educational programs and seminars. **Awards:** Most Outstanding Asian Artists Award. **Frequency:** annual. **Type:** recognition. **Publications:** *Chinese-American Art News*. Newsletter. **Price:** free for members. **Circulation:** 600. **Advertising:** accepted. **Conventions/Meetings:** annual Chinatown Cultural Festival - meeting.

9609 ■ Filipinas Americas Science and Art Foundation (FASAF)
1209 Park Ave.
New York, NY 10128
Ph: (212)427-6930
Fax: (212)427-6931
Founded: 1976. **Members:** 150. **Staff:** 15. **Budget:** $750,000. **Languages:** English, Spanish, Tagalog. **Description:** Resource center and sponsor of activities designed to increase the appreciation for North and South American, Philippine, and Asian cultures. Sponsors little-known artists in the fields of art, music, sciences, and tourism. Conducts specialized education, children's services, and charitable programs. Offers courses in travel and tourism, accounting and bookkeeping, and tax and preparation. Operates speakers' bureau. Maintains hall of fame. **Libraries: Type:** reference. **Holdings:** 2,500. **Subjects:** music, art, sciences, travel, tourism, management, taxation, art, cultures. **Awards:** Service Awards. **Frequency:** semiannual. **Type:** scholarship. **Recipient:** for students, staff, and the public. **Computer Services:** database, on-site training programs. **Committees:** Parent Advisory. **Also Known As:** (1993) Town

House International School. **Publications:** *THIS Play House*, quarterly. Features school events and general public activities. **Price:** free. **Circulation:** 1,000. **Advertising:** accepted. Alternate Formats: online ● *Town House International School Newsletter*, monthly ● Brochures. **Conventions/Meetings:** quarterly dinner, with awards ceremony (exhibits) - held in April, June, August, and December, in New York City.

9610 ■ Leonardo, The International Society for the Arts, Sciences and Technology
211 Sutter St., Ste.501
San Francisco, CA 94108
Ph: (415)391-1110
Fax: (415)391-2385
E-mail: isast@leonardo.info
URL: http://www.leonardo.info
Contact: Roger Malina, Chm.
Founded: 1968. **Members:** 700. **Membership Dues:** subscription, $80 (annual) ● student/retiree, $50 (annual) ● organizational, corporate, $1,000-$1,500 (annual). **Staff:** 5. **Budget:** $250,000. **Multinational. Description:** Serves the international arts community by promoting and documenting work at the intersection of the arts, sciences, and technology, and by encouraging and stimulating collaboration between artists, scientists, and technologists. **Libraries: Type:** reference. **Awards:** F.J. Malina-Leonardo Prize. **Type:** recognition ● Leonardo Award for Excellence. **Type:** recognition ● New Horizons Award for Innovation. **Type:** recognition. **Telecommunication Services:** electronic mail, rmalina@alum.mit.edu. **Working Groups:** Leonardo/College Art Association. **Formerly:** (1982) International Society of Scientist-Artists. **Publications:** *Leonardo Music Journal*, annual. Features scholarly and theoretical writings by and about contemporary musicians, composers and sound artists using science and technology. **Price:** $30.00/year ● Journal, bimonthly. Features scholarly and theoretical writings by and about contemporary artists. **Price:** $72.00/year. ISSN: 0024-094X. **Circulation:** 3,000. **Advertising:** accepted. **Conventions/Meetings:** annual Refresh! New Media History - conference ● annual Space and the Arts Workshop.

9611 ■ Mexican Arts and Technology Network
Address Unknown since 2007
Founded: 1994. **Languages:** English, French, Russian, Spanish. **Description:** Encourages the exchange of ideas in the fields of arts, technology, and business between Mexico and other countries. Promotes innovation and development in arts, technology, and business. **Libraries: Type:** lending. **Holdings:** articles, articles, artwork, books, periodicals. **Subjects:** Mexican arts, technology, business. **Publications:** *Mexican Journals Partnerships*. **Conventions/Meetings:** competition.

9612 ■ World Academy of Art and Science (WAAS)
301 19th Ave. S
Minneapolis, MN 55455
Ph: (612)624-5592
Fax: (612)625-3513
E-mail: kvargo@hhh.umn.edu
URL: http://www.worldacademy.org
Contact: Dr. Walter T. Anderson, Pres.
Founded: 1960. **Members:** 500. **Staff:** 2. **Budget:** $200,000. **Regional Groups:** 2. **Description:** Network of not more than 500 individual Fellows from diverse cultures, nationalities, and intellectual disciplines, "chosen for eminence in art, the natural and social sciences, and the humanities". Activities focus on "the social consequences and policy implications of knowledge". Serves as a forum for reflective scientists, artists, scholars, and practitioners of public affairs to discuss the vital opportunities of humankind, independent of political boundaries or limits, whether spiritual or physical. Strives to discuss these opportunities objectively, constructively, scientifically, in global perspective free from vested interests or regional attachments. **Libraries: Type:** reference. **Holdings:** 400; archival material, books, monographs, periodicals. **Awards: Type:** recognition. **Foreign language name:** Academie Mondiale de l'Art et de la Science. **Publications:** *Directory of Fellows* ● *World Academy of Art and Science Newsletter*, 2-3/year. Alternate Formats: online ● Books ● Monographs. **Conventions/Meetings:** quinquennial Assembly of Fellows - general assembly.

Asian

9613 ■ Allies Building Community (ABC)
PO Box 57250
Washington, DC 20037-0250
Ph: (202)496-1555 (202)625-2244
Fax: (202)338-2918
E-mail: abcallies3@gmail.com
URL: http://www.archway2.org
Contact: Dr. Dwan Tai, Pres./Founder
Founded: 1963. **Members:** 3,000. **Description:** Organized for artistic, cultural, educational, economic development, and community service activities. **Formerly:** (2003) Asian Benevolent Corps. **Publications:** *Asian Voice*, periodic. Magazine.

9614 ■ American Oriental Society (AOS)
Univ. of Michigan
Hatcher Graduate Lib.
Ann Arbor, MI 48109-1205
Ph: (734)647-4760
E-mail: jrodgers@umich.edu
URL: http://www.umich.edu/~aos
Contact: Jonathan Rodgers, Sec.-Treas.
Founded: 1842. **Members:** 1,250. **Membership Dues:** student, retired, $25 (annual) ● regular, $70 (annual). **Staff:** 3. **Description:** Represents professional and amateur Orientalists united to promote research in Oriental languages, history, and civilizations. **Libraries: Type:** reference. **Holdings:** 22,413; monographs, periodicals. **Subjects:** Oriental culture. **Awards:** The Louise Wallace Hackney Fellowship for the Study of Chinese Art. **Frequency:** annual. **Type:** fellowship. **Recipient:** for postdoctoral and doctoral students, who are U.S. citizens, studying Chinese art. **Affiliated With:** American Council of Learned Societies. **Publications:** *American Oriental Series*, periodic. Monographs ● *American Oriental Series Essays*, periodic ● *Journal of the American Oriental Society*, quarterly. Includes book reviews. **Price:** included in membership dues; $80.00 /year for institutions; $50.00 /year for individuals. ISSN: 0003-0279. **Advertising:** accepted. **Conventions/Meetings:** annual conference (exhibits).

9615 ■ American Schools of Oriental Research (ASOR)
656 Beacon St., 5th Fl.
Boston, MA 02215-2006
Ph: (617)353-6570
Free: (888)847-8753
Fax: (617)353-6575
E-mail: asor@bu.edu
URL: http://www.asor.org
Contact: Andrew G. Vaughn PhD, Exec. Dir.
Founded: 1900. **Members:** 1,500. **Membership Dues:** professional, $110 (annual) ● student/retired, $85 (annual) ● associate, $50 (annual) ● sustaining, $250 (annual) ● corporate/institutional, $1,000 (annual). **Staff:** 6. **Regional Groups:** 4. **Local Groups:** 2. **National Groups:** 11. **Multinational. Description:** Represents colleges, universities, theological seminaries, libraries, and research institutes; scholars working in archaeological, historical and biblical fields; interested others. Promotes public understanding of the peoples and cultures of the Near East and their wider spheres of interaction. Conducts archaeological research on the peoples and cultures of the Near East, from the early to modern periods. Offers visiting professorships. Supports archaeological field projects. Maintains libraries and hostels in Amman, Jordan, Nicosia, Cyprus, Jerusalem and Israel. **Awards: Frequency:** annual. **Type:** fellowship ● **Type:** grant. **Recipient:** for study and travel in the Middle East. **Telecommunication Services:** electronic mail, asored@bu.edu. **Committees:** Archaeological Policy; Baghdad; Damascus; Development; Outreach; Personnel; Program; Publications. **Publications:** *Bulletin of the American Schools of Oriental Research*, quarterly. Journal ● *Journal of Cuneiform Studies*, annual ● *Near Eastern Archaeology*, quarterly. Bulletin ● Newsletter, quarterly ● Monograph, annual. **Conventions/Meetings:** annual conference (exhibits) ● annual meeting (exhibits).

9616 ■ Asia Society
725 Park Ave., 70th St.
New York, NY 10021
Ph: (212)327-9217
Fax: (212)794-1223
E-mail: info@asiasoc.org
URL: http://www.asiasociety.org
Contact: Vishakha N. Desai, Pres.
Founded: 1956. **Members:** 6,500. **Membership Dues:** individual, $65 (annual) ● senior citizen, student, teacher, associate, $40 (annual) ● dual/family, $120 (annual) ● dual associate/dual senior citizen, $80 (annual) ● contributing, $250 (annual) ● sustaining, $500 (annual). **Staff:** 100. **Budget:** $14,000,000. **Regional Groups:** 5. **Description:** Fosters understanding of Asia and communication between Americans and the people of Asia and the Pacific. Presents a wide range of programs including high-level conferences, symposia, international study missions, press briefings, publications, major art exhibitions and performing arts productions. **Awards:** Osborn Elliot Prize for Excellence in Asia Journalism. **Frequency:** annual. **Type:** recognition. **Recipient:** for an individual who has produced the best example of journalism about Asia in any media channel, including print, broadcast and online sources. **Departments:** Asia Society Store; Contemporary Affairs and Corporate Program; Education; Galleries. **Programs:** Cultural. **Absorbed:** (1990) China Council. **Publications:** *Archives of Asian Art*, annual. Book ● *Asia Newsletter*, 3/year. Contains chapter news and calendar of events. **Price:** included in membership dues. **Circulation:** 8,000 ● *Asian Update*. Reports ● *China Briefing*, annual ● *India Briefing*, annual ● *Korea Briefing*, annual ● Annual Report, annual. **Price:** free ● Brochures ● Catalogs ● Monographs ● Videos. **Conventions/Meetings:** annual conference, business and economics - in Asia.

9617 ■ Conference on Asian History (CAH)
c/o Prof. George M. Wilson, Chm.
Indiana Univ.
East Asian Stud. Center
Memorial Hall West 207
1021 E Third St.
Bloomington, IN 47405
Ph: (812)855-3765
Free: (800)441-3272
Fax: (812)855-7762
E-mail: easc@indiana.edu
URL: http://www.indiana.edu/~easc
Contact: Prof. George M. Wilson, Chm.
Founded: 1953. **Members:** 100. **Description:** Historians of Asia at North American universities and colleges. Dedicated to the exchange of information on Asia. Sponsors luncheon and panel discussions on Asian history during American Historical Association (see separate entry) meeting. **Telecommunication Services:** electronic mail, gmiv@indiana.edu. **Affiliated With:** American Historical Association.

9618 ■ Cultural Integration Fellowship (CIF)
360 Cumberland St.
San Francisco, CA 94114
Ph: (415)626-2442 (415)386-9590
E-mail: info@culturalintegration.org
Contact: Mrs. Bina Chaudhuri, Pres.
Founded: 1951. **Members:** 85. **Membership Dues:** student/senior, $20 (annual) ● sponsoring, $250 (annual) ● contributing, $50 (annual) ● general, $35 (annual) ● sustaining, $100 (annual). **Staff:** 4. **Description:** Individuals interested in the concepts of universal religion, cultural harmony, and creative self-fulfillment. Promotes intercultural understanding between Asia and America; emphasizes the "spiritual oneness of the human race"; applies fundamental spiritual principles in daily living. Operates small, spiritually-oriented bookstore. **Libraries: Type:** reference. **Holdings:** 3,000; books, monographs. **Sub-**

jects: philosophy, psychology, religion. **Awards:** Haridas Chaudhuri Scholarship. **Frequency:** annual. **Type:** scholarship. **Recipient:** for current students from the California Institute of Integral Studies. **Committees:** Universal Religion. **Publications:** *Ashram Bulletin*, quarterly ● *Special Cultural Events*, quarterly. Report. **Conventions/Meetings:** weekly meeting, with lectures - always Sunday ● quarterly seminar, covers oriental philosophy - always summer.

9619 ■ East-West Cultural Center (EWCC)
12329 Marshall St.
Culver City, CA 90230
Ph: (310)390-9083
Fax: (310)390-7763
E-mail: ewcc@sriaurobindocenter-la.org
URL: http://www.sriaurobindocenter-la.org
Founded: 1953. **Staff:** 4. **Languages:** English, Sanskrit. **Description:** Artists, philosophers, scientists, musicians, dancers, and teachers of other spiritual movements and religions. Seeks to relate and integrate the cultural and spiritual values of the East (primarily India) with those of Western civilization. Conducts lectures; holds performances. Sponsors study groups based on the teachings of Sri Aurobindo, an Indian mystic. Offers classes in Hindi, Punjabi, Sanskrit, and Yoga. Sponsors the work at Auroville, the City of Human Unity being built in Pondicherry, and Tamil Nadu, India. **Libraries: Type:** reference. **Holdings:** 2,000. **Subjects:** Eastern religion, philosophy, history, literature, language, culture. **Publications:** *First Lessons in Sanskrit Grammar and Reading* ● *JYOTI- An Informational and Cultural*. Journal. Alternate Formats: CD-ROM ● Booklets.

9620 ■ Indonesian Studies Committee
c/o Dr. Karl Heider
Off. of Provost
Univ. of South Carolina
Columbia, SC 29208
Ph: (803)777-2808
Fax: (803)777-9502
Contact: Dr. Karl Heider, Contact
Members: 100. **Membership Dues:** $12 (annual). **Budget:** $2,000. **Languages:** English, Indonesian. **Description:** Promotes Indonesian studies. Organizes or sponsors panels at the Association for Asian Studies. **Computer Services:** Electronic publishing. **Telecommunication Services:** electronic bulletin board. **Publications:** *Antara Kita*, 3/year. Newsletter. Addresses Indonesian studies. **Circulation:** 200. Alternate Formats: online ● *International Directory of Indonesianists*. **Conventions/Meetings:** biennial Suma Indonesia Conference - meeting - spring.

9621 ■ Leadership Education for Asian Pacifics (LEAP)
327 E 2nd St., Ste.226
Los Angeles, CA 90012
Ph: (213)485-1422
Fax: (213)485-0050
E-mail: leap@leap.org
URL: http://www.leap.org
Contact: J.D. Hokoyama, Pres./CEO
Founded: 1982. **Members:** 20,000. **Membership Dues:** corporate, $1,000 ● patron, $500 ● sponsor, $250 ● community/nonprofit, $150 ● sustaining, $100 ● individual, $50 ● student, $25. **Staff:** 15. **Budget:** $2,213,500. **Description:** Strives to achieve full participation and equality for Asian Pacific Americans through leadership, empowerment, and policy. Works to mobilize the talent and resources of the Asian Pacific community. Conducts workshops. Publishes original policy research. **Awards:** David R. Barclay Leadership Award. **Frequency:** annual. **Type:** recognition. **Recipient:** to individuals who embody the values of David Barclay ● Leap Leadership Award. **Frequency:** annual. **Type:** recognition. **Subgroups:** Asian Pacific American Public Policy Institute; Community Development Institute; Leadership Management Institute. **Publications:** *Reapportionment and Redistricting in Los Angeles: Implications for Asian Pacific Americans*. Pamphlets. Covers the issues of reapportionment and redistricting. **Price:** $10.00/set ● *The State of Asian Pacific America: Economic Diversity, Issues & Policies*. Report. Documents the historic labor, immigration, and education patterns that have shaped the current status of Asian Pacific Americans. **Price:** $15.00 ● *The State of Asian Pacific America: Policy Issues to the Year 2020*. Report. Forecasts a near tripling of the Asian Pacific American population by the year 2020 and examines the implications of these demographic changes. **Price:** $15.00 ● *The State of Asian Pacific America: Reframing the Immigration Debate*. **Price:** $17.00 ● *The State of Asian Pacific America: Transforming Race Relations*. **Price:** $20.00 ● The State of Asian Pacific America: Reframing the Immigration Debate. See enclosed publication list for report description and price.

9622 ■ Mai Wah Society
PO Box 404
Butte, MT 59703
Ph: (406)723-3231 (406)782-4867
E-mail: info@maiwah.org
URL: http://www.maiwah.org
Contact: Jim Griffin, Pres.
Founded: 1991. **Membership Dues:** regular, $10 (annual). **Multinational. Description:** Preserves and interprets the history and culture of Asian people in the Rocky Mountain West. Collects and preserves artifacts. Preserves historic buildings and sites. Presents public exhibits and supports research and publication of materials of scholarly and general interest. Raises funds and encourages volunteers in the local and global community. **Publications:** *Mai Wah News*. Newsletter. Alternate Formats: online. **Conventions/Meetings:** annual meeting, celebration of Chinese New Year - always February.

Asian-American

9623 ■ National Association of Asian American Professionals (NAAAP)
PO Box 52030
Boston, MA 02205
Ph: (206)619-8427
E-mail: pr@naaap.org
URL: http://www.naaap.org
Contact: Brad Baldia, Exec. VP
Founded: 1982. **Members:** 600. **Membership Dues:** single, $35 (annual) ● family, $55 (annual) ● student, $25 (annual). **Regional Groups:** 5. **Description:** Works to enhance cultural and educational awareness of the Asian community in the U.S. Provides resources and assistance to the Asian community. Develops social and professional networking programs. Maintains mentor program targeting underprivileged high school students. **Awards:** Scholarship and Leadership Award. **Frequency:** annual. **Type:** scholarship. **Recipient:** for two high school senior students from Greater Metropolitan New York area. **Formerly:** National Association of Young Asian Professionals. **Publications:** *NAAAP Times*, monthly. Newsletter. Includes articles, book and movie reviews, community news, member news and updates. **Price:** included in membership dues. **Advertising:** accepted. **Conventions/Meetings:** annual conference.

Assyrian

9624 ■ Bet-Nahrain (BN)
PO Box 4116
Modesto, CA 95352
Ph: (209)538-4130 (209)537-0933
Fax: (209)538-2795
E-mail: betnahrain@hotmail.com
URL: http://www.betnahrain.org
Contact: Dr. Sargon Dadisho, Pres.
Founded: 1974. **Members:** 5,000. **Membership Dues:** regular, $25 (annual). **Description:** Individuals united internationally to perpetuate the heritage of the Assyrian people through radio, television, printed material, and athletic and cultural programs. Conducts seminars and classes in ancient Assyrian language. Sponsors Assyrian broadcasting radio station and television network. **Libraries: Type:** open to the public. **Holdings:** 1,000. **Subjects:** Assyrian history and language. **Awards:** Bet Nahrain National Awards. **Frequency:** annual. **Type:** monetary. **Recipient:** for excellence in education, arts, literature, etc. **Computer Services:** Information services, Assyrian language. **Committees:** Athletic; Educational; Khamatit Bet Nahrain (Women's Auxiliary); Mass Media; Radio and TV. **Publications:** Magazine (in Arabic, Assyrian, and English), monthly. Features events, programs and activities of Assyrian organizations and institutions all over the world. **Price:** $25.00/year. ISSN: 0748-2906. **Circulation:** 3,000. Alternate Formats: online. **Conventions/Meetings:** monthly meeting.

Austrian

9625 ■ Austrian Cultural Forum (ACFNY)
Austrian Cultural Inst.
11 E 52nd St.
New York, NY 10022
Ph: (212)319-5300
Fax: (212)644-8660
E-mail: desk@acfny.org
URL: http://www.acfny.org
Contact: Andreas Stadler, Dir.
Founded: 1962. **Staff:** 11. **Description:** Serves as Austrian government agency in charge of cultural and scientific relations between the United States of America and Austria. **Libraries: Type:** reference. **Holdings:** 10,000. **Subjects:** Austrian history, art, literature. **Formerly:** (1989) Austrian Institute; (2003) Austrian Cultural Institute. **Publications:** *Austria.Culture*, bimonthly. Magazine. **Price:** free. Alternate Formats: online.

9626 ■ Center for Austrian Studies (CAS)
Univ. of Minnesota
314 Social Sci. Bldg.
267 19th Ave. S
Minneapolis, MN 55455
Ph: (612)624-9811
Fax: (612)626-9004
E-mail: casahy@umn.edu
URL: http://www.cas.umn.edu
Contact: Dr. Gary B. Cohen, Dir.
Founded: 1977. **Staff:** 6. **Budget:** $150,000. **Description:** Provides a forum for the multi-disciplinary study of Austria within the context of central Europe. Holds international conferences, artistic performances, concerts, lectures, and exhibitions. Sponsors student and faculty exchanges with Austrian universities. Promotes research and coursework in Austrian history, culture, and current affairs. The center was a gift from the Austrian people to the U.S. on its bicentennial in 1976. **Awards:** Center for Austrian Studies Graduate Travel Grant. **Frequency:** annual. **Type:** grant. **Recipient:** to a graduate student at the University of Minnesota to do research in Austria or in neighboring countries formerly part of the Habsburg monarchy ● Voices of Vienna Award. **Frequency:** biennial. **Type:** scholarship. **Recipient:** to an undergraduate senior or graduate student of the University of Minnesota in the social sciences or humanities who proposes to do research in Austria or one of the other former Habsburg lands in Central Europe. **Publications:** *Austrian History Yearbook*, annual. Scholarly journal in Austrian and Habsburg history. ISSN: 0667-2378. **Circulation:** 450 ● *Austrian Studies Newsletter*, semiannual ● *CAS Annual Report*, annual. Alternate Formats: online ● *Monographs Arising from the Annual Symposia* ● *Working Papers in Austrian Studies*, 6-9/year. Proceedings. **Conventions/Meetings:** lecture ● seminar, on Austrian studies ● biennial symposium.

9627 ■ Federation of Alpine and Schuhplattler Clubs in North America (FASCNA)
N21 W26682 Cattail Ct.
Pewaukee, WI 53072
Ph: (262)695-2112

Fax: (262)695-0556
Contact: John Schaefer, Contact
Founded: 1966. **Members:** 4,800. **Membership Dues:** chapter, $60 (annual). **Local Groups:** 80. **Languages:** English, German. **Description:** Fosters and promotes Bavarian and Austrian culture and dance. Conducts charitable program and service for children. Offers specialized education. Sponsors biennial Schuhplattler Group Competitive Dancing. Compiles statistics. **Libraries: Type:** reference. **Awards:** Meistpreis. **Frequency:** periodic. **Type:** recognition ● Wander Prize. **Frequency:** biennial. **Type:** recognition. **Recipient:** for 1st place prize in dance competition ● Weitpreis. **Frequency:** periodic. **Type:** recognition. **Also Known As:** Gauverband Nordamerika. **Publications:** *Gauzeitung* (in English and German), 10/year. Newsletter. Contains association news, information on Bavarian and Austrian costumes and alpine flowers, calendar of events, and obituaries. **Price:** $15.00/year. **Circulation:** 1,000. **Advertising:** accepted ● *Trachten Kalender*, biennial. Directory. **Conventions/Meetings:** biennial Gaufest - convention, for delegates, members and the public (exhibits) - always odd-numbered years ● biennial General Delegates Meeting - meeting and workshop, for delegates and alternates - always even-numbered years.

9628 ■ Society for Austrian and Habsburg History (SAHH)
c/o Gary B. Cohen
Center for Austrian Stud.
Univ. of Minnesota
314 Social Sci. Bldg.
267 19th Ave. S
Minneapolis, MN 55455
Ph: (612)624-9811
Fax: (612)626-9004
E-mail: casahy@umn.edu
URL: http://www.cas.umn.edu
Contact: Gary B. Cohen, Contact
Founded: 1957. **Members:** 200. **Membership Dues:** individual, $35 (annual). **Description:** Represents scholars interested in Central and East Central European history. **Affiliated With:** American Historical Association. **Formerly:** (1989) United States Committee to Promote Studies of the History of the Hapsburg Monarchy. **Publications:** *Austrian History Yearbook*, annual. **Price:** included in membership dues; $60.00 for institutions. ISSN: 0667-2378. **Advertising:** accepted ● *Austrian Studies Newsletter*, semiannual. **Price:** free. **Circulation:** 3,000.

Authors

9629 ■ American Boccaccio Association (ABA)
c/o Dr. Janet Smarr, Pres.
Univ. of California at San Diego
Dept. of Theatre - 0344
9500 Gilman Dr.
La Jolla, CA 92093-0344
Ph: (858)454-7683
Fax: (858)454-7687
E-mail: jsmarr@ucsd.edu
URL: http://www.heliotropia.org/aba/about.shtml
Contact: Dr. Janet Smarr, Pres.
Members: 100. **Membership Dues:** regular, $5 (annual). **Languages:** English, Italian. **Description:** Represents university professors and other scholars of the Middle Ages and the Renaissance who are interested in the life and work of Italian author Giovanni Boccaccio (1313-75). Conducts seminars and regional meetings in conjunction with literary and historical conventions; disseminates information of interest to Boccaccio scholars; organizes ongoing Lectura Boccacci lecture and publication series. **Publications:** *Boccaccio Newsletter*, annual. Contains news on any aspect of Boccaccio studies plus bibliography. Alternate Formats: online ● *Heliotropia*, annual. Journal. Contains articles on any aspect of Boccaccio studies. Alternate Formats: online. **Conventions/Meetings:** annual Lectura Boccacci - lecture, analyses of tales from Boccaccio's "Decameron"; usually held in conjunction with MLA ● annual meeting, held in conjunction with Modern Language Association of America, American Association of Italian Studies, Renaissance Society of America or the Medieval Congress.

9630 ■ American Chesterton Society
4117 Pebblebrook Cir.
Minneapolis, MN 55437
Ph: (952)831-3096
Fax: (952)831-0387
E-mail: info@chesterton.org
URL: http://www.chesterton.org
Contact: Dale Ahlquist, Pres.
Founded: 1996. **Members:** 2,400. **Membership Dues:** individual in U.S., $42 (annual) ● individual in Canada, $50 (annual) ● individual outside U.S. and Canada, $58 (annual). **Staff:** 6. **Budget:** $120,000. **Local Groups:** 20. **Description:** Promotes interest in the life and ideas of Chesterton; circulates information about Chesterton and sponsors a variety of lectures around the country. Offers scholarships to high school and college students. **Libraries: Type:** reference. **Awards:** Lifetime Achievement Award. **Frequency:** annual. **Type:** recognition ● Outline of Sanity Award. **Frequency:** annual. **Type:** recognition. **Computer Services:** database, Chesterton's complete works. **Publications:** *Gilbert Magazine*, 8/year. Focuses on Chesterton's perspective. **Price:** $35.00. **Circulation:** 2,400. **Advertising:** accepted. **Conventions/Meetings:** annual G.K. Chesterton Conference, includes paper presentations and discussions - usually mid-June in St. Paul, MN.

9631 ■ American Hobbit Association (AHA)
6068 Tarn Cir.
Mason, OH 45040
Ph: (513)398-8058
E-mail: reneegen@cinci.rr.com
Contact: Renee (Arwen) Alper, Exec. Dir.
Founded: 1977. **Description:** Fans of British writer J.R.R. Tolkien (1892-1973) and his works, including *The Hobbit* and *The Lord of the Rings* trilogy. Seeks to inform and unite Tolkien fans worldwide; encourages members to form local subgroups. Sponsors trips to local Tolkien events. Holds monthly council to discuss Tolkien's works and related topics, play Tolkien games, and have costume parties. Publishes The Rivendell Review and Annuminas that contains stories, poems, art, puzzles, jokes and more, all with a Tolkien/Middle-Earth theme; copies of the its one-time fanzine, The Tales of Aragorn and Arwen, are also available upon request; this 77-page booklet contains stories, poems, songs, and artwork, dealing with the royal couple and their families, including out of print works by Darkover/Mists of Avalon author, Marion Zimmer Bradley. **Libraries: Type:** not open to the public. **Holdings:** 300; artwork, audio recordings, books, periodicals, photographs, video recordings. **Subjects:** Tolkien's collection. **Publications:** *The Rivendell Review*. Includes reviews of Tolkien-related merchandise, short stories, artwork, and association news. **Price:** included in membership dues. **Circulation:** 200. Also Cited As: *Annuminas* ● *The Tales of Aragorn and Arwen*. **Price:** $20.00 plus shipping and handling ($3) ● Back issue list available upon request.

9632 ■ American Teilhard Association (ATA)
PO Box 280
Lewisburg, PA 17837
Ph: (570)523-0929
E-mail: donna@religionandecology.org
URL: http://www.teilharddechardin.org
Contact: John Grim, Pres.
Founded: 1964. **Members:** 450. **Membership Dues:** student, $10 (annual) ● regular, $35 (annual) ● household, international, $40 (annual) ● contributing, $100 (annual) ● sponsor, $250 (annual) ● life, $400. **Description:** Seeks to bring an "encompassing vision" of its purposes through the writings of Teilhard. Maintains speakers' bureau. Holds regular lecture series. An international committee sponsors publication of his collected works. **Formerly:** (1975) American Teilhard de Chardin Association; (1986) American Teilhard Association for the Future of Man. **Publications:** *Teilhard Perspective*, semiannual. Newsletter. **Price:** included in membership dues ● *Teilhard Studies*, semiannual. Newsletter. **Price:** included in membership dues. **Conventions/Meetings:** annual meeting (exhibits) - always April or May, New York City.

9633 ■ Angela Thirkell Society (ATS)
PO Box 7109
San Diego, CA 92167
Ph: (619)222-8143
Fax: (619)255-3612
E-mail: joinats@aol.com
URL: http://www.angelathirkell.org
Contact: Barbara Houlton, Sec.
Founded: 1985. **Members:** 500. **Membership Dues:** individual, $15 (annual). **Description:** Individuals interested in the life and work of British author Angela Thirkell (1890-1961). Promotes increased appreciation of Thirkell's novels. Gathers and disseminates information. **Computer Services:** Mailing lists. **Publications:** *ATS Journal*, annual. **Price:** included in membership dues ● *Bulletin*, 3/year. Newsletter ● Books. **Conventions/Meetings:** meeting - every 18 months.

9634 ■ August Derleth Society (ADS)
PO Box 481
Sauk City, WI 53583
Ph: (608)643-3242
Fax: (608)643-3143
E-mail: kprice2@charter.net
URL: http://www.derleth.org
Contact: Kay Price, Exec. Sec.
Founded: 1978. **Members:** 450. **Membership Dues:** individual, $15 (annual) ● family, $20 (annual) ● business/library, $30 (annual). **Multinational. Description:** Individuals interested in the works of August Derleth (1909-71), American author of over 150 books including: history, science fiction, fantasy, romance, children's, poetry, and nature journals. Founder of Arkham House Publishing; editor, publisher, naturalist, and environmentalist. Provides information about Derleth and his work and his contribution to American literature. Conducts speakers' bureau and programs. **Libraries: Type:** by appointment only. **Holdings:** 300. **Subjects:** August Derleth. **Awards:** August Derleth Writers Awards. **Frequency:** annual. **Type:** monetary. **Recipient:** for promising writers in grade, high school and college levels. **Publications:** *Atmosphere of Houses*. Journal. Contains profiles of the houses of Sac Prairie and their inhabitants. **Price:** $6.00 ● *August Derleth Society Newsletter*, quarterly. Contains original Derleth writings, ADS activities, and board member profiles. **Price:** included in membership dues. ISSN: 0272-9911. **Circulation:** 600 ● *Remembering Derleth*. Book. **Price:** $10.00 ● *Return to Derleth*. Book. **Price:** $7.00 ● *Return to Derleth II*. Book. **Price:** $7.00 ● Bibliography. **Price:** $10.00. **Conventions/Meetings:** annual Walden West Festival, open to the public; features speakers, films, plays, skits, and book sales (exhibits) - always 2nd weekend of October.

9635 ■ Barbara Pym Society (BPS)
c/o Ellen Miller
145 Indian Hill Rd.
Carlisle, MA 01741
Ph: (978)287-4776
E-mail: ellen@ellenmiller.net
URL: http://www.barbara-pym.org
Contact: Ellen Miller, Contact
Founded: 1994. **Membership Dues:** individual, $22 (annual) ● family, $34 (annual) ● senior citizen, $12 (annual) ● senior family, $18 (annual). **Multinational. Description:** Fosters the appreciation and wider knowledge of the life and works of Barbara Pym. Secures the preservation of the manuscripts, letters and memorabilia of Barbara Pym. Encourages and supports publications and theses on Barbara Pym, her life and work. Provides a program of literary events and regular communications concerning the works of Barbara Pym. **Publications:** *Green Leaves*, semiannual. Newsletter. **Price:** included in membership dues. Alternate Formats: online.

9636 ■ Bernard Shaw Society (BSS)
PO Box 1159
Madison Square Sta.
New York, NY 10159-1159
Ph: (212)982-9885
E-mail: irarhoda@rcn.com
URL: http://chuma.cas.usf.edu/~dietrich/shawsociety.html
Contact: Rhoda Nathan, Pres.
Founded: 1962. **Members:** 300. **Membership Dues:** individual, $30 (annual). **Staff:** 6. **Description:** Individuals and libraries. Presents, studies, and explains the dramas and social philosophy of Bernard Shaw (1856-1950) through lectures, readings, performances, discussions, and publications. Presents dramatic readings of Bernard Shaw plays at the American Irish Historical Society's Fifth Avenue mansion. Conducts theater parties to Shavian productions. **Publications:** *The Independent Shavian*, 3/year. Journal. Features book and theatre reviews, illustrations, critical articles, and other material relating to the life and work of Bernard Shaw. **Price:** $30.00/year. ISSN: 0019-3763. **Circulation:** 600. **Advertising:** accepted. Alternate Formats: microform. **Conventions/Meetings:** lecture and symposium, covers Shaw as a dramatist, social philosopher, and critic of the arts ● monthly meeting - always in New York City, NY.

9637 ■ Bertrand Russell Society (BRS)
c/o Dennis Darland
1406 26th St.
Rock Island, IL 61201-2837
E-mail: dlhesq@rochester.rr.com
URL: http://www.users.drew.edu/~jlenz/brs.html
Contact: David Henehan, Sec.
Founded: 1974. **Members:** 150. **Membership Dues:** individual, $35 (annual) ● individual in Canada or Mexico, $39 (annual) ● individual outside North America, $45 (annual) ● couple, $40 (annual) ● couple in Canada or Mexico, $44 (annual) ● couple outside North America, $50 (annual) ● student, $20 (annual) ● student in Canada and Mexico, $24 (annual) ● student outside North America, $30 (annual) ● limited income, $20 (annual) ● limited income in Canada and Mexico, $24 (annual) ● limited income outside North America, $30 (annual). **Description:** Seeks to foster a better understanding of the life, work and writings of Bertrand Russell (1872-1970), and how his contributions relate to today's world. **Libraries: Type:** reference. **Holdings:** articles, audio recordings, books, video recordings. **Awards:** Bertrand Russell Society Award. **Frequency:** annual. **Type:** recognition. **Recipient:** for an individual or organization representing a cause or idea advocated by Russell ● Book Award. **Frequency:** annual. **Type:** recognition. **Recipient:** for the best book on Bertrand Russell published in the past year ● Lee Eisler BRS Service Award. **Frequency:** periodic. **Type:** recognition. **Recipient:** for service to the Russell Society ● Prizes for Papers. **Frequency:** annual. **Type:** recognition. **Recipient:** for the best two new papers on Bertrand Russell's life, work, or influence, one by an undergraduate, one by a graduate student. **Committees:** Philosophers; Science. **Publications:** *The Bertrand Russell Society Quarterly*. Journal. **Price:** included in membership dues. **Conventions/Meetings:** annual conference and workshop (exhibits) - usually June.

9638 ■ Betsy-Tacy Society (BTS)
PO Box 94
Mankato, MN 56002-0094
Ph: (507)345-9777
E-mail: membership@betsy-tacysociety.org
URL: http://www.betsy-tacysociety.org
Contact: Ms. Julie Schrader, Dir.
Founded: 1990. **Members:** 1,500. **Membership Dues:** individual, $15 (annual) ● patron, $25 (annual) ● life, $200 ● business, $30 (annual). **Staff:** 1. **Regional Groups:** 2. **Multinational. Description:** Admirers of author Maud Hart Lovelace and her work, especially the Betsy-Tacy series. Promotes the career of Lovelace and encourages readership of her work. Advocates maintaining the publication of Betsy-Tacy and related titles. Works to preserve existing landmarks and sites associated with the real people and places portrayed in the Betsy-Tacy books. The group has to purchased Lovelace's childhood home and that of her friend Frances Kirch (Tacy) to establish a museum, visitor center, and gift shop. Conducts educational programs. **Libraries: Type:** by appointment only. **Holdings:** archival material, biographical archives, books, papers, periodicals, photographs. **Publications:** *The Betsy-Tacy Society Journal*, periodic. **Price:** included in membership dues. **Circulation:** 1,500 ● *The Deep Valley Sun*, quarterly. Newsletters. **Price:** included in membership dues. **Circulation:** 1,500. **Conventions/Meetings:** quinquennial convention, tour of Betsy's and Tacy's houses and the surrounding Deep Valley area; also includes speakers, banquet, and children's program (exhibits).

9639 ■ Bram Stoker Memorial Association (BSMA)
29 Washington Sq. W, Penthouse N
New York, NY 10011
E-mail: countdracula145@hotmail.com
URL: http://www.benecke.com/stoker.html
Contact: Jeanne Keyes Youngson, Pres./Founder
Founded: 1985. **Members:** 189. **Multinational. Description:** Seeks to preserve the works and memory of Bram Stoker (1847-1912), Irish author noted for his use of Gothic tradition with supernatural themes (as in his book, *Dracula*).Maintains an extensive collection of Stoker memorabilia. (Research library open to authors under contract. Advance reservations necessary.). **Libraries: Type:** reference; by appointment only. **Holdings:** 250; archival material, papers, photographs. **Subjects:** Bram Stoker, his family, friends, and works; Henry Irving. **Telecommunication Services:** electronic mail, vampireprez@benecke.com ● electronic mail, bramstoker145@yahoo.com. **Affiliated With:** American Friends of Henry Irving; Bram Stoker Society - Ireland; International Frankenstein Society; The Vampire Empire; Vampire Information Exchange. **Formerly:** (2000) Count Dracula Fan Club.

9640 ■ Burroughs Bibliophiles (BB)
c/o George T. McWhorter, Treas.
Univ. of Louisville
Rare Book Rm., Ekstrom Lib.
Louisville, KY 40292
Ph: (502)852-8729
E-mail: gtmcwh01@gwise.louisville.edu
URL: http://www.burroughsbibliophiles.com
Contact: George T. McWhorter, Treas.
Founded: 1960. **Members:** 900. **Membership Dues:** regular, in U.S., $35 (annual) ● regular, outside U.S., $45 (annual). **Staff:** 1. **Budget:** $12,000. **Regional Groups:** 7. **State Groups:** 5. **Local Groups:** 1. **National Groups:** 2. **Languages:** English, French, German. **Multinational. Description:** Enthusiasts and collectors of the works of Edgar Rice Burroughs (1875-1950), best known as creator of the Tarzan books and as a writer of science fiction. Encourages reading and reprinting of his works; seeks to "correct the misinterpretations given the author's works by motion pictures and comic art forms." Personal libraries of members contain first editions, reprints, variant volumes in English and foreign languages, original art, motion pictures, cartoon strips, and books based on Burroughs' works. Maintains museum; conducts research programs. **Libraries: Type:** open to the public. **Holdings:** 10,000; archival material, films, periodicals. **Subjects:** biography, bibliography, art. **Awards:** Edgar Rice Burroughs Life Achievement Award. **Frequency:** annual. **Type:** recognition. **Recipient:** for outstanding service to the memory of Edgar Rice Burroughs ● Golden Lion Award. **Frequency:** annual. **Type:** recognition. **Computer Services:** Mailing lists. **Telecommunication Services:** electronic mail, george.mcwhorter@louisville.edu. **Publications:** *The Burroughs Bulletin*, quarterly. Contains bibliographies, biographical information, current events, book and film reviews. **Price:** $45.00 libraries and institutions (domestic); $55.00 libraries and institutions (international). **Circulation:** 900 ● *Edgar Rice Burroughs Memorial Collection Catalog: 1991* ● *The Gridley Wave*, monthly. Newsletter. **Price:** included in membership dues ● *House of Greystoke* ● *Roster and Dum-Dum*, annual. Directory. Includes club report. ● Directory, periodic. **Conventions/Meetings:** annual congress, huckster room displays (exhibits).

9641 ■ Byron Society of America (BSA)
c/o Charles E. Robinson, Exec. Dir.
Univ. of Delaware
Dept. of English
Newark, DE 19716-2537
Ph: (302)831-3654
Fax: (302)831-1586
E-mail: robinson@udel.edu
URL: http://www.english.udel.edu/byron
Contact: Charles E. Robinson, Exec. Dir.
Founded: 1971. **Members:** 400. **Membership Dues:** student, $15 (annual) ● active, $30 (annual) ● sustaining, $50 (annual) ● contributing, $100 (annual) ● donor, $250 (annual) ● sponsor, $500 (annual) ● benefactor, $1,000 (annual). **Staff:** 1. **Description:** University professors of romantic literature; graduate students studying romantic literature; public and university libraries and individuals interested in the works of George Gordon Byron (1788-1824), better known as Lord Byron, English romantic poet. Conducts annual tour of a country or literary association connected with Byron. Develops lecture series, dramatic readings, and concerts by the national committees. **Libraries: Type:** open to the public; by appointment only; reference. **Holdings:** 5,000; articles, books, periodicals. **Subjects:** Byron and the Romantics. **Awards:** Travel Grant Program for Young Scholars. **Frequency:** annual. **Type:** grant. **Recipient:** for graduate students with scholarly interest in Byron. **Computer Services:** Bibliographic search ● database ● mailing lists. **Councils:** International. **Formerly:** (1997) American Byron Society. **Publications:** *Byron Journal*, semiannual. Covers the life and works of Lord Byron and his literary circle. Includes book reviews. **Price:** included in membership dues; $30.00 for nonmembers. **Circulation:** 2,000. **Advertising:** accepted. **Conventions/Meetings:** annual International Byron Society Conference - conference and seminar - usually late summer ● annual Leslie A. Marchand Memorial Lecture - in October, at University of Delaware ● annual MLA Byron Session - lecture, in conjunction with Modern Language Association of America convention - always December.

9642 ■ Charles S. Peirce Society (CPS)
c/o Robert Lane, Sec.-Treas.
Philosophy Prog.
Univ. of West Georgia
1601 Maple St.
Carrollton, GA 30118
Ph: (678)839-4745
E-mail: rlane@westga.edu
URL: http://www.peircesociety.org
Contact: Robert Lane, Sec.-Treas.
Founded: 1946. **Members:** 514. **Membership Dues:** individual, $35 (annual) ● institution, $60 (annual) ● sustaining, $100 (annual) ● special, $20 (annual). **Multinational. Description:** College and university teachers and others interested in the study of, and communication about, the life and work of Charles Sanders Peirce and its ongoing influence in the many fields of intellectual endeavor to which the scientist had contributed. (Peirce, 1839-1914, a U.S. scientist, mathematician, and logician, is considered the founder of philosophical pragmatism and modern semiotics.) Prepares a museum of Peirce's home with the National Park Service in Milford, PA. **Awards:** C.S. Peirce Essay Contest Award. **Frequency:** annual. **Type:** monetary. **Recipient:** for graduate students and those who have earned their PhD degree within five years. **Affiliated With:** American Philosophical Association. **Publications:** *Transactions of the Charles S. Peirce Society: A Quarterly Journal in American Philosophy*. Includes articles and book reviews. **Price:** included in membership dues. ISSN: 0009-1774. **Circulation:** 600. **Advertising:** accepted. **Conventions/Meetings:** annual meeting, held in conjunction with Eastern Division of American Philosophical Association - always December 28,

usually in New York, Boston, Washington, or Atlanta ● periodic meeting, in conjunction with other scholarly organizations.

9643 ■ Christopher Morley Knothole Association (CMKA)
c/o Bryant Library
2 Paper Mill Rd.
Roslyn, NY 11576
E-mail: robertbsargent@aol.com
URL: http://christophermorley.org/index.html
Contact: Peter Cohn, Pres.
Founded: 1961. **Members:** 180. **Description:** Friends and admirers of author Christopher Morley (1890-1957). The association was organized with the specific purpose of preserving Morley's log cabin writing studio (known as The Knothole) as a memorial to the author and a center of interest for literary people. The building was bought and presented to Nassau County, NY, which installed it in the Christopher Morley Park, where it is open to the public during the summer. The association now concentrates on activities designed to keep alive Morley's reputation and introduce his works to young readers. Maintains Christopher Morley Alcove of the Bryant Library at Roslyn, NY, which contains reading copies and first editions of Morley's books as well as letters, manuscript material, clippings, and memorabilia. Sponsors readings. **Libraries: Type:** open to the public. **Holdings:** photographs. **Publications:** *Knothole*, irregular. Newsletter. **Conventions/Meetings:** meeting - always Bryant Library, Roslyn, NY.

9644 ■ Dante Society of America (DSA)
PO Box 711
Framingham, MA 01701-0711
E-mail: dsa@dantesociety.org
URL: http://www.dantesociety.org
Contact: Todd Boli, Sec.-Treas.
Founded: 1881. **Members:** 450. **Membership Dues:** regular, $30 (annual). **Description:** Teachers, scholars, and others interested in the study of Dante Alighieri (Italian poet, 1265-1321, author of the *Divine Comedy*) and in furthering scholarship in the field. **Libraries: Type:** reference. **Holdings:** 200; books. **Subjects:** Dante. **Awards:** Charles Hall Grandgent Award. **Frequency:** annual. **Type:** monetary. **Recipient:** for the best essay submitted by an American or Canadian graduate student enrolled in any graduate program ● Dante Prize. **Frequency:** annual. **Type:** monetary. **Recipient:** to individuals at undergraduate and graduate levels for the best student essay in competition on a subject related to the life or works of Dante. **Computer Services:** Mailing lists. **Formerly:** (1954) Dante Society. **Publications:** *American Dante Bibliography*, annual. Alternate Formats: online ● *Dante Society Newsletter*, semiannual. Alternate Formats: online ● *Dante Studies*, annual. Journal. Contains literary criticism relating to the works of Dante. Includes membership list and annotated bibliography. **Price:** included in membership dues; $30.00/issue for institutions. **Circulation:** 700 ● *International Dante Directory*. **Conventions/Meetings:** semiannual meeting.

9645 ■ D.H. Lawrence Society of North America (DHLSNA)
c/o Julianne Newmark, Sec.
New Mexico Tech
Humanities Dept.
801 Leroy Pl.
Socorro, NM 87801
Ph: (505)835-5190
E-mail: jnewmark@nmt.edu
URL: http://www.wsu.edu/~hydev/dhl/dhlsna.htm
Contact: Julianne Newmark, Sec.
Founded: 1975. **Members:** 200. **Membership Dues:** regular, $25 (annual) ● student, retired, $10 (annual). **Description:** Persons interested in studying the works of D.H. Lawrence (1885-1930), English novelist. Sponsors symposia and meetings concerned with the literature of Lawrence. **Awards:** Harry T. Moore Award. **Frequency:** biennial. **Type:** recognition. **Recipient:** to an individual who has made an outstanding contribution to the development of D.H. Lawrence studies ● New Scholar Award. **Frequency:** biennial. **Type:** monetary. **Recipient:** for excellence in research and promise of future scholarship. **Publications:** *D.H. Lawrence Society of North America Newsletter*, semiannual. Contains information on Lawrence studies (worldwide) and activities of the society. **Price:** included in membership dues. **Circulation:** 200. **Conventions/Meetings:** periodic conference, with its affiliate CILC ● quinquennial International Conference in North America ● annual meeting, held in conjunction with Modern Language Association of America.

9646 ■ Dickens Society (DS)
Wilkes Univ.
English Dept.
170 S Franklin St.
Wilkes-Barre, PA 18766
Ph: (570)408-4533
Free: (800)945-5378
Fax: (717)408-7860
E-mail: heaman23@msn.com
URL: http://www.lang.nagoya-u.ac.jp/~matsuoka/CD-Society.html
Contact: Robert J. Heaman, Sec.-Treas.
Founded: 1970. **Members:** 500. **Membership Dues:** in North America, $25 (annual) ● outside North America, $30 (annual) ● life, $400. **Staff:** 3. **Budget:** $13,500. **Description:** Represents individuals interested in the life and work of Charles Dickens (1812-70), English novelist. Works to conduct, encourage, further, and support research, publication, instruction, and general interest in the life, times, and literature of Dickens. **Awards:** Robert B. Partlow, Jr. Prize. **Frequency:** annual. **Type:** recognition. **Recipient:** for best essay submitted to Dickens Quarterly by a graduate student enrolled in a degree program. **Publications:** *Dickens Quarterly*. Journal. Provides information for scholars interested in the life, times, and works of Dickens. Includes annual index and bibliographies. **Price:** included in membership dues; $20.00 /year for individuals and institutions in U.S.; $25.00 /year for individuals and institutions (overseas). ISSN: 0742-5473. **Circulation:** 500. **Advertising:** accepted. **Conventions/Meetings:** annual Dickens Symposium - conference and dinner - always in the fall.

9647 ■ Edgar Allan Poe Society of Baltimore (EAPSB)
c/o Mr. Jeffrey A. Savoye, Sec.-Treas.
1610 Dogwood Hill Rd.
Towson, MD 21286-1506
Ph: (410)821-1285
URL: http://www.eapoe.org
Contact: Mr. Jeffrey A. Savoye, Sec.-Treas.
Founded: 1923. **Members:** 300. **Membership Dues:** student, $2 (annual) ● regular, $5 (annual) ● sustaining, $8 (annual). **Description:** Persons interested in the life and works of Edgar Allan Poe (1809-49), U.S. poet, critic, and short story writer. Functions as clearinghouse for information on Poe and his works. Serves in an advisory capacity to the Poe Museum, operated by the city of Baltimore, MD at 203 Amity St., where Poe lived and wrote from 1832 to 1835. Maintains archives at University of Baltimore library. Sponsors annual lecture and commemorative program in October on the anniversary of Poe's death; seeks to protect memorials of Poe in Baltimore, MD, especially his place of burial. **Libraries: Type:** reference. **Holdings:** archival material. **Publications:** *Annual Lectures*. Pamphlet. **Conventions/Meetings:** annual lecture, commemorative lecture on the life and works of Poe - always first Sunday in October.

9648 ■ Eugene O'Neill Society (EOS)
PO Box 402
Danville, CA 94526
Ph: (925)828-0659
Fax: (925)828-0265
E-mail: dmsdds@aol.com
Contact: Diane Schinnerer, Sec.-Treas.
Founded: 1978. **Members:** 300. **Multinational. Description:** Individuals interested in the life and works of American playwright Eugene O'Neill (1888-1953). Encourages the production of O'Neill's plays throughout the world. Studies O'Neill's works by means of: historical and critical writing; artistic performances on stage, film, television, and radio. Collects historical documentation and publications. **Publications:** *Eugene O'Neill Review*, annual. Journal. Includes book and play reviews and bibliography, articles, photographs. **Price:** included in membership dues; $15.00 /year for nonmembers. ISSN: 1040-9483. **Circulation:** 400. **Advertising:** accepted. **Conventions/Meetings:** periodic International O'Neill Conference and Tours - meeting, in conjunction with the Modern Language Association of America.

9649 ■ F. Scott Fitzgerald Society
c/o Prof. Ruth Prigozy, Exec. Dir.
107 Hofstra Univ.
Hempstead, NY 11549
E-mail: engrmp@hofstra.edu
URL: http://www.fitzgeraldsociety.org
Contact: Jackson R. Bryer, Pres.
Membership Dues: full, $25 (annual) ● student, $20 (annual). **Multinational. Description:** Assists and coordinates F. Scott Fitzgerald studies through conferences, publications and activities approved by the society. Disseminates accurate information and bibliographies about the life and works of Fitzgerald. Offers individuals interested in self-teaching and teachers of highschool and college a variety of materials to assist their study and appreciation of Fitzgerald, his work, and his times. **Affiliated With:** American Literature Association. **Publications:** Newsletter, annual. **Price:** included in membership dues.

9650 ■ Francis Bacon Foundation (FBF)
100 Corson St.
Pasadena, CA 91103
URL: http://www.sirfrancisbacon.org
Contact: Walter Arensberg, Co-Founder
Founded: 1937. **Staff:** 4. **Budget:** $130,000. **Description:** Educational and research institution affiliated with the Claremont Colleges. Promotes study in science, literature, religion, history, and philosophy, with special reference to the works of Francis Bacon, his character, his life, and his influence on his own and succeeding times. (Bacon, 1561-1626, was an English philosopher, essayist, and statesman.) Provides bibliographies and reading lists for persons engaged in research in fields covered by the foundation library. Conducts special exhibits; maintains speakers' bureau. **Libraries: Type:** reference. **Holdings:** 14,700; books. **Subjects:** Francis Bacon, Elizabethan and Jacobean background, English Renaissance 1470-1643, early cryptography, early Rosicrucian, early to modern Dante, anti-Shakespeareana, 18th Century American political theory, 16th and 17th Centuries emblem literature, Arensberg archive. **Awards: Type:** grant. **Recipient:** for private colleges and universities to enable them to hire outstanding scholars as visiting professors and lecturers. **Divisions:** Francis Bacon Library. **Publications:** *Francis Bacon Foundation—Annual Report*. **Price:** available to members only. **Conventions/Meetings:** annual Bacon Seminar - meeting - always January ● annual meeting - always third Wednesday of March, Claremont, CA.

9651 ■ Gene Stratton Porter Memorial Society
1205 Pleasant Point
Box 639
Rome City, IN 46784-9644
Ph: (260)854-3790
Fax: (260)854-9102
E-mail: gsporter@kuntrynet.com
URL: http://www.genestratton-porter.com
Contact: Fran Umbaugh, Pres.
Founded: 1976. **Members:** 240. **Membership Dues:** single, $10 (annual) ● family, $15 (annual) ● sustaining, $20 (annual) ● non-profit organization, business, $25 (annual) ● life, single, $100 ● life, husband and wife, $150. **Description:** Perpetuates the memory of American author Gene Stratton-Porter (1868-1924). Endeavors to further and promote the purposes, activities, and programs of the Gene Stratton-Porter State Historic Site on Sylvan Lake at Rome City, IN.

Publications: Newsletter, 3-4/year. **Conventions/ Meetings:** annual meeting - always in May.

9652 ■ George Sand Association
c/o Annabelle M. Rea, Pres.
Occidental Coll.
Spanish and French Literary Stud.
1600 Campus Rd.
Los Angeles, CA 90041
Ph: (818)244-0487
E-mail: rea@oxy.edu
URL: http://www.hofstra.edu/georgesand
Contact: Annabelle M. Rea, Pres.
Founded: 1976. **Members:** 225. **Membership Dues:** student/emeritus, $15 (annual) ● regular, $25 (annual) ● institution, $30 (annual). **Languages:** English, French. **Multinational. Description:** Scholars, writers, libraries, organizations, students, and other individuals interested in the works of French writer George Sand, pseudonym of Amantine Aurore Lucile Dupin Dudevant (1804-76). Purposes are to coordinate research and scholarship; to serve as clearinghouse for information; to publicize and encourage events that would interest scholars and potential scholars; to facilitate English translations of Sand's works; to examine aspects of her life that augment an appreciation of her work and her time. Organizes conferences. **Awards:** George Sand Association Memorial Prize. **Frequency:** periodic. **Type:** recognition. **Recipient:** for best doctoral dissertation, in French or in English. **Affiliated With:** Modern Language Association of America. **Formerly:** (1999) Friends of George Sand. **Publications:** *The George Sand Association Newsletter*, annual ● *George Sand Studies—Journal*, annual. **Price:** $25.00 /year for individuals; $15.00/year for students; $30.00 /year for institutions. ISSN: 0161-6544. **Advertising:** accepted. **Conventions/Meetings:** periodic international conference.

9653 ■ George Sand Society
c/o Linda E. Odenborg, Chair
PO Box 1333
Portland, OR 97207
Ph: (360)693-4785 (503)497-9163
Fax: (360)693-4785
E-mail: lodenborg@comcast.net
URL: http://leopro.com
Contact: Linda E. Odenborg, Chair
Founded: 1991. **Members:** 35. **Membership Dues:** individual, $12 (annual). **Regional Groups:** 1. **State Groups:** 1. **Local Groups:** 1. **Languages:** English, French. **Description:** Links individuals with an interest in French author Amantine-Lucille-Aurore Dupin (1804-76), who wrote under the pseudonym George Sand. Promotes study of her life and works and seeks to make them better understood. **Libraries: Type:** not open to the public. **Holdings:** 250. **Publications:** Journal, annual ● Newsletter, semiannual. **Conventions/Meetings:** annual meeting - every last Saturday of June, Portland, OR.

9654 ■ Goethe Society of North America (GSNA)
c/o Prof. Astrida Tantillo, Exec. Sec./Ed.
Dept. of Germanic Stud.
Univ. of Illinois at Chicago
601 S Morgan St.
Chicago, IL 60607
Ph: (312)413-2374
Fax: (312)413-2377
E-mail: tantillo@uic.edu
URL: http://www.goethesociety.org
Contact: Prof. Astrida Tantillo, Exec. Sec./Ed.
Founded: 1979. **Members:** 225. **Membership Dues:** individual, institutional, $25 (annual). **Languages:** English, German. **Description:** Represents the interests of individuals dedicated to the encouragement of research on Johann Wolfgang von Goethe (1749-1832), German poet and dramatist. Seeks to stimulate interest in Goethe's works and the eighteenth-century literature and culture. Promotes lectures and symposia about Goethe and his times. Seeks to develop research opportunities for the study of 18th century literature and culture. **Awards:** Gloria Flaherty Scholarship. **Frequency:** annual. **Type:** scholarship ● GSNA Essay Prize. **Frequency:** annual. **Type:** monetary. **Affiliated With:** American Society for Eighteenth-Century Studies; Modern Language Association of America. **Publications:** *Goethe News and Notes* (in English and German), semiannual. Newsletter. Includes calendar of events, recent publications, and research updates. **Price:** included in membership dues. **Circulation:** 275 ● *Goethe Yearbook*, annual. **Conventions/Meetings:** annual meeting and seminar, in conjunction with the Modern Language Association of America, American Society for 18th Century Studies, and the German Studies Association.

9655 ■ Harriet Beecher Stowe Center (SDF)
77 Forest St.
Hartford, CT 06105
Ph: (860)522-9258
Fax: (860)522-9259
E-mail: kane@stowecenter.org
URL: http://www.HarrietBeecherStowe.org
Contact: Katherine Kane, Exec. Dir.
Founded: 1941. **Members:** 200. **Membership Dues:** individual, $25 (annual) ● household, $45 (annual) ● HBS society, $1,000 (annual) ● international, $50 (annual) ● student, $15 (annual) ● sustaining, $100 (annual) ● associate, $250 (annual) ● benefactor, $500 (annual) ● library, $175 (annual). **Staff:** 29. **Budget:** $1,100,000. **Description:** Owns and maintains the Harriet Beecher Stowe House and the Stowe Center Library. Offers Stowe House tours, seasonal Garden tours, Children's tours; exhibits on 19th-century American life and culture; and scholarly, family programs. Covers collections of: Harriet Beecher Stowe; Isabella Beecher Hooker; Charles Dudley Warner; architecture; decorative arts; literature of 19th-century America; abolitionism; women's suffrage; William Gillette; other Nook Farm genealogy. Conducts educational programs. **Libraries: Type:** by appointment only; open to the public. **Holdings:** 15,000; archival material, audiovisuals, books, photographs. **Subjects:** Stowe and Beecher families, 19th century decorative arts and architecture, African-American history, women's history, religion, theater, genealogy. **Awards:** CT History Day Awards. **Frequency:** annual. **Type:** monetary. **Recipient:** for best women's history projects ● Good Citizen Award. **Frequency:** annual. **Type:** monetary ● Newspaper In Education Awards. **Frequency:** annual. **Type:** monetary. **Programs:** Children's Activities; Exhibits; Workshops, Lectures and Symposia. **Formerly:** (1994) Stowe-Day Foundation. **Publications:** *The American Woman's Home*. Reprints ● *Harriet Beecher Stowe in Europe*. Book ● *The Harriet Beecher Stowe Reader* ● *The Journal*, 3/year. Newsletter. **Price:** included in membership dues. **Circulation:** 1,500 ● *Victorian Blossoms: Gardens of the Harriet Beecher Stowe Center*, annual. Book. Includes floral guide of the Victorian flowers at the Harriet Beecher Stowe Center. **Price:** $15.00 ● Books ● Papers.

9656 ■ Harry Stephen Keeler Society
c/o Richard Polt, Ed.
4745 Winton Rd.
Cincinnati, OH 45232
Ph: (513)591-1226 (513)745-3274
E-mail: polt@xavier.xu.edu
URL: http://keelersociety.mondoplex.com
Contact: Richard Polt, Ed.
Founded: 1997. **Members:** 60. **Membership Dues:** North America, $10 (annual) ● outside North America, $15 (annual). **Staff:** 1. **Budget:** $700. **Languages:** English, French, Icelandic, Spanish, Swedish. **Multinational. Description:** Promotes the work of author Harry Stephen Keeler. **Libraries: Type:** reference. **Holdings:** 100; articles, books. **Subjects:** material by and about Keeler. **Awards:** Imitate Keeler Contest. **Frequency:** annual. **Type:** recognition. **Recipient:** for skill and wit in imitating Keeler's style. **Publications:** *Keeler News*, 5/year. Newsletter. Features Keeler novels for sale, articles, reviews, letters, and other items. **Price:** included in membership dues. ISSN: 1524-323. **Circulation:** 60. **Advertising:** accepted. Alternate Formats: online. Also Cited As: *Bulletin of the Harry Stephen Keeler Society*.

9657 ■ Hegel Society of America (HSA)
c/o Philosophy Documentation Center
PO Box 7147
Charlottesville, VA 22906-7147
Ph: (804)220-3300
Free: (800)444-2419
Fax: (804)220-3301
E-mail: acollin@luc.edu
URL: http://www.hegel.org
Contact: Dr. Ardis B. Collins, Treas.
Founded: 1968. **Members:** 329. **Membership Dues:** regular, $35 (annual) ● student, $17 (annual). **Staff:** 10. **Description:** Promotes the study of the philosophy of Hegel, its relationship to social, political, and cultural movements since the philosopher's time, and its relevance to contemporary issues and fields of knowledge. **Computer Services:** Mailing lists. **Subgroups:** Hegel Society Executive. **Publications:** *The Owl of Minerva*, semiannual. Journal. **Price:** included in membership dues; $25.00 /year for nonmembers; $35.00 /year for institutions and libraries; $10.00 for students. ISSN: 0030-7580. **Circulation:** 610. **Advertising:** accepted. **Conventions/Meetings:** biennial conference (exhibits) - early October, even-numbered years ● biennial meeting - late December; odd-numbered years.

9658 ■ Hemingway Foundation and Society
c/o Susan F. Beegel, Ed.
14 Terhune Dr.
Phippsburg, ME 04562
Ph: (207)389-2839
Fax: (207)389-2839
E-mail: president@hemingwaysociety.org
URL: http://www.hemingwaysociety.org
Contact: James H. Meredith, Pres.
Founded: 1980. **Members:** 650. **Membership Dues:** regular, $30 (annual) ● student, $20 (annual) ● retired, $25 (annual). **Languages:** English, Spanish. **Description:** Scholars, teachers, and other individuals interested in Ernest Hemingway (1899-1961), American journalist, novelist, and short story writer. Promotes and publicizes items of interest to teachers and scholars about Hemingway. Maintains bibliographic archives in the Kennedy Library, Boston, MA. Sponsors conferences. **Awards:** PEN/Hemingway Award. **Type:** recognition. **Recipient:** for best first work of fiction, U.S. ● Smith-Reynolds Founders Fellowships. **Type:** fellowship. **Recipient:** for research. **Publications:** *The Hemingway Newsletter*, semiannual. Contains short news items for those interested in the Writings and life of Ernest Hemingway. Includes notices of awards and publications. **Price:** included in membership dues. **Circulation:** 600 ● *The Hemingway Review*, semiannual. Journal. Contains critical, bibliographical, and textual articles on the writings and life of Ernest Hemingway. Includes bibliographies and book reviews. **Price:** included in membership dues; $15.00 for nonmembers; $20.00 for institutions. ISSN: 0276-3362. **Circulation:** 1,150. Alternate Formats: microform. **Conventions/Meetings:** biennial International Congress ● annual meeting, held in conjunction with the American Literature Association and the Modern Language Association of America; holds sessions for papers and discussions (exhibits).

9659 ■ Horatio Alger Society (HAS)
PO Box 70361
Richmond, VA 23255
E-mail: rkasper@hotmail.com
URL: http://www.thehoratioalgersociety.org
Contact: Robert E. Kasper, Sec.
Founded: 1961. **Members:** 225. **Membership Dues:** senior, $20 (annual) ● regular, $25 (annual). **Description:** Persons interested in the life and writings of Horatio Alger, Jr. (1832-99), American author whose novels featured the meteoric rise from rags to riches of boys who were "honest, loyal, industrious and with religious principles". Conducts research on Alger's life and works. Works closely with Northern Illinois University in Dekalb, Illinois, site of Horatio Alger Society Archives. **Libraries: Type:** open to the public. **Holdings:** 2,000; articles, books, periodicals. **Awards:** Newsboy Award. **Frequency:** annual. **Type:** recognition. **Recipient:** to publishers and authors for

best publication in sympathy with Alger's rags to riches theme ● **Type:** recognition. **Recipient:** for outstanding society member ● Strive and Succeed Award. **Frequency:** annual. **Type:** recognition. **Recipient:** to a boy or a girl who lives up to the Alger image. **Computer Services:** Online services, forum for discussing the work and word of Horatio Alger, Jr. **Committees:** Awards; Research. **Formerly:** (1961) Horatio Alger Newsboy Club. **Publications:** *Membership Roster,* annual. Booklet. Lists all members and their other collecting interests. **Price:** included in membership dues. **Circulation:** 300 ● *Newsboy,* bimonthly. Newsletter. Provides articles and research on Alger and other authors of the same period. Includes book reviews. **Price:** included in membership dues; $3.00 for nonmembers. ISSN: 0028-9396. **Circulation:** 300 ● Also publishes bibliography. **Conventions/Meetings:** annual meeting and convention (exhibits).

9660 ■ Ibsen Society of America (ISA)

c/o Prof. Arne Lunde
Dept. of German, Scandinavian, and Dutch
Univ. of Minnesota
205 Folwell Hall
Minneapolis, MN 55455
E-mail: joantmp@aol.com
URL: http://www.ibsensociety.liu.edu
Contact: Joan Templeton, Pres.

Founded: 1978. **Members:** 200. **Membership Dues:** regular, $15 (annual) ● student, $7 (annual). **Multinational. Description:** Individuals interested in the works of Henrik Ibsen (1828-1906), Norwegian poet and dramatist. Promotes informed study of Ibsen writings. **Awards:** Honorary Membership. **Frequency:** periodic. **Type:** recognition. **Recipient:** for contribution to Ibsen studies. **Computer Services:** Mailing lists, of members. **Councils:** The Council of the ISA. **Affiliated With:** Society for the Advancement of Scandinavian Study. **Publications:** *Ibsen News and Comment, Journal of The Ibsen Society of America,* annual, published in spring. Includes feature articles, interviews, theater and book reviews and member news. Also contains ISA session abstracts. **Price:** included in membership dues; $15.00 /year for libraries. ISSN: 1089-6171. **Circulation:** 200. **Advertising:** accepted. **Conventions/Meetings:** annual Business and Program Meeting - conference, in conjunction with the annual SASS meeting (exhibits).

9661 ■ International Brecht Society (IBS)

c/o Paula Hanssen, Sec.-Treas.
Webster Univ.
470 E Lockwood
St. Louis, MO 63119
Ph: (314)968-6900
Fax: (314)963-6926
E-mail: hanssen@webster.edu
URL: http://german.lss.wisc.edu/brecht
Contact: Paula Hanssen, Sec.-Treas.

Founded: 1970. **Members:** 300. **Membership Dues:** sustaining, institution, $50 (annual) ● student, emeritus, $20 (annual) ● regular (based on annual income), $30-$40 (annual) ● life, $200. **Languages:** English, German. **Description:** Represents individuals working in theatre and filmmaking, university teachers, graduate students, editors, writers, and libraries in 6 countries. Encourages free and open discussion on the relationship of the arts to the contemporary world, placing emphasis on the work of Bertolt Brecht (1898-1956), German playwright and poet. **Libraries: Type:** reference. **Holdings:** archival material. **Foreign language name:** Sociedad Internacional Brecht; Societe Internationale de Brecht. **Publications:** *Brecht Yearbook* (in English and German), annual. Features a collection of critical essays on research concerning modern drama, especially in the works of Bertolt Brecht. **Price:** included in membership dues. ISSN: 0734-8665. **Circulation:** 300. **Advertising:** accepted ● *Communications,* annual. Journal. Covers all areas related to the German playwright Bertolt Brecht, his times, and political theater, as well as society news. Includes reviews. **Price:** included in membership dues. ISSN: 0740-8943. **Circulation:** 300. **Advertising:** accepted. **Conventions/Meetings:** annual meeting, in conjunction with Modern Language Association of America ● biennial meeting and symposium.

9662 ■ International Lawrence Durrell Society (ILDS)

c/o Paul H. Lorenz, Sec.-Treas.
3201 S Beech St., No. 40
Pine Bluff, AR 71603
Ph: (870)575-8618
Fax: (870)575-8040
E-mail: paullorenz@sbcglobal.net
URL: http://www.lawrencedurrell.org
Contact: Paul H. Lorenz, Sec.-Treas.

Founded: 1977. **Members:** 300. **Membership Dues:** regular, $15 (annual) ● student, $10 (annual) ● joint, $20 (annual). **Multinational. Description:** Represents admirers of author Lawrence Durrell (1912-90), whose most notable work was The Alexandria Quartet. Promotes the "study, understanding, and appreciation" of Durrell's work. Conducts critical study on Durrell's writings and works to "establish his place in the canon of world literature." Sponsors educational programs. **Awards:** Durrell Prize for New Scholarship. **Frequency:** annual. **Type:** monetary. **Recipient:** for best scholarly essay written (or published) by scholar who has not previously published on Durrell. **Publications:** *Deus Loci,* periodic. Journal. **Price:** $10.00/issue. ISSN: 0707-9141 ● *The International Lawrence Durrell Society Herald.* Membership Directory. **Conventions/Meetings:** periodic meeting ● biennial On Miracle Ground - conference ● periodic seminar.

9663 ■ International Spenser Society (ISS)

c/o Prof. Craig Berry, Sec.-Treas.
1518 W Thorndale, No. 2W
Chicago, IL 60660
E-mail: craigberry@mac.com
URL: http://www.english.cam.ac.uk/spenser/society
Contact: Prof. Craig Berry, Sec.-Treas.

Founded: 1976. **Members:** 350. **Membership Dues:** regular in U.S. and Canada, $28 (annual) ● regular outside U.S. and Canada, $34 (annual) ● student emeritus/independent in U.S. and Canada, $18 (annual) ● student emeritus/independent outside U.S. and Canada, $24 (annual). **Multinational. Description:** University professors specializing in 16th-century English literature, especially the poetry of Edmund Spenser (1552-99), author of *The Faerie Queene* and creator of the Spenserian stanza. Maintains and encourages Spenserian scholarship. Provides a forum for members to meet and discuss common interests. **Awards:** Isabel MacCaffrey Award. **Frequency:** annual. **Type:** recognition. **Recipient:** for article on Spenser. **Publications:** *The Spenser Review,* 3/year. Journal. **Price:** included in membership dues; $14.00 for nonmembers in U.S. and Canada; $19.00 for nonmembers outside U.S. and Canada. Alternate Formats: online. **Conventions/Meetings:** annual meeting and luncheon, held in conjunction with Modern Language Association of America - always December.

9664 ■ International Theodore Dreiser Society

c/o Donna Packer-Kinlaw, Sec.-Treas.
Univ. of Maryland
Dept. of English
3101 Susquehanna Hall
College Park, MD 20742
E-mail: sndkinlaw@yahoo.com
URL: http://www.uncwil.edu/dreiser
Contact: Stephen Brennan, Pres.

Founded: 1991. **Membership Dues:** regular, $20 (annual) ● student, $10 (annual) ● foreign, $30 (annual). **Multinational. Description:** Promotes interest in the life and works of American naturalist author Theodore Dreiser. Provides a forum for formal and informal exchange of ideas among Dreiser scholars. Sponsors educational sessions. **Telecommunication Services:** electronic mail, stephencbrennan@bellsouth.net. **Publications:** *Studies in American Naturalism,* semiannual. Journal. Contains essays, documents, notes, bibliographies and reviews pertaining to American literary naturalism. **Price:** included in membership dues; $35.00 institution; $25.00 individual. ISSN: 1931-2555. **Advertising:** accepted.

9665 ■ International Thomas Merton Society (ITMS)

Bellarmine Univ.
Thomas Merton Center
2001 Newburg Rd.
Louisville, KY 40205-0671
Ph: (502)452-8177 (502)452-8187
Free: (800)274-4723
Fax: (502)452-8452
E-mail: merton@bellarmine.edu
URL: http://www.merton.org/ITMS
Contact: Dr. Paul M. Pearson, Sec.

Founded: 1987. **Members:** 1,600. **Membership Dues:** student, $15 (annual) ● regular (includes the Merton Seasonal), $25 (annual) ● enhanced (includes both the Merton Seasonal and the Merton Annual), $40 (annual). **Staff:** 3. **Regional Groups:** 14. **Local Groups:** 37. **Multinational. Description:** Admirers of author Thomas Merton. Promotes appreciation Merton's contributions to American literature, the literature of spirituality, social criticism, and theology. Encourages study and research into Merton's writings; assists in the designing of undergraduate and graduate courses covering Merton and his works. Conducts educational programs; maintains speakers' bureau. Publishes a quarterly journal, the Merton Seasonal and organizes conferences. **Libraries: Type:** reference; open to the public. **Holdings:** archival material, articles, artwork, audio recordings, books, photographs. **Subjects:** Thomas Merton, spirituality, theology, literature. **Awards:** Daggy Youth/Student Scholarships. **Frequency:** biennial. **Type:** scholarship. **Recipient:** to enable young people (ages 14-29) to participate in an international Thomas Merton Society conference by covering costs of meals, accommodation and registration ● The Louie. **Frequency:** biennial. **Type:** recognition. **Recipient:** to an individual who has made a significant contribution on an international level to the promotion of Merton's writings (in English or in translation) and to the presentation of his ideas ● The Louie - Society Award. **Frequency:** biennial. **Type:** recognition. **Recipient:** to a member of the ITMS whose distinguished service has contributed to the aims of the society and to furthering its goals ● Shannon Fellowships. **Frequency:** annual. **Type:** grant. **Recipient:** to enable qualified researchers to visit the Thomas Merton center archives at Bellarmine University in Louisville, Kentucky. **Computer Services:** Bibliographic search, electronic access to finding aids for the archives of the Thomas Merton center ● database ● mailing lists. **Publications:** *The Merton Annual: Studies in Culture, Spirituality and Social Concerns,* annual. Book. Contains articles about Thomas Merton and about related matters of major concern to his life and work. **Price:** $19.95 for nonmembers; $15.00 for members; included in enhanced membership dues ● *Merton Seasonal,* quarterly. Journal. **Price:** included in membership dues. ISSN: 0988-4927. **Circulation:** 1,600. **Advertising:** accepted. **Conventions/Meetings:** biennial conference, these forums produce lively exchanges, spiritual renewal and new scholarly Merton research on an international scale - 2009 June 11-14, Rochester, NY - **Avg. Attendance:** 350; 2011 June 9-12, Chicago, IL - **Avg. Attendance:** 350.

9666 ■ International Virginia Woolf Society (IVWS)

c/o Bonnie Kime Scott, Pres.
Dept. of Women's Stud.
San Diego State Univ.
5500 Campanile Dr.
San Diego, CA 92182-8138
Ph: (619)594-6460
Fax: (619)594-5218
E-mail: bkscott@mail.sdsu.edu
URL: http://www.utoronto.ca/IVWS
Contact: Bonnie Kime Scott, Pres.

Founded: 1975. **Members:** 600. **Membership Dues:** full time, $20 (annual) ● student, part-time, retired, $10 (annual). **Staff:** 7. **Description:** Critics, scholars, teachers, readers, and students. Fosters and encourages the study of, critical attention to, and general interest in the work, career and cultural context of Virginia Woolf (1882-1941), English author. Presents panels at MLA conventions and endorses an annual Woolf conference. **Libraries: Type:** reference. **Subjects:** Virginia Woolf, Leonard Woolf, Hogarth Press, Bloomsbury Group, Leslie Stephen, Vanessa Bell, modernism, feminism, pacifism, imperialism. **Awards: Type:** recognition ● Travel Awards. **Frequency:** annual. **Type:** monetary. **Recipient:** assistance with travel expenses, for students and others in need during annual conference via conference organizers. **Telecommunication Services:** electronic mail, mhussey@pace.edu. **Formerly:** (1997) Virginia Woolf Society. **Publications:** *Virginia Woolf Miscellany*, biennial. Newsletter. **Price:** included in membership dues; $10.00 /year for nonmembers; $15.00 /year for libraries and institutions ● Bibliography, annual. **Price:** included in membership dues. Alternate Formats: online. **Conventions/Meetings:** annual conference, held in conjunction with Modern Language Association of America, with organization panels and society party ● annual meeting and conference, held in conjunction with the annual conference on Virginia Woolf - always in June.

9667 ■ International Vladimir Nabokov Society (IVNS)
c/o Prof. Stephen Jan Parker, Sec.-Treas./Ed.
Dept. of Slavic Languages and Literatures
Univ. of Kansas - Wescoe Hall
1445 Jayhawk Blvd., Rm. 2134
Lawrence, KS 66045-7590
Ph: (785)864-3313
Fax: (785)864-4298
E-mail: sjp@ku.edu
URL: http://www.libraries.psu.edu/nabokov/nabsoc.htm
Contact: Prof. Stephen Jan Parker, Sec.-Treas./Ed.
Founded: 1978. **Members:** 290. **Multinational. Description:** Individuals and institutions dedicated to the appreciation of the writings of Vladimir Nabokov (1899-1977), Russian-born American author and poet. Promotes the exchange of views and information concerning Nabokov's writings and encourages fellowship among readers. **Formerly:** (2006) Vladimir Nabokov Society. **Publications:** *The Nabokovian*, semiannual. Journal. Includes abstracts of books, articles, and dissertations, annotations to Nabokov's works, previously unpublished interviews, and other writings. **Price:** $17.00 /year for individuals; $22.00 /year for institutions; $10.00 for back issues (individuals); $15.00 for back issues (institutions). **Circulation:** 290. **Conventions/Meetings:** annual meeting, held in conjunction with Modern Language Association of America - always December.

9668 ■ International Wizard of Oz Club (IWOC)
PO Box 2657
Alameda, CA 94501
E-mail: info@ozclub.org
URL: http://www.ozclub.org
Contact: Angelica Carpenter, Pres.
Founded: 1957. **Members:** 1,300. **Membership Dues:** basic, in U.S., $25 (annual) ● youth, in U.S., $15 (annual) ● basic, outside U.S., $35 (annual) ● youth, outside U.S., $25 (annual) ● contributing, in U.S., $50 (annual) ● contributing, outside U.S., $60 (annual) ● sustaining, in U.S., $100 (annual) ● sustaining, outside U.S., $110 (annual) ● patron, in U.S., $250 (annual) ● patron, outside U.S., $260 (annual) ● Wizard's Circle, in U.S., $500 (annual) ● Wizard's Circle, outside U.S., $510 (annual). **Staff:** 1. **Description:** Persons interested in the fantasy novels about the Land of Oz and in L. Frank Baum (1856-1919) who created it in *The Wonderful Wizard of Oz*, published in 1900. Promotes preservation and study of books, plays, motion pictures, songs, and other by-products of Oz; conducts research on persons other than Baum who contributed to Oz, including Ruth Plumly Thompson, W.W. Denslow, and John R. Neill. Offers opportunity for members to exchange or auction books and other items. **Awards:** L. Frank Baum Memorial Award. **Frequency:** annual. **Type:** recognition. **Telecommunication Services:** electronic mail, angelica@csufresno.edu. **Publications:** *The Baum Bugle*, 3/year. Journal. Contains articles and reports on the utopian land of Oz; includes book reviews, bibliography, MGM scrapbook, and "Oz in the News". **Price:** included in membership dues; $8.00 for nonmembers. **Circulation:** 2,500 ● *Bibliographia Oziana*. Book. Contains a detailed checklist of all the Oz books. **Price:** $25.00 ● *Bibliographia Oziana: A Bibliographic Checklist of Baum's Other Fantasy Novels*. Book ● *The Enchanted Island of Oz*. Book. **Price:** $12.00 ● *The Forbidden Fountain of Oz*. Book. **Price:** $12.00 ● *The Hidden Prince of Oz*. Book. **Price:** $100.00 ● *The Hidden Valley of Oz*. Book. **Price:** $12.00 ● *Oziana*, annual. Magazine. Contains stories, games, and puzzles. **Price:** $5.00. **Circulation:** 1,000 ● *The Scarecrow of Oz*. Book. **Price:** $30.00 ● *Unexplored Territory in Oz*. Booklet. Contains essays on Oz. ● Also publishes maps of Oz and gazetteer of Oz; selected reprints of original Oz books. **Conventions/Meetings:** annual meeting and convention (exhibits) - always third weekend in June for Midwest, July for West Coast, August for East Coast.

9669 ■ Jack London Research Center (JLRC)
PO Box 337
Glen Ellen, CA 95442
Ph: (707)996-2888
Fax: (707)996-4107
E-mail: jlondon@vom.com
URL: http://jacklondonfdn.org
Contact: Winifred Kingman, Exec. Off.
Founded: 1976. **Membership Dues:** student/senior, $15 (annual) ● family, $20 (annual) ● supporting, $50 (annual) ● sponsor, $100 (annual) ● patron, $200 (annual) ● fellow, $500 (annual) ● life, $1,000. **Description:** Serves as resource center providing authentic information on Jack London (1876-1916), American writer of short stories, popular fiction, essays, and works on socialism. Provides advisory bibliographical and historical information covering all secondary research material on Jack London. Maintains speakers' bureau. Compiles statistics. Operates the Jack London Foundation. **Libraries: Type:** reference. **Holdings:** archival material. **Awards: Type:** recognition. **Publications:** Newsletter, quarterly. **Conventions/Meetings:** annual competition, descriptive writing contests in high schools.

9670 ■ James A. Michener Society
c/o A. Richard Boera, Treas.
PO Box 1126
Lyndonville, VT 05851
Ph: (505)296-9047
E-mail: joybliss2@comcast.net
URL: http://webpages.charter.net/boerad/michener.htm
Contact: Ms. Joy V. Bliss, Sec.
Founded: 1999. **Members:** 225. **Membership Dues:** individual, $12 (annual) ● life, $500 ● benefactor, $2,500 (annual) ● couple, $18 (annual) ● institutional, $50 (annual). **Description:** Friends, associates, readers of James A. Michener. Endeavors to preserve the intellectual legacy of James A. Michener as a writer, teacher, historian, public servant, patriot and philanthropist; ensure that future generations have full access to all of his writings; to promote the exchange of ideas and information about his writings and encourage fellowship among readers of his writings; and to inform his devotees and members about recent publications and critiques of his writings. **Publications:** *James A. Michener Society Newsletter*, semiannual. Contains reviews of Michener related books, quotations from Michener's writings, Michener memories. **Price:** included in membership dues. **Circulation:** 200. **Conventions/Meetings:** annual meeting - September or October.

9671 ■ James Joyce Society (JJS)
c/o A. Nicholas Fargnoli, Pres.
26 Varick Ct.
Rockville Centre, NY 11570
E-mail: info@joycesociety.org
URL: http://www.joycesociety.org
Contact: A. Nicholas Fargnoli, Pres.
Founded: 1947. **Members:** 125. **Membership Dues:** individual, $20 (annual). **Staff:** 2. **Description:** Readers and admirers of Irish literary figure James Joyce (1882-1941) and his work, including academics, students, and others. Makes available Joycean interpretations and commentaries by inviting Joyce scholars and enthusiasts to give addresses. Promotes activity within the membership through the presentation of papers, discussions, and periodic publication of material. Encourages the presentation of Joyce's work in theatre, radio, television, motion pictures, readings, and concerts. **Study Groups:** James Joyce Society Reading. **Publications:** *James Joyce Journal and Hoon Publications*, annual. Contains essays and other materials related to Joyce. **Advertising:** accepted. **Conventions/Meetings:** quarterly meeting.

9672 ■ James Joyce Society of Southern Colorado
PO Box 62482
Colorado Springs, CO 80962
Ph: (719)594-9164
Contact: John Holiday, Founder
Founded: 1993. **Staff:** 2. **Description:** Promotes appreciation of the works of Irish literary figure James Joyce (1882-1941). Supports writers' rights and intellectual freedom. Exhibits works by and about Joyce at libraries. Houses the John Socia Memorial Library. **Libraries: Type:** not open to the public. **Holdings:** 1,500; audiovisuals, books, periodicals, photographs. **Subjects:** studies and works of James Joyce. **Conventions/Meetings:** James Joyce-Life and Works - lecture (exhibits).

9673 ■ Jane Austen Society of North America (JASNA)
c/o Bobbie Gay, Membership Sec.
7230 N San Blas Dr.
Tucson, AZ 85704
Free: (800)836-3911
E-mail: info@jasna.org
URL: http://www.jasna.org
Contact: Ms. Marsha Huff, Pres.
Founded: 1979. **Members:** 3,000. **Membership Dues:** family in Canada, C$56 (annual) ● individual in Canada, C$38 (annual) ● life in U.S., $350 ● life in Canada, C$500 ● family in U.S., $45 (annual) ● individual in U.S., $30 (annual). **Budget:** $127,000. **Local Groups:** 60. **Multinational. Description:** Encourages and promotes interest, discussion, and scholarship relating to the works and life of Jane Austen, English novelist, 1775-1817. Aims are achieved through annual literary conference, publication of journals and other materials, student essay contest, and local group meetings. **Awards:** Student Essay Contest. **Frequency:** annual. **Type:** recognition. **Recipient:** for high school, college, and graduate student levels. **Computer Services:** Mailing lists. **Telecommunication Services:** electronic mail, hettyb@comcast.net. **Publications:** *JASNA News*, 3/year. Newsletter. Reports on new works about Austen; includes book reviews and news of society activities. **Price:** included in membership dues. ISSN: 0892-8665. **Circulation:** 4,000. **Advertising:** accepted ● *Persuasions and Persuasions On-Line*, annual. Journals. **Price:** included in membership dues; $30.00. ISSN: 0821-0314. Alternate Formats: online ● *Persuasions: Occasional Papers*, periodic. **Conventions/Meetings:** annual conference, with lectures, workshops, and banquet.

9674 ■ Jesse Stuart Foundation (JSF)
1645 Winchester Ave.
PO Box 669
Ashland, KY 41105
Ph: (606)326-1667
Free: (800)504-0209
Fax: (606)325-2519
E-mail: jsf@jsfbooks.com
URL: http://www.jsfbooks.com
Contact: James M. Gifford PhD, CEO/Sr. Ed.
Founded: 1979. **Members:** 7,000. **Membership Dues:** senior, $15 (annual) ● individual, $20 (annual) ● family, $30 (annual). **Staff:** 4. **Budget:** $300,000. **Description:** Promotes the literary works of Jesse Stuart (1906-84), American educator, writer, and author of poems and stories; preserves Stuart's W-Hollow home in Kentucky. Projects include:

promoting the 726-acre Jesse Stuart nature preserve as a resource for public school and college programs; encouraging educational courses related to the life and works of Stuart and the study of related American, Anglo-American, and international literature; promoting cultural, natural, recreational, and educational programs that relate to Stuart's life and works. **Telecommunication Services:** electronic mail, gifford@jsfbooks.com. **Publications:** *A Sketch in the Life and Character of Daniel Boone*. Book. **Price:** $15.95 ● *A Sorrow in Our Heart*. Book. **Price:** $7.99 ● *A True Man of God*. Book. Contains a portrait of a unique missionary priest who brought hope to many needy people in one of the isolated places in America. **Price:** $22.00 ● *Appalachian Mountain Religion: History*. Book. **Price:** $24.95 ● *Cradle of Copperheads*. Book. **Price:** $22.00 ● *Dandelion on the Acropolis—Journal of Greece*. Book. **Price:** $10.00 ● *The Jesse Stuart Foundation Newsletter*, quarterly ● Monographs. **Conventions/Meetings:** annual Jesse Stuart Weekend - meeting (exhibits) ● annual meeting and symposium.

9675 ■ Joseph Conrad Society of America (JCSA)

c/o Prof. Mary Morzinski, Ed.
Dept. of English
Univ. of Wisconsin-La Crosse
1725 State St.
La Crosse, WI 54601
E-mail: morzinsk.mary@uwlax.edu
URL: http://www.engl.unt.edu/~jgpeters/Conrad
Contact: Prof. Mary Morzinski, Ed.

Founded: 1974. **Members:** 350. **Membership Dues:** individual in U.S. and Canada, $25 (annual) ● institution in U.S. and Canada, individual outside U.S. and Canada, $29 (annual) ● institution outside U.S. and Canada, $35 (annual) ● student in U.S. and Canada, $15 (annual) ● student outside U.S. and Canada, $18 (annual) ● life, $250. **Description:** Professors of English and graduate students; college and university libraries; interested others. Promotes interest in and knowledge of the life, times, and works of Joseph Conrad (1857-1924), English novelist born in Poland. **Awards:** The Bruce Harkness Young Conrad Scholar Award. **Frequency:** annual. **Type:** monetary. **Recipient:** for outstanding graduate student or assistant professor ● The Ian P. Watt Prize for Excellence in Conrad Scholarship. **Frequency:** annual. **Type:** monetary. **Recipient:** for outstanding scholarship of member ● Juliet McLauchlan Prize. **Frequency:** annual. **Type:** monetary. **Recipient:** for new Conradians and emergent scholars, including undergraduates, postgraduates and independent scholars of any age ● Young Scholars Travel Awards. **Frequency:** periodic. **Type:** grant. **Recipient:** for young scholars who attend the conference and present a paper on Conrad. **Affiliated With:** Modern Language Association of America. **Publications:** *Joseph Conrad Today*, semiannual. Newsletter. Presents abstracts of papers and lectures given by Conrad scholars; includes meeting announcements and book reviews. **Price:** $12.00 /year for individuals; $15.00 /year for libraries. ISSN: 0162-413X. **Circulation:** 400. **Advertising:** accepted. **Conventions/Meetings:** annual international conference (exhibits) ● annual meeting, held in conjunction with Modern Language Association of America - last week in December.

9676 ■ Kafka Society of America and Journal (KSA)

c/o Dr. Marie Luise Caputo-Mayr, Dir.
160 E 65th St., 2C
New York, NY 10021
Ph: (212)744-0821
Fax: (212)744-0821
E-mail: mlcaputo@kafkasocietyofamerica.org
URL: http://www.kafkasocietyofamerica.org
Contact: Dr. Marie Luise Caputo-Mayr, Dir.

Founded: 1975. **Members:** 500. **Membership Dues:** individual, $25 (annual) ● student, retired, $10 (annual) ● institution, $45 (annual) ● executive committee, $100 (annual) ● sponsor, $500 (annual) ● donor, $1,000 (annual). **Staff:** 2. **Languages:** English, German. **Multinational. Description:** Students, teachers, scholars, and departments of modern literature; readers of Franz Kafka's works; psychologists and academicians; university and public libraries with holdings in modern literature. Presents and publishes papers of Kafka (1883-1924); Austrian/Jewish/Czech writer. Informs members of ongoing research and events concerning Kafka such as exhibitions, meetings, publications, performances, and congresses. Operates speakers' bureau. **Committees:** Editorial Advisory. **Affiliated With:** Modern Language Association of America. **Publications:** *Journal of the Kafka Society of America* (in English and German), semiannual. Covers Kafka and the era he lived in and international notes and announcements of conferences, bibliography, and meeting programs at the MLA. **Price:** included in membership dues; $4.00/journal for nonmembers in Canada, plus $3 in U.S.; $5.00 surface mail to Europe; $10.00 international postage/handling (airmail). ISSN: 0894-6388. **Circulation:** 500. **Advertising:** accepted. Alternate Formats: CD-ROM. Also Cited As: *JKSA* ● Bibliographies. Features Kafka and his works in 3 volumes. ● Papers. **Conventions/Meetings:** annual convention, with presentation of papers - always in December.

9677 ■ Keats-Shelley Association of America (KSAA)

476 5th Ave.
New York Public Lib., Rm. 226
New York, NY 10018
Ph: (212)764-0655 (631)470-5737
Fax: (631)470-5737
E-mail: rhartley@optonline.net
URL: http://www.rc.umd.edu/ksaa/ksaa.html
Contact: Dr. Robert A. Hartley, Sec.-Treas.

Founded: 1948. **Members:** 1,000. **Membership Dues:** active, $20 (annual) ● sustaining, $25-$49 (annual) ● contributing, $50-$99 (annual) ● donor, $100-$249 (annual) ● sponsor, $250-$499 (annual) ● benefactor, $500-$999 (annual) ● patron, $1,000 (annual) ● student (requires confirmation from teacher), $10 (annual). **Multinational. Description:** Promotes the study and appreciation of Keats, Shelley and Byron and members of their circles. **Awards:** Carl H. Pforzheimer, Jr. Research Grants. **Frequency:** annual. **Type:** grant ● Distinguished Scholar Awards. **Frequency:** annual. **Type:** recognition. **Recipient:** for contribution to scholarship on younger romantics ● Essay Award. **Frequency:** annual. **Type:** recognition. **Publications:** *Keats-Shelley Journal*, annual. Covers poets Keats, Shelley, Byron, and Hunt, and their literary circles. Includes bibliography, book reviews, and obituaries. **Price:** included in membership dues. ISSN: 0453-4387. **Circulation:** 1,000. Also Cited As: *KSJ*. **Conventions/Meetings:** annual dinner, to present Distinguished Scholar Award(s), Essay Prize, and Research Grant(s) - held during MLA convention in December ● annual meeting, for general membership - held in May.

9678 ■ Langston Hughes Society

c/o Institute for African American Studies
312 Holmes/Hunter Academic Bldg.
Univ. of Georgia
Athens, GA 30602
Ph: (706)542-5197
Fax: (706)542-3071
E-mail: afam@arches.uga.edu
URL: http://www.csuohio.edu/english/langston/society.html
Contact: Dr. R. Baxter Miller, Exec. Ed./Dir.

Founded: 1981. **Members:** 200. **Membership Dues:** regular, in U.S., $14 (annual) ● regular, outside U.S., $18 (annual) ● life, $500. **Staff:** 5. **Budget:** $5,000. **Description:** Promotes the work of Langston Hughes. **Libraries: Type:** reference. **Holdings:** 17. **Awards:** Langston Hughes Award. **Frequency:** periodic. **Type:** recognition. **Computer Services:** database. **Additional Websites:** http://www.uga.edu/~iaas/lhr/index.html. **Publications:** *The Langston Hughes Review*. **Price:** included in membership dues; $20.00 /year for nonmembers in U.S.; $14.00 for nonmembers in U.S.

9679 ■ Laura Ingalls Wilder Memorial Society (LIWMS)

PO Box 426
De Smet, SD 57231
Free: (800)880-3383
E-mail: laura@discoverlaura.org
URL: http://www.discoverlaura.org
Contact: Cheryl Palmlund, Dir.

Founded: 1957. **Members:** 675. **Membership Dues:** general, $10 (annual) ● general, $25 (triennial) ● life, $500. **Staff:** 16. **Description:** Dedicated to the preservation and restoration of the Ingalls-Wilder heritages in De Smet and to educate and enhance the experience of learning to all interested people. **Telecommunication Services:** electronic mail, info@discoverlaura.org. **Publications:** *Lore*, semiannual. Newsletter. **Price:** included in membership dues.

9680 ■ Lessing Society (LS)

Germanic Languages Dept.
Univ. of Cincinnati
733 Old Chem
Cincinnati, OH 45221-0372
Ph: (513)556-2752
Fax: (513)556-1991
E-mail: lessing.society@uc.edu
URL: http://asweb.artsci.uc.edu/german/lessing
Contact: Richard E. Schade, Managing Ed.

Founded: 1966. **Members:** 350. **Membership Dues:** regular, $35 (annual) ● student, $15 (annual). **Staff:** 4. **Languages:** English, German. **Description:** Individuals interested in the life and works of Gotthold Ephraim Lessing (1729-81), German dramatist and author of numerous critical and theological writings, and active in the literature, philosophy, and aesthetics of the 18th century. Encourages research on Lessing in order to stimulate a "reappraisal of the pertinence of his thought in modern times." Develops research facilities; reemphasizes Lessing's "cosmopolitan humanism and his continuing importance throughout the world.". **Committees:** Editorial. **Formerly:** (1974) American Lessing Society. **Publications:** *Lessing Society—Notes and Notices*, semiannual. Newsletter. Publishes calls for papers and announcements concerning Lessing's life and works. ● *Lessing Yearbook*. Scholarly journal containing research on Lessing and his contemporaries, and on the 18th-century Enlightenment in Germany. Includes book reviews. **Price:** included in membership dues. **Circulation:** 300 ● *Proceedings of International Lessing Conferences*. **Conventions/Meetings:** semiannual lecture.

9681 ■ Lewis Carroll Society of North America (LCSNA)

c/o Clare Imholtz, Sec.
11935 Beltsville Dr.
Beltsville, MD 20705
E-mail: imholtz99@lantech.net
URL: http://www.lewiscarroll.org
Contact: Clare Imholtz, Sec.

Founded: 1974. **Members:** 380. **Membership Dues:** regular, $25 (annual) ● sustaining, $50 (annual). **Multinational. Description:** Collectors, authors, publishers, rare book dealers, and others interested in the life and works of Charles Lutwidge Dodgson (1832-98), who wrote under the pen name of Lewis Carroll. Encourages the study of life, works, times, and influence of Dodgson. Aims to become a center for Carroll studies. **Committees:** Nominating; Publications. **Funds:** Maxine Schaefer Memorial; Stan Marx Memorial. **Publications:** *Chapbook Series*, periodic. Pamphlet ● *Knight Letter*, semiannual. Magazine. Serves as a medium of communication for collectors, authors, publishers, rare-book dealers, and others interested in Dodgson's life and works. **Price:** free for members. ISSN: 0193-886X ● Plans to publish scholarly journals. **Conventions/Meetings:** semiannual meeting - always spring and fall.

9682 ■ Louisa May Alcott Memorial Association (LMAMA)

c/o Orchard House
399 Lexington Rd.
PO Box 343
Concord, MA 01742-0343
Ph: (978)369-4118
Fax: (978)369-1367

E-mail: info@louisamayalcott.org
URL: http://www.louisamayalcott.org
Contact: Jan Turnquist, Exec. Dir.
Founded: 1911. **Members:** 800. **Membership Dues:** individual, $40 (annual) ● household, $60 (annual) ● student, senior, $25 (annual) ● philosopher's group, $250 (annual) ● transcendentalist's circle, $500 (annual) ● life, $2,500 ● library, $100 (annual) ● writer's guild, $125 (annual) ● youth (through age 17), $10 (annual). **Staff:** 35. **Budget:** $525,000. **Languages:** Chinese, English, Esperanto, French, German, Japanese, Spanish. **Description:** Maintains former home of Louisa May Alcott (1832-88) as a museum for the display of memorabilia of Alcott and Bronson Alcott's School of Philosophy. Sponsors summer children's program; offers lecture series at School of Philosophy; maintains library. **Libraries: Type:** by appointment only. **Holdings:** 350; books. **Subjects:** the Alcotts. **Also Known As:** Orchard House. **Publications:** *Alcott Newsnotes U.S.A.*, quarterly. Newsletter. Features information on current and upcoming activities of the historic house. **Price:** included in membership dues. **Circulation:** 1,500. Also Cited As: *Orchard House Newsletter* ● *Gift Shop Catalogue* ● *Story of the Alcotts.* **Conventions/Meetings:** annual Summer Conversational Series - workshop, adult education workshop - mid-July.

9683 ■ Lowell Celebrates Kerouac! (LCK!)

c/o Lawrence Carradini, Pres.
PO Box 1111
Lowell, MA 01853-1111
Free: (877)KER-OUAC
E-mail: lcarradini@earthlink.net
URL: http://lckorg.tripod.com
Contact: Lawrence Carradini, Pres.
Founded: 1985. **Members:** 95. **Membership Dues:** individual, $25 (annual) ● student/senior citizen, $20 (annual) ● family, $35 (annual). **Budget:** $10,000. **Description:** Individuals who share an appreciation and enthusiasm for the literary works of American author, Jack Kerouac. Promotes the study and enjoyment of Jack Kerouac's works by sponsoring events, educational programs, performance, and art. **Awards:** Barbara Concannon - Crete Memorial High School Poetry Prize. **Frequency:** annual. **Type:** monetary ● Jack Kerouac Literary Prize. **Frequency:** periodic. **Type:** monetary. **Recipient:** for the winner of the literary competition for new and established writers. **Committees:** Events Planning. **Also Known As:** (2002) Corporation for the Celebration of Jack Kerouac in Lowell. **Publications:** *Beat Notes*, semiannual. Newsletter. **Price:** included in membership dues. **Conventions/Meetings:** annual festival and symposium, readings, musical features (exhibits) - early October ● annual March Celebration - festival, readings, musical features, tours (exhibits) - mid-March.

9684 ■ Mark Twain Boyhood Home Associates (MTBHA)

120 N Main St.
Hannibal, MO 63401
Ph: (573)221-9010
Fax: (573)221-7975
E-mail: henry.sweets@marktwainmuseum.org
URL: http://www.marktwainmuseum.org
Contact: Henry H. Sweets III, Curator
Founded: 1981. **Members:** 520. **Membership Dues:** student, $25 (annual) ● individual, $50 (annual) ● couple, $75 (annual) ● family, $100 (annual) ● apprentice, $250 (annual) ● journeyman, $500 (annual). **Staff:** 1. **Description:** Operates as the membership branch of the Mark Twain Home Foundation. Seeks to perpetuate the memory of American author Mark Twain (pen name for Samuel Clemens, 1835-1910) and his literary works by contributing to and assisting in maintaining the Mark Twain Home and Museum in Hannibal, MO. Sponsors special programs at the museum. **Publications:** *Fence Painter*, bimonthly. Newsletter. Contains articles on Mark Twain, Hannibal, MO, and the Mark Twain Museum. **Price:** included in membership dues. ISSN: 0891-4958. **Circulation:** 650. **Conventions/Meetings:** annual meeting - always near November 30 (Twain's birthday), in Hannibal, MO.

9685 ■ Mark Twain Circle of New York (MTC)

c/o Salwen Business Communications
156 5th Ave., Ste.517
New York, NY 10010-7002
Ph: (212)242-5546 (212)384-8081
Fax: (212)242-5670
E-mail: mtc@salwen.com
URL: http://www.salwen.com/mtahome.html
Contact: Peter Salwen, Contact
Founded: 1926. **Members:** 200. **Description:** Individuals united in appreciation of the works of Mark Twain (pseudonym of American author Samuel Clemens, 1835-1910). Aims to study and to promote awareness of Twain's life and writings. **Formerly:** (1999) Mark Twain Association of New York. **Publications:** *Information Sheet*, annual. **Conventions/Meetings:** meeting - 3-4/year.

9686 ■ Mark Twain Home Foundation (MTHF)

120 N Main St.
Hannibal, MO 63401
Ph: (573)221-9010
Fax: (573)221-7975
E-mail: regina.faden@marktwainmuseum.org
URL: http://www.marktwainmuseum.org
Contact: Dr. Regina Faden, Exec. Dir.
Founded: 1974. **Members:** 15. **Staff:** 5. **Budget:** $692,000. **Description:** Responsible for the care, restoration, and operation of the Interpretive Center, Mark Twain Boyhood Home, John Marshall Clemens' Justice of the Peace Office, Grant's Drug Store, Becky Thatcher House, and the Museum Gallery, all buildings related to the life of Samuel Clemens (1835-1910), who wrote under the pen name of Mark Twain. Clemens lived in Hannibal from 1839 to 1853. Offers speakers and programs on Mark Twain. **Libraries: Type:** reference. **Holdings:** 1,900. **Subjects:** Mark Twain. **Publications:** *The Fence Painter*, quarterly. Newsletter. **Price:** $15.00/year. ISSN: 0891-4948. **Circulation:** 740.

9687 ■ Mark Twain House and Museum (MTH)

351 Farmington Ave.
Hartford, CT 06105-4401
Ph: (860)247-0998
Fax: (860)278-8148
E-mail: info@marktwainhouse.org
URL: http://www.marktwainhouse.org
Contact: Debra Petke, Exec. Dir.
Founded: 1929. **Members:** 800. **Membership Dues:** individual, $50 (annual) ● household (couple and children under 17), $75 (annual) ● sustaining (household admitted with up to 4 guests), $150 (annual) ● national (individual living outside Connecticut), $40 (annual). **Staff:** 30. **Budget:** $3,000,000. **Description:** Fosters appreciation of the legacy of Samuel L. Clemens (1835-1910) as a national defining cultural figure and to demonstrate the continuing relevance of his work, life and times. Designated a National Historic Landmark by the U.S. Department of the Interior. **Libraries: Type:** by appointment only. **Holdings:** 5,000; books, clippings, photographs. **Subjects:** life and works of Mark Twain. **Committees:** Clemens Circle; Friends; Friends of The Mark Twain House. **Formerly:** (1998) Mark Twain Memorial. **Publications:** *Mark Twain News*, quarterly. Newsletter. **Price:** included in membership dues. **Circulation:** 2,000.

9688 ■ Mark Twain Research Foundation (MTRF)

c/o Mark Twain Birthplace
37352 Shrine Rd.
Florida, MO 65283
Ph: (573)565-3449
Fax: (573)565-3718
E-mail: mark.twain.birthplace.state.historic.site@dnr.mo.gov
Contact: John Huffman, Administrator
Founded: 1939. **Members:** 400. **Membership Dues:** regular, $20 (annual). **Description:** Teachers of English and American literature and others interested in the life and writings of Samuel Clemens (1835-1910), who used the pen name Mark Twain; colleges and universities. Promotes restoration of the village of Florida, MO, where Clemens was born. Collects and distributes newly discovered facts about the life and writings of Twain; maintains collection of personal items associated with the author. Cooperates with Mark Twain Birthplace State Historic Site, Florida, MO, and Missouri Department of Natural Resources. **Convention/Meeting:** none. **Publications:** *The Twainian*, quarterly. Newsletter. Reports on the life and writings of Mark Twain. **Price:** included in membership dues. **Circulation:** 400.

9689 ■ Marlowe Lives! Association (ML!A)

402 S Illinois Ave.
Carbondale, IL 62901-2813
Ph: (618)549-3495
E-mail: marlovian@aol.com
URL: http://www.marlovian.com
Contact: David A. More, Ed.
Founded: 1993. **Members:** 25. **Membership Dues:** regular, $15 (annual). **Description:** Individuals interested in the life and works of 16th century poet-dramatist named Christopher Marlowe. Promotes the claim that Marlowe is the author of the works attributed to William Shakespeare. Conducts research. **Libraries: Type:** not open to the public. **Holdings:** 257; books. **Subjects:** Christopher Marlowe, William Shakespeare. **Awards:** The Shakespeare Prize. **Frequency:** annual. **Type:** recognition. **Recipient:** for best essay on Marlowe's contribution to Shakespeare canon. **Formerly:** (1997) Shakespeare Authorship Society. **Publications:** *The Marlovian*, 3/year. Newsletter. **Price:** included in membership dues.

9690 ■ Marlowe Society of America (MSA)

c/o Prof. Bruce E. Brandt, Pres.
South Dakota State Univ.
Dept. of English
Box 504
Brookings, SD 57007-1397
Ph: (605)688-4058
Fax: (605)688-5192
E-mail: bruce.brandt@sdstate.edu
Contact: Prof. Bruce E. Brandt, Pres.
Founded: 1976. **Members:** 150. **Membership Dues:** individual, $25 (annual). **Description:** Scholars and laypeople interested in the life and works of Christopher Marlowe (1564-93), English dramatist. Sponsors panels at the MLA Convention and holds international conferences on the plays, poems, and biography of Marlowe. **Awards:** Roma Gill Award. **Frequency:** biennial. **Type:** recognition. **Recipient:** for the best publication on Christopher Marlowe. **Affiliated With:** Modern Language Association of America. **Publications:** Newsletter, semiannual. Includes book reviews. Alternate Formats: online. **Conventions/Meetings:** quinquennial international conference ● annual meeting, held in conjunction with Modern Language Association of America - always December 27-30.

9691 ■ Melville Society (MS)

c/o Christopher Sten, Sec.
Dept. of English
George Washington Univ.
Washington, DC 20052
E-mail: csten@gwu.edu
URL: http://people.hofstra.edu/faculty/john_L_bryant/Melville/AboutMelville.html
Contact: Christopher Sten, Sec.
Founded: 1945. **Members:** 800. **Membership Dues:** individual, library, $25 (annual). **Staff:** 15. **Description:** Persons interested in the life, times, and writings of the American author, Herman Melville (1819-91). **Libraries: Type:** open to the public. **Holdings:** articles, artwork, books, periodicals. **Subjects:** Herman Melville. **Awards:** Hennig Cohen Prize. **Frequency:** annual. **Type:** monetary. **Recipient:** for best article/essay on Melville. **Telecommunication Services:** electronic mail, listserv@pride.hofstra.edu. **Publications:** *Leviathan*, semiannual. Journal ● *Melville Society Extracts*, semiannual. Newsletter. **Price:** included in membership dues. **Advertising:** accepted ● Pamphlets, occasional. **Conventions/Meetings:** annual Modern Language Association conference (exhibits).

9692 ■ Mencken Society (MS)
PO Box 16218
Baltimore, MD 21210
E-mail: president@mencken.org
URL: http://www.mencken.org
Contact: Edward A. Martin, Pres.
Founded: 1976. **Members:** 300. **Membership Dues:** individual, $25 (annual). **Description:** Mencken scholars and enthusiasts. Provides a forum for people who enjoy reading and discussing the writings of Henry Louis Mencken (1880-1956), American editor and satirist. **Projects:** Mencken Transcription. **Publications:** *Menckeniana*, quarterly. Journal. Published by Enoch Pratt Free Library. **Price:** included in membership dues ● *President's Letter*, periodic. **Conventions/Meetings:** meeting - 3/year ● annual Mencken Day - meeting (exhibits) - always first or second Saturday of September, in Baltimore, MD.

9693 ■ Milton Society of America (MSA)
Duquesne Univ.
English Dept.
Pittsburgh, PA 15282
Ph: (412)396-6420
Fax: (412)396-1112
E-mail: labriola@duq.edu
URL: http://www.urich.edu/~creamer/milton/society.html
Contact: Albert C. Labriola, Sec.
Founded: 1948. **Members:** 550. **Description:** Professors, graduate students, and others interested in the study of English poet John Milton (1608-74). Occasionally honors an outstanding Milton scholar. **Affiliated With:** Modern Language Association of America. **Publications:** *Milton Society of America—Bulletin*, annual. Contains a membership directory. **Price:** included in membership dues. **Circulation:** 550. **Conventions/Meetings:** annual meeting - always December 28.

9694 ■ Nathaniel Hawthorne Society (NHS)
c/o Mr. Leland S. Person, Treas.
Dept. of English
Univ. of Cincinnati
Cincinnati, OH 45221-0069
Ph: (513)556-5924
Fax: (513)556-5960
E-mail: lee.person@uc.edu
URL: http://asweb.artsci.uc.edu/english/Hawthorne-Society/nh.html
Contact: Mr. Leland S. Person, Treas.
Founded: 1974. **Members:** 500. **Membership Dues:** regular, $15 (annual) ● student, $5 (annual) ● international, $15 (annual). **Description:** Scholars, collectors, students, and librarians united to promote the study and appreciation of Nathaniel Hawthorne (1804-64), American author. **Publications:** *Nathaniel Hawthorne Review*, semiannual. Journal. Contains society news, abstracts of program papers, book reviews, current bibliographies, articles, and research updates. **Price:** included in membership dues. **Circulation:** 500. **Advertising:** accepted. **Conventions/Meetings:** semiannual conference - even-numbered years ● semiannual symposium.

9695 ■ National Steinbeck Center
1 Main St.
Salinas, CA 93901
Ph: (831)796-3833 (831)775-4721
Fax: (831)796-3828
E-mail: info@steinbeck.org
URL: http://www.steinbeck.org
Contact: Tiffany DiTullio, Dir. of Development
Founded: 1983. **Members:** 2,500. **Membership Dues:** individual, $45 (annual) ● family, $65 (annual). **Staff:** 12. **Budget:** $1,800,000. **Description:** Provides and supports educational experiences that inspire audiences to learn about human nature, literature, history, agriculture, and arts. Promotes Steinbeck's works and philosophy through interactive, multisensory exhibits for all ages and backgrounds, priceless artifacts, entertaining displays, educational programs and research archives. Maintains museum and archive of John Steinbeck's birthplace in Oldtown Salinas. **Libraries: Type:** reference. **Holdings:** archival material, artwork, books. **Subjects:** Steinbeck, agriculture, local history. **Affiliated With:** Monterey County Convention and Visitors Bureau; Monterey Peninsula Chamber of Commerce; Salinas Valley Chamber of Commerce. **Formerly:** (1997) Steinbeck Center Foundation. **Publications:** *National Steinbeck Center News*, quarterly. Newsletter. Includes events and museum news. **Price:** included in membership dues. **Circulation:** 2,500. **Conventions/Meetings:** annual Steinbeck Festival - festival and tour, with literary speakers - first weekend of August.

9696 ■ New York C.S. Lewis Society (NYCSLS)
c/o Clara Sarrocco, Sec.
84-23 77th Ave.
Glendale, NY 11385-7706
Ph: (718)846-7858
E-mail: csarrocco@aol.com
URL: http://www.nycslsociety.com
Contact: Clara Sarrocco, Sec.
Founded: 1969. **Members:** 600. **Membership Dues:** in U.S., $10 (annual) ● outside U.S., $15 (annual). **Description:** Individuals united to foster and share an enthusiasm for the works of C.S. Lewis (1898-1963), English novelist and essayist. Although its name implies otherwise, the organization is an international group. **Libraries: Type:** open to the public. **Subjects:** literature, philosophy, religion. **Publications:** *CSL: The Bulletin of the New York C.S. Lewis Society*, bimonthly. **Price:** $10.00 in U.S.; $15.00 outside U.S. ISSN: 0883-9980. **Circulation:** 600 ● Also publishes articles and reviews. **Conventions/Meetings:** quadrennial C.S. Lewis Symposium, with speakers.

9697 ■ Nockian Society (NS)
42 Leathers Rd.
Fort Mitchell, KY 41017
URL: http://alumnus.caltech.edu/~ckank/FultonsLair/013/nock/society.html
Contact: Robert M. Thornton, Founder
Founded: 1963. **Members:** 750. **Description:** Informal fellowship of persons who admire the writings of Albert Jay Nock (1883-1945), American essayist and editor. Encourages interest in Nock's books and helps members locate out-of-print books. Sponsors reprinting of Nock's books. **Convention/Meeting:** none. **Publications:** *Memorandum*, periodic.

9698 ■ Paul Claudel Society (PCS)
Address Unknown since 2008
Founded: 1969. **Members:** 65. **Membership Dues:** regular, $10 (annual). **Languages:** English, French. **Multinational. Description:** College professors and high school teachers. Unites individuals interested in the life and works of Paul Claudel (1868-1955), French diplomat, poet, and dramatist. Provides a forum for discussion; encourages and supports critical studies; provides research materials; promotes performance of dramatic works; discusses related authors and works. **Publications:** *Paul Claudel Papers* (in English and French), annual. Journal. Contains monographs, research papers, and reviews. **Price:** $20.00 for members. ISSN: 1496-4813. **Circulation:** 500. Alternate Formats: online. **Conventions/Meetings:** annual convention, held in conjunction with the Modern Language Association of America (exhibits) ● symposium.

9699 ■ Pearl S. Buck Birthplace Foundation (PSBBF)
c/o Pearl S. Buck Museum
PO Box 126
Hillsboro, WV 24946
Ph: (304)653-4430
E-mail: info@pearlsbuckbirthplace.com
URL: http://www.pearlsbuckbirthplace.com/aboutus.html
Contact: Mrs. Rose Anderson, Pres.
Founded: 1966. **Members:** 100. **Staff:** 3. **Budget:** $25,000. **Description:** Individuals and organizations supporting the ideals of Pearl S. Buck (1892-1973), American novelist. Seeks to establish a center for arts and humanities and to promote educational and cultural development. Maintains Buck's birthplace as the Historic House Museum of 1892. Conducts museum tours; provides information and referrals concerning Buck's life and work. Maintains library of Buck books and manuscripts; provides researchers with limited access to original manuscripts. **Publications:** *Between Two Worlds*. Book. **Price:** $29.95 ● *The Dragon Seed*. Book. **Price:** $75.00 ● *The Kennedy Woman*. Book. **Price:** $50.00 ● *My Mother's House*. Book. **Price:** $100.00/copy ● *Our Live and Work in China*. Book. **Price:** $5.00 paperback. **Conventions/Meetings:** annual meeting - always second Sunday of October, in White Sulphur Springs, WV.

9700 ■ Philip Jose Farmer Society (PJFS)
Address Unknown since 2008
Founded: 1978. **Members:** 150. **Description:** Enthusiasts and collectors of the works of Philip Jose Farmer (1918-), writer of adventure and speculative fiction. Acts as clearinghouse of information on and forum for discussion of Farmer's life and works. Conventions/Meetings: none. **Publications:** *Farmerage*, periodic. Journal ● Books ● Directory, periodic.

9701 ■ Pirandello Society of America (PSA)
CNL Anne and Henry Paolucci Intl. Conf. Center
68-02 Metropolitan Ave.
Middle Village, NY 11379
Ph: (718)821-3916
E-mail: anneandhenrypaolucci@yahoo.com
URL: http://www.pirandello.homestead.com
Contact: Nishan Parlakian, Pres.
Founded: 1958. **Members:** 500. **Membership Dues:** individual in U.S. and outside U.S., $25 (annual) ● library in U.S., $35 (annual) ● library outside U.S., $40 (annual). **Staff:** 5. **Languages:** English, Italian. **Description:** Encourages the study of the works of Italian author Luigi Pirandello (1867-1936), particularly his plays and his varied influence on the contemporary theatre. Forms speakers' bureau. **Awards:** Pirandello Scholar and Dramatist Influence Awards. **Frequency:** annual. **Type:** recognition. **Recipient:** to Pirandello member or theater people who have featured Pirandello. **Publications:** Journal, annual. Covers the work of Pirandello and contemporary literature in general. Includes reviews of books, plays, films, and special programs. **Price:** included in membership dues; $20.00 back issues (individual); $35.00 back issues (library). ISSN: 1042-4822. **Circulation:** 500. **Advertising:** accepted. **Conventions/Meetings:** annual board meeting, held in conjunction with Modern Language Association of America.

9702 ■ P.N. Elrod Fan Club (PNEFC)
c/o The Teeth in the Neck Gang
PO Box 60391
Fort Worth, TX 76115
E-mail: pnelrod@vampwriter.com
URL: http://www.vampwriter.com
Founded: 1993. **Staff:** 2. **Nonmembership. Multinational. Description:** Admirers of author P.N. Elrod. Promotes appreciation of Elrod's works and seeks to advance her career. Keeps public informed of Elrod's future plans and appearance itinerary; facilitates communication and good fellowship among members. **Also Known As:** Teeth In the Neck Gang.

9703 ■ Poe Foundation (PF)
c/o Poe Museum
1914-16 Main St.
Richmond, VA 23223
Ph: (804)648-5523
Free: (888)21E-APOE
Fax: (804)648-8729
E-mail: info@poemuseum.org
URL: http://www.poemuseum.org
Contact: Katarina Spears, Exec. Dir.
Founded: 1922. **Members:** 450. **Membership Dues:** student teacher, $15 (annual) ● individual, $25 (annual) ● family, $35 (annual) ● contributing, $100 (annual) ● benefactor, $250 (annual). **Staff:** 10. **Budget:** $150,000. **Description:** Persons who contribute to the operation and maintenance of the Edgar Allan Poe Museum. Encourages student research, and serves as a source of information for persons interested in the Poe era in American literature. Conducts internship arrangement with local colleges.

Libraries: Type: reference. **Holdings:** 1,500. **Subjects:** material on and by Edgar Allan Poe. **Formerly:** (1934) The Poe Shrine. **Publications:** *Evermore*, quarterly. Newsletter. Includes articles and features on activities/events at the museum. **Price:** $1.00. **Circulation:** 2,000.

9704 ■ Poe Studies Association (PSA)
c/o Paul C. Jones, Sec.-Treas.
Dept. of English
360 Ellis Hall
Ohio Univ.
Athens, OH 45701
E-mail: jonesp2@ohio.edu
URL: http://www.an.psu.edu/psa
Contact: Paul C. Jones, Sec.-Treas.
Founded: 1971. **Members:** 330. **Membership Dues:** individual, $20 (annual) ● international, $25 (annual). **Description:** College teachers and other persons concerned with the works of Edgar Allan Poe (1809-49), American poet and storywriter. Promotes exchange of information and ideas related to Poe's biography and criticism; works to establish a sense of community among Poe scholars worldwide. Informs members of current Poe studies; encourages publication and research. Bestows honorary membership to persons who have made significant contributions to the Poe scholarship. **Awards:** Gargano Quinn. **Frequency:** annual. **Type:** monetary. **Recipient:** for best essay or best book on Poe. **Publications:** *The Edgar Allan Poe Review*, semiannual. Journal. Includes book reviews and recent dissertations. **Price:** included in membership dues. ISSN: 1051-743X. **Circulation:** 330 ● Newsletter. Alternate Formats: online. **Conventions/Meetings:** annual conference, in conjunction with Modern Language Association of America and American Literature Association - MLA-December, ALA-late May, alternatively Boston and San Diego.

9705 ■ Powys Society of North America (PSNA)
c/o Nicholas Birns, Exec. Sec.
205 E 10th St.
New York, NY 10003-7634
Ph: (212)533-8397
E-mail: kate.kavanagh@virgin.net
URL: http://members.aol.com/nicbirns/powys.html
Contact: Nicholas Birns, Exec. Sec.
Founded: 1983. **Members:** 150. **Membership Dues:** regular, $15 (annual). **Staff:** 3. **Description:** Individuals interested in the lives and literary works of brothers John Cowper Powys (1872-1963), Theodore Francis Powys (1875-1953), and Llewelyn Powys (1884-1939). Promotes study and appreciation of their writings, especially with regard to their impact on North American literature. Encourages research in collections of Powys papers located in North America. **Publications:** *Powys Notes*, semiannual. Journal. Includes book reviews, essays, and symposia. **Price:** included in membership dues. ISSN: 1058-7691. **Circulation:** 250. **Advertising:** accepted. **Conventions/Meetings:** annual Powys and the Canon - conference (exhibits).

9706 ■ Ralph Waldo Emerson Memorial Association (RWEMA)
Address Unknown since 2008
Founded: 1930. **Members:** 15. **Staff:** 2. **Description:** Seeks to promote and maintain public interest in the literary works of Ralph Waldo Emerson (1803-82). Operates and maintains the home of Emerson in Concord, MA, a national historic landmark open to the public April through October. **Publications:** none. **Awards: Frequency:** annual. **Type:** grant. **Recipient:** bestowed to editors and scholars for projects that further interest in and knowledge of Emerson's works. **Conventions/Meetings:** annual meeting.

9707 ■ Richard Wright Circle (RWC)
c/o James A. Miller
George Washington Univ.
Dept. of English
Washington, DC 20052
Ph: (202)994-6743
Fax: (202)994-7915
E-mail: jam@gwu.edu
Contact: James A. Miller, Contact
Founded: 1991. **Members:** 125. **Membership Dues:** individual, $10 (annual). **Staff:** 1. **Description:** Encourages study and teaching of the life and works of Richard Wright, African American author. **Publications:** Newsletter, annual. **Price:** included in membership dues.

9708 ■ Rousseau Association
c/o Sally H. Campbell, Sec.-Treas.
Dept. of Political Sci.
Concord Univ.
PO Box 1000
Athens, WV 24712
E-mail: scampbell@concord.edu
URL: http://www.rousseauassociation.org
Contact: Byron Wells, Pres.
Founded: 1979. **Members:** 175. **Multinational. Description:** History, philosophy, political science, and French literature and language scholars interested in the life and works of Jean-Jacques Rousseau (1712-78), French philosopher and author. Seeks to advance the study of the life and works of Rousseau. Provides a reprint exchange; conducts research and educational programs. **Libraries: Type:** lending. **Formerly:** (1982) Society for Rousseau Studies; (2006) North American Association for the Study of Jean-Jacques Rousseau. **Publications:** *North American Association for the Study of Jean-Jacques Rousseau—Newsletter*, quarterly. Includes book reviews and research reports. ● *North American Association for the Study of Jean-Jacques Rousseau—Proceedings*, periodic ● *Pensie Libre*. **Conventions/Meetings:** biennial conference.

9709 ■ Shakespeare Oxford Society (SOS)
PO Box 808
Yorktown Heights, NY 10598
Ph: (914)962-1717
E-mail: matthew@ovations.com
URL: http://www.shakespeare-oxford.com
Contact: Matthew Cossolotto, Pres.
Founded: 1957. **Members:** 650. **Membership Dues:** regular, in U.S. and Canada, $50 (annual) ● regular, outside U.S. and Canada, $60 (annual) ● student, in U.S. and Canada, $30 (annual) ● student, outside U.S. and Canada, $40 (annual) ● family, in U.S. and Canada, $75 (annual) ● family, outside U.S. and Canada, $85 (annual) ● sponsor, $100 (annual) ● contributor, $250 (annual) ● patron, $500 (annual) ● benefactor, $1,000 (annual). **Regional Groups:** 6. **Description:** Persons interested in the humanities, especially research into the history of the Elizabethan period of English literature. Explores and attempts to verify evidence bearing on the authorship of works attributed to Shakespeare, particularly evidence indicating that Edward de Vere, the 17th Earl of Oxford, was their author. Searches for original manuscripts in England to support its theories. Conducts research and educational programs; maintains Speaker's Bureau. **Libraries: Type:** reference. **Holdings:** 2,000; books, periodicals. **Subjects:** authorship question, Shakespeare, Elizabethan history. **Awards:** Oxfordian of the Year. **Frequency:** annual. **Type:** recognition ● Shakespeare Oxford Society Lifetime Achievement Award. **Frequency:** periodic. **Type:** recognition. **Publications:** *The Ever Reader*. Magazine. Features sampling of news, articles and essays drawn from recent issues of the Shakespeare Oxford Newsletter. Alternate Formats: online ● *The Oxfordian*, annual. Journal. **Price:** $10.00 /year for members; $20.00 /year for nonmembers. ISSN: 1521-3641 ● *Shakespeare Oxford Newsletter*, quarterly. **Price:** included in membership dues. ISSN: 1525-6863. **Circulation:** 700. **Advertising:** accepted. Alternate Formats: online ● Brochures ● Pamphlets. **Conventions/Meetings:** annual conference - always fall.

9710 ■ Shakespeare Society
45 E 78th St.
New York, NY 10021
Ph: (212)327-3399
Fax: (212)327-3377
E-mail: bard@shakespearesociety.org
URL: http://www.shakespearesociety.org
Contact: Barbara Tracey, Admin. Dir.
Founded: 1997. **Members:** 650. **Membership Dues:** patron (couple), $310 (annual) ● sponsor (couple), $175 (annual) ● student (single, under 21), $50 (annual) ● benefactor (couple), $650 (annual) ● player king (couple), $1,500 (annual) ● Bard's Circle (couple), $2,500 (annual). **Staff:** 5. **Description:** Dedicated to increasing the enjoyment, understanding, and appreciation of William Shakespeare's works through performance, commentary, and adult education activities. **Awards:** The Shakespeare Medal. **Frequency:** annual. **Type:** medal. **Publications:** *Shakespeare Newsletter*, quarterly. **Price:** included in membership dues. **Conventions/Meetings:** Monday Evening Events - meeting - 5/year ● Shakespeare Study Seminars ● Speak-the-Verse Seminars.

9711 ■ Swedenborg Foundation (SF)
320 N Church St.
West Chester, PA 19380
Ph: (610)430-3222
Free: (800)355-3222
Fax: (610)430-7982
E-mail: info@swedenborg.com
URL: http://www.swedenborg.com
Contact: Ms. Dana Bateman, Admin. Asst.
Founded: 1849. **Members:** 700. **Membership Dues:** regular, $40 (annual). **Staff:** 8. **Budget:** $1,440,000. **Description:** Publishes the theological writings of Emanuel Swedenborg (1688-1772) and related literature. Swedenborg was an eighteenth century Swedish scientist, philosopher, civil engineer, nobleman, and religious visionary. Also sponsors annual lecture program; translates all Swedenborg's works and occasionally produces videos. **Libraries: Type:** reference; by appointment only. **Holdings:** 2,000; archival material, books, periodicals, video recordings. **Subjects:** theology, philosophy, psychology, biography. **Awards: Frequency:** annual. **Type:** grant. **Recipient:** for translators and scholarly research projects. **Additional Websites:** http://www.newcenturytv.com/swedenborg. **Publications:** *Light in My Darkness*. Book. **Circulation:** 11,500 ● *Logos*, 3/year. Newsletter. Contains news and events. **Price:** included in membership dues. **Circulation:** 700 ● *The Presence of Other Worlds*. Book ● *Splendors of the Spirit: Swedenborg's Quest for Insight*. Video. **Conventions/Meetings:** annual meeting - held in May.

9712 ■ The Thomas Hardy Association (TTHA)
c/o Rosemarie Morgan, Pres./Ed.
124 Bishop St.
New Haven, CT 06511
E-mail: hardy-association@mailman.yale.edu
URL: http://www.yale.edu/hardysoc/Welcome/welcomet.htm
Contact: Rosemarie Morgan, Pres./Ed.
Founded: 1997. **Membership Dues:** individual, $40 (annual) ● couple, $55 (annual) ● student, $30 (annual) ● institutional, $65 (annual) ● life, $450. **Multinational. Description:** Promotes the study and appreciation of Hardy's work. Encourages an interest in and appreciation of the works of Thomas Hardy. Promotes the study of Thomas Hardy's writings. Publishes information about Hardy. Engages its members in discussion of and inquiry into all aspects of Hardy's life and work. **Telecommunication Services:** electronic mail, rm82@pantheon.yale.edu ● electronic mail, rosemarie.morgan@yale.edu. **Publications:** *The Hardy Review*, annual. Journal. **Price:** included in membership dues. Alternate Formats: online.

9713 ■ Thomas Wolfe Society (TWS)
c/o David Strange, Membership Coor.
PO Box 1146
Bloomington, IN 47402-1146
E-mail: twostrange2000@yahoo.com
URL: http://www.thomaswolfe.org
Contact: David Strange, Membership Coor.
Founded: 1979. **Members:** 500. **Membership Dues:** individual, institution, $30 (annual). **Staff:** 12. **De-**

scription: Scholars, critics, teachers, students, and admirers of American novelist Thomas C. Wolfe (1900-38). Seeks "to encourage scholarly study of, critical attention to, and general interest in the work and career of Thomas Wolfe." Sponsors Thomas Wolfe Society Student Essay Prize Literary Contest for undergraduate and graduate students. **Libraries: Type:** reference. **Holdings:** 100; archival material. **Subjects:** Thomas Wolfe, Aline Bernstein, Belinda Jellife, University of North Carolina: Chapel Hill. **Awards:** Richard S. Kennedy Student Essay Prize. **Frequency:** annual. **Type:** grant ● William B. Wisdom Grant. **Frequency:** annual. **Type:** grant. **Recipient:** for travel to Wolfe Collections at Harvard, UNC ● Zelda and Paul Gitlin Literary Prize. **Frequency:** annual. **Type:** monetary. **Recipient:** to the most important published article on Thomas Wolfe. **Computer Services:** Mailing lists. **Committees:** Gitlin Prize; Publications; Student Essay Prize; Wisdom Grant. **Publications:** *The Proceedings and Membership List of the Thomas Wolfe Society*, annual. Journal. Contains listing of Zelda Gitlin Literary Prize winners and Thomas Wolfe Society Citation of Merit winners. Includes list of society publications. **Price:** included in membership dues. **Circulation:** 500 ● *The Thomas Wolfe Review*, annual. Journal. Contains information on the life and writings of American novelist Thomas C. Wolfe. **Price:** included in membership dues; $12.00 /year for nonmembers. ISSN: 0276-5683. **Circulation:** 750. **Advertising:** accepted ● Book, annual. Contains previously unpublished Wolfe material or a monograph about Wolfe or his work. **Price:** included in membership dues. **Conventions/Meetings:** annual meeting, with awards banquet (exhibits) - always May.

9714 ■ Thoreau Society (TS)

55 Old Bedford Rd.
Concord, MA 01742
Ph: (978)369-5310
Fax: (978)369-5382
E-mail: info@thoreausociety.org
URL: http://www.thoreausociety.org
Contact: Mr. Michael Frederick, Exec. Dir.

Founded: 1941. **Members:** 2,000. **Membership Dues:** individual in U.S., Canada, Mexico, $40 (annual) ● individual overseas, contributing, institutional in U.S., Canada, Mexico, $50 (annual) ● family in U.S., Canada, Mexico, $55 (annual) ● family overseas, institutional overseas, library overseas, $65 (annual) ● student in U.S., Canada, Mexico, $20 (annual) ● student overseas, $30 (annual) ● sustaining, $75 (annual) ● library in U.S., Canada, Mexico, $60 (annual). **Staff:** 2. **Budget:** $300,000. **Description:** College professors, students, and laymen interested in the life and writings of Henry David Thoreau (1817-62), American philosopher, poet, and naturalist. Collaborates with the Walden Woods Project on the Thoreau Institute (see separate entry), a learning center, museum, and library in Lincoln, MA. Supports efforts to preserve the Walden Pond Reservation. Owns the largest and most comprehensive research collection in the world. **Libraries: Type:** open to the public. **Holdings:** 20,000; articles, books. **Subjects:** Thoreau, transcendentalism. **Awards:** Thoreau Society Medal. **Frequency:** periodic. **Type:** medal. **Recipient:** for significant contribution to Thoreauvian principles. **Computer Services:** database, listserv. **Committees:** Annual Gathering; Collections; Nominations and Elections; Publications. **Publications:** *Concord Saunterer*, annual. Journal. **Price:** included in membership dues ● *Thoreau Society—Bulletin*, quarterly. Includes bibliographies and book reviews. **Price:** included in membership dues. ISSN: 0040-6406. **Circulation:** 2,000. Alternate Formats: CD-ROM ● Concord Saunterer-annual journal. Essays and articles on Thoreau and his significance today. **Conventions/Meetings:** annual conference and workshop - always July in Concord, MA.

9715 ■ Thorne Smith Society

Address Unknown since 2008

Founded: 1992. **Staff:** 1. **Description:** Enthusiasts and collectors of the works of Thorne Smith (1892-1934). Serves as a forum for exchange of information on Smith's life and works. Smith was "perhaps the most critically neglected popular author of the twentieth century". Smith was the author of humorous supernatural fantasy fiction literature such as *Rain in the Doorway*, *The Stray Lamb*, and *Topper*, and was "the master of the pointless conversation". The "Thorne Smith touch" has inspired several motion pictures and television series, including "Bewitched". **Convention/Meeting:** none.

9716 ■ Trollope Society

c/o Mercantile Library
17 E 47th St.
New York, NY 10017
Ph: (212)758-1355
Fax: (212)758-1387
E-mail: info@trollopeusa.org
URL: http://www.trollopeusa.org
Contact: Randolph L. Williams, Pres.

Founded: 1989. **Members:** 750. **Membership Dues:** individual, $48 (annual) ● benefactor, $300 (annual). **For-Profit. Description:** Promotes awareness of and interest in the work of Victorian novelist Anthony Trollope (1815-1882). Sponsors annual programs of lectures, seminars, dinners with speakers, trips, occasional exhibits, receptions and lawn parties. **Awards:** Short Story Prize. **Frequency:** annual. **Type:** monetary ● Trollope Essay Prize. **Frequency:** annual. **Type:** monetary. **Publications:** *Trollopiana*, quarterly. Magazine. **Price:** included in membership dues. **Circulation:** 3,000. **Advertising:** accepted. **Conventions/Meetings:** annual lecture, by leading scholars on aspects of Trollope's life and work ● annual party and lecture, festive cocktail party with occasional entertainments - every winter.

9717 ■ Uncle Remus Museum (URM)

PO Box 184
Eatonton, GA 31024
Ph: (706)485-6856
E-mail: brerfox@uncleremus.com
URL: http://www.uncleremus.com/museum.html
Contact: Grainger McKoy Jr., Contact

Founded: 1962. **Staff:** 3. **Description:** Persons interested in Joel Chandler Harris (1848-1908) and his folklore tales of Uncle Remus. Purposes are to: honor the memory of Harris; keep his works before the public; distribute the Uncle Remus stories. Maintains museum in an old slave cabin depicting an antebellum Southern plantation and the imaginary world of Uncle Remus. **Convention/Meeting:** none. **Libraries: Type:** reference. **Holdings:** photographs, reports.

9718 ■ Vachel Lindsay Association (VLA)

603 S Fifth St.
PO Box 9357
Springfield, IL 62791
Ph: (217)528-9254
URL: http://vachel.blogspot.com
Contact: Larry Stevens, Sec.

Founded: 1946. **Members:** 300. **Membership Dues:** individual, $25 (annual) ● family, $35 (annual) ● patron, $50 (annual) ● sustaining, $100 (annual). **Local Groups:** 1. **Description:** Persons interested in the life and writings of U.S. poet Vachel Lindsay (1879-1931). Conducts educational programs and poetry readings. Maintains speakers' bureau, and art collection. **Libraries: Type:** reference. **Holdings:** archival material. **Publications:** *Look into Your Heart: The Challenge of Vachel*. Video. **Price:** $20.00/copy ● *Vachel*. Book. Features poetry and art work of Vachel Lindsay; book for young people. **Price:** $9.95/copy ● *Vachel Lindsay Association Newsletter*, quarterly. **Price:** included in membership dues. **Circulation:** 300. **Conventions/Meetings:** annual meeting - always fall, Springfield, IL.

9719 ■ Vergilian Society (VS)

c/o Bee English, Sec.
Lake Travis High Scholarship
3324 Ranch Rd., 620 S
Lakeway, TX 78738
Ph: (210)685-0157
E-mail: vergsoc@yahoo.com
URL: http://www.vergil.clarku.edu
Contact: Bee English, Sec.

Founded: 1937. **Members:** 1,200. **Membership Dues:** student, $18 (annual) ● retired, $35 (annual) ● regular, $45 (annual) ● regular, outside U.S., $50 (annual) ● regular, $100 (triennial) ● supporting, $60 (annual) ● supporting, $170 (triennial) ● contributing, institutional, $110 (annual) ● contributing, $330 (triennial) ● life, $750 ● life, benefactor, $1,500. **Languages:** English, Greek, Latin. **Description:** Teachers, students, and others interested in ancient Roman culture; schools and libraries. Seeks to develop interest in classical studies and Latin literature, history, and Roman life, with special attention to the Roman epic poet Vergil (70-19 B.C.). Promotes effective teaching, particularly in secondary schools and colleges, and provides teaching aids and illustrative materials to members. Holds annual summer school (July and August) at Villa Vergiliana in Cuma, Italy, for Latin teachers and students; conducts classical tour of Sicily, Rome, and other historical areas. Promotes and distributes classical books and articles. **Publications:** *Vergilian Society—Monographs*, periodic ● *Vergilian Society—Newsletter*, semiannual. **Price:** included in membership dues. **Advertising:** accepted ● *Vergilius*, annual. Journal. Contains articles on Roman culture and civilization. Includes book reviews. **Price:** included in membership dues; $25.00 /year for nonmembers. **Circulation:** 1,250. **Advertising:** accepted. **Conventions/Meetings:** annual meeting, held in conjunction with the American Philological Association - always December.

9720 ■ W. T. Bandy Center for Baudelaire and Modern French Studies (CBS)

c/o Central Library, Vanderbilt University
Jean and Alexander Heard Lib.
Box 6325, Sta. B
Nashville, TN 37235
Ph: (615)343-0372 (615)322-6284
Fax: (615)343-7451
E-mail: baudelaire@library.vanderbilt.edu
URL: http://www.library.vanderbilt.edu/bandy
Contact: Tracy Sharpley-Whiting, Dir.

Founded: 1968. **Members:** 250. **Staff:** 3. **Description:** Serves as scholarly research center for the study of the works of Charles-Pierre Baudelaire (1821-67), French poet. **Libraries: Type:** reference. **Holdings:** articles, periodicals. **Subjects:** materials by and about Baudelaire. **Computer Services:** database. **Formerly:** (1998) W. T. Bandy Center for Baudelaire Studies. **Publications:** Also publishes studies.

9721 ■ Walt Whitman Birthplace Association (WWBA)

246 Old Walt Whitman Rd.
Huntington Station, NY 11746-4148
Ph: (631)427-5240
Fax: (631)427-5247
E-mail: wwba@optonline.net
URL: http://www.waltwhitman.org
Contact: Cynthia Shor, Exec. Dir.

Founded: 1949. **Members:** 500. **Membership Dues:** student, senior, teacher, $20 (annual) ● individual, $30 (annual) ● family, $40 (annual) ● friend, $50-$99 (annual) ● patron, $100-$149 (annual) ● patron plus, $150-$249 (annual) ● sponsor, $250-$499 (annual) ● donor, $500-$999 (annual) ● benefactor, $1,000-$2,499 (annual). **Staff:** 12. **Budget:** $200,000. **Description:** Seeks to further understand the American poet Walt Whitman (1819-92) and his works. Works for the preservation and operation of the Walt Whitman Birthplace, a state-owned historic site in Huntington, NY. Maintains museum at birthplace Interpretive Center. Sponsors lectures, concerts, exhibits, and tours. Works with school, literary, and poetry groups. **Libraries: Type:** reference. **Holdings:** 350. **Subjects:** Walt Whitman. **Awards:** Poet in Residence. **Frequency:** annual. **Type:** recognition. **Recipient:** for distinguished contemporary poets. **Publications:** *Starting from Paumanok*, quarterly. Newsletter. Carries information on exhibits and events at the association's library and museum. Includes association reports and calendar of events. **Price:** included in membership dues. **Circulation:** 700. **Advertising:** accepted. **Conventions/Meetings:** monthly Poetry Workshops and Readings - meeting (exhibits).

9722 ■ Willa Cather Pioneer Memorial and Educational Foundation (WCPM)
413 N Webster St.
Red Cloud, NE 68970-2466
Ph: (402)746-2653
Free: (866)731-7304
Fax: (402)746-2652
E-mail: info@willacather.org
URL: http://www.willacather.org
Contact: Betty Kort, Exec. Dir.
Founded: 1955. **Members:** 1,000. **Membership Dues:** general, $50 (annual) ● friend, $250 (annual) ● sustaining, $125 (annual) ● student/educational institution, $20 (annual) ● patron, $500 (annual) ● benefactor, $1,000 (annual) ● Cather Circle, $2,500 (annual). **Staff:** 12. **Description:** Persons interested in the preservation of the life, times, and works of American author Willa Cather (1873-1947). Identifies places made famous in Cather's writings. Conducts tours through "Catherland" (western half of Webster County, NE). Seeks to perpetuate a worldwide interest in the work of Willa Cather. Maintains research archives and educational programs. **Libraries: Type:** reference. **Holdings:** archival material. **Awards:** Leslie and Helen Wilson Scholarship. **Frequency:** annual. **Type:** scholarship. **Recipient:** for residents of Red Cloud, upper one-third of class enrolled in agricultural or secondary educational pursuit while being active in community and church ● Norma Ross Walter Scholarship. **Frequency:** annual. **Type:** scholarship. **Recipient:** for Nebraskan girls majoring in English. **Computer Services:** database. **Boards:** Governors. **Also Known As:** Willa Cather Society; Willa Cather Foundation. **Publications:** *Newsletter and Review*, 3/year. **Price:** included in membership dues. **Circulation:** 1,750. **Conventions/Meetings:** triennial Willa Cather International Seminar (exhibits) ● annual Willa Cather Spring Festival - conference - always first weekend of May in Red Cloud, NE.

9723 ■ William Allen White Foundation (WAWF)
c/o William Allen White Library
Emporia State Univ.
1200 Commercial St.
Emporia, KS 66801-5092
Ph: (316)341-5038
Fax: (316)341-5997
E-mail: egazette@valu-line.com
URL: http://www.emporia.com/waw/foundation.html
Contact: Dana Leibengood, Dir.
Founded: 1944. **Description:** Trustees are editors, publishers, and advertising and broadcast executives, together with other communications professionals and non-journalists who knew William Allen White or who are especially interested in perpetuating his memory. (White, 1868-1944, was an author and longtime editor of the Emporia, KS "Gazette".) Established to widen the scope and services of the William Allen White School of Journalism and Mass Communications at the University of Kansas. **Awards:** Burton Marvin Award. **Frequency:** annual. **Type:** recognition. **Recipient:** for citations of journalistic merit to a Kansas journalist ● Inland Daily Press Association Editorial Excellence Award. **Type:** recognition ● William Allen White Citation Award. **Frequency:** annual. **Type:** recognition. **Recipient:** for citations of journalistic merit to an American journalist. **Committees:** National Citation Selection. **Conventions/Meetings:** competition ● annual meeting - always in Lawrence, KS.

9724 ■ William Dean Howells Society (WDHS)
c/o Prof. Elsa Nettels, Treas.
211 Indian Springs Rd.
Williamsburg, VA 23185
E-mail: sgoodman@sigurd.english.udel.edu
URL: http://www.wsu.edu/~campbelld/howells
Contact: Susan Goodman, Pres.
Founded: 1997. **Membership Dues:** regular, $10 (annual). **Description:** Promotes the study of the life and works of American realist author, editor, and literary critic William Dean Howells. Facilitates the exchange of facts, ideas, and texts concerning Howells and those authors significantly associated with him. Serves as an information resource for studies and research pertaining to William Dean Howells. **Telecommunication Services:** electronic mail, exnett@wm.edu ● electronic mail, campbelld@wsu.edu. **Publications:** *The Howellsian*, semiannual. Journal. **Price:** included in membership dues. Alternate Formats: online ● Membership Directory. **Price:** included in membership dues.

9725 ■ William Morris Society in the United States (WMS/US)
c/o Florence Boos, Pres.
PO Box 53263
Washington, DC 20009
E-mail: us@morrissociety.org
URL: http://www.morrissociety.org
Contact: Florence Boos, Pres.
Founded: 1956. **Members:** 350. **Membership Dues:** individual, $45 (annual) ● family, $50 (annual) ● corporate, $55 (annual) ● life, $550. **Staff:** 2. **Description:** Persons interested in the life, activities, ideas, and influence of William Morris (1834-96), an Englishman known through his work as a poet, writer, designer, craftsman, printer, pioneer, and socialist. Seeks to deepen understanding and stimulate a wider appreciation of Morris, his friends, and their work. **Libraries: Type:** reference. **Holdings:** 300. **Subjects:** William Morris, the Pre-Raphaelites. **Awards:** Joseph R. Dunlap Memorial Fellowship. **Frequency:** annual. **Type:** grant. **Recipient:** for individuals ● William Morris Society Fellowship. **Frequency:** annual. **Type:** monetary. **Computer Services:** Mailing lists, of members. **Formerly:** (1986) William Morris Society, North American Branch; (1987) William Morris Society, American Branch. **Publications:** *A Note by William Morris on His Aims in Founding the Kelmscott Press*. Reprint of 1898 publication, by William S. Peterson. **Price:** $45.00 ● *The After Summer Seed*. Book. Collection of essays on Sigurd the Volsung. ● *The Golden Chain*. Book. Collection of essays on Morris's early writings. ● *The Juvenilia of William Morris*. Book ● *The Widow's House by the Water*. Book ● *William Morris: The Collector as Creator*. Catalog. **Price:** $15.00 ● Journal, semiannual. **Price:** included in membership dues. **Circulation:** 4,000. **Advertising:** accepted ● Newsletter, biennial. **Price:** included in membership dues. **Circulation:** 3,000. **Advertising:** accepted ● Also publishes collections of essays; makes available special editions of works by Morris. **Conventions/Meetings:** annual meeting, held in conjunction with the Modern Language Association of America ● periodic meeting.

9726 ■ The Wodehouse Society (TWS)
c/o Amy Plofker, Corresponding Sec.
111 Rice Ave., Fl. 1
Sleepy Hollow, NY 10591-1937
Ph: (914)631-2554
E-mail: amyplf@verizon.net
URL: http://www.wodehouse.org
Contact: Amy Plofker, Corresponding Sec.
Founded: 1979. **Members:** 600. **Membership Dues:** individual or two names at one address, $25 (annual). **Budget:** $15,000. **Local Groups:** 18. **Multinational. Description:** Persons interested in the writings of P.G. Wodehouse (1881-1975), English humor novelist. Facilitates the exchange of information on Wodehouse and his writings and strives to keep his literary legacy fresh in the public mind. Local chapters in the U.S. and Canada sponsor exhibits, dramatic readings and informal gatherings. **Publications:** *Plum Lines*, quarterly. Newsletter. Includes articles, chapter news, book reviews, and announcements. **Price:** included in membership dues. **Circulation:** 600. **Conventions/Meetings:** biennial convention, scholarly talks, banquet, cricket match, book dealers, souvenirs (exhibits).

9727 ■ Wolfe Pack (WP)
PO Box 230822
New York, NY 10023
E-mail: webmaster@nerowolfe.org
URL: http://www.nerowolfe.org
Contact: Mary Glasscock, Membership Chair
Founded: 1978. **Members:** 400. **Membership Dues:** general, $35 (biennial). **Description:** Admirers of Rex Stout (1886-1975), American writer of detective stories and creator of the characters Nero Wolfe and Archie Goodwin. Promotes fellowship and extends friendship to those who enjoy the great literary works of mystery through a series of events, and book discussions. **Awards:** Archie Goodwin. **Frequency:** semiannual. **Type:** recognition. **Recipient:** for writers who have impressed a significant majority of Wolfe Pack members worldwide ● Nero Wolfe. **Frequency:** annual. **Type:** recognition. **Recipient:** to an author for literature excellence in the mystery genre. **Telecommunication Services:** electronic mail, glascock@panix.com. **Publications:** *The Gazette: The Journal of the Wolfe Pack*, semiannual. Includes membership news. **Price:** included in membership dues. ISSN: 0193-533X. **Circulation:** 350. **Conventions/Meetings:** annual Black Orchid Banquet - always first Saturday of December, New York City.

9728 ■ Zane Grey's West Society (ZGWS)
PO Box 34
Elizabethton, TN 37644-0034
Ph: (928)775-8960
E-mail: tbolin3194@aol.com
URL: http://www.zgws.org
Contact: Terry Bolinger, VP
Founded: 1983. **Members:** 375. **Membership Dues:** regular active in U.S., associate outside U.S., $25 (annual) ● regular active outside U.S., $35 (annual) ● associate in U.S., $15 (annual) ● student in U.S., $10 (annual) ● student outside U.S., $20 (annual). **Regional Groups:** 3. **Description:** People interested in American author Zane Grey (1872-1939), best known for his adventure stories of the American West. Works to promote interest in and knowledge of Grey and his writings. **Awards:** Heritage of the West. **Frequency:** annual. **Type:** recognition ● Purple Sage Awards. **Frequency:** annual. **Type:** recognition. **Publications:** *Zane Grey Review*, bimonthly. Newsletter. ISSN: 1083-7140. **Circulation:** 375. **Advertising:** accepted ● Books ● Pamphlets. **Conventions/Meetings:** annual conference (exhibits).

9729 ■ Zora Neale Hurston Society
c/o Dolan Hubbard, Chair
Morgan State Univ.
1700 E Cold Spring Ln.
Baltimore, MD 21251
Ph: (443)885-3435
Fax: (443)319-3166
E-mail: english@morgan.edu
URL: http://jewel.morgan.edu/~english/blackboard/vol2iss1/page13.html
Contact: Dolan Hubbard, Chair
Membership Dues: regular, $35 (annual) ● student, $25 (annual). **Description:** Promotes the work of Zora Neale Hurston and African studies. **Awards: Type:** recognition. **Recipient:** to graduate student. **Conventions/Meetings:** annual conference.

Baltic

9730 ■ Association for the Advancement of Baltic Studies (AABS)
14743 Braemar Crescent Way
Darnestown, MD 20878-3911
Ph: (301)977-8491
Fax: (301)977-8492
E-mail: aabs@washington.edu
URL: http://depts.washington.edu/aabs
Contact: Anita Juberts, Admin. Exec. Dir.
Founded: 1968. **Members:** 700. **Membership Dues:** student, Baltic resident, $25 (annual) ● emeritus/retired, $35 (annual) ● regular, $60 (annual) ● sponsor, $100 (annual) ● patron, $500 (annual) ● life, $2,000. **Staff:** 3. **Languages:** English, Estonian, Latvian, Lithuanian. **Description:** Promotes scholarly interest in research on the Baltic area and people of Estonia, Latvia, and Lithuania. Encourages intrar-

egional, cross-disciplinary, and specialized studies of the Baltic area. **Awards:** Saltups Postgraduate Fellowship. **Frequency:** annual. **Type:** fellowship. **Recipient:** to Latvian students for furthering their studies at the graduate level in the United States ● Vilis Vitols Award. **Frequency:** annual. **Type:** recognition. **Recipient:** for best article written for the *Journal of Baltic Studies*. **Computer Services:** database. **Committees:** Academic Program; Bibliography; Research; Student Affairs. **Funds:** Baltic Studies. **Programs:** University of Latvia Baltic Studies; University of Tartu Baltic Studies; Vytautas Magnus University Baltic Studies. **Publications:** *Baltic Studies Newsletter*. Highlights current activities in Baltic studies for AABS members and the entire international scholarly community interested in Baltic studies. Alternate Formats: online ● *Journal of Baltic Studies* (in English and German), quarterly. **Price:** $60.00 /year for libraries and institutions. ISSN: 0162-9778. **Circulation:** 1,100. **Advertising:** accepted. Alternate Formats: online. **Conventions/Meetings:** biennial Conference on Baltic Studies - meeting.

Barbados

9731 ■ National Association of Barbados Organizations (NABO)
PO Box 11764
Atlanta, GA 30355
Ph: (954)917-5469
Fax: (404)365-9275
E-mail: bajan5425@aol.com
URL: http://members.aol.com/naboamerica
Contact: Bonita Ebb, Exec. Dir.
Founded: 1993. **Membership Dues:** regular, $100 (annual). **Multinational. Description:** Provides a forum of communication among different Barbadian and Caribbean communities residing in U.S. Preserves and promotes Barbadian cultural heritage.

Basque

9732 ■ Basque Educational Organization (BEO)
PO Box 31861
San Francisco, CA 94131-0861
E-mail: info@basqueed.org
URL: http://www.basqueed.org
Contact: Nicole Sorhondo, Sec.
Founded: 1983. **Nonmembership. Description:** Attempts to preserve, teach, and share Basque culture, language, and traditions through educational and charitable activities. (Basques are members of an ethnic group originating in the French-Spanish area of Europe where the Pyrenees Mountains meet the Cantabrian coast; they maintain a distinct culture and language.) Conducts Basque language, folk dance, costume design, music, and sports classes. Sponsors concerts, theater events, educational programs, and book series. Maintains museum in Basque Cultural Center, South San Francisco, CA. **Libraries: Type:** reference. **Holdings:** 2,000; biographical archives, video recordings. **Computer Services:** Mailing lists. **Committees:** Audio-visual; Library; Mailing; Mass Media; Research; Teaching. **Conventions/Meetings:** monthly meeting.

9733 ■ Society of Basque Studies in America (SBSA)
19 Colonial Gardens
Brooklyn, NY 11209
E-mail: sbsany@aol.com
URL: http://www.basque.ws
Founded: 1978. **Members:** 1,000. **Membership Dues:** regular, $25 (annual) ● special, $35 (annual) ● benefactor, $50-$99 (annual) ● special benefactor, $100-$249 (annual) ● distinguished benefactor, $250 (annual). **Languages:** Basque, English, Spanish. **Multinational. Description:** Individuals interested in Basque culture. Seeks to stimulate interest in Basque culture. Conducts research on Basque culture and heritage; promotes Basque ethnic values. Sponsors artistic exhibit. Maintains speakers' bureau and hall of fame. **Publications:** *Journal of Basque Studies in America* (in English, French, and Spanish), annual. Contains information about Basque culture. **Price:** $25.00. **Conventions/Meetings:** biennial symposium.

Belarussian

9734 ■ Belarusian Institute of Arts and Science (BIAS)
166-34 Gothic Dr.
Jamaica, NY 11432
Ph: (201)244-0776
Fax: (732)557-0095
Contact: Vitaut Kipel, Chm.
Founded: 1951. **Members:** 73. **Staff:** 2. **Regional Groups:** 2. **State Groups:** 1. **Local Groups:** 1. **Description:** Scholars, writers, and artists interested in research on the land, history, and culture of the Belorussian people and Americans of Belorussian descent and in creative activities in Belorussian literature and the arts. Provides reference and information services on Belarus. **Libraries: Type:** reference. **Holdings:** 6,500; books, periodicals. **Subjects:** Belarusian research. **Divisions:** Bibliography. **Formerly:** (1975) Whiteruthenian Institute of Arts and Science. **Publications:** *Belarusian Poets and Writers Abroad*. Monographs. **Price:** $25.00 ● *History of Belarusian Immigration Series* ● *Zapisy/Annals*, annual. Journal. Contains research information and bibliographic surveys. Includes calendar of events and English summaries. **Price:** $25.00 ● *Zapisy-Transactions*, annual. Contains history literature. ● Books. Features a series of Belarusian poets and writers. ● Monographs. **Conventions/Meetings:** biennial meeting - always November, in New York City.

9735 ■ North American Association for Belarusian Studies (NAABS)
c/o Curt Woolhiser, Sec.-Treas.
Dept. of Slavic Languages and Literatures
Harvard Univ.
Barker Ctr. 327
12 Quincy St.
Cambridge, MA 02138-3804
E-mail: maria.survilla@wartburg.edu
URL: http://www.belarusianstudies.org
Contact: Maria Paula Survilla, Pres.
Membership Dues: academic (from Belarus and the FSU), $5 (annual) ● student, $15 (annual) ● supporting, educator, $30 (annual) ● institutional, $50 (annual) ● patron, $100 (annual). **Multinational. Description:** Seeks to promote research, study, and teaching in all aspects of Belarusian studies. Fosters the exchange of information among scholars engaged in various aspects of Belarusian studies. Supports the publication of research by North American Belarusianists. **Telecommunication Services:** electronic mail, webmaster@belarusianstudies.org. **Affiliated With:** American Association for the Advancement of Slavic Studies. **Publications:** *Naviny*, semiannual. Newsletter. Includes information about association's business, Belarusian studies-related events and new publications. **Price:** included in membership dues. Alternate Formats: online.

Belgian

9736 ■ Belgian American Educational Foundation (BAEF)
195 Church St.
New Haven, CT 06510
Ph: (203)777-5765 (203)785-4055
Fax: (203)777-5765
E-mail: emile.boulpaep@yale.edu
URL: http://www.baef.be
Contact: Emile L. Boulpaep, Pres.
Founded: 1920. **Members:** 250. **Staff:** 2. **Budget:** $2,927,000. **Description:** Promotes closer relations and the exchange of intellectual ideas between Belgium and the U.S. through fellowships granted to graduate students of one country for study and research in the other. Assists higher education and scientific research and commemorates the work of the Commission for Relief in Belgium and associated organizations during the First World War, 1914-1918. **Awards:** Alumni Award. **Frequency:** annual. **Type:** recognition. **Recipient:** to a Belgian researcher or a researcher who is affiliated with a Belgian university for at least two years ● B.A.E.F. Fellowships. **Frequency:** annual. **Type:** fellowship. **Recipient:** for U.S. and Belgian citizens. **Committees:** American Fellowship; Belgian Fellowship. **Formerly:** (1938) CRB Educational Foundation, Inc. **Publications:** *Belgian American Educational Foundation—Directory of Fellows*, quinquennial. Membership Directory. **Conventions/Meetings:** annual meeting - always January in New York City.

Bengal

9737 ■ Cultural Association of Bengal (CAB)
143 Grymes Hill Rd.
Staten Island, NY 10301
Ph: (718)815-1401 (201)433-6245
E-mail: tulsi-sengupta@att.net
URL: http://www.os4e.com/osnp/teachers/nony/index.asp?teacher_id=764
Contact: Pranab Das, Pres.
Founded: 1971. **Members:** 1,000. **Membership Dues:** regular, $20 (annual). **Languages:** Bengali, English. **Description:** Individuals interested in Bengali language, culture, history, and heritage. (Bengal is a region encompassing Bangladesh and part of India.) Promotes Bengali language and culture. Offers children's services. **Libraries: Type:** reference. **Holdings:** 5,000; archival material, books. **Subjects:** Bengal. **Awards:** Distinguished Service Award. **Frequency:** annual. **Type:** recognition. **Recipient:** for service and promotion of Bengali culture. **Publications:** Magazine, bimonthly. **Conventions/Meetings:** annual North American Bengali Conference - conference and general assembly (exhibits) - always July in New York.

Book Clubs

9738 ■ Association of Book Group Readers and Leaders (ABGRL)
Box 885
Highland Park, IL 60035
Ph: (312)337-8810
E-mail: rachelj1@comcast.net
Contact: Rachel Jacobsohn, Contact
Founded: 1994. **Members:** 1,000. **Membership Dues:** individual/group/organization in U.S. and Canada, $20 (annual) ● individual/group/organization outside U.S. and Canada, $27 (annual). **Staff:** 3. **For-Profit. Multinational. Description:** Individual readers, groups, librarians, educators, and bookstore associates. Works to provide an information clearinghouse for enthusiastic readers. Provides literary commentary and analysis of classic and contemporary novels; offers an open forum for leaders, educators and librarians; provides reading lists; conducts educational programs; maintains speakers' bureau. **Computer Services:** database, available to members only ● mailing lists, insert flyer program. **Publications:** *Reverberations*, 3/year. Newsletter. ISSN: 1534-2999. **Advertising:** accepted. **Conventions/Meetings:** regional meeting ● workshop.

9739 ■ Society of Phantom Friends (SPF)
c/o Kate Emburg
4100 Cornelia Way
North Highlands, CA 95660
E-mail: dolladopt@aol.com
URL: http://www.nancydrewsleuth.com/tww.html
Contact: Kate Emburg, Contact
Founded: 1985. **Members:** 300. **Membership Dues:** individual in U.S., $30 (annual) ● individual outside U.S. and Canada, $40 (annual) ● individual in Canada, $33 (annual). **Staff:** 5. **Budget:** $1,000. **For-Profit. Multinational. Description:** Readers, authors, and collectors of popular fiction written for girls

between 8 and 18 years old. Maintains book collection. **Libraries: Type:** by appointment only. **Holdings:** 5,000; books. **Subjects:** fiction for girls. **Publications:** *Whispered Watchword*, 10/year. Magazine. Features book reviews, collecting tips, interviews, short fiction, and book classifieds. **Price:** included in membership dues. **Circulation:** 300. **Advertising:** accepted. **Conventions/Meetings:** annual Phantom Friends Reunion - convention and lecture, with book sales, sightseeing (exhibits) - usually August.

Books

9740 ■ Antiquarian Booksellers Association of America (ABAA)

20 W 44th St., 4th Fl.
New York, NY 10036-6604
Ph: (212)944-8291
Fax: (212)944-8293
E-mail: sbenne@abaa.org
URL: http://www.abaa.org
Contact: Susan Benne, Exec. Dir.

Founded: 1949. **Members:** 475. **Membership Dues:** general, $575 (annual). **Staff:** 2. **Regional Groups:** 8. **Description:** Dealers and appraisers of fine, rare and out-of-print books, manuscripts, and related materials. Sponsors two annual regional international book fairs and four biennial regional international book fairs. Promotes ethical standards in the industry. Sponsors educational programs for members, librarians, archivists, and the public. Administers the Antiquarian Booksellers' Benevolent Fund. **Publications:** Membership Directory, annual. Includes subject, geographic, and personal name indexes. **Price:** free ● Directories ● Newsletter, quarterly. **Price:** $25.00/year in U.S.; $35.00/year outside U.S. ● Plans to publish *ABAA Handbook*.

9741 ■ Bibliographical Society of America (BSA)

PO Box 1537
Lenox Hill Sta.
New York, NY 10021
Ph: (212)452-2710
Fax: (212)452-2710
E-mail: bsa@bibsocamer.org
URL: http://www.bibsocamer.org
Contact: Michele E. Randall, Exec. Sec.

Founded: 1904. **Members:** 1,200. **Membership Dues:** individual, $65 (annual) ● student, $20 (annual) ● institutional, $75 (annual) ● life, $1,250 ● sustaining, $250 (annual) ● contributing, $100 (annual). **Staff:** 1. **Description:** Scholars, collectors, librarians, rare book dealers, and others interested in books and descriptive bibliography. Promotes bibliographical research and issues bibliographical publications. Maintains Fellowship Program which supports bibliography inquiries and research in the history of publishing and book trades. **Libraries: Type:** open to the public. **Holdings:** 4. **Awards:** BSA Fellowship. **Frequency:** annual. **Type:** monetary. **Recipient:** for scholars of any nationality ● William L. Mitchell Prize for Research on Early British Serials. **Frequency:** triennial. **Type:** recognition. **Recipient:** for scholars engaged in bibliographical scholarship on 18th century periodicals. **Publications:** *Bibliographical Society of America—List of Members*, annual. Membership Directory. **Price:** included in membership dues. **Circulation:** 1,300 ● *The Papers of the Bibliographical Society of America*, quarterly. Journal. Provides information for scholars of English and Continental literature, historians, and all those interested in the history of book production. **Price:** included in membership dues; $20.00/year for students; $65.00 /year for nonmembers. ISSN: 0006-128X. **Circulation:** 1,300. **Advertising:** accepted. **Conventions/Meetings:** annual meeting - always fourth Friday in January, New York City.

9742 ■ Bibliographical Society of the University of Virginia (BSUVA)

c/o Anne Ribble, Sec.-Treas.
Alderman Lib.
PO Box 400152
Charlottesville, VA 22904
Ph: (434)924-7013 (434)924-7951
Fax: (434)924-1431
E-mail: bibsoc@virginia.edu
URL: http://etext.lib.virginia.edu/bsuva
Contact: Anne Ribble, Sec.-Treas.

Founded: 1947. **Members:** 400. **Membership Dues:** individual, $55 (annual) ● student, $27 (annual) ● contributing, $150 (annual). **Multinational. Description:** Serves as an international society of bibliographers, book collectors, librarians, scholars, and others interested in books and bibliographies. **Awards:** Student Book Collecting Award. **Frequency:** biennial. **Type:** monetary. **Recipient:** for best book collection of undergraduate or graduate student. **Publications:** *Studies in Bibliography*, annual. **Price:** $45.00. Alternate Formats: online. **Conventions/Meetings:** annual meeting - always in Charlottesville, VA.

9743 ■ Binders' Guild (BG)

2925 Powell St.
Eugene, OR 97405
Ph: (541)485-6527
E-mail: editor@bindersguild.org
URL: http://www.bindersguild.org
Contact: Susan Lunas, Sec.

Founded: 1977. **Members:** 45. **Staff:** 1. **Description:** Amateur and professional hand bookbinders and other interested persons. Facilitates exchange of information among members concerning techniques and sources of supplies. **Convention/Meeting:** none.

9744 ■ Books For Africa (BFA)

253 E 4th St., Ste.200
St. Paul, MN 55101
Ph: (651)602-9844
Fax: (651)602-9848
E-mail: bfa@booksforafrica.org
URL: http://www.booksforafrica.org
Contact: Patrick Plonski, Exec. Dir.

Founded: 1988. **Staff:** 6. **Budget:** $405,800. **Nonmembership. Multinational. Description:** Seeks to ensure the availability of books and educational materials throughout Africa.

9745 ■ Center for Book Arts (CBA)

28 W 27th St., 3rd Fl.
New York, NY 10001-6906
Ph: (212)481-0295
Fax: (212)481-9853
E-mail: info@centerforbookarts.org
URL: http://www.centerforbookarts.org
Contact: Alexander Campos, Exec. Dir.

Founded: 1974. **Members:** 650. **Membership Dues:** associate, $50 (annual) ● friend, $100 (annual) ● patron, $250 (annual) ● supporter, $500 (annual) ● sustainer, $1,000 (annual) ● benefactor, $2,500 (annual) ● master benefactor, $5,000 (annual). **Staff:** 3. **Budget:** $375,000. **Description:** Dedicated to the preservation of the traditional crafts of bookmaking, as well as encouraging contemporary interpretations of the book as an art object. Organizes exhibitions related to the art of the book and offers an extensive selection of educational courses, workshops and seminars in traditional and contemporary bookbinding, letterpress printing, fine press publishing, and other associated arts. Other programs include Artist-in-Residence, Broadsides Reading Series, and the Poetry Chapbook Competition. Supported by local businesses, various foundations including the Lenrow Fund, the Milton and Sally Avery Arts Foundation, the NY State Council on the Arts, the National Endowment for the Arts, and its members. **Libraries: Type:** reference. **Awards:** Poetry Chapbook Competition, Artist Residency Program. **Frequency:** annual. **Type:** monetary. **Telecommunication Services:** electronic mail, acampos@centerforbookarts.org. **Committees:** Exhibition. **Publications:** *Koob Stra, Book Arts Review*, quarterly. Newsletter. Lists news opportunities and event for book artists. **Price:** included in membership dues. **Circulation:** 3,000. **Advertising:** accepted ● *Poetry Broadsides* ● *Poetry Chapbooks* ● Books ● Catalogs. **Conventions/Meetings:** annual meeting (exhibits) - usually December.

9746 ■ Children's Book Council (CBC)

12 W 37th St., 2nd Fl.
New York, NY 10018-7480
Ph: (212)966-1990
Free: (800)807-9355
Fax: (212)966-2073
E-mail: info@cbcbooks.org
URL: http://www.cbcbooks.org
Contact: Simon Boughton, Chm.

Founded: 1945. **Members:** 79. **Membership Dues:** associate, $400 (annual) ● affiliate, initiating, $1,200 (annual). **Staff:** 8. **Description:** Members are publishers of trade books for children and young adults. Encourages the reading and enjoyment of children's books. Sponsors Young People's Poetry Week in April and Children's Book Week in November. Develops children's book programs related to various disciplines through joint committees with library, bookselling, and education associations. Maintains examination library of professional reference works and children's trade books published within the past 2 years. **Libraries: Type:** open to the public. **Holdings:** 10,000; books. **Subjects:** children's book publishing. **Computer Services:** database, awards and prizes online. **Publications:** *CBC Features*, semiannual. Newsletter. Includes listing of free and inexpensive materials. **Price:** $60.00 one-time only fee for placement on mailing list. ISSN: 0008-0721 ● *Children's Books: Awards & Prizes*, annual. Features domestic and international awards given to children's literature. **Price:** $150.00 ● Bibliographies ● Brochures ● Report, annual. Contains an overview of the organization's programs and projects. ● Also publishes information sheets and other educational and promotional materials for parents, teachers, librarians, and booksellers. **Conventions/Meetings:** periodic meeting.

9747 ■ Dictionary Society of North America (DSNA)

c/o Lisa Berglund, Exec. Sec.
Buffalo State Coll.
Dept. of English
Ketchum Hall 326
1300 Elmwood Ave.
Buffalo, NY 14222
Ph: (716)878-4049
E-mail: berglul@buffalostate.edu
URL: http://polyglot.lss.wisc.edu/dsna/index.html
Contact: Lisa Berglund, Exec. Sec.

Founded: 1975. **Members:** 550. **Membership Dues:** regular/joint/institutional in North America, student/retired outside North America, $30 (annual) ● student/retired in North America, $20 (annual) ● life, in North America, $600 ● regular/joint/institutional outside North America, $40 (annual). **Description:** Lexicographers, librarians, dictionary editors, curators of dictionary collections, professors of linguistics, and other individuals interested in the manufacture, use, collection, or history of dictionaries. Aims to foster scholarly, professional, and amateur activities relating to dictionaries. **Awards:** Laurence Urdang-DSNA Award. **Frequency:** annual. **Type:** recognition. **Recipient:** for member lexicographical project. **Formerly:** (1977) Society for the Study of Dictionaries and Lexicography. **Publications:** *Dictionaries*, annual. Journal. Discusses the composition of dictionaries and the critique, use, collection, and descriptions of significant dictionaries collections. **Price:** included in membership dues; $30.00 /year for nonmembers; $30.00 /year for libraries; $10.00/back issues for members. ISSN: 0197-6745. **Circulation:** 550. **Advertising:** accepted ● *Dictionary Society of North America—Membership Directory*, biennial. **Price:** included in membership dues, non-institutional. **Circulation:** 500 ● *Dictionary Society of North America—Newsletter*, semiannual. Provides information on society's membership and activities, dictionaries or lexicographic research in progress or recently published, other topics. **Price:** included in membership dues; $3.00/issue for nonmembers. **Circulation:** 500. **Advertising:** accepted. **Conventions/Meetings:** biennial conference, book publishers of dictionaries and works on lexicography (exhibits).

9748 ■ Great Books Foundation (GBF)
35 E Wacker Dr., Ste.400
Chicago, IL 60601-2205
Free: (800)222-5870
Fax: (312)407-0334
E-mail: tr@greatbooks.org
URL: http://www.greatbooks.org
Contact: Alex J. Pollock, Chm.
Founded: 1947. **Members:** 800,000. **Membership Dues:** individual, $38 (annual) ● international, $59 (annual). **Staff:** 83. **Budget:** $7,200,000. **Description:** Provides people of all ages with the opportunity to read, discuss, and learn from outstanding works of literature. Publishes the Junior Great Books Curriculum, a daily program of interpretive reading, writing, and discussion with the goal of bringing higher literacy within reach of all students, K-12. The curriculum includes the Junior Great Books Read-Aloud program for grades K-1, Junior Great Books for grades 2-9, and Introduction to Great Books for grades 10-12. Publishes the Great Books Reading and Discussion Program, which provides adults with the opportunity to discuss the ideas of the great thinkers and writers. Conducts courses in shared inquiry, the method of reading and discussion central to all Great Books programs throughout the U.S. and abroad. **Libraries: Type:** open to the public. **Holdings:** books, video recordings. **Publications:** *The Common Review*, quarterly. Magazine. Features published books, sponsored seminars and cultural events. **Price:** $17.95 /year for nonmembers in U.S.; included in membership dues; $24.95 /year for nonmembers outside U.S. ● Also publishes reader and leader aids, curriculum materials, and activity books.

9749 ■ Grolier Club (GC)
c/o Mr. Eric Holzenberg, Dir.
47 E 60th St.
New York, NY 10022
Ph: (212)838-6690
Fax: (212)838-2445
E-mail: ejh@grolierclub.org
URL: http://www.grolierclub.org
Contact: Mr. Eric Holzenberg, Dir.
Founded: 1884. **Members:** 729. **Staff:** 6. **Description:** Persons concerned with the book arts. Named after Jean Grolier (1489-1565), French bibliophile. Conducts free public exhibitions per year. **Libraries: Type:** reference. **Holdings:** 100,000; books. **Subjects:** history of printing, bibliography, book collecting. **Publications:** *Gazette of the Grolier Club*, annual. **Price:** included in membership dues; $20.00 for nonmembers ● Books. Designed to illustrate and encourage arts of book production. ● Yearbook, annual.

9750 ■ Guild of Book Workers (GBW)
521 5th Ave.
New York, NY 10175-0038
Ph: (212)292-4444
E-mail: publicity@guildofbookworkers.allmail.net
URL: http://palimpsest.Stanford.edu/byorg/gbw
Contact: James Reid-Cunningham, Pres.
Founded: 1906. **Members:** 950. **Membership Dues:** individual in U.S., $75 (annual) ● individual in Canada, $85 (annual) ● individual outside U.S. and Canada, $90 (annual) ● student, $40 (triennial) ● chapter, $10 (annual). **Regional Groups:** 10. **Multinational. Description:** Amateur and professional workers in the handbook crafts such as bookbinding, calligraphy, illuminating, fine presswork, and decorative papermaking. Works to improve standards by the sponsorship of exhibitions, field trips, lectures, workshops, and discussion groups. **Libraries: Type:** reference; lending. **Holdings:** 1,500; books, video recordings. **Subjects:** bookcrafts. **Computer Services:** Mailing lists. **Committees:** Exhibition; Standards. **Publications:** *Directory of Study Opportunities*. Lists schools and individuals who teach book arts; includes catalogs listing publications of guild-sponsored exhibitions. **Price:** included in membership dues. Alternate Formats: online ● *Guild of Book Workers—Journal*, semiannual. Each issue covers a specific theme in the book arts field, such as exhibitions, training, and history. **Price:** included in membership dues; $15.00 for nonmembers. ISSN: 0434-9245 ● *Guild of Book Workers—Membership Directory*, annual. Lists guild members. **Price:** included in membership dues ● *Guild of Book Workers—Newsletter*, bimonthly. Provides information on events in the book arts field, special publications, and occasional serials pertaining to methodology. Includes book reviews. **Price:** included in membership dues; $5.00/issue for nonmembers. **Advertising:** accepted ● *Supply Directory*, irregular. Lists suppliers of materials used by book artists. **Price:** included in membership dues; $15.00 for nonmembers. Alternate Formats: online. **Conventions/Meetings:** annual seminar, with educational sessions, tours, lectures - always fall.

9751 ■ Jewish Book Council (JBC)
520 8th Ave., 4th Fl.
New York, NY 10018
Ph: (212)201-2920
Fax: (212)532-4952
E-mail: jbc@jewishbooks.org
URL: http://www.jewishbookcouncil.org
Contact: Lawrence J. Krule, Pres.
Founded: 1942. **Staff:** 3. **Description:** Disseminates information about Jewish books in English, Hebrew, and Yiddish. Encourages the publication and distribution of such books. Sponsors Jewish Book Month (November/December). **Awards:** National Jewish Book Awards. **Frequency:** annual. **Type:** recognition. **Recipient:** for best books in 14 categories. **Formerly:** Jewish Book Council of the Jewish Community Center Association of North America; (1991) JWB Jewish Book Council. **Publications:** *Jewish Book Annual: The American Yearbook of Jewish Literary Creativity*, annual. Contains literary criticism and bibliographies of Judaica published in the past year in the United States in English, Hebrew, and Yiddish. **Price:** $44.00 each. **Circulation:** 2,000 ● *Jewish Book World*, 3/year. Newsletter. Lists and reviews books of Jewish interest. **Price:** $28.00/year. **Circulation:** 3,300. **Advertising:** accepted. **Conventions/Meetings:** annual meeting.

9752 ■ Miniature Book Society (MBS)
c/o Kathy King, Treas.
402 York Ave.
Delaware, OH 43015
Free: (877)627-1983
E-mail: miniaturebooks@yahoogroups.com
URL: http://www.mbs.org
Contact: Kathy King, Treas.
Founded: 1983. **Members:** 300. **Membership Dues:** in U.S., $40 (annual) ● outside U.S., $55 (annual). **Multinational. Description:** Individuals, libraries, book collectors, miniaturists, antiquarian book dealers, and others with an interest in miniature books. (Miniature books are less than three inches in height, are often produced with hand-set type and released in very limited editions, and are recognized as one of the highest expressions of the printer's and binder's arts.) Promotes interest in miniature books; facilitates communication among members. Holds miniature book competition; sponsors traveling exhibit. **Awards:** Anderson-Yarnell Award. **Frequency:** annual. **Type:** recognition ● Glasgow Cup Award. **Frequency:** annual. **Type:** recognition ● Miniature Book Society Exhibition Award. **Frequency:** annual. **Type:** recognition ● Norman W. Forgue Award. **Frequency:** annual. **Type:** recognition. **Publications:** *Miniature Book Society Newsletter*, quarterly. Magazine. **Price:** $30.00 in U.S.; $40.00 outside U.S. **Advertising:** accepted. **Conventions/Meetings:** annual Conclave - meeting, displays of miniature books (exhibits) - usually Labor Day weekend.

9753 ■ National Book Critics Circle (NBCC)
360 Park Ave. S
New York, NY 10010
Ph: (973)744-9045
E-mail: jfreeman4@nyc.rr.com
URL: http://www.bookcritics.org
Contact: John Freeman, Pres.
Founded: 1974. **Members:** 480. **Membership Dues:** regular, $40 (annual) ● individual associate, $25 (annual) ● student, $15 (annual). **Description:** Nationwide professional book critics and book review editors. Purposes are to: elevate standards of book reviewing and book criticism; encourage public appreciation of criticism. **Awards:** Ivan Sandrof Life Achievement Award. **Frequency:** annual. **Type:** recognition. **Recipient:** for dedication to book culture both longstanding and outstanding ● National Book Critics Circle Award. **Frequency:** annual. **Type:** recognition. **Recipient:** for outstanding books on fiction, general nonfiction, poetry, criticism, autobiography/memoir, and biography ● Nona Balakian Citation for Excellence in Reviewing. **Frequency:** annual. **Type:** recognition. **Recipient:** for an outstanding book reviewer. **Computer Services:** Online services, journal ● online services, membership and renewal. **Publications:** *The Journal*, 5/year. Contains general information on book reviewing and the activities of the Board of Directors. Alternate Formats: online. **Conventions/Meetings:** annual meeting, for members, board of directors; public awarding - usually in New York City.

9754 ■ Society for the History of Authorship, Reading and Publishing (SHARP)
PO Box 30
Wilmington, NC 28402-0030
Ph: (910)254-0308
Fax: (910)254-1065
E-mail: membership@sharpweb.org
URL: http://www.sharpweb.org
Contact: Barbara A. Brannon PhD, Membership Sec.
Founded: 1991. **Members:** 1,100. **Membership Dues:** regular in U.S. and Canada, $55 (annual) ● regular outside U.S. and Canada, $60 (annual) ● student/unwaged outside U.S. and Canada, $25 (annual) ● student/unwaged in U.S. and Canada, $20 (annual) ● supporting, $75 (annual) ● sustaining, $100 (annual). **Budget:** $10,000. **Multinational. Description:** Promotes teaching, research, and publication in the field of book history. **Awards:** Graduate Essay Prize. **Frequency:** annual. **Type:** monetary. **Recipient:** to best graduate student essay published in book history during previous year ● SHARP/DeLong Book History Prize. **Frequency:** annual. **Type:** monetary. **Recipient:** to the best book-length monograph on the history of the book published during the previous year. **Computer Services:** Mailing lists, of qualified mailers. **Publications:** *Book History*, annual. Journal. **Price:** included in membership dues. ISSN: 1098-7371. **Circulation:** 1,200. **Advertising:** accepted ● *SHARP News*, quarterly. Newsletter. **Price:** included in membership dues (individual and student members); $25.00 /year for libraries and institutions in U.S. and Canada; $30.00 /year for libraries and institutions outside U.S. and Canada. ISSN: 1073-1725. **Circulation:** 1,300 ● Directory, annual. Contains listing of members and book history periodicals. **Price:** included in membership dues. **Circulation:** 1,300. **Conventions/Meetings:** annual conference (exhibits) - 2008 June 24-28, Oxford, United Kingdom.

9755 ■ Taurine Bibliophiles of America (TBA)
c/o Gil Arruda
59 Pearl Ave.
North Providence, RI 02904
Ph: (401)353-6326
E-mail: sconrad@mundo-taurino.org
URL: http://mundo-taurino.org/tba2.html
Contact: Gil Arruda, Contact
Founded: 1964. **Members:** 165. **Membership Dues:** in U.S., $30 (annual) ● outside U.S., $40 (annual). **Description:** Represents persons interested in books (and other cultural materials such as film and art) concerning tauromaquia (Spanish-style "bullfighting"). Aims to bring together, through correspondence, aficionados of tauromaquia who collect literature on the subject (primarily in English); and to publicize taurine books and articles. Maintains a bibliography of taurine books in English, and a filmography of taurine movies, and conducts research on taurine literature, past and present, in all languages. **Awards:** Honorary Life Member Award. **Frequency:** annual. **Type:** recognition. **Publications:** *El Clarin de la Busca*, quarterly. Newsletter ● *La Busca*, quarterly. Journal. Includes bibliography of bullfighting books

printed in English, book reviews, and list of new members. **Price:** included in membership dues; $25.00 /year for nonmembers. **Circulation:** 165. **Advertising:** accepted.

9756 ■ U.S. Board on Books for Young People (USBBY)
800 Barksdale Rd.
Newark, DE 19714-8139
Ph: (302)731-1600
Fax: (302)731-1057
E-mail: usbby@reading.org
URL: http://www.usbby.org
Contact: Alida von Krogh Cutts, Exec. Sec.
Founded: 1985. **Members:** 400. **Membership Dues:** individual, $25 (annual) ● student, $15 (annual) ● organization, $75 (annual) ● sponsor, $500 (annual) ● patron, $1,000 (annual). **Staff:** 2. **Budget:** $25,000. **Description:** U.S. national section of the International Board on Books for Young People. Persons and institutions united to promote reading material of merit for young people and to increase interest in international children's literature. Facilitates international exchange of information on aspects of books and reading encouragement. **Awards:** Bridge to Understanding. **Frequency:** annual. **Type:** monetary. **Recipient:** for the most original and creative program that uses books to build bridges between children in the U.S. and other parts of the world. **Affiliated With:** International Board on Books for Young People. **Formed by Merger of:** Friends of IBBY; U.S. National Section of IBBY. **Publications:** *Bookbird*, quarterly. Journal. **Circulation:** 1,000 ● *USBBY Newsletter*, semiannual. Covers children's literature from around the world. Includes articles on the need for children's literature in developing countries. **Price:** included in membership dues. **Circulation:** 1,000. **Conventions/Meetings:** biennial IBBY Regional - conference - always held in odd years ● lecture - 3/year; always January, May, and November ● annual meeting, held in conjunction with the American Library Association, International Reading Association, or National Council of Teachers of English annual conferences.

Brazilian

9757 ■ Brazilian-American Cultural Institute (BACI)
4719 Wisconsin Ave. NW
Washington, DC 20016
Ph: (202)362-8334
Fax: (202)362-8337
E-mail: info@bacidc.org
URL: http://www.bacidc.org
Contact: Dr. Jose M. Neistein PhD, Exec. Dir.
Founded: 1964. **Members:** 700. **Membership Dues:** single, $40 (annual) ● couple, $45 (annual) ● family, $50 (annual). **Staff:** 7. **Description:** Persons interested in fostering understanding between Brazil and the United States through cultural exchange. Offers courses for children and adults in Portuguese language and Brazilian literature. Operates art gallery for American and Brazilian works. Presents movies, lectures, and concerts. **Convention/Meeting:** none. **Libraries: Type:** reference. **Holdings:** 8,000; audio recordings, audiovisuals, books, photographs. **Subjects:** fiction and nonfiction in Portuguese, English, French, Spanish, German. **Publications:** Books (in English and Portuguese).

Breton

9758 ■ U.S. Branch of the International Committee for the Defense of the Breton Language (U.S. ICDBL)
c/o Lois Kuter, Sec.-Treas./Ed.
169 Greenwood Ave., B-4
Jenkintown, PA 19046
Ph: (215)886-6361
E-mail: lkuter@fast.net
URL: http://www.breizh.net/icdbl/saozg
Contact: Lois Kuter, Sec.-Treas./Ed.
Founded: 1981. **Members:** 150. **Membership Dues:** in U.S., $20 (annual) ● outside U.S., $25 (annual). **Languages:** Breton, English, French. **Description:** Supports Breton language education in its native land of Brittany, France, and educates Americans on Breton language and culture. Through their support, members show to the people of Brittany that their language is of interest and value to people all over the world. **Publications:** *A Guide to Music in Brittany*. Papers. **Price:** $5.00 ● *Bro Nevez: Newsletter of the U.S. ICDBL*, quarterly. Includes information about the current state of the Breton language, book and music CD reviews, and short notes on Breton history and culture. **Price:** included in membership dues. ISSN: 0895-3074. **Circulation:** 170 ● *Chronology of Breton History*. Papers ● *Introduction to the Breton Language* ● *Learning Materials for Breton*. Papers.

British

9759 ■ Cornish American Heritage Society (CAHS)
c/o Jim Thomas, Treas.
8494 Wesley Dr.
Flushing, MI 48433-1165
E-mail: jim_jeanne2000@hotmail.com
URL: http://www.cousinjack.org
Contact: Vivianne Trevithick Bradley, Pres.
Founded: 1982. **Members:** 500. **Membership Dues:** individual in U.S., $10 (annual) ● family in U.S., $15 (annual) ● life, in U.S., $150 ● individual in Canada, $14 (annual) ● family in Canada, $21 (annual) ● life, in Canada, $210 ● junior in U.S., $5 (annual) ● junior in Canada, $7 (annual). **Local Groups:** 26. **Description:** Individuals with an interest in the history of Cornish migration to North America, and in the accomplishments of Cornish Americans. Promotes increased awareness of the history and achievements of Cornish Americans. Facilitates formation of local Cornish heritage associations. Gathers and disseminates information on Cornish migration and history; conducts research and educational programs. Identifies and gains protected status for Cornish historical sites. Maintains speakers' bureau. **Libraries: Type:** reference. **Holdings:** articles, books, clippings. **Subjects:** Cornwall, Cornish history, genealogy, Cornish people overseas especially in North America. **Awards:** Ambassador's Trophy. **Frequency:** annual. **Type:** recognition. **Recipient:** to individuals working for the betterment of Cornwall and Cornish people overseas ● Cornish Heritage Certificate. **Frequency:** annual. **Type:** recognition. **Recipient:** for individuals whose ancestors emigrated from Cornwall to North America ● Paul Smales Award. **Frequency:** biennial. **Type:** monetary. **Recipient:** for individuals or groups presenting workshops at the biennial meeting ● Stephen R. Curnow Memorial. **Frequency:** annual. **Type:** recognition. **Recipient:** for the best penned essay by high school juniors and seniors. **Publications:** *The Cornish Circle*, quarterly. Newsletter. Given to officers of local Cornish groups in North America. ISSN: 1522-1636. **Circulation:** 130 ● *Directory of Some Cornish Resources in North America and Cornwall*, periodic. Lists of organizations, businesses, and sources of information on Cornwall and the Cornish People. ● *Tam Kernewek*, quarterly. Newsletter. ISSN: 1085-1267. **Circulation:** 500. **Advertising:** accepted ● Brochure. **Conventions/Meetings:** biennial Gathering of Cornish Cousins - conference and workshop, music, speakers on Cornish topics - always held in North America.

9760 ■ North American Conference on British Studies (NACBS)
c/o Dr. Andrew August, Exec. Sec.
Pennsylvania State Univ.
1600 Woodland Rd.
Abington, PA 19001
Ph: (215)881-7584
Fax: (215)881-7333
E-mail: axa24@psu.edu
URL: http://www.nacbs.org
Contact: Dr. Andrew August, Exec. Sec.
Founded: 1951. **Members:** 1,100. **Membership Dues:** individual, $66 (annual) ● sustaining, $114 (annual) ● student, $38 (annual). **Regional Groups:** 7. **Description:** Represents North American scholars specializing in British studies including history, art history, literature, and political science. **Awards:** NACBS Dissertation Year. **Frequency:** annual. **Type:** fellowship. **Recipient:** for individuals ● NACBS-Huntington Library. **Frequency:** annual. **Type:** fellowship. **Recipient:** for graduate students. **Affiliated With:** American Historical Association. **Formerly:** (1982) Conference on British Studies. **Publications:** *Journal of British Studies*, quarterly. **Price:** $227.00 /year for institutions in U.S.; $62.00 /year for individuals in U.S.; $241.00 /year for institutions outside U.S.; $76.00 /year for individuals outside U.S. ISSN: 0021-9371. **Circulation:** 1,600. **Advertising:** accepted. Also Cited As: *JBS*. **Conventions/Meetings:** annual meeting (exhibits) - always October or November.

Broadcasting

9761 ■ Catholic Academy for Communication Arts Professionals
1645 Brook Lynn Dr., Ste.2
Dayton, OH 45432-1933
Ph: (937)458-0265 (301)740-3929
Fax: (937)458-0263
E-mail: admin@catholicacademy.org
URL: http://www.CatholicAcademy.org
Contact: Jeanean Merkel, Pres.
Founded: 2002. **Members:** 325. **Membership Dues:** individual, $210 (annual) ● student, $45 (annual) ● organization, $575 (annual). **Staff:** 2. **Regional Groups:** 4. **Description:** Brings together media professionals to nurture the Christian and professional development of members. Advances the communications mission of the Church. Supports and recognizes excellence in media through the Gabriel Awards. Includes individual members such as: Catholic broadcasters, allied communicators, filmmakers, and those of all faiths who support the aims and objectives of the organization; group members such as dioceses, syndicated program-producing groups, individual radio and television stations, and allied agencies in the field of communications. Promotes cooperation among those involved in communications; seeks to develop a discerning audience for social communications; assesses the sources and influences of media and the impact of U.S. media upon other nations and peoples; strives to preserve freedom of expression and foster good relations between media and government; works to develop mutual understanding among people of various cultures. Conducts training workshop for members; compiles statistics. **Awards:** Gabriel Award. **Frequency:** annual. **Type:** recognition. **Recipient:** to commercial and religious broadcasters for their ability to "uplift and nourish the human spirit and affirming the dignity of human beings". **Computer Services:** Mailing lists ● online services. **Telecommunication Services:** electronic mail, jmerkel@illumicom.org. **Committees:** Awards; General Assemblies; Multi-Cultural/Ethnic; Research and Planning. **Affiliated With:** Catholic Press Association. **Formerly:** (2002) UNDA U.S.A. National Catholic Association for Communicators. **Supersedes:** Catholic Broadcasters Association. **Publications:** *Catholic Academy Membership Directory*, annual. **Price:** $50.00. **Circulation:** 300. **Advertising:** accepted ● Newsletter, quarterly. **Price:** included in membership dues. Alternate Formats: online. **Conventions/Meetings:** annual general assembly and conference (exhibits).

9762 ■ Corporation for Public Broadcasting (CPB)
401 9th St. NW
Washington, DC 20004-2129
Ph: (202)879-9600
Free: (800)272-2190
Fax: (202)879-9700
E-mail: comments@cpb.org
URL: http://www.cpb.org
Contact: Patricia De Stacy Harrison, Pres./CEO
Founded: 1968. **Staff:** 90. **Budget:** $405,000,000. **Description:** Promotes and finances the growth and

development of noncommercial radio and television. Makes grants to local public television and radio stations, program producers, and program distribution networks; studies emerging technologies; works to provide adequate long-range financing from the U.S. government and other sources for public broadcasting. Supports children's services; compiles statistics; sponsors training programs. **Awards:** Edward R. Murrow Award. **Frequency:** annual. **Type:** recognition. **Recipient:** for individuals who have contributed to the growth of public radio ● Fred Rogers Award. **Frequency:** annual. **Type:** trophy. **Recipient:** for an individual or organization who has contributed to educational media ● Ralph Lowell Award. **Frequency:** annual. **Type:** medal. **Recipient:** for individuals with outstanding contributions to public television. **Publications:** *CPB Annual Report* ● Also publishes statistical and other research reports on public broadcasting.

9763 ■ Educational Broadcasting Corporation (EBC)
c/o Thirteen/WNET
450 W 33rd St.
New York, NY 10001
Ph: (212)560-1313
Fax: (212)560-1314
E-mail: programming@thirteen.org
URL: http://www.thirteen.org/index.php
Contact: William F. Baker, CEO
Founded: 1961. **Members:** 315,000. **Staff:** 482. **Budget:** $107,000,000. **Description:** Owner and licensee of WNET/Channel 13, the principal public television station in New York City. Produces programs distributed by the Public Broadcasting Service to 350 noncommercial television stations in the U.S., Hawaii, Guam, and Puerto Rico. Conducts educational and cultural broadcasts; operates outreach programs to schools and community groups. **Convention/Meeting:** none. **Divisions:** Development; Educational Resources Center; Marketing and Communications; Program Service. **Absorbed:** (1972) National Educational Television. **Publications:** *Program Guide*, monthly.

9764 ■ National Black Programming Consortium (NBPC)
68 E 131st St., 7th Fl.
New York, NY 10037
Ph: (212)234-8200
Fax: (212)234-7032
E-mail: info@nbpc.tv
URL: http://www.nbpc.tv
Contact: Jacquie Jones, Exec. Dir.
Founded: 1979. **Members:** 250. **Membership Dues:** student, $20 (annual) ● producer, $60 (annual) ● individual, $35 (annual) ● organizational, $300 (annual). **Staff:** 7. **Budget:** $1,200,000. **Description:** Public telecommunications systems and television stations, academic institutions, and interested individuals. Objectives are to: assist the public broadcasting system in supplying programming that serves the needs of all population segments of the U.S; serve as a collection, distribution, and archival center for black-oriented television programming; coproduce black programming; serve as a liaison between the black community and telecommunications systems with regard to black programming; provide funds for and encourage more and better black productions. Participates in the acquisition and distribution of programs for the cable and international markets. Sponsors children's programs. Operates clearinghouse. **Libraries: Type:** reference. **Holdings:** 2,500; archival material, films, video recordings. **Awards:** Best Black Independent Producer. **Frequency:** annual. **Type:** recognition ● Best Student Film/Videomaker. **Frequency:** annual. **Type:** recognition ● Emerging Artist. **Frequency:** annual. **Type:** recognition ● Oscar Micheaux Award. **Frequency:** annual. **Type:** recognition. **Computer Services:** Mailing lists ● online services. **Committees:** Prized Pieces, Community Outreach, Screening, Program Advisory. **Divisions:** Programming; Public Relations/ Services. **Publications:** *TAKE II*, 3/year. Newsletter ● *Take One*, annual. Newsletter ● Catalog. **Advertising:** accepted ● Pamphlet. **Conventions/Meetings:** biennial Film/Video Festival, includes awards ceremony - always November in Columbus, OH ● biennial Prized Pieces - competition, film and video competition.

9765 ■ National Public Radio (NPR)
635 Massachusetts Ave. NW
Washington, DC 20001
Ph: (202)513-2000 (202)513-2300
Fax: (202)513-3329
E-mail: nprhelp@npr.org
URL: http://www.npr.org
Contact: Kevin Klose, Pres.
Founded: 1970. **Members:** 727. **Staff:** 650. **Budget:** $100,000,000. **Description:** Funded principally by its member stations, with additional support from foundations and corporations. Originates and disseminates news and cultural programming through live satellite distribution and via the Internet. **Libraries: Type:** reference. **Holdings:** 2,800; archival material. **Subjects:** general reference. **Divisions:** Communications; Cultural Programming; Development; Distribution; Finance and Administration; General Counsel; Human Resources; Information Technology; Member Services; News and Information Programming. **Absorbed:** (1977) Association of Public Radio Stations. **Publications:** Catalog, quarterly. Includes a program description guide. **Conventions/Meetings:** annual Public Radio Conference (exhibits).

9766 ■ National Telemedia Council (NTC)
c/o Marieli Rowe, Exec. Dir.
120 E Wilson St.
Madison, WI 53703
Ph: (608)257-7712
Fax: (608)257-7714
E-mail: ntc@danenet.wicip.org
URL: http://danenet.wicip.org/ntc
Contact: Marieli Rowe, Exec. Dir.
Founded: 1953. **Members:** 24,000. **Membership Dues:** basic, $30 (annual) ● contributing, $50 (annual) ● patron, $100 (annual) ● school, $40 (annual) ● organization/library, $60 (annual) ● corporate sponsor, $500 (annual). **Staff:** 2. **Budget:** $28,000. **State Groups:** 1. **Description:** Promotes media literacy and the development of critical viewing skills. Provides educators with support information to help them teach and integrate media literacy concepts into the classroom. **Awards:** Jessie McCanse Media Literacy Award. **Frequency:** annual. **Type:** recognition. **Recipient:** for long term (at least ten years) individual contribution to the field of media literacy. **Absorbed:** Television Action Committee for Today and Tomorrow. **Formerly:** (1983) American Council for Better Broadcasts. **Publications:** *Managing Television is a Family Affair*. Booklet. **Price:** $10.00 ● *Telemedium*, 3/year. Journal. Contains information regarding the field of media education and available resources for teachers. **Price:** included in membership dues. **Circulation:** 700. **Advertising:** accepted. Also Cited As: *Better Broadcasts News (former name)* ● Brochures ● Also publishes teaching aids. **Conventions/Meetings:** periodic workshop and conference.

9767 ■ Native American Public Telecommunications (NAPT)
1800 N 33rd St.
Lincoln, NE 68503
Ph: (402)472-3522
Fax: (402)472-8675
E-mail: native@unl.edu
URL: http://www.nativetelecom.org
Contact: Shirley K. Sneve, Exec. Dir.
Founded: 1977. **Staff:** 8. **Description:** Supports the creation, promotion and distribution of Native public media. Works to: produce and develop educational telecommunications programs for all media including television and public radio; distribute and encourage the broadest use of such educational telecommunications programs; provide training opportunities to encourage increasing numbers of American Indians and Alaska Natives to produce quality programs; promote increased control and use of information technologies by American Indians and Alaska Natives; provide leadership in creating awareness of and developing telecommunications policies favorable to American Indians and Alaska Natives; and build partnerships to develop and implement telecommunications projects with tribal nations, Indian organizations and native communities. **Awards:** NAPT Public Television Fund. **Frequency:** annual. **Type:** grant. **Recipient:** for project proposals from native independent or public television producers. **Telecommunication Services:** electronic mail, ssneve2@unl.edu. **Formerly:** Native American Public Broadcasting Consortium. **Publications:** *AIROS Native Network E-Newsletter*, monthly. Alternate Formats: online ● *NAPT Producer E-Newsletter*, monthly. Alternate Formats: online ● *Native American Public Telecommunications E-Newsletter*, monthly. Alternate Formats: online ● *Three Decades*, periodic. Brochure.

9768 ■ Public Broadcasting Service (PBS)
2100 Crystal Dr.
Arlington, VA 22202
Ph: (703)739-5000
Fax: (703)739-0775
E-mail: viewer@pbs.org
URL: http://www.pbs.org
Contact: Paula Kerger, Pres./CEO
Founded: 1969. **Members:** 350. **Staff:** 485. **Budget:** $313,000,000. **Description:** Strives to enrich the lives of Americans through quality programs and education services on non-commercial television, the Internet and other media. Owned and operated by the nation's 350 public television stations. **Publications:** Annual Report.

Buddhist

9769 ■ Cambodian Buddhist Society (CBS)
13800 New Hampshire Ave.
Silver Spring, MD 20904
Ph: (301)622-6544 (301)384-3319
Fax: (301)622-6544
E-mail: sovantun@cambodian-buddhist.org
URL: http://www.cambodian-buddhist.org
Contact: Dr. Tun Sovan, VP
Founded: 1978. **Members:** 1,000. **Staff:** 15. **Languages:** English, Khmer. **Description:** Aims to preserve the Cambodian Buddhist religion and the Cambodian tradition and culture. Counsels Cambodian refugees and organizes Cambodian religious and traditional ceremonies. Maintains Cambodian Buddhist Temple. Organizes classes on Khmer (Cambodian) language for children, Cambodian music and Cambodian dance. **Libraries: Type:** reference. **Holdings:** 400. **Subjects:** Buddhism, Cambodian culture. **Computer Services:** Mailing lists. **Committees:** Ceremonies; Cultural Affairs; Maintenance; Public Relations. **Publications:** *Vatt Khmer* (in English and Khmer), quarterly. Newsletter. Features topics on Buddhism and Cambodian tradition and culture. **Price:** included in membership dues. **Conventions/Meetings:** annual general assembly - always August, Silver Spring, MD.

Byzantine

9770 ■ American Institute for Patristic and Byzantine Studies (AIPBS)
12 Minuet Ln.
Kingston, NY 12401
Ph: (845)336-8797
Fax: (845)331-1002
Contact: Prof. Constantine N. Tsirpanlis PhD, Founder/Pres.
Founded: 1967. **Members:** 390. **Membership Dues:** individual, $95 (annual) ● library, institute, $174 (annual). **Staff:** 3. **Languages:** English, French, German, Greek, Italian, Spanish. **Multinational. Description:** Professors, authors, historians, theologians, journalists, and intellectuals. Promotes knowledge and scholarly research concerning Greek, Christian, and Byzantine civil patristics, literature, history, theology, philosophy, art, science, and folklore. Conducts specialized education and research programs. **Libraries: Type:** reference. **Holdings:** 11,000; books. **Subjects:** world cultures and religions, Byzantine and

Greek history, theology, science, philosophy, philology, classics, modern Greek literature, language, folklore, poetry, art. **Awards:** The Byzantine-Patristic Medal and Certificate. **Frequency:** annual. **Type:** medal. **Recipient:** for professional excellence in the fields of humanities, Byzantine-Greek and Ecumenical scholarship, authorship, teaching, and church leadership, and journalism. **Committees:** Conferences; Editorial; Lecture. **Formerly:** (1981) American Society for Neo-Hellenic Studies. **Publications:** *Eastern Orthodox Theology (12 Vols.)* ● *Greek Patristic Theology (16 Vols.)* (in English, French, German, Greek, Italian, and Spanish), triennial. Book. **Advertising:** accepted. Alternate Formats: CD-ROM; online ● *Hellenism in America, Inc.* (in English, French, German, Greek, and Italian), monthly. Newspaper ● *Orthodox Thought and Life* ● *The Patristic and Byzantine Review*, triennial ● *Studies in Byzantine History (30 Vols.)*. **Conventions/Meetings:** biennial International Byzantino-Patepiko Symposium - meeting (exhibits) ● annual symposium, covers patristics, theology, history of religion, eastern Christianity, humanities, Byzantine history, culture, ancient and modern Greek language, literature and folklore.

9771 ■ U.S. National Committee for Byzantine Studies (USNCBS)
214 St. Mark's Sq.
Philadelphia, PA 19104
Ph: (215)387-1447 (802)457-2043
Fax: (215)387-1447
E-mail: nsevcenko@aol.com
URL: http://www.aiebnet.gr
Contact: Nancy P. Sevcenko, Pres.

Founded: 1962. **Members:** 225. **Description:** Members of the academic profession, institutions of higher learning, research institutions, and museums who devote half or more of their professional activity to the study of, and writing on, Byzantine history, art history, literature, theology, and other disciplines constituting Byzantinology. Works for exchange of information among members, and communications with international affiliation. **Computer Services:** Mailing lists, listserv. **Publications:** *Directory of American Byzantinists (1996)*. **Price:** $15.00 plus shipping and handling ($2.50). **Conventions/Meetings:** quinquennial international conference (exhibits).

Canals

9772 ■ American Canal Society (ACS)
c/o Charles W. Derr, Sec.-Treas.
117 Main St.
Freemansburg, PA 18017
Ph: (610)691-0956 (508)478-4918
E-mail: dgbarber@cs.com
URL: http://www.americancanals.org
Contact: David G. Barber, Pres.

Founded: 1972. **Members:** 900. **Membership Dues:** regular, $20 (annual) ● dual, $25 (annual) ● sustaining, $35 (annual) ● patron, $50 (annual) ● life, $200. **National Groups:** 3. **Multinational. Description:** Persons interested in historic and operating canals of the Americas. Encourages the preservation, restoration, and use of navigation canals of the Americas; works to save threatened canals; provides an exchange of canal information on an international basis. Collects and disseminates historical and engineering information on canals. Conducts detailed research on the indexing of canals and canal structures of North America. **Committees:** Canal Archeology; Canal Boat; Canal Indexing; Canal Operations and Maintenance; Canal Parks; Engineering Design; Literature Sales; Navigable Canals. **Publications:** *American Canal Guide*, periodic. Journal ● *American Canals*, quarterly. Newsletter. Includes book reviews and calendar of events. **Price:** included in membership dues; $3.00 for nonmembers. **Circulation:** 850. Alternate Formats: online ● *The Best From American Canal*, triennial. Journal ● Also publishes index sheets on many canals. **Conventions/Meetings:** annual meeting.

9773 ■ Canal Society of New York State (CSNYS)
c/o Michele D. Beilman, Exec. Dir.
2527 Cherry Valley Tpke.
Marcellus, NY 13108
Ph: (315)730-4495
Fax: (315)673-1864
E-mail: info@canalsnys.org
URL: http://www.canalsnys.org
Contact: Michele D. Beilman, Exec. Dir.

Founded: 1956. **Members:** 500. **Membership Dues:** individual, $30 (annual) ● family (husband and wife/parent and child), $40 (annual) ● institutional, $55 (annual) ● sustaining, $45 (annual). **Description:** Persons and organizations interested in the history of New York State waterways. Financially assists canal-related research and projects. Conducts one to two field trips per year. **Libraries: Type:** reference. **Holdings:** archival material, artwork, books, periodicals. **Subjects:** New York canals and waterways. **Telecommunication Services:** electronic mail, mbeilman@twcny.rr.com. **Publications:** *Bottoming Out*, periodic. Journal. **Price:** included in membership dues ● *Godfrey Letters* ● *Mohawk River Boats and Navigation Before 1820*. Book ● Also publishes guidebooks from field trips. **Conventions/Meetings:** annual meeting.

Caribbean

9774 ■ Caribbean American Intercultural Organization (CAIO)
PO Box 55395
Washington, DC 20040
Ph: (202)720-3900
E-mail: service@caribamerican.org
URL: http://www.caribamerican.org
Contact: Cordell Deane, Pres.

Founded: 1958. **Members:** 170. **Membership Dues:** regular, $30 (annual) ● organizational affiliation, $100 (annual) ● regular (life), $300 ● student, $20 (annual) ● organizational affiliation (life), $500. **Description:** Citizens of the Caribbean-American community in the Washington, DC metropolitan area. Aims to promote, encourage, and maintain intercultural relations between the various peoples of the Caribbean and the people of the U.S. Sponsors exhibitions, forums, and audiovisual educational programs. Conducts charitable programs. Presents awards to outstanding individuals of Caribbean ancestry who made significant contributions to the development of the U.S., Caribbean, or Third World. Maintains speakers' bureau. **Awards:** Independence. **Frequency:** annual. **Type:** recognition. **Publications:** *CAIO Courier*, quarterly. Newsletter ● Books. **Conventions/Meetings:** quarterly meeting.

9775 ■ Caribbean Culture Center
408 W 58th St.
New York, NY 10019
Ph: (212)307-7420
Fax: (212)315-1086
E-mail: mmvega@cccadi.org
URL: http://www.cccadi.org/node/83
Contact: Marta Moreno Vega PhD, Pres./Founder

Founded: 1976. **Members:** 500. **Membership Dues:** individual, $50 ● family, $75 ● patron, $250 ● senior citizen, student, $25 ● benefactor, $500. **Staff:** 5. **Budget:** $800,000. **Description:** Works for cultural diversity and Diaspora. Sponsors educational activities and research. Maintains resource center. **Convention/Meeting:** none. **Libraries: Type:** reference; open to the public. **Holdings:** archival material, books, periodicals, photographs, video recordings. **Subjects:** African Diaspora. **Programs:** Oral Traditions Literacy. **Projects:** In-Class International Museum. **Publications:** *Under the Sun*. Newsletter. Alternate Formats: online.

Catholic

9776 ■ Catholic Theological Society of America (CTSA)
c/o Dr. Dolores Christie, Exec. Dir.
John Carroll Univ.
20700 N Park Blvd.
University Heights, OH 44118
Ph: (216)397-1631
Fax: (216)397-1804
E-mail: dlchristie@aol.com
URL: http://www.jcu.edu/ctsa
Contact: Margaret O'Gara, Pres.

Founded: 1946. **Members:** 1,600. **Membership Dues:** regular, $30-$120 (annual). **Staff:** 2. **Description:** Seeks to promote an exchange of views among Catholic theologians. Furthers studies and research in Catholic theology. Relates theological science to current problems. **Libraries: Type:** reference. **Holdings:** archival material. **Awards:** John Courtney Murray Award. **Frequency:** annual. **Type:** recognition. **Publications:** *Catholic Theological Society of America—Directory*, quinquennial. Membership Directory. **Price:** included in membership dues; $25.00/copy, for nonmembers ● *Catholic Theological Society of America—Proceedings*, annual. **Price:** included in membership dues; $25.00 for nonmembers. Also Cited As: *Microform* ● Reports. **Conventions/Meetings:** annual convention (exhibits).

9777 ■ Fellowship of Catholic Scholars (FCS)
c/o Dr. J. Brian Benestad, VP/Ed.
PO Box 495
Notre Dame, IN 46556
Ph: (574)631-5825
E-mail: benestadjl@cranton.edu
URL: http://www.catholicscholars.org
Contact: Dr. Bernard Dobranski, Pres.

Founded: 1974. **Members:** 900. **Membership Dues:** regular, $40 (annual) ● associate, $35 (annual) ● perpetual, $500. **Staff:** 2. **National Groups:** 4. **Description:** Roman Catholic professors and scholars. Acts as a forum for Catholic intellectuals; applies intellectual abilities to service of the Roman Catholic Church. Seeks to identify significant moral issues and problems and formulate responses for individual worshipers and leaders in the Roman Catholic Church. Provides bibliographies and book reviews. **Awards:** Cardinal Wright Award. **Frequency:** annual. **Type:** recognition. **Recipient:** for outstanding Catholic scholarship and service. **Computer Services:** Mailing lists. **Committees:** Higher Education; Social Action. **Publications:** *Convention Proceedings*, annual. **Circulation:** 1,600 ● *Fellowship of Catholic Scholars Quarterly*. Journal. **Price:** included in membership dues. **Circulation:** 1,600. Alternate Formats: online ● Also publishes works by individual authors. **Conventions/Meetings:** semiannual board meeting - April and September ● annual conference - always September ● Interdisciplinary Seminars.

9778 ■ Jesuit Philosophical Association (JPA)
c/o Rev. Joseph Koterski, SJ, Sec.
Fordham Univ.
Dept. of Philosophy
Bronx, NY 10458
Ph: (718)817-3291
Fax: (718)817-3300
E-mail: koterski@fordham.edu
Contact: Rev. Joseph Koterski SJ, Sec.

Founded: 1935. **Members:** 120. **Membership Dues:** restricted, $15 (annual). **Description:** Represents Jesuits in the U.S. and Canada who are engaged in, or interested in, the teaching and study of philosophy. Seeks to further philosophical interchange among Jesuits in the field of philosophy. **Formerly:** Jesuit Philosophical Association of the United States and Canada. **Publications:** Proceedings, annual. Includes member list and financial report. **Price:** included in membership dues; $4.00 for nonmembers. **Conventions/Meetings:** annual conference, in conjunction with the American Catholic Philosophical Association.

Celtic

9779 ■ Southwest Celtic Music Association (SCMA)
833 Exposition Ave., Ste.101
Dallas, TX 75226-2490

E-mail: lybolynn@hotmail.com
URL: http://www.scmatx.org
Contact: Betsy Cummings, Pres.
Founded: 1983. **Membership Dues:** family, $15 (annual) ● organization, $25 (annual) ● friendship, $50 (annual) ● sponsor, $100 (annual) ● life, $300. **Description:** Promotes Celtic music, dance, and culture in the southwest United States. Provides referrals for entertainers, organizes regular sessions, supports other cultural associations with similar purposes. Sponsors Ceili dance series. **Publications:** *Ceili*, bimonthly. Newsletter. **Advertising:** accepted. Alternate Formats: online. **Conventions/Meetings:** annual meeting ● workshop, music and dance.

Ceramics

9780 ■ Potters Council
735 Ceramic Pl., Ste.100
Westerville, OH 43081
Free: (866)721-3322
Fax: (614)794-5842
E-mail: info@ceramics.org
URL: http://ceramicartsdaily.org/potterscouncil
Contact: David Hendley, Pres.
Founded: 2001. **Members:** 2,500. **Membership Dues:** general, $35 (annual). **Multinational. Description:** Serves the needs of potters, ceramic artists and interested individuals. Provides forums for knowledge exchange and professional enhancement. Supports ACerS efforts to promote ceramic awareness. **Computer Services:** database, studio directory. **Programs:** Mentoring. **Publications:** *Potter's Pages*, quarterly. Newsletter. Alternate Formats: online ● Brochure. Alternate Formats: online.

Children

9781 ■ Children's Art Foundation (CAF)
PO Box 83
Santa Cruz, CA 95063
Ph: (831)426-5557
Free: (800)447-4569
Fax: (831)426-1161
E-mail: editor@stonesoup.com
URL: http://www.stonesoup.com
Contact: Ms. Gerry Mandel, Co-Dir.
Founded: 1973. **Members:** 20,000. **Membership Dues:** individual, $34 (annual). **Staff:** 3. **Budget:** $400,000. **Description:** Publishes Stone Soup and maintains a collection of children's art from around the world. **Libraries: Type:** by appointment only. **Holdings:** 200; books. **Subjects:** writing by children, child art education. **Computer Services:** database ● mailing lists. **Publications:** *Stone Soup: The Magazine by Young Writers and Artists*, bimonthly. Contains fiction, poetry, and art created by children ages eight through 13. Includes book reviews. **Price:** included in membership dues; $34.00 /year for nonmembers. ISSN: 0094-579X. **Circulation:** 20,000. **Advertising:** accepted.

9782 ■ Sesame Workshop
1 Lincoln Plz.
New York, NY 10023
Ph: (212)595-3456
E-mail: privacy@sesameonline.org
URL: http://www.sesameworkshop.com
Contact: Gary E. Knell, Pres./CEO
Founded: 1968. **Staff:** 250. **Description:** Develops innovative and engaging educational content for television, radio, books, magazines, interactive media and outreach both in the U.S. and elsewhere in the world. Makes meaningful difference in the lives of children by addressing their critical developmental needs through research-intensive approach. **Formerly:** (2001) Children's Television Workshop. **Publications:** *Sesame Workshop Family Newsletter*, weekly. Contains new online features and promotional offers. **Price:** free. Alternate Formats: online ● Annual Report, annual. Alternate Formats: online.

Chinese

9783 ■ Center for Chinese Research Materials (CCRM)
PO Box 3090
Oakton, VA 22124
Ph: (703)715-2688
Fax: (703)715-7913
E-mail: ccrm703@aol.com
Contact: Pingfeng Chi, Dir.
Founded: 1967. **Staff:** 5. **Description:** Locates, reproduces, and distributes rare materials on contemporary China in order to assist libraries in maintaining complete records of Chinese language publications and to encourage scholars in Chinese study. Original materials needed for reproduction are obtained through loan arrangements with libraries or private collections in the U.S. and abroad. Provides bibliographic services to students and scholars. Assists libraries in building collections of items such as newspapers, government publications, and foreign archival materials. **Convention/Meeting:** none. **Publications:** Newsletter, 2-3/year.

9784 ■ Center for United States-China Arts Exchange
423 W 118th St., No. 1E
New York, NY 10027
Ph: (212)280-4648
Fax: (212)662-6346
E-mail: us_china_arts@yahoo.com
URL: http://www.columbia.edu/cu/china
Contact: Chou Wen-chung, Dir.
Founded: 1978. **Staff:** 6. **For-Profit. Description:** Promotes and facilitates exchanges of materials and specialists in the visual, literary, and performing arts between the U.S. and the People's Republic of China in an effort to stimulate public interest in the arts of both countries. Fosters collaborative projects between American and Chinese artists. Arranges professional activities for exchange artists including lectures, conferences, performances and exhibitions, and research opportunities in their respective fields. **Publications:** *U.S.-China Arts Exchange* (in Chinese and English), annual. Newsletter.

9785 ■ China Institute in America (CI)
125 E 65th St.
New York, NY 10021
Ph: (212)744-8181
Fax: (212)628-4159
E-mail: info@chinainstitute.org
URL: http://chinainstitute.org
Contact: Sara Judge McCalpin, Pres.
Founded: 1926. **Members:** 1,000. **Membership Dues:** individual, $55 (annual) ● dual/family, $95 (annual) ● special, $1,500-$25,000 (annual) ● supporting, $250-$2,300 (annual) ● corporate, $2,500-$25,000 (annual) ● young associate, $100 (annual). **Staff:** 25. **Budget:** $2,700,000. **Languages:** Cantonese, English, Mandarin. **Description:** Promotes the understanding of Chinese civilization, culture, heritage and current affairs through classroom teaching and seminars, art exhibitions, public programs, teacher education, lectures and symposia. **Libraries: Type:** reference. **Programs:** Discover China Through Art (student tours of gallery); Language Exchange. **Formerly:** China Institute. **Publications:** *Art Exhibition Catalogs*, semiannual. Accompanies art exhibitions with object (China Institute Gallery listings and scholarly essays). **Price:** $50.00 ● *Program Courses & Catalog*, quarterly ● Catalog, 3/year. **Price:** free upon request ● Annual Report. **Price:** free upon request ● Newsletter, monthly. **Price:** free.

9786 ■ Chinese American Forum (CAF)
Address Unknown since 2008
Founded: 1982. **Members:** 280. **Membership Dues:** regular, sponsor, charter, patron, $30 (annual). **Description:** Individuals 18 years of age or older with Chinese-American bicultural heritage or interest. Cultivates understanding among U.S. citizens of the Chinese-American cultural heritage and the American public; promotes the interest, active participation, and contribution of Chinese-Americans in American society; serves as an open and constructive forum on issues of national, international, and general interest as well as those related to China from the standpoint of Chinese-Americans. **Libraries: Type:** open to the public. **Subgroups:** Advisers; Editorial; Regional Representatives. **Publications:** *Chinese American Forum*, quarterly. Journal. Contains book reviews. **Price:** $14.00 /year for individuals; $18.00 /year for institutions. ISSN: 0895-4690. **Circulation:** 1,200. **Advertising:** accepted. **Conventions/Meetings:** annual board meeting.

9787 ■ Chinese Culture Association (CCA)
Address Unknown since 2008
Founded: 1966. **Members:** 2,000. **Description:** A worldwide organization of professors, scientists, engineers, artists, physicians, and businessmen. Promotes communication among members and mutual understanding between the Chinese and people of other countries. Sponsors social meetings, lectures, concerts, painting and dancing exhibitions, films, and discussions. **Publications:** *Chinese Culture Association—Journal*, periodic. **Price:** included in membership dues. **Advertising:** accepted ● Newsletter, 4-5/year. **Conventions/Meetings:** periodic regional meeting ● seminar.

9788 ■ Chinese Culture Foundation of San Francisco (CCFSF)
750 Kearny St., 3rd Fl.
San Francisco, CA 94108-1809
Ph: (415)986-1822
Fax: (415)986-2825
E-mail: info@c-c-c.org
URL: http://www.c-c-c.org
Contact: Tzu-Chen Lee, Pres.
Founded: 1965. **Members:** 500. **Membership Dues:** senior, student, $25 (annual) ● regular, $35 (annual) ● family, $50 (annual) ● not-for-profit, $75 (annual) ● sponsor, $1,000 (annual) ● benefactor, $500 (annual) ● contributor, $200 (annual). **Staff:** 10. **Budget:** $400,000. **Languages:** Chinese, English. **Description:** Promotes understanding and appreciation of Chinese and Chinese-American art, culture and history in the U.S. Offers educational and cultural programs, including art exhibitions, lecture and film series, performances, classes, research projects, and Chinatown walks. Also sponsors events in conjunction with academic and cultural organizations in the Bay Area. **Also Known As:** Chinese Culture Center of San Francisco. **Publications:** *Chinese Culture Center Newsletter*, quarterly. Contains cultural calendar, exhibition news, "Who's News", and "What's New in Our Gallery Shop" photos. **Price:** free for members ● Catalogs (in Chinese and English). Provides information on exhibitions. **Conventions/Meetings:** weekly Chinese Music and Painting - workshop.

9789 ■ Chinese Historical Society of America (CHSA)
965 Clay St.
San Francisco, CA 94108
Ph: (415)391-1188
Fax: (415)391-1150
E-mail: info@chsa.org
URL: http://www.chsa.org
Contact: Sue Lee, Exec. Dir.
Founded: 1963. **Members:** 500. **Membership Dues:** individual, $50 (annual) ● student, senior, educator, $30 (annual) ● family, foreign, $60 (annual) ● institutional, contributing, $100 (annual) ● sponsor, $250 (annual) ● patron, $500 (annual) ● President's Circle, $1,000 (annual). **Staff:** 5. **Budget:** $512,000. **Languages:** Chinese, English. **Description:** Works on documentation, study, and presentation of Chinese-American history and culture. Operates a Museum and Learning Center located in the landmark Julia Morgan-designed Chinatown YWCA building. Promotes the contributions of Chinese-Americans and preserves the legacy of Chinese-America through exhibitions, publications, and educational and public programming. **Libraries: Type:** not open to the public. **Holdings:** 500. **Subjects:** Chinese-American culture, history, immigration. **Committees:** Field Trips; Grants and Fundraising; Oral History; Public

Relations; Research; Speakers' Forum. **Affiliated With:** American Association of Museums; American Association for State and Local History. **Publications:** *Chinese America: History and Perspectives*, annual, every February. Journal. Includes research reports. **Price:** included in membership dues; $15.00 for nonmembers. **Circulation:** 800 ● *Chinese Historical Society of America Bulletin*, bimonthly. Newsletter. Reports on CHSA events, activities, and news in Chinese-American history and culture. Includes calendar of events and annual report. **Price:** included in membership dues. **Circulation:** 800. Alternate Formats: online ● *The Chinese in America*. Catalog ● *CHSA Bulletin*, monthly. Alternate Formats: online ● *The Repeal and Its Legacy: Proceedings of the Conference on the 50th Anniversary of the Repeal of the Exclusion Acts*, periodic. Features a compilation of Chinese-American history. Includes conference papers. **Price:** $23.00/copy for members; $25.00/copy for nonmembers ● Books ● Also publishes a historical syllabus, museum exhibition catalogues. **Conventions/Meetings:** monthly meeting - except July and August.

9790 ■ Conference for Chinese Oral and Performing Literature (CHINOPERL)
c/o Shu-Chu Wei, Pres.
Whitman Coll.
Dept. of Foreign Languages and Literature
Walla Walla, WA 99362
Ph: (509)527-5891 (509)529-8121
Fax: (509)527-5039
E-mail: weipeng@whitman.edu
Contact: Shu-Chu Wei, Pres.
Founded: 1969. **Members:** 200. **Languages:** Chinese, English. **Description:** Seeks to foster knowledge of Chinese oral and performing literature. Provides a written and/or taped record of such literature and of papers written concerning it. Conducts research programs and specialized education. **Affiliated With:** Association for Asian Studies. **Publications:** *CHINOPERL Papers*, annual. Journal. **Price:** $25.00 /year for individuals; $30.00 /year for institutions. ISSN: 0193-7774. **Circulation:** 200. **Conventions/Meetings:** annual conference.

9791 ■ Institute of Chinese Culture (ICC)
10550 Westoffice Dr.
Houston, TX 77042
Ph: (281)980-5172
URL: http://members.aol.com/icchouston
Contact: Jeanne Ma, Contact
Founded: 1944. **Members:** 100. **Staff:** 4. **Description:** Represents scholars, community leaders, and others interested in China. Works to further cultural relations between the U.S. and Taiwan. Promotes cultural and educational programs and activities between the American and Chinese people. Sponsors Chinese Forum and art exhibits; holds cultural classes in Chinese art and language; offers lecture service. **Awards:** Junior Achievement. **Type:** recognition. **Recipient:** for scholarly achievements. **Conventions/Meetings:** annual conference.

9792 ■ Press Division, Taipei Economic and Cultural Office in New York (TECO-NY)
1 E 42nd St., 11th Fl.
New York, NY 10017
Ph: (212)557-5122
Fax: (212)557-3043
E-mail: roctaiwan@taipei.org
URL: http://www.taiwanembassy.org/US/NYC/mp.asp?mp=62
Contact: Mr. Ben Shao, Dir.
Founded: 1941. **Staff:** 18. **Languages:** Chinese, English. **Description:** Promotes cultural exchanges between the U.S. and Taiwan. Provides informational materials on Taiwan to interested groups or individuals. Sponsors art exhibitions. Maintains gallery and theater. Conducts children's services and educational programs. Offers Chinese cultural studies programs. **Libraries: Type:** reference; open to the public. **Holdings:** 40,000; archival material, books, periodicals. **Subjects:** social sciences, humanities. **Computer Services:** Online services, news service. **Formerly:** (1966) Chinese News Service; (1979) Chinese Information Service; (1991) Chinese Cultural Center; (2006) Information Division, Taipei Economic and Cultural Office in New York. **Publications:** *CICC Currents*, bimonthly. Newsletter. Reports on cultural activities of the CICC and in Taiwan, such as exhibitions in the Taipei Gallery. **Price:** free. **Circulation:** 5,000. Alternate Formats: online ● *The Republic of China Yearbook*, annual. Includes Chinese culture, leaders, politics, education, and economy. **Price:** $45.00 ● *Selections from Chinese Scholarship in the United States* (in Chinese and English), bimonthly. **Circulation:** 5,700 ● *Sinorama* (in Chinese and English), monthly. Contains commentaries on social and cultural aspects of the Republic of China. **Circulation:** 67,000. **Advertising:** accepted ● *Taipei Journal*, weekly. Contains information of the Republic of China. **Circulation:** 40,000. **Advertising:** accepted ● *Taipei Review*, monthly.

9793 ■ Sino-American Cultural Society (SACS)
Address Unknown since 2008
Founded: 1958. **Members:** 400. **Description:** Educational organization formed to arrange educational and cultural programs related to the Republic of China and the U.S; to encourage the performance of Chinese music, drama, and opera; to assist Chinese educational leaders visiting Washington, DC; to organize Sino-American social functions. Works to: increase public awareness of the cultural and intellectual heritage of Chinese civilization and cultivate mutual understanding between peoples of the East and West; promote cooperation in educational and cultural services; provide a forum for leading figures of China and the U.S. Sponsors Chinese art exhibits and concerts. **Awards:** P.W. Kuo Scholarship. **Frequency:** annual. **Type:** scholarship. **Formerly:** (1961) Sino-American Cultural Committee. **Publications:** Books ● Brochures. **Conventions/Meetings:** bimonthly Friendship Dinner.

9794 ■ Wildflowers Institute
354 Pine St., 7th Fl.
San Francisco, CA 94104
Ph: (415)399-1199
Fax: (415)399-1599
E-mail: nectar@wildflowers.org
URL: http://www.wildflowers.org
Contact: Dr. Hanmin Liu, Pres./CEO
Founded: 1978. **Members:** 150. **Membership Dues:** corporate, $5,000 (annual) ● patron, $3,000 (annual) ● benefactor, $1,000 (annual) ● friend, $300 (annual) ● family, $200 (annual) ● individual, $100 (annual) ● student, $25 (annual). **Staff:** 3. **Budget:** $400,000. **Multinational. Description:** Promotes leadership development and community building in the U.S. and abroad; works to assist communities to uncover and utilize the strengths of various cultures within the community, including planning, growing economically and by becoming more socially sustainable. **Libraries: Type:** reference. **Holdings:** 200. **Formerly:** (2004) United States-China Educational Institute. **Publications:** *A Pearl in the Orient: A Profile of the Meiyuan Community*. Paper. Alternate Formats: online ● *A Wildflowers Lens: Cultural Dynamics and the Social Health of Families and Communities*. Paper. Alternate Formats: online ● *African American and Hispanic Communities in East Palo Alto*. Paper. Alternate Formats: online ● *Balancing Self-interest and Solidarity: Community Development and Civic Engagement in the Enterprise Culture*. Paper. Alternate Formats: online ● *Cultural Assets for Latino Community Building in East Palo Alto*. Paper. Alternate Formats: online ● *The Essential Book of Traditional Chinese Medicine (Vol. I and II)* ● *Outside In, Inside Out: Seeing San Francisco's Filipino Community*. Paper. Alternate Formats: online ● *Studies 2000: Discovering the Cultural Formations of Asian and Pacific Island Communities*. Report ● *Vision-Building: Discovering Invisible Cultural Premises*. Paper. Alternate Formats: online ● *The Wildflowers Approach*. Paper. Alternate Formats: online. **Conventions/Meetings:** annual seminar ● annual workshop.

Circus

9795 ■ American Youth Circus Organization (AYCO)
PO Box 96
Temple, NH 03084
Ph: (603)654-5523
Fax: (208)977-4342
E-mail: info@americanyouthcircus.org
URL: http://www.americanyouthcircus.org
Contact: Kevin O'Keefe, Founder/Pres.
Founded: 1998. **Membership Dues:** kinker, $25 (biennial) ● roustabout, $60 (biennial) ● acrobat, $120 (biennial) ● aerialist, $200 (biennial) ● ringmaster, $500 (annual) ● producer, $1,000 (biennial). **Description:** Promotes the participation of youth in circus arts. Fosters communication among circus arts educators. Provides circus arts coaches with training procedures and guidelines for safety standards. Provides circus-related educational materials to schools and educators. **Computer Services:** Online services, community board postings. **Publications:** Newsletter, biennial. **Price:** included in membership dues.

9796 ■ Circus Education Specialists (CES)
56 Lion Ln.
Westbury, NY 11590
Ph: (516)334-2123
Fax: (516)334-2249
E-mail: info@nationalcircusproject.com
URL: http://nationalcircusproject.com
Contact: Jean Paul Jenack, Exec. Off.
Founded: 1976. **Staff:** 18. **Budget:** $400,000. **Description:** Promotes the circus arts. Seeks to revive the skills and arts practiced by members of the family-operated traveling shows that were forerunners of modern circuses. Aims to establish grass roots programs presenting circus artists to the public in order to stimulate interest and enthusiasm for preserving the circus arts. Maintains: National Circus Project, which incorporates circus skills training into existing school curricula to promote physical education, recreation, and fitness activities for students; International Circus Exchange, through which circus artists from other nations conduct performances in American schools. Conducts lectures, and events at schools, libraries, and parks; sponsors artist-in-residence programs. Maintains Circus Information/Referral Center which compiles statistics; operates biographical archives and information and referral service for fact-checking. Plans to operate a National Circus Academy offering novice, preprofessional, and professional-level training for circus performers. **Libraries: Type:** not open to the public. **Holdings:** 20,000; articles, books, periodicals. **Subjects:** circus, theater, allied arts. **Publications:** Fact sheets. **Conventions/Meetings:** workshop.

9797 ■ Circus Fans Association of America (CFA)
2704 Marshall Ave.
Lorain, OH 44052-4315
Ph: (440)960-2811
Fax: (440)960-2866
E-mail: deptulascircus@centurytel.net
URL: http://www.circusfans.org
Contact: Cheryl Deptula, Exec. Sec.-Treas.
Founded: 1926. **Members:** 2,500. **Membership Dues:** individual (includes subscription to The White Tops magazine), $35 (annual) ● junior (includes subscription to The White Tops magazine), $20 (annual) ● international (includes subscription to The White Tops magazine), $50 (annual) ● institutional (includes subscription to The White Tops magazine), $55 (annual). **Staff:** 2. **Budget:** $50,000. **State Groups:** 48. **Local Groups:** 156. **Description:** Seeks to create an enthusiasm for the circus as an institution and preserve it for future generations. **Computer Services:** Mailing lists. **Committees:** Jurisprudence; Long Term Planning; Public Relations. **Affiliated With:** National Circus Preservation Society. **Publications:** *CFA Roster*, biennial. Directory ● *White Tops*, bimonthly. Magazine. **Price:** $35.00. ISSN: 0043-499X. **Circulation:** 2,500. **Advertising:** accepted. **Conventions/Meetings:** annual convention (exhibits) - 2009 June 11-14, Palm Springs, CA.

9798 ■ Circus Historical Society (CHS)
c/o Alan Campbell, Sec.-Treas.
600 Kings Peak Dr.
Alpharetta, GA 30022-7844

E-mail: circushistory@gmail.com
URL: http://www.circushistory.org
Contact: Alan Campbell, Sec.-Treas.
Founded: 1939. **Members:** 1,400. **Membership Dues:** in U.S., $40 (annual) ● in Canada, $42 (annual) ● sustaining, $50 (annual) ● contributing, $70 (annual) ● concessionary club, $100 (annual) ● ringmaster club, $250 (annual). **Description:** Represents circus managers, employees, and fans interested in collecting and preserving historical material on circuses throughout the world. Members cooperate with other groups to select performers to be honored by the Circus Hall of Fame, Sarasota, FL; maintains collections of circusiana. **Publications:** *Bandwagon*, bimonthly. Journal ● *Membership Roster*, biennial. Membership Directory. **Conventions/Meetings:** annual convention.

9799 ■ National Circus Preservation Society (NCPS)
c/o Cheryl Deptula, Exec. Sec.-Treas.
2704 Marshall Ave.
Lorain, OH 44052
Ph: (440)960-2811
Fax: (440)960-5932
E-mail: deptulascircus@centurytel.net
URL: http://www.circusfans.org/res.php
Contact: Cheryl Deptula, Exec. Sec.-Treas.
Founded: 1980. **Members:** 2,000. **Membership Dues:** individual, $35 (annual). **Regional Groups:** 16. **State Groups:** 50. **Description:** Works to develop and advance information for a better understanding of American circuses; to foster the captive propagation of endangered species and other performing and exhibition animals; to encourage humane handling of all circus animals; to promote reasonable and practical legislation, rules, and regulations that affect the health and well-being of circus animals; to promote favorable public opinion to the objectives and purposes of the society. **Libraries: Type:** reference. **Committees:** Education. **Formerly:** National Circus Fund. **Publications:** *The White Taps*, bimonthly. Magazine. **Price:** included in membership dues; $35.00 for nonmembers. ISSN: 0043-499X. **Circulation:** 2,200. **Advertising:** accepted. **Conventions/Meetings:** annual conference, held in conjunction with the Circus Fans Association of America (exhibits).

Classical Studies

9800 ■ National Committee for Latin and Greek (NCLG)
c/o Nancy McKee, Chair
239 Eacker Dr.
Jeffersonville, VT 05464
Ph: (802)644-6434
E-mail: mckeena@aol.com
URL: http://www.promotelatin.org
Contact: Nancy McKee, Chair
Founded: 1978. **Members:** 15. **Staff:** 4. **Budget:** $18,000. **Regional Groups:** 7. **State Groups:** 12. **Local Groups:** 10. **National Groups:** 4. **Description:** Works to initiate and coordinate efforts to promote the study of Latin and Greek on behalf of all cooperating classical organizations by developing a variety of appropriate projects and activities. Serves as a forum for the sharing of information and experience, and for cooperation and discussion within the classics profession for the identification of nationwide needs and priorities in the classics. Acts as Clearinghouse and resource center for enrollment figures, and the value of a classical education for the news media, school administrators, and the profession. Sponsors the Classics Action Network, which notifies member organizations of upcoming federal legislation affecting languages, and initiates constituent action. **Committees:** Advocacy. **Subgroups:** Classics Action Network. **Formerly:** (1986) National Coordinating Office for Latin and Greek. **Publications:** *Exemplary Latin programs for Elementary and Middle Schools*. Brochure. Includes 2 curriculum packets describing innovative programs. **Price:** $7.00 ● *Latin for the Elementary and Middle Schools*. Brochure. Contains information about Latin in elementary and middle schools. **Price:** $5.00 ● *Latin for the 90's*. Includes an information packet containing facts, benefits figures, brochures and news articles. **Price:** $6.20 ● *Pro Bono*, semiannual. Newsletter. Alternate Formats: online ● *Prospects*, semiannual. Newsletter ● Also provides promotional materials. **Conventions/Meetings:** semiannual meeting, held in conjunction with American Classical League in June and held in conjunction with American Philological Association in December - last week of June and last week of December.

9801 ■ Women's Classical Caucus (WCC)
c/o Prof. Maryline Parca, Sec.-Treas.
Univ. of Illinois
Dept. of the Classics
4080 Languages Bldg.
707 S Matthews Ave.
Urbana, IL 61801
E-mail: mparca@uiuc.edu
URL: http://www.wccaucus.org/index.html
Contact: Prof. Maryline Parca, Sec.-Treas.
Founded: 1972. **Members:** 500. **Membership Dues:** student, retired, $5 (annual) ● life, $150 ● regular, $15 (annual). **Description:** Represents ancient historians, archaeologists, art historians and classicists. Works to support the professional status of women in Classics and related fields, and facilitates research on women in the areas of archaeology, ancient history and ancient literature. Maintains an Equity Fund to promote just and equitable treatment in hiring, promotion and working conditions within the profession. Makes available outlines for courses on Women in Antiquity and syllabi for other courses. **Awards:** Best Oral Paper. **Frequency:** annual. **Type:** monetary. **Recipient:** to a paper that represents a feminist perspective on some aspects of classical antiquity ● Best Published Article. **Frequency:** annual. **Type:** monetary. **Recipient:** to an article that represents a feminist perspective on some aspects of classical antiquity ● **Frequency:** annual. **Type:** recognition. **Recipient:** for feminist research on classical antiquity. **Computer Services:** Mailing lists. **Publications:** *CLOELIA*, semiannual. Newsletter. **Price:** $5.00 for students; $15.00 /year for individuals; $15.00 /year for institutions. **Circulation:** 600. **Advertising:** accepted. **Conventions/Meetings:** annual conference, held in conjunction with American Philological Association and Archaeological Institute of America (exhibits) - always 1st week of January.

Community

9802 ■ North American Sankethi Association (NASA)
34 Longwood Dr.
Clifton Park, NY 12065
E-mail: president@sankethi.org
URL: http://www.sankethi.org
Contact: Dr. S. Sridhara, Pres.
Founded: 1984. **Membership Dues:** general, $25 (annual) ● life, $200. **Description:** Provides a forum for the members of the Sankethi community to meet frequently and maintain religious, cultural, charitable, educational and social activities. Encourages the younger generation to understand the culture, language and family relationships of the Sankethis. Increases public awareness and understanding of the contribution of Sankethis to the society and country. **Computer Services:** Information services, Sankethi resources. **Telecommunication Services:** electronic mail, vice-president@sankethi.org ● electronic mail, secretary@sankethi.org ● electronic mail, assistant-secretary1@sankethi.org ● electronic mail, treasurer@sankethi.org. **Publications:** Newsletter. **Price:** included in membership dues. Alternate Formats: online.

Composers

9803 ■ American Beethoven Society (ABS)
c/o Ira F. Brilliant Center for Beethoven Studies
San Jose State Univ.
1 Washington Sq.
San Jose, CA 95192-0171
Ph: (408)808-2058
Fax: (408)808-2060
E-mail: lvb@email.sjsu.edu
URL: http://www.sjsu.edu/depts/beethoven/abs/abso-ciety.html
Contact: Dr. William Meredith, Dir./Ed.
Founded: 1985. **Members:** 400. **Membership Dues:** pastoral, $45 (annual) ● student in U.S., $25 (annual) ● student outside U.S., teacher in U.S., $35 (annual) ● Eroica, $100 (annual) ● Fidelio, $250 (annual) ● Appassionata, $500 (annual) ● Emperor, $1,000 (annual). **Staff:** 7. **Regional Groups:** 1. **Description:** Individuals and organizations that support the activities of the Ira F. Brilliant Center for Beethoven Studies. Supports research and publication in Beethoven studies. Promotes performances of Beethoven's compositions on musical instruments of the type that existed during his life. Seeks to increase public understanding and appreciation of Beethoven's life and music through lectures, studies, and musical performances. Celebrates Beethoven's ideals and achievements. Sponsors annual piano competition for California high school students. Develops an online bibliography of materials relating to Beethoven. **Libraries: Type:** reference. **Holdings:** 20,000; archival material, articles, audio recordings, books, periodicals. **Subjects:** life and music of Ludwig van Beethoven. **Awards:** Young Pianists Beethoven Competition. **Frequency:** annual. **Type:** monetary. **Recipient:** for California high school students. **Computer Services:** database, Beethoven Bibliography. **Telecommunication Services:** electronic mail, meredith@email.sjsu.edu. **Formerly:** (1986) Friends of Beethoven in America. **Publications:** *The Beethoven Journal*, semiannual. Includes bibliographies, reviews, conference reports, and full-length articles. **Price:** included in membership dues; $25.00 /year for institutions in U.S.; $35.00 /year for institutions outside U.S. ISSN: 1087-8262. **Circulation:** 1,000. Alternate Formats: online. **Conventions/Meetings:** annual Beethoven Birthday Open House - meeting, continuous exhibits at the Center for Beethoven Studies (exhibits) - always December ● annual Beethoven Summer Party - meeting - always July.

9804 ■ American Brahms Society (ABS)
c/o George S. Bozarth, Exec. Dir.
School of Music
Univ. of Washington
Box 353450
Seattle, WA 98195-3450
Ph: (206)543-0400
Fax: (206)284-0111
E-mail: brahms@u.washington.edu
URL: http://brahms.unh.edu
Contact: George S. Bozarth, Exec. Dir.
Founded: 1983. **Members:** 250. **Membership Dues:** retired/senior citizen, $20 (annual) ● regular, $25 (annual) ● student, $15 (annual). **Staff:** 1. **Description:** Musicians, educators, and other individuals with an interest in the life and work of German composer Johannes Brahms. Seeks to advance the study of Brahms's life and music. Facilitates exchange of information about research. **Libraries: Type:** by appointment only. **Holdings:** articles, audio recordings, books. **Subjects:** Brahms. **Awards:** Karl Geiringer Scholarship in Brahms Research. **Frequency:** annual. **Type:** scholarship. **Recipient:** to a PhD candidate in final stage of work on dissertation on Brahm's related topic. **Publications:** *American Brahms Society Newsletter*, semiannual. Contains articles, reviews of recent publications and recordings. **Price:** free for members. ISSN: 8756-8357. **Circulation:** 1,000 ● *Brahms Studies*. Book. **Conventions/Meetings:** annual board meeting.

9805 ■ American Composers Forum (ACF)
332 Minnesota St., Ste.E-145
St. Paul, MN 55101-1300
Ph: (651)228-1407 (651)251-2811
Fax: (651)291-7978
E-mail: mail@composersforum.org
URL: http://www.composersforum.org
Contact: John Nuechterlein, Pres./CEO
Founded: 1973. **Members:** 1,700. **Membership Dues:** student/senior in U.S., $35 (annual) ● indi-

vidual in U.S., $55 (annual) ● individual outside U.S., $65 (annual) ● student/senior outside U.S., $45 (annual). **Staff:** 16. **Regional Groups:** 10. **Description:** Composers, performers, and ensembles; nonmusicians with an interest in composition. Seeks to "link communities with composers and performers, encouraging the making, playing, and enjoyment of new music". Facilitates communication and cooperation among members; conducts educational programs; sponsors competitions. Organizes church and synagogue residency and musical exchange programs. Makes available music software and hardware discounts to members; provides financial support to composers. **Awards:** McKnight Composer Fellowships. **Frequency:** annual. **Type:** grant. **Publications:** *American Composers Forum User's Guide*, annual. Handbook. Includes description of programs, chapters, and organizational structure. ● *Sounding Board*, bimonthly. Newsletter. **Price:** $10.00 for members. ISSN: 1090-1868. **Circulation:** 1,800 ● Report, annual. Contains survey of organization's programs and projects. **Conventions/Meetings:** annual Sonic Circuits Electronic Music Festival.

9806 ■ American Handel Society (AHS)
Univ. of Maryland
School of Music
College Park, MD 20742
Ph: (909)607-3568
Fax: (909)621-8645
E-mail: info@americanhandelsociety.org
URL: http://www.americanhandelsociety.org
Contact: Graydon Beeks, Pres.
Founded: 1986. **Members:** 150. **Membership Dues:** regular, $25 (annual) ● subscriber, joint, $30 (annual) ● donor, $40 (annual) ● sponsor, $65 (annual) ● life, $400 ● student, retired, $15 (annual) ● patron, $130 (annual). **Description:** Individuals interested in the life and works of German composer George Friderich Handel. Promotes study of Handel's life and performance of his music. Conducts research; serves as a clearinghouse on Handel and his music. **Awards:** J. Merrill Knapp Research Fellowship. **Frequency:** biennial. **Type:** fellowship. **Recipient:** for an advanced graduate student or a scholar in the early stage of his or her career. **Publications:** *Newsletter of the American Handel Society*, 3/year. Contains reports on scholarly developments, notices of upcoming conferences and performances, reviews of books and an annual discography. **Price:** included in membership dues. ISSN: 0888-8701. **Circulation:** 170. **Advertising:** accepted. **Conventions/Meetings:** biennial conference.

9807 ■ American Liszt Society (ALS)
c/o Justin Kolb, Exec. Membership Sec.
1136 Hog Mountain Rd.
Fleischmanns, NY 12430
Ph: (845)586-4457
E-mail: mellon@catskill.net
URL: http://www.americanlisztsociety.org
Contact: Justin Kolb, Exec. Membership Sec.
Founded: 1964. **Members:** 550. **Membership Dues:** student, $20 (annual) ● individual, $40 (annual) ● library/school/organization, $60 (annual) ● family, $50 (annual) ● contributing, $100 (annual) ● supporting, $250 (annual) ● life, $400. **Regional Groups:** 8. **Local Groups:** 7. **Languages:** English, Greek. **Description:** Scholars, professional musicians, students, and others interested in the life and works of Franz Liszt (1811-86), Hungarian pianist and composer. Seeks to develop increased interest in Liszt's music, particularly that which is seldom played, through performances, recordings, publications, and forums for presentation of scholarly papers. Maintains archive of tapes of festival performances, papers, programs and other Lisztiana at the Library of Congress. **Awards:** ALS Medal for Excellence. **Frequency:** annual. **Type:** medal. **Recipient:** for scholarship, performance, and administration. **Computer Services:** Mailing lists. **Committees:** Research. **Publications:** *American Liszt Society Newsletter*, semiannual, in April and September ● *Journal of the American Liszt Society*, semiannual ● Monograph. **Conventions/Meetings:** annual board meeting ● annual conference and festival, a Library of Congress exhibit of Liszt in America (exhibits).

9808 ■ Christian Fellowship of Art Music Composers (CFAMC)
Greatbatch Scholarship of Music
Houghton Coll.
Houghton, NY 14744
Ph: (585)567-9424
E-mail: cfamc@cfamc.org
URL: http://www.cfamc.org
Contact: Dr. Mark Hijleh, Pres.
Founded: 1994. **Members:** 60. **Membership Dues:** student, $20 (annual) ● composer, $35 (annual). **Staff:** 5. **Description:** Composers of music, music students, and other individuals with an interest in music. Seeks to "glorify the Lord Jesus Christ and help build His kingdom." Encourages the "work and witness of Christian composers of symphonic and chamber music, opera, and other concert works." Provides peer review of classical music written by Christian composers. Sponsors performances. **Libraries:** **Type:** reference. **Holdings:** archival material, audio recordings. **Subjects:** music by Christian composers. **Awards:** CFAMC Scholarship. **Frequency:** biennial. **Type:** scholarship. **Recipient:** for student composers. **Computer Services:** Mailing lists. **Publications:** *CONCERTed Offering*, quarterly. Newsletter. **Conventions/Meetings:** biennial conference.

9809 ■ Gilbert and Sullivan Society
Community Church of New York
40 E 35th St.
New York, NY 10016
Ph: (212)757-5804
E-mail: gspresident@g-and-s.org
URL: http://www.g-and-s.org
Contact: Sara Ruderman, Pres.
Founded: 1936. **Members:** 400. **Membership Dues:** individual, $30 (annual) ● joint, $40 (annual) ● student/junior, $15 (annual) ● non-resident, $20 (annual) ● joint non-resident, $27 (annual). **Staff:** 30. **Description:** Represents persons interested in the operas of William S. Gilbert (1836-1911) and Sir Arthur S. Sullivan (1842-1900). Seeks to bring Gilbert and Sullivan fans together and to encourage the production of the operas in a traditional manner. Maintains collection of more than 100 volumes, donated to the library of the General Society of Mechanics and Tradesmen (see separate entry), including biographies of Gilbert and Sullivan, various editions of operas, and plays by Gilbert. **Publications:** *The Palace Peeper*, 10/year, published September - June. Newsletter. Includes reviews and calendar of events. **Price:** included in membership dues. **Circulation:** 400. **Conventions/Meetings:** convention - 10/year, always in New York City.

9810 ■ International Percy Grainger Society (IPGS)
c/o Lucinda Hess
7 Cromwell Pl.
White Plains, NY 10601
Ph: (914)582-1237 (870)950-3493
Fax: (870)950-3494
E-mail: info@percygrainger.org.uk
URL: http://www.percygrainger.org
Contact: Lucinda Hess, Contact
Founded: 1964. **Members:** 400. **Membership Dues:** regular, $28 (annual) ● life, $100. **Staff:** 2. **Budget:** $26,000. **Regional Groups:** 3. **Languages:** English, French, German, Norwegian. **Description:** Musicians, music instructors, musicologists, and others interested in the music of Percy Grainger (1882-1961), Australian-born pianist and composer. Promotes acceptance of Grainger's works by encouraging orchestras and ensembles to perform his music. Maintains museum at the Grainger home in White Plains, NY. **Libraries:** **Type:** by appointment only. **Holdings:** archival material, articles, artwork, audio recordings, books, papers. **Awards:** Grainger Medallion. **Frequency:** annual. **Type:** recognition. **Computer Services:** Information services. **Additional Websites:** http://www.percygrainger.org.uk. **Formerly:** (1980) Percy Grainger Library Society. **Publications:** *The Grainger Journal*, semiannual. **Price:** available to members only. **Circulation:** 400 ● *In a Nutshell*, quarterly. Newsletter ● *Random Round*, periodic. Newsletter. **Conventions/Meetings:** annual meeting - always May, White Plains, NY.

9811 ■ Jack Point Preservation Society (JPPS)
PO Box 179
New Ellenton, SC 29809
Ph: (803)652-3492 (803)652-7932
E-mail: pandro42@yahoo.com
URL: http://www.hostultra.com/~daisybtoes/Koko.html
Contact: Cheryl W. Duval, Exec. Off.
Founded: 1985. **Staff:** 1. **Description:** Fans of the playwright/composer team of William S. Gilbert (1836-1911) and Sir Arthur S. Sullivan (1842-1900). Fosters appreciation of the works of Gilbert and Sullivan; promotes communication among members. Group derives its name from the character Jack Point in the Gilbert and Sullivan opera Yeomen of the Guard. **Telecommunication Services:** electronic mail, jackpointlives@yahoo.com. **Publications:** *Ko-ko's Corner*. Newsletter. Includes news items and discussions. Alternate Formats: online.

9812 ■ Leopold Stokowski Club
3900 SE 33 Ave.
Ocala, FL 34480
E-mail: ad@classical.net
URL: http://www.classical.net/music/guide/society/lssa/index.html
Contact: Robert M. Stumpf II, Pres.
Founded: 1983. **Members:** 1,982. **Membership Dues:** individual, $20 (annual) ● sustaining, $40 (annual). **Description:** Persons interested in classical music, particularly the work of Leopold Stokowski (1882-1977), American conductor who helped popularize classical music. Promotes study and appreciation of Stokowski's work. **Libraries:** **Type:** reference. **Holdings:** 2,000; audiovisuals, video recordings. **Subjects:** Stokowski. **Formerly:** (2005) Leopold Stokowski Society of America. **Publications:** *Maestrino*, semiannual. Newsletter. Presents articles on Stokowski's life and work. Reviews recordings and audio equipment. **Price:** included in membership dues. **Circulation:** 2,000. **Advertising:** accepted ● Also publishes annotated discography of Stokowski compositions; produces Annual recording of compositions by Stokowski.

9813 ■ Midwestern Gilbert and Sullivan Society (MGS)
c/o Sarah Cole, Sec.
613 W State St.
North Aurora, IL 60542-1538
Ph: (630)896-8860
Fax: (630)896-4422
E-mail: midwestgs@yahoo.com
Contact: Sarah Cole, Sec.
Founded: 1984. **Members:** 150. **Description:** Individuals interested in the works of Sir William Schwenck Gilbert (1836-1911) and Sir Arthur Seymour Sullivan (1842-1900), whose collaborative compositions include comic operas such as H.M.S. Pinafore, The Pirates of Penzance, and The Mikado. Promotes knowledge of Gilbert and Sullivan and encourages production of their works. Keeps members abreast of current productions and news relating to Gilbert and Sullivan. Conducts charitable activities; donates materials related to Gilbert and Sullivan to libraries. **Publications:** *Precious Nonsense*, quarterly. Newsletter. Contains new findings related to Gilbert and Sullivan and announcements of productions of their works. **Circulation:** 200. **Conventions/Meetings:** annual meeting.

9814 ■ Mozart Society of America
Univ. of Nevada
Dept. of Music
4505 S Maryland Pkwy.
Las Vegas, NV 89154-5025
Ph: (702)732-4391
Fax: (702)895-4239

E-mail: msa@nevada.edu
URL: http://www.unlv.edu/mozart
Contact: Isabelle Emerson, Pres.
Membership Dues: regular, $40 (annual) ● full-time student, emeritus, $25 (annual) ● sustaining, $80 (annual) ● patron, $200 (annual) ● life, $1,000. **Description:** Promotes studies and research pertaining to the life, works, historical context, and reception of Wolfgang Amadeus Mozart. Provides a forum for communication among scholars. Supports educational projects and offers assistance to graduate student researchers. **Publications:** Newsletter, semiannual. **Price:** included in membership dues. Alternate Formats: online.

9815 ■ Roger Sessions Society (RSS)

c/o Department of Music
Univ. of North Carolina Wilmington
601 S Coll. Rd.
Wilmington, NC 28403-5975
Ph: (910)962-3890
Fax: (910)962-7106
E-mail: salwenb@uncw.edu
URL: http://www.uncw.edu/music/sessionssociety
Contact: Dr. Barry D. Salwen, Exec. Dir.
Founded: 1988. **Membership Dues:** individual, $20 (annual) ● institution, $30 (annual). **Description:** Promotes the dissemination and performance of the works of American composer Roger Sessions (1896-1985). Provides information and reference, and sometimes hands-on assistance to individuals and groups interested in performing Sessions' music, obtaining scores and recordings, or learning more about this leading composer. **Publications:** Newsletter, periodic. Features events and articles covering the sessions. **Price:** included in membership dues. **Advertising:** accepted.

9816 ■ Schubert Society of the USA (SSUSA)

c/o Dr. Janet I. Wasserman, Founder/Exec. Dir.
752 W End Ave., No. 5H
New York, NY 10025-6231
Ph: (212)222-2015
Fax: (212)222-2015
E-mail: execdir@schubertsocietyusa.org
URL: http://www.schubertsocietyusa.org
Contact: Dr. Janet I. Wasserman, Founder/Exec. Dir.
Membership Dues: regular, $35 (annual) ● student, senior citizen, $20 (annual) ● sustaining, $50 (annual) ● institutional, patron, $125 (annual) ● life, $500. **Description:** Aims to advance and cultivate studies and research about the life, works, historical context and musical influence of Austrian composer Franz Peter Schubert. Offers assistance to scholars for research and related projects. Encourages exploration of new ideas concerning Schubert and his era. Provides a forum for communication among members. Serves as a central clearinghouse for information about Schubert materials in the USA. **Publications:** *ARPEGGIONE*. Journal. Contains scholarly articles, reviews, essays, forums, and working notes pertaining to Franz Schubert. ● *SSUSA Newsletter*, 3/year. Contains news and information about the society and its members. Alternate Formats: online.

9817 ■ Society of Composers, Inc. (SCI)

Box 450
New York, NY 10013-0450
E-mail: wells.7@osu.edu
URL: http://www.societyofcomposers.org
Contact: Thomas Wells, Pres.
Founded: 1966. **Members:** 1,200. **Membership Dues:** full, $50 (annual) ● joint/proxy, $65 (annual) ● senior/student/institutional/associate, $25 (annual) ● student chapter, $15 (annual) ● life, $950. **Staff:** 2. **Regional Groups:** 8. **Description:** Professional composers. Subjects of concern include: exchange of music and performers; the printing and recording of music; exchange of technical data and discoveries in the electronic and computer field as they relate to music and composition; coordination in fundraising. Cosponsors with Society of European Stage Authors and Composers the SCI/SESAC Student Composition Contest. **Formerly:** (1987) American Society of University Composers. **Publications:** *CD Series*, semiannual ● *Journal of Music Scores*, semiannual ● Newsletter, bimonthly. **Price:** $50.00. **Circulation:** 1,350. Alternate Formats: online. **Conventions/Meetings:** annual conference.

9818 ■ Songwriters of Wisconsin International (SOWI)

PO Box 1027
Neenah, WI 54957-1027
Ph: (920)725-5129
Fax: (920)720-0195
E-mail: sowi@new.rr.com
URL: http://www.songwritersofwisconsin.org
Contact: Tony Ansems, Pres.
Founded: 1983. **Members:** 175. **Membership Dues:** individual, $30 (annual). **State Groups:** 1. **Languages:** Dutch, English. **Description:** Songwriters. Promotes collective exploration of the craft of songwriting among members. Facilitates communication and exchange of information among members; sponsors educational programs. **Awards:** Songwriter of the Year. **Frequency:** annual. **Type:** recognition. **Publications:** Newsletter, quarterly. **Price:** included in membership dues. **Circulation:** 200. **Conventions/Meetings:** annual Songwriting Contest - competition ● monthly Songwriting Meeting - meeting and seminar.

9819 ■ Wilhelm Furtwangler Society of America (WFSA)

PO Box 620702
Woodside, CA 94062-0702
Contact: Dade Thieriot, Pres.
Founded: 1989. **Members:** 350. **Membership Dues:** regular, in U.S., $25 (annual) ● regular, outside U.S., $30 (annual). **Description:** Classical music enthusiasts. Promotes the music and art of German conductor Wilhelm Furtwangler (1886-1954). **Publications:** Newsletter, quarterly. Includes book reviews and information about newly released recordings; reports on association activities. **Price:** $30.00 in U.S.; $35.00 outside U.S. **Circulation:** 350.

9820 ■ Yrjo Kilpinen Society of North America (YKSNA)

c/o Paul Rowe
PO Box 2092
Madison, WI 53701-2092
E-mail: info@kilpinen.org
URL: http://www.kilpinen.org
Contact: Rolliana Scheckler, Pres.
Founded: 1999. **Multinational. Description:** Honors and cherishes the artistic memory of the Finnish composer Yrjo Kilpinen. Promotes the performance of the vocal literature of Kilpinen. Promotes the singing in original languages of Kilpinen repertoire with songs from Opus 100 and other songs and song cycles. Encourages and assists research, recording, and publication of lied music to promote the publicity of lied. **Publications:** *Audio Cassette Recording of the 64 Lyric Poems in Finnish*. Audiotape. **Price:** $8.50 ● Video. **Price:** $16.00.

Costumes

9821 ■ Costume Collection (CC)

601 W 26th St., 3rd Fl., Ste.325
New York, NY 10001
Ph: (212)989-5855
Fax: (212)206-0922
E-mail: costume@tdf.org
URL: http://www.tdf.org
Contact: Gregory A. Poplyk, Dir.
Founded: 1969. **Staff:** 7. **Description:** Serves as Project of the Theatre Development Fund; provides low-cost costume rental and related service to not-for-profit performing arts organizations, universities, schools, etc. Offers three fully equipped workrooms for rental for making costumes, a small research library and a collection of antique costumes available to designers for research and study. **Publications:** Newsletter, quarterly. Alternate Formats: online.

9822 ■ Costume Society of America (CSA)

203 Towne Centre Dr.
Hillsborough, NJ 08844
Ph: (908)359-1471
Free: (800)272-9447
Fax: (908)359-7619
E-mail: national.office@costumesocietyamerica.com
URL: http://www.costumesocietyamerica.com
Contact: Kaye Kittle Boyer, Exec. Dir.
Founded: 1973. **Members:** 1,600. **Membership Dues:** library, student (electronic publications), $45 (annual) ● individual, $75 (annual) ● sustaining, business/corporate, $150 (annual) ● non-profit institution, $115 (annual). **Staff:** 2. **Budget:** $175,000. **Regional Groups:** 7. **Multinational. Description:** Represents museum and historical society personnel; college/university faculty of costume history, retailing, material culture, apparel design, social-psychological aspects, economics; theatre/film fashion designers; conservators; costume and textile collectors/dealers; and re-enactors. Focuses on the scholarly study of all aspects of dress and appearance. Promotes the study of dress through education, research, preservation, and design. Supports scholarship and its dissemination through research papers and publications; collects and disseminates information on the preservation, interpretation, and exhibition of costumes; provides referrals for the identification and conservation of costumes, sponsors international study tours. **Awards:** Adele Filene Student Travel Award. **Frequency:** annual. **Type:** monetary. **Recipient:** for members currently enrolled as students to assist their travel to CSA national symposia ● College and University Collection Grant. **Frequency:** biennial. **Type:** monetary ● Costume Design Award. **Frequency:** biennial. **Type:** recognition ● Evelyn Welch Livingstone Award. **Frequency:** annual. **Type:** monetary. **Recipient:** for a member who undertakes research that furthers understanding of the history of fashion industry and/or fashion journalism in the United States ● Fellow. **Frequency:** annual. **Type:** recognition ● Grant to Support Costume in Small Museums. **Frequency:** annual. **Type:** monetary. **Recipient:** to small museums ● Millia Davenport Publication Award. **Frequency:** annual. **Type:** monetary. **Recipient:** to a published book or exhibition catalog that makes a significant contribution to the study of costume ● Richard Martin Award for Excellence in the Exhibition of Costume. **Frequency:** biennial. **Type:** recognition. **Recipient:** for outstanding achievement in the area of costume exhibition ● Scholars Roundtable. **Frequency:** annual. **Type:** recognition ● Stella Blum Research Grant. **Frequency:** annual. **Type:** grant. **Recipient:** for a student member working in the field of North American costume ● Travel Research Grants. **Frequency:** biennial. **Type:** monetary. **Recipient:** for non-student members to further an on-going research project. **Computer Services:** database ● mailing lists. **Telecommunication Services:** electronic bulletin board, for members only. **Publications:** *Costume Society of America—Membership Directory*, annual. **Price:** included in membership dues. **Advertising:** accepted ● *CSA E-News*, monthly. Newsletter. Alternate Formats: online ● *CSA News*, 3/year. Newsletter. Includes membership activities and calendar of events. **Price:** included in membership dues. **Circulation:** 1,600. **Advertising:** accepted ● *DRESS*, annual. Journal. Includes book reviews. **Price:** included in membership dues. ISSN: 0361-2112. **Conventions/Meetings:** annual symposium and meeting (exhibits) - always spring. 2009 May 27-31, Phoenix, AZ.

Crafts

9823 ■ Alliance for American Quilts (AAA)

PO Box 6521
Louisville, KY 40206
Ph: (502)897-3819
Fax: (502)897-3819
E-mail: info@quiltalliance.org
URL: http://www.quiltalliance.org
Contact: Shelly Zegart, Founding Dir.
Founded: 1993. **Membership Dues:** student, $35 (annual) ● friend, $50 (annual) ● family, $70 (annual)

● contributor, $125 (annual) ● patron, $250 (annual) ● associate, $1,000 (annual). **Description:** Documents and preserves the American quilt heritage. Collects rich stories that historic and contemporary quilts tell about the nation's diverse people and communities. Encourages people from the quilt world to find common ground and build collaborative ventures. **Computer Services:** Online services, quilt index. **Committees:** Development; National Support; Projects; Publicity. **Projects:** Boxers Under the Bed; Quilt Treasures; Quilters' SOS- Save our Stories.

9824 ■ American Arts and Crafts Alliance (AACA)
PO Box 250826
New York, NY 10025
Ph: (212)866-2239
Contact: Simon Gaon, Dir.
Founded: 1979. **Members:** 900. **Description:** Brings together craftspeople who exhibit their handmade goods at the alliance's six crafts festivals held in New York City. Promotes American craft-making.

9825 ■ American Association of Woodturners (AAW)
222 Landmark Ctr.
75 W 5th St.
St. Paul, MN 55102
Ph: (651)484-9094
Fax: (651)484-1724
E-mail: inquiries@woodturner.org
URL: http://woodturner.org
Contact: Larry Sommer, Exec. Dir.
Founded: 1986. **Members:** 13,000. **Membership Dues:** general (individual), $45 (annual) ● youth, $18 (annual) ● family, general in Canada and Mexico, $50 (annual) ● supporting individual/foreign, $100 (annual) ● benefactor, $500 (annual) ● patron (individual), $1,000 (annual) ● general (business/professional), business/professional (foreign), $70 (annual) ● supporting (business/professional), $250 (annual) ● benefactor (business/professional), $650 (annual) ● patron (business/professional), $1,500 (annual) ● general (overseas), $60 (annual). **Staff:** 7. **Local Groups:** 273. **Multinational. Description:** Amateur and professional woodturners, gallery owners, wood and equipment suppliers, and collectors. Provides educational and organizational leadership in the art of woodturning. **Libraries: Type:** open to the public. **Holdings:** photographs. **Awards: Type:** scholarship. **Computer Services:** database ● mailing lists. **Publications:** *AAW Resource Directory*, annual. Membership Directory. **Advertising:** accepted ● *American Woodturner*, quarterly. Journal. Features information, articles and other materials relating to woodturning. **Advertising:** accepted. **Conventions/Meetings:** annual symposium (exhibits).

9826 ■ American Bladesmith Society (ABS)
PO Box 1481
Cypress, TX 77410-1481
Ph: (281)225-9159
E-mail: info@americanbladesmith.com
URL: http://www.americanbladesmith.com
Contact: Joe Keeslar, Chm.
Founded: 1976. **Members:** 500. **Membership Dues:** regular, $60 (annual) ● associate/collector, $30 (annual) ● youth, $15 (annual). **Description:** Working bladesmiths (apprentice, journeymen, and master) dedicated to the preservation of hand-forged and art blades; associate members are collectors and other interested people. Encourages and promotes interest in the traditional blade; seeks to educate the public on the forged blade's quality and art value. Has established Bladesmith School in Washington, AR. Provides courses in basic bladesmithing and Damascus steel making, handle making, folding-knife making, and engraving. Holds lectures and demonstrations on forging, blade design, frontier bladesmithing, and blacksmith techniques. Bestows bladesmith ratings. **Publications:** *ABS Newsletter*, quarterly. **Price:** available to members only ● *American Bladesmith*, 3/year. Journal. **Advertising:** accepted. Alternate Formats: online ● *Membership List*, periodic. Membership Directory ● Also publishes booklet on ABS history. **Conventions/Meetings:** annual Knife Show, in conjunction with the Blade Super Show (exhibits) ● annual seminar (exhibits).

9827 ■ American Craft Council (ACC)
72 Spring St., 6th Fl.
New York, NY 10012-4019
Ph: (212)274-0630
Free: (800)836-3470
Fax: (212)274-0650
E-mail: council@craftcouncil.org
URL: http://www.craftcouncil.org
Contact: Carmine Branagan, Exec. Dir.
Founded: 1943. **Members:** 30,000. **Membership Dues:** regular, in U.S., $40 (annual) ● regular, outside U.S., $55 (annual) ● professional, $50 (annual). **Staff:** 21. **Budget:** $6,494,000. **Description:** Promotes understanding and appreciation of contemporary American craft. **Libraries: Type:** reference. **Holdings:** 10,000; books, periodicals, video recordings. **Subjects:** 20th century American craft. **Awards:** Aileen Osborn Webb Awards. **Frequency:** annual. **Type:** recognition. **Recipient:** for outstanding achievement in the craft field ● American Craft Council Fellow. **Frequency:** annual. **Type:** fellowship. **Recipient:** to an artist having outstanding ability in the craft field. **Computer Services:** database. **Telecommunication Services:** electronic mail, branagan@craftcouncil.org. **Formerly:** American Crafts Council; American Craftsmen's Council. **Publications:** *American Craft*, bimonthly. Magazine. Celebrates the excellence of contemporary craft, focusing on masterful achievements in the craft media. Emphasis is on American subject matter. **Price:** included in membership dues. ISSN: 0194-8008. **Circulation:** 43,000. **Advertising:** accepted. Alternate Formats: microform. Also Cited As: *Craft Horizons*.

9828 ■ American Quilt Study Group (AQSG)
1610 L St.
Lincoln, NE 68508-2509
Ph: (402)477-1181
Fax: (402)477-1183
E-mail: aqsg2@alltel.net
URL: http://www.h-net.org/~aqsg
Contact: Judy J. Brott Buss PhD, Exec. Dir.
Founded: 1980. **Members:** 1,000. **Membership Dues:** senior/student, $45 (annual) ● friend, $55 (annual) ● associate/guild, $100 (annual) ● benefactor, $250-$999 (annual) ● sponsor, $1,000-$1,999 (annual) ● patron, $2,000-$4,999 (annual) ● pacesetter, $5,000-$9,999 (annual) ● master's circle (minimum), $10,000 (annual). **Staff:** 2. **Budget:** $150,000. **Description:** Persons interested in the documenting aspects of quilts, textiles, quiltmaking, and quiltmakers. Promotes the development of a quilt-related research library for students of quilt history; encourages and sponsors research into quilts and quilting, conducts educational programs. **Libraries: Type:** reference. **Holdings:** 5,000; articles, books, periodicals. **Subjects:** quilts, quilt-related subjects, fiber arts, women's history. **Awards:** Lucy Hilty Award. **Frequency:** annual. **Type:** grant. **Recipient:** for research ● Meredith Scholar Award. **Frequency:** annual. **Type:** grant. **Recipient:** for research ● Seminar Scholarship. **Type:** scholarship. **Recipient:** to an individual who attends AQSG seminars. **Computer Services:** Mailing lists. **Publications:** *Blanket Statements*, quarterly. Newsletter. **Price:** included in membership dues ● *Collecting Stories*. Pamphlet. **Price:** $5.00 plus $2 shipping ● *Dating Antique Quilts*. Pamphlet. **Price:** $5.00 plus $2 shipping ● *In Your Care We Trust*. Pamphlet. **Price:** $5.00 plus $2 shipping ● *Quilt Documentation*. Pamphlet. **Price:** $5.00 plus $2 shipping ● *Tracing the Quiltmaker*. Pamphlet. **Price:** $5.00 plus $2 shipping ● *Uncoverings*, annual. Journal. Contains research papers on quilts and quiltmakers. **Price:** $20.00 plus $4 shipping (book rate for nonmembers); included in membership dues. ISSN: 0277-0628. **Advertising:** accepted ● Membership Directory, annual. **Conventions/Meetings:** annual seminar, includes presentation of research papers (exhibits).

9829 ■ Caricature Carvers of America (CCA)
PO Box 565
Derby, KS 67037
E-mail: vicotto@clearwire.net
URL: http://www.cca-carvers.org
Contact: Tom Brown, Pres.-Elect
Description: Promotes the art of caricature woodcarving. Raises awareness and appreciation of the art of caricature woodcarving within both the woodcarving community and the general public. Provides an environment that encourages growth in skill, creativity and excellence among members. **Publications:** *Carving the Caricature Carvers of America Circus*, periodic. Book ● *Carving the Full Moon Saloon*, periodic. Book ● *CCA Signature Collection*, periodic. Book.

9830 ■ Firearms Engravers Guild of America (FEGA)
1452 Ivanhoe Rd.
Ludington, MI 49431
Ph: (231)843-4895
E-mail: fegainfo@fega.com
URL: http://www.fega.com
Founded: 1981. **Membership Dues:** regular, $50 (annual) ● associate, $35 (annual) ● international, certified professional, $75 (annual). **Multinational. Description:** Provides opportunities for engravers to exchange ideas and knowledge. Assists in improving individual skills. Promotes firearms engraving as an art form. Raises public interest and appreciation of quality firearms engraving. **Awards:** Engravers Choice Award. **Frequency:** annual. **Type:** recognition. **Recipient:** to outstanding exhibiting members in the art of firearms engraving. **Computer Services:** Online services, message board. **Publications:** *Engraver*, quarterly. Magazine. Contains information about events, how-to's, photographs of engraving, guild activities and general engraving information. **Price:** included in membership dues. **Advertising:** accepted.

9831 ■ International Guild of Candle Artisans (IGCA)
1640 Garfield St.
Fremont, NE 68025
E-mail: contact@igca.net
URL: http://www.igca.net
Contact: Alice Marguardt, Ed.
Founded: 1961. **Members:** 800. **Membership Dues:** individual, $40 (annual) ● associate, $10 (annual). **Staff:** 2. **Description:** Persons and companies involved in candlemaking. Encourages the study of candlemaking and candle design. Fosters fellowship and exchange of ideas among members; seeks to raise and maintain standards of craftsmanship and design. Cooperates with agencies and individuals to increase participation in and appreciation of the art. Conducts demonstrations and regional workshops. **Awards: Type:** recognition. **Recipient:** for excellence at competitive exhibit. **Telecommunication Services:** electronic mail, president@igca.net. **Publications:** *The Candlelighter*, monthly. Newsletter. **Circulation:** 600 ● *Candlelighter Yearbook and Buyers' Guide*, annual, in January. **Conventions/Meetings:** annual convention (exhibits).

9832 ■ International Ivory Society (IIS)
c/o Robert Weisblut, Founder
11109 Nicholas Dr.
Wheaton, MD 20902
Contact: Robert Weisblut, Founder
Founded: 1996. **Members:** 165. **Staff:** 2. **Budget:** $3,000. **Description:** Individuals interested in ivory, scrimshaw, ivory carving, and related crafts. Promotes ivory carving; seeks to insure respect for laws governing international trade in ivory. Serves as a network linking members; conducts educational programs. **Libraries: Type:** reference; by appointment only. **Holdings:** 300; books, clippings, periodicals. **Subjects:** ivory, international trade regulations governing ivory sales, ivory carving, scrimshaw. **Publications:** *International Ivory Society Newsletter*, monthly. **Conventions/Meetings:** annual conference and convention ● monthly regional meeting.

9833 ■ International String Figure Association (ISFA)
PO Box 5134
Pasadena, CA 91117
Ph: (626)398-1057

Fax: (626)398-1057
E-mail: webweavers@isfa.org
URL: http://www.isfa.org/isfa.htm
Contact: Mark A. Sherman PhD, Acting Pres.

Founded: 1978. **Members:** 200. **Membership Dues:** individual in U.S., $25 (annual) ● overseas, $35 (annual). **Staff:** 5. **Budget:** $9,000. **Languages:** English, German, Japanese. **Multinational. Description:** Promotes the preservation and study of string figures or "cat's cradles" (designs woven on the hands with a loop of string). Conducts research of interest to anthropologists, folklorists, linguists, mathematicians, performance artists (mimes, storytellers), physical therapists, and educators. Encourages the invention of new figures. **Libraries: Type:** reference. **Holdings:** archival material, books, periodicals. **Subjects:** string figures. **Computer Services:** Bibliographic search ● database; comprehensive string figure bibliography. **Publications:** *Bulletin of the International String Figure Association*, annual. Journal. Features original material that advances understanding and enhances enjoyment of string figures. **Price:** included in membership dues; $15.00 /year for libraries. ISSN: 1076-7886. **Circulation:** 1,500 ● *ISFA News*, semiannual. Newsletter. **Price:** free for members. Alternate Formats: online ● *String Figure Magazine*, quarterly. **Price:** included in membership dues; $12.00 /year for libraries. ISSN: 1087-1527. **Conventions/Meetings:** annual general assembly and workshop.

9834 ■ Knifemakers' Guild (KG)

c/o Gil Hibben, Pres.
2914 Winters Ln.
La Grange, KY 40031
Ph: (502)222-1937
Fax: (502)222-2676
E-mail: gil_hibben@bellsouth.net
URL: http://www.knifemakersguild.com
Contact: Gil Hibben, Pres.

Founded: 1971. **Members:** 1,500. **Membership Dues:** voting, probationary, new applicant, $125 (annual) ● associate, $75 (annual) ● honorary, $25 (annual). **Description:** Knifemakers and interested others. Promotes knives and knifemakers; provides technical assistance to knifemakers; encourages ethical and professional business conduct. **Publications:** Brochure ● Membership Directory, periodic ● Newsletter, periodic. Alternate Formats: online ● Also publishes guide to handmade knives. **Conventions/Meetings:** annual show (exhibits).

9835 ■ Lock Museum of America (LMA)

230 Main St., Rte. 6
PO Box 104
Terryville, CT 06786-0104
Ph: (860)589-6359
Fax: (860)589-6359
E-mail: thomasnsc@aol.com
URL: http://www.lockmuseum.com
Contact: Thomas F. Hennessy Jr., Pres./Asst. Curator

Founded: 1971. **Members:** 500. **Membership Dues:** single, $20 (annual) ● family, $25 (annual) ● company, $100 (annual) ● individual (life), $200 ● company (life), $1,000. **Description:** Locksmiths, lock collectors, lock and key manufacturers, and builders. Seeks to preserve and exhibit the colonial American craft of lock, key, and security device making. Maintains hall of fame and museum. **Libraries: Type:** reference. **Holdings:** 1,000. **Publications:** *Newsletter and Historical Research Series*, quarterly. **Price:** free for members. **Circulation:** 500. **Conventions/Meetings:** annual Lock Collection Show - always October in Terryville, CT.

9836 ■ National Council on Education for the Ceramic Arts (NCECA)

77 Erie Village Sq., Ste.280
Erie, CO 80516-6996
Ph: (303)828-2811
Free: (866)266-2322
Fax: (303)828-0911
E-mail: office@nceca.net
URL: http://www.nceca.net
Contact: Robert Harrison, Pres.

Founded: 1967. **Members:** 3,700. **Membership Dues:** regular in U.S., $70 (annual) ● regular in Canada, $75 (annual) ● regular outside U.S. and Canada, $85 (annual) ● student in U.S., $40 (annual) ● student in Canada, $45 (annual) ● student outside U.S. and Canada, $55 (annual) ● institutional, $100 (annual) ● sustaining, $750 (annual) ● patron, $1,000 (annual). **Staff:** 5. **Description:** Educators, ceramic historians, museum curators, artists, potters, collectors, craft magazine editors, and craft center directors. Works to promote and improve ceramic art education through the exchange of information among artists, teachers, and individuals in the ceramic arts community. Gathers and disseminates information and ideas that are vital to the teacher, the studio artist, and individuals throughout the creative studies community. Presents new processes and information, debates current issues and concerns, and discusses new perspectives through lectures, panels, workshops, and seminars. Conducts ceramic and traveling exhibitions. Compiles statistics and develops archives. **Awards: Frequency:** annual. **Type:** fellowship ● NCECA Excellence in Teaching. **Type:** recognition. **Computer Services:** database, U.S. Ceramic Education Programs ● mailing lists, of members. **Programs:** International; National. **Publications:** Journal, annual. Covers spring conferences. ● Newsletter, quarterly. **Advertising:** accepted. Alternate Formats: online ● Membership Directory, annual. Lists the names, addresses, phone numbers and email addresses of current NCECA members. **Advertising:** accepted. **Conventions/Meetings:** annual conference (exhibits).

9837 ■ Pomegranate Guild of Judaic Needlework (PGJN)

c/o Randy Paul Heskins, Membership VP
PO Box 132
Fair Lawn, NJ 07410
Ph: (856)667-5609
E-mail: pomguild@verizon.net
URL: http://www.pomegranateguild.org
Contact: Sybil Bernstein, Co-Pres.

Founded: 1977. **Members:** 685. **Membership Dues:** individual, $36 (annual). **State Groups:** 20. **Description:** Nonsectarian group of individuals interested in Judaic needlework, which involves Jewish needle art techniques applied to traditional ritual objects. Purposes are to: disseminate information on Judaic needlework and weaving; promote high standards of artistry techniques, Judaic knowledge and its application, craftsmanship, and use of materials; stimulate creativity and originality; popularize and create modern Judaic art. Offers training courses in Judaic needlework; exhibits artists' works. Strives to keep the Judaic arts alive; to teach and therefore hand down the arts to the next generation. Seeks to educate communities by way of exhibits and workshops; provides networking for those seeking the skills and products of members. **Computer Services:** Online services, forum, member classifieds. **Telecommunication Services:** electronic mail, eberns@netreach.com. **Committees:** Education; Newsletter; Special Projects. **Publications:** *Paper Pomegranate Magazine*, quarterly. Includes articles, projects with charted designs, chapter news, and national news. **Price:** included in membership dues ● Newsletter. Includes local chapter/affiliations news. **Conventions/Meetings:** semiannual conference ● monthly meeting.

9838 ■ Potters for Peace (PFP)

PO Box 1043
Bisbee, AZ 85603
Ph: (520)432-4616
E-mail: peter@pottersforpeace.org
URL: http://www.pottersforpeace.org
Contact: Peter Chartrand, Dir.

Founded: 1986. **Membership Dues:** general, $25 (annual). **Languages:** English, Spanish. **Multinational. Description:** Represents the interests of potters concerned with peace and justice issues. Provides assistance to pottery groups and individuals. Seeks to build tolerance, understanding and cross-cultural relationships around the world. **Publications:** Newsletter, semiannual. Includes updates on recent and ongoing projects, events and other articles by PFP members. Alternate Formats: online.

9839 ■ Professional Knifemakers Association (PKA)

2905 N Montana Ave., Ste.30027
Helena, MT 59601
Ph: (618)753-2147
E-mail: craig@camererknives.com
URL: http://www.proknifemakers.com
Contact: Craig Camerer, Sec.-Treas.

Founded: 1993. **Membership Dues:** active, $100 (annual) ● associate, $60 (annual) ● support, $15 (annual). **Multinational. Description:** Aims to increase awareness of the art and science of hand-crafted knives. Advances excellence and professional standards in the art, science and industry of the hand-crafted knife. Provides educational opportunities for people who are interested in making custom knives.

9840 ■ Roycrofters-at-Large Association (RALA)

21 S Grove St., Ste.110
East Aurora, NY 14052
Ph: (716)655-7252 (716)649-4052
E-mail: info@ralaweb.com
URL: http://www.ralaweb.com
Contact: Dorothy Markert, Contact

Founded: 1976. **Members:** 290. **Membership Dues:** individual, $30 (annual) ● patron, $50 (annual). **Staff:** 1. **Description:** Individuals interested in the life and work of Elbert Hubbard (1856-1915). Works to preserve the Roycroft Campus and raise funds for modern-day craftsmen. Maintains speakers' bureau. Conducts arts and crafts exhibits. **Libraries: Type:** reference. **Holdings:** biographical archives. **Awards: Type:** scholarship. **Recipient:** for craftsmen. **Formerly:** (1991) Roycrofters-At-Large Association/Elbert Hubbard Foundation. **Publications:** *Roycroft Campus Chronicle*, quarterly. Newsletter. Includes information on current news, events and interviews on Roycroft. **Price:** included in membership dues. **Circulation:** 500. **Conventions/Meetings:** competition ● annual festival - always last weekend in June ● annual festival - always first weekend in December.

9841 ■ Society of North American Goldsmiths (SNAG)

540 Oak St., Ste.A
Eugene, OR 97401
Ph: (541)345-5689 (541)345-5691
Fax: (541)345-1123
E-mail: dsinger@snagmetalsmith.org
URL: http://www.snagmetalsmith.org
Contact: Dana Singer, Exec. Dir.

Founded: 1969. **Members:** 6,000. **Membership Dues:** silver, in North America, $29 (annual) ● silver (international), $41 (annual) ● gold, in North America, $69 (annual) ● gold (international), $85 (annual) ● gold (student in North America), $45 (annual) ● gold (international student), $58 (annual) ● platinum, in North America, $131 (biennial) ● platinum (international), $161 (biennial) ● platinum, in North America, $186 (triennial) ● platinum (international), $230 (triennial). **Staff:** 3. **Budget:** $600,000. **Multinational. Description:** Individuals working in any aspect of jewelry, design and metalsmithing. Supports education in the jewelry and metals field; promotes a supportive environment for all metalsmiths working with any metals on any scale; works to advance the awareness and appreciation of this work to the general public. **Computer Services:** Mailing lists. **Departments:** Circulation. **Divisions:** Audio-Visual; Book. **Publications:** *Metalsmith*, 5/year. Journal. Contains information on exhibitions. Includes profiles and interviews with artists, essays, technical papers, and book and exhibition catalog reviews. **Price:** $29.00 /year for nonmembers in North America; $41.00 /year for nonmembers outside North America; free for gold and platinum members or multi-year. ISSN: 0270-1146. **Circulation:** 12,000. **Advertising:** accepted. Also Cited As: *Goldsmith Journal* ● *SNAG News*, 5/year. Newsletter ● Membership Directory, annual. Lists the contact information of all individual and institutional members. **Price:** free for gold and platinum members. **Conventions/Meetings:** annual conference, with trade vendors (exhibits) - 2009 May 20-23, Philadelphia, PA; 2010 Mar. 10-13, Houston, TX.

9842 ■ United Chainsaw Carvers Guild (UCCG)
PO Box 255
Ridgway, PA 15853-0255
E-mail: gschieffer@wi.rr.com
URL: http://www.uccg.org
Contact: Jerry Schieffer, Pres.
Membership Dues: regular, in U.S., $20 (annual) ● international, $25 (annual). **Multinational. Description:** Promotes the art of chainsaw carving. Acts as a bridge for national and international cooperative programs and educational opportunities. Serves as a resource for international communication and cooperation among professional and novice chainsaw carvers. Enhances the enjoyment and skills of chainsaw carvers by sharing knowledge, experience and friendship. **Publications:** *The Chainsaw Letter*, bimonthly. Newsletter.

9843 ■ Wood Engravers Network (WEN)
c/o James Horton
3999 Waters Rd.
Ann Arbor, MI 48103
E-mail: jimhorton@sbcglobal.net
URL: http://www.woodengravers.net
Contact: James Horton, Contact
Founded: 1994. **Members:** 200. **Membership Dues:** regular, in U.S., $30 (annual) ● overseas, $35 (annual). **Multinational. Description:** Promotes printmaking and engraving upon end-grain wood. Pursues communication, encouragement and education in the historic and contemporary relief medium of wood engraving. **Libraries: Type:** lending. **Holdings:** audio recordings, books, video recordings. **Subjects:** wood engraving. **Computer Services:** Information services, wood engraving resources ● mailing lists. **Publications:** *Block and Burin*, biennial. Newsletter. Features articles, events, news and announcements.

Croatian

9844 ■ CFU Junior Cultural Federation (CFUJCF)
c/o Croatian Fraternal Union
100 Delaney Dr.
Pittsburgh, PA 15235
Ph: (412)843-0380
Fax: (412)823-1594
E-mail: cfuofa@usaor.net
URL: http://www.croatianfraternalunion.org
Contact: Joan Kutz, Pres.
Founded: 1966. **Description:** Promotes Croatian culture, especially music and the use of the tamburitza. **Affiliated With:** Croatian Fraternal Union of America. **Publications:** *Junior Magazine*, bimonthly ● *Zajednicar*, weekly. Newsletter. Alternate Formats: online. **Conventions/Meetings:** annual festival - 4th weekend of July.

Cuban

9845 ■ Center for Cuban Studies/Cuban Art Space (CCS)
124 W 23rd St.
New York, NY 10011
Ph: (212)242-0559
Fax: (212)242-1937
E-mail: curators@cubanartspace.net
URL: http://www.cubanartspace.net
Contact: Sandra Levinson, Exec. Dir.
Founded: 1972. **Members:** 2,000. **Membership Dues:** individual, $60 (annual) ● foreign/institutional, $70 (annual) ● supporting, $100 (annual) ● sustaining, $150-$250 (annual) ● student/senior, $40 (annual). **Staff:** 5. **Budget:** $500,000. **Description:** Individuals and institutions organized to provide resource materials on Cuba to educational and cultural institutions. Sponsors film showings, lectures, and seminars; organizes tours of Cuba. Maintains an art collection with photographic archives, paintings, drawings, ceramics, and posters; sponsors art exhibits. **Libraries: Type:** reference. **Holdings:** 3,000; artwork, books, periodicals, video recordings. **Subjects:** post 1959 period. **Additional Websites:** http://www.cubaupdate.org. **Telecommunication Services:** electronic mail, cubanctr@igc.org ● electronic mail, slevinson@cubanartspace.net. **Formerly:** (2002) Center for Cuban Studies. **Publications:** *Bilingual Books and Document Series*, periodic. Journal. **Price:** $35.00/year. **Advertising:** accepted ● Pamphlets. Alternate Formats: online. **Conventions/Meetings:** weekly Havana Wednesdays - lecture, film showings and lectures.

Cultural Centers

9846 ■ American Community Cultural Center Association (ACCCA)
149 Cannongate III
Nashua, NH 03063-1953
Ph: (603)886-2748 (603)886-7944
Fax: (603)886-7944
E-mail: mjanz@ix.netcom.com
Contact: Milli Janz, Exec. Dir.
Founded: 1978. **Description:** Encourages people in all communities to develop cultural centers for the purpose of presenting cultural possibilities for everyone, regardless of economic status or geographic location; promotes the idea that cultural activities can be accomplished without spending large sums of money. Offers programs and courses on history of culture for schools, libraries, art galleries, and institutions including: An Evening With George Sand 19th Century in Words and Music; Culture Without Pain - European History Told in Words, Music, and Art; Our Natural Earth-Touch-and-Tell - An Earth Science Exhibition. Offers children's services; maintains speakers' bureau; operates placement service. Maintains Theater Arts Group in Nashua, NH. Sponsors training and scholarship programs. **Libraries: Type:** reference. **Subjects:** the culture spot. **Committees:** Education; International; Theater. **Publications:** *The Culture Spot*. Book ● *Culture Without Pain or Money*. Book. **Conventions/Meetings:** periodic competition ● annual convention and symposium (exhibits).

9847 ■ Ethnic Cultural Preservation Council (ECPC)
6500 S Pulaski Rd.
Chicago, IL 60629
Ph: (773)582-5143
Fax: (773)582-5133
Contact: Stanley Balzekas Jr., Dir.
Founded: 1977. **Members:** 100. **Membership Dues:** regular, $25 (annual). **Staff:** 4. **Budget:** $10,000. **Languages:** English, Lithuanian, Polish, Russian. **Description:** Membership includes North American ethnic museums, other museums, historical societies, libraries, archives, fraternal organizations, universities, university libraries, and cultural centers. Functions as vehicle for other ethnic and non-ethnic groups to become viable art and education centers in their communities; aids in the exchange of ideas and helps to facilitate development of arts and humanities programs in other institutions. Provides information on grants; disseminates information on ethnic activities to other individuals and institutions. Offers referrals to information on artists, ethnic groups, and institutions. Sponsors exhibits. Operates on a national level, with primary concentration in Illinois, Indiana, Wisconsin, and Michigan. **Libraries: Type:** reference. **Holdings:** 1,000. **Subjects:** folk art. **Conventions/Meetings:** seminar ● workshop, cultural and artistic.

Cultural Exchange

9848 ■ American Telugu Association (ATA)
PO Box 4496
Naperville, IL 60567
Ph: (630)783-2250
Fax: (630)783-2251
E-mail: info@ataworld.org
URL: http://www.ataworld.org
Contact: Mohan Mallam, Pres.
Founded: 1990. **Membership Dues:** grand patron, $5,000 ● patron, $1,000 ● life, $100. **Description:** Addresses the interests and preserves the heritage of people of Telugu origin in North America. Assists and promotes literary, cultural, educational, religious, social, economic, health and community activities of people of Telugu origin. **Telecommunication Services:** electronic mail, drmallam@aol.com. **Publications:** *America Bharathi*, quarterly. Magazine. **Advertising:** accepted ● Membership Directory, biennial. **Advertising:** accepted.

9849 ■ Butimar Productions
PO Box 609
Menlo Park, CA 94026-0609
Ph: (650)327-7908
Fax: (650)322-1359
E-mail: info@butimarproductions.org
URL: http://www.butimarproductions.org
Contact: Marjaneh Moghimi, Founder/Exec. Dir.
Description: Represents the interests of individuals dedicated to the preservation of the artistic and cultural traditions of the East. Seeks to promote cultural diversity through the production of documentary films, musical recordings, performances, presentations of visual art, translations of literary works and the organization of intercultural activities.

9850 ■ Cultural Arts in Progress (CAPS)
1250 Dolington Rd.
Yardley, PA 19067
Ph: (215)493-3124
E-mail: groya@capsart.org
Contact: Cynthia Groya, Founder
Multinational. Description: Children, adults, students, and teachers. Provides students with presentations into worldly cultures through art.

9851 ■ Friends of Malawi (FOM)
c/o Lance Cole, Treas.
7940 SW 11th
Portland, OR 97219
E-mail: questions@friendsofmalawi.org
URL: http://www.friendsofmalawi.org
Contact: John Staub, Pres.
Founded: 1987. **Membership Dues:** supporting, $15 (annual) ● life, $1,000. **Multinational. Description:** Seeks to initiate and implement programs, activities and publications related to Malawi. Supports projects and organizations in Malawi in the fields of education, health/human services, agriculture, environment, small business development and others as appropriate. Promotes cultural and commercial relations between the people of Malawi and the United States. **Telecommunication Services:** electronic mail, president@friendsofmalawi.org.

9852 ■ Global Routes
1 Short St.
Northampton, MA 01060
Ph: (413)585-8895
Fax: (413)585-8810
E-mail: mail@globalroutes.org
URL: http://www.globalroutes.org
Contact: Kenneth Hahn, Co-Exec. Dir.
Multinational. Description: Supports volunteerism to encourage global community building. **Awards: Type:** scholarship. **Funds:** Diversity. **Programs:** College-level Internship. **Projects:** Belize; China; Costa Rica; Dominican Republic; Ecuador; Ghana.

9853 ■ Tamizdat
PO Box 20618
New York, NY 10009
Ph: (212)260-8444
Fax: (413)513-1157
E-mail: matthew@tamizdat.org
URL: http://www.tamizdat.org
Contact: Heather Mount, Pres.
Multinational. Description: Fosters the free exchange of information and ideas between artists and

audiences worldwide. Works to build international communities by bridging the cultural and economic gaps that separate American and Western Europe from Central and Eastern Europe. Facilitates the cultural cross-pollination between artists, music industry personnel and audiences from around the world.

9854 ■ World Association for Vedic Studies (WAVES)
c/o Prof. BhuDev Sharma, Pres.
Clark Atlanta Univ., CAU Box 764
223 James P. Brawley Dr. SW
Atlanta, GA 30314
Ph: (404)880-6912 (404)248-9494
E-mail: bsharma@cau.edu
URL: http://www.umassd.edu/indic/waves
Contact: Prof. BhuDev Sharma, Pres.
Founded: 1996. **Membership Dues:** ordinary, $50 (annual) ● life, $500. **Multinational. Description:** Promotes Vedic and ancient Indian studies in all its forms. Conducts multidisciplinary activities for research and study of Vedic and ancient Indian traditions. Encourages research in developing all aspects of Vedic and ancient Indian traditions. **Telecommunication Services:** electronic mail, sharma-waves@yahoo.co.in. **Publications:** Journals ● Proceedings.

9855 ■ World Council of Elders (WCOE)
PO Box 7915
Boulder, CO 80306
Ph: (303)444-9263
Free: (877)750-4162
E-mail: wcoe4peace@earthlink.net
URL: http://www.worldcouncilofelders.org
Founded: 2000. **Multinational. Description:** Aims to preserve, share, and integrate traditional indigenous wisdom with modern cultures toward worldwide healing, peace, and sustainable living for future generations. Facilitates the gathering of the world's indigenous wisdom-keepers.

Cultural Resources

9856 ■ Alliance of National Heritage Areas (ANHA)
221 Essex St., Ste.41
Salem, MA 01970
Ph: (202)528-7549
Free: (866)546-6152
E-mail: anha.cosgrove@adelphia.net
URL: http://www.nationalheritageareas.com
Contact: John W. Cosgrove, Exec. Dir.
Membership Dues: full, $3,500 (annual) ● associate, $1,500 (annual) ● partner, $500 (annual) ● individual, $100 (annual). **Description:** Promotes the heritage development movement in America. Encourages the formation of local, private, state, and federal partnerships in the field of heritage development. Develops educational conferences, programs, and workshops concerning heritage development. **Conventions/Meetings:** biennial International Heritage Development Conference.

9857 ■ Association for Cultural Evolution (ACE)
PO Box 2382
Mill Valley, CA 94942
Ph: (415)409-3220
E-mail: info@ace.to
URL: http://www.ace.to/new
Contact: Faustin Bray, Event Coor.
Description: Gathers information for education, entertainment and service to the unfolding of the emerging planetary community of individuals. Documents and archives significant contributions toward mental and physical well-being, while popularizing the ecological, globally pan cultural, mobility enhancing, interdisciplinary, futuristic, links between arts and sciences that foster human compassion, generosity and creativity. Publishes and disseminates materials of association's collection, articles, and other relevant collections. Provides an inclusive, interdisciplinary forum and philosophical meeting ground for state-of-the-arts technology and life-asart integration. **Libraries: Type:** lending. **Holdings:** video recordings. **Telecommunication Services:** electronic mail, faustin@ace.to. **Publications:** *Bits and Pieces—from Richard's Life and Times*. Audiotape. Includes Richard Feynman lectures. ● *Computers From The Inside Out*. Audiotape. Includes lectures of Richard Feynman. ● *Computers From The Inside Out*. Video ● *Idiosyncratic Thinking Workshop*. Audiotape ● *Idiosyncratic Thinking Workshop*. Video ● *Last Journey of a Genius and No Ordinary Genius*. Video ● *No Ordinary Genius: The Complete Illustrated Feynman*. Book ● *The Pleasure of Finding Things Out and Fun To Imagine*. Video. Includes science stories. ● *Quantum Mechanical View of Reality: Workshop at Esalen*. Audiotape ● *Quantum Mechanical View of Reality: Workshop at Esalen*. Video ● *Tiny Machines - The Feynman Lecture on Nanotechnology*. Video. **Conventions/Meetings:** conference.

9858 ■ National Initiative for a Networked Cultural Heritage (NINCH)
21 Dupont Cir., NW
Washington, DC 20036
Ph: (202)296-5346
Fax: (202)872-0886
E-mail: ninch@ninch.org
URL: http://www.ninch.org
Contact: David Green, Exec. Dir.
Founded: 1993. **Membership Dues:** smaller organization level, $500 (annual) ● medium-sized organization level, $2,000 (annual) ● larger organization level, corporate friend, $5,000 (annual) ● corporate sponsor, $10,000 (annual). **Description:** Assures leadership from the arts and humanities community in the rapidly evolving digital world. Reiterates the role of the cultural community in modern society. Creates a forum for information exchange for an integrated and accessible body of cultural material. Provides a framework for the development of programs, projects and partnerships that benefit the cultural community. **Publications:** *NINCH Guide to Good Practice in the Digital Representation and Management of Cultural Heritage Materials*. Book. Contains methods and techniques for all sectors in the cultural community who are digitizing and networking cultural resources. Alternate Formats: online.

9859 ■ Wordcraft Circle of Native Writers and Storytellers (WC)
2801 Cabernet St. SW
Albuquerque, NM 87121
Ph: (505)259-3682
E-mail: nativerealities@comcast.net
URL: http://www.wordcraftcircle.org
Contact: Lee Francis IV, Natl. Dir.
Founded: 1993. **Membership Dues:** regular (Native and non-Native), $40 (annual) ● student, elder (Native and non-Native), $25 (annual) ● individual (publisher/literary agent/publicist), $50 (annual) ● organization (library/educational institution), $75 (annual) ● sponsor, $100 (annual). **Multinational. Description:** Develops and maintains on-going formal and informal relations among Indigenous Native American, Alaska Native, Native Hawaii'an, First Nations of Canada and Indigenous People of Mexico, Central and South America. Seeks to bring the oral storytelling and written traditions of Indigenous Native literature to students at all educational levels. Promotes the emphasis of Indigenous Native traditions through the writings and story-tellings by beginning, emerging and established Native and non-Native writers and storytellers. **Awards:** Intern of the Year. **Frequency:** annual. **Type:** recognition. **Recipient:** for commitment and contribution to the organization's vision ● Mentor of the Year. **Frequency:** annual. **Type:** recognition. **Recipient:** for individual who has worked zealously to help younger writers ● Publisher of the Year. **Frequency:** annual. **Type:** recognition. **Recipient:** for publisher who has demonstrated commitment and contribution to the organization's vision ● Wordcrafter of the Year. **Frequency:** annual. **Type:** recognition. **Recipient:** to a writer who has demonstrated commitment and contribution to the organization's vision ● Writer of the Year. **Frequency:** annual. **Type:** recognition. **Recipient:** to a writer in a specific category. **Projects:** Previews and Reviews; STaR. **Publications:** *Native Realities*. Journal. Alternate Formats: online.

Czech

9860 ■ Czechoslovak Society of Arts and Sciences (SVU)
c/o Dr. Karel Raska, Jr., Pres.
254 Easton Ave.
New Brunswick, NJ 08901
Ph: (732)745-8504 (202)396-8108
Fax: (732)828-3858
E-mail: kraska@saintpetersuh.com
URL: http://www.svu2000.org
Contact: Dr. Karel Raska Jr., Pres.
Founded: 1958. **Members:** 2,300. **Membership Dues:** student, $5 (annual) ● individual (in Czech Republic and Slovakia), $10 (annual) ● individual (additional $5 for spouse), $35 (annual) ● institution, $100 (annual). **Budget:** $60,000. **Regional Groups:** 20. **Multinational. Description:** College professors, writers, artists, and scientists interested in Czech or Slovak matters. Activities are conducted in cultural, educational, literary, artistic, and scientific fields through lectures, concerts, and exhibitions. **Libraries: Type:** reference. **Holdings:** archival material, books, periodicals. **Subjects:** arts, sciences. **Awards:** Presidential Citations. **Frequency:** annual. **Type:** recognition. **Recipient:** for contributions to the Czechoslovak Society of Arts and Sciences ● Stephen Fiala Cultural Heritage Award. **Frequency:** annual. **Type:** recognition. **Recipient:** for contributions toward preserving Czech and/or Slovak heritage abroad ● Student Awards. **Frequency:** annual. **Type:** recognition. **Recipient:** for best undergraduate or graduate paper dealing with some aspect of Czech or Slovak culture ● SVU Elias Human Tolerance Award. **Frequency:** annual. **Type:** recognition. **Recipient:** for an individual whose life and work symbolize the living value of human tolerance. **Also Known As:** Spolecnost pro Vedy a Umeni. **Formerly:** (1979) Czechoslovak Society of Arts and Sciences in America. **Publications:** *Educators With Czechoslovak Roots* ● *KOSMAS*, semiannual. Journal ● *Zpravy SVU*, bimonthly ● Membership Directory, periodic ● Books ● Bulletin, quarterly ● Newsletter, bimonthly. **Price:** free ● Monographs. **Conventions/Meetings:** biennial congress (exhibits) ● annual general assembly.

9861 ■ International Association of Teachers of Czech (IATC-NAATC)
c/o Prof. Hana Pichova, Exec. Off.
Univ. of Texas
PO Box 7217
Austin, TX 78713
E-mail: n.bermel@sheffield.ac.uk
URL: http://www.language.brown.edu/iatc/index.html
Contact: Prof. Hana Pichova, Exec. Off.
Founded: 1991. **Members:** 200. **Membership Dues:** regular, $20 (annual) ● student, $8 (annual) ● institutional, $75 (annual). **Multinational. Description:** Promotes study of the Czech language. Facilitates contacts among teachers of Czech in North America. Encourages research in language learning pedagogy. Publishes a newsletter to serve as a forum for the exchange of ideas and information. Coordinates teaching programs of the Czech language among North American institutions. Seeks contacts and affiliations with Czech academic institutions. Raises funds for scholarships and teaching programs. **Computer Services:** Mailing lists, of members. **Affiliated With:** American Association of Teachers of Slavic and East European Languages. **Formerly:** (2002) North American Association of Teachers of Czech. **Publications:** *Czech Language News*, semiannual. Newsletter. Serves as a forum for the exchange of ideas. ISSN: 1085-2950. **Advertising:** accepted. Alternate Formats: online ● Report. Alternate Formats: online. **Conventions/Meetings:** semiannual meeting, scholarly panels at the National

Meeting of the American Association of Teachers of Slavic and East European Languages.

Dance

9862 ■ American Ballet Competition (ABC)
c/o Dance Affiliates
4701 Bath St., No. 46
Philadelphia, PA 19137-2229
Ph: (215)636-9000
Fax: (215)672-2912
E-mail: info@danceaffiliates.org
URL: http://www.dancecelebration.org
Contact: F. Randolph Swartz, Artistic Dir.

Founded: 1979. **Members:** 40. **Staff:** 4. **Budget:** $750,000. **Regional Groups:** 40. **Description:** Selects and prepares the U.S. team for participation in the annual International Ballet Competition (the "Olympics of Dance"). Works to establish the U.S. as a major force in ballet; to stimulate interest in international competitions and festivals; to encourage young American dancers to strive for world-class excellence; and to build an ongoing program to finance and support further international competitions. Raises funds from private and corporate sources; secures federal grants and sells promotional items. Sponsors trips to observe performing arts in other countries. **Awards: Type:** monetary. **Recipient:** for qualified dancers in international competition. **Telecommunication Services:** electronic mail, randy@danceaffiliates.org. **Committees:** National Selection. **Publications:** Brochures ● Newsletter, periodic. **Conventions/Meetings:** annual International Competition - meeting.

9863 ■ American Bop Association (ABA)
c/o Jim Laux, Pres.
125 Red River Dr.
Sherwood, AR 72120
Ph: (501)834-8609
E-mail: jimlaux@att.net
URL: http://www.americanbopassociation.com
Contact: Jim Laux, Pres.

Description: Promotes and preserves bop, swing, shag and jitterbug dance styles and the heritage of those styles of music. Strives to enhance communication and promotional coordination of activities throughout the membership. **Awards:** A.B.A. Hall of Fame. **Frequency:** periodic. **Type:** recognition. **Recipient:** to individuals and couples who have demonstrated exceptional dancing skills or exceptional dedication to the dance community served by the association. **Publications:** *ABA News*, quarterly. Newsletter. Provides member clubs with dance news and communication. **Price:** free. Alternate Formats: online.

9864 ■ American College Dance Festival Association (ACDFA)
225 Rockville Pike, Ste.L10-B
Rockville, MD 20850
Ph: (301)251-1848
Fax: (301)762-7599
E-mail: acdfa@verizon.net
URL: http://www.acdfa.org
Contact: Diane DeFries, Exec. Dir.

Founded: 1973. **Members:** 300. **Membership Dues:** individual, $50 (annual) ● institution ($300 after October 31st), $250 (biennial) ● life, $500. **Staff:** 1. **Budget:** $80,000. **Regional Groups:** 9. **Description:** Colleges, universities, individuals, and dance organizations. Works to provide regional and national visibility for dance works produced in colleges and universities and to recognize excellence in performance and choreography. Offers master classes and lectures. **Computer Services:** Mailing lists, college and university dance programs. **Publications:** *ACDFA Annual Report*, annual. Provides information on college dance festivals throughout the United States. **Price:** available to members only. **Conventions/Meetings:** annual festival, regional college dance ● biennial festival, national college dance ● workshop.

9865 ■ American Dance Festival (ADF)
Box 90772
Durham, NC 27708-0772
Ph: (919)684-6402 (212)586-1925
Fax: (919)684-5459
E-mail: adf@americandancefestival.org
URL: http://americandancefestival.org

Founded: 1934. **Members:** 100. **Staff:** 12. **Budget:** $2,500,000. **Description:** A modern dance producing and service organization for modern dancers and modern dance choreographers. Seeks to create greater public awareness of the field of modern dance and its particular needs. Sponsors American and foreign artists performing in the U.S. Conducts choreography projects and national television productions. Maintains six-week school, young dancers' school, and professional workshops. Maintains speakers' bureau. Collaborates with France, the People's Republic of China, Japan, and others. Operates the National Choreography Project, which includes the Young Choreographers and Composers in Residence Program. The program provides the opportunity for participants to create new works together and present them before a large audience. **Libraries: Type:** reference. **Holdings:** archival material, books, photographs, video recordings. **Subjects:** modern dance. **Awards:** National Competitive Scholarship. **Frequency:** annual. **Type:** scholarship. **Recipient:** for students with technical ability, creative potential, and financial need ● **Type:** recognition. **Recipient;** to a visual artist ● Samuel H. Scripps American Dance Festival Award. **Frequency:** annual. **Type:** recognition. **Recipient:** for lifetime achievement in modern dance ● Scripps/ADF Humphrey-Weidman-Limon Fellowship for Choreography. **Frequency:** annual. **Type:** fellowship. **Recipient:** for young choreographers. **Formerly:** (1989) American Dance Festival; (1998) Association for the American Dance Festival. **Publications:** *African American Genius in Modern Dance* ● *Black Tradition in American Modern Dance*. **Conventions/Meetings:** annual festival, modern dance performance festival - always summer ● workshop.

9866 ■ American Dance Guild (ADG)
PO Box 2006
Lenox Hill Sta.
New York, NY 10021
Ph: (212)932-2789
E-mail: info@americandanceguild.org
URL: http://www.americandanceguild.org
Contact: Ms. Deborah Mauldin, Pres.

Founded: 1956. **Members:** 400. **Membership Dues:** student, retired, $25 (annual) ● regular, $50 (annual) ● supporter, $100 (annual) ● sponsor, $250 (annual) ● patron, $500 (annual) ● life, $600 ● organization/institution (based on annual budget), $80-$125 (annual). **Description:** Serves the dance professional by providing: a networking system between dance artists and dance educators; an informed voice on behalf of the dance field to governmental, educational and corporate institutions and the general public; international dance festivals, conferences and dance film festivals; educational publications and videos; the ADG Fannie Weiss Scholarship; the ADG Harkness Resource for Dance Study. **Libraries: Type:** open to the public. **Holdings:** 300; books, periodicals, video recordings. **Subjects:** dance. **Awards:** Award of Artistry. **Frequency:** annual. **Type:** scholarship ● Fannie Weiss Student Scholarship. **Frequency:** annual. **Type:** scholarship. **Recipient:** for dancers and students between ages 16 to 25 ● **Frequency:** annual. **Type:** recognition. **Recipient:** for outstanding achievement in dance and/or outstanding service in the field of dance. **Computer Services:** Online services, members community website with the ability to web chat, blog, post events, resumes and jobs. **Telecommunication Services:** electronic mail, americandanceguild@hotmail.com. **Formerly:** (1956) Dance Teachers Guild; (1966) National Dance Teachers Guild; (1968) National Dance Guild. **Publications:** *ADG Newsletter*, semiannual. Contains ADG notices and articles; announcements, award news, conference notes, member news, scholarship information, and dance reviews. **Price:** free to conference attendees. **Circulation:** 500. **Advertising:** accepted ● *American Dance*, semiannual. Magazine. Deals with contemporary issues in the field. **Price:** included in membership dues. **Advertising:** accepted ● *Souvenir Journal*, annual. Contains program of annual conference. **Price:** free to conference attendees. **Circulation:** 700. **Advertising:** accepted ● Videos ● Books. **Conventions/Meetings:** annual conference (exhibits) - usually June ● festival, film festival, presents the creative work of dance artists ● seminar ● workshop.

9867 ■ Art Resources in Collaboration (ARC)
123 W 18th St., 7th Fl.
New York, NY 10011-4127
Ph: (212)206-6492
Fax: (212)627-2838
E-mail: info@eyeondance.org
URL: http://www.eyeondance.org
Contact: Ms. Celia Ipiotis, Dir.

Founded: 1975. **Staff:** 3. **Description:** Produces dance videotapes ranging from collaborations with choreographers to introductory segments on videotaping techniques and the art of Baroque dancing. Produces Eye on Dance, aired on Public Broadcasting Service stations that seek to explore topics in dance such as: history; health problems of dancers; post-career options; relationships between the arts, business, and politics; Third World dance; the growing dance and choreography industry of music-video performance. Conducts research for its productions; holds lectures at universities. Provides information on video and the arts. **Libraries: Type:** reference. **Holdings:** 324; video recordings. **Subjects:** dance. **Also Known As:** ARC Videodance. **Conventions/Meetings:** periodic conference ● workshop.

9868 ■ Ballet Theatre Foundation (BTF)
890 Broadway
New York, NY 10003-1278
Ph: (212)477-3030
Fax: (212)254-5938
E-mail: ltheriault@abt.org
URL: http://www.abt.org
Contact: Rachel S. Moore, Exec. Dir.

Founded: 1940. **Members:** 5,500. **Membership Dues:** friend, $75 (annual) ● golden circle, $1,000 (annual). **Staff:** 130. **Budget:** $25,000,000. **Description:** Parent organization of American Ballet Theatre. Offers special events, open rehearsals, priority ticket buying, and telephone reservations for members. ABT consists of 75 dancers, conducts an annual national tour, has toured overseas, and maintains a repertoire of more than 100 classic, contemporary, humorous, serious, story, and abstract ballets. **Convention/Meeting:** none. **Also Known As:** American Ballet Theatre. **Publications:** *On Pointe*, semiannual. Newsletter. Features company news. **Price:** included in membership dues. **Circulation:** 6,000. **Advertising:** accepted ● *Souvenir*, annual. Book. Includes photos of dancers and company information. **Price:** $15.00. **Advertising:** accepted.

9869 ■ Callerlab - International Association of Square Dance Callers
467 Forrest Ave., Ste.118
Cocoa, FL 32922
Ph: (321)639-0039
Fax: (321)639-0851
E-mail: info@callerlab.org
URL: http://www.callerlab.org
Contact: Jerry Reed, Exec. Dir.

Founded: 1974. **Members:** 2,000. **Membership Dues:** individual, $95 (annual). **Staff:** 4. **Budget:** $500,000. **Description:** Square dance callers in 15 countries who call on an average of at least once a week. Promotes and perpetuates square dancing and aims to improve the quality of square dance callers throughout the world. Seeks to: standardize dance figures and terms; select new movements; set guidelines for public relations and construction of square dance halls. Provides guidance to outstanding leaders in the field. Conducts research on ways to teach and publicize square dancing and has developed a caller training curriculum and a program of caller school accreditation. Has established Foundation for the Promotion and Preservation of

Square Dancing. Maintains speakers' bureau. **Awards:** George White Memorial Scholarship. **Frequency:** annual. **Type:** scholarship. **Recipient:** for callers who have been calling for more than three years at the time of application ● Heyman Scholarship. **Frequency:** annual. **Type:** scholarship. **Recipient:** for a caller who has a background of calling or dancing and has indicated a desire to learn, to call or a desire to improve his calling ● Jerry Schatzer Scholarship. **Frequency:** annual. **Type:** scholarship. **Recipient:** for any person interested in learning to call or in improving calling skills ● Tex Hencerling Memorial Scholarship. **Frequency:** annual. **Type:** scholarship. **Recipient:** for callers who are from overseas and who have been calling for more than five years at the time of application. **Additional Websites:** http://www.callerlabfoundation.org. **Committees:** Planning and Research; Programming and Coordinating; Special Interest; Ways and Means. **Publications:** *Choreographic Guidelines*, bimonthly. Newsletter ● *The Community Dance Program*. Journal. Contains information and dances relative to the CDP. ● *Curriculum Guidelines for Caller Training*. Manual. Serves as a training manual. ● *Direction*, bimonthly. Newsletter ● *Selection of Experimental Figures and Basics*, quarterly ● *Square Dance Building Guidelines* ● *Standard Mainstream Applications* ● *Standard Plus Applications* ● *Technical Supplement to Curriculum Guidelines*. **Conventions/Meetings:** annual convention (exhibits) - always March or April.

9870 ■ Committee for Handicapable Dancers (CHD)
9354 Johnson Rd.
Mobile, AL 36695
Ph: (251)633-8212
Fax: (251)633-8212
E-mail: ush2@ushandicapable.org
URL: http://www.usda.org/handicap.htm
Contact: Dean Emery, Pres./Founder
Founded: 1984. **Members:** 225. **Description:** Square dance clubs; square dance callers specializing in calling for "handicapable" dancers. Promotes square dancing for individuals with physical and/or mental disabilities. Acts as a network and referral system of local square dance organizations for the disabled and for individuals who are interested in starting square dancing activity for disabled people. Handicapable clubs are located both in the United States and several foreign countries. **Publications:** Directory, periodic. Lists local clubs for disabled dancers. ● Newsletter, periodic. **Conventions/Meetings:** biennial Square Dance Convention.

9871 ■ Congress on Research in Dance (CORD)
State Univ. of New York
Dept. of Dance
350 New Campus Dr.
Brockport, NY 14420
Ph: (585)395-2590
Fax: (585)395-5413
E-mail: gcarlson@brockport.edu
URL: http://www.cordance.org
Contact: Virgina Carlson, Contact
Founded: 1965. **Members:** 800. **Membership Dues:** retired, student in U.S., Canada and Mexico, $35 (annual) ● retired, student outside North America, $50 (annual) ● regular in U.S., Canada and Mexico, $75 (annual) ● regular outside North America, $90 (annual) ● institutional in U.S., Canada and Mexico, $115 (annual) ● institutional outside North America, $127 (annual). **Staff:** 1. **Description:** Represents colleges, universities, and libraries around the world as well as from the United States. Works to encourage research in all aspects of dance and related fields. Fosters the exchange of ideas, resources, and methodologies through publications, international and regional conferences, and workshops. Promotes the accessibility of research materials. Works with other professional organizations to provide members unique opportunities to network with others in and outside the field of dance. Provides vehicles for the dissemination of scholarship over the years; has provided and continues to provide leadership in dance scholarship by defining the standards for the field. **Awards:** Award for Outstanding Publications. **Frequency:** annual. **Type:** recognition ● Graduate Student Research Award. **Frequency:** annual. **Type:** recognition ● Outstanding Contribution to Dance Research. **Frequency:** annual. **Type:** recognition ● Outstanding Leadership in Dance Research. **Frequency:** annual. **Type:** recognition ● Outstanding Service to Dance Research. **Frequency:** annual. **Type:** recognition ● Trust for Dance Scholarship. **Frequency:** annual. **Type:** scholarship. **Recipient:** for outstanding teachers and scholars. **Computer Services:** Mailing lists. **Formerly:** (1979) Committee on Research in Dance. **Publications:** *CORD Conference Proceedings*. Contains a collection of papers presented at the conference. ● *CORD Newsletter*, semiannual, published in fall and spring. Provides information pertaining to the organization, its current officers, awardees honored and its workings. **Price:** $75.00 /year for individuals in North America; $90.00 /year for individuals outside North America; $115.00 /year for institutions in North America. ISSN: 0734-4856 ● *Dance Research Journal*, semiannual. Includes book reviews, reports on conferences, and bibliographies. **Price:** $75.00 /year for individuals in North America; $90.00 /year for individuals outside North America; $127.00 /year for institutions in North America. ISSN: 0149-7677 ● Membership Directory, biennial. **Conventions/Meetings:** annual conference.

9872 ■ Connolly Dance Foundation (CDF)
PO Box 573
Madison, WI 53701-0573
Ph: (608)244-4328
E-mail: connolly@msn.fullfeed.com
URL: http://www.silwikdesign.com/clients/connolly/profile.htm
Contact: Kristanne Connolly, Artistic Dir./Choreographer
Founded: 1994. **Members:** 6. **Staff:** 1. **Budget:** $250,000. **Description:** Promotes increased appreciation and understanding of modern dance. Conducts performances, lecture demonstrations, workshops, and master classes. **Affiliated With:** American Cancer Society. **Also Known As:** Connolly Dance Company. **Publications:** Newsletter, semiannual. **Price:** free for members. **Advertising:** accepted. Alternate Formats: online. **Conventions/Meetings:** workshop and lecture - year-round.

9873 ■ Country Dance and Song Society (CDSS)
132 Main St.
PO Box 338
Haydenville, MA 01039-0338
Ph: (413)268-7426
Fax: (413)268-7471
E-mail: office@cdss.org
URL: http://www.cdss.org
Contact: Bradley R. Foster, Exec. and Artistic Dir.
Founded: 1915. **Members:** 3,800. **Membership Dues:** student/limited income individual, $25 (annual) ● student/limited income family, $35 (annual) ● individual, $45 (annual) ● family, $65 (annual) ● group affiliate, $85 (annual). **Staff:** 10. **Budget:** $700,000. **Regional Groups:** 200. **Description:** Amateur and professional musicians; dance historians and recreational dancers. Promotes modern use of English and Anglo-American folk dances, songs, and music. Holds 11 week-long adult camps per year and 3 week-long family camps. **Programs:** Dance; Family; Music; Special. **Formerly:** Country Dance Society of America; (1996) Country Dance and Song Society of America. **Publications:** *A Choice Selection of American Country Dances of the Revolutionary Era*. Book. **Price:** $12.50 ● *Balance and Swing*. Book. **Price:** $19.50 ● *Country Dance and Song Society—Group Directory*, annual. **Price:** included in membership dues; $7.00 /year for nonmembers. **Circulation:** 3,000. **Advertising:** accepted ● *Country Dance and Song Society—Newsletter*, bimonthly. Contains special events listing and features on new dances. **Price:** $20.00/year. ISSN: 1070-8251. **Advertising:** accepted. Alternate Formats: online ● *Family and Community Dances*. Pamphlet ● *Legacy: 50 Years of Dance and Song*. Book. **Price:** $25.00 ● *Members List*, annual. Membership Directory. **Price:** available to members only ● *The Playford Ball: 103 Early English Country Dances*. Book. **Price:** $19.00 ● *Swing the Next*. Book. **Price:** $28.00 ● *Twenty-four Early American Country Dances: Cotillions and Reels*. Book. **Price:** $14.00 ● Also issues recordings. **Conventions/Meetings:** periodic meeting.

9874 ■ Cross-Cultural Dance Resources
518 S Agassiz St.
Flagstaff, AZ 86001-5711
Ph: (928)774-8108
Fax: (928)774-8108
E-mail: jwk3@jan.ucc.nau.edu
URL: http://www.ccdr.org
Contact: Pegge Vissicaro, Pres.
Founded: 1981. **Members:** 250. **Membership Dues:** individual, $50 (annual) ● family, $75 (annual) ● student, $25 (annual) ● life, $1,000 ● business, organization, library, $125 (annual) ● donor, $250 (annual) ● sustaining, $500 (annual). **Staff:** 3. **Multinational. Description:** Promotes dance performances; preserves and researches dance materials; fosters a dynamic environment for dance events; provides rehearsal space. Offers consultation in areas such as dance theory and methods, ethnomusicology, cultural dynamics, and ethics. Awards internships. Sponsors concerts, visiting artists, and lecture demonstrations. Maintains museum of musical instruments and costumes. Archive includes material of Gertrude Prokosch Kurath, Eleanor King. **Libraries: Type:** reference. **Holdings:** 12,000; artwork, audiovisuals, books, clippings, monographs, periodicals. **Subjects:** performance, especially dance, Eleanor King Collection, Gertrude Prokosch Kurath collection. **Computer Services:** Online services, library. **Boards:** Directors. **Programs:** Capitol Drive. **Affiliated With:** Dance Critics Association. **Also Known As:** CCDR. **Publications:** *CCDR Newsletter*, 3/year. Provides information on dance research, news, and upcoming events. **Price:** included in membership dues. ISSN: 1069-7241. **Advertising:** accepted ● *Half a Century of Dance Research: Essays by Gertrude Prokosch Kurath*. Book. **Price:** $15.00 for members; $20.00 for nonmembers ● *Tibet Week in Flagstaff*. Booklet. **Price:** $5.00 ● Brochure. **Conventions/Meetings:** quarterly board meeting ● annual meeting - always August ● periodic workshop.

9875 ■ Dance Critics Association (DCA)
PO Box 1882
Old Chelsea Sta.
New York, NY 10011
E-mail: dancecritics@hotmail.com
URL: http://www.dancecritics.org
Contact: Kena Herod, Co-Chair
Founded: 1973. **Members:** 300. **Membership Dues:** voting, associate, $50 (annual) ● student, senior, senior voting, $25 (annual) ● institutional, $75 (annual) ● benefactor, $100 (annual). **Description:** Critics who review dance as a major professional responsibility either on a regular basis or as a freelance reviewer, in print and/or broadcast media; teachers, historians, publicists, and other individuals interested in dance writing. Encourages excellence in dance criticism through education, research, and the exchange of ideas. Conducts clinics on practical topics of interest to critics. **Computer Services:** Mailing lists. **Committees:** Critics' Training. **Publications:** *DCA Newsletter*, quarterly. **Price:** included in membership dues ● Membership Directory, periodic. **Conventions/Meetings:** annual conference - usually June ● symposium ● workshop.

9876 ■ Dance/Drill Team Directors of America (DTDA)
10604 Whispering Pines Dr.
Frisco, TX 75034
E-mail: president@dtda.org
URL: http://www.dtda.org
Contact: Michelle McGaughy, Pres.
Membership Dues: active, $50 (annual) ● associate, $45 (annual) ● student, $25 (annual). **Description:** Aims to unite directors of dance/drill teams, pep squads and song leaders of public, private and parochial schools and dance studios. Works toward

achieving the highest standards possible for the profession. **Programs:** Mentor. **Publications:** *Insights*, quarterly. Magazine. Alternate Formats: online. **Conventions/Meetings:** annual convention - spring.

9877 ■ Dance Heritage Coalition (DHC)
1111 16th St. NW, Ste.300
Washington, DC 20036
Ph: (202)223-8393
Fax: (202)833-2686
E-mail: projects@danceheritage.org
URL: http://www.danceheritage.org
Contact: Barbara Drazin, Exec. Dir.
Founded: 1992. **Staff:** 1. **Description:** Serves as a national alliance of institutions holding significant collections of materials documenting the history of dance. Aims to preserve, make accessible, enhance and augment the materials that document the artistic accomplishments in dance of the past, present and future. **Computer Services:** Information services, cataloging ● online services, tutorial for in-depth dance research. **Publications:** Papers. Alternate Formats: online.

9878 ■ Dance Notation Bureau (DNB)
151 W 30th St., Ste.202
New York, NY 10001-4007
Ph: (212)564-0985
Fax: (212)216-9027
E-mail: dnbinfo@dancenotation.org
URL: http://www.dancenotation.org
Contact: Lynne Weber, Exec. Dir.
Founded: 1940. **Members:** 300. **Membership Dues:** student, $40 (annual) ● regular, $60 (annual) ● institution, $95 (annual) ● sponsor, $100 (annual) ● patron, $250 (annual) ● benefactor, $500 (annual) ● angel, $1,000 (annual) ● student outside North America, $45 (annual) ● regular outside North America, $65 (annual) ● institution outside North America, $100 (annual). **Staff:** 8. **Multinational. Description:** Documents and preserves dance works through the use of graphic notation. Conducts research into movement-related analysis techniques and programs. Maintains extension at Ohio State University, Columbus. Maintains placement service; assists choreographers in copyrighting, licensing, and restaging of their dance works. Offers service for dance reconstructors and circulating library materials to members. Maintains archive of original Labanotated dance scores in the world. **Libraries: Type:** reference. **Holdings:** 3,000; archival material, articles, audio recordings, books, periodicals, video recordings. **Subjects:** dance and movement. **Awards:** Dance Service Award. **Frequency:** annual. **Type:** recognition. **Boards:** Examiners. **Publications:** *DNBulletin*, quarterly. Newsletter. Alternate Formats: online ● *Notated Theatrical Dances*, periodic ● Also publishes texts on Labanotation, effort/shape and dance applications, and the collected works of Doris Humphrey. **Conventions/Meetings:** biennial Professional Advisory Committee - meeting - always in New York City.

9879 ■ Dance/U.S.A.
1111 16th St. NW, Ste.300
Washington, DC 20036
Ph: (202)833-1717
Fax: (202)833-2686
E-mail: asnyder@danceusa.org
URL: http://www.danceusa.org
Contact: Andrea Snyder, Exec. Dir.
Founded: 1982. **Members:** 375. **Membership Dues:** company (based on revenue), $150-$8,700 (annual) ● service organization, $350 (annual) ● individual, $100 (annual) ● presenter (based on artists fee), business affiliate, $350-$550 (annual) ● affiliate outside U.S. (based on revenue), $150-$1,000 (annual) ● education affiliate, $350 (annual) ● agent/artist representative, $150-$350 (annual) ● dancer affiliate, student, $30 (annual). **Staff:** 6. **Regional Groups:** 1. **State Groups:** 4. **Local Groups:** 10. **Description:** Dancers, dance companies, artists, and others involved in non-profit professional dance. Seeks to advance dance as an art form by encouraging higher standards; works to further knowledge, appreciation, and support of dance. Provides a forum for the discussion of issues of concern to members; supports network for exchange of information; compiles statistics. Assists dance professionals in improving their capabilities. Administers two regranting programs and other special projects. **Awards:** Dance/USA Ernie. **Frequency:** biennial. **Type:** recognition. **Recipient:** for unsung heroes who have led exemplary lives in dance ● Dance/USA Honors. **Frequency:** biennial. **Type:** recognition. **Recipient:** for outstanding lifetime contributions to dance. **Computer Services:** Mailing lists, of members. **Publications:** *AIDS in the Dance/Arts Workplace*. Journal. **Price:** $5.00 ● *Dance and AIDS*. Journal. **Price:** $5.00 ● *Dance Presenting*. Journal. **Price:** $2.00 ● *Dance/USA Journal*, quarterly. **Price:** $40.00 in U.S.; $50.00 in Canada; $70.00 overseas. **Circulation:** 1,600 ● *Dance/USA Member Profiles*, biennial. Directory. **Price:** $40.00/issue ● *Data and Personnel Compensation Surveys*. Available to participating companies only. **Price:** $30.00 ● *Member Bulletin*, 11/year. Distributed via fax or mail. **Price:** $11.00 ● *Widening the Circle Towards a New Vision for Dance Education*, monthly. Report. **Price:** $6.00 in U.S.; $8.00 in Canada; $15.00 overseas ● Also issues performance calendar and roundtable documentation. **Conventions/Meetings:** biennial Dance: The Art - roundtable (exhibits).

9880 ■ Dancers Without Borders
Address Unknown since 2008
Description: Uses movement, spoken word and music to mobilize resistance to human rights abuses, state and personal violence, corporate culture and environmental destruction. Collaborates with anti-war, human rights, community groups and other artists to choreograph dance-theater for public events.

9881 ■ Exotic Dancers League of America (EDLA)
c/o Burlesque Hall of Fame
PO Box 1437
Las Vegas, NV 89125
E-mail: info@exoticworldusa.org
URL: http://www.burlesquehall.com
Founded: 1955. **Members:** 636. **Staff:** 4. **Budget:** $5,000. **Regional Groups:** 4. **Local Groups:** 2. **Description:** Women who perform in night clubs and theaters as exotic dancers (also known as ecdysiasts, strippers, or burlesque dancers). Strives to promote and improve the image of "a fine old American tradition"; to fight the trend of pornography. Holds annual contest to choose "Miss Exotic World" on the basis of beauty of face and figure, talent, personality, and showmanship. Collects photographs, playbills, books, costumes, and historical material about burlesque. Maintains speakers' bureau. Conducts charitable activities. **Libraries: Type:** reference. **Holdings:** archival material, video recordings. **Subjects:** exotic dancing. **Awards:** Fanny Award. **Frequency:** annual. **Type:** recognition. **Affiliated With:** American Guild of Variety Artists; Burlesque Historical Society. **Publications:** Newsletter, periodic. **Conventions/Meetings:** annual meeting - every October ● annual reunion (exhibits) - every April.

9882 ■ Foundation for Pacific Dance (PDA)
Address Unknown since 2008
Founded: 1987. **Staff:** 25. **Budget:** $750,000. **Multinational. Description:** Seeks to preserve and promote traditional authentic Hawaiian and Pacific dance and culture. Maintains speakers' bureau and performing group. Also hosts workshops and seminars. **Awards:** Ka'Uhane Oka Hula. **Frequency:** annual. **Type:** scholarship. **Recipient:** for summer seminar in Honolulu. **Formerly:** (1991) Pacific Dance Association. **Conventions/Meetings:** annual Pacific Dance Seminar, taught by Kumu Hula (Hawaiian master instructors) for intermediate to advanced dancers (exhibits) - always July ● workshop, provided for individuals interested in refining their dance skills and learning new dances.

9883 ■ International Association for Creative Dance (IACD)
c/o Douglas R. Victor
103 Princeton Ave.
Providence, RI 02907
Ph: (401)521-0546
E-mail: iacd@dancecreative.org
URL: http://www.dancecreative.org
Contact: Douglas R. Victor, Contact
Founded: 1996. **Members:** 140. **Membership Dues:** individual, $15 (annual) ● organization, $20 (annual) ● individual, $25 (biennial). **Multinational. Description:** Represents individuals with an interest in Mettler-based creative dance. Works to advance the field of creative dance and sponsors opportunities for the study and teaching of creative dance. **Telecommunication Services:** electronic mail, membership@dancecreative.org. **Affiliated With:** National Dance Education Association; Sacred Dance Guild. **Publications:** *Newsletter for the People in the Field of Creative Dance*, semiannual. **Price:** included in membership dues. **Circulation:** 1,250. **Conventions/Meetings:** annual Creative Dance Congress, creative dance instruction for those with some previous Mettler-based creative dance experience.

9884 ■ International Association of Gay/Lesbian Country Western Dance Clubs (IAGLCWDC)
PMB 107
5543 Edmondson Pike
Nashville, TN 37211
E-mail: information@iaglcwdc.org
URL: http://www.iaglcwdc.org
Contact: Charlie Monroe, Chm.
Founded: 1993. **Members:** 33. **Membership Dues:** organization, $100 (annual). **Regional Groups:** 33. **Description:** Promotes appreciation of gay and lesbian country western dance throughout the world. **Awards:** Club Service Award. **Frequency:** annual. **Type:** recognition. **Recipient:** for a club that fosters the spirit of gay and lesbian country western dancing ● Individual Service Award/The Dancing Boots Award. **Frequency:** annual. **Type:** recognition. **Recipient:** for an individual who fosters the spirit of gay and lesbian country western dancing. **Committees:** Dance Competitions; Internet. **Publications:** *Roundup*, quarterly. Newsletter. Covers the organization's status and contains an events calendar. **Price:** free for members. **Conventions/Meetings:** annual convention ● semiannual convention.

9885 ■ International Association of Gay Square Dance Clubs (IAGSDC)
PO Box 9176
Denver, CO 80209-0176
Ph: (303)722-5276
Free: (800)835-6462
E-mail: information@iagsdc.org
URL: http://www.iagsdc.org
Contact: John Mckinstry, Chm.
Founded: 1983. **Members:** 2,400. **Membership Dues:** full and associate, $1 (annual) ● affiliate, $25 (annual). **Local Groups:** 57. **Multinational. Description:** All square dancers regardless of age, race, gender, religion, ethnic background, or sexual orientation. Offers educational programs. **Computer Services:** Electronic publishing. **Conventions/Meetings:** annual convention (exhibits).

9886 ■ International Association of Round Dance Teachers
176 S Cole Rd.
Boise, ID 83709-0932
Ph: (208)377-1232
Free: (800)346-7522
Fax: (208)377-1236
E-mail: roundalab@roundalab.org
URL: http://www.roundalab.org
Contact: Bruce Nelson, Gen. Chm.
Founded: 1977. **Members:** 1,320. **Membership Dues:** individual (depends on the number of sessions per year), $169-$206 (annual) ● in U.S. (without ASCAP/BMI), $100 (annual) ● in Canada (without ASCAP/BMI), $71 (annual) ● outside U.S. and Canada (without ASCAP/BMI), $138 (annual) ● emeritus, $66 (annual) ● regular, U.S. affiliate organization, $105 (annual) ● overseas, $77 (annual). **Staff:** 1. **Budget:** $215,000. **Description:** Professional round dance teachers. Seeks to promote, protect, and perpetuate the art of round dancing

(choreographed ballroom dancing), and to foster the round dance as a complement to overall square dance activity. Encourages professional competence, accreditation, standardization, and ethics in round dancing. Sponsors teacher seminars and clinics. Maintains hall of fame. **Libraries: Type:** reference. **Awards: Frequency:** annual. **Type:** recognition. **Committees:** Education; Technology. **Also Known As:** International Association of Round Dance Teachers. **Formerly:** (2000) ROUNDALAB. **Publications:** *Manual for Callers Using Rounds in Square Dance Program*, annual ● *Phase Booklet*, annual. Includes description of figures, Phase I through Phase VI. ● *Round Dance Manual for New Teachers*, annual ● *ROUNDALAB—Directory*, annual. Membership Directory. **Price:** included in membership dues ● *ROUNDALAB—Journal*, quarterly. Contains feature articles on round dancing; includes member news, board and committee reports, and obituaries. **Price:** included in membership dues ● Videos ● Also publishes glossary and index. **Conventions/Meetings:** annual convention, includes clinic - always late June, prior to the National Square Dance Convention.

9887 ■ International Council of Kinetography Laban (ICKL)
c/o Valerie Mockabee, Treas.
2801 Northwest Blvd.
Columbus, OH 43221
Ph: (614)469-9984
Fax: (614)469-9984
E-mail: secretary@ickl.org
URL: http://www.ickl.org
Contact: Richard Allan Ploch, Sec.
Founded: 1959. **Members:** 100. **Membership Dues:** regular, $50 (annual) ● student, $35 (annual) ● regular, EUR 42 (annual) ● student, EUR 29 (annual). **Multinational. Description:** Professional dancers, teachers, and others in 20 countries using the Labanotation system for recording dance movements. Supports Kinetography Laban/Labanotation by: guiding the unified development of the system; encouraging consistent standards of practice; acting as the authoritative body with regard to orthography; promoting research into notation matters likely to increase the efficiency and usage of the system. Maintains archive of papers and conference reports. **Committees:** Research Panel. **Publications:** *International Council of Kinetography Laban—Conference Proceedings*, biennial. Contains technical reports, papers presented, and reports from notation centers. **Price:** $35.00/copy. ISSN: 1013-4468. **Circulation:** 100 ● *Laban Notation Scores: An International Bibliography (Vols. 1, 2, 3 and 4)* ● Also publishes Indexes of Technical Matters and Technical and Nontechnical Papers from the biennial conferences of the International Council of Kinetography Laban and Conference Proceedings 1959-1977. **Conventions/Meetings:** biennial conference.

9888 ■ International Tap Association (ITA)
PO Box 356
Boulder, CO 80306
Ph: (303)443-7989
Fax: (303)443-7992
E-mail: ita@tapdance.org
URL: http://www.tapdance.org/tap/ita/index.html
Contact: Marda Kirn, Dir.
Founded: 1987. **Members:** 930. **Membership Dues:** regular in U.S., $35 (annual) ● regular in Canada and Mexico, $45 (annual) ● international, $50 (annual). **Staff:** 6. **Regional Groups:** 47. **Multinational. Description:** Represents the interests of tap dancers, performers, studios, choreographers, teachers, scholars, historians, students, and other tap enthusiasts. Promotes understanding, preservation, and development of tap dance as an art form. Encourages the creation of new tap performance venues and touring circuits. Preserves the history of tap through archival documentation and research. Establishes support mechanisms and communication networks for tap. **Libraries: Type:** by appointment only. **Holdings:** papers. **Computer Services:** database ● mailing lists. **Publications:** *On Tap*, 5/year. Magazine. Includes calendar of events, historical articles, practical articles, articles from and about leaders in the field. **Price:** $5.00 for members; $7.00 for nonmembers. **Advertising:** accepted.

9889 ■ Israeli Dance Institute (IDI)
JCRC, 12th Fl.
711 Third Ave.
New York, NY 10017
Ph: (212)983-4806
Fax: (212)983-4084
E-mail: idi_nirkoda@juno.com
URL: http://www.madwomb.com/web/dance/nirkoda.html
Contact: Danny Uziel, Dir.
Founded: 1969. **Staff:** 3. **Description:** International educational and cultural foundation. Maintains information service; sponsors skills workshops, leadership training seminar, and annual Folk Dance Festival. **Publications:** *The Chassidic Dance*. Book ● *Harikud*. Book ● *HORA: A Review of Israel Folk Dance News*, semiannual. Includes articles and feature columns; lists new records and books. **Price:** $3.00/year. ISSN: 0741-9384. **Circulation:** 5,000 ● *Israeli Folk Dance Clearinghouse Calendar*, bimonthly. Listing of Israeli folk dance events. **Price:** $9.00/year ● *Machol Ha'am*. Book ● *Nirkoda*. Magazine. Contains review of Israeli and Jewish dance news. **Price:** $15.00/year in U.S.; $18.00/year outside U.S. ● *100 Israeli Folk Dances*. Book.

9890 ■ Junior Shag Association (JSA)
c/o Keith Dallas, Pres.
437 Palmer Ct.
Eden, NC 27288
Ph: (336)635-1353
E-mail: kdallas@triad.rr.com
URL: http://www.juniorshaggers.com
Contact: Keith Dallas, Pres.
Members: 343. **Membership Dues:** junior, $5 (annual) ● adult, $10 (annual) ● corporate, $50 (annual) ● sponsor, $1,000 (annual). **Description:** Promotes and perpetuates beach and shag dance music, and shag dancing. Works to help junior shaggers who might want to learn about shagging and shag dance music. Facilitates communication and cooperation among members. **Telecommunication Services:** electronic mail, rlalexander@bellsouth.net. **Publications:** Newsletter. **Price:** free for members. Alternate Formats: online.

9891 ■ Laban/Bartenieff Institute of Movement Studies (LIMS)
520 8th Ave., Rm. 304
New York, NY 10018
Ph: (212)643-8888
Fax: (212)643-8388
E-mail: info@limsonline.org
URL: http://www.limsonline.org
Contact: Ms. Regina Miranda CMA, Exec. Dir./Hd. of Arts and Culture
Founded: 1978. **Members:** 250. **Membership Dues:** benefactor (minimum), $2,500 (annual) ● individual, $75 (annual) ● friend, $76-$249 (annual) ● advocate, $250-$499 (annual) ● sponsor, $500-$999 (annual) ● sustainer, $1,000-$2,499 (annual). **Staff:** 11. **Budget:** $347,000. **Multinational. Description:** Professional movement educators, dancers, choreographers, dance therapists, behavioral researchers, teachers, fitness and athletic trainers, health practitioners, and students. Devoted to the study of human movement. Studies the role of movement in human behavior through training, research, and practical application. Offers certificate program in Laban movement studies, workshops, and seminars. Supports research and development projects of practicing movement analysts. **Libraries: Type:** reference. **Holdings:** 250; archival material, books. **Subjects:** movement, psychology, art. **Computer Services:** Mailing lists, of members. **Boards:** Advisory. **Committees:** Artistic; Education; Program Development. **Formerly:** (1981) Laban Institute of Movement Studies. **Publications:** *Movement News*. Newsletter ● *Movement Studies*, annual. Journal ● Membership Directory, annual. **Conventions/Meetings:** biennial conference ● Laban In the Performing Arts at Bratislava in Movement - conference.

9892 ■ National Clogging Organization (CLOG)
c/o David Phillips, Co.-Exec. Dir.
2986 Mill Park Ct.
Dacula, GA 30019
Ph: (770)985-5557 (678)889-4355
Fax: (603)925-0967
E-mail: clog@clog.org
URL: http://www.clog.org
Contact: David Phillips, Co-Exec. Dir.
Membership Dues: regular, in U.S., $30 (annual) ● regular, in Canada, $35 (annual) ● foreign, $40 (annual). **Description:** Represents the interests and concerns of individuals dedicated to the promotion, education, enhancement and preservation of American Clog Dance. Supports worldwide clogging activities, communications and events. **Computer Services:** Online services, discussion forum. **Committees:** Communications; Competition; Education; Global; Merchandising; Traditional. **Programs:** Certified Clogging Instructor. **Publications:** *CLOG Today*. Newsletter ● Bulletin. Alternate Formats: online. **Conventions/Meetings:** annual convention.

9893 ■ National Dance Association (NDA)
1900 Assn. Dr.
Reston, VA 20191
Ph: (703)476-3400
Free: (800)213-7193
Fax: (703)476-9527
E-mail: nda@aahperd.org
URL: http://www.aahperd.org/nda
Contact: Ms. Colleen Hearn Dean MA, Program Admin.
Founded: 1932. **Members:** 2,500. **Membership Dues:** professional, graduating senior, $125 (annual) ● institutional, $200 (annual) ● retired, $45 (annual) ● graduate/undergraduate, $45 (annual) ● life (payable in 4 payments within one year), $2,000. **Staff:** 3. **Regional Groups:** 6. **State Groups:** 50. **Description:** Dance educators, choreographers, schools and dance/arts administrators, researchers, performers, dance medicine/science specialists, technologists, therapists and others associated with dance/arts education. Works with 160 federal and state agencies, arts and education associations, foundations, and businesses and corporations to ensure that: (1) quality dance/arts education is available to all Americans regardless of age, sex, ability, interest, or culture; and (2) quality dance/arts education becomes a part of U.S. education for all children. **Awards:** Dance Educators of the Year. **Frequency:** annual. **Type:** recognition. **Recipient:** for outstanding teacher of dance K-12 ● Heritage Award. **Frequency:** annual. **Type:** recognition. **Recipient:** for outstanding contributions to the field of dance ● NDA Scholar/Artist Award. **Frequency:** annual. **Type:** recognition. **Recipient:** for current production of scholarly materials or other creative works ● NDA Student Literary Award. **Frequency:** annual. **Type:** recognition. **Recipient:** for professional writing on dance and dance education by collegiate students of dance ● Outstanding Dance Student Award. **Frequency:** annual. **Type:** recognition. **Recipient:** for outstanding dance student from colleges and universities. **Divisions:** Dance Education; Dance Medicine, Science, and Technology; Dance Performance. **Affiliated With:** American Alliance for Health, Physical Education, Recreation and Dance. **Formerly:** (1972) Dance Division (of AAHPER). **Publications:** *Brain-Compatible Dance Education*. Book ● *Creative Dance for All Ages*. Book ● *Dance Movement Therapy: A Healing Book*. Includes information that every young American should know and be able to do in dance. ● *The National Standards for Dance Education*. Book. Includes information that every young American should know and be able to do in dance. ● *Reminiscence of a Dancing Man*. Book ● *Seeing While Being Seen: Dance Photography & the Creative Process*. Book ● *Spotlight on Dance*. Newsletter. **Conventions/Meetings:** annual convention (exhibits) ● Dance Science & Somatics - conference ● semiannual Dancing with the Mouse Technology/Dance Conference ● semiannual From the Page to Stage: Making the Dance Standards Work for You - meeting ● semiannual Pedagogy - conference.

9894 ■ National Fastdance Association (NFA)
c/o Bill Maddox, Pres.
3371 Debussy Rd.
Jacksonville, FL 32277
Ph: (904)744-2424
Free: (877)NFA-CLUB
E-mail: nfainfo@attbi.com
URL: http://www.fastdancers.com
Contact: Bill Maddox, Pres.
Description: Preserves and promotes various fastdance styles and musics. Encourages communication among member clubs. Serves as a coordinating body for member club activities. **Telecommunication Services:** electronic mail, mtstech@mediaone.net. **Publications:** *NFA News*, quarterly. Newsletter.

9895 ■ National Square Dance Convention (NSDC)
c/o Jack Cauble, Registration and Housing Chm.
3430 Statesville Blvd.
Salisbury, NC 28145
Ph: (704)633-9147
E-mail: registration@56thnsdc.com
URL: http://www.56thnsdc.com
Contact: Jack Cauble, Registration and Housing Chm.
Founded: 1952. **Members:** 25,000. **Description:** Liaison organization of square dance clubs and dancers. Principal activity is sponsorship of the convention which includes: square and round dancing; folk dancing; contra and old-time dancing. **Committees:** Business; Education; Program; Publicity; Registration and Housing; Services; Social and Special Events. **Publications:** *National Square Dance Convention—Membership Directory*, annual. Lists more than 10,000 square, round, contra, and clogging clubs. **Price:** $7.00/copy ● *National Squares*, quarterly. Journal. Promotes square dancing and the convention. **Price:** $7.00/year. **Circulation:** 4,500. **Advertising:** accepted. **Conventions/Meetings:** annual convention (exhibits) - 2008 June 25-28, Wichita, KS.

9896 ■ Royal Academy of Dance (RAD)
1412 17th St., Ste.259
Bakersfield, CA 93301
Ph: (661)336-0160 (661)336-0161
Fax: (661)336-0162
E-mail: info@radusa.org
URL: http://www.radusa.org
Contact: Mrs. Patti Ashby, Contact
Founded: 1920. **Members:** 700. **Membership Dues:** student, full (over 65 years of age and no longer teaching; F/T education but not teaching), $60 (annual) ● full, corporate, $100 (annual) ● teaching, $140 (annual) ● individual, $45 (annual). **Staff:** 3. **Multinational. Description:** International examining body working to maintain a high standard of classical ballet training. Provides teachers with an examination syllabus. Conducts teachers' courses and summer schools for children and teachers. **Libraries: Type:** open to the public; lending. **Holdings:** archival material, books, periodicals, photographs, video recordings. **Subjects:** dance, ballet education. **Formerly:** (2001) Royal Academy of Dancing, United States Branch. **Publications:** *Dance Gazette*, triennial. Journal. **Price:** $2.50. **Circulation:** 18,000. **Advertising:** accepted ● The Foundations of Classical Ballet Technique, Royal Academy of Dancing, 1996, ISBN: 095248482X; Dictionary of Classical Ballet Terminology, Royal Academy of Dancing, 1995, ISBN: 0952484803, author R. Ryman. **Conventions/Meetings:** annual meeting - always first week in January, London, England ● annual Teachers' Workshop - workshop and meeting, for training purposes.

9897 ■ Sacred Dance Guild (SDG)
PO Box 1046
Laurel, MD 20725-1046
Free: (877)422-8678
Fax: (301)725-5323
E-mail: sdg@marinermanagement.com
URL: http://www.sacreddanceguild.org
Contact: Peggy Hoffman, Admin. Asst.
Founded: 1958. **Members:** 700. **Membership Dues:** student, $25 (annual) ● senior, $30 (annual) ● international, $42 (annual) ● international, $70 (biennial) ● group, $85 (annual) ● life, $1,000. **Staff:** 1. **Regional Groups:** 30. **Multinational. Description:** Promotes sacred dance as prayer and as a means of spiritual growth, connection to the Creator, and integration of mind, body and spirit. Represents students, directors, dancers, choreographers, sponsors and others in multicultural and interfaith atmosphere, which are interested in dance. Works to stimulate interest in dance as a religious art form and to provide a means of communication and training for dance choirs. Supports and encourages workshops. Maintains information clearinghouse, including lists of children's dance teachers, workshop leaders, and performers in sacred dance. Conducts local, regional, and national workshops for training in dance technique, religious theme, and application to worship service and religious occasions. Sponsors research on the origins of the many styles of sacred dance. Compiles history of the guild. Operates talent resource bank, and agency network for career opportunities. Maintains limited scholarship program and sacred dancers' bureau. **Awards: Frequency:** annual. **Type:** scholarship. **Computer Services:** database ● mailing lists ● online services. **Committees:** Development; Reciprocal Arrangements; Scholarship. **Affiliated With:** American Alliance for Health, Physical Education, Recreation and Dance; American Dance Guild; National Dance Association. **Formerly:** (1958) Eastern Regional Dance Association. **Publications:** *Directory of Publications*, 3/year. Journal. ISSN: 1043-5328. **Advertising:** accepted ● *SDG Calendar*, 3/year. Newsletter. Informs members of workshops, meetings, and other guild activities with respect to dance as a language of worship and celebration, part of journal. **Price:** included in membership dues. **Circulation:** 800. **Advertising:** accepted ● *SDG Directory*, annual. Membership Directory. Includes lists of professional liturgical dance groups, dance choirs, and workshop leaders. **Price:** available to members only. **Circulation:** 800. **Advertising:** accepted ● Journal, 3/year. Contains chapter and regional news with recommended reading and articles of interest. **Price:** included in membership dues; $35.00/year for corporate members. ISSN: 1043-5328. **Circulation:** 800. **Advertising:** accepted. **Conventions/Meetings:** annual Paths of Radiance - festival and workshop ● periodic regional meeting and conference.

9898 ■ United Square Dancers of America (USDA)
c/o Si Kittle, Co-Pres.
320 Maynard Dr.
Sun Prairie, WI 53590
Ph: (608)837-6958
E-mail: usda@usda.org
URL: http://www.usda.org
Contact: Si Kittle, Co-Pres.
Founded: 1981. **Members:** 250,000. **Membership Dues:** affiliate, $100 (annual). **Regional Groups:** 4. **State Groups:** 57. **Local Groups:** 2,766. **Description:** Square dancers united to provide a forum for integration between dancers and leaders. Represents dancer's views to callers, instructors, commercial enterprises, national and international organizations, and other dancers. Assists groups with material for teaching square dancing to the handicapped. Provides moderators and panelists for educational programs; prepares educational literature; conducts charitable program; assists groups interested in teaching square dancing to youth. Provides liability insurance to member groups. **Libraries: Type:** reference. **Holdings:** archival material, audiovisuals, clippings, periodicals. **Subjects:** square dancing, round dancing, clogging, line dancing, traditional dancing. **Awards:** Youth Scholarship. **Frequency:** annual. **Type:** scholarship. **Recipient:** to square dancing junior/senior in high school. **Computer Services:** Mailing lists. **Telecommunication Services:** electronic mail, usda.president@usda.org ● electronic mail, usda.information.officer@usda.org. **Committees:** Badges; Credit Card; Education; Facilities; Handicapable Dancers; Insurance; Publications; Youth. **Publications:** *Class Graduation*. Pamphlet ● *Club Erosion*. Pamphlet ● *Club Newsletters*. Pamphlet ● *Games, Gimmicks, Skits*. Booklet ● *Recruiting and Keeping New Dancers*. Booklet ● *Take the First Step*. Booklet ● *USDA News*, quarterly. Newsletter. **Price:** $5.00/year. **Circulation:** 850. **Advertising:** accepted ● Also publishes information sheets and training literature of interest to dancers. **Conventions/Meetings:** annual executive committee meeting (exhibits) - every January ● annual meeting - always fourth Wednesday in June.

9899 ■ United States National Institute of Dance (USNID)
38 S Arlington Ave.
PO Box 245
East Orange, NJ 07019
Ph: (973)673-9225
Contact: Trevor Cox, Dir. Gen.
Founded: 1979. **Staff:** 25. **Description:** Participants include dance teachers, students, colleges and universities, dance companies, and local and international dance teachers' organizations. Seeks to: provide dance teachers with international variations and techniques for improving artistic qualities and teaching methods; establish a uniform method of teaching all forms of dance at the highest professional level; provide an international network of consultation and counseling services for dance teachers and dancers. Maintains speakers' bureau; offers placement and children's services; sponsors competitions. Conducts demonstrations, lectures, and certificate correspondence courses. Produces new correspondence course "How to Prevent and Care for Dance Injuries". **Libraries: Type:** reference. **Holdings:** books, video recordings. **Awards: Type:** recognition. **Recipient:** for outstanding contributions to the dance field. **Affiliated With:** World Congress of Teachers of Dancing. **Conventions/Meetings:** workshop and seminar.

9900 ■ USA Dance
PO Box 152988
Cape Coral, FL 33915-2988
Ph: (239)242-0805
Free: (800)447-9047
Fax: (239)573-0946
E-mail: central-office@usadance.org
URL: http://www.usabda.org
Contact: Ms. Esther Freeman, Pres.
Founded: 1965. **Members:** 23,000. **Membership Dues:** social dancer, $25 (annual) ● adult dance sport athlete (competitor), $60 (annual) ● associate, manager, organizer, trainer, official, $50 (annual) ● junior, $15 (annual) ● ballroom dancer, $35 (annual) ● student, $20 (annual). **Staff:** 1. **Budget:** $600,000. **Regional Groups:** 6. **National Groups:** 150. **Description:** Individuals interested in participating in or observing ballroom dancing. Promotes ballroom dancing as a social recreational activity as well as a competitive sport at local and national levels. Emphasizes the physical, mental, and social benefits of dancing. Includes the expansion of ballroom dancing skills for all ages. **Awards: Frequency:** annual. **Type:** recognition. **Recipient:** for recognition of competitive proficiency. **Committees:** DanceSport; Youth and College. **Formerly:** (2005) United States Amateur Ballroom Dancers Association. **Publications:** *Amateur Dancers*, bimonthly. Magazine. Contains competition results, letters, financial and developmental reports, calendar of events, and articles relating to ballroom dance. **Price:** included in membership dues; $30.00 /year for nonmembers. **Circulation:** 23,000. **Advertising:** accepted. **Conventions/Meetings:** biennial Intercontinental DanceSport Festival, with competition, workshops, and social dancing (exhibits) ● annual National Championship - competition (exhibits) - in August.

9901 ■ World Dance Alliance (WDA)
433 W 34th St., Apt. No. 8L
New York, NY 10001-1524
Ph: (212)695-3925
Fax: (212)268-4229
E-mail: wdaamericas@juno.com
URL: http://www.yorku.ca/wda
Contact: Judie Janney, Coor.
Founded: 1993. **Membership Dues:** individual (earning under $25000), $10 (annual) ● individual

(earning $25001-50000), $35 (annual) ● individual (earning $50001-75000), $50 (annual) ● individual (earning above $75001), $70 (annual) ● President's Circle, $1,000 (annual) ● Hemisphere Club, $500 (annual) ● partner, $200 (annual) ● sponsor, $100 (annual) ● organization, $70 (annual). **Multinational**. **Description:** Support group for dance. Goals are: to establish a Center of information, advocacy and communication for dance organizations and individuals, a forum for the exchange of ideas, information expertise and resources, all in the areas of dance; to encourage an awareness of access to and understanding of dance as an art, a ritual, and traditional expression, and as a leisure-time activity in diverse communities throughout the world; to assist in the identification and promotion of all dance traditions, styles, and approaches in recognition of their cultural, artistic and social importance; to coordinate, support and enhance the work of existing dance organizations, and to collaborate with other organizations working in other art forms, related disciplines, education and community activity. **Telecommunication Services:** information service, member information. **Special Interest Groups:** Archival Development; Choreography; Exchange; Health and Welfare; Training and Education of Dancers. **Publications:** *WDA Americas CHANNELS* (in English and Spanish). Newsletter. Contains news and reports on other status of dance and general information. **Price:** included in membership dues. Alternate Formats: online ● Membership Directory. **Price:** included in membership dues. **Conventions/Meetings:** biennial general assembly ● biennial Global Assemblies - assembly - opposite years of General Assemblies ● Interest Group Meetings.

9902 ■ World Swing Dance Council (WSDC)
c/o Cathy Tigges
4401 E Janice Way
Phoenix, AZ 85032
Ph: (602)482-2828
E-mail: ctigges@cox.net
URL: http://www.swingdancecouncil.com
Contact: Cathy Tigges, Contact
Founded: 1993. **Membership Dues:** professional, $200 (annual) ● associate professional, $150 (annual) ● gold, $100 (annual) ● friend, $35 (annual). **Multinational**. **Description:** Promotes, encourages and enhances swing dancing on a national and world level. Serves as a clearinghouse of information for all aspects of swing dance events, competitions, club formation, instruction and judging. Addresses the concerns and needs of individuals, clubs, competitors, instructors, judges, DJs and promoters, for the betterment of the entire swing dance community. **Awards:** Swing Dance Hall of Fame. **Frequency:** annual. **Type:** recognition. **Recipient:** to swing dance enthusiasts whose long-time accomplishments have contributed to the growth and prestige of swing dancing.

Danish

9903 ■ Danish American Heritage Society (DAHS)
4105 Stone Brooke Rd.
Ames, IA 50010
Ph: (515)232-7479 (480)816-8725
E-mail: iversenji@qwest.net
URL: http://www.danishamericanheritagesociety.org
Contact: Dr. James Iversen, Pres.
Founded: 1977. **Members:** 700. **Membership Dues:** general, $30 (annual) ● associate, $50 (annual) ● patron, $100 (annual) ● student, $15 (annual). **Staff:** 1. **Budget:** $20,000. **Description:** Individuals and institutions interested in Danish American culture and history. Goals are to encourage research in the life, culture, and history of Danish Americans; serve as an agency for the publication of studies of Danish American history; provide a means of communicating with and informing people interested in the activities of North Americans of Danish descent; support the related activities of other Danish American and Danish Canadian associations; encourage and assist with conferences, meetings, and endeavors to stimulate interest in Danish culture, heritage, and language. Promotes research. **Awards:** Bodiker Fellowship. **Frequency:** periodic. **Type:** scholarship ● Edith and Arnold N. Bodtker Grant for Research or Internship. **Frequency:** annual. **Type:** grant. **Recipient:** for applicants from Denmark, Canada, or the United States. **Computer Services:** database, membership list. **Publications:** *The Bridge*, semiannual. Journal. Includes articles on the history of Danes in North America and book reviews. **Price:** included in membership dues; $8.00 /year for nonmembers. ISSN: 0741-1200. **Circulation:** 800 ● *Newsletter of the DAHS*, semiannual. Reports on the activities of the organization and its members. ● Brochure. **Conventions/Meetings:** periodic Danish Immigration - convention.

Design

9904 ■ Feng Shui Institute of America (FSIA)
7547 Bruns Ct.
Canal Winchester, OH 43110
Ph: (614)837-8370
Fax: (614)834-9760
E-mail: connie@windwater.com
URL: http://www.windwater.com
Contact: Connie Spruill, Contact
Description: Professional feng shui designers and advisors. (Feng shui is "an information system that reveals how a home or workplace can affect health, relationships, and self-actualization"). Promotes professionalization of the practice of feng shui; seeks to expand career opportunities available to professional feng shui practitioners. Establishes standards of training and practice for feng shui professionals. Serves as a clearinghouse on feng shui; conducts educational and training programs; sponsors feng shui certification courses and examinations; makes available home study packages. **Publications:** *Windwater*, quarterly. Newsletter. **Price:** $20.00/year. **Conventions/Meetings:** semiannual Interdisciplinary Minds Converging to Advance Feng Shui - conference.

9905 ■ International Design Conference in Aspen (IDCA)
Address Unknown since 2008
URL: http://www.idca.org
Founded: 1950. **Staff:** 2. **Description:** Exists solely to stage an annual conference to further an appreciation of art, design, communication, and the environment. Consists of those individuals who attend this meeting in Aspen, Colorado. **Publications:** Makes available conference programs on cassette. **Conventions/Meetings:** annual The More Things Change - conference - always Aspen, CO.

9906 ■ International Feng Shui Guild (IFSG)
6663 SW Beaverton Hillsdale Hwy., Ste.333
Portland, OR 97225-1403
Free: (888)881-IFSG
Fax: (503)525-2999
E-mail: membership@internationalfengshuiguild.org
URL: http://www.internationalfengshuiguild.org
Contact: Rosalie Prinzivalli, Chair
Members: 457. **Membership Dues:** professional, $108 (annual) ● associate, $89 (annual). **Multinational**. **Description:** Advances the practice, teaching and use of Feng Shui globally. Encourages Feng Shui students and professional practitioners to develop their craft. Increases public awareness and understanding of the ancient Asian art and science of Feng Shui. **Telecommunication Services:** electronic mail, rosalieprinzivalli@internationalfengshuiguild.org. **Publications:** *Feng Shui Quarterly*. Newsletter. **Advertising:** accepted. Alternate Formats: online ● *Grapevine*, quarterly. Newsletter. **Price:** included in membership dues. Alternate Formats: online.

9907 ■ Organization of Black Designers (OBD)
300 M St. SW, Ste.N110
Washington, DC 20024
Ph: (202)659-3918
Fax: (202)488-3838
E-mail: obdesign@aol.com
URL: http://www.core77.com/OBD/welcome.html
Contact: David H. Rice, Founder/Chm.
Founded: 1990. **Members:** 10,000. **Membership Dues:** professional/affiliate, $175 (annual) ● corporate, $500 (annual) ● student, $75 (annual). **Staff:** 5. **Budget:** $622,000. **Regional Groups:** 10. **Description:** African American designers holding college degrees who are practicing graphic advertising, industrial, fashion, textile, and interior design. Provides forum for discussion and educational programs, business, career and economic development. Sponsors competitions and speakers' bureau. **Libraries: Type:** reference. **Holdings:** archival material, articles. **Subjects:** design issues that impact black design professionals. **Awards:** OBD Design Award. **Frequency:** annual. **Type:** recognition. **Recipient:** for outstanding designers ● OBD Scholarship. **Frequency:** annual. **Type:** scholarship. **Recipient:** for design school students. **Computer Services:** database ● electronic publishing. **Additional Websites:** http://www.obd.org. **Publications:** *DesigNation*, biennial. Journal. **Price:** $10.00/issue. **Circulation:** 100,000. **Advertising:** accepted. Alternate Formats: diskette ● *OBData*. Newsletter. **Conventions/Meetings:** annual DesigNation - conference, covers business, professional development, design education, design technology and career development (exhibits) - last weekend in October.

Dutch

9908 ■ Association for the Advancement of Dutch-American Studies (AADAS)
The Joint Archives of Holland
Hope Coll.
PO Box 9000
Holland, MI 49422-9000
Ph: (616)395-7798
Fax: (616)395-7197
E-mail: archives@hope.edu
URL: http://www.jointarchives.org
Contact: Geoffrey Reynolds, Appointed Dir.
Founded: 1979. **Members:** 150. **Membership Dues:** individual, couple, institution, $20 (annual) ● student, $10 (annual). **Description:** Seeks to record the achievements and influence of North American Dutch and Americans of Dutch ancestry in government, industry, science, religion, education, and the arts. Serves as a forum for interested individuals. Analyzes North American-Netherlandic relations. Encourages research and disseminates results. Holds a biennial conference on Dutch American Studies. **Additional Websites:** http://www.aadas.net. **Publications:** *AADAS News*. Newsletter. Alternate Formats: online ● Papers. Includes Conference papers. **Price:** included in membership dues; $20.00 for nonmembers. **Conventions/Meetings:** biennial conference.

9909 ■ Holland Historical Trust
31 W 10th St.
Holland, MI 49423
Ph: (616)394-1362 (616)392-9084
Free: (888)200-9123
Fax: (616)394-4756
E-mail: hollandmuseum@hollandmuseum.org
URL: http://www.hollandmuseum.org
Contact: Paula Dunlap, Operations Mgr.
Founded: 1937. **Members:** 948. **Membership Dues:** family, $35 (annual) ● senior couple, $30 (annual) ● senior individual, $20 (annual) ● individual, $25 (annual) ● builder, $60 (annual) ● sponsor, $100 (annual) ● patron, $250 (annual) ● benefactor, $500 (annual) ● Wichers' Circle, $1,000 (annual). **Staff:** 24. **Budget:** $504,000. **Local Groups:** 1. **Description:** Collects, preserves, and interprets material that documents the traditional Dutch and multicultural history of the Holland, MI, area. Operates the Holland Museum and the Cappon & Settlers House Museums. **Libraries: Type:** reference. **Holdings:** archival material. **Subjects:** 19th century Dutch materials related to the establishment of the Holland area. **Awards:** Friend of History. **Frequency:** annual. **Type:** recogni-

tion. **Recipient:** for preservation or communication of community's heritage fostering understanding and pride in its entire people. **Formerly:** (1961) Netherlands Pioneer and Historical Foundation; (1986) Netherlands Museum. **Publications:** *Review*, quarterly. Newsletter. Presents historical articles and museum news.

Economics

9910 ■ Foundation Francisco Marroquin (FFM)
c/o Mrs. Rosa Gutierrez, Admin. Mgr.
PO Box 2422
Stuart, FL 34995-2422
Ph: (772)286-6450
Fax: (772)288-0670
E-mail: rosa@ffmnet.org
URL: http://www.ffmnet.org
Contact: Mrs. Rosa Gutierrez, Admin. Mgr.
Description: Works to raise money to give to Latin America schools, centers and institutes that are effective in terms of its goals and grant them whatever could be raised. **Awards: Frequency:** annual. **Type:** fellowship.

English

9911 ■ English First
8001 Forbes Pl., Ste.102
Springfield, VA 22151
Ph: (703)321-8818
Fax: (703)321-8408
E-mail: info@englishfirst.org
URL: http://www.englishfirst.org
Contact: Jim Boulet Jr., Exec. Dir.
Founded: 1986. **Members:** 150,000. **Membership Dues:** regular, $28 (annual). **Description:** Works to make English the America's official language. Gives every child the chance to learn English and eliminates "costly and ineffective" multilingual policies. **Publications:** Report, bimonthly. **Price:** included in membership dues.

9912 ■ ProEnglish
1601 N Kent St., Ste.1100
Arlington, VA 22209
Ph: (703)816-8821
Fax: (703)816-8824
E-mail: mail@proenglish.org
URL: http://www.proenglish.org
Contact: K.C. McAlpin, Exec. Dir.
Founded: 1994. **Membership Dues:** regular, $20. **Description:** Educates the public about protecting English as a common language and as the official language of the United States. Defends the right of individual states to make English the official language of government operations. Seeks to end bilingual education programs in public schools. Repeals federal mandates for the translation of government documents and voting ballots into languages other than English. **Publications:** *ProEnglish Advocate*, quarterly. Newsletter. Contains updates on legislative activity regarding English and other languages. **Price:** included in membership dues. Alternate Formats: online.

Environment

9913 ■ Tree of Peace Society
326 Cook Rd.
Hogansburg, NY 13655
Ph: (518)358-2641
Fax: (518)358-2641
E-mail: treeofpeace@earthlink.net
URL: http://www.treeofpeacesociety.info
Contact: Jake Swamp, Founder/Pres./Chm.
Founded: 1984. **Description:** Aims to address current topics in environmental and cultural education. Promotes environmental and social ethics. Works to preserve the culture and languages of the Haudenosaunee. Builds cross-cultural understanding between Native and non-Native people. **Publications:** *Tree of Peace Society Newsletter*. Alternate Formats: online.

Esperanto

9914 ■ Esperanto League for North America (ELNA)
PO Box 1129
El Cerrito, CA 94530
Ph: (510)653-0998
Free: (800)377-3726
Fax: (510)653-1468
E-mail: elna@esperanto-usa.org
URL: http://www.esperanto-usa.org
Contact: Phil Dorcas, Pres.
Founded: 1952. **Members:** 700. **Membership Dues:** individual, $40 (annual) ● family, $60 (annual) ● sustaining, $80 (annual) ● life (individual), $800 ● youth (under 27 years old), limited income, $20 (annual) ● friend of Esperanto, $10 (annual) ● life (sustaining), $1,800 ● life (patron), $2,400 ● life (family), $1,200 ● friendship doubler, $250 (annual) ● life (friendship doubler), $5,000 ● patron, $120 (annual). **Staff:** 1. **Budget:** $98,000. **Languages:** English, Esperanto. **Description:** Persons interested in promoting and using the international language Esperanto in the U.S. Seeks to introduce Esperanto into schools as the basic course for students learning foreign languages; sponsors Esperanto courses by mail. Cooperates with specialist organizations such as American Association of Teachers of Esperanto, Mensa, Institute for Esperanto in Commerce and Industry, and World Scout Organization. Maintains Esperanto Information Center; operates book service that sells literature in Esperanto, textbooks, recordings, dictionaries, and promotional materials. Sponsors teacher-training courses, including one at the North American Summer Esperanto Workshop. **Libraries: Type:** reference. **Holdings:** archival material. **Subjects:** history of language planning in the U.S. and elsewhere. **Awards:** Honorary Member. **Frequency:** periodic. **Type:** recognition. **Recipient:** for outstanding contribution to information, education, or culture of Esperanto in US. **Committees:** Education; Intercultural; Literary; Publishing. **Affiliated With:** Universal Esperanto Association. **Publications:** *Catalog of ELNA Esperanto Book Service*, annual ● *Comprehensive English-Esperanto Dictionary*. Book. **Price:** $27.00 ● *Esperanto: Learning and Using the International Language*. Book. **Price:** $15.00 ● *Esperanto USA*, bimonthly. Newsletter. Includes book reviews, calendar of events, and regional reports. **Price:** included in membership dues. ISSN: 1056-0297. **Circulation:** 1,100. Also Cited As: *ELNA Newsletter: News of the Language Problem and Esperanto as a Solution* ● *Handbook for New Members of ELNA* ● *Plena Manlibro de Esperanta Gramatiko*. Book. **Price:** $27.00 ● Membership Directory (in English and Esperanto), annual. **Price:** included in membership dues. **Circulation:** 1,000 ● Bibliography. **Conventions/Meetings:** annual Landa Kongreso - congress, allows Esperantists to get together and discuss the state of Esperanto learning and usage in the U.S. ● annual North American Summer Esperanto Workshop, language workshop.

9915 ■ International Catholic Esperanto Association (IKUE)
Address Unknown since 2007
Founded: 1910. **Members:** 1,300. **Languages:** English, Spanish. **Description:** International organization of Roman Catholics in 43 countries. Promotes the study and use of Esperanto as the international language. Seeks to introduce Esperanto as a regular accredited subject in Catholic institutions of learning. **Divisions:** Ecumenical; Esperanto Section of Vatican Radio; Liturgy; Mission Activity; Youth. **Affiliated With:** Universal Esperanto Association. **Also Known As:** Internacia Katolika Unio Esperantista. **Formerly:** International Catholic Esperanto Union. **Publications:** *Espero Katolika* (in Esperanto), monthly. Magazine. Contains Christian, ecumenical, interfaith, and Esperanto-movement information. **Price:** included in membership dues. **Circulation:** 1,300. **Advertising:** accepted ● *Jarlibro*, periodic. Yearbook ● Also publishes works concerning Esperanto and the Catholic church. **Conventions/Meetings:** annual congress (exhibits).

9916 ■ International Naturist Organisation for Esperanto (INOE)
c/o Leif Heilberg, Pres.
Viking Photography, Inc.
PO Box 22159
San Francisco, CA 94122
Fax: (415)759-6958
Contact: Leif Heilberg, Pres.
Founded: 1961. **Members:** 237. **Membership Dues:** individual, $16 (annual) ● couple, $23 (annual). **Budget:** EUR 26,600. **Regional Groups:** 2. **Languages:** English, Esperanto. **Description:** Naturists in 38 countries who speak Esperanto. Disseminates the ideas of naturists in Esperantist circles and promotes the use of Esperanto in naturist circles. Maintains correspondence network. **Study Groups:** Catholic. **Affiliated With:** International Naturist Federation; Universal Esperanto Association. **Publications:** *Naturista Vivo* (in Esperanto), quarterly. Journal. **Circulation:** 200. **Advertising:** accepted. **Conventions/Meetings:** annual Principal Convention, in conjunction with UEA - always July or August.

9917 ■ International Society of Friendship and Good Will (ISFGW)
c/o D. Gary Grady, Pres.
3119 Lassiter St.
Durham, NC 27707-3888
E-mail: dgary@mindspring.com
URL: http://www.friendshipandgoodwill.org
Contact: D. Gary Grady, Pres.
Founded: 1978. **Members:** 3,480. **Membership Dues:** college student, limited income, $15 (annual) ● patron, $90 (annual) ● senior, $20 (annual) ● individual, $30 (annual) ● sustaining, $60 (annual) ● life, $600. **Staff:** 2. **Budget:** $15,000. **Languages:** English, Esperanto. **Description:** Persons who speak or have an interest in the language of Esperanto, as well as others who are united to foster international understanding, peace, friendship, and goodwill among people of all nations. Promotes: Peace, Friendship, and Good Will Week; International Friendship Week; United Nations Week; Human Rights Month; Universal Women's Week; Universal Children's Week; International Amateur Radio Month; Freedom Week; Self-Improvement Month; Universal Letter-Writing Week; World Communication Week; International Volunteers Week; International Language Week; Universal Family Week; Celebration of Love Week. Maintains hall of fame honoring persons who have made significant contributions to humanity through their service in government, business, industry, education, and the arts and sciences. Operates speakers' bureau. **Libraries: Type:** reference. **Holdings:** 676; books. **Subjects:** Esperanto. **Awards:** Certificates of Commendation and Recognition. **Frequency:** annual. **Type:** recognition. **Affiliated With:** Esperanto League for North America. **Publications:** *Essentials of Esperanto*. **Price:** $20.00 ● *Friendship and Good Will* (in English and Esperanto), quarterly. Newsletter. Covers society activities and international issues involving the betterment of mankind; includes obituaries. **Price:** included in membership dues; $3.00/copy for nonmembers. **Circulation:** 3,000. **Advertising:** accepted. Alternate Formats: CD-ROM ● *International Society of Friendship and Good Will—Bulletin in Esperanto*, periodic. Provides information for people who speak or have an interest in the language of Esperanto. **Price:** included in membership dues. **Advertising:** accepted. **Conventions/Meetings:** annual World Esperanto Congress - meeting (exhibits) - always last full week in July.

Ethnic Studies

9918 ■ American Society for Ethnohistory (ASE)
c/o Duke University Press
PO Box 906660
Durham, NC 27708-0660

Ph: (919)687-3602
Free: (888)387-5687
Fax: (919)687-3602
E-mail: lesleyt@dukeupress.edu
URL: http://www.ethnohistory.org
Contact: Frank Salomon, Pres.

Founded: 1954. **Members:** 1,300. **Membership Dues:** retired person, student, $25 (annual) ● individual, $45 (annual) ● institution, $99 (annual) ● life, $700. **Budget:** $50,000. **Description:** Anthropologists, historians, art historians, geographers, libraries, universities and colleges, and research institutions in the social sciences. Promotes and encourages original research relating to the cultural history of ethnic groups worldwide. **Libraries: Type:** reference. **Holdings:** archival material. **Awards:** Erminie Wheeler-Voegelin Award. **Frequency:** annual. **Type:** recognition. **Recipient:** for best book length work in ethnohistory ● Robert F. Heizer Award. **Frequency:** annual. **Type:** recognition. **Recipient:** for best article concerning ethnohistory. **Formerly:** (1966) American Indian Ethnohistoric Conference. **Publications:** *Annual Meeting Program and Abstracts*, annual. Proceedings. **Advertising:** accepted ● *Ethnohistory*, quarterly. Journal. Covers historical and anthropological studies; includes book reviews. **Price:** included in membership dues. ISSN: 0014-1801. **Circulation:** 1,300. **Advertising:** accepted. Alternate Formats: online. **Conventions/Meetings:** annual conference (exhibits) - always November.

9919 ■ National Association for Ethnic Studies (NAES)

Western Washington Univ.
516 High St., MS 9113
Bellingham, WA 98225
Ph: (360)650-2349
Fax: (360)650-2690
E-mail: naes@wwu.edu
URL: http://www.ethnicstudies.org
Contact: Larry Estrada, Pres.

Founded: 1975. **Members:** 300. **Membership Dues:** regular (based on annual income), $35-$85 (annual) ● institution (department or library), $65 (annual) ● patron, $150 (annual) ● life, $500 ● associate, $40 (annual). **Description:** Individuals, libraries, and institutions. Promotes research, study, and curriculum design in the field of ethnic studies. **Awards:** Charles C. Irby Distinguished Service Award. **Frequency:** annual. **Type:** recognition. **Recipient:** for services to NAES and the field of ethnic studies ● Cortland Auser Undergraduate Student Paper Award. **Frequency:** annual. **Type:** recognition. **Recipient:** for best undergraduate student paper on ethnic studies ● Ernest M. Pon Memorial Award. **Frequency:** annual. **Type:** recognition. **Recipient:** for allocation of monies to Asian and Asian American organizations dedicated to human rights and equal justice ● Philips G. Davies Graduate Student Paper Award. **Frequency:** annual. **Type:** recognition. **Recipient:** for best graduate student paper on ethnic studies. **Computer Services:** Mailing lists. **Formerly:** (1976) National Association of Interdisciplinary Studies for Native American, Black, Chicano, Puerto Rican, Asian Americans; (1985) National Association of Interdisciplinary Ethnic Studies. **Publications:** *The Ethnic Reporter*, semiannual. Newsletter. Monitors developments in the field, discusses educational issues and reports on activities of the association. **Price:** included in membership dues. **Circulation:** 300. **Advertising:** accepted. Alternate Formats: microform; online ● *Ethnic Studies Review*. Journal. **Price:** included in membership dues. Also Cited As: *ESR* ● Monographs ● Proceedings. **Conventions/Meetings:** annual international conference (exhibits).

9920 ■ National Association of Hispanic and Latino Studies (NAHLS)

c/o National Association of African American Studies and Affiliates
PO Box 6670
Scarborough, ME 04070-6670
Ph: (207)839-8004 (207)283-0170
Fax: (207)839-3776
E-mail: naaasconference@earthlink.net
URL: http://www.naaas.org
Contact: Dr. Isela Almaguer, Contact

Founded: 1994. **Members:** 75. **Membership Dues:** individual, $125 (annual) ● institution, $500 (annual) ● student and sustaining, $100 (annual) ● life, $3,000. **Staff:** 15. **Budget:** $17,000. **Regional Groups:** 4. **State Groups:** 7. **Local Groups:** 25. **Languages:** English, Spanish. **Description:** Works to advance research about Hispanics and Latinos. Provides a forum for research presentations; conducts educational programs. Maintains speakers' bureau. **Awards:** Executive Directors Award. **Frequency:** annual. **Type:** recognition. **Recipient:** for excellence in research related to Hispanics and Latinos and a major contribution to education, community or research. **Computer Services:** Mailing lists, zip order. **Publications:** *Journal of Intercultural Disciplines*. **Price:** $30.00 /year for individuals; $50.00 /year for institutions; $18.00/copy ● *NAHLS-Bringing the World Together*. Proceedings. **Price:** $46.50/year ● *NAHLS News Notes* (in English and Spanish), 3/year. Newsletter. **Price:** free. **Circulation:** 2,000. **Advertising:** accepted ● *Network*. Journal. **Conventions/Meetings:** annual conference, book exhibits and educational materials (exhibits) - always second week of February.

European

9921 ■ Historians of German and Central European Art and Architecture (HGCEA)

c/o Rose-Carol Washton Long, Treas.
Prog. in Art History
CUNY Graduate Center
365 Fifth Ave.
New York, NY 10016-4309
E-mail: pchamet@siu.edu
URL: http://www.hgcea.org
Contact: Peter Chametzky, Pres.

Founded: 1997. **Membership Dues:** regular, $25 (annual) ● student, $15 (annual). **Multinational. Description:** Fosters the study of visual and material culture of Central Europe. Enhances communication and cooperation among scholars working on the art and architecture of the region. Organizes and supports scholarly endeavors and events focused on Central European topics. **Telecommunication Services:** electronic mail, rcwlong@aol.edu. **Affiliated With:** College Art Association. **Publications:** *Eurotexture*. Newsletter. Contains news, announcements, short essays, and reports that are of interest to members. **Price:** included in membership dues. Alternate Formats: online.

Exploration

9922 ■ Prince Henry Sinclair Society of the United States

c/o Delane Coleman
5044 W New World Dr.
Glendale, AZ 85302-5024
E-mail: princehssp@aol.com
Contact: Delane Coleman, Contact

Founded: 1993. **Members:** 500. **Budget:** $5,000. **Description:** Promotes research early transatlantic explorations to the new world, especially Prince Henry Sinclair's expedition in 1398.

Feminism

9923 ■ Committee on the Status of Women in Sociology (CSWS)

c/o American Sociological Association
1307 New York Ave. NW, Ste.700
Washington, DC 20005
Ph: (202)383-9005
Fax: (202)638-0882
E-mail: executive.office@asanet.org
URL: http://www.asanet.org
Contact: Sally Hillsman, Exec. Off.

Founded: 1970. **Members:** 6. **Staff:** 1. **Description:** A standing committee of the American Sociological Association. Aims to monitor and further the status of women in the sociological profession. **Telecommunication Services:** TDD, (202)638-0981. **Affiliated With:** American Sociological Association. **Conventions/Meetings:** annual conference, held in conjunction with ASA (exhibits).

9924 ■ Sociologists for Women in Society (SWS)

c/o Jessica Holden Sherwood, PhD, Exec. Off.
Univ. of Akron
Chafee Social Sci. Center
Kingston, RI 02881
Ph: (401)874-9510
Fax: (401)874-2588
E-mail: sws@etal.uri.edu
URL: http://www.socwomen.org
Contact: Jessica Holden Sherwood PhD, Exec. Off.

Founded: 1970. **Members:** 1,100. **Membership Dues:** income less than 15000, $14 (annual) ● with income of 15000-19999, $21 (annual) ● with income of 20000-29999, $31 (annual) ● with income of 30000-39999, $41 (annual) ● with income of 40000-49999, $46 (annual) ● income more than 50000, $51 (annual) ● sustaining, $100 (annual) ● life, $1,800. **Staff:** 3. **Local Groups:** 20. **Description:** Members are mainly national and international professional social scientists, sociologists and students of sociology, though membership is open to anyone interested in the purposes of the organization. Maximizes the effectiveness of and professional opportunities for women in sociology. Explores the contributions which sociology can, does, and should make to the investigation of and improvement in the status of women in society. Acts as watchdog of the American Sociological Association to ensure that it does not ignore the special needs of women in the profession; has organized a job market service to bring potential jobs and applicants together; established a discrimination committee offering advice and organizational support for women who pursue cases charging sex discrimination; has aided women to establish social, professional, and intellectual contacts with each other. Supports minority scholarships, breast cancer research and academic mentoring activities. **Awards:** Barbara Rosenblum Cancer Dissertation Scholarship. **Frequency:** annual. **Type:** scholarship. **Recipient:** for best cancer dissertation ● The Beth B. Hess Memorial Scholarship. **Frequency:** annual. **Type:** scholarship. **Recipient:** to a new or continuing graduate student who began her or his study in a community college or technical school ● Cheryl Allyn Miller Award. **Frequency:** annual. **Type:** recognition. **Recipient:** to sociology graduate student or a recent doctorate whose research or activism constitutes an outstanding contribution to the field of women and work ● Feminist Activism Award. **Frequency:** annual. **Type:** recognition. **Recipient:** to a member who has made notable contributions to improving the lives of women in society, especially through activism ● Feminist Lecturer Award. **Frequency:** annual. **Type:** recognition. **Recipient:** for outstanding scholarship in sociology of gender ● Mentor Award. **Frequency:** annual. **Type:** recognition. **Recipient:** to a member who is an outstanding feminist mentor. **Computer Services:** Mailing lists. **Committees:** Awards; Career Development; Discrimination; International; Nominations; Publications; Scholarship and Human Rights; Social Action; Student Concerns. **Publications:** *Gender and Society*, bimonthly. Journal. Includes articles, research reports and book reviews. **Price:** free for members; $246.00 /year for institutions. ISSN: 0891-2432. **Advertising:** accepted ● *Network News*, quarterly. Newsletter. Includes articles, letters to Editor, columns, minutes of meetings, job announcements, committee reports, and financial reports. **Price:** free for members; $17.00 /year for libraries. **Circulation:** 1,000. **Advertising:** accepted ● *The Social Construction of Gender*. Book ● *SWS Membership Directory*, semiannual. **Price:** $5.00 for members. Alternate Formats: online ● Brochures. **Con-**

ventions/Meetings: annual Summer Meeting (exhibits) - always August ● annual Winter Meeting - conference - always February.

Film

9925 ■ Academy of Science Fiction, Fantasy, and Horror Films (ASFFHF)
334 W 54th St.
Los Angeles, CA 90037-3806
Ph: (323)752-5811
Fax: (323)752-5811
E-mail: scifiacademy@comcast.net
URL: http://www.saturnawards.org
Contact: Robert Holguin, Pres.
Founded: 1972. **Members:** 3,000. **Membership Dues:** out-of-state, $40 (annual) ● regular, $120 (annual) ● friend, $500 (biennial) ● gold circle single supporter, $1,000 (annual) ● gold circle corporate, $5,000 (annual) ● gold circle elite, $10,000 (annual) ● gold circle patron, $50,000 (annual) ● gold circle stellar, $100,000 (annual). **State Groups:** 12. **Description:** Actors, writers, producers, directors, special effects people, and other individuals connected with the film industry; persons in the field of education. Recognizes artists in these genres in the fields of acting, music, direction, writing, cinematography, special effects, makeup, film criticism, set decoration and design, stop motion animation, publicity, and advertising. Conducts lectures and seminars. Maintains hall of fame. Sponsors Science Fiction Film Awards, a nationally syndicated television program. **Awards:** Golden Scroll Awards. **Frequency:** monthly. **Type:** recognition ● Saturn Awards. **Frequency:** annual. **Type:** recognition. **Recipient:** for outstanding science fiction, fantasy, and horror films of the year. **Telecommunication Services:** electronic mail, rholguin@saturnawards.com. **Committees:** Acting; Costume; Direction; Make-up; Music; Special Effects; Writing. **Divisions:** Art; Literature; Television; Theater. **Formerly:** Academy of Horror Films and Science Fiction Films. **Publications:** *Academy of Science Fiction, Fantasy, and Horror Films—Newsletter*, quarterly. Contains book and film reviews and calendar of events. **Price:** included in membership dues. **Circulation:** 3,500 ● *Saturn*, quarterly. **Conventions/Meetings:** annual banquet.

9926 ■ African American Cinema Society (AACS)
3617 Monclair St.
Los Angeles, CA 90018
Ph: (626)794-4677
Fax: (626)794-4677
E-mail: aclayton@wsbrec.org
URL: http://www.wsbrec.org
Contact: Avery Clayton, Exec. Dir.
Founded: 1976. **Members:** 1,350. **Membership Dues:** Carter G. Woodson (adult), $30 ● Emmitt Till (young adult), $20 ● Booker T. Washington (corporate), $5,000 ● Harriet Tubman (underground railroad), $100 ● Langston Hughes Literary (bronze), $500 ● George Washington Carver Science (silver), $750 ● Frederick Douglass Freedom (gold), $1,500 ● Thurgood Marshall Justice (platinum), $2,500. **Budget:** $32,000. **Description:** Faculty members, students, senior citizens, and film and jazz enthusiasts. Works to bring about an awareness of the contributions made by blacks to the motion picture industry in silent films, early talkies, and short and feature films. Feels that by viewing these films, black children can see the sacrifice and humiliation endured by black actors and actresses, directors, film writers, and producers while making films. Maintains collection of early black films owned by the Western States Black Research Center. Conducts research projects, film shows, and Black History Month seminars. Provides financial support to and student independent black filmmakers. Compiles statistics; maintains speakers' bureau, and charitable program; traveling film festival. **Libraries: Type:** reference. **Holdings:** 30,000; archival material, books, clippings, films, periodicals, photographs. **Subjects:** black history, literature. **Awards:** Black American Cinema Society Award. **Frequency:** annual. **Type:** monetary. **Formerly:** (2003) Black American Cinema Society. **Publications:** *Black Talkies Souvenir Book*, annual. **Price:** $3.50. **Advertising:** accepted ● *Mayme Clayton Golf Tournament Souvenir Book*, annual. **Price:** $100.00. **Advertising:** accepted. **Conventions/Meetings:** annual banquet, includes awards presentation ● annual Black Film Festival - meeting - always Los Angeles, CA ● competition.

9927 ■ American Film Institute (AFI)
2021 N Western Ave.
Los Angeles, CA 90027-1625
Ph: (323)856-7600
Fax: (323)467-4578
URL: http://www.afi.com
Contact: Jean Picker Firstenberg, Pres./CEO
Founded: 1967. **Members:** 135,000. **Membership Dues:** basic (minimum), $50 (annual) ● basic (maximum), $1,000 (annual) ● premiere circle (minimum), corporate circle (minimum), $2,500 (annual) ● premiere circle (maximum), corporate circle (maximum), $50,000 (annual). **Staff:** 114. **Description:** Preserves and develops the nation's artistic and cultural resources in film and video. Catalogs and preserves America's film heritage. Acts as a bridge between learning a craft and practicing a profession, through an intensive two-year course in filmmaking and film theory. Promotes the study of film as an art form with its own aesthetics, history, and techniques, through seminars for film teachers and special materials. Brings outstanding classic and contemporary films to public attention at a national film theater through The American Film Institute Theatre in the Kennedy Center in Washington, DC. Maintains exhibition services to produce touring film series; conducts television and video services to develop new audiences for the video arts; spotlights innovations; works with other organizations concerned with the television and video arts. Maintains the Center for Advanced Film and Television Studies. **Libraries: Type:** reference; open to the public. **Holdings:** 86,350; books, clippings, papers, periodicals, photographs. **Awards:** AFI Maya Deren Award for Independent Film and Video Artists. **Frequency:** annual. **Type:** recognition. **Recipient:** for artists whose visions have challenged the art form ● **Type:** grant. **Recipient:** for independent film and video makers ● Life Achievement Award. **Frequency:** annual. **Type:** recognition. **Recipient:** to an individual whose talent has advanced the filmmaking art ● Robert M. Bennett Award. **Frequency:** annual. **Type:** recognition. **Recipient:** for outstanding achievement in local and regional television programming. **Computer Services:** database, National Moving Image. **Publications:** *The AFI Catalog of Feature Films* ● *Catalog of Motion Pictures Produced in the United States* ● *Getting Started in Film*. **Conventions/Meetings:** Directing Workshop for Women, provides an opportunity for women in media arts to explore their talents in the art and craft of screen directing ● Gary Hendler Minority Filmmakers Program - meeting, a ten-month intensive program giving talented minority filmmakers an opportunity to pursue their creative vision ● annual Patricia Doyle Wise Lecture, delivered by a distinguished scholar or writer outside the field of moving image scholarship in locations across the country ● Television Writers Workshop, provides a learning environment for promising new talent ● Visions of U.S. Home Video Competition, recognizes original video production using small-video format.

9928 ■ Anthology Film Archives (AFA)
32 2nd Ave.
New York, NY 10003
Ph: (212)505-5181
Fax: (212)477-2714
E-mail: john@anthologyfilmarchives.org
URL: http://www.anthologyfilmarchives.org
Contact: Jonas Mekas, Artistic Dir.
Founded: 1970. **Members:** 600. **Membership Dues:** individual, $50 (annual) ● dual, $75 (annual) ● contributor, $100 (annual) ● donor, $250 (annual) ● preservation donor, $1,000 (annual) ● archival donor, $3,000 (annual) ● student, senior, $30 (annual) ● sponsor, $500 (annual) ● partner, $10,000 (annual). **Staff:** 5. **Budget:** $600,000. **Description:** Museum funded by foundations including the New York State Council on the Arts and National Endowment for the Arts. Maintains research facilities open to scholars and the public. Facilities include visual and written research library, publication of texts on film, nightly public screenings of films in the collection, and presentation of video works. Is concerned with the preservation of New American Cinema and European avant-garde and encourages presentation of new work. Operates two theatres that run films from the AFA collection as well as new material. Conducts research programs. **Libraries: Type:** by appointment only. **Holdings:** 12,400; audio recordings, books, clippings, periodicals, photographs. **Subjects:** history and practice of independent film and video. **Awards:** Preservation Honors. **Frequency:** annual. **Type:** recognition. **Recipient:** for preservation of cinema. **Divisions:** Film Collection; Library; Preservation; Video Library. **Supersedes:** Film-Makers' Cinematheque. **Publications:** *Film Preservation Honors Journal* ● *Legend of Maya Deren, Vol. I*. Book. Multi-volume book. ● Catalog.

9929 ■ Art Directors Guild (ADG)
11969 Ventura Blvd., 2nd Fl.
Studio City, CA 91604
Ph: (818)762-9995
Fax: (818)762-9997
E-mail: lydia@artdirectors.org
URL: http://www.artdirectors.org
Contact: Scott Roth, Exec. Dir.
Founded: 1937. **Members:** 840. **Staff:** 5. **Description:** Represents supervisors of the design, construction, and decor of motion pictures and settings. **Libraries: Type:** reference. **Holdings:** archival material, reports. **Awards:** Excellence in Production Design. **Frequency:** annual. **Type:** recognition. **Telecommunication Services:** electronic mail, scott@artdirectors.org. **Affiliated With:** International Alliance of Theatrical Stage Employees, Moving Picture Technicians, Artists and Allied Crafts of the United States, Its Territories and Canada. **Formerly:** (1968) Society of Motion Picture Art Directors; (2000) Society of Motion Picture and Television Art Directors. **Publications:** *Trace*, monthly. Newsletter. **Price:** included in membership dues. **Circulation:** 840.

9930 ■ Asian CineVision (ACV)
133 W 19th St., Ste.300
New York, NY 10011-4117
Ph: (212)989-1422
Fax: (212)727-3584
E-mail: info@asiancinevision.org
URL: http://www.asiancinevision.org
Contact: John C. Woo, Exec. Dir.
Founded: 1976. **Members:** 200. **Membership Dues:** media fan, $45 ● student, senior, media artist, $30 ● institution, organization, film fanatic, $75 ● new media sponsor, $150 ● director's club, $250 ● movie angel, $500 ● cinema circle, $1,000. **Staff:** 4. **Description:** Promotes and preserves Asian and Asian-American media expressions by: helping to develop and support both emerging and experienced Asian-American film and videomakers and other media artists working in a range of genres and styles; helping to ensure that the full spectrum of Asian and Asian-American media works reach diverse audiences in Asian-American communities and beyond. **Libraries: Type:** reference. **Holdings:** video recordings. **Awards:** Asian-American Media Award. **Frequency:** annual. **Type:** recognition. **Recipient:** for contribution to the field of Asian American media. **Publications:** *CineVue*, annual. Catalog. ISSN: 0895-805X ● *CineVue Journal*, quarterly ● *Out of the Shadows: Asians in American Cinema*. Book. **Conventions/Meetings:** annual Asian American International Film Festival, includes film and video (exhibits) - last 2 weekends of July.

9931 ■ Association of Independent Video and Filmmakers (AIVF)
Address Unknown since 2008
URL: http://www.aivf.org
Founded: 1974. **Members:** 5,000. **Membership Dues:** student, $40 (annual) ● individual, $70 (an-

nual) ● library, $80 (annual) ● dual, $110 (annual) ● non-profit/school, $200 (annual) ● business, $300 (annual). **Staff:** 12. **Budget:** $700,000. **Description:** Represents independent media artists working at all levels across all genres. Mission is to increase the creative and professional opportunities for independent video and filmmakers and to enhance the growth of independent media by providing services, advocacy, and information. Goals are to create new opportunities for the field; to engender a strong sense of community among the very diverse constituencies of independent media artists; and to promote media arts to a broader public. **Libraries: Type:** open to the public. **Holdings:** 450. **Computer Services:** Mailing lists. **Publications:** *The AIVF Film and Video Exhibitor's Guide*. Book. Contains a road map for navigating venues. **Price:** $25.00 for members; $30.00 for nonmembers ● *The AIVF Self-Distribution Toolkit*. Book. Contains articles and interviews by industry professionals. **Price:** $20.00 for members; $25.00 for nonmembers ● *Guide to Film and Video Distributors*. Book. Contains views of film and video distributors of North America. **Price:** $25.00 for members; $35.00 for nonmembers ● *Guide to International Film and Video Festivals*. Book. Contains contact information and profile of film and video festivals. **Price:** $25.00 for members; $35.00 for nonmembers ● *The Independent Film and Video Monthly*, 10/year. Magazine. **Price:** $3.95/issue. ISSN: 0731-5198. **Circulation:** 300,000. **Advertising:** accepted ● *The Next Step: Distributing Independent Films and Videos*. Books. Contains information on distribution. **Price:** $24.00 ● Journal ● Pamphlets.

9932 ■ Association of Moving Image Archivists (AMIA)
1313 N Vine St.
Hollywood, CA 90028
Ph: (323)463-1500
Fax: (323)463-1506
E-mail: amia@amianet.org
URL: http://www.amianet.org
Contact: Janice Simpson, Pres./Dir.
Founded: 1991. **Members:** 750. **Membership Dues:** individual, $75 (annual) ● nonprofit institution, $250 (annual) ● for-profit institution, $500 (annual) ● student, $50 (annual). **Staff:** 3. **Multinational. Description:** Works to advance the field of moving image archiving by fostering cooperation among individuals and institutions concerned with the collection, description, preservation, exhibition, and use of moving image materials (film and video). Seeks to improve public awareness of preservation needs through educational programs. **Libraries: Type:** reference. **Holdings:** books, business records, clippings, monographs, periodicals. **Subjects:** moving image conservation. **Awards:** Dan and Kathy Leab Award. **Frequency:** annual. **Type:** recognition. **Recipient:** for individuals who have made significant contributions to the field ● Silver Light Award. **Frequency:** annual. **Type:** recognition. **Recipient:** for distinguished contributions to the field. **Computer Services:** Mailing lists. **Committees:** Access; Cataloging and Documentation; Preservation. **Special Interest Groups:** Academic/Archival; Digital Archives; Independent Media; Lesbian, Gay, Bisexual, and Transgender; News and Documentary Collections; Regional Archives. **Formerly:** (1990) Film and Television Archives Advisory Committee. **Publications:** *AMIA Newsletter*, quarterly. **Price:** included in membership dues; $35.00 /year for nonmembers. ISSN: 1075-6477. **Circulation:** 750. **Advertising:** accepted ● *The Moving Image*, semiannual. Journal. **Price:** included in membership dues. **Conventions/Meetings:** annual conference (exhibits).

9933 ■ Black Filmmaker Foundation (BFF)
11 W 42nd St., 9th Fl.
New York, NY 10036
Ph: (212)253-1690
E-mail: info@dvrepublic.org
URL: http://www.dvrepublic.org
Contact: Mr. Warrington Hudlin, Pres.
Founded: 1978. **Members:** 1,500. **Staff:** 5. **Budget:** $300,000. **Description:** Assists emerging filmmakers and builds audiences for their work. Administers the DV Republic online community which hosts public discussion and social critiques of film and television. Administers a laboratory that develops digital films and interactive online filmmaking that is entertainment driven and socially concerned. **Libraries: Type:** reference. **Awards:** Webby Award for Weapons of Misdirection. **Frequency:** annual. **Type:** recognition. **Telecommunication Services:** electronic mail, hudlin@dvrepublic.org. **Conventions/Meetings:** monthly Networking Salon - meeting ● seminar ● workshop.

9934 ■ Center for Independent Documentary (CID)
680 S Main St.
Sharon, MA 02067
Ph: (781)784-3627
Fax: (781)784-8254
E-mail: info@documentaries.org
URL: http://www.documentaries.org/index.html
Contact: Susan Walsh, Exec. Dir.
Founded: 1981. **Membership Dues:** individual, $30 (annual). **Staff:** 2. **Budget:** $1,500,000. **Description:** Works to create films and videos on issues of contemporary social and cultural concerns. **Additional Websites:** http://documentaries.wordpress.com. **Telecommunication Services:** electronic mail, susi@documentaries.org.

9935 ■ Council on International Nontheatrical Events (CINE)
1112 16th St. NW, Ste.510
Washington, DC 20036
Ph: (202)785-1136
Fax: (202)785-4114
E-mail: info@cine.org
URL: http://www.cine.org
Contact: David L. Weiss, Exec. Dir.
Founded: 1957. **Staff:** 3. **Budget:** $300,000. **Description:** Works to present a realistic view of the U.S., its people, products, and philosophy, through showcasing the best of American documentary films to overseas audiences. Recognizes and fosters overall excellence in film and video production and provides educational and programmatic services to supports its goals. **Libraries: Type:** not open to the public. **Holdings:** 1,500; video recordings. **Awards:** CINE Golden Eagle Award. **Frequency:** annual. **Type:** trophy. **Recipient:** for high quality professional production in a variety of content categories, as well as in student and amateur works ● CINE Leadership Award. **Frequency:** annual. **Type:** recognition. **Recipient:** for a distinguished person in the film and video industry who has advanced or enhanced the quality of the media through outstanding leadership ● CINE Lifetime Achievement Award. **Frequency:** annual. **Type:** recognition. **Recipient:** for pinnacle leaders in the world of film and video whose lifetime contribution and great service are continuing to leave a profound impact on the culture ● CINE Special Jury Award. **Frequency:** annual. **Type:** recognition. **Recipient:** for excellence in four divisions. **Subgroups:** Adult; Agriculture; Art; Avant-Garde; Business and Industry; Education; Entertainment; Environment; Experimental; History; Human Relations; Medical; Religious; Safety; Science; Sports; Travel; TV and Government Documentary; Youth and Student Amateur. **Formerly:** (1963) Committee on International Non-Theatrical Events. **Publications:** *CINE Yearbook of Golden Eagle Winners*, annual. **Price:** $25.00. **Advertising:** accepted. Alternate Formats: online; CD-ROM. **Conventions/Meetings:** annual Gala Awards Event - workshop, an awards ceremony and reception, includes demos and speakers - always April in Washington, DC.

9936 ■ Film Advisory Board (FAB)
c/o Janet Stokes, Chair/CEO
263 W Olive Ave., No. 377
Burbank, CA 91502
Ph: (323)461-6541
Fax: (323)469-8541
URL: http://www.filmadvisoryboard.org
Contact: Janet Stokes, Chair/CEO
Founded: 1975. **Members:** 150. **Membership Dues:** charter, $50 (annual). **Local Groups:** 1. **Description:** Previews and evaluates films in all media and promotes better family entertainment on television and in motion pictures and videocassettes. Advocates the use of a rating system designed mainly for the home video market with 6 basic ratings, including C for Children, ages 10 and under; F for Family, all ages; PD for Parental Discretion; PD-M for Parental Discretion-Mature, ages 13 and over; EM for Extremely Mature, ages 17 and over; and AO for Adults Only, ages 18 and over; features X rating when appropriate. (The "PD" and "PD-M" categories are replacements for the M for Mature and the VM for Very Mature categories respectively. Though the M and VM are no longer in use they can be found on many videos in the video stores along with the others.) Maintains speakers' bureau. **Awards:** Award of Excellence. **Frequency:** annual. **Type:** recognition. **Recipient:** for entertainment products suitable for viewing and use by families and children. **Boards:** Family Entertainment Advisory. **Committees:** Award of Excellence Review; Review; Telephone. **Publications:** *Film Advisory Board Monthly*. Newsletter. **Advertising:** accepted. Alternate Formats: CD-ROM ● Also publishes list of "Award of Excellence" winners and list of Video Ratings. **Conventions/Meetings:** annual Awards Ceremony - conference.

9937 ■ Film Arts Foundation (FAF)
145 9th St., Ste.101
San Francisco, CA 94103
Ph: (415)552-8760 (415)552-0882
Fax: (415)552-0882
E-mail: info@filmarts.org
URL: http://www.filmarts.org
Founded: 1976. **Members:** 3,400. **Membership Dues:** filmmaker, $65 (annual). **Staff:** 16. **Budget:** $1,400,000. **Description:** Independent film- and video-makers. Supports and encourages artistic expression through the film and video media. Offers technical, educational, and information services. Makes available equipment for film and video production, editing, and screening. **Libraries: Type:** reference. **Holdings:** audio recordings, books, films, periodicals, video recordings. **Awards:** Film Arts Foundation Grant. **Frequency:** annual. **Type:** grant. **Recipient:** for artists in San Francisco, CA, and surrounding counties who plan to produce a film or video. **Computer Services:** database, festival, funding and other opportunities for independent filmmakers ● mailing lists ● online services. **Publications:** *Business Directory*. Alternate Formats: online ● *Film Arts Magazine*, bimonthly. Contains news and information for independent films and video-makers. **Price:** $65.00/year. **Circulation:** 10,000. **Advertising:** accepted. Alternate Formats: online. **Conventions/Meetings:** annual meeting - always January ● seminar, covers artistic, technical, legal, and business aspects of film and video making.

9938 ■ Film/Video Arts (F/VA)
270 W 96th St.
New York, NY 10025
Ph: (212)941-8787
E-mail: mariopaoli@fva.com
URL: http://www.fva.com
Contact: Mario Paoli, Exec. Dir.
Founded: 1968. **Members:** 1,200. **Membership Dues:** individual, $95 (annual) ● corporate, $349 (annual) ● associate, $450 (annual) ● Director's Chair, $1,000 (annual) ● Founder's Council, $2,000 (annual). **Staff:** 15. **Budget:** $950,000. **Description:** Seeks to encourage media production as an artistic, educational, and vocational experience for people who might not otherwise find such opportunities. Services include film and video workshops for individuals and organizations. Provides the use of postproduction facilities for film and video editing. Offers scholarship assistance to African-Americans, Asians, Latinos, and Native Americans pursuing careers in media arts. Offers fiscal sponsorship to individual artists. **Convention/Meeting:** none. **Computer Services:** Mailing lists. **Departments:** Education. **Programs:** Filmmakers in Residence; Fiscal Sponsorship; Membership Discount. **Projects:** Artist Mentor. **Absorbed:** Youth Film Distribution Center. **Formerly:** (1967) Film Club; (1984) Young Filmmakers Foundation. **Publications:** Newsletter, quarterly.

Price: included in membership dues. Alternate Formats: online.

9939 ■ Historians Film Committee/Film and History Magazine (HFC/Film & History)
c/o Peter C. Rollins, Ed.-in-Chief
Popular Culture Center
RR 3, Box 80
Cleveland, OK 74020-0515
Ph: (918)243-7637
Fax: (918)243-5995
E-mail: rollinspc@aol.com
URL: http://www.h-net.org/~filmhis
Contact: Peter C. Rollins, Ed.-in-Chief
Founded: 1970. **Members:** 1,000. **Description:** Individuals and institutions with an interest in the media and the impact of feature films, propaganda, documentaries, and television on popular perception. Promotes study of the film and broadcast media and their influence. Serves as a clearinghouse on the media; conducts educational programs; maintains speakers' bureau. Produces CD-ROMs, journals, proceedings, etc. for sale to libraries and individuals. **Awards:** John E. O'Connor Award. **Frequency:** annual. **Type:** monetary. **Recipient:** for service to journal. **Telecommunication Services:** electronic bulletin board. **Formerly:** (2003) Historians Film Committee. **Publications:** *Film and History: An Interdisciplinary Journal of Film and Television Studies*, semiannual. **Price:** $50.00 /year for individuals; $80.00 /year for institutions outside U.S., plus shipping and handling ($20). ISSN: 0360-3695. **Circulation:** 1,000. **Advertising:** accepted. **Conventions/Meetings:** biennial The Documentary Tradition: Documentary as a Force in Film and History - conference, scholars discuss the role of documentary as film and as historical force—from early classics up to the most recent (exhibits).

9940 ■ International Film Seminars (IFS)
6 E 39th St., 12th Fl.
New York, NY 10016
Ph: (212)448-0457
Fax: (212)448-0458
E-mail: ifs@flahertyseminar.org
URL: http://www.flahertyseminar.org
Contact: Mary Kerr, Exec. Dir.
Founded: 1960. **Staff:** 2. **Budget:** $300,000. **Description:** Promotes the annual Robert Flaherty Seminar, an international convocation of persons professionally active in independent film and video production, distribution, and exhibition. Seminars are named for the late Robert Flaherty, a pioneer in documentary film production. Fosters the study of film and video with emphasis on independent works created in the spirit of exploration and discovery. **Awards:** Charles Samu Award. **Frequency:** annual. **Type:** recognition. **Recipient:** for animators ● Leo Dratfield Award. **Frequency:** annual. **Type:** recognition. **Recipient:** to individuals or organizations who most exemplify the commitment and spirit of Leo Dratfield and who show a sustained ability to introduce innovative approaches into the media arts field ● Ronder Award. **Frequency:** annual. **Type:** fellowship ● Sol Worth Award. **Frequency:** annual. **Type:** fellowship. **Supersedes:** Robert Flaherty Foundation. **Conventions/Meetings:** annual Robert Flaherty Seminar - conference (exhibits) - always June.

9941 ■ National Board of Review of Motion Pictures (NBR)
40 W 37th St., Ste.501
New York, NY 10018
Ph: (212)465-9166
Fax: (212)465-9168
E-mail: nbr@nyc.rr.com
URL: http://www.nbrmp.org
Contact: Annie Schulhof, Pres.
Founded: 1909. **Members:** 8,500. **Membership Dues:** $250 (annual). **Staff:** 15. **Local Groups:** 3. **Description:** Persons interested in all phases of the motion picture industry and specialists interested in the technical and artistic phases of movies. **Libraries: Type:** reference. **Holdings:** biographical archives. **Awards:** Career Achievement Award. **Type:** recognition. **Publications:** *Films in Review*, bimonthly. Journal. Features television, film, video, and book reviews. **Price:** $18.00/year in U.S.; $22.00/year outside U.S. **Circulation:** 50,000.

9942 ■ National Center for Film and Video Preservation (NCFVP)
c/o American Film Institute
2021 N Western Ave.
Los Angeles, CA 90027-1657
Ph: (323)856-7600 (323)856-7708
Free: (800)774-4234
Fax: (323)467-4578
URL: http://www.afi.com
Contact: Jean Picker Firstenberg, Pres./Chm.
Founded: 1984. **Staff:** 15. **Budget:** $900,000. **Description:** Works to preserve the art of film, television and other forms of the moving image. Its mission is to: coordinate American moving image preservation activities on a national scale. Locate and acquire films and television programs for inclusion in the AFI Collection at the Library of Congress and other archives. **Libraries: Type:** reference. **Holdings:** 7,000; archival material. **Subjects:** film, television. **Computer Services:** database, lists the film and video holdings of U.S. Archives. **Affiliated With:** American Film Institute. **Publications:** *AFI Catalog of Feature Films*, periodic. Provides filmographies on feature-length motion pictures produced in the U.S. Alternate Formats: online; CD-ROM ● *American Film Institute Catalog of Feature Films: Meet Frank Capra* ● Has also published fact sheets and press releases.

9943 ■ National Center for Jewish Film (NCJF)
Brandeis Univ.
Lown 102 MS053
Waltham, MA 02454
Ph: (781)899-7044 (781)736-8600
Fax: (781)736-2070
E-mail: jewishfilm@brandeis.edu
URL: http://www.jewishfilm.org
Contact: Sharon Pucker Rivo, Exec. Dir.
Founded: 1976. **Staff:** 6. **Description:** Aims to gather, restore, circulate, and distribute film material relevant to the Jewish experience. Maintains speakers' bureau. Offers educational programs. Maintains archives and study center. Distributes over 250 Jewish theme films and videos. **Libraries: Type:** reference. **Holdings:** 8,000; films, video recordings. **Subjects:** the Holocaust, Nazi-made anti-Semitic propaganda, Yiddish, Jewish-themed films. **Formerly:** (1981) Rutenberg and Everett Yiddish Film Library. **Publications:** Catalogs. Alternate Formats: online. **Conventions/Meetings:** periodic meeting.

9944 ■ Outfest
3470 Wilshire Blvd., Ste.1022
Los Angeles, CA 90010
Ph: (213)480-7088
Fax: (213)480-7099
E-mail: outfest@outfest.org
URL: http://www.outfest.org
Contact: Stephen Gutwillig, Exec. Dir.
Founded: 1986. **Members:** 1,500. **Membership Dues:** family crew, $75 (annual) ● best boy/best girl, $100 (annual) ● assistant director, $200 (annual) ● director, $400 (annual) ● producer, $725 (annual) ● executive producer, $1,350 (annual) ● studio executive, $2,500 (annual) ● mogul, $5,000 (annual) ● legend, $10,000 (annual) ● crew, $50 (annual) ● student/senior/low income, $35 (annual). **Staff:** 35. **Budget:** $1,200,000. **Description:** Individuals and organizations. Serves as a programming group focusing on independent fiction, documentary, and short films and videos dealing with gay and lesbian situations. Promotes positive portrayal of gays and lesbians and avoidance of stereotypes. Offers year-round gay and lesbian-themed weekly screening series as well as a screenwriting lab. **Libraries: Type:** reference. **Holdings:** 650; audiovisuals, films, video recordings. **Subjects:** gay and lesbian. **Awards:** Audience and Juried Awards. **Frequency:** annual. **Type:** monetary. **Recipient:** for acceptance in outfest film festival ● Outfest Achievement Award. **Frequency:** annual. **Type:** recognition. **Recipient:** for a body of work that significantly contributes to LGBT film ● Outfest Honors. **Frequency:** annual. **Type:** recognition. **Recipient:** to individuals and companies for their committed support to Outfest and their outstanding contributions to LGBT media visibility ● Outfest Screenwriting Lab. **Frequency:** annual. **Type:** recognition. **Recipient:** for screen writers ● Screen Idol Awards. **Frequency:** annual. **Type:** recognition. **Recipient:** to individuals for gay, lesbian, bisexual and transgendered roles in feature films or films made for television. **Computer Services:** database, 13000 names ● mailing lists. **Projects:** Legacy for LGBT Film Preservation. **Formerly:** Gay and Lesbian Media Coalition; (1998) Out on the Screen. **Publications:** *Outfest: The Los Angeles Gay & Lesbian Film Festival Catalogue*, annual. **Price:** free. **Circulation:** 10,000. **Advertising:** accepted. **Conventions/Meetings:** annual festival, features Gay and Lesbian International Film Festival - always July.

9945 ■ San Francisco Camerawork
657 Mission St., 2nd Fl.
San Francisco, CA 94105-4104
Ph: (415)512-2020
Fax: (415)512-7109
E-mail: sfcamera@sfcamerawork.org
URL: http://www.sfcamerawork.org
Contact: Sharon Tanenbaum, Exec. Dir.
Founded: 1974. **Members:** 1,500. **Membership Dues:** subscribing, $50 ● student, $30 ● foreign, $40 ● sponsor, $200 ● collector, $350 ● benefactor, $650 ● patron, $1,250 ● platinum, $5,000. **Staff:** 4. **Budget:** $300,000. **Description:** Represents nationally recognized artists' organization whose purpose is to stimulate dialogue, encourage inquiry, and communicate ideas about contemporary photography and related media through a variety of artistic and professional programs. **Libraries: Type:** open to the public. **Holdings:** 3,000; articles, books, monographs, periodicals. **Subjects:** photography, art theory. **Publications:** *Camerawork: A Journal of Photographic Arts*, semiannual. Contains photography, essays, and critiques. **Price:** $8.00 for nonmembers; included in membership dues. **Circulation:** 5,000. **Advertising:** accepted.

9946 ■ Society for Cinema and Media Studies (SCMS)
729 Elm Ave.
Hester Hall, Rm. 170
Norman, OK 73019
Ph: (405)325-8075
Fax: (405)325-7135
E-mail: office@cmstudies.org
URL: http://www.cmstudies.org
Contact: Ms. Jane Dye, Admin. Coor.
Founded: 1959. **Members:** 1,000. **Membership Dues:** unemployed, underemployed, $25 (annual) ● student, $30 (annual) ● assistant professor, $55 (annual) ● associate professor, $65 (annual) ● full professor, joint regular, $75 (annual) ● independent scholar, $50 (annual) ● joint student, $40 (annual) ● institutional, $125 (annual) ● sustaining (minimum), $800 (annual). **Budget:** $40,000. **Description:** College and university professors, film scholars, critics, archivists, and others concerned with the history and criticism of the moving image. Provides exchange of ideas and information; encourages and publishes serious writing about film; assists students in film research and criticism. **Awards:** Honorary Lifetime Membership Award. **Frequency:** annual. **Type:** monetary. **Recipient:** for outstanding contributions to the field of cinema and media studies ● Katherine Singer Kovacs Book Award. **Frequency:** annual. **Type:** monetary. **Recipient:** for outstanding book on film and media studies ● Katherine Singer Kovacs Essay Award. **Frequency:** annual. **Type:** monetary. **Recipient:** for outstanding essay in scholarship and writing ● SCMS Dissertation Award. **Frequency:** annual. **Type:** monetary. **Recipient:** for the best dissertation in the field of cinema and/or media studies ● SCMS Pedagogy Award. **Frequency:** annual. **Type:** monetary. **Recipient:** for pedagogical achievement in instruction, publication and development of education materials and service in cinema and media studies pedagogy ● Student Writing Award. **Frequency:** annual. **Type:** monetary. **Recipient:** for

outstanding student writing in the field of film, television and other media studies. **Computer Services:** Mailing lists. **Telecommunication Services:** electronic mail, njdye@ou.edu. **Formerly:** Society of Cinematologists; (2005) Society for Cinema Studies. **Publications:** *Cinema Journal*, quarterly, every November, February, May, and August. ISSN: 0009-7101. **Advertising:** accepted. Alternate Formats: online. **Conventions/Meetings:** annual conference (exhibits).

9947 ■ Society for Cinephiles/Cinecon
3727 W Magnolia Blvd., No. 760
Burbank, CA 91505
Free: (800)411-0455
E-mail: cinecon@hollywoodtimemachine.com
URL: http://www.cinecon.org
Contact: Bob Birchard, Pres.
Membership Dues: regular, $20 (annual). **Description:** Persons interested in the historic preservation and showing of classic film. **Publications:** *Cinephiles*. Newsletter. **Conventions/Meetings:** annual convention, showing of rare preserved film, and memorabilia vendors (exhibits) ● annual festival and banquet (exhibits) - 2008 Aug. 28-Sept. 1, Los Angeles, CA.

9948 ■ Sundance Institute (SI)
PO Box 684426
Park City, UT 84068
Ph: (801)328-3456
Fax: (801)575-5175
E-mail: institute@sundance.org
URL: http://www.sundance.org
Contact: Robert Redford, Pres./Founder
Founded: 1981. **Membership Dues:** premier benefactor, $10,000 (annual) ● benefactor, $5,000 (annual) ● supporter, $2,500 (annual) ● contributor, $1,250 (annual). **Staff:** 39. **Budget:** $2,000,000. **Description:** Resource center for independent filmmakers and other artists. Works to support the development of well-crafted, independent films for a variety of markets; educate individuals on aspects of their craft; provide a disciplined and professional environment for participants, including the opportunity to collaborate with professionals. Sponsors programs in film, theater, writing, and music. **Funds:** Sundance Documentary. **Programs:** Documentary Film; Feature Film; Film Music; Native American. **Publications:** Newsletter, monthly. **Price:** included in membership dues. Alternate Formats: online.

9949 ■ U.S.A. Film Festival (USAFF)
6116 N Central Expy., Ste.105
Dallas, TX 75206
Ph: (214)821-6300
Fax: (214)821-6364
E-mail: usafilmfestival@aol.com
URL: http://www.usafilmfestival.com
Contact: Ann Alexander, Managing Dir.
Founded: 1970. **Members:** 3,000. **Membership Dues:** general, $20 (annual) ● associate individual, $85 (annual) ● associate dual, $115 (annual) ● sponsor, $350 (annual) ● patron, $1,000 (annual). **Staff:** 4. **Budget:** $400,000. **Description:** Organizes a national film festival. **Awards:** Great Director Award. **Frequency:** annual. **Type:** recognition ● Master Screen Artist Award. **Type:** recognition ● National Short Film/Video Competition Awards. **Frequency:** annual. **Type:** monetary. **Recipient:** for the best film or video (must be made in the USA, under 60 minutes, and produced during the previous year). **Publications:** *Program Book*, annual. **Advertising:** accepted. **Conventions/Meetings:** annual Kid Film festival, for children ● annual USA Film Festival - always spring.

9950 ■ Visual Studies Workshop (VSW)
31 Prince St.
Rochester, NY 14607
Ph: (585)442-8676
E-mail: info@vsw.org
URL: http://www.vsw.org
Contact: Kris Merola, Education Coor.
Founded: 1969. **Members:** 2,500. **Staff:** 15. **Description:** Individuals interested in the study and creation of visual media including illustrated books, films and videos, and photography. Offers MFA program in visual studies in conjunction with State University of New York; conducts community education classes; sponsors lectures with film and video screenings; holds exhibitions. Makes available facilities for the production of visual artworks to qualified individuals. Maintains Research Center containing 100,000 photographic and photomechanical prints, books, periodicals, independent films, and videotapes. **Libraries: Type:** open to the public. **Holdings:** 16,000; audio recordings, books, periodicals, photographs, video recordings. **Subjects:** photography, visual arts, mass media. **Computer Services:** Mailing lists ● online services. **Committees:** Book Service; Exhibitions; Traveling Exhibitions. **Programs:** Educational; Master of Fine Arts; Media; Media Access; Media Installation. **Formerly:** (1970) Photographic Studies Workshop. **Publications:** *Afterimage*, bimonthly. Journal. Covers photography and experimental film and video. Focuses on cultural politics, feminism, and critical theory. Includes reviews and job listings. **Price:** included in membership dues; $33.00 /year for individuals; $90.00 /year for libraries and institutions; $20.00/year for students. ISSN: 0300-7472. **Circulation:** 4,000. **Advertising:** accepted. Alternate Formats: microform; online ● Books. **Price:** $3.00 in U.S.; $4.50 outside U.S. ● Also publishes artists' books and other materials. **Conventions/Meetings:** periodic seminar and symposium ● periodic workshop.

Finnish

9951 ■ Finnish American Historical Archives (FAHA)
c/o Gary Kaunonen, Archivist
Finlandia Univ.
601 Quincy St.
Hancock, MI 49930
Ph: (906)487-7347
Fax: (906)487-7557
E-mail: archives@finlandia.edu
URL: http://www.finlandia.edu/Department/FAHC/fahc.html
Contact: Gary Kaunonen, Archivist
Founded: 1932. **Membership Dues:** individual, $50 (annual) ● family, $75 (annual). **Staff:** 2. **Languages:** English, Finnish. **Description:** Promotes the collection and preservation of materials related to the history and culture of Finns in the United States. Maintains archives. **Libraries: Type:** open to the public. **Holdings:** 20,000. **Subjects:** Finns in North America, Finnish history and culture. **Conventions/Meetings:** conference ● seminar.

9952 ■ International Order of Runeberg (IOR)
6094 Myrtle Ave.
Eureka, CA 95503
Ph: (707)445-2364
E-mail: swede.finn@humboldt1.com
Contact: Janet Anderson, Contact
Founded: 1920. **Members:** 1,430. **Staff:** 3. **Regional Groups:** 3. **Local Groups:** 28. **Description:** Promotes the preservation of Pan-Scandinavian culture and traditions, with special emphasis on Finland. Conducts student exchange program. **Awards:** Runeberg Student Scholarship. **Frequency:** annual. **Type:** recognition. **Supersedes:** Swedish-Finnish Benevolent and Aid Association of America and Swedish-Finnish Temperance Association. **Publications:** *Leading Star*, monthly. Newsletter. **Price:** $10.00/year. **Circulation:** 1,350. **Advertising:** accepted. Also Cited As: *Ledstjaran*. **Conventions/Meetings:** quadrennial congress.

Folk

9953 ■ American Folklore Society (AFS)
c/o Timothy Lloyd, Exec. Dir.
Ohio State Univ.
Mershon Center
1501 Neil Ave.
Columbus, OH 43201-2602
Ph: (614)292-3375
Fax: (614)292-2407
E-mail: lloyd.100@osu.edu
URL: http://www.afsnet.org
Contact: Timothy Lloyd, Exec. Dir.
Founded: 1888. **Members:** 2,200. **Membership Dues:** regular, $100 (annual) ● student, partner, $35 (annual) ● independent, retired, $80 (annual) ● new professional, $65 (annual) ● sustainer, $150 (annual) ● sponsor, $250 (annual). **Budget:** $600,000. **Multinational. Description:** Represents individuals and institutions interested in the collection, discussion, and publication of folklore throughout the world. **Awards:** The American Folklore Society Lifetime Scholarly Achievement Award. **Frequency:** biennial. **Type:** recognition. **Recipient:** for outstanding accomplishments over a career of scholarship ● The Americo Paredes Prize. **Type:** recognition. **Recipient:** for excellence in integrating scholarship and engagement with the people and communities ● The Benjamin A. Botkin Prize. **Frequency:** annual. **Type:** recognition. **Recipient:** for outstanding achievement in public folklore ● The Chicago Folklore Prize. **Frequency:** annual. **Type:** recognition. **Recipient:** to the best folklore book of the year ● The Kenneth Goldstein Award for Lifetime Academic Leadership. **Frequency:** biennial. **Type:** recognition. **Recipient:** for outstanding achievement in the building and strengthening of academic programs in folklore ● The Zora Neale Hurston Prize. **Frequency:** annual. **Type:** recognition. **Recipient:** for the best student work in any medium on African American folklore. **Computer Services:** Online services, web site resources. **Publications:** *American Folklore Society News*, bimonthly. Newsletter. Features book notices, calendar of events, calls for papers, employment opportunities, meeting news, and publication news. **Price:** included in membership dues; $25.00 /year for nonmembers. ISSN: 0745-5178. **Circulation:** 1,600 ● *Journal of American Folklore*, quarterly. Contains scholarly articles, notes, and film, record, exhibition and book reviews of interest to folklorists. **Price:** included in membership dues; $85.00 /year for nonmembers. ISSN: 0021-8715. **Circulation:** 2,600. **Advertising:** accepted. **Conventions/Meetings:** annual conference (exhibits) ● meeting (exhibits) - always October.

9954 ■ Baidarka Historical Society
PO Box 5454
Bellingham, WA 98227-5454
Ph: (360)734-9226
Contact: George B. Dyson, Pres.
Founded: 1984. **Members:** 250. **Membership Dues:** individual, $20 (annual). **Staff:** 1. **Description:** Strives to further knowledge of the Aleut baidarka and its role in Russian-American history. (The baidarka is a type of kayak made of animal skins.) Encourages the evolution of the skin boat. **Libraries: Type:** reference. **Publications:** Papers.

9955 ■ Folk Alliance
510 S Main St., 1st Fl.
Memphis, TN 38103
Ph: (901)522-1170
Fax: (901)522-1172
E-mail: fa@folk.org
URL: http://www.folk.org
Contact: Dan Navarro, Pres.
Founded: 1989. **Members:** 2,000. **Membership Dues:** individual, $70 (annual) ● sustaining, $100 (annual) ● partner, $95 (annual) ● small organization, $150 (annual) ● medium organization, $230 (annual) ● large organization, $505 (annual) ● life, $1,000 ● affiliate, $50 (annual) ● student, $35 (annual). **Staff:** 5. **Budget:** $400,000. **Regional Groups:** 6. **Multinational. Description:** Promotes multicultural, traditional, and contemporary folk music, dance, and related performing arts. Believes that through folk music and dance, living cultural expressions and traditions are shared. Provides opportunities for participation and appreciation of folk music and dance. Conducts educational and research programs. Compiles statistics. **Libraries: Type:** reference. **Holdings:** audio recordings, periodicals. **Subjects:** folk music and dance. **Awards:** Lifetime Achievement

Award. **Frequency:** annual. **Type:** recognition. **Recipient:** for contributions to the field. **Computer Services:** database ● mailing lists. **Also Known As:** North American Folk Music and Dance Alliance. **Publications:** Newsletter, bimonthly. **Price:** included in membership dues. **Circulation:** 2,500. **Advertising:** accepted. Alternate Formats: online ● Membership Directory, annual. **Conventions/Meetings:** annual conference (exhibits) - always February. 2009 Feb. 19-22, Memphis, TN.

9956 ■ Folk Art Society of America (FASA)
PO Box 17041
Richmond, VA 23226-7041
Ph: (804)285-4532
Free: (800)527-FOLK
E-mail: fasa@folkart.org
URL: http://www.folkart.org
Contact: Ann F. Oppenhimer, Pres.
Founded: 1987. **Members:** 1,200. **Membership Dues:** family, $50 (annual) ● foreign, $60 (annual) ● individual, gift, $35 (annual) ● contributing, $100 (annual) ● bronze star, $250 (annual) ● gold star, $1,000 (annual) ● silver star, $500 (annual). **Staff:** 3. **Languages:** English, French, Italian. **Description:** Individuals and institutions interested in the discovery, study, promotion, preservation, exhibition, and documentation of folk art; folk artists, and folk art environments. Conducts educational programs. **Libraries: Type:** by appointment only; not open to the public. **Holdings:** 500; archival material, audio recordings, books, clippings, periodicals. **Subjects:** American folk and outsider art. **Awards:** Award of Distinction. **Frequency:** annual. **Type:** recognition. **Recipient:** for contribution to American art and culture. **Publications:** *Contemporary American Folk Art: A Collector's Guide, 1996*. Book. **Price:** $29.95 for nonmembers; $22.00 for members ● *Folk Art Messenger*, 3/year. Magazine. **Price:** $22.00/year in U.S.; $50.00/year foreign. ISSN: 1043-5026. **Circulation:** 1,000. Alternate Formats: online. **Conventions/Meetings:** annual conference.

9957 ■ Independent Scholars of Asia (ISA)
c/o Dr. Ruth-Inge Heinze, Natl. Dir.
2321 Russell, No. 3C
Berkeley, CA 94705-1959
Ph: (510)849-3791
Fax: (510)849-3791
E-mail: riheinze@juno.com
URL: http://www.hypersphere.com/isa
Contact: Dr. Ruth-Inge Heinze, Natl. Dir.
Founded: 1981. **Members:** 138. **Membership Dues:** general, $18 (annual) ● student, supporter, $12 (annual). **Staff:** 4. **Budget:** $1,000. **Regional Groups:** 4. **State Groups:** 1. **Local Groups:** 4. **Multinational. Description:** Institutions of higher learning and scholars of anthropology, geography, history, linguistics, literature, political sciences, psychology, religion, and social sciences interested in Asian culture. Promotes the study of Asian affairs through dissemination of information about research conducted in Asian countries, information on grants and fellowships, essays, and book reviews. Organizes local, state, national, and international workshops and conferences. Maintains Speaker's Bureau. **Libraries: Type:** reference. **Subjects:** biographical files on Asian scholars. **Affiliated With:** Association for Asian Studies. **Formerly:** Asian Folklore Studies Group. **Publications:** *Annual International Conference on Shamanism and Alternative Healing*, annual. Proceedings. Contains 40 essays and discussions from conferences. **Price:** $23.95 ● Newsletter, 3/year, every April, August, and December. Features information on Asian studies. **Price:** $18.00. **Circulation:** 138. **Conventions/Meetings:** annual conference and meeting (exhibits).

9958 ■ Jargon Society (JS)
PO Box 15458
Winston-Salem, NC 27113
E-mail: mail@jargonbooks.com
URL: http://www.jargonbooks.com/jargon.html
Contact: Mr. Thorns Craven, Treas.
Founded: 1951. **Members:** 100. **Staff:** 2. **Budget:** $150,000. **Description:** Deals in contemporary poetry, literature, and visual art, particularly nontraditional folk art, environmental art, and the avant-garde. Issues limited editions of selected works. Strives to preserve such works. Aids artists occasionally in obtaining fellowships and grants. Organizes authors' lectures, poetry readings, and art exhibits. **Formerly:** (1968) Jargon Press. **Conventions/Meetings:** annual board meeting.

9959 ■ Maine Folklife Center (MFC)
5773 S Stevens Hall, Rm. 112B
Orono, ME 04469-5773
Ph: (207)581-1891
Fax: (207)581-1823
E-mail: folklife@maine.edu
URL: http://www.umaine.edu/folklife
Contact: James Moreira PhD, Dir.
Founded: 1957. **Members:** 325. **Membership Dues:** basic, $25 (annual) ● friend, $50 (annual) ● sponsor, $100 (annual) ● patron, $500 (annual) ● benefactor, $1,000 (annual). **Staff:** 3. **Budget:** $90,000. **Description:** Seeks to strengthen communities through promotion of folklife, folklore, and history of Maine and Atlantic Canada; encourages appreciation of diverse cultures and heritage of the region. **Libraries: Type:** reference; open to the public. **Holdings:** 12,443; articles, audio recordings, books, periodicals, photographs, video recordings. **Computer Services:** Online services. **Publications:** *A Catalog of the First 1800 Accessions*. Alternate Formats: online ● *Northeast Folklore*, annual. Monograph ● Newsletter. Alternate Formats: online. **Conventions/Meetings:** biennial board meeting.

9960 ■ The Mountain Institute (TMI)
1707 L St. NW, Ste.1030
Washington, DC 20036
Ph: (202)452-1636
Fax: (202)452-1635
E-mail: summit@mountain.org
URL: http://www.mountain.org
Contact: Bob Davis, Pres./CEO
Founded: 1972. **Staff:** 25. **Budget:** $3,700,000. **Description:** Educational and scientific organization dedicated to advancing mountain cultures and preserving mountain environments. Promotes public education about mountain environments; develops mountain community leadership roles; creates international nature preserves in mountainous regions; develops sustainable businesses for mountain communities. Conducts field research. Operates charitable program. **Convention/Meeting:** none. **Libraries: Type:** reference. **Holdings:** 1,000. **Telecommunication Services:** electronic mail, assistant@mountain.org. **Programs:** Andes; Appalachian; Himalayan; Peak Enterprise; Research and Education; Sacred Mountains. **Formerly:** Woodlands Institute; Woodlands Mountain Institute. **Publications:** Annual Report, annual. Alternate Formats: online.

9961 ■ National Council for the Traditional Arts (NCTA)
1320 Fenwick Ln., Ste.200
Silver Spring, MD 20910
Ph: (301)565-0654
Fax: (301)565-0472
E-mail: info@ncta.net
URL: http://www.ncta.net
Contact: Julia Olin, Exec. Dir.
Founded: 1933. **Staff:** 6. **Budget:** $1,350,000. **Description:** Producers and presenters of festivals, national and international performing arts tours, concerts, recordings, films, and radio and television programs that feature the authentic folk, ethnic and tribal arts and artists. Assists the National Park Service, U.S. Information Agency, the National Endowment for the Arts, and state and local organizations in planning and directing cultural presentations. **Publications:** none. **Convention/Meeting:** none. **Libraries: Type:** reference. **Formerly:** National Folk Festival Association.

9962 ■ Slavic and East European Folklore Association (SEEFA)
c/o Jeanmarie Rouhier-Willoughby, Sec.-Treas.
Russian and Eastern Stud. and Linguistics
1055 Patterson Off. Tower
Univ. of Kentucky
Lexington, KY 40506-0027
E-mail: jrouhie@pop.uky.edu
URL: http://www.arts.ualberta.ca/SEEFA
Contact: Jeanmarie Rouhier-Willoughby, Sec.-Treas.
Membership Dues: student, $10 (annual) ● individual, $25 (annual) ● institution, $35 (annual). **Multinational. Description:** Facilitates the exchange of knowledge among scholars interested in Slavic and East European folklore. Seeks to promote instruction and to encourage the preparation of teaching materials and translations. Fosters exchanges, summer programs, and research in Slavic and East European Folklore and related fields such as anthropology, ethnic studies, history, literature, and musicology. **Publications:** *FOLKLORICA: Journal of the Slavic and East European Folklore Association*, semiannual. Alternate Formats: online.

9963 ■ Society for Folk Arts Preservation (SFAP)
75 Timberhill Ln.
South Fallsburg, NY 12779
Ph: (845)436-7314
E-mail: info@societyforfolkarts.com
Contact: Kalika Stern, Exec. Dir.
Founded: 1977. **Members:** 200. **Description:** Museums, craft groups, anthropologists, filmmakers, artists, and travelers. Preserves living folk art and craft traditions throughout the world; documents and disseminates traditional craft techniques for the use of artists, anthropologists, social scientists and others; develops projects to allow for the survival of traditional crafts and cultural values despite changing surroundings or political upheaval; and assists the public in locating fine craft items. Sponsors exhibitions, seminars, workshops, lectures, slide presentations, and working expeditions to folk art areas around the world. Serves as clearinghouse for living folk arts and crafts information and events. **Convention/Meeting:** none. **Libraries: Type:** reference. **Holdings:** 18,000; photographs, video recordings. **Subjects:** Asian craft traditions and techniques. **Committees:** Exhibition; Film. **Publications:** *Society for Folk Arts Preservation—Newsletter: In Support of Living Art and Craft Traditions*, 3/year. Includes book reviews and listing of events and exhibitions. **Price:** included in membership dues. **Circulation:** 500.

9964 ■ Tennessee Folklore Society (TFS)
PO Box 201
Middle Tennessee State Univ.
Murfreesboro, TN 37132
Ph: (615)898-2573
E-mail: info@tennesseefolklore.org
URL: http://tennesseefolklore.org
Contact: Dr. Kenneth R. DeShane, Ed.
Founded: 1934. **Members:** 400. **Membership Dues:** student, $10 (annual) ● individual, $20 (annual) ● joint, library, institution, $30 (annual). **Staff:** 3. **Budget:** $6,000. **Description:** Professional educators, government employees, and others. Promotes the study, collection, and use of traditional expressive culture in Tennessee and the mid-South. Produces records; audio, and video tapes; acts as adviser on folklore media projects. Serves as conduit for folklore project grants. Maintains research files, unpublished material, and publication back issues. **Libraries: Type:** reference. **Holdings:** 300; archival material. **Computer Services:** Mailing lists. **Publications:** *Tennessee Folklore Society—Bulletin*, quarterly. Journal. Covers the traditional folk culture of the upper South. Includes book reviews, calendar of events, and record reviews. **Price:** included in membership dues. ISSN: 0040-3253. **Circulation:** 400. Alternate Formats: microform. Also Cited As: *TFSB* ● Also publishes indexes to journal and issues phonograph record series and videotapes. **Conventions/Meetings:** annual conference (exhibits) - always November.

Folk Dance

9965 ■ North American Federation of German Folk Dance Groups (NAFGFDG)
c/o Doug Hall, Treas.
515 Marquis St.
San Antonio, TX 78216-5217

E-mail: ebarneysmith@hotmail.com
URL: http://www.germandance.org/NAFGFDG
Contact: Doug Hall, Treas.
Founded: 1994. **Membership Dues:** association, $25 (annual) ● group, $15 (annual) ● individual, $10 (annual). **Multinational. Description:** Promotes and preserves the traditional dance, music, folklore and crafts of Germany and German speaking countries. Practices and cultivates German folk dance forms. Preserves and disseminates related aspects of folklore in their historical and cultural context including costumes, needlecrafts and music. Documents the cultural and historical background of members. **Publications:** *German Folkdancer*, 5/year. Newsletter. Provides news and educational articles. **Price:** included in membership dues.

Food

9966 ■ Kitchen Gardeners International (KGI)
3 Powderhorn Dr.
Scarborough, ME 04074
Ph: (207)883-5341
E-mail: info@kitchengardeners.org
URL: http://www.kitchengardeners.org
Contact: Roger Doiron, Contact
Founded: 2003. **Membership Dues:** basic, $30 (annual) ● supporting, $50 (annual) ● sustaining, $100 (annual) ● patron, $500 (annual). **Description:** Seeks to empower individuals, families, and communities to achieve greater levels of food self-reliance through the promotion of kitchen gardening, home-cooking, and sustainable local food systems. Works to connect, serve and expand the global community of people who grow their own food. Promotes public awareness of the benefits of participating and contributing in food production and preparation. **Publications:** Newsletter, monthly. Alternate Formats: online.

French

9967 ■ American Society of the French Order of Merit
Address Unknown since 2007
Founded: 1996. **Members:** 150. **Staff:** 8. **National Groups:** 1. **Languages:** French. **Description:** Members of the French Order of Merit. Seeks to promote French culture in the United States and American Culture in France. Strives to strengthen the traditional friendship and goodwill existing between the peoples of the two countries. Makes donations to organizations involved in Franco-American exchange. **Publications:** Newsletter, semiannual. **Price:** for members. **Conventions/Meetings:** annual assembly - always December.

9968 ■ French Institute Alliance Francaise (FIAF)
22 E 60th St.
New York, NY 10022
Ph: (212)355-6100 (646)388-6646
Fax: (212)935-4119
E-mail: reception@fiaf.org
URL: http://www.fiaf.org
Contact: Ms. Marie Monique Steckel, Pres.
Founded: 1971. **Members:** 7,500. **Membership Dues:** senior and academic, $70 (annual) ● individual, $90 (annual) ● family, $140 (annual) ● senior and academic family, $100 (annual) ● contributing, $250 (annual) ● supporting, $750 (annual) ● patron, $1,500 (annual). **Staff:** 45. **Budget:** $7,000,000. **Languages:** English, French. **Description:** Works to: promote and enhance knowledge of French and Francophone culture; encourage interaction and better understanding between French-speaking and American communities by creating programs in the arts and education that provide appealing, accessible, and innovative experiences; make an important contribution to the broad spectrum of arts events that nourish and enrich New York City's diverse audiences; serve those who look to it for leadership, acumen, and guidance in the exploration and presentation of the arts of Francophone cultures; feature a full season of film screenings, literary events, live performances of music, theater, and dance, as well as series and workshops developed for students and children. **Libraries: Type:** reference; lending. **Holdings:** 50,000; audio recordings, audiovisuals, books, films, periodicals, video recordings. **Formed by Merger of:** Alliance Francaise de New York; French Institute in the United States.

9969 ■ Order of the Noble Companions of the Swan
c/o William de Alabona-Ostrogojsk, Exec. Off.
PO Box 404
Milltown, NJ 08850
E-mail: swanorder@aol.com
URL: http://www.swanorder.org
Contact: William de Alabona-Ostrogojsk, Exec. Off.
Founded: 1983. **Members:** 350. **Multinational. Description:** Multinational Order of Christian Chivalry. Serves the chivalric tradition and continues the tradition of knighthood. Perpetuates the memory of the first Swan Knight, Godfrey de Bouillon (French leader of the 1st Crusade after the capture of Jerusalem in 1099, he was elected to the first ruler of the Latin Kingdom of Jerusalem) and his Crusader Knights of Jerusalem. **Awards:** Order of Merit of Saint Angilbert. **Frequency:** annual. **Type:** recognition. **Recipient:** for service rendered to The Order of the Noble Companions of the Swan. **Publications:** *Brevery of the Order Prayerbook* ● *Handbook of the Order of the Noble Companions of the Swan*, bimonthly ● *Swan Bulletin*, bimonthly. Newsletter. **Conventions/Meetings:** biennial congress and banquet, knighting ceremony.

Furniture

9970 ■ Society of American Period Furniture Makers (SAPFM)
c/o Brian Coe, Ed.
2865 Friendship-Ledford Rd.
Winston-Salem, NC 27107
E-mail: slashheh@aol.com
URL: http://www.sapfm.org
Contact: Steven M. Lash, Pres.
Founded: 1999. **Membership Dues:** individual, $35 (annual) ● joint, $50 (annual) ● student, $20 (annual) ● institutional, $50 (annual) ● business, benefactor, $100 (annual). **Description:** Represents the interests of amateur and professional woodworkers, educators, collectors, curators, conservators and individuals interested in making, restoring, and conserving American period furniture. **Awards:** Cartouche Award. **Frequency:** annual. **Type:** recognition. **Recipient:** lifetime achievement in period furniture making. **Publications:** *American Period Furniture*, annual. Journal. **Price:** free for members.

Gastronomy

9971 ■ Slow Food USA
20 Jay St., Ste.313
Brooklyn, NY 11201
Ph: (718)260-8000
Fax: (718)260-8068
E-mail: info@slowfoodusa.org
URL: http://www.slowfoodusa.org
Contact: Erika Lesser, Exec. Dir.
Founded: 1986. **Members:** 14,000. **Membership Dues:** individual, $60 (annual) ● couple, $75 (annual) ● student, $30 (annual). **Local Groups:** 150. **Description:** Individuals and corporations in 27 countries committed to traditions that bring family and friends together to share great food and wine in a spirit of conviviality and civility. "Slow food" is defined as food prepared slowly and lovingly by time-honored methods, using fresh ingredients, and consumed at leisure in gracious surroundings. Believes that meals should be an opportunity for communication. Maintains that fast food is detrimental to health, jeopardizes the gastronomic heritage of regions around the world, is responsible for the eradication of family life, and is an important factor in the deforestation of the Amazon because of the increasing demand for cheap meat. Encourages public education about: folklore and local traditions; health benefits of wholesome foods and beverages; the degradation of quality that comes from excessive processing and packaging of food; the ecological benefits that come from respecting the lands and waters and by abandoning pesticides and additives. Works to establish a worldwide reputation for the U.S. as a first-class culinary capital and wine-producing country, not a country of fast food and soft drinks. Founded in Italy in response to the opening of a McDonald's in Rome. **Awards:** Betsy Lyndon Award. **Frequency:** annual. **Type:** monetary ● **Type:** scholarship. **Recipient:** to chefs, winemakers, and others studying culinary arts. **Computer Services:** Online services, forums. **Telecommunication Services:** electronic mail, erika@slowfoodusa.org. **Programs:** Ark of Taste; Corporate Matching Gift; Presidia; Slow Food in Schools. **Publications:** *Slow* (in English, French, German, Italian, Japanese, and Spanish), quarterly. Journal. Features in-depth stories about food culture across the globe. ● *The Slow Food Guide to Chicago*. Handbook. Serves as a guidebook on the best Slow restaurants, markets and bars in Chicago. Alternate Formats: online ● *The Slow Food Guide to New York*. Handbook. Serves as a guidebook on the best Slow restaurants, markets and bars in New York City. Alternate Formats: online ● *The Snail*, bimonthly. Magazine. Contains articles on important food issues such as genetically modified foods and sustainable fisheries. Alternate Formats: online ● Brochure. Alternate Formats: online. **Conventions/Meetings:** periodic dinner and seminar.

Gay/Lesbian

9972 ■ National Latina/o Lesbian, Gay, Bisexual, and Transgender Organization (LLEGO)
Address Unknown since 2008
Members: 172. **Membership Dues:** individual, $35 (annual) ● companion, $50 ● activist, $250 ● champion, $500. **Multinational. Description:** Strives to organize Latina/o lesbian, gay, bisexual and transgender communities on local, regional, national, and international levels; promotes understanding of social, health, and political barriers due to sexual orientation, gender identity and ethnic background. Sponsors training sessions. **Computer Services:** Mailing lists. **Telecommunication Services:** electronic mail, gnieto@llego.org. **Programs:** ACCION LLEGO; Avanzado; Horizontes; Proyecto Fenix. **Publications:** *AIDSida Info*, quarterly. Newsletter. **Price:** included in membership dues ● *AquiLLEGO* (in English and Spanish), quarterly. Newsletter. **Price:** included in membership dues ● *4th Annual Latina Lesbian Leadership Breakfast*. Booklet. Alternate Formats: online ● Annual Report, annual. **Conventions/Meetings:** annual conference ● retreat and workshop.

Genealogy

9973 ■ Hispanic Genealogical Society
PO Box 231271
Houston, TX 77223-1271
Fax: (281)449-4020
E-mail: joguerra@hispanicgs.com
URL: http://www.hispanicgs.com
Contact: Lydia Zermeno Chavarria, Pres.
Founded: 1983. **Members:** 300. **Membership Dues:** household, $25 (annual). **Description:** People interested in Hispanic genealogy. Aims to increase awareness in the field of Hispanic genealogical research. Produces newsletters and annual journal. Holds meetings. **Publications:** Journal, annual. **Price:** included in membership dues ● Newsletters. **Conventions/Meetings:** monthly meeting - always 3rd Wednesday in Houston, TX.

9974 ■ Irish Family History Forum (IFHF)
PO Box 67
Plainview, NY 11803-0067
URL: http://www.ifhf.org
Contact: James J. McDonald, Pres.
Founded: 1991. **Membership Dues:** individual in U.S., $20 (annual) ● family, individual outside U.S.,

$30 (annual) ● corporate in U.S., $50 (annual) ● corporate outside U.S., $60 (annual). **Description:** Family historians and genealogists interested in Irish family history. **Libraries: Type:** by appointment only; reference. **Holdings:** 300; books, video recordings. **Publications:** *Forum*, bimonthly. Newsletter.

9975 ■ Puerto Rican Hispanic Genealogical Society (PRHGS)
PO Box 260118
Bellerose, NY 11426-0118
Ph: (914)941-4920
E-mail: prhgs@yahoo.com
URL: http://www.rootsweb.com/~prhgs
Contact: Patricia Montalvo Calandra, Pres.

Founded: 1996. **Members:** 125. **Membership Dues:** individual, $20 (annual) ● family, $30 (annual). **Description:** People interested in Hispanic genealogy. Aims to develop and enhance skills, knowledge, and ability to conduct a competent genealogical search. Sponsors conferences, seminars, training sessions, and originates print and electronic publications. **Publications:** *Apellidos Familiares*. Directory. Contains entries from current and new members. **Price:** $10.00 ● *El Coqui de Ayer*, bimonthly. Newsletter. **Price:** included in membership dues; $2.50 for nonmembers. **Conventions/Meetings:** conference ● seminar.

German

9976 ■ American Institute for Contemporary German Studies (AICGS)
1755 Massachusetts Ave. NW, Ste.700
Washington, DC 20036-2121
Ph: (202)332-9312
Fax: (202)265-9531
E-mail: info@aicgs.org
URL: http://www.aicgs.org
Contact: Dr. Jackson Janes, Exec. Dir.

Founded: 1983. **Staff:** 12. **Budget:** $2,000,000. **Languages:** English, German. **Multinational. Description:** Strengthens the German-American relationship in an evolving Europe and changing world. Produces objective and original analyses of developments and trends in Germany, Europe and the United States; creates new transatlantic networks; and facilitates dialogue among the business, political, and academic communities to manage differences and define and promote common interests. **Awards:** Global Leadership Award. **Frequency:** annual. **Type:** recognition. **Recipient:** for a German business leader. **Computer Services:** Mailing lists. **Conventions/Meetings:** periodic conference and seminar.

9977 ■ Goethe-Institut Inter Nationes
1014 5th Ave.
New York, NY 10028
Ph: (212)439-8700
Fax: (212)439-8705
E-mail: info@newyork.goethe.org
URL: http://www.goethe.de/ins/us/ney/deindex.htm
Contact: Gabriele Becker, Dir.

Founded: 1957. **Staff:** 21. **Languages:** English, German. **Nonmembership. Description:** Promotes knowledge of the German language abroad and fosters international cultural cooperation. Conveys a comprehensive picture of Germany by providing information on Germany's cultural, social and political life. Aims to shape and revise the image of Germany in the United States. Fosters German language and culture within the American educational system. Develops a transatlantic network for the exchange of culture and ideas. **Libraries: Type:** reference; lending; open to the public. **Holdings:** 9,000; audio recordings, books, periodicals, video recordings. **Subjects:** German civilization with emphasis on literature, film, arts. **Formerly:** Goethe Institut. **Publications:** *Calendar of Events*, quarterly. **Circulation:** 5,000. **Advertising:** accepted ● *GAPP Magazine* (in English and German), semiannual ● *GAPP Newsletter*, annual.

9978 ■ Gottscheer Heritage and Genealogy Association (GHGA)
PO Box 725
Louisville, CO 80027-0725
E-mail: snancy@centurytel.net
URL: http://www.gottschee.org
Contact: Elizabeth Nick, Pres.

Founded: 1992. **Members:** 500. **Membership Dues:** individual, $22 (annual) ● family, $27 (annual). **Description:** Descendants of the Gottschee Region of Slovenia, which was inhabited by German-speaking people from the 14th century until 1941, when they were relocated to Untersteiermark (lower Syria) and the Gottschee Region was transferred to Italian rule. Gottschee is now a part of Slovenia. Seeks to preserve the history of the Gottschee region and its German-speaking inhabitants. Conducts historical and genealogical research on the Gottschee Region and its German-speaking inhabitants; assists family historians and genealogists. Provides support to agencies maintaining historic properties in the Gottschee Region; organizes tours to view Gottschee historic sites. **Publications:** *The Gottschee Tree*, quarterly. Journal. Contains historical articles. **Price:** included in membership dues ● *The Gottscheer Connection*, 3/year. Newsletter. **Price:** included in membership dues. **Conventions/Meetings:** annual meeting, business meeting with speakers (exhibits) - always June.

9979 ■ Society for German-American Studies (SGAS)
c/o Dr. LaVern J. Rippley, Newsletter Ed.
St. Olaf Coll.
German Dept.
Northfield, MN 55057-1098
Ph: (507)786-3233
E-mail: rippleyl@stolaf.edu
URL: http://www.ulib.iupui.edu/collections/kade/sgasin.html
Contact: William D. Keel, Pres.

Founded: 1968. **Members:** 500. **Membership Dues:** regular, in North America, $25 (annual) ● regular, outside North America, $40 (annual) ● student, $10 (annual) ● joint (in same address), $35 (annual) ● institution in North America, $30 (annual) ● institution outside North America, $40 (annual) ● sustaining, $40 (annual) ● donor, $75 (annual) ● affiliated organization, $150 (annual) ● life, $500. **Regional Groups:** 25. **Languages:** English, German. **Description:** Academicians, students, and individuals and organizations interested in German-American studies. Works to advance the field, improve cross-cultural relations, and to assist those interested in studying, researching, or teaching German-Americana. Conducts and disseminates studies on German-American history, literature, and culture. **Awards:** Special Recognition Award. **Frequency:** annual. **Type:** recognition. **Computer Services:** Mailing lists, of members. **Publications:** *Newsletter of the Society for German-American Studies*, quarterly. **Price:** $25.00/year. ISSN: 0741-5733. **Circulation:** 700 ● *Yearbook of German-American Studies*, annual. Includes bibliographies and book reviews. **Price:** $35.00. ISSN: 0741-2827. **Conventions/Meetings:** annual meeting and symposium - always April.

9980 ■ Society for the History of the Germans in Maryland (SHGM)
c/o German-American Citizens Association of Maryland
PO Box 22367
Baltimore, MD 21203
Ph: (410)522-4144
Fax: (410)522-1146
E-mail: dbm@md-germans.org
Contact: Gerald William Wittstadt, Pres.

Founded: 1886. **Members:** 350. **Membership Dues:** single, $20 (annual) ● married couple, $25 (annual). **Staff:** 1. **Description:** Individuals interested in German-American relations and in the preservation and publication of historical material relative to the activities of Americans of German descent in Maryland and other states. Society does not maintain genealogical records and does not act as a genealogical society. **Libraries: Type:** not open to the public. **Holdings:** 44. **Subjects:** German-American history. **Publications:** Journal, annual. **Price:** $20.00 for nonmembers; included in membership dues. **Circulation:** 1,000 ● Also publishes literature on German-American history. **Conventions/Meetings:** annual banquet - always in April or May.

Gifted

9981 ■ American Mensa
1229 Corporate Dr. W
Arlington, TX 76006-6103
Ph: (817)607-0060
Free: (800)66-MENSA
Fax: (817)649-5232
E-mail: nationaloffice@americanmensa.org
URL: http://www.us.mensa.org
Contact: Pamela L. Donahoo CAE, Exec. Dir.

Founded: 1960. **Members:** 50,000. **Membership Dues:** individual, $52 (annual). **Staff:** 19. **Budget:** $2,200,000. **Regional Groups:** 10. **Local Groups:** 139. **Description:** Individuals who have scored in the top two percent of the general population on a standardized intelligence test. Strives to identity and foster human intelligence for the benefit of humanity; to encourage research into intelligence; and to provide a stimulating and social environment for its members. **Awards:** Awards for Excellence. **Frequency:** annual. **Type:** recognition. **Recipient:** for research on human intelligence ● Distinguished Teacher. **Frequency:** annual. **Type:** recognition. **Recipient:** for teachers ● Group of the Year. **Frequency:** annual. **Type:** recognition. **Recipient:** for a group ● Hall of Fame. **Frequency:** annual. **Type:** recognition. **Recipient:** for individuals ● Lifetime Achievement. **Frequency:** annual. **Type:** recognition. **Recipient:** for individuals ● Local Group Owls. **Frequency:** annual. **Type:** recognition. **Recipient:** for a local group. **Computer Services:** Mailing lists, of members. **Committees:** Communications; Electronic Voting; Leadership Development; Marketing; National Awards; Nominating; Research Review; Risk Management. **Also Known As:** Mensa, the High IQ Society. **Publications:** *InterLoc*, 10/year. Newsletter. Serves as the channel of communication for local and national officers. **Price:** free for members and officers. **Circulation:** 2,200 ● *Mensa Bulletin*, 10/year. Magazine. **Price:** free for members; $12.00 for guests. **Circulation:** 40,675. **Advertising:** accepted ● *Mensa International Journal*, 10/year. Magazine. Contains additional articles and advertisements of interest to members worldwide. ● *Mensa Research*, 3/year. Journal. **Price:** $7.00 sample; $21.00 3 issues; $42.00 6 issues. **Conventions/Meetings:** annual convention, organized by local group, which receives bid from American Mensa Committee - usually July.

9982 ■ Hollingworth Center for Highly Gifted Children (HCHGC)
827 Central Ave., No. 282
Dover, NH 03820-2506
Ph: (207)655-3767 (303)554-7895
E-mail: kkearney@midcoast.com
URL: http://www.hollingworth.org
Contact: Kathi Kearney, Founder

Founded: 1983. **Members:** 300. **Membership Dues:** individual, $30 (annual) ● individual, $55 (biennial) ● individual, $75 (triennial) ● life, $300. **Description:** Exceptionally gifted children and their families and teachers; interested others. (Exceptionally gifted children have an IQ above 140 or exhibit prodigious talent in areas such as mathematics or music.) Functions as a resource and support network for members; provides information to members seeking solutions to the problems of raising and educating a gifted child. Offers referral service. **Publications:** *Highly Gifted Children*, quarterly. Newsletter. Includes book reviews and calendar of events. **Price:** $25.00/year. **Circulation:** 300. **Conventions/Meetings:** annual National Conference on the Exceptionally Gifted - conference and workshop, includes student conference (exhibits).

9983 ■ International Society for Philosophical Enquiry (ISPE)
c/o John A. Kosinski, PhD, Acting Admissions Off.
1200 Remsen Mill Rd.
Wall Township, NJ 07753-7206
Ph: (732)280-8799
E-mail: j.a.kosinski@ieee.org
URL: http://www.thethousand.com
Contact: John A. Kosinski PhD, Acting Admissions Off.
Founded: 1974. **Members:** 600. **Membership Dues:** regular, $50 (annual). **Budget:** $20,000. **Multinational.** **Description:** Individuals in 35 countries ranked in the top 1/10 of 1 percentile of intellect, as determined by standardized adult intelligence and linguistic ability tests. Helps members enrich their education and experience in an environment of intellectual research, accomplishment, and high achievement; members progress through various levels within the organization according to their achievements and are encouraged to make original contributions to society. Conducts specialized education and research programs; creates ad hoc committees to examine special philosophical and ethical issues. Compiles statistics. Provides accreditation for titles achieved and worldwide publicity for recipients. **Libraries: Type:** reference. **Holdings:** 80; archival material, books. **Awards:** Whiting Memorial Award. **Frequency:** annual. **Type:** recognition. **Recipient:** for unique contribution to humanity using high intelligence. **Committees:** President's Committee on Membership; Psychometrics; Whiting Memorial Fund. **Formerly:** (1974) Thousand. **Publications:** *International Society for Philosophical Enquiry—Membership Roster*, annual. Membership Directory. Includes cross-references. **Price:** available to members only. **Circulation:** 650 ● *The ISPE*. Brochures ● *Telicom*, monthly. Journal. Contains articles, poems, biographies of members, and society news. **Price:** included in membership dues. ISSN: 1087-6456. **Circulation:** 500 ● Also publishes statement of goals. **Conventions/Meetings:** annual breakfast - every 14th of July.

9984 ■ INTERTEL
PO Box 1083
Tulsa, OK 74101
Ph: (918)583-2928
Fax: (918)583-2928
E-mail: interteloffice@aol.com
URL: http://www.intertel-iq.org
Contact: Kort Patterson, Pres.
Founded: 1966. **Members:** 1,700. **Membership Dues:** individual, $39 (annual). **Staff:** 1. **Budget:** $60,000. **Regional Groups:** 8. **Description:** Individuals who have proven to have an intelligence quotient at or above the 99th percentile on a valid supervised test acceptable to the Intertel Acceptance Committee (INTERTEL is an acronym for International Legion of Intelligence.) Encourages a meaningful and lasting intellectual fellowship; fosters an exchange of ideas on any and all subjects; assists in research relating to high intelligence. **Telecommunication Services:** electronic mail, kort@overalltech.net. **Committees:** Audit; Election; Intertel Acceptance; Publications. **Publications:** *Integra, the Journal of Intertel*, monthly. Includes commentaries, short stories, poetry, and puzzles. **Price:** included in membership dues; $35.00 /year for nonmembers. ISSN: 0279-9995. **Circulation:** 1,700. **Advertising:** accepted ● *The One-Percent Solution: A Short History of INTERTEL, 1966-1988*. Book ● Membership Directory, annual. **Conventions/Meetings:** annual general assembly - usually July.

9985 ■ Lewis M. Terman Society
PO Box 539
New York, NY 10101-0539
URL: http://www.toponesociety.com
Contact: Ronald K. Hoeflin PhD, Founder
Membership Dues: individual, $30 (annual). **Staff:** 3. **Description:** Comprises of the One-in-a-Thousand Society, Top One Percent Society, Epimetheus Society, and the Omega Society. Members are persons with intelligence in the 99th percentile (top 1&percent;). Members share ideas and opinions through their journal. **Additional Websites:** http://www.oathsociety.com, http://www.epimetheussociety.com, http://www.theomegasociety.com. **Formed by Merger of:** (2004) Top One Percent Society; (2004) One-in-a-Thousand Society. **Publications:** *Termite*, monthly. Journal.

9986 ■ Mega Society (MS)
13155 Wimberly Sq., No. 284
San Diego, CA 92128
E-mail: ward-jeff@san.rr.com
URL: http://www.megasociety.org
Contact: Jeff Ward, Admin.
Founded: 1982. **Members:** 35. **Membership Dues:** regular, $15 (annual). **Description:** Individuals who have proven by test to have an intelligence quotient higher than that of 99.9999&percent; of the general population. Works to provide a forum for individuals of extremely high intellectual ability; seeks to increase knowledge about these intelligence levels. Derives its name from the prefix mega-, meaning million; theoretically, on any given test or combination of tests accepted for admission purposes by the society, only one person in one million can qualify for membership. **Convention/Meeting:** none. **Absorbed:** One-in-a-Million Society; Noetic Society. **Supersedes:** 501 Society; 606 Society. **Publications:** *Noesis*, quarterly. Journal. Contains official business, articles, and correspondence. **Price:** $15.00/year. **Circulation:** 50. Alternate Formats: online.

9987 ■ Prometheus Society
PO Box 24513
Federal Way, WA 98093
E-mail: prometheus@iquadrivium.org
URL: http://www.prometheussociety.org
Contact: Fred Britton, Pres.
Founded: 1982. **Members:** 60. **Membership Dues:** in North America, $25 (annual) ● outside North America, $35 (annual). **Description:** Persons exceeding the 99.997th percentile of general intelligence. Conducts research; provides for the exchange of ideas and opinions. Membership aids the society in identifying the norms for high ability intelligence tests. **Computer Services:** Mailing lists. **Formed by Merger of:** (1985) Titan Society; Xenophon Society. **Publications:** *Gift of Fire*, 10/year. Journal. **Price:** included in membership dues; $20.00 /year for nonmembers. **Circulation:** 80. **Advertising:** accepted. Alternate Formats: online.

9988 ■ Triple Nine Society (TNS)
c/o Ed Schreiber, Membership Off.
4046 S Magnolia Way
Denver, CO 80237
E-mail: info@triplenine.org
URL: http://www.triplenine.org
Contact: Ed Schreiber, Membership Off.
Founded: 1978. **Members:** 540. **Membership Dues:** full, in U.S. and Canada, $25 (annual) ● full, outside U.S. and Canada, $30 (annual). **Staff:** 10. **Description:** Individuals who can produce certified evidence of a score in the 99.9th percentile on specific standardized intelligence tests. Promotes free exchange of ideas among persons of proven high intelligence. Fosters development of an intellectual community based on inquiry into broad rather than narrow fields of knowledge. Compiles statistics. **Publications:** *Vidya*, monthly. Journal. Includes roster of members, index of past articles, and Correspondence Group directory. **Price:** $25.00 /year for nonmembers in U.S. and Canada; $30.00 /year for nonmembers outside U.S. and Canada; $10.00 internet; included in membership dues. **Circulation:** 400. **Advertising:** accepted. **Conventions/Meetings:** annual conference.

Graphic Arts

9989 ■ American Printing History Association (APHA)
PO Box 4519
Grand Central Sta.
New York, NY 10163-4519
Ph: (212)930-9220
Fax: (212)930-0079
E-mail: sgcrook@printinghistory.org
URL: http://www.printinghistory.org
Contact: Stephen Crook, Exec. Sec.
Founded: 1974. **Members:** 750. **Membership Dues:** individual, $45 (annual) ● contributing, $90 (annual) ● institutional, $55 (annual) ● sustaining, $200 (annual) ● benefactor, $500 (annual) ● student, $20 (annual). **Staff:** 1. **Regional Groups:** 5. **Description:** Bibliophiles, booksellers, book and artifact collectors, designers, editors, educators, historians, librarians, library school professors, printers, publishers, museum curators, private press proprietors, and researchers; students in these and related fields. Works to record and preserve the heritage of printing and publishing and their related arts and skills. Seeks to encourage the preservation of the artifacts of printing including presses, equipment, type specimens, and records; the study of printing history, especially American printing history, from a world context to national, regional, state, and local contexts; the development and maintenance of libraries and museums for the preservation and use of oral, written, and printed records, and other source materials for printing history, including the artifacts of printing. Sponsors exhibits; compiles statistics; conducts censuses of artifacts and archives. Assists in publications on printing history. **Awards: Frequency:** annual. **Type:** recognition. **Recipient:** for an institution and an individual for outstanding contribution to printing history. **Committees:** Artifacts Preservation; Education; Exhibits; Relationships; Research. **Publications:** *Printing History Journal*, semiannual. **Price:** free for members. ISSN: 0192-9275. **Circulation:** 800. **Advertising:** accepted ● Newsletter, quarterly. **Price:** free for members. **Circulation:** 800. **Advertising:** accepted ● Membership Directory, periodic. **Conventions/Meetings:** annual conference ● annual meeting - always January.

9990 ■ American Typecasting Fellowship (ATF)
PO Box 263
Terra Alta, WV 26764
Ph: (304)789-2455
E-mail: wvtypenut@aol.com
Contact: Richard L. Hopkins, Coor.
Founded: 1978. **Members:** 350. **Multinational.** **Description:** Persons interested in preserving the arts of metal typecasting, letter design, and letterpress printing. **Publications:** Newsletter, periodic. **Price:** $4.00 in U.S. and Canada; $8.00 outside U.S. and Canada. **Circulation:** 350. **Advertising:** accepted. **Conventions/Meetings:** biennial conference.

9991 ■ International Institute for Frame Study (IIFS)
Address Unknown since 2008
URL: http://www.iifs.org
Founded: 1992. **Description:** A public archive devoted exclusively to the history of picture frames, comprising hundreds of photographs, drawings, out-of-print books, auction and frame makers' catalogues, articles, videotapes of public and private collections, and other frame-related ephemera. Conducts frame surveys of public and private collections and special exhibitions. Provides educational programs which include exhibitions, lectures and workshops. **Libraries: Type:** open to the public. **Holdings:** archival material, photographs. **Subjects:** frames, gilding. **Computer Services:** Mailing lists. **Publications:** *IIFS Journal*, annual. **Price:** included in membership dues ● Membership Directory, annual. **Conventions/Meetings:** annual workshop.

9992 ■ Society of American Graphic Artists (SAGA)
32 Union Sq., Rm. 1214
New York, NY 10003
E-mail: tbaker@monmouth.edu
URL: http://www.clt.astate.edu/elind/sagamain.htm
Contact: Linda Adato, Pres.
Founded: 1915. **Members:** 250. **Membership Dues:** regular, $40 (annual). **Description:** Workers in the print media (etching, lithography, engraving, woodcut,

wood engraving); also offers associate membership. Sponsors exhibitions and traveling shows. **Awards:** Lifetime Achievement. **Type:** recognition. **Formerly:** (1931) Society of Brooklyn Etchers; (1947) Society of American Etchers; (1951) Society of American Etchers, Gravers, Lithographers and Woodcutters. **Publications:** *Sagazine*, quarterly. Newsletter. Contains lists of exhibition opportunities, member activities and other items of interest to printmakers. **Advertising:** accepted. Alternate Formats: online. **Conventions/Meetings:** dinner, for members ● Juried Shows ● annual meeting, for members ● biennial Print Competition.

9993 ■ Typophiles
30 E 23rd St., 8th Fl.
New York, NY 10010
E-mail: info@typophiles.org
URL: http://www.typophiles.org
Contact: Mr. Paul Romaine, Sec.-Treas.
Founded: 1930. **Members:** 300. **Membership Dues:** active, $25 (annual). **Description:** Represents designers, printers, book collectors, artists, calligraphers, private press owners, wood engravers, librarians and others interested in graphic arts. Promotes the love and appreciation of fine graphic design and printing. Conducts quarterly meeting-luncheons and maintains publications. **Awards:** Honorary Membership. **Frequency:** periodic. **Type:** recognition. **Recipient:** for contributions to the art of fine printing and to the association. **Publications:** *Typophile Chapbooks*, irregular. Monograph. **Price:** included in membership dues ● *The Typophiles Newsletter*, quarterly. Contains news about the association's activities and other activities, and exhibitions relating to printing and graphic arts. **Price:** included in membership dues. **Advertising:** accepted ● Also publishes chapbooks on graphic arts and keepsakes. **Conventions/Meetings:** quarterly luncheon, with program ● quarterly meeting and lecture.

Great Plains

9994 ■ Institute of the Great Plains (IGP)
PO Box 68
Lawton, OK 73502
Ph: (580)581-3460
Fax: (580)581-3458
E-mail: archeoly@museumgreatplains.org
URL: http://institutegreatplains.tripod.com
Contact: Joe Anderson, Contact
Founded: 1960. **Members:** 814. **Staff:** 3. **Budget:** $50,000. **Description:** Historians, geographers, and sociologists; libraries and archives. Seeks to further the study and understanding of the history, ecology, anthropology, archaeology, and sociology of the Great Plains of North America. Conducts research in human adaptation in an arid and semiarid environment. Affiliated with the Museum of the Great Plains, and Great Plains Archives. **Libraries: Type:** reference. **Holdings:** 25,000; photographs. **Subjects:** history, archaeology, natural history of the Great Plains. **Awards:** BOR Archaeological Research. **Frequency:** annual. **Type:** grant. **Divisions:** Anthropology; Archaeological Research; Education; Exhibits; Special Collections. **Formerly:** (1970) Great Plains Historical Association. **Publications:** *Great Plains Journal*, annual. Covers prehistory, history, and natural history of the Great Plains of North America. **Price:** included in membership dues. **Circulation:** 800. Alternate Formats: microform ● Catalog ● Monographs ● Booklets. **Price:** $24.95 each. **Conventions/Meetings:** annual meeting - always in Lawton, OK.

Greek

9995 ■ Hellenic American National Council (HANC)
2155 W 80th St.
Chicago, IL 60620
Ph: (773)994-2222
Fax: (773)994-4682
E-mail: hanc@hellasusa.com
URL: http://www.hellasusa.com/hanc
Contact: Mr. Ted G. Spyropoulos, Pres.
Founded: 1992. **Multinational. Description:** Seeks to honor, protect and preserve the democratic Hellenic and American ideals. Encourages, protects and promotes the Hellenic culture and language. Promotes the Hellenic culture to all United States people through the educational process. Protects and preserves Hellenic human rights internationally. Promotes friendship and better understanding of Hellenism. Fosters a better understanding and respect for the constitutional government of the United States and Hellas.

9996 ■ Modern Greek Studies Association (MGSA)
Box 622
Kent, OH 44240
Ph: (330)672-0910
Fax: (330)672-4025
E-mail: mgsa@kent.edu
URL: http://www.hnet.uci.edu/classics/MGSA
Contact: Prof. S. Victor Papacosma, Exec. Dir.
Founded: 1968. **Members:** 350. **Membership Dues:** regular, $50 (annual) ● student, $30 (annual) ● institutional, $95 (annual) ● joint, $60 (annual) ● patron, $100-$499 (annual) ● life, $750. **Budget:** $30,000. **Description:** Scholars in the field of Modern Greek studies; friends of Greece; institutions and libraries. Seeks to foster and advance Modern Greek studies and assist in the establishment of chairs and programs of Modern Greek studies. Serves as a center for dissemination of information in the field and about professional opportunities. Maintains speakers' bureau. **Awards:** Best Book Prize. **Frequency:** biennial. **Type:** monetary. **Recipient:** for academic book ● Best Dissertation Prize. **Frequency:** biennial. **Type:** monetary. **Recipient:** for best English-language dissertation on a Greek subject ● Elizabeth Constantinides Memorial Translation Prize. **Frequency:** biennial. **Type:** monetary. **Recipient:** for translator of Modern Greek literature into English. **Boards:** Executive. **Committees:** Administration; Computers and Technology; Elizabeth Constantinides Translation Prize; Endowment Funds; Fund Raising and Long-Term Planning; Graduate Studies; Greek Diaspora; Nominations; Publications; Standing; Undergraduate Studies. **Affiliated With:** American Association for the Advancement of Slavic Studies; American Council on the Teaching of Foreign Languages; American Historical Association; American Philological Association; International Studies Association; Modern Language Association of America. **Publications:** *Journal of Modern Greek Studies*, semiannual. **Price:** $20.00 each ● *Modern Greek Society: A Social Science Newsletter*, semiannual. Includes an extensive bibliography of books, articles, reviews, and dissertations on modern Greece; calendar of events; and research updates. **Price:** $15.00/year. ISSN: 0147-0779. **Circulation:** 600 ● Bulletin, semiannual. **Price:** $15.00/issue ● Books ● Proceedings. Features proceedings of symposia. **Conventions/Meetings:** biennial conference ● annual seminar - always summer ● symposium.

9997 ■ Society for the Preservation of the Greek Heritage (SPGH)
5125 MacArthur Blvd. NW, Ste.11B
Washington, DC 20016
Ph: (202)363-4337
Fax: (202)363-4658
E-mail: classic.heritage@verizon.net
URL: http://spghworld.org
Contact: Mr. Costas Carras, Chm.
Founded: 1974. **Members:** 700. **Membership Dues:** individual, $35 (annual) ● family, $50 (annual) ● sustaining, $100 (annual) ● donor, $500 (annual) ● sponsor, $1,000 (annual) ● patron, $2,000 (annual) ● benefactor, $5,000 (annual). **Staff:** 2. **Languages:** English, Greek. **Description:** Represents professional, business leaders, academic, classicists, university students and individuals interested in the promotion and preservation of the classical Greek heritage. Aims to increase awareness of and appreciation for ancient and Modern Greek culture and philosophy, and exploring the interrelationship between Greek heritage and contemporary society worldwide. Works to establish a Classics program at The Seed Public Charter School in Washington, DC that covers mythology, ancient Greek history, philosophy, and classical art and architecture. Collaborates with Greek affiliate on projects in Greece to restore and preserve historic buildings and contents. **Libraries: Type:** reference. **Holdings:** 50; books. **Subjects:** philosophy, archeology, architecture, art, politics relative to democratic history. **Publications:** *Destiny of the Parthenon Marbles (1999)*. Book. **Price:** included in membership dues; $10.00 for nonmembers. **Circulation:** 1,000 ● *The Meaning of Classical Theatre Through the Ages*. Book. Includes seminar proceedings. **Price:** included in membership dues; $10.00 for nonmembers. **Circulation:** 1,000 ● *Odysseus Across the Centuries (2001)*. Book. Includes book reviews and excerpts from speeches. **Price:** included in membership dues; $10.00 for nonmembers. **Circulation:** 1,000. **Conventions/Meetings:** semiannual lecture and seminar.

Hinduism

9998 ■ Brahman Samaj of North America (BSNA)
PO Box 716
Belle Mead, NJ 08502
Ph: (908)431-9845
E-mail: shuklafamily@earthlink.net
URL: http://www.bsna.org
Contact: Dr. Umesh Shukla, Gen. Sec.
Founded: 1994. **Membership Dues:** family, $35 (annual) ● life, $350 ● patron, $5,000 (annual) ● benefactor, $1,000 (annual) ● foreign student, $5 (annual). **Multinational. Description:** Represents Brahmans of Indian origin residing in North America. Educates its members and others about the history, culture, geography, and religious customs of Brahmans. Promotes studies of the literature, culture, traditions and the values of Brahmans at schools, colleges and universities. Educates the younger generation to integrate the traditional Brahman (Vedic) values with modern scientific attitude and contemporary technological development. **Publications:** *Brahma Bharati*, quarterly. Newsletter. Alternate Formats: online ● *Brahma-Vani*, annual. Magazine. Alternate Formats: online ● *Brahmakulum*. Directory.

Hispanic

9999 ■ Association of Hispanic Arts (AHA)
PO Box 1169
New York, NY 10029
Ph: (212)876-1242
Free: (888)876-1240
Fax: (212)876-1285
E-mail: informacion@latinoarts.org
URL: http://www.latinoarts.org
Contact: Julia L. Gutierrez-Rivera, Interim Exec. Dir.
Founded: 1975. **Members:** 8,000. **Staff:** 4. **Description:** Promotes Hispanic arts as an integral part of the arts community in the U.S. Offers services to all non-profit, Hispanic arts organizations, and individual artists; also promotes the activities of related Hispanic arts organizations. Assists community presentations of dance and music concerts, theatrical performances, and art exhibitions that reflect Hispanic history, culture, social conditions, beliefs, and attitudes. Maintains central information office and a mailing list of active arts organizations, individual artists, and media sources. Offers individual technical assistance and referral services on administrative, financial management, and fundraising matters. **Awards:** JP Morgan Chase. **Frequency:** annual. **Type:** grant. **Recipient:** to Latino arts organization. **Computer Services:** database, Latino artist/arts organizations. **Publications:** *AHA! - Hispanic Arts News*, quarterly. Newsletter. Covers Hispanic cultural activities. Includes calendar of events, people page, and opportunities for artists. **Price:** $25.00 /year for individu-

als; $40.00 /year for institutions. **Circulation:** 6,000. **Advertising:** accepted ● *Directory of Latino Arts Organizations*, semiannual. Provides thousands of Latino arts and cultural groups in communities throughout the USA.

10000 ■ Feministas Unidas (FU)
c/o Candyce Leonard, Treas./Membership Recorder
Wake Forest Univ.
PO Box 7332
Winston-Salem, NC 27109
E-mail: leonaca@wfu.edu
URL: http://titan.iwu.edu/~hispanic/femunidas
Contact: Candyce Leonard, Treas./Membership Recorder
Founded: 1979. **Members:** 300. **Membership Dues:** professor/associate professor, $20 (annual) ● assistant professor, $15 (annual) ● instructor/graduate student/other, $10 (annual) ● institution, $25 (annual). **Languages:** English, Spanish. **Description:** Feminist scholars in Hispanic, Luso-Brazilian, Chicano, or Puerto Rican studies. Serves as a forum for discussion and workshops of women and women's issues in Hispanic and Luso-Brazilian cultures. Conducts panel discussions in conjunction with the Modern Language Association of America and with the Midwest Modern Language Association. **Absorbed:** (1979) Women in Spanish. **Publications:** *The Children's Revolt Against Structures of Repression in Cristina Peri Rossi's La Rebellion De Los Ninos*. Article. Analyzes three stories from Peri Rossi's collection entitled La rebellion de los ninos. ● *Feministas Unidas Newsletter*, semiannual, always April and December. Contains reports on current research, job postings, and other items of interest to Hispanic feminists and feminist Hispanists. **Price:** available to members only. **Circulation:** 300. **Advertising:** accepted ● *Spanish Women Writers and the Essay: Gender, Politics and the Self*. Book. Consists of twelve critical essays on Spanish women essayists from late nineteenth century to the present. **Conventions/Meetings:** annual convention, held in conjunction with the MLA and the Midwest MLA.

10001 ■ Hispanic Organization of Latin Actors (HOLA)
107 Suffolk St., Ste.302
New York, NY 10002
Ph: (212)253-1015
Fax: (212)253-9651
E-mail: holagram@hellohola.org
URL: http://www.hellohola.org
Contact: Manny Alfaro, Exec. Dir.
Founded: 1975. **Members:** 500. **Membership Dues:** individual, $65 (annual). **Staff:** 3. **Budget:** $100,000. **Languages:** English, Spanish. **Description:** Represents Hispanic artists in the fields of theatre, film, television, radio, dance, video, and music; interested individuals, organizations, and corporations. Fosters an image of Hispanic cultural diversity, richness, and vitality through the American media by promoting the work of Hispanic actors and actresses. Maintains Career Development Center that offers adult theatre training and orientation seminars. Provides referral service to casting agents. **Awards:** Gala Hola Awards for Excellence in Theater. **Frequency:** annual. **Type:** recognition. **Computer Services:** database ● mailing lists. **Also Known As:** Hispanic Organization of Latin Actors. **Publications:** *Directory of Hispanic Talent*, annual. Alternate Formats: online ● *HOLA Brochure*. Alternate Formats: online ● *La Nueva Ola*, semiannual. Newsletter. Provides information about casting, members' activities, commercial and nonprofit projects, sponsorship opportunities, and marketing data. **Circulation:** 2,800. Alternate Formats: online.

10002 ■ Hispanic Society of America (HSA)
613 W 155th St.
New York, NY 10032
Ph: (212)926-2234
Fax: (212)690-0743
E-mail: info@hispanicsociety.org
URL: http://www.hispanicsociety.org
Contact: Dr. Mitchell A. Codding, Exec. Dir.
Founded: 1904. **Members:** 400. **Staff:** 40. **Languages:** English, Portuguese, Spanish. **Multinational. Description:** Represents persons who have made distinguished contributions to the fields of Hispanic art, literature, history, and general culture, which includes music, social customs, costumes, and bullfighting. Maintains museum, which is representative of Hispanic development from prehistoric days to the present, including collections of paintings, drawings, sculpture, furniture, metalwork, pottery, glass, lace, textiles, prints and photographs. **Libraries: Type:** reference. **Holdings:** 500,000; archival material, artwork, books, maps, papers, photographs. **Subjects:** art, history, literature, linguistics, culture of Spain, Portugal, and Colonial Hispanic America, fine and decorative arts, costumes of Spain and Portugal. **Publications:** Books ● Brochures ● Catalogs. Lists museum and library holdings and publications.

10003 ■ Hispanic Women's Corporation (HWC)
4545 N 36th St., Ste.108
Phoenix, AZ 85018-3473
Ph: (602)954-7995
Free: (888)388-4HWC
Fax: (602)954-7563
E-mail: marketing@hispanicwomen.org
URL: http://www.hispanicwomen.org
Contact: Linda Mazon-Guitierrez, Pres.
Founded: 1981. **Description:** Acts as proactive leader in the development of Hispanic women. **Programs:** Youth. **Publications:** Newsletter. Alternate Formats: online.

10004 ■ National Hispanic Institute (NHI)
PO Box 220
Maxwell, TX 78656-0020
Ph: (512)357-6137
Fax: (512)357-2206
E-mail: nietoe@aol.com
URL: http://www.nhi-net.org
Contact: Ernesto Nieto, Pres.
Founded: 1920. **Members:** 189. **Staff:** 2. **Description:** Provides research programs; offers lectures and concerts. **Libraries: Type:** reference. **Holdings:** archival material, books. **Subjects:** Spanish and Portuguese literature. **Awards:** Vernon Prize. **Frequency:** annual. **Type:** recognition. **Recipient:** for best literary essay by a college student. **Formerly:** Instituto de las Espanas; (1988) Hispanic Institute in the United States. **Publications:** *Revista Hispanica Moderna* (in English, Portuguese, and Spanish), semiannual. Journal. Includes literary articles and book reviews. **Price:** $30.00/volume; $3,150.00 complete set. ISSN: 0034-9593. **Circulation:** 1,892 ● Monographs.

10005 ■ Spanish Colonial Arts Society
PO Box 5378
Santa Fe, NM 87502-5378
Ph: (505)982-2226
Fax: (505)982-4585
E-mail: museum@spanishcolonial.org
URL: http://www.spanishcolonial.org
Contact: Joseph Moure, Pres.
Founded: 1925. **Members:** 850. **Membership Dues:** Spanish market artist, $35 (annual) ● family/dual (Sagrada Familia), $60 (annual) ● supporter, $100 (annual) ● sponsor, $300 (annual) ● sustainer, business, $500 (annual) ● patron, $1,000 (annual) ● benefactor, $2,500 (annual) ● chairman's council, $5,000 (annual). **Staff:** 11. **Budget:** $1,000,000. **Languages:** English, Spanish. **Description:** Aims to preserve and perpetuate Spanish colonial art; as sponsor of the annual Spanish Market and Winter Spanish Market exhibitions, the society today is a key resource in the education of traditional Spanish media, design, and techniques. Operates the Museum of Spanish Colonial Art. **Libraries: Type:** reference. **Holdings:** 1,093. **Subjects:** New Mexico, Spanish, world art, local history. **Awards:** Spanish Market Awards. **Frequency:** annual. **Type:** monetary. **Recipient:** judged panel. **Publications:** *Adobe Notes*. Book ● *Chispas*, triennial. Newsletter. Describes Spanish Market programs and activities. ● *Conexiones: Connections in Spanish Colonial Art*. Book. **Price:** $50.00 ● *Hispanic Arts and Ethnohistory in the Southwest*. Book ● *Spanish New Mexico*. Book. **Price:** $65.00 ● Books ● Also produces posters and postcards. **Conventions/Meetings:** assembly, inauguration of Museum of Spanish Colonial Art.

Historic Preservation

10006 ■ Accokeek Foundation (AF)
3400 Bryan Point Rd.
Accokeek, MD 20607
Ph: (301)283-2113
Fax: (301)283-2049
E-mail: accofound@accokeek.org
URL: http://www.accokeek.org
Contact: Wilton Corkern, Pres.
Founded: 1957. **Members:** 500. **Membership Dues:** individual, $25 (annual) ● family, $45 (annual) ● sustaining, $100 (annual). **Staff:** 13. **Budget:** $750,000. **Description:** Located at the Southern end of Prince Georges County, MD, across the Potomac River from Mt. Vernon. Ongoing programs in history (National Colonial Farm, a living museum), agriculture (Robert Ware Straus Ecosystem Farm) and education. Offers tours and educational programs to children and adults alike. Maintains several trails through woodlands, marshes, and along the shoreline. **Libraries: Type:** reference. **Holdings:** books. **Subjects:** agriculture, U.S. history of the mid-18th century. **Publications:** *Agricultural History Research Reports*, periodic ● *The Nation's River Toward the Twenty First Century* ● Newsletter, quarterly. **Conventions/Meetings:** annual board meeting - always May or October, Accokeek, MD.

10007 ■ Advisory Council on Historic Preservation (ACHP)
1100 Pennsylvania Ave. NW, Ste.803
Old Post Off. Bldg.
Washington, DC 20004
Ph: (202)606-8503
Fax: (202)606-8647
E-mail: achp@achp.gov
URL: http://www.achp.gov
Contact: John M. Fowler, Exec. Dir.
Founded: 1966. **Members:** 20. **Staff:** 41. **Budget:** $4,600,000. **Description:** Promotes the preservation, enhancement, and productive use of the nation's historic resources. Advises the President and Congress on national historic preservation policy. Provides a forum for influencing Federal activities, programs, and policies that impact historic properties. **Awards:** Chairman's Award for Federal Achievement in Historic Preservation. **Frequency:** quarterly. **Type:** recognition. **Recipient:** for significant contributions to historic preservation in the Federal Government ● The National Trust for Historic Preservation/ACHP Federal Partnerships in Historic Preservation. **Frequency:** annual. **Type:** recognition. **Recipient:** for outstanding partnerships that promote the preservation of important historic resources ● Preserve America Presidential Awards. **Frequency:** annual. **Type:** recognition. **Recipient:** to organizations, businesses, government entities, or individuals with exemplary accomplishments in the sustainable use and preservation of cultural or natural heritage assets. **Telecommunication Services:** electronic mail, jfowler@achp.gov. **Committees:** Federal Agency Programs; Outreach; Preservation Initiatives. **Task Forces:** Affordable Housing and Historic Preservation; Archaeology; Department of Defense Historic Buildings. **Conventions/Meetings:** quarterly board meeting.

10008 ■ American Antiquarian Society (AAS)
185 Salisbury St.
Worcester, MA 01609-1634
Ph: (508)755-5221
Fax: (508)753-3311
E-mail: edunlap@mwa.org
URL: http://www.americanantiquarian.org
Contact: Ellen S. Dunlap, Pres.
Founded: 1812. **Members:** 733. **Staff:** 55. **Budget:** $2,000,000. **Description:** Gathers, preserves, and promotes serious study of the materials of early

American history and life. Conducts program on the history of the book in American culture. Maintains research library specializing in the period of American history through 1876. Sponsors fellowships, educational programs, and research. **Libraries: Type:** reference. **Holdings:** 5,000,000; articles, books, maps, periodicals. **Subjects:** American history through 1876. **Publications:** *Almanac: AAS Newsletter*, semiannual. Covers Society activities, grants, and special programs concerning the preservation of materials of early American history and life. ISSN: 1098-7878. **Circulation:** 1,525 ● *American Antiquarian Society Proceedings*, semiannual. Journal. Contains bibliographies, research aids, and edited primary documents covering early American history and culture. **Price:** $45.00/year in U.S.; $53.00/year outside U.S. ISSN: 0044-751X. **Circulation:** 1,070 ● *The Book: Newsletter of the Program in the History of the Book in American Culture*, 3/year. Includes book reviews, notes on collections at libraries in the United States and abroad, research notes, and seminar and conference announcements. **Price:** free. ISSN: 0740-8439. **Circulation:** 2,600. Alternate Formats: online ● Also publishes books and pamphlets. **Conventions/Meetings:** semiannual meeting - always third week of April ● annual meeting - always third week of October.

10009 ■ American Friends of St. David's Cathedral (AFSDC)
St. David's Episcopal Church
5150 Macomb St. NW
Washington, DC 20016
Ph: (434)978-4552 (703)528-8192
Fax: (434)974-1880
E-mail: afsdc@verizon.net
URL: http://www.afsdc.org
Contact: Ms. Beverly A. Bivins, Sec.
Founded: 1998. **Budget:** $20,000. **Nonmembership. Description:** Individuals interested in St. David's Cathedral in Pembrokeshire, Wales. Promotes preservation of the cathedral, which sits on the site of the original monastery of St. David, the patron saint of Wales. Raises funds for the maintenance of St. David's Cathedral; conducts educational programs, including pilgrimages to Cathedral and Wales; has sponsored tour of the United States by the cathedral's choir. **Computer Services:** database ● mailing lists.

10010 ■ American Highway Project (AHP)
15 Church St.
Le Roy, NY 14482
Ph: (585)768-8354
Fax: (585)768-9484
E-mail: info@highwayproject.org
URL: http://www.highwayproject.org
Contact: Edgar G. Praus, Founder
Founded: 1998. **Description:** Works to preserve the architecture and cultural landscapes along U.S. highways. **Libraries: Type:** reference. **Subjects:** road culture. **Telecommunication Services:** electronic mail, praus@highwayproject.org.

10011 ■ American Institute for Conservation of Historic and Artistic Works (AIC)
1717 K St. NW, Ste.200
Washington, DC 20036
Ph: (202)452-9545
Fax: (202)452-9328
E-mail: info@aic-faic.org
URL: http://www.aic-faic.org
Contact: Ms. Eryl Wentworth, Exec. Dir.
Founded: 1972. **Members:** 3,000. **Membership Dues:** fellow, professional associate, associate, $127 (annual) ● institutional, $197 (annual) ● student, retired, $57 (annual). **Staff:** 6. **Budget:** $800,000. **Multinational. Description:** Professionals, scientists, administrators, and educators in the field of art conservation; interested individuals. Advances the practice and promotes the importance of the preservation of cultural property. Coordinates the exchange of knowledge, research, and publications. Establishes and upholds professional standards. Publishes conservation literature. Compiles statistics. Represents membership to allied professional associations and advocates on conservation-related issues. Solicits and dispenses money exclusively for charitable, scientific, and educational objectives. **Libraries: Type:** reference; not open to the public. **Computer Services:** Mailing lists. **Telecommunication Services:** electronic mail, ewentworth@aic-faic.org. **Subgroups:** Architecture; Book and Paper; Conservators in Private Practice; Electronic Media; Objects; Paintings; Photographic Materials; Research and Technical Studies; Textiles; Wooden Artifacts. **Supersedes:** (1959) International Institute for Conservation of Historic and Artistic Works—American Group. **Publications:** *AIC Directory*, annual. Lists names, addresses, and specialties of all members, arranged alphabetically and by geographical location. **Price:** included in membership dues; $25.00 for nonprofit individuals, plus $6 postage; $50.00 for commercial companies, plus $6 postage. **Advertising:** accepted ● *AIC News*, bimonthly. Newsletter. Reports on the latest news on conservation and related issues, specialties, new products and techniques; also includes Institute news. **Price:** included in membership dues. **Circulation:** 3,500. **Advertising:** accepted ● *Journal of the American Institute for Conservation*, 3/year. Includes book reviews. **Price:** $75.00 in U.S.; $95.00 outside U.S. **Circulation:** 3,600. **Advertising:** accepted ● A publications list is available from the AIC office. **Conventions/Meetings:** annual meeting and conference, with specialty group sessions and special events (exhibits) - always June.

10012 ■ American Overseas Schools Historical Society (AOSHS)
PO Box 1500
Wichita, KS 67201
Ph: (316)265-6837
E-mail: overseasschools@aoshs.org
URL: http://aoshs.wichita.edu
Contact: Scarlett Rehrig, Pres.
Founded: 1995. **Membership Dues:** individual, $25 (annual). **Description:** Collects, records and preserves the history of educating American children and youth abroad. Enhances public knowledge, understanding and appreciation of the contributions of American educators and their students in the advancement of democracy around the world. **Publications:** *AOSHS Quarterly*. Journal. **Price:** included in membership dues.

10013 ■ APVA Preservation Virginia (APVA)
204 W Franklin St.
Richmond, VA 23220
Ph: (804)648-1889
Fax: (804)775-0802
E-mail: efuccella@apva.org
URL: http://www.apva.org
Contact: Betty Fuccella, Membership Coor.
Founded: 1889. **Members:** 6,000. **Membership Dues:** individual associate, $30 (annual) ● family associate, individual, $40 (annual) ● teacher, student (full-time), $25 (annual) ● individual (plus one), organizational, $50 (annual) ● family, $60 (annual) ● individual (plus one associate), $35 (annual) ● benefactor, $500 (annual) ● century, $100 (annual) ● sponsor, $250 (annual). **Staff:** 20. **Budget:** $2,000,000. **State Groups:** 23. **Description:** Owns and/or maintains over 35 historical properties, some of which are open to the public. Conducts seminars; offers professional training for docents. Sponsors research programs; maintains museum. **Libraries: Type:** reference. **Holdings:** 5,000. **Subjects:** American and English decorative arts and architecture. **Awards:** Gabriella Page Historic Preservation Award. **Frequency:** annual. **Type:** recognition. **Recipient:** for an outstanding preservation effort on the part of a business or civic organization ● Mary Mason Anderson William Award. **Frequency:** annual. **Type:** recognition. **Recipient:** for outstanding contribution to historic preservation. **Computer Services:** Mailing lists, of members. **Formerly:** (2006) Association for the Preservation of Virginia Antiquities. **Publications:** *APVA Newsletter*, 3/year. Includes calendar of events, photographs, and announcements. ● Also publishes properties brochure. **Conventions/Meetings:** annual meeting.

10014 ■ Architectural Heritage Foundation (AHF)
Old City Hall
45 School St.
Boston, MA 02108-3204
Ph: (617)523-8678
Fax: (617)523-3782
E-mail: info@ahfboston.com
URL: http://www.ahfboston.com
Contact: Sean McDonnell, Pres.
Founded: 1966. **Staff:** 7. **Nonmembership. Description:** Specializes in the adaptive reuse of historic structures.

10015 ■ Association for Gravestone Studies (AGS)
278 Main St., Ste.207
Greenfield, MA 01301-3230
Ph: (413)772-0836
E-mail: info@gravestonestudies.org
URL: http://www.gravestonestudies.org
Contact: Andrea Carlin, Admin.
Founded: 1977. **Members:** 1,200. **Membership Dues:** student, $20 (annual) ● senior, $40 (annual) ● individual, $50 (annual) ● institutional, $50 (annual) ● supporting, $80 (annual) ● life, $1,000 ● family, dual, library, $60 (annual) ● contributing, $250 (annual). **Staff:** 2. **Budget:** $110,000. **Description:** Historians, archaeologists, anthropologists, genealogists, folklorists, art historians, and other individuals and organizations interested in the study and preservation of old gravestones. Seeks to promote public awareness of and education on the preservation of gravestones. Serves as an information clearinghouse for the public. Aids community restoration programs by fostering orderly and systematic recording practices and conducting restoration workshops. Conducts research and has developed position statements on stone conservation, the recording of cemetery data, and model legislation. Maintains archives and speakers' bureau. **Libraries: Type:** open to the public. **Holdings:** 900; archival material, articles, books, periodicals. **Subjects:** study and preservation of gravemarkers. **Awards:** Forbes Award. **Frequency:** annual. **Type:** recognition. **Recipient:** for exceptional service of an individual, institution or organization ● Oakley Certificate of Merit. **Frequency:** periodic. **Type:** recognition. **Recipient:** for exceptional individuals and groups. **Publications:** *AGS Quarterly: Bulletin of the Association for Gravestone Studies*. Presents information about projects, literature, and research concerning gravestones. **Price:** included in membership dues. ISSN: 0146-5783. **Circulation:** 1,200. **Advertising:** accepted ● *Markers*, annual. Journal. Contains articles relating to the study of gravestones from colonial times to the present. Also contains scholarly articles relating to funerary art. **Price:** free for members. ISSN: 0277-8726. **Circulation:** 500 ● Also publishes regional cemetery guides and material on preservation of gravestones and graveyards. **Conventions/Meetings:** annual conference and meeting, features conservation workshops, scholarly papers, participating sessions and tours of area cemeteries (exhibits) - always June.

10016 ■ Association for Preservation Technology International (APT)
3085 Stevenson Dr., Ste.200
Springfield, IL 62703
Ph: (217)529-9039
Free: (888)723-4242
E-mail: info@apti.org
URL: http://www.apti.org
Contact: Nathela Chatara, Admin. Dir.
Founded: 1968. **Members:** 2,000. **Membership Dues:** full (in U.S. and international), $125 (annual) ● full, in Canada, $150 (annual) ● student (in U.S. and international), $55 (annual) ● institution (in U.S. and international), $200 (annual) ● institution in Canada, $250 (annual) ● student in Canada, $70 (annual) ● corporate (in U.S. and international), $425 (annual) ● corporate in Canada, $525 (annual) ● patron (in U.S. and international), $1,500 (annual) ● patron, in Canada, $1,850 (annual) ● sponsor, overseas, $1,500 (annual) ● life (in U.S. and over-

seas), $3,750 ● life - in Canada, $4,600. **Regional Groups:** 8. **Multinational. Description:** Professional preservationists, architects, furnishings consultants, museum curators, architectural educators, archaeologists, craftsmen, and other persons directly or indirectly involved in preservation activities. Promotes improved quality of professional practice in the field of historic preservation worldwide; promotes research and gathers technical information in all aspects of historic preservation; encourages the training of craftsmen in the traditional techniques and skills required for historic preservation; encourages the establishment of national and local collections of reference materials, tools, and artifacts for study purposes; encourages governmental and private participation and support of the activities described above; maintains a listing of professional restorationists, consultants, curators, conservationists, craftsmen, and sources of supply or other services related to historic preservation. Maintains speakers' bureau. **Awards:** Anne de Fort-Menares Award. **Type:** recognition. **Recipient:** for the most outstanding article ● College of Fellows. **Type:** recognition ● Harley J. McKee Award. **Type:** recognition. **Recipient:** for individuals who have made outstanding contributions to the field of preservation technology ● Lee Nelson Award. **Type:** recognition. **Recipient:** for outstanding and influential publications ● Oliver Torrey Fuller Award. **Type:** recognition. **Recipient:** for the most outstanding article ● Student Scholarships. **Frequency:** annual. **Type:** scholarship. **Committees:** Awards; International; Special Interest. **Formerly:** (1988) Association for Preservation Technology. **Publications:** *APT Bulletin: The Journal of Preservation Technology*, 3/year. Features new developments in preservation technology. ● *Association for Preservation Technology—Communique*, quarterly. Newsletter. Includes calendar of events, periodical abstracts, and research updates. **Price:** included in membership dues. ISSN: 0319-4558. **Circulation:** 2,000. Alternate Formats: online. **Conventions/Meetings:** annual conference.

10017 ■ Capitol Hill Restoration Society (CHRS)

420 10th St. SE
PO Box 15264
Washington, DC 20003-0264
Ph: (202)543-0425
Fax: (202)543-0425
E-mail: info@chrs.org
URL: http://www.chrs.org
Contact: Mr. Dick Wolf, Pres.

Founded: 1955. **Members:** 800. **Membership Dues:** household, $30 (annual) ● single, $25 (annual) ● household patron, $60 (annual) ● household sponsor, $120 (annual) ● life, $1,000. **Staff:** 1. **Budget:** $70,000. **Description:** Individuals interested in the restoration and preservation of the Capitol Hill section of Washington, DC, as a residential area. Active in city planning, zoning, traffic, historic, and other civic matters. Sponsors historical research. **Committees:** City Planning; Communications; Community Development; Environment; Grants; Historic Preservation; House and Garden Tour; Newsletter; Public Safety; Transportation; Zoning. **Publications:** *CHRS News*, monthly. Newsletter. **Circulation:** 700. **Conventions/Meetings:** monthly meeting ● annual tour, of house and garden.

10018 ■ Carpenters' Company (CC)

c/o Carpenters' Hall
320 Chestnut St.
Philadelphia, PA 19106
Ph: (215)925-0167
E-mail: carphall@carpentershall.com
URL: http://www.carpentershall.org
Contact: Christy Thompson, Admin.

Founded: 1724. **Members:** 175. **Staff:** 2. **Description:** Architects and builders. Seeks to preserve Carpenters' Hall (where the First Continental Congress met). The hall has been open to the public as a museum since 1857. **Libraries: Type:** reference. **Holdings:** 5,500; books, periodicals. **Subjects:** fiction, travel, history, art, architecture. **Computer Services:** database. **Telecommunication Services:** electronic mail, christythompson@carpentershall.com. **Also Known As:** Carpenters' Company of the City and County of Philadelphia. **Publications:** *Building Early America*. Book ● *1786 Rule Book* ● Brochures. **Conventions/Meetings:** annual meeting - always held in Philadelphia, PA ● quarterly meeting - always held in Philadelphia, PA.

10019 ■ Civil War Preservation Trust (CWPT)

1331 H St. NW, Ste.1001
Washington, DC 20005
Ph: (202)367-1861
Free: (888)606-1400
Fax: (202)367-1865
E-mail: info@civilwar.org
URL: http://www.civilwar.org
Contact: James Lighthizer, Pres.

Founded: 1998. **Members:** 46,000. **Membership Dues:** bugler, $35 (annual) ● sentry, $50 (annual) ● quartermaster, $100 (annual) ● cavalryman, $250 (annual) ● cannoneer, $500 (annual) ● regimental color bearer, $1,000 (annual) ● brigade color bearer, $2,500 (annual) ● division color bearer, $5,000 (annual) ● corps color bearer, $10,000 (annual) ● national color bearer, $25,000 (annual) ● classroom, $25 (annual). **Description:** Individuals and organizations with an interest in the battlefields of the American Civil War. Promotes preservation of Civil War battlefields and other historic sites from the Civil War Era. Works with public and private agencies to raise funds to preserve Civil War battlefields; conducts educational programs to raise public awareness of the Civil War and of the importance of preserving historic sites; purchases land on Civil War battlefields at risk for commercial development. **Formed by Merger of:** (2000) Civil War Trust; (2000) Association for the Preservation of Civil War Sites. **Publications:** *Hallowed Ground*, quarterly. Magazine. Contains updates on historical preservation and leading historians. **Conventions/Meetings:** annual conference.

10020 ■ Communal Studies Association (CSA)

PO Box 122
Amana, IA 52203
Ph: (319)622-6446
Fax: (319)622-6446
E-mail: csa@netins.net
URL: http://www.communalstudies.info
Contact: Kathleen Fernandez, Exec. Dir.

Founded: 1975. **Members:** 354. **Membership Dues:** individual, $50 (annual) ● community, institution, $90 (annual) ● friend, $200 (annual) ● life, $600 ● student, $20 (annual) ● couple, sustaining, $75 (annual) ● regular, outside North America, $60 (annual) ● retired, $30 (annual). **Staff:** 1. **Regional Groups:** 1. **Description:** Historians, museum directors, and other individuals; institutions. Encourages the study, restoration, preservation, and public interpretation of American communal societies and intentional communities, both past and present. (Communal societies and intentional communities are groups that agree to share property rights equally among themselves due to a shared religious or political philosophy.) Seeks to: facilitate communication and cooperation among members; increase public awareness of the communal heritage. **Awards:** Distinguished Scholar Award. **Frequency:** annual. **Type:** recognition. **Recipient:** to persons who have contributed greatly to the study of communal societies ● Donald E. Pitzer Distinguished Service Award. **Frequency:** annual. **Type:** recognition. **Recipient:** to persons who have contributed greatly to the organization ● Outstanding Contribution Award. **Frequency:** annual. **Type:** recognition. **Recipient:** to persons or groups who promote the understanding of communal societies ● Starting Scholar Award. **Frequency:** annual. **Type:** recognition. **Recipient:** to authors who are new to the field of communal studies. **Computer Services:** database. **Formerly:** (1991) National Historic Communal Societies Association. **Publications:** *Communal Societies*, annual. Journal. Includes scholarly articles, photographs, and book reviews on past and present communal groups. **Price:** $15.00 for nonmembers; included in membership dues. ISSN: 0739-1250. **Circulation:** 380 ● *Communique*, semiannual, January and July. Newsletter. Contains announcements, featured articles, news from communal sites, and calendar of events. **Conventions/Meetings:** annual Communal Studies Conference (exhibits) - October or late September. 2008 Oct. 2-4, Estero, FL; 2009 Oct. 1-3, Aurora, OR.

10021 ■ Council on America's Military Past (CAMP)

PO Box 1151
Fort Myer, VA 22211
E-mail: counterscarp@comcast.net
URL: http://www.campjamp.org
Contact: Mr. Dale Floyd, Sec.

Founded: 1966. **Members:** 1,200. **Membership Dues:** family, $10 (annual) ● individual, $40 (annual) ● corporate, $50 (annual) ● contributing, $60 (annual) ● sustaining, $100 (annual) ● patron, $250 (annual). **Staff:** 6. **Budget:** $50,000. **Regional Groups:** 20. **Description:** Individuals and organizations interested in identification, location, restoration, preservation, and memorialization of old military installations and units. Actively works for the cause of historic preservation, and, in particular, endorses efforts to prevent treasure and souvenir hunters from destroying historic sites. Endorses restoration or memorialization programs for certain fort sites. **Awards:** Yount-Windsor Grant. **Frequency:** annual. **Type:** grant. **Recipient:** for students who express interest in attending annual conference. **Computer Services:** Mailing lists, of members. **Telecommunication Services:** electronic mail, reynoldsrg@earthlink.net. **Formerly:** (1982) Council on Abandoned Military Posts - USA. **Publications:** *Headquarters Heliogram*, monthly. Newspaper. Covers military history and historic preservation. **Price:** included in membership dues. **Circulation:** 1,400. **Advertising:** accepted ● *Journal of America's Military Past*, quarterly. Covers America's military past with articles on famous battles and military personnel and the bases where they served. **Price:** included in membership dues. **Advertising:** accepted ● Directory, triennial. **Conventions/Meetings:** annual Military History - conference, with papers on military history and visits to military history sites - usually held every 2nd Wednesday through Saturday of May. 2009 May 6-10, Pittsburgh, PA.

10022 ■ Czech Heritage Preservation Society (CHPS)

PO Box 199
Tyndall, SD 57066-0199
URL: http://www.sdhistory.org/soc/Hist_Orgs/czech.htm
Contact: Mildred Cimpl, Treas.

Founded: 1974. **Members:** 230. **Membership Dues:** adult, $3 (annual) ● juvenile, $1 (annual). **Description:** Works to preserve the history of contributions made by persons of Czechoslovakian descent to the building of the United States. Disseminates information; maintains a museum, Hall of Fame, and the Vancura Memorial Park; conducts charitable programs. **Libraries: Type:** reference. **Holdings:** archival material, periodicals. **Boards:** Directors. **Publications:** Newsletter. **Conventions/Meetings:** board meeting - 5/year.

10023 ■ Frank Lloyd Wright Preservation Trust (FLWPT)

931 Chicago Ave.
Oak Park, IL 60302
Ph: (708)848-1976
Fax: (708)848-1248
E-mail: info@wrightplus.org
URL: http://www.wrightplus.org
Contact: Joan B. Mercuri, Pres./CEO

Founded: 1974. **Members:** 3,000. **Membership Dues:** individual, $45 (annual) ● family, $55 (annual) ● Prairie Society, $100 (annual) ● Octagon Society, $250 (annual) ● Inglenook Society, $500 (annual) ● Skylight Society, $1,000 (annual) ● Cornerstone Society, $2,500 (annual) ● Wright Society, $5,000 (annual). **Staff:** 64. **Budget:** $5,000,000. **Languages:** English, French, German, Italian, Japanese, Spanish. **Description:** Individuals interested in the work of architect Frank Lloyd Wright (1867-1959), architecture, and history. Founded as a co-stewardship site with the National Trust for Historic Preservation to restore and preserve Wright's Oak Park, IL home and studio, where he developed what is known as the Prairie style of architecture. Operates Home and Studio Museum, Robie House Museum in Hyde Park, and Research center. Conducts tours; maintains research center; operates speaker's bureau and bookshops; presents education programs; restores and preserves its historic sites. **Libraries: Type:** reference. **Holdings:** 1,800; archival material, books, photographs. **Subjects:** Wright and other Prairie school architects, each phase of the restoration program. **Telecommunication Services:** electronic mail, flwpr@wrightplus.org. **Publications:** *Building a Legacy - Restoration of Frank Lloyd Wright's Oak Park Home and Studio*. Book. **Price:** $30.00/copy ● *Frank Lloyd Wright and the Prairie*. Book. Features color photography of 12 magnificent buildings, archival photographs and drawings, accompanied by quotes from the architect's writings. **Price:** $18.95/copy ● *Frank Lloyd Wright Home and Studio for Children Coloring Book*. Provides a room-by-room tour of the buildings given by the Wright children themselves. **Price:** $4.95/copy ● *Frank Lloyd Wright Oak Park Home and Studio*. Brochure ● *Frederick C. Robie House Tour Information*. Brochure ● *Oak Park Home and Studio of Frank Lloyd Wright*. Book. Focuses on the history of the buildings and how they embody Wright's principles. **Price:** $11.95/copy ● *Wright Angles*, quarterly. Magazine. **Price:** included in membership dues ● Also publishes educational materials. **Conventions/Meetings:** workshop.

10024 ■ French Heritage Society (FHS)

14 E 60th St., Ste.605
New York, NY 10022
Ph: (212)759-6846
Fax: (212)759-9632
E-mail: fhs@frenchheritagesociety.org
URL: http://www.frenchheritagesociety.org
Contact: Jessica W. London, Exec. Dir.

Founded: 1982. **Members:** 2,000. **Membership Dues:** individual, $100 (annual) ● dual/family, $175 (annual) ● contributing, $250 (annual) ● sponsor, $500 (annual) ● patron, $1,000 (annual) ● donor alliance, $2,500 (annual) ● President's Circle, $5,000 (annual) ● corporate partner, $500-$5,000 (annual) ● associate, $300 (annual). **Description:** Seeks to provide American students with the opportunity to learn about the history and preservation of the French architectural heritage. Offers financial assistance to the Vieilles Maisons Francaises, a French society that works to preserve historical sites in France. Solicits donations through its 13 American chapters and a Paris, France chapter, and sponsors cultural and student exchange programs, including meetings between French and American artisans. American chapters conduct local activities such as educational lectures. Hosts FVMF members in cultural visits to France and VMF members visiting the U.S. Encourages the French to make donations to preserve American historical sites. **Formerly:** (2003) Friends of Vieilles Maisons Francaises. **Publications:** *Au Courant*, quarterly. Newsletter. Contains FVMF calendar of events. **Price:** free for members. Alternate Formats: online ● *VMF Magazine*, 5/year ● Report, biennial. Provides information on member activities.

10025 ■ Friends of Cast Iron Architecture (FCIA)

Address Unknown since 2008

Founded: 1970. **Description:** Preservationists, architectural historians, architects, and laymen interested in historic buildings and urban amenities. Major objective is to promote the preservation of 19th century cast-iron architecture throughout the country. Seeks to arouse public interest and appreciation of this uniquely American form and advocates for local landmark commissions to protect it officially. Urges owners to maintain these iron buildings and to avoid making what the group considers inappropriate renovations. Provides information to architects and architectural students. **Convention/Meeting:** none. **Libraries: Type:** by appointment only. **Affiliated With:** National Trust for Historic Preservation; Society of Architectural Historians; Society for Industrial Archeology; Victorian Society in America.

10026 ■ Friends of French Art (FoFA)

Address Unknown since 2007

Founded: 1979. **Members:** 600. **Membership Dues:** $100 (annual). **Staff:** 2. **Budget:** $250,000. **Local Groups:** 1. **Languages:** French. **Description:** Individuals with an interest in preserving French art in peril. Funds art conservation in France and French art in the U.S. Sponsors annual art conservation houseparty to France. **Awards: Type:** scholarship. **Recipient:** bestowed to French students in the U.S. and American students in France for art conservation. **Subgroups:** La Coterie. **Publications:** *Friends of French Art Annual Magazine*. Journal. Provides information on the FoFA's conservation and restoration projects in progress and completed. **Price:** included in membership dues; $50.00 for nonmembers. **Advertising:** not accepted. **Conventions/Meetings:** annual Houseparty to France - meeting - always spring.

10027 ■ Friends of Lindenwald

PO Box 64
Kinderhook, NY 12106
Ph: (518)758-2249 (518)758-3061
URL: http://www.nps.gov/mava
Contact: Robert Worsfold, Pres.

Founded: 1983. **Members:** 200. **Description:** Individuals interested in the preservation of Lindenwald the Martin VanBuren National Historic Site, estate of Martin Van Buren (1782-1862), eighth President of the United States. Conducts tours and educational programs. **Publications:** *Van Buren Chronicles*, quarterly. Newsletter ● Also publishes calendar of events. **Conventions/Meetings:** monthly meeting.

10028 ■ Friends of the National Parks at Gettysburg (FNPG)

PO Box 4622
Gettysburg, PA 17325
Ph: (717)334-0772
Fax: (717)334-3118
E-mail: fnpgmembership@friendsofgettysburg.org
URL: http://www.friendsofgettysburg.org
Contact: Barbara J. Finfrock, Chair

Founded: 1989. **Members:** 25,000. **Membership Dues:** regular, $25 (annual) ● sustaining, $50 (annual) ● supporting, $75 (annual) ● patron, $100 (annual) ● first corps, $150 (annual) ● first corps headquarters guard, $250 (annual) ● first corps standard bearer, $500 (annual) ● first corps commander's staff, $1,000 (annual). **Staff:** 8. **Budget:** $1,200,000. **Description:** Citizens interested in protecting, preserving, and maintaining the two national parks at Gettysburg: Gettysburg National Military Park and the Eisenhower National Historic Site. **Telecommunication Services:** electronic mail, dneil@friendsofgettysburg.org. **Publications:** Newsletter, quarterly. **Price:** free for members.

10029 ■ Friends of Terra Cotta (FOTC)

c/o Susan Tunick, Pres.
771 W End Ave., No. 10E
New York, NY 10025
Ph: (212)932-1750
URL: http://www.preserve.org/fotc
Contact: Susan Tunick, Pres.

Founded: 1981. **Members:** 625. **Membership Dues:** Terra Cat-ta, $30 (annual) ● Terra Cotta Smile, $50 (annual) ● Terra Cotta Capitol, $100 (annual) ● Terra Cotta Angel, $250 (annual). **Regional Groups:** 2. **Description:** Represents architects, engineers, contractors, historians, conservators, and preservationists. Raises awareness of architects, engineers, owners of terra cotta-clad buildings, and the public about the value of and the difficulties associated with the preservation of terra cotta. **Libraries: Type:** reference. **Holdings:** archival material, articles. **Computer Services:** database, archives. **Publications:** *American Decorative Tile*. Booklet. **Price:** $6.50 includes postage ● *Field Guide to Apartment Building Architecture*. Booklet. **Price:** $6.50 includes postage ● *George and Edward Blum: Texture and Design in New York Apartment House Architecture*. Book. **Price:** $18.00 includes postage ● *Paris and The Legacy of French Architectural Ceramics*. Book. **Price:** $22.00 includes postage ● *Sites 18: Architectural Terra Cotta*. Book. **Price:** $10.00 includes postage ● *Terra Cotta: Don't Take it for Granite*. Book. **Price:** $12.00 includes postage ● *Terra Cotta Skyline: NY's Architectural Ornament*. Book. **Price:** $48.50 postpaid ● *Tile Roofs of Alfred*. Book. **Price:** $7.00 plus postage ● Also publishes posters. **Conventions/Meetings:** lecture ● seminar ● tour ● workshop.

10030 ■ Great Lakes Lighthouse Keepers Association (GLLKA)

PO Box 219
Mackinaw City, MI 49701-0219
Ph: (231)436-5580
Fax: (231)436-5466
E-mail: info@gllka.com
URL: http://www.gllka.com
Contact: Mr. Terry Pepper, Exec. Dir.

Founded: 1982. **Members:** 1,600. **Membership Dues:** individual, $35 (annual) ● individual, $65 (biennial) ● family, $50 (annual) ● family, $90 (biennial) ● life, $1,500 ● keeper, $125 (annual) ● keeper, $235 (biennial) ● inspector, $250 (annual) ● inspector, $475 (biennial) ● superintendent, beacon, $500 (annual) ● superintendent, beacon, $950 (biennial) ● small business, $1,000 (annual) ● corporate, $2,000 (annual). **Staff:** 2. **Description:** Brings together people who are interested in the historic preservation and restoration of lighthouses on the Great Lakes and those seeking contact with the descendants of lighthouse keepers on the Great Lakes. Conducts teacher workshops and supplies education materials for those wishing to teach students about Great Lakes maritime heritage. Acts as a clearinghouse of information concerning restoration projects; sponsors seminars; conducts research programs; compiles statistics. Holds annual conferences and cruises. **Formerly:** (1983) Lighthouse Keepers Association. **Publications:** *The Beacon*, quarterly. Newsletter. Provides a forum for the exchange of information on the history of Great Lakes lighthouses, lighthouse keepers, and historic preservation activities. **Price:** included in membership dues. **Circulation:** 2,000. **Advertising:** accepted ● Also publishes calendars and reprints of historical books. **Conventions/Meetings:** Great Lakes Conference and Workshop, on each of the Great Lakes (exhibits) - 5/year ● annual Maritime Heritage Educator - workshop.

10031 ■ Gungywamp Society (GS)

PO Box 592
Colchester, CT 06415-0592
E-mail: gungywamp@ctol.net
URL: http://www.gungywamp.com
Contact: Paulette Buchanan, Corresponding Sec./Researcher

Founded: 1979. **Members:** 775. **Staff:** 1. **Budget:** $3,000. **Description:** Avocational archaeologists, anthropologists, historians, geologists, astronomers, and interested individuals. Seeks to protect and preserve sites throughout the Northeastern United States that show evidence of ancient and pre-Columbian cultures. Investigates and studies lithic features, architecture, artifacts, ancient inscriptions, and historic records. Has discovered an archaeological site in Connecticut that shows evidence of serial occupancy since 3000 B.C. Conducts tours through the Gungywamp Complex, an archaeological area preserved by the group. Sponsors educational and charitable programs. Maintains speakers' bureau. **Libraries: Type:** reference. **Holdings:** 762; archival material, artwork, audiovisuals, books, clippings, periodicals. **Subjects:** archaeology, epigraphy, ancient history, lithic sites. **Awards:** H.W. Nelson Award. **Frequency:** annual. **Type:** recognition. **Recipient:** for excellence in writing, drama, history ● President's Citation. **Frequency:** annual. **Type:** recognition ● **Frequency:** annual. **Type:** scholarship ● Trustees Award. **Frequency:** annual. **Type:** recognition. **Computer Services:** database ● mailing lists. **Publications:** *The Greater Gungywamp: A Guide*. Book. **Price:** $12.50 ● *Stonewatch*, annual. Newsletter. Contains information on archaeological discoveries, ancient inscriptions, translations, and membership updates. **Price:** $10.00/year. ISSN: 0892-1741. **Circulation:** 400. Alternate Formats: online.

10032 ■ Harmonie Associates (HA)

c/o Pennsylvania Historical and Museum Commission
Old Economy Village
270 16th St.
Ambridge, PA 15003-2225
Ph: (724)266-1803 (724)266-4500
Free: (800)732-0999
Fax: (724)266-7506
URL: http://www.oldeconomyvillage.org
Contact: Rebecca Matsco, Contact

Founded: 1956. **Members:** 120. **Membership Dues:** student, $15 (annual) ● family/grand family, $40 (annual) ● sustaining, friend, $100 (annual) ● benefactor, $500 (annual) ● individual, $25 (annual) ● patron, $250 (annual). **Description:** Individuals concerned with the history, preservation, and development of New Harmony, Harmony Township, and the tri-state region of Indiana, Illinois, and Kentucky. (New Harmony was the site of an experimental cooperative community in the 19th century and is now a national historical landmark and state park.) Collects cultural artifacts; maintains exhibits. Raises funds and provides financial assistance for historical, cultural, and educational development. **Computer Services:** Mailing lists, of members. **Publications:** *Harmonist Rose*, periodic. Newsletter. **Conventions/Meetings:** bimonthly dinner and seminar.

10033 ■ Heritage Conservation Network (HCN)

1557 North St.
Boulder, CO 80304
Ph: (303)444-0128
Fax: (775)320-6837
E-mail: info@heritageconservation.net
URL: http://www.heritageconservation.net
Contact: Judith Broeker, Co-Founder/Program Dir.

Languages: English, Italian, Spanish. **Multinational.** **Description:** Promotes the conservation of historic architecture and sites around the world by organizing hands-on building conservation workshops. Strives to increase awareness of the significance of historic sites. Stimulates each community's interest in and knowledge of appropriate conservation skills. **Computer Services:** Mailing lists. **Publications:** *Update*. Newsletter. Alternate Formats: online ● Annual Report. Alternate Formats: online.

10034 ■ Historic Deerfield (HD)

PO Box 321
Deerfield, MA 01342
Ph: (413)774-5581 (413)775-7214
Fax: (413)775-7220
E-mail: info@historic-deerfield.org
URL: http://www.historic-deerfield.org
Contact: Philip Zea, Pres.

Founded: 1952. **Members:** 2,000. **Membership Dues:** individual, $40 (annual) ● family, $60 (annual) ● active, $100 (annual) ● contributing, $150 (annual) ● patron, $500 (annual). **Staff:** 155. **Budget:** $5,400,000. **Languages:** English, French, German, Italian, Japanese, Russian, Spanish. **Description:** Owns and maintains 52 buildings on 93 acres in Deerfield, MA, including the Deerfield Inn (1884), 14 houses open daily to the public and furnished with antique furniture, textiles, ceramics, and other early American decorative arts. Offers educational programs and special events for families. **Libraries:** **Type:** reference. **Holdings:** 25,000; books, periodicals. **Subjects:** New England history, arts. **Awards:** Historic Deerfield Summer Fellowships in Early American History and Material Culture. **Frequency:** annual. **Type:** fellowship. **Recipient:** for college students interested in professional careers in the fields of preservation and interpretation of early American culture. **Additional Websites:** http://www.deerfielddescendants.org. **Boards:** Trustees. **Committees:** Advisory Committee for Historic Deerfield. **Formerly:** (1971) Heritage Foundation. **Publications:** *A Walking Tour of Deerfield*. Brochures ● *Historic Deerfield: A Portrait of Early America*. Book ● *Historic Deerfield: An Introduction*. Book ● *Old Deerfield, Massachusetts*. Book ● Magazine, semiannual ● Annual Report, annual. **Circulation:** 2,500. **Conventions/Meetings:** annual Dublin Seminar for New England Folklife - weekend in June ● annual Historic Deerfield - Wellesley College Symposium in American Art - weekend in October or November.

10035 ■ Historic New England

141 Cambridge St.
Boston, MA 02114
Ph: (617)227-3956 (617)227-3957
Fax: (617)227-9204
E-mail: membership@historicnewengland.org
URL: http://www.historicnewengland.org
Contact: Jane Nylander, Pres.

Founded: 1910. **Members:** 3,600. **Membership Dues:** individual, $45 ● household, $55 ● contributing, $100 ● garden and landscape, $75 ● historic homeowner, $200 ● supporting, $250 ● national, $35 ● institutional, $85. **Staff:** 90. **Budget:** $5,000,000. **State Groups:** 6. **Description:** Seeks to preserve, interpret, and collect building, landscapes, and objects reflecting New England's daily life from the 17th century to the present. Owns and operates 35 historic properties in five states which tell about the people and stories of New England. Offers educational programs. **Libraries:** **Type:** reference; by appointment only. **Holdings:** 1,500,000; archival material, clippings, photographs. **Subjects:** architecture, decorative arts; historic buildings, people, and places. **Awards:** SPNEA Book Prize. **Frequency:** annual. **Type:** recognition. **Formerly:** (2004) Society for the Preservation of New England Antiquities. **Publications:** *Beauport* ● *Historic Houses in New England*, annual. Directory. Lists 22 house museums in New England that are open to the public. **Price:** free. **Circulation:** 45,000 ● *Oldtime New England: New England Furniture*. Journal. Features illustrated essays that focus on the material evidence of the region's social history, craftsmanship and daily life. Alternate Formats: online ● *SPNEA News*, quarterly. Newsletter. Reports on SPNEA historic conservation and preservation projects with updates on historical properties owned by the society. Includes calendar. **Price:** included in membership dues. **Circulation:** 6,500 ● *Wallpaper in New England*. Catalog. Contains comprehensive listings of conservators, reproduction wallpaper manufacturers, suppliers, and other historic wallpaper collections. **Conventions/Meetings:** annual meeting - always spring, New England.

10036 ■ Historic Pullman Foundation (HPF)

614 E 113th St.
Chicago, IL 60628
Ph: (773)785-8181 (773)785-8901
Fax: (773)785-8182
E-mail: foundation@pullmanil.org
URL: http://www.pullmanil.org
Contact: Michael Shymanski, Pres.

Founded: 1973. **Members:** 750. **Membership Dues:** general, $20 (annual) ● associate, $30 (annual) ● supporting, $50 (annual) ● friend, $100 (annual) ● donor, $500 (annual) ● patron, $1,000 (annual) ● resident, $15 (annual). **Staff:** 3. **Budget:** $450,000. **Description:** Individuals interested in preserving the town of Pullman, IL. The town was built in the 1880's by railroad baron George Pullman (1831-97) for Pullman Palace Car Company employees, and was considered a model industrial community and "the world's most perfect town" at the time of its construction. Fosters historic preservation of properties. Sponsors educational programs; maintains museum. **Libraries:** **Type:** reference. **Holdings:** artwork, audiovisuals, books, clippings, monographs, periodicals. **Subjects:** Pullman, the company and town. **Awards:** Pullman Essay Contest Awards. **Type:** recognition. **Recipient:** for best essay of students grade 7 to 12. **Committees:** House Tour; Publicity; Tours/Education; Volunteers. **Publications:** *Update: Historic Pullman*, quarterly. Newsletter. **Price:** included in membership dues ● Books ● Brochures. **Conventions/Meetings:** annual Candlelight House Walk and Buffet - dinner (exhibits) ● First Sunday Guided Walking Tours (exhibits) - always first Sunday, May through October, in Chicago, IL ● Golf Open - competition ● periodic lecture ● Pullman Essay Contest Awards Ceremony - competition, with guest speaker.

10037 ■ Historic Winslow House Association

634 Careswell St.
Marshfield, MA 02050-5623
Ph: (781)837-5753
E-mail: info@winslowhouse.org
URL: http://www.winslowhouse.org
Contact: Mark A. Schmidt, Exec. Dir.

Founded: 1920. **Members:** 500. **Membership Dues:** student/senior, $25 (annual) ● individual, $40 (annual) ● family, $75 (annual) ● corporate, $300 (annual) ● life, $250. **Staff:** 2. **Regional Groups:** 7. **State Groups:** 4. **Local Groups:** 5. **Multinational.** **Description:** Represents individuals who are interested in restoration and preservation of the Isaac Winslow House, circa 1699, in Marshfield, Massachusetts. Created to preserve the ancestral home of the founding family of Marshfield and used to sustain cultural climate of South Shore. Promotes interest in local, regional and national history. Maintains the Isaac Winslow House and its outbuildings and operates them as a museum. Conducts social and educational programs, social outreach and community betterment. **Libraries:** **Type:** reference; not open to the public. **Awards:** Mayflower Award. **Frequency:** periodic. **Type:** recognition. **Recipient:** to the person who has best exemplified what it means to be a member of the Winslow House Association and preserves the integrity of the historic Winslow House ● Winslow House Book Award. **Frequency:** annual. **Type:** monetary. **Recipient:** to the best book published in the calendar year that focuses on the Winslow House and/or local history between 1620-1850. **Boards:** Governors. **Publications:** *Careswell Chronicles*, semiannual. Newsletters. **Price:** free for members; $1.00 for nonmembers. Alternate Formats: online.

10038 ■ Hudson River Sloop Clearwater (HRSC)

112 Market St.
Poughkeepsie, NY 12601
Ph: (845)454-7673
Free: (800)67-SLOOP
Fax: (845)454-7953
E-mail: office@clearwater.org
URL: http://www.clearwater.org
Contact: Jeff Rumpf, Exec. Dir.

Founded: 1964. **Members:** 6,000. **Membership Dues:** individual, $40 ● family, $55 ● contributor, $100 ● sponsor, $200 ● mariner, $500 ● sailing master, $1,000. **Staff:** 20. **Budget:** $1,300,000. **Regional Groups:** 12. **Description:** Owners of the 106-foot sloop Clearwater. Promotes interest in the restoration and preservation of the Hudson River and related waters. Promotes environmental education and action programs; sponsors waterfront festivals, school programs, and day sails for camps and scouts, schools, community groups, historical societies, and individuals. **Libraries:** **Type:** reference. **Holdings:** audiovisuals, biographical archives, books, periodicals. **Subjects:** Hudson River history and ecology. **Telecommunication Services:** electronic mail, jeff@clearwater.org. **Formerly:** (1977) Hudson River Sloop Restoration, Inc. **Publications:** *Clearwater Navigator*, bimonthly. Newsletter ● *Down by the Riverside*. Book ● *The Hudson: An Illustrated Guide to the Living River*. Book. **Price:** $23.95 softcover; $44.95 hardcover ● Also publishes curriculum materials and an annotated map of the Hudson River; has also produced two record albums of river songs and sea chanties. **Conventions/Meetings:** annual Great Hudson River Revival Festival, features ethnic, folk, and popular music (exhibits) - always third weekend of June ● annual meeting - usually third Sunday of September.

10039 ■ International Catacomb Society (ICS)

50 Cross St.
Winchester, MA 01890
Ph: (781)729-1150
Fax: (781)729-1170

E-mail: ahirschfeld@catacombsociety.org
URL: http://www.catacombsociety.org
Contact: Amy Hirschfeld, Exec. Dir.
Founded: 1980. **Members:** 200. **Membership Dues:** individual, $50 (annual) ● student, $25 (annual) ● institution, $100 (annual). **Languages:** English, French, Italian. **Description:** Provides and promotes awareness of the need for preservation, restoration, and maintenance of certain catacombs in Rome, other sites in Italy, and elsewhere, which house archival paintings, epigraphy, and artifacts depicting the culture and customs of early religions under the Roman Empire. Circulates exhibits and disseminates publications and information that will encourage an interreligious understanding through studying the relationships among religions of this period. Cooperates with educational institutions in order to establish collections and displays of artifacts, photographs, maps, plans, replicas, and other materials of historical, archaeological, and religious significance. **Libraries: Type:** by appointment only. **Holdings:** 1,000; articles, books, maps, monographs, periodicals, photographs. **Subjects:** catacombs, Greek, Roman, near Eastern history. **Awards:** Shohet Scholars Program. **Frequency:** annual. **Type:** grant. **Recipient:** for research in the fields of archeology, art history, classical studies, history, comparative religions, or related subjects. **Computer Services:** Bibliographic search, catacomb studies ● database, photographic image of catacombs and Greek, Roman, and near eastern art and archaeology. **Formerly:** International Committee to Preserve Catacombs in Italy. **Publications:** *ICS Newsletter*, periodic. Covers the ICS-sponsored exhibits and activities, which involve the preservation of catacombs. **Price:** included in membership dues; available to others upon request ● *Vaults of Memory: Jewish and Christian Imagery in the Catacombs of Rome*. Catalog.

10040 ■ International Garden Club (IGC)
Bartow-Pell Mansion Museum
895 Shore Rd.
Pelham Bay Park
Bronx, NY 10464
Ph: (718)885-1461
Fax: (718)885-9164
E-mail: bartowpell@aol.com
URL: http://www.BartowPellMansionMuseum.org
Contact: Clarissa Cylich, Exec. Dir.
Founded: 1914. **Members:** 400. **Staff:** 3. **Budget:** $100,000. **Description:** Preserves, maintains, and manages Bartow-Pell Mansion Museum, a national landmark at Pelham Bay Park, NY. Conducts educational programs. Operates speakers' bureau and museum. Maintains Bartow-Pell Landmark Fund. **Libraries: Type:** reference. **Holdings:** 1,500. **Committees:** Benefits; Carriage House; Development; Education; Grants and Foundations; Lecture Series; Library; Museum; Tours. **Publications:** *Barton-Pell Mansion Museum Newsletter*, 3/year. **Price:** free. **Circulation:** 550 ● Yearbook, annual. **Price:** free for members. **Circulation:** 400.

10041 ■ International Time Capsule Society (ITCS)
c/o Oglethorpe University
4484 Peachtree Rd. NE
Atlanta, GA 30319
Ph: (404)261-1441
Free: (800)428-4484
URL: http://www.oglethorpe.edu/about_us/crypt_of_civilization
Contact: Paul Hudson, Contact
Founded: 1990. **Multinational. Description:** Educates the general public and the academic community on the value of time capsules. Maintains a registry of all known time capsules. Encourages the study of the history, variety and motivation behind time capsule projects. **Computer Services:** Information services, crypt of civilization resources ● information services, time capsule resources.

10042 ■ John Marshall Foundation (JMF)
c/o Lynn Brackenridge, Exec. Dir.
209 W Franklin St.
Richmond, VA 23220
Ph: (804)775-0861
Fax: (804)775-0862
E-mail: lynnb@johnmarshallfoundation.org
URL: http://www.johnmarshallfoundation.org
Contact: Lynn Brackenridge, Exec. Dir.
Founded: 1987. **Staff:** 3. **Budget:** $400,000. **Nonmembership. Description:** Acts as the steward of the legacy of the Great Chief Justice (Chief Justice of the United States Supreme Court, 1801-1835). Sponsors educational and public interest programs or other activities in the fields of law, government, history and public affairs to promote a greater public understanding of Chief Justice John Marshall and his many contributions and accomplishments related to the foundation of the nation. Supports the preservation of a permanent collection of well-maintained sites related to John Marshall's life and legacy that provide public access and interpretation appropriate to the nature of each site. **Libraries: Type:** reference. **Awards:** Award for Excellence in Teaching the U.S. Constitution. **Frequency:** annual. **Type:** recognition. **Recipient:** to Virginia secondary school teachers of the U.S. Constitution who showed knowledge of and enthusiasm for the Constitution as evidenced through activities inside and outside the classroom ● Medal-in-Law Award. **Frequency:** biennial. **Type:** recognition. **Recipient:** to a deserving leader in United States Jurisprudence. **Affiliated With:** APVA Preservation Virginia. **Publications:** *The Marshall Family*. Book. **Price:** $24.50 ● *Mr. Chief Justice*. Video. **Conventions/Meetings:** competition.

10043 ■ Lincoln Highway Association (LHA)
PO Box 308
Franklin Grove, IL 61031
Ph: (815)456-3030
E-mail: president@lincolnhighwayassoc.org
URL: http://www.lincolnhighwayassoc.org
Contact: Jan Shupert-Arick, Pres.
Founded: 1992. **Members:** 1,150. **Membership Dues:** individual/non-profit organization/city or county government, $30 (annual) ● family, $40 (annual) ● student, $15 (annual) ● supporting/business, $50 (annual) ● patron/corporate, $100 (annual) ● life, $750. **Staff:** 5. **State Groups:** 12. **Description:** Individuals, businesses, and organizations with an interest in the Lincoln Highway, the first transcontinental highway in the United States (the Lincoln Highway was completed in 1913 and linked New York, NY with San Francisco, CA). Promotes preservation of the Highway and associated landmarks; seeks to raise public awareness of the Highway and its history. Conducts research and educational programs; sponsors promotional activities to encourage travel along the Lincoln Highway; creates and develops historical markers and other interpretive sites along the Highway. **Libraries: Type:** open to the public. **Holdings:** books, periodicals. **Subjects:** Lincoln Highway, related items. **Publications:** *The Lincoln Highway Forum*, quarterly. Magazine. Contains historical photos and articles on Lincoln Hwy. **Price:** $6.50 for nonmembers; included in membership dues. **Circulation:** 1,200. **Advertising:** accepted. **Conventions/Meetings:** annual Lincoln Highway - conference and lecture, with displays of Lincoln Highway/bus trips on Lincoln Highway in Indiana.

10044 ■ Mamie Doud Eisenhower Birthplace Foundation
709 Caroll St.
Boone, IA 50036
Ph: (515)432-1907
E-mail: mamiedoud@opencominc.com
URL: http://www.mamiesbirthplace.homestead.com
Contact: Larry Adams, Curator
Founded: 1970. **Members:** 350. **Membership Dues:** single, $15 (annual) ● couple, $30 (annual) ● sponsor, $50 (annual) ● patron, $100 (annual) ● sustaining, $500-$1,000 (annual). **Staff:** 3. **Budget:** $50,000. **Description:** Seeks to restore, preserve, and maintain the Mamie Doud Eisenhower Birthplace. Offers educational and research programs, a museum, and a speakers bureau. **Libraries: Type:** reference; open to the public. **Holdings:** 1,500; archival material, artwork, audiovisuals, books, clippings, periodicals. **Subjects:** Eisenhower, local history, White House and genealogy. **Publications:** Newsletter, periodic ● Brochure. **Conventions/Meetings:** quarterly board meeting - always January, April, June, and October in Boone, IA.

10045 ■ Memorial Foundation of the Germanna Colonies in Virginia
PO Box 279
Locust Grove, VA 22508-0279
Ph: (540)423-1700
Fax: (540)423-1747
E-mail: office@germanna.org
URL: http://www.germanna.org
Contact: Thomas Wallace Faircloth, Pres.
Founded: 1956. **Members:** 2,000. **Membership Dues:** individual, $20 (annual) ● family, $30 (annual). **Staff:** 1. **Description:** Seeks to preserve and make known the history of the Germanna Colonies in Virginia, their operations under the patronage of Governor Alexander Spotswood, and his residence and activities in Germanna and the surrounding areas. Aims to purchase and improve real estate that was part of the original Germanna tract. Donated 100 acres of the original Germanna tract in 1969 to establish Germanna Community College. Encourages members to conduct genealogical and historical research on the original Germanna colonies and their descendants. Conducts research, archaeology, and educational programs; maintains speakers' bureau. **Libraries: Type:** reference; open to the public. **Holdings:** 500; archival material, artwork, books, clippings, monographs, periodicals. **Subjects:** genealogy, history, archaeology. **Computer Services:** database ● electronic publishing ● mailing lists. **Affiliated With:** National Genealogical Society; National Trust for Historic Preservation. **Also Known As:** Germanna Foundation. **Publications:** *Clore, Yager, and Utz Descendants - 1717 Colonists*. Book. Contains information on the first four generations of the Clore, Yager, and Utz families. **Price:** $15.00. Also Cited As: *Germanna Record No. 10* ● *Culpeper: A Virginia County's History Through 1920*. **Price:** $35.00 ● *Genealogical and Historical Notes on Culpeper County, Virginia*. **Price:** $35.00 ● *Germanna*. Newsletter. **Price:** included in membership dues ● *The Germanna Foundation: The First Decade, 1956-1966*. Book. Describes the objectives and achievements of the foundation. Includes information on genealogical research and a chronology of Germanna history. **Price:** $15.00. Also Cited As: *Germanna Record No. 9* ● *Germanna Heritage Book 1714-1999 (Germanna Record No. 15)*. **Price:** $65.00 ● *Germanna, Outpost of Adventure, 1714-1956*. Book. Includes a history of the Germanna Colonies of 1714 and 1717, Lt. Gov. Spotswood's ironworks, John Fontaine, the Knights of the Golden Horseshoe, etc. **Price:** $15.00 for members; free to new members. Also Cited As: *Germanna Record No. 7* ● *Germantown Revived*. Book. Features an account of the Germantown in Fauquier County, VA, where the first Germanna colony of 1714 resettled in 1719 after leaving Germanna. **Price:** $15.00. Also Cited As: *Germanna Record No. 2* ● *Historic Culpeper*. **Price:** $10.00 ● *The Holtzclaw Genealogy, 1540-1935*. Book. Includes reprint of a 1930s work on the families of the 1714 Germanna Colony. **Price:** $15.00. Also Cited As: *Germanna Record No. 14* ● *John Carpenter and Thomas Wayland Descendants*. Book. Features information on Germanna pioneers of the Second Germanna Colony through the 1850s. **Price:** $15.00. Also Cited As: *Germanna Record No. 11* ● *John Hoffman, 1714*. Book. Contains information on Hoffman and his descendants. **Price:** $15.00. Also Cited As: *Germanna Record No. 3* ● *John Jacob Rector, 1714*. Book. Contains information on the Germanna Colonist and his descendants. **Price:** $15.00. Also Cited As: *Germanna Record No. 4* ● *Peter Hitt, John Joseph Martin and Tillman Weaver*. Book. Features an account of Hitt, Martin, and Weaver of the 1714 Colony and their descendants. **Price:** $15.00. Also Cited As: *Germanna Record No. 1* ● *Second Germanna Colony, 1717*. Book. Contains an account of the 1717 Germanna Colony that initially settled on the Rapidan River and later settled on the Robinson River. **Price:** $15.00. Also Cited As: *Germanna Record No. 6*. **Conventions/Meetings:** semiannual board meeting - every spring and fall ● annual

reunion (exhibits) - always third Sunday in July ● annual seminar (exhibits) - always 3rd Saturday in July.

10046 ■ Mount Rushmore National Memorial Society (MR)
13000 Hwy. 244, Bldg. 31, Ste.1
Keystone, SD 57751-0268
Ph: (605)574-2523 (605)574-3171
Fax: (605)574-2307
E-mail: mrnms@mtrushmore.org
URL: http://www.nps.gov/moru
Founded: 1930. **Members:** 250. **Membership Dues:** life, $200. **Staff:** 3. **Local Groups:** 1. **Description:** Individuals dedicated to preservation of Mount Rushmore national monument. Conducts fundraising activities; gathers and disseminates information on Mount Rushmore. Conducts research activities; sponsors educational programs; collects related artifacts. Operates in cooperation with the National Park Service. **Libraries: Type:** reference. **Holdings:** archival material. **Formerly:** Mount Rushmore Society. **Publications:** *America's Shrine of Democracy*. Book. **Price:** $9.95 soft cover; $12.95 hard cover ● *The Four Faces of Freedom* ● *Mount Rushmore - The Shrine*. Video ● Newsletter, quarterly. **Conventions/Meetings:** annual meeting ● semiannual meeting - always spring and fall.

10047 ■ National Association of Tribal Historic Preservation Officers (NATHPO)
PO Box 19189
Washington, DC 20036-9189
Ph: (202)628-8476
Fax: (202)628-2241
E-mail: info@nathpo.org
URL: http://www.nathpo.org
Contact: Ms. D. Bambi Kraus, Pres.
Founded: 1998. **Membership Dues:** associate, $250 (annual). **Description:** Supports the preservation, maintenance and revitalization of the culture and traditions of native people of the United States. Provides a forum for discussion and dissemination of ideas. Assists in the preservation of historic and cultural properties.

10048 ■ National Preservation Institute (NPI)
PO Box 1702
Alexandria, VA 22313
Ph: (703)765-0100
E-mail: info@npi.org
URL: http://www.npi.org
Contact: Jere Gibber, Exec. Dir.
Founded: 1980. **Nonmembership**. **Description:** Dedicated to the preservation of historic, cultural, and environmental resources; provides professional training, customized training, and technical assistance. **Awards: Type:** scholarship. **Recipient:** to attend seminars. **Publications:** *Seminars in Historic Preservation and Cultural Resource Management*, semiannual. Catalog. Alternate Formats: online. **Conventions/Meetings:** seminar, for professional skills development in the preservation, protection, and interpretation of historic, archaeological, cultural and environmental resources - 45/year.

10049 ■ National Society for the Preservation of Covered Bridges (NSPCB)
PO Box 267
Jericho, VT 05465-0267
Ph: (802)899-2093 (802)722-4040
E-mail: jcnelson@together.net
URL: http://www.vermontbridges.com/nspcb1st.htm
Contact: Mr. David W. Wright, Pres.
Founded: 1950. **Members:** 1,202. **Membership Dues:** individual, family, $15 (annual) ● student, $5 (annual) ● life, $250 ● couple (life), $300 ● corporate, $500 (annual). **Description:** Individuals, historical societies, and libraries with an interest in preservation of historic covered bridges. Contacts public officials regarding covered bridges. **Libraries: Type:** reference. **Publications:** *Covered Bridge Topics*, quarterly ● *National Society for the Preservation of Covered Bridges Newsletter*, quarterly ● *World Guide to Covered Bridges*. **Price:** $8.00. **Conventions/Meetings:** annual meeting - usually last weekend in October.

10050 ■ National Temple Hill Association (NTHA)
PO Box 315
Vails Gate, NY 12584
Ph: (845)561-5073
E-mail: swaddell@hvc.rr.com
URL: http://www.nationaltemplehill.org
Contact: Daniel S. Lucia, Pres.
Founded: 1933. **Members:** 225. **Membership Dues:** individual, $15 (annual) ● couple, $25 (annual) ● life, $1,000. **Staff:** 6. **Description:** Works to restore and maintain the Revolutionary War headquarters of Generals Horatio Gates and Arthur St. Clair at Edmonston House, New Windsor, NY. Temple Hill, a New York state historic site, was the final campground of George Washington's Continental army in the winter of 1782-83. Interprets and develops site of the last encampment of the continental army, with authentically reconstructed soldiers huts. **Libraries: Type:** by appointment only; reference. **Holdings:** 100. **Subjects:** revolutionary, local history. **Subcommittees:** Last Encampment of the Continental Army. **Publications:** *18th Century Houses in New Windsor*. Book ● *Washington's Last Cantonment: High Time for a Peace*. Book ● Newsletter, quarterly. **Conventions/Meetings:** annual meeting and dinner - always March 15, New Windsor, NY.

10051 ■ National Trust for Historic Preservation (NTHP)
1785 Massachusetts Ave. NW
Washington, DC 20036-2117
Ph: (202)588-6000
Free: (800)944-6847
Fax: (202)588-6038
E-mail: feedback@nthp.org
URL: http://www.nationaltrust.org
Contact: Richard Moe, Pres.
Founded: 1949. **Members:** 200,000. **Membership Dues:** individual, $20 (annual) ● family, $30 (annual) ● contributing, $50 (annual) ● sustaining, $100 (annual) ● participating, $250 (annual) ● heritage society, $1,000 (annual) ● forum, $115 (annual). **Staff:** 275. **Budget:** $50,000,000. **Regional Groups:** 6. **Description:** Facilitates public participation in the preservation of buildings, sites, and objects significant in American history and culture. Gives direct assistance in the form of low-interest loans, matching grants, and expert counsel. Monitors legislation and regulations. Acts as a clearinghouse for information on state, local, and federal and private preservation programs. Takes direct legal action in prototypical cases; develops and tests new approaches to preservation. Maintains historic properties. **Libraries: Type:** not open to the public. **Holdings:** 14,325. **Awards:** Crowninshield Award. **Frequency:** annual. **Type:** recognition. **Recipient:** for outstanding achievement in preservation ● National Presentation Honor Award. **Frequency:** annual. **Type:** recognition. **Recipient:** for projects demonstrating outstanding commitment to excellence in historic preservation. **Additional Websites:** http://www.nthp.org. **Telecommunication Services:** teletype, (202)588-6200. **Subgroups:** Finance and Merchandising; Law and Public Policy; Programs, Services, and Information; Resources Development; Stewardship of Historic Sites. **Absorbed:** (1954) National Council for Historic Sites and Buildings; (1985) Historic House Association of America. **Publications:** *Preservation*, bimonthly. Magazine. Reports on the preservation of America's architectural heritage. Includes articles on the people and organizations working in the field. **Price:** included in membership dues. ISSN: 0018-2419. **Circulation:** 250,000. **Advertising:** accepted. Alternate Formats: microform ● *Preservation Forum*, bimonthly. Journal ● *Preservation Law Reporter*, periodic. Journal. Contains laws that protect community's character. **Price:** available to members only. **Conventions/Meetings:** annual National Preservation Conference - conference and seminar (exhibits) - 2008 Oct. 21-26, Tulsa, OK.

10052 ■ Newport Restoration Foundation (NRF)
51 Touro St.
Newport, RI 02840
Ph: (401)849-7300 (401)849-7301
Fax: (401)849-0125
E-mail: geninfo@newportrestoration.org
URL: http://www.newportrestoration.com
Contact: Pieter N. Roos, Exec. Dir.
Founded: 1969. **Members:** 5. **Staff:** 33. **Budget:** $3,800,000. **Description:** Established to preserve and restore 18th and 19th century colonial buildings in the resort town of Newport, RI. The foundation has purchased over 79 dwellings, which have been restored to look as they did in colonial times, but with modernized plumbing and electricity; the homes are rented after restoration. Maintains a museum (the Samuel Whitehorne House) in Newport, RI and Prescott Farm Complex, Middletown, RI and Rough Point Mansion Museum (a former home of the late Doris Duke).

10053 ■ Noah Webster House (NWH)
227 S Main St.
West Hartford, CT 06107
Ph: (860)521-5362
Fax: (860)521-4036
E-mail: comments@noahwebster.org
URL: http://www.noahwebsterhouse.org
Contact: Chris Dobbs, Exec. Dir.
Founded: 1965. **Members:** 500. **Membership Dues:** senior, student, $25 (annual) ● individual, $30 (annual) ● family/household, grandparent, $40 (annual) ● sustainer, $500 (annual) ● contributor, $100 (annual) ● sponsor, $250 (annual) ● benefactor, $1,000 (annual). **Staff:** 21. **Budget:** $250,000. **Description:** Individuals interested in the preservation of the birthplace of Noah Webster (1758-1843), American lexicographer, author, and teacher, who is known as the "father of his country's language". Maintains Webster's childhood home and the West Hartford Historical Society as a museum. Sponsors educational programs. **Libraries: Type:** reference. **Holdings:** archival material. **Subjects:** Noah Webster, 18th century, West Hartford and Connecticut history. **Awards:** Freeman & Mary Meyer Prize For Excellence in History. **Frequency:** annual. **Type:** monetary. **Recipient:** for best local history research paper by a West Hartford High School student. **Programs:** Education; Public; Scout. **Formerly:** (1995) Noah Webster Foundation. **Publications:** *Spectator*, quarterly. Newsletter. Includes organization and event news. **Price:** included in membership dues. **Circulation:** 500. **Conventions/Meetings:** annual meeting (exhibits) - May ● periodic tour.

10054 ■ North American Araucanian Royalist Society
c/o Daniel Morrison, Gen. Sec.
205 Loetscher Pl., Ste.1-A
Princeton, NJ 08540
E-mail: tourtoirac@yahoo.com
URL: http://www.geocities.com/tourtoirac
Contact: Daniel Morrison, Gen. Sec.
Founded: 1995. **Members:** 80. **Membership Dues:** regular in North America, $20 (annual) ● regular outside North America, $30 (annual). **Staff:** 1. **Budget:** $1,750. **Description:** Promotes the study of the Mapuche and the Kingdom of Araucania and Patagonia, which they founded in 1861. Sponsors educational programs and a speakers' bureau. **Libraries: Type:** open to the public. **Holdings:** 400; artwork, audio recordings, books. **Subjects:** Mapuche Indians, the Kingdom of Araucania and Patagonia. **Publications:** *The Steel Crown*, quarterly. Journal. ISSN: 1098-5506. **Circulation:** 120. **Advertising:** accepted. **Conventions/Meetings:** annual board meeting - usually in December.

10055 ■ North American Voyageur Council (NAVC)
c/o Northwest Co. Fur Post
PO Box 51
Pine City, MN 55063
E-mail: director@navoyageur.org
URL: http://www.navoyageur.org
Contact: Terry Haas, Contact
Founded: 1978. **Members:** 250. **Membership Dues:** family, $10 (annual) ● associate, $12 (annual). **Description:** Individuals and groups (brigades) who reenact the life and work of the voyageurs, fur trad-

ers and trappers of French Canadian descent who created or discovered trails and routes that were later used for westward expansion and settlement. Promotes interest in the canoe men and women of the fur trade. **Publications:** Newsletter, quarterly. Includes calendar of events and articles on costuming, skills development, historical information, songs, and folklore. **Conventions/Meetings:** annual meeting.

10056 ■ Oregon-California Trails Association (OCTA)
PO Box 1019
Independence, MO 64051-0519
Ph: (816)252-2276
Free: (888)811-6282
Fax: (816)836-0989
E-mail: octa@octa-trails.org
URL: http://www.octa-trails.org
Contact: Mr. F. Travis Boley, Mgr.

Founded: 1982. **Members:** 3,000. **Membership Dues:** emigrant, educator, $45 (annual) ● pioneer, $60 (annual) ● trail patron, $125 (annual) ● Mattes Society, $250 (annual) ● institution, $300 (annual) ● life, $1,000 ● corporate, $1,250 (annual) ● student (college), $20 (annual).. **Staff:** 3. **Budget:** $300,000. **State Groups:** 11. **Description:** Individuals interested in the history of overland emigrant trails in the trans-Mississippi west. Preserves and interprets trails and emigrant burial sites. Develops educational material for students. Conducts trail mapping and marking programs. Distributes educational material. Conducts field trip programs. Promotes Trail Preservation. **Libraries: Type:** reference. **Holdings:** 3,000; archival material. **Subjects:** emigrant trails 1830-1890. **Awards:** Education, Friend of the Trails. **Frequency:** annual. **Type:** recognition. **Recipient:** for teacher's performance and trail preservation. **Computer Services:** Mailing lists, internet discussion list for questions about westward emigrant trails. **Committees:** Archaeology; Census of Overland Emigrant Documents; Education; Friends of the Trail; Fund Raising; Graves and Sites; Legislative Action; Trail Marking and Mapping. **Publications:** *Emigrant Names Search Software*. Directory. Alternate Formats: CD-ROM ● *News from the Plains*, quarterly. Newsletter. **Price:** included in membership dues. **Circulation:** 3,000. **Advertising:** accepted ● *The 1854 Oregon Trail Diary of Winfield Scott Ebey*. Books ● *The 1849 California Trail Diaries of Elisah Preston Howell*, quarterly. Books. Features scholarly articles and book reviews. **Price:** $40.00/year. **Circulation:** 3,000. **Advertising:** accepted ● *Overland Journal*, quarterly. Magazine. Features scholarly articles and book reviews. **Price:** $40.00/year. **Circulation:** 3,000. **Advertising:** accepted ● *The Overland Memoir of Charles Frederick True*. Books. **Conventions/Meetings:** annual meeting and tour, includes speakers, trips, trail hikes (exhibits) - always second week of August. 2008 Aug. 8-11, Elko, NV - **Avg. Attendance:** 350; 2009 Aug. 7-10, Denver, CO - **Avg. Attendance:** 500; 2010 Aug. 13-16, Nampa, ID - **Avg. Attendance:** 500.

10057 ■ Patriots of Fort McHenry-Living Classrooms
Ft. McHenry Natl. Monument and Historic Shrine
802 S Caroline St.
Baltimore, MD 21231
Ph: (410)396-3453
E-mail: heather@patriotsoffortmchenry.org
URL: http://www.patriotsoffortmchenry.org
Contact: Heather Armstrong, Contact

Founded: 1984. **Members:** 1,000. **Membership Dues:** student, $25 (annual) ● individual, $35 (annual) ● family, $65 (annual) ● contributor, $100 (annual) ● patron, $500 (annual) ● patriot, $1,000 (annual). **Staff:** 2. **Budget:** $250,000. **Description:** Raises funds to restore Ft. McHenry, MD, site of the War of 1812 Battle of Baltimore during which Francis Scott Key wrote the Star-Spangled Banner. **Awards: Type:** recognition. **Computer Services:** database. **Formerly:** (1998) Patriots of Fort McHenry. **Publications:** Newsletter, quarterly. Alternate Formats: online. **Conventions/Meetings:** periodic meeting.

10058 ■ Preservation Action (PA)
401 F St. NW, Ste.324
Washington, DC 20001
Ph: (202)637-7873
Fax: (202)637-7874
E-mail: mail@preservationaction.org
URL: http://www.preservationaction.org
Contact: Heather MacIntosh, Pres.

Founded: 1974. **Members:** 700. **Membership Dues:** individual, $55 (annual) ● advocate, $250 (annual) ● preservation ally, $100 (annual) ● patron, $500 (annual) ● Sponsors' Circle, $1,000 (annual) ● student, $25 (annual). **Staff:** 3. **Budget:** $250,000. **State Groups:** 51. **Description:** Primary objective is to lobby for funding and program support in order to maintain and enhance the historic built environment of America. Successes in Congress include: initiating and securing tax incentives to save and utilize older buildings profitably and sensibly; retaining federal funding for state preservation programs; adapting government buildings for community use; uniting retail, commercial, and residential communities to restore vitality to older neighborhoods and central business districts; preservation issues; and lobbying to ensure no changes are made in historic rehabilitation tax incentives. **Publications:** *Alert*, quarterly. Newsletter ● *Preservation Action Legislative Watch*, weekly. Sent by email. Alternate Formats: online. Also Cited As: *PalWatch* ● Also publishes brochure. **Conventions/Meetings:** annual Lobby Day - conference.

10059 ■ Preservation Volunteers (PV)
232 E 11th St.
New York, NY 10003
Ph: (212)769-2900
E-mail: dexter@vandenbergnyc.com
URL: http://www.preservationvolunteers.com
Contact: Dexter Guerrieri, Pres.

Founded: 1978. **Description:** Seeks to preserve historic monuments, buildings and sites. Provides opportunities and support for preservation education, preservation craft trade skills and preservation community action to restore and maintain local heritage structures and sites. **Committees:** Advisory. **Projects:** Fairview School House Association; The Green-Wood Cemetery; The Huguenot Historical Society.

10060 ■ Royal Oak Foundation (ROF)
26 Broadway, Ste.950
New York, NY 10004-1715
Ph: (212)480-2889
Free: (800)913-6565
Fax: (212)785-7234
E-mail: general@royal-oak.org
URL: http://www.royal-oak.org
Contact: Mr. John James Oddy, Exec. Dir.

Founded: 1973. **Members:** 30,000. **Membership Dues:** individual, $55 (annual) ● family, $90 (annual) ● conservator, $150 (annual) ● art and design, $250 (annual) ● sponsor, $500 (annual) ● benefactor, $1,000 (annual) ● guardian, $5,000 (annual) ● patron (life), $10,000 ● steward, $2,500 (annual) ● dual, $80 (annual). **Staff:** 7. **Budget:** $750,000. **Regional Groups:** 9. **Description:** Professionals, students, and laypeople who are interested in architecture, nature conservation, and historic preservation areas. Seeks to further the preservation and understanding of Anglo-American cultural and architectural heritage. Conducts symposia; presents lecture series and special lectures given by foreign speakers visiting the U.S; sponsors exhibits emphasizing historic preservation. Maintains charitable program. **Convention/Meeting:** none. **Libraries: Type:** reference. **Holdings:** 800; books, films. **Computer Services:** database, membership. **Telecommunication Services:** electronic mail, lectures@royal-oak.org. **Publications:** Newsletter, quarterly. **Price:** free. **Circulation:** 15,000.

10061 ■ Save the Battlefield Coalition (SBC)
PO Box 110
Catharpin, VA 20143
Ph: (803)329-8626
Fax: (803)329-8626
E-mail: jrankin421@aol.com
Contact: Betty Rankin, Pres.

Founded: 1988. **Description:** Individuals and organizations interested in the preservation and restoration of Manassas National Battlefield Park. (Manassas, or Bull Run, is the historical site of 2 Confederate victories during the Civil War.) Successfully worked for federal acquisition of the Stuart Hill land tract adjacent to the Manassas National Battlefield Park to stop proposed commercial development projects; is involved in clean-up program and restoration project of this area. Was catalyst for the formation of other preservation groups to save civil war battlefields and adjacent lands.

10062 ■ Shenandoah National Park Association (SNPA)
3655 US Hwy. 211 E
Luray, VA 22835
Ph: (540)999-3582 (540)999-3581
Fax: (540)999-3583
E-mail: snpa@shentel.net
URL: http://www.snpbooks.org

Founded: 1950. **Members:** 900. **Membership Dues:** individual, $20 (annual) ● family, $25 (annual) ● life, $250 ● student, $8 (annual) ● supporting individual/small business/tourism bureau, $50 (annual) ● corporate, $500 (annual). **Staff:** 6. **Budget:** $600,000. **Description:** Individuals united to promote, support, and maintain the beauty and history of the Shenandoah National Park in Virginia. Furthers their cause through the sale of educational materials at the park's visitors' centers. **Formerly:** (2002) Shenandoah Natural History Association. **Publications:** *Overlook*, annual. Newsletter ● *The Trillium*, semiannual. Newsletter. Contains information about the association as well as special events in the parks. **Price:** included in membership dues. **Conventions/Meetings:** quarterly board meeting.

10063 ■ Society of the Founders and Friends of Norwich, Connecticut (SFFNC)
PO Box 13
Norwich, CT 06360-0013
Ph: (860)889-9440
E-mail: info@leffingwellhousemuseum.org
URL: http://www.leffingwellhousemuseum.org
Contact: Ann-etta Cannon, Pres.

Founded: 1901. **Members:** 425. **Membership Dues:** student, $10 (annual) ● senior (over 65), $15 (annual) ● individual, $20 (annual) ● family, $30 (annual) ● sustaining, $60 (annual) ● patron, $150 (annual) ● life, $500. **Staff:** 1. **Description:** Descendants of early setters of Norwich, CT; interested others. Fosters the preservation and promotion of historical sites and the early history surrounding Norwich, CT. Conducts slide and lecture presentations on topics such as Homes in the Norwichtown Historic District and Rebels and Tories: the Leffingwell Family in Norwich. Maintains restored 18th century house, small library, and museum. **Libraries: Type:** not open to the public. **Holdings:** 60; books. **Subjects:** local history. **Programs:** Interpreter Training. **Formerly:** (1990) Society of the Founders of Norwich, Connecticut. **Publications:** *Leffingwell Inn News*, quarterly. Newsletter. Contains information on activities at the museum. **Circulation:** 325. **Conventions/Meetings:** annual meeting.

10064 ■ Society for the Preservation of Natural History Collections (SPNHC)
c/o Barbara Brown, Treas.
PO Box 797
Washington, DC 20044-0797
Ph: (212)769-5864
E-mail: bbrown@amnh.org
URL: http://www.spnhc.org
Contact: Barbara Brown, Treas.

Founded: 1985. **Members:** 600. **Membership Dues:** individual, $25 (annual) ● library, $30 (annual) ● associate/institution, $50 (annual) ● life, $625. **Budget:** $30,000. **Description:** Individuals interested in the development and preservation of natural history collections. (Natural history collections include specimens and supporting documentation such as audiovisual materials, labels, library materials, field data, and archives.) Encourages research on the requirements for preserving, storing, and displaying natural history collections; provides and maintains an international association of persons who study and care for natural history collections. Conducts educational programs. **Awards:** Faber Award. **Frequency:** annual. **Type:** monetary. **Recipient:** for a competitive research proposal, intended to encourage innovative projects that promote the objectives of the Society in collections management, conservation, or other collection-oriented aspects of natural history ● President's Award. **Frequency:** annual. **Type:** recognition. **Recipient:** for an individual who has made a significant contribution to the society ● SPNHC Award. **Frequency:** annual. **Type:** recognition. **Recipient:** for an individual who has made a significant contribution to the objectives of the society. **Telecommunication Services:** electronic mail, rabeler@umich.edu. **Publications:** *Collection Forum*, semiannual. Journal. **Price:** included in membership dues; $11.00 for back issues. ISSN: 0831-4985 ● *SPNHC Newsletter*, semiannual. **Price:** included in membership dues; $2.50 for back issues. ISSN: 1071-2887 ● *Storage of Natural History Collections: A Preventive Conservation Approach*. Book. **Price:** $36.00 includes shipping and handling ● *Storage of Natural History Collections: Ideas and Practical Solutions*. Book. **Price:** $36.00 includes shipping and handling. **Conventions/Meetings:** annual conference (exhibits).

10065 ■ Society for the Preservation of Old Mills (SPOOM)
5667 Leisure South Dr. SE
Kentwood, MI 49548-6851
Ph: (616)455-0609 (704)365-9857
Free: (866)362-6277
E-mail: eamedit@aol.com
URL: http://www.spoom.org
Contact: Esther A. Middlewood, Ed.
Founded: 1972. **Members:** 1,500. **Membership Dues:** regular, in U.S., $21 (annual) ● regular, outside U.S., $24 (annual) ● family in U.S., $25 (annual) ● sustaining, $30 (annual) ● sustaining organization, patron, $50 (annual) ● corporate, $250 (annual). **Staff:** 1. **Budget:** $26,000. **Regional Groups:** 7. **Description:** Works to promote interest, both public and private, in old mills of all types. Helps in the preservation or reconstruction of such structures and honors individuals whose work and ideas made these mills possible. Acts as a clearinghouse on mill information. Compiles rosters of old mills still standing and of those still in operation (by states); also compiles statistics regarding specialty mills such as cider mills, B&Bs, mill museums, etc. Operates bookstore and publishes both reprints of classic texts and original research. **Libraries: Type:** reference; open to the public; by appointment only. **Holdings:** archival material, audio recordings, books, papers, photographs, video recordings. **Subjects:** mills, equipment, technical information, milling. **Awards:** SPOOM Mill Restoration Grant. **Frequency:** annual. **Type:** grant. **Recipient:** for restoration of nonprofit mills. **Computer Services:** database. **Committees:** Technical Advisory. **Affiliated With:** The International Molinological Society. **Publications:** *Old Mill News*, quarterly. Magazine. Covers news of old mills and mill restoration. Includes index for 1972-2001, book reviews, and listing of mill machinery to sell, buy, or trade. **Price:** included in membership dues. ISSN: 0276-3338. **Circulation:** 1,500. **Advertising:** accepted. **Conventions/Meetings:** annual conference, with mill tours (exhibits) - always fall ● semiannual Regional Chapter Meetings, with mill tours - usually spring and fall.

10066 ■ Statue of Liberty - Ellis Island Foundation (SOLEIF)
c/o History Center
17 Battery Pl., No. 210
New York, NY 10004-3507
Ph: (212)561-4588
E-mail: historycenter@ellisisland.org
URL: http://www.ellisisland.org
Contact: Stephen A. Briganti, Pres./CEO
Founded: 1982. **Membership Dues:** sustaining, $45 (annual). **Staff:** 25. **Budget:** $5,000,000. **Description:** Works to foster and promote public knowledge of and interest in the history of the Statue of Liberty and Ellis Island and to restore both monuments. More than $500 million has been raised for the restoration, which included the creation of an exhibit on the Statue's history and construction. The restored Main Registry Building on Ellis Island contains a 100,000 square foot museum telling the story of the peopling of America. The museum contains four exhibit areas, two theatres, an oral history studio, a library for immigration studies, and a learning center which features a 16-screen interactive video wall. Plans to sponsor educational and scholarly seminars, special interest tours and changing exhibits. **Awards:** Ellis Island Family Heritage Awards. **Frequency:** annual. **Type:** recognition. **Recipient:** to Ellis Island immigrants or their descendants. **Committees:** History. **Divisions:** Public Affairs. **Publications:** *Between Race and Ethnicity*. Book ● *The Butte Irish*. Book ● *Century of European Migrations, 1830-1930*. Book ● *Family, Church, and Market*. Book ● *Germans in the New World*. Book ● *Immigrant World of Ybor City*. Book ● *Labor and Community*. Book ● *Les Icariens*. Book ● *Liberty Highlights*. Newsletter ● *Liberty: The Statue and the American Dream*. Book ● *Making of an American Pluralism*. Book ● *The Persistence of Ethnicity*. Book ● Annual Report. **Conventions/Meetings:** quarterly board meeting.

10067 ■ Surratt Society (SS)
c/o Laurie Verge, Dir.
9118 Brandywine Rd.
Box 427
Clinton, MD 20735
Ph: (301)868-1121
Fax: (301)868-8177
E-mail: surratt@surratt.org
URL: http://www.surratt.org
Contact: Laurie Verge, Dir.
Founded: 1975. **Members:** 1,500. **Membership Dues:** individual, $7 (annual) ● life, $125. **Staff:** 7. **Budget:** $130,000. **Description:** Individuals dedicated to the preservation and interpretation of historic Surratt House and Tavern in Clinton, MD. Encourages research into the historical aspects of the house with special focus on the Lincoln assassination conspiracy. Conducts museum tours and educational programs. Operates speaker's bureau and gift shop. **Libraries: Type:** reference. **Holdings:** 1,500; archival material. **Subjects:** Lincoln assassination, Civil War, 19th-century life. **Awards:** T.S. Gwynn History Award. **Frequency:** annual. **Type:** monetary. **Recipient:** for an outstanding community college student in history field. **Computer Services:** Information services, "Ask the Historians". **Publications:** *The Body in the Barn*. Book. **Price:** $12.00 ● *From War Department Files*. Book. **Price:** $22.00 ● *In Pursuit Of.Continuing Research in the Field of the Lincoln Assassination*. Book. **Price:** $25.00 ● *The Lincoln Assassination*, monthly. Newsletter. Covers society news; includes historical articles. **Price:** included in membership dues ● *On the Way to Garrett's Farm*. Book. **Price:** $20.00 ● *Surratt Courier*, monthly. Newsletter. Covers society news; includes historical articles. **Price:** included in membership dues. **Conventions/Meetings:** biennial banquet and lecture - May and September in Clinton, MD.

10068 ■ Tangier American Legation Museum Society (TALMS)
c/o Stephan Eastman, Treas.
PO Box 43
Merrimac, MA 01860
Ph: (978)346-9078
Fax: (978)346-7498
E-mail: seeastman@wellmanage.com
Contact: Stephan Eastman, Treas.
Founded: 1976. **Members:** 300. **Membership Dues:** regular, $10 (annual). **Staff:** 3. **Budget:** $40,000. **Description:** Individuals and organizations. Maintains the American Legation, former chancery and residence of American diplomats, in Tangier, Morocco, as a historic landmark of the United States. Operates a museum and educational center. Fosters goodwill between the U.S. and Morocco. **Libraries: Type:** reference. **Holdings:** 7,000. **Subjects:** American/Moroccan diplomatic history. **Publications:** *Legation*, annual. Newsletter ● Catalog. Lists library holdings. **Conventions/Meetings:** periodic conference and seminar.

10069 ■ Thomas Jefferson's Poplar Forest (CJPF)
PO Box 419
Forest, VA 24551-0419
Ph: (434)525-1806
Fax: (434)525-7252
E-mail: media@poplarforest.org
URL: http://www.poplarforest.org
Contact: Anna McAlpine, Dir. of Public Relations and Marketing
Founded: 1983. **Staff:** 32. **Budget:** $2,310,000. **Regional Groups:** 16. **Description:** Seeks to preserve and restore Poplar Forest, the house Thomas Jefferson (1743-1826), third president of the U.S., built as his year-round retreat on his plantation in Bedford County, VA. **Libraries: Type:** open to the public. **Holdings:** 800; books. **Subjects:** Thomas Jefferson and the poplar forest retreat/plantation community. **Committees:** National; Virginia. **Publications:** *Thomas Jefferson's Poplar Forest: Campaign Newsletter*, 2-3/year. Reports on current developments in the restoration, archeology, and educational programs at Poplar Forest. ● Annual Report. **Conventions/Meetings:** board meeting - 5/year.

10070 ■ Touro Synagogue Foundation
85 Touro St.
Newport, RI 02840
Ph: (401)847-4794
Fax: (401)845-6790
E-mail: info@tourosynagogue.org
URL: http://www.tourosynagogue.org
Contact: Steven Sitrin, Exec. Dir.
Founded: 1948. **Members:** 4,300. **Membership Dues:** individual, $25 (annual) ● founder, $500 (annual) ● family, $50 (annual) ● contributing, $100 (annual) ● sustaining, $180 (annual). **Staff:** 4. **Budget:** $200,000. **Description:** Works to help maintain Touro Synagogue, the oldest Jewish house of worshiping in the United States, as a National Historic Site. Promotes religious freedom in America. Sponsors tour program and other cultural activities. **Libraries: Type:** reference. **Awards:** Aaron and Rita Slom Scholarship. **Frequency:** annual. **Type:** scholarship ● Alexander G. Teitz Award. **Frequency:** annual. **Type:** recognition. **Recipient:** for demonstration of a commitment to religious freedom and tolerance. **Formerly:** (2004) Society of Friends of Touro Synagogue. **Publications:** *Society Update*, quarterly. Newsletter. Includes stories on religious freedom. **Price:** free for members. **Circulation:** 5,000. Alternate Formats: online. **Conventions/Meetings:** annual meeting - always August.

10071 ■ United States Historical Society
7433 Whitepine Rd.
Richmond, VA 23237
Ph: (804)648-4736
Free: (800)788-4478
Fax: (804)648-0002
E-mail: administrator@ushs.org
URL: http://www.ushs.org
Contact: Samuel Eliot Morison, Trustee
Founded: 1972. **Members:** 250,000. **Staff:** 15. **Description:** Dedicated to historical research and the sponsorship of projects that are artistically and historically significant. Works with museums, educational institutions, foundations, and other organizations to authorize reproduction of objects that have significance, artistic value and authenticity.

10072 ■ U.S. Life-Saving Service Heritage Association (USLSSHA)
c/o John Galluzzo, Exec. Dir.
PO Box 213
Hull, MA 02045-0213
Ph: (781)724-7131

E-mail: mo72506@mail.nantucket.net
URL: http://www.uslife-savingservice.org
Contact: John Galluzzo, Exec. Dir.
Founded: 1995. **Membership Dues:** life-saver, $35 (annual) ● life-saver family, $40 (annual) ● institution, $50 (annual) ● station keeper, $100 (annual) ● assistant inspector, $250 (annual) ● district superintendent, $500 (annual). **Description:** Seeks to preserve the stations, history, boats, and equipment of the U.S. Life-Saving Service and U.S. Coast Guard. Facilitates communication and cooperation among many preservation-minded individuals and organizations. Raises awareness of the importance of preserving America's architectural lifesaving and lifeboat stations, watercraft, and unique artifacts. **Telecommunication Services:** electronic mail, johnj-galluzzo@hotmail.com. **Publications:** *Life Lines*, quarterly. Newsletter. **Price:** included in membership dues. Alternate Formats: online ● *They Had to Go Out: True Stories of America's Coastal Life-Savers From the Pages of Wreck & Rescue Journal.* Book. **Price:** $19.45/copy, plus shipping and handling ● *Wreck & Rescue*, quarterly. Journal. **Price:** included in membership dues.

10073 ■ United States Lighthouse Society (USLHS)
244 Kearny St., 5th Fl.
San Francisco, CA 94108
Ph: (415)362-7255
E-mail: info@uslhs.org
URL: http://www.uslhs.org
Contact: Wayne C. Wheeler, Pres./Exec. Dir.
Founded: 1984. **Members:** 12,000. **Membership Dues:** family, $50 (annual) ● commissioner's circle, $500 (annual) ● patron of pharos, $1,000 (annual) ● deputy engineer, $100 (annual) ● keeper, $35 (annual) ● district inspector, $75 (annual) ● deputy commissioner, $250 (annual). **Staff:** 4. **Budget:** $350,000. **Regional Groups:** 5. **Description:** Promotes restoration and preservation of America's lighthouses. Seeks to unite public agencies, private corporations, and individuals interested in preserving lighthouses and promoting maritime heritage. Collects lore and artifacts for maritime and lighthouse museums. Researches individual lighthouse restoration projects and provides the history of those stations. Assists with interpreting lighthouse details (such things as period furniture and color information). Organizes seminars and funding drives. Compiles statistics; offers speakers' bureau; sponsors tours and photography contest. Conducts regional and international tours of lighthouses. **Libraries: Type:** reference. **Holdings:** 1,000; archival material, films, photographs. **Subjects:** lighthouses/lightships and aids to navigation, 75 rolls of microfilm. **Awards:** Keeper of the Quarter. **Frequency:** quarterly. **Type:** recognition. **Recipient:** for outstanding leaders ● President's Award. **Frequency:** annual. **Type:** recognition. **Recipient:** for history preservation. **Computer Services:** Bibliographic search, lighthouse books and articles ● database, lighthouse research facilities. **Projects:** Lightship LV 605 Restoration; New Dungeness, WA Light Station. **Publications:** *The Keeper's Log*, quarterly. Journal. Includes information on lighthouses that are open to the public and for sale. Contains historical articles on U.S. and foreign lighthouses. **Price:** included in membership dues. ISSN: 0883-0061. **Circulation:** 8,500. **Advertising:** accepted ● Bulletin, quarterly. News of chapters, projects, tours foreign and regional. **Price:** included in membership dues ● Also publishes information regarding local lighthouse restoration groups.

10074 ■ United States National Committee of the International Council on Monuments and Sites (US/ICOMOS)
401 F St. NW, Ste.331
Washington, DC 20001-2728
Ph: (202)842-1866
Fax: (202)842-1861
E-mail: info@usicomos.org
URL: http://www.icomos.org/usicomos
Contact: Gustavo F. Araoz AIA, Exec. Dir.
Founded: 1965. **Members:** 550. **Membership Dues:** student, $30 (annual) ● national affiliate, $80 (annual) ● international, $135 (annual) ● institutional, $425 (annual) ● supporting, $850 (annual) ● sponsor, benefactor, $1,500 (annual). **Staff:** 2. **Languages:** English, French, Spanish. **Description:** Represents professionals and supporters of historic preservation and related fields. Includes over 100 national committees worldwide. Promotes the study and preservation of historic buildings, sites, and districts. Provides consulting and technical services to government and private institutions. Conducts international summer intern program. Provides access to the ICOMOS Documentation Centre in Paris, France. **Libraries: Type:** reference. **Subjects:** historic preservation in other countries. **Computer Services:** Mailing lists, of members. **Telecommunication Services:** electronic mail, garaoz@usicimos.org. **Affiliated With:** International Council on Monuments and Sites - France. **Publications:** *Historic Preservation in Other Countries.* Books ● Newsletter, bimonthly. Contains president's report, membership activities, and calendar of events. ● Also publishes a series of occasional papers, booklist, and a list of short courses in historic preservation abroad. **Conventions/Meetings:** triennial General Assembly and International Symposium - meeting and symposium, world meeting of national committees' delegates and members (exhibits) ● Inter-American Symposium on Authenticity in Preservation, hemispheric conference of preservation professionals ● annual meeting - always April.

10075 ■ Victorian Homeowner's Association and Old House Lovers
Address Unknown since 2007
Founded: 1991. **Members:** 1,000. **Membership Dues:** household, $30 (annual) ● sustaining, $50 ● contributing, $100 ● life, $1,000. **Staff:** 3. **For-Profit. Description:** Victorian and old house owners. Promotes the rehabilitation, historical documentation, and exchange of information on these homes. Lifestyle, sources, poetry, classified and display ads. Membership includes a brass plaque for your home. **Publications:** *Victorian Homeowner's and Old House Lover's Newsletter*, 6/year. **Price:** $30.00/year. **Advertising:** accepted. Also Cited As: *Victorian Tymes Newsletter.*

10076 ■ Walden Woods Project (WWP)
44 Baker Farm Rd.
Lincoln, MA 01773-3004
Ph: (781)259-4700
Free: (800)554-3569
Fax: (781)259-4710
E-mail: wwproject@walden.org
URL: http://www.walden.org
Contact: John H. Adams, Exec. Dir.
Founded: 1990. **Members:** 15,000. **Staff:** 3. **Description:** Works to protect 2 historical land tracts surrounding Walden Pond, in Concord, Massachusetts, where author Henry David Thoreau (1817-62) conducted his conservation studies from 1845-47. (The areas where Thoreau maintained a retreat during his stay at Walden are currently protected by the state of Massachusetts as historical landmarks). Disseminates information. **Convention/Meeting:** none. **Publications:** *Walden Woods Project Newsletter*, semiannual. **Price:** included in membership dues. **Circulation:** 18,000. **Advertising:** accepted.

10077 ■ World Heritage Alliance (WHA)
c/o United Nations Foundation
1225 Connecticut Ave., 4th Fl.
Washington, DC 20036
Ph: (202)887-9040
E-mail: agough@unfoundation.org
URL: http://www.worldheritagealliance.org
Contact: Andrea Gough, Contact
Founded: 2005. **Multinational. Description:** Promotes and preserves sustainable tourism and awareness of world heritage sites and communities around the world. Educates travellers on responsible tourism in and around world heritage sites. Fosters economic development and encourages travel industry to promote world heritage sites and communities.

Historical Societies

10078 ■ Gay, Lesbian, Bisexual, Transgender Historical Society (GLBTHS)
657 Mission St., No. 300
San Francisco, CA 94105
Ph: (415)777-5455
Fax: (415)777-5576
E-mail: terence@glbthistory.org
URL: http://www.glbthistory.org
Contact: Terence Kissack, Exec. Dir.
Membership Dues: philanthropist, $1,000 (annual) ● benefactor, $500 (annual) ● patron, $250 (annual) ● sustainer, $100 (annual) ● supporter, $75 (annual) ● regular, $50 (annual) ● student/low income, $30 (annual) ● gift, $15 (annual). **Description:** Aims to collect, preserve and exhibit public historical, cultural and artistic materials related to gay, lesbian, bisexual, transgender communities, identities and practices. Aims to build the world's first full-scale, professional quality museum devoted to Gay, Lesbian, Bisexual, Transgender (GLBT) history and culture. **Publications:** *OurStories.* Newsletter.

History

10079 ■ Academy of Accounting Historians (AAH)
Univ. of Alabama
Culverhouse School of Accountancy
Box 870220
Tuscaloosa, AL 35487
Ph: (205)348-6131
Fax: (205)348-8453
E-mail: mstone@cba.ua.edu
URL: http://accounting.rutgers.edu/raw/aah
Contact: Tiffany Welch, Admin.
Founded: 1973. **Members:** 800. **Membership Dues:** individual, $45 (annual) ● institution, $95 (annual) ● student, $10 (annual). **Staff:** 1. **Description:** Accounting institutions, accountants, university libraries, and individuals interested in accounting and/or business history. Encourages research, publication, teaching, and personal exchange in all facets of accounting history and its relationship to business and economic history. Issues scholarly historical papers at regional and national meetings of the American Accounting Association (see separate entry). Maintains: Tax History Center, in conjunction with the University of Mississippi, to promote research in tax history and Garner Center, in conjunction with the University of Alabama, to promote research in accounting history. **Libraries: Type:** reference. **Awards:** Vangermeersch Manuscript Award. **Frequency:** annual. **Type:** monetary. **Recipient:** for outstanding manuscript in accounting history. **Publications:** *Accounting Historians' Journal*, semiannual ● *Accounting Historians' Notebook*, semiannual. Newsletter ● Monographs, periodic ● Also publishes classic reprint series. **Conventions/Meetings:** annual conference and meeting, research conference with papers presented, followed by business meeting (exhibits).

10080 ■ Agricultural History Society (AHS)
c/o C. Fred Williams, Exec. Sec.-Treas.
Univ. of Arkansas at Little Rock
Dept. of History
2801 S Univ. Ave.
Little Rock, AR 72204
Ph: (501)569-8782
Fax: (501)569-3059
E-mail: cfwilliams@ualr.edu
URL: http://www.aghistorysociety.org
Contact: C. Fred Williams, Exec. Sec.-Treas.
Founded: 1919. **Members:** 900. **Membership Dues:** individual, $49 (annual) ● student/retired, $23 (annual) ● institution, $172 (annual) ● life, $1,000. **Budget:** $5,000. **Description:** Historians, geographers, agricultural economists, farmers, agricultural scientists, and other interested individuals. Promotes the study and publication of research in the history of agriculture. **Awards:** Everett E. Edwards Memorial Award. **Frequency:** annual. **Type:** recognition. **Re-**

cipient: for the best article in agricultural history by a student ● Gilbert C. Fite Dissertation Award. **Frequency:** annual. **Type:** recognition. **Recipient:** for the best dissertation in agricultural history ● National History Day History of Agriculture and Rural Life Award. **Frequency:** annual. **Type:** recognition. **Recipient:** for a secondary student interested in history ● Theodore Saloutos Memorial Award. **Frequency:** annual. **Type:** recognition. **Recipient:** for the best book published in the field of agricultural history ● Vernon Carstensen Memorial Award. **Frequency:** annual. **Type:** recognition. **Recipient:** for the best article published in *Agricultural History* ● Wayne D. Rasmussen Award. **Frequency:** annual. **Type:** recognition. **Recipient:** for the best article in agricultural journal other than Agricultural History. **Computer Services:** Mailing lists. **Committees:** Art Peterson Art Fund; Carstensen Award; Edwards Award; Executive; Fellowship; Fite Award; Rasmussen Award; Saloutos Award. **Publications:** *Agricultural History*, quarterly, every January, April, July and October. Journal. **Price:** included in membership dues. ISSN: 0002-1482. **Advertising:** accepted ● *Symposium Proceedings*, annual. **Conventions/Meetings:** annual conference, held in conjunction with Organization of American Historians - always March or April ● annual meeting and symposium (exhibits) - always June. 2008 June 19-21, Reno, NV.

10081 ■ American Academy of Research Historians of Medieval Spain (AARHMS)

c/o Helen Nader, Sec.-Treas.
Univ. of Arizona
Dept. of History
PO Box 210027
Tucson, AZ 85721
E-mail: naderh@email.arizona.edu
URL: http://www.uca.edu/divisions/academic/history/aarhms
Contact: Helen Nader, Sec.-Treas.

Founded: 1974. **Members:** 200. **Membership Dues:** ordinary, $10 (annual). **Languages:** English, Spanish. **Description:** Professional historians conducting research on Medieval Spain. Promotes study of Medieval Iberia. Serves as a clearinghouse; conducts educational programs. **Computer Services:** Online services, publication. **Publications:** Newsletter, semiannual. Alternate Formats: online. **Conventions/Meetings:** semiannual convention - always January and May.

10082 ■ American Association for the History of Medicine (AAHM)

c/o Chris Crenner, MD, Sec.-Treas.
Univ. of Kansas Medical Center
Dept. of History and Philosophy
3901 Rainbow Blvd.
MS 1025
Kansas City, KS 66160
Ph: (913)588-7040 (913)588-7098
Fax: (913)588-7060
E-mail: aahm@kumc.edu
URL: http://www.histmed.org
Contact: Chris Crenner MD, Sec.-Treas.

Founded: 1925. **Members:** 1,300. **Membership Dues:** student, $25 (annual) ● regular, $85 (annual) ● family, Constituent Society, $95 (annual) ● with income or pension under $30,000 per year, $50 (annual) ● life, $1,500. **Staff:** 1. **Description:** Physicians, historians and others with professional or vocational interest in the history of medicine. Promotes research, study, interest, and writing in history of medicine, including public health, dentistry, pharmacy, nursing, medical social work, and allied sciences and professions. **Awards:** Estes Award. **Frequency:** annual. **Type:** monetary. **Recipient:** for best article in history of pharmacology in the past 2 years ● Lifetime Achievement Award. **Frequency:** annual. **Type:** trophy. **Recipient:** for support and for distinguished scholarship in the history of medicine ● Osler Medal. **Frequency:** annual. **Type:** medal. **Recipient:** for outstanding essays by medical students ● Pressman-Burroughs Welcome Award. **Frequency:** biennial. **Type:** monetary. **Recipient:** for the best proposal to turn dissertation into book ● Shryock Medal. **Frequency:** annual. **Type:** medal. **Recipient:** for outstanding essays by graduate students ● Welch Medal. **Frequency:** annual. **Type:** medal. **Recipient:** for outstanding book. **Computer Services:** Mailing lists. **Affiliated With:** American Council of Learned Societies; American Historical Association. **Publications:** *Bulletin of the History of Medicine*, quarterly. Journal. **Price:** included in membership dues. **Advertising:** accepted. Alternate Formats: online ● Directory, biennial ● Newsletter, 3/year. Provides information on membership activities. **Conventions/Meetings:** annual meeting (exhibits) - 2009 Apr. 23-26, Cleveland, OH.

10083 ■ American Association for the History of Nursing (AAHN)

PO Box 175
Lanoka Harbor, NJ 08734-0175
Ph: (609)693-7250
Fax: (609)693-1037
E-mail: aahn@aahn.org
URL: http://www.aahn.org
Contact: Janet L. Fickeissen, Exec. Sec.

Founded: 1980. **Members:** 600. **Membership Dues:** reduced, $50 (annual) ● individual, $100 (annual) ● agency, supporting, $150 (annual). **Staff:** 1. **Description:** Fosters the importance of history in understanding the present and guiding the future of nursing. **Awards:** H 15 Grant. **Frequency:** annual. **Type:** grant. **Recipient:** for new researchers; must be members of AAHN and holds a doctorate degree ● H 31 - Pre-doctoral Research Grant. **Frequency:** annual. **Type:** grant. **Recipient:** to encourage and support graduate training and historical research at the masters and doctoral levels ● Lavinia L. Dock Award. **Frequency:** annual. **Type:** recognition. **Recipient:** for exemplary historical research and writing produced by an experienced scholar in nursing history ● M. Adelaide Nutting Award. **Frequency:** annual. **Type:** recognition. **Recipient:** for exemplary historical research and writing ● **Type:** recognition ● Teresa E. Christy Award. **Frequency:** annual. **Type:** recognition. **Recipient:** to a doctoral student for exemplary historical research and writing. **Committees:** Abstract Review; Awards; Bylaws and Policies; Nominating; Strategic Planning. **Publications:** *Bulletin of AAHN*, quarterly. Newsletter. Includes association news and research reports. **Price:** included in membership dues. ISSN: 0898-6622. **Circulation:** 650. **Advertising:** accepted ● *Nursing History Review*, annual. Journal. **Price:** included in membership dues. ISSN: 1062-8061. **Circulation:** 1,000. **Conventions/Meetings:** annual conference, for researchers interested in sharing new research that addresses events, issues, and topics pertinent to the history of the nursing profession (exhibits) - usually September or October.

10084 ■ American Association for State and Local History (AASLH)

1717 Church St.
Nashville, TN 37203-2921
Ph: (615)320-3203
Fax: (615)327-9013
E-mail: membership@aaslh.org
URL: http://www.aaslh.org
Contact: Terry L. Davis, Pres./CEO

Founded: 1940. **Members:** 6,400. **Membership Dues:** individual sustaining, $125 (annual) ● individual supporting, $85 (annual) ● individual basic, $60 (annual) ● individual retired, $40 (annual) ● individual student, $30 (annual) ● institutional basic, $100 (annual) ● institutional contributing, $250 (annual) ● institutional supporting, $500 (annual) ● institutional sustaining, $750 (annual) ● individual patron, $250 (annual) ● institutional partner, $1,000 (annual). **Staff:** 7. **Budget:** $1,200,000. **Description:** Works to preserve and promote history. Ensures the highest-quality expressions of state and local history in publications, exhibitions, and public programs through its diverse services. Represents more than 6,400 individual and institutional members. **Awards:** Albert B. Corey Award. **Frequency:** annual. **Type:** recognition ● Award of Distinction. **Frequency:** annual. **Type:** recognition. **Recipient:** for an individual ● Award of Merit. **Frequency:** annual. **Type:** recognition. **Recipient:** for an individual ● Certificate of Commendation. **Frequency:** annual. **Type:** recognition. **Recipient:** for an individual. **Computer Services:** Mailing lists. **Committees:** Awards; Education; Standards, Ethics, and Tenure. **Absorbed:** (1963) Association of Historic Sites Officials. **Formerly:** Council of Historical Societies. **Publications:** *Dispatch*, monthly. Newsletter. Keeps members informed of all of AASLH's programs and benefits. ● *History News*, quarterly. Magazine. Includes a handy technical leaflet in each issue. **Conventions/Meetings:** annual conference and meeting (exhibits) - usually September ● seminar ● workshop.

10085 ■ American Catholic Historical Association (ACHA)

Mullen Lib., Rm. 320
Catholic Univ. of Am.
Washington, DC 20064
Ph: (202)319-5079
Fax: (202)319-5079
E-mail: cua-chracha@cua.edu
URL: http://research.cua.edu/acha
Contact: Robert Trisco, Sec.-Treas.

Founded: 1919. **Members:** 1,006. **Membership Dues:** student, $30 (annual) ● ordinary, $50 (annual) ● retired (after 20 consecutive years of membership), $40 (annual) ● life, $1,000 ● associate, $5 (annual). **Staff:** 1. **Budget:** $58,000. **Description:** Professional society of historians, educators, students, and others interested in the history of the Catholic Church in the United States and abroad and in the promotion of historical scholarship among Catholics. Has sponsored the publication of the papers of John Carroll, first Bishop and Archbishop of Baltimore, MD. **Awards:** Howard R. Marraro Prize. **Frequency:** annual. **Type:** recognition. **Recipient:** for a book or essay on Italian history or Italo-American history or relations ● John Gilmary Shea Prize. **Frequency:** annual. **Type:** recognition. **Recipient:** for a book on the history of the Catholic Church broadly considered ● John Tracy Ellis Dissertation Award. **Frequency:** annual. **Type:** recognition. **Recipient:** for a graduate student working on some aspect of the history of the Catholic Church ● Peter Guilday Prize. **Frequency:** annual. **Type:** recognition. **Recipient:** for an article in the *Catholic Historical Review* which is the author's first scholarly publication. **Publications:** *Catholic Historical Review*, quarterly. Journal. Includes scholarly articles on the history of the Catholic Church, book reviews, and professional news. **Price:** included in membership dues. ISSN: 0008-8080. **Circulation:** 1,976. **Advertising:** accepted. **Conventions/Meetings:** annual meeting, sessions, business meeting, presidential luncheon (exhibits) - always January. 2009 Jan. 2-5, New York, NY; 2010 Jan. 7-10, San Diego, CA; 2011 Jan. 6-9, Chicago, IL.

10086 ■ American Catholic Historical Society (ACHS)

263 S 4th St.
Philadelphia, PA 19106
Ph: (856)424-4728
E-mail: e_mcmerty@yahoo.com
URL: http://www.amchs.org
Contact: Louis M. Ferraro, VP

Founded: 1884. **Members:** 720. **Membership Dues:** individual, $40 (annual). **Budget:** $40,000. **Multinational. Description:** Interested individuals. Collects and seeks to preserve materials relevant to the historical role of Catholics in the building of the Americas. Presents lectures on Catholic history. Maintains museum. **Convention/Meeting:** none. **Libraries: Type:** reference. **Holdings:** 40,000; archival material, papers. **Awards:** Barry Award. **Frequency:** annual. **Type:** recognition. **Recipient:** for distinguished professional, church, and community services. **Committees:** Historical Research. **Publications:** *American Catholic Studies*, quarterly. Journal. Contains historical items and book reviews. **Price:** $40.00 /year for members. ISSN: 002 7790. **Circulation:** 720. **Advertising:** accepted ● Books ● Newsletter, annual ● Pamphlets.

10087 ■ American Civil War Association (ACWA)

c/o Debi Casey, Treas.
547C Morse Ave.
Sacramento, CA 95864

Ph: (301)399-3702
E-mail: debi.casey@comcast.net
URL: http://acwa.org
Contact: Debi Casey, Treas.

Founded: 1988. **Members:** 10. **Membership Dues:** single, $40 (annual) ● couple, $45 (annual) ● family, sutler, guild, $50 (annual) ● visitor (combatant), $15 (annual) ● visitor (non-combatant), $5 (annual) ● supporting, $20 (annual). **Staff:** 2. **Budget:** $50. **Description:** Individuals interested in the American Civil War. Encourages understanding and appreciation of the American Civil War; fosters patriotism. Preserves and protects American Civil War property; cooperates with government representatives, public agencies, and historical societies in developing living history programs for the public; encourages research in American history of the Civil War era. Assists individuals and organizations that reenact Civil War battles; helps members attend reenactments. **Committees:** Advisors for Civil War Movies; Historical Preservations; Living History. **Publications:** *Courier*, bimonthly. Newsletter. Alternate Formats: online ● *The Old Guard Regular*, monthly. Newsletter. Contains short list of Civil War re-enactments and personal stories after each event. **Price:** $15.00.

10088 ■ American Historical Association (AHA)

400 A St. SE
Washington, DC 20003-3889
Ph: (202)544-2422
Fax: (202)544-8307
E-mail: info@historians.org
URL: http://www.historians.org
Contact: Arnita A. Jones, Exec. Dir.

Founded: 1884. **Members:** 15,800. **Membership Dues:** student, $37 (annual) ● joint spouse, partner, $42 (annual) ● emeritus, retired, associate, $52 (annual) ● regular (based on income), $42-$141 (annual) ● contributing, $177 (annual) ● life, $2,600. **Staff:** 20. **Budget:** $1,200,000. **Description:** Professional historians, educators, and others interested in promoting historical studies and collecting and preserving historical manuscripts. Conducts research and educational programs. **Awards:** Eugene Asher Award. **Frequency:** annual. **Type:** recognition. **Recipient:** for distinguished post secondary history teaching ● Troyer Steele Anderson Prize. **Frequency:** annual. **Type:** recognition. **Recipient:** for contributions to the advancement of AHA. **Computer Services:** Mailing lists. **Committees:** Albert J. Beveridge Award and the John H. Dunning Prize; Clarence H. Haring Prize; Committee on Affiliated Societies; George Louis Beer Prize; Harmsworth Professorship; Herbert Baxter Adams Prize; Herbert Feis Award; Howard and Helen Marraro Prize; International Historical Activities; J. Franklin Jameson Prize; James H. Breasted Prize; James Harvey Robinson Prize; Joan Kelly Prize for Women's History; John K. Fairbank Prize; Joint Committee of the Canadian Historical Association and the American Historical Association; Joint Committee on Historians and Archivists; Leo Gershoy Award; Littleton-Griswold Prize; Minority Historians; Morris D. Forkosch Prize; Paul Birdsall Prize; Waldo G. Leland Prize; Women Historians. **Divisions:** Professional; Research; Teaching. **Affiliated With:** Immigration and Ethnic History Society. **Publications:** *American Historical Association—Perspectives*, monthly. Newsletter. Contains news and information concerning historical profession. **Price:** included in membership dues. ISSN: 0745-0516. **Circulation:** 16,000. **Advertising:** accepted ● *American Historical Review*, 5/year, published every February, April, June, October, and December. Journal. Includes annual and advertisers indexes, book reviews, documents, and bibliographies. **Price:** included in membership dues. ISSN: 0002-8762. **Advertising:** accepted ● *Careers for Students of History* ● *Directory of Affiliated Societies* ● *Directory of History Departments and Organizations in the United States and Canada*, annual ● *Grants, Fellowships, and Prizes of Interest to Historians*, annual ● Pamphlets ● Proceedings, annual. **Conventions/Meetings:** annual conference and meeting (exhibits) - every Thursday through Sunday. 2009 Jan. 2-5, New York, NY; 2010 Jan. 7-10, San Diego, CA; 2011 Jan. 6-9, Boston, MA.

10089 ■ American Society for Eighteenth-Century Studies (ASECS)

Wake Forest Univ.
PO Box 7867
Winston-Salem, NC 27109
Ph: (336)727-4694
Fax: (336)727-4697
E-mail: asecs@wfu.edu
URL: http://asecs.press.jhu.edu
Contact: Byron R. Wells, Exec. Dir.

Founded: 1969. **Members:** 2,600. **Membership Dues:** student, $30 (annual) ● sponsor, $100 (annual) ● patron, $150 (annual) ● individual (based on the income), $50-$75 (annual) ● emeritus, $50 (annual) ● joint, $85-$175 (annual) ● life, $500-$1,250. **Staff:** 2. **Budget:** $250,000. **Regional Groups:** 9. **Description:** Scholars and others interested in the cultural history of the 18th century. Encourages and advances study and research in this area; promotes the interchange of information and ideas among scholars from different disciplines (such as librarianship and bibliography) who are interested in the 18th century. Co-sponsors seven fellowship programs; sponsors Graduate Student Caucus. **Awards:** Clifford Prize. **Frequency:** annual. **Type:** monetary. **Recipient:** for the best article on 18th century subjects ● Gottschalk Prize. **Frequency:** annual. **Type:** monetary. **Recipient:** for the best book on 18th century subjects. **Computer Services:** Mailing lists, of members. **Committees:** Article Prizes; Editorial. **Sections:** Ancillary Disciplines; Classics; Comparative Literature; Economics and Political Science; English and American Literature; Fine Arts; History; Linguistics; Other Modern Languages and Literatures; Philosophy, Religion and History of Ideas; Science, Medicine and Technology; Speech and Drama. **Affiliated With:** American Council of Learned Societies. **Publications:** *American Society for Eighteenth-Century Studies—News Circular*, quarterly. Newsletter. **Price:** included in membership dues; $4.75 each, for nonmembers. **Circulation:** 2,600. **Advertising:** accepted ● *American Society for Eighteenth-Century Studies—Program for Annual Meeting*. Lists seminar topics and speakers. **Price:** included in membership dues; price varies for nonmembers. **Circulation:** 2,600. **Advertising:** accepted ● *Eighteenth-Century Studies*, quarterly. Journal. Contains articles and reviews on eighteenth century subjects including English and American literature. **Price:** included in membership dues; $52.00 /year for institutions. ISSN: 0013-2586. **Circulation:** 4,000. **Advertising:** accepted ● *Studies in Eighteenth-Century Culture*, annual. Contains selected papers presented at the meetings of ASECS and its affiliates. **Price:** $30.00/ issue for members. ISSN: 0360-2370. **Circulation:** 1,000. **Conventions/Meetings:** annual conference, for table top (exhibits).

10090 ■ American Society for Legal History (ASLH)

c/o William P. LaPiana, Treas.
New York Law School
57 Worth St.
New York, NY 10013
Ph: (212)431-1830
E-mail: wlapiana@nyls.edu
URL: http://www.aslh.net
Contact: William P. LaPiana, Treas.

Founded: 1956. **Members:** 1,300. **Membership Dues:** individual (based on annual income), $60-$125 (annual) ● student (emeritus), $20 (annual) ● life, $1,000. **Staff:** 1. **Budget:** $50,000. **Description:** Judges, lawyers, law educators; history, political science, and economics professors; historians, students, and others. Interested in legal history and its uses in formulating legal policy, decisions, and actions; unearthing historical items; and preserving legal and legislative records. Promotes and recognizes excellence in the field of legal history; preserves legal records; encourages scholarly research and study; exchanges information and holds discussions; a member organization of the American Council of Learned Societies (see separate entry). **Awards:** Surrency Prize. **Frequency:** annual. **Type:** monetary. **Recipient:** for best journal article ● Sutherland Prize. **Frequency:** annual. **Type:** monetary. **Recipient:** for best article in English legal history. **Computer Services:** Mailing lists, labels, print-outs. **Telecommunication Services:** electronic mail, jreader@law.harvard.edu. **Committees:** Documentary Preservation; Honors; Prizes. **Affiliated With:** American Council of Learned Societies; American Historical Association; National Humanities Alliance. **Publications:** *ASLH Newsletter*, 3/year. Includes general info, grants available, and recent publications. **Circulation:** 1,300 ● *Law and History Review*, 3/year. Journal. Covers topics in American, English, European, and ancient legal history. Includes essays, commentaries, and book reviews. **Price:** included in membership dues. **Circulation:** 1,300. **Advertising:** accepted. Alternate Formats: microform ● *Studies in Legal History*. Monograph. Book-length series. **Conventions/Meetings:** annual meeting, lectures, panel sessions, social events (exhibits) - always October/ November.

10091 ■ American Spelean Historical Association (ASHA)

6304 Kaybro St.
Laurel, MD 20707
Ph: (301)725-5877
E-mail: asha@caves.org
URL: http://www.caves.org/section/asha
Contact: Robert Hoke, Sec.-Treas.

Founded: 1968. **Members:** 100. **Membership Dues:** regular, $4 (annual). **Description:** Individuals interested in the history of caves and their influence on man's history. Encourages and conducts historical research. **Affiliated With:** National Speleological Society. **Publications:** *Journal of Spelean History*, semiannual. Contains articles on the history of caves. **Price:** included in membership dues. ISSN: 0022-4693. **Circulation:** 125. **Conventions/Meetings:** annual Spelean History Session - meeting, presentations on Spelean history.

10092 ■ Arabian Horse Historians Association (AHHA)

Address Unknown since 2007

Membership Dues: associate, $20 (annual) ● lifetime general, $20. **Description:** Currently Inactive. Individuals who have authored or coauthored three published works on Arabian horses and their history; other admirers of Arabian horses are associate members. Seeks to encourage interest in the history of Arabian horses; maintains standards of ethics for equine historical researchers and authors. Serves as a forum for the exhange of information among historians; facilitates scholarship on Arabian horses and their history; sponsors research and educational programs. **Awards:** Certificate of Merit. **Frequency:** annual. **Type:** recognition. **Recipient:** outstanding Arabian horse periodicals.

10093 ■ Association of Ancient Historians (AAH)

c/o Prof. Jennifer T. Roberts, Pres.
Dept. of Foreign Languages and Literatures
City Coll. of New York
NAC 5-223
Convent Ave. and 138th St.
New York, NY 10031
Ph: (212)650-6731
Fax: (718)796-4392
E-mail: robertsjt@aol.com
URL: http://www.associationofancienthistorians.org
Contact: Prof. Jennifer T. Roberts, Pres.

Founded: 1974. **Members:** 800. **Membership Dues:** associate, $5 (annual) ● individual, $7 (annual). **Description:** Ancient historians, either university faculty or graduate students; other interested individuals. Seeks to further the teaching and research of ancient history worldwide. **Awards: Frequency:** annual. **Type:** monetary. **Recipient:** for younger members of the association who will attend the annual meeting. **Affiliated With:** American Historical Association; American Philological Association. **Publications:** Monographs, biennial. Covers current state of study in particular areas of ancient history. **Price:** free to members ● Newsletter, 3/year. **Conventions/Meetings:** annual conference and general assembly (exhibits) - usually first weekend of May.

10094 ■ Association for the Bibliography of History (ABH)
c/o Charles A. D'Aniello, Exec. Sec.-Treas.
State Univ. of New York at Buffalo
Lockwood Memorial Lib., Rm. 321
Buffalo, NY 14260
Ph: (716)645-2817 (716)645-2323
Fax: (716)645-3859
E-mail: lclcharl@acsu.buffalo.edu
URL: http://www.h-net.msu.edu/~histbibl/abh.html
Contact: Charles A. D'Aniello, Exec. Sec.-Treas.
Founded: 1978. **Members:** 200. **Description:** Historians, bibliographers, librarians, and others wishing to promote the development of bibliographical skills and tools to facilitate the study of history. Seeks to: uphold professional standards in the dissemination of information through bibliography; support education and building of careers in historical bibliography; act as a clearinghouse for bibliographic activity; function as a liaison among professional societies; organize sessions and workshops. **Affiliated With:** American Historical Association. **Publications:** Bulletin, semiannual. **Price:** included in membership dues. ISSN: 0892-4600. **Circulation:** 400. **Conventions/Meetings:** annual conference and symposium, held in conjunction with American Historical Association.

10095 ■ Association of Personal Historians (APH)
c/o Gloria Nussbaum, Membership Chair
870 NW 178th Ave.
Beaverton, OR 97006-4044
Ph: (503)645-0616
E-mail: president@personalhistorians.org
URL: http://www.personalhistorians.org
Contact: Jeanne Archer, Pres.
Founded: 1995. **Members:** 600. **Membership Dues:** individual, $145 (annual) ● individual in Canada, C$155 (annual). **Multinational. Description:** Seeks to "help people preserve their life stories and memories". Advances the efforts of personal historians through networking and training. Encourages personal history activities and projects. Conducts classes in memoir writing, the organization of memorabilia, life writing and presentations. **Telecommunication Services:** electronic bulletin board, listserv, members only. **Publications:** *APH Brochure*. **Price:** free upon request. Alternate Formats: online ● *APH Newsletter*, quarterly. **Price:** free for members ● *APH Online Membership Directory and Resource Guide*, annual. **Price:** free for members. Alternate Formats: online. **Conventions/Meetings:** annual conference (exhibits).

10096 ■ Baronial Order of Magna Charta and the Military Order of Crusades (BOMCMOC)
14115 41st Ave. N
Plymouth, MN 55446
E-mail: bomcadmin@magnacharta.com
URL: http://magnacharta.com
Contact: Tracy Ashley Crocker, Contact
Founded: 1898. **Members:** 554. **Membership Dues:** regular, $40 (annual) ● life, $600. **Regional Groups:** 6. **Description:** Lineal descendants, male and female, of the 25 earls and barons and five nonsurety supporters who forced England's King John to seal the Magna Charta and were elected to be the first official guardians of adherence to the charter by the Magna Charta Earls and Barons in 1215. (The original Magna Charta, or Magna Carta, was a definitive statement of feudal law and general charter of liberties. It became a symbol of protection against oppression and was adopted, in part, into succeeding charters of England and other English colonies; it is an integral part of U.S. constitutional law and legislation.) Promotes literary study and social intercourse among members and fosters admiration and respect for related principles of constitutional government. Promotes awareness of the Magna Charta's history and perpetuates the memory of the 25 earls and barons and five supporters of the Magna Charta; observes June 15 as the anniversary of the granting of the charter. Holds annual commemorative events. Conducts research, educational and charitable programs. The order has a seat on the Board of Trustees of the Magna Carta Trust in London, England. Membership is comprised of individuals of proven lineal descent from one or more Crusaders of Knightly or Higher Rank who participate in one or more of the regular and/or interim Crusades between 1096 and 1291 and who made great personal sacrifices, endured great hardship, performed heroically, and died in great numbers during the Crusades. **Libraries: Type:** reference; not open to the public. **Holdings:** 200; archival material. **Subjects:** genealogy, history, Western law, Magna Charta. **Awards:** Magna Charta Day Award. **Frequency:** annual. **Type:** recognition. **Recipient:** for individuals who have demonstrated belief in the purposes of the Magna Charta. **Computer Services:** database ● online services. **Committees:** Magna Charta Day Award. **Formerly:** (1945) Baronial Order of Runnemede. **Publications:** *Herald*, quarterly. Newsletter. Includes directory. **Price:** free. **Circulation:** 1,000. **Advertising:** accepted ● *Magna Carta in America*. Book. Contains information about the project of Magna Carta Research Foundation. **Conventions/Meetings:** semiannual general assembly (exhibits) - always January and June, middle Atlantic.

10097 ■ Bostonian Society (TBS)
Old State House
206 Washington St.
Boston, MA 02109-1713
Ph: (617)720-1713
Fax: (617)720-3289
E-mail: oldstatehouse@bostonhistory.org
URL: http://www.bostonhistory.org
Contact: Brian W.J. LeMay, Exec. Dir.
Founded: 1881. **Members:** 1,600. **Membership Dues:** senior, $40 (annual) ● student, teacher, $25 (annual) ● individual, $50 (annual) ● family, $80 (annual) ● supporter, $150 (annual) ● benefactor, $500 (annual) ● Bostonian fellow, $25,000 (annual) ● Liberty fellow, $24,999 (annual) ● Golden Lion Club, $5,000 (annual) ● Pennant Circle, $3,500-$4,999 (annual) ● benefactor (corporate), $2,000-$2,499 (annual) ● supporter (corporate), $1,000-$1,999 (annual). **Description:** Students, writers, and others interested in the history of Boston. Housed in the Old State House built in 1713, the society maintains a museum with exhibitions relating to the American Revolution, all aspects of Boston history, and themes of related interest; also has a marine collection, showing Boston's relation to the sea, with models and pictures. Conducts educational programs. **Libraries: Type:** reference. **Holdings:** 37,850; archival material, books, clippings, photographs. **Subjects:** history, architecture, maritime history of Boston. **Awards:** Boston History Award. **Frequency:** annual. **Type:** recognition. **Publications:** *News*, quarterly. Newsletter ● Proceedings, periodic. **Conventions/Meetings:** annual meeting - always in Boston, MA.

10098 ■ Business History Conference (BHC)
c/o Roger Horowitz, Sec.-Treas.
Hagley Museum and Lib.
PO Box 3630
Wilmington, DE 19807-0630
Ph: (302)658-2400
Fax: (302)655-3188
E-mail: rh@udel.edu
URL: http://www.h-net.org/~business/bhcweb
Contact: Roger Horowitz, Sec.-Treas.
Founded: 1954. **Members:** 740. **Membership Dues:** student, $30 (annual) ● individual, $55 (annual) ● sustaining, $100 (annual). **Description:** Business historians and economic historians (most are from the academic community but a number of business firms are represented through their corporate historians). Brings together persons who are active historians of American and international business, with interests ranging from writing biographies of businessmen and histories of firms to the application of economic theory to analysis of the evolution of American business. **Awards:** Business History Conference Lifetime Achievement Award. **Frequency:** periodic. **Type:** recognition. **Recipient:** for an individual who has contributed most to the Business History Conference and to scholarship in business history ● Hagley Prize. **Frequency:** annual. **Type:** recognition. **Recipient:** for the best book in business history ● Harold F. Williamson Prize. **Frequency:** periodic. **Type:** recognition. **Recipient:** for a mid-career scholar who has made significant contributions to the field of business history ● Herman E. Krooss Prize. **Frequency:** annual. **Type:** recognition. **Recipient:** for the best dissertation in business history ● K. Austin Kerr Prize. **Frequency:** periodic. **Type:** recognition. **Recipient:** for the best first paper delivered at the annual meeting ● Newcomen Article Prize. **Frequency:** annual. **Type:** recognition. **Recipient:** for the author of an article published in any BHC publication. **Computer Services:** Mailing lists. **Publications:** *Enterprise and Society: The International Journal of Business History*, quarterly. **Conventions/Meetings:** annual Political Economy of Enterprise - conference (exhibits) - between March and June.

10099 ■ Center for Socialist History (CSH)
PO Box 626
Alameda, CA 94501-8626
Ph: (510)601-6460
E-mail: mlipow@pacbell.net
URL: http://csh.gn.apc.org
Contact: Ernest Haberkern, Exec. Dir.
Founded: 1981. **Description:** Promotes research and publication in the history of socialism. **Conventions/Meetings:** periodic conference.

10100 ■ Charles Babbage Institute for the History of Information Technology (CBI)
Univ. of Minnesota
211 Andersen Lib.
222 21st Ave. S
Minneapolis, MN 55455
Ph: (612)624-5050
Fax: (612)625-8054
E-mail: cbi@umn.edu
URL: http://www.cbi.umn.edu
Contact: Thomas J. Misa PhD, Dir.
Founded: 1978. **Members:** 2,853. **Staff:** 6. **Description:** Associates, founders, corporate sponsors, and subscribers, including business administrators in the computing industry, scholars studying the history of data processing and its social implications, technical people using computers, pioneers in the computing field, and government officials representing agencies that let many of the first contracts for computers. Purposes are to study the development of information processing, including technical and socioeconomic aspects, and to promote increased awareness of the impact of that development on society. Offers annual fellowship to a graduate student working in the history of information processing. Provides counsel and research assistance to other scholars in the field. Maintains archives, including 320 oral histories of computing pioneers. **Convention/Meeting:** none. **Publications:** *Iterations: Interdisciplinary Journal of Software History*, publishes continuously. Contains information on software application in industry. **Price:** free. Alternate Formats: online ● Newsletter, quarterly. Features news, conferences, and other developments. Alternate Formats: online.

10101 ■ Chemical Heritage Foundation (CHF)
315 Chestnut St.
Philadelphia, PA 19106-2702
Ph: (215)925-2222 (215)873-8245
Fax: (215)925-1954
E-mail: info@chemheritage.org
URL: http://www.chemheritage.org
Contact: Arnold Thackray, Pres.
Founded: 1982. **Members:** 27. **Staff:** 40. **Budget:** $6,000,000. **Description:** Serves as the primary source for the history of chemical science and technology. Encourages research, scholarship, and writing on history of chemical science, chemical engineering, and the chemical process industries. Houses archival records of organizations and individuals important in the history of chemistry and chemical engineering. Records oral histories of pioneers of modern chemical developments. Operates large historical research library. Creates travel-

ing exhibits. Founding members are the American Chemical Society and the American Institute of Chemical Engineers. **Libraries: Type:** reference. **Holdings:** 75,000; archival material, books, periodicals. **Subjects:** history of chemistry, chemical technology from the 15th to the 20th centuries. **Awards:** Biotechnology Heritage Award. **Frequency:** annual. **Type:** recognition. **Recipient:** for an outstanding individual of CHF ● Petrochemical Heritage Award. **Frequency:** annual. **Type:** recognition. **Recipient:** for outstanding individuals in the petrochemical society ● Pittcon Heritage Award. **Frequency:** annual. **Type:** recognition. **Recipient:** for an outstanding individual in the world of economy ● Travel Grants and Fellowships. **Frequency:** annual. **Type:** grant. **Recipient:** for an essay describing a research topic. **Affiliated With:** Alpha Chi Sigma; American Association for Clinical Chemistry; American Association of Textile Chemists and Colorists; American Chemical Society; American Chemistry Council; American Institute of Chemical Engineers; American Institute of Chemists; American Oil Chemists' Society; American Society for Mass Spectrometry; Chemists' Club; Electrochemical Society; International Society for Pharmaceutical Engineering; Societe de Chimie Industrielle, American Section; Society for Applied Spectroscopy. **Formerly:** (1987) Center for History of Chemistry; (1989) Arnold and Mabel Beckman Center for History of Chemistry; (1992) National Foundation for History of Chemistry. **Publications:** *Chemical Heritage*, quarterly. Magazine. Contains the history of chemistry, chemical engineering, and the chemical process industries; also includes book reviews and calendar of events. **Price:** $5.00 in U.S.; $10.00 outside U.S. ISSN: 0736-4555. **Circulation:** 30,000. **Advertising:** accepted. Also Cited As: *Beckman Center for the History of Chemistry; CHOC News* ● *Chemical Heritage Foundation Series, Innovation and Entrepreneurship*, quarterly. Monographs ● Brochures ● Pamphlets. **Conventions/Meetings:** periodic conference and workshop ● seminar.

10102 ■ Civil War Round Table Associates (CWRTA)
PO Box 7281
Little Rock, AR 72217
E-mail: milhistory@aristotle.net
Contact: Charles Olin Durnette, Contact

Founded: 1968. **Members:** 1,575. **Membership Dues:** regular, $15 (annual). **Staff:** 1. **Local Groups:** 325. **Description:** Individuals and organizations interested in the history of the American Civil War. Promotes preservation of Civil War historical sites; develops local round tables. Holds periodic Civil War studies forums; and tours. **Publications:** *Civil War Round Table Digest*, periodic. Newsletter. Covers contemporary events relating to the study and preservation of Civil War history and historic sites. **Price:** included in membership dues. **Circulation:** 1,500 ● *CWRT Organization Guide*. Details instructions on organizing a new CWRT. **Conventions/Meetings:** semiannual Congress of CWRTs, Confederate Historical Institute ● semiannual meeting and symposium (exhibits) - April and October, near a Civil War battlefield.

10103 ■ Civil War Society (CWS)
33756 Black Mountain Rd.
Tollhouse, CA 93667
Ph: (559)855-8637
Free: (800)546-6707
Fax: (559)855-8639
E-mail: kathypoulter@northandsouthmagazine.com
URL: http://www.northandsouthmagazine.com
Contact: Keith Poulter, Publisher

Founded: 1983. **Members:** 8,600. **Membership Dues:** regular, $39 (annual). **Staff:** 4. **Budget:** $600,000. **Description:** Professionals, retired professionals, educators, re-enactors, and others interested in the history of the U.S. Civil War. Raises funds for the preservation of Civil War battlefields; has helped preserve battlefields at Perryville, KY, Shiloh, TN, and Cedar Creek, VA. Sponsors lecture series, workshops, and walking tours of battlefields; conducts high school essay contest and bestows preservation awards. **Libraries: Type:** open to the public. **Holdings:** 54. **Formerly:** (1988) Virginia Country Civil War Society. **Publications:** *North & South*, 7/year. Magazine. Features Civil War conflict. **Price:** $5.99/copy. ISSN: 1522-9742. **Circulation:** 40,000. **Advertising:** accepted ● *Society Newsletter*, semiannual. **Conventions/Meetings:** annual convention (exhibits) ● seminar and tour - 5/year.

10104 ■ Colonial Society of Massachusetts (CSM)
87 Mt. Vernon St.
Boston, MA 02108
Ph: (617)227-2782
E-mail: info@colonialsociety.org
URL: http://www.colonialsociety.org
Contact: Celeste Walker, Membership Chair

Founded: 1892. **Members:** 320. **Membership Dues:** resident, $25 ● non-resident, $15. **Description:** Individuals interested in the publication of documents and monographs on the history of Plymouth and Massachusetts Bay colonies and the New England area in the period preceding the American Revolution and immediately thereafter. **Awards:** Whitehill Prize. **Frequency:** annual. **Type:** scholarship. **Recipient:** for best essay in topics related to early New England history. **Publications:** *Aristotelian & Cartesian Logic at Harvard* ● *The Glorious Revolution in Massachusetts*. **Price:** $40.00 ● *New England Quarterly*. Journal ● *Sermon Notebook of Samuel Parris, 1689-1694*. **Price:** $50.00 ● Also publishes 65 volumes dating back to 1896. **Conventions/Meetings:** competition ● quarterly meeting.

10105 ■ Confederate Memorial Literary Society (CMLS)
The Museum of the Confederacy
1201 E Clay St.
Richmond, VA 23219
Ph: (804)649-1861
Fax: (804)644-7150
E-mail: info@moc.org
Contact: Mr. S. Waite Rawls III, Exec. Dir.

Founded: 1890. **Members:** 3,500. **Staff:** 25. **Budget:** $1,600,000. **Description:** Authors, educators, students, and others interested in the study of Confederate history and culture. Maintains museum of Confederate uniforms, weapons, flags, and equipage. Owns the restored "White House of the Confederacy" (Confederate Executive Mansion, 1861-65). Conducts special tours for school classes. **Libraries: Type:** reference. **Holdings:** 11,000. **Subjects:** bonds, currency, Jefferson Davis collection. **Doing business as:** (2002) Museum and White House of the Confederacy. **Publications:** *Museum Journal*, annual. Focuses on collections. ● Newsletter, quarterly. Features articles on the Civil War. **Price:** included in membership dues. **Circulation:** 3,500.

10106 ■ Custer Battlefield Historical and Museum Association (CBHMA)
PO Box 902
Hardin, MT 59034-0902
URL: http://www.cbhma.org
Contact: Jon Custer, Pres.

Founded: 1953. **Members:** 2,300. **Membership Dues:** regular, in U.S., $30 (annual) ● regular, in U.S., $50 (biennial) ● regular, outside U.S., $40 (annual) ● regular, outside U.S., $70 (biennial) ● sustaining, $40 (annual) ● junior, $20 (annual). **Staff:** 2. **Budget:** $56,000. **Description:** Represents individuals interested in the history of the Custer Battlefield, the Battle of the Little Big Horn, and the general study of the Plains Indian Wars. Disseminates information. Provides funds to help protect the Little Big Horn Battlefield National Monument. **Awards:** CBHMA Book Award. **Type:** recognition. **Publications:** *Battlefield Dispatch*, quarterly. Newsletter ● *Greasy Grass*, annual. Journal. **Conventions/Meetings:** annual symposium, three-day weekend with field trips, membership meeting and auction (exhibits) - always the weekend closest to June 25 in Hardin, Montana.

10107 ■ Daniel Boone and Frontier Families Research Association
c/o Ken Kamper, Historian
1770 Little Bay Rd.
Hermann, MO 65041
Ph: (573)943-6423
E-mail: kenbeakamper@juno.com
Contact: Ken Kamper, Historian

Founded: 1996. **Members:** 302. **Membership Dues:** individual, $10 (annual) ● family, sustaining, $15 (annual) ● supporting, $20 (annual) ● senior, student, $8 (annual). **Staff:** 3. **Budget:** $1,200. **Description:** Individuals with an interest in the history of the American frontier, Daniel Boone, and the genealogy of the Trans-Allegheny frontier families. Promotes the study of, and interest in, frontier history, genealogy and historical site preservation. Seeks to discover historical and genealogical materials pertaining to the settlement of Kentucky and Missouri. Documents and preserves frontier historical and genealogical materials; conducts research and educational programs; participates in charitable activities; compiles statistics. **Libraries: Type:** reference. **Holdings:** 500; archival material, articles. **Subjects:** frontier family genealogy, frontier history. **Computer Services:** Information services, answering inquiries. **Committees:** Genealogy; Historical Site. **Publications:** *Boone and Frontier Families Research Letter*, quarterly. Newsletter. **Price:** included in membership dues.

10108 ■ Facing History and Ourselves National Foundation (FHAO)
16 Hurd Rd.
Brookline, MA 02445
Ph: (617)232-1595
Fax: (617)232-0281
E-mail: info@facing.org
URL: http://www.facinghistory.org
Contact: Sophia Balakian, Contact

Founded: 1976. **Staff:** 110. **Budget:** $11,000,000. **Regional Groups:** 8. **Multinational. Description:** Assists teachers and administrators in educating students about 20th century genocide, racism, human rights, and related issues of human behavior. Has developed curricula geared to junior high and high school levels that take an interdisciplinary approach to citizenship education, based on the methods of the humanities - inquiry, analysis, and interpretation. Dedicated to the belief that students must be trusted to examine history in all of its complexities, including its legacies of prejudice and discrimination, resilience and courage. This trust encourages young people to develop a voice in the conversations of their peer culture, as well as in the critical discussions and debates of their community and nation. Involves the community, parents, teachers, police officers, community activists, and other citizens. Created the "Choosing to Participate" initiative, which includes an exhibition, study guide, and community programs that highlight stories that illuminate the power of individual civic choices decisions that people make everyday about others in their community and nation. Operates resource center containing films, media kits, posters, tapes, periodicals, and books for use during the academic year. Sponsors adult education, teacher in-service programs, and summer institute for educators in the United States, Canada, Europe, and South Africa. **Libraries: Type:** open to the public. **Holdings:** 15,000; books, video recordings. **Subjects:** American and European history, sociology, holocaust, psychology. **Formerly:** (1982) Facing History and Ourselves. **Publications:** *Facing History and Ourselves: Annotated Bibliography* ● *Facing History and Ourselves: Choosing to Participate*. Book. Focuses on a time in American history when people were struggling to expand democratic traditions and strengthen democratic ideals. ● *Facing History and Ourselves: Elements of Time*. Book. **Price:** $18.00 1-4 copies, plus shipping and handling; $15.00 5 copies and above, plus shipping and handling ● *Facing History and Ourselves: Holocaust and Human Behavior, 1982, 1994*. Book. Provides an interdisciplinary approach to citizenship education. **Price:** $25.00 1-4 copies, plus shipping and handling; $21.00 5 copies and above, plus shipping and handling ● *Facing History and Ourselves News*, periodic. Newsletter. Reports on programs and activities of the foundation; discusses issues involved in genocide and human behavior. **Price:** free. **Circulation:** 60,000 ● *Facing History and Ourselves: Race and Membership in American*

History: The Eugenics Movement. Book ● *Facing History and Ourselves: Race and Membership in American History: The Eugenics Movement, 2001.* Book ● *Facing History and Ourselves: The Jews of Poland.* Book. **Conventions/Meetings:** annual Benefits Dinner ● annual Human Rights and Justice - conference ● seminar ● workshop.

10109 ■ Forest History Society (FHS)
701 William Vickers Ave.
Durham, NC 27701-3162
Ph: (919)682-9319
Fax: (919)682-2349
E-mail: stevena@duke.edu
URL: http://www.foresthistory.org
Contact: Steven Anderson, Pres.
Founded: 1946. **Members:** 1,200. **Membership Dues:** individual, $60 (annual) ● friend of society, $100 (annual) ● basic corporate, patron, $250 (annual) ● basic joint, $85 (annual) ● benefactor, $500 (annual) ● basic institution, $140 (annual). **Staff:** 11. **Description:** Historians, geographers, political scientists, foresters, botanists, ecologists, educators, business executives of forest products industries, librarians, archivists, and curators of manuscripts and museums (includes 100 corporate members, 1,100 individuals, and 300 library and institutional members). Leads a continental search for sources of North American forest history. Aids scholars and writers in the fields of conservation, forestry, and forest industry history. Serves as clearinghouse for manuscripts, personal papers, company records, pictures, and museum objects related to forest history; conducts special sessions at meetings of scholarly and professional associations. Cooperates with regional repositories. **Libraries: Type:** reference. **Holdings:** 9,000; archival material, books, periodicals, photographs. **Subjects:** forest history, forest industries, land policy, American economic history, government forestry, conservation of natural resources. **Awards:** Alfred D. Bell Travel Grants. **Frequency:** 5/year. **Type:** grant. **Recipient:** for scholars who can benefit from in depth research in the library and archives of the Forest History Society ● Charles A. Wayehaeuser Book Award. **Frequency:** annual. **Type:** recognition. **Recipient:** to an author who has exhibited fresh insight into a topic and whose narrative analysis is clear and inventive ● John M. Collier Forest History Journalism Award. **Type:** recognition. **Computer Services:** database, forest history collections in North American repositories, bibliography of forest and conservation history. **Departments:** Library; Research; Service. **Formerly:** (1952) Forest Products History Foundation of Minnesota Historical Society; (1954) American Forest History Foundation; (1955) Forest History Foundation. **Publications:** *American Forests: A History of Resiliency and Recovery.* Pamphlets ● *America's Fires: Management on Wildlands and Forests.* Pamphlets ● *Environmental History*, quarterly. Journal. Contains international articles that portray human interactions with the natural world over time. **Price:** included in membership dues; $130.00 /year for libraries. ISSN: 1084-5453. **Advertising:** accepted ● *Forest and Wildlife Science in America: A History.* Book ● *Forest History Today*, semiannual. Magazine ● *Forest Pharmacy: Medicinal Plants in American Forests.* Pamphlets ● *Guides to Forest and Conservation History of North America*, periodic ● *Newsprint: Canadian Supply and American Demand.* Pamphlets. **Conventions/Meetings:** annual conference (exhibits).

10110 ■ German Historical Institute (GHI)
1607 New Hampshire Ave. NW
Washington, DC 20009-2562
Ph: (202)387-3355
Fax: (202)483-3430
E-mail: info@ghi-dc.org
URL: http://www.ghi-dc.org
Contact: Dr. Christof Mauch, Dir.
Founded: 1987. **Staff:** 34. **Nonmembership. Description:** Serves as center for research and advanced studies in German and American history. Promotes exchange of ideas between American and German historians and political scientists. Supports research on topics including: origin and development of Western democracy and society; American history and American-German relations; transatlantic migration; the roles played by the U.S. and Germany in international history. Provides information on German and American archives. **Libraries: Type:** reference; open to the public. **Holdings:** 37,000; archival material, monographs, periodicals. **Subjects:** German history, German-American relations, American history. **Awards:** Dissertation Prize, Friends of the GHI. **Frequency:** annual. **Type:** scholarship. **Recipient:** for research on dissertation. **Computer Services:** Mailing lists ● online services, catalog. **Councils:** Academic Advisory. **Also Known As:** Deutsches Historisches Institut. **Publications:** *German Studies in North America: A Directory of Scholars.* Alternate Formats: online ● *Publications of the German Historical Institute.* Monographs ● *Reference Guide*, periodic. **Price:** free ● *Transatlantische Historische Studien.* Monograph ● Bulletin, semiannual. Contains information on upcoming events and lectures, scholarships, and research facilities in Federal Republic of Germany and the U.S. **Price:** free. **Circulation:** 4,000. Alternate Formats: online ● Papers, periodic. **Price:** free. **Conventions/Meetings:** conference and workshop - 10-15/year ● annual lecture ● semiannual lecture - always spring and fall ● seminar.

10111 ■ Gluckstal Colonies Research Association (GCRA)
611 Esplanade
Redondo Beach, CA 90277-4130
Ph: (310)540-1872
Fax: (310)792-8058
E-mail: gcra31@aol.com
URL: http://www.glueckstal.org
Contact: Margaret Freeman, Exec. Dir.
Founded: 1986. **Members:** 400. **Membership Dues:** standard, $20 (annual). **Budget:** $5,000. **Description:** Historians and other individuals with an interest in the early European settlement of North American German-speaking individuals from Russia. Seeks to locate, gather, and organize all primary sources pertaining to the so-called Gluckstal colonies of South Russia. Serves as a clearinghouse on the Gluckstal colonies; conducts historical and genealogical research; sponsors educational programs. **Libraries: Type:** by appointment only; reference. **Holdings:** archival material, audio recordings, books, periodicals, video recordings. **Subjects:** Gluckstal Colonies, early European settlement of the Dakotas, settlement records from Ukraine. **Affiliated With:** American Historical Society of Germans From Russia; Germans From Russia Heritage Society. **Publications:** *Bicentennial Volume on the Gluckstal Colonies.* Book. Comes with companion video. **Price:** $95.00 each with 2 CDR and DVD; $29.95 VHS version only; $29.95 DVD version only. Alternate Formats: CD-ROM ● *GCRA Newsletter*, semiannual. Includes research information. **Price:** $7.50/issue for nonmembers; included in membership dues ● *Gluckstal Colonies, Births and Marriages: 1833-1900.* Book. Contains births and marriages found in the microfilm of the St. Petersburg Consistory for the Gluckstal Colonies parishes. **Price:** $50.00 for members (softcover); $75.00 for members (hardcover); $70.00 for nonmembers (softcover); $95.00 for nonmembers (hardcover) ● *Gluckstal Colonies Deaths 1833-1900.* Book. Includes extractions of almost 10,000 death events for the Lutheran Colonies of Bergdorf, Gluckstal, Kassel and Neudorf, Imperial Russia. **Price:** $45.00 for members (softcover); $70.00 for members (hardcover); $65.00 for nonmembers (softcover); $90.00 for nonmembers (hardcover) ● *Gluckstal Kolonien Geburten und Eheschliebungen: 1833-1900* (in German). Book. **Price:** $50.00 for members (softcover); $75.00 for members (hardcover); $70.00 for nonmembers (softcover); $95.00 for nonmembers (hardcover) ● *Gluckstal Kolonien Todesfalle: 1833-1900* (in German). Book. **Price:** $45.00 for members (softcover); $70.00 for members (hardcover); $65.00 for nonmembers (softcover); $90.00 for nonmembers (hardcover) ● *Marienberg: Schicksal eines Dorfes - Fate of a Village.* Book. Features a chronicle of the daughter colony of the Glueckstal group of villages written by Johann Bollinger. **Price:** $35.00 softcover; $55.00 hardcover.

10112 ■ Group for the Use of Psychology in History (GUPH)
c/o Charles B. Strozier, Exec. Off.
John Jay Coll., CUNY
555 W 57th St., Ste.601
New York, NY 10019
Ph: (212)237-8432
E-mail: strozier2@aol.com
URL: http://www.historians.org/affiliates/group_use_psychology_his.htm
Contact: Charles B. Strozier, Exec. Off.
Founded: 1971. **Members:** 400. **Membership Dues:** regular, $22 (annual). **Description:** Historians, sociologists, psychologists, psychoanalysts, and political scientists interested in the uses of psychology in humanistic and social science disciplines. **Awards:** William L. Langer Award. **Type:** recognition. **Recipient:** for the best article written in the field. **Affiliated With:** American Historical Association. **Publications:** *Psychohistory Review*, quarterly. Journal. Reports on recent developments in the field. Includes essays, book reviews, and news notes. **Price:** included in membership dues; $22.00 /year for nonmembers. ISSN: 0363-891X. **Circulation:** 400. **Advertising:** accepted. Alternate Formats: microform. Also Cited As: *Group for the Use of Psychology in History Newsletter.* **Conventions/Meetings:** annual conference.

10113 ■ Historical Society of the United Methodist Church (HSUMC)
c/o Bill Bakeman
1178 County Rd. B.W.
Roseville, MN 55113-4301
E-mail: pajt8817@aol.com
URL: http://www.historicalsocietyunitedmethodistchurch.org
Contact: Patricia Thompson, Pres.
Founded: 1988. **Members:** 350. **Membership Dues:** individual, $30 (annual) ● family, $36 (annual) ● institution, $43 (annual) ● benefactor, $100 (annual) ● life, $500 ● student, $20 (annual). **Budget:** $13,000. **Multinational. Description:** Individuals interested in the history of the United Methodist church. Promotes the study, preservation, and dissemination of information on the history of the United Methodist church and its antecedent bodies. Serves as a forum for exchange of information among members; monitors research projects involving United Methodist Church history. Assists in expanding the archival collections of the General Commission on Archives and History of the United Methodist Church. Makes available to members discounts on publications and admissions to convocations and meetings. **Awards:** Saddlebag Selection. **Frequency:** annual. **Type:** recognition. **Recipient:** to the outstanding book on United Methodist history or a related subject published during a given calendar year. **Publications:** *Historian's Digest*, quarterly. Newsletter. **Circulation:** 800. Alternate Formats: online ● *Methodist History*, quarterly. Journal. **Price:** included in membership dues; $20.00 for nonmembers. **Conventions/Meetings:** annual conference.

10114 ■ Historical Society of Washington, DC (HSW)
Mt. Vernon Sq.
801 K St. NW
Washington, DC 20001
Ph: (202)383-1850 (202)383-1810
Fax: (202)383-1872
E-mail: info@historydc.org
URL: http://www.historydc.org
Contact: Ms. Bell Clement, Exec. Dir.
Founded: 1894. **Members:** 3,000. **Membership Dues:** individual, $50 (annual) ● family, $75 (annual) ● contributing, $100 (annual) ● benefactor, $500 (annual) ● patron, $1,000 (annual) ● President's Circle, $2,500 (annual) ● Chairman's Circle, $5,000 (annual). **Staff:** 3. **Budget:** $1,000,000. **State Groups:** 1. **Description:** Individuals, libraries, corporations, and organizations. Historical society that collects, preserves, and disseminates information on the history, biography, geography, and topography of the District of Columbia. The society's collection of Washington history and its Research Library is cur-

rently housed in old Carnegie Library building on Mount Vernon Square. Conducts annual teacher training workshop on District of Columbia history. Holds local history exhibitions, lectures, and educational outreach program to district area schools. **Libraries: Type:** open to the public; reference. **Holdings:** 20,000; archival material, articles, books, clippings, maps, photographs. **Subjects:** Washington, DC history and its people. **Awards:** Renchard Prize. **Frequency:** annual. **Type:** recognition. **Recipient:** for outstanding historic preservation projects. **Computer Services:** database, library holdings. **Committees:** Collections; Exhibitions; Historic House. **Formerly:** (1989) Columbia Historical Society. **Publications:** *Metro History News*, quarterly. Newsletter. Contains activity updates. **Circulation:** 2,000. Alternate Formats: online ● *Records of the Columbia Historical Society* ● *Washington at Home: History of Neighborhoods* ● *Washington History*, semiannual. Magazine. Includes articles on Washington, D.C. history, photo essays, and reviews of books, exhibitions, films, and videos. **Price:** $7.95/issue. ISSN: 1042-9719. **Circulation:** 2,500. **Conventions/Meetings:** annual Washington DC Historical Studies Conference, two-day public forum (exhibits) - always fall in Washington, DC.

10115 ■ History of Dermatology Society (HDS)
1760 Market St., No. 301
Philadelphia, PA 19103-4106
Ph: (215)563-8333
Fax: (215)563-3044
E-mail: larryderm@yahoo.com
URL: http://www.dermato.med.br/hds
Contact: Lawrence C. Parish MD, Pres.
Founded: 1973. **Members:** 120. **Membership Dues:** regular, $75 (annual). **Staff:** 2. **Description:** Represents dermatologists interested in promoting the history of dermatology. **Awards:** Zakon Award. **Frequency:** annual. **Type:** recognition. **Recipient:** for best paper on the history of dermatology. **Publications:** *Program Guide*, annual. **Conventions/Meetings:** annual meeting.

10116 ■ History of Earth Sciences Society (HESS)
c/o Emma Rainforth, Treas.
Ramapo Coll. of New Jersey
505 Ramapo Valley Rd.
Mahwah, NJ 07430
E-mail: treasurer@historyearthscience.org
URL: http://www.historyearthscience.org
Contact: Emma Rainforth, Treas.
Founded: 1982. **Members:** 500. **Membership Dues:** individual in U.S., $48 (annual) ● individual outside U.S., $50 (annual) ● institutional in U.S., $78 (annual). **National Groups:** 3. **Description:** Science historians, geologists, and interested individuals. Promotes the discipline of the history of geology. Encourages interest in the earth sciences through publications and organization of meetings. Supports scholarly and scientific endeavors and other associations having similar interests. **Publications:** *Earth Sciences History*, semiannual. Journal. Covers a variety of topics from the biographical to the analytical perspective. Includes book reviews. **Price:** included in membership dues; $30.00 /year for nonmembers in U.S.; $35.00 /year for nonmembers outside U.S.; $76.00 /year for institutions in U.S. ISSN: 0736-6234. **Circulation:** 500 ● Monograph, periodic. **Conventions/Meetings:** annual conference.

10117 ■ History of Economics Society (HES)
c/o Neil B. Niman, Treas.
Univ. of New Hampshire
McConnell Hall
15 Coll. Rd.
Durham, NH 03824
Ph: (603)862-3336
E-mail: hes@orbit.unh.edu
URL: http://www.historyofeconomics.org
Contact: Neil B. Niman, Treas.
Founded: 1974. **Members:** 600. **Membership Dues:** individual, $30 (annual). **Description:** Scholars whose primary or secondary interest is the history of economics. Purposes are to: promote interest and inquiry into the history of economics and related parts of intellectual history; facilitate communication and discourse among scholars working in the field; acquaint members of the profession, especially young people, with the scientific, literary, and philosophical tradition of economics today. **Awards:** Award for the Best Article. **Frequency:** annual. **Type:** recognition. **Recipient:** for the best article in the history of Economics ● Distinguished Fellow Award. **Frequency:** annual. **Type:** recognition. **Recipient:** for those who have contributed a lifetime of study to the history of Economics ● Joseph Dorfman Award. **Frequency:** annual. **Type:** recognition. **Recipient:** for the best dissertation in the history of Economics ● Joseph J. Spengler Award. **Frequency:** annual. **Type:** recognition. **Recipient:** for the best book in the history of Economics. **Computer Services:** Online services. **Programs:** Young Scholars. **Publications:** *Journal of the History of Economic Thought*, quarterly. Covers HES activities including meetings, annual programs, and contributed papers on the history of economic thought. **Price:** included in membership dues; $426.00 /year for institutions (print subscription); $404.00 /year for institutions (online subscription); $170.00 /year for individuals (print subscription). ISSN: 1042-7716. **Circulation:** 600. **Advertising:** accepted. **Conventions/Meetings:** annual conference (exhibits).

10118 ■ History of Education Society (HES)
c/o History of Education Quarterly
Univ. of Illinois at Urbana - Champaign
Educational Policy Stud.
360 Educ. Bldg., MC-708
1310 S Sixth St.
Champaign, IL 61820
Ph: (213)333-2446
Fax: (217)244-7064
E-mail: heq@ed.uiuc.edu
URL: http://www.ed.uiuc.edu/hes
Contact: Nancy Beadie, Pres.
Founded: 1960. **Members:** 450. **Membership Dues:** individual, $50 (annual) ● student, $25 (annual). **Staff:** 2. **Budget:** $50,000. **Description:** Seeks to advance interest, study, and research in the history of education in the U.S. and throughout the world. **Awards:** Claude A. Eggertsen Dissertation Prize. **Frequency:** annual. **Type:** monetary. **Recipient:** to the most outstanding individual in the field of history of education ● Henry Barnard Prize. **Frequency:** biennial. **Type:** recognition. **Recipient:** for best essay by a graduate student ● HES Award. **Frequency:** biennial. **Type:** recognition. **Recipient:** for best essay published in the History of Education Quarterly ● Outstanding Book Award. **Frequency:** biennial. **Type:** scholarship. **Recipient:** to the author of the best book published in the preceding year. **Publications:** *History of Education Quarterly*. Journal. Contains articles, documents and debates on important issues in the history of education. ISSN: 0018-2680. **Conventions/Meetings:** annual meeting, with book exhibits (exhibits).

10119 ■ History of Science Society (HSS)
PO Box 117360
Gainesville, FL 32611-7360
Ph: (352)392-1677
Fax: (352)392-2795
E-mail: info@hssonline.org
URL: http://www.hssonline.org
Contact: Robert Jay Malone, Exec. Dir.
Founded: 1924. **Members:** 4,000. **Membership Dues:** individual, $91 (annual) ● student, $30 (annual) ● family, $119 (annual) ● institution, $348 (annual) ● retired, $55 (annual). **Staff:** 5. **Budget:** $254,000. **Regional Groups:** 5. **Multinational. Description:** Serves as professional society of educators, historians, scientists, and others interested in the history and cultural influence of science. **Awards:** Derek Price/Rod Webster Prize. **Frequency:** annual. **Type:** monetary ● History of Women in Science Prize. **Frequency:** annual. **Type:** monetary ● Joseph H. Hazen Education Prize. **Frequency:** annual. **Type:** monetary ● Margaret W. Rossiter Women in Science Prize. **Frequency:** annual. **Type:** recognition. **Recipient:** to an outstanding article in even-numbered years and an outstanding book in odd-numbered years on women in science ● Pfizer Award. **Frequency:** annual. **Type:** monetary. **Recipient:** for an outstanding book in the history of science ● Sarton Medal. **Frequency:** annual. **Type:** recognition ● Watson Davis, and Helen Miles Davis Prize. **Frequency:** annual. **Type:** monetary. **Recipient:** for best books in the history of science directed to a general public. **Caucuses:** Women's. **Committees:** Education; Finance; Honors and Prizes; Meetings and Programs; Publications; Research and the Profession. **Programs:** K-12 Teacher Workshops. **Affiliated With:** American Association for the Advancement of Science; American Council of Learned Societies; American Historical Association; Consortium of Social Science Associations; National Coalition for History; National Humanities Alliance; National Science Foundation. **Publications:** *Guide to the History of Science*, periodic. Book. **Price:** $39.00 soft; $50.00 cloth. **Circulation:** 3,000. **Advertising:** accepted ● *History of Science Society Newsletter*, quarterly. Includes society news, list of current literature, and statistics. **Price:** included in membership dues; $20.00 /year for nonmembers. **Circulation:** 3,000. **Advertising:** accepted ● *Isis*, quarterly. Journal. Includes book reviews, news in the profession, and annual *Current Bibliography of the History of Science*. **Price:** included in membership dues; $176.00 /year for institutions. **Circulation:** 4,500. **Advertising:** accepted ● *Osiris*, annual. Contains topical essays. **Circulation:** 4,500. **Conventions/Meetings:** annual conference and meeting (exhibits) - always fall. 2008 Nov. 6-9, Pittsburgh, PA; 2009 Nov. 18-22, Phoenix, AZ.

10120 ■ Illinois Central Railroad Historical Society (ICHS)
PO Box 288
Paxton, IL 60957
E-mail: membership@icrrhistorical.org
URL: http://icrrhistorical.org
Contact: George Walterhausen, 2nd VP
Founded: 1979. **Members:** 1,034. **Membership Dues:** regular, $35 (annual) ● sustaining, $45 (annual). **Regional Groups:** 1. **Description:** Individuals interested in the history of the Illinois Central Railroad. Dedicated to the preservation of historical and educational information about the Illinois Central Railroad and its predecessor lines. Strives to preserve the memories of the people who worked for the railroad, the places it went, and the effect it had on the communities through which it passed. Purchased the former Lake Erie & Western Railway freighthouse to house the group's headquarters and archives. Conducts educational programs. **Libraries: Type:** reference. **Holdings:** archival material, audio recordings, business records, video recordings. **Subjects:** Illinois Central Railroad history. **Departments:** Company Store; Depot at Paxton; Internet Operations; Publications. **Publications:** *Green Diamond*, quarterly. Magazine. Contains articles and stories about the railroad. **Price:** $6.50/issue for nonmembers; included in membership dues. **Circulation:** 2,000 ● Newsletter, quarterly. Includes information on upcoming society events. **Price:** included in membership dues. **Conventions/Meetings:** annual meeting and show.

10121 ■ Immigration and Ethnic History Society (IEHS)
c/o Betty A. Bergland, Sec.
Univ. of Wisconsin
Dept. of History
River Falls, WI 54022
Ph: (715)425-3164
Fax: (715)425-0657
E-mail: betty.a.bergland@uwrf.edu
URL: http://www.iehs.org
Contact: Betty A. Bergland, Sec.
Founded: 1965. **Members:** 900. **Membership Dues:** student, $25 (annual) ● individual in U.S. and Canada, $45 (annual) ● institution/organization, $190 (annual). **Description:** Scholars interested in the study of human migration, particularly immigration to the United States and Canada. Provides a means of

communication for historians, sociologists, economists, and others engaged in researching this field. Disseminates information on current research projects and available publications. **Awards:** Carlton C. Qualey Article Award. **Frequency:** biennial. **Type:** monetary. **Recipient:** for articles published in Journal of American Ethnic History ● George E. Pozzetta Dissertation Research Award. **Frequency:** annual. **Type:** monetary. **Recipient:** for dissertation research ● Theodore Saloutos Memorial Book Award in Immigration History. **Frequency:** annual. **Type:** monetary. **Recipient:** for the outstanding book of the year in American immigration and ethnic history. **Boards:** Executive. **Affiliated With:** American Historical Association; Organization of American Historians. **Formerly:** (1998) Immigration and History Society. **Publications:** *Immigration and Ethnic History Newsletter*, semiannual. Includes society business. **Price:** included in membership dues. **Circulation:** 900 ● *Journal of American Ethnic History*, quarterly. Features scholarly articles. **Price:** included in membership dues. **Circulation:** 830. **Advertising:** accepted. **Conventions/Meetings:** annual meeting and dinner, held in conjunction with the annual convention of the Organization of American Historians - usually spring.

10122 ■ Indochina Center (IC)
c/o Center for Southeast Asia Studies
Univ. of California, Berkeley
2223 Fulton St., Rm. 617, MC2318
Berkeley, CA 94720-2318
Ph: (510)642-3609
Fax: (510)643-7062
E-mail: cseas@berkeley.edu
URL: http://www.ocf.berkeley.edu/~sdenney
Founded: 1979. **Description:** Scholars, writers, journalists, businesspeople, clergy, and interested individuals. Collects and disseminates information on Indochina. Conducts research on Indochina and the Vietnam War. Encourages the teaching of updated courses on that period of history. Sponsors lectures, seminars, musical performances, art exhibitions, poetry readings, and video and slide presentations. **Libraries: Type:** reference; open to the public. **Holdings:** 1,000; books, periodicals. **Subjects:** Vietnam, Laos, Cambodia, Indochina. **Absorbed:** Project on the Vietnam Generation. **Formerly:** (2000) IndoChina Institute. **Publications:** Also publishes directories, information sheet, proceedings, reports, occasional papers, self-learning packets; also makes available Back in the World: Writing After Viet Nam (audiocassette). **Conventions/Meetings:** conference and symposium.

10123 ■ Institute for Psychohistory (IP)
140 Riverside Dr.
New York, NY 10024-2605
Ph: (212)799-2294 (303)442-1735
Fax: (212)799-2294
E-mail: psychhst@tiac.net
URL: http://www.psychohistory.com
Contact: Lloyd deMause, Dir.
Founded: 1976. **Members:** 50. **Staff:** 2. **Budget:** $100,000. **Description:** Historians, psychotherapists, sociologists, political scientists, and other scholars; fifteen branches in the U.S. and other countries. Promotes research and educational activities in psychohistory. (Psychohistory is the application of the principles of psychology to the study of history). **Libraries: Type:** reference. **Holdings:** 2,000; books, periodicals. **Subjects:** psychohistory. **Affiliated With:** International Psychohistorical Association. **Also Known As:** Association for Psychohistory. **Publications:** *Foundations of Psychohistory*. Books ● *Journal of Psychohistory*, quarterly. Includes book reviews. **Price:** $54.00 /year for individuals; $129.00 /year for institutions. ISSN: 0145-3378. **Circulation:** 3,000. **Advertising:** accepted. Alternate Formats: microform; online. **Conventions/Meetings:** periodic meeting and seminar ● seminar ● workshop.

10124 ■ International Association for the History of Glass
c/o Jane Shadel Spillman, Gen. Sec.
Corning Museum of Glass
1 Museum Way
Corning, NY 14830
Ph: (607)974-8357
Fax: (607)974-8470
E-mail: spillmanjs@cmog.org
URL: http://www.aihv.org
Contact: Jane Shadel Spillman, Gen. Sec.
Founded: 1958. **Members:** 420. **Membership Dues:** institutional, EUR 50 (annual) ● individual, EUR 32 (annual). **National Groups:** 15. **Languages:** English, French, German. **Multinational. Description:** Promotes the historic, archaeological, and artistic study of glass in 30 countries. Facilitates international scientific collaboration among members and specialists in examining the cultural aspects of glass heritage within a larger historical context. Examines problems of conservation and technology, excluding those regarding the industrial production of contemporary glass; studies all periods in the history of glass. **Publications:** *Annales de l'AIHV* (in English, French, and German), triennial. Proceedings. Also Cited As: *AIHV or Annales AIHV* ● Monographs. **Conventions/Meetings:** triennial congress (exhibits).

10125 ■ International Psychohistorical Association (IPA)
PO Box 314
New York, NY 10024
E-mail: hwlipa@gmail.com
URL: http://www.psychohistory.us
Contact: Henry Lawton, Sec.
Founded: 1977. **Members:** 350. **Membership Dues:** individual, $25 (annual) ● life, $1,000. **Staff:** 4. **Budget:** $10,000. **Multinational. Description:** Represents professional scholars, academicians, and laypeople interested in psychohistory (the application of psychological and psychoanalytical methods to the interpretation of history). Promotes the study and discussion of psychohistory. Sponsors speakers' bureau. **Libraries: Type:** reference. **Holdings:** 450; archival material, books. **Awards:** Azar Kalbache and Zara Ben Hamou Memorial Award. **Type:** recognition ● Emilio Bernabi Memorial Award. **Type:** recognition ● Evelyn Bauer Memorial Award. **Type:** recognition ● Roger Lorenz Award. **Type:** recognition ● Rose and Michael David Elovitz Memorial Award. **Type:** recognition ● William K. Joseph Award for Economics. **Type:** recognition. **Affiliated With:** Institute for Psychohistory; Psychohistory Forum. **Publications:** *Directory of Convention Participants*, annual. **Price:** included in membership dues ● *Psychohistorical Bibliography*, periodic. **Price:** included in membership dues ● *Psychohistory News*, quarterly. Bulletin. **Price:** included in membership dues. Alternate Formats: online ● Membership Directory, annual. **Price:** included in membership dues. **Conventions/Meetings:** annual convention, three days of scholarly presentations.

10126 ■ International Society for Intellectual History (ISIH)
c/o Mr. Steven Lestition, PhD, Membership Sec.
B41 Holder Hall
Mathey Coll.
Princeton, NJ 08544
Ph: (609)258-3317
Fax: (609)258-2889
E-mail: sol@princeton.edu
URL: http://www.history.upenn.edu/isih
Contact: Mr. Steven Lestition PhD, Membership Sec.
Founded: 1994. **Members:** 400. **Membership Dues:** Europe, Africa and Indian subcontinent, EUR 30 (annual) ● Europe, Africa and Indian subcontinent, EUR 50 (biennial) ● student, Europe, Africa and Indian subcontinent, EUR 40 (biennial) ● individual, Americas, Australia and the Far East, $35 (annual) ● individual, Americas, Australia and the Far East, $55 (biennial) ● graduate student, Americas, Australia and the Far East, $45 (biennial). **Multinational. Description:** Fosters communication and interaction among the international community of intellectual historians and scholars. **Committees:** Standing. **Publications:** *Intellectual News*, semiannual. Journal. Contains articles, reviews, and summaries of books by members. **Price:** included in membership dues ● Membership Directory. **Price:** included in membership dues. **Conventions/Meetings:** annual conference ● annual international conference.

10127 ■ Judson Welliver Society (JWS)
c/o Gordon Stewart, Sec.
Insurance Info. Inst.
110 William St.
New York, NY 10038
Ph: (212)346-5501
Fax: (212)267-6623
E-mail: gordons@iii.org
Contact: Gordon Stewart, Sec.
Founded: 1984. **Members:** 60. **Description:** Former principal presidential speechwriters; derives name from Judson Welliver, who became the first full-time presidential speechwriter in 1921, during the administration of Warren Harding. Recognizes speechwriters as an inevitable, essential, and formerly invisible part of U.S. presidential administrations. Facilitates discussion among members. **Publications:** Plans to publish book tracing the writing of famous presidential speeches. **Conventions/Meetings:** annual meeting and dinner.

10128 ■ Lewis and Clark Trail Heritage Foundation (LCTHF)
4201 Giant Springs Rd.
Great Falls, MT 59405
Ph: (406)454-1234 (406)761-3950
Free: (888)701-3434
Fax: (406)771-9237
E-mail: membership@lewisandclark.org
URL: http://www.lewisandclark.org
Contact: Carol A. Bronson, Exec. Dir.
Founded: 1969. **Members:** 3,500. **Membership Dues:** individual, library, non-profit, $49 (annual) ● student, $30 (annual) ● family, international, $68 (annual) ● heritage club, $100 (annual) ● explorer club, $150 (annual) ● Jefferson club, $250 (annual) ● discovery club, $500 (annual) ● expedition club, $1,000 (annual) ● leadership, $2,500 (annual) ● business, $150 (annual). **Staff:** 5. **Budget:** $400,000. **Regional Groups:** 40. **State Groups:** 11. **Description:** Provides national leadership as keepers of the story, stewards of the Lewis and Clark National Historic Trail, and its vibrant, engaged membership promotes inclusiveness and cultural diversity. Comprised of federal, state, and local government officials; historical societies; schools; libraries; students; historians; interested individuals. Encourages public interest in the Lewis and Clark Expedition and the Native Americans they met and preservation and protection of the Lewis and Clark National Historic Trail and related sites. Also contributions to American history made by expedition members and the Native Americans they met, and events of time and place concerning and following the Expeditions that are of historical importance. Meriwether Lewis (1774-1809) and William Clark (1770-1838) were selected by President Thomas Jefferson in 1803 to explore the Louisiana Purchase (which included lands from the Mississippi River to the Rocky Mountains), and the watershed of the Columbia River (located in Idaho, Washington, and Oregon). The Expedition provided the first real documentation of lands, peoples, and resources within these areas. Supports activities that enhance the enjoyment and understanding of the Lewis and Clark Expedition and Trail. Encourages the study of the history of the Expedition within the context of local geographical settings; promotes cooperative long-range planning focusing upon historic sites and scenic and recreational resources within the Trail; complements and supplements activities of state and local interest groups. Provides annual meeting papers, interpretive (on-site) talks, and annual banquet addresses. **Libraries: Type:** reference. **Holdings:** 1,000; archival material. **Subjects:** Lewis and Clark Expedition, President Thomas Jefferson, Western Expansion, Native Americans. **Awards:** Monetary Grants. **Frequency:** annual. **Type:** scholarship. **Recipient:** for expedition, research, museum exhibits and interpretive markers related to expeditions ● **Frequency:** annual. **Type:** recognition. **Recipient:** to individuals or groups for acts of distinction or achievement in Lewis and Clark historical research, writing, or deed. **Telecommunication Services:** electronic mail, discovery@lewisandclark.org. **Committees:** Archives; Awards; Bylaws; Diversity; Education; Governance; Monetary

Grants; Reinactors; Trail Stewardship. **Publications:** *Lewis and Clark Trail Heritage Foundation—Members Handbook*, annual. Covers the Lewis and Clark expedition, related topics, foundation news, and book reviews. **Price:** included in membership dues; $5.00/ issue for nonmembers. ISSN: 0275-6706. **Circulation:** 3,000 ● *The Orderly Report*, quarterly. Newsletter. **Price:** included in membership dues. **Circulation:** 3,500. Alternate Formats: online ● *We Proceeded On*, quarterly. Magazine. Covers the Lewis and Clark expedition, related topics, foundation news, book reviews. **Price:** included in membership dues. ISSN: 0275-6706. **Circulation:** 3,500. Also Cited As: *We Proceeded On Publications* ● *WPO Publications*, periodic. Reprints. Contains collections of topical essays and papers presented at the foundation's annual meetings. Also Cited As: *We Proceeded On Publications* ● Monographs. **Conventions/Meetings:** annual meeting (exhibits) - always August.

10129 ■ MARHO: The Radical Historians' Organization

c/o American Historical Association
400 A St. SE
Washington, DC 20003-3889
Ph: (202)544-2422 (212)998-2632
Fax: (202)544-8307
E-mail: rhr@igc.org
URL: http://www.theaha.org/affiliates/marho.htm
Contact: Marc Goulding, Managing Ed.

Founded: 1973. **Members:** 1,500. **Membership Dues:** student/senior, $20 (annual) ● regular, $32 (annual). **Staff:** 2. **Description:** Collective comprising leftist historians and others interested in radical perspectives on the study, teaching, and public presentation of history. Opposes the concept that academic historians can isolate themselves from social and political concerns. Resists the confines of conventional history by stimulating theoretical discussion and political analysis. Seeks to develop a critical history of capitalism. Encourages controversy over current historical questions. **Formerly:** Mid-Atlantic Radical Historians Organization. **Publications:** *History from South Africa: Alternative Visions and Practices* ● *Presenting the Past* ● *Radical History Review*, 3/year. Journal. **Price:** $28.00/year in U.S.; $32.00/ year outside U.S. ISSN: 0163-6545. **Circulation:** 5,000. **Advertising:** accepted. Alternate Formats: microform ● *Resisting Images: Essays on Cinema and History* ● *Visions of History*. **Conventions/Meetings:** periodic meeting.

10130 ■ Mexican Epigraphic Society (MES)

Address Unknown since 2007

Founded: 1982. **Members:** 300. **Staff:** 13. **Regional Groups:** 4. **For-Profit. Description:** Specialists in the field of ancient American epigraphy and archaeology and interested others. Translates and studies epigraphs left by ancient North Americans in order to support a theory of Pre-Columbian transoceanic contact with European and Asian cultures. Sponsors educational programs. Maintains library and museum. **Also Known As:** Sociedad de Epigraphia. **Publications:** *Diffusionist Quarterly*. Magazine. Contains articles on the group's findings. **Price:** $20.00/year. **Circulation:** 300. **Advertising:** accepted. **Conventions/Meetings:** periodic conference (exhibits).

10131 ■ Mining History Association (MHA)

PO Box 552
Sedalia, CO 80135
Ph: (707)785-3814
E-mail: doubledllc@aol.com
URL: http://www.mininghistoryassociation.org
Contact: Eleanor Swent, Pres.

Founded: 1989. **Members:** 320. **Membership Dues:** general, $25 (annual) ● general, outside U.S., $35 (annual) ● sustaining, $50 (annual) ● patron, $100 (annual) ● corporate, $500 (annual). **Staff:** 15. **Budget:** $15,000. **Multinational. Description:** Academics, educators, students, and other individuals with an interest in the history of mining. Promotes teaching and scholarship in the field; promotes increased interest in mining history. Conducts educational programs. **Awards:** Clark Spence Award. **Frequency:** biennial. **Type:** recognition. **Recipient:** to the authors of the most significant, recently published book on mining history ● John Townley Award. **Frequency:** annual. **Type:** recognition. **Recipient:** to the contributor of best essay appearing in the MHA Journal ● Rodman Paul Award. **Frequency:** annual. **Type:** recognition. **Recipient:** for the outstanding contributor to the study of mining history. **Publications:** *Mining History Journal*, annual. Contains journal with 10 essays and book reviews. ● *Mining History News*, quarterly. Newsletter. Alternate Formats: online. **Conventions/Meetings:** annual conference, with book dealer and mining collectibles (exhibits).

10132 ■ Museum of the Fur Trade

6321 Hwy. 20
Chadron, NE 69337
Ph: (308)432-3843
E-mail: museum@furtrade.org
URL: http://www.furtrade.org
Contact: Gail DeBuse Potter, Dir.

Founded: 1949. **Members:** 3,000. **Membership Dues:** regular, in U.S., $15 (annual) ● regular, outside U.S., $18 (annual). **Staff:** 7. **Budget:** $70,000. **Multinational. Description:** Universities, historical societies, and individuals with primary interest in North American history. Acts as a clearinghouse for the dissemination of information and operation of Museum of the Fur Trade, which is devoted to the material aspects of the North American fur trade. Serves as a consulting service for museums, artists, writers, and publishers; provides professional training for persons in specialized museums; conducts lectures, research program, and other programs for schools at all levels. **Libraries: Type:** reference. **Holdings:** 8,000; archival material, artwork, audiovisuals, books, periodicals. **Subjects:** North American fur trade. **Awards:** Distinguished Service Award. **Frequency:** periodic. **Type:** recognition. **Recipient:** for volunteer service of exceptional quality. **Computer Services:** Mailing lists, of members. **Formerly:** (2001) Museum Association of the American Frontier. **Publications:** *David Adams Journal*. Book. **Price:** $20.00 hardbound ● *The Hawken Rifle: Its Place in History*. Book. **Price:** $12.00 each ● *Museum of the Fur Trade Quarterly*. Journal. Includes book reviews. **Price:** included in membership dues; $320.00 complete set (U.S. postpaid), for nonmembers; $340.00 complete set (foreign), for nonmembers. $18.00 special issue (hardbound), for nonmembers. ISSN: 0027-4135. **Circulation:** 3,000 ● *The Northwest Gun*. Book. **Price:** $8.00 each ● *The Plains Rifle*. Book. **Price:** $42.00 hardbound ● Monographs. **Conventions/Meetings:** annual conference.

10133 ■ National Capital Historical Museum of Transportation (NCHMT)

c/o National Capital Trolley Museum
1313 Bonifant Rd.
Colesville, MD 20905-5955
Ph: (301)384-6088
Fax: (301)384-2865
URL: http://dctrolley.org
Contact: Kenneth Rucker, Dir. of Administration

Founded: 1959. **Members:** 150. **Staff:** 4. **Budget:** $61,000. **Description:** People interested in the preservation of historic European and American streetcars and historic items pertaining to street rail transportation. Operates the National Capital Trolley Museum, which runs 17 antique trolley cars on a one-mile track. Offers opportunity to learn all aspects of operating a full-scale trolley line through volunteer work. Presents public programs on transportation history. **Libraries: Type:** reference. **Holdings:** 350. **Subjects:** electric railways. **Affiliated With:** American Association for State and Local History; Association of Railway Museums. **Publications:** *Headway Recorder*, bimonthly. Newsletter ● Membership Directory, annual. **Conventions/Meetings:** annual meeting.

10134 ■ National Center for the American Revolution

435 Devon Park Dr.
Wayne, PA 19087
Ph: (610)975-4939
Fax: (610)917-3188
E-mail: sswigart@ix.netcom.com
Contact: Tom Daly, Exec. Dir.

Description: Provides information about the events that took place during the American Revolution, the people who participated, and the legacy of this period in American history. **Conventions/Meetings:** lecture.

10135 ■ National Coalition for History (NCH)

400 A St. SE
Washington, DC 20003
Ph: (202)544-2422
Fax: (202)544-8307
E-mail: lwhite@historycoalition.org
URL: http://historycoalition.org
Contact: Lee White, Exec. Dir.

Founded: 1977. **Members:** 72. **Staff:** 1. **Budget:** $125,000. **State Groups:** 24. **Description:** Archival and historical organizations such as: American Historical Association; Organization of American Historians; Phi Alpha Theta; Society of American Archivists; Western History Association. Serves as central advocacy office and information clearinghouse for history/archival related topics affecting government agencies, legislative aides, and professional history and archival associations; develops network of constituent contacts in districts and states; testifies before congressional committees; monitors employment opportunities. **Convention/Meeting:** none. **Libraries: Type:** reference. **Holdings:** archival material. **Formerly:** (2002) National Coordinating Committee for the Promotion of History. **Publications:** *NCH Washington Update*, weekly. Newsletter. **Price:** free. **Circulation:** 60,000. Alternate Formats: online ● Also publishes special reports.

10136 ■ National Council on Public History (NCPH)

327 Cavanaugh Hall - IUPUI
425 Univ. Blvd.
Indianapolis, IN 46202
Ph: (317)274-2716 (512)389-4464
Fax: (317)278-5230
E-mail: ncph@iupui.edu
URL: http://www.ncph.org
Contact: John R. Dichtl PhD, Exec. Dir.

Founded: 1979. **Members:** 1,700. **Membership Dues:** student (add $20 if outside U.S.), $25 (annual) ● new professional (add $20 if outside U.S.), $35 (annual) ● individual (add $20 if outside U.S.), $65 (annual) ● institution (paper and electronic - add $20 if outside U.S.), $150 (annual) ● institution (electronic only - add $20 if outside U.S.), $128 (annual). **Staff:** 2. **Budget:** $140,000. **Description:** Aims to encourage a broader interest in professional history and to stimulate national interest in public history by promoting its use at all levels of society. (Public history deals with nonacademic history. History is brought to the public rather than the classroom through museum work, public displays, and federal, local, and corporate historians.) Serves as an information clearinghouse; sponsors training programs, local and regional colloquia, projects, and panels. Offers advice to departments of history, historical associations, and others seeking information on public history, professional standards, opportunities, and internships. Conducts surveys and analyses. **Awards:** G. Wesley Johnson Award. **Frequency:** annual. **Type:** recognition. **Recipient:** for best article in *The Public Historian* ● NCPH Book Award. **Frequency:** annual. **Type:** recognition. **Recipient:** for books about public history, including those that address the theory and/or practice of public history and books "growing out of" public history - such as the products of public history work, exhibition catalogs or an agency history ● New Professional Award. **Frequency:** annual. **Type:** recognition. **Recipient:** for new professional in the field of public history ● Robert Kelley Memorial Award. **Frequency:** annual. **Type:** recognition. **Recipient:** for outstanding contribution to the field of public history ● Student Project Award. **Frequency:** annual. **Type:** recognition. **Recipient:** for the best student project in public history. **Computer Services:** database, continuing education opportunity ● database, contract history services. **Telecommunication Services:** electronic mail, jdichtl@iupui.edu. **Com-**

mittees: Advocacy; Cultural Resource Management; Curriculum and Training; Electronic Communications and Publications; Endowment; History and the National Parks Collaboration; Pre-Collegiate Education. **Publications:** *Careers for Students of History*. Published in conjunction with American Historical Association. **Price:** $6.00 ● *Guide to Graduate Programs in Public History* ● *The Public Historian*, quarterly. Journal. Covers all aspects of public history including policy, archives, education, cultural resources management, and business history. **Price:** included in membership dues. ISSN: 0272-3433. **Circulation:** 1,500. **Advertising:** accepted ● *Public History News*, quarterly. Newsletter. Provides a historical understanding of contemporary issues, policies, problems, and trends. Provides information on NCPH activities. **Price:** included in membership dues. ISSN: 0891-2610. **Circulation:** 1,500. **Conventions/Meetings:** annual conference (exhibits) - always spring ● annual meeting.

10137 ■ New Canaan Historical Society (NCHS)

13 Oenoke Ridge
New Canaan, CT 06840
Ph: (203)966-1776
Fax: (203)972-5917
E-mail: newcanaan.historical@snet.net
URL: http://www.nchistory.org
Contact: Janet Lindstrom, Exec. Dir.

Founded: 1889. **Members:** 860. **Membership Dues:** individual, $35 (annual) ● family, $50 (annual) ● supporting, $100 (annual) ● sustaining, $250 (annual) ● patron, $500 (annual) ● benefactor, $1,000 (annual). **Staff:** 3. **Budget:** $296,000. **Description:** Individuals interested in the history of New Canaan, CT. Seeks to "bring together and arrange the historical events of the town of New Canaan and the genealogies of the families who have lived in town." Sponsors research and educational programs; serves as a clearinghouse on the history of New Canaan, CT; maintains six historical structures; operates museums within these structures. **Libraries: Type:** reference. **Holdings:** 5,000. **Subjects:** New Canaan and New England history, genealogy of New Canaan families, colonial architecture. **Publications:** Books, annual. Contains local history. **Conventions/Meetings:** annual Ice Cream Social - party and seminar, varied history exhibits (exhibits) - second Sunday in June.

10138 ■ Newcomen Society of the United States (NSUS)

211 Welsh Pool Rd., Ste.240
Exton, PA 19341-1321
Ph: (610)363-6600
Free: (800)466-7604
Fax: (610)363-0612
E-mail: info@newcomen.org
URL: http://www.newcomen.org
Contact: Jill R. Felix Colton, Pres./CEO

Founded: 1923. **Members:** 5,000. **Membership Dues:** individual, $125 (annual) ● institutional/corporate (contributing), $700 (annual) ● contributing, $150 (annual) ● sustaining, $625 (annual) ● special, $50 (annual) ● life, $1,200-$5,000 ● institutional/corporate (sustaining), $1,300 (annual). **Staff:** 7. **Description:** Business and professional people in education and industry in the United States and Canada. Studies material history, as distinguished from political history, in terms of the beginnings, growth, and contributions of industry, transportation, communication, mining, agriculture, banking, insurance, medicine, education, invention, law, and related historical fields. Maintains Thomas Newcomen Memorial Museum in Steam Technology and Industrial History in Chester County, PA. Society named for Thomas Newcomen (1663-1729), British pioneer who invented the first atmospheric steam engine. **Libraries: Type:** reference. **Holdings:** 3,000. **Subjects:** steam technology, industrial history. **Awards:** Harvard-Newcomen Postdoctoral Fellowship. **Frequency:** annual. **Type:** recognition. **Recipient:** for graduate students for essays and theses in industrial history and for proficiency in mathematics, chemistry, and physics ● Newcomen-Harvard Awards in Business History. **Frequency:** annual. **Type:** monetary. **Recipient:** for outstanding articles published in Business History Review. **Telecommunication Services:** electronic mail, jcolton@newcomen.org. **Also Known As:** American Newcomen. **Formerly:** (1982) Newcomen Society in North America. **Publications:** *Newcomen Now*, quarterly. Magazine. **Advertising:** accepted. Alternate Formats: online ● *1500 Corporate Histories*, semiannual. Newsletter ● Has issued more than 1400 studies of business, industrial, educational, and other institutions.

10139 ■ North American Society for Sport History (NASSH)

c/o Ronald A. Smith, Sec.-Treas.
PO Box 1026
121 Dale St.
Lemont, PA 16851-1026
E-mail: secretary-treasurer@nassh.org
URL: http://nassh.org
Contact: Mark Dyreson, Pres.

Founded: 1972. **Members:** 900. **Membership Dues:** regular, in U.S. and Canada, $50 (annual) ● regular, outside U.S. and Canada, $55 (annual) ● institution in U.S. and Canada, $70 (annual) ● institution outside U.S. and Canada, $75 (annual). **Budget:** $40,000. **Multinational. Description:** Individuals interested in sport history, social history, or physical education; research and general libraries; athletic clubs; halls of fame. Purposes are: to promote and stimulate study, research, and writing of the history of sport; to support and cooperate with local, national, and international organizations of similar purpose. **Libraries: Type:** reference. **Holdings:** archival material. **Awards:** NASSH Book Award. **Frequency:** annual. **Type:** monetary. **Recipient:** for the best sport history book; published in English the previous year ● NASSH Book Award - Anthology. **Frequency:** annual. **Type:** monetary. **Recipient:** for the best sport history book anthology; published in English the previous year ● NASSH Recognition Award. **Frequency:** annual. **Type:** recognition ● NASSH Service Award. **Frequency:** annual. **Type:** recognition. **Telecommunication Services:** electronic mail, president@nassh.org. **Publications:** *Directory of Scholars Identifying with the History of Sport*, periodic. Lists sport historians, their interests, addresses, email addresses, telephone numbers, and publications. **Circulation:** 900. **Advertising:** accepted ● *Journal of Sport History*, 3/year. Contains journal articles, book reviews, journal surveys, film, media, and museum reviews. ISSN: 0094-1700. **Circulation:** 900. **Advertising:** accepted ● Newsletter, periodic. Includes annual conference program, news, and future program information. **Circulation:** 900. **Advertising:** accepted ● Proceedings, annual. Contains annual conference proceedings, including abstracts of papers, books displayed, minutes of meetings, by-laws, and photos. ISSN: 0093-6235. **Circulation:** 900. **Advertising:** accepted. **Conventions/Meetings:** annual conference - always May.

10140 ■ Omohundro Institute of Early American History and Culture (OIEAHC)

PO Box 8781
Williamsburg, VA 23187-8781
Ph: (757)221-1114 (757)221-1110
Fax: (757)221-1047
E-mail: ieahc1@wm.edu
URL: http://oieahc.wm.edu
Contact: Ronald Hoffman, Dir.

Founded: 1943. **Membership Dues:** student, $25-$35 (annual) ● regular, $60-$84 (annual) ● contributing, $85-$99 (annual) ● perpetuating, $100-$149 (annual) ● supporting, $150-$249 (annual) ● sustaining, $250-$499 (annual) ● conserving, $500-$999 (annual) ● patron, $1,000 (annual). **Staff:** 15. **Description:** Seeks to further the study, research and publication about American history to the year 1815. Covers geographical scope of interest that reaches back into European and African origins and influences and also includes the imperial domains in North America. Awards postdoctoral fellowships. Sponsors and co-sponsors conferences on early American history. Cosponsored by The Colonial Williamsburg Foundation and the College of William and Mary, Williamsburg, VA. **Libraries: Type:** reference. **Holdings:** 7,480. **Subjects:** pre-1800 American newspapers, early American history and culture. **Awards:** Andrew W. Mellon Postdoctoral Research Fellowship. **Frequency:** annual. **Type:** fellowship. **Recipient:** for completion of revisions to first-book manuscript for publication by the institute ● Institute/NEH Postdoctoral Fellowship. **Frequency:** annual. **Type:** fellowship. **Recipient:** for the revision of dissertation into a significant first book to be published by the institute ● Jamestown Award. **Frequency:** periodic. **Type:** monetary. **Recipient:** for best first-book manuscript. **Formerly:** (1996) Institute of Early American History and Culture. **Publications:** *Uncommon Sense*, semiannual. Newsletter. **Price:** free to William and Mary Quarterly subscribers; $15.00/year to others. **Circulation:** 2,200. Alternate Formats: online ● *William and Mary Quarterly*. Journal ● Monographs, 3-4/year. **Conventions/Meetings:** The Atlantic World and Virginia - conference, in honor of David Beers Quinn ● annual conference.

10141 ■ Oral History Association (OHA)

c/o Madelyn Campbell, Exec. Sec.
Dickinson Coll.
PO Box 1773
Carlisle, PA 17013-2896
Ph: (717)245-1036 (804)752-3218
Fax: (717)245-1046
E-mail: oha@dickinson.edu
URL: http://www.dickinson.edu/oha
Contact: Alphine Jefferson, Pres.

Founded: 1966. **Members:** 1,400. **Membership Dues:** student, $35 (annual) ● regular, $65 (annual) ● contributing, $80 (annual) ● life, $500 ● regular institution, $116 (annual) ● sponsoring institution, $140 (annual). **Budget:** $104,000. **Regional Groups:** 5. **State Groups:** 5. **Local Groups:** 1. **Description:** Historians, medical scholars, archivists, librarians, authors, oral history interviewers, and editors, directors, and their institutions. Membership figure includes 140 institutions. Works to: foster the growth of oral history and the exchange of information on practical and intellectual problems connected therewith; encourage the use of oral history materials; improve techniques. (Oral history involves recording, transcribing, and preserving conversations with persons who have participated in important political, cultural, economic, and social developments in modern times, for use by historians, biographers, teachers, and students.). **Awards:** Elizabeth B. Mason Project Award. **Frequency:** biennial. **Type:** recognition. **Recipient:** to an outstanding oral history project ● Martha Rose Teaching Award. **Frequency:** biennial. **Type:** recognition. **Recipient:** to a distinguished primary or secondary school teacher ● Outstanding Article. **Frequency:** biennial. **Type:** recognition. **Recipient:** to a published article or essay that uses oral history ● Outstanding Book. **Frequency:** biennial. **Type:** recognition. **Recipient:** to a published book that uses oral history ● Outstanding Postsecondary Teaching. **Frequency:** biennial. **Type:** recognition. **Recipient:** to a distinguished postsecondary educator ● Outstanding Use of Oral History in a Nonprint Format. **Frequency:** biennial. **Type:** recognition. **Recipient:** to a film, video, performance pieces, radio program or series, exhibition, or drama that uses oral history. **Telecommunication Services:** electronic mail, awjefferson@rmc.edu. **Publications:** *Oral History and the Law*. Pamphlet. Provides an introduction to the many legal issues relating to oral history practice. **Price:** $15.00 ● *Oral History Evaluation Guidelines*. Booklet. Outlines professional standards for the practice of oral history. **Price:** $5.00/copy ● *Oral History for the Family Historian: A Basic Guide*. Pamphlet. **Price:** $15.00 ● *Oral History in the Secondary School Classroom* ● *Oral History Review*, semiannual. Journal. **Price:** included in membership dues; $34.00/copy for nonmembers student/individual; $69.00/copy for nonmembers institution. ISSN: 0094-0798 ● *Using Oral History in Community History Projects*. Pamphlet. Offers concrete suggestions for planning, organizing, and undertaking oral history in community settings. **Price:** $4.00 available in photocopy ● Newsletter, 3/year. Includes book reviews and research updates. **Price:** included in membership dues; $3.00/back issue. ISSN: 0474-

3253. **Circulation:** 1,900. Alternate Formats: microform. **Conventions/Meetings:** annual meeting (exhibits) - 2008 Oct. 15-18, Pittsburgh, PA.

10142 ■ Organization of American Historians (OAH)

PO Box 5457
Bloomington, IN 47407-5457
Ph: (812)855-9852 (812)855-7311
Fax: (812)855-0696
E-mail: oah@oah.org
URL: http://www.oah.org
Contact: Lee W. Formwalt, Exec. Dir.

Founded: 1907. **Members:** 12,000. **Membership Dues:** dual, $40 (annual) ● student, $35 (annual) ● history educator, $50 (annual) ● emeritus/retired, $50 (annual) ● associate, $55 (annual) ● contributing, $250 (annual) ● regular (based on income), $40-$190 (annual). **Staff:** 26. **Budget:** $2,000,000. **Description:** Professional historians, including college faculty members, secondary school teachers, graduate students, and other individuals in related fields; institutional subscribers are college, university, high school and public libraries, and historical agencies. Promotes historical research and study. Sponsors 12 prize programs for historical writing; maintains speakers' bureau. Conducts educational programs. **Awards:** ABC-CLIO America: History and Life Award. **Type:** monetary. **Recipient:** for scholarship in American history ● Erik Barnouw Award. **Type:** recognition. **Recipient:** for outstanding reporting or programming on network or cable television. **Computer Services:** Mailing lists, of members. **Boards:** Executive; Journal of American History; Magazine of History; OAH Newsletter. **Committees:** Community Colleges; Employment of Part-Time and Adjunct Faculty; Historians and Archivists; History Teaching Alliance; National Historical Publication and Records Commission; National Park Service; Program; Public History; Research and Access to Historical Documentation; Status of ALANA History and ALANA Historians; Status of Women in the Historical Profession; Teaching. **Affiliated With:** American Council of Learned Societies; National Coalition for History; National History Day. **Formerly:** (1965) Mississippi Valley Historical Association. **Publications:** *Journal of American History*, quarterly. Covers various areas of American history including oral history, museum exhibits, book and film reviews. **Price:** $275.00 /year for institutions. ISSN: 0021-8723. **Circulation:** 12,000. **Advertising:** accepted ● *OAH Magazine of History*, quarterly. Covers scholarships, lesson plans, feature articles, and news of the profession for teachers of history and social studies. **Price:** $25.00 for nonmembers; $15.00 for members. ISSN: 0882-228X. **Advertising:** accepted ● *OAH Newsletter*, quarterly. Covers news of the organization and the profession. **Price:** included in membership dues. ISSN: 0196-3341. **Conventions/Meetings:** annual conference (exhibits) - 2009 Mar. 26-29, Seattle, WA; 2010 Apr. 7-10, Washington, DC; 2011 Mar. 17-20, Houston, TX.

10143 ■ Peace History Society (PHS)

c/o Christy Snider, Treas.
Dept. of History
Berry Coll.
5010 Mt. Berry Sta.
Mount Berry, GA 30149
Ph: (706)368-5652
E-mail: csnider@berry.edu
URL: http://www.peacehistorysociety.org
Contact: Scott H. Bennett, Pres.

Founded: 1964. **Members:** 330. **Membership Dues:** regular, $40 (annual) ● student, retired, unemployed, $25 (annual) ● institutional, $45 (annual) ● sustaining, $55 (annual) ● life, $350. **Description:** Historians and others interested in peace research. Seeks to encourage historical research to clarify the causes of international peace and difficulties in creating it. Members are individually engaged in research on: the history of peace, peacemaking, disarmament, pacifism, and peace movements; origins and dynamics of war; war endings and crises resolved without war; dilemmas of power and law in United States foreign policy; internationalism; other historical subjects relating to problems of securing or maintaining peace. **Awards:** DeBenedetti Prize. **Frequency:** biennial. **Type:** monetary. **Recipient:** to the best journal article in English on peace history topic ● Scott Bills Memorial Prize. **Frequency:** biennial. **Type:** monetary. **Recipient:** for an outstanding English-language work in the field of peace history. **Committees:** Charles DeBenedetti Prize; Nominations. **Affiliated With:** American Historical Association; United Nations. **Absorbed:** Society for the Study of Internationalism. **Formerly:** Council on Peace Research in History. **Publications:** *Biographical Dictionary of Modern Peace Leaders* ● *Peace and Change: A Journal of Peace Research*, quarterly. Publishes scholarly and interpretive articles on the achievement of a peaceful, just, and humane society. **Price:** $69.00 /year for members; $86.00 /year for nonmembers; $339.00 /year for institutions. ISSN: 0149-0508. **Circulation:** 1,500 ● *PHS News*, 2-3/year. Newsletter. Carries updates of interest to members. Alternate Formats: online. **Conventions/Meetings:** annual board meeting, in conjunction with American Historical Association (winter) ● biennial conference, covering different aspects of peace history.

10144 ■ Pearl Harbor History Associates (PHHA)

PO Box 1007
Stratford, CT 06615
Ph: (203)378-2353
URL: http://www.pearlharbor-history.org
Contact: Ernest Arroyo, Pres.

Founded: 1982. **Members:** 300. **Membership Dues:** general, $10 (annual) ● sustaining, $100 (annual). **Description:** Historians, teachers, students, and others with an interest in the history of World War II. Aims to educate, research, and promulgate historical data regarding the Japanese attack on Pearl Harbor on Dec. 7, 1941. Compiles statistics. Maintains speaker's bureau; conducts educational programs. **Libraries:** **Type:** reference. **Holdings:** 300; archival material, books, clippings, monographs, periodicals. **Subjects:** Pearl Harbor attack, the Pacific War, ships' histories. **Publications:** *Air Raid, Pearl Harbor - This is Not a Drill!*. Book. Includes map with ship locations on December 7, 1941. **Price:** $6.00 plus shipping and handling ($1.50) ● *East Wind Rain - A Pictorial History of the Attack on Pearl Harbor*. Book. **Price:** $16.95 plus shipping and handling ($3.50) ● *The Newsletter*, 3/year. **Price:** included in membership dues. **Circulation:** 350. **Advertising:** accepted ● *Pearl Harbor Collector's set - The Pearl Harbor Story*. Brochure. Contains 25 2-sided 5x7 cards. **Price:** $9.95 plus shipping and handling ($2.50) ● *Remembering Pearl Harbor*. Brochure. Includes facts, statistics, and data. **Price:** free. **Circulation:** 60,000. **Conventions/Meetings:** annual board meeting (exhibits) ● annual lecture (exhibits).

10145 ■ Pony Express Historical Association (PEHA)

1202 Penn St.
PO Box 1022
St. Joseph, MO 64502
Ph: (816)232-8206
Fax: (816)232-3717
E-mail: patee@ponyexpress.net
URL: http://stjoseph.net/ponyexpress
Contact: Gary Chilcote, Museum Dir.

Founded: 1964. **Members:** 425. **Membership Dues:** regular, $10 (annual) ● corporate, $30 (annual) ● associate, $50 (annual) ● sponsor, $100 (annual) ● life, $500 ● sustaining, $25 (annual) ● junior (under 16), $5 (annual). **Staff:** 10. **Budget:** $150,000. **Description:** Individuals interested in the history of St. Joseph, MO. Supports and operates the Patee House Museum, a national landmark which served as headquarters for the Pony Express in 1860, and the Jesse James Home, the site where the outlaw was killed. Maintains restored 1917 Oriental Tea House and ice cream parlor. Researches history of the Pony Express and Jesse James (1860-1882). Helps National Pony Express Association stage annual Pony Express Rerun between St. Joseph and Sacramento, CA. Presents new exhibit, a 1941 vintage, and operating carousel. **Libraries:** **Type:** reference. **Holdings:** 4,887; periodicals. **Subjects:** bound volumes of *St. Joseph News-Press and Gazette* 1903-1950, local history. **Also Known As:** Patee House Museum. **Publications:** *Pony Express Mail*, monthly. Newsletter. Contains information on the Patee House Museum and the Jesse James Home. **Price:** included in membership dues. **Circulation:** 400. **Conventions/Meetings:** annual meeting, held in conjunction with the National Pony Express Association - last weekend in September ● annual Pony Express Rerun - meeting (exhibits) - usually 2nd week in June.

10146 ■ Public Works Historical Society (PWHS)

c/o American Public Works Association
2345 Grand Blvd., Ste.700
Kansas City, MO 64108
Ph: (816)472-6100 (816)595-5224
Free: (800)848-APWA
Fax: (816)472-1610
E-mail: thon@apwa.net
URL: http://www.apwa.net/about/sig/pwhs
Contact: Ms. Teresa Hon, Staff Liaison

Founded: 1975. **Members:** 420. **Membership Dues:** individual, $35 (annual) ● individual, C$52 (annual). **Staff:** 2. **Description:** Individuals, corporations, and institutions united to promote public understanding of the role of public works in the growth and development of civilization through the collection, preservation, and dissemination of public works history. Documents and recognizes the achievements of the public works profession. Fosters scholarly research and publication; promotes collaboration among public works officials, historians, and educators; maintains bibliography of public works history; recognizes and encourages the preservation of historically significant public works; collects and preserves records of selected individuals and groups involved in public works activities; finds suitable repositories in which such records can be preserved, processed, and made available to scholars. Has developed an oral history program. **Libraries:** **Type:** by appointment only. **Holdings:** 2; articles, audio recordings, books, business records, periodicals. **Subjects:** politics, history. **Awards:** Abel Wolman Award. **Frequency:** annual. **Type:** monetary. **Recipient:** for historians whose research and publications have made outstanding contribution to the history of public works ● Michael Robinson Award. **Frequency:** annual. **Type:** monetary. **Recipient:** for the best essay or article published in the field of public works history. **Telecommunication Services:** electronic mail, keyre@greeley-hansen.com. **Affiliated With:** American Public Works Association. **Publications:** *An Interview With (Oral History)*, annual. Books. **Price:** $12.00 for members; $15.00 for nonmembers ● *Essay Series*, annual. Books. Provides a forum for historians and practitioners to publish historical papers on public works topics. **Price:** cost varies per title, members receive discount. **Circulation:** 500 ● *Public Works History*, 3/year. Newsletter. **Price:** included in membership dues; $35.00 for nonmembers. **Circulation:** 500. Alternate Formats: online. **Conventions/Meetings:** annual meeting, held in conjunction with International Public Works Congress and Equipment Show.

10147 ■ Quiet Valley Living Historical Farm (QVLHF)

1000 Turkey Hill Rd.
Stroudsburg, PA 18360
Ph: (570)992-6161
Fax: (570)992-9587
E-mail: farm@quietvalley.org
URL: http://www.quietvalley.org
Contact: Kenneth Lee, Pres.

Founded: 1971. **Members:** 1,200. **Membership Dues:** individual, $20 (annual) ● junior, $10 (annual) ● senior, $15 (annual) ● family, $50 (annual) ● contributing, $75 (annual) ● sustaining, $125 (annual) ● donor, $500 (annual) ● life, $1,000. **Budget:** $177,700. **Description:** Individuals interested in education, history, and family activities. Seeks to demonstrate how families lived on Pennsylvania

Dutch farms in the 18th and 19th centuries; operates the Quiet Valley Living Historical Farm. Although members are concentrated in Pennsylvania, membership is open to interested individuals nationwide. **Formerly:** (1998) Historical Farm Association. **Publications:** *The Roosters Tale*, 5/year. Newsletter. **Price:** included in membership dues. **Conventions/Meetings:** annual dinner.

10148 ■ Ranching Heritage Association (RHA)
c/o Whitney Barron, Business Mgr.
PO Box 43201
Lubbock, TX 79409-3201
Ph: (806)742-0497
E-mail: whitney.barron@ttu.edu
URL: http://www.depts.ttu.edu/ranchhc/body_rha.htm
Contact: Whitney Barron, Business Mgr.
Founded: 1969. **Members:** 680. **Membership Dues:** individual in U.S., $30 (annual) ● corporate, $500 (annual) ● family, individual outside U.S., $50 (annual) ● patron, $250 (annual) ● Society of the Brand, $1,000 (annual) ● Junior Rough Rider, $15 (annual). **Staff:** 2. **Description:** Individuals and businesses interested in promoting the history and heritage of ranching in the US. Preserves historical buildings and sites. Maintains the Ranching Heritage Center. Operates speakers' bureau. **Awards:** National Golden Spur Award. **Frequency:** annual. **Type:** recognition. **Recipient:** for lifetime contribution to ranching and livestock industry. **Boards:** Overseers. **Committees:** Executive. **Formerly:** Ranch Headquarters Association. **Publications:** *Ranch Record*, quarterly. Magazine. Features ranching heritage and special activities. **Price:** included in membership dues ● Brochures. **Conventions/Meetings:** annual meeting - every fall.

10149 ■ Social Welfare History Group (SWHG)
c/o Iris Carlton-LaNey, Pres.
Univ. of North Carolina at Chapel Hill
School of Social Work
CB No. 3550
301 Pittsboro St.
Chapel Hill, NC 27516
Ph: (919)962-6536
Fax: (919)962-7557
E-mail: ibc9717@email.unc.edu
URL: http://depts.washington.edu/sswweb/swhg/index.html
Contact: Iris Carlton-LaNey, Pres.
Founded: 1956. **Members:** 262. **Membership Dues:** regular, $20 (annual) ● student/retired, $10 (annual) ● contributing, $25 (annual). **Description:** Historians, social workers, and others interested in research, teaching, and preservation of the history and historical records of social welfare. Holds program meetings in conjunction with Council on Social Work Education and other historical associations. **Affiliated With:** Council on Social Work Education. **Formerly:** Committee on the History of Social Welfare. **Publications:** *Social Welfare History Group Newsletter*, triennial. Includes annual bibliography. **Price:** included in membership dues. **Conventions/Meetings:** annual conference and meeting, held in conjunction with Council on Social Work Education (exhibits) - usually in March.

10150 ■ Society of Architectural Historians (SAH)
1365 N Astor St.
Chicago, IL 60610-2144
Ph: (312)573-1365
Fax: (312)573-1141
E-mail: info@sah.org
URL: http://www.sah.org
Contact: Pauline Saliga, Exec. Dir.
Founded: 1940. **Members:** 3,600. **Membership Dues:** student, $45 (annual) ● individual, $115 (annual) ● joint, $155 (annual) ● patron, $350 (annual) ● supporting, $175 (annual) ● donor, $500 (annual) ● life, $2,500 ● benefactor, $7,500 ● institutional - active, $300 (annual) ● institutional - sustaining, $400 (annual) ● institutional - corporate, $1,000 (annual). **Staff:** 6. **Local Groups:** 27. **Description:** Architects and city planners, educators, scholars, libraries, historical societies, interior designers, museum personnel, students, and others interested in architecture. Promotes the preservation of buildings of historical and aesthetic significance. Encourages scholarly research in the field. Conducts tours in the U.S. and abroad. **Libraries: Type:** reference; not open to the public. **Holdings:** 200; books. **Subjects:** architecture, landscape design. **Awards:** Alice Davis Hitchcock Book Award. **Frequency:** annual. **Type:** recognition. **Recipient:** for the most distinguished work of scholarship in the history of architecture ● Antoinette Forrester Downing Award. **Type:** recognition. **Recipient:** for excellence in published architectural surveys ● Carroll L.V. Meeks Fellowship. **Frequency:** annual. **Type:** scholarship. **Recipient:** for an outstanding student to participate in the annual SAH domestic tour ● The Edilia de Montequin Fellowship. **Frequency:** annual. **Type:** fellowship. **Recipient:** for travel costs associated with research on Iberian and Latin American architecture ● Founders' Award. **Frequency:** annual. **Type:** recognition. **Recipient:** for the best article on the history of architecture published each year in the Journal of the Society of Architectural Historians by a young scholar ● George R. Collins Memorial Fund Travel Stipends. **Frequency:** annual. **Type:** grant. **Recipient:** for a foreign speaker to attend the annual meeting ● Keepers Preservation Education Fund Fellowship. **Frequency:** annual. **Type:** fellowship. **Recipient:** for a student in historic preservation to attend the annual meeting ● Philip Johnson Award. **Frequency:** annual. **Type:** recognition. **Recipient:** for excellence in published exhibition catalogues ● Rosann Berry Fellowship. **Frequency:** annual. **Type:** fellowship. **Recipient:** for a student engaged in advanced graduate study to attend the annual meeting of the Society of Architectural Historians ● Spiro Kostof Book Award for Architecture and Urbanism Citation. **Frequency:** annual. **Type:** recognition. **Recipient:** to a publication providing the greatest contribution to the understanding of the physical environment. **Computer Services:** Mailing lists, of members. **Committees:** Book Awards; Chapters; Development; Education; Electronic Media; Investment; Nominating; Preservation; Publications; Standing; Study Tours. **Publications:** *Buildings of Alaska*. Book ● *Buildings of Colorado*. Book ● *Buildings of Iowa*. Book ● *Buildings of Michigan*. Book ● *Buildings of the United States*. Book ● *Buildings of Washington D.C.*. Book ● *Journal of the Society of Architectural Historians*, quarterly. Covers architectural and art history. Includes information on awards and book reviews. **Price:** included in membership dues. ISSN: 0037-9808. **Circulation:** 3,600. **Advertising:** accepted. Alternate Formats: online. Also Cited As: *JSAH* ● *Newsletter of the Society of Architectural Historians*, bimonthly. Provides information on national and international architecture schools, courses, conferences, exhibitions, and tours. Includes bibliography. **Price:** included in membership dues. **Circulation:** 3,600. **Advertising:** accepted. Alternate Formats: online ● *Society of Architectural Historians—The Forum*, semiannual. Newsletter. Provides articles on historic preservation of architecture. **Price:** included in membership dues. **Circulation:** 3,600 ● Also publishes occasional tour guides. **Conventions/Meetings:** annual meeting (exhibits) - usually April.

10151 ■ Society of Civil War Historians
Dept. of History
Florida Atlantic Univ.
Boca Raton, FL 33431
Ph: (561)297-2621
Fax: (561)297-2704
E-mail: engle@fau.edu
Contact: Stephen D. Engle, Exec. Treas.
Founded: 1984. **Members:** 250. **Membership Dues:** regular, $10 (annual). **Staff:** 1. **Description:** Individuals interested in the Civil War. Fosters the teaching of Civil War history. **Publications:** Newsletter, quarterly. **Price:** included in membership dues. **Circulation:** 250. **Conventions/Meetings:** annual conference.

10152 ■ Society for the Comparative Study of Society and History (CSSH)
c/o Dr. David Akin, Managing Ed.
Univ. of Michigan
1007 E Huron
Ann Arbor, MI 48109-1690
Ph: (734)764-6362
Fax: (734)647-2105
E-mail: cssh@umich.edu
URL: http://www.lsa.umich.edu/history/cssh
Contact: Dr. David Akin, Managing Ed.
Founded: 1958. **Staff:** 6. **Description:** Participants include social scientists and historians. Its journal serves as a forum for debate among historians, social scientists, and humanists and for presentation of significant new research. **Telecommunication Services:** electronic mail, csshwebadmin@umich.edu. **Publications:** *Book Series*, periodic. Books ● *Comparative Studies in Society and History*, quarterly. Journal. Includes book series containing information on research in social sciences. **Price:** $49.00 /year for individuals; $119.00 /year for institutions (online only); $133.00 /year for institutions (print and online); $12.00/article. ISSN: 0010-4175. **Advertising:** accepted. **Conventions/Meetings:** periodic conference.

10153 ■ Society for Coptic Archaeology (North America)
914 E Lemon St., Ste.108
Tempe, AZ 85281
Ph: (480)731-3201
E-mail: haflele@imap4.asu.edu
Contact: Leslie MacCoull, Contact
Founded: 1984. **Staff:** 1. **Description:** Scholars, teachers, and researchers. Promotes the study, research, and teaching of Coptic language, literature, history, and culture. Provides a forum for discussion of work in progress; facilitates the coordination of research projects between members and scholars in related disciplines. **Publications:** Monographs, periodic. **Conventions/Meetings:** quadrennial meeting, held in conjunction with the International Congress of Coptic Studies.

10154 ■ Society of Dance History Scholars (SDHS)
3416 Primm Ln.
Birmingham, AL 35216
Ph: (205)978-1404
Fax: (205)823-2760
E-mail: sdhs@primemanagement.net
URL: http://www.sdhs.org
Contact: Ginnine Cocuzza, Treas.
Founded: 1983. **Members:** 500. **Membership Dues:** regular, in U.S., $75 (annual) ● regular, in Canada and Mexico, $83 (annual) ● regular, outside North America, $87 (annual) ● student in U.S., $40 (annual) ● student in Canada and Mexico, $48 (annual) ● student outside North America, $52 (annual) ● retired/senior in U.S., $45 (annual) ● retired/senior in Canada and Mexico, $53 (annual) ● retired/senior outside North America, $57 (annual) ● institution in U.S., $130 (annual) ● institution in Canada and Mexico, $138 (annual) ● institution outside North America, $142 (annual) ● benefactor in U.S., $500 (annual) ● benefactor in Canada and Mexico, $508 (annual) ● benefactor outside North America, $512 (annual). **Description:** Scholars, writers, and teachers in the field of dance. Dedicated to historical research in dance. **Awards:** Gertrude Lippincott Award. **Frequency:** annual. **Type:** recognition. **Recipient:** for best English language article of the year on dance, dance history, or theory ● Selma Jeanne Cohen Award. **Frequency:** annual. **Type:** scholarship. **Recipient:** to graduate students for dance history and related subjects including aesthetics and philosophy. **Working Groups:** Dance History Teachers; Early Dance; Ethnicity and Dance; Reconstruction; Strategies for Doctoral Education; Students in SDHS. **Formerly:** (1983) Dance History Scholars. **Publications:** *Society of Dance History Scholars—Newsletter*, semiannual. **Price:** included in membership dues. **Advertising:** accepted ● *Society of Dance History Scholars—Proceedings*, annual. **Price:** free for members; $20.00 for nonmembers ● *Studies in Dance History*, semiannual, every spring and autumn. Monographs. **Price:** free for members; $45.00 /year for nonmembers ● Membership Directory, annual, usually in autumn. **Price:** included in membership dues ● Also publishes membership list. **Conventions/Meetings:** annual conference and lecture,

paper presentations, demonstrations, and movement workshops - usually February or June.

10155 ■ Society for French Historical Studies (SFHS)
c/o Jeremy D. Popkin, Exec. Dir.
Univ. of Kentucky
Dept. of History, 1725 POT
Lexington, KY 40506-0027
Ph: (859)335-6254
E-mail: popkin@uky.edu
URL: http://www.h-france.net/sfhs/sfhshome.html
Contact: Jeremy D. Popkin, Exec. Dir.
Founded: 1956. **Members:** 1,450. **Membership Dues:** individual, $35 (annual) ● student/retiree, $18 (annual). **Staff:** 1. **Description:** Professional historians and people interested in French history. Seeks to further the study of French history in the United States and Canada. **Awards:** David Pinkney Prize. **Frequency:** annual. **Type:** monetary. **Recipient:** for the best book on French history by a citizen of the United States or Canada or an author with a full-time appointment at U.S. or Canadian college or university ● Gilbert Chinard Prize. **Frequency:** annual. **Type:** monetary. **Recipient:** for distinguished scholarly books in the history of themes shared by France and North, Central, and South America ● John B. and Theta H. Wolf Travel Fellowship. **Frequency:** annual. **Type:** monetary. **Recipient:** for research travel ● Marjorie M. Farrar Award. **Frequency:** annual. **Type:** monetary. **Recipient:** to a doctoral student in French history at a North American university to support work on an outstanding dissertation in progress ● Research-Travel Award. **Frequency:** annual. **Type:** monetary. **Recipient:** for a scholarly work in progress ● William Koren, Jr. Prize. **Frequency:** annual. **Type:** monetary. **Recipient:** to the outstanding journal article on any era in French history by a North American author in an American, European, or a Canadian journal. **Publications:** *French Historical Studies*, quarterly. Journal. **Price:** included in membership dues. ISSN: 0016-1071. **Advertising:** accepted. **Conventions/Meetings:** annual conference (exhibits) - every spring.

10156 ■ Society for Historians of American Foreign Relations (SHAFR)
Dept. of History
Ohio State Univ.
106 Dulles Hall
230 W 17th Ave.
Columbus, OH 43210
Ph: (614)292-1951 (614)292-7200
Fax: (614)292-2282
E-mail: shafr@osu.edu
URL: http://www.shafr.org
Contact: Richard H. Immerman, Pres.
Founded: 1967. **Members:** 1,650. **Membership Dues:** regular, $50 (annual) ● student, unemployed, $20 (annual). **Description:** Professional scholars and others interested in the historical approach to American diplomatic history and foreign relations in general. Membership is open to anyone, including diplomatic historians of other countries. Fosters study of diplomatic history through cooperation with the National Archives and other federal agencies. Sponsors programs and meetings of the American Historical Association and the Organization of American Historians. **Awards:** Betty M. Unterberger Dissertation Prize. **Frequency:** biennial. **Type:** recognition. **Recipient:** for a graduate student with distinguished research and writing in the field of diplomatic history ● Michael J. Hogan Fellowship. **Frequency:** annual. **Type:** fellowship. **Recipient:** for a graduate student member of SHAFR ● Norman and Laura Graebner Award. **Frequency:** biennial. **Type:** recognition. **Recipient:** for a senior historian of United States foreign relations ● Robert H. Ferrell Book Prize. **Frequency:** annual. **Type:** recognition. **Recipient:** for a distinguished scholar in the history of American foreign relations ● Stuart L. Bernath Book Prize. **Frequency:** annual. **Type:** recognition. **Recipient:** for best book and article ● Stuart L. Bernath Dissertation Grant. **Frequency:** annual. **Type:** grant. **Recipient:** for a doctoral student who is a member of SHAFR ● Stuart L. Bernath Lecture Prize. **Frequency:** annual. **Type:** recognition. **Recipient:** for a young scholar with excellence in teaching and research in the field of foreign relations ● Stuart L. Bernath Scholarly Article Prize. **Frequency:** annual. **Type:** recognition. **Recipient:** for a young scholar with distinguished research and writing in the field of diplomatic relations. **Affiliated With:** American Historical Association; Organization of American Historians. **Publications:** *Diplomatic History*, quarterly. Journal. Covers American foreign relations; contains scholarly articles and reviews. **Price:** included in membership dues. **Circulation:** 2,450. **Advertising:** accepted ● *Guide to American Foreign Relations* ● *Passport*, quarterly. Newsletter. Contains personal notices, publication announcements, calls for papers employment advertisements, fellowship notices and obituaries. ● *Roster and Research List*, biennial. **Conventions/Meetings:** annual Bernath Memorial Lecture ● annual conference.

10157 ■ Society for Historians of the Early American Republic (SHEAR)
3355 Woodland Walk
Philadelphia, PA 19104-4531
Ph: (215)746-5393
Fax: (215)573-3391
E-mail: info@shear.org
URL: http://www.shear.org
Contact: Amy L. Baxter-Bellamy, Exec. Coor.
Founded: 1977. **Members:** 1,100. **Membership Dues:** student, $30 (annual) ● individual (with $45,000 income or less), $40 (annual) ● individual (with above $45,000 income), $70 (annual) ● institution, $110 (annual). **Staff:** 3. **Budget:** $78,000. **Description:** Represents individuals interested in the study of U.S. history between 1789-1848. **Awards:** Ralph Gray Article Prize. **Frequency:** annual. **Type:** monetary. **Recipient:** for best article in the Journal of Early Republic ● SHEAR Book Prizes. **Frequency:** annual. **Type:** monetary. **Computer Services:** Mailing lists, of members. **Publications:** *Journal of the Early Republic*, quarterly. Covers early American history. Includes book reviews and recent dissertations. **Price:** included in membership dues; $60.00 /year for institutions. ISSN: 0275-1275. **Circulation:** 1,100. **Advertising:** accepted. **Conventions/Meetings:** annual conference (exhibits) - always July. 2008 July 17-20, Philadelphia, PA.

10158 ■ Society for the History of Discoveries (SHD)
c/o George Chalou, Treas.
3348 Sheffield Ct.
Falls Church, VA 22042
Ph: (612)788-6570
Fax: (612)626-9353
E-mail: chalou@erols.com
URL: http://www.sochistdisc.org
Contact: Ralph E. Ehrenberg, Pres.
Founded: 1960. **Members:** 290. **Membership Dues:** regular, $30 (annual) ● contributing, $50 (annual) ● student/retiree, $15 (annual). **Staff:** 10. **Multinational. Description:** College and university professors, librarians, antiquarians and others who are interested in the history of geographical exploration. Seeks to stimulate interest in teaching, research, and publishing in the history of geographical exploration. Initiative for the organization grew out of the International Congress for the History of Discoveries, held in Lisbon, Portugal, in 1960. Concentrates on the expansion of Europe, including the allied fields of cartography, economic expansion, geographic thought, and beginnings of colonialism, to the extent that these subjects pertain to the age of discoveries. **Libraries: Type:** reference. **Holdings:** articles. **Awards:** Essay Contest. **Frequency:** annual. **Type:** monetary. **Recipient:** for students. **Telecommunication Services:** electronic mail, goodwin@uta.edu. **Affiliated With:** American Historical Association. **Publications:** *Terra Cognita*, annual. Newsletter. Alternate Formats: online ● *Terrae Incognitae: The Journal for the History of Discoveries*, annual. **Price:** $30.00 /year for members and institutions, in U.S. and Canada; $35.00 /year for members and institutions, outside U.S. and Canada. ISSN: 0082-2884. Alternate Formats: online ● Annual Report, annual ● Membership Directory, annual ● Monograph. **Conventions/Meetings:** annual conference - usually fall.

10159 ■ Society for History in the Federal Government (SHFG)
Box 14139
Benjamin Franklin Sta.
Washington, DC 20044
Ph: (301)451-4344 (301)402-6134
E-mail: foxbro@mail.nih.gov
URL: http://www.shfg.org
Contact: John W. Roberts, Pres.
Founded: 1979. **Members:** 250. **Membership Dues:** sustaining, $75 (annual) ● patron, institutional, $100 (annual) ● student, $20 (annual) ● retired, $25 (annual) ● regular, $35 (annual). **Description:** Public and private historians, archivists, curators, editors, consultants, and preservationists. Seeks to promote and foster historical and archival activities of the U.S. government. Provides a forum for professionals concerned with the practice of history in the branches of the federal system. Coordinates activities with other groups. **Awards:** Charles Thomson Prizes. **Frequency:** annual. **Type:** recognition. **Recipient:** for excellence in an article or essay that deals with any aspect of the federal government's history written in or for a federal history program ● Franklin Delano Roosevelt Prize. **Frequency:** triennial. **Type:** recognition. **Recipient:** for outstanding contributions to the study of federal government history ● George Pendleton Prizes. **Frequency:** annual. **Type:** recognition. **Recipient:** for an outstanding major publication, on the federal government's history produced by or for a federal history program ● Henry Adams Prize. **Frequency:** annual. **Type:** recognition. **Recipient:** for a superior book length narrative history ● James Madison Prize. **Frequency:** annual. **Type:** recognition. **Recipient:** for a distinguished article ● John Wesley Powell Prize. **Frequency:** annual. **Type:** recognition. **Recipient:** for historical preservation or historical display ● Maryellen Trautman Award. **Type:** recognition. **Recipient:** for outstanding service to the society ● Thomas Jefferson Prize. **Frequency:** annual. **Type:** recognition. **Recipient:** for documentary editions and reference material. **Computer Services:** Mailing lists, of members. **Telecommunication Services:** electronic mail, rothfea@mail.nih.gov. **Committees:** Membership; Professional Development; Program; Publications. **Affiliated With:** American Historical Association. **Publications:** *Directory of Federal Historical Programs and Activities*, periodic. Serves as a reference guide. **Price:** included in membership dues; $24.00 for nonmembers. ISSN: 1048-0110. **Circulation:** 500 ● *The Federalist*, quarterly. Newsletter. Prints news of recent activities of the society, its membership, and of important issues affecting federal history programs. ● *Historical Programs in the Federal Government: A Guide, 1998*. Alternate Formats: online ● Bulletin, monthly. Alternate Formats: online. **Conventions/Meetings:** annual conference (exhibits) - always March/April ● annual dinner - always fall ● annual Members Reception - meeting - always December.

10160 ■ Society for the History of Technology (SHOT)
618 Ross Hall
Dept. of History
Iowa State Univ.
Ames, IA 50011
Ph: (515)294-8469
Fax: (515)294-6390
E-mail: shot@iastate.edu
URL: http://www.historyoftechnology.org
Contact: Dr. Amy Bix, Sec.
Founded: 1958. **Members:** 1,800. **Membership Dues:** individual, $50 (annual) ● institution, $130 (annual) ● student, $30 (annual) ● emeritus, $40 (annual). **Staff:** 1. **Multinational. Description:** Academicians in science, engineering, history, sociology, economics, and anthropology; practicing engineers, industrialists, institutions, libraries, and museums. Promotes the study of the development of technology and its relations with society and culture. Cooperates with other societies and professional organizations in arranging educational programs on the history of

technology. Sponsors special interest groups in numerous technological fields. Encourages preservation of technological artifacts and documents. **Awards:** Abbott Payson Usher Prize. **Frequency:** annual. **Type:** recognition. **Recipient:** to the best publication by the society ● Brooke Hindle Postdoctoral Fellowship. **Frequency:** annual. **Type:** fellowship. **Recipient:** for the postdoctoral fellowship in history of technology ● DaVinci Medal. **Frequency:** annual. **Type:** medal. **Recipient:** for outstanding individual with great contribution to the history of technology, through research, teaching, publications, and other activities ● Dibner Prize. **Frequency:** annual. **Type:** recognition. **Recipient:** for excellence in museum exhibitry ● Edelstein Prize. **Frequency:** annual. **Type:** recognition. **Recipient:** for the author of an outstanding scholarly book on the history of technology ● Eugene S. Ferguson Prize. **Frequency:** biennial. **Type:** recognition. **Recipient:** for the outstanding reference work supporting scholarship in history of technology ● IEEE Life Members Prize. **Frequency:** annual. **Type:** recognition. **Recipient:** to the best paper in electrical history ● International Scholars. **Frequency:** annual. **Type:** recognition. **Recipient:** for non-U.S. scholars in history of technology ● Joan Cahalin Robinson Prize. **Frequency:** annual. **Type:** recognition. **Recipient:** to the best presented paper at the SHOT annual meeting ● Levinson Prize. **Frequency:** annual. **Type:** recognition. **Recipient:** to the best unpublished essay on the history of technology ● Melvin Kranzberg Dissertation Fellowship. **Frequency:** annual. **Type:** fellowship. **Recipient:** for doctoral student preparing dissertation on the history of technology ● Sally Hacker Prize. **Frequency:** annual. **Type:** recognition. **Recipient:** to the best popular book on the history of technology. **Computer Services:** Mailing lists, of members. **Committees:** Awards; Editorial; Education; Finance; International; International Scholars; Local Arrangements; Nominating; Program; Sites. **Affiliated With:** American Association for the Advancement of Science; American Council of Learned Societies; American Historical Association; International Committee for the History of Technology. **Publications:** *SHOT-AHA Booklet Series*, periodic. Booklets. Features various topics focusing on the history of technology. ● *SHOT Newsletter*, quarterly. Provides information on the development of technology and its relations with society and culture. **Price:** included in membership dues; $15.00 /year for nonmembers. **Circulation:** 1,800. **Advertising:** accepted ● *Technology and Culture*, quarterly. Journal. Covers the history of technological devices and processes as well as the relationship of technology to other aspects of the world. **Price:** included in membership dues; $37.00 /year for nonmembers; $85.00 /year for institutions. ISSN: 0040-165X. **Circulation:** 2,800. **Advertising:** accepted. Alternate Formats: microform ● Directory. **Conventions/Meetings:** annual conference (exhibits) - 2008 Oct. 9-12, Lisbon, Portugal ● periodic symposium, tackles topics relating to the history of technology.

10161 ■ Supreme Court Historical Society (SCHS)

Opperman House
224 E Capitol St. NE
Washington, DC 20003
Ph: (202)543-0400
Free: (888)539-4438
Fax: (202)547-7730
E-mail: micelischs@aol.com
URL: http://www.supremecourthistory.org
Contact: Frank G. Jones Esq., Pres.

Founded: 1974. **Members:** 4,200. **Membership Dues:** regular, gift, $50 (annual) ● contributing, $100 (annual) ● sustaining, $1,000 (annual) ● life, $5,000. **Staff:** 6. **Description:** Students, individuals, and libraries engaged in historical research and acquisition of memorabilia and artifacts concerning the history of the Supreme Court of the United States and the dissemination of such information to scholars, historians, and the public. Sponsors special research projects, including Documentary History of the Supreme Court 1789-1800 and Index of Opinions by Justice, which indexes each justice's written opinions and statements. Bestows triennial book prize. **Committees:** Acquisitions; Journal Board of Editors; Student Chapters. **Publications:** *Annual Lecture Reprints* ● *SCHS Journal of Supreme Court History*, 3/year. **Price:** $20.00. **Circulation:** 5,000 ● Annual Report ● Newsletter, quarterly. Contains information on activities and meetings of the organization. **Circulation:** 5,000. **Conventions/Meetings:** annual meeting - always May or June.

10162 ■ Surveyors Historical Society (SHS)

300 W High St.
Lawrenceburg, IN 47025-1912
Ph: (812)537-2000
E-mail: ingram@cfw.com
URL: http://www.surveyhistory.org/surveyor's_historical_society.htm
Contact: Roger Woodfill, Admin.

Founded: 1977. **Members:** 400. **Membership Dues:** individual, $45 (annual). **Budget:** $15,000. **State Groups:** 5. **Description:** Persons interested in the history of surveying. Dedicated to the preservation of surveying instruments, records, memorabilia, and relics. Seeks to educate the public about the history of surveying. Organizes displays of surveying memorabilia and instruments. Conducts research projects. Operates speakers' bureau and museum; compiles statistics. **Libraries: Type:** reference. **Holdings:** 100; books. **Subjects:** land surveying, mapping. **Computer Services:** database, archives ● mailing lists ● online services, artifact collection catalog. **Committees:** Artifact Acquisition Evaluation; Artifacts; Exhibitions; Historical Writing; Publication and Public Relations. **Affiliated With:** American Congress on Surveying and Mapping. **Publications:** *Backsights*, semiannual. Newsletter. **Price:** free. **Circulation:** 850. **Advertising:** accepted ● *Insights*, quarterly. Newsletter. Includes short features and society news. ● Brochure, annual ● Membership Directory, annual. **Conventions/Meetings:** annual congress - in spring ● annual The Surveyor's Rendezvous - meeting and congress, held in conjunction with continuing education meeting (exhibits) - in fall.

10163 ■ Treasury Historical Association (THA)

PO Box 28118
Washington, DC 20038-8118
Ph: (202)298-0550
E-mail: info@treasuryhistoricalassn.org
URL: http://www.treasuryhistoricalassn.org
Contact: Thomas P. O'Malley, Chm.

Founded: 1973. **Members:** 300. **Membership Dues:** general, $12 (annual) ● supporting, $50 (annual) ● patron, $100 (annual) ● sustaining, $250 (annual) ● life - sponsor, $500 ● life - donor, $1,000. **Description:** Private citizens, present and former Treasury employees, former Treasury officials, including all former Secretaries of the Treasury. Aims to preserve Treasury history and economic history relating to the Treasury Department. Includes major project which is the preservation and enhancement of the Main Treasury Building, a national historic landmark. Has completed a pilot oral history program regarding Treasury history. Conducts field trips, tours, and lectures. Produces and markets commemorative products, with accompanying educational brochures. **Libraries: Type:** reference. **Holdings:** archival material. **Committees:** Capital Development; Commemorative Products; Communications; Programs; Publications. **Publications:** *Annual Report of the Treasury Historical Association*, annual. **Price:** included in membership dues. **Circulation:** 250. **Conventions/Meetings:** annual meeting - every second Wednesday of December in Washington, DC.

10164 ■ United States Capitol Historical Society (USCHS)

200 Maryland Ave. NE
Washington, DC 20002
Ph: (202)543-8919
Free: (800)887-9318
Fax: (202)544-8244
E-mail: uschs@uschs.org
URL: http://www.uschs.org
Contact: Hon. Ronald A. Sarasin, Pres.

Founded: 1962. **Members:** 3,000. **Membership Dues:** charter, $35-$49 (annual) ● Freedom Society, $50-$99 (annual) ● Cornerstone Society, $100-$249 (annual) ● Rotunda Society, $250-$499 (annual) ● architect of history, $500-$999 (annual) ● capitol circle, $1,000-$2,499 (annual) ● capitol benefactor, $2,500-$4,999 (annual) ● capitol founder, $5,000-$9,999 (annual) ● Brumidi Society donor, $10,000 (annual) ● Leadership Council, $25,000 (annual). **Staff:** 26. **Budget:** $3,800,000. **Description:** Preserves and communicates the history and heritage of the U.S. Capital, its institutions, and the individuals who have served in Congress. Activities include educational programs, popular and scholarly symposia and publications, enhancement of the Capitol's collection of art and artifacts, and research in the U.S. Capitol and the U.S. Congress. **Libraries: Type:** by appointment only. **Holdings:** books. **Subjects:** Capitol and Congressional history. **Awards:** Capitol Fellowship. **Frequency:** 3/year. **Type:** fellowship. **Recipient:** for individuals conducting research on the art and architectural history of the capitol ● The Freedom Award. **Frequency:** annual. **Type:** recognition. **Recipient:** for individuals and organizations that have advanced greater public understanding and appreciation for freedom. **Telecommunication Services:** electronic mail, dwailes@uschs.org. **Publications:** *The Capitol Dome*, quarterly. Newsletter. **Price:** included in membership dues. **Circulation:** 3,000 ● *We, the People: The Story of the United States Capitol* ● We, the People annual Calendar; gift catalog free upon request.

10165 ■ White House Historical Association (WHHA)

PO Box 27624
Washington, DC 20038-7624
Ph: (202)737-8292 (202)789-0440
Free: (800)555-2451
Fax: (202)789-0440
E-mail: edu@whha.org
URL: http://www.whitehousehistory.org
Contact: Neil W. Horstman, Pres.

Founded: 1961. **Staff:** 25. **Nonmembership. Description:** Seeks to enhance appreciation, understanding, and enjoyment of the White House through educational programs. **Libraries: Type:** reference. **Holdings:** reports. **Publications:** *Art In The White House: A Nation's Pride*. Book ● *The First Ladies*. Book ● *The Living White House*. Book ● *The President's House*. Book ● *The Presidents of the United States*. Book ● *Where History Lives: A Tour of the White House*. Video ● *The White House: A Historic Guide*. Book ● *White House Glassware: Two Centuries of Presidential Entertaining*. Book ● *The White House: Its Historic Furnishings and First Families*. Book. Tells the story of the historic objects and decorative arts in the White House. **Price:** $39.95. ISSN: 7892-0624 ● Also makes available slides, prints, and postcards.

10166 ■ World History Association (WHA)

Univ. of Hawaii at Manoa
Sakamaki Hall A-203
2530 Dole St.
Honolulu, HI 96822
Ph: (808)956-7688
Fax: (808)956-9600
E-mail: thewha@hawaii.edu
URL: http://www.thewha.org
Contact: Heidi Roupp, Exec. Dir.

Founded: 1982. **Members:** 1,400. **Membership Dues:** regular, $60 (annual) ● student/independent scholar, $30 (annual) ● new professional, $45 (annual) ● life, $1,200. **Staff:** 2. **Regional Groups:** 7. **Multinational. Description:** Promotes the study of world history through support of research, teaching, collegial communication, and publication in world history. **Awards:** Phi Alpha Theta History Society, Inc. & World History Association Student Paper Prize. **Frequency:** annual. **Type:** monetary. **Recipient:** to the best graduate and graduate paper written in world history ● World History Association Book Award. **Fre-**

quency: annual. **Type:** monetary. **Recipient:** for new scholarly studies ● World History Association Teaching Prize. **Frequency:** annual. **Type:** monetary. **Recipient:** for best classroom lesson plan inspired by or directly related to world history scholarship. **Computer Services:** database ● mailing lists, of labels and members. **Affiliated With:** American Historical Association. **Publications:** *Journal of World History*, quarterly. **Price:** $75.00/yfs (from UHP, 10&percent; off to agents); $60.00 /year for individuals (from WHA only); $25.00/year, student (from WHA only, with ID); $20.00 back issues (through 2003). ISSN: 1045-6007. **Circulation:** 1,700. **Advertising:** accepted. Alternate Formats: online ● *World History Bulletin*, semiannual. ISSN: 0886-117X. **Circulation:** 1,700. **Advertising:** accepted. **Conventions/Meetings:** annual conference, discussions concerning world history and teaching world history (exhibits) - late June ● annual Sessions at the American Historical Association - conference, held at the American Historical Association's annual meeting (exhibits) - always January.

10167 ■ World War Two Studies Association (WWTSA)
c/o Prof. Mark Parillo
Dept. of History
Kansas State Univ.
Eisenhower Hall
Manhattan, KS 66506-1002
Ph: (913)532-0374
Fax: (913)532-7004
URL: http://www.h-net.org/~war/wwtsa
Contact: Prof. Mark Parillo, Contact
Founded: 1967. **Members:** 368. **Membership Dues:** regular, $15 (annual) ● student (with special circumstances), $5 (annual). **Description:** Academic and government historians and others interested in the history of World War II. One of 32 national committees that form the International Committee for the History of the Second World War. Promotes historical research on all aspects of the Second World War era. Disseminates information. **Libraries: Type:** reference. **Holdings:** articles, books, periodicals. **Affiliated With:** American Historical Association. **Formerly:** (1992) American Committee on the History of the Second World War. **Publications:** Newsletter, semiannual. Covers new items on World War II studies, with emphasis on archival and bibliographical resources. Includes book reviews. **Price:** included in membership dues. ISSN: 0885-5668. **Circulation:** 400. **Conventions/Meetings:** annual meeting and symposium, held in conjunction with American Historical Association (exhibits).

Human Development

10168 ■ American Creativity Association (ACA)
Drexel Univ.
Goodwin Coll.
3001 Market St.
Philadelphia, PA 19104
Free: (866)616-4492
Fax: (215)259-3842
E-mail: info@amcreativityassoc.org
URL: http://www.amcreativityassoc.org
Contact: Mr. William Wurtz, Pres.
Founded: 1989. **Members:** 200. **Membership Dues:** $75 (annual). **Staff:** 1. **Description:** Seeks to promote and develop creativity on personal and professional levels. Works to increase awareness of the importance of creativity in society. Promotes the idea that creativity is the foundation of innovation, and essential for individuals and organizations to stay competitive. **Publications:** *Creativity: Global Correspondents*, annual. Covers latest research in 20 different countries in the field of creativity. **Price:** included in membership dues ● *Focus*, bimonthly. Newsletter. Contains articles in the field of creativity. **Price:** included in membership dues. **Advertising:** accepted. **Conventions/Meetings:** annual convention, includes leaders from business education, engineers, scientists, the arts sharing their expertise; presents the latest trends in the field (exhibits).

10169 ■ Arica Institute (AI)
PO Box 645
Kent, CT 06757-0645
Ph: (860)927-1006
Fax: (860)927-1007
E-mail: info@arica.org
URL: http://www.arica.org
Contact: Oscar Ichazo, Founder
Founded: 1971. **Members:** 800. **Membership Dues:** regular, $180 (annual). **Staff:** 5. **Budget:** $520,000. **Local Groups:** 30. **Languages:** English, French, German, Greek, Portuguese, Spanish. **Multinational. Description:** Teaches a theory and method, developed by Oscar Ichazo, that seeks a better society through the development of self-fulfilled individuals. Offers training programs, short courses, and self-study courses. **Libraries: Type:** reference. **Holdings:** articles. **Telecommunication Services:** electronic mail, orders@aricaschool.org. **Formerly:** (1973) Arica Institute in America. **Publications:** *Arica Day of Unity Report*, monthly. Newsletter ● Audiotapes ● Books ● Journals ● Magazines. **Conventions/Meetings:** periodic seminar and workshop.

10170 ■ Association for Transpersonal Psychology (ATP)
PO Box 50187
Palo Alto, CA 94303
Ph: (650)424-8764
Fax: (650)618-1851
E-mail: info@atpweb.org
URL: http://www.atpweb.org
Contact: David Lukoff, Co-Pres.
Founded: 1971. **Members:** 1,500. **Membership Dues:** general, $75 (annual) ● professional, $95 (annual) ● student, $55 (annual) ● organizational, $150 (annual) ● supporting, $175 (annual) ● recent graduate/alumni, $60 (annual) ● international, $50 (annual) ● life, $99 ● library, $500 (annual). **Description:** Membership branch of the Transpersonal Institute. Professional and nonprofessional individuals interested in the development of the transpersonal orientation. Encourages theoretical and applied scientific transpersonal research as a "vital part of psychology, education, religion, philosophy and other related fields." Concerned with "transpersonal values, unitive consciousness, and transcendence of the self." Interests include education, psychological research, and therapy. **Telecommunication Services:** electronic mail, stuartcs@jps.net. **Publications:** *Journal of Transpersonal Psychology*, semiannual. Contains information on theory, research application in transpersonal psychology, psychotherapy, spiritual disciplines, and consciousness research. **Price:** included in membership dues; $32.00 /year for libraries and institutions; $24.00 /year for nonmembers. ISSN: 0022-524X. **Circulation:** 3,000. Alternate Formats: microform ● *Listing of Professional Members*, annual ● *Listing of Schools and Programs*, annual ● Newsletter, quarterly.

10171 ■ Cultural Survival (CS)
215 Prospect St.
Cambridge, MA 02139
Ph: (617)441-5400 (617)441-5404
Fax: (617)441-5417
E-mail: culturalsurvival@cs.org
URL: http://www.cs.org
Contact: Ellen Lutz, Exec. Dir.
Founded: 1972. **Members:** 3,000. **Membership Dues:** student/senior, $25 (annual) ● individual, $45 (annual) ● library, $60 (annual) ● high donor-sponsor, $100-$249 (annual) ● high donor-sustainer, $250-$499 (annual) ● high donor-patron, $500-$999 (annual) ● high donor-benefactor, $1,000 (annual) ● major donor (maximum), $99,999. **Staff:** 8. **Budget:** $400,000. **Languages:** Danish, English, French, Polish, Portuguese, Russian, Spanish. **Description:** Indigenous people, ethnic groups, anthropologists, and academics interested in the Developing World; research institutes, museums, government agencies, and individuals. Helps indigenous people survive, both physically and culturally, the rapid changes brought on by contact with an expanding industrial society. Sponsors projects, primarily in the areas of human rights, land, and resource management, designed to help tribal societies become successful ethnic minorities. Maintains filing system that serves as a center for research and documentation on the problems of threatened societies. Maintains speakers' bureau; compiles statistics; conducts research on problems confronting indigenous peoples. **Libraries: Type:** reference. **Holdings:** 1,500; books, clippings, periodicals. **Subjects:** indigenous peoples, development, human rights. **Computer Services:** database, scholars and specialists network, global information service for indigenous peoples. **Telecommunication Services:** electronic mail, membership@cs.org. **Publications:** *Cultural Survival Quarterly*. Journal. Addresses issues of both immediate and long-term concern to indigenous peoples throughout the world. **Price:** included in membership dues. ISSN: 0740-3291. **Circulation:** 8,000. **Advertising:** accepted. Alternate Formats: CD-ROM. **Conventions/Meetings:** semiannual seminar, public forum and student conference on Innuland rights (exhibits).

10172 ■ Esalen Institute (EI)
55000 Hwy. 1
Big Sur, CA 93920-9546
Ph: (831)667-3000 (831)667-3005
Fax: (831)667-2724
E-mail: info@esalen.org
URL: http://www.esalen.org
Contact: Gordon Wheeler, Pres./CEO
Founded: 1962. **Budget:** $8,000,000. **Description:** Works to explore trends in the sciences, art, religion, and philosophy, with emphasis on the potentialities and values of human existence. Activities include weekend seminars, five-day workshops, one-to four-week workshops, four-week work-study programs, and consulting and research programs; sponsors Transformation Project, invitational conferences, and a school for early childhood education. **Telecommunication Services:** electronic mail, workstudy@esalen.org. **Publications:** Catalog, 3/year. Provides a listing of workshops/programs. **Price:** $5.00. **Circulation:** 11,000. Alternate Formats: online.

10173 ■ Inner Peace Movement (IPM)
PO Box 681757
San Antonio, TX 78268
Free: (877)475-7792
Fax: (210)641-7871
E-mail: ipmtx@aaahawk.com
URL: http://innerpeacemovement.org
Contact: Ben Dreese, Pres.
Founded: 1964. **Members:** 750,000. **Staff:** 8. **Description:** A leadership training program designed "to help man identify and balance the physical, mental and spiritual forces in life so he can mold his own destiny and become the architect of his own success." Believes that meditation and inner guidance will help individuals make mature decisions. The nature of the program evolves with the changing needs of the members. **Computer Services:** Mailing lists, of members. **Publications:** *Expression*, quarterly. Magazine. **Conventions/Meetings:** annual meeting ● periodic workshop.

10174 ■ Institute of HeartMath (IHM)
14700 W Park Ave.
Boulder Creek, CA 95006
Ph: (831)338-8500
Fax: (831)338-8504
E-mail: ihminquiry@heartmath.org
URL: http://www.heartmath.org
Contact: Sara Paddison, Pres./CEO
Founded: 1991. **Membership Dues:** charter, $25 (annual). **Staff:** 18. **Budget:** $900,000. **Regional Groups:** 53. **Description:** Works to create a cultural shift in how organizations view people, and how people view each other and themselves. Seeks to scientifically validate the intelligence of the heart. Conducts biomedical research programs on the sources of stress, including work with post-cardiac patients, people interested in emotional management, educators serving child populations of at risk, learning disabled, at risk for violence, and in all sectors of

society. **Libraries: Type:** not open to the public. **Holdings:** articles, books, monographs, papers. **Subjects:** stress, intuition, education. **Boards:** Scientific Advisory. **Councils:** Physics of Humanity. **Publications:** *Heartmath Solution*. Book. Details the pioneering program developed at the Institute of HeartMath. **Price:** $12.60 for members; $14.00 for nonmembers ● *Research Overview*, annual. Booklets. Provides an overview of IHM's research exploring the role of the heart in health and performance. **Price:** $10.00. **Circulation:** 4,000. Alternate Formats: online ● Newsletter, quarterly. **Price:** included in membership dues. Alternate Formats: online.

10175 ■ Institute for the Study of Human Knowledge (ISHK)
PO Box 176
Los Altos, CA 94023
Ph: (650)948-9428
Free: (800)222-4745
Fax: (650)948-2687
E-mail: ishkhelp@aol.com
URL: http://www.ishkbooks.com
Contact: Robert E. Ornstein PhD, Pres.
Founded: 1969. **Description:** Provides a communication center for the human sciences through lectures, symposia, donation of books to libraries, book and cassette tape service, and publication of articles. Focuses on interdisciplinary approach to human ecology, integrative health and medical policies, functional specialization of the brain, and the development of the human capacity to learn. Supports research. **Libraries: Type:** reference. **Holdings:** books.

10176 ■ Lama Foundation (LF)
PO Box 240
San Cristobal, NM 87564
Ph: (505)586-1269 (505)758-8622
Fax: (206)984-0916
E-mail: info@lamafoundation.org
URL: http://www.lamafoundation.org
Contact: Jan Cross, Coor.
Founded: 1967. **Members:** 50. **Staff:** 15. **Budget:** $150,000. **Description:** Spiritual community and educational center dedicated to awakening of consciousness. Conducts program of regular meditation, communal living, work projects, silk screening, and gardening. Offers educational programs in music, healing, meditation, and the study of various religious traditions. Provides hermitage cabins (for a fee) for individuals that wish complete solitude. Serves as a Retreat Center during the summer months. **Libraries: Type:** reference; by appointment only; open to the public. **Holdings:** 7,500; archival material, artwork, biographical archives, books, periodicals, photographs. **Computer Services:** Online services, staff and retreatants have access to the Internet. **Telecommunication Services:** electronic mail, taosoffice@lamafoundation.org. **Boards:** Trustees. **Committees:** Curriculum; Physical Plane. **Councils:** Lama. **Publications:** *Lama Alive!*, annual. Newsletter ● *Lama Summer Program*, annual. Brochure. Includes general information on Lama plus retreat schedule and description. **Circulation:** 12,000. Alternate Formats: online ● Also makes available prayer flags, cards and rubber stamps with sacred symbols. **Conventions/Meetings:** annual meeting - mid-May to mid-September.

10177 ■ Learning Light Foundation (LLF)
1212 E Lincoln Ave.
Anaheim, CA 92805-4249
Ph: (714)533-2311
E-mail: info@learninglight.net
URL: http://www.learninglight.org
Contact: Kerri Ramaley, Gen. Mgr.
Founded: 1962. **Members:** 600. **Membership Dues:** individual, $40 ● family, $60. **Staff:** 20. **Description:** Men and women dedicated to a positive, unbiased and unprejudiced mission to discover and recognize valid and scientific principles as proclaimed by existing agencies or individuals and an open-minded search for new and advanced ideas, opinions and methods that may be accepted and used for the betterment of humanity. Engages in study and research in an atmosphere free from tradition, dogma and doctrine to discover truths that are based on natural law and to discover the methods by which those truths may be used for the advancement and betterment of man in the physical, mental, emotional and spiritual aspects of his life experiences. Sponsors lectures, demonstrations, workshops, classes, and social and recreational programs. Operates Learning Light Adult Development Program which provides learning programs for students whose learning disabilities, behavior, or age makes them unsuited for public school programs. **Libraries: Type:** reference. **Holdings:** articles, reports. **Telecommunication Services:** electronic mail, kerri@learninglight.net. **Formerly:** (1994) Psynetics Foundation. **Publications:** *Learning Light*, monthly. Magazine. Covers Foundation activities in psychic, self, and spiritual development. Includes calendar of events. **Price:** free. **Circulation:** 20,000. **Advertising:** accepted. **Conventions/Meetings:** annual congress - always October in Anaheim, CA.

10178 ■ School of Living (SOL)
215 Julian Woods Ln.
Julian, PA 16844
Ph: (814)353-0130
E-mail: office@schoolofliving.org
URL: http://schoolofliving.org
Contact: Ann Wilken, Office Mgr.
Founded: 1934. **Members:** 125. **Membership Dues:** regular, $20 (annual) ● contributing, $50 (annual) ● sustaining, $100 (annual) ● life, $500. **Staff:** 2. **Description:** Demonstrates, organizes, and promotes adult education using 17 distinguishable, major problems of living. Espouses organic lifestyle and permaculture environment. Administers Community Land Trust and fosters alternative education. **Committees:** Building without Banks; Education; Land Trust; Membership; Permaculture; Publications. **Projects:** Geonomics. **Affiliated With:** Council of Georgist Organizations. **Publications:** *Green Revolution*, quarterly. Journal. Covers decentralism, geonomics, alternative schools, community living, homesteading, land trusts, and permaculture. **Price:** $20.00/year. ISSN: 0017-3983. **Circulation:** 400 ● *Ralph Borsodi: Reshaping Modern Culture*. **Conventions/Meetings:** quarterly board meeting and meeting, also holds committee meetings ● annual meeting and general assembly, for members ● seminar ● symposium.

10179 ■ Well-Springs Foundation (WSF)
c/o Pat Kinnamon, Exec. Dir.
550 W Butternut Rd.
Summerville, SC 29483
Ph: (843)873-1960
E-mail: spkinnamon@aol.com
URL: http://www.well-springs.org
Contact: Pat Kinnamon, Exec. Dir.
Founded: 1966. **Staff:** 2. **Description:** Educational foundation that conducts workshops combining music, movement, color, art, meditation, and massage, allowing individuals to relieve tension and become more aware of their spiritual and creative abilities. Presents lecture demonstrations; offers individual spiritual counseling with music. **Formerly:** (1960) Relax Tension Centre; (1966) Relax and Rebound Centre. **Publications:** Audiotapes ● Booklets ● Newsletter, periodic ● Videos.

10180 ■ Wilbur Hot Springs Health Sanctuary (WHSHS)
3375 Wilbur Springs Rd.
Williams, CA 95987-9709
Ph: (530)473-2306
Fax: (530)473-2497
E-mail: info@wilburhotsprings.com
URL: http://www.wilburhotsprings.com
Contact: Dr. Richard Louis Miller PhD, Founder/Pres.
Founded: 1972. **Staff:** 10. **For-Profit. Description:** Promotes holistic lifestyle. Sponsors working retreats to creative persons. Offers retreat for healthy people. **Libraries: Type:** not open to the public. **Holdings:** 800; articles, books, periodicals. **Formerly:** (1975) Gestalt Community.

Human Potential

10181 ■ Association for the Development of Human Potential (ADHP)
406 S Coeur d'Alene St., No. T
Spokane, WA 99204
Ph: (509)838-3575
Free: (800)251-9273
Fax: (509)838-6652
E-mail: radhayoga@comcast.net
URL: http://www.timeless.org
Contact: Swami Radha, Founder
Founded: 1970. **Members:** 35. **Membership Dues:** associate, $15 (annual) ● sponsoring, $25 (annual). **Staff:** 5. **Budget:** $50,000. **State Groups:** 3. **Description:** Promotes personal growth and awareness through the study of the interrelationship of the physical, mental, emotional and spiritual aspects of human existence as set forth in the teachings of Swami Sivananda Radha. Consists of a publishing house, teaching centers, and conducts outreach seminars and workshops. **Additional Websites:** http://www.radha.org/spokane. **Divisions:** Ascent Magazine; Radha Yoga Center; Timeless Books. **Affiliated With:** Yasodhara Ashram Society. **Publications:** *Ascent*, quarterly. Magazine ● Books ● Also produces audiovisual educational materials and audio cassette and CD-ROM educational materials. **Conventions/Meetings:** annual conference.

10182 ■ Feldenkrais Guild of North America (FGNA)
5436 N Albina Ave.
Portland, OR 97217
Ph: (503)221-6612
Free: (800)775-2118
Fax: (503)221-6616
E-mail: executivedirector@feldenkraisguild.com
URL: http://www.feldenkrais.com/guild
Contact: Barbara Greenfield, Exec. Dir.
Founded: 1977. **Members:** 1,800. **Membership Dues:** professional in U.S., $300 (annual) ● professional in Canada, $255 (annual) ● international, $160 (annual) ● associate, $165 (annual) ● student, $75 (annual). **Staff:** 8. **Regional Groups:** 10. **Multinational. Description:** Practitioners and teachers and students of the Feldenkrais Method(TM) who have been trained by the late Dr. Moshe Feldenkrais or guild-certified trainers. The Feldenkrais Method(TM) provides a technique for bringing about better maturation of the nervous system through integrated movement using the reversible relationship of the muscular and nervous system. Seeks to provide training, information, and increased public awareness regarding Feldenkrais Method(TM); protect the quality of the method. Offers research and continuing education programs for members. **Libraries: Type:** open to the public. **Holdings:** 50; articles, audio recordings, books, video recordings. **Computer Services:** database, members only ● electronic publishing, "SenseAbility": newsletter for public available on website. **Boards:** Training Accreditation. **Publications:** *Feldenkrais Journal*, annual ● *In Touch*, quarterly. Newsletter ● Membership Directory, annual. Alternate Formats: online ● Directory, annual. Contains educational materials. **Circulation:** 2,000. Alternate Formats: online ● Also distributes taped lessons and educational materials. **Conventions/Meetings:** annual The Paradox of Simplicity - conference (exhibits).

10183 ■ International Imagery Association (IIA)
c/o Leslie J. Dagnall, Dir. of Training
18 Edgeclif Terr.
Yonkers, NY 10705
Ph: (914)476-0781
Fax: (914)476-5796
E-mail: jldag@aol.com
URL: http://www.imagery-iia.com
Contact: Akhter Ahsen PhD, Chm./Founder
Founded: 1979. **Description:** Represents individuals interested in the phenomenon of mental imagery. (Imagery conducts the central creative and expressive core of the individual, involving concentration, thought, language, behavior, and progression of hu-

man consciousness.) Seeks to integrate a multidiscipline focus into the imagery field. Fosters communication and discussion on how imagery can aid in fulfilling human potential. Encourages mental imagery research. **Libraries: Type:** reference. **Holdings:** archival material, books, monographs, periodicals. **Subjects:** mental imagery. **Publications:** *Imagery Today*, semiannual. Newsletter ● *International Imagery Bulletin*, semiannual ● *Journal of Mental Imagery*, quarterly. Contains new evidence and applications arising out of the increased attention to imagery and its manifestations. **Price:** $40.00 /year for individuals; $90.00 /year for institutions. **Conventions/Meetings:** annual conference ● annual international conference.

10184 ■ Macro Society (MS)
PO Box 26880
Tempe, AZ 85285-6880
Fax: (602)991-7076
E-mail: lise@macrosociety.com
URL: http://www.donalexander.com
Contact: Ann Conley, Mgr.

Founded: 1975. **Members:** 8,000. **Membership Dues:** contributor, $20 (annual). **Multinational. Description:** Individuals interested in self-determination through the development of a positive mental attitude and individual responsibility for life choices, experiences. Strives to provide "happy and healthy alternatives for daily life choices" through positive thinking; believes one's thoughts determine one's realities. Sponsors study groups, classes, and correspondence courses on developing a positive mental attitude. Organizes social activities to reinforce these values. Maintains speakers' bureau. **Awards: Type:** scholarship. **Recipient:** to high school and college students. **Publications:** *How to Develop Your Macro Awareness.* Booklet. **Price:** $10.00 ● *How to Do Personal Evolution Tutoring.* Booklet. **Price:** $10.00 ● *How to Live a Macro Lifestyle.* Booklet. **Price:** $10.00 ● *The Macro Study Guide and Workbook.* Booklet. **Price:** $30.00 ● *The Macro Use of Your Dream State.* Booklet. **Price:** $10.00 ● *Simultaneous Time: Twin Souls, Soul Mates, and Parallel Lives.* Booklet. **Price:** $10.00 ● *2150 A.D. (Original Ed. 1971).* Book. **Price:** $10.00 ● *2150 A.D., (Revised Ed. 1976).* Book. **Price:** $10.00. **Conventions/Meetings:** annual conference and seminar - usually Labor Day weekend in Arizona ● seminar.

Human Relations

10185 ■ Giraffe Heroes Project
PO Box 759
Langley, WA 98260
Ph: (360)221-7989
Fax: (360)221-7817
E-mail: office@giraffe.org
URL: http://www.giraffe.org
Contact: John Graham, Pres.

Founded: 1984. **Members:** 2,500. **Membership Dues:** individual, $35 (annual). **Staff:** 11. **Budget:** $400,000. **Description:** Honors and publicizes the acts of individuals who "stick their necks out" for the common good in a manner that involves physical, financial, or social risk. Develops character education programs for schools and youth organizations. **Awards:** Giraffe Award. **Frequency:** quarterly. **Type:** recognition. **Telecommunication Services:** electronic mail, graham@giraffe.org. **Publications:** *Everyday Heroes: A Giraffe Story for Each Weekday of the Year* ● *Giraffe News*, semiannual. Journal. Includes inspirational stories. **Price:** included in membership dues. **Circulation:** 3,500 ● *The Giraffe Project Handbook: How to Stick Your Neck Out* ● *Voices of Hope*. Book. Tells kids that individuals can impact their world for the better and that they themselves can do that too. **Price:** $12.95 student book; $21.95 teacher guide; $34.90 1 student book and 1 teacher guide; $151.45 10 student books and 1 teacher guide ● Also makes available radio scripts and teaching kits. **Conventions/Meetings:** periodic lecture ● periodic seminar.

10186 ■ Golden Rule Foundation (GRF)
PO Box 658
Camden, ME 04843
Ph: (207)236-4104
E-mail: goldenrule@goldrule.org
URL: http://www.goldrule.org
Contact: Laurel Frye, Admin.

Founded: 1937. **Staff:** 1. **Description:** Individuals and groups dedicated to securing liberty, freedom, and justice for all people by respecting individual rights. Aims to work towards a more perfect world via the Applied Eclectic Rational Empiricism philosophy. **Libraries: Type:** reference. **Publications:** *Towards a More Perfect World*, periodic.

10187 ■ Human Relations Area Files (HRAF)
755 Prospect St.
New Haven, CT 06511-1225
Ph: (203)764-9401
Free: (800)520-4723
Fax: (203)764-9404
E-mail: hraf@yale.edu
URL: http://www.yale.edu/hraf
Contact: Melvin Ember, Pres.

Founded: 1949. **Members:** 300. **Membership Dues:** sponsor, $5,000 (annual) ● associate (minimum), $2,900 (annual) ● associate (maximum), $3,900 (annual). **Staff:** 13. **Budget:** $1,000,000. **Description:** A research organization with a world membership of universities, libraries, and museums. Seeks "to encourage and facilitate area studies and the worldwide comparative study of human behavior and culture, thereby promoting a general understanding of the people of the world, their ways of life, their problems, values, and ideas. . . ." Develops programs and services that aid in this study, particularly a worldwide cultural data archive and retrieval system available on microfiche, CD-ROM and World Wide Web. Offers workshops on use of information system and summer training sessions in cross-cultural research. Conducts grant and contract research. **Libraries: Type:** reference. **Holdings:** 4,000; archival material. **Computer Services:** database, collection of Archaeology ● database, collection of Ethnography ● database, on CD-ROM and World Wide Web. **Telecommunication Services:** electronic mail, hrafmem@hrafmem.mail.yale.edu. **Publications:** *Cross-Cultural Research*, annual. Journal. Covers cross-cultural/comparative issues in the social/behavioral sciences. Contains research articles and reports. **Price:** $54.00 /year for individuals; $125.00 /year for institutions. ISSN: 0094-3673. **Circulation:** 900. **Advertising:** accepted ● Newsletter, semiannual. Contains current cross-cultural research and upcoming events. Alternate Formats: online. **Conventions/Meetings:** annual board meeting - always April in New Haven, CT.

10188 ■ International Laughter Society (ILS)
16000 Glen Una Dr.
Los Gatos, CA 95030
Ph: (408)354-3456
Contact: L. Katherine Ferrari, Pres.

Founded: 1981. **Members:** 4,800. **State Groups:** 2. **For-Profit. Description:** Professionals and others interested in therapeutic humor for stress management, motivation, and enjoyment. Promotes positive, wholesome humor; sponsors humor support groups, workshops, and training programs. **Publications:** *Humor First Aid Kit.*

10189 ■ International Organization for the Study of Group Tensions (IOSGT)
c/o Dr. Herbert Krauss, PhD, Co-Pres.
Pace Univ.
1 Pace Plz.
New York, NY 10038
Ph: (212)346-1506
E-mail: hkrauss@pace.edu
Contact: Dr. Herbert Krauss PhD, Co-Pres.

Founded: 1970. **Members:** 150. **Membership Dues:** individual, $30 (annual). **Description:** Behavioral scientists and scholars including anthropologists, economists, historians, political scientists, psychiatrists, psychoanalysts, psychologists, and sociologists. Seeks to bring about new and clearer understanding of and solutions to the problems of human conflict and violence. Conducts research into the causes of group tension in the hope that such research may make a contribution to the alleviation of the phenomenon and to its replacement by mutual understanding and tolerance. Has formed study groups and regional group centers. **Awards:** Benjamin B. Wolman Award. **Frequency:** annual. **Type:** monetary. **Recipient:** for contributions to the field. **Committees:** Education; Membership; Proposal Writing and Funding; Public Relations and Fund Raising; Research; Speakers' Bureau; Study-Research Groups. **Publications:** *International Journal of Group Tensions*, quarterly. **Conventions/Meetings:** biennial conference ● seminar.

10190 ■ Joygerms Unlimited (JU)
PO Box 555
Syracuse, NY 13206
Ph: (315)472-2779
Contact: Joan E. White, Founder

Founded: 1981. **Members:** 109,500. **Staff:** 1. **Local Groups:** 1. **Multinational. Description:** Churches, schools, organizations, health and wholeness centers, and interested individuals dedicated to "spreading joy and cheer" throughout the world. Seeks to "eliminate doom and gloom" and "rid the world of gruff and grumpy grouches" by promoting goodwill and humor. Conducts Smile Check Up Clinics in hospitals, nursing homes, schools, and fraternal organizations. Maintains speakers' bureau; conducts children's services and charitable and educational programs. **Awards:** Eckard 100 Women. **Frequency:** annual. **Type:** recognition ● Joygerm Joan Awarded Post Standard Achievement Award. **Frequency:** annual. **Type:** recognition. **Recipient:** for significant or unusual ongoing contribution to the welfare of the community. **Publications:** *Infectionately Yours*, quarterly. Newsletter. Includes updates on local and national activities, member feedback, poetry, and material on hope, inspiration, and living life to the fullest. **Price:** $9.50/year; $5.00/year (senior); $7.00/year (gift). **Circulation:** 1,000. **Conventions/Meetings:** Owed to Joy Rally - competition and rally.

10191 ■ Simply Love Foundation
PO Box 8888
Albuquerque, NM 87198
E-mail: michaelb@simplylove.net
URL: http://www.simplylove.net
Contact: Michael Bischoff LPCC, Clinical Therapist

Founded: 1986. **Members:** 200. **Staff:** 2. **Description:** Promotes love, romance, friendship, and healthy, supportive and affirming relationships among all people as life's highest priority. Sponsors educational programs. Offers individual, group, couples, and family counseling in local offices or via e-mail/over the Internet; maintains speakers' bureau. **Convention/Meeting:** none. Broadcasts radio-show "Simply Love". **Formerly:** Love Notes; (1998) Simply Love. **Publications:** *Simply Love*, quarterly. Newsletter. Discusses relationships. **Price:** available on request.

Human Rights

10192 ■ U.S. Copts Association
529 14th St. NW, Ste.1081
Washington, DC 20045
Ph: (202)737-3660
Fax: (202)737-3661
E-mail: copts@copts.com
URL: http://www.copts.net
Contact: Michael Meunier, Pres.

Founded: 1996. **Multinational. Description:** Raises public awareness of the plight of Copts within Egypt. Educates the Coptic community on issues of human rights, democracy and religious freedom. Seeks to reverse the state of affairs imposed upon Copts within their homeland. **Computer Services:** Information services, Copts resources ● mailing lists. **Publications:** *Copts Daily Digest*. Newsletter. Alternate Formats: online.

Humanism

10193 ■ Alliance of Secular Humanist Societies (ASHS)
c/o Council for Secular Humanism
PO Box 664
Amherst, NY 14226-0664
Ph: (716)636-7571
Fax: (716)636-1733
E-mail: info@secularhumanism.org
URL: http://www.secularhumanism.org
Contact: Erika Hedberg, Natl. Coor.
Membership Dues: individual, $20 (annual) ● family, $34 (annual) ● life, $1,000. **Description:** Secular humanists. Unites to create mutual support among local and regional societies of secular humanists.

10194 ■ Aspen Institute
One Dupont Cir. NW, Ste.700
Washington, DC 20036-1133
Ph: (202)736-5800 (202)736-3849
Free: (800)525-6618
Fax: (202)467-0790
E-mail: info@aspeninst.org
URL: http://www.aspeninstitute.org
Contact: Walter Isaacson, Pres./CEO
Founded: 1949. **Staff:** 120. **Budget:** $22,000,000. **Multinational. Description:** A global forum for leveraging the power of leaders to improve the human condition. Through seminars and policy programs, fosters enlightened, morally responsible leadership and convenes leaders and policy makers to address the foremost challenges of the new century. Have principal offices in Aspen, CO; Chicago, IL; Washington, DC; and on the Wye River on Maryland's Eastern shore. Operates internationally through a network of partners in Europe and Asia. **Computer Services:** Mailing lists, of members. **Telecommunication Services:** electronic mail, jim.spiegelman@aspeninstitute.org ● additional toll-free number, events information, (800)410-3463. **Formerly:** (1988) Aspen Institute for Humanistic Studies. **Publications:** *Aspen Idea*. Magazine. Covers about the people, ideas, and diverse going-on of the Organization. Alternate Formats: online ● Catalog ● Also publishes books.

10195 ■ Family of Humanists (FOH)
PO Box 4153
Salem, OR 97302
E-mail: peter@familyofhumanists.org
URL: http://www.familyofhumanists.org/index.html
Contact: Peter Wernick, Pres.
Founded: 1978. **Members:** 215. **Membership Dues:** general, $10 (annual). **State Groups:** 2. **Description:** Families with young children; interested others. Promotes modern humanism as a life philosophy. Conducts research and educational programs; maintains speakers' bureau. Sponsors children's activities. **Awards: Type:** recognition. **Publications:** *Humanism for Kids*. Book. **Price:** $6.00/copy ● *Starwalker*, bimonthly. Includes articles by and for youth ages 12 to 16. **Price:** $6.00/year. **Circulation:** 30 ● *Why Evolution*. Book. **Price:** $6.00/copy ● Newsletter, monthly. Includes articles for parents. **Price:** $10.00/year. **Circulation:** 80. **Conventions/Meetings:** annual meeting.

Humanities

10196 ■ American Academy of Arts and Letters (AAAL)
633 W 155 St.
New York, NY 10032
Ph: (212)368-5900
URL: http://www.artsandletters.org
Contact: Ezra Laderman, Pres.
Founded: 1898. **Members:** 250. **Staff:** 9. **Description:** U.S. artists, writers, and composers qualified by notable achievement in their field (membership limited to 250); honorary members are American choreographers, filmmakers, photographers, and foreign artists, writers, and composers. Promotes literature and the fine arts in the United States. **Libraries: Type:** open to the public; by appointment only. **Holdings:** 40,000; books. **Awards:** Academy Awards. **Frequency:** annual. **Type:** monetary. **Recipient:** for artists, writers, composers, and architects ● Marc Blitzstein Award. **Frequency:** periodic. **Type:** monetary. **Recipient:** for a composer, lyricist, or librettist. **Publications:** *A Century of Arts and Letters*. Book. **Price:** $39.00 ● Brochure ● Proceedings, annual. **Price:** $15.00. **Conventions/Meetings:** annual meeting, includes induction and award ceremony (exhibits) - always May, in New York City.

10197 ■ American Council of Learned Societies (ACLS)
633 3rd Ave.
New York, NY 10017-6795
Ph: (212)697-1505 (212)838-0641
Fax: (212)949-8058
E-mail: bhenning@acls.org
URL: http://www.acls.org
Contact: Pauline Yu, Pres.
Founded: 1919. **Members:** 67. **Membership Dues:** Constituent Learned Society (based on the number of members), $440-$4,400 (annual) ● institution (granting PhD in the humanities and social sciences), $6,000 (annual) ● institution (granting MA in the humanities and social sciences), $2,500 (annual) ● associate, $1,500 (annual) ● affiliate, $1,000 (annual). **Staff:** 26. **Description:** Seeks to advance humanistic studies in all fields of learning in the Humanities and the related social sciences and to maintain and strengthen relations among the national societies devoted to such studies. **Libraries: Type:** reference. **Holdings:** archival material. **Telecommunication Services:** electronic mail, paulineyu@acls.org. **Publications:** *American Council of Learned Societies Annual Report*. **Price:** free. **Circulation:** 2,000. Alternate Formats: online ● *American Council of Learned Societies—Occasional Paper Series*. Monograph. Monograph series reprinting selected ACLS speeches and presentations. **Price:** free. **Circulation:** 6,000. Alternate Formats: online. **Conventions/Meetings:** annual meeting - always May. 2009 May 7-9, Philadelphia, PA.

10198 ■ Federation of State Humanities Councils (FSHC)
1600 Wilson Blvd., Ste.902
Arlington, VA 22209
Ph: (703)908-9700
Fax: (703)908-9706
E-mail: emackintosh@statehumanities.org
URL: http://www.statehumanities.org
Contact: Esther Mackintosh, Pres.
Founded: 1977. **Members:** 56. **Staff:** 4. **Budget:** $700,000. **Description:** Humanities councils in each state and the District of Columbia, Guam, American Samoa, Northern Marianas, Puerto Rico, and the Virgin Islands. Encourages public understanding and utilization of the humanities; promotes the application of the humanities in American life. Utilizes the media to disseminate information; sponsors reading and discussion programs, traveling exhibits, seminars, workshops, institutes, lecture series, and speakers' bureau. **Awards:** Schwartz Prize. **Frequency:** annual. **Type:** recognition. **Programs:** African American Heritage; Arizona History Traveler; Bleeding Kansas: Where the Civil War Began; Capitol Forum on America's Future; Louisiana Crossroads Season 4; One Book Montana. **Projects:** The Odyssey. **Formerly:** (1986) National Federation of State Humanities Councils. **Conventions/Meetings:** annual National Humanities Conference.

10199 ■ National Humanities Alliance (NHA)
21 Dupont Cir. NW, Ste.800
Washington, DC 20036
Ph: (202)296-4994 (202)265-3808
Fax: (202)872-0884
E-mail: jessica@cni.org
URL: http://www.nhalliance.org
Contact: Jessica Jones Irons, Exec. Dir.
Founded: 1981. **Members:** 90. **Membership Dues:** associate, $500 (annual) ● active, $1,000 (annual). **Staff:** 2. **Budget:** $225,000. **Description:** Organizations interested in broadening support for the humanities. Acts as liaison between members and Congress, federal agencies, and national institutions in the humanities. Seeks to foster an understanding of the importance of the humanities in American life and to develop awareness of the need for public support of the humanities. Conducts research. Organizes congressional testimonies and grass roots campaigns. **Telecommunication Services:** electronic mail, esmith@nhalliance.org. **Publications:** Reports, 15-20/year. Covers federal policies affecting humanities. **Conventions/Meetings:** annual meeting, business meeting - late April/early May.

10200 ■ National Humanities Center (NHC)
PO Box 12256
Research Triangle Park, NC 27709-2256
Ph: (919)549-0661
Fax: (919)990-8535
E-mail: lmorgan@ga.unc.edu
URL: http://www.nhc.rtp.nc.us
Contact: Geoffrey Harpham, Pres./Dir.
Founded: 1976. **Members:** 900. **Staff:** 25. **Budget:** $5,000,000. **Description:** Professional and nonprofessional scholars in the humanities. Encourages advanced study in the humanities. Brings together humanistic scholars with people in various fields. Members pursue individual research, participate in seminars and conferences, and present lectures. Offers extensive programs to strengthen collegiate and pre-collegiate teaching of the humanities. **Libraries: Type:** reference. **Holdings:** 2,000. **Subjects:** humanities. **Awards:** Richard W. Lyman Award. **Frequency:** annual. **Type:** fellowship. **Recipient:** to outstanding Humanities scholars. **Telecommunication Services:** electronic mail, dsolomon@nhc.rtp.nc.us. **Publications:** *National Humanities Center Report*, annual. Newsletter. ISSN: 1040-130X ● *News of the National Humanities Center*, semiannual. Newsletter. Alternate Formats: online ● Papers.

10201 ■ National Society of Arts and Letters (NSAL)
4227 46th St. NW
Washington, DC 20016
Ph: (202)363-5443
Fax: (202)686-8287
E-mail: ruthalbright@yahoo.com
URL: http://www.arts-nsal.org
Contact: Ruth Albright, Pres.
Founded: 1944. **Members:** 1,773. **Local Groups:** 35. **Description:** Individuals professionally engaged in arts and letters who are interested in becoming involved in activities that support the work of young artists. Encourages and assists young people pursuing careers in art, dance, drama, literature, and music (Membership is by invitation only). **Awards:** Estelle Campbell Award. **Frequency:** annual. **Type:** recognition. **Recipient:** for long time members and benefactors. **Telecommunication Services:** electronic mail, caltstet@uiuc.edu. **Committees:** Career Opportunities and Development; Education. **Publications:** *The Record*, annual ● *Roster of Members*, biennial. Membership Directory ● Newsletter, periodic. **Conventions/Meetings:** annual competition ● convention.

10202 ■ Renaissance Artists and Writers Association (RAWA)
c/o RAWA New York Sector
97-38 42nd Ave., 1st Fl.
Corona, NY 11368
Ph: (718)898-1603
E-mail: rawa@nys.amps.org
URL: http://www.ru.org/rawa
Founded: 1958. **Members:** 150. **Staff:** 5. **Description:** Seeks to unite artists and writers who desire to utilize their talents to serve humanity and to accelerate human spiritual progress. Objectives are: to support and promote art that leads to the all-around development of the individual and society; to encourage art that is created in the spirit of service to humanity; to arrest the trend of excessive commercialization of the arts and literature; to attend to the various social, political, and economic handicaps confronting talented artists and writers; to actively

encourage and coordinate artists working towards a rebirth of the arts. Offers children's programs. **Additional Websites:** http://rawanys.ru.org. **Publications:** *New Renaissance*, quarterly. Magazine. Features social and spiritual awakening. **Price:** $4. 00. **Circulation:** 2,000. **Advertising:** accepted. **Conventions/Meetings:** semiannual meeting - usually December/January and July/August.

10203 ■ Society for the Humanities (SH)
Andrew D. White House
27 East Ave.
Cornell Univ.
Ithaca, NY 14853-1101
Ph: (607)255-9274 (607)255-4086
Fax: (607)255-1422
E-mail: humctr-mailbox@cornell.edu
URL: http://www.arts.cornell.edu/sochum
Contact: Mary Ahl, Admin. Mgr.
Founded: 1966. **Staff:** 4. **Description:** Teachers and scholars in the humanities. Supports and encourages creative research in the humanities, especially investigations that deal with essential humanistic concepts, stress the methods common to the several branches of the humanities, or explore the role that the humanities may play in the solution of human problems. The fellows of the Society are invited to conduct one seminar each term. **Awards:** Mellon Postdoctoral Fellowship. **Frequency:** annual. **Type:** fellowship. **Recipient:** for promising humanists. **Telecommunication Services:** electronic mail, mea4@cornell.edu.

10204 ■ Southern Humanities Council (SHC)
c/o Mark Ledbetter, Exec. Dir.
1204 Jackson Springs Rd.
Macon, GA 31211
Ph: (478)992-9110
E-mail: shcouncil@bellsouth.net
URL: http://www.southernhumanities.org
Contact: Mark Ledbetter, Exec. Dir.
Founded: 1947. **Members:** 200. **Membership Dues:** regular, $25 (annual). **Staff:** 15. **Description:** Learned societies in the humanities; colleges and universities; interested individuals. Promotes the study and development of the humanities; coordinates activities of members; encourages cooperation between business and academia in humanities work. **Formerly:** (1989) Southern Humanities Conference. **Publications:** *Humanities in the South*, annual. Newsletter. **Advertising:** accepted ● *Southern Humanities Review*, quarterly. Journal. **Conventions/Meetings:** annual Rhetoric in Culture: Relations, Rights and Responsibilities - conference (exhibits).

10205 ■ Wilbur Foundation
PO Box 3370
Santa Barbara, CA 93130-3370
Fax: (805)563-1082
E-mail: info@wilburfoundation.org
URL: http://www.wilburfoundation.org
Contact: Gary R. Ricks Esq., Pres.
Description: Strives to enhance, preserve, and protect the transcendent and permanent values of civilization and society through the support of humanities. **Awards: Frequency:** periodic. **Type:** grant. **Recipient:** to foundations that reflect a concern for historical continuity and studies of a traditional nature.

10206 ■ Woodrow Wilson International Center for Scholars
1 Woodrow Wilson Plz.
1300 Pennsylvania Ave. NW
Washington, DC 20004-3027
Ph: (202)691-4000
Fax: (202)691-4001
E-mail: wwics@wilsoncenter.org
URL: http://www.wilsoncenter.org
Contact: Lee H. Hamilton, Pres./Dir.
Founded: 1968. **Staff:** 100. **Budget:** $8,000,000. **Description:** Aims to commemorate Woodrow Wilson's (the 28th President of the United States) service to the nation. Serves as a nonpartisan institution of advanced study - a neutral forum for open, serious and informed dialogue that promotes scholarship in public affairs. Convenes the "thinkers and doers" scholars and policymakers, journalists and businesspeople - in the hope that through shared research and dialogue, "better understanding and wiser policy will emerge". Supports research in social sciences and humanities, with an emphasis on history, political science, and international relations. Includes discussions that draw from the perspectives of history while promoting inquiry into the future. **Libraries: Type:** not open to the public; reference. **Holdings:** 20,000; books. **Subjects:** general reference. **Awards:** Residential Fellowships. **Frequency:** annual. **Type:** fellowship. **Councils:** Wilson. **Publications:** *Centerpoint*, monthly. Newsletter. Alternate Formats: online ● *China Environment Series*. Report. Alternate Formats: online ● *Climate Action in the U.S. and China* ● *CWIHP Book Series*. Books ● *CWIHP Working Papers* ● *East European Studies Newsletter* ● *EES Occasional Papers*. Alternate Formats: online ● *EES Special Reports*. Alternate Formats: online ● *Environmental Change and Security Project Report*, annual. Journal. Alternate Formats: online ● *Noticias*. Newsletter ● *Population, Environmental Change & Security News*, quarterly. Newsletter. Also Cited As: *PECS News* ● *Wilson Center Update*, monthly. Newsletter. Alternate Formats: online ● *Wilson Quarterly*. Magazine. **Price:** $20.00/year in U.S.; $35.00/year outside U.S. **Circulation:** 60,000. **Advertising:** accepted. **Conventions/Meetings:** periodic meeting ● seminar.

Humor

10207 ■ American Humor Studies Association (AHSA)
c/o Janice McIntire-Strasburg, PhD, Exec. Dir.
St. Louis Univ.
Dept. of English
3800 Lindell Blvd.
St. Louis, MO 63108-3414
E-mail: mcintire@slu.edu
URL: http://www.americanhumor.org
Contact: Janice McIntire-Strasburg PhD, Exec. Dir.
Founded: 1974. **Members:** 400. **Membership Dues:** full, $20 (annual). **Description:** Academics, general readers, and professional humorists. Encourages the study and appreciation of American humor from interdisciplinary perspectives. **Libraries: Type:** reference. **Holdings:** papers. **Awards:** The Charlie. **Type:** recognition. **Recipient:** for outstanding contribution to the study of American humor. **Telecommunication Services:** electronic mail, jalvarez@carolina.rr.com. **Affiliated With:** Modern Language Association of America. **Publications:** *Studies in American Humor*, annual. Magazine. Contains articles and reviews on topics in American humor. **Price:** included in membership dues. ISSN: 0095-280X. **Circulation:** 400. **Advertising:** accepted ● *To Wit*, semiannual. Newsletter. **Conventions/Meetings:** quadrennial seminar, held in conjunction with Modern Language Association of America and American Literature Association (exhibits) - always May or December ● annual seminar, held in conjunction with American Literature Association - always May/June.

10208 ■ Humor Helps! (HH)
14224 SE 88th Ave.
Summerfield, FL 34491
Ph: (352)307-7993
E-mail: haroldharris18@aol.com
Contact: Harold Harris, Pres.
Founded: 1987. **Members:** 200. **Membership Dues:** life, $15. **Staff:** 1. **Local Groups:** 2. **Description:** Individuals interested in introducing humor into the home and workplace on a regular basis. **Formerly:** (1992) Humor Association.

10209 ■ HUMOR Project
480 Broadway, Ste.210
Saratoga Springs, NY 12866-2288
Ph: (518)587-8770
E-mail: info@humorproject.com
URL: http://www.humorproject.com
Contact: Dr. Joel Goodman, Founder/Dir.
Founded: 1977. **Members:** 160,000. **Staff:** 4. **For-Profit. Multinational. Description:** Works to make a difference in helping people to get more "smileage" out of their lives and jobs. Consists of health care professionals, educators, counselors, therapists, business executives, and others interested in developing their sense of humor. Operates the HUMOResources mail-order and on-line bookstore with a wealth of books, videos, and fun props to amuse and amaze. Sponsors international humor conference in April and international humor workshop in October. Operates media clearinghouse. Provides grants to 400 non-profit organizations, schools, hospitals, and human service agencies to help them develop projects and services that tap the positive power of humor. **Libraries: Type:** by appointment only; reference. **Holdings:** 10,000; archival material, articles, audio recordings, books, periodicals, video recordings. **Subjects:** humor, creativity, stress management, resilience, aging, innovation, play, keys to business success, laughing and learning, the humor-health connection, the role of humor in world peace, love and laughter, innovation, coaching, public speaking. **Awards:** Corporate Compassion Humor and Creativity Award. **Frequency:** annual. **Type:** recognition ● Humor and Altruism Award. **Frequency:** annual. **Type:** recognition ● Making a Difference Award. **Frequency:** annual. **Type:** recognition. **Recipient:** for humor in action ● National Humor Treasure Award. **Frequency:** annual. **Type:** recognition. **Computer Services:** Mailing lists, of members. **Telecommunication Services:** electronic mail, webmaster@humorproject.com. **Publications:** *HUMOResources*. Videos. Alternate Formats: online ● *Laffirmations: 1,001 Ways to Add Humor to Your Life and Work*. Book ● *Laughing Matters*. Magazine. Examines the serious implications and applications of humor. Includes interviews with famous humorists and comedians. ISSN: 0731-1788. **Circulation:** 10,000 ● *Playfair: Everybody's Guide to Noncompetitive Play*. Book ● *Some Days You're the Pigeon. . .Some Days You're the Statue*. Book ● *2005 Humor Sourcebook*, annual. Catalogs. Describes the programs and services offered by The Humor Project. **Circulation:** 160,000. Alternate Formats: online. **Conventions/Meetings:** HUMOResilience (TM): Tickling Stress Before It Tackles You - workshop ● annual International Conference on the Positive Power of Humor, Hope and Healing (exhibits) - always in Saratoga Springs, NY.

10210 ■ International Society for Humor Studies (ISHS)
c/o Martin D. Lampert, PhD, Exec. Sec.-Treas.
Holy Names Univ.
Psychology Dept.
3500 Mountain Blvd.
Oakland, CA 94619-1627
Ph: (510)436-1532
E-mail: ishs@hnu.edu
URL: http://www.humorstudies.org
Contact: Rod Martin, Pres.
Founded: 1988. **Members:** 500. **Membership Dues:** student, $75 (annual) ● regular, $85 (annual) ● associate, $30 (annual). **Multinational. Description:** Works for the advancement of humor research. Represents university and college professors in the disciplines of psychology, philosophy, linguistics, literature, religion, biology, fine arts, anthropology, and education; also includes professionals in areas such as counseling, management, journalism, nursing, and theater. Studies the many facets of humor, including its role in entertainment, business, and health care as well as how humor varies according to culture, age, gender, situation, and historical context. **Libraries: Type:** reference. **Holdings:** 1,000; archival material. **Awards:** Graduate Student Award. **Frequency:** annual. **Type:** recognition ● Scholarly Contribution Award. **Frequency:** annual. **Type:** scholarship. **Recipient:** to a recent PhD who has conducted research in the area of humor studies. **Computer Services:** database, bibliographies of humor research ● database, teaching resources for humor courses ● database, test bank of tools for humor research ● mailing lists, directories of current and recent members. **Telecommunication Services:** electronic mail, ramartin@uwo.ca. **Committees:** Nominations. **Formerly:** (1985) Western Humor and

Irony Membership; (1988) World Humor and Irony Membership; (1989) World Humor and Irony Movement. **Publications:** *Humor: International Journal of Humor Research*, quarterly. Covers interdisciplinary humor research, including studies in humor theory, research methodologies, and applications of humor studies. **Price:** included in membership dues; $80.00 previous year's volume from the society; EUR 168.00 volume purchased from the publisher. ISSN: 0933-1719. **Circulation:** 500 ● *The Humorous Times: Newsletter of the International Society for Humor Studies*, quarterly. Newsletters. **Price:** free for members. Alternate Formats: online. **Conventions/Meetings:** annual International Humor Conference - convention and conference, forum for scholarly and professional papers on humor research presented in plenary, breakout, and workshop formats - 2008 June 28-July 1, Newport, RI.

10211 ■ Jokewriters Guild
Address Unknown since 2008
Founded: 1977. **Membership Dues:** individual, $24 (annual). **For-Profit. Multinational. Description:** Offers assistance to comedy writers in creating and marketing their work. Compiles statistics. Does not book jobs for performers, but endeavors to help them creatively. **Libraries: Type:** reference. **Holdings:** 100. **Subjects:** humor. **Absorbed:** (1996) Humor Correspondence Club. **Formerly:** (2003) Comedy Writers and Performers Association. **Publications:** *Comedy Buyer's Bulletin*, annual ● *How to Write Jokes* ● *Jokewriters Guild Newsletter*, semiannual ● *Short Jokes*, quarterly. **Conventions/Meetings:** annual meeting - always New York City.

10212 ■ Secret Society of Happy People (SOHP)
1315 Riverchase Dr., Ste.2316
Coppell, TX 75019
Ph: (972)471-1485
E-mail: webmaster@sohp.com
URL: http://www.sohp.com
Contact: Pamela Gail Johnson, Founder
Founded: 1998. **Members:** 6,000. **Membership Dues:** cheerful, $10 (annual). **Description:** Seeks to provide a voice for those who experience happiness and want to express it. Strives to encourage the expression of happiness and discourage parade raining. Raises awareness of recognizing different types of happiness through insightful stories and witty pieces. Inspires people to lead better lives by forming the habit of expressing happiness as much as possible. **Awards:** Happy (Campaign) Trails Award. **Frequency:** periodic. **Type:** recognition. **Recipient:** for a positive campaign media philosophy. **Publications:** *Happy Attitudes*, monthly. Newsletter. **Price:** included in membership dues.

Hungarian

10213 ■ American Hungarian Folklore Centrum (AHFC)
178 Oakdene Ave.
Teaneck, NJ 07666
Ph: (201)836-4869
Fax: (201)836-1590
E-mail: magyar@centrummanagement.org
URL: http://hungaria.org
Contact: Kalman Magyar, Dir.
Founded: 1978. **Members:** 600. **Staff:** 2. **Regional Groups:** 15. **Languages:** English, Hungarian. **Description:** A division of the American Hungarian Educators' Association (see separate entry). Persons interested in the support and promotion of Hungarian studies and folk culture within the scholarly and public life of America. Activities include researching and collecting American-Hungarian folklore, sponsoring folk dance festivals, and organizing folklore projects and Hungarian folk culture exhibits within American-Hungarian communities. Conducts charitable programs and children's services. Maintains museum. **Libraries: Type:** reference. **Holdings:** audio recordings, biographical archives, video recordings. **Telecommunication Services:** electronic mail, magyar@magyar.org. **Affiliated With:** American Hungarian Educators' Association. **Publications:** Articles ● Books. **Conventions/Meetings:** biennial meeting and symposium.

10214 ■ American Hungarian Foundation (AHF)
PO Box 1084
New Brunswick, NJ 08903
Ph: (732)846-5777
Fax: (732)249-7033
E-mail: info@ahfoundation.org
URL: http://www.ahfoundation.org
Contact: Dr. Zsolt Harsanyi, Chm.
Founded: 1954. **Description:** Contributors interested in furthering the understanding and appreciation of the Hungarian cultural and historical heritage in the U.S. Aids persons and organizations of Hungarian origin; supports and promotes publications, research, educational programs, and academic studies of Hungarian culture in American universities, colleges, and high schools. Maintains library and museum collection of books and 500 paintings, rare volumes, and manuscripts; conducts 3-4 special museum exhibits per year. Maintains Hungarian Heritage Center, a research center for the Foundation's library, archives and manuscripts, museum collection, and exhibits open to the public. **Libraries: Type:** open to the public. **Holdings:** 50,000. **Subjects:** Hungarian studies, Hungarians in America. **Awards:** Abraham Lincoln Award. **Frequency:** annual. **Type:** recognition. **Recipient:** for persons who have aided Hungary or Hungarian people and for people of Hungarian descent who have achieved success in the U.S. ● **Type:** fellowship. **Recipient:** for Hungarian studies and Hungarian immigration history ● George Washington Award. **Frequency:** annual. **Type:** recognition. **Computer Services:** database, Research Libraries Information Network ● mailing lists, of members. **Formerly:** (1977) American Hungarian Studies Foundation. **Publications:** *Hungarian Heritage*, 3/year ● *Hungarian Reference Shelf Series*. Contains five volumes per set. ● *Hungarian Studies Newsletter*, 3/year ● Report. **Conventions/Meetings:** annual meeting and dinner, includes awards presentation.

10215 ■ American Hungarian Library and Historical Society (AHLHS)
213 E 82nd St.
New York, NY 10028-2701
Ph: (212)249-9360
URL: http://magyarhaz.org/index.php?&menuid=4
Contact: Charles Vamossy, Pres.
Founded: 1955. **Members:** 200. **Membership Dues:** lending library, $15 (annual). **Staff:** 3. **Description:** Maintains collection of Hungariana; promotes research and study in the contribution of Hungarian culture to that of the U.S. Presents scientific and cultural lectures. **Libraries: Type:** reference. **Holdings:** 4,000; books. **Affiliated With:** American Hungarian Foundation. **Conventions/Meetings:** annual general assembly.

Immigration

10216 ■ Center for Equal Opportunity (CEO)
7700 Leesburg Pike, Ste.2341
Falls Church, VA 22043
Ph: (703)442-0066
Fax: (703)442-0449
E-mail: lchavez@ceousa.org
URL: http://www.ceousa.org
Contact: Linda Chavez, Chair
Description: Promotes the assimilation of immigrants into the society and conducts research on their economic and social impact on the United States. **Publications:** *Linda's Memo*, monthly. Newsletter. Contains monthly updates of CEO activities, programs and events.

India

10217 ■ India American Cultural Association (IACA)
1281 Cooper Lake Rd. SE
Smyrna, GA 30082
Ph: (770)436-3719
Fax: (770)436-4272
E-mail: komalbatra@gmail.com
URL: http://www.myiaca.org
Contact: Komal Batra, Sec.
Founded: 1971. **Membership Dues:** family, $50 (annual) ● donor, $150 (annual) ● single, $25 (annual) ● student, $10 (annual) ● life, $1,200. **Multinational. Description:** Provides cultural shows, exhibits, seminars, and introduction to arts, crafts and foods of India. Organizes The Festival of India. **Publications:** *Voice of India*. Newsletter.

10218 ■ Patidar Cultural Association of USA (PCA)
32 Stevenson Dr.
Marlboro, NJ 07746
Ph: (732)761-9829 (732)422-0429
E-mail: bhalodia@verizon.net
URL: http://www.pca1.com
Contact: Jayant Dadhania, Pres.
Membership Dues: life, $250. **Multinational. Description:** Works to preserve and promote Indian-Gujarat heritage. Promotes friendship and understanding between India and the USA. Aims to promote excellence among the youth as they grow up to be valued citizens of the USA. **Awards:** Student Excellence Award. **Frequency:** annual. **Type:** monetary. **Recipient:** for students who top the Student Excellence Index (SEI). **Publications:** Newsletter. Alternate Formats: online.

10219 ■ Uttaranchal Association of North America (UANA)
10560 Main St., Ste.LL-1
Fairfax, VA 22030
Ph: (703)273-7982
Fax: (703)385-3346
E-mail: info@uttaranchal.org
URL: http://www.uttaranchal.org
Contact: Mr. Deepak Nautiyal, Pres.
Founded: 1998. **Membership Dues:** regular, $25 (annual) ● life, $250. **Multinational. Description:** Preserves and promotes culture and heritage of Uttaranchalis in North America. Organizes social activities to bring the community closer and to make people aware of the issues of Uttaranchal. Provides a forum for Uttaranchalis in North America. **Awards:** UANA Award for Academic Excellence. **Frequency:** annual. **Type:** recognition. **Recipient:** to top two students from each of the 13 districts of Uttaranchal attaining the highest grade in class 12th and 10th examinations. **Publications:** *Uttharanchal Patrika*, semiannual. Newsletter. Contains articles on Uttaranchal news and special achievements of Uttaranchalis in America and other countries. **Advertising:** accepted. Alternate Formats: online.

Indian

10220 ■ Bihar Association of North America (BANA)
1823 Mustang Crossing
Missouri City, TX 77459
Ph: (281)416-2234
Fax: (832)204-8433
E-mail: admin@biharassociation.net
URL: http://www.biharassociation.net
Contact: Dr. Madhusudan Choudhary, Pres.
Founded: 1992. **Membership Dues:** single, $15 (annual) ● family, $25 (annual) ● life (single), $100 ● life (family), $125. **Multinational. Description:** Preserves and promotes the social and cultural heritage of Bihar in North America. Provides a forum for cultural and social interactions between members. Promotes the welfare of people of Bihar origin and ancestry. Facilitates communication and cooperation among members. **Publications:** *Biharika*. Magazine. Alternate Formats: online.

10221 ■ Leuva Patidar Samaj of USA (LPS of USA)
c/o Gunvant Prema
Knights Inn
1111B Bell Rd.
Antioch, TN 37013

Ph: (615)731-3205 (562)761-1275
Fax: (615)620-9900
E-mail: info@leuvapatidarsamaj.com
URL: http://www.leuvapatidarsamaj.com
Contact: Bhagubhai N. Patel, Pres.

Membership Dues: regular, $60 (annual) ● regular, $100 (biennial). **Description:** Aims to unite the Leuva Patidar community in the United States. Seeks to preserve the history of the Leuva Patidar community. Promotes the culture, religion and heritage of the Leuva Patidar community. **Telecommunication Services:** electronic mail, bnjasu@aol.com.

10222 ■ Milan Cultural Association
75 Ruff Cir.
Glastonbury, CT 06033
Ph: (860)657-4271
E-mail: milanusa2@aol.com
URL: http://www.milanusa.org
Contact: Suresh Sharma, Pres.

Multinational. Description: Promotes awareness of Indian culture, heritage and tradition. Protects the social and cultural ideology of India. Provides a bridge that connects Indian and American culture.

10223 ■ Punjabi-American Cultural Association (PACA)
5055 Bus. Center Dr., Ste.108, No. 165
Fairfield, CA 94534
E-mail: info@pacassociation.org
URL: http://www.pacassociation.org
Contact: Gaggandeep Singh Sooch, Contact

Founded: 2002. **Multinational. Description:** Encourages public appreciation of the Punjabi culture. Seeks to protect the Punjabi-American culture. Raises public awareness and understanding of the Punjabi culture and Sikh religion. **Publications:** *Punjabi Heritage*, annual. Newsletter. Contains news on the activities of the organization. **Price:** free. Alternate Formats: online.

Indigenous Peoples

10224 ■ First Peoples Worldwide (FPW)
3307 Bourbon St.
Fredericksburg, VA 22408
Ph: (540)899-6545
Fax: (540)899-6501
E-mail: infofpw@firstnations.org
URL: http://www.firstpeoples.org
Contact: Rebecca L. Adamson, Pres.

Multinational. Description: Seeks to assist indigenous peoples to control and develop their assets and build the capacity to direct their economic futures in ways that fit their cultures. Aims to develop indigenous capacity to manage money and invest in their own communities and businesses.

10225 ■ Igorot Global Organization (IGO)
PO Box 4471
West Covina, CA 91791
Ph: (626)919-1094
Fax: (626)919-5144
E-mail: hwprillsr@aol.com
URL: http://www.igorotglobal.org
Contact: Rosalynda Callagan, CEO

Founded: 2000. **Multinational. Description:** Preserves for future generations the diverse heritage of the Igorot people. Promotes the advancement and interests of the Igorots and those of related people. Seeks to be the advocate of Igorot rights and causes - linking Igorots and related people worldwide. **Awards:** Indigenous Peoples Leadership Award. **Frequency:** annual. **Type:** recognition. **Recipient:** for the most outstanding indigenous leaders. **Publications:** *The Igorot*, 3/year. Newsletter. **Price:** $20.00 per year in U.S.; $21.00 per year in Canada; $35.00 per year (overseas). **Circulation:** 1,000. **Advertising:** accepted. Also Cited As: *TI* ● Proceedings. Alternate Formats: online.

10226 ■ Saq' Be': Organization for Mayan and Indigenous Spiritual Bodies
PO Box 31111
Santa Fe, NM 87594
Ph: (505)466-4044
E-mail: saqbe@sacredroad.org
URL: http://www.sacredroad.org
Contact: Adam Rubel, Co-Dir.

Multinational. Description: Seeks to educate the public on current indigenous struggles. Assists indigenous communities in the preservation of their spiritual traditions. Arranges for meetings and exchanges between spiritual leaders of indigenous communities and the general public. **Computer Services:** Information services, Mayan calendar ● online services, forum. **Publications:** *SacredRoad Runner Newsletter* (in English and Spanish), 1-2/month. Alternate Formats: online.

Interdisciplinary Studies

10227 ■ Association for Integrative Studies (AIS)
c/o Prof. William H. Newell, Exec. Dir.
Miami Univ.
School of Interdisciplinary Stud.
Oxford, OH 45056
Ph: (513)529-2213 (513)260-3750
Fax: (513)529-5849
E-mail: newellwh@muohio.edu
URL: http://www.units.muohio.edu/aisorg
Contact: Prof. William H. Newell, Exec. Dir.

Founded: 1979. **Members:** 1,200. **Membership Dues:** student, $25 (annual) ● regular, $50 (annual) ● institutional, $200 (annual). **Staff:** 1. **Budget:** $20,000. **Description:** Faculty and administrators of integrative colleges, schools, programs, and courses; those interested in integrative (interdisciplinary) topics. Promotes the exchange of ideas and information among scholars and administrators in all arts and sciences and professional fields in order to encourage and improve integrative study. Provides consultants to institutions that plan to initiate or modify existing interdisciplinary programs; offers assistance in the resolution of problems concerning methodology, interdisciplinary research, and curriculum design. Seeks the development of interdisciplinary theory and standards of excellence in integrative studies research and teaching. Maintains National Archives of Undergraduate Interdisciplinary Programs, whose holdings include questionnaires, syllabi, brochures, and other documents for 750 programs. **Awards:** Kenneth E. Boulding Award. **Frequency:** periodic. **Type:** recognition. **Recipient:** for lifetime achievement and contributions to interdisciplinarity. **Computer Services:** Mailing lists, Interdis. **Affiliated With:** American Association for the Advancement of Science; Association of American Colleges and Universities. **Publications:** *AIS Newsletter*, quarterly. **Price:** included in membership dues. ISSN: 1081-647X. **Circulation:** 500 ● *Interdisciplinary Undergraduate Programs: A Directory*. Book ● *Issues in Integrative Studies*, annual. Journal. **Price:** included in membership dues. ISSN: 1081-4760. **Circulation:** 500. **Advertising:** accepted. **Conventions/Meetings:** annual conference (exhibits).

10228 ■ Educational Center for Applied Ekistics (ECAE)
1900 DeKalb Ave. NE
Atlanta, GA 30307
Ph: (404)378-2219
Fax: (404)378-8946
E-mail: horizonsschool@mindspring.com
URL: http://www.horizonsschool.com
Contact: Les Garber, Admin.

Founded: 1977. **Members:** 135. **Staff:** 12. **Description:** Generates awareness and interest in ekistics, particularly among people engaged in education. (Ekistics is a science dealing with human settlements drawing on the research and experience of professionals in various fields, such as architecture, sociology, and city planning.) Aims to provide educational resources to assist in the study, understanding, and application of ekistics. Extends applied ekistics to educators through the production and dissemination of educational materials and relevant research. Maintains an arena for cross-cultural exchange and collective global planning in the field. Provides a forum for meaningful dialogue on planned and alternative futures. Maintains Horizons School (multicultural demonstration school); offers seminars, symposia, technical assistance, and teacher education programs; acts as educational consultant. **Publications:** Also publishes educational materials, teachers' guides, audiovisual materials, and research reports.

10229 ■ Salzburg Seminar
c/o The Marble Works
152 Maple St., Ste.102
Box 886
Middlebury, VT 05753
Ph: (802)388-0007
Fax: (802)388-1030
E-mail: info@salzburgglobal.org
URL: http://www.salzburgseminar.org
Contact: Stephen Salyer, Pres./CEO

Founded: 1947. **Staff:** 60. **Budget:** $4,700,000. **Multinational. Description:** Promotes intercultural, interdisciplinary dialogue among conceptual thinkers and policymakers and mid-career professionals of demonstrated performance and potential. Fosters the development of a global community through the widening of personal, intellectual, and cultural horizons. Encourages a deepened respect for the experience and perceptions of others. **Libraries: Type:** reference. **Holdings:** 10,000. **Telecommunication Services:** electronic mail, ssalyer@salzburgglobal.org. **Publications:** *eView*, periodic. Newsletter. Alternate Formats: online ● Annual Report, annual ● Brochure ● Reports ● Annual Reports. **Conventions/Meetings:** periodic seminar, on business, government, the humanities, international relations, and law - always in Salzburg, Austria.

10230 ■ Society for Cross-Cultural Research (SCCR)
c/o David Cournoyer, Sec.-Treas.
43 O'Connell Rd.
Colchester, CT 06415
Ph: (860)570-9155 (860)537-3733
Fax: (860)537-3733
E-mail: david.cournoyer@uconn.edu
URL: http://www.sccr.org
Contact: David Cournoyer, Sec.-Treas.

Founded: 1971. **Members:** 250. **Membership Dues:** regular (single), $50 (annual) ● regular (joint), $60 (annual) ● retired, student (single), $35 (annual) ● retired, student (joint), $45 (annual) ● corresponding (single), $15 (annual) ● corresponding (joint), $45 (annual) ● retired, student (joint), $85 (biennial) ● retired, student (single), $65 (biennial). **Description:** Individuals representing the fields of anthropology, education, political science, psychology, and sociology. Supports and encourages interdisciplinary and comparative research to establish scientifically derived generalizations about human behavior. Sponsors charitable programs. **Awards: Type:** recognition. **Publications:** *Cross-Cultural Research*, periodic. Journal. Reports empirical cross-cultural studies. **Price:** $45.00. ISSN: 1069-3971. **Advertising:** accepted ● *SCCR Newsletter*, 3-4/year. Contains articles on psychological, anthropological, social science, and cross-cultural issues. Includes abstracts of research and book reviews. **Price:** included in membership dues. **Circulation:** 300. Alternate Formats: online. **Conventions/Meetings:** annual conference and meeting (exhibits) - always February.

10231 ■ Society of Educators and Scholars (SES)
c/o Prof. Sounny Slitine, Dir.
1801 MLK
San Antonio, TX 78203
Ph: (210)531-3396 (828)299-4604
Fax: (210)531-3396

E-mail: sounny@ses-online.org
URL: http://www.ses-online.org
Contact: Richard Kruse, Pres.
Founded: 1975. **Members:** 175. **Membership Dues:** general, $50 (annual). **Multinational. Description:** Professionals in fields such as humanities, social sciences, natural and physical sciences, technology, business, education, and administration. Seeks to advance human well-being through advancement of interdisciplinary understanding, expression, interchange, and dissemination of knowledge and reports on the purposes, foundations, and environments of leadership and education in society. Promotes participation in conferences, research projects, and related publications. **Telecommunication Services:** electronic mail, rak4818@cs.com. **Publications:** *Scholar and Educator*, semiannual. Journal ● *Voicer*, 3/year. Newsletter ● Also publishes and distributes scholarly books and monographs. **Conventions/Meetings:** annual conference, provides a unique exchange among specialists and generalists from all fields (exhibits).

International Cooperation

10232 ■ Trust for Mutual Understanding (TMU)
6 W 48th St., 12th Fl.
New York, NY 10036
Ph: (212)843-0404
Fax: (212)843-0344
E-mail: tmu@tmuny.org
URL: http://www.tmuny.org
Contact: Mr. Richard S. Lanier, Dir.
Founded: 1984. **Staff:** 6. **Multinational. Description:** Works to support cultural and environmental exchange between the U.S., Russia, and Eastern and Central Europe.

International Studies

10233 ■ Central Eurasian Studies Society (CESS)
c/o Harvard Program on Central Asia and the Caucasus
1730 Cambridge St. - CGIS S, Rm. S-326
Cambridge, MA 02138
Ph: (617)496-2643
Fax: (617)495-8319
E-mail: cess@fas.harvard.edu
URL: http://www.cess.fas.harvard.edu
Contact: John Schoeberlein, Dir.
Founded: 2000. **Membership Dues:** regular (based on annual income), $15-$50 (annual). **Multinational. Description:** Represents scholars who are interested in the study of Central Eurasia and its history, languages, cultures, modern states and societies. Promotes high standards of research and teaching about Central Eurasia. Fosters cooperation among persons and organizations concerned with the scholarly study of Central Eurasia. **Awards:** CESS Award for Best Graduate Student Paper. **Frequency:** annual. **Type:** recognition. **Recipient:** for a paper to be read by a graduate student at the CESS annual conference. **Telecommunication Services:** electronic mail, schoeber@fas.harvard.edu. **Publications:** *Central Eurasian Studies Review*, semiannual. Journal. Contains review of research, resources, events, publications and developments in scholarship and teaching on Central Eurasia. **Price:** $50.00 institution in North America; $65.00 institution (elsewhere); included in membership dues. ISSN: 1538-5043. **Advertising:** accepted. Alternate Formats: online. Also Cited As: *CESR*. **Conventions/Meetings:** annual conference.

10234 ■ Institute for Intercultural Studies (IIS)
67A E 77th St.
New York, NY 10021-1813
Ph: (212)737-1011
E-mail: institute@interculturalstudies.org
URL: http://www.interculturalstudies.org
Contact: Dr. Mary Catherine Bateson, Pres.
Founded: 1943. **Members:** 3. **Staff:** 1. **Description:** Conducts and encourages scholarly or scientific research and writing dealing with the behavior, customs, psychology and social organization of the various peoples and nations of the world, with special attention to those peoples and those aspects of their life, which are most likely to affect intercultural and international relations. Supports director initiated projects only and does not accept application. **Libraries: Type:** reference. **Holdings:** archival material, books, films. **Formerly:** (1944) Council on Intercultural Relations.

10235 ■ International Studies Association (ISA)
Univ. of Arizona
324 Social Sciences Bldg.
Tucson, AZ 85721
Ph: (520)621-7715 (319)335-2358
Fax: (520)621-5780
E-mail: isa@u.arizona.edu
URL: http://www.isanet.org
Contact: Thomas J. Volgy, Exec. Dir.
Founded: 1959. **Members:** 3,000. **Membership Dues:** individual (based on annual income), $40-$120 (annual) ● additional family, $20 (annual) ● institutional, $1,000 (annual) ● student (electronic journal only), $25 (annual) ● student (hard copy journal), $35 (annual) ● region (for ISA members only), $2 (annual). **Staff:** 6. **Budget:** $500,000. **Regional Groups:** 6. **Description:** Social scientists and other scholars from a wide variety of disciplines who are specialists in international affairs and cross-cultural studies; academicians; government officials; officials in international organizations; business executives; students. Promotes research, improved teaching, and the orderly growth of knowledge in the field of international studies; emphasizes a multidisciplinary approach to problems. Conducts conventions, workshops and discussion groups. **Libraries: Type:** reference. **Holdings:** archival material. **Telecommunication Services:** electronic mail, meyermk@eckerd.edu. **Committees:** Carl Beck Award; Federal Relations; Harold and Margaret Sprout Award; Karl Deutsch Award; Professional Responsibilities and Rights; Transnational Activities. **Sections:** American-Soviet Successor-State Relations; Comparative Interdisciplinary Studies; Environmental Studies; Feminist Theory and Gender Studies; Foreign Policy Analysis; Intelligence Studies; International Education; International Ethics; International Law; International Organization; International Political Economy; International Security Studies; Peace Studies; Scientific Study of International Processes. **Affiliated With:** American Association for the Advancement of Science; Consortium of Social Science Associations; International Social Science Council; Modern Greek Studies Association; Peace and Justice Studies Association. **Publications:** *International Studies Newsletter*, 10/year. Contains information on awards, grants, and fellowships. **Price:** included in membership dues; $25.00 /year for nonmembers. **Circulation:** 2,900 ● *International Studies Notes*, 3/year. Contains research, curricular, and program reports on international affairs. **Price:** $20.00/year; $36.00/2 years; $10.00/issue. **Advertising:** accepted ● *International Studies Quarterly*. Journal. **Price:** $110.00 /year for nonmembers; $30.00/issue for nonmembers; free for members. ISSN: 0020-8833. Alternate Formats: microform. **Conventions/Meetings:** competition ● annual convention (exhibits).

10236 ■ Island Resources Foundation (IRF)
1718 P St. NW, Ste.T-4
Washington, DC 20036
Ph: (202)265-9712
Fax: (202)232-0748
E-mail: irf@irf.org
URL: http://www.irf.org
Contact: Bruce Potter, Pres.
Founded: 1971. **Members:** 200. **Staff:** 6. **Budget:** $450,000. **Description:** Individuals interested in and concerned about islands and island resource management problems. Seeks to establish a research and educational center for the study of small island systems. Operates internationally. Conducts technical assistance programs for island governments and other educational and research programs; maintains speakers' bureau. Compiles statistics. **Convention/Meeting:** none. **Libraries: Type:** reference. **Holdings:** 10,000; archival material, audiovisuals, books, periodicals. **Subjects:** Oceanic Islands, development strategies, environmental planning. **Awards:** Euan P. McFarlane Fellowship Award. **Type:** fellowship. **Recipient:** for outstanding environmental leadership by young West Indians. **Computer Services:** Mailing lists, of members. **Telecommunication Services:** electronic mail, bpotter@irf.org. **Publications:** *NGO News for the Eastern Caribbean*, quarterly. Newsletter ● Annual Report ● Books ● Papers, periodic ● Has also published manuscripts.

Iranian

10237 ■ American Institute of Iranian Studies (AIIrS)
c/o Dr. Erica Ehrenberg, Exec. Dir.
118 Riverside Dr., No. 13A
New York, NY 10024
E-mail: aiis@nyc.rr.com
URL: http://www.simorgh-aiis.org
Contact: Dr. Erica Ehrenberg, Exec. Dir.
Founded: 1967. **Members:** 25. **Membership Dues:** institutional, $750 (annual). **Languages:** English, Persian. **Description:** Represents educational institutions. Seeks to facilitate research on Iran by both North American and Iranian scholars by promoting and supporting language study and scholarly exchange between Iran and the U.S. Aids scholars by supporting visa applications, facilitating appropriate contacts, and generally enhancing the work of such scholars while in the U.S. or Iran. **Awards: Frequency:** annual. **Type:** grant. **Recipient:** for advanced scholarly research in Iranian studies. **Telecommunication Services:** electronic mail, flewis@uchicago.edu. **Conventions/Meetings:** annual board meeting and symposium.

10238 ■ International Society for Iranian Studies (ISIS)
c/o Hamid Akbari, Exec. Dir.
Northeastern Illinois Univ.
5500 N St. Louis Ave.
Chicago, IL 60625
Ph: (773)442-6126
E-mail: h-akbari@neiu.edu
URL: http://www.iranian-studies.com
Contact: Hamid Akbari, Exec. Dir.
Founded: 1967. **Members:** 450. **Membership Dues:** student, $30 (annual) ● institution, $243 (annual) ● individual, $55 (annual). **Staff:** 1. **Description:** Scholars and students working in the field of Iranian studies, including historians, economists, sociologists, anthropologists, psychologists, and literary critics. Promotes scholarship in the field. Conducts seminars and conferences. **Libraries: Type:** open to the public. **Holdings:** 35. **Subjects:** Iranian studies. **Awards:** Saidi-Sirjani Memorial Book Prize. **Frequency:** annual. **Type:** monetary. **Recipient:** for excellent book on topic of Persian studies. **Committees:** Executive. **Formerly:** (1969) Society For Iranian Cultural and Social Studies; (2004) Society for Iranian Studies. **Publications:** *Iranian Studies*, quarterly. Journal. Contains research articles, book reviews, and bibliographies. **Price:** included in membership dues; $81.00 /year for individuals. ISSN: 0450-0862. **Advertising:** accepted. Alternate Formats: online ● *SIS Newsletter*, periodic. **Conventions/Meetings:** periodic conference (exhibits).

Irish

10239 ■ American Conference for Irish Studies (ACIS)
c/o Prof. Jose Lanters, Pres.
Univ. of Wisconsin-Milwaukee
Dept. of English
PO Box 413
Milwaukee, WI 53201

Ph: (912)871-1755
E-mail: lanters@uwm.edu
URL: http://www.acisweb.com/index.php
Contact: Prof. Jose Lanters, Pres.
Founded: 1962. **Members:** 1,200. **Membership Dues:** individual, $30 (annual) ● library/institution, $35 (annual) ● student, $15 (annual) ● European individual, EUR 38 (annual). **Staff:** 4. **Budget:** $30,000. **Regional Groups:** 5. **Description:** Scholars interested in Irish arts, folklore, history, language, literature, and social sciences. Sponsors microfilm project. Maintains archives of information concerning teaching and research in Irish studies. **Libraries: Type:** reference. **Holdings:** archival material. **Awards:** Book Awards. **Frequency:** annual. **Type:** monetary. **Recipient:** for books on Irish subjects published worldwide. **Telecommunication Services:** electronic mail, byronk@msu.edu. **Affiliated With:** American Historical Association; Modern Language Association of America. **Formerly:** (1987) American Committee for Irish Studies. **Publications:** *ACIS Newsletter*, 3/year. Alternate Formats: online ● *Irish Literary Supplement*, semiannual. Newsletter. **Advertising:** accepted. **Conventions/Meetings:** annual convention (exhibits) - usually April.

10240 ■ American Irish Historical Society (AIHS)
991 5th Ave.
New York, NY 10028
Ph: (212)288-2263
Fax: (212)628-7927
E-mail: info@aihs.org
URL: http://www.aihs.org
Contact: Mr. William D. Cobert, Exec. Dir.
Founded: 1897. **Members:** 700. **Membership Dues:** household, $100 (annual). **Staff:** 2. **Regional Groups:** 1. **Description:** Persons interested in American-Irish cultural and historical affairs. **Libraries: Type:** reference. **Holdings:** 11,000; articles, books, periodicals, reports. **Subjects:** Irish biography, literature, poetry, history and genealogy, the Irish in America. **Awards:** Gold Medal. **Frequency:** annual. **Type:** medal. **Recipient:** to an outstanding American of Irish lineage. **Computer Services:** database, library. **Telecommunication Services:** electronic mail, research@aihs.org. **Publications:** *The Recorder*, semiannual. Journal. Contains articles on the Irish in the U.S. and Ireland. **Price:** included in membership dues; $22.50 /year for nonmembers; $34.00 /year for institutions. ISSN: 0885-7741. **Circulation:** 2,000. **Advertising:** accepted. **Conventions/Meetings:** annual banquet - always first Thursday of November.

10241 ■ Irish American Cultural Institute (IACI)
1 Lackawanna Pl.
Morristown, NJ 07960
Ph: (973)605-1991
Fax: (973)605-8875
E-mail: info@iaci-usa.org
URL: http://www.iaci-usa.org
Contact: Jackie Walsh, Exec. Dir.
Founded: 1962. **Membership Dues:** student (must be currently enrolled), $25 (annual) ● basic, $50 (annual) ● sponsor, $75 (annual) ● patron, $150 (annual) ● benefactor, $500 (annual) ● corporate benefactor, $1,000 (annual). **Local Groups:** 21. **Description:** Individuals and firms contributing to the institute's programs. Works to stimulate creativity in the arts in Ireland. Encourages research in all aspects of Irish civilization, in Ireland and abroad. Sponsored first Irish symphony performed in the U.S; has imported Irish theater groups to tour the U.S. **Awards:** Bernard Croke Memorial Traditional Music Award. **Frequency:** annual. **Type:** recognition. **Recipient:** for young Irish musicians from the Society of Uillean Pipers who have participated in the world renowned Willie Clancy Summer School ● Butler Literary Award. **Frequency:** annual. **Type:** recognition. **Recipient:** for writers in Irish language ● Heritage Award. **Frequency:** annual. **Type:** monetary. **Recipient:** for Irish efforts to interpret Irish history ● Irish Research Funds. **Frequency:** annual. **Type:** grant. **Recipient:** for a graduate research in Irish-American studies. **Telecommunication Services:** electronic mail, jackiewalsh@iaci-usa.org. **Programs:** Irish Perception Series; Irish Way Program in Ireland for American High School Students. **Publications:** *Ducas*, 3/year. Newsletter. **Price:** included in membership dues. **Advertising:** accepted ● *Eire - Ireland*, quarterly. Journal. ISSN: 0013-2683. **Circulation:** 5,000. **Advertising:** accepted.

10242 ■ Irish American Partnership
33 Broad St.
Boston, MA 02109
Ph: (617)723-2707
Free: (800)722-3893
Fax: (617)723-5478
E-mail: info@irishap.org
URL: http://www.irishap.org
Contact: John P. Murray, Chm.
Membership Dues: associate, $35 ● benefactor, $250 ● founder, $500. **Languages:** English, Irish. **Description:** Enlists the financial support of Irish Americans to fund advanced degree scholarships in the sciences and technology in Ireland, North and South, as well as skills training, projects and programs that lead to job creation in Ireland, North and South. **Publications:** Newsletters.

10243 ■ Irish Arts Center - An Claidheamh Soluis
553 W 51st St.
New York, NY 10019
Ph: (212)757-3318
Fax: (212)247-0930
E-mail: info@irishartscenter.org
URL: http://www.irishartscenter.org
Contact: Pauline Turley, Exec. Dir.
Founded: 1972. **Members:** 3,500. **Membership Dues:** basic (minimum), $50 (annual) ● patron (minimum), $250 (annual) ● Claddagh Scholar (minimum), $10,000 (annual) ● sponsor (minimum), $100 (annual) ● benefactor (minimum), $500 (annual) ● Claddagh Circle of Friends (minimum), $1,000 (annual) ● Claddagh Angel (minimum), $5,000 (annual) ● Claddagh Guardian (minimum), $25,000 (annual). **Staff:** 6. **Budget:** $210,000. **Description:** Seeks to develop in America an awareness of the artistic expression of the Irish people. Provides a forum for the education, research, exploration, and development of Irish art forms, and for communication through art with people of other national backgrounds. An Claidheamh Soluis means "The Sword of Light". In Irish mythology this sword appeared to the Irish people when they were in great danger. Strives to ensure that the Irish culture not only survives, but again becomes the everyday expression of the Irish people. Sponsors concerts, Irish dances, and an Off-Broadway theater. Maintains speakers' bureau. **Telecommunication Services:** electronic mail, bridin@irishartscenter.org. **Divisions:** Language; Library; Music/Dance; Theatre. **Publications:** *Irish Arts*, quarterly. Newsletter. Covers Irish and Irish-American life. Includes book, record, theater, and concert reviews, and obituaries. **Price:** $30.00/year. **Circulation:** 5,000. **Advertising:** accepted. **Conventions/Meetings:** workshop, free instruction on traditional Irish music, dance, theatre, and language.

10244 ■ Irish Special Interest Group of Mensa (ISIG)
c/o Shirley Starke, Coor.
Box 230, Rte. 2
Valley City, ND 58072
Ph: (701)845-2382
E-mail: valkyriepub@hotmail.com
URL: http://www.lisashea.com/irish
Contact: Shirley Starke, Coor.
Founded: 1977. **Members:** 140. **Membership Dues:** regular, $5 (annual). **Staff:** 2. **Languages:** English, Gaelic, Irish. **Description:** Represents Mensa members and non-Mensans interested in Irish history, literature, language, genealogy, Northern Ireland. **Libraries: Type:** not open to the public. **Subjects:** Irish history, literature, language, genealogy, cooking, Northern Ireland, dance, music, folklore. **Affiliated With:** American Mensa. **Publications:** *Danta*. Features collection of creative work by members. ● *Litir Sceala* (in English and Gaelic), bimonthly. Newsletter. **Price:** $5.00/year. **Circulation:** 140. **Advertising:** accepted. Alternate Formats: online.

Islam

10245 ■ American Society for Muslim Advancement (ASMA)
475 Riverside Dr., Ste.248
New York, NY 10115
Ph: (212)870-2552
Fax: (212)870-2540
URL: http://www.asmasociety.org
Contact: Daisy Khan, Exec. Dir.
Founded: 1997. **Description:** Represents individuals dedicated to fostering an American-Muslim identity and building bridges between American Muslims and the American public. Encourages spiritual evolution in Muslim and non-Muslim Americans. Helps non-Muslims overcome "biases and negative perceptions by dismantling the common stereotypes and myths surrounding Muslims and Islam". Empowers young American Muslims to become spokespeople for a tolerant, harmonious, and authentic Islam.

Islamic

10246 ■ Committee for Crescent Observation International (CFCO)
1069 Ellis Hollow Rd.
Ithaca, NY 14850
Ph: (607)277-6706
E-mail: omarafzal1@yahoo.com
URL: http://www.islamicmoon.com
Contact: Dr. Omar Afzal, Chm.
Founded: 1979. **Members:** 431. **Membership Dues:** general, $10 (annual). **Staff:** 4. **Budget:** $14,000. **Regional Groups:** 10. **State Groups:** 37. **Local Groups:** 170. **Languages:** Arabic, English. **Description:** Disseminates information on the Lunar calendar and Islamic observance dates. Conducts research and educational programs; maintains speakers' bureau; compiles statistics. **Libraries: Type:** reference. **Holdings:** books, clippings, monographs, periodicals. **Subjects:** lunar calendar. **Computer Services:** database. **Publications:** *Islamic Lunar Calendars*, quarterly. Newsletter. **Conventions/Meetings:** quarterly meeting (exhibits).

10247 ■ International Institute of Islamic Thought (IIIT)
500 Grove St.
Herndon, VA 20170
Ph: (703)471-1133
Fax: (703)471-3922
E-mail: iiit@iiit.org
URL: http://www.iiit.org
Contact: Dr. Fathi Malkawi, Exec. Dir.
Founded: 1981. **Languages:** Arabic, English, French. **Description:** Restores and promotes Islamic thought and its integration into the social sciences. Promotes research in the social sciences, particularly in methodology and on the philosophy of science, in an effort to address the problems pertinent to Islam, the Muslim community, and the world through the principles, concepts, and values of the Islamic model. Offers guidance and supervision to graduate students. Maintains speakers' bureau. Conducts educational and research programs. **Libraries: Type:** reference. **Holdings:** 1,000; books. **Subjects:** Islamic social sciences, history, jurisprudence. **Computer Services:** Mailing lists. **Departments:** Overseas; Publications; Seminars and Research; Translation. **Affiliated With:** Association of Muslim Social Scientists. **Publications:** *American Journal of Islamic Social Sciences*, quarterly. Contains information in the field of Islamic social sciences and human studies. **Advertising:** accepted ● *IIIT/AMSS Newsbulletin* (in Arabic and English), quarterly. Books ● Books (in Arabic and English) ● Also publishes scholarly

works in Arabic and English. **Conventions/Meetings:** periodic conference and seminar.

10248 ■ International Islamic Federation of Student Organizations (IIFSO)
Address Unknown since 2007
Founded: 1969. **Regional Groups:** 5. **Multinational. Description:** Islamic student and youth groups in 45 countries, who seek to create "Ummah, the global Islamic brotherhood." Works to develop Islamic awareness among students; fosters "the attainment of an Islamic personality through providing students moral, ideological, social, and behavioral training." Encourages Muslim youth to participate in the development of their home countries and to use Islamic alternatives in addressing contemporary problems; supports social services for those in need; promotes study and understanding of Islam. Coordinates activities of and provides aid to Islamic youth organizations; promotes "productive work" for members as opposed to "propaganda and publicity." Presently inactive. **Publications:** *A Critical Look at the Theory*. Book ● *Forty Hadiths*. Book ● *IIFSO Connection*, periodic. Newsletter ● *The Individual and the State*. Book ● *Islam and Christianity*. Book ● *Islam and the World*. Book ● *Islam: The Religion of the Future*. Book ● *Islam Today*. Book ● *Milestones*. Book ● *The Muslim's Character*. Book ● *This Religion of Islam*. Book. **Conventions/Meetings:** periodic conference ● periodic seminar.

10249 ■ Islamic Society of North America (ISNA)
PO Box 38
Plainfield, IN 46168
Ph: (317)839-8157
Fax: (317)839-1840
E-mail: imattson@hartsem.edu
URL: http://www.isna.com
Contact: Dr. Ingrid Mattson, Pres.
Founded: 1963. **Members:** 10,000. **Membership Dues:** regular, $50 (annual). **Staff:** 25. **Local Groups:** 200. **Description:** Muslim organizations and individuals. Provides a common platform for presenting Islam, supporting Muslim communities, developing educational, social and outreach programs; fosters good relations with other religious communities, civic and service organizations. **Computer Services:** Mailing lists. **Committees:** Education; Family; Religious Affairs. **Divisions:** Education and Information; Professional Associations. **Publications:** *Islamic Horizons*, bimonthly. Magazine. Contains news about Muslims in North America. **Price:** $24.00/year in U.S.; $29.95/year in Canada; $60.00/year outside U.S. and Canada. ISSN: 0875-2367. **Circulation:** 35,000. **Advertising:** accepted. Alternate Formats: online ● Also publishes books and manuals. **Conventions/Meetings:** annual conference - always summer ● annual convention and lecture (exhibits) - always Labor Day weekend.

10250 ■ North American Islamic Trust (NAIT)
745 McClintock Dr., Ste.114
Burr Ridge, IL 60527
Ph: (630)789-9191
Fax: (630)789-9455
E-mail: info@nait.net
URL: http://www.nait.net
Contact: Dr. Muzammil Siddiqi, Board of Trustee
Founded: 1973. **Staff:** 20. **Budget:** $1,500,000. **Description:** Distributes Islamic books and religious supplies. **Libraries: Type:** reference. **Subjects:** Islam. **Divisions:** American Trust Publications; Islamic Book Service; Islamic Centers. **Affiliated With:** Islamic Society of North America.

Israeli

10251 ■ America-Israel Cultural Foundation (AICF)
51 E 42nd St., Ste.400
New York, NY 10017
Ph: (212)557-1600
Fax: (212)557-1611
E-mail: info@aicf.org
URL: http://www.aicf.org
Contact: William Schwartz, Pres.
Founded: 1939. **Staff:** 4. **Budget:** $2,000,000. **Nonmembership. Description:** Encourages, promotes, and sustains cultural excellence in Israel. Provides scholarships in music, the visual and design arts, filmmaking, dance, and theater to gifted students; advanced-study fellowships to teachers and young professionals; and grants to arts institutions and special projects in Israel. Allocates approximately $2.3 million for underwriting over 800 scholarships, projects, and institutions. Sponsors Israel Philharmonic Orchestra, Tel Aviv Museum of Art, Jerusalem Film and Television School, Batsheva Dance Company, and the Beit Zvi School of Drama. **Awards: Type:** scholarship. **Recipient:** for young Israelis to study the arts in Israel and occasionally abroad. **Computer Services:** database. **Telecommunication Services:** electronic mail, scholarships@aicf.co.il. **Absorbed:** (1965) America-Israel Society. **Formerly:** American Fund for Israel Institutions; American Fund for Palestine Institutions; American Palestine Fund. **Publications:** Newsletter, semiannual. **Price:** included in membership dues. **Circulation:** 5,000. **Advertising:** accepted. **Conventions/Meetings:** annual Gala Concert - show.

10252 ■ America-Israel Friendship League (AIFL)
134 E 39th St.
New York, NY 10016
Ph: (212)213-8630 (520)322-9544
Fax: (212)683-3475
E-mail: aifl@aifl.org
URL: http://www.aifl.org
Contact: Mr. William H. Behrer III, Chief Operating Off.
Founded: 1971. **Members:** 15,000. **Membership Dues:** individual, $60 (annual). **Staff:** 11. **Regional Groups:** 3. **Description:** Strengthens ties between the people of the United States and Israel; bridges distance to reveal the beauty, humanity, and modern democratic values that define both nations. **Awards:** America-Israel Friendship Award. **Type:** recognition. **Telecommunication Services:** electronic mail, volunteer@aifl.org. **Departments:** Education; Information. **Publications:** *Birth of Two Nations* ● *Israel and the U.S.A.: A Comparison of Two Allies* ● Newsletter, semimonthly ● Also publishes scholarly works on the Middle East.

10253 ■ American Friends of Beth Hatefutsoth (AFBH)
633 3rd Ave., 21st Fl.
New York, NY 10017
Ph: (212)339-6034
Fax: (212)318-6176
E-mail: ggolan@aol.com
URL: http://www.bh.org.il
Contact: Gloria Bloch Golan, Exec. Dir.
Founded: 1976. **Membership Dues:** regular, $25 (annual) ● associate, $50 (annual) ● patron/supporting, $100 (annual) ● sustaining, $500 (annual) ● Director's Circle, $1,000 (annual). **Staff:** 1. **Multinational. Description:** American supporters of Beth Hatefutsoth (the Nahum Goldmann Museum of the Jewish Diaspora in Tel Aviv, Israel).

10254 ■ American-Israel Environmental Council
c/o Perry Davis Associates, Inc.
25 W 45th St., Ste.1405
New York, NY 10036
Ph: (212)840-1166
Fax: (212)840-1514
E-mail: info@perrydavis.com
URL: http://www.perrydavis.com/index.shtml
Contact: Mrs. Aura Herzog, Contact
Founded: 1976. **Staff:** 4. **Nonmembership. Description:** Assists town planners, architects, botanists, and educators, in their efforts to preserve Israel's past and present; improves the ecological and environmental quality of life in Israel. Sponsors CBI Center for Environmental Studies in Tel Aviv. **Awards:** CBI International Environmental Award. **Frequency:** annual. **Type:** recognition. **Recipient:** for an individual who has exhibited interest and help in environmental causes. **Formerly:** (1987) Council for a Beautiful Israel. **Publications:** *Calendar Appointment Book*, annual. **Price:** $25.00. **Conventions/Meetings:** periodic meeting.

10255 ■ Friends of Bezalel Academy of Arts
501 5th Ave., Ste.909
New York, NY 10017-6107
Ph: (212)687-0542
Fax: (212)687-1140
E-mail: bezalel@earthlink.net
URL: http://www.bezalelfriends.org
Contact: Ari Kissiloff, Contact
Founded: 1980. **Members:** 3,000. **Membership Dues:** general, $250 (annual) ● friend, $500 (annual) ● scholar, $1,500 (annual). **Staff:** 3. **Description:** Individuals interested in culture or the Bezalel Academy of Arts. Raises funds to support the Bezalel Academy of Arts in Jerusalem. Conducts annual mission to Israel. **Libraries: Type:** reference. **Publications:** *Bezalel News*, semiannual. Magazine. **Price:** included in membership dues. **Conventions/Meetings:** annual meeting.

Italian

10256 ■ American Italian Historical Association (AIHA)
c/o The John D. Calandra Italian American Institute
Queens Coll./City Univ. of New York
25 W 43rd St., 17th Fl.
New York, NY 10036
Ph: (708)756-7168
Fax: (708)756-7168
E-mail: gguida@citytech.cuny.edu
URL: http://www.aihaweb.org
Contact: Mary Jo Bona, Pres.
Founded: 1966. **Members:** 500. **Membership Dues:** individual, foreign, $40 (annual) ● student, $20 (annual) ● senior (65 and over), $25 (annual) ● family, $60 (annual) ● institutional, $80 (annual) ● life, $800. **Staff:** 1. **Local Groups:** 3. **Description:** Academicians (historians, sociologists, anthropologists, writers, artists and educators) and lay persons interested in collecting, preserving, publishing, and popularizing material about the settlement and history of the Italians in the U.S. and Canada. Maintains AIHA Memorial Scholarship Fund and speakers' bureau. **Libraries: Type:** reference. **Holdings:** archival material. **Subjects:** Italian-American history and culture. **Computer Services:** Information services, H-ITAM listserv (email: lawton@purdue.edu to join). **Telecommunication Services:** electronic mail, mbona@notes.cc.sunysb.edu. **Publications:** *AIHA Newsletter*, semiannual. Contains association news, research in progress, conference notes, and book reviews. ● Bibliography. Contains information on the Italian-American experience. ● Proceedings, annual. **Conventions/Meetings:** annual conference, with photographic and other art displays (exhibits) ● seminar.

10257 ■ Istituto Italiano di Cultura
686 Park Ave.
New York, NY 10021-5009
Ph: (212)879-4242
Fax: (212)861-4018
E-mail: iicnewyork@esteri.it
URL: http://www.iicnewyork.esteri.it
Contact: Dr. Claudio Angelini, Dir.
Founded: 1950. **Membership Dues:** individual, $40 (annual). **Staff:** 13. **Languages:** English, Italian. **Description:** The cultural agency of the Italian Ministry of Foreign Affairs; serves as a center of documentation and information on Italy. Promotes cultural relations between Italy and the U.S. Organizes cultural events alone and in cooperation with other institutions. **Libraries: Type:** open to the public; by appointment only. **Holdings:** books. **Subjects:** literature, history, tourism, art, politics. **Telecommunication Services:** electronic mail, claudio.angelini@esteri.it. **Departments:** Audio-visual; Information Services; Italian Language; Library; Literature; Music;

Performing Arts; Scholarships; Students Office; Visual Arts. **Also Known As:** Italian Cultural Institute.

10258 ■ Italian Culture Council (ICC)
c/o Patricia A. McDorman, Exec.Dir.
35 W Sumner Ave., Apt. 105
Union, NJ 07083-9414
Ph: (908)206-1288
E-mail: patmcdorman@juno.com
Contact: Patricia A. McDorman, Exec.Dir.
Founded: 1963. **Languages:** English, Italian. **Description:** Professors, teachers, and other individuals and groups concerned with the Italian language and culture. Disseminates information on Italian language and culture; serves as an information center for teachers, students, Italian/Italian-American social groups, and the public. Provides speakers in New Jersey or the New York City area for informal talks on Italian history and culture. **Libraries: Type:** not open to the public. **Holdings:** books, periodicals. **Subjects:** Italian culture, cooking.

10259 ■ Italian Folk Art Federation of America (IFAFA)
PO Box 1192
Rockford, IL 61105
Free: (800)601-6888
E-mail: mark.desanctis@gmail.com
URL: http://www.italian-american.com/ifafa/welcome.htm
Contact: Mark DeSanctis, Pres.
Founded: 1979. **Members:** 800. **Membership Dues:** performing group/supporting organization, $25 (annual) ● individual, $10 (annual) ● senior/student, $5 (annual). **National Groups:** 25. **Languages:** English, Italian. **Description:** Represents Italian folk art performing groups, cultural organizations, and individuals. Works to preserve and encourage interest in Italian folk art and to highlight Italian folk art as a part of American culture. Researches Italian folk art, including folklore, traditions and customs, crafts, costumes, dances, music, and instruments. Trains leaders in Italian folk dance, songs, and crafts; collects and disseminates information. **Awards:** IFAFA Award. **Frequency:** biennial. **Type:** recognition. **Recipient:** for services pertaining to Italian involvement in community. **Computer Services:** Online services. **Publications:** *Educational Video on Folk Dance and Folk Singing*. **Price:** $25.00 for members, plus shipping and handling; $40.00 for nonmembers, plus shipping and handling ● *Folk Dances, Costumes and Customs of Italy*. Book. Includes seventeen dances with description and music, illustrations (some in color), information about Italy, costumes and traditions. **Price:** $25.00 for members, plus shipping and handling; $40.00 for nonmembers, plus shipping and handling ● *Tradizioni*, semiannual. Newsletter. **Price:** included in membership dues. **Circulation:** 1,000. **Conventions/Meetings:** biennial conference and workshop, cultural (exhibits).

10260 ■ Italian Genealogical Society of America (IGSA)
PO Box 3572
Peabody, MA 01961-3572
E-mail: mdmelnyk@comcast.net
URL: http://www.italianroots.org
Contact: Marcia Ianizzi D. Melnyk, Pres.
Founded: 1994. **Members:** 140. **Membership Dues:** individual, $15 (annual) ● family, $20 (annual) ● student, organization, $10 (annual). **Staff:** 2. **Description:** People interested in Italian genealogy. Aims to increase awareness in the field of Italian genealogical research. Holds meetings and assists in finding others with same areas of research interests. **Publications:** *Lo Specchio*, quarterly. Newsletter. **Price:** included in membership dues. **Circulation:** 150. **Advertising:** accepted ● Membership Directory, annual. **Price:** included in membership dues.

10261 ■ Italian Historical Society of America (IHS)
410 Park Ave., Ste.1530
New York, NY 10022
Ph: (718)852-2929
E-mail: society2@italianhistorical.org
URL: http://www.italianhistorical.org
Contact: Dr. John J. LaCorte, Pres.
Founded: 1949. **Members:** 100. **Staff:** 1. **Description:** Perpetuates Italian heritage in America and gathers historical data on Americans of Italian descent. Sponsored the First Italian Heritage Cultural Festival in New York City of June, 1972, in order to promote greater appreciation of basic human values and to encourage youth to become more involved in the enhancement of man's dignity. **Libraries: Type:** reference. **Holdings:** 300. **Awards:** Meucci Award. **Frequency:** annual. **Type:** recognition. **Recipient:** for exceptional contributions to improve human condition ● Varrazano Award. **Frequency:** annual. **Type:** recognition. **Recipient:** for exceptional contributions to improve human condition. **Telecommunication Services:** electronic mail, geraldpottier@gmail.com. **Also Known As:** American Italian Historical Society.

10262 ■ Italic Institute of America
PO Box 818
Floral Park, NY 11001
Ph: (516)488-7400
Fax: (516)488-4889
E-mail: italicone@aol.com
URL: http://www.italic.org
Contact: John Mancini, Chm.
Founded: 1987. **Members:** 1,000. **Membership Dues:** general, $20 (annual) ● Core Council, $150 (annual). **Staff:** 5. **Budget:** $150,000. **Languages:** English, Italian. **Description:** Conducts research and educational programs on Roman, Etruscan, and Italian culture, language, and civilization. Offers youth education program in Italian language and culture. **Libraries: Type:** reference. **Holdings:** 1,000. **Subjects:** Italian history, Italian-American history. **Awards:** ARA Pacis Award (Altar of Peace) and Silver Medallion. **Frequency:** annual. **Type:** recognition. **Recipient:** for significant contributions by Italic individual. **Councils:** Midwest. **Formerly:** (1989) Society for Italic Studies; (2000) Italic Studies Institute. **Publications:** *Italic Way*, quarterly. Magazine. Contains current events, biographies, history and analysis. **Price:** included in membership dues. **Circulation:** 3,500. **Advertising:** accepted ● Catalog ● Newsletter, bimonthly ● Also produces documentary videos and educational products. **Conventions/Meetings:** Awards Luncheon - usually in New York, NY.

Japanese

10263 ■ Japan-America Society of Washington, D.C. (JASW)
1819 L St. NW, 1B Level
Washington, DC 20036
Ph: (202)833-2210
Fax: (202)833-2456
E-mail: jaswdc@us-japan.org
URL: http://www.us-japan.org/dc
Contact: Ambassador John R. Malott, Pres./CEO
Founded: 1957. **Members:** 1,000. **Membership Dues:** student, $25 (annual) ● senior citizen, $40 (annual) ● individual, $60 (annual) ● family, $80 (annual) ● sustaining, $150 (annual) ● corporate, $500-$5,000 (annual). **Staff:** 4. **Budget:** $800,000. **Languages:** English, Japanese. **Description:** Aims to promote a greater understanding of Japan and Japanese culture, and to strengthen the relationship between the American and Japanese people. Provides a forum in Washington, DC, where distinguished Japanese visitors may meet with Americans for an exchange of ideas and offers cultural, public affairs, and educational programs and activities relating to Japan. Operates a Japanese Language School for adults and a traveling educational outreach program called "Japan-in-a-Suitcase" for elementary school children. Fosters educational exchanges and promotes a wide variety of cultural activities; arranges programs and talks on Japan and U.S.-Japan relations. Operates a resume circulation service. Holds annual events such as the Sakura Matsuri - Japanese Street Festival, National Japan Bowl Competition for high school students, and Public Affairs Dinner and Silent Auctions. **Libraries: Type:** reference. **Holdings:** 1,000. **Subjects:** Japan, Japanese-American relations. **Telecommunication Services:** electronic mail, jisdc@us-japan.org. **Committees:** Education. **Programs:** Cultural and Performing Arts; Public Affairs. **Publications:** *Nichi-Bei News*, monthly. Newsletter. Contains information about upcoming events. Alternate Formats: online. **Conventions/Meetings:** annual National Japanese Language Competition (Japan Bowl), for 300 United States' high school students ● annual Public Affairs Dinner - always in Washington, DC ● annual Sakura Matsuri (Japanese Street Festival) - always in Washington, DC.

10264 ■ Japan Foundation (JF)
New York Off.
152 W 57th St., 17th Fl.
New York, NY 10019
Ph: (212)489-0299 (213)621-2267
Fax: (212)489-0409
E-mail: info@jfny.org
URL: http://www.jfny.org
Contact: Isao Tsujimoto, Dir. Gen.
Founded: 1972. **Members:** 15. **Staff:** 15. **Languages:** English, Japanese. **Description:** Promotes international cultural and educational exchange between Japan and other countries. Provides fellowships for scholars, professionals, and doctoral candidates in the social sciences and humanities to conduct research in Japan. Offers institutional project support programs, whereby U.S. organizations can receive financial assistance for educational programs on Japan-related research. Maintains a library support program, which makes books and other materials relating to Japan available to U.S. institutions. **Libraries: Type:** reference. **Holdings:** audiovisuals, films. **Subjects:** Japan. **Awards: Frequency:** annual. **Type:** fellowship ● **Frequency:** annual. **Type:** grant. **Recipient:** for projects that will further the understanding of Japanese arts and culture. **Computer Services:** Mailing lists. **Committees:** American Advisory; Japan Studies. **Also Known As:** Kokusai Koryu Kikin. **Publications:** *Awards Announcement*, annual ● *Bridges*, semiannual. Newsletter. Provides latest information on the Foundation's activities, grants, and publications. **Price:** free. Alternate Formats: online ● *Programs Available in the U.S.*, annual ● Annual Report, annual. **Conventions/Meetings:** annual meeting.

10265 ■ Japan Information Access Project
2000 P St. NW, Ste.620
Washington, DC 20036-6920
Ph: (202)822-6040
Fax: (202)822-6044
E-mail: access@jiaponline.org
URL: http://www.jiaponline.org
Contact: Ms. Mindy L. Kotler, Dir.
Founded: 1991. **Members:** 900. **Membership Dues:** individual, $100 (annual) ● institutional, $500 (annual) ● government, academic, journalist, $65 (annual) ● corporate (minimum), $3,000 (annual). **Staff:** 2. **Languages:** English, Japanese. **Multinational. Description:** Business executives, scientists, engineers, educators, legislators, and journalists interested in Japan. Educates professionals on how to access, use, and evaluate Japanese information in science, technology, business, and management. Operates clearinghouse. **Also Known As:** Japan Project; JIAP. **Publications:** *A Guide to Japan's Patent System*, bimonthly. Newsletter. Includes reports on new sources, new legislation and regulations, and a calendar of events. **Price:** $50.00 for members; $75.00 for nonmembers. ISSN: 1065-528X ● *Asia Policy Calendar*, weekly. Report. **Price:** $50.00 for members; $75.00 for nonmembers. Alternate Formats: online ● *Japan Access Alert Bulletin*, bimonthly. Newsletter. Includes reports on new sources, new legislation and regulations, and a calendar of events. **Price:** $125.00 for nonmembers; $75.00 for members. ISSN: 1065-528X ● *Japan-U.S. Trade and Technology Primer*, annual. Directory. **Price:** $125.00 for nonmembers; $75.00 for members ● *Japan Washington Watch*, weekly. Report. **Price:** $75.00 for members; $125.00 for nonmembers ●

Japan Washington Watch, weekly. Newsletter. Reviews upcoming hearings, events and conferences with special emphasis on science and technology issue. Alternate Formats: online ● *Japanese Intellectual Property: Japanese Patent System and Strategies for Competitiveness*. Proceedings. **Price:** $75.00 for members; $125.00 for nonmembers ● *Japanese Nuclear Energy Policy and Public Opinion*. Papers. Contains information on East Asian energy markets and Energy Cooperation in Northeast Asia. **Price:** $10.00 ● Papers. Contains information on East Asian energy markets and Energy Cooperation in Northeast Asia. **Price:** $10.00 ● Reports. Alternate Formats: online. **Conventions/Meetings:** annual conference and workshop, on topics such as financial services, biomedical technology and pharmaceuticals, chemicals and materials, security and economic issues, intellectual property, and trade and technology policy.

10266 ■ Japan Society (JS)
333 E 47th St.
New York, NY 10017
Ph: (212)832-1155 (212)715-1258
Fax: (212)755-6752
E-mail: hr@japansociety.org
URL: http://www.japansociety.org
Contact: Richard J. Wood, Pres.
Founded: 1907. **Members:** 6,000. **Membership Dues:** student, senior, associate, $40 ● individual, $60 ● family/dual, $95 ● contributing, $150 ● sustaining, $250 ● sponsor, $500. **Staff:** 50. **Budget:** $5,000,000. **Description:** Individuals, institutions, and corporations representing the business, professional, and academic worlds in Japan and the United States. Promotes the exchange of ideas between Americans and Japanese in order to enhance their mutual understanding. Organizes exchange programs and offers courses in Japanese and English. Sponsors U.S.-Japan Program Outreach Service. Conducts lectures, art exhibitions, theatrical performances, film showings, and concerts. Maintains Japan Society Gallery and Japan Film Center. **Libraries: Type:** reference. **Holdings:** 7,000; biographical archives, books, periodicals. **Subjects:** Japan. **Awards:** Japan Society Award. **Frequency:** annual. **Type:** recognition. **Telecommunication Services:** electronic mail, register@japansociety.org. **Publications:** *Research Reports*, annual. Monographs. Based on research projects on issues of bilateral importance. ● *U.S.-Japan Media Dialogue*, annual. Monographs. Covers U.S.-Japan policy issues. ● Annual Report. Alternate Formats: online ● Books ● Catalogs ● Newsletters. Alternate Formats: online ● Also publishes a public affairs series based on corporate seminars and conferences. **Conventions/Meetings:** annual meeting - always fall/winter.

10267 ■ National Japanese American Historical Society (NJAHS)
1684 Post St.
San Francisco, CA 94115
Ph: (415)921-5007
Fax: (415)921-5087
E-mail: njahs@nikkeiheritage.org
URL: http://www.nikkeiheritage.org
Contact: Rosalyn Tonai, Exec. Dir.
Founded: 1980. **Membership Dues:** basic, $40 (annual) ● family, nonprofit, $50 (annual) ● supporting, $60 (annual) ● contributing, $100 (annual) ● corporation, $250 (annual) ● life, $1,000 ● patron, $500 (annual) ● student, $25 (annual). **Description:** Strives to promote and preserve the history and culture of Japanese Americans. **Publications:** *Nikkei Heritage*, quarterly. Journal ● *Rabbit in the Moon*. Video. **Price:** $29.95.

10268 ■ U.S.-Japan Culture Center (USJCC)
2600 Virginia Ave. NW, Ste.512
Washington, DC 20037
Ph: (202)342-5800 (202)342-5801
Fax: (202)342-5803
E-mail: mkanfs6295@aol.com
Contact: Mikio Kanda, Exec. Dir.
Founded: 1978. **Staff:** 5. **Description:** Seeks to promote mutual understanding between the U.S. and Japan. Helps the public, scholars, government officials, and businessmen of both countries to increase their knowledge of U.S.-Japan relations. Sponsors cultural activities that extend into the areas of education, economics, and politics. Provides information and research material services; Japanese and English language classes; exchange programs for students, teachers, and specialists; intern and work-study programs for American and Japanese university students; exchange programs for state and local government officers; and national speech contest in Japanese. **Libraries: Type:** reference. **Holdings:** 10,000; books, periodicals. **Committees:** American; Japanese. **Publications:** Newsletter, bimonthly. **Conventions/Meetings:** competition, essay contest on U.S.-Japan relations ● competition, speech contest in Japanese ● monthly lecture ● monthly seminar.

10269 ■ Urasenke Tea Ceremony Society (UTCS)
Address Unknown since 2008
Founded: 1980. **Members:** 150. **Staff:** 4. **Description:** Purpose is to introduce the Japanese culture through the centuries-old tradition of the tea ceremony. Aids students in mastering the highly structured form of the tea ceremony. Conducts lectures and demonstrations throughout the U.S.

Jazz

10270 ■ American Federation of Jazz Societies (AFJS)
c/o Jim Jones, Pres.
1400 16th St., Ste.420
Washington, DC 20036
Ph: (310)831-3372
Fax: (310)831-3372
E-mail: jjbanjo@juno.com
URL: http://www.afjs.org
Contact: Jim Jones, Pres.
Founded: 1985. **Members:** 5,000. **Membership Dues:** individual, $36 (annual) ● organization/institution, $95 (annual) ● Jazz Society (based on size), $50-$150 (annual) ● band, $50 (annual). **Staff:** 1. **Budget:** $10,000. **Local Groups:** 230. **Multinational. Description:** Helps support and sustain the promotion, performance, preservation, and perpetuation of jazz. Works for the advancement of all forms of jazz as one music. Covers the entire jazz spectrum from traditional and Dixieland through be-bop, Latin and avant-garde. **Libraries: Type:** reference. **Awards:** Benny Carter Award. **Frequency:** annual. **Type:** recognition. **Recipient:** to a standout in the jazz spectrum. **Boards:** Directors. **Publications:** *Federation Jazz*, periodic. Journal. Features sections for reports of successes and activities of societies, an ombudsman feature, cogent articles and historic recountings. **Price:** included in membership dues. **Circulation:** 500. **Conventions/Meetings:** annual convention and conference.

Jewelry

10271 ■ American Society of Jewelry Historians (ASJH)
1333A North Ave., No. 103
New Rochelle, NY 10804
Ph: (914)235-0983 (212)302-6636
Fax: (914)235-0983
E-mail: info@jewelryhistorians.org
URL: http://www.jewelryhistorians.org
Contact: Ms. Meg Selig, Sec.
Founded: 1986. **Members:** 500. **Membership Dues:** student, $25 (annual) ● individual in U.S., $65 (annual) ● individual outside U.S., $55 (annual) ● dual, $110 (annual) ● company, $135 (annual) ● corporate, $2,500 (annual). **Regional Groups:** 3. **Multinational. Description:** Promotes study of the history of jewelry through lectures, field trips and informational newsletters for members. **Publications:** *Newsletter of the American Society of Jewelry Historians*, semiannual. Contains synopsis of Jewelry Society lectures, jewelry-related book reviews, museum exhibitions and independent articles ancient to modern jewelry. **Price:** included in membership dues. **Circulation:** 500. **Conventions/Meetings:** annual party and lecture, with auction ● seminar.

Jewish

10272 ■ American Jewish Historical Society (AJHS)
15 W 16th St.
New York, NY 10011
Ph: (212)294-6160 (617)559-8880
Fax: (212)294-6161
E-mail: info@ajhs.cjh.org
URL: http://www.ajhs.org
Contact: Kenneth J. Bialkin, Chm.
Founded: 1892. **Members:** 2,300. **Membership Dues:** sponsor, $500 (annual) ● patron, $1,000 (annual) ● friend, $50 (annual). **Staff:** 13. **Budget:** $1,500,000. **Languages:** English, Hebrew, Yiddish. **Description:** Individuals and institutions interested in American Jewish history. Seeks to collect, display, preserve, and publish material on the history of the American Jewish community. Maintains speakers' bureau. **Libraries: Type:** reference. **Holdings:** 50,000; archival material, articles, books, papers, photographs. **Subjects:** American Jewish history. **Awards:** Emma Lazarus Award. **Frequency:** annual. **Type:** recognition. **Recipient:** for contribution to improve the human condition ● Hank Greenberg Sportsmanship. **Frequency:** annual. **Type:** recognition. **Recipient:** for Jewish-American contribution to the world of sports ● Lee Max Friedman Memorial Award. **Frequency:** annual. **Type:** recognition. **Recipient:** for contributions to American-Jewish history ● Ruth Fein Fellowship. **Frequency:** annual. **Type:** fellowship. **Recipient:** for graduate research using the holdings of the American-Jewish Historical Society ● Saul Viener Prize. **Frequency:** biennial. **Type:** monetary. **Recipient:** for best book in American-Jewish history ● Sidney Lapidus Fellowship. **Frequency:** annual. **Type:** fellowship. **Recipient:** for graduate research using the holdings of the American-Jewish Historical Society ● Wasserman Prize. **Frequency:** annual. **Type:** recognition. **Recipient:** for best student essay, best article, and best local history article submitted for publication. **Computer Services:** Mailing lists, of members. **Telecommunication Services:** electronic mail, dsolomon@ajhs.cjh.org. **Committees:** Academic; Award. **Affiliated With:** American Historical Association; Council of American Jewish Museums; Council of Archives and Research Libraries in Jewish Studies. **Publications:** *America Stands with Israel*. Book. Provides a record, in photographs and text, of the rally in support of Israel in Washington, D.C., on April 15, 2002. ● *American Jewish History*, quarterly. Journal. Contains articles about settlement, history, and life of Jews on the American continent. Includes book reviews. **Price:** included in membership dues. ISSN: 0164-0178. **Circulation:** 3,700. **Advertising:** accepted. Alternate Formats: online ● *Blessings of Freedom*. Book. Includes chapters in American-Jewish history. **Price:** $35.00 ● *Facing the New World*. Book. **Price:** $20.00 ● *Heritage*, quarterly. Newsletter. Presents information concerning the history of the Jews in the United States. Includes research updates. **Price:** included in membership dues. ISSN: 0732-0914. **Circulation:** 8,000 ● *History of Jewish Women in America*. Book. Contains 2 volumes. **Price:** $200.00 ● *Hoopskirts and Huppas*. Book. **Price:** $20.00 ● *Jewish Justices Supreme Court*. Book. **Price:** $20.00 ● *The Jewish People in America*. Books. Multivolume study of American-Jewish history, 1654 to post World War II. ● *Lehman: A Family History*. Book. **Price:** $20.00 ● *Levy Family and Montecillo*. Book. **Price:** $20.00 ● Videos. **Conventions/Meetings:** biennial Academic Council Scholars' Conference (exhibits).

10273 ■ American Society for Jewish Heritage in Poland (ASJHIP)
1202 Lexington Ave., No. 121
New York, NY 10028-1425
Ph: (212)330-6588

E-mail: info@asjhip.org
URL: http://www.asjhip.org
Contact: Nancy Brumm, Pres./Founder

Founded: 1997. **Multinational. Description:** Aims to advance the understanding of Jews and the Jewish community in Poland. Provides information about the Jews and the Jewish community in Poland, their past and current history, and their contributions and impact throughout the world. Promotes Jewish heritage by preserving documents, archives, books, and similar artifacts.

10274 ■ Athra Kadisha: The Society for the Preservation of Jewish Holy Sites
203 Penn St.
Brooklyn, NY 11211
Ph: (845)783-9626
Fax: (845)782-6283
E-mail: jstern1@frontiernet.net
Contact: Rabbi Zvi Kestenbaum, Pres.

Founded: 1942. **Description:** Works to "protect and preserve the sanctity and integrity" of Jewish cemeteries around the world. Appeals to government agencies and other groups to preserve the cemeteries. Cemeteries in Israel and Europe have been preserved.

10275 ■ Central Yiddish Culture Organization (CYCO)
Publishing House and Book Distribution Ctr.
25 E 21st St.
New York, NY 10010
Ph: (212)505-8305
Fax: (212)505-8044
E-mail: cycobooks@aol.com
Contact: Hy Wolfe, Exec. Dir.

Founded: 1938. **Members:** 1,000. **Staff:** 3. **Languages:** English, Yiddish. **Description:** Publishes and distributes Yiddish books. **Libraries: Type:** open to the public. **Holdings:** 2; books. **Subjects:** Yiddish literature in America. **Affiliated With:** Congress for Jewish Culture. **Publications:** *The World of Yiddish Books 2003* (in English and Yiddish). Catalog. Contains a partial listing of more than 50,000 books. **Conventions/Meetings:** annual meeting.

10276 ■ Committee for the Implementation of the Standardized Yiddish Orthography (CISYO)
c/o League for Yiddish, Inc.
45 E 33 St., No. 203
New York, NY 10016
Ph: (212)889-0380
Fax: (212)889-0380
E-mail: info@leagueforyiddish.org

Founded: 1958. **Description:** Promotes the implementation of the standardized Yiddish orthography. (Currently there are several different ways of spelling many Yiddish words.) Conducts a wide-range correspondence on standard Yiddish orthography. Conventions/Meetings: none. **Boards:** Editorial. **Publications:** *Guide to Standardized Yiddish Orthography* (in English and Yiddish). Book. **Price:** $15.00 ● *Yiddish Orthography: An Outline for a Course* (in English and Yiddish).

10277 ■ Congregation Bina
600 W End Ave., Ste.1C
New York, NY 10024-1643
Ph: (212)873-4261
E-mail: shmueldivekar@aol.com

Founded: 1981. **Members:** 90. **Membership Dues:** individual, $25 (annual) ● family, $50 (annual). **Staff:** 9. **Description:** Seeks to preserve and foster interest in the customs, liturgy, music, and folklore of Jews who settled in India. Works to establish and maintain synagogues. Sponsors educational, charitable, and research programs and children's services. Maintains speakers' bureau. Holds religious services. **Publications:** *Kol Bina*, semiannual. Includes information on members' activities and articles on the Jews of India. **Price:** free. **Circulation:** 750.

10278 ■ Congress for Jewish Culture (CJC)
25 E 21st St.
New York, NY 10010
Ph: (212)505-8040
E-mail: kongres@earthlink.net
Contact: Dr. Barnett Zumoff, Co-Pres.

Founded: 1948. **Members:** 3,500. **Staff:** 5. **Regional Groups:** 30. **Languages:** English, Yiddish. **Description:** Federation of organizations of writers, educators, publishers, cultural departments, and fraternal organizations promoting Jewish cultural activities such as literary events, concerts of Jewish music, and art exhibits and publication of works in Yiddish. Conducts research programs. Maintains speakers' bureau. **Libraries: Type:** reference. **Holdings:** archival material. **Awards:** Communal Award. **Frequency:** annual. **Type:** recognition. **Recipient:** for excellence and achievement ● Literary Award. **Type:** recognition. **Recipient:** for excellence and achievement. **Publications:** *Anthology of Yiddish Literature* (in English and Yiddish). Contains two volumes per set. ● *Biographical Dictionary of Yiddish Literature* (in English and Yiddish). Contains eight volumes per set. ● *Encyclopedia of Education* (in English and Yiddish). Contains three volumes per set. ● *Grammar of Standard Yiddish* ● *History of Yiddish Literature* ● *ZUKUNFT (The Future)*, quarterly. Magazine. Contains literary material. ● Also has published more than 100 volumes on Jewish history, literary criticism, and the Holocaust.

10279 ■ Congress of Secular Jewish Organizations (CSJO)
320 Claymore Blvd.
Cleveland, OH 44143-1730
Ph: (216)481-0850 (216)373-3262
Free: (866)333-2756
Fax: (216)481-0964
E-mail: rifke@adelphia.net
Contact: Ms. Roberta E. Feinstein, Exec. Dir.

Founded: 1970. **Members:** 3,500. **Membership Dues:** individual, family, group, $35 (annual). **Staff:** 1. **National Groups:** 24. **Description:** Promotes the interests of Secular Jewish organization members. Conducts holiday programs; sponsors adult education and Sunday schools; makes available children's services. **Libraries: Type:** reference. **Awards:** Andrews Foundation Grant. **Type:** grant. **Recipient:** for an outstanding holiday book. **Computer Services:** Mailing lists, of members and publications. **Publications:** *Apples and Honey: A Compendium of Music and Readings for the New Year Festival* ● *CSJO Newsletter*, quarterly. Includes compilation of board minutes and member group activities. **Price:** included in membership dues. **Circulation:** 2,000 ● *Festivals, Folklore and Philosophy* ● *The Jewish New Year Festival* ● *Mame Loshn - A History of Yiddish Culture* ● *New Yorkish* ● *Passover Haggadah* ● *Pushcarts and Dreamers* ● *We Rejoice in Our Heritage* ● *Yiddish Short Story Sampler.* **Conventions/Meetings:** annual conference, with new publications/teaching supplies and curricula (exhibits) - Memorial Day weekend.

10280 ■ Eleanor Leff Jewish Women's Resource Center (JWRC)
820 2nd Ave., 2nd Fl.
New York, NY 10017-4504
Ph: (212)687-5030
Fax: (212)687-5032
E-mail: alandau@ncjwny.org
URL: http://www.ncjwny.org
Contact: Annette Henkin Landau, Coor.

Founded: 1978. **Members:** 3,000. **Membership Dues:** individual, $50 (annual) ● life, $350. **Staff:** 2. **Description:** Dedicated to the documentation of the modern Jewish feminist movement through programs, lectures, publications, and a library that can reach an international network of women and men connected and concerned with Jewish women. **Libraries: Type:** reference; open to the public. **Holdings:** 18,051; archival material, articles, audio recordings, books, papers, periodicals. **Subjects:** birth ceremonies, egalitarian marriage contracts, Passover Haggadot, Jewish women's history, Rosh Hodesh ceremonies, healing ceremonies, poetry publications. **Awards:** The Ellie. **Frequency:** semiannual. **Type:** trophy. **Recipient:** for best film, advancement of women, etc. **Computer Services:** Information services, catalog-ing. **Committees:** Film Festival; Library; Poetry; Programming. **Formerly:** (2002) Jewish Women's Resource Center. **Publications:** *Di Froyen, Conference Proceedings on Women and Yiddish.* Book. **Price:** $5.00 ● *Jewish Women's Literary Annual*, annual. Book. **Price:** $18.00 ● *Sarah's Daughters Sing.* Book. Features poetry anthology. **Price:** $12.00 ● *Which Lilith? Feminist Writers Re-Create The World's First Woman.* Book. **Price:** $20.00. **Conventions/Meetings:** periodic Transforming the Jewish World: A Feminist View - conference.

10281 ■ Hineni
232 W End Ave.
New York, NY 10023
Ph: (212)496-1660
Fax: (212)496-1908
E-mail: hineni@hineni.org
URL: http://www.hineni.org
Contact: Barbara Janov, Exec. Dir.

Founded: 1973. **Members:** 26,000. **Staff:** 14. **Multinational. Description:** Jewish families and individuals. Seeks to make Jews aware of and knowledgeable about their heritage. Conducts classes, seminars, and study sessions on the Bible and Talmud; maintains a crisis center for individual and family counseling. Operates singles center that sponsors social gatherings and programs. Maintains the Hineni World Heritage Center, designed to preserve the Jewish community and to give young Jews a sense of pride in their heritage. Sponsors semiannual leadership training program. Maintains placement service and speakers' bureau; broadcasts WEE television program. Maintains a museum. **Libraries: Type:** open to the public. **Holdings:** 1,500; audio recordings, video recordings. **Subjects:** Judaic. **Awards: Frequency:** periodic. **Type:** recognition. **Computer Services:** Online services, dating service - Computerized Matchmaking Services. **Publications:** *The Committed Life.* Books. Contains ancient teachings of the past. **Price:** $11.00 ● *The Committed Marriage.* Books. Features a guide on how to find a soulmate, strengthen a relationship, heal past hurts and build a new life. **Price:** $16.77 ● *The Jewish Soul on Fire.* Books. Contains the personal story of Rebbetzin Esther Jungreis and compelling actions for Jews everywhere. **Price:** $15.00 ● *Prayer Works.* Videos. Covers the Bible and related Jewish subject matter. **Price:** $20.00 ● *Wisdom from the Torah.* Audiotapes. Covers the Bible and related Jewish subject matter. **Price:** $60.00. **Conventions/Meetings:** weekly lecture ● annual retreat.

10282 ■ Historical Society of Jews from Egypt (HSJE)
PO Box 230445
Brooklyn, NY 11223
Fax: (718)998-2497
E-mail: information@hsje.org
URL: http://www.hsje.org
Contact: Desire L. Sakkal, Pres.

Description: Seeks to preserve the culture and history of the Jews from Egypt as well as Jewish historical sites and monuments in Egypt, including cemeteries, synagogues, schools, hospitals, social welfare buildings; provides genealogical research; sponsors educational programs. **Libraries: Type:** reference. **Publications:** *Second Exodus*, quarterly. Newsletter. Includes scholarly reports and community announcements. Provides forum for renewal of contacts. **Price:** $1.00. **Conventions/Meetings:** lecture.

10283 ■ Jewish Publication Society (JPS)
2100 Arch St., 2nd Fl.
Philadelphia, PA 19103-4599
Ph: (215)832-0608 (215)832-0600
Free: (800)234-3151
Fax: (215)568-2017
E-mail: jewishbook@jewishpub.org
URL: http://www.jewishpub.org
Contact: Dr. Ellen Frankel, Ed.-in-Chief/CEO

Founded: 1888. **Members:** 15,000. **Membership Dues:** copper circle, $108 (annual) ● contributing,

$36 (annual) ● supporting, $54 (annual) ● sustaining, $108 (annual) ● bronze circle, $500 (annual) ● silver circle, $1,000 (annual) ● gold circle, $2,500 (annual) ● platinum circle, $5,000 (annual). **Staff:** 24. **Description:** Individuals and institutions, predominantly Jewish, interested in publication and dissemination of books on Jewish history, religion, and literature. **Telecommunication Services:** electronic mail, development@jewishpub.org. **Formerly:** (1985) Jewish Publication Society of America. **Supersedes:** American Jewish Publication Society. **Publications:** *And Hannah Wept*. Book. Provides information and emotional support from a Jewish perspective for situations ranging from pregnancy loss to genetic engineering. **Price:** $5.98 ● *Celebration and Renewal*. Book. Contains 10 essays about Jewish perspective on the life cycle and contemporary applications of Jewish law and tradition. **Price:** $7.98 ● *Coat of Many Cultures*. Book. Presents seven works based on the biblical story, drawn from writers of different backgrounds and faiths. **Price:** $12.00 ● *The Court Jesters*. Book. **Price:** $6.80 ● *Documentors of the Dream*. Book. Contains black and white pictures of the origin and development of Eretz Israel. **Price:** $20.00 ● *JPS Torah Commentary* ● *Publications Catalog*, semiannual ● *Tanakh*. The English-language Jewish Bible. **Conventions/Meetings:** annual meeting - usually late May or early June in Philadelphia, PA.

10284 ■ Leo Baeck Institute (LBI)
15 W 16th St.
New York, NY 10011
Ph: (212)744-6400
Fax: (212)988-1305
E-mail: lbaeck@lbi.cjh.org
URL: http://www.lbi.org
Contact: Carol Kahn Strauss, Exec. Dir.
Founded: 1955. **Members:** 1,200. **Membership Dues:** student, $50 (annual) ● general, $100 (annual) ● university, university department, $150 (annual) ● corporate, $250 (annual) ● sponsor, $1,000-$2,999 (annual) ● patron, $3,000-$4,999 (annual) ● benefactor, $5,000-$10,000 (annual). **Staff:** 18. **Budget:** $600,000. **Languages:** English, German. **Description:** Documents and preserves the history and culture of German-speaking Jewry in Central Europe. Maintains The Institute's library, archives, photo and art collections that are used free of charge by researchers, historians, genealogists and journalists around the world. **Libraries: Type:** reference. **Holdings:** 60,000; archival material, artwork, books, periodicals, photographs, reports. **Subjects:** German speaking Jewish history and culture. **Awards:** David Baumgardt Memorial Fellowship. **Frequency:** annual. **Type:** fellowship. **Recipient:** for research done at LBI ● Fritz Halbers Fellowship. **Frequency:** annual. **Type:** fellowship. **Recipient:** for students enrolled in a PhD program at an accredited institution of higher education ● LBI/DAAD Award. **Frequency:** annual. **Type:** monetary. **Recipient:** for doctoral students and recent PhDs. **Computer Services:** Online services, catalog listing library and archives. **Telecommunication Services:** electronic mail, carol@lbi.cjh.org. **Publications:** *Bulletin des Leo Baeck Instituts*. **Price:** $12.00 ● *Judischer Almanach des LBI, Vol. 10*. Book. **Price:** $25.00 ● *LBI News*, periodic. Newsletter. Reports on activities of the institute and on LBI collections of interest to the public. **Price:** included in membership dues ● *Leo Baeck Institute List of Publications*. Catalog ● *Leo Baeck Memorial Lecture*, annual. **Price:** included in membership dues; $12.00 for nonmembers ● Yearbook, annual. Contains studies and essays on the political, cultural, economic, and social history of Jews in German-speaking countries; includes bibliography. **Price:** included in membership dues; $45.00 for nonmembers. Alternate Formats: CD-ROM ● Also has published over 100 books of historical and cultural focus.

10285 ■ Marcus Center of the American Jewish Archives (AJA)
3101 Clifton Ave.
Cincinnati, OH 45220
Ph: (513)221-1875 (513)221-7444
Fax: (513)221-7812
E-mail: gzola@huc.edu
URL: http://www.americanjewisharchives.org/aja
Contact: Gary P. Zola PhD, Exec. Dir.
Founded: 1947. **Staff:** 12. **Description:** Gathers and catalogues letters, congregational records, and other documents pertaining to the history of Jews in America. Located on campus of Hebrew Union College-Jewish Institute of Religion in Cincinnati, OH, which acts as patron. **Libraries: Type:** open to the public; reference. **Holdings:** archival material, biographical archives, reports. **Awards:** Bernard and Audre Rapoport Fellowships. **Frequency:** annual. **Type:** fellowship ● Ethel Marcus Memorial Fellowship. **Frequency:** annual. **Type:** fellowship ● Loewenstein-Wiener Fellowship Award. **Frequency:** annual. **Type:** fellowship ● Marguerite R. Jacobs Memorial Post-Doctoral Award. **Frequency:** annual. **Type:** fellowship ● Rabbi Frederic A. Doppelt Memorial Fellowship. **Frequency:** annual. **Type:** fellowship ● Rabbi Theodore S. Levy Tribute Fellowship. **Frequency:** annual. **Type:** fellowship ● Starkoff Fellowship. **Frequency:** annual. **Type:** fellowship. **Telecommunication Services:** electronic mail, rkreimer@huc.edu. **Formerly:** (2003) American Jewish Archives. **Publications:** *American Jewish Archives Journal*, semiannual. Includes information on American Jewish life, history, and culture; book reviews; and archival information. ISSN: 0002-905X. **Circulation:** 6,125. Alternate Formats: microform ● Books ● Brochures ● Monographs ● Pamphlets.

10286 ■ Memorial Foundation for Jewish Culture (MFJC)
c/o Dr. Jerry Hochbaum, Exec. VP
50 Broadway, 34th Fl.
New York, NY 10004-1690
Ph: (212)425-6606
Fax: (212)425-6602
E-mail: office@mfjc.org
URL: http://www.mfjc.org
Contact: Dr. Jerry Hochbaum, Exec. VP
Founded: 1965. **Staff:** 8. **Multinational. Description:** Aims to encourage and contribute to Jewish scholarship, culture, and education. Provides aid for professional training to serve Jewish communities overseas and sponsors individual and team projects in institutions in areas of Jewish education, research, scholarship, and publication. **Convention/Meeting:** none. **Libraries: Type:** reference. **Holdings:** archival material. **Awards:** Ephraim E. Urbach Post-Doctoral Fellowships. **Frequency:** annual. **Type:** fellowship ● International Community Service Scholarship. **Frequency:** annual. **Type:** scholarship. **Recipient:** for Jewish educational, religious, and communal workers to help obtain advanced training for leadership positions ● International Doctoral Scholarship for Studies Specializing in Jewish Fields. **Frequency:** annual. **Type:** scholarship. **Recipient:** to graduate students specializing in a Jewish field who are enrolled in a doctoral program at a recognized university and engaged in doctoral dissertation research ● International Fellowships in Jewish Studies. **Frequency:** annual. **Type:** fellowship. **Recipient:** to individuals engaged in independent Jewish research or cultural projects ● Post-Rabbinic Scholarship Program. **Frequency:** annual. **Type:** scholarship.

10287 ■ National Center for Jewish Healing (NCJH)
120 W 57th St.
New York, NY 10019
Ph: (212)399-2320
Fax: (212)399-2475
E-mail: info@ncjh.org
URL: http://www.ncjh.org
Founded: 1994. **Staff:** 3. **Description:** Helps communities to meet the spiritual needs of Jews living with illness, loss and other significant life challenges. **Libraries: Type:** reference. **Holdings:** 50; articles, books, video recordings. **Subjects:** health, spiritual healing, Jewish resources on spiritual healing. **Also Known As:** (1999) Jewish Healing Center. **Publications:** *Guide Me Along the Way: A Jewish Spiritual Companion for Surgery*. Book. **Price:** $11.95 ● *The Outstretched Arm*, quarterly. Newsletter. **Price:** included in membership dues; $1.50/copy. **Circulation:** 10,000 ● *When the Body Hurts the Soul Still Longs to Sing*. Booklet. **Price:** $4.00/copy; $3.25/copy (minimum of 10); $2.75/copy (minimum of 50).

10288 ■ National Yiddish Book Center (NYBC)
Harry and Jeanette Weinberg Bldg.
1021 West St.
Amherst, MA 01002-3375
Ph: (413)256-4900
Fax: (413)256-4700
E-mail: yiddish@bikher.org
URL: http://www.yiddishbookcenter.org
Contact: Aaron Lansky, Pres./Founder
Founded: 1980. **Members:** 30,000. **Membership Dues:** regular, $36 (annual) ● supporter, $54 (annual) ● patron, $180 (annual) ● President's Circle, $360 (annual) ● Editor's Council, $1,000 (annual) ● Publisher's Society, $5,000 (annual). **Staff:** 21. **Budget:** $3,000,000. **Languages:** English, Yiddish. **Description:** Jewish cultural activists; students and scholars of Yiddish literature; other interested persons. Dedicated to the revitalization of Jewish life through the preservation and promotion of Yiddish culture and contemporary Jewish literature. Collects discarded Yiddish books; catalogs, digitizes and makes the books available to teachers, students, and university and institution libraries. Offers a comprehensive program of cultural activities and courses in Yiddish language and contemporary Jewish literature; exhibits on Yiddish culture and conferences, readings, lectures, and film screenings. Offers student internship in Yiddish language and culture. Maintains searchable online database of available English and Yiddish titles. **Libraries: Type:** reference. **Holdings:** 1,500,000; biographical archives, books, films, periodicals. **Subjects:** fiction, non-fiction, poetry, drama, social science. **Awards:** Student Internships. **Frequency:** annual. **Type:** recognition. **Recipient:** to eighteen students. **Computer Services:** database, of Yiddish books. **Telecommunication Services:** electronic mail, members@bikher.org. **Formerly:** (1982) National Yiddish Book Exchange. **Publications:** *An Hour in Paradise*. Book. **Price:** $13.95 ● *The Curse of the Appropriate Man*. Book. **Price:** $13.00 ● *Natasha and Other Stories*. Book ● *Outwitting History: The Amazing Adventures of a Man Who Rescued a Million Yiddish Books*. Booklets. **Price:** $30.95 large printed edition; $24.95 hard cover ● *Pakn Treger*, periodic. Magazine. Contains fiction essays, photos and arts about Jewish culture. **Price:** included in membership dues; $6.00 for nonmembers. **Circulation:** 30,000. **Advertising:** accepted. Alternate Formats: online ● *The Place Will Comfort You*. Book. **Price:** $23.00. **Conventions/Meetings:** periodic conference.

10289 ■ Society for the History of Czechoslovak Jews (SHCJ)
Address Unknown since 2008
Founded: 1961. **Members:** 240. **Membership Dues:** $25 (annual). **Description:** Persons united to study the economic, religious, social, and cultural aspects of the history of Jews from Czechoslovakia and to increase public knowledge of such history. **Publications:** *The Jews of Czechoslovakia*. Book. **Price:** $12.00 per volume of the book; $6.00 per volume of the review ● *Review I*. Book ● *Review II*. Book ● *Review III*. Book ● *Review IV*. Book ● *Review V*. Book ● *Review VI*. Book. **Conventions/Meetings:** annual meeting, with memorial service - early March, always New York City.

10290 ■ Tzivos Hashem (TH)
792 Eastern Pkwy.
Brooklyn, NY 11213
Ph: (718)467-6630
Fax: (718)467-8527
E-mail: info@tzivoshashem.org
URL: http://www.tzivos-hashem.org
Contact: Rabbi Yerachmiel Benjaminson, Exec. Dir.
Founded: 1980. **Members:** 420,000. **Staff:** 21. **Budget:** $2,500,000. **Local Groups:** 200. **Description:** Children under 13 years of age. Seeks to foster among Jewish youth an appreciation of their Jewish heritage. Established the first ever Jewish Children's

Museum. Maintains educational resource center, educational toy and book store, Tzivos Hashem Book Club, and Hachai (a publishing house). Offers pen pal introduction service; sponsors athletic teams, guidance programs, bar-mitzvah preparation, and crafts programs. Conducts rallies for youth groups. Maintains charitable program. (The group's title translates from Hebrew as "Hosts of God"). **Publications:** *Moshiach Times*, 5/year. Magazine ● *Tzivos Hashem Newsletter*, 5/year ● Books. **Conventions/Meetings:** periodic competition.

10291 ■ Yiddisher Kultur Farband (YKUF)
Address Unknown since 2008
Founded: 1937. **Staff:** 2. **Budget:** $100,000. **Description:** Promotes Jewish culture through publishing works of contemporary and classical Jewish authors, conducting cultural forums, and exhibiting historical materials and works of contemporary Jewish artists. **Libraries: Type:** reference. **Holdings:** 30,000. **Subjects:** literature, literary criticism. **Awards: Frequency:** annual. **Type:** recognition. **Recipient:** for literature. **Publications:** *Yiddishe Kultur* (in Yiddish), bimonthly. Magazine. **Price:** $25.00 in U.S.; $30.00 in Canada. ISSN: 0044-0426. **Circulation:** 1,800. **Advertising:** accepted. **Conventions/Meetings:** annual conference; **Avg. Attendance:** 300.

10292 ■ YIVO Institute for Jewish Research (YIVO)
15 W 16th St.
New York, NY 10011-6301
Ph: (212)246-6080 (212)294-6126
Fax: (212)292-1892
E-mail: yivomail@yivo.cjh.org
URL: http://www.yivo.org
Contact: Dr. Carl J. Rheins, Exec. Dir.
Founded: 1925. **Members:** 17,000. **Membership Dues:** regular, $54 (annual) ● senior, student, $36 (annual). **Staff:** 35. **Budget:** $4,400,000. **Local Groups:** 2. **National Groups:** 2. **Languages:** English, Yiddish. **Description:** Engages in research in East European Jewish social and historical studies, and in Yiddish language, literature, and folklore as they relate to East European Jews and their descendants. Collects and preserves documentary and archival material pertaining to Ashkenazic Jewish life in Eastern and Central Europe and the U.S; trains young scholars through the Max Weinreich Center for Advanced Jewish Studies, in Jewish history, folklore, ethnography; Yiddish language, literature, and linguistics; disseminates information to universities, organizations, and the public. Offers public programs, symposia and adult education classes. **Libraries: Type:** reference. **Holdings:** 350,000; archival material, artwork, audiovisuals, books, monographs, periodicals. **Subjects:** Yiddish language and literature, Eastern European Jewish history and culture, Jews in the USA. **Awards:** Abraham and Rachela Melezin Fellowship. **Type:** fellowship ● Abram and Fannie Gottlieb Immerman and Abraham Nathan and Bertha Daskal Weinstein Memorial Fellowship. **Type:** fellowship ● Aleksander and Alicja Hertz Memorial Fellowship. **Type:** fellowship ● Dina Abromowicz Emerging Scholar Fellowship. **Type:** fellowship ● Dora and Meyer Tendler Fellowship. **Type:** fellowship ● Maria Salit-Gitelson Tell Memorial Fellowship. **Type:** fellowship ● The Natalie and Mendel Racolin Memorial Fellowship. **Frequency:** annual. **Type:** recognition. **Recipient:** for post-doctoral research ● Prof. Bernard Choseed Research Fellowship. **Frequency:** annual. **Type:** fellowship. **Recipient:** for post-doctoral research ● Rose and Isidore Drench Fellowship. **Frequency:** annual. **Type:** fellowship. **Recipient:** for post-doctoral research ● Vivian Lefsky Hort Fellowship. **Frequency:** annual. **Type:** fellowship. **Recipient:** for post-doctoral research ● Vladimir and Pearl Heifetz Memorial Fellowship. **Frequency:** annual. **Type:** fellowship. **Recipient:** for undergraduate, graduate or post graduate researcher at the YIVO archives and library ● Workmen's Circle/Dr. Emanuel Patt Visiting Professorship in Eastern European Jewish Studies. **Type:** fellowship. **Telecommunication Services:** electronic mail, crheins@yivo.cjh.org. **Affiliated With:** American Historical Association; Association for Jewish Studies; Society of American Archivists. **Publications:** *Guide to the YIVO Archives*. Journal. **Price:** $130.00 ● *The Last Days of the Jerusalem of Lithuania: Chronicles from Vilna Ghetto and the Camps, 1939-1944*. Book. **Price:** $39.02 ● *YIVO Annual*, annual. Journal ● *YIVO Bleter* (in English and Yiddish), periodic ● *YIVO News/Yedies* (in English and Yiddish), semiannual. **Circulation:** 17,000. Alternate Formats: online ● Books. **Conventions/Meetings:** periodic conference.

10293 ■ Yugntruf - Youth for Yiddish (YYY)
45 E 33rd St., No. 203
New York, NY 10016
Ph: (212)889-0381
E-mail: yugntruf@yugntruf.org
URL: http://www.yugntruf.org
Contact: Ms. Myra Mniewski, Exec. Dir.
Founded: 1964. **Members:** 1,053. **Membership Dues:** full-time student, $18 (annual) ● regular, $36 (annual). **Staff:** 1. **Local Groups:** 7. **Languages:** English, Yiddish. **Multinational. Description:** College and high school students, young adults and those young at heart, with an interest in Yiddish. Promotes the Yiddish language. Perpetuates Yiddish cultural heritage. Develops contemporary Yiddish literature and culture. Creates environments where Yiddish is the spoken language in the members' respective countries, especially among young people, by sponsoring retreats, picnics, concerts, lectures, discussions and day-long workshops and events conducted entirely in Yiddish. Makes available: "Vaserl", a record of Yiddish songs, "Vidervuks", an anthology of young Yiddish writers, "Dos Kleyne Vekerl", a children's book, children's T-shirts and buttons with Yiddish in Hebrew lettering written on them. **Libraries: Type:** reference. **Holdings:** 300; books, papers, periodicals. **Subjects:** Yiddish language, literature, history, philosophy. **Telecommunication Services:** electronic mail, yugntrufreshime-request@yugntruf.org. **Committees:** Editorial. **Sections:** Leyenkrayzn (reading groups); Shmueskrayzn (conversation groups); Shraybkrayz (Yiddish writers workshop); Yiddish classes. **Publications:** *Vidervuks: An Anthology of 20 Young Yiddish Writers* (in English and Yiddish). Book. **Price:** $20.00 ● *Yiddish Source Finder*. Directory. Lists Yiddish schools, publishing houses, publications, records, radio programs, clubs, and reading circles. **Price:** $3.00/issue ● *Yugntruf* (in English and Yiddish), periodic. Journal. Contains Yiddish stories, poems, and articles; includes Yugntruf news. **Price:** $4.00 for nonmembers or for extra copy; included in membership dues. ISSN: 0098-3640. **Circulation:** 1,000. **Advertising:** accepted ● Brochures. **Conventions/Meetings:** monthly Yiddish Conversation Group - workshop, activities range from speakers to discussions of social events marking the Jewish holidays and event outings ● monthly Yiddish Writers Workshop, with Yiddish writers reading and discussing their work ● annual Yidish-tog - symposium, day-long event with lectures, workshops, and entertainment around a particular theme (exhibits) ● annual Yidish-vokh - retreat, includes lectures, discussions, sports, singing and other cultural activities; conducted entirely in Yiddish - one week in late summer.

Korean

10294 ■ World Kouk Sun Do Society
45 S Main St., Ste.90
West Hartford, CT 06107-2402
Ph: (860)523-5260
E-mail: question@sundo.org
URL: http://www.sundo.org
Contact: Al Passacantando, Contact
Founded: 1983. **Members:** 200. **State Groups:** 1. **National Groups:** 8. **Languages:** English, Korean. **Multinational. Description:** Represents the interests of individuals committed to educating people around the world to help them attain a more healthful way of life. Fosters a personal sense of peace and contentment that affects peoples' lives and their work within the society. **Also Known As:** Sun Do Mountain Taoist Breathing Meditation Center. **Publications:** *Sun Do News*, quarterly. Newsletter ● *Tao of Life*. Book. **Conventions/Meetings:** Sun Do Retreats - 6/year.

Labor

10295 ■ Eugene V. Debs Foundation
PO Box 843
Terre Haute, IN 47808
Ph: (812)232-2163
URL: http://www.eugenevdebs.com
Contact: Michael J. Sullivan, Pres.
Founded: 1962. **Members:** 750. **Membership Dues:** student, limited income, $5 (annual) ● regular, $10 (annual) ● supporting, $25 (annual) ● sustaining, $100 (annual) ● life, $250. **Budget:** $20,000. **Description:** Seeks to preserve as a museum the home of Eugene V. Debs (1855-1926), American labor leader and political figure. Collects documents and other materials pertaining to Eugene V. Debs, his brother, Theodore Debs, and the labor and reform movements in general. Mural of Debs' life by artist John Joseph Laska is in Debs House. Promotes labor education programs and conferences. Maintains hall of fame for labor leaders in Debs Memorial Gardens. **Libraries: Type:** reference. **Holdings:** 1,000. **Subjects:** labor, social reform movements. **Awards:** Debs Award. **Frequency:** annual. **Type:** recognition. **Recipient:** for an outstanding person in the field of labor, education, or public service ● Eugene V. Debs Award. **Frequency:** annual. **Type:** recognition. **Publications:** *Debs Foundation Newsletter*, semiannual. **Price:** free for members. Alternate Formats: online ● Brochure. **Conventions/Meetings:** annual dinner - always October or November in Terre Haute, IN ● semiannual meeting - always spring and fall.

Language

10296 ■ American Philological Association (APA)
c/o University of Pennsylvania
292 Logan Hall
249 S 36th St.
Philadelphia, PA 19104-6304
Ph: (215)898-4975
Free: (800)548-1784
Fax: (215)573-7874
E-mail: apaclassics@sas.upenn.edu
URL: http://www.apaclassics.org
Contact: Adam D. Blistein PhD, Exec. Dir.
Founded: 1869. **Members:** 3,300. **Membership Dues:** regular (based on annual salary), $28-$196 (annual) ● student, $25 (annual) ● joint, $25 (annual) ● life, $2,000 ● joint life, $2,500. **Staff:** 4. **Budget:** $600,000. **Description:** Teachers of Latin and Greek, classical archaeologists with literary interests, and comparative linguists. Works for the advancement and diffusion of philological information. Sponsors placement service and campus advisory service to provide advice on instructional programs in classical studies. **Awards:** Charles J. Goodwin Award of Merit. **Frequency:** annual. **Type:** recognition. **Recipient:** for an outstanding contribution to classical scholarship published by the member within a period of three years ● Excellence in Teaching the Classics. **Frequency:** annual. **Type:** recognition. **Recipient:** for excellence in the teaching of the Classics. **Computer Services:** database ● online services. **Telecommunication Services:** electronic mail, blistein@sas.upenn.edu. **Committees:** Ancient History; Classical Tradition; Computer Activities; Education; Finance; Joint Commission on Classics in American Education; Performance of Classical Texts; Placement; Publications; Research; Status of Women and Minority Groups. **Publications:** *Amphora*, semiannual, spring and fall. Includes literature, language, mythology, history, culture, classical tradition and the arts, and by featuring reviews of current books, films. **Price:** free. Alternate Formats: online ● *Positions for Classicists and Archaeologists*, monthly ● *Transactions of the American Philological Association*,

semiannual. Journal. **Price:** included in membership dues. Alternate Formats: online ● Membership Directory, biennial. **Advertising:** accepted ● Monographs ● Newsletter, bimonthly. ISSN: 0569-6941. Alternate Formats: online. **Conventions/Meetings:** annual meeting (exhibits) - 2009 Jan. 8-11, Philadelphia, PA.

10297 ■ Assyrian Academic Society (AAS)
8324 N Lincoln Ave.
Skokie, IL 60077
Ph: (847)982-5800
E-mail: info@aas.net
URL: http://www.aas.net
Contact: Dr. John C. Michael, Committee Advisor
Membership Dues: regular, $100 (annual). **Multinational. Description:** Devoted to an interdisciplinary study of research on Assyrians and Sureth-speaking villages. **Libraries: Type:** reference. **Computer Services:** Mailing lists. **Publications:** *Assyrians in Armenia*. Video. **Price:** $25.00 plus shipping and handling ● *The Journal of the Assyrian Academic Society*, semiannual. Contains cultural studies, comparative and cross-disciplinary historical literature, national and religious diversification. ● *The Tablet*. Newsletter. Alternate Formats: online ● Papers. Alternate Formats: online.

10298 ■ AUI Peace Language International (aPLI)
Address Unknown since 2007
Founded: 1982. **Members:** 100. **Staff:** 2. **Languages:** German. **Description:** Currently Inactive. Individuals interested in studying aUI (the language of space) and its philosophy. Purpose is to promote the teaching and spread of aUI. Advocates use of aUI as a method of communication, creativity, and self-expression, and as a guide to emotional and mental health and peace within the individual, and ultimately, the world. Believes that this international language may dissolve the slogans and divisiveness of conventional language. Seeks to educate the public about what the group believes are the linguistic and psychological advantages of aUI, and its potential as an international language. Provides technical support for educational activities and sessions. Trains health professionals in the use of logotherapy, or the use of symbols, in their treatment of the mentally and emotionally disturbed. **Libraries: Type:** reference. **Holdings:** 20; books. **Subjects:** communication, creativity, mental health. **Telecommunication Services:** electronic mail, weilgart@oneota.net. **Formerly:** aUI Peace Language International. **Publications:** *aUI, The Language of Space*. Book. Textbook to study the language of space and its philosophy. **Price:** $14.95. **Advertising:** not accepted ● *Cosmic Elements of Meaning*.

10299 ■ Bhojpuri Association of North America (BANA)
50 Tennyson Rd.
East Windsor, NJ 08520
Ph: (972)948-0996
E-mail: info@bhojpuri.us
URL: http://www.bhojpuri.us
Contact: Shri. Sailesh Mishra, Founder/Pres.
Membership Dues: regular, $25 (annual) ● student, $10 (annual) ● life, $250. **Multinational. Description:** Brings together the Bhojpuri-speaking community in the United States and Canada. Promotes Bhojpuri language, culture and traditions in North America. Provides a platform for American Bhojpuriyas to interact with each other. Popularizes Bhojpuri Music and Arts in various forms in USA/Canada. Adopts common Bhojpuri Grammar standards across the globe.

10300 ■ Endangered Language Fund (ELF)
300 George St., Ste.900
New Haven, CT 06511
E-mail: elf@haskins.yale.edu
URL: http://www.endangeredlanguagefund.org
Contact: Douglas H. Whalen, Founder/Pres.
Membership Dues: regular, $50-$99 ● sustaining, $500 ● supporting, $100-$499 ● Friend of the Fund, $50. **Description:** Devoted to the scientific study of endangered languages; supports native efforts to maintain endangered languages; disseminates findings to the native and scholarly communities; strives to preserve texts of native cultures, prepare videotaped instruction in languages, support "generation skipping" language learning. **Awards: Frequency:** annual. **Type:** grant. **Recipient:** for language maintenance and linguistic fieldwork. **Computer Services:** Online services, ELFIALA: The Endangered Language Fund Internet Algonquian Language Archive. **Publications:** Reports. **Conventions/Meetings:** workshop.

10301 ■ Hankes Foundation (HF)
1768 Colfax Ave. S
Minneapolis, MN 55403
Ph: (612)374-2453 (612)377-6412
E-mail: e.hankes@att.net
URL: http://www.elmhansynd.com
Contact: Camilla R. Hempleman, Pres.
Founded: 1982. **Members:** 4. **Staff:** 8. **Description:** Participants are academics engaged in phonetic studies relative to invented languages. Promotes studies of various aspects of languages for developing a universal second language known as Emaygheecha. Emaygheecha was originated by Elmer Hankes, based on a special abstract binary code, and is intended for use in future international communication. Foundation activities are centered in Minneapolis, MN, and Hengyang, China. **Publications:** none. **Convention/Meeting:** none. **Awards: Type:** grant. **Recipient:** for studies in universal languages. **Telecommunication Services:** electronic mail, elmhansynd@att.net.

10302 ■ International Society for Language Studies (ISLS)
c/o OSBORN
Fordham Univ.
Graduate School of Educ.
113 W 60th St., Rm. 1102
New York, NY 10023
E-mail: info@isls-inc.org
URL: http://www.isls-inc.org
Contact: Lisa Patel Stevens, Pres.
Founded: 2002. **Membership Dues:** regular, $75 (annual) ● student, $45 (annual). **Multinational. Description:** Aims to bridge the gap between arbitrary academic disciplines pertaining to language studies. Provides a forum for both theoretical and empirical research for exploring the relationships among language, power, discourses, and social practices. Disseminates post-positivistic research in language matters. **Publications:** *Critical Inquiry in Language Studies: An International Journal*, quarterly. Covers critical discourse and research in language matters. **Price:** included in membership dues. Also Cited As: *CILS* ● *Emergent Scholars in Language Studies Volume Series*. Book. Features the work of authors engaged in advanced graduate studies and newly minted graduates of doctoral programs. ● *Language Studies Course and Practice-Based Series*. Book. Contains texts that will be used for teaching purposes in the area of language studies. ● *Readings in Language Studies Volume Series*. Book. Contains writings featuring a range of stylistic and research approaches to language studies. **Conventions/Meetings:** annual conference.

10303 ■ Joint National Committee for Languages (JNCL)
4646 40th St. NW, Ste.310
Washington, DC 20016
Ph: (202)966-8477 (202)833-7522
Fax: (202)966-8310
E-mail: info@languagepolicy.org
URL: http://www.languagepolicy.org
Contact: J. David Edwards PhD, Exec. Dir.
Founded: 1972. **Members:** 61. **Membership Dues:** organization, association, $1,500 (annual). **Staff:** 3. **Budget:** $200,000. **Description:** Language organizations concerned with the pedagogy and use of languages for education, cultural communication, government, and trade. Monitors and assists in development of language-related policies and administrative issues at the federal level; educates members of constituent organizations to enhance their participation in national policy. **Telecommunication Services:** electronic mail, jde@languagepolicy.org. **Affiliated With:** National Council for Languages and International Studies. **Publications:** *Annual State Survey in Cooperation with the National Council of State Foreign Language Supervisors*, periodic. Report ● Also publishes policy summaries. **Conventions/Meetings:** annual Delegate Assembly - always spring.

10304 ■ Logical Language Group (LLG)
2904 Beau Ln.
Fairfax, VA 22031
Ph: (703)385-0273
E-mail: lojban@lojban.org
URL: http://www.lojban.org
Contact: Arnt Richard Johansen, Pres.
Founded: 1987. **Members:** 750. **Budget:** $8,000. **Description:** Individuals studying Loglan/Lojban (an artificial human language); persons interested in the artificial language movement. Fosters research, development, and education relating to logical languages, especially Loglan/Lojban. Aims to promote the scientific study of the relationships between language, thought, and human culture; investigate the nature of language and determine the requirements for an artificially engineered natural language; implement and experiment with such a language and devise and promote its applications in fields including anthropology, computer science, education, and human biology. Develops educational materials; holds classes; conducts research on foreign language teaching methods, artificial intelligence, and linguistics. Maintains speakers' bureau. **Libraries: Type:** reference. **Holdings:** 100; archival material, books. **Subjects:** linguistics, Loglan/Lojban history and description/text. **Telecommunication Services:** electronic mail, president@lojban.org. **Publications:** *Ju'i Lobypli*, periodic. Journal. **Price:** $28.00. **Circulation:** 100 ● *Le Lojbo Karni*, periodic. Newsletter. **Price:** $5.00. **Circulation:** 750 ● *Lojban Reference Grammar*. Book ● Also publishes language education software; plans to publish textbook and dictionary. **Conventions/Meetings:** annual meeting - usually July, Fairfax, VA.

10305 ■ National Alliance to Save Native Languages
1455 Pennsylvania Ave. NW
Washington, DC 20004
Ph: (206)420-4638
Fax: (202)659-1340
E-mail: r_lakota@hotmail.com
URL: http://www.savenativelanguages.org
Contact: Ryan Wilson, Pres.
Founded: 2006. **Description:** Promotes the revitalization of Native Languages. Comprised of stakeholders including tribes, schools, individuals, and regional and national organizations. Aims to reclaim and revitalize America's Native Languages. Assists in the rallying of resources on all levels to preserve Native languages as a vital part of contemporary Native society.

10306 ■ National Council for Languages and International Studies (NCLIS)
4646 40th St. NW, Ste.310
Washington, DC 20016
Ph: (202)966-8477 (202)833-7522
Fax: (202)966-8310
E-mail: info@languagepolicy.org
URL: http://www.languagepolicy.org
Contact: J. David Edwards PhD, Exec. Dir.
Founded: 1988. **Members:** 57. **Membership Dues:** organization/association, $1,500 (annual). **Staff:** 3. **Budget:** $200,000. **Regional Groups:** 5. **State Groups:** 26. **National Groups:** 33. **Description:** Language and international education associations, and organizations concerned with foreign language education, international studies, international exchanges, and global affairs. Aims to maintain contact with legislators and policymakers in order to sensitize them to concerns of the language and international studies communities, and to acquire and disseminate information. Objectives are: to broaden and improve the learning and teaching of languages and other

international studies; to increase cooperation and dialogue among foreign language, classical, English-as-a-second-language, bilingual, and international studies associations; to inform others of the importance and value of language and international studies to the political, economic, and intellectual security of the U.S; to foster international exchange and foreign study programs that stress development of full proficiency in languages and international studies. Supports legislation and policies that promote languages and international studies. Conducts political action workshops. **Telecommunication Services:** electronic mail, jde@languagepolicy.org. **Affiliated With:** Joint National Committee for Languages. **Formerly:** (1987) Council for Languages and Other International Studies. **Publications:** *Legislative Update*, periodic ● Brochure. **Conventions/Meetings:** annual conference.

10307 ■ Society for New Language Study
c/o Dr. Peter J. Fields, Sec./Ed.
English Dept.
Midwestern State Univ.
3410 Taft Blvd.
Wichita Falls, TX 76308
Ph: (940)397-4246
Fax: (940)397-4931
E-mail: peter.fields@mwsu.edu
Contact: Dr. Peter J. Fields, Sec./Ed.
Founded: 1972. **Members:** 60. **Staff:** 1. **Budget:** $550. **Multinational. Description:** Aims to stimulate consideration, evaluation, and cultivation of the study of language, literature, and philosophy from a perennial perspective. **Libraries: Type:** reference. **Holdings:** archival material. **Publications:** *In Geardagum: Essays on Old and Middle English Language and Literature*, annual. Journal. Contains literary and philosophical criticism. **Price:** $10.00. **Circulation:** 50 ● *Poetry Series*, periodic ● Monographs, annual ● Also publishes volumes on literary topics and poetry occasionally. **Conventions/Meetings:** annual convention.

10308 ■ Society for the Study of Indigenous Languages of the Americas (SSILA)
PO Box 555
Arcata, CA 95518
E-mail: gerdts@sfu.ca
URL: http://www.ssila.org
Contact: Donna Gerdts, Pres.
Founded: 1981. **Members:** 850. **Membership Dues:** individual in U.S., $20 (annual) ● individual in Canada, C$21 (annual). **Staff:** 1. **Budget:** $10,000. **Description:** All persons interested in the scientific study of the languages of the native peoples of North, Central, and South America. Promotes the study of indigenous linguistics in the Americas. **Awards:** Ken Hale Prize. **Frequency:** annual. **Type:** monetary. **Recipient:** for achievements in community-based work on indigenous languages ● Mary R. Haas Award. **Frequency:** annual. **Type:** recognition. **Recipient:** for the author of a significant unpublished work on an American Indian language ● Wick R. Miller Travel Award. **Frequency:** annual. **Type:** monetary. **Recipient:** for scholars residing outside the U.S. or Canada. **Computer Services:** Mailing lists. **Publications:** *SSILA Directory*, annual. Includes an index of the languages of specialization of members, and listing of e-mail addresses. **Price:** $3.50 for members; C$5.00 for members ● *SSILA Newsletter*, quarterly. Contains news, announcements, notices of recent publications, and a listing of recent dissertations. **Price:** included in membership dues; $20.00 /year for nonmembers; $5.00/issue for nonmembers. ISSN: 1046-4476. **Circulation:** 900 ● *Studies in the Indigenous Languages of the Americas*. Monograph. **Conventions/Meetings:** annual conference and meeting, held in conjunction with American Anthropological Association or Linguistic Society of America.

Latin American

10309 ■ Association of Teachers of Latin American Studies (ATLAS)
58th Ave., Level 1, Ste.252
Little Neck, NY 11362
Ph: (718)428-1237
Fax: (718)428-1237
E-mail: atlas0754@aol.com
Contact: Daniel J. Mugan, Exec. Dir.
Founded: 1970. **Members:** 727. **Membership Dues:** $12 (annual). **Staff:** 5. **Budget:** $85,000. **Languages:** English, Portuguese, Spanish. **Description:** Represents educators, graduate students, and others interested in promoting teaching about Latin America in U.S. educational institutions. Conducts teacher training and lectures. Sponsors low-cost flights to Latin America. Has conducted nine Fulbright and one Tinker Foundation program for the U.S. Department of Education in Latin America. Operates speakers' bureau. **Libraries: Type:** reference. **Holdings:** 1,000. **Subjects:** Latin America. **Awards:** Fulbright-Hayes. **Frequency:** annual. **Type:** grant. **Recipient:** for high school and college teachers only. **Committees:** International Programs; Studies Program. **Publications:** *Association of Teachers of Latin American Studies—Perspective*, quarterly. Newsletter. Covers information on meetings, grant and job opportunities, media reviews, and news from colleges. **Price:** included in membership dues. **Circulation:** 700. **Advertising:** accepted ● Also publishes course outlines and curriculum guides on Chile, Ecuador, Brazil, Argentina, Peru, and Venezuela. **Conventions/Meetings:** semiannual conference, features media items (exhibits) - always October in various locations ● biennial symposium ● workshop and seminar.

10310 ■ Conference on Latin American History (CLAH)
c/o U.S. Department of of History and Program in Latin American Studies
Univ. of North Carolina at Charlotte
9201 Univ. City Blvd.
Charlotte, NC 28223
Ph: (704)687-2027
Fax: (704)687-3218
E-mail: clah@uncc.edu
URL: http://www.h-net.org/~clah/index.php
Contact: Dr. Thomas Holloway, Sec.
Founded: 1926. **Members:** 775. **Membership Dues:** retired, $25 (annual) ● professional, $40 (annual) ● life, $700 ● student, $15 (annual). **Staff:** 3. **Description:** Individuals and institutions with an interest in the history and civilization of the countries of Latin origin in the Americas. Fosters study and dissemination of information about Latin American history. **Libraries: Type:** reference. **Holdings:** 36; books, clippings, periodicals. **Subjects:** Latin American history. **Awards:** Bolton-Johnson Memorial Prize. **Frequency:** annual. **Type:** monetary. **Recipient:** for best book in English on Latin American history ● Conference on Latin American History Prize. **Frequency:** annual. **Type:** monetary. **Recipient:** for best article on Latin American history ● Distinguished Service Award. **Type:** monetary. **Recipient:** for lifetime contribution to the study of Latin America ● Howard F. Cline Memorial Prize. **Frequency:** biennial. **Type:** monetary ● James A. Robertson Memorial Prize. **Frequency:** annual. **Type:** monetary. **Recipient:** for best article in HAHR ● James R. Scobie Memorial Award. **Type:** monetary ● Lydia Cabrera Award. **Frequency:** annual. **Type:** monetary. **Recipient:** for best project on Cuban history, pre-1868 ● TIBESAR Prize. **Frequency:** annual. **Type:** monetary. **Recipient:** for best article in The Americas. **Computer Services:** Mailing lists, available for purchase. **Committees:** Andean Studies; Borderlands; Brazilian Studies; Caribe Studies; Centro America Studies; Chile-Rio de la Plata Studies; Colonial Studies; Gran Columbian Studies; International Scholarly Relations; Mexican Studies; Social Science History; Teaching and Teaching Materials. **Affiliated With:** American Historical Association. **Publications:** *CLAH Newsletter*, semiannual ● *Conference Series Publications*, periodic ● *Membership List*, annual. Membership Directory. **Conventions/Meetings:** annual meeting, held in conjunction with American Historical Association (exhibits).

10311 ■ Latin American Studies Association (LASA)
Univ. of Pittsburgh
416 Bellefield Hall
Pittsburgh, PA 15260
Ph: (412)648-7929
Fax: (412)624-7145
E-mail: lasa@pitt.edu
URL: http://lasa.international.pitt.edu
Contact: Mr. Charles R. Hale, Pres.
Founded: 1966. **Members:** 5,500. **Membership Dues:** student, Latin-American (permanent resident of Latin America or Caribbean, including Puerto Rico, with income of under $20000), $27 (annual) ● joint, $32 (annual) ● regular (based on gross calendar year income), $35-$110 (annual) ● Latin-American (permanent resident of Latin America or Caribbean, including Puerto Rico, with income of over $20000), $40 (annual) ● life, $2,500. **Staff:** 4. **Budget:** $200,000. **Languages:** English, Portuguese, Spanish. **Description:** Persons and institutions with scholarly interests in Latin America, inclusive of non-U.S. nationals. Encourages more effective training, teaching, and research in Latin American studies; aids in interchange of professional personnel; works to improve library resource materials in this field; provides centralized information services; fosters research and publications. **Awards:** Bryce Wood Book Award. **Frequency:** periodic. **Type:** recognition. **Recipient:** for an outstanding book on Latin America in the social sciences and humanities published in English ● Kalman Silvert Award. **Frequency:** periodic. **Type:** recognition. **Recipient:** for lifetime contribution to the study of Latin America ● LASA Media Award. **Frequency:** periodic. **Type:** recognition. **Recipient:** for outstanding media coverage of Latin America. **Funds:** Congress Travel; General Endowment; Humanities Endowment; Student Travel. **Publications:** *Bulletin of Latin American Research*, quarterly. **Price:** $51.00 ● *Journal of Latin American Studies*. **Price:** $50.00 ● *LASA Forum*, quarterly. Newsletter. Reports on anthropology, economics, geography, political science, human rights, literature, the arts, and Spanish and Portuguese languages. **Price:** included in membership dues; $30.00 /year for nonmembers. **Circulation:** 4,900. **Advertising:** accepted ● *Latin American Research Review*, 3/year. Journal. Provides articles, research reports and notes, and review essays. **Price:** included in membership dues; $25.00 /year for nonmembers. **Advertising:** accepted ● Brochure (in English, Portuguese, and Spanish), annual. **Price:** free ● Membership Directory. Provides information on all current LASA members. ● Also issues special reports, reprints. **Conventions/Meetings:** International Congress - conference, with book and film exhibits (exhibits) - every 18 months.

10312 ■ Panamerican Cultural Circle (PCC)
PO Box 469
Cedar Grove, NJ 07009-0469
Ph: (973)239-3125
Fax: (973)239-3125
E-mail: circulodecultura@aol.com
URL: http://www.circulodeculturapanamericano.org
Contact: Dr. Elio Alba-Buffill PhD, Exec. Sec.
Founded: 1963. **Members:** 800. **Membership Dues:** college professor, writer, poet, $20 (annual). **Regional Groups:** 5. **Languages:** English, Spanish. **Description:** Professors, scholars, writers, poets, artists, and others interested in the culture and democratic ideals of Panamerica. Seeks to: promote the ideals of Panamericanism; disseminate information on Latin American culture; stimulate literary activity and the study of Spanish and Latin American literature. **Awards:** Alberto Gutierrez de la Solana (Novels & Theatre). **Frequency:** annual. **Type:** monetary. **Recipient:** for the best unpublished novel or play ● Enrique Labrador Ruiz Award (Short Stories). **Frequency:** annual. **Type:** monetary. **Recipient:** for literary value ● Eugenio Florit Award (Poetry). **Frequency:** annual. **Type:** monetary. **Recipient:** for the best unpublished collection of poetry ● **Type:** recognition. **Also Known As:** Circulo de Cultura Panamericano. **Publications:** *Circulo: Poetico* (in English and Spanish), annual. Journal. Contains poetry. **Price:** $15.00. ISSN: 0009-2349. **Circulation:** 800 ● *Circulo: Revista de Cultura* (in English and Spanish), annual. Journal. Contains scholarly works on Latin American and Spanish literature and culture. **Price:** $25.00. ISSN: 0009-7349. **Circulation:** 800. **Adver-**

tising: accepted. Also Cited As: *Circulo* ● *Estudios Literarios Sobre Hispanoamerica.* Proceedings ● *Jose Marti en el Centenario de su Muerte.* Proceedings ● *Marti Ante la Critica Actual.* Proceedings. **Conventions/Meetings:** annual convention, lectures on Hispanic literature and culture - always fall, in New York metropolitan area ● annual Summer Cultural Convention, critical essays on Hispanic literatures (exhibits) - always summer in Miami, FL.

10313 ■ Tinker Foundation
55 E 59th St.
New York, NY 10022
Ph: (212)421-6858
Fax: (212)223-3326
E-mail: tinker@tinker.org
URL: http://foundationcenter.org/grantmaker/tinker
Contact: Renate Rennie, Pres.

Founded: 1959. **Staff:** 6. **Nonmembership. Multinational. Description:** Works to promote projects related to Antarctica, Latin America, Spain, and Portugal, with a focus on environmental, economic and governance policies in those regions. **Awards:** Tinker Field Research Grant. **Frequency:** annual. **Type:** grant. **Recipient:** for graduate students who wish to acquire a comprehensive knowledge of language and culture ● Tinker Institutional Grant. **Frequency:** annual. **Type:** grant. **Recipient:** for an institutional entity geographically focused on Latin America, Iberia or Antarctica. **Publications:** Annual Report, annual.

Libraries

10314 ■ AFL-CIO/ALA Joint Committee on Library Service to Labor Groups
c/o American Library Association
50 E Huron St.
Chicago, IL 60611
Ph: (312)280-4395 (312)280-5273
Free: (800)545-2433
Fax: (312)944-8085
E-mail: dvicha@ala.org
URL: http://www.ala.org/rusa
Contact: Donavan Vicha, Exec. Dir.

Description: Representatives of the American Library Association and the AFL-CIO. Promotes cooperation between librarian and labor organizations and their constituencies. Disseminates information on books, audiovisual materials, and service programs to better serve labor union members. **Awards:** John Sessions Memorial Award. **Frequency:** annual. **Type:** recognition. **Recipient:** for recognition of work with the labor community. **Conventions/Meetings:** annual conference, held in conjunction with ALA.

10315 ■ Alternatives in Publication Task Force (AIP)
c/o American Library Association
Social Responsibilities Round Table
50 E Huron St.
Chicago, IL 60611
Ph: (312)344-7072
E-mail: cgulyas@colum.edu
URL: http://www.libr.org/AIP
Contact: Carol Gulyas, Coor.

Founded: 1970. **Members:** 150. **Description:** Members of the Social Responsibilities Round Table of the American Library Association (see separate entry) concerned with increasing awareness of and responsiveness to small and alternative press publications. Serves as a liaison between librarians and alternative press publishers; compiles directories of small and alternative press publishers, bookstores, and distributors; arranges programs and exhibits. **Awards:** Jackie Eubanks Memorial Award. **Frequency:** annual. **Type:** recognition. **Recipient:** to a library professional who has shown outstanding achievement in promoting the use of alternative information resources in libraries. **Formerly:** (2002) Task Force on Alternatives in Print. **Publications:** *Alternative Publishers of Books in North America.* Directory. Contains list and description of over 150 small and alternative presses. **Conventions/Meetings:** semiannual conference.

10316 ■ American Association of Law Libraries (AALL)
53 W Jackson Blvd., Ste.940
Chicago, IL 60604
Ph: (312)939-4764 (314)244-2660
Fax: (312)431-1097
E-mail: aallhq@aall.org
URL: http://www.aallnet.org
Contact: Kate Hagan, Exec. Dir.

Founded: 1906. **Members:** 5,000. **Membership Dues:** active, associate, $208 (annual) ● student, retired, $52 (annual). **Staff:** 13. **Regional Groups:** 30. **Description:** Librarians who serve the legal profession in the courts, bar associations, law societies, law schools, private law firms, federal, state, and county governments, and business; associate members are legal publishers and other interested persons. Seeks to advance the profession of law librarianship. Conducts continuing professional development programs for members; maintains placement service. **Awards: Type:** recognition ● **Type:** scholarship. **Computer Services:** Mailing lists, of members. **Telecommunication Services:** electronic mail, membership@aall.org. **Committees:** Awards; Continuing Professional Education; Copyright; Diversity; Government Relations; Index to Foreign Legal Periodicals; Indexing of Periodical Literature; Public Relations; Relations with Information Vendors; Scholarships. **Publications:** *AALL Directory and Handbook*, annual ● *AALL Spectrum*, monthly. Magazine. Contains substantive articles of interest to law libraries and other legal information professionals, plus association news. **Price:** free for members; $75.00 for nonmembers. ISSN: 1089-8689. **Circulation:** 5,000. **Advertising:** accepted ● *Index to Foreign Legal Periodicals*, quarterly ● *Law Library Journal*, quarterly. **Price:** $110.00 /year for nonmembers. **Circulation:** 5,500. **Advertising:** accepted ● *Salary Survey*, biennial. **Price:** $110.00 for members, 2005 Edition; $175.00 for nonmembers, 2005 Edition; $95.00 for members, 2003 Edition; $150.00 for nonmembers, 2003 Edition. Alternate Formats: online ● Also publishes manuals and institute proceedings dealing with law library administration and techniques. **Conventions/Meetings:** annual conference (exhibits) - 2008 July 12-15, Portland, OR.

10317 ■ American Association of School Librarians (AASL)
50 E Huron St.
Chicago, IL 60611-2729
Ph: (312)280-4382
Free: (800)545-2433
Fax: (312)280-5276
E-mail: aasl@ala.org
URL: http://www.aasl.org
Contact: Julie A. Walker, Exec. Dir.

Founded: 1951. **Members:** 9,100. **Membership Dues:** student, $20 (annual) ● retired, $25 (annual) ● regular, $50 (annual) ● corporate, organizational, $75 (annual). **Staff:** 10. **State Groups:** 57. **Description:** Elementary and secondary school library media specialists and others interested in the general improvement and extension of school library media services for children and young people, and in interpreting the need for and function of school library media programs for educational and lay groups. **Awards:** AASL ABC-CLIO Leadership Grant. **Frequency:** annual. **Type:** grant. **Recipient:** for an affiliate organization for the creation of an outstanding leadership program held at the state level ● AASL Distinguished School Administrators Award. **Frequency:** annual. **Type:** monetary. **Recipient:** for outstanding and sustained contribution to the advancement of school library media programs in the American educational system ● AASL Distinguished Service Award. **Frequency:** annual. **Type:** monetary. **Recipient:** for outstanding contributions to librarianship and school library development ● AASL Frances Henne Award. **Frequency:** annual. **Type:** monetary. **Recipient:** for a school library media specialist, with five or fewer years of experience, to attend the ALA/AASL Conference ● AASL Highsmith Research Grant. **Frequency:** annual. **Type:** grant. **Recipient:** for an individual conducting innovative research aimed at measuring and evaluating the impact of school library media programs on learning and education ● AASL Information Technology Pathfinder. **Frequency:** annual. **Type:** monetary. **Recipient:** for innovative approaches to information technology in the school library media center ● AASL National School Library Media Program of the Year. **Frequency:** annual. **Type:** monetary. **Recipient:** for the most outstanding achievement, excellence, and innovative services in providing an exemplary school library media program ● AASL School Librarian's Workshop Scholarship. **Frequency:** annual. **Type:** scholarship. **Recipient:** for an individual studying to become a school library media specialist in preschool, elementary, or secondary schools ● American Association of School Librarians (AASL) SIRS Intellectual Freedom Award. **Frequency:** annual. **Type:** monetary. **Recipient:** for upholding the principles of intellectual freedom as set forth by the AASL and the American Library Association. **Telecommunication Services:** electronic mail, jwalker@ala.org. **Committees:** American University Press Services; Annual Conference; Awards; Bylaws and Organization; Competencies for School Library Media Specialists in the 21st Century; Continuing Education/Professional Development; General Conference; Intellectual Freedom; Legislation; Nominating; Publications; Research and Statistics. **Councils:** National Council for the Accreditation of Teacher Education. **Sections:** Educators of School Library Media Specialists; Independent School; Supervisors. **Task Forces:** ICENNECT; Implementation of the New National Guidelines and Standards; Non-Conference Year Programming; Teaching for Learning. **Formerly:** (1941) Section of the Division of Libraries for Children and Young People of the American Library Association; (1951) School Libraries Division of the American Library Association. **Publications:** *Knowledge Quest*, bimonthly. Journal. Provides the latest in research and best practices. **Price:** $40.00 for nonmembers. Alternate Formats: online ● *School Library Media Research.* Journal. Provides the latest in research and best practices. **Price:** included in membership dues; $40.00 for nonmembers. ISSN: 1094-9046. **Circulation:** 9,100. **Advertising:** accepted. Alternate Formats: online. **Conventions/Meetings:** biennial conference and meeting, national division conference (exhibits).

10318 ■ American Friends of the Vatican Library (AFVL)
3535 Indian Trail
Orchard Lake, MI 48324
Ph: (248)683-0311
E-mail: info@afvl.org
URL: http://www.afvl.org
Contact: Rev. Charles G. Kosanke, Pres.

Founded: 1981. **Members:** 600. **Membership Dues:** friend, $25 (annual) ● contributing, $50 (annual) ● sustaining, $100 (annual) ● patron, $500 (annual) ● founder, $1,000 (annual). **Budget:** $10,000. **Description:** Clergy and laypeople. Purpose is to raise funds for the Vatican Library in Rome, Italy, which is open to qualified scholars and houses cultural material including 75,000 manuscripts, 65,000 units of archival material, 100,000 prints, maps, and engravings, 330,000 coins and medals, and more than two million books and serials. Seeks to restore and maintain the manuscripts and books, and to expand the collection of reference materials needed in the study and use of manuscripts. Assists in the publication of scholarly studies undertaken by the Vatican Library. **Affiliated With:** Catholic Library Association. **Publications:** *Amici*, semiannual. Newsletter. Includes book reviews and statistics. **Price:** included in membership dues. **Circulation:** 700 ● *The Popes and The Vatican Library.* Booklet. **Conventions/Meetings:** annual board meeting.

10319 ■ American Indian Library Association (AILA)
c/o Ms. Rhonda Harris Taylor, Newsletter Ed.
Univ. of Oklahoma
School of Lib. and Info. Stud.
401 W Brooks
Norman, OK 73019

Ph: (405)325-3921
Fax: (405)325-7648
E-mail: rtaylor@ou.edu
URL: http://aila.library.sd.gov
Contact: Ms. Rhonda Harris Taylor, Newsletter Ed.

Founded: 1979. **Members:** 300. **Membership Dues:** student, $10 (annual) ● individual, $15 (annual) ● library, $30 (annual). **Description:** Individuals and institutions interested in promoting the development, maintenance, and improvement of libraries, library systems, and cultural and information services on reservations and in communities of Native Americans and Native Alaskans. Develops and encourages adoption of standards for Indian libraries; provides technical assistance to Indian tribes on establishing and maintaining archives systems. Works to enhance the capability of libraries to assist Indians who are writing tribal histories and to perpetuate knowledge of Indian language, history, legal rights, and culture. Seeks support for the establishment of networks for exchange of information among Indian tribes. Communicates the needs of Indian libraries to legislators and the library community. Coordinates development of courses, workshops, institutes, and internships on Indian library services. **Awards: Frequency:** annual. **Type:** scholarship. **Recipient:** for American Indian and Alaskan Native students who are enrolled in or have been accepted to enroll in a master's degree program in an American Library Association accredited library. **Affiliated With:** American Library Association. **Publications:** *American Indian Libraries Newsletter*, quarterly. **Price:** included in membership dues. ISSN: 0139-8207. **Circulation:** 300. **Advertising:** accepted. Alternate Formats: CD-ROM; online; magnetic tape. **Conventions/Meetings:** annual conference, held during American Library Association conference (exhibits).

10320 ■ American Library Association (ALA)

50 E Huron St.
Chicago, IL 60611
Ph: (312)944-6780 (312)280-1392
Free: (800)545-2433
Fax: (312)440-9374
E-mail: ala@ala.org
URL: http://www.ala.org
Contact: Mr. Keith Michael Fiels, Exec. Dir.

Founded: 1876. **Members:** 64,989. **Membership Dues:** individual - first year, $55 ● individual - second year, $83 ● individual - third year and later, $110 ● trustee, associate, $50 (annual) ● student, $28 (annual) ● foreign individual, $66 (annual) ● library support staff, $39 (annual). **Staff:** 275. **Budget:** $43,839,000. **Regional Groups:** 4. **State Groups:** 50. **Local Groups:** 3. **Description:** Librarians, libraries, trustees, friends of libraries, and others interested in the responsibilities of libraries in the educational, social, and cultural needs of society. Promotes and improves library service and librarianship. Establishes standards of service, support, education, and welfare for libraries and library personnel; promotes the adoption of such standards in libraries of all kinds; safeguards the professional status of librarians; encourages the recruiting of competent personnel for professional careers in librarianship; promotes popular understanding and public acceptance of the value of library service and librarianship. Works in liaison with federal agencies to initiate the enactment and administration of legislation that will extend library services. Offers placement services. **Libraries: Type:** reference; by appointment only. **Holdings:** 10,000; archival material, audio recordings, books, periodicals, photographs, video recordings. **Subjects:** library science. **Awards:** Caldecott Medal. **Frequency:** annual. **Type:** medal. **Recipient:** to the artist of the most distinguished American picture book for children ● Michael L. Printz Award. **Frequency:** annual. **Type:** recognition. **Recipient:** for a book that exemplifies literary excellence in young adult literature ● Newbery Medal. **Frequency:** annual. **Type:** medal. **Recipient:** to the author of the most distinguished contribution to American literature for children ● Theodor Seuss Geisel Award. **Frequency:** annual. **Type:** recognition. **Recipient:** to the author and illustrator of the most distinguished contribution to the body of American children's literature known as beginning reader books published in the united states during the preceding year. **Telecommunication Services:** electronic mail, membership@ala.org ● TDD, (888)-814-7692 ● additional toll-free number, Washington, (800)941-8478. **Committees:** Accreditation; Awards; Chapter Relations; Freedom and Equality of Access to Information; Intellectual Freedom; International Relations; Legislation; Library Education; Library Outreach Services; Library Personnel Resources; Minority Concerns and Cultural Diversity; Pay Equity; Policy Monitoring; Professional Ethics; Program Evaluation and Support; Public Information; Publishing; Research and Statistics; Review, Inquiry, and Mediation; Standards; Status of Women in Librarianship; User Instruction for Information Literacy. **Departments:** Office for Human Resource Development and Recruitment. **Divisions:** American Association of School Librarians; American Library Trustee Association; Association for Library Collections and Technical Services; Association for Library Service to Children; Association of College and Research Libraries; Association of Specialized and Cooperative Library Agencies; Library Administration and Management Association; Library and Information Technology Association; Public Library Association; Reference and Adult Services; Young Adult Library Services Association. **Subgroups:** Armed Forces Libraries; Continuing Library Education Network and Exchange; Ethnic Materials; Exhibits; Federal Librarians; Government Documents; Independent Librarians Exchange; Intellectual Freedom; Library History; Library Instruction; Library Research; Map and Geography; New Members; Social Responsibilities; Staff Organizations; Support Staff Interests; Video. **Affiliated With:** American Association of Law Libraries; American Indian Library Association; Asia/Pacific American Librarians Association; Association for Library and Information Science Education; Association of Research Libraries; Black Caucus of the American Library Association; Chinese American Librarians Association; Council on Library-Media Technicians; Friends of Libraries U.S.A.; Medical Library Association; Music Library Association; ProLiteracy Worldwide; REFORMA: National Association to Promote Library Services to the Spanish-Speaking; Urban Libraries Council. **Publications:** *ALA Handbook of Organization and Membership Directory*, annual. Serves as a guide to the structure of the ALA. Includes names of current officials, committee members, councilors, and representatives. **Price:** $25.00. ISSN: 0273-4605 ● *American Libraries*, 11/year. Magazine. Provides articles on issues that shape the library profession. Includes calendar of events, and list of employment opportunities. **Price:** included in membership dues; $60.00 /year for libraries; $70.00 for foreign subscription. ISSN: 0002-9769. **Advertising:** accepted. Alternate Formats: microform; online ● *Book Links*, bimonthly. Magazine. Designed for teachers, librarians, library media specialists, booksellers, parents, and other adults interested in connecting children with books. **Price:** $25.95/year in U.S., Canada and Mexico; $32.00 in all other countries. ISSN: 1055-4742. **Advertising:** accepted ● *Booklist*, biweekly. Journal. Provides a guide to current print and nonprint materials worthy of consideration for purchase by libraries and schools. **Price:** $74.00/year; $87.50 for foreign subscription. ISSN: 0006-7385. **Advertising:** accepted. **Conventions/Meetings:** annual conference (exhibits) - 2008 June 26-July 2, Anaheim, CA; 2009 July 9-15, Chicago, IL ● annual meeting (exhibits) - 2009 Jan. 23-28, Chicago, IL; 2010 Jan. 15-20, Boston, MA.

10321 ■ American Merchant Marine Library Association (AMMLA)

635 Fourth Ave.
Brooklyn, NY 11232
Ph: (718)369-3818 (212)269-0711
E-mail: ussammla@ix.netcom.com
URL: http://www.uss-ammla.com
Contact: Edward R. Morgan, Pres.

Founded: 1921. **Membership Dues:** regular, $25 (annual) ● special, $50 (annual) ● sponsor, $100 (annual) ● patron, $300 (annual) ● benefactor special grant, $500 (annual). **Staff:** 10. **Budget:** $172,000. **Description:** Furnishes free library services to officers and crews of U.S.-flag oceangoing vessels, Great Lakes vessels, the Coast Guard, and other waterborne operations of the U.S. government. Maintains shoreside dispatch offices. Collects books from publishers and the public and places boxed collections aboard ships in their ports. Supplies other U.S. ships and ports by mail. Conducts Ship's Literary Club, which supplies current best-sellers to more than 100 ships. Sponsors Merchant Marine Book Week in New York City. **Awards:** Great Lakes Crew Award of Merit. **Frequency:** annual. **Type:** recognition. **Recipient:** for donation to ship's literary club ● Honorable Mention Award. **Frequency:** annual. **Type:** recognition ● Ocean Crew Award of Merit. **Frequency:** annual. **Type:** recognition. **Recipient:** for donation to ship's literary club. **Also Known As:** Public Library of the High Seas. **Publications:** *USS Reports*, annual. Newsletter. Contains information on the association's activities. **Price:** free. **Circulation:** 3,000 ● Annual Report, annual. Includes statistics and descriptions of the association's activities and events. **Price:** free. **Circulation:** 2,500 ● Also publishes book reviews and articles. **Conventions/Meetings:** annual meeting - usually second Wednesday in May, New York City.

10322 ■ American Society of Indexers (ASI)

10200 W 44th Ave., Ste.304
Wheat Ridge, CO 80033
Ph: (303)463-2887
Fax: (303)422-8894
E-mail: info@asindexing.org
URL: http://www.asindexing.org
Contact: Francine Butler, Exec. Dir.

Founded: 1968. **Members:** 1,000. **Membership Dues:** retired, $130 (annual) ● regular, $150 (annual) ● organizational, $500 (annual) ● sustaining organizational, $1,000 (annual). **Budget:** $200,000. **Regional Groups:** 20. **Description:** Professional indexers, librarians, editors, publishers, and organizations employing indexers. Works to improve the quality of indexing and adherence to indexing standards; to encourage members to increase their professional indexing capabilities and performance; to advise authors, editors, and publishers on the qualifications and remuneration of indexers; to protect the professional interests of indexers; to facilitate communication among members concerning methods and developments in the field; to maintain liaison with related organizations. Members' activities include indexing books, databases, and periodicals, teaching indexing courses, and conducting research on indexing problems. **Awards:** H.W. Wilson Award. **Frequency:** annual. **Type:** recognition. **Recipient:** for excellence in indexing ● Hines Award. **Frequency:** annual. **Type:** recognition. **Recipient:** for members who have made contributions to the organization. **Telecommunication Services:** electronic mail, treasurer@asindexing.org. **Committees:** Chapter Relations; Jobs Hotline; Locator Publicity; Professional Development/Speakers Bureau. **Affiliated With:** Indexing and Abstracting Society of Canada; National Information Standards Organization; Society of Indexers. **Publications:** *A Guide to Indexing Software*. Booklet. Evaluates nine standalone indexing programs for IBM PC and compatible computers and one program for Macintosh. **Price:** $10.00 for members; $15.00 for nonmembers ● *Directory of Indexing and Abstracting Courses and Seminars*. Assists people interested in starting a career as an indexer to find courses or seminars in their region. **Price:** $10.00 for members; $15.00 for nonmembers ● *Generic Markup of Electronic Index Manuscripts*. Booklet. Provides tips on generic markup to help freelancers who submit indexes to publishers on diskette or by modem. **Price:** $10.00 for members; $15.00 for nonmembers ● *The Indexer*, semiannual. Journal. Devotes specifically to all aspects of indexing. **Price:** $25.00 /year for members. ISSN: 0019-4131. **Advertising:** accepted ● *Indexing from A to Z*. Booklet. Covers basic indexing techniques, author-publisher-indexer relations, business considerations, editing and proofreading, and many other topics. **Price:** $35.00 ● *Key Words: American Society of Indexers*, bimonthly. Bulletin. **Price:** included in membership dues; $40.00 /year for nonmembers.

ISSN: 1064-1211. **Circulation:** 1,000. **Advertising:** accepted ● Articles ● Books ● Also publishes guidelines, and is a sponsor of *Information Science Abstracts*. **Conventions/Meetings:** annual conference (exhibits) - always summer ● annual meeting ● seminar ● workshop.

10323 ■ American Theological Library Association (ATLA)

300 S Wacker Dr., Ste.2100
Chicago, IL 60606-6701
Ph: (312)454-5100 (214)768-1867
Free: (888)665-2852
Fax: (312)454-5505
E-mail: atla@atla.com
URL: http://www.atla.com
Contact: Dennis A. Norlin, Exec. Dir.

Founded: 1946. **Members:** 1,000. **Membership Dues:** individual (based on annual gross income), $15-$150 (annual) ● affiliate, $100 (annual) ● institutional (based on annual expenditures), $100-$1,000 (annual). **Staff:** 42. **Budget:** $4,920,000. **Regional Groups:** 19. **Description:** Professional theological librarians; persons interested in theological librarianship; institutions. Studies problems of theological libraries, increase professional competence of the membership and improve the quality of library service to theological education. Seeks to: foster professional growth of members; provide continuing education programs; publish, preserve, and disseminate theological literature, research tools, and aids; develop and implement standards for theological libraries; promote theological research; facilitate communication among members. Provides consultation service to member institutions. Compiles statistics. **Awards:** Bibliographic/Indexing Project. **Type:** grant ● Minority Scholarship. **Type:** scholarship. **Computer Services:** database, ATLA Religion ● database, ATLA Senals ● mailing lists, of members. **Telecommunication Services:** electronic mail, memberrep@atla.com. **Projects:** Cooperative Digital Resources Initiative; NEH Microfilm Preservation; Retrospective Indexing. **Subgroups:** Collection Evaluation and Development; College and University Librarians; Judaica; OCLC Users; Public Services; Special Collections; Technical Services; World Christianity. **Affiliated With:** American Library Association; Association of Theological Schools in the United States and Canada; Council on Library and Information Resources; National Federation of Abstracting and Information Services; National Information Standards Organization. **Publications:** *The American Theological Library Association: Essays in Celebration of the First Fifty Years*. Features eighteen essays documenting all programs and projects. **Price:** $25.00/copy ● *American Theological Library Association—Summary of Proceedings*, annual. Includes directory and member statistics. **Price:** included in membership dues; $55.00 for nonmembers. ISSN: 0066-0868. **Circulation:** 750. **Advertising:** accepted ● *ATLASerials*, quarterly. Contains collection of major religion and theology journals from 1924 to present. **Price:** $2,226.00 for nonmembers; $2,115.00 for members. Alternate Formats: online. Also Cited As: *ATLAS* ● *Bonhoeffer Bibliography*. Indexes all primary sources and secondary literature in English by or about Dietrich Bonhoeffer. **Price:** $20.00/copy ● *Catholic Periodical and Literature Index*. Lists periodicals, books, newspapers and papal documents dealing with the practice of Catholic faith and lifestyle. **Price:** $1,055.00 for institutions; $265.00 for individuals ● *Chinese-Language Christian Collection*. Contains 307 monograph titles and 55 serial titles. **Price:** $100.00 for members (per reel); $7,700.00 for members (collection); $130.00 for nonmembers (per reel); $10,010.00 for nonmembers (collection). Alternate Formats: microform ● *Christianity's Encounter with World Religions, 1850-1950*. Features the 19th and 20th century global missions, Christian and non-Christian, with emphasis on Asia, India and Middle East. **Price:** $100.00 for members (per reel); $116,400.00 for members (collection); $130.00 for nonmembers (per reel); $151,320.00 for nonmembers (collection) ● *Denominational Documentation Series*. Drawn from Phases 6 and 7 of the Monographs on Microfiche collection. Two broad categories: Histories and Liturgies; Doctrine and Work. Alternate Formats: microform ● *Index to Book Reviews in Religion*, quarterly. Bibliography. Features citations for book reviews. Comprises indexing from 1960-2003. **Price:** $318.00 for institutions; $159.00 for subscribers of RDB in any format; $106.00 for individuals. ISSN: 0887-1574. Alternate Formats: online; CD-ROM ● *International Christian Literature Documentation Project*. Indexes 18,600 monographs, pamphlets and other documents, along with 6,700 essays in 1,800 multi-author works. **Price:** $200.00 ● *Monographs on Microfilm*. Contains three collections: General; Corpus of American Lutheranism; Yale Day Missions Collection. International; 18th to 21st century titles. **Price:** $100.00 for members; $130.00 for nonmembers ● *New Testament Abstracts*. Contains more than 38,000 articles and more than 13,500 book summaries. **Price:** $398.00 for institutions; $106.00 for individuals ● *Old Testament Abstracts*. Includes journal articles, books, and essays. **Price:** $398.00 for institutions; $106.00 for individuals; $375.00 network, 2-5 simultaneous user nodes. ISSN: 0364-8591. Alternate Formats: CD-ROM; online ● *Religion Database*, quarterly. Contains religious information. **Price:** $2,147.00 standard (1-5 members); $2,039.00 institutional member; $375.00 each, additional user. Alternate Formats: CD-ROM; online ● *Religion Index One: Periodical Literature*, semiannual. Indexes articles in and related to the field of religion from 640 fully and selectively indexed journals and 5 scanned journals. **Price:** $610.00/copy. ISSN: 0149-8428 ● *Religion Indexes Thesaurus*. Contains 14,400 valid subject headings and cross-references from 5,400 unused subject headings. **Price:** $50.00/copy ● *Research in Ministry*, quarterly. Indexes and abstracts project reports and theses from more than 50 Doctors of Ministry programs accredited by Association of Theological Schools. **Price:** free. Alternate Formats: online ● *Serials on Microfilm*. Includes more than 2,500 fully cataloged serial titles. **Price:** $100.00 for members; $130.00 for nonmembers. Alternate Formats: microform ● *Theology Cataloging Bulletin*, quarterly ● *Yale Day Missions Collection: Selection from Asia and the Pacific Rim*. Monographs. Documents missionary activities of American, British and German denominations and missionary societies during 19th/early 20th centuries. **Price:** $100.00 for members (per reel); $20,200.00 for members (collection); $130.00 for nonmembers (per reel); $26,260.00 for nonmembers (collection). **Conventions/Meetings:** annual conference, with professional development workshops, programs and papers (exhibits) - always in June. 2008 June 25-28, Ottawa, ON, Canada - **Avg. Attendance:** 300; 2009 June 17-20, St. Louis, MO; 2010 June 16-18, Louisville, KY.

10324 ■ Americans for Libraries Council (ALC)

27 Union Sq. W, Ste.204
New York, NY 10003
Ph: (646)336-6236
Free: (800)542-1918
Fax: (646)336-6318
E-mail: info@lff.org
URL: http://www.americansforlibraries.org
Contact: Diantha Dow Schull, Pres.

Founded: 1992. **Staff:** 14. **Nonmembership**. **Description:** Champions the role of libraries in American life and promotes new approaches to sustaining and developing libraries in the 21st Century. **Formerly:** (2003) Libraries for the Future. **Publications:** *ALC Update*, quarterly. Newsletter. Alternate Formats: online.

10325 ■ AMIGOS Library Services

14400 Midway Rd.
Dallas, TX 75244-3509
Ph: (972)851-8000
Free: (800)843-8482
Fax: (972)991-6061
E-mail: amigos@amigos.org
URL: http://www.amigos.org
Contact: Bonnie Juergens, Exec. Dir.

Founded: 1974. **Members:** 800. **Membership Dues:** general, $350 (annual) ● full user, $1,450 (annual). **Staff:** 50. **Description:** Aims to provide resource-sharing opportunities and information technology to libraries. Has 800 library and cultural institution members that share resources through collaborative programs and services, including cataloging, reference, collections, preservation, imaging, consulting, and training. **Computer Services:** database ● mailing lists, broadcast internet. **Committees:** Amigos Conference Advisory; Amigos Training Advisory. **Departments:** Marketing and Library Relations. **Programs:** Amigos Fellowship. **Formerly:** (2001) AMIGOS Bibliographic Council. **Publications:** *Amigos Agenda and OCLC Connection*, monthly. Bulletin. Contains answers to frequently asked questions and offers timely tips and knowledgeable advice on a variety of subjects. Alternate Formats: online ● *AMIGOS Annual Report*, annual. Annual Reports. Alternate Formats: online ● *Annual Survey Report*, annual. Annual Report. Alternate Formats: online ● *Que Pasa*, quarterly. Newsletter. Contains updates about the organization. **Price:** free. Alternate Formats: online ● *Telecommunications and Equipment* ● Brochure. **Conventions/Meetings:** annual conference, for members.

10326 ■ Archivists and Librarians in the History of the Health Sciences (ALHHS)

c/o Brooke Fox, Sec.-Treas.
PO Box 250403
Charleston, SC 29425
Ph: (843)792-2288
E-mail: ebf2@musc.edu
URL: http://www.alhhs.org
Contact: Micaela Sullivan-Fowler, Pres.

Founded: 1975. **Members:** 168. **Membership Dues:** individual in U.S., $15 (annual) ● individual outside U.S., $21 (annual). **Budget:** $7,000. **Description:** Medical librarians and archivists working with rare book collections, archives, and artifacts related to the history of the health sciences; book collectors, physicians, medical historians, booksellers, and other interested people. Fosters rare book librarianship within the history of the health sciences field. Promotes continuing education programs. **Awards:** ALHHS Recognition of Merit. **Frequency:** periodic. **Type:** recognition. **Recipient:** to individuals who have made significant gifts to health sciences libraries ● Curatorship Award. **Frequency:** periodic. **Type:** recognition. **Recipient:** to an individual member who has made outstanding achievement in the field of medical historical curatorship ● Lisabeth M. Holloway Award. **Frequency:** biennial. **Type:** recognition. **Recipient:** for outstanding service to the organization and the profession ● Publication Award. **Frequency:** biennial. **Type:** recognition. **Recipient:** to a member for a significant publication. **Committees:** Archivist; Local Arrangements; Nominating; Program; Publications; Recruiting. **Formerly:** (1992) Association of Librarians in the History of the Health Sciences. **Publications:** *ALHHS Directory*, biennial. Membership Directory. **Price:** included in membership dues ● *The Watermark*, quarterly. Newsletter. **Price:** included in membership dues. **Advertising:** accepted. **Conventions/Meetings:** annual conference, held in conjunction with the American Association for the History of Medicine (exhibits) - usually April or May.

10327 ■ Asia/Pacific American Librarians Association (APALA)

c/o Michelle Baildon, VP
MIT Humanities Lib.
77 Massachusetts Ave., Rm. 14S-222
Cambridge, MA 02139
Ph: (617)253-9352 (419)530-4485
Fax: (617)253-3109
E-mail: baildon@mit.edu
URL: http://www.apalaweb.org
Contact: Buenaventura B. Basco, Pres.

Founded: 1980. **Members:** 302. **Membership Dues:** personal, $20 (annual) ● student, $10 (annual) ● institutional, $50 (annual) ● life, $300. **Staff:** 1. **Description:** Librarians and information specialists of Asian Pacific descent working in the U.S; interested persons. Provides a forum for discussing problems and concerns; supports and encourages library services to Asian Pacific communities; recruits and supports Asian Pacific Americans in the library and information science professions. Offers placement service; compiles statistics. Conducts fundraising for scholarships. **Awards:** APALA Scholarship Award. **Frequency:** annual. **Type:** scholarship. **Recipient:** to a student of Asian or Pacific background who has been accepted into a master's or doctoral degree program in library and/or information science at a library school accredited by the ALA ● APALA Sheila S. Lai Research Grant Award. **Frequency:** annual. **Type:** grant. **Computer Services:** Mailing lists, of members. **Telecommunication Services:** electronic mail, skumar@utnet.utoledo.edu. **Affiliated With:** American Library Association. **Publications:** Newsletter, quarterly. Includes book reviews, list of employment opportunities, notices of conferences and programs, and news of members, exhibits, and publications. **Price:** included in membership dues. **Circulation:** 350. **Advertising:** accepted. Alternate Formats: online ● Membership Directory, annual ● Proceedings, annual. **Conventions/Meetings:** annual conference, held in conjunction with the American Library Association annual conference (exhibits) ● semiannual meeting (exhibits) - usually June/July and January/February.

10328 ■ Association of Architecture School Librarians (AASL)

c/o Jennifer Benedetto Beals, Sec.-Treas.
Art and Architecture Librarian
Univ. of Tennessee
145 Hodges Lib.
Knoxville, TN 37996-1000
Ph: (865)974-0014
Fax: (865)974-9242
E-mail: jbeals@utk.edu
URL: http://www.architecturelibrarians.org
Contact: Jennifer Benedetto Beals, Sec.-Treas.

Founded: 1979. **Members:** 60. **Membership Dues:** individual, institutional, $15 (annual). **Description:** Advances the academic architectural librarianship. Develops and increases the usefulness of architecture school librarians in the advancement of architecture education, and promotes a spirit of cooperation within the profession. **Awards:** Conference Travel Award and Conference Student Award. **Frequency:** annual. **Type:** monetary. **Telecommunication Services:** electronic mail, ma1f@andrew.cmu.edu. **Affiliated With:** Association of Collegiate Schools of Architecture. **Conventions/Meetings:** annual conference (exhibits).

10329 ■ Association of Caribbean University, Research and Institutional Libraries

PO Box 23317
San Juan, PR 00931-3317
Ph: (787)790-8054 (787)764-0000
Fax: (787)764-2311
E-mail: acuril@uprrp.edu
URL: http://acuril.rrp.upr.edu
Contact: Mrs. Oneida Rivera de Ortiz, Exec. Sec.

Founded: 1969. **Members:** 250. **Membership Dues:** individual, $25 (annual) ● associate individual, $20 (annual) ● student, retired/non-salaried, $10 (annual) ● associate student, associate retired/non-salaried, $7 (annual). **Staff:** 2. **Budget:** $15,000. **Regional Groups:** 5. **Languages:** English, French, Spanish. **Multinational. Description:** Libraries serving universities and research institutions. Promotes growth and development of libraries and archives; encourages high standards of ethics and practice among library personnel. Encourages communication and cooperation among members. **Additional Websites:** http://acuril.uprrp.edu. **Telecommunication Services:** electronic mail, acurilt@yahoo.com. **Also Known As:** ACURIL. **Publications:** *Carta Informativa, Proceedings of Annual Conferences, Cybernotes* (in English, French, and Spanish), annual. Newsletter. **Price:** included in membership dues. **Conventions/Meetings:** annual conference (exhibits).

10330 ■ Association of Christian Librarians (ACL)

PO Box 4
Cedarville, OH 45314
Ph: (937)766-2255
Fax: (937)766-5499
E-mail: info@acl.org
URL: http://www.acl.org
Contact: Linda Poston, Pres.

Founded: 1957. **Members:** 400. **Multinational. Description:** Represents Evangelical Christian academic libraries that promote the professional and spiritual growth of the association's members and provides services to the academic library community worldwide. **Libraries: Type:** reference. **Holdings:** archival material. **Awards:** Emily Russel Award. **Type:** recognition. **Additional Websites:** http://acl.org/cpi.cfm. **Commissions:** International Library Assistance. **Committees:** Bible College; Index; Journal; Liberal Arts College. **Formerly:** Christian Librarians' Fellowship. **Publications:** *Christian Librarian*, 3/year. **Advertising:** accepted ● *Christian Periodical Index*, semiannual. Includes annual cumulation. Alternate Formats: CD-ROM; online ● *The Librarians Manual.* **Conventions/Meetings:** annual conference (exhibits) - always second week of June.

10331 ■ Association of College and Research Libraries (ACRL)

50 E Huron St.
Chicago, IL 60611-2795
Ph: (312)280-2523 (312)280-3248
Free: (800)545-2433
Fax: (312)280-2520
E-mail: acrl@ala.org
URL: http://www.ala.org/acrl
Contact: Mary Ellen K. Davis, Exec. Dir.

Founded: 1889. **Members:** 13,000. **Membership Dues:** institutional, personal, $45 (annual) ● organizational (based on budget), $110-$1,415 (annual) ● corporate contributor, $350 (annual) ● corporate patron, $1,000 (annual) ● corporate benefactor, $2,500 (annual) ● library champion, $5,000 (annual) ● international, associate, library support staff, $55 (annual) ● continuing, retired, $35 (annual) ● life, $55. **Staff:** 36. **Budget:** $5,000,000. **State Groups:** 42. **Description:** A division of the American Library Association. Academic and research librarians seeking to improve the quality of service in academic libraries; promotes the professional and career development of academic and research librarians; represent the interests and support the programs of academic and research libraries. Operates placement services; sponsors specialized education and research grants and programs; gathers, compiles, and disseminates statistics. Establishes and adopts standards; maintains publishing program; offers professional development courses. **Awards:** ACRL Academic or Research Librarian of the Year. **Frequency:** annual. **Type:** recognition. **Recipient:** for outstanding contribution to academic/research librarianship ● ACRL Best Practices in Marketing Academic and Research Libraries Award. **Frequency:** annual. **Type:** recognition. **Recipient:** for the academic/research library in each category (community college, college, and university) that demonstrates an outstanding best practices marketing program ● Coutts Nijhoff International West European Specialists Study Grant. **Frequency:** annual. **Type:** grant ● DLS Haworth Press Distance Learning Librarian Conference Sponsorship. **Frequency:** annual. **Type:** recognition ● Doctoral Dissertation Fellowship. **Frequency:** annual. **Type:** fellowship ● EBSCO Community College Learning Resources Achievement Awards. **Frequency:** annual. **Type:** recognition. **Recipient:** for program development and leadership at two-year institutions ● EBSS Distinguished Education and Behavioral Science Librarian Award. **Frequency:** annual. **Type:** recognition. **Recipient:** for outstanding contribution in education/behavioral sciences librarianship ● Excellence in Academic Libraries. **Frequency:** annual. **Type:** recognition ● Hugh Atkinson Memorial Award. **Frequency:** annual. **Type:** recognition. **Recipient:** for significant contributions in the area of library automation and/or library development ● Ilene Rockman IS Publication Award. **Frequency:** annual. **Type:** recognition. **Recipient:** for outstanding publication related to instruction in a library environment ● IS Innovation Award. **Frequency:** annual. **Type:** recognition ● Katherine Kyes Leab and Daniel J. Leab American Book Prices Current Exhibition Catalog Award. **Frequency:** annual. **Type:** recognition ● LPSS Marta Lange/CQ Award. **Frequency:** annual. **Type:** recognition ● Marta Lange/CQ Award. **Frequency:** annual. **Type:** recognition. **Recipient:** for contributions to law or political science librarianship ● Miriam Dudley Award. **Frequency:** annual. **Type:** recognition. **Recipient:** for bibliographic instruction ● Oberly Award. **Frequency:** biennial. **Type:** recognition. **Recipient:** for bibliography in agricultural sciences ● Samuel Lazerow Fellowship. **Frequency:** annual. **Type:** fellowship. **Recipient:** for research in acquisitions or technical services ● Women's Study Section Awards. **Frequency:** annual. **Type:** recognition. **Computer Services:** Mailing lists, available through the American Library Association. **Telecommunication Services:** electronic mail, mdavis@ala.org. **Committees:** Academic or Research Librarian of the Year Award; Academic Status; ACRL/Harvard Leadership Institute Advisory; Appointments; Budget and Finance; Bylaws; Colleagues; Conference Program Planning; Copyright; Doctoral Dissertation Award; Effective Practices; Ethics; Excellence in Academic Libraries Awards; Government Relations; Hugh C. Atkinson Memorial Award; Information Literacy Advisory; Institute for Information Literacy Executive; Intellectual Freedom; International Relations; Liaisons; Membership; National Conference Executive; President's Program; Professional Development; Publications; Racial and Ethnic Diversity; Research; Samuel Lazerow Fellowship for Research in Acquisitions or Technical Services; Scholarly Communications; Standards and Accreditation; Statistics. **Sections:** Afro-American Studies Librarian; Anthropology and Sociology; Arts; Asian, African, and Middle Eastern; College Libraries; Community and Junior College Libraries; Distance Learning Services; Education and Behavioral Sciences; Friends Fund; Instruction; Law and Political Science; Literatures in English; Marketing Academic and Research Libraries; Rare Books and Manuscripts; Science and Technology; Slavic and East European; Spectrum Scholars Mentor; University Libraries; Western European Specialists; Women's Studies. **Affiliated With:** American Library Association. **Formerly:** (1938) Association of College and Reference Libraries. **Publications:** *Choice: Current Reviews for College Libraries*, 11/year. Journal. Provides a reference and advisory guide on significant current publications. **Price:** $270.00/year in U.S.; $320.00/year outside U.S. ISSN: 0009-4978. **Advertising:** accepted. Alternate Formats: CD-ROM; online ● *Choice Reviews-on-Cards* ● *College & Research Libraries*, bimonthly. Journal. Includes book reviews and information on recent publications. **Price:** included in membership dues; $65.00 /year for nonmembers in U.S.; $75.00 /year for nonmembers outside U.S. ISSN: 0010-0870. **Advertising:** accepted ● *College & Research Libraries News*, 11/year. Journal. Contains news and articles on college, research, and other libraries. Includes calendar of events, job opportunities, member news, and acquisitions. **Price:** included in membership dues; $44.00 /year for nonmembers in U.S.; $55.00 /year for nonmembers outside U.S. ISSN: 0099-0086. **Circulation:** 13,000. **Advertising:** accepted. Also Cited As: *C & RL News* ● *Publications in Librarianship*, periodic ● *RBM: A Journal of Rare Books, Manuscripts and Cultural Heritage*, semiannual. **Price:** $40.00/year in U.S. and Canada; $55.00/year outside U.S. and Canada; $20.00/year for single issue. ISSN: 0884-450X ● Books ● Directories ● Manuals. **Conventions/Meetings:** biennial Sailing into the Future - Charting our Destiny - conference (exhibits) - 2009 Mar. 12-15, Seattle, WA; 2011 Mar. 30-Apr. 2, Philadelphia, PA; 2013 Apr. 4-7, Indianapolis, IN.

10332 ■ Association of Jewish Libraries (AJL)

c/o NFJC
330 7th Ave., 21st Fl.
New York, NY 10001
Ph: (212)725-5359 (513)487-3282
Fax: (513)221-0519
E-mail: ajlibs@osu.edu
URL: http://www.jewishlibraries.org
Contact: Laurel Wolfson, VP

Founded: 1965. **Members:** 1,200. **Membership Dues:** individual, institutional, $50 (annual) ● retiree, student, friend of AJL, $30 (annual). **Budget:** $82,000. **Local Groups:** 19. **Multinational. Description:** Devoted to the educational, informational, and networking needs of librarians responsible for collections of Judaica and to the promotion of Judaic librarianship. **Libraries: Type:** reference. **Holdings:** archival material. **Awards:** AJL Judaica Bibliography Award. **Frequency:** annual. **Type:** recognition. **Recipient:** for bibliography books with Jewish content ● AJL Judaica Reference Book Award. **Frequency:** annual. **Type:** recognition. **Recipient:** for reference books with Jewish content ● AJL Scholarship. **Frequency:** annual. **Type:** scholarship. **Recipient:** for library school student ● Fanny Goldstein Merit Award. **Frequency:** annual. **Type:** recognition. **Recipient:** for outstanding contributions to the association and the field of Judaica Librarianship ● Life Achievement Award. **Frequency:** annual. **Type:** recognition. **Recipient:** for outstanding contributions to the association and the field of Judaica Librarianship ● Sydney Taylor Body of Work Award. **Type:** recognition ● Sydney Taylor Book Award. **Frequency:** annual. **Type:** recognition. **Recipient:** for contributions in picture books for young children and in older children's books ● Sydney Taylor Manuscript Award. **Frequency:** annual. **Type:** recognition. **Recipient:** for best fiction manuscript for readers ages eight to 12 with positive Jewish focus. **Computer Services:** Mailing lists, of members. **Telecommunication Services:** electronic mail, galron.1@osu.edu. **Committees:** Automation; Book Awards; Continuing Education; Job Clearinghouse; Manuscript Competition; Recruitment to the Judaica Library Profession; Scholarship. **Divisions:** Research and Special Library; School, Synagogue, and Center. **Formed by Merger of:** (1965) Jewish Librarians Association; Jewish Library Association. **Publications:** *Conference Proceedings*, annual. Records of Judaica librarianship papers presented at the annual AJL conventions. Alternate Formats: online ● *Judaica Librarianship*, periodic. Focuses on library and information science, Judaic religions and theology and computer application in Judaic and Hebrew studies. **Circulation:** 1,300 ● Newsletter, quarterly. Focuses on activities related to the Judaica Library. Includes book and media reviews and job listings. **Price:** included in membership dues. ISSN: 0747-6175. **Circulation:** 1,200. **Advertising:** accepted ● Membership Directory, annual ● Bibliographies ● Monographs ● Also publishes classification schemes and subject heading lists. **Conventions/Meetings:** annual convention (exhibits) - 2008 June 22-25, Cleveland, OH.

10333 ■ Association for Library Collections and Technical Services (ALCTS)

50 E Huron St.
Chicago, IL 60611
Ph: (312)280-5037
Free: (800)545-2433
Fax: (312)280-5033
E-mail: alcts@ala.org
URL: http://www.ala.org/ala/alcts/alcts.htm
Contact: Charles Wilt, Exec. Dir.

Founded: 1957. **Members:** 4,800. **Membership Dues:** organization, corporate, $65 (annual) ● personal, $55 (annual) ● student, $15 (annual). **Staff:** 3. **Regional Groups:** 47. **Description:** Offers well-integrated and forward-looking services to library and information specialists in acquisitions, cataloging, classification, preservation, and collection development and management. Offers extensive programming, regional educational events, and practical publications. **Awards:** Best of LRTS Award. **Frequency:** annual. **Type:** recognition. **Recipient:** for the best paper published in Library Resources and Technical Services ● Blackwell's. **Frequency:** annual. **Type:** scholarship. **Recipient:** for outstanding monograph, article or original paper in acquisitions or collection development ● Bowker/Ulrich's Serials Librarianship Award. **Frequency:** annual. **Type:** monetary. **Recipient:** for distinguished contributions to serials ● Esther J. Piercy Award. **Frequency:** annual. **Type:** grant. **Recipient:** for contributions and leadership ● First Step Award. **Frequency:** annual. **Type:** grant. **Recipient:** for individuals with less than 5 years experience in serials ● Leadership in Library Acquisitions Award. **Frequency:** annual. **Type:** grant. **Recipient:** for outstanding leadership and contribution ● Margaret Mann Citation. **Frequency:** annual. **Type:** scholarship. **Recipient:** for outstanding professional achievement ● Sage Library Support Staff Travel Grant. **Frequency:** annual. **Type:** grant. **Recipient:** for library support travel to the American Library Association's annual conference. **Boards:** LRTS Editorial. **Committees:** Budget and Finance; Education; Fundraising; International Relations; Leadership Development; Membership; Nominating; Organization and Bylaws; Planning; Program; Publications. **Sections:** Acquisitions; Cataloging and Classification; Collection Management and Development; Preservation and Reformatting; Serials. **Formed by Merger of:** (1957) Division of Cataloging and Classification - of ALA; (1957) Serials Round Table - of ALA; (1957) Board of Acquisitions of Library Materials - of ALA. **Formerly:** (1989) Resources and Technical Services Division - of ALA. **Publications:** *ALCTS Newsletter Online*, bimonthly. Contains news of activities of the division and news items of interest to members. ISSN: 1047-949X. **Circulation:** 5,000. **Advertising:** accepted. Alternate Formats: online. Also Cited As: *ANO* ● *Library Resources and Technical Services*, quarterly. Journal. Includes research articles in acquisitions, collection development, preservation, and classification and cataloging. **Price:** included in membership dues; $75.00 for nonmembers; $85.00 for institutions. ISSN: 0024-2527. **Circulation:** 6,500. **Advertising:** accepted. Alternate Formats: online. Also Cited As: *LRTS* ● Monographs. **Conventions/Meetings:** semiannual meeting, held in conjunction with ALA (exhibits) ● annual meeting - January or June.

10334 ■ Association for Library Service to Children (ALSC)

50 E Huron St.
Chicago, IL 60611-2795
Ph: (312)280-2163 (312)280-2162
Free: (800)545-2433
Fax: (312)280-5271
E-mail: alsc@ala.org
URL: http://www.ala.org/alsc
Contact: Diane Foote, Exec. Dir.

Founded: 1901. **Members:** 3,700. **Membership Dues:** regular, organizational, corporate, $55 (annual) ● retired, library support staff, $39 (annual) ● student, $28 (annual) ● associate, trustee, $50 (annual) ● international, $66 (annual). **Staff:** 6. **Budget:** $850,000. **Description:** An activity division of the American Library Association. Represents persons interested in the improvement and extension of services to children in all types of libraries. Responsible for the evaluation and selection of book and non-book materials, and for the improvement of techniques of library service to children from preschool through the eighth grade or junior high school age. Maintains numerous committees including Intellectual Freedom, and Notable Children's books, videos, and recordings. **Awards:** Book Wholesalers Summer Reading Program Grant. **Frequency:** annual. **Type:** grant. **Recipient:** for summer reading program ● Bound to Stay Bound Books. **Frequency:** annual. **Type:** scholarship. **Recipient:** for individuals pursuing graduate and postgraduate library degrees who plan to work with children ● Caldecott Medal. **Frequency:** annual. **Type:** recognition. **Recipient:** for outstanding picture book in U.S. ● Carnegie Medal. **Frequency:** annual. **Type:** recognition. **Recipient:** for outstanding video for children produced in the U.S. ● Frederic G. Melcher. **Frequency:** annual. **Type:** scholarship. **Recipient:** for individuals pursuing a masters degree in library science and intend on working with children ● Louise Seaman Bechtel Fellowship. **Frequency:** annual. **Type:** grant. **Recipient:** for mid-career librarians interested in research ● Mildred L. Batchelder Award. **Frequency:** annual. **Type:** recognition. **Recipient:** for best foreign children's book, subsequently translated into English ● Newbery Medal. **Frequency:** annual. **Type:** recognition. **Recipient:** for greatest contribution to children's literature ● Pura Belpre Medal. **Frequency:** biennial. **Type:** recognition. **Recipient:** for the most outstanding children's book by a Latino/a author or illustrator ● Robert F. Sibert Medal. **Frequency:** annual. **Type:** recognition. **Recipient:** for the most distinguished children's informational book ● Wilder Medal. **Frequency:** biennial. **Type:** recognition. **Recipient:** for outstanding body of work by children's author or illustrator. **Computer Services:** Online services, electronic discussion list. **Telecommunication Services:** electronic mail, dfoote@ala.org. **Affiliated With:** American Library Association. **Formerly:** (1958) Children's Library Association; (1977) Children's Services Division. **Publications:** *ALSConnect*, quarterly. Newsletter. Publishes news of the association, and its activities, meetings, and conferences. Provides information on awards, grants, and scholarships. **Price:** included in membership dues. ISSN: 0162-6612. **Circulation:** 3,700 ● *Children and Libraries: The Journal of The Association for Library Service to Children*, 3/year. Covers trends and issues in librarianship for children. **Price:** included in membership dues; $40.00 for nonmembers in U.S. and Canada; $50.00 for nonmembers outside North America. ISSN: 1542-9806. **Circulation:** 4,000. **Advertising:** accepted ● Books ● Brochures ● Monographs. **Conventions/Meetings:** annual meeting, held in conjunction with American Library Association - always midwinter ● biennial National Institute - meeting - 2008 Sept. 18-20, Salt Lake City, UT ● regional meeting - 2-4/year.

10335 ■ Association for Library Trustees and Advocates (ALTA)

50 E Huron St.
Chicago, IL 60611
Ph: (312)280-2160
Free: (800)545-2433
Fax: (312)280-3256
E-mail: dthorn@ala.org
URL: http://www.ala.org/ala/alta/alta.htm
Contact: Doll Thorn, Program/Event Coor.

Founded: 1890. **Members:** 1,300. **Membership Dues:** personal, $95 (annual). **Staff:** 2. **Budget:** $122,000. **Description:** A division of the American Library Association consisting of librarians, members of library boards, and interested individuals. Conducts continuing and comprehensive educational program for library trustees. Sponsors workshops and institutes in library leadership. **Awards:** ALTA/GALE Outstanding Trustee Conference Grant. **Frequency:** annual. **Type:** grant. **Recipient:** to two public library trustees who have demonstrated qualitative interests and efforts in supportive service of the local public library ● Literacy Award. **Frequency:** annual. **Type:** recognition. **Recipient:** to volunteer with major contribution to support literacy ● Major Benefactors Honor Award. **Frequency:** annual. **Type:** recognition. **Recipient:** for members' benefactions to public libraries ● Trustee Citation. **Frequency:** annual. **Type:** recognition. **Recipient:** to public library trustees for distinguished service to library development. **Committees:** Action Development; Education of Trustees; Fund Raising and Financial Development; Intellectual Freedom; Jury on Trustee Citations; Legislation; Services to Specialized Clientele; White House Conference. **Affiliated With:** American Library Association. **Formerly:** American Association of Library Trustees; (1941) Trustee Division (of ALA); (2000) American Library Trustee Association. **Publications:** *The Voice*, quarterly. Newsletter. Covers membership activities; includes articles on the responsibilities of library trustees and public library trusteeship. **Price:** included in membership dues. ISSN: 0734-8991. Alternate Formats: online. **Conventions/Meetings:** annual meeting, in conjunction with ALA.

10336 ■ Association for Population/Family Planning Libraries and Information Centers-International (APLIC-I)

c/o Kiet Bang, Membership Sec.
The Pennsylvania State Univ.
Population Res. Inst.
706 Oswald Tower
University Park, PA 16802
Ph: (814)863-6703 (919)960-5636
Fax: (814)863-8342

E-mail: bang@pop.psu.edu
URL: http://www.aplici.org
Contact: Katherine Willson, Pres.

Founded: 1968. **Members:** 80. **Membership Dues:** individual, $50 (annual) ● developing country/student, $15 (annual) ● institution, $125 (annual). **Regional Groups:** 3. **Multinational. Description:** Population/family planning agencies and their librarians, information scientists, educators, and communicators. Works to professionally develop effective documentation, information systems, and services in the field of population/family planning. Aims to strengthen professional contact among members. Establishes a cooperative network of population/family planning libraries and information centers. Institutes a program of continuing education in the field. Sponsors Duplicate Books Exchange Program. **Libraries: Type:** reference. **Holdings:** archival material. **Telecommunication Services:** electronic mail, kwillson@constellagroup.com. **Commissions:** Discussion Lists. **Committees:** Archives; Webmasters. **Programs:** Duplicates. **Publications:** *APLIC International Communicator*, quarterly. Newsletter. **Price:** included in membership dues. Alternate Formats: online. **Conventions/Meetings:** annual meeting, with focus on current issues in communication, information, and technology (exhibits) - 2009 Apr. 27-29, Detroit, MI.

10337 ■ Association for Recorded Sound Collections (ARSC)

c/o Peter Shambarger, Exec. Dir.
PO Box 543
Annapolis, MD 21404-0543
Ph: (410)757-0488 (310)392-3777
Fax: (410)349-0175
E-mail: execdir@arsc-audio.org
URL: http://www.arsc-audio.org
Contact: Peter Shambarger, Exec. Dir.

Founded: 1966. **Members:** 1,100. **Membership Dues:** student, $20 (annual) ● individual, $36 (annual) ● institutional, $40 (annual) ● sustaining, $72 (annual) ● donor, $200 (annual) ● patron, $500 (annual) ● benefactor, $1,000 (annual). **Budget:** $55,000. **Regional Groups:** 2. **Local Groups:** 2. **Multinational. Description:** Persons in the broadcasting and recording industries, librarians, curators, and private collectors; archivists connected with museums, libraries, and audio archives; institutional and corporate members include university and public libraries, national libraries, and research foundations. Aims to: communicate with libraries, recording archives, and collectors; act as a central information center; encourage cooperation among sound archivists; provide research grants in projects related to the documentation and preservation of recorded sound. Aids in exchange of information about holdings of members' collections and their findings with respect to techniques of preservation, storage, playback use, and restoration of sound recordings. **Awards:** Awards for Excellence in Recorded Sound Research. **Frequency:** annual. **Type:** recognition. **Computer Services:** Mailing lists. **Telecommunication Services:** electronic mail, shambarger@sprynet.com. **Committees:** Associated Audio Archives; Dealers; Discographic Access; Education; Fair Practices; Technical. **Affiliated With:** International Association of Sound and Audiovisual Archives. **Publications:** *Audio Preservation: A Planning Study*. Monograph ● *Rigler and Deutsch Record Index* ● *Rules for Cataloging of Archival Sound Recordings*. Book ● *V-Discs, A History and Discography*. Monograph ● Journal, semiannual. Contains association news, research results, and information on technical developments, unusual discoveries, and discographies. Includes book reviews. **Price:** included in membership dues; $5.00/back issue. ISSN: 0004-5438. **Circulation:** 1,100. **Advertising:** accepted ● Membership Directory, biennial. Includes information on members' collections. **Price:** included in membership dues ● Newsletter, 3/year. Covers association activities and provides notices of information desired and items offered or wanted. **Price:** included in membership dues. Alternate Formats: online ● Bulletin, annual. Includes information and reports concerning ARSC's governance and activities. **Conventions/Meetings:** annual conference (exhibits).

10338 ■ Association of Research Libraries (ARL)

21 Dupont Cir. NW, Ste.800
Washington, DC 20036
Ph: (202)296-2296
Fax: (202)872-0884
E-mail: webmgr@arl.org
URL: http://www.arl.org
Contact: Duane E. Webster, Exec. Dir.

Founded: 1932. **Members:** 123. **Membership Dues:** regular, $21,580 (annual). **Staff:** 35. **Description:** Works to influence the changing environment of scholarly communication and the public policies that affect research libraries and the communities. Promotes equitable access and effective use of recorded knowledge in support of higher education, research, and community service. **Computer Services:** database, research library statistics. **Committees:** Membership; Public Policies Affecting Research Libraries; Research, Teaching, and Learning; Scholarly Communication; Statistics and Assessment. **Projects:** Coalition for Networked Information; Scholarly Publishing and Academic Resources Coalition. **Working Groups:** Diversity Initiatives; Fair Use and Related Exemptions. **Publications:** *ARL: A Bimonthly Report on Research Library Issues & Actions from ARL, CNI, and SPARC*. Newsletter. Summarizes current issues on trends and development in scholarly communication, federal relations, collection management diversity and other topics. **Price:** $25.00 for members; $50.00 for nonmembers; $60.00 outside North America. ISSN: 1050-6098. Alternate Formats: online ● *ARL Academic Health Sciences Library Statistics*, annual. Presents data on collections, expenditures, personnel and services for more than 65 medical libraries. **Price:** $65.00 for members; $135.00 for nonmembers. ISSN: 1538-9006. Alternate Formats: online ● *ARL Academic Law Library Statistics*, annual. Presents data on collections, expenditures, personnel and services for more than 75 law libraries. **Price:** $65.00 for members; $135.00 for nonmembers. ISSN: 1538-8999 ● *ARL Annual Salary Survey*, annual. Contains compilation of data covering over 12,000 professional positions in ARL libraries. **Price:** $75.00 for members; $150.00 for nonmembers. ISSN: 0361-5669. Alternate Formats: online ● *ARL Preservation Statistics*, annual. Includes statistics on library preservation programs, staffs, and materials preserved. **Price:** $60.00 for members; $120.00 for nonmembers. ISSN: 1050-7442 ● *ARL Statistics*, annual. Presents data on a wide range of topics including collection size and growth, expenditures and services. **Price:** $85.00 for members; $170.00 for nonmembers. ISSN: 0147-2135 ● *SPEC Kits*, bimonthly. Survey. Contains a survey and review of practices and policies of ARL libraries; also available by single issues. **Price:** $215.00 for members; $285.00 for nonmembers. ISSN: 0160-3582. **Conventions/Meetings:** semiannual meeting and workshop - always May and October.

10339 ■ Association of Seventh-Day Adventist Librarians (ASDAL)

Columbia Union Coll. Lib.
7600 Flower Ave.
Takoma Park, MD 20912-7796
Ph: (301)891-4222
Fax: (301)891-4204
E-mail: lwisel@cuc.edu
URL: http://www.asdal.org
Contact: Lee Marie Wisel, Treas.

Founded: 1981. **Members:** 150. **Membership Dues:** regular, $20 (annual) ● student, retiree, $10 (annual). **Description:** Librarians belonging to the Seventh-Day Adventist church. Aims to: enhance communication among members; serve as a forum for discussion of mutual problems and professional concerns; promote librarianship and library services to Seventh-Day Adventist institutions. Sponsors D. Glenn Hilts Scholarship for graduate studies. Maintains placement service. Compiles statistics. **Awards:** D. Glenn Hilts. **Frequency:** annual. **Type:** scholarship. **Recipient:** to a Seventh-day Adventist pursuing a master's degree at an American Library Association accredited library school. **Committees:** Scholarship and Awards; Secondary Schools; Seventh-Day Adventist Periodical Index. **Sections:** Adventist Heritage; School Librarians. **Publications:** *ASDAL Action*, 3/year. Newsletter. **Circulation:** 150 ● *Seventh-Day Adventist Periodical Index*, annual. ISSN: 0270-3599. **Conventions/Meetings:** annual conference ● annual meeting.

10340 ■ Association of Specialized and Cooperative Library Agencies (ASCLA)

c/o American Library Association
50 E Huron St.
Chicago, IL 60611
Ph: (312)280-4395 (312)280-5273
Free: (800)545-2433
Fax: (312)944-8085
E-mail: ascla@ala.org
URL: http://www.ala.org/ala/ascla/ascla.htm
Contact: Barbara Macikas, Exec. Dir.

Founded: 1978. **Members:** 992. **Membership Dues:** individual, $95 (annual) ● student, $43 (annual) ● retired, $54 (annual) ● trustee, associate, $90 (annual) ● organization, $50 (annual). **Staff:** 4. **Budget:** $82,000. **Description:** A division of the American Library Association. Represents the interests of state and specialized library agencies, and multitype library organizations, and independent librarians. Develops and evaluates goals and plans for types of libraries represented. Represents and interprets their role, functions, and services. Establishes, evaluates, and promotes standards and service guidelines. Identifies the interests and needs of all persons, encouraging the creation of services to meet their needs. Stimulates professional growth and promotes the specialized training and continuing education of library personnel at all levels, and encourages membership participation in appropriate type-of-activity divisions within the ALA. **Awards:** ASCLA/KLAS/NOD Award. **Frequency:** annual. **Type:** recognition. **Recipient:** for successfully developing or expanding services for people with disabilities ● ASCLA Leadership Award. **Frequency:** annual. **Type:** recognition. **Recipient:** for leadership in consulting, multitype library cooperation, and state library development ● Exceptional Service Award. **Frequency:** annual. **Type:** recognition. **Recipient:** for exceptional service to homebound patients, medical, nursing and other professional staff in hospitals and prisons ● Francis Joseph Campbell Award. **Type:** recognition ● Professional Achievement Award. **Frequency:** annual. **Type:** recognition. **Recipient:** for achievement in consulting, networking and statewide services and programs. **Telecommunication Services:** TDD, (312)944-7298 ● TDD, (888)814-7692. **Committees:** Awards; Continuing Education; Legislation; Research; Standards. **Sections:** Independent Librarian Exchange; Interlibrary Cooperation and Networks; Libraries Serving Special Populations; State Library Agencies. **Affiliated With:** American Library Association. **Formed by Merger of:** Association of Cooperative Library Organizations; Association of State Library Agencies; Health and Rehabilitative Library Services. **Conventions/Meetings:** semiannual meeting, held in conjunction with ALA.

10341 ■ Association of Vision Science Librarians (AVSL)

c/o Fong Optometry and Health Sciences Library
School of Optometry
490 Minor Hall
Berkeley, CA 94720-2020
Ph: (510)642-1020
E-mail: banton@library.berkeley.edu
URL: http://optometry.berkeley.edu/~library/avslint.htm
Contact: Pamela C. Sieving, Chair

Founded: 1968. **Members:** 141. **Multinational. Description:** Works to foster collective and individual acquisition and dissemination of vision science information. Improves services for persons seeking vision science information. Develops standards among member-affiliated libraries. **Telecommunication Services:** electronic mail, sievingp@ors.od.nih.gov. **Formerly:** Association of Visual Science Librarians. **Publications:** *Guidelines for Vision Science Libraries*, annual. Provides quantitative information about the collections and services of vision science libraries. **Circulation:** 75. Alternate Formats: online ● *International Directory of Members*, 3/year. Membership Directory ● *Opening Day Book, Journal and A-V Collection: Vision Science*. Alternate Formats: online ● *Union List of Vision-Related Serials*. Alternate Formats: online. **Conventions/Meetings:** annual conference, held in conjunction with American Academy of Optometry - always December ● annual meeting - always May, in conjunction with the Medical Library Association.

10342 ■ Athenaeum of Philadelphia (PAT)
219 S 6th St.
Philadelphia, PA 19106-3794
Ph: (215)925-2688
Fax: (215)925-3755
E-mail: rwmoss@athenaonline.org
URL: http://www.philaathenaeum.org
Contact: Dr. Roger W. Moss, Exec. Dir.
Founded: 1814. **Members:** 1,500. **Membership Dues:** stockholder, $100 (annual) ● subscriber, $125 (annual). **Staff:** 15. **Budget:** $1,500,000. **Description:** Founded as a member-supported special collections library and housed in the National Historic Landmark Athenaeum Building. Encourages study, research, and publications relating to American cultural history from 1814 to 1950, particularly in the areas of architecture and decorative arts. Conducts exhibitions and lectures. Offers information services. **Convention/Meeting:** none. **Libraries: Type:** reference. **Holdings:** 75,000; archival material, biographical archives, photographs. **Subjects:** American architecture and design. **Awards:** Atheaneum Literary Award. **Frequency:** annual. **Type:** recognition. **Recipient:** for outstanding work of fiction or non-fiction by a Philadelphia area author ● Charles E. Peterson Fellowships. **Frequency:** annual. **Type:** fellowship. **Recipient:** to support research in American architecture and building technology prior to 1860 ● Peterson HABS Prize. **Frequency:** annual. **Type:** monetary. **Recipient:** for best set of architectural drawings submitted to the historic American buildings survey by a graduate student. **Computer Services:** database, American Architects and Buildings. **Publications:** *Athenaeum Annotations*, periodic. Newsletter ● *Book List*, monthly ● Also publishes reprint series of rare Victorian materials and original monographs on 19th century cultural history.

10343 ■ Black Caucus of the American Library Association (BCALA)
c/o Karolyn S. Thompson, VP
118 Coll. Dr., No. 5053
Hattiesburg, MS 39406-0001
Ph: (601)266-5111
Fax: (601)266-4410
E-mail: karolyn.thompson@usm.edu
URL: http://www.bcala.org
Contact: Karolyn S. Thompson, VP
Founded: 1970. **Members:** 1,000. **Membership Dues:** regular, $45 (annual) ● institution, $60 (annual) ● corporate, $200 (annual) ● student, $10 (annual) ● library support staff, $20 (annual) ● life, $500. **Staff:** 20. **Budget:** $20,000. **Description:** Black librarians; blacks interested in library services. Promotes librarianship; encourages active participation of blacks in library associations and boards and all levels of the profession. Monitors activities of the American Library Association (see separate entry) with regard to its policies and programs and how they affect black librarians and library users. Reviews, analyzes, evaluates, and recommends to the ALA actions that influence the recruitment, development, advancement, and general working conditions of black librarians. Facilitates library services that meet the informational needs of black people including increased availability of materials related to social and economic concerns. **Awards:** BCALA Literary Award. **Frequency:** annual. **Type:** monetary. **Recipient:** for excellence in adult fiction and non-fiction by black authors ● DEMCO/BCALA Award for Excellence in Librarianship. **Frequency:** annual. **Type:** monetary. **Recipient:** for a librarian who has made significant contributions in promoting the status of blacks in the library profession ● Distinguished Service Award. **Frequency:** annual. **Type:** recognition ● E.J. Josey Scholarship Award. **Frequency:** annual. **Type:** monetary. **Recipient:** for future librarians ● Trailblazer's Award. **Frequency:** quinquennial. **Type:** recognition. **Recipient:** for an individual with pioneering contributions in the library profession. **Telecommunication Services:** electronic bulletin board, bcala@listserv.kent.edu. **Committees:** Affiliates/Chapters; Affirmative Action; ALA Relations; Awards; Budget/Audit; Constitution and Bylaws; Fundraising; History; International Relations; Membership; Nominations and Elections; Program; Public Relations; Publications; Recruitment and Professional Development; Services to Children and Families of African Descent; Technology Advisory. **Publications:** *BCALA Newsletter*, bimonthly. Represents news of interest about black librarians. Recurring features include notices of professional opportunities and activities of individuals. **Price:** included in membership dues. **Circulation:** 900. **Advertising:** accepted. Alternate Formats: online ● *Conference Proceedings of National Conference of African American Librarians* ● *Directory of the Black Caucus of the American Library Association*, biennial. **Conventions/Meetings:** biennial Culture Keepers - conference, books, journals, library products (exhibits) ● semiannual meeting - January and June.

10344 ■ Catholic Library Association (CLA)
100 North St., Ste.224
Pittsfield, MA 01201-5109
Ph: (413)443-2252
Fax: (413)442-2252
E-mail: cla@cathla.org
URL: http://www.cathla.org
Contact: Jean R. Bostley SSJ, Exec. Dir.
Founded: 1921. **Members:** 1,000. **Membership Dues:** corporate, $300 (annual) ● individual (based on salary), $45-$75 (annual) ● retired, library science student, $25 (annual) ● institution (based on library budget), $100-$300 (annual) ● sustaining, $150 (annual). **Staff:** 9. **Budget:** $200,000. **Local Groups:** 29. **Description:** Librarians, teachers, and booksellers concerned with Catholic libraries and their specialized problems and the writing, publishing, and distribution of Catholic literature. Members represent lay and clergy in both Catholic and non-Catholic institutions. **Awards:** John Brubaker Memorial Award. **Frequency:** annual. **Type:** recognition. **Recipient:** for outstanding work of literary merit in Catholic Library World ● Regina Medal Award. **Frequency:** annual. **Type:** medal. **Recipient:** for best children's literature ● Rev. Andrew L. Bouwhuis Memorial Scholarship. **Frequency:** annual. **Type:** scholarship. **Recipient:** for graduate study toward a master's degree in library science ● World Book Scholarship. **Frequency:** annual. **Type:** scholarship. **Recipient:** for study in children's or school librarianship for CLA national member. **Roundtables:** Bibliographic Instruction; Cataloging and Classification; Preservation of American Catholic Materials. **Sections:** Academic Library Services; Children's Library Services; High School/Young Adult Library Services; Parish and Community Library Services. **Publications:** *Catholic Library World*, quarterly. Journal. Reports on library activities and professionals; includes new product information, print and non-print media reviews, and bibliographies. **Price:** included in membership dues; $60.00 for nonmembers. ISSN: 0008-820X. **Circulation:** 3,000. **Advertising:** accepted. Alternate Formats: microform; online ● *Catholic Periodical and Literature Index*, quarterly. Contains subject and author index to Catholic periodicals and newspapers; includes an author/title/subject bibliography of books. ISSN: 0008-8285. Alternate Formats: CD-ROM; online. **Conventions/Meetings:** annual conference and convention, held in conjunction with the National Catholic Educational Association (exhibits) - 2009 Apr. 14-17, Anaheim, CA.

10345 ■ Center for Research Libraries (CRL)
6050 S Kenwood Ave.
Chicago, IL 60637-2804
Ph: (773)955-4545
Free: (800)621-6044
Fax: (773)955-4339
E-mail: breilly@crl.edu
URL: http://www.crl.edu
Contact: Bernard F. Reilly, Pres.
Founded: 1949. **Members:** 206. **Staff:** 65. **Budget:** $5,000,000. **Description:** Primarily universities, colleges and research libraries. Provides an organizational framework for cooperative collection development and resource sharing. **Libraries: Type:** reference. **Holdings:** 4,000,000. **Formerly:** (1965) Midwest Interlibrary Center. **Publications:** *FOCUS: On The Center for Research Libraries*, quarterly. Newsletter. Alternate Formats: online ● Handbook, biennial ● Annual Report. Contains an overview of events and activities of specific year, as well as detailed financial statements. Alternate Formats: online ● Apply for list of other publications. **Conventions/Meetings:** annual Council of Voting Members - meeting, membership meeting - usually April, Chicago, IL.

10346 ■ Chief Officers of State Library Agencies (COSLA)
201 E Main St., Ste.1405
Lexington, KY 40507
Ph: (859)514-9151 (859)514-9210
Fax: (859)514-9166
E-mail: ttucker@amrms.com
URL: http://www.cosla.org
Contact: Tracy Tucker, Dir.
Founded: 1973. **Members:** 50. **Membership Dues:** state head of library agency, $3,000 (annual). **Staff:** 1. **Budget:** $149,000. **Description:** State and territorial librarians, directors, commissioners, or officials who head state and territorial agencies that are responsible for statewide library development. Works to provide a continuing mechanism for dealing with problems in library development. **Publications:** Directory, annual. **Price:** $25.00/year ● Membership Directory. Alternate Formats: online. **Conventions/Meetings:** quarterly meeting.

10347 ■ Chinese American Librarians Association (CALA)
c/o Jian Anna Xiong, Membership Chair
Southern Illinois Univ. - Carbondale
Morris Lib.
605 Agriculture Dr.
Mailcode 6632
Carbondale, IL 62901
E-mail: shixingwen@yahoo.com
URL: http://www.cala-web.org
Contact: Shixing Wen, Exec. Dir.
Founded: 1973. **Members:** 500. **Membership Dues:** student, non-salaried, overseas, $15 (annual) ● individual, $30 (annual) ● institutional, affiliated, $100 (annual) ● life, $300. **Regional Groups:** 5. **Description:** Promotes better communication among Chinese American librarians in the U.S., serves as a forum for the discussion of mutual problems, and supports the development and promotion of librarianship. Maintains placement referral service. **Awards:** C.C. Seetoo/CALA Conference Travel Scholarship. **Frequency:** annual. **Type:** monetary. **Recipient:** for library school students ● CALA Distinguished Service Award. **Frequency:** annual. **Type:** recognition. **Recipient:** for outstanding service to the librarianship profession ● CALA President's Recognition Award. **Frequency:** periodic. **Type:** recognition ● Sheila Suen Lai Scholarship. **Frequency:** annual. **Type:** monetary. **Recipient:** for library school students. **Committees:** Annual Conference Program Planning; Awards; Books to China; Constitution and Bylaws; International Relations; Local Arrangement; Newsletter Editors; Nominating; Public Relations/Fund Raising; Publications; Scholarship. **Affiliated With:** American Library Association. **Absorbed:** (1983) Chinese Librarians Association. **Formerly:** Mid-West Chinese American Librarians Association. **Publications:** *CALA E-Journal*, semiannual ● *CALA Membership Directory*, annual. **Advertising:** accepted ● *Chinese American Librarians Association—Newsletter*, periodic. Includes calendar of events, list of employment opportunities, and new member news. **Price:** included in membership dues. ISSN: 0736-8887. **Circulation:** 300. **Advertising:** accepted ● *Directory of Chinese*

American Libraries in the U.S. ● *Journal of Library and Information Science* (in Chinese and English), semiannual. Covers problems common to librarians and information scientists; new concepts, systems, and technology; and leading events worldwide. **Price:** included in membership dues; $15.00 /year for nonmembers; $45.00 for institutions. ISSN: 0363-3640. **Circulation:** 500 ● Newsletter, 3/year, February, June, September. **Conventions/Meetings:** semiannual board meeting ● annual conference and board meeting, held in conjunction with American Library Association, also includes membership meeting (exhibits).

10348 ■ Church and Synagogue Library Association (CSLA)
2920 SW Dolph Ct., Ste.3A
Portland, OR 97219
Ph: (503)244-6919
Free: (800)LIB-CSLA
Fax: (503)977-3734
E-mail: csla@worldaccessnet.com
URL: http://cslainfo.org
Contact: Judith Janzen, Admin.
Founded: 1967. **Members:** 1,800. **Membership Dues:** individual in U.S., $35 (annual) ● individual outside U.S., $40 (annual) ● church in U.S., $55 (annual) ● church outside U.S., $60 (annual). **Staff:** 2. **Budget:** $92,000. **Regional Groups:** 33. **Description:** Provides educational guidance in the establishment and maintenance of congregational libraries. **Libraries: Type:** open to the public. **Holdings:** 20. **Awards: Frequency:** annual. **Type:** recognition. **Recipient:** for outstanding congregational libraries and librarians ● **Type:** recognition. **Recipient:** for contributors to congregational libraries and children's literature. **Computer Services:** Mailing lists. **Committees:** Awards; Chapters; Conference; Continuing Education; Library Services. **Publications:** *Church and Synagogue Libraries*, bimonthly. Newsletter. Covers library methods and training opportunities for religious librarians. **Price:** included in membership dues; $25.00 /year for nonmembers in U.S.; $35.00 /year for nonmembers in Canada; $55.00 /year for nonmembers foreign. ISSN: 0009-6342. **Circulation:** 3,000. **Advertising:** accepted. Alternate Formats: microform ● Also publishes planning materials. **Conventions/Meetings:** annual conference (exhibits).

10349 ■ Committee on Research Materials on Southeast Asia (CORMOSEA)
Harvard Coll. Lib.
Harvard Univ.
Cambridge, MA 02138
Ph: (617)495-0585 (617)495-2425
Fax: (617)496-8704
E-mail: comments@cormosea.org
URL: http://www.cormosea.org
Contact: Dr. Raymond Lum, Chm.
Founded: 1969. **Members:** 12. **Description:** Committee of the Southeast Asia Council of the Association for Asian Studies. Programs and objectives include: supporting research for bibliographical and other reference aids for Southeast Asian studies; proposing changes in basic cataloging procedures for the management of Southeast Asian language materials; working with national and international organizations in developing research materials on microfilm. **Subcommittees:** Collection Development; Technical Processes. **Affiliated With:** Association for Asian Studies. **Formerly:** Committee on American Library Resources on South Asia; Committee on American Library Resources on Southeast Asia. **Publications:** *CORMOSEA Bulletin*, semiannual. Newsletter. Provides information on bibliographies, microforms, archives, and other research materials on Southeast Asia. **Price:** included in membership dues. ISSN: 0734-449X. **Circulation:** 150. **Advertising:** accepted. **Conventions/Meetings:** annual meeting, held in conjunction with AAS.

10350 ■ Continuing Library Education Network and Exchange Round Table (CLENE)
c/o Jasmine Posey, Programming Chair
Greenwich Lib.
101 W Putnam Ave.
Greenwich, CT 06830-4328
Ph: (203)622-7941
Fax: (203)622-7939
E-mail: jposey@greenwichlibrary.org
URL: http://www.ala.org/ala/clenert/clenert.htm
Contact: Pat Taviss, Pres.
Founded: 1984. **Members:** 350. **Membership Dues:** individual, $15 (annual) ● organization, $50 (annual). **Staff:** 5. **Budget:** $25,000. **Description:** Roundtable unit of the American Library Association (see separate entry). State agencies, associations, individuals, and institutions interested in continuing education programs for library, media, and information science personnel. Works to: provide a forum for the exchange of concerns and ideas among library and information personnel responsible for continuing library education programs, training, and staff development; provide learning activities and material to maintain the competency of those who provide continuing library education; initiate and support programs to increase the availability of quality continuing library education programs; develop an awareness of the need for continuing library education on the part of employers and employees. **Telecommunication Services:** electronic mail, pat@taviss.com. **Supersedes:** (1983) Continuing Library Education Network and Exchange. **Publications:** *A Focus Group Interview*. Manual. **Price:** $10.00 each ● *CLENExchange*, quarterly. Newsletter. Provides information on continuing library education program: staff development, program ideas, and new concepts. Includes reviews of books. **Price:** included in membership dues; $20.00 /year for nonmembers. **Circulation:** 400. Alternate Formats: online ● *Self Assessment for Children's Services*. Manual. **Price:** $11.00 each ● *Workshop Evaluation: Forms Follow Function*. **Price:** $6.00 each. **Conventions/Meetings:** semiannual conference, in conjunction with the ALA Annual Conference and Midwinter Meeting.

10351 ■ Council of Archives and Research Libraries in Jewish Studies (CARLJS)
c/o National Foundation for Jewish Culture
330 7th Ave., 21st Fl.
New York, NY 10001
Ph: (212)629-0500
Fax: (212)629-0508
E-mail: nfjc@jewishculture.org
URL: http://www.jewishculture.org/archives/archives_libraries.html
Contact: David Gilner, Pres.
Founded: 1970. **Members:** 35. **Membership Dues:** full, $100 (annual) ● associate, $50 (annual). **Staff:** 1. **Description:** Jewish libraries and archives, theological seminaries, and major university libraries. Seeks to encourage, support, and further the growth and development of North American archives and research libraries having major collections in the field of Jewish studies; facilitates optimum use of these collections by scholars in Jewish studies; raises public and private support and understanding for their work; and promotes information exchange among members. Undertakes projects in the areas of cataloging and description of archival materials; is concerned with the preservation of manuscripts, local community records, newspapers, films, and other materials vital to Jewish studies. **Computer Services:** database, members ● mailing lists, of members. **Conventions/Meetings:** annual meeting - always in June on Father's Day.

10352 ■ Council on Botanical and Horticultural Libraries (CBHL)
c/o Ms. Gayle Bradbeer, Sec.
Auraria Lib.
1100 Lawrence St.
Denver, CO 80204-2095
Ph: (303)556-2791
Fax: (303)556-3528
E-mail: gayle.bradbeer@auraria.edu
URL: http://www.cbhl.net
Contact: Ms. Gayle Bradbeer, Sec.
Founded: 1970. **Members:** 250. **Membership Dues:** individual, $55 (annual) ● institutional, $105 (annual) ● student, retiree, $35 (annual) ● commercial, $150 (annual). **Multinational. Description:** Libraries with collections of or interest in botanical or horticultural materials; librarians, bibliographers, booksellers, publishers, researchers, and administrators interested in these fields. Initiates and improves communication between persons and institutions concerned with the development, maintenance, and use of botanical and horticultural libraries. Assists in the organization and coordination of activities of benefit and interest to these libraries; promotes communication among members. **Awards:** CBHL Annual Literature Award. **Frequency:** annual. **Type:** recognition. **Recipient:** for both author and publisher of a work that makes a significant contribution to the literature of botany or horticulture ● Charles Robert Long Award. **Frequency:** periodic. **Type:** recognition. **Recipient:** for outstanding contribution and meritorious service to the organization or to the field of botanical and horticultural libraries or literature. **Committees:** Electronic Communications; Preservation and Access; Public Relations. **Also Known As:** CBHL. **Publications:** Newsletter, quarterly ● Membership Directory ● Also publishes membership brochure. **Conventions/Meetings:** annual meeting, with lectures, tours, and programs business meeting - usually spring.

10353 ■ Council on Library and Information Resources (CLIR)
1755 Massachusetts Ave. NW, Ste.500
Washington, DC 20036
Ph: (202)939-4750 (202)939-4752
Fax: (202)939-4765
E-mail: chenry@clir.org
URL: http://www.clir.org
Contact: Dr. Charles Henry, Pres.
Founded: 1956. **Staff:** 13. **Description:** Dedicated to improving the management of information for research, teaching and learning. **Libraries: Type:** reference. **Awards:** A.R. Zipf Fellowship in Information Management. **Frequency:** annual. **Type:** monetary. **Recipient:** for a student in the early stages of graduate school, who has shown exceptional promise for leadership and technical achievement in information management ● Mellon Fellowships for Dissertation Research in Original Sources. **Frequency:** annual. **Type:** grant. **Recipient:** for junior scholars in the humanities and related social science fields ● Postdoctoral Fellowship in Scholarly Information Resources. **Frequency:** annual. **Type:** fellowship. **Recipient:** for recent PhDs who believe there are opportunities to develop meaningful linkages among disciplinary scholarship, libraries, archives, and evolving digital tools ● Rovelstad Scholarship in International Librarianship. **Frequency:** annual. **Type:** scholarship. **Recipient:** for a student of library and information science. **Formed by Merger of:** (1998) Council on Library Resources and Commission on Preservation and Access. **Publications:** *CLIR Issues*, bimonthly. Newsletter. **Price:** free. ISSN: 0892-0605. **Circulation:** 4,000. Alternate Formats: online ● Annual Report. **Price:** free. ISSN: 0070-1181. **Circulation:** 4,000 ● Publications also include technical reports.

10354 ■ Ethnic and Multicultural Information Exchange Roundtable (EMIERT)
c/o American Library Association
50 E Huron
Chicago, IL 60611
Ph: (312)280-4295
Free: (800)545-2433
Fax: (312)280-3256
E-mail: sorange@ala.org
URL: http://www.ala.org/ala/emiert/aboutemiert/aboutemiert.htm
Contact: Dr. Plummer Alston Jones Jr., Chm.
Founded: 1972. **Members:** 600. **Membership Dues:** student, $10 (annual) ● organization, $25 (annual) ● individual, $20 (annual). **Description:** A round table of the ALA. Exchanges information about minority materials and library services for minority groups in the U.S. Conducts educational programs with a focus on multicultural librarianship. **Awards:** Coretta Scott King Book Award. **Frequency:** annual. **Type:** recognition. **Recipient:** for African-American author and illustrator with outstanding inspirational and educational contribution ● David Cohen/EMIERT Award. **Frequency:** annual. **Type:** monetary. **Recipient:** to a

work that promotes increase in understanding of multiculturalism in libraries of North America ● GALE/EMIERT Multicultural Award. **Frequency:** annual. **Type:** monetary. **Recipient:** for outstanding achievement in the area of multicultural librarianship. **Committees:** Armenian-American Librarians; Children's Services; Collection Development; Coretta Scott King Book Award; EMIE Bulletin; Jewish Information; Library Education; Publishing and Multicultural Materials. **Formerly:** (1983) Ethnic Materials Information Exchange Task Force (SRRT); (2001) Ethnic Materials and Information Exchange Round Table; (2002) Ethnic and Multicultural Information Exchange. **Publications:** *Directory of Ethnic & Multicultural Publishers, Distributors and Resource Organizations, 5th Edition*, periodic. Contains over 500 publishers, etc. including 45 ethnic groups. **Circulation:** 500. **Advertising:** accepted ● *EMIE Bulletin*, quarterly. Insert in quarterly issues of MultiCultural Review. **Price:** $20.00 /year for individuals; $25.00 /year for institutions; $10.00/year for students. ISSN: 0737-9021. **Circulation:** 600 ● *Ventures Into Culture: A Resource Book of Multicultural Materials and Programs, 2nd Edition (2001)*, periodic. Handbook. Contains bibliography of multicultural materials for libraries, arranged by ethnic and minority groups. **Conventions/Meetings:** annual conference, held in conjunction with ALA (exhibits) ● annual meeting, held in conjunction with ALA (exhibits) - always midwinter.

10355 ■ Evangelical Church Library Association (ECLA)

PO Box 353
Glen Ellyn, IL 60138
Ph: (630)375-7865
Fax: (847)296-0754
E-mail: judi@eclalibraries.org
URL: http://www.eclalibraries.org
Contact: Judi Turek, Sec.

Founded: 1970. **Members:** 475. **Membership Dues:** church, individual, school in U.S., $35 (annual) ● church, individual, school in Canada, $40 (annual) ● church, individual, school outside U.S. and Canada, $50 (annual). **Staff:** 1. **Regional Groups:** 1. **Local Groups:** 1. **Description:** Church libraries, special libraries, schools, organizations, and concerned individuals. Promotes the development and maintenance of church libraries and media centers. **Publications:** *Church Libraries*, quarterly. Magazine. Covers library organization and operation; includes promotional ideas, book reviews, and list of recommended books. **Price:** included in membership dues. ISSN: 0739-0297. **Circulation:** 500. **Advertising:** accepted. **Conventions/Meetings:** annual conference, includes book exchange (exhibits) - always October or November, Wheaton, IL ● workshop.

10356 ■ Federal Library and Information Center Committee (FLICC)

c/o The Library of Congress
101 Independence Ave. SE, Adams Bldg., Rm. 217
Washington, DC 20540-4935
Ph: (202)707-4800
Fax: (202)707-4818
E-mail: flicc@loc.gov
URL: http://www.loc.gov/flicc
Contact: Roberta I. Shaffer, Exec. Dir.

Founded: 1965. **Members:** 57. **Staff:** 45. **Budget:** $3,300,000. **Description:** Representatives of departments and agencies of the federal government. Makes recommendations on federal library and information policies, programs, and procedures; coordinates cooperative activities and services among federal libraries and information centers. Serves as a forum to focus on issues and policies that affect libraries and information centers; needs and priorities in providing information services to the government and to the public; efficient and cost-effective use of federal library and information resources and services. Promotes improved access to information and continued development and use of FEDLINK (Federal Library and Information Network); advocates research and development in the applications of new technologies for federal libraries. Seeks improvement in the management of federal libraries and information centers. Conducts educational programs. Provides training as OCLC (Online Computer Library Center) network. **Libraries: Type:** reference. **Awards:** Federal Librarian. **Frequency:** annual. **Type:** recognition ● Federal Librarian of the Year. **Frequency:** annual. **Type:** recognition ● Federal Library Technician. **Frequency:** annual. **Type:** recognition. **Computer Services:** database, access offered by 65 vendors and two bibliographic utilities. **Telecommunication Services:** electronic mail, rsha@loc.gov. **Working Groups:** Awards; Competitive Sourcing; Content Management; Department of Homeland Security Libraries; Education; Federal Depository Libraries/GPO Partnership; Membership and Governance; Nominating. **Formerly:** (1984) Federal Library Committee. **Publications:** *Federal Library and Information Center Committee Annual Report*, annual. Includes statistics and graphs. Included with FLICC Newsletter. **Price:** free ● *FEDLINK Technical Notes*, bimonthly. ISSN: 0737-4178 ● *FLICC Federal Information Policies*, annual. Contains a summary of forum proceedings. Included with FLICC Newsletter. **Price:** free. ISSN: 1061-7485 ● *FLICC/FEDLINK Course Catalog* ● *FLICC Newsletter*, quarterly. ISSN: 0882-908X. **Conventions/Meetings:** annual Forum on Federal Information Policies - meeting ● annual Information Technology Update - meeting ● annual Joint Spring Workshop.

10357 ■ Friends of Libraries for Blind and Physically Handicapped Individuals in North America

Address Unknown since 2007

Description: Individuals and libraries supporting programs designed to enhance accessibility of library facilities and holdings to people who are blind or physically handicapped. Assists federally sponsored programs for the acquisition, cataloging, and distribution of braille materials in the U.S. and Canada; produces video programs featuring authors, poets, and other guest lecturers; holds special events in conjunction with national meetings of organizations representing people who are blind or physically handicapped. **Publications:** *International Yearbook* ● Brochures.

10358 ■ Friends of Libraries U.S.A. (FOLUSA)

1420 Walnut St., Ste.450
Philadelphia, PA 19102
Ph: (215)790-1674
Free: (800)936-5872
Fax: (215)545-3821
E-mail: folusa@folusa.org
Contact: Sally G. Reed, Exec. Dir.

Founded: 1979. **Members:** 2,000. **Membership Dues:** friend, $40-$100 (annual) ● library, $50-$100 (annual) ● all-in-one, $100-$250 (annual). **Staff:** 4. **Budget:** $400,000. **State Groups:** 30. **Local Groups:** 3,000. **Description:** Groups, trustees, libraries and individuals committed to supporting libraries. Provides training, consultation, and resources to further the development of support for libraries; specializes in Friends group development, trustee development, library advocacy, fundraising for libraries, and early childhood literacy and libraries. **Libraries: Type:** not open to the public. **Awards:** Porter Award. **Frequency:** annual. **Type:** recognition. **Recipient:** for the best essay about libraries. **Computer Services:** Mailing lists. **Affiliated With:** American Library Association. **Formerly:** Literary Landmarks Association; (2000) Books for Babies. **Publications:** *Getting Grants in Your Community*. **Price:** $42.00 each ● *Making Our Voices Heard: Citizens Speak Out for Libraries*. Alternate Formats: online ● *News Update*, bimonthly. Newsletter ● *101 Great Ideas for Libraries and Friends* ● Also publishes fact sheets and sourcebook. **Conventions/Meetings:** semiannual conference, held in conjunction with the American Library Association annual and mid-winter conferences (exhibits).

10359 ■ Independent Research Libraries Association (IRLA)

c/o Dr. Charles F. Bryan, Jr., Pres.
PO Box 7311
Richmond, VA 23221-0311
Ph: (804)342-9656 (804)358-4901
Fax: (804)355-2399
E-mail: cbryan@vahistorical.org
URL: http://irla.lindahall.org
Contact: Dr. Charles F. Bryan Jr., Pres.

Founded: 1972. **Members:** 19. **Description:** Research libraries that are autonomous institutions holding nationally significant collections. Seeks to provide consultation to members concerning mutual problems, and to develop a common foundation for thinking about funding, organization, operational, legislative, and other matters of joint concern. **Publications:** Directory, periodic. **Conventions/Meetings:** annual meeting.

10360 ■ Interagency Council on Information Resources for Nursing (ICIRN)

c/o Richard J. Barry, Pres.
Amer. Nurses Assn. Lib.
8515 Georgia Ave., Ste.400
Silver Spring, MD 20910-3492
Ph: (301)628-5143
Fax: (301)628-5008
E-mail: richard.barry@ana.org
URL: http://www.icirn.org
Contact: Richard J. Barry, Pres.

Founded: 1960. **Members:** 25. **Membership Dues:** voluntary, $100 (annual). **Description:** Representatives of agencies and organizations concerned with providing and improving access to library and information resources and services for nurses. Member representatives network, consult, or learn about the products, programs, and services of other organizations, publicize their products, programs, and services, and collaborate in providing, promoting, and/or developing informational programs, services, and tools for nurses or information specialists who provide services to nurses. The Executive Committee is composed of representatives from the American Nurses Association, National Library of Medicine, Medical Library Association, American Public Health Association and the American Library Association (see separate entries). **Publications:** *Essential Nursing Resources*, biennial. Catalog. Alternate Formats: online ● Also publishes fact sheet. **Conventions/Meetings:** semiannual meeting - always March and October in New York City.

10361 ■ International Association of Aquatic and Marine Science Libraries and Information Centers (IAMSLIC)

c/o Janet Webster, Librarian
Hatfield Marine Sci. Center
Oregon State Univ.
2030 S Marine Sci. Dr.
Newport, OR 97365
E-mail: butler@uoregon.edu
URL: http://www.iamslic.org
Contact: Barbara Butler, Pres.

Founded: 1975. **Members:** 300. **Membership Dues:** individual and institution in the developed world, $50 (annual) ● individual and institution in the developing world, $20 (annual). **Languages:** English, French, Spanish. **Description:** Marine-related libraries and information centers; university and government research libraries; librarians; information specialists; managers of special libraries. Encourages members to exchange scientific and technical information and explore issues of mutual concern. **Computer Services:** Mailing lists, of members. **Telecommunication Services:** electronic mail, iamwebcomment@ucdavis.edu. **Committees:** Electronic Mail Network; Union List of Oceanographic Atlases. **Absorbed:** (1976) East Coast Marine Science Librarians. **Formerly:** International Association of Marine Sciences Libraries and Information Centers; (1978) Marine Science Libraries Association. **Publications:** *Directory of Marine Science Libraries and Information Centers*, periodic ● Newsletter, quarterly. ISSN: 0193-9254. **Circulation:** 250. Alternate Formats: online ● Proceedings, annual. **Price:** $15.00 for members, plus shipping and handling; $40.00 for nonmembers, plus shipping and handling. ISSN: 8755-6332. Alternate Formats: online ● Also publishes selected readings on the ocean and maintains a union list of serials in marine science libraries on microfiche. **Conventions/Meetings:** annual conference (exhibits) - always fall ● workshop.

10362 ■ International Association of Music Libraries, Archives and Documentation Centers, U.S. Branch (IAML-US)
c/o Mary Wallace Davidson, Pres.
Indiana Univ.
620 S Park Ave.
Bloomington, IN 47401
Ph: (812)334-1410
E-mail: mdavidso@indiana.edu
URL: http://www.iamlus.org
Contact: Mary Wallace Davidson, Pres.
Founded: 1955. **Members:** 268. **Membership Dues:** individual, $48 (annual) ● institutional, $68 (annual). **Description:** Libraries, educational institutions, publishers, dealers, and interested individuals. U.S. members of the International Association of Music Libraries, which has its headquarters in Kassel, Germany, and has members in 39 countries. **Awards:** Lenore Coral Travel Award. **Frequency:** periodic. **Type:** monetary. **Recipient:** for members to attend IAML meetings abroad. **Formerly:** (1999) International Association of Music Libraries, United States Branch. **Publications:** *Fontes Artis Musicae*, quarterly. Journal. Includes book reviews, research reports, and bibliographies. **Price:** included in membership dues; $33.00 for nonmembers; $48.00 for institutions. ISSN: 0015-6191. **Advertising:** accepted ● Directory, triennial. **Conventions/Meetings:** annual conference and meeting, held in conjunction with Music Library Association (exhibits).

10363 ■ International Friends of the London Library
c/o John W. Spurdle, Sec.
515 Madison Ave., Ste.3702
New York, NY 10022
Ph: (212)644-4858
E-mail: jspurdle@aol.com
URL: http://www.londonlibrary.co.uk/legacy/legacy.html
Contact: John W. Spurdle, Sec.
Description: Admirers of the London, England private library founded by Thomas Carlyle in 1841. Promotes appreciation of, and contribution to, the operation of this institution serving authors and bibliophiles. **Libraries: Type:** not open to the public. **Holdings:** 1,500,000.

10364 ■ International Survey Library Association (ISLA)
c/o Roper Center for Public Opinion Research
Univ. of Connecticut
Homer Babbidge Lib.
369 Fairfield Way, Unit 2164
Storrs Mansfield, CT 06269-2164
Ph: (860)486-4440
Fax: (860)486-6308
E-mail: lois@ropercenter.uconn.edu
URL: http://www.ropercenter.uconn.edu
Contact: Lois Timms-Ferrara, Assoc. Dir.
Founded: 1964. **Members:** 57. **Staff:** 20. **Description:** Serves educational institutions and nonprofit research organizations and the corporate community. Encourages the use of survey data by educational and other nonprofit organizations, and provides the media and corporate community with polling data on public policy and social issues. Member institutions obtain data acquisition publications and other descriptive materials from the Roper Center. The Roper Center also provides services such as data analysis and interpretation, and customized searches of the archive. **Computer Services:** Online services, iPOLL (Public Opinion Location Library), an information retrieval service available from the Roper Center or through DIALOG and Lexis/Nexis. **Publications:** *Data Acquisitions Catalog*, semiannual.

10365 ■ John F. Kennedy Library Foundation (JFKLF)
Columbia Point
Boston, MA 02125
Ph: (617)514-1600
Free: (866)JFK-1960
Fax: (617)436-3395
E-mail: membership@jfklfoundation.org
URL: http://www.jfklibrary.org
Contact: John Shattuck, CEO
Founded: 1984. **Membership Dues:** individual, $40 (annual) ● family, $60 (annual) ● contributor, $100 (annual) ● benefactor, $250 (annual) ● Leadership Circle, $500 (annual) ● President's Circle, $1,000 (annual). **Staff:** 19. **Description:** Supports the educational programs and activities of the John F. Kennedy Library and Museum. Offers educational programs which encourage leadership and community service in urban youth. Awards archival internships and research grants, and holds forums. **Libraries: Type:** open to the public. **Holdings:** 21,135; articles. **Subjects:** mid-20th Century U.S. history, politics, government centering on life, career, administration of President John F. Kennedy, also Ernest Hemingway. **Awards: Type:** fellowship. **Recipient:** for research ● **Type:** grant. **Recipient:** for teachers ● Profile in Courage Award. **Frequency:** annual. **Type:** recognition. **Recipient:** for elected officials exhibiting political courage and leadership. **Publications:** *John F. Kennedy Presidential Library Newsletter*, semiannual. Features library activities and reminiscences about President Kennedy. **Price:** included in membership dues. **Circulation:** 12,000. Alternate Formats: online.

10366 ■ Library Administration and Management Association (LAMA)
c/o American Library Association
50 E Huron St.
Chicago, IL 60611-2729
Ph: (312)280-5032
Free: (800)545-2433
Fax: (312)280-5033
E-mail: lama@ala.org
URL: http://www.ala.org/ala/lama/lama.htm
Contact: Fred Reuland, Marketing Specialist
Founded: 1957. **Members:** 5,000. **Membership Dues:** individual, $50 (annual) ● corporate/organizational, $65 (annual) ● student, $15 (annual). **Staff:** 2. **Budget:** $400,000. **Description:** A type-of-activity division of the American Library Association (see separate entry). Works to improve and develop all aspects and levels of administration in all types of libraries, covering library administration in general, human resources administration, training, public relations and marketing, fundraising, financial development and administration, buildings and equipment, organization and management, measurement and evaluation, and management of library systems and services. Offers regional institutes on subjects of interest to library managers, such as diversity, leadership, building design, emergency preparedness, staff recruitment and development, marketing and customer service. **Awards:** AIA/ALA-LAMA Library Buildings Award Program. **Frequency:** biennial. **Type:** recognition. **Recipient:** for distinguished accomplishment in library architecture ● John Cotton Dana Library Public Relations Award. **Frequency:** annual. **Type:** recognition. **Recipient:** for outstanding library public relations ● LAMA Cultural Diversity Grant. **Frequency:** annual. **Type:** grant. **Recipient:** for LAMA members or LAMA units ● LAMA Group Achievement Award. **Frequency:** annual. **Type:** recognition. **Recipient:** to LAMA committees or task forces, recognizing outstanding teamwork supporting the goals of LAMA ● LAMA President's Award. **Frequency:** annual. **Type:** recognition. **Recipient:** for nonmember or organization that has made significant contributions to the goals of LAMA ● LAMA/YBP Student Writing and Development Award. **Frequency:** annual. **Type:** recognition. **Recipient:** to the best article on a topic in the area of library administration and management. **Boards:** Editorial Advisory. **Committees:** Cultural Diversity; Education; Governmental Affairs; Leadership Development; Recognition of Achievement; Small Libraries Publications; Special Conference and Programs. **Programs:** ALA Library Buildings Award. **Sections:** Buildings and Equipment; Fund Raising and Financial Development; Human Resources; Library Organization and Management; Measurement, Assessment and Evaluation; Public Relations and Marketing; Systems and Services. **Affiliated With:** American Library Association. **Formerly:** Library Administration Division of ALA. **Publications:** *Leads from LAMA*, periodic. Newsletter. Includes news relevant to librarians interested in management and administration. Alternate Formats: online ● *Library Administration and Management*, quarterly. Magazine. Covers the organization and management of libraries, public relations, personnel administration, buildings and equipment and automated systems. **Price:** included in membership dues; $65.00 for nonmembers in U.S.; $75.00 for nonmembers outside U.S. ISSN: 0888-4463. **Advertising:** accepted. Alternate Formats: online. Also Cited As: *LA&M* ● *Library Building Consultant List*. Alternate Formats: online ● Bibliographies ● Monographs ● Pamphlets. **Conventions/Meetings:** annual conference, held in conjunction with ALA ● biennial National Institute - meeting, held in conjunction with ALA - always midwinter.

10367 ■ Library Cat Society (LCS)
PO Box 274
Moorhead, MN 56560
Ph: (218)236-7205
E-mail: lahtiph2003@yahoo.com
Contact: Ms. Phyllis Lahti, Dir.
Founded: 1987. **Members:** 165. **Membership Dues:** individual, $6 (annual). **Staff:** 1. **Budget:** $1,000. **Description:** Represents librarians who have, or wish to have, cats-in-residence in their libraries; individuals who advocate library cats. Objectives are to encourage the establishment of a cat or cats in a library environment; improve the well-being and image of the library cat; promote camaraderie among library staffs who have cats, or hope to, and with those persons not in libraries who advocate library cats. **Convention/Meeting:** none. **Libraries: Type:** lending. **Holdings:** 150. **Awards: Type:** grant. **Publications:** *Cats, Librarians, and Libraries*, one edition only. Booklet. Essays by and for librarians. **Price:** $3.50/copy. ISSN: 1071-2593. **Advertising:** accepted ● *The Library Cat*, 3/year. Newsletter. **Price:** $1.00 sample copy; $6.00/year.

10368 ■ Library and Information Technology Association (LITA)
c/o American Library Association
50 E Huron St.
Chicago, IL 60611-2795
Ph: (312)280-4268 (312)280-4267
Free: (800)545-2433
Fax: (312)280-3257
E-mail: lita@ala.org
URL: http://www.lita.org
Contact: Mary C. Taylor, Exec. Dir.
Founded: 1966. **Members:** 5,400. **Membership Dues:** regular, rejoin, joint, $60 (annual) ● student, $25 (annual) ● organizational, $90 (annual). **Staff:** 4. **Budget:** $435,000. **Description:** A division of the American Library Association concerned with the planning, development, design, application and integration of technologies within the library and information environment, with the impact of emerging technologies on library service, and with the effect of automated technologies on people. **Awards:** Frederick G. Kilgour Award. **Frequency:** annual. **Type:** recognition. **Recipient:** for research in library and information technology ● Hugh C. Atkinson Memorial Award. **Frequency:** annual. **Type:** recognition. **Recipient:** for an academic librarian who has contributed significant improvements in the area of library automation, library management or development or research ● LITA/Endeavor Student Writing Award. **Frequency:** annual. **Type:** recognition. **Recipient:** for the best unpublished manuscript on a topic in the area of libraries and information technology ● LITA/Library Hi Tech Award for Outstanding Communication for Continuing Education in Library and Information Science. **Frequency:** annual. **Type:** recognition. **Recipient:** for a single seminal work, or body of work that has shown outstanding achievement in educating practitioners within the library field ● LITA/LSSI Minority Scholarship. **Frequency:** annual. **Type:** scholarship. **Recipient:** for minority students who have planned to follow a career in library automation ● LITA/OCLC Minority Scholarship. **Frequency:** an-

nual. **Type:** scholarship. **Recipient:** for minority students who have demonstrated potential in and have a strong commitment to the use of automated systems in libraries ● LITA/Sirsi Scholarship. **Type:** scholarship. **Recipient:** for a beginning student on the master's degree level in an American Library Association-accredited program in library information science. **Committees:** Bylaws and Organization; Distance Learning; Education; Endeavor Student Writing Award; Gaylord Award; International Relations; ITAL Editorial; Legislation and Regulation; LSSI and OCLC Minority Scholarships; Machine-Readable Bibliographic Information; Membership Development; National Forum; Nominating; OCLC Kilgour Award; Program Planning; Publications; Regional Institutes; Sirsi and Christian Larew Scholarships; Technology and Access; Technology Electronic Reviews; Top Tech Trends; Web Coordinating. **Special Interest Groups:** Authority Control; Digital Libraries Technology; Electronic Publishing/Electronic Journals; Emerging Technologies; Heads of Library Technology; Human/Machine Interface; Imagineering; Internet Resources; Library Consortia/Automated Systems; Library Hi Tech Award; MARC Formats; Microcomputer Users; Open Source Systems; Secure Systems and Services; Technical Services Workstations; Technology and the Arts. **Affiliated With:** American Library Association. **Formerly:** (1978) Information Science and Automation Division. **Publications:** *Information Technology and Libraries*, quarterly. Journal. Covers material related to all aspects of library and information technology. Includes book and software reviews. **Price:** included in membership dues; $55.00 /year for nonmembers in U.S.; $60.00 /year for nonmembers in Canada, Mexico, Spain and other PUAS countries; $65.00 /year for nonmembers in other foreign countries. ISSN: 0730-9295. **Circulation:** 7,500. **Advertising:** accepted. Alternate Formats: microform; online. Also Cited As: *ITAL* ● Monographs. **Conventions/Meetings:** annual National Forum - conference, impact and management of future technologies.

10369 ■ Library Public Relations Council (LPRC)

2576 Broadway, No. 532
New York, NY 10025
E-mail: info@libprcouncil.org
URL: http://www.libprcouncil.org
Contact: Kay Ann Cassell, Membership Chair

Founded: 1940. **Members:** 300. **Membership Dues:** regular, $40 (annual). **Description:** Library directors and public relations specialists from related fields of business interested in promoting effective communication for libraries. Strives to develop awareness and understanding of the vital importance of public relations to library service. Provides packets of publicity material from library sources. Conducts educational programs. **Awards:** L. Percy Award. **Frequency:** annual. **Type:** recognition. **Recipient:** for printed items produced by libraries in specific subject categories ● Share the Wealth. **Frequency:** annual. **Type:** recognition. **Recipient:** for effective public relations and publicity pieces. **Committees:** Awards; Packets; Publicity Program. **Publications:** Membership Directory, annual. **Price:** included in membership dues. **Circulation:** 300. **Conventions/Meetings:** triennial dinner - always in metropolitan New York area ● annual meeting, held in conjunction with American Library Association.

10370 ■ Library Users of America (LUA)

c/o American Council of the Blind
1155 15th St. NW, Ste.1004
Washington, DC 20005
Ph: (202)467-5081
Free: (800)424-8666
Fax: (202)467-5085
E-mail: info@acb.org
URL: http://www.acb.org
Contact: Barry Levine, Pres.

Founded: 1987. **Members:** 200. **Description:** Blind and visually impaired persons interested in improved library services for the visually impaired. **Affiliated With:** American Council of the Blind. **Conventions/Meetings:** annual conference.

10371 ■ Major Orchestra Librarians' Association (MOLA)

c/o Patrick McGinn, Admin.
Milwaukee Symphony Orchestra
700 N Water St., Ste.700
Milwaukee, WI 53202
E-mail: admin@mola-inc.org
URL: http://www.mola-inc.org
Contact: Patrick McGinn, Admin.

Founded: 1983. **Members:** 225. **Membership Dues:** regular, $175-$250 (annual). **Multinational. Description:** Aims to help improve communication among orchestra librarians. Educates and assists librarians, presenting a unified voice in publisher relations, and providing education, support, and information to performing art and other music service organizations. **Libraries: Type:** not open to the public. **Publications:** *Marcato*, quarterly. Newsletter. **Price:** $20.00/ year. Alternate Formats: online. **Conventions/Meetings:** annual conference (exhibits) - spring.

10372 ■ Medical Library Association (MLA)

65 E Wacker Pl., Ste.1900
Chicago, IL 60601-7246
Ph: (312)419-9094
Fax: (312)419-8950
E-mail: info@mlahq.org
URL: http://www.mlanet.org
Contact: Carla J. Funk, Exec. Dir.

Founded: 1898. **Members:** 5,000. **Membership Dues:** institutional (based on the total library expenditures, excluding any grants or contracts), $255-$600 (annual) ● international, $110 (annual) ● affiliate, $100 (annual) ● student, $40 (annual) ● regular, $165 (annual). **Staff:** 15. **Budget:** $2,500,000. **Regional Groups:** 14. **National Groups:** 23. **Description:** Educational organization of more than 1,200 institutions and 3,800 individual members in the health sciences information field. Members serve society by developing new health information delivery systems, fostering educational and research programs for health sciences information professionals, and encouraging an enhanced public awareness of health care issues. **Awards:** Donald A.B. Lindberg Research Fellowship. **Frequency:** annual. **Type:** grant. **Recipient:** to fund research aimed at expanding the research knowledge base ● Majors/MLA Chapter Project of the Year. **Frequency:** annual. **Type:** recognition. **Recipient:** for excellence, innovation and contribution to the profession of health sciences librarianship ● Marcia C. Noyes Award. **Frequency:** annual. **Type:** recognition. **Recipient:** for outstanding contributions to health sciences librarianship ● MLA Fellowship. **Frequency:** annual. **Type:** fellowship. **Recipient:** for sustained and outstanding contributions to health sciences librarianship; elected by the board of directors. **Computer Services:** Mailing lists, based on membership type. **Committees:** Awards; Books Panel; Bylaws; Continuing Education; Credentialing; Governmental Relations; Grants and Scholarship; JMLA Editorial; Membership; MLANET Editorial; Oral History; Publication. **Sections:** Cancer Librarians; Chiropractic Libraries; Collection Development; Consumer and Patient Health Information; Dental; Educational Media and Technologies; Federal Libraries; Health Association Libraries; History of the Health Sciences; Hospital Libraries; International Cooperation; Leadership and Management; Medical Informatics; Medical Library Education; Nursing and Allied Health Resources; Pharmacy and Drug Information; Public Health/Health Administration; Public Services; Relevant Issues; Research; Technical Services; Veterinary Medical Libraries. **Publications:** *Journal of the Medical Library Association*, quarterly. Contains articles on technical, administrative, and biomedical information research. Includes book reviews and obituaries. Also includes index. **Price:** included in membership dues; $210.00 /year for nonmembers outside North America; $163.00 /year for nonmembers (in U.S., Canada, and Mexico). ISSN: 1536-5050. **Circulation:** 5,000. **Advertising:** accepted. Alternate Formats: online. Also Cited As: *JMLA* ● *MLA BibKit Series*. Bibliographies. Contains selective and annotated bibliographies of discrete subject areas in the health sciences literature. ● *MLA DocKit Series*. Collections of representative, unedited Library documents from variety of institutions. ● *MLA News*, 10/year. Newsletters. Includes calendar of events, member news, legislative news, media and software news, and personals. **Price:** included in membership dues; $58.00 for nonmembers in U.S., Canada, and Mexico; $74.00 /year for nonmembers outside North America. **Circulation:** 5,100. **Advertising:** accepted. Alternate Formats: online ● Monographs. **Conventions/Meetings:** annual meeting, a forum in which the diverse members of the library medical community come together in a professional atmosphere of a focused, educational, and networking meeting (exhibits) - always in May. 2009 May 15-20, Honolulu, HI; 2010 May 21-26, Washington, DC.

10373 ■ Middle East Librarians Association (MELA)

c/o Mr. William J. Kopycki, Sec.-Treas.
Univ. of Pennsylvania Lib.
3420 Walnut St.
Philadelphia, PA 19104-6206
Ph: (215)898-2196
Fax: (215)898-0559
E-mail: secretary@mela.us
URL: http://www.mela.us
Contact: Mr. William J. Kopycki, Sec.-Treas.

Founded: 1972. **Members:** 141. **Membership Dues:** general, $30 (annual). **Description:** Librarians and others interested in aspects of librarianship that support the study or dissemination of information about the Middle East since the rise of Islam. Facilitates communication among members through meetings and publications. Improves the quality of area librarianship through the development of standards for the profession and education of Middle East library specialists. Compiles and disseminates information concerning Middle East libraries and collections and represents the judgment of the members in matters affecting them. Encourages cooperation among members and Middle East libraries, especially in the acquisition of materials and the development of bibliographic controls. **Awards:** David H. Partington Award. **Frequency:** annual. **Type:** recognition. **Recipient:** for excellent contributions to Middle East librarianship ● George Atiyeh Prize. **Frequency:** annual. **Type:** monetary. **Recipient:** for students who are currently enrolled in an accredited library education program and have an interest in Middle East librarianship. **Computer Services:** Mailing lists. **Committees:** Cataloging; David H. Partington Award; Education; George Atiyeh Prize; Iraqi Libraries; Legal Affairs. **Publications:** *MELA Notes: Journal of Middle Eastern Librarianship*, biennial. Contains articles on Middle Eastern librarianship, bibliography, book reviews and association news. **Price:** $30.00/year. ISSN: 0364-2410. **Circulation:** 300. **Advertising:** accepted. **Conventions/Meetings:** annual meeting, held in conjunction with Middle East Studies Association of North America (exhibits) - always November/ December.

10374 ■ Music Library Association (MLA)

8551 Res. Way, Ste.180
Middleton, WI 53562-3567
Ph: (608)836-5825
Fax: (608)831-8200
E-mail: mla@areditions.com
URL: http://www.musiclibraryassoc.org
Contact: Philip Vandermeer, Pres.

Founded: 1931. **Members:** 1,800. **Membership Dues:** individual in U.S., $90 (annual) ● individual outside U.S., $100 (annual) ● institutional in U.S., $125 (annual) ● institutional outside U.S., $135 (annual) ● associate, retired in U.S., $60 (annual) ● associate, retired outside U.S., $70 (annual) ● student in U.S., $35 (annual) ● student outside U.S., $45 (annual) ● corporate patron in U.S., $750 (annual) ● corporate patron outside U.S., $760 (annual) ● corporate in U.S., $450 (annual) ● corporate outside U.S., $460 (annual) ● sustaining in U.S., $180 (annual) ● sustaining outside U.S., $190 (annual). **Regional Groups:** 12. **Description:** Promotes the establishment, growth, and use of music libraries and collection of music, musical instruments, musical literature, and audio-visual aids. Maintains placement service. **Awards:** Carol June Bradley Award. **Fre-**

quency: annual. **Type:** recognition. **Recipient:** to support studies that involve the history of music libraries or special collections ● Dena Epstein Award. **Frequency:** annual. **Type:** grant. **Recipient:** to support research in archives or libraries ● Kevin Freeman Travel Grant. **Frequency:** annual. **Type:** grant. **Recipient:** to support travel and hotel expenses to attend the Music Library Association annual meeting ● Walter Gerboth Award. **Frequency:** annual. **Type:** recognition. **Recipient:** to members of MLA who are in the first five years of their professional library careers. **Committees:** Awards; Bibliographic Control; Development; Education; Preservation; Program; Reference and Public Service; Resource Sharing and Collection Development. **Affiliated With:** International Federation of Library Associations and Institutions. **Publications:** *Index and Bibliography Series*, periodic ● *Music Cataloging Bulletin*, monthly. **Price:** $35.00/year ● *Music Library Association—Notes*, quarterly. Journal. Covers music bibliography; provides information on events and trends in music publishing. Includes CD, book, record, and music reviews. **Price:** included in membership dues; $85.00 /year for individuals; $100.00 /year for institutions. ISSN: 0027-4380. **Advertising:** accepted. Alternate Formats: microform ● *Technical Reports*, periodic ● Newsletter, quarterly. Alternate Formats: online. **Conventions/Meetings:** annual meeting (exhibits) - always February/March.

10375 ■ National Church Library Association (NCLA)

275 S 3rd St., Ste.101A
Stillwater, MN 55082-4996
Ph: (651)430-0770
E-mail: info@churchlibraries.org
URL: http://www.churchlibraries.org
Contact: Susan Benish, Exec. Dir.

Founded: 1958. **Members:** 1,750. **Membership Dues:** church (with 500 or more members), $55 (annual) ● individual, church (with less than 500 members), $40 (annual) ● corporate, $185 (annual). **Staff:** 2. **Budget:** $75,000. **Regional Groups:** 35. **Description:** Represents individuals, church libraries, and church organizations. Seeks to further the growth of church libraries. Assists members in establishing and operating a church library; furnishes lists of books and audiovisuals recommended for church libraries. Maintains speakers' bureau; conducts specialized education program; offers children's services; compiles statistics. Conducts workshops for church librarians and other parish educational staff. **Boards:** Advisory; Finance; Library Services; Publications. **Formerly:** (2005) Lutheran Church Library Association. **Publications:** *Libraries Alive*, quarterly. Journal. Contains news, education, resources, and reviews. **Price:** included in membership dues. ISSN: 0024-7472. **Circulation:** 3,000. **Advertising:** accepted ● Bibliographies, semiannual ● Also publishes guidelines.

10376 ■ National Serials Data Program (NSDP)

Lib. of Cong.
101 Independence Ave. SE
Washington, DC 20540-4160
Ph: (202)707-6452 (202)707-6379
Fax: (202)707-6333
E-mail: issn@loc.gov
URL: http://www.loc.gov/issn
Contact: Regina R. Reynolds, Hd.

Founded: 1972. **Staff:** 13. **Description:** Works to implement a system for the control and identification of serial publications through the use of the International Standard Serial Number (ISSN) and its associated "key title". Enters ISSN into national and international machine-readable databases of bibliographic descriptions of serial publications to be utilized in responding to the needs of publishers, libraries, abstracting and indexing services, subscription agencies, the U.S. Postal Service, and the community at large. **Convention/Meeting:** none. **Telecommunication Services:** electronic mail, rrey@loc.gov. **Also Known As:** U.S. ISSN Center. **Publications:** *ISSN is for Serials*. Brochures. Alternate Formats: online.

10377 ■ Natural Resources Information Council (NRIC)

c/o Beth Thomsett-Scott, Science Librarian
Sci. and Tech. Lib.
Univ. of North Texas
PO Box 305190
Denton, TX 76203-5190
E-mail: bscott@library.unt.edu
URL: http://www.nric.info/2005.html
Contact: Beth Thomsett-Scott, Science Librarian

Founded: 1991. **Members:** 30. **Membership Dues:** ordinary, $10 (annual). **Description:** Natural resources librarians and information specialists in the United States and Canada. Seeks to advance the practice of natural resources librarianship; promotes increased public awareness of natural resources and environmental protection issues. Facilitates communication and cooperation among members; functions as a network for the collection and dissemination of natural resources information; conducts continuing education programs for natural resources librarians. **Publications:** *Fish and Game/Natural Resources Library Survey*, annual. Journal ● *NRIC Newsletter*, 1-2/year. **Conventions/Meetings:** annual conference - usually mid-summer.

10378 ■ North American Serials Interest Group (NASIG)

c/o Ms. Joyce Tenney, Sec.
PMB 214
2103 N Decatur Rd.
Decatur, GA 30033
E-mail: info@nasig.org
URL: http://www.nasig.org
Contact: Ms. Joyce Tenney, Sec.

Founded: 1985. **Members:** 1,274. **Membership Dues:** student/retiree in U.S. and Canada, $25 (annual) ● regular in U.S., $75 (annual) ● regular in Canada, $60 (annual) ● regular in Mexico, $18 (annual) ● regular outside North America, $75 (annual). **Description:** Promotes communication, information exchange, and continuing education about serials and the broader issues of scholarly communication. Represents librarians; subscription vendors; publishers; serial automation vendors; serials binders; library science educators; others involved in serials management. Promotes educational and social networking among members. **Awards:** Fritz Schwartz Serials Education Scholarship. **Type:** scholarship ● Horizon Award. **Frequency:** annual. **Type:** grant. **Recipient:** for beginning serials professional ● Marcia Tuttle International Award. **Type:** grant ● NASIG Student Grant. **Frequency:** annual. **Type:** grant. **Recipient:** for library and information science students ● Serials Specialist Award. **Frequency:** annual. **Type:** grant. **Recipient:** for a promising paraprofessional. **Computer Services:** Mailing lists, membership directory, available to members only ● online services. **Publications:** *NASIG Newsletter*, 4-5/year. **Price:** available to members only. ISSN: 0892-1733. **Circulation:** 1,200. Alternate Formats: online ● Proceedings, annual ● Membership Directory, annual. **Conventions/Meetings:** annual conference.

10379 ■ Online Audiovisual Catalogers (OLAC)

c/o Vicki Toy-Smith, Pres.
Univ. of Nevada
Mail Stop 322
Reno, NV 89557-0044
Ph: (775)682-5601
Fax: (775)784-1751
E-mail: vicki@unr.edu
URL: http://www.olacinc.org
Contact: Vicki Toy-Smith, Pres.

Founded: 1980. **Members:** 700. **Membership Dues:** personal, $20 (annual) ● institutional outside U.S., $25 (annual) ● contributing, $50 (annual). **Description:** Librarians interested in the cataloging and processing of audiovisual materials, computer files, electronic resources, and other non-book materials. Works to increase knowledge and understanding of the cataloging of non-book materials. **Awards:** Nancy B. Olson Award. **Frequency:** annual. **Type:** recognition. **Recipient:** for a librarian who made significant contributions to the advancement and understanding of audiovisual cataloging. **Computer Services:** Mailing lists. **Committees:** Cataloging Policy. **Affiliated With:** American Library Association. **Formerly:** (1986) On-line Audiovisual Catalogers. **Publications:** Handbook. Alternate Formats: online ● Newsletter, quarterly. Includes cumulative index. **Price:** $12.00 /year for individuals in North America; $18.00 /year for institutions in North America; $20.00/year outside North America. ISSN: 0739-1153. Alternate Formats: online. **Conventions/Meetings:** biennial conference and workshop, with two keynote speakers - 2008 Sept. 26-28, Cleveland, OH ● semiannual convention and meeting, in conjunction with American Library Association.

10380 ■ Polar Libraries Colloquy (PLC)

c/o Betty Galbraith, Sec.-Treas.
1915 NW Valhalla Dr.
Washington State Univ.
Pullman, WA 99163
Ph: (509)335-7930
E-mail: bettyg@wsu.edu
URL: http://arcticcentre.ulapland.fi/polarweb/plc/cmte.asp
Contact: Betty Galbraith, Sec.-Treas.

Founded: 1994. **Members:** 80. **Membership Dues:** individual, $20 (biennial) ● institution, $40 (biennial). **Multinational. Description:** Organized group of individuals affiliated with libraries that have collections pertaining to cold regions, particularly the Polar Regions. Facilitates international communication between polar scholars and information specialists. Conducts educational programs. **Awards:** Hubert Wenger Award. **Frequency:** biennial. **Type:** monetary. **Recipient:** for delegates. **Computer Services:** Mailing lists, of members ● online services, publications. **Formerly:** (1988) Northern Libraries Colloquy. **Publications:** *Polar and Cold Regionals Library Resources*, periodic. Directory. Lists 6 contact details and provides brief description of libraries and archives with relevant collections. **Price:** $25.00/copy. Alternate Formats: online ● *Polar Libraries Bulletin*, periodic. Newsletter. **Conventions/Meetings:** biennial congress (exhibits) - alternately in Western Europe and North America.

10381 ■ Progressive Librarians Guild (PLG)

Rider Univ. Lib.
2083 Lawrenceville Rd.
Lawrenceville, NJ 08648
Ph: (425)831-8155
E-mail: eharger@agoron.net
URL: http://libr.org/PLG
Contact: Elaine Harger, Ed.

Founded: 1990. **Multinational. Description:** Provides a forum for discussion of the responsibilities of librarians in relation to the important problems of social change that face educational institutions and libraries. **Awards:** Miriam Braverman Award. **Frequency:** annual. **Type:** recognition. **Recipient:** for the student winner in essay contest. **Computer Services:** Online services, listserv: PLGnet. **Boards:** Editorial. **Committees:** Coordinating. **Affiliated With:** American Library Association; Social Responsibilities Round Table of the American Library Association. **Publications:** *Progressive Librarian*, semiannual. Journal. **Price:** $30.00 /year for institutions in U.S.; $40.00 /year for institutions overseas; included in membership dues. ISSN: 1052-5726. **Circulation:** 400.

10382 ■ Public Library Association (PLA)

c/o American Library Association
50 E Huron St.
Chicago, IL 60611
Ph: (312)280-5028
Free: (800)545-2433
Fax: (312)280-5029
E-mail: pla@ala.org
URL: http://www.pla.org
Contact: Susan Hildreth, Pres.

Founded: 1944. **Members:** 9,043. **Membership Dues:** individual, $50 (annual). **Staff:** 8. **Budget:** $900,000. **Description:** A division of the American Library Association. Librarians, trustees, and friends of libraries interested in the general improvement and expansion of public library services to readers of all ages. Plans programs on current public library issues and concerns; develops and distributes publications for public librarians; compiles and disseminates statistics on public libraries and public library service. Conducts research; provides continuing education program for public librarians; represents the library profession at national levels. Maintains 82 committees, including: Intellectual Freedom; International Relations; Multicultural Library Services; Planning Process; Research; Technology. **Awards:** Advancement of Literacy Award. **Frequency:** annual. **Type:** recognition. **Recipient:** for publisher, bookseller, hardware and/or software dealer, foundation, or similar group that has made a significant contribution to the advancement of adult literacy ● Allie Beth Martin Award. **Frequency:** annual. **Type:** recognition. **Recipient:** for a public librarian who has demonstrated extraordinary knowledge on books or other library materials and has distinguished ability to share this knowledge ● Baker and Taylor Entertainment Audio Music/Video Product Award. **Frequency:** annual. **Type:** grant. **Recipient:** for a public library to provide the opportunity to build or expand a collection of either or both formats ● Charlie Robinson Award. **Frequency:** annual. **Type:** recognition. **Recipient:** for public library director who, over a period of seven years, has been a risk taker and/or a change agent in a public library ● Excellence in Small and/or Rural Public Library Service Award. **Frequency:** annual. **Type:** recognition. **Recipient:** to a public library that has demonstrated excellence of service to its community as exemplified by an overall service program ● Highsmith Library Innovation Award. **Frequency:** annual. **Type:** recognition. **Recipient:** for a public library's innovative and creative service program to the community. **Committees:** Assessing for Results Book Review; Conference Program Coordinating; Electronic Communications Advisory; Leadership Development. **Programs:** E-Learning@ PLA. **Sections:** Issues and Concerns Cluster; Library Development Cluster; Library Services Cluster. **Affiliated With:** American Library Association. **Formerly:** (1958) Public Libraries Division. **Publications:** *Public Libraries*, bimonthly. Journal. Includes book reviews. **Price:** included in membership dues; $50.00 /year for nonmembers in U.S.; $60.00 /year for nonmembers outside U.S. ISSN: 0163-5506. **Circulation:** 9,803. **Advertising:** accepted. Alternate Formats: microform ● Brochures ● Monographs. **Conventions/Meetings:** biennial conference, with continuing education programs (exhibits).

10383 ■ Reference and User Services Association of American Library Association (RUSA)

c/o Barbara Macikas, Exec. Dir.
50 E Huron St.
Chicago, IL 60611
Ph: (312)280-4395 (312)280-5273
Free: (800)545-2433
Fax: (312)944-8085
E-mail: rusa@ala.org
URL: http://www.ala.org/rusa
Contact: Barbara Macikas, Exec. Dir.

Founded: 1972. **Members:** 5,000. **Membership Dues:** individual, $60 (annual) ● library organization, $80 (annual) ● student, $25 (annual). **Staff:** 3. **Budget:** $450,000. **Description:** Works to stimulate and support excellence in the delivery of general library services and materials to adults, and the provision of reference and information services, collection development, and resource sharing for all ages, in every type of library. **Awards:** Dartmouth Medal. **Frequency:** annual. **Type:** medal. **Recipient:** for the creation of a reference work with outstanding quality and significance, presented by the collection development and evaluation section (codes) of RUSA ● Genealogical Publishing Company Award. **Frequency:** annual. **Type:** monetary. **Recipient:** for a librarian, library or a publisher to encourage professional achievement in historical reference and research librarianship ● Isadore Gilbert Mudge - R.R. Bowker Award. **Frequency:** annual. **Type:** monetary. **Recipient:** to an individual who has made a distinguished contribution to reference librarianship ● John Sessions Memorial Award. **Frequency:** annual. **Type:** recognition. **Recipient:** to a library or library system for significant work with the labor community ● Margaret E. Monroe Award. **Frequency:** annual. **Type:** recognition. **Recipient:** for a librarian who has made significant contributions to library adult services ● Reference Service Press Award. **Frequency:** annual. **Type:** monetary. **Recipient:** to the most outstanding article published in RUSA during the preceding two-volume year. **Committees:** Adult Services; Cooperative Reference; Interlibrary Loan; Library Services to the Spanish Speaking; Outstanding Reference Sources; Reference Services in Large Research Libraries; Standards; Virtual Reference Services; Wilson Indexes. **Councils:** Notable Books. **Sections:** Business Reference and Services; Collection Development and Evaluation; History; Machine Assisted Reference; Reference Services; Sharing and Transforming Access to Resources. **Affiliated With:** American Library Association. **Formed by Merger of:** (1992) Reference Services Division of ALA; Adult Services Division of ALA. **Formerly:** (1997) Reference and Adult Services Division of ALA. **Publications:** *Reference and User Services Quarterly*. Journal. Contains articles on a broad range of library-related topics. Includes reviews of books, databases, and professional library sources. **Price:** included in membership dues; $50.00 /year for nonmembers. ISSN: 1094-9054. **Advertising:** accepted. Alternate Formats: microform. **Conventions/Meetings:** semiannual meeting, in conjunction with the American Library Association conferences.

10384 ■ REFORMA: National Association to Promote Library Services to the Spanish-Speaking

c/o Sandra Rios Balderrama
PO Box 4386
Fresno, CA 93744
Ph: (480)734-4460
E-mail: reformaoffice@riosbalderrrama.com
URL: http://www.reforma.org
Contact: Mario Ascencio, Pres.

Founded: 1971. **Members:** 700. **Membership Dues:** librarian (based on annual income), $25-$40 (annual) ● library trustee/commissioner, $20 (annual) ● library science student, $5 (annual) ● library support staff/community supporter/retiree, $15 (annual) ● library/library school/non-profit organization, $50 (annual) ● corporation, $200 (annual) ● life (individual), $400. **Regional Groups:** 18. **Description:** Librarians and institutions interested in improving library service to the Spanish-speaking populations of the United States. Maintains speakers' bureau. **Awards:** REFORMA Librarian of the Year Award. **Frequency:** annual. **Type:** monetary. **Recipient:** to a librarian who has outstanding contributions to the organization and who has promoted and advocated services to the Spanish-speaking and Latino communities ● REFORMA Scholarship. **Frequency:** annual. **Type:** scholarship. **Recipient:** for a library science student interested in working with the Spanish speaking community. **Computer Services:** Mailing lists, of members. **Telecommunication Services:** TDD, (212)-340-0044. **Committees:** Legislative Education; Public Relations; Scholarship. **Programs:** Mentoring. **Formerly:** (1983) REFORMA: National Association of Spanish-Speaking Librarians; (1983) REFORMA: National Association of Library Services to the Spanish-Speaking. **Publications:** *The English-Only Movement: A Selected Bibliography* ● *REFORMA Membership Directory*, biennial ● *REFORMA Newsletter*, quarterly. Provides information about REFORMA activities, programs, and local projects. Includes chapter reports, new publication news, and committee reports. **Price:** included in membership dues; $20.00 /year for nonmembers; $35.00 /year for institutions. ISSN: 0891-8880. **Advertising:** accepted ● *REFORMA/UCLA Mentor Program: A Mentoring Manual*. **Conventions/Meetings:** semiannual meeting, held in conjunction with the American Library Association.

10385 ■ Research Libraries Group (RLG)

2029 Stierlin Ct., Ste.100
Mountain View, CA 94043-4684
Ph: (650)691-2333
Free: (800)537-7546
Fax: (650)964-0943
E-mail: ric@rlg.org
URL: http://www.rlg.org
Contact: James P. Michalko, Pres./CEO

Founded: 1974. **Members:** 150. **Staff:** 100. **Multinational. Description:** Universities, archives, historical societies, museums, and related institutions devoted to improving access to information that supports research and learning. Maintains the Research Libraries Information Network (RLIN), an online bibliographic database of more than 22 million items, including books, serials, archival materials, maps, music scores, sound recordings, films, photographs, and computer-readable files. RLIN contains the Library of Congress Name Authority and Subject Authority Files, the Art and Architecture thesaurus, and special databases for 18th-century printed material, art auction catalogs, and library collection management. CitaDel, a citation and document-delivery service, is available through RLIN. **Committees:** Art and Architecture Group Steering. **Projects:** Digital Preservation and Ensured Long-term Access; Expanded Online Access to Research Resources; Global Resource Sharing. **Task Forces:** Digital Repository Certification; SCIPIO Advisory. **Working Groups:** Preservation Metadata: Implementation Strategies; Special Collections Resource Sharing. **Publications:** *Research Libraries Group News*, quarterly. Magazine. **Price:** free. Alternate Formats: online ● *RLG DigiNews*, bimonthly. Newsletter. Focuses on digitization and digital preservation. ISSN: 1093-5371. Alternate Formats: online ● *RLG Focus*, bimonthly. Newsletter. Alternate Formats: online ● *RLG TopShelf*, monthly. Newsletter. Contains news about the organization and the latest member projects and initiatives. Alternate Formats: online ● Brochures ● Monographs ● Papers.

10386 ■ Seminar on the Acquisition of Latin American Library Materials (SALALM)

Tulane Univ.
The Latin Amer. Lib.
422 Howard-Tilton Memorial Lib.
7001 Freret St.
New Orleans, LA 70118
Ph: (504)247-1366
Fax: (504)247-1367
E-mail: salalm@tulane.edu
URL: http://library.lib.binghamton.edu/salalm
Contact: Hortensia Calvo, Exec. Sec.

Founded: 1956. **Members:** 500. **Membership Dues:** personal, $60 (annual) ● institutional, $110 (annual) ● supporting institutional, $500 (annual) ● student, emeritus, individual (in Latin America, Caribbean and Puerto Rico), $30 (annual) ● retired, student (in Latin America, Caribbean and Puerto Rico), $15 (annual). **Staff:** 2. **Budget:** $40,000. **Languages:** English, French, Portuguese, Spanish. **Description:** Individuals and institutions interested in acquiring library materials from Latin America and building Latin American library collections. Collects, organizes, and disseminates bibliographic information; develops Latin American library services; addresses problems and seeks further development of libraries in Latin America and the Caribbean; provides library materials serving needs of Spanish- and Portuguese-speaking populations in the U.S; offers information on career development for librarians; sponsors educational field trips, library tours, and international book exhibits. **Libraries: Type:** reference. **Subjects:** Latin-American materials. **Awards:** Enlace Travel Awards. **Frequency:** annual. **Type:** grant. **Recipient:** for selected Latin-Americans attending the organization's annual conference ● Jose Toribio Medina Award. **Frequency:** annual. **Type:** recognition. **Recipient:** for the best reference tool or bibliography published by a member ● Marietta Daniels Shepard Award. **Frequency:** annual. **Type:** scholarship. **Recipient:** for students from Latin America at University of Texas at Austin Graduate School of Library and Information Science ● Presidential Travel Fellowships. **Frequency:** annual. **Type:** fellowship. **Recipient:** to defray the expenses of attending the organization's annual meeting. **Committees:** Access and

Bibliography; Acquisitions; Constitution and Bylaws; Interlibrary Cooperation; Library Operations and Services; Outreach/Enlace; Policy, Research and Investigation. **Publications:** *Afro-Brazilian Religions: A Selective, Annotated*, annual. Bibliography ● *Directory of Bookdealers*, periodic ● *Index to Spanish Language Short Stories in Anthologies*, annual. Monograph. Contains papers presented at the annual conference. **Price:** included in membership dues. **Circulation:** 500 ● *Latin American Publications Available by Gift or Exchange*. Directory ● *Membership List*, annual. Newsletter. Covers Latin American library collection development and service; includes annual index. **Price:** included in membership dues; $25.00 /year for nonmembers. ISSN: 0098-6275. **Circulation:** 580. **Advertising:** accepted ● *Microfilming Projects Newsletter*, annual. Lists original microreproduction projects recently completed or in progress. **Price:** $8.50/year. **Circulation:** 350 ● *Papers of the Seminar on the Acquisition of Latin American Library Materials*, annual. Monograph. Contains papers presented at the annual conference. **Price:** included in membership dues. **Circulation:** 500 ● *SALALM Newsletter*, bimonthly. Covers Latin American library collection development and service; includes annual index. **Price:** included in membership dues; $25.00 /year for nonmembers. ISSN: 0098-6275. **Circulation:** 580. **Advertising:** accepted ● *Seminar of the Acquisition of Latin American Library Materials*, 2-3/year. Monograph. **Price:** included in membership dues ● *Sendero Luminoso: An Annotated Bibliography of the Shining Path Guerrilla Movement*, annual. Lists original microreproduction projects recently completed or in progress. **Price:** $8.50/year. **Circulation:** 350 ● Books ● Papers. **Conventions/Meetings:** annual conference and seminar (exhibits) - always spring.

10387 ■ Social Responsibilities Round Table of the American Library Association (SRRT)

c/o American Library Association
50 E Huron St.
Chicago, IL 60611
Ph: (312)280-4294
Free: (800)545-2433
Fax: (312)280-3255
E-mail: aml44@drexel.edu
URL: http://libr.org/srrt
Contact: Alison Lewis, Coor.

Founded: 1969. **Members:** 1,500. **Membership Dues:** individual, $12 (annual) ● institution, $20 (annual). **State Groups:** 7. **Description:** Round table of the American Library Association. Provides a forum for discussion of the responsibilities of libraries in relation to the important problems of social change that face institutions and librarians; provides for exchange of information with the goal of increasing understanding of current social problems; acts as a stimulus to the ALA and its various units in making libraries more responsive to current social needs. **Awards:** Coretta Scott King Book Award. **Frequency:** annual. **Type:** recognition ● Eubanks Memorial Award. **Frequency:** annual. **Type:** recognition ● Gay, Lesbian and Bisexual Book Award. **Frequency:** annual. **Type:** recognition. **Telecommunication Services:** electronic mail, rlitwin@earthlink.net ● additional toll-free number, in Illinois, (800)545-2444 ● additional toll-free number, in Canada, (800)545-2455. **Task Forces:** Alternatives In Publication; Environment; Feminist; Hunger, Homelessness and Poverty; Information Policy in the Public Interest; International Responsibilities; Martin Luther King, Jr. Holiday. **Publications:** Newsletter, quarterly. **Price:** included in membership dues; $15.00 /year for nonmembers. ISSN: 0749-1670. **Circulation:** 1,900. Alternate Formats: online. **Conventions/Meetings:** semiannual meeting, held in conjunction with ALA (exhibits).

10388 ■ Society of School Librarians International (SSLI)

19 Savage St.
Charleston, SC 29401
Ph: (843)577-5351
E-mail: sbssteve@aol.com
URL: http://falcon.jmu.edu/~ramseyil/sslihome.htm
Contact: Jeanne Schwartz, Exec. Dir.

Founded: 1985. **Members:** 1,000. **Membership Dues:** retired, student, $25 (annual) ● regular, $45 (annual) ● corporate, $75 (annual) ● life, $400. **Staff:** 2. **Budget:** $152,000. **Multinational. Description:** Seeks to serve elementary and secondary school librarians at the school and district level. Works for the improvement of school library programs. Develops study courses in school library management. Maintains liaison with other educational societies; operates information network. Conducts international study tours and leadership development programs and seminars. **Awards:** Book Awards for K-12 Grades. **Frequency:** annual. **Type:** recognition. **Publications:** *SSLI Reports*, bimonthly. Contains school library news, association's activity news, legislative information, and recommended book lists. **Conventions/Meetings:** annual conference (exhibits).

10389 ■ Special Libraries Association (SLA)

331 S Patrick St.
Alexandria, VA 22314-3501
Ph: (703)647-4900
Fax: (703)647-4901
E-mail: sla@sla.org
URL: http://www.sla.org
Contact: Janice R. Lachance, CEO

Founded: 1909. **Members:** 12,000. **Membership Dues:** full (based on annual salary), $99-$160 (annual) ● organizational, $650 (annual) ● student, $35 (annual) ● virtual, $65 (annual). **Staff:** 28. **Budget:** $9,000,000. **Regional Groups:** 57. **Multinational. Description:** International association of information professionals who work in special libraries serving business, research, government, universities, newspapers, museums, and institutions that use or produce specialized information. Seeks to advance the leadership role of special librarians. Offers consulting services to organizations that wish to establish or expand a library or information services. Conducts strategic learning and development courses, public relations, and government relations programs. Provides employment services. Operates knowledge exchange on topics pertaining to the development and management of special libraries. Maintains Hall of Fame. **Libraries: Type:** reference. **Holdings:** 3,000; archival material, books. **Awards:** Diversity Leadership Development Program Award. **Frequency:** annual. **Type:** recognition. **Recipient:** to active members who are interested in learning more about SLA and have the potential for leadership responsibilities ● Factiva Leadership Award. **Frequency:** annual. **Type:** recognition. **Recipient:** to an individual member who exemplifies leadership as a special librarian ● Honorary Member Award. **Frequency:** annual. **Type:** recognition. **Recipient:** to an individual who is not a member of SLA ● John Cotton Dana Award. **Frequency:** annual. **Type:** recognition. **Recipient:** to an individual member in recognition of exceptional service to special librarianship ● President's Award. **Type:** recognition. **Recipient:** to an individual member for a notable or important contribution that enhanced the Association or furthered its goals and objectives ● Professional Award. **Type:** recognition. **Recipient:** to an individual or group in recognition of a specific major achievement in, or a specific significant contribution to, the field of librarianship or information science ● SLA Scholarship. **Frequency:** annual. **Type:** scholarship. **Recipient:** for graduate study in librarianship ● Steven I. Goldspeil Memorial Research Fund. **Frequency:** annual. **Type:** grant. **Recipient:** to support projects which promote research on and advancement of library sciences. **Computer Services:** database, CONSULT ● mailing lists, of division or chapter members. **Caucuses:** Association Information Services; Baseball; Gay and Lesbian Issues; Information Futurists; International Information Exchange; Labor Issues; Natural History; Non-Traditional Careers; Retired Members; Women's Issues. **Committees:** Awards and Honors; Bylaws; Cataloging; Consultation Service; Diversity Leadership Development; Networking; Professional Development; Public Policy; Public Relations; Research; SLA Endowment Fund Grants; Strategic Planning; Student and Academic Relations; Technical Standards. **Divisions:** Advertising and Marketing; Biomedical and Life Sciences; Business and Finance; Chemistry; Education; Engineering; Environmental and Resource Management; Food, Agriculture, and Nutrition; Geography and Map; Information Technology; Insurance and Employee Benefits; Leadership Management; Legal; Materials Research and Manufacturing; Military Librarians; Museums, Arts and Humanities; News; Petroleum and Energy Resources; Pharmaceutical and Health Technology; Physics-Astronomy-Mathematics; Science-Technology; Social Science; Solo Librarians; Transportation. **Programs:** Fund Development; Knowledge Exchange; Professional Development; Public Policy; Public Relations. **Publications:** *Information Outlook*, monthly. Magazine. Provides coverage of issues related to the information profession. Includes feature articles, international news, and association information. **Price:** included in membership dues; $125.00 /year for nonmembers in U.S. ISSN: 1091-0808. **Circulation:** 17,000. **Advertising:** accepted. Alternate Formats: online ● *SLA Connections*, monthly. Newsletter. Alternate Formats: online ● Books ● Brochures ● Also publishes information kits, and papers. **Conventions/Meetings:** annual conference (exhibits) - 2008 July 27-30, Seattle, WA; 2009 June 14-17, Washington, DC ● annual meeting - always winter ● annual Winter Education Conference - always winter.

10390 ■ Substance Abuse Librarians and Information Specialists (SALIS)

PO Box 9513
Berkeley, CA 94709-0513
Ph: (510)597-3440
Fax: (510)985-6459
E-mail: salis@salis.org
URL: http://www.salis.org
Contact: Andrea Mitchell, Exec. Dir.

Founded: 1978. **Members:** 136. **Membership Dues:** full (without Addiction Professional magazine), $100 (annual) ● full (with Addiction Professional magazine), $106 (annual) ● associate, $50 (annual) ● institutional, $30 (annual) ● sponsor, $500 (annual) ● full (ELISAD member; without Addiction Professional magazine), $60 (annual) ● full (ELISAD member; with Addiction Professional magazine), $66 (annual). **Staff:** 1. **Multinational. Description:** Individuals and organizations interested in the collection, organization, dissemination, exchange, and retrieval of materials concerning substance abuse, including alcohol, tobacco, and other drugs. Provides professional development and exchange of information and concerns about access to and dissemination of information on substance abuse. Offers information on films, books, articles, pamphlets, reports, government publications, libraries, clearinghouses, and information centers. **Computer Services:** database. **Subgroups:** Canada; Southeast Asia. **Affiliated With:** Alcohol and Other Drugs Council of Australia. **Publications:** *SALIS News*, quarterly. Newsletter. Contains reviews, books list, government documents, and periodical updates. **Price:** included in membership dues; $25.00 /year for nonmembers. **Circulation:** 250. **Conventions/Meetings:** annual conference, addresses changes in drug use, drug policy, and information delivery (exhibits) ● workshop.

10391 ■ Theatre Library Association (TLA)

c/o The New York Public Library for the Performing Arts
40 Lincoln Center Plz.
New York, NY 10023
E-mail: dnochimson100@qc.cuny.edu
URL: http://tla.library.unt.edu
Contact: David Nochimson, Exec. Sec.

Founded: 1937. **Members:** 500. **Membership Dues:** personal, $30 (annual) ● student/non-salaried, $20 (annual) ● institutional, $40 (annual). **Description:** Curators, librarians, scene designers, actors, booksellers, writers, and others interested in performing arts research and the extension of performing arts library facilities. Furthers the interests of gathering, preserving, and making available through libraries, museums, and private collections any records (books, photographs, playbills) of theatre. **Awards:** George Freedley Memorial Award. **Frequency:** annual. **Type:** recognition. **Recipient:** for an outstanding published work in the field of legitimate theatre ● Theatre Library Association Award. **Frequency:** annual. **Type:** recognition. **Recipient:** for an outstanding published work in the field of cinema, television, or radio. **Committees:** Awards; Programs; Publications; Strategic Planning. **Affiliated With:** American Library Association; American Society for Theatre Research; International Federation for Theatre Research. **Publications:** *Broadside*, quarterly. Newsletter. Covers TLA-sponsored events including exhibits and collections related to the performing arts. Includes book reviews and calendar of events. **Price:** included in membership dues. ISSN: 0068-2748. **Circulation:** 500 ● *Performing Arts Resources*, annual. Monograph. Contains articles on resource materials relating to theatre, film, television, radio, and popular entertainment. **Price:** included in membership dues; $30.00 for nonmembers. ISSN: 0360-3814. **Circulation:** 500. Also Cited As: *PAR*. **Conventions/Meetings:** annual conference, held in conjunction with ALA.

10392 ■ United States Book Exchange (USBE)

2969 W 25th St.
Cleveland, OH 44113
Ph: (216)241-6960
Fax: (216)241-6966
E-mail: usbe@usbe.com
URL: http://www.usbe.com
Contact: John T. Zubal, Pres.

Founded: 1948. **Members:** 2,200. **Membership Dues:** library, $150 (annual). **Staff:** 12. **Description:** Represents libraries and institutions with library installations throughout the world. Serves as a clearinghouse for the redistribution of a wide range of duplicate publications on a self-supporting basis, and on a national and international scale. Maintains a revolving stock of between 3 and 4 million periodical issues in 16,000 titles and 600,000 books on all research fields. **Also Known As:** USBE. **Formerly:** (1948) American Book Center for War Devastated Libraries; (1975) United States Book Exchange; (1990) Universal Serials and Book Exchange. **Publications:** *Shelf List*, annual. Catalog. Contains alphabetic listing of most periodicals kept in stock. **Price:** $7.00/issue. **Circulation:** 16,000. **Conventions/Meetings:** annual meeting (exhibits).

10393 ■ Urban Libraries Council (ULC)

125 S Wacker Dr., Ste.1050
Chicago, IL 60606
Ph: (312)676-0999
Fax: (312)676-0950
E-mail: info@urbanlibraries.org
URL: http://www.urbanlibraries.org
Contact: Mr. Martin Gomez, Pres./CEO

Founded: 1971. **Members:** 165. **Staff:** 8. **Description:** Public libraries in cities with over 100,000 people. Identifies and makes known the expanded role of the urban public library. Develops legislation supporting urban library programs. Disseminates information on sources of financial support. Organizes for collective action on matters that affect urban libraries. Facilitates the exchange of ideas and programs. Develops programs that enable libraries to act as a focus of community development. Conducts research and training of importance to urban libraries. **Awards:** Award of Excellence. **Frequency:** annual. **Type:** monetary. **Recipient:** for a member library ● Joey Rodger Fund for Library Leadership. **Frequency:** annual. **Type:** scholarship ● Urban Player Award. **Frequency:** annual. **Type:** monetary. **Recipient:** to a member library. **Formerly:** (1975) Urban Library Trustees Council. **Publications:** *Frequent Fast Facts Survey Reports*, periodic. **Price:** included in membership dues; $45.00 for nonmembers, plus shipping and handling ● *ULC Exchange*. Newsletter. Covers developments of interest to urban public libraries. **Price:** free for members; $50.00 /year for nonmembers. **Circulation:** 230. **Conventions/Meetings:** annual Leadership Symposium ● annual meeting, held in conjunction with American Library Association ● annual meeting, held in conjunction with ALA - always midwinter.

10394 ■ Western Association of Map Libraries (WAML)

c/o Mary Douglass, Pres.
Seattle Public Lib.
History, Travel, Maps Dept.
1000 4th Ave.
Seattle, WA 98104
Ph: (206)386-4627
E-mail: mary.douglass@spl.org
URL: http://www.waml.org
Contact: Mary Douglass, Pres.

Founded: 1967. **Members:** 225. **Membership Dues:** individual, $30 (annual) ● life, $500. **Description:** Map librarians, government publications librarians, curators of map collections, collectors, teachers of geography and cartography, libraries, commercial firms, and publishers of cartographic materials. (Maps include all forms of cartographic materials, including spatial data, aerial photos, atlases, remote sensing, globes, cartobibliographies, and geographies.) Seeks to encourage high standards in every phase of the organization and administration of map libraries by: providing for the discussion of mutual problems and interests through meetings and publications; exchanging information on experiences, ideas, and methods; encouraging higher production standards of map manufacturers; establishing and improving standards of professional service. Bestows honorary memberships. **Committees:** Continuing Education; Membership/Hospitality; Publications Advisory. **Publications:** *Information Bulletin*, 3/year. **Price:** $30.00 /year for individuals outside U.S.; included in membership dues; $35.00 /year for nonmembers. ISSN: 0049-7282. **Advertising:** accepted ● *WAML Electronic News and Notes*. Newsletter. Alternate Formats: online ● Also publishes occasional papers. **Conventions/Meetings:** semiannual conference - always spring and fall.

10395 ■ Young Adult Library Services Association (YALSA)

c/o American Library Association
50 E Huron St.
Chicago, IL 60611
Ph: (312)280-4390
Free: (800)545-2433
Fax: (312)280-5276
E-mail: yalsa@ala.org
URL: http://www.ala.org/ala/yalsa/yalsa.htm
Contact: Ms. Beth Yoke, Exec. Dir.

Founded: 1930. **Members:** 5,013. **Membership Dues:** regular, $50 (annual) ● student, $20 (annual). **Staff:** 3. **Multinational. Description:** A division of the American Library Association (see separate entry). Responsible for the evaluation and selection of books and nonbook materials and the interpretation and use of materials for young adults ages 12 to 18. Advocates, promotes and strengthens library services to young adults. Offers Frances Henne/VOYA Research Grant, YALSA/Baker and Taylor Conference grants, Great Book Giveaway, YALSA/Book Wholesalers Inc. Collection Development Grant, YALSA/Sagebrush Corporation Award for a Young Adult Reading or Literature Program. Annually selects the following lists: Best Books for Young Adults, Quick Picks for Reluctant Young Adult Readers, Popular Paperbacks for Young Adults, Selected DVDs and Videos for Young Adults, Alex Awards and Michael Printz Award. Maintains 35 committees, task forces and discussion groups. **Awards:** Alex Awards. **Frequency:** annual. **Type:** recognition. **Recipient:** to literary achievements in books for adults with potential appeal to teens ● BWI/YALSA Collection Development Grant. **Frequency:** annual. **Type:** monetary. **Recipient:** for collection development to YALSA members who represent a public library and work directly with young adults ages 12 to 18 ● Frances Henne/YALSA/VOYA Research Grant. **Frequency:** annual. **Type:** monetary. **Recipient:** for small-scale projects that encourage research and respond to the YALSA research agenda applications ● Michael L. Printz Award. **Frequency:** annual. **Type:** recognition. **Recipient:** to honor the highest literary achievement in books for young adults. **Affiliated With:** American Library Association. **Publications:** *ALA's Guide to Best Reading*. With ALA, ALSC, RUSA and Booklist. Camera-ready art. ● *Bare Bones: Young Adult Services*. Book ● *Best Books for Young Adults* ● *The Fair Garden and The Swarm of Beasts*. Book ● *Hit List for Young Adults: Frequently Challenged Books* ● *New Directions for Library Service to Young Adults*. Book ● *100 All-Start Choices for Teens: The Best of the Best Books for Young Adults*. Pamphlet ● *Outstanding Books for the College Bound and Lifelong Learners*. Pamphlet ● *Sizzling Summer Reading Programs for Young Adults*. Book ● *Teen Read Week Manual*. Book ● *YAttitudes*, quarterly. Newsletter. **Price:** free, for members only. **Circulation:** 5,000. Alternate Formats: online ● *Young Adult Library Services*, quarterly. Journal. Covers current practices information, young adult literature, research, and new services and technology. Includes book reviews. **Price:** included in membership dues; $50.00 /year for nonmembers. ISSN: 1541-4302. **Circulation:** 5,000. **Advertising:** accepted ● *Youth Participation in School and Public Libraries: It Works*. Book. **Conventions/Meetings:** annual meeting, in conjunction with ALA - midwinter.

Lighting

10396 ■ Rushlight Club (RC)

c/o Mrs. Jane Rausch, Corresponding Sec.
20132 Metzger Dr.
Rockwood, MI 48173
Ph: (734)379-3119
E-mail: info@rushlight.org
URL: http://www.rushlight.org
Contact: Mrs. Jane Rausch, Corresponding Sec.

Founded: 1932. **Members:** 600. **Membership Dues:** individual in U.S., $35 (annual) ● individual in Canada, $40 (annual) ● individual outside U.S. and Canada, $45 (annual). **Description:** International membership of individuals and museums interested in the study of early lighting, including the use of early lighting fuels and devices. Traces the origin and development of lighting through written articles. Offers educational programs. **Libraries: Type:** reference. **Holdings:** audiovisuals, books, periodicals. **Awards:** Thwing Award. **Frequency:** annual. **Type:** recognition. **Publications:** *Early Lighting - A Pictorial Guide*. **Price:** $20.00 for members; $30.00 for nonmembers ● *Flickerings*, quarterly. Newsletter. **Price:** included in membership dues ● *The Rushlight*, quarterly. Journal. **Price:** included in membership dues ● Directory, annual. **Price:** included in membership dues. **Advertising:** accepted ● Also publishes material on early lighting, and reprints of early pamphlets; also makes available slide series. **Conventions/Meetings:** triennial conference ● periodic lecture.

Linguistics

10397 ■ American Association for Applied Linguistics (AAAL)

3416 Primm Ln.
Birmingham, AL 35216
Ph: (205)824-7700
Free: (866)821-7700
Fax: (205)823-2760
E-mail: aaal@primemanagement.net
URL: http://www.aaal.org
Contact: Kathleen Bardovi-Harlig, Pres.

Founded: 1977. **Members:** 700. **Membership Dues:** regular, in North America, $85 (annual) ● regular, outside North America, $100 (annual) ● student in North America, $50 (annual) ● student outside North America, $65 (annual) ● institution in North America, $150 (annual) ● institution outside North America, $165 (annual) ● emeritus, retired in North America, $45 (annual) ● joint in North America, $135 (annual) ● emeritus, retired outside North America, $60 (annual) ● joint outside North America, $150 (annual) ● publisher, $215 (annual) ● publisher, $230 (annual).

Budget: $50,000. **Description:** Represents the interests of individuals who are interested in and actively contributing to the advancement of applied linguistics (multidisciplinary approaches to language problems and issues) as a science and profession. Promotes study and research and disseminates information in the field of applied linguistics. **Awards:** Award for Distinguished Scholarship and Service. **Frequency:** annual. **Type:** recognition. **Recipient:** to a distinguished scholar for her/his scholarship and service to the organization ● Graduate Student Travel Grants. **Frequency:** annual. **Type:** grant. **Recipient:** to support travel (and some expenses) of 6 graduate student members of AAAL to the annual meeting ● Jacqueline A. Ross Dissertation Award. **Frequency:** annual. **Type:** recognition. **Recipient:** for a doctoral dissertation research that makes a significant and original contribution to knowledge about second/ foreign language tests and testing ● TOEFL Outstanding Young Scholar Award. **Frequency:** annual. **Type:** recognition. **Recipient:** for outstanding contribution to the field of second or foreign language assessment by a scholar under the age of 40 ● TOEFL Partners in Excellence Award. **Frequency:** annual. **Type:** recognition. **Recipient:** to international students, faculty, staff and administrators who work together to initiate and develop a program involving international education ● TOEFL Small Grants For Doctoral Research in Second/Foreign Language Assessment. **Frequency:** annual. **Type:** grant. **Recipient:** for promising students to facilitate the timely completion of their dissertations. **Publications:** *AAALetter*, 3/year. Newsletter. Covers research and exchange of information in the field of applied linguistics. Includes abstracts of papers, and conference reports. **Price:** included in membership dues. **Circulation:** 700 ● *Applied Linguistics*, 3/year. Journal. **Conventions/Meetings:** annual conference (exhibits).

10398 ■ American Dialect Society (ADS)
c/o Allan A. Metcalf, Exec. Sec.
MacMurray Coll.
Dept. of English
Jacksonville, IL 62650-2590
Ph: (217)479-7117
Fax: (217)245-0405
E-mail: americandialect@mac.edu
URL: http://www.americandialect.org
Contact: Allan A. Metcalf, Exec. Sec.
Founded: 1889. **Members:** 500. **Membership Dues:** individual, $50 (annual) ● student, $25 (annual). **Staff:** 2. **Budget:** $25,000. **Regional Groups:** 4. **Description:** Educators and others who study the English language in North America and its interaction with other languages. Sponsors the *Dictionary of American Regional English.* Awards three Presidential Honorary Memberships each year to students interested in the work of the society. **Awards:** Presidential Honorary Memberships. **Frequency:** annual. **Type:** recognition. **Recipient:** to a student, graduate or undergraduate, who shows outstanding aptitude for and interest in the field. **Committees:** New Words; Non-English Dialects; Teaching; Usage. **Affiliated With:** American Council of Learned Societies. **Publications:** *American Speech*, quarterly. Journal. Features scholarly articles and book reviews. **Price:** included in membership dues; $123.00 institutional (print); $122.00 institutional (online); $137.00 institutional (print and online). ISSN: 0003-1283. **Advertising:** accepted. Alternate Formats: online ● *Newsletter of the American Dialect Society*, 3/year. Reports on society news and activities and announces national and regional meetings. Notifies members of deadline dates for papers to be given. **Price:** included in membership dues. ISSN: 0002-8193. **Circulation:** 700. Alternate Formats: online. Also Cited As: *NADS* ● *Publication of the American Dialect Society*, annual. Monograph. Serves as a supplement to American Speech. Also Cited As: *PADS*. **Conventions/ Meetings:** annual meeting, held in conjunction with Linguistic Society of America (exhibits) - early January.

10399 ■ American Society of Geolinguistics (ASG)
c/o Prof. Wayne Finke, Ed.
Dept. of Modern Languages
Baruch Coll., B6-280
17 Lexington Ave.
New York, NY 10010-5585
Ph: (646)312-4420 (646)312-4210
Fax: (646)312-4211
E-mail: wayne_finke@baruch.cuny.edu
Contact: Prof. Wayne Finke, Ed.
Founded: 1964. **Members:** 200. **Membership Dues:** individual, $35 (annual) ● student, retiree, $25 (annual). **Staff:** 1. **Budget:** $2,500. **Languages:** English, French, Spanish. **Multinational. Description:** Professionals in the field of languages. Seeks to promote the exchange of ideas and information; foster research and study of the world's present-day languages; advance the study of linguistics and modern languages; cooperate with other organizations established for similar purposes. Conducts study groups. Areas of special interest include linguistic geography, languages in contact and conflict, sociolinguistics, language planning, education and politics. **Libraries: Type:** open to the public. **Holdings:** 30. **Publications:** *Geolinguistics* (in English and French), annual. Journal. Contains articles, professional notes, book reviews, and language notes. **Price:** included in membership dues. ISSN: 0190-4671. **Circulation:** 150. **Conventions/Meetings:** periodic banquet ● quarterly meeting ● seminar.

10400 ■ Association for Computational Linguistics (ACL)
c/o Priscilla Rasmussen, Business Mgr.
209 N Eighth St.
Stroudsburg, PA 18360-1721
Ph: (570)476-8006
Fax: (570)476-0860
E-mail: acl@aclweb.org
URL: http://www.aclweb.org
Contact: Priscilla Rasmussen, Business Mgr.
Founded: 1962. **Members:** 2,000. **Membership Dues:** regular/student-employed, $60 (annual) ● student/retired/unemployed, $30 (annual) ● joint, $70 (annual). **Staff:** 3. **Description:** Individuals interested in computational linguistics. Deals with algorithms, models, and computer systems or components of systems for research on language, applications (translation, documentation, and lexicography), and scholarly investigation (stylistics and content analysis). **Awards:** Best Paper and Best Student Paper Awards. **Frequency:** annual. **Type:** recognition. **Recipient:** to authors who have submitted conference papers judged by the program committee to be the best representation of the work ● Donald and Betty Walker Scholarship Fund. **Frequency:** annual. **Type:** scholarship ● Lifetime Achievement Award. **Frequency:** annual. **Type:** recognition. **Recipient:** to a person who has made significant contributions to the field throughout his or her career. **Formerly:** (1968) Association for Machine Translation and Computational Linguistics. **Publications:** *ACL Conference Proceedings*, annual. **Price:** $30.00 for members; $60.00 for nonmembers ● *ACL Newsletter.* Alternate Formats: online ● *Coling Proceedings*, biennial ● *Computational Linguistics*, quarterly. Journal. **Price:** included in membership dues. ISSN: 0891-2017. **Advertising:** accepted ● *EACL Conference Proceedings*, biennial. Contains European chapter proceedings. **Price:** $30.00 for members; $60.00 for nonmembers ● *NAACL Conference Proceedings*, annual. **Price:** $35.00 for members; $70.00 for nonmembers. Alternate Formats: CD-ROM ● *Workshop Proceedings.* **Conventions/Meetings:** annual conference (exhibits).

10401 ■ Center for Applied Linguistics (CAL)
4646 40th St. NW
Washington, DC 20016-1859
Ph: (202)362-0700
Fax: (202)362-3740
E-mail: info@cal.org
URL: http://www.cal.org
Contact: Donna Christian, Pres.
Founded: 1959. **Staff:** 75. **Budget:** $7,000,000. **Languages:** Arabic, Chinese, English, French, German, Spanish. **Nonmembership. Description:** Serves as a national and international resource center in the application of linguistic science to social, cultural, and educational problems. Principal areas of emphasis are education in English as a second language, and literacy, foreign language, and bilingual education; cross-cultural communication; language variation; testing and assessment. Provides evaluation, training and technical assistance for teachers and program administrators through its school services as well as for those serving adults and others in the multicultural workforce. Conducts research and collaborates with universities and other institutions, public and private. Operates information and technical assistance services including: Cultural Orientation Resource Center; National Center for ESL Literacy Education; Center for Research on Education, Diversity and Excellence. Hosts public lectures on language policy and education. **Libraries: Type:** reference. **Telecommunication Services:** electronic mail, donna@cal.org. **Divisions:** Foreign Language Education; Language and Culture Resources; Language and Literacy; Language Education and Academic Development; Language in Society; Language Testing. **Publications:** *CAL Reporter*, semiannual. Newsletter ● Offers materials in areas of ESL, bilingual education, foreign language education, refugee resettlement, language testing, and sociolinguistics. Co-publishes professional reference materials for educators with Delta Systems, Inc. and also distributes reports, tests, manuals, videos and other materials in these areas. **Conventions/Meetings:** annual conference.

10402 ■ Elvish Linguistic Fellowship (ELF)
c/o Carl F. Hostetter, Hd.
2509 Ambling Cir.
Crofton, MD 21114
E-mail: aelfwine@elvish.org
URL: http://www.elvish.org
Contact: Carl F. Hostetter, Hd.
Founded: 1971. **Members:** 125. **Staff:** 4. **Budget:** $750. **Regional Groups:** 2. **Description:** Linguists and other individuals interested in the invented languages of J.R.R. Tolkien (1892-1973). Promotes the study and use of Tolkien's languages. Conducts research and educational programs. **Libraries: Type:** reference. **Committees:** Scholars. **Affiliated With:** Mythopoeic Society. **Formerly:** (1978) Mythopoeic Linguistic Fellowship. **Publications:** *Parma Eldalamberon*, annual. Journal. Includes articles, letters, book reviews, and art works. **Price:** $20.00/copy. **Circulation:** 100 ● *Vinyar Tengwar* (in English and Spanish), quarterly. Journal. Includes articles, columns, letters, book reviews, and art works. ISSN: 1054-7606. **Circulation:** 125. Alternate Formats: online.

10403 ■ International Clinical Phonetics and Linguistics Association (ICPLA)
c/o Nicole Mueller
Univ. of Louisiana at Lafayette
Dept. of Communicative Disorders
PO Box 43107
Lafayette, LA 70504-3170
Ph: (337)482-1077
Fax: (337)482-6195
E-mail: nmueller@louisiana.edu
URL: http://www.ucs.louisiana.edu/%7Emjb0372/ICPLA.html
Contact: Sara Howard, Pres.
Founded: 1990. **Members:** 150. **Membership Dues:** full, $20 (annual) ● student, retired, $10 (annual). **Multinational. Description:** Promotes the study of the interaction of the language sciences and the study of communication disorders. **Additional Websites:** http://www.icpla.org. **Telecommunication Services:** electronic mail, s.howard@sheffield.ac.uk. **Publications:** *Clinical Linguistics & Phonetics*, monthly. Journal. **Price:** $1,118.00 /year for institutions; $441.00 /year for individuals. ISSN: 0269-9206. **Advertising:** accepted. Alternate Formats: online. **Conventions/Meetings:** biennial meeting (exhibits).

10404 ■ International Maledicta Society (IMS)
PO Box 14123
Santa Rosa, CA 95402-6123
Ph: (707)795-8178
E-mail: aman@sonic.net
URL: http://www.sonic.net/maledicta
Contact: Reinhold A. Aman PhD, Pres.
Founded: 1975. **Members:** 3,000. **Membership Dues:** individual, $20 (annual). **Staff:** 1. **Languages:**

Arabic, Burmese, Chinese, English, French, German, Hebrew, Italian, Polish, Russian, Spanish, Yiddish. **For-Profit**. **Description:** Professors of linguistics, English, folklore, sociology, philology, anthropology, psychology, and foreign languages; others interested in these fields. Seeks to promote, conduct, and support interdisciplinary research on verbal aggression, pejoration, value judgments, and related subjects in all languages, dialects, cultures, religions, and ethnic groups. Maintains the International Research Center for Verbal Aggression. **Libraries: Type:** reference. **Holdings:** 3,000; articles, books, clippings. **Subjects:** insults, curses, slurs, epithets and other maledicta, including items from 200 cultures and ranging from about 3000 B.C. to the present. **Computer Services:** database, restricted to members. **Publications:** *Maledicta Press Publications*, periodic. Book. Contains essays and glossaries of insults, curses, blasphemies, slurs, etc. ISSN: 0363-9037. **Circulation:** 2,000 ● *Maledicta: The International Journal of Verbal Aggression*, periodic. Specializes in uncensored studies and glossaries of offensive and negatively-valued words and expressions from all languages and cultures. **Price:** included in membership dues; $18.00/year. ISSN: 0363-3659.

10405 ■ Linguistic Association of Canada and the United States (LACUS)
c/o Lilly Lee Chen, Sec.-Treas.
Rice Univ.
Center for the Stud. of Languages, MS 36
Houston, TX 77251-1892
Ph: (713)348-2820
Fax: (713)348-5846
E-mail: lchen@rice.edu
URL: http://www.ruf.rice.edu/~lacus
Contact: Lilly Lee Chen, Sec.-Treas.
Founded: 1974. **Members:** 300. **Membership Dues:** professional, $50 (annual) ● student, $30 (annual) ● emeritus, $40 (annual) ● life, $600. **Languages:** English, French, Spanish. **Multinational**. **Description:** Linguists and other interested individuals from 50 countries. Purpose is to support and promote applied and theoretical linguistic studies. **Awards:** Honorary Lifetime Memberships. **Type:** recognition. **Recipient:** for senior scholars in the field ● **Frequency:** annual. **Type:** recognition. **Recipient:** for two best papers presented at the LACUS Forum by young scholars. **Also Known As:** Association de Linguistique du Canada et des Etats Unis. **Publications:** *LACUS Forum*, annual. Proceedings. **Price:** included in membership dues. **Circulation:** 600 ● *LACUS Newsletter*, semiannual. **Conventions/Meetings:** annual conference, on university campuses alternating between Canada and the United States (exhibits) - always August.

10406 ■ Linguistic Society of America (LSA)
1325 18th St. NW, Ste.211
Washington, DC 20036-6501
Ph: (202)835-1714
Fax: (202)835-1717
E-mail: lsa@lsadc.org
URL: http://www.lsadc.org
Contact: Margaret W. Reynolds, Exec. Dir.
Founded: 1924. **Members:** 6,500. **Membership Dues:** student in U.S., $30 (annual) ● student outside U.S., $40 (annual) ● regular in U.S., $75 (annual) ● regular outside U.S., $85 (annual) ● institution in U.S., $110 (annual) ● institution outside U.S., $120 (annual) ● life, $1,500. **Staff:** 3. **Budget:** $600,000. **Description:** Educators and linguists devoted to the furtherance of research and the publication of scientific analysis of language and languages. Cosponsors with a host university the Linguistic Institute, a biennial summer school of theoretical and applied linguistics on both the graduate and undergraduate levels. **Awards:** Kenneth L. Hale Award. **Frequency:** periodic. **Type:** recognition. **Recipient:** for outstanding linguistic scholarship that documents a particular endangered or no longer spoken language or language family ● Leonard Bloomfield Book Award. **Frequency:** biennial. **Type:** recognition ● Linguistics, Language, and the Public Award. **Frequency:** biennial. **Type:** recognition ● Victoria A. Fromkin Prize. **Frequency:** periodic. **Type:** recognition. **Recipient:** for individuals who have performed extraordinary service to the society and the discipline. **Computer Services:** Mailing lists. **Committees:** Language in the School Curriculum; Linguistic Institutes and Fellowships; Social and Political Concerns; Status of Women in Linguistics; Undergraduate Program Advisory. **Affiliated With:** American Council of Learned Societies; Consortium of Social Science Associations; National Humanities Alliance. **Publications:** *Language*, quarterly. Journal. Contains technical articles dealing with the scientific analysis of language and languages. Includes book reviews. **Price:** included in membership dues. ISSN: 0097-8507. **Circulation:** 6,500. **Advertising:** accepted. Alternate Formats: online ● *LSA Meeting Handbook*, annual. Contains schedule for and abstracts of papers presented at the society's annual meeting. **Price:** free to meeting registrants; $8.50/copy for non-registrants. **Advertising:** accepted. **Conventions/Meetings:** annual meeting (exhibits).

10407 ■ Mend Our Tongues Society (MOTS)
Address Unknown since 2007
Founded: 1982. **Members:** 64. **Description:** A special interest group of Mensa (see separate entry). Seeks to invent new words for the English language. Conducts linguistic research. **Affiliated With:** American Mensa. **Publications:** *Ferment*, periodic. Newsletter. **Price:** included in membership dues; $5.00/4 issues. **Circulation:** 70. **Advertising:** not accepted. **Conventions/Meetings:** periodic conference.

10408 ■ North American Chapter of the Association for Computational Linguistics (NAACL)
c/o Lillian Lee, Sec.
Dept. of Cmpt. Sci.
Cornell Univ.
4152 Upson Hall
Ithaca, NY 14853
Ph: (607)255-8119
Fax: (607)255-4428
E-mail: llee@cs.cornell.edu
URL: http://www.cs.cornell.edu/home/llee/naacl
Contact: Lillian Lee, Sec.
Membership Dues: regular, student, unemployed, retired, $30 (annual) ● student-employed, $60 (annual) ● joint, $70 (annual). **Multinational**. **Description:** Provides a regional focus for members of the Association for Computational Linguistics (ACL) in North America. Encourages and facilitates ACL membership by people and institutions in North America. Establishes banking facilities in North America that simplify financial transactions with the ACL by its North American members. Promotes cooperation and information exchange among related scientific and professional societies within North America. **Publications:** Newsletter. Alternate Formats: online.

Literature

10409 ■ American Comparative Literature Association (ACLA)
Univ. of Texas at Austin
Prog. in Comparative Literature
1 Univ. Sta. B5003
Austin, TX 78712-0196
Ph: (512)471-8020
E-mail: info@acla.org
URL: http://www.acla.org
Contact: Susan Kaczmarczik, Admin. Asst.
Founded: 1960. **Members:** 800. **Membership Dues:** regular, faculty, $55 (annual) ● student, $25 (annual) ● institution, $100 (annual) ● emeritus, $30 (annual) ● emeritus (ACLA/ICLA), $40 (annual) ● student (ACLA/ICLA), $35 (annual). **Staff:** 1. **Description:** College and university professors, graduate students, and others interested in comparative literature. Works to strengthen and support the study and teaching of comparative literature in American colleges and universities. **Awards:** A. Owen Aldridge Prize. **Frequency:** annual. **Type:** recognition. **Recipient:** for an outstanding paper by a graduate student ● Charles Bernheimer Prize. **Frequency:** annual. **Type:** recognition. **Recipient:** for an outstanding dissertation in comparative literature ● Harry Levin Prize. **Frequency:** biennial. **Type:** recognition. **Recipient:** for a work of literary history ● Horst Frenz Prize. **Frequency:** annual. **Type:** recognition. **Recipient:** for an outstanding paper by a graduate student ● Rene Wellek Prize. **Frequency:** biennial. **Type:** recognition. **Recipient:** for a work of literary theory. **Committees:** Constitution; Student Affairs; Travel Grants. **Affiliated With:** American Council of Learned Societies; International Comparative Literature Association; National Humanities Alliance. **Conventions/Meetings:** annual meeting ● annual meeting and conference, scholarly.

10410 ■ American Friends of the Hakluyt Society
c/o Clare Flemming
Explorers Club
46 E 70th St.
New York, NY 10021
E-mail: collections@explorers.org
URL: http://www.hakluyt.com/hak-soc-amer-top.htm
Contact: Dr. Ross MacPhee, Pres.
Founded: 1996. **Members:** 750. **Description:** National branch of the international organization (see separate entry, International Organizations). Promotes and helps provide financial support for the publication of scholarly editions of records of voyages, travels, and other geographical material of the past, and cooperates with other organizations having similar objectives, in particular, the Hakluyt Society.

10411 ■ American Literature Association (ALA)
c/o Alfred Bendixen, Exec. Dir.
Dept. of English
Texas A&M Univ.
College Station, TX 77843-4227
E-mail: abendixen@tamu.edu
URL: http://www.calstatela.edu/academic/english/ala2
Contact: Alfred Bendixen, Exec. Dir.
Founded: 1989. **Membership Dues:** regular, $10 (annual). **Description:** Focuses on the study of American authors. **Publications:** *Directory of Affiliated Societies*. Alternate Formats: online ● *Directory of Scholars*. Alternate Formats: online. **Conventions/Meetings:** annual conference.

10412 ■ Association of American Collegiate Literary Societies (AACLS)
Address Unknown since 2008
Founded: 1978. **Members:** 300. **Staff:** 1. **Regional Groups:** 10. **Description:** Works with literary societies in the U.S. to promote the creation of new societies, maintain existing societies, and revive old societies. Conducts research programs for new societies. Compiles statistics. Organizes debates between member societies; maintains speakers' bureau. **Libraries: Type:** reference. **Holdings:** 100; archival material. **Subjects:** literary societies of U.S. **Computer Services:** database. **Publications:** *AACLS Report*, annual ● Brochures, annual ● Newsletter, periodic ● Papers ● Also publishes data bank printouts. **Conventions/Meetings:** annual congress - always spring ● annual RHETOR - meeting and workshop, features desktop publishing, poetry/fiction readings, debates, public speaking, writing - always fall.

10413 ■ Association of Literary Scholars and Critics (ALSC)
650 Beacon St., Ste.510
Boston, MA 02215
Ph: (617)358-1990
Fax: (617)358-1995
E-mail: alsc@bu.edu
URL: http://www.bu.edu/literary
Contact: Mr. Michael Gouin-Hart, Exec. Dir.
Founded: 1994. **Members:** 2,200. **Staff:** 2. **Budget:** $200,000. **Description:** Professors of literature and language, writers, scholars, and grad students. Seeks to promote the appreciation and value of literary study. Conducts research programs. **Computer**

Services: database ● mailing lists. **Additional Websites:** http://www.thevalve.org. **Committees:** Curriculum; Nominations; Program; Publications. **Publications:** *ALSC Newsletter*, quarterly. **Circulation:** 2,200. **Advertising:** accepted ● *Literary Imagination*, 3/year. Journal. **Price:** $25.00 /year for individuals; $40.00 /year for institutions. ISSN: 1523-9012. **Conventions/Meetings:** annual conference.

10414 ■ Association for the Study of Literature and Environment (ASLE)
c/o Amy McIntyre, Managing Dir.
PO Box 502
Keene, NH 03431
Ph: (603)357-7411
Fax: (603)357-7411
E-mail: asle.us@verizon.net
URL: http://www.asle.umn.edu
Contact: Amy McIntyre, Managing Dir.
Founded: 1992. **Members:** 1,000. **Membership Dues:** patron, $150 (annual) ● sustaining, $100-$149 (annual) ● regular (based on annual income), $20-$80 (annual) ● couple, $10 (annual) ● inside Canada/ Mexico, $5 (annual) ● international, $10 (annual). **Staff:** 1. **Budget:** $45,000. **Description:** Seeks to promote the exchange of ideas and information on literature that considers the relationship between human beings and the natural world and to facilitate new nature writing. **Libraries: Type:** reference. **Computer Services:** Bibliographic search. **Caucuses:** Diversity. **Working Groups:** Graduate Student. **Affiliated With:** American Studies Association; Modern Language Association of America. **Publications:** *ASLE News*, semiannual. Newsletter. Contains news about conferences, forthcoming publications, and work-in-progress. ● *ISLE: Interdisciplinary Studies in Literature and the Environment*, semiannual. Journal. **Price:** $6.50 1990-93 edition; $5.00 1994 edition; $6.00 1995 edition. ISSN: 1076-0962 ● Membership Directory, annual. **Conventions/Meetings:** biennial conference (exhibits) ● meeting.

10415 ■ Augustan Reprint Society (ARS)
c/o AMS Press Inc.
63 Flushing Ave., Unit No. 221, Bldg. 292, Ste.417
Brooklyn, NY 11205-1005
Ph: (718)875-8100
Fax: (718)875-3800
E-mail: amserve@earthlink.net
URL: http://amspressinc.com
Contact: Mr. Gabriel Hornstein, Pres.
Founded: 1946. **Members:** 700. **Description:** Individuals and institutions interested in 17th- and 18th-century English literary history. Makes available reprints (usually facsimile reproductions) of rare Restoration and 18th-century works. **Convention/ Meeting:** none.

10416 ■ Before Columbus Foundation (BCF)
655-13th St., Ste.302
Oakland, CA 94612
Ph: (510)268-9775
URL: http://www.ankn.uaf.edu/IEW/BeforeColumbus
Contact: Gundars Strads, Contact
Founded: 1976. **Staff:** 4. **Description:** Participants are individuals interested in promoting contemporary, American multicultural literature. (Group defines American multicultural literature as the evolution of African-American, Asian-American, Native American, Latin American, and European American literary traditions in North America.) Derives its name from the book *They Came Before Columbus*, which maintains that American literature was already evolving in each American ethnic group before they actually came to North America. Aims to educate the public. Provides information, research, and educational services. Sponsors lectures, classes, and readings. **Awards:** American Book Award. **Frequency:** annual. **Type:** recognition.

10417 ■ Center for the Book (CBLC)
c/o Library of Congress
101 Independence Ave. SE
Washington, DC 20540-4920
Ph: (202)707-5221
Fax: (202)707-0269
E-mail: cfbook@loc.gov
URL: http://www.loc.gov/loc/cfbook
Contact: John Y. Cole, Dir.
Founded: 1977. **Staff:** 4. **State Groups:** 50. **National Groups:** 85. **Description:** Uses resources and prestige of Library of Congress to stimulate public interest in books, reading, literacy, and libraries, and encourage the study of books and the printed word. Sponsors lectures, symposia, reading promotion projects, and publications. Develops partnerships with state center for the book affiliates and national organizations. **Computer Services:** database. **Programs:** Mother Goose. **Projects:** Books & Beyond; The International Community of the Book; Letters About Literature; Read More About It; Reading Powers the Mind; River of Words; Telling America's Stories. **Publications:** Books.

10418 ■ Children's Literature Association (ChLA)
PO Box 138
Battle Creek, MI 49016-0138
Ph: (269)965-8180
Fax: (269)965-3568
E-mail: info@childlitassn.org
URL: http://www.childlitassn.org
Contact: Kathryn Kiessling, Admin.
Founded: 1972. **Members:** 975. **Membership Dues:** individual in U.S., $75 (annual) ● individual in Canada, $90 (annual) ● individual outside U.S. and Canada, $105 (annual) ● institution in U.S., $135 (annual) ● institution in Canada, $150 (annual) ● institution outside U.S. and Canada, $165 (annual) ● retired, in U.S., $50 (annual) ● retired, in Canada, $65 (annual) ● retired outside U.S. and Canada, $80 (annual) ● student in U.S., $30 (annual) ● student in Canada, $45 (annual) ● student outside U.S. and Canada, $60 (annual). **Staff:** 1. **Budget:** $100,000. **Description:** Represents College teachers of children's literature, librarians, parents, authors, publishers, and college faculty in sociology, psychology, and art who are interested in children's literature. Encourages serious scholarship and research in the area of children's literature; provides an outlet for scholarship through conferences and publications; works in conjunction with other organizations, publishers, and the public to disseminate information about children's literature. **Awards:** Carol Gay. **Frequency:** annual. **Type:** recognition. **Recipient:** for paper ● Children's Literature Association Research Fellowship. **Frequency:** annual. **Type:** scholarship. **Recipient:** for members doing innovative research in the field ● ChLA Article Award. **Frequency:** annual. **Type:** recognition. **Recipient:** for outstanding published criticism of children's literature ● ChLA Book Award. **Frequency:** annual. **Type:** recognition. **Recipient:** for outstanding published criticism of children's literature ● Hannah Beitr Graduate Research. **Frequency:** annual. **Type:** recognition. **Recipient:** for individual ● International Sponsorship. **Frequency:** annual. **Type:** grant. **Recipient:** for paper ● Phoenix. **Frequency:** annual. **Type:** recognition. **Recipient:** for book ● Research. **Frequency:** annual. **Type:** grant. **Recipient:** for individual. **Telecommunication Services:** electronic mail, kkiessling@childlitsassn.org. **Committees:** Awards; Publications; Scholarship. **Affiliated With:** Modern Language Association of America; National Coalition Against Censorship. **Publications:** *Children's Literature*, annual. Journal. **Price:** included in membership dues. ISSN: 0092-8208. **Circulation:** 850 ● *Children's Literature Association Quarterly*. Journal. **Price:** included in membership dues; $10.00/back issue. ISSN: 0885-0429. **Circulation:** 850 ● *Festchrift: A Ten Year Retrospective*. **Price:** $3.00 plus shipping and handling ● *The First Steps: Best of the Early ChLA Quarterly*. **Price:** $3.75 plus shipping and handling. **Conventions/Meetings:** annual international conference.

10419 ■ Council on National Literatures (CNL)
6802 Metropolitan Ave.
Middle Village, NY 11379
Ph: (718)821-3916
E-mail: anneandhenrypaolucci@yahoo.com
URL: http://annehenrypaolucci.homestead.com/CNL1.html
Contact: Anne Paolucci PhD, Pres.
Founded: 1974. **Members:** 1,200. **Staff:** 3. **Budget:** $50,000. **Description:** Libraries and academic and nonacademic private members interested in both Western and non-Western literatures. Discusses ways and means of expanding comparative study of literature to include new programs in the humanities, translation, new definitions of comparative studies, outlines of pilot programs to expand existing literature courses, and questions of critical terminology. Sponsors meetings with related organizations. Plans to launch an annual fundraising event at which the council will honor a person who has furthered the integration of Western and non-Western literature. **Libraries: Type:** reference. **Holdings:** 2,000; articles, books, video recordings. **Subjects:** comparative literature. **Awards:** CNL Poetry. **Frequency:** annual. **Type:** grant ● Fiction. **Frequency:** annual. **Type:** grant. **Committees:** Contributing Editors; Editorial; Policy; Special Events. **Publications:** *CNL/World Report*. Monographs. **Price:** $15.00 each. ISSN: 0145-6783 ● *Review of National Literatures*. Monographs. **Price:** $25.00 each. ISSN: 0034-6640. Also Cited As: *RNL* ● Also publishes press releases. **Conventions/ Meetings:** annual conference, held in conjunction with Modern Language Association of America - always in December ● periodic conference.

10420 ■ Count Dracula Society (CDS)
Address Unknown since 2007
Founded: 1962. **Members:** 1,000. **Description:** Academicians, teachers, writers, librarians, movie producers, and others devoted to the serious study of horror films and Gothic literature. Named for the character of Bram Stoker's novel *Dracula*. Maintains Horror Hall of Fame. **Awards:** Horace Walpole Gold Medal. **Type:** recognition ● International Cinema Achievement Award. **Frequency:** annual. **Type:** recognition ● Mrs. Ann Radcliffe Award. **Type:** recognition. **Recipient:** for achievement in literature, movies, and television ● Rev. Dr. Montague Summers Memorial Award. **Type:** recognition. **Affiliated With:** Academy of Science Fiction, Fantasy, and Horror Films. **Publications:** *The Count Dracula Quarterly* ● *Tana Leaflet*, semiannual. **Conventions/Meetings:** bimonthly meeting.

10421 ■ Elizabethan Club of Yale University (ECYU)
459 Coll. St.
New Haven, CT 06511
Ph: (203)432-0172
Fax: (203)432-8767
Contact: Stephen R. Parks, Librarian
Founded: 1911. **Members:** 2,300. **Description:** Promotes appreciation of literary, aesthetic, and intellectual works. Possesses Elizabethan collection. Occasionally underwrites publication of scholarly books.

10422 ■ International Arthurian Society, North American Branch (IAS/NAB)
c/o Logan E. Whalen, Sec.-Treas.
Univ. of Oklahoma
Dept. of Modern Languages, Literatures, and Linguistics
780 Van Vleet Oval, Rm. 206
Norman, OK 73019-2032
Ph: (405)325-6181
Fax: (405)325-0103
E-mail: lwhalen@ou.edu
URL: http://faculty.smu.edu/arthuriana
Contact: Logan E. Whalen, Sec.-Treas.
Founded: 1948. **Members:** 350. **Membership Dues:** student, $30 (annual) ● emeritus, $40 (annual) ● regular, $50 (annual) ● contributing, joint, $60 (annual) ● patron, $75 (annual) ● life, $500. **Languages:** English, French, German. **Description:** University professors and other individuals interested in Arthurian literature; libraries of universities, seminars, and research institutes. Seeks to further Arthurian studies and encourage exchange of information among members. **Publications:** *Arthuriana*, quarterly. Journal. Features scholarly articles. **Price:** included

in membership dues. **Circulation:** 350. **Advertising:** accepted ● *Bibliographical Bulletin/Bulletin Bibliographique of the International Arthurian Society de la Societe Internationale Arthurienne* (in English, French, and German), annual. Includes abstracts of studies on Arthurian subjects published in previous year, news of various IAS branches and articles. **Price:** included in membership dues; $25.00 /year for institutions. ISSN: 0074-1388. **Circulation:** 475. Also Cited As: *BBIAS and BBSIA*. **Conventions/Meetings:** annual conference and symposium (exhibits) - always May in Kalamazoo, MI ● triennial international conference.

10423 ■ International Comparative Literature Association (ICLA)
Brigham Young Univ.
HRCB
Provo, UT 84602-4538
Ph: (801)422-5598
Fax: (801)422-0307
E-mail: iclaweb@byu.edu
URL: http://icla.byu.edu/www
Contact: Dr. Steven P. Sondrup, Sec.

Founded: 1955. **Members:** 4,500. **Membership Dues:** $10 (annual). **Staff:** 30. **National Groups:** 65. **Languages:** English, French, German, Italian, Spanish. **Multinational. Description:** National associations in 70 countries; scholars and professors. Promotes worldwide study of comparative literature. **Telecommunication Services:** electronic mail, sondrup@byu.edu. **Committees:** Comparative History Coordinating; Procedures; Research; Theory; Translation. **Publications:** *Comparative History of Literatures in European Languages* (in English and French). Covers areas such as Expressionism and the Renaissance. ● *Literary Research/Recherche Litteraire*, annual. Journal. **Price:** free for members ● Bulletin, annual. Covers association activities. Includes obituaries and meeting and publications information. **Price:** free for members. Alternate Formats: online ● Pamphlets. Contains research. ● Proceedings, triennial ● Directory. Provides comparatists with information on research interests and main publications of colleagues around the world. **Conventions/Meetings:** triennial congress.

10424 ■ International Courtly Literature Society (ICLS)
c/o Maureen Boulton, North American Branch Pres.
Univ. of Notre Dame
343 O'Shaughnessy Hall
Notre Dame, IN 46556
E-mail: boulton1@nd.edu
URL: http://www.clas.ufl.edu/icls
Contact: June Hall McCash, VP

Founded: 1973. **Members:** 700. **Membership Dues:** $20 (annual). **National Groups:** 13. **Languages:** English, French, German. **Multinational. Description:** Professors, librarians, and students in 16 countries interested in literature created at royal courts from medieval to modern time. Fosters study and research of the nature and significance of courtly literature. Encourages cooperation between members; sponsors scholarly papers. **Telecommunication Services:** electronic mail, jmcash@mtsu.edu. **Committees:** MLA Seminar Presentation. **Publications:** *Encomia: Bibliographical Bulletin of the International Courtly Literature Society* (in English, French, and German), annual. Features reviews, directory, and membership list. **Price:** included in membership dues; $40.00 /year for libraries and agencies. ISSN: 0363-4841. **Circulation:** 900 ● *Selected Congress Proceedings*, triennial. **Conventions/Meetings:** triennial congress (exhibits).

10425 ■ International Institute of Iberoamerican Literature (IILI)
Univ. of Pittsburgh
1312 Cathedral of Learning
Pittsburgh, PA 15260
Ph: (412)624-3359
Fax: (412)624-0829
E-mail: iili@pitt.edu
URL: http://www.pitt.edu/AFShome/h/i/hispan/public/html/iili
Contact: Prof. Mabel Morana, Dir. of Publications

Founded: 1938. **Members:** 2,200. **Staff:** 2. **Languages:** English, Portuguese, Spanish. **Description:** Professors of Iberoamerican literature from 37 countries. Seeks to: promote the study of Iberoamerican literature; strengthen cultural relations among people of the Americas; encourage the establishment of chairs of Iberoamerican literature in the United States and chairs of American literature in South American countries. Coordinates linguistic and literary research. **Libraries: Type:** reference. **Holdings:** 210. **Computer Services:** Mailing lists. **Committees:** Editorial. **Publications:** *Congress Proceedings* (in English, Portuguese, and Spanish), biennial. **Advertising:** accepted ● *Revista Iberoamericana* (in English and Spanish), quarterly. **Advertising:** accepted. **Conventions/Meetings:** biennial meeting.

10426 ■ Lord Ruthven Assembly International Conference on the Fantastic in the Arts (LRA)
Address Unknown since 2008

Founded: 1988. **Members:** 75. **Membership Dues:** $15 (annual). **Staff:** 6. **Budget:** $500. **Description:** College and university scholars who research and publish information about the revenant archetype in the disciplines of literature, history, sociology, folklore, psychology, cinema, and the arts. (The term revenant, which means "one who returns after death or long absence," is used by the assembly primarily to refer to vampires, but can also refer to ghosts and zombies.) (The assembly's title is derived from the vampire Lord Ruthven, the major character in John Polidori's novel *The Vampyr*.). **Awards:** Lord Ruthven Award. **Frequency:** annual. **Type:** recognition. **Recipient:** for best article or book on revenant research. **Formerly:** (2005) Lord Ruthven Assembly. **Publications:** *Horror Gems* ● *The Ruthven Literary Bulletin*, quarterly. Includes book reviews and current research sources. **Conventions/Meetings:** annual International Conference on the Fantastic - meeting - always mid-March.

10427 ■ Mythopoeic Society (MS)
PO Box 320486
San Francisco, CA 94132-0486
E-mail: correspondence@mythsoc.org
URL: http://www.mythsoc.org
Contact: Edith Crowe, Corresponding Sec.

Founded: 1967. **Members:** 350. **Membership Dues:** regular in U.S., $20 (annual) ● regular outside U.S., $10 (annual). **Budget:** $25,000. **Local Groups:** 17. **Description:** Educational and literary organization devoted to the study, discussion, and enjoyment of myth, fantasy, and imaginative literature, especially the works of J.R.R. Tolkien, C.S. Lewis, and Charles Williams. **Awards:** Mythopoeic Fantasy Award. **Frequency:** annual. **Type:** recognition. **Recipient:** for adult and juvenile fantasy literature ● Mythopoeic Scholarship Award. **Frequency:** annual. **Type:** scholarship. **Recipient:** for scholarly work relating to Inklings studies or myth and fantasy studies. **Telecommunication Services:** information service, email discussion group. **Publications:** *Mythic Circle*, annual. Magazine. Contains fiction, fantasy, and science fiction. Functions as a writers' roundtable. Features art and poetry. **Price:** $10.00 for members; $8.00 for nonmembers and institutions. **Circulation:** 120 ● *Mythlore: A Journal of J.R.R. Tolkien, C.S. Lewis, Charles Williams, General Fantasy and Mythic Studies*, annual. Covers the genres of myth and fantasy. **Price:** $28.00 2 double issues (for nonmembers and institutions); $20.00 2 double issues (for members). ISSN: 0146-9339. **Circulation:** 569. Alternate Formats: online ● *Mythprint*, monthly. Newsletter. Covers conferences and other society activities in the genres of myth, fantasy, and imaginative literature. Includes calendar of events and reviews. **Price:** $20.00 /year for nonmembers. ISSN: 0146-9347. **Circulation:** 300 ● Proceedings. **Conventions/Meetings:** annual Mythcon - convention, with papers and panel discussions - always July or August.

10428 ■ Philolexian Society
Columbia Univ.
515 Lerner Hall
2920 Broadway
New York, NY 10027
Fax: (212)854-3434
E-mail: philo@philo.org
URL: http://www.columbia.edu/cu/philo
Contact: Allen Ginsberg, Pres.

Founded: 1802. **Description:** Individuals affiliated with Columbia University and interested in rhetoric and literary studies. Holds events, including open debates, the Annual Joyce Kilmer Memorial Bad Poetry Contest, lectures, and symposia. Compiles statistics. Operates speakers' bureau. **Libraries: Type:** by appointment only; open to the public. **Holdings:** 2,000; archival material, artwork, books, clippings, papers, photographs. **Awards:** Philolexian Centennial Washington Prize in Oratory. **Frequency:** quadrennial. **Type:** monetary. **Recipient:** to a student who delivered the best oration on a selected topic ● The Thomas Vinciguerra Award. **Frequency:** annual. **Type:** monetary. **Recipient:** to a graduating Philo senior who best exemplifies the spirit and commitment to the society evinced by its namesake. **Telecommunication Services:** electronic mail, philo@columbia.edu. **Committees:** Intersocietal Relations and Vigilante Justice; Nomenclature; Oatmeal; Obscure Etymology; Search-and-Destroy; Self-Aggrandizement. **Affiliated With:** Association of American Collegiate Literary Societies. **Publications:** *Surgam*, annual. Magazine. **Conventions/Meetings:** periodic congress ● weekly meeting - always New York City.

10429 ■ Philomathean Society of the University of Pennsylvania (PS)
Coll. Hall
Box H
Philadelphia, PA 19104
Ph: (215)898-8907
E-mail: moderator@philomathean.org
URL: http://www.philomathean.org/Welcome_to_Philo%21
Contact: Ramon Miyar, Moderator

Founded: 1813. **Members:** 3,000. **Membership Dues:** collegiate, $50 (biennial). **Staff:** 9. **Budget:** $20,000. **Description:** Literary society. Promotes interest in books and reading. Sponsors readings, lectures, debates, and symposia. Operates art gallery. Houses William Henry Harrison Presidential Library. Conducts research and education programs. **Libraries: Type:** reference. **Holdings:** 6,000; archival material, books, monographs, periodicals. **Subjects:** literature. **Awards:** Philomathean Book Award. **Frequency:** annual. **Type:** recognition. **Recipient:** for authors associated with the University of Pennsylvania or who are Philadelphia residents. **Computer Services:** database, membership records. **Boards:** Alumni Association; 175th Anniversary Endowment Trust. **Publications:** *Apocrypha of Etiquette: A Gentlemen's Guide*. Book. Contains information on manners and care of antiques. **Circulation:** 250 ● *Margin to Mainstream: The Broadening of the American Literary Canon*. Book ● *Old Philo*, annual. Newsletter. Includes society events/calendar. **Price:** free. **Circulation:** 3,000. **Advertising:** accepted ● *The Philomathean Anthology of Poetry in Honor of Daniel Hoffman*. Book. **Circulation:** 2,000 ● *Philomel*, annual. Magazine. **Price:** $5.00/copy. ISSN: 1052-4878. **Circulation:** 2,000. **Advertising:** accepted. **Conventions/Meetings:** biennial congress, for the Association of American Collegiate Literary Societies ● annual Edgar Allan Poe Vespertil - meeting ● biweekly meeting - during academic year ● meeting - 16/year ● annual Open Poetry Reading - meeting, for high school students - always March.

10430 ■ Society for the Study of Midwestern Literature (SSML)
c/o Mr. Roger J. Bresnahan, PhD, Sec.-Treas.
Michigan State Univ.
Dept. of Writing, Rhetoric and Amer. Cultures
235 Bessey Hall
East Lansing, MI 48824-1033

E-mail: bresnaha@msu.edu
URL: http://www.ssml.org
Contact: Mr. Roger J. Bresnahan PhD, Sec.-Treas.
Founded: 1971. **Members:** 500. **Membership Dues:** regular, $45 (annual) ● student, $25 (annual) ● emeritus, $35 (annual) ● institution, $90 (annual). **Staff:** 2. **Description:** Scholars, academics, poets, writers, journalists, and others interested in producing or studying Midwestern American literature. Supports members who study or contribute to the body of Midwestern literature; recognizes individuals who have made significant literary or scholarly contributions to the field. **Awards:** Gwendolyn Brooks Poetry Prize. **Frequency:** annual. **Type:** monetary. **Recipient:** for best poem read at annual conference ● Mark Twain. **Frequency:** annual. **Type:** recognition. **Recipient:** for significant contribution to Midwestern literature ● Mid-America Award. **Frequency:** annual. **Type:** recognition. **Recipient:** for significant contribution to study of Midwestern literature ● Midwestern Heritage Essay Prize. **Frequency:** annual. **Type:** monetary. **Recipient:** for best scholarly paper read at annual conference ● Paul Somers Creative Prose Prize. **Frequency:** annual. **Type:** monetary. **Recipient:** for best fiction or creative prose read at annual conference. **Publications:** *Mid America*, annual. Journal ● *Midwestern Miscellany*, semiannual. Journal. **Conventions/Meetings:** annual The Cultural Heritage of the Midwest & The Midwest Poetry Festival with the Midwest Independent Film Festival, readings of academic papers, poetry, fiction, and creative non-fiction; screening of student-made and independent films from the Midwest - always May, East Lansing, MI.

10431 ■ Society for the Study of Southern Literature (SSSL)
c/o Jeff Abernathy, Dean/Sec.-Treas.
Augustana Coll.
639 38th St.
Rock Island, IL 61201
E-mail: abernathy@augustana.edu
Contact: Jeff Abernathy, Dean/Sec.-Treas.
Founded: 1968. **Members:** 550. **Description:** Scholars and other interested persons. Seeks to encourage and enhance the study of Southern literature. Sponsors bibliographical projects, including a checklist of published writings by a representative group of Southern authors. Encourages publication of editions of Southern authors. **Awards:** C. Hugh Holman Award. **Frequency:** annual. **Type:** recognition. **Recipient:** for the best book of literary scholarship or literary criticism in the field of Southern literature ● Richard Beale Davis Award. **Frequency:** biennial. **Type:** recognition. **Recipient:** for distinguished lifetime contributions to Southern letters. **Committees:** Awards; Bibliography. **Publications:** *Society for the Study of Southern Literature—Newsletter*, semiannual. Includes bibliography. **Price:** included in membership dues. ISSN: 0197-8071. **Circulation:** 550. **Advertising:** accepted. Alternate Formats: online. **Conventions/Meetings:** biennial conference (exhibits) ● annual meeting, held in conjunction with American Literature Association and Modern Language Association of America.

10432 ■ Society for Textual Scholarship (STS)
c/o Prof. Robin G. Schulze, Exec. Dir.
Penn State Univ.
Dept. of English
117 Burrowes Bldg.
State College, PA 16802-6200
Ph: (814)863-0258
E-mail: rgs3@psu.edu
URL: http://www.textual.org
Contact: Prof. Robin G. Schulze, Exec. Dir.
Founded: 1979. **Members:** 600. **Membership Dues:** basic, $80. **Multinational. Description:** Scholars interested in interdisciplinary discussion of textual theory and practice. (Textual scholarship involves the discovery and cataloging of documents and establishment of and commentary on texts; scholarly editing involves examining various editions of works, how they have been changed from edition to edition, and determining how to best reflect an author's original intent.) Serves as a forum for interchange among textual scholars. **Awards:** Fredson Bowers Memorial Prize. **Frequency:** biennial. **Type:** monetary. **Recipient:** for the best article published in the fields of textual scholarship, textual editing, or editorial theory ● Richard Finneran Award. **Frequency:** biennial. **Type:** monetary. **Recipient:** for the best edition or book about editorial theory and/or practice. **Affiliated With:** Modern Language Association of America. **Publications:** *Textual Cultures*, biennial. Journal. Covers the fields of textual scholarship, editorial theory and practice. **Price:** free for members; $59.00 for nonmembers, and institutions. **Circulation:** 600. **Conventions/Meetings:** biennial conference (exhibits).

10433 ■ Vietnamese Nom Preservation Foundation (VNPF)
229 Beachers Brook Ln.
Cary, NC 27511
E-mail: info@nomfoundation.org
URL: http://nomfoundation.org
Contact: John Balaban, Pres.
Founded: 1999. **Languages:** English, Vietnamese. **Multinational. Description:** Preserves 1,000 years of writing in Chu Nom, the Chinese-like script that the Vietnamese used to record their own language and its vast heritage of poetry, history, medicine and religion. Seeks assistance in funding for projects supporting Chu Nom. **Awards:** Nom Scholarships in Vietnam. **Frequency:** annual. **Type:** scholarship. **Recipient:** for American PhD candidates including Nom in their dissertation work and for high school and college students in Vietnam who wish to learn Nom. **Telecommunication Services:** electronic mail, tbalaban@earthlink.net.

10434 ■ Western Literature Association (WLA)
Utah State Univ.
English Dept.
3200 Old Main Hill
Logan, UT 84322-3200
Ph: (435)797-1603
Fax: (435)797-4099
E-mail: wal@cc.usu.edu
URL: http://www.usu.edu/westlit
Contact: Robert Thacker, Exec. Sec.-Treas.
Founded: 1966. **Members:** 550. **Membership Dues:** student, $25 (annual) ● individual, $30 (annual) ● couple, $35 (annual) ● sustaining, $50 (annual) ● patron, $100 (annual) ● sponsor, $75 (annual) ● compatriot, $500 (annual) ● friend, $1,000 (annual). **Staff:** 6. **Description:** Persons interested in the scholarly study of Western American literature. **Awards:** Delbert and Edith Wylder Award. **Frequency:** annual. **Type:** recognition. **Recipient:** for distinguished longtime service to Western studies ● Distinguished Achievement Award. **Frequency:** annual. **Type:** recognition ● Don D. Walker Prize. **Frequency:** annual. **Type:** recognition. **Recipient:** for the best essay published in Western American Studies ● Frederick Manfred Creative Writing Award. **Frequency:** annual. **Type:** recognition. **Recipient:** for best submission to the conference in creative writing ● J. Golden Taylor Award. **Frequency:** annual. **Type:** recognition. **Recipient:** for the best essay by a graduate student, submitted to WLA Conference ● Thomas J. Lyon Book Award. **Frequency:** annual. **Type:** recognition. **Recipient:** for outstanding book in American literary criticism. **Computer Services:** Mailing lists. **Publications:** *Literary History of the American West*. Book. Alternate Formats: online ● *Updating the Literary West*. Book. **Price:** $25.00 ordered direct from WLA ● *Western American Literature*, quarterly. Journal. Contains literary criticism; includes book reviews and annual bibliography of research on Western American literature; also includes Western art. **Price:** included in membership dues; $22.00 /year for nonmembers; $65.00 /year for institutions. ISSN: 0043-3462. **Circulation:** 1,200. **Advertising:** accepted. Alternate Formats: microform ● *Western Literature Association—Directory*, biennial. **Price:** available to members only. **Conventions/Meetings:** annual conference, includes book exhibits by publishers of books concerning the American West (exhibits) - always October.

Lithuanian

10435 ■ Institute of Lithuanian Studies (ILS)
5600 S Claremont Ave.
Chicago, IL 60636-1039
Ph: (773)434-4545
Fax: (773)434-9363
URL: http://www.lithuanianresearch.org/eng/lithinstitute/lithinstitutehome.htm
Contact: Jonas Rackauskas PhD, Pres.
Founded: 1951. **Members:** 135. **Membership Dues:** $10 (annual). **Description:** Seeks to sponsor and encourage research on Lithuanian language, literature, folklore, history, and other fields related to Lithuania and its culture. **Committees:** Bibliography; History; Linguistics; Literature; Psychology. **Divisions:** Ethnography; Lithuanian Language; Lithuanian Pre-history. **Publications:** *Lithuanian Studies*, periodic. Booklets. Contains studies and archival materials in Lithuanian. **Price:** $10.00 for Vol. II; $15.00 for Vol. III, IV, and V ● Proceedings, biennial. **Price:** $15.00 for 1971 papers; $20.00 for 1981 papers ● Bibliographies. **Price:** $10.00 paperback; $20.00 hardcover ● Monographs. **Price:** $10.00 ● Also publishes scholarly books on Lithuanian literature, and history. **Conventions/Meetings:** biennial meeting (exhibits).

10436 ■ Lituanus Foundation
47 W Polk St., Ste.100-300
Chicago, IL 60605
Ph: (312)341-9396
Fax: (312)341-9396
E-mail: admin@lituanus.org
URL: http://www.lituanus.org
Contact: Mr. Arvydas Tamulis, Managing Ed.
Founded: 1954. **Members:** 11. **Languages:** English, Lithuanian. **Description:** Organizes, sponsors, and publishes research material on the language, history, politics, geography, economics, folklore, literature, and arts of Lithuania and the Baltic States. **Awards: Type:** fellowship ● **Type:** grant ● **Type:** scholarship. **Publications:** *Lituanus: Lithuanian Quarterly Journal of Arts and Sciences*. Includes articles, poetry, photographs of art, book reviews, a current events feature, conference news, research reports, and statistics. **Price:** $15.00 /year for institutions; $10.00/ year for others. ISSN: 0024-5089. **Circulation:** 3,500. Alternate Formats: microform. **Conventions/Meetings:** annual conference.

Macedonian

10437 ■ Macedonian Arts Council
PO Box 23905
New York, NY 10023
Ph: (212)799-0009
Fax: (815)301-3893
E-mail: info@macedonianarts.org
URL: http://www.macedonianarts.org
Contact: Pavlina Proevska, Exec. Dir./Founder
Founded: 1991. **Membership Dues:** individual, $35 (annual) ● family, $75 (annual) ● non-profit, $150 (annual) ● corporate, $1,000 (annual). **Multinational. Description:** Represents individuals dedicated to the promotion and affirmation of the Macedonian cultural heritage. Raises public awareness and understanding of the cultural tradition, art, language and literature of Macedonia. **Telecommunication Services:** electronic mail, pproevska@macedonianarts.org. **Publications:** Newsletter. Alternate Formats: online.

Marine

10438 ■ Great Lakes Historical Society (GLHS)
c/o Inland Seas Maritime Museum
PO Box 435
Vermilion, OH 44089-0435

Ph: (440)967-3467
Free: (800)893-1485
Fax: (440)967-1519
E-mail: glhs1@inlandseas.org
URL: http://www.inlandseas.org
Contact: Christopher H. Gillcrist, Exec. Dir.
Founded: 1944. **Members:** 3,000. **Membership Dues:** regular (family), $49 (annual) ● senior couple (over 65), $32 (annual) ● contributing, $100 (annual) ● sustaining, $64 (annual) ● benefactor, $200 (annual) ● patron, $500 (annual) ● life, $2,500 ● student, $15 (annual). **Staff:** 8. **Description:** Libraries, historical societies, museums, schools, and individuals interested in the Great Lakes region. Promotes interest in discovering and preserving material on the Great Lakes and the Great Lakes area of the U.S. and Canada, such as books, documents, records, and objects relating to the history, geology, commerce, and folklore of the Great Lakes. Conducts research programs; maintains museum. **Libraries: Type:** reference. **Holdings:** 6,000; business records, papers, photographs. **Subjects:** Great Lakes and shipping. **Publications:** *The Chadburn*, quarterly. Newsletter. **Price:** included in membership dues. **Circulation:** 3,000. **Advertising:** accepted ● *Inland Seas*, quarterly. Journal. Includes articles relating to the past and present history of the Great Lakes. Includes Great Lakes calendar, book reviews, and roundtable. **Price:** included in membership dues. ISSN: 0020-1537. **Circulation:** 3,000. **Advertising:** accepted. Alternate Formats: CD-ROM. **Conventions/Meetings:** semiannual meeting (exhibits) - always May and October in Vermilion, OH ● annual Model Shipwrights Competition.

10439 ■ Great Lakes Maritime Institute (GLMI)
PO Box 1990
Dearborn, MI 48121
Ph: (313)852-4051
URL: http://www.glmi.org
Contact: John Polacsek, Coordinating Dir.
Founded: 1952. **Members:** 500. **Membership Dues:** regular, $40 (annual) ● benefactor, $100 (annual) ● life, $350 ● library/school/association, $20 (annual). **Description:** Amateur and professional marine historians. Collects information, records, photographs, and memorabilia of Great Lakes marine history and fosters an interest in the subject through publication. Supports accession and promotion program of the Dossin Great Lakes Museum, Belle Isle, Detroit, MI which maintains Ship Information Center data and research resources on Great Lakes history, including information on over 5000 ships and a photograph and negative collection. **Convention/Meeting:** none. **Libraries: Type:** not open to the public. **Publications:** *Telescope Magazine*, biennial.

10440 ■ Historic Naval Ships Association (HNSA)
PO Box 401
Smithfield, VA 23431-0401
Ph: (757)356-9422
Fax: (757)356-9433
E-mail: info@hnsa.org
URL: http://hnsa.org/index.htm
Contact: Jeffrey S. Nilsson, Exec. Dir.
Founded: 1966. **Members:** 608. **Membership Dues:** regular, $25 (annual) ● friend, $75 (annual) ● patron, $150 (annual) ● life, $500. **Staff:** 7. **Budget:** $84,100. **Multinational. Description:** Seeks to enhance the abilities of each of its member ship museums and memorials to educate the public on the rich naval maritime heritage for which the ships serve as living testimony. Provides services to benefit all of the ships that they could not begin to realize as single entities; this support is provided by means of printed materials, telephonic and internet communication, publications, annual conferences and personal visits. **Libraries: Type:** not open to the public. **Holdings:** 100; books, periodicals. **Subjects:** historic naval ships. **Awards:** Casper J. Knight Award. **Frequency:** annual. **Type:** recognition. **Recipient:** for support to the association and its objectives ● Educator Award. **Frequency:** annual. **Type:** recognition. **Recipient:** to a staff member who performed at a superior level in furthering the education program of the organization ● Henry A. Vadnais, Jr. Award. **Frequency:** annual. **Type:** recognition. **Recipient:** to a staff person working in the areas of curatorship, collections management, exhibits or registration with outstanding service ● Historic Naval Ship Maintenance Award. **Frequency:** annual. **Type:** recognition. **Recipient:** to staff or volunteer person who has provided exemplary work on a daily or part time maintenance and preservation of a historic naval ship ● Old Walrus Award. **Frequency:** annual. **Type:** recognition. **Recipient:** for demonstrated knowledge of the Historic Naval Ship Fleet ● William J. Diffey Award. **Frequency:** annual. **Type:** recognition. **Recipient:** to a departing director of the organization. **Computer Services:** Mailing lists. **Formerly:** (1994) Historic Naval Ships Association of North America. **Publications:** *Anchor Watch*, quarterly. Newsletter. Reports on the naval museums and memorial sites that house ships of historic value. Seeks to preserve and present naval history. **Price:** included in membership dues. **Circulation:** 650. **Advertising:** accepted ● *Historic Naval Ships Association Executive Director Memorandums*, periodic ● *Historic Naval Ships Visitors' Guide*, biennial. Contains a listing of historic naval ship museums in U.S., U.K., Australia, Canada, France, Greece, The Netherlands, Germany, Norway, Russia & Turkey. **Price:** $10.50 ● *Membership Application Brochure* ● *Museum Operations Handbook*, periodic. **Conventions/Meetings:** annual conference, four-day conference covering topics pertaining to management of historic naval ship museums (exhibits).

10441 ■ Mystic Seaport
PO Box 6000
Mystic, CT 06355-0990
Ph: (860)572-0711 (860)572-5315
Free: (888)973-2767
E-mail: info@mysticseaport.org
URL: http://www.mysticseaport.org
Contact: Douglas H. Teeson, Pres.
Founded: 1929. **Members:** 25,000. **Membership Dues:** individual, $34 (annual) ● dual, $54 (annual) ● family/grandparent, $70 (annual) ● mariner, $94 (annual) ● sustaining, $199 (annual) ● associate, $300 (annual) ● benefactor/library, $500 (annual) ● America and the Sea Society (minimum), $1,000 (annual). **Staff:** 325. **Budget:** $20,000,000. **Description:** Presents the American experience from a maritime perspective. Maintains recreated seaport community reminiscent of Age of Sail; 500 vessels and small craft; 19th century sailing ships; planetarium; displays of small boats, many of which are the only surviving examples of such craft; working preservation shipyard. **Libraries: Type:** reference. **Holdings:** 70,000; artwork, photographs. **Subjects:** maritime history, boats, buildings, ship plans, models, tools. **Awards:** Founder's Award. **Frequency:** annual. **Type:** recognition. **Recipient:** for exceptional record of service to the museum. **Telecommunication Services:** TDD, (860)572-5319. **Committees:** Audit; Communications; Curatorial; Development; Education; Exhibitions; Higher Education; Information Management; Information Services; Interpretation; Investment; Library; Maritime Studies; Museum Store; Photography; Publications; Watercraft; Yachting. **Departments:** Development/Membership; Food Services; Watercraft Preservation. **Programs:** Summer Seamanship Training; Williams College - Mystic Seaport Studies. **Formerly:** (1997) Mystic Seaport Museum. **Publications:** Magazine, quarterly. **Price:** available to members only. **Circulation:** 25,000 ● Books. **Conventions/Meetings:** semiannual Maritime History Symposium - festival ● annual meeting - always in Mystic, CT ● annual Small Craft Weekend - meeting.

10442 ■ National Aquarium Society (NAS)
U.S. Department of Commerce Bldg., Rm. B-077
14th St. and Constitution Ave. NW
Washington, DC 20230
Ph: (202)482-2825
Fax: (202)482-4946
E-mail: info@nationalaquarium.com
URL: http://www.nationalaquarium.com
Contact: Mr. Robert Ramin, Exec. Dir.
Founded: 1873. **Members:** 500. **Membership Dues:** family, $40 (annual) ● individual, $15 (annual) ● couple, $25 (annual) ● family plus, $50 (annual). **Staff:** 5. **Description:** Operates The National Aquarium, which was previously administered by the U.S. Federal Government. Develops educational programs for the public; provide information regarding aquariums. Cooperates with other aquarium and wildlife societies. Conducts school tours. Sponsors Shark Day. **Libraries: Type:** reference. **Publications:** *Fish Lines*, quarterly. Newsletter. **Price:** included in membership dues.

10443 ■ North American Society for Oceanic History (NASOH)
Dept. of History
Texas Christian Univ.
Box 297260
Fort Worth, TX 76129
E-mail: hattendj@nwc.navy.mil
URL: http://www.nasoh.org
Contact: Dr. John B. Hattendorf, Pres.
Founded: 1974. **Members:** 200. **Membership Dues:** dual, $25 (annual) ● student, $18 (annual) ● regular, institutional, $65 (annual). **Description:** Professional historians and laypeople interested in the history of the sea, with emphasis on North America. Promotes the dissemination of information among individuals in North America who are interested in the history of the sea and inland waterways. Fosters a general awareness of historical matters pertaining to the sea and its relationship to North America. Encourages marine education. Protects marine archaeological sites. **Awards:** John Lyman Book Award in American Naval Biography. **Frequency:** annual. **Type:** recognition. **Recipient:** for significant contribution to naval and maritime literature ● John Lyman Book Award in American Naval History. **Frequency:** annual. **Type:** recognition. **Recipient:** for significant contribution to naval and maritime literature ● John Lyman Book Award in Canadian Maritime History. **Frequency:** annual. **Type:** recognition. **Recipient:** for significant contribution to naval and maritime literature ● John Lyman Book Award in U.S. Maritime History. **Frequency:** annual. **Type:** recognition. **Recipient:** for significant contribution to naval and maritime literature ● K. Jack Baver Award for Distinguished Service. **Frequency:** annual. **Type:** recognition. **Recipient:** for meritorious contribution to the aims of the society. **Affiliated With:** American Historical Association. **Publications:** *Membership Roster*, periodic. Membership Directory ● *NASOH Newsletter*, 3/year. Includes book reviews. **Price:** included in membership dues. **Conventions/Meetings:** annual conference and symposium - always spring.

10444 ■ Oceanic Navigation Research Society (ONRS)
PO Box 1641
Palm Springs, CA 92263-1641
Ph: (760)325-5398
E-mail: onrs@earthlink.net
Contact: Charles Ira Sachs, Pres.
Founded: 1977. **Members:** 300. **Membership Dues:** regular, $35 (annual) ● regular, outside North America (surface mail), $40 (annual) ● regular, outside North America (air mail), $45 (annual) ● student, $30 (annual). **Staff:** 1. **Budget:** $14,000. **Regional Groups:** 1. **Local Groups:** 1. **Multinational. Description:** Works for the preservation of the history of the ocean liner and the Golden Era of transatlantic run. Focuses on the Atlantic routes traveled from 1840's to the 1930's and conducts research, educational, and charitable programs. Maintains speakers' bureau and schedules periodic ship tours and lecture cruises. **Libraries: Type:** reference; by appointment only. **Holdings:** archival material, books, clippings, periodicals, video recordings. **Subjects:** history of steamship and ocean liner passenger travel. **Publications:** *Ship to Shore*, quarterly. Journal. Contains articles concerning transatlantic travel. **Price:** included in membership dues. ISSN: 0738-6575. **Circulation:** 1,000. **Advertising:** accepted.

10445 ■ Penobscot Marine Museum (PMM)
PO Box 498
Searsport, ME 04974-0498
Ph: (207)548-2529

Fax: (207)548-2520
E-mail: museumoffices@penobscotmarinemuseum.org
URL: http://www.penobscotmarinemuseum.org
Contact: Niles Parker, Exec. Dir.

Founded: 1936. **Members:** 900. **Membership Dues:** student, $20 (annual) ● friend, $35 (annual) ● supporter, $50 (annual) ● contributor, $125 (annual) ● sponsor, $250 (annual) ● patron, $500 (annual) ● benefactor, $1,000 (annual) ● President's Circle, $2,000 (annual). **Staff:** 25. **Budget:** $600,000. **Description:** Works to preserve, exhibit, and document the maritime history of Penobscot Bay. Maintains exhibit buildings: Old Town Hall (exhibits on Downeaster Sailing Ships); Captain Merithew House (ship portraits and models, whaling memorabilia, and Working the Bay, a permanent exhibit of marine paintings of Thomas and James Buttersworth); Fowler-True-Ross House (American and Oriental furnishings of the 19th and 20th century); Douglas and Margaret Carver Memorial Art Gallery; Classroom Building; Small Craft Barn (work boats of the Penobscot Bay); Stephen Phillips Memorial Library Building. Offers specialized education program and children's services. **Libraries: Type:** open to the public. **Holdings:** 7,000. **Subjects:** maritime and genealogical history. **Telecommunication Services:** electronic mail, nparker@penobscotmarinemuseum.org. **Publications:** *Bay Chronicle*, 3/year. Newsletter. **Price:** included in membership dues ● *Forty-Four Ship Portraits at PMM*. Monograph ● *Lace and Leaves*. Catalog ● *Seaport Sea Captains*. Annual Report. **Conventions/Meetings:** annual Penobscot Bay History Conference.

10446 ■ South Street Seaport Museum (SSSM)

12 Fulton St.
New York, NY 10038
Ph: (212)748-8600 (212)748-8750
Fax: (212)748-8610
E-mail: membership@southstseaport.org
URL: http://www.southstseaport.org
Contact: Frank J. Sciame, Chm.

Founded: 1967. **Members:** 4,000. **Membership Dues:** senior citizen/student, $45 (annual) ● individual, $60 (annual) ● dual, $75 (annual) ● national/international, $50 (annual) ● family, $125 (annual) ● captain, $500 (annual) ● Cape Horn Society, $1,000 (annual) ● Navigators' Society, $2,500 (annual) ● Boatswain, $300 (annual) ● Pilot Society, $5,000 (annual) ● Commodore Society, $10,000 (annual). **Staff:** 50. **Budget:** $3,000,000. **Description:** Individuals and families interested in maritime history and the history of New York City. The state maritime museum of New York preserves and interprets the maritime history of New York City and state. Maintains 11 blocks of 19th century commercial, port-related buildings, five historic ships at Piers 15 and 16, and maritime art and artifacts. To date, the museum includes piers, ships, exhibition galleries, a children's center, boat building shop, a maritime crafts center, and shops. Conducts schooner sails, internships, teacher orientations, and special programs. Operates book publishing program. **Libraries: Type:** reference. **Holdings:** 7,000; photographs. **Committees:** Curatorial; Education; Library and Archives; Marketing; Operations; Programming; Public Affairs; Visitor Services; Volunteers; Waterfront. **Publications:** *Beacon*, semiannual. Newsletter ● *The Broadside*, 3/year ● *Seaport Magazine*, quarterly. **Conventions/Meetings:** periodic lecture ● periodic seminar ● periodic tour.

10447 ■ Titanic Historical Society (THS)

208 Main St.
PO Box 51053
Indian Orchard, MA 01151-0053
Ph: (413)543-4770
Fax: (413)583-3633
E-mail: titanicinfo@titanichistoricalsociety.org
URL: http://www.titanic1.org
Contact: Edward S. Kamuda, Pres.

Founded: 1963. **Members:** 6,000. **Membership Dues:** gold, $100 (annual) ● silver, $60 (annual) ● bronze, $50 (annual). **Multinational. Description:** Commits to preserve the history of RMS Titanic and the White Star Line; maintains the Titanic Museum archive of pre-discovery artifacts and documents relating to the disaster. **Formerly:** (1975) Titanic Enthusiasts of America. **Publications:** *Echoes In The Night*. Book. Features biography of a third class survivor. ● *Titanic Commutator*, quarterly. Journal. Provides information on the wreck of the Titanic; contains survivor stories, research notes, and information on other passenger vessels. **Price:** included in membership dues. **Circulation:** 7,000. **Advertising:** accepted ● *The White Star Line An Illustrated History 1869-1934*. Book. Contains biographical information. **Conventions/Meetings:** annual conference (exhibits) - summer and/or April.

10448 ■ Titanic International Society

c/o Robert Bracken, Treas.
47 Van Blarcom Ave.
Midland Park, NJ 07432
Ph: (814)899-5438
E-mail: dshuttle401@aol.com
URL: http://www.titanicinternationalsociety.org
Contact: Charles Haas, Pres.

Founded: 1989. **Members:** 1,000. **Membership Dues:** individual in U.S., $45 (annual) ● individual outside U.S., $50 (annual). **Staff:** 10. **Description:** Works to preserve the history of the Titanic and the people who sailed aboard Her. Provides research/reference materials to all deep ocean dives to Titanic's wreck site; assists in artifact recovery identification and educational displays. Sponsors research, educational, and charitable programs. **Libraries: Type:** reference. **Holdings:** archival material. **Subjects:** RMS Titanic and other ocean liners. **Awards:** Lifetime Achievement. **Frequency:** annual. **Type:** recognition. **Formerly:** (1998) Titanic International. **Publications:** *Voyage*, quarterly. Journal. Profiles a range of topics regarding nautical history; includes research and photographs of the Titanic and its passengers and crew. **Price:** included in membership dues. ISSN: 1054-9269. **Circulation:** 1,000. **Advertising:** accepted. **Conventions/Meetings:** annual convention (exhibits) - usually East Coast.

10449 ■ USS Constellation Museum

301 E Pratt St.
Pier 1
Baltimore, MD 21202-3134
Ph: (410)539-1797
Fax: (410)539-6238
E-mail: administration@constellation.org
URL: http://www.constellation.org
Contact: Christopher Rowsom, Exec. Dir.

Founded: 1970. **Members:** 700. **Membership Dues:** individual (Petty Officer), $30 (annual) ● family (Ship's Crew), $50 (annual) ● family (Sailing Master), $100 (annual) ● family (Captain), $250 (annual) ● family (Commodore), $500 (annual) ● family (Admiral), $1,000 (annual). **Staff:** 24. **Budget:** $1,200,000. **Description:** Serves as the steward of the sloop-of-war USS Constellation, the last all sail warship built by the US Navy, the only US Navy ship active during the Civil War still afloat, the largest example of Chesapeake Bay shipbuilding in existence, and one of the largest wooden sailing ships remaining in the world. Built in 1854, the Constellation is a National Historic Landmark, is on the official national registry of historic places, and is open to the public daily as a museum and historic shrine in Baltimore's Inner Harbor. **Computer Services:** database ● online services. **Telecommunication Services:** electronic mail, daldridge@constellation.org. **Formerly:** Constellation Historical Preservation Corp.; (1997) USF Constellation Foundation; (2004) Constellation Foundation. **Publications:** *The Deck Log*, quarterly. Newsletter. **Price:** included in membership dues. **Circulation:** 3,500. **Conventions/Meetings:** quarterly board meeting.

10450 ■ USS St. Louis CL-49 Association

c/o Jack R. Jones, Ed.
1112 N 18th St.
Cambridge, OH 43725
Ph: (740)432-5305
E-mail: jriones79@roadrunner.com
URL: http://ussstlouis.com
Contact: Jack R. Jones, Ed.

Founded: 1976. **Members:** 500. **Membership Dues:** ship crew, associate, $10 (annual) ● life, $50. **Staff:** 10. **Budget:** $3,000. **Description:** Individuals who were aboard the USS St. Louis during its U.S. Navy lifetime (1939-46), their families, and other supporters. Exhibits presented at Soldiers Memorial in St. Louis, MO, U.S. Marine Corps Historical Museum, U.S. Navy Academy Museum, and USS Arizona Memorial Visitors Center in Pearl Harbor. Maintains speakers' bureau, Nimitz Museum. **Publications:** *Hubble Bubble*, quarterly. Newsletter. **Price:** available to members only. **Circulation:** 500. **Conventions/Meetings:** annual conference and reunion (exhibits).

10451 ■ Whaling Museum Society (WMS)

PO Box 25
Cold Spring Harbor, NY 11724
Ph: (631)367-3418
Fax: (631)692-7037
E-mail: info@cshwhalingmuseum.org
URL: http://www.cshwhalingmuseum.org
Contact: Paul B. De Orsay, Exec. Dir.

Founded: 1936. **Members:** 1,000. **Membership Dues:** individual, $35 (annual) ● family, $45 (annual) ● associate, $250 (annual) ● sponsor, $500 (annual) ● benefactor, $5,000 (annual) ● life, $1,000 ● patron, $100 (annual) ● business, $100-$499 (annual) ● corporate, $500-$2,499 (annual) ● guardian, $2,500-$5,000 (annual). **Staff:** 10. **Budget:** $500,000. **Description:** Maintains a whaling museum containing a 19th century whale boat, whaling irons, vessel equipment, prints, photographs, and oil portraits relating to whaling and whalemen, dioramas, a collection of 300 sailors' knots, splices, and working knots, 700 pieces of scrimshaw and models of whaling vessels, and a permanent exhibition on the history of Long Island whaling. Sponsors educational programs and maritime workshops for schools and adult groups, and in-service workshops for teachers. **Libraries: Type:** reference. **Holdings:** 8,500; books. **Subjects:** zoological, historical, statistical, narrative accounts of actual and fictional whaling cruises and incidents, logbooks of whaling vessels, books of account, other similar material. **Also Known As:** Cold Spring Harbor Whaling Museum. **Publications:** *A Whaling Account*, 3/year. Newsletter. **Price:** included in membership dues ● *Calendar of Events*, periodic ● *Cold Spring Harbor: Rediscovering History in Streets* ● *In Their Hours of Ocean Leisure: Scrimshaw in the Cold Spring Harbor Whaling Museum*. Monograph ● Annual Report, annual. **Conventions/Meetings:** annual meeting - usually October in Cold Spring Harbor, NY.

Marxism

10452 ■ Society for the Philosophical Study of Marxism (SPSM)

c/o Peter Amato, Coor.
Drexel Univ.
3141 Chestnut St.
Dept. of English and Philosophy
5030 MacAlister Hall
Philadelphia, PA 19104
Ph: (215)382-1448
E-mail: peterama@drexel.edu
URL: http://www.pages.drexel.edu/~pa34/spsm_website.htm
Contact: Peter Amato, Coor.

Founded: 1962. **Members:** 125. **Description:** Individuals interested in research and discussion of Marxism. Seeks to provide a forum for interested philosophers to clarify issues and discuss problems pertaining to Marxism. Organizes panel discussions and promotes research on topics related to Marxism including humanism, ethics, alienation, anthropology, social and political theory, capitalism, socialism, and peace.

Mathematics

10453 ■ Euler Society
c/o Mary Ann McLoughlin, Treas.
Dept. of Mathematics
Coll. of St. Rose
432 Western Ave.
Albany, NY 12203
E-mail: mcloughm@mail.strose.edu
URL: http://www.eulersociety.org
Contact: Robert E. Bradley, Pres.
Membership Dues: regular, $50 (annual). **Description:** Encourages scholarly contributions analyzing the life and works of the Swiss mathematician and physicist Leonhard Euler. Promotes translations of his writings into English. Explores current studies in the mathematical sciences that were built upon Euler's work. **Telecommunication Services:** electronic mail, bradley@adelphi.edu. **Publications:** Newsletter, 3-4 times a year. Alternate Formats: online.

Media

10454 ■ Independent Media Arts Preservation (IMAP)
c/o Electronic Arts Intermix
535 W 22nd St., 5th Fl.
New York, NY 10011
Ph: (212)560-7259
Fax: (212)337-0679
E-mail: imap@imappreserve.org
URL: http://www.imappreserve.org
Contact: Dara Meyers-Kingsley, Exec. Dir.
Founded: 2002. **Membership Dues:** individual, $25 (annual) ● nonprofit (budget up to $150K), $50 (annual) ● nonprofit (budget from $151-500K), $75 (annual) ● nonprofit (budget from $501K-$1M), $125 (annual) ● nonprofit (budget over $1M), $175 (annual). **Description:** Works for the preservation of non-commercial electronic media. **Projects:** Catalog-ing. **Conventions/Meetings:** Introduction to Media Preservation - workshop.

10455 ■ Pacific Islanders in Communications (PIC)
1221 Kapiolani Blvd., Ste.6A-4
Honolulu, HI 96814
Ph: (808)591-0059
Fax: (808)591-1114
E-mail: info@piccom.org
URL: http://www.piccom.org
Contact: Ruth Bolan, Exec. Dir.
Founded: 1991. **Multinational. Description:** Aims to support, advance and develop Pacific Island media content and talent. Promotes deeper understanding of the history, culture and contemporary challenges of Pacific Island. Funds and distributes film, video and new media. Provides training and professional development to media talent. Conducts broadcast services and community outreach. **Awards: Frequency:** annual. **Type:** scholarship. **Recipient:** for students pursuing certifications or degrees in media/and or communications from accredited schools, colleges and universities. **Telecommunication Services:** electronic mail, rbolan@piccom.org. **Publications:** *StoryBoard*, 3/year. Magazine. Features information about digital technology and insights into industry happenings. Alternate Formats: online.

Medieval

10456 ■ Center for Medieval and Renaissance Studies (CEMERS)
PO Box 6000
Binghamton, NY 13902-6000
Ph: (607)777-2730
E-mail: ssticca@binghamton.edu
URL: http://www.binghamton.edu/cemers
Contact: Sandro Sticca, Dir./Ed.
Founded: 1966. **Members:** 75. **Staff:** 3. **Description:** Medievalists on the staff of Binghamton University and individuals from other campuses. Seeks to foster Medieval and Renaissance studies through research and academic programs. Sponsors seminars, faculty research projects, and special courses of instruction. Awards B.A. for Medieval Studies to undergraduates and certificates to graduate students completing the special program. Has purchased microfilms of the entire Vatican Arabic Collection with St. Louis Vatican Library, 800 documents of the special archives of a Tyrolian family, and slides from the Bodleian, Morgan, and other libraries; also maintains microfilm holdings of Medieval English public records. Holds public records. **Libraries: Type:** reference. **Holdings:** archival material. **Subjects:** Tyrolian family, Medieval English. **Formerly:** (1998) Center for Medieval and Early Renaissance Studies. **Publications:** *Mediaevalia*, biennial. Journal. **Price:** $25.00 institution; $20.00 individual; $15.00 student ● Brochures ● Manuals. **Conventions/Meetings:** annual meeting (exhibits) - usually late October/early November in Binghamton, NY.

10457 ■ Center for Medieval and Renaissance Studies (CMRS)
Ohio State Univ.
308 Dulles Hall
230 W 17th Ave.
Columbus, OH 43210-1361
Ph: (614)292-7495
Fax: (614)292-1599
E-mail: cmrs@osu.edu
URL: http://cmrs.osu.edu
Contact: Richard Firth Green, Dir.
Founded: 1965. **Members:** 110. **Staff:** 4. **Description:** Faculty members at Ohio State University who teach or conduct research in medieval and/or Renaissance studies. Teaches graduate students in special interdisciplinary seminars. Instructs undergraduates in interdisciplinary courses; also offers undergraduates a course of major study. Sponsors coordinated lecture services each year. **Awards:** Stanley J. Kahrl Award. **Frequency:** annual. **Type:** recognition. **Recipient:** for best undergraduate and graduate papers on a Medieval or Renaissance topic. **Affiliated With:** Centers and Regional Associations. **Publications:** *Nouvelles/Nouvelles*, 2/quarter. Newsletter. Reports on the "humanistic disciplines pertaining to the Medieval and Renaissance periods." Includes calendar of events and faculty publications. **Price:** free. **Circulation:** 450. Alternate Formats: online. **Conventions/Meetings:** annual conference.

10458 ■ Centers and Regional Associations (CARA)
c/o The Medieval Academy of America
104 Mt. Auburn St., 5th Fl.
Cambridge, MA 02138-5019
Ph: (617)491-1622
Fax: (617)492-3303
E-mail: speculum@medievalacademy.org
URL: http://www.medievalacademy.org/committees/committee_cara.htm
Contact: Prof. Robert E. Bjork, Chm.
Founded: 1968. **Members:** 101. **Membership Dues:** regular, $70 (annual) ● contributing, $100 (annual) ● student, unemployed/part-time, $30 (annual) ● retired, $50 (annual) ● life, $1,500 ● regular outside U.S., $80 (annual) ● contributing outside U.S., $110 (annual) ● sustaining outside U.S., $160 (annual) ● student, unemployed/part-time outside U.S., $40 (annual) ● retired outside U.S., $60 (annual) ● life (in U.S.), $1,600. **Description:** Represents institutes, graduate and undergraduate centers, programs, committees, research libraries and regional associations specializing in medieval studies. Promotes and transmits the scholarly research and pedagogical innovations carried on by its member groups. Seeks to promote institutional cooperation among its member institutions and associations. Sponsors the re-issue of out-of-print texts for medieval and Renaissance programs through the Subcommittee on Medieval Academy Reprints for Teaching. **Affiliated With:** Medieval Academy of America. **Supersedes:** Association of Centers of Medieval and Renaissance Studies. **Conventions/Meetings:** annual meeting - fall ● annual Working Session - meeting - always fall.

10459 ■ Charles Homer Haskins Society (CHHS)
c/o Frederick Suppe, Treas.
Ball State Univ.
Dept. of History
Muncie, IN 47306
Ph: (765)285-8783
Fax: (765)285-5612
E-mail: fsuppe@bsu.edu
URL: http://www.haskins.cornell.edu
Contact: Frederick Suppe, Treas.
Founded: 1982. **Members:** 200. **Membership Dues:** regular, $50 (annual) ● student, $30 (annual) ● sustaining, $65 (annual) ● student, 20 (annual) ● regular, 30 (annual) ● sustaining, 40 (annual) ● student, 4,500 (annual) ● regular, 6,000 (annual) ● sustaining, 9,000 (annual). **Multinational. Description:** International society of medieval historians. Named in honor of Charles Homer Haskins (1870-1937), leading scholar of medieval studies in America. Promotes the study of Viking, Anglo-Saxon, Anglo-Norman, and early Angevin history and the history of neighboring areas and peoples. Organizes and sponsors scholarly sessions and annual reception at the International Congress on Medieval Studies. **Awards:** Denis Bethell Award. **Frequency:** annual. **Type:** recognition. **Recipient:** to a junior scholar ● **Frequency:** annual. **Type:** recognition. **Recipient:** for the best paper by a junior scholar. **Affiliated With:** American Historical Association. **Formerly:** (1983) Haskins Society for Viking, Anglo-Saxon, Anglo-Norman, and Angevin History. **Publications:** *Anglo-Norman Anonymous*, quarterly. Newsletter. Includes directory. **Price:** free for members ● *The Haskins Society Journal*, annual. Includes scholarly papers. **Price:** $50.00 per issue (with Newsletter included). **Conventions/Meetings:** annual conference (exhibits).

10460 ■ International Anchoritic Society (IAS)
c/o Susannah Mary Chewning, Founder
Union County Coll.
Dept. of English
1033 Springfield Ave.
Cranford, NJ 07016
Ph: (908)709-7182
E-mail: chewning@ucc.edu
URL: http://www.swan.ac.uk/english/gender/IAS%20home.htm
Contact: Susannah Mary Chewning, Founder
Founded: 2003. **Multinational. Description:** Promotes the study of medieval religious enclosure, eremeticism, and anchoritism. Encourages scholarly research related to anchoritic literature, devotion, mysticism, and other subjects. Provides a forum for interchange of ideas and new research pertaining to medieval enclosure. **Publications:** Newsletter, annual.

10461 ■ International Center of Medieval Art (ICMA)
The Cloisters
Ft. Tryon Park
New York, NY 10040
Ph: (212)928-1146
Fax: (212)928-9946
E-mail: icma@medievalart.org
URL: http://www.medievalart.org
Contact: Mary B. Shepard, Pres.
Founded: 1956. **Members:** 1,300. **Membership Dues:** student, $20 (annual) ● institution, $75 (annual) ● individual outside U.S., $60 (annual) ● individual in U.S., $55 (annual) ● independent scholar/retiree, $45 (annual) ● joint, $80 (annual) ● contributor, $150 (annual) ● patron, $300 (annual) ● sustainer, $600 (annual) ● benefactor, $1,200 (annual) ● council, $5,000 (annual). **Staff:** 2. **Languages:** English, French, German, Italian, Spanish. **Description:** Scholars, students, and others from 30 countries interested in medieval art and civilization; libraries and other institutions. Promotes the study and understanding of medieval art and civilization between 325 and 1500 A.D. Facilitates interchange of ideas on medieval art. Makes available results of new research. Sponsors excavation of medieval sites. Conducts lectures and symposia. **Awards:** Comput-

erization in the Visual Arts. **Frequency:** annual. **Type:** monetary ● Travel Stipends. **Frequency:** annual. **Type:** monetary. **Publications:** *Gesta* (in English, French, and German), semiannual. Journal. Contains scholarly writings on art of the Middle Ages. **Price:** included in membership dues. ISSN: 0016-920X. **Circulation:** 1,100. **Advertising:** accepted ● *International Census of Doctoral Dissertations in Medieval Art, 1982-93.* Book. **Price:** $9.50/copy for members ● *Romanesque and Gothic Sculpture in American Public Collections.* Book. **Price:** $82.00/volume ● Newsletter, 3/year. Provides information on medieval art exhibits, conferences, and publications. **Price:** included in membership dues. **Circulation:** 1,400. **Conventions/Meetings:** annual meeting, in conjunction with the College Art Association of America.

10462 ■ Medieval Academy of America (MAA)
104 Mt. Auburn St., 5th Fl.
Cambridge, MA 02138
Ph: (617)491-1622
Fax: (617)492-3303
E-mail: speculum@medievalacademy.org
URL: http://www.medievalacademy.org
Contact: Paul E. Szarmach, Exec. Dir./Ed.
Founded: 1925. **Members:** 4,400. **Membership Dues:** active in North America, $70 (annual) ● contributing in North America, $100 (annual) ● student, unemployed, part-time employed, retired, or joint in North America, $30 (annual) ● life in North America, $1,500 ● contributing outside North America, $110 (annual) ● active outside North America, $80 (annual) ● sustaining in North America, $150 (annual) ● sustaining outside North America, $160 (annual) ● student, unemployed, part-time employed outside North America, $40 (annual) ● retired in North America, $50 (annual) ● retired outside North America, $60 (annual) ● joint in North America, $25 (annual) ● joint outside North America, $35 (annual) ● life outside North America, $1,600. **Staff:** 5. **Description:** Educators, scholars, and others with an avocational interest in the study of the Middle Ages (A.D. 500-1500). Promotes research, publication, and instruction in medieval records, art, archaeology, history, law, literature, music, philosophy, and science, social and economic institutions, and other aspects of medieval civilization. **Awards:** CARA Award for Excellence in Teaching. **Frequency:** annual. **Type:** recognition. **Recipient:** for a member teacher ● Elliot Prize. **Frequency:** annual. **Type:** recognition. **Recipient:** for best first article by a medievalist in the U.S. or Canada ● Haskins Medal. **Frequency:** annual. **Type:** medal. **Recipient:** for a distinguished publication in medieval studies ● John Leyerle - CARA Prize. **Frequency:** annual. **Type:** recognition. **Recipient:** for doctoral research of a Medieval Academy member ● John Nicholas Brown Prize. **Frequency:** annual. **Type:** recognition. **Recipient:** for best first book. **Computer Services:** Mailing lists, individuals or institutions (international). **Telecommunication Services:** electronic mail, pes@medievalacademy.org. **Publications:** *Medieval Academy Books* ● *Speculum: A Journal of Medieval Studies*, quarterly. **Price:** included in membership dues. ISSN: 0038-7134. **Circulation:** 5,770. **Advertising:** accepted ● *Speculum Anniversary Monographs.* **Conventions/Meetings:** annual meeting (exhibits) - always spring.

10463 ■ Society for Creative Anachronism (SCA)
PO Box 360789
Milpitas, CA 95036-0789
Ph: (408)263-9305
Free: (800)789-7486
Fax: (408)263-0641
E-mail: directors@sca.org
URL: http://www.sca.org
Contact: Jason Williams, Chm.
Founded: 1966. **Members:** 25,000. **Membership Dues:** sustaining/international, $35 (annual) ● associate, $20 (annual) ● family (minimum), $10 (annual). **Regional Groups:** 12. **Local Groups:** 700. **Description:** People interested in learning about the Middle Ages by means of theoretical and practical research into various aspects of the culture and technology of the time. Primary activity is staging events that provide an opportunity for members to exercise and display skills in medieval music, dancing, cooking, and martial arts, and to display artifacts such as clothing, manuscripts, armor, pavilions, and furniture which members have created or commissioned. Seeks to provide a total environment in which everyone can be a participant rather than a spectator. Encourages private research into pre-17th life and publishes the results; conducts classes, and seminars as well as living history events such as revels, tournaments, and "wars". Provides exhibits and demonstrations for schools and other groups. **Awards: Type:** recognition. **Recipient:** for general excellence and specific achievement in craftsmanship and performance, martial arts, and administration. **Telecommunication Services:** electronic mail, chairman@sca.org. **Divisions:** College of Arms; Office of the Arts and Sciences; Office of the Marshal; Office of the Steward. **Publications:** *Compleat Anachronist*, quarterly. Pamphlet. **Price:** $15.00 for members ● *The Known World Handbook of the Current Middle Ages* ● *Monthly Regional Newsletter* ● *Tournaments Illuminated*, quarterly. Magazine. **Price:** $15.00 for members. **Advertising:** accepted ● Books.

10464 ■ Society for Medieval and Renaissance Philosophy (SMRP)
c/o Prof. Jeremiah Hackett, Sec.-Treas.
Univ. of South Carolina
Dept. of Philosophy
Columbia, SC 29208
E-mail: hackettj@gwm.sc.edu
URL: http://www.smrphil.org
Contact: Prof. Jeremiah Hackett, Sec.-Treas.
Founded: 1979. **Members:** 318. **Membership Dues:** regular, $10 (annual) ● contributing (minimum), $15 (annual) ● life, $150 ● associate/student, $5 (annual). **Budget:** $2,000. **Description:** Professors and scholars of medieval philosophy, literature, history, and theology; sponsors sessions at major philosophy conferences. Presents scholarly papers on medieval philosophy. **Publications:** *John Wippel, The Metaphysical Thought of Thomas Aquinas: From Finite Being to Uncreated Being* ● Newsletter, semiannual. Alternate Formats: online. **Conventions/Meetings:** annual executive committee meeting and meeting, held in conjunction with American Philosophical Association.

Meditation

10465 ■ Foundation of Human Understanding (FHU)
PO Box 1000
Grants Pass, OR 97528
Ph: (541)956-6700
Free: (800)877-3227
Fax: (541)956-6705
E-mail: fhusupport@fhu.com
URL: http://www.fhu.com
Contact: Roy Masters, Pres./Founder
Founded: 1963. **Staff:** 25. **Description:** Religious/educational organization. Provides instruction, through books and recordings, in a Judeo-Christian meditation exercise. Operates a call-in radio program nationwide and throughout Europe and Canada known as "How Your Mind Can Keep You Well." Maintains ranch-retreat in Oregon, where spiritual guidance and training in practical skills are provided. Offers audiotapes of lectures and books (by Roy Masters) on subjects such as "controlling negative emotions" and "healing through understanding one's relationship to stress". **Publications:** *Adam & Eve SINdrome.* Book. **Price:** $20.00 ● *Beyond the Known.* Book. **Price:** $20.00 ● *Eat No Evil.* Book. **Price:** $20.00 ● *Finding God in Physics.* Book. **Price:** $20.00 ● *How to Conquer Negative Emotions.* Book. **Price:** $20.00 ● *How to Conquer Suffering Without Doctors.* Book. **Price:** $20.00 ● *How to Survive Your Parents.* Book. **Price:** $20.00 ● *How Your Mind Can Keep You Well.* Book. **Price:** $20.00 ● *The Hypnosis of Life.* Book. **Price:** $20.00 ● *New Insights*, monthly. Newsletter. Provides self-help for the human condition. **Price:** $35.00/year; $20.00/year (online). Alternate Formats: online ● *The Secret Power of Words.* Book. **Price:** $20.00 ● *Secrets of a Parallel Universe.* Book. **Price:** $20.00 ● *Surviving the Comfort Zone.* Book. **Price:** $20.00 ● *Understanding Sexuality.* Book. **Price:** $20.00.

Mediterranean

10466 ■ Mediterranean Studies Association (MSA)
PO Box 212
East Sandwich, MA 02537
E-mail: btaggie@umassd.edu
URL: http://www.mediterraneanstudies.org
Contact: Benjamin F. Taggie, Exec. Dir./Treas.
Founded: 1994. **Membership Dues:** regular, $50 (annual) ● editorial board, $40 (annual). **Multinational. Description:** Promotes the scholarly study of the Mediterranean region in all aspects and disciplines. Encourages particular studies in the ideas and ideals of Western Mediterranean cultures from Late Antiquity to the Enlightenment. Provides a forum for scholarly meetings, classes, and workshops. **Telecommunication Services:** electronic mail, sousa@ku.edu. **Publications:** *Mediterranean Studies*, annual. Journal. **Price:** included in membership dues. **Conventions/Meetings:** annual international conference.

Methodist

10467 ■ General Commission on Archives and History of the United Methodist Church (GCAH)
PO Box 127
Madison, NJ 07940
Ph: (973)408-3189
Fax: (973)408-3909
E-mail: research@gcah.org
URL: http://www.gcah.org
Contact: Robert Williams PhD, Gen. Sec.
Founded: 1968. **Staff:** 4. **Budget:** $850,000. **Regional Groups:** 5. **Local Groups:** 64. **Description:** Seeks to gather and preserve historical data, records, books, archives, and other property related to the origin and development of the United Methodist Church; to stimulate and encourage historical research and appreciation. Provides genealogical service. Operates museum on the Methodist Church, the Evangelical United Brethren Church, and their antecedents. **Libraries: Type:** reference; open to the public. **Holdings:** 70,000; archival material, books. **Subjects:** the Methodist Church, Evangelical United Brethren Church and their antecedents, documents from general church agencies of the United Methodist Church and from general church leaders. **Awards:** The Jesse Lee Prize. **Frequency:** quadrennial. **Type:** monetary. **Recipient:** for a winning book-length monograph in Methodist history ● John H. Ness Memorial Award. **Frequency:** annual. **Type:** monetary. **Recipient:** for seminary students who have been enrolled in the United Methodist courses and who have produced the best manuscripts on a United Methodist history subject ● Racial/Ethnic History Research Grant. **Frequency:** annual. **Type:** grant. **Recipient:** for research in the history and heritage of ethnic groups in the American United Methodist tradition ● Women in United Methodist History Research Grant. **Frequency:** annual. **Type:** grant. **Recipient:** for research projects relating specifically to the history of women in the United Methodist Church or its antecedents ● Women in United Methodist History Writing Award. **Frequency:** annual. **Type:** monetary. **Recipient:** for original manuscript (not longer than 20 pages) on history of women in the United Methodist Church or its antecedents. **Telecommunication Services:** electronic mail, rwilliams@gcah.org. **Committees:** Archives and Libraries; Heritage Landmarks; History and Interpretation. **Affiliated With:** Historical Society of the United Methodist Church; World Methodist Historical Society. **Formed by Merger of:**

Historical Society of the Evangelical United Brethren Church; Association of Methodist Historical Societies. **Formerly:** (1981) Commission on Archives and History of the United Methodist Church. **Publications:** *Methodist History*, quarterly. Journal. **Price:** $20.00/year in U.S.; $22.00/year outside U.S.; $10.00/year for students in U.S.; $12.00/year for students outside U.S. ISSN: 0026-1238. **Circulation:** 700 ● *Methodist Union Catalog* ● Booklets ● Directory, quadrennial. **Conventions/Meetings:** quadrennial Historical Convocation - conference and meeting.

Migration

10468 ■ Center for Migration Studies of New York (CMS)

27 Carmine St.
New York, NY 10014
Ph: (718)351-8800 (718)351-0232
Fax: (718)667-4598
E-mail: jfugolo@cmsny.org
URL: http://www.cmsny.org
Contact: Rev. Joseph Fugolo, Exec. Dir.

Founded: 1964. **Membership Dues:** friend, $75 (annual). **Staff:** 12. **Budget:** $550,000. **Languages:** English, French, German, Italian, Portuguese, Spanish. **Description:** Encourages and facilitates the study of sociological, demographic, economic, historical, legislative, and pastoral aspects of human migration, refugee movements, and ethnic group relations. Conducts research projects on contemporary immigration problems. **Libraries: Type:** open to the public. **Holdings:** 27,000; archival material, papers, periodicals. **Subjects:** migration, ethnicity, refugees. **Awards:** CMS Immigration and Refugee Policy Award. **Frequency:** annual. **Type:** recognition. **Telecommunication Services:** electronic mail, sales@cmsny.org. **Publications:** *CMS Newsletter*, semiannual. Covers the activities in the center's programs; reports on research projects, publications, conferences, library/archives developments, and grants. **Price:** free. ISSN: 8756-4467. **Circulation:** 950 ● *In Defense of the Alien*. Proceedings. Focuses on issues affecting U.S. immigration legislation, legal practice, immigration laws reform, refugee policy, and U.S. foreign policy. **Price:** $19.95. ISSN: 0275-634X. **Circulation:** 1,200 ● *International Migration Review*, quarterly. Journal. Covers the sociodemographic, economic, historical, political, and legislative aspects of human migration and refugee movements. **Price:** $42.00 /year for individuals (the Americas); 33.00 /year for individuals (rest of the world); $250.00 /year for institutions (the Americas); 153.00 /year for institutions (rest of the world). ISSN: 0197-9183. **Circulation:** 2,500. **Advertising:** accepted. Alternate Formats: microform ● Papers ● Offers various volumes and occasional papers on immigration policy, immigrant groups, and refugees. **Conventions/Meetings:** annual Legal Conference on Immigration and Refugee Policy (exhibits) ● periodic seminar.

10469 ■ Research Foundation for Jewish Immigration (RFJI)

570 7th Ave.
New York, NY 10018
Ph: (212)921-3871
Fax: (212)575-1918
Contact: Dennis Rohr, Archivist

Founded: 1971. **Staff:** 1. **Languages:** English, German. **Description:** Educational foundation established for the preparation, research, writing, and editing of the history of German-speaking immigrants of the Nazi period and their world-wide resettlement and acculturation. Holds jointly with the Institut fur Zeitgeschichte in Munich, Federal Republic of Germany, archives of 25,000 biographies of outstanding emigres of the Nazi period. Maintains oral history collection on German-Jewish immigration to the U.S. since 1933. Maintains master file. **Affiliated With:** American Federation of Jews From Central Europe. **Publications:** *International Biographical Dictionary of Central European Emigres, 1933-1945* ● *Jewish Immigrants of the Nazi Period in the U.S.A.*.

Military History

10470 ■ Air Force Historical Foundation (AFHF)

1535 Command Dr., Ste.A-122
Andrews AFB, MD 20762-7002
Ph: (301)736-1959
Fax: (301)981-3574
E-mail: afhf@earthlink.net
URL: http://www.afhistoricalfoundation.com
Contact: Lt. Gen. (Ret.) Michael A. Nelson USAF, Pres.

Founded: 1953. **Members:** 2,500. **Membership Dues:** individual, friend/gift, $45 (annual) ● institutional, $55 (annual) ● college student, cadet, junior officer, enlisted personnel, $35 (annual) ● life (age 55 and older), $300 ● life (age 45-54), $600 ● life (age 35-44), $900 ● life (age 35 under), $1,200. **Staff:** 3. **Description:** Preserves the history of American air power and the annals of the U.S. Air Force, its components, subsidiaries, and affiliates. Collects and disseminates historical information on air subjects. **Awards:** Air Force Academy Air Power History Award. **Frequency:** annual. **Type:** recognition. **Recipient:** for outstanding article on the history of air power ● Air Force ROTC Scholarship Award. **Frequency:** annual. **Type:** scholarship. **Recipient:** for outstanding academic and military achievement ● Air Water College Award, Research and Writing. **Frequency:** annual. **Type:** monetary. **Recipient:** to a student at the Air Water College who writes the best aerospace report ● The General Bryce Poe II AFIT Award. **Frequency:** annual. **Type:** monetary. **Recipient:** to the author(s) of the thesis having the most significant contribution to the understanding of the historical factors affecting an Air Force or DOD problem ● Logistics Lessons Learned Award. **Frequency:** annual. **Type:** recognition. **Recipient:** for best article in the Air Force Journal of Logistics ● School of Advanced Air and Space Studies Thesis Award. **Frequency:** annual. **Type:** monetary. **Recipient:** to a student who writes the best aerospace report of major historical interest to the United States Air Force during the year. **Publications:** *A Few Great Captains*. Book. Presents an accurate and detailed history of United States military air power from its genesis through 1939. **Price:** $19.95/copy, plus shipping and handling ● *The Air Force*. Book. Features highly illustrated history of the United States Air Force. **Price:** $60.00/copy for members; $75.00/copy for nonmembers ● *Air Power History*, quarterly. Journal. Covers all aspects of aerospace history and air power. **Price:** $35.00 /year for individuals; $45.00 /year for institutions. **Circulation:** 7,000. **Advertising:** accepted. Also Cited As: *Aerospace Historian* ● *Chasing the Silver Bullet: USAF Weapons Development from Vietnam to Desert Storm*. Book. Features the unprecedented detail of the evolution of the Air Force's principal weapons systems since the Korean War. **Price:** $37.95/copy. **Conventions/Meetings:** annual Guide Post for the US Military - conference and symposium - always mid-September.

10471 ■ Army Historical Foundation (AHF)

2425 Wilson Blvd.
Arlington, VA 22201
Ph: (703)522-7901
Free: (800)506-2672
Fax: (703)522-7929
E-mail: ahfdirector@aol.com
URL: http://www.armyhistory.org
Contact: Creighton W. Abrams, Exec. Dir.

Founded: 1983. **Members:** 3,000. **Membership Dues:** charter, $100 (annual) ● sustaining, $50 (annual) ● individual, $25 (annual) ● life, $1,500. **Staff:** 5. **Budget:** $290,000. **Description:** Seeks to preserve the history of the American soldier by building a National Army Museum at Fort Belvoir, Virginia, that will house artifacts, the Army Art Collection, and the Center for Military History. Supports Army historical research programs, museums and artifact conservation. **Libraries: Type:** open to the public. **Holdings:** 1,000; books, periodicals. **Subjects:** US Army history. **Awards:** Distinguished Article Award. **Frequency:** annual. **Type:** grant ● Distinguished Book Award. **Frequency:** annual. **Type:** grant. **Recipient:** nomination to selection committee ● Museum of Excellence Award. **Frequency:** annual. **Type:** grant. **Computer Services:** Online services, research information on US Army history. **Publications:** *On Point*, quarterly. Magazine. Contains coverage of foundation sponsored events, news pieces, and historical anecdotes. **Price:** free. **Circulation:** 3,500. **Conventions/Meetings:** annual meeting.

10472 ■ Black Military History Institute of America (BMHIA)

c/o Col. William A. De Shields, Exec. Off.
PO Box 1134
Fort Meade, MD 20755
Ph: (410)757-4250
Contact: Col. William A. De Shields, Exec. Off.

Founded: 1987. **Members:** 60. **Budget:** $50,000. **Regional Groups:** 1. **Description:** Individuals interested in promoting the military achievements of black Americans and publicizing other aspects of black history. Seeks to: provide archival facilities to collect, preserve, and exhibit materials pertaining to military history; motivate and support underprivileged youths by using military role models as a source of inspiration; foster a spirit of camaraderie and goodwill among all persons sharing an interest in community involvement programs for the underprivileged. Sponsors slide lectures and photographic exhibit. Maintains speakers' bureau. **Publications:** Newsletter, quarterly. **Conventions/Meetings:** monthly meeting - always third Thursday.

10473 ■ Coast Defense Study Group (CDSG)

634 Silver Dawn Ct.
Zionsville, IN 46077-9088
E-mail: berhowma@insightbb.com
URL: http://www.cdsg.org
Contact: Glen Williford, Trustee

Founded: 1985. **Members:** 500. **Membership Dues:** regular, in U.S., $35 (annual) ● regular, outside U.S. (air mail), $68 (annual). **Description:** Individuals and organizations. Promotes the study of coast defense, fortifications and artillery and their history, architectural technology, strategic and tactical employment, personnel, military units, and evolution. Encourages related education, technical research and documentation, preservation, and accurate site interpretation. Assists groups interested in the preservation and interpretation of coast defense sites. Conducts tours. Reprints historic volumes on coast defense. **Awards:** CDSG Fund. **Frequency:** periodic. **Type:** grant. **Recipient:** for preservation and interpretation efforts concerning seacoast defenses around the United States. **Computer Services:** Online services, historical information. **Publications:** *Coast Defense Journal*, quarterly. Contains assorted articles on coast defense and coast artillery. **Price:** included in membership dues. ISSN: 1085-9675. **Circulation:** 500. Alternate Formats: CD-ROM. Also Cited As: *CD Journal* ● Also publishes conference notes from previous study conferences and reprint of key historical books. **Conventions/Meetings:** annual conference, covers coast defense and related subjects (exhibits).

10474 ■ De Re Militari: The Society for Medieval Military History

c/o Carroll Gillmor, Sec.-Treas.
PO Box 784
Salt Lake City, UT 84111
E-mail: deremilitari@hotmail.com
URL: http://www.deremilitari.org
Contact: Stephen Morillo, Pres.

Founded: 1991. **Members:** 200. **Membership Dues:** individual, $35 (annual). **Languages:** English, French, Italian, Spanish. **Multinational. Description:** Represents professors, graduate students, publishers, and scholars with interest in medieval and early modern warfare. Promotes the study of military affairs and warfare in the Middle Ages and the Early Modern Period. Facilitates exchange of information and ideas on pre-modern military affairs. **Awards:** Verbruggen Prize. **Frequency:** annual. **Type:** recognition. **Recipient:** for the best book on medieval military history. **Publications:** *Journal of Medieval Military History*, annual. **Price:** included in membership dues.

10475 ■ Great War Association (GWA)
c/o Rob Zienta, Pres.
4601 Embassy Cir., No. 203
Owings Mills, MD 21117
Ph: (443)394-7605
E-mail: rzienta@comcast.net
URL: http://www.great-war-assoc.org
Contact: Rob Zienta, Pres.
Description: Strives to keep alive the history of the Great War. Fosters and perpetuates the memory of all those who served in the first World War from all nations. Educates members and the general public through the sponsoring of living history re-creations and encouraging research into the lives and culture of the armies of 1914-1918. **Publications:** *On the Wire*, published 2 to 3 times a year. Newsletter. Contains general announcements for the members and upcoming events. Alternate Formats: online.

10476 ■ International Naval Research Organization (INRO)
5905 Reinwood Dr.
Toledo, OH 43613-5605
Ph: (419)472-1331
E-mail: info@warship.org
URL: http://www.warship.org
Contact: David Sullivan, Business Office Mgr.
Founded: 1963. **Members:** 2,500. **Membership Dues:** in U.S., $29 (annual) ● in Canada, $31 (annual) ● outside U.S. and Canada, $37 (annual) ● contributing, in U.S., $32 (annual) ● sustaining, in U.S., $34 (annual) ● benefactor, in U.S., $42 (annual) ● patron, in U.S., $50 (annual) ● contributing, in Canada, $34 (annual) ● sustaining, in Canada, $36 (annual). **Staff:** 18. **Multinational. Description:** Individuals interested in warships and the world's navies; maritime and historical libraries. Provides exchange of information, history, and pictures of all navies and their ships. Sells books and photographs. **Departments:** Book Service; Information Service; Warship Photo Negative Bank; Warship Photo Service. **Formerly:** (1976) Naval Records Club. **Publications:** *Warship International*, quarterly. Journal. Covers naval history and warships from 1860 to the present. Includes summaries of the careers of various classes of warships; contains book reviews. **Price:** included in membership dues; $5.00/issue, for nonmembers in U.S.; $6.25/issue, for nonmembers in Canada. ISSN: 0043-0374. **Circulation:** 3,000. **Advertising:** accepted. **Conventions/Meetings:** biennial meeting.

10477 ■ Marine Corps Heritage Foundation (MCHF)
307 5th Ave.
Quantico, VA 22134
Ph: (703)640-7965
Free: (800)397-7585
Fax: (703)640-9546
E-mail: info@marineheritage.org
URL: http://www.marineheritage.org
Contact: Lt. Gen. Ron Christmas USMC, Pres.
Founded: 1979. **Members:** 80,000. **Membership Dues:** first to fight, $35 (annual) ● eagle, globe, anchor, $50 (annual) ● flag raiser, $100 (annual) ● esprit de corp, $250 (annual) ● Semper Fidelis Society, $500 (annual). **Staff:** 24. **Budget:** $13,700,000. **Description:** Individuals and institutions interested in the preservation of Marine Corps history. Promotes the Marine Corps' historical role and encourages the study of its history and traditions. Works to preserve, perpetuate, and fund publications and displays of manuscripts, books, relics, and pictures focusing on the history and tradition of the Marine Corps. Supports museum; sponsors Research Grant Fund and educational programs such as the annual doctoral dissertation and masters theses fellowships. Construction funding and program support for the National Museum of the Marine Corps, Quantico, VA. **Libraries: Type:** not open to the public. **Awards:** Geiger Award. **Frequency:** annual. **Type:** recognition. **Recipient:** to the author of the best article published during the preceding year in Marine Corps gazette in the field of Marine Corps aviation ● Greene Award. **Frequency:** annual. **Type:** recognition. **Recipient:** to the author of the outstanding nonfiction book published during the preceding year pertinent to Marine Corps history ● Hatch Award. **Frequency:** annual. **Type:** recognition. **Recipient:** for the best videotape dealing with historical or current Marine Corps subjects ● Heinl Award. **Frequency:** annual. **Type:** recognition. **Recipient:** to the author of the best article pertinent to Marine Corps history published in a newspaper, magazine, journal or other periodical during the preceding year ● Magruder Award. **Frequency:** annual. **Type:** recognition. **Recipient:** to an individual, institution, or organization for excellence in depicting Marine Corps history in exhibits or displays in a museum ● Thomason Award. **Frequency:** annual. **Type:** recognition. **Recipient:** for excellence in the fine or applied arts, including photography, in depicting the historic or contemporary Marine Corps. **Committees:** Awards; Museum Store; Volunteer Services. **Formerly:** (1998) Marine Corps Historical Foundation. **Publications:** *Legacy*, quarterly. Newsletter. **Conventions/Meetings:** annual meeting.

10478 ■ Naval Historical Foundation (NHF)
1306 Dahlgren Ave. SE
Washington Navy Yard
Washington, DC 20374-5055
Ph: (202)678-4333 (202)678-4431
Free: (888)880-0102
Fax: (202)889-3565
E-mail: nhfwny@navyhistory.org
URL: http://www.navyhistory.org
Contact: Capt. Charles T. Creekman USN, Exec. Dir.
Founded: 1926. **Members:** 1,020. **Membership Dues:** life, $500 ● active, $25 (annual). **Staff:** 8. **Budget:** $750,000. **Description:** Dedicated to preserving and promoting the Navy's proud heritage, including the principal donation point for personal papers relating to naval history, a dynamic nationwide oral history program, a means for supporting the Navy's historical collections and programs, especially the Navy Museum. Provides historic research, and document and photo reproduction services. **Awards:** National History Day. **Frequency:** annual. **Type:** monetary. **Telecommunication Services:** information service, research inquiries can be made by phone. **Publications:** *History Monograph Series*, periodic. Monographs. Includes Navy-related history. ● *Naval Historical Foundation Manuscript Collection Catalog* ● *Pull Together*, semiannual. Newsletter. **Price:** included in membership dues. **Circulation:** 2,300 ● Pamphlets. **Conventions/Meetings:** annual meeting (exhibits) - always June, Washington, DC.

10479 ■ Order of the Indian Wars (OIW)
PO Box 1650
Johnstown, CO 80534
E-mail: majorreno@sbcglobal.net
URL: http://www.indianwars.com
Contact: Mike Koury, Chm.
Founded: 1979. **Members:** 200. **Membership Dues:** individual, $30 (annual). **Description:** Represents professional and informal historians interested in the study of the frontier conflicts between the Indians and the white settlers, the Indians and the US Army and the conflicts among Indian tribes themselves; the period of interest includes the time from the early settlement of the United States to 1890. Provides the opportunity for individuals to meet and discuss common areas of interest concerning the Indian Wars. **Publications:** *Special Orders*, semiannual. Newsletter. Covers contemporary news and historical material relating to the Indian Wars of North America. **Price:** included in membership dues. **Conventions/Meetings:** annual assembly and lecture (exhibits) - late summer or early fall, always near Indian Wars site.

10480 ■ Sharkhunters International
PO Box 1539
Hernando, FL 34442
Ph: (352)637-2917
Free: (866)258-2188
Fax: (352)637-6289
E-mail: sharkhunters@earthlink.net
URL: http://www.sharkhunters.com
Contact: Harry Cooper, Pres./Founder
Founded: 1983. **Members:** 7,000. **Membership Dues:** regular, $50 (annual). **Staff:** 45. **For-Profit. Description:** Dedicated to finding and preserving the history of the submarine services of all nations. Conducts research programs; compiles statistics; operates museum; maintains speakers' bureau. **Libraries: Type:** reference. **Holdings:** 3,000; archival material, audio recordings, books, clippings, periodicals, video recordings. **Subjects:** submarine history. **Publications:** *KTB Magazine*, monthly. Contains facts and figures, questions and answers, and diagrams and specs of submarines. **Price:** included in membership dues. ISSN: 1046-7335. **Circulation:** 6,600. **Advertising:** accepted. **Conventions/Meetings:** annual convention.

10481 ■ Society of Ancient Military Historians (SAMH)
c/o Dr. Lee L. Brice, Pres.
Morgan Hall 445
Dept. of History
Western Illinois Univ.
Macomb, IL 61455-1390
Ph: (309)298-1053
Fax: (309)298-2540
E-mail: ll-brice@wiu.edu
URL: http://ccat.sas.upenn.edu/rrice/samh.html
Contact: Dr. Lee L. Brice, Pres.
Membership Dues: individual, $5 (annual). **Description:** Promotes the study of warfare in the Ancient World. **Telecommunication Services:** electronic mail, jroth@email.sjsu.edu. **Publications:** *Res Militares*, annual. Newsletter.

10482 ■ Society for Military History (SMH)
c/o Journal of Military History
George C. Marshall Lib.
Virginia Military Inst.
Lexington, VA 24450
Ph: (540)464-7468
Fax: (540)464-7330
E-mail: jmhsmh@vmi.edu
URL: http://www.smh-hq.org
Contact: Dr. Robert H. Berlin, Exec. Dir.
Founded: 1933. **Members:** 2,400. **Membership Dues:** individual in U.S., Canada, Mexico, $50 (annual) ● student in U.S., Canada, Mexico, $25 (annual) ● sustaining in U.S., Canada, Mexico, $100 (annual) ● individual - overseas, $60 (annual) ● student - overseas, $35 (annual) ● sustaining - overseas, $110 (annual). **Staff:** 9. **Budget:** $90,000. **Description:** Persons interested in the writing and study of military history and the preservation of manuscripts, publications, relics, and other materials related to military history. Maintains book review, editorial, and membership offices at the George C. Marshall Library, Virginia Military Institute in Lexington, VA. **Awards:** Distinguished Book Award. **Frequency:** annual. **Type:** recognition. **Recipient:** for the two best books in military history ● Moncado Prizes. **Frequency:** annual. **Type:** recognition. **Recipient:** for the four most significant articles in the Society's journal ● Russel F. Weigley Graduate Student Travel Grant Award. **Frequency:** annual. **Type:** grant. **Recipient:** to support participation in the Society's annual meeting ● Samuel Eliot Morrison Prize. **Frequency:** annual. **Type:** recognition. **Recipient:** for contribution to military history ● Victor Gondos Memorial Service Award. **Frequency:** annual. **Type:** recognition. **Recipient:** for service to the SMH. **Committees:** Automation; Awards; Finance; Long-Range Planning; Nominating; Program; Tellers. **Affiliated With:** American Historical Association; National Coalition for History; Organization of American Historians. **Absorbed:** Order of Indian Wars of the United States. **Formerly:** American Military History Foundation; (1991) American Military Institute. **Publications:** *Headquarters Gazette*, quarterly. Newsletter. **Price:** included in membership dues ● *Journal of Military History*, quarterly. Contains articles, book reviews, and bibliographic materials. **Price:** included in membership dues. **Circulation:** 2,500.

Advertising: accepted. Alternate Formats: online ● *Symposia Proceedings*, periodic ● Bibliographies ● Membership Directory, biennial. **Price:** included in membership dues ● Also publishes indexes. **Conventions/Meetings:** annual meeting and conference (exhibits).

10483 ■ Trireme Trust U.S.A. (TTUSA)
c/o Ford Weiskittel, Pres.
803 S Main St.
Geneva, NY 14456
E-mail: dudhia@atm.ox.ac.uk
URL: http://www.atm.ox.ac.uk/rowing/trireme
Contact: Ford Weiskittel, Pres.
Founded: 1987. **Members:** 500. **Staff:** 2. **Description:** Represents historians, engineers, rowers, classicists, and others interested in ancient oared ships and naval power. Encourages historical research and experimental archaeology on the Greek Navy's reconstructed trireme warship, Olympias, dated 5th century BC. (A trireme is an ancient galley having 3 banks of oars.) Promotes participation in the semiannual sea trials of the Olympias. Sponsors exhibitions at archaeological conferences. Maintains speakers' bureau. **Publications:** *Newsletter, Trireme Trust USA*, semiannual. Includes historical research and reports on the sea trials of the Olympias trireme. **Price:** included in membership dues. **Circulation:** 500 ● Also distributes books, slides, and educational materials. **Conventions/Meetings:** seminar.

10484 ■ U.S. Cavalry Association and Memorial Research Library
PO Box 2325
Fort Riley, KS 66442-0325
Ph: (785)784-5797
Fax: (785)784-5797
E-mail: cavalry@flinthills.com
URL: http://www.uscavalry.org
Contact: Robert J. Smith, Acting Exec. Dir.
Founded: 1976. **Members:** 2,000. **Membership Dues:** regular, charter, heritage, modern cavalry, living history, $30 (annual) ● overseas, $60 (annual) ● organization, $45 (annual) ● corporate, $500 (annual) ● life - individual, $400 ● life - overseas, $600. **Staff:** 4. **Description:** Former horse cavalrymen and their descendants; horsemen and others interested in the history of the cavalry. Seeks to obtain and preserve the uniforms, weapons, and equipment used by the cavalry soldier, as well as the traditions and customs of the horse cavalry. Sponsors the U.S. Cavalry Museum and the U.S. Cavalry Memorial Research Library at Ft. Riley, KS, and other museums that are cavalry-oriented. Operates BIOCAV, which uses a data bank to record and analyze the wide range of cavalry and lore. Maintains informational services. Plans to collect biographies of horse cavalrymen and the history of cavalry regiments. **Libraries: Type:** open to the public. **Holdings:** 5,000; archival material, artwork, books, periodicals. **Subjects:** U.S. Cavalry. **Awards:** ROTC Cavalry Award. **Frequency:** annual. **Type:** recognition ● U.S. Cavalry Associations Pony Club Award. **Frequency:** annual. **Type:** recognition. **Recipient:** for highest placed members. **Committees:** Artifact; Field Artillery; Historical; Library; Medical Support; Museum; Veterinary. **Formerly:** (1993) U.S. Horse Cavalry Association. **Publications:** *The Cavalry Journal*, quarterly. Magazine. **Price:** included in membership dues. ISSN: 1074-0252 ● *Crossed Sabers*, quarterly. Newsletter. **Conventions/Meetings:** Annual Bivouac, National Cavalry Competition - conference and competition, reenactors from around the country participate - always September.

10485 ■ Western Front Association - U.S. Branch (WFA)
96 Coll. Ave.
Poughkeepsie, NY 12603
Ph: (845)486-6189
Fax: (845)486-6190
E-mail: gagin1@aol.com
URL: http://www.wfa-usa.org
Contact: Rear Admiral T.J. Johnson USN, Pres.
Founded: 1980. **Members:** 4,000. **Membership Dues:** regular, in England, $55 (annual) ● regular, in U.S., $25 (annual). **Regional Groups:** 5. **Description:** Honors veterans of WWI from all countries who fought in France and Flanders. Seeks to preserve the memories and comradeship of those who served their countries from 1914-1918, and to promote scholarship of the WWI era. **Awards:** Norman Thomlinson, Jr. Prize. **Frequency:** annual. **Type:** monetary. **Recipient:** for best work of history in English on WWI ● Undergraduate Essay Prize. **Frequency:** annual. **Type:** monetary. **Recipient:** for impact of WWI on the U.S.A. **Publications:** *Camaraderie*, 3/year. Journal. **Price:** included in membership dues ● *The Field Memo*, 3/year. Newsletter. **Price:** included in membership dues. **Advertising:** accepted ● *Stand To! (U.K.)*, 3/year. Journal. **Price:** included in membership dues ● *The WFA Bulletin (UK)*. **Conventions/Meetings:** annual seminar (exhibits).

Minorities

10486 ■ Minorities in Agriculture, Natural Resources and Related Sciences (MANRRS)
PO Box 381017
Germantown, TN 38183-1017
Ph: (901)757-9700
Fax: (901)757-9706
E-mail: exec.office@manrrs.org
URL: http://www.manrrs.org
Contact: Dr. Alvin Larke Jr., Natl. Pres.
Membership Dues: professional, $75 (annual) ● student, $10 (annual). **Description:** Promotes natural and agricultural sciences and other related fields among ethnic minorities in all phases of career preparation and participation. Provides a network to support the professional development of minorities. **Conventions/Meetings:** annual conference.

Mongolian

10487 ■ Mongolia Society (MONGSOC)
Indiana Univ.
322 Goodbody Hall
1011 E 3rd St.
Bloomington, IN 47405-7005
Ph: (812)855-4078
Fax: (812)855-7500
E-mail: monsoc@indiana.edu
URL: http://www.indiana.edu/~mongsoc
Contact: Susie Drost, Treas.
Founded: 1961. **Members:** 475. **Membership Dues:** student, $25 (annual) ● regular, $35 (annual) ● ethnic Mongolian, $25 (annual) ● library, $50 (annual) ● corporate, $100 (annual) ● sustaining, $250 (annual) ● life, $500. **Description:** Individuals, libraries, and other organizations interested in furthering the study of Mongolia and adjacent areas of inner Asia. Promotes the history, language, and culture of the region. Sponsors films and exhibits. **Libraries: Type:** reference. **Holdings:** periodicals. **Awards:** Dr. Gombojab Hangin Memorial Scholarship. **Frequency:** annual. **Type:** scholarship. **Recipient:** for a Mongolian student pursuing Mongolian studies in the US. **Additional Websites:** http://www.mongoliasociety.org. **Publications:** *Mongolia Survey*, semiannual. Newsletter ● *Mongolian Studies*, annual. Journal. Contains scholarly research articles, book reviews, and "embraces cross-Asian and multi disciplinary approaches to Mongolia, past and present". ● *Special Papers*, periodic. Contains text in Old Script Mongolian. ● Papers, periodic. Important Mongolian publications translated into English. ● Also publishes dictionaries and textbook of Mongolian language. **Conventions/Meetings:** annual lecture and meeting.

Museums

10488 ■ African American Museums Association (AAMA)
PO Box 427
Wilberforce, OH 45384
Ph: (937)376-4944
Fax: (937)376-2007
E-mail: billingsley@blackmuseums.org
URL: http://www.blackmuseums.org
Contact: William Billingsley, Exec. Dir.
Founded: 1978. **Members:** 430. **Membership Dues:** individual, $55 (annual) ● institutional (depends upon the annual budget), $125-$1,000 (annual) ● trustee/scholar, $75 (annual) ● student, $25 (annual) ● affiliate, $500 (annual) ● corporate sponsor, $1,000 (annual). **Budget:** $180,000. **Regional Groups:** 6. **State Groups:** 28. **Description:** Represents museums, museum professionals, and scholars concerned with preserving, restoring, collecting, and exhibiting African-American history and culture. Provides technical information to African-American museums. Conducts professional training workshops, surveys, evaluations, and consultant and referral services. Compiles statistics. **Affiliated With:** American Association of Museums; International Council of Museums. **Publications:** *Black Museums Calendar*, monthly. Newsletter. **Price:** free ● *Blacks in Museums*, biennial. Directory ● *Profile of Black Museums*. Directory ● *Scrip*, quarterly. Newsletter ● Also publishes *Profile of Black Museums* (statistical survey) and brochures. **Conventions/Meetings:** annual conference.

10489 ■ American Association for Museum Volunteers (AAMV)
c/o Victoria B. Wilson, Membership Sec.
PO Box 9494
Washington, DC 20016
E-mail: kuter@acnatsci.org
URL: http://www.aamv.org
Contact: Victoria B. Wilson, Membership Sec.
Founded: 1979. **Members:** 480. **Membership Dues:** individual, $35 (annual) ● sponsor, $100 (annual) ● volunteer group, $75 (annual). **Budget:** $25,000. **State Groups:** 2. **Description:** Serves as forum and source of information, on national and international levels, for museum volunteers. Aims to establish a resource center for disseminating information on museum volunteers and volunteer programs; strengthen national and international reciprocity among volunteers. Works to establish professional standards for museum volunteers. Informs and represents museum volunteers in legislative matters affecting volunteer service. Offers continuing education in the form of workshops and panel discussions. An affiliate committee of the American Association of Museums. **Computer Services:** Mailing lists. **Telecommunication Services:** electronic mail, vwilson@bowdoin.edu. **Formerly:** (1986) United States Association of Museum Volunteers. **Publications:** *AAMV Newsletter*, quarterly. Features news of volunteer activities in cultural institutions. **Price:** included in membership dues. Alternate Formats: online ● *Directory of Museum Volunteer Programs*, periodic. **Price:** $18.00 ● *Volunteer Program Administration*. Handbook. **Price:** $19.00. **Conventions/Meetings:** annual meeting, held in conjunction with AAM annual meeting.

10490 ■ American Association of Museums (AAM)
1575 Eye St. NW, Ste.400
Washington, DC 20005
Ph: (202)289-1818
Fax: (202)289-6578
E-mail: membership@aam-us.org
URL: http://www.aam-us.org
Contact: Ford Bell, Pres.
Founded: 1906. **Members:** 16,000. **Membership Dues:** museum staff/independent professional/non-profit organization staff (over $40000 income), $110 (annual) ● museum staff/independent professional/non-profit organization staff (below $40000 income), $75 (annual) ● museum trustee, $150 (annual) ● student, $35 (annual) ● museum/associate member, $100-$15,000 (annual) ● commercial firm, $650 (annual). **Staff:** 63. **Budget:** $8,000,000. **Regional Groups:** 6. **Description:** Represents directors, curators, registrars, educators, exhibit designers, public relations officers, development officers, security managers, trustees, and volunteers in museums as well as all museums, including art, history, science,

military and maritime, and youth, as well as aquariums, zoos, botanical gardens, arboretums, historic sites, and science and technology centers. Dedicated to promoting excellence within the museum community. Assists museum staff, boards, and volunteers through advocacy, professional education, information exchange, accreditation, and guidance. **Awards:** AAM/ICOM International Service Citation. **Frequency:** annual. **Type:** recognition. **Recipient:** for individual professionals, museums, and organizations that have made a long-term commitment to advance the cause of museum-based international relations ● AAM Medal for Distinguished Philanthropy. **Frequency:** annual. **Type:** medal. **Recipient:** for altruism and extraordinary museum patronage ● Award for Distinguished Service to Museums. **Frequency:** annual. **Type:** medal. **Recipient:** for museum professionals who have sustained excellence and extraordinary service ● Excellence in Peer Review Service Award. **Frequency:** annual. **Type:** recognition. **Recipient:** for peer reviewers ● Nancy Hanks Memorial Award for Professional Excellence. **Frequency:** annual. **Type:** recognition. **Recipient:** for museum professionals. **Committees:** Audience Research and Evaluation; Curators; Development and Membership; Diversity in Museums; Education; Exhibition; Media and Technology; Museum Administration and Finance; Museum Association Security; Museum Management; Museum Professional Training; P.R. and Marketing; Public Relations and Marketing; Registrars; Security; Small Museum Administrators; Standing Professional; Visitor Research and Evaluation. **Councils:** Affiliates; Regional Associations. **Programs:** Accreditation; Bookstore; Government Affairs; Museum Assessment. **Affiliated With:** International Council of Museums. **Publications:** *Aviso*, monthly. Newsletter. **Price:** included in membership dues. **Advertising:** accepted ● *Bookstore Catalog*, semiannual. Features organizations self-titles. Alternate Formats: online ● *Museum News (TM)*, bimonthly. Magazine. **Price:** included in membership dues. **Advertising:** accepted. **Conventions/Meetings:** annual Meeting & MuseumExpo - meeting and symposium (exhibits) - 2009 Apr. 30-May 4, Philadelphia, PA.

10491 ■ American Friends of the Israel Museum (AFIM)
500 5th Ave., Ste.2540
New York, NY 10110
Ph: (212)997-5611
Fax: (212)997-5536
E-mail: mail@afimnyc.org
URL: http://www.imj.org.il/eng/about/friends.html
Contact: James S. Snyder, Dir.

Founded: 1972. **Members:** 400. **Staff:** 10. **Description:** Represents individuals and organizations supporting the Israel Museum in Jerusalem. Sponsors programs and development at the Israel Museum and exhibitions and activities of the museum in the U.S. **Publications:** *The Israel Museum, Jerusalem Magazine*, periodic. Reports on exhibitions and recent acquisitions. **Price:** free. **Circulation:** 11,000. **Conventions/Meetings:** annual International Council - meeting - always in Jerusalem, Israel.

10492 ■ American Friends of the National Gallery of Australia (AFANG)
c/o American Australian Association
599 Lexington Ave., 17th Fl.
New York, NY 10022
Ph: (212)338-6860
Fax: (212)338-6864
E-mail: information@aaanyc.org
URL: http://www.americanaustralian.org/Cultural/afang.php
Contact: Ms. Frances M. Cassidy, Pres.

Founded: 1982. **Members:** 38. **Staff:** 1. **Description:** U.S. citizens interested in aiding the Australian National Gallery in Canberra, Australia. Seeks financial contributions or works of art. Assists the Australian National Gallery in staging exhibitions in the U.S. **Formerly:** (1998) American Friends of the Australian National Gallery Foundation.

10493 ■ Association of Art Museum Curators (AAMC)
174 E 80th St.
New York, NY 10021
Ph: (212)879-5701
Fax: (212)628-3146
E-mail: aamc@artcurators.org
URL: http://www.artcurators.org
Contact: George T.M. Shackelford, Pres.

Founded: 2001. **Members:** 500. **Membership Dues:** curator (based on annual salary), $30-$100 (annual). **Multinational. Description:** Serves as an advocacy group for the curatorial profession. Raises public understanding of the curator's role through lectures, symposia and published materials. Promotes research and scholarship by developing educational programs. Provides a collegial forum for discussion about museum issues in North America. **Awards:** AAMC Awards. **Frequency:** annual. **Type:** recognition. **Recipient:** for outstanding book, article and exhibition of the year. **Publications:** Newsletter, monthly. Alternate Formats: online. **Conventions/Meetings:** annual meeting - held each May.

10494 ■ Association of Art Museum Directors (AAMD)
120 E 56th St., Ste.520
New York, NY 10022
Ph: (212)754-8084
Fax: (212)754-8087
E-mail: eroberts@aamd.org
URL: http://www.aamd.org
Contact: Millicent Hall Gaudieri, Exec. Dir.

Founded: 1916. **Members:** 200. **Budget:** $275,000. **Description:** Represents chief staff officers of major art museums. **Committees:** Art Issues; Education and Community Issues; Ethics and Standards; Future Directions; Government Affairs; Museum Operations; Professional Issues; Program; Public Affairs; Works of Art. **Task Forces:** Collecting; Nazi Looted Art. **Publications:** *Professional Practices in Art Museums*. **Price:** $10.00 ● *Salary Survey*, annual. **Price:** $45.00 for members; $75.00 for nonmembers ● Proceedings. **Conventions/Meetings:** semiannual conference.

10495 ■ Association of Children's Museums (ACM)
1300 L St. NW, No. 975
Washington, DC 20005
Ph: (202)898-1080
Fax: (202)898-1086
E-mail: acm@childrensmuseums.org
URL: http://www.childrensmuseums.org
Contact: Janet Rice Elman, Exec. Dir.

Founded: 1962. **Members:** 500. **Membership Dues:** associate, independent professional, $250 (annual) ● children museum in U.S. (based on annual income), $300-$1,600 (annual) ● sponsor museum, $2,100 (annual) ● affiliate museum, $800 (annual) ● children's museum outside U.S., $550 (annual) ● emerging children's museum, $300 (annual) ● museum member staff, student, $50 (annual) ● corporate leader, $1,000 (annual) ● corporate supporter, $600 (annual) ● individual consultant, $400 (annual). **Staff:** 9. **Budget:** $900,000. **Description:** Serves as professional service organization for museums maintaining interactive exhibits and programs aimed at family or child audiences. Compiles statistics. **Libraries: Type:** reference. **Holdings:** 200; audiovisuals. **Subjects:** children's museums from around the world. **Awards:** Great Friend to Kids Award. **Frequency:** annual. **Type:** recognition. **Recipient:** for promotion of child advocacy ● Promising Practice Award. **Frequency:** annual. **Type:** grant. **Recipient:** for innovative and creative practices in U.S. children's museums. **Computer Services:** database, membership ● mailing lists. **Committees:** Program. **Programs:** Reciprocal. **Formerly:** American Association of Youth Museums; (2002) Association of Youth Museums. **Publications:** *ACM Forum*, bimonthly. Newsletter. **Price:** free for members. **Circulation:** 400. **Advertising:** accepted ● *Capturing the Vision: A Companion Volume to Collective Vision*. Book. **Price:** $55.00 for members; $85.00 for nonmembers. Alternate Formats: CD-ROM ● *Collective Vision: Starting & Sustaining a Children's Museum*. Book. **Price:** $100.00 for nonmembers; $65.00 for members ● *Hand to Hand*, quarterly. Journal. Highlights national issues and trends in the youth museum field. **Price:** $20.00/issue for members; $25.00/issue for nonmembers; $15.00/issue for members (volume 6); $20.00/issue for nonmembers (volume 6). **Circulation:** 420 ● *Salary Survey*. Surveys. Provides compensation data of the children's museum field. **Price:** $45.00 for members; $100.00 for nonmembers ● *The 21st Century Learner Symposium Report*. **Price:** $10.00 ● Membership Directory, semiannual. Lists telephone numbers and addresses of members. **Price:** $130.00 for nonmembers; $80.00 for members. **Conventions/Meetings:** annual InterActivity - conference, three-day meeting for children's museum professionals (exhibits) - always spring.

10496 ■ Association of College and University Museums and Galleries (ACUMG)
c/o Philip and Muriel Berman Museum of Art
Ursinus Coll.
601 E Main St.
Collegeville, PA 19426
Ph: (610)409-3500
Fax: (610)409-3664
E-mail: lhanover@ursinus.edu
URL: http://www.acumg.org
Contact: Lisa Tremper Hanover, Pres.

Founded: 1980. **Members:** 325. **Membership Dues:** individual, $25 (annual) ● institution, $50 (annual) ● corporate, $75 (annual) ● student, $10 (annual). **Staff:** 1. **Budget:** $10,000. **Regional Groups:** 6. **Description:** Institutions and individuals professionally involved with college and university museums and galleries. Represents the needs, interests, and concerns of college and university museum and gallery professionals. **Awards:** Student Scholarships. **Frequency:** annual. **Type:** scholarship. **Computer Services:** database ● mailing lists. **Boards:** Directors. **Affiliated With:** American Association of Museums. **Publications:** *News and Issues*, quarterly. Newsletter. **Price:** free for members. **Circulation:** 400. **Advertising:** accepted. Alternate Formats: online. **Conventions/Meetings:** annual conference ● annual regional meeting and conference.

10497 ■ Association for Living History, Farm and Agricultural Museums (ALHFAM)
8774 Rte. 45 NW
North Bloomfield, OH 44450
Ph: (440)685-4410
Fax: (440)685-4410
E-mail: sheridan@orwell.net
URL: http://www.alhfam.org
Contact: Judith M. Sheridan, Sec.-Treas.

Founded: 1970. **Members:** 1,000. **Membership Dues:** basic, $30 (annual) ● supporting, business associate, $50 (annual) ● joint, $55 (annual) ● student, retired, $25 (annual) ● small institution, library, $60 (annual) ● large institution, $120 (annual) ● patron, $100 (annual). **Budget:** $50,000. **Regional Groups:** 9. **Multinational. Description:** Acts as a clearinghouse of information on plants, animals, tools, and implements used in farming in the past; assists farms and museums in securing information about living history programs and historical accuracy. **Awards:** ALHFAM Conference Fellowship. **Frequency:** annual. **Type:** scholarship. **Recipient:** for professional development benefits by attending conference. **Computer Services:** Information services, publications ● information services, resource list ● mailing lists. **Committees:** Collections; Education; Electronic Resources; First Person Interpretation; Historic Clothing; Historic Foodways; Livestock Resources; Machinery; Replica Resources; Seeds and Plants. **Affiliated With:** American Association of Museums. **Formerly:** (1998) Association for Living Historical Farms and Agricultural Museums. **Publications:** *Living Historical Farms Bulletin*, quarterly. **Price:** $15.00 regular membership; $50.00 /year for institutions; $7.00/year for students. ISSN: 0047-4851. **Circulation:** 1,000. **Advertising:** accepted ● Proceedings, annual. **Price:** $12.00. **Circulation:** 500 ● Also publishes an index; 25 years of conference proceedings. **Conventions/Meetings:** annual conference (exhibits).

10498 ■ Association of Science Museum Directors (ASMD)
c/o Bonnie W. Styles, Sec.-Treas.
Illinois State Museum
502 S Spring St.
Springfield, IL 62706-5000
Ph: (217)782-7011
Fax: (217)782-1254
E-mail: director@museum.state.il.us
URL: http://www.asmd.org
Contact: Bonnie W. Styles, Sec.-Treas.
Founded: 1960. **Members:** 100. **Membership Dues:** institution (based on operating budget), $100-$200 (annual). **Description:** Chief administrative officers of museums whose research, education, exhibition, collection, and publication programs are in the physical, biological, geological and anthropological sciences. **Conventions/Meetings:** semiannual conference ● annual meeting, held in conjunction with American Association of Museums.

10499 ■ Association of Science-Technology Centers (ASTC)
1025 Vermont Ave. NW, Ste.500
Washington, DC 20005-6310
Ph: (202)783-7200
Fax: (202)783-7207
E-mail: info@astc.org
URL: http://www.astc.org
Contact: Bonnie VanDorn, Exec. Dir.
Founded: 1973. **Members:** 550. **Membership Dues:** science center/museum, $500-$4,000 (annual) ● sustaining, $750 (annual). **Staff:** 21. **Budget:** $3,000,000. **Description:** Science centers and related institutions, including zoos, nature centers, aquaria, planetariums and space theaters, and natural history and children's museums. Supports and stimulates excellence and innovation in science museums, and strengthens their capacity to serve as effective community resources in promoting public understanding of science and technology to an increasingly diverse audience. **Libraries: Type:** reference. **Awards:** ASTC Conference Fellowship. **Frequency:** annual. **Type:** fellowship. **Recipient:** for people of color in the science center field ● ASTC Fellow Award. **Frequency:** annual. **Type:** recognition. **Recipient:** to individuals for significant contributions to the advancement of public understanding and appreciation of science and technology or ASTC ● Leading Edge Awards. **Frequency:** annual. **Type:** recognition. **Recipient:** to ASTC members and/or their employees in recognition of extraordinary accomplishments in visitor experience, business practice, and leadership in the field. **Committees:** Advocacy; Conference Program Planning; International Development; Nominating; Professional Development. **Programs:** Conference Fellowship; Passport. **Publications:** *ASTC Catalog of Publications*, annual. **Price:** free. Alternate Formats: online ● *ASTC Dimensions*, bimonthly. Journal. Provides information on trends, best practices, perspectives and news of significance to the science and technology center field programs. **Price:** $35.00 /year for members in U.S.; $45.00 /year for members outside U.S.; $50.00 /year for nonmembers in U.S.; $66.00 /year for nonmembers outside U.S. ISSN: 0895-7371. **Circulation:** 3,000 ● *ASTC Directory*, annual. Membership Directory. Lists science museums and related institutions. **Price:** $25.00/copy for members; $35.00/copy for nonmembers. **Circulation:** 500. **Advertising:** accepted ● *Science-Center Statistics*, periodic. Reports. Contains science center information including attendance, floor space, revenues, etc. **Price:** $25.00 for members; $40.00 for nonmembers. **Circulation:** 500 ● Brochures. **Conventions/Meetings:** annual conference, with speakers (exhibits) - usually October. 2008 Oct. 18-21, Philadelphia, PA; 2009 Oct. 31-Nov. 3, Fort Worth, TX.

10500 ■ Council of American Jewish Museums (CAJM)
c/o Center for Judaic Studies
2000 E Asbury Ave. Ste.157
Denver, CO 80208
Ph: (303)871-3015
E-mail: jkauvar@jewishculture.org
URL: http://www.jewishculture.org/museums/museums.html
Contact: Joanne Marks Kauvar, Exec. Dir.
Founded: 1977. **Members:** 75. **Membership Dues:** general, $75 (annual) ● contributing, $250 (annual) ● sustaining, $500 (annual) ● student, $36 (annual) ● patron, $1,000 (annual) ● affiliate, $100 (annual) ● institutional, $250-$1,000 (annual). **Staff:** 1. **Description:** Administered by the National Foundation for Jewish Culture. Jewish museums, historical societies, and nonprofit galleries. Supports, encourages, and promotes the development of American Jewish museums in collecting, preserving, and interpreting Jewish art and artifacts for public education and the advancement of scholarship. Fosters cooperation among institutions maintaining Judaica collections. Facilitates the best utilization of collections concerning Jewish aspects of the arts, humanities, and social sciences. Acts as clearinghouse and network for the museums and advocates projects aimed at advancing the field of Jewish musicology. Develops a comprehensive sourcebook for use by docents. **Computer Services:** database, members ● mailing lists ● online services. **Committees:** Steering. **Publications:** *CAJM Newsletter*, semiannual. **Circulation:** 1,500. Alternate Formats: online. **Conventions/Meetings:** annual conference.

10501 ■ Council of American Maritime Museums (CAMM)
c/o The Whaling Museum at Cold Spring Harbor
PO Box 25
Cold Spring Harbor, NY 11724
E-mail: president@councilofamericanmaritimemuseums.org
URL: http://www.councilofamericanmaritimemuseums.org
Contact: Anne B. Brengle, Pres.
Founded: 1974. **Members:** 70. **Description:** Museums located in the U.S. and Canada that are devoted primarily to maritime history. Seeks to uphold, promote, and further the welfare, programs, and activities of American maritime museums. **Telecommunication Services:** electronic mail, abrengle@whalingmuseum.com. **Publications:** *Meeting Minutes*, periodic. **Conventions/Meetings:** annual meeting.

10502 ■ Council for Museum Anthropology (CMA)
c/o Catherine S. Fowler, PhD, Pres.
Univ. of Nevada
Dept. of Anthropology
Reno, NV 89557
Ph: (775)682-7687
Fax: (775)327-2226
E-mail: csfowler@unr.edu
URL: http://unparallel.com/cma
Contact: Catherine S. Fowler PhD, Pres.
Founded: 1975. **Members:** 411. **Membership Dues:** individual, $25 (annual) ● institution, $47 (annual) ● student, $18 (annual). **Description:** Anthropologists and individuals interested in museum anthropology; institutions with large anthropological collections. Seeks to: preserve and improve anthropological collections in museums; facilitate the use of collections for research and education; assist in developing policies for acquisition, exchange, loan, and exhibition of anthropological specimens; improve and modernize museum facilities and train museum personnel; develop and standardize guides, indexes, catalogs, and sources for the location and description of existing anthropological collections. Supports the collection of new materials and the advancement of conservation and storage techniques; has developed a formal policy dealing with the repatriation of Native American ceremonial objects and human remains. **Computer Services:** Mailing lists. **Publications:** *Museum Anthropology*, annual. Journal. **Price:** included in membership dues; $30.00 for nonmembers; $45.00 for institution. ISSN: 0892-8339. **Circulation:** 600. **Advertising:** accepted. Alternate Formats: online ● Reports. **Conventions/Meetings:** semiannual meeting, held in conjunction with American Association of Museums in spring and American Anthropological Association in fall (exhibits).

10503 ■ Edna Hibel Society
PO Box 9721
Coral Springs, FL 33075
Ph: (954)731-6699 (954)978-3188
E-mail: hibelsoc@aol.com
URL: http://www.hibel.com/society.htm
Contact: Ralph Burg, Pres.
Founded: 1976. **Members:** 3,000. **Membership Dues:** individual, $35 (annual). **Staff:** 2. **Description:** Supports the endeavors of the Hibel Museum of Art. **Computer Services:** Mailing lists, of members. **Publications:** *Hibeletter*, quarterly. **Price:** free. Alternate Formats: online. **Conventions/Meetings:** annual meeting - always March in Jupiter, FL.

10504 ■ Fudan Museum Foundation (FMF)
4206 73rd Terr. E
Sarasota, FL 34243-5112
Ph: (941)351-8208
Fax: (941)951-8208
E-mail: fmfsafsa@juno.com
URL: http://www.geocities.com/fmfsafsa
Contact: Alfonz Lengyel PhD, Pres.
Founded: 1988. **Languages:** Chinese, English. **Description:** Strives to help transfer the latest methods of museum operation, exhibition, and restoration and to develop a student and scholarly exchange program. Organizes the Sino-American Field School of Archaeology in Xian, China. Offers professional training in museum studies; plans to establish a videotape library of past temporary exhibitions in Shanghai. Maintains speakers' bureau. **Computer Services:** database. **Study Groups:** Sino-American Field School of Archaeology. **Publications:** *Archaeology for Museologists*. Book. **Advertising:** accepted ● *Chinese Chronological History: From Pre-history to 1950*. Book ● *Museum Study Series*, periodic. **Price:** $20.00. ISSN: 1050-4346. **Advertising:** accepted. **Conventions/Meetings:** annual meeting - always July, Shanghai, China.

10505 ■ Intermuseum Conservation Association (ICA)
2915 Detroit Ave.
Cleveland, OH 44113
Ph: (216)658-8700
Fax: (216)658-8709
E-mail: ica@ica-artconservation.org
URL: http://www.ica-artconservation.org
Contact: Albert Albano, Exec. Dir.
Founded: 1952. **Members:** 30. **Membership Dues:** organization (based on the organization's budget), $100-$500 (annual) ● business, $600 (annual) ● individual/dual, $75 (annual) ● student, $25 (annual). **Staff:** 7. **Budget:** $550,000. **Description:** Performs the examination and treatment of works of art, inspection and maintenance of collections, and research and education in art conservation technology. Conducts seminars for museum professionals. **Libraries: Type:** open to the public. **Holdings:** 2,000. **Subjects:** art conservation materials, methods and research. **Computer Services:** Information services, member conservation information network. **Programs:** Third Year Graduate Conservation Internship. **Publications:** *ICA News*, quarterly. Newsletter. **Price:** included in membership dues. Alternate Formats: online. **Conventions/Meetings:** annual meeting.

10506 ■ International Congress of Maritime Museums (ICMM)
c/o Stuart Parnes, Sec. Gen.
PO Box 326
Mystic, CT 06355
Ph: (860)767-8269
Fax: (860)767-7028
E-mail: sparnes@ctrivermuseum.org
URL: http://www.icmmonline.org
Contact: Morten Hahn-Pedersen, Pres.
Founded: 1972. **Membership Dues:** full, $140 (annual) ● associate, $40 (annual). **Multinational. Description:** Maritime museums, individuals, and universities. Establishes, maintains, and promotes close liaison between museums and other permanent

institutions concerned with matters of maritime history. **Computer Services:** database, directory information update. **Telecommunication Services:** electronic mail, mhp@fimus.dk. **Committees:** Ship Preservation. **Affiliated With:** International Council of Museums. **Publications:** Newsletter. Alternate Formats: online ● Directory. Alternate Formats: online. **Conventions/Meetings:** triennial congress and workshop ● annual Interim Congress.

10507 ■ International Museum Theatre Alliance (IMTAL)
c/o Putnam Museum
1717 W 12th St.
Davenport, IA 52804
E-mail: membership@imtal.org
URL: http://www.imtal.org
Contact: Christina Myatt, Membership Chair
Founded: 1990. **Membership Dues:** institution, $80 (annual) ● individual, $40 (annual) ● student, $25 (annual). **Multinational**. **Description:** Represents museum and theatre professionals. **Publications:** *Insights*, quarterly. Newsletter.

10508 ■ Museum of American Finance (MAF)
26 Broadway, Ste.947
New York, NY 10004
Ph: (212)908-4110
Fax: (212)908-4601
E-mail: kaguilera@financialhistory.org
URL: http://www.financialhistory.org
Contact: Kristin Aguilera, Communications Dir.
Founded: 1988. **Members:** 2,876. **Membership Dues:** individual, $55 (annual) ● student, senior (65 or over), $45 (annual) ● international, $65 (annual) ● institutional, $75 (annual) ● Smithsonian affiliate, $150 (annual) ● Alexander Hamilton Society, $500 (annual) ● donor, $1,000 (annual) ● corporate, $1,000 (annual). **Staff:** 7. **Budget:** $700,000. **Description:** Works to collect and preserve historical financial artifacts, to display them in a permanent display with special exhibits for the public, and to use material as an educational resource for the nation. Gathers and disseminates information on financial history; conducts public educational programs. **Libraries: Type:** open to the public; by appointment only. **Holdings:** 1,250. **Subjects:** finance, history, stock market, wall street, money, banking, entrepreneurship, business. **Formerly:** (2005) Museum of American Financial History. **Publications:** *Financial History*, quarterly. Magazine. Covers American financial history, economics, banking, corporate history, and entrepreneurship. **Price:** $4.00/issue; $40.00/year in U.S. and Canada. ISSN: 1520-4723. **Circulation:** 6,000. **Advertising:** accepted. Alternate Formats: online.

10509 ■ Museum Education Roundtable (MER)
PO Box 15727
Washington, DC 20003
Ph: (202)547-8378
Fax: (202)547-8344
E-mail: info@mer-online.org
URL: http://www.mer-online.org
Contact: Rose Stapp, Office Mgr.
Founded: 1969. **Members:** 770. **Membership Dues:** individual, $40 (annual) ● student/senior, $30 (annual) ● contributor, $1-$99 (annual) ● patron, $100-$199 (annual) ● sponsor, $200-$499 (annual) ● benefactor (minimum), $500 (annual). **Description:** Represents museum educators, museums, cultural organizations, schools, and teachers. Promotes the use of museums and cultural institutions as educational resources. Acts as a communications network encouraging leadership, scholarship, and personal development among educators and museum professionals. Conducts panels, roundtable discussions, workshops, training programs, and research forum. **Boards:** Board of Directors. **Committees:** Membership; Nominations; Programs; Publication; Technology. **Publications:** *Journal of Museum Education*, 3/year. Presents an anthology of practice and theory. **Price:** included in membership dues. ISSN: 1059-8650. **Circulation:** 1,000 ● *Museum Education Anthology: Perspectives on Informal Learning/A Decade of Roundtable Reports, 1973-1983*. Book ● *Network*, 3/year. Newsletter. **Price:** included in membership dues ● *Patterns in Practice: Selections from the Journal of Museum Education*. Book ● *Transforming Practice: Selections from the Journal of Museum Education 1992-1999*. Book. **Conventions/Meetings:** quadrennial meeting and workshop, on audiovisuals, interpretation techniques, docent training, interpretation, theory and practice of museum education, professional development, museum-school programming, learning and behavioral philosophy ● workshop and symposium - usually held in May and August.

10510 ■ Museum Trustee Association (MTA)
4633 E Broadway Blvd., Ste.101
Tucson, AZ 85711
Ph: (520)322-5555
Free: (866)640-7555
Fax: (520)323-3399
E-mail: office@mta-hq.org
URL: http://www.mta-hq.org
Contact: Aaron M. Milrad, Chm.
Founded: 1986. **Members:** 7,100. **Membership Dues:** friend, $100-$249 (annual) ● contributor, $250-$499 (annual) ● donor, $500-$999 (annual) ● patron, $1,000-$2,499 (annual) ● major patron, $2,500-$4,999 (annual) ● distinguished patron, $5,000-$9,999 (annual) ● benefactor (minimum), $10,000 (annual) ● museum, $200-$1,000 (annual) ● university museum, $250 (annual). **Staff:** 2. **Budget:** $545,000. **Description:** Museum trustees and boards of trustees. Provides continuing education and training programs for museum trustees, and directors. **Awards:** George C. Seybolt Award. **Frequency:** annual. **Type:** recognition. **Recipient:** for outstanding and meritorious trusteeship by making a contribution to museums and their missions. **Councils:** Advisory Council of Directors. **Formerly:** (1988) Museum Trustee Committee for Research and Development. **Publications:** *MTA Briefings*, quarterly. Newsletter. **Price:** included in membership dues. **Circulation:** 7,100. **Advertising:** accepted. Alternate Formats: online. **Conventions/Meetings:** annual conference and workshop, includes social events - always fall.

10511 ■ National Association of Automobile Museums (NAAM)
PO Box 271
Auburn, IN 46706
Ph: (260)925-1444
Fax: (260)925-6266
E-mail: jfrady@automuseum.org
URL: http://naam.museum
Contact: Jackie Frady, Contact
Membership Dues: individual, $25 (annual) ● institutional (based on operating budget), $35-$150 (annual). **Description:** Aims to link auto museums, enabling them to foster education, share exhibits, and exchange vital data about collections. Strives to elevate standards for automobile museums in the areas of registration and documentation, conservation, and preservation. Promotes and markets member museums' programs and exhibits through the media and on the internet. Engages in collaborative marketing of products in museum stores. **Awards:** NAAMY Awards of Excellence. **Frequency:** annual. **Type:** recognition. **Recipient:** to recognize automotive/transportation museum leaders for achievement, professionalism, and creativity. **Publications:** *NAAM News*, quarterly. Newsletter. **Price:** included in membership dues. Alternate Formats: online ● Membership Directory. **Price:** included in membership dues. **Conventions/Meetings:** annual conference.

10512 ■ National Automotive and Truck Museum of United States (NATMUS)
1000 Gordon M. Buehrig Pl.
Auburn, IN 46706
Ph: (260)925-9100
Fax: (260)925-8695
E-mail: info@natmus.org
URL: http://www.natmus.org
Contact: David J. Turner, Contact
Founded: 1988. **Members:** 1,000. **Membership Dues:** family, $30 (annual) ● student, senior, $25 (annual) ● life, $1,000. **Staff:** 5. **Budget:** $200,000. **Multinational**. **Description:** Represents individuals and corporations interested in preserving automotive and truck history. Conducts various activities. Focuses with post WWII automobiles, trucks of all eras, automotive toys and models. **Libraries: Type:** reference; by appointment only; open to the public. **Holdings:** 25,000; archival material, articles, books, periodicals, reports, video recordings. **Subjects:** automotive and truck history. **Awards:** Volunteer of the Year. **Frequency:** periodic. **Type:** recognition. **Recipient:** to individuals who have been most productive in accomplishing goals of the museum. **Publications:** *Futurliner News*, biennial. Newsletter. Features news and events pertaining to the historic restoration and preservation of Futurliner No. 10. **Price:** $5.00. Alternate Formats: online ● *PAST-LANE*, quarterly. Newsletter. **Price:** included in membership dues. **Circulation:** 1,000.

10513 ■ San Francisco Maritime National Park Association
PO Box 470310
San Francisco, CA 94147-0310
Ph: (415)561-6662
Fax: (415)561-6660
E-mail: info@maritime.org
URL: http://www.maritime.org
Contact: Eamon O'Byrne, Exec. Dir.
Founded: 1950. **Members:** 1,750. **Membership Dues:** shipmate, $60 (annual) ● crew, $100 (annual) ● mariner, $125 (annual) ● master mariner, $250 (annual) ● captain, $500 (annual) ● commodore, $1,000 (annual) ● admiral (minimum), $2,500 (annual). **Staff:** 60. **Budget:** $3,000,000. **Description:** Works to promote maritime preservation, history and education. Operates the USS Pampanito, a WWII submarine museum and supports the San Francisco Maritime National Historical Park. **Formerly:** (2001) National Maritime Museum Association. **Publications:** *Sea Letter*, semiannual. Magazine. Contains articles of maritime interest, mostly related to Maritime Park collection and west coast history. **Price:** free for members ● *Update*. Newsletter. **Price:** free for members ● *USS Pampanito: A Submarine and Her Crew*. Book. **Price:** $14.95/copy. **Conventions/Meetings:** annual Gala and Maritime Heritage Award - party.

10514 ■ Small Museum Association (SMA)
c/o Michael DiPaolo
Lewis Historical Soc.
110 Shipcarpenter St.
Lewes, DE 19958
Ph: (302)645-7670
E-mail: mike@historiclewes.org
URL: http://www.smallmuseum.org
Contact: Michael DiPaolo, Contact
Membership Dues: regular, $20 (annual). **Description:** Promotes small museums. **Libraries: Type:** lending. **Computer Services:** Online services, listserv. **Publications:** *SMAll Talk*. Newsletter. **Price:** included in membership dues. **Conventions/Meetings:** board meeting ● conference and workshop ● annual conference.

10515 ■ U.S. National Committee of the International Council of Museums (AAM/ICOM)
1575 Eye St. NW, Ste.400
Washington, DC 20005
Ph: (202)289-9115
Fax: (202)289-6578
E-mail: aam-icom@aam-us.org
URL: http://www.aam-us.org/museumresources/icom/index.cfm
Contact: Mr. Erik Ledbetter, Sr. Mgr. of Intl. Programs
Founded: 1973. **Members:** 750. **Staff:** 2. **Budget:** $40,000. **Description:** U.S. national committee of International Council of Museums (see separate

entry); similar groups function in 106 member countries. Members include individuals and institutions. Disseminates information on activities, programs, and issues related to the global museum community to museum professionals in the U.S. and abroad. Conducts meetings, programs, and exchanges concerning international museum activities and cooperation, museum education, exhibitions, architecture, publications, research materials, documentation, and conservation techniques. Sponsors International Museum Day annually on May 18. **Awards:** AAM/ICOM International Service Citation. **Frequency:** annual. **Type:** recognition. **Affiliated With:** American Association of Museums. **Publications:** *ICOM News*, quarterly. Newsletter. Discusses issues of concern to international museum personnel, supporters, and professional members. Includes list of educational opportunities. **Price:** included in membership dues. **Circulation:** 8,000.

10516 ■ Volunteer Committees of Art Museums of Canada and the United States (VCAM)

c/o Nancy Rosenbloom, Pres.
400 Loring Ave.
Los Angeles, CA 90024
E-mail: president@vcam.org
URL: http://www.vcam.org
Contact: Nancy Rosenbloom, Pres.

Founded: 1952. **Members:** 116. **Membership Dues:** individual, $150 (triennial). **Staff:** 17. **Regional Groups:** 10. **National Groups:** 4. **Multinational. Description:** Represents art museum volunteers. Shares information and ideas pertaining to museums of all sizes across Canada and the United States. Commits to strengthen the volunteer programs of visual art museums. **Formerly:** (1959) Association of Women's Committees of Art Museums. **Publications:** *Conference Report*, triennial. Booklet. Features comprehensive descriptions of panels and workshops. **Price:** $25.00. **Circulation:** 200. **Advertising:** accepted ● *VCAM Conference Handbook*, triennial ● Newsletter, 3/year. **Circulation:** 700. Alternate Formats: online. **Conventions/Meetings:** triennial Art Gallery of Ontario and Royal Ontario Museum - conference (exhibits).

10517 ■ Wyckoff House and Association (WH&A)

5816 Clarendon Rd.
Brooklyn, NY 11203
Ph: (718)629-5400
Fax: (718)629-3125
E-mail: info@wyckoffassociation.org
URL: http://www.wyckoffassociation.org
Contact: Maryann M. Feeney, Exec. Dir.

Founded: 1937. **Members:** 1,350. **Membership Dues:** individual, $35 (annual) ● family, $50 (annual) ● individual (supporter), $60 (annual) ● patron (individual), $500 (annual) ● patron (family), $750 (annual) ● individual (Brooklyn community), $25 (annual) ● family (Brooklyn community), $40 (annual) ● benefactor (individual), $100 (annual) ● benefactor (family), $150 (annual). **Staff:** 3. **Budget:** $200,000. **Description:** Promotes interest in Wyckoff House Museum and in the history of the Pieter Claesen Wyckoff family. Disseminates materials and information on the museum and the Wyckoff descendants. Conducts educational program for school groups and visitors to the Wyckoff House Museum. Provides charitable services. **Libraries: Type:** not open to the public. **Subjects:** Wyckoff family. **Awards: Frequency:** annual. **Type:** recognition. **Recipient:** for major donors. **Computer Services:** Information services, membership list with genealogy data. **Publications:** *Huisvriend*, quarterly. Newsletter. **Price:** included in membership dues ● *Wyckoff Family in America*, annual. Bulletin. **Price:** included in membership dues ● *Wyckoff House and Association Bulletin*, annual. **Conventions/Meetings:** annual meeting and reunion.

Music

10518 ■ Academy of Country Music (ACM)

5500 Balboa Blvd., Ste.200
Encino, CA 91316
Ph: (818)788-8000
Fax: (818)788-0999
E-mail: info@acmcountry.com
URL: http://www.acmcountry.com
Contact: Bob Romero, Exec. Dir.

Founded: 1964. **Members:** 4,000. **Membership Dues:** professional, $75 (annual). **Staff:** 5. **Description:** Record company personnel, music publishers, radio stations, artists/entertainers, composers, and other affiliates of the country music industry. Promotes country music worldwide. Produces country music shows several times a year. Sponsors annual Celebrity Golf Classic. **Awards:** Academy of Country Music Awards. **Frequency:** annual. **Type:** recognition. **Computer Services:** database ● mailing lists. **Formerly:** (1974) Academy of Country and Western Music. **Publications:** *Souvenir Awards Book*, annual ● *The Tempo*, quarterly. Newsletter. Contains list of festivals and awards. **Price:** included in membership dues. **Circulation:** 4,000. **Conventions/Meetings:** quarterly meeting.

10519 ■ Accordion Federation of North America (AFNA)

1101 W Orangethorpe Ave.
Fullerton, CA 92833-4735
Ph: (714)447-9163
E-mail: afna@musician.org
Contact: Madeleine D'Ablaing, Pres.

Founded: 1957. **Members:** 70. **Staff:** 1. **Description:** Represents music school operators, teachers, instrument wholesalers, music publishers, and professional accordionists dedicated to the advancement of the accordion in all areas (teaching, performing, and, particularly, acquainting the public with its possibilities and advantages). Seeks to recognize outstanding ability and conspicuous service to the accordion industry. **Awards: Type:** scholarship. **Recipient:** for winners of music competitions at annual festival. **Committees:** Bylaws; Festival; Judging. **Formerly:** (1972) Accordion Association of Southern California. **Publications:** *Roster of Members*, annual. Membership Directory ● Brochures, annual. Alternate Formats: online ● Newsletter, monthly. **Conventions/Meetings:** annual Music Festival - festival and competition.

10520 ■ African American Art Song Alliance (AASA)

c/o Darryl Taylor, Founder
15 Newton Ct.
Irvine, CA 92604
Ph: (949)468-8031
Fax: (949)824-4914
E-mail: taylord@uci.edu
URL: http://www.darryltaylor.com/alliance
Contact: Darryl Taylor, Founder

Founded: 1997. **Description:** Represents individuals interested in art song by African-American composers. Encourages performance and scholarship related to African-American art song. Serves the needs of scholars, teachers, and performers seeking information about African-American art song.

10521 ■ African-American Music Society (AAMS)

PO Box 2522
Springfield, MA 01101-2522
Ph: (413)734-2555
Fax: (413)734-2288
E-mail: jeri231@cs.com
Contact: Rick Grant, Pres.

Founded: 1988. **Members:** 311. **Membership Dues:** board, $5 (monthly) ● ordinary, $15 (annual). **Local Groups:** 1. **Description:** Admirers of African-American classical music (jazz). Seeks to present and preserve the history of jazz and its leading exponents. Conducts educational programs; sponsors concerts.

10522 ■ Alternative Health and Fitness Association (AHFA)

Lafferty Rd., Ste.205
Pasadena, TX 77502
Ph: (713)378-9612
E-mail: rcthomas007@juno.com
Contact: R.C. Thomas, Dir.

Founded: 2000. **Membership Dues:** charter, $25 (annual). **Staff:** 7. **Budget:** $100,000. **Description:** People who chose natural healing as a method of well-being. Health and fitness; no chemicals, drugs or medications, study and practice of healing methods from around the world. Sponsors discussions, seminars, chats and events to promote well being on the planet. Covers subjects in Iridology, reflexology, herbs, meditation, aromatheraphy, homeophaty, feng shui, spiritual healings, etc. as well as how-to information on food preparation and cooking, and information on harvesting food. **Libraries: Type:** by appointment only; not open to the public; reference. **Holdings:** articles, artwork, books, clippings, periodicals. **Computer Services:** database, e-mail communications.

10523 ■ Amateur Chamber Music Players (ACMP)

1123 Broadway, Rm. 304
New York, NY 10010-2007
Ph: (212)645-7424
Fax: (212)741-2678
E-mail: webmaster@acmp.net
URL: http://www.acmp.net
Contact: Daniel Nimetz, Exec. Dir.

Founded: 1947. **Members:** 5,400. **Staff:** 1. **Budget:** $90,000. **Multinational. Description:** Amateur and professional musicians who play chamber music as a hobby. **Publications:** *Catalog of the Helen Rice Collection at Hartford Connecticut Public Library* ● *Helen Rice: The Great Lady of Chamber Music*. Book ● *International Directory*, biennial ● *Ledger Lines*, 3/year. Newsletter. **Price:** included in membership dues. **Circulation:** 7,000. Alternate Formats: online ● *List of Recommended Books on Chamber Music* ● *List of Recommended Chamber Music*. Book.

10524 ■ America Sings!

904 Polaris Way
Missoula, MT 59803
Free: (800)372-1222
E-mail: info@americasings.org
URL: http://www.americasings.org
Contact: John Jacobson, Pres./Founder

Founded: 1988. **Staff:** 3. **Description:** Creates choral music festivals featuring school and community singing groups. **Computer Services:** Mailing lists. **Telecommunication Services:** electronic mail, john@americasings.org. **Conventions/Meetings:** annual festival - spring.

10525 ■ American Accordion Musicological Society (AAMS)

c/o Joanna Arnold Darrow
322 Haddon Ave.
Westmont, NJ 08108
Ph: (856)854-6628
E-mail: accordion1@comcast.net
URL: http://www.aamsaccordionfestival.com
Contact: Joanna Arnold Darrow, Contact

Founded: 1970. **Members:** 980. **Membership Dues:** regular, $10 (annual). **Staff:** 5. **Budget:** $5,000. **Description:** Enthusiasts of the accordion. Promotes study, research, and knowledge related to accordions. Maintains museum of antique accordions. Sponsors annual composition contest and bestows cash prize. **Libraries: Type:** reference. **Holdings:** 500; audio recordings, books, papers. **Subjects:** music, accordions, accordion history. **Awards:** Virtuoso Scholarship Award. **Frequency:** annual. **Type:** monetary. **Publications:** *Compendium*, annual. Journal. Features articles on accordions from around the world. **Conventions/Meetings:** annual seminar (exhibits) - always first weekend in March.

10526 ■ American Accordionists' Association (AAA)

152 Home Fair Dr.
Fairfield, CT 06825
Ph: (203)335-2045
Fax: (203)335-2048

E-mail: aaa1938@aol.com
URL: http://www.ameraccord.com
Contact: Linda Soley Reed, Pres.
Founded: 1938. **Members:** 17,000. **Membership Dues:** full, in U.S., $65 (annual) ● associate in U.S., $35 (annual) ● full, outside U.S., $72 (annual) ● associate outside U.S., $42 (annual). **Staff:** 22. **Budget:** $200,000. **Description:** Certified accordion instructors, students, manufacturers and importers of accordions, and publishers and arrangers of accordion music. Promotes the accordion through contests, concerts, granting of scholarships, and commissioning of contemporary American composers to write for the accordion. Conducts research programs. **Telecommunication Services:** electronic mail, lsoleyreed@aol.com. **Affiliated With:** International Confederation of Accordionists; International Music Council; National Music Council. **Publications:** Journal, annual ● Newsletter, quarterly. **Conventions/Meetings:** competition ● symposium.

10527 ■ American Bandmasters Association (ABA)

c/o Dr. William J. Moody, Sec.-Treas.
4250 Shorebrook Dr.
Columbia, SC 29206
Ph: (803)787-6540
E-mail: wmoody@sc.rr.com
URL: http://www.americanbandmasters.org
Contact: Dr. William J. Moody, Sec.-Treas.
Founded: 1929. **Members:** 390. **Description:** Represents band directors, composers, and arrangers, music publishers and instrument manufacturers. Maintains a Research Center at the University of Maryland. Sponsors a foundation. **Awards:** ABA-Ostwald Concert Band Composition Award. **Frequency:** biennial. **Type:** recognition. **Recipient:** for original composition for band. **Committees:** Associate/Liaison; Convention Resource; Educational Projects; Edwin Franko Goldman Memorial Citation; Enrichment; International Relations; Research Center; School Bands. **Publications:** *Journal of Band Research*, semiannual. **Price:** $10.00/year in U.S.; $12.00/year outside U.S.; $18.00 2-year in U.S.; $22.00 2-year outside U.S. Alternate Formats: CD-ROM; microform. **Conventions/Meetings:** annual convention - in March.

10528 ■ American Banjo Fraternity (ABF)

636 Pelis Rd.
Newark, NY 14513
Ph: (315)331-6717
E-mail: msmith07@rochester.rr.com
URL: http://www.abfbanjo.org
Contact: Mary E. Smith, Exec. Sec.
Founded: 1948. **Members:** 400. **Membership Dues:** individual, $10 (annual). **Multinational. Description:** Represents players, collectors, and historians of the classic standard five-string banjo. Seeks to perpetuate the instrument's music and performing technique as it was used for entertainment and concert purposes from 1885 to 1915. Conducts social activities. **Libraries: Type:** reference. **Holdings:** 5,000; articles, audio recordings, books. **Subjects:** banjo history. **Publications:** *Five Stringer*, quarterly. Magazine. Includes banjo music transcriptions, historical articles and pictures. **Price:** included in membership dues. **Circulation:** 400 ● Membership Directory, biennial. **Price:** included in membership dues. **Conventions/Meetings:** semiannual Banjo Rally, with memorabilia, photo, and instruments (exhibits) - always May and October ● seminar and workshop, educational.

10529 ■ American Berlin Opera Foundation (ABOF)

c/o Mannheim LLC
712 5th Ave., 32nd Fl.
New York, NY 10019
Ph: (212)664-8843
Fax: (212)664-8415
E-mail: abof@operafoundation.org
URL: http://www.operafoundation.org
Contact: Mr. Bernhard Koepp, Pres.
Founded: 1986. **Description:** Individuals who support the Deutsche Oper Berlin, Berlin, Germany. Conducts fundraising activities for scholarships that send young American artists to Germany to study with the opera. **Awards:** Scholarships. **Frequency:** annual. **Type:** monetary. **Recipient:** to an American singer under 30 years old. **Publications:** Newsletter, 3/year. **Conventions/Meetings:** annual meeting.

10530 ■ American Children of SCORE

8031 Great Run Ln.
PO Box 3423
Warrenton, VA 20188
Ph: (540)428-2313
Fax: (540)428-2314
E-mail: scoreweb@earthlink.net
URL: http://scoremusicensemble.org
Contact: Mr. J Krumich, Artistic Dir.
Founded: 1994. **Members:** 50. **Staff:** 3. **Budget:** $60,000. **Regional Groups:** 3. **Local Groups:** 1. **Description:** Children participating in SCORE (String, Choral, Orff, and Recorder Ensemble) programs. Seeks to involve children aged 8-12 in ensemble music and early childhood music classes ages 4-7. **Libraries: Type:** reference. **Holdings:** archival material, articles, audio recordings, video recordings. **Subjects:** children's ensemble music. **Awards:** Financial Assistance. **Frequency:** 5/year. **Type:** scholarship. **Recipient:** for qualifying families (needs based). **Publications:** *SCORE Notes*, semiannual. Newsletter. **Conventions/Meetings:** quarterly board meeting.

10531 ■ American Choral Directors Association (ACDA)

PO Box 2720
Oklahoma City, OK 73101-2720
Ph: (405)232-8161
Fax: (405)232-8162
E-mail: acda@acdaonline.org
URL: http://www.acdaonline.org
Contact: Dr. Jerry Warren, Interim Exec. Dir.
Founded: 1959. **Members:** 20,000. **Membership Dues:** active in U.S. and Canada, associate, $85 (annual) ● student, $35 (annual) ● retired, $45 (annual) ● institutional, foreign active (airmail), $110 (annual) ● industry, $135 (annual) ● foreign active (surface), $100 (annual) ● life, $2,000. **Staff:** 12. **Budget:** $1,000,000. **Regional Groups:** 7. **State Groups:** 50. **Description:** Choral directors for elementary and secondary schools, colleges, universities, church, community and industrial organizations, radio, television, the concert stage, and the recording industry; associate members are publishers and dealers in choral music, manufacturers of choral accessories, and interested individuals. Seeks to foster choral singing. Encourages compositions of superior quality through commissions. **Awards:** Julius Herford Award. **Frequency:** annual. **Type:** recognition. **Recipient:** for prominent scholars, pianists, and teachers ● Raymond Brock Student Composition Award. **Frequency:** annual. **Type:** monetary. **Recipient:** for students through age 27. **Computer Services:** Mailing lists. **Telecommunication Services:** electronic mail, jwarren@cdaonline.org. **Committees:** Research and Publications. **Subcommittees:** Advisory; Herford Prize; Monograph and Composer Series; Technology. **Publications:** *ACDA National Convention Survey*. Alternate Formats: online ● *Choral Journal*, monthly. ISSN: 0009-5028. **Circulation:** 18,000. **Advertising:** accepted. Alternate Formats: online ● Monographs. **Conventions/Meetings:** annual convention (exhibits).

10532 ■ American Composers Alliance (ACA)

648 Broadway, Rm. 803
New York, NY 10012
Ph: (212)362-8900 (212)925-0458
Fax: (212)925-6798
E-mail: info@composers.com
URL: http://www.composers.com
Contact: Jasna Radonjic, Exec. Dir.
Founded: 1937. **Members:** 300. **Membership Dues:** individual, $100 (annual). **Staff:** 3. **Description:** Represents American composers of concert music. Promotes the music of the working composer. Provides career advice to composers and information to the public, as well as services in the areas of copyrights, licenses, contracts, and legal protection. Prints and sells scores, available online. **Awards:** Laurel Leaf Award. **Frequency:** annual. **Type:** recognition. **Recipient:** for distinguished achievement in fostering and encouraging American music. **Computer Services:** database, searchable online database with score information. **Telecommunication Services:** electronic mail, jasna@composers.com. **Conventions/Meetings:** annual Laurel Leaf Awards - meeting - always in New York City.

10533 ■ American Festival of Microtonal Music (AFMM)

c/o Johnny Reinhard, Dir.
318 E 70th St., Ste.5FW
New York, NY 10021
Ph: (212)517-3550
Fax: (212)517-5495
E-mail: info@afmm.org
URL: http://www.afmm.org
Contact: Johnny Reinhard, Dir.
Founded: 1981. **Description:** Musicians, composers, music students, scholars, and others interested in microtonal music. (Microtonal music uses alternative tunings based on principles of sound that differ from the standard Western 12-tone equal tempered scale.) Develops, organizes, and produces concerts of microtonal music. Conducts research; compiles information for an encyclopedia of microtonal music. Sponsors radio broadcasts; organizes educational programs. **Libraries: Type:** reference. **Holdings:** archival material. **Publications:** *Pitch*, quarterly. Magazine. Provides information on microtonal exploration. Back issues only are available. **Circulation:** 2,000 ● *Pitch for the International Microtonalist* ● *Pressbook*.

10534 ■ American Flute Guild (AFG)

PO Box 1515
South Pasadena, CA 91031
Ph: (626)441-6314
E-mail: info@americanfluteguild.com
URL: http://www.americanfluteguild.com
Contact: Catherine Thompson, Ed.
Description: Represents flutists and individuals interested in the flute. Promotes and furthers appreciation of the flute. Provides information about the many aspects of the flute industry in North America. **Publications:** Articles. Alternate Formats: online.

10535 ■ American Guild of English Handbell Ringers (AGEHR)

1055 E Centerville Sta. Rd.
Dayton, OH 45459
Ph: (937)438-0085
Free: (800)878-5459
Fax: (937)438-0434
E-mail: membership@agehr.org
URL: http://www.agehr.org
Contact: Mr. Dan Virzi, Membership and Marketing Dir.
Founded: 1954. **Members:** 9,000. **Membership Dues:** regular, $65 (annual) ● senior, $40 (annual). **Staff:** 7. **Regional Groups:** 12. **State Groups:** 50. **Description:** Church and school groups and individual musicians interested in the art of English handbell ringing. Encourages participation in area and national festivals. **Committees:** Festivals; Music. **Publications:** *Handbell Music* ● *Handbell Notation*. Book ● *Overtones*, bimonthly. Journal. **Circulation:** 9,000. **Advertising:** accepted. **Conventions/Meetings:** festival - 8/year ● workshop.

10536 ■ American Guild of Music (AGM)

PO Box 599
Warren, MI 48090-0599
Ph: (248)686-1975
E-mail: agm@americanguild.org
URL: http://www.americanguild.org
Contact: Mr. Lorelei Eccleston Dart, 1st VP
Founded: 1901. **Members:** 400. **Membership Dues:** professional, $40 (annual) ● studio-store, $65 (annual) ● professional associate, $30 (annual) ● music publisher, $75 (annual) ● trade, $150 (annual) ● college student, $20 (annual). **Staff:** 12. **Description:** Professional musicians, students, and trade groups interested in competing on the piano, guitar, key-

board, drum, accordion, banjo, mandolin, and other instruments. Dedicated to the advancement of musical talent throughout North America and Canada. Sponsors music contests, concerts, and displays of musical instruments and music. **Awards:** Mark Peel Memorial Award. **Frequency:** annual. **Type:** recognition. **Recipient:** to a guitarist who accumulates the most all-around points in plectrum guitar at the annual AGM national convention and competition. **Divisions:** Test List. **Programs:** Examination. **Formerly:** (1953) American Guild of Banjoists, Mandolinists and Guitarists. **Publications:** *Allegro Vivo*. Newsletter. Alternate Formats: online ● *News*, quarterly. Magazine. **Price:** included in membership dues; $25.00 /year for nonmembers. **Circulation:** 400. **Advertising:** accepted ● Also publishes student help folders. **Conventions/Meetings:** annual competition - 3/year ● annual meeting (exhibits) ● workshop, for teachers.

10537 ■ American Guild of Organists (AGO)
475 Riverside Dr., Ste.1260
New York, NY 10115
Ph: (212)870-2310
Free: (800)AGO-5115
Fax: (212)870-2163
E-mail: info@agohq.org
URL: http://www.agohq.org
Contact: James E. Thomashower, Exec. Dir.
Founded: 1896. **Members:** 22,000. **Membership Dues:** regular, independent, $88 (annual) ● special independent, special voting, partner voting, $64 (annual) ● student, $36 (annual) ● dual voting, $35 (annual) ● student, dual, $14 (annual). **Staff:** 12. **Budget:** $2,000,000. **Regional Groups:** 9. **Local Groups:** 342. **Multinational**. **Description:** Educational and service organization organized to advance the cause of organ and choral music and to maintain standards of artistic excellence of organists and choral conductors. Offers professional certification in organ playing, choral and instrumental training, and theory and general knowledge of music. **Awards:** AGO/ECS Publishing Award in Choral Composition. **Frequency:** biennial. **Type:** monetary. **Recipient:** for unpublished chorus and organ piece ● AGO/Quimby Regional Competition for Young Organists. **Frequency:** biennial. **Type:** monetary. **Recipient:** to organist under age of 23 ● Holtkamp-AGO Award in Organ Competition. **Frequency:** biennial. **Type:** monetary. **Recipient:** for unpublished organ solo ● National Competition in Organ Improvisation. **Frequency:** biennial. **Type:** monetary. **Recipient:** to members of American Guild of Organists and Royal Canadian College of Organists ● National Young Artists Competition in Organ Performance. **Frequency:** biennial. **Type:** monetary. **Recipient:** to organists ages 22-32. **Computer Services:** Mailing lists, rentals available to members and advertisers. **Telecommunication Services:** electronic mail, jet@agohq.org. **Committees:** Budget and Finance; Career Development and Support; Competition; Convention; Development; Educational Resources; Executive; Membership; National Nominating; New Music; New Organist; Professional Certification; Professional Concerns; Professional Education; Professional Networking and Public Relations; Seminary and Denominational Relations. **Publications:** *The American Organist*, monthly. Magazine. **Price:** $52.00 /year for nonmembers in U.S.; $70.00 /year for nonmembers outside U.S.; included in membership dues. ISSN: 0164-3150. **Circulation:** 23,000. **Advertising:** accepted. **Conventions/Meetings:** biennial convention (exhibits) - even numbered years. 2008 June 22-26, Minneapolis, MN - **Avg. Attendance:** 2000.

10538 ■ American Harp Society (AHS)
c/o Kathleen Moon, Exec. Sec.
PO Box 38334
Los Angeles, CA 90038-0334
Ph: (323)469-3050
Fax: (323)469-3050
E-mail: kmoon@uclalumni.net
URL: http://www.harpsociety.org
Contact: Kathleen Moon, Exec. Sec.
Founded: 1962. **Members:** 3,700. **Membership Dues:** student, $36 (annual) ● regular, in U.S., $51 (annual) ● regular, outside U.S., $66 (annual) ● contributing, $81 (annual) ● sustaining, $115 (annual) ● sponsor, $151 (annual) ● patron, $201 (annual) ● benefactor, $2,025 (annual) ● life, $1,025. **Regional Groups:** 12. **Local Groups:** 73. **Description:** Harpists, harp students, music educators, researchers, composers, and others interested in the realities, lore and literature of the harp. Works to: improve the quality of the instrument and performance; establish regional and national competitions and encourage composers to write material designed for the harp. **Libraries: Type:** reference. **Holdings:** audio recordings, video recordings. **Subjects:** harp classics. **Awards:** Grandjany Prize. **Frequency:** annual. **Type:** recognition. **Recipient:** for performance of a work by Marcel Grandjany ● Karl Carlson Awards. **Frequency:** annual. **Type:** recognition. **Recipient:** for students of any age who have showed musical promise and who have studied the harp for less than six years ● Mildred Biehn Johnson Award. **Frequency:** annual. **Type:** scholarship. **Recipient:** for students with financial need and musical promise in the study of the harp ● Prix Renie. **Frequency:** annual. **Type:** recognition. **Recipient:** for performance of a work by Henriette Renie ● Wickersham Award. **Frequency:** annual. **Type:** scholarship. **Recipient:** for students pursuing study in the field of music therapy using the harp. **Working Groups:** Administrative; Competitions; Conference; Education; Media; Regional Directors. **Publications:** *American Harp Journal*, semiannual. Features music, record reviews, obituaries, book reviews and video reviews. **Price:** included in membership dues. ISSN: 0000-869X. **Circulation:** 3,500. **Advertising:** accepted ● *American Harp Society—Regional Newsletter*, semiannual. **Price:** included in membership dues ● *Teacher's Forum*. Newsletter ● *Uncle Knuckles' Knews*. Newsletter ● Membership Directory, annual. **Price:** included in membership dues. **Conventions/Meetings:** annual National Conference/Summer Student Institute, conference and Summer Student Institute alternate years (exhibits) - 2008 June 23-26, Dearborn, MI.

10539 ■ American Institute for Verdi Studies (AIVS)
Dept. of Music
Faculty of Arts and Sci.
24 Waverly Pl., Rm. 268
New York, NY 10003
Ph: (212)998-2587
Fax: (212)995-4147
E-mail: verdi.institute@nyu.edu
URL: http://www.nyu.edu/projects/verdi
Contact: Martin Chusid, Dir.
Founded: 1976. **Members:** 300. **Membership Dues:** student, $25 (annual) ● regular, $50 (annual) ● contributing, $65 (annual) ● friend, $75 (annual) ● sponsor, $100 (annual) ● benefactor, $250 (annual) ● patron, $500-$2,000 (annual). **Description:** Persons interested in the life and works of Giuseppe Verdi (1813-1901), Italian composer. Resources include archive of letters, documents, stage designs, librettos, scores, costumes and secondary literature relating to the works of Verdi. Sponsors lectures and conferences. Presents concerts; sponsors occasional courses at New York University. Maintains Speaker's Bureau. **Libraries: Type:** reference. **Holdings:** 20,000; archival material, books, periodicals. **Subjects:** Verdi, Italian 19th century opera. **Computer Services:** database. **Boards:** Advisory; Executive. **Formerly:** (1977) AIVS Newsletter. **Publications:** *Verdi America* (in English and Italian), semiannual. Newsletter. Includes articles, book and video reviews, bibliographies, and lists of archive materials. **Price:** included in membership dues; $25.00/copy for nonmembers. **Circulation:** 500. **Advertising:** accepted ● *Verdi Forum*, annual. Journal. **Conventions/Meetings:** periodic congress and conference ● annual meeting and conference.

10540 ■ American Lithuanian Musicians Alliance (ALMA)
7310 S California Ave.
Chicago, IL 60629
Ph: (708)687-1430
Founded: 1911. **Members:** 350. **Membership Dues:** individual, $10 (annual). **Staff:** 6. **Regional Groups:** 5. **Local Groups:** 5. **Languages:** English, Lithuanian. **Description:** Musicians and singers of Lithuanian birth or descent. Promotes new Lithuanian music; sponsors concerts, musicals, operas, seminars, and conferences on church music and Lithuanian folklore and music literature. **Libraries: Type:** reference. **Holdings:** 33,000; archival material. **Subjects:** Lithuanian musicology. **Computer Services:** Mailing lists. **Commissions:** Music. **Formerly:** (1970) American Lithuanian Roman Catholic Organist Alliance; (1985) American Lithuanian Organist Musicians Alliance. **Publications:** *Music News - Muzikos Zinios* (in English and Lithuanian), periodic. Bulletin. **Price:** included in membership dues. **Circulation:** 350. Alternate Formats: online. **Conventions/Meetings:** semiannual conference and workshop, with new and old music (exhibits).

10541 ■ American Music Center (AMC)
30 W 26th St., Ste.1001
New York, NY 10010-2011
Ph: (212)366-5260
Fax: (212)366-5265
E-mail: center@amc.net
URL: http://www.amc.net
Contact: Joanne Hubbard Cossa, CEO
Founded: 1939. **Members:** 2,500. **Membership Dues:** individual, $55 (annual) ● student/senior, $35 (annual) ● organization, $85-$135 (annual) ● individual outside U.S., $65 (annual) ● student/senior outside U.S., $45 (annual). **Staff:** 9. **Budget:** $1,177,750. **Description:** Represents composers, performers, students and other music professionals. Appointed official U.S. Information Center for American Music in October 1962 by National Music Council. Seeks to encourage the creation, performance and appreciation of contemporary American music. Maintains information center. **Libraries: Type:** reference. **Holdings:** 60,000; archival material, audio recordings, books. **Subjects:** new American concert music and jazz. **Awards:** Letter of Distinction. **Frequency:** annual. **Type:** recognition. **Recipient:** for distinction in the field of contemporary American music. **Computer Services:** database, music score collection ● mailing lists, of members. **Additional Websites:** http://www.newmusicbox.org. **Telecommunication Services:** electronic mail, joanne@amc.net. **Programs:** Aaron Copland Fund for Music Performing Ensembles; Aaron Copland Fund for Music Recording; Composer Assistance; Live Music for Dance. **Publications:** *Contemporary Ensembles Directory*, annual. **Price:** $15.00 for members; $30.00 for nonmembers ● *Opportunities in New Music*, annual. Directory. **Price:** $30.00 for nonmembers; $15.00 for members ● *Opportunity Updates*, monthly. Directory. **Price:** included in membership dues.

10542 ■ American Music Conference (AMC)
5790 Armada Dr.
Carlsbad, CA 92008-4391
Ph: (760)431-9124
Fax: (760)438-7327
E-mail: info@amc-music.org
URL: http://www.amc-music.org
Contact: Danny Rocks, Pres.
Founded: 1947. **Members:** 250. **Membership Dues:** $50. **Staff:** 3. **Budget:** $250,000. **Description:** Represents associations, companies, and individuals supported by instrument manufacturers, publishers, wholesalers and retailers, educators, music industry and educator associations and other interested individuals. Promotes the importance of music, music making and music education to the general public. **Publications:** *Adult Attitudes Toward Music Making and Music Education*. Brochure ● *American Attitudes Toward Music*. Reports. Covers attitude and instrument usage research. ● *Music and Your Child: The Importance of Music to Children Development*. Brochure ● *Yes You Can! Learn to Play a Musical Instrument as an Adult*. Brochure. **Conventions/Meetings:** annual meeting (exhibits) - usually July, Nashville, TN.

10543 ■ American Music Festival Association (AMFA)
10 N 2nd St., Ste.401
Harrisburg, PA 17101
Ph: (717)255-3020
Fax: (717)255-6554
E-mail: cschulz@harrisburgevents.com
URL: http://www.americanmusicfest.org
Contact: Tina Manoogian-King, Department Dir.
Founded: 1981. **Membership Dues:** music association/organization, $495 (annual) ● music festival association, $395 (annual) ● professional/educational, $195 (annual) ● general, $95 (annual). **Staff:** 12. **Regional Groups:** 6. **State Groups:** 50. **Local Groups:** 93. **Languages:** English, Spanish. **Description:** Music festival founders, recording artists, songwriters, lyricists, music publishers, recording music executives, and all those interested in music. Recognizes and preserves American music achievements in each major field. Sponsors the American Music Festival Tour to attract national attention and interest to independent music festivals throughout the country. Conducts research, educational, and charitable activities. Compiles statistics. Plans to establish library, museum, hall of fame, and publish newsletter. **Libraries: Type:** reference; not open to the public. **Holdings:** 100,000; films, video recordings. **Subjects:** American music performances of the 20th century. **Awards:** Achievement and Hall of Fame Award. **Frequency:** annual. **Type:** recognition. **Recipient:** for significant musical achievement ● Music Education/Scholarship Programs. **Type:** scholarship. **Recipient:** for music performers. **Committees:** AMF-Tour Steering; AMFA Theme Site; Foundation; Membership and Sponsorships; Research. **Publications:** *Developing AMFA Newsletter*, annual. Features past, present, and future festival events. **Advertising:** accepted. **Conventions/Meetings:** annual tour - always in April through October.

10544 ■ American Musical Instrument Society (AMIS)
389 Main St., Ste.202
Malden, MA 02148
Ph: (781)397-8870
Fax: (781)397-8887
E-mail: amis@guildassoc.com
URL: http://www.amis.org
Contact: Kathryn Shanks Libin, Pres.
Founded: 1971. **Members:** 600. **Membership Dues:** student in U.S., joint international, $20 (annual) ● student outside U.S., $30 (annual) ● institution in U.S., $60 (annual) ● institution outside U.S., $70 (annual) ● joint in U.S., $10 (annual) ● regular in U.S., $45 (annual) ● regular outside U.S., $55 (annual). **Description:** Individuals, museums, and other institutions interested in all aspects of musical instruments. Disseminates information on all types of instruments (both Western and non-Western) through demonstrations, papers, slides, and meetings. **Awards:** Curt Sachs. **Frequency:** annual. **Type:** recognition. **Recipient:** for important contributions toward the goals of the society ● Frances Densmore Prize. **Frequency:** biennial. **Type:** monetary. **Recipient:** for most significant article-length publication in English (awarded in even years) ● Nicholas Bessaraboff Prize. **Frequency:** biennial. **Type:** monetary. **Recipient:** for most distinguished book-length publication (awarded in odd years) ● William E. Gribbon Memorial Award for Student Travel. **Frequency:** annual. **Type:** scholarship. **Recipient:** for students whose course of academic study and career interests relate to the purposes of the society. **Publications:** Journal, annual. Includes articles on all aspects of musical instruments. **Price:** included in membership dues. ISSN: 0362-3300. **Circulation:** 850. **Advertising:** accepted ● Newsletter, 3/year. Includes events of interest to the society, accessions made by various museums, and research information about American makers. **Price:** included in membership dues. ISSN: 0160-2365. **Advertising:** accepted ● Membership Directory, biennial. **Price:** included in membership dues. **Conventions/Meetings:** annual meeting, a wide variety of papers, panels, and performances are given.

10545 ■ American Musicological Society (AMS)
6010 College Sta.
Brunswick, ME 04011
Ph: (207)798-4243
Free: (877)679-7648
Fax: (207)798-4254
E-mail: ams@ams-net.org
URL: http://www.ams-net.org
Contact: Robert Judd, Exec. Dir.
Founded: 1934. **Members:** 3,500. **Staff:** 2. **Budget:** $600,000. **Regional Groups:** 15. **Description:** Professional musicologists, educators, and other interested persons. Works to advance research in the various fields of music as a branch of learning and scholarship. Sponsors scholarly editions of old music and musicological monographs. **Awards:** The Alfred Einstein Award. **Frequency:** annual. **Type:** recognition. **Recipient:** for journal article ● Alvin H. Johnson AMS 50 Dissertation-year Fellowships. **Frequency:** annual. **Type:** fellowship. **Recipient:** for outstanding student with a doctorate degree at a North American University ● The Claude V. Palisca Award. **Frequency:** annual. **Type:** monetary. **Recipient:** for an outstanding scholarly edition or translation in the field of musicology ● The Eugene K. Wolf Travel Fund. **Frequency:** annual. **Type:** monetary. **Recipient:** for students in any field of musical scholarship planning to undertake research in Europe ● The H. Colin Slim Award. **Frequency:** annual. **Type:** monetary. **Recipient:** for an outstanding musicological article by a scholar ● The Howard Mayer Brown Fellowship. **Frequency:** annual. **Type:** monetary. **Recipient:** for graduate program ● The Lewis Lockwood Award. **Frequency:** annual. **Type:** monetary. **Recipient:** for an author of a musicological book published during the previous year in any language ● The Noah Greenberg Award. **Frequency:** annual. **Type:** recognition. **Recipient:** for historical performance ● The Otto Kinkeldey Award. **Frequency:** annual. **Type:** monetary. **Recipient:** for the author of a musicological book published during the previous year in any language ● The Paul A. Pisk Prize. **Frequency:** annual. **Type:** recognition. **Recipient:** for the best student paper at AMS annual meeting ● The Philip Brett Award. **Frequency:** annual. **Type:** monetary. **Recipient:** for an exceptional musicological work in the field of gay, lesbian, bisexual or transgender/transsexual studies ● The Robert M. Stevenson Award. **Frequency:** annual. **Type:** monetary. **Recipient:** for an outstanding scholarship in Iberian music. **Committees:** American Music; Career-Related Issues; Publications. **Publications:** *AMS Directory*, annual. **Price:** included in membership dues. **Advertising:** accepted ● *AMS Newsletter*, semiannual. Provides research updates and information on awards, grants, and fellowships. **Price:** included in membership dues. **Circulation:** 4,500 ● *Journal of the American Musicological Society*, 3/year. Includes book reviews. **Price:** included in membership dues; $65.00 /year for libraries. ISSN: 0003-0139. **Advertising:** accepted ● Also publishes studies and documents. **Conventions/Meetings:** annual conference, scholarly meeting (exhibits).

10546 ■ American Nyckelharpa Association (ANA)
c/o John Wendell, Sec.-Treas.
1486 Ulupuni St.
Kailua, HI 96734
E-mail: info@nyckelharpa.org
URL: http://www.nyckelharpa.org
Contact: Tim Rued, Pres.
Members: 149. **Membership Dues:** digital, $10 (annual) ● snail mail in U.S., $15 (annual) ● snail mail (international), $20 (annual). **Multinational. Description:** Conducts educational programs and activities to promote knowledge of and interest in the nyckelharpa. Provides instruction in playing the instrument and the musical tradition associated with it. **Computer Services:** Information services, Nyckelharpa resources. **Telecommunication Services:** electronic mail, cd.sales@nyckelharpa.org ● electronic mail, string.sales@nyckelharpa.org ● electronic mail, timrued@aol.com. **Publications:** *Nyckel Notes*, quarterly. Newsletter. **Price:** included in membership dues. Alternate Formats: online.

10547 ■ American Orff-Schulwerk Association (AOSA)
PO Box 391089
Cleveland, OH 44139-8089
Ph: (440)543-5366
Fax: (440)543-2687
E-mail: info@aosa.org
URL: http://www.aosa.org
Contact: Ms. Katherine P. Johnson, Exec. Dir.
Founded: 1968. **Members:** 5,000. **Membership Dues:** regular, $70 (annual) ● student, $35 (annual) ● retired, $47 (annual) ● music industry, $98 (annual) ● regular, $180 (triennial). **Staff:** 5. **Budget:** $800,000. **Local Groups:** 97. **Description:** Music and movement educators, music therapists, and church choir directors united to promote and encourage the philosophy of Carl Orff's (1895-1982, German composer) Schulwerk (Music for Children) in America. Distributes information on the activities and growth of Orff Schulwerk in America. Conducts research; offers information on teacher training. Operates clearinghouse. **Libraries: Type:** reference. **Holdings:** biographical archives. **Subjects:** Orff-Schulwerk and music education. **Awards:** AOSA Research. **Frequency:** annual. **Type:** grant. **Recipient:** to members who show documented evidence of expertise in Orff Schulwerk training and work experience ● Distinguished Service Award. **Frequency:** annual. **Type:** recognition. **Recipient:** for service to the association and to Orff-Schulwerk in the United States ● Gunild Keetman Assistance Fund. **Frequency:** annual. **Type:** scholarship. **Recipient:** to members who need financial assistance to further their education in Orff Schulwerk ● Industry Service Award. **Frequency:** annual. **Type:** recognition ● Shields-Gillespie Scholarship. **Frequency:** annual. **Type:** scholarship. **Recipient:** to a member who is actively involved in preschool or kindergarten programs for low-income and racially diverse populations ● TAP Fund. **Type:** scholarship. **Recipient:** for members needing financial assistance for Orff instruments. **Computer Services:** Mailing lists. **Committees:** Conference; Financial Assistance; Professional Development; Publicity; Research. **Affiliated With:** MENC: The National Association for Music Education. **Publications:** *The Orff Echo*, quarterly. Magazine. Discusses the uses of the Orff-Schulwerk approach. **Price:** included in membership dues. **Circulation:** 5,400. **Advertising:** accepted ● *Reverberations*, quarterly. Newsletter. Contains news and lesson plans. **Price:** included in membership dues. **Circulation:** 5,400. **Advertising:** accepted ● Directory, annual ● Videos. **Conventions/Meetings:** annual conference (exhibits) - always November. 2008 Nov. 12-15, Charlotte, NC - **Avg. Attendance:** 2500.

10548 ■ American Recorder Society (ARS)
1129 Ruth Dr.
St. Louis, MO 63122-1019
Ph: (314)966-4082
Free: (800)491-9588
Fax: (314)966-4649
E-mail: ars.recorder@americanrecorder.org
URL: http://www.americanrecorder.org
Contact: Letitia Berlin, Pres.
Founded: 1939. **Members:** 2,400. **Membership Dues:** individual in U.S. and Canada, $40 (annual) ● individual in U.S. and Canada, $75 (biennial) ● organization, business, $120 (annual) ● sustaining in U.S. and Canada, $70 (annual) ● student in U.S. and Canada, $20 (annual) ● individual outside U.S. and Canada, $50 (annual) ● student outside U.S. and Canada, $25 (annual) ● workshop, $60 (annual). **Staff:** 1. **Budget:** $185,000. **Local Groups:** 95. **National Groups:** 34. **Description:** Works to promote recorder players in the U.S., Canada and 34 other countries. Includes amateurs, professionals, teachers and students. Playing under expert direction, short performances or lecture demonstrations are presented. **Awards:** Distinguished Achievement Award. **Frequency:** annual. **Type:** recognition. **Recipient:** for significant achievement in and contributions to the North American recorder movement. **Publications:**

American Recorder/ARS Newsletter, 5/year. Magazine. Reports on recorder technique, the care and making of recorders. Contains recorder music, literature, and reports of worldwide recorder events. **Price:** included in membership dues; $6.00/copy for nonmembers. ISSN: 0003-0724. **Circulation:** 4,500. **Advertising:** accepted. Alternate Formats: microform ● *American Recorder Society—International Directory of Members*, biennial. Membership Directory. **Price:** included in membership dues. **Circulation:** 2,400. **Advertising:** accepted ● *American Recorder Society—Members' Library*, semiannual. Booklets. Music for recorder ensembles. **Price:** included in membership dues. **Circulation:** 2,400 ● Booklets.

10549 ■ American-Slovenian Polka Foundation (ASPF)
605 E 222nd St.
Euclid, OH 44123
Ph: (216)261-3263
Free: (866)66P-OLKA
Fax: (216)261-4134
E-mail: polkashop@aol.com
URL: http://www.clevelandstyle.com
Contact: Cecilia Dolgan, Pres.
Founded: 1988. **Members:** 1,600. **Membership Dues:** regular, $15 (annual) ● life, $150. **Staff:** 2. **Budget:** $100,000. **Description:** Works to preserve and promote Cleveland-style or Slovenian-American-style polka music. Maintains the National Cleveland-Style Polka Hall of Fame and Museum; collects artifacts and memorabilia concerning the history of polka. **Awards:** Annual Achievement Awards. **Frequency:** annual. **Type:** recognition. **Recipient:** for band of the year ● Lifetime Achievement Award. **Frequency:** annual. **Type:** recognition. **Recipient:** for lifetime contribution ● Trustees' Honor Roll. **Frequency:** annual. **Type:** recognition. **Recipient:** for lifetime contribution. **Publications:** Newsletter, quarterly. **Price:** free. **Circulation:** 1,500 ● Catalog. **Conventions/Meetings:** annual Induction/Awards Ceremony and Show - usually Thanksgiving weekend ● meeting, for members only.

10550 ■ American Society for Jewish Music (ASJM)
Center for Jewish History
15 W 16th St.
New York, NY 10011
Ph: (212)294-8328
Fax: (212)294-6161
E-mail: info@jewishmusic-asjm.org
URL: http://www.jewishmusic-asjm.org
Contact: Michael Leavitt, Pres.
Founded: 1974. **Members:** 500. **Membership Dues:** individual, $40 (annual) ● organization/synagogue, $100 (annual) ● foreign, $45 (annual) ● student, $20 (annual) ● university library, $15 (annual). **Staff:** 1. **Budget:** $20,000. **Description:** Composers, musicians, cantors, educators, and concerned laypersons devoted to the performance, scholarship, and perpetuation of all forms of Jewish music including new, old, art, folk, secular, and liturgical. Informs the general music public of the wide and rich dimensions of Jewish music. Sponsors several public concerts each year. **Libraries: Type:** not open to the public. **Holdings:** 16. **Boards:** Governors. **Committees:** Concert; Panel of Judges. **Publications:** *ASJM Matters*. Newsletter. Alternate Formats: online ● *In Honor of Cantor Moshe Ganchoff*. Audiotape ● *Musica Judaica*, annual. Journal. Includes topics on Jewish music. Features book reviews and obituaries. **Price:** included in membership dues. **Circulation:** 1,000. Alternate Formats: online.

10551 ■ American Society of Music Arrangers and Composers (ASMAC)
PO Box 17840
Encino, CA 91416
Ph: (818)994-4661
Fax: (818)994-6181
E-mail: syd@theproperimageevents.com
URL: http://www.asmac.org
Contact: Scherr Lillico, Dir.
Founded: 1938. **Members:** 500. **Membership Dues:** active, $50 (annual). **Staff:** 1. **Local Groups:** 1. **Description:** Arrangers, composers and orchestrators. Organizes regularly scheduled workshop sessions to present experimental performance of orchestral and vocal writings by members that demonstrate new techniques in creative music. Conducts monthly membership luncheons. Works with the American Federation of Musicians of the United States and Canada to insure fair compensation and welfare for those persons engaged in music preparation in the U.S. and Canada. Conducts educational workshops and professional clinics. **Awards:** Golden Score Award. **Frequency:** annual. **Type:** recognition. **Recipient:** to leading composer, to recognize high caliber work ● President's Award. **Frequency:** annual. **Type:** recognition. **Recipient:** for individual. **Computer Services:** Mailing lists, of members. **Committees:** Archives; Awards; Clinic; Workshop. **Formerly:** (1991) American Society of Music Arrangers. **Publications:** Newsletter, periodic. **Circulation:** 1,000. **Advertising:** accepted. **Conventions/Meetings:** annual meeting.

10552 ■ American Symphony Orchestra League
33 W 60th St., 5th Fl.
New York, NY 10023
Ph: (212)262-5161
Fax: (212)262-5198
E-mail: league@symphony.org
URL: http://www.symphony.org
Contact: Henry Fogel, CEO/Pres.
Founded: 1942. **Members:** 5,330. **Membership Dues:** individual, $50 (annual) ● professional, $100 (annual) ● student, $25 (annual) ● student professional, $75 (annual) ● orchestra (based on total expenses), $150-$325 (annual) ● collegiate/community orchestra, $150 (annual) ● youth orchestra, $124 (annual) ● business, $385 (annual) ● professional business, $215 (annual). **Staff:** 30. **Budget:** $5,000,000. **Description:** Symphony orchestras; associate members include educational institutions, arts councils, public libraries, business firms, orchestra professionals, and individuals interested in symphony orchestras. Engages in extensive research on diverse facets of symphony orchestra operations and development. Provides consulting services for orchestras, their boards, and volunteer organizations. Sponsors management seminars and workshops for professional symphony orchestra administrative and artistic staff, volunteers, and prospective management personnel. Maintains employment services; collects and distributes resource materials, financial data, and statistical reports on many aspects of orchestra operations. Compiles statistics; sponsors educational programs; maintains resource center. **Awards: Type:** recognition. **Publications:** *The Gold Book: Directory of Successful Projects for Volunteers*, annual. **Price:** $32.50 for members; $37.50 for nonmembers ● *Orchestra/Business Directory*, annual. **Price:** $11.00 for members; $13.00 for nonmembers ● *SYMPHONY*, bimonthly. Magazine. Includes association news, feature articles, orchestras, people, public sector, recordings, and repertoire. **Price:** $35.00/year. **Circulation:** 17,000. **Advertising:** accepted. **Conventions/Meetings:** annual conference (exhibits) - 2009 June 9-13, Chicago, IL.

10553 ■ American Theatre Organ Society (ATOS)
c/o Jim Merry, Exec. Sec.
PO Box 5327
Fullerton, CA 92838-0327
Ph: (714)773-4354
Fax: (714)773-4829
E-mail: merry@atos.org
URL: http://www.atos.org
Contact: Jim Merry, Exec. Sec.
Founded: 1955. **Members:** 5,000. **Membership Dues:** basic, $40 (annual) ● student, $25 (annual) ● contributing, $75 (annual) ● sustaining, $100 (annual) ● patron, $200 (annual) ● benefactor, $500 (annual). **Budget:** $300,000. **Local Groups:** 74. **Description:** Dedicated to the preservation, restoration and presentation of the theatre pipe organ and its music. Chapters sponsor local and regional meetings and concerts to play or rebuild theatre organs and exchange information on organ music, restoration and history. Annual Young Artist Competition encourages youth to learn the instrument. Student scholarships available as well as funds for theatre pipe organ restoration. Annually votes living or deceased former theatre organists into hall of fame. Operates committee that gathers history and old music from silent film days and information on theatre organists, theaters and organ installations of the silent film era. **Libraries: Type:** reference. **Holdings:** archival material, books, films, periodicals. **Subjects:** arrangements to back silent films and recordings. **Awards:** Honorary Member Award. **Frequency:** annual. **Type:** recognition. **Recipient:** for a member who has contributed the most to the progress of the society ● Organist of the Year. **Frequency:** annual. **Type:** recognition. **Formerly:** American Association of Theatre Organ Enthusiasts; (1970) American Theatre Organ Enthusiasts. **Publications:** *ATOS International News*, bimonthly. Newsletter ● *Theatre Organ*, bimonthly. Journal. **Advertising:** accepted ● Membership Directory, periodic ● Journal, weekly. Alternate Formats: online. **Conventions/Meetings:** annual convention (exhibits) ● Young Organist Competition.

10554 ■ American Viola Society (AVS)
14070 Proton Rd., Ste.100
Dallas, TX 75244-3601
Ph: (972)233-9107
Fax: (972)490-4219
E-mail: info@avsnationaloffice.org
URL: http://www.americanviolasociety.org
Contact: Madeleine Crouch, Gen. Mgr.
Founded: 1971. **Members:** 1,400. **Membership Dues:** regular, $42 (annual) ● student, emeritus, $21 (annual) ● joint, Canadian, $52 (annual) ● regular (group), $36 (annual) ● student (group), $18 (annual). **Staff:** 1. **Budget:** $40,000. **Description:** Professional violists, amateur string players, and viola conservatories; university and secondary school teachers. Encourages the performance, research, and pedagogical aspects of the viola. Has established the Primrose International Viola Archive, housed at Brigham Young University, Provo, UT. Sponsors viola competitions. Assists in publishing viola music. **Formerly:** (1978) Viola Research Society. **Publications:** Journal, semiannual. Covers the history of the viola and its music. Announces and reviews new viola recordings, music, and concerts. Features book reviews. **Price:** included in membership dues; $5.00/copy (back issue); $50.00 collection of all issues. **Circulation:** 1,000 ● Directory, annual ● Membership Directory, annual ● Booklets. **Conventions/Meetings:** annual International Viola Congress, with concerts, lectures (exhibits).

10555 ■ Americana Music Association
PO Box 128077
Nashville, TN 37212
Ph: (615)386-6936
Fax: (615)386-6937
E-mail: info@americanamusic.org
URL: http://www.americanamusic.org
Contact: Danna Strong, Operations Mgr.
Founded: 1999. **Membership Dues:** industry, $75 (annual) ● artist, $35 (annual). **Description:** Provides a forum for the advocacy of Americana music. Promotes public awareness of the genre to support the creative and economic viability of professionals in this field. Encourages long-term growth, creating continually expanding opportunities at artistic and financial levels. **Awards:** Americana Honors and Awards. **Frequency:** annual. **Type:** recognition. **Recipient:** for outstanding achievements in Americana music. **Telecommunication Services:** electronic mail, danna@americanamusic.org. **Publications:** Newsletter, monthly. **Price:** included in membership dues ● Membership Directory. **Price:** included in membership dues. Alternate Formats: online.

10556 ■ Asian American Music Society (AAMS)
39 Eton Overlook
Rockville, MD 20850
Ph: (301)424-3379
Fax: (301)424-8694

E-mail: webmaster@aamsopera.com
URL: http://www.aamsopera.com
Founded: 1993. **Description:** Promotes the cultural diversity of the Asian American music community. Arranges music and dance entertainment presentations. Provides artist management to individuals who want to pursue their career in music.

10557 ■ Asiatic Philharmonia Society
PO Box 2799
Sunnyvale, CA 94087
Ph: (408)331-4909
Fax: (408)331-4909
E-mail: info@asiaticphilharmonia.org
URL: http://asiaticphilharmonia.org
Contact: Jindong Cai, Music Dir./Conductor
Multinational. Description: Strives to help Chinese and Asian music emerge into the American mainstream. Promotes cultural understanding/appreciation and social interaction between Asian and American musicians. Employs renowned Chinese/Asian musicians for high culture performing events and music education.

10558 ■ Association for the Advancement of Creative Musicians (AACM)
410 S Michigan Ave., Ste.943
Chicago, IL 60680
Ph: (312)922-1900
Fax: (312)922-1900
E-mail: greatblackmusic@aacmchicago.org
Contact: Muata Bowden, Pres.
Founded: 1965. **Members:** 48. **Staff:** 3. **Description:** Professional musicians united to create music "of a high artistic level" for the public through the presentation of programs designed to magnify the importance of creative music. Seeks to provide a source of employment for worthy, creative musicians and to showcase their original compositions. Cultivates young musicians through a free inner-city training program. Conducts workshops and concerts. Maintains library of music literature and recordings. **Conventions/Meetings:** annual conference - always May, Chicago, IL.

10559 ■ Association of Armenian Church Choirs of America (AACCA)
c/o Ms. Mary Selvinazian, Treas./Ed.
5636 196th Pl.
Flushing, NY 11365-2310
Ph: (718)423-5680
E-mail: maryamsel@worldnet.att.net
URL: http://sograd.com/aacca
Contact: Ms. Mary Selvinazian, Treas./Ed.
Description: Promotes the teaching of the sacred music of the Armenian church. Encourages the choirs to learn and adhere to the liturgical rites, canons and doctrines of the Armenian church. Promotes the appreciation and use of Armenian music. **Publications:** Bulletin. Alternate Formats: online.

10560 ■ Association of Concert Bands (ACB)
c/o Nada Vencl, Sec.
6613 Cheryl Ann Dr.
Independence, OH 44131-3718
Ph: (216)524-1897
Free: (800)726-8720
E-mail: acbsec@sbcglobal.net
URL: http://www.acbands.org
Contact: Nada Vencl, Sec.
Founded: 1977. **Members:** 850. **Membership Dues:** individual, $30 (annual) ● family, $45 (annual) ● organizational, $50 (annual) ● corporate, $150 (annual) ● life, $1,000 ● organization (with BMI/ASCAP Performance Licensing Agreement), $208 (annual). **Staff:** 1. **Budget:** $36,000. **Description:** Adult musicians; concert and community bands; corporations. Works to: promote concert band music and concert bands; foster appreciation of concert bands; provide the public with the opportunity to hear and see performances of the best selection of concert band compositions. Seeks to enable adult concert bands to qualify for and obtain national and state funding; disseminates information on funding policies and practices of music projects. Regularly surveys community bands in America. Cooperates with the Public Broadcasting Service in programming television broadcasts of adult concert bands. Encourages organization of new bands. Conducts composition contest. **Computer Services:** Mailing lists, of members. **Affiliated With:** American Federation of Musicians of the United States and Canada. **Formerly:** (1981) Association of Concert Bands of America. **Publications:** *ACB Membership Roster*, biennial. Membership Directory. **Price:** included in membership dues ● *ACB National Band Directory*, biennial. **Price:** included in membership dues of corporate and organization; $35.00 for individual members ● *Advance*, 3/year. Magazine. Promotes concert and community bands for adult musicians. Includes conference reports and fundraising appeals. **Price:** included in membership dues; $3.00/issue for nonmembers. **Circulation:** 4,000. **Advertising:** accepted ● *The Band Builders*. Manual ● *National Convention of the Association of Concert Bands*, annual. Contains program guide. **Price:** free to convention participants ● Articles ● Books. **Conventions/Meetings:** annual convention (exhibits).

10561 ■ Association for Korean Music Research (AKMR)
c/o Prof. Okon Hwang, Sec.-Treas.
Eastern Connecticut State Univ.
Performing Arts Dept.
Willimantic, CT 06226
Ph: (860)465-5109
E-mail: hwango@easternct.edu
URL: http://www.akmr.org
Contact: Prof. Okon Hwang, Sec.-Treas.
Founded: 1995. **Membership Dues:** student, $5 (annual) ● non-student, $10 (annual). **Multinational. Description:** Aims to promote and advance the in-depth study of Korean music as a distinctive cluster of traditions. Supports research on Korean music studies and its impact on world culture. Fosters exchange of information among scholars and performers. **Awards:** AKMR Prize. **Frequency:** annual. **Type:** monetary. **Recipient:** for the most distinguished student paper on Korean music presented during society for ethnomusicology annual conference. **Publications:** Newsletter. Alternate Formats: online.

10562 ■ Association of Music Writers and Photographers (AMWP)
PO Box 79
Oak Lawn, IL 60454
Fax: (801)327-4735
E-mail: amwp@amwp.org
URL: http://www.musicpressreport.com
Membership Dues: professional/associate, $55 (annual) ● student, $35 (annual). **Multinational. Description:** Defends the interests of music writers and photographers. Establishes the first music press community. Offers networking opportunities, job listings, industry directories, guides and contests. **Computer Services:** Online services, discussion forum. **Publications:** *Music Press Report*, weekly. Newsletter. **Price:** free. Alternate Formats: online.

10563 ■ Balalaika and Domra Association of America (BDAA)
2801 Warner St.
Madison, WI 53713-2160
Ph: (608)259-9440
Fax: (608)259-9440
E-mail: execdir@bdaa.com
URL: http://www.bdaa.com
Contact: Maxwell B. McCullough, Exec. Dir.
Founded: 1978. **Members:** 500. **Membership Dues:** individual in U.S. and Canada, $25 (annual) ● family in U.S. and Canada, $30 (annual) ● individual outside U.S. and Canada, $30 (annual) ● family outside U.S. and Canada, $35 (annual). **Budget:** $38,000. **Regional Groups:** 14. **Local Groups:** 56. **Multinational. Description:** Orchestras, ensembles, dancers, singers, musicians, and non-performing individuals interested in Eastern European music and musical instruments. Promotes performances of music written for traditional Eastern European musical instruments, particularly the balalaika (a three-stringed, lute-like instrument with a triangular body) and the domra (a three-stringed, mandolin-like instrument). Disseminates information regarding the musical and cultural heritage of Eastern Europe; serves as a forum for discussing musical possibilities of and developments concerning the balalaika and domra. Offers musical instruction; acts as a clearinghouse for members' collections of materials pertaining to Eastern European music and culture. Maintains hall of fame. **Awards: Type:** recognition ● **Type:** scholarship. **Publications:** *BDAA Newsletter*, quarterly. Features articles of current interest, listings of concert schedules, music, historical references and information on upcoming conferences and tours. **Price:** included in membership dues. ISSN: 0897-2907. **Advertising:** accepted ● *BDAA Newsletter Reprint Series*, periodic ● *Membership List*, annual. Membership Directory. **Conventions/Meetings:** annual convention, musical instruments, Russian souvenirs, tapes, CDs (exhibits) - always June/July ● periodic workshop.

10564 ■ Bands of America (BOA)
39 W Jackson Pl., Ste.150
Indianapolis, IN 46225
Ph: (317)636-2263
Free: (800)848-2263
Fax: (317)524-6200
E-mail: info@musicforall.org
URL: http://www.bands.org
Contact: L. Scott McCormick, Pres.
Founded: 1975. **Staff:** 15. **Budget:** $2,500,000. **Description:** Works to create, support, and serve the experience of the school band and orchestra; to provide the opportunity for acknowledgement of young participants; and to promote excellence and participation in young people. Acts as a voice for high school bands across the country. **Awards:** Hall of Fame. **Frequency:** annual. **Type:** recognition. **Recipient:** for individual. **Formerly:** (1984) Marching Bands of America. **Publications:** Newsletter, quarterly. **Circulation:** 25,000. **Advertising:** accepted. Alternate Formats: online. **Conventions/Meetings:** annual Grand National Championship - competition (exhibits) - 2008 Nov. 12-15, Indianapolis, IN; 2009 Nov. 11-14, Indianapolis, IN ● Summer Band Symposium - workshop.

10565 ■ Big Band Academy of America (BBAA)
c/o David Bernhart, Pres.
1438 N Pepper St.
Burbank, CA 91505-1835
Ph: (818)559-1313
E-mail: miltbernhart@email.com
Contact: David Bernhart, Pres.
Founded: 1983. **Members:** 500. **Membership Dues:** individual, $25 (annual). **Staff:** 15. **Budget:** $75,000. **Local Groups:** 1. **Description:** Big band enthusiasts. Seeks to perpetuate the memory and sound of the big band and to introduce big band music to younger generations; big band music in the style of Glenn Miller and Tommy Dorsey attained popularity during the 1930s and 1940s. Promotes big band music by seeking to increase public awareness of the big band sound. **Libraries: Type:** reference. **Holdings:** 20,000; archival material, audio recordings, books. **Awards: Type:** recognition. **Affiliated With:** International Association for Jazz Education. **Publications:** *The Bandstand*, quarterly. Newsletter. Features updates in the world of big bands. **Price:** included in membership dues. **Conventions/Meetings:** annual Big Band Reunion - banquet, also features concert (exhibits) - every first Sunday of March.

10566 ■ The Blues Foundation (TBF)
49 Union Ave.
Memphis, TN 38103
Ph: (901)527-2583
Fax: (901)529-4030
E-mail: jay@blues.org
URL: http://www.blues.org
Contact: Jay Sieleman, Exec. Dir.
Founded: 1980. **Members:** 4,000. **Membership Dues:** fan, $25 (annual) ● friend, $50 (annual) ● partner, corporate, affiliate, $100 (annual) ● supporter, $250 (annual) ● patron, $500 (annual) ● V.I. P., $1,000 (annual) ● charter, $5,000 (annual) ● V.I.

P., life, $5,000. **Staff:** 5. **Budget:** $800,000. **Regional Groups:** 12. **Local Groups:** 88. **Description:** Educational and cultural organization that celebrates Blues music as the common thread in American popular music and promotes Blues music to foster understanding across socioeconomic lines. Individual members and grass roots societies around the globe support the Foundation's mission to preserve Blues history, celebrate Blues excellence and support Blues education. **Awards:** Blues Hall of Fame. **Type:** recognition. **Recipient:** to individuals, literature, and recordings that have been selected by a committee of music authorities ● Keeping the Blues Alive Award. **Frequency:** annual. **Type:** recognition. **Recipient:** to individuals, literature, and recordings that have been selected by ballot of 20,000 voters ● **Type:** recognition ● W.C. Handy Blues Awards. **Frequency:** annual. **Type:** recognition. **Recipient:** for the best in Blues recordings and performance. **Committees:** Blues in the School; Blues on Radio. **Publications:** *Blues at the Foundation*, quarterly. Newsletter. **Price:** free for members. **Circulation:** 5,000. **Advertising:** accepted. Alternate Formats: online. **Conventions/Meetings:** annual International Blues Challenge - competition (exhibits) ● annual W.C. Handy Blues Awards Show - dinner.

10567 ■ Blues Heaven Foundation (BHF)

2120 Michigan Ave.
Chicago, IL 60616
Ph: (312)808-1286
Fax: (312)808-0273
E-mail: info@bluesheaven.com
URL: http://www.bluesheaven.com

Founded: 1981. **Description:** Supporters are individuals involved with the documentation, performance, and preservation of blues music and music history. Conducts harmonica clinics during Black History Month. Promotes copyright and publication protection. Maintains an audiovisual archive. **Convention/Meeting:** none. **Awards:** The Muddy Waters Scholarship. **Type:** scholarship. **Recipient:** for full time Chicago college student studying music.

10568 ■ Bohemia Ragtime Society (BRS)

4501 Palm Ave.
Des Moines, IA 50310-3790
E-mail: theragtimer@juno.com
URL: http://www.ragtimer.com
Contact: Nick Taylor, Admin.

Founded: 1990. **Staff:** 1. **Description:** Seeks to preserve and promote ragtime music, both as a musical art form and an historical cultural element. Encourages the preservation of classic ragtime music, as well as the development of contemporary ragtime styles. Serves as a forum for the performance and discussion of ragtime music. Maintains information on ragtime music, including history, composers, recordings, artists, and ragtime events worldwide. **Conventions/Meetings:** periodic meeting.

10569 ■ Broadcast Music, Inc. (BMI)

320 W 57th St.
New York, NY 10019-3790
Ph: (212)586-2000
Fax: (212)956-2059
E-mail: newyork@bmi.com
URL: http://bmi.com
Contact: Del Bryant, Pres./CEO

Founded: 1940. **Members:** 300,000. **Staff:** 1,500. **Regional Groups:** 12. **Description:** Consists of more than 90,000 writers and 50,000 publisher affiliates. Acts as steward for the performing rights of the works of its affiliates by collecting license fees from music users and making payments to the creators of the music used (based on a published schedule of payments). Maintains reciprocal agreements with 41 sister licensing organizations worldwide. **Awards:** BMI Pop. **Frequency:** annual. **Type:** recognition. **Recipient:** for songwriters ● Charlie Parker Jazz Composition Prize. **Frequency:** annual. **Type:** recognition. **Recipient:** for songwriters ● Christian Music. **Frequency:** annual. **Type:** recognition. **Recipient:** for songwriters ● Student Composer Awards for Classical Compositions. **Frequency:** annual. **Type:** recognition. **Recipient:** for student composers to encourage young writers of concert music. **Publications:** *BMI Music World*, quarterly. Magazine. Includes profiles of songwriters and coverage of music events. **Price:** free. **Circulation:** 75,000. Alternate Formats: online ● Booklets ● Brochures. Contains information on concert music affiliates. ● Pamphlets. **Conventions/Meetings:** competition ● seminar, on music business ● workshop ● workshop, on film, television, and jazz composers.

10570 ■ Caledonian Foundation USA (CF)

PO Box 1242
Edgartown, MA 02539-1242
URL: http://www.caledonianfoundationusa.org
Contact: Ms. Duncan MacDonald, Exec. VP/Treas.

Founded: 1976. **Membership Dues:** regular, $10 (annual). **Multinational. Description:** Individuals interested in building U.S. support for Scottish arts. Promotes the establishment of an endowment that will enable the Scottish Opera Company to maintain high standards of excellence and continue to improve all aspects of its program, including opera performances, expansion of touring schedule, educational programs and services, and the training of young singers. Seeks support in the U.S. for the operation and maintenance of the Balnain House in Inverness and the Theatre Royal in Glasgow, Scotland, which houses the performances of Scottish Opera and the Edinburgh Festival Theatre. Identifies outstanding persons of Scottish birth or descent. Offers travel program to Scotland; maintains speakers' bureau. **Awards:** Gavin Boyd Memorial Scholarship. **Frequency:** annual. **Type:** scholarship ● Nestor J. MacDonald Scholarship. **Frequency:** annual. **Type:** scholarship ● Teddy Hawkins Scholarship. **Frequency:** annual. **Type:** scholarship. **Projects:** Great Scots; Scottish Information Network. **Formerly:** (1976) American Friends of Scottish Opera. **Publications:** *Caledonian News*, quarterly. Newsletter. Includes president's message and meeting and production information. **Price:** included in membership dues. Also Cited As: *News from Caledonian Foundation*. **Conventions/Meetings:** annual symposium.

10571 ■ CAS Forum of the Violin Society of America

c/o Violin Society of America
48 Acad. St.
Poughkeepsie, NY 12601
Ph: (845)452-7557
Fax: (845)452-7618
E-mail: info@vsa.to
URL: http://www.catgutacoustical.org
Contact: Julius J. VandeKopple, Pres.

Founded: 1963. **Members:** 1,700. **Membership Dues:** individual (in U.S., Canada and Mexico), library, $85 (annual) ● individual (in other countries), $105 (annual) ● full time student (in U.S., Canada and Mexico), $30 (annual) ● full time student (other countries), $45 (annual). **Staff:** 1. **Description:** Physicists, engineers, instrument makers, musicians, and others interested in violin acoustics. Congregates for periodic discussions of plate vibrations, varnish, damping factors, tap tones, air resonance, special properties of the slip-stick action of the bowed string, and other aspects of violin construction and sound. Studies factors affecting the quality of old Italian violins and modern instruments. Has developed and constructed eight new instruments of the violin family. Sponsors musical compositions for new instruments. Individual members have published research studies. **Libraries:** **Type:** open to the public. **Holdings:** 62. **Subjects:** violin. **Committees:** Projects. **Formerly:** (2004) CAS Forum. **Publications:** *VSA Papers*, semiannual. Journal. Contains research articles and book reviews. **Price:** included in membership dues; $26.00/issue for nonmembers (1967 to 1987). ISSN: 0882-2212. **Circulation:** 1,700. **Advertising:** accepted. Alternate Formats: online. Also Cited As: *Newsletter of the Catgut Acoustical Society*. **Conventions/Meetings:** biennial International Forum on Musical Acoustics - symposium (exhibits).

10572 ■ Center for Contemporary Opera (CCO)

PO Box 258
New York, NY 10044-0205
Ph: (212)785-2757
Fax: (212)758-0389
E-mail: mail@conopera.org
URL: http://conopera.org
Contact: Richard Marshall, Gen. Dir.

Founded: 1982. **Members:** 110. **Membership Dues:** individual (minimum), $50 (annual) ● friend (minimum), $100 (annual) ● donor (minimum), $250 (annual) ● patron (minimum), $500 (annual) ● benefactor (minimum), $1,000 (annual) ● angel (minimum), $2,500 (annual). **Staff:** 4. **Budget:** $250,000. **Description:** Adults interested in promoting the creation and production of modern opera written in English. Produces 2-3 operas annually; sponsors the International Opera Singers Competition; presents winners in a recital. Presents lectures and panel discussions on American Opera. **Telecommunication Services:** electronic mail, esalzman@aba.org. **Affiliated With:** National Opera Association; OPERA America. **Publications:** *Opera Today*, semiannual. Newsletter. Includes news of modern opera performances and group's activities. **Circulation:** 18,000. **Advertising:** accepted. **Conventions/Meetings:** periodic conference.

10573 ■ Chamber Music America (CMA)

305 7th Ave.
New York, NY 10001-6008
Ph: (212)242-2022
Fax: (212)242-7955
E-mail: mlioi@chamber-music.org
URL: http://www.chamber-music.org
Contact: Margaret M. Lioi, CEO

Founded: 1977. **Members:** 11,000. **Membership Dues:** organization (based on gross income), $125-$375 (annual) ● professional, $85 (annual) ● advocate, $60 (annual) ● student, $35 (annual) ● business, $95 (annual). **Staff:** 11. **Budget:** $3,000,000. **Description:** Professional chamber music ensembles and presenters; organizations, foundations, and individuals actively supporting chamber music performances. Purposes are to: promote artistic excellence and economic stability within the profession, and to ensure that chamber music, in its broadest sense, is a vital part of American life. Disseminates information on organization, repertoire, fundraising, fiscal management, and touring. Conducts workshops and conferences on management of chamber ensembles. Offers consultation services. Compiles statistics; conducts research programs. **Libraries:** **Type:** reference. **Holdings:** archival material. **Awards:** Recognition of Merit. **Frequency:** annual. **Type:** recognition ● Richard J. Bogomolny National Service Award. **Frequency:** annual. **Type:** recognition. **Computer Services:** Mailing lists, for members only. **Publications:** *Accent*, monthly. Newsletter. Alternate Formats: online ● *Chamber Music*, bimonthly. Magazine. Offers news and commentary for and about chamber music artists, concert presenters, music schools, and music enthusiasts. **Price:** included in membership dues. ISSN: 8775-0725. **Circulation:** 12,000. **Advertising:** accepted ● *CMA Matters*, quarterly. Bulletin. Focuses on professional development and "how-to" articles for ensembles and presenters in the chamber music field. **Price:** included in membership dues ● *Directory of Summer Chamber Music Workshops, Schools, and Festivals*, annual. Lists training programs and concert series in the U.S. and abroad for adult amateurs, professionally oriented students, and young people. **Price:** $15.00/year. **Circulation:** 12,000. **Advertising:** accepted ● Membership Directory, annual. Includes descriptions of performing groups and concert presenters, indexes of professional members and types of ensembles. **Price:** included in membership dues. **Circulation:** 12,000. **Advertising:** accepted. **Conventions/Meetings:** annual conference (exhibits) - always January.

10574 ■ Charles Ives Society

c/o Indiana University
School of Music
Bloomington, IN 47405
Ph: (812)855-7097
Fax: (812)855-4936

E-mail: jsinclair@charlesives.org
URL: http://www.charlesives.org
Contact: James B. Sinclair, Exec. Ed.
Founded: 1973. **Description:** Seeks to further the preparation, along scholarly-critical lines, of new and revised performing editions of the works of Charles E. Ives (1874-1954), American composer who was awarded the Pulitzer Prize for his Third Symphony and is credited with the early use of atonality, polyharmony, and polyrhythms. Commissions editions of Ives' music from scholar-musicians. Supports projects that promote Ives' music. **Convention/Meeting:** none. **Publications:** Bulletin, every 1-2 years. Lists works by Ives. **Price:** free.

10575 ■ Chinese Music Society of North America (CMSNA)

PO Box 5275
Woodridge, IL 60517
Ph: (630)910-1551
Fax: (630)910-1561
URL: http://www.chinesemusic.net
Contact: Sin-Yan Shen, Pres.
Founded: 1976. **Members:** 15,600. **Membership Dues:** individual, $30 (annual) ● institution, $54 (annual). **Staff:** 17. **Budget:** $1,200,000. **State Groups:** 5. **National Groups:** 165. **Description:** Provides current information based on the society's research. Supports scholars and musicians; promotes opportunities for individuals in culture, instrumental and vocal music, theater and dance, composition, performance and theory. Sponsors the U.S. and European Concert Tour of the Chinese Classical Orchestra, the Silk and Bamboo Ensemble, and Concerts and Lectures for communities, museums and university campuses annually. **Libraries: Type:** reference. **Holdings:** 2,400; archival material, audiovisuals, books. **Subjects:** scores of Chinese music. **Awards: Type:** grant ● **Type:** monetary ● **Type:** recognition ● **Type:** scholarship. **Computer Services:** Mailing lists, of members. **Divisions:** Library. **Subgroups:** International Center for Musical and Cultural Exchange; Music Research Institute. **Publications:** *Chinese Music*, quarterly. Journal. Covers Chinese music performance, archaeological discoveries, musical instruments, regional art forms, composition, theory, and reviews. **Price:** included in membership dues; $30.00 /year for nonmembers; $53.75 /year for institutions. ISSN: 0192-3749. **Circulation:** 12,000. **Advertising:** accepted. Alternate Formats: microform ● *Chinese Music Masterpiece Series*, Audiotapes ● *Chinese Music Monograph Series*. ISSN: 1071-5649. **Advertising:** accepted. **Conventions/Meetings:** competition ● annual conference (exhibits) ● lecture.

10576 ■ Chopin Foundation of the United States

1440 79th St. Causeway, Ste.117
Miami, FL 33141
Ph: (305)868-0624
Fax: (305)865-5150
E-mail: info@chopin.org
URL: http://www.chopin.org
Contact: Jadwiga Gewert, Exec. Dir.
Founded: 1977. **Description:** Aims to support young American classical musicians; promotes classical music. **Awards: Frequency:** annual. **Type:** scholarship. **Councils:** Florida Chopin; New York Chopin; Northwest Chopin; San Francisco Chopin. **Programs:** Exchange. **Affiliated With:** Frederick Chopin Society. **Publications:** *Polonaise*, semiannual, spring/fall. Magazine. **Price:** included in membership dues. **Conventions/Meetings:** annual festival ● Membership Musicales - festival, series of free monthly concerts, with Master Classes - held in South Florida ● quinquennial National Chopin Piano Competition, exclusive for American pianists - held in Miami, Florida ● Public Concerts - show.

10577 ■ Chorus America

1156 15th St. NW, Ste.310
Washington, DC 20005
Ph: (202)331-7577
Fax: (202)331-7599
E-mail: service@chorusamerica.org
URL: http://www.chorusamerica.org
Contact: Ann Meier Baker, Pres./CEO
Founded: 1977. **Members:** 1,600. **Membership Dues:** individual, $65 (annual) ● chorus (based on budget), $135-$800 (annual) ● library, $75 (annual) ● business, $300 (annual) ● affiliate, $200 (annual) ● contributing, $165 (annual) ● student, $25 (annual). **Staff:** 8. **Budget:** $1,000,000. **Description:** Individuals and non-profit organizations united to promote the professional growth, quality, and expansion of vocal ensembles and to encourage appreciation and enjoyment of vocal music. Acts as liaison between federal and state arts agencies and the choral industry. Surveys the choral industry on audiences, office administration, budgets, repertoire, touring, and other matters of concern to professional ensembles. Communicates with professional musicians' unions; sponsors media presentations. Provides consulting services, relocation assistance, group liability insurance for member ensembles, and group health insurance for professional singers and conductors. **Libraries: Type:** reference. **Holdings:** 27. **Subjects:** music. **Awards:** ASCAP/Chorus America Awards for Adventuresome Programs. **Frequency:** annual. **Type:** grant. **Recipient:** for member ● Chorus America Philanthropy. **Frequency:** annual. **Type:** recognition. **Recipient:** for individual, corporation or foundation ● Education Outreach. **Frequency:** annual. **Type:** recognition. **Recipient:** for education outreach program ● Louis Botto Award for Innovative Action and Entrepreneurial Spirit. **Frequency:** biennial. **Type:** recognition. **Recipient:** for individual ● Margaret Hillis Achievement Award for Choral Excellence. **Frequency:** annual. **Type:** grant. **Recipient:** for professional chorus, a volunteer chorus and a children or youth chorus ● Michael Korn Founders Award for Development of the Professional Choral Art. **Frequency:** annual. **Type:** recognition. **Recipient:** for individual. **Computer Services:** Mailing lists, of members. **Formerly:** (1987) Association of Professional Vocal Ensembles; (1990) Chorus America: Association of Professional Vocal Ensembles. **Publications:** *Education and Outreach (1997)*. Video. **Price:** $10.00 each ● *2005 Business*. Directory. **Price:** $10.00 for members; $15.00 for nonmembers ● *Voice*, quarterly. Newsletter. Features book reviews, profiles of member organizations, member news, dateline listing of concert performances of members, and publications list. **Price:** included in membership dues; $75.00 /year for nonmembers. ISSN: 1074-0805. **Circulation:** 7,500. **Advertising:** accepted. **Conventions/Meetings:** annual conference (exhibits) - always first week in June ● annual workshop, conductor training.

10578 ■ Classical Music Lovers' Exchange (CMLE)

PO Box 275
Santa Barbara, CA 93102-0275
E-mail: info@cmle.com
URL: http://www.cmle.com
Contact: Mr. Stewart Neill, Pres.
Founded: 1980. **Members:** 16,000. **Membership Dues:** individual, $65 (semiannual). **Staff:** 1. **For-Profit. Description:** A nationwide exchange for professional and amateur musicians and others interested in classical music. Seeks to unite unattached classical music lovers for the purpose of sharing musical interests and friendship. Fosters appreciation of the genre. **Publications:** *Membership List*, monthly. Membership Directory ● Newsletter, monthly. **Price:** $65.00 for 6 months.

10579 ■ Cobbett Association for Chamber Music Research

601 Timber Trail
Riverwoods, IL 60015-3846
Ph: (847)374-1800
E-mail: cobbettassociation@sbcglobal.net
URL: http://www.cobbettassociation.org
Contact: Raymond Silvertrust, Pres./Dir.
Founded: 1990. **Membership Dues:** regular, in U.S. (check payment), $20 (annual) ● regular, in U.S. (credit card payment), $23 (annual) ● regular, outside U.S. (check payment), $25 (annual) ● regular, outside U.S. (credit card payment), $28 (annual). **Description:** Aims to preserve recordings of rare and neglected chamber music of merit. Cultivates public interest in and appreciation for chamber music. Maintains a copying library for members. **Libraries: Type:** open to the public. **Holdings:** 1,300. **Subjects:** chamber music. **Publications:** *The Chamber Music Journal*, quarterly. Contains informative articles on chamber music, evaluation of recommended works and record reviews. **Price:** included in membership dues.

10580 ■ Company of Fifers and Drummers (CFD)

PO Box 277
Ivoryton, CT 06442-0277
Ph: (860)767-2237 (860)399-6519
Fax: (860)767-9765
E-mail: companyhq@companyoffifeanddrum.org
URL: http://companyoffifeanddrum.org
Contact: Sylvia Hooghkirk, Pres.
Founded: 1965. **Members:** 4,000. **Membership Dues:** individual in U.S., $25 (annual) ● corps, $100 (annual) ● family, $40 (annual) ● individual in Canada, $30 (annual) ● individual outside U.S. and Canada, $35 (annual) ● junior, $10 (annual). **Staff:** 15. **Budget:** $60,000. **Multinational. Description:** Drum Corps, individuals, and institutions interested in drum and fife activities and music. Perpetuates and preserves colonial, military, and traditional forms of American fife and drum music. Seeks to insure the continued existence and growth of the sounds of the fife and drum by fostering greater understanding and appreciation of field music. Serves as a headquarters for members. Assists in the formation of new fife and drum corps by providing information regarding instruction, music, and uniforms. Provides service to towns, musical units, and organizations in conducting parades, pageants, and muster type activities upon request. Maintains speakers' bureau and Museum of Fife and Drum which holds memorabilia of the Ancient Drum Corps such as uniforms, drums, fifes, music and awards dating back to 18th century and displays featuring earlier European Fife & Drum Culture. **Libraries: Type:** reference; by appointment only. **Holdings:** 400; archival material, articles, audio recordings, books, periodicals, photographs. **Subjects:** fife and drum corps history. **Affiliated With:** Corps of Drums Society. **Publications:** *The Ancient Times*, quarterly. Newsletter. **Price:** included in membership dues. **Circulation:** 1,300. **Advertising:** accepted ● Also publishes material dealing with the history and development of traditional fife and drum activity.

10581 ■ Conductors Guild

5300 Glenside Dr., Ste.2207
Richmond, VA 23228
Ph: (804)553-1378
Fax: (804)553-1876
E-mail: guild@conductorsguild.net
URL: http://www.conductorsguild.org
Contact: Amanda Burton Winger, Exec. Dir.
Founded: 1975. **Members:** 2,000. **Membership Dues:** regular, associate, institutional, $100 (annual) ● student, $50 (annual) ● life, $2,000. **Staff:** 4. **Budget:** $210,000. **For-Profit. Description:** Conductors and institutions involved with music. Works to advance the art of conducting and serving the artistic and professional needs of conductors. Conducts educational programs. **Awards:** Theodore Thomas Award. **Frequency:** annual. **Type:** recognition. **Recipient:** for outstanding service to the profession. **Publications:** *Conductor Opportunities Bulletin*, monthly. Alternate Formats: online; CD-ROM ● *Journal of the Conductors Guild*, semiannual. **Price:** included in membership dues. Alternate Formats: CD-ROM ● *Podium Notes*, quarterly. Newsletter. Alternate Formats: online; CD-ROM ● Membership Directory, annual. Alternate Formats: online; CD-ROM. **Conventions/Meetings:** annual Conference for Conductors, discusses topics of interest to all conductors (exhibits) ● periodic seminar ● quarterly workshop.

10582 ■ Contemporary A Cappella Society of America (CASA)

681 10th Ave.
San Francisco, CA 94118

Ph: (415)358-8067
E-mail: julia@casa.org
URL: http://www.casa.org
Contact: Jonathan Minkoff, Pres.

Founded: 1990. **Members:** 6,000. **Membership Dues:** silver, $25 (annual) ● gold/patron, $100 (annual). **Staff:** 50. **Description:** High school, collegiate, professional, and recreational a cappella groups, and interested individuals. Promotes the advancement of a cappella (a singing style without instrumental accompaniment.) Negotiates discounts on recordings, offers services for individuals looking to start or join a group, encourages collegiate a cappella groups, helps locate agents and venues around the country, and offers free concert listings. **Libraries: Type:** reference. **Holdings:** 1,500; audio recordings. **Subjects:** a cappella, vocal music. **Awards:** A Cappella Community Awards. **Frequency:** annual. **Type:** recognition. **Recipient:** for an a cappella group ● Contemporary A Cappella Recording Awards. **Frequency:** annual. **Type:** recognition. **Recipient:** for an a cappella group. **Computer Services:** database, lists of groups and organizations. **Subgroups:** A Capella Ambassadors. **Also Known As:** The Contemporary A Cappella Society. **Publications:** *The Contemporary A Cappella News*, bimonthly. Newsletter. Includes reviews of concerts and albums, interviews, classifieds, and calendar. **Price:** included in membership dues. **Circulation:** 2,000. **Advertising:** accepted. Also Cited As: *The CAN*. **Conventions/Meetings:** annual A Cappella Summit - conference and workshop (exhibits) - always fall in Boston, MA and San Rafael, CA.

10583 ■ Country Legends Association (CLA)

942 89th Ave. W, No. 102
Duluth, MN 55808
Ph: (218)626-9044
Fax: (218)626-2796
E-mail: cla@clalonestar.com
URL: http://www.clalonestar.com
Contact: Frank Dell, Pres.

Founded: 1997. **Membership Dues:** senior citizen, veteran, $15 (annual) ● songwriter, musician, disc jockey, $25 (annual) ● talent agency, radio station, television, advertising agency, record/video, theater/venue, merchandiser, affiliated, $100 (annual) ● fan, $20 (annual) ● artist, personal manager, country comedy, promoter, publication, $50 (annual) ● life, $500. **Description:** Seeks to promote and preserve Original Country, Gospel and Bluegrass and Western music. Raises public awareness of Traditional Country Music. **Telecommunication Services:** electronic mail, presfd@clalonestar.com.

10584 ■ Country Music Association (CMA)

1 Music Cir. S
Nashville, TN 37203-4312
Ph: (615)244-2840
Fax: (615)726-0314
E-mail: communications@cmaworld.com
URL: http://www.cmaworld.com
Contact: Clarence Spalding, Pres.

Founded: 1958. **Members:** 6,000. **Membership Dues:** regular, $50 (annual) ● sterling, $100 (annual) ● basic - organizational, $125 (annual) ● bronze - organizational, $200 (annual) ● silver - organizational, bronze - patron, $500 (annual) ● gold - organizational, $1,250 (annual) ● gold - patron, $2,500 (annual) ● silver - patron, $1,000 (annual). **Staff:** 30. **Description:** Artists, musicians, artist managers or agents, advertising representatives, talent buyers or promoters, disc jockeys, publishers, radio-television personnel, record company personnel, record merchandisers, composers, and authors. Promotes and publicizes country music. Established Country Music Hall of Fame, library, and Country Music Foundation (see separate entry). Promotes October as International Country Music Month. Conducts annual surveys in U.S. and Canada to determine the number of radio stations broadcasting country music on a part- or full-time basis. Co-sponsors International Country Music Fan Fair in June. **Awards:** Connie B. Gay. **Frequency:** annual. **Type:** recognition. **Recipient:** for individual ● Jo Walker-Meador International. **Frequency:** annual. **Type:** recognition. **Recipient:** for individual or company ● Media Achievement. **Frequency:** annual. **Type:** recognition. **Recipient:** for print journalist, author, and editor ● **Frequency:** annual. **Type:** recognition. **Recipient:** for 12 categories of achievement of performance for country music entertainers ● **Frequency:** annual. **Type:** recognition. **Recipient:** for broadcasting and newly elected hall of fame members ● Special President's Award. **Frequency:** annual. **Type:** recognition. **Recipient:** for individual. **Committees:** Awards; Broadcasters; Country Music Month; Hall of Fame; International; Legislative Affairs; Merchandising; Public Relations; Radio; Talent Buyers Seminar; Television. **Publications:** *Close-Up*, bimonthly. Magazine. Includes calendar of events, media updates, obituaries, and songwriter, artist, and broadcaster profiles. **Price:** included in membership dues ● *CMA 2002*. Directory. Lists every country radio station, syndicator, satellite and internet radio, artist reference guide includes record labels, managers, booking agents. **Price:** included in membership dues; $75.00 for nonmembers. **Conventions/Meetings:** quarterly meeting.

10585 ■ Country Music Foundation (CMF)

222 Fifth Ave. S
Nashville, TN 37203
Ph: (615)416-2001
Free: (800)852-6437
E-mail: info@countrymusichalloffame.com
URL: http://www.countrymusichalloffame.com
Contact: Kyle Young, Dir.

Founded: 1964. **Membership Dues:** museum, $125 (annual) ● general, adult, $25 (annual) ● friend, $100-$500 (annual) ● circle, $1,000 (annual) ● child (6 to 17 years old), $10 (annual). **Staff:** 35. **Budget:** $3,500,000. **Description:** Educational foundation. Collects, preserves, interprets, displays, and disseminates items, artifacts, and information related to the history and development of country music and encourages scholarly research in the field of country music and related areas. Operates the Country Music Hall of Fame and Museum, a historic recording studio (formerly RCA's Studio B), and Hatch Show Print (one of the South's oldest-known show poster print shop). Maintains artifact and photograph storage vaults, a reading room, and a gift shop. Operates CMF Records, a re-issue record label of historically important recordings distributed internationally and Country Music Foundation Press, which publishes scholarly reprints and books on Anglo-American music. **Libraries: Type:** reference. **Holdings:** 5,000; archival material, audio recordings, books, clippings, periodicals, video recordings. **Subjects:** development and history of country, traditional, folk, American music. **Publications:** *A Good Natured Riot: The Birth of the Grand Ole Opry*. Book. **Price:** $29.95 hardcover ● *BMI 50th Anniversary: The Explosion of American Music* ● *Bob Wills: Hubbin' It*. Book. **Price:** $10.95 softcover ● *The Country Music Catalog*, 3/year ● *The Country Music Hall of Fame and Museum: A Pictorial Journey*. Book. **Price:** $24.95 hardcover ● *Country Music Legends in the Hall of Fame*. Book ● *The Country Reader: 25 Years of the Journal of Country Music*. Book ● *Country: The Music and the Musicians*. Book. **Price:** $45.00 each ● *The Delmore Brothers: Truth is Stranger Than Publicity*. Book. **Price:** $12.98 softcover ● *Devil's Box: Masters of Southern Fiddling*. Book. **Price:** $18.95 softcover ● *The Encyclopedia of Country Music*. Book. **Price:** $29.95 softcover ● *Hatch Show Print: The History of a Great American Poster Shop*. Book ● *Journal of Country Music*, 3/year. **Price:** $18.00 /year for individuals in U.S.; $23.00 /year for individuals outside U.S.; $28.00 /year for libraries. **Advertising:** accepted ● *My Husband Jimmie Rodgers*. Book. **Price:** $12.95 softcover ● *The Nashville Sound: Authenticity, Commercialization, and Country Music*. Book. **Price:** $29.95 hardcover ● *The Official Country Calendar*, annual ● *The Official Hall of Fame Souvenir Book* ● *Ramblin' Rose: The Life and Career of Rose Maddox*. Book. **Price:** $29.95 hardcover ● *Sing Your Heart Out, Country Boy*. Book ● *True Adventures with the King of Bluegrass - Jimmy Martin*. Book. **Price:** $17.95 hardcover.

10586 ■ Country Music Showcase International (CMSI)

PO Box 368
Carlisle, IA 50047-0368
Ph: (515)989-3748
E-mail: haroldl@cmshowcase.org
URL: http://www.cmshowcase.org
Contact: Harold L. Luick, CEO/Dir.

Founded: 1984. **Members:** 900. **Staff:** 5. **Budget:** $25,000. **Description:** Helps songwriters and entertainers learn more about songwriting and the general music industry. Sponsors Song Evaluation and Critiques Service, songwriting seminars and workshops and songwriter showcases. Operates a BMI Music Publishing Company for the benefit of members whose songs qualify for publishing. Configures specially made computers for songwriters, musicians, and entertainers to use. Owns and operates: Country Music Showcase International, Inc; Attraction Booking Agency, which serves fairs, festivals, and corporate fund raising events providing them access to all 14 Art Forms of Country Music Entertainers and Stage Shows. Serves as the trustee for the Iowa/Midwest Country Music Heritage "Virtual" Museum, Library and Hall Of Fame. **Libraries: Type:** reference. **Holdings:** 18,000. **Subjects:** songwriting, recording, music business, industry. **Awards:** Hall of Fame Songwriter. **Frequency:** annual. **Type:** recognition. **Recipient:** for individuals who have helped others to become successful. **Computer Services:** Bibliographic search, "virtual" museum on the internet. **Subgroups:** Iowa/Midwest Music Heritage Research. **Affiliated With:** National Traditional Country Music Association. **Publications:** *Iowa/Midwest Consumer Behavior Report*, semiannual. **Price:** $100.00 for nonmembers ● *Iowa/Midwest Music Heritage Journal*, quarterly. **Price:** free for members ● *Midwest Entertainment News*, monthly. Magazine. Contains news in the entertainment world. **Price:** $25.00/year. **Circulation:** 10,000. **Advertising:** accepted. Alternate Formats: CD-ROM; online ● Also publishes information packets about seminars, 190 different workshop subjects on song writing and the music industry in general, and the Country Music Showcase International, Inc. CyberNews and Views. **Conventions/Meetings:** annual Iowa/Midwest Country Music Expo and Trade Show - festival and trade show, with competition and music contests (exhibits) ● annual Iowa/Midwest Songwriter, Entertainer, Record Artist, Music Business Expo - seminar and workshop (exhibits).

10587 ■ Creative Music Foundation (CMF)

PO Box 671
Woodstock, NY 12498
Ph: (845)679-8847
E-mail: creativemusic@verizon.net
URL: http://www.creativemusicstudio.org
Contact: Karl H. Berger, Founder/Dir.

Founded: 1971. **Members:** 1,700. **Staff:** 3. **Description:** Musicians, composers, artists, and interested individuals. Strives to further the knowledge and technical skills of composers and musicians and to aid the public in developing an appreciation of all types of music, from jazz to classical. Sponsors seminars, professional training workshops, public service programs, and recordings.

10588 ■ Drinker Library of Choral Music (DLCM)

Free Lib. of Philadelphia
1901 Vine St.
Philadelphia, PA 19103
Ph: (215)686-5364 (215)686-5322
Fax: (215)686-5326
E-mail: shelkrote@library.phila.gov
URL: http://www.library.phila.gov
Contact: Elliot L. Shelkrot, Pres./Dir.

Founded: 1943. **Members:** 338. **Membership Dues:** literati, $35 (annual) ● scholar, $50 (annual) ● conservator, $100 (annual) ● bibliophile, $250 (annual) ● rare edition, $500 (annual). **Staff:** 2. **Description:** Professional and amateur choral organizations in schools, colleges, and churches; symphony orchestras; symphonic choruses; community organizations; glee clubs. Makes available multiple copies of choral music for use by organized singing groups. Collection includes music from 16th through 20th centuries and comprises sacred and secular cantatas and motets, masses, requiems, madrigals, art songs, and folk songs. Most works have been prepared in a modern singable English translation and orchestra parts for accompaniment are available for many works in the collection. Drinker Library is a department of the Free Library of Philadelphia and subscription is required to borrow the choral music. **Convention/Meeting:** none. **Publications:** none. **Absorbed:** (1970) American Choral Foundation Library. **Formerly:** (1965) Association of American Choruses.

10589 ■ Drum Corps International (DCI)
470 S Irmen Dr.
Addison, IL 60101
Ph: (630)628-7888
Free: (800)495-7469
Fax: (630)628-7971
E-mail: dci@dci.org
URL: http://www.dci.org
Contact: Daniel E. Acheson, Exec. Dir./CEO

Founded: 1972. **Members:** 25. **Staff:** 11. **Budget:** $5,000,000. **Multinational**. **Description:** Drum and bugle corps. Functions as the promotional, educational, and service arm of North American drum and bugle corps activity. Establishes rules and regulations; sponsors competitions and judging seminars, and produces events. Maintains a hall of fame. **Publications:** Magazine, 3/year. Includes updates on progress of competitive drum corps units. **Price:** $15.00 /year for individuals in U.S.; $17.00 /year for individuals in Canada; $21.00 /year for individuals outside U.S. and Canada. **Advertising:** accepted. **Conventions/Meetings:** periodic seminar, management and promotion - January ● annual Summer Music Games World Championship - competition (exhibits) ● annual World Championships - competition, on rules.

10590 ■ The Duke Ellington Society (TDES)
PO Box 31
Church St. Sta.
New York, NY 10008-0031
E-mail: duke-lym@concordia.ca
URL: http://museum.media.org/duke
Contact: David Hajdu, Pres.

Founded: 1959. **Members:** 400. **Membership Dues:** individual, $25 (annual) ● life, $500. **Description:** Represents persons interested in furthering appreciation of the music of Duke Ellington (1899-1974), American jazz band leader and composer. Conducts critical research. Holds several concerts each season. Participates in the annual international conference on the music of Duke Ellington. **Libraries: Type:** reference. **Holdings:** archival material. **Computer Services:** Mailing lists, online. **Committees:** Annual Concert; Archives; Audio and Equipment; Discography; Journalism; Social Activities. **Formerly:** (1968) Duke Ellington Jazz Society; (1995) The Duke Ellington Society - New York Chapter. **Publications:** *Jazziz*, monthly. Newsletter. Includes calendar of events and record and CD reviews. **Circulation:** 700. **Conventions/Meetings:** annual conference (exhibits) - always spring ● monthly meeting - between September and June in New York, NY.

10591 ■ Early Music Network (EMN)
PO Box 854
Atlanta, GA 30301
Ph: (770)638-7554
Free: (866)327-5968
Fax: (770)638-7554
E-mail: office@earlymusic.net
URL: http://www.earlymusic.net
Contact: Predrag Gosta PGCE, Founder/Pres.

Founded: 1998. **Membership Dues:** organization (EMN visionary), $5,000 (annual) ● organization (sponsor), $2,000 (annual) ● organization (benefactor), individual (EMN visionary), $1,000 (annual) ● organization (supporter), individual (sponsor), $500 (annual) ● organization (patron), individual (benefactor), $300 (annual) ● organization (donor), individual (supporter), $200 (annual) ● organization (sustaining/income over 100,000), individual (patron), $125 (annual) ● organization (contributing/income of 50,000-100,000), individual (donor), $95 (annual) ● organization (regular/instrument maker/library), individual (sustaining), $68 (annual) ● individual (contributing), $48 (annual) ● individual (regular), $35 (annual) ● individual (over age 65), $29 (annual) ● individual (full-time student under age 27, second in household), $19 (annual). **Multinational**. **Description:** Aims to promote, revive and support historical performance practice of early music. Seeks to connect all early music organizations around the world through the internet. Provides information about early music in general and events around the world. **Publications:** Newsletter, monthly. **Price:** included in membership dues. Alternate Formats: online ● Yearbook, annual. **Price:** included in membership dues ● Membership Directory. **Price:** included in membership dues.

10592 ■ Electronic Music Foundation (EMF)
PO Box 8748
Albany, NY 12208
Ph: (518)434-4110
Free: (888)749-9998
Fax: (518)434-0308
E-mail: emf@emf.org
URL: http://www.emf.org
Contact: Benjamin Chadabe, Exec. Dir.

Founded: 1994. **Membership Dues:** life, $100. **Description:** Promotes the work of electronic music pioneers. Fosters public access to the expressive potential of electronic technology used for electronic music. **Computer Services:** database, EMF/SEAMUS opportunities list ● mailing lists, of members. **Programs:** Media. **Projects:** Institute. **Publications:** *EMF Network*. Newsletter.

10593 ■ Ernst Bacon Society
8 Johnson Rd.
Sharon, MA 02067
E-mail: mail@ernstbacon.org
URL: http://www.ernstbacon.org
Contact: Ellen Bacon, Pres.

Founded: 1996. **Description:** Promotes awareness and appreciation of the music and other works of Ernst Bacon. Provides information about the life and works Ernst Bacon. Facilitates the exchange of ideas concerning the American composer and his literary works. Arranges series of concerts and other events.

10594 ■ European American Musical Alliance (EAMA)
1160 Fifth Ave., Ste.201
New York, NY 10029
Ph: (212)831-7424
E-mail: info@eamusic.org
URL: http://www.eamusic.org
Contact: Dr. Philip Lasser, Pres.

Founded: 1996. **Nonmembership**. **Multinational**. **Description:** Promotes musical endeavors between America and Europe. Aims to teach and to broaden interest in the arts. Seeks out and promotes craft, study and integrity in all the arts regardless of style. **Programs:** Summer Music.

10595 ■ Film Music Society (FMS)
1516 S Bundy Dr., Ste.305
Los Angeles, CA 90025
Ph: (310)820-1909
Fax: (310)820-1301
E-mail: info@filmmusicsociety.org
URL: http://www.filmmusicsociety.org
Contact: David Newman, Pres.

Founded: 1982. **Members:** 800. **Membership Dues:** domestic, $50 (annual) ● international, $75 (annual) ● underscore, $100 (annual) ● love theme, $250 (biennial) ● main title theme, $1,000 (quinquennial). **Budget:** $150,000. **National Groups:** 2. **Description:** Interested individuals and groups. Promotes the preservation of film music scores, recordings, and documents; coordinates donations of film music collections to libraries; encourages publication of serious writing about film music. Profiles and interviews film music composers; disseminates film music discographies and information on events relating to film music. **Libraries: Type:** open to the public. **Holdings:** 1,000; papers. **Subjects:** film music. **Awards:** Career Achievement Award. **Frequency:** annual. **Type:** recognition. **Recipient:** for a composer's contribution to film and television music. **Committees:** Preservation. **Formerly:** (1997) Society for the Preservation of Film Music. **Publications:** *The Cue Sheet*, quarterly. Journal. Includes articles of historical interest and interviews with the influential music makers of yesteryear. **Price:** included in membership dues. **Circulation:** 700 ● *Film Music I*. Book ● *Film Music Notebook* ● *Film Music 2: History, Theory, Practice*. Book. Features works by some of the leading writers and theorists on the subject of film music. **Conventions/Meetings:** annual International Film Music Conference (exhibits).

10596 ■ Fischoff National Chamber Music Association
Univ. of Notre Dame
303 Brownson Hall
Notre Dame, IN 46556
Ph: (574)631-0984 (574)631-0599
Fax: (574)631-2903
E-mail: info@fischoff.org
URL: http://fischoff.org
Contact: Ann Divine, Exec. Dir.

Founded: 1973. **Staff:** 3. **Description:** Provides opportunity for education and development of young people through chamber music competition, residencies, and concerts. **Awards:** Competition Prizes and Scholarships. **Frequency:** annual. **Type:** scholarship. **Programs:** Artist-of-the-Month; Arts-in-Education Residency; Peanut Butter and Jelly Jam; Peer Ambassadors for Chamber Music; S.A.M. I Am. **Projects:** Chamber Music Mentoring. **Affiliated With:** Chamber Music America. **Conventions/Meetings:** annual competition, chamber music competition.

10597 ■ Fretted Instrument Guild of America (FIGA)
2501 Saddleback Dr.
Edmond, OK 73034
E-mail: allfrets@aol.com
URL: http://www.frettedinstrumentguildofamerica.org
Contact: Johnny Baier, Sec.-Treas.

Founded: 1957. **Members:** 2,000. **Membership Dues:** regular, in U.S., $30 (annual) ● life, $500 ● student and associate in U.S., $20 (annual) ● student and associate in Canada, $24 (annual) ● student and associate overseas, $31 (annual) ● regular, in Canada, $36 (annual) ● regular, outside U.S. and Canada, $47 (annual). **Staff:** 2. **Description:** Professional and avocational players of the banjo, mandolin, guitar, and other fretted instruments. Sponsors workshops, lectures, concerts, and exhibitions. **Libraries: Type:** reference. **Subjects:** musical arrangements (many of which are out of print). **Committees:** Music Writing. **Departments:** Historian; Orchestra; Reception. **Publications:** *All Frets*, bimonthly. Newsletter. Covers news of the guild and musical pieces for fretted instruments, including the banjo, guitar, violin, fiddle, mandolin, lute, and bass. **Price:** included in membership dues; $3.00 sample issue. **Advertising:** accepted ● Directory, periodic. **Advertising:** accepted. **Conventions/Meetings:** annual convention and meeting (exhibits).

10598 ■ Future of Music Coalition (FMC)
1325 13th St. NW, No. 34
Washington, DC 20005
Ph: (202)518-4117
E-mail: jenny@futureofmusic.org
URL: http://www.futureofmusic.org
Contact: Jenny Toomey, Exec. Dir.

Description: Represents the interests of the music, technology, public policy, and intellectual property law communities. Educates the media, the policymakers, and the public about music/technology issues. Aims to identify and promote innovative business models that will help musicians and citizens benefit from new technologies. **Publications:** Newsletter, monthly. Alternate Formats: online.

10599 ■ Gay and Lesbian Association of Choruses (GALA Choruses)
PO Box 99998
Pittsburgh, PA 15233
Ph: (412)999-4489
Fax: (412)322-1814
E-mail: info@galachoruses.org
URL: http://www.galachoruses.org
Contact: Sonelius Kendrick-Smith, Pres.
Founded: 1982. **Members:** 10,000. **Membership Dues:** individual, $50 (annual) ● professional, affiliate (non-U.S. based), $100 (annual). **Staff:** 6. **Budget:** $409,000. **Regional Groups:** 188. **Multinational. Description:** Aims to support gay, lesbian, bisexual and transgender (GLBT) choruses. Serves US GLBT choruses while embracing multi-national participation in its programs. Conducts programs such as international and regional festivals, leadership conferences, conductors and managers programs, and small ensemble festivals. Provides production of choral festivals, conferences, and institutes; publishes a quarterly newsletter, reference materials, and membership rosters; offers grants; and consultations on management and artistic issues. **Libraries: Type:** reference. **Holdings:** audio recordings, audiovisuals, periodicals. **Subjects:** concert programs from choruses. **Awards:** Commission Matching Grants. **Frequency:** annual. **Type:** monetary. **Recipient:** to choruses engaging in commissioning new musical works either independently or in conjunction with other choruses ● Legacy Award. **Frequency:** quadrennial. **Type:** recognition. **Recipient:** for leadership in the gay and lesbian choral movement. **Computer Services:** Online services, membership roster ● online services, resource library for members. **Committees:** Quadrennial Festival. **Also Known As:** GALA Choruses. **Formerly:** (1982) GALA Performing Arts. **Publications:** *Chorus Handbook*, annual. Guide to chorus management. **Price:** $50.00 ● *Compensation Survey*. Handbook ● *Diversity Handbook*. Newsletter ● *GALAgram*, 3/year. Directory. **Circulation:** 8,500. **Advertising:** accepted. Alternate Formats: online ● *Membership Roster*, annual. Directory ● *Repertoire Listings*. **Conventions/Meetings:** annual conference (exhibits) - not in festival years ● quadrennial festival (exhibits) ● biennial Small Ensemble Festival.

10600 ■ Gospel Music Association (GMA)
1205 Div. St.
Nashville, TN 37203
Ph: (615)242-0303
Fax: (615)254-9755
E-mail: info@gospelmusic.org
URL: http://www.gospelmusic.org
Contact: John Styll, Pres.
Founded: 1964. **Members:** 5,000. **Membership Dues:** associate, $60 (annual) ● professional, $85 (annual) ● college student, $25 (annual) ● platinum, $1,450 (annual) ● gold, $750 (annual) ● affiliate, $350 (annual). **Staff:** 15. **Description:** Supports, encourages, and promotes the development of all forms of gospel music. **Libraries: Type:** reference. **Holdings:** archival material, books, clippings, periodicals. **Awards:** Dove Award. **Frequency:** annual. **Type:** recognition. **Recipient:** for excellence in gospel music. **Publications:** *Christian Music Networking Guide*, annual. **Price:** $14.95 for student and associate member; $19.95 for nonmembers; free to professional member. **Advertising:** accepted. Alternate Formats: online ● *GMA Today*, quarterly. Newsletter ● *GMAIL*, weekly. Newsletter. Includes weekly music sales, charts, news, links to valuable resources, and information about upcoming industry events. **Price:** free for members. Alternate Formats: online. **Conventions/Meetings:** annual Gospel Music Week - meeting (exhibits) - always April, Nashville, TN.

10601 ■ Gospel Music Workshop of America (GMWA)
PO Box 38842
Detroit, MI 48238
Ph: (313)491-9980
Fax: (313)491-1288
E-mail: gmwanational@hotmail.com
URL: http://www.gmwanational.org
Contact: Dr. Albert L. Jamison Sr., Chm.
Founded: 1967. **Members:** 75,000. **Description:** Individuals interested in gospel music. Promotes the enjoyment and performance of gospel and spiritual music. Offers musical instruction in performance and composition. **Publications:** Bulletin, annual. **Conventions/Meetings:** annual convention - always August. 2008 Aug. 9-15, Nashville, TN.

10602 ■ GRAMMY Foundation
3402 Pico Blvd.
Santa Monica, CA 90405
Ph: (310)392-3777
Free: (877)GRAMMYED
Fax: (310)392-2188
E-mail: grammyfoundation@grammy.com
URL: http://www.grammy.com/grammy_foundation
Contact: Neil Portnow, Pres.
Founded: 1989. **Membership Dues:** regular, $100 (annual) ● regular, $180 (biennial) ● regular, $260 (triennial). **Description:** Promotes the value of music and arts education; aims to preserve the rich cultural legacy of music for future generations. **Awards:** Grammy Hall of Fame. **Type:** recognition. **Recipient:** to honor early recordings of lasting significance ● Latin GRAMMY. **Frequency:** annual. **Type:** recognition ● Legend. **Type:** recognition. **Recipient:** to music groups ● Lifetime Achievement. **Type:** recognition. **Recipient:** to performers ● Tech. **Type:** recognition. **Recipient:** to individuals or companies who have made contributions of technical significance to the recording field ● Trustees. **Type:** recognition. **Recipient:** to individuals. **Computer Services:** database, GRAMMY Search.

10603 ■ Guam Symphony Society
PO Box 4069
Hagatna, GU 96932
Ph: (671)477-1959 (671)734-9039
E-mail: symphony@ite.net
URL: http://www.guamsymphony.org
Contact: Ms. Karen A. Carpenter, Pres.
Founded: 1967. **Members:** 200. **Membership Dues:** friend, $25 (annual) ● supporter, $50 (annual) ● sponsor, $100 (annual) ● patron, $250 (annual) ● benefactor, $500 (annual) ● guarantor, $1,000 (annual). **Description:** Individual and corporate members. Aims to provide the opportunity for musicians and listeners to experience quality music. Conducts concerts.

10604 ■ Guild of Carillonneurs in North America (GCNA)
PO Box 221
Gladwyne, PA 19035-0221
E-mail: dccarillon@aol.com
URL: http://www.gcna.org
Contact: Dennis Curry, Pres.
Founded: 1936. **Members:** 490. **Membership Dues:** associate in U.S., $40 (annual) ● carillonneur in U.S., $50 (annual) ● sustaining in U.S., $75 (annual) ● associate outside U.S., $47 (annual) ● carillonneur outside U.S., $59 (annual) ● associate outside U.S., $89 (annual). **Multinational. Description:** Players of carillons and chimes; persons interested in bells as musical instruments; bell manufacturers. Aims to: promote the development of proficient carillonneurs by the dissemination of information and discussion of problems; improve the quality of carillon music by issuing music and encouraging new composition; encourage improvement in carillon design and construction; advance the art, literature, and science of the carillon in North America. Bestows honorary membership for distinguished service to the art of the carillon. Maintains archives at Historic Bok Tower, Lake Wales, Florida. **Awards:** Carillonneur Status. **Frequency:** annual. **Type:** recognition. **Committees:** Archives; Examinations; Library; Music Publication; Public Relations; Statistics; Tower and Carillon Design. **Publications:** *Carillon News*, semiannual. Newsletter. **Price:** included in membership dues; $2.00/back issue. **Circulation:** 490. Alternate Formats: online ● *Music by Series of Compositions*, annual ● Bulletin, annual. **Conventions/Meetings:** annual congress.

10605 ■ Guitar Foundation of America (GFA)
PO Box 4909
Garden Grove, CA 92842
Ph: (909)624-7730
Free: (877)570-3409
E-mail: info@guitarfoundation.org
URL: http://www.guitarfoundation.org
Contact: Brian Head, Pres.
Founded: 1973. **Members:** 2,600. **Membership Dues:** regular, $50 (annual) ● student, $30 (annual). **Staff:** 2. **Description:** Guitarists, teachers, students, and others interested in and supportive of the classic guitar. Supports (as funds permit) the serious study of the guitar in its historic and performance aspects; promotes the guitar as an ensemble instrument; encourages composition and arrangements of ensemble music involving the guitar; and preserves and make available literature on the guitar. **Libraries: Type:** reference. **Holdings:** 29; books. **Subjects:** historic guitar music and memorabilia. **Awards:** International Solo Guitar Competition. **Frequency:** annual. **Type:** monetary. **Recipient:** for winner of international competition. **Computer Services:** Mailing lists, of members. **Committees:** Editorial. **Publications:** *Cooperating Collections*, periodic ● *Facsimile Series*, annual ● *Soundboard*, quarterly. Journal. Contains historical articles, reviews of compositions and arrangements for the guitar, and information on guitar festivals and other events. **Price:** included in membership dues. **Circulation:** 3,000 ● *Soundboard Magazine*, quarterly. Journal. **Price:** $7.00/issue; $7.90 for back issues; $12.00 current issue. ISSN: 0145-6237. **Circulation:** 3,000. **Advertising:** accepted ● Membership Directory. **Conventions/Meetings:** annual convention (exhibits) - 2008 Aug. 5-10, San Francisco, CA ● annual meeting (exhibits) ● seminar.

10606 ■ Hardanger Fiddle Association of America (HFAA)
PO Box 23046
Minneapolis, MN 55423-0046
E-mail: info@hfaa.org
URL: http://www.hfaa.org
Contact: Loretta Kelley, Pres.
Founded: 1983. **Members:** 300. **Membership Dues:** individual in U.S., $30 (annual) ● individual outside U.S., $40 (annual) ● family/institutional in U.S., $35 (annual) ● family/institutional outside U.S., $45 (annual) ● life, $500. **Description:** Dedicated to preserving and promoting the Norwegian Hardanger fiddle (hardingfele in Norwegian) and related traditions of Norwegian music and dance.(The Hardanger fiddle, which is now recognized as the national folk instrument of Norway, was originally made in 1651 by Olav Jonsson Jastad from Hardanger, Norway. Differs from the conventional fiddle in that has eight strings, bridge and fingerboard are flatter, can be tuned in over 20 ways, and certain features of the fiddle are artistically designed.) Produces an annual workshop featuring master teachers in both Hardanger fiddle and the related dance traditions, a quarterly newsletter, and maintains a specialized merchandise catalog of strings, educational materials and CDs. **Libraries: Type:** reference. **Subjects:** Hardanger fiddle, immigrants, early fiddlers. **Awards:** Bernt Balchen, Jr. Hardanger Fiddle Scholarship. **Frequency:** annual. **Type:** scholarship. **Recipient:** to a promising fiddler in order for them to attend the annual workshop. **Committees:** Educational Materials; Fundraising; Scholarship. **Publications:** *Sound Post*, quarterly. Journal. Features events, people, and music. **Price:** included in membership dues. **Advertising:** accepted ● Manual, annual. **Conventions/Meetings:** annual meeting and workshop (exhibits) - always June/July, Midwestern U.S.

10607 ■ Harmony Foundation
225 W Washington St., Ste.2330
Chicago, IL 60606
Ph: (312)701-1001
Free: (800)876-7464

Fax: (312)701-1005
E-mail: hf@harmonyfoundation.org
URL: http://www.harmonyfoundation.org
Contact: Clarke Caldwell, Pres./CEO
Founded: 1959. **Regional Groups:** 16. **Local Groups:** 850. **Description:** Serves as a philanthropic force dedicated to perpetuating the barbershop harmony art form for present and future generations to enjoy. **Telecommunication Services:** electronic mail, ccaldwell@harmonyfoundation.org.

10608 ■ Historic Brass Society (HBS)
148 W 23rd St., No. 5F
New York, NY 10011
Ph: (212)627-3820
Fax: (212)627-3820
E-mail: president@historicbrass.org
URL: http://www.historicbrass.org
Contact: Jeffrey Nussbaum, Pres.
Founded: 1988. **Members:** 800. **Membership Dues:** individual, $35 (annual) ● student, senior, library/institution, $25 (annual) ● individual, $90 (triennial). **Budget:** $20,000. **Description:** Seeks to preserve and promote all aspects of early brass music. Provides a forum for the exchange of ideas. **Awards:** Christopher Monk Award. **Frequency:** annual. **Type:** recognition. **Recipient:** for senior scholars, performers or teachers who have made life-long contributions to the early brass field. **Computer Services:** database. **Publications:** *Bucina: The Historic Brass Society Series*. Books ● *Historic Brass Society Journal*, annual. Contains articles on historic brass instruments. ISSN: 1045-4616 ● *Historic Brass Society Newsletter*, annual. Provides information on all aspects of brass music. **Price:** $25.00 /year for individuals; $25.00 /year for libraries. ISSN: 1045-4594. **Circulation:** 800. **Advertising:** accepted ● *Mozart's Use of Horns in Bb and the Question of Alto-Basso in the Eighteenth Century*. Article. Alternate Formats: online. **Conventions/Meetings:** annual Early Brass Festival - conference and lecture, discussion sessions, informal playing sessions, concerts (exhibits) - last week of July or first week of August.

10609 ■ Historical Harp Society (HHS)
c/o Anne Humphrey, Project Chair
631 N 3rd Ave.
St. Charles, IL 60174
E-mail: harpnhorse@sonic.net
URL: http://www.historicalharps.org
Contact: Cheryl Ann Fulton, Pres.
Founded: 1990. **Members:** 150. **Membership Dues:** individual, $25 (annual). **Description:** Cultivates, fosters, sponsors, and develops love and appreciation of the art, history, literature, and uses of historical harps. Also promotes appreciation of and to raise the level of proficiency in the performance and use of historical harps. Collects and disseminates information regarding the construction of and performance upon historical harps. **Publications:** *Journal of the Historical Harp Society*, annual. Contains reviews of publications and academic articles. **Price:** included in membership dues ● Newsletter, quarterly. Contains information on the association and its members. Alternate Formats: online ● Bulletin, quarterly. Contains news, activities and practical information. **Price:** included in membership dues.

10610 ■ Institute of the American Musical (IAM)
121 N Detroit St.
Los Angeles, CA 90036-2915
Ph: (323)934-1221
Fax: (323)934-1221
Contact: Miles Kreuger, Pres./Curator
Founded: 1972. **Description:** Works for the acquisition and safekeeping of musical theatre and film materials. Established the first study center and archives expressly devoted to the American art form, the musical. Produces film retrospectives and exhibitions for the public. **Convention/Meeting:** none. **Libraries: Type:** reference; by appointment only. **Holdings:** 300,000; archival material, audio recordings, films, photographs. **Subjects:** American stage and film musicals. **Publications:** Plans to publish periodical on American musical theatre, films and recordings.

10611 ■ Intercollegiate Men's Choruses, An International Association of Male Choruses (IMC)
c/o Gerald Polich, Exec. Sec.
Dept. of Music
McCain Auditorium
Kansas State Univ.
Manhattan, KS 66506-4706
Ph: (913)532-5740
Fax: (913)532-5709
E-mail: polich@ksu.edu
URL: http://www.cco.caltech.edu/~dgc/imc.html
Contact: Gerald Polich, Exec. Sec.
Founded: 1915. **Members:** 1,000. **Membership Dues:** collegiate chorus, adult/affiliated chorus, secondary school chorus (minimum), supporting, $40 (annual) ● student - secondary school chorus, $0 (annual) ● director, $20 (annual) ● student - collegiate or adult/affiliated chorus, $1 (annual). **Description:** Collegiate and secondary school male choruses. Aims to encourage and improve male choruses and group male singing in universities, colleges, and preparatory schools in the U.S. Promotes the research, publication, and production of quality music for male choruses. Seeks to facilitate communication among members and resolve problems affiliated with male chorus singing. Encourages adoption of professional standards in concert singing and music performance. Sponsors seminars and lectures on male chorus singing and promotion. Provides male chorus music to member choruses. **Libraries: Type:** reference. **Holdings:** archival material. **Awards:** Marshall Bartholomew Award. **Frequency:** annual. **Type:** recognition. **Recipient:** for outstanding male chorus conductors. **Computer Services:** Mailing lists, of members. **Formerly:** (1987) Intercollegiate Musical Council, A National Association of Male Choruses; (1992) Inter-collegiate Men's Chorus, A National Association of Male Choruses. **Publications:** *IMC Handbook*, annual ● *Quodlibet*, semiannual. Newsletter. Covers the practice and theory of chorus music for men. Includes award and lecture news and music reviews. **Price:** included in membership dues. **Advertising:** accepted. **Conventions/Meetings:** biennial meeting and seminar ● annual meeting and seminar.

10612 ■ International Alliance for Women in Music (IAWM)
Univ. of Maryland/Baltimore County
Dept. of Music, FA 509
1000 Hilltop Cir.
Baltimore, MD 21250
Ph: (623)556-2276
E-mail: ehinkle@unt.edu
URL: http://www.iawm.org
Contact: Dr. Anne Kilstofte PhD, Pres.
Founded: 1995. **Members:** 500. **Membership Dues:** student, $30 (annual) ● individual, $55 (annual) ● senior, $30 (annual) ● life, $1,000. **Multinational. Description:** Professional composers, conductors, performers, musicologists, educators, librarians, and other individuals with a love of music. Promotes participation by women in music. Facilitates communication and cooperation among members. Supports performances and recordings of the works of women composers; fosters research on topics pertaining to the contributions made by women to music; works to increase the presence of minority women in all phases of the music industry. Conducts advocacy campaigns; sponsors competitions. **Libraries: Type:** reference. **Holdings:** archival material, audio recordings. **Awards:** Ellen Taaffe Zwilich Prize. **Frequency:** annual. **Type:** monetary. **Recipient:** for outstanding women composers less than 21 years old ● Judith Lang Zaimont Prize. **Frequency:** annual. **Type:** monetary. **Recipient:** for women in or out of school, age 30 and up, whose music has not yet been published ● Libby Larsen Prize. **Frequency:** annual. **Type:** monetary. **Recipient:** for those enrolled in music schools ● Miriam Gideon Prize. **Frequency:** annual. **Type:** monetary. **Recipient:** for women age 50 and above (solo voice and 1-5 instruments) ● New Genre Prize. **Frequency:** annual. **Type:** monetary. **Recipient:** for innovation in form or style, including improv, multimedia and use of non-traditional notation ● Pauline Alderman Award. **Frequency:** annual. **Type:** monetary. **Recipient:** for outstanding research work on women in music ● Pauline Oliveros Prize. **Frequency:** annual. **Type:** monetary. **Recipient:** for individuals working for the electro-acoustic media ● Sylvia Glickman Prize. **Frequency:** annual. **Type:** monetary. **Recipient:** for string or piano trio that is unperformed and unpublished ● Theodore Front Prize. **Frequency:** annual. **Type:** monetary. **Recipient:** for chamber and orchestral works (minimum age 22). **Computer Services:** Mailing lists ● online services. **Committees:** Administrative; Advocacy; Awards; Communication; Congress; Development; Nominations/Elections. **Publications:** *IAWM Journal*, semiannual. **Price:** included in membership dues. ISSN: 1082-1872. **Conventions/Meetings:** annual meeting - always June.

10613 ■ International Association of African-American Music (IAAAM)
PO Box 382
Gladwyne, PA 19035
Ph: (610)664-8292
Fax: (610)664-5940
E-mail: iaaam1@aol.com
URL: http://www.iaaam.com
Contact: Dyana Williams, Co-Founder
Founded: 1990. **Multinational. Description:** Promotes and preserves America's indigenous music. Promotes education within the music industry. **Projects:** Literacy Lyric. **Subgroups:** IAAM Executive Consortium.

10614 ■ International Association for Research in Vietnamese Music
2005 Willow Ridge Cir.
Kent, OH 44240
Ph: (330)673-3763
Fax: (330)673-4434
E-mail: ivm@vietnamesemusic.us
URL: http://www.vietnamesemusic.us
Contact: Phong Nguyen PhD, Exec. Dir.
Founded: 1989. **Members:** 255. **Staff:** 6. **Budget:** $1,500. **Regional Groups:** 4. **Description:** Promotes the study and understanding of the music of Vietnam, overseas Vietnamese communities, and the relationship between Vietnamese and Asian music. **Libraries: Type:** reference. **Holdings:** archival material, business records, periodicals. **Subjects:** music of Vietnam and Asia. **Awards:** Vietnam Musical Heritage. **Frequency:** annual. **Type:** scholarship. **Recipient:** for individuals and institutions in Vietnam. **Computer Services:** Mailing lists. **Funds:** Vietnam Musical Heritage. **Publications:** *Nhac Viet*, periodic. Monograph.

10615 ■ International Bluegrass Music Association (IBMA)
2 Music Cir. S, Ste.100
Nashville, TN 37203
Ph: (615)256-3222
Free: (888)438-4262
Fax: (615)256-0450
E-mail: info@ibma.org
URL: http://www.ibma.org
Contact: Greg Cahill, Pres./Chm.
Founded: 1985. **Members:** 2,600. **Membership Dues:** fan, $40 (annual) ● individual, $70 (annual) ● organization/group, $200 (annual) ● youth, $15 (annual) ● life (individual), $1,000 ● life (organization), $2,500. **Staff:** 4. **Budget:** $485,000. **Multinational. Description:** Composers, performers, agents, music publishers, organizations, and enthusiasts involved in bluegrass and related genres of music. Works to promote unity within the bluegrass music industry; enhance the industry's public image and recognition; establish rosters of bluegrass media, venues, organizations, and businesses, thereby increasing awareness within the industry; encourage new markets for bluegrass music. Maintains Bluegrass Music Trust Fund to assist industry professionals in emergency need. Seeks to assist local associations, promoters, and performers in their activities; acts as a central

communication resource within the industry; encourages all festivals, shows, and media outlets to feature bluegrass music. Surveys the industry and radio stations with regard to bluegrass music. Compiles marketing statistics. **Awards:** Distinguished Achievement Award. **Frequency:** annual. **Type:** recognition. **Recipient:** for individuals who have distinguished contributions to bluegrass music ● Hall of Honor. **Frequency:** annual. **Type:** recognition. **Recipient:** for individuals with outstanding contributions to bluegrass music ● International Bluegrass Music Award. **Frequency:** annual. **Type:** recognition. **Computer Services:** database, bluegrass record companies, retailers and distributors, event producers, press, and related association's membership. **Committees:** Bluegrass in the Schools; Bluegrass Newservice; Distinguished Achievement Awards; Education; Executive; Hall of Honor; International; Internet; Leadership Bluegrass; Marketing; Radio; Wellness. **Publications:** *Blue Hot!*, monthly. Newsletter. **Price:** free to retail buyers and distributors. ISSN: 1097-3117. **Circulation:** 600 ● *International Bluegrass*, bimonthly. Newsletter. Contains a list of new members, member news, obituaries, record reviews, and industry news. **Price:** included in membership dues. **Circulation:** 5,000. **Conventions/Meetings:** annual International Bluegrass Music Awards - assembly ● seminar ● annual World of Bluegrass Week - convention and festival (exhibits).

10616 ■ International Clarinet Association (ICA)

PO Box 1310
Lyons, CO 80540
Ph: (801)867-4335
Fax: (212)457-6124
E-mail: membership@clarinet.org
URL: http://www.clarinet.org
Contact: Ms. So Rhee, Exec. Dir.

Founded: 1990. **Members:** 3,900. **Membership Dues:** student, $25 (annual) ● regular, institutional, $50 (annual). **Staff:** 1. **Budget:** $50,000. **Regional Groups:** 8. **State Groups:** 50. **National Groups:** 11. **Description:** Students, teachers, and manufacturers interested in all aspects of clarinetistry. Seeks to focus attention on the importance of the clarinet and to foster communication and fellowship between clarinetists. **Libraries: Type:** reference. **Holdings:** archival material. **Subjects:** clarinet music. **Awards:** Young Artist and High School Competitions. **Frequency:** annual. **Type:** monetary. **Recipient:** merit. **Computer Services:** Mailing lists, mailing labels for sale. **Telecommunication Services:** electronic mail, execdirector@clarinet.org. **Committees:** Library; Research; Sound Archives. **Formed by Merger of:** (1957) International Clarinet Society; Clarinet International. **Formerly:** (1992) International Clarinet Society/Clarinetwork International. **Publications:** *The Clarinet*, quarterly. Journal. **Price:** $45.00 in U.S., Canada, Mexico; $50.00 international. ISSN: 0361-5553. **Circulation:** 3,900. **Advertising:** accepted ● Membership Directory ● CD compilations. **Conventions/Meetings:** annual ClarinetFest - symposium, with competitions, concerts, lectures (exhibits).

10617 ■ International Concert Alliance (ICA)

47 W 85th St., Ste.2B
New York, NY 10024
E-mail: info@concertalliance.org
URL: http://www.concertalliance.org
Contact: Thomas J. Cuffari, Dir., Keyboard Division

Multinational. Description: Provides exposure and guidance to talented young musicians. Promotes and fosters the careers of the next generation of major concert artists. Offers competitions, performances and educational opportunities to young musicians.

10618 ■ International Conference of Symphony and Opera Musicians (ICSOM)

c/o Leonard Leibowitz
120 W 86th St., Ste.9B
New York, NY 10024
Ph: (917)863-2897
Fax: (212)877-4287
E-mail: bruceridge@earthlink.net
URL: http://www.icsom.org
Contact: Mr. Bruce Ridge, Chm.

Founded: 1960. **Members:** 4,200. **Staff:** 9. **Budget:** $300,000. **Description:** Represents professional symphony, opera, and ballet musicians. Aims to promote the welfare of and make more rewarding the livelihood of the orchestral performer. Disseminates inter-orchestra information. **Libraries: Type:** reference. **Subjects:** union related. **Awards:** Mendelsohn Award Minority Scholarship. **Frequency:** annual. **Type:** scholarship. **Recipient:** to promising young musicians (minority) pursuing an orchestral career. **Affiliated With:** American Federation of Musicians of the United States and Canada. **Publications:** *Senza Sordino*, bimonthly. Newsletter. **Circulation:** 7,000. Alternate Formats: online ● Bulletin, periodic ● Directory, annual. **Conventions/Meetings:** annual conference, union/labor management discussions - always August.

10619 ■ International Double Reed Society (IDRS)

c/o Norma R. Hooks, Exec. Sec.-Treas.
2423 Lawndale Rd.
Finksburg, MD 21048-1401
Ph: (410)871-0658
Fax: (410)871-0659
E-mail: norma4idrs@verizon.net
URL: http://www.idrs.org
Contact: Norma R. Hooks, Exec. Sec.-Treas.

Founded: 1972. **Members:** 4,500. **Membership Dues:** library, institution, regular, $50 (annual) ● benefactor, $400 (annual) ● patron, $300 (annual) ● donor, $150 (annual) ● sustaining, $75 (annual) ● student, $35 (annual). **Staff:** 1. **Budget:** $70,000. **National Groups:** 11. **Multinational. Description:** Professional and student bassoonists and oboists, instructors, and businesses that service musical instruments, musicians, and music school librarians in 56 countries. Disseminates information on all aspects of double reed performance and study. **Libraries: Type:** reference. **Holdings:** audio recordings. **Subjects:** double reeds. **Computer Services:** Mailing lists. **Publications:** *The Double Reed*, quarterly. Journal. ISSN: 0741-7659. **Circulation:** 4,500. **Advertising:** accepted. **Conventions/Meetings:** annual conference (exhibits) - usually June or August ● annual Fernand Gillet - Hugo Fox Competition (exhibits).

10620 ■ International Horn Society (IHS)

PO Box 630158
Lanai City, HI 96763-0158
Ph: (808)565-7273
Fax: (808)565-7273
E-mail: exec-secretary@hornsociety.org
URL: http://www.hornsociety.org
Contact: Heidi Vogel, Exec. Sec.

Founded: 1970. **Members:** 3,600. **Membership Dues:** regular, $35 (annual) ● individual, $90 (triennial) ● student, $25 (annual) ● club, $30 (annual) ● life, $750. **Staff:** 2. **Budget:** $100,000. **Multinational. Description:** Represents professors and professional and student players of the French horn, horn and brass musical instrument manufacturers and libraries. Seeks to further knowledge and literature concerning the horn. Promotes musical and personal communication among horn players. Recommends that the term horn be recognized and used as the proper name for this instrument in the English language rather than the term French horn. Disseminates information on: playing techniques; acoustical studies; improvisational, jazz, and ensemble performance; horn development, care, and maintenance; classical and modern music composition and transcription. Reviews books, music, and records; reports on activities of notable horn players. Conducts clinics, lectures, master classes, and recitals. **Awards:** Barry Tuckwell Scholarship. **Frequency:** annual. **Type:** scholarship. **Recipient:** to worthy horn students to pursue education and performance by attending and participating in master classes and workshops throughout the world ● Dorothy Frizelle Memorial Awards. **Frequency:** annual. **Type:** monetary. **Recipient:** for students to support study of orchestral horn playing at the IHS workshops ● Farkas Performance Awards. **Frequency:** annual. **Type:** recognition. **Recipient:** for individual who has not reached the age of twenty-five ● Jon Hawkins Memorial Scholarship. **Frequency:** annual. **Type:** scholarship. **Recipient:** for deserving, highly motivated horn students to attend the annual IHS workshops. **Publications:** *Horn Call*, 3/year. Journal. Covers all aspects of horn playing and music for horns. Includes advertisers index and annual author and title index. **Price:** included in membership dues. ISSN: 0046-7928. **Circulation:** 3,600. **Advertising:** accepted. Alternate Formats: online. **Conventions/Meetings:** annual International Workshop, with horn performances, competitions, lectures, exhibits, and master classes by world known artists (exhibits).

10621 ■ International Manuel Ponce Society (IMPS)

PO Box 59152
Dallas, TX 75229
Ph: (972)293-5360
Fax: (940)387-6897
E-mail: leslieenlow@hotmail.com
URL: http://www.imps.org
Contact: Leslie Enlow, Pres.

Founded: 1997. **Members:** 75. **Membership Dues:** ordinary, $100 (annual). **Budget:** $10,000. **Languages:** English, Spanish. **Description:** Individuals with an interest in classical music written by composers of Hispanic descent. Promotes appreciation of Hispanic classical music. Sponsors educational programs and performances of Hispanic classical music. **Libraries: Type:** not open to the public; lending. **Holdings:** audio recordings. **Subjects:** Hispanic classical recordings.

10622 ■ International Native American Flute Association (INAFA)

3351 Mintonville Point Dr.
Suffolk, VA 23435
Ph: (757)538-0468
Fax: (757)538-2937
E-mail: inafa@aol.com
URL: http://worldflutes.org
Contact: Dr. Kathleen Joyce-Grendahl, Exec. Dir.

Membership Dues: general, $25-$35 (annual). **Multinational. Description:** Fosters the preservation, appreciation and advancement of the Native American flute. **Programs:** INAFA Outreach.

10623 ■ International Piano Guild (IPG)

Address Unknown since 2008
URL: http://www.pianoguild.com

Description: Sponsored by the American College of Musicians to enable piano dealers and manufacturers to join with piano teachers in plans for stimulating widespread interest in the study of piano. **Affiliated With:** National Fraternity of Student Musicians; National Guild of Piano Teachers.

10624 ■ International Polka Association (IPA)

4608 S Archer Ave.
Chicago, IL 60632-2932
Free: (800)TO-POLKA
E-mail: webmaster@internationalpolka.com
URL: http://www.internationalpolka.com
Contact: Dave Ulczycki, Pres.

Founded: 1968. **Members:** 1,300. **Membership Dues:** regular, $15 (annual) ● life, $200. **Description:** Educational organization concerned with the preservation and advancement of polka music. Promotes, maintains, and advances interest in polka entertainment; pursues the study of polka music, dancing, and traditional folklore. Maintains Polka Music Hall of Fame and museum. **Awards:** IPA Polka Music Hall of Fame. **Frequency:** annual. **Type:** recognition. **Recipient:** to personalities who have made outstanding contributions to the advancement and promotion of polka music ● Polka Music Awards, Favorite Album. **Frequency:** annual. **Type:** recognition ● Polka Music Awards, Favorite Female Vocalist. **Frequency:** annual. **Type:** recognition ● Polka Music Awards, Favorite Instrumental Group. **Frequency:** annual. **Type:** recognition ● Polka Music Awards, Favorite Male Vocalist. **Frequency:** annual. **Type:**

recognition ● Polka Music Awards, Favorite Song. **Frequency:** annual. **Type:** recognition. **Committees:** Hall of Fame. **Publications:** *IPA News*, monthly. Newsletter. Provides information on membership activities. **Price:** included in membership dues. **Circulation:** 1,300. **Advertising:** accepted. **Conventions/Meetings:** annual meeting and festival (exhibits) - first weekend in August.

10625 ■ International Society of Bassists (ISB)
14070 Proton Rd., Ste.100
Dallas, TX 75244
Ph: (972)233-9107
Fax: (972)490-4219
E-mail: info@isbworldoffice.com
URL: http://www.isbworldoffice.com
Contact: Madeleine Crouch, Gen. Mgr.
Founded: 1967. **Members:** 3,000. **Membership Dues:** regular, $60 (annual) ● student in U.S., $30 (annual) ● regular, outside U.S., $65 (annual) ● senior in U.S., $45 (annual) ● student outside U.S., $35 (annual) ● senior outside U.S., $50 (annual) ● life, $750. **Staff:** 1. **Budget:** $64,000. **Description:** Professional and amateur players of the string bass in 45 countries; teachers, repairmen, students; libraries. Acts as central clearinghouse. **Divisions:** Educational; Performance. **Formerly:** (1975) International Institute for the String Bass. **Publications:** *Bass Line*, biennial. Newsletter. Contains bass happening around the world. **Price:** $15.00 for members; $30.00 for nonmembers ● *Bass World*, 3/year. Magazine. **Circulation:** 2,500. **Advertising:** accepted. **Conventions/Meetings:** competition and workshop ● biennial conference (exhibits).

10626 ■ International Society for Contemporary Music - USA (ISCM)
c/o David Mcmullin
332 Jamaicaway, No. 208
Boston, MA 02130
Ph: (617)901-1677
E-mail: mcmullin@league-iscm.org
URL: http://www.iscm.org
Contact: David Mcmullin, Contact
Founded: 1922. **Members:** 35. **Staff:** 2. **Budget:** $30,000. **Multinational. Description:** Has national sections in 30 countries. Seeks to propagate and develop contemporary music. Has contemporary works that are considered without regard to nationality, race, religion, or political affiliations of composers. (In the early history of the society, contemporary music was rarely performed and was at that time "a cause to fight for." Music festival was often the only opportunity to perform the works of such "radicals" as Bartok, Schoenberg, and others, which have since become 20th century classics.) Sponsors annual World Music Days. Conducts annual four concert series in New York. **Committees:** Journal; Programming; Recording. **Also Known As:** League of Composers - International Society for Contemporary Music, U.S. Section; League/ISCM. **Conventions/Meetings:** competition, for new music performers ● annual festival ● annual National Composers Competition, for composers.

10627 ■ International Society of Folk Harpers and Craftsmen (ISFHC)
1614 Pittman Dr.
Missoula, MT 59803
Ph: (406)542-1976
E-mail: clem@in-tch.com
URL: http://www.folkharpsociety.org
Contact: Mr. David Woodworth, Pres.
Founded: 1980. **Members:** 1,100. **Membership Dues:** regular in U.S., $30 (annual) ● regular in Canada and Mexico, $32 (annual) ● regular outside U.S., Canada and Mexico, $38 (annual) ● sustaining, $50 (annual) ● patron, $100 (annual). **Budget:** $80,000. **Local Groups:** 10. **Multinational. Description:** Folk harpers, folk harp makers, concert artists, and craftsmen in 16 countries. Conducts technical and artistic programs, and promotes craft exchange. Collects and distributes historical and current information regarding folk harps and harpers. Organizes concerts. **Computer Services:** database, index to Folk Harp Journal (available on Internet). **Publications:** *Folk Harp Journal*, quarterly. Includes book and record reviews, chapter news, and calendar of events. **Price:** included in membership dues; $16.00 /year for institutions. ISSN: 0094-8934. **Circulation:** 1,400. **Advertising:** accepted ● *International Society of Folk Harpers and Craftsmen—Directory of Members*, annual. Membership Directory. Contains list of members arranged alphabetically and geographically. **Price:** included in membership dues. **Circulation:** 1,400. **Conventions/Meetings:** Conference of Folk Harpers and Craftsmen, players and builders of folk harp (exhibits).

10628 ■ International Society for Organ History and Preservation (ISOHP)
Address Unknown since 2007
Founded: 1975. **Staff:** 1. **Description:** Promotes the documentation and preservation of pipe organs in all countries. Conducts historical and descriptive research in conjunction with the Organ Historical Society. **Libraries: Type:** reference. **Holdings:** 400. **Subjects:** American and international organ history. **Affiliated With:** Organ Historical Society. **Publications:** *The Diapason*, monthly. Journal. **Price:** $20.00 in U.S.; $30.00 outside U.S. ISSN: 0012-2378. **Advertising:** accepted.

10629 ■ International Steel Guitar Convention (ISGC)
9535 Midland Blvd.
St. Louis, MO 63114-3314
Ph: (314)427-7794
Fax: (314)427-0516
E-mail: scotty@scottysmusic.com
URL: http://scottysmusic.com
Contact: Scott DeWitt, Founder
Founded: 1971. **Members:** 3,000. **Membership Dues:** individual, $60 (annual). **Budget:** $65,000. **For-Profit. Multinational. Description:** Musicians and music fans in 32 countries united to promote the steel guitar through sponsorship of a convention. Provides fans with entertainment from steel guitarists and various instruments including the bass guitar, drums, piano, and fiddle. Offers continuous 30-minute performances by steel guitarists throughout the convention. Conducts seminars on the steel guitar and related products, and holds clinics on music performance. Maintains hall of fame. **Libraries: Type:** reference. **Holdings:** audio recordings, video recordings. **Subjects:** music performances. **Awards:** The Steel Guitar Hall of Fame. **Frequency:** annual. **Type:** recognition. **Computer Services:** Mailing lists. **Formerly:** Annual Steel Guitar Convention. **Publications:** *The Steel Guitar Hall of Fame*, annual. Bulletin. **Price:** free. **Conventions/Meetings:** annual convention (exhibits).

10630 ■ International Trumpet Guild (ITG)
c/o Dixie Burress, Treas.
PO Box 2688
Davenport, IA 52809-2688
Fax: (413)403-8899
E-mail: info@trumpetguild.org
URL: http://www.trumpetguild.org
Contact: Jeffrey Piper, Pres.
Founded: 1974. **Members:** 7,000. **Membership Dues:** regular, $50 (annual) ● senior, student, $30 (annual). **Budget:** $200,000. **Description:** Promotes communication among trumpet players around the world. Seeks to improve the artistic level of performance, teaching, and literature associated with the trumpet. Compiles statistics. **Libraries: Type:** reference. **Holdings:** archival material. **Computer Services:** Mailing lists, of members. **Telecommunication Services:** electronic mail, president@trumpetguild.org. **Committees:** Commissions; Competitions; Organizing Conference; State Planning. **Publications:** *ITG Journal*, quarterly. Includes book, music, and record reviews; lists new publications and recordings. Refereed. **Price:** included in membership dues. **Circulation:** 6,000. **Advertising:** accepted. Alternate Formats: CD-ROM ● Directory, biennial ● Books. Alternate Formats: CD-ROM. **Conventions/Meetings:** annual conference (exhibits).

10631 ■ International Tuba-Euphonium Association (ITEA)
c/o Kathy Aylsworth Brantigan, Treas.
2253 Downing St.
Denver, CO 80205
Ph: (303)832-4676
Fax: (303)832-0839
E-mail: itea@denverbrass.org
URL: http://www.iteaonline.org
Contact: Kathy Aylsworth Brantigan, Treas.
Founded: 1972. **Members:** 2,100. **Membership Dues:** professional, amateur, associate, $50 (annual) ● student, retired, $35 (annual) ● life, $930. **Staff:** 2. **Budget:** $107,000. **Description:** Musicians who serve as liaison among those who take a significant interest in the instruments of the tuba and euphonium family and in their development, literature, pedagogy, and performance. Aims to: expand performance and job opportunities; redefine the image and role of euphoniumists, tubists, and their instruments; explore pedagogical approaches through new teaching materials; promote activity in new instrument design; generate new compositions for the tuba and euphonium; explore new directions in technique; establish appropriate libraries of recorded and printed materials; coordinate and cosponsor tuba-euphonium symposia/workshops on the local, regional, national, and international levels. Commissions new musical compositions for tuba and euphonium; conducts research and educational programs. Compiles statistics. **Libraries: Type:** reference. **Holdings:** 500; archival material. **Computer Services:** Mailing lists. **Committees:** Commissions; Conferences. **Formerly:** (2001) Tubists Universal Brotherhood Association. **Publications:** Journal, quarterly. Contains articles, music and record reviews, and news on subjects of interest to members. **Price:** included in membership dues; $40.00 for nonmembers in U.S.; $50.00 for nonmembers outside U.S. **Circulation:** 2,100. **Advertising:** accepted ● Membership Directory, annual. Includes list of members. **Price:** included in membership dues. **Circulation:** 2,700 ● Brochures ● Pamphlets. **Conventions/Meetings:** biennial conference, with competitions and concerts (exhibits) - even-numbered years ● biennial regional meeting and conference, with competitions and concerts - odd-numbered years.

10632 ■ Jazz World Society (JWS)
PO Box 35
New York, NY 10018
Fax: (212)253-4160
E-mail: jws@jazzsociety.com
URL: http://www.jazzsociety.com
Contact: Jan A. Byrczek, Pres./Founder
Founded: 1983. **Members:** 3,500. **Staff:** 3. **Description:** Professionals involved in jazz, including musicians, composers, record producers, distributors, collectors, and journalists; individuals actively supporting jazz music. Promotes the development of jazz music in its various interpretations and fosters communication among jazz participants. Operates library of records, publications, books, and photographs. Organizes competitions; offers specialized education programs, seminars, and placement service. Maintains hall of fame and biographical archives. **Awards: Type:** recognition. **Computer Services:** database, jazz world ● mailing lists, of members. **Councils:** International Advisory. **Affiliated With:** International Music Council. **Formerly:** (1975) European Jazz Federation; (1983) International Jazz Federation. **Publications:** *European Jazz Directory*, biennial ● *Jazz Festivals International Directory*, periodic ● *Jazz World*, bimonthly. Newsletter. Serves as a communications source for the entire jazz industry including advertisers, booking agents, producers, and record labels. **Price:** included in membership dues; $25.00 /year for nonmembers. ISSN: 0749-4564. **Circulation:** 6,000 ● *USA Jazz Directory*, periodic ● Also publishes jazz reference books. **Conventions/Meetings:** semiannual general assembly.

10633 ■ Jazzmobile
154 W 127th St.
New York, NY 10027
Ph: (212)866-4900

E-mail: jazzy@jazzmobile.org
URL: http://www.jazzmobile.org
Contact: Robin Bell-Stevens, Exec. Dir./CEO
Founded: 1964. **Description:** Represents persons involved in the musical, dramatic, and graphic arts fields who are interested in bringing jazz music to neighborhoods by means of mobile units. Conducts tour in New York, during the summer months, giving regular free jazz concerts. Provides free jazz workshop program in New York City using professional jazz musicians as instructors. Presents free lecture/demonstrations about jazz in public schools. Currently studying expansion of the program.

10634 ■ Jew's Harp Guild
69954 Hidden Valley Ln.
Cove, OR 97824
E-mail: newsletter@jewsharpguild.org
URL: http://www.jewsharpguild.org
Contact: Wayland Harman, Exec. Dir.
Founded: 1996. **Description:** Represents individuals interested in Jew's harp. Promotes and furthers appreciation of the Jew's harp. Preserves the history and art of Jew's harp and other ancient, unique, or culturally significant acoustic instruments. **Publications:** *The Pluck-n-Post.* Newsletter. Alternate Formats: online.

10635 ■ Kurt Weill Foundation for Music (KWFM)
7 E 20th St.
New York, NY 10003-1106
Ph: (212)505-5240
Fax: (212)353-9663
E-mail: kwfinfo@kwf.org
URL: http://www.kwf.org
Contact: Carolyn Weber, Dir./VP
Founded: 1962. **Staff:** 7. **Languages:** English, German. **Multinational. Description:** Promotes the study and performance of music by Kurt Weill (1900-50), naturalized American composer of symphonic, chamber, and vocal works, musical theater works, and scores for motion pictures. Conducts grant and prize programs. Administers Weill/Lenya Research Center. **Libraries: Type:** reference. **Holdings:** archival material, audiovisuals, books, clippings, photographs. **Awards:** Kurt Weill Foundation for Music Grants Program. **Frequency:** annual. **Type:** grant. **Recipient:** for research, travel, and performances in support of projects related to Weill ● Kurt Weill Prize. **Type:** recognition. **Recipient:** for Distinguished Scholarship in Music Theatre. **Computer Services:** database, Weill performances and research materials. **Telecommunication Services:** electronic mail, cweber@kwf.org. **Publications:** *A Guide to the New Weill/Lenya Research Center* ● *Kurt Weill: A Guide to His Works* ● *Kurt Weill Newsletter*, semiannual. Includes grants announcement, research reports, and reviews of books, recordings, and performances. **Price:** free. ISSN: 0899-6407. **Circulation:** 5,000. Alternate Formats: online.

10636 ■ Latin American Art Song Alliance (LAASA)
18204 NE 23rd St.
Vancouver, WA 98684
E-mail: allison@laasa.org
URL: http://www.laasa.org
Contact: Allison Weiss, Pres.
Membership Dues: regular, $15 (annual) ● regular, $28 (biennial) ● regular, $39 (triennial). **Description:** Represents musicians, musician-scholars, and music appreciators. Promotes Latin American art song. Assists teachers and students of singing who are trying to access the published repertoire. Seeks to publish, perform, record, and promote solo vocal music by Latin American composers. **Publications:** *LAASA Inside*, annual. Newsletter. **Price:** free. Alternate Formats: online.

10637 ■ Latvian Choir Association of the U.S. (LCAUS)
Address Unknown since 2007
Founded: 1958. **Members:** 30. **Description:** Latvian choirs. Supplies music material to choirs; organizes and sponsors song festivals to preserve and promote Latvian national heritage. Conducts choir directors' seminars. Compiles statistics on members. **Libraries: Type:** reference. **Holdings:** archival material. **Publications:** *Latvju Muzika* (in Latvian), annual. Journal. **Advertising:** not accepted. **Conventions/Meetings:** quinquennial meeting.

10638 ■ Lesbian and Gay Band Association (LGBA)
PO Box 14874
San Francisco, CA 94114-0874
E-mail: lgbainfo@aol.com
URL: http://www.gaybands.org
Contact: Judy Ames, Pres.
Founded: 1982. **Members:** 26. **Membership Dues:** family, $1,000 (annual) ● best friend, $500 (annual) ● close friend, $250 (annual) ● dear friend, $100 (annual) ● good friend, $50 (annual) ● friend, $25 (annual). **Staff:** 14. **Multinational. Description:** Represents gay and lesbian concert and marching bands from cities across America and the world. Encourages the formation of new bands, and shares the gift of music with gay and non-gay audiences. **Libraries: Type:** reference. **Holdings:** 500; audio recordings. **Telecommunication Services:** electronic mail, lgbaprez@rochester.rr.com. **Divisions:** Fundraising; National Librarian; Outreach; Special Events. **Formerly:** (2004) Lesbian and Gay Bands of America. **Publications:** *How to Form a Lesbian and Gay Community Band* ● *LGBA Roster*, semiannual. Newsletter ● *TieLine*, monthly. Newsletter. **Price:** included in membership dues. Alternate Formats: online. **Conventions/Meetings:** annual Benefit Concert - conference.

10639 ■ Leschetizky Association (LA)
c/o Ms. Young Drago, Treas./Registrar/Corresponding Sec.
37-21 90th St., Apt. 2R
Jackson Heights, NY 11372
Ph: (718)205-8271
Fax: (718)205-8271
E-mail: tonyoungdrago@aol.com
URL: http://www.leschetizky.org
Contact: Ms. Young Drago, Treas./Registrar/Corresponding Sec.
Founded: 1942. **Members:** 295. **Membership Dues:** individual, $40 (annual) ● life, $350. **Regional Groups:** 5. **State Groups:** 2. **Local Groups:** 1. **Description:** Pianists whose training derives from Theodor Leschetizky (1830-1915), a world-famous Polish teacher and composer whose students included Paderewski, Gabrilowitsch, Horszowski, Brailowsky, and Schnabel; professional musicians and other individuals who support the ideals and principles that Leschetizky brought to piano playing and teaching. Sponsors a concert series, youth concerts, an adult players group, a triennial piano competition and a biannual Gifted Young Pianists Concerto Competition. **Libraries: Type:** reference. **Holdings:** biographical archives. **Subjects:** Theodore Leschetizky (1830-1915). **Awards:** Recital Debut. **Frequency:** triennial. **Type:** recognition. **Computer Services:** Mailing lists. **Councils:** Advisory. **Publications:** *News Bulletin*, annual. Includes calendar of events. **Price:** included in membership dues. **Advertising:** accepted ● Membership Directory. **Conventions/Meetings:** annual meeting, business meeting with concert, elections if necessary - always June.

10640 ■ Liederkranz Foundation (LF)
6 E 87th St.
New York, NY 10128
Ph: (212)534-0880
Fax: (212)828-5372
E-mail: info@liederkranznycity.org
URL: http://www.liederkranznycity.org
Contact: Dr. Hans G. Hachmann, Pres.
Founded: 1847. **Members:** 135. **Membership Dues:** resident, $350 (annual) ● non-resident, $150 (annual) ● chorus, $175 (annual). **Staff:** 5. **Budget:** $50,000. **Description:** Seeks to achieve and maintain high musical standards in America by giving recognition and encouragement to talented young singers. Finances and administers cultural, musical, and educational programs of The Liederkranz (a musical society founded in New York City in 1847 by German-Americans) to give as many people as possible an opportunity to hear and participate in fine music and to further close cultural ties between the United States and the German-speaking countries. In the past century, Liederkranz choral groups and the Liederkranz Orchestra have participated in numerous concerts and musical events. Encourages amateur and professional participation in choral groups, stages professionally coached operas and operettas, and sponsors a variety of concerts, most notably its Musicale Series. Establishes a scholarship fund for singers to enable them to attend accredited music schools and conservatories or to study privately. Sponsors competition. **Convention/Meeting:** none. **Awards: Frequency:** annual. **Type:** scholarship. **Publications:** *L K News*, bimonthly.

10641 ■ Lute Society of America (LSA)
c/o Garald Farnham, Treas.
255 W 98th St., No. 5C
New York, NY 10025-7282
Ph: (925)686-5800
E-mail: d.hoban@tcu.edu
URL: http://www.cs.dartmouth.edu/~lsa
Contact: Dick Hoban, Pres.
Founded: 1966. **Members:** 700. **Membership Dues:** individual, $45 (annual) ● life, $500. **Description:** Represents musicians, musicologists, teachers, and manufacturers of instruments and related items. Seeks to cultivate, promote, and foster interest in the lute and related string instruments; coordinate groups of lutenists and furnish them with information. Conducts educational programs. Maintains 700 item microfilm library. **Libraries: Type:** lending. **Holdings:** archival material, audio recordings, books, papers. **Subjects:** source material for lute and other related instruments. **Computer Services:** Mailing lists, of members. **Publications:** *LSA Quarterly.* Newsletter. **Advertising:** accepted ● Directory, annual ● Journal, annual. ISSN: 0076-1526. **Circulation:** 650. **Advertising:** accepted. **Conventions/Meetings:** annual seminar - always summer.

10642 ■ Maple Leaf Club (MLC)
15522 Ricky Ct.
Grass Valley, CA 95949
URL: http://www.rag-time.com/mlc
Founded: 1967. **Members:** 550. **Membership Dues:** regular in U.S. and Canada, $17 (annual) ● regular outside U.S. and Canada, $24 (annual). **Description:** Individuals dedicated to the preservation of classic ragtime music, a style of American music featuring rhythmic complexity and syncopation that originated at the end of the 19th century. **Publications:** *The Rag Times*, bimonthly. Newsletter. **Price:** included in membership dues. ISSN: 0090-4570. **Conventions/Meetings:** bimonthly show.

10643 ■ Meet the Composer (MTC)
75 9th Ave., Fl. 3R, Ste.C
New York, NY 10011-7006
Ph: (212)645-6949
Fax: (212)645-9669
E-mail: mtc@meetthecomposer.org
URL: http://www.meetthecomposer.org
Contact: Ed Harsh, Pres.
Founded: 1974. **Staff:** 8. **Regional Groups:** 7. **Nonmembership. Description:** Arts service organization supporting the entire spectrum of new music. Seeks to: promote the music of living American composers; encourage the creation, commissioning, performing, and recording of new music; develop new audiences for contemporary music. **Awards: Type:** grant. **Recipient:** for American composers for commissions, performances, residencies, and collaboration. **Programs:** Composer/Choreographer; Composers Performance Fund/National Affiliate Network; Education; Jazz; Meet The Composer/Reader's Digest Commissioning; New Residencies. **Publications:** *Commissioning Music.* Handbook ● *Composers in the Marketplace: How to Earn a Living Writing Music.* Handbook.

10644 ■ Melodious Accord (MA)
c/o Alice Parker, Artistic Dir./Founder
96 Middle Rd.
Hawley, MA 01339
Ph: (413)339-8508
Fax: (413)339-6609
E-mail: aparker@melodiousaccord.org
URL: http://www.melodiousaccord.org
Contact: Alice Parker, Artistic Dir./Founder
Founded: 1984. **Staff:** 2. **Budget:** $69,000. **Description:** Unites composers, professional and amateur performers, and music enthusiasts by involving them in the process of music-making. Seeks to build a sense of community resulting from the enjoyment of singing and benefit society through the power of music. Encourages composers. Presents professional chamber music concerts that include audience participation. Offers master classes in performance and composition, and internships and fellowships for professional musicians. Conducts workshops and biennial composition search. **Committees:** Composition Search; Fellowship. **Projects:** Alice Parker Recording. **Publications:** *Melodious Accord Newsletter*, 3/year. Contains information on music education, surveys and calendar of events. **Circulation:** 5,400. Alternate Formats: online ● Brochure ● Also publishes songbooks, and produces recordings for the Musical Heritage Society. **Conventions/Meetings:** periodic Community Sing - meeting.

10645 ■ Metropolitan Opera Association
Lincoln Center
New York, NY 10023
Ph: (212)799-3100 (212)362-6000
E-mail: metinfo@metopera.org
URL: http://www.metoperafamily.org/metopera/index.aspx
Contact: Peter Gelb, Gen. Mgr.
Founded: 1883. **Staff:** 750. **Description:** Supporters include individuals, foundations, and corporations. Aims to produce and make available, through tours, radio, and television, fully staged operas at the Metropolitan Opera House in New York City; increase public understanding and appreciation of opera. Sponsors seminars, professional training programs, and in-school programs. Maintains historic archives of photographs and costumes. **Affiliated With:** Metropolitan Opera Guild. **Also Known As:** Metopera. **Publications:** *Opera News*, semimonthly.

10646 ■ Metropolitan Opera Guild (MOG)
70 Lincoln Center Plz.
New York, NY 10023
Ph: (212)769-7000 (212)769-7010
E-mail: info@metguild.org
URL: http://www.metoperafamily.org/guild
Contact: William S. Morris, Pres./CEO
Founded: 1935. **Members:** 70,000. **Membership Dues:** national, $65 (annual) ● supporting, $125 (annual) ● contributing, $200 (annual) ● donor, $350 (annual) ● sponsor, $600 (annual) ● fellow, $1,000 (annual). **Staff:** 68. **Budget:** $17,500,000. **Description:** Seeks to promote greater interest in opera; further musical education and appreciation; broaden the base of support for the Metropolitan Opera. Conducts educational programs including in-school opera program, in-service teacher courses, evening lecture series, and student performances at Opera House. Operates three retail outlets and extensive mail order business as well as member travel program. Stages various membership and fundraising events during the year. **Affiliated With:** Metropolitan Opera Association. **Publications:** *Metropolitan Opera Season Souvenir Book*, annual ● *Opera News*, monthly. Magazine. Serves as a guide to broadcasts and covers news of the opera world, reviews, and articles. **Price:** $30.00/year. ISSN: 0030-3607. **Circulation:** 110,000. **Advertising:** accepted.

10647 ■ Mexican American Music Association (MAMA)
103 Broadway Ave.
Dodson, TX 79230
Ph: (806)493-4938
E-mail: pbsmama@gmail.com
URL: http://www.pbsmama.com
Contact: Pete Salmeron, Pres.
Multinational. Description: Provides opportunities and exposure for aspiring Mexican American musicians and vocalists. Works to eliminate the "prevailing prejudices and biases" that exist in the music industry. Provides promoters, managers, and record labels with talented budding artists.

10648 ■ Mixed Harmony Barbershop Quartet Association (MHBQA)
c/o Kim Orloff, Coor./Co-Founder
PO Box 1209
Aptos, CA 95001
E-mail: korloff@ix.netcom.com
URL: http://mixedbarbershop.com
Contact: Kim Orloff, Coor./Co-Founder
Founded: 1995. **Membership Dues:** quartet/individual in U.S., $15 (annual) ● quartet/individual in Canada, $16 (annual) ● quartet/individual outside U.S. and Canada, $20 (annual). **Description:** Acts as a clearinghouse for the exchange of ideas and experiences unique to the mixed quartet performing code. Seeks potential resources for assisting with barbershop harmony exposure in school systems. Fosters camaraderie among its members. Maintains a roster of active mixed quartets. **Publications:** Newsletter. **Price:** included in membership dues.

10649 ■ Moravian Music Foundation (MMF)
457 S Church St.
Winston-Salem, NC 27101
Ph: (336)725-0651
Fax: (336)725-4514
E-mail: bwall@mcsp.org
URL: http://www.moravianmusic.org
Contact: Karen E. Hyland, Exec. Asst.
Founded: 1956. **Staff:** 4. **Budget:** $300,000. **Nonmembership. Multinational. Description:** Works to advance early American Moravian music and complementary music through research, publications, recordings and education. Holds copyrights to the music collections of the Moravian Church in America and makes available its musical and documentary materials to accredited scholars and graduate students. Assists in and occasionally sponsors concerts of Moravian music; supported by contributions from individuals, church congregations and others. **Libraries: Type:** reference; lending. **Holdings:** 6,000; archival material, articles, books, periodicals, video recordings. **Subjects:** hymnology, Church music, early American music, early and contemporary Moravian music. **Awards:** James V. Salzwedel Award for Excellence in Church Music. **Frequency:** periodic. **Type:** recognition. **Recipient:** for individuals with significant contributions to the musical life of the congregations(s) they have served, over an extended period of time ● Moramus Award for Distinguished Service to American Music. **Frequency:** periodic. **Type:** recognition. **Recipient:** to scholars and others whose activities and achievements have resulted in outstanding contributions to American Moravian music and have furthered the work of the MMF. **Boards:** Trustees. **Publications:** *Moravian Music Foundation Newsletter*, quarterly. **Circulation:** 1,800 ● Also publishes bibliographical-historical reprints on the music of the American Moravians, catalogs of manuscript, and early printed music. **Conventions/Meetings:** semiannual board meeting ● annual festival ● seminar and workshop, for Church musicians.

10650 ■ Music Critics Association of North America (MCANA)
722 Dulaney Valley Rd., No. 259
Baltimore, MD 21204
Ph: (410)435-3881
Fax: (410)435-3881
E-mail: musiccritics@aol.com
URL: http://mcana.org
Contact: Tim Smith, Pres.
Founded: 1957. **Members:** 150. **Membership Dues:** regular, $100 (annual) ● student, $35 (annual) ● active critic, journalist, editor, book author, program annotator, retired, $100 (annual). **Staff:** 1. **Description:** Classical music critics for newspapers, magazines, and broadcast media. Promotes improved standards and quality of music criticism in the U.S. and Canada; fosters public interest in music. **Computer Services:** Mailing lists, only to not-for-profit groups. **Committees:** Education of Music Critics. **Formerly:** (1995) Music Critics Association. **Publications:** *Critical Issues*, quarterly. Newsletter. Contains information about the organization. **Price:** free for members. **Circulation:** 750. **Conventions/Meetings:** annual conference.

10651 ■ Music Performance Fund (MPF)
1501 Broadway, Ste.518
New York, NY 10036
Ph: (212)391-3950
Fax: (212)221-2604
E-mail: info@musicpf.org
URL: http://www.musicpf.org
Contact: Mr. John C. Hall, Trustee
Founded: 1948. **Description:** Public service organization created and financed by the recording industries under agreements with the American Federation of Musicians of the U.S. and Canada. Spends its funds to provide admission to free, live, instrumental musical performances throughout the U.S. and Canada, on occasions which will contribute to the public knowledge and appreciation of music in connection with patriotic, charitable, educational, and public activities. About $15,000,000 is spent each year for approximately 25,000 musical presentations. **Formerly:** Recording Industries Music Performance Trust Funds; (2005) Music Performance Trust Funds. **Publications:** Annual Report. Alternate Formats: online.

10652 ■ Musicians Foundation (MF)
875 6th Ave., Ste.2303
New York, NY 10001-3507
Ph: (212)239-9137
Fax: (212)239-9138
E-mail: info@musiciansfoundation.org
URL: http://www.musiciansfoundation.org
Contact: B.C. Vermeersch, Exec. Dir.
Founded: 1914. **Staff:** 1. **Description:** Represents the interests and advances the condition and social welfare of professional musicians and their families; does not bestow scholarships. **Convention/Meeting:** none.

10653 ■ NAMM Foundation Research Division
5790 Armada Dr.
Carlsbad, CA 92008
E-mail: info@nammfoundation.org
URL: http://www.music-research.org
Contact: Joe Lamond, Pres./CEO
Founded: 1997. **Multinational. Description:** Promotes scientific research into the relationship between music and physical and emotional well being, focusing on the elderly population, impact of music on at-risk youth, effects of music and music making. **Awards:** Fellowships/Assistanceships. **Type:** fellowship. **Formerly:** (2006) International Foundation for Music Research. **Publications:** Newsletter.

10654 ■ Nashville Songwriters Association International (NSAI)
1710 Roy Acuff Pl.
Nashville, TN 37203
Ph: (615)256-3354
Free: (800)321-6008
Fax: (615)256-0034
E-mail: nsai@nashvillesongwriters.com
URL: http://www.nashvillesongwriters.com
Contact: Barton Herbison, Exec. Dir.
Founded: 1967. **Members:** 4,500. **Membership Dues:** active/associate outside U.S., student, professional, $100 (annual) ● active/associate in U.S., $150 (annual) ● life, $2,000. **Staff:** 10. **Regional Groups:** 95. **National Groups:** 101. **Description:** Professional and amateur songwriters; individuals in the songwriting industry. Works to advance the art of musical composition and promote the growth of creative leadership for artistic, cultural, and educational progress in the field; helps songwriters gain

recognition for their work; participates in legislative work for songwriter benefits. Maintains hall of fame. **Libraries: Type:** open to the public. **Holdings:** 200. **Subjects:** craft of songwriting, music business education, career management. **Awards:** Song of the Year Award. **Frequency:** annual. **Type:** recognition ● Songwriter/Artist of the Year Award. **Frequency:** annual. **Type:** recognition ● Songwriter of the Year Award. **Frequency:** annual. **Type:** recognition. **Computer Services:** Online services, chatroom and forum. **Formerly:** (1976) Nashville Songwriters Association. **Publications:** *NSAI Newswire*, quarterly. Newsletter. **Circulation:** 4,500 ● *ProUpdate*, quarterly. Newsletter ● Books. **Conventions/Meetings:** annual Music Row Songwriters Symposium ● weekly Nashville Workshop, for songwriters unable to travel to major recording centers - every Thursday evenings ● annual Tin Pan South - festival - always April.

10655 ■ National Academy of Popular Music (NAPM)

330 W 58th St., Ste.411
New York, NY 10019-1827
Ph: (212)957-9230
Fax: (212)957-9227
E-mail: info@songhall.org
URL: http://www.songwritershalloffame.org/about_napm.asp
Contact: Hal David, Chm./CEO

Founded: 1969. **Members:** 1,300. **Membership Dues:** associate, $25 (annual) ● professional, $50 (annual) ● executive (music industry), $100 (annual) ● life, $1,000. **Staff:** 2. **Description:** Songwriters, record producers, publishers, performers, and others involved in popular music. Seeks to highlight the role of popular music in American life and history. Honors artists, composers, and entertainers for their contributions to the entertainment field. **Libraries: Type:** reference. **Holdings:** 50,000; archival material, audio recordings, books, papers, video recordings. **Subjects:** sheet music. **Awards:** Induction Award. **Frequency:** annual. **Type:** recognition ● Industry Award. **Frequency:** annual. **Type:** recognition. **Additional Websites:** http://www.songhall.org. **Publications:** *Words about Music*, semiannual. Newsletter. Contains reports on organizational activities. **Price:** free. **Circulation:** 2,500. **Conventions/Meetings:** annual dinner (exhibits) ● seminar, songwriting ● quarterly workshop.

10656 ■ National Alliance for Musical Theatre (NAMT)

520 8th Ave., 3rd Fl., Ste.301
New York, NY 10018
Ph: (212)714-6668
Fax: (212)714-0469
E-mail: info@namt.org
URL: http://namt.org
Contact: Kathy Evans, Exec. Dir.

Founded: 1985. **Members:** 130. **Staff:** 4. **Budget:** $500,000. **Description:** Professional institutions and theaters. Promotes the production and development of stage musicals. **Awards: Type:** grant. **Recipient:** to a member who is interested in writing an original musical. **Telecommunication Services:** electronic mail, kathy@namt.org. **Publications:** *Little Black Book*, annual. Directory. **Price:** $25.00 ● Newsletter, weekly. Provides information about show openings, industry news, review quotes and other announcements. **Conventions/Meetings:** semiannual meeting.

10657 ■ National Association of Composers, U.S.A. (NACUSA)

PO Box 49256
Barrington Sta.
Los Angeles, CA 90049
Ph: (818)274-6048
E-mail: nacusa@music-usa.org
URL: http://www.music-usa.org/nacusa
Contact: Dr. Daniel Kessner, Pres.

Founded: 1975. **Members:** 500. **Membership Dues:** student, senior, newsletter subscriber, $15 (annual) ● regular, $25 (annual) ● friend, $50-$74 (annual) ● patron, $75-$99 (annual) ● benefactor, $100 (annual). **Budget:** $5,000. **Regional Groups:** 5. **Local Groups:** 4. **Description:** Composers, conductors, professional performers, and patrons of music. Sponsors several free concerts each season for presentation of members' works; also sponsors contests for young composers. **Awards:** NACUSA Young Composers' Competition. **Frequency:** annual. **Type:** monetary. **Recipient:** for quality of the music. **Committees:** Public Relations. **Supersedes:** National Association for Composers and Conductors. **Publications:** *Composer/U.S.A.*, 3/year. Newsletter. Contains listings of awards competitions, opportunities, commissions, and recordings; includes concert and performance calendar. **Price:** included in membership dues; $20.00 for nonmembers. ISSN: 1086-1998. **Circulation:** 700. **Advertising:** accepted ● Bulletin. Alternate Formats: online ● Catalog. Alternate Formats: online.

10658 ■ National Association of Negro Musicians (NANM)

PO Box 43053
Chicago, IL 60643
Ph: (773)568-3818
Fax: (773)785-5388
E-mail: rcarter600@aol.com
URL: http://www.nanm.org
Contact: Roland M. Carter, Pres.

Founded: 1919. **Members:** 2,500. **Membership Dues:** individual, $40 (annual) ● youth, $15 (annual) ● junior, collegiate, $10 (annual) ● life, $500 ● affiliate, $85 (annual). **Budget:** $150,000. **Regional Groups:** 5. **Local Groups:** 43. **Description:** Amateur, professional, and retired musicians; interested individuals. Promotes the advancement of all types of music, especially among young black musicians. Also sponsors concerts by recognized musicians. **Awards:** Music. **Frequency:** annual. **Type:** scholarship. **Recipient:** for competition. **Divisions:** Life Member Guild; Patrons of Art; Valentine Loan Fund. **Publications:** *NANM Newsletter*, quarterly ● *Post-Convention Newsletter*, annual. **Conventions/Meetings:** annual competition, regional winners compete for scholarships ● annual convention (exhibits) - always August.

10659 ■ National Association of Rhythm and Blues Dee Jay's

c/o Berni McKenna, Sec.
3331 Saratoga Dr.
Belleville, IL 62221-6633
Ph: (618)257-9638 (662)342-6413
E-mail: thepresident@randbdeejays.com
URL: http://www.randbdeejays.com
Contact: Tom Polzin, Pres.

Membership Dues: regular/associate/supporter, $25 (annual). **Description:** Promotes, preserves and perpetuates the rhythm and blues music. Provides a national network of communication between DeeJay's with similar interests. Encourages mutual cooperation and camaraderie between all types of DeeJay's and R&B associations. **Awards:** Blue Note Award. **Frequency:** annual. **Type:** recognition. **Recipient:** to the members for their effort in the promotion, preservation and perpetuation of rhythm & blues music with distinction ● Rufus Oates Award. **Frequency:** annual. **Type:** recognition. **Recipient:** to the members who volunteer their time and effort in a professional manner for the advancement, prestige and growth of the association. **Telecommunication Services:** electronic mail, secretary@randbdeejays.com.

10660 ■ National Band Association (NBA)

PO Box 25136
Baton Rouge, LA 70894
Ph: (225)578-2259
Fax: (225)578-4693
E-mail: info@nationalbandassociation.org
URL: http://www.nationalbandassociation.org
Contact: Dr. Linda Moorhouse, Exec. Sec.

Founded: 1960. **Members:** 3,000. **Membership Dues:** retired, student, $25 (annual) ● individual, $45 (annual) ● Canadian, $50 (annual) ● institutional, international, $55 (annual) ● spousal, $70 (annual) ● corporate, $120 (annual) ● life, $300 ● student bridge, $10 (annual). **Staff:** 1. **Description:** Directors of school, college, professional, military, and community bands; music publishers; manufacturers of musical instruments and others interested in development of bands and band music. Sponsors clinics and other educational functions for band directors. Offers program exchange service and research projects. Maintains Academy of Wind and Percussion Arts which recognizes persons who promote the musical and educational significance of bands and band music throughout the world. Conducts Hall of Fame of Distinguished Band Conductors. **Awards:** Certificate of Merit for Marching Excellence. **Frequency:** annual. **Type:** recognition. **Recipient:** for outstanding marching band directors ● Citation of Excellence. **Frequency:** annual. **Type:** recognition. **Recipient:** for outstanding concert band directors ● High School Jazz Student Award. **Frequency:** annual. **Type:** recognition. **Recipient:** for outstanding jazz student ● Outstanding Band Musician. **Frequency:** annual. **Type:** recognition. **Recipient:** for outstanding members of band musician ● Outstanding Jazz Educator. **Frequency:** annual. **Type:** recognition. **Recipient:** for outstanding jazz teacher. **Committees:** Composition Contests; Jazz; Marching Band; Music Camps; Music Education; Music Publications. **Projects:** Research Grants; Young Composer Mentor; Young Conductor Mentor. **Affiliated With:** MENC: The National Association for Music Education. **Publications:** *The Instrumentalist*, monthly. Magazine ● *NBA Journal*, 3/year. **Advertising:** accepted. **Conventions/Meetings:** biennial convention.

10661 ■ National Catholic Band Association (NCBA)

c/o John Badsing, Sec.-Treas.
3334 N Normandy Ave.
Chicago, IL 60634-3716
E-mail: info@catholicbands.org
URL: http://www.catholicbands.org
Contact: John Badsing, Sec.-Treas.

Founded: 1953. **Members:** 200. **Membership Dues:** active, associate retail, $40 (annual) ● commercial, $50 (annual). **Description:** Catholic bandmasters and non-Catholic members who teach in Catholic schools. Seeks to: coordinate Catholic band activities on a national level; present a factual composite of the program to the clergy; work with teacher training organizations to emphasize techniques to be used in Catholic bands; assist in placing competent Catholic bandmasters in Catholic schools. Sponsors competitions; compiles statistics; provides educational evaluations. **Libraries: Type:** reference. **Holdings:** archival material, periodicals. **Subjects:** liturgical music. **Awards:** Adam P. Lesinsky Award. **Frequency:** annual. **Type:** recognition. **Recipient:** for distinguished service and dedication given to the Catholic band movement and to the NCBA ● Charles R. Winking Award. **Frequency:** annual. **Type:** recognition. **Recipient:** for outstanding contributions to the field of wind band conducting ● NCBA Service Award. **Frequency:** annual. **Type:** recognition. **Recipient:** for notable achievement in leadership involving service to other members ● President's Award. **Frequency:** annual. **Type:** recognition. **Recipient:** for outstanding contributions in a singular event to the work of the NCBA ● Rev. George Wiskirchen Jazz Award. **Type:** recognition. **Recipient:** for outstanding jazz musician in a band program ● Robert F. O'Brien Award. **Frequency:** annual. **Type:** recognition. **Recipient:** for a graduating student who, over the years, has demonstrated continual development in outstanding musicianship. **Committees:** Development; Evaluation; Honor Band; Liturgical Music; Live Contest. **Formerly:** (1993) National Catholic Bandmasters' Association. **Publications:** *NCBA Newsletter*, bimonthly. Reports on liturgical music involvements, members' bands, and the activities of the association. **Price:** included in membership dues. **Circulation:** 200. Alternate Formats: online ● *Update*. Contains special information regarding current activities. ● Membership Directory, annual. **Conventions/Meetings:** annual board meeting ● annual conference.

10662 ■ National Federation of Music Clubs (NFMC)

1336 N Delaware St.
Indianapolis, IN 46202-2481

Ph: (317)638-4003
Fax: (317)638-0503
E-mail: info@nfmc-music.org
URL: http://www.nfmc-music.org
Contact: Jennifer Keller, Admin. Mgr.
Founded: 1898. **Members:** 200,000. **Membership Dues:** junior, $12 (annual) ● student, $15 (annual) ● senior, $20 (annual) ● contributing, $25 (annual) ● life, $200. **Staff:** 3. **State Groups:** 50. **Local Groups:** 6,000. **Description:** Represents local music clubs, state associations, and individuals directly or indirectly connected with musical activities, such as amateur opera groups, elementary and high school music departments, and music conservatories. Aids young musicians; encourages the use of stringed instruments; promotes higher television and radio musical standards and legislation to improve status of musicians. Commissions symphonic works; conducts junior festivals, in which entrants have the opportunity to be rated on individual merits and work toward a designated objective with criteria for evaluation. Sponsors Parade of American Music and National Music Week, annually; has organized or assisted in promotion of numerous amateur, semi-professional, and professional opera companies operating nationwide. Maintains music therapy program in hospitals. Conducts young artist and student auditions biennially. **Awards:** Composition Competitions. **Type:** monetary ● Duo-Piano Award Competition. **Frequency:** biennial. **Type:** monetary. **Recipient:** for pianists ages 18-36 ● Junior Special Awards. **Frequency:** biennial. **Type:** monetary. **Recipient:** for high school musicians ● Student Auditions, Competitive. **Frequency:** biennial. **Type:** monetary. **Recipient:** for instrumentalists ages 16-26 and vocalists ages 18-26 ● Young Artist Award. **Frequency:** biennial. **Type:** monetary. **Recipient:** for instrumentalists ages 18-30 and vocalists ages 23-35, ready for concert career. **Divisions:** Administrative; American Music; Arts; Competitions and Awards; Education; Junior; National Affiliates; Public Relations; Student. **Publications:** *Junior Keynotes*, 3/year. Magazine. **Price:** $5.00. **Circulation:** 9,000. **Advertising:** accepted ● *Music Clubs Magazine*, 3/year. **Price:** included in membership dues (for seniors); $6.00 for nonmembers. **Conventions/Meetings:** biennial convention.

10663 ■ National Flute Association (NFA)
26951 Ruether Ave., Ste.H
Santa Clarita, CA 91351
Ph: (661)713-6013 (661)250-8920
Fax: (661)299-6681
E-mail: ceo@nfaonline.org
URL: http://www.nfaonline.org
Contact: Phyllis T. Pemberton, Exec. Dir./CEO
Founded: 1972. **Members:** 4,500. **Membership Dues:** active, affiliate, $65 (annual) ● active, affiliate (electronic), $55 (annual) ● student, $35 (annual) ● student (electronic), $30 (annual) ● contributing, $110 (annual) ● contributing (electronic), $90 (annual) ● sustaining, $150 (annual) ● sustaining (electronic), $135 (annual) ● life, $1,500 ● library, $45 (annual). **Budget:** $210,600. **Description:** Flutists and individuals interested in the flute including professionals, amateurs, students, flute clubs, flute makers, and music publishers. Aims to: promote and further appreciation of the flute; contribute to the musical enrichment of all peoples through the performance of flute music; create or sponsor worthwhile projects relative to the flute and flute playing; establish guidelines for the upgrading of flute teaching. Encourages development of increasingly high standards of artistic excellence for the flute, flutists, and flute literature; promotes helpfulness and fellowship among members. Sponsors annual Young Artist Competition, High School Soloist Competition, and New Music Competition for best new works published for the flute each year. Maintains library of music for flute. **Libraries: Type:** lending; reference. **Holdings:** 1,000; archival material. **Committees:** Jazz; New Music Advisory; Nominating; Oral History; Pedagogy; Performance Health Care; Piccolo; Special Publication. **Publications:** *The Flutist Quarterly*. Newsletter ● *National Flute Association Music Library Catalog*. Alternate Formats: online ● Membership Directory, annual. **Conventions/Meetings:** annual convention (exhibits) - 2008 Aug. 14-17, Kansas City, MO; 2009 Aug. 13-16, New York, NY; 2010 Aug. 12-15, Anaheim, CA.

10664 ■ National Music Council (NMC)
425 Park St.
Upper Montclair, NJ 07043
Ph: (973)655-7974
Fax: (973)655-5432
E-mail: sandersd@mail.montclair.edu
URL: http://www.musiccouncil.org
Contact: Dr. David Sanders, Dir.
Founded: 1940. **Members:** 50. **Staff:** 1. **Description:** Federation of 50 nationally active music organizations; chartered by U.S. Congress. Functions as a national forum for the discussion of nationwide musical problems. Compiles statistics. **Awards:** American Eagle Award. **Frequency:** annual. **Type:** recognition. **Recipient:** for classical and popular music categories. **Computer Services:** Mailing lists. **Committees:** International Affairs; Music Education; Music Industry; Professional Performance. **Affiliated With:** International Music Council. **Publications:** Newsletter. Alternate Formats: online. **Conventions/Meetings:** annual meeting - always May or June.

10665 ■ National Oldtime Fiddlers' Association (NOTFA)
c/o National Oldtime Fiddlers' Contest and Festival
115 W Idaho St.
Weiser, ID 83672
Ph: (208)414-0255
Free: (800)437-1280
Fax: (208)414-0256
E-mail: director@fiddlecontest.com
URL: http://www.fiddlecontest.com
Contact: Karen Penner, Exec. Dir./Contest Dir.
Founded: 1967. **Members:** 2,000. **Membership Dues:** regular, $15 (annual). **Staff:** 2. **Description:** Works for the coordination of the states in the revival and preservation of old time fiddle music. **Publications:** *National Oldtime Fiddler*, bimonthly. Newspaper. **Price:** $1.25. **Circulation:** 1,000. **Advertising:** accepted. **Conventions/Meetings:** annual meeting.

10666 ■ National Opera Association (NOA)
c/o Robert Hansen, Exec. Dir.
PO Box 60869
Canyon, TX 79016-0869
Ph: (806)651-2857
Fax: (806)651-2958
E-mail: rhansen@mail.wtamu.edu
URL: http://www.noa.org
Contact: Robert Hansen, Exec. Dir.
Founded: 1955. **Members:** 600. **Membership Dues:** individual, $60 (annual) ● organization, $75 (annual) ● library (journal only), $45 (annual) ● Goldovsky Foundation, $65 (annual). **Staff:** 1. **Budget:** $60,000. **Description:** Opera composers, conductors, directors, singers, managers, and producers; publishers of operatic music; librettists, teachers, translators, and others connected with or interested in opera; opera companies, colleges and universities, schools of music, and workshops. Advances the appreciation, composition, and production of opera. Provides opportunities for operatic talent and supports special projects that improve the scope and quality of opera. Provides a forum for the discussion of ideas and presentation of practical solutions to problems encountered in all areas of opera production. Maintains score and tape library of contemporary American operas at the American Music Center. **Computer Services:** database, chamber opera, freelance artist, production. **Committees:** Awards; Chamber Opera Competition; College Preparation; Convention; Endowment Development; Nominations; Opera Production/Theatre; Opera Production Video; Regional Companies; Research Development; Scholarly Papers; Special Education Projects; Vocal Competitions. **Absorbed:** Opera for Youth. **Publications:** *NOA Goldovsky Studies*, periodic. Books. Contains information on the history and practice of opera. **Advertising:** accepted ● *NOA Membership Directory*, annual. **Price:** $10.00/copy for members; $20.00/copy for nonmembers ● *NOA Newsletter*, bimonthly. Includes membership activities and annual convention report. **Price:** included in membership dues. **Advertising:** accepted ● *Opera Journal*, quarterly. Contains scholarly articles on operatic subjects; includes book reviews and reviews of operatic productions. **Price:** included in membership dues; $10.00/issue for nonmembers. **Advertising:** accepted ● Papers ● Reports. **Conventions/Meetings:** annual convention (exhibits).

10667 ■ National Orchestral Association (NOA)
PO Box 7016
New York, NY 10150-7016
Ph: (212)208-4691
Fax: (212)208-4691
E-mail: info@nationalorchestral.org
URL: http://www.nationalorchestral.org
Contact: Matthew J. Trachtenberg, Chm./Pres./CEO
Founded: 1930. **Description:** Has fostered the training of American classical musicians and conductors, as well as supporting organizations that provide American musicians and composers with an opportunity to reach wider audiences. Sponsors musical performances and conductor and orchestral training. Provides support for initiatives undertaken by other organizations to promote the work of American classical musicians, conductors and composers. Offers assistance for musical outreach programs for schools and senior citizens. **Libraries: Type:** open to the public. **Publications:** *Notes*. Newsletter. Alternate Formats: online. **Conventions/Meetings:** annual Orchestral and Chamber Concert - meeting.

10668 ■ National Sheet Music Society (NSMS)
Address Unknown since 2008
Founded: 1958. **Members:** 400. **Membership Dues:** $20 (annual). **Description:** Songwriters and sheet music collectors; members of the American Society of Composers, Authors and Publishers (see separate entry); and institutions including Songwriters Hall of Fame, universities, colleges, and public libraries. Seeks to advance knowledge of the historical and cultural value of American music by promoting interest in collecting sheet music. Disseminates information; conducts research and educational programs. Find out-of-print music. **Publications:** *N.S.M.S. Membership*, annual. Directory. **Price:** included in membership dues ● *The Song Sheet*, 5/year. Newsletter. Provides information on society activities, the history of song sheets, and the history of song sheet illustration and composers. **Price:** available to members only. **Conventions/Meetings:** annual luncheon, with awards ceremony - always November ● monthly meeting - always 2nd Saturday except July and August.

10669 ■ National Symphony Orchestra Association (NSO)
John F. Kennedy Center for the Performing Arts
2700 F St. NW
Washington, DC 20566
Ph: (202)416-8000 (202)467-4600
Free: (800)444-1324
E-mail: comments@kennedy-center.org
URL: http://www.kennedy-center.org/nso
Contact: Rita Shapiro, Exec. Dir.
Founded: 1931. **Members:** 7,000. **Description:** Represents persons who contribute more than $50 to sustain the National Symphony Orchestra, located in Washington, DC. **Conventions/Meetings:** annual meeting.

10670 ■ National Traditional Country Music Association (NTCMA)
PO Box 492
Anita, IA 50020
Ph: (712)762-4363
E-mail: bobeverhart@yahoo.com
URL: http://www.oldtimemusic.bigstep.com
Contact: Bob Everhart, Founder/Pres.
Founded: 1976. **Members:** 3,500. **Membership Dues:** individual, $25 (annual). **Staff:** 3. **Budget:** $100,000. **Regional Groups:** 12. **State Groups:** 8.

National Groups: 8. **Description:** Individuals interested in the preservation, presentation, and perpetuation of traditional acoustic country, folk, honky-tonk, ragtime, mountain, and bluegrass music celebrating contributions of U.S. settlers and pioneers; country music associations. Supports what the association views as related, traditional values. Holds jam sessions; sponsors booths and offers hands-on music and craft experiences; operates charitable program; offers children's services; maintains placement service. Sponsors championship contests in numerous categories, including: Great Plains Story Telling; Hank Williams Songwriting; International Country Singer; Jimmie Rodgers Yodeling; National Bluegrass Band; National Harmonica Playing. Programs are taped and televised by various local, national, and international stations. Established the "Old-Time Music Hour" radio program at the Walnut Country Opera House, Pioneer Music Museum, America Old-Time Fiddlers Hall of Fame, and America Country Music Hall of Fame. **Libraries: Type:** open to the public. **Holdings:** periodicals. **Subjects:** old time country music. **Awards:** International Traditional Country and Bluegrass Music Award. **Frequency:** annual. **Type:** recognition. **Recipient:** for European residents. **Formerly:** National Traditional Music Association; (1982) Cornhusker Country Music Club; (1989) Traditional Country Music Association; (1989) National Traditional Country Music Association. **Publications:** *Tradition Magazine*, bimonthly. Includes book, festival, and record reviews; provides news about employment opportunities in traditional music and current travel information. **Price:** included in membership dues. ISSN: 1071-1864. **Circulation:** 3,500. **Advertising:** accepted ● Also publishes songbooks. **Conventions/Meetings:** annual American Traditional Music and Dance Festival - conference and international conference, with music, dance, and seminars (exhibits) ● bimonthly meeting ● annual National Old-Time Country Music Contest and Festival - conference and festival (exhibits) - always Labor Day weekend in Missouri Valley, Iowa.

10671 ■ New Orleans Jazz Club (NOJC)

828 Royal St., Ste.265
New Orleans, LA 70116
Ph: (504)887-9839
Fax: (504)779-7806
E-mail: info@nojazzclub.com
URL: http://www.nojazzclub.com
Contact: Sharon Anderson, Treas.

Founded: 1948. **Members:** 2,000. **Membership Dues:** individual, $20 (annual). **Description:** Represents persons interested in jazz music, especially Dixieland or New Orleans style. Believes that jazz is the only art form to have originated in the United States. Provides activities such as: jam sessions, concerts, and a radio show. Conducts charitable programs and specialized education programs. Sponsors speakers' bureau. **Libraries: Type:** reference. **Holdings:** archival material. **Subjects:** jazz. **Awards: Type:** recognition. **Publications:** *The Second Line*, quarterly. Magazine. **Price:** included in membership dues. **Advertising:** accepted. **Conventions/Meetings:** annual conference and workshop, with speakers, presentations including lectures and labs (exhibits) - always March ● annual Musical Program - meeting - always in New Orleans, LA.

10672 ■ New Violin Family Association (NVFA)

42 Taylor Dr.
Wolfeboro, NH 03894
Ph: (603)569-7946
E-mail: online@newviolinfamily.org
URL: http://www.newviolinfamily.org
Contact: Dr. Carleen M. Hutchins, Exec. Dir./Founder

Founded: 1999. **Membership Dues:** regular, $35 (annual). **Multinational. Description:** Seeks to educate the public about the new Octet Violins through writings, concerts, lectures and demonstrations. Encourages the use of new Octet Violins in public performances and in teaching. Sponsors the collection and preservation of documents and other materials pertaining to these violins. **Telecommunication Services:** electronic mail, music@newviolinfamily.org. **Publications:** *Violin Octet*, semiannual. Newsletter. **Price:** included in membership dues. Alternate Formats: online.

10673 ■ New Wilderness Foundation (NWF)

c/o Charles Morrow Associates, Inc.
307 Seventh Ave., Ste.1402
New York, NY 10001
Ph: (212)989-2400
Fax: (212)989-2697
E-mail: info@cmorrow.com
Contact: Charlie Morrow, Pres.

Founded: 1974. **Staff:** 6. **Budget:** $100,000. **Description:** Artists and contributors. Aims to promote public appreciation of innovative music and to offer support services to sound artists including radio broadcasts, audio facilities, special events, and publications. Maintains a listening room with unpublished and independent-label tapes of ethnic and new music and literary arts; also maintains an eight-track audio studio available to artists, independent producers, and non-profit organizations for noncommercial audio projects. Current studio interest is in experimental, public broadcast, and sound art projects. **Convention/Meeting:** none. **Publications:** *New Wilderness Letter: Journal of Poetry*, annual ● Audiotape.

10674 ■ North America Country Music Associations, International (NACMAI)

PO Box 1145
Maynardville, TN 37807
E-mail: octpc3@aol.com
URL: http://www.geocities.com/nacmai
Contact: Peggy Franck, Chm./Pres./CEO/Founder

Founded: 1997. **Multinational. Description:** Promotes the development of the country and gospel music industry. Promotes and informs members of the industry and the public about resources available in the various states and countries for country/gospel music production. Creates opportunities for the discovery, showcasing and promotion of emerging and aspiring country and gospel music artists, musicians and songwriters. **Awards:** NACMAI Hall of Fame. **Frequency:** annual. **Type:** recognition. **Recipient:** to an individual who has influenced the evolution of country music ● NACMAI Industry Awards. **Frequency:** annual. **Type:** recognition. **Recipient:** for distinguished members of the association ● NACMAI Katie Brandenburg Music Scholarship. **Frequency:** annual. **Type:** scholarship. **Recipient:** to a young person from an affiliated state association. **Telecommunication Services:** electronic mail, mdebills@aol.com. **Conventions/Meetings:** annual general assembly, with competition and award show.

10675 ■ North American Brass Band Association (NABBA)

c/o Rusty Morris, Pres.
5 Big Stone Ct.
Little Rock, AR 72227
E-mail: rjmorris61@comcast.net
URL: http://www.nabba.org
Contact: Rusty Morris, Pres.

Founded: 1983. **Members:** 700. **Membership Dues:** individual, $30 (annual) ● student (21 and under), $15 (annual) ● senior (65 and older), $20 (annual) ● family, $50 (annual) ● life - individual, $400-$600 ● life - family, $600. **Description:** Fosters the establishment and development of adult amateur British-type brass bands throughout the U.S. and Canada. Supports continued musical education of members; seeks to advance public appreciation of British-style brass bands. Sponsors international band competitions. Holds workshops. **Publications:** *The Cyber Brass Band Bridge*, quarterly. Journal. Provides brass band information, contest dates, and record and music reviews. **Price:** available to members only. **Advertising:** accepted. Alternate Formats: online ● *How to Start a British Brass Band*. **Conventions/Meetings:** annual competition (exhibits).

10676 ■ North American British Music Studies Association (NABMSA)

c/o Deborah Heckert, Sec.
Music Dept.
3304 Staller Ctr.
SUNY Stony Brook
Stony Brook, NY 11794-5475
E-mail: dheckert@notes.cc.sunysb.edu
URL: http://www.nabmsa.org
Contact: Deborah Heckert, Sec.

Membership Dues: regular, $20 (annual) ● student, $10 (annual). **Multinational. Description:** Promotes the study of British Music from all time periods on the North American continent. Provides a collegial and supportive forum for discussion through electronic and other means. Provides a clearinghouse of information on the study of such music. **Publications:** Newsletter, semiannual ● Books ● Articles.

10677 ■ North American Dhrupad Association (NADA)

PO Box 361
Agoura Hills, CA 91376
Ph: (818)991-0825 (714)998-1447
E-mail: dhrupad@pobox.com
URL: http://www.raga.com/text/nada.html
Contact: Sunil Dutta, Founder

Founded: 1996. **Multinational. Description:** Supports and disseminates Dhrupad music in India and the U.S. Maintains an archive of important materials related to Dhrupad music. Supports artists and students of Dhrupad music.

10678 ■ North American Guild of Change Ringers (NAGCR)

c/o A. Thomas Miller, Membership Sec.
229 Howard Ave.
Woodstown, NJ 08098-1249
Ph: (856)769-7264
E-mail: membership@nagcr.org
URL: http://www.nagcr.org
Contact: Mr. Porter Brownlee, Pres.

Founded: 1972. **Members:** 500. **Membership Dues:** resident, associate in U.S., $20 (annual) ● resident, associate in Canada, C$22 (annual) ● student in U.S., $6 (annual) ● student in Canada, C$7 (annual) ● senior in U.S., $10 (annual) ● senior in Canada, C$11 (annual). **Local Groups:** 50. **Description:** Represents the interests of change ringers and those interested in English-style change ringing. (Change ringing is the art of ringing a set of tuned bells in continually varying order according to set methods or principles, as in the bell tower of a church or in a set of handbells.) Draws together ringers from throughout the country. Offers courses and instruction on a local level. Sponsors tours of American and English bell towers. Maintains archives of bellringing activities. **Publications:** *Bells of Kalamazoo*. Videos ● *Bells of North America*. Audiotape ● *The Change Ringers* ● *Change Ringing*. Pamphlet ● *The Clapper*, quarterly. Newsletter. Covers membership activities; includes annual report. **Price:** $15.00 in U.S.; $18.00 in Canada; $30.00 for all other countries. **Circulation:** 400. **Advertising:** accepted ● *Elementary Minor Methods on Handbells*. Booklet ● *NAGCR Book Service*. Books ● Report, annual. **Price:** $5.00. **Circulation:** 400. **Advertising:** accepted ● Films. **Conventions/Meetings:** annual meeting, with ringing course (exhibits) ● monthly regional meeting.

10679 ■ North American Saxophone Alliance (NASA)

c/o Kenneth Tse, Membership Dir.
Univ. of Iowa
School of Music
2046 Voxman Music Bldg.
Iowa City, IA 52242
E-mail: kenneth-tse@uiowa.edu
URL: http://www.saxalliance.org
Contact: Kenneth Tse, Membership Dir.

Members: 900. **Membership Dues:** professional, $35 (annual) ● student, senior citizen, $25 (annual) ● institution, overseas, $50 (annual). **Staff:** 17. **Budget:** $10,000. **Regional Groups:** 10. **Description:** Professional performers, university professors, schoolteachers, music students, and others with an interest in the saxophone. Promotes scholarship and performance involving the saxophone. **Awards:** North American Saxophone Alliance Performance Competitions. **Frequency:** biennial. **Type:** monetary. **Recipient:** for competition in jazz and classical performance. **Computer Services:** Mailing lists, one time use labels for sale. **Publications:** *NASA Update*, bimonthly. Newsletter. Contains information on the activities of the association and its members. **Price:** included in membership dues. **Circulation:** 900. **Advertising:** accepted ● *The Saxophone Symposium*, annual. Journal. Includes articles of interest to members. **Price:** included in membership dues. **Advertising:** accepted. **Conventions/Meetings:** biennial convention, for U.S./Canada (exhibits) - spring, even years ● biennial Regional Conferences - regional meeting - spring, odd years, usually 5 or 6 held the same year ● triennial World Saxophone Congress (exhibits).

10680 ■ North American Singers Association (NASA)

c/o Mrs. Lois Lynch, Sec.
1828 Pinecrest Dr.
Dayton, OH 45414
Ph: (937)278-4606
Fax: (937)278-4606
E-mail: loislynch@ameritech.net
Contact: Mrs. Lois Lynch, Sec.

Founded: 1848. **Members:** 3,000. **Membership Dues:** active singer, $2 (annual). **Regional Groups:** 9. **Local Groups:** 105. **Languages:** English, German. **Description:** Active singers belonging to German-American women's, men's, and mixed choruses. Promotes pride in German-American heritage and traditions; works to foster German ethnic pride by encouraging observance of German customs and use of German language and songs. Presents benefit choral concerts. **Computer Services:** database ● mailing lists. **Committees:** Music. **Also Known As:** Nord Amerikanischer Sangerbund. **Formerly:** (1983) North American Singers Union. **Publications:** Newsletters. **Conventions/Meetings:** triennial Delegate Meeting, with National Song Festival ● triennial National Song Festival - meeting, national delegates meeting.

10681 ■ OPERA America

330 Seventh Ave., 16th Fl.
New York, NY 10001
Ph: (212)796-8620
Fax: (212)796-8631
E-mail: frontdesk@operaamerica.org
URL: http://www.operaamerica.org
Contact: Marc A. Scorca, Pres./CEO

Founded: 1970. **Members:** 2,500. **Membership Dues:** professional, $90 (annual) ● individual (basic), $60 (annual) ● educational institution, $125-$350 (annual) ● affiliate, $250 (annual) ● business, $300 (annual) ● premium, $85 (annual). **Staff:** 20. **Budget:** $290,000. **Languages:** English, French, Spanish. **Description:** Professional opera companies, allied international companies, other producing, presenting, and educational institutions, individual performing and creative artists, arts administrators and consultants, affiliated businesses, libraries, trustees, volunteers, and patrons. Promotes the growth and expansion of the operatic form; assists in the development of resident professional opera companies through provision of cooperative artistic management services; fosters and improve the education, training, and development of operatic composers, singers, and other talented persons; encourages and assists in the improvement of the quality of operatic presentations; encourages greater appreciation and enjoyment of opera by all segments of society. Provides arts service through intercompany communications. Offers special consulting services; compiles statistics. **Libraries: Type:** reference. **Holdings:** archival material. **Awards:** Bravo Awards. **Frequency:** annual. **Type:** recognition. **Recipient:** for corporate support of opera companies ● **Type:** grant ● Opera America Award. **Frequency:** annual. **Type:** recognition. **Computer Services:** database, contains statistics, member season schedules, sets and costumes for rent, artists ● mailing lists, for sale to public and members. **Telecommunication Services:** electronic mail, mscorca@operaamerica.org. **Committees:** Annual Conference; Canadian; Communications; Development; Education; Executive; Fellowship. **Absorbed:** (1990) Central Opera Service. **Publications:** *List of Education Resource Materials*, semiannual ● *Music!Words!Opera!*. Directory. Three-level set of instructional resource materials designed for classroom use. ● *Opera America—Career Guide for Singers*, biennial. Directory. Lists professional singers' training programs, apprenticeships, and competitions operated by opera companies. Includes audition information. **Price:** $25.00 for members; $45.00 for nonmembers ● *Opera America Newsline*, 10/year. Newsletter. Reports on what is going on in the opera field and other news that affects it. **Price:** included in membership dues. ISSN: 1062-7243. **Circulation:** 2,700. **Advertising:** accepted ● *Opera America—Season Schedule of Performances*, annual. Lists productions and performance dates for Opera America companies. **Price:** $9.00 for members; $15.00 for nonmembers ● *Register*, annual. Membership Directory. Contains contact information for OPERA America Business, Affiliate, and Company members. **Price:** $25.00 for members; $20.00 for nonmembers ● *Sets, Costumes, and Title Projections Directory*. Lists company-owned property available for rent; also includes a listing of commercial costume houses and title projection establishments. Alternate Formats: online ● Report, annual. Provides information on the professional opera field including annual survey of attendance, repertoire, and fiscal data. **Price:** $9.00 for members; $15.00 for nonmembers. **Conventions/Meetings:** annual conference (exhibits) ● seminar ● workshop.

10682 ■ Organ Clearing House LLC (OCHLLC)

PO Box 290786
Charlestown, MA 02129-0214
Ph: (617)241-8550
Free: (866)827-3055
Fax: (617)241-8551
E-mail: john@organclearinghouse.com
URL: http://www.organclearinghouse.com
Contact: John Bishop, Exec. Dir.

Founded: 1959. **Staff:** 3. **For-Profit. Description:** Facilitates the relocation of used pipe organs that might otherwise be discarded, and provides interested churches with information about such instruments. According to the group, a used pipe organ can be purchased, moved, renovated, and installed for about the same cost as an electronic substitute and for considerably less than the cost of a new pipe organ. Maintains and disseminates list of old organs for sale. Recommends organ builders and consultants on request. Supplies historical information about particular organs and their builders through the Organ Historical Society (see separate entry). Offers educational slide and tape program. **Affiliated With:** International Society for Organ History and Preservation; Organ Historical Society. **Publications:** *Lists of Organs for Sale*, annual ● *Recent Projects*, annual. Newsletter.

10683 ■ Organ Historical Society (OHS)

PO Box 26811
Richmond, VA 23261
Ph: (804)353-9226
Fax: (804)353-9266
E-mail: mail@organsociety.org
URL: http://www.organsociety.org
Contact: Daniel N. Colburn II, Exec. Dir.

Founded: 1956. **Members:** 4,000. **Membership Dues:** regular, $57 (annual) ● over age 65 or 2nd person in household, $45 (annual) ● age 25 and under, $20 (annual) ● contributing, $75 (annual) ● sustaining, $100 (annual) ● donor, $150 (annual) ● patron, $200 (annual) ● supporter, $250 (annual) ● benefactor, $350 (annual) ● sponsor, $500 (annual) ● President's Circle, $1,000 (annual). **Staff:** 7. **Budget:** $360,000. **Regional Groups:** 16. **Description:** Persons interested in the heritage of American organ building, including scholars, historians, enthusiasts, organists, organ builders, clergymen, and libraries. Encourages the study of the pipe organ and its builders in North America; preserves or restores significant organs. Issues sound recordings of historically important American pipe organs. Conducts audio-visual demonstration of American organs to interested groups, including organ music, color slides, and commentary. Sponsors concert series on historic organs. Bestows citations on historic instruments. Maintains archive of 17th, 18th, 19th, and 20th century organ publications and memorabilia. **Libraries: Type:** reference. **Holdings:** archival material, books, monographs, periodicals. **Subjects:** American and European organ building. **Telecommunication Services:** electronic mail, dcolburn@organsociety.org. **Committees:** Extant Organs; Historic Organs; International Interests; Recital Series; Research. **Publications:** *Organ Handbook*, annual. **Price:** included in membership dues. **Circulation:** 4,200. **Advertising:** accepted ● *The Tracker*, quarterly. Journal. Includes news and articles about the organ and its history, organ builders, exemplary organs, and the music played on the organ. **Price:** included in membership dues. **Circulation:** 4,000. **Advertising:** accepted ● Books ● Monographs ● Also publishes lists of organs built by Americans. **Conventions/Meetings:** annual convention - usually in June, July or August. 2008 July 13-18, Seattle, WA; 2009 July 26-31, Cleveland, OH.

10684 ■ Other Minds (OM)

333 Valencia St., Ste.303
San Francisco, CA 94103-3552
Ph: (415)934-8134
Fax: (415)934-8136
E-mail: otherminds@otherminds.org
URL: http://www.otherminds.org
Contact: Charles Amirkhanian, Exec. Dir.

Multinational. Description: Promotes innovative music by composers from all over the world. Provides audio and video recordings of composers, artists and musicians. Launches a web radio station that encourages and commissions the composition of new Internet audio works. Offers visual online galleries and text documentation on selected subjects. **Telecommunication Services:** electronic mail, charles@otherminds.org. **Publications:** *MindAlert*, periodic. Newsletter. Contains notice of events, news, announcements, interviews and projects. **Price:** free ● *MindReader*. Newsletter. Contains feature articles and in depth information about Other Minds projects. Alternate Formats: online.

10685 ■ Pedal Steel Guitar Association (PSGA)

PO Box 20248
Floral Park, NY 11002-0248
Ph: (516)616-9214
Fax: (516)616-9214
E-mail: bobpsga@optonline.net
URL: http://www.psga.org
Contact: Bob Maickel, Pres.

Founded: 1973. **Members:** 1,521. **Membership Dues:** regular, $30 (annual). **Staff:** 10. **Description:** Professional and amateur steel guitarists. Aims to share information on playing the pedal steel guitar; help others improve playing abilities; to inform the public of the potential of the instrument. Conducts workshops. **Libraries: Type:** reference. **Holdings:** 31. **Subjects:** playing steel guitar, record reviews, instruction course reviews, events. **Awards:** Steel Guitarist Appreciation Award. **Frequency:** annual. **Type:** recognition. **Recipient:** for contributions made to improve playing skills on the steel guitar. **Publications:** *Pedal Steel Newsletter*, 10/year. Includes calendar of events and member profiles. **Price:** included in membership dues. ISSN: 1088-7954. **Circulation:** 1,600. **Advertising:** accepted. **Conventions/Meetings:** annual Steel Guitar Celebration - seminar and convention, includes concert (exhibits).

10686 ■ Percussive Arts Society (PAS)

32 E Washington, Ste.1400
Indianapolis, IN 46204
Ph: (317)974-4488
Fax: (317)974-4499
E-mail: percarts@pas.org
URL: http://www.pas.org
Contact: Michael Kenyon, Exec. Dir.

Founded: 1961. **Members:** 8,500. **Membership Dues:** individual friend, $150 (annual) ● library, $100 (annual) ● professional, $90 (annual) ● senior citizen (65 or older), $65 (annual) ● full-time student, $60 (annual) ● ePAS professional, $50 (annual) ● ePAS student, $28 (annual). **Staff:** 10. **Regional Groups:**

20. **State Groups:** 50. **National Groups:** 20. **Multinational. Description:** Promotes percussion education, research, performance and appreciation worldwide. Accomplishes goals through publications, a worldwide network of chapters, website, workshops, museum, and convention. **Libraries: Type:** reference. **Holdings:** 500; archival material, audio recordings, books, periodicals, video recordings. **Subjects:** percussion instruments, music reference. **Awards:** Fred Sanford Award. **Frequency:** annual. **Type:** recognition. **Recipient:** to the highest scoring ensemble in the annual marching percussion competition ● Hall of Fame Award. **Frequency:** annual. **Type:** recognition ● Lifetime Achievement in Education Award. **Frequency:** annual. **Type:** recognition. **Recipient:** for the contributions of leaders in percussion education ● Outstanding Chapter President Award. **Frequency:** annual. **Type:** recognition. **Recipient:** for individuals who have increased PAS chapter membership ● Outstanding PAS Supporter Award. **Frequency:** annual. **Type:** recognition. **Computer Services:** database, percussion music and reviews, journal article archives ● online services, drum rudiments and percussion practice exercises. **Committees:** Audition; Composition Contest; Education; International; Marching Percussion; New Music; Pedagogy; Publications; Scholarly Papers. **Publications:** *Percussion News*, bimonthly, odd-numbered months. Newsletter. Includes updates on society research and special education programs, chapter news, and lists of employment opportunities. **Price:** included in membership dues. **Circulation:** 6,500. **Advertising:** accepted ● *Percussive Notes*, bimonthly, even-numbered months. Magazine. Includes society news, index of advertisers, and articles on education, performance and individual artists. **Price:** included in membership dues; $85.00/year for professionals; $55.00/year for students; $90.00 /year for libraries. ISSN: 0553-6502. **Circulation:** 6,500. **Advertising:** accepted. **Conventions/Meetings:** annual international conference, with concerts, clinics, master classes and events, plus expo and marching percussion festival (exhibits) - always in November.

10687 ■ Polish Singers Alliance of America (PSAA)
c/o Mrs. Teresa Krenglicki, Pres.
208 Caesar Blvd.
Williamsville, NY 14221
Ph: (716)827-1722
E-mail: psaausa@aol.com
URL: http://www.polishsingersalliance.dnswh.com
Contact: Mrs. Teresa Krenglicki, Pres.
Founded: 1889. **Members:** 1,200. **Membership Dues:** regular, $6 (annual) ● life, $50. **State Groups:** 46. **Local Groups:** 15. **National Groups:** 6. **Languages:** English, Polish. **Multinational. Description:** Amateur Polish choruses (male, female, mixed, and children). Seeks to: promulgate Polish culture through song; acquaint Americans with the work of Polish composers; encourage Polish-American youth to take pride in their ethnic heritage. Holds triennial concert and choral contest, and arranges concerts and accepts invitations to sing at public events by the local groups. **Libraries: Type:** not open to the public. **Holdings:** periodicals. **Subjects:** history of choruses and activities. **Awards:** Honorary Membership. **Frequency:** triennial. **Type:** recognition. **Recipient:** for outstanding service to the Polish community, local chorus, and PSAA. **Publications:** *Singers Bulletin* (in English and Polish), quarterly. Newsletter. Includes district reports and obituaries. **Price:** included in membership dues. **Conventions/Meetings:** triennial Award Banquet, with sessions, competitions, dinner/dance, choruses - usually Memorial Day weekend ● Concert and Choral Contest - meeting.

10688 ■ Positive Music Association (PMA)
c/o Scott Johnson
4593 Maple Ct.
Boulder, CO 80301
Ph: (303)581-9083
E-mail: scott@positivemusicassociation.com
URL: http://www.positivemusicassociation.com
Contact: Scott Johnson, Contact
Membership Dues: professional, $35 (annual). **Description:** Promotes interest in and appreciation of positive music, also known as "poz" music. Provides resources and networking opportunities for its members to grow and market their music. Gives its members a chance to have their music heard online through its poz radio.

10689 ■ Professional Women Singers Association (PWSA)
PO Box 884
New York, NY 10159
Ph: (212)969-0590
E-mail: info@womensingers.org
URL: http://www.womensingers.org
Contact: Beatrice Broadwater, Pres.
Founded: 1982. **Members:** 44. **Membership Dues:** performing, $85 (annual) ● affiliate, $50 (annual) ● friend, $25 (annual). **Budget:** $5,000. **Description:** Professional women singers. Promotes career advancement of women singers. Serves as a network for singers looking for career support. **Libraries: Type:** reference. **Holdings:** archival material. **Publications:** *PWSAWorks*, quarterly. Newsletter. Includes an email letter about project status. **Conventions/Meetings:** periodic meeting.

10690 ■ Raissa Tselentis Memorial Johann Sebastian Bach International Competitions
c/o James Marra, Dir.
569 Legacy Pride Dr.
Herndon, VA 20170
Ph: (703)787-9652
Contact: James Marra, Dir.
Founded: 1958. **Nonmembership. Multinational. Description:** Promotes the study and performance of the music of German composer Johann Sebastian Bach (1685-1750), especially among young people, ages 15 to 42. Conducts superbly designed education and performance programs for advanced music students, beginner and intermediate music students (ages 15-18), amateur musicians, and teachers from around the world. **Awards:** J.S. Bach International Competition Awards (Piano, Organ, Strings). **Frequency:** periodic. **Type:** monetary. **Recipient:** for excellence in renditions of the compositions of J.S. Bach. **Formerly:** (1994) American Bach Foundation. **Conventions/Meetings:** annual J.S. Bach International Competitions ● Music Academy - meeting ● periodic Piano Competition (All Bach).

10691 ■ Reed Organ Society (ROS)
c/o Carol Kuhn, Sec.
70 William Blaydes St.
Atoka, TN 38004
E-mail: carolon81@earthlink.net
URL: http://www.reedsoc.org
Contact: Wayne T. Warren, Pres.
Founded: 1981. **Members:** 650. **Membership Dues:** corporate, individual, joint, $12 (annual) ● contributing, $24 (annual) ● supporting, $25-$49 (annual) ● sustaining, $50-$99 (annual) ● patron, $100 (annual). **Description:** Musicians, enthusiasts, owners, collectors, and restorers interested in the reed organ. Aims to make the reed organ and its music better known to the public; to promote preservation and restoration of reed organs; to foster research and publication in the field; document and survey extant reed organs; encourage public performances of reed organ music and offer advice on performance techniques. (Reed organs include instruments such as harmonicas, accordions, concertinas, and lap organs.) **Convention/Meeting:** none. **Telecommunication Services:** electronic mail, w8047@cs.com. **Formerly:** (1982) Reed Organ Society of America. **Publications:** *Reed Organ Society—Bulletin*, quarterly. Includes articles on reed organ history, membership activities news, book reviews, and lists of patents. **Price:** included in membership dues; $2.50/issue for nonmembers. ISSN: 0736-9549. **Circulation:** 600. **Advertising:** accepted ● *Reed Organ Society—Membership Directory*, annual. Includes lists of members' interests and specialties and organ parts and memorabilia availability. **Circulation:** 800 ● Brochure ● Monographs ● Reprints.

10692 ■ Rhythm and Blues Rock and Roll Society, Inc. (RBRRSI)
PO Box 1949
New Haven, CT 06510
Ph: (203)924-1079
URL: http://www.bluesfestivalguide.com/directory/societies.shtml
Contact: William J. Nolan, Dir.
Founded: 1974. **Members:** 50,000. **Regional Groups:** 13. **Description:** Record collectors, disc jockeys, record dealers, performing artists, and others dedicated to the preservation and promotion of rhythm and blues music and its counterparts (blues, gospel, and jazz) as a part of U.S. cultural heritage. Sponsors benefit concerts for prisoners, fundraising programs for amateur talent, and music concerts and festivals. Conducts workshops on R and B culture with lectures and films on the history of black music. Seeks to encourage the employment of minorities in jobs related to blues music and hopes to offer training programs in the production of educational television shows and films. Sponsors Antique Blues, a cultural radio program presenting, live gospel, blues, and rhythm and blues performing groups. Cooperates with the annual W.C. Handy Blues Music Awards ceremony. Maintains international record review panel. Compiles statistics and conducts research. Operates record and tape-book library and archive; plans to maintain hall of fame and museum. **Committees:** Grants; Lobbying; Research. **Publications:** Bulletin, periodic ● Newsletter, periodic. Includes reports on the society's concerts, fundraising events and festivals; calendar of events and interviews with musicians. **Price:** free. **Circulation:** 45,000. **Conventions/Meetings:** annual conference.

10693 ■ Science Songwriters' Association (SSA)
PO Box 3531
Vista, CA 92085-3531
E-mail: lynda@sing-smart.com
URL: http://www.science-groove.org/SSA
Contact: Lynda Jones, Pres./Co-Founder
Founded: 1999. **Membership Dues:** basic, $7 (annual) ● commercial, $30 (annual). **Multinational. Description:** Aims to advance the use of music in the science classroom. Promotes the use of science as the major theme in music composition. Sponsors student science songwriting contests. **Telecommunication Services:** electronic mail, scimusic@tranquility.net.

10694 ■ Scott Joplin International Ragtime Foundation
321 S Ohio Ave.
Sedalia, MO 65301
Ph: (660)826-2271
Free: (866)218-6258
E-mail: ragtimer@scottjoplin.org
URL: http://www.scottjoplin.org
Contact: Jo Ann Neher, Pres.
Founded: 1974. **Members:** 14. **Membership Dues:** individual, $20 (annual) ● friend, $30 (annual) ● family, $50 (annual) ● patron, $100 (annual) ● advisor, $250 (annual) ● sponsor, $500 (annual) ● producer, $1,000 (annual) ● angel, $5,000 (annual). **Staff:** 2. **Budget:** $90,000. **Description:** Fans of ragtime composer and musician Scott Joplin (1868-1917) and of ragtime music. Sponsors concerts featuring ragtime artists. Offers children's services; conducts annual research trips to other festivals and historically affiliated sites in the U.S. and Canada. Maintains speakers' bureau; conducts educational and charitable programs; operates museum. **Libraries: Type:** reference. **Holdings:** archival material, artwork, books, clippings. **Awards:** Scott Joplin Foundation of Sedalia Lifetime Achievement Award. **Frequency:** annual. **Type:** recognition. **Recipient:** for research and achievements in ragtime. **Computer Services:** Mailing lists. **Councils:** Advisory. **Formerly:** (1966) Scott Joplin Commemorative Committee; (1983) Scott Joplin Ragtime Festival Committee; (1991) Scott Joplin Ragtime Festival; (2002) Scott Joplin Foundation of Sedalia. **Publications:** *Cradle of Ragtime*. Brochure ● *Sedalia Rag*, 2-4/year. Newsletter. **Price:** free for members. **Circulation:** 3,000. **Adver-**

tising: accepted. **Conventions/Meetings:** competition ● annual Scott Joplin Ragtime Festival (exhibits).

10695 ■ Scottish Harp Society of America (SHSA)

PO Box 250504
Plano, TX 75025-0504
E-mail: membership.shsa@gmail.com
URL: http://scottishharpsociety.net
Contact: Beth Richard, Membership Committee Chair

Founded: 1983. **Members:** 250. **Membership Dues:** regular, in U.S., $18 (annual) ● life, $350 ● regular, outside U.S., $21 (annual). **Budget:** $2,200. **Description:** Players of nonpedal Celtic (Scottish) harps interested in Scottish traditional music. Promotes interest in the Scottish harp. Conducts workshops on the history and playing techniques of the Scottish harp. Sponsors competitions; offers scholarships. **Awards:** National Award. **Frequency:** annual. **Type:** monetary. **Recipient:** for study of Scottish Harp. **Publications:** *Competitor's Handbook*. Alternate Formats: online ● *Kilt and Harp*, quarterly. Journal. **Price:** included in membership dues. **Circulation:** 250. **Advertising:** accepted. **Conventions/Meetings:** competition - first weekend of June ● annual meeting - fourth Saturday of June.

10696 ■ Scriabin Society of America

44 W 62nd St.
Penthouse 31D
New York, NY 10023-7014
URL: http://www.scriabinsociety.com
Contact: Edith Finton Rieber, Pres./Dir.

Founded: 1995. **Members:** 150. **Membership Dues:** supporter, $300 (annual) ● donor, $100 (annual) ● institution, $75 (annual) ● regular, $40 (annual) ● student, $25 (annual) ● patron (minimum), $1,000 (annual) ● benefactor, $500 (annual). **Staff:** 3. **Languages:** English, Russian. **Description:** Represents Alexander Scriabin fans, and pianists. Provides facts and information about Alexander Scriabin. Holds concerts. **Libraries: Type:** reference. **Holdings:** 250. **Subjects:** Russian music. **Awards:** Prize in Honor of Alexander Scriabin. **Frequency:** quadrennial. **Type:** monetary. **Recipient:** for outstanding performance. **Publications:** *Alexander and Julian Scriabin*. Reprint. **Price:** $30.00 for members; $40.00 for nonmembers ● *Alexander Scriabin*. Bibliography. **Price:** $5.00 ● *Journal of the Scriabin Society of American*, annual. Contains scholarly articles and essays. **Price:** included in membership dues. **Circulation:** 200. **Advertising:** accepted. **Conventions/Meetings:** semiannual Gala Concert in Honor of Scriabin - show - every spring and fall.

10697 ■ Sir Thomas Beecham Society (TBS)

85 Morningside Dr.
Falling Waters, WV 25419-4052
E-mail: beecham3@juno.com
URL: http://www.geocities.com/b_wehrung/beecham.html
Contact: Charles Niss, Exec. Sec.

Founded: 1964. **Members:** 300. **Membership Dues:** regular, $20 (annual). **Description:** Record collectors, music lovers, and interested individuals. Works to preserve the memory of Sir Thomas Beecham (1879-1961) and supports the music of Frederick Delius (1862-1934). Encourages the release of new commercial recordings and the re-issuance of recordings no longer in the catalog, and discourages deletions from the current recordings catalog. Seeks to preserve the memory of other composers and conductors of the past, such as Arturo Toscanini, Kousseuitzky, etc. **Libraries: Type:** reference. **Holdings:** archival material, audio recordings, films. **Subjects:** Sir Thomas Beecham and his music. **Publications:** *Le Grand Baton*, annual. Journal ● Has also published discography list of Beecham's recordings.

10698 ■ Society for American Music (SAM)

Univ. of Pittsburgh
Stephen Foster Memorial
Pittsburgh, PA 15260
Ph: (412)624-3031
Fax: (412)624-7447
E-mail: sam@american-music.org
URL: http://www.american-music.org
Contact: Mariana Whitmer, Exec. Dir.

Founded: 1975. **Members:** 1,000. **Membership Dues:** individual, $75 (annual) ● retiree, $38 (annual) ● student (full time, in residence), $35 (annual) ● spouse/partner, $30 (annual) ● institution, $137 (annual). **Staff:** 1. **Budget:** $80,000. **Description:** Represents musicologists, ethnomusicologists, composers, conductors, performers, sheet music collectors, librarians, museum curators, institutions, students, music critics, and publishers. (Named for Oscar Sonneck (1873-1928), American musician, historian, and librarian.) Encourages study and interest in musical American music in all its historical and contemporary styles and contexts. **Awards:** Irving Lowens Memorial Awards. **Frequency:** annual. **Type:** recognition. **Recipient:** for a book and an article that made outstanding contributions to American music studies. **Formerly:** (1999) Sonneck Society. **Publications:** *American Music*, quarterly. Journal. Includes scholarly reviews of books, music, recordings, and other media relevant to its central mission. **Price:** included in membership dues ● *The Bulletin of the Society for American Music*, 3/year. Newsletter. Includes news of the Society, upcoming conferences of interest, recent research and reviews and other communications of interest to members. **Price:** included in membership dues ● *Society for American Music Membership Directory*, annual. Includes members' addresses, important information concerning the Society such as officers, appointments, committees, and interest group listing. **Price:** included in membership dues. **Conventions/Meetings:** annual conference (exhibits).

10699 ■ Society for Asian Music (SAM)

PO Box 7819
Austin, TX 78713-7819
Ph: (512)232-7621
Fax: (512)232-7178
E-mail: mfh2@cornell.edu
URL: http://asianmusic.skidmore.edu
Contact: Marty Hatch, Treas.

Founded: 1959. **Members:** 525. **Membership Dues:** individual, $32 (annual) ● student, $26 (annual) ● sustaining, $50 (annual) ● patron, $100 (annual) ● life, $600 ● benefactor, $1,000 (annual). **Staff:** 1. **Budget:** $20,000. **Description:** Encourages scholarship and appreciation of all types of Asian music in historical and cultural contexts, including music from the Middle to the Far East and Asian diaspora. **Publications:** *Asian Music*, semiannual. Journal. Contains general and scholarly articles on Asian performing arts and other aspects of Asian culture. Includes book and record reviews. **Price:** included in membership dues. ISSN: 0044-9202. **Circulation:** 500. **Conventions/Meetings:** periodic conference.

10700 ■ Society for Electro-Acoustic Music in the United States (SEAMUS)

c/o Mark Zaki, VP for Membership
PO Box 272
Milltown, NJ 08850
Ph: (408)924-4632
Fax: (408)924-4773
E-mail: seamus_membership@earthlink.net
URL: http://www.seamusonline.org
Contact: Mark Zaki, VP for Membership

Founded: 1984. **Members:** 450. **Membership Dues:** individual, international associate, $45 (annual) ● student, $25 (annual) ● senior (age over 65), $35 (annual) ● library/institution, $50 (annual) ● friend, $75 (annual) ● donor, $150 (annual) ● sponsor, $300 (annual) ● patron, $600 (annual). **Description:** Individuals involved or interested in the composition or instruction of electro-acoustic music (music reproduced or modified by electronic means and requiring electronic amplification). Promotes the research and performance of electro-acoustic music in the U.S. Seeks to: improve licensing procedures for electro-acoustic music; publicize activities of electro-acoustic music composers; develop a network for technical support. Encourages radio broadcasting of electro-acoustic music; appeals to the U.S. Information Service and Voice of America to broadcast more electro-acoustic music. Solicits grants for development of electro-acoustic music. **Libraries: Type:** reference. **Holdings:** archival material. **Subjects:** electro-acoustic recordings. **Awards:** ASCAP/SEAMUS. **Frequency:** annual. **Type:** recognition. **Recipient:** for young composers ● SEAMUS Award for Lifetime Achievement. **Frequency:** annual. **Type:** recognition. **Recipient:** for contribution to the art and craft of electro-acoustic music. **Publications:** *SEAMUS Journal*, semiannual. **Price:** included in membership dues. ISSN: 0897-6473. **Advertising:** accepted ● *SEAMUS Membership Directory*, periodic ● *SEAMUS Newsletter*, quarterly. **Price:** included in membership dues ● Also publishes Audio CDs-annual and President's Communique-quarterly. **Conventions/Meetings:** annual conference (exhibits) - usually March or April.

10701 ■ Society for Ethnomusicology (SEM)

Morrison Hall 005
1165 E 3rd St.
Bloomington, IN 47405-3700
Ph: (812)855-6672
Fax: (812)855-6673
E-mail: sem@indiana.edu
URL: http://webdb.iu.edu/sem/scripts/home.cfm
Contact: Alan Burdette, Exec. Dir.

Founded: 1955. **Members:** 2,500. **Membership Dues:** institution, $95 (annual) ● student (full-time only), $40 (annual) ● spouse/partner (life), $1,100 ● life, $900 ● individual/emeritus (earning $25,000 or less), $60 (annual) ● individual/emeritus (earning $25,000-$40,000), $75 (annual) ● individual/emeritus (earning $40,000-$60,000), $85 (annual) ● individual/emeritus (earning $60,000-$80,000), $95 (annual) ● individual/emeritus (earning $80,000 above), $105 (annual) ● spouse/partner (individual/emeritus category above plus $35), $35 (annual). **Staff:** 2. **Budget:** $145,400. **Regional Groups:** 6. **Multinational. Description:** Represents ethnomusicologists, anthropologists, musicologists, and laypeople interested in the study of music as a human activity with a special focus on its cultural dimensions. **Awards:** Alan Merriam Prize. **Type:** recognition ● Ida Halpern Award. **Type:** recognition ● Jaap Kunst Prize. **Type:** recognition ● Klaus Wachsmann Prize. **Type:** recognition ● Lois Ibsen al-Faruqi Award. **Type:** recognition ● The Nadia and Nicholas Nahumck Fellowship and Award. **Frequency:** semiannual. **Type:** fellowship. **Recipient:** to help support research on dance-related subject and its subsequent publication ● Seeger Prize. **Frequency:** annual. **Type:** recognition ● Stevenson Prize. **Frequency:** biennial. **Type:** monetary. **Recipient:** to ethnomusicologists who are also composers; for encouraging research, and recognizing a book, dissertation, or paper on their compositional oeuvre. **Sections:** African Music; Applied Ethnomusicology; Dance; Education; Popular Music; Status of Women. **Special Interest Groups:** Archiving; European Music; Historical Ethnomusicology; Medical Ethnomusicology; The Music of Iran and Central Asia; The Society for Arab Music Research; South Asian Performing Arts. **Task Forces:** Gender and Sexualities. **Publications:** *An Invitation to Join the Society for Ethnomusicology*. Brochure. Provides information on the history, purpose, publications, and membership benefits of the organization. ● *Ethnomusicology*, 3/year. Journal. Includes annual index; book, film, and record reviews; current bibliography, discography, and filmography. **Price:** included in membership dues; $75.00 /year for institutions. ISSN: 0014-1836. Alternate Formats: microform ● *SEM Newsletter*, quarterly. Contains news of the society and of its members, of conferences, of research topics and grant possibilities, obituaries. **Price:** included in membership dues. **Circulation:** 2,100. **Conventions/Meetings:** annual meeting (exhibits) - always fall. 2008 Oct. 25-28, Middletown, CT.

10702 ■ Society for Music Theory (SMT)

Dept. of Music
Univ. of Chicago
1010 E 59th St.
Chicago, IL 60637
Ph: (773)834-3821

E-mail: vlong@uchicago.edu
URL: http://www.societymusictheory.org
Contact: Victoria L. Long, Exec. Dir.
Founded: 1977. **Members:** 1,050. **Membership Dues:** regular, $75 (annual) ● dual, $85 (annual) ● student, $35 (annual) ● student, dual, $45 (annual) ● emeritus, $45 (annual). **Multinational. Description:** Promotes music theory as a scholarly and a pedagogical discipline. **Awards:** Emerging Scholar Award. **Frequency:** annual. **Type:** recognition. **Recipient:** to a book or article by an author in an early stage of her/his career ● Outstanding Publication Award. **Frequency:** annual. **Type:** recognition. **Recipient:** to a distinguished article by an author of any age or career stage ● Wallace Berry Award. **Frequency:** annual. **Type:** recognition. **Recipient:** to a distinguished book by an author of any age or career stage. **Subgroups:** Analysis and Performance; Jazz (SMT-Jz); Music and Philosophy; Music Cognition; Music Informatics; Music Theory Pedagogy; Popular Music; Queer Resource. **Publications:** *Music Theory Online*. Journal. **Price:** included in membership dues. Alternate Formats: online ● *Music Theory Spectrum*, semiannual. Journal. **Price:** $129.00 for library and institutional subscriptions; $25.00/back issue for regular members; $20.00/back issue for students and emeritus ● *SMT Newsletter*, semiannual. Alternate Formats: online. **Conventions/Meetings:** annual meeting - 2008 Nov. 6-9, Nashville, TN; 2009 Oct. 28-Nov. 2, Montreal, QC, Canada; 2010 Nov. 4-7, Indianapolis, IN.

10703 ■ Society for the Preservation and Advancement of the Harmonica (SPAH)

Dept. W
PO Box 865
Troy, MI 48099-0865
Ph: (586)771-4866
E-mail: harpspah@spah.org
URL: http://www.spah.org
Contact: Eugene Hansen, Treas.
Founded: 1963. **Members:** 1,000. **Membership Dues:** individual, $35 (annual) ● family, $50 (annual). **Staff:** 7. **Multinational. Description:** Harmonica enthusiasts who wish to advance and preserve harmonicas and harmonica music. Arranges harmonica instruction for hobbyists. Members regularly perform for service organizations. **Awards:** Harmonica Player of the Year. **Frequency:** annual. **Type:** recognition. **Publications:** *Harmonica Happenings*, quarterly. Magazine. **Price:** included in membership dues. **Circulation:** 1,200. **Advertising:** accepted. **Conventions/Meetings:** annual convention (exhibits).

10704 ■ Society for the Preservation and Encouragement of Barber Shop Quartet Singing in America (SPEBSQSA)

110 Seventh Ave. N
Nashville, TN 37203-3704
Ph: (615)823-3993
Free: (800)876-SING
E-mail: info@barbershop.org
URL: http://www.barbershop.org
Contact: Ed Watson, Exec. Dir./CEO
Founded: 1938. **Members:** 30,000. **Membership Dues:** individual, $87 (annual) ● senior, student, $43 (annual) ● dual, $10 (annual). **Staff:** 30. **Budget:** $6,000,000. **Regional Groups:** 16. **Local Groups:** 820. **Multinational. Description:** Serves as the fraternity of barbershop-style singers. Encourages vocal music in schools and communities while preserving a traditional form of American music. **Libraries: Type:** reference; by appointment only. **Holdings:** 650,000; archival material, audio recordings. **Subjects:** old songs, historical material regarding barbershop harmony. **Awards:** Award of Harmony. **Frequency:** annual. **Type:** recognition. **Recipient:** to a person selected from the community, not a barbershopper, who best represents, through his or her life and efforts, the truest meaning of harmony. **Also Known As:** (2005) Barbershop Harmony Society. **Formerly:** Society for the Preservation and Propagation of Barber Shop Quartet Singing in the United States. **Publications:** *Harmonizer*, bimonthly. Newsletter. **Price:** $21.00/year. ISSN: 0017-7849. **Circulation:** 37,000. **Advertising:** accepted. Alternate Formats: online ● Audiotapes ● Also publishes barbershop arrangements and songbooks. **Conventions/Meetings:** annual convention (exhibits) - 2008 June 29-July 6, Nashville, TN; 2009 June 28-July 5, Anaheim, CA; 2010 June 27-July 4, Philadelphia, PA.

10705 ■ Society for Seventeenth-Century Music (SSCM)

c/o Prof. Stefanie Tcharos, Treas.
Dept. of Music
Univ. of California
Santa Barbara, CA 93106-6070
Ph: (805)893-4027
Fax: (805)893-7194
E-mail: sscmtreasurer@yahoo.com
URL: http://www.arts.uci.edu/sscm
Contact: Georgia Cowart, Pres.
Founded: 1991. **Members:** 280. **Membership Dues:** regular, $20 (annual). **Description:** Promotes the study and performance of seventeenth-century music and related arts. Facilitates communication among individual scholars and performers. Encourages communication among existing and future organizations devoted to the study and performance of specific aspects of seventeenth-century music and related arts. Sponsors conferences, festivals, workshops, seminars, study sessions and other activities. **Awards:** Irene Alm Memorial Prize. **Frequency:** annual. **Type:** recognition. **Recipient:** for a scholarly presentation or lecture-demonstration given by a student. **Telecommunication Services:** electronic mail, georgia.cowart@case.edu. **Publications:** *Journal of Seventeenth-Century Music*. Alternate Formats: online. Also Cited As: *JSCM* ● *17th-Century Music*, semiannual. Newsletter. Contains news, reports, programs and scholarly articles. **Price:** included in membership dues. **Conventions/Meetings:** annual meeting, held in conjunction with the annual meeting of the American Musicological Society.

10706 ■ Society for Strings (SS)

c/o Mary McGowan-Welp, Admissions Dir.
Meadowmount School of Music
1424 County Rte. 10
Westport, NY 12993
Ph: (518)962-2400
Fax: (518)962-2310
E-mail: admissions@meadowmount.com
URL: http://www.meadowmount.com
Contact: Prof. Owen Carman, Dir./Pres.
Founded: 1944. **Budget:** $500,000. **Description:** Promotes the art of string playing in America. Operates Meadowmount School of Music, a 7-week summer school, located near Westport, NY, for students (ages 12 to 25) of violin, viola, and cello. **Convention/Meeting:** none. **Telecommunication Services:** electronic mail, director@meadowmount.com. **Publications:** Brochure.

10707 ■ Southeastern Composers' League (SCL)

c/o Betty Wishart, Pres.
209 Maple Dr.
Erwin, NC 28339
E-mail: wishartb@campbell.edu
URL: http://www.radford.edu/~scl-web
Contact: Betty Wishart, Pres.
Founded: 1952. **Members:** 130. **Membership Dues:** student, $10 (annual) ● composer, $30 (annual) ● associate, $20 (annual). **Regional Groups:** 1. **Description:** Composers of solo, chamber, and orchestral music. Promotes the performance of the music of regional composers; assists in the performance of contemporary music in general. Supports symposia of members' and nonmembers' compositions. **Awards:** Arnold Salop Memorial Undergraduate Student Composition Award. **Frequency:** annual. **Type:** monetary ● Philip Slates Memorial Graduate Student Composition Award. **Frequency:** annual. **Type:** monetary. **Publications:** *Music Now*, quarterly. Newsletter. Features member activities, composer opportunities, articles on theory and composition. **Price:** free for members. **Circulation:** 200. **Conventions/Meetings:** periodic competition and meeting, with 4 to 6 concerts of contemporary music, mostly by member composers - spring ● annual conference, includes concert series ● periodic meeting, with forum.

10708 ■ Southern Appalachian Dulcimer Association (SADA)

Address Unknown since 2007
Founded: 1974. **Members:** 57. **Regional Groups:** 4. **State Groups:** 3. **Local Groups:** 1. **Description:** Dulcimer players and makers; individuals interested in the dulcimer. Seeks to preserve and foster the playing and crafting of the traditional Appalachian dulcimer and hammered dulcimer. **Conventions/Meetings:** annual festival ● quarterly meeting - always first Sunday in February, April, June, and October.

10709 ■ Southwest Bluegrass Association (SWBA)

5206 Calle de Ricardo
Torrance, CA 90505
E-mail: swba@s-w-b-a.com
URL: http://www.s-w-b-a.com
Contact: Jon Labrum, Pres.
Membership Dues: single, married, family, $18 (annual) ● band, business, $20 (annual) ● single, married, family, $36 (biennial). **Description:** Represents and promotes bluegrass music, pickers and grinners in Southwest U.S. **Computer Services:** Online services. **Publications:** *The Bluegrass Soundboard*, bimonthly. Newsletter. **Advertising:** accepted ● *SWBA - Bluegrass Recipe Book*. **Price:** $7.00 ● *SWBA Directory*. **Price:** $5.00 for members.

10710 ■ Sphinx Organization

400 Renaissance Ctr., Ste.2550
Detroit, MI 48243
Ph: (313)877-9100
Fax: (313)877-0164
E-mail: info@sphinxmusic.org
URL: http://www.sphinxmusic.org
Contact: Aaron P. Dworkin, Founder/Pres.
Founded: 1996. **Description:** Focuses on the involvement of youth and minorities in classical music. Increases the participation of Blacks and Latinos in music schools, as professional musicians and classical music audiences. Enhances K-12 music education. **Funds:** Instrument Fund; Music Assistance Fund. **Programs:** Classical Connections; Musical Encounters; Sphinx Competition; Sphinx Symphony. **Publications:** *The Quarter Note*, quarterly. Newsletter ● Articles. Alternate Formats: online.

10711 ■ Sweet Adelines International

PO Box 470168
Tulsa, OK 74147-0168
Ph: (918)622-1444
Free: (800)992-7464
Fax: (918)665-0894
E-mail: admin@sweetadelineintl.org
URL: http://www.sweetadelineintl.org
Contact: Pat LeVezu, Pres.
Founded: 1945. **Members:** 30,113. **Staff:** 33. **Budget:** $3,500,000. **Regional Groups:** 31. **Local Groups:** 610. **Multinational. Description:** Women singers committed to advancing the musical art form of barbershop harmony through education and performances. Provides education, training, and coaching in the development of women's four-part barbershop harmony. **Awards:** Internal Champion Quartet. **Frequency:** annual. **Type:** recognition. **Recipient:** for best of adjudicated contests ● International Champion Chorus. **Frequency:** annual. **Type:** recognition. **Telecommunication Services:** phone referral service, worldwide access, (732)544-2866 ● additional toll-free number, in U.S. and Canada, (800)223-3482. **Boards:** Editorial Review; International Board of Directors. **Committees:** Educational Direction; International Bylaws and Rules Specialist; International Faculty Coordinators; International Music Arrangers Program Coordinators; Worldwide Liaison. **Formerly:** (1991) Sweet Adelines, Inc. **Publications:** *Arrangers' Newsletter* ● *Chapter President's Newsletter* ● *Judges' Newsletter* ● *Pitch Pipe*, quarterly. Magazine. Includes articles on quartet and chorus competitions, association news, and vocal,

music and leadership skills. **Price:** included in membership dues; $12.00 for nonmembers in U.S.; $24.00 for nonmembers outside U.S. **Circulation:** 30,000. **Advertising:** accepted ● *Young Women in Harmony Newsletter*. **Conventions/Meetings:** annual convention and competition, includes education classes, quartet and chorus competitions (exhibits) - 2008 Nov. 4-8, Honolulu, HI; 2009 Nov. 3-7, Nashville, TN; 2010 Oct. 19-23, Seattle, WA; 2011 Oct. 18-22, Houston, TX.

10712 ■ Tamburitza Association of America (TAA)

c/o Joseph R. Novosel, Esq., Pres.
3894 Spartan Dr.
Fort Gratiot, MI 48059
Ph: (810)385-9667
E-mail: novoselnorth@aol.com
URL: http://www.tamburitza.org/TAA
Contact: Joseph R. Novosel Esq., Pres.

Founded: 1967. **Members:** 2,500. **Membership Dues:** regular, $10 (annual) ● regular, $35 (quinquennial). **Staff:** 31. **Description:** Musicians, teachers, and enthusiasts of tamburitza music. (The tamburitza is a stringed instrument native to former Yugoslavia, now the Balkan region, similar to the guitar in shape and the mandolin in sound.) Aims to promote and perpetuate Yugoslavian tamburitza music and Slavic culture. Conducts concerts; maintains hall of fame exhibit of tamburitza performers; encourages participation of youth groups in tamburitza music; sponsors competitions. **Libraries: Type:** reference. **Holdings:** audio recordings, photographs. **Subjects:** music, instruments, other related artifacts. **Awards:** Anniversary Awards. **Frequency:** annual. **Type:** recognition. **Recipient:** for those who have celebrated their 50-year anniversary as a tambura musician ● Founder's Award. **Frequency:** annual. **Type:** recognition. **Recipient:** to a young person who demonstrates an outstanding devotion to the preservation of tambura music and the Slavic culture ● President's Award. **Frequency:** annual. **Type:** recognition. **Recipient:** for individual's contribution to the Tamburitza Association of America. **Committees:** Band Selection; Historical Audit; Media; Site Selection; Transportation. **Publications:** *Annual Program* ● *Tamburitza Extravaganza Bulletin*, semiannual ● *Tamburitza Times*, quarterly. Newsletter ● Directory, periodic. **Conventions/Meetings:** annual Tamburitza Extravaganza - meeting.

10713 ■ TRI-M Music Honor Society (TRI-M)

1806 Robert Fulton Dr.
Reston, VA 20191
Ph: (703)860-4000
Free: (800)336-3768
Fax: (703)860-9143
E-mail: mbrserv@menc.org
URL: http://www.menc.org/information/trim/main_trim.html
Contact: Betty Cook, Dir. of Membership

Founded: 1936. **Members:** 45,000. **Staff:** 3. **National Groups:** 1,500. **Description:** A program of the National Association for Music Education (MENC)(see separate entry). Seeks to motivate secondary music students and recognize their effort and honor their accomplishments. Provides an appropriate method of recognizing musical achievement, strengthens school music programs, helps students reach their full musical potential, encourages instrumental and vocal students to work toward the same goals, challenges and inspires, and focuses public attention on school music programs. **Libraries: Type:** reference; not open to the public. **Awards:** Honor Ensemble Participation. **Frequency:** annual. **Type:** recognition. **Recipient:** for member who is selected to represent their school in any music honor ensemble ● Tri-M Leadership. **Frequency:** annual. **Type:** recognition. **Recipient:** for member who is a prominent leader for school, chapter, and community organizations and activities in addition to his or her involvement with music ● Tri-M Master Musician. **Frequency:** annual. **Type:** recognition. **Recipient:** for member who excels in music, has achieved success in the performance field, and has been active in performing in school and community functions ● Tri-M Outstanding Service. **Frequency:** annual. **Type:** recognition. **Recipient:** for member who has demonstrated exceptional examples of service through school, chapter, and community organizations and activities in addition to their involvement with music. **Programs:** Chapter of the Year Summer Music Scholarship Award. **Formerly:** (1983) Modern Music Masters. **Publications:** *TRI-M News*, semiannual. Newsletter. **Conventions/Meetings:** biennial National In-Service Conference - convention (exhibits).

10714 ■ The Unconservatory

8035 SW 26th St.
Miami, FL 33155
Ph: (305)266-9673 (305)461-4970
Fax: (305)266-9673
E-mail: pianistas2@aol.com
URL: http://www.unconservatory.org
Contact: Ubaldo Henriquez, Pres.

Description: Represents the interests of individuals dedicated to creation, performance, recording and education in the musical arts. Promotes the work of historic musicians and musical educators. Presents events in local communities. Produces limited national and international touring projects. Offers forums, articles and other educational resources related to musical arts. **Telecommunication Services:** electronic mail, ubaldohenriquez@yahoo.com.

10715 ■ United in Group Harmony Association (UGHA)

PO Box 185
Clifton, NJ 07015-0185
Ph: (973)365-0049 (973)470-UGHA
Fax: (201)365-2665
E-mail: ronniei@ugha.org
URL: http://www.ugha.org
Contact: Ronald Italiano, Founder/Pres.

Founded: 1976. **Members:** 2,000. **Membership Dues:** domestic, $25 (annual) ● foreign, $30 (annual). **Staff:** 5. **Budget:** $35,000. **Description:** Persons interested in vintage rhythm and blues vocal group harmony. Preserves vocal group harmony music by encouraging its performance by pioneer and modern groups and promote group harmony music as an important part of American music history. Conducts educational programs; supports charitable programs. Maintains hall of fame. Sponsors weekly radio program in New York City. **Libraries: Type:** reference. **Holdings:** archival material, audiovisuals, books, business records, clippings, periodicals. **Subjects:** R&B vocal group history. **Awards:** UGHA Classic Group of the Year (The Charles Moffit Memorial Award). **Frequency:** annual. **Type:** recognition. **Recipient:** for groups who have recorded during the 1950s and/or 1960s, and who have performed for UGHA over the last 12 months ● UGHA Hall of Fame Award. **Frequency:** annual. **Type:** recognition. **Recipient:** for pioneer group singers of membership voted inductees who have played significant roles in the history of the given group ● UGHA Rookie Group of the Year (The Gus Gossert Memorial Award). **Frequency:** annual. **Type:** recognition. **Recipient:** for local acappella groups or vocal bands who have performed for UGHA for the first time during the last 12 months ● UGHA Veteran Group of the Year (The Sonny Til Memorial Award). **Frequency:** annual. **Type:** recognition. **Recipient:** for local acappella groups or vocal group bands who have performed for UGHA over the last 24 months or more. **Publications:** *UGHA Newsletter*, monthly. **Price:** included in membership dues. **Circulation:** 2,000. **Conventions/Meetings:** competition ● annual Hall of Fame Induction Ceremony - meeting ● monthly meeting and show - usually last Friday or Saturday, North Bergen, NJ.

10716 ■ U.S. Scottish Fiddling Revival (SFIRE)

c/o Jan Tappan, VP
1938 Rose Villa St.
Pasadena, CA 91107
Ph: (626)793-3716
E-mail: fiddlers@earthlink.net
URL: http://www.scottishfiddling.org
Contact: Jan Tappan, VP

Founded: 1976. **Members:** 225. **Membership Dues:** individual, $15 (annual) ● family, $30 (annual) ● organization, $75 (annual) ● life (individual), $300 ● life (family), $600 ● life (organization), $1,500. **Budget:** $2,500. **Regional Groups:** 5. **Local Groups:** 12. **Description:** Fiddlers and other musicians; Scottish clan and Highland games organizations; Scottish country dance groups; other interested individuals. Seeks to foster the growth of traditional Scottish fiddle (violin) music playing and performance. Sponsors Jink and Diddle Scottish Fiddling School, held annually in mid-July, encourages local performing groups and facilitates communication among them. Supports and sanctions local performance groups and competitions at Highland games. **Committees:** Judges Panel. **Also Known As:** Scottish FIRE. **Publications:** *Scottish Fiddling Revival Newsletter*, quarterly. Includes periodic membership list. **Price:** $15.00 /year for individuals; $30.00/year for families; $75.00/ year for organizations. **Circulation:** 225. **Advertising:** accepted. **Conventions/Meetings:** annual meeting - always the weekend of the US National Fiddle Competition ● U.S. National Fiddling Competition, awards scholarships to fiddling schools in the U.S. and Scotland.

10717 ■ Villa-Lobos Music Society (VLMS)

153 E 92nd St., No. 4R
New York, NY 10128-2479
Ph: (212)427-5103
E-mail: villobosms@aol.com
Contact: Dr. Alfred Heller, Pres.

Founded: 1986. **Multinational. Description:** Seeks to revitalize an interest in the life and music of Brazilian composer Heitor Villa-Lobos (1887-1959) and other composers of like musical philosophy. Organizes concerts and recordings. **Convention/Meeting:** none.

10718 ■ Viola d'Amore Society of America (VDSA)

10917 Pickford Way
Culver City, CA 90230
Ph: (310)838-5509
E-mail: altviool@sbcglobal.net
URL: http://www.violadamoresocietyofamerica.org
Contact: Dr. Daniel Thomason, Co-Dir.

Founded: 1977. **Members:** 150. **Membership Dues:** general, $23 (annual) ● overseas, $28 (annual). **Description:** Professional and amateur performers; college, university, and conservatory teachers; institutions. Promotes the music, performance, and history of the viola d'amore (a 14-stringed—seven playing and seven sympathetic—instrument that combines traits of the violin and viol families). Holds conferences and meetings. Makes available viola d'amore music. **Telecommunication Services:** electronic mail, roseviola@earthlink.net. **Publications:** *Viola d'Amore Society of America—Newsletter* (in English and German), semiannual. Includes book and record reviews. **Price:** included in membership dues. **Circulation:** 150. **Advertising:** accepted. **Conventions/ Meetings:** biennial congress, music, instruments (exhibits).

10719 ■ Viola da Gamba Society of America (VdGSA)

c/o Mr. Ken Perlow, Treas.
131 S Humphrey Ave.
Oak Park, IL 60302
Ph: (708)383-4608
E-mail: post@vdgsa.org
URL: http://vdgsa.org
Contact: Mr. Ken Perlow, Treas.

Founded: 1962. **Members:** 1,100. **Membership Dues:** in U.S. and Canada ($20 for first year), $30 (annual) ● outside U.S. and Canada, $35 (annual) ● student in U.S. and Canada, $25 (annual). **Budget:** $200,000. **Regional Groups:** 30. **Multinational. Description:** Musicians, teachers, dealers, and libraries. Aims to promote interest in the viola da gamba (bass of the viol family, having a range and tone similar to the violoncello) and its music. Encourages formation of local groups, known as consorts, in communities and educational institutions. Engages in historical research and supports amateur and professional players. **Libraries: Type:** reference. **Holdings:** 200. **Subjects:** music manuscripts, theoretical treatises. **Publications:** *Journal of the Viola da Gamba Society of America*, annual. Contains articles on the viola de gamba, compositions written for the instrument, notable original instruments, composers, and performers. **Price:** included in membership dues. ISSN: 0607-0252. **Circulation:** 1,200 ● *List of Members*, annual. Membership Directory ● *VdGSA News*, quarterly. Newsletter. **Price:** included in membership dues. ISSN: 0506-306X. **Circulation:** 1,200. **Advertising:** accepted. **Conventions/Meetings:** annual Conclave - meeting and workshop, intensive, weeklong - usually late July or early August.

10720 ■ Violin Society of America (VSA)
48 Acad. St.
Poughkeepsie, NY 12601
Ph: (845)452-7557
Fax: (845)452-7618
E-mail: info@vsa.to
URL: http://www.vsa.to
Contact: Mr. Robert Martinez, Exec. Dir.
Founded: 1973. **Members:** 1,800. **Membership Dues:** regular (in U.S., Canada, and Mexico), $120 (biennial) ● regular (in U.S., Canada, and Mexico), library/institution, $85 (annual) ● regular (in other country), $105 (annual) ● full-time student (in U.S., Canada, and Mexico), $30 (annual) ● full-time student (in other country), $45 (annual) ● regular (in other country), $150 (biennial). **Staff:** 1. **Description:** Musicians, violin dealers, craftsmen, restorers of stringed instruments, music teachers, and individuals interested in the violin, viola, and cello. Sponsors biennial international competition among violin, viola, cello, and bow makers. Maintains VSA-H.K. Goodkind Library at Oberlin College, Oberlin, OH. **Awards:** Instrument/Bow Making. **Frequency:** biennial. **Type:** recognition. **Recipient:** for outstanding craftsmanship and/or tone of new instruments and bows ● Kaplan-Goodkind Memorial Scholarship. **Frequency:** semiannual. **Type:** scholarship. **Recipient:** for worthy students interested in learning how to make and restore instruments. **Formerly:** American Society for the Advancement of Violin Making. **Publications:** *Newsletter of the Violin Society of America*, 3/year. **Price:** included in membership dues; $100.00 for nonmembers. **Advertising:** accepted ● *VSA Journal*, 1-2/year. **Price:** included in membership dues. **Circulation:** 1,500. **Advertising:** accepted ● *VSA Papers*, semiannual. Journal. **Price:** $100.00 for members. **Conventions/Meetings:** annual meeting and symposium, with lectures on violin making related subjects, instrument making; includes competition on even years (exhibits).

10721 ■ Violoncello Society (VS)
Address Unknown since 2008
Founded: 1956. **Members:** 300. **Membership Dues:** tri-state, NY, NJ, and CT, $35 (annual) ● outside of tri-state area, $30 (annual) ● student, $15 (annual). **Staff:** 1. **Local Groups:** 1. **Description:** Amateur and professional cellists, educators, musicians, music lovers, and composers. Objectives are to promote the art of violoncello playing in the U.S; provide an opportunity for performances by composers and other artists; advance interest in the cello as a solo instrument; develop a better understanding of the art of the instrument; further members' artistic development; offer a meeting ground for professional and amateur cellists. Sponsors guest artists and speakers. **Publications:** Newsletter, 3/year. **Conventions/Meetings:** meeting - 4/year.

10722 ■ Wagner Society of New York (WSNY)
PO Box 230949
Ansonia Sta.
New York, NY 10023-0949
Ph: (212)749-4561
Fax: (212)749-1542
E-mail: wagnerring@aol.com
URL: http://www.wagnersocietyny.org
Contact: Nathalie D. Wagner, Pres./Chair
Founded: 1977. **Members:** 1,300. **Membership Dues:** regular in Canada, $50 (annual) ● dual, $70 (annual) ● student/senior, $25 (annual) ● nonresident (more than 100 miles from New York City) and Canadian, $30 (annual) ● individual outside U.S., $60 (annual) ● patron, $100 (annual) ● donor, $150 (annual) ● sponsor, $275 (annual) ● benefactor, $500 (annual). **Budget:** $100,000. **Description:** Opera and vocal music enthusiasts. Seeks to foster the performance and appreciation of the music of German composer Richard Wagner (1813-83). Sponsors recitals and lectures, receptions for opera performers, and panel discussions. Offers films and video presentations; disseminates information. Although members are primarily from New York and surrounding states, membership is open internationally. Provides ticket services for selected events for members. **Awards:** Robert Lauch Memorial Grant. **Frequency:** annual. **Type:** grant. **Recipient:** for outstanding promising Wagner singer ● Student and Young Professional Grant. **Frequency:** semiannual. **Type:** grant. **Recipient:** for potential in singing Wagner repertoire. **Computer Services:** database ● mailing lists, not for rental, except by special arrangement with exchange of service ● online services, membership, event reservations, and catalogue items. **Boards:** Advisory. **Committees:** Development; Finance; Program; Publications; Singers. **Publications:** *Wagner Notes*, bimonthly. Newsletter. Features international coverage of all aspects of Wagner: reviews of performances and books. Includes society news. **Price:** included in membership dues. **Circulation:** 1,300 ● *Wagner Society of New York Catalogue.* Lists Wagner-related books and materials for sale through society. Alternate Formats: online ● Also publishes librettos of Wagner operas. **Conventions/Meetings:** monthly lecture, with films or slide lectures or interviews; recitals by outstanding grantees - September through May ● annual seminar, in-depth study of a Wagner opera; several speakers and metropolitan opera cast members.

10723 ■ Western Music Association (WMA)
c/o Roger S. Banks, Exec. Dir.
3342 Cedarhill Dr.
San Angelo, TX 76904
Ph: (325)234-4306
Free: (877)588-3747
Fax: (325)949-6870
E-mail: rogerbanks@cox.net
URL: http://www.westernmusic.org
Contact: Roger S. Banks, Exec. Dir.
Founded: 1989. **Members:** 900. **Membership Dues:** sponsoring, $1,000 (annual) ● life - individual, $600 ● corporate, $500 (annual) ● business, patron, $100 (annual) ● family, family performing, $65 (annual) ● individual, individual performing, $40 (annual) ● performing group (based on number of members), $65-$150 (annual) ● chapter, $10-$25 (annual). **Staff:** 1. **State Groups:** 10. **Description:** Seeks to advance and to preserve western music, and the history, literature and musical tradition of the West. **Awards:** Western Music Association Female Vocalist of the Year. **Frequency:** annual. **Type:** trophy. **Recipient:** for female vocalist selected by professionals in the music business ● Western Music Association Male Vocalist of the Year. **Frequency:** annual. **Type:** trophy. **Recipient:** for male vocalist selected by professionals in the music business. **Committees:** Chapters; Education; Festival. **Formerly:** (1997) Western Music Association; (2001) International Western Music Association. **Publications:** *Western Way*, quarterly. Magazine. **Price:** included in membership dues. **Circulation:** 1,500. **Advertising:** accepted. **Conventions/Meetings:** annual Western Music Festival - festival and workshop, with showcases, vendors, concerts.

10724 ■ Women in Music National Network (WIMNN)
1450 Oddstad Dr.
Redwood City, CA 94063
Free: (866)305-7963
Fax: (510)234-7272
E-mail: info@womeninmusic.com
URL: http://www.womeninmusic.com
Founded: 1993. **Members:** 5,000. **Membership Dues:** silver, $9 (monthly) ● gold, $14 (monthly) ● platinum, $19 (monthly). **Description:** Networking and resource services for professional writers, performers, management, booking agents, publishers, producers, attorneys, engineers, publicists, record company personnel, distributors, individuals, and students. Connects women in music with other women who can become mentors and business associates, and other opportunities in the music industry. **Publications:** Newsletter, monthly. Contains music, industry, and organization's news information. **Price:** included in membership dues. Alternate Formats: online. **Conventions/Meetings:** seminar ● workshop.

10725 ■ World Folk Music Association (WFMA)
PO Box 40553
Washington, DC 20016
Ph: (202)362-2225
E-mail: webmaster@wfma.net
URL: http://www.wfma.net
Contact: Richard A. Cerri, Pres.
Founded: 1983. **Membership Dues:** friend of folk music, $35 (annual). **Description:** Promotes folk music; acts as a clearinghouse for information on folk music and musicians. Sponsors Friends of Folk Music; holds concerts and showcases. **Awards:** Kate Wolf Memorial Award. **Frequency:** annual. **Type:** recognition. **Recipient:** to a singer/songwriter who best represents qualities of Kate Wolf. **Publications:** *Folk News*, quarterly. Newsletter. **Price:** free. **Circulation:** 3,500 ● *Folk Notes*, 2-3/year. **Price:** free. **Circulation:** 3,500. **Conventions/Meetings:** seminar.

10726 ■ World Piano Competition (WPC)
441 Vine St., Ste.1030
Cincinnati, OH 45202
Ph: (513)421-5342 (513)421-2672
Fax: (513)421-2672
E-mail: info@amsa-wpc.org
Contact: Ms. Gloria Ackerman, Founder/CEO
Founded: 1956. **Members:** 2,500. **Membership Dues:** teacher, $35 (annual). **Staff:** 4. **Budget:** $600,000. **Regional Groups:** 25. **State Groups:** 10. **Local Groups:** 6. **National Groups:** 20. **Description:** Seeks to expose young pianists, ages five to 30, to the influence of performances by great musicians; strives to foster greater music appreciation through public exposure of talented artists. Works to establish standards for teaching technical mastery and artistic excellence. Sponsors international piano competition and master classes; coordinates music festivals and recitals. **Libraries: Type:** open to the public. **Subjects:** piano. **Awards: Frequency:** annual. **Type:** recognition. **Committees:** Community Group; Donor Group; Piano Club. **Programs:** Bach-Beethoven-Brahms Club Educational Outreach; International Festival Educational; Junior Ambassador Educational; Master Class and Joint Recital Educational. **Formerly:** (1968) Cincinnati Music Scholarship Association; (2004) American Music Scholarship Association. **Publications:** *Friend Letter*, periodic ● *Membership Letter*, annual ● *Piano Guides*, periodic ● *Piano Guides 1-4* ● *Teacher's Piano Syllabus* ● Newsletter, periodic. Alternate Formats: online. **Conventions/Meetings:** annual competition - always July, Cincinnati, OH.

10727 ■ Young Concert Artists (YCA)
250 W 57th St., Ste.1222
New York, NY 10107
Ph: (212)307-6655
Fax: (212)581-8894
E-mail: yca@yca.org
URL: http://www.yca.org
Contact: Susan Wadsworth, Dir.
Founded: 1961. **Members:** 15. **Staff:** 10. **Budget:** $950,000. **Description:** Aims to discover and launch the careers of extraordinary classical musicians. Holds annual Young Concert Artists International Auditions; presents the winners in Young Concert Artists Series in New York City, Boston, and Washington, DC; books concert engagements throughout the U.S. and abroad. Provides publicity materials, debut recordings, management services, and career guid-

ance, at no cost to the artists, until they go to a commercial manager, usually in three to five years. **Awards:** Young Concert Artists International Auditions. **Frequency:** annual. **Type:** recognition. **Recipient:** for exceptional talent, virtuosity, artistic individuality, projection as a performer.

Muslim

10728 ■ American Muslims Intent on Learning and Activism (AMILA)
PO Box 2216
Los Gatos, CA 95031
E-mail: director@amila.org
URL: http://www.amila.org
Contact: Moina Noor, Dir.
Founded: 1992. **Members:** 100. **Membership Dues:** $40 (annual). **Description:** Strives to strengthen the American Muslim community through activism, Islamic education, spirituality, and networking with other Muslim groups. Works to encourage Muslim youth to make Islam a priority. **Publications:** Newsletter, bimonthly. **Conventions/Meetings:** monthly meeting ● annual picnic.

Mythology

10729 ■ Society for the Study of Myth and Tradition (SSMT)
135 E 15 St.
New York, NY 10003
Ph: (212)505-6200
Free: (800)560-MYTH
Fax: (212)979-7325
E-mail: editors@parabola.org
URL: http://www.parabola.org
Contact: Arthur Kurzweil, Publisher
Founded: 1976. **Staff:** 9. **Budget:** $1,300,000. **Description:** Dedicated to exploring the wisdom and beauty of traditional cultures in relation to myth and the modern quest for meaning. **Publications:** *Parabola*, quarterly. Magazine. Contains myth, tradition, and the search for meaning. **Price:** $7.50/single copy; $26.00/year in U.S.; $30.00/year in Canada. ISSN: 0362-1596. **Advertising:** accepted ● Audiotapes ● Videos ● Newsletter, monthly. **Conventions/Meetings:** annual symposium - always in New York City.

Native American

10730 ■ American Indian Arts Council (AIAC)
725 Preston Forest Shopping Ctr., Ste.B
Dallas, TX 75230
Ph: (214)891-9640
Fax: (214)891-0221
E-mail: aiac@flash.net
URL: http://www.AmericanIndianArtFestival.org
Contact: Pat Peterson, Exec. Dir.
Founded: 1989. **Members:** 175. **Membership Dues:** silver, $50 (annual) ● gold, $100 (annual) ● turquoise, $250 (annual) ● platinum, $500 (annual). **Staff:** 3. **Budget:** $200,000. **State Groups:** 1. **Local Groups:** 1. **Description:** Promotes American Indian visual and performing arts. Preserves the art, history, and culture of American Indians. Maintains speakers' bureau, Cultural Presenters Program. Conducts cultural programs such as annual American Indian Art Festival and Market in October. **Convention/Meeting:** none. **Libraries: Type:** reference. **Holdings:** artwork, audio recordings, books, video recordings. **Subjects:** history, art. **Awards:** American Indian Arts Council Scholarship. **Frequency:** semiannual. **Type:** scholarship. **Recipient:** for American Indian majoring in fine arts at an accredited college or university with a 2.5 GPA minimum. **Computer Services:** Mailing lists. **Publications:** Newsletter, quarterly. **Price:** $3.00/year. **Circulation:** 800.

10731 ■ American Indian Culture Research Center (AICRC)
PO Box 98
Marvin, SD 57251-0098
Ph: (605)398-9200
Fax: (605)398-9201
E-mail: indian@bluecloud.org
URL: http://www.bluecloud.org/dakota.html
Contact: Ms. Coleen Cordell, Dir.
Founded: 1967. **Staff:** 2. **Budget:** $60,000. **Description:** Corporation that supports Indian leaders and Indian educators in their ambitions for rebuilding the Indian community. Aids in teaching the non-Indian public about the culture and philosophy of the Indian. Serves as a resource for guidance and funding in Indian self-help programs. Has compiled an oral history and a photographic collection. Conducts workshops and seminars; compiles statistics. Maintains speakers' bureau and a small museum. **Libraries: Type:** reference. **Holdings:** 3,000; photographs.

10732 ■ American Indian Heritage Foundation (AIHF)
PO Box 6301
Falls Church, VA 22040
Ph: (703)819-0979
Fax: (703)532-1921
E-mail: wilrose@indians.org
URL: http://www.indians.org
Contact: Dr. Wil Rose, CEO
Founded: 1973. **Members:** 1,000. **Membership Dues:** friend, $25 (annual). **Staff:** 3. **Budget:** $500,000. **Description:** Informs and educates non-Indians concerning the culture and heritage of the American Indian. Seeks to respond to the spiritual and physical needs of American Indians and to inspire Indian youth. Sponsors food and clothing distribution program. Presents cultural concerts for children. Operates speakers' bureau and museum. Sponsors American Indian Heritage Month and Seminars; also sponsors annual National Indian Awards Night, Miss Indian U.S.A. Scholarship Pageant, the National Endowment for the American Indian and annual children's show. **Libraries: Type:** reference. **Holdings:** 50. **Subjects:** American Indian history and culture. **Awards:** American Indian Education Fund. **Frequency:** annual. **Type:** scholarship. **Recipient:** for Indian youths ● National Youth Achievement Awards. **Frequency:** annual. **Type:** recognition. **Recipient:** for outstanding achievement in 10 categories. **Computer Services:** database, Indian Information clearinghouse. **Telecommunication Services:** electronic mail, palemoon@indians.org. **Councils:** Inter-Tribal Advisory. **Also Known As:** Native American Heritage Foundation. **Publications:** Brochure, periodic. **Price:** included in membership dues. Alternate Formats: online. **Conventions/Meetings:** annual festival, includes pow-wow (exhibits) - always July 4 in Washington, DC.

10733 ■ American Indian Institute (AII)
Univ. of Oklahoma
Coll. of Continuing Educ.
555 Constitution St., Ste.227
Norman, OK 73072-7820
Ph: (405)325-4127
Fax: (405)325-7757
E-mail: aii@ou.edu
URL: http://www.aii.outreach.ou.edu
Contact: Ernest Clark, Dir.
Founded: 1951. **Staff:** 32. **Description:** Promotes American Indian education and research, training and career development opportunities, perpetuation of tribal cultures, traditions, and histories, and development of human and natural resources. Works to bring together representatives of North American Indian tribes and bands to provide leadership and strategies for dealing with social and human problems. Provides training to child welfare, school, mental health, and other professional personnel. Conducts research and educational programs in substance abuse prevention, cultural resource identification, and leadership training. Develops cultural curriculum and multicultural training programs. Designs and develops seminars and workshops. Provides on-site consultation and technical assistance. **Libraries: Type:** reference. **Holdings:** archival material, audio recordings, books, clippings, periodicals, video recordings. **Subjects:** Native American issues. **Computer Services:** Information services, Native American Research Information System. **Telecommunication Services:** electronic mail, erclark@ou.edu. **Publications:** *Child Abuse and Neglect Conference Proceedings*, annual. **Price:** $15.00 each (for 1987-90 editions); $10.00 each (for 1985-86 editions); $8.50 each (for 1983-84 editions) ● *Mental Health Conference Proceedings*, annual. **Price:** $15.00 each (for 1989-90 editions); $10.00 each (for 1988 edition). **Conventions/Meetings:** annual Early Childhood Intervention Conference ● annual National American Indian Conference on Child Abuse and Neglect ● annual National Conference on Gifted and Talented Education for Native People ● annual National Native American, Alaska Native, First Nations Cultural Curriculum Development Workshop.

10734 ■ Association for the Study of American Indian Literatures (ASAIL)
c/o Siobhan Senier
Univ. of New Hampshire
Dept. of English
Hamilton Smith Hall
95 Main St.
Durham, NH 03824
E-mail: rnelson@richmond.edu
URL: http://oncampus.richmond.edu/faculty/ASAIL
Contact: Robert Nelson, Historian
Founded: 1972. **Members:** 500. **Membership Dues:** regular individual in U.S., $30 (annual) ● regular individual outside U.S., $55 (annual) ● limited income in U.S., $20 (annual) ● limited income outside U.S., $40 (annual) ● sponsor in U.S., $50 (annual) ● sponsor outside U.S., $70 (annual) ● patron in U.S., $100 (annual) ● patron outside U.S., $120 (annual). **Description:** Promotes study, criticism, research on the oral traditions and written literatures of Native Americans; teaching such traditions and literatures. **Publications:** *Studies in American Indian Literatures*, quarterly. Journal. Focuses exclusively on American Indian cultures. **Conventions/Meetings:** annual Native American Literatures Symposium - conference.

10735 ■ Cherokee National Historical Society (CNHS)
PO Box 515
Tahlequah, OK 74465-0515
Ph: (918)456-6007
Fax: (918)456-6165
URL: http://www.powersource.com/heritage
Contact: Mac R. Harris, Exec. Dir.
Founded: 1963. **Members:** 1,600. **Membership Dues:** regular, $30 (annual) ● sustaining, $100 (annual) ● Sequoyah, $500 (annual) ● Chairman's Heritage Council, $1,000 (annual) ● charter archive, $5,000 (annual). **Staff:** 50. **Budget:** $3,000,000. **Description:** Persons and organizations interested in preserving the history and tradition of the Cherokee Indian Nation. Seeks to interest the public in Cherokee history. Plans to mark locations of historic significance to the Cherokees, including graves of officials and other prominent persons of the Nation. Sponsors educational, charitable, and benevolent activities for Cherokees and their descendants. Operates Cherokee Heritage Center, which includes the Cherokee National Museum, and Cherokee Arboretum and Herb Garden (including trees and plants used traditionally by Cherokees for food, fiber, and medicines). Maintains a "living" Indian Village, circa 1700-50 and a Rural Cherokee Museum Village, circa 1875-90; annually presents The Trail of Tears, an outdoor epic symphonic drama relating to Cherokee history in the southeast and forced migration to Indian territory. Maintains Cherokee Hall of Fame for persons of Cherokee descent who have made distinguished contributions to the nation; also maintains the Ho-Chee-Nee Trail of Tears Memorial Chapel. **Libraries: Type:** reference. **Holdings:** 1,200; archival material, papers. **Subjects:** Cherokee history and development. **Also Known As:** Cherokee Heritage Center. **Publications:** *The Columns*, quarterly. Newsletter. **Price:** free. **Circulation:** 900. Alternate Formats: online ● *Trail of Tears Drama Program*, annual. Includes theater company bibliographical information and description of programs at the Cherokee Heritage Center. **Conventions/Meetings:** lecture, on Cherokee history and culture ● annual Trail of Tears Art Show.

10736 ■ Comanche Language and Cultural Preservation Committee (CLCPC)
1375 NE Cline Rd.
Elgin, OK 73538-3086
Ph: (580)492-5126
Fax: (580)492-5119
E-mail: clcpc@comanchelanguage.org
URL: http://www.comanchelanguage.org
Contact: Barbara Goodin, Treas.
Founded: 1993. **Members:** 400. **Staff:** 2. **Budget:** $100,000. **Local Groups:** 1. **Description:** Seeks to revive the Comanche language into a "living language"; aims to provide opportunity for Comanche people of all ages to speak, write and understand the language in order to continue the culture. **Publications:** *Comanche Dictionary*. Book. Contains over 6,000 Comanche words with Comanche to English, and English to Comanche sections. **Price:** $35.00 plus shipping and handling ● *Comanche Hymns*. Book. Contains 116 Comanche songs with English translation; includes 3 CDs. **Price:** $25.00 plus shipping and handling. Alternate Formats: CD-ROM ● *Comanche Language Flash Cards Set*. Paper. Contains three sets of 48 flash cards featuring simple Comanche words; includes CDs. **Price:** $15.00 plus shipping and handling ● *Comanche Language Newsletter*, quarterly. Provides language news, activities and stories. **Circulation:** 600. Alternate Formats: online ● *Comanche Lessons*. Booklet. Includes four written Comanche lessons with CD. **Price:** $25.00 plus shipping and handling. Alternate Formats: CD-ROM ● *Picture Dictionary*. Booklet. Explains Comanche alphabet and the sound of each letter; includes CDs. **Price:** $15.00 plus shipping and handling. **Conventions/Meetings:** annual Comanche Language Conference ● annual Comanche Nation Fair - festival, with contests, dancing (traditional), storytelling, carnival (exhibits).

10737 ■ Continental Confederation of Adopted Indians (CCAI)
960 Walhonding Ave.
Logan, OH 43138
Ph: (740)385-7136
E-mail: lelandconner@webtv.net
Contact: Leland L. Conner, Chief
Founded: 1950. **Members:** 150. **Description:** Non-Indians who have been presented with honorary tribal chieftainship, an official Indian name, or recipients of any other Indian-oriented awards. Persons so honored include Wayne Newton, Reginald Laubin, and Ann Miller. Membership also open to blooded Indians. Maintains Indian Lore Hall of Fame. Maintains speakers' bureau. **Awards:** National Catlin Peace Pipe Achievement Award. **Frequency:** annual. **Type:** recognition.

10738 ■ Council for Native American Indians (CNAIP)
Address Unknown since 2007
Founded: 1974. **Members:** 843. **Description:** Individuals interested in the holistic philosophies and teachings of the earlier indigenous groups of North and Central America. Conducts research on the social, economic, and political relationships between the indigenous groups and the 16th century settlers in New York City and Long Island, NY areas. Conducts educational series for children that teaches concepts of discipline through the methods and techniques of the ancient peoples. Sponsors charitable programs; compiles statistics. **Councils:** Medicine People. **Publications:** *Earth Walk and Four Directions for Peace* ● *Medicine Lodge* ● Newsletter, periodic. **Conventions/Meetings:** annual meeting - usually New York City or Los Angeles, CA.

10739 ■ Crazy Horse Memorial Foundation (CHMF)
12151 Ave. of the Chiefs
Crazy Horse, SD 57730-9506
Ph: (605)673-4681
Fax: (605)673-2185
E-mail: memorial@crazyhorse.org
URL: http://www.crazyhorse.org
Contact: Ruth Ziolkowski, Pres./CEO
Founded: 1948. **Members:** 23. **Membership Dues:** Grass Root Club, $41 (annual) ● Korczack club, $174 (annual) ● Driller Club, $250 (annual) ● Blaster Club, $500 (annual) ● Ruth Club, $1,000 (annual) ● Bronze Club, $1,500 (annual) ● Granite Club, $2,500 (annual) ● Crazy Horse Circle, $5,000 (annual) ● Crazy Horse League, $10,000 (annual). **Staff:** 50. **Description:** Seeks completion of the memorial to North American Indians begun by sculptor Korczak Ziolkowski (1908-82). (This memorial is to be a statue, 563 feet high and 641 feet long, depicting the Sioux leader Crazy Horse astride his pony and pointing to the lands of his people. Ziolkowki's wife and children are continuing to work on the statue, which is being carved from Thunderhead Mountain in South Dakota.) Maintains museum of art and artifacts of Indian tribes from many areas of the United States, a museum-studio of American and European antiques, art objects, marble, bronze, and mahogany sculpture. Plans to establish a university and medical center for Native Americans. **Libraries: Type:** reference. **Holdings:** 22,000. **Subjects:** Indian culture, heritage, arts, crafts, history. **Awards:** Crazy Hoarse Teacher of the Year Award. **Frequency:** annual. **Type:** recognition ● Native American Scholarship Fund. **Type:** scholarship. **Recipient:** to Native Americans. **Telecommunication Services:** electronic mail, info@crazyhorse.org. **Publications:** *Crazy Horse and Korczak* ● *Crazy Horse Memorial 50th Anniversary Booklet* ● *Crazy Horse Progress*, quarterly. Newsletter ● *Korczak, Sage of Sitting Bull's Bones* ● *Korczak: Storyteller in Stone*. **Conventions/Meetings:** annual meeting.

10740 ■ Creek Indian Memorial Association (CIMA)
Creek Coun. House Museum
Town Sq.
106 W 6th
Okmulgee, OK 74447
Ph: (918)756-2324
Fax: (918)756-3671
E-mail: creekmuseum@sbcglobal.net
Founded: 1923. **Members:** 113. **Staff:** 3. **Description:** Operates museum of Creek Indian culture containing displays of Indian artifacts, archaeology artifacts, Indian murals, and paintings. Conducts fundraising, provides educational programs. **Libraries: Type:** reference. **Holdings:** 200; audiovisuals, books, clippings, monographs, periodicals. **Subjects:** Creek history and legend, Native Americans. **Formerly:** (1923) Indian Historical Society. **Publications:** Booklets ● Brochures. **Conventions/Meetings:** annual Council House Indian Art Market - meeting - first Saturday in October ● monthly meeting - always third Tuesday.

10741 ■ Cultural Conservancy
PO Box 29044
San Francisco, CA 94129-0044
Ph: (415)561-6594
Fax: (415)561-6482
E-mail: mknelson@igc.org
URL: http://www.nativeland.org
Contact: Melissa Nelson, Pres.
Membership Dues: regular, $25-$49 (annual) ● associate, $50-$99 (annual) ● friend, $100-$249 (annual) ● contributor, $250-$999 (annual) ● donor, $1,000 (annual). **Staff:** 2. **Description:** Promotes the preservation and revitalization of indigenous culture and ancestral lands of Native Americans. Provides mediation, legal information, referral and audio recording services. Produces educational programs and trainings on native land conservation and rights, cultural and ecological restoration, traditional indigenous arts and spiritual values. **Projects:** Artist in Residence; Kashaya; Presidio; Story Scape; Tibetan. **Publications:** Newsletter.

10742 ■ Gathering of Nations (GN)
3301 Coors Blvd. NW, Ste.R300
Albuquerque, NM 87120-1229
Ph: (505)836-2810
Fax: (505)839-0475
E-mail: website@gatheringofnations.com
URL: http://www.gatheringofnations.com
Founded: 1983. **Description:** Native Americans. Promotes the expression of Native American culture and religion, including Native American song and dance. Sponsors pow wows and periodic song, dance, and Miss Indian World competitions. **Libraries: Type:** open to the public. **Holdings:** 3; books. **Subjects:** Native American culture and lifestyle. **Awards: Frequency:** annual. **Type:** monetary. **Publications:** *Program Book*, annual. Magazine. Contains information about pow wows and Native American culture. **Price:** $3.00 plus $1 postage. **Advertising:** accepted. **Conventions/Meetings:** annual Gathering of Nations Pow Wow - meeting (exhibits) - always 4th weekend of April, Albuquerque, NM.

10743 ■ Indian Arts and Crafts Association (IACA)
4010 Carlisle NE, Ste.C
Albuquerque, NM 87107
Ph: (505)265-9149
Fax: (505)265-8251
E-mail: info@iaca.com
URL: http://www.iaca.com
Contact: Michael Garcia, Pres.
Founded: 1974. **Members:** 700. **Membership Dues:** student, $15 (annual) ● collector (individual), subsequent location for retail, $50 (annual) ● artist/craftsperson, $60 (annual) ● associate, $85 (annual) ● sustaining, $110 (annual) ● wholesale business, retail business, $195 (annual) ● collector/artist/craftsperson (joint), $60 (annual) ● museum, $55 (annual) ● retail/wholesale business, tribal enterprise, cooperative, guild, $215 (annual). **Staff:** 3. **Budget:** $300,000. **Description:** Indian craftspeople and artists, museums, dealers, collectors, and others. Works to promote, preserve, protect, and enhance the understanding of authentic American Indian arts and crafts. Sets code of ethics for members and standards for the industry. Conducts consumer education seminars, meetings, and display programs; works with related government groups. Operates speakers' bureau. **Awards:** Artist of the Year. **Frequency:** annual. **Type:** recognition. **Recipient:** for IACA member artists/craftspeople. **Publications:** *Indian Arts and Crafts Association—Directory*, annual ● *Indian Arts and Crafts Association—Newsletter*, quarterly ● *Membership Directory/Buyer's Guide*, annual. **Price:** $10.00 plus shipping and handling. **Conventions/Meetings:** annual Artist of the Year - competition ● semiannual Wholesale Market - meeting - always April/May in Albuquerque, CO, and October/November in Phoenix, AZ.

10744 ■ Indian Heritage Council (IHC)
Address Unknown since 2007
Founded: 1988. **Members:** 10,000. **Membership Dues:** individual, $10 (annual). **Regional Groups:** 3. **State Groups:** 3. **Local Groups:** 6. **National Groups:** 2. **Languages:** English, Spanish. **Description:** American Indians and interested others. Promotes and supports American Indian endeavors. Seeks a deeper understanding between American Indians and others of the cultural, educational, spiritual, and historical aspects of Native Americans. Conducts research and educational programs. Sponsors charitable events; operates speakers' bureau. Publishes books, poems, manuscripts written by members or Native Americans. **Libraries: Type:** reference. **Holdings:** 5,000. **Subjects:** Indian concerns, Indian literature. **Awards:** Native American Literary Award. **Frequency:** annual. **Type:** monetary. **Publications:** *Crazy Horse's Philosophy of Riding Rainbows*. Book. **Price:** $19.95. **Advertising:** accepted ● *Great American Indian Bible*. **Price:** $20.00. **Circulation:** 5,000. **Advertising:** accepted ● *Indian Drug Usage*. **Price:** $15.00 ● *Indian Heritage Quarterly*. Newsletter. Reports actions taken on behalf of American Indian causes and promotions. **Price:** $10.00/year. **Advertising:** accepted ● *Native American Play*. **Price:** $10.00 ● *Native American Poetry* ● *Native American Poets' Anthology*. **Price:** $19.95 ● *Native American Prophecies*. **Price:** $10.00 ● *Native Letters to the People*. **Price:** $19.95 ● *Vision Quest*. Epic poem. **Price:** $15.00 ● *The Vision Quest Preparation*. **Price:** $12.00. **Conventions/Meetings:** monthly International Writers Conference and Festival ● annual Pow-Wow and Conference (exhibits).

10745 ■ Institute of American Indian Arts (IAIA)
83 Avan Nu Po Rd.
Santa Fe, NM 87508
Ph: (505)424-2300 (505)424-2323
Free: (800)804-6423
Fax: (505)424-3900
E-mail: setzel@iaia.edu
URL: http://www.iaia.edu
Contact: Dr. Robert Martin, Pres.
Founded: 1962. **Membership Dues:** individual, national friend (dual), $40 (annual) ● dual, $50-$99 (annual) ● sponsor, $100-$249 (annual) ● contributor, $250-$499 (annual) ● patron, $500-$999 (annual) ● benefactor, $1,000-$2,499 (annual) ● director's friend (minimum), $2,500 (annual) ● business/corporate (minimum), $1,000 (annual) ● national friend (individual), $30 (annual). **Staff:** 50. **Budget:** $3,180,000. **Description:** Federally chartered private institution. Offers learning opportunities in the arts and crafts to Native American youth (Indian, Eskimo, or Aleut). Emphasis is placed upon Indian traditions as the basis for creative expression in fine arts including painting, sculpture, museum studies, creative writing, printmaking, photography, communications, design, and dance, as well as training in metal crafts, jewelry, ceramics, textiles, and various traditional crafts. Students are encouraged to identify with their heritage and to be aware of themselves as members of a race rich in architecture, the fine arts, music, pageantry, and the humanities. All programs are based on elements of the Native American cultural heritage that emphasizes differences between Native American and non-Native American cultures. Sponsors Indian arts-oriented junior college offering Associate of Fine Arts degrees in various fields as well as seminars, an exhibition program, and traveling exhibits. Maintains extensive library, museum, and biographical archives. Provides placement service. **Convention/Meeting:** none. **Libraries: Type:** open to the public. **Holdings:** 20,000; audio recordings, books, periodicals, photographs, video recordings. **Subjects:** Native Americans, arts. **Telecommunication Services:** electronic mail, rmartin@iaia.edu ● additional toll-free number, admission, records and enrollment, (800)804-6422. **Divisions:** College; Guidance; Research; Special Services. **Formerly:** (1962) Sante Fe Indian School. **Publications:** *New Work from IAIA*, annual. Book. Contains students' prose and poetry. ● *Newswinds*, quarterly. Newsletter ● *School Catalog*, annual.

10746 ■ Institute for the Study of American Cultures (ISAC)
PO Box 2707
Columbus, GA 31902
Founded: 1983. **Members:** 100. **Membership Dues:** general, $60 (annual). **Staff:** 1. **Description:** Supports and promotes unbiased research into the origin and history of the American Indians and their pre-Columbian ancestors. Promotes a revisionist examination of the discovering of America by Columbus. Uses research technology in the fields of archaeology, anthropology, linguistics, epigraphy, music, and history to determine the "truth and relevancy of new discoveries without allegiance to any historical or ethnological paradigm." Sponsors projects. **Libraries: Type:** reference. **Holdings:** 400; books, periodicals. **Subjects:** pre-Columbian history, archaeology, epigraphy. **Awards:** Root Cutter Award. **Frequency:** annual. **Type:** recognition. **Publications:** *Columbus, the Man.* Book ● *Dene and NaDene Ingian Migration 1233 A.D., Escape from Genghis Khan to America* ● *ISAC Report*, quarterly. Newsletter ● *Lost America: The Story of Pre-Columbian Iron Age in America* ● *The Nexus: Spoken Language Connection between the Mayar Asemetic During Pre-Columbian Times* ● *The Norse Discovery of America* ● *North American Sun Kings: Keeper of the Flame* ● *The Primeval Middle East and Greece* ● *The Rediscovery of Lost America* ● *The Yuchi-Yuki: Nonplus.* **Conventions/Meetings:** annual conference, speakers and presentations - October.

10747 ■ Inter-Tribal Indian Ceremonial Association (ITIC)
Address Unknown since 2008
Founded: 1921. **Members:** 350. **Membership Dues:** in India, $40 (annual). **Staff:** 3. **Budget:** $600,000. **Languages:** English, Navajo. **Description:** Indian people, businessmen, dealers and collectors of Indian arts and crafts, and individuals interested in the annual Inter-Tribal Indian Ceremonial sponsored by the association to promote and preserve American Indian culture. The four-day program includes Indian dances, sports, arts and crafts, rituals, and a rodeo. Conducts correspondence and other activities in connection with legislation affecting Indian arts and crafts. Conducts specialized education and children's services; provides educational materials on Indian crafts; produces color slides of Indian ceremonies. Maintains Red Rock Park as a museum. Active in maintaining the highest standards in Native American hand made art. **Libraries: Type:** reference. **Holdings:** archival material. **Awards: Frequency:** annual. **Type:** recognition. **Committees:** Dance Production; Exhibit; Parade; Rodeo. **Publications:** *A Measure of Excellence.* Book. Features top visual artists of each annual ceremonial. **Price:** $19.95. **Conventions/Meetings:** annual meeting (exhibits) - always Gallup, NM.

10748 ■ Iroquois Studies Association (ISA)
28 Zevan Rd.
Johnson City, NY 13790
Ph: (607)729-0016
Fax: (607)770-9610
E-mail: isa1@otsiningo.com
URL: http://www.otsiningo.com
Membership Dues: regular, $5 (annual). **Description:** Provides educational and cultural programs about American Indians, particularly the Six Nations of the Iroquois. **Publications:** *Flights of Fancy: An Introduction to Iroquois Beadwork, 2nd Edition.* Book. **Price:** $25.00 ● *The Otsiningo Circle*, semiannual. Newsletter. Covers Indian exhibits and events within a 200 mile radius.

10749 ■ National Indian Youth Council (NIYC)
c/o Norman Ration, Exec. Dir.
318 Elm St. SE
Albuquerque, NM 87102
Ph: (505)247-2251 (505)678-6275
Fax: (505)247-4251
E-mail: nration@niyc-alb.org
URL: http://www.niyc-alb.org
Contact: Norman Ration, Exec. Dir.
Founded: 1961. **Members:** 12,000. **Description:** Aims to protect Indian natural resources; protect Indian religious freedom and other tribal and individual civil liberties; protect and enhance treaty rights and federal government's trust relationship and responsibilities; improve Indian health and education; preserve the Indian family unit and community. Operates educational and employment programs and sponsors action-related research projects. Compiles statistics on the Indian electorate. **Libraries: Type:** reference. **Holdings:** archival material. **Publications:** *Americans Before Columbus*, quarterly. Newsletter. **Price:** included in membership dues; $20.00 for nonmembers. **Conventions/Meetings:** annual meeting - always late June, on Indian-owned land.

10750 ■ National Native American (Indian) Cooperative (NNAC)
c/o Carole J. Garcia, International Rep.
PO Box 27626
Tucson, AZ 85726-7626
Ph: (520)622-4900
Fax: (520)622-3525
E-mail: info@usaindianinfo.org
URL: http://www.usaindianinfo.org
Contact: Fred Synder, Dir./Consultant
Founded: 1969. **Members:** 2,700. **Staff:** 2. **Budget:** $100,000. **For-Profit. Description:** Native American artists and craftsmen, cultural presenters, dance groups, and individuals interested in preserving American Indian crafts, culture, and traditional education. Provides incentives to Native Americans to encourage the preservation of their culture; offers assistance marketing American Indian crafts and locating material that is difficult to find. Supplies referral information on public health, education, career counseling, scholarships and funding sources, marketing, models, and dance. Sponsors crafts and cultural demonstrations. Is currently developing a North American Indian Trade and Information Center. Compiles statistics; operates speakers' bureau. Maintains museum. **Libraries: Type:** reference. **Holdings:** 3,000; archival material. **Subjects:** Native Americans, American Indians. **Computer Services:** Mailing lists, American Indians and their crafts, culture, and education. **Publications:** *Indian Information Packets.* Includes maps, brochures, newspapers, magazines, etc. **Price:** $10.00. **Advertising:** accepted ● *Native American Directory: Alaska, Canada, U.S.*, quinquennial. Lists organizations, events, and tribal offices and reserves. **Price:** $65.95 in U.S.; $131.00 library edition; $80.95 in Canada. **Circulation:** 35,000 ● *Pow Wow on the Red Road.* Includes calendar of major American Indian events in the U.S. and Canada from 2003 to 2008. **Price:** $25.00. **Circulation:** 25,000. **Advertising:** accepted ● Also make available copies of material related to Native American crafts. **Conventions/Meetings:** annual meeting, held in conjunction with the North American Native American Indian Information and Trade Center ● Pow Wow - competition, with dancers from over 50 tribes (exhibits) - always Thanksgiving and New Year's Eve weekend.

10751 ■ Native American Institute (NAI)
220 W Central Ave., No. 314
Brea, CA 92821
Ph: (714)256-4945
Fax: (714)879-1337
E-mail: runningbear001@yahoo.com
Contact: Dr. John E. Collins, Contact
Founded: 1957. **Membership Dues:** individual, $25 (annual) ● couple, $30 (annual) ● student (under 21 with school ID), $15 (annual). **Description:** Students and patrons of the Indian arts, crafts, and history. **Awards:** Catlin Peace Pipe Award. **Frequency:** annual. **Type:** recognition. **Formerly:** (2005) American Indian Lore Association. **Publications:** Newsletter. Alternate Formats: online.

10752 ■ North America Native American (Indian) Information and Trade Center
PO Box 27626
Tucson, AZ 85726-7626
Ph: (520)622-4900
Fax: (520)622-3525
E-mail: info@usaindianinfo.org
URL: http://www.usaindianinfo.org
Contact: Fred Synder, Dir.
Founded: 1991. **Staff:** 3. **Budget:** $100,000. **Description:** A project of the National Native American Cooperative. Provides educational programs to individuals interested in Native American culture. Serves as a clearinghouse of information on American Indians including special events and sales of arts and crafts. Maintains trading post of Indian crafts. Also maintains speakers' bureau and museum. Compiles statistics. **Libraries: Type:** reference. **Holdings:** 5,000; archival material. **Subjects:** American Indians. **Computer Services:** Mailing lists. **Affiliated With:** National Native American (Indian) Cooperative. **Publications:** *American Indian Information Packet.* Contains pow wows, brochures, newspapers and maps. **Price:** $15.00. **Circulation:** 30,000. **Advertising:** accepted ● *Cherokee Ceremonial Songs & Dances, Vol. 1.* Audiotape. Sung in Cherokee. **Price:** $15.00 first tape, plus shipping and handling; $12.00 each additional tape; $21.00 first CD, plus shipping and handling; $18.00 each additional CD ● *Cherokee Ceremonial Songs & Dances, Vol. 2.* Audiotape. **Price:** $15.00 first tape, plus shipping and handling; $12.00 each additional tape; $21.00 first CD, plus shipping and handling; $18.00 each additional CD ● *Indian America*, periodic. **Price:** $10.00. **Circulation:** 100,000. **Advertising:** accepted ● *Intertribal Peyote Songs, Vol. 1.* Audiotape. **Price:** $15.00 first tape, plus shipping and handling; $12.00 each additional tape; $21.00 first CD, plus shipping and handling; $18.00 each additional CD ● *Intertribal Songs, Vol. 2.* Audiotape. **Price:** $15.00 first tape, plus shipping and handling; $12.00 each additional tape; $21.00 first CD, plus shipping and handling; $18.00 each additional CD ● *Native American Directory: Alaska, Canada, U.S..* **Price:** $59.95 for individuals, plus

shipping and handling ($6); $131.00 for libraries, plus shipping and handling ($6) ● *Native American Veterans Pow-Wow*. Audiotape. Contains 20 songs. **Price:** $15.00 first tape, plus shipping and handling; $12.00 each additional tape; $21.00 first CD, plus shipping and handling; $18.00 each additional CD ● *Navajo Peyote Songs, Vol. 1*. Audiotape. Contains 20 songs. **Price:** $15.00 first tape, plus shipping and handling; $12.00 each additional tape; $21.00 first CD, plus shipping and handling; $18.00 additional CD (each) ● *Navajo Peyote Songs, Vol. 2*. Audiotape. **Price:** $15.00 first tape, plus shipping and handling; $12.00 each additional tape; $21.00 first CD, plus shipping and handling; $18.00 additional CD (each) ● *Oklahoma Pow-Wow & Specialty Dance Songs*. Audiotape. Contains 18 songs, including Eagle Dance. **Price:** $15.00 first tape, plus shipping and handling; $12.00 each additional tape; $21.00 first CD, plus shipping and handling; $18.00 additional CD (each) ● *Pow Wow on the Red Road*. Contains more than 700 Indian events in the U.S. and Canada. **Price:** $25.00 ● *Songs of the Native American Church, Vol. 1*. Audiotape. Contains Peyote songs. **Price:** $15.00 first tape, plus shipping and handling; $12.00 each additional tape; $21.00 first CD, plus shipping and handling; $18.00 additional CD (each) ● *Songs of the Native American Church, Vol. 2*. Audiotape. **Price:** $15.00 first tape, plus shipping and handling; $12.00 each additional tape; $21.00 first CD, plus shipping and handling; $18.00 each additional CD. **Conventions/Meetings:** annual American Indian Exposition - meeting (exhibits) ● semiannual Pow Wow - meeting (exhibits) - always Thanksgiving weekend and New Years weekend, Tucson, AZ.

10753 ■ Pan American Indian Association (PAIA)
c/o Loving Hands Institute
639 11th St.
Fortuna, CA 95540
Ph: (707)725-9627
Fax: (707)725-2471
E-mail: skyhawk@northcoast.com
URL: http://www.lovinghandsinstitute.com/htm/paia.htm
Contact: Skyhawk Ojala, Contact
Founded: 1984. **Members:** 4,232. **Membership Dues:** life, $25. **Staff:** 4. **Regional Groups:** 20. **State Groups:** 3. **Local Groups:** 2. **National Groups:** 10. **Description:** Americans of Native American descent; students and other interested individuals. Assists persons with Native American heritage in researching their tribal roots. Provides genealogical and historical aids. Provides speakers' bureau and educational programs. **Libraries: Type:** reference. **Holdings:** 76; books, periodicals. **Subjects:** Native American spiritual ways and teaching. **Awards:** Appreciation-Spiritual. **Type:** recognition. **Recipient:** for individuals. **Publications:** *Whirling Rainbow-Voice of the People*, quarterly. Journal. Contains information on Native American storytelling, Powwow and spiritual guidance. **Price:** $15.00/5 issues (member renewal); $20.00 for nonmembers. ISSN: 1078-7297. **Circulation:** 5,000. **Advertising:** accepted. **Conventions/Meetings:** monthly meeting.

10754 ■ Thunderbird American Indian Dancers (TAID)
c/o Louis Mofsie, Dir.
204 W Central Ave.
Maywood, NJ 07607
Ph: (201)587-9633
Fax: (201)587-9633
Contact: Louis Mofsie, Dir.
Founded: 1956. **Members:** 30. **Description:** Indians and non-Indians who raise money for the Thunderbird Indian Scholarship Fund for Indian Students. Offers cultural classes in crafts, singing, dancing, and language. Sponsors Indian studies program for Indian youngsters. **Conventions/Meetings:** monthly Powwow - meeting - always New York City.

10755 ■ Tribal Preservation Program
c/o Heritage Preservation Services
Natl. Park Ser.
1201 Eye St. NW, 2255
Washington, DC 20005
Ph: (202)354-1837
Fax: (202)371-1794
E-mail: nps_hps-info@nps.gov
URL: http://www.cr.nps.gov/hps/tribal
Contact: James Bird, Contact
Founded: 1990. **Description:** Protects resources and traditions of importance to Native Americans. Works with Indian tribes, Alaska Natives, Native Hawaiians and other national organizations. **Awards: Type:** grant. **Programs:** American Indian Liaison Office; Archeology and Ethnography; Historic Preservation Internship Training; National Register of Historic Places.

10756 ■ United National Indian Tribal Youth (UNITY)
PO Box 800
Oklahoma City, OK 73101
Ph: (405)236-2800
Fax: (405)971-1071
E-mail: unity@unityinc.org
URL: http://www.unityinc.org
Contact: Loretta Tuell, Chair
Founded: 1976. **Members:** 211. **Membership Dues:** Unity Network Youth Council affiliate, $25 (annual) ● Unity Network individual affiliate, $5 (annual) ● supporter, $100 (annual). **Staff:** 5. **Description:** Youth councils and individuals. Strives to foster the spiritual, mental, physical, and social development of American Indian and Alaska Native youth and to help build a strong, unified, and self-reliant Native America through involvement of its youth. Works to combat negative peer pressure and develop and use talents of Native youth. Conducts youth leadership seminars; assists in the development of tribal, village, and community youth councils; helps youth to formally voice their concerns and opinions at Congressional and Senate hearings. Sponsors Unity Network and National UNITY Council. **Publications:** *UNITY News*, quarterly. Newsletter. Promotes activities of the organization as well as youth council projects. **Circulation:** 15,000. **Advertising:** accepted ● Newsletters, semiannual, fall and winter. Contains information on the activities of the organization. Alternate Formats: online. **Conventions/Meetings:** annual National Unity Conference, for youth leadership development (exhibits) - 2008 July 11-15, Reno, NV.

10757 ■ White Bison
6145 Lehman Dr., Ste.200
Colorado Springs, CO 80918
Ph: (719)548-1000
Fax: (719)548-9407
E-mail: info@whitebison.org
URL: http://www.whitebison.org
Contact: Don Coyhis, Pres./Founder
Founded: 1988. **Description:** Indian communities. Strives to bring 100 Indian communities into healing by the year 2010; aims to bring the message of sobriety and physical, mental, emotional and spiritual wellness to Native communities. Provides programs and resources for recovery from ancient traditions, teachings and ceremonies, including treatment, prevention, recovery and intervention strategies that will lead to sobriety and wellness. Hosts Circles of Recovery program. Produces t-shirts, mugs, kits, videotapes, audiocassettes, and posters. **Programs:** Coalition Building; Conflict Resolution; Diversity; Healing Forest; Leadership Training; Servant Leadership. **Publications:** *Wellbriety!*. Magazine. Provides news of the Wellbriety Movement. Alternate Formats: online ● Books. **Conventions/Meetings:** annual Circles of Recovery - conference.

Nature Religions

10758 ■ Hedonic Society of America (HSA)
Address Unknown since 2008
Founded: 2001. **Membership Dues:** individual, $30 (annual) ● student, low income, $15 (annual) ● family (2 adults & children under 16), $45 (annual). **Description:** Promotes enlightened hedonism, a naturalistic lifestance based on the following general principles: knowledge is gained through reasoned study of all available evidence; in the absence of conclusive evidence for a supernatural, ethics and morality must be based on living in the natural world; pleasure and pain are the natural means for determining what is beneficial or harmful to life; those actions best which lead to the greatest pleasure and happiness, or the least pain and suffering, in the long term for all concerned; lives are made most happy and fulfilling by cultivating the higher pleasures of intellectual development, aesthetic appreciation and creativity, and social bonds of friendship, family and romantic love; happiness is best attained in an atmosphere of freedom, tolerance, nonviolence and diversity; enlightened hedonism is a positive worldview, rooted in the teachings of the Carvaka school of India, the Greek philosophers Democritus and Epicurus, the Renaissance and Enlightenment, and the utilitarians of the modern era. **Publications:** *Enjoy Life! The Case for Enlightened Hedonism*. **Conventions/Meetings:** meeting.

Norwegian

10759 ■ Norwegian-American Historical Association (NAHA)
1510 St. Olaf Ave.
Northfield, MN 55057-1097
Ph: (507)646-3221
Fax: (507)646-3734
E-mail: naha@stolaf.edu
URL: http://www.naha.stolaf.edu
Contact: Kim Holland, Admin. Dir.
Founded: 1925. **Members:** 1,900. **Membership Dues:** associate, $55 (annual) ● sustaining, $125 (annual) ● patron, $250 (annual) ● student, $40 (annual) ● sustaining, $550 (quinquennial). **Staff:** 3. **Description:** Individuals and institutions. Locates, collects, preserves, and interprets Norwegian-American history. **Libraries: Type:** reference. **Holdings:** 8,000; archival material, books, papers, periodicals. **Subjects:** Norwegian-American life. **Awards:** Einar and Eva Lund Haugen Memorial Scholarship. **Frequency:** annual. **Type:** scholarship. **Recipient:** for graduate level work in a Scandinavian-American topic. **Publications:** *Authors Series* ● *Special Publications* ● *Studies and Records* ● *Topical Studies* ● *Travel and Description Series*, periodic. Newsletter ● Newsletter, periodic ● Also publishes manuscript guide. **Conventions/Meetings:** triennial meeting.

Nudism

10760 ■ American Association for Nude Recreation (AANR)
1703 N Main St., Ste.E
Kissimmee, FL 34744
Ph: (407)933-2064
Free: (800)879-6833
Fax: (407)933-7577
E-mail: try-nude@aanr.com
URL: http://www.aanr.com
Contact: Erich E. Schuttauf JD, Exec. Dir.
Founded: 1931. **Members:** 50,000. **Membership Dues:** associate (for individual), $52 (annual) ● dual associate (for family and couple), $81 (annual) ● individual premier, $112 (annual) ● dual premier, $224 (annual) ● introductory national, $35 (annual) ● internet, $19 (annual) ● student, $24 (annual). **Staff:** 15. **Budget:** $1,700,000. **Regional Groups:** 7. **Local Groups:** 226. **Description:** Aims to promote, enhance and protect, in appropriate settings, nude recreation and nude living in the Americas. **Libraries: Type:** reference. **Holdings:** periodicals. **Subjects:** nudism. **Committees:** Government Affairs. **Affiliated With:** International Naturist Federation. **Formerly:** American Sunbathing Association. **Publications:** *The Bulletin*, monthly. Newspaper. Provides information on nudists clubs/nude recreation organizations, and the nudist movement worldwide. **Price:** included in membership dues. **Circulation:** 30,000. **Advertising:** accepted ● *Management Guide*, periodic. Newsletter. **Price:** free. **Circulation:** 500 ● *North American Guide to Nude Recreation*. Directory.

Alternate Formats: CD-ROM ● *Try-Nude Journal.* Magazine. Contains articles and interesting news used to introduce clothes-free recreation to non-nudists and prospective members. **Advertising:** accepted. Alternate Formats: online. **Conventions/Meetings:** annual convention, for AANR members only (exhibits) - held in August ● Nude Recreation Week - meeting.

10761 ■ Beach Education Advocates for Culture, Health, Environment and Safety (BEACHES)
PO Box 530702
Miami Shores, FL 33153
Ph: (305)620-7090
Fax: (305)620-7091
E-mail: exdirbeaches@aol.com
URL: http://www.beachesfoundation.org
Contact: Shirley Mason, Exec. Dir./Sec.
Founded: 1999. **Membership Dues:** chapter group, $500 (annual). **Staff:** 5. **Regional Groups:** 2. **State Groups:** 4. **Local Groups:** 1. **National Groups:** 2. **Description:** Naturist activists and supporters. Promotes clothing-optional beaches and public sites. **Libraries: Type:** open to the public. **Holdings:** 13. **Subjects:** culture, health, environment, safety, legal. **Also Known As:** (1999) B.E.A.C.H.E.S. Foundation Institute. **Publications:** *Beach Buzz,* quarterly. Journal. **Price:** $30.00/year. **Circulation:** 25,000. **Advertising:** accepted. **Conventions/Meetings:** annual board meeting ● annual conference ● tour and workshop - 2-4/year.

10762 ■ BeachFront USA (BFUSA)
PO Box 328
Moreno Valley, CA 92556
Ph: (949)240-3183
E-mail: info@bfusa.org
URL: http://www.bfusa.org
Contact: Bill Roe, Dir.
Founded: 1973. **Members:** 82. **Membership Dues:** individual, $15 (annual) ● family, $20 (annual). **Staff:** 7. **Budget:** $2,000. **Description:** Individuals advocating the concept of nudism as "wholesomeness of the human body and its natural functions and activities." Promotes the legalization of clothes-optional recreation at designated beaches and other public sites. Represents the nudist and freebeach communities. Seeks to educate the public on nudist culture. Maintains the Callen-Davis Memorial Fund to provide funding for legal action to secure nudist rights. Provides speakers for radio and television talk shows. Markets items of interest to supporters. Compiles statistics. **Libraries: Type:** not open to the public. **Holdings:** 1,800; books, periodicals. **Subjects:** Nudism. **Funds:** Callen-Davis Memorial. **Absorbed:** (1985) Free Beaches Coalition. **Publications:** *Free Beach News,* bimonthly. Newsletter. Contains association news, updates on California free beaches, worldwide items about civil rights and news of the Callen-Davis Memorial Fund. **Price:** $15.00 /year for individuals; $20.00/year for families. **Circulation:** 125 ● Also publishes a guide to nudist beaches and resorts in southern California, free for SASE. **Conventions/Meetings:** annual meeting - always last Saturday of January.

10763 ■ The Naturist Society (TNS)
PO Box 132
Oshkosh, WI 54903
Ph: (920)426-5009
Free: (800)886-7230
Fax: (920)426-5184
E-mail: naturist@naturistsociety.com
URL: http://www.naturistsociety.com
Contact: Ms. Nicky Hoffman Lee, Co-Owner
Founded: 1976. **Members:** 20,000. **Membership Dues:** regular in U.S., $53 (annual) ● senior, student, $43 (annual) ● in Canada, $58 (annual) ● foreign, $68 (annual). **Staff:** 7. **Budget:** $1,050,000. **Regional Groups:** 280. **State Groups:** 4. **Local Groups:** 1. **National Groups:** 86. **For-Profit. Multinational. Description:** Provides communication and coordination for the clothes-optional recreation movement as a natural solution to many problems of modern living. Believes that "body acceptance is the idea, nude recreation is the way". Conducts research programs, Speaker's Bureau, and specialized education. **Libraries: Type:** reference. **Holdings:** 10,000; archival material, audiovisuals, books, clippings, monographs, periodicals. **Subjects:** nudism, body acceptance, health, travel. **Awards:** Baxandall Award. **Frequency:** annual. **Type:** recognition. **Recipient:** to members ● Lifetime Achievement Award. **Frequency:** annual. **Type:** recognition. **Recipient:** for outstanding achievements towards body acceptance. **Committees:** Naturist Action; Naturist Education Foundation. **Formerly:** (1979) Free Beaches Information Center; (1980) Free Beaches Documentation Center; (1983) The Naturists. **Publications:** *N: Nude and Natural,* quarterly. Journal. **Price:** $8.00. ISSN: 0883-4325. **Circulation:** 26,000. **Advertising:** accepted. Alternate Formats: online ● *Naturist Action Committee Newsletter,* monthly. ISSN: 1075-735X. **Circulation:** 2,000 ● *Nude and Natural,* quarterly. Magazine. Contains information for the serious naturist and the newcomer to clothing-optional living and recreation. **Advertising:** accepted ● *World Guide to Nude Beaches and Resorts.* Book. **Conventions/Meetings:** annual Eastern Naturist Gathering - meeting (exhibits).

Onomatology

10764 ■ American Name Society (ANS)
c/o Dr. Michael F. McGoff, Vice Provost/Treas.
Off. of the Provost
Binghamton Univ.
State Univ. of New York
Binghamton, NY 13902-6000
Ph: (607)777-2143
Fax: (607)777-4831
E-mail: mmcgoff@binghamton.edu
URL: http://www.wtsn.binghamton.edu/ans
Contact: Dr. Michael F. McGoff, Vice Provost/Treas.
Founded: 1951. **Members:** 800. **Membership Dues:** individual, $40 (annual) ● individual outside U.S., $45 (annual) ● individual in Canada, $42 (annual). **Staff:** 1. **Budget:** $20,000. **Regional Groups:** 5. **Local Groups:** 5. **Multinational. Description:** Professional society of onomatologists, including linguists, geographers, literary historians, and others interested in the study of the etymology, origin, meaning, and application of place names; personal names; scientific, popular, and commercial nomenclature and the publication of dictionaries, monographs, and pamphlets in the field of onomastics. Conducts research on the origin and meaning of names. **Libraries: Type:** reference; not open to the public. **Holdings:** 52; archival material, periodicals. **Subjects:** all aspects of personal, geographic and literary names. **Committees:** Literary Onomastics; Personal Names Study; Toponymic Interest Group. **Affiliated With:** American Dialect Society; Linguistic Society of America. **Publications:** *Names: A Journal of Onomastics,* quarterly. Contains articles on onomastics; includes book reviews. **Price:** included in membership dues; $40.00 /year for nonmembers in U.S.; $45.00 /year for nonmembers outside U.S. ISSN: 0027-7728. **Circulation:** 800 ● *Names Bulletin,* 3/year. **Conventions/Meetings:** annual conference, held in conjunction with Modern Language Association of America (exhibits) ● annual lecture (exhibits).

Opera

10765 ■ Gerda Lissner Foundation
135 E 55th St.
New York, NY 10022
Ph: (212)826-6100
Fax: (212)826-0366
E-mail: mail@gerdalissner.com
URL: http://gerdalissner.com
Contact: Betty Smith, Pres.
Founded: 1994. **Members:** 5. **Multinational. Description:** Works to help gifted singers develop their talent into an international career in opera, including coaches; teachers for opera languages, acting, dance, etc; guidance in makeup and etiquette grants for stage clothing, domestic and foreign travel, etc. **Awards:** Encouragement Grants. **Frequency:** annual. **Type:** monetary. **Conventions/Meetings:** annual competition, open to men and women upon completion of vocal study, regardless of age, nationality, professional experience, repertoire, or recommendation - usually mid-July, in New York City, NY.

Orchestras

10766 ■ World Federation of Amateur Orchestras (WFAO)
c/o Steve Hobson
811 Essex Cir.
Grayslake, IL 60030
Ph: (847)548-6443
Fax: (847)492-3872
E-mail: info@wfao.org
URL: http://www.wfao.org
Contact: Steve Hobson, Contact
Founded: 1991. **Languages:** English, French, Japanese, Spanish. **Multinational. Description:** Aims to establish and develop a worldwide amateur orchestra network. Fosters mutual communication among amateur and youth orchestras and their associations throughout the world. Promotes and encourages the creation and development of amateur orchestras. Supports worldwide amateur and youth orchestra activities. **Telecommunication Services:** electronic mail, shobson@wfao.org ● electronic mail, shobson@dist113.org.

Pacific

10767 ■ Pacific Islanders' Cultural Association (PICA)
1016 Lincoln Blvd., No. 5
San Francisco, CA 94129
Ph: (415)281-0221
E-mail: info@pica-org.org
URL: http://www.pica-org.org
Contact: Shirley Avilla, Pres.
Founded: 1995. **Description:** Works to develop the histories, cultures, and traditions of Pacific Islanders through educational and social activities.

Paganism

10768 ■ Pagan/Occult/Witchcraft Special Interest Group (POWSIG)
c/o American Mensa, Ltd.
1229 Corporate Dr. W
Arlington, TX 76006-6103
Ph: (817)607-0060
Free: (800)66-MENSA
Fax: (817)649-5232
E-mail: nationaloffice@americanmensa.org
URL: http://www.us.mensa.org
Contact: Jonathan Elliot, SIG Off.
Founded: 1975. **Members:** 50. **Membership Dues:** regular, $52 (annual). **Staff:** 3. **Budget:** $500. **Description:** A special interest group of Mensa (see separate entry). Individuals sharing a practical or academic interest in witchcraft, nature religions, mythological traditions of various cultures, or related topics. Promotes communication and contact among members; disseminates information about paganism and related topics; fosters spiritual exploration with a view to a "healthy community on a healthy planet". Provides consultation to law enforcement and other public officials. **Publications:** *Interloc,* 10/year. Newsletter. Serves as a communications link for sharing thought-provoking ideas, suggestions and concerns relative to Mensa. **Price:** free for members ● *POW!,* quarterly. Newsletter. Includes book, recording, and film reviews, poetry, how-to materials, obituaries and rites of passage. **Price:** $10.00 /year for nonmembers; included in membership dues. **Circulation:** 50. **Advertising:** accepted.

Papyrology

10769 ■ American Society of Papyrologists (ASP)
c/o University of Cincinnati
U.S. Department of of Classics ML 226
410 Blegen Lib.
Cincinnati, OH 45221-0226
Ph: (513)556-4366
Fax: (513)556-4366
E-mail: asp@papyrology.org
URL: http://classics.uc.edu/asp
Contact: Maryline Parca, Pres.

Founded: 1961. **Members:** 325. **Membership Dues:** regular, $30 (annual) ● student, $15 (annual) ● spouse, $10 (annual). **Description:** Represents University professors and others with a special interest in the field of papyrology (the study of papyrus, writing paper of the ancient Egyptians made from the papyrus plant, and of manuscripts written on this material). Promotes and facilitates research in papyrology and provides aid to students in this field. **Publications:** *American Studies in Papyrology*, periodic. Monograph. **Price:** $35.00 for institutions; $5.00 outside U.S. **Circulation:** 325. **Advertising:** accepted ● *Bulletin of the American Society of Papyrologists*, quarterly. Journal ● Also publishes supplements. **Conventions/Meetings:** annual meeting - usually in early January.

Parliaments

10770 ■ American Institute of Parliamentarians (AIP)
550M Richie Hwy. No. 271
Severna Park, MD 21146
Free: (888)664-0428
Fax: (410)544-4640
E-mail: aip@parliamentaryprocedure.org
URL: http://www.parliamentaryprocedure.org
Contact: Mary D. Smith, Pres.

Founded: 1958. **Members:** 1,350. **Membership Dues:** full-time student (June through May), $20 (annual) ● regular, $55 (annual). **Staff:** 1. **Budget:** $80,000. **Regional Groups:** 8. **National Groups:** 40. **Description:** Parliamentarians and others interested in parliamentary procedure. Promotes the preparation and use of parliamentary literature. Conducts certification program qualifying members in two classes: Certified Parliamentarian and Certified Professional Parliamentarian. Encourages teaching of and provides speakers on parliamentary procedure in universities, colleges, and high schools. Conducts research. Sponsors practicums (four day seminars in different parts of the country; scholarships available). Offers correspondence courses. **Libraries: Type:** reference. **Holdings:** 400. **Subjects:** parliamentary procedure. **Awards:** Practicum Scholarship. **Frequency:** annual. **Type:** scholarship. **Recipient:** for college students. **Telecommunication Services:** electronic mail, parliamary@insight.rr.com. **Committees:** Accrediting; Education; Ethics; Member Service; Parliamentary Opinions; Public Relations; Publications and Marketing; Scholarships; Youth. **Publications:** *Communicator*, quarterly. Newsletter. Contains information about upcoming events and includes parliamentary procedure information and resources. ● *Parliamentary Journal*, quarterly. Features articles on parliamentary procedures and meetings. **Price:** $60.00 in U.S. and Canada; $6.00/issue. ISSN: 0048-2994. **Circulation:** 1,600. **Conventions/Meetings:** annual assembly and workshop (exhibits) ● semiannual Practicums - workshop, offers practical experience with parliamentary procedure - every January and June.

10771 ■ National Association of Parliamentarians (NAP)
213 S Main St.
Independence, MO 64050-3850
Ph: (816)833-3892
Free: (888)NAP-2929
Fax: (816)833-3893
E-mail: hq@nap2.org
URL: http://www.parliamentarians.org
Contact: Sarah Nieft, Exec. Dir.

Founded: 1930. **Members:** 4,000. **Membership Dues:** regular, $62 (annual). **Staff:** 3. **Budget:** $250,000. **State Groups:** 42. **Local Groups:** 285. **Multinational. Description:** Represents persons interested in parliamentary procedure. Works to study, teach, promote, and disseminate the democratic principles of parliamentary law and procedure. Conducts examination and awards title of Registered Parliamentarian. Maintains referral service of Professional Registered Parliamentarians. **Libraries: Type:** reference. **Holdings:** 600. **Subjects:** parliamentary law. **Computer Services:** Mailing lists. **Telecommunication Services:** electronic mail, sarah@nap2.org. **Publications:** *Membership Manual of National Association of Parliamentarians*, biennial. Membership Directory. Includes listings of state and local groups. Also contains association rules, bylaws, and ethical standards. **Circulation:** 4,000 ● *National Parliamentarian*, quarterly. Magazine. Includes articles on parliamentary procedure, convention information, and notices of proposed changes in NAP bylaws. **Price:** $20.00/year. ISSN: 8755-7592 ● Books ● Also publishes training guides. **Conventions/Meetings:** biennial convention (exhibits) - odd-numbered years ● biennial National Training Conference - even-numbered years.

Pennsylvania Dutch

10772 ■ Folk Heritage Institute (FHI)
PO Box 141
Glenville, PA 17329
Ph: (717)235-4235
Contact: Marsha McKnight, Pres.

Founded: 1975. **Members:** 95. **Description:** Craftsmen, farmers, musicians, folk dancers, historians, government officials, and other persons interested in preserving Pennsylvania Dutch culture, including music, customs, beliefs, and farming and cooking techniques. Conducts educational programs on construction techniques for musical instruments, pottery, animal care, and the collecting of oral history. Offers musical presentations and activities for senior citizens. **Publications:** Newsletter, periodic.

Performing Arts

10773 ■ Global Alliance of Performers (GAP)
19924 Aurora Ave. N, Ste.101
Seattle, WA 98133
Ph: (206)264-5072
E-mail: info@gap.org
URL: http://www.gap.org

Founded: 1991. **Multinational. Description:** Represents the interests of performers, artists, charities, technicians, businesses and the general public dedicated to creating a better world through music, education and community. Increases public awareness of important social and environmental concerns.

10774 ■ International Guild of Musicians in Dance (IGMID)
c/o Larry Attaway, Sec.-Treas.
5144 Boulevard Pl.
Indianapolis, IN 46208
E-mail: lattaway@butler.edu
URL: http://www.dancemusician.org
Contact: Larry Attaway, Sec.-Treas.

Founded: 1990. **Membership Dues:** regular, $35 (annual). **Multinational. Description:** Aims to establish standards of excellence for musicians involved in the field of art dance. Fosters collaborative relationships between dancers and musicians. Documents the history of musicians in dance. Develops training programs for musicians in dance. **Telecommunication Services:** electronic mail, jt@dancemusician.org. **Publications:** Journal. Alternate Formats: online ● Newsletter.

10775 ■ National New Deal Preservation Association (NNDPA)
PO Box 602
Santa Fe, NM 87504-0602
Ph: (505)473-3985
Fax: (505)473-3985
E-mail: newdeal@cybermesa.com
URL: http://www.newdeallegacy.org
Contact: Kathy Flynn, Exec. Dir.

Membership Dues: individual, $25 (annual) ● life, $300 ● institutional/group, $100 (annual) ● family, $45 (annual). **Description:** Aims to identify, document, and preserve the New Deal visual and performing arts, literature, crafts, structures, and environmental projects and to educate people about these legacies. **Publications:** Newsletter. Alternate Formats: online.

10776 ■ Sword Swallowers Association International (SSAI)
3729 Belle Oaks Dr.
Antioch, TN 37013
E-mail: ssai@swordswallow.org
URL: http://www.swordswallow.org
Contact: Dan Meyer, Exec. Dir.

Founded: 2001. **Membership Dues:** regular, $25 (annual). **Multinational. Description:** Promotes and preserves the art of sword swallowing worldwide. Encourages safe sword swallowing practices and techniques. Promotes dialogue between sword swallowers. Works in conjunction with the international medical community to encourage the free exchange of medical knowledge and information on the health risks, complications and treatments associated with sword swallowing. **Additional Websites:** http://www.swordswallow.com. **Telecommunication Services:** electronic mail, dan@swordswallow.org.

Philanthropy

10777 ■ Andrew W. Mellon Foundation (AWMF)
140 E 62nd St.
New York, NY 10065-8124
Ph: (212)838-8400 (609)924-9424
Fax: (212)500-2302
E-mail: inquiries@mellon.org
URL: http://www.mellon.org
Contact: Don Michael Randel, Pres.

Founded: 1969. **Description:** Provides aid and support to religious, charitable, scientific, literary, and educational purposes to further the well-being of mankind. **Publications:** Annual Report, annual. Alternate Formats: online.

Philatelic

10778 ■ Journalists, Authors and Poets on Stamps Study Unit (JAPOS)
800 E River Dr., Unit B
De Pere, WI 54115-4159
Ph: (920)339-9117
E-mail: cdelvaux@msn.com
Contact: Clete Delvaux, Pres.

Founded: 1974. **Members:** 50. **Membership Dues:** regular, in U.S., $7 (annual) ● regular, outside U.S., $10 (annual). **Multinational. Description:** Studies writers on stamps; researches history and biographies of individual writers portrayed on postal stamps and postal and philatelic history, including fairy tales on stamps. **Libraries: Type:** reference. **Holdings:** archival material. **Affiliated With:** American First Day Cover Society; American Philatelic Society; American Topical Association. **Publications:** *JAPOS Bulletin*, quarterly. Newsletter. **Price:** free for members. **Circulation:** 60. **Advertising:** accepted. **Conventions/Meetings:** periodic meeting.

Philippine

10779 ■ Filipino American National Historical Society (FANHS)
810 18th Ave., Rm. 100
Seattle, WA 98122

Ph: (206)322-0203
E-mail: fanhsnational@earthlink.net
URL: http://www.fanhs-national.org
Contact: Dr. Dorothy Laigo Cordova, Exec. Dir./Founder

Founded: 1982. **Members:** 1,000. **Membership Dues:** individual, $35 (annual) ● family, $50 (annual) ● student, senior, $15 (annual) ● individual (life), $500 ● family (life), $600. **Description:** Gathers, maintains, and disseminates Filipino American history. Conducts research programs, public forums and is currently developing a museum. **Libraries: Type:** reference. **Holdings:** archival material. **Awards: Type:** grant. **Recipient:** for research ● **Type:** recognition. **Publications:** *Filipino Americans: Discovering Their Past for the Future*. Video. **Price:** $31.79 for members in Washington State; $29.50 for members outside Washington State; $36.09 for nonmembers in Washington State; $33.45 for nonmembers outside Washington State ● Bibliography ● Journal, biennial. **Price:** $8.00 for members, plus shipping and handling; $10.00 for nonmembers, plus shipping and handling. **Conventions/Meetings:** biennial conference.

10780 ■ National Federation of Filipino American Associations
2607 24th St. NW, Ste.4
Washington, DC 20008-2600
Ph: (202)986-1153
Fax: (202)478-5109
E-mail: admin@naffaa.org
URL: http://www.naffaa.org
Contact: Jonathan Melegrito, Natl. Communications Dir.

Founded: 1997. **Members:** 600. **Membership Dues:** individual (charter), $50 (annual) ● organization, $100 (annual) ● individual, $25 (annual). **Staff:** 3. **Budget:** $100,000. **Regional Groups:** 10. **State Groups:** 32. **Local Groups:** 520. **National Groups:** 12. **Languages:** English, Tagalog. **Description:** Filipino American individuals and organizations. Seeks to promote the interests and well-being of the 3 million Filipinos and Filipino Americans residing in the United States by getting them involved as leaders and participants in United States society. Major programs include citizenship and leadership development, voter education, entrepreneurial training, and community development. **Libraries: Type:** by appointment only. **Holdings:** archival material, clippings, periodicals. **Awards:** Azores Fellowship Award. **Frequency:** annual. **Type:** fellowship. **Recipient:** for community leadership and summer internship. **Conventions/Meetings:** annual convention and trade show, with photo exhibits (exhibits).

Philosophy

10781 ■ Aesthetic Realism Foundation (ARF)
141 Greene St.
New York, NY 10012
Ph: (212)777-4490
Fax: (212)777-4426
URL: http://www.aestheticrealism.org
Contact: Ellen Reiss, Class Chair/Ed.

Founded: 1973. **Staff:** 50. **Languages:** English, French, German, Hebrew, Italian, Portuguese, Spanish. **Nonmembership. Description:** Teaches Aesthetic Realism, the philosophy founded in 1941 by American poet and educator Eli Siegel (1902-78). Aesthetic Realism is defined as "the art of liking the world and oneself at the same time by seeing the world and oneself as aesthetic opposites". Believes that the aesthetic method of criticism, including criticism of contempt, results in knowledge, real justice to things and people, and true self-respect. Conducts: classes in poetry, education, art, music, anthropology; weekly public seminars and dramatic presentations; and individual consultations in person and by telephone. Offers classes for children and talks titled "The Aesthetic Realism of Eli Siegel Shows How Art Answers the Questions of Your Life!". Operates the Terrain Gallery with permanent collection and exhibitions. **Libraries: Type:** reference. **Holdings:** 29,800; audio recordings, books. **Subjects:** aesthetics, approaches to mind, art and literary criticism, drama, history, labor and economics, philosophy, poetry, the sciences, world literature. **Affiliated With:** Nonprofit Coordinating Committee of New York. **Publications:** *A Rosary of Evil* ● *The American Family Versus American Art* ● *Eleven Aesthetic Realism Essays* ● *The Furious Aesthetics of Marriage* ● *The Opposites Class* ● *The Right of Aesthetic Realism to Be Known*, biweekly. Journal. Contains works by Eli Siegel, commentary by Ellen Reiss, and articles by Aesthetic Realism consultants. **Price:** $18.00/6 months, in U.S.; $14.00/6 months, in Canada and Mexico; $20.00/6 months, outside North America. ISSN: 0882-3731. Alternate Formats: online ● *Ten More Aesthetic Realism Essays*. Book ● *The Two Selves of Jessica Throckmorton*. Book.

10782 ■ American Maritain Association (AMA)
c/o John Trapani, Jr., Pres.
Walsh Univ.
2020 Easton St. NW
North Canton, OH 44720-3336
E-mail: jtrapani@walsh.edu
URL: http://www.jacquesmaritain.org
Contact: John Trapani Jr., Pres.

Founded: 1977. **Members:** 500. **Membership Dues:** regular, $40 (annual). **Staff:** 5. **Languages:** English, French. **Description:** Academicians and other individuals interested in the philosophy of Jacques Maritain (1882-1973), French philosopher and Catholic intellectual interpreter of the philosophy of St. Thomas Aquinas. Seeks to develop a social and formative cultural movement based on research, study, and critical interpretation of all aspects of Maritain's life and work, particularly with regard to the broader areas of Thomism. Works to apply these studies as practical and viable solutions to problems of contemporary society and culture. Annual volumes are distributed by the University of Notre Dame Press and the Catholic University of American Press, Washington, D.C. Sponsors annual conference. **Libraries: Type:** not open to the public. **Holdings:** 500; books, periodicals. **Subjects:** works by Jacques Maritain and contemporaries. **Awards:** Maritain Medal Award. **Frequency:** annual. **Type:** recognition. **Committees:** Research and Publications. **Publications:** *Beauty, Art and The Polis*, annual. Book. **Price:** $15.00 ● *The Common Things: Essays on Thomism and Education*. Book. **Price:** $14.00 ● *Freedom in the Modern World: Jacques Maritain, Yves R. Simon, Mortimer Adler*. Book. **Price:** $14.00 ● *Freedom, Virtue, and the Common Good*. Book. **Price:** $14.00 ● *From Twilight to Dawn: The Cultural Vision of Jacques Maritain*. Book ● *The Future of Thomism*. Book. **Price:** $14.00 ● *Jacques Maritain and the Jews*. Book. **Price:** $14.00 ● *Jacques Maritain: The Man and His Metaphysics*. Book. **Price:** $14.00 ● *Jacques Maritain & The Many Ways of Knowing, 2002*. Book. **Price:** $14.00 ● *Maritain Notebook*, quarterly. Newsletter. **Price:** included in membership dues. **Circulation:** 500. **Advertising:** accepted ● *Postmodernism and Christian Philosophy*. Book. **Price:** $14.00 ● *Truth Matters: Essays in Honor of Jacques Maritain*. Book. **Conventions/Meetings:** annual conference and symposium (exhibits).

10783 ■ American Philosophical Association (APA)
Univ. of Delaware
31 Amstel Ave.
Newark, DE 19716-4797
Ph: (302)831-1112
Fax: (302)831-8690
E-mail: apaonline@udel.edu
URL: http://www.apa.udel.edu/apa/index.html
Contact: David Schrader, Exec. Dir.

Founded: 1900. **Members:** 11,000. **Membership Dues:** regular (based on annual income), $45-$250 (annual) ● life, $2,500 ● international associate, student associate in U.S. and Canada, $35 (annual) ● student associate overseas, $45 (annual). **Staff:** 9. **Budget:** $800,000. **Regional Groups:** 3. **Description:** College and university teachers of philosophy and others with an interest in philosophy. Facilitates exchange of ideas in philosophy, encourages creative and scholarly activity in philosophy, and fosters the professional work of teachers of philosophy. Participates in international congresses of philosophy and maintains affiliations with national and international philosophical organizations. Maintains placement service; sponsors competitions. Oversees selection of Romanell, Schutz and Carus lecturers and other prizes and awards. **Computer Services:** database ● mailing lists. **Telecommunication Services:** electronic mail, dschrade@udel.edu. **Committees:** Academic Career Opportunities and Placement; American Indians; Asian and Asian-American Philosophers and Philosophies; Blacks in Philosophy; Computers; Defense of Professional Rights of Philosophers; Hispanics; International Cooperation; Law; Lectures, Publications, and Research; Lesbian, Gay, Bisexual, and Transgender People in the Profession; Medicine; Non-Academic Careers; Pre-College Instruction in Philosophy; Status and Future of the Profession; Teaching of Philosophy; Two-Year Colleges; Women. **Publications:** *APA Newsletter*, semiannual, fall and spring. Published by the Committee of Philosophy and Medicine. **Price:** included in membership dues. ISSN: 1067-9464. **Advertising:** accepted. Alternate Formats: online ● *Guidebook to Graduate Programs in Philosophy*, biennial ● *Jobs for Philosophers*, quarterly, October, November, February, May. Features ads for available philosophy positions. **Advertising:** accepted. Alternate Formats: online ● *Proceedings & Address of the American Philosophical Association*, 5/year, September, November, January, February, May. Features news and events of the association. Alternate Formats: online. **Conventions/Meetings:** annual Eastern, Central, Pacific Divisional Meetings - conference and meeting, book exhibits (exhibits) - usually March (Pacific Division), April (Central Division), and December (Eastern Division).

10784 ■ American Society for Value Inquiry (ASVI)
c/o Joram G. Haber, Sec.-Treas.
Dept. of Philosophy
Bergen Community Coll.
400 Paramus Rd.
Paramus, NJ 07652-1595
Ph: (201)447-9282
E-mail: jghaber@rockland.net
URL: http://www.mindspring.com/~mfpatton/asvinlet3.htm
Contact: Joram G. Haber, Sec.-Treas.

Founded: 1970. **Members:** 200. **Membership Dues:** $53 (annual). **Regional Groups:** 3. **Description:** Represents University and college professors; persons with an MA or PhD interested in the study of values. **Affiliated With:** American Philosophical Association. **Publications:** *Journal of Value Inquiry*, quarterly. Seeks work in meta-disciplinary value inquiry that includes value theory and meta-ethics. ISSN: 0022-5363 ● Newsletter, semiannual. **Conventions/Meetings:** annual Conference on Value Inquiry - convention (exhibits) - spring.

10785 ■ Association for Informal Logic and Critical Thinking (AILACT)
c/o Donald Hatcher, Treas.
Ctr. for Critical Thinking
Baker Univ.
Baldwin City, KS 66006
E-mail: don.hatcher@bakeru.edu
URL: http://www.humanities.mcmaster.ca/~ailact
Contact: Donald Hatcher, Treas.

Founded: 1983. **Members:** 250. **Membership Dues:** individual, $6 (annual). **Staff:** 2. **Description:** University and college professors of philosophy and the humanities who teach informal logic and critical thinking; researchers of the theory of reasoning; interested individuals. Seeks to encourage research, scholarly exchange, and improved teaching. Sponsors sessions and meetings in conjunction with the American Philosophical Association and Canadian Philosophical Association. **Additional Websites:** http://ailact.mcmaster.ca. **Publications:** Papers. Contain information on symposia. ● Also makes available bibliographic materials on critical thinking.

10786 ■ Association for Philosophy of the Unconscious (APU)
Dept. of Philosophy
Georgetown Univ.
Washington, DC 20057
Ph: (202)687-7613
Fax: (202)687-4493
E-mail: vereeckw@georgetown.edu
Contact: Prof. W. Ver Eecke, Pres.
Founded: 1971. **Members:** 150. **Membership Dues:** individual, $5 (annual) ● student, $2 (annual). **Description:** Individuals interested in philosophy and psychoanalysis. Conducts philosophical discussions on the conceptual problems of psychoanalysis. Members prepare papers for presentation at meetings. **Publications:** Newsletter, annual. Contains information and suggested reading for the annual meeting. **Price:** included in membership dues. **Conventions/Meetings:** annual meeting, held in conjunction with American Philosophical Association, Eastern Division - always December, between Christmas and New Year.

10787 ■ Ayn Rand Institute (ARI)
2121 Alton Pkwy., Ste.250
Irvine, CA 92606-4926
Ph: (949)222-6550
Fax: (949)222-6558
E-mail: mail@aynrand.org
URL: http://www.aynrand.org
Contact: Dr. Yaron Brook, Pres./Exec. Dir.
Founded: 1985. **Members:** 4,000. **Staff:** 28. **Budget:** $3,500,000. **Description:** Works to promote increased awareness and understanding of Objectivism as defined by philosopher, essayist, and novelist Ayn Rand (1905-82), author of *The Fountainhead, Atlas Shrugged*, and other books. (Rand's philosophy of Objectivism upholds the supremacy of individual rights through advocacy of reason as the ultimate source of knowledge, self-interest as the proper code of ethics, and laissez-faire capitalism as the ideal political-economic system.) Believes that "historical trends are the inescapable product of philosophy." Seeks to change current political and economic trends in the U.S. by changing underlying philosophies, primarily by introducing Rand's Objectivism into university courses and classrooms. Establishes Objectivist clubs at colleges and universities to foster an increased interest in Objectivist philosophy among students. Disseminates literature and teaching aids on Objectivism. Maintains college campus speakers' bureau. Holds workshops; conducts seminars for graduate students in philosophy. **Awards: Type:** grant. **Recipient:** for university students attending conferences or Objectivist Academic Center ● **Type:** scholarship. **Recipient:** for high school and college students. **Publications:** *Impact: Newsletter of the Ayn Rand Institute*, monthly. Bulletin. Covers events and activities. **Price:** $35.00 contribution. **Circulation:** 3,500. **Conventions/Meetings:** annual conference - 2008 June 28-July 6, Newport Beach, CA; 2009 July 3-11, Boston, MA.

10788 ■ Ayn Rand Society (ARS)
c/o Prof. Allan Gotthelf, Chm.
Univ. of Pittsburgh
Dept. of History and Philosophy of Sci.
1017 Cathedral of Learning
Pittsburgh, PA 15260
E-mail: ars@aynrandsociety.org
URL: http://www.aynrandsociety.org
Contact: Prof. Allan Gotthelf, Chm.
Founded: 1987. **Membership Dues:** regular, $20 (annual) ● student, $10 (annual) ● contributor, $30 (annual). **Description:** Fosters scholarly study by philosophers of philosophical thought and writings of Ayn Rand. **Committees:** Steering. **Publications:** Papers. Contain information on the society's program in advance of the meeting. **Price:** included in membership dues ● Books ● Journal. **Conventions/Meetings:** annual meeting, held in conjunction with the annual meeting of the APA Eastern Division.

10789 ■ Center for Process Studies (CPS)
1325 N Coll. Ave.
Claremont, CA 91711
Ph: (909)621-5330
Fax: (909)621-2760
E-mail: process@ctr4process.org
URL: http://www.ctr4process.org
Contact: John Quiring PhD, Program Dir.
Founded: 1973. **Members:** 540. **Membership Dues:** international, $60 (annual) ● contributing, $150 (annual) ● general, $40 (annual) ● sustaining, $300 (annual) ● associate, $500 (annual) ● Hartshorne, $1,000 (annual) ● participating, $50 (annual). **Staff:** 10. **Budget:** $220,000. **Languages:** Chinese, English, German, Japanese, Korean. **Description:** Encourages exploration of the relevance of process thought to many fields of reflection and action. Promotes a new way of thinking based on the work of philosophers Alfred North Whitehead (1861-1947) and Charles Hartshorne (1897-2000) through seminars, conferences, publications and a library. **Libraries: Type:** reference; lending; open to the public. **Holdings:** 10,000; archival material, audiovisuals, books, clippings, monographs, periodicals. **Subjects:** process thought, feminism, ecology, environment, science, religion, philosophy. **Computer Services:** Mailing lists. **Telecommunication Services:** electronic mail, johnq@ctr4process.org. **Programs:** Process and Faith. **Projects:** China. **Publications:** *Process Perspectives: Newsletter of the Center of Process Studies*, 3/year. Reports on events and publications of interest to scholars of Whiteheadian and process thought. **Price:** $15.00 /year for individuals in U.S.; $22.00 /year for individuals outside U.S. ISSN: 0360-618X. **Circulation:** 600 ● *Process Studies*, semiannual. Journal. Contains articles of interest to scholars on the work of Whitehead, Hartshorne and related thinkers. **Price:** $26.00 /year for individuals in U.S.; $33.00 /year for individuals outside U.S.; $50.00 /year for institutions in U.S.; $60.00 /year for institutions outside U.S. ISSN: 0360-6503. **Circulation:** 880. **Advertising:** accepted. **Conventions/Meetings:** conference - 1-3/year ● seminar, with a one-hour presentation and a one-hour discussion period - 12-15/year.

10790 ■ Conference of Philosophical Societies (CoPS)
c/o G. John M. Abbarno, Pres.
Div. of Liberal Arts
D'Youville Coll.
Buffalo, NY 14201-2486
E-mail: abbarnojo@dyc.edu
URL: http://216.25.45.103/Philosophical_Calendar
Contact: G. John M. Abbarno, Pres.
Founded: 1976. **Membership Dues:** society, $10 (annual). **Description:** Acts as an umbrella organization for philosophical societies or associations whose membership is composed primarily of doctors of philosophy or educators in the field. Seeks to present North American professional philosophy to the public, agencies and foundations, and international bodies. Disseminates information; provides a forum for discussion; facilitates joint action. **Publications:** *Directory of Philosophical Societies*, periodic. Lists philosophical societies; includes information on their purposes, activities, and officers. **Price:** included in membership dues; $4.50 for nonmembers. **Circulation:** 150 ● *Philosophical Calendar*, bimonthly. Lists philosophical meetings throughout North America and selected international conferences. **Price:** included in membership dues; $6.00 /year for nonmembers. ISSN: 1090-3240. **Circulation:** 550. Alternate Formats: online ● Newsletter, semiannual. **Price:** included in membership dues. **Circulation:** 150. **Conventions/Meetings:** conference, held in conjunction with the American Philosophical Association - 3/year ● seminar ● workshop.

10791 ■ Council for Research in Values and Philosophy (RVP)
PO Box 261, Cardinal Sta.
Washington, DC 20064
Ph: (202)319-6089
Free: (800)659-9962
Fax: (202)319-6089
E-mail: cua-rvp@cua.edu
URL: http://www.crvp.org
Contact: George F. McLean, Sec.-Treas.
Founded: 1980. **Members:** 450. **Regional Groups:** 83. **Local Groups:** 7. **National Groups:** 52. **Multinational. Description:** Works to identify human and social issues in philosophy that need researching. Promotes international cooperation among scholars on problems of man and society, man and nature, man and God, and good and evil. Conducts research on cultural heritage and contemporary life in Asia, Africa, Eastern Europe and Latin America and publishes results. Sponsors continuing research seminars and colloquia annually. **Libraries: Type:** reference. **Holdings:** 140. **Subjects:** philosophy, culture. **Publications:** *Cultural Heritage and Contemporary Change*, 25/year. Book. **Price:** $45.00 clothbound; $17.50 paperbound. Alternate Formats: online. **Conventions/Meetings:** Challenges and Prospects of the Dialogue of Cultural Traditions - general assembly.

10792 ■ ERIS Roundtable for Independent Study (ERIS)
Address Unknown since 2007
Founded: 1994. **Members:** 4. **Staff:** 1. **Description:** An independent organization for the discussion of philosophy and its relation to an emerging global society. Focuses on the question, "Why has philosophy failed to resolve its problems?" Discusses the underlying structure of traditional philosophical systems, the transformation to a new structure, and its meaning for cultural evolution and the development of an open world community. **Publications:** *The Controlling Image*. Book. **Conventions/Meetings:** periodic roundtable.

10793 ■ Foundation for Philosophy of Creativity (SPC)
c/o Dr. Larry Cobb, Exec. Dir.
250 Slippery Rock Rd.
Slippery Rock, PA 16057
Ph: (724)794-2938
Fax: (413)604-3279
E-mail: ethicsworks@aol.com
Contact: Dr. Larry Cobb, Exec. Dir.
Founded: 1951. **Members:** 150. **Membership Dues:** academic, $10 (annual). **Regional Groups:** 4. **Description:** Functions as a research group in a cooperative relationship with the American Philosophical Association for the development of philosophy of creativity. Conducts special studies of creativity in the philosophies of Charles Hartshorne, Henry Nelson Wieman, Alfred North Whitehead, George Herbert Mead, William James, John Dewey, Paul Tillich, Henri Bergson, Josiah Royce, William Ernest Hocking, Charles Sanders Peirce, Ernest Cassirer, Richard McKeon, Robert S. Hartman, Paul Weiss, and others. Supports and conducts research on the role of creativity in metaphysics, epistemology, axiology, ethics, aesthetics, religion, science, and the possible function of these philosophical disciplines in both personal and institutional policymaking. **Libraries: Type:** reference. **Subjects:** manuscripts, tapes, and symposia on creativity at the Morris Library, Southern Illinois University, Carbondale, IL. **Awards:** Distinguished Service Award. **Type:** recognition. **Recipient:** for contributions to the study and understanding of creativity. **Affiliated With:** American Philosophical Association. **Formerly:** Society for Philosophy of Creativity; (1958) Creative Ethics Group; (1966) Society for Creative Ethics. **Publications:** *Foundation for Philosophy of Creativity-Monograph Series*, periodic. **Price:** $16.00/copy ● *Foundation for Philosophy of Creativity-Newsletter*, semiannual. Contains book reviews. **Price:** available to members only. **Circulation:** 200. **Conventions/Meetings:** annual meeting, held for each APA division.

10794 ■ Gabriel Marcel Society (GMS)
c/o Prof. Brendan Sweetman, PhD, Pres.
Rockhurst Univ.
1100 Rockhurst Rd.
Kansas City, MO 64110-2561
Ph: (816)501-4681
E-mail: brendan.sweetman@rockhurst.edu
URL: http://www.lemoyne.edu/gms
Contact: Prof. Brendan Sweetman PhD, Pres.
Founded: 1987. **Members:** 100. **Membership Dues:** regular, $10 (annual). **Description:** College and university professors of philosophy, literature, and

theology; ministers and priests. Objective is to encourage scholarship and the exchange of ideas among scholars of French philosopher Gabriel Marcel (1889-1973). Establishes communication with Marcel groups in other countries. **Publications:** Newsletter, semiannual. **Price:** included in membership dues. **Conventions/Meetings:** annual conference, held in conjunction with the American Catholic Philosophical Association.

10795 ■ Institute of Advanced Philosophic Research (IAPR)
PO Box 805
Moultonborough, NH 03254
Ph: (603)253-3311
Fax: (603)253-3311
E-mail: realia@cyberportal.net
Contact: Ms. Lydia Eaton, Exec.Dir.
Founded: 1957. **Members:** 200. **Membership Dues:** individual, $37 (annual) ● individual, $68 (biennial) ● individual, $94 (triennial) ● student, $33 (annual) ● library, $44 (annual). **Staff:** 1. **Description:** Represents professors and students of philosophy, humanities, and social sciences, individuals dedicated to the discovery, clarification, and solution of contemporary and future reality-oriented philosophic problems. Seeks to bring the results of philosophic research into harmony with the findings of scientific principles. Conducts research projects in education, social organization, and humanistic society. Compiles statistics. **Awards: Type:** recognition. **Also Known As:** Realia - Philosophy in Service to Humanity. **Publications:** *Contemporary Philosophy: Philosophic Research, Analysis, and Solutions*, 3/year. Journal. Contains philosophic papers by professionals on contemporary philosophic problems. **Price:** $44.00 /year for libraries; $37.00 /year for individuals; $68.00 2 years for individuals; $94.00 3 years for individuals. **Circulation:** 200. **Advertising:** accepted ● *Philosophic Works*, 3/year. Book. **Price:** $30.00/year student; $17.00 foreign add (for surface mail). **Circulation:** 200. **Advertising:** accepted ● *Philosophy of the Humanistic Society*. Book. **Conventions/Meetings:** competition ● annual conference - always August ● seminar - always summer.

10796 ■ Institute for the Advancement of Philosophy for Children (IAPC)
c/o Montclair State University
Univ. Hall 2151
Montclair, NJ 07043
Ph: (973)655-7049 (973)655-4278
Fax: (973)655-7834
E-mail: gregorym@mail.montclair.edu
URL: http://cehs.montclair.edu/academic/iapc
Contact: Maughn Gregory, Dir.
Founded: 1974. **Staff:** 8. **Budget:** $75,000. **Multinational. Description:** Works to teach children to think independently, logically, and ethically. Encourages recognition of imaginative and intellectual skills and demonstrates how children can be given opportunities to practice them. Seeks to increase children's ability to draw valid inferences, see connections and make distinctions, and discover alternatives. Stresses the need for objectivity and consistency and the importance of giving reasons for opinions. Conducts educational experiments and in-service education for teachers; develops specialized curricula, including the Philosophy for Children program. **Publications:** *Philosophy for Children Curriculum*. Manual. Contains conceptual explanations for teachers as well as discussion exercises and activities that can be used to supplement the students' inquiry. **Price:** $20.00 ● *Thinking: The Journal of Philosophy for Children*, quarterly. Magazine. Contains verbatim transcripts of children discussing philosophical issues, research reports of experimental results, and other articles. **Price:** $45.00 /year for individuals, in U.S. (includes shipping); $70.00 /year for institutions, in U.S.; $60.00 /year for individuals, foreign; $85.00 /year for institutions, foreign. ISSN: 0190-3330. **Circulation:** 350. **Conventions/Meetings:** semiannual international conference.

10797 ■ International Association for Philosophy and Literature (IAPL)
c/o Prof. Hugh J. Silverman, Exec. Dir.
Stony Brook Univ.
Philosophy Dept.
Stony Brook, NY 11794-3750
Ph: (631)331-4598
Fax: (631)331-0142
E-mail: execdir@iapl.info
URL: http://www.iapl.info
Contact: Prof. Hugh J. Silverman, Exec. Dir.
Founded: 1976. **Members:** 1,800. **Membership Dues:** student and retired, $50 (annual) ● regular, $85 (annual) ● life, $700 ● life, supporting, $900 ● institutional, $1,500. **Description:** Represents University and college professors of philosophy, literature, history, and the arts. Encourages study of the relationships between philosophy and literature. Supports contemporary research in literary theory, method, and interpretation. **Computer Services:** Mailing lists. **Publications:** *Call for Papers*, annual ● *Conference Program*, annual ● *Series in Philosophy, Literature and Culture*, annual. Book ● Newsletter, periodic. **Conventions/Meetings:** periodic European Conference ● seminar.

10798 ■ International Berkeley Society (IBS)
Dept. of Philosophy
Texas A and M Univ.
College Station, TX 77843
Ph: (979)845-5660
E-mail: sdaniel@philisophy.tamu.edu
URL: http://georgeberkeley.tamu.edu
Contact: Stephen Daniel, Pres.
Founded: 1975. **Members:** 150. **Membership Dues:** regular, $15 (annual). **Multinational. Description:** Promotes interest in the life and work of the philosopher Bishop George Berkeley. **Libraries: Type:** reference. **Holdings:** 120; articles, books, periodicals. **Subjects:** George Berkeley. **Awards:** Turbayne Berkeley Essay Prize. **Frequency:** biennial. **Type:** monetary. **Recipient:** for scholars who wrote unpublished treatments of some aspect of Berkeley's philosophy. **Publications:** *Berkeley Briefs*, semiannual. Newsletter. Includes news items and other announcements of interest to the Society and its members. **Price:** included in membership dues. Alternate Formats: online ● *Berkeley Newsletter*, annual. Journal. Contains scholarly articles, research notes, abstracts of conference papers, book reviews, and bibliographic updates of the latest work on Berkeley. Alternate Formats: online ● Booklets ● Monographs. **Conventions/Meetings:** annual conference.

10799 ■ International Boethius Society (IBS)
c/o Noel Harold Kaylor, Jr., Exec. Dir.
Dept. of English
Univ. of Northern Iowa
Cedar Falls, IA 50614-0502
Fax: (319)273-5807
E-mail: noel.kaylor@uni.edu
URL: http://ccat.sas.upenn.edu/jod/boethius.society.html
Contact: J. Keith Atkinson, Pres.
Membership Dues: regular in U.S., student outside U.S., $30 (annual) ● regular outside U.S., $32 (annual) ● student in U.S., $28 (annual). **Multinational. Description:** Promotes scholarship on all aspects of the work, influence, and age of Boethius. **Publications:** *Carmina Philosophiae*, annual. Journal. **Price:** included in membership dues ● *IBS Newsletter*, semiannual. **Price:** included in membership dues.

10800 ■ International Federation of Philosophical Societies
c/o William L. McBride, Sec. Gen.
Purdue Univ.
Dept. of Philosophy
100 N Univ. St.
West Lafayette, IN 47907-2098
Ph: (765)494-4285
Fax: (765)496-1616
E-mail: wmcbride@purdue.edu
URL: http://www.fisp.org
Contact: William L. McBride, Sec. Gen.
Founded: 1948. **Members:** 102. **Membership Dues:** national or international philosophy society, 200 SFr (annual). **Budget:** $12,000. **Languages:** English, French, German, Russian, Spanish. **Multinational. Description:** Represents national and international philosophical societies, academies, and unions. Promotes international cooperation in the field of philosophy. **Committees:** Congresses and Meetings; Intercultural Research in Philosophy. **Publications:** *Congress Proceedings*, quinquennial ● *FISP Newsletter*, semiannual. Alternate Formats: online ● *The Idea of Values: A Short History of the International Federation of Philosophical Societies* ● *Ideas Underlying World Problems*, periodic. Book. Features a series of books. ● *Les philosophes et la technique* ● *Socrates for Everybody*. **Conventions/Meetings:** quinquennial congress ● World Congress of Philosophy (exhibits).

10801 ■ International Husserl and Phenomenological Research Society (IHPRS)
c/o World Phenomenology Institute
1 Ivy Pointe Way
Hanover, NH 03755
Ph: (802)295-3487
Fax: (802)295-5963
E-mail: info@phenomenology.org
URL: http://www.phenomenology.org
Contact: Anna-Teresa Tymieniecka PhD, Sec. Gen.
Founded: 1968. **Members:** 550. **Membership Dues:** regular in U.S., $32 (annual) ● regular outside U.S., $39 (annual). **Staff:** 5. **Budget:** $25,000. **Regional Groups:** 4. **Description:** Represents professional philosophers and scholars from diverse backgrounds specializing in phenomenology. (Phenomenology is the study of life and of the human condition as a center to all philosophical queries.) Serves primarily as a research program and forum for the exchange of information and scholarly concerns in phenomenology. Conducts seminars and symposia. Organization's name is derived from German philosopher and founder of phenomenology, Edmund Husserl (1859-1938). **Libraries: Type:** reference. **Holdings:** 1,500. **Affiliated With:** World Institute for Advanced Phenomenological Research and Learning. **Publications:** *Analecta Husserliana: The Yearbook of Phenomenological Research* (in English, French, and German), 3-5/year. Includes the society's research material. **Circulation:** 800 ● *Les Travaux de Recherches de l'Institut Mondial de Hautes Etudes Phenomenologiques*, periodic. **Price:** $43.00 in U.S.; $50.00 outside U.S. ● *Phenomenological Inquiry: A Review of Philosophical Ideas and Trends*, annual. Journal. Includes book review, and information on scholarly events. **Price:** $43.00 /year for individuals in North America; $50.00 /year for individuals in other country; $37.00/year for agency in North America; $44.00/ year for agency in other country. ISSN: 0885-3886. **Circulation:** 900. **Conventions/Meetings:** World Congress of Phenomenology: The Phenomenology and Existentialism of the 20th Century - 2008 Aug. 17-20, Krakow, Poland.

10802 ■ International New Thought Alliance (INTA)
5003 E Broadway Rd.
Mesa, AZ 85206
Ph: (480)830-2461
Fax: (480)830-2561
E-mail: azinta@qwest.net
URL: http://newthoughtalliance.org
Contact: Dr. Blaine C. Mays, Pres.
Founded: 1914. **Membership Dues:** individual, $50 (annual) ● group, $100 (annual) ● life, $600. **Budget:** $225,000. **Description:** Represents individuals and groups interested in religious-educational philosophy and metaphysics. **Publications:** *New Thought*, quarterly. Magazine. Contains articles on enlarging and enriching one's way of life, universalizing vision and consciousness, and developing transcendental faculties. **Price:** included in membership dues; $3.75/ copy for nonmembers; $15.00 /year for nonmembers. ISSN: 0146-7832. **Circulation:** 3,000. **Advertising:** accepted. **Conventions/Meetings:** annual congress - always July.

10803 ■ International Phenomenological Society (IPS)
c/o Brown University
54 Coll. St.
Box 1947
Providence, RI 02912
Ph: (401)863-3215

Fax: (401)863-2719
E-mail: ppr@brown.edu
Contact: Prof. Ernest Sosa, Pres.
Founded: 1940. **Description:** Philosophers and philosophically minded persons from other fields, such as psychologists, scientists, and humanists in 60 countries. Originally founded to further study of the works of Edmund Husserl (1859-1938), founder of the philosophical school of phenomenology. **Publications:** *Philosophy and Phenomenological Research*, bimonthly. Journal. Contains articles in the fields of philosophy of mind, epistemology, ethics, metaphysics, and philosophical history. Includes reviews. **Price:** $48.00 /year for individuals; $210.00 /year for institutions and library. ISSN: 0031-8205. **Advertising:** accepted.

10804 ■ International Society for Neoplatonic Studies (ISNS)

c/o Michael Wagner, Sec.-Treas.
Univ. of San Diego
5998 Alcala Park
San Diego, CA 92110-2492
Ph: (619)260-4600
Fax: (619)260-4227
E-mail: john-finamore@uiowa.edu
URL: http://www.isns.us
Contact: John F. Finamore, Pres.
Founded: 1973. **Members:** 600. **Membership Dues:** regular, $60 (annual) ● student, retired, $20 (annual). **Regional Groups:** 6. **National Groups:** 8. **Languages:** English, French, German, Italian, Polish, Russian, Spanish. **Multinational. Description:** Scholars from 21 countries involved in the study of Neoplatonism, including philosophers, classicists, historians, and literary persons. Supports academic studies; facilitates communication among members. Operates research center at Vanderbilt University in Nashville, TN. **Publications:** *Journal of Neoplatonic Studies*, quarterly. **Price:** $15.00 /year for individuals; $10.00/year for students; $25.00 /year for institutions ● *Studies in Neoplatonism: Ancient and Modern*. Available in seven volumes. ● Newsletter, biennial. **Price:** included in membership dues. **Conventions/Meetings:** annual international conference and congress ● annual Neoplatonism - conference.

10805 ■ International Society for Phenomenological Studies

c/o Prof. William Blattner, Dir.
Georgetown Univ.
Dept. of Philosophy
240 New North Bldg.
Washington, DC 20057-1133
Ph: (202)687-4528
Fax: (202)687-4493
E-mail: blattnew@georgetown.edu
URL: http://www.intsocphenom.org
Contact: Prof. William Blattner, Dir.
Founded: 1998. **Multinational. Description:** Promotes the study of phenomenology, existentialism and hermeneutics. Seeks to develop and explore the style of phenomenology called "California phenomenology." Facilitates discussion of current philosophical research through an annual workshop-style meeting where invited participants present their respective works for feedback from other participants. Attendance of Society meetings is by invitation only.

10806 ■ International Society for Phenomenology and Literature (ISPL)

c/o World Phenomenology Institute
1 Ivy Pointe Way
Hanover, NH 03755
Ph: (802)295-3487
Fax: (802)295-5963
E-mail: info@phenomenology.org
URL: http://www.phenomenology.org
Contact: Anna-Teresa Tymieniecka, Pres.
Founded: 1974. **Members:** 300. **Membership Dues:** in U.S., $43 (annual) ● outside U.S., $50 (annual). **Staff:** 10. **Budget:** $15,000. **Regional Groups:** 1. **Multinational. Description:** Literary scholars, philosophers, and specialists in the theory of literature and phenomenology. Seeks to develop dialogue between philosophy and literature. Conducts research. **Affiliated With:** World Institute for Advanced Phenomenological Research and Learning. **Formerly:** (1976) International Association for Philosophy and Literature. **Publications:** *Analecta Husserliana, The Yearbook of Phenomenological Research* ● *Phenomenological Inquiry, A Review of Philosophical Ideas and Trends*, periodic. Journal. Includes articles, book reviews, and scholarly information. **Price:** $43.00 /year for individuals in U.S.; $50.00 /year for individuals outside U.S.; $35.00/year for agencies in U.S.; $44.00/year for agencies outside U.S. ISSN: 0885-3886. **Circulation:** 600. **Advertising:** accepted. **Conventions/Meetings:** annual meeting (exhibits) - in Cambridge, MD.

10807 ■ International Society for Phenomenology and the Sciences of Life (ISPSL)

c/o World Phenomenology Institute
1 Ivy Pointe Way
Hanover, NH 03755
Ph: (802)295-3487
Fax: (802)295-5963
E-mail: info@phenomenology.org
URL: http://www.phenomenology.org
Contact: Anna-Teresa Tymieniecka, Pres.
Founded: 1976. **Members:** 250. **Membership Dues:** in U.S., $43 (annual) ● outside U.S., $50 (annual). **Staff:** 3. **Languages:** English, French, Italian, Russian, Spanish. **Description:** Professors and scholars in the sciences of life. Seeks to reestablish communication among the sciences of life. **Libraries: Type:** reference. **Subjects:** phenomenology, history of philosophy. **Affiliated With:** World Institute for Advanced Phenomenological Research and Learning. **Formerly:** International Society for Phenomenology and the Human Sciences. **Publications:** *Analecta Husserliana, The Yearbook of Phenomenological Research* (in English, French, German, and Spanish) ● *Phenomenological Inquiry, a Review of Philosophical Ideas and Trends*, periodic. Includes articles, book reviews, and scholarly information. **Price:** $43.00 in U.S.; $50.00 outside U.S. ISSN: 0885-3886. **Circulation:** 900. **Conventions/Meetings:** International Congress of Philosophy and The Sciences of Life, held in conjunction with World Institute for Advanced Phenomenological Research and Learning in collaboration with the Department of Philosophy and Human Sciences, Macerata University (exhibits).

10808 ■ Karl Jaspers Society of North America (KJSNA)

c/o Andrew Gluck, Sec.-Treas.
3145 Rte. 44/55
Gardiner, NY 12525
E-mail: andy_gluck@msn.com
URL: http://www.bu.edu/paideia/kjsna/index.html
Contact: Andrew Gluck, Sec.-Treas.
Founded: 1980. **Members:** 81. **Membership Dues:** general, $20 (annual) ● life, $200. **Description:** Individuals interested in the works and studies of German existentialist philosopher Karl Jaspers (1883-1969). Promotes study and research in the thought of Jaspers and related thought for philosophical, educational, and research aims. Provides a forum for reporting and exchanging views on research. **Affiliated With:** Conference of Philosophical Societies. **Publications:** *Proceedings and Information*, periodic. **Conventions/Meetings:** semiannual conference, held in conjunction with American Philosophical Association ● periodic international conference.

10809 ■ Leibniz Society of North America

c/o Glenn A. Hartz, Ed.
Philosophy Dept.
Ohio State Univ.
1680 Univ. Dr.
Mansfield, OH 44906
Ph: (419)755-4354
Fax: (419)755-4367
E-mail: hartz.1@osu.edu
URL: http://philosophy2.ucsd.edu/~rutherford/Leibniz/leibrev.htm
Contact: Glenn A. Hartz, Ed.
Founded: 1991. **Members:** 120. **Membership Dues:** regular, $25 (annual) ● student, $15 (annual). **Description:** Promotes international scholarship on the philosophy of G.W. Leibniz. **Publications:** *The Leibniz Review*, annual. Journal. Contains articles and book reviews of recent works on the philosophy of G.W. Leibniz. **Price:** $40.00 /year for libraries and institutions in U.S. and Canada; $50.00 /year for libraries and institutions outside U.S. and Canada. ISSN: 1524-1556. **Circulation:** 160 ● *Leibniz Society News*. Newsletter.

10810 ■ Libertarian SIG (LibSIG)

c/o American Mensa
1229 Corporate Dr. W
Arlington, TX 76006-6103
Ph: (817)607-0060
Free: (800)66-MENSA
Fax: (817)649-5232
E-mail: nationaloffice@americanmensa.org
URL: http://www.us.mensa.org
Contact: Russ Bakke, Chm.
Founded: 1970. **Members:** 230. **Membership Dues:** regular, $52 (annual). **Staff:** 1. **Description:** Special interest group of Mensa dedicated to the discussion of personal liberty and the political theory of libertarianism. Provides a forum for the discussion of personal liberty and libertarianism, and the interchange of ideas and experiences. **Affiliated With:** American Mensa. **Publications:** Newsletter, bimonthly. **Price:** free to participating members. **Circulation:** 230. **Advertising:** accepted.

10811 ■ Merleau-Ponty Circle (MPC)

c/o Prof. Galen A. Johnson, Gen. Sec.
Univ. of Rhode Island
Dept. of Philosophy
Lippitt Hall, No. 206
Kingston, RI 02881
E-mail: merleaufan@yahoo.com
URL: http://www.uri.edu/artsci/phl/impc
Contact: Prof. Galen A. Johnson, Gen. Sec.
Founded: 1974. **Members:** 750. **Languages:** English, French, German, Italian, Japanese, Spanish. **Description:** Individuals interested in studying the theories of French philosopher, Maurice Merleau-Ponty (1908-61), a leading proponent of phenomenology and author of *Phenomenology of Perception, The Visible and the Invisible, Sense and Non-Sense*, and *Signs*. **Awards:** M.C. Dillon Annual Lectureship. **Frequency:** annual. **Type:** monetary. **Recipient:** to the submitter of the best graduate student paper. **Computer Services:** database, membership list. **Publications:** Newsletter, annual. Alternate Formats: online. **Conventions/Meetings:** annual conference - always September.

10812 ■ Metaphysical Society of America (MSA)

c/o Department of Philosophy
Univ. of Alabama—Huntsville
Huntsville, AL 35899
Ph: (205)895-6555
Fax: (205)895-6949
E-mail: martineb@email.uah.edu
URL: http://www.acls.org/metaphys.htm
Contact: Brian J. Martine, Sec.
Founded: 1950. **Members:** 600. **Membership Dues:** individual, $600 (annual). **Description:** Represents professors, scholars, and laymen interested in metaphysics. Seeks to "turn the attention of the philosophical community from more limited objectives to concern with the ultimate questions of philosophy, which are questions about the nature of reality". **Affiliated With:** American Council of Learned Societies; International Federation of Philosophical Societies. **Publications:** *Announcements*, annual ● *Presidential Address*, annual ● Membership Directory, periodic. **Conventions/Meetings:** annual conference.

10813 ■ Natural Law Society (NLS)

c/o Dr. Robert L. Chapman, Ed.
Dept. of Philosophy and Religious Stud.
Pace Univ.
41 Park Row, Rm. 310
New York, NY 10038

Ph: (212)346-1460 (212)346-1453
Free: (800)874-PACE
Fax: (212)346-1113
E-mail: veralex@pace.edu
URL: http://www.pace.edu
Contact: Dr. Robert L. Chapman, Ed.
Founded: 1979. **Members:** 400. **Membership Dues:** individual, $25 (annual) ● institution, $45 (annual). **Staff:** 3. **Budget:** $6,000. **Regional Groups:** 2. **Multinational. Description:** Individuals and institutions interested in the ongoing philosophical debate between those who believe in natural law and those who question its existence. (Natural law refers to a system of universal, usually reason-based, objective moral and physical laws that describe both the way in which physical events occur in the universe and the development of philosophical ideas, especially civil laws and systems of morality.) Seeks to strengthen philosophies that incorporate natural law. Comments on and clarifies ideas supporting the existence of natural law; studies the history of natural law. Encourages interest in natural law philosophies and their use in discussions of morality, rights, and law. **Libraries: Type:** reference. **Holdings:** archival material, books, periodicals. **Subjects:** natural law, rights, legal philosophy, political, social philosophy. **Publications:** *Cumulative Index*, quinquennial. Journal. Includes directory. **Circulation:** 400. **Advertising:** accepted. Alternate Formats: CD-ROM; online ● *Vera Lex*, annual. Journal. Includes natural law, morality, rights, justice, and positive law. **Price:** $25.00 /year for individuals; $40.00 /year for institutions and libraries; $10.00/copy (back issue); $115.00 complete set (back issue). ISSN: 0893-4851. **Circulation:** 450. **Conventions/Meetings:** biennial conference, in conjunction with International Association for Philosophy of Law and Social Philosophy and the American Philosophical Association, Maritian Society, and the American Catholic Philosophical Association.

10814 ■ Nietzsche Society (NS)

c/o Babette E. Babich, Exec. Sec.
Fordham Univ.
Dept. of Philosophy
113 W 60th St.
New York, NY 10023
Ph: (212)636-6297
Fax: (212)636-7153
E-mail: babich@fordham.edu
URL: http://www.fordham.edu/gsas/phil/nns/new_nietzsche_society.html
Contact: Babette E. Babich, Exec. Sec.
Founded: 1979. **Members:** 580. **Membership Dues:** individual, $40 (annual). **Description:** Represents scholars interested in the works and influence of Friedrich Nietzsche (1844-1900), German philosopher and poet. Conducts scholarly research. Holds an annual meeting. Publishes a journal, New Nietzsche Studies. **Committees:** Executive Program. **Publications:** *New Nietzsche Studies*, annual. Journal. Features new European and American reflections on Nietzsche's thought. **Price:** included in membership dues; $50.00 /year for institutions and libraries. ISSN: 1091-0239. **Conventions/Meetings:** annual international conference, held in conjunction with Society for Phenomenology and Existential Philosophy - on the morning of the first Thursday of Society for Phenomenology and Existential Philosophy meeting.

10815 ■ North American Fichte Society (NAFS)

c/o Daniel Breazeale, Ed./Co-Founder
Dept. of Philosophy
Univ. of Kentucky
Lexington, KY 40506
Ph: (859)257-4376 (859)252-5048
Fax: (859)257-3285
E-mail: breazeal@uky.edu
URL: http://www.phil.upenn.edu/~cubowman/fichte
Contact: Daniel Breazeale, Ed./Co-Founder
Founded: 1991. **Description:** Scholars. Dedicated to the study of the German philosopher Johann Gottlieb Fichte and his work. **Publications:** *Fichteana*, periodic. Newsletter. Contains bibliography of recent and announced publications that relate to Fichte in some fashion. Alternate Formats: online ● Proceedings. Features various meetings and conferences of the NAFS. ● Books ● Articles. **Conventions/Meetings:** biennial conference.

10816 ■ North American Kant Society (NAKS)

c/o Patricia Kitcher, Pres.
Columbia Univ.
Dept. of Philosophy
708 Philosophy Hall
1150 Amsterdam Ave.
New York, NY 10027
Ph: (314)935-6670
Fax: (314)935-7349
E-mail: pk206@columbia.edu
URL: http://www.sandiego.edu/naks
Contact: Patricia Kitcher, Pres.
Founded: 1985. **Members:** 300. **Membership Dues:** individual, $20 (annual) ● student, retired, unemployed, $10 (annual). **Regional Groups:** 2. **Description:** Scholars promoting the study of the work of Immanuel Kant (1724-1804), a German philosopher who attempted to discern the limits of human knowledge in such works as *Critique of Pure Reason*, *Critique of Practical Reason*, and *Critique of Judgement*. Conducts academic programs. **Publications:** *North American Kant Society Newsletter*, quarterly. **Circulation:** 300 ● *North American Kant Society Studies in Philosophy*, annual. Monographs. **Conventions/Meetings:** meeting, held in conjunction with American Philosophical Association and American Society for 18th Century Studies - 3/year.

10817 ■ North American Levinas Society (NALS)

c/o Sol Neely, Sec./Webmaster
Dept. of English
Purdue Univ.
500 Oval Dr.
West Lafayette, IN 47907-2038
Fax: (765)494-3780
E-mail: secretary@levinas-society.org
URL: http://web.ics.purdue.edu/~sjneely/levinas.htm
Contact: Sol Neely, Sec./Webmaster
Description: Promotes the study and research on the works of Lithuanian-born French philosopher and Talmudic commentator, Emmanuel Levinas. Fosters interest and appreciation of Levinas' works. Facilitates collaboration between Levinas scholars. **Telecommunication Services:** electronic mail, aporia@purdue.edu. **Publications:** Bulletin, quarterly. Contains book reviews and announcements concerning conference schedules and academic advancement in Levinas studies. ● Newsletter. Alternate Formats: online.

10818 ■ North American Nietzsche Society (NANS)

Univ. of Illinois
Dept. of Philosophy
105 Gregory Hall
810 S Wright St.
Urbana, IL 61801
Ph: (217)333-1939 (217)333-2889
Fax: (217)244-8355
E-mail: nans@uiuc.edu
URL: http://www.phil.uiuc.edu/nietzsche
Contact: Prof. Richard Schacht, Exec. Dir.
Founded: 1980. **Members:** 350. **Membership Dues:** student, retired, $20 (annual) ● individual, $30 (annual). **Multinational. Description:** Professors of philosophy, literature, and other disciplines; graduate students; other interested persons. (Friedrich Nietzsche, 1844-1900, was a German philosopher and poet.) Promotes the exchange of ideas among Nietzsche scholars and encourages scholarly research and creative work concerning Nietzsche. **Publications:** *International Studies in Philosophy, NANS issue*, quarterly. Journal. **Price:** included in membership dues ● *Nietzcheana*, occasional ● *Nietzsche News*, semiannual. Newsletter. **Conventions/Meetings:** semiannual conference, held in conjunction with American Philosophical Association.

10819 ■ North American Sartre Society (NASS)

c/o Berghahn Books
150 Broadway, Ste.812
New York, NY 10038
E-mail: kanders@emory.edu
URL: http://sartresociety.org
Contact: Adrian Mirvish, Pres.
Founded: 1985. **Members:** 300. **Membership Dues:** full, $55 (annual) ● student/adjunct, $18 (annual). **Description:** Scholars and other individuals interested in the work of Jean-Paul Sartre (1905-80), a French philosopher noted for the existential themes in his novels, plays, and philosophical works. **Formerly:** (2003) Sartre Society. **Publications:** *Berghahn Journal*, semiannual. **Price:** $125.00 /year for institutions; $45.00 /year for individuals. ISSN: 1357-1559. Alternate Formats: online. **Conventions/Meetings:** meeting - every 18 months.

10820 ■ North American Society for Social Philosophy (NASSP)

c/o Philosophy Documentation Center
PO Box 7147
Charlottesville, VA 22906-7147
Ph: (434)220-3300
Free: (800)444-2419
Fax: (434)220-3301
E-mail: order@pdcnet.org
URL: http://www.pitt.edu/~nassp/nassp.html
Contact: Alistair Macleod, Pres.
Founded: 1983. **Members:** 300. **Membership Dues:** regular, $40 (annual) ● student/low income (includes SPT), $25 (annual) ● student/low income (without SPT), $12 (annual). **Budget:** $5,000. **Regional Groups:** 5. **Description:** Professors of philosophy, political science, sociology, law, history, and philosophical theology. Facilitates exchange of ideas and information among social philosophers. Sponsors an annual international conference, of which peer-reviewed proceedings are published annually, as well as sessions in conjunction with the meetings of other academic organizations throughout the year. **Awards:** Social Philosophy Book Award. **Frequency:** annual. **Type:** recognition. **Recipient:** to the book that makes the most significant contribution to social philosophy. **Affiliated With:** American Catholic Philosophical Association; American Philosophical Association; American Political Science Association; International Federation of Philosophical Societies. **Publications:** *Journal of Social Philosophy*, quarterly. **Price:** $58.00 /year for nonmembers in U.S. and Canada; $52.00 /year for nonmembers outside U.S. and Canada; $44.00 /year for members in U.S. and Canada; $62.00 /year for members outside U.S. and Canada. ISSN: 0047-2786. **Circulation:** 400 ● *Social Philosophy Today Series*, annual. Book. **Price:** $65.00 /year for institutions; $40.00 for nonmembers. ISSN: 1543-4044. **Conventions/Meetings:** annual meeting - July or August ● regional meeting - 5/year ● annual Social Philosophy Conference - international conference.

10821 ■ The Objectivist Center (TOC)

1001 Connecticut Ave. NW, Ste.425
Washington, DC 20036
Ph: (202)296-7263
Free: (800)374-1776
Fax: (202)296-0771
E-mail: toc@objectivistcenter.org
URL: http://www.objectivistcenter.org
Contact: Edward L. Hudgins, Exec. Dir.
Founded: 1990. **Members:** 2,500. **Membership Dues:** patron, $10,000 ● benefactor, $5,000-$9,999 ● sponsor, $1,000-$2,499 ● sustaining, $250-$999 ● regular, $100-$249 ● student, $25-$49. **Staff:** 11. **Budget:** $1,200,000. **Description:** A center for research and public advocacy of Objectivism, a philosophy originated by Ayn Rand, which promotes reason, individualism, and capitalism. **Formerly:** (1999) Institute for Objectivist Studies. **Publications:** *A Life of One's Own: Individual Rights in the Welfare State*. Book. Criticizes the doctrine of "rights" to welfare benefits. Discusses consequences of privatizing philanthropy and social insurance. **Price:** $16.75 ● *The Contested Legacy of Ayn Rand*. Book. **Price:** $21.95 ● *The Fountainhead — A Fiftieth An-*

niversary Celebration. Booklet. Commemorates the anniversary of Ayn Rand's novel *The Fountainhead*. **Price:** $7.95 ● *Greed and Achievement in the 1980s*. Pamphlet. Refutes the myth of the 1980s as a decade of greed. ● *The Green Machine*. Pamphlet. Discusses the environmental movement. **Price:** $4.50 ● *Navigator*, 11/year. Journal. **Price:** free, for members only. **Circulation:** 2,500 ● *Reason and Value: Aristotle vs. Rand*. Book. **Price:** $14.95 ● *Truth and Toleration*. Monograph. Covers the history of the organized Objectivist movement and the proper means of advocating a philosophy of reason and individualism. ● *Unrugged Individualism: The Selfish Basis of Benevolence*. Book. Analyzes benevolence as a moral virtue from Objectivist standpoint. **Price:** $11.95 ● Brochure. Covers the mission and projects of the Institute. **Conventions/Meetings:** annual dinner, for members at sponsor level and above - always July ● annual Objectivism: Theory and Practice - conference - always summer.

10822 ■ Pacific Society for Women in Philosophy (P-SWIP)
c/o Amy Coplan, Exec. Sec.
California State Univ. Fullerton
Dept. of Philosophy
PO Box 6868
Fullerton, CA 92834-6868
E-mail: acoplan@fullerton.edu
URL: http://www.csus.edu/org/pswip
Contact: Christina Bellon, Treas.

Founded: 1975. **Members:** 140. **Membership Dues:** full-time professional, $30 (annual) ● part-time professional, $20 (annual) ● student, underemployed, $5 (annual). **Description:** Represents women and men employed as philosophers or with degrees in philosophy. Facilitates the discussion of issues concerning philosophers, philosophy and academia, and related job issues; disseminates information involving women in philosophy. Offers career advice, support for women in the field, and a channel for socializing. **Telecommunication Services:** electronic mail, bellon@csus.edu. **Publications:** *Hypatia: A Journal of Feminist Philosophy*, quarterly. **Price:** $40.00/year ● Newsletter, semiannual. **Conventions/Meetings:** semiannual meeting - always spring in Southern California, and fall in Northern California ● annual meeting, held in conjunction with American Philosophical Association.

10823 ■ Philosophical Research Society (PRS)
3910 Los Feliz Blvd.
Los Angeles, CA 90027
Ph: (323)663-2167
Free: (800)548-4062
Fax: (323)663-9443
E-mail: info@prs.org
URL: http://www.prs.org
Contact: Dr. Obadiah S. Harris, Pres./Chm. of the Board

Founded: 1934. **Staff:** 6. **Budget:** $500,000. **Nonmembership. Multinational. Description:** Investigates the essential teachings of scientific, spiritual, and cultural leaders and further clarify and integrate man's body of knowledge; applies the knowledge to the present needs of mankind using modern skills and the cooperation of outstanding experts; makes available vital concepts to the public through lectures, publications, and other media; increases public awareness of the usefulness of these ideas and ideals in solving the personal and collective problems of modern man. Maintains a collection of art. Sponsors research projects. **Libraries: Type:** reference; open to the public. **Holdings:** 30,000; archival material, books, papers, periodicals, photographs. **Subjects:** religion, comparative religion, ancient and modern philosophy, mythology, Asian studies, Egyptology, Baconiana, astrology, Theosophy, masonry and secret societies, Divination, popular metaphysics, history and archeology, Christianity, Judaism and Kabbalah, inspirational literature. **Additional Websites:** http://www.uprs.edu. **Programs:** University of Philosophical Research. **Publications:** *PRS Publications Book Catalog*. Alternate Formats: online ● *Secret Teachings of All Ages*. Books ● Audiotapes ● Books.

10824 ■ Philosophy Documentation Center (PDC)
PO Box 7147
Charlottesville, VA 22906-7147
Ph: (434)220-3300
Free: (800)444-2419
Fax: (434)220-3301
E-mail: order@pdcnet.org
URL: http://www.pdcnet.org
Contact: George Leaman, Dir.

Founded: 1966. **Staff:** 9. **Languages:** English, German. **Description:** Acts as a clearinghouse for bibliographic and other information regarding philosophy and philosophers. Offers computer typesetting, journal production, instructional software, subscription fulfillment, mailing lists, advertising, and conference exhibits. **Convention/Meeting:** none. **Awards:** APA/PDC Award for Excellence and Innovation in Philosophy Programs. **Frequency:** annual. **Type:** monetary. **Recipient:** for programs with successful initiatives. **Computer Services:** Mailing lists, philosophers, philosophy departments in Canada, the U.S. and international, and philosophers by specialty. **Publications:** *American Catholic Philosophical Quarterly*. Journal. Features articles, topical discussions, and book reviews dealing with all philosophical areas and approaches. **Price:** $65.00 for institutions; $25.00/issue for nonmembers. ISSN: 1051-3558 ● *Business Ethics Quarterly*. Journal. Contains articles from variety of disciplinary orientations and business community. **Price:** $165.00 /year for institutions; $60.00 /year for individuals; $30.00/year for retirees and students; $20.00/issue for individuals. ISSN: 1052-150X ● *Directory of American Philosophers*, biennial. Journal. ISSN: 0070-508X ● *Idealistic Studies* (in English and French), 3/year. Journal. Provides a peer-reviewed forum for the discussion of themes and topics that relate to the tradition and legacy of philosophical idealism. **Price:** $55.00 /year for institutions; $32.00 /year for individuals; $20.00/issue for institutions; $12.00/issue for individuals. ISSN: 0046-8541 ● *International Directory of Philosophy and Philosophers* (in English and Italian), semiannual. Journal. ISSN: 0074-4603 ● *International Journal of Applied Philosophy*, semiannual. Contains philosophical articles. **Price:** $55.00 /year for institutions; $28.00 /year for individuals; $28.00/issue for institutions; $14.00/issue for individuals. ISSN: 0739-098X ● *International Philosophical Quarterly*. Journal. Provides an international peer reviewed forum in English for the exchange of basic philosophical ideas. **Price:** $60.00 /year for institutions; $32.00 /year for individuals; $15.00/issue for institutions; $10.00/issue for individuals. ISSN: 0019-0365 ● *Journal of Philosophical Research* (in English and French), annual. Contains articles from any philosophical orientation. **Price:** $70.00 for institutions; $32.00 for individuals. ISSN: 1053-8364 ● *New Vico Studies* (in English and Italian), annual. Journal. Contains articles, translations, notes, reports, and book reviews that reflect the current state of the study of the works of Giambattista Vico. **Price:** $50.00 for institutions; $28.00 for individuals. ISSN: 0733-9542 ● *Philosophy and Theology*, semiannual. Journal. Includes articles devoted to critical contact with the thought and legacy of the theologian Karl Rahner. **Price:** $40.00 /year for institutions and individuals; $20.00/issue for institutions and individuals. ISSN: 0890-2461 ● *Proceedings of the American Catholic Philosophical Association*, annual. Journal. Includes topical papers delivered by invited speakers, and the President's address. **Price:** $40.00. ISSN: 0065-7638 ● *Questions: Philosophy for Young People*, annual. Journal. Contains philosophical discussions, drawings, philosophical writing by students, and articles. **Price:** $25.00 for individuals; $50.00 for schools. ISSN: 1541-4760 ● *Social Philosophy Today*, annual. Journal. Contains a selection of papers presented at the International Social Philosophy Conference. **Price:** $65.00 for institutions; $40.00 for individuals. ISSN: 1543-4044 ● *Teaching Philosophy*, quarterly. Journal. Contains articles, discussions, reports, case studies, and reviews. **Price:** $75.00 /year for institutions; $30.00 /year for individuals; $20.00/issue for institutions; $8.00/issue for individuals. ISSN: 0145-5788.

10825 ■ Philosophy of Science Association (PSA)
c/o University of Chicago Press
Journals Div.
PO Box 37005
Chicago, IL 60637
Ph: (773)753-3347
Free: (877)705-1878
Fax: (773)753-0811
E-mail: subscriptions@press.uchicago.edu
URL: http://philsci.org
Contact: George Gale, Exec. Sec.

Founded: 1934. **Members:** 1,000. **Budget:** $100,000. **Description:** Represents philosophers, educators, scientists and others interested in the relationship of philosophy and science. **Affiliated With:** American Association for the Advancement of Science. **Publications:** *Philosophy of Science Association Directory*, biennial ● *Philosophy of Science Journal*, quarterly. **Price:** included in membership dues; $60.00 /year for nonmembers. ISSN: 0031-8248. **Circulation:** 2,200. **Advertising:** accepted ● *Proceedings of the Biennial Meeting* ● Newsletter, quarterly. Includes employment opportunities and lists of grants awarded. **Price:** included in membership dues. **Circulation:** 1,500. Alternate Formats: online. **Conventions/Meetings:** biennial meeting (exhibits).

10826 ■ Polanyi Society (PS)
c/o Phil Mullins, Ed.
Missouri Western State Univ.
4525 Downs Dr.
St. Joseph, MO 64507
Ph: (816)271-4386
Fax: (816)271-5680
E-mail: mullins@missouriwestern.edu
URL: http://www.missouriwestern.edu/orgs/polanyi
Contact: Phil Mullins, Ed.

Founded: 1972. **Members:** 350. **Membership Dues:** regular, $25 (annual) ● student, $12 (annual). **Budget:** $3,600. **Multinational. Description:** College and university faculty, graduate students, and other individuals interested in the thought of Michael Polanyi (1891-1976), British chemist and philosopher. (Polanyi did important scientific research in X-ray analysis, thermodynamics, and reaction kinetics; he later turned to economics and philosophy and published works including *Personal Knowledge*, *The Tacit Dimension*, and *The Study of Man*.) Serves as a communication network among members and a scholarly society. **Libraries: Type:** reference. **Holdings:** archival material, business records, periodicals. **Subjects:** Polanyi Society. **Formerly:** (1974) Society of Explorers. **Publications:** *Tradition and Discovery*, 3/year. Journal. **Price:** $20.00 for members. ISSN: 1057-1027. **Circulation:** 350. **Advertising:** accepted. **Conventions/Meetings:** annual conference, with academic paper discussions - 2008 June 13-15, Chicago, IL ● periodic Interpretation of Polanyi - conference.

10827 ■ Resources for Independent Thinking (RIT)
484 Lake Park Ave., No. 24
Oakland, CA 94610-2730
Ph: (925)228-0565
Fax: (925)891-3515
E-mail: askrit@rit.org
URL: http://www.rit.org
Contact: Sharon Presley PhD, Exec. Dir.

Founded: 1993. **Staff:** 3. **Nonmembership. Description:** Seeks to promote self-empowerment and personal autonomy through critical thinking. Conducts educational programs to encourage critical thinking, independent thinking, questioning of cultural stereotypes, and development of compassionate moral values. Operates speakers' bureau; produces audiotapes. **Publications:** *How to Avoid Being Manipulated, Bamboozled and Seduced by Experts and Authorities*. Brochure ● Articles ● Pamphlets ● Reports.

10828 ■ Society for the Advancement of American Philosophy (SAAP)
c/o Dr. Thomas Alexander, Pres.
Dept. of Philosophy
Southern Illinois Univ.
Faner Hall, Rm. 3065
Mailcode 4505
Carbondale, IL 62901
Ph: (618)536-6641
Fax: (618)453-7428
E-mail: mleldrid@email.uncc.edu
URL: http://www.american-philosophy.org
Contact: Dr. Michael Eldridge, Sec.
Founded: 1972. **Members:** 900. **Membership Dues:** regular (with earnings of less than $50,000 annually), $40 (annual) ● regular (with earnings of $50,000 or more annually), $60 (annual) ● sustaining, $90 (annual) ● benefactor, $140 (annual). **Description:** Scholars and others interested in American philosophy. Promotes research and interest in the history of American philosophy and original creative works in the field. Provides a forum for the exchange of information and ideas. **Awards:** Douglas Greenlee Prize. **Frequency:** annual. **Type:** recognition. **Recipient:** to the best paper ● Herbert Schneider Award. **Frequency:** annual. **Type:** recognition. **Recipient:** for a career-long achievement of distinguished contributions to the understanding of American Philosophy ● Ila and John Mellow Prize. **Frequency:** annual. **Type:** monetary. **Recipient:** for excellence in advancing the American philosophical tradition toward the resolution of current personal, social and political problems ● Joseph J. Blau Prize. **Frequency:** annual. **Type:** monetary. **Recipient:** to the author of the paper that makes the most significant contribution to the history of American Philosophy from colonial times to the recent present. **Committees:** Greenlee Prize; Program. **Publications:** Newsletter, 3/year. Includes calendar of events, book reviews, and calls for papers. **Price:** included in membership dues. **Circulation:** 900. **Advertising:** accepted ● Membership Directory, quadrennial. **Conventions/Meetings:** annual meeting (exhibits).

10829 ■ Society for Analytical Feminism (SAF)
c/o Sharon Crasnow, Pres.
925 Archer St.
San Diego, CA 92109
E-mail: sharon.crasnow@rcc.edu
URL: http://www.ku.edu/~acudd/safhomepage.htm
Contact: Sharon Crasnow, Pres.
Founded: 1991. **Members:** 100. **Membership Dues:** student/unemployed, $5 (annual) ● retired, $5 (annual) ● regular, $15 (annual). **Staff:** 4. **Regional Groups:** 1. **Description:** Sponsors paper sessions at divisional meetings of the American Philosophical Association. **Awards:** Graduate Student/Underfunded Professional Travel Stipend. **Frequency:** annual. **Type:** monetary. **Recipient:** for the best paper in this category. **Conventions/Meetings:** annual American Philosophical Association Central Division - convention ● periodic American Philosophical Association Eastern Division - conference ● annual American Philosophical Association Pacific Division - conference.

10830 ■ Society for Ancient Greek Philosophy (SAGP)
c/o Anthony Preus, Sec.-Treas.
Binghamton Univ.
Dept. of Philosophy
Binghamton, NY 13902-6000
Ph: (607)777-2886 (607)777-2646
Fax: (607)777-6255
E-mail: apreus@binghamton.edu
URL: http://sagp.binghamton.edu
Contact: Anthony Preus, Sec.-Treas.
Founded: 1953. **Members:** 500. **Membership Dues:** regular, in U.S., $10 (annual) ● regular, in Canada, outside North America, $15 (annual). **Staff:** 2. **Description:** Persons, mainly from universities, interested in ancient philosophy. Promotes closer cooperation between philosophers and classical scholars. Sponsors meetings with other scholarly organizations. **Affiliated With:** American Philological Association; American Philosophical Association. **Publications:** *Essays in Ancient Greek Philosophy, Volume VI*. Book ● Newsletter, quarterly. Includes papers presented at the meetings with the American Philological Association and divisions of the American Philosophical Association. **Circulation:** 500. **Advertising:** accepted. **Conventions/Meetings:** periodic conference (exhibits) ● annual conference, with the Society for the Study of Islamic Philosophy and Science and other groups (exhibits).

10831 ■ Society for Asian and Comparative Philosophy (SACP)
c/o Michiko Yusa, Pres.
516 High St.
Dept. of Modern And Classical Languages and Literatures
Western Washington Univ.
Bellingham, WA 98225-9057
Ph: (360)650-4851
Fax: (360)650-6110
E-mail: yusa@wwu.edu
URL: http://www.sacpweb.org
Contact: Michiko Yusa, Pres.
Founded: 1968. **Members:** 400. **Membership Dues:** regular, $35 (annual) ● student, emeritus, $20 (annual) ● sustaining, $50 (annual). **Description:** Professors, graduate students, and Asian scholars. Works to advance the development of Asian and comparative philosophies and to bring Asian and Western philosophers together for a mutually beneficial exchange of ideas. Sponsors panels and workshops in themes of both scholarly and topical interest. **Publications:** *Forum*, semiannual. Newsletter ● *Monograph Series* ● *Philosophy East and West*, quarterly. Journal. **Price:** $60.00 /year for institutions; $35.00 /year for individuals; $18.00/year for students; $7.50 back issues. ISSN: 0031-8221 ● Directory, quinquennial. **Conventions/Meetings:** annual meeting, in conjunction with the Association for Asian Studies, the American Philosophical Association, and the American Academy of Religion (exhibits).

10832 ■ Society of Christian Philosophers (SCP)
c/o Kelly James Clark, Sec.-Treas.
Calvin Coll.
Dept. of Philosophy
3201 Burton St. SE
Grand Rapids, MI 49546-4388
Ph: (616)526-6421
Fax: (616)957-8551
E-mail: kclark@calvin.edu
URL: http://www.siu.edu/~scp
Contact: Dr. Kelly James Clark, Sec.-Treas.
Founded: 1978. **Members:** 1,100. **Membership Dues:** regular, $45 (annual) ● student/retired/unemployed, $25 (annual). **Budget:** $50,000. **Regional Groups:** 4. **Multinational. Description:** Professional philosophers, graduate students, and theologians. Seeks to foster fellowship among Christian philosophers and to provide a forum for discussion of issues arising from their joint Christian and philosophical commitments. **Awards:** Konyndyk Memorial Lectureship. **Frequency:** annual. **Type:** monetary. **Computer Services:** Mailing lists, philosophical discussion. **Publications:** *Faith and Philosophy*, quarterly. Journal. **Price:** $45.00 /year for individuals in U.S.; $75.00 /year for institutions in U.S.; $90.00 /year for individuals in Canada; $60.00 /year for institutions in Canada. ISSN: 0739-7046. **Circulation:** 1,600 ● Brochure ● Newsletter, quarterly. Alternate Formats: online. **Conventions/Meetings:** periodic meeting (exhibits) - always spring.

10833 ■ Society for Exact Philosophy (SEP)
Univ. of Florida
Dept. of Philosophy
300 Griffin-Floyd Hall
Gainesville, FL 32611-8545
Ph: (352)392-2084
Fax: (352)392-5577
E-mail: sep@phil.ufl.edu
URL: http://www.phil.ufl.edu/SEP
Contact: Greg Ray, Sec.
Founded: 1971. **Members:** 150. **Membership Dues:** individual, C$5 (annual) ● individual, $5 (annual). **Multinational. Description:** American and Canadian academics in philosophy, computer science, linguistics, and mathematics. Purpose is to sponsor conferences at which papers are read. **Telecommunication Services:** electronic mail, gray@phil.ufl.edu. **Also Known As:** La Societe de Philosophie Exacte. **Conventions/Meetings:** annual meeting.

10834 ■ Society for Phenomenology and Existential Philosophy (SPEP)
c/o John M. Rose, Sec.-Treas.
Philosophy Dept.
Goucher Coll.
1021 Dulany Valley Rd.
Baltimore, MD 21204
Ph: (410)337-6258
Fax: (410)337-6405
E-mail: spep@goucher.edu
URL: http://www.spep.org
Contact: James Risser, Co-Dir.
Founded: 1962. **Members:** 2,200. **Membership Dues:** student, retired, $20 (annual) ● full, $60 (annual). **Budget:** $40,000. **Description:** Represents University and college professors and students of philosophy, psychology, literature, the arts, social studies, and psychiatry. Develops contemporary continental philosophy and phenomenological studies in the areas of cultural, literary, human, or behavioral sciences. **Computer Services:** Mailing lists. **Publications:** *Selected Studies in Phenomenology and Existential Philosophy*, annual. Journal. Contains a special edition of "Philosophy Today". **Circulation:** 1,100 ● *Volume of Essays: Selected Studies in Phenomenology and Existential Philosophy*, periodic. **Price:** $10.00 back issue, in U.S.; $12.00 back issue, outside U.S. **Conventions/Meetings:** annual conference (exhibits) - always October.

10835 ■ Society for the Philosophical Study of Genocide and the Holocaust (SPSGH)
c/o Prof. James R. Watson, PhD, Pres.
Loyola Univ. - New Orleans
Dept. of Philosophy
New Orleans, LA 70118
Ph: (504)865-3940 (601)799-4476
Fax: (504)865-3948
E-mail: jrwatson@ametro.net
URL: http://www.loyno.edu/~spsgh
Contact: Prof. James R. Watson PhD, Pres.
Founded: 1978. **Members:** 50. **Membership Dues:** all, $10 (annual). **Staff:** 10. **Budget:** $400. **Regional Groups:** 3. **State Groups:** 2. **Multinational. Description:** Philosophers with an interest in intellectual reactions to genocide, with particular emphasis on philosophical responses to the Holocaust. Promotes philosophical discussion of genocide. Works to sensitize individuals and governments worldwide regarding the value of human life; seeks to create a "transformation of the way we think and proceed in this murderous, business-as-usual world." Conducts research and educational programs. **Telecommunication Services:** electronic mail, watson@loyno.edu. **Divisions:** European; USA. **Conventions/Meetings:** annual Feminism and Genocide - conference.

10836 ■ Society for the Philosophy of Sex and Love (SPSL)
c/o Dr. Carol Caraway
Dept. of Philosophy
Indiana Univ. of Pennsylvania
452 Sutton Hall
Indiana, PA 15705-0001
Ph: (724)357-2310 (724)357-5617
Fax: (724)357-4039
E-mail: caraway@iup.edu
Contact: Adrianne Leigh McEvoy, Exec.Pres.
Founded: 1977. **Members:** 70. **Membership Dues:** regular, $7 (annual). **Budget:** $500. **Description:** Philosophy instructors and others affiliated with colleges and universities; privately employed profes-

sionals; students. Presents and distributes philosophy papers on the topics of sex and love. **Publications:** *Sex, Love, and Friendship, Studies of the Society for the Philosophy of Sex and Love, 1977-1992.* Book ● Newsletter, annual. Contains membership list. **Conventions/Meetings:** semiannual conference, with session held in conjunction with American Philosophical Association.

10837 ■ Society for Philosophy and Technology (SPT)
c/o Philosophy Documentation Center
PO Box 7147
Charlottesville, VA 22906-7147
Ph: (434)220-3300
Free: (800)444-2419
Fax: (434)220-3301
E-mail: john.sullins@sonoma.edu
URL: http://www.spt.org
Contact: John Sullins, Sec.-Treas.
Founded: 1975. **Members:** 300. **Membership Dues:** general, $20 (annual) ● student, $15 (annual). **Multinational. Description:** Encourages, supports and facilitates philosophically significant considerations of technology. Maintains an association with the American Philosophical Association. **Affiliated With:** American Philosophical Association. **Publications:** *Philosophy and Technology*, annual. Journal. Alternate Formats: online ● Newsletter, quarterly. Alternate Formats: online. **Conventions/Meetings:** biennial conference ● regional meeting, in conjunction with the American Philosophical Association - 3/year.

10838 ■ Society for the Study of Process Philosophies (SSPP)
c/o Dr. Jude Jones, Dir.
Fordham Univ.
Dept. of Philosophy
Collins Hall
441 E Fordham Rd.
Bronx, NY 10458
Ph: (718)817-4721
Fax: (718)817-3300
E-mail: jujones@fordham.edu
URL: http://faculty.msmary.edu/henning/sspp
Contact: Dr. Jude Jones, Dir.
Founded: 1966. **Members:** 350. **Membership Dues:** regular (earning $25,000 or more annually), $5 (annual) ● sustaining, $50 (annual) ● benefactor, $100 (annual). **Description:** Represents scholars in philosophy and related fields with a specialty or interest in process thought. Conducts meetings with conjunction in other national professional meetings, such as the American Philosophical Association and the Metaphysical Society of America (see separate entries). Circulates through its mailing list, papers to be discussed, other papers of interest, and information concerning relevant projects. **Affiliated With:** American Philosophical Association; Metaphysical Society of America. **Conventions/Meetings:** periodic meeting ● semiannual seminar and symposium.

10839 ■ Society for Utopian Studies (SUS)
c/o Dr. Carrie Hintz, Pres.
Queens/CUNY
65-30 Kissena Blvd.
Flushing, NY 11367
Ph: (718)997-4677
Fax: (718)997-4677
E-mail: carriehintz@hotmail.com
URL: http://www.utoronto.ca/utopia
Contact: Dr. Carrie Hintz, Pres.
Founded: 1975. **Members:** 315. **Membership Dues:** regular in U.S., $55 (annual) ● regular in U.S., $100 (biennial) ● regular outside U.S., $60 (annual) ● regular outside U.S., $110 (biennial) ● student/retired/unemployed in U.S., $30 (annual) ● student/retired/unemployed outside U.S., $40 (annual) ● institution in U.S., $85 (annual) ● institution outside U.S., $95 (annual) ● sponsor, $100 (annual) ● benefactor, $250 (annual) ● patron, $500 (annual). **Staff:** 2. **Description:** Academics from a variety of disciplines; architects, futurists, urban planners, and environmentalists; interested others. Promotes the study of experimental and literary utopias and utopian thought through the exchange of information. **Libraries: Type:** reference. **Holdings:** archival material. **Awards:** Arthur O. Lewis Award. **Frequency:** annual. **Type:** monetary. **Recipient:** for best paper by a young scholar ● Distinguished Scholar Award. **Type:** recognition. **Recipient:** for academic accomplishments ● Eugenio Battisti Award. **Frequency:** annual. **Type:** monetary. **Recipient:** to the author of best article ● Larry E. Hough Distinguished Service Award. **Type:** recognition. **Recipient:** for substantial achievement in support of Utopian studies. **Committees:** Awards; Nominating; Steering. **Formerly:** Conference on Utopian Studies. **Publications:** *Utopian Studies*, semiannual. Journal. Contains scholarly articles and book reviews. **Price:** included in membership dues. **Circulation:** 370. **Advertising:** accepted ● *Utopus Discovered*, 3/year. Newsletter. **Price:** included in membership dues. Alternate Formats: online. **Conventions/Meetings:** annual conference, presents formal papers and presentations.

10840 ■ World Institute for Advanced Phenomenological Research and Learning
1 Ivy Pointe Way
Hanover, NH 03755
Ph: (802)295-3487
Fax: (802)295-5963
E-mail: info@phenomenology.org
URL: http://www.phenomenology.org
Contact: Anna-Teresa Tymieniecka, Founder/Pres.
Founded: 1976. **Members:** 2,000. **Membership Dues:** regular, in U.S., $43 (annual) ● regular, outside U.S., $50 (annual). **Staff:** 5. **Budget:** $90,000. **Regional Groups:** 8. **Local Groups:** 1. **Multinational. Description:** Serves as umbrella organization for, and carries out work through, the International Husserl and Phenomenological Research Society, the International Society for Phenomenology and the Sciences of Life, and the International Society of Phenomenology and Literature. Scholars and university and college professors. Aims to: promote research in the phenomenology of man and of the human condition; develop the phenomenological groundwork for interdisciplinary communication; unite scholars for the exchange of views and research. Disseminates book reviews, research articles, and related information. **Libraries: Type:** reference. **Holdings:** 1,000. **Subjects:** phenomenology. **Divisions:** Phenomenological Theory; Phenomenology and Fine Arts; Phenomenology and Literature; Phenomenology and The Sciences of Life. **Affiliated With:** International Husserl and Phenomenological Research Society; International Society for Phenomenology and the Sciences of Life. **Also Known As:** World Phenomenology Institute. **Formerly:** (1976) International Association of Philosophy and Literature. **Publications:** *Analecta Husserliana: The Yearbook of Phenomenological Research*, annual. Journal ● *Impetus and Equipoise in the Life-Strategies of Reason*. Yearbook. Describes the intrinsic law of the primogenital logos that operate in the working of the indivisible dyad of impetus and equipoise. **Price:** $135.00 hardbound (in Great Britain); $198.00 hardbound (in U.S.); $236.00 hardbound (in Europe); $47.00 softcover (in Great Britain) ● *Phenomenological Inquiry: A Review of Philosophical Ideas and Trends*, 1-2/year. Journal. **Price:** $43.00 /year for individuals in North America; $50.00 /year for institutions in North America; $37.00/year for agencies in North America; $50.00 /year for individuals outside North America. ISSN: 0885-3886. **Circulation:** 900. **Advertising:** accepted ● Books. **Conventions/Meetings:** International Phenomenology Conference, held in conjunction with World Congress of Philosophy ● Official Roundtables at the World Congress of Philosophy ● symposium and congress, fine arts and books (exhibits) - 3/year ● World Congress of Phenomenology.

10841 ■ Yves R. Simon Institute (YRSI)
3921 Glenview Dr.
South Bend, IN 46628
Ph: (574)271-1187
Fax: (574)271-1292
E-mail: aos1936@comcast.net
Contact: Anthony O. Simon, Dir.
Founded: 1988. **Members:** 500. **Staff:** 2. **Languages:** English, French. **Description:** Individuals interested in the works and studies of philosopher Yves R. Simon (1903-1961). Works to make Simon's ideas available to the public. Seeks to apply philosophical realism to social issues. Sponsors lectures and conferences. **Libraries: Type:** reference. **Holdings:** 500; articles, biographical archives, books. **Subjects:** Simon's works and contemporaries. **Publications:** *A Conscience as Large as the World: Yves R. Simon Versus the Catholic Neoconservatives*. Book ● *Acquaintance with the Absolute: The Philosophy of Yves R. Simon*. Book. ISSN: 8232-1751 ● *Critique of Moral Knowledge, 2002*. Book ● *Definition of Moral Virtue* ● *Democracy by Vukan Kuic* ● *Foresight and Knowledge* ● *Introduction to the Metaphysics of Knowledge* ● *Philosopher at Work: Essays by Yves R. Simon*. Book ● *Practical Knowledge* ● *Work, Society, and Culture* ● *Yves R. Simon: Real Philosophy*. ISSN: 0847-6961 ● Newsletter, periodic. **Conventions/Meetings:** annual lecture (exhibits).

Phonetics

10842 ■ American Association of Phonetic Sciences (AAPS)
Dept. of Commun. Disorders
3750 Lindell Blvd.
St. Louis, MO 63108
Ph: (314)977-2825
Fax: (314)977-3360
E-mail: mcguirra@slu.edu
Contact: Richard McGuire PhD, Exec. Sec.
Founded: 1973. **Members:** 150. **Membership Dues:** professional, $15 (annual). **Staff:** 7. **Budget:** $2,000. **Description:** Individuals who work in phonetics and have a fundamental interest in the field, and students enrolled in academic programs leading to a degree in phonetics or related fields. Aims to: encourage research in the phonetic sciences; provide a forum for exchange and development of information about the phonetic sciences. **Committees:** Constitution. **Affiliated With:** International Society of Phonetic Sciences. **Publications:** *AAPS Newsletter*, semiannual. **Price:** $15.00. **Advertising:** accepted. **Conventions/Meetings:** annual Business and Scientific Program - conference (exhibits).

Photography

10843 ■ American Photographic Historical Society (APHS)
28 Marksman Ln.
Levittown, NY 11756-5110
Ph: (516)796-7280
Contact: Larry Berke, Treas.
Founded: 1969. **Members:** 500. **Membership Dues:** $30 (annual). **Description:** Historians, collectors, curators, and authors. Operates speakers' bureau; conducts educational programs. **Libraries: Type:** reference. **Holdings:** 300; audiovisuals, books. **Subjects:** photographic history, personalities, patents, events. **Awards:** Rudolf and Hertha Benjamin Photo History Award. **Frequency:** annual. **Type:** monetary. **Recipient:** for relevant history of photography material. **Computer Services:** database ● mailing lists. **Formerly:** (1980) Photographic Historical Society of New York. **Publications:** *In Focus*, 8/year. Newsletter. **Price:** included in membership dues. **Circulation:** 500. **Advertising:** accepted ● *Photographica*, quarterly. Magazine. **Price:** included in membership dues. **Circulation:** 500. **Advertising:** accepted. **Conventions/Meetings:** semiannual general assembly - always in spring/fall in New York, NY.

10844 ■ American Society of Camera Collectors (ASCC)
6445 Antiqua Pl.
West Hills, CA 91307
Ph: (818)888-1125
Contact: Dr. Stuart R. Cole, Pres.
Founded: 1978. **Members:** 100. **Description:** Professional and amateur photographers; collectors of photographica; individuals interested in antique cameras, photo history, motion pictures, and camera

restoration and repairs. Seeks to collect, restore, and preserve antique still and motion picture cameras, photographs, and films and to establish their significance in the history of photography. **Formerly:** (1980) Valley Camera and Movie Collectors. **Publications:** *The Machine That Froze History* ● *Membership Roster*, annual. **Conventions/Meetings:** semiannual Antique Camera Show - always September and March ● monthly meeting (exhibits) - always second Wednesday.

10845 ■ American Society of Photographers (ASP)
c/o Doug Box, Exec. Dir.
PO Box 1120
Caldwell, TX 77836-6120
Ph: (979)272-5555
Free: (800)638-9609
Fax: (979)272-5201
E-mail: dougbox@aol.com
URL: http://www.asofp-online.com
Contact: Doug Box, Exec. Dir.
Founded: 1937. **Members:** 900. **Membership Dues:** active, $125 (annual). **Staff:** 1. **Budget:** $75,000. **Description:** Photographers who have earned the degrees of Master of Photography, Photographic Craftsman, and Photographic Specialist through the Professional Photographers of America (see separate entry). Sponsors annual traveling exhibit of Masters' photographs and annual National Student Competition and Exhibit. **Committees:** Fellowship Judging; Student Exhibit; Traveling Masters Exhibit. **Affiliated With:** Professional Photographers of America. **Publications:** *American Society of Photographers—Newsletter*, quarterly. Includes directory, how-to articles on photography, obituaries, and awards information. **Price:** available to members only. **Circulation:** 1,000. **Advertising:** accepted. **Conventions/Meetings:** annual meeting, held in conjunction with PPA.

10846 ■ Association of International Photography Art Dealers (AIPAD)
1767 P St. NW, Ste.200
Washington, DC 20036-1421
Ph: (202)986-0105
Fax: (202)986-0448
E-mail: info@aipad.com
URL: http://www.aipad.com
Contact: Kathleen Ewing, Exec. Dir.
Founded: 1979. **Members:** 127. **Membership Dues:** regular, $600 (annual). **Staff:** 4. **Budget:** $500,000. **Description:** Galleries and private dealers in fine art and photography, who have been in business for at least 5 years. Promotes a greater understanding of photography as an art form. Fosters communication within the photographic community. Encourages public support of art photography. Seeks to increase the public's confidence in responsible photography dealers. **Awards:** Lifetime Achievement Award. **Frequency:** annual. **Type:** recognition. **Computer Services:** Mailing lists, of members. **Publications:** *AIPAD Membership Directory and Illustrated Catalogue*, annual. **Price:** $25.00 for members, in U.S.; $45.00 for members, outside U.S. **Advertising:** accepted ● *On Collecting Photographs*. Booklet. **Price:** $10.00 in U.S., plus shipping and handling; $15.00 outside U.S., plus shipping and handling. **Conventions/Meetings:** annual The Photography Show - conference and trade show, exhibits by AIPAD members - usually March or February ● seminar (exhibits).

10847 ■ Blue Earth Alliance (BEA)
PO Box 94388
Seattle, WA 98124-6688
E-mail: info@blueearth.org
URL: http://www.blueearth.org
Contact: Adam L. Weintraub, Co-Pres.
Founded: 1996. **Membership Dues:** general, $50 (annual) ● student, $35 (annual) ● supporting, $150 (annual) ● patron, $300 (annual) ● sustaining, $500 (annual) ● benefactor, $1,500 (annual). **Description:** Seeks to educate the public about threatened cultures, environments, and other social concerns through photography. Grants and sponsors various photographic projects. Provides opportunities for photographers to pursue personal photographic projects. **Publications:** *Shooting from the Heart*, periodic. Handbook. Collaborative resource book for artists pursuing not-for-profit projects. **Price:** included in membership dues ● Newsletter, periodic. **Price:** included in membership dues.

10848 ■ Daguerreian Society
3043 W Liberty Ave.
Pittsburgh, PA 15216-2460
Ph: (412)221-0306
E-mail: dagsocpgh@comcast.net
URL: http://www.daguerre.org
Contact: Matthew Isenburg, Pres.
Founded: 1988. **Members:** 1,035. **Membership Dues:** individual, $75-$80 (annual) ● household, $90-$95 (annual) ● student, $50 (annual). **Description:** Daguerreotypists, photo historians, collectors, dealers, institutions, and others interested in daguerreotype photography. Dedicated to the history, science, and art of the daguerreotype. (A daguerreotype is an early photograph produced on a silver or a silver-covered copper plate). **Computer Services:** Information services, galleries and resources about daguerreotype ● record retrieval services, past messages of DagNews. **Publications:** *The Daguerreian Annual*, annual. Book. Compilation of unique research by society members; includes reproductions and historical reprints. **Price:** $40.00 for members (softcover); $55.00 for nonmembers (softcover); $70.00 for members (hardcopy); $85.00 for nonmembers (hardcopy) ● *The Daguerreian Membership Directory*, annual, always August. Contains members' names, addresses, phones, and interests. Alternate Formats: online ● *The Daguerreian Society Newsletter*, quarterly. Contains previously unpublished daguerreotypes, articles, and publication reviews. **Price:** included in membership dues. **Advertising:** accepted. Alternate Formats: online. **Conventions/Meetings:** annual symposium and trade show, with presentations and discussions (exhibits) - always fall.

10849 ■ En Foco
1738 Hone Ave.
Bronx, NY 10461
Ph: (718)584-7718
Fax: (718)584-7718
E-mail: info@enfoco.org
URL: http://www.enfoco.org
Contact: Miriam Romais, Exec. Dir.
Founded: 1974. **Members:** 610. **Membership Dues:** photographer, $45 (annual) ● art professional, $80 (annual) ● collector, $300 (annual) ● corporate, $1,000 (annual). **Staff:** 3. **Budget:** $100,000. **Languages:** English, Spanish. **Description:** Hispanic photographers and other artists of color. Aids and promotes photographers; conducts art exhibitions; maintains slide registry and print collectors program. **Libraries: Type:** reference. **Holdings:** artwork, books, clippings, periodicals. **Subjects:** photography. **Awards:** New Works Competition. **Frequency:** annual. **Type:** recognition. **Recipient:** honorarium for members who are photographers of color. **Publications:** *Nueva Luz* (in English and Spanish), 3/year. Journal. Contains information on photography competitions, exhibitions, and employment opportunities in the photography field. **Price:** $7.00 for nonmembers, plus $3 for shipping and handling; $15.00 for nonmembers, commemorative issue; included in membership dues. ISSN: 0887-5855. **Circulation:** 5,000. **Advertising:** accepted. Alternate Formats: online ● Brochure. **Price:** free for members ● Catalogs. **Conventions/Meetings:** Gallery Opening - meeting (exhibits).

10850 ■ International Kodak Historical Society (IKHS)
PO Box 21
Flourtown, PA 19031
URL: http://www.kodakhistoricalsociety.org
Contact: Dr. George S. Layne, Dir.
Founded: 1985. **Members:** 100. **Description:** Persons interested in the history of photography, particularly history related to Eastman Kodak Company. Makes available information on Kodakiana and Kodak cameras. **Publications:** *Journal of the International Kodak Historical Society*, quarterly. Contains articles on Kodakiana. **Price:** $20.00/year.

10851 ■ International Photographic Historical Organization (InPHO)
PO Box 16074
San Francisco, CA 94116
Ph: (415)681-4356
E-mail: silver@photographyhistory.com
URL: http://www.well.com/user/silver
Contact: David F. Silver, Pres.
Founded: 1985. **Members:** 500. **Description:** Resource center for groups or individuals seeking information pertaining to the history of photography. Services include: research and resource acquisition, peer review of new photohistorical literature and media presentations, aid to museums and photohistorical exhibits. Appraises classic/antique cameras and photographic materials. Operates speakers' bureau. **Libraries: Type:** reference. **Holdings:** archival material. **Subjects:** history of photography. **Awards:** Talbot Award. **Frequency:** annual. **Type:** recognition. **Recipient:** for excellence in photo historical writing. **Absorbed:** (1994) Bay Area Photographica Association. **Publications:** *Directory of Photographic Collectors, Organizations, and Historians*, periodic. Lists individuals who wish to share information on photographic history.

10852 ■ International Society of Fine Art Photographers (ISOFAP)
Address Unknown since 2008
Founded: 1996. **Membership Dues:** individual, $75 (annual). **Staff:** 3. **Budget:** $180,000. **Languages:** English, Spanish. **Description:** Promotes the collection, creation, understanding, and publishing of fine art photography. Sponsors workshops, fine art exhibits, competitions, publishing projects and educational programs. **Libraries: Type:** reference. **Holdings:** books, monographs, periodicals. **Subjects:** photography. **Awards:** Focused. **Frequency:** annual. **Type:** monetary. **Recipient:** for excellence in documentary photography. **Publications:** *Fototeque*, bimonthly. Directory. **Price:** $12.95. **Circulation:** 10,000. **Advertising:** accepted ● Books. **Conventions/Meetings:** annual convention and trade show (exhibits).

10853 ■ National Stereoscopic Association (NSA)
PO Box 86708
Portland, OR 97286
Ph: (951)736-8918
E-mail: strwld@teleport.com
URL: http://www.stereoview.org
Contact: Mr. Lawrence Kaufman, Pres.
Founded: 1974. **Members:** 3,500. **Membership Dues:** in U.S., $32 (annual) ● outside U.S., $44 (annual). **Staff:** 3. **Regional Groups:** 12. **Description:** Museums, libraries, institutions, and individuals with an interest in history as recorded by the stereo photographer and in the present day uses of stereoscopy, the science dealing with stereographic (three dimensional photographic) equipment. Goals are: to promote the study and collection of stereographs and related materials; to encourage the appreciation of the stereograph as a visual record of more than 120 years of U.S. history; to foster the use of stereoscopy in the visual arts and technology; to provide a forum for collectors and students of stereoscopic history. Maintains the Oliver Wendell Holmes Library containing important early catalogs and trade lists of 19th century stereo photographers and publishers and a collection of stereographs and books on stereoscopy and related photographic techniques. Sponsors competitions; compiles statistics; conducts research programs. **Telecommunication Services:** electronic mail, kaufman3d@earthlink.net. **Committees:** Contemporary Stereoscopy. **Formerly:** (2001) Stereo Photographers, Collectors and Enthusiasts Club. **Publications:** *Stereo World*, bimonthly. Magazine. Contains calendar of events. **Price:** included in membership dues. ISSN: 0191-4030. **Circulation:** 3,500. **Advertising:** accepted ●

Membership Directory, annual. **Conventions/Meetings:** annual meeting.

10854 ■ Nikon Historical Society (NHS)
RJR Publishing Inc.
PO Box 3213
Munster, IN 46321
E-mail: rotoloni@msn.com
URL: http://www.nikonhs.org
Contact: Robert J. Rotoloni, Founder/Pres.
Founded: 1983. **Members:** 400. **Membership Dues:** regular in U.S. and Canada, $35 (annual) ● regular outside U.S. and Canada, $45 (annual). **For-Profit. Description:** Persons interested in Nikon cameras. Facilitates research into the history and development of the Nikon camera and its manufacturer Nippon Kogaku. Compiles statistics. **Libraries: Type:** not open to the public. **Holdings:** 200; biographical archives. **Computer Services:** database, Nikon serial numbers. **Publications:** *History of the Nikon Camera*. Monograph ● *Nikon Journal*, quarterly. Contains articles on research of Nikon cameras, and membership information. **Price:** $7.00 in U.S. (back issues); $9.00 in Canada (back issues). **Advertising:** accepted. **Conventions/Meetings:** semiannual meeting (exhibits).

10855 ■ The Photographic Historical Society (TPHS)
350 Whiting Rd.
Webster, NY 14580
E-mail: tphs@rochester.rr.com
URL: http://www.tphs.org
Contact: Andrew Davidhazy, Contact
Founded: 1965. **Members:** 150. **Membership Dues:** regular, $20 (annual) ● family, $30 (annual). **Description:** Photograph historians, photographers, and camera and image collectors. Works to bring together individuals interested in preserving the historical objects that depict the history of photography and to share knowledge and experience with other members. **Awards:** Fellow of the Society. **Type:** recognition. **Recipient:** for individual contribution to photo history. **Publications:** *Photographic History Society Newsletter*, quarterly. **Price:** included in membership dues. **Circulation:** 150. **Conventions/Meetings:** triennial PhotoHistory - symposium, lectures and talks by recognized experts in all aspects of the history of photography, informal gatherings, trade show (exhibits).

10856 ■ Pictorial Photographers of America (PPA)
c/o Jack Levy, Treas.
300 E 74th St., Apt. 35G
New York, NY 10021-3717
Ph: (212)243-0273
Fax: (212)206-7640
E-mail: info@ppa-photoclub.org
URL: http://www.ppa-photoclub.org
Contact: Kathryn Buck, Pres.
Founded: 1916. **Members:** 25. **Membership Dues:** regular, $50 (annual). **Description:** Amateur and professional photographers. Aids members in perfecting their photographic techniques. Sponsors individual print and slide analysis, exhibitions, and field trips. **Publications:** *Light and Shade*, monthly. Newsletter. Includes calendar of events, photography contests, and book reviews. **Price:** available to members only. **Circulation:** 100. Alternate Formats: online ● Membership Directory, annual. **Conventions/Meetings:** competition (exhibits) ● annual dinner, includes awards presentation ● seminar.

10857 ■ Student Photographic Society (SPS)
229 Peachtree St. NE, Ste.2200
Atlanta, GA 30303
Free: (866)886-5325
Fax: (404)614-6400
E-mail: info@studentphoto.com
URL: http://www.studentphoto.com
Contact: Joy Tribble, Contact
Founded: 1999. **Membership Dues:** student, $29 (annual). **Description:** Represents photography students and educators. Provides career building resources, networking opportunities, and information resources to photography students. Conducts photography contests. **Telecommunication Services:** electronic mail, jtribble@studentphoto.com. **Publications:** *Student Photo Newsletter*. **Price:** included in membership dues.

Play

10858 ■ The Association for the Study of Play (TASP)
c/o Dana Gross, Sec.
St. Olaf Coll.
1520 St. Olaf Ave.
Northfield, MN 55057-1098
Ph: (507)646-3624
E-mail: aguilmette@brocku.ca
URL: http://www.csuchico.edu/kine/tasp
Contact: Anne Marie Guilmette, Pres.
Founded: 1973. **Members:** 230. **Membership Dues:** retiree and student (with TASP Annual), $65 (annual) ● professional in U.S. (includes TASP Annual), $75 (annual) ● professional outside U.S. (includes TASP Annual), $80 (annual) ● institutional in U.S. (with TASP Annual), $85 (annual) ● retiree, student, institutional (without TASP Annual), $25 (annual). **Description:** Scholars in the social and behavioral sciences (anthropology, psychology, sociology, physical education, folklore, kinesiology, the arts, philosophy, dance, recreation, history, communication, cultural studies and musicology); college and university libraries. Promotes, stimulates, and encourages the study of play; supports and cooperates with other organizations having similar purposes; organizes meetings and publications that facilitate the sharing and dissemination of information related to the field. **Awards: Type:** recognition. **Recipient:** for pioneers in play research and theory. **Formerly:** (1987) Association for the Anthropological Study of Play. **Publications:** *TASP Annual: Play and Culture Studies Edited Volume*, annual. Contains peer-reviewed articles on play theory and research. **Price:** included in membership dues ● Newsletter, 3/year. Contains book reviews and research reports. **Price:** included in membership dues. **Circulation:** 250. Alternate Formats: online. **Conventions/Meetings:** annual meeting (exhibits) ● Olympic Scientific Congress.

Poetry

10859 ■ Academy of American Poets
584 Broadway, Ste.604
New York, NY 10012-5243
Ph: (212)274-0343
Fax: (212)274-9427
E-mail: academy@poets.org
URL: http://www.poets.org
Contact: Tree Swenson, Exec. Dir.
Founded: 1934. **Members:** 8,500. **Membership Dues:** contributing, $35 (annual) ● associate, $55 (annual) ● sustaining, $100 (annual). **Staff:** 10. **Budget:** $1,800,000. **Description:** Fosters the appreciation of contemporary poetry and supports American poets at all stages of their careers. Offers programs such as Poets.org, National Poetry Month, Poetry Audio Archives, American Poet magazine, Academy Book Awards, poetry readings and events, and high-school workshops for New York City students. **Awards:** College Prizes. **Frequency:** annual. **Type:** monetary. **Recipient:** for students of more than 170 colleges and universities ● Harold Morton Landon Translation Award. **Frequency:** annual. **Type:** recognition. **Recipient:** for an American poet for published translation of poetry from any language into English ● James Laughlin Award. **Frequency:** annual. **Type:** recognition. **Recipient:** for publication of a second manuscript by a previously published poet ● Lenora Marshall Poets Prize. **Frequency:** annual. **Type:** monetary. **Recipient:** for best book poetry ● Walt Whitman Award. **Frequency:** annual. **Type:** recognition. **Recipient:** for publication of a first manuscript by a previously published poet. **Publications:** *American Poet*, semiannual. Journal. Contains poems, essays and articles on academy programs. **Price:** included in membership dues. **Circulation:** 10,000. **Advertising:** accepted ● *Poetry Audio Archives*. Audiotapes. Contains a series of poets reading their work. Alternate Formats: CD-ROM.

10860 ■ Friends of Robert Frost (FoRF)
c/o Robert Frost Stone House Museum
121 Historic Rte. 7A
Shaftsbury, VT 05262
Ph: (802)447-6200
E-mail: stopping@frostfriends.org
URL: http://www.frostfriends.org
Contact: Carole Thompson, Pres.
Membership Dues: friend, $25 (annual) ● sponsor, $50 (annual) ● patron, $100 (annual) ● benefactor, $500 (annual). **Description:** Promotes interest in the poet Robert Frost's life and art, and the historic preservation of the Frost farms in New England where he lived and wrote. **Publications:** Newsletter. Contains book reviews, mailbag, feature stories, and a letter from the association president. Alternate Formats: online. **Conventions/Meetings:** meeting, with poetry readings.

10861 ■ Haiku Society of America (HSA)
c/o Lane Parker, Sec.
578 3rd Ave.
San Francisco, CA 94118-3903
E-mail: lstparker@cs.com
URL: http://www.hsa-haiku.org
Contact: Lane Parker, Sec.
Founded: 1968. **Members:** 600. **Membership Dues:** regular in U.S., $33 (annual) ● regular in Canada and Mexico, $35 (annual) ● all other area, $45 (annual) ● senior/full-time student in North America, $30 (annual). **Budget:** $13,000. **Regional Groups:** 7. **Description:** Individuals interested in the writing and enjoyment of Haiku. **Publications:** *A Haiku Path*. Book. **Price:** $27.95 ● *Frogpond*, 3/year. Magazine. Contains Haiku and related forms of poetry, criticism, and theoretical articles. **Price:** included in membership dues; $7.00/issue for nonmembers in U.S. and Canada; $9.00/issue for nonmembers in other countries. ISSN: 8755-156X. **Circulation:** 600 ● *Information Sheet*, annual ● *Members' Anthology*, annual ● Newsletter, quarterly. Reports minutes of quarterly meetings, and news items about Haiku groups. **Conventions/Meetings:** meeting - always fall.

10862 ■ International Poetry Forum (IPF)
c/o Grace Library
3333 5th Ave.
Pittsburgh, PA 15213
Ph: (412)621-9893
Fax: (412)621-9898
E-mail: ipf1@earthlink.net
URL: http://www.thepoetryforum.org
Contact: Dr. Samuel Hazo, Pres./Dir./Founder
Founded: 1966. **Members:** 126. **Staff:** 2. **Description:** Sponsors poetry readings. Maintains biographical archives.

10863 ■ Longfellow Society
c/o Dawn L. Stewart, Pres.
106 Richard Rd.
Holliston, MA 01746
E-mail: dawnstewart@dlstewart.com
URL: http://www.dlstewart.com/longfellow
Contact: Dawn L. Stewart, Pres.
Founded: 1971. **Members:** 30. **Membership Dues:** adult, $20 (annual). **Local Groups:** 1. **Description:** Poets, writers, educators, artists. Encourages discussion and exchange of ideas in the literary arts. Conducts regular meetings for recitation, review, criticism, and exercise in poetic and literary expression. Special interest in the life and works of Henry Wadsworth Longfellow (1807-82). **Libraries: Type:** reference. **Holdings:** archival material, books, clippings, periodicals. **Subjects:** Longfellow, contemporaries, speakers, visitors, members. **Awards: Type:** recognition. **Committees:** Literature; Poetry. **Formerly:** (1973) Wayside Club; (1977) Longfellow Club; (1987) Longfellow Poetry Society; (2003) Longfellow Society of Sudbury at the Wayside Inn. **Publications:** Journal, annual. **Price:** included in membership dues;

$8.50 /year for nonmembers. **Conventions/Meetings:** annual conference.

10864 ■ Mirage Group (MG)
PO Box 803282
Santa Clarita, CA 91380-3282
Ph: (661)799-0694
URL: http://hometown.aol.com/mrg291/myhomepage/business.html
Founded: 1997. **Members:** 32. **Membership Dues:** associate, $24 (annual) ● general, $70 (annual) ● family, $120 (annual). **Staff:** 2. **Budget:** $2,000. **Regional Groups:** 2. **Description:** Individuals with an interest in poetry. Promotes appreciation and writing of poetry. Provides support and promotional assistance to poets; sponsors competitions; maintains speakers' bureau. Publishes monograph series as a resource for members. **Awards:** Mirage Award. **Frequency:** annual. **Type:** recognition. **Publications:** *Mirage*, periodic. Monograph. **Circulation:** 100. **Advertising:** accepted. Alternate Formats: online ● *New Mirage Quarterly*. Journal. Contains poetry submitted by its readers. **Price:** $26.00. **Circulation:** 150. **Advertising:** accepted ● Also publishes a special series of monographs. **Conventions/Meetings:** annual meeting.

10865 ■ National Federation of State Poetry Societies (NFSPS)
c/o Ms. Doris Stengel, Pres.
1510 S 7th St.
Brainerd, MN 56401
Ph: (218)829-9072
Fax: (218)829-9072
E-mail: dpoet@brainerd.net
URL: http://nfsps.com
Contact: Ms. Doris Stengel, Pres.
Founded: 1959. **Members:** 7,000. **Membership Dues:** individual, $1 (annual). **Staff:** 28. **Budget:** $40,000. **State Groups:** 39. **Description:** Educational, literary, and cultural organization dedicated to the promulgation of poetry. Seeks to unite all poets in the bond of fellowship and understanding. Sponsors annual national poetry contest; state groups conduct student poetry contests. **Libraries: Type:** reference. **Holdings:** archival material, books, business records, clippings, monographs, periodicals. **Subjects:** poetry. **Awards:** Manningham Youth Awards. **Frequency:** annual. **Type:** monetary. **Recipient:** for previous winners of member states, students in grades 6-12 ● NFSPS Poetry Awards (50 categories). **Frequency:** annual. **Type:** monetary. **Recipient:** for the winner of NSPS poetry manuscript competition ● NFSPS University-Level Poetry Competition. **Frequency:** annual. **Type:** monetary. **Recipient:** for the winner of the NFSPS university-level poetry competition ● Stevens Poetry Manuscript Prize. **Frequency:** annual. **Type:** monetary. **Recipient:** for the winner of NSPS poetry manuscript competition. **Publications:** *ENCORE*, annual. Journal. Contains collection of prize poems from annual contest. **Price:** $10.00 ● *Strophes*, quarterly. Newsletter. Covers the activities of state poetry groups; includes contest news. **Price:** free, for members only; $1.00 for nonmembers. **Circulation:** 7,000 ● Brochures, annual. Contains a listing of 50 contests. **Price:** free for SASE. **Circulation:** 7,000. **Conventions/Meetings:** annual conference and convention, with 5 days of poetry programs and awards (exhibits) - weekend in June.

10866 ■ National Poetry Foundation (NPF)
c/o University of Maine
5752 Neville Hall, Rm. 400
Orono, ME 04469-5752
Ph: (207)581-3814 (207)581-3813
Fax: (207)581-3886
E-mail: hatlen@maine.edu
URL: http://www2.umaine.edu/npf/NPF1.html
Contact: Burton Hatlen, Dir.
Founded: 1971. **Members:** 950. **Staff:** 4. **Description:** Individuals and organizations concerned with promoting poets and poetry. **Publications:** *Paideuma: Studies on American and British Modernist Poetry*, 3/year. Journal. Includes book reviews, poetry-related events and activities, and reports on Pound conferences. **Price:** $20.00 /year for individuals; $37.00 /year for institutions. ISSN: 0090-5674. **Circulation:** 700. **Advertising:** accepted ● *Sagetrieb: Poetry and Poetics after Modernism*, 3/year. Journal. Contains book reviews, poetry-related activities and events, conference reports, and review essays on contemporary poetry presses. **Price:** $20.00 /year for individuals; $37.00 /year for institutions. ISSN: 0735-4665. **Circulation:** 400. **Advertising:** accepted ● Books. **Conventions/Meetings:** annual conference (exhibits) - usually June or August in Orono, ME.

10867 ■ Poetry Foundation
444 N Michigan Ave., Ste.1850
Chicago, IL 60611-4034
Ph: (312)787-7070
Fax: (312)787-6650
E-mail: mail@poetryfoundation.org
URL: http://www.poetrymagazine.org
Contact: John Barr, Pres.
Founded: 1941. **Staff:** 8. **Multinational. Description:** Serves as a private operating foundation devoted to poetry. **Awards:** Ruth Lilly Poetry Fellowship. **Frequency:** annual. **Type:** monetary. **Recipient:** to two young poets for one year of poetry study and practice ● Ruth Lilly Poetry Prize. **Frequency:** annual. **Type:** monetary. **Recipient:** to an American poet whose accomplishments warrant extraordinary recognition. **Additional Websites:** http://www.poetryfoundation.org. **Formerly:** (2003) Modern Poetry Association. **Publications:** *Poetry*, monthly. Magazine. Contains original poems and prose about poetry. **Price:** included in membership dues; $35.00 /year for nonmembers. ISSN: 0032-2032. **Circulation:** 12,000. **Advertising:** accepted. **Conventions/Meetings:** annual meeting.

10868 ■ Poetry Project (PP)
St. Mark's Church
131 E 10th St.
New York, NY 10003
Ph: (212)674-0910
Fax: (212)529-2318
E-mail: info@poetryproject.com
URL: http://www.poetryproject.com
Contact: Anselm Berrigan, Artistic Dir.
Founded: 1966. **Members:** 6,000. **Membership Dues:** individual, $50 (annual) ● supporting, $85 (annual) ● sustaining, $125 (annual) ● donor, $250 (annual) ● benefactor, $500 (annual) ● patron, $1,000 (annual). **Staff:** 3. **Budget:** $250,000. **Description:** Represents poets and individuals interested in poetry. Promotes poetry and foster contemporary as well as traditional forms of poetry. Serves as a learning institution for poetry writing. Sponsors three weekly reading series in which poets are paid for reading their work. Conducts weekly poetry workshops. Maintains tape archives of readings. Holds New Years marathon in which over 120 poets, writers, dancers, musicians, and artists perform. **Libraries: Type:** reference. **Holdings:** archival material, audio recordings. **Subjects:** poetry readings. **Computer Services:** Mailing lists. **Publications:** *The World*, annual. Magazine. **Price:** $10.00/issue; $35.00 for 4 issues. ISSN: 0043-8154 ● Newsletter, bimonthly, from October-July. Includes regular features and interviews, announcements, regional updates, poetry, short fiction, as well as various other poetical pieces. **Price:** $25.00 /year for nonmembers; included in membership dues. **Circulation:** 6,000. **Advertising:** accepted. Alternate Formats: online. **Conventions/Meetings:** annual symposium.

10869 ■ Poetry Society of America (PSA)
15 Gramercy Park
New York, NY 10003
Ph: (212)254-9628
Fax: (212)673-2352
E-mail: tom@poetrysociety.org
URL: http://www.poetrysociety.org
Contact: Alice Quinn, Exec. Dir.
Founded: 1910. **Members:** 2,900. **Membership Dues:** individual, $45 (annual) ● student, $25 (annual) ● sustainer, $100 (annual) ● patron, $250 (annual) ● benefactor, $500 (annual) ● angel, $1,000 (annual) ● supporter, $65 (annual). **Staff:** 6. **Budget:** $500,000. **Description:** Represents professional and practicing poets, critics, lecturers, librarians, educators, and patrons. Aims to aid poets and poetry. Sponsors competitions. Conducts poetry workshops, readings, lectures, and symposia. **Libraries: Type:** not open to the public. **Holdings:** 5,000. **Subjects:** poetry. **Awards: Frequency:** annual. **Type:** recognition. **Boards:** Directors. **Publications:** *Crossroads*, semiannual. Journal. Includes interviews, conference dates, grants, and information on new members. **Price:** free, for members only. **Circulation:** 3,000. **Advertising:** accepted. Alternate Formats: online ● *Poetry in Motion: 100 Poems from the Subways and Buses* ● *The Poetry in Motion Postcard Book*. **Conventions/Meetings:** annual meeting, with awards ceremony (exhibits).

10870 ■ Poets and Writers (PW)
72 Spring St., Ste.301
New York, NY 10012
Ph: (212)226-3586
Fax: (212)226-3963
E-mail: admin@pw.org
URL: http://www.pw.org
Contact: Elliot Figman, Exec. Dir.
Founded: 1970. **Staff:** 21. **Budget:** $3,000,000. **Description:** Provides support, information, and publications to help writers in their professional lives. **Libraries: Type:** reference. **Holdings:** archival material. **Computer Services:** Information services, for writers ● mailing lists ● online services, publication. **Publications:** *Directory of American Poets and Fiction Writers*, biennial. **Price:** $29.95/issue for individuals; $34.95/issue for institutions. ISSN: 0734-0605. **Advertising:** accepted. Alternate Formats: online ● *IntoPrint: Guides to the Writing Life* ● *Literary Agents: The Essential Guide for Writers* ● *Writers' Resources* ● Magazine, bimonthly. Includes information on such topics as copyright, taxes, grants and awards, translation, and agents. Includes essays by and interviews with poets. **Price:** $14.97/year. **Circulation:** 50,000. **Advertising:** accepted. Alternate Formats: microform; online ● Newsletter, monthly. Alternate Formats: online.

10871 ■ Tanka Society of America (TSA)
c/o Carole MacRury, Sec.-Treas.
1636 Edwards Dr.
Point Roberts, WA 98281
E-mail: macrury@whidbey.com
URL: http://www.tankasocietyofamerica.com
Contact: Carole MacRury, Sec.-Treas.
Founded: 2000. **Membership Dues:** in U.S., $25 (annual) ● in Canada, $30 (annual) ● outside U.S. and Canada, $35 (annual). **Multinational. Description:** Represents individuals interested in tanka poetry. Aims to further the writing, reading, study and appreciation of tanka poetry in English. Facilitates collaboration and cooperation among members. **Telecommunication Services:** electronic mail, mchlmcclintock@aol.com. **Publications:** *Ribbons*, quarterly. Journal. Features articles, essays, translations, book reviews, and contest results. **Price:** included in membership dues; $5.00 per back issue for members in U.S.; $9.00 per back issue for members outside U.S. and Canada; $10.00 per back issue for nonmembers. Alternate Formats: online ● *TSA Newsletter*. Contains news and announcements pertaining to Tanka Society of America business, its members, and events in the tanka community in general. **Price:** included in membership dues; $3.50 per back issue for members in U.S.; $4.00 per back issue for members outside U.S. and Canada; $5.00 per back issue for nonmembers.

10872 ■ Theodore Roethke Memorial Foundation (TRMF)
c/o John Shek
11 W Hannum Blvd.
Saginaw, MI 48602
Ph: (989)792-5567
Fax: (989)792-5567
E-mail: patriciashek2004@yahoo.com
Contact: Patricia Shek, Pres.
Founded: 1967. **Members:** 5. **Description:** Gives a triennial award for a published work of poetry in

English. (Organization is named for Theodore Roethke, who was born in Saginaw, MI in 1908 and who received more prizes for his work than any other contemporary poet). **Awards:** Theodore Roethke Memorial Poetry Prize. **Frequency:** triennial. **Type:** monetary. **Recipient:** for a published work of poetry in English.

10873 ■ World Congress of Poets
c/o Michelle Wang, Treas.
4423 Pitch Pine Court
San Jose, CA 95136
Ph: (408)281-8041
Contact: Michelle Wang, Treas.
Founded: 1969. **Members:** 1,200. **Membership Dues:** poet, $40 (annual) ● life, $300. **Languages:** Arabic, Chinese, English, French, German, Greek, Spanish. **Multinational. Description:** Published and unpublished poets. Seeks to unite nations in achieving world peace and understanding through poetry and "substitute peace for war in the minds of men." Fosters the interchange of culture and poetic works and translations between members. **Awards: Frequency:** annual. **Type:** recognition. **Recipient:** given to 3 major and 3 minor poets. **Publications:** Newsletter (in Chinese, English, French, German, Greek, and Spanish), annual. **Conventions/Meetings:** annual congress - India; Mongolia.

10874 ■ Yuki Teikei Haiku Society (YTHS)
5135 Cribari Pl.
San Jose, CA 95135
E-mail: kdkaaacg@aol.com
URL: http://www.youngleaves.org
Contact: Ann Bendixen, Sec.
Founded: 1975. **Members:** 145. **Membership Dues:** regular, in U.S., $26 ● regular, outside U.S., $31. **Description:** Promotes the study and enjoyment of the Japanese tradition of Yuki Teikei Haiku (a Japanese poetic form that consists of 5, 7, and 5 syllable count and a kigo, or season-word). Facilitates intellectual and cultural interchange among English language haikuists. Conducts Yuki Teikei Haiku workshops and retreats. Sponsors annual international competition in collaboration with distinguished judges from Japan. Conducts group lectures on haiku history and practice. Operates speakers' bureau. **Awards:** Kiyoshi Tokutomi Memorial Haiku Contest. **Type:** recognition. **Supersedes:** Yukuhara Haiku Society, English Language Division. **Publications:** *Geppo Haiku Journal*, bimonthly. Includes calendar of events, member news, and information on society workshops and competitions. **Price:** included in membership dues. **Circulation:** 170 ● *Haiku Journal*, periodic ● *Members Anthology*, annual. **Price:** included in membership dues. **Conventions/Meetings:** monthly meeting ● annual retreat - always first weekend after Labor Day, Pacific Grove, CA.

Poets

10875 ■ James Dickey Society
c/o Prof. William B. Thesing, Dir./Ed.
Univ. of South Carolina
Dept. of English
1620 Coll. St.
Columbia, SC 29208
Fax: (803)777-9064
E-mail: thesingw@gwm.sc.edu
URL: http://www.jamesdickey.org
Contact: Prof. William B. Thesing, Dir./Ed.
Founded: 1990. **Description:** Represents scholars and other individuals interested in the study of the life and literary works of James Lafayette Dickey III, an American poet, novelist, essayist, and critic. Aims to advance scholarship and dissemination of knowledge pertaining to the life and work of James Dickey. Supports research and other scholarly activities concerning the author's primary and secondary works. **Publications:** *James Dickey Newsletter*, semiannual. **Price:** $12.00 /year for individuals; $14.00 /year for institutions in U.S.; $15.50 /year for institutions outside U.S.; $8.00/issue for individuals and institutions.

Polish

10876 ■ American Institute of Polish Culture (AIPC)
1440 79th St. Causeway, Ste.117
Miami, FL 33141
Ph: (305)864-2349
Fax: (305)865-5150
E-mail: info@ampolinstitute.org
URL: http://www.ampolinstitute.org
Contact: Blanka A. Rosenstiel, Pres./Founder
Founded: 1972. **Members:** 350. **Membership Dues:** individual, $50 (annual) ● family, $75 (annual) ● patron, $150 (annual) ● benefactor, $500 (annual) ● sponsor, $1,000 (annual). **Staff:** 3. **Budget:** $260,000. **Languages:** English, Polish. **Description:** Represents professionals, students, artists, writers, and members of other cultural organizations. Advances the knowledge of and appreciation for the history, science, art, and culture of Poland. Sponsors seminars, exhibitions, concerts, poetry readings, and Polish culture weeks (at universities). **Libraries: Type:** reference. **Holdings:** 2,000; books. **Subjects:** Polish literature, culture, art, fiction, non-fiction, history, biography, science, poetry. **Awards:** Gold Medal Award. **Frequency:** annual. **Type:** recognition ● Harriet Irsay Scholarship Grant. **Frequency:** annual. **Type:** grant. **Recipient:** for the fields of journalism, communication and/or public relations. **Committees:** Educational; Social. **Councils:** Chopin Foundation. **Formerly:** (1974) Polish-American Cultural Institute of Miami. **Publications:** *Good News*, annual. Magazine. Contains articles, photos, reports on activities. **Price:** free for members. **Circulation:** 3,000. **Advertising:** accepted. Alternate Formats: online; diskette ● Also publishes books. **Conventions/Meetings:** annual International Polonaise Ball - dinner, gala honoring ties between Poland and different nations always held in Miami Beach, FL - first weekend of February.

10877 ■ Federation of Polish Americans (FPA)
2000 L St. NW, Ste.200
Washington, DC 20036
Fax: (800)466-4850
E-mail: fpamembers@usa.net
URL: http://www.polishwashington.com/fpa
Contact: Mark Lazar, Pres.
Membership Dues: President's Club, $1,200 (annual) ● regular, $36 (annual) ● supporting, $24 (annual) ● student, $12 (annual). **Description:** Brings together persons of Polish heritage and those supportive of the Polish American community's issues and concerns. Promotes the interests of Polish Americans in civic affairs. **Publications:** Newsletter. **Conventions/Meetings:** meeting.

10878 ■ Jozef Pilsudski Institute of America for Research in the Modern History of Poland
180 2nd Ave.
New York, NY 10003-5778
Ph: (212)505-9077
Fax: (212)505-9052
E-mail: info@pilsudski.org
URL: http://www.pilsudski.org
Contact: Mr. Jacek Galazka, Pres.
Founded: 1943. **Members:** 1,000. **Membership Dues:** sustaining, $100 (annual) ● student/retired, $25 (annual) ● regular, $50 (annual) ● life, $1,000. **Staff:** 2. **Budget:** $250,000. **Languages:** English, French, German, Polish, Russian. **Description:** Collects documents and publishes works connected with the modern history of Poland, particularly the history of Poland's fight for independence. Named for Jozef Pilsudski (1867-1935), Polish marshal and first head of state, 1918-22. Founded in Warsaw, Poland, in 1923, as the Institute for Research in Modern History of Poland; reorganized in the United States after most of the institute's archives were destroyed in World War II. **Libraries: Type:** reference. **Holdings:** 25,000; books, clippings, films, papers, periodicals, photographs. **Subjects:** diplomatic, political and military documents, personal accounts and letters, history. **Awards: Type:** recognition ● **Type:** scholarship. **Recipient:** for research. **Computer Services:** database, archive inventory ● database, Polish history from 1863-present and the experiences of Poles living in the Soviet Union from 1939-present ● mailing lists. **Publications:** *Biuletyn Instytutu J. Pilsudskiego*, annual. **Price:** available to members only. **Advertising:** accepted ● *Niepodleglosc*, annual. Presents a historical review covering modern history of Poland and Polish-American relations since 1918; includes book reviews. **Price:** $15.00/issue for members. **Advertising:** accepted. Also Cited As: *Independence* ● Books (in English and Polish) ● Brochures ● Monographs. **Conventions/Meetings:** monthly lecture.

10879 ■ Kosciuszko Foundation (KF)
15 E 65th St.
New York, NY 10021-6595
Ph: (212)734-2130
Fax: (212)628-4552
E-mail: info@thekf.org
URL: http://www.kosciuszkofoundation.org
Contact: Joseph E. Gore Esq., Pres./Exec. Dir.
Founded: 1925. **Members:** 3,000. **Membership Dues:** associate, $30 (annual) ● full, $50 (annual) ● sustaining, $100 (annual) ● Friends' Circle, $250 (annual) ● patron, $500 (annual) ● President's Club, $1,000 (annual) ● Chairman's Club, $2,500 (annual) ● benefactor, $5,000 (annual) ● supporting, $75 (annual). **Staff:** 16. **Budget:** $1,200,000. **Regional Groups:** 7. **Languages:** English, Polish. **Description:** International foundation which funds scholarly and cultural exchange programs between Poland and the U.S. Conducts summer sessions at Polish universities annually and a medical studies program in Poland for Americans of Polish descent. Maintains a permanent collection of Polish art - open to the public - and hosts exhibits of Polish and Polish American artists. **Libraries: Type:** not open to the public. **Holdings:** 5,000. **Awards:** Chopin Scholarship in Piano Accomplishment. **Frequency:** annual. **Type:** scholarship. **Recipient:** for winner of nationwide competition ● **Frequency:** annual. **Type:** scholarship. **Recipient:** for American graduate students of Polish descent, students engaged in Polish studies, and scholars from Poland doing postgraduate work at U.S. universities. **Additional Websites:** http://www.thekf.org. **Also Known As:** American Center for Polish Culture. **Publications:** Newsletter, quarterly. Includes book reviews, president's report, and articles on all programs and activities of the KFO. **Price:** included in membership dues. **Circulation:** 4,000 ● Books. Features Polish subjects. ● Brochures. **Conventions/Meetings:** semiannual meeting - always spring and fall, in New York City ● annual meeting - always September.

10880 ■ Polish American Historical Association (PAHA)
Central Connecticut State Univ.
1615 Stanley St.
New Britain, CT 06050
Ph: (860)832-3010 (248)683-1743
E-mail: paha@polishamericanstudies.org
URL: http://www.polishamericanstudies.org
Contact: Dr. Karen Majewski, Exec. Dir.
Founded: 1941. **Members:** 700. **Membership Dues:** individual, $30 (annual) ● institution, $50 (annual) ● student, senior citizen, $15 (annual) ● household, $45 (annual) ● patron, $100 (annual) ● life - individual, $500. **Staff:** 1. **State Groups:** 1. **Languages:** English, Polish. **Description:** Concerned with Polish Americana and the history of Poles in the U.S. Conducts research programs and Polish-American studies. **Libraries: Type:** open to the public. **Holdings:** archival material. **Subjects:** Poland, Polish, history. **Awards:** Amicus Poloniae Award. **Frequency:** periodic. **Type:** recognition. **Recipient:** for significant contributions to knowledge of Polish and Polish American heritage by a non-Polish American ● Civic Achievement Award. **Frequency:** periodic. **Type:** recognition. **Recipient:** for individuals or groups promoting research and awareness of the Polish experience in the America ● Creative Arts Award. **Frequency:** annual. **Type:** recognition. **Recipient:** for outstanding creative work dealing with Polish experience in the Americas ● Distinguished

Service Award. **Frequency:** periodic. **Type:** recognition. **Recipient:** for valuable and sustained service to the organization ● Kulczycki Prize. **Frequency:** annual. **Type:** recognition. **Recipient:** for a young scholar who has written an important dissertation on the Polish experience in the United States ● Mieczyslaw Haiman Award. **Frequency:** annual. **Type:** recognition. **Recipient:** for sustained contribution to the study of Polish Americans ● Oskar Halecki Prize. **Frequency:** annual. **Type:** recognition. **Recipient:** for outstanding book or monograph on the Polish experience in the United States ● Swastek Prize. **Frequency:** annual. **Type:** recognition. **Recipient:** for outstanding article in PAHA journal, Polish American studies. **Computer Services:** Mailing lists. **Committees:** Local Arrangements; Publicity; Special Projects. **Affiliated With:** American Historical Association. **Formerly:** (1948) Polish American Historical Commission of the Polish Institute of Arts and Sciences in America. **Publications:** *Polish American Studies*, semiannual. Journal. **Price:** $20.00 individual; $35.00 institutional. ISSN: 0032-2806. **Circulation:** 750. **Advertising:** accepted. **Conventions/Meetings:** annual conference, held in conjunction with American Historical Association (exhibits).

10881 ■ Polish Institute of Arts and Sciences of America (PIASA)
208 E 30th St.
New York, NY 10016
Ph: (212)686-4164
Fax: (212)545-1130
E-mail: piasany@verizon.net
URL: http://www.piasa.org
Contact: Dr. Thaddeus V. Gromada, Exec. Dir./VP

Founded: 1942. **Members:** 1,500. **Membership Dues:** supporting, $100 (annual) ● sustaining, regular, $50 (annual) ● student, $20 (annual) ● donor, $500 (annual) ● patron, $1,000 (annual) ● benefactor, $5,000 (annual). **Staff:** 4. **Languages:** English, Polish. **Description:** Dedicated to the maintenance of a strong center of learning and culture; concerned with advancing knowledge about Poland's humanistic heritage and the Polish-American contribution to the life, culture and history of the U.S. **Libraries: Type:** reference. **Holdings:** 25,000; archival material, books, monographs, periodicals. **Subjects:** history, religion, social problems, art, music relating to Poland and Poles (in English and Polish). **Awards:** Bronislaw Malinowski Social Science Award. **Frequency:** annual. **Type:** recognition. **Recipient:** for scholarly achievement in the field of sociology ● Casimir Funk Natural Science Award. **Frequency:** annual. **Type:** recognition. **Recipient:** for scholarly achievement in the field of natural science ● Oskar Halecki Polish and East Central European History Award. **Frequency:** annual. **Type:** monetary. **Recipient:** for scholarly achievement in the field of history ● Tadeusz Sendzimir Applied Sciences Award. **Frequency:** annual. **Type:** recognition. **Recipient:** for scholarly achievement in the field of applied sciences. **Computer Services:** database. **Telecommunication Services:** electronic mail, piasany@bellatlantic.net. **Formerly:** (1984) Polish Institute of Arts and Science of America. **Publications:** *Guide to the Archives of the Polish Institute of Arts and Sciences in America*, annual. Newsletter. **Price:** available to members only ● *Polish Review*, quarterly. Journal. **Price:** included in membership dues; $35.00 /year for institutions in U.S., /year for individuals outside U.S.; $40.00 /year for institutions outside U.S.; $30.00 /year for individuals in U.S. **Circulation:** 1,500. **Advertising:** accepted ● Monographs ● Newsletter, quarterly. **Conventions/Meetings:** annual Multidisciplinary Conference on Polish and Polish American Studies - meeting, for scholars interested in Polish and Polish-American Studies, with occasional book exhibits (exhibits) - June.

10882 ■ Polish Museum of America (PMA)
984 N Milwaukee Ave.
Chicago, IL 60622-4101
Ph: (773)384-3352
Fax: (773)384-3799
E-mail: pma@prcua.org
URL: http://pma.prcua.org
Contact: Mr. Michael McCally, Exec. Dir.

Founded: 1935. **Members:** 800. **Membership Dues:** regular, $25 (annual) ● patron, $50 (annual) ● benefactor, $100 (annual) ● institutional, $250 (annual) ● life (individual only), $2,500 ● family, $65 (annual). **Staff:** 7. **Budget:** $200,000. **Languages:** English, Polish. **Description:** Gathers and preserves records of Polish activities in the U.S. and displays Polish culture through its archives and museum. Sponsors lectures and seminars on Polish culture, Polish immigration, and Eastern European studies. Maintains art gallery. **Libraries: Type:** lending; open to the public; reference. **Holdings:** 60,000; archival material, books, business records, clippings, monographs, periodicals. **Subjects:** Polish and Polish-American history, culture. **Awards:** Polish Spirit Award. **Frequency:** annual. **Type:** recognition. **Recipient:** for service to Polish-American community. **Computer Services:** database ● mailing lists. **Telecommunication Services:** electronic mail, info@prcua.org. **Affiliated With:** Polish American Historical Association; Polish Roman Catholic Union of America. **Formerly:** Archives and Museum of the Polish Catholic Union of America. **Publications:** Newsletter, quarterly. Contains eight-pages informational letter.

Polynesian

10883 ■ Institute for the Advancement of Hawaiian Affairs (IAHA)
86-649 Puuhulu Rd.
Waianae, HI 96792-2723
Ph: (808)696-5157
Fax: (808)696-7774
E-mail: plaenui@pixi.com
URL: http://www.opihi.com/sovereignty
Contact: Poka Laenui, Contact

Founded: 1985. **Description:** Works to raise awareness of all aspects of Hawaiian culture. Promotes discussion on such issues as traditional healing practices, self-determination of indigenous peoples, national independence, and the impact of tourism on Hawaiian people. **Publications:** Papers, periodic. Contains information on Hawaiian sovereignty.

10884 ■ Native Hawaiian Culture and Arts Program (NHCAP)
Bishop Museum
1525 Bernice St.
Honolulu, HI 96817
Ph: (808)847-3511
Fax: (808)841-8968
E-mail: membership@bishopmuseum.org
Contact: Dr. Bill Brown, Contact

Founded: 1986. **Members:** 13. **Staff:** 1. **Budget:** $72,000. **Local Groups:** 1. **Description:** Individuals, organizations, and agencies interested in the preservation and perpetuation of traditional Native Hawaiian culture, arts, and values. Works to research, recover, and develop native practices and ceremonies; fosters personal pride among Native Hawaiians and enhances awareness and appreciation of Native Hawaiian history among all people. Sponsors cultural research with emphasis on values, language, lore, ceremony, and protocol. Facilitates access to natural and cultural resources; disseminates information on current research and findings. Encourages improved psychological, social, cultural, and economic well-being of Native Hawaiians. Promotes and assists in the development of Native Hawaiian professionals; operates speakers' bureau. Maintains museum. **Libraries: Type:** reference. **Holdings:** 15; books. **Awards: Type:** recognition. **Publications:** Annual Report, annual.

10885 ■ Polynesian Cultural Center (PCC)
55-370 Kamehameha Hwy.
Laie, HI 96762
Ph: (808)293-3333 (808)293-3005
Free: (800)367-7060
Fax: (808)293-3022
E-mail: internetrez@polynesia.com
URL: http://www.polynesia.com
Contact: Von Orgill, CEO

Founded: 1963. **Staff:** 1,025. **Description:** Presents, preserves, and perpetuates the arts, crafts, culture, and lore of Fijian, Hawaiian, Maori, Marquesan, Tahitian, Tongan, Samoan, and other Polynesian peoples. Seeks to preserve and dramatize ancient cultures in a manner that is entertaining, informative, and educational. Offers visitors guided tours, extemporaneous dancing by Tahitian and other Polynesian peoples, crafts demonstrations, and an evening show featuring up to 150 performers. Shares cultural information and experience with approximately one million visitors per year. Maintains collection of Polynesian artifacts. Funds the Institute for Polynesian Studies, located at Brigham Young University Hawaii campus. **Awards:** David O. McKay Award. **Frequency:** annual. **Type:** recognition ● President's Council Teacher of the Year. **Frequency:** annual. **Type:** recognition ● Seven District Teacher of the Year. **Frequency:** annual. **Type:** recognition ● State Teacher of the Year. **Frequency:** annual. **Type:** recognition ● Sterling Scholar Awards. **Frequency:** annual. **Type:** recognition. **Recipient:** for the 13 top high school academic achievers.

Popular Culture

10886 ■ American Culture Association (ACA)
c/o John F. Bratzel, Exec. Dir.
Michigan State Univ.
276 Bessey Hall
East Lansing, MI 48824
Ph: (517)355-6660
Fax: (517)355-5250
E-mail: bratzel@msu.edu
URL: http://pcaaca.org
Contact: John F. Bratzel, Exec. Dir.

Founded: 1978. **Members:** 1,300. **Membership Dues:** academic, $50 (annual). **Staff:** 1. **Regional Groups:** 7. **Description:** College and university students, professors, and others interested in popular culture. Provides a multi- and interdisciplinary study of past and present popular culture in North and South America. Conducts workshops. **Libraries: Type:** reference. **Holdings:** 23. **Publications:** *Journal of American Culture* (in English and Spanish), quarterly. Published in conjunction with Popular Culture Association. **Price:** $50.00 /year for individuals; $100.00 /year for institutions. **Circulation:** 1,300. **Advertising:** accepted. **Conventions/Meetings:** annual conference, held in conjunction with PCA (exhibits) - week before Easter ● international conference.

10887 ■ Hip-Hop Association (H2A)
PO Box 1181
New York, NY 10035
Ph: (212)500-5970
Fax: (212)300-4895
E-mail: info@hiphopassociation.org
URL: http://www.hiphopassociation.org
Contact: Rolando Brown, Exec. Dir.

Founded: 2002. **Description:** Facilitates, fosters and preserves the Hip-Hop culture. Works to utilize Hip-Hop culture as a tool to effectively encourage critical thinking, social change and unity. Raises awareness about Hip-Hop culture and social issues through educational and cultural initiatives. **Publications:** Report. Alternate Formats: online.

10888 ■ Popular Culture Association (PCA)
c/o Michael K. Schoenecke, Exec. Dir.
Texas Tech Univ.
English Dept., Box 43091
Lubbock, TX 79409-3091
Ph: (806)742-2500
Fax: (806)742-0989
E-mail: mkschoene@aol.com
URL: http://www.h-net.org/~pcaaca
Contact: Michael K. Schoenecke, Exec. Dir.

Founded: 1969. **Members:** 4,500. **Membership Dues:** individual, $55 (annual) ● joint, $80 (annual) ●

combined (PCA and American Culture Association), $90 (annual). **Staff:** 1. **Regional Groups:** 10. **Description:** Academics and others interested in popular culture. Unites cultures around the world through the study of the aspects of society and the everyday culture. Promotes respect and understanding of all cultures worldwide. Studies topics include television, motion pictures, editorial cartoons, pulp fiction, underground culture, folklore, American humor, popular and protest music, black culture, Indian and Chicano popular culture, and the social significance of soap opera. **Libraries: Type:** reference. **Holdings:** 500,000. **Computer Services:** Mailing lists. **Committees:** Popular Culture Association Advisory Faculty. **Publications:** *Journal of American Culture*, quarterly. Includes book reviews. **Price:** included in membership dues. **Circulation:** 1,100. **Advertising:** accepted. Alternate Formats: microform ● *Journal of Cultural Geography*, semiannual ● *Journal of Popular Culture*, bimonthly. Features the study of mass culture. Contains book reviews. **Price:** $209.00 /year for individuals (print and premium online); $190.00 /year for individuals (print and standard online); $181.00 /year for individuals (premium online only). ISSN: 0022-3840. **Circulation:** 3,300. **Advertising:** accepted. Alternate Formats: microform ● *PCA/ACA Joint Newsletter*, periodic. **Conventions/Meetings:** annual conference (exhibits) - usually March/April ● periodic international conference.

Portuguese

10889 ■ American Portuguese Society (APS)

Address Unknown since 2008

Founded: 1959. **Members:** 200. **Staff:** 2. **Description:** Individuals and companies interested in Portugal; foundations and corporations interested in financially supporting the society's aims. Promotes friendship and understanding between Portugal and the U.S. Arranges art shows, concerts, lectures, business seminars, and luncheon briefings. **Formerly:** (1972) American Portuguese Cultural Society. **Publications:** Journal, annual.

10890 ■ Luso-American Education Foundation (LAEF)

PO Box 2967
Dublin, CA 94568
Ph: (925)828-3883
Fax: (925)828-3883
E-mail: odom@luso-american.org
URL: http://www.luso-american.org/laef
Contact: Cecelia Souza PhD, Pres.

Founded: 1963. **Members:** 275. **Membership Dues:** sustaining, $25 (annual) ● sponsor, $50 (annual) ● legal entity, $500 (annual) ● benefactor, $1,000 ● perpetual, $2,500. **Budget:** $50,600. **Description:** Seeks to perpetuate the ethnic and national culture brought to America by emigrants from Portugal; assists qualified students and others in studying and understanding Portuguese culture. Develops high school and college courses for the teaching of Portuguese language, history, and culture. Conducts summer study program. Maintains library. **Awards: Type:** grant. **Recipient:** for qualified California residents ● **Frequency:** annual. **Type:** scholarship. **Committees:** Annual Celebration of Portuguese Day; Grants to Teachers and College Students; Scholarship. **Formerly:** (1963) Luso-American Fraternal Federation Scholarship Committee. **Conventions/Meetings:** annual Conference on Portuguese American Education - meeting (exhibits) ● annual meeting and convention (exhibits) - usually March or April.

Presbyterian

10891 ■ Presbyterian Historical Society (PHS)

425 Lombard St.
Philadelphia, PA 19147-1516
Ph: (215)627-1852
Fax: (215)627-0509
E-mail: refdesk@history.pcusa.org
URL: http://www.history.pcusa.org
Contact: Frederick J. Heuser Jr., Dir./Assoc. Stated Clerk

Founded: 1852. **Staff:** 27. **Budget:** $2,300,000. **Description:** National archives of the Presbyterian Church (U.S.A.). Documents the history of American Presbyterian and Reformed traditions. Contains archival records, monographs, and museum objects. **Libraries: Type:** open to the public. **Also Known As:** Department of History and Records Management Services of the Presbyterian Church (U.S.A.). **Formerly:** (1987) Presbyterian Historical Society; (1990) Presbyterian Historical Association. **Publications:** *Journal of Presbyterian History*, semiannual. **Price:** $70.00. ISSN: 1521-9216. **Circulation:** 700 ● *Presbyterian Heritage*, 3/year. Newsletter. **Conventions/Meetings:** annual Local Church History Seminar - workshop.

Press

10892 ■ Alternative Press Center (APC)

PO Box 33109
Baltimore, MD 21218
Ph: (410)243-2471
Fax: (410)235-5325
E-mail: altpress@altpress.org
URL: http://www.altpress.org
Contact: Chuck D'Adamo, Co-Ed.

Founded: 1969. **Staff:** 5. **Budget:** $175,000. **Description:** Indexes over 300 radical and alternative magazines and newspapers, including numerous English-language foreign publications. Also maintains reading library of about 1,400 books and approximately 400 periodical subscriptions. **Libraries: Type:** reference. **Holdings:** 2,300; books, periodicals. **Subjects:** socialism, feminism, ecology, labor, anarchism, gay/lesbianism, third world. **Formerly:** (1972) Radical Research Center. **Publications:** *Alternative Press Index*, semiannual. Journal. Articles are indexed by subject. Contains book and film reviews. **Price:** $75.00 /year for individuals; $425.00 /year for institutions. ISSN: 0002-662X. **Circulation:** 650. Alternate Formats: CD-ROM; online.

10893 ■ Council of Literary Magazines and Presses (CLMP)

154 Christopher St., Ste.3-C
New York, NY 10014-9110
Ph: (212)741-9110
Fax: (212)741-9112
E-mail: info@clmp.org
URL: http://www.clmp.org
Contact: Jeffrey Lependorf, Exec. Dir.

Founded: 1967. **Members:** 350. **Membership Dues:** organization (based on annual budget), $75-$750 (annual). **Staff:** 4. **Description:** Provides services to noncommercial literary magazines and presses in support of continued publication. Receives funds from the National Endowment for the Arts, the New York State Council on the Arts, foundations, corporations, and individuals. Provides information resources for members. Makes available a bibliography of resource information on publishing non-commercial literary magazines, a list of small press distributors, references for legal assistance for the arts. **Telecommunication Services:** electronic mail, jlependorf@clmp.org. **Publications:** *CLMPages*, quarterly. Newsletter. Contains informative articles relevant to literary publishing. **Price:** free, for members only ● *Directory of Literary Magazines and Presses*, annual. **Price:** free for members; $19.00 for nonmembers in U.S.; $20.00 for nonmembers outside U.S.

Professions

10894 ■ International Association of Torch Clubs (IATC)

749 Boush St.
Norfolk, VA 23510-1517
Ph: (757)622-3927
Free: (888)622-4101
Fax: (757)623-9740
E-mail: iatc@infionline.net
URL: http://www.torch.org
Contact: James V. Strickland Jr., Exec. Sec.

Founded: 1924. **Members:** 2,550. **Staff:** 2. **Budget:** $101,400. **Local Groups:** 73. **Description:** Men and women of diverse professions who meet monthly to present and discuss papers related to these fields. Seeks to: stimulate a broader growth of thought and understanding; prevent narrowing tendencies of specialization; foster high standards of professional ethics and civic well-being. **Awards:** The Best Club in a Region. **Frequency:** annual. **Type:** recognition. **Recipient:** for a local torch club ● Editor's Quill Award. **Frequency:** annual. **Type:** recognition. **Recipient:** for excellence in torch papers ● Golden and Silver Torch Awards. **Frequency:** annual. **Type:** recognition. **Recipient:** to an outstanding member and those members nominated by their club for outstanding club service ● The Outstanding Torch Club. **Frequency:** annual. **Type:** recognition. **Recipient:** for a local torch club ● Paxton Award. **Frequency:** annual. **Type:** recognition. **Recipient:** to the author of the most outstanding paper of the past year among all the torch clubs. **Publications:** *Torch Magazine*, 3/year. Alternate Formats: online ● *The Torchlight*, annual. Newsletter. Alternate Formats: online. **Conventions/Meetings:** annual convention - always June. 2008 June 26-29, Lancaster, PA.

10895 ■ International Doctors Society (IDS)

PO Box 21088
Detroit, MI 48221
Ph: (313)368-8701 (313)368-4572
Contact: Dr. Jabari V. Prempeh, Exec. Dir.

Founded: 1984. **Staff:** 4. **Regional Groups:** 5. **State Groups:** 50. **Local Groups:** 12. **For-Profit. Description:** Serves as a social support organization for nonmedical doctors who graduated from accredited institutions. Aims to protect the title, employment, income, and political interests of members. Assists members in gaining recognition for their doctorates. Represents members' interests before Congress and governmental agencies; keeps members informed of state and federal legislation relevant to their fields. Works with graduate schools in setting standards for doctoral programs. Provides a professional insurance plan to the public enabling them to use members' services. Offers job placement services; conducts professional training seminars. Encourages nonmedical doctors to enter politics on a local, state, national, or international level. Maintains biographical archives; compiles statistics. **Publications:** *Journal of IDS*, periodic. **Conventions/Meetings:** annual meeting.

Public Information

10896 ■ American Guild of Town Criers (AGTC)

c/o John Karsten, Pres.
121 S Div. Ave.
Holland, MI 49424
Ph: (616)396-1943
E-mail: johnkarsten@yahoo.com
URL: http://www.americantowncriers.com
Contact: John Karsten, Pres.

Founded: 1997. **Description:** Represents town criers. Aims to rebuild the relevance of the town crier profession. Serves as a venue for modern day town criers to meet and compete.

10897 ■ American Library Association - Public Information Office (PIO)

50 E Huron St.
Chicago, IL 60611
Free: (800)545-2433
Fax: (312)280-5274
E-mail: pio@ala.org
URL: http://www.ala.org/ala/pio/publicinformation.htm
Contact: Mark Gould, Dir.

Description: Develops and implements strategic communication plans tied to American Library Association. Provides public relations counsel, coordinates national media relations efforts, maintains an advocacy network and develops support materials to help librarians promote their programs and services. **Telecommunication Services:** electronic mail, mgould@ala.org.

Public Speaking

10898 ■ Gavel Clubs (GC)
c/o Toastmasters International
PO Box 9052
Mission Viejo, CA 92690-9052
Ph: (949)858-8255
Fax: (949)858-1207
E-mail: newclubs@toastmasters.org
URL: http://www.gavelclub.org
Founded: 1957. **Members:** 3,200. **Membership Dues:** individual, $48 (annual). **Local Groups:** 80. **Description:** Persons desiring speech training who cannot participate in the complete Toastmasters Club program. Promotes self-improvement through study and practice of public speaking and parliamentary procedure. Provides education and training in communications and leadership in schools, prisons, and other institutions. **Affiliated With:** Toastmasters International. **Publications:** *Directory of Clubs*, annual ● *Toastmaster Magazine*, monthly. **Conventions/Meetings:** annual meeting - always August.

10899 ■ Genealogical Speakers Guild
PO Box 38314
Olmsted Falls, OH 44138-0314
E-mail: hodgessj@hotmail.com
URL: http://www.genealogicalspeakersguild.org
Contact: Shirley Gage Hodges, Pres.
Founded: 1991. **Membership Dues:** individual, $40 (annual) ● family, $45 (annual). **Description:** Aims to facilitate better communication between speakers and societies in the field of genealogy. Promotes speakers' interests by providing a forum for the discussion of topics of concern to genealogical speakers. Raises professional lecture standards. Aids speakers in understanding and fulfilling their obligations to program planners and to audiences. **Publications:** *Genealogical Speakers Guild Member Directory*. Membership Directory. **Price:** $10.00/copy ● *SPEAK!*, 03Y. Newsletter.

10900 ■ International Association of Speakers Bureaus (IASB)
7150 Winton Dr., Ste.300
Indianapolis, IN 46268
Ph: (317)328-7790
Free: (866)880-IASB
Fax: (317)280-8527
E-mail: info@iasbweb.org
URL: http://www.iasbweb.org
Contact: James Montoya CAE, Exec. VP
Founded: 1986. **Members:** 150. **Membership Dues:** general, $500 (annual). **Staff:** 5. **Budget:** $178,000. **Multinational. Description:** Maintains Speaker's Bureau representing 15 countries. Focuses on continuing education for its members, promotes awareness among meeting planners and raises the bar on accepted practices in the speakers' bureau industry. **Committees:** Education; Ethics; Legislation; Programs. **Affiliated With:** Convention Industry Council. **Formerly:** (2001) International Group of Agencies and Bureaus. **Publications:** *Bureau Talk*, monthly. Book. **Circulation:** 150. **Advertising:** accepted. Alternate Formats: online. **Conventions/Meetings:** annual convention.

10901 ■ International Platform Association (IPA)
Address Unknown since 2007
Founded: 1831. **Members:** 5,000. **Membership Dues:** $65 (annual). **Staff:** 5. **Description:** Professional lecturers, musicians, actors, and others who appear in person before live audiences to inform or entertain; lecture bureaus; program chairmen; booking agents; former performers and others in the fields of politics, diplomacy, writing, journalism, and entertainment who are interested in the medium of the platform. Seeks to improve the quality of the American lecture platform. Promotes educational interests of members; seeks to increase their scope of contacts. **Libraries: Type:** by appointment only. **Holdings:** 1,000; periodicals. **Subjects:** public speaking and opinions. **Awards:** Silver Bowl. **Frequency:** annual. **Type:** recognition. **Recipient:** public service or public speaking and news media. **Committees:** Art; Monologue; Poetry; Storytelling; Theatre. **Formerly:** American Chautauquas; American Lyceum Association; International Lyceum Association. **Publications:** *How to Get Started in Professional Public Speaking* ● *The Podium*, quarterly. Newsletter. **Price:** $65.00/year. **Circulation:** 5,000. **Advertising:** accepted ● *Secrets of Successful Public Speaking: The Public Speaker's Handbook*. **Conventions/Meetings:** annual meeting (exhibits) - always first week of August, Washington, DC ● meeting.

10902 ■ National Capital Speakers Association (NCSA)
2020 Pennsylvania Ave. NW
Washington, DC 20006
Ph: (301)459-0738
Fax: (301)552-0225
E-mail: shardiman@aol.com
URL: http://www.expertcenter.com/nsa/ncsa
Contact: Tom Antion, Pres.
Founded: 1980. **Members:** 200. **Membership Dues:** professional, $110 (annual) ● associate, $185 (annual). **Staff:** 1. **Description:** Provides a platform for those seeking to improve the quality, integrity, and visibility of professional speakers in the Washington, DC metropolitan area. Conducts idea-exchange showcases and seminars. Maintains speakers' bureau. **Libraries: Type:** reference. **Holdings:** audiovisuals, books. **Subjects:** public speaking. **Committees:** Program; Publicity; Showcase. **Affiliated With:** National Speakers Association. **Publications:** *Speaking of Speaking*, monthly. Newsletter. **Advertising:** accepted. **Conventions/Meetings:** annual convention ● monthly seminar (exhibits) - always second Saturday in Washington, DC.

10903 ■ National Speakers Association (NSA)
1500 S Priest Dr.
Tempe, AZ 85281
Ph: (480)968-2552
Fax: (480)968-0911
E-mail: info@nsaspeaker.org
URL: http://www.nsaspeaker.org
Contact: Mark LeBlanc, Pres.
Founded: 1973. **Members:** 4,000. **Membership Dues:** professional, $600 (annual). **Staff:** 20. **Budget:** $2,800,000. **Regional Groups:** 37. **Description:** Professional speakers. Works to increase public awareness of the speaking profession, advance the integrity and visibility of professional speakers, and provide a learning and communication vehicle to professional speakers. Sponsors workshops, conventions, and labs. **Awards:** Certified Speaking Professional. **Type:** recognition. **Recipient:** for achievement through a proven record of speaking experience ● Council of Peers Award of Excellence - Speaker Hall of Fame. **Frequency:** annual. **Type:** recognition. **Recipient:** for demonstrated platform excellence and professionalism. **Special Interest Groups:** Bureaus; Consultants; Diversity; Educators; Facilitators; Health/Fitness; Humorists; International; Motivational; Sales Trainers; Technology; Workshop/Seminar Leaders; Writing/Publishing. **Publications:** *Professional Speaker*, monthly. Magazine. **Advertising:** accepted ● *Voices of Experience*, 10/year. Magazine. Audio tape magazine. ● *Who's Who in Professional Speaking: The Meeting Planner's Guide*, annual. Directory ● Survey. Alternate Formats: online. **Conventions/Meetings:** annual convention (exhibits) - always July/August. 2008 Aug. 2-5, New York, NY; 2009 July 18-21, Phoenix, AZ; 2010 July 17-20, Orlando, FL.

10904 ■ Toastmasters International (TI)
PO Box 9052
Mission Viejo, CA 92690-9052
Ph: (949)858-8255 (949)835-1300
Free: (800)993-7732
Fax: (949)858-1207
E-mail: tminfo@toastmasters.org
URL: http://www.toastmasters.org
Contact: Donna H. Groh, Exec. Dir.
Founded: 1924. **Members:** 210,000. **Membership Dues:** regular, $27 (semiannual). **Staff:** 50. **Budget:** $6,000,000. **Description:** Men and women who wish to improve their communication and leadership skills. Sponsors clubs in corporate, government, and military facilities, as well as local communities in over 90 countries. Sponsors annual World Championship of Public Speaking. Special activities include: advanced communication and leadership program; youth leadership programs for junior and senior high school students; Gavel Clubs in schools, prisons, and other institutions. **Awards:** Golden Gavel Award. **Frequency:** annual. **Type:** recognition. **Recipient:** for prominent communicators. **Programs:** Communication and Leadership; Distinguished Area and Division; Distinguished District; Youth Leadership. **Publications:** *The Toastmaster* (in English and Spanish), monthly. Magazine. **Price:** included in membership dues. ISSN: 0040-8263. **Circulation:** 180,000. **Advertising:** accepted. Alternate Formats: online ● *Toastmasters International-District Newsletter*, 11/year. Provides management suggestions and organizational information for district officers. Contains district performance statistics. **Price:** available to district officers only. Alternate Formats: online ● *Toastmasters International-Tips*, bimonthly. Newsletter. Covers association activities and program suggestions for club officers. **Price:** available to club officers only ● Manuals (in English, French, and Spanish). Also available in Braille. **Conventions/Meetings:** annual conference - always August.

10905 ■ Walters International Speakers Bureau
PO Box 398
Glendora, CA 91740
Ph: (626)335-8069
Fax: (626)335-6127
E-mail: info@walters-intl.com
URL: http://www.walters-intl.com
Contact: Dottie Walters, Pres./CEO
Founded: 1978. **Membership Dues:** $100 (semiannual). **Staff:** 8. **Description:** Provides news, tips, and trends regarding public speaking for speakers, meeting planners, agents, bureaus, trainers, and consultants. Conducts educational programs; maintains speakers' bureau. **Convention/Meeting:** none. **Formerly:** (2005) Sharing Ideas Society. **Publications:** *Sharing Ideas*, quarterly, winter, spring, summer, fall. Magazine. Publication for professional speakers, meeting planners, consultants, and bureau owners. **Price:** $100.00/2 years in U.S.; $124.00/2 years in Canada and Mexico; $175.00/2 years outside North America. ISSN: 0886-1501. **Circulation:** 2,500. **Advertising:** accepted. Alternate Formats: online.

Racing

10906 ■ Godolphin Society
c/o National Museum of Racing and Hall of Fame
191 Union Ave.
Saratoga Springs, NY 12866-3566
Ph: (518)584-0400
Free: (800)JOCKEY-4
Fax: (518)584-4574
E-mail: nmrdev@racingmuseum.net
URL: http://www.racingmuseum.org/donations/godolphin.asp
Contact: Mr. Mike Kane, Communications Off.
Founded: 1950. **Membership Dues:** individual, $35 (annual). **Budget:** $35. **Description:** Displays fine art, artifacts and memorabilia relating to Thoroughbred racing in America. The collection includes paintings, bronzes, trophies, pictures and memorabilia. The Official National Throughbred Racing Hall of Fame enshrines horses, jockeys and trainers who are deemed to be the top performers in the sport. An annual election is held with voting by a panel of turf writers. Candidates who receive 75&percent; of more

of the votes cast are elected. **Libraries: Type:** by appointment only. **Holdings:** 5,000; archival material, books, business records, films, periodicals, photographs. **Subjects:** research materials relating to the sport of Thoroughbred racing in America from the 18th century to the present. **Publications:** Annual Report. **Conventions/Meetings:** annual Appreciation Reception - meeting.

Railroads

10907 ■ Anthracite Railroads Historical Society (ARHS)
PO Box 519
Lansdale, PA 19446-0519
E-mail: arjay3@comcast.net
URL: http://arhs.railfan.net
Contact: Walter Hoffmann, Pres.
Founded: 1975. **Members:** 1,600. **Membership Dues:** individual, $25 (annual) ● individual outside U.S., $35 (annual). **Budget:** $100,000. **Description:** Individuals interested in the history of the Lehigh Valley Railroad; Delaware, Lackawanna and Western Railroad; Lehigh and Hudson River Railroad; Lehigh and New England Railroad; the Central Railroad of New Jersey; and the Reading Railroad. Promotes historical study of railroads serving the coal-mining regions of the Northeastern United States. **Libraries: Type:** reference. **Holdings:** archival material, artwork, photographs. **Subjects:** anthracite railroads. **Publications:** *Anthracite Extra*, periodic. Newsletter. Contains information on the society's activities and products. ● *Flags, Diamonds and Statues*, 3/year. Magazine. Contains historical articles, diagrams and old photos. **Price:** $20.00/year; $7.00/issue. **Circulation:** 2,400. **Conventions/Meetings:** annual conference.

10908 ■ Association of Railway Museums (ARM)
1016 Rosser St.
Conyers, GA 30012
Ph: (770)278-0088
Fax: (770)388-7772
E-mail: secretary@railwaymuseums.org
URL: http://www.railwaymuseums.org
Contact: Molly Butterworth, Pres.
Founded: 1961. **Members:** 100. **Membership Dues:** full (voting), $125 (annual) ● institutional affiliate, $75 (annual) ● commercial affiliate, $200 (annual) ● individual affiliate, $20 (annual). **Staff:** 1. **Description:** Works for the preservation of railway equipment, artifacts, and history. **Telecommunication Services:** electronic mail, rmq@railwaymuseums.org. **Committees:** Parts. **Affiliated With:** American Association of Museums. **Publications:** *Railway Museum Quarterly*. Newsletter. Highlights major projects at member museums and features articles of interest to railway museums. **Price:** included in membership dues. **Circulation:** 1,000. **Advertising:** accepted. Alternate Formats: online. Also Cited As: *RMQ* ● *Recommended Practices for Railway Museums*. Booklet. Alternate Formats: online. **Conventions/Meetings:** annual convention (exhibits).

10909 ■ Baltimore and Ohio Railroad Historical Society (B&ORRHS)
PO Box 24225
Baltimore, MD 21227-0725
E-mail: info@borhs.org
URL: http://www.borhs.org
Contact: Nicholas Fry, Dir.
Founded: 1979. **Members:** 1,750. **Membership Dues:** regular in U.S., $35 (annual) ● regular outside U.S., sustaining in U.S., $47 (annual) ● sustaining outside U.S., $63 (annual) ● associate, $125 (annual) ● institutional, $25 (annual). **Budget:** $60,000. **Description:** Gathers and disseminates information on America's first common carrier transportation company, the Baltimore & Ohio (B&O) railroad. **Libraries: Type:** reference; not open to the public. **Holdings:** 100; archival material, articles. **Subjects:** Baltimore and Ohio railroad. **Computer Services:** database ● mailing lists. **Publications:** *The B&O Modeler*. Magazine. Alternate Formats: online ● *Sentinel*, quarterly. Magazine. Features historical articles. **Price:** $6.00. **Circulation:** 2,500. **Advertising:** accepted ● Books ● Monographs. **Conventions/Meetings:** annual conference (exhibits) - normally Columbus Day weekend.

10910 ■ Chesapeake and Ohio Historical Society (C&OHS)
PO Box 79
Clifton Forge, VA 24422
Ph: (540)862-2210
Free: (800)453-2647
E-mail: cohs@cohs.org
URL: http://www.cohs.org
Contact: Thomas W. Dixon Jr., Chm./Pres. Emeritus
Founded: 1969. **Members:** 2,500. **Membership Dues:** regular, $39 (annual) ● sustaining, $50 (annual) ● contributing, $75 (annual) ● Cando club, $100 (annual) ● Allegheny associate, $250 (annual) ● Chessie club, $500 (annual) ● Commander-in-Chief Leadership Circle, $1,000 (annual). **Staff:** 4. **Budget:** $500,000. **Description:** Railroad enthusiasts, former railroad employees and officials, historians, libraries, and model railroaders. Collects and preserves Chesapeake and Ohio Railway, Pere Marquette Railway, Hocking Valley Railroad, Chessie System railroads, and CSX Transportation Companies' historical data, equipment, and artifacts, encourage research into C&O and related subjects, and exchange information. Researches specific questions on C&O history upon request. **Libraries: Type:** reference. **Holdings:** 5,000; archival material, artwork, periodicals, photographs, reports. **Subjects:** C&O Railway. **Computer Services:** database. **Additional Websites:** http://www.chessieshop.com. **Publications:** *C&O History*, monthly. Magazine. Includes book reviews. **Price:** free for members. ISSN: 0886-6287. **Advertising:** accepted. Alternate Formats: microform. Also Cited As: *Chesapeake and Ohio Historical Newsletter* ● *Chesapeake and Ohio, Coal, and Color*. Book ● *Chessie's Road*. Book ● *Modeling the C&O*. Book ● Also publishes calendars. **Conventions/Meetings:** annual conference.

10911 ■ Electric Railroaders' Association (ERA)
PO Box 3323
Grand Central Sta.
New York, NY 10163-3323
Ph: (212)986-4482
Fax: (212)986-4482
E-mail: info@electricrailroaders.org
URL: http://www.electricrailroaders.org
Contact: Frank Miklos, Pres.
Founded: 1934. **Members:** 2,000. **Membership Dues:** regular in U.S., $25 (annual) ● regular in Canada and Mexico, $28 (annual) ● other country, $30 (annual). **Staff:** 12. **Budget:** $40,000. **Local Groups:** 1. **Description:** Individuals interested in history and progress of electric railways. Provides information to members and the public. **Libraries: Type:** reference. **Holdings:** 2,500; books, papers, photographs. **Subjects:** historical, technical, economic data on electric railways. **Publications:** *Electric Railroads*, periodic. Magazine. **Price:** free for members ● *50 Years of Progressive Transit*. Book ● *Headlights*, semiannual. Magazine. Contains articles on technical data and current and past traction systems worldwide. Includes book reviews. **Price:** included in membership dues; $20.00 /year for nonmembers in U.S. **Circulation:** 1,850 ● *Pioneers of Electric Railroading*. Book ● *Tracks of New York*. Book. Discusses specific company or division of New York City Rail Transit. **Price:** $20.00. **Conventions/Meetings:** annual convention - always late August.

10912 ■ Friends of the Valley Railroad
PO Box 452
1 Railroad Ave.
Essex, CT 06426
Ph: (860)767-0103
Free: (800)377-3987
Fax: (860)377-3987
E-mail: valleyrailroad@net.net
URL: http://www.essexsteamtrain.com/friends.html
Contact: Brendan Matthews, Membership Chm.
Founded: 1991. **Members:** 50. **Membership Dues:** regular, $25. **Staff:** 1. **Description:** Preserves the history and restores equipment of railroads. Concentrates activities on the history of New York, New Haven, and Hartford railroads, primarily the Connecticut Valley Line. Conducts research and educational programs. Maintains speakers' bureau; operates museum. **Libraries: Type:** not open to the public.

10913 ■ Lexington Group in Transportation History (LGTH)
c/o Don L. Hofsommer, Treas./Ed.
Dept. of History
St. Cloud State Univ.
St. Cloud, MN 56301
Ph: (320)308-4906
URL: http://www.lexingtongroup.org
Contact: H. Roger Grant, Pres.
Founded: 1942. **Members:** 500. **Membership Dues:** $25 (annual). **Description:** Historians, economists, railroaders, writers, librarians, and others interested in the study of railroad and transportation history. Founded in Lexington, KY, at annual meeting of the Mississippi Valley Historical Association (now the Organization of American Historians, see separate entry); hence the group's name. Exchanges information about research activities and opportunities in the field of transportation history. **Publications:** *Lexington Quarterly*. Newsletter. Contains book reviews. **Price:** $25.00/year. ISSN: 0888-7837. **Circulation:** 500 ● *Membership List*, annual. **Conventions/Meetings:** annual meeting - last full weekend in September.

10914 ■ Mystic Valley Railway Society (MVRS)
PO Box 365486
Hyde Park, MA 02136-0009
Ph: (617)361-4445
Fax: (617)361-4451
E-mail: contactus@mysticvalleyrs.org
URL: http://www.mysticvalleyrs.org
Contact: Dorothy Dear, Corresponding Sec.
Founded: 1970. **Members:** 5,600. **Membership Dues:** individual, $6 (annual) ● family, $8 (annual) ● life, $100. **Budget:** $40,000. **Description:** Individuals, families, and others dedicated to educating the public about mass transportation with emphasis on railroads. Maintains Discover New England By Train, an informational program for members. Conducts rail tours; sponsors meetings with guest speakers. **Libraries: Type:** reference. **Holdings:** audiovisuals, photographs. **Awards:** New England Railroading Color Slide Contest. **Frequency:** annual. **Type:** recognition. **Recipient:** for members. **Committees:** Mailing; Outreach; Social; Trip Team; Waybill. **Publications:** *New England Railroading Calendar*, annual. Features New England and railway topics. **Price:** $8.00. **Circulation:** 10,000 ● *WayBill*, quarterly. Includes society news and activities, calendar of events, member news, and trains on stamps feature. **Price:** included in membership dues. ISSN: 0897-7577. **Circulation:** 14,000. **Advertising:** accepted. **Conventions/Meetings:** annual Christmas Dinner - every first Saturday (evening) in December ● semiannual Rail-A-Rama - trade show (exhibits) - usually February and November ● seminar ● annual Slide Contest - competition.

10915 ■ National Railway Historical Society (NRHS)
100 N 17th St., Ste.1203
Philadelphia, PA 19103-2767
Ph: (215)557-6606
Fax: (215)557-6740
E-mail: info@nrhs.com
URL: http://www.nrhs.com
Contact: Ellen D. Pinsky, Asst. Sec.
Founded: 1935. **Members:** 14,000. **Membership Dues:** member-at-large, $34 (annual) ● student, $16 (annual) ● additional family, $5 (annual) ● chapter, $33 (annual). **Staff:** 1. **Local Groups:** 173. **Descrip-**

tion: Persons interested in North American rail transportation. Preserves historical information on railroad subjects and sponsors railroad inspection trips to points of interest. Conducts research on railroads. **Libraries: Type:** reference. **Holdings:** 5,000; archival material, books, business records, clippings, periodicals. **Subjects:** North American railroad history. **Projects:** Amtrak Trails and Rails; Historic Structures Surveys; Operation Lifesaver; Rail Landmark Recognition; RailCamp; Railway Heritage Grants. **Formed by Merger of:** (1935) Lancaster (Pennsylvania) Railway and Locomotive Historical Society; Interstate Trolley Club of New York. **Publications:** *National Railway Bulletin*, bimonthly. Journal. Covers subjects on railroad history, and NRHS business for information to the members. **Price:** included in membership dues. ISSN: 0885-5099. **Conventions/Meetings:** annual convention and general assembly - 2008 June 16-22, Fort Worth, TX.

10916 ■ Ontario and Western Railway Historical Society (OWRHS)
PO Box 713
Middletown, NY 10940
E-mail: agentgs@aol.com
URL: http://owrhs.org
Contact: George S. Shammas, Pres.

Founded: 1963. **Members:** 735. **Membership Dues:** regular, $27 (annual) ● sustaining, $38 (annual). **Staff:** 25. **Description:** Promotes interest in the Ontario and Western Railway. Collects and preserves artifacts and data related to the railroad. Maintains an archive center. **Libraries: Type:** reference. **Holdings:** archival material, books, business records. **Subjects:** Ontario and Western Railway. **Awards:** Member of the Year. **Frequency:** annual. **Type:** recognition. **Recipient:** for outstanding service to the society. **Affiliated With:** National Railway Historical Society. **Formerly:** (1999) Ontario and Western Railroad Historical Society. **Publications:** *Observer*, quarterly. Newsletter. Contains information about the society as well as historical information. **Price:** included in membership dues ● *Yearly Calendar*. **Conventions/Meetings:** annual dinner ● monthly meeting - every first Friday except July, August, November.

10917 ■ Pacific Railroad Society (PRS)
PO Box 80726
San Marino, CA 91118-8726
Ph: (562)692-4858
Fax: (626)570-8651
E-mail: info@pacificrailroadsociety.org
URL: http://www.pacificrailroadsociety.org
Contact: Vir Carlucci, Pres.

Founded: 1936. **Members:** 650. **Membership Dues:** individual, $35 (annual) ● sustaining, $50 (annual) ● corporate, $100 (annual) ● life, $500. **Description:** Educates the public about railroads and rail transit; seeks to preserve railway history, equipment, and artifacts. Maintains 10 railroad passenger cars. Conducts excursions; arranges displays of artifacts and equipment. Operates the Pacific Railroad Museum located in San Dimas, CA. **Libraries: Type:** reference. **Holdings:** 2,000; archival material, artwork, books, business records, clippings, periodicals. **Subjects:** railroad, rail transit. **Telecommunication Services:** electronic mail, pacificrrsociety@sbcglobal.net. **Committees:** Pacific Railroad Museum. **Publications:** *50 Years of Railroading in Southern California, 1936-1986*. Report. Includes updates through 1996. ● *For The Love of Trains, PRS, 1936-1961*. Video ● *Wheel Clicks*, monthly. Journal. **Price:** included in membership dues. ISSN: 0043-4744. **Circulation:** 650 ● Also publishes railroad historical materials. **Conventions/Meetings:** annual banquet - always December ● meeting - 11/year, always second Friday (except December), Alhambra, CA.

10918 ■ Pacific Southwest Railway Museum (PSRM)
4695 Nebo Dr.
La Mesa, CA 91941-5259
Ph: (619)465-7776
E-mail: reservations@psrm.org
URL: http://www.psrm.org
Contact: Mr. Jim Lundquist, Pres.

Founded: 1961. **Members:** 700. **Membership Dues:** individual, $30 (annual) ● student, senior, $20 (annual) ● family, $40 (annual) ● contributing, $50 (annual) ● supporting, $75 (annual) ● sustaining, $150 (annual) ● senior (life), $300 ● life, $750 ● gold spike (life), $1,000 ● benefactor, $5,000. **Budget:** $300,000. **Languages:** English, Spanish. **Description:** Maintains public museum of railroading in Campo, CA and is actively engaged in the preservation, restoration, and operation of steam and diesel locomotives and related items representing the railroad heritage of the U.S. Runs restored equipment on 20 miles of standard gauge railroad track, and maintains several railroad buildings, a depot, and a museum building for indoor exhibits. Offers escorted private railway excursions in Mexico and in the U.S. Has restored the 1894 La Mesa Depot, operated as the La Mesa Depot Railroad Museum in La Mesa, CA. Provides information on local railroad history; tours for schools. Maintains speakers' bureau; conducts research programs. **Libraries: Type:** open to the public. **Holdings:** 10,000; articles, books, periodicals. **Subjects:** railroads. **Awards: Type:** recognition. **Committees:** Library; Museum Development. **Departments:** Equipment; Facilities; Interpretation; Maintenance; Operations; Public Services. **Formerly:** San Diego County Railway Museum; (2003) San Diego Railroad Museum. **Publications:** *Hotscoop*, monthly. Newsletter. **Price:** $1.00. **Circulation:** 1,100. **Conventions/Meetings:** monthly board meeting.

10919 ■ Railroad Enthusiasts (RRE)
PO Box 96
Peabody, MA 01960-0896
E-mail: represent@massbayrre.org
URL: http://www.massbayrre.org

Founded: 1934. **Members:** 1,400. **Regional Groups:** 7. **Description:** Persons interested in the railroad industry, including hobbyists, photographers, railroad employees, and model builders. Divisions hold meetings for slide presentations, movies, discussions of railroading and railroad history, and exchange of information about railroads. Divisions sponsor special passenger excursion trains and rail trips. **Formerly:** National Association of Railroad Enthusiasts. **Conventions/Meetings:** annual workshop - midwinter.

10920 ■ Railroad Station Historical Society (RSHS)
c/o Jim Dent, Business Mgr.
26 Thackeray Rd.
Oakland, NJ 07436-3312
Ph: (212)818-8085
E-mail: jdent1@optonline.net
URL: http://www.rrshs.org
Contact: Jim Dent, Business Mgr.

Founded: 1967. **Members:** 400. **Membership Dues:** 3rd class mailing in U.S., $12 (annual) ● regular in Canada, first class mailing in U.S., $16 (annual) ● regular outside U.S. and Canada, $25 (annual). **Description:** Persons interested in railroad stations and other railroad buildings and structures from historical and architectural perspectives. Preserves photographs and data on railroad stations. Conducts research on the care and maintenance of depots of historical interest. **Libraries: Type:** reference; by appointment only; open to the public. **Holdings:** 20,000; archival material, artwork, photographs. **Committees:** Archives. **Publications:** *Bulletin of the Railroad Station Historical Society*, bimonthly. Contains book reviews. **Price:** $10.00/year in U.S.; $15.00/year outside U.S. ISSN: 0147-0027. **Circulation:** 450 ● Monograph, periodic. **Conventions/Meetings:** annual convention - usually June.

10921 ■ Railway and Locomotive Historical Society (R&LHS)
c/o William H. Lugg, Jr., Membership Sec.
PO Box 292927
Sacramento, CA 95829-2927
Ph: (916)383-4711
Fax: (916)383-2503
E-mail: bilugg@mindspring.com
URL: http://rlhs.org
Contact: William H. Lugg Jr., Membership Sec.

Founded: 1921. **Members:** 2,500. **Membership Dues:** regular, $25 (annual) ● family in U.S., $30 (annual) ● contributing in U.S., $50 (annual) ● sustaining in U.S., $75 (annual) ● patron in U.S., $250 (annual) ● additional for all levels in Canada, $7 (annual) ● additional for all levels outside U.S. and Canada, $18 (annual). **Staff:** 5. **Regional Groups:** 8. **Description:** Represents persons interested in preserving documents and records of railway history. Maintains museum; conducts research programs. **Awards:** Railroad History. **Frequency:** annual. **Type:** recognition. **Recipient:** for photography, best railroad book, and best railroad article. **Committees:** Awards; Program; Research. **Publications:** *Membership Roster*, biennial. Journal. Includes railroad history. **Price:** included in membership dues. ISSN: 0090-7847. **Circulation:** 2,800. **Advertising:** accepted ● *Railroad History*, semiannual. Journal. **Price:** $7.50/back issue for members; $12.50/back issue for nonmembers ● Newsletter, quarterly. Addresses topics of current interest in the Society and in railroading. Offers brief articles on railroad history. Alternate Formats: online. **Conventions/Meetings:** annual congress ● annual meeting.

10922 ■ Society of Freight Car Historians (SFCH)
PO Box 2480
Monrovia, CA 91017
E-mail: dgcasdorph@msn.com
URL: http://dgcasdorph.com
Contact: David G. Casdorph, Pres.

Founded: 1980. **Members:** 400. **Description:** Railway freight car enthusiasts, modelers, historians, and those individuals interested in railway freight car history and technical development. Aims to promote and disseminate the interests of freight car history both past and present. **Libraries: Type:** not open to the public. **Holdings:** clippings, photographs. **Computer Services:** database. **Additional Websites:** http://intermodaltransport.com. **Telecommunication Services:** electronic mail, fr8cars@aol.com. **Formerly:** (1986) Modern Transport Technical and Historical Society. **Publications:** *Freight Car News and Notes*, periodic. Journal. **Price:** $5.00. ISSN: 1548-4629. Alternate Formats: online; CD-ROM ● *Freight Cars Today*, periodic. Journal. **Price:** $5.00. ISSN: 1548-4610. Alternate Formats: online; CD-ROM ● *Intermodal Transport History and Technology*, periodic. Journal. **Price:** $5.00. ISSN: 1550-4824. Alternate Formats: CD-ROM; online.

10923 ■ Soo Line Historical and Technical Society (SLHTS)
c/o C. David Pulse, Treas.
39105 Fishermans Ln.
Chassell, MI 49916
E-mail: membership@sooline.org
URL: http://www.sooline.org
Contact: C. David Pulse, Treas.

Founded: 1977. **Members:** 1,300. **Membership Dues:** regular, $30 (annual) ● contributing, $40 (annual) ● corporate, $150 (annual). **Description:** Railroad enthusiasts. Collects, researches, and publishes the history of the Soo Line Railroad and its predecessors. **Publications:** *The SOO*, quarterly. Magazine. Features articles on varying subjects. **Price:** $7.00 for nonmembers; included in membership dues. **Circulation:** 1,300. **Advertising:** accepted ● Membership Directory. **Conventions/Meetings:** annual meeting, membership (exhibits).

10924 ■ Spokane, Portland and Seattle Railway Historical Society (SP&SHS)
c/o Duane Cramer, Treas.
2618 NW 113th St.
Vancouver, WA 98685
E-mail: cramer@pacifier.com
URL: http://www.spshs.org
Contact: Duane Cramer, Treas.

Founded: 1981. **Members:** 380. **Membership Dues:** regular, $25 (annual) ● sustaining, family, $35 (annual) ● overseas, $40 (annual). **Budget:** $5,000. **Description:** Individuals interested in the history of the Spokane Portland and Seattle Railway. Disseminates historical and technical information about the S.P. & S. Railway to members. Sponsors competitions; conducts educational programs. **Libraries: Type:** reference. **Holdings:** archival material, business records. **Subjects:** engineering data, financial records, descriptions of the physical plant. **Publications:** *The Northwest's Own Railway*, quarterly. Newsletter. **Price:** $4.50/issue. **Circulation:** 400. **Advertising:** accepted. **Conventions/Meetings:** annual conference (exhibits).

10925 ■ Terminal Railroad Association Historical and Technical Society (TRRA H&TS)
c/o Larry Thomas, Sec.-Treas./Ed.
PO Box 1688
St. Louis, MO 63188-1688
Ph: (314)535-3101
E-mail: webmaster@trra-hts.railfan.net
URL: http://trra-hts.railfan.net
Contact: Larry Thomas, Sec.-Treas./Ed.

Founded: 1986. **Members:** 250. **Membership Dues:** regular, $25 (annual) ● sustaining/foreign, $45 (annual) ● contributing, $100 (annual) ● life, $350 ● corporate, $1,000 (annual). **Staff:** 3. **Budget:** $10,000. **Description:** Promotes and disseminates information on the history of the Terminal Railroad, St. Louis Union Station, and the general rail history of the Metro St. Louis area and Southwestern Illinois. **Libraries: Type:** reference. **Holdings:** archival material. **Subjects:** Terminal Railroad, St. Louis Union Station. **Also Known As:** TRRA Historical Society. **Publications:** Magazine, quarterly. Contains features on St. Louis and its rail history, and the Terminal Railroad and St. Louis Union Station. **Price:** $5.00. **Circulation:** 1,000. **Advertising:** accepted. Alternate Formats: online. **Conventions/Meetings:** annual meeting (exhibits) - always last Saturday of July.

10926 ■ Transport Museum Association (TMA)
2967 Barret Sta. Rd.
St. Louis, MO 63122
Ph: (314)965-6885
Fax: (314)965-0288
URL: http://www.transportmuseumassociation.org
Contact: James M. Schloeman, Pres.

Founded: 1944. **Members:** 1,000. **Membership Dues:** coachman, $40 (annual) ● conductor, $55 (annual) ● navigator, $100 (annual) ● pilot, $250 (annual) ● captain, $500 (annual) ● engineer, $1,000 (annual). **Staff:** 18. **Budget:** $511,500. **Description:** Serves as a cultural and educational organization for museum housing a collection of more than 140 locomotives and assorted rolling stock, a city transit display representing periods from the horsecar to the motorbus, highway vehicles, and many smaller related items. Houses relics tracing the growth of communications and waterway, pipeline, animal-powered, and air transportation. **Libraries: Type:** reference. **Subjects:** automobiles, modes of transportation. **Formerly:** St. Louis Railway Historical Society; Museum of Transport; (1980) National Museum of Transport. **Publications:** *Transport Museum—News and Views*, quarterly ● Brochures. **Conventions/Meetings:** annual meeting - always September in St. Louis, MO.

10927 ■ Wabash, Frisco and Pacific Association (WF&P)
c/o Mr. Michael Lorance, Treas.
17238 Hilltop Ridge Dr.
Eureka, MO 63025
Ph: (636)587-3538 (636)296-4492
E-mail: teddytrain@sbcglobal.net
URL: http://www.wfprr.com
Contact: Jim Strain, Pres.

Founded: 1939. **Members:** 150. **Membership Dues:** active, $25 (annual) ● student, junior, $10 (annual) ● associate, $20 (annual) ● family, $35 (annual). **Description:** Individuals interested in the theory and practice of constructing, maintaining, and operating a mini-steam tourist railway (12 inch gauge). Members participate in all phases of railroading: surveying and grading right-of-way, laying rail, designing and building cars, and maintaining and improving the steam locomotives. Runs a 1 mile line (2 miles roundtrip) miniature railroad along the Meramec River at Glencoe, in southeastern Wildwood, MO. The system comprises regulation switches and sidings, machine shop, ticket office, water tower and fuel tanks, and coaling bunker, 3 turntables on the line and a WYE at the other (and a 3-stall 8-track roundhouse with another turntable for locomotives completed in 1992), and carbarn for equipment. Scheduled hours of operation: Sunday afternoon 11:15 am to 4:15 pm only (May through October). The line hauls 14,000 people annually. Also have 10 steam locomotives; 4 burn coal and 6 burn jet fuel. Also have 4 gasoline locomotives/44 cars. Two trains are operated, hauled consecutively by three different locomotives dispatched by radio. **Computer Services:** database ● mailing lists. **Publications:** *Whiffenpoof*, 3/year. Newsletter. Contains details of operating the railway, maintenance and general railway news. **Price:** included in membership dues. **Circulation:** 150 ● Also publishes photo brochure for the general public. **Conventions/Meetings:** monthly board meeting ● annual meeting - always January in St. Louis, MO.

Recordings

10928 ■ Musical Heritage Society (MHS)
1710 Hwy. 35
Oakhurst, NJ 07755
Ph: (732)531-7003
Fax: (732)517-0438
E-mail: memberservices@musicalheritage.org
URL: http://www.musicalheritage.com
Contact: Robert Nissim, Contact

Membership Dues: individual, $150 (annual). **For-Profit. Description:** Mail order clearinghouse for classical music recordings.

10929 ■ National Academy of Recording Arts and Sciences (NARAS)
3402 Pico Blvd.
Santa Monica, CA 90405
Ph: (310)392-3777
Fax: (310)399-3090
E-mail: memservices@grammy.com
URL: http://www.grammy.com
Contact: Jimmy Jam, Chm.

Founded: 1957. **Members:** 18,000. **Membership Dues:** regular, $100 (annual) ● regular, $180 (biennial) ● regular, $260 (triennial). **Staff:** 200. **Regional Groups:** 3. **State Groups:** 12. **Description:** Musicians, producers and other recording professionals. Dedicated to improving the cultural environment and quality of life for music and its makers. The Recording Academy is internationally known for the Grammy Awards and is responsible for numerous groundbreaking outreach, professional development, cultural enrichment, education and human service programs. **Awards:** The Grammy Awards. **Frequency:** annual. **Type:** recognition. **Recipient:** for commercially released recordings for that year ● **Type:** scholarship. **Recipient:** for music and related fields. **Also Known As:** (2005) The Recording Academy. **Publications:** *Grammy Magazine*, periodic. Alternate Formats: online ● *The Grammy Winners Book*, annual ● *Program Book*, annual ● Journal, semiannual. **Conventions/Meetings:** annual The Grammy Awards - meeting.

Reformation

10930 ■ Center for Reformation Research (CRR)
801 Seminary Pl.
St. Louis, MO 63105-3168
Contact: Robert Rosin, Exec. Dir.

Founded: 1957. **Staff:** 2. **Description:** Encourages the study of the 16th century, particularly the Reformation, through programs, seminars, and publications and by serving as the administrative headquarters of other scholarly associations. Sponsors summer institute in paleography and research skills. **Convention/Meeting:** none. **Libraries: Type:** open to the public. **Holdings:** 16,000; biographical archives, books. **Subjects:** history, theology (15th-16th centuries). **Formerly:** (1974) Foundation for Reformation Research. **Publications:** *Sixteenth Century Bibliography Series*, periodic ● Books ● Monographs ● Newsletter, quarterly.

10931 ■ Society for Reformation Research (SRR)
c/o Jeffery Tyler, Treas.
Hope Coll.
PO Box 9000
Holland, MI 49422-9000
E-mail: tyler@hope.edu
URL: http://www.reformationresearch.org
Contact: Jeffery Tyler, Treas.

Founded: 1947. **Members:** 200. **Membership Dues:** individual, $20 (annual). **Description:** Professors of history, church history, and religion; research libraries and publishers; graduate students and others with a special interest in the history of the Reformation. Fosters historical research and promotes the writing of scholarly articles and monographs in the field of the Reformation. Encourages the translation into English of significant documents, books, and articles; facilitates exchange of ideas among members and among similar groups in other countries. **Awards:** Bodo Nischan Award. **Frequency:** biennial. **Type:** recognition. **Recipient:** for individual scholarship and civility ● Miriam U. Chrisman Travel Fellowship. **Frequency:** biennial. **Type:** fellowship. **Recipient:** for graduate students who need to travel abroad to do research. **Telecommunication Services:** electronic mail, gibbs@hope.edu. **Formerly:** (1986) American Society for Reformation Research. **Publications:** *Archive for Reformation History* (in English and German), annual. Journal. Published in cooperation with the German Verein fur Reformationsgeschichte. **Price:** $43.00. ISSN: 0003-9381. **Conventions/Meetings:** semiannual conference ● periodic meeting, held in conjunction with the 16th Century Studies Conference.

Renaissance

10932 ■ Renaissance English Text Society (RETS)
c/o Arthur F. Kinney, Dir.
Univ. of Massachusetts
Dept. of English
Center for Renaissance Stud.
PO Box 2300
Amherst, MA 01004
Ph: (413)577-3600
Fax: (413)577-3605
E-mail: renaissance@english.umass.edu
URL: http://www.umass.edu/renaissance
Contact: Arthur F. Kinney, Dir.

Founded: 1959. **Members:** 250. **Membership Dues:** institutional, individual, $35 (annual). **Multinational. Description:** Publishes scarce early modern texts, both from printed book and manuscript, chiefly nondramatic, of the period 1475-1660. Thirty-seven volumes, some double, have appeared; publication is now annual. Current publisher is Arizona Center for Medieval and Early Renaissance Studies. A cloth volume is distributed with membership each year. **Affiliated With:** Bibliographical Society of America; Malone Society; Modern Language Association of America; Renaissance Society of America. **Publications:** *Anatomie of Abuses*, annual. Book. Hardbound letter press. **Price:** $45.00 each ● *Lady Mary Wroth's Urania*. Book. **Price:** $40.00 paperback ● *Poems of Sir Walter Raleigh*. Book. **Price:** $35.00 each. **Conventions/Meetings:** annual meeting, with forums held in conjunction with Modern Language Association of America, Renaissance Society of America, Sixteenth-Century Studies Conference and Medieval Congress at Kalamazoo (exhibits) - always December.

10933 ■ Renaissance Society of America (RSA)
c/o CUNY
365 5th Ave., Rm. 5400
New York, NY 10016-4309
Ph: (212)817-2130
Fax: (212)817-1544
E-mail: rsa@rsa.org
URL: http://www.rsa.org
Contact: John Monfasani, Exec. Dir.
Founded: 1954. **Members:** 2,500. **Membership Dues:** individual, $60 (annual) ● student, $30 (annual) ● dual, $70 (annual) ● patron, $100 (annual) ● benefactor, $2,500 (annual) ● institutional, $100 (annual) ● subscription, $100 (annual) ● retiree, $45 (annual) ● life, $2,500. **Staff:** 3. **Budget:** $340,000. **Local Groups:** 34. **Multinational. Description:** Educators, scholars, antiquarians, book dealers, institutional members (libraries), collectors, art historians, and musicologists. Promotes research and publication in the field of Renaissance studies, especially of interchanges among various fields of specialization such as art, music, the modern literatures, classical scholarship, sciences, law, philosophy, religion and theology, and political, economic, and social history. Sponsors summer institute for high school teachers. **Awards:** Paul Oskar Kristeller Lifetime Achievement Award. **Frequency:** periodic. **Type:** recognition. **Recipient:** for a living scholar ● Phyllis Goodhard Gordan Book Prize. **Frequency:** annual. **Type:** recognition. **Recipient:** for the best book ● Research Grants. **Type:** grant. **Recipient:** for research projects in all subjects and language areas within Renaissance studies ● William Nelson Prize. **Frequency:** annual. **Type:** recognition. **Recipient:** for the best essay submitted to the *Renaissance Quarterly*. **Computer Services:** Mailing lists, Avery 5164 labels only. **Committees:** Development; Electronic Media; International Cooperation; Publications. **Publications:** *Renaissance News and Notes*, semiannual. Newsletter. **Price:** included in membership dues. Alternate Formats: online ● *Renaissance Quarterly*. Journal. Includes lists of new bibliographic tools and obituaries. **Price:** included in membership dues. ISSN: 0034-4338. **Circulation:** 3,200. **Advertising:** accepted. Alternate Formats: microform; online ● Membership Directory. **Price:** included in membership dues. Alternate Formats: online. **Conventions/Meetings:** annual meeting (exhibits) - 2009 Mar. 26-28, Los Angeles, CA.

Research

10934 ■ American Library Association - Office for Research and Statistics (ORS)
50 E Huron St.
Chicago, IL 60611-2795
Ph: (312)280-4273
Free: (800)545-2433
Fax: (312)280-4392
E-mail: ors@ala.org
URL: http://www.ala.org/ala/ors/researchstatistics.htm
Contact: Denise M. Davis, Dir.
Description: Provides leadership and advice to American Library Association staff, members and public on matters related to research and statistics of libraries and librarians.

Rhetoric

10935 ■ Alliance of Rhetoric Societies (ARS)
c/o David Henry, Exec. Sec.
Univ. of Nevada
Greenspun School of Commun.
Box 454052
Las Vegas, NV 89154-4052
Ph: (702)895-3030
E-mail: dhenry@ccmail.nevada.edu
URL: http://www.rhetoricalliance.org
Contact: David Henry, Exec. Sec.
Founded: 2001. **Membership Dues:** organization, $200 (annual) ● institution, $50 (annual). **Description:** Aims to advance research and teaching in the art of rhetoric. Fosters collaboration among different scholarly organizations and communities whose members' work includes the traditions and techniques of rhetorical studies. Facilitates dialogue, promotes intellectual community, and provides advocacy in support of the continuing development of the art.

10936 ■ International Society for the History of Rhetoric (ISHR)
c/o Dr. Stephen McKenna, Sec. Gen.
The Catholic Univ. of Am.
Dept. of Media Stud.
Washington, DC 20064
Ph: (202)319-5488
Fax: (202)319-4188
E-mail: mckennas@cua.edu
URL: http://ishr.cua.edu
Contact: Dr. Stephen McKenna, Sec. Gen.
Founded: 1975. **Members:** 800. **Membership Dues:** regular, $46 (annual) ● student/special, $20 (annual). **Multinational. Description:** Promotes the study of both the theory and practice of rhetoric (effective and persuasive speaking and writing) in all periods and languages and the relationship of rhetoric to poetics, literary theory and criticism, philosophy, politics, religion, law and other aspects of the cultural context. **Awards:** Biennial Prize for Best Article in Rhetorica. **Frequency:** biennial. **Type:** monetary. **Recipient:** for best article published in Rhetorica Journal over the two previous years. **Publications:** *Rhetorica* (in English, French, German, Italian, Latin, and Spanish), quarterly. Journal. **Price:** included in membership dues; $135.00/year - electronic subscription; $12.00/issue for nonmembers and students; $37.00/issue for institutions. ISSN: 0734-8584. **Advertising:** accepted. Alternate Formats: online ● Newsletter, periodic. Alternate Formats: online. **Conventions/Meetings:** biennial congress and conference.

10937 ■ Rhetoric Society of America (RSA)
c/o David Henry, Exec. Dir.
Univ. of Nevada, Las Vegas
4505 Maryland Pkwy.
Las Vegas, NV 89154
Ph: (801)378-3581
E-mail: rhetoric-society@byu.edu
URL: http://rhetoricsociety.org
Contact: David Zarefsky, Pres.
Founded: 1968. **Members:** 900. **Membership Dues:** student, $30 (annual) ● regular, $60 (annual) ● life, $1,000 ● enhanced life, $1,600 ● sustaining, $100 (annual) ● international, $70 (annual). **Staff:** 1. **Budget:** $80,000. **Languages:** English, French, German, Greek, Italian, Latin. **Description:** Works to gather from all relevant fields of study, and to disseminate among its members, current knowledge of rhetoric, broadly construed; to identify new areas within the subject of rhetoric in which research is especially needed, and to stimulate such research; to encourage experimentation in the teaching of rhetoric; to facilitate professional cooperation among its members, to organize meetings at which members may exchange findings and ideas; and to sponsor the publication of such materials dealing with rhetoric. **Awards:** Charles Kneupper Award. **Frequency:** annual. **Type:** recognition. **Recipient:** for the best piece published in RSQ ● Dissertation Award. **Frequency:** biennial. **Type:** recognition. **Recipient:** for the best PhD dissertation on rhetoric completed by a student member of the Society within the past two years ● Distinguished Book Award. **Frequency:** biennial. **Type:** recognition. **Recipient:** for the best book on rhetoric authored by a member of the Society and published within the past two years ● George Yoos Award. **Frequency:** biennial. **Type:** recognition. **Recipient:** for service and research in the field of rhetoric by a member of the Society ● Gerard A. Hauser Award. **Frequency:** biennial. **Type:** recognition. **Recipient:** for outstanding graduate student research presented at the biennial conference ● RSA Fellow. **Frequency:** periodic. **Type:** fellowship. **Recipient:** for distinguished scholarship, teaching, and/or service to the field of rhetorical studies. **Telecommunication Services:** electronic mail, d-zarefsky@northwestern.edu. **Publications:** *Rhetoric Society Quarterly*, every January, April, July and October. Journal. Contains scholarly articles, book reviews, and bibliographies. **Price:** included in membership dues; $100.00 /year for institutions. **Advertising:** accepted. Alternate Formats: microform. Also Cited As: *Rhetoric Society Newsletter* ● Book, biennial. Contains proceedings of biennial conferences. **Conventions/Meetings:** biennial conference and roundtable, week-long seminars and three-day workshops on specialized topics in rhetoric (exhibits) - odd-numbered years ● biennial conference, plenary sessions and break-out sessions for research presentations (exhibits) - even-numbered years.

Romanian

10938 ■ Romanian Studies Association of America (RSAA)
c/o Dr. Nicolae Harsanyi, Ed.
6937 Bay Dr., Ste.210
Miami Beach, FL 33141
Ph: (305)994-1419
E-mail: niki@thewolf.fiu.edu
URL: http://www.uwo.ca/modlang/RSAA
Contact: Dr. Nicolae Harsanyi, Ed.
Founded: 1972. **Members:** 60. **Membership Dues:** regular, $15 (annual). **Description:** Organizes sessions on Romanian literature, culture, history, and politics, and promotes Romanian studies within an East European context. Facilitates the exchange of information within the discipline and in the field of comparative literature. Conducts research and publicizes the cultural contributions of Romanian writers and other cultural figures. Encourages dialogue and collaboration among Romanian and American scholars of Romanian studies and academics specializing in European and American studies. **Affiliated With:** Modern Language Association of America. **Publications:** Journal ● Newsletter, semiannual. **Conventions/Meetings:** board meeting, also includes members ● annual meeting - always December 27-30.

10939 ■ Society for Romanian Studies (SRS)
c/o Paul E. Michelson, Pres.
Huntington Coll.
Dept. of History
Huntington, IN 46750
Ph: (260)359-4242 (260)356-5518
Fax: (260)356-4086
E-mail: pmichelson@huntington.edu
URL: http://www.huntington.edu/srs
Contact: Paul E. Michelson, Pres.
Founded: 1973. **Members:** 200. **Membership Dues:** regular, $15 (annual) ● full time student, $10 (annual) ● joint, $33 (annual) ● joint student, $19 (annual) ● life, $100. **Languages:** English, Romanian. **Description:** Provides communication among scholars of Romanian history, language, culture, politics, and economics; promotes the study of Romania and Moldova. **Computer Services:** Mailing lists. **Affiliated With:** American Association for the Advancement of Slavic Studies; American Historical Association; American Political Science Association. **Formerly:** (1978) Romanian Studies Group. **Publications:** *SRS Newsletter*, 3/year. Contains news of society activities and research projects; includes book reviews and calendar of events. **Price:** $15.00/year. **Circulation:** 600. **Advertising:** accepted. Alternate Formats: online. **Conventions/Meetings:** annual conference.

Romany

10940 ■ Gypsy Lore Society (GLS)
c/o Sheila Salo, Treas.
5607 Greenleaf Rd.
Cheverly, MD 20785
Ph: (301)341-1261
Fax: (301)341-1261

E-mail: headquarters@gypsyloresociety.org
URL: http://www.gypsyloresociety.org
Contact: Sheila Salo, Treas.
Founded: 1888. **Members:** 300. **Membership Dues:** individual, $35 (annual) ● contributing, $100 (annual) ● sustaining, $75 (annual) ● supporting, $50 (annual). **Budget:** $10,000. **Multinational. Description:** Anthropologists, linguists, sociologists, folklorists, educators, and others interested in the study of the Gypsy peoples and analogous itinerant or nomadic groups. Works to disseminate information aimed at increasing understanding of Gypsy culture in its diverse forms. Seeks to establish closer contacts among scholars in the U.S. and Canada. Maintains Victor Weybright Archives of Gypsy Studies. **Libraries: Type:** by appointment only. **Holdings:** 500; articles, audio recordings, books, periodicals, video recordings. **Subjects:** Gypsies, travelers and analogous groups. **Awards:** Young Scholar's Prize in Romani Studies. **Frequency:** annual. **Type:** monetary. **Recipient:** for papers written in English by graduate students beyond their first year of study and those holding the PhD no more than 3 years beyond awarding of degree. **Formerly:** (1989) Gypsy Lore Society, North American Chapter. **Publications:** *Gypsies and Travelers in North America: An Annotated Bibliography*. Paper. **Price:** $20.00 for nonmembers in U.S. and Canada; $23.00 for nonmembers elsewhere; $15.00 for members in U.S. and Canada; $18.00 for members elsewhere ● *100 Years of Gypsy Studies*. Paper. **Price:** $20.00 for nonmembers in U.S. and Canada; $23.00 for nonmembers elsewhere; $15.00 for members in U.S. and Canada; $18.00 for members elsewhere ● *Romani Studies (Continuing Journal of the Gypsy Lore Society)*, semiannual. Contains articles and book reviews in any discipline dealing with various aspects of Gypsy Studies. **Price:** included in membership dues; $35.00 /year for individuals; $10.00 each, for nonmembers. ISSN: 1528-0748. **Circulation:** 300. **Advertising:** accepted ● Membership Directory, annual. Includes bibliography. **Price:** $3.00 /year for members. **Circulation:** 90 ● Newsletter, quarterly. Contains calls for papers, research and conference news, and bibliography. **Price:** included in membership dues; $35.00 /year for individuals. ISSN: 1070-4604. **Circulation:** 300. **Advertising:** accepted. **Conventions/Meetings:** annual conference and meeting, scholarly, on Gypsy studies (exhibits).

Russian

10941 ■ Association of Russian-American Scholars in the United States of America (ARASUSA)

PO Box 180035
Richmond Hill, NY 11418
E-mail: webmaster@russamscholars.org
URL: http://www.russamscholars.org
Contact: Prof. Nadja Jernakoff, Pres.
Founded: 1948. **Members:** 150. **Membership Dues:** individual, $40 (annual) ● retiree, $20 (annual). **Regional Groups:** 1. **Languages:** English, Russian. **Description:** Persons of Russian descent or others interested in Russian studies who hold a master's degree or higher from an American institution of higher learning, or its equivalent from an educational institution outside the U.S., and have been teaching in an institution of higher learning, or have published works. Functions as a Russian scholarly center aimed at: cooperating with Russian scholars in their pedagogical work and in their research projects in the U.S; uniting persons involved in the study of Russian culture. Believes in complete freedom of scholarly inquiry. **Divisions:** Washington, DC Branch. **Publications:** *Transactions/Zapiski* (in English and Russian), annual. Journal. Covers Russian literature, arts, history, and culture. **Price:** included in membership dues; $34.00 /year for nonmembers, plus shipping and handling; $38.00 outside U.S. ISSN: 0066-9717. **Circulation:** 500. **Conventions/Meetings:** periodic lecture ● periodic seminar.

Scandinavian

10942 ■ American-Scandinavian Foundation (ASF)

58 Park Ave.
New York, NY 10016
Ph: (212)879-9779 (212)847-9717
Fax: (212)686-2115
E-mail: info@amscan.org
URL: http://www.amscan.org
Contact: Edward P. Gallagher, Pres./CEO
Founded: 1910. **Members:** 6,000. **Membership Dues:** national/international associate, $35 (annual) ● Scandinavia House associate, $50 (annual) ● family associate, $65 (annual) ● contributing associate, $150 (annual) ● supporting associate, $300 (annual) ● sustaining associate, $500 (annual) ● patron, $1,000 (annual) ● President's Circle, $2,500 (annual) ● senior, student associate, $25 (annual). **Staff:** 20. **Budget:** $3,500,000. **Regional Groups:** 20. **Description:** Americans, Scandinavians, and Americans of Scandinavian descent. Seeks to further understanding between the U.S. and the Scandinavian countries through educational and cultural exchanges, publications, and public programs such as art exhibitions and lectures. Provides a foreign training program in both the U.S. and Nordic countries. **Convention/Meeting:** none. **Libraries: Type:** open to the public. **Holdings:** 1,200; books, periodicals. **Subjects:** Scandinavian-related topics, travel, history, fiction, biography. **Awards: Type:** fellowship ● Public Project Grants. **Type:** grant ● **Type:** recognition. **Computer Services:** Mailing lists. **Telecommunication Services:** electronic mail, mem@amscan.org. **Committees:** Fellowships and Grants. **Divisions:** Exchange; Public Programs; Publishing. **Publications:** *The Longboat*, annual. Newsletter. Alternate Formats: online ● *Scan*, quarterly. Newsletter. **Price:** included in membership dues. **Circulation:** 6,000 ● *Scandinavian Review*, 3/year. Magazine. Covers culture and society of Denmark, Finland, Iceland, Norway, and Sweden. **Price:** $15.00/year. ISSN: 0098-857X. **Circulation:** 5,000. **Advertising:** accepted ● Annual Report, annual. Alternate Formats: online.

Science Fiction

10943 ■ Fan Tek

1610 Lee Rd.
Fort Washington, MD 20744
Ph: (301)292-5231
E-mail: fantek@obscure.org
URL: http://www.fantek.org
Contact: Bruce Evry, Exec. Off.
Founded: 1982. **Members:** 3,000. **Description:** A group based on friendship, made up of individuals with interests in science fiction, fantasy, gaming, computers, art, writing, historical reenactment, costuming, videos, making bad movies, attention deficit disorder, post traumatic stress disorder, fun technology, and chocolate. **Computer Services:** Mailing lists. **Publications:** *The Castle*. Newsletter. Contains articles, editorials, science fiction and fantasy art, classified ads, and convention and meeting updates. **Price:** included in membership dues. **Circulation:** 1,500. **Advertising:** accepted.

10944 ■ Gaylactic Network (GN)

Address Unknown since 2008
Founded: 1987. **Members:** 85. **Membership Dues:** $10 (annual). **Staff:** 7. **Regional Groups:** 1. **State Groups:** 13. **Local Groups:** 13. **Multinational. Description:** Gay, lesbian, and bisexual individuals and others interested in science fiction, fantasy, and horror. Promotes the genres in all media, specifically material dealing with homosexuality. Provides a network for shared information and interests. **Conventions/Meetings:** annual Gaylaxicon - convention (exhibits).

10945 ■ International Association for the Fantastic in the Arts (IAFA)

c/o Stacie L. Hanes, Membership/Registration Coor.
PO Box 3701
Youngstown, OH 44513
E-mail: esmeraldus@earthlink.net
URL: http://www.iafa.org
Contact: Stacie L. Hanes, Membership/Registration Coor.
Founded: 1979. **Members:** 450. **Membership Dues:** regular in North America, $75 (annual) ● overseas, $90 (annual) ● joint, $110 (annual) ● student, $50 (annual). **Description:** Scholars, educators, writers, critics, and artists sharing an interest in the fantastic, science fiction, horror, and fantasy and their impact on literature, the visual and performing arts, cinema, and other art forms. Serves as a forum for the dissemination of scholarship and the exchange of ideas among members. Encourages work in the field through publications and professional support service. **Awards:** IAFA Graduate Award. **Frequency:** annual. **Type:** scholarship. **Recipient:** for graduate students for scholarship and/or fiction writing ● Robert A. Collins Service Award. **Frequency:** annual. **Type:** recognition. **Recipient:** to an officer, board member, or division head for outstanding service to the organization. **Divisions:** The Fantastic in Film, Fine Arts, and Popular Culture; Fantasy Literature in English; Horror Literature; Interdisciplinary Approaches to Fantastic Literature; International Fantastic Literature; Science Fiction Literature. **Publications:** *IAFA Membership Directory*, annual. **Price:** included in membership dues ● *IAFA Newsletter*, quarterly. **Price:** included in membership dues ● *Journal of the Fantastic in the Arts*, quarterly. Contains critical commentaries and reviews. **Price:** included in membership dues ● Papers. **Conventions/Meetings:** annual International Conference on the Fantastic in the Arts, book and art exhibits (exhibits) - 3rd week of March.

10946 ■ National Fantasy Fan Federation (N3F)

c/o Dennis L. Davis, Chm./Sec.
25549 Byron St.
San Bernardino, CA 92404-6403
E-mail: n3f_info@yahoo.com
URL: http://www.n3f.org
Contact: Dennis L. Davis, Chm./Sec.
Founded: 1941. **Members:** 300. **Membership Dues:** individual, $18 (annual) ● joint, $22 (annual). **Multinational. Description:** Correspondence club of persons interested in reading, writing, viewing, and collecting science fiction and fantasy books, magazines, articles, movies, and other materials. Activities include an annual short story contest. **Awards:** Kaymar Award. **Frequency:** annual. **Type:** recognition. **Recipient:** for outstanding service to club ● Speculative Fiction Awards. **Frequency:** annual. **Type:** recognition. **Recipient:** for honor to the broad spectrum of speculative fiction creativity. **Computer Services:** Online services, information and discussion groups ● online services, list of member's email addresses. **Telecommunication Services:** electronic mail, ruthiechan@ruthiechan.net. **Special Interest Groups:** N'APA. **Supersedes:** Strangers Club. **Publications:** *The National Fantasy Fan*, quarterly. Magazine. Covers federation activities, includes letters and reviews. **Price:** included in membership dues. Alternate Formats: online ● *Tightbeam*, bimonthly. Includes letters from members, reviews, poetry, fiction, convention reports, N3F History, puzzles, contests, and artwork. **Conventions/Meetings:** annual meeting, held in conjunction with the World Science Fiction Convention.

10947 ■ Parallax Society

744 Arkansas St.
Tallahassee, FL 32304-2060
URL: http://www.firebyrd.com/parallax
Contact: Sonia M. James, Admin.
Founded: 1993. **Members:** 50. **Membership Dues:** individual in U.S. and Canada, Mexico, $15 (annual) ● household (2 people) in U.S. and Canada, Mexico, $20 (annual) ● household (3-5 people) in U.S. and Canada, Mexico, $30 (annual). **Staff:** 4. **Multinational. Description:** Science fiction, fantasy, and horror enthusiasts. Promotes enjoyment of these literary genres. Collects and disseminates information. **Also Known As:** Gems and Aces. **Publications:** *The Convergence*, monthly. Magazine. **Price:** free for members. **Advertising:** accepted.

10948 ■ Science Fiction Poetry Association (SFPA)

c/o Helena Bell, Treas.
1225 W Freeman St., Apt. 12
Carbondale, IL 62901

E-mail: sfpattreasurer@gmail.com
URL: http://www.sfpoetry.com
Contact: Deborah P. Kolodji, Pres.
Founded: 1978. **Members:** 150. **Membership Dues:** in U.S. and Canada, $21 (annual) ● overseas, $25 (annual) ● life, $300. **Multinational. Description:** Professional writers, "poetic dabblers", general readers, and others interested in science fiction poetry, poets, writers, and libraries. Seeks to: promote communication among people interested in science fiction and fantasy; serve as a forum for the exchange of information and views; facilitate the sharing of poetry and art. Operates placement service and shares marketing news; reviews current science fiction publications. Sponsors workshops; conducts seminars, panel discussions, and readings at World Science Fiction Society (see separate entry) conventions. Publishes anthologies such as the annual Rhysling Anthologies and The Alchemy of Stars: Rhysling Award Winners Showcase. **Libraries: Type:** reference. **Subjects:** reviewed poetry material. **Awards:** Grand Master Award. **Type:** recognition. **Recipient:** for lifetime achievement in speculative poetry ● Rhysling Award. **Frequency:** annual. **Type:** recognition. **Recipient:** for the best long and short poems in the field of speculative poetry, voted on by the entire membership. **Publications:** *Rhysling Anthology*, annual. Book. Contains collection of poems nominated for the Rhysling Award by the SFPA membership. ● *Star Line*, bimonthly. Newsletter. Includes award presentations, annual index, and anthology of the best poetry of the year. **Price:** included in membership dues; $8.00 /year for nonmembers. **Circulation:** 200 ● Also publishes poetry cassette anthology. **Conventions/Meetings:** annual convention, with poetry reading/award presentation.

10949 ■ Starships of the Third Fleet (SS/3F)
10358 Aquilla Dr.
Lakeside, CA 92040-2236
E-mail: ss3f@cox.net
URL: http://www.ss3f.com
Contact: T.E. Lawrence, Contact
Founded: 1988. **Members:** 30. **Description:** Represents individuals interested in writing science fiction based on Star Trek. Works through an online group of writers' who create characters from their own imaginations. These characters "fill positions aboard USS PHOENIX (NCC-2315) while the Captain of the PHOENIX publishes a "mission prologue" which outlines, in broad terms, what the ship's mission will be. Members develop a plot and story line, using their characters and the other characters aboard the ship, and complete the mission".

10950 ■ World Science Fiction Society (WSFS)
PO Box 426159
Cambridge, MA 02142
E-mail: webmaster@wsfs.org
URL: http://www.wsfs.org
Contact: Pat McMurray, Sec.
Founded: 1939. **Members:** 10,000. **Membership Dues:** attending, $225 (annual) ● supporting, $45 (annual) ● child, $50 (annual). **Multinational. Description:** Represents professionals and amateurs involved in all aspects of science fiction (books, magazines, movies, and radio-television) united to sustain interest in science fiction. **Awards:** Hugo Award. **Frequency:** annual. **Type:** recognition. **Recipient:** for Best Novel, Best Short Story, Best Novella, Best Novelette, Best Science Fiction Book, Best Dramatic Research and Best Artist. **Publications:** *Program Book*, annual. Provides information on the World Science Fiction Convention. **Advertising:** accepted ● *Progress Reports*, quarterly. **Conventions/Meetings:** annual World Science Fiction Convention (exhibits) - 2008 Aug. 6-10, Denver, CO.

Scottish

10951 ■ Armstrong Clan Society (ACS)
c/o Peter A. Armstrong, Membership Chm./Treas./Dir.
128 Essex Dr.
Summerville, SC 29485
E-mail: parmstrong@sc.rr.com
URL: http://www.armstrong.org
Contact: Peter A. Armstrong, Membership Chm./Treas./Dir.
Founded: 1981. **Membership Dues:** individual or family in U.S. and Canada, $25 (annual) ● individual or family outside U.S. and Canada, $35 (annual). **Multinational. Description:** People who are descendants of or bear the name of Armstrong. Seeks friendship and unity among Armstrongs and associated families. Maintains library, genealogical and historical recorder. **Libraries: Type:** reference. **Publications:** *Armstrong Chronicles*, 3/year. Newsletter. **Price:** included in membership dues. ISSN: 0898-1329 ● Newsletter, quarterly.

10952 ■ Bruce International, USA Branch
c/o Polly Tilford, Sec.
5561 Earl Young Rd.
Bloomington, IN 47408
E-mail: pollytilford@insightbb.com
URL: http://www.brucefamily.com
Contact: John Carlisle FSA, Pres.
Founded: 1984. **Members:** 140. **Membership Dues:** individual, family, $20 (annual) ● life (based on age), $200-$350. **Budget:** $3,500. **Multinational. Description:** People who are descendents of or bear the name of Bruce. Promotes kinship among its family members and encourages interest in the family of Bruce and its history. **Publications:** *The Blue Lion*, 2-3/year. Newsletter. **Price:** included in membership dues. **Circulation:** 175. **Conventions/Meetings:** annual general assembly.

10953 ■ Clan Anderson Society
c/o H. Wesley Weaver, Pres.
19411 Center St.
Cornelius, NC 28031
Ph: (704)892-5608
E-mail: hweaver1@bellsouth.net
URL: http://showcase.netins.net/web/clanande
Contact: H. Wesley Weaver, Pres.
Members: 500. **Membership Dues:** individual or family, $20 (annual) ● life, $150. **Description:** People who are descendents of or bear the name of Anderson. Seeks to promote and to share the pride and kinship of Anderson ancestry. Attends Scottish Highland games and Scottish festivals, sponsors tents, publishes quarterly newsletter. **Publications:** *Armstrong Chronicles*. Book. **Price:** included in membership dues ● Newsletter, quarterly.

10954 ■ An Comunn Gaidhealach America (ACGA)
PO Box 103069
Denver, CO 80250
E-mail: ruadh@idirect.com
URL: http://www.acgamerica.org
Contact: Janice Chan, Pres.
Founded: 1984. **Members:** 300. **Membership Dues:** individual, $35 (annual) ● family, $45 (annual) ● club, $50 (annual) ● corporate, $100 (annual). **Languages:** English, Gaelic, Scottish. **Description:** Individuals interested in preserving the Scottish Gaelic language and culture. Studies, promotes, and perpetuates the Scottish Gaelic language and culture, including Gaelic history, music, and art. Works to help Scottish-Americans and Canadians maintain awareness of their cultural heritage. Coordinates activities and cooperates with similar organizations in the U.S. and abroad; organizes Gaelic study groups and sponsors Gaelic classes; provides representation at Scottish games and festivals. Sponsors choral music group which performs traditional and contemporary music in Gaelic. Maintains charitable program. **Awards: Frequency:** periodic. **Type:** recognition ● **Frequency:** annual. **Type:** scholarship. **Recipient:** for members to learn Gaelic in short course settings. **Telecommunication Services:** electronic mail, jdgressett@verizon.net. **Committees:** Administrative; Education; Election; Gaidhealtachd Support; Immersion; Mod; Outreach; Publications. **Publications:** *Naidheachd*, quarterly. Newsletter. Includes news of events in Scotland and America, Gaelic-related articles, book reviews, and lessons in Gaelic. **Price:** included in membership dues ● Annual Reports, annual. **Conventions/Meetings:** annual general assembly.

10955 ■ Scottish Historic and Research Society of Delaware Valley (SHRSDV)
102 St. Paul's Rd.
Ardmore, PA 19003-2811
Ph: (610)649-4144
Contact: Blair C. Stonier, Pres.
Founded: 1964. **Members:** 200. **Membership Dues:** regular, $15 (annual) ● family, $20 (annual). **Local Groups:** 3. **Description:** Individuals interested in Scottish history and culture. Provides educational activities and programs. Maintains speakers' bureau. **Libraries: Type:** reference; open to the public; by appointment only. **Holdings:** 5,000; audiovisuals, books, clippings, monographs, periodicals. **Subjects:** Scottish history, genealogy, travel, literature, fiction. **Awards:** The Eagle Award. **Type:** recognition. **Recipient:** for service to Scottish community. **Committees:** Education. **Also Known As:** Scottish Historic and Research Society. **Publications:** *How to Search for Scottish Ancestors*. Monograph. **Price:** $2.00 ● *The Rampant Lion Newsletter*, quarterly. **Price:** included in membership dues. ISSN: 1076-4658. **Advertising:** accepted ● *Scotland: Fact and Fancy*. **Price:** $3.50. **Conventions/Meetings:** annual Kirkin O' the Tartan - festival ● meeting - always second Friday, September-June ● Robert Burns Dinner - always Saturday closest to January 25.

Sculpture

10956 ■ Anonymous Arts Recovery Society (AARS)
Address Unknown since 2008
Founded: 1960. **Staff:** 4. **Budget:** $35,000. **Local Groups:** 6. **Description:** Persons interested in rescuing architectural ornaments and sculpture (such as heads, caryatids, columns, capitals, carvings, and bas-relief figures) from buildings being demolished or remodeled in the older districts of American cities, particularly New York City. Concentrates on saving pieces from the years 1875 to 1910, generally works of unknown artisans and sculptors (hence, the "anonymous" of the society's name), as a means of preserving objects of aesthetic merit and historical importance and because of the contention that the objects represent the last applications of ornament to classically oriented buildings. The society purchases some of the sculptures and encourages demolition contractors to donate others to the collection, some of which have been placed in a specially-designed garden at the Brooklyn Museum. Conducts research; has contributed works to several New York state museums. Provides appraisals and assists in processing gifts to pertinent institutions. Offers technical information for conservation of works in collections. Operates Anonymous Arts Museum of Architectural Sculpture and History of Charlotteville Museum in Charlotteville, NY. Engages in cemetery restoration; maintains 1832 church. Maintains speakers' bureau. Acquired site of 1850 seminary ruin. Excavations in progress. Recovered artifacts on view in church exhibition room. **Libraries: Type:** reference. **Holdings:** 300; archival material, photographs. **Subjects:** history of American architecture, NY state history, local history, village of Charlotteville.

10957 ■ Association of Lifecasters International (ALI)
c/o Edmund McCormick, Dir.
18 Bank St.
Summit, NJ 07901
Ph: (908)273-5600
Fax: (908)273-9256
E-mail: info@lifecasting.org
URL: http://www.lifecasting.org
Contact: Edmund McCormick, Dir.
Founded: 2000. **Members:** 300. **Multinational. Description:** Promotes life-casting and represents the interests of life-casting artists from around the world. Educates new artists to the life-casting medium.

Certifies life-casting teachers to ensure consistent and safe instruction in this art form. **Libraries: Type:** reference. **Subjects:** lifecasting and related subjects. **Telecommunication Services:** electronic mail, ali@artmolds.com.

10958 ■ International Sculpture Center (ISC)
14 Fairgrounds Rd., Ste.B
Hamilton, NJ 08619-3447
Ph: (609)689-1051
Fax: (609)689-1061
E-mail: isc@sculpture.org
URL: http://www.sculpture.org
Contact: Beverly Bancroft, Office Mgr.
Founded: 1960. **Members:** 10,000. **Membership Dues:** basic, in U.S., Canada and Mexico, $95 (annual) ● basic (international), $115 (annual) ● professional in U.S., Canada and Mexico, $350 (annual) ● professional (international), $370 (annual) ● senior, student, young professional in U.S., Canada and Mexico, $60 (annual) ● senior, student, young professional (international), $80 (annual) ● associate in U.S., Canada and Mexico, $200 (annual) ● library in U.S., Canada and Mexico, $100 (annual) ● library (international), $120 (annual) ● university in U.S., Canada and Mexico, $170 (annual) ● university (international), $190 (annual) ● associate (international), $220 (annual) ● corporate level, $2,500 (annual). **Staff:** 12. **Multinational. Description:** Sculptors, architects, developers, journalists, curators, historians, critics, educators, foundries, galleries, and museums committed to the field of sculpture. **Awards:** Lifetime Achievement in Contemporary Sculpture. **Frequency:** annual. **Type:** recognition. **Recipient:** for achievement in sculpture field ● Outstanding Sculpture Educator. **Frequency:** annual. **Type:** recognition. **Recipient:** for achievement in sculpture field ● Outstanding Student Achievement in Contemporary Sculpture. **Frequency:** annual. **Type:** recognition. **Recipient:** for achievement in sculpture field ● Patron's Recognition Award. **Frequency:** annual. **Type:** recognition. **Recipient:** for achievement in sculpture field. **Computer Services:** Information services, portfolio registry and referral system. **Programs:** ISC Sculpture. **Affiliated With:** College Art Association. **Publications:** *Insider*, 10/year. Newsletter. Provides opportunities for artists. **Price:** included in membership dues ● *ISC Sculpture Destinations Directory*. Alternate Formats: online ● *ISC Sculpture Parks and Gardens Directory*. Alternate Formats: online ● *ISC Technical Resources Directory*. Alternate Formats: online ● *Portfolio*. Directory. Alternate Formats: online ● *Sculpture Magazine*. Features criticism, reviews, studio visits, interviews, and technical information of interest. **Price:** included in membership dues; $50.00 for nonmembers in U.S., Canada and Mexico; $70.00 for nonmembers outside U.S., Canada and Mexico. **Advertising:** accepted. Alternate Formats: online. **Conventions/Meetings:** biennial conference.

10959 ■ National Sculpture Society (NSS)
237 Park Ave.
New York, NY 10017
Ph: (212)764-5645
Fax: (212)764-5651
E-mail: info@nationalsculpture.org
URL: http://www.nationalsculpture.org
Contact: Gwen Pier, Exec. Dir.
Founded: 1893. **Members:** 4,000. **Membership Dues:** associate in U.S., $65 (annual) ● associate outside U.S., $75 (annual) ● subscriber, $24 (annual) ● patron, fellow, $250 ● sculptor, $175 ● benefactor, $25,000 ● sustaining, $15,000 ● donor, $10,000 ● supporting, $5,000 ● life, $2,000. **Staff:** 4. **Budget:** $500,000. **Languages:** English, Spanish. **Description:** Sculptors throughout the U.S. as well as the general public. Rotating exhibitions at its headquarters in New York City provide a venue for people to view some of America's best contemporary figurative sculpture. Conducts educational programs. **Libraries: Type:** reference; open to the public. **Holdings:** 3,300; archival material, audiovisuals, books, clippings, monographs, periodicals. **Subjects:** sculpture—general, American, foreign, members, technical, historical. **Awards:** Alex Ettl Grant. **Frequency:** annual. **Type:** monetary. **Recipient:** to an accomplished sculptor for a life's body of work ● Annual Exhibition Awards. **Frequency:** annual. **Type:** monetary. **Recipient:** for meritorious work of sculpture ● Dexter Jones Award. **Frequency:** annual. **Type:** monetary. **Recipient:** for outstanding work of sculpture in bas-relief ● Emerging Artists Award. **Type:** recognition. **Recipient:** for a young artist ● Henry Hering - Art and Architecture Award. **Frequency:** periodic. **Type:** recognition. **Recipient:** for outstanding collaboration among architect, owner and sculptor in the distinguished use of sculpture in an architectural project ● **Type:** monetary ● Williams Scholarship. **Frequency:** annual. **Type:** scholarship. **Recipient:** for a figurative sculptor ● Young Sculptors Awards. **Type:** monetary. **Recipient:** for meritorious work of sculpture. **Telecommunication Services:** electronic mail, gwen@nationalsculpture.org. **Committees:** Delegates to the Fine Arts Federation of New York; Education; Exhibition. **Publications:** *Exhibition Catalogs*, annual. **Price:** $10.00 ● *NSS News Bulletin*, bimonthly. Journal. Contains articles of interest for sculptors of all levels of ability. ● *Sculpture Review*, quarterly. Magazine. Deals primarily with representational sculpture; provides information on upcoming exhibits, contemporary, and art historical articles. **Price:** $24.00/year. ISSN: 0747-5284. **Circulation:** 8,000. **Advertising:** accepted. Alternate Formats: microform ● Videos. **Conventions/Meetings:** competition - 3/year (January, May and October), always in New York City ● monthly meeting - always third Tuesday in New York City.

10960 ■ Rogers Group (RG)
Address Unknown since 2008
Founded: 1970. **Members:** 110. **Membership Dues:** $10 (annual). **Description:** Lawyers, doctors, artists, corporate professionals, professors, and others interested in the life and works of John Rogers (1829-1904), American sculptor. **Libraries: Type:** reference. **Holdings:** archival material. **Publications:** Newsletter, semiannual. **Conventions/Meetings:** semiannual meeting.

10961 ■ Sculptors Guild (SG)
110 Greene St., Ste.601
New York, NY 10012
Ph: (212)431-5669
Fax: (212)431-5669
E-mail: sculptorsguild@gmail.com
URL: http://www.sculptorsguild.org
Contact: Jerelyn Hanrahan, Pres.
Founded: 1937. **Members:** 124. **Membership Dues:** regular, in U.S., $200 (annual) ● regular, outside U.S., $225 (annual). **Staff:** 1. **Description:** Professional sculptors. Seeks to further the artistic goals of sculptors and the art community. Sponsors annual exhibitions of members' works; has assembled numerous traveling exhibitions for circulation by the American Federation of Arts, the Carnegie Corporation of New York (see separate entries), and the Board of Education of New York. **Libraries: Type:** open to the public. **Holdings:** archival material, video recordings. **Subjects:** Sculptors Guild activities and exhibitions. **Publications:** *Sculptors Guild—Guild Reporter*, semiannual. Newsletter. Covers occupational health hazards, sculpture exhibitions, competitions, activities and honors guild members. **Price:** free. **Advertising:** accepted ● Catalogs, varies ● Newsletter, varies. **Conventions/Meetings:** annual meeting (exhibits).

Semantics

10962 ■ Institute of General Semantics (IGS)
2260 Coll. Ave.
Fort Worth, TX 76110
Ph: (817)922-9950
Fax: (817)922-9903
E-mail: igs@time-binding.org
URL: http://www.time-binding.org
Contact: Mr. Steve Stockdale, Exec. Dir.
Founded: 1938. **Members:** 700. **Membership Dues:** student, $25 (annual) ● regular, $50 (annual) ● contributor, $100 (annual) ● supporter, $250 (annual) ● sponsor, $500 (annual) ● time-binder, $1,000 (annual). **Staff:** 3. **Budget:** $300,000. **Regional Groups:** 2. **Multinational. Description:** Professional or nonprofessional persons, libraries, and business and government organizations. Activities include training, publishing, and consulting in the field of general semantics and non-Aristotelian systems. Sponsors five day seminar-workshops, weekend seminars, and one-day conferences. Annual Alfred Korzybski Memorial Lecture. **Libraries: Type:** by appointment only; reference. **Holdings:** 3,000; archival material, audio recordings, books, clippings, periodicals, photographs. **Subjects:** general semantics, linguistics, language, arts, philosophy, science. **Awards:** J. Talbot Winchell Award. **Frequency:** annual. **Type:** recognition. **Computer Services:** Online services, book sales. **Publications:** *General Semantics Bulletin*, annual. **Price:** $15.00 ● *Manhood of Humanity*. Book ● *Science & Sanity*. Book ● *Time-Bindings*, quarterly. Newsletter ● Articles ● Monographs, quarterly. **Conventions/Meetings:** annual Alfred Korzybski Memorial Lecture - seminar and workshop, intensive educational seminar.

Shakers

10963 ■ Friends of the Shakers (FS)
c/o The Shaker Society
707 Shaker Rd.
New Gloucester, ME 04260
Ph: (207)926-4597 (207)926-4865
Fax: (207)926-3559
E-mail: usshakers@aol.com
URL: http://www.maineshakers.com/friends
Contact: Terry Barry, Contact
Founded: 1974. **Members:** 400. **Membership Dues:** individual, $15 (annual) ● family, $25 (annual) ● contributor, $35 (annual) ● sponsor, $50 (annual) ● patron, $100 (annual) ● benefactor, $200 (annual) ● life, $500 ● corporate, $1,000 (annual). **Description:** Assists Shakers at Sabbathday Lake, ME in continuing their enrichment programs, including their museum and library of original manuscripts and photographs. (The United Society of Believers in Christ's Second Appearing, commonly referred to as the Shakers, came to the U.S. in 1774. The Shakers believe in celibacy, the equality of the sexes, and self-sufficiency. Sabbathday Lake, a 1900-acre village of 17 buildings, was built 200 years ago and is the only extant Shaker community.) Provides financial assistance to the Shakers. **Libraries: Type:** reference. **Holdings:** 3,000; archival material, clippings, films, maps, photographs, video recordings. **Telecommunication Services:** electronic mail, brooks1@shaker.lib.me.us. **Committees:** Friends' Weekend; Work Day. **Publications:** *The Clarion*, 3-4/year. Newsletter. **Price:** included in membership dues. **Conventions/Meetings:** annual Friends Weekend - assembly (exhibits) - usually second weekend of August at Sabbathday Lake, ME.

Sherlock Holmes

10964 ■ Baker Street Irregulars (BSI)
2 Dettling Rd.
Maynard, MA 01754
Ph: (717)633-8911
E-mail: email@bakerstreetjournal.com
URL: http://www.bakerstreetjournal.com
Contact: Steven Rothman, Ed.
Founded: 1934. **Members:** 300. **Local Groups:** 300. **Multinational. Description:** Serves as literary society for Sherlock Holmes. **Libraries: Type:** reference. **Holdings:** archival material. **Awards:** Irregular Shillings. **Frequency:** periodic. **Type:** recognition. **Recipient:** for members who have shown serious interest over a period of years ● Morley-Montgomery Award. **Frequency:** annual. **Type:** recognition. **Recipient:** to the most outstanding article to appear in the Baker Street Journal in a given year. **Telecommunication Services:** electronic mail, bsj.editor@gmail.com. **Publications:** *The Baker Street Irregulars*

Archival Series, periodic. Books. **Price:** $25.00 ● *The Baker Street Irregulars International Series*, periodic. Books. Features Sherlockian scholarship from a variety of countries that have not previously published in English. **Price:** $39.95 ● *Baker Street Journal: An Irregular Quarterly of Sherlockiana.* Contains articles on literary criticism of Sherlock Holmes. **Price:** $23.00/year in U.S.; $25.00/year outside U.S. **Advertising:** accepted ● *The Baker Street Irregulars Manuscript Series*, periodic. Books. Covers original manuscript of the Sherlock Holmes stories, with commentary from Sherlockian scholars worldwide. **Price:** $35.00. Also Cited As: *The Hound of the Baskervilles: Chapter XI The Angels of Darkness G.K. Chesterton's Sherlock Holmes The Napoleon Bust Business Again.* **Conventions/Meetings:** annual dinner.

Skiing

10965 ■ International Skiing History Association (ISHA)
530 Cheese Factory Rd.
South Burlington, VT 05403
Ph: (802)863-2511
E-mail: isha@snet.net
URL: http://skiinghistory.org
Contact: Hugh Harley, Pres.
Founded: 1991. **Membership Dues:** associate, $40 (annual) ● life, $1,000. **Description:** Preserves the knowledge of ski history. Increases public awareness of the ski heritage. Acts as a clearinghouse for information about skiing history and public and private collections in every country. **Computer Services:** Information services, ski resources ● online services, forum. **Publications:** *Skiing Heritage*, quarterly. Journal. Features serious and popular ski history and skiing heritage. **Price:** included in membership dues.

Slavic

10966 ■ American Association for the Advancement of Slavic Studies (AAASS)
8 Story St.
Cambridge, MA 02138
Ph: (617)495-0677 (617)496-9412
Fax: (617)495-0680
E-mail: aaass@fas.harvard.edu
URL: http://www.aaass.org
Contact: Dmitry P. Gorenburg PhD, Exec. Dir.
Founded: 1948. **Members:** 2,500. **Membership Dues:** individual (dues scaled based on income level), $35-$180 (annual) ● institutional (dues scaled based on type of organization), $150-$600 (annual) ● affiliate, $40 (annual). **Staff:** 5. **Regional Groups:** 7. **Multinational. Description:** Scholars and others in teaching, research, administration, and government. Seeks to advance study, publication, and teaching relating to Russia, Eurasia, and Eastern Europe. **Awards:** AAASS/Orbis Books Prize for Polish Studies. **Frequency:** annual. **Type:** recognition. **Recipient:** for the best book in any discipline, on any aspect of Polish affairs ● Barbara Jelavich Book Prize. **Frequency:** annual. **Type:** recognition. **Recipient:** for a distinguished monograph published on any aspect of Southeast European or Habsburg studies since 1600 ● Ed A. Hewett Book Prize. **Frequency:** annual. **Type:** recognition. **Recipient:** for an outstanding publication on the political economy of the centrally planned economies of the former Soviet Union and East Central Europe and their transitional successors ● Marshall Shulman Book Prize. **Frequency:** annual. **Type:** recognition. **Recipient:** for an outstanding monograph dealing with the international relations, foreign policy, or foreign-policy decision-making of any of the states of the former Soviet Union or Eastern Europe ● W. Bruce Lincoln Book Prize. **Frequency:** biennial. **Type:** recognition. **Recipient:** for an author's first published monograph or scholarly synthesis that is of exceptional merit and lasting significance for the understanding of Russia's past ● Wayne S. Vucinich Book Prize. **Frequency:** annual. **Type:** recognition. **Recipient:** for the most important contribution to Russian, Eurasian, and East European studies in any discipline of the humanities or social sciences. **Telecommunication Services:** electronic mail, gorenbur@fas.harvard.edu. **Committees:** Bibliography and Documentation; Education; Language; Slavic Review; Status of Women in the Profession. **Publications:** *NewsNet*, 5/year, January, March, May, August, and October. Newsletter. Features news of the profession and association. **Price:** $25.00 in U.S.; $40.00 outside U.S. ISSN: 1074-3057. **Circulation:** 2,500. **Advertising:** accepted ● *Slavic Review*, quarterly. Journal. **Price:** $150.00 in U.S.; $170.00 in Canada or Mexico; $190.00 outside North America. ISSN: 0037-6779. **Circulation:** 3,500. **Advertising:** accepted. **Conventions/Meetings:** annual convention (exhibits) - 2008 Nov. 20-23, Boston, MA.

10967 ■ American Committee of Slavists (ACS)
c/o Prof. Michael S. Flier, Chm.
Harvard Univ.
Dept. of Slavic Languages and Literatures
12 Quincy St., Barker Ctr.
Cambridge, MA 02138
E-mail: flier@fas.harvard.edu
URL: http://www.fas.harvard.edu/~slavic/acs
Contact: Prof. Michael S. Flier, Chm.
Founded: 1957. **Members:** 23. **Description:** Chairs of university departments granting the PhD degree in Slavic languages and literatures. Activity limited to organizing American participation in the International Congress of Slavists, organized by the International Committee of Slavists. Submits scholarly papers to ICS Congress. **Telecommunication Services:** electronic mail, rar@slavic.umass.edu. **Publications:** *American Contributions to the International Congress of Slavists*, quinquennial. **Conventions/Meetings:** annual meeting, in conjunction with the American Association for the Advancement of Slavic Studies.

10968 ■ National Council for Eurasian and East European Research (NCEEER)
2601 4th Ave., Ste.310
Seattle, WA 98121
Ph: (206)441-6433
Fax: (206)753-0066
E-mail: danochka@nceeer.org
URL: http://www.nceeer.org
Contact: Robert Huber, Pres.
Founded: 1978. **Staff:** 5. **Budget:** $2,000,000. **Languages:** English, Russian. **Description:** Conducts peer reviews of funding proposals for postdoctoral research (U.S. only). Aims to develop and sustain long-term and high-quality research programs dealing with major policy issues and questions of Eastern Europe, the USSR, and its successor states' social, political, economic, and historical development. Awards research contracts and grants on the basis of national, annual competitions; conducts occasional seminars in connection with research contracts. Distributes final reports from research contracts to governmental subscribers. **Libraries: Type:** reference. **Holdings:** 1,000; books, periodicals. **Subjects:** Eastern European history, sociology, economics, politics. **Awards: Frequency:** annual. **Type:** fellowship. **Telecommunication Services:** electronic mail, bth@nceeer.org. **Formerly:** (1999) National Council for Soviet and East European Research. **Publications:** *Research Report*, periodic. **Price:** free ● Newsletter, quarterly. **Price:** free. **Circulation:** 250. **Conventions/Meetings:** annual meeting.

10969 ■ Slavic Heritage Coalition (SHC)
51 W 14th St., Ste.4R
New York, NY 10011
Ph: (212)366-5406
Free: (888)699-7531
E-mail: info@slavicheritagecoalition.com
URL: http://www.slavicheritagecoalition.com
Contact: Mira Zivkovich, Contact
Description: Advances the interests of Slavic-American communities. Aims to unite, support and promote the importance of Slavic heritage, culture and tradition. Increases awareness of Slavic history and educates about the contributions of Slavic Americans to American institutions and cultural life. **Telecommunication Services:** electronic mail, survey@slavicheritagecoalition.com ● electronic mail, mira@mziglobal.com.

Slovak

10970 ■ Slovak-American Cultural Center (SACC)
Address Unknown since 2008
Founded: 1967. **Members:** 200. **Membership Dues:** individual, $15 (annual). **Languages:** English, Slovak. **Description:** Slovaks and others interested in Slovak culture. Wishes to maintain and extend Slovak national and cultural history. Sponsors cultural programs in music and art in addition to social and sporting events. Sponsors Heart to Heart project to train Slovak doctors in children's heart diseases. **Awards:** Milan R. Stefanik Award. **Frequency:** annual. **Type:** recognition ● Muse of the Tatra Award. **Type:** recognition. **Commissions:** Art and Science; Cultural; Education; Entertainment; Sports. **Formerly:** Slovensko-Americke Kulturne Stredisko. **Publications:** *Ozvena*, quarterly. Newsletter. **Conventions/Meetings:** biennial general assembly.

10971 ■ Slovak Studies Association (SSA)
c/o Dr. Carol Skalnik Leff, Pres.
Univ. of Illinois
Dept. of Political Sci.
361 Lincoln Hall
702 S Wright St.
Urbana, IL 61801
Ph: (217)244-2270
Fax: (217)244-5712
E-mail: leffc@uiuc.edu
URL: http://www.as.uky.edu/ssa
Contact: Dr. Carol Skalnik Leff, Pres.
Founded: 1977. **Members:** 149. **Membership Dues:** individual, $5 (annual). **Description:** Represents scholars in Slovak studies organized to promote and foster interdisciplinary research on Slovak culture. Issues papers on Slovak topics. **Awards: Type:** recognition. **Publications:** *SSA Newsletter*, semiannual. Contains information and articles in the area of Slovak studies. **Price:** included in membership dues. Alternate Formats: online. **Conventions/Meetings:** annual meeting, held in conjunction with the American Association for the Advancement of Slavic Studies.

Slovenian

10972 ■ Slovenian Research Center of America (SRCA)
29227 Eddy Rd.
Willoughby Hills, OH 44092
Ph: (440)944-7237
Fax: (440)944-0461
E-mail: gobedslo@aol.com
Contact: Dr. Edward Gobetz, Exec.Dir.
Founded: 1951. **Languages:** Croatian, English, French, German, Italian, Slovene, Spanish. **Description:** Conducts worldwide research on Slovenian heritage, culture, and history; promotes the study of Slovenian language, culture, and ethnic contributions to the U.S. and the world. Presents lectures and exhibits at universities, museums, libraries, festivals, and symposia. Organizes and provides assistance in Slovenian language courses. Operates speakers' bureau; compiles statistics. Offers educational programs. **Libraries: Type:** reference. **Holdings:** archival material. **Subjects:** Slovenian heritage and historical contributions. **Awards:** Slovenian Studies Award. **Frequency:** annual. **Type:** recognition. **Recipient:** for excellence in Slovenian Studies. **Committees:** Art and Exhibits; International Advisory; Language; Research and Publications. **Formerly:** Slovenian Research Project. **Publications:** *Ohio's Lincoln, From Carniola to Carnegie Hall, etc..* Monographs ● *Slovenian Heritage, Adjustment and Assimilation, translations of Slovenian Literature.* Books ● *Slovenian Language Manuals (Textbooks)* ● *SRCA Newsletter*, periodic. **Price:** free for members and those with special needs. **Circulation:** 3,000. Also

Cited As: *Porocila* ● Also publishes articles on Slovenian Americans in Encyclopedias, journals, magazines, and newspapers, and creates flyers and posters on Slovenian culture, language, art, and history. **Conventions/Meetings:** conference and workshop.

Spanish

10973 ■ Queen Sofia Spanish Institute
684 Park Ave.
New York, NY 10021
Ph: (212)628-0420
Fax: (212)734-4177
URL: http://www.spanishinstitute.org
Contact: Oscar de la Renta, Chm.

Founded: 1954. **Members:** 1,000. **Membership Dues:** individual, $60 (annual) ● friend, $500 (annual) ● patron, $1,000 (annual) ● sponsor, corporate, $5,000 (annual) ● benefactor, $15,000 (annual) ● golden benefactor, $25,000 (annual). **Staff:** 10. **Languages:** English, Spanish. **Description:** Represents persons and corporations interested in promoting and increasing knowledge of the culture, life, history, and customs of Spain and Spanish-speaking countries. Conducts language courses, concerts, dance programs, theatre productions, poetry readings, film showings, and art exhibitions. Conducts: language class program with classes in Castilian Spanish, Catalan, business Spanish, Spanish for the medical profession, and Spanish for children; art history and Spanish dance classes. Spanish and American business leaders, experts, and government officials exchange views via corporate and public affairs program. Maintains a gallery for exhibits of paintings, drawings, and sculpture by Spanish artists. Makes available translation services. **Libraries: Type:** reference. **Holdings:** 5,000; periodicals. **Subjects:** 20th century Spain. **Awards:** Gold Medal Award. **Frequency:** annual. **Type:** medal. **Recipient:** for Americans and Spaniards who have made significant contributions towards the betterment of relations between Spain and the U.S. **Publications:** Annual Report, annual ● Brochures ● Catalogs. **Conventions/Meetings:** annual Gold Medal Award Gala - dinner - always November ● lecture.

10974 ■ Society of Spanish and Spanish-American Studies (SSSAS)
Univ. of Colorado
Dept. of Spanish and Portuguese
134 McKenna Languages Bldg., 278 UCB
Boulder, CO 80309-0278
Ph: (303)492-5900
Fax: (303)492-3699
E-mail: sssas@colorado.edu
URL: http://www.colorado.edu/spanish/sssas
Contact: Luis T. Gonzalez-del-Valle, Gen. Ed.

Founded: 1976. **Members:** 1,000. **Staff:** 3. **Languages:** English, Spanish. **Description:** Spanish and Spanish-American creative writers, critics, and teachers at institutions of higher learning and specialists in Spanish and Spanish-American literature throughout the world. Studies Spanish and Spanish-American literature, art, and pedagogy. Promotes bibliographical, critical, and pedagogical research in Spanish and Spanish-American studies by publishing meritorious works. Organizes lecture tours. Recognizes outstanding contributions to Hispanism and the humanities by naming distinguished individuals honorary fellows. Sponsors the Twentieth Century Spanish Association of America. **Libraries: Type:** open to the public. **Holdings:** 2. **Councils:** Editorial Advisory. **Affiliated With:** Twentieth Century Spanish Association of America. **Publications:** *Anales de la Literatura Espanola Contemporanea* (in English and Spanish), 3/year. Journal. Examines all aspects of twentieth-century Spanish literature. Includes book reviews. **Price:** $30.00 /year for individuals; $100.00 /year for institutions. ISSN: 0272-1635. **Circulation:** 900. **Advertising:** accepted ● *Journal of Spanish Studies, Twentieth Century*. **Price:** $20.00/volume; $1.00/copy. ISSN: 0092-1807 ● *Siglo XX/20th Century* (in English and Spanish), semiannual. Journal. Contains essays on twentieth-century Spanish and Spanish-American literature. **Price:** included in membership dues; $35.00 for nonmembers. ISSN: 0740-946X. **Circulation:** 550 ● Books ● Catalog, annual.

10975 ■ Twentieth Century Spanish Association of America (TCSAA)
Univ. of Colorado at Boulder
Dept. of Spanish and Portuguese
Boulder, CO 80309-0278
Ph: (303)492-5900
Fax: (303)492-3699
E-mail: sssas@colorado.edu
Contact: Dr. Luis T. Gonzalez-del-Valle, Exec.Sec.

Founded: 1981. **Members:** 1,000. **Staff:** 2. **Languages:** English, Spanish. **Description:** A division of the Society of Spanish and Spanish-American Studies. Individuals interested in the study of 20th century Spanish literature. Sponsors lecture tours; coordinates meetings of professional organizations. **Libraries: Type:** open to the public. **Subjects:** Spanish, Spanish American literature. **Computer Services:** database ● mailing lists. **Affiliated With:** Society of Spanish and Spanish-American Studies. **Publications:** *Annals of Contemporary Spanish Literature*, periodic. Journal. Contains scholarly essays. **Price:** $90.00 /year for institutions; $170.00/2 years for institutions; $30.00 /year for individuals; $53.00/2 years for individuals. ISSN: 0272-1635. **Circulation:** 900.

Spiritual Life

10976 ■ IONS - Institute of Noetic Sciences (IONS)
101 San Antonio Rd.
Petaluma, CA 94952
Ph: (707)775-3500 (707)779-8240
Free: (877)769-4667
Fax: (707)781-7420
E-mail: membership@noetic.org
URL: http://www.noetic.org
Contact: James O'Dea, Pres.

Founded: 1973. **Members:** 20,000. **Membership Dues:** income-sensitive, $35 (annual) ● regular, $55 (annual) ● Shift in Action Partners Program, $10 (monthly) ● circle, $1,000-$5,000 (annual). **Staff:** 30. **Local Groups:** 200. **Multinational. Description:** Promotes research and education on "Noetic Sciences" and the study of human consciousness. (Noetic sciences encompass diverse ways of knowing including intellectual, sensate, and intuitive.) Seeks to broaden knowledge of the nature and abilities of the mind and consciousness and to apply that knowledge toward the enhancement of human well-being and the quality of life. Encourages scientific research into the mind-body relationship; provides network of communication and discourse between scientists and scholars. **Libraries: Type:** reference. **Holdings:** 7,500; books, periodicals, reports. **Awards:** Temple Award for Creative Altruism. **Type:** recognition. **Recipient:** for altruism. **Computer Services:** database, case histories of spontaneous remission of disease. **Telecommunication Services:** electronic mail, stephendinan@noetic.org. **Departments:** Research. **Programs:** Altruistic Spirit; Bioenergy Medicine; Emerging Paradigms in Science and Society; Exceptional Abilities; Inner Mechanisms of the Healing Response; Meditation; Monthly Intention. **Publications:** *Shift: At the Frontiers of Consciousness*, quarterly. Magazine. Includes book reviews, essays, interviews, and research updates. **Price:** included in membership dues. **Circulation:** 30,000 ● *Technical Reports*, periodic. **Conventions/Meetings:** annual conference ● biennial International Membership Conference (exhibits).

10977 ■ Vedic Friends Association (VFA)
PO Box 15082
Detroit, MI 48215
E-mail: srinandan@aol.com
URL: http://www.vedicfriends.org
Contact: Stephen Knapp, Pres./Treas.

Multinational. Description: Promotes the truths found in Vedic Dharma, the ancient cultural knowledge of India. **Libraries: Type:** reference. **Subjects:** Vedic culture. **Computer Services:** Online services, email newsgroup. **Committees:** Dharma Defense. **Departments:** Ayurveda; Vedic Astrology; Vedic Spiritual Advisors and Writers; Vegetarianism. **Programs:** Donor Membership. **Publications:** Journals, monthly.

Storytelling

10978 ■ By Word of Mouth Storytelling Guild (BWMS)
c/o Truman Coggswell, Sr.
PO Box 56
Frankford, MO 63441
Ph: (573)784-2589
Fax: (573)784-2364
E-mail: gladcogg@nemonet.com
URL: http://shorock.com/folk/bwom
Contact: Truman Coggswell Sr., Contact

Founded: 1991. **Members:** 480. **Membership Dues:** individual, $25 (annual). **Staff:** 5. **Budget:** $15,000. **Regional Groups:** 2. **State Groups:** 4. **Local Groups:** 3. **Description:** Storytellers and interested individuals. Promotes the preservation of traditional and nontraditional storytelling. Conducts workshops and performances; maintains speakers' bureau; offers placement service. Conducts educational and professional development seminars. Offers member referral services. **Libraries: Type:** reference. **Holdings:** audio recordings, books, video recordings. **Subjects:** children's storytelling, storytelling as a business. **Awards:** Langston Hughes Award. **Frequency:** annual. **Type:** recognition. **Recipient:** for individuals involved in storytelling for at least five years ● Mark Twain Award. **Frequency:** annual. **Type:** recognition. **Recipient:** for individuals involved in storytelling for at least five years ● Story Teller of the Year Award. **Frequency:** annual. **Type:** recognition. **Recipient:** for individuals involved in storytelling for at least five years. **Committees:** Education Professional Development; Multiculturalism. **Publications:** *Storylines*, semiannual. Newsletter. Contains stories, resources, book reviews and member news. **Price:** free for members. **Circulation:** 500. **Advertising:** accepted ● *Storytelling 101*. Video. **Price:** $69.95 each (video); $29.95 each (audio) ● *Why There Are No Dragons*. Book. **Price:** $4.95. **Conventions/Meetings:** annual Oral and Moral Storytelling Conference/Festival and Retreat - conference and workshop (exhibits).

10979 ■ International Order of E.A.R.S.
PO Box 17141
Louisville, KY 40217
Ph: (502)245-0643
E-mail: cornisland@insightbb.com
URL: http://www.cornislandstorytellingfestival.org
Contact: Heather Dotson, Exec. Dir.

Founded: 1983. **Membership Dues:** single, $20 (annual) ● family, $30 (annual). **Regional Groups:** 1. **Description:** Storytellers and listeners. Promotes interest in storytelling. Conducts storytelling performances. Operates the Storytelling Resource Center of books and 2000 cataloged stories on video and audiotape. Sponsors storytelling weekends and radio and television programs. Plans to build Storytelling Theatre. Produces Tale Trader, an International quarterly storytelling newspaper. **Libraries: Type:** reference. **Holdings:** 500; archival material. **Subjects:** storytelling, oral history. **Awards:** Director's Award. **Frequency:** annual. **Type:** recognition. **Recipient:** for service to the organization/storytelling ● Distinguished Service Citation. **Frequency:** annual. **Type:** recognition ● Volunteer of the Year. **Frequency:** annual. **Type:** recognition. **Recipient:** for volunteers. **Subgroups:** Tale Talk. **Also Known As:** (1975) Corn Island Storytelling Festival. **Publications:** *Corn Island Storytelling Festival*. Brochure ● *Tale Trader*, quarterly. Newspaper. Includes calendar of events. **Price:** included in membership dues; $15.00 /year for nonmembers. **Circulation:** 15,000. **Advertising:** accepted. **Conventions/Meetings:** annual Corn Island Storytelling Festival - meeting -

always third weekend in September, Louisville, KY ● periodic workshop.

10980 ■ Jewish Storytelling Coalition (JSC)
63 Gould Rd.
Waban, MA 02468
Ph: (617)244-2884
E-mail: bbonnieg@aol.com
URL: http://www.jewishstorytelling.org
Contact: Bonnie Greenberg, Co-Chair

Founded: 1989. **Members:** 50. **Membership Dues:** individual, $10 (annual). **Description:** Jewish storytellers and listeners. Promotes Jewish storytelling and the sharing of Jewish values and traditions. Sponsors story sharings and events; offers story-swaps; maintains speakers' bureau. **Telecommunication Services:** electronic mail, cmars13@aol.com. **Publications:** *Directory of Jewish Storytelling Coalition Performers*, annual. **Price:** free. **Conventions/Meetings:** annual Chanukah Storytelling Concert - meeting.

10981 ■ National Association of Black Storytellers (NABS)
PO Box 67722
Baltimore, MD 21215
Ph: (410)947-1117 (410)489-6747
Fax: (410)489-2428
E-mail: questions@nabsinc.org
URL: http://nabsinc.org
Contact: Linda J. Brown, Exec. Dir.

Founded: 1984. **Members:** 700. **Membership Dues:** elder, $25 (annual) ● youth, $15 (annual) ● regular, $50 (annual) ● contributing, $100 (annual) ● organization, $200 (annual) ● life, $500. **Staff:** 7. **State Groups:** 7. **Description:** Storytellers, scholars, and enthusiasts. Seeks to establish a forum to promote the African oral tradition. Conducts educational services and educational programs. Preserves and passes on the folklore, legends, myths, and fables of Africans and their descendants and ancestors. **Awards:** Zora Neale Hurston Award. **Frequency:** annual. **Type:** recognition. **Recipient:** for pioneers in African oral tradition and cultural heritage. **Telecommunication Services:** electronic mail, ljbrownnabs@comcast.net. **Subgroups:** Youth Development. **Formerly:** (1990) Association of Black Storytellers. **Publications:** *Membership Handbook*, annual. Contains listings of membership, officers, and committees. **Price:** included in membership dues. **Circulation:** 650. **Advertising:** accepted ● *NABS Brochure* ● *Spread the Word*, semiannual. Newsletter. **Circulation:** 1,000. **Advertising:** accepted. Alternate Formats: online. **Conventions/Meetings:** annual National Festival of Black Storytelling (exhibits).

10982 ■ National Story League (NSL)
Address Unknown since 2008

Founded: 1903. **Members:** 600. **Membership Dues:** storyteller, $20 (annual). **Regional Groups:** 3. **Local Groups:** 40. **Description:** Teachers, librarians, social workers, students and others interested in storytelling to all ages, pre-school to Sr. Citizens, provide "Service Through Storytelling". Strives "to encourage the creation and appreciation of the good and beautiful in life and literature through the art of storytelling". Seeks to discover the best stories in the world's literature and tell them to all audiences with talent and conviction. Members volunteer to tell and record stories at schools (pre-school-college), service and social clubs, libraries, community events, churches and church groups, camps, Sr. Citizens groups, retirement homes and Storytelling Festivals. Operates National Junior Story League. Conducts seminars and writing and telling workshops; sponsors writing contest. Maintains speakers' bureau. **Awards:** Adlyn M. Keffer Short Story Writing Contest. **Frequency:** annual. **Type:** recognition. **Committees:** Publicity. **Formerly:** Story Tellers' League. **Publications:** *Story Art: A Magazine for Storytellers*, quarterly. Publishes award-winning oral stories; also provides news of the league and its chapters. Includes obituaries. **Price:** included in membership dues; $12.00/year. **Circulation:** 850 ● *Story Art Yearbook* ● Also publishes roster and brochures. **Conventions/Meetings:** annual conference - during summer months.

10983 ■ National Storytelling Network (NSN)
132 Boone St., Ste.5
Jonesborough, TN 37659
Ph: (423)913-8201
Free: (800)525-4514
Fax: (423)753-9331
E-mail: nsn@storynet.org
URL: http://www.storynet.org
Contact: Bobbie Morgan, Exec. Dir.

Founded: 1975. **Members:** 3,000. **Membership Dues:** individual, standard, $55 (annual) ● elder (65 and older), $40 (annual) ● international, family, $75 (annual) ● life, $1,100 ● school/library in U.S., $80 (annual) ● business/association, $200 (annual) ● associate guild, $85 (annual) ● affiliate guild, $180 (annual) ● youth, $35 (annual). **Staff:** 7. **Description:** Individuals and organizations interested in the art of storytelling, as both an entertainment and educational tool. Seeks to provide opportunities to learn about the art business. Sponsors educational programs for teachers, librarians, and others interested in applying storytelling in their work. Currently conducting a search to locate all storytelling organizations, centers, and events in the U.S. **Libraries: Type:** reference; not open to the public. **Holdings:** articles, audio recordings, books, periodicals. **Subjects:** storytelling material. **Awards:** J.J. Reneaux Mentorship Grant. **Frequency:** annual. **Type:** grant. **Recipient:** for a gifted younger teller (18-30 years of age) to work with a seasoned teller as mentor. **Additional Websites:** http://www.tellabration.org. **Telecommunication Services:** electronic mail, bmorgan@storynet.org. **Committees:** Review. **Formerly:** (1993) National Association for the Preservation and Perpetuation of Storytelling; (2000) National Storytelling Association. **Publications:** *National Catalog of Storytelling*, semiannual ● *National Directory of Storytelling*, annual. **Price:** $35.00 for members (basic subscription); $40.00 for nonmembers (basic subscription); $75.00 for members (enhanced subscription); $85.00 for nonmembers (enhanced subscription). Alternate Formats: online ● *Storytelling Magazine*, bimonthly. Contains news, stories and articles on storytelling community. **Price:** included in membership dues; $6.50 for nonmembers. ISSN: 0743-1104. **Advertising:** accepted. **Conventions/Meetings:** annual conference, educational conference - always July ● annual festival - always first full weekend of October in Jonesborough, TN.

10984 ■ Spellbinders
PO Box 128
Woody Creek, CO 81656
Ph: (970)922-1444
Fax: (970)923-2396
E-mail: info@spellbinders.org
URL: http://www.spellbinders.org
Contact: Al Dietsch, Exec. Dir.

Local Groups: 19. **Multinational. Description:** Nurtures character, community and the spirit of humanity through the art of oral storytelling. Promotes oral storytelling to young and old everywhere by training volunteers to be tellers. **Publications:** *Spellbinder Newsletter*, quarterly. Alternate Formats: online.

10985 ■ Story Circle Network (SCN)
PO Box 500127
Austin, TX 78750-0127
Ph: (512)454-9833
E-mail: storycircle@storycircle.org
URL: http://www.storycircle.org
Contact: Peggy Moody, Exec. Dir.

Founded: 1997. **Members:** 575. **Membership Dues:** regular in U.S., $35 (annual) ● regular in Canada and Mexico, $45 (annual) ● elsewhere, $50 (annual) ● supporter, $70 (annual) ● sponsor, $125 (annual) ● patron, $200 (annual) ● benefactor, $400 (annual) ● internet chapter, Austin chapter (in addition to national dues), $18 (annual). **Staff:** 1. **Multinational. Description:** Strives to raise public awareness of the importance of women's personal histories. Represents the interests of women who want to explore their lives and their souls through lifewriting. Seeks to "empower women to tell their stories, discover their identities, and choose to be the authors of their own lives". **Computer Services:** database, list of authors ● database, list of speakers ● database, reviews of books by, for, and about women. **Additional Websites:** http://www.storycirclebookreviews.org. **Projects:** Older Women's Legacy Circle. **Publications:** *The Story Circle Journal*, quarterly, every March, June, September and December. Contains poetry and prose submitted by members. **Price:** free for members; $6.00 for nonmembers. Alternate Formats: online ● *True Words*, annual. Journal. **Price:** free for members; $6.00 for nonmembers. **Circulation:** 575.

10986 ■ Story Rhymes for Education (SRE)
PO Box 416
Denver, CO 80201-0416
Ph: (303)575-5676
Fax: (303)575-1187
E-mail: mail@storytimestoriesthatrhyme.net
URL: http://www.storytimestoriesthatrhyme.com
Contact: A. Doyle, Contact

Founded: 1998. **Staff:** 1. **For-Profit. Description:** Promotes understanding and appreciation of the therapeutic and educational effects of storytelling. Provides educational materials to schools and health care providers. **Libraries: Type:** reference. **Holdings:** 300; books. **Awards:** Story Rhyme Award. **Frequency:** annual. **Type:** recognition. **Recipient:** for the person who makes regular contributions in storytelling in rhyme. **Additional Websites:** http://www.kidsrhymenewsletter.com, http://www.storiesforschools.com. **Publications:** *Kids Rhyme Newsletter; Stories, Games and More*, annual. Features educational story rhymes. **Price:** $5.00. ISSN: 0738-7431. **Advertising:** accepted ● *Story Rhyme Newsletter for Schools*, annual. Contains educational stories for schools. **Price:** $2.00/year. ISSN: 1087-755X. **Circulation:** 10,000 ● Booklets. **Price:** $29.95 each. **Conventions/Meetings:** annual Story Rhymes for Education Week - meeting, available online.

Swedish

10987 ■ American Swedish Historical Museum (ASHM)
1900 Pattison Ave.
Philadelphia, PA 19145-5901
Ph: (215)389-1776
Fax: (215)389-7701
E-mail: info@americanswedish.org
URL: http://www.americanswedish.org
Contact: Ms. Tracey R. Beck, Exec. Dir.

Founded: 1926. **Members:** 770. **Membership Dues:** individual, $45 (annual) ● senior, full-time student, $35 (annual) ● family, $55 (annual) ● organizational, $75 (annual) ● contributor, $1,000 (annual) ● patron, $500 (annual) ● friend, $100 (annual) ● sustaining, $250 (annual). **Staff:** 6. **Budget:** $350,000. **Languages:** English, Swedish. **Description:** Galleries. Focuses on the history of Swedes in America from the establishment of the new Sweden Colony in 1638 to modern day Swedish technology, art and glass. Offers Swedish language classes and educational programs. **Libraries: Type:** reference. **Holdings:** 5,000; archival material. **Subjects:** history, culture of Sweden, Scandinavia, Swedish America, New Sweden Colony, genealogy. **Telecommunication Services:** electronic mail, development@americanswedish.org. **Affiliated With:** Swedish Council of America. **Publications:** *ASHM Newsletter*, quarterly. **Price:** free for members. **Circulation:** 770. **Conventions/Meetings:** annual History Conference, a Jenny Lind Commemoration (concert, lecture) ● workshop, on Swedish crafts.

10988 ■ American Swedish Institute (ASI)
2600 Park Ave.
Minneapolis, MN 55407-1090
Ph: (612)871-4907
Fax: (612)871-8682

E-mail: information@americanswedishinst.org
URL: http://www.americanswedishinst.org
Contact: Bruce Karstadt, Pres./CEO
Founded: 1929. **Members:** 6,000. **Membership Dues:** individual, non-resident, $35 (annual) ● full-time student, $20 (annual) ● household, $50 (annual). **Staff:** 25. **Budget:** $2,600,000. **Regional Groups:** 10. **State Groups:** 6. **Local Groups:** 21. **Languages:** English, Swedish. **Multinational. Description:** Promotes and preserves Swedish immigrant cultural heritage and develops close relations between the U.S. and Sweden. Maintains museum with art, culture, and history exhibits. Offers instruction in Swedish language and holds folk art classes; sponsors concerts and lectures; maintains historic Turnblad mansion (1908) on National Register of Historic Places. **Libraries: Type:** reference. **Holdings:** 15,000; archival material. **Subjects:** Swedish-American history, genealogy, immigration. **Awards:** Lilly Lorenzen Scholarship. **Frequency:** annual. **Type:** scholarship. **Recipient:** for a member to study in Sweden ● Malmberg Fellowship. **Frequency:** annual. **Type:** fellowship. **Recipient:** for a work or research at ASI ● Malmberg Scholarship. **Frequency:** annual. **Type:** scholarship. **Recipient:** for members; will be granted up to one academic year of study in Sweden. **Formerly:** American Institute of Swedish Arts, Literature, and Science. **Publications:** *The American Swedish Institute: Turnblad's Castle*. Book. **Price:** $19.95 ● *ASI Posten*, 11/year. Newsletter. **Price:** included in membership dues. **Circulation:** 7,000. Also Cited As: *ASI Happenings* ● *To Amerika*. Book ● *Var Sa God Cookbook*.

10989 ■ Swedish-American Historical Society (SAHS)
3225 W Foster Ave.
Box 48
Chicago, IL 60625
Ph: (773)583-5722
E-mail: info@swedishamericanhist.org
URL: http://www.swedishamericanhist.org
Contact: Ronald J. Johnson, Chm.
Founded: 1948. **Members:** 950. **Membership Dues:** regular, $25 (annual) ● sustaining, $50 (annual) ● donor, $100 (annual) ● benefactor, $250 (annual) ● life, $1,000. **Staff:** 1. **Description:** Persons interested in the history of the Swedish people in America. Aims to record the achievements of the Swedish pioneers in America through the publication of historical studies, immigrant history, biographical sketches, and translations. **Libraries: Type:** reference. **Holdings:** 3,000; archival material, audiovisuals, books, clippings, monographs, periodicals. **Subjects:** Swedes in America from 1638 to present. **Telecommunication Services:** electronic mail, ellen@swedishamericanhist.org. **Committees:** Finance; Membership; Preservation; Publication. **Formerly:** (1983) Swedish Pioneer Historical Society. **Supersedes:** Swedish Pioneer Centennial Committee. **Publications:** *The Swedish-American Historical Quarterly*. Journal. Illustrates and discusses Swedish roots. **Price:** free for members; $8.50 for nonmembers plus shipping and handling. Alternate Formats: online. **Conventions/Meetings:** annual meeting - always fall, in Chicago, IL ● annual meeting - always spring.

10990 ■ Swedish American Museum Association of Chicago (SAMAC)
5211 N Clark St.
Chicago, IL 60640
Ph: (773)728-8111
Fax: (773)728-8870
E-mail: museum@samac.org
URL: http://www.samac.org
Contact: Kerstin Lane, Exec. Dir.
Founded: 1976. **Members:** 1,600. **Membership Dues:** student/senior, $15 (annual) ● student/senior couple, $25 (annual) ● individual, $35 (annual) ● spouse/family, $50 (annual) ● sustaining/nonprofit organization, $75 (annual) ● corporate, $250 (annual) ● Sandburg Society, $100-$249 (annual) ● Linnaeus Society, $250-$520 (annual) ● club, $521-$999 (annual) ● 3 Crowns Group (minimum), $1,000 (annual). **Staff:** 6. **Budget:** $600,000. **Languages:** English, Swedish. **Description:** Americans of Swedish descent; other interested Swedes. Group is national in scope, but membership is concentrated in the Chicago, IL area. Seeks to preserve the history and culture of Swedish Americans. Maintains speakers' bureau and Swedish Museum and Cultural Center; offers genealogy classes, craft lessons, and language instruction; provides children's services. Sponsors concerts; observes Swedish holidays; holds exhibits. **Awards:** Swedish American Museum Award. **Frequency:** annual. **Type:** recognition. **Publications:** *FLAGGAN*, quarterly. Newsletter. **Price:** included in membership dues. **Circulation:** 1,500. **Advertising:** accepted.

10991 ■ Swedish Colonial Society (SCS)
c/o Doriney Seagers, Registrar
371 Devon Way
West Chester, PA 19380
Ph: (215)389-1513 (856)778-7137
E-mail: dorineyseagers@colonialswedes.org
URL: http://www.ColonialSwedes.org
Contact: Doriney Seagers, Registrar
Founded: 1909. **Members:** 400. **Membership Dues:** individual, $30 (annual) ● family, $35 (annual) ● life, individual, $400. **Description:** Historical society. Erects monuments to honor early Swedes. Preserves landmarks. Maintains historical and genealogical archives. Publishes works and furthers research about New Sweden. Conducts annual History Conference in the Philadelphia area every fall. Sponsors cultural exchanges and guided travel to Sweden and Finland. Publishes semi-annual magazine "Swedish Colonial News". **Libraries: Type:** by appointment only; open to the public; reference. **Holdings:** archival material, articles, artwork, biographical archives, books, maps. **Subjects:** history of Swedes in America, Swedish historic sites and churches, genealogical records, institutional records, colonial history. **Awards:** Amandus Johnson Award. **Frequency:** annual. **Type:** recognition. **Recipient:** for a student at the University of Pennsylvania for outstanding scholarship in Swedish language ● Fellow of the Swedish Colonial Society. **Frequency:** biennial. **Type:** recognition. **Recipient:** for distinguished service to the Society. **Computer Services:** Information services, basic reference only. **Committees:** Gloria Dei Church; Heritage; Jubilee; Publications, Library and Collections. **Sections:** Forefather Members. **Publications:** *Swedish Colonial News*, biennial. Journal. Includes news of organization, genealogy, and historical research of Colonial New Sweden. **Price:** free for members. **Circulation:** 700 ● Books. **Conventions/Meetings:** annual conference ● annual Forefather's Luncheon - usually April.

Swiss

10992 ■ Swiss American Historical Society (SAHS)
c/o Marianne Burkhard
5521 Rosalie Dr.
Peoria, IL 61614
URL: http://www.swissgenealogy.com/SAHS.htm
Contact: Marianne Burkhard, Contact
Founded: 1927. **Members:** 300. **Membership Dues:** institution, $75 (annual) ● individual, $50 (annual) ● student, $25 (annual) ● life, $500. **National Groups:** 2. **Multinational. Description:** Represents the interests of academicians and others interested in Swiss American matters; people of Swiss descent in the U.S. Records with "accuracy and scholarly expertise" Swiss involvement in American life and the relations between Switzerland and the U.S. Provides connections with experts in Swiss American genealogy. Maintains Speaker's Bureau. **Awards:** SAHS Grants. **Frequency:** annual. **Type:** grant. **Recipient:** for Swiss or Swiss American topics. **Publications:** *Swiss American Historical Society Review*, 3/year. Magazine. Contains Swiss American history and Swiss topics of interest to Swiss Americans. ISSN: 0883-4814. **Circulation:** 400. **Conventions/Meetings:** annual meeting - early October.

Tattooing

10993 ■ Empire State Tattoo Club of America (ESTCA)
Address Unknown since 2008
URL: http://www.tattooequipment.com
Founded: 1974. **Members:** 6,000. **Membership Dues:** $1,000 (annual). **Staff:** 3. **Description:** International organization of tattoo artists and individuals with tattoos. Works to increase public awareness of tattoo art. **Awards:** Achievement Award. **Frequency:** monthly. **Type:** recognition. **Computer Services:** Mailing lists, tattoo artists and fans. **Affiliated With:** Professional Tattoo Artists Guild. **Conventions/Meetings:** annual competition (exhibits).

10994 ■ National Tattoo Association (NTA)
485 Bus. Park Ln.
Allentown, PA 18109-9120
Ph: (610)433-7261
Fax: (610)433-7294
E-mail: curt@nationaltattoo.com
URL: http://www.nationaltattooassociation.com
Contact: Florence Makofske, Sec.-Treas.
Founded: 1976. **Members:** 1,324. **Membership Dues:** single, $50 (annual) ● couple, $60 (annual). **Staff:** 10. **Budget:** $46,000. **Languages:** English, German, Spanish. **Multinational. Description:** Tattoo artists and enthusiasts. Promotes tattooing as a viable contemporary art form; seeks to upgrade standards and practices of tattooing. Offers advice on selecting a tattoo artist and studio. Holds seminars for tattoo artists to improve skills and learn better hygienic practices. Operates museum and biographical archives. **Libraries: Type:** not open to the public. **Holdings:** 6. **Subjects:** tattoo. **Awards:** Best Black and Gray Design Sheet. **Frequency:** annual. **Type:** recognition. **Recipient:** for entries done on paper in black and gray ● Best Black/Gray Back Piece. **Frequency:** annual. **Type:** recognition ● Best Black/Gray Tattoo. **Frequency:** annual. **Type:** recognition. **Recipient:** for a black and gray tattoo ● Best Colored Back Piece. **Frequency:** annual. **Type:** recognition ● Best Colored Design Sheet. **Frequency:** annual. **Type:** recognition. **Recipient:** for entries done on paper in colored ● Best Cover-Up Tattoo. **Frequency:** annual. **Type:** recognition ● Best Large Tattoo. **Frequency:** annual. **Type:** recognition ● Best Portrait Tattoo. **Frequency:** annual. **Type:** recognition ● Best Sleeve. **Frequency:** annual. **Type:** recognition. **Recipient:** for males or females with 75&percent; or greater sleeve coverage ● Best Tattooed Female. **Frequency:** annual. **Type:** recognition. **Recipient:** for females whose total work coverage is 2 points or higher ● Best Tattooed Male. **Frequency:** annual. **Type:** recognition. **Recipient:** for males whose total work coverage is 4 points or higher ● Best Tattooist. **Frequency:** annual. **Type:** recognition ● Best Traditional Style Tattoo. **Frequency:** annual. **Type:** recognition. **Recipient:** for tattoo done in traditional style of 1960's or earlier ● Best Unique Tattoo. **Frequency:** annual. **Type:** recognition ● Bob Show Golden Age Award. **Frequency:** annual. **Type:** recognition. **Recipient:** for 40 years in the business ● Elizabeth Weinzirl Award. **Frequency:** annual. **Type:** recognition. **Recipient:** for enthusiast of the year ● Fine Art Award. **Frequency:** annual. **Type:** recognition. **Recipient:** for fine art drawings or paintings and sculpture ● Most Realistic Tattoo. **Frequency:** annual. **Type:** recognition. **Recipient:** for tattoo of flowers, animals, buildings, cars, except for portraits ● Nicest Tattoo Studio. **Frequency:** annual. **Type:** recognition. **Computer Services:** Information services, lists of members and tattoo studios. **Formerly:** (1984) National Tattoo Club of the World. **Publications:** *National Tattoo Association—Newsletter*, bimonthly. **Price:** included in membership dues. **Circulation:** 1,300. **Conventions/Meetings:** annual competition and convention (exhibits).

Theatre

10995 ■ Actors Studio (AS)
8341 Delongpre Ave.
West Hollywood, CA 90069-2601

Ph: (323)654-7125
Fax: (323)654-8266
Contact: Harry Governick, Artistic Dir.

Founded: 1947. **Members:** 800. **Staff:** 6. **Budget:** $300,000. **Description:** Professional actors, playwrights, and directors. Conducts theatre workshop for professional actors to continue their development and experiment with new forms in theatre work; scenes are rehearsed, performed, and evaluated by members and artistic directors. **Libraries: Type:** reference. **Holdings:** 500. **Subjects:** theatre. **Sections:** Actors; Directors; Playwrights.

10996 ■ Alliance for Inclusion in the Arts
1560 Broadway, Ste.1600
New York, NY 10036
Ph: (212)730-4750
Fax: (212)730-4820
E-mail: info@ntcp.org
URL: http://www.inclusioninthearts.org
Contact: Sharon Jensen, Exec. Dir.

Founded: 1986. **Description:** Advocates the elimination of discrimination in theatre, film, and television. Works to increase the employment of artists of color and artists with disabilities by encouraging cultural diversity throughout the artistic process and all levels of production and administration, and offering consultative services. Maintains the Artist Files containing pictures and resumes of 3,000 actors, directors, writers, designers, and stage managers of color as well as those with disabilities. Sponsors forums. **Computer Services:** database, of NTCP's artist files. **Formerly:** (2007) Non-Traditional Casting Project. **Publications:** *Beyond Tradition*. Book. **Conventions/Meetings:** seminar ● periodic symposium.

10997 ■ Alliance of Resident Theatres/New York (ART/NY)
575 8th Ave., Ste.1720
New York, NY 10018-3054
Ph: (212)244-6667
Fax: (212)714-1918
E-mail: lstevenson@art-newyork.com
URL: http://www.offbroadwayonline.com
Contact: Robert LuPone, Pres.

Founded: 1972. **Members:** 425. **Membership Dues:** associate, $100 (annual) ● professional, $150 (annual) ● joint (based on budget), $85-$195 (annual) ● organization (with 250000 annual income or less in the last fiscal year), $125 (annual) ● organization (with income over 1500000 in the last fiscal year), $750 (annual). **Staff:** 14. **Budget:** $2,600,000. **Regional Groups:** 425. **Description:** Nonprofit professional theatres in New York City and interested theatre-related associations. Promotes recognition of the nonprofit theatre community. Provides members with administrative services and resources pertinent to their field. Facilitates discussion among the theatres; helps to solve real estate problems; serves as a public information source. Acts as advocate on behalf of members with government, corporate, and foundation funders to encourage greater support for New York's not-for-profit theatres. Sponsors seminars, roundtables, and individual consultations for members in areas such as financial management, board development and marketing. Organizes Passports to Off Broadway, an industry-wide marketing campaign. **Awards:** Nancy Quinn Fund and JP Morgan Chase Fund for Small Theatres. **Frequency:** annual. **Type:** grant. **Recipient:** for participating theatre companies. **Publications:** *How to Run a Small Box Office* ● *Rehearsal and Performance Space Lists* ● *Theatre Member Directory*, periodic. Membership Directory ● Handbooks. **Conventions/Meetings:** annual Curtain Call - meeting - usually June in New York City.

10998 ■ American Alliance for Theatre and Education (AATE)
7475 Wisconsin Ave., Ste.300A
Bethesda, MD 20814
Ph: (301)951-7977 (517)629-0327
Fax: (301)968-0144
E-mail: info@aate.com
URL: http://www.aate.com
Contact: Betsy Quinn, Pres.

Founded: 1987. **Members:** 1,000. **Membership Dues:** individual, $110 (annual) ● student, $60 (annual) ● organizational, $220 (annual) ● retired, $70 (annual). **Staff:** 1. **Budget:** $125,000. **Description:** Promotes standards of excellence in theatre and theatre education. Achieves this by disseminating quality practices in theatre and theatre education, connecting artists, educators, researchers and scholars with each other, and by providing opportunities for members to learn, exchange, and diversity their work, their audiences and their perspectives. **Libraries: Type:** reference. **Holdings:** archival material. **Awards:** Alliance Award. **Frequency:** annual. **Type:** recognition. **Recipient:** for long-term and sustained service to the organization ● Anne Flagg Multicultural Award. **Frequency:** annual. **Type:** recognition. **Recipient:** for significant contributions to the field of theatre/drama for youth or arts education dealing with multicultural issues ● Barbara Salisbury Wills Award. **Frequency:** annual. **Type:** recognition. **Recipient:** for long-term and sustained service to the organization ● Campton Bell Lifetime Achievement Award. **Frequency:** annual. **Type:** recognition. **Recipient:** for outstanding lifetime contributions to the field ● Charlotte B. Chorpenning Playwright Award. **Frequency:** annual. **Type:** recognition. **Recipient:** for a nationally known writer of outstanding plays for children ● Creative Drama Award. **Frequency:** annual. **Type:** recognition. **Recipient:** to a member for outstanding achievement and service as a creative drama specialist ● Dina Rees Evans Theatre in Our Schools Award. **Frequency:** annual. **Type:** recognition. **Recipient:** for exemplary programs and individuals in support of Theatre in Our Schools ● Distinguished Book Award. **Frequency:** annual. **Type:** recognition. **Recipient:** to an author and publisher for the outstanding book relating to any aspect of the field published during the past calendar year ● Distinguished Play Award. **Frequency:** annual. **Type:** recognition. **Recipient:** for the playwright(s) and publisher(s) of the most outstanding plays for young people published during the past calendar year ● F. Loren Winship Secondary School Theatre Award. **Frequency:** annual. **Type:** recognition. **Recipient:** to an individual or organization for long-term outstanding contribution to the mission of secondary school theatre ● John C. Barner Teacher of the Year Award. **Frequency:** annual. **Type:** recognition. **Recipient:** for an individual member who is currently teaching Theatre on the secondary school level and who has developed an exemplary program ● Lin Wright Special Recognition Awards. **Frequency:** annual. **Type:** recognition. **Recipient:** for persons who have established special programs, developed experimental works, made distinctive educational contributions or provided meritorious service thus furthering theatre and drama for young people ● Monte Meacham Award. **Frequency:** annual. **Type:** recognition. **Recipient:** to a nonmember person or organization for outstanding contribution to children's theatre ● Sara Spencer Artistic Achievement Award. **Frequency:** annual. **Type:** recognition. **Recipient:** for artistic theatre practice of long duration and wide recognition ● Winifred Ward Award for Outstanding New Children's Theatre Company. **Frequency:** annual. **Type:** recognition. **Recipient:** for a member theatre company serving young audiences which has been in operation at least two fall years, but not more than five years ● Youth Theatre Director of the Year. **Frequency:** annual. **Type:** recognition. **Recipient:** to an individual for outstanding achievement as a director in Youth Theatre. **Computer Services:** database. **Telecommunication Services:** electronic mail, tallerimcrae@hotmail.com. **Committees:** Curriculum; Playwriting; Professional Theatre; Research. **Publications:** *A Bibliography on the Mask*. Contains annotated bibliography of books which feature making and using masks in the classroom. **Price:** $6.50 for members; $9.00 for nonmembers ● *A Model Drama/Theatre Curriculum: Philosophy, Goals and Objectives*. Book. Provides guidance for developing curricular and co-curricular drama/theatre programs based upon the individual needs of the learners (K-12). **Price:** $10.00 for members; $12.50 for nonmembers ● *AATE Dialogue*, quarterly. Newsletter. Alternate Formats: online ● *AATE Membership Directory*, annual. Alternate Formats: online ● *Adjudication*. Monograph. Tells how adjudication can be a positive experience, with the emphasis on responding rather than judging. **Price:** $6.50 for members; $9.00 for nonmembers ● *Award-Winning Plays from the Playwrights Network of The American Alliance for Theatre and Education*, annual. Bibliography. Contains annotated bibliography of all plays that have won the AATE Awards. **Price:** $3.50 ● *Drama/Theatre Teacher*. Book. Features practical articles on theatre education with an emphasis on classroom instruction K-12. **Price:** $7.50 ● *Education Centerstage! Education/Outreach Programs in Professional Theatres*. Monograph. Profiles the education/outreach programs of ten American professional theatre companies. **Price:** free for members; $7.50 for nonmembers ● *Freedom of Artistic Expression in Educational Theatre*. Article. Clarifies the rights and responsibilities of theatre artist/educators, students, parents and administrators. ● *High School Network: A Directory of Playwrights and Plays that Work*. Contains plays recommended by the AATE High School Network that have been proven to be successful for use with secondary school students. **Price:** $5.00 ● *National Standards for Theatre Education*. Book. Addresses issues of curriculum sequencing, staffing, materials and equipment for Pre K-12 in theatre, designed for both advocates and educators. **Price:** $7.00 for members; $12.00 for nonmembers ● *1996 Script Resource Directory*. Features useful and up-to-date resource of scripts for young audiences with information on target audience and other useful data. **Price:** $5.00 ● *Opportunity to Learn Standards*. Book. Addresses issues of curriculum, staffing, materials for K-12 in Dance, Music, Theatre and Visual Arts. **Price:** $10.00 for members; $15.00 for nonmembers ● *Perspectives on Dramatic Literacy*. Article. Contains essays authored by Roger Bedard, Robert Coly and Lowell Swortzell, discussing issues influencing the design and analysis of the research. **Price:** $5.00 ● *Stage of the Art*, quarterly. Manual. Features resource information for the classroom theatre teacher. **Price:** included in membership dues; $28.00 /year for nonmembers in U.S.; $35.00 /year for nonmembers outside U.S. **Circulation:** 1,000. **Advertising:** accepted ● *Standards For High School Theatre Education*. Pamphlet. Contains detailed description of the standards for successful curricular and extra curricular programs in high school theatre. **Price:** free ● *Technical Report Available from 3-Year Study*. Informs AATE members and others of the progress of a study of the Student and Teacher Theaters Literacy Project. ● *Theatre Safety*. Monograph. Guides administrators and theatre arts teachers in establishing and maintaining a safe environment for actors, technicians and audience. **Price:** $6.50 for members; $9.00 for nonmembers ● *Youth Theatre Journal*, annual. Includes updates on research in the field and reviews of books and plays. **Price:** included in membership dues; $25.00 /year for nonmembers in U.S.; $30.00 /year for nonmembers outside U.S. **Circulation:** 1,100. **Advertising:** accepted ● Also publishes free flyers. **Conventions/Meetings:** annual Honoring Our Mentors and Celebrating Our Students - conference, dramatic publishers, and textbooks (exhibits) - 2008 July 22-28, Atlanta, GA.

10999 ■ American Association of Community Theatre (AACT)
8402 Briar Wood Cir.
Lago Vista, TX 78645
Ph: (512)267-0711
Free: (866)687-2228
Fax: (512)267-0712
E-mail: info@aact.org
URL: http://www.aact.org
Contact: Julie Angelo, Exec. Dir.

Founded: 1986. **Members:** 1,800. **Staff:** 4. **Budget:** $240,000. **Description:** Community theatre organizations and individuals involved in community theatre. Promotes excellence in community theatre through networking, workshops, publications, and festivals of community theatre productions. **Computer Services:** Mailing lists, for 6,000 community theatre groups and 4,000 individuals in community theatre. **Supersedes:** American Community Theatre Association. **Publications:** *AACT/Fest Handbook*, biennial. Includes rules, procedures and guidelines for conducting a community theater festival. **Price:** $8.00 ● *AACT Membership and Resource Directory*, annual. Membership Directory. **Price:** included in membership dues. **Circulation:** 1,800. **Advertising:** accepted ● *Spotlight*, bimonthly. Magazine. **Price:** included in membership dues. **Circulation:** 10,000. **Advertising:** accepted. **Conventions/Meetings:** biennial convention (exhibits) ● biennial festival, showcases winners of 10 regional festivals; conducts workshops and networking (exhibits).

11000 ■ American Conservatory Theater Foundation (ACT)
30 Grant Ave., 6th Fl.
San Francisco, CA 94109-5800
Ph: (415)834-3200 (415)749-2250
Fax: (415)749-2291
E-mail: tickets@act-sf.org
URL: http://www.act-sf.org
Contact: Heather Kitchen, Exec. Dir.
Founded: 1965. **Staff:** 150. **Budget:** $10,000,000. **Description:** Provides resources for the American Conservatory Theater which functions as a repertory theatre and accredited acting school, offering a Master of Fine Arts degree. Holds national auditions for the MFA program in Chicago, IL, New York City, and Los Angeles, CA, usually in February. Holds student matinees, school outreach programs, and in-theatre discussions between artist and audiences. Conducts professional actor-training programs, a summer training congress, and a young conservatory evening academy program for children aged 8-18. Offers children's services. Operates speakers' bureau and placement service. **Libraries: Type:** reference. **Holdings:** 8,000; archival material, books. **Subjects:** plays. **Telecommunication Services:** electronic mail, mbechtold@act-sf.org. **Publications:** *ACT Bulletin*, periodic ● *Words On Plays*, 8/year. Magazine. Offers insights into the plays, playwrights, and productions of the ACT subscription season. **Price:** $10.00 each; $70.00 full season. Alternate Formats: online.

11001 ■ American Russian Theatrical Alliance (ARTA)
1409 Midvale Ave., Ste.105
Los Angeles, CA 90024
Ph: (310)312-4989
Fax: (310)312-4989
E-mail: info@arta-la.com
URL: http://www.arta-la.com
Contact: Elmar Mamedov, CEO/Co-Founder
Description: Represents artistic professionals committed to building the bridge between theater and film. Creates social and cultural alliances through theatre, film, and educational outreach services. Unites American and Russian cultures through the collaboration of dedicated artists and teachers in diverse projects and performances of local and international significance.

11002 ■ American Society for Theatre Research (ASTR)
PO Box 1798
Boulder, CO 80306-1798
Ph: (303)530-1838
Free: (888)530-1838
Fax: (303)530-1839
E-mail: nericksn@aol.com
URL: http://www.astr.org
Contact: Nancy J. Erickson, Admin.
Founded: 1956. **Members:** 730. **Membership Dues:** regular, in North America, $60 (annual) ● retired, in North America, $40 (annual) ● student, in North America, $35 (annual) ● regular, outside North America, $65 (annual) ● retired, outside North America, $45 (annual) ● student, outside North America, $40 (annual) ● IFTR regular, $80 (annual) ● IFTR student, $30 (annual). **Staff:** 1. **Description:** Scholars of the theatre. Aims to promote better knowledge of the history of the theatre. Sponsors research projects. **Awards: Frequency:** annual. **Type:** scholarship. **Recipient:** for graduate students in theatre. **Computer Services:** Mailing lists. **Telecommunication Services:** electronic mail, kencerni@hotmail.com. **Committees:** Ad-Hoc; Publications; Regular; Research Fellowship; Standing. **Affiliated With:** International Federation for Theatre Research; Theatre Library Association. **Publications:** *ASTR News*, semiannual. Newsletter. Alternate Formats: online ● *Membership List*, annual. Directory ● *Theatre Survey*, semiannual. Journal. ISSN: 0040-5574. Alternate Formats: online ● Books. Contains information on the stage and theatre. **Conventions/Meetings:** annual conference (exhibits) - usually November in Toronto, ON, Canada.

11003 ■ American Theatre Arts for Youth (ATAFY)
1429 Walnut St.
Philadelphia, PA 19102
Ph: (215)563-3501
Free: (800)523-4540
Fax: (215)563-1588
E-mail: atafyinfo@atafy.org
URL: http://www.atafy.org
Contact: Laurie Wagman, Founder/Chm.
Founded: 1970. **Description:** Produces professional, curriculum-related theatre, which serve teachers' instructional goals and the cultural-enrichment needs of students. Believes that theatre arts is an important educational medium that extends language development, motivates students, and stimulates learning. Focuses on original musicals including: literature, history, and current events and are performed in over 400 cities for 1,200,000 students annually.

11004 ■ American Theatre Critics Association (ATCA)
c/o Kathryn Burger, Admin.
773 Nebraska Ave. W
St. Paul, MN 55117
Ph: (651)261-7804
E-mail: atca_admin@msn.com
URL: http://www.americantheatrecritics.org
Contact: Kathryn Burger, Admin.
Founded: 1975. **Members:** 300. **Membership Dues:** individual, $55 (annual). **Budget:** $25,000. **Description:** Theater critics. Works to support critics in their professional development and the theater community. **Libraries: Type:** not open to the public. **Holdings:** archival material, articles, clippings, papers, periodicals. **Awards:** Francesca Primus Prize. **Frequency:** annual. **Type:** monetary. **Recipient:** to support emerging women artists ● M. Elizabeth Osborn Award For an Emerging Playwright. **Frequency:** annual. **Type:** monetary. **Recipient:** to a playwright whose plays have not yet received a major production ● Steinberg New Play Award. **Frequency:** annual. **Type:** monetary. **Recipient:** to an outstanding new play. **Committees:** Conference; Ethical Standards; International; New Plays; Professional Development; Regional Theatre Award. **Conventions/Meetings:** annual conference.

11005 ■ American Theatre and Drama Society (ATDS)
c/o Ken Bright, Membership Sec.
325 Clearview Ave., Apt. No. 2
Crafton, PA 15205
E-mail: kbright@ohio.net
URL: http://www.athe.org/atds
Contact: John Frick, Pres.
Members: 200. **Membership Dues:** student, adjunct, $20 (annual) ● general, $30 (annual). **Multinational. Description:** Promotes the study of U.S. theatre and drama, its varied histories, traditions, literatures, and performances within cultural contexts. Furthers the understanding of the cross-cultural aspects of American theatre and drama. Encourages the evolving debate exploring national identities and experiences through research, pedagogy and practice. **Awards:** Betty Jean Jones Award. **Frequency:** annual. **Type:** recognition. **Recipient:** to an outstanding teacher of American theatre and drama. **Telecommunication Services:** electronic mail, jwf8f@cms.mail.virginia.edu. **Publications:** *Journal of American Drama and Theatre*. **Price:** included in membership dues. Also Cited As: *JADT* ● Membership Directory. **Price:** included in membership dues ● Newsletter, semiannual. **Price:** included in membership dues.

11006 ■ Audience Development Committee (AUDELCO)
PO Box 30
New York, NY 10027
Ph: (212)368-6906
Fax: (212)368-6906
E-mail: audelco@aol.com
URL: http://www.audelco.net
Contact: Lou Myers, Co-Chair
Founded: 1973. **Members:** 1,000. **Membership Dues:** friend, $35 (annual). **Staff:** 3. **Description:** Individuals interested in or pursuing a career in black theatre. Aims to develop a greater appreciation of theatrical productions among blacks and to build an audience for black theatrical and dance companies. Operates black theatre archives; maintains speakers' bureau. Offers a low-cost ticket program for senior citizens, children, and those who are unable to afford tickets at box office prices. **Publications:** *Black Theatre Directory*, periodic ● *Intermission*, monthly. Newsletter ● *Overture*, semiannual. Magazine. **Conventions/Meetings:** annual Black Theatre Festival - always June.

11007 ■ Bilingual Foundation of the Arts (BFA)
421 North Ave. 19
Los Angeles, CA 90031
Ph: (323)225-4044
Fax: (323)225-1250
E-mail: bfa99@earthlink.net
URL: http://www.bfatheatre.org
Contact: Carmen Zapata, Pres.
Founded: 1973. **Membership Dues:** friend, $25 (annual) ● benefactor, $500 (annual) ● patron, $1,000 (annual) ● fan, $100 (annual) ● companion, $50 (annual) ● padrino, $250 (annual). **Staff:** 10. **Budget:** $975,000. **Languages:** English, Spanish. **Description:** Hispanics, non-Hispanics, instructors, students, interested individuals, and artists who perform in the foundation's programs. Actors are bilingual and conduct Spanish and English performances. Seeks to: produce and perform (in Los Angeles, CA and on tour) professional Hispanic-American theatre, drawing from contemporary and classic Hispanic and Hispanic-American dramatic literature, in Spanish and English; present these theatre offerings to Hispanic and non-Hispanic audiences, celebrating the Hispanic cultural heritage and sharing it with non-Hispanic Americans. Produces 3-4 plays yearly. Develops new translations; offers training for theatre technicians and actors; maintains playwrights' and directors' residencies. Sponsors Para Los Ninos, a touring children's theatre program, Teatro Para Los Jovenes in school theatre program for teens, a reader's theatre, a translation program, and Senior Sunday, a program that offers low-cost admission to BFA productions for senior citizens. **Publications:** none. **Awards:** El Angel Award. **Frequency:** annual. **Type:** recognition. **Recipient:** for outstanding Hispanic-American artists and corporations that have contributed to the Hispanic arts. **Computer Services:** Mailing lists.

11008 ■ Black Theatre Network (BTN)
c/o Dr. La Tanya Reese, Business Mgr.
2609 Douglas Rd. SE, Ste.102
Washington, DC 20020-6540
Ph: (202)274-5667
E-mail: lreese@udc.edu
URL: http://www.blacktheatrenetwork.org
Contact: Dr. Sandra G. Shannon, Pres.
Founded: 1986. **Members:** 500. **Membership Dues:** retired/student, $35 (annual) ● individual, $75 (annual) ● organization, $110 (annual). **Description:** Individuals involved in higher education and professionals in black theatre. Serves as a networking organization for those with interests in black theater either in academia or at the professional level.

Organizes workshops. **Awards:** Judy Dearing Design Competition. **Frequency:** annual. **Type:** recognition ● Randolph Edmond Young Scholars. **Frequency:** annual. **Type:** scholarship. **Computer Services:** Mailing lists. **Publications:** *Black Theatre Connections*, quarterly. Bulletin ● *Black Theatre Directory*, annual. Lists artists, scholars, and theater competitions. **Price:** $15.00 ● *Dissertation Concerning Black Theatre*, annual. Journal. **Conventions/Meetings:** annual conference (exhibits) - 2008 Aug. 3-7, Orlando, FL.

11009 ■ Burlesque Historical Society (BHS)
c/o Burlesque Hall of Fame
PO Box 1437
Las Vegas, NV 89125
URL: http://www.burlesquehall.com
Contact: Dixie Evans, Exec. Off.

Founded: 1963. **Members:** 500. **Regional Groups:** 4. **Description:** Supported by donations of materials and funds from persons interested in maintaining a museum of burlesque, which includes books, magazines, photographs, newspaper clippings, films, costumes, displays, posters, and other items relating to burlesque shows and dancers. Conducts specialized education program and placement service. Maintains Burlesque Hall of Fame, museum, and school for strippers. **Libraries: Type:** reference. **Holdings:** 50; video recordings. **Subjects:** striptease dance, chorus lines, comedy. **Awards:** Miss Exotic World. **Frequency:** annual. **Type:** recognition. **Recipient:** for performance, costume, personality. **Boards:** Directors. **Affiliated With:** Exotic Dancers League of America. **Publications:** *Jennie Lee, The Bazoom Girl*, periodic. Magazine ● *Legend of Jennie Lee*, periodic. Booklet ● Newsletter, annual. **Price:** free. **Circulation:** 2,000. **Advertising:** accepted. **Conventions/Meetings:** semiannual board meeting ● annual reunion - always May, in conjunction with EDLA.

11010 ■ Drama Desk (DD)
c/o Lester Schecter
244 W 54th St., 9th Fl.
New York, NY 10019
Ph: (212)586-2600 (212)354-5124
Fax: (212)695-1519
E-mail: lester.schecter@verizon.net
URL: http://www.dramadesk.com
Contact: Lester Schecter, Contact

Founded: 1949. **Members:** 200. **Description:** Drama critics, editors, and reporters who cover the New York theatre for newspapers, radio and television stations, and magazines. Holds press conferences; gives after-theater salutes to personalities and organizations. **Awards:** Drama Desk Award. **Frequency:** annual. **Type:** recognition. **Recipient:** for outstanding performances and creative efforts, on or off Broadway. **Conventions/Meetings:** monthly luncheon.

11011 ■ Drama League (DL)
520 8th Ave., Ste.320
New York, NY 10018
Ph: (212)244-9494
Free: (877)NYC-PLAY
Fax: (212)244-9191
E-mail: audienceproject@dramaleague.org
URL: http://www.dramaleague.org
Contact: Jano Herbosch, Pres.

Founded: 1916. **Members:** 2,000. **Membership Dues:** individual, $85 (annual) ● friend, $125 (annual) ● benefactor, $500 (annual) ● patron, $1,000 (annual) ● sponsor, $2,500 (annual) ● star, $5,000 (annual). **Staff:** 6. **Budget:** $700,000. **Description:** Theater artists and audiences. Works to strengthen and enrich American theater. Sponsors the nationally recognized Directors Project for emerging theater directors. **Awards:** Drama League. **Frequency:** annual. **Type:** recognition. **Recipient:** for outstanding contribution to theatre. **Publications:** *Theatre Today*, 10/year. Newsletter. Contains articles, interviews, updates and ticket opportunities; a primary information source for members.

11012 ■ Dramatists Guild of America (DGA)
1501 Broadway, Ste.701
New York, NY 10036
Ph: (212)398-9366
Fax: (212)944-0420
E-mail: rsevush@dramatistsguild.com
URL: http://www.dramatistsguild.com
Contact: Ralph Sevush, Exec. Dir.

Founded: 1920. **Members:** 7,000. **Membership Dues:** student, $35 (annual) ● associate, $95 (annual) ● active, $150 (annual). **Staff:** 8. **Description:** Playwrights, lyricists, and composers; corporate member of the Authors League of America. Offers use of the guild's contracts; advises members on business problems. Conducts symposia and other programs. **Libraries: Type:** reference. **Holdings:** archival material, books, business records, periodicals. **Subjects:** theatre playwriting, business/ contracts. **Awards:** Hull-Warriner Award. **Frequency:** annual. **Type:** recognition. **Computer Services:** database, playwrights, composers, and lyricists. **Telecommunication Services:** electronic mail, jminore@dramatistsguild.com. **Formerly:** (1998) Dramatist Guild. **Publications:** *The Dramatist*, bimonthly. Magazine. Contains announcements of all Guild activities, as well as industry news of interest. **Price:** $25.00 /year for individuals; $35.00 /year for institutions; $200.00/ year for business. **Circulation:** 7,000. **Advertising:** accepted. Alternate Formats: online ● *The Dramatists Guild Resource Directory*, annual. Contains up-to-date information on agents, attorneys, grants, producers, conferences, and workshops. ● Newsletter, bimonthly. Contains articles by members and staff focusing on craft, business and contract tips, and updates on opportunities. **Conventions/Meetings:** symposium.

11013 ■ Episcopal Actors' Guild of America (EAGA)
Little Church Around the Corner
1 E 29th St.
New York, NY 10016-7405
Ph: (212)685-2927
Fax: (212)685-8793
E-mail: actors_guild@msn.com
URL: http://www.actorsguild.org
Contact: Marius J. Hulswit, Exec. Dir.

Founded: 1923. **Members:** 750. **Membership Dues:** performing arts professional, $20 (annual) ● associate, $35 (annual) ● life, professional, $300 ● life, associate, $500. **Staff:** 2. **Budget:** $320,000. **Description:** Actors, members of allied arts, clergymen, and others interested in bringing together the people of the theatre with the church in order to promote social interchange and general welfare and to provide help for sick, needy, and indigent members of the theatrical profession. Membership is interdenominational. Offers emergency aid and relief and scholarship program. **Libraries: Type:** reference. **Holdings:** 400; archival material, books. **Subjects:** theatre. **Awards:** Claire Strakosh Scholarship. **Frequency:** semiannual. **Type:** scholarship. **Recipient:** for students of American Academy of Dramatic Arts ● Episcopal Actors' Guild's Scholarship Program. **Frequency:** annual. **Type:** scholarship. **Recipient:** for students of Hornet Foundation ● George C. Scott Memorial Scholarship. **Frequency:** annual. **Type:** scholarship. **Recipient:** for Theatre Arts student at the University of Missouri ● **Frequency:** annual. **Type:** recognition. **Recipient:** for an individual who has made a distinguished contribution to the performing arts or service to the guild. **Committees:** Archives; Development; Events; Grants; Publications; Scholarships; Strategic Planning. **Publications:** *The Eaglet*, quarterly. Newsletter. **Price:** included in membership dues. **Circulation:** 650. Alternate Formats: online. **Conventions/Meetings:** annual meeting - always June, in New York City.

11014 ■ Eugene O'Neill Memorial Theater Center (EOMTC)
305 Great Neck Rd.
Waterford, CT 06385
Ph: (860)443-5378 (860)443-7139
Fax: (860)443-9653
E-mail: info@theoneill.org
URL: http://www.oneilltheatercenter.org
Contact: Preston Whiteway, Exec. Dir.

Founded: 1964. **Members:** 1,000. **Membership Dues:** O'Neill, $50 (annual) ● O'Neill dual, $75 (annual) ● The Edith, $125 (annual) ● Blue Gene's, $250 (annual) ● The Rose Barn, $500 (annual) ● The Dina, $1,000 (annual) ● Monte Cristo, $2,500 (annual) ● Walnut Grove, $5,000 (annual). **Staff:** 28. **Budget:** $2,500,000. **Description:** Persons interested in supporting the center's projects: a museum, theater, library, and school in Waterford, CT; established as a permanent memorial to Eugene O'Neill (1888-1953), U.S. playwright. The Theater Collection includes memorabilia, books, pictures, and reference materials dealing with O'Neill and the American theatre. In April 1974, the center acquired the Monte Cristo cottage, boyhood home of O'Neill, which is used to house the center's library and museum collection. **Telecommunication Services:** electronic mail, shendrix@theoneill.org. **Also Known As:** O'Neill Theater Center. **Formerly:** Eugene O'Neill Memorial Theater Foundation. **Publications:** *The O'Neill*, quarterly. Newsletter. Alternate Formats: online. **Conventions/Meetings:** annual O'Neill Music Theater Conference - retreat - August ● annual O'Neill Playwrights Conference - retreat - July ● annual O'Neill Puppetry Conference - retreat - June.

11015 ■ Ford's Theatre Society (FTS)
511 10th St. NW
Washington, DC 20004
Ph: (202)638-2941 (202)638-2367
Free: (800)899-2367
Fax: (202)347-6269
E-mail: onstage@fordtheatre.org
URL: http://www.fordstheatre.org
Contact: Paul R. Tetreault, Producing Dir.

Founded: 1968. **Staff:** 30. **Description:** Supports theatre program at the restored Ford's Theatre in Washington, DC., performing from September through June; produces musicals and plays that illuminate the eclectic character of American life. **Telecommunication Services:** electronic mail, membership@fordstheatre.org.

11016 ■ Friars Club (FC)
57 E 55th St.
New York, NY 10022
Ph: (212)751-7272
Fax: (212)355-0217
E-mail: webmonk@friarsclub.com
URL: http://www.friarsclub.com
Contact: Robert B. Fields, Pres.

Founded: 1904. **Members:** 1,500. **Membership Dues:** theatrical and non-theatrical personnel, $2,100 (annual). **Staff:** 65. **Budget:** $5,000,000. **Description:** Theatrical writers, movie, television, and radio performers, motion picture and television executives, theatrical agents, and public relations executives. Activities include: Semiannual Roast; Friars Blood Bank; hospital shows; welfare programs. Dispenses approximately $200,000 annually in gifts, clothing, and toys to underprivileged children. **Libraries: Type:** reference. **Holdings:** 3,000; photographs. **Awards:** Friars Roast Award. **Frequency:** annual. **Type:** scholarship. **Recipient:** to students attending colleges and universities for the performing arts. **Telecommunication Services:** electronic mail, liz.nieves@friarsclub.com. **Committees:** Cemetery; Christmas Distribution; Entertainment. **Also Known As:** Friars National Association. **Publications:** *Friars Epistle*, quarterly. **Price:** $5.00. **Circulation:** 5,000. **Advertising:** accepted. **Conventions/Meetings:** annual meeting.

11017 ■ Hospital Audiences (HAI)
548 Broadway, 3rd Fl.
New York, NY 10012
Ph: (212)575-7676 (212)575-7696
Fax: (212)575-7669
E-mail: hai@hospaud.org
URL: http://www.hospitalaudiences.org
Contact: Michael Jon Spencer, Founder/Exec. Dir.

Founded: 1969. **Staff:** 50. **Description:** HAI service recipients include people with mental and physical disabilities, the frail elderly, youth at risk of HIV and violence or in detention, mentally retarded/developmental disabled persons, homeless single adults and families, and persons with HIV/AIDS. Promotes the cultural enrichment of these individuals by arranging access to cultural experiences, and by presenting music, dance, and theater events for people from health/human service facilities. Develops daily living skills through hands-on participation in the arts. Provides prevention education/skill building to persons at high risk regarding critical public health issues, such as HIV/AIDS and youth violence. **Computer Services:** database ● mailing lists ● online services. **Boards:** Clinical Advisory. **Publications:** *Access for All: A Guide for People with Disabilities to New York City Cultural Institutions*. Book. Covers theaters, museums, concert venues, galleries, public institutions, historical sites, zoos, gardens and sporting arenas. **Price:** $5.00 ● *HAI-News*, periodic. Newsletter. Covers HAI news and profiling HAI services. **Circulation:** 50,000 ● *The Healing Role of the Arts: A European Perspective*. Book ● *The Healing Role of the Arts: Working Papers*. Book ● *Hope and Inspiration through the Arts (A 25th Anniversary Report)* ● *Live Arts Experiences: Their Impact on Health and Wellness* ● *The Provision of Cultural Services to Physically and Mentally Impaired Aged in Long Term Care Facilities*. Booklet.

11018 ■ Institute of Outdoor Drama (IOD)

UNC-Chapel Hill
1700 Martin Luther King Jr. Blvd.
CB No. 3240
Chapel Hill, NC 27599-3240
Ph: (919)962-1328
Fax: (919)962-4212
E-mail: outdoor@unc.edu
URL: http://www.unc.edu/depts/outdoor
Contact: Rob Franklin Fox, Dir.

Founded: 1963. **Staff:** 3. **Description:** Public service, research and advisory agency of the University of North Carolina for all phases of planning, production, and management of historical drama produced in outdoor theaters. Currently serves 120 operating dramas, community planning groups, government agencies, the media, and the public. Conducts feasibility studies. Assists writers and academic researchers. Maintains archives containing correspondence, photographs, slides, playscripts, brochures and programs, press releases, and news clippings. **Libraries: Type:** reference. **Holdings:** archival material, artwork, audiovisuals, books, business records, clippings. **Subjects:** outdoor historical drama. **Awards:** Mark R. Sumner Award. **Frequency:** annual. **Type:** recognition. **Recipient:** for significant achievement and service. **Publications:** *More than 50*. Bulletins ● *U.S. Outdoor Drama*, quarterly. Newsletter ● Reports ● Surveys. **Conventions/Meetings:** annual conference, interactive sessions for outdoor theatre managers, artists, staff, board members, directors, playwrights, composers (exhibits) - always October ● annual meeting - always March.

11019 ■ The Lambs

3 W 51st St.
New York, NY 10019
Ph: (212)586-0306
Fax: (212)586-0306
E-mail: information@the-lambs.org
URL: http://www.the-lambs.org
Contact: Mr. Bruce Brown, Pres.

Founded: 1874. **Members:** 220. **Membership Dues:** non-theatrical, $500 (annual) ● theatrical, $400 (annual) ● junior theatrical (under 30), $200 (annual). **Description:** Social organization of men and women connected with the theatre, radio, television, motion pictures, and other branches of the entertainment industry. **Libraries: Type:** by appointment only. **Holdings:** archival material, articles, artwork, biographical archives, books, business records. **Awards:** Honorary Membership. **Frequency:** periodic. **Type:** recognition. **Recipient:** to persons in the arts; includes free membership ● Shepherds Award. **Frequency:** periodic. **Type:** recognition. **Recipient:** for outstanding contribution of a member. **Telecommunication Services:** electronic mail, membership@the-lambs.org. **Publications:** *The Lambs' Script*, quarterly. Newsletter. **Conventions/Meetings:** periodic Gambols - show ● weekly Low Jinks (Happy Hour) - party ● periodic Shepherd's Luncheons.

11020 ■ League of American Theatres and Producers (LATP)

226 W 47th St.
New York, NY 10036
Ph: (212)764-1122
Fax: (212)944-2136
E-mail: league@broadway.org
URL: http://www.livebroadway.com
Contact: Charlotte St. Martin, Exec. Dir.

Founded: 1930. **Members:** 500. **Staff:** 30. **Description:** Producers, theatre owners, and presenters of Broadway theatre throughout North America. Negotiates labor contracts and government relations. Compiles statistics; conducts audience development, research, marketing, and educational programs. **Awards:** Antoinette Perry (Tony) Award. **Frequency:** annual. **Type:** recognition. **Recipient:** for theatre productions. **Telecommunication Services:** electronic mail, cstmartin@broadway.org. **Committees:** Education; Financial; Labor; Marketing and Promotion; Membership Services; Production; Tony Administration. **Formerly:** League of New York Theatres; (1985) League of New York Theatres and Producers. **Publications:** *Broadway's Economic Contribution to New York City*. Report. **Price:** $25.00 for nonmembers; $15.00 for members ● *League Line*, bimonthly. **Price:** free for members. **Circulation:** 700 ● *Stage Specs*. Features backstage technical touring of Broadway houses across the U.S. and Canada. **Price:** $125.00 ● *Who Goes to Broadway? A Demographic Study of the Audience*. Report. Contains annual demographic study of the New York Broadway audience. **Price:** $25.00 for nonmembers; $15.00 for members. **Conventions/Meetings:** biennial Industry Conference ● annual Spring Road - conference.

11021 ■ League of Historic American Theatres (LHAT)

334 N Charles St., 2nd Fl.
Baltimore, MD 21201
Ph: (410)659-9533
Free: (877)627-0833
Fax: (410)837-9664
E-mail: info@lhat.org
URL: http://www.lhat.org
Contact: Dulcie C. Gilmore, Pres.

Founded: 1976. **Members:** 500. **Membership Dues:** service provider, $475-$945 (annual) ● theatre, $290-$840 (annual) ● government agency, $105-$210 (annual) ● individual, $105 (annual) ● student, $60 (annual). **Staff:** 3. **Budget:** $400,000. **Description:** Restored theaters and those in the process of restoration; professional managers of theaters; community organizations, art councils, and other groups involved in community development or renewal projects; scholars, writers, and individuals involved in restoration of historic theatres. The group defines a historic theatre as one built 50 or more years ago, which is architecturally significant, or has played an important role in the history of the American stage or the community, and can still be used as a performing arts or movie facility. Provides members with a network of contacts to help them preserve, protect, and program their historic facilities. **Awards:** Outstanding Historic Theatre Award. **Frequency:** annual. **Type:** recognition. **Recipient:** for a theatre that demonstrates the highest standards of excellence ● Outstanding Individual Contribution Award. **Frequency:** annual. **Type:** recognition. **Recipient:** for individuals who have a remarkable effort and contribute significantly in achieving the mission of the league. **Telecommunication Services:** electronic mail, fholden@lhat.org. **Programs:** Education. **Publications:** *InLeague*, quarterly. Newsletter. Contains articles relevant to restoring and operating historic theatres; includes regional reports, theatre profiles, reviews and events calendar. **Price:** included in membership dues. **Circulation:** 1,000. **Advertising:** accepted ● *Publications List*, annual. Brochure. Lists books on arts management, theatres, and historic preservation available through LHAT. ● Membership Directory, annual. **Price:** included in membership dues. **Conventions/Meetings:** annual conference, four-day event focused upon education, speakers, and social events designed to help communities to re-develop their historic theatres and help restoration specialists communicate their services to potential users (exhibits) - 2008 July 16-19, Atlanta, GA ● seminar ● tour.

11022 ■ League of Resident Theatres (LORT)

c/o Adam Knight, Management Assoc.
1501 Broadway, Ste.2401
New York, NY 10036
Ph: (212)944-1501
Fax: (212)768-0785
E-mail: adam@lort.org
URL: http://www.lort.org
Contact: Adam Knight, Management Assoc.

Founded: 1965. **Members:** 76. **Description:** Promotes the general welfare of resident theatres in the U.S. and its territories; promotes community interest in and support of resident theatres. **Conventions/Meetings:** semiannual meeting.

11023 ■ Literary Managers and Dramaturgs of the Americas (LMDA)

PO Box 728
New York, NY 10014
Ph: (212)561-0315
E-mail: lmdanyc@hotmail.com
URL: http://www.lmda.org
Contact: Liz Engelman, Chair

Founded: 1985. **Members:** 300. **Membership Dues:** student, intern, $25 (annual) ● voting, $60 (annual) ● institutional, $200 (annual). **Staff:** 1. **Regional Groups:** 12. **Description:** Literary managers, dramaturgs, and others interested in the field. Conducts dramaturg programs; offers script exchange. **Awards:** Elliot Hayes Award. **Frequency:** annual. **Type:** monetary. **Recipient:** for exemplary work of an LMDA member and nonmember dramaturgs in the USA and Canada. **Caucuses:** University. **Funds:** New Dramatures. **Programs:** Residency. **Projects:** The Production Diaries. **Publications:** *The Dramaturgy Bibliography*, annual. **Price:** $4.00 ● *Full Spectrum: The Expanded Script Exchange*, annual. **Price:** $12.00 ● *The LMDA Guide to Dramatology Training Programs*, annual. **Price:** $3.00 ● *The LMDA University Caucus Sourcebook*. **Price:** $13.00 ● Newsletter, 3/year. **Conventions/Meetings:** annual conference.

11024 ■ The Masquers

105 Park Pl.
Point Richmond, CA 94801-3922
Ph: (510)232-3888 (510)232-3889
E-mail: info@masquers.org
URL: http://www.masquers.org
Contact: Bob Goshay, Pres.

Founded: 1955. **Members:** 110. **Budget:** $150,000. **Description:** Social organization of actors and others associated with the theatre, motion pictures, and television. Sponsors annual Christmas party for underprivileged schoolchildren. **Telecommunication Services:** electronic mail, president@masquers.org. **Publications:** *Wicked Stage*, quarterly. **Conventions/Meetings:** annual meeting.

11025 ■ Movement Theatre International (MTI)

50 Bernard Dr.
Yardley, PA 19067
Ph: (215)519-0321
E-mail: mapedretti@aol.com
Contact: Michael Pedretti, Pres.

Founded: 1979. **Staff:** 1. **Budget:** $25,000. **Regional Groups:** 1. **Description:** Promotes increased appreciation and support of movement artists. Seeks to increase public awareness of movement theatre. Provides opportunities for movement artists to produce and perform. Rents theater space for theater, dance and movement theater productions. **Libraries: Type:** reference. **Awards:** Red Skelton Award. **Type:** recognition. **Recipient:** for best artists in clowning and miming.

11026 ■ National Association of Dramatic and Speech Arts (NADSA)
c/o Dr. Wendy R. Coleman, VP
504 Coll. Dr.
Albany, GA 31705
Ph: (229)430-4840 (318)247-0686
Fax: (229)430-1617
E-mail: wendy.coleman@asurams.edu
URL: http://www.nadsainc.com
Contact: Dr. Wendy R. Coleman, VP
Founded: 1936. **Members:** 1,000. **Membership Dues:** individual, $35 (annual) ● organization, $100 (annual). **Staff:** 5. **Budget:** $35,000. **Regional Groups:** 6. **State Groups:** 3. **Local Groups:** 1. **Description:** Persons interested in educational, community, children's, and professional theater; area of interest is black and ethnic theater and writers. Provides placement service. Sponsors competitions and educational programs. **Libraries: Type:** reference. **Holdings:** 1,000; monographs, periodicals. **Subjects:** black theatre, theatre and speech arts. **Awards:** Life Time Achievement. **Type:** recognition ● Play Festival. **Type:** recognition ● Playwriting Contest. **Frequency:** annual. **Type:** recognition ● Redder's Theatre. **Type:** recognition. **Computer Services:** Mailing lists. **Divisions:** Children's Theatre; Community Theatre; Professional Theatre; Secondary School; University and College Theatre. **Also Known As:** SADSA. **Publications:** *Encore*, semiannual. Journal. Includes research articles, reports, and scripts of new plays. **Price:** included in membership dues; $10.00/copy for nonmembers. **Circulation:** 5,000. **Advertising:** accepted ● *NADSA Conference Directory*, annual ● *NADSA Monogram*, annual ● *NADSA Newsletter*, quarterly ● *NADSA UPDATE*, semiannual. **Conventions/Meetings:** annual conference and convention, books, supplies - always late March or early April.

11027 ■ National Corporate Theatre Fund (NCTF)
505 8th Ave., Ste.2303
New York, NY 10018
Ph: (212)750-6895
Fax: (212)750-6977
E-mail: bwhitacre@nctf.org
URL: http://www.nctf.org
Contact: Bruce E. Whitacre, Exec. Dir.
Founded: 1977. **Members:** 11. **Staff:** 4. **Budget:** $750,000. **Description:** Fosters national corporate support for regional theatres. Acts as a central national development office for member theaters. Provides broad recognition for corporate contributors. **Awards:** Chairman's Awards. **Frequency:** annual. **Type:** recognition. **Recipient:** for artists, managers, and corporations that contribute to the health of nonprofit professional theatres. **Programs:** Concierge Ticket Service; New York's Best Kept Secret; Save My Seat; Theatre Party Planning. **Formerly:** (1981) Corporate Theatre Fund. **Publications:** *NCTF News*, quarterly. Newsletter. Includes theatre schedules. **Price:** free. **Circulation:** 2,000. **Conventions/Meetings:** semiannual board meeting.

11028 ■ National Movement Theatre Association (NMTA)
Address Unknown since 2007
Founded: 1984. **Members:** 145. **Membership Dues:** individual, $30 (annual) ● company, $50 (annual) ● benefactor, $100 (annual) ● patron, $250 (annual). **Budget:** $10,000. **Description:** Movement theatre artists. Purpose is to promote the development of movement theatre through the publication of materials for and about movement theatre artists. Seeks to heighten public awareness of movement theatre and to improve the quality of work by offering networking opportunities. Acts as clearinghouse of information in the field of movement theatre. Operates speakers' bureau; compiles statistics. **Libraries: Type:** reference. **Holdings:** 10; archival material. **Subjects:** American contemporary artists. **Computer Services:** http://www.bluefin.net/~pontine. **Formerly:** (1990) National Mime Association. **Publications:** *Directory of Movement Theatre Training*, annual ● *Movement Theatre quarterly*, quarterly. Newsletter. Includes book reviews and conference and workshop information. **Price:** $20.00/year. ISSN: 1065-1519. **Circulation:** 400. **Advertising:** accepted ● Membership Directory, annual. **Conventions/Meetings:** annual conference - always summer.

11029 ■ National Music Theater Network (NMTN)
242 W 38th St., No. 1102
New York, NY 10018
Ph: (212)664-0979
Fax: (212)664-0978
E-mail: info@nmtn.org
URL: http://www.nmtn.org
Contact: Tim Jerome, Founder/Pres.
Founded: 1983. **Staff:** 5. **Description:** Professional stage and musical directors. Promotes the works of "unknown" American writers and composers by acting as a clearinghouse for new musicals. Works to provide theaters and producers "reliable access to works of superior merit." Encourages public awareness of and enthusiasm for new music theater productions. Provides writers and composers with objective evaluations of their work. Solicits submissions from writers and composers of manuscripts to be evaluated. Produces concerts, staged readings, and entertainment of works, which have been recommended for publication or production. **Libraries: Type:** open to the public. **Awards:** Directors' Choice Award. **Frequency:** annual. **Type:** recognition. **Recipient:** for wonderful musicals submitted to the evaluators. **Also Known As:** Broadway Dozen. **Publications:** *Catalogue of Recommended Works*, periodic. Contains current information and specifications for all NMTN-recommended musicals and operas. **Price:** free. Alternate Formats: online. **Conventions/Meetings:** bimonthly Broadway Dozen - meeting.

11030 ■ National New Play Network (NNPN)
c/o David Golston, Gen. Mgr.
InterAct Theatre
2030 Sansom St.
Philadelphia, PA 19103
Ph: (215)568-8077
Fax: (215)568-8095
E-mail: nnpn@unicorntheatre.org
URL: http://www.nnpn.org
Contact: David Golston, Gen. Mgr.
Founded: 1998. **Members:** 21. **Description:** Promotes the development, production, and continued life of new plays for the American theatre. Supports its members' efforts in producing new works for the American theatre by creating and developing innovative programs. Strives to cultivate an informed, passionate, and supportive audience for new works of theatre in the future. **Awards:** Smith Prize. **Frequency:** annual. **Type:** monetary. **Recipient:** for a play that best illuminates issues focusing on civic institutions, particularly democratic institutions. **Telecommunication Services:** electronic mail, davidg@nnpn.org.

11031 ■ National Performance Network (NPN)
900 Camp St., 2nd Fl.
New Orleans, LA 70130
Ph: (504)595-8008
Fax: (504)595-8006
E-mail: info@npnweb.org
URL: http://www.npnweb.org
Contact: M.K. Wegmann, Pres./CEO
Founded: 1985. **Members:** 60. **Staff:** 12. **Budget:** $1,200,000. **Description:** Sixty diverse cultural organizers, including artists, working to create meaningful partnerships and to provide leadership that enables the practice and public experience of the performing arts in the U.S. Supports artists' residencies through its fee support program, commission's new work through the Creation Fund, and extended residency support through the Community Fund. **Programs:** Community Fund; Creation Fund; Residencies. **Publications:** *NAAMP Executive Summary*. Report. Contains synopsis of full NAAMP report. Alternate Formats: online ● *National Arts Administration Mentorship Program: A Report to the Field: A Record and Reflection of Value-Based Learning*. Book. **Price:** $15.00. Alternate Formats: online ● *National Performance Network Directory*, annual. Booklet. Contains descriptions of programs and partner organization. **Price:** free. Alternate Formats: online ● *NPN Brochure*, annual. Booklet. **Price:** $15.00 ● *Reaffirming the Tradition of the New*. Booklet. **Price:** $15.00. **Conventions/Meetings:** annual meeting, by invitation only.

11032 ■ National Theatre Conference (NTC)
c/o Jack B. Wright, Pres.
4513 Turnberry Dr.
Lawrence, KS 66047
Ph: (785)864-4110
Fax: (785)864-5251
E-mail: kujack@ku.edu
URL: http://www.nationaltheatreconference.org/index.htm
Contact: Jack B. Wright, Pres.
Founded: 1925. **Members:** 120. **Description:** Leaders of the noncommercial theatre in the U.S; membership is limited to 120 voting members, divided between academic and nonacademic theatre professionals. Collaborates on matters of policy and action with other major organizations and federal government agencies concerned with the welfare and advance of drama and theatre arts. Maintains archives in the Eli Lilly Library of rare books and original documents at Indiana University, Bloomington, IN, and in the Theatre Collection, Baldwin-Wallace College, Berea, OH. **Affiliated With:** American Association of Community Theatre. **Conventions/Meetings:** meeting - always December, in New York City.

11033 ■ National Theatre Workshop of the Handicapped (NTWH)
535 Greenwich St.
New York, NY 10013
Ph: (212)206-7789
Fax: (212)206-0200
E-mail: admission@ntwh.org
URL: http://www.ntwh.org
Contact: Rick Curry PhD, Founder/Artistic Dir.
Founded: 1977. **Staff:** 7. **Budget:** $500,000. **Description:** Offers workshops in New York City that provides training in the theatre arts to physically disabled adults in preparation for professional acting or other careers. Offers a comprehensive program in theatre arts for the physically disabled. **Libraries: Type:** open to the public. **Holdings:** 100. **Subjects:** disability issues.

11034 ■ New Dramatists (ND)
424 W 44th St.
New York, NY 10036
Ph: (212)757-6960
Fax: (212)265-4738
E-mail: newdramatists@newdramatists.org
URL: http://newdramatists.org
Contact: Joel K. Ruark, Exec. Dir.
Founded: 1949. **Members:** 50. **Staff:** 7. **Budget:** $800,000. **Description:** Works to promote and develop new playwriting talent for the American theatre. Serves as a laboratory where writers can develop their craft through a comprehensive program that includes: script distribution; play panels; discount theatre tickets; readings of works in progress. Provides information on awards, scholarships, and grants to members. Offers playwriting classes taught by members to the public on a trimester basis. **Convention/Meeting:** none. **Libraries: Type:** open to the public. **Holdings:** 2,000; periodicals. **Subjects:** playwrighting. **Awards:** Van Lier Fellowship. **Frequency:** annual. **Type:** fellowship. **Recipient:** for play submission; by nomination only. **Departments:** Program; Script-Share. **Divisions:** Literary Services. **Formerly:** New Dramatists Committee. **Publications:** *Members Bulletin*, monthly. Updates on organization activities and member activities. ● *New Dramatist*, semiannual. Newsletter.

11035 ■ New England Theatre Conference (NETC)
215 Knob Hill Dr.
Hamden, CT 06518
Ph: (617)851-8535
Fax: (203)288-5938

E-mail: mail@netconline.org
URL: http://netconline.org
Contact: Jim Quinn, Pres.
Founded: 1952. **Members:** 2,000. **Membership Dues:** individual, $45 (annual) ● student, $30 (annual) ● group, $95 (annual). **Staff:** 1. **Budget:** $145,000. **Description:** Individuals and theatre-producing groups in New England who are actively engaged in or have a particular interest in theatre activity either professionally or as an avocation. Aims to develop, expand, and assist theatre activity on community, educational, and professional levels in New England. Activities include: auditions for jobs in New England summer theatres; workshops on performance, administrative, and technical aspects of production. **Awards:** Aurand Harris Memorial Play Writing Award. **Frequency:** annual. **Type:** monetary. **Recipient:** to new scripts for young audiences ● Award for Outstanding Creative Achievement in the American Theatre. **Frequency:** annual. **Type:** recognition. **Recipient:** for theatre achievement nationally and regionally ● John Gassner Memorial Play Writing Award. **Frequency:** annual. **Type:** monetary. **Recipient:** for new full-length plays ● Moss Hart Memorial Award. **Frequency:** annual. **Type:** recognition. **Recipient:** for outstanding production of a full-length play with positive values. **Computer Services:** Mailing lists. **Telecommunication Services:** electronic mail, jquinn@bridgew.edu. **Divisions:** Children's and Youth; College and University; Community; Professional Theatre; Secondary School. **Publications:** *NETC News*, quarterly. Newsletter ● *New England Theatre Journal*, annual. Contains articles and reviews. **Price:** $10.00. ISSN: 1050-9720. **Circulation:** 1,000. **Advertising:** accepted. **Conventions/Meetings:** annual The New England Region: An Inexhaustible Theatrical Resource - convention and workshop (exhibits) - always November.

11036 ■ O'Neill Critics Institute (OCI)
c/o Dan Sullivan, Dir.
Eugene O'Neill Theater Ctr.
305 Great Neck Rd.
Waterford, CT 06385
Ph: (860)443-5378 (612)522-9053
Fax: (860)443-9653
E-mail: critics@theoneill.org
URL: http://www.oneilltheatercenter.org
Contact: Dan Sullivan, Dir.
Founded: 1968. **Staff:** 2. **Budget:** $50,000. **Description:** A project of the Eugene O'Neill Memorial Theater Center (see separate entry). Seeks to improve the state of arts coverage in American journalism, particularly in regards to the theater. **Telecommunication Services:** electronic mail, sulli008@yahoo.com. **Formerly:** (2002) National Critics Institute. **Conventions/Meetings:** annual meeting, operates in tandem with the O'Neill Playwrights Conference - June-July ● annual Summer Program - workshop, with a boot camp for critics ● workshop, critical writing - during academic year.

11037 ■ Outer Critics Circle (OCC)
c/o Marjorie Gunner, Pres. Emerita
101 W 57th St.
New York, NY 10019
Ph: (212)765-8557
Fax: (212)765-7979
URL: http://www.outercriticscircle.org
Contact: Simon Saltzman, Pres.
Founded: 1950. **Members:** 70. **Description:** Writers who cover the New York theatre for out-of-town newspapers and other media. **Awards:** John Gassner Award. **Frequency:** annual. **Type:** recognition. **Recipient:** for the author of a preferably new outstanding American play ● **Frequency:** annual. **Type:** recognition. **Recipient:** for outstanding work in the New York theatre. **Conventions/Meetings:** annual Awards Supper Party - dinner - always late May or early June ● periodic meeting.

11038 ■ The Players
16 Gramercy Park S
New York, NY 10003
Ph: (212)475-6116
Fax: (212)473-2701
E-mail: info@theplayersnyc.org
URL: http://www.theplayersnyc.org
Contact: Timothy Hutton, Pres.
Founded: 1888. **Members:** 650. **Description:** Private social club for actors, dramatists, writers, publishers, journalists, editors, musicians, artists, cartoonists, composers, and other professionals and patrons of the arts. Maintains and houses the Hampden-Booth Theatre Library, a research facility relating to the history of American and British theatre. **Libraries: Type:** reference. **Publications:** *Brief Chronicles*, monthly. Newsletter.

11039 ■ Playwrights Conference
Address Unknown since 2007
Founded: 1965. **Staff:** 3. **Description:** Strives to create a supportive environment that empowers the playwright to discover a play off the page. Conference gathers a team of working professionals to support each project and playwright through a month-long residency that includes a four-day rehearsal period culminating in two staged readings. Conference is held yearly at the Eugene O'Neill Theater Center. **Affiliated With:** Eugene O'Neill Memorial Theater Center. **Formerly:** (2002) National Playwrights Conference.

11040 ■ Puerto Rican Traveling Theatre Company (PRTT)
304 W 47th St.
New York, NY 10036
Ph: (212)354-1293
Fax: (212)307-6769
E-mail: prtt@prtt.org
URL: http://www.prtt.org
Contact: Miriam Colon Valle, Artistic Dir./Pres.
Founded: 1967. **Members:** 700. **Membership Dues:** individual, $50 (annual). **Description:** Individuals interested in bilingual theater. Promotes and supports bilingual theater and Latino playwrights. Sponsors educational activities, including an acting unit for children and a playwriting unit for minority writers. Engages in community outreach activities, including free outdoor drama performances. Performs season of drama by U.S.-based and internationally known Latino writers. Conducts search service to locate Latino actors and actresses for performances. Maintains permanent theater. **Libraries: Type:** reference. **Holdings:** archival material, photographs. **Subjects:** Latino actors and actresses. **Awards: Frequency:** annual. **Type:** monetary. **Recipient:** for students in training unit. **Publications:** Bulletins. **Price:** available to members only. **Conventions/Meetings:** meeting, held for subscribers and group leaders.

11041 ■ Rites and Reason Theatre
Box 1148
Brown Univ.
155 Angell St.
Providence, RI 02912
Ph: (401)863-3558
Fax: (401)863-3559
E-mail: karen_baxter@brown.edu
URL: http://www.brown.edu/Departments/African_American_Studies/RitesandReason
Contact: Karen Allen Baxter, Managing Dir./Producer
Staff: 7. **Description:** Aims to develop new works for the American stage which analyze and articulate the African Diaspora.

11042 ■ Shakespeare Theatre Association of America (STAA)
c/o Laura Cole, Sec.
499 Peachtree St. NE
Atlanta, GA 30308
Ph: (404)874-5299
Fax: (404)874-9219
URL: http://www.staaonline.org
Contact: Laura Cole, Sec.
Founded: 1991. **Membership Dues:** organization, $100 (annual) ● associate, $50 (annual). **Multinational. Description:** Acts as an advocate for Shakespearean productions and training in North America. Provides a forum for the artistic and managerial leadership of theatres whose central activity is the production of Shakespeare's plays. Discusses issues and facilitates the sharing of ideas, resources, and information related to an American production approach to Shakespeare. **Publications:** *Quarto*, semiannual. Newsletter. **Price:** included in membership dues ● Membership Directory, annual. **Price:** included in membership dues.

11043 ■ Southeastern Theatre Conference (SETC)
PO Box 9868
Greensboro, NC 27429
Ph: (336)272-3645
Fax: (336)272-8810
E-mail: setc@setc.org
URL: http://www.setc.org
Contact: Elizabeth N. Baun, Exec. Dir.
Founded: 1949. **Members:** 4,200. **Membership Dues:** individual, $60 (annual) ● organization, $70 (annual) ● student, $30 (annual) ● senior, $40 (annual) ● life, $1,200. **Staff:** 4. **Budget:** $400,000. **State Groups:** 10. **Description:** Serves the needs of individuals and theatre organizations involved in professional, university/college, community, children/youth, and secondary school theatres. Brings together people interested in theatre and theatre artists and craftsmen from 10 southeastern states of the U.S., across the nation and internationally in order to promote high standards and to stimulate creativity in all phases of theatrical endeavor. Services include: job contact service for technical hiring and job listings, resume service, etc; playwriting projects for new plays; scholarships for a variety of theatre interests; and annual auditions (spring and fall) for professional, dinner, repertory, summer indoor and outdoor theatres, cruise lines and entertainment venues. **Libraries: Type:** reference. **Holdings:** 43; archival material. **Subjects:** popular theater. **Awards:** Distinguished Career Award. **Frequency:** annual. **Type:** recognition. **Recipient:** for individuals in the South who have become nationally or internationally renowned ● Getchell New Play Award. **Frequency:** annual. **Type:** monetary. **Recipient:** for writing of a new play ● Leighton M. Ballew Award. **Frequency:** annual. **Type:** scholarship. **Recipient:** to a graduate student studying directing ● Marian A. Smith Award. **Frequency:** annual. **Type:** scholarship. **Recipient:** for a graduate study in costume design or costume technology ● Polly Holliday Award. **Frequency:** annual. **Type:** monetary. **Recipient:** to a graduating high school student going on to study theatre ● Robert Porterfield Award. **Frequency:** annual. **Type:** scholarship. **Recipient:** to a graduate student of merit for study in theatre ● Sara Spencer Award. **Frequency:** annual. **Type:** recognition. **Recipient:** for superior service and accomplishment in theatre for youth ● Secondary School Scholarship. **Frequency:** annual. **Type:** scholarship. **Recipient:** to a high school senior who is planning to attend a college or university in the SETC region with the intent of majoring in theatre arts ● Suzanne M. Davis Memorial Award. **Frequency:** annual. **Type:** recognition. **Recipient:** for distinguished service to theatre in the South ● William E. Wilson. **Frequency:** annual. **Type:** scholarship. **Recipient:** to a secondary school teacher who is pursuing a graduate degree in theatre or speech and theatre. **Computer Services:** database, current members ● online services, job contact bulletin; online listing of jobs in theatre ● online services, registration and application for events sponsored by the organization. **Telecommunication Services:** electronic mail, betsey@setc.org. **Subgroups:** American College Theatre; Children's Theatre/Theatre for Youth; College and University Theatre; Community Theatre; Professional Theatre; Secondary School Theatre. **Affiliated With:** American Association of Community Theatre. **Publications:** *Job Contact Bulletin*, monthly. Lists jobs available in theatres. **Price:** included in membership dues. **Circulation:** 10,000. **Advertising:** accepted ● *Journal of the Southeastern Theatre Conference*, annual. ISSN: 1065-4917 ● *Southeastern Theatre Conference—Newsletter*, bimonthly. Includes news of conferences and conventions; contains directory of affairs. **Price:** included in membership dues. **Circulation:** 3,570 ● *Southern Theatre*, quarterly. Magazine. Includes

featured articles, theatre survey, and new play reviews. **Price:** $17.50 /year for nonmembers; included in membership dues. ISSN: 0584-4738. **Circulation:** 3,600. **Advertising:** accepted. **Conventions/Meetings:** annual convention and competition, auditions, workshops, commercial and non-commercial exhibits, theatre festivals (exhibits) - always the first full Wednesday-Sunday of March.

11044 ■ Stage Directors and Choreographers Foundation (SDCF)
1501 Broadway, Ste.1701
New York, NY 10036-5600
Ph: (212)302-5359
Free: (800)541-5204
Fax: (212)302-6195
E-mail: foundation@ssdc.org
URL: http://www.ssdc.org/sdcf.php
Contact: Barbara Hauptman, Exec. Dir.
Founded: 1965. **Staff:** 2. **Description:** Serves directors, choreographers, artists, educators, students, and other professionals working to develop the craft and careers of theatrical directors and choreographers. Dedicated exclusively to supporting the craft and artistry of theatrical directors and choreographers. Represents a one-of-a-kind nexus between great masters, mid-career professionals, and rising artists. Sponsors core programs in Chicago, Los Angeles, San Francisco, and Seattle. Offers critical career-building initiative, such as craft workshops, mentoring programs, professional observerships, and artistic fellowships. **Libraries:** **Type:** by appointment only. **Holdings:** books, periodicals. **Subjects:** theatre, dance. **Awards:** Mr. Abbott Award. **Frequency:** annual. **Type:** recognition. **Recipient:** for lifetime achievement. **Publications:** *The Journal for Stage Directors and Choreographers*, semiannual. Magazine. **Price:** $12.00/issue. ISSN: 1078-4802. **Circulation:** 1,600. **Advertising:** accepted.

11045 ■ Texas International Theatrical Arts Society (TITAS)
3625 N Hall St., Ste.740
Dallas, TX 75219
Ph: (214)528-6112 (214)528-5576
Fax: (214)528-2617
E-mail: csantos@titas.org
URL: http://www.titas.org
Contact: Charles Santos, Exec. Dir.
Founded: 1982. **Staff:** 13. **Budget:** $2,100,000. **Description:** Theatrical agencies working to book entertainers and international acts into all live music venues. Provides placement service; conducts educational seminars. **Libraries:** **Type:** open to the public. **Computer Services:** Information services, linking theatrical agencies. **Telecommunication Services:** electronic mail, srozsa@titas.org. **Publications:** Newsletter, 3/year. Alternate Formats: online. **Conventions/Meetings:** annual meeting.

11046 ■ Theatre Authority (TA)
Address Unknown since 2008
Founded: 1934. **Members:** 12. **Staff:** 2. **Description:** Represents entertainers that perform at charity sponsored benefits or telethons. **Publications:** *A Performers Guide* ● *A Sponsor's Guide*.

11047 ■ Theatre Communications Group (TCG)
520 8th Ave., 24th Fl.
New York, NY 10018-4156
Ph: (212)609-5900
Fax: (212)609-5901
E-mail: tcg@tcg.org
URL: http://www.tcg.org
Contact: Teresa Eyring, Exec. Dir.
Founded: 1961. **Members:** 446. **Membership Dues:** individual, $39 (annual) ● student, $20 (annual) ● affiliate, $500 (annual). **Staff:** 55. **Budget:** $6,000,000. **Description:** Works to strengthen, nurture and promote the not-for-profit American theatre. Offers career development programs for artists and provides professional development opportunities for theatre leaders. Conducts research; assists theatres in the areas of budgeting, long-range planning, fundraising, and advocacy. Operates play distribution service; offers advisory and consultation services; sponsors symposia, workshops, conferences, and seminars. Maintains artist and theatre resource files. **Awards:** Alan Schneider Director Award. **Frequency:** biennial. **Type:** grant. **Recipient:** for talented freelance directors. **Computer Services:** Information services, data bank on financial, statistical, and salary information. **Telecommunication Services:** electronic mail, teyring@tcg.org. **Affiliated With:** American Arts Alliance. **Publications:** *American Theatre Magazine*, monthly. **Price:** included in membership dues. ISSN: 8750-3255. **Circulation:** 70,000. **Advertising:** accepted ● *ARTSEARCH*, bimonthly. Bulletin. Alternate Formats: online ● *Dramatists Sourcebook*, biennial ● *Fiscal Survey*, annual. Report ● *Theatre Directory*, annual ● Also publishes plays, anthologies, and reference, criticism, theory, and management books. **Conventions/Meetings:** biennial conference, by invitation only - always June ● workshop.

11048 ■ Theatre Development Fund (TDF)
1501 Broadway, 21st Fl.
New York, NY 10036-5652
Ph: (212)221-0885
Fax: (212)768-1563
E-mail: info@tdf.org
URL: http://www.tdf.org
Contact: Victoria Bailey, Exec. Dir.
Founded: 1968. **Members:** 80,000. **Membership Dues:** regular, $25 (annual). **Staff:** 50. **Budget:** $11,000,000. **Description:** Stimulates the production of plays in the commercial and not-for-profit theatre. Provides support for almost every area of professional theatre, dance, and music. Offers low-cost admissions to a wide variety of plays, dance, and musical events for the benefit of those who might otherwise be unable to attend. Programs include: subsidized and non-subsidized ticket distribution; a performing arts voucher for Off-Off Broadway, dance and music groups; Costume Collection (see separate entry); discount tickets on the day of performance at the Times Square, and Lower Manhattan Theatre TKTS Centres; a Theatre Access Project for the disabled; national services to assist other cities; and several Arts Education Programs. **Awards:** The Robert Whitehead Award. **Frequency:** annual. **Type:** recognition. **Recipient:** for excellence in commercial producing ● TDF Irene Sharaff Award. **Frequency:** annual. **Type:** recognition. **Recipient:** for best costume design. **Programs:** Education. **Projects:** Accessibility Services. **Affiliated With:** Costume Collection. **Publications:** *Play By Play*, quarterly. Magazine. Student theatre magazine written for and by high school students. **Circulation:** 35,000. Alternate Formats: online ● Annual Report.

11049 ■ Theatre Guild (TG)
135 Central Park W, Ste.4S
New York, NY 10023
Ph: (212)873-0676
Fax: (212)873-5972
E-mail: theatguild@aol.com
Contact: Philip Langner, Pres.
Founded: 1919. **Members:** 105,000. **Staff:** 50. **Local Groups:** 5. **Description:** Theatrical producing organization. Encourages and promotes attendance at dramatic, musical, and theatrical performances "of an artistic character and high standard of excellence." Sponsors American Theatre Society, a national subscription service for major Broadway attractions touring principal cities throughout the United States, and Theatre Guild Abroad, which enables participants to travel on cultural exchange programs.

11050 ■ Theatre Historical Society of America (THSA)
York Theatre Bldg.
152 N York, 2nd Fl.
Elmhurst, IL 60126-2889
Ph: (630)782-1800
Fax: (630)782-1802
E-mail: thrhistsoc@aol.com
URL: http://www.historictheatres.org
Contact: Richard J. Sklenar, Exec. Dir.
Founded: 1969. **Members:** 1,000. **Membership Dues:** student, $30 (annual) ● regular, $55 (annual) ● patron, $500 (annual). **Staff:** 2. **Budget:** $200,000. **Description:** Individual hobbyists, college and public libraries, historical societies, and architects. Aims: to preserve the history of popular theatre in the U.S; to make available information relating to American theatres; to encourage study in this field; to promote preservation of important theatre buildings. Emphasizes on theater architecture, management, advertising, and publicity and includes movie houses and legitimate, vaudeville, and stock company houses. Collects archive material from various individuals and corporations such as Loew's. Maintains speakers' bureau and museum; conducts research program; all research by appointment. **Libraries:** **Type:** open to the public; by appointment only. **Holdings:** 650; archival material, photographs. **Subjects:** theatre buildings, blueprints. **Awards:** Honorary Member of the Year Award. **Frequency:** annual. **Type:** recognition. **Recipient:** for an individual or organizational member who has demonstrated outstanding efforts outside the organization ● Jeffrey Weiss Literary. **Frequency:** annual. **Type:** monetary. **Recipient:** for individuals who have an interest in research and writing in historic theatre ● Member of the Year Award. **Frequency:** annual. **Type:** recognition. **Recipient:** for an individual or organizational member who has continuously demonstrated outstanding leadership, achievement and contribution to the organization ● President's Award. **Frequency:** annual. **Type:** recognition. **Recipient:** for individuals who have made exemplary contributions to the society. **Formerly:** Theatre Historical Society of America. **Publications:** *Marquee*, quarterly. Journal. Contains news and feature stories on theatre buildings. **Price:** $45.00. ISSN: 0025-3928. **Circulation:** 1,000. **Advertising:** accepted ● Also publishes special material pertinent to the field. **Conventions/Meetings:** annual Conclave - meeting and tour, tours various theatres (exhibits).

11051 ■ Theatre for Young Audiences/USA (TYA/USA)
1602 Belle View Blvd., No. 810
Alexandria, VA 22307
Ph: (202)416-8837
Fax: (202)416-8297
E-mail: info@assitej-usa.org
URL: http://www.assitej-usa.org
Contact: Kim Peter Kovac, Pres.
Founded: 1965. **Members:** 500. **Membership Dues:** student (with I.D.), $35 (annual) ● individual, $75 (annual) ● retiree, $40 (annual) ● library (non-voting), $60 (annual) ● individual/organization outside U.S., $95 (annual) ● organizational (based on budget), $150-$425 (annual). **Staff:** 1. **Budget:** $52,000. **Description:** Promotes the power of professional theatre for young audiences through excellence, collaboration and innovation across cultural and international boundaries. **Awards:** Ann Shaw Fellowship. **Frequency:** annual. **Type:** fellowship. **Recipient:** to fund career development opportunities for theater artists and administrators committed to Theatre for Young Audiences. **Formerly:** (2007) ASSITEJ/USA. **Publications:** *International Hotline*, quarterly. Newsletter. Alternate Formats: online ● *Marquee*, annual. Directory. Includes seasons listings for member theaters. ● *Next*, periodic. Newsletter. Features emerging artists. Alternate Formats: online ● *TYA Today*, semiannual. Journal. Includes book reviews, articles, updates of news in the field and theater reviews. **Price:** included in membership dues. **Circulation:** 500. **Advertising:** accepted. **Conventions/Meetings:** triennial International Congresses, productions from various countries are seen and discussed ● One Theatre World - festival - every two or three years.

11052 ■ United States Institute for Theatre Technology (USITT)
6443 Ridings Rd.
Syracuse, NY 13206-1111
Ph: (315)463-6463
Free: (800)938-7488
Fax: (866)398-7488
E-mail: info@office.usitt.org
URL: http://www.usitt.org
Contact: Sylvia Hillyard Pannell, Pres.
Founded: 1960. **Members:** 3,500. **Membership Dues:** student, $60 (annual) ● senior, $80 (annual) ●

individual, $102 (annual) ● professional, $150 (annual) ● organizational, $200 (annual) ● sustaining, $660 (annual) ● contributing, $1,100 (annual). **Staff:** 6. **Budget:** $500,000. **Regional Groups:** 18. **Description:** Design production and technology professionals in the performing arts industry. Promotes the advancement of the knowledge and skills of its members through a variety of publications and activities. **Libraries: Type:** reference. **Holdings:** archival material. **Subjects:** design productions. **Awards:** Barbizon Award for Lighting Design. **Frequency:** annual. **Type:** recognition. **Recipient:** for graduate students in lighting ● Clear-Com Intercom Systems Sound Achievement Award. **Frequency:** annual. **Type:** recognition. **Recipient:** for graduate students in sound ● Golden Hammer Scenic Technology Award. **Frequency:** annual. **Type:** recognition. **Recipient:** for graduate students in stage engineering, shop management, scene painting, scenery or properties construction and craft ● The KM Fabrics Technical Production Award. **Frequency:** annual. **Type:** recognition. **Recipient:** for graduate students in technical direction or production management ● Kryolon Makeup Design Award. **Frequency:** annual. **Type:** recognition. **Recipient:** for graduate students in makeup design ● Rose Brand Award for Scenic Lighting. **Frequency:** annual. **Type:** recognition. **Recipient:** for graduate student in scene design ● USITT Architecture Design Award. **Frequency:** annual. **Type:** recognition. **Recipient:** for excellence in design of large and small projects for old and new theatres ● USITT/Edward Kook Endowment Fund. **Frequency:** annual. **Type:** recognition ● Zelma H. Weisfeld Costume Design and Technology Award. **Frequency:** annual. **Type:** recognition. **Recipient:** for graduate students in costume design or costume technology. **Computer Services:** Mailing lists, available to members only. **Telecommunication Services:** electronic mail, hillyard@uga.edu. **Commissions:** Costume Design and Technology; Education; Engineering; Health and Safety; Lighting and Sound Design; Publications; Scenography; Sound; Technical Production; Theatre; Theatre Architecture. **Publications:** *AMX/DMX Standards* ● *Backstage Handbook.* **Price:** $13.00 for members; $15.00 for nonmembers ● *Practical Projects for Teaching Lighting Design, A Compendium.* **Price:** $18.00 for members; $24.00 for nonmembers ● *Recommended Practice for DMX 512.* Provides users and installers with needed information to build a successful DMX system. **Price:** $8.00 for members; $11.00 for nonmembers ● *Scenic Modeler's Sourcebook.* Contains bibliographic and supplier listing for scenic modelers. **Price:** $15.00 for members; $20.00 for nonmembers ● *Sightlines*, monthly. Newsletter. **Price:** included in membership dues. **Circulation:** 4,000. **Advertising:** accepted ● *The TD in Educational Theatre.* Magazine. **Price:** $3.00 for members; $5.00 for nonmembers ● *Theatre Design and Technology*, quarterly. Catalog. Contains articles on theatrical lighting, acoustics, costuming, architecture, health, safety, and education. Includes book reviews and new products. **Price:** included in membership dues; $48.00 /year for libraries in U.S.; $58.00 /year for libraries outside U.S. **Circulation:** 4,100. **Advertising:** accepted ● *Theatre Technology Exhibit Catalog*, biennial. **Price:** $10.00 for members; $14.00 for nonmembers ● *Theatre Words.* Membership Directory. Contains translations of theatre terminology into nine languages. ● *U.S. Institute for Theatre Technology—Annual Membership Directory.* **Price:** included in membership dues. **Circulation:** 4,000. **Advertising:** accepted ● *USITT Guidelines for a Standard Technical Information Package.* **Price:** $5.00 for members; $7.00 for nonmembers. **Conventions/Meetings:** annual conference and workshop (exhibits) ● annual Costume Symposium ● biennial Design/Tech Expo - meeting (exhibits).

11053 ■ Yiddish Theatrical Alliance (YTA)
c/o Yablokoff Chapels
31 E 7th St.
New York, NY 10003
Ph: (212)674-3437
E-mail: yta18@aol.com
Contact: Ruth Harris, Sec.
Founded: 1917. **Members:** 275. **Description:** Cares for the sick, poor, and indigent members of the Yiddish theatre and their families. Maintains own cemetery and supplies burial funds for indigent members. Conducts charitable programs. Operates museum. **Libraries: Type:** reference. **Holdings:** archival material. **Awards: Type:** recognition. **Conventions/Meetings:** annual meeting.

11054 ■ Ziegfeld Club (ZC)
593 Park Ave.
New York, NY 10021
Ph: (212)751-6688 (212)986-0362
Fax: (212)751-6688
URL: http://www.thenationalziegfeldclubinc.com
Contact: Paula Lamont, Pres.
Founded: 1936. **Members:** 350. **Membership Dues:** regular, $40 (annual) ● non-voting associate, $35. **National Groups:** 2. **Description:** Performers from the original Ziegfeld Follies; professionals in the theatre business and allied arts; honorary celebrities. (In 1907 theatrical producer Florenz Ziegfeld (1869-1932) first produced the Follies, a series of annual revues featuring a chorus line and striking costumes and settings.) Provides financial assistance to needy women in show business. **Awards:** Miss Ziegfeld of the Year Award. **Frequency:** annual. **Type:** recognition. **Publications:** Newsletter, quarterly. **Price:** available to members only. **Conventions/Meetings:** annual Charity Ball - meeting.

Tibetan

11055 ■ Tibet Fund (TF)
241 E 32nd St.
New York, NY 10016
Ph: (212)213-5011
Fax: (212)213-1219
E-mail: tibetfund@tibetfund.org
URL: http://www.tibetfund.org
Contact: Mr. Rinchen Dharlo, Pres./Dir.
Founded: 1982. **Staff:** 4. **Budget:** $3,000,000. **Languages:** English, Tibetan. **Description:** Assists in the preservation of Tibetan culture; furthers on-going development of Tibetan arts and sciences; promotes Tibetan contributions to the modern world. Funds Tibetan institutions in exile such as the Tibetan Medical Institute, the Institute of Higher Tibetan Studies, and the Tibetan Institute of Performing Arts, in addition to Tibetan Buddhist monastic institutions now reestablished in India and Nepal. Maintains speakers' bureau; conducts charitable program; compiles statistics. **Libraries: Type:** reference. **Holdings:** archival material, books. **Subjects:** Tibetan history, art, religion. **Programs:** Community Development; Cultural Preservation; Education; Fostering Growth of Other Organizations; Health Care; Old People's Homes; Rehabilitation of New Refugees. **Supersedes:** (1968) Tibetan Foundation. **Publications:** *The Tibet Fund - 10 Year Report*, annual. Brochure.

Time

11056 ■ International Society for the Study of Time (ISST)
442 Brookhurst Ave.
Narberth, PA 19072
E-mail: isst@studyoftime.org
URL: http://www.studyoftime.org
Contact: Dr. Thomas Weissert, Exec. Sec.
Founded: 1966. **Members:** 200. **Membership Dues:** individual, $80 (annual) ● student, $55 (annual). **Multinational. Description:** Scientists and humanists. Explores the idea and experience of time and the role time plays in the physical, organic, intellectual, and social worlds. Encourages interdisciplinary study; provides a forum for exchange of ideas among members. **Awards:** J.T. Fraser Prize. **Frequency:** triennial. **Type:** monetary. **Recipient:** for the author of an outstanding time-related book published during the preceding three years. **Computer Services:** Bibliographic search, Timeline is an online bibliography of time-related books and articles ● database, Kronopedia (Wiki Ticki Tocki) is an encyclopedia of time open to edit by members of the ISST ● mailing lists, ISST-D is for focused discussions of interdisciplinary topics related to the subject of time ● mailing lists, ISST-L is for the dissemination of information among ISST members. **Publications:** *KronoScope*, semiannual. Journal. **Price:** $124.00 for nonmembers (institution); $82.00 for nonmembers (individual); free for members. Alternate Formats: online ● *The Study of Time*, triennial. Book. Contains a series of select and peer-reviewed conference papers. **Price:** $110.00 ● *Time's News*, annual. Newsletter. Contains member news, election ballots, information about upcoming conferences, and council meeting minutes, etc. **Price:** included in membership dues. **Circulation:** 200. Alternate Formats: online. **Conventions/Meetings:** triennial conference, six-day conference of about 100 people usually held at a resort hotel in Europe, Canada, or the United States (exhibits).

Trails

11057 ■ Trail of Tears Association (TOTA)
1100 N Univ., Ste.143
Little Rock, AR 72207
Ph: (501)666-9032
Fax: (501)666-5875
E-mail: totajerra@aol.com
URL: http://www.nationaltota.org
Contact: Jack Baker, Pres.
Membership Dues: general, $25 (annual). **State Groups:** 9. **Description:** Supports the creation, development and interpretation of the Trail of Tears National Historic Trail. Promotes and engages in the protection and preservation of the Trail resources. Promotes awareness of the Trail's legacy, including the effects of the US Government's Indian Removal Policy on the Cherokees and other tribes. Perpetuates the management and development techniques that are consistent with the National Park Service's trail plan. **Computer Services:** database, Geographic Information System. **Publications:** *Trail News*, semiannual. Newsletter.

Translation

11058 ■ American Literary Translators Association (ALTA)
Univ. of Texas at Dallas
PO Box 830688
Richardson, TX 75083-0688
Ph: (972)883-2093
Fax: (972)883-6303
E-mail: lindy.jolly@utdallas.edu
URL: http://www.literarytranslators.org
Contact: Mrs. Lindy Jolly, Admin. Asst.
Founded: 1978. **Members:** 800. **Membership Dues:** library in U.S. and Canada, $75 (annual) ● foreign library, $100 (annual) ● institutional, $150 (annual) ● student, $20 (annual) ● individual in U.S. and Canada, $65 (annual) ● foreign individual, $70 (annual) ● senior (65 and over), $50 (annual) ● joint household, $80 (annual). **Staff:** 2. **Description:** Literary translators who translate from any language into English, and institutions who wish to support such efforts. Works to improve the quality of literary translation; to expand the market and expedite contact between translators and publishers; to upgrade the profession and increase respect in the academic world; to facilitate the exchange of information among translators. **Libraries: Type:** reference. **Holdings:** 1,000; books. **Subjects:** translations and their originals. **Awards:** ALTA Travel Fellowship Award. **Frequency:** annual. **Type:** fellowship. **Recipient:** to beginning translators ● National Translation Award. **Frequency:** annual. **Type:** monetary. **Recipient:** for outstanding translation of a literary work into English. **Publications:** *Translation Review*, semiannual. Journal. Includes reviews of translations, interviews with translators, and articles on translation. ISSN: 0737-4836. **Circulation:** 1,000. **Advertising:** accepted ● Newsletter, 3/year. **Price:** included in membership dues. Alternate Formats: online. **Conventions/Meetings:** annual conference, books (exhibits) - always fall.

11059 ■ Swedish Translators in North America (STiNA)
c/o Laura A. Wideburg, Sec.-Treas.
6008 Corliss Ave. N
Seattle, WA 98103
E-mail: wideburg@ix.netcom.com
URL: http://www.swedishtranslators.org
Contact: Laura A. Wideburg, Sec.-Treas.
Founded: 2004. **Membership Dues:** regular, $15 (annual). **Multinational. Description:** Represents Swedish translators in North America. Promotes and encourages the translation of Swedish literature in all genres into English. Provides a forum for communication and exchange among translators in North America. **Publications:** *Swedish Book Review*. **Price:** included in membership dues.

Turkish

11060 ■ American Research Institute in Turkey (ARIT)
c/o University of Pennsylvania Museum
3260 South St.
Philadelphia, PA 19104-6324
Ph: (215)898-3474
Fax: (215)898-0657
E-mail: leinwand@sas.upenn.edu
URL: http://ccat.sas.upenn.edu/ARIT
Contact: Dr. Nancy Leinwand, Exec. Dir.
Founded: 1964. **Members:** 32. **Membership Dues:** individual, $25 (annual) ● institutional (sliding scale up to $2500), $500 (annual). **Staff:** 6. **Budget:** $600,000. **Description:** Members are institutions of higher learning in the U.S. and Canada. Works to advance knowledge of Turkey and enhance mutual understanding between the U.S. and Turkey by supporting and promoting research and study of the country in all fields of the humanities and social sciences. Research support includes maintaining two research centers in Turkey and administering a program of research fellowships and language study. **Libraries: Type:** reference. **Holdings:** 19,500. **Subjects:** Archaeology; Byzantine, Islamic, Ottoman, modern Turkish studies. **Awards:** ARIT. **Frequency:** annual. **Type:** scholarship. **Recipient:** for scholarly excellence ● ARIT/Department of State, Educational and Cultural Affairs. **Frequency:** annual. **Type:** scholarship. **Recipient:** for scholarly excellence ● ARIT/Mellon. **Frequency:** annual. **Type:** scholarship. **Recipient:** for scholarly excellence ● ARIT/NEH. **Frequency:** annual. **Type:** scholarship. **Recipient:** for scholarly excellence. **Computer Services:** database. **Publications:** *ARIT Newsletter*, semiannual. Provides information on research conditions and institute-sponsored research in Turkey. **Price:** free. **Circulation:** 1,800 ● Monographs ● Also publishes research work of fellows.

11061 ■ Institute of Turkish Studies (ITS)
Intercultural Center, Georgetown Univ.
Box 571033
Washington, DC 20057-1033
Ph: (202)687-0295
Fax: (202)687-3780
E-mail: dcc@turkishstudies.org
URL: http://www.turkishstudies.org
Contact: David C. Cuthelli, Exec. Dir.
Founded: 1982. **Staff:** 2. **Budget:** $350,000. **Description:** Provides funding to research centers and scholars interested in Turkish studies; encourages development of Turkish studies in university curricula. **Awards:** Grant Program in Ottoman and Modern Turkish Studies. **Frequency:** annual. **Type:** scholarship. **Recipient:** for academic and scholarly qualifications. **Publications:** *Multi-Year Report*. Reprint. Alternate Formats: online ● Brochures. **Conventions/Meetings:** periodic conference.

11062 ■ Turkish Studies Association (TSA)
c/o Andras Riedlmayer, Pres.
Fine Arts Lib.
Harvard Univ.
32 Quincy St.
Cambridge, MA 02138
Ph: (617)495-3372
Fax: (617)496-4889
E-mail: riedlmay@fas.harvard.edu
URL: http://www.h-net.org/~thetsa
Contact: Paul Kaldjian, Sec.-Treas.
Founded: 1971. **Members:** 400. **Membership Dues:** regular, associate, $30 ● joint, $40 ● student, $15 ● institutional, $50. **Staff:** 1. **Multinational. Description:** Individual scholars, professional associations, and university libraries interested in Turkish language, history, and culture. Seeks to facilitate communication among members; encourages cooperation with Turkish scholars outside the U.S; promotes high standards of scholarship in the field. **Awards:** Adivar Award. **Frequency:** annual. **Type:** scholarship. **Recipient:** to a qualified undergraduate in any discipline in support of travel to Turkey for the purpose of study or research ● James W. Redhouse Turkish Language Prize. **Frequency:** annual. **Type:** recognition. **Recipient:** for best progress in Turkish language study ● M. Fuat Koprulu Book Prize. **Frequency:** biennial. **Type:** recognition. **Recipient:** for best scholarly book in Turkish studies ● Omer Lutfi Barkan Article Prize. **Frequency:** biennial. **Type:** recognition. **Recipient:** best scholarly article in Turkish studies ● Sydney N. Fisher Graduate Student Paper Prize. **Frequency:** annual. **Type:** recognition. **Affiliated With:** United Nations Educational, Scientific and Cultural Organization. **Publications:** *Turkish Studies Association Journal*, semiannual. Provides research on Turkey and the Ottoman empire. **Price:** included in membership dues. **Circulation:** 300. **Advertising:** accepted. **Conventions/Meetings:** annual meeting, held in conjunction with Middle East Studies Association of North America (exhibits) - always November.

Ukrainian

11063 ■ Ukrainian Academy of Arts and Sciences in the U.S. (UVAN)
206 W 100 St.
New York, NY 10021-1018
Ph: (212)222-1866
Fax: (212)864-3977
URL: http://wotan.liu.edu/~lyudvin
Contact: Dr. Oleska-Myron Bilaniuk, Pres.
Founded: 1950. **Members:** 196. **Membership Dues:** individual, $50 (annual). **Staff:** 2. **Budget:** $60,000. **State Groups:** 2. **Languages:** English, Ukrainian. **Description:** Unites scholars interested in studies pertaining to the Ukraine and Eastern Europe; promotes the development of Ukrainian scholarship in the free world. Maintains museum and archives. **Libraries: Type:** reference. **Holdings:** 70,000; archival material, artwork, books, clippings, periodicals. **Subjects:** Ukrainian scholarship in the free world. **Commissions:** For the Preservation of the Literary Inheritance by Vynnychenko; For the Study of History of Ukrainian-Jewish Relations. **Sections:** Ancient History; Bibliographical; Biological; Economics; Fine Arts; Historical; Literature. **Publications:** *Annals of the Ukrainian Academy of Arts and Sciences in the U.S.* (in English and Ukrainian), periodic. Journal. ISSN: 0503-1001. **Circulation:** 500 ● *Collection of Essays*. Articles. **Price:** $40.00 ● *Fedir Vovk*. Book. **Price:** $35.00 ● *George Shevelov*. Bibliography. **Price:** $25.00 ● *Kulish, Bayda and the Cossacks*. **Price:** $20.00 ● *Language, Nationality, Denationalization*. Brochure. **Price:** $18.00 ● *News of the Academy, Vol. II*, periodic. Contains documents for the study of literature and ideological trends. **Price:** $25.00 ● *125 Years of the Kievan Ukrainian Academic Tradition 1861-1986*. **Price:** $98.00 ● *Ostap Luckyj and His Contemporaries*. **Price:** $20.00 ● *Sources of Modern History of Ukraine Vol. I, II, III and IV*, periodic. Contains annals for the study of literature and ideological trends. **Price:** $98.00 Vol. 17, 18, and 19 in one volume. **Conventions/Meetings:** annual conference (exhibits) - always in New York City.

11064 ■ Ukrainian Educational Council
PO Box 391
Cooper Sta.
New York, NY 10276-0391
Ph: (212)477-1200
Fax: (212)777-7201
E-mail: rada@ridnashkola.org
URL: http://www.ridnashkola.org
Contact: Dr. Eugene Fedorenko, Chm.
Founded: 1969. **Members:** 156. **Description:** Promotes study of history, problems, and present status of people of Ukrainian origin in their demographic, cultural, social, economic, and related aspects; fosters a better understanding of these people, regardless of their religious or political affiliations. Conducts research through questionnaires, interviews, seminars, symposia, and conferences. Arranges special study groups to follow the development and changes of various aspects of cultural and political life of Ukrainian people and disseminates information about their culture. **Formerly:** Ukrainian Center for Social Research. **Publications:** Bulletin, periodic ● Directories ● Has also published a map of the Ukraine.

11065 ■ Ukrainian Institute of America (UIA)
2 E 79th St.
New York, NY 10021
Ph: (212)288-8660
Fax: (212)288-2918
E-mail: programs@ukrainianinstitute.org
URL: http://www.ukrainianinstitute.org
Contact: Walter Nazarewicz, Pres.
Founded: 1948. **Members:** 450. **Membership Dues:** life, with yearly assessments, $1,000. **Staff:** 3. **Budget:** $150,000. **Languages:** English, Polish, Russian, Ukrainian. **Description:** Individuals interested in providing philanthropic, research, educational, and cultural activities. Maintains the collection of the Gritchenko Foundation, church and religious relics, ceramic and woodwork collection, and portraits from the Ukrainian Historical Gallery; sponsors exhibits and concerts. Conducts courses in English language; sponsors Music at the Institute program. Performs community services. Sponsors lectures and presentations for young working professionals. Provides assistance to Ukrainian intellectuals, artists, and musicians immigrating to the U.S. Conducts cultural interchange programs. Sponsors theatrical productions. Maintains Ukrainian Research and Documentation Center. **Libraries: Type:** reference. **Holdings:** 22,000; archival material, books, clippings, periodicals. **Awards:** Ukrainian of the Year Award. **Frequency:** annual. **Type:** recognition. **Computer Services:** database. **Committees:** Arts; Education; Exhibitions; Music; Patents Exhibition; Public Relations. **Publications:** Brochures ● Catalogs ● Newsletter, periodic. **Conventions/Meetings:** annual Art Auction - party - always October or November ● lecture, topics include Ukrainian culture, music, and literature ● annual New Years Gala - meeting.

Urban Affairs

11066 ■ Center for Urban and Regional Studies (CURS)
108 Battle Ln.
Campus Box 3410, UNC
Chapel Hill, NC 27599-3410
Ph: (919)962-3074 (919)962-3076
Fax: (919)962-2518
E-mail: brohe@unc.edu
URL: http://curs.unc.edu
Contact: William M. Rohe, Dir.
Founded: 1957. **Staff:** 10. **Budget:** $5,700,000. **Multinational. Description:** Founded by the Institute for Research in Social Science of the University of North Carolina to facilitate research in urban and regional affairs. Center is concerned with: the investigation of underlying processes responsible for rapid growth and change in the urban scene; the study of problems and issues associated with these processes; the development of systems for the stimulation of urban processes so that policy and program alternatives for achieving local objectives can be tested and their implications studied before putting them into effect. Current research projects include: studies of urban and regional problems such as housing and com-

munity development; coastal zone management; flood hazard management; land use management; urban growth management; water source protection in urbanizing watersheds, brown fields redevelopment, sustainable development and poverty and equity issues. **Libraries: Type:** reference. **Holdings:** 2,500; artwork, books, reports. **Subjects:** housing, community development, economic development, environmental protection, sustainable development, transportation. **Awards:** CURS Scholar in Residence Award. **Frequency:** semiannual. **Type:** scholarship. **Programs:** Carolina Transportation; Smart Growth/New Economy. **Publications:** *Center for Urban and Regional Studies Annual Report*, annual ● *Curs Update*, semiannual. Newsletter ● *Working Paper Series*. Pamphlets ● Monographs ● Also publishes project reports.

Vegetarianism

11067 ■ American Vegan Society (AVS)
56 Dinshah Ln.
PO Box 369
Malaga, NJ 08328
Ph: (856)694-2887
Fax: (856)694-2288
Contact: Freya Dinshah, Pres.

Founded: 1960. **Membership Dues:** regular, $20 (annual) ● low income, student, $10 (annual). **Description:** "Individuals interested in the compassionate, harmless way of life found in Veganism and Ahimsa." Defines Veganism as reverence for all life, especially avoiding cruelty and exploitation of the animal kingdom, including use of a total vegetarian diet and non-animal clothing; Ahimsa is a Sanskrit word for non-killing, non-harming. Outlines six guides, each beginning with a letter of Ahimsa: Abstinence from animal products; Harmlessness with reverence for life; Integrity of thought, word, and deed; Mastery over oneself; Service to humanity, nature, and creation; Advancement of understanding and truth. Conducts lectures, meetings, and training programs on how to live a better life. Maintains educational center. **Affiliated With:** International Vegetarian Union; North American Vegetarian Society. **Publications:** *American Vegan*, quarterly. Magazine. Includes articles on compassionate living, health, nutrition, recipes, reviews, notices, etc. **Price:** $20.00/year; $10.00 low income, students. ISSN: 1536-3767 ● Books. **Conventions/Meetings:** annual Going Vegan - meeting and lecture, with classes, meals, and social entertainment.

11068 ■ Jewish Vegetarian Society - North America (JVSNA)
PO Box 5722
Baltimore, MD 21282-5722

Founded: 1982. **Members:** 2,300. **National Groups:** 13. **Languages:** English, Esperanto, Hebrew, Russian. **Description:** Jewish vegetarians. Objectives are to promote vegetarianism among Jews through education and consciousness-raising activities and to initiate practical plans for dissemination of vegetarian information to governmental agencies and other groups such as the World Health Organization. Publicizes citations in Jewish scripture and Talmudic literature advocating vegetarianism; researches dietetic effects and means of utilization, preparation, and production of vegetarian foods; disseminates information on what the society sees as the cruelty of the meat industry; points out the wholesomeness and healthiness of vegetarian foods; fosters the concept of respect for all life; advances vegetarianism as a solution to world hunger. Organizes related cultural and social activities; provides information on vegetarian culinary, health, travel, and other facilities and services worldwide; sponsors booths at Jewish fairs; produces five-minute vegetarian news broadcasts; offers bibliographies and book reviews; secures health, life, and disability insurance discounts for members. Conducts educational classes on topics such as cruelty to animals, cookery, religious precepts, health, and diet. Participates in projects including establishing homes for elderly vegetarians, developing training for naturopaths, and promoting related youth congresses. Maintains Jewish Vegetarian Matchmaking Service for persons seeking a spouse. Organization is distinct from Jewish Vegetarians of North America. **Libraries: Type:** reference. **Holdings:** 50; books, clippings. **Subjects:** Jewish vegetarianism. **Formerly:** (1982) American Jewish Vegetarian Society; (1989) Jewish Vegetarian Society - America. **Publications:** *Directory of Vegetarian Restaurants and Hotels*, periodic ● *The Jewish Vegetarian*, quarterly ● Membership Directory, periodic ● Newsletter, monthly. **Conventions/Meetings:** annual meeting ● seminar, religious study ● seminar, weekends in cities with a high population of Jewish vegetarians.

11069 ■ Jewish Vegetarians of North America (JVNA)
6938 Reliance Rd.
Federalsburg, MD 21632-2722
Ph: (410)754-5550
E-mail: mail@jewishveg.com
URL: http://www.jewishveg.com
Contact: Israel Mossman, Admin.

Founded: 1984. **Members:** 800. **Staff:** 5. **Description:** Individuals interested in promoting vegetarianism within the Judaic tradition and exploring the relationship between Judaism, dietary law, and vegetarianism; distinct from the Jewish Vegetarian Society - North America. **Affiliated With:** Vegetarian Resource Group. **Also Known As:** Jewish Vegetarians. **Publications:** *Low Fat Jewish Vegetarian Cooking* ● *No Cholesterol Passover Recipes* ● Newsletter, 3/year. Provides dietary information. Includes articles about animal rights, world hunger, and major Jewish holidays, as well as vegetarian and vegan recipes. **Price:** $12.00 /year for nonmembers; $9.00/year for students; included in membership dues. ISSN: 0883-1904. **Circulation:** 1,000. Alternate Formats: online ● Five titles sold by mail order.

11070 ■ North American Vegetarian Society (NAVS)
PO Box 72
Dolgeville, NY 13329
Ph: (518)568-7970
E-mail: navs@telenet.net
URL: http://www.navs-online.org
Contact: Jennie O. Kerwood, Pres.

Founded: 1974. **Members:** 3,800. **Membership Dues:** individual in U.S., $22 (annual) ● family in U.S., $28 (annual) ● individual outside U.S., $29 (annual) ● family outside U.S., $35 (annual) ● life, $600 ● benefactor, $2,500 (annual). **Staff:** 4. **Local Groups:** 155. **Description:** Individual vegetarians and vegetarian organizations. Educates the public and the media about the nutritional, economical, ecological, and ethical benefits of a vegetarian diet. Provides a support network for vegetarians and related groups. Founded World Vegetarian Day (Oct. 1st). Hosts the annual Vegetarian Summerfest Conference. **Awards:** Vegetarian Hall of Fame. **Frequency:** annual. **Type:** recognition. **Publications:** *Good Nutrition* ● *Vegetarian Voice*, quarterly. Magazine. Covers health, dietary cooking and lifestyle, plus issues related to environmental and animal protection; healthful recipes in every issue. **Price:** included in membership dues. ISSN: 0271-1591. **Circulation:** 6,500. Alternate Formats: online ● Also publishes Eat Light, Eat Right: Tips & Recipes: Great-Tasting meals with a fraction of the fat; The Care & Feeding of Vegetarians: A How to Guide for Non-Vegetarians; Heart Smart: Recipes & Tips for Healthier Lifestyle. **Conventions/Meetings:** annual Vegetarian Summerfest - meeting and seminar, educational social event open to vegetarians and interested public (exhibits).

11071 ■ Vegan Action
PO Box 4288
Richmond, VA 23220
Ph: (804)502-8736
Fax: (804)254-8346
E-mail: information@vegan.org
URL: http://www.vegan.org
Contact: Kristine Vandenberg, Exec. Dir.

Founded: 1993. **Members:** 1,600. **Membership Dues:** student, $10 (annual) ● basic, $40 (annual) ● supporter, $100 (annual). **Budget:** $19,000. **Description:** Promotes the vegan diet and lifestyle. Seeks to increase the availability of vegan food. Works to inspire more individuals to become involved in the vegan movement. (A vegan consumes only plant foods, and avoids such foods as dairy and egg products.) Offers educational programs. Sponsors the Vegan Certification Logo (a registered trademark for vegan foods and products). **Libraries: Type:** reference; by appointment only. **Holdings:** articles, books, clippings, periodicals. **Subjects:** health, environment, animal welfare, animal rights. **Awards:** Farm Animal Reform Movement, The Nalith Foundation. **Frequency:** annual. **Type:** grant. **Also Known As:** Vegan Awareness Foundation. **Publications:** *Vegan News*, quarterly. Newsletter. **Price:** free. **Circulation:** 1,000. **Advertising:** accepted. Alternate Formats: online. **Conventions/Meetings:** monthly board meeting.

11072 ■ Vegetarian Awareness Network (VEGANET)
PO Box 321
Knoxville, TN 37901
Free: (800)280-8343
Fax: (865)693-8329
Contact: Lige Weill, Exec. Dir.

Founded: 1980. **Description:** Networks nationally with consumers, communities, and companies. Goals are to encourage eco-friendliness, kindness, and healthfulness for products, people, and the planet; to advance public awareness of the benefits of a vegetarian lifestyle; to assist consumers in making informed dietary decisions; to enhance the visibility and accessibility of vegetarian products and services; to facilitate the formation and expansion of local vegetarian groups; to promote healthful living, environmental healing, and respect for all life. Vegetarian Awareness Month in October. Maintains speakers' bureau; offers information and referral services. **Libraries: Type:** reference. **Awards:** Vegetarian Awareness Month Awards. **Frequency:** annual. **Type:** recognition. **Recipient:** for event promotion achievement. **Computer Services:** database. **Telecommunication Services:** additional toll-free number, from Canada, (800)EAT-VEGE.

11073 ■ Vegetarian Resource Group (VRG)
PO Box 1463
Baltimore, MD 21203
Ph: (410)366-8343
Fax: (410)366-8804
E-mail: vrg@vrg.org
URL: http://www.vrg.org
Contact: Charles Stahler, Co-Dir.

Founded: 1982. **Members:** 20,000. **Membership Dues:** individual in U.S., $20 (annual) ● individual in Canada and Mexico, $32 (annual) ● individual outside U.S., Canada and Mexico, $42 (annual) ● contributor, $30 (annual) ● supporter, $50 (annual) ● sustaining, $100 (annual) ● life, $500. **Staff:** 10. **Description:** Health professionals, activists, and educators working with businesses and individuals to bring about healthy changes in schools, workplaces, and communities. Educates the public about vegetarianism (abstinence from meat, fish, and fowl) and veganism (abstinence from meat, fish, and fowl, and other animal products such as dairy products, eggs, wool and leather). Examines vegetarian issues as they relate to issues of health, nutrition, animal rights, ethics, world hunger, and ecology. Promotes World Vegetarian Day (October 1). Offers internships and children's services. Provides information and referral services. Conducts research. Operates speakers' bureau. Holds cooking demonstrations. **Awards:** Vegetarian Essay Contest. **Frequency:** annual. **Type:** monetary. **Recipient:** for best essay on vegetarianism written by a person, 18 years old or younger ● Vegetarian Resource Group College Scholarship. **Frequency:** annual. **Type:** monetary. **Recipient:** for high school students who have promoted vegetarianism. **Formerly:** (1989) Baltimore Vegetarians. **Publications:** *Conveniently Vegan*. Book. **Price:** $15.00/copy ● *I Love Animals and Broccoli Activity Book* ● *Leprechaun Cake and Other Tales*. Book ● *The Low-fat Jewish Vegetarian Cookbook* ● *Meatless Meals for Working People*. Book. **Price:** $12.00/copy ● *Simply Vegan*. Book. Includes recipes, tips, general information, nutrition data, and shopping sources. **Price:** $12.95/copy ● *Vegan Handbook*. **Price:** included in membership dues; $19.95/copy for nonmembers ● *Vegan in Volume*. Book. **Price:** $20.00/copy ● *Vegan Meals for 1 or 2*. Book. **Price:** $15.00/copy ● *Vegetarian Journal*, quarterly. Contains informative articles, recipes, book reviews, notices about vegetarian events and product evaluations. **Price:** $25.00 for nonmembers; included in membership dues. ISSN: 0885-7636 ● *Vegetarian Journal's Food Service Update*, quarterly. Newsletter. **Price:** $10.00. ISSN: 1072-0820. **Conventions/Meetings:** annual conference (exhibits) ● annual Essay Contest - competition, for students.

Vexillology

11074 ■ Flag Research Center (FRC)
c/o Dr. Whitney Smith, Dir.
PO Box 580
Winchester, MA 01890-0880
Ph: (781)729-9410
Fax: (781)721-4817
E-mail: vexor@comcast.net
URL: http://www.crwflags.com/fotw/flags/vex-frc.html
Contact: Dr. Whitney Smith, Dir.

Founded: 1962. **Members:** 1,370. **Staff:** 3. **Budget:** $200,000. **Description:** Professional and amateur vexillologists (flag historians) seeking to coordinate flag research activities and promote vexillology as a historical discipline and hobby and to increase knowledge of and appreciation for flags of all kinds. Provides data and gives lectures on flag history, etiquette, design, symbolism, and uses. Operates speakers' bureau; offers children's services and placement service; compiles statistics. Plans to establish museum. **Libraries: Type:** reference. **Holdings:** 18,000; archival material, books. **Subjects:** flags, heraldry, posters, charts. **Awards: Type:** recognition. **Affiliated With:** International Federation of Vexillological Associations; North American Vexillological Association. **Publications:** *The Flag Bulletin*, bimonthly. Provides current news and historical articles on flags including their symbolism, usage, and design. Includes book reviews. **Price:** included in membership dues; $32.00 /year for nonmembers; $40.00 /year for institutions. ISSN: 0015-3370. **Circulation:** 1,370. **Advertising:** accepted. Alternate Formats: microform; CD-ROM ● *News from the Vexillarium*, bimonthly ● Books. Contains information on U.S. flags and flags of the world. ● Bibliography. Lists foreign flag items. ● Also publishes flag charts. **Conventions/Meetings:** competition ● annual meeting.

11075 ■ International Federation of Vexillological Associations (FIAV)
c/o Mr. Charles A. Spain, Jr., Sec. Gen.
504 Branard St.
Houston, TX 77006-5018
Ph: (713)529-2545 (713)655-2742
Fax: (713)752-2304
E-mail: sec.gen@fiav.org
URL: http://www.fiav.org
Contact: Mr. Charles A. Spain Jr., Sec. Gen.

Founded: 1969. **Members:** 52. **Staff:** 3. **National Groups:** 52. **Languages:** English, French, German, Spanish. **Multinational. Description:** Unites those associations and institutions throughout the world whose object is the pursuit of vexillology, which is the creation and development of a body of knowledge about flags of all types, their forms and functions, and of scientific theories and principles based on that knowledge. **Awards:** Best Paper Award. **Frequency:** biennial. **Type:** recognition. **Recipient:** for the best paper presented at an International Congress of Vexillology ● Fellow of the Federation. **Frequency:** periodic. **Type:** recognition. **Recipient:** for significant contributions to vexillology and/or significant service to the federation or a federation member ● Laureate of the Federation. **Frequency:** periodic. **Type:** recognition. **Recipient:** for an outstanding, original contribution to the science of vexillology ● Vexillon Award. **Frequency:** biennial. **Type:** recognition. **Recipient:** for the most important contribution to vexillology during the two years preceding an International Congress of Vexillology. **Also Known As:** (1999) Federacion Internacional de Asociaciones Vexilologicas; (1999) Internationale Foderation Vexillologischer Gesellschaften. **Publications:** *Info-FIAV*, semiannual. Newsletter. Includes summaries of the work of the general assembly and board. ISSN: 1560-9979 ● *Report of the International Congress of Vexillology*, biennial. Annual Reports. **Conventions/Meetings:** biennial International Congress of Vexillology, with presentation of papers in the field of vexillology (exhibits) - 2009 July 12-17, Yokohama, Japan - **Avg. Attendance:** 100.

11076 ■ National Flag Foundation (NFF)
Flag Plz.
1275 Bedford Ave.
Pittsburgh, PA 15219
Ph: (412)261-1776
Free: (800)615-1776
Fax: (412)261-9132
E-mail: flag@americanflags.org
URL: http://www.americanflags.org
Contact: Joyce J. Doody, Exec. Dir.

Founded: 1968. **Members:** 4,000. **Membership Dues:** patriot, $50 (annual) ● citizen, $25 (annual) ● Stars and Stripes, $250 (annual) ● Old Glory, $500 (annual) ● Grand Union, $100 (annual). **Staff:** 4. **Budget:** $300,000. **Languages:** English, German. **Description:** Unites to inspire all Americans, especially young people, to have greater respect for the flag and be more responsible citizens. Offers a patriotic education program entitled Young Patriots for use by schools, with Web site, teacher's guide, and three 20-minute video programs with teacher's guides addressing topics of The Pledge of Allegiance, The History of the U.S. Flag, and Flag Etiquette; program can be placed in schools by sponsors paying $100 annual fee for the school. Provides a program called Flags Across America, which is a grassroots initiative to erect a 30-foot by 60-foot flag on a 120-foot pole in every county in the U.S. **Libraries: Type:** open to the public; by appointment only. **Holdings:** 1,000. **Subjects:** flags of select American history. **Awards:** New Constellation Award. **Frequency:** periodic. **Type:** recognition. **Recipient:** for distinguished services rendered on the Flag of America. **Additional Websites:** http://www.youngpatriots.org. **Affiliated With:** International Federation of Vexillological Associations; North American Vexillological Association; United States Flag Foundation. **Formerly:** (1972) Flag Plaza Foundation. **Publications:** *Broad Stripes and Bright Stars*. Book ● *Flag Facts*, quarterly. Newsletter. **Price:** included in membership dues ● *Historic Flags of America*, quarterly. Newsletter. **Circulation:** 3,000. Also Cited As: *Flag Plaza Standard* ● *The New Constellation*, quarterly. Newsletter. **Price:** included in membership dues. **Circulation:** 3,000 ● *Our Flag*. Brochure. Provides informational brochure. ● *Stars, Stripes and Statutes*. Pamphlet ● *You are the Flag*. Pamphlet.

11077 ■ North American Vexillological Association (NAVA)
1977 N Olden Ave. Extension
PMB 225
Trenton, NJ 08618-2193
E-mail: pres@nava.org
URL: http://www.nava.org
Contact: Peter Ansoff, Pres.

Founded: 1967. **Members:** 415. **Membership Dues:** active, $40 (annual) ● organization, $60 (annual) ● associate (spouse, youth, student), $20 (annual). **Budget:** $25,000. **Multinational. Description:** Individuals, organizations, and companies with an interest in history, symbolism, design, manufacture, etiquette, and other aspects of flags. (Vexillology is the scientific and scholarly study of flag history and symbolism). Cooperates with other national, regional, and international associations. Encourages flag scholarship. **Awards:** Vexillonnaire. **Frequency:** annual. **Type:** recognition ● Whitney Award. **Frequency:** periodic. **Type:** recognition. **Recipient:** for outstanding contributions to vexillology ● William Driver Award. **Frequency:** annual. **Type:** monetary. **Recipient:** for best original, previously unpublished paper in the field of vexillology presented at the annual convention. **Computer Services:** Mailing lists. **Affiliated With:** International Federation of Vexillological Associations. **Publications:** *NAVA News*, quarterly. Newsletter. Contains association and vexillological news. **Price:** included in membership dues. ISSN: 1053-3338. **Circulation:** 450. **Advertising:** accepted ● *Raven: A Journal of Vexillology*, annual. Includes juried scholarly articles about flags. **Price:** included in membership dues; $25.00 for nonmembers in North America; $30.00 for nonmembers outside North America. ISSN: 1071-0043. **Circulation:** 450. **Conventions/Meetings:** annual convention (exhibits) - usually October.

11078 ■ United States Flag Foundation (USFF)
Flag Plz.
1275 Bedford Ave.
Pittsburgh, PA 15219
Ph: (412)261-1776
Free: (800)615-1776
Fax: (412)261-9132
E-mail: flag@americanflags.org
URL: http://www.americanflags.org
Contact: Joyce J. Doody, Exec. Dir.

Founded: 1942. **Members:** 4,000. **Membership Dues:** citizen, $25 (annual) ● patriot, $50 (annual) ● grand union, $100 (annual). **Staff:** 5. **Budget:** $300,000. **Languages:** English, German. **Description:** A service mark of National Flag Foundation. Encourages daily and proper display of the flag of the U.S; disseminates information and literature on the origin, history, and significance of the American flag to schools, libraries, teachers, and civic organizations to encourage respect for the flag, responsible citizenship and love of country. **Libraries: Type:** reference. **Subjects:** nationalism. **Affiliated With:** International Federation of Vexillological Associations; National Flag Foundation. **Publications:** *The New Constellation*, 3/year. Newsletter. **Price:** $2.00/copy. **Circulation:** 7,000.

Victorian

11079 ■ North American Victorian Studies Association (NAVSA)
c/o Prof. Dino Franco Felluga, Chm.
Purdue Univ.
Dept. of English
500 Oval Dr.
West Lafayette, IN 47907
Fax: (765)494-3780
E-mail: navsa@purdue.edu
URL: http://www.cla.purdue.edu/academic/engl/navsa
Contact: Prof. Dino Franco Felluga, Chm.

Founded: 2002. **Membership Dues:** student/retired/unaffiliated in U.S., $35 (annual) ● student/retired/unaffiliated outside U.S., $47 (annual) ● regular in U.S., $50 (annual) ● regular outside U.S., $62 (annual) ● joint in U.S., $67 (annual) ● joint outside U.S., $79 (annual). **Multinational. Description:** Provides a forum for the discussion of the Victorian period. Encourages a wide variety of theoretical and disciplinary approaches to the field. Facilitates the networking of Victorianists across regional and national boundaries. Furthers the interests of scholars of the Victorian period. **Awards:** Donald Gray Prize. **Frequency:** annual. **Type:** recognition. **Recipient:** for best essay published in the field of Victorian Studies ● Graduate Paper Prize. **Frequency:** annual. **Type:** recognition. **Recipient:** for the best paper submitted by a graduate student for the annual NAVSA conference ● Student Travel Grant. **Frequency:** annual. **Type:** grant. **Recipient:** for students who have no support for conference attendance from their institutions or other sources. **Telecommunication Services:** electronic mail, felluga@purdue.edu. **Publications:** *Victorian Studies*, quarterly. Journal. Includes interdisciplinary articles on comparative literature, social and political history. **Price:** included in membership dues. Alternate Formats: online. Also Cited As: *VS* ● Newsletter. Alternate Formats: online. **Conventions/Meetings:** annual conference - 2008 Nov. 14-16, New Haven, CT.

11080 ■ Research Society for Victorian Periodicals (RSVP)
c/o Carol Martin, Sec.
English Dept., B 307
Boise State Univ.
Boise, ID 83725
Ph: (208)426-1179
Fax: (208)426-4373
E-mail: secretary@rs4vp.org
URL: http://www.rs4vp.org
Contact: Carol Martin, Sec.

Founded: 1968. **Members:** 700. **Membership Dues:** individual outside Canada, $32 (annual) ● student outside Canada, $25 (annual) ● institution outside Canada, $53 (annual) ● individual in Canada, C$44 (annual) ● student in Canada, C$35 (annual) ● institution in Canada, $64 (annual). **Staff:** 2. **Budget:** $14,000. **Multinational**. **Description:** Scholars from universities in Australia, Canada, Finland, France, Germany, Great Britain, Israel, Japan, Netherlands, New Zealand, South Africa, Spain, Sweden, and the United States. Founded to foster cooperative scholarship necessary to make Victorian periodicals accessible. Hopes to consolidate and improve research by encouraging liaison among all those engaged in the study of Victorian periodicals and to increase awareness of Victorian journals, proprietors, editors, illustrators, and authors. **Awards:** Barbara Quinn Schmidt and Josef Altholz Memorial Travel Award. **Frequency:** annual. **Type:** monetary. **Recipient:** for graduate student members of the society to help defray the cost of travel to the RSVP conference ● VanArsdel Prize. **Frequency:** annual. **Type:** recognition. **Recipient:** for graduate student paper. **Publications:** *Victorian Periodicals Review*, quarterly. Journal. Includes bibliography and book reviews. **Price:** included in membership dues; $30.00 /year for nonmembers; $40.00 /year for libraries. ISSN: 0709-4698. **Circulation:** 750. **Advertising:** accepted ● Membership Directory, biennial ● Also publishes special issues. **Conventions/Meetings:** annual conference, book displays (exhibits).

11081 ■ Victorian Society in America (VSA)
205 S Camac St.
Philadelphia, PA 19107
Ph: (215)545-8340
Fax: (215)545-8379
E-mail: info@victoriansociety.org
URL: http://www.victoriansociety.org
Contact: Bruce Davies, Pres.

Founded: 1966. **Members:** 2,800. **Membership Dues:** individual, $50 (annual) ● household, $60 (annual) ● student, $30 (annual) ● historical society/university/library/historic home/museum, $45 (annual) ● sustaining, $100 (annual) ● contributing/business partner, $250 (annual) ● life, $1,500. **Staff:** 1. **Regional Groups:** 17. **Local Groups:** 17. **Description:** Professionals in the field of museum work; teachers of art, art history, and architecture; preservationists, architects, and laymen. Dedicated to fostering appreciation and understanding of 19th century America and encouraging the protection and preservation of things Victorian. Activities include: public lectures, slide programs, and exhibits; discussion groups; tours of Victorian architecture and art exhibits; summer schools in the U.S. and England. **Libraries: Type:** reference. **Holdings:** 300. **Subjects:** architecture, art, culture. **Awards:** Book Awards. **Frequency:** annual. **Type:** recognition. **Recipient:** for books that best advance an understanding or appreciation of the decorative arts or architecture of the 19th century ● Preservation Awards. **Frequency:** annual. **Type:** recognition. **Recipient:** for preservation excellence ● President's Award. **Frequency:** periodic. **Type:** recognition. **Recipient:** for an individual with an outstanding service or contribution to VSA. **Computer Services:** Mailing lists. **Committees:** Decorative Arts Licensing Program; Development; Education; Preservation; Travel. **Publications:** *19th Century*, semiannual. Magazine. **Price:** $45.00/year. **Circulation:** 3,000. **Advertising:** accepted ● *The Victorian*, quarterly. Newsletter. Provides information on decorative arts and architecture. **Price:** $45.00/year. **Advertising:** accepted ● *Victorian Furniture*. Contains information from symposium papers. ● *Victorian Resorts and Hotels*. Contains information published from symposium papers. **Price:** $25.00 ● *The Victorian Traveler's Companion*. **Conventions/Meetings:** annual conference and meeting ● annual seminar - always spring ● annual symposium - always fall.

Vietnamese

11082 ■ Champa Cultural Preservation Association of USA
PO Box 62061
Sunnyvale, CA 94088-2061
Ph: (408)258-4202 (916)395-3754
Fax: (916)395-3754
E-mail: ccpaoffice@ilimochampa.org
URL: http://www.ilimochampa.org
Contact: Dang Chanh Anh, Pres.

Multinational. **Description:** Seeks to unite all ethnic minorities of Champa people who are currently living in the United States. Preserves, develops, and promulgates the culture and art of Champa people. Researches, studies, and develops the native language of Champa.

Welsh

11083 ■ North American Association for the Study of Welsh Culture and History (NAASWCH)
c/o John S. Ellis, Sec.-Treas.
Dept. of History
Univ. of Michigan
Flint, MI 48502
Ph: (810)762-3366 (810)632-6194
E-mail: ellisjs@umflint.edu
URL: http://spruce.flint.umich.edu/~ellisjs/naaswch.html
Contact: John S. Ellis, Sec.-Treas.

Multinational. **Description:** Promotes scholarship on all aspects of Welsh history and culture. Develops connections between teachers and scholars who are committed to the study of Welsh culture, history, and language in the United States, Canada and the United Kingdom. Provides a forum in which teachers and scholars of Welsh culture and history can share their research and teaching experiences. Provides support for the study of Welsh-North American culture and history. **Publications:** *North American Journal of Welsh Studies*, semiannual. Alternate Formats: online.

Women

11084 ■ Business and Professional Women's Foundation (BPWF)
1900 M St. NW, Ste.310
Washington, DC 20036
Ph: (202)293-1100
Fax: (202)861-0298
E-mail: foundation@bpwusa.org
URL: http://www.bpwfoundation.org
Contact: Deborah L. Frett, CEO

Founded: 1919. **Staff:** 15. **Nonmembership**. **Description:** Dedicated to improving the economic status of working women through their integration into all occupations. Conducts and supports research on women and work, with special emphasis on economic issues. Maintains Marguerite Rawalt Resource Center of 20,000 items on economic issues involving women and work and provides public reference and referral service. **Libraries: Type:** open to the public. **Holdings:** 5,000. **Subjects:** women's issues, economics, social issues. **Awards:** Career Advancement Scholarship. **Frequency:** annual. **Type:** scholarship. **Recipient:** for women in all fields and industries. **Telecommunication Services:** electronic mail, dfrett@bpwusa.org. **Affiliated With:** Business and Professional Women/USA. **Publications:** *Business Woman*, quarterly. Magazine. Features articles reflecting member's concerns including issues affecting working women. **Price:** $12.00/year. **Advertising:** accepted ● *Headquarters News*. Newsletter. Contains up-to-date happenings at the national level and important developments in issues and trends affecting workplace equity. Alternate Formats: online ● *Legislative Hotline*. Report. Provides member current information concerning legislative priorities. Alternate Formats: online ● *Workingwomen Speak Out*. Survey. Provides answers to questions about what is important to workingwomen. Alternate Formats: online ● Also issues publications list. **Conventions/Meetings:** annual Policy and Action Conference, expo with products geared to working women (exhibits).

11085 ■ Catalyst
120 Wall St., 5th Fl.
New York, NY 10005-3904
Ph: (212)514-7600
Fax: (212)514-8470
E-mail: info@catalyst.org
URL: http://www.catalystwomen.org
Contact: Ilene H. Lang, Pres.

Founded: 1962. **Members:** 270. **Membership Dues:** corporate affiliation in U.S., $10,000 (annual) ● corporate affiliation in Canada, C$7,500 (annual) ● business school/professional association, $3,500 (annual). **Staff:** 75. **Budget:** $8,000,000. **For-Profit**. **Multinational**. **Description:** Works to advance women in Business and the professions. Serves as a source of information on women in business for past four decades. Helps companies and women maximize their potential. Holds current statistics, print media, and research materials on issues related to women in business. **Libraries: Type:** by appointment only. **Holdings:** 6,000; articles, books, periodicals. **Subjects:** women in the workforce, women's issues. **Awards:** The Catalyst Award. **Frequency:** annual. **Type:** recognition. **Recipient:** for corporations or professional firms with exemplary initiatives for women's advancement. **Telecommunication Services:** electronic mail, ilenelang@catalyst.org. **Publications:** *Catalyst Census of Women Board Directors of Canada*. Report ● *Catalyst Census of Women Corporate Officers and Top Earners of Canada*. Report. Contains detailed statistics about the women officers in leading Canadian companies. **Price:** $30.00 for nonmembers; $20.00 for members ● *Catalyst Census of Women Corporate Officers and Top Earners of the Fortune 500*. Report ● *Catalyst Census of Women Directors of the Fortune 500*, annual. Report. Lists numbers and names of women on Fortune 1000 boards. **Price:** free for members; $90.00 for nonmembers. Alternate Formats: online ● *The CEO View: Women on Corporate Boards*. Report. Highlights America's Fortune 1000 CEOs expectation on women directors and insights into the written and unwritten criteria for board nomination. **Price:** $90.00 for nonmembers; $60.00 for members ● *Cracking the Glass Ceiling: Strategies for Success, 2000*. Book. Provides up-to-date cases detailing how leading corporations remove barriers to women's advancement to senior leadership. **Price:** $90.00 for nonmembers; $60.00 for members ● *MBA Grads in Info Tech: Women and Men in the Information Technology Industry*. Reports. Contains personal and unique insight into the high tech world. **Price:** $20.00 for nonmembers; $13.34 for members ● *Perspective*, monthly. Newsletter. Covers different human resource topics pertaining to women and information from recent research in today's corporate world. **Price:** free by request. Alternate Formats: online ● *2003 Catalyst Member Benchmarking Report*. Reports. **Price:** $36.00 for nonmembers; $20.00 for members ● A variety of research reports, practical guides and fact sheets examining issues related to women's career advancement and work/life balance are available for purchase. Publication's brochure is available upon request. **Conventions/Meetings:** annual Catalyst Awards Conference - convention, representatives from winning companies provide examinations of initiatives; prominent women in business discuss their paths to leadership - March, in New York City ● annual dinner, includes conference and awards ● regional meeting ● Women, Business and the Media - convention.

11086 ■ Iris Films/Iris Feminist Collective
2600 Tenth St., Ste.413
Berkeley, CA 94710
Ph: (510)845-5414
Fax: (510)841-3336
E-mail: irisweb@aol.com
URL: http://www.irisfilms.org
Contact: Frances Reid, Dir./Producer
Founded: 1975. **Members:** 5. **Staff:** 2. **Budget:** $250,000. **Description:** Produces realistic, entertaining films with strong positive images of women including: "Skin Deep" and "Long Night's Journey Into Day": South Africa's Search for Truth and Reconciliation. **Divisions:** Production. **Formerly:** (1978) Iris Films. **Publications:** *Skin Deep*. Film. Documents race relations on college campuses. **Price:** $195.00 for colleges, universities, large nonprofit; $78.00 for K-12 schools, libraries, small nonprofit; $495.00 for corporations ● *Talking About Race*. Film. **Price:** $110.00 for colleges, universities, large nonprofit; $78.00 for K-12 schools, libraries, small nonprofit. **Conventions/Meetings:** seminar and workshop.

11087 ■ Ladyslipper
PO Box 3124
Durham, NC 27715
Ph: (919)383-8773
Free: (800)634-6044
Fax: (919)383-3525
E-mail: info@ladyslipper.org
URL: http://www.ladyslipper.org
Contact: Laurie Fuchs, Dir.
Founded: 1976. **Staff:** 10. **Description:** Seeks to increase public awareness of the achievements of women artists and musicians and expand the scope and availability of musical and literary recordings by women. Makes available information on recordings by female musicians, writers, and composers. **Computer Services:** Mailing lists. **Publications:** *Ladyslipper Catalog: Resource Guide to Records, Tapes, Compact Discs, and Videos by Women*, triennial. Includes music reviews arranged by artist. **Price:** free. **Advertising:** accepted.

11088 ■ Lesbian Herstory Educational Foundation (LHEF)
PO Box 1258
New York, NY 10116
Ph: (718)768-3953
Fax: (718)768-4663
URL: http://www.lesbianherstoryarchives.org
Contact: Lucinda R. Zoe, Contact
Founded: 1980. **Budget:** $30,000. **Languages:** Dutch, English, French, German, Spanish. **Nonmembership. Multinational. Description:** Works to gather, preserve, and share information on the lives and activities of historical and present day lesbians worldwide. Makes available guest speakers and offers slide shows for schools and community groups. Offers tours and visits on site. Answers research questions. **Libraries: Type:** by appointment only. **Holdings:** 30,000; archival material, audio recordings, books, papers, photographs. **Subjects:** lesbian history and culture, diaries, poetry, prose, memorabilia. **Also Known As:** Lesbian Herstory Archives. **Publications:** *Lesbian Herstory Archives Newsletter*, periodic. Lists lesbian cultural material, bibliographies and reviews; includes research updates. **Price:** $10.00/2 issues. **Circulation:** 10,000 ● Bibliographies.

11089 ■ National Black Herstory Task Force (NBHTF)
PO Box 55021
Atlanta, GA 30308
Ph: (770)369-2700
E-mail: public-relations@blackherstory.org
URL: http://www.blackherstory.org
Contact: Mozella Galloway, Pres./Co-Founder
Founded: 1997. **Membership Dues:** student, $15 (annual) ● general, comrade, ally, $35 (annual) ● chapter affiliate, organizational, $500 (annual) ● life, $2,000. **Description:** Promotes the study and research about women of African descent. Provides vehicles to collect, research, authenticate, document, archive and celebrate the legacies and lives of women of African descent and their alliances. Strives to correct invalid and inaccurate information in the stories of these women through proper documentation. **Telecommunication Services:** electronic mail, herstorian@blackherstory.org. **Publications:** *The Herstorian*, quarterly. Newsletter.

11090 ■ National Women's History Project (NWHP)
3343 Indus. Dr., Ste.4
Santa Rosa, CA 95403
Ph: (707)636-2888
Fax: (707)636-2909
E-mail: nwhp@aol.com
URL: http://www.nwhp.org
Contact: Ms. Molly Murphy MacGregor, Co-Founder/Exec. Dir.
Founded: 1980. **Members:** 4,600. **Membership Dues:** general, $30 (annual) ● sustaining, institutional, $100 (annual) ● sustaining supporter, $500 (annual) ● sustaining sponsor, $1,000 (annual) ● student, $20 (annual). **Staff:** 12. **Budget:** $1,250,000. **Description:** Publishers of semiannual catalog of materials promoting awareness of the history of American women. Encourages multicultural study of women to reclaim contributions and impact of all groups of women and to persuade constructive and expansive social change. Sponsors annual National Women's History Month. Maintains archive for National Women's History Month. Conducts educational training sessions introducing women into curricula and offers educational consulting for teachers, teacher trainers, administrators, and workplace organizers. Sponsors Women's History Network. **Libraries: Type:** reference. **Holdings:** 6,000; archival material, audiovisuals, books, clippings, monographs. **Subjects:** history of women in U.S. **Awards:** National Women's History Honorees. **Frequency:** annual. **Type:** recognition. **Recipient:** for American women with outstanding roles in the transformation of culture, history, and politics. **Formerly:** (1980) National Women's History Week Project. **Publications:** *A History of Women in the United States: State-by-State Reference*. Book. Provides a documentation of women's history in each individual states and a compilation of U.S. and women's history information. **Price:** $399.00 ● *A Reader's Companion*. Book. Provides 400 articles of a diverse, rich panorama of a neglected part of the nation's past. **Price:** $20.00 ● *Enterprising Women*. Book. Contains history of women entrepreneurs in America from the colonial era up the end of 20th century. **Price:** $25.00 ● *The Equal Rights Amendment: Unfinished Business for the Constitution*. Video. **Price:** $24.95 ● *Lesson Plans* ● *Sewing Woman*. Book. **Price:** $135.00 ● *Women's History Catalog*, semiannual. Lists publications, videos, CD-ROMs, and curriculum materials on women's history. **Circulation:** 250,000 ● *Women's History Network Directory*, semiannual. Lists network participants; includes a brief biographical sketch and/or a description of women's history activities. **Circulation:** 650 ● *Women's History Network News*, quarterly. Newsletter. Covers educational resources, commemorative holidays, traveling exhibits, and activities. Includes calendar of events and news of participants. **Circulation:** 650. **Conventions/Meetings:** annual A Woman's Place is in the Curriculum - conference, for teacher training - always July or August.

11091 ■ Red Hat Society (RHS)
431 S Acacia Ave.
Fullerton, CA 92831
Ph: (714)738-0001
Free: (866)FUN-AT50
E-mail: info@redhatsociety.com
URL: http://www.redhatsociety.com
Contact: Sue Ellen Cooper, Exalted Queen Mother
Membership Dues: chapter, $39 (annual) ● individual, $20 (annual). **Description:** Offers nurturing network for women over age 50 with agenda of humor and laughter; promotes visibility of women in that age group. **Computer Services:** Information services, Queen's List broadcasts ● online services, Queen Mother Board postings. **Telecommunication Services:** electronic mail, memberservices@redhatsociety.com. **Publications:** *LifeStyle*, semiannual. Magazine. Contains how-to-crafts, travel excursions, party theme ideas, inspiration on fun and friendship, and much more. **Price:** $19.98/year ● *Red Hat Matters*, quarterly, winter, spring, summer, fall. Magazine. **Price:** $20.00 /year for members; $25.00 /year for nonmembers in U.S.; $40.00 for chapters outside U.S.; $50.00 /year for nonmembers outside U.S. **Conventions/Meetings:** annual convention.

11092 ■ Sisterhood Agenda
524 Ridge St.
Newark, NJ 07104
Ph: (973)230-2765
E-mail: administrator@sisterhoodagenda.com
URL: http://www.sisterhoodagenda.com
Contact: Angela D. Coleman, Pres./CEO
Founded: 1994. **Staff:** 7. **Budget:** $250,000. **Local Groups:** 1. **Description:** Seeks to uplift and aid in the self-development of women and girls of African descent. Addresses the health, cultural, social and economic concerns of women and girls. Offers educational programs, a speakers' bureau, and children's services. **Awards:** Foundation Grants. **Type:** grant. **Recipient:** for state, federal and individuals. **Computer Services:** database ● mailing lists. **Telecommunication Services:** electronic mail, streetteam@sisterhoodagenda.com. **Boards:** Advisory. **Programs:** A Journey Toward Womanhood; Sister Slumber Party; Sisters Healthy and Empowered. **Publications:** Newsletter, bimonthly. **Advertising:** accepted ● Brochure. **Conventions/Meetings:** monthly board meeting.

11093 ■ Women in the Arts (WIA)
PO Box 1427
Indianapolis, IN 46206-1427
Ph: (317)713-1144
E-mail: wia@wiaonline.org
URL: http://www.wiaonline.org
Contact: Sandra Cockerham, Pres.
Founded: 1974. **Members:** 300. **Membership Dues:** individual, $40 (annual) ● family, $60 (annual) ● senior, student, $20 (annual). **Description:** Women artists and women interested in the arts. Works to overcome discrimination against women artists, arrange exhibits of the work of women artists, and protest the under-representation of women artists in museums and galleries. Conducts specialized education programs, and compiles statistics. **Libraries: Type:** reference. **Holdings:** archival material. **Telecommunication Services:** electronic mail, info@wiaonline.org. **Publications:** *Women in the Arts Newsletter*, 3-4/year. Includes book reviews, calendar of events, exhibit announcements, and lists of employment opportunities. **Price:** included in membership dues; $9.00 /year for nonmembers; $15.00 /year for institutions; $19.00/year for foreign institutions. **Circulation:** 400. **Advertising:** accepted. **Conventions/Meetings:** competition ● monthly meeting - always second Wednesday (except January, February, July and August) in New York City.

11094 ■ Women Make Movies (WMM)
462 Broadway, Ste.500WS
New York, NY 10013
Ph: (212)925-0606
Fax: (212)925-2052
E-mail: info@wmm.com
URL: http://www.wmm.com
Contact: Debra Zimmerman, Exec. Dir.
Founded: 1972. **Members:** 400. **Membership Dues:** friend, $50 (annual) ● contributor, $100 (annual) ● sponsor, $250 (annual) ● benefactor, $500 (annual) ● Donor's Circle, $1,000 (annual). **Staff:** 15. **Budget:**

$750,000. **Description:** Individuals devoted to the development of a strong multicultural feminist media that accurately reflects the lives of women. Aims the universal distribution of woman-made productions that encourage audiences to explore the changing and diverse roles women play in the society. Conducts sale or rental of films and videos made by women about issues important to women; filmmakers are available to attend screenings and to speak with audiences about the films and film making process. Distributes more than 300 films and videotapes on topics such as health, gender, equity, and cultural identity. Operates Production Assistance Program designed to assist emerging women artists. **Libraries: Type:** reference. **Computer Services:** Mailing lists, of members. **Telecommunication Services:** electronic mail, dzimmerman@wmm.com. **Publications:** Catalog, annual. Contains up-to-date listings of films/videos. **Price:** $5.00 each; free for institutions, organizations, programmers ● Video. **Price:** $15.00 for academic institutions; $89.00 for K-12 school, public library. **Conventions/Meetings:** workshop and seminar.

11095 ■ Women's History Network (WHN)
c/o National Women's History Project
3343 Indus. Dr., Ste.4
Santa Rosa, CA 95403-2060
Ph: (707)636-2888
Fax: (707)636-2909
E-mail: admin@womenshistorynetwork.org
URL: http://www.nwhp.org
Contact: Molly Murphy MacGregor, Pres./Co-Founder

Founded: 1983. **Members:** 500. **Membership Dues:** individual, $30 (annual) ● student, $20 (annual) ● sustaining supporter, $500 (annual) ● sustaining, institutional, $100 (annual) ● sustaining sponsor, $1,000 (annual). **Staff:** 2. **Description:** A project of the National Women's History Project (see separate entry). Coordinates the recognition and celebration of the contributions of women in U.S. history. Furnishes information, materials, referrals, technical assistance, and support services to aid those who seek to recognize and promote women's achievements. Develops, discovers, and collects ideas and resources for women's history activities for educators, historians, community organizers, workplace activists, and unaffiliated individuals. Maintains a women's history performers' bureau. **Libraries: Type:** reference. **Holdings:** 6,000; archival material, biographical archives, photographs. **Subjects:** women in U.S. history. **Telecommunication Services:** electronic mail, ednasmolly@aol.com. **Publications:** *Network News*, quarterly. Newsletter. Covers multicultural U.S. women's history. **Price:** included in membership dues. ISSN: 1097-0657. **Circulation:** 650 ● *Network Participant Directory*, semiannual.

11096 ■ Women's Interart Center (WIC)
549 W 52nd St.
New York, NY 10019
Ph: (212)246-1050
URL: http://www.ncrw.org/digest/interart.htm
Contact: Margot Lewitin, Artistic Dir.

Founded: 1969. **Members:** 250. **Budget:** $310,000. **Description:** Professional women artists (painters, sculptors, actors, poets, photographers, filmmakers, video artists, writers, ceramists, and serigraphers). Offers opportunities for members to practice their crafts or explore new ones; exchange ideas; meet and work with other artists. Encourages members to explore new areas of expertise. Activities include film and video festival, panels, lectures, demonstrations, and workshops. Facilities include a theatre and a gallery which house events such as poetry readings, theatrical performances, painting, sculpture and photography exhibitions, and seminars and lectures. Maintains video documentary archives of women visual artists and a Fine Arts Museum. **Publications:** *Interart News*, quarterly. Newsletter.

World Notables

11097 ■ Aaron Burr Accord (ABA)
8311 54th Ave. S
Seattle, WA 98118-4702
Ph: (206)725-0873
Contact: Gene Buck PhD, Founder/Pres.

Founded: 1985. **Members:** 505. **Membership Dues:** regular, associate, $30 (annual) ● non-voting, $15 (annual). **Staff:** 3. **Budget:** $475,000. **Regional Groups:** 7. **State Groups:** 50. **Local Groups:** 1. **Multinational. Description:** Seeks to preserve and promote the memory of the Revolutionary War hero and 3rd Vice President, Aaron Burr. Lobbies the U.S. Postal Service to issue a commemorative stamp in memory of Aaron Burr. Conducts educational and research programs. Maintains speakers' bureau. Seeks the exhumation of Aaron Burr and Martin Van Buren to discover if President Van Buren is Aaron Burr's illegitimate son through scientific DNA testing. Strives for posthumous promotion of Aaron Burr to General. Celebrates Col. Burr's birthday each year on February 6 (1756). **Libraries: Type:** not open to the public. **Holdings:** 1,827; archival material, articles, artwork, books, clippings. **Subjects:** Aaron Burr historical events and documents. **Awards:** Aaron Burr Humanitarian Award. **Frequency:** semiannual. **Type:** recognition. **Recipient:** for outstanding contributions to humanity, in general; and to the memory of Aaron Burr, specifically. **Committees:** Aaron Burr Commemorative Stamp League; Aaron Burr Legacy Project. **Formerly:** (1985) Aaron Burr Commemorative Stamp Committee; (1985) Empire of Burravia. **Publications:** *Ye Fitful Mudsling.* Newsletter. Contains news of the activities of the Aaron Burr Accord, and historical notes. **Price:** free for members. **Circulation:** 642. **Advertising:** accepted ● News Releases sent to the media and membership several times each year, as needed. **Conventions/Meetings:** annual conference - always February.

11098 ■ Aaron Burr Association (ABA)
1004 Butterworth Ln.
Upper Marlboro, MD 20774-2205
Ph: (301)641-0494
Free: (800)990-2870
E-mail: peterjtj@aol.com
URL: http://www.aaronburrassociation.org
Contact: Stuart Johnson, Pres.

Founded: 1946. **Members:** 250. **Membership Dues:** interested party of Aaron Burr, $25 (annual). **Staff:** 4. **Description:** Relatives and others interested in the life and career of Colonel Aaron Burr (1756-1836), American political figure who served as Vice President of the U.S. from 1801-05. Conducts historical and genealogical research; Works to correct popular misconceptions about Burr. Disseminates information on related history, publicity, publications, and genealogy. **Libraries: Type:** reference. **Holdings:** archival material, books, clippings, periodicals. **Subjects:** Aaron Burr-life and times. **Publications:** *The Chronicle*, quarterly. Newsletter. Contains members' activities, notice and information on annual meetings and special events. **Price:** included in membership dues. **Conventions/Meetings:** annual meeting, with luncheon and speaker (exhibits).

11099 ■ Abigail Adams Historical Society Inc. (AAHS)
Address Unknown since 2007

Founded: 1947. **Members:** 200. **Membership Dues:** regular, $5 (annual) ● donor, $10 (annual) ● patron, $25 (annual) ● benefactor, $50 (annual) ● life, $100 (annual) ● jounor, $5 (annual). **Description:** Individuals interested in restoring, preserving, and exhibiting, with period furnishings, the birthplace of Abigail Adams (1744-1818), wife of U.S. President John Adams and mother of John Quincy Adams. Maintains library. Membership centered in Weymouth, MA, and nearby towns. **Libraries: Type:** reference; not open to the public. **Publications:** *Abigail's Almanac*, semiannual. Newsletter. Includes information on association activities. **Price:** free. **Advertising:** not accepted. **Conventions/Meetings:** annual dinner and meeting; **Avg. Attendance:** 60.

11100 ■ Abraham Lincoln Association (ALA)
One Old State Capitol Plz.
Springfield, IL 62701-1507
Free: (866)865-8500
E-mail: rhart1213@aol.com
URL: http://www.abrahamlincolnassociation.org
Contact: Richard E. Hart, Pres.

Founded: 1908. **Members:** 850. **Membership Dues:** student, $25 (annual) ● railsplitter, $50 (annual) ● postmaster, $100 (annual) ● lawyer, $250 (annual) ● congressman, $500 (annual) ● president, $1,000 (annual). **Description:** Individuals and organizations interested in Abraham Lincoln (1809-65). Seeks to further the collection, preservation, and dissemination of information on the life of Abraham Lincoln, 16th president of the U.S. **Awards:** Abraham Lincoln Association Student Award. **Frequency:** annual. **Type:** monetary. **Recipient:** for Lincoln essay projects ● Hay-Nicolay Dissertation Prize. **Frequency:** annual. **Type:** monetary. **Recipient:** for best dissertation in Lincoln studies ● Lincoln The Lawyer Award. **Frequency:** periodic. **Type:** recognition. **Recipient:** for lawyers who reflect the character and ideals of Abraham Lincoln in their legal careers ● Logan-Hay Medal. **Frequency:** periodic. **Type:** medal. **Recipient:** for individuals who have made noteworthy contributions to the mission of the association. **Formerly:** (1923) Lincoln Centennial Association. **Publications:** *Abraham Lincoln Association—Journal*, semiannual. Contains presentations made by Lincoln scholars at the symposium. Includes award news, conference news, and book and periodical listing. **Price:** included in membership dues; $70.00 /year for nonmembers in U.S.; $185.00 /year for institutions in U.S. ISSN: 0890-4212. **Circulation:** 750. **Advertising:** accepted ● *The Collected Works of Abraham Lincoln.* Alternate Formats: online ● *For the People*, quarterly. Newsletter. Contains information about Abraham Lincoln and member news. ● Monographs ● Also publishes speeches. **Conventions/Meetings:** annual symposium and banquet - always February 12 in Springfield, IL.

11101 ■ Albert Schweitzer Fellowship (ASF)
330 Brookline Ave.
Boston, MA 02215
Ph: (617)667-5111
Fax: (617)667-7989
E-mail: info@schweitzerfellowship.org
URL: http://www.schweitzerfellowship.org
Contact: Dr. Lachlan Forrow MD, Pres.

Founded: 1939. **Members:** 1,000. **Staff:** 5. **Regional Groups:** 7. **Languages:** English, French. **Description:** Provides year-long community service fellowships for graduate students in health-related disciplines. Makes available fellowships for New England and New York area medical students to work at the Schweitzer Hospital in Lambarene, Gabon. Supports the Schweitzer Hospital in Gabon and its Community Health Program, and distributes publications by and about Dr. Albert Schweitzer; community service fellowships for 2003 are in Baltimore, Boston, Chicago, New Hampshire/Vermont, North Carolina, and Pittsburgh. **Telecommunication Services:** electronic mail, lforrow@bidmc.harvard.edu. **Publications:** *Reverence*, 3/year. Newsletter. Includes publication lists; describes activities of the U.S. and Lambarene Schweitzer Fellows Programs and information on Albert Schweitzer. **Price:** free. Also Cited As: *The Courier* ● Books ● Pamphlets.

11102 ■ American Friends of Lafayette (AFL)
316 Markle Hall
Lafayette Coll.
Easton, PA 18042
E-mail: blkbooks@comcast.net
URL: http://www.friendsoflafayette.org
Contact: William Kirchner, Pres.

Founded: 1932. **Members:** 125. **Membership Dues:** active, $20 (annual) ● sustaining, $30 (annual) ● student, $5 (annual) ● family, $35 (annual) ● individual, life, $200 ● institutional, life, $250 ● corporate, $250 (annual) ● benefactor, $1,000 (annual). **Description:** Individuals, historical societies, universities, and colleges interested in the study of the Marquis de Lafayette (1757-1834), Frenchman who fought in the American Revolution. Promotes historical research relative to Lafayette through the collection of books, manuscripts, documents, and other associated material. Promotes the traditional friendship between the U.S. and France of which Lafayette is a symbol. Maintains collection at Lafayette College, Easton, PA. **Libraries: Type:** open to the public. **Holdings:** 2,500; biographical archives, books, papers. **Subjects:** Marquis de Lafayette. **Awards:** Liberty Award. **Frequency:** annual. **Type:** recognition. **Recipient:** for service in the spirit of the Marquis de LaFayette. **Publications:** *Gazette* (in English and French), annual. Newsletter. **Price:** included in membership dues. **Circulation:** 150. **Conventions/Meetings:** annual conference.

11103 ■ Bolivarian Society of the United States
Address Unknown since 2007
Founded: 1941. **Members:** 60. **Membership Dues:** individual, $25 (annual) ● corporate, $100 (annual) ● life, $500. **Staff:** 1. **Budget:** $5,000. **Description:** Currently inactive. Businessmen, college faculty and students, and others interested in the "contributions of Simon Bolivar (1783-1830) to independence and unity in the Americas. " Maintains library. **Convention/Meeting:** none. **Libraries: Type:** not open to the public. **Subjects:** Simon Bolivar.

11104 ■ Buckminster Fuller Institute (BFI)
181 N 11th St., Ste.402
Brooklyn, NY 11211
Ph: (718)290-9280
Free: (800)967-6277
Fax: (718)290-9281
E-mail: contact@bfi.org
URL: http://www.bfi.org
Contact: Elizabeth Thompson, Exec. Dir.
Founded: 1983. **Members:** 1,200. **Membership Dues:** student/senior/fixed income, $20 (annual) ● basic, $35-$99 (annual) ● associate, $100-$249 (annual) ● supporter, $250-$499 (annual) ● patron, $500-$999 (annual) ● benefactor (minimum), $1,000 (annual). **Staff:** 3. **Description:** Individuals committed to a successful and sustainable future for 100&percent; of humanity; inspired by the design science principles pioneered by the late Buckminster Fuller. Serves as an information resource to students, educators, authors, designers, and concerned citizens working to advance humanity's option for success. Provides educational and networking assistance; archives reside at Stanford University in Palo Alto, CA. **Libraries: Type:** reference. **Holdings:** archival material, articles, books. **Computer Services:** database ● information services, Fuller Information Exchange. **Absorbed:** (1983) Friends of Buckminster Fuller Foundation. **Publications:** *Trimtab Bulletin*, quarterly. Newsletter. Features news and resources related to whole systems solutions to humanity's challenges. **Price:** free, for members only. **Circulation:** 1,600 ● Bulletin, monthly. Alternate Formats: online. **Conventions/Meetings:** annual board meeting and general assembly.

11105 ■ Buffalo Bill Historical Center (BBHC)
720 Sheridan Ave.
Cody, WY 82414-3428
Ph: (307)587-4771
Free: (800)533-3838
E-mail: bobs@bbhc.org
URL: http://www.bbhc.org
Contact: Robert E. Shimp PhD, Exec. Dir.
Founded: 1927. **Members:** 6,805. **Membership Dues:** student, $20 (annual) ● Pahaska League, $2,000 (annual) ● Cody Firearms Museum, $150-$1,000 (annual) ● business friend, $150 (annual) ● individual, $35 (annual) ● family/household, $60 (annual) ● centennial, grand centennial, $100 (annual) ● sponsor, corporate sponsor, $250 (annual) ● sustainer, corporate sustainer, $500 (annual) ● benefactor, corporate benefactor, $1,000 (annual) ● corporate, corporate associate, $2,500 (annual) ● corporate contributor, $5,000 (annual) ● corporate founder, $10,000 (annual). **Staff:** 89. **Languages:** English, French, German, Italian, Japanese, Spanish. **Description:** Operates five separate museums: The Buffalo Bill Museum, Whitney Gallery of Western Art, Cody Firearms Museum, the Plains Indian Museum and the Draper Museum of Natural History, as well as the McCracken Research Library. **Libraries: Type:** by appointment only; reference. **Holdings:** 30,000; archival material, articles, audio recordings, books, periodicals, photographs. **Subjects:** American Western history and art, Plains Indian ethnography and art, firearms technology, photography, music. **Awards:** Cody Award for Western Design. **Frequency:** annual. **Type:** recognition. **Recipient:** to leaders in the field of Western design. **Publications:** *Points West*, quarterly. Journal. Alternate Formats: online ● Annual Report, annual. **Price:** free. **Circulation:** 6,805.

11106 ■ C.A.L./N-X-211 Collectors Society
Address Unknown since 2008
Founded: 1988. **Members:** 232. **Membership Dues:** regular, $20 (annual). **Staff:** 4. **Description:** Individuals interested in the life of Charles A. Lindbergh (1902-74), American aviator who made the first solo nonstop transatlantic flight from New York to Paris, France in his monoplane, The Spirit of St. Louis. Perpetuates the memory of Lindbergh through the collection of Lindbergh and N-X-211 memorabilia. This includes the study of the development (before and after the flight) of the aircraft, the Spirit of St. Louis, and later models. Offers appraisal services. **Awards:** Lone Eagle Award. **Frequency:** annual. **Type:** recognition. **Recipient:** for outstanding continued efforts for the society. **Publications:** *Spirit of St. Louis*, quarterly. Newsletter. Contains member profiles and activities, and C.A.L/N-X-211 history. **Price:** included in membership dues. **Circulation:** 310. **Advertising:** accepted. **Conventions/Meetings:** annual symposium (exhibits).

11107 ■ Calvin Coolidge Memorial Foundation (CCMF)
PO Box 97
Plymouth, VT 05056
Ph: (802)672-3389
Fax: (802)672-3369
E-mail: info@calvin-coolidge.org
URL: http://www.calvin-coolidge.org
Contact: Cynthia D. Bittinger, Exec. Dir.
Founded: 1960. **Members:** 680. **Membership Dues:** individual, $35 (annual) ● family, $50 (annual) ● contributing, $100 (annual) ● supporting, $250 (annual) ● sustaining, $500 (annual) ● benefactor, $1,000 (annual). **Staff:** 2. **Budget:** $70,000. **Description:** Individuals interested in Calvin Coolidge (1872-1933), the 30th President of the United States. Seeks to perpetuate the memory of Coolidge and to interpret his life, times, and presidential administration. Provides educational programs; maintains museum. Maintains speakers' bureau. Maintains the Union Christian Church. Foundation is located in Plymouth, VT, Coolidge's birthplace and site of his 1923 presidential inauguration. **Libraries: Type:** reference. **Holdings:** 300; archival material, audiovisuals, books, periodicals. **Subjects:** Coolidge and his era. **Awards:** Calvin Coolidge Notary Award. **Frequency:** annual. **Type:** recognition. **Recipient:** for government officials ● Coolidge Scholarship. **Frequency:** annual. **Type:** monetary. **Recipient:** for Vermont or Massachusetts college student. **Telecommunication Services:** electronic mail, cbittinger@calvin-coolidge.org. **Publications:** *Calvin Coolidge Memorial Foundation—Newsletter*, periodic. **Price:** included in membership dues. Alternate Formats: online ● *News Bulletins*, periodic ● *The Real Calvin Coolidge*, annual. Journal. Provides rare photographs and original research, both current and reprinted, on President Calvin Coolidge. Includes book reviews. **Price:** $5.95. **Circulation:** 700 ● Books ● Also publishes educational materials. **Conventions/Meetings:** annual convention - usually July 4, Coolidge's birthday ● annual Plymouth Old Home Day - meeting - always first weekend of August in Plymouth, VT.

11108 ■ Captain Eddie Premier Gala
Address Unknown since 2007
Founded: 1988. **Staff:** 14. **Nonmembership. Description:** Admirers of Captain Edward Vernon Rickenbacker (18901973), U.S. air ace of World War I and president of Eastern Air Lines. Seeks to commemorate Rickenbacker's life and times, and to "educate future generations of the United States of America about the freedoms this man believed in." Successfully campaigned to have Rickenbacker's likeness placed on a U.S. postage stamp in 1995; currently works to construct Rickenbacker's boyhood home replica in Columbus, OH upon a museum campus. Conducts educational programs; operates museum; maintains speakers' bureau. " Capt. Eddie Rickenbacker, a patriot of these United States of America, who sincerely believed that if we do not, selfishly and with great strength, defend this nation (morally, politically, and militarily), we, as a people, will lose forever the precious freedoms we now enjoy.". **Conventions/Meetings:** annual board meeting - always January.

11109 ■ Churchill Centre
1150 17th St. NW, Ste.307
Washington, DC 20036
Ph: (202)223-5511
Free: (888)WSC-1874
Fax: (202)223-4944
E-mail: dmyers@winstonchurchill.org
URL: http://www.winstonchurchill.org
Contact: Daniel Myers, Exec. Dir.
Founded: 1968. **Members:** 3,000. **Membership Dues:** friend in North America, $50 (annual) ● friend outside North America, $A 60 (annual) ● undergraduate, C$10 (annual) ● contributor, $100 (annual) ● sustainer, $150 (annual) ● supporter, $250 (annual) ● benefactor, $500 (annual) ● fellow, $1,000 (annual) ● Number Ten Club, $10,000 (annual). **Staff:** 2. **Budget:** $500,000. **State Groups:** 8. **Local Groups:** 20. **Multinational. Description:** Historians, students, and individuals interested in the life and times of Rt. Hon. Sir Winston Spencer Churchill (1874-1965), British statesman and historian. Preserves the memory and legacy of Churchill and his theme of unity among the English-speaking peoples. Develops and sponsors teacher and student seminars; symposia, conferences, and colloquia; and, sponsors the annual Churchill Lecture on topics of current import. Publishes a quarterly journal, periodic membership newsletter, and biennial Conference Proceedings. **Libraries: Type:** not open to the public. **Holdings:** 2,500. **Subjects:** Sir Winston Churchill. **Awards:** Blenheim. **Frequency:** periodic. **Type:** recognition ● Emery Reves. **Frequency:** periodic. **Type:** recognition. **Recipient:** for literary achievement ● Farrow. **Frequency:** annual. **Type:** recognition. **Recipient:** for excellence in Churchill studies ● Finest Hour Journal Award. **Frequency:** annual. **Type:** recognition. **Recipient:** for the best article published in the centre's journal within the last 4 issues. **Computer Services:** Bibliographic search, works by and about Churchill. **Affiliated With:** American Philatelic Society; American Topical Association. **Formerly:** (1981) Winston S. Churchill Study Unit; (1998) International Churchill Society - United States. **Publications:** *The Dream.* Book ● *Finest Hour*, quarterly. Journal. **Price:** available to members only. ISSN: 0882-3715. **Circulation:** 3,500. Alternate Formats: online ● *The Orders, Decorations and Medals of Sir Winston Churchill.* Book ● *Thoughts and Adventures*, periodic. Book. Consists of 23 essays. ● Proceedings, semiannual. **Price:** available to members only ● Pamphlets. **Conventions/Meetings:** annual conference ● annual International Churchill Conference (exhibits) - 2008 Sept. 30, Boston, MA; 2009 Sept. 30, San Francisco, CA ● annual international conference ● semiannual seminar.

11110 ■ Edison Birthplace Association (EBA)
c/o Edison Birthplace Museum
PO Box 451
Milan, OH 44846
Ph: (419)499-2135
Fax: (419)499-2135
E-mail: rwheeler@accnorwalk.com
URL: http://www.tomedison.org
Contact: Robert K.L. Wheeler, Pres.
Founded: 1950. **Members:** 97. **Membership Dues:** student, $5 (annual) ● individual, $25 (annual) ● family, $50 (annual) ● special friend, $100 (annual) ● life, $1,000 ● corporate sponsor, $5,000 (annual). **Staff:** 2. **Budget:** $70,000. **Description:** Persons who contribute to an endowment fund for the purpose

of perpetuating the Thomas Alva Edison Birthplace Museum, which opened in 1947 in Milan, OH. Edison (1847-1931), the inventor, was born in Milan, and the museum has been designated as a National Historic Landmark. Provides specialized education program. **Conventions/Meetings:** annual meeting, for trustees ● tour.

11111 ■ Franklin and Eleanor Roosevelt Institute (FERI)
4079 Albany Post Rd.
Hyde Park, NY 12538
Ph: (845)486-1150
Fax: (845)486-1151
E-mail: info@feri.org
URL: http://www.feri.org
Contact: Christopher N. Breiseth, Pres./CEO
Founded: 1987. **Membership Dues:** individual, $35 (annual) ● family, $60 (annual) ● new dealer, $100 (annual) ● Cuff Links Club, $250 (annual) ● Brains Trust, $500 (annual) ● student (17-22), $15 (annual). **Staff:** 6. **Budget:** $1,000,000. **Description:** Initiates and cosponsors projects that celebrate and perpetuate the heritage and values of Franklin (1882-1945) and Eleanor Roosevelt (1884-1962), especially in the fields of social studies, human rights, youth, and social policy. **Awards:** FDR Four Freedoms Medals. **Frequency:** annual. **Type:** medal. **Recipient:** to individual contributions for promoting one or more of FDR's four freedoms ● FDR International Disability Award. **Frequency:** annual. **Type:** monetary. **Recipient:** for nations who have made significant progress toward meeting the needs of citizens with disabilities ● Grants-in-Aid to Scholars. **Frequency:** semiannual. **Type:** grant. **Recipient:** to scholars for research at the FDR Library. **Supersedes:** Eleanor Roosevelt Institute; Franklin D. Roosevelt Four Freedoms Foundation. **Publications:** *The View From Hyde Park*, semiannual. Newsletter. Includes news of the Roosevelt Institute and the FDR Library and Museum, brief historical articles, and lists of grant recipients. **Price:** included in membership dues. **Conventions/Meetings:** annual board meeting.

11112 ■ Frederick A. Cook Society (FACS)
c/o Russell W. Gibbons, Exec. Dir./Ed.
207 Grandview Dr. S
Pittsburgh, PA 15215
Ph: (412)782-0171
Fax: (412)784-8801
E-mail: frederick@cookpolar.org
URL: http://www.cookpolar.org
Contact: Russell W. Gibbons, Exec. Dir./Ed.
Founded: 1940. **Members:** 278. **Membership Dues:** individual, $15 (annual) ● couple, $20 (annual) ● family, $25 (annual) ● life, $100. **Staff:** 1. **Description:** Persons who are interested in the contention that Dr. Frederick A. Cook (1865-1940) led the first expedition to reach the North Pole. Seeks to gain official recognition for the scientific and geographic accomplishments of the American physician and explorer, including his arrival at the North Pole on Apr. 21, 1908. Questions the popular belief that Robert E. Peary reached the North Pole first; calls this view a distortion of history. Conducts research and corresponds with geographers, historians, and scholars interested in polar exploration. Maintains Dr. Frederick A. Cook Exhibit Room in the Sullivan County Museum, Art and Cultural Center in Hurleyville, NY, and collections at the Library of Congress and at the Byrd Polar Research Center including archives and collections of photographs from Dr. Cook's Mt. McKinley Expeditions (1903 and 1906), North Pole Expedition (1907-09), and the Belgian Antarctic Expedition (1897-99). **Libraries: Type:** reference. **Holdings:** 200; archival material, audiovisuals, books, clippings, monographs, periodicals. **Subjects:** polar history and geography. **Awards:** Ruth Cook Hamilton Scholarship. **Frequency:** annual. **Type:** scholarship. **Publications:** *Frederick A. Cook Society Membership News*, semiannual. Newsletter. Features up-to-date information and news. **Price:** included in membership dues ● *Polar Priorities*, annual. Journal. Contains professional papers and commentary. **Price:** included in membership dues; $25.00 /year for nonmembers. ISSN: 1086-4881. **Circulation:** 460. **Advertising:** accepted ● Also publishes historical studies, technical abstracts, and reprints of Cook papers. **Conventions/Meetings:** annual meeting and symposium - usually September or October.

11113 ■ Friends of the Abraham Lincoln Museum (FLC)
c/o Abraham Lincoln Museum
Lincoln Memorial Univ.
6965 Cumberland Gap Pkwy.
Harrogate, TN 37752
Ph: (423)869-6235 (423)869-3611
Free: (800)325-0900
Fax: (423)869-6350
E-mail: thomas.mackie@lmunet.edu
URL: http://www.lmunet.edu
Contact: Dr. Thomas Mackie, Dir.
Founded: 1898. **Staff:** 6. **Budget:** $150,000. **Description:** Sponsored by the Abraham Lincoln Museum of Lincoln Memorial University. Conducts general studies, as well as historical, biographical, and bibliographic writing. Examines other phases of research on the life of Abraham Lincoln (1809-65), President of the U.S. during the Civil War, 1861-65. Research includes study of the Civil War, nineteenth century America, and the biographical study of Abraham Lincoln. Sponsors speakers' bureau; conducts specialized education program. Maintains museum of more than 25,000 Lincoln and Civil War items. **Convention/Meeting:** none. **Libraries: Type:** reference. **Holdings:** 700; archival material, artwork, audiovisuals, books, clippings, periodicals. **Subjects:** Civil War, Abraham Lincoln, Lincolniana, Civil War sheet music. **Awards:** Lincoln Diploma of Honor. **Frequency:** annual. **Type:** recognition. **Recipient:** for individuals who have major and significant contribution to the study of Abraham Lincoln. **Computer Services:** Online services. **Formerly:** (1988) National Lincoln Civil War Council. **Publications:** *Lincoln Herald*, quarterly. Journal. Contains information on Abraham Lincoln and the Civil War. **Price:** $20.00/year in U.S.; $30.00/year outside U.S. ISSN: 0024-3671. **Circulation:** 1,000. **Advertising:** accepted ● *Lincoln Letters*, quarterly. Newsletter.

11114 ■ Friends of Franklin (FOF)
PO Box 40048
Philadelphia, PA 19106
Ph: (856)833-1771
Fax: (856)854-0773
E-mail: info@benfranklin2006.org
URL: http://friendsoffranklin.org
Contact: Roy E. Goodman, Pres.
Founded: 1990. **Members:** 235. **Membership Dues:** Franklin, $100 (annual) ● corporate, $1,000 (annual) ● Ben For Life, $1,500. **Multinational. Description:** Individuals and organizations with an interest in the life and work of American philosopher, inventor, and diplomat Benjamin Franklin (1706-90). Promotes the study of Franklin and his times; works to "translate and promote the spirit of Benjamin Franklin." Serves as a clearinghouse on Franklin and his work. Facilitates exchange of information among members. Sponsors educational programs. **Libraries: Type:** reference. **Subjects:** Benjamin Franklin. **Publications:** *Benjamin Franklin 1706-1790*. Book. **Price:** $9.95/copy ● *The Franklin Gazette*, quarterly. Newsletter. **Price:** included in membership dues. **Conventions/Meetings:** Benjamin Franklin Tour - tour and lecture.

11115 ■ Friends of Patrick Henry (FPH)
PO Box 1776
Hanford, CA 93232
Ph: (559)582-8534 (559)584-5209
Fax: (559)584-4084
E-mail: liberty89@libertygunrights.com
URL: http://www.libertygunrights.com
Contact: Bernadine Smith, Dir.
Founded: 1983. **Staff:** 5. **Description:** Promotes the teachings of Patrick Henry (1736-99), renowned orator and American Revolutionary War leader, and defends the U.S. Constitution. Promotes responsible citizenship. Sponsors lectures and seminars. **Convention/Meeting:** none. **Publications:** *Patrick Henry Letter*, periodic.

11116 ■ Friends of Peace Pilgrim (FoPP)
PO Box 2207
Shelton, CT 06484-1207
Ph: (203)926-1581
E-mail: info@peacepilgrim.org
URL: http://www.peacepilgrim.org
Contact: Bruce Nichols, Board Member
Founded: 1982. **Budget:** $45,000. **Nonmembership. Description:** Aims to provide information about the life and work of a woman who called herself Peace Pilgrim (Mildred Norman Ryder 1908-1981). Publishes and freely distributes books, booklets, and other materials about Peace Pilgrim's life and message. **Publications:** *Friends of Peace Pilgrim Newsletter*, 3/year. Alternate Formats: online.

11117 ■ Gabriel Garcia Moreno Memorial Association (GGMMA)
PO Box 826
Prentiss, MS 39474
Ph: (601)792-5708
Contact: John C. Moran, Dir.
Founded: 1975. **Members:** 32. **Staff:** 3. **Languages:** English, Spanish. **Multinational. Description:** Works to commemorate the martyrdom and defend the memory of Dr. Garcia Moreno (1821-75), President of Ecuador and to work for his canonization. Also encourages and promotes Catholic social and moral principles in the public order. Maintains speakers' bureau. **Convention/Meeting:** none. **Libraries: Type:** reference. **Holdings:** 27; archival material. **Subjects:** Garcia Moreno. **Publications:** *In Memoriam: Gabriel Garcia Moreno 1875-1975*. Book.

11118 ■ George C. Marshall Foundation (GCMF)
c/o VMI Parade
PO Drawer 1600
Lexington, VA 24450
Ph: (540)463-7103
Free: (800)578-8524
Fax: (703)464-5229
E-mail: marshallfoundation@marshallfoundation.org
URL: http://www.marshallfoundation.org
Contact: Wesley B. Taylor Jr., Pres.
Founded: 1953. **Membership Dues:** individual, $25-$49 (annual) ● friend, $50-$99 (annual) ● sponsor, $100-$499 (annual) ● President's Club, $500-$999 (annual) ● associate, $1,000-$2,499 (annual) ● society, $2,500-$4,999 (annual) ● five-star, $5,000 (annual). **Staff:** 25. **Description:** Formed to honor General George Catlett Marshall (1880-1959) through preservation of documents and memorabilia bearing on his 50 years of public service. (General Marshall was chief of staff of the U.S. Army in World War II, envoy to China in 1946, U.S. Secretary of State from 1947-49, President of the Red Cross from 1949-50, and Secretary of Defense from 1950-51. Under President Harry S. Truman's direction, he proposed what became the Marshall Plan for postwar aid to Europe and in 1953 he was awarded the Nobel Peace Prize.) The Foundation's building, completed in 1964, is situated between Virginia Military Institute, where Marshall was a cadet and First Captain graduating in the class of 1901, and Washington and Lee University. The museum section, open to the public, includes Marshall's personal possessions, photographs, cartoons, clippings, flags, an electric map of allied progress in World War II, and various exhibits. Leading a project to edit the papers of George Catlett Marshall is an ongoing special project. Sponsors special exhibits. **Libraries: Type:** reference. **Holdings:** 30,000; archival material, audio recordings, books, papers, periodicals. **Subjects:** twentieth-century U.S. military, political and diplomatic history, General Marshall. **Awards:** George C. Marshall/Baruch Fellowship. **Frequency:** annual. **Type:** fellowship. **Recipient:** for doctoral/postdoctoral work ● Marshall Undergraduate Scholarship. **Frequency:** annual. **Type:** scholarship. **Recipient:** for undergraduates. **Computer Services:** Online services, library catalog. **Publications:** *The Authorized Biography of George C. Marshall*. Book. Contains four-volume work. **Price:** $67.50 soft cover ● *The Edited Papers of George Catlett Marshall*. Book. Contains four-volume work. ● *George C. Marshall Founda-*

tion—Topics, quarterly. Newsletter. **Price:** free. **Circulation:** 9,000. Alternate Formats: online ● *George C. Marshall ROTC Award Seminar Report*, annual. Contains texts of speeches and roundtables presented during the annual three-day seminar for outstanding ROTC cadets. **Price:** free. **Circulation:** 3,500 ● *George C. Marshall's Mediation Mission to China, December 1945-January 1947* ● *Interviews and Reminiscences for Forrest Pogue*. Book. Features an edited transcription of George C. Marshall's interviews with Dr. Forrest Pogue, official biographer. ● Report, annual. **Price:** free. **Circulation:** 1,000. **Conventions/Meetings:** quarterly Marshall - meeting and lecture ● annual ROTC Award Seminar, covers the national security of the U.S; winners of the George C. Marshall Army ROTC Award (College Seniors) - always spring.

11119 ■ Hall of Fame for Great Americans (HFGA)
c/o Bronx Community College
Univ. Ave. at W 181st St.
Bronx, NY 10453
Ph: (718)289-5161
URL: http://www.bcc.cuny.edu/halloffame
Contact: Susan Zuckerman, Contact
Founded: 1900. **Staff:** 3. **Budget:** $50,000. **Description:** Honors distinguished Americans by an election process. Displays the bronze bust and inscribed plaque (98 installed) of each elected person in the Colonnade of the Hall of Fame at Bronx Community College, Bronx, NY. Conducts guided tours; provides children's services; sponsors educational programs. **Libraries: Type:** not open to the public. **Holdings:** 100,000. **Subjects:** college education. **Awards:** Municipal Arts Society of N.Y. **Type:** recognition ● 1999 N.Y. Landmarks Conservancy. **Type:** recognition. **Publications:** *Hall of Fame Face-to-Face History*. Brochure. Alternate Formats: online. **Conventions/Meetings:** quarterly N.Y. State Division of Tourism Halls of Fame - meeting.

11120 ■ Harry S. Truman Library Institute for National and International Affairs
500 W U.S. Hwy. 24
Independence, MO 64050
Ph: (816)268-8248 (816)268-8200
Free: (800)833-1225
Fax: (816)268-8295
E-mail: truman.library@nara.gov
URL: http://www.trumanlibrary.org
Contact: Ms. Lisa A. Sullivan, Admin. Dir.
Founded: 1957. **Members:** 1,250. **Membership Dues:** basic, $35 (annual) ● family, $50 (annual) ● associate, $120 (annual) ● diplomat, $250 (annual) ● ambassador, $500 (annual) ● benefactor, $750 (annual) ● presidential, $1,000 (annual). **Staff:** 9. **Description:** Individuals from all types of backgrounds interested in the objectives of the institute. Supports the Truman Library and promotes its interests as a research center; named for the 33rd President of the U.S. Harry S. Truman (1884-1972). Provides grants-in-aid to scholars working in the Truman period; fosters scholarly publications; supports special research projects; and sponsors conferences at which some aspect of the Truman administration or research of the Truman years is examined. **Libraries: Type:** open to the public. **Awards:** Dissertation Year Fellowship. **Frequency:** annual. **Type:** grant. **Recipient:** for graduate students ● Harry S. Truman Book Award. **Frequency:** biennial. **Type:** recognition. **Recipient:** for the best book on Harry S. Truman or the period of his presidency ● Research Grant. **Frequency:** semiannual. **Type:** grant. **Recipient:** for graduate students and postdoctoral scholars ● Scholars Award. **Frequency:** annual. **Type:** grant. **Recipient:** for postdoctoral scholars. **Committees:** Research, Scholarship and Academic Relations. **Publications:** *Whistle Stop*, quarterly. Newsletter.

11121 ■ Henry Clay Memorial Foundation (HCMF)
120 Sycamore Rd.
Lexington, KY 40502
Ph: (859)266-8581
Fax: (859)268-7266
E-mail: info@henryclay.org
URL: http://www.henryclay.org
Contact: Ann Hagan-Michel, Exec. Dir.
Founded: 1926. **Membership Dues:** friend of Ashland (family), $45 (annual) ● friend of Ashland (donor), $50 (annual) ● friend of Ashland (contributing), $100 (annual) ● friend of Ashland (supporting), $500 (annual) ● friend of Ashland (sustaining), $1,000 (annual) ● Henry Clay Society, $5,000 (annual) ● friend of Ashland (individual), $25 (annual). **Staff:** 10. **Budget:** $300,000. **Description:** Maintains Ashland, The Henry Clay Estate in Lexington, KY, as a historic house museum and National Historic Landmark. Open to the public since 1950. Clay (1777-1852) was a statesman, senator, Whig candidate for President, Secretary of State, and a leading figure in the development of fiscal policies and the concept of Pan-Americanism. **Libraries: Type:** reference. **Holdings:** archival material, artwork, books, business records, periodicals, photographs. **Subjects:** Clay family. **Awards:** Henry Clay Award for Distinguished Service. **Frequency:** annual. **Type:** medal. **Telecommunication Services:** electronic mail, ahmichel@henryclay.org. **Also Known As:** (2006) Ashland, The Henry Clay Estate. **Publications:** *Newsletter of Ashland, the Henry Clay Estate*, quarterly. **Price:** included in membership dues. **Circulation:** 2,000. **Advertising:** accepted. **Conventions/Meetings:** quarterly board meeting.

11122 ■ Herbert Hoover Presidential Library Association (HHPLA)
PO Box 696
West Branch, IA 52358
Ph: (319)643-5327
Free: (800)828-0475
Fax: (319)643-2391
E-mail: info@hooverassociation.org
URL: http://www.hooverassociation.org
Contact: Rebeckah Allgood, Exec. Dir.
Founded: 1954. **Members:** 1,000. **Membership Dues:** individual, $45 (annual) ● dual, $65 (annual) ● family, $80 (annual) ● sponsor, $125 (annual) ● associate, $250 (annual) ● patron, $500 (annual) ● benefactor, $1,000 (annual) ● President's Circle, $5,000 (annual). **Staff:** 5. **Description:** Fosters the collection, interpretation, and preservation of historical resources relating to the life, ideas, and times of Herbert Hoover (1874-1964), 31st President of the U.S. Promotes public education about appreciation for Herbert Hoover. Supports the Hoover Presidential Library-Museum and the National Historic Site at West Branch, Iowa. **Awards:** Herbert Hoover Book Award. **Frequency:** annual. **Type:** monetary. **Recipient:** for a scholarly publication on history between 1914 and 1964 ● Herbert Hoover Travel Grant. **Frequency:** annual. **Type:** grant. **Recipient:** for specific research projects at the Hoover Presidential Library ● Hoover Uncommon Student Award. **Frequency:** annual. **Type:** scholarship. **Recipient:** for Iowa high school students ● Hoover Young Engineer Award. **Frequency:** annual. **Type:** recognition. **Recipient:** for the best engineering project at state and regional middle school and high schools' science fairs. **Formerly:** Herbert Hoover Birthplace Foundation. **Publications:** *The American Road*, quarterly. Newsletter. Contains membership information. **Price:** included in membership dues ● Also publishes Hoover's writings. In 1996, published the revised edition of The Herbert Hoover Family Genealogy by Hulda Hoover McLean. **Conventions/Meetings:** periodic seminar.

11123 ■ Houdini Historical Center/Outagamie County Historical Society (HHC/OCHS)
330 E Coll. Ave.
Appleton, WI 54911-5715
Ph: (920)733-8445 (920)735-9370
E-mail: terry@myhistorymuseum.org
URL: http://www.foxvalleyhistory.org
Contact: Terry Bergen, Exec. Dir.
Founded: 1872. **Members:** 365. **Membership Dues:** individual, $25 (annual) ● student, senior, $15 (annual) ● family, $50 (annual) ● professional, $75 (annual) ● contributor, $125 (annual) ● life, $1,000. **Staff:** 10. **Description:** Inspires people to discover the history of the Fox River Valley through exhibition, collections, and educational programs. Holds strong collection of material relating to the history of magician Harry Houdini (born Ehrich Weiss, 1874-1926). Gathers, interprets, and disseminates information and preserves artifacts on the life and times of Houdini. Sponsors permanent exhibition, a tour of downtown Appleton (Houdini's home town), and related special events. Conducts research and educational programs; offers children's services. Maintains museum; conducts youth magic workshops. **Libraries: Type:** reference. **Holdings:** archival material, clippings, maps, papers, photographs. **Subjects:** history of Outagamie County and the Lower Fox River Valley, Harry Houdini. **Awards:** Carolyn Kellogg Historic Preservation Award. **Frequency:** annual. **Type:** recognition. **Recipient:** to a person who has demonstrated exemplary effort to maintain, restore, or reuse a historic structure or object ● Lillian Mackesy Historian of the Year Award. **Frequency:** annual. **Type:** recognition. **Recipient:** to a research project about some aspect of Outagamie County history that results in a visual, oral, or written presentation to the public. **Publications:** *History Today*, quarterly. Newsletter. Includes scholarly information on Fox River Valley history. **Price:** included in membership dues. **Circulation:** 365.

11124 ■ International Society for Hildegard Von Bingen Studies (ISHBS)
c/o Prof. Pozzi Escot, Pres.
24 Avon Hill
Cambridge, MA 02140
Ph: (617)868-0215 (765)285-8456
Fax: (617)868-0215
E-mail: pescot@newenglandconservatory.edu
Contact: Prof. Pozzi Escot, Pres.
Founded: 1984. **Members:** 420. **Membership Dues:** individual, $10 (annual) ● student, $5 (annual). **Staff:** 3. **Multinational. Description:** Scholars worldwide interested in the study of Hildegard Von Bingen (1098-1179), a 12th century German mystic who wrote texts concerning theology, the arts, and the sciences, composed music, and served as an adviser to various kings and popes. Researches Von Bingen's works; disseminates information. **Publications:** *Qualelibet*, semiannual. Newsletter. Contains news of members' activities and essays. **Price:** included in membership dues. **Circulation:** 500. **Advertising:** accepted. **Conventions/Meetings:** annual Bridges to Infinity - festival, with plenary speakers, exhibit, poetry, banquet, presenters and concerts (exhibits) ● annual conference, with concerts (exhibits) - always May, Kalamazoo, MI.

11125 ■ James Beard Foundation (JBF)
167 W 12th St.
New York, NY 10011
Ph: (212)675-4984 (212)627-2308
Free: (800)36-BEARD
Fax: (212)645-1438
E-mail: info@jamesbeard.org
URL: http://www.jamesbeard.org
Contact: Izabela Wojcik, Dir. of House Programming
Founded: 1986. **Members:** 4,400. **Membership Dues:** associate, $125 (annual) ● fellow, $150-$250 (annual) ● professional, $175-$275 (annual) ● Chairman's Circle, $500 (annual) ● corporate, $600 (annual) ● student, $35 (annual) ● donor, $1,000-$4,999 (annual) ● patron, $5,000-$9,999 (annual) ● benefactor, $10,000 (annual). **Staff:** 25. **Description:** Seeks to honor James Beard (1903-85), the "Father of Fine Cooking in America", and advance the recognition and appreciation of the culinary arts in the U.S. Maintains Beard's house in New York City for use as a culinary resource space, library, and archive. Activities include: special dinners from around the world; demonstrations and workshops with guest cooking teachers; wine tastings and wine maker dinners; monthly professional networking luncheons; monthly Italian luncheons. Offers scholarship program. **Libraries: Type:** reference. **Holdings:** 2,000. **Subjects:** fine cooking, James Beard. **Awards:** The James Beard Awards. **Frequency:** annual. **Type:** medal. **Computer Services:** Mailing lists, of members. **Committees:** Development; Garden; Kitchen; Library; President; Scholarship and Apprenticeship.

Publications: *Beard House*, quarterly ● *Calendar and Newsletter*, monthly ● *The James Beard Foundation Directory of Fine Food and Beverage Professionals*, annual ● *The James Beard Foundation Restaurant Directory*, annual.

11126 ■ James Buchanan Foundation for the Preservation of Wheatland (JBF)
1120 Marietta Ave.
Lancaster, PA 17603
Ph: (717)392-8721
Fax: (717)295-8825
E-mail: marketing@wheatland.org
URL: http://www.wheatland.org
Contact: Timothy A. Mackey, Pres.
Founded: 1936. **Members:** 500. **Membership Dues:** individual, $40 (annual) ● family/grandfamily, $60 (annual) ● Legislator, $175 (annual) ● Congressman, $250 (annual) ● Cabinet, $1,000 (annual) ● Presidential, $2,500 (annual). **Staff:** 10. **Description:** Maintains and operates Wheatland mansion in Lancaster, PA, former home of James Buchanan (1791-1868), 15th President of the United States. Operates tours April through November. **Formerly:** (2003) James Buchanan Foundation. **Publications:** Newsletter, quarterly. **Price:** included in membership dues.

11127 ■ James K. Polk Memorial Association (JKPMA)
c/o Polk Home
PO Box 741
Columbia, TN 38402
Ph: (931)388-2354
Fax: (931)388-5971
E-mail: jameskpolk@bellsouth.net
URL: http://www.jameskpolk.com
Contact: Mr. John Holtzapple, Dir.
Founded: 1924. **Members:** 1,200. **Membership Dues:** individual/family, $40 (annual) ● benefactor, $100 (annual). **Staff:** 2. **Budget:** $150,000. **Description:** Works to the preserve the memory of James K. Polk (1795-1849), 11th president of the United States. Conducts educational programs about Polk and his contributions to the U.S. Maintains historic Polk Home in Columbia, TN. **Publications:** *Polk Notes*, semiannual. Newsletter. **Conventions/Meetings:** annual luncheon.

11128 ■ James Monroe Memorial Foundation (JMMF)
1009 Bainbridge St.
Richmond, VA 23224
Ph: (804)231-1827
E-mail: pres@monroefoundation.org
URL: http://www.monroefoundation.org
Contact: G. William Thomas Jr., Pres.
Founded: 1928. **Description:** Aims to increase the size and scope of the James Monroe Law Office Museum and Memorial Library and the James Monroe Freedom Scholarship Program. Promotes adherence to the Monroe Doctrine through public education. James Monroe (1758-1831) was fifth President of the United States, 1817-25. Museum contains relics and papers relating to Monroe; extensive library contains manuscripts, pamphlets, and other materials on Monroe and his contemporaries, the Monroe Doctrine, U.S. diplomatic relations with Latin America from Monroe's time to the present, Virginiana, and Americana. Museum is housed in the original building in which Monroe practiced law from 1786-89 and contains personal possessions of Monroe and his family, including Louis XVI furniture (the first furniture used in the White House after its burning by the British in War of 1812). Conducts research, provides specialized education program, and promotes educational activities. Sponsors competitions. On Apr. 1, 1964, the museum and library were deeded to the state of Virginia by the foundation, which continues to manage the property through the Foundation's secretary. **Publications:** *James Monroe: An Appreciation* ● *The People, The Sovereigns* ● Books ● Pamphlets. **Conventions/Meetings:** annual Garden Reception - meeting - always April 28 (President Monroe's birthday).

11129 ■ Jefferson Davis Association (JDA)
Rice Univ., MS 43
PO Box 1892
Houston, TX 77251-1892
Ph: (713)348-4990
Fax: (713)348-4383
E-mail: davis@rice.edu
URL: http://jeffersondavis.rice.edu
Contact: Bertram Hayes-Davis, Pres.
Founded: 1963. **Staff:** 3. **Description:** Cosponsors (with Rice University) of the preparation and publication of *The Papers of Jefferson Davis*, a 15-volume edition of the letters, papers, and speeches of Jefferson Davis (1808-89), president of the Confederacy, 1861-65. The project is endorsed by the National Historical Publications and Records Commission, which has contributed several grants to the association, supported by the National Endowment for the Humanities, the State of Mississippi, and other corporate and individual donations; a recipient of the Centennial Medallion of the Civil War Centennial Commission and the Founders Award of the Museum of the Confederacy. Published by the Louisiana State University Press. **Also Known As:** The Papers of Jefferson Davis. **Publications:** Book, periodic.

11130 ■ John Ericsson Society (JES)
c/o Mr. Leif Brisfjord, Pres.
5 E 48th St.
New York, NY 10017
Ph: (973)464-2038 (973)746-0074
E-mail: info@johnericsson.org
URL: http://www.johnericsson.org
Contact: Mr. Leif Brisfjord, Pres.
Founded: 1907. **Members:** 140. **Membership Dues:** individual, $20 (annual) ● life, $200. **Languages:** English, Swedish. **Description:** Engineers and others interested in perpetuating and honoring the memory of Captain John Ericsson (1803-89), Swedish-American inventor of the screw propeller for marine navigation and designer of the Civil War vessel, Monitor. Promotes historical research of and disseminates information on Ericsson's life and works. Gathers and preserves books, manuscripts, papers, and relics; marks places of historical interest. **Libraries: Type:** open to the public; by appointment only. **Holdings:** 15; archival material, articles, books, business records, photographs, video recordings. **Subjects:** John Ericsson, USS monitor, inventions, civil war. **Awards:** Achievement Award in Memory of John Ericsson. **Frequency:** annual. **Type:** monetary. **Recipient:** for students of John Ericsson Junior High School in Brooklyn, New York. **Computer Services:** Mailing lists. **Publications:** *John Ericsson Society Newsletter*, quarterly. Contains information on society and Ericsson. **Price:** included in membership dues. **Circulation:** 200. Alternate Formats: diskette. **Conventions/Meetings:** meeting and dinner (exhibits) - 4-6/year.

11131 ■ John Pelham Historical Association (JPHA)
c/o Bill Gilmore, Treas.
210 Old Gabblettville Rd.
West Point, GA 31833
E-mail: info@gallantpelham.org
URL: http://www.gallantpelham.org
Contact: Brett Bradshaw, Pres.
Founded: 1982. **Members:** 200. **Membership Dues:** individual, $20 (annual) ● family and international, $25 (annual). **Description:** Individuals interested in the life of Lt. Col. John Pelham (1838-1863), the Cavalry campaigns of the Army of Northern Virginia, and other aspects of the American Civil War (1861-65). (Pelham was a major in the Confederate army who fought at the battles of Manassas, Antietam, and Fredericksburg. He was awarded the rank of Lieutenant Colonel posthumously.) Seeks to establish and maintain a museum. Preserves and erects monuments to Col. Pelham; promotes education and interest in the Colonel's life. **Libraries: Type:** open to the public. **Holdings:** archival material, books, maps, papers, photographs. **Subjects:** Lt. Col. John Pelham (1838-1863). **Committees:** Archives; Monuments. **Publications:** *The Cannoneer*, bimonthly. Newsletter ● Booklets. **Conventions/Meetings:** annual dinner - usually early September.

11132 ■ Kahlil Gibran Memorial Foundation (KGMF)
The Carriage House
1 St. Matthews Ct. NW
Washington, DC 20036
Ph: (202)331-7738
Fax: (202)331-7739
E-mail: anawaty@aol.com
Contact: William Anawaty, Legal Counsel
Founded: 1983. **Staff:** 1. **Description:** Strives to foster intercultural communication and understanding through the commemoration of Kahlil Gibran (1883-1931), Lebanese-born philosopher, poet, novelist, and artist. Supports creation of an archive in the U.S. to house the work and related memorabilia of Gibran. Donated a Kahlil Gibran memorial garden to the American people in Washington, DC in 1991. Plans to organize cultural and educational activities in the future. **Convention/Meeting:** none. **Committees:** Honorary. **Formerly:** Kahlil Gibran Centennial Foundation.

11133 ■ Ladies' Hermitage Association (LHA)
4580 Rachel's Ln.
Hermitage, TN 37076
Ph: (615)889-2941
Fax: (615)889-9289
E-mail: info@thehermitage.com
URL: http://www.thehermitage.com
Contact: Patricia Leach, Pres./CEO
Founded: 1889. **Members:** 1,500. **Membership Dues:** individual, $45 (annual) ● family, household, $60 (annual) ● Congressman's Circle, $200 (annual) ● Senator's Circle, $500 (annual) ● General's Circle, $1,000 (annual) ● President's Circle, $2,500 (annual) ● student, teacher, $20 ● senior, $40 ● dual, $50. **Staff:** 75. **Budget:** $2,500,000. **Description:** Individuals interested in Andrew Jackson (1767-1845), 7th President of the U.S., 1829-37, the Jackson family, and preservation of related historic properties. His Tennessee residence is known as The Hermitage. Maintains 700-acre historic Jackson plantation including the Hermitage mansion, Tulip Grove mansion, Old Hermitage Church, other historic buildings, and Andrew Jackson Visitors Center. Conducts archaeological excavations on the grounds of The Hermitage. Sponsors Andrew Jackson Papers Project which publishes all of Jackson's papers. Maintains museum of artifacts owned by Jackson, his wife Rachel, and other family members. **Awards:** Lewis Donelson Award. **Frequency:** annual. **Type:** recognition. **Recipient:** for outstanding preservation efforts for The Hermitage. **Programs:** Adult Education; Scout Patch. **Publications:** *Guide Book to Jackson Properties* ● *The Jacksonian*, 3/year. Newsletter. **Price:** included in membership dues. **Circulation:** 2,500. **Conventions/Meetings:** semiannual meeting - always in Hermitage, TN.

11134 ■ Leif Ericson Viking Ship (LEVS)
PO Box 393
Swarthmore, PA 19081-0393
Ph: (410)275-8516
Fax: (410)275-8516
E-mail: info@vikingship.org
URL: http://www.vikingship.org
Contact: Steven A. Clarke, Pres.
Founded: 1992. **Members:** 200. **Membership Dues:** Leif, $1,000 (annual) ● sustaining, $500 (annual) ● contributing, $100 (annual) ● Norstead, $50 (annual) ● voting, $30 (annual) ● friend, $20 (annual). **Multinational. Description:** Aims to educate all Americans about Leif Ericson as the first European known to have discovered and settled on the North American Continent. Promotes knowledge and a realistic historic image of Viking people as merchants, navigators, shipbuilders, artists, explorers and warriors. Provides sail training and practice in recreating the experience of traveling on water as the Vikings did a thousand years ago. **Libraries: Type:** reference. **Holdings:** archival material. **Subjects:** Leif Ericson's discovery of North America, early North American settlements. **Awards:** Viking of the Year Award. **Fre-**

quency: annual. **Type:** recognition. **Computer Services:** Information services, an FAQ section for school kids and others to learn more about Vikings, Vikingships and Leif Ericson. **Committees:** Education; Vikingship. **Formerly:** (1968) Leif Ericson Society International. **Publications:** *The Norseman News*, 3/year. Newsletter. **Price:** free for members. **Advertising:** accepted. Alternate Formats: online. **Conventions/Meetings:** monthly board meeting, with exhibits and a sale of "Viking" items (exhibits) ● competition, involving the group Viking ship, The Norseman.

11135 ■ Little Bighorn History Alliance (LBHA)
PO Box 1752
Niceville, FL 32588
Ph: (850)897-4505
Fax: (850)897-4505
E-mail: lbha@cox.net
URL: http://www.LittleBighorn.info
Contact: Mrs. Diane Merkel, Founder
Founded: 1967. **Members:** 575. **Staff:** 0. **Multinational. Description:** Consists of students, historians, collectors, writers, and others who are invited to explore the history of the Battle of the Little Bighorn without bias or bigotry. **Libraries: Type:** not open to the public. **Computer Services:** Information services, answers questions from the public. **Telecommunication Services:** electronic bulletin board, message boards. **Formerly:** (2007) Little Big Horn Associates.

11136 ■ Martin Van Buren Fan Club (MVBFC)
c/o Gary L. Holloway, Pres.
778 14th St.
San Francisco, CA 94114
Ph: (415)626-0676
E-mail: cepi@aol.com
URL: http://members.aol.com/litpulp/mvbfc/marty.html
Contact: Gary L. Holloway, Pres.
Founded: 1975. **Members:** 1,000. **Membership Dues:** life, $15 ● life (senior and junior), $5. **Description:** Individuals interested in preserving the history and promoting highlights of the life of Martin Van Buren (1782-1862), 8th President of the U.S. **Libraries: Type:** reference. **Holdings:** archival material. **Awards:** Marty Award. **Frequency:** annual. **Type:** recognition. **Publications:** *OK News*, periodic. **Price:** included in membership dues. **Circulation:** 700. **Conventions/Meetings:** annual dinner - always Saturday closest to Martin Van Buren's birthday (December 5), San Francisco, CA.

11137 ■ Morris-Jumel Mansion
65 Jumel Terr.
New York, NY 10032
Ph: (212)923-8008
URL: http://www.morrisjumel.org
Contact: James L. Kerr Esq., Pres.
Founded: 1904. **Members:** 500. **Membership Dues:** friend, $35 (annual) ● family, $55 (annual) ● Madame Jumel Circle, $100 (annual) ● Roger Morris Circle, $250 (annual) ● Aaron Burr Circle, $500 (annual) ● George Washington Circle, $1,000 (annual) ● Octagon Society, $2,500 (annual) ● student, senior, $25 (annual). **Staff:** 7. **Budget:** $230,000. **Description:** Represents the interests of persons interested in maintaining as a historic house museum the Morris-Jumel Mansion, which was General George Washington's headquarters in New York in September and October of 1776. Conducts tours for adult education groups, school classes, and other interested groups; sponsors art and history lectures, exhibits, and workshops; offers internship programs; maintains speakers' bureau and children's services. **Libraries: Type:** reference. **Holdings:** 250; biographical archives. **Subjects:** history of mansion. **Committees:** Development; Historic Preservation; Interiors; Programs. **Programs:** Adult; Children's; School. **Formerly:** (1990) Washington Headquarters Association. **Publications:** *Calendar of Events*, quarterly ● *Morris-Jumel Mansion: A Historical View*. Book. Contains photographs and analysis of history, architecture, programs and collections. ● Newsletter, semiannual. Covers topics related to the Morris-Jumel Mansion including research, history, and upcoming events. **Price:** included in membership dues. **Circulation:** 500 ● Brochures. **Price:** free. **Circulation:** 2,500 ● Catalogs. **Conventions/Meetings:** annual meeting - always third Tuesday of September.

11138 ■ Mount Vernon Ladies' Association (MVLA)
PO Box 110
Mount Vernon, VA 22121
Ph: (703)780-2000 (703)799-8606
Fax: (703)799-8609
E-mail: info@mountvernon.org
URL: http://www.mountvernon.org
Contact: Mr. James C. Rees, Exec. Dir.
Founded: 1853. **Membership Dues:** Palladian society, $50-$99 ● Piazza society, $100-$249 ● Colonnade society, $250-$499 ● Cupola society, $500-$999 ● Regent's circle, $1,000-$4,999 ● Mount Vernon one hundred, $5,000-$9,999 ● Washington council, $10,000. **Budget:** $12,000,000. **Description:** Dedicated to the preservation of the home and tomb of George Washington (1732-99), the first President of the U.S. and his wife Martha (1731-1802) at Mount Vernon, VA. Restores and maintains home of George Washington; open to public every day of year. Promotes returning to Mount Vernon all objects related to the domestic life of George and Martha Washington. Conducts research and educational programs; operates children's programs. **Libraries: Type:** by appointment only. **Holdings:** 12,000; books, photographs. **Subjects:** George Washington, Mount Vernon, 18th-Century history, decorative arts. **Telecommunication Services:** TDD, (703)799-8121. **Also Known As:** Mount Vernon Ladies' Association of the Union; Mount Vernon Estate and Gardens. **Publications:** *The Gardens and Grounds at Mount Vernon: How George Washington Planned and Planted Them*. Book ● *George Washington: A Brief Biography*. Book ● *Mount Vernon: A Handbook*. **Price:** $4.00 ● *Yesterday, Today, Tomorrow*, semiannual. Newsletter. **Circulation:** 6,000 ● Annual Report, annual. **Circulation:** 4,000 ● Also publishes cookbooks, children's activity and coloring books, and other books about George Washington and Mount Vernon. **Conventions/Meetings:** semiannual meeting - always in Mount Vernon, VA.

11139 ■ Napoleonic Historical Society (NHS)
6000A W Irving Park Rd.
Chicago, IL 60634
Ph: (610)581-0280
Fax: (810)581-0400
E-mail: staff@napoleonic-society.com
URL: http://www.napoleonic-society.com
Contact: Douglas J. Allan, Pres./CEO
Founded: 1983. **Members:** 465. **Membership Dues:** student, in U.S., $24 (annual) ● regular, $48 (annual) ● chevalier, $100 (annual) ● officer, $250 (annual) ● commander, $500 (annual) ● grand officer, $750 (annual) ● Grand Cross, $1,000 (annual) ● regular Canada, $52 (annual) ● student, Canada, $26 (annual) ● regular (all other countries), $62 (annual) ● student (all other countries), $31 (annual). **Budget:** $60,000. **Multinational. Description:** Individuals interested in the life and times of Napoleon Bonaparte (1769-1821), Emperor of France. Facilitates exchange among individuals interested in Napoleon. Offers reprints and synopses of works on Napoleon and provides bibliographical information; reports on auctions and private sales of Napoleonic memorabilia; announces museum shows, movies, and television documentaries; provides travel tours to Malmaison, Versaille, Paris, Fontainebleau, Corsica, Elba, St. Helena, Waterloo, Austerlitz, and other battlefields. Conducts annual conferences. **Libraries: Type:** reference. **Holdings:** 800; articles, books, periodicals. **Awards:** Napoleonic Historical Society Annual Literary Award. **Frequency:** annual. **Type:** recognition. **Recipient:** for the best book on the Napoleonic period published in the prior year ● Napoleonic Society Literary Award. **Frequency:** annual. **Type:** recognition. **Recipient:** to the single best book published in the prior year on the Napoleonic period. **Formerly:** (1999) Napoleonic Society; (2007) Napoleonic Society of America. **Publications:** *First Empire*, bimonthly. Magazine. **Circulation:** 3,500. **Advertising:** accepted. **Conventions/Meetings:** annual conference (exhibits).

11140 ■ National Register of Prominent Americans and International Notables (NRPA&IN)
Drawer 1375
Washington, DC 20013-1375
Ph: (301)565-5155
Contact: Geoffery Parsons PhD, Exec. Dir.
Founded: 1956. **Members:** 7,600. **Staff:** 3. **Description:** Individuals who have made outstanding achievements and contributions to their professions, communities, businesses, states, or countries. Supports preservation of national historic landmarks; worldwide conservation and environmental efforts. Addresses future status of recognized arts and sciences. **Libraries: Type:** reference. **Also Known As:** National Register Association. **Publications:** Bulletin, periodic.

11141 ■ Patton Society (PS)
c/o Charles M. Province, Pres./Founder
17010 S Potter Rd.
Oregon City, OR 97045
E-mail: pattonhq@hotmail.com
URL: http://www.pattonhq.com
Contact: Charles M. Province, Pres./Founder
Founded: 1970. **Members:** 300. **Membership Dues:** corporal, $15 (annual) ● sergeant, $20 (annual) ● warrant officer, $25 (annual) ● captain, $50 (annual) ● major, $75 (annual) ● colonel, $100 (annual) ● general (life), $1,000. **Staff:** 3. **Description:** Retired military personnel and civilians interested in the life of George S. Patton, Jr. (1885-1945), American general who commanded the Third U.S. Army during World War II. Seeks to perpetuate the history and achievements of Patton. Goals are to: carry on the responsibility of the U.S. to guarantee the freedom of the individual and family, and to secure the common good of all U.S. citizens in accordance with the Constitution; uphold the Constitution according to its original meaning; avoid war by assisting in military preparedness; defend the peace by protecting citizens against external and internal enemies; promote among the civilian population an understanding of the military community; oppose socialism, communism, and those ideologies that the society believes threaten to destroy personal freedom and hinder individual initiative. Operates speakers' bureau. **Libraries: Type:** reference. **Holdings:** 500; audio recordings, books, periodicals, video recordings. **Subjects:** military, military science, ancient history. **Computer Services:** Bibliographic search, Patton and Third U.S. Army. **Also Known As:** George Smith Patton, Jr. Historical Society. **Publications:** *Articles and Essays by G.S. Patton, Jr.*, semiannual. Newsletter. **Circulation:** 150. **Advertising:** accepted ● *The Desert Training Center* ● *Gallipoli: An Essay by G.S. Patton, Jr.* ● *General S. Patton Jr.: A Historical Primer*. Pamphlet ● *Intelligence for Patton*. Book ● Also publishes Patton speeches. **Conventions/Meetings:** Patton's One-Minute Messages - seminar, on Patton, Third Army history, military history, quality control and leadership.

11142 ■ President Benjamin Harrison Foundation (PBHF)
1230 N Delaware St.
Indianapolis, IN 46202
Ph: (317)631-1898
Fax: (317)632-5488
E-mail: harrison@presidentbenjaminharrison.org
Contact: Phyllis D. Geeslin, Dir.
Founded: 1966. **Members:** 400. **Membership Dues:** voter, $25 (annual) ● elector, $35 (annual) ● delegate, $50 (annual) ● representative, $100 (annual) ● senator, $250 (annual) ● justice, $500 (annual) ● cabinet, $1,000 (annual). **Staff:** 10. **Languages:** English, French, German, Japanese, Portuguese, Russian, Spanish. **Description:** Individuals and corporate supporters interested in the life and times of Benjamin Harrison (1833-1901), president of the U.S. from 1889-93. Works to preserve Harrison's memory and maintain artifacts of his life. Operates Harrison's home in Indianapolis, IN, as a museum;

maintains speaker's bureau. Offers educational programs to schools. Holds quarterly first-person living history presentations entitled, "Live From Delaware Street". **Libraries: Type:** reference. **Holdings:** 9,859. **Telecommunication Services:** TDD, (317)-631-1888. **Publications:** *The Statesman*, quarterly. Newsletter ● Brochures ● Pamphlets ● Makes available slide show. **Conventions/Meetings:** lecture ● tour ● workshop.

11143 ■ Rachel Carson Homestead Association (RCHA)

613 Marion Ave.
PO Box 46
Springdale, PA 15144-0046
Ph: (724)274-5459
Fax: (724)275-1259
E-mail: info@rachelcarsonhomestead.org
URL: http://www.rachelcarsonhomestead.org
Contact: Patricia M. DeMarco PhD, Exec. Dir.

Founded: 1975. **Members:** 300. **Membership Dues:** individual, $30 (annual) ● family/household, $50 (annual) ● supporting, $125 (annual) ● sustaining, $275 (annual) ● patron, $500 (annual) ● benefactor, $1,000 (annual) ● student/senior, $15 (annual) ● kid's club, $10 (annual). **Staff:** 3. **Budget:** $90,000. **Regional Groups:** 1. **Description:** Persons and organizations interested in carrying on the principles of Rachel Carson (1907-64), ecologist and nature writer whose 1962 book "Silent Spring" launched the modern environmental movement. Seeks to preserve, restore, and interpret Rachel Carson's birthplace and home; to design and implement environmental education programs in keeping with the precepts of Rachel Carson. Functions as a clearinghouse on Carson and her work. Maintains museum and offers guided tours of Carson's house and grounds; conducts environmental education classes and school and outreach programs. **Libraries: Type:** reference. **Holdings:** books, clippings, periodicals. **Subjects:** environment, education, pesticides, oceanography, Rachel Carson. **Awards:** Rachel Carson Scholarship. **Frequency:** annual. **Type:** scholarship. **Recipient:** for student at Springdale High School ● Ruth Scott Scholarship. **Type:** scholarship. **Recipient:** for local children to attend educational programs. **Telecommunication Services:** electronic mail, pmdemarco@rachelcarsonhomestead.org. **Committees:** Bibliographic; Calendar of Museum Activities; Development; Education; House and Grounds; Membership; Press Releases; Rachel Carson Biography; Visit Planner. **Publications:** *The Spring*, quarterly. Newsletter. Details association activities and provides historical information. **Price:** included in membership dues. **Circulation:** 1,500. Alternate Formats: online. **Conventions/Meetings:** annual Public Program - conference ● annual Rachel Carson Day - meeting (exhibits) - always May.

11144 ■ Richard the III Foundation

9067 Vintage Wine Ave.
Las Vegas, NV 89148
E-mail: richard3foundation@yahoo.com
URL: http://www.richard111.com
Contact: Mary Kelly, Mgr.

Founded: 1994. **Membership Dues:** regular in U.S., $35 (annual) ● regular single in UK, 20 (annual) ● regular family in UK, 26 (annual). **Staff:** 30. **Regional Groups:** 8. **State Groups:** 5. **Multinational. Description:** Specializes in the advancement of the education and research of the medieval period, with emphasis on King Richard III, his contemporaries, and the era in which he lived. Sponsors and encourages research utilizing primary and secondary sources, works in conjunction with universities and colleges offering medieval programs. Promotes conferences, lectures, and publication projects. **Libraries: Type:** lending. **Holdings:** 150; archival material, audio recordings, audiovisuals, books, clippings, periodicals. **Subjects:** medieval/15th century history, biography, battles. **Awards:** Richard III Collegiate Scholarship Fund. **Frequency:** annual. **Type:** scholarship. **Recipient:** for studies pertaining to 15th century. **Computer Services:** database ● electronic publishing. **Subgroups:** Historic Preservation; Literary; Public Relations; Research; Travel. **Publications:** *The Medelai Gazette: The Chronicles of King Richard III*, 3/year. Journal. Offers researched materials focusing on the 15th century. **Price:** free for members; $6.95/back issue, in U.S.; 4.95/back issue, in UK. **Advertising:** accepted. **Conventions/Meetings:** annual convention, includes medieval conferences, meetings, and special presentations (exhibits).

11145 ■ Richard III Society, American Branch

c/o Pamela J. Butler
11000 Anaheim Ave. NE
Albuquerque, NM 87122
E-mail: membership@r3.org
URL: http://www.r3.org
Contact: Pamela J. Butler, Contact

Founded: 1924. **Members:** 800. **Membership Dues:** regular, in U.S., $35 (annual) ● regular, outside U.S., $40 (annual) ● honorary Fotheringhay, $75 (annual) ● honorary Middleham, $180 (annual) ● honorary Bosworth, $300 (annual) ● plantagenet angel, $500 (annual). **Description:** Teachers, historians, students, and others interested in historical research into the life and times of Richard III (1452-85, King of England, 1483-85). Seeks "to secure a reassessment of the historical material relating to this period and of the role in English history of this monarch," especially in regard to the fate of the two young "Princes in the Tower" and the character of their uncle, Richard, who was accused of murdering his nephews to claim the throne. Writes letters and prepares articles to correct "misinformation" about Richard III; conducts research; publishes annual memorial in the New York Times and London Times. In England, maintains several memorials and historic sites and conducts expeditions to places of interest connected with Richard III. English parent society has erected a life-size sculpture of Richard III by noted British sculptor James Butler, RA, in Leicester, city nearest Bosworth Field, where Richard died in battle. **Libraries: Type:** not open to the public; lending. **Holdings:** articles, books. **Awards:** Schallek Memorial Graduate Fellowship Awards. **Frequency:** annual. **Type:** fellowship. **Recipient:** for graduate students working in field of 15th Century English history and culture. **Absorbed:** Friends of Richard III. **Formerly:** (1959) Fellowship of the White Boar. **Publications:** *The Ricardian*, quarterly. Journal. Includes book reviews. **Price:** included in membership dues; $5.00/copy for nonmembers. **Circulation:** 8,500. **Advertising:** accepted ● *The Ricardian Bulletin*, quarterly. Includes minutes of the annual general meeting, reports on branch activities, information on upcoming Ricardian gatherings and conferences. ISSN: 0308-4337 ● *Ricardian Register*, quarterly. Newsletter. Includes book review section and regular updates on Branch programs and projects. **Advertising:** accepted ● Has also published critical editions of 15th Century source documents, as well as collections of essays by 20th Century scholars. **Conventions/Meetings:** annual conference - always Saturday nearest October 2 ● triennial conference, on 15th Century England in partnership with University of Illinois at Urbana-Champaign ● annual tour, tour of Ricardian Britain.

11146 ■ Robert E. Lee Memorial Association (RELMA)

c/o Stratford Hall Plantation
483 Great House Rd.
Stratford, VA 22558-0001
Ph: (804)493-8038 (804)493-8371
Fax: (804)493-0333
E-mail: info@stratfordhall.org
URL: http://www.stratfordhall.org
Contact: Mr. Paul C. Reber, Exec. Dir.

Founded: 1929. **Members:** 3,000. **Membership Dues:** friend of Stratford, $35 (annual). **Staff:** 35. **Budget:** $3,200,000. **Regional Groups:** 13. **State Groups:** 46. **Local Groups:** 10. **National Groups:** 25. **Description:** Supported by membership and contributions to restore, preserve, and maintain Stratford Hall Plantation as a living memorial to the Lees of Virginia and to honor other famous men who lived there such as General Robert E. Lee (1807-70). Stratford Hall Plantation in Virginia was the birthplace of General Lee and ancestral home of the Lee family, including Richard Henry Lee and Francis Lightfoot Lee, the only brothers to sign the Declaration of Independence. Offers full meeting support for gatherings of up to sixty people, and twenty guest rooms. **Libraries: Type:** reference. **Holdings:** 9,000; archival material, artwork, audiovisuals, books, clippings, periodicals. **Subjects:** related Virginia history, the Lee family. **Awards:** Lee Integrity Award. **Type:** recognition. **Telecommunication Services:** electronic mail, preber@stratfordhall.org. **Formerly:** Robert E. Lee Memorial Foundation. **Publications:** *Growing Up in the 1850s: The Journal of Agnes Lee* ● *Jessie Ball DuPont, 1884-1970* ● *The Manner House Before Stratford*. Book ● *Stratford Hall Plantation and the Lees of Virginia*. Book ● *Stratford Journal*, quarterly ● Annual Report, annual ● Newsletter, annual. **Conventions/Meetings:** tour.

11147 ■ Ronald Reagan Home Preservation Foundation (RRHPF)

PO Box 816
Dixon, IL 61021
Ph: (815)288-5176
Fax: (815)288-3642
E-mail: raegan1@grics.net
Contact: Jim Burke, Pres.

Founded: 1981. **Members:** 15. **Staff:** 4. **Budget:** $100,000. **Description:** Aims to raise funds and restore the boyhood home of Ronald Reagan (1911-2004), president of the United States of America from 1980-88. Distributes films, literature, and other works depicting Reagan's youth. Plans to establish a library and museum at the home. **Convention/Meeting:** none. **Formerly:** (1982) Ronald Reagan Restoration and Preservation Association. **Publications:** Brochure.

11148 ■ Rutherford B. Hayes Presidential Center (RBHPC)

Spiegel Grove
Fremont, OH 43420-2796
Ph: (419)332-2081
Free: (800)998-7737
Fax: (419)332-4952
E-mail: nkleinhenz@rbhayes.org
URL: http://www.rbhayes.org
Contact: Thomas J. Culbertson, Exec. Dir.

Founded: 1916. **Members:** 1,000. **Membership Dues:** student, $20 (annual) ● individual, $30 (annual) ● individual plus, $45 (annual) ● family, grandparent, $50 (annual) ● patron, $100 (annual) ● representative, $250 (annual) ● cabinet, $500 (annual) ● advisor, $1,000 (annual) ● executive, $1,500 (annual). **Staff:** 43. **Description:** Site of the nation's first presidential library. Commemorates the life of Rutherford B. Hayes (1822-93), 19th President of the United States, and serves as a center for the study of the Gilded Age (1865-1916). Staff guides lead tours of the 31-room Hayes residence filled with family furnishings. Self-guided tours are offered through the Hayes Museum, containing exhibits on Hayes, the Civil War and life in 19th century America. The Hayes Research Library is open free of charge six days a week and contains extensive Gilded Age, local history and genealogy collections. Spiegel Grove grounds are part of the Hayes estate and include the Hayes tomb and two historic trails. Special events take place year-round including lectures, educational classes, school programs, and musical presentations. Professional staff available for public meetings via speakers' bureau. **Libraries: Type:** reference; open to the public. **Holdings:** 100,000; archival material, books, maps, papers, periodicals, photographs. **Subjects:** about Rutherford B. Hayes, American history 1860-1914, Ohio and local history, genealogy. **Computer Services:** database, Hayes manuscript collections, regional obituary index, library catalog, shopping cart ● information services, facts about the Hayes family. **Telecommunication Services:** electronic mail, hayeslib@rbhayes.org ● electronic mail, tculbertson@rbhayes.org. **Departments:** Administration; Buildings and Grounds; Computer Systems; Development; Genealogy; Hayes Home; Museum; Public Relations. **Affiliated With:** Ohio Historical Society. **Formerly:** (1981) Rutherford B. Hayes Library and Museum. **Publications:** *The Billet*, monthly. Newsletters. **Circulation:** 1,000. Alternate

Formats: online ● *The Statesman*, quarterly. Newsletter. Includes calendar of events. **Price:** free. **Conventions/Meetings:** periodic conference ● annual Lecture on the Presidency - Sunday of Presidents' Day weekend ● symposium ● tour, nature.

11149 ■ Sam Davis Memorial Association (SDMA)
1399 Sam Davis Rd.
Smyrna, TN 37167
Ph: (615)459-2341
Fax: (615)459-2341
E-mail: director@samdavishome.org
URL: http://www.samdavishome.org
Contact: Bethany Hawkins, Dir.
Founded: 1930. **Members:** 450. **Membership Dues:** Stewart's Creek Society, $25 (annual) ● Charles Louis Davis Society, $100 (annual) ● Coleman Scout, $500 (annual) ● honor guard, $50 (annual) ● Jane Simmons Davis Society, $250 (annual) ● Sam Davis Society, $1,000 (annual). **Staff:** 8. **Budget:** $165,000. **Description:** Persons interested in preserving the home of and spreading information about Sam Davis. Maintains original plantation home, outbuildings, and museum of Davis family artifacts and Civil War relics. Conducts annual activities, including Easter and Christmas. Conducts Heritage Days every October, and Days on the Farm school field trip. **Publications:** *The Courier*, quarterly. Newsletter ● Also makes available biographical movie for a fee. **Conventions/Meetings:** annual meeting and picnic.

11150 ■ San Martin Society of United States of America, Washington DC (SMS)
19385 Cypress Ridge Terr., Unit 601
Leesburg, VA 20176-5166
Ph: (703)883-0950
Fax: (703)883-0950
E-mail: cggodoy@msn.com
Contact: Christian Garcia-Godoy, Pres.
Founded: 1977. **Members:** 319. **Regional Groups:** 2. **Languages:** English, Spanish. **Description:** Individuals interested in the study of Argentine General Jose de San Martin (1778-1850) and the South American liberation movements which he led. Purposes are to pool efforts in order to make available in the English language the ideals held by San Martin; to promote understanding and solidarity between the peoples of the Americas; and to stimulate study and historic research on San Martin's life and work. Sponsors periodic commemorative ceremonies including San Martin's birthday (Feb. 25), Argentine Independence Day (July 9, 1816), and the anniversary of San Martin's death (Aug. 17). Conducts historical research; recognizes achievements in dissemination of San Martin's ideals and feats; sponsors competitions. **Libraries: Type:** reference. **Holdings:** biographical archives, books, papers. **Subjects:** General Jose de San Martin. **Awards:** San Martin Bicentennial Medal. **Frequency:** periodic. **Type:** medal. **Recipient:** for distinguished Samaritans ● San Martin Palms. **Frequency:** periodic. **Type:** recognition. **Recipient:** for distinguished Samaritans. **Formerly:** (2003) San Martin Society of Washington, DC. **Publications:** *The Essential San Martin*. A maxim written by General San Martin for his daughter Marcedes Tomasa. ● *Jefes Espanolas en la formacion militar de San Martin*. A maxim written by General San Martin for his daughter Marcedes Tomasa. ● *San Martin News* (in English and Spanish), periodic. Newsletter. **Price:** free. **Advertising:** accepted ● *The San Martin Papers*. Book ● *Tomas Godoy Cruz*. Book ● *Tomas Godoy Cruz: Dictamen Federalista*. A maxim written by General San Martin for his daughter Marcedes Tomasa. ● Pamphlets ● Books ● Also publishes short documents and essays. **Conventions/Meetings:** Ceremonies - meeting, to celebrate birthday, commemorate death, honor independence and remember National Day ● annual meeting, to lay wreath on monument - always September or October, Washington, DC.

11151 ■ Tesla Memorial Society (TMS)
c/o William H. Terbo, Exec. Sec.
Southwyck Village
21 Maddaket
Scotch Plains, NJ 07076-3136
Ph: (732)396-8852
E-mail: teslamemorialsociety@sicaproductions.com
URL: http://www.teslamemorialsociety.org
Contact: William H. Terbo, Exec. Sec.
Founded: 1979. **Members:** 400. **Membership Dues:** individual, $25 (annual) ● supporter, $100 (annual) ● patron, $250 (annual) ● benefactor, $1,000 (annual). **Staff:** 2. **Multinational. Description:** Serves as a scientific, educational, and cultural society dedicated to commemorating and popularizing the life and works of Nikola Tesla (1856-1943). Tesla was a Yugoslav-American electrical scientist and inventor who introduced the first practical application of alternating current and formed the system for the generation and use of power from Niagara Falls. Tesla invented the radio antenna/ground system, tuned circuits and resonant frequency tuning. Maintains speakers' bureau and museum. Compiles statistics related to Tesla's work. **Libraries: Type:** reference. **Holdings:** 1,000; archival material, books, papers. **Subjects:** Tesla's writings. **Awards:** Tesla Memorial Scholarship. **Frequency:** annual. **Type:** scholarship. **Recipient:** for advanced students in electroscience. **Computer Services:** Mailing lists. **Committees:** Cultural; Editorial; Education; Scholarship; Science and Technology. **Publications:** Newsletter, quarterly. Includes book reviews. **Price:** free for members; $1.50/copy for nonmembers ● Articles ● Books ● Newsletter, quarterly. **Conventions/Meetings:** annual conference ● symposium.

11152 ■ Theodore Roosevelt Association (TRA)
PO Box 719
Oyster Bay, NY 11771
Ph: (516)921-6319
Fax: (516)921-6481
E-mail: info@theodoreroosevelt.org
URL: http://www.theodoreroosevelt.org
Contact: Mr. Norman Parsons, Acting Pres.
Founded: 1919. **Members:** 2,200. **Membership Dues:** Sagamore Hill, $35 (annual) ● Badlands Rancher, $65 (annual) ● Rough Rider, $150 (annual) ● conservationist, $350 (annual) ● gubernatorial, $700 (annual) ● bull moose, $1,200 (annual) ● presidential, $1,500 (annual) ● corporate sponsor, $5,000 (annual). **Staff:** 4. **Budget:** $378,000. **Regional Groups:** 4. **Description:** Persons interested in the life and principles of Theodore Roosevelt (1858-1919), 26th President of the U.S. Restored Theodore Roosevelt House, his birthplace, in New York City and presented it to the National Park Service; restored Sagamore Hill, his home at Oyster Bay, NY, used as the summer White House and presented it to the National Park Service; enlisted a million subscribers in the purchase of Theodore Roosevelt Island, Washington, DC and gave it as a national memorial and wilderness park to the government; presented a memorial park to the town of Oyster Bay; presented to Harvard University books, letters, and photographs relating to President Roosevelt. Maintains speakers' bureau. **Libraries: Type:** reference. **Holdings:** archival material. **Subjects:** history of TRA, TR reference. **Awards:** T.R.A. Police Award. **Frequency:** annual. **Type:** recognition. **Recipient:** for police officer who overcame handicap or physical problem and is on active duty with good record ● Theodore Roosevelt Distinguished Service Medal. **Frequency:** periodic. **Type:** medal. **Telecommunication Services:** electronic mail, trinfo@cs.com. **Committees:** Sagamore Hill; Theodore Roosevelt Birthplace. **Absorbed:** Women's Theodore Roosevelt Memorial Association. **Formerly:** (1953) Roosevelt Memorial Association. **Publications:** *Collected Letters*. Book ● *Collected Works of Theodore Roosevelt*. Book ● *Theodore Roosevelt Association—Journal*, quarterly. Contains historical articles about Theodore Roosevelt and his times; also includes association news and book reviews. **Price:** included in membership dues. **Circulation:** 2,200. **Advertising:** accepted. Alternate Formats: microform ● *Theodore Roosevelt Cyclopedia*. Book ● Books ● Has also published quotations from Roosevelt's writings and speeches. **Conventions/Meetings:** annual meeting - usually October ● annual Public Speaking Contest - competition, in New York City high schools and Nassau County NY High Schools.

11153 ■ Thomas Paine National Historical Association (TPNHA)
983 North Ave.
New Rochelle, NY 10804-3609
Ph: (914)434-7270 (914)740-5343
URL: http://www.thomaspaine.org
Contact: Mr. Brian McCartin, Pres.
Founded: 1884. **Members:** 150. **Membership Dues:** individual, $25 (annual) ● family, $40 (annual) ● international, $50 (annual) ● organization/business, $100 (annual) ● sponsor, $250 (annual) ● life, $1,000 ● benefactor, $500 (annual). **Staff:** 1. **Budget:** $30,000. **Description:** Individuals interested in Thomas Paine (1737-1809), American political philosopher and author. Educates the world about the life, times, and works of Thomas Paine. **Libraries: Type:** reference. **Holdings:** 3,000; archival material, books, clippings. **Subjects:** Thomas Paine, roles in American revolution, French revolution, modern democratic movements worldwide. **Boards:** Trustees. **Conventions/Meetings:** annual general assembly, with trustee's annual meeting.

11154 ■ Ulysses S. Grant Association (USGA)
Southern Illinois Univ.
Morris Lib.
Carbondale, IL 62901
Ph: (618)453-2773
Fax: (618)453-6119
E-mail: jsimon@lib.siu.edu
URL: http://twister.lib.siu.edu/projects/usgrant
Contact: John Y. Simon, Exec. Dir.
Founded: 1962. **Members:** 300. **Membership Dues:** life, $200. **Staff:** 4. **Description:** Organized by the Civil War Centennial Commissions of Illinois, Ohio, and New York for publication of a complete edition of the papers of Ulysses S. Grant (1822-85), U.S. general during the Civil War and 18th President of the U.S., 1869-77, and for general dissemination of information about Grant. Prepares new edition of *Grant's Memoirs* and a comprehensive bibliography. **Libraries: Type:** reference. **Holdings:** clippings. **Subjects:** Grant's documents. **Publications:** *The Papers of Ulysses S. Grant*, periodic. Book. Covers Grant's career through 1875.

11155 ■ Woodrow Wilson Presidential Library Foundation (WWPL)
18-24 N Coalter St.
PO Box 24
Staunton, VA 24402-0024
Ph: (540)885-0897
Free: (888)496-6376
Fax: (540)886-9874
E-mail: info@woodrowwilson.org
URL: http://www.woodrowwilson.org
Contact: Eric Vettel PhD, Exec. Dir.
Founded: 1938. **Members:** 500. **Membership Dues:** associate, $50-$99 (annual) ● diplomat, $100-$199 (annual) ● ambassador, $200-$499 (annual) ● statesman, $500-$999 (annual) ● cabinet, $1,000 (annual). **Staff:** 20. **Budget:** $550,000. **Description:** Persons interested in the preservation, restoration, maintenance, and interpretation of the birthplace of Woodrow Wilson (1856-1924), 28th President of the United States, 1913-21. Conducts research and interprets the life and times of President Wilson. Manages a historic house and museum. Sponsors educational programs. Shows exhibits; conducts tours and sponsors lectures, symposia and institutes. **Libraries: Type:** by appointment only. **Holdings:** 4,500; archival material, books, photographs. **Subjects:** Woodrow Wilson's life and times. **Committees:** Advancement; Board Resources; Collections and Library; Education and Interpretation; Finance; Marketing and Promotion; Properties. **Formerly:** (2004) Woodrow Wilson Birthplace Foundation. **Publications:** *Woodrow Wilson Matters*, quarterly. Newsletter. Covers activities of the presidential museum. **Price:** included in membership dues. **Circulation:** 1,000. **Conventions/Meetings:** annual Woodrow Wilson Luncheon - November in Staunton, VA.

Writers

11156 ■ American Christian Fiction Writers (ACFW)
PO Box 101066
Palm Bay, FL 32910-1066
E-mail: president@acfw.com
URL: http://www.acfw.com
Contact: Rachel Hauck, Pres.
Founded: 2000. **Members:** 900. **Membership Dues:** regular, $35 (annual). **Description:** Encourages writers of Christian fiction to develop their skills. Provides education and offers services that will benefit its members. Fosters fellowship among members and writers with the same interests. **Awards:** ACFW Book of the Year. **Frequency:** annual. **Type:** recognition. **Recipient:** for outstanding works in Christian fiction ● ACFW Genesis Contest. **Frequency:** annual. **Type:** recognition. **Recipient:** for unpublished works in Christian fiction. **Telecommunication Services:** electronic mail, sectry@acfw.com. **Publications:** *Aficionado*, monthly. Magazine. Alternate Formats: online.

11157 ■ American Friends of the Shakespeare Birthplace Trust
c/o John Chwat, Pres.
625 Slaters Ln., Ste.103
Alexandria, VA 22314-1176
Ph: (703)684-7703
Fax: (703)684-7594
E-mail: john.chwat@chwatco.com
URL: http://www.shakespeare.org.uk
Contact: John Chwat, Pres.
Founded: 1999. **Staff:** 2. **Nonmembership. Multinational. Description:** Supports the preservation of William Shakespeare's heritage through educational programs, cultural projects, sculpture placement on behalf of the Shakespeare Birthplace Trust, Stratford-Upon-Avon, UK. Assists the trustees in US fundraising efforts. **Awards:** Columbia University Gilman Summer Graduate Fellowships. **Frequency:** annual. **Type:** fellowship ● Tree Garden Young Artist Sculpture Placement Program at Anne Hathaway's Cottege. **Frequency:** annual. **Type:** scholarship.

11158 ■ American Society of Journalists and Authors (ASJA)
1501 Broadway, Ste.302
New York, NY 10036
Ph: (212)997-0947
Fax: (212)937-2315
E-mail: execdir@asja.org
URL: http://www.asja.org
Contact: Anne Peace, Exec. Dir.
Founded: 1948. **Members:** 1,100. **Membership Dues:** individual, $195 (annual). **Staff:** 2. **Budget:** $300,000. **Regional Groups:** 6. **Description:** Represents freelance writers of nonfiction magazine articles and books. Seeks to elevate the professional and economic position of nonfiction writers, provide a forum for discussion of common problems among writers and editors, and promote a code of ethics for writers and editors. Operates writer referral service for individuals, institutions, or companies seeking writers for special projects; sponsors Llewellyn Miller Fund to aid professional writers who no longer able to work due to age, disability, or extraordinary professional crisis. **Awards:** The Arlenes. **Frequency:** annual. **Type:** recognition. **Recipient:** for the best article ● Career Achievement. **Frequency:** annual. **Type:** recognition. **Recipient:** for members ● Donald Robinson Memorial Award for Investigative Journalism. **Frequency:** annual. **Type:** recognition. **Recipient:** for members ● Extraordinary Service. **Frequency:** annual. **Type:** recognition. **Recipient:** for members ● June Roth Memorial. **Frequency:** triennial. **Type:** recognition. **Recipient:** for eligible book ● Outstanding Articles. **Frequency:** annual. **Type:** recognition. **Recipient:** for members ● Outstanding Book. **Frequency:** annual. **Type:** recognition. **Recipient:** for members ● Robert C. Anderson Memorial. **Frequency:** annual. **Type:** recognition. **Recipient:** for individual magazine editor. **Computer Services:** Mailing lists, of members. **Committees:** Awards; Contracts; Editor-Writer Relations; Editorial Liaison; Professional Rights. **Formerly:** (1975) Society of Magazine Writers. **Publications:** *American Society of Journalists and Authors—Directory of Writers*, annual. Membership Directory. Provides brief biography on each member, including area of expertise, subject specialty, books written, and pseudonyms. **Price:** $98.00/year. ISSN: 0278-8829 ● Newsletter, monthly. Includes confidential market information. **Price:** available to members only. **Circulation:** 1,500 ● Books. Covers nonfiction writing. **Price:** $15.95. **Conventions/Meetings:** annual ASJA Writers Conference - convention and conference (exhibits) - April or May, New York City ● meeting - 8/year, always in New York City.

11159 ■ Arthur Miller Society
c/o Stephen Marino, Sec.-Treas./Ed.
100-14 160th Ave.
Howard Beach, NY 11414
E-mail: smarino@stfranciscollege.edu
URL: http://www.ibiblio.org/miller
Contact: Stephen Marino, Sec.-Treas./Ed.
Membership Dues: individual, $25 (annual) ● student, $10 (annual) ● overseas, $30 (annual). **Description:** Encourages the study of the life and works of Arthur Miller, American author, essayist and playwright. Fosters continued interest in Miller's work. Promotes the production of Miller's plays. **Publications:** *Arthur Miller Journal*, semiannual. **Price:** $20.00 /year for individuals in U.S. and Canada; $30.00 /year for institutions and overseas subscribers.

11160 ■ Association of Writers and Writing Programs (AWP)
George Mason Univ.
Mail Stop 1E3
Fairfax, VA 22030-4444
Ph: (703)993-4301
Fax: (703)993-4302
E-mail: awp@awpwriter.org
URL: http://www.awpwriter.org
Contact: David W. Fenza, Exec. Dir.
Founded: 1967. **Members:** 25,000. **Membership Dues:** individual, $65 (annual) ● institutional (based on the number of students), $395-$815 (annual) ● writer's conference and center, $175 (annual) ● affiliate, $225 (annual) ● student, $40 (annual) ● international (based on geographical region), $72-$94 (annual). **Staff:** 12. **Budget:** $1,500,000. **Local Groups:** 340. **Description:** Writers; students and teachers in creative writing programs in university departments of English; editors, publishers, and freelance creative and professional writers. Fosters literary talent and achievement; advocates the craft of writing as primary to a liberal and humane education; provides publications and services to the makers and readers of contemporary literature. Operates career services and job listings; sponsors literary competitions. **Libraries: Type:** open to the public. **Holdings:** 28; articles. **Subjects:** creative writing. **Awards:** AWP Award Series. **Frequency:** annual. **Type:** monetary. **Recipient:** for the excellent new book-length works of poetry, fiction, and creative nonfiction. **Computer Services:** Mailing lists, of members ● online services, forums. **Telecommunication Services:** electronic mail, services@awpwriter.org ● electronic mail, advertising@awpwriter.org ● electronic mail, conference@awpwriter.org ● electronic mail, jobs@awpwriter.org. **Committees:** Advocacy; Programs; Undergraduate Creative Writing. **Formerly:** (2005) Associated Writing Programs. **Publications:** *AWP Job List*, 7/year. Newsletter. Contains position descriptions for teachers of creative writing. Also includes descriptions of editing, publishing, and technical writing jobs. **Price:** available to members only. Alternate Formats: online ● *AWP Official Guide to Writing Programs*, biennial. Directory. Describes creative writing offerings in more than 330 institutions in the U.S. and Canada. **Price:** $28.45 plus shipping and handling ● *The Writer's Chronicle*, periodic. Journal. Includes essays, critiques, and interviews. **Price:** $20.00 /year for nonmembers. **Circulation:** 25,000. **Advertising:** accepted. **Conventions/Meetings:** annual conference (exhibits) - 2009 Feb. 11-14, Chicago, IL ● annual meeting and symposium, offers panels, presentations, and readings about writing, editing, and teaching as well as a bookfair (exhibits).

11161 ■ Authors Guild (AG)
31 E 32nd St., 7th Fl.
New York, NY 10016-7923
Ph: (212)563-5904
Fax: (212)564-5363
E-mail: staff@authorsguild.org
URL: http://www.authorsguild.org
Contact: Paul Aiken, Exec. Dir.
Founded: 1912. **Members:** 8,100. **Membership Dues:** regular/member-at-large/associate, $90 (annual). **Description:** Professional book and magazine writers. Maintains legal staff to provide book and magazine contract reviews for members. Group health insurance available. Members of the guild are also members of the Authors League of America. **Committees:** Book Contract; Children's Book; Copyright; Freedom of Expression; Lobbying. **Affiliated With:** Authors League of America; Dramatists Guild of America. **Publications:** *Authors Guild—Bulletin*, quarterly. Journal. Covers the business interests of professional authors including copyright protection, contract problems, freedom of expression, and taxation. **Price:** included in membership dues. **Circulation:** 7,000 ● *Model Trade Book Contract & Guide*. **Price:** included in membership dues. **Conventions/Meetings:** annual meeting - always February in New York City.

11162 ■ Authors League of America (ALA)
c/o The Authors Guild
31 E 32nd St., 7th Fl.
New York, NY 10016-7923
Ph: (212)563-5904
Fax: (212)564-5363
E-mail: staff@authorsguild.org
URL: http://www.authorsguild.org
Contact: Paul Aiken, Exec. Dir.
Founded: 1912. **Members:** 14,700. **Membership Dues:** general (based on writing income), $90-$500 (annual). **Description:** Serves as a professional organization of authors of books, magazine material, and plays. **Sections:** Authors Guild; Dramatists Guild. **Publications:** *Dramatists Guild Quarterly*. Newsletter ● Bulletin, quarterly. Contains contracts, copyright, electronic changes, agents and publishers. **Conventions/Meetings:** annual meeting.

11163 ■ Bread Loaf Writers Conference (BLWC)
Middlebury Coll.
Middlebury, VT 05753
Ph: (802)443-5286
Fax: (802)443-2087
E-mail: blwc@middlebury.edu
URL: http://www.middlebury.edu/~blwc
Contact: Noreen Cargill, Admin. Mgr.
Founded: 1926. **Description:** Participants are writers of fiction, nonfiction and poetry. Provides an opportunity for sustained dialogue among writers through lectures, workshops, discussion groups, panels, and informal conversation. Maintains an Endowment Fund, which awards fellowships and makes available scholarship assistance to enable writers to attend a session of the conference. **Awards:** Fellowships and Scholarships. **Frequency:** annual. **Type:** fellowship. **Recipient:** for quality of writing. **Telecommunication Services:** electronic mail, ncargill@middlebury.edu. **Publications:** *Crumb*, daily. Newsletter. Alternate Formats: online. **Conventions/Meetings:** annual Writers' Conference - always in August in Ripton, Vermont.

11164 ■ Carson McCullers Society
c/o James Mayo
Dept. of English and Foreign Languages
Jackson State Community Coll.
2046 N Pkwy.
Jackson, TN 38301
Free: (800)355-5722

E-mail: jmayo@jscc.edu
URL: http://www.mccullerssociety.org
Contact: Carlos L. Dews, Charter Pres.
Founded: 1997. **Membership Dues:** regular, $10 (annual). **Description:** Promotes interest in the works and life of Carson McCullers, an American writer. Provides a forum for the scholarly and informal exchange of information on Carson McCullers' life, works, and influences. Coordinates and sponsors McCuller sessions at the MLA and ALA annual conferences. **Telecommunication Services:** electronic mail, cdews@uwf.edu. **Publications:** Newsletter, annual. Includes articles, reviews, bibliography, and information concerning Carson McCullers. **Price:** included in membership dues. Alternate Formats: online.

11165 ■ Catharine Maria Sedgwick Society (CMSS)
c/o Deborah Gussman, VP - Membership and Finance
619 Wayne Ave.
Haddonfield, NJ 08033
E-mail: ldamonba@salemstate.edu
URL: http://www.salemstate.edu/imc/sedgwick
Contact: Lucinda Damon-Bach, Pres./Founder
Founded: 1997. **Membership Dues:** regular, $10 (annual) ● institutional, $25 (annual) ● international, $15 (annual) ● student, $5 (annual) ● life, $200. **Description:** Promotes the study and awareness of Sedgwick's life and works. Aims to increase availability and access to the author's writings. Provides a forum for established and emerging scholars, and others who are interested in Sedgwick, to exchange ideas, research, and pedagogical strategies. **Telecommunication Services:** electronic mail, lucinda.damonbach@salemstate.edu ● electronic mail, wa.gu@verizon.net. **Publications:** *The Catharine Maria Sedgwick Society Newsletter*. **Price:** included in membership dues. Alternate Formats: online.

11166 ■ Charles W. Chesnutt Association
c/o Susan Prothro Wright
Clark Atlanta Univ.
Dept. of English
Atlanta, GA 30314
E-mail: smcfatt@cau.edu
URL: http://www.charleswaddellchesnutt.com/pages/1/index.htm
Contact: Viktor Osinubi, Pres.
Founded: 1996. **Membership Dues:** individual, $20 (annual) ● institution, $50 (annual) ● student, $10 (annual). **Description:** Promotes the life and work of author Charles W. Chesnutt, the first African-American writer to receive widespread attention during his lifetime as a literary artist. **Awards:** Sylvia Lyons Render Award. **Frequency:** annual. **Type:** recognition. **Publications:** *Chesnutt Grapevine*, annual. Newsletter. **Price:** included in membership dues.

11167 ■ Committee on Scholarly Editions (CSE)
c/o Modern Language Association of America
26 Broadway, 3rd Fl.
New York, NY 10004
Ph: (646)576-5000 (646)576-5102
Fax: (646)458-0030
E-mail: cse@mla.org
URL: http://www.mla.org
Contact: David G. Nicholls, Staff Liaison
Founded: 1976. **Members:** 8. **Budget:** $10,000. **Languages:** English, Spanish. **Description:** Provides consulting services for editors producing scholarly editions. Presents emblems of approval to completed editions that meet its standards; any editor may apply for advice and information. Formerly acted as coordinating body for Center for Scholarly Editions, which superseded Center for Editions of American Authors (founded 1966). **Libraries: Type:** not open to the public. **Holdings:** 200; books. **Subjects:** literature, history. **Awards:** MLA Prize for a Scholarly Edition. **Frequency:** biennial. **Type:** monetary. **Recipient:** for excellence in producing a scholarly edition. **Affiliated With:** Modern Language Association of America. **Conventions/Meetings:** annual workshop - always in September.

11168 ■ Cormac McCarthy Society
13850 SW 100th Ave.
Miami, FL 33176
E-mail: info@cormacmccarthy.com
URL: http://www.cormacmccarthy.com
Contact: Rick Wallach, Sec.-Treas.
Founded: 1995. **Membership Dues:** regular in U.S., $35 (annual) ● student/military in U.S., $25 (annual) ● regular (in Canada, Mexico and Latin America), $41 (annual) ● regular (in Europe), $44 (annual) ● regular (in Asia, Africa and the Pacific), $48 (annual) ● student/military (in Canada, Mexico and Latin America), $31 (annual) ● student/military (in Europe), $34 (annual) ● student/military (in Asia, Africa, and the Pacific), $38 (annual). **Multinational. Description:** Aims to further the scholarship and general appreciation of Cormac McCarthy's writings. Facilitates the gathering of scholars and enthusiastic lay readers who share a common interest in Cormac McCarthy and his work. Assists scholars worldwide who are researching the work of Cormac McCarthy. Provides information about McCarthy and his work. Facilitates communication and cooperation among members. **Publications:** *Cormac McCarthy Journal*, annual. Alternate Formats: online ● Newsletter, semiannual ● Proceedings, periodic.

11169 ■ Don DeLillo Society
c/o Marni Gauthier, Sec.
PO Box 2000
Cortland, NY 13045-0900
E-mail: gauthierm@cortland.edu
URL: http://www.k-state.edu/english/nelp/delillo
Contact: Marni Gauthier, Sec.
Description: Encourages the scholarly study of and general interest in the works of Don DeLillo. Facilitates exchange of ideas and information between scholars, critics, teachers, and general readers. Promotes matters of interest to Don DeLillo scholars and readers. **Publications:** Newsletter, annual.

11170 ■ Evelyn Scott Society
c/o Dr. Tim Edwards, VP/Treas.
Univ. of West Alabama
Dept. of Languages and Literature
Sta. 22
Livingston, AL 35470
E-mail: tedwards@uwa.edu
URL: http://www.wtamu.edu/~ptyrer/Organizations/EvelynScottSociety/scottindex.htm
Contact: Dr. Tim Edwards, VP/Treas.
Founded: 2003. **Members:** 2. **Membership Dues:** faculty, independent scholar, $10 (annual) ● student, $5 (annual) ● life, $100. **Description:** Promotes the study of the life and works of American modernist writer, Evelyn Scott. Facilitates the exchange of scholarly ideas concerning the American writer and her literary works. Serves as an information resource for studies and research pertaining to Evelyn Scott. **Affiliated With:** American Literature Association; Society for the Study of American Women Writers. **Publications:** Newsletter, annual. **Price:** included in membership dues. Alternate Formats: online.

11171 ■ Friends of American Writers (FAW)
506 Rose Ave.
Des Plaines, IL 60016
Ph: (847)827-8339
E-mail: vmortens@parkridge.lib.il.us
Contact: Vivian Mortensen, Chm.
Founded: 1922. **Members:** 200. **Membership Dues:** individual, $12 (annual). **Description:** Individuals in the Chicago, IL, area who are interested in the study of American literature and in encouraging and promoting high standards among writers of the Midwest. Recognizes publishers of award-winning books. **Awards:** Friends of American Writers Awards. **Frequency:** annual. **Type:** grant. **Recipient:** for books chosen each spring ● **Type:** monetary. **Recipient:** to authors of adult and juvenile books ● **Frequency:** annual. **Type:** monetary. **Recipient:** to published authors who are at least five-year residents of the Midwest or those who have used the Midwest as their books' locales, and have not published more than three books. **Publications:** *Friends of American Writers Bulletin*, monthly ● *Friends of American Writers Yearbook and Friends of American Writers 75 Year History*. **Conventions/Meetings:** annual luncheon, includes awards ● monthly meeting, includes speakers on literary topics.

11172 ■ Georgia Writers Association and Young Georgia Writers (GWA)
Kennesaw State Univ.
English Dept. Bldg., No. 2701
1000 Chastain Rd.
Kennesaw, GA 30144
Ph: (770)420-4736
Fax: (770)420-4736
E-mail: lmrussell@georgiawriters.org
URL: http://www.georgiawriters.org
Contact: Kevin Cantwell, Pres.
Founded: 1964. **Members:** 500. **Membership Dues:** student, $30 (annual) ● individual, $45 (annual) ● professional, $75-$200 (annual) ● affiliate, $150 (annual) ● supporting, $250 (annual) ● sponsor, $500 (annual) ● patron, $2,000 (annual) ● Olympian, $5,000 (annual). **Staff:** 1. **Budget:** $45,000. **Languages:** English, French, Spanish. **Description:** Serves as an organization for all writers; writing professionals, new writers - youth group and adults and other interested individuals. Promotes high standards in writing and formal critique groups (commitments necessary). Encourages interest in writers and their books, and other literary works. Disseminates information, provides opportunity, and improves library skills. Conducts new initiatives like: formal Writing In The Schools (WitS) and Young Georgia Writers program, partnered by State Board of PTA and supported by writer/members and other organizations across the state of Georgia. **Libraries: Type:** open to the public. **Holdings:** 150; audio recordings, books, periodicals, video recordings. **Awards:** Georgia Author of the Year Award. **Frequency:** annual. **Type:** trophy. **Recipient:** for books published by authors living and working in Georgia ● Georgia Writers' High School Writing Competition. **Type:** recognition ● **Frequency:** annual. **Type:** scholarship. **Recipient:** for a high school student in Georgia. **Computer Services:** Mailing lists, of members. **Boards:** Critique Groups; Junior. **Formerly:** (1988) Dixie Council of Authors and Journalists; (1994) Council of Authors and Journalists; (2002) Georgia Writers. **Publications:** *Branch Water Review*, annual. Book ● *Georgia Writers News/Magazine*, bimonthly. Newsletter. Contains articles, features and submissions from members. **Circulation:** 700. **Advertising:** accepted. Alternate Formats: online; CD-ROM ● *On My Mind*, annual. Book. **Conventions/Meetings:** periodic competition ● annual Dwight E. Humphries Memorial Young Poets Competition ● annual Georgia Author of the Year Awards - dinner, private reception, awards ceremony (exhibits) ● annual Nora Deloach Memorial Young Mystery Writers Competition (exhibits) ● annual Spring Festival - workshop, with 20 workshops and author signings (exhibits).

11173 ■ Harriet Beecher Stowe Society
c/o Nancy Lusignan Schultz, Treas.
Dept. of English
Salem State Coll.
352 Lafayette St.
Salem, MA 01970-5333
E-mail: rcc8j@virginia.edu
URL: http://www.people.virginia.edu/~rcc8j/Stowe_Society/Home.html
Contact: Joan Hedrick, Pres.
Founded: 1996. **Membership Dues:** student, independent, $10 (annual) ● faculty, $15 (annual) ● life, $150. **Description:** Promotes the study and appreciation of the works and life of Harriet Beecher Stowe. Provides a forum for studies about the author through presentations of scholarly work and roundtable discussions. Serves as an information resource for related works pertaining to Harriet Beecher Stowe. **Publications:** Newsletter. Alternate Formats: online.

11174 ■ Horror Writers Association (HWA)
244 5th Ave., Ste.2767
New York, NY 10001-7604
E-mail: hwa@horror.org
URL: http://www.horror.org
Contact: Nancy Etchemendy, Admin. Dir.
Founded: 1987. **Members:** 560. **Membership Dues:** active, associate, affiliate, $65 (annual) ● corporate, $110 (annual) ● family, $85 (annual). **Budget:** $40,000. **Regional Groups:** 13. **Multinational. Description:** Horror writers, including creators of comic strips, screenplays, and role-playing games, who have sold at least one work at professional rates are active members; horror writers who have sold something but not at professional rates are affiliate members. Non-writing professionals are associate members. Seeks to assist aspiring and accomplished horror writers in advancing their art and careers. Facilitates networking among members; gathers and disseminates information on horror fiction markets; serves as liaison between members and writers' agents and publishers. **Libraries: Type:** reference. **Holdings:** archival material. **Subjects:** horror, writing, publishing. **Awards:** Bram Stoker Awards for Superior Achievement. **Frequency:** annual. **Type:** trophy. **Recipient:** for outstanding achievement in written horror (8 categories) ● Bram Stoker Lifetime Achievement Award. **Frequency:** annual. **Type:** trophy. **Recipient:** for outstanding body of work in horror over a lifetime ● HWA Specialty Press Award. **Frequency:** annual. **Type:** trophy. **Recipient:** to a specialty publisher whose work has contributed substantially to the horror genre. **Computer Services:** Mailing lists, information for some members ● online services, information and private message board, available to members only. **Telecommunication Services:** electronic bulletin board, available to members only. **Special Interest Groups:** HWA Children's Horror Group; HWA Graphic Novelists Group; HWA Poets Group; HWA Screenwriters Group. **Also Known As:** Horror Writers of America. **Publications:** *Handbook/Directory*, annual. **Circulation:** 820. **Advertising:** accepted. Alternate Formats: online ● Newsletter, monthly. **Circulation:** 820. **Advertising:** accepted. **Conventions/Meetings:** annual Bram Stoker Awards Ceremony - banquet ● annual conference, with panels, readings, workshops, discussion groups and a business meeting.

11175 ■ International Association of Crime Writers, North American Branch (IACW/NA)
PO Box 8674
New York, NY 10116-8674
E-mail: info@crimewritersna.org
URL: http://www.crimewritersna.org
Contact: Mary A. Frisque, Exec. Dir.
Members: 250. **Membership Dues:** regular, $60 (annual). **Multinational. Description:** Aims to encourage communication among writers of all nationalities. Promotes crime writing as an influential and significant art form. Supports the translation of crime writing into other languages. Serves as the voice of authors against censorship. **Awards:** Hammett Prize. **Frequency:** annual. **Type:** recognition. **Recipient:** for literary excellence in the field of crime writing. **Affiliated With:** International Association of Crime Writers. **Publications:** *Border Patrol*, quarterly. Newsletter.

11176 ■ International Association of Media Tie-in Writers (IAMTW)
PO Box 8212
Calabasas, CA 91372
E-mail: info@iamtw.org
URL: http://www.iamtw.org
Contact: Max Allan Collins, Co-Founder/Pres.
Membership Dues: regular, $35 (annual). **Multinational. Description:** Enhances the professional and public image of tie-in writers. Works with the media to review tie-in novels and publicize their authors. Raises public awareness of media tie-in writers. Provides a forum for tie-in writers to share information and discuss issues related to the field of tie-in writing. **Awards:** Scribe Awards. **Frequency:** annual. **Type:** recognition. **Recipient:** for the most outstanding novels written. **Publications:** Newsletter, monthly. Alternate Formats: online.

11177 ■ International Black Writers and Artists (IBWA)
PO Box 43576
Los Angeles, CA 90043
Ph: (213)964-3721
E-mail: ibwa_la@yahoo.com
URL: http://members.tripod.com/~ibwa/home.htm
Founded: 1974. **Members:** 1,800. **Membership Dues:** regular, $50 (annual) ● senior citizen, student, $35 (annual) ● sustaining, organization, $100 (annual). **Budget:** $40,000. **Regional Groups:** 5. **State Groups:** 4. **Local Groups:** 1. **Description:** Seeks to discover and support new black writers. Conducts research and monthly seminars in poetry, fiction, nonfiction, music, and jazz. Provides writing services and children's services. Maintains speakers' bureau. Offers referral service. Plans to establish hall of fame, biographical archives, and museum. **Libraries: Type:** not open to the public; lending. **Holdings:** 500; articles, books, periodicals. **Subjects:** writing, Black history, Black art, writing resources. **Awards:** Alice Browning Award for Excellence in Writing. **Frequency:** annual. **Type:** recognition. **Recipient:** for recently published work ● **Type:** recognition. **Recipient:** for journalism and poetry. **Committees:** Jazz; Poetry; Youth. **Formerly:** (1982) International Black Writers Conference; (2005) International Black Writers. **Publications:** *Black Expressions*, bimonthly. Newsletter. **Price:** included in membership dues; $25.00 for nonmembers ● *The Black Writer*, quarterly. Magazine. **Price:** $3.00 ● *Directory of Afro-American Writers*, periodic ● *Griots Benaate, the Baobab: Tales From Los Angeles*. Book. **Price:** $15.00 ● *In Touch Newsletter*, monthly ● *Poetry Contest*, annual ● *River Crossings: Voices of the Diaspora*. Book. **Price:** $14.95 ● *Urban Voices Poetry*, annual ● Bulletin, periodic. **Conventions/Meetings:** periodic competition ● annual conference and workshop (exhibits) - always July ● monthly workshop, includes panel discussions - every 3rd Sunday.

11178 ■ International Rebecca West Society
c/o Helen Macleod, Sec.-Treas.
129 Columbia Heights, No. 42
Brooklyn, NY 11202
E-mail: anorton@anselm.edu
URL: http://www.rebeccawestsociety.org
Contact: Ann Norton, VP
Founded: 2003. **Membership Dues:** regular, $30 (annual) ● reduced (graduate student, retired, part-time employee), $10 (annual). **Multinational. Description:** Encourages and creates interest in the life and works of Rebecca West, a British-Irish feminist and writer. Fosters conversation among all people who are interested in her work. Maintains a bibliographic listing of recent works about Rebecca West.

11179 ■ International Thriller Writers (ITW)
PO Box 311
Eureka, CA 95502
Fax: (707)442-9251
E-mail: info@thrillerwriters.org
URL: http://www.thrillerwriters.org
Contact: Steve Berry, Exec. VP
Founded: 2004. **Membership Dues:** active/associate, $50 (annual) ● charter, $500 (annual) ● charter sponsor, $1,000 (annual) ● founding sponsor, $5,000 (annual). **Multinational. Description:** Promotes suspense or thriller novels. Enhances the prestige and raises the profile of thriller writers. Provides opportunities for collegiality among authors and other industry professionals. **Awards:** Best First Novel. **Frequency:** annual. **Type:** recognition. **Recipient:** for a debut novelist ● Best Novel. **Frequency:** annual. **Type:** recognition. **Recipient:** for the most outstanding novel written ● Best Paperback Original. **Frequency:** annual. **Type:** recognition. **Recipient:** for the most outstanding piece of work in a paperback format ● Best Script. **Frequency:** annual. **Type:** recognition. **Recipient:** for the most outstanding script written for a screen or stage production ● Distinguished Literature Award. **Frequency:** annual. **Type:** recognition. **Recipient:** for an author whose body of work in books or film had a significant impact on literature over a sustained period of time. **Publications:** *Thriller Readers*, monthly. Newsletter. Contains author interviews, book reviews and excerpts. **Price:** free. Alternate Formats: online.

11180 ■ International Women's Writing Guild (IWWG)
PO Box 810
Gracie Sta.
New York, NY 10028-0082
Ph: (212)737-7536
Fax: (212)737-9469
E-mail: dirhahn@iwwg.org
URL: http://www.iwwg.org
Contact: Hannelore Hahn, Founder/Exec. Dir.
Founded: 1976. **Members:** 3,500. **Membership Dues:** regular, $45 (annual) ● youth, $30 (annual). **Staff:** 2. **Multinational. Description:** Women writers in 24 countries interested in expressing themselves through the written word professionally and for personal growth regardless of portfolio. Seeks to empower women personally and professionally through writing. Facilitates manuscript submissions to literary agents and independent presses. Participates in international network. Maintains dental and vision program at group rates. **Publications:** *Network*, bimonthly. Journal. Helps women writers publish their work. Includes calendar of events; lists awards, and information on environmental issues, contests and member news. **Price:** included in membership dues. **Advertising:** accepted. **Conventions/Meetings:** annual conference (exhibits) - every summer in Saratoga Springs, NY ● workshop, writing.

11181 ■ Mystery Writers of America (MWA)
17 E 47th St., 6th Fl.
New York, NY 10017
Ph: (212)888-8171
Fax: (212)888-8107
E-mail: mwa@mysterywriters.org
URL: http://www.mysterywriters.org
Contact: Margery Flax, Admin. Mgr.
Founded: 1945. **Members:** 3,000. **Membership Dues:** individual, $95 (annual). **Staff:** 1. **Regional Groups:** 11. **Local Groups:** 1. **Description:** Professional writers in the mystery-crime field; publishers and agents are associate members. **Libraries: Type:** not open to the public. **Holdings:** 1,100; biographical archives, books. **Awards:** Edgar Allan Poe Award. **Frequency:** annual. **Type:** recognition. **Recipient:** for the author of the book that is published in 13 different categories ● Ellery Queen Award. **Type:** recognition ● Grand Master Award. **Type:** recognition. **Recipient:** for lifetime achievement ● Raven Award. **Type:** recognition. **Publications:** *Mystery Writers of America Edgar Awards Annual*, annual. Journal. Features a collection of articles on a general theme; includes listing of nominees for the Edgar Allan Poe Awards. **Price:** included in membership dues; $10.00/issue for nonmembers. **Circulation:** 3,500. **Advertising:** accepted ● *Regional Chapter Newsletters*, periodic. **Price:** included in membership dues ● *The Third Degree*, 10/year. Newsletter. Includes market news and other issues of interest to writers. **Price:** included in membership dues. **Circulation:** 2,700. **Conventions/Meetings:** annual Edgar Allan Poe Awards Banquet - always late April or early May in New York City ● annual Edgar Symposium - symposium and workshop - always held on day before annual awards banquet.

11182 ■ National Alliance of Short Fiction Authors (NASFA)
c/o Timson Edwards, Co.
PO Box 58-0898
Jacksonville, FL 32255-0898
E-mail: publisher@short-fiction.com
URL: http://www.short-fiction.com
Contact: Alex Gonzalez, Exec. Dir.
Founded: 1996. **Membership Dues:** individual, $45 (annual). **Description:** Authors, editors, professors, publishers, and others interested in the short story as a form of writing. Promotes the writing and reading of short stories with a particular emphasis on fiction and new writers. Holds quarterly publishing competitions

and offers educational programs. **Libraries: Type:** reference; by appointment only. **Holdings:** books, monographs, periodicals. **Subjects:** the short story. **Awards:** Bronze Quill. **Frequency:** annual. **Type:** recognition. **Recipient:** for excellence in short story fiction by a new writer. **Publications:** *The Bayside Bench Anthology*, quarterly. Directory. **Circulation:** 5,000. **Advertising:** accepted. **Conventions/Meetings:** annual convention.

11183 ■ National Association of Women Writers (NAWW)
24165 IH-10 W, Ste.217-637
San Antonio, TX 78257
Free: (866)821-5829
Fax: (866)821-5829
E-mail: naww@onebox.com
URL: http://www.naww.org
Contact: Sheri McConnell, Founder/Pres.
Founded: 2001. **Members:** 3,000. **Membership Dues:** regular, $120 (annual). **Description:** Promotes appreciation of the work of women writers. Serves as a support and assistance network for women writers. Aims to create opportunities for its members to excel and become more prolific individuals in their own respective fields of writing. **Publications:** *101 Best Resources for Writers.* Booklet. Alternate Formats: online ● Newsletter, weekly. **Price:** included in membership dues. **Advertising:** accepted. Alternate Formats: online ● Membership Directory. **Price:** included in membership dues.

11184 ■ North American Jules Verne Society (NAJVS)
c/o Brian Kutzera, Sec.-Treas.
1632 N 54th St.
Seattle, WA 98103-6120
E-mail: info@najvs.org
URL: http://www.najvs.org
Contact: Jean-Michel Margot, Pres.
Founded: 1993. **Membership Dues:** in U.S. and Canada, $20 (annual) ● outside North America, $25 (semiannual). **Multinational. Description:** Promotes interest in Jules Verne and his writings. Provides a forum for the interchange of information and materials about and/or relating to Jules Verne and his works. Seeks to stimulate Jules Verne research. **Publications:** *Extraordinary Voyages*, quarterly. Newsletter. Contains articles about Jules Verne and society related issues. **Price:** included in membership dues. Alternate Formats: online.

11185 ■ PEN American Center (PEN)
588 Broadway, Ste.303
New York, NY 10012
Ph: (212)334-1660
Fax: (212)334-2181
E-mail: pen@pen.org
URL: http://www.pen.org
Contact: Ana Bozicevic-Bowling, Exec. Asst.
Founded: 1922. **Members:** 3,300. **Membership Dues:** associate, $40 (annual) ● student associate, $20 (annual) ● full, $100 (annual). **Staff:** 12. **Description:** Seeks to "promote and maintain friendship and intellectual cooperation between people of letters in all countries in the interests of literature, freedom of expression, and international goodwill. Stands for the principle of unhampered transmission of thought within each nation and between all nations and members pledge themselves to oppose any form of suppression of freedom of expression in the country and community to which they belong." (The acronym PEN stands for poets, playwrights, editors, essayists, and novelists.) Membership is by invitation to qualified writers, editors, and translators. Approximately 141 such autonomous centers in 99 countries are associated with the international organization. Sponsors writing competitions for prisoners prisoned in U.S. **Committees:** Censorship; Emergency Fund for Writers; Freedom to Write; Translation; Writers-in-Prison. **Publications:** *Grants & Awards Available to American Writers*, periodic. Directory. **Price:** $12.00 /year for nonmembers; $10.00 /year for members; $200.00 /year for institutions. Alternate Formats: online ● *PEN America*, annual. Journal. **Price:** $10.00/copy; $18.00 /year for individuals; $28.00 /year for institutions. ISSN: 1536-0261 ● *PEN Newsletter*, monthly. Contains PEN news and updates. **Conventions/Meetings:** annual PEN World Voices: The New York Festival of International Literature, one week annual festival that aims to bring together hundreds of writers from around the world - in April.

11186 ■ PEN Center U.S.A.
c/o Antioch University
400 Corporate Pointe
Culver City, CA 90230
Ph: (310)862-1555
Fax: (310)862-1556
E-mail: pen@penusa.org
URL: http://penusa.org
Contact: Adam Somers, Exec. Dir.
Founded: 1952. **Members:** 1,000. **Membership Dues:** full, $79 (annual) ● associate, $50 (annual) ● student, $25 (annual). **Staff:** 5. **Budget:** $550,000. **Regional Groups:** 5. **State Groups:** 2. **Description:** Poets, playwrights, essayists, editors, and novelists (PEN). Promotes freedom of expression nationally and internationally; works to effect the release of writers imprisoned because of their writings. Encourages awareness of the western U.S. as a vital literary and journalistic community. Conducts educational and charitable programs. **Awards:** PEN Center West Literary Award. **Frequency:** annual. **Type:** monetary. **Recipient:** for authors living in West of the Mississippi; awarded in 10 categories ● PEN USA Freedom to Write Domestic Award. **Frequency:** annual. **Type:** monetary. **Recipient:** to a person or organization whose work defends the First Amendment as it relates to the freedom to write ● PEN USA Freedom to Write International Award. **Frequency:** annual. **Type:** monetary. **Recipient:** to a writer who has faced and overcome attempts to silence him/her and his/her work ● PEN USA Lifetime Achievement Award. **Frequency:** annual. **Type:** monetary. **Telecommunication Services:** electronic mail, asomers@penusa.org. **Committees:** Emerging Voices; Freedom to Write; Pen in the Classroom. **Affiliated With:** International P.E.N. - England. **Formerly:** (1989) International PEN - U.S.A West. **Publications:** *Author Access.* Features a roster of writers for the community. **Price:** $5.00 ● *PEN Center U.S.A. West Membership*, annual. Membership Directory. **Price:** $1,000.00/year. **Circulation:** 1,000. **Conventions/Meetings:** annual International Congress ● annual PEN USA Literary Awards Festival - dinner, awards presentation and gala dinner.

11187 ■ Philip Roth Society
c/o Derek Parker Royal, Pres./Exec. Ed.
Texas A&M University-Commerce
Dept. of Literature and Languages
2600 S Neal St.
Commerce, TX 75429-3011
Ph: (903)886-5260
Fax: (903)886-5980
E-mail: derek_royal@tamu-commerce.edu
URL: http://orgs.tamu-commerce.edu/rothsoc
Contact: Derek Parker Royal, Pres./Exec. Ed.
Founded: 2002. **Membership Dues:** individual, $15 (annual) ● institution, $30 (annual). **Multinational. Description:** Promotes the study and the appreciation of the writings of American novelist Philip Milton Roth. Encourages the exchange of ideas and texts concerning the author. Maintains a list of bibliographical resources pertaining to Philip Roth and his works. Facilitates communication and cooperation among members. **Publications:** *Philip Roth Society Newsletter*, semiannual. Contains short articles and reviews pertaining to Philip Roth's writings. **Price:** included in membership dues. ISSN: 1543-1347. Alternate Formats: online ● *Philip Roth Studies*, semiannual. Journal. **Price:** $30.40 /year for members (individual); $38.00 /year for nonmembers (individual); $70.40 /year for members (institutional); $88.00 /year for nonmembers (institutional). ISSN: 1547-3929.

11188 ■ Philippine American Writers and Artists (PAWA)
PO Box 31928
San Francisco, CA 94131-0928
E-mail: pawa@pawainc.com
URL: http://www.pawainc.com
Contact: Edwin Agustin Lozada, Pres.
Founded: 1994. **Membership Dues:** friend, $25 ● supporting, $50 ● sustaining, $100 ● life, $500. **Description:** Seeks to create and encourage literature and arts for the preservation and enrichment of Filipino and Filipino-American historical, cultural and spiritual values. Encourages the writing of Philippine and Philippine American literature and the arts among its members. Supports and encourages Filipino-American writers and artists in their creative efforts of bringing and disseminating Filipino culture to various levels of readership audiences. **Awards:** PAWA Young Writers Award. **Frequency:** annual. **Type:** recognition. **Recipient:** for aspiring writers 15-25 years of age.

11189 ■ Poets Against the War (PAW)
Box 1614
Port Townsend, WA 98368
E-mail: info@poetsagainstwar.net
URL: http://www.poetsagainstthewar.org
Contact: Sam Hamill, Dir.
Description: Provides information and resources to aid poets in creating strong networks and taking action in opposing war. Publishes poetry via website. **Computer Services:** Mailing lists.

11190 ■ Robinson Jeffers Association (RJA)
c/o Mr. Robert Kafka, Treas.
UCLA Extension, Rm. 214
10995 LeConte Ave.
Los Angeles, CA 90024-2400
E-mail: rkafka@unex.ucla.edu
URL: http://www.jeffers.org/rja/index.html
Contact: Mr. Robert Kafka, Treas.
Founded: 1990. **Membership Dues:** student, $10 (annual) ● regular, $25 (annual) ● sustaining, $50 (annual) ● patron, $100 (annual) ● life, $500. **Multinational. Description:** Promotes the life and work of Robinson Jeffers (1887-1962), the California poet. **Computer Services:** Online services, email list. **Affiliated With:** American Literature Association. **Publications:** *Jeffers Studies*, semiannual. Journal. Contains articles and notes about the life and work of Robinson Jeffers and his circle. **Price:** included in membership dues; $35.00 for institutions; $5.00/back issue. ISSN: 1096-5076. **Circulation:** 250. Alternate Formats: online ● *Robinson Jeffers Newsletter*. **Price:** $4.00/back issue; $250.00 complete back file of 100 numbers; $175.00 issues 1-79; $80.00 issues 80-100. **Conventions/Meetings:** annual conference ● periodic meeting.

11191 ■ Romance Writers of America (RWA)
16000 Stuebner Airline Rd., Ste.140
Spring, TX 77379
Ph: (832)717-5200
Fax: (832)717-5201
E-mail: info@rwanational.org
URL: http://www.rwanational.org
Contact: Allison Kelley CAE, Exec. Dir.
Founded: 1980. **Members:** 9,500. **Membership Dues:** general and associate, $75 (annual) ● affiliate, $10 (annual). **Budget:** $1,700,000. **Regional Groups:** 6. **Local Groups:** 144. **Description:** Writers, editors, and publishers of romance novels. Aims to support beginning, intermediate, and advanced romance writers; promotes recognition of the genre of romance writing as a serious literary form. Conducts workshops. **Awards:** Golden Heart Award. **Frequency:** annual. **Type:** recognition. **Recipient:** for best unpublished romance novel ● RITA Award. **Frequency:** annual. **Type:** recognition. **Recipient:** for best published romance novel. **Telecommunication Services:** hotline, (281)440-8081. **Committees:** Agent Standards of Practice; Contest; Editorial; Insurance; Professional Relations. **Affiliated With:** American Society of Association Executives. **Publications:** *Romance Writers Report*, monthly. Magazine. **Conventions/Meetings:** periodic regional meeting ● annual conference, for romance writers to meet and network with industry professionals to improve their craft - 2008 July 30-Aug. 2, San Francisco, CA; 2009

July 15-18, Washington, DC; 2010 July 28-31, Nashville, TN; 2011 July 27-30, New York, NY.

11192 ■ Saint Andrew Abbey
10510 Buckeye Rd.
Cleveland, OH 44104-3725
Ph: (216)721-5300
Fax: (216)721-1253
URL: http://csnmail.net/~bocohio/index.htm
Contact: Fr. Andrew Pier, Dir.
Founded: 1954. **Members:** 57. **Description:** Persons of Slovak birth or descent, living in the U.S., Canada, South America, and Europe, who are authors, intellectuals, journalists, painters, editors, composers, or musicians. Promotes Christian Slovak culture abroad by publishing the works of Slovak authors and helping them in their creative efforts. Maintains Slovak Institute, which contains library on Slovak history, art, and literature and the cultural achievements of Americans of Slovak ancestry. **Publications:** *Most*, quarterly. Also Cited As: *Bridge*. **Conventions/Meetings:** periodic meeting.

11193 ■ Science Fiction and Fantasy Writers of America (SFWA)
PO Box 877
Chestertown, MD 21620
Fax: (410)778-3052
E-mail: execdir@sfwa.org
URL: http://www.sfwa.org
Contact: Jane Jewell, Exec. Dir.
Founded: 1965. **Members:** 1,450. **Membership Dues:** active/associate/estate, $70 (annual) ● affiliate, $55 (annual) ● institutional, $80 (annual). **Staff:** 1. **Budget:** $70,000. **Description:** Professional writers of science fiction stories, novels, radio plays, teleplays, or screenplays. Works to achieve the best working conditions possible for writers. Maintains legal fund and emergency medical fund to help members in time of need. Helps mediate between writers and publishers. Encourages public interest in science fiction literature through use of school and public library facilities; produces and disseminates science fiction literature of high quality. Conducts discussions, lectures, and seminars. Maintains speakers' bureau. **Libraries: Type:** reference. **Awards:** SFWA Nebula Award. **Frequency:** annual. **Type:** recognition. **Recipient:** for authors of the best science fiction novel, novella, novelette, and short story of the year as determined by poll of active membership; winners and runners-up are published in *Nebula Awards Anthology*. **Computer Services:** Mailing lists, on labels or directory only. **Committees:** Anthologies; Contracts; E-Piracy; Grants and Fellowships; Grievance; Outreach; Publicity; Random Audit. **Formerly:** (1991) Science Fiction Writers of America. **Publications:** *The Bulletin*, quarterly. Magazine. Contains news, articles and organization's activities. **Price:** $18.00/year; $4.99/issue. **Advertising:** accepted ● *Forum*, bimonthly. Newsletter ● *Science Fiction and Fantasy Writers of America Handbook*. Handbooks ● Brochures ● Directory, annual. **Conventions/Meetings:** annual Nebula Awards - banquet.

11194 ■ Society of Children's Book Writers and Illustrators (SCBWI)
8271 Beverly Blvd.
Los Angeles, CA 90048
Ph: (323)782-1010
Fax: (323)782-1892
E-mail: scbwi@scbwi.org
URL: http://www.scbwi.org
Contact: Stephen Mooser, Pres.
Founded: 1971. **Members:** 20,000. **Membership Dues:** full, associate, $60 (annual) ● one time-initiation fee, $15. **Staff:** 5. **Budget:** $1,000,000. **Regional Groups:** 65. **For-Profit. Description:** Individuals with an active interest in children's literature. Acts as a network for the exchange of information among children's writers, editors, publishers, illustrators, and agents. Serves as a consolidated voice for children's writers and illustrators to effect changes within the field. **Awards:** Golden Kite Awards. **Frequency:** annual. **Type:** recognition. **Recipient:** for SCBWI member who has published a book (within year of the award) ● **Frequency:** 8/year. **Type:** grant. **Formerly:** (1992) Society of Children's Book Writers. **Publications:** *SCBWI Bulletin*, bimonthly. Newsletter. Includes market news, writing and illustrating tips, and items on member activities. **Price:** included in membership dues. **Circulation:** 14,000. Alternate Formats: online ● Monographs. **Conventions/Meetings:** annual conference - every summer. 2008 Aug. 1-4, Los Angeles, CA; 2009 Aug. 7-10, Los Angeles, CA ● semiannual National Conference on Writing and Illustrating for Children - early August and February.

11195 ■ Society for the Study of American Women Writers (SSAWW)
c/o Prof. Melissa J. Homestead, Membership and Finances Off.
PO Box 88033
Lincoln, NE 68588-0333
E-mail: mhomestead2@unl.edu
URL: http://www.lehigh.edu/~dek7/SSAWW
Contact: Karen Kilcup, Pres.
Membership Dues: regular, $15 (annual) ● retired, independent scholar, student, $5 (annual) ● life, $150. **Multinational. Description:** Promotes the study of American women writers through research, teaching, and publication. Aims to strengthen relations among persons and institutions who are devoted to such studies. Seeks to broaden knowledge among the general public about American women writers. **Telecommunication Services:** electronic mail, academic@karenkilcup.org. **Affiliated With:** Association for the Study of Literature and Environment; Society for the History of Authorship, Reading and Publishing. **Publications:** *LEGACY: A Journal of Women Writers*, semiannual. **Price:** $33.00 institutions in U.S.; $38.00 institutions outside U.S.; $20.00 per year for regular with SSAWW member discount; $13.60 per year for student with SSAWW member discount. ISSN: 0748-4321 ● Newsletter, semiannual. Provides information on events, issues, and concerns of interest to scholars of American women writers. **Price:** included in membership dues.

11196 ■ Space Coast Writers' Guild (SCWG)
PO Box 262
Melbourne, FL 32902-0262
E-mail: scwg-jm@cfl.rr.com
URL: http://www.scwg.org
Contact: Judy Mammay, Pres.
Founded: 1982. **Members:** 173. **Membership Dues:** individual, $35 (annual) ● student, $25 (annual). **Staff:** 3. **Description:** Professional and aspiring writers in all media. Trains, develops, and promotes individuals in the writing professions. Supports and conducts community and educational activities of advancing the literary art of writing. **Libraries: Type:** not open to the public. **Awards:** Distinguished Service. **Frequency:** annual. **Type:** recognition ● Michael Shaara Writer's Award. **Frequency:** annual. **Type:** recognition. **Recipient:** for outstanding author. **Computer Services:** Mailing lists, membership and conference list. **Formerly:** (1991) Florida Space Coast Writers Conference. **Publications:** *Organization, Events, Awards and Membership (SCWG)*, annual. Membership Directory. **Price:** included in membership dues. **Conventions/Meetings:** annual Writers' Conference, features Richard Lederer.

11197 ■ Susan Glaspell Society
c/o Martha C. Carpentier, VP
Dept. of English
Seton Hall Univ.
400 S Orange Ave.
South Orange, NJ 07079
E-mail: glaspellsociety@shu.edu
URL: http://academic.shu.edu/glaspell
Contact: Martha C. Carpentier, VP
Founded: 2003. **Membership Dues:** regular, $20 (annual) ● student, part-time/retired faculty, $10 (annual). **Description:** Promotes the study of the life and works of American writer Susan Glaspell. Fosters continued growth of Glaspell scholarship. Facilitates exchange of information pertaining to Susan Glaspell and her literary works. **Telecommunication Services:** electronic mail, ozieblo@uma.es. **Affiliated With:** American Literature Association.

11198 ■ Tall Grass Writers Guild (TWG)
c/o Outrider Press
2036 N Winds Dr.
Dyer, IN 46311
Ph: (219)322-7270
Free: (800)933-4680
Fax: (219)322-7085
E-mail: outriderpress@sbcglobal.net
URL: http://www.outriderpress.com
Contact: Whitney Scott, Pres.
Founded: 1980. **Members:** 150. **Membership Dues:** ordinary, $45 (annual) ● student, $25 (annual) ● international, $60 (annual). **Staff:** 3. **Budget:** $18,000. **Regional Groups:** 1. **Description:** Writers including individuals who write for publication or as a recreational pursuit. Seeks to promote personal and literary development of members. Facilitates communication among members. Sponsors formal readings; makes available leadership training opportunities; conducts writing development courses. **Libraries: Type:** not open to the public. **Holdings:** archival material. **Subjects:** poetry/prose on nature, animals, food. **Awards:** Tall Grass Writers Guild Award. **Frequency:** annual. **Type:** monetary. **Recipient:** for best poetry/best prose in anthology contest. **Formerly:** (1998) Feminist Writers Guild. **Publications:** *A Kiss is Still a Kiss (2001)*, annual. Book. Deals with romantic love. **Price:** $22.50/copy ● *A Walk Through My Garden (2007)*, annual. Book. **Price:** $18.95. **Advertising:** accepted ● *Alternatives (1997)*, annual. Book. Contains poetry, fiction, and creative nonfiction on counter culture. **Price:** $20.30/copy ● *Earth Beneath, Sky Beyond - Nature and Our Planet (2000)*, annual. Book. Contains poetry, fiction, and creative nonfiction on nature. **Price:** $22.50/copy ● *Falling in Love Again - The 2nd Time Around (2005)*, annual. Book ● *Family Gatherings (2003)*, annual. Book. Contains poetry, essays, and fiction on human and non-human family gatherings. **Price:** $23.50 ● *Feathers, Fins and Fur (1999)*, annual. Book. Contains poetry, fiction, and creative nonfiction on animals. **Price:** $21.50/copy ● *Freedom's Just Another Word (1998)*, annual. Book. Contains poetry, fiction, and creative nonfiction dealing with concepts and limitations of freedom. **Price:** $20.30/copy ● *Prairie Hearts-Women View the Midwest (1996)*, annual. Book. **Price:** $20.30/copy ● *Take Two, They're Small - Writings on Food (2002)*, annual. Book. Contains poetry, essays, and fiction on human and non-human family gatherings. **Price:** $23.50 ● *Things That Go Bump in the Night - The Supernatural from the Horrific to the Hilarious (2004)*, annual. Book. Contains poetry and fiction. **Price:** $23.50 ● *Vacations: the Good, the Bad and the Ugly (2006)*, annual. Book. **Conventions/Meetings:** bimonthly board meeting ● semiannual Formal Themed Reading - show ● annual Kick-Off Reading - show ● monthly Open Mic Night - show.

11199 ■ Text and Academic Authors Association (TAA)
PO Box 76477
St. Petersburg, FL 33734-6477
Ph: (727)563-0020
Fax: (727)230-2409
E-mail: text@tampabay.rr.com
URL: http://www.taaonline.net
Contact: John Wakefield, Pres.
Founded: 1987. **Members:** 1,000. **Membership Dues:** graduate student, instructor, postdoctoral fellow, $15 (annual) ● assistant professor, textbook author (with royalties under $5000 per year), $30 (annual) ● emeritus, $35 (annual) ● associate professor, $55 (annual) ● professor, textbook author (with royalties above $5000 per year), $75 (annual). **Staff:** 5. **Description:** Authors of text and academic materials as well as software authors, text editors, and other academic authors. Promotes professionalism among textbook authors; seeks to improve working conditions. **Awards:** Texty Excellence Award. **Frequency:** annual. **Type:** recognition. **Recipient:** for an association author ● William Holmes McGuffey Longevity Award. **Frequency:** annual. **Type:** recognition. **For-**

merly: Textbook Authors Association. **Publications:** *Academic Author*, quarterly. Newsletter. **Price:** included in membership dues; $30.00 /year for nonmembers. ISSN: 1041-1453. **Advertising:** accepted. Alternate Formats: online. **Conventions/ Meetings:** annual convention (exhibits) - always June.

11200 ■ Thornton Wilder Society
Coll. of New Jersey
PO Box 7718
Ewing, NJ 08628-0718
Ph: (609)771-2346
Fax: (609)637-5112
E-mail: wilder@tcnj.edu
URL: http://www.tcnj.edu/~wilder
Contact: Dr. Lincoln Konkle, Exec. Dir.
Founded: 2000. **Membership Dues:** regular, $25 (annual). **Multinational. Description:** Represents scholars, teachers, professionals, and members of the public who are interested in the life and legacy of American playwright and novelist Thornton Wilder. Seeks to preserve and enhance the values of Thornton Wilder's works. Provides an international registry service for scholars, professionals and amateurs who produce Wilder's plays and operas. **Publications:** *The Thornton Wilder Society Newsletter*, published once or twice a year. Includes insightful and provocative articles about Wilder's life and works. **Price:** included in membership dues. Alternate Formats: online ● Bulletin, periodic.

11201 ■ Western Writers of America (WWA)
c/o Rod Miller
1665 E Julio St.
Sandy, UT 84093
E-mail: wwa@unm.edu
URL: http://www.westernwriters.org
Contact: Paul Andrew Hutton, Exec. Dir./Sec.-Treas.
Founded: 1952. **Members:** 650. **Membership Dues:** active/associate, $75 (annual) ● sustaining, $150 (annual) ● patron, $250 (annual). **Staff:** 2. **Description:** Represents freelance writers of Western fiction and nonfiction, editors, literary agents, historians, romance writers, screenplay and scriptwriters, and journalists. Sponsors competitions; maintains speakers' bureau, hall of fame, and library. **Awards:** Owen Wister Awards. **Frequency:** annual. **Type:** recognition. **Recipient:** for lifetime achievement and contributions to the field of Western literature ● Spur Awards. **Frequency:** annual. **Type:** recognition. **Recipient:** for distinguished writing about the American West. **Committees:** Marketing; Nominations; Publicity; Roundup Magazine; Spur Award. **Publications:** *Roundup*, bimonthly. Magazine. Provides information on writing, marketing, and publishing books and stories about the American West. Includes association and member news. **Price:** included in membership dues; $30.00 /year for nonmembers. ISSN: 0035-844X. **Circulation:** 800. **Advertising:** accepted. Alternate Formats: online. **Conventions/ Meetings:** annual convention.

11202 ■ Writers-in-Exile Center, American Branch, International PEN Club
c/o Clara Gyorgyey, Pres.
42 Derby Ave.
Orange, CT 06477
Ph: (203)397-1479 (203)785-4744
Fax: (203)397-5439
E-mail: gyorgyey@aol.com
Contact: Clara Gyorgyey, Pres.
Founded: 1951. **Members:** 125. **Membership Dues:** individual, $45 (annual). **Staff:** 2. **Description:** Writers in exile from their native lands who are now living in the western hemisphere. Goals are global communication among writers and fight for freedom of expression. Activities include recitals and promotion of publishing and translation, especially from lesser known literatures. **Committees:** Political Action; Writers-in-Prison. **Affiliated With:** PEN American Center. **Publications:** *Writers-in-Exile Center, American Branch, International PEN Club—Newsletter*, quarterly. Reports on writers who are in prison or forced exile; includes conference reports. **Price:** included in membership dues. **Circulation:** 200. **Conventions/ Meetings:** annual Borderless World/Literacy - congress (exhibits) ● periodic roundtable and congress ● symposium, literary.

11203 ■ Writers Workshop (WW)
c/o University of Illinois at Urbana-Champaign
608 S Wright St., 208 English Bldg.
Urbana, IL 61801
Ph: (217)333-8796 (217)333-1919
E-mail: wow@uiuc.edu
URL: http://www.english.uiuc.edu/cws/wworkshop
Contact: Elizabeth Morley, Dir.
Founded: 1978. **Members:** 125. **Membership Dues:** support group, $35 (annual). **Staff:** 2. **Budget:** $100,000. **Local Groups:** 1. **Description:** Seeks to critically evaluate and provide feedback on screenplays submitted for consideration in its two annual screenwriting contests. Works to act as a support group for new screenwriters; provide, through a network of major production studios and agents, critical screenplay analysis, career counseling, and studio exposure for new talent. Sponsors charitable activities. **Libraries: Type:** reference. **Holdings:** audio recordings. **Awards:** Ethnic Minority Award. **Frequency:** annual. **Type:** monetary. **Recipient:** for best ethnic minority script ● National Award. **Frequency:** annual. **Type:** monetary. **Formerly:** (1991) American Film Institute Alumni Association Writers Workshop. **Conventions/Meetings:** annual Ethnic Minority Screenwriters Development Program - seminar ● annual From Concept to Screenplay in 12 Weeks - workshop ● annual Writers Workshop Ethnic Minority Contest - competition ● annual Writer's Workshop National Screenplay Contest - competition.

11204 ■ Writing Academy (WA)
c/o Inez Schneider, New Member Coor.
4010 Singleton Rd.
Rockford, IL 61114
Ph: (815)877-9675
E-mail: info@wams.org
URL: http://www.wams.org
Contact: Inez Schneider, New Member Coor.
Founded: 1979. **Members:** 80. **Membership Dues:** associate, $50 (annual) ● active, charter, $360 (annual) ● reserve, $10 (annual). **Description:** Christian writers. Provides motivation and instruction for Christian writers who want to learn to write for church or secular publications. Offers courses designed to improve writing skills; sponsors individual and group writing projects; provides professional and peer group critiques. Offers fellowship among members. **Awards:** Annual Writing Contests. **Frequency:** annual. **Type:** monetary. **Recipient:** for members only. **Computer Services:** Mailing lists, roster ● online services, MorningStar. **Divisions:** Development; Instructional Writing; Project Writing. **Publications:** *Writing Academy News*, quarterly. Newsletter. Contains news of organization and work by members. **Price:** included in membership dues; $10.00 /year for nonmembers. **Circulation:** 180 ● Also plans to develop *Devotionals*, *Interstamental Period Study*, and *Vocation Bible School Curriculum*. **Conventions/Meetings:** annual seminar, 4 or 5 days of lectures, workshops, fellowship (exhibits) - usually August.

Writing

11205 ■ American Association of Handwriting Analysts (AAHA)
c/o Ed Jackson, Pres.
1060 Grandeview Blvd., Apt. 622
Huntsville, AL 35824
Ph: (256)772-5326
Free: (800)826-7774
E-mail: aahaemail@aol.com
URL: http://www.handwriting.org/aaha/aahamain.html
Contact: Ed Jackson, Pres.
Founded: 1962. **Members:** 350. **Membership Dues:** senior, $10 (annual) ● affiliate, $45 (annual) ● certified, associate, $50 (annual) ● life, $500. **Regional Groups:** 8. **Description:** Persons who have completed recognized courses in handwriting analysis, passed examinations by a committee of the Association, and displayed proficiency in the science of analyzing character from handwriting are certified members; individuals who have passed an exam on the guiding principles of graphology are associate members. Those who are interested in graphology are affiliate members. Serves as a forum for the exchange of information on graphology and research in the field. Promotes professionalism in the "science of analyzing character through examination of all forms of writing." Seeks public recognition of handwriting analysis as an important aid in the solution of problems involving personality and identification of signatures or writing. Promotes research in handwriting analysis. **Libraries: Type:** reference. **Holdings:** 750; articles, books. **Subjects:** handwriting analysis; psychology in English, German and French. **Awards:** Honorary Membership. **Type:** recognition. **Recipient:** for outstanding service. **Committees:** Accreditation; Education; Research. **Publications:** *AAHA Dialogue*, bimonthly. Newsletter. Contains 16-20 page document dedicated to organizational business and educational articles. **Advertising:** accepted. **Conventions/Meetings:** annual convention - usually in July or August ● semiannual workshop and regional meeting - usually in October/November and April/May.

11206 ■ American Handwriting Analysis Foundation (AHAF)
PO Box 6201
San Jose, CA 95150-6201
Free: (800)826-7774
E-mail: ahaf@iwhome.com
URL: http://www.handwritingfoundation.org
Contact: Heidi H. Harralson CG, Pres.
Founded: 1968. **Members:** 251. **Membership Dues:** in U.S., $50 (annual) ● in Canada and Mexico, $60 (annual) ● international, $70 (annual). **Staff:** 5. **Regional Groups:** 7. **Multinational. Description:** Individuals interested in handwriting analysis. Seeks to advance graphology (the art and science of determining qualities of the personality from the script) as a helping profession; provide certification program for members; establish a code of ethics; foster research in handwriting analysis and cooperation among all handwriting analysts and handwriting societies. Maintains research and educational programs. Maintains speakers' bureau. Disseminates resource information. **Libraries: Type:** reference; lending. **Holdings:** 800; books, monographs, periodicals. **Subjects:** handwriting analysis, questioned document work, psychology. **Awards:** Honorary Membership Award. **Frequency:** periodic. **Type:** recognition. **Recipient:** for service and special contributions to graphology ● Michael-Flandrin Award. **Type:** recognition. **Recipient:** for individuals who have made special contributions. **Committees:** Certification; Conference; Education; Ethics; Finance; Librarian; Parliamentarian; Public Relations; Research. **Affiliated With:** American Association of Handwriting Analysts. **Publications:** *AHAF Journal*, bimonthly. Newsletter. Includes book reviews, calendar of events, research updates, graphological articles and statistics. **Price:** included in membership dues; $50. 00/year in U.S.; $60.00/year in Canada and Mexico; $70.00/year outside North America. **Circulation:** 500. **Advertising:** accepted ● *Cursive vs. Printing Report*. **Price:** $9.95/copy ● *Cursive vs. Printing Study*. Book. **Price:** $9.95/copy ● *Guide to Self-Published Papers, 1978-1988*, annual. Directory. **Price:** $6.95/copy ● *Guide to Self-Published Papers, 1979*. **Price:** $6.95/ copy ● *International Bibliography of Graphological Journal Articles, 1968-1988*. **Price:** $19.95/copy ● *International Index of Graphological Journal Articles, 1968-1988*. **Price:** $6.95/copy ● *Manual for Graphological Researchers*. **Price:** $6.95/copy ● *Recommended Reading Dossier*. Book ● *Research Trilogy*. Book. **Price:** $32.95/copy ● *Standard Terms for Handwriting Analysts: English Terms, Document Examination Terms, Health Terms, International Terms*. Book. **Price:** $15.95/copy ● *Tattle Tale T's*. Book. **Price:** $20.00/copy ● *Write Learning*. Book. **Price:** $15.00/copy ● Directory, annual ● Publishes many brochures on handwriting analysis. **Conventions/Meetings:** annual Writing Out of the Box -

conference, in conjunction with the American Association of Handwriting Analysts (exhibits) - summer.

11207 ■ American Society of Greek and Latin Epigraphy (ASGLE)
c/o Prof. Paul Iversen, Sec.-Treas.
CWRU Dept. of Classics
111 Mather House
11201 Euclid Ave.
Cleveland, OH 44106-7111
E-mail: paul.iversen@cwru.edu
URL: http://www.case.edu/artsci/clsc/asgle
Contact: Prof. Paul Iversen, Sec.-Treas.
Founded: 1996. **Membership Dues:** college/university faculty, $30 (annual) ● student, retired, independent, $10 (annual) ● student, retired, independent (include membership in AIEGL), $30 (annual). **Description:** Works to further research in, and the teaching of, Greek and Latin epigraphy in North America. Fosters collaboration in the field. Facilitates the exchange of scholarly research and discussion, both in the public forum and in published form.

11208 ■ Center for Sutton Movement Writing
PO Box 517
La Jolla, CA 92038-0517
Ph: (858)456-0098
Fax: (858)456-0020
E-mail: sutton@signwriting.org
URL: http://www.dancewriting.org
Contact: Valerie J. Sutton, Founder/Dir./Webmaster
Founded: 1973. **Members:** 300. **Membership Dues:** regular, $15 (annual). **Staff:** 3. **Description:** Aims to promote Sutton Movement Writing and Shorthand, an international handwriting used to record on paper the movements of all forms of dance, deaf sign languages, physical therapy, classic pantomime, martial arts, science, and sports. Conducts teacher certification courses. Maintains speakers' bureau and placement service for teachers of Sutton Writing; offers specialized education. Has developed Sign Writer Software for personal computers. **Convention/Meeting:** none. **Libraries: Type:** reference. **Holdings:** articles, books, periodicals. **Computer Services:** Online services, seven web sites that provide lessons online archive of documents on Sutton Movement Writing software developed to type movement. **Additional Websites:** http://www.signwriting.org. **Telecommunication Services:** electronic mail, sutton@dancewriting.org. **Formerly:** (1984) Movement Shorthand Society. **Publications:** Also publishes notated sheet dance and sign literature for the deaf; makes available computer signwriting software.

11209 ■ Council of Graphological Societies (COGS)
c/o Louie Seibert, Treas.
PO Box 615
Hardy, AR 72542
E-mail: graphex@copper.net
URL: http://www.handwriting.org/cogs/cogsmain.htm
Contact: Ellen Bowers, Pres.
Founded: 1974. **Members:** 246. **Membership Dues:** individual, $5 (annual). **Regional Groups:** 7. **Description:** Graphological associations, including the Handwriting Analysts International, International Graphological Society, National Society for Graphology, Great Lakes Association of Handwriting Examiners, Rhode Island Study Group, Saskatchewan Handwriting Analysis Club, and Special Interest Group promoting the profession of handwriting analysis and related fields. **Committees:** Accreditation; Education; Ethics; Public Relations; Research. **Affiliated With:** International Graphological Society; National Society for Graphology. **Publications:** *Council of Graphological Sciences Newsletter Communicator*, 1-2/year. Includes articles and research reports about handwriting analyses and related fields. **Circulation:** 600 ● *Graphological Sciences*, annual. Journal ● *Information Bulletins*, periodic ● *Research Bulletins*, periodic. **Conventions/Meetings:** triennial conference.

11210 ■ International Graphoanalysis Society (IGAS)
842 5th Ave.
New Kensington, PA 15068
Ph: (724)472-9701
Fax: (267)501-1931
E-mail: greg@igas.com
URL: http://www.igas.com
Contact: Greg Greco, Pres.
Founded: 1929. **Members:** 50,000. **Membership Dues:** regular (pro-rated), $90 (annual). **Staff:** 50. **Description:** Represents handwriting analysts and identification experts. Maintains hall of fame and speakers' bureau. Compiles statistics; conducts research programs, specialized education, and placement service. **Libraries: Type:** reference. **Holdings:** 500. **Subjects:** psychology and identification. **Awards:** International Graphoanalyst of the Year. **Frequency:** annual. **Type:** recognition. **Absorbed:** (1949) American Institute of Grapho Analysis. **Publications:** *Journal of Graphoanalysis*, monthly ● Also publishes books, monographs, and dictionaries. **Conventions/Meetings:** annual international conference.

11211 ■ International Graphological Society (IGS)
Address Unknown since 2007
Founded: 1983. **Members:** 183. **Staff:** 6. **Description:** Graphologists, document examiners, and other individuals interested in handwriting analysis. Promotes graphology as a means to better self-understanding, and as an instrument for subjective personality assessment. **Libraries: Type:** reference. **Publications:** *Document Examiner*, quarterly ● *The Quill and NQDA*, quarterly. **Price:** $10.00/year in the U.S.; $12.00/year outside the U.S. **Circulation:** 1,846. **Advertising:** accepted. **Conventions/Meetings:** annual conference and seminar.

11212 ■ National Society for Graphology (NSG)
250 W 57th St., Ste.1228A
New York, NY 10107
Ph: (212)265-1148
E-mail: irenicnyc@aol.com
URL: http://www.handwriting.org/nsg/nsgmain.html
Contact: Janice Klein, Contact
Founded: 1972. **Members:** 300. **Membership Dues:** regular, $65 (annual). **Description:** Professionally certified graphologists and individuals interested in Gestalt graphology. (Graphology is the study of handwriting for purposes of character analysis.) Promotes the study of graphology. Encourages individuals to train in graphology and seek professional status within the organization. **Libraries: Type:** reference. **Holdings:** 400; books, clippings, monographs, periodicals. **Subjects:** graphology, psychology. **Publications:** *Write-Up*, bimonthly. Newsletter. **Price:** included in membership dues. **Circulation:** 300. **Conventions/Meetings:** meeting and seminar - 6/year, always in New York City.

11213 ■ Society for Calligraphy (SfC)
PO Box 64174
Los Angeles, CA 90064-0174
E-mail: president@societyforcalligraphy.org
URL: http://www.societyforcalligraphy.org
Contact: Carrie Imai, Pres.
Founded: 1974. **Members:** 1,194. **Membership Dues:** regular, $42 (annual) ● patron, $100 (annual) ● supporting, family, $60 (annual) ● student with full-time verification, $25 (annual). **Budget:** $55,000. **Regional Groups:** 5. **Description:** Calligraphers, illustrators, graphic artists, curators, book artists, and students and teachers of calligraphy; calligraphy associations. (Calligraphy is the art of producing beautiful or elegant handwriting and lettering.) Promotes the study and practice of calligraphy; fosters exchange of information and ideas about calligraphy. Conducts workshops, symposia, and seminars; holds art auction, annual retreat, and biennial exhibit; sponsors lectures, with slide shows or demonstrations. Maintains library of books and audiovisual materials. **Committees:** Activities; Communications; Exhibit; Programs; Public Relations; Regionals; Resources; Special Projects. **Publications:** *The Calligraph*, 3/year. Journal. Provides information on letterforms, pens, inks, papers, and the history of letters; includes interviews with well-known calligraphers. ● *Calligraphers Guide to Los Angeles* ● Bulletin ● Membership Directory, annual. **Conventions/Meetings:** annual International Calligraphy Conference ● annual meeting - always May.

11214 ■ Society of Scribes (SOS)
PO Box 933
New York, NY 10150
Ph: (212)452-0139
E-mail: info@societyofscribes.org
URL: http://www.societyofscribes.org
Contact: Eva J. Kokoris, Pres.
Founded: 1974. **Members:** 700. **Membership Dues:** basic (in U.S.), $40 (annual) ● basic (outside U.S.), $45 (annual) ● supporting, $75 (annual) ● patron, $100 (annual). **Staff:** 9. **Description:** Calligraphers, bookbinders, lettering artists, and individuals with an interest in book arts. Promotes calligraphy and related lettering arts. Collects and disseminates information. Conducts exhibitions, workshops, lecturers, programs, and publications. **Libraries: Type:** reference. **Holdings:** business records, periodicals. **Subjects:** calligraphy and lettering arts. **Committees:** Exhibitions; Programs; Workshops. **Publications:** *Classes and Workshops*, semiannual, every fall/winter and winter/spring. Brochure. Contains offerings of classes and workshops. ● *Letters from New York*, semiannual. Journal. Contains articles, reviews and discussions relating to calligraphy. **Price:** $10.00 ● *NewSOS*, semiannual. Newsletter. Includes book and workshop reviews, meeting announcements, professional information, technical notes, and artwork. **Price:** included in membership dues. **Circulation:** 1,000. **Advertising:** accepted. **Conventions/Meetings:** annual Holiday Fair - meeting (exhibits) - always 1st Sunday of December ● lecture ● annual meeting (exhibits) - always last Saturday of February ● periodic meeting ● seminar ● workshop.

11215 ■ Washington Calligraphers Guild (WCG)
PO Box 3688
Merrifield, VA 22116-3688
E-mail: info@calligraphersguild.org
URL: http://www.calligraphersguild.org
Contact: Gretchen Elson, Pres.
Founded: 1976. **Members:** 500. **Membership Dues:** supporting, $50 (annual) ● patron, $100 (annual) ● sustaining, $150 (annual). **Multinational. Description:** Calligraphers and individuals interested in calligraphy. Promotes the appreciation of calligraphy and its applications and history. Seeks to foster a greater understanding of calligraphy as an art. Conducts studies on calligraphy; sponsors charitable and educational programs. **Libraries: Type:** reference; lending. **Holdings:** 300; books, periodicals. **Subjects:** lettering and book arts. **Awards:** Hermann Zapf Educational Fund Scholarship. **Frequency:** biennial. **Type:** scholarship. **Recipient:** to a student of calligraphy to aid in furthering his study and education in this art. **Publications:** *Scripsit*, 3/year. Journal. Contains articles and interviews; includes book and workshop reviews. **Price:** included in membership dues. **Circulation:** 750 ● Newsletter, monthly. Contains class schedules, exhibit notices, and calendar of events. ● Membership Directory, annual. **Conventions/Meetings:** annual Art Exhibit - meeting, with invitational exhibit of artwork (exhibits) ● periodic Letterforum - international conference, gathering of lettering artists and instructors from various countries for an intense, week-long study and exploration in the calligraphic arts (exhibits) ● seminar ● workshop.

Yoga

11216 ■ American Yoga Association (AYA)
PO Box 19986
Sarasota, FL 34276
Ph: (941)927-4977
Fax: (941)921-9844

E-mail: info@americanyogaassociation.org
URL: http://www.americanyogaassociation.org
Contact: Alice Christensen, Founder/Dir.

Founded: 1968. **Staff:** 7. **National Groups:** 2. **Nonmembership**. **Description:** Promotes the practice of Yoga as a practical and effective tool for physical, mental, and emotional health and well-being. Teaches all facets of classical Yoga with emphasis on breathing, exercise, and relaxation/meditation. Designs programs for the elderly ("Easy Does It Yoga"), which includes workshops for health professionals and other fitness trainers throughout the country. Offers a Stress Management Program to businesses and organizations throughout the country. Conducts classes, seminars, lectures, and workshops. Distributes instructional materials on teaching safe beginner Yoga practices and practical nutrition and the benefits of Yoga in treating common health problems. Has engaged in local, state, and federally funded research to evaluate the effects of classical Yoga practice. Maintains center in Cleveland, OH. Conventions/Meetings: none. **Formerly:** (1983) Light of Yoga Society. **Publications:** *American Yoga Association Beginner's Manual*. Book. **Price:** $16.00 ● *The American Yoga Association's Desk Meditation*. Audiotape. Alternate Formats: online ● *The American Yoga Associations Easy Does It Yoga*. Book ● *The American Yoga Association's New Yoga Challenge*. Book. Alternate Formats: CD-ROM ● *The American Yoga Association's Wellness Book* ● *The American Yoga Association's Yoga for Sports*. Book ● *Arthritis: An American Yoga Association Wellness Guide*. Book ● *Basic Yoga*. Video ● *Complete Relaxation and Meditation*. Audiotape. **Price:** $16.00. Alternate Formats: CD-ROM ● *The Easy Does It Yoga Trainer's Guide*. Book ● *Heart Health: An American Yoga Association Wellness Guide*. Book ● *The 'I Love You' Meditation Technique*. Audiotape. Alternate Formats: CD-ROM ● *Light of Yoga*. Book ● *Meditation*. Book ● *Reflections of Love*. Book ● *20-Minute Yoga Workouts*. Book ● *Weight Management: An American Yoga Association Wellness Guide*. Book ● *Yoga of the Heart*. Book.

11217 ■ Ananda Yoga Teachers Association (AYTA)

c/o The Expanding Light
14618 Tyler Foote Rd.
Nevada City, CA 95959
Ph: (530)478-7518
E-mail: info@anandayoga.org
URL: http://www.anandayoga.org
Contact: Brook Dunwoody, Contact

Membership Dues: regular, $40 (annual) ● regular (couple), $60 (annual) ● associate, $25 (annual). **Description:** Represents individuals interested in the practice or teaching of Ananda Yoga. Explores and supports the practice or teaching of Ananda Yoga. Provides certification to teachers of Ananda Yoga. **Publications:** *Awake & Ready!*, 3/year. Newsletter. Contains articles to support the practice and teaching of Ananda Yoga. **Price:** included in membership dues. Alternate Formats: online.

11218 ■ Association of Himalayan Yoga Meditation Societies (AHYMS)

631 Univ. Ave. NE
Minneapolis, MN 55413
Ph: (612)379-2386
Fax: (612)379-2456
E-mail: info@ahyms.org
URL: http://www.bindu.org
Contact: Pandit Hari Shankar Dabral, Spiritual Dir.

Multinational. **Description:** Promotes the practice of yoga as an effective tool for physical, mental, and emotional health and well being. Aims to teach yoga and meditation, its texts, history, and philosophy in accordance with the tradition of the Himalayan masters. Helps and serves the needy in all parts of the world.

11219 ■ North American Yoga Federation (NAYF)

114 E 28th St., 2A
New York, NY 10016
Ph: (212)696-9642
Fax: (212)696-9642
E-mail: info@nayf.org
URL: http://www.nayf.org
Contact: Guru Dileepji, Pres.

Membership Dues: individual (member of United States Yoga Federation, Mexican Yoga Federation, and Canadian Yoga Alliance), $50 (annual) ● organization (member of International Yoga Federation), $50 (annual) ● individual, $90 (annual) ● organization (member of United States Yoga Federation, Mexican Yoga Federation, and Canadian Yoga Alliance), $100 (annual) ● association/organization, $150 (annual). **Multinational**. **Description:** Provides support, standards and international recognition for yoga teachers, yoga masters, yoga therapists, and yoga schools, organizations, and associations. Promotes the practice of yoga. Provides certification to members.

11220 ■ Yoga Alliance (YA)

PO Box 369
Clinton, MD 20735
Ph: (301)868-4700
Free: (877)964-2255
Fax: (301)868-7909
E-mail: info@yogaalliance.org
URL: http://www.yogaalliance.org
Contact: Terri Kennedy PhD, Interim Pres./CEO

Founded: 1999. **Description:** Supports yoga teachers. Promotes the diversity and integrity of yoga. Aims to lead the yoga community, set standards, provide resources and uphold the teachings of yoga.